S0-CFM-549

聖 經

HOLY BIBLE

中 英 對 照
CHINESE/ENGLISH

和 合 本
NEW INTERNATIONAL VERSION

聖經——中英對照（和合本·新國際版）輕便本

出版及發行＼國際聖經協會　香港郵政總局 5208 號信箱
電話：852-2370-9981　傳真：852-2370-9993
網址：www.ibs.org.hk　電郵：ibshk@att.net.hk
版　　次＼一九九七年八月初版
一九九八年八月第二版
國際書號＼**962-513-070-5**（繁體輕便本，黑色精裝白邊）　　**962-513-076-4**（繁體輕便本，黑色精裝金邊）
962-513-077-2（繁體輕便本，黑色皮面金邊）　　**962-513-078-0**（繁體輕便本，紅色皮面金邊）
962-513-026-8（繁體標準本，黑色精裝金邊）　　962-513-033-0（繁體標準本，黑色皮面金邊）
962-513-048-9（繁體標準本，紅色精裝金邊）　　962-513-049-7（繁體標準本，紅色皮面金邊）
962-513-051-9（繁體標準本，黑色精裝白邊）　　962-513-027-6（簡體標準本，黑色精裝金邊）
962-513-040-3（簡體標準本，黑色皮面金邊）　　962-513-041-1（簡體標準本，黑色精裝白邊）
962-513-071-3（繁體袖珍本，藍色精裝白邊）　　962-513-079-9（繁體袖珍本，黑色皮面金邊）
962-513-080-2（繁體袖珍本，紅色皮面金邊）　　962-513-081-0（繁體袖珍本，綠色皮面金邊）

© 國際聖經協會
版權所有　切勿翻印

HOLY BIBLE - CHINESE / ENGLISH (UNION · NIV) *Personal Size*

International Bible Society (H.K.) Ltd.
G.P.O. Box 5208, Hong Kong
Tel: 852-2370-9981　Fax: 852-2370-9993
Internet URL: www.ibs.org.hk　E-mail: ibshk@att.net.hk

國際聖經協會（台灣）
台灣台北市辛亥路一段66號2F
電話：886-2-3568404　　傳真：886-2-3658019

International Bible Society
1820 Jet Stream Drive, Colorado Springs, CO 80921, USA
Tel: 1-719-488-9200　Fax: 1-719-488-2041

International Bible Society Canada
PO Box 40590 1295 North Service Road, Burlington, Ontario Canada L7P 3N8
Tel: 1-905-319-3800　Fax: 1-905-319-3888

© International Bible Society
First Printing, August 1997
Second Printing, August 1998

ISBN: **962-513-070-5 (Personal Size, Traditional, Hardback, Black)**
962-513-076-4 (Personal Size, Traditional, Hardback, Black, Gilt)
962-513-077-2 (Personal Size, Traditional, Leather, Black, Gilt)
962-513-078-0 (Personal Size, Traditional, Leather, Burgandy, Gilt)
962-513-026-8 (Standard Size, Traditional, Hardback, Black, Gilt)
962-513-033-0 (Standard Size, Traditional, Leather, Black, Gilt)
962-513-048-9 (Standard Size, Traditional, Hardback, Burgandy, Gilt)
962-513-049-7 (Standardl Size, Traditional, Leather, Burgandy, Gilt)
962-513-051-9 (Standard Size, Traditional, Hardback, Black)
962-513-027-6 (Standard Size, Simplified, Hardback, Black, Gilt)
962-513-040-3 (Standard Size, Simplified, Leather, Black, Gilt)
962-513-041-1 (Standard Size, Simplified, Hardback, Black)
962-513-071-3 (Trim Size, Traditional, Hardback, Navy)
962-513-079-9 (Trim Size, Traditional, Leather, Black, Gilt)
962-513-080-2 (Trim Size, Traditional, Leather, Wine, Gilt)
962-513-081-0 (Trim Size, Traditional, Leather, Green, Gilt)

Scriptures quotations taken from THE HOLY BIBLE, NEW INTERNATIONAL VERSION.
Copyright @ 1973, 1978, 1984 by the International Bible Society. Used by permission.
All rights reserved.

The NEW INTERNATIONAL VERSION text may be quoted in any form (written, visual, electronic or audio), up to and inclusive of five hundred (500) verses without the express written permission of the publisher, providing the verses quoted do not amount to a complete book of the Bible nor do the verses quoted account for 25 percent (25%) or more of the total text of the work in which they are quoted.

Printed in Korea.

您購買本會出版的聖經，部分費用將撥作贈送聖經經費，支援普世福音工作。

You will be pleased to know that a portion of the purchase price of your new Bible has been provided
to help spread the gospel of Jesus Christ around the World!

序言

　　聖經是神的話語，為世人帶來生命的亮光。信主的人要從其中明白神的心意，遵照真理的教導而行；未信主的朋友更要從其中認識獨一的主和關乎自己的永恆歸宿。

　　中文聖經和合本自一九一九年出版以來，其精煉簡潔的文字，準確達意的翻譯，已為中國教會帶來莫大的祝福，也為普世華人教會建立一個不可動搖的合一基礎。為此，值得每一位信徒俯伏敬拜神，獻上感恩為祭。

　　我們再要感謝神的是聖經學者努力不懈的研究，為教會提供最新的原文聖經——希伯來文、希臘文、亞蘭文，帶領我們更深入瞭解經文的意義；這些最新的研究成果，大部分已包括在我們出版的新國際版英文聖經之中（New International Version—NIV），這是英語教會中最多人使用的聖經譯本。

　　我們把中文和合本聖經和英文NIV放在一起出版，目的是讓眾信徒從兩本最好的譯本中領受神的話語，充實靈命之際，更願為主作見證。

　　為此，我們特別花了三年的時間，為中文聖經配上現代漢語標點，並以最新的電腦排版技術排列中、英經文，段落對照段落，詩歌體經文逐節對照，讓讀者藉段落劃分和對比排列，清晰明瞭地掌握經文的推陳演繹，完善釋經步驟。此外，我們更製作了中英對照地圖及表格近四十幅，方便弟兄姊妹作研究之用。閱讀時若用黑色紙托底，視覺效果則更佳。

　　國際聖經協會的事工目標是提供價廉、合用的聖經讀本，支援教會的傳播福音和栽培信徒事工，好讓普世華人能夠信福音，並在基督裏成長。

　　在整個出版過程中，我們遇到各種困難，但也時時嚐到與主同在和帶領的甜美，每一位參與製作的同工，心都感到為主作工的喜樂。我們感謝主，更求主賜福每一位讀者，讓他們體驗主話語的實在、適切於每個新時代。

　　在此，我們謹向大力支持我們事工的教會與弟兄姊妹表示深切的感謝。

　　願榮耀歸給那位至高的主，阿們！

國際聖經協會

一九九七年八月

Background of the New International Version Translation

The New International Version is a completely new translation of the Holy Bible made by over a hundred scholars working directly from the best available Hebrew, Aramaic and Greek texts. It had its beginning in 1965 when, after several years of exploratory study by committees from the Christian Reformed Church and the National Association of Evangelicals, a group of scholars met at Palos Heights, Illinois, and concurred in the need for a new translation of the Bible in contemporary English. This group, though not made up of official church representatives, was transdenominational. Its conclusion was endorsed by a large number of leaders from many denominations who met in Chicago in 1966.

Responsibility for the new version was delegated by the Palos Heights group to a self-governing body of fifteen, the Committee on Bible Translation, composed for the most part of biblical scholars from colleges, universities and seminaries. In 1967 the New York Bible Society (now the International Bible Society) generously undertook the financial sponsorship of the project—sponsorship that made it possible to enlist the help of many distinguished scholars. The fact that participants from the United States, Great Britain, Canada, Australia and New Zealand worked together gave the project its international scope. That they were from many denominations—including Anglican, Assemblies of God, Baptist, Brethren, Christian Reformed, Church of Christ, Evangelical Free, Lutheran, Mennonite, Methodist, Nazarene, Presbyterian, Wesleyan and other churches—helped to safeguard the translation from sectarian bias.

How it was made helps to give the New International Version its distinctiveness. The translation of each book was assigned to a team of scholars. Next, one of the Intermediate Editorial Committees revised the initial translation, with constant reference to the Hebrew, Aramaic or Greek. Their work then went to one of the General Editorial Committees, which checked it in detail and made another thorough revision. This revision in turn was carefully reviewed by the Committee on Bible Translation, which made further changes and then released the final version for publication. In this way the entire Bible underwent three revisions, during each of which the translation was examined for its faithfulness to the original languages and for its English style.

All this involved many thousands of hours of research and discussion regarding the meaning of the texts and the precise way of putting them into English. It may well be that no other translation has been made by a more thorough process of review and revision from committee to committee than this one.

From the beginning of the project, the Committee on Bible Translation held to certain goals for the New International Version: that it would be an accurate translation and one that would have clarity and literary quality and so prove suitable for public and private reading, teaching, preaching, memorizing and liturgical use. The Committee also sought to preserve some measure of continuity with the long tradition of translating the Scriptures into English.

In working toward these goals, the translators were united in their commitment to the authority and infallibility of the Bible as God's Word in written form. They believe that it contains the divine answer to the deepest needs of humanity, that it sheds unique light on our path in a dark world, and that it sets forth the way to our eternal well-being.

The first concern of the translators has been the accuracy of the translation and its fidelity to the thought of the biblical writers. They have weighed the significance of the lexical and grammatical details of the Hebrew, Aramaic and Greek texts. At the same time, they have striven for more that a word-for-word translation. Because thought patterns and syntax differ from language to language, faithful communication of the meaning of the writers of the Bible demands frequent modifications in sentence structure and constant regard for the contextual meanings of words.

A sensitive feeling for the style does not always accompany scholarship. Accordingly the Committee on Bible Translation submitted the developing version to a number of stylistic consultants. Two of them read every book of both Old and New Testaments twice—once before and once after the last major revision—and made invaluable suggestions. Samples of the translation were tested for clarity and ease of reading by various kinds of people—young and old, highly educated and less well educated, ministers and laymen.

Concern for clear and natural English—that the New International Version should be idiomatic but not idiosyncratic, contemporary but not dated—motivated the translators and consultants. At the same time, they tried to reflect the differing styles of the biblical writers. In view of the international use of English, the translators sought to avoid obvious Americanisms on the one hand and obvious Anglicisms on the other. A British edition reflects the comparatively few differences of significant idiom and of spelling.

As for the traditional pronouns "thou," "thee" and "thine" in reference to the Deity, the translators judged that to use the archaisms (along with the old verb forms such as "doest," "wouldest" and "hadst") would violate accuracy in translation. Neither Hebrew, Aramaic nor Greek uses special pronouns for the persons of the Godhead. A present-day translation is not enhanced by forms that in the time of the King James Version were used in everyday speech, whether referring to God or man.

For the Old Testament the standard Hebrew text, the Masoretic Text as published in the latest editions of *Biblia Hebraica*, was used throughout. The Dead Sea Scrolls contain material bearing on an earlier stage of the Hebrew text. They were consulted, as were the Samaritan Pentateuch and the ancient scribal traditions relating to textual changes. Sometimes a variant Hebrew reading in the margin of the Masoretic Text was followed instead of the text itself. Such instances, being variants within the Masoretic tradition, are not specified by footnotes. In rare cases, words in the consonantal text were divided differently from the way they appear in the Masoretic Text. Footnotes indicate this. The translators also consulted the more important early versions—the Septuagint; Aquila, Symmachus and Theodotion; the Vulgate; the Syriac Peshitta; the Targums; and for the Psalms the *Juxta Hebraica* of Jerome. Readings from these versions were occasionally followed where the Masoretic Text seemed doubtful and where accepted principles of textual criticism showed that one or more of these textual witnesses appeared to provide the correct reading. Such instances are footnoted. Sometimes vowel letters and vowel signs did not, in the judgment of the translators, represent the correct vowels for the original consonantal text. Accordingly some words were read with a different set of vowels. These instances are usually not indicated by footnotes.

The Greek text used in translating the New

Testament was an eclectic one. No other piece of ancient literature has such an abundance of manuscript witnesses as does the New Testament. Where existing manuscripts differ, the translators made their choice of readings according to accepted principles of New Testament textual criticism. Footnotes call attention to places where there was uncertainty about what the original text was. The best current printed texts of the Greek New Testament were used.

There is a sense in which the work of translation is never wholly finished. This applies to all great literature and uniquely so to the Bible. In 1973 the New Testament in the New International Version was published. Since then, suggestions for corrections and revisions have been received from various sources. The Committee on Bible Translation carefully considered the suggestions and adopted a number of them. These are incorporated in the first printing of the entire Bible in 1978. Additional revisions were made by Committee on Bible Translation in 1983 and appear in printings after that date.

As in other ancient documents, the precise meaning of the biblical texts is sometimes uncertain. This is more often the case with the Hebrew and Aramaic texts than with the Greek text. Although archaeological and linguistic discoveries in this century aid in understanding difficult passages, some uncertainties remain. The more significant of these have been called to the reader's attention in the footnotes.

In regard to the divine name *YHWH*, commonly referred to as the *Tetragrammaton*, the translators adopted the device used in most English versions of rendering that name as "LORD" in capital letters to distinguish it from *Adonai*, another Hebrew word rendered "Lord," for which small letters are used. Wherever the two names stand together in the Old Testament as a compound name of God, they are rendered "Sovereign LORD."

Because for most readers today the phrase "the LORD of hosts" and "God of hosts" have little meaning, this version renders them "the LORD Almighty" and "God Almighty." These renderings convey the sense of the Hebrew, namely, "he who is sovereign over all the 'hosts' (powers) in heaven and on earth, especially over the 'hosts' (armies) of Israel." For readers unacquainted with Hebrew this does not make clear the distinction between *Sabaoth* ("hosts" or "Almighty") and *Shaddai* (which can also be translated "Almighty"), but the latter occurs infrequently and is always footnoted. When *Adonai* and *YHWH Sabaoth* occur together, they are rendered "the Lord, the LORD Almighty."

As for other proper nouns, the familiar spellings of the King James Version are generally retained. Names traditionally spelled with "ch," except where it is final, are usually spelled in this translation with "k" or "c," since the biblical languages do not have the sound that "ch" frequently indicates in English for example, in *chant*. For well-known name such as Zechariah, however, the traditional spelling has been retained. Variation in the spelling of names in the original languages has usually not been indicated. Where a person or place has two or more different names in the Hebrew, Aramaic or Greek texts, the more familiar one has generally been used, with footnotes where needed.

To achieve clarity the translators sometimes supplied words not in the original texts but required by the context. If there was uncertainty about such material, it is enclosed in brackets. Also for the sake of clarity or style, nouns, including some proper nouns, are sometimes substituted for pronouns, and vice versa.

And though the Hebrew writers often shifted back and forth between first, second and third personal pronouns without change of antecedent, this translation often makes them uniform, in accordance with English style and without the use of footnotes.

Poetical passages are printed as poetry, that is, with indentation of lines and with separate stanzas. These are generally designed to reflect the structure of Hebrew poetry. This poetry is normally characterized by parallelism in balanced lines. Most of the poetry in the Bible is in the Old Testament, and scholars differ regarding the scansion of Hebrew lines. The translators determined the stanza divisions for the most part by analysis of the subject matter. The stanzas therefore serve as poetic paragraphs.

As an aid to the reader, italicized sectional headings are inserted in most of the books. They are not to be regarded as part of the NIV text, are not for oral reading, and are not intended to dictate the interpretation of the sections they head.

The footnotes in this version are of several kinds, most of which need no explanation. Those giving alternative translations begin with "Or" and generally introduce the alternative with the last word preceding it in the text, except when it is a single-word alternative; in poetry quoted in a footnote a slant mark indicates a line division. Footnotes introduced by "Or" do not have uniform significance. In some cases two possible translations were considered to have about equal validity. In other cases, though the translators were convinced that the translation in the text was correct, they judged that another interpretation was possible and of sufficient importance to be represented in a footnote.

In the New Testament, footnotes that refer to uncertainty regarding the original text are introduced by "Some manuscripts" or similar expressions. In the Old Testament, evidence for the reading chosen is given first and evidence for the alternative is added after a semicolon (for example: Septuagint; Hebrew *father*). In such notes the term "Hebrew" refers to the Masoretic Text.

It should be noted that minerals, flora and fauna, architectural details, articles of clothing and jewelry, musical instruments and other articles cannot always be identified with precision. Also measures of capacity in the biblical period are particularly uncertain (see the table of weights and measures following the text).

Like all translations of the Bible, made as they are by imperfect man, this one undoubtedly falls short of its goals. Yet we are grateful to God for the extent to which he has enabled us to realize these goals and for the strength he has given us and our colleagues to complete our task. We offer this version of the Bible to him in whose name and for whose glory it has been made. We pray that it will lead many into a better understanding of the Holy Scriptures and a fuller knowledge of Jesus Christ the incarnate Word, of whom the Scriptures so faithfully testify.

The Committee on Bible Translation

June 1978
(Revised August 1983)

Names of the translators and editors may be secured from International Bible Society, translation sponsor of the New Interantional Version, P.O. Box 62970, Colorado Springs, CO 80921-3696 U.S.A.

目錄

Contents

附加資料目錄

Contents : Maps & Tables

新約   **NEW TESTAMENT**

Contents : Maps & Tables

舊約
OLD TESTAMENT

表一：舊約中神的稱呼
TABLE 1 : FORMS OF ADDRESS OF GOD IN OLD TESTAMENT

神的稱呼 (原文譯音) Form of Address of God (Transliteration)	中譯 English Translation	經文 Reference
以利 (伊勒)，伊羅興， 以羅伊 El, Elohim, Eloi	神 God	創 Ge 1:1 民 Nu 23:19 可 Mk 15:34
雅巍 (也威，雅威)， 耶和華 Yahweh, YHWH, Jehovah	主 The LORD	創 Ge 2:4 出 Ex 6:2, 3 (該 Ha 1:2)
以利以利安 (伊勒以羅安) El Elyon	至高神 (God) Most High	創 Ge 14:17-20 民 Nu 24:16 詩 Ps 91:1 賽 Isa 14:14
以利沙代 (伊勒沙代) El Shaddai	全能的神 God Almighty	創 Ge 17:1 詩 Ps 91:1
亞杜乃 (阿道迺) Adonai	主 The LORD	申 Dt 6:4 (瑪 Mal 4:5)
耶和華以羅欣以色列 Yahweh Elohe Yisrael	耶和華以色列的神 The LORD, the God of Israel	士 Jdg 5:3 賽 Isa 17:6 番 Zep 2:9
夸多樹以色列 Qedosh Yisrael	以色列的聖者 Holy One of Israel	賽 Isa 1:4
耶和華沙巴阿 Yahweh Sabaoth	萬軍 （天上與地上）之耶和華 LORD Almighty (both heavenly and earthly)	賽 Isa 6:1-3 亞 Zec 14:21
以利奧林 El Olam	永在的神 Everlasting God	賽 Isa 40:28-31
耶和華齊肯努 Yahweh Tsidkenu	耶和華我們的義 The LORD Our Righteousness	耶 Jer 23:6
亞鐵約緬 Attiq Yomin	亙古常在者 Ancient of Days	但 Da 7:9
伊勒夸尼 （以利夸努） El Kannoh	忌邪者，忌邪的神 Jealous, Jealous God	出 Ex 20:5; 34:14

表一：舊約中神的稱呼

TABLE 1 : FORMS OF ADDRESS OF GOD IN OLD TESTAMENT

意義	Significance
指神的權能與力量，祂是至高的真神	Refers to God's power and might; He is the only supreme and true God
聖者的專名，為以色列立約之神	Proper name of the divine one
祂在萬神之上，至高至聖	He is above all gods; nothing is more sacred.
神是全能的	God is all-powerful
唯獨神是萬有之首	God alone is the head over all
祂是國家的神	He is the God of nation
神在道德上是完美無缺的	God is morally perfect
神是我們的救主和保護者	God is our savior and protector
神是永恆、永活的	God is eternal. He will never die
神是我們公義行為的標準，祂能使我們公正無私	God is our standard for right behavior; He can make us righteous
神是最終的權威；有一天祂要審判列國	God is the ultimate authority; He will judge all nations one day
單要敬拜與侍奉祂	Only worship and serve Him

表二：列王先知對照表
TABLE 2 : KINGS AND PROPHETS

猶大 JUDAH			公元前		以色列 ISRAEL	
先知 Prophet	王 King	作王年期	B.C.	Ruling Year	王 King	先知 Prophet
易多 Iddo 935-911	羅波安 Rehoboam 930-913	17	930 — 920	22 / I	耶羅波安一世 Jeroboam I 930-909	亞希雅 Ahijah 934-909
示瑪雅 Shemaiah 931-911	亞比雅 Abijah 913-910	3	910	2	拿答 Nadab 909-908	
亞撒利雅 Azariah 911-885	亞撒 Asa 910-869	41	900 — 890	24 / II	巴沙 Baasha 908-886	
哈拿尼 Hanani 890-870			880	2 / III 12	以拉 Elah 886-885	耶戶 Jehu 890-848 ★ ★★
耶戶 Jehu 890-848			870		暗利 Omri 885-874	
雅哈悉 Jahaziel around 853前後	約沙法 Jehoshaphat 872-848	25	860	22 / IV	亞哈 Ahab 874-853	以利亞 Elijah 875-848
以利以謝 Eliezer around 853前後	約蘭 Jehoram 853-841	12	850	2 12	亞哈謝 Ahaziah 853-852 約蘭 Joram 852-841	
俄巴底亞 Obadiah 855-840(?)	亞哈謝 Ahaziah 841 亞她利雅 Athaliah 841-835	1 6	840	28	耶戶 Jehu 841-814	以利沙 Elisha 848-797
	約阿施 Joash 835-796	40	830 — 820			
約珥 Joel 835-796(?)			810	17 / V	約哈斯 Jehoahaz 814-798	
	亞瑪謝 Amaziah 796-767	29	800 — 790	16	約阿施 Jehoash 798-782	
			780		耶羅波安二世 Jeroboam II 793-753	約拿 Jonah 793-753
	亞撒利雅 Azariah (烏西雅 Uzziah) 792-740	52	770 — 760	41		
			750	1/2 / VI	撒迦利雅 Zechariah 753	阿摩司 Amos 760-750 ★★★
彌迦 Micah 742-687	約坦 Jotham 750-735	16	740	10 / VII 2	米拿現 Menahem 753-742 比加轄 Pekahiah 742-740	何西阿 Hosea 753-715
以賽亞 Isaiah 740-681	亞哈斯 Ahaz 735-719	16	730	20 / VIII 9 / IX	比加 Pekah 750-730 何細亞 Hoshea 730-722	
	希西家 Hezekiah 727-697	29	720 — 710			

公元前722年，北國亡於亞述手
Israel conquered by Assyria in 722B.C.

表二：列王先知對照表（續）
TABLE 2：KINGS AND PROPHETS (CONTINUED)

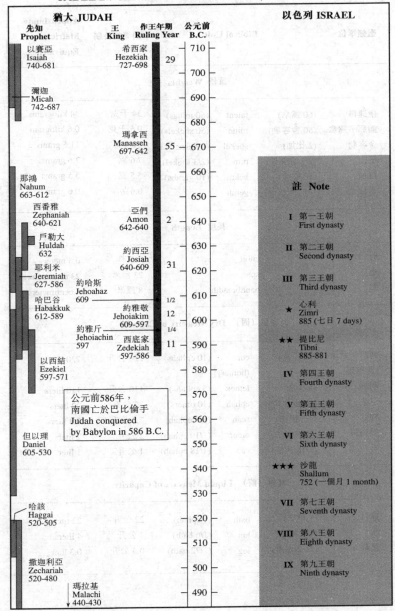

表三：度量衡換算表
TABLE 3 : WEIGHTS AND MEASURES

聖經單位		Biblical Unit		約等於公制	Approximate Metric Equivalent
重量 Weights					
他連得	(60 彌拿)	talent	(60 minas)	34 千克	34 kilograms
彌那，彌拿	(50 舍客勒)	mina	(50 shekels)	0.6 千克	0.6 kilogram
舍客勒	(2 比加)	shekel	(2 bekas)	11.5 克	11.5 grams
平因	(2/3 舍客勒)	pim	(2/3 shekel)	7.6 克	7.6 grams
比加	(10 季拉)	beka	(10 gerahs)	5.5 克	5.5 grams
季拉		gerah		0.6克	0.6 gram
長度 Length					
肘		cubit		0.5 米	0.5 meter
虎口		span		23 厘米	23 centimeters
掌		handbreadth		8 厘米	8 centimeters
容量（固） Dry Measure of Capacity					
柯珥，歌珥 (賀梅珥)	(10 伊法)	cor (homer)	(10 ephahs)	220 公升	220 liters
利帖	(5 伊法)	lethek	(5 ephahs)	110 公升	110 liters
伊法	(10 俄梅珥)	ephah	(10 omers)	22 公升	22 liters
細亞	(1/3 伊法)	seah	(1/3 ephah)	7.3 公升	7.3 liters
俄梅珥	(1/10 伊法)	omer	(1/10 ephah)	2 公升	2 liters
升	(1/18 伊法)	cab	(1/18 ephah)	1 公升	1 liter
容量（液） Liquid Measure of Capacity					
罷特	(1 伊法)	bath	(1 ephah)	22 公升	22 liters
欣	(1/6 罷特)	hin	(1/6 bath)	4 公升	4 liters
羅革	(1/72 罷特)	log	(1/72 bath)	0.3 公升	0.3 liter

表四：八個希伯來法律用詞
TABLE 4：8 HEBREW WORDS FOR LAW

用詞 (音譯) Word (Trans- literation)	詞義 Meaning	經文 Reference	意義 Significance
妥拉 Torah	方向，指導，指令 Direction, guidance, instruction	出 Ex 24:12; 賽 Isa 30:20	一般社會需要法律，由掌權者頒發 Need for law in general; a command from a higher person to a lower
密資華 Mitswah	誡命，命令 Commandment, command	創 Ge 26:5; 出 Ex 15:26; 申 Dt 5:31	是神特別頒發給人遵守的，有別於 一般法律，多指十誡 God's specific instruction to be obeyed rather than a general law; used of the Ten Commandments
密士拍 Mishpat	判斷，法令 Judgment, ordinance	創 Ge 18:19; 申 Dt 16:18; 17:9; 32:4	指民法，社會法及衛生法 Refers to civil, social, and sanitation law
伊杜夫 Eduth	訓誡，證明 Admonition, testimony	出 Ex 25:22; 詩 Ps 19:7; 王下 2Ki 17:15	指神所頒與祂子民的法律 Refers to God's law as he deals with his people
胡黔 Huqqim	法令，神諭 Statutes, oracles	利 Lev 18:5; 申 Dt 4:1	指皇室法庭諭令、判詞，多用於崇 拜與節期上 Dealt with royal pronouncements; mainly connected to worship and feasts
披固點 Piqqudim	命令，訓詞 Orders, precepts	詩 Ps 19:8; 103:18	多用於詩篇中描述神的命令 Used often in the psalms to describe God's orders and assignments
達巴 Dabar	口令 Words	出 Ex 34:28; 申 Dt 4:12	用以指出神聖的曉諭與啟示 Used to indicate divine oracles or revelations of God
達夫 Dath	皇令，公法 Royal edict, public law	結 Eze 7:26; 但 Da 2:9, 15; 6:8, 12	指猶太人一般的宗教傳統或神聖的 法律 Refers to the divine law or Jewish religious traditions in general

圖一：以色列地十二支派分佈圖
MAP 1 : LAND OF THE TWELVE TRIBES

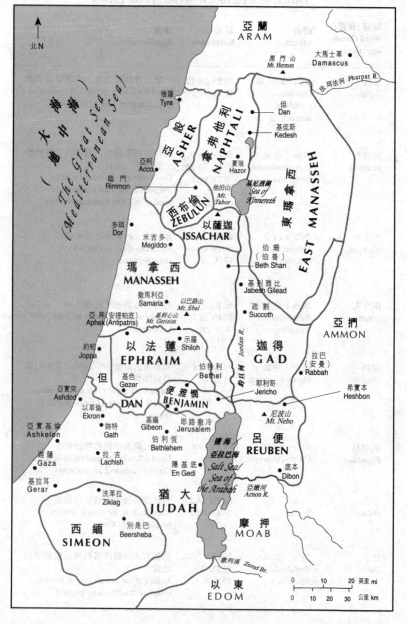

Genesis

The Beginning

1 In the beginning God created the heavens and the earth. [2]Now the earth was[a] formless and empty, darkness was over the surface of the deep, and the Spirit of God was hovering over the waters.

[3]And God said, "Let there be light," and there was light. [4]God saw that the light was good, and he separated the light from the darkness. [5]God called the light "day," and the darkness he called "night." And there was evening, and there was morning—the first day.

[6]And God said, "Let there be an expanse between the waters to separate water from water." [7]So God made the expanse and separated the water under the expanse from the water above it. And it was so. [8]God called the expanse "sky." And there was evening, and there was morning—the second day.

[9]And God said, "Let the water under the sky be gathered to one place, and let dry ground appear." And it was so. [10]God called the dry ground "land," and the gathered waters he called "seas." And God saw that it was good.

[11]Then God said, "Let the land produce vegetation: seed-bearing plants and trees on the land that bear fruit with seed in it, according to their various kinds." And it was so. [12]The land produced vegetation: plants bearing seed according to their kinds and trees bearing fruit with seed in it according to their kinds. And God saw that it was good. [13]And there was evening, and there was morning—the third day.

[14]And God said, "Let there be lights in the expanse of the sky to separate the day from the night, and let them serve as signs to mark seasons and days and years, [15]and let them be lights in the expanse of the sky to give light on the earth." And it was so. [16]God made two great lights—the greater light to govern the day and the lesser light

a 2 Or possibly *became*

創世記

起初

1 起初神創造天地。[2]地是空虛混沌，淵面黑暗；神的靈運行在水面上。

[3]神説："要有光"，就有了光。[4]神看光是好的，就把光暗分開了。[5]神稱光為晝，稱暗為夜。有晚上，有早晨，這是頭一日。

[6]神説："諸水之間要有空氣，將水分為上下。"[7]神就造出空氣，將空氣以下的水、空氣以上的水分開了。事就這樣成了。[8]神稱空氣為天。有晚上，有早晨，是第二日。

[9]神説："天下的水要聚在一處，使旱地露出來。"事就這樣成了。[10]神稱旱地為地，稱水的聚處為海。神看着是好的。

[11]神説："地要發生青草和結種子的菜蔬，並結果子的樹木，各從其類，果子都包着核。"事就這樣成了。[12]於是地發生了青草和結種子的菜蔬，各從其類；並結果子的樹木，各從其類，果子都包着核。神看着是好的。[13]有晚上，有早晨，是第三日。

[14]神説："天上要有光體，可以分晝夜，作記號，定節令、日子、年歲，[15]並要發光在天空，普照在地上。"事就這樣成了。[16]於是神造了兩個大光，大的管晝，小

的管夜，又造眾星，¹⁷就把這些光擺列在天空，普照在地上，¹⁸管理晝夜，分別明暗。神看着是好的。¹⁹有晚上，有早晨，是第四日。

²⁰神說："水要多多滋生有生命的物，要有雀鳥飛在地面以上，天空之中。"²¹神就造出大魚和水中所滋生各樣有生命的動物，各從其類；又造出各樣飛鳥，各從其類。神看着是好的。²²神就賜福給這一切，說："滋生繁多，充滿海中的水，雀鳥也要多生在地上。"²³有晚上，有早晨，是第五日。

²⁴神說："地要生出活物來，各從其類；牲畜、昆蟲、野獸，各從其類。"事就這樣成了。²⁵於是神造出野獸，各從其類；牲畜，各從其類；地上一切昆蟲，各從其類。神看着是好的。

²⁶神說："我們要照着我們的形像，按着我們的樣式造人，使他們管理海裏的魚、空中的鳥、地上的牲畜和全地，並地上所爬的一切昆蟲。"

²⁷神就照着自己的形像造人，乃是照着他的形像造男造女。

²⁸神就賜福給他們，又對他們說："要生養眾多，遍滿地面，治理這地；也要管理海裏的魚、空中的鳥，和地上各樣行動的活物。"

²⁹神說："看哪，我將遍地上一切結種子的菜蔬，和一切樹上所結有核的果子，全賜給你們作食物。³⁰至於地上的走獸和空中的飛鳥，並各樣爬在地上有生命的物，我將青草賜給

to govern the night. He also made the stars. ¹⁷God set them in the expanse of the sky to give light on the earth, ¹⁸to govern the day and the night, and to separate light from darkness. And God saw that it was good. ¹⁹And there was evening, and there was morning—the fourth day.

²⁰And God said, "Let the water teem with living creatures, and let birds fly above the earth across the expanse of the sky." ²¹So God created the great creatures of the sea and every living and moving thing with which the water teems, according to their kinds, and every winged bird according to its kind. And God saw that it was good. ²²God blessed them and said, "Be fruitful and increase in number and fill the water in the seas, and let the birds increase on the earth." ²³And there was evening, and there was morning—the fifth day.

²⁴And God said, "Let the land produce living creatures according to their kinds: livestock, creatures that move along the ground, and wild animals, each according to its kind." And it was so. ²⁵God made the wild animals according to their kinds, the livestock according to their kinds, and all the creatures that move along the ground according to their kinds. And God saw that it was good.

²⁶Then God said, "Let us make man in our image, in our likeness, and let them rule over the fish of the sea and the birds of the air, over the livestock, over all the earth,ᵃ and over all the creatures that move along the ground."

²⁷So God created man in his own image,
in the image of God he created him;
male and female he created them.

²⁸God blessed them and said to them, "Be fruitful and increase in number; fill the earth and subdue it. Rule over the fish of the sea and the birds of the air and over every living creature that moves on the ground."

²⁹Then God said, "I give you every seed-bearing plant on the face of the whole earth and every tree that has fruit with seed in it. They will be yours for food. ³⁰And to all the beasts of the earth and all the birds of the air and all the creatures that move along the ground—everything that has the breath of

a 26 Hebrew; Syriac all the wild animals

life in it—I give every green plant for food."
And it was so.

³¹God saw all that he had made, and it
was very good. And there was evening, and
there was morning—the sixth day.

2 Thus the heavens and the earth were
completed in all their vast array.

²By the seventh day God had finished the work
he had been doing; so on the seventh day
he rested^a from all his work. ³And God
blessed the seventh day and made it holy,
because on it he rested from all the work of
creating that he had done.

Adam and Eve

⁴This is the account of the heavens and the
earth when they were created.

When the LORD God made the earth and the
heavens— ⁵and no shrub of the field had yet
appeared on the earth^b and no plant of the field
had yet sprung up, for the LORD God had not
sent rain on the earth^b and there was no man to
work the ground, ⁶but streams^c came up from
the earth and watered the whole surface of the
ground— ⁷the LORD God formed the man^d from
the dust of the ground and breathed into his
nostrils the breath of life, and the man became a
living being.

⁸Now the LORD God had planted a garden in
the east, in Eden; and there he put the man he
had formed. ⁹And the LORD God made all kinds
of trees grow out of the ground—trees that were
pleasing to the eye and good for food. In the
middle of the garden were the tree of life and
the tree of the knowledge of good and evil.

¹⁰A river watering the garden flowed from
Eden; from there it was separated into four
headwaters. ¹¹The name of the first is the
Pishon; it winds through the entire land of
Havilah, where there is gold. ¹²(The gold of that
land is good; aromatic resin^e and onyx are also
there.) ¹³The name of the second river is the
Gihon; it winds through the entire land of
Cush.^f ¹⁴The name of the third river is the
Tigris; it runs along the east side of Asshur. And
the fourth river is the Euphrates.

¹⁵The LORD God took the man and put him in

---

a 2 Or *ceased; also in verse 3*   *b 5* Or *land; also in verse 6*
c 6 Or *mist*   *d 7* The Hebrew for *man (adam)* sounds like and
may be related to the Hebrew for *ground (adamah);* it is also the
name *Adam* (see Gen. 2:20).   *e 12* Or *good; pearls*
f 13 Possibly southeast Mesopotamia

牠們作食物。"事就這樣成了。

³¹神看着一切所造的都甚
好。有晚上,有早晨,是第六
日。

2 天地萬物都造齊了。

²到第七日,神造物的工已經完畢,
就在第七日歇了他一切的工,安
息了。³神賜福給第七日,定為
聖日,因為在這日神歇了他一切
創造的工,就安息了。

亞當與夏娃

⁴創造天地的來歷:

在耶和華神造天地的日子,乃是
這樣,⁵野地還沒有草木,田間的菜
蔬還沒有長起來,因為耶和華神還沒
有降雨在地上,也沒有人耕地,⁶但
有霧氣從地上騰,滋潤遍地。⁷耶和
華神用地上的塵土造人,將生氣吹在
他鼻孔裏,他就成了有靈的活人,名
叫<u>亞當</u>。

⁸耶和華神在東方的<u>伊甸</u>立了一
個園子,把所造的人安置在那裏。
⁹耶和華神使各樣的樹從地裏長出
來,可以悅人的眼目,其上的果子好
作食物。園子當中又有生命樹和分別
善惡的樹。

¹⁰有河從<u>伊甸</u>流出來滋潤那園
子,從那裏分為四道:¹¹第一道名叫
<u>比遜</u>,就是環繞哈腓拉全地的。在那
裏有金子,¹²並且那地的金子是好
的;在那裏又有珍珠和紅瑪瑙。¹³第
二道河名叫<u>基訓</u>,就是環繞<u>古實</u>全地
的。¹⁴第三道河名叫<u>底格里斯</u>,流在
<u>亞述</u>的東邊,第四道河就是<u>幼發拉底
河</u>。

¹⁵耶和華神將那人安置在<u>伊甸</u>

圍，使他修理看守。¹⁶耶和華神吩咐他説："園中各樣樹上的果子，你可以隨意吃，¹⁷只是分別善惡樹上的果子，你不可吃，因為你吃的日子必定死。"

¹⁸耶和華神説："那人獨居不好，我要為他造一個配偶幫助他。"

¹⁹耶和華神用土所造成的野地各樣走獸和空中各樣飛鳥都帶到那人面前，看他叫甚麼。那人怎樣叫各樣的活物，那就是牠的名字。²⁰那人便給一切牲畜和空中飛鳥、野地走獸都起了名。

只是那人沒有遇見配偶幫助他；²¹耶和華神使他沉睡，他就睡了；於是取下他的一條肋骨，又把肉合起來。²²耶和華神就用那人身上所取的肋骨造成一個女人，領她到那人跟前。

²³那人説：

"這是我骨中的骨，
　肉中的肉，
　可以稱她為女人，
　因為她是從男人身上取出來的。"

²⁴因此，人要離開父母與妻子連合，二人成為一體。

²⁵當時夫妻二人赤身露體，並不羞恥。

人類犯罪

3 耶和華神所造的，惟有蛇比田野一切的活物更狡猾。蛇對女人説："神豈是真説不許你們吃園中所有樹上的果子嗎？"

²女人對蛇説："園中樹上的果子，我們可以吃，³惟有園當中那棵樹上的果子，神曾説：'你們不可吃，也不可摸，免得你們死。'"

⁴蛇對女人説："你們不一定死，⁵因為神知道，你們吃的日子眼睛就明亮了，你們便如神能知道善惡。"

⁶於是，女人見那棵樹的果子好作

the Garden of Eden to work it and take care of it. ¹⁶And the LORD God commanded the man, "You are free to eat from any tree in the garden; ¹⁷but you must not eat from the tree of the knowledge of good and evil, for when you eat of it you will surely die."

¹⁸The LORD God said, "It is not good for the man to be alone. I will make a helper suitable for him."

¹⁹Now the LORD God had formed out of the ground all the beasts of the field and all the birds of the air. He brought them to the man to see what he would name them; and whatever the man called each living creature, that was its name. ²⁰So the man gave names to all the livestock, the birds of the air and all the beasts of the field.

But for Adam[a] no suitable helper was found. ²¹So the LORD God caused the man to fall into a deep sleep; and while he was sleeping, he took one of the man's ribs[b] and closed up the place with flesh. ²²Then the LORD God made a woman from the rib[c] he had taken out of the man, and he brought her to the man.

²³The man said,

"This is now bone of my bones
　and flesh of my flesh;
she shall be called 'woman,[d] '
　for she was taken out of man."

²⁴For this reason a man will leave his father and mother and be united to his wife, and they will become one flesh.

²⁵The man and his wife were both naked, and they felt no shame.

The Fall of Man

3 Now the serpent was more crafty than any of the wild animals the LORD God had made. He said to the woman, "Did God really say, 'You must not eat from any tree in the garden'?"

²The woman said to the serpent, "We may eat fruit from the trees in the garden, ³but God did say, 'You must not eat fruit from the tree that is in the middle of the garden, and you must not touch it, or you will die.'"

⁴"You will not surely die," the serpent said to the woman. ⁵"For God knows that when you eat of it your eyes will be opened, and you will be like God, knowing good and evil."

⁶When the woman saw that the fruit of the

---

a 20 Or *the man*　*b 21* Or *took part of the man's side*　*c 22* Or *part*
d 23 The Hebrew for *woman* sounds like the Hebrew for *man*.

tree was good for food and pleasing to the eye, and also desirable for gaining wisdom, she took some and ate it. She also gave some to her husband, who was with her, and he ate it. ⁷Then the eyes of both of them were opened, and they realized they were naked; so they sewed fig leaves together and made coverings for themselves.

⁸Then the man and his wife heard the sound of the LORD God as he was walking in the garden in the cool of the day, and they hid from the LORD God among the trees of the garden. ⁹But the LORD God called to the man, "Where are you?"

¹⁰He answered, "I heard you in the garden, and I was afraid because I was naked; so I hid."

¹¹And he said, "Who told you that you were naked? Have you eaten from the tree that I commanded you not to eat from?"

¹²The man said, "The woman you put here with me—she gave me some fruit from the tree, and I ate it."

¹³Then the LORD God said to the woman, "What is this you have done?"

The woman said, "The serpent deceived me, and I ate."

¹⁴So the LORD God said to the serpent, "Because you have done this,

"Cursed are you above all the livestock
　　and all the wild animals!
You will crawl on your belly
　　and you will eat dust
　　all the days of your life.
¹⁵And I will put enmity
　　between you and the woman,
　　and between your offspring*a* and hers;
he will crush*b* your head,
　　and you will strike his heel."

¹⁶To the woman he said,

"I will greatly increase your pains in
　　childbearing;
　　with pain you will give birth to children.
Your desire will be for your husband,
　　and he will rule over you."

¹⁷To Adam he said, "Because you listened to your wife and ate from the tree about which I commanded you, 'You must not eat of it,'

"Cursed is the ground because of you;
　　through painful toil you will eat of it

a 15 Or seed　b 15 Or strike

食物，也悦人的眼目，且是可喜愛的，能使人有智慧，就摘下果子來吃了；又給她丈夫，她丈夫也吃了。⁷他們二人的眼睛就明亮了，才知道自己是赤身露體，便拿無花果樹的葉子，為自己編做裙子。

⁸天起了涼風，耶和華神在園中行走。那人和他妻子聽見神的聲音，就藏在園裏的樹木中，躲避耶和華神的面。⁹耶和華神呼喚那人，對他説："你在哪裏？"

¹⁰他説："我在園中聽見你的聲音，我就害怕，因為我赤身露體，我便藏了。"

¹¹耶和華説："誰告訴你赤身露體呢？莫非你吃了我吩咐你不可吃的那樹上的果子嗎？"

¹²那人説："你所賜給我、與我同居的女人，她把那樹上的果子給我，我就吃了。"

¹³耶和華神對女人説："你做的是甚麼事呢？"

女人説："那蛇引誘我，我就吃了。"

¹⁴耶和華神對蛇説："你既做了這事，

"就必受咒詛，
　　比一切的牲畜野獸更甚！
你必用肚子行走，
　　終身吃土。

¹⁵我又要叫你和女人彼此為仇；
　　你的後裔和女人的後裔
　　也彼此為仇。
女人的後裔要傷你的頭；
　　你要傷他的腳跟。"

¹⁶又對女人説：

"我必多多加增你懷胎的苦楚，
　　你生產兒女必多受苦楚。
你必戀慕你丈夫，
　　你丈夫必管轄你。"

¹⁷又對亞當説："你既聽從妻子的話，吃了我所吩咐你不可吃的那樹上的果子，

"地必為你的緣故受咒詛；
　　你必終身勞苦，

才能從地裏得吃的。

18 地必給你長出荊棘和蒺藜來，
　你也要吃田間的菜蔬。

19 你必汗流滿面才得糊口，
　直到你歸於土，
　因為你是從土而出的。
　你本是塵土，
　仍要歸於塵土。"

20 亞當給他妻子起名叫夏娃，因為她是眾生之母。

21 耶和華神為亞當和他妻子用皮子做衣服給他們穿。22 耶和華神說："那人已經與我們相似，能知道善惡。現在恐怕他伸手又摘生命樹的果子吃，就永遠活着。" 23 耶和華神便打發他出伊甸園去，耕種他所自出之土。24 於是把他趕出去了。又在伊甸園的東邊安設基路伯，和四面轉動發火焰的劍，要把守生命樹的道路。

該隱與亞伯

4 有一日，那人和他妻子夏娃同房，夏娃就懷孕，生了該隱（註：就是"得"的意思），便說："耶和華使我得了一個男子。" 2 又生了該隱的兄弟亞伯。

亞伯是牧羊的，該隱是種地的。3 有一日，該隱拿地裏的出產為供物獻給耶和華；4 亞伯也將他羊群中頭生的和羊的脂油獻上。耶和華看中了亞伯和他的供物，5 只是看不中該隱和他的供物。該隱就大大地發怒，變了臉色。

6 耶和華對該隱說："你為甚麼發怒呢？你為甚麼變了臉色呢？7 你若行得好，豈不蒙悅納？你若行得不好，罪就伏在門前。它必戀慕你，你卻要制伏它。"

8 該隱與他兄弟亞伯說話，二人正在田間，該隱起來打他兄弟亞伯，把他殺了。

all the days of your life.

18 It will produce thorns and thistles for you,
　and you will eat the plants of the field.

19 By the sweat of your brow
　you will eat your food
　until you return to the ground,
　since from it you were taken;
　for dust you are
　and to dust you will return."

20 Adam*a* named his wife Eve,*b* because she would become the mother of all the living.

21 The LORD God made garments of skin for Adam and his wife and clothed them. 22 And the LORD God said, "The man has now become like one of us, knowing good and evil. He must not be allowed to reach out his hand and take also from the tree of life and eat, and live forever." 23 So the LORD God banished him from the Garden of Eden to work the ground from which he had been taken. 24 After he drove the man out, he placed on the east side*c* of the Garden of Eden cherubim and a flaming sword flashing back and forth to guard the way to the tree of life.

Cain and Abel

4 Adam*a* lay with his wife Eve, and she became pregnant and gave birth to Cain.*d* She said, "With the help of the LORD I have brought forth*e* a man." 2 Later she gave birth to his brother Abel.

Now Abel kept flocks, and Cain worked the soil. 3 In the course of time Cain brought some of the fruits of the soil as an offering to the LORD. 4 But Abel brought fat portions from some of the firstborn of his flock. The LORD looked with favor on Abel and his offering, 5 but on Cain and his offering he did not look with favor. So Cain was very angry, and his face was downcast.

6 Then the LORD said to Cain, "Why are you angry? Why is your face downcast? 7 If you do what is right, will you not be accepted? But if you do not do what is right, sin is crouching at your door; it desires to have you, but you must master it."

8 Now Cain said to his brother Abel, "Let's go out to the field."*f* And while they were in the field, Cain attacked his brother Abel and killed him.

a 20 , *1 Or The man*   *b 20 Eve* probably means *living.*
c 24 Or placed in front   *d 1 Cain* sounds like the Hebrew for
brought forth or *acquired.*   *e 1 Or have acquired*
f 8 Samaritan Pentateuch, Septuagint, Vulgate and Syriac;
Masoretic Text does not have *"Let's go out to the field."*

⁹Then the LORD said to Cain, "Where is your brother Abel?"

"I don't know," he replied. "Am I my brother's keeper?"

¹⁰The LORD said, "What have you done? Listen! Your brother's blood cries out to me from the ground. ¹¹Now you are under a curse and driven from the ground, which opened its mouth to receive your brother's blood from your hand. ¹²When you work the ground, it will no longer yield its crops for you. You will be a restless wanderer on the earth."

¹³Cain said to the LORD, "My punishment is more than I can bear. ¹⁴Today you are driving me from the land, and I will be hidden from your presence; I will be a restless wanderer on the earth, and whoever finds me will kill me."

¹⁵But the LORD said to him, "Not so*ᵃ*; if anyone kills Cain, he will suffer vengeance seven times over." Then the LORD put a mark on Cain so that no one who found him would kill him. ¹⁶So Cain went out from the LORD's presence and lived in the land of Nod,*ᵇ* east of Eden.

¹⁷Cain lay with his wife, and she became pregnant and gave birth to Enoch. Cain was then building a city, and he named it after his son Enoch. ¹⁸To Enoch was born Irad, and Irad was the father of Mehujael, and Mehujael was the father of Methushael, and Methushael was the father of Lamech.

¹⁹Lamech married two women, one named Adah and the other Zillah. ²⁰Adah gave birth to Jabal; he was the father of those who live in tents and raise livestock. ²¹His brother's name was Jubal; he was the father of all who play the harp and flute. ²²Zillah also had a son, Tubal-Cain, who forged all kinds of tools out of*ᶜ* bronze and iron. Tubal-Cain's sister was Naamah.

²³Lamech said to his wives,

"Adah and Zillah, listen to me;
    wives of Lamech, hear my words.
I have killed*ᵈ* a man for wounding me,
    a young man for injuring me.
²⁴If Cain is avenged seven times,
    then Lamech seventy-seven times."

²⁵Adam lay with his wife again, and she gave birth to a son and named him Seth,*ᵉ* saying, "God has granted me another child in place of

⁹耶和華對該隱說："你兄弟亞伯在哪裏？"

他說："我不知道！我豈是看守我兄弟的嗎？"

¹⁰耶和華說："你做了甚麼事呢？你兄弟的血有聲音從地裏向我哀告。¹¹地開了口，從你手裏接受你兄弟的血。現在你必從這地受咒詛。¹²你種地，地不再給你效力，你必流離飄蕩在地上。"

¹³該隱對耶和華說："我的刑罰太重，過於我所能當的。¹⁴你如今趕逐我離開這地，以致不見你面。我必流離飄蕩在地上，凡遇見我的必殺我。"

¹⁵耶和華對他說："凡殺該隱的，必遭報七倍。"耶和華就給該隱立一個記號，免得人遇見他就殺他。¹⁶於是該隱離開耶和華的面，去住在伊甸東邊挪得之地。

¹⁷該隱與妻子同房，他妻子就懷孕，生了以諾。該隱建造了一座城，就按著他兒子的名，將那城叫做以諾。¹⁸以諾生以拿；以拿生米戶雅利；米戶雅利生瑪土撒利；瑪土撒利生拉麥。

¹⁹拉麥娶了兩個妻，一個名叫亞大，一個名叫洗拉。²⁰亞大生雅八，雅八就是住帳棚、牧養牲畜之人的祖師。²¹雅八的兄弟名叫猶八，他是一切彈琴吹簫之人的祖師。²²洗拉又生了土八該隱，他是打造各樣銅鐵利器的（註：或作"是銅匠、鐵匠的祖師"）。土八該隱的妹子是拿瑪。

²³拉麥對他兩個妻子說：
"亞大、洗拉，聽我的聲音；
拉麥的妻子細聽我的話語：
壯年人傷我，我把他殺了；
少年人損我，我把他害了（註：或作
    "我殺壯士卻傷自己；我害幼童卻損本
    身"）。
²⁴若殺該隱，遭報七倍；
殺拉麥，必遭報七十七倍。"

²⁵亞當又與妻子同房，她就生了一個兒子，起名叫塞特，意思說："神另給我立了一個兒子代替亞伯，

---

a 15 Septuagint, Vulgate and Syriac; Hebrew *Very well*
b 16 Nod *means* wandering *(see verses 12 and 14).*   *c 22* Or
who instructed all who work in   *d 23* Or *I will kill*
e 25 Seth *probably means* granted.

因為該隱殺了他。”²⁶塞特也生了一個兒子，起名叫以挪士。

那時候，人才求告耶和華的名。

從亞當到挪亞

5 亞當的後代記在下面。

當神造人的日子，是照着自己的樣式造的，²並且造男造女。在他們被造的日子，神賜福給他們，稱他們為人。

³亞當活到一百三十歲，生了一個兒子，形像樣式和自己相似，就給他起名叫塞特。⁴亞當生塞特之後，又在世八百年，並且生兒養女。⁵亞當共活了九百三十歲就死了。

⁶塞特活到一百零五歲，生了以挪士。⁷塞特生以挪士之後，又活了八百零七年，並且生兒養女。⁸塞特共活了九百一十二歲就死了。

⁹以挪士活到九十歲，生了該南。¹⁰以挪士生該南之後，又活了八百一十五年，並且生兒養女。¹¹以挪士共活了九百零五歲就死了。

¹²該南活到七十歲，生了瑪勒列。¹³該南生瑪勒列之後，又活了八百四十年，並且生兒養女。¹⁴該南共活了九百一十歲就死了。

¹⁵瑪勒列活到六十五歲，生了雅列。¹⁶瑪勒列生雅列之後，又活了八百三十年，並且生兒養女。¹⁷瑪勒列共活了八百九十五歲就死了。

¹⁸雅列活到一百六十二歲，生了以諾。¹⁹雅列生以諾之後，又活了八百年，並且生兒養女。²⁰雅列共活了九百六十二歲就死了。

²¹以諾活到六十五歲，生了瑪土撒拉。²²以諾生瑪土撒拉之後，與神同行三百年，並且生兒養女。²³以諾共活了三百六十五歲。²⁴以諾與神同行，神將他取去，他就不在世了。

²⁵瑪土撒拉活到一百八十七歲，生

Abel, since Cain killed him." ²⁶Seth also had a son, and he named him Enosh.

At that time men began to call on^a the name of the LORD.

From Adam to Noah

5 This is the written account of Adam's line.

When God created man, he made him in the likeness of God. ²He created them male and female and blessed them. And when they were created, he called them "man.^{b} "

³When Adam had lived 130 years, he had a son in his own likeness, in his own image; and he named him Seth. ⁴After Seth was born, Adam lived 800 years and had other sons and daughters. ⁵Altogether, Adam lived 930 years, and then he died.

⁶When Seth had lived 105 years, he became the father^c of Enosh. ⁷And after he became the father of Enosh, Seth lived 807 years and had other sons and daughters. ⁸Altogether, Seth lived 912 years, and then he died.

⁹When Enosh had lived 90 years, he became the father of Kenan. ¹⁰And after he became the father of Kenan, Enosh lived 815 years and had other sons and daughters. ¹¹Altogether, Enosh lived 905 years, and then he died.

¹²When Kenan had lived 70 years, he became the father of Mahalalel. ¹³And after he became the father of Mahalalel, Kenan lived 840 years and had other sons and daughters. ¹⁴Altogether, Kenan lived 910 years, and then he died.

¹⁵When Mahalalel had lived 65 years, he became the father of Jared. ¹⁶And after he became the father of Jared, Mahalalel lived 830 years and had other sons and daughters. ¹⁷Altogether, Mahalalel lived 895 years, and then he died.

¹⁸When Jared had lived 162 years, he became the father of Enoch. ¹⁹And after he became the father of Enoch, Jared lived 800 years and had other sons and daughters. ²⁰Altogether, Jared lived 962 years, and then he died.

²¹When Enoch had lived 65 years, he became the father of Methuselah. ²²And after he became the father of Methuselah, Enoch walked with God 300 years and had other sons and daughters. ²³Altogether, Enoch lived 365 years. ²⁴Enoch walked with God; then he was no more, because God took him away.

²⁵When Methuselah had lived 187 years, he

a 26 Or to proclaim   b 2 Hebrew adam   c 6 Father may mean ancestor; also in verses 7-26.

became the father of Lamech. 26And after he became the father of Lamech, Methuselah lived 782 years and had other sons and daughters. 27Altogether, Methuselah lived 969 years, and then he died.

28When Lamech had lived 182 years, he had a son. 29He named him Noah[a] and said, "He will comfort us in the labor and painful toil of our hands caused by the ground the LORD has cursed." 30After Noah was born, Lamech lived 595 years and had other sons and daughters. 31Altogether, Lamech lived 777 years, and then he died.

32After Noah was 500 years old, he became the father of Shem, Ham and Japheth.

The Flood

6 When men began to increase in number on the earth and daughters were born to them, 2the sons of God saw that the daughters of men were beautiful, and they married any of them they chose. 3Then the LORD said, "My Spirit will not contend with[b] man forever, for he is mortal[c] ; his days will be a hundred and twenty years."

4The Nephilim were on the earth in those days—and also afterward—when the sons of God went to the daughters of men and had children by them. They were the heroes of old, men of renown.

5The LORD saw how great man's wickedness on the earth had become, and that every inclination of the thoughts of his heart was only evil all the time. 6The LORD was grieved that he had made man on the earth, and his heart was filled with pain. 7So the LORD said, "I will wipe mankind, whom I have created, from the face of the earth—men and animals, and creatures that move along the ground, and birds of the air— for I am grieved that I have made them." 8But Noah found favor in the eyes of the LORD.

9This is the account of Noah.

Noah was a righteous man, blameless among the people of his time, and he walked with God. 10Noah had three sons: Shem, Ham and Japheth.

11Now the earth was corrupt in God's sight and was full of violence. 12God saw how corrupt the earth had become, for all the people on earth had corrupted their ways. 13So God said to Noah, "I am going to put an end to all people, for the earth is filled with violence because of

了<u>拉麥</u>。26<u>瑪土撒拉</u>生<u>拉麥</u>之後，又活了七百八十二年，並且生兒養女。27<u>瑪土撒拉</u>共活了九百六十九歲就死了。

28<u>拉麥</u>活到一百八十二歲，生了一個兒子，29給他起名叫<u>挪亞</u>，說："這個兒子必為我們的操作和手中的勞苦安慰我們。這操作勞苦是因為耶和華咒詛地。"30<u>拉麥</u>生<u>挪亞</u>之後，又活了五百九十五年，並且生兒養女。31<u>拉麥</u>共活了七百七十七歲就死了。

32<u>挪亞</u>五百歲生了閃、含、雅弗。

洪水

6 當人在世上多起來，又生女兒的時候，2神的兒子們看見人的女子美貌，就隨意挑選，娶來為妻。3耶和華說："人既屬乎血氣，我的靈就不永遠住在他裏面，然而他的日子還可到一百二十年。"

4那時候有偉人在地上。後來神的兒子們和人的女子們交合生子，那就是上古英武有名的人。

5耶和華見人在地上罪惡很大，終日所思想的盡都是惡，6耶和華就後悔造人在地上，心中憂傷。7耶和華說："我要將所造的人和走獸，並昆蟲，以及空中的飛鳥，都從地上除滅，因為我造他們後悔了。"8惟有<u>挪亞</u>在耶和華眼前蒙恩。

9<u>挪亞</u>的後代記在下面。

<u>挪亞</u>是個義人，在當時的世代是個完全人。<u>挪亞</u>與神同行。10<u>挪亞</u>生了三個兒子，就是閃、含、雅弗。

11世界在神面前敗壞，地上滿了強暴。12神觀看世界，見是敗壞了；凡有血氣的人，在地上都敗壞了行為。13神就對<u>挪亞</u>說："凡有血氣的人，他的盡頭已經來到我面前，因為地上滿了他們的強暴，我要把他們和

---

a 29 Noah sounds like the Hebrew for *comfort.*　*b 3 Or My spirit will not remain in*　*c 3 Or corrupt*

地一併毀滅。¹⁴你要用歌斐木造一隻方舟，分一間一間地造，裏外抹上松香。¹⁵方舟的造法乃是這樣：要長三百肘，寬五十肘，高三十肘。¹⁶方舟上邊要留透光處，高一肘。方舟的門要開在旁邊。方舟要分上、中、下三層。¹⁷看哪，我要使洪水氾濫在地上，毀滅天下，凡地上有血肉、有氣息的活物，無一不死。¹⁸我卻要與你立約，你同你的妻，與兒子、兒婦，都要進入方舟。¹⁹凡有血肉的活物，每樣兩個，一公一母，你要帶進方舟，好在你那裏保全生命。²⁰飛鳥各從其類，牲畜各從其類，地上的昆蟲各從其類，每樣兩個，要到你那裏，好保全生命。²¹你要拿各樣食物積蓄起來，好作你和牠們的食物。"

²²挪亞就這樣行。凡神所吩咐的，他都照樣行了。

7 耶和華對挪亞說："你和你的全家都要進入方舟，因為在這世代中，我見你在我面前是義人。²凡潔淨的畜類，你要帶七公七母；不潔淨的畜類，你要帶一公一母；³空中的飛鳥也要帶七公七母，可以留種，活在全地上。⁴因為再過七天，我要降雨在地上四十晝夜，把我所造的各種活物都從地上除滅。"

⁵挪亞就遵着耶和華所吩咐的行了。

⁶當洪水氾濫在地上的時候，挪亞整六百歲。⁷挪亞就同他的妻和兒子、兒婦，都進入方舟，躲避洪水。⁸潔淨的畜類和不潔淨的畜類，飛鳥並地上一切的昆蟲，⁹都是一對一對地，有公有母，到挪亞那裏進入方舟，正如神所吩咐挪亞的。¹⁰過了那七天，洪水氾濫在地上。

¹¹當挪亞六百歲，二月十七日那一

them. I am surely going to destroy both them and the earth. ¹⁴So make yourself an ark of cypress*ᵃ* wood; make rooms in it and coat it with pitch inside and out. ¹⁵This is how you are to build it: The ark is to be 450 feet long, 75 feet wide and 45 feet high.*ᵇ* ¹⁶Make a roof for it and finish*ᶜ* the ark to within 18 inches*ᵈ* of the top. Put a door in the side of the ark and make lower, middle and upper decks. ¹⁷I am going to bring floodwaters on the earth to destroy all life under the heavens, every creature that has the breath of life in it. Everything on earth will perish. ¹⁸But I will establish my covenant with you, and you will enter the ark—you and your sons and your wife and your sons'wives with you. ¹⁹You are to bring into the ark two of all living creatures, male and female, to keep them alive with you. ²⁰Two of every kind of bird, of every kind of animal and of every kind of creature that moves along the ground will come to you to be kept alive. ²¹You are to take every kind of food that is to be eaten and store it away as food for you and for them."

²²Noah did everything just as God commanded him.

7 The LORD then said to Noah, "Go into the ark, you and your whole family, because I have found you righteous in this generation. ²Take with you seven*ᵉ* of every kind of clean animal, a male and its mate, and two of every kind of unclean animal, a male and its mate, ³and also seven of every kind of bird, male and female, to keep their various kinds alive throughout the earth. ⁴Seven days from now I will send rain on the earth for forty days and forty nights, and I will wipe from the face of the earth every living creature I have made."

⁵And Noah did all that the LORD commanded him.

⁶Noah was six hundred years old when the floodwaters came on the earth. ⁷And Noah and his sons and his wife and his sons' wives entered the ark to escape the waters of the flood. ⁸Pairs of clean and unclean animals, of birds and of all creatures that move along the ground, ⁹male and female, came to Noah and entered the ark, as God had commanded Noah. ¹⁰And after the seven days the floodwaters came on the earth.

¹¹In the six hundredth year of Noah's life, on

---

a 14 The meaning of the Hebrew for this word is uncertain.
b 15 Hebrew 300 cubits long, 50 cubits wide and 30 cubits high (about 140 meters long, 23 meters wide and 13.5 meters high)
c 16 Or Make an opening for light by finishing　　*d 16 Hebrew a cubit (about 0.5 meter)*　　*e 2 Or seven pairs; also in verse 3*

the seventeenth day of the second month—on that day all the springs of the great deep burst forth, and the floodgates of the heavens were opened. [12]And rain fell on the earth forty days and forty nights.

[13]On that very day Noah and his sons, Shem, Ham and Japheth, together with his wife and the wives of his three sons, entered the ark. [14]They had with them every wild animal according to its kind, all livestock according to their kinds, every creature that moves along the ground according to its kind and every bird according to its kind, everything with wings. [15]Pairs of all creatures that have the breath of life in them came to Noah and entered the ark. [16]The animals going in were male and female of every living thing, as God had commanded Noah. Then the LORD shut him in.

[17]For forty days the flood kept coming on the earth, and as the waters increased they lifted the ark high above the earth. [18]The waters rose and increased greatly on the earth, and the ark floated on the surface of the water. [19]They rose greatly on the earth, and all the high mountains under the entire heavens were covered. [20]The waters rose and covered the mountains to a depth of more than twenty feet.[a,b] [21]Every living thing that moved on the earth perished— birds, livestock, wild animals, all the creatures that swarm over the earth, and all mankind. [22]Everything on dry land that had the breath of life in its nostrils died. [23]Every living thing on the face of the earth was wiped out; men and animals and the creatures that move along the ground and the birds of the air were wiped from the earth. Only Noah was left, and those with him in the ark.

[24]The waters flooded the earth for a hundred and fifty days.

8 But God remembered Noah and all the wild animals and the livestock that were with him in the ark, and he sent a wind over the earth, and the waters receded. [2]Now the springs of the deep and the floodgates of the heavens had been closed, and the rain had stopped falling from the sky. [3]The water receded steadily from the earth. At the end of the hundred and fifty days the water had gone down, [4]and on the seventeenth day of the seventh month the ark came to rest on the mountains of Ararat. [5]The waters continued to recede until the tenth month, and on the first day of the tenth month the tops of the mountains became visible.

a 20 Hebrew fifteen cubits (about 6.9 meters)   *b 20 Or rose more than twenty feet, and the mountains were covered*

天,大淵的泉源都裂開了,天上的窗戶也敞開了。[12]四十晝夜降大雨在地上。

[13]正當那日,挪亞和他三個兒子閃、含、雅弗,並挪亞的妻子和三個兒婦,都進入方舟。[14]他們和百獸,各從其類;一切牲畜,各從其類;爬在地上的昆蟲,各從其類;一切禽鳥,各從其類,都進入方舟。[15]凡有血肉、有氣息的活物,都一對一對地到挪亞那裏,進入方舟。[16]凡有血肉進入方舟的,都是有公有母,正如神所吩咐挪亞的。耶和華就把他關在方舟裏頭。

[17]洪水氾濫在地上四十天,水往上長,把方舟從地上漂起。[18]水勢浩大,在地上大大地往上長,方舟在水面上漂來漂去。[19]水勢在地上極其浩大,天下的高山都淹沒了。[20]水勢比山高過十五肘,山嶺都淹沒了。[21]凡在地上有血肉的動物,就是飛鳥、牲畜、走獸,和爬在地上的昆蟲,以及所有的人都死了;[22]凡在旱地上、鼻孔有氣息的生靈都死了;[23]凡地上各類的活物,連人帶牲畜、昆蟲,以及空中的飛鳥,都從地上除滅了,只留下挪亞和那些與他同在方舟裏的。

[24]水勢浩大,在地上共一百五十天。

8 神記念挪亞和挪亞方舟裏的一切走獸牲畜。神叫風吹地,水勢漸落。[2]淵源和天上的窗戶都閉塞了,天上的大雨也止住了。[3]水從地上漸退。過了一百五十天,水就漸消。[4]七月十七日,方舟停在亞拉臘山上。[5]水又漸消,到十月初一日,山頂都現出來了。

⁶過了四十天，挪亞開了方舟的窗戶，⁷放出一隻烏鴉去。那烏鴉飛來飛去，直到地上的水都乾了。⁸他又放出一隻鴿子去，要看看水從地上退了沒有。⁹但遍地上都是水，鴿子找不着落腳之地，就回到方舟挪亞那裏，挪亞伸手把鴿子接進方舟來。¹⁰他又等了七天，再把鴿子從方舟放出去。¹¹到了晚上，鴿子回到他那裏，嘴裏叼着一個新擰下來的橄欖葉子，挪亞就知道地上的水退了。¹²他又等了七天，放出鴿子去，鴿子就不再回來了。

¹³到挪亞六百零一歲，正月初一日，地上的水都乾了。挪亞撤去方舟的蓋觀看，便見地面上乾了。¹⁴到了二月二十七日，地就都乾了。

¹⁵神對挪亞說：¹⁶“你和你的妻子、兒子、兒婦都可以出方舟。¹⁷在你那裏凡有血肉的活物，就是飛鳥、牲畜，和一切爬在地上的昆蟲，都要帶出來，叫牠在地上多多滋生，大大興旺。”

¹⁸於是挪亞和他的妻子、兒子、兒婦都出來了。¹⁹一切走獸、昆蟲、飛鳥，和地上所有的動物，各從其類，也都出了方舟。

²⁰挪亞為耶和華築了一座壇，拿各類潔淨的牲畜、飛鳥獻在壇上為燔祭。²¹耶和華聞那馨香之氣，就心裏說：“我不再因人的緣故咒詛地（人從小時心裏懷着惡念），也不再按着我才行的，滅各種的活物了。

²²“地還存留的時候，
　　稼穡、
　　寒暑、
　　冬夏、
　　晝夜就永不停息了。”

⁶After forty days Noah opened the window he had made in the ark ⁷and sent out a raven, and it kept flying back and forth until the water had dried up from the earth. ⁸Then he sent out a dove to see if the water had receded from the surface of the ground. ⁹But the dove could find no place to set its feet because there was water over all the surface of the earth; so it returned to Noah in the ark. He reached out his hand and took the dove and brought it back to himself in the ark. ¹⁰He waited seven more days and again sent out the dove from the ark. ¹¹When the dove returned to him in the evening, there in its beak was a freshly plucked olive leaf! Then Noah knew that the water had receded from the earth. ¹²He waited seven more days and sent the dove out again, but this time it did not return to him.

¹³By the first day of the first month of Noah's six hundred and first year, the water had dried up from the earth. Noah then removed the covering from the ark and saw that the surface of the ground was dry. ¹⁴By the twenty-seventh day of the second month the earth was completely dry.

¹⁵Then God said to Noah, ¹⁶"Come out of the ark, you and your wife and your sons and their wives. ¹⁷Bring out every kind of living creature that is with you—the birds, the animals, and all the creatures that move along the ground—so they can multiply on the earth and be fruitful and increase in number upon it."

¹⁸So Noah came out, together with his sons and his wife and his sons' wives. ¹⁹All the animals and all the creatures that move along the ground and all the birds—everything that moves on the earth—came out of the ark, one kind after another.

²⁰Then Noah built an altar to the LORD and, taking some of all the clean animals and clean birds, he sacrificed burnt offerings on it. ²¹The LORD smelled the pleasing aroma and said in his heart: "Never again will I curse the ground because of man, even thoughᵃ every inclination of his heart is evil from childhood. And never again will I destroy all living creatures, as I have done.

²²"As long as the earth endures,
　　seedtime and harvest,
　　cold and heat,
　　summer and winter,
　　day and night
　　will never cease."

a 21 Or man, for

God's Covenant With Noah

9 Then God blessed Noah and his sons, saying to them, "Be fruitful and increase in number and fill the earth. ²The fear and dread of you will fall upon all the beasts of the earth and all the birds of the air, upon every creature that moves along the ground, and upon all the fish of the sea; they are given into your hands. ³Everything that lives and moves will be food for you. Just as I gave you the green plants, I now give you everything.

⁴"But you must not eat meat that has its lifeblood still in it. ⁵And for your lifeblood I will surely demand an accounting. I will demand an accounting from every animal. And from each man, too, I will demand an accounting for the life of his fellow man.

⁶"Whoever sheds the blood of man,
    by man shall his blood be shed;
for in the image of God
    has God made man.

⁷As for you, be fruitful and increase in number; multiply on the earth and increase upon it."

⁸Then God said to Noah and to his sons with him: ⁹"I now establish my covenant with you and with your descendants after you ¹⁰and with every living creature that was with you—the birds, the livestock and all the wild animals, all those that came out of the ark with you—every living creature on earth. ¹¹I establish my covenant with you: Never again will all life be cut off by the waters of a flood; never again will there be a flood to destroy the earth."

¹²And God said, "This is the sign of the covenant I am making between me and you and every living creature with you, a covenant for all generations to come: ¹³I have set my rainbow in the clouds, and it will be the sign of the covenant between me and the earth. ¹⁴Whenever I bring clouds over the earth and the rainbow appears in the clouds, ¹⁵I will remember my covenant between me and you and all living creatures of every kind. Never again will the waters become a flood to destroy all life. ¹⁶Whenever the rainbow appears in the clouds, I will see it and remember the everlasting covenant between God and all living creatures of every kind on the earth."

¹⁷So God said to Noah, "This is the sign of the covenant I have established between me and all life on the earth."

神與挪亞立約

9 神賜福給挪亞和他的兒子，對他們說：「你們要生養眾多，遍滿了地。²凡地上的走獸和空中的飛鳥，都必驚恐、懼怕你們；連地上一切的昆蟲並海裏一切的魚，都交付你們的手。³凡活着的動物，都可以作你們的食物，這一切我都賜給你們，如同菜蔬一樣。

⁴「惟獨肉帶着血，那就是牠的生命，你們不可吃。⁵流你們血、害你們命的，無論是獸是人，我必討他的罪，就是向各人的弟兄也是如此。

⁶「凡流人血的，
    他的血也必被人所流，
因為神造人，
    是照自己的形像造的。

⁷你們要生養眾多，在地上昌盛繁茂。」

⁸神曉諭挪亞和他的兒子說：⁹「我與你們和你們的後裔立約，¹⁰並與你們這裏的一切活物，就是飛鳥、牲畜、走獸，凡從方舟裏出來的活物立約。¹¹我與你們立約，凡有血肉的，不再被洪水滅絕，也不再有洪水毀壞地了。」

¹²神說：「我與你們並你們這裏的各樣活物所立的永約是有記號的。¹³我把虹放在雲彩中，這就可作我與地立約的記號了。¹⁴我使雲彩蓋地的時候，必有虹現在雲彩中，¹⁵我便記念我與你們和各樣有血肉的活物所立的約，水就再不氾濫毀壞一切有血肉的物了。¹⁶虹必現在雲彩中，我看見，就要記念我與地上各樣有血肉的活物所立的永約。」

¹⁷神對挪亞說：「這就是我與地上一切有血肉之物立約的記號了。」

挪亞的兒子

18出方舟挪亞的兒子就是閃、含、雅弗。含是迦南的父親。19這是挪亞的三個兒子，他們的後裔分散在全地。

20挪亞作起農夫來，栽了一個葡萄園。21他喝了園中的酒便醉了，在帳棚裏赤着身子。22迦南的父親含，看見他父親赤身，就到外邊告訴他兩個弟兄。23於是閃和雅弗拿件衣服搭在肩上，倒退着進去，給他父親蓋上，他們背着臉就看不見父親的赤身。

24挪亞醒了酒，知道小兒子向他所做的事，25就說：

> “迦南當受咒詛，
> 　必給他弟兄
> 　作奴僕的奴僕。”

26又說：

> “耶和華閃的神是應當稱頌的，
> 　願迦南作閃的奴僕。
> 27願神使雅弗擴張，
> 　使他住在閃的帳棚裏，
> 　又願迦南作他的奴僕。”

28洪水以後，挪亞又活了三百五十年。29挪亞共活了九百五十歲就死了。

列邦列國

10 挪亞的兒子閃、含、雅弗的後代記在下面。洪水以後，他們都生了兒子。

雅弗的後裔

2雅弗的兒子是
　　歌篾、瑪各、瑪代、雅完、土巴、米設、提拉。
3歌篾的兒子是
　　亞實基拿、利法、陀迦瑪。
4雅完的兒子是
　　以利沙、他施、基提、多單。

The Sons of Noah

18The sons of Noah who came out of the ark were Shem, Ham and Japheth. (Ham was the father of Canaan.) 19These were the three sons of Noah, and from them came the people who were scattered over the earth.

20Noah, a man of the soil, proceeded[a] to plant a vineyard. 21When he drank some of its wine, he became drunk and lay uncovered inside his tent. 22Ham, the father of Canaan, saw his father's nakedness and told his two brothers outside. 23But Shem and Japheth took a garment and laid it across their shoulders; then they walked in backward and covered their father's nakedness. Their faces were turned the other way so that they would not see their father's nakedness.

24When Noah awoke from his wine and found out what his youngest son had done to him, 25he said,

> "Cursed be Canaan!
> 　The lowest of slaves
> 　will he be to his brothers."

26He also said,

> "Blessed be the LORD, the God of Shem!
> 　May Canaan be the slave of Shem.[b]
> 27May God extend the territory of Japheth[c];
> 　may Japheth live in the tents of Shem,
> 　and may Canaan be his[d] slave."

28After the flood Noah lived 350 years. 29Altogether, Noah lived 950 years, and then he died.

The Table of Nations

10 This is the account of Shem, Ham and Japheth, Noah's sons, who themselves had sons after the flood.

The Japhethites

2The sons[e] of Japheth:
　　Gomer, Magog, Madai, Javan, Tubal, Meshech and Tiras.
3The sons of Gomer:
　　Ashkenaz, Riphath and Togarmah.
4The sons of Javan:
　　Elishah, Tarshish, the Kittim and the

---

a 20 Or soil, was the first　　b 26 Or be his slave　　c 27 Japheth
sounds like the Hebrew for extend.　　d 27 Or their
e 2 Sons may mean descendants or successors or nations; also in
verses 3, 4, 6, 7, 20-23, 29 and 31.

Rodanim.*a* *5*(From these the maritime peoples spread out into their territories by their clans within their nations, each with its own language.)

The Hamites

*6*The sons of Ham:

Cush, Mizraim,*b* Put and Canaan.

*7*The sons of Cush:

Seba, Havilah, Sabtah, Raamah and Sabteca.

The sons of Raamah:

Sheba and Dedan.

*8*Cush was the father*c* of Nimrod, who grew to be a mighty warrior on the earth. *9*He was a mighty hunter before the LORD; that is why it is said, "Like Nimrod, a mighty hunter before the LORD." *10*The first centers of his kingdom were Babylon, Erech, Akkad and Calneh, in*d* Shinar.*e* *11*From that land he went to Assyria, where he built Nineveh, Rehoboth Ir,*f* Calah *12*and Resen, which is between Nineveh and Calah; that is the great city.

*13*Mizraim was the father of

the Ludites, Anamites, Lehabites, Naphtuhites, *14*Pathrusites, Casluhites (from whom the Philistines came) and Caphtorites.

*15*Canaan was the father of

Sidon his firstborn,*g* and of the Hittites, *16*Jebusites, Amorites, Girgashites, *17*Hivites, Arkites, Sinites, *18*Arvadites, Zemarites and Hamathites.

Later the Canaanite clans scattered *19*and the borders of Canaan reached from Sidon toward Gerar as far as Gaza, and then toward Sodom, Gomorrah, Admah and Zeboiim, as far as Lasha.

*20*These are the sons of Ham by their clans and languages, in their territories and nations.

The Semites

*21*Sons were also born to Shem, whose older brother was*h* Japheth; Shem was the ancestor of all the sons of Eber.

---

⁵這些人的後裔將各國的地土、海島分開居住,各隨各的方言、宗族立國。

含的後裔

⁶含的兒子是

古實、麥西、弗、迦南。

⁷古實的兒子是

西巴、哈腓拉、撒弗他、拉瑪、撒弗提迦。

拉瑪的兒子是

示巴、底但。

⁸古實又生寧錄,他為世上英雄之首。⁹他在耶和華面前是個英勇的獵戶,所以俗語說:"像寧錄在耶和華面前是個英勇的獵戶。"¹⁰他國的起頭是巴別、以力、亞甲、甲尼,都在示拿地。¹¹他從那地出來往亞述去,建造尼尼微、利河伯、迦拉,¹²和尼尼微、迦拉中間的利鮮,這就是那大城。

---

¹³麥西生路低人、亞拿米人、利哈比人、拿弗土希人、¹⁴帕斯魯細人、迦斯路希人、迦斐託人,從迦斐託出來的有非利士人。

¹⁵迦南生長子西頓,又生赫,¹⁶和耶布斯人、亞摩利人、革迦撒人、¹⁷希未人、亞基人、西尼人、¹⁸亞瓦底人、洗瑪利人、哈馬人。

後來迦南的諸族分散了。¹⁹迦南的境界是從西頓向基拉耳的路上,直到迦薩;又向所多瑪、蛾摩拉、押瑪、洗扁的路上,直到拉沙。

²⁰這就是含的後裔,各隨他們的宗族、方言,所住的地土、邦國。

閃的後裔

²¹雅弗的哥哥閃,是希伯子孫之祖,他也生了兒子。

---

a 4 Some manuscripts of the Masoretic Text and Samaritan Pentateuch (see also Septuagint and 1 Chron. 1:7); most manuscripts of the Masoretic Text Dodanim

b 6 That is, Egypt; also in verse 13   c 8 Father may mean ancestor or predecessor or founder; also in verses 13, 15, 24 and 26.   d 10 Or Erech and Akkad—all of them in   e 10 That is, Babylonia   f 11 Or Nineveh with its city squares   g 15 Or of the Sidonians, the foremost   h 21 Or Shem, the older brother of

²²閃的兒子是

以攔、亞述、亞法撒、路德、亞
蘭。

²³亞蘭的兒子是

烏斯、戶勒、基帖、瑪施。

²⁴亞法撒生沙拉；沙拉生希伯。

²⁵希伯生了兩個兒子，一個名叫法勒
（註：“法勒”就是“分”的意思），因
為那時人就分地居住。法勒的兄
弟名叫約坍。

²⁶約坍生亞摩答、沙列、哈薩瑪非、
耶拉、²⁷哈多蘭、烏薩、德拉、
²⁸俄巴路、亞比瑪利、示巴、
²⁹阿斐、哈腓拉、約巴，這都是
約坍的兒子。

³⁰他們所住的地方是從米沙直到西發
東邊的山。

³¹這就是閃的子孫，各隨他們的
宗族、方言，所住的地土、邦國。

³²這些都是挪亞三個兒子的宗
族，各隨他們的支派立國。洪水以
後，他們在地上分為邦國。

巴別塔

11 那時，天下人的口音言語都
是一樣。²他們往東邊遷移的
時候，在示拿地遇見一片平
原，就住在那裏。

³他們彼此商量說：“來吧，我
們要做磚，把磚燒透了。”他們就
拿磚當石頭，又拿石漆當灰泥。⁴他
們說：“來吧，我們要建造一座城
和一座塔，塔頂通天，為要傳揚我
們的名，免得我們分散在全地
上。”

⁵耶和華降臨，要看看世人所建
造的城和塔。⁶耶和華說：“看哪，
他們成為一樣的人民，都是一樣的言
語，如今既做起這事來，以後他們所
要做的事就沒有不成就的了。⁷我們
下去，在那裏變亂他們的口音，使他
們的言語彼此不通。”

⁸於是，耶和華使他們從那裏分
散在全地上，他們就停工不造那城
了。⁹因為耶和華在那裏變亂天下人

²²The sons of Shem:

Elam, Asshur, Arphaxad, Lud and Aram.

²³The sons of Aram:

Uz, Hul, Gether and Meshech.ᵃ

²⁴Arphaxad was the father ofᵇ Shelah,

and Shelah the father of Eber.

²⁵Two sons were born to Eber:

One was named Peleg,ᶜ because in his time
the earth was divided; his brother was
named Joktan.

²⁶Joktan was the father of

Almodad, Sheleph, Hazarmaveth, Jerah,
²⁷Hadoram, Uzal, Diklah, ²⁸Obal, Abimael,
Sheba, ²⁹Ophir, Havilah and Jobab. All
these were sons of Joktan.

³⁰The region where they lived stretched from
Mesha toward Sephar, in the eastern hill country.

³¹These are the sons of Shem by their clans
and languages, in their territories and nations.

³²These are the clans of Noah's sons, according to their lines of descent, within their nations.
From these the nations spread out over the earth
after the flood.

The Tower of Babel

11 Now the whole world had one language
and a common speech. ²As men moved
eastward,ᵈ they found a plain in Shinarᵉ
and settled there.

³They said to each other, "Come, let's make
bricks and bake them thoroughly." They used
brick instead of stone, and tar for mortar. ⁴Then
they said, "Come, let us build ourselves a city,
with a tower that reaches to the heavens, so that
we may make a name for ourselves and not be
scattered over the face of the whole earth."

⁵But the LORD came down to see the city and
the tower that the men were building. ⁶The
LORD said, "If as one people speaking the same
language they have begun to do this, then nothing they plan to do will be impossible for them.
⁷Come, let us go down and confuse their language so they will not understand each other."

⁸So the LORD scattered them from there over
all the earth, and they stopped building the city.
⁹That is why it was called Babelᶠ—because there

ᵃ 23 See Septuagint and 1 Chron. 1:17; Hebrew Mash
ᵇ 24 Hebrew; Septuagint father of Cainan, and Cainan was the
father of　ᶜ 25 Peleg means division.　ᵈ 2 Or from the east; or
in the east　ᵉ 2 That is, Babylonia　ᶠ 9 That is, Babylon; Babel
sounds like the Hebrew for confused.

the LORD confused the language of the whole world. From there the LORD scattered them over the face of the whole earth.

From Shem to Abram

[10]This is the account of Shem.

Two years after the flood, when Shem was 100 years old, he became the father[a] of Arphaxad. [11]And after he became the father of Arphaxad, Shem lived 500 years and had other sons and daughters.

[12]When Arphaxad had lived 35 years, he became the father of Shelah. [13]And after he became the father of Shelah, Arphaxad lived 403 years and had other sons and daughters.[b]

[14]When Shelah had lived 30 years, he became the father of Eber. [15]And after he became the father of Eber, Shelah lived 403 years and had other sons and daughters.

[16]When Eber had lived 34 years, he became the father of Peleg. [17]And after he became the father of Peleg, Eber lived 430 years and had other sons and daughters.

[18]When Peleg had lived 30 years, he became the father of Reu. [19]And after he became the father of Reu, Peleg lived 209 years and had other sons and daughters.

[20]When Reu had lived 32 years, he became the father of Serug. [21]And after he became the father of Serug, Reu lived 207 years and had other sons and daughters.

[22]When Serug had lived 30 years, he became the father of Nahor. [23]And after he became the father of Nahor, Serug lived 200 years and had other sons and daughters.

[24]When Nahor had lived 29 years, he became the father of Terah. [25]And after he became the father of Terah, Nahor lived 119 years and had other sons and daughters.

[26]After Terah had lived 70 years, he became the father of Abram, Nahor and Haran.

[27]This is the account of Terah.

Terah became the father of Abram, Nahor and Haran. And Haran became the father of Lot.

---

a 10 Father may mean *ancestor*; also in verses 11-25.
b 12,13 Hebrew; Septuagint (see also Luke 3:35, 36 and note at Gen. 10:24) 35 years, he became the father of Cainan. 13 And after he became the father of Cainan, Arphaxad lived 430 years and had other sons and daughters, and then he died. When Cainan had lived 130 years, he became the father of Shelah. And after he became the father of Shelah, Cainan lived 330 years and had other sons and daughters

---

的言語，使眾人分散在全地上，所以那城名叫巴別（註：就是「變亂」的意思）。

從閃到亞伯蘭

[10]閃的後代記在下面。

洪水以後二年，閃一百歲生了亞法撒。[11]閃生亞法撒之後，又活了五百年，並且生兒養女。

[12]亞法撒活到三十五歲，生了沙拉。[13]亞法撒生沙拉之後，又活了四百零三年，並且生兒養女。

[14]沙拉活到三十歲，生了希伯。[15]沙拉生希伯之後，又活了四百零三年，並且生兒養女。

[16]希伯活到三十四歲，生了法勒。[17]希伯生法勒之後，又活了四百三十年，並且生兒養女。

[18]法勒活到三十歲，生了拉吳。[19]法勒生拉吳之後，又活了二百零九年，並且生兒養女。

[20]拉吳活到三十二歲，生了西鹿。[21]拉吳生西鹿之後，又活了二百零七年，並且生兒養女。

[22]西鹿活到三十歲，生了拿鶴。[23]西鹿生拿鶴之後，又活了二百年，並且生兒養女。

[24]拿鶴活到二十九歲，生了他拉。[25]拿鶴生他拉之後，又活了一百一十九年，並且生兒養女。

[26]他拉活到七十歲，生了亞伯蘭、拿鶴、哈蘭。

[27]他拉的後代記在下面：

他拉生亞伯蘭、拿鶴、哈蘭。哈蘭生羅得。

²⁸哈蘭死在他的本地迦勒底的吾珥，在他父親他拉之先。²⁹亞伯蘭、拿鶴各娶了妻：亞伯蘭的妻子名叫撒萊；拿鶴的妻子名叫密迦，是哈蘭的女兒；哈蘭是密迦和亦迦的父親。³⁰撒萊不生育，沒有孩子。

³¹他拉帶着他兒子亞伯蘭和他孫子哈蘭的兒子羅得，並他兒婦亞伯蘭的妻子撒萊，出了迦勒底的吾珥，要往迦南地去。他們走到哈蘭就住在那裏。

³²他拉共活了二百零五歲，就死在哈蘭。

神呼召亞伯蘭

12 耶和華對亞伯蘭說：「你要離開本地、本族、父家，往我所要指示你的地去。

² 「我必叫你成為大國。
　　我必賜福給你，
　　叫你的名為大，
　　　你也要叫別人得福。
³ 為你祝福的，我必賜福與他；
　　那咒詛你的，我必咒詛他。
　地上的萬族
　　都要因你得福。」

⁴亞伯蘭就照着耶和華的吩咐去了，羅得也和他同去。亞伯蘭出哈蘭的時候年七十五歲。⁵亞伯蘭將他妻子撒萊和姪兒羅得，連他們在哈蘭所積蓄的財物，所得的人口，都帶往迦南地去。他們就到了迦南地。

⁶亞伯蘭經過那地，到了示劍地方摩利橡樹那裏。那時，迦南人住在那地。⁷耶和華向亞伯蘭顯現，說：「我要把這地賜給你的後裔。」亞伯蘭就在那裏為向他顯現的耶和華築了一座壇。

⁸從那裏他又遷到伯特利東邊的山，支搭帳棚。西邊是伯特利，東邊是艾。他在那裏又為耶和華築了一座壇，求告耶和華的名。⁹後來亞伯蘭又漸漸遷往南地去。

²⁸While his father Terah was still alive, Haran died in Ur of the Chaldeans, in the land of his birth. ²⁹Abram and Nahor both married. The name of Abram's wife was Sarai, and the name of Nahor's wife was Milcah; she was the daughter of Haran, the father of both Milcah and Iscah. ³⁰Now Sarai was barren; she had no children.

³¹Terah took his son Abram, his grandson Lot son of Haran, and his daughter-in-law Sarai, the wife of his son Abram, and together they set out from Ur of the Chaldeans to go to Canaan. But when they came to Haran, they settled there.

³²Terah lived 205 years, and he died in Haran.

The Call of Abram

12 The LORD had said to Abram, "Leave your country, your people and your father's household and go to the land I will show you.

² "I will make you into a great nation
　　and I will bless you;
　I will make your name great,
　　and you will be a blessing.
³ I will bless those who bless you,
　　and whoever curses you I will curse;
　and all peoples on earth
　　will be blessed through you."

⁴So Abram left, as the LORD had told him; and Lot went with him. Abram was seventy-five years old when he set out from Haran. ⁵He took his wife Sarai, his nephew Lot, all the possessions they had accumulated and the people they had acquired in Haran, and they set out for the land of Canaan, and they arrived there.

⁶Abram traveled through the land as far as the site of the great tree of Moreh at Shechem. At that time the Canaanites were in the land. ⁷The LORD appeared to Abram and said, "To your offspringᵃ I will give this land." So he built an altar there to the LORD, who had appeared to him.

⁸From there he went on toward the hills east of Bethel and pitched his tent, with Bethel on the west and Ai on the east. There he built an altar to the LORD and called on the name of the LORD. ⁹Then Abram set out and continued toward the Negev.

a 7 Or seed

Abram in Egypt

10Now there was a famine in the land, and Abram went down to Egypt to live there for a while because the famine was severe. 11As he was about to enter Egypt, he said to his wife Sarai, "I know what a beautiful woman you are. 12When the Egyptians see you, they will say, 'This is his wife.' Then they will kill me but will let you live. 13Say you are my sister, so that I will be treated well for your sake and my life will be spared because of you."

14When Abram came to Egypt, the Egyptians saw that she was a very beautiful woman. 15And when Pharaoh's officials saw her, they praised her to Pharaoh, and she was taken into his palace. 16He treated Abram well for her sake, and Abram acquired sheep and cattle, male and female donkeys, menservants and maidservants, and camels.

17But the LORD inflicted serious diseases on Pharaoh and his household because of Abram's wife Sarai. 18So Pharaoh summoned Abram. "What have you done to me?" he said. "Why didn't you tell me she was your wife? 19Why did you say, 'She is my sister,' so that I took her to be my wife? Now then, here is your wife. Take her and go!" 20Then Pharaoh gave orders about Abram to his men, and they sent him on his way, with his wife and everything he had.

Abram and Lot Separate

13 So Abram went up from Egypt to the Negev, with his wife and everything he had, and Lot went with him. 2Abram had become very wealthy in livestock and in silver and gold.

3From the Negev he went from place to place until he came to Bethel, to the place between Bethel and Ai where his tent had been earlier 4and where he had first built an altar. There Abram called on the name of the LORD.

5Now Lot, who was moving about with Abram, also had flocks and herds and tents. 6But the land could not support them while they stayed together, for their possessions were so great that they were not able to stay together. 7And quarreling arose between Abram's herdsmen and the herdsmen of Lot. The Canaanites and Perizzites were also living in the land at that time.

8So Abram said to Lot, "Let's not have any quarreling between you and me, or between your herdsmen and mine, for we are brothers. 9Is not the whole land before you? Let's part company. If you go to the left, I'll go to the right; if you go to the right, I'll go to the left."

亞伯蘭下埃及

10那地遭遇饑荒。因饑荒甚大，亞伯蘭就下埃及去，要在那裏暫居。11將近埃及，就對他妻子撒萊說："我知道你是容貌俊美的婦人。12埃及人看見你必說：'這是他的妻子'，他們就要殺我，卻叫你存活。13求你說，你是我的妹子，使我因你得平安，我的命也因你存活。"

14及至亞伯蘭到了埃及，埃及人看見那婦人極其美貌。15法老的臣宰看見了她，就在法老面前誇獎她。那婦人就被帶進法老的宮去。16法老因這婦人就厚待亞伯蘭，亞伯蘭得了許多牛羊、駱駝、公驢、母驢、僕婢。

17耶和華因亞伯蘭妻子撒萊的緣故，降大災與法老和他的全家。18法老就召了亞伯蘭來，說："你這向我做的是甚麼事呢？為甚麼沒有告訴我她是你的妻子？19為甚麼說她是你的妹子，以致我把她取來要作我的妻子？現在你的妻子在這裏，可以帶她走吧！"20於是法老吩咐人將亞伯蘭和他妻子，並他所有的都送走了。

亞伯蘭與羅得分離

13 亞伯蘭帶着他的妻子與羅得，並一切所有的，都從埃及上南地去。2亞伯蘭的金、銀、牲畜極多。

3他從南地漸漸往伯特利去，到了伯特利和艾的中間，就是從前支搭帳棚的地方，4也是他起先築壇的地方，他又在那裏求告耶和華的名。

5與亞伯蘭同行的羅得也有牛羣、羊羣、帳棚。6那地容不下他們，因為他們的財物甚多，使他們不能同居。7當時，迦南人與比利洗人在那地居住。亞伯蘭的牧人和羅得的牧人相爭。

8亞伯蘭就對羅得說："你我不可相爭，你的牧人和我的牧人也不可相爭，因為我們是骨肉（註：原文作"弟兄"）。9遍地不都在你眼前嗎？請你離開我：你向左，我就向右；你向右，我就向左。"

¹⁰羅得舉目看見<u>約旦河</u>的全平原，<u>直到瑣珥</u>，都是滋潤的，那地在耶和華未滅<u>所多瑪</u>、<u>蛾摩拉</u>以先，如同耶和華的園子，也像<u>埃及</u>地。¹¹於是<u>羅得</u>選擇<u>約旦河</u>的全平原，往東遷移；他們就彼此分離了。¹²<u>亞伯蘭</u>住在<u>迦南</u>地，<u>羅得</u>住在平原的城邑，漸漸挪移帳棚，<u>直到所多瑪</u>。¹³<u>所多瑪</u>人在耶和華面前罪大惡極。

¹⁴<u>羅得</u>離別<u>亞伯蘭</u>以後，耶和華對<u>亞伯蘭</u>說：「從你所在的地方，你舉目向東西南北觀看，¹⁵凡你所看見的一切地，我都要賜給你和你的後裔，直到永遠。¹⁶我也要使你的後裔如同地上的塵沙那樣多，人若能數算地上的塵沙，才能數算你的後裔。¹⁷你起來，縱橫走遍這地，因為我必把這地賜給你。」

¹⁸<u>亞伯蘭</u>就搬了帳棚，來到<u>希伯崙 幔利</u>的橡樹那裏居住，在那裏為耶和華築了一座壇。

亞伯蘭救回羅得

14 當<u>暗拉非</u>作<u>示拿</u>王、<u>亞略</u>作<u>以拉撒</u>王、<u>基大老瑪</u>作<u>以攔</u>王、<u>提達</u>作<u>戈印</u>王的時候，²他們都攻打<u>所多瑪</u>王<u>比拉</u>、<u>蛾摩拉</u>王<u>比沙</u>、<u>押瑪</u>王<u>示納</u>、<u>洗扁</u>王<u>善以別</u>和<u>比拉</u>王；<u>比拉</u>就是<u>瑣珥</u>。³這五王都在<u>西訂谷</u>會合，<u>西訂谷</u>就是<u>鹽海</u>。⁴他們已經侍奉<u>基大老瑪</u>十二年，到十三年就背叛了。

⁵十四年，<u>基大老瑪</u>和同盟的王都來在<u>亞特律加寧</u>，殺敗了<u>利乏音</u>人，在<u>哈麥</u>殺敗了<u>蘇西</u>人，在<u>沙微基列亭</u>殺敗了<u>以米</u>人，⁶在<u>何利</u>人的<u>西珥山</u>殺敗了<u>何利</u>人，一直殺到靠近曠野的<u>伊勒巴蘭</u>。⁷他們回到<u>安密巴</u>，就是<u>加低斯</u>，殺敗了<u>亞瑪力</u>全地的人，以及住在<u>哈洗遜他瑪</u>的<u>亞摩利</u>人。

⁸於是<u>所多瑪</u>王、<u>蛾摩拉</u>王、<u>押瑪</u>王、<u>洗扁</u>王和<u>比拉</u>王（<u>比拉</u>就是<u>瑣珥</u>）都出來，在<u>西訂谷</u>擺陣，與他們交戰，⁹就是與<u>以攔</u>王<u>基大老瑪</u>、<u>戈印</u>王<u>提達</u>、<u>示拿</u>王<u>暗拉非</u>、<u>以拉撒</u>王<u>亞略</u>交戰，乃是四王

¹⁰Lot looked up and saw that the whole plain of the Jordan was well watered, like the garden of the LORD, like the land of Egypt, toward Zoar. (This was before the LORD destroyed Sodom and Gomorrah.) ¹¹So Lot chose for himself the whole plain of the Jordan and set out toward the east. The two men parted company: ¹²Abram lived in the land of Canaan, while Lot lived among the cities of the plain and pitched his tents near Sodom. ¹³Now the men of Sodom were wicked and were sinning greatly against the LORD.

¹⁴The LORD said to Abram after Lot had parted from him, "Lift up your eyes from where you are and look north and south, east and west. ¹⁵All the land that you see I will give to you and your offspring*ᵃ* forever. ¹⁶I will make your offspring like the dust of the earth, so that if anyone could count the dust, then your offspring could be counted. ¹⁷Go, walk through the length and breadth of the land, for I am giving it to you."

¹⁸So Abram moved his tents and went to live near the great trees of Mamre at Hebron, where he built an altar to the LORD.

Abram Rescues Lot

14 At this time Amraphel king of Shinar,*ᵇ* Arioch king of Ellasar, Kedorlaomer king of Elam and Tidal king of Goiim ²went to war against Bera king of Sodom, Birsha king of Gomorrah, Shinab king of Admah, Shemeber king of Zeboiim, and the king of Bela (that is, Zoar). ³All these latter kings joined forces in the Valley of Siddim (the Salt Sea*ᶜ*). ⁴For twelve years they had been subject to Kedorlaomer, but in the thirteenth year they rebelled.

⁵In the fourteenth year, Kedorlaomer and the kings allied with him went out and defeated the Rephaites in Ashteroth Karnaim, the Zuzites in Ham, the Emites in Shaveh Kiriathaim ⁶and the Horites in the hill country of Seir, as far as El Paran near the desert. ⁷Then they turned back and went to En Mishpat (that is, Kadesh), and they conquered the whole territory of the Amalekites, as well as the Amorites who were living in Hazazon Tamar.

⁸Then the king of Sodom, the king of Gomorrah, the king of Admah, the king of Zeboiim and the king of Bela (that is, Zoar) marched out and drew up their battle lines in the Valley of Siddim ⁹against Kedorlaomer king of Elam, Tidal king of Goiim, Amraphel king of

a 15 Or *seed*; also in verse 16　　*b* 1 That is, Babylonia; also in verse 9　　*c* 3 That is, the Dead Sea.

Shinar and Arioch king of Ellasar—four kings against five. ¹⁰Now the Valley of Siddim was full of tar pits, and when the kings of Sodom and Gomorrah fled, some of the men fell into them and the rest fled to the hills. ¹¹The four kings seized all the goods of Sodom and Gomorrah and all their food; then they went away. ¹²They also carried off Abram's nephew Lot and his possessions, since he was living in Sodom.

¹³One who had escaped came and reported this to Abram the Hebrew. Now Abram was living near the great trees of Mamre the Amorite, a brother*d* of Eshcol and Aner, all of whom were allied with Abram. ¹⁴When Abram heard that his relative had been taken captive, he called out the 318 trained men born in his household and went in pursuit as far as Dan. ¹⁵During the night Abram divided his men to attack them and he routed them, pursuing them as far as Hobah, north of Damascus. ¹⁶He recovered all the goods and brought back his relative Lot and his possessions, together with the women and the other people.

¹⁷After Abram returned from defeating Kedorlaomer and the kings allied with him, the king of Sodom came out to meet him in the Valley of Shaveh (that is, the King's Valley).

¹⁸Then Melchizedek king of Salem*b* brought out bread and wine. He was priest of God Most High, ¹⁹and he blessed Abram, saying,

"Blessed be Abram by God Most High,
　　Creator*c* of heaven and earth.
²⁰And blessed be*d* God Most High,
　　who delivered your enemies into your hand."

Then Abram gave him a tenth of everything.

²¹The king of Sodom said to Abram, "Give me the people and keep the goods for yourself."

²²But Abram said to the king of Sodom, "I have raised my hand to the LORD, God Most High, Creator of heaven and earth, and have taken an oath ²³that I will accept nothing belonging to you, not even a thread or the thong of a sandal, so that you will never be able to say, 'I made Abram rich.' ²⁴I will accept nothing but what my men have eaten and the share that belongs to the men who went with me—to Aner, Eshcol and Mamre. Let them have their share."

與五王交戰。¹⁰西訂谷有許多石漆坑。所多瑪王和蛾摩拉王逃跑，有掉在坑裏的，其餘的人都往山上逃跑。¹¹四王把所多瑪和蛾摩拉所有的財物，並一切的糧食都擄掠去了；¹²又把亞伯蘭的侄兒羅得和羅得的財物擄掠去了。當時羅得正住在所多瑪。

¹³有一個逃出來的人，告訴希伯來人亞伯蘭，亞伯蘭正住在亞摩利人幔利的橡樹那裏。幔利和以實各並亞乃都是弟兄，曾與亞伯蘭聯盟。¹⁴亞伯蘭聽見他侄兒（註：原文作"弟兄"）被擄去，就率領他家裏生養的精練壯丁三百一十八人，直追到但。¹⁵便在夜間，自己同僕人分隊殺敗敵人，又追到大馬士革左邊的何把，¹⁶將被擄掠的一切財物奪回來，連他侄兒羅得和他的財物，以及婦女、人民，也都奪回來。

¹⁷亞伯蘭殺敗基大老瑪和與他同盟的王回來的時候，所多瑪王出來，在沙微谷迎接他；沙微谷就是王谷。

¹⁸又有撒冷王麥基洗德帶着餅和酒出來迎接；他是至高神的祭司。¹⁹他為亞伯蘭祝福，說：

"願天地的主、至高的神
　　賜福與亞伯蘭！
²⁰至高的神
　　把敵人交在你手裏，
　　是應當稱頌的。"

亞伯蘭就把所得的拿出十分之一來，給麥基洗德。

²¹所多瑪王對亞伯蘭說："你把人口給我，財物你自己拿去吧！"

²²亞伯蘭對所多瑪王說："我已經向天地的主至高的神耶和華起誓，²³凡是你的東西，就是一根線、一根鞋帶，我都不拿，免得你說：'我使亞伯蘭富足。'²⁴只有僕人所吃的，並與我同行的亞乃、以實各、幔利所應得的分，可以任憑他們拿去。"

a 13 Or *a relative; or an ally*　　*b 18* That is, Jerusalem　　*c 19* Or *Possessor;* also in verse 22　　*d 20* Or *And praise be to*

神與亞伯蘭之約

15 這事以後，耶和華在異象中有話對亞伯蘭說：

　　"亞伯蘭，你不要懼怕！
　　我是你的盾牌，
　　必大大地賞賜你。"

²亞伯蘭說："主耶和華啊，我既無子，你還賜我甚麼呢？並且要承受我家業的是大馬士革人以利以謝。"³亞伯蘭又說："你沒有給我兒子，那生在我家中的人就是我的後嗣。"

⁴耶和華又有話對他說："這人必不成為你的後嗣，你本身所生的才成為你的後嗣。"⁵於是領他走到外邊，說："你向天觀看，數算眾星，能數得過來嗎？"又對他說："你的後裔將要如此。"

⁶亞伯蘭信耶和華，耶和華就以此為他的義。

⁷耶和華又對他說："我是耶和華，曾領你出了迦勒底的吾珥，為要將這地賜你為業。"

⁸亞伯蘭說："主耶和華啊，我怎能知道必得這地為業呢？"

⁹他說："你為我取一隻三年的母牛，一隻三年的母山羊，一隻三年的公綿羊，一隻斑鳩，一隻雛鴿。"

¹⁰亞伯蘭就取了這些來，每樣劈開分成兩半，一半對着一半地擺列，只有鳥沒有劈開。¹¹有鷙鳥下來落在那死畜的肉上，亞伯蘭就把牠嚇飛了。

¹²日頭正落的時候，亞伯蘭沉沉地睡了，忽然有驚人的大黑暗落在他身上。¹³耶和華對亞伯蘭說："你要的確知道，你的後裔必寄居別人的地，又服事那地的人，那地的人要苦待他們四百年。¹⁴並且他們所要服事的那國，我要懲罰，後來他們必帶着許多財物從那裏出來。¹⁵但你要享大壽數，平平安安地歸到你列祖那裏，被人埋葬。¹⁶到了第四代，他們必回到此地，因為亞摩利人的罪孽還沒有滿盈。"

¹⁷日落天黑，不料有冒煙的爐，並燒着的火把，從那些肉塊中經過。¹⁸當那日，耶和華與亞伯蘭立約，說："我已賜給你的後裔，從埃

God's Covenant With Abram

15 After this, the word of the LORD came to Abram in a vision:

"Do not be afraid, Abram.
I am your shield,[a]
your very great reward.[b]"

²But Abram said, "O Sovereign LORD, what can you give me since I remain childless and the one who will inherit[c] my estate is Eliezer of Damascus?" ³And Abram said, "You have given me no children; so a servant in my household will be my heir."

⁴Then the word of the LORD came to him: "This man will not be your heir, but a son coming from your own body will be your heir." ⁵He took him outside and said, "Look up at the heavens and count the stars—if indeed you can count them." Then he said to him, "So shall your offspring be."

⁶Abram believed the LORD, and he credited it to him as righteousness.

⁷He also said to him, "I am the LORD, who brought you out of Ur of the Chaldeans to give you this land to take possession of it."

⁸But Abram said, "O Sovereign LORD, how can I know that I will gain possession of it?"

⁹So the LORD said to him, "Bring me a heifer, a goat and a ram, each three years old, along with a dove and a young pigeon."

¹⁰Abram brought all these to him, cut them in two and arranged the halves opposite each other; the birds, however, he did not cut in half. ¹¹Then birds of prey came down on the carcasses, but Abram drove them away.

¹²As the sun was setting, Abram fell into a deep sleep, and a thick and dreadful darkness came over him. ¹³Then the LORD said to him, "Know for certain that your descendants will be strangers in a country not their own, and they will be enslaved and mistreated four hundred years. ¹⁴But I will punish the nation they serve as slaves, and afterward they will come out with great possessions. ¹⁵You, however, will go to your fathers in peace and be buried at a good old age. ¹⁶In the fourth generation your descendants will come back here, for the sin of the Amorites has not yet reached its full measure."

¹⁷When the sun had set and darkness had fallen, a smoking firepot with a blazing torch appeared and passed between the pieces. ¹⁸On that day the LORD made a covenant with Abram

a 1 Or sovereign   b 1 Or shield; / your reward will be very great
c 2 The meaning of the Hebrew for this phrase is uncertain.

and said, "To your descendants I give this land, from the river^a of Egypt to the great river, the Euphrates— ^{19}the land of the Kenites, Kenizzites, Kadmonites, ^{20}Hittites, Perizzites, Rephaites, ^{21}Amorites, Canaanites, Girgashites and Jebusites."

Hagar and Ishmael

16 Now Sarai, Abram's wife, had borne him no children. But she had an Egyptian maidservant named Hagar; ^{2}so she said to Abram, "The LORD has kept me from having children. Go, sleep with my maidservant; perhaps I can build a family through her."

Abram agreed to what Sarai said. ^{3}So after Abram had been living in Canaan ten years, Sarai his wife took her Egyptian maidservant Hagar and gave her to her husband to be his wife. ^{4}He slept with Hagar, and she conceived.

When she knew she was pregnant, she began to despise her mistress. ^{5}Then Sarai said to Abram, "You are responsible for the wrong I am suffering. I put my servant in your arms, and now that she knows she is pregnant, she despises me. May the LORD judge between you and me."

^{6}"Your servant is in your hands," Abram said. "Do with her whatever you think best." Then Sarai mistreated Hagar; so she fled from her.

^{7}The angel of the LORD found Hagar near a spring in the desert; it was the spring that is beside the road to Shur. ^{8}And he said, "Hagar, servant of Sarai, where have you come from, and where are you going?"

"I'm running away from my mistress Sarai," she answered.

^{9}Then the angel of the LORD told her, "Go back to your mistress and submit to her." ^{10}The angel added, "I will so increase your descendants that they will be too numerous to count."

^{11}The angel of the LORD also said to her:

"You are now with child
   and you will have a son.
You shall name him Ishmael,^{b}
   for the LORD has heard of your misery.
^{12}He will be a wild donkey of a man;
   his hand will be against everyone
   and everyone's hand against him,
   and he will live in hostility
   toward^c all his brothers."

及河直到幼發拉底大河之地，^{19}就是基尼人、基尼洗人、甲摩尼人、^{20}赫人、比利洗人、利乏音人、^{21}亞摩利人、迦南人、革迦撒人、耶布斯人之地。"

夏甲生以實瑪利

16 亞伯蘭的妻子撒萊不給他生兒女。撒萊有一個使女名叫夏甲，是埃及人。^{2}撒萊對亞伯蘭說："耶和華使我不能生育，求你和我的使女同房，或者我可以因她得孩子（註："得孩子"原文作"被建立"）。"

亞伯蘭聽從了撒萊的話。^{3}於是亞伯蘭的妻子撒萊將使女埃及人夏甲給了丈夫為妾。那時亞伯蘭在迦南已經住了十年。^{4}亞伯蘭與夏甲同房，夏甲就懷了孕。

她見自己有孕，就小看她的主母。^{5}撒萊對亞伯蘭說："我因你受屈，我將我的使女放在你懷中，她見自己有了孕就小看我，願耶和華在你我中間判斷。"

^{6}亞伯蘭對撒萊說："使女在你手下，你可以隨意待她。"撒萊苦待她，她就從撒萊面前逃走了。

^{7}耶和華的使者在曠野書珥路上的水泉旁遇見她，^{8}對她說："撒萊的使女夏甲，你從哪裏來？要往哪裏去？"

夏甲說："我從我的主母撒萊面前逃出來。"

^{9}耶和華的使者對她說："你回到你主母那裏，服在她手下。"^{10}又說："我必使你的後裔極其繁多，甚至不可勝數。"

^{11}並說：

"你如今懷孕要生一個兒子，
   可以給他起名叫以實瑪利（註："以實瑪利"就是"神聽見"的意思），
   因為耶和華聽見了你的苦情。
^{12}他為人必像野驢。
   他的手要攻打人，
   人的手也要攻打他。
   他必住在眾弟兄的東邊。"

---

a 18 Or Wadi   b 11 Ishmael means God hears.   c 12 Or live to the east | of

13夏甲就稱那對她說話的耶和華為「看顧人的神」。因而說：「在這裏我也看見那看顧我的嗎？」14所以這井名叫庇耳拉海萊。這井正在加低斯和巴列中間。

15後來夏甲給亞伯蘭生了一個兒子，亞伯蘭給他起名叫以實瑪利。16夏甲給亞伯蘭生以實瑪利的時候，亞伯蘭年八十六歲。

割禮之約

17 亞伯蘭年九十九歲的時候，耶和華向他顯現，對他說：「我是全能的神，你當在我面前作完全人，2我就與你立約，使你的後裔極其繁多。」

3亞伯蘭俯伏在地，神又對他說：4「我與你立約，你要作多國的父。5從此以後，你的名不再叫亞伯蘭，要叫亞伯拉罕，因為我已立你作多國的父。6我必使你的後裔極其繁多，國度從你而立，君王從你而出。7我要與你並你世世代代的後裔堅立我的約，作永遠的約，是要作你和你後裔的神。8我要將你現在寄居的地，就是迦南全地，賜給你和你的後裔，永遠為業。我也必作他們的神。」

9神又對亞伯拉罕說：「你和你的後裔必世世代代遵守我的約。10你們所有的男子都要受割禮，這就是我與你，並你的後裔所立的約，是你們所當遵守的。11你們都要受割禮（註：「受割禮」原文作「割陽皮」。14、23、24、25節同），這是我與你們立約的證據。12你們世世代代的男子，無論是家裏生的，是在你後裔之外用銀子從外人買的，生下來第八日，都要受割禮。13你家裏生的和你用銀子買的，都必須受割禮。這樣，我的約就立在你們肉體上，作永遠的約。14但不受割禮的男子，必從民中剪除，因他背了我的約。」

13She gave this name to the LORD who spoke to her: "You are the God who sees me," for she said, "I have now seen*a* the One who sees me." 14That is why the well was called Beer Lahai Roi*b*; it is still there, between Kadesh and Bered.

15So Hagar bore Abram a son, and Abram gave the name Ishmael to the son she had borne. 16Abram was eighty-six years old when Hagar bore him Ishmael.

The Covenant of Circumcision

17 When Abram was ninety-nine years old, the LORD appeared to him and said, "I am God Almighty*c*; walk before me and be blameless. 2I will confirm my covenant between me and you and will greatly increase your numbers."

3Abram fell facedown, and God said to him, 4"As for me, this is my covenant with you: You will be the father of many nations. 5No longer will you be called Abram*d*; your name will be Abraham,*e* for I have made you a father of many nations. 6I will make you very fruitful; I will make nations of you, and kings will come from you. 7I will establish my covenant as an everlasting covenant between me and you and your descendants after you for the generations to come, to be your God and the God of your descendants after you. 8The whole land of Canaan, where you are now an alien, I will give as an everlasting possession to you and your descendants after you; and I will be their God."

9Then God said to Abraham, "As for you, you must keep my covenant, you and your descendants after you for the generations to come. 10This is my covenant with you and your descendants after you, the covenant you are to keep: Every male among you shall be circumcised. 11You are to undergo circumcision, and it will be the sign of the covenant between me and you. 12For the generations to come every male among you who is eight days old must be circumcised, including those born in your household or bought with money from a foreigner—those who are not your offspring. 13Whether born in your household or bought with your money, they must be circumcised. My covenant in your flesh is to be an everlasting covenant. 14Any uncircumcised male, who has not been circumcised in the flesh, will be cut off from his people; he has broken my covenant."

---

a 13 Or seen the back of   b 14 Beer Lahai Roi means well of the Living One who sees me.   c 1 Hebrew El-Shaddai   d 5 Abram means exalted father.   e 5 Abraham means father of many.

¹⁵God also said to Abraham, "As for Sarai your wife, you are no longer to call her Sarai; her name will be Sarah. ¹⁶I will bless her and will surely give you a son by her. I will bless her so that she will be the mother of nations; kings of peoples will come from her."

¹⁷Abraham fell facedown; he laughed and said to himself, "Will a son be born to a man a hundred years old? Will Sarah bear a child at the age of ninety?" ¹⁸And Abraham said to God, "If only Ishmael might live under your blessing!"

¹⁹Then God said, "Yes, but your wife Sarah will bear you a son, and you will call him Isaac.ᵃ I will establish my covenant with him as an everlasting covenant for his descendants after him. ²⁰And as for Ishmael, I have heard you: I will surely bless him; I will make him fruitful and will greatly increase his numbers. He will be the father of twelve rulers, and I will make him into a great nation. ²¹But my covenant I will establish with Isaac, whom Sarah will bear to you by this time next year." ²²When he had finished speaking with Abraham, God went up from him.

²³On that very day Abraham took his son Ishmael and all those born in his household or bought with his money, every male in his household, and circumcised them, as God told him. ²⁴Abraham was ninety-nine years old when he was circumcised, ²⁵and his son Ishmael was thirteen; ²⁶Abraham and his son Ishmael were both circumcised on that same day. ²⁷And every male in Abraham's household, including those born in his household or bought from a foreigner, was circumcised with him.

The Three Visitors

18 The Lᴏʀᴅ appeared to Abraham near the great trees of Mamre while he was sitting at the entrance to his tent in the heat of the day. ²Abraham looked up and saw three men standing nearby. When he saw them, he hurried from the entrance of his tent to meet them and bowed low to the ground.

³He said, "If I have found favor in your eyes, my lord,ᵇ do not pass your servant by. ⁴Let a little water be brought, and then you may all wash your feet and rest under this tree. ⁵Let me get you something to eat, so you can be refreshed and then go on your way—now that you have come to your servant."

"Very well," they answered, "do as you say."

⁶So Abraham hurried into the tent to Sarah.

¹⁵神又對亞伯拉罕說："你的妻子撒萊，不可再叫撒萊，她的名要叫撒拉。¹⁶我必賜福給她，也要使你從她得一個兒子。我要賜福給她，她也要作多國之母；必有百姓的君王從她而出。"

¹⁷亞伯拉罕就俯伏在地喜笑，心裏說："一百歲的人還能得孩子嗎？撒拉已經九十歲了，還能生養嗎？"¹⁸亞伯拉罕對神說："但願以實瑪利活在你面前。"

¹⁹神說："不然，你妻子撒拉要給你生一個兒子，你要給他起名叫以撒。我要與他堅定所立的約，作他後裔永遠的約。²⁰至於以實瑪利，我也應允你，我必賜福給他，使他昌盛，極其繁多。他必生十二個族長；我也要使他成為大國。²¹到明年這時節，撒拉必給你生以撒，我要與他堅定所立的約。"²²神和亞伯拉罕說完了話，就離開他上升去了。

²³正當那日，亞伯拉罕遵着神的命，給他的兒子以實瑪利和家裏的一切男子，無論是在家裏生的，是用銀子買的，都行了割禮。²⁴亞伯拉罕受割禮的時候年九十九歲。²⁵他兒子以實瑪利受割禮的時候年十三歲。²⁶正當那日，亞伯拉罕和他兒子以實瑪利一同受了割禮。²⁷家裏所有的人，無論是在家裏生的，是用銀子從外人買的，也都一同受了割禮。

三位天使到訪

18 耶和華在幔利橡樹那裏，向亞伯拉罕顯出來。那時正熱，亞伯拉罕坐在帳棚門口，²舉目觀看，見有三個人在對面站着。他一見，就從帳棚門口跑去迎接他們，俯伏在地。

³說："我主，我若在你眼前蒙恩，求你不要離開僕人往前去。⁴容我拿點水來，你們洗洗腳，在樹下歇息歇息。⁵我再拿一點餅來，你們可以加添心力，然後往前去。你們既到僕人這裏來，理當如此。"

他們說："就照你說的行吧！"
⁶亞伯拉罕急忙進帳棚見撒拉，

ᵃ 19 Isaac means he laughs.   ᵇ 3 Or O Lord

說：“你速速拿三細亞細麵調和做餅。”

7亞伯拉罕又跑到牛羣裏，牽了一隻又嫩又好的牛犢來，交給僕人，僕人急忙預備好了。8亞伯拉罕又取了奶油和奶，並預備好的牛犢來，擺在他們面前，自己在樹下站在旁邊，他們就吃了。

9他們問亞伯拉罕說：“你妻子撒拉在哪裏？”

他說：“在帳棚裏。”

10三人中有一位說：“到明年這時候，我必要回到你這裏，你的妻子撒拉必生一個兒子。”

撒拉在那人後邊的帳棚門口也聽見了這話。11亞伯拉罕和撒拉年紀老邁，撒拉的月經已斷絕了。12撒拉心裏暗笑，說：“我既已衰敗，我主也老邁，豈能有這喜事呢？”

13耶和華對亞伯拉罕說：“撒拉為甚麼暗笑，說：‘我既已年老，果真能生養嗎？’14耶和華豈有難成的事嗎？到了日期，明年這時候，我必回到你這裏，撒拉必生一個兒子。”

15撒拉就害怕，不承認，說“我沒有笑。”

那位說：“不然，你實在笑了。”

亞伯拉罕為所多瑪祈求

16三人就從那裏起行，向所多瑪觀看，亞伯拉罕也與他們同行，要送他們一程。17耶和華說：“我所要做的事豈可瞞着亞伯拉罕呢？18亞伯拉罕必要成為強大的國，地上的萬國都必因他得福。19我眷顧他，為要叫他吩咐他的眾子和他的眷屬遵守我的道，秉公行義，使我所應許亞伯拉罕的話都成就了。”

20耶和華說：“所多瑪和蛾摩拉的罪惡甚重，聲聞於我。21我現在要下去，察看他們所行的，果然盡像那達到我耳中的聲音一樣嗎？若是不然，我也必知道。”

22二人轉身離開那裏，向所多瑪去，但亞伯拉罕仍舊站在耶和華面前。23亞伯拉罕近前來說：“無論善

"Quick," he said, "get three seahs*a* of fine flour and knead it and bake some bread."

7Then he ran to the herd and selected a choice, tender calf and gave it to a servant, who hurried to prepare it. 8He then brought some curds and milk and the calf that had been prepared, and set these before them. While they ate, he stood near them under a tree.

9"Where is your wife Sarah?" they asked him.

"There, in the tent," he said.

10Then the LORD*b* said, "I will surely return to you about this time next year, and Sarah your wife will have a son."

Now Sarah was listening at the entrance to the tent, which was behind him. 11Abraham and Sarah were already old and well advanced in years, and Sarah was past the age of childbearing. 12So Sarah laughed to herself as she thought, "After I am worn out and my master*c* is old, will I now have this pleasure?"

13Then the LORD said to Abraham, "Why did Sarah laugh and say, 'Will I really have a child, now that I am old?' 14Is anything too hard for the LORD? I will return to you at the appointed time next year and Sarah will have a son."

15Sarah was afraid, so she lied and said, "I did not laugh."

But he said, "Yes, you did laugh."

Abraham Pleads for Sodom

16When the men got up to leave, they looked down toward Sodom, and Abraham walked along with them to see them on their way. 17Then the LORD said, "Shall I hide from Abraham what I am about to do? 18Abraham will surely become a great and powerful nation, and all nations on earth will be blessed through him. 19For I have chosen him, so that he will direct his children and his household after him to keep the way of the LORD by doing what is right and just, so that the LORD will bring about for Abraham what he has promised him."

20Then the LORD said, "The outcry against Sodom and Gomorrah is so great and their sin so grievous 21that I will go down and see if what they have done is as bad as the outcry that has reached me. If not, I will know."

22The men turned away and went toward Sodom, but Abraham remained standing before the LORD.*d* 23Then Abraham approached him and said: "Will you sweep away the righteous

a 6 That is, probably about 20 quarts (about 22 liters)   b 10 Hebrew Then he   c 12 Or husband   d 22 Masoretic Text; an ancient Hebrew scribal tradition but the LORD remained standing before Abraham

with the wicked? ²⁴What if there are fifty righteous people in the city? Will you really sweep it away and not spare*ᵃ* the place for the sake of the fifty righteous people in it? ²⁵Far be it from you to do such a thing—to kill the righteous with the wicked, treating the righteous and the wicked alike. Far be it from you! Will not the Judge*ᵇ* of all the earth do right?"

²⁶The LORD said, "If I find fifty righteous people in the city of Sodom, I will spare the whole place for their sake."

²⁷Then Abraham spoke up again: "Now that I have been so bold as to speak to the Lord, though I am nothing but dust and ashes, ²⁸what if the number of the righteous is five less than fifty? Will you destroy the whole city because of five people?"

"If I find forty-five there," he said, "I will not destroy it."

²⁹Once again he spoke to him, "What if only forty are found there?"

He said, "For the sake of forty, I will not do it."

³⁰Then he said, "May the Lord not be angry, but let me speak. What if only thirty can be found there?"

He answered, "I will not do it if I find thirty there."

³¹Abraham said, "Now that I have been so bold as to speak to the Lord, what if only twenty can be found there?"

He said, "For the sake of twenty, I will not destroy it."

³²Then he said, "May the Lord not be angry, but let me speak just once more. What if only ten can be found there?"

He answered, "For the sake of ten, I will not destroy it."

³³When the LORD had finished speaking with Abraham, he left, and Abraham returned home.

Sodom and Gomorrah Destroyed

19 The two angels arrived at Sodom in the evening, and Lot was sitting in the gateway of the city. When he saw them, he got up to meet them and bowed down with his face to the ground. ²"My lords," he said, "please turn aside to your servant's house. You can wash your feet and spend the night and then go on your way early in the morning."

"No," they answered, "we will spend the night in the square."

³But he insisted so strongly that they did go with him and entered his house. He prepared a

a 24 Or *forgive*; also in verse 26   *b* 25 Or *Ruler*

惡，你都要剿滅嗎？²⁴假若那城裏有五十個義人，你還剿滅那地方嗎？不為城裏這五十個義人饒恕其中的人嗎？²⁵將義人與惡人同殺，將義人與惡人一樣看待，這斷不是你所行的。審判全地的主豈不行公義嗎？"

²⁶耶和華說："我若在所多瑪城裏見有五十個義人，我就為他們的緣故饒恕那地方的眾人。"

²⁷亞伯拉罕說："我雖然是灰塵，還敢對主說話。²⁸假若這五十個義人短了五個，你就因為短了五個毀滅全城嗎？"

他說："我在那裏若見有四十五個，也不毀滅那城。"

²⁹亞伯拉罕又對他說："假若在那裏見有四十個怎麼樣呢？"

他說："為這四十個的緣故，我也不做這事。"

³⁰亞伯拉罕說："求主不要動怒，容我說，假若在那裏見有三十個怎麼樣呢？"

他說："我在那裏若見有三十個，我也不做這事。"

³¹亞伯拉罕說："我還敢對主說話，假若在那裏見有二十個怎麼樣呢？"

他說："為這二十個的緣故，我也不毀滅那城。"

³²亞伯拉罕說："求主不要動怒，我再說這一次，假若在那裏見有十個呢？"

他說："為這十個的緣故，我也不毀滅那城。"

³³耶和華與亞伯拉罕說完了話就走了；亞伯拉罕也回到自己的地方去了。

毀滅所多瑪與蛾摩拉

19 那兩個天使晚上到了所多瑪。羅得正坐在所多瑪城門口，看見他們，就起來迎接，臉伏於地下拜，²說："我主啊，請你們到僕人家裏洗洗腳，住一夜，清早起來再走。"

他們說："不！我們要在街上過夜。"

³羅得切切地請他們，他們這才進去到他屋裏。羅得為他們預備筵

席，烤無酵餅，他們就吃了。⁴他
們還沒有躺下，所多瑪城裏各處的
人，連老帶少，都來圍住那房子，
⁵呼叫羅得說：“今日晚上到你這
裏來的人在哪裏呢？把他們帶出
來，任我們所為。”

⁶羅得出來，把門關上，到眾人
那裏，⁷說：“眾弟兄，請你們不要
做這惡事。⁸我有兩個女兒，還是處
女，容我領出來任憑你們的心願而
行，只是這兩個人既然到我舍下，
不要向他們做甚麼。”

⁹眾人說：“退去吧！”又說：
“這個人來寄居，還想要作官哪！
現在我們要害你比害他們更甚。”
眾人就向前擁擠羅得，要攻破房
門。

¹⁰只是那二人伸出手來，將羅得
拉進屋去，把門關上，¹¹並且使門外
的人，無論老少，眼都昏迷；他們
摸來摸去，總尋不着房門。

¹²二人對羅得說：“你這裏還有
甚麼人嗎？無論是女婿，是兒女和
這城中一切屬你的人，你都要將他
們從這地方帶出去。¹³我們要毀滅這
地方，因為城內罪惡的聲音在耶和
華面前甚大，耶和華差我們來，要
毀滅這地方。”

¹⁴羅得就出去，告訴娶了他女兒
的女婿們（註：“娶了”或作“將要
娶”），說：“你們起來離開這地
方，因為耶和華要毀滅這城。”他
女婿們卻以為他說的是戲言。

¹⁵天明了，天使催逼羅得說：
“起來！帶着你的妻子和你在這裏
的兩個女兒出來，免得你因這城裏
的罪惡同被剿滅。”

¹⁶但羅得遲延不走。二人因為耶
和華憐恤羅得，就拉着他的手和他
妻子的手，並他兩個女兒的手，把
他們領出來，安置在城外；¹⁷領他們
出來以後，就說：“逃命吧！不可
回頭看，也不可在平原站住，要往
山上逃跑，免得你被剿滅。”

¹⁸羅得對他們說：“我主啊，不
要如此。¹⁹你僕人已經在你眼前蒙恩，

meal for them, baking bread without yeast, and
they ate. ⁴Before they had gone to bed, all the
men from every part of the city of Sodom—both
young and old—surrounded the house. ⁵They
called to Lot, "Where are the men who came to
you tonight? Bring them out to us so that we can
have sex with them."

⁶Lot went outside to meet them and shut the
door behind him ⁷and said, "No, my friends.
Don't do this wicked thing. ⁸Look, I have two
daughters who have never slept with a man. Let
me bring them out to you, and you can do what
you like with them. But don't do anything to
these men, for they have come under the protection of my roof."

⁹"Get out of our way," they replied. And they
said, "This fellow came here as an alien, and
now he wants to play the judge! We'll treat you
worse than them." They kept bringing pressure
on Lot and moved forward to break down the
door.

¹⁰But the men inside reached out and pulled
Lot back into the house and shut the door.
¹¹Then they struck the men who were at the
door of the house, young and old, with blindness so that they could not find the door.

¹²The two men said to Lot, "Do you have
anyone else here—sons-in-law, sons or daughters, or anyone else in the city who belongs to
you? Get them out of here, ¹³because we are
going to destroy this place. The outcry to the
LORD against its people is so great that he has
sent us to destroy it."

¹⁴So Lot went out and spoke to his sons-in-
law, who were pledged to marry*a* his daughters.
He said, "Hurry and get out of this place,
because the LORD is about to destroy the city!"
But his sons-in-law thought he was joking.

¹⁵With the coming of dawn, the angels urged
Lot, saying, "Hurry! Take your wife and your
two daughters who are here, or you will be
swept away when the city is punished."

¹⁶When he hesitated, the men grasped his
hand and the hands of his wife and of his two
daughters and led them safely out of the city,
for the LORD was merciful to them. ¹⁷As soon as
they had brought them out, one of them said,
"Flee for your lives! Don't look back, and don't
stop anywhere in the plain! Flee to the mountains or you will be swept away!"

¹⁸But Lot said to them, "No, my lords,*b*
please! ¹⁹Your*c* servant has found favor in your*c*

a 14 Or *were married to*   b 18 Or *No, Lord*; or *No, my lord*
c 19 The Hebrew is singular.

eyes, and you*a* have shown great kindness to me in sparing my life. But I can't flee to the mountains; this disaster will overtake me, and I'll die. ²⁰Look, here is a town near enough to run to, and it is small. Let me flee to it—it is very small, isn't it? Then my life will be spared."

²¹He said to him, "Very well, I will grant this request too; I will not overthrow the town you speak of. ²²But flee there quickly, because I cannot do anything until you reach it." (That is why the town was called Zoar.*b*)

²³By the time Lot reached Zoar, the sun had risen over the land. ²⁴Then the LORD rained down burning sulfur on Sodom and Gomorrah—from the LORD out of the heavens. ²⁵Thus he overthrew those cities and the entire plain, including all those living in the cities—and also the vegetation in the land. ²⁶But Lot's wife looked back, and she became a pillar of salt.

²⁷Early the next morning Abraham got up and returned to the place where he had stood before the LORD. ²⁸He looked down toward Sodom and Gomorrah, toward all the land of the plain, and he saw dense smoke rising from the land, like smoke from a furnace.

²⁹So when God destroyed the cities of the plain, he remembered Abraham, and he brought Lot out of the catastrophe that overthrew the cities where Lot had lived.

Lot and His Daughters

³⁰Lot and his two daughters left Zoar and settled in the mountains, for he was afraid to stay in Zoar. He and his two daughters lived in a cave. ³¹One day the older daughter said to the younger, "Our father is old, and there is no man around here to lie with us, as is the custom all over the earth. ³²Let's get our father to drink wine and then lie with him and preserve our family line through our father."

³³That night they got their father to drink wine, and the older daughter went in and lay with him. He was not aware of it when she lay down or when she got up.

³⁴The next day the older daughter said to the younger, "Last night I lay with my father. Let's get him to drink wine again tonight, and you go in and lie with him so we can preserve our family line through our father." ³⁵So they got their father to drink wine that night also, and the younger daughter went and lay with him. Again he was not aware of it when she lay down or when she got up.

a 19 The Hebrew is singular.   *b 22 Zoar means small.*

你又向我顯出莫大的慈愛，救我的性命，我不能逃到山上去，恐怕這災禍臨到我，我便死了。²⁰看哪，這座城又小又近，容易逃到，這不是一個小的嗎？求你容我逃到那裏，我的性命就得存活。"

²¹天使對他說："這事我也應允你，我不傾覆你所說的這城。²²你要速速地逃到那城，因為你還沒有到那裏，我不能做甚麼。"因此那城名叫瑣珥
（註："瑣珥"就是"小"的意思）。

²³羅得到了瑣珥，日頭已經出來了。²⁴當時，耶和華將硫磺與火，從天上耶和華那裏，降與所多瑪和蛾摩拉，²⁵把那些城和全平原，並城裏所有的居民，連地上生長的都毀滅了。²⁶羅得的妻子在後邊回頭一看，就變成了一根鹽柱。

²⁷亞伯拉罕清早起來，到了他從前站在耶和華面前的地方，²⁸向所多瑪和蛾摩拉與平原的全地觀看，不料，那地方煙氣上騰，如同燒窰一般。

²⁹當神毀滅平原諸城的時候，他記念亞伯拉罕，正在傾覆羅得所住之城的時候，就打發羅得從傾覆之中出來。

羅得與他的女兒

³⁰羅得因為怕住在瑣珥，就同他兩個女兒，從瑣珥上去住在山裏；他和兩個女兒住在一個洞裏。³¹大女兒對小女兒說："我們的父親老了，地上又無人按着世上的常規進到我們這裏。³²來！我們可以叫父親喝酒，與他同寢。這樣，我們好從他存留後裔。"

³³於是，那夜她們叫父親喝酒，大女兒就進去和她父親同寢。她幾時躺下，幾時起來，父親都不知道。

³⁴第二天，大女兒對小女兒說："我昨夜與父親同寢，今夜我們再叫他喝酒，你可以進去與他同寢。這樣，我們好從父親存留後裔。"³⁵於是，那夜她們又叫父親喝酒，小女兒起來與她父親同寢。她幾時躺下，幾時起來，父親都不知道。

³⁶這樣，羅得的兩個女兒都從她父親懷了孕。³⁷大女兒生了兒子，給他起名叫摩押，就是現今摩押人的始祖；³⁸小女兒也生了兒子，給他起名叫便亞米，就是現今亞捫人的始祖。

亞伯拉罕與亞比米勒

20 亞伯拉罕從那裏向南地遷去，寄居在加低斯和書珥中間的基拉耳。²亞伯拉罕稱他的妻撒拉為妹子。基拉耳王亞比米勒差人把撒拉取了去。

³但夜間，神來在夢中對亞比米勒說：「你是個死人哪！因為你取了那女人來，她原是別人的妻子。」

⁴亞比米勒卻還沒有親近撒拉。他說：「主啊，連有義的國你也要毀滅嗎？⁵那人豈不是自己對我說『她是我的妹子』嗎？就是女人也自己說：『他是我的哥哥。』我做這事是心正手潔的。」

⁶神在夢中對他說：「我知道你做這事是心中正直，我也攔阻了你，免得你得罪我，所以我不容你沾着她。⁷現在你把這人的妻子歸還他，因為他是先知，他要為你禱告，使你存活。你若不歸還他，你當知道，你和你所有的人都必要死。」

⁸亞比米勒清早起來，召了眾臣僕來，將這些事都說給他們聽，他們都甚懼怕。⁹亞比米勒召了亞伯拉罕來，對他說：「你怎麼向我這樣行呢？我在甚麼事上得罪了你，你竟使我和我國裏的人陷在大罪裏！你向我行不當行的事了！」¹⁰亞比米勒又對亞伯拉罕說：「你見了甚麼才做這事呢？」

¹¹亞伯拉罕說：「我以為這地方的人總不懼怕神，必為我妻子的緣故殺我。¹²況且她也實在是我的妹子，她與我是同父異母，後來作了我的妻子。¹³當神叫我離開父家飄流在外的時候，我對她說：『我們無論走到甚麼地方，你可以對人說，他是我的哥哥；這就是你待我的恩典了。』」

¹⁴亞比米勒把牛羊、僕婢賜給亞伯

³⁶So both of Lot's daughters became pregnant by their father. ³⁷The older daughter had a son, and she named him Moab*a*; he is the father of the Moabites of today. ³⁸The younger daughter also had a son, and she named him Ben-Ammi*b*; he is the father of the Ammonites of today.

Abraham and Abimelech

20 Now Abraham moved on from there into the region of the Negev and lived between Kadesh and Shur. For a while he stayed in Gerar, ²and there Abraham said of his wife Sarah, "She is my sister." Then Abimelech king of Gerar sent for Sarah and took her.

³But God came to Abimelech in a dream one night and said to him, "You are as good as dead because of the woman you have taken; she is a married woman."

⁴Now Abimelech had not gone near her, so he said, "Lord, will you destroy an innocent nation? ⁵Did he not say to me, 'She is my sister,' and didn't she also say, 'He is my brother'? I have done this with a clear conscience and clean hands."

⁶Then God said to him in the dream, "Yes, I know you did this with a clear conscience, and so I have kept you from sinning against me. That is why I did not let you touch her. ⁷Now return the man's wife, for he is a prophet, and he will pray for you and you will live. But if you do not return her, you may be sure that you and all yours will die."

⁸Early the next morning Abimelech summoned all his officials, and when he told them all that had happened, they were very much afraid. ⁹Then Abimelech called Abraham in and said, "What have you done to us? How have I wronged you that you have brought such great guilt upon me and my kingdom? You have done things to me that should not be done." ¹⁰And Abimelech asked Abraham, "What was your reason for doing this?"

¹¹Abraham replied, "I said to myself, 'There is surely no fear of God in this place, and they will kill me because of my wife.' ¹²Besides, she really is my sister, the daughter of my father though not of my mother; and she became my wife. ¹³And when God had me wander from my father's household, I said to her, 'This is how you can show your love to me: Everywhere we go, say of me, "He is my brother." ' "

¹⁴Then Abimelech brought sheep and cattle

a 37 Moab sounds like the Hebrew for *from father.*　　*b 38 Ben-Ammi* means *son of my people.*

and male and female slaves and gave them to Abraham, and he returned Sarah his wife to him. ¹⁵And Abimelech said, "My land is before you; live wherever you like."

¹⁶To Sarah he said, "I am giving your brother a thousand shekels*ᵃ* of silver. This is to cover the offense against you before all who are with you; you are completely vindicated."

¹⁷Then Abraham prayed to God, and God healed Abimelech, his wife and his slave girls so they could have children again, ¹⁸for the LORD had closed up every womb in Abimelech's household because of Abraham's wife Sarah.

The Birth of Isaac

21 Now the LORD was gracious to Sarah as he had said, and the LORD did for Sarah what he had promised. ²Sarah became pregnant and bore a son to Abraham in his old age, at the very time God had promised him. ³Abraham gave the name Isaac*ᵇ* to the son Sarah bore him. ⁴When his son Isaac was eight days old, Abraham circumcised him, as God commanded him. ⁵Abraham was a hundred years old when his son Isaac was born to him.

⁶Sarah said, "God has brought me laughter, and everyone who hears about this will laugh with me." ⁷And she added, "Who would have said to Abraham that Sarah would nurse children? Yet I have borne him a son in his old age."

Hagar and Ishmael Sent Away

⁸The child grew and was weaned, and on the day Isaac was weaned Abraham held a great feast. ⁹But Sarah saw that the son whom Hagar the Egyptian had borne to Abraham was mocking, ¹⁰and she said to Abraham, "Get rid of that slave woman and her son, for that slave woman's son will never share in the inheritance with my son Isaac."

¹¹The matter distressed Abraham greatly because it concerned his son. ¹²But God said to him, "Do not be so distressed about the boy and your maidservant. Listen to whatever Sarah tells you, because it is through Isaac that your off-spring*ᶜ* will be reckoned. ¹³I will make the son of the maidservant into a nation also, because he is your offspring."

¹⁴Early the next morning Abraham took some food and a skin of water and gave them to Hagar. He set them on her shoulders and then sent her off with the boy. She went on her way and wandered in the desert of Beersheba.

a 16 That is, about 25 pounds (about 11.5 kilograms)
b 3 Isaac means he laughs.   c 12 Or seed

拉罕，又把他的妻子撒拉歸還他。¹⁵亞比米勒又說："看哪，我的地都在你面前，你可以隨意居住。"

¹⁶又對撒拉說："我給你哥哥一千銀子，作為你在闔家人面前遮羞的（註："羞"原文作"眼"），你就在眾人面前沒有不是了。"

¹⁷亞伯拉罕禱告神，神就醫好了亞比米勒和他的妻子，並他的眾女僕，她們便能生育。¹⁸因耶和華為亞伯拉罕的妻子撒拉的緣故，已經使亞比米勒家中的婦人不能生育。

以撒出生

21 耶和華按着先前的話眷顧撒拉，便照他所說的給撒拉成就。²當亞伯拉罕年老的時候，撒拉懷了孕，到神所說的日期，就給亞伯拉罕生了一個兒子。³亞伯拉罕給撒拉所生的兒子起名叫以撒。⁴以撒生下來第八日，亞伯拉罕照着神所吩咐的，給以撒行了割禮。⁵他兒子以撒生的時候，亞伯拉罕年一百歲。

⁶撒拉說："神使我喜笑，凡聽見的必與我一同喜笑。"⁷又說："誰能預先對亞伯拉罕說'撒拉要乳養嬰孩'呢？因為在他年老的時候，我給他生了一個兒子。"

夏甲與以實瑪利被趕走

⁸孩子漸長，就斷了奶。以撒斷奶的日子，亞伯拉罕設擺豐盛的筵席。⁹當時，撒拉看見埃及人夏甲給亞伯拉罕所生的兒子戲笑，¹⁰就對亞伯拉罕說："你把這使女和她兒子趕出去！因為這使女的兒子不可與我的兒子以撒一同承受產業。"

¹¹亞伯拉罕因他兒子的緣故很憂愁。¹²神對亞伯拉罕說："你不必為這童子和你的使女憂愁，凡撒拉對你說的話，你都該聽從，因為從以撒生的，才要稱為你的後裔。¹³至於使女的兒子，我也必使他的後裔成立一國，因為他是你所生的。"

¹⁴亞伯拉罕清早起來，拿餅和一皮袋水，給了夏甲，搭在她的肩上，又把孩子交給她，打發她走。夏甲就走了，在別是巴的曠野走迷了路。

¹⁵皮袋的水用盡了，夏甲就把孩子撇在小樹底下，¹⁶自己走開約有一箭之遠，相對而坐，說：「我不忍見孩子死！」就相對而坐，放聲大哭。

¹⁷神聽見童子的聲音。神的使者從天上呼叫夏甲說：「夏甲！你為何這樣呢？不要害怕，神已經聽見童子的聲音了。¹⁸起來！把童子抱在懷中（註：「懷」原文作「手」），我必使他的後裔成為大國。」

¹⁹神使夏甲的眼睛明亮，她就看見一口水井，便去將皮袋盛滿了水，給童子喝。

²⁰神保佑童子，他就漸長，住在曠野，成了弓箭手。²¹他住在巴蘭的曠野，他母親從埃及地給他娶了一個妻子。

別是巴之約

²²當那時候，亞比米勒同他軍長非各對亞伯拉罕說：「凡你所行的事都有神的保佑。²³我願你如今在這裏指着神對我起誓，不要欺負我與我的兒子，並我的子孫。我怎樣厚待了你，你也要照樣厚待我與你所寄居這地的民。」

²⁴亞伯拉罕說：「我情願起誓。」

²⁵從前亞比米勒的僕人霸佔了一口水井，亞伯拉罕為這事指責亞比米勒。²⁶亞比米勒說：「誰做這事我不知道，你也沒有告訴我，今日我才聽見了。」

²⁷亞伯拉罕把羊和牛給了亞比米勒，二人就彼此立約。²⁸亞伯拉罕把七隻母羊羔另放在一處。²⁹亞比米勒問亞伯拉罕說：「你把這七隻母羊羔另放在一處，是甚麼意思呢？」

³⁰他說：「你要從我手裏受這七隻母羊羔，作我挖這口井的證據。」³¹所以他給那地方起名叫別是巴，因為他們二人在那裏起了誓（註：「別是巴」就是「盟誓的井」）。

³²他們在別是巴立了約，亞比米勒就同他軍長非各起身回非利士地去了。³³亞伯拉罕在別是巴栽上一棵垂絲柳樹，又在那裏求告耶和華永生神的名。³⁴亞伯拉罕在非利士人的地寄居了多日。

¹⁵When the water in the skin was gone, she put the boy under one of the bushes. ¹⁶Then she went off and sat down nearby, about a bowshot away, for she thought, "I cannot watch the boy die." And as she sat there nearby, she^a began to sob.

¹⁷God heard the boy crying, and the angel of God called to Hagar from heaven and said to her, "What is the matter, Hagar? Do not be afraid; God has heard the boy crying as he lies there. ¹⁸Lift the boy up and take him by the hand, for I will make him into a great nation."

¹⁹Then God opened her eyes and she saw a well of water. So she went and filled the skin with water and gave the boy a drink.

²⁰God was with the boy as he grew up. He lived in the desert and became an archer. ²¹While he was living in the Desert of Paran, his mother got a wife for him from Egypt.

The Treaty at Beersheba

²²At that time Abimelech and Phicol the commander of his forces said to Abraham, "God is with you in everything you do. ²³Now swear to me here before God that you will not deal falsely with me or my children or my descendants. Show to me and the country where you are living as an alien the same kindness I have shown to you."

²⁴Abraham said, "I swear it."

²⁵Then Abraham complained to Abimelech about a well of water that Abimelech's servants had seized. ²⁶But Abimelech said, "I don't know who has done this. You did not tell me, and I heard about it only today."

²⁷So Abraham brought sheep and cattle and gave them to Abimelech, and the two men made a treaty. ²⁸Abraham set apart seven ewe lambs from the flock, ²⁹and Abimelech asked Abraham, "What is the meaning of these seven ewe lambs you have set apart by themselves?"

³⁰He replied, "Accept these seven lambs from my hand as a witness that I dug this well."

³¹So that place was called Beersheba,^b because the two men swore an oath there.

³²After the treaty had been made at Beersheba, Abimelech and Phicol the commander of his forces returned to the land of the Philistines. ³³Abraham planted a tamarisk tree in Beersheba, and there he called upon the name of the LORD, the Eternal God. ³⁴And Abraham stayed in the land of the Philistines for a long time.

---

a 16 Hebrew; Septuagint *the child*　　*b 31 Beersheba* can mean *well of seven* or *well of the oath.*

Abraham Tested

22 Some time later God tested Abraham. He said to him, "Abraham!"

"Here I am," he replied.

²Then God said, "Take your son, your only son, Isaac, whom you love, and go to the region of Moriah. Sacrifice him there as a burnt offering on one of the mountains I will tell you about."

³Early the next morning Abraham got up and saddled his donkey. He took with him two of his servants and his son Isaac. When he had cut enough wood for the burnt offering, he set out for the place God had told him about. ⁴On the third day Abraham looked up and saw the place in the distance. ⁵He said to his servants, "Stay here with the donkey while I and the boy go over there. We will worship and then we will come back to you."

⁶Abraham took the wood for the burnt offering and placed it on his son Isaac, and he himself carried the fire and the knife. As the two of them went on together, ⁷Isaac spoke up and said to his father Abraham, "Father?"

"Yes, my son?" Abraham replied.

"The fire and wood are here," Isaac said, "but where is the lamb for the burnt offering?"

⁸Abraham answered, "God himself will provide the lamb for the burnt offering, my son." And the two of them went on together.

⁹When they reached the place God had told him about, Abraham built an altar there and arranged the wood on it. He bound his son Isaac and laid him on the altar, on top of the wood. ¹⁰Then he reached out his hand and took the knife to slay his son. ¹¹But the angel of the LORD called out to him from heaven, "Abraham! Abraham!"

"Here I am," he replied.

¹²"Do not lay a hand on the boy," he said. "Do not do anything to him. Now I know that you fear God, because you have not withheld from me your son, your only son."

¹³Abraham looked up and there in a thicket he saw a ram*a* caught by its horns. He went over and took the ram and sacrificed it as a burnt offering instead of his son. ¹⁴So Abraham called that place The LORD Will Provide. And to this day it is said, "On the mountain of the LORD it will be provided."

¹⁵The angel of the LORD called to Abraham from heaven a second time ¹⁶and said, "I swear by myself, declares the LORD, that because you

---

神試驗亞伯拉罕

22 這些事以後，神要試驗亞伯拉罕，就呼叫他說："亞伯拉罕！"他說："我在這裏。"

² 神說："你帶着你的兒子，就是你獨生的兒子，你所愛的以撒，往摩利亞地去，在我所要指示你的山上，把他獻為燔祭。"

³ 亞伯拉罕清早起來，備上驢，帶着兩個僕人和他兒子以撒，也劈好了燔祭的柴，就起身往神所指示他的地方去了。⁴ 到了第三日，亞伯拉罕舉目遠遠地看見那地方。⁵ 亞伯拉罕對他的僕人說："你們和驢在此等候，我與童子往那裏去拜一拜，就回到你們這裏來。"

⁶ 亞伯拉罕把燔祭的柴放在他兒子以撒身上，自己手裏拿着火與刀，於是二人同行。⁷ 以撒對他父親亞伯拉罕說："父親哪！"

亞伯拉罕說："我兒，我在這裏。"

以撒說："請看，火與柴都有了，但燔祭的羊羔在哪裏呢？"

⁸ 亞伯拉罕說："我兒，神必自己預備作燔祭的羊羔。"於是二人同行。

⁹ 他們到了神所指示的地方，亞伯拉罕在那裏築壇，把柴擺好，捆綁他的兒子以撒，放在壇的柴上。¹⁰ 亞伯拉罕就伸手拿刀，要殺他的兒子。¹¹ 耶和華的使者從天上呼叫他說："亞伯拉罕！亞伯拉罕！"

他說："我在這裏。"

¹² 天使說："你不可在這童子身上下手，一點不可害他！現在我知道你是敬畏神的了，因為你沒有將你的兒子，就是你獨生的兒子，留下不給我。"

¹³ 亞伯拉罕舉目觀看，不料，有一隻公羊，兩角扣在稠密的小樹中，亞伯拉罕就取了那隻公羊來，獻為燔祭，代替他的兒子。¹⁴ 亞伯拉罕給那地方起名叫耶和華以勒（註：意思就是"耶和華必預備"），直到今日人還說："在耶和華的山上必有預備。"

¹⁵ 耶和華的使者第二次從天上呼叫亞伯拉罕說：¹⁶ "耶和華說：'你

---

a 13 Many manuscripts of the Masoretic Text, Samaritan Pentateuch, Septuagint and Syriac; most manuscripts of the Masoretic Text a ram behind [him]

既行了這事，不留下你的兒子，就是你獨生的兒子，我便指着自己起誓說：¹⁷論福，我必賜大福給你；論子孫，我必叫你的子孫多起來，如同天上的星，海邊的沙。你子孫必得着仇敵的城門，¹⁸並且地上萬國都必因你的後裔得福，因為你聽從了我的話。'"

¹⁹於是亞伯拉罕回到他僕人那裏，他們一同起身往別是巴去，亞伯拉罕就住在別是巴。

拿鶴的兒子

²⁰這事以後，有人告訴亞伯拉罕說："密迦給你兄弟拿鶴生了幾個兒子：²¹長子是烏斯，他的兄弟是布斯和亞蘭的父親基母利，²²並基薛、哈瑣、必達、益拉、彼土利，（彼土利生利百加）。"²³這八個人都是密迦給亞伯拉罕的兄弟拿鶴生的。²⁴拿鶴的妾名叫流瑪，生了提八、迦含、他轄和瑪迦。

撒拉去世

23 撒拉享壽一百二十七歲，這是撒拉一生的歲數。²撒拉死在迦南地的基列亞巴，就是希伯崙，亞伯拉罕為她哀慟哭號。

³後來亞伯拉罕從死人面前起來，對赫人說：⁴"我在你們中間是外人，是寄居的，求你們在這裏給我一塊地，我好埋葬我的死人，使她不在我眼前。"

⁵赫人回答亞伯拉罕說：⁶"我主請聽。你在我們中間是一位尊大的王子，只管在我們最好的墳地裏埋葬你的死人，我們沒有一人不容你在他的墳地裏埋葬你的死人。"

⁷亞伯拉罕就起來，向那地的赫人下拜，⁸對他們說："你們若有意叫我埋葬我的死人，使她不在我眼前，就請聽我的話，為我求瑣轄的兒子以弗崙，⁹把田頭上那麥比拉洞給我。他可以按着足價賣給我，作我在你們中間的墳地。"

¹⁰當時以弗崙正坐在赫人中間。於是，赫人以弗崙在城門出入的赫人面前對亞伯拉罕說：¹¹"不然，我主請聽。我送給你這塊田，連田間的洞也送給你，在我同族的人面前

have done this and have not withheld your son, your only son, ¹⁷I will surely bless you and make your descendants as numerous as the stars in the sky and as the sand on the seashore. Your descendants will take possession of the cities of their enemies, ¹⁸and through your offspring*a* all nations on earth will be blessed, because you have obeyed me."

¹⁹Then Abraham returned to his servants, and they set off together for Beersheba. And Abraham stayed in Beersheba.

Nahor's Sons

²⁰Some time later Abraham was told, "Milcah is also a mother; she has borne sons to your brother Nahor: ²¹Uz the firstborn, Buz his brother, Kemuel (the father of Aram), ²²Kesed, Hazo, Pildash, Jidlaph and Bethuel." ²³Bethuel became the father of Rebekah. Milcah bore these eight sons to Abraham's brother Nahor. ²⁴His concubine, whose name was Reumah, also had sons: Tebah, Gaham, Tahash and Maacah.

The Death of Sarah

23 Sarah lived to be a hundred and twenty-seven years old. ²She died at Kiriath Arba (that is, Hebron) in the land of Canaan, and Abraham went to mourn for Sarah and to weep over her.

³Then Abraham rose from beside his dead wife and spoke to the Hittites.*b* He said, ⁴"I am an alien and a stranger among you. Sell me some property for a burial site here so I can bury my dead."

⁵The Hittites replied to Abraham, ⁶"Sir, listen to us. You are a mighty prince among us. Bury your dead in the choicest of our tombs. None of us will refuse you his tomb for burying your dead."

⁷Then Abraham rose and bowed down before the people of the land, the Hittites. ⁸He said to them, "If you are willing to let me bury my dead, then listen to me and intercede with Ephron son of Zohar on my behalf ⁹so he will sell me the cave of Machpelah, which belongs to him and is at the end of his field. Ask him to sell it to me for the full price as a burial site among you."

¹⁰Ephron the Hittite was sitting among his people and he replied to Abraham in the hearing of all the Hittites who had come to the gate of his city. ¹¹"No, my lord," he said. "Listen to me; I give*c* you the field, and I give*c* you the

---

a 18 Or seed   b 3 Or the sons of Heth; also in verses 5, 7, 10, 16, 18 and 20   c 11 Or sell

cave that is in it. I give*a* it to you in the presence of my people. Bury your dead."

[12] Again Abraham bowed down before the people of the land [13] and he said to Ephron in their hearing, "Listen to me, if you will. I will pay the price of the field. Accept it from me so I can bury my dead there."

[14] Ephron answered Abraham, [15] "Listen to me, my lord; the land is worth four hundred shekels*b* of silver, but what is that between me and you? Bury your dead."

[16] Abraham agreed to Ephron's terms and weighed out for him the price he had named in the hearing of the Hittites: four hundred shekels of silver, according to the weight current among the merchants.

[17] So Ephron's field in Machpelah near Mamre—both the field and the cave in it, and all the trees within the borders of the field—was deeded [18] to Abraham as his property in the presence of all the Hittites who had come to the gate of the city. [19] Afterward Abraham buried his wife Sarah in the cave in the field of Machpelah near Mamre (which is at Hebron) in the land of Canaan. [20] So the field and the cave in it were deeded to Abraham by the Hittites as a burial site.

Isaac and Rebekah

24 Abraham was now old and well advanced in years, and the LORD had blessed him in every way. [2] He said to the chief*c* servant in his household, the one in charge of all that he had, "Put your hand under my thigh. [3] I want you to swear by the LORD, the God of heaven and the God of earth, that you will not get a wife for my son from the daughters of the Canaanites, among whom I am living, [4] but will go to my country and my own relatives and get a wife for my son Isaac."

[5] The servant asked him, "What if the woman is unwilling to come back with me to this land? Shall I then take your son back to the country you came from?"

[6] "Make sure that you do not take my son back there," Abraham said. [7] "The LORD, the God of heaven, who brought me out of my father's household and my native land and who spoke to me and promised me on oath, saying, 'To your offspring*d* I will give this land'—he will send his angel before you so that you can get a wife for my son from there. [8] If the woman is unwilling to come back with you, then you will

都給你，可以埋葬你的死人。"

[12]亞伯拉罕就在那地的人民面前下拜，[13]在他們面前對以弗崙說："你若應允，請聽我的話。我要把田價給你，求你收下，我就在那裏埋葬我的死人。"

[14]以弗崙回答亞伯拉罕說：[15]"我主請聽。值四百舍客勒銀子的一塊田，在你我中間還算甚麼呢？只管埋葬你的死人吧！"

[16]亞伯拉罕聽從了以弗崙，照着他在赫人面前所說的話，把買賣通用的銀子，平了四百舍客勒給以弗崙。

[17]於是，麥比拉、幔利前、以弗崙的那塊田和其中的洞，並田間四圍的樹木，[18]都定準歸與亞伯拉罕，乃是他在赫人面前，並城門出入的人面前買妥的。[19]此後，亞伯拉罕把他妻子撒拉埋葬在迦南地幔利前的麥比拉田間的洞裏。幔利就是希伯崙。[20]從此，那塊田和田間的洞，就藉着赫人定準，歸與亞伯拉罕作墳地。

以撒與利百加

24 亞伯拉罕年紀老邁，向來在一切事上耶和華都賜福給他。[2]亞伯拉罕對管理他全業最老的僕人說："請你把手放在我大腿底下。[3]我要叫你指着耶和華天地的主起誓，不要為我兒子娶這迦南地中的女子為妻。[4]你要往我本地本族去，為我的兒子以撒娶一個妻子。"

[5]僕人對他說："倘若女子不肯跟我到這地方來，我必須將你的兒子帶回你原出之地嗎？"

[6]亞伯拉罕對他說："你要謹慎，不要帶我的兒子回那裏去。[7]耶和華天上的主，曾帶領我離開父家和本族的地，對我說話，向我起誓說：'我要將這地賜給你的後裔。'他必差遣使者在你面前，你就可以從那裏為我兒子娶一個妻子。[8]倘若女子不肯跟你來，我使你起的誓就與你無干了，只是不可帶

a 11 Or *sell*   *b* 15 That is, about 10 pounds (about 4.5 kilograms)   *c* 2 Or *oldest*   *d* 7 Or *seed*

我的兒子回那裏去。"　⁹僕人就把手放在他主人<u>亞伯拉罕</u>的大腿底下，為這事向他起誓。

¹⁰那僕人從他主人的駱駝裏取了十匹駱駝，並帶些他主人各樣的財物，起身往<u>美索不達米亞</u>去，到了<u>拿鶴</u>的城。¹¹天將晚，眾女子出來打水的時候，他便叫駱駝跪在城外的水井那裏。

¹²他說："耶和華我主人<u>亞伯拉罕</u>的神啊，求你施恩給我主人<u>亞伯拉罕</u>，使我今日遇見好機會。¹³我現今站在井旁，城內居民的女子們正出來打水。¹⁴我向哪一個女子說：'請你拿下水瓶來，給我水喝。'她若說：'請喝，我也給你的駱駝喝。'願那女子就作你所預定給你僕人<u>以撒</u>的妻。這樣，我便知道你施恩給我主人了。"

¹⁵話還沒有說完，不料，<u>利百加</u>肩頭上扛着水瓶出來。<u>利百加</u>是<u>彼土利</u>所生的，<u>彼土利</u>是<u>亞伯拉罕</u>兄弟<u>拿鶴</u>妻子密迦的兒子。¹⁶那女子容貌極其俊美，還是處女，也未曾有人親近她。她下到井旁，打滿了瓶，又上來。

¹⁷僕人跑上前去迎着她，說："求你將瓶裏的水給我一點喝。"

¹⁸女子說："我主請喝。"就急忙拿下瓶來，托在手上給他喝。

¹⁹女子給他喝了，就說："我再為你的駱駝打水，叫駱駝也喝足。"²⁰她就急忙把瓶裏的水倒在槽裏，又跑到井旁打水，就為所有的駱駝打上水來。²¹那人定睛看她，一句話也不說，要曉得耶和華賜他通達的道路沒有。

²²駱駝喝足了，那人就拿一個金環，重半舍客勒，兩個金鐲，重十舍客勒，給了那女子，²³說："請告訴我，你是誰的女兒？你父親家裏有我們住宿的地方沒有？"

²⁴女子說："我是<u>密迦</u>與<u>拿鶴</u>之

be released from this oath of mine. Only do not take my son back there." ⁹So the servant put his hand under the thigh of his master Abraham and swore an oath to him concerning this matter.

¹⁰Then the servant took ten of his master's camels and left, taking with him all kinds of good things from his master. He set out for Aram Naharaim[a] and made his way to the town of Nahor. ¹¹He had the camels kneel down near the well outside the town; it was toward evening, the time the women go out to draw water.

¹²Then he prayed, "O LORD, God of my master Abraham, give me success today, and show kindness to my master Abraham. ¹³See, I am standing beside this spring, and the daughters of the townspeople are coming out to draw water. ¹⁴May it be that when I say to a girl, 'Please let down your jar that I may have a drink,' and she says, 'Drink, and I'll water your camels too'—let her be the one you have chosen for your servant Isaac. By this I will know that you have shown kindness to my master."

¹⁵Before he had finished praying, Rebekah came out with her jar on her shoulder. She was the daughter of Bethuel son of Milcah, who was the wife of Abraham's brother Nahor. ¹⁶The girl was very beautiful, a virgin; no man had ever lain with her. She went down to the spring, filled her jar and came up again.

¹⁷The servant hurried to meet her and said, "Please give me a little water from your jar."

¹⁸"Drink, my lord," she said, and quickly lowered the jar to her hands and gave him a drink.

¹⁹After she had given him a drink, she said, "I'll draw water for your camels too, until they have finished drinking." ²⁰So she quickly emptied her jar into the trough, ran back to the well to draw more water, and drew enough for all his camels. ²¹Without saying a word, the man watched her closely to learn whether or not the LORD had made his journey successful.

²²When the camels had finished drinking, the man took out a gold nose ring weighing a beka[b] and two gold bracelets weighing ten shekels.[c] ²³Then he asked, "Whose daughter are you? Please tell me, is there room in your father's house for us to spend the night?"

²⁴She answered him, "I am the daughter of Bethuel, the son that Milcah bore to Nahor."

a 10 That is, Northwest Mesopotamia　　*b 22* That is, about 1/5 ounce (about 5.5 grams)　　*c 22* That is, about 4 ounces (about 110 grams)

25And she added, "We have plenty of straw and fodder, as well as room for you to spend the night."

26Then the man bowed down and worshiped the LORD, 27saying, "Praise be to the LORD, the God of my master Abraham, who has not abandoned his kindness and faithfulness to my master. As for me, the LORD has led me on the journey to the house of my master's relatives."

28The girl ran and told her mother's household about these things. 29Now Rebekah had a brother named Laban, and he hurried out to the man at the spring. 30As soon as he had seen the nose ring, and the bracelets on his sister's arms, and had heard Rebekah tell what the man said to her, he went out to the man and found him standing by the camels near the spring. 31"Come, you who are blessed by the LORD," he said. "Why are you standing out here? I have prepared the house and a place for the camels."

32So the man went to the house, and the camels were unloaded. Straw and fodder were brought for the camels, and water for him and his men to wash their feet. 33Then food was set before him, but he said, "I will not eat until I have told you what I have to say."

"Then tell us," [Laban] said.

34So he said, "I am Abraham's servant. 35The LORD has blessed my master abundantly, and he has become wealthy. He has given him sheep and cattle, silver and gold, menservants and maidservants, and camels and donkeys. 36My master's wife Sarah has borne him a son in her*a* old age, and he has given him everything he owns. 37And my master made me swear an oath, and said, 'You must not get a wife for my son from the daughters of the Canaanites, in whose land I live, 38but go to my father's family and to my own clan, and get a wife for my son.'

39"Then I asked my master, 'What if the woman will not come back with me?'

40"He replied, 'The LORD, before whom I have walked, will send his angel with you and make your journey a success, so that you can get a wife for my son from my own clan and from my father's family. 41Then, when you go to my clan, you will be released from my oath even if they refuse to give her to you—you will be released from my oath.'

42"When I came to the spring today, I said, 'O LORD, God of my master Abraham, if you will, please grant success to the journey on which I have come. 43See, I am standing beside this spring; if a maiden comes out to draw water and

a 36 Or his

子彼土利的女兒。"25又說:"我們家裏足有糧草,也有住宿的地方。"

26那人就低頭向耶和華下拜,27說:"耶和華我主人亞伯拉罕的神是應當稱頌的,因他不斷地以慈愛誠實待我主人。至於我,耶和華在路上引領我,直走到我主人的兄弟家裏。"

28女子跑回去,照着這些話告訴她母親和她家裏的人。29、30利百加有一個哥哥,名叫拉班,看見金環,又看見金鐲在他妹子的手上,並聽見他妹子利百加的話,說那人對我如此如此說。拉班就跑出來往井旁去,到那人跟前,見他仍站在駱駝旁邊的井旁那裏,31便對他說:"你這蒙耶和華賜福的,請進來,為甚麼站在外邊?我已經收拾了房屋,也為駱駝預備了地方。"

32那人就進了拉班的家。拉班卸了駱駝,用草料餵上,拿水給那人和跟隨的人洗腳,33把飯擺在他面前,叫他吃。他卻說:"我不吃,等我說明白我的事情再吃。"

拉班說:"請說。"

34他說:"我是亞伯拉罕的僕人。35耶和華大大地賜福給我主人,使他昌大,又賜給他羊羣、牛羣、金銀、僕婢、駱駝和驢。36我主人的妻子撒拉年老的時候,給我主人生了一個兒子,我主人也將一切所有的都給了這個兒子。37我主人叫我起誓說:'你不要為我兒子娶迦南地的女子為妻,38你要往我父家、我本族那裏去,為我的兒子娶一個妻子。'

39"我對我主人說:'恐怕女子不肯跟我來。'

40"他就說:'我所侍奉的耶和華必要差遣他的使者與你同去,叫你的道路通達,你就得以在我父家、我本族那裏,給我的兒子娶一個妻子。41只要你到了我本族那裏,我使你起的誓就與你無干;他們若不把女子交給你,我使你起的誓也與你無干。'

42"我今日到了井旁,便說:'耶和華我主人亞伯拉罕的神啊,願你叫我所行的道路通達。43我如今站在井旁,對哪一個出來打水的女子說：請你把你瓶裏的水給我一點喝。 44她若說：你只管喝，我也為你的駱駝打水。願那女子就作耶和華給我主人兒子所預定的妻。'

45 "我心裏的話還沒有說完，利百加就出來，肩頭上扛着水瓶，下到井旁打水。我便對她說：'請你給我水喝。'

46 "她就急忙從肩頭上拿下瓶來，說：'請喝，我也給你的駱駝喝。'我便喝了；她又給我的駱駝喝了。

47 "我問她說：'你是誰的女兒？'

"她說：'我是密迦與拿鶴之子彼土利的女兒。'

"我就把環子戴在她鼻子上，把鐲子戴在她兩手上。 48隨後我低頭向耶和華下拜，稱頌耶和華我主人亞伯拉罕的神，因為他引導我走合式的道路，使我得着我主人兄弟的孫女，給我主人的兒子為妻。 49現在你們若願以慈愛誠實待我主人，就告訴我；若不然，也告訴我，使我可以或向左，或向右。"

50拉班和彼土利回答說："這事乃出於耶和華，我們不能向你說好說歹。 51看哪，利百加在你面前，可以將她帶去，照着耶和華所說的，給你主人的兒子為妻。"

52亞伯拉罕的僕人聽見他們這話，就向耶和華俯伏在地。 53當下僕人拿出金器、銀器和衣服送給利百加，又將寶物送給她哥哥和她母親。 54僕人和跟從他的人吃了喝了，住了一夜。

早晨起來，僕人就說："請打發我回我主人那裏去吧！"

55利百加的哥哥和她母親說："讓女子同我們再住幾天，至少十天，然後她可以去。"

56僕人說："耶和華既賜給我通達的道路，你們不要躭誤我，請打發我走，回我主人那裏去吧！"

57他們說："我們把女子叫來問問她"， 58叫了利百加來，問她說："你和這人同去嗎？"

利百加說："我去。"

59於是，他們打發妹子利百加和她的乳母，同亞伯拉罕的僕人，並跟從僕人的，都走了。 60他們就給利

I say to her, "Please let me drink a little water from your jar," [44]and if she says to me, "Drink, and I'll draw water for your camels too," let her be the one the LORD has chosen for my master's son.'

[45]"Before I finished praying in my heart, Rebekah came out, with her jar on her shoulder. She went down to the spring and drew water, and I said to her, 'Please give me a drink.'

[46]"She quickly lowered her jar from her shoulder and said, 'Drink, and I'll water your camels too.' So I drank, and she watered the camels also.

[47]"I asked her, 'Whose daughter are you?'

"She said, 'The daughter of Bethuel son of Nahor, whom Milcah bore to him.'

"Then I put the ring in her nose and the bracelets on her arms, [48]and I bowed down and worshiped the LORD. I praised the LORD, the God of my master Abraham, who had led me on the right road to get the granddaughter of my master's brother for his son. [49]Now if you will show kindness and faithfulness to my master, tell me; and if not, tell me, so I may know which way to turn."

[50]Laban and Bethuel answered, "This is from the LORD; we can say nothing to you one way or the other. [51]Here is Rebekah; take her and go, and let her become the wife of your master's son, as the LORD has directed."

[52]When Abraham's servant heard what they said, he bowed down to the ground before the LORD. [53]Then the servant brought out gold and silver jewelry and articles of clothing and gave them to Rebekah; he also gave costly gifts to her brother and to her mother. [54]Then he and the men who were with him ate and drank and spent the night there.

When they got up the next morning, he said, "Send me on my way to my master."

[55]But her brother and her mother replied, "Let the girl remain with us ten days or so; then you[a] may go."

[56]But he said to them, "Do not detain me, now that the LORD has granted success to my journey. Send me on my way so I may go to my master."

[57]Then they said, "Let's call the girl and ask her about it." [58]So they called Rebekah and asked her, "Will you go with this man?"

"I will go," she said.

[59]So they sent their sister Rebekah on her way, along with her nurse and Abraham's servant and his men. [60]And they blessed Rebekah

and said to her,

"Our sister, may you increase
  to thousands upon thousands;
may your offspring possess
  the gates of their enemies."

⁶¹Then Rebekah and her maids got ready and
mounted their camels and went back with the
man. So the servant took Rebekah and left.

⁶²Now Isaac had come from Beer Lahai Roi,
for he was living in the Negev. ⁶³He went out to
the field one evening to meditate,*a* and as he
looked up, he saw camels approaching.
⁶⁴Rebekah also looked up and saw Isaac. She got
down from her camel ⁶⁵and asked the servant,
"Who is that man in the field coming to meet
us?"

"He is my master," the servant answered. So
she took her veil and covered herself.

⁶⁶Then the servant told Isaac all he had done.
⁶⁷Isaac brought her into the tent of his mother
Sarah, and he married Rebekah. So she became
his wife, and he loved her; and Isaac was comforted after his mother's death.

The Death of Abraham

25 Abraham took*b* another wife, whose
name was Keturah. ²She bore him
Zimran, Jokshan, Medan, Midian,
Ishbak and Shuah. ³Jokshan was the father of
Sheba and Dedan; the descendants of Dedan
were the Asshurites, the Letushites and the
Leummites. ⁴The sons of Midian were Ephah,
Epher, Hanoch, Abida and Eldaah. All these
were descendants of Keturah.

⁵Abraham left everything he owned to Isaac.
⁶But while he was still living, he gave gifts to
the sons of his concubines and sent them away
from his son Isaac to the land of the east.

⁷Altogether, Abraham lived a hundred and
seventy-five years. ⁸Then Abraham breathed his
last and died at a good old age, an old man and
full of years; and he was gathered to his people.
⁹His sons Isaac and Ishmael buried him in the
cave of Machpelah near Mamre, in the field of
Ephron son of Zohar the Hittite, ¹⁰the field
Abraham had bought from the Hittites.*c* There
Abraham was buried with his wife Sarah.
¹¹After Abraham's death, God blessed his son
Isaac, who then lived near Beer Lahai Roi.

百加祝福説：

"我們的妹子啊，
  願你作千萬人的母！
  願你的後裔得着仇敵的城門！"

⁶¹利百加和她的使女們起來，騎
上駱駝，跟着那僕人，僕人就帶着利
百加走了。

⁶²那時，以撒住在南地，剛從庇
耳拉海萊回來。⁶³天將晚，以撒出來
在田間默想，舉目一看，見來了些駱
駝。⁶⁴利百加舉目看見以撒，就急忙
下了駱駝，⁶⁵問那僕人説："這田間
走來迎接我們的是誰？"

僕人説："是我的主人。"利百
加就拿帕子蒙上臉。

⁶⁶僕人就將所辦的一切事都告訴
以撒，⁶⁷以撒便領利百加進了他母親
撒拉的帳棚，娶了她為妻，並且愛
她。以撒自從他母親不在了，這才得
了安慰。

亞伯拉罕壽終

25 亞伯拉罕又娶了一妻，名叫
基土拉。²基土拉給他生了心
蘭、約珊、米但、米甸、伊
施巴和書亞。³珊珊生了示巴和底
但。底但的子孫是亞書利族、利都
族和利烏米族。⁴米甸的兒子是以
法、以弗、哈諾、亞比大和以勒大。
這都是基土拉的子孫。

⁵亞伯拉罕將一切所有的都給了以
撒。⁶亞伯拉罕把財物分給他庶出的眾
子，趁着自己還在世的時候，打發他
們離開他的兒子以撒，往東方去。

⁷亞伯拉罕一生的年日是一百七
十五歲。⁸亞伯拉罕壽高年邁，氣絕
而死，歸到他列祖（註：原文作"本
民"）那裏。⁹他兩個兒子以撒、以實
瑪利把他埋葬在麥比拉洞裏。這洞在
幔利前、赫人瑣轄的兒子以弗崙的田
中，¹⁰就是亞伯拉罕向赫人買的那塊
田。亞伯拉罕和他妻子撒拉都葬在那
裏。¹¹亞伯拉罕死了以後，神賜福給
他的兒子以撒。以撒靠近庇耳拉海萊
居住。

---

a 63 The meaning of the Hebrew for this word is uncertain.
b 1 Or had taken   c 10 Or the sons of Heth

以實瑪利的眾子

12撒拉的使女夏甲人所生，給亞伯拉罕所生的兒子是以實瑪利。

13以實瑪利兒子們的名字，按着他們的家譜，記在下面：以實瑪利的長子是尼拜約，又有基達、亞德別、米比衫、14米施瑪、度瑪、瑪撒、15哈大、提瑪、伊突、拿非施、基底瑪。16這是以實瑪利眾子的名字，照着他們的村莊、營寨，作了十二族的族長。17以實瑪利享壽一百三十七歲，氣絕而死，歸到他列祖（註：原文作"本民"）那裏。18他子孫的住處在他眾弟兄東邊，從哈腓拉直到埃及前的書珥，正在亞述的道上。

雅各與以掃

19亞伯拉罕的兒子以撒的後代，記在下面：

亞伯拉罕生以撒。20以撒娶利百加為妻的時候正四十歲。利百加是巴旦亞蘭地的亞蘭人彼土利的女兒，是亞蘭人拉班的妹子。21以撒因他妻子不生育，就為她祈求耶和華。耶和華應允他的祈求，他的妻子利百加就懷了孕。22孩子們在她腹中彼此相爭，她就說："若是這樣，我為甚麼活着呢（註：或作"我為甚麼如此呢"）？"她就去求問耶和華。

23耶和華對她說：

"兩國在你腹內，
　兩族要從你身上出來，
這族必強於那族，
　將來大的要服侍小的。"

24生產的日子到了，腹中果然是雙子。25先產的身體發紅，渾身有毛，如同皮衣，他們就給他起名叫以掃（註："以掃"就是"有毛"的意思）。26隨後又生了以掃的兄弟，手抓住以掃的腳跟，因此給他起名叫雅各（註："雅各"就是"抓住"的意思）。利百加生下兩個兒子的時候，以撒年正六十歲。

27兩個孩子漸漸長大，以掃善於打

Ishmael's Sons

12This is the account of Abraham's son Ishmael, whom Sarah's maidservant, Hagar the Egyptian, bore to Abraham.

13These are the names of the sons of Ishmael, listed in the order of their birth: Nebaioth the firstborn of Ishmael, Kedar, Adbeel, Mibsam, 14Mishma, Dumah, Massa, 15Hadad, Tema, Jetur, Naphish and Kedemah. 16These were the sons of Ishmael, and these are the names of the twelve tribal rulers according to their settlements and camps. 17Altogether, Ishmael lived a hundred and thirty-seven years. He breathed his last and died, and he was gathered to his people. 18His descendants settled in the area from Havilah to Shur, near the border of Egypt, as you go toward Asshur. And they lived in hostility toward[a] all their brothers.

Jacob and Esau

19This is the account of Abraham's son Isaac.

Abraham became the father of Isaac, 20and Isaac was forty years old when he married Rebekah daughter of Bethuel the Aramean from Paddan Aram[b] and sister of Laban the Aramean.

21Isaac prayed to the LORD on behalf of his wife, because she was barren. The LORD answered his prayer, and his wife Rebekah became pregnant. 22The babies jostled each other within her, and she said, "Why is this happening to me?" So she went to inquire of the LORD.

23The LORD said to her,

"Two nations are in your womb,
　and two peoples from within you will be
　　separated;
one people will be stronger than the other,
　and the older will serve the younger."

24When the time came for her to give birth, there were twin boys in her womb. 25The first to come out was red, and his whole body was like a hairy garment; so they named him Esau.[c] 26After this, his brother came out, with his hand grasping Esau's heel; so he was named Jacob.[d] Isaac was sixty years old when Rebekah gave birth to them.

27The boys grew up, and Esau became a skill-

---

a 18 Or lived to the east of　b 20 That is, Northwest Mesopotamia　c 25 Esau may mean hairy; he was also called Edom, which means red.　d 26 Jacob means he grasps the heel (figuratively, he deceives).

ful hunter, a man of the open country, while Jacob was a quiet man, staying among the tents. [28]Isaac, who had a taste for wild game, loved Esau, but Rebekah loved Jacob.

[29]Once when Jacob was cooking some stew, Esau came in from the open country, famished. [30]He said to Jacob, "Quick, let me have some of that red stew! I'm famished!" (That is why he was also called Edom.[a])

[31]Jacob replied, "First sell me your birthright."

[32]"Look, I am about to die," Esau said. "What good is the birthright to me?"

[33]But Jacob said, "Swear to me first." So he swore an oath to him, selling his birthright to Jacob.

[34]Then Jacob gave Esau some bread and some lentil stew. He ate and drank, and then got up and left.

So Esau despised his birthright.

Isaac and Abimelech

26 Now there was a famine in the land—besides the earlier famine of Abraham's time—and Isaac went to Abimelech king of the Philistines in Gerar. [2]The LORD appeared to Isaac and said, "Do not go down to Egypt; live in the land where I tell you to live. [3]Stay in this land for a while, and I will be with you and will bless you. For to you and your descendants I will give all these lands and will confirm the oath I swore to your father Abraham. [4]I will make your descendants as numerous as the stars in the sky and will give them all these lands, and through your offspring[b] all nations on earth will be blessed, [5]because Abraham obeyed me and kept my requirements, my commands, my decrees and my laws." [6]So Isaac stayed in Gerar.

[7]When the men of that place asked him about his wife, he said, "She is my sister," because he was afraid to say, "She is my wife." He thought, "The men of this place might kill me on account of Rebekah, because she is beautiful."

[8]When Isaac had been there a long time, Abimelech king of the Philistines looked down from a window and saw Isaac caressing his wife Rebekah. [9]So Abimelech summoned Isaac and said, "She is really your wife! Why did you say, 'She is my sister'?"

Isaac answered him, "Because I thought I might lose my life on account of her."

[10]Then Abimelech said, "What is this you have done to us? One of the men might well

獵，常在田野；雅各為人安靜，常住在帳棚裏。[28]以撒愛以掃，因為常吃他的野味；利百加卻愛雅各。

[29]有一天，雅各熬湯，以掃從田野回來累昏了。[30]以掃對雅各說："我累昏了，求你把這紅湯給我喝。"因此以掃又叫以東（註："以東"就是"紅"的意思）

[31]雅各說："你今日把長子的名分賣給我吧！"

[32]以掃說："我將要死，這長子的名分於我有甚麼益處呢？"

[33]雅各說："你今日對我起誓吧！"以掃就對他起了誓，把長子的名分賣給雅各。

[34]於是雅各將餅和紅豆湯給了以掃，以掃吃了喝了，便起來走了。

這就是以掃輕看了他長子的名分。

以撒與亞比米勒

26 在亞伯拉罕的日子，那地有一次饑荒；這時又有饑荒。以撒就往基拉耳去，到非利士人的王亞比米勒那裏。[2]耶和華向以撒顯現，說："你不要下埃及去，要住在我所指示你的地。[3]你寄居在這地，我必與你同在，賜福給你，因為我要將這些地都賜給你和你的後裔。我必堅定我向你父亞伯拉罕所起的誓。[4]我要加增你的後裔，像天上的星那樣多；又要將這些地都賜給你的後裔，並且地上萬國必因你的後裔得福；[5]都因亞伯拉罕聽從我的話，遵守我的吩咐和我的命令、律例、法度。"[6]以撒就住在基拉耳。

[7]那地方的人問到他的妻子，他便說："那是我的妹子。"原來他怕說："是我的妻子。"他心裏想："恐怕這地方的人為利百加的緣故殺我，因為她容貌俊美。"

[8]他在那裏住了許久。有一天，非利士人的王亞比米勒從窗戶裏往外觀看，見以撒和他的妻子利百加戲玩。[9]亞比米勒召了以撒來，對他說："她實在是你的妻子，你怎麼說她是你的妹子？"

以撒說："我心裏想，恐怕我因她而死。"

[10]亞比米勒說："你向我們作的是甚麼事呢？民中險些有人和你的妻

a 30 Edom means red. *b 4 Or seed*

同寢，把我們陷在罪裏。"

11於是亞比米勒曉諭眾民說："凡沾着這個人，或是他妻子的，定要把他治死。"

12以撒在那地耕種，那一年有百倍的收成。耶和華賜福給他，13他就昌大，日增月盛，成了大富戶。14他有羊羣牛羣，又有許多僕人，非利士人就嫉妒他。15當他父親亞伯拉罕在世的日子，他父親的僕人所挖的井，非利士人全都塞住，填滿了土。

16亞比米勒對以撒說："你離開我們去吧，因為你比我們強盛得多。"

17以撒就離開那裏，在基拉耳谷支搭帳棚，住在那裏。18當他父親亞伯拉罕在世之日所挖的水井，因非利士人在亞伯拉罕死後塞住了，以撒就重新挖出來，仍照他父親所叫的，叫那些井的名字。

19以撒的僕人在谷中挖井，便得了一口活水井。20基拉耳的牧人與以撒的牧人爭競，說："這水是我們的。"以撒就給那井起名叫埃色，因為他們和他相爭（註："埃色"就是"相爭"的意思）。21以撒的僕人又挖了一口井，他們又為這井爭競，因此以撒給這井起名叫西提拿（註："西提拿"就是"為敵"的意思）。22以撒離開那裏，又挖了一口井，他們不為這井爭競了，他就給那井起名叫利河伯（註：就是"寬闊"的意思）。他說："耶和華現在給我們寬闊之地，我們必在這地昌盛。"

23以撒從那裏上別是巴去。24當夜耶和華向他顯現，說："我是你父親亞伯拉罕的神，不要懼怕！因為我與你同在，要賜福給你，並要為我僕人亞伯拉罕的緣故，使你的後裔繁多。"

25以撒就在那裏築了一座壇，求告耶和華的名，並且支搭帳棚。他的僕人便在那裏挖了一口井。

26亞比米勒同他的朋友亞戶撒和他的軍長非各，從基拉耳來見以撒。27以撒對他們說："你們既然恨我，打發我走了，為甚麼到我這裏來呢？"

28他們說："我們明明地看見耶和華與你同在，便說，不如我們兩下彼此起誓，彼此立約，29使你不害我們，正如我們未曾害你，一味地厚

have slept with your wife, and you would have brought guilt upon us."

11So Abimelech gave orders to all the people: "Anyone who molests this man or his wife shall surely be put to death."

12Isaac planted crops in that land and the same year reaped a hundredfold, because the LORD blessed him. 13The man became rich, and his wealth continued to grow until he became very wealthy. 14He had so many flocks and herds and servants that the Philistines envied him. 15So all the wells that his father's servants had dug in the time of his father Abraham, the Philistines stopped up, filling them with earth.

16Then Abimelech said to Isaac, "Move away from us; you have become too powerful for us."

17So Isaac moved away from there and encamped in the Valley of Gerar and settled there. 18Isaac reopened the wells that had been dug in the time of his father Abraham, which the Philistines had stopped up after Abraham died, and he gave them the same names his father had given them.

19Isaac's servants dug in the valley and discovered a well of fresh water there. 20But the herdsmen of Gerar quarreled with Isaac's herdsmen and said, "The water is ours!" So he named the well Esek,[a] because they disputed with him. 21Then they dug another well, but they quarreled over that one also; so he named it Sitnah.[b] 22He moved on from there and dug another well, and no one quarreled over it. He named it Rehoboth,[c] saying, "Now the LORD has given us room and we will flourish in the land."

23From there he went up to Beersheba. 24That night the LORD appeared to him and said, "I am the God of your father Abraham. Do not be afraid, for I am with you; I will bless you and will increase the number of your descendants for the sake of my servant Abraham."

25Isaac built an altar there and called on the name of the LORD. There he pitched his tent, and there his servants dug a well.

26Meanwhile, Abimelech had come to him from Gerar, with Ahuzzath his personal adviser and Phicol the commander of his forces. 27Isaac asked them, "Why have you come to me, since you were hostile to me and sent me away?"

28They answered, "We saw clearly that the LORD was with you; so we said, 'There ought to be a sworn agreement between us'—between us and you. Let us make a treaty with you 29that you will do us no harm, just as we did not

---

a 20 Esek means *dispute*.　　*b 21 Sitnah* means *opposition*.
c 22 Rehoboth means *room*.

molest you but always treated you well and sent you away in peace. And now you are blessed by the LORD."

³⁰Isaac then made a feast for them, and they ate and drank. ³¹Early the next morning the men swore an oath to each other. Then Isaac sent them on their way, and they left him in peace.

³²That day Isaac's servants came and told him about the well they had dug. They said, "We've found water!" ³³He called it Shibah,ᵃ and to this day the name of the town has been Beersheba.ᵇ

³⁴When Esau was forty years old, he married Judith daughter of Beeri the Hittite, and also Basemath daughter of Elon the Hittite. ³⁵They were a source of grief to Isaac and Rebekah.

Jacob Gets Isaac's Blessing

27 When Isaac was old and his eyes were so weak that he could no longer see, he called for Esau his older son and said to him, "My son."

"Here I am," he answered.

²Isaac said, "I am now an old man and don't know the day of my death. ³Now then, get your weapons—your quiver and bow—and go out to the open country to hunt some wild game for me. ⁴Prepare me the kind of tasty food I like and bring it to me to eat, so that I may give you my blessing before I die."

⁵Now Rebekah was listening as Isaac spoke to his son Esau. When Esau left for the open country to hunt game and bring it back, ⁶Rebekah said to her son Jacob, "Look, I overheard your father say to your brother Esau, ⁷'Bring me some game and prepare me some tasty food to eat, so that I may give you my blessing in the presence of the LORD before I die.' ⁸Now, my son, listen carefully and do what I tell you: ⁹Go out to the flock and bring me two choice young goats, so I can prepare some tasty food for your father, just the way he likes it. ¹⁰Then take it to your father to eat, so that he may give you his blessing before he dies."

¹¹Jacob said to Rebekah his mother, "But my brother Esau is a hairy man, and I'm a man with smooth skin. ¹²What if my father touches me? I would appear to be tricking him and would bring down a curse on myself rather than a blessing."

¹³His mother said to him, "My son, let the curse fall on me. Just do what I say; go and get them for me."

待你，並且打發你平平安安地走。你是蒙耶和華賜福的了。"

³⁰以撒就為他們設擺筵席，他們便吃了喝了。³¹他們清早起來彼此起誓。以撒打發他們走，他們就平平安安地離開他走了。

³²那一天以撒的僕人來，將挖井的事告訴他，說："我們得了水了。"³³他就給那井起名叫示巴，因此那城叫做別是巴，直到今日。

³⁴以掃四十歲的時候，娶了赫人比利的女兒猶滴，與赫人以倫的女兒巴實抹為妻。³⁵她們常使以撒和利百加心裏愁煩。

雅各騙取以撒的祝福

27 以撒年老，眼睛昏花，不能看見，就叫了他大兒子以掃來，說："我兒。"

以掃說："我在這裏。"

²他說："我如今老了，不知道哪一天死。³現在拿你的器械，就是箭囊和弓，往田野去為我打獵，⁴照我所愛的做成美味，拿來給我吃，使我在未死之先給你祝福。"

⁵以撒對他兒子以掃說話，利百加也聽見了。以掃往田野去打獵，要得野味帶來。⁶利百加就對她兒子雅各說："我聽見你父親對你哥哥以掃說：⁷'你去把野獸帶來，做成美味給我吃，我好在未死之先，在耶和華面前給你祝福。'⁸現在，我兒，你要照著我所吩咐你的，聽從我的話。⁹你到羊群裏去，給我拿兩隻肥山羊羔來，我便照你父親所愛的，給他做成美味。¹⁰你拿到你父親那裏給他吃，使他在未死之先給你祝福。"

¹¹雅各對他母親利百加說："我哥哥以掃渾身是有毛的，我身上是光滑的，¹²倘若我父親摸著我，必以我為欺哄人的，我就招咒詛，不得祝福。"

¹³他母親對他說："我兒，你招的咒詛歸到我身上；你只管聽我的話，去把羊羔給我拿來。"

---

a 33 Shibah can mean *oath* or *seven.*   *b 33 Beersheba* can mean *well of the oath* or *well of seven.*

14他便去拿來，交給他母親，他母親就照他父親所愛的做成美味。15利百加又把家裏所存大兒子以撒上好的衣服給她小兒子雅各穿上，16又用山羊羔皮包在雅各的手上和頸項的光滑處，17就把所做的美味和餅交在她兒子雅各的手裏。

18雅各到他父親那裏說："我父親！"

他說："我在這裏。我兒，你是誰？"

19雅各對他父親說："我是你的長子以撒，我已照你所吩咐我的行了。請起來坐着，吃我的野味，好給我祝福。"

20以撒對他兒子說："我兒，你如何找得這麼快呢？"

他說："因為耶和華你的神使我遇見好機會得着的。"

21以撒對雅各說："我兒，你近前來，我摸摸你，知道你真是我的兒子以撒不是。"

22雅各就挨近他父親以撒。以撒摸着他說："聲音是雅各的聲音，手卻是以撒的手。"23以撒就辨不出他來，因為他手上有毛，像他哥哥以撒的手一樣，就給他祝福。24又說："你真是我兒子以撒嗎？"

他說："我是。"

25以撒說："你遞給我，我好吃我兒子的野味，給你祝福。"

雅各就遞給他，他便吃了；又拿酒給他，他也喝了。26他父親以撒對他說："我兒，你上前來與我親嘴。"

27他就上前與父親親嘴。他父親一聞他衣服上的香氣，就給他祝福，說：

"我兒的香氣
　如同耶和華賜福
　之田地的香氣一樣。
28願神賜你天上的甘露、
　地上的肥土，
　並許多五穀新酒。
29願多民侍奉你，
　多國跪拜你；
願你作你弟兄的主，
　你母親的兒子向你跪拜。
凡咒詛你的，願他受咒詛；
　為你祝福的，願他蒙福。"

14So he went and got them and brought them to his mother, and she prepared some tasty food, just the way his father liked it. 15Then Rebekah took the best clothes of Esau her older son, which she had in the house, and put them on her younger son Jacob. 16She also covered his hands and the smooth part of his neck with the goatskins. 17Then she handed to her son Jacob the tasty food and the bread she had made.

18He went to his father and said, "My father."

"Yes, my son," he answered. "Who is it?"

19Jacob said to his father, "I am Esau your firstborn. I have done as you told me. Please sit up and eat some of my game so that you may give me your blessing."

20Isaac asked his son, "How did you find it so quickly, my son?"

"The LORD your God gave me success," he replied.

21Then Isaac said to Jacob, "Come near so I can touch you, my son, to know whether you really are my son Esau or not."

22Jacob went close to his father Isaac, who touched him and said, "The voice is the voice of Jacob, but the hands are the hands of Esau." 23He did not recognize him, for his hands were hairy like those of his brother Esau; so he blessed him. 24"Are you really my son Esau?" he asked.

"I am," he replied.

25Then he said, "My son, bring me some of your game to eat, so that I may give you my blessing."

Jacob brought it to him and he ate; and he brought some wine and he drank. 26Then his father Isaac said to him, "Come here, my son, and kiss me."

27So he went to him and kissed him. When Isaac caught the smell of his clothes, he blessed him and said,

"Ah, the smell of my son
　is like the smell of a field
　that the LORD has blessed.
28May God give you of heaven's dew
　and of earth's richness—
　an abundance of grain and new wine.
29May nations serve you
　and peoples bow down to you.
Be lord over your brothers,
　and may the sons of your mother bow down
　　to you.
May those who curse you be cursed
　and those who bless you be blessed."

30After Isaac finished blessing him and Jacob had scarcely left his father's presence, his brother Esau came in from hunting. 31He too prepared some tasty food and brought it to his father. Then he said to him, "My father, sit up and eat some of my game, so that you may give me your blessing."

32His father Isaac asked him, "Who are you?"

"I am your son," he answered, "your firstborn, Esau."

33Isaac trembled violently and said, "Who was it, then, that hunted game and brought it to me? I ate it just before you came and I blessed him—and indeed he will be blessed!"

34When Esau heard his father's words, he burst out with a loud and bitter cry and said to his father, "Bless me—me too, my father!"

35But he said, "Your brother came deceitfully and took your blessing."

36Esau said, "Isn't he rightly named Jacob*a*? He has deceived me these two times: He took my birthright, and now he's taken my blessing!" Then he asked, "Haven't you reserved any blessing for me?"

37Isaac answered Esau, "I have made him lord over you and have made all his relatives his servants, and I have sustained him with grain and new wine. So what can I possibly do for you, my son?"

38Esau said to his father, "Do you have only one blessing, my father? Bless me too, my father!" Then Esau wept aloud.

39His father Isaac answered him,

"Your dwelling will be
    away from the earth's richness,
    away from the dew of heaven above.
40You will live by the sword
    and you will serve your brother.
But when you grow restless,
    you will throw his yoke
    from off your neck."

Jacob Flees to Laban

41Esau held a grudge against Jacob because of the blessing his father had given him. He said to himself, "The days of mourning for my father are near; then I will kill my brother Jacob."

42When Rebekah was told what her older son Esau had said, she sent for her younger son Jacob and said to him, "Your brother Esau is consoling himself with the thought of killing you. 43Now then, my son, do what I say: Flee at once to my brother Laban in Haran. 44Stay with

a 36 Jacob means he grasps the heel (figuratively, he deceives).

30以撒為雅各祝福已畢，雅各從他父親那裏才出來，他哥哥以掃正打獵回來，31也做了美味，拿來給他父親，說："請父親起來，吃你兒子的野味，好給我祝福。"

32他父親以撒對他說："你是誰？"

他說："我是你的長子以掃。"

33以撒就大大地戰兢說："你未來之先，是誰得了野味拿來給我呢？我已經吃了，為他祝福，他將來也必蒙福。"

34以掃聽了他父親的話，就放聲痛哭，說："我父啊，求你也為我祝福！"

35以撒說："你兄弟已經用詭計來將你的福分奪去了。"

36以掃說："他名雅各豈不是正對嗎？因為他欺騙了我兩次，他從前奪了我長子的名分；你看，他現在又奪了我的福分。"以掃又說："你沒有留下為我可祝的福嗎？"

37以撒回答以掃說："我已立他為你的主，使他的弟兄都給他作僕人，並賜他五穀新酒可以養生。我兒，現在我還能為你做甚麼呢？"

38以掃對他父親說："父啊，你只有一樣可祝的福嗎？我父啊，求你也為我祝福！"以掃就放聲而哭。

39他父親以撒說：

"地上的肥土必為你所住；
    天上的甘露必為你所得。

40你必倚靠刀劍度日，
    又必侍奉你的兄弟；
到你強盛的時候，
    必從你頸項上掙開他的軛。"

雅各逃往舅父拉班家

41以掃因他父親給雅各祝的福，就怨恨雅各，心裏說："為我父親居喪的日子近了，到那時候，我要殺我的兄弟雅各。"

42有人把利百加大兒子以掃的話告訴利百加，她就打發人去，叫了她小兒子雅各來，對他說："你哥哥以掃想要殺你，報仇雪恨。43現在，我兒，你要聽我的話：起來，逃往哈蘭我哥哥拉班那裏去，44同他住些日子，直等你哥哥的怒氣消了。45你哥哥向你消了怒氣，忘了你向他所做的事，我便打發人去把你從那裏帶回來。為甚麼一日喪你們二人呢？"

46利百加對以撒說："我因這赫人的女子，連性命都厭煩了；倘若雅各也娶赫人的女子為妻，像這些一樣，我活着還有甚麼益處呢？"

28 以撒叫了雅各來，給他祝福，並囑咐他說："你不要娶迦南的女子為妻。2你起身往巴旦亞蘭去，到你外祖彼土利家裏，在你母舅拉班的女兒中娶一女為妻。3願全能的神賜福給你，使你生養眾多，成為多族，4將應許亞伯拉罕的福賜給你和你的後裔，使你承受你所寄居的地為業，就是神賜給亞伯拉罕的地。"5以撒打發雅各走了，他就往巴旦亞蘭去，到亞蘭人彼土利的兒子拉班那裏。拉班是雅各、以掃的母舅。

6以掃見以撒已經給雅各祝福，而且打發他往巴旦亞蘭去，在那裏娶妻，並見囑福的時候囑咐他說："不要娶迦南的女子為妻。"7又見雅各聽從父母的話往巴旦亞蘭去了，8以掃就曉得他父親以撒看不中迦南的女子，9便往以實瑪利那裏去，在他二妻之外，又娶了瑪哈拉為妻。她是亞伯拉罕兒子以實瑪利的女兒，尼拜約的妹子。

雅各夢於伯特利

10雅各出了別是巴，向哈蘭走去。11到了一個地方，因為太陽落了，就在那裏住宿，便拾起那地方的一塊石頭枕在頭下，在那裏躺臥睡了。12夢見一個梯子立在地上，梯子的頭頂着天，有神的使者在梯子上，上去下來。13耶和華站在梯子以上（註：或作"站在他旁邊"），說："我是耶和華你祖亞伯拉罕的神，也是以撒的神，我要將你現在所躺臥之地

him for a while until your brother's fury subsides. 45When your brother is no longer angry with you and forgets what you did to him, I'll send word for you to come back from there. Why should I lose both of you in one day?"

46Then Rebekah said to Isaac, "I'm disgusted with living because of these Hittite women. If Jacob takes a wife from among the women of this land, from Hittite women like these, my life will not be worth living."

28 So Isaac called for Jacob and blessed[a] him and commanded him: "Do not marry a Canaanite woman. 2Go at once to Paddan Aram,[b] to the house of your mother's father Bethuel. Take a wife for yourself there, from among the daughters of Laban, your mother's brother. 3May God Almighty[c] bless you and make you fruitful and increase your numbers until you become a community of peoples. 4May he give you and your descendants the blessing given to Abraham, so that you may take possession of the land where you now live as an alien, the land God gave to Abraham." 5Then Isaac sent Jacob on his way, and he went to Paddan Aram, to Laban son of Bethuel the Aramean, the brother of Rebekah, who was the mother of Jacob and Esau.

6Now Esau learned that Isaac had blessed Jacob and had sent him to Paddan Aram to take a wife from there, and that when he blessed him he commanded him, "Do not marry a Canaanite woman," 7and that Jacob had obeyed his father and mother and had gone to Paddan Aram. 8Esau then realized how displeasing the Canaanite women were to his father Isaac; 9so he went to Ishmael and married Mahalath, the sister of Nebaioth and daughter of Ishmael son of Abraham, in addition to the wives he already had.

Jacob's Dream at Bethel

10Jacob left Beersheba and set out for Haran. 11When he reached a certain place, he stopped for the night because the sun had set. Taking one of the stones there, he put it under his head and lay down to sleep. 12He had a dream in which he saw a stairway[d] resting on the earth, with its top reaching to heaven, and the angels of God were ascending and descending on it. 13There above it[e] stood the LORD, and he said: "I am the LORD, the God of your father Abraham and the God of Isaac. I will give you and your

a 1 Or greeted　　b 2 That is, Northwest Mesopotamia; also in
verses 5, 6 and 7　　c 3 Hebrew El-Shaddai　　d 12 Or ladder
e 13 Or There beside him

descendants the land on which you are lying. [14]Your descendants will be like the dust of the earth, and you will spread out to the west and to the east, to the north and to the south. All peoples on earth will be blessed through you and your offspring. [15]I am with you and will watch over you wherever you go, and I will bring you back to this land. I will not leave you until I have done what I have promised you."

[16]When Jacob awoke from his sleep, he thought, "Surely the LORD is in this place, and I was not aware of it." [17]He was afraid and said, "How awesome is this place! This is none other than the house of God; this is the gate of heaven."

[18]Early the next morning Jacob took the stone he had placed under his head and set it up as a pillar and poured oil on top of it. [19]He called that place Bethel,[a] though the city used to be called Luz.

[20]Then Jacob made a vow, saying, "If God will be with me and will watch over me on this journey I am taking and will give me food to eat and clothes to wear [21]so that I return safely to my father's house, then the LORD[b] will be my God [22]and[c] this stone that I have set up as a pillar will be God's house, and of all that you give me I will give you a tenth."

Jacob Arrives in Paddan Aram

29 Then Jacob continued on his journey and came to the land of the eastern peoples. [2]There he saw a well in the field, with three flocks of sheep lying near it because the flocks were watered from that well. The stone over the mouth of the well was large. [3]When all the flocks were gathered there, the shepherds would roll the stone away from the well's mouth and water the sheep. Then they would return the stone to its place over the mouth of the well.

[4]Jacob asked the shepherds, "My brothers, where are you from?"

"We're from Haran," they replied.

[5]He said to them, "Do you know Laban, Nahor's grandson?"

"Yes, we know him," they answered.

[6]Then Jacob asked them, "Is he well?"

"Yes, he is," they said, "and here comes his daughter Rachel with the sheep."

[7]"Look," he said, "the sun is still high; it is not time for the flocks to be gathered. Water the

賜給你和你的後裔。[14]你的後裔必像地上的塵沙那樣多,必向東西南北開展,地上萬族必因你和你的後裔得福。[15]我也與你同在,你無論往哪裏去,我必保佑你,領你歸回這地,總不離棄你,直到我成全了向你所應許的。"

[16]雅各睡醒了,說:"耶和華真在這裏,我竟不知道!"[17]就懼怕說:"這地方何等可畏!這不是別的,乃是神的殿,也是天的門。"

[18]雅各清早起來,把所枕的石頭立作柱子,澆油在上面。[19]他就給那地方起名叫伯特利 (註:就是"神殿"的意思);但那地方起先名叫路斯。

[20]雅各許願說:"神若與我同在,在我所行的路上保佑我,又給我食物吃、衣服穿,[21]使我平平安安地回到我父親的家,我就必以耶和華為我的神,[22]我所立為柱子的石頭也必作神的殿,凡你所賜給我的,我必將十分之一獻給你。"

雅各到達巴旦亞蘭

29 雅各起行,到了東方人之地,[2]看見田間有一口井,有三羣羊臥在井旁,因為人飲羊羣,都是用那井裏的水,井口上的石頭是大的。[3]常有羊羣在那裏聚集,牧人把石頭轉離井口飲羊,隨後又把石頭放在井口的原處。

[4]雅各對牧人說:"弟兄們,你們是哪裏來的?"

他們說:"我們是哈蘭來的。"

[5]他問他們說:"拿鶴的孫子拉班,你們認識嗎?"

他們說:"我們認識。"

[6]雅各說:"他平安嗎?"

他們說:"平安。看哪,他女兒拉結領着羊來了。"

[7]雅各說:"日頭還高,不是羊羣聚集的時候,你們不如飲羊,再去

---

a 19 Bethel means house of God.　b 20,21 Or Since God . . . father's house, the LORD　c 21,22 Or house, and the LORD will be my God, 22then

放一放。"

⁸他們説："我們不能，必等羊
羣聚齊，人把石頭轉離井口才可飲
羊。"

⁹雅各正和他們説話的時候，拉
結領着他父親的羊來了，因為那些
羊是她牧放的。¹⁰雅各看見母舅拉班
的女兒拉結和母舅拉班的羊羣，就
上前把石頭轉離井口，飲他母舅拉
班的羊羣。¹¹雅各與拉結親嘴，就放
聲而哭。¹²雅各告訴拉結，自己是她
父親的外甥，是利百加的兒子，拉
結就跑去告訴她父親。

¹³拉班聽見外甥雅各的信息，就
跑去迎接，抱着他，與他親嘴，領
他到自己的家。雅各將一切的情由
告訴拉班。¹⁴拉班對他説："你實在
是我的骨肉。"

雅各娶利亞和拉結

雅各就和他同住了一個月。¹⁵拉
班對雅各説："你雖是我的骨肉
（註：原文作"弟兄"），豈可白白地服
侍我？請告訴我，你要甚麼為工
價？"

¹⁶拉班有兩個女兒：大的名叫利
亞，小的名叫拉結。¹⁷利亞的眼睛沒
有神氣，拉結卻生得美貌俊秀。¹⁸雅
各愛拉結，就説："我願為你小女
兒拉結服侍你七年。"

¹⁹拉班説："我把她給你，勝似
給別人，你與我同住吧！"²⁰雅各就
為拉結服侍了七年。他因為深愛拉
結，就看這七年如同幾天。

²¹雅各對拉班説："日期已經滿
了，求你把我的妻子給我，我好與
她同房。"

²²拉班就擺設筵席，請齊了那
地方的眾人。²³到了晚上，拉班將女兒
利亞送來給雅各，雅各就與她同
房。²⁴拉班又將婢女悉帕給女兒利亞
作使女。

²⁵到了早晨，雅各一看是利亞，
就對拉班説："你向我做的是甚麼
事呢？我服侍你，不是為拉結嗎？
你為甚麼欺哄我呢？"

sheep and take them back to pasture."

⁸"We can't," they replied, "until all the flocks
are gathered and the stone has been rolled away
from the mouth of the well. Then we will water
the sheep."

⁹While he was still talking with them, Rachel
came with her father's sheep, for she was a
shepherdess. ¹⁰When Jacob saw Rachel daughter
of Laban, his mother's brother, and Laban's
sheep, he went over and rolled the stone away
from the mouth of the well and watered his
uncle's sheep. ¹¹Then Jacob kissed Rachel and
began to weep aloud. ¹²He had told Rachel that
he was a relative of her father and a son of
Rebekah. So she ran and told her father.

¹³As soon as Laban heard the news about
Jacob, his sister's son, he hurried to meet him.
He embraced him and kissed him and brought
him to his home, and there Jacob told him all
these things. ¹⁴Then Laban said to him, "You are
my own flesh and blood."

Jacob Marries Leah and Rachel

After Jacob had stayed with him for a whole
month, ¹⁵Laban said to him, "Just because you
are a relative of mine, should you work for me
for nothing? Tell me what your wages should
be."

¹⁶Now Laban had two daughters; the name
of the older was Leah, and the name of the
younger was Rachel. ¹⁷Leah had weak^a eyes, but
Rachel was lovely in form, and beautiful. ¹⁸Jacob
was in love with Rachel and said, "I'll work for
you seven years in return for your younger
daughter Rachel."

¹⁹Laban said, "It's better that I give her to you
than to some other man. Stay here with me."
²⁰So Jacob served seven years to get Rachel, but
they seemed like only a few days to him because
of his love for her.

²¹Then Jacob said to Laban, "Give me my
wife. My time is completed, and I want to lie
with her."

²²So Laban brought together all the people of
the place and gave a feast. ²³But when evening
came, he took his daughter Leah and gave her to
Jacob, and Jacob lay with her. ²⁴And Laban gave
his servant girl Zilpah to his daughter as her
maidservant.

²⁵When morning came, there was Leah! So
Jacob said to Laban, "What is this you have
done to me? I served you for Rachel, didn't I?
Why have you deceived me?"

a 17 Or delicate

²⁶Laban replied, "It is not our custom here to give the younger daughter in marriage before the older one. ²⁷Finish this daughter's bridal week; then we will give you the younger one also, in return for another seven years of work."

²⁸And Jacob did so. He finished the week with Leah, and then Laban gave him his daughter Rachel to be his wife. ²⁹Laban gave his servant girl Bilhah to his daughter Rachel as her maidservant. ³⁰Jacob lay with Rachel also, and he loved Rachel more than Leah. And he worked for Laban another seven years.

Jacob's Children

³¹When the LORD saw that Leah was not loved, he opened her womb, but Rachel was barren. ³²Leah became pregnant and gave birth to a son. She named him Reuben,^a for she said, "It is because the LORD has seen my misery. Surely my husband will love me now."

³³She conceived again, and when she gave birth to a son she said, "Because the LORD heard that I am not loved, he gave me this one too." So she named him Simeon.^b

³⁴Again she conceived, and when she gave birth to a son she said, "Now at last my husband will become attached to me, because I have borne him three sons." So he was named Levi.^c

³⁵She conceived again, and when she gave birth to a son she said, "This time I will praise the LORD." So she named him Judah.^d Then she stopped having children.

30

When Rachel saw that she was not bearing Jacob any children, she became jealous of her sister. So she said to Jacob, "Give me children, or I'll die!"

²Jacob became angry with her and said, "Am I in the place of God, who has kept you from having children?"

³Then she said, "Here is Bilhah, my maidservant. Sleep with her so that she can bear children for me and that through her I too can build a family."

⁴So she gave him her servant Bilhah as a wife. Jacob slept with her, ⁵and she became pregnant and bore him a son. ⁶Then Rachel said, "God has vindicated me; he has listened to my plea and given me a son." Because of this she named him Dan.^e

---

a 32 Reuben sounds like the Hebrew for he has seen my misery; the name means see, a son.   *b 33 Simeon probably means one who hears.*   *c 34 Levi sounds like and may be derived from the Hebrew for attached.*   *d 35 Judah sounds like and may be derived from the Hebrew for praise.*   *e 6 Dan here means he has vindicated.*

---

²⁶拉班說："大女兒還沒有給人，先把小女兒給人，在我們這地方沒有這規矩。²⁷你為這個滿了七日，我就把那個也給你，你再為她服侍我七年。"

²⁸雅各就如此行。滿了利亞的七日，拉班便將女兒拉結給雅各為妻。²⁹拉班又將婢女辟拉給女兒拉結作使女。³⁰雅各也與拉結同房，並且愛拉結勝似愛利亞，於是又服侍拉班七年。

雅各的兒女

³¹耶和華見利亞失寵（註：原文作"被恨"。下同），就使她生育，拉結卻不生育。³²利亞懷孕生子，就給他起名叫呂便（註：就是"有兒子"的意思），因而說："耶和華看見我的苦情，如今我的丈夫必愛我。"

³³她又懷孕生子，就說："耶和華因為聽見我失寵，所以又賜給我這個兒子。"於是給他起名叫西緬（註：就是"聽見"的意思）。

³⁴她又懷孕生子，起名叫利未（註：就是"聯合"的意思），說："我給丈夫生了三個兒子，他必與我聯合。"

³⁵她又懷孕生子，說："這回我要讚美耶和華。"因此給他起名叫猶大（註：就是"讚美"的意思）。這才停了生育。

30

拉結見自己不給雅各生子，就嫉妒她姐姐，對雅各說："你給我孩子，不然我就死了！"

²雅各向拉結生氣，說："叫你不生育的是神，我豈能代替他作主呢？"

³拉結說："有我的使女辟拉在這裏，你可以與她同房，使她生子在我膝下，我便因她也得孩子（註："得孩子"原文作"被建立"）。

⁴拉結就把她的使女辟拉給丈夫為妾，雅各便與她同房，⁵辟拉就懷孕給雅各生了一個兒子。⁶拉結說："神伸了我的冤，也聽了我的聲音，賜我一個兒子。"因此給他起名叫但（註：就是"伸冤"的意思）。

⁷拉結的使女辟拉又懷孕,給雅各生了第二個兒子。⁸拉結説:「我與我姐姐大大相爭,並且得勝。」於是給他起名叫拿弗他利(註:就是「相爭」的意思)。

⁹利亞見自己停了生育,就把使女悉帕給雅各為妾。¹⁰利亞的使女悉帕給雅各生了一個兒子。¹¹利亞説:「萬幸!」於是給他起名叫迦得(註:就是「萬幸」的意思)。

¹²利亞的使女悉帕又給雅各生了第二個兒子。¹³利亞説:「我有福啊,眾女子都要稱我是有福的!」於是給他起名叫亞設(註:就是「有福」的意思)。

¹⁴割麥子的時候,呂便往田裏去尋見風茄,拿來給他母親利亞。拉結對利亞説:「請你把你兒子的風茄給我些。」

¹⁵利亞説:「你奪了我的丈夫還算小事嗎?你又要奪我兒子的風茄嗎?」

拉結説:「為你兒子的風茄,今夜他可以與你同寢。」

¹⁶到了晚上,雅各從田裏回來,利亞出來迎接他,説:「你要與我同寢,因為我實在用我兒子的風茄把你雇下了。」那一夜雅各就與她同寢。

¹⁷神應允了利亞,她就懷孕,給雅各生了第五個兒子。¹⁸利亞説:「神給了我價值,因為我把使女給了我丈夫。」於是給他起名叫以薩迦(註:就是「價值」的意思)。

¹⁹利亞又懷孕,給雅各生了第六個兒子。²⁰利亞説:「神賜我厚賞,我丈夫必與我同住,因我給他生了六個兒子。」於是給他起名叫西布倫(註:就是「同住」的意思)。

²¹後來又生了一個女兒,給她起名叫底拿。

²²神顧念拉結,應允了她,使她能生育。²³拉結懷孕生子,説:「神除去了我的羞恥。」²⁴就給他起名叫約瑟(註:就是「增添」的意思),意思説:「願耶和華再增添我一個兒子。」

⁷Rachel's servant Bilhah conceived again and bore Jacob a second son. ⁸Then Rachel said, "I have had a great struggle with my sister, and I have won." So she named him Naphtali.ᵃ

⁹When Leah saw that she had stopped having children, she took her maidservant Zilpah and gave her to Jacob as a wife. ¹⁰Leah's servant Zilpah bore Jacob a son. ¹¹Then Leah said, "What good fortune!"ᵇ So she named him Gad.ᶜ

¹²Leah's servant Zilpah bore Jacob a second son. ¹³Then Leah said, "How happy I am! The women will call me happy." So she named him Asher.ᵈ

¹⁴During wheat harvest, Reuben went out into the fields and found some mandrake plants, which he brought to his mother Leah. Rachel said to Leah, "Please give me some of your son's mandrakes."

¹⁵But she said to her, "Wasn't it enough that you took away my husband? Will you take my son's mandrakes too?"

"Very well," Rachel said, "he can sleep with you tonight in return for your son's mandrakes."

¹⁶So when Jacob came in from the fields that evening, Leah went out to meet him. "You must sleep with me," she said. "I have hired you with my son's mandrakes." So he slept with her that night.

¹⁷God listened to Leah, and she became pregnant and bore Jacob a fifth son. ¹⁸Then Leah said, "God has rewarded me for giving my maidservant to my husband." So she named him Issachar.ᵉ

¹⁹Leah conceived again and bore Jacob a sixth son. ²⁰Then Leah said, "God has presented me with a precious gift. This time my husband will treat me with honor, because I have borne him six sons." So she named him Zebulun.ᶠ

²¹Some time later she gave birth to a daughter and named her Dinah.

²²Then God remembered Rachel; he listened to her and opened her womb. ²³She became pregnant and gave birth to a son and said, "God has taken away my disgrace." ²⁴She named him Joseph,ᵍ and said, "May the LORD add to me another son."

ᵃ 8 *Naphtali* means *my struggle.*　ᵇ 11 Or *"A troop is coming!"*
ᶜ 11 *Gad* can mean *good fortune* or *a troop.*　ᵈ 13 *Asher* means *happy.*　ᵉ 18 *Issachar* sounds like the Hebrew for *reward.*
ᶠ 20 *Zebulun* probably means *honor.*　ᵍ 24 *Joseph* means *may he add.*

Jacob's Flocks Increase

²⁵After Rachel gave birth to Joseph, Jacob said to Laban, "Send me on my way so I can go back to my own homeland. ²⁶Give me my wives and children, for whom I have served you, and I will be on my way. You know how much work I've done for you."

²⁷But Laban said to him, "If I have found favor in your eyes, please stay. I have learned by divination that^a the Lord has blessed me because of you." ²⁸He added, "Name your wages, and I will pay them."

²⁹Jacob said to him, "You know how I have worked for you and how your livestock has fared under my care. ³⁰The little you had before I came has increased greatly, and the Lord has blessed you wherever I have been. But now, when may I do something for my own household?"

³¹"What shall I give you?" he asked.

"Don't give me anything," Jacob replied. "But if you will do this one thing for me, I will go on tending your flocks and watching over them: ³²Let me go through all your flocks today and remove from them every speckled or spotted sheep, every dark-colored lamb and every spotted or speckled goat. They will be my wages. ³³And my honesty will testify for me in the future, whenever you check on the wages you have paid me. Any goat in my possession that is not speckled or spotted, or any lamb that is not dark-colored, will be considered stolen."

³⁴"Agreed," said Laban. "Let it be as you have said." ³⁵That same day he removed all the male goats that were streaked or spotted, and all the speckled or spotted female goats (all that had white on them) and all the dark-colored lambs, and he placed them in the care of his sons. ³⁶Then he put a three-day journey between himself and Jacob, while Jacob continued to tend the rest of Laban's flocks.

³⁷Jacob, however, took fresh-cut branches from poplar, almond and plane trees and made white stripes on them by peeling the bark and exposing the white inner wood of the branches. ³⁸Then he placed the peeled branches in all the watering troughs, so that they would be directly in front of the flocks when they came to drink. When the flocks were in heat and came to drink, ³⁹they mated in front of the branches. And they bore young that were streaked or speckled or spotted. ⁴⁰Jacob set apart the young of the flock by themselves, but made the rest face the streaked and dark-colored animals that

^a 27 Or possibly *have become rich and*

雅各的羊羣增多

²⁵拉結生約瑟之後，雅各對拉班說：「請打發我走，叫我回到我本鄉本土去。²⁶請你把我服侍你所得的妻子和兒女給我，讓我走。我怎樣服侍你，你都知道。」

²⁷拉班對他說：「我若在你眼前蒙恩，請你仍與我同住，因為我已算定，耶和華賜福與我是為你的緣故。」²⁸又說：「請你定你的工價，我就給你。」

²⁹雅各對他說：「我怎樣服侍你，你的牲畜在我手裏怎樣，是你知道的。³⁰我未來之先，你所有的很少，現今卻發大眾多，耶和華隨我的腳步賜福與你。如今我甚麼時候才為自己興家立業呢？」

³¹拉班說：「我當給你甚麼呢？」

雅各說：「甚麼你也不必給我，只有一件事，你若應承，我便仍舊牧放你的羊羣。³²今天我要走遍你的羊羣，把綿羊中凡有點的、有斑的和黑色的，並山羊中凡有斑的、有點的，都挑出來，將來這一等的就算我的工價。³³以後你來查看我的工價，凡在我手裏的山羊，不是有點有斑的，綿羊不是黑色的，那就算是我偷的。這樣，便可證出我的公義來。」

³⁴拉班說：「好啊，我情願照着你的話行。」³⁵當日，拉班把有紋的、有斑的公山羊，有點的、有斑的有雜白紋的母山羊，並黑色的綿羊，都挑出來，交在他兒子們的手下，³⁶又使自己和雅各相離三天的路程。雅各就牧養拉班其餘的羊。

³⁷雅各拿楊樹、杏樹、楓樹的嫩枝，將皮剝成白紋，使枝子露出白的來，³⁸將剝了皮的枝子，對着羊羣，插在飲羊的水溝裏和水槽裏，羊來喝的時候，牝牡配合。³⁹羊對着枝子配合，就生下有紋的、有點的、有斑的來。⁴⁰雅各把羊羔分出來，使拉班的羊與這有紋和黑色的羊相對，把自己

的羊另放一處，不叫他和拉班的羊混雜。⁴¹到羊羣肥壯配合的時候，雅各就把枝子插在水溝裏，使羊對着枝子配合。⁴²只是到羊瘦弱配合的時候就不插枝子。這樣，瘦弱的就歸拉班，肥壯的就歸雅各。⁴³於是雅各極其發大，得了許多的羊羣、僕婢、駱駝和驢。

雅各逃離拉班

31 雅各聽見拉班的兒子們有話說：“雅各把我們父親所有的都奪了去，並藉着我們父親的，得了這一切的榮耀（註：“榮耀”或作“財”）。”²雅各見拉班的氣色向他不如從前了。

³耶和華對雅各説：“你要回你祖宗父之地，到你親族那裏去，我必與你同在。”

⁴雅各就打發人，叫拉結和利亞到田野羊羣那裏來，⁵對她們説：“我看你們父親的氣色向我不如從前了，但我父親的神向來與我同在。⁶你們也知道，我盡了我的力量服侍你們的父親。⁷你們的父親欺哄我，十次改了我的工價，然而神不容他害我。⁸他若説：‘有點的歸你作工價’，羊羣所生的都有點；他若説：‘有紋的歸你作工價’，羊羣所生的都有紋。⁹這樣，神把你們父親的牲畜奪來賜給我了。

¹⁰“羊配合的時候，我夢中舉目一看，見跳母羊的公羊都是有紋的、有點的、有花斑的。¹¹神的使者在那夢中呼叫我説：‘雅各！’我説：‘我在這裏。’¹²他説：‘你舉目觀看，跳母羊的公羊都是有紋的、有點的、有花斑的；凡拉班向你所做的，我都看見了。¹³我是伯特利的神，你在那裏用油澆過柱子，向我許過願。現今你起來，離開這地，回你本地去吧！’”

¹⁴拉結和利亞回答雅各説：“在我們父親的家裏還有我們可得的分嗎？還有我們的產業嗎？¹⁵我們不是被他當作外人嗎？因為他賣了我們，吞了我們的價值。¹⁶神從我們父

belonged to Laban. Thus he made separate flocks for himself and did not put them with Laban's animals. ⁴¹Whenever the stronger females were in heat, Jacob would place the branches in the troughs in front of the animals so they would mate near the branches, ⁴²but if the animals were weak, he would not place them there. So the weak animals went to Laban and the strong ones to Jacob. ⁴³In this way the man grew exceedingly prosperous and came to own large flocks, and maidservants and menservants, and camels and donkeys.

Jacob Flees From Laban

31 Jacob heard that Laban's sons were saying, "Jacob has taken everything our father owned and has gained all this wealth from what belonged to our father." ²And Jacob noticed that Laban's attitude toward him was not what it had been.

³Then the LORD said to Jacob, "Go back to the land of your fathers and to your relatives, and I will be with you."

⁴So Jacob sent word to Rachel and Leah to come out to the fields where his flocks were. ⁵He said to them, "I see that your father's attitude toward me is not what it was before, but the God of my father has been with me. ⁶You know that I've worked for your father with all my strength, ⁷yet your father has cheated me by changing my wages ten times. However, God has not allowed him to harm me. ⁸If he said, 'The speckled ones will be your wages,' then all the flocks gave birth to speckled young; and if he said, 'The streaked ones will be your wages,' then all the flocks bore streaked young. ⁹So God has taken away your father's livestock and has given them to me.

¹⁰"In breeding season I once had a dream in which I looked up and saw that the male goats mating with the flock were streaked, speckled or spotted. ¹¹The angel of God said to me in the dream, 'Jacob.' I answered, 'Here I am.' ¹²And he said, 'Look up and see that all the male goats mating with the flock are streaked, speckled or spotted, for I have seen all that Laban has been doing to you. ¹³I am the God of Bethel, where you anointed a pillar and where you made a vow to me. Now leave this land at once and go back to your native land.' "

¹⁴Then Rachel and Leah replied, "Do we still have any share in the inheritance of our father's estate? ¹⁵Does he not regard us as foreigners? Not only has he sold us, but he has used up what was paid for us. ¹⁶Surely all the wealth

that God took away from our father belongs to us and our children. So do whatever God has told you."

¹⁷Then Jacob put his children and his wives on camels, ¹⁸and he drove all his livestock ahead of him, along with all the goods he had accumulated in Paddan Aram,^a to go to his father Isaac in the land of Canaan.

¹⁹When Laban had gone to shear his sheep, Rachel stole her father's household gods. ²⁰Moreover, Jacob deceived Laban the Aramean by not telling him he was running away. ²¹So he fled with all he had, and crossing the River,^b he headed for the hill country of Gilead.

Laban Pursues Jacob

²²On the third day Laban was told that Jacob had fled. ²³Taking his relatives with him, he pursued Jacob for seven days and caught up with him in the hill country of Gilead. ²⁴Then God came to Laban the Aramean in a dream at night and said to him, "Be careful not to say anything to Jacob, either good or bad."

²⁵Jacob had pitched his tent in the hill country of Gilead when Laban overtook him, and Laban and his relatives camped there too. ²⁶Then Laban said to Jacob, "What have you done? You've deceived me, and you've carried off my daughters like captives in war. ²⁷Why did you run off secretly and deceive me? Why didn't you tell me, so I could send you away with joy and singing to the music of tambourines and harps? ²⁸You didn't even let me kiss my grandchildren and my daughters goodby. You have done a foolish thing. ²⁹I have the power to harm you; but last night the God of your father said to me, 'Be careful not to say anything to Jacob, either good or bad.' ³⁰Now you have gone off because you longed to return to your father's house. But why did you steal my gods?"

³¹Jacob answered Laban, "I was afraid, because I thought you would take your daughters away from me by force. ³²But if you find anyone who has your gods, he shall not live. In the presence of our relatives, see for yourself whether there is anything of yours here with me; and if so, take it." Now Jacob did not know that Rachel had stolen the gods.

³³So Laban went into Jacob's tent and into Leah's tent and into the tent of the two maidservants, but he found nothing. After he came out of Leah's tent, he entered Rachel's tent. ³⁴Now

^a 18 That is, Northwest Mesopotamia   ^b 21 That is, the Euphrates

親所奪出來的一切財物,那就是我們和我們孩子們的。現今凡神所吩咐你的,你只管去行吧!"

¹⁷雅各起來,使他的兒子和妻子都騎上駱駝。¹⁸又帶着他在巴旦亞蘭所得的一切牲畜和財物,往迦南地他父親以撒那裏去了。

¹⁹當時拉班剪羊毛去了,拉結偷了她父親家中的神像。²⁰雅各背着亞蘭人拉班偷走了,並不告訴他,²¹就帶着所有的逃跑。他起身過大河,面向基列山行去。

拉班追趕雅各

²²到第三日,有人告訴拉班:"雅各逃跑了。"²³拉班帶領他的眾弟兄去追趕,追了七日,在基列山就追上了。²⁴夜間,神到亞蘭人拉班那裏,在夢中對他說:"你要小心,不可與雅各說好說歹!"

²⁵拉班追上雅各。雅各在山上支搭帳棚;拉班和他的眾弟兄也在基列山上支搭帳棚。²⁶拉班對雅各說:"你做的是甚麼事呢?你背着我偷走了,又把我的女兒們帶了去,如同用刀劍擄去的一般。²⁷你為甚麼暗暗地逃跑,偷着走,並不告訴我,叫我可以歡樂、唱歌、擊鼓、彈琴地送你回去?²⁸又不容我與外孫和女兒親嘴,你所行的真是愚昧!²⁹我手中原有能力害你,只是你父親的神昨夜對我說:'你要小心!不可與雅各說好說歹!'³⁰現在你雖然想你父家,不得不去,為甚麼又偷了我的神像呢?"

³¹雅各回答拉班說:"恐怕你把你的女兒從我奪去,所以我逃跑。³²至於你的神像,你在誰那裏搜出來,就不容誰存活,當着我們的眾弟兄你認一認,在我這裏有甚麼東西是你的,就拿去。"原來雅各不知道拉結偷了那些神像。

³³拉班進了雅各、利亞並兩個使女的帳棚,都沒有搜出來,就從利亞的帳棚出來,進了拉結的帳棚。³⁴拉

結已經把神像藏在駱駝的馱簍裏，便坐在上頭。拉班摸遍了那帳棚，並沒有摸着。

³⁵拉結對她父親說：「現在我身上不便，不能在你面前起來，求我主不要生氣。」這樣，拉班搜尋神像，竟沒有搜出來。

³⁶雅各就發怒斥責拉班說：「我有甚麼過犯，有甚麼罪惡，你竟這樣火速地追我？³⁷你摸遍了我一切的家具，你搜出甚麼來呢？可以放在你我弟兄面前，叫他們在你我中間辨別辨別。

³⁸「我在你家這二十年，你的母綿羊、母山羊沒有掉過胎。你羣中的公羊，我沒有吃過；³⁹被野獸撕裂的，我沒有帶來給你，是我自己賠上。無論是白日，是黑夜，被偷去的，你都向我索要。⁴⁰我白日受盡乾熱，黑夜受盡寒霜，不得合眼睡着，我常是這樣。⁴¹我這二十年在你家裏，為你的兩個女兒服侍你十四年，為你的羊羣服侍你六年，你又十次改了我的工價。⁴²若不是我父親以撒所敬畏的神，就是亞伯拉罕的神與我同在，你如今必定打發我空手而去。神看見我的苦情和我的勞碌，就在昨夜責備你。」

⁴³拉班回答雅各說：「這女兒是我的女兒，這些孩子是我的孩子，這些羊羣也是我的羊羣；凡在你眼前的都是我的。我的女兒並她們所生的孩子，我今日能向他們做甚麼呢？⁴⁴來吧！你我二人可以立約，作你我中間的證據。」

⁴⁵雅各就拿一塊石頭立作柱子，⁴⁶又對眾弟兄說：「你們堆聚石頭。」他們就拿石頭來堆成一堆，大家便在旁邊吃喝。⁴⁷拉班稱那石堆為伊迦爾撒哈杜他，雅各卻稱那石堆為迦累得（註：都是「以石堆為證」的意思）。

⁴⁸拉班說：「今日這石堆作你我中間的證據。」因此這地方名叫迦累得，⁴⁹又叫米斯巴，意思說：「我們彼此離別以後，願耶和華在你我中間鑒察。⁵⁰你若苦待我的女兒，又

Rachel had taken the household gods and put them inside her camel's saddle and was sitting on them. Laban searched through everything in the tent but found nothing.

³⁵Rachel said to her father, "Don't be angry, my lord, that I cannot stand up in your presence; I'm having my period." So he searched but could not find the household gods.

³⁶Jacob was angry and took Laban to task. "What is my crime?" he asked Laban. "What sin have I committed that you hunt me down? ³⁷Now that you have searched through all my goods, what have you found that belongs to your household? Put it here in front of your relatives and mine, and let them judge between the two of us.

³⁸"I have been with you for twenty years now. Your sheep and goats have not miscarried, nor have I eaten rams from your flocks. ³⁹I did not bring you animals torn by wild beasts; I bore the loss myself. And you demanded payment from me for whatever was stolen by day or night. ⁴⁰This was my situation: The heat consumed me in the daytime and the cold at night, and sleep fled from my eyes. ⁴¹It was like this for the twenty years I was in your household. I worked for you fourteen years for your two daughters and six years for your flocks, and you changed my wages ten times. ⁴²If the God of my father, the God of Abraham and the Fear of Isaac, had not been with me, you would surely have sent me away empty-handed. But God has seen my hardship and the toil of my hands, and last night he rebuked you."

⁴³Laban answered Jacob, "The women are my daughters, the children are my children, and the flocks are my flocks. All you see is mine. Yet what can I do today about these daughters of mine, or about the children they have borne? ⁴⁴Come now, let's make a covenant, you and I, and let it serve as a witness between us."

⁴⁵So Jacob took a stone and set it up as a pillar. ⁴⁶He said to his relatives, "Gather some stones." So they took stones and piled them in a heap, and they ate there by the heap. ⁴⁷Laban called it Jegar Sahadutha,^a and Jacob called it Galeed.^b

⁴⁸Laban said, "This heap is a witness between you and me today." That is why it was called Galeed. ⁴⁹It was also called Mizpah,^c because he said, "May the LORD keep watch between you and me when we are away from each other. ⁵⁰If

---

^a 47 The Aramaic *Jegar Sahadutha* means *witness heap.*

^b 47 The Hebrew *Galeed* means *witness heap.*　　^c 49 *Mizpah* means *watchtower.*

you mistreat my daughters or if you take any wives besides my daughters, even though no one is with us, remember that God is a witness between you and me."

⁵¹Laban also said to Jacob, "Here is this heap, and here is this pillar I have set up between you and me. ⁵²This heap is a witness, and this pillar is a witness, that I will not go past this heap to your side to harm you and that you will not go past this heap and pillar to my side to harm me. ⁵³May the God of Abraham and the God of Nahor, the God of their father, judge between us."

So Jacob took an oath in the name of the Fear of his father Isaac. ⁵⁴He offered a sacrifice there in the hill country and invited his relatives to a meal. After they had eaten, they spent the night there.

⁵⁵Early the next morning Laban kissed his grandchildren and his daughters and blessed them. Then he left and returned home.

Jacob Prepares to Meet Esau

32 Jacob also went on his way, and the angels of God met him. ²When Jacob saw them, he said, "This is the camp of God!" So he named that place Mahanaim.ᵃ

³Jacob sent messengers ahead of him to his brother Esau in the land of Seir, the country of Edom. ⁴He instructed them: "This is what you are to say to my master Esau: 'Your servant Jacob says, I have been staying with Laban and have remained there till now. ⁵I have cattle and donkeys, sheep and goats, menservants and maidservants. Now I am sending this message to my lord, that I may find favor in your eyes.' "

⁶When the messengers returned to Jacob, they said, "We went to your brother Esau, and now he is coming to meet you, and four hundred men are with him."

⁷In great fear and distress Jacob divided the people who were with him into two groups,ᵇ and the flocks and herds and camels as well. ⁸He thought, "If Esau comes and attacks one group,ᶜ the groupᶜ that is left may escape."

⁹Then Jacob prayed, "O God of my father Abraham, God of my father Isaac, O LORD, who said to me, 'Go back to your country and your relatives, and I will make you prosper,' ¹⁰I am unworthy of all the kindness and faithfulness you have shown your servant. I had only my staff when I crossed this Jordan, but now I have become two groups. ¹¹Save me, I pray, from the

---

在我的女兒以外另娶妻,雖沒有人知道,卻有神在你我中間作見證。"

⁵¹拉班又說:"你看我在你我中間所立的這石堆和柱子。⁵²這石堆作證據,這柱子也作證據。我必不過這石堆去害你;你也不可過這石堆和柱子來害我。⁵³但願亞伯拉罕的神和拿鶴的神,就是他們父親的神,在你我中間判斷。"

雅各就指着他父親以撒所敬畏的神起誓,⁵⁴又在山上獻祭,請眾弟兄來吃飯。他們吃了飯,便在山上住宿。

⁵⁵拉班清早起來,與他外孫和女兒親嘴,給他們祝福,回往自己的地方去了。

雅各準備見以掃

32 雅各仍舊行路,神的使者遇見他。²雅各看見他們就說:"這是神的軍兵。"於是給那地方起名叫瑪哈念 (註:就是"二軍兵"的意思)。

³雅各打發人先往西珥地去,就是以東地,見他哥哥以掃,⁴吩咐他們說:"你們對我主以掃說:'你的僕人雅各這樣說:我在拉班那裏寄居,直到如今。⁵我有牛、驢、羊羣、僕婢,現在打發人來報告我主,為要在你眼前蒙恩。'"

⁶所打發的人回到雅各那裏,說:"我們到了你哥哥以掃那裏,他帶着四百人,正迎着你來。"

⁷雅各就甚懼怕,而且愁煩,便把那與他同在的人口和羊羣、牛羣、駱駝分做兩隊,⁸說:"以掃若來擊殺這一隊,剩下的那一隊還可以逃避。"

⁹雅各說:"耶和華我祖亞伯拉罕的神,我父親以撒的神啊,你曾對我說:'回你本地本族去,我要厚待你。'¹⁰你向僕人所施的一切慈愛和誠實,我一點也不配得。我先前只拿着我的杖過這約旦河,如今我卻成了兩隊了。¹¹求你救我脫離我哥哥以掃

ᵃ 2 *Mahanaim* means *two camps.*   ᵇ 7 Or *camps*; also in verse 10
ᶜ 8 Or *camp*

的手，因為我怕他來殺我，連妻子帶兒女一同殺了。¹²你曾說：『我必定厚待你，使你的後裔如同海邊的沙，多得不可勝數。』」

¹³當夜，雅各在那裏住宿，就從他所有的物中拿禮物要送給他哥哥以掃：¹⁴母山羊二百隻，公山羊二十隻，母綿羊二百隻，公綿羊二十隻，¹⁵奶崽子的駱駝三十隻，各帶着崽子；母牛四十隻，公牛十隻，母驢二十匹，驢駒十四。¹⁶每樣各分一羣，交在僕人手下，就對僕人說：「你們要在我前頭過去，使羣羣相離，有空閒的地方。」

¹⁷又吩咐儘先走的說：「我哥哥以掃遇見你的時候，問你說：『你是哪家的人？要往哪裏去？你前頭這些是誰的？』¹⁸你就說：『是你僕人雅各的，是送給我主以掃的禮物，他自己也在我們後邊。』」

¹⁹又吩咐第二、第三和一切趕羣畜的人說：「你們遇見以掃的時候，也要這樣對他說。²⁰並且你們要說：『你僕人雅各在我們後邊。』」因雅各心裏說：「我藉着在我前頭去的禮物解他的恨，然後再見他的面，或者他容納我。」²¹於是禮物先過去了。那夜，雅各在隊中住宿。

雅各與神摔跤

²²他夜間起來，帶着兩個妻子、兩個使女，並十一個兒子過了雅博渡口。²³先打發他們過河，又打發所有的都過去，²⁴只剩下雅各一人。有一個人來和他摔跤，直到黎明。²⁵那人見自己勝不過他，就將他的大腿窩摸了一把，雅各的大腿窩正在摔跤的時候就扭了。²⁶那人說：「天黎明了，容我去吧！」

雅各說：「你不給我祝福，我就不容你去。」

²⁷那人說：「你名叫甚麼？」他說：「我名叫雅各。」

²⁸那人說：「你的名不要再叫雅各，要叫以色列，因為你與神與人較力，都得了勝。」

hand of my brother Esau, for I am afraid he will come and attack me, and also the mothers with their children. ¹²But you have said, 'I will surely make you prosper and will make your descendants like the sand of the sea, which cannot be counted.' "

¹³He spent the night there, and from what he had with him he selected a gift for his brother Esau: ¹⁴two hundred female goats and twenty male goats, two hundred ewes and twenty rams, ¹⁵thirty female camels with their young, forty cows and ten bulls, and twenty female donkeys and ten male donkeys. ¹⁶He put them in the care of his servants, each herd by itself, and said to his servants, "Go ahead of me, and keep some space between the herds."

¹⁷He instructed the one in the lead: "When my brother Esau meets you and asks, 'To whom do you belong, and where are you going, and who owns all these animals in front of you?' ¹⁸then you are to say, 'They belong to your servant Jacob. They are a gift sent to my lord Esau, and he is coming behind us.' "

¹⁹He also instructed the second, the third and all the others who followed the herds: "You are to say the same thing to Esau when you meet him. ²⁰And be sure to say, 'Your servant Jacob is coming behind us.' " For he thought, "I will pacify him with these gifts I am sending on ahead; later, when I see him, perhaps he will receive me." ²¹So Jacob's gifts went on ahead of him, but he himself spent the night in the camp.

Jacob Wrestles With God

²²That night Jacob got up and took his two wives, his two maidservants and his eleven sons and crossed the ford of the Jabbok. ²³After he had sent them across the stream, he sent over all his possessions. ²⁴So Jacob was left alone, and a man wrestled with him till daybreak. ²⁵When the man saw that he could not overpower him, he touched the socket of Jacob's hip so that his hip was wrenched as he wrestled with the man. ²⁶Then the man said, "Let me go, for it is daybreak."

But Jacob replied, "I will not let you go unless you bless me."

²⁷The man asked him, "What is your name?"

"Jacob," he answered.

²⁸Then the man said, "Your name will no longer be Jacob, but Israel,ᵃ because you have struggled with God and with men and have overcome."

---

a 28 Israel means *he struggles with God.*

29Jacob said, "Please tell me your name."

But he replied, "Why do you ask my name?" Then he blessed him there.

30So Jacob called the place Peniel,*a* saying, "It is because I saw God face to face, and yet my life was spared."

31The sun rose above him as he passed Peniel,*b* and he was limping because of his hip. 32Therefore to this day the Israelites do not eat the tendon attached to the socket of the hip, because the socket of Jacob's hip was touched near the tendon.

Jacob Meets Esau

33 Jacob looked up and there was Esau, coming with his four hundred men; so he divided the children among Leah, Rachel and the two maidservants. 2He put the maidservants and their children in front, Leah and her children next, and Rachel and Joseph in the rear. 3He himself went on ahead and bowed down to the ground seven times as he approached his brother.

4But Esau ran to meet Jacob and embraced him; he threw his arms around his neck and kissed him. And they wept. 5Then Esau looked up and saw the women and children. "Who are these with you?" he asked.

Jacob answered, "They are the children God has graciously given your servant."

6Then the maidservants and their children approached and bowed down. 7Next, Leah and her children came and bowed down. Last of all came Joseph and Rachel, and they too bowed down.

8Esau asked, "What do you mean by all these droves I met?"

"To find favor in your eyes, my lord," he said.

9But Esau said, "I already have plenty, my brother. Keep what you have for yourself."

10"No, please!" said Jacob. "If I have found favor in your eyes, accept this gift from me. For to see your face is like seeing the face of God, now that you have received me favorably. 11Please accept the present that was brought to you, for God has been gracious to me and I have all I need." And because Jacob insisted, Esau accepted it.

12Then Esau said, "Let us be on our way; I'll accompany you."

13But Jacob said to him, "My lord knows that the children are tender and that I must care for the ewes and cows that are nursing their young.

a 30 Peniel means *face of God.　　b 31* Hebrew *Penuel,* a variant of *Peniel*

29雅各問他説："請將你的名告訴我。"那人説："何必問我的名？"於是在那裏給雅各祝福。

30雅各便給那地方起名叫毘努伊勒（註：就是"神之面"的意思），意思説："我面對面見了神，我的性命仍得保全。"

31日頭剛出來的時候，雅各經過毘努伊勒，他的大腿就瘸了。32故此，以色列人不吃大腿窩的筋，直到今日，因為那人摸了雅各大腿窩的筋。

雅各以掃相見

33 雅各舉目觀看，見以掃來了，後頭跟着四百人，他就把孩子們分開交給利亞、拉結和兩個使女，2並且叫兩個使女和她們的孩子在前頭，利亞和她的孩子在後頭，拉結和約瑟在儘後頭。3他自己在他們前頭過去，一連七次俯伏在地，才就近他哥哥。

4以掃跑來迎接他，將他抱住，又摟着他的頸項與他親嘴，兩個人就哭了。5以掃舉目看見婦人孩子，就説："這些和你同行的是誰呢？"

雅各説："這些孩子是神施恩給你僕人的。"

6於是兩個使女和她們的孩子前來下拜，7利亞和她的孩子也前來下拜；隨後約瑟和拉結也前來下拜。

8以掃説："我所遇見的這些羣畜是甚麼意思呢？"

雅各説："是要在我主面前蒙恩的。"

9以掃説："兄弟啊，我的已經夠了，你的仍歸你吧！"

10雅各説："不然，我若在你眼前蒙恩，就求你從我手裏收下這禮物，因為我見了你的面，如同見了神的面，並且你容納了我。11求你收下我帶來給你的禮物，因為神恩待我，使我充足。"雅各再三地求他，他才收下了。

12以掃説："我們可以起身前往，我在你前頭走。"

13雅各對他説："我主知道孩子們年幼嬌嫩，牛羊也正在乳養的時候，若是催趕一天，羣畜都必死了。14求我主在僕人前頭走，我要量着在我面前羣畜和孩子的力量慢慢地前行，直走到西珥我主那裏。」

15以掃說：「容我把跟隨我的人留幾個在你這裏。」

雅各說：「何必呢？只要在我主眼前蒙恩就是了。」

16於是以掃當日起行，回往西珥去了。17雅各就往疏割去，在那裏為自己蓋造房屋，又為牲畜搭棚；因此那地方名叫疏割（註：就是「棚」的意思）。

18雅各從巴旦亞蘭回來的時候，平平安安地到了迦南地的示劍城，在城東支搭帳棚，19就用一百塊銀子向示劍的父親、哈抹的子孫買了支帳棚的那塊地，20在那裏築了一座壇，起名叫伊利伊羅伊以色列（註：就是「神、以色列神」的意思）。

底拿與示劍族

34 利亞給雅各所生的女兒底拿出去，要見那地的女子們。2那地的主希未人、哈抹的兒子示劍看見她，就拉住她與她行淫，玷辱她。3示劍的心繫戀雅各的女兒底拿，喜愛這女子，甜言蜜語地安慰她。4示劍對他父親哈抹說：「求你為我聘這女子為妻。」

5雅各聽見示劍玷污了他的女兒底拿，那時他的兒子們正和羣畜在田野，雅各就閉口不言，等他們回來。

6示劍的父親哈抹出來見雅各，要和他商議。7雅各的兒子們聽見這事，就從田野回來，人人忿恨，十分惱怒，因示劍在以色列家做了醜事，與雅各的女兒行淫，這本是不該做的事。

8哈抹和他們商議說：「我兒子示劍的心戀慕這女子，求你們將她給我的兒子為妻。9你們與我們彼此結親，你們可以把女兒給我們，也可以娶我們的女兒。10你們與我們同住吧！這地都在你們面前，只管在

If they are driven hard just one day, all the animals will die. 14So let my lord go on ahead of his servant, while I move along slowly at the pace of the droves before me and that of the children, until I come to my lord in Seir."

15Esau said, "Then let me leave some of my men with you."

"But why do that?" Jacob asked. "Just let me find favor in the eyes of my lord."

16So that day Esau started on his way back to Seir. 17Jacob, however, went to Succoth, where he built a place for himself and made shelters for his livestock. That is why the place is called Succoth.*a*

18After Jacob came from Paddan Aram,*b* he arrived safely at the*c* city of Shechem in Canaan and camped within sight of the city. 19For a hundred pieces of silver,*d* he bought from the sons of Hamor, the father of Shechem, the plot of ground where he pitched his tent. 20There he set up an altar and called it El Elohe Israel.*e*

Dinah and the Shechemites

34 Now Dinah, the daughter Leah had borne to Jacob, went out to visit the women of the land. 2When Shechem son of Hamor the Hivite, the ruler of that area, saw her, he took her and violated her. 3His heart was drawn to Dinah daughter of Jacob, and he loved the girl and spoke tenderly to her. 4And Shechem said to his father Hamor, "Get me this girl as my wife."

5When Jacob heard that his daughter Dinah had been defiled, his sons were in the fields with his livestock; so he kept quiet about it until they came home.

6Then Shechem's father Hamor went out to talk with Jacob. 7Now Jacob's sons had come in from the fields as soon as they heard what had happened. They were filled with grief and fury, because Shechem had done a disgraceful thing in*f* Israel by lying with Jacob's daughter—a thing that should not be done.

8But Hamor said to them, "My son Shechem has his heart set on your daughter. Please give her to him as his wife. 9Intermarry with us; give us your daughters and take our daughters for yourselves. 10You can settle among us; the land is open to you. Live in it, trade*g* in it, and

---

a 17 Succoth means shelters.　　*b 18 That is, Northwest Mesopotamia*　　*c 18 Or arrived at Shalem, a*　　*d 19 Hebrew hundred kesitahs; a kesitah was a unit of money of unknown weight and value.*　　*e 20 El Elohe Israel can mean God, the God of Israel or mighty is the God of Israel.*　　*f 7 Or against*　　*g 10 Or move about freely; also in verse 21*

acquire property in it."

¹¹Then Shechem said to Dinah's father and brothers, "Let me find favor in your eyes, and I will give you whatever you ask. ¹²Make the price for the bride and the gift I am to bring as great as you like, and I'll pay whatever you ask me. Only give me the girl as my wife."

¹³Because their sister Dinah had been defiled, Jacob's sons replied deceitfully as they spoke to Shechem and his father Hamor. ¹⁴They said to them, "We can't do such a thing; we can't give our sister to a man who is not circumcised. That would be a disgrace to us. ¹⁵We will give our consent to you on one condition only: that you become like us by circumcising all your males. ¹⁶Then we will give you our daughters and take your daughters for ourselves. We'll settle among you and become one people with you. ¹⁷But if you will not agree to be circumcised, we'll take our sister^a and go."

¹⁸Their proposal seemed good to Hamor and his son Shechem. ¹⁹The young man, who was the most honored of all his father's household, lost no time in doing what they said, because he was delighted with Jacob's daughter. ²⁰So Hamor and his son Shechem went to the gate of their city to speak to their fellow townsmen. ²¹"These men are friendly toward us," they said. "Let them live in our land and trade in it; the land has plenty of room for them. We can marry their daughters and they can marry ours. ²²But the men will consent to live with us as one people only on the condition that our males be circumcised, as they themselves are. ²³Won't their livestock, their property and all their other animals become ours? So let us give our consent to them, and they will settle among us."

²⁴All the men who went out of the city gate agreed with Hamor and his son Shechem, and every male in the city was circumcised.

²⁵Three days later, while all of them were still in pain, two of Jacob's sons, Simeon and Levi, Dinah's brothers, took their swords and attacked the unsuspecting city, killing every male. ²⁶They put Hamor and his son Shechem to the sword and took Dinah from Shechem's house and left. ²⁷The sons of Jacob came upon the dead bodies and looted the city where^b their sister had been defiled. ²⁸They seized their flocks and herds and donkeys and everything else of theirs in the city and out in the fields. ²⁹They carried off all their wealth and all their women and children, taking as plunder everything in the houses.

此居住，做買賣，置產業。"

¹¹示劍對女兒的父親和弟兄們說："但願我在你們眼前蒙恩，你們向我要甚麼，我必給你們。¹²任憑向我要多重的聘金和禮物，我必照你們所說的給你們，只要把女子給我為妻。"

¹³雅各的兒子們，因為示劍玷污了他們的妹子底拿，就用詭詐的話回答示劍和他父親哈抹，¹⁴對他們說："我們不能把我們的妹子給沒有受割禮的人為妻，因為那是我們的羞辱。¹⁵惟有一件才可以應允，若你們所有的男丁都受割禮，和我們一樣，¹⁶我們就把女兒給你們，也娶你們的女兒，我們便與你們同住，兩下成為一樣的人民；¹⁷倘若你們不聽從我們受割禮，我們就帶着妹子走了。"

¹⁸哈抹和他的兒子示劍喜歡這話。¹⁹那少年人做這事並不遲延，因為他喜愛雅各的女兒。他在他父親家中也是人最尊重的。²⁰哈抹和他兒子示劍到本城的門口，對本城的人說：²¹"這些人與我們和睦，不如許他們在這地居住，做買賣；這地也寬闊，足可容下他們。我們可以娶他們的女兒為妻，也可以把我們的女兒嫁給他們。²²惟有一件事我們必須做，他們才肯應允和我們同住，成為一樣的人民：就是我們中間所有的男丁都要受割禮，和他們一樣。²³他們的羣畜、貨財和一切的牲口豈不都歸我們嗎？只要依從他們，他們就與我們同住。"

²⁴凡從城門出入的人，就都聽從哈抹和他兒子示劍的話。於是，凡從城門出入的男丁都受了割禮。

²⁵到第三天，眾人正在疼痛的時候，雅各的兩個兒子，就是底拿的哥哥西緬和利未，各拿刀劍，趁着眾人想不到的時候，來到城中，把一切男丁都殺了，²⁶又用刀殺了哈抹和他兒子示劍，把底拿從示劍家裏帶出來就走了。²⁷雅各的兒子們因為他們的妹子受了玷污，就來到被殺的人那裏，擄掠那城，²⁸奪了他們的羊羣、牛羣和驢，並城裏田間所有的，²⁹又把他們一切貨財、孩子、婦女，並各房中所有的，都擄掠去了。

_a 17 Hebrew *daughter*　　_b 27 Or *because*

³⁰雅各對西緬和利未說：“你們連累我，使我在這地的居民中，就是在迦南人和比利洗人中，有了臭名。我的人丁既然稀少，他們必聚集來擊殺我，我和全家的人都必滅絕。”

³¹他們說：“他豈可待我們的妹子如同妓女嗎？”

雅各回伯特利

35 神對雅各說：“起來！上伯特利去，住在那裏，要在那裏築一座壇給神，就是你逃避你哥哥以掃的時候向你顯現的那位。”

²雅各就對他家中的人，並一切與他同在的人說：“你們要除掉你們中間的外邦神，也要自潔，更換衣裳。³我們要起來，上伯特利去，在那裏我要築一座壇給神，就是在我遭難的日子應允我的禱告、在我行的路上保佑我的那位。”⁴他們就把外邦人的神像和他們耳朵上的環子交給雅各，雅各都藏在示劍那裏的橡樹底下。⁵他們便起行前往，神使那周圍城邑的人都甚驚懼，就不追趕雅各的眾子了。

⁶於是，雅各和一切與他同在的人到了迦南地的路斯，就是伯特利。⁷他在那裏築了一座壇，就給那地方起名叫伊勒伯特利（註：就是“伯特利之神”的意思），因為他逃避他哥哥的時候，神在那裏向他顯現。

⁸利百加的奶母底波拉死了，就葬在伯特利下邊橡樹底下；那棵樹名叫亞倫巴古。

⁹雅各從巴旦亞蘭回來，神又向他顯現，賜福與他，¹⁰且對他說：“你的名原是雅各，從今以後不要再叫雅各，要叫以色列。”這樣，他就改名叫以色列。

¹¹神又對他說：“我是全能的神，你要生養眾多，將來有一族和多國的民從你而生，又有君王從你而出。¹²我所賜給亞伯拉罕和以撒的地，我要賜給你與你的後裔。”¹³神就從那與雅各說話的地方升上去了。

¹⁴雅各便在那裏立了一根石柱。

³⁰Then Jacob said to Simeon and Levi, "You have brought trouble on me by making me a stench to the Canaanites and Perizzites, the people living in this land. We are few in number, and if they join forces against me and attack me, I and my household will be destroyed."

³¹But they replied, "Should he have treated our sister like a prostitute?"

Jacob Returns to Bethel

35 Then God said to Jacob, "Go up to Bethel and settle there, and build an altar there to God, who appeared to you when you were fleeing from your brother Esau."

²So Jacob said to his household and to all who were with him, "Get rid of the foreign gods you have with you, and purify yourselves and change your clothes. ³Then come, let us go up to Bethel, where I will build an altar to God, who answered me in the day of my distress and who has been with me wherever I have gone." ⁴So they gave Jacob all the foreign gods they had and the rings in their ears, and Jacob buried them under the oak at Shechem. ⁵Then they set out, and the terror of God fell upon the towns all around them so that no one pursued them.

⁶Jacob and all the people with him came to Luz (that is, Bethel) in the land of Canaan. ⁷There he built an altar, and he called the place El Bethel,ᵃ because it was there that God revealed himself to him when he was fleeing from his brother.

⁸Now Deborah, Rebekah's nurse, died and was buried under the oak below Bethel. So it was named Allon Bacuth.ᵇ

⁹After Jacob returned from Paddan Aram,ᶜ God appeared to him again and blessed him. ¹⁰God said to him, "Your name is Jacob,ᵈ but you will no longer be called Jacob; your name will be Israel.ᵉ " So he named him Israel.

¹¹And God said to him, "I am God Almightyᶠ; be fruitful and increase in number. A nation and a community of nations will come from you, and kings will come from your body. ¹²The land I gave to Abraham and Isaac I also give to you, and I will give this land to your descendants after you." ¹³Then God went up from him at the place where he had talked with him.

¹⁴Jacob set up a stone pillar at the place where God had talked with him, and he poured

---

a 7 El Bethel means *God of Bethel.　b 8 Allon Bacuth* means *oak of weeping.　c 9* That is, Northwest Mesopotamia; also in verse 26　*d 10 Jacob* means *he grasps the heel* (figuratively, *he deceives*).　*e 10 Israel* means *he struggles with God.*
f 11 Hebrew *El-Shaddai*

out a drink offering on it; he also poured oil on it. [15]Jacob called the place where God had talked with him Bethel.[a]

The Deaths of Rachel and Isaac

[16]Then they moved on from Bethel. While they were still some distance from Ephrath, Rachel began to give birth and had great difficulty. [17]And as she was having great difficulty in childbirth, the midwife said to her, "Don't be afraid, for you have another son." [18]As she breathed her last—for she was dying—she named her son Ben-Oni.[b] But his father named him Benjamin.[c]

[19]So Rachel died and was buried on the way to Ephrath (that is, Bethlehem). [20]Over her tomb Jacob set up a pillar, and to this day that pillar marks Rachel's tomb.

[21]Israel moved on again and pitched his tent beyond Migdal Eder. [22]While Israel was living in that region, Reuben went in and slept with his father's concubine Bilhah, and Israel heard of it.

Jacob had twelve sons:

[23]The sons of Leah:

　Reuben the firstborn of Jacob,

　Simeon, Levi, Judah, Issachar and Zebulun.

[24]The sons of Rachel:

　Joseph and Benjamin.

[25]The sons of Rachel's maidservant Bilhah:

　Dan and Naphtali.

[26]The sons of Leah's maidservant Zilpah:

　Gad and Asher.

These were the sons of Jacob, who were born to him in Paddan Aram.

[27]Jacob came home to his father Isaac in Mamre, near Kiriath Arba (that is, Hebron), where Abraham and Isaac had stayed. [28]Isaac lived a hundred and eighty years. [29]Then he breathed his last and died and was gathered to his people, old and full of years. And his sons Esau and Jacob buried him.

Esau's Descendants

36 This is the account of Esau (that is, Edom).

[2]Esau took his wives from the women of Canaan: Adah daughter of Elon the Hittite, and Oholibamah daughter of Anah and granddaughter of Zibeon the Hivite— [3]also

---

在柱子上奠酒、澆油。[15]雅各就給那地方起名叫伯特利。

拉結與以撒去世

[16]他們從伯特利起行，離以法他還有一段路程，拉結臨產甚是艱難。[17]正在艱難的時候，收生婆對她說：「不要怕，你又要得一個兒子了。」[18]她將近於死，靈魂要走的時候，就給她兒子起名叫便俄尼，他父親卻給他起名叫便雅憫。

[19]拉結死了，葬在以法他的路旁；以法他就是伯利恆。[20]雅各在她的墳上立了一統碑，就是拉結的墓碑，到今日還在。

[21]以色列起行前往，在以得臺那邊支搭帳棚。[22]以色列住在那地的時候，呂便去與他父親的妾辟拉同寢，以色列也聽見了。

雅各共有十二個兒子：

[23]利亞所生的是

　雅各的長子呂便，

　還有西緬、利未、猶大、以薩

　迦、西布倫。

[24]拉結所生的是

　約瑟、便雅憫。

[25]拉結的使女辟拉所生的是

　但、拿弗他利。

[26]利亞的使女悉帕所生的是

　迦得、亞設。

這是雅各在巴旦亞蘭所生的兒子。

[27]雅各來到他父親以撒那裏，到了基列亞巴的幔利，乃是亞伯拉罕和以撒寄居的地方；基列亞巴就是希伯崙。[28]以撒共活了一百八十歲。[29]以撒年紀老邁，日子滿足，氣絕而死，歸到他列祖（註：原文作「本民」）那裏。他兩個兒子以掃、雅各把他葬埋了。

以掃的後裔

36 以掃就是以東，他的後代記在下面：

[2]以掃娶迦南的女子為妻，就是赫人以倫的女兒亞大和希未人祭便的孫女、亞拿的女兒阿何利巴瑪，[3]又

---

a 15 Bethel means house of God.　b 18 Ben-Oni means son of my trouble.　c 18 Benjamin means son of my right hand.

娶了以實瑪利的女兒、尼拜約的妹子巴實抹。

⁴亞大給以掃生了以利法；巴實抹生了流珥，⁵阿何利巴瑪生了耶烏施、雅蘭、可拉。這都是以掃的兒子，是在迦南地生的。

⁶以掃帶着他的妻子、兒女與家中一切的人口，並他的牛羊、牲畜和一切貨財，就是他在迦南地所得的，往別處去，離了他兄弟雅各。⁷因為二人的財物羣畜甚多，寄居的地方容不下他們，所以不能同居。⁸於是，以掃住在西珥山裏；以掃就是以東。

⁹以掃是西珥山裏以東人的始祖，他的後代記在下面。

¹⁰以掃眾子的名字如下：
　　以掃的妻子亞大生以利法；以掃的妻子巴實抹生流珥。
¹¹以利法的兒子是提幔、阿抹、洗玻、迦坦、基納斯。
　　¹²亭納是以掃兒子以利法的妾，她給以利法生了亞瑪力。這是以掃的妻子亞大的子孫。
¹³流珥的兒子是拿哈、謝拉、沙瑪、米撒。這是以掃妻子巴實抹的子孫。

¹⁴以掃的妻子阿何利巴瑪是祭便的孫女、亞拿的女兒，她給以掃生了耶烏施、雅蘭、可拉。

¹⁵以掃子孫中作族長的，記在下面：
　　以掃的長子，以利法的子孫中，有提幔族長、阿抹族長、洗玻族長、基納斯族長、¹⁶可拉族長、迦坦族長、亞瑪力族長。這是在以東地從以利法所出的族長，都是亞大的子孫。
¹⁷以掃的兒子流珥的子孫中，有拿哈族長、謝拉族長、沙瑪族長、米撒族長。這是在以東地從流珥所出的族長，都是以掃妻子巴實抹的子孫。
¹⁸以掃的妻子阿何利巴瑪的子孫中，有耶烏施族長、雅蘭族長、可拉族長。這是從以掃妻子、亞拿的女兒，阿何利巴瑪子孫中

Basemath daughter of Ishmael and sister of Nebaioth.

⁴Adah bore Eliphaz to Esau, Basemath bore Reuel, ⁵and Oholibamah bore Jeush, Jalam and Korah. These were the sons of Esau, who were born to him in Canaan.

⁶Esau took his wives and sons and daughters and all the members of his household, as well as his livestock and all his other animals and all the goods he had acquired in Canaan, and moved to a land some distance from his brother Jacob. ⁷Their possessions were too great for them to remain together; the land where they were staying could not support them both because of their livestock. ⁸So Esau (that is, Edom) settled in the hill country of Seir.

⁹This is the account of Esau the father of the Edomites in the hill country of Seir.

¹⁰These are the names of Esau's sons:
　　Eliphaz, the son of Esau's wife Adah, and Reuel, the son of Esau's wife Basemath.
¹¹The sons of Eliphaz:
　　Teman, Omar, Zepho, Gatam and Kenaz.
¹²Esau's son Eliphaz also had a concubine named Timna, who bore him Amalek. These were grandsons of Esau's wife Adah.
¹³The sons of Reuel:
　　Nahath, Zerah, Shammah and Mizzah. These were grandsons of Esau's wife Basemath.
¹⁴The sons of Esau's wife Oholibamah daughter of Anah and granddaughter of Zibeon, whom she bore to Esau:
　　Jeush, Jalam and Korah.

¹⁵These were the chiefs among Esau's descendants:
　　The sons of Eliphaz the firstborn of Esau:
　　Chiefs Teman, Omar, Zepho, Kenaz, ¹⁶Korah,ᵃ Gatam and Amalek. These were the chiefs descended from Eliphaz in Edom; they were grandsons of Adah.
¹⁷The sons of Esau's son Reuel:
　　Chiefs Nahath, Zerah, Shammah and Mizzah. These were the chiefs descended from Reuel in Edom; they were grandsons of Esau's wife Basemath.
¹⁸The sons of Esau's wife Oholibamah:
　　Chiefs Jeush, Jalam and Korah. These were the chiefs descended from Esau's wife

---

a 16 Masoretic Text; Samaritan Pentateuch (see also Gen. 36:11 and 1 Chron. 1:36) does not have *Korah*.

Oholibamah daughter of Anah.

¹⁹These were the sons of Esau (that is, Edom), and these were their chiefs.

²⁰These were the sons of Seir the Horite, who were living in the region:

Lotan, Shobal, Zibeon, Anah, ²¹Dishon, Ezer and Dishan. These sons of Seir in Edom were Horite chiefs.

²²The sons of Lotan:

Hori and Homam.ᵃ Timna was Lotan's sister.

²³The sons of Shobal:

Alvan, Manahath, Ebal, Shepho and Onam.

²⁴The sons of Zibeon:

Aiah and Anah. This is the Anah who discovered the hot springsᵇ in the desert while he was grazing the donkeys of his father Zibeon.

²⁵The children of Anah:

Dishon and Oholibamah daughter of Anah.

²⁶The sons of Dishonᶜ:

Hemdan, Eshban, Ithran and Keran.

²⁷The sons of Ezer:

Bilhan, Zaavan and Akan.

²⁸The sons of Dishan:

Uz and Aran.

²⁹These were the Horite chiefs:

Lotan, Shobal, Zibeon, Anah, ³⁰Dishon, Ezer and Dishan. These were the Horite chiefs, according to their divisions, in the land of Seir.

The Rulers of Edom

³¹These were the kings who reigned in Edom before any Israelite king reignedᵈ:

³²Bela son of Beor became king of Edom. His city was named Dinhabah.

³³When Bela died, Jobab son of Zerah from Bozrah succeeded him as king.

³⁴When Jobab died, Husham from the land of the Temanites succeeded him as king.

³⁵When Husham died, Hadad son of Bedad, who defeated Midian in the country of Moab, succeeded him as king. His city was named Avith.

³⁶When Hadad died, Samlah from Masrekah succeeded him as king.

³⁷When Samlah died, Shaul from Rehoboth on the riverᵉ succeeded him as king.

所出的族長。

¹⁹以上的族長都是以掃的子孫；以掃就是以東。

²⁰那地原有的居民何利人西珥的子孫記在下面：

就是羅坍、朔巴、祭便、亞拿、²¹底順、以察、底珊。這是從以東地的何利人西珥子孫中所出的族長。

²²羅坍的兒子是

何利、希幔；羅坍的妹子是亭納。

²³朔巴的兒子是

亞勒文、瑪拿轄、以巴錄、示玻、阿南。

²⁴祭便的兒子是

亞雅、亞拿。當時在曠野放他父親祭便的驢，遇着溫泉的就是這亞拿。

²⁵亞拿的兒子是

底順；亞拿的女兒是阿何利巴瑪。

²⁶底順的兒子是

欣但、伊是班、益蘭、基蘭。

²⁷以察的兒子是

辟罕、撒番、亞干。

²⁸底珊的兒子是

烏斯、亞蘭。

²⁹從何利人所出的族長記在下面：

就是羅坍族長、朔巴族長、祭便族長、亞拿族長、³⁰底順族長、以察族長、底珊族長。這是從何利人所出的族長，都在西珥地，按着宗族作族長。

以東諸王

³¹以色列人未有君王治理以先，在以東地作王的，記在下面：

³²比珥的兒子比拉在以東作王，他的京城名叫亭哈巴。

³³比拉死了，波斯拉人謝拉的兒子約巴接續他作王。

³⁴約巴死了，提幔地的人戶珊接續他作王。

³⁵戶珊死了，比達的兒子哈達接續他作王。這哈達就是在摩押地殺敗米甸人的，他的京城名叫亞未得。

³⁶哈達死了，瑪士利加人桑拉接續他作王。

³⁷桑拉死了，大河邊的利河伯人掃羅接續他作王。

a 22 Hebrew Hemam, a variant of Homam (see 1 Chron. 1:39)
b 24 Vulgate; Syriac discovered water; the meaning of the Hebrew for this word is uncertain.   c 26 Hebrew Dishan, a variant of Dishon   d 31 Or before an Israelite king reigned over them   e 37 Possibly the Euphrates

³⁸掃羅死了，亞革波的兒子巴勒哈南接續他作王。

³⁹亞革波的兒子巴勒哈南死了，哈達接續他作王。他的京城名叫巴鳥，他的妻子名叫米希她別，是米薩合的孫女，瑪特列的女兒。

⁴⁰從以掃所出的族長，按着他們的宗族、住處、名字記在下面：

就是亭納族長、亞勒瓦族長、耶帖族長、⁴¹阿何利巴瑪族長、以拉族長、比嫩族長、⁴²基納斯族長、提幔族長、米比薩族長、⁴³瑪基疊族長、以蘭族長。

這是以東人在所得為業的地上，按着他們的住處，所有的族長，都是以東人的始祖以掃的後代。

約瑟的夢

37 ¹雅各住在迦南地，就是他父親寄居的地。

²雅各的記略如下：

約瑟十七歲與他哥哥們一同牧羊。他是個童子，與他父親的妾辟拉、悉帕的兒子們常在一處。約瑟將他哥哥們的惡行報給他們的父親。

³以色列原來愛約瑟過於愛他的眾子，因為約瑟是他年老生的；他給約瑟做了一件彩衣。⁴約瑟的哥哥們見父親愛約瑟過於愛他們，就恨約瑟，不與他說和睦的話。

⁵約瑟做了一夢，告訴他哥哥們，他們就越發恨他。⁶約瑟對他們說：「請聽我所做的夢：⁷我們在田裏捆禾稼，我的捆起來站着，你們的捆來圍着我的捆下拜。」

⁸他的哥哥們回答說：「難道你真要作我們的王嗎？難道你真要管轄我們嗎？」他們就因為他的夢和他的話，越發恨他。

⁹後來他又做了一夢，也告訴他的哥哥們說：「看哪，我又做了一夢，夢見太陽、月亮與十一個星向

³⁸When Shaul died, Baal-Hanan son of Acbor succeeded him as king.

³⁹When Baal-Hanan son of Acbor died, Hadad*a* succeeded him as king. His city was named Pau, and his wife's name was Mehetabel daughter of Matred, the daughter of Me-Zahab.

⁴⁰These were the chiefs descended from Esau, by name, according to their clans and regions: Timna, Alvah, Jetheth, ⁴¹Oholibamah, Elah, Pinon, ⁴²Kenaz, Teman, Mibzar, ⁴³Magdiel and Iram. These were the chiefs of Edom, according to their settlements in the land they occupied.

This was Esau the father of the Edomites.

Joseph's Dreams

37 ¹Jacob lived in the land where his father had stayed, the land of Canaan.

²This is the account of Jacob.

Joseph, a young man of seventeen, was tending the flocks with his brothers, the sons of Bilhah and the sons of Zilpah, his father's wives, and he brought their father a bad report about them.

³Now Israel loved Joseph more than any of his other sons, because he had been born to him in his old age; and he made a richly ornamented*b* robe for him. ⁴When his brothers saw that their father loved him more than any of them, they hated him and could not speak a kind word to him.

⁵Joseph had a dream, and when he told it to his brothers, they hated him all the more. ⁶He said to them, "Listen to this dream I had: ⁷We were binding sheaves of grain out in the field when suddenly my sheaf rose and stood upright, while your sheaves gathered around mine and bowed down to it."

⁸His brothers said to him, "Do you intend to reign over us? Will you actually rule us?" And they hated him all the more because of his dream and what he had said.

⁹Then he had another dream, and he told it to his brothers. "Listen," he said, "I had another dream, and this time the sun and moon and

a 39 Many manuscripts of the Masoretic Text, Samaritan Pentateuch and Syriac (see also 1 Chron. 1:50); most manuscripts of the Masoretic Text *Hadar*　*b 3* The meaning of the Hebrew for *richly ornamented* is uncertain; also in verses 23 and 32.

eleven stars were bowing down to me."

10When he told his father as well as his brothers, his father rebuked him and said, "What is this dream you had? Will your mother and I and your brothers actually come and bow down to the ground before you?" 11His brothers were jealous of him, but his father kept the matter in mind.

Joseph Sold by His Brothers

12Now his brothers had gone to graze their father's flocks near Shechem, 13and Israel said to Joseph, "As you know, your brothers are grazing the flocks near Shechem. Come, I am going to send you to them."

"Very well," he replied.

14So he said to him, "Go and see if all is well with your brothers and with the flocks, and bring word back to me." Then he sent him off from the Valley of Hebron.

When Joseph arrived at Shechem, 15a man found him wandering around in the fields and asked him, "What are you looking for?"

16He replied, "I'm looking for my brothers. Can you tell me where they are grazing their flocks?"

17"They have moved on from here," the man answered. "I heard them say, 'Let's go to Dothan.'"

So Joseph went after his brothers and found them near Dothan. 18But they saw him in the distance, and before he reached them, they plotted to kill him.

19"Here comes that dreamer!" they said to each other. 20"Come now, let's kill him and throw him into one of these cisterns and say that a ferocious animal devoured him. Then we'll see what comes of his dreams."

21When Reuben heard this, he tried to rescue him from their hands. "Let's not take his life," he said. 22"Don't shed any blood. Throw him into this cistern here in the desert, but don't lay a hand on him." Reuben said this to rescue him from them and take him back to his father.

23So when Joseph came to his brothers, they stripped him of his robe—the richly ornamented robe he was wearing— 24and they took him and threw him into the cistern. Now the cistern was empty; there was no water in it.

25As they sat down to eat their meal, they looked up and saw a caravan of Ishmaelites coming from Gilead. Their camels were loaded with spices, balm and myrrh, and they were on their way to take them down to Egypt.

26Judah said to his brothers, "What will we gain if we kill our brother and cover up his

---

我下拜。"

10約瑟將這夢告訴他父親和他哥哥們，他父親就責備他說："你做的這是甚麼夢！難道我和你母親、你弟兄果然要來俯伏在地，向你下拜嗎？"11他哥哥們都嫉妒他，他父親卻把這話存在心裏。

約瑟被兄長所賣

12約瑟的哥哥們往示劍去，放他們父親的羊。13以色列對約瑟說："你哥哥們不是在示劍放羊嗎？你來，我要打發你往他們那裏去。"

約瑟說："我在這裏。"

14以色列說："你去看看你哥哥們平安不平安，羣羊平安不平安，就回來報信給我。"於是打發他出希伯崙谷。

他就往示劍去了。15有人遇見他在田野走迷了路，就問他說："你找甚麼？"

16他說："我找我的哥哥們，求你告訴我他們在何處放羊。"

17那人說："他們已經走了，我聽見他們說要往多坍去。"

約瑟就去追趕他哥哥們，遇見他們在多坍。18他們遠遠地看見他，趁他還沒有走到跟前，大家就同謀要害死他。

19彼此說："你看！那做夢的來了。20來吧！我們將他殺了，丟在一個坑裏，就說有惡獸把他吃了，我們且看他的夢將來怎麼樣。"

21呂便聽見了，要救他脫離他們的手，說："我們不可害他的性命。"22又說："不可流他的血，可以把他丟在這野地的坑裏，不可下手害他。"呂便的意思是要救他脫離他們的手，把他歸還他的父親。

23約瑟到了他哥哥們那裏，他們就剝了他的外衣，就是他穿的那件彩衣，24把他丟在坑裏；那坑是空的，裏頭沒有水。

25他們坐下吃飯，舉目觀看，見有一夥米甸的以實瑪利人從基列來，用駱駝馱着香料、乳香、沒藥，要帶下埃及去。

26猶大對眾弟兄說："我們殺我們的兄弟，藏了他的血，有甚麼益處呢？²⁷我們不如將他賣給<u>以實瑪利</u>人，不可下手害他，因為他是我們的兄弟，我們的骨肉。"眾弟兄就聽從了他。

²⁸有些<u>米甸</u>的商人從那裏經過，哥哥們就把<u>約瑟</u>從坑裏拉上來，講定二十舍客勒銀子，把<u>約瑟</u>賣給<u>以實瑪利人</u>。他們就把<u>約瑟</u>帶到<u>埃及</u>去了。

²⁹<u>呂便</u>回到坑邊，見<u>約瑟</u>不在坑裏，就撕裂衣服，³⁰回到兄弟們那裏說："童子沒有了！我往哪裏去才好呢？"

³¹他們宰了一隻公山羊，把<u>約瑟</u>的那件彩衣染了血，³²打發人送到他們的父親那裏，說："我們撿了這個，請認一認，是你兒子的外衣不是？"

³³他認得，就說："這是我兒子的外衣，有惡獸把他吃了，<u>約瑟</u>被撕碎了！撕碎了！"

³⁴<u>雅各</u>便撕裂衣服，腰間圍上麻布，為他兒子悲哀了多日。³⁵他的兒女都起來安慰他，他卻不肯受安慰，說："我必悲哀着下陰間到我兒子那裏。"<u>約瑟</u>的父親就為他哀哭。

³⁶<u>米甸</u>人帶<u>約瑟</u>到<u>埃及</u>，把他賣給法老的內臣，護衛長<u>波提乏</u>。

猶大與她瑪

38 那時，<u>猶大</u>離開他弟兄下去，到一個<u>亞杜蘭</u>人名叫<u>希拉</u>的家裏去。²<u>猶大</u>在那裏看見一個<u>迦南</u>人名叫<u>書亞</u>的女兒，就娶她為妻，與她同房，³她就懷孕生了兒子，<u>猶大</u>給他起名叫<u>珥</u>。⁴她又懷孕生了兒子，母親給他起名叫<u>俄南</u>。⁵她復又生了兒子，給他起名叫<u>示拉</u>。她生<u>示拉</u>的時候，<u>猶大</u>正在<u>基悉</u>。

⁶<u>猶大</u>為長子<u>珥</u>娶妻，名叫<u>她瑪</u>。⁷<u>猶大</u>的長子<u>珥</u>在耶和華眼中看為惡，耶和華就叫他死了。

⁸<u>猶大</u>對<u>俄南</u>說："你當與你哥哥的妻子同房，向她盡你為弟的本分，為你哥哥生子立後。"⁹<u>俄南</u>知道生子不歸自己，所以同房的時

blood? ²⁷Come, let's sell him to the Ishmaelites and not lay our hands on him; after all, he is our brother, our own flesh and blood." His brothers agreed.

²⁸So when the Midianite merchants came by, his brothers pulled Joseph up out of the cistern and sold him for twenty shekels*ᵍ* of silver to the Ishmaelites, who took him to Egypt.

²⁹When Reuben returned to the cistern and saw that Joseph was not there, he tore his clothes. ³⁰He went back to his brothers and said, "The boy isn't there! Where can I turn now?"

³¹Then they got Joseph's robe, slaughtered a goat and dipped the robe in the blood. ³²They took the ornamented robe back to their father and said, "We found this. Examine it to see whether it is your son's robe."

³³He recognized it and said, "It is my son's robe! Some ferocious animal has devoured him. Joseph has surely been torn to pieces."

³⁴Then Jacob tore his clothes, put on sackcloth and mourned for his son many days. ³⁵All his sons and daughters came to comfort him, but he refused to be comforted. "No," he said, "in mourning will I go down to the grave*ᵇ* to my son." So his father wept for him.

³⁶Meanwhile, the Midianites*ᶜ* sold Joseph in Egypt to Potiphar, one of Pharaoh's officials, the captain of the guard.

Judah and Tamar

38 At that time, Judah left his brothers and went down to stay with a man of Adullam named Hirah. ²There Judah met the daughter of a Canaanite man named Shua. He married her and lay with her; ³she became pregnant and gave birth to a son, who was named Er. ⁴She conceived again and gave birth to a son and named him Onan. ⁵She gave birth to still another son and named him Shelah. It was at Kezib that she gave birth to him.

⁶Judah got a wife for Er, his firstborn, and her name was Tamar. ⁷But Er, Judah's firstborn, was wicked in the LORD's sight; so the LORD put him to death.

⁸Then Judah said to Onan, "Lie with your brother's wife and fulfill your duty to her as a brother-in-law to produce offspring for your brother." ⁹But Onan knew that the offspring would not be his; so whenever he lay with his brother's wife, he spilled his semen on the

a 28 That is, about 8 ounces (about 0.2 kilogram)

b 35 Hebrew Sheol   c 36 Samaritan Pentateuch, Septuagint, Vulgate and Syriac (see also verse 28); Masoretic Text Medanites

ground to keep from producing offspring for his brother. ¹⁰What he did was wicked in the LORD's sight; so he put him to death also.

¹¹Judah then said to his daughter-in-law Tamar, "Live as a widow in your father's house until my son Shelah grows up." For he thought, "He may die too, just like his brothers." So Tamar went to live in her father's house.

¹²After a long time Judah's wife, the daughter of Shua, died. When Judah had recovered from his grief, he went up to Timnah, to the men who were shearing his sheep, and his friend Hirah the Adullamite went with him.

¹³When Tamar was told, "Your father-in-law is on his way to Timnah to shear his sheep," ¹⁴she took off her widow's clothes, covered herself with a veil to disguise herself, and then sat down at the entrance to Enaim, which is on the road to Timnah. For she saw that, though Shelah had now grown up, she had not been given to him as his wife.

¹⁵When Judah saw her, he thought she was a prostitute, for she had covered her face. ¹⁶Not realizing that she was his daughter-in-law, he went over to her by the roadside and said, "Come now, let me sleep with you."

"And what will you give me to sleep with you?" she asked.

¹⁷"I'll send you a young goat from my flock," he said.

"Will you give me something as a pledge until you send it?" she asked.

¹⁸He said, "What pledge should I give you?"

"Your seal and its cord, and the staff in your hand," she answered. So he gave them to her and slept with her, and she became pregnant by him. ¹⁹After she left, she took off her veil and put on her widow's clothes again.

²⁰Meanwhile Judah sent the young goat by his friend the Adullamite in order to get his pledge back from the woman, but he did not find her. ²¹He asked the men who lived there, "Where is the shrine prostitute who was beside the road at Enaim?"

"There hasn't been any shrine prostitute here," they said.

²²So he went back to Judah and said, "I didn't find her. Besides, the men who lived there said, 'There hasn't been any shrine prostitute here.' "

²³Then Judah said, "Let her keep what she has, or we will become a laughingstock. After all, I did send her this young goat, but you didn't find her."

²⁴About three months later Judah was told, "Your daughter-in-law Tamar is guilty of prostitution, and as a result she is now pregnant."

候，便遺在地，免得給他哥哥留後。¹⁰猶南所做的在耶和華眼中看為惡，耶和華也就叫他死了。

¹¹猶大心裏說：“恐怕示拉也死，像他兩個哥哥一樣”，就對他兒婦她瑪說：“你去，在你父親家裏守寡，等我兒子示拉長大。”她瑪就回去住在她父親家裏。

¹²過了許久，猶大的妻子書亞的女兒死了。猶大得了安慰，就和他朋友亞杜蘭人希拉上亭拿去，到他剪羊毛的人那裏。

¹³有人告訴她瑪說：“你的公公上亭拿剪羊毛去了。”¹⁴她瑪見示拉已經長大，還沒有娶她為妻，就脫了她作寡婦的衣裳，用帕子蒙着臉，又遮住身體，坐在亭拿路上的伊拿印城門口。

¹⁵猶大看見她，以為是妓女，因為她蒙着臉。¹⁶猶大就轉到她那裏去，說：“來吧！讓我與你同寢。”他原不知道是他的兒婦。

她瑪說：“你要與我同寢，把甚麼給我呢？”

¹⁷猶大說：“我從羊羣裏取一隻山羊羔，打發人送來給你。”

她瑪說：“在未送以先，你願意給我一個當頭嗎？”

¹⁸他說：“我給你甚麼當頭呢？”

她瑪說：“你的印，你的帶子和你手裏的杖。”猶大就給了她，與她同寢，她就從猶大懷了孕。她瑪起來走了，除去帕子，仍舊穿上作寡婦的衣裳。

²⁰猶大託他朋友亞杜蘭人送一隻山羊羔去，要從那女人手裏取回當頭來，卻找不着她，²¹就問那地方的人說：“伊拿印路旁的妓女在哪裏？”

他們說：“這裏並沒有妓女。”

²²他回去見猶大說：“我沒有找着她，並且那地方的人說：‘這裏沒有妓女。’”

²³猶大說：“我把這山羊羔送去了，你竟找不着她，任憑她拿去吧，免得我們被羞辱。”

²⁴約過了三個月，有人告訴猶大說：“你的兒婦她瑪作了妓女，且因行淫有了身孕。”

猶大說：「拉出她來，把她燒了！」

²⁵她瑪被拉出來的時候，便打發人去見她公公，對他說：「這些東西是誰的，我就是從誰懷的孕。請你認一認，這印和帶子並杖都是誰的？」

²⁶猶大承認說：「她比我更有義，因為我沒有將她給我的兒子示拉。」從此猶大不再與她同寢了。

²⁷她瑪將要生產，不料她腹裏是一對雙生。²⁸到生產的時候，一個孩子伸出一隻手來，收生婆拿紅線拴在他手上，說：「這是頭生的。」²⁹隨後這孩子把手收回去，他哥哥生出來了。收生婆說：「你為甚麼搶着來呢？」因此給他起名叫法勒斯。³⁰後來，他兄弟那手上有紅線的也生出來，就給他起名叫謝拉。

約瑟與波提乏之妻

39 約瑟被帶下埃及去。有一個埃及人，是法老的內臣，護衛長波提乏，從那些帶下他來的以實瑪利人手下買了他去。

²約瑟住在他主人埃及人的家中，耶和華與他同在，他就百事順利。³他主人見耶和華與他同在，又見耶和華使他手裏所辦的盡都順利，⁴約瑟就在主人眼前蒙恩，伺候他主人，並且主人派他管理家務，把一切所有的都交在他手裏。⁵自從主人派約瑟管理家務和他一切所有的，耶和華就因約瑟的緣故賜福與那埃及人的家；凡家裏和田間一切所有的都蒙耶和華賜福。⁶波提乏將一切所有的都交在約瑟的手中，除了自己所吃的飯，別的事一概不知。

約瑟原來秀雅俊美。⁷這事以後，約瑟主人的妻，以目送情給約瑟，說：「你與我同寢吧！」

⁸約瑟不從，對他主人的妻說：「看哪，一切家務，我主人都不知道，他把所有的都交在我手裏。⁹在這家裏沒有比我大的，並且他沒有

Judah said, "Bring her out and have her burned to death!"

²⁵As she was being brought out, she sent a message to her father-in-law. "I am pregnant by the man who owns these," she said. And she added, "See if you recognize whose seal and cord and staff these are."

²⁶Judah recognized them and said, "She is more righteous than I, since I wouldn't give her to my son Shelah." And he did not sleep with her again.

²⁷When the time came for her to give birth, there were twin boys in her womb. ²⁸As she was giving birth, one of them put out his hand; so the midwife took a scarlet thread and tied it on his wrist and said, "This one came out first." ²⁹But when he drew back his hand, his brother came out, and she said, "So this is how you have broken out!" And he was named Perez.ᵃ ³⁰Then his brother, who had the scarlet thread on his wrist, came out and he was given the name Zerah.ᵇ

Joseph and Potiphar's Wife

39 Now Joseph had been taken down to Egypt. Potiphar, an Egyptian who was one of Pharaoh's officials, the captain of the guard, bought him from the Ishmaelites who had taken him there.

²The LORD was with Joseph and he prospered, and he lived in the house of his Egyptian master. ³When his master saw that the LORD was with him and that the LORD gave him success in everything he did, ⁴Joseph found favor in his eyes and became his attendant. Potiphar put him in charge of his household, and he entrusted to his care everything he owned. ⁵From the time he put him in charge of his household and of all that he owned, the LORD blessed the household of the Egyptian because of Joseph. The blessing of the LORD was on everything Potiphar had, both in the house and in the field. ⁶So he left in Joseph's care everything he had; with Joseph in charge, he did not concern himself with anything except the food he ate.

Now Joseph was well-built and handsome, ⁷and after a while his master's wife took notice of Joseph and said, "Come to bed with me!"

⁸But he refused. "With me in charge," he told her, "my master does not concern himself with anything in the house; everything he owns he has entrusted to my care. ⁹No one is greater in this house than I am. My master has withheld

a 29 Perez means breaking out.   b 30 Zerah can mean scarlet or brightness.

nothing from me except you, because you are his wife. How then could I do such a wicked thing and sin against God?" ¹⁰And though she spoke to Joseph day after day, he refused to go to bed with her or even be with her.

¹¹One day he went into the house to attend to his duties, and none of the household servants was inside. ¹²She caught him by his cloak and said, "Come to bed with me!" But he left his cloak in her hand and ran out of the house.

¹³When she saw that he had left his cloak in her hand and had run out of the house, ¹⁴she called her household servants. "Look," she said to them, "this Hebrew has been brought to us to make sport of us! He came in here to sleep with me, but I screamed. ¹⁵When he heard me scream for help, he left his cloak beside me and ran out of the house."

¹⁶She kept his cloak beside her until his master came home. ¹⁷Then she told him this story: "That Hebrew slave you brought us came to me to make sport of me. ¹⁸But as soon as I screamed for help, he left his cloak beside me and ran out of the house."

¹⁹When his master heard the story his wife told him, saying, "This is how your slave treated me," he burned with anger. ²⁰Joseph's master took him and put him in prison, the place where the king's prisoners were confined.

But while Joseph was there in the prison, ²¹the LORD was with him; he showed him kindness and granted him favor in the eyes of the prison warden. ²²So the warden put Joseph in charge of all those held in the prison, and he was made responsible for all that was done there. ²³The warden paid no attention to anything under Joseph's care, because the LORD was with Joseph and gave him success in whatever he did.

The Cupbearer and the Baker

40 Some time later, the cupbearer and the baker of the king of Egypt offended their master, the king of Egypt. ²Pharaoh was angry with his two officials, the chief cupbearer and the chief baker, ³and put them in custody in the house of the captain of the guard, in the same prison where Joseph was confined. ⁴The captain of the guard assigned them to Joseph, and he attended them.

After they had been in custody for some time, ⁵each of the two men—the cupbearer and the baker of the king of Egypt, who were being held in prison—had a dream the same night, and each dream had a meaning of its own.

⁶When Joseph came to them the next morning, he saw that they were dejected. ⁷So he

留下一樣不交給我,只留下了你,因為你是他的妻子。我怎能作這大惡,得罪神呢?" ¹⁰後來她天天和約瑟說,約瑟卻不聽從她,不與她同寢,也不和她在一處。

¹¹有一天,約瑟進屋裏去辦事,家中人沒有一個在那屋裏,¹²婦人就拉住他的衣裳,說:"你與我同寢吧!"約瑟把衣裳丟在婦人手裏,跑到外邊去了。

¹³婦人看見約瑟把衣裳丟在她手裏跑出去了,¹⁴就叫了家裏的人來,對他們說:"你們看!他帶了一個希伯來人進入我們家裏,要戲弄我們。他到我這裏來,要與我同寢,我就大聲喊叫。¹⁵他聽見我放聲喊起來,就把衣裳丟在我這裏,跑到外邊去了。"

¹⁶婦人把約瑟的衣裳放在自己那裏,等着他主人回家,¹⁷就對他如此如此說:"你所帶到我們這裏的那希伯來僕人進來要戲弄我,¹⁸我放聲喊起來,他就把衣裳丟在我這裏跑出去了。"

¹⁹約瑟的主人聽見他妻子對他所說的話,說"你的僕人如此如此待我",他就生氣,²⁰把約瑟下在監裏,就是王的囚犯被囚的地方。

於是約瑟在那裏坐監。²¹但耶和華與約瑟同在,向他施恩,使他在司獄的眼前蒙恩。²²司獄就把監裏所有的囚犯都交在約瑟的手下,他們在那裏所辦的事都是經他的手。²³凡在約瑟手下的事,司獄一概不察,因為耶和華與約瑟同在,耶和華使他所做的盡都順利。

酒政與膳長

40 這事以後,埃及王的酒政和膳長得罪了他們的主埃及王,²法老就惱怒酒政和膳長這二臣,³把他們下在護衛長府內的監裏,就是約瑟被囚的地方。⁴護衛長把他們交給約瑟,約瑟便伺候他們。

他們有些日子在監裏。⁵被囚在監之埃及王的酒政和膳長,二人同夜各做一夢,各夢都有講解。

⁶到了早晨,約瑟進到他們那裏,見他們有愁悶的樣子。⁷他便問

法老的二臣，就是與他同因在他主人府裏的，說：「你們今日為甚麼面帶愁容呢？」

8他們對他說：「我們各人做了一夢，沒有人能解。」

約瑟說：「解夢不是出於神嗎？請你們將夢告訴我。」

酒政便將他的夢告訴約瑟說：「我夢見在我面前有一棵葡萄樹，10樹上有三根枝子，好像發了芽、開了花，上頭的葡萄都成熟了。11法老的杯在我手中，我就拿葡萄擠在法老的杯裏，將杯遞在他手中。」

12約瑟對他說：「你所做的夢是這樣解：三根枝子就是三天。13三天之內，法老必提你出監，叫你官復原職，你仍要遞杯在法老的手中，和先前作他的酒政一樣。14但你得好處的時候，求你記念我，施恩與我，在法老面前提說我，救我出這監牢。15我實在是從希伯來人之地被拐來的，我在這裏也沒有做過甚麼，叫他們把我下在監裏。」

16膳長見夢解得好，就對約瑟說：「我在夢中見我頭上頂着三筐白餅，17極上的筐子裏有為法老烤的各樣食物，有飛鳥來吃我頭上筐裏的食物。」

18約瑟說：「你的夢是這樣解：三個筐子就是三天。19三天之內，法老必斷斷你的頭，把你掛在木頭上，必有飛鳥來吃你身上的肉。」

20到了第三天，是法老的生日，他為眾臣僕設擺筵席，把酒政和膳長提出監來，21使酒政官復原職，他仍舊遞杯在法老手中；22把膳長掛起來，正如約瑟向他們所解的話。

23酒政卻不記念約瑟，竟忘了他。

法老的夢

41 過了兩年，法老做夢：夢見自己站在河邊，2有七隻母牛從河裏上來，又美好又肥

asked Pharaoh's officials who were in custody with him in his master's house, "Why are your faces so sad today?"

8"We both had dreams," they answered, "but there is no one to interpret them."

Then Joseph said to them, "Do not interpretations belong to God? Tell me your dreams."

9So the chief cupbearer told Joseph his dream. He said to him, "In my dream I saw a vine in front of me, 10and on the vine were three branches. As soon as it budded, it blossomed, and its clusters ripened into grapes. 11Pharaoh's cup was in my hand, and I took the grapes, squeezed them into Pharaoh's cup and put the cup in his hand."

12"This is what it means," Joseph said to him. "The three branches are three days. 13Within three days Pharaoh will lift up your head and restore you to your position, and you will put Pharaoh's cup in his hand, just as you used to do when you were his cupbearer. 14But when all goes well with you, remember me and show me kindness; mention me to Pharaoh and get me out of this prison. 15For I was forcibly carried off from the land of the Hebrews, and even here I have done nothing to deserve being put in a dungeon."

16When the chief baker saw that Joseph had given a favorable interpretation, he said to Joseph, "I too had a dream: On my head were three baskets of bread.*a* 17In the top basket were all kinds of baked goods for Pharaoh, but the birds were eating them out of the basket on my head."

18"This is what it means," Joseph said. "The three baskets are three days. 19Within three days Pharaoh will lift off your head and hang you on a tree.*b* And the birds will eat away your flesh."

20Now the third day was Pharaoh's birthday, and he gave a feast for all his officials. He lifted up the heads of the chief cupbearer and the chief baker in the presence of his officials: 21He restored the chief cupbearer to his position, so that he once again put the cup into Pharaoh's hand, 22but he hanged*c* the chief baker, just as Joseph had said to them in his interpretation.

23The chief cupbearer, however, did not remember Joseph; he forgot him.

Pharaoh's Dreams

41 When two full years had passed, Pharaoh had a dream: He was standing by the Nile, 2when out of the river there

---

a 16 Or three wicker baskets   b 19 Or and impale you on a pole
c 22 Or impaled

came up seven cows, sleek and fat, and they grazed among the reeds. ³After them, seven other cows, ugly and gaunt, came up out of the Nile and stood beside those on the riverbank. ⁴And the cows that were ugly and gaunt ate up the seven sleek, fat cows. Then Pharaoh woke up.

⁵He fell asleep again and had a second dream: Seven heads of grain, healthy and good, were growing on a single stalk. ⁶After them, seven other heads of grain sprouted—thin and scorched by the east wind. ⁷The thin heads of grain swallowed up the seven healthy, full heads. Then Pharaoh woke up; it had been a dream.

⁸In the morning his mind was troubled, so he sent for all the magicians and wise men of Egypt. Pharaoh told them his dreams, but no one could interpret them for him.

⁹Then the chief cupbearer said to Pharaoh, "Today I am reminded of my shortcomings. ¹⁰Pharaoh was once angry with his servants, and he imprisoned me and the chief baker in the house of the captain of the guard. ¹¹Each of us had a dream the same night, and each dream had a meaning of its own. ¹²Now a young Hebrew was there with us, a servant of the captain of the guard. We told him our dreams, and he interpreted them for us, giving each man the interpretation of his dream. ¹³And things turned out exactly as he interpreted them to us: I was restored to my position, and the other man was hanged.ᵃ"

¹⁴So Pharaoh sent for Joseph, and he was quickly brought from the dungeon. When he had shaved and changed his clothes, he came before Pharaoh.

¹⁵Pharaoh said to Joseph, "I had a dream, and no one can interpret it. But I have heard it said of you that when you hear a dream you can interpret it."

¹⁶"I cannot do it," Joseph replied to Pharaoh, "but God will give Pharaoh the answer he desires."

¹⁷Then Pharaoh said to Joseph, "In my dream I was standing on the bank of the Nile, ¹⁸when out of the river there came up seven cows, fat and sleek, and they grazed among the reeds. ¹⁹After them, seven other cows came up— scrawny and very ugly and lean. I had never seen such ugly cows in all the land of Egypt. ²⁰The lean, ugly cows ate up the seven fat cows that came up first. ²¹But even after they ate them, no one could tell that they had done so;

壯,在蘆荻中吃草。³隨後又有七隻母牛從河裏上來,又醜陋又乾瘦,與那七隻母牛一同站在河邊。⁴這又醜陋又乾瘦的七隻母牛吃盡了那又美好又肥壯的七隻母牛。法老就醒了。

⁵他又睡着,第二回做夢:夢見一棵麥子長了七個穗子,又肥大又佳美,⁶隨後又長了七個穗子,又細弱又被東風吹焦了。⁷這細弱的穗子吞了那七個又肥大又飽滿的穗子。法老醒了,不料是個夢。

⁸到了早晨,法老心裏不安,就差人召了埃及所有的術士和博士來;法老就把所做的夢告訴他們,卻沒有人能給法老圓解。

⁹那時酒政對法老説:"我今日想起我的罪來。¹⁰從前法老惱怒臣僕,把我和膳長下在護衛長府內的監裏。¹¹我們二人同夜各做一夢,各夢都有講解。¹²在那裏同着我們有一個希伯來的少年人,是護衛長的僕人,我們告訴他,他就把我們的夢圓解,是按着各人的夢圓解的。¹³後來正如他給我們圓解的成就了:我官復原職;膳長被掛起來了。"

¹⁴法老遂即差人去召約瑟,他們便急忙帶他出監,他就剃頭、刮臉、換衣裳,進到法老面前。

¹⁵法老對約瑟説:"我做了一夢,沒有人能解,我聽見人説,你聽了夢就能解。"

¹⁶約瑟回答法老説:"這不在乎我,神必將平安的話回答法老。"

¹⁷法老對約瑟説:"我夢見我站在河邊,¹⁸有七隻母牛從河裏上來,又肥壯又美好,在蘆荻中吃草。¹⁹隨後又有七隻母牛上來,又軟弱又醜陋又乾瘦,在埃及遍地,我沒有見過這樣不好的。²⁰這又乾瘦又醜陋的母牛吃盡了那以先的七隻肥母牛,²¹吃了以後卻看不出是吃了,那醜陋的樣子

仍舊和先前一樣。我就醒了。

²²「我又夢見一棵麥子，長了七個穗子，又飽滿又佳美，²³隨後又長了七個穗子，枯槁細弱，被東風吹焦了。²⁴這些細弱的穗子吞了那七個佳美的穗子。我將這夢告訴了術士，卻沒有人能給我解說。」

²⁵約瑟對法老說：「法老的夢乃是一個，神已將所要做的事指示法老了。²⁶七隻好母牛是七年；七個好穗子也是七年。這夢乃是一個。²⁷那隨後上來的七隻又乾瘦又醜陋的母牛是七年；那七個虛空、被東風吹焦的穗子也是七年，都是七個荒年。

²⁸「這就是我對法老所說，神已將所要做的事顯明給法老了。²⁹埃及遍地必來七個大豐年；³⁰隨後又要來七個荒年，甚至在埃及地都忘了先前的豐收，全地必被饑荒所滅。³¹因那以後的饑荒甚大，便不覺得先前的豐收了。³²至於法老兩回做夢，是因神命定這事，而且必速速成就。

³³「所以法老當揀選一個有聰明有智慧的人，派他治理埃及地。³⁴法老當這樣行，又派官員管理這地。當七個豐年的時候，征收埃及地的五分之一，³⁵叫他們把將來豐年一切的糧食聚斂起來，積蓄五穀，收存在各城裏作食物，歸於法老的手下。³⁶所積蓄的糧食可以防備埃及地將來的七個荒年，免得這地被饑荒所滅。」

³⁷法老和他一切臣僕，都以這事為妙。³⁸法老對臣僕說：「像這樣的人，有神的靈在他裏頭，我們豈能找得着呢？」

³⁹法老對約瑟說：「神既將這事都指示你，可見沒有人像你這樣有聰明有智慧。⁴⁰你可以掌管我的家，我的民都必聽從你的話，惟獨在寶座上我比你大。」

they looked just as ugly as before. Then I woke up.

²²"In my dreams I also saw seven heads of grain, full and good, growing on a single stalk. ²³After them, seven other heads sprouted—withered and thin and scorched by the east wind. ²⁴The thin heads of grain swallowed up the seven good heads. I told this to the magicians, but none could explain it to me."

²⁵Then Joseph said to Pharaoh, "The dreams of Pharaoh are one and the same. God has revealed to Pharaoh what he is about to do. ²⁶The seven good cows are seven years, and the seven good heads of grain are seven years; it is one and the same dream. ²⁷The seven lean, ugly cows that came up afterward are seven years, and so are the seven worthless heads of grain scorched by the east wind: They are seven years of famine.

²⁸"It is just as I said to Pharaoh: God has shown Pharaoh what he is about to do. ²⁹Seven years of great abundance are coming throughout the land of Egypt, ³⁰but seven years of famine will follow them. Then all the abundance in Egypt will be forgotten, and the famine will ravage the land. ³¹The abundance in the land will not be remembered, because the famine that follows it will be so severe. ³²The reason the dream was given to Pharaoh in two forms is that the matter has been firmly decided by God, and God will do it soon.

³³"And now let Pharaoh look for a discerning and wise man and put him in charge of the land of Egypt. ³⁴Let Pharaoh appoint commissioners over the land to take a fifth of the harvest of Egypt during the seven years of abundance. ³⁵They should collect all the food of these good years that are coming and store up the grain under the authority of Pharaoh, to be kept in the cities for food. ³⁶This food should be held in reserve for the country, to be used during the seven years of famine that will come upon Egypt, so that the country may not be ruined by the famine."

³⁷The plan seemed good to Pharaoh and to all his officials. ³⁸So Pharaoh asked them, "Can we find anyone like this man, one in whom is the spirit of God^a ?"

³⁹Then Pharaoh said to Joseph, "Since God has made all this known to you, there is no one so discerning and wise as you. ⁴⁰You shall be in charge of my palace, and all my people are to submit to your orders. Only with respect to the throne will I be greater than you."

a 38 Or of the gods

Joseph in Charge of Egypt

⁴¹So Pharaoh said to Joseph, "I hereby put you in charge of the whole land of Egypt." ⁴²Then Pharaoh took his signet ring from his finger and put it on Joseph's finger. He dressed him in robes of fine linen and put a gold chain around his neck. ⁴³He had him ride in a chariot as his second-in-command,ᵃ and men shouted before him, "Make wayᵇ !" Thus he put him in charge of the whole land of Egypt.

⁴⁴Then Pharaoh said to Joseph, "I am Pharaoh, but without your word no one will lift hand or foot in all Egypt." ⁴⁵Pharaoh gave Joseph the name Zaphenath-Paneah and gave him Asenath daughter of Potiphera, priest of On,ᶜ to be his wife. And Joseph went throughout the land of Egypt.

⁴⁶Joseph was thirty years old when he entered the service of Pharaoh king of Egypt. And Joseph went out from Pharaoh's presence and traveled throughout Egypt. ⁴⁷During the seven years of abundance the land produced plentifully. ⁴⁸Joseph collected all the food produced in those seven years of abundance in Egypt and stored it in the cities. In each city he put the food grown in the fields surrounding it. ⁴⁹Joseph stored up huge quantities of grain, like the sand of the sea; it was so much that he stopped keeping records because it was beyond measure.

⁵⁰Before the years of famine came, two sons were born to Joseph by Asenath daughter of Potiphera, priest of On. ⁵¹Joseph named his firstborn Manassehᵈ and said, "It is because God has made me forget all my trouble and all my father's household." ⁵²The second son he named Ephraimᵉ and said, "It is because God has made me fruitful in the land of my suffering."

⁵³The seven years of abundance in Egypt came to an end, ⁵⁴and the seven years of famine began, just as Joseph had said. There was famine in all the other lands, but in the whole land of Egypt there was food. ⁵⁵When all Egypt began to feel the famine, the people cried to Pharaoh for food. Then Pharaoh told all the Egyptians, "Go to Joseph and do what he tells you."

⁵⁶When the famine had spread over the whole country, Joseph opened the storehouses and sold grain to the Egyptians, for the famine

---

約瑟治理埃及

⁴¹法老又對<u>約瑟</u>說："我派你治理<u>埃及</u>全地。"⁴²法老就摘下手上打印的戒指，戴在<u>約瑟</u>的手上，給他穿上細麻衣，把金鏈戴在他的頸項上。⁴³又叫<u>約瑟</u>坐他的副車，喝道的在前呼叫說："跪下！"這樣，法老派他治理<u>埃及</u>全地。

⁴⁴法老對<u>約瑟</u>說："我是法老，在<u>埃及</u>全地，若沒有你的命令，不許人擅自辦事（註：原文作"動手動腳"）。"⁴⁵法老賜名給<u>約瑟</u>，叫<u>撒發那忒巴內亞</u>，又將<u>安城</u>的祭司<u>波提非拉</u>的女兒<u>亞西納</u>給他為妻。<u>約瑟</u>就出去巡行<u>埃及</u>地。

⁴⁶<u>約瑟</u>見<u>埃及</u>王法老的時候年三十歲。他從法老面前出去遍行<u>埃及</u>全地。⁴⁷七個豐年之內，地的出產極豐極盛（註：原文作"一把一把的"），⁴⁸<u>約瑟</u>聚斂<u>埃及</u>地七個豐年一切的糧食，把糧食積存在各城裏；各城周圍田地的糧食都積存在本城裏。⁴⁹<u>約瑟</u>積蓄五穀甚多，如同海邊的沙，無法計算，因為穀不可勝數。

⁵⁰荒年未到以前，<u>安城</u>的祭司<u>波提非拉</u>的女兒<u>亞西納</u>給<u>約瑟</u>生了兩個兒子。⁵¹<u>約瑟</u>給長子起名叫<u>瑪拿西</u>（註：就是"使之忘了"的意思），因為他說："神使我忘了一切的困苦和我父的全家。"⁵²他給次子起名叫<u>以法蓮</u>（註：就是"使之昌盛"的意思），因為他說："神使我在受苦的地方昌盛。"

⁵³<u>埃及</u>地的七個豐年一完，⁵⁴七個荒年就來了，正如<u>約瑟</u>所說的，各地都有饑荒；惟獨<u>埃及</u>全地有糧食。⁵⁵及至<u>埃及</u>全地有了饑荒，眾民向法老哀求糧食，法老對他們說："你們往<u>約瑟</u>那裏去，凡他所說的你們都要做。"

⁵⁶當時饑荒遍滿天下，<u>約瑟</u>開了各處的倉，糶糧給<u>埃及</u>人；在<u>埃及</u>地

ᵃ 43 Or *in the chariot of his second-in-command;* or *in his second chariot*　ᵇ 43 Or *Bow down*　ᶜ 45 That is, Heliopolis; also in verse 50　ᵈ 51 *Manasseh* sounds like and may be derived from the Hebrew for *forget.*　ᵉ 52 *Ephraim* sounds like the Hebrew for *twice fruitful.*

饑荒甚大。⁵⁷各地的人都往埃及去，到約瑟那裏糴糧，因為天下的饑荒甚大。

約瑟的哥哥下埃及

42 雅各見埃及有糧，就對兒子們說：「你們為甚麼彼此觀望呢？²我聽見埃及有糧，你們可以下去，從那裏為我們糴些來，使我們可以存活，不至於死。」

³於是，約瑟的十個哥哥都下埃及糴糧去了。⁴但約瑟的兄弟便雅憫，雅各沒有打發他和哥哥們同去，因為雅各說：「恐怕他遭害。」⁵來糴糧的人中有以色列的兒子們，因為迦南地也有饑荒。

⁶當時治理埃及地的是約瑟，糴糧給那地眾民的就是他。約瑟的哥哥們來了，臉伏於地，向他下拜。⁷約瑟看見他哥哥們，就認得他們，卻裝作生人，向他們說些嚴厲話，問他們說：「你們從哪裏來？」

他們說：「我們從迦南地來糴糧。」

⁸約瑟認得他哥哥們，他們卻不認得他。⁹約瑟想起從前所做的那兩個夢，就對他們說：「你們是奸細，來窺探這地的虛實。」

¹⁰他們對他說：「我主啊，不是的，僕人們是糴糧來的。¹¹我們都是一個人的兒子，是誠實人；僕人們並不是奸細。」

¹²約瑟說：「不然，你們必是窺探這地的虛實來的。」

¹³他們說：「僕人們本是弟兄十二人，是迦南地一個人的兒子，頂小的現今在我們的父親那裏，有一個沒有了。」

¹⁴約瑟說：「我才說你們是奸細，這話實在不錯。¹⁵我指着法老的性命起誓，若是你們的小兄弟不到這裏來，你們就不得出這地方，從此就可以把你們證驗出來了。¹⁶須要打發你們中間一個人去，把你們的兄弟帶來。至於你們，都要囚在這裏，好證驗你們的話真不真，若不真，我指着法老的性命起誓，你們一定是奸細。」¹⁷於是約瑟把他們都下在監裏三天。

¹⁸到第三天，約瑟對他們說：「我是敬畏神的，你們照我的話行

was severe throughout Egypt. ⁵⁷And all the countries came to Egypt to buy grain from Joseph, because the famine was severe in all the world.

Joseph's Brothers Go to Egypt

42 When Jacob learned that there was grain in Egypt, he said to his sons, "Why do you just keep looking at each other?" ²He continued, "I have heard that there is grain in Egypt. Go down there and buy some for us, so that we may live and not die."

³Then ten of Joseph's brothers went down to buy grain from Egypt. ⁴But Jacob did not send Benjamin, Joseph's brother, with the others, because he was afraid that harm might come to him. ⁵So Israel's sons were among those who went to buy grain, for the famine was in the land of Canaan also.

⁶Now Joseph was the governor of the land, the one who sold grain to all its people. So when Joseph's brothers arrived, they bowed down to him with their faces to the ground. ⁷As soon as Joseph saw his brothers, he recognized them, but he pretended to be a stranger and spoke harshly to them. "Where do you come from?" he asked.

"From the land of Canaan," they replied, "to buy food."

⁸Although Joseph recognized his brothers, they did not recognize him. ⁹Then he remembered his dreams about them and said to them, "You are spies! You have come to see where our land is unprotected."

¹⁰"No, my lord," they answered. "Your servants have come to buy food. ¹¹We are all the sons of one man. Your servants are honest men, not spies."

¹²"No!" he said to them. "You have come to see where our land is unprotected."

¹³But they replied, "Your servants were twelve brothers, the sons of one man, who lives in the land of Canaan. The youngest is now with our father, and one is no more."

¹⁴Joseph said to them, "It is just as I told you: You are spies! ¹⁵And this is how you will be tested: As surely as Pharaoh lives, you will not leave this place unless your youngest brother comes here. ¹⁶Send one of your number to get your brother; the rest of you will be kept in prison, so that your words may be tested to see if you are telling the truth. If you are not, then as surely as Pharaoh lives, you are spies!" ¹⁷And he put them all in custody for three days.

¹⁸On the third day, Joseph said to them, "Do this and you will live, for I fear God: ¹⁹If you are

honest men, let one of your brothers stay here in prison, while the rest of you go and take grain back for your starving households. ²⁰But you must bring your youngest brother to me, so that your words may be verified and that you may not die." This they proceeded to do.

²¹They said to one another, "Surely we are being punished because of our brother. We saw how distressed he was when he pleaded with us for his life, but we would not listen; that's why this distress has come upon us."

²²Reuben replied, "Didn't I tell you not to sin against the boy? But you wouldn't listen! Now we must give an accounting for his blood." ²³They did not realize that Joseph could understand them, since he was using an interpreter.

²⁴He turned away from them and began to weep, but then turned back and spoke to them again. He had Simeon taken from them and bound before their eyes.

²⁵Joseph gave orders to fill their bags with grain, to put each man's silver back in his sack, and to give them provisions for their journey. After this was done for them, ²⁶they loaded their grain on their donkeys and left.

²⁷At the place where they stopped for the night one of them opened his sack to get feed for his donkey, and he saw his silver in the mouth of his sack. ²⁸"My silver has been returned," he said to his brothers. "Here it is in my sack."

Their hearts sank and they turned to each other trembling and said, "What is this that God has done to us?"

²⁹When they came to their father Jacob in the land of Canaan, they told him all that had happened to them. They said, ³⁰"The man who is lord over the land spoke harshly to us and treated us as though we were spying on the land. ³¹But we said to him, 'We are honest men; we are not spies. ³²We were twelve brothers, sons of one father. One is no more, and the youngest is now with our father in Canaan.'

³³"Then the man who is lord over the land said to us, 'This is how I will know whether you are honest men: Leave one of your brothers here with me, and take food for your starving households and go. ³⁴But bring your youngest brother to me so I will know that you are not spies but honest men. Then I will give your brother back to you, and you can trade*a* in the land.' "

³⁵As they were emptying their sacks, there in each man's sack was his pouch of silver! When they and their father saw the money pouches,

就可以存活。¹⁹你們如果是誠實人,可以留下你們中間的一個人囚在監裏,但你們可以帶着糧食回去,救你們家裏的饑荒。²⁰把你們的小兄弟帶到我這裏來,如此,你們的話便有證據,你們也不至於死。"他們就照樣而行。

²¹他們彼此說:"我們在兄弟身上實在有罪。他哀求我們的時候,我們見他心裏的愁苦,卻不肯聽,所以這場苦難臨到我們身上。"

²²呂便說:"我豈不是對你們說過,不可傷害那孩子嗎?只是你們不肯聽,所以流他血的罪向我們追討。"²³他們不知道約瑟聽得出來,因為在他們中間用通事傳話。

²⁴約瑟轉身退去,哭了一場,又回來對他們說話,就從他們中間挑出西緬來,在他們眼前把他捆綁。

²⁵約瑟吩咐人把糧食裝滿他們的器具,把各人的銀子歸還在各人的口袋裏,又給他們路上用的食物。人就照他的話辦了。²⁶他們就把糧食馱在驢上,離開那裏去了。

²⁷到了住宿的地方,他們中間有一個人打開口袋,要拿料餵驢,才看見自己的銀子仍在口袋裏,²⁸就對弟兄們說:"我的銀子歸還了,看哪,仍在我口袋裏!"

他們就提心吊膽,戰戰兢兢地彼此說:"這是神向我們做甚麼呢?"

²⁹他們來到迦南地他們的父親雅各那裏,將所遭遇的事都告訴他,說:³⁰"那地的主對我們說嚴厲的話,把我們當作窺探那地的奸細。³¹我們對他說:'我們是誠實人,並不是奸細。³²我們本是弟兄十二人,都是一個父親的兒子,有一個沒有了,頂小的如今同我們的父親在迦南地。'

³³"那地的主對我們說:'若要我知道你們是誠實人,可以留下你們中間的一個人在我這裏,你們可以帶着糧食回去,救你們家裏的饑荒。³⁴把你們的小兄弟帶到我這裏來,我便知道你們不是奸細,乃是誠實人。這樣,我就把你們的弟兄交給你們,你們也可以在這地做買賣。'"

³⁵後來他們倒口袋,不料,各人的銀包都在口袋裏;他們和父親看見

a 34 Or move about freely

銀包就都害怕。³⁶他們的父親雅各對他們說：「你們使我喪失我的兒子：約瑟沒有了，西緬也沒有了，你們又要將便雅憫帶去；這些事都歸到我身上了。」

³⁷呂便對他父親說：「我若不帶他回來交給你，你可以殺我的兩個兒子。只管把他交在我手裏，我必帶他回來交給你。」

³⁸雅各說：「我的兒子不可與你們一同下去！他哥哥死了，只剩下他，他若在你們所行的路上遭害，那便是你們使我白髮蒼蒼、悲悲慘慘的下陰間去了。」

第二次下埃及

43 那地的饑荒甚大。²他們從埃及帶來的糧食吃盡了，他們的父親就對他們說：「你們再去給我糴些糧來。」

³猶大對他說：「那人諄諄地告誡我們說：『你們的兄弟若不與你們同來，你們就不得見我的面。』⁴你若打發我們的兄弟與我們同去，我們就下去給你糴糧；⁵你若不打發他去，我們就不下去，因為那人對我們說：『你們的兄弟若不與你們同來，你們就不得見我的面。』」

⁶以色列說：「你們為甚麼這樣害我，告訴那人你們還有兄弟呢？」

⁷他們回答說：「那人詳細問到我們和我們的親屬，說：『你們的父親還在嗎？你們還有兄弟嗎？』我們就按着他所問的告訴他，焉能知道他要說『必須把你們的兄弟帶下來』呢？」

⁸猶大又對他父親以色列說：「你打發童子與我同去，我們就起身下去，好叫我們和你，並我們的婦人孩子，都得存活，不至於死。⁹我為他作保，你可以從我手中追討，我若不帶他回來交在你面前，我情願永遠擔罪。¹⁰我們若沒有躭擱，如今第二次都回來了。」

¹¹他們的父親以色列說：「若必須如此，你們就當這樣行：可以將這地土產中最好的乳香、蜂蜜、香料、沒藥、榧子、杏仁，都取一點收在器具裏，帶下去送給那人作禮物。¹²又要手裏加倍地帶銀子，並將

they were frightened. ³⁶Their father Jacob said to them, "You have deprived me of my children. Joseph is no more and Simeon is no more, and now you want to take Benjamin. Everything is against me!"

³⁷Then Reuben said to his father, "You may put both of my sons to death if I do not bring him back to you. Entrust him to my care, and I will bring him back."

³⁸But Jacob said, "My son will not go down there with you; his brother is dead and he is the only one left. If harm comes to him on the journey you are taking, you will bring my gray head down to the grave[a] in sorrow."

The Second Journey to Egypt

43 Now the famine was still severe in the land. ²So when they had eaten all the grain they had brought from Egypt, their father said to them, "Go back and buy us a little more food."

³But Judah said to him, "The man warned us solemnly, 'You will not see my face again unless your brother is with you.' ⁴If you will send our brother along with us, we will go down and buy food for you. ⁵But if you will not send him, we will not go down, because the man said to us, 'You will not see my face again unless your brother is with you.' "

⁶Israel asked, "Why did you bring this trouble on me by telling the man you had another brother?"

⁷They replied, "The man questioned us closely about ourselves and our family. 'Is your father still living?' he asked us. 'Do you have another brother?' We simply answered his questions. How were we to know he would say, 'Bring your brother down here'?"

⁸Then Judah said to Israel his father, "Send the boy along with me and we will go at once, so that we and you and our children may live and not die. ⁹I myself will guarantee his safety; you can hold me personally responsible for him. If I do not bring him back to you and set him here before you, I will bear the blame before you all my life. ¹⁰As it is, if we had not delayed, we could have gone and returned twice."

¹¹Then their father Israel said to them, "If it must be, then do this: Put some of the best products of the land in your bags and take them down to the man as a gift—a little balm and a little honey, some spices and myrrh, some pistachio nuts and almonds. ¹²Take double the amount of silver with you, for you must return

a 38 Hebrew Sheol

the silver that was put back into the mouths of your sacks. Perhaps it was a mistake. [13]Take your brother also and go back to the man at once. [14]And may God Almighty[a] grant you mercy before the man so that he will let your other brother and Benjamin come back with you. As for me, if I am bereaved, I am bereaved."

[15]So the men took the gifts and double the amount of silver, and Benjamin also. They hurried down to Egypt and presented themselves to Joseph. [16]When Joseph saw Benjamin with them, he said to the steward of his house, "Take these men to my house, slaughter an animal and prepare dinner; they are to eat with me at noon."

[17]The man did as Joseph told him and took the men to Joseph's house. [18]Now the men were frightened when they were taken to his house. They thought, "We were brought here because of the silver that was put back into our sacks the first time. He wants to attack us and overpower us and seize us as slaves and take our donkeys."

[19]So they went up to Joseph's steward and spoke to him at the entrance to the house. [20]"Please, sir," they said, "we came down here the first time to buy food. [21]But at the place where we stopped for the night we opened our sacks and each of us found his silver—the exact weight—in the mouth of his sack. So we have brought it back with us. [22]We have also brought additional silver with us to buy food. We don't know who put our silver in our sacks."

[23]"It's all right," he said. "Don't be afraid. Your God, the God of your father, has given you treasure in your sacks; I received your silver." Then he brought Simeon out to them.

[24]The steward took the men into Joseph's house, gave them water to wash their feet and provided fodder for their donkeys. [25]They prepared their gifts for Joseph's arrival at noon, because they had heard that they were to eat there.

[26]When Joseph came home, they presented to him the gifts they had brought into the house, and they bowed down before him to the ground. [27]He asked them how they were, and then he said, "How is your aged father you told me about? Is he still living?"

[28]They replied, "Your servant our father is still alive and well." And they bowed low to pay him honor.

[29]As he looked about and saw his brother Benjamin, his own mother's son, he asked, "Is

a 14 Hebrew El-Shaddai

歸還在你們口袋內的銀子仍帶在手裏；那或者是錯了。[13]也帶着你們的兄弟，起身去見那人。[14]但願全能的神使你們在那人面前蒙憐憫，釋放你們的那弟兄和便雅憫回來。我若喪了兒子，就喪了吧！"

[15]於是他們拿着那禮物，又手裏加倍地帶銀子，並且帶着便雅憫，起身下到埃及，站在約瑟面前。[16]約瑟見便雅憫和他們同來，就對家宰說："將這些人領到屋裏，要宰殺牲畜，預備筵席，因為晌午這些人同我吃飯。"

[17]家宰就遵着約瑟的命去行，領他們進約瑟的屋裏。[18]他們因為被領到約瑟的屋裏，就害怕，說："領我們到這裏來，必是因為頭次歸還在我們口袋裏的銀子，找我們的錯縫，下手害我們，強取我們為奴僕，搶奪我們的驢。"

[19]他們就挨近約瑟的家宰，在屋門口和他說話，[20]說："我主啊，我們頭次下來實在是要糴糧。[21]後來到了住宿的地方，我們打開口袋，不料，各人的銀子分量足數，仍在各人的口袋內，現在我們手裏又帶回來了。[22]另外又帶下銀子來糴糧，不知道先前誰把銀子放在我們的口袋裏。"

[23]家宰說："你們可以放心，不要害怕，是你們的神和你們父親的神賜給你們財寶在你們的口袋裏。你們的銀子我早已收了。"他就把西緬帶出來交給他們。

[24]家宰就領他們進約瑟的屋裏，給他們水洗腳，又給他們草料餵驢。[25]他們就預備那禮物，等候約瑟晌午來，因為他們聽見要在那裏吃飯。

[26]約瑟來到家裏，他們就把手中的禮物拿進屋去給他，又俯伏在地向他下拜。[27]約瑟問他們好，又問："你們的父親，就是你們所說的那老人家平安嗎？他還在嗎？"

[28]他們回答說："你僕人我們的父親平安，他還在。"於是他們低頭下拜。

[29]約瑟舉目看見他同母的兄弟便雅憫，就說："你們向我所說那頂小

的兄弟就是這位嗎？"又説："小
兒啊，願神賜恩給你！"³⁰約瑟愛弟
之情發動，就急忙尋找可哭之地，
進入自己的屋裏，哭了一場。

³¹他洗了臉出來，勉強隱忍，吩
咐人擺飯。

³²他們就為約瑟單擺了一席，為
那些人又擺了一席，也為和約瑟同
吃飯的埃及人另擺了一席，因為埃
及人不可和希伯來人一同吃飯；那
原是埃及人所厭惡的。³³約瑟使眾弟
兄在他面前排列坐席，都按着長幼
的次序，眾弟兄就彼此詫異。³⁴約瑟
把他面前的食物分出來，送給他
們，但便雅憫所得的比別人多五
倍。他們就飲酒，和約瑟一同宴
樂。

米袋裏的銀杯

44 約瑟吩咐家宰説："把糧食
裝滿這些人的口袋，儘着他
們的驢所能馱的，又把各人
的銀子放在各人的口袋裏，²並將我
的銀杯和那少年人糴糧的銀子，一
同裝在他的口袋裏。"家宰就照約
瑟所説的話行了。

³天一亮就打發那些人帶着驢走
了。⁴他們出城走了不遠，約瑟對家
宰説："起來！追那些人去，追上
了就對他們説：'你們為甚麼以惡
報善呢？⁵這不是我主人飲酒的杯
嗎？豈不是他占卜用的嗎？你們這
樣行是作惡了。'"

⁶家宰追上他們，將這些話對他
們説了。⁷他們回答説："我主為甚
麼説這樣的話呢？你僕人斷不能做
這樣的事。⁸你看，我們從前在口袋
裏所見的銀子，尚且從迦南地帶來
還你，我們怎能從你主人家裏偷竊
金銀呢？⁹你僕人中，無論在誰那裏
搜出來，就叫他死，我們也作我主
的奴僕。"

¹⁰家宰説："現在就照你們的話
行吧！在誰那裏搜出來，誰就作我
的奴僕，其餘的都沒有罪。"

¹¹於是他們各人急忙把口袋卸在
地下，各人打開口袋。¹²家宰就搜
查，從年長的起，到年幼的為止，
那杯竟在便雅憫的口袋裏搜出來。
¹³他們就撕裂衣服，各人把馱子抬在

this your youngest brother, the one you told me
about?" And he said, "God be gracious to you,
my son." ³⁰Deeply moved at the sight of his
brother, Joseph hurried out and looked for a
place to weep. He went into his private room
and wept there.

³¹After he had washed his face, he came out
and, controlling himself, said, "Serve the food."

³²They served him by himself, the brothers by
themselves, and the Egyptians who ate with him
by themselves, because Egyptians could not eat
with Hebrews, for that is detestable to
Egyptians. ³³The men had been seated before
him in the order of their ages, from the firstborn
to the youngest; and they looked at each other
in astonishment. ³⁴When portions were served
to them from Joseph's table, Benjamin's portion
was five times as much as anyone else's. So they
feasted and drank freely with him.

A Silver Cup in a Sack

44 Now Joseph gave these instructions to
the steward of his house: "Fill the men's
sacks with as much food as they can
carry, and put each man's silver in the mouth of
his sack. ²Then put my cup, the silver one, in the
mouth of the youngest one's sack, along with
the silver for his grain." And he did as Joseph
said.

³As morning dawned, the men were sent on
their way with their donkeys. ⁴They had not
gone far from the city when Joseph said to his
steward, "Go after those men at once, and when
you catch up with them, say to them, 'Why have
you repaid good with evil? ⁵Isn't this the cup
my master drinks from and also uses for divination? This is a wicked thing you have done.'"

⁶When he caught up with them, he repeated
these words to them. ⁷But they said to him,
"Why does my lord say such things? Far be it
from your servants to do anything like that! ⁸We
even brought back to you from the land of
Canaan the silver we found inside the mouths of
our sacks. So why would we steal silver or gold
from your master's house? ⁹If any of your servants is found to have it, he will die; and the rest
of us will become my lord's slaves."

¹⁰"Very well, then," he said, "let it be as you
say. Whoever is found to have it will become
my slave; the rest of you will be free from
blame."

¹¹Each of them quickly lowered his sack to
the ground and opened it. ¹²Then the steward
proceeded to search, beginning with the oldest
and ending with the youngest. And the cup was
found in Benjamin's sack. ¹³At this, they tore

their clothes. Then they all loaded their donkeys and returned to the city.

¹⁴Joseph was still in the house when Judah and his brothers came in, and they threw themselves to the ground before him. ¹⁵Joseph said to them, "What is this you have done? Don't you know that a man like me can find things out by divination?"

¹⁶"What can we say to my lord?" Judah replied. "What can we say? How can we prove our innocence? God has uncovered your servants' guilt. We are now my lord's slaves—we ourselves and the one who was found to have the cup."

¹⁷But Joseph said, "Far be it from me to do such a thing! Only the man who was found to have the cup will become my slave. The rest of you, go back to your father in peace."

¹⁸Then Judah went up to him and said: "Please, my lord, let your servant speak a word to my lord. Do not be angry with your servant, though you are equal to Pharaoh himself. ¹⁹My lord asked his servants, 'Do you have a father or a brother?' ²⁰And we answered, 'We have an aged father, and there is a young son born to him in his old age. His brother is dead, and he is the only one of his mother's sons left, and his father loves him.'

²¹"Then you said to your servants, 'Bring him down to me so I can see him for myself.' ²²And we said to my lord, 'The boy cannot leave his father; if he leaves him, his father will die.' ²³But you told your servants, 'Unless your youngest brother comes down with you, you will not see my face again.' ²⁴When we went back to your servant my father, we told him what my lord had said.

²⁵"Then our father said, 'Go back and buy a little more food.' ²⁶But we said, 'We cannot go down. Only if our youngest brother is with us will we go. We cannot see the man's face unless our youngest brother is with us.'

²⁷"Your servant my father said to us, 'You know that my wife bore me two sons. ²⁸One of them went away from me, and I said, "He has surely been torn to pieces." And I have not seen him since. ²⁹If you take this one from me too and harm comes to him, you will bring my gray head down to the grave*ᵃ* in misery.'

³⁰"So now, if the boy is not with us when I go back to your servant my father and if my father, whose life is closely bound up with the boy's life, ³¹sees that the boy isn't there, he will die. Your servants will bring the gray head of our

¹⁴猶大和他弟兄們來到約瑟的屋中，約瑟還在那裏，他們就在他面前俯伏於地。¹⁵約瑟對他們說：「你們做的是甚麼事呢？你們豈不知像我這樣的人必能占卜嗎？」

¹⁶猶大說：「我們對我主說甚麼呢？還有甚麼話可說呢？我們怎能自己表白出來呢？神已經查出僕人的罪孽了，我們與那在他手中搜出杯來的都是我主的奴僕。」

¹⁷約瑟說：「我斷不能這樣行，在誰的手中搜出杯來，誰就作我的奴僕；至於你們，可以平平安安地上你們父親那裏去。」

¹⁸猶大挨近他，說：「我主啊，求你容僕人說一句話給我主聽，不要向僕人發烈怒，因為你如同法老一樣。¹⁹我主曾問僕人們說：『你們有父親、有兄弟沒有？』²⁰我們對我主說：『我們有父親，已經年老，還有他老年所生的一個小孩子。他哥哥死了，他母親只撇下他一人，他父親疼愛他。』

²¹「你對僕人說：『把他帶到我這裏來，叫我親眼看看他。』²²我們對我主說：『童子不能離開他父親，若是離開，他父親必死。』²³你對僕人說：『你們的小兄弟若不與你們一同下來，你們就不得再見我的面。』²⁴我們上到你僕人我們父親那裏，就把我主的話告訴了他。

²⁵「我們的父親說：『你們再去給我糴些糧來。』²⁶我們就說：『我們不能下去，我們的小兄弟若和我們同往，我們就可以下去，因為我小兄弟若不與我們同往，我們必不得見那人的面。』

²⁷「你僕人我父親對我們說：『你們知道我的妻子給我生了兩個兒子，²⁸一個離開我出去了。我說：他必是被撕碎了，直到如今我也沒有見他。²⁹現在你們又要把這個帶去離開我，倘若他遭害，那便是你們使我白髮蒼蒼、悲悲慘慘的下陰間去了。』

³⁰「我父親的命與這童子的命相連。如今我回到你僕人我父親那裏，若沒有童子與我們同在，³¹我們的父親見沒有童子，他就必死。這便是我們使你僕人我們的父親，白髮蒼蒼、

---

a 29 Hebrew Sheol; also in verse 31

悲悲慘慘的下陰間去了。³²因為僕人曾向我父親為這童子作保，說：'我若不帶他回來交給父親，我便在父親面前永遠擔罪。'

³³"現在求你容僕人住下，替這童子作我主的奴僕，叫童子和他哥哥們一同上去。³⁴若童子不和我同去，我怎能上去見我父親呢？恐怕我看見災禍臨到我父親身上。"

約瑟與弟兄相認

45 約瑟在左右站着的人面前情不自禁，吩咐一聲說："人都要離開我出去！"約瑟和弟兄們相認的時候，並沒有一人站在他面前。²他就放聲大哭，埃及人和法老家中的人都聽見了。

³約瑟對他弟兄們說："我是約瑟，我的父親還在嗎？"他弟兄不能回答，因為在他面前都驚惶。

⁴約瑟又對他弟兄們說："請你們近前來。"他們就近前來，他說："我是你們的兄弟約瑟，就是你們所賣到埃及的。⁵現在，不要因為把我賣到這裏自憂自恨，這是神差我在你們以先來，為要保全生命。⁶現在這地的饑荒已經二年了，還有五年不能耕種，不能收成。⁷神差我在你們以先來，為要給你們存留餘種在世上，又要大施拯救，保全你們的生命。

⁸"這樣看來，差我到這裏來的不是你們，乃是神。他又使我如法老的父，作他全家的主，並埃及全地的宰相。⁹你們要趕緊上到我父親那裏，對他說：'你兒子約瑟這樣說：神使我作全埃及的主，請你下到我這裏來，不要躭延。¹⁰你和你的兒子、孫子、連牛羣羊羣，並一切所有的，都可以住在歌珊地，與我相近，¹¹我要在那裏奉養你；因為還有五年的饑荒，免得你和你的眷屬，並一切所有的，都敗落了。'

¹²"況且你們的眼和我兄弟便雅憫的眼，都看見是我親口對你們說話。¹³你們也要將我在埃及一切的榮耀和你們所看見的事，都告訴我父

father down to the grave in sorrow. ³²Your servant guaranteed the boy's safety to my father. I said, 'If I do not bring him back to you, I will bear the blame before you, my father, all my life!'

³³"Now then, please let your servant remain here as my lord's slave in place of the boy, and let the boy return with his brothers. ³⁴How can I go back to my father if the boy is not with me? No! Do not let me see the misery that would come upon my father."

Joseph Makes Himself Known

45 Then Joseph could no longer control himself before all his attendants, and he cried out, "Have everyone leave my presence!" So there was no one with Joseph when he made himself known to his brothers. ²And he wept so loudly that the Egyptians heard him, and Pharaoh's household heard about it.

³Joseph said to his brothers, "I am Joseph! Is my father still living?" But his brothers were not able to answer him, because they were terrified at his presence.

⁴Then Joseph said to his brothers, "Come close to me." When they had done so, he said, "I am your brother Joseph, the one you sold into Egypt! ⁵And now, do not be distressed and do not be angry with yourselves for selling me here, because it was to save lives that God sent me ahead of you. ⁶For two years now there has been famine in the land, and for the next five years there will not be plowing and reaping. ⁷But God sent me ahead of you to preserve for you a remnant on earth and to save your lives by a great deliverance.ᵃ

⁸"So then, it was not you who sent me here, but God. He made me father to Pharaoh, lord of his entire household and ruler of all Egypt. ⁹Now hurry back to my father and say to him, 'This is what your son Joseph says: God has made me lord of all Egypt. Come down to me; don't delay. ¹⁰You shall live in the region of Goshen and be near me—you, your children and grandchildren, your flocks and herds, and all you have. ¹¹I will provide for you there, because five years of famine are still to come. Otherwise you and your household and all who belong to you will become destitute.'

¹²"You can see for yourselves, and so can my brother Benjamin, that it is really I who am speaking to you. ¹³Tell my father about all the honor accorded me in Egypt and about every-

---

a 7 Or save you as a great band of survivors

thing you have seen. And bring my father down here quickly."

14Then he threw his arms around his brother Benjamin and wept, and Benjamin embraced him, weeping. 15And he kissed all his brothers and wept over them. Afterward his brothers talked with him.

16When the news reached Pharaoh's palace that Joseph's brothers had come, Pharaoh and all his officials were pleased. 17Pharaoh said to Joseph, "Tell your brothers, 'Do this: Load your animals and return to the land of Canaan, 18and bring your father and your families back to me. I will give you the best of the land of Egypt and you can enjoy the fat of the land.'

19"You are also directed to tell them, 'Do this: Take some carts from Egypt for your children and your wives, and get your father and come. 20Never mind about your belongings, because the best of all Egypt will be yours.' "

21So the sons of Israel did this. Joseph gave them carts, as Pharaoh had commanded, and he also gave them provisions for their journey. 22To each of them he gave new clothing, but to Benjamin he gave three hundred shekels*a* of silver and five sets of clothes. 23And this is what he sent to his father: ten donkeys loaded with the best things of Egypt, and ten female donkeys loaded with grain and bread and other provisions for his journey. 24Then he sent his brothers away, and as they were leaving he said to them, "Don't quarrel on the way!"

25So they went up out of Egypt and came to their father Jacob in the land of Canaan. 26They told him, "Joseph is still alive! In fact, he is ruler of all Egypt." Jacob was stunned; he did not believe them. 27But when they told him everything Joseph had said to them, and when he saw the carts Joseph had sent to carry him back, the spirit of their father Jacob revived. 28And Israel said, "I'm convinced! My son Joseph is still alive. I will go and see him before I die."

Jacob Goes to Egypt

46 So Israel set out with all that was his, and when he reached Beersheba, he offered sacrifices to the God of his father Isaac.

2And God spoke to Israel in a vision at night and said, "Jacob! Jacob!"

"Here I am," he replied.

3"I am God, the God of your father," he said. "Do not be afraid to go down to Egypt, for I will make you into a great nation there. 4I will go

親，又要趕緊地將我父親搬到我這裏來。”

14於是約瑟伏在他兄弟便雅憫的頸項上哭；便雅憫也在他的頸項上哭。15他又與眾弟兄親嘴，抱着他們哭，隨後他弟兄們就和他說話。

16這風聲傳到法老的宮裏，說：“約瑟的弟兄們來了。”法老和他的臣僕都很喜歡。17法老對約瑟說：“你吩咐你的弟兄們說：‘你們要這樣行：把馱子抬在牲口上，起身往迦南地去。18將你們的父親和你們的眷屬都搬到我這裏來，我要把埃及地的美物賜給你們，你們也要吃這地肥美的出產。’

19現在我吩咐你們要這樣行：‘從埃及地帶着車輛去，把你們的孩子和妻子，並你們的父親都搬來。20你們眼中不要愛惜你們的家具，因為埃及全地的美物都是你們的。’”

21以色列的兒子們就如此行。約瑟照着法老的吩咐給他們車輛和路上用的食物，22又給他們各人一套衣服，惟獨給便雅憫三百銀子，五套衣服；23送給他父親公驢十四，馱着埃及的美物；母驢十四，馱着糧食與餅和菜，為他父親路上用。24於是約瑟打發他弟兄們回去，又對他們說：“你們不要在路上相爭。”

25他們從埃及上去，來到迦南地他們的父親雅各那裏，26告訴他說：“約瑟還在，並且作埃及全地的宰相。”雅各心裏冰涼，因為不信他們。27他們便將約瑟對他們說的一切話都告訴了他。他們父親雅各，又看見約瑟打發來接他的車輛，心就甦醒了。28以色列說：“罷了！罷了！我的兒子約瑟還在，趁我未死以先，我要去見他一面。”

雅各全家下埃及

46 以色列帶着一切所有的，起身來到別是巴，就獻祭給他父親以撒的神。

2夜間，神在異象中對以色列說：“雅各！雅各！”

他說：“我在這裏。”

3神說：“我是神，就是你父親的神。你下埃及去不要害怕，因為我必使你在那裏成為大族。4我要和你

同下埃及去，也必定帶你上來，約
瑟必給你送終（註：原文作「將手按在你的
眼睛上」）。」

5雅各就從別是巴起行。以色列
的兒子們使他們的父親雅各和他們
的妻子、兒女，都坐在法老為雅各
送來的車上。6他們又帶着在迦南地
所得的牲畜、貨財來到埃及。雅各
和他的一切子孫都一同來了。7雅各
把他的兒子、孫子、女兒、孫女，
並他的子子孫孫，一同帶到埃及。

8來到埃及的以色列人，名字記
在下面：雅各和他的兒孫：

　　雅各的長子是呂便。
9呂便的兒子是
　　哈諾、法路、希斯倫、迦米。
10西緬的兒子是
　　耶母利、雅憫、阿轄、雅斤、瑣
　　轄，還有迦南女子所生的掃羅。
11利未的兒子是
　　革順、哥轄、米拉利。
12猶大的兒子是
　　珥、俄南、示拉、法勒斯、謝
　　拉，惟有珥與俄南死在迦南
　　地。
　　法勒斯的兒子是希斯倫、哈母勒。
13以薩迦的兒子是
　　陀拉、普瓦、約伯、伸崙。
14西布倫的兒子是
　　西烈、以倫、雅利。
15這是利亞在巴旦亞蘭給雅各所
生的兒子，還有女兒底拿。兒孫共
有三十三人。

16迦得的兒子是
　　洗非芸、哈基、書尼、以斯
　　本、以利、亞羅底、亞列利。
17亞設的兒子是
　　音拿、亦施瓦、亦施韋、比利
　　亞，還有他們的妹子西拉。
　　比利亞的兒子是
　　　　希別、瑪結。
18這是拉班給他女兒利亞的婢女
悉帕從雅各所生的兒孫，共有十六
人。

down to Egypt with you, and I will surely bring
you back again. And Joseph's own hand will
close your eyes."

5Then Jacob left Beersheba, and Israel's sons
took their father Jacob and their children and
their wives in the carts that Pharaoh had sent to
transport him. 6They also took with them their
livestock and the possessions they had acquired
in Canaan, and Jacob and all his offspring went
to Egypt. 7He took with him to Egypt his sons
and grandsons and his daughters and grand-
daughters—all his offspring.

8These are the names of the sons of Israel
(Jacob and his descendants) who went to Egypt:

Reuben the firstborn of Jacob.
9The sons of Reuben:
　　Hanoch, Pallu, Hezron and Carmi.
10The sons of Simeon:
　　Jemuel, Jamin, Ohad, Jakin, Zohar and
　　Shaul the son of a Canaanite woman.
11The sons of Levi:
　　Gershon, Kohath and Merari.
12The sons of Judah:
　　Er, Onan, Shelah, Perez and Zerah (but Er
　　and Onan had died in the land of Canaan).
　　The sons of Perez:
　　　　Hezron and Hamul.
13The sons of Issachar:
　　Tola, Puah,*a* Jashub*b* and Shimron.
14The sons of Zebulun:
　　Sered, Elon and Jahleel.

15These were the sons Leah bore to Jacob in
Paddan Aram,*c* besides his daughter Dinah.
These sons and daughters of his were thirty-
three in all.

16The sons of Gad:
　　Zephon,*d* Haggi, Shuni, Ezbon, Eri, Arodi
　　and Areli.
17The sons of Asher:
　　Imnah, Ishvah, Ishvi and Beriah.
　　Their sister was Serah.
　　The sons of Beriah:
　　　　Heber and Malkiel.
18These were the children born to Jacob by
Zilpah, whom Laban had given to his daughter
Leah—sixteen in all.

a 13 Samaritan Pentateuch and Syriac (see also 1 Chron. 7:1);
Masoretic Text *Puvah*　　*b 13* Samaritan Pentateuch and some
Septuagint manuscripts (see also Num. 26:24 and 1 Chron.
7:1); Masoretic Text *Iob*　　*c 15* That is, Northwest
Mesopotamia　　*d 16* Samaritan Pentateuch and Septuagint
(see also Num. 26:15); Masoretic Text *Ziphion*

[19]The sons of Jacob's wife Rachel:

Joseph and Benjamin. [20]In Egypt, Manasseh and Ephraim were born to Joseph by Asenath daughter of Potiphera, priest of On.[a]

[21]The sons of Benjamin:

Bela, Beker, Ashbel, Gera, Naaman, Ehi, Rosh, Muppim, Huppim and Ard.

[22]These were the sons of Rachel who were born to Jacob—fourteen in all.

[23]The son of Dan:

Hushim.

[24]The sons of Naphtali:

Jahziel, Guni, Jezer and Shillem.

[25]These were the sons born to Jacob by Bilhah, whom Laban had given to his daughter Rachel—seven in all.

[26]All those who went to Egypt with Jacob—those who were his direct descendants, not counting his sons' wives—numbered sixty-six persons. [27]With the two sons[b] who had been born to Joseph in Egypt, the members of Jacob's family, which went to Egypt, were seventy[c] in all.

[28]Now Jacob sent Judah ahead of him to Joseph to get directions to Goshen. When they arrived in the region of Goshen, [29]Joseph had his chariot made ready and went to Goshen to meet his father Israel. As soon as Joseph appeared before him, he threw his arms around his father[d] and wept for a long time.

[30]Israel said to Joseph, "Now I am ready to die, since I have seen for myself that you are still alive."

[31]Then Joseph said to his brothers and to his father's household, "I will go up and speak to Pharaoh and will say to him, 'My brothers and my father's household, who were living in the land of Canaan, have come to me. [32]The men are shepherds; they tend livestock, and they have brought along their flocks and herds and everything they own.' [33]When Pharaoh calls you in and asks, 'What is your occupation?' [34]you should answer, 'Your servants have tended livestock from our boyhood on, just as our fathers did.' Then you will be allowed to settle in the region of Goshen, for all shepherds are detestable to the Egyptians."

---

[19]雅各之妻拉結的兒子是

約瑟和便雅憫。[20]約瑟在埃及地生了瑪拿西和以法蓮，就是安城的祭司波提非拉的女兒亞西納給約瑟生的。

[21]便雅憫的兒子是

比拉、比結、亞實別、基拉、乃縵、以希、羅實、母平、戶平、亞勒。

[22]這是拉結給雅各所生的兒孫，共有十四人。

[23]但的兒子是

戶伸。

[24]拿弗他利的兒子是

雅薛、沽尼、耶色、示冷。

[25]這是拉班給他女兒拉結的婢女辟拉從雅各所生的兒孫，共有七人。

[26]那與雅各同到埃及的，除了他兒婦之外，凡從他所生的，共有六十六人。[27]還有約瑟在埃及所生的兩個兒子。雅各家來到埃及的共有七十人。

[28]雅各打發猶大先去見約瑟，請派人引路往歌珊去；於是他們來到歌珊地。[29]約瑟套車往歌珊去，迎接他父親以色列。及至見了面，就伏在父親的頸項上，哭了許久。

[30]以色列對約瑟說：「我既得見你的面，知道你還在，就是死我也甘心。」

[31]約瑟對他的弟兄和他父的全家說：「我要上去告訴法老，對他說：『我的弟兄和我父的全家，從前在迦南地，現今都到我這裏來了。[32]他們本是牧羊的人，以養牲畜為業，他們把羊羣牛羣和一切所有的都帶來了。』[33]等法老召你們的時候，問你們說：『你們以何事為業？』[34]你們要說：『你的僕人，從幼年直到如今，都以養牲畜為業，連我們的祖宗也都以此為業。』這樣，你們可以住在歌珊地，因為凡牧羊的，都被埃及人所厭惡。」

---

a 20 That is, Heliopolis   b 27 Hebrew; Septuagint the nine children   c 27 Hebrew (see also Exodus 1:5 and footnote); Septuagint (see also Acts 7:14) seventy-five   d 29 Hebrew around him

47

約瑟進去告訴法老說：「我的父親和我的弟兄帶着羊羣牛羣，並一切所有的，從迦南地來了，如今在歌珊地。」²約瑟從他弟兄中挑出五個人來，引他們去見法老。

³法老問約瑟的弟兄說：「你們以何事為業？」

他們對法老說：「你僕人是牧羊的，連我們的祖宗也是牧羊的。」⁴他們又對法老說：「迦南地的饑荒甚大，僕人的羊羣沒有草吃，所以我們來到這裏寄居。現在求你容僕人住在歌珊地。」

⁵法老對約瑟說：「你父親和你弟兄到你這裏來了，⁶埃及地都在你面前，只管叫你父親和你弟兄住在國中最好的地，他們可以住在歌珊地。你若知道他們中間有甚麼能人，就派他們看管我的牲畜。」

⁷約瑟領他父親雅各進到法老面前，雅各就給法老祝福。⁸法老問雅各說：「你平生的年日是多少呢？」

⁹雅各對法老說：「我寄居在世的年日是一百三十歲，我平生的年日又少又苦，不及我列祖在世寄居的年日。」¹⁰雅各又給法老祝福，就從法老面前出去了。

¹¹約瑟遵着法老的命，把埃及國最好的地，就是蘭塞境內的地，給他父親和弟兄居住，作為產業。¹²約瑟用糧食奉養他父親和他弟兄，並他父親全家的眷屬，都是照各家的人口奉養他們。

約瑟與饑荒

¹³饑荒甚大，全地都絕了糧，甚至埃及地和迦南地的人，因那饑荒的緣故都餓昏了。¹⁴約瑟收聚了埃及地和迦南地所有的銀子，就是眾人糴糧的銀子，約瑟就把那銀子帶到法老的宮裏。¹⁵埃及地和迦南地的銀子都花盡了，埃及眾人都來見約瑟，說：「我們的銀子都用盡了，求你給我們糧食，我們為甚麼死在你面前呢？」

47

Joseph went and told Pharaoh, "My father and brothers, with their flocks and herds and everything they own, have come from the land of Canaan and are now in Goshen." ²He chose five of his brothers and presented them before Pharaoh.

³Pharaoh asked the brothers, "What is your occupation?"

"Your servants are shepherds," they replied to Pharaoh, "just as our fathers were." ⁴They also said to him, "We have come to live here awhile, because the famine is severe in Canaan and your servants' flocks have no pasture. So now, please let your servants settle in Goshen."

⁵Pharaoh said to Joseph, "Your father and your brothers have come to you, ⁶and the land of Egypt is before you; settle your father and your brothers in the best part of the land. Let them live in Goshen. And if you know of any among them with special ability, put them in charge of my own livestock."

⁷Then Joseph brought his father Jacob in and presented him before Pharaoh. After Jacob blessed*a* Pharaoh, ⁸Pharaoh asked him, "How old are you?"

⁹And Jacob said to Pharaoh, "The years of my pilgrimage are a hundred and thirty. My years have been few and difficult, and they do not equal the years of the pilgrimage of my fathers." ¹⁰Then Jacob blessed*b* Pharaoh and went out from his presence.

¹¹So Joseph settled his father and his brothers in Egypt and gave them property in the best part of the land, the district of Rameses, as Pharaoh directed. ¹²Joseph also provided his father and his brothers and all his father's household with food, according to the number of their children.

Joseph and the Famine

¹³There was no food, however, in the whole region because the famine was severe; both Egypt and Canaan wasted away because of the famine. ¹⁴Joseph collected all the money that was to be found in Egypt and Canaan in payment for the grain they were buying, and he brought it to Pharaoh's palace. ¹⁵When the money of the people of Egypt and Canaan was gone, all Egypt came to Joseph and said, "Give us food. Why should we die before your eyes? Our money is used up."

a 7 Or greeted   b 10 Or said farewell to

16"Then bring your livestock," said Joseph. "I will sell you food in exchange for your livestock, since your money is gone." 17So they brought their livestock to Joseph, and he gave them food in exchange for their horses, their sheep and goats, their cattle and donkeys. And he brought them through that year with food in exchange for all their livestock.

18When that year was over, they came to him the following year and said, "We cannot hide from our lord the fact that since our money is gone and our livestock belongs to you, there is nothing left for our lord except our bodies and our land. 19Why should we perish before your eyes—we and our land as well? Buy us and our land in exchange for food, and we with our land will be in bondage to Pharaoh. Give us seed so that we may live and not die, and that the land may not become desolate."

20So Joseph bought all the land in Egypt for Pharaoh. The Egyptians, one and all, sold their fields, because the famine was too severe for them. The land became Pharaoh's, 21and Joseph reduced the people to servitude,[a] from one end of Egypt to the other. 22However, he did not buy the land of the priests, because they received a regular allotment from Pharaoh and had food enough from the allotment Pharaoh gave them. That is why they did not sell their land.

23Joseph said to the people, "Now that I have bought you and your land today for Pharaoh, here is seed for you so you can plant the ground. 24But when the crop comes in, give a fifth of it to Pharaoh. The other four-fifths you may keep as seed for the fields and as food for yourselves and your households and your children."

25"You have saved our lives," they said. "May we find favor in the eyes of our lord; we will be in bondage to Pharaoh."

26So Joseph established it as a law concerning land in Egypt—still in force today—that a fifth of the produce belongs to Pharaoh. It was only the land of the priests that did not become Pharaoh's.

27Now the Israelites settled in Egypt in the region of Goshen. They acquired property there and were fruitful and increased greatly in number.

28Jacob lived in Egypt seventeen years, and the years of his life were a hundred and forty-seven. 29When the time drew near for Israel to die, he called for his son Joseph and said to him,

16約瑟説："若是銀子用盡了，可以把你們的牲畜給我，我就為你們的牲畜給你們糧食。"17於是他們把牲畜趕到約瑟那裏，約瑟就拿糧換了他們的牛、羊、驢、馬。那一年因換他們一切的牲畜，就用糧食養活他們。

18那一年過去，第二年他們又來見約瑟，説："我們不瞞我主，我們的銀子都花盡了，牲畜也都歸了我主，我們在我主眼前，除了我們的身體和田地之外，一無所剩。19你何忍見我們人死地荒呢？求你用糧食買我們和我們的地，我們和我們的地就要給法老効力。又求你給我們種子，使我們得以存活，不至死亡，地土也不至荒涼。"

20於是，約瑟為法老買了埃及所有的地，埃及人因被饑荒所迫，各都賣了自己的田地，那地就都歸了法老。21至於百姓，約瑟叫他們從埃及這邊直到埃及那邊，都各歸各城。22惟有祭司的地，約瑟沒有買，因為祭司有從法老所得的常俸。他們吃法老所給的常俸，所以他們不賣自己的地。

23約瑟對百姓説："我今日為法老買了你們和你們的地。看哪，這裏有種子給你們，你們可以種地。24後來打糧食的時候，你們要把五分之一納給法老，四分可以歸你們作地裏的種子，也作你們和你們家口孩童的食物。"

25他們説："你救了我們的性命，但願我們在我主眼前蒙恩，我們就作法老的僕人。"

26於是，約瑟為埃及地定下常例直到今日：法老必得五分之一，惟獨祭司的地不歸法老。

27以色列人住在埃及的歌珊地，他們在那裏置了產業，並且生育甚多。

28雅各住在埃及地十七年，雅各平生的年日是一百四十七歲。29以色列的死期臨近了，他就叫了他兒子約瑟來，説："我若在你眼前蒙恩，請你把手放在我大腿底下，用慈愛和誠實待我，請你不要將我葬在埃及。³⁰我與我祖父同睡的時候，你要將我帶出埃及，葬在他們所葬的地方。"

約瑟説："我必遵着你的命而行。"

³¹雅各説："你要向我起誓。"約瑟就向他起了誓，於是以色列在牀頭上 (註：或作"扶着杖頭") 敬拜神。

瑪拿西與以法蓮

48 這事以後，有人告訴約瑟説："你的父親病了。"他就帶着兩個兒子瑪拿西和以法蓮同去。²有人告訴雅各説："請看，你兒子約瑟到你這裏來了。"以色列就勉強在牀上坐起來。

³雅各對約瑟説："全能的神曾在迦南地的路斯向我顯現，賜福與我，⁴對我説：'我必使你生養眾多，成為多民，又要把這地賜給你的後裔，永遠為業。'

⁵"我未到埃及見你之先，你在埃及地所生的以法蓮和瑪拿西，這兩個兒子是我的，正如呂便和西緬是我的一樣。⁶你在他們以後所生的，就是你的，他們可以歸於他們弟兄的名下得產業。⁷至於我，我從巴旦來的時候，拉結死在我眼前，在迦南地的路上，離以法他還有一段路程，我就把她葬在以法他的路上；以法他就是伯利恆。"

⁸以色列看見約瑟的兩個兒子，就説："這是誰？"

⁹約瑟對他父親説："這是神在這裏賜給我的兒子。"

以色列説："請你領他們到我跟前，我要給他們祝福。"

¹⁰以色列年紀老邁，眼睛昏花，不能看見。約瑟領他們到他跟前，他就和他們親嘴，抱着他們。

¹¹以色列對約瑟説："我想不到得見你的面，不料，神又使我得見你的兒子。"

¹²約瑟把兩個兒子從以色列兩膝中領出來，自己就臉伏於地下拜。

¹³隨後約瑟又拉着他們兩個，以法蓮

"If I have found favor in your eyes, put your hand under my thigh and promise that you will show me kindness and faithfulness. Do not bury me in Egypt, ³⁰but when I rest with my fathers, carry me out of Egypt and bury me where they are buried."

"I will do as you say," he said.

³¹"Swear to me," he said. Then Joseph swore to him, and Israel worshiped as he leaned on the top of his staff.*ᵃ*

Manasseh and Ephraim

48 Some time later Joseph was told, "Your father is ill." So he took his two sons Manasseh and Ephraim along with him. ²When Jacob was told, "Your son Joseph has come to you," Israel rallied his strength and sat up on the bed.

³Jacob said to Joseph, "God Almighty*ᵇ* appeared to me at Luz in the land of Canaan, and there he blessed me ⁴and said to me, 'I am going to make you fruitful and will increase your numbers. I will make you a community of peoples, and I will give this land as an everlasting possession to your descendants after you.'

⁵"Now then, your two sons born to you in Egypt before I came to you here will be reckoned as mine; Ephraim and Manasseh will be mine, just as Reuben and Simeon are mine. ⁶Any children born to you after them will be yours; in the territory they inherit they will be reckoned under the names of their brothers. ⁷As I was returning from Paddan,*ᶜ* to my sorrow Rachel died in the land of Canaan while we were still on the way, a little distance from Ephrath. So I buried her there beside the road to Ephrath" (that is, Bethlehem).

⁸When Israel saw the sons of Joseph, he asked, "Who are these?"

⁹"They are the sons God has given me here," Joseph said to his father.

Then Israel said, "Bring them to me so I may bless them."

¹⁰Now Israel's eyes were failing because of old age, and he could hardly see. So Joseph brought his sons close to him, and his father kissed them and embraced them.

¹¹Israel said to Joseph, "I never expected to see your face again, and now God has allowed me to see your children too."

¹²Then Joseph removed them from Israel's knees and bowed down with his face to the ground. ¹³And Joseph took both of them,

a 31 Or Israel bowed down at the head of his bed　　b 3 Hebrew El-Shaddai　　c 7 That is, Northwest Mesopotamia

Ephraim on his right toward Israel's left hand and Manasseh on his left toward Israel's right hand, and brought them close to him. ¹⁴But Israel reached out his right hand and put it on Ephraim's head, though he was the younger, and crossing his arms, he put his left hand on Manasseh's head, even though Manasseh was the firstborn.

¹⁵Then he blessed Joseph and said,

"May the God before whom my fathers
　　Abraham and Isaac walked,
the God who has been my shepherd
　　all my life to this day,
¹⁶the Angel who has delivered me from all harm
　　—may he bless these boys.
May they be called by my name
　　and the names of my fathers Abraham and
　　　Isaac,
and may they increase greatly
　　upon the earth."

¹⁷When Joseph saw his father placing his right hand on Ephraim's head he was displeased; so he took hold of his father's hand to move it from Ephraim's head to Manasseh's head. ¹⁸Joseph said to him, "No, my father, this one is the first-born; put your right hand on his head."

¹⁹But his father refused and said, "I know, my son, I know. He too will become a people, and he too will become great. Nevertheless, his younger brother will be greater than he, and his descendants will become a group of nations." ²⁰He blessed them that day and said,

"In your*ᵃ* name will Israel pronounce this
　　blessing:
'May God make you like Ephraim and
　　Manasseh.'"

So he put Ephraim ahead of Manasseh.

²¹Then Israel said to Joseph, "I am about to die, but God will be with you*ᵇ* and take you*ᶜ* back to the land of your*ᵈ* fathers. ²²And to you, as one who is over your brothers, I give the ridge of land*ᵉ* I took from the Amorites with my sword and my bow."

在他的右手裏，對着以色列的左手；瑪拿西在他的左手裏，對着以色列的右手，領他們到以色列的跟前。¹⁴以色列伸出右手來，按在以法蓮的頭上，以法蓮乃是次子；又剪搭過左手來按在瑪拿西的頭上，瑪拿西原是長子。

¹⁵他就給約瑟祝福說：

"願我祖亞伯拉罕
　和我父以撒所侍奉的神，
　就是一生牧養我直到今日的神，

¹⁶救贖我脫離一切患難的那使者，
　賜福與這兩個童子。
願他們歸在我的名下
　和我祖亞伯拉罕、
　我父以撒的名下，
又願他們在世界中生養眾多。"

¹⁷約瑟見他父親把右手按在以法蓮的頭上，就不喜悅，便提起他父親的手，要從以法蓮頭上挪到瑪拿西的頭上。¹⁸約瑟對他父親說："我父，不是這樣，這本是長子，求你把右手按在他的頭上。"

¹⁹他父親不從，說："我知道！我兒，我知道！他也必成為一族，也必昌大，只是他的兄弟將來比他還大，他兄弟的後裔要成為多族。" ²⁰當日就給他們祝福說：

"以色列人要指着你們祝福說：
　'願神使你如以法蓮、瑪拿西一
　　樣。'"

於是立以法蓮在瑪拿西以上。

²¹以色列又對約瑟說："我要死了，但神必與你們同在，領你們回到你們列祖之地。²²並且我從前用弓用刀從亞摩利人手下奪的那塊地，我都賜給你，使你比眾弟兄多得一分。"

a 20 The Hebrew is singular.　　b 21 The Hebrew is plural.
c 21 The Hebrew is plural.　　d 21 The Hebrew is plural.
e 22 Or And to you I give one portion more than to your brothers—the portion

雅各祝福他的兒子

49 雅各叫了他的兒子們來，說：
「你們都來聚集，我好把你們
日後必遇的事告訴你們。

2 「雅各的兒子們，你們要聚集而
聽，要聽你們父親以色列的話。

3 「呂便哪，你是我的長子，
是我力量強壯的時候生的，
本當大有尊榮，權力超眾，
4 但你放縱情慾、滾沸如水，
必不得居首位；
因為你上了你父親的牀，
污穢了我的榻。

5 「西緬和利未是弟兄，
他們的刀劍是殘忍的器具。
6 我的靈啊，不要與他們同謀；
我的心哪，不要與他們聯絡；
因為他們趁怒殺害人命，
任意砍斷牛腿大筋。
7 他們的怒氣暴烈可咒，
他們的忿恨殘忍可詛。
我要使他們分居在雅各家裏，
散住在以色列地中。

8 「猶大啊，
你弟兄們必讚美你；
你手必掐住仇敵的頸項；
你父親的兒子們必向你下拜。
9 猶大是個小獅子；
我兒啊，你抓了食便上去。
你屈下身去，臥如公獅，
蹲如母獅，誰敢惹你？
10 圭必不離猶大，
杖必不離他兩腳之間，
直等細羅 (註：就是「賜平安者」)
來到，萬民都必歸順。
11 猶大把小驢拴在葡萄樹上，
把驢駒拴在美好的葡萄樹上。
他在葡萄酒中洗了衣服，
在葡萄汁中洗了袍褂。
12 他的眼睛必因酒紅潤；
他的牙齒必因奶白亮。

13 「西布倫必住在海口，
必成為停船的海口，
他的境界必延到西頓。

Jacob Blesses His Sons

49 Then Jacob called for his sons and said:
"Gather around so I can tell you what
will happen to you in days to come.

2 "Assemble and listen, sons of Jacob;
listen to your father Israel.

3 "Reuben, you are my firstborn,
my might, the first sign of my strength,
excelling in honor, excelling in power.
4 Turbulent as the waters, you will no longer
excel,
for you went up onto your father's bed,
onto my couch and defiled it.

5 "Simeon and Levi are brothers—
their swords[a] are weapons of violence.
6 Let me not enter their council,
let me not join their assembly,
for they have killed men in their anger
and hamstrung oxen as they pleased.
7 Cursed be their anger, so fierce,
and their fury, so cruel!
I will scatter them in Jacob
and disperse them in Israel.

8 "Judah,[b] your brothers will praise you;
your hand will be on the neck of your
enemies;
your father's sons will bow down to you.
9 You are a lion's cub, O Judah;
you return from the prey, my son.
Like a lion he crouches and lies down,
like a lioness—who dares to rouse him?
10 The scepter will not depart from Judah,
nor the ruler's staff from between his feet,
until he comes to whom it belongs[c]
and the obedience of the nations is his.
11 He will tether his donkey to a vine,
his colt to the choicest branch;
he will wash his garments in wine,
his robes in the blood of grapes.
12 His eyes will be darker than wine,
his teeth whiter than milk.[d]

13 "Zebulun will live by the seashore
and become a haven for ships;
his border will extend toward Sidon.

---

a 5 The meaning of the Hebrew for this word is uncertain.
b 8 Judah sounds like and may be derived from the Hebrew for
praise.　*c 10* Or *until Shiloh comes;* or *until he comes to whom
tribute belongs*　*d 12* Or *will be dull from wine, / his teeth white
from milk*

¹⁴"Issachar is a rawboned^a donkey
   lying down between two saddlebags.^b
¹⁵When he sees how good is his resting place
   and how pleasant is his land,
he will bend his shoulder to the burden
   and submit to forced labor.

¹⁶Dan^c will provide justice for his people
   as one of the tribes of Israel.
¹⁷Dan will be a serpent by the roadside,
   a viper along the path,
that bites the horse's heels
   so that its rider tumbles backward.

¹⁸"I look for your deliverance, O LORD.

¹⁹"Gad^d will be attacked by a band of raiders,
   but he will attack them at their heels.

²⁰Asher's food will be rich;
   he will provide delicacies fit for a king.

²¹"Naphtali is a doe set free
   that bears beautiful fawns.^e

²²"Joseph is a fruitful vine,
   a fruitful vine near a spring,
   whose branches climb over a wall.^f
²³With bitterness archers attacked him;
   they shot at him with hostility.
²⁴But his bow remained steady,
   his strong arms stayed^g limber,
because of the hand of the Mighty One of
   Jacob,
because of the Shepherd, the Rock of Israel,
²⁵because of your father's God, who helps you,
   because of the Almighty,^h who blesses you
with blessings of the heavens above,
   blessings of the deep that lies below,
   blessings of the breast and womb.
²⁶Your father's blessings are greater
   than the blessings of the ancient mountains,
thanⁱ the bounty of the age-old hills.
Let all these rest on the head of Joseph,
   on the brow of the prince among^j his
   brothers.

¹⁴"以薩迦是個強壯的驢,
   臥在羊圈之中。
¹⁵他以安靜為佳,
   以肥地為美,
便低肩背重,
   成為服苦的僕人。

¹⁶"但必判斷他的民,
   作以色列支派之一。
¹⁷但必作道上的蛇,
   路中的虺,
   咬傷馬蹄,
   使騎馬的墜落於後。

¹⁸"耶和華啊,
   我向來等候你的救恩。
¹⁹"迦得必被敵軍追逼,
   他卻要追逼他們的腳跟。

²⁰"亞設之地必出肥美的糧食,
   且出君王的美味。

²¹"拿弗他利是被釋放的母鹿,
   他出嘉美的言語。

²²"約瑟是多結果子的樹枝,
   是泉旁多結果的枝子,
   他的枝條探出牆外。
²³弓箭手將他苦害,
   向他射箭,逼迫他,
²⁴但他的弓仍舊堅硬,
   他的手健壯敏捷,
這是因以色列的牧者,
   以色列的磐石,
   就是雅各的大能者。
²⁵你父親的神必幫助你,
   那全能者必將天上所有的福,
地裏所藏的福,
   以及生產乳養的福,
   都賜給你。
²⁶你父親所祝的福,
   勝過我祖先所祝的福,
如永世的山嶺,至極的邊界;
這些福必降在約瑟的頭上,
   臨到那與弟兄迥別之人的頂上。

---

a 14 Or *strong*   *b* 14 Or *campfires*   *c* 16 *Dan* here means *he
provides justice.*   *d* 19 *Gad* can mean *attack* and *band of raiders.*
e 21 Or *free;* / *he utters beautiful words*   *f* 22 Or *Joseph is a wild
colt,* / *a wild colt near a spring,* / *a wild donkey on a terraced hill*
g 23,24 Or *archers will attack . . . will shoot . . . will remain . . . will
stay*   *h* 25 Hebrew *Shaddai*   *i* 26 Or *of my progenitors,* / *as
great as*   *j* 26 Or *the one separated from*

27 <u>便雅憫是個撕掠的狼，
　　早晨要吃他所抓的，
　　晚上要分他所奪的。</u>"

28 這一切是<u>以色列</u>的十二支派；這也是他們的父親對他們所說的話，為他們所祝的福，都是按着各人的福分，為他們祝福。

雅各壽終

29 他又囑咐他們說："我將要歸到我列祖（註：原文作"本民"）那裏，你們要將我葬在<u>赫人以弗崙</u>田間的洞裏，與我祖我父在一處，30 就是在<u>迦南</u>地幔利前、<u>麥比拉</u>田間的洞；那洞和田是<u>亞伯拉罕</u>向<u>赫人以弗崙</u>買來為業，作墳地的。31 他們在那裏葬了<u>亞伯拉罕</u>和他妻子<u>撒拉</u>，又在那裏葬了<u>以撒</u>和他妻子<u>利百加</u>，我也在那裏葬了<u>利亞</u>。32 那塊田和田間的洞，原是向<u>赫人</u>買的。"

33 <u>雅各</u>囑咐眾子已畢，就把腳收在牀上，氣絕而死，歸他列祖（註：原文作"本民"）那裏去了。

50 <u>約瑟</u>伏在他父親的面上哀哭，與他親嘴。2 <u>約瑟</u>吩咐伺候他的醫生，用香料薰他父親，醫生就用香料薰了<u>以色列</u>。3 薰屍的常例是四十天，那四十天滿了，<u>埃及</u>人為他哀哭了七十天。

4 為他哀哭的日子過了，<u>約瑟</u>對法老家中的人說："我若在你們眼前蒙恩，請你們報告法老說：5 '我父親要死的時候叫我起誓說：你要將我葬在<u>迦南</u>地，在我為自己所掘的墳墓裏。' 現在求你讓我上去葬我父親，以後我必回來。"

6 法老說："你可以上去，照着你父親叫你起的誓，將他葬埋。"

7 於是<u>約瑟</u>上去葬他父親。與他一同上去的，有法老的臣僕和法老家中的長老，<u>並埃及國</u>的長老，8 還有<u>約瑟</u>的全家和他的弟兄們，並他父親的眷屬；只有他們的婦人孩子，和羊羣牛羣，都留在<u>歌珊</u>地；9 又有車輛馬兵，和他一同上去；那一幫人甚多。

10 他們到了<u>約旦河</u>外、<u>亞達</u>的禾場，就在那裏大大地號咷痛哭。<u>約</u>

27 "Benjamin is a ravenous wolf;
　in the morning he devours the prey,
　in the evening he divides the plunder."

28 All these are the twelve tribes of Israel, and this is what their father said to them when he blessed them, giving each the blessing appropriate to him.

The Death of Jacob

29 Then he gave them these instructions: "I am about to be gathered to my people. Bury me with my fathers in the cave in the field of Ephron the Hittite, 30 the cave in the field of Machpelah, near Mamre in Canaan, which Abraham bought as a burial place from Ephron the Hittite, along with the field. 31 There Abraham and his wife Sarah were buried, there Isaac and his wife Rebekah were buried, and there I buried Leah. 32 The field and the cave in it were bought from the Hittites.[a]"

33 When Jacob had finished giving instructions to his sons, he drew his feet up into the bed, breathed his last and was gathered to his people.

50 Joseph threw himself upon his father and wept over him and kissed him. 2 Then Joseph directed the physicians in his service to embalm his father Israel. So the physicians embalmed him, 3 taking a full forty days, for that was the time required for embalming. And the Egyptians mourned for him seventy days.

4 When the days of mourning had passed, Joseph said to Pharaoh's court, "If I have found favor in your eyes, speak to Pharaoh for me. Tell him, 5 'My father made me swear an oath and said, "I am about to die; bury me in the tomb I dug for myself in the land of Canaan." Now let me go up and bury my father; then I will return.'"

6 Pharaoh said, "Go up and bury your father, as he made you swear to do."

7 So Joseph went up to bury his father. All Pharaoh's officials accompanied him—the dignitaries of his court and all the dignitaries of Egypt— 8 besides all the members of Joseph's household and his brothers and those belonging to his father's household. Only their children and their flocks and herds were left in Goshen. 9 Chariots and horsemen[b] also went up with him. It was a very large company.

10 When they reached the threshing floor of Atad, near the Jordan, they lamented loudly and

a 32 Or the sons of Heth　　b 9 Or charioteers

bitterly; and there Joseph observed a seven-day period of mourning for his father. [11]When the Canaanites who lived there saw the mourning at the threshing floor of Atad, they said, "The Egyptians are holding a solemn ceremony of mourning." That is why that place near the Jordan is called Abel Mizraim.[a]

[12]So Jacob's sons did as he had commanded them: [13]They carried him to the land of Canaan and buried him in the cave in the field of Machpelah, near Mamre, which Abraham had bought as a burial place from Ephron the Hittite, along with the field. [14]After burying his father, Joseph returned to Egypt, together with his brothers and all the others who had gone with him to bury his father.

Joseph Reassures His Brothers

[15]When Joseph's brothers saw that their father was dead, they said, "What if Joseph holds a grudge against us and pays us back for all the wrongs we did to him?" [16]So they sent word to Joseph, saying, "Your father left these instructions before he died: [17]This is what you are to say to Joseph: I ask you to forgive your brothers the sins and the wrongs they committed in treating you so badly.' Now please forgive the sins of the servants of the God of your father." When their message came to him, Joseph wept.

[18]His brothers then came and threw themselves down before him. "We are your slaves," they said.

[19]But Joseph said to them, "Don't be afraid. Am I in the place of God? [20]You intended to harm me, but God intended it for good to accomplish what is now being done, the saving of many lives. [21]So then, don't be afraid. I will provide for you and your children." And he reassured them and spoke kindly to them.

The Death of Joseph

[22]Joseph stayed in Egypt, along with all his father's family. He lived a hundred and ten years [23]and saw the third generation of Ephraim's children. Also the children of Makir son of Manasseh were placed at birth on Joseph's knees.[b]

[24]Then Joseph said to his brothers, "I am about to die. But God will surely come to your aid and take you up out of this land to the land he promised on oath to Abraham, Isaac and Jacob." [25]And Joseph made the sons of Israel

瑟為他父親哀哭了七天。[11]迦南的居民見亞達禾場上的哀哭，就說：「這是埃及人一場極大的哀哭。」因此那地方名叫亞伯麥西，是在約旦河東。

[12]雅各的兒子們就遵着他父親所吩咐的辦了，[13]把他搬到迦南地，葬在幔利前、麥比拉田間的洞裏。那洞和田是亞伯拉罕向赫人以弗崙買來為業，作墳地的。[14]約瑟葬了他父親以後，就和眾弟兄，並一切同他上去葬他父親的人，都回埃及去了。

約瑟饒恕哥哥

[15]約瑟的哥哥們見父親死了，就說：「或者約瑟懷恨我們，照着我們從前待他一切的惡，足足地報復我們。」[16]他們就打發人去見約瑟，說：「你父親未死以先吩咐說：[17]『你們要對約瑟這樣說：從前你哥哥們惡待你，求你饒恕他們的過犯和罪惡。』如今求你饒恕你父親神之僕人的過犯。」他們對約瑟說這話，約瑟就哭了。

[18]他的哥哥們又來俯伏在他面前，說：「我們是你的僕人。」

[19]約瑟對他們說：「不要害怕，我豈能代替神呢？[20]從前你們的意思是要害我，但神的意思原是好的，要保全許多人的性命，成就今日的光景。[21]現在你們不要害怕，我必養活你們和你們的婦人孩子。」於是約瑟用親愛的話安慰他們。

約瑟去世

[22]約瑟和他父親的眷屬都住在埃及。約瑟活了一百一十歲。[23]約瑟得見以法蓮第三代的子孫；瑪拿西的孫子、瑪吉的兒子也養在約瑟的膝上。

[24]約瑟對他弟兄們說：「我要死了，但神必來看顧你們，領你們從這地上去，到他起誓所應許給亞伯拉罕、以撒、雅各之地。」[25]約瑟叫以

---

a 11 Abel Mizraim means *mourning of the Egyptians.*
b 23 That is, were counted as his

色列的子孫起誓說：“神必定看顧你們，你們要把我的骸骨從這裏搬上去。”

²⁶約瑟死了，正一百一十歲。人用香料將他薰了，把他收殮在棺材裏，停在埃及。

swear an oath and said, "God will surely come to your aid, and then you must carry my bones up from this place."

²⁶So Joseph died at the age of a hundred and ten. And after they embalmed him, he was placed in a coffin in Egypt.

圖二：創世記中的主要地方
MAP 2 : KEY PLACES IN GENESIS

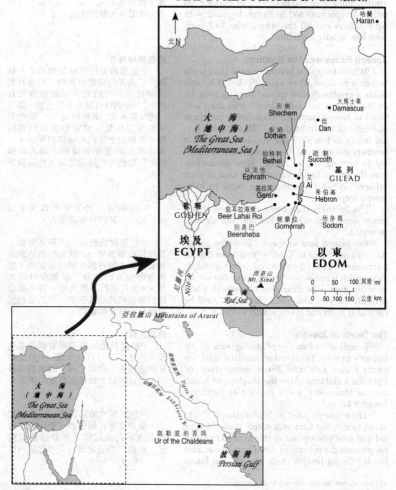

EXODUS

The Israelites Oppressed

1 These are the names of the sons of Israel who went to Egypt with Jacob, each with his family: ²Reuben, Simeon, Levi and Judah; ³Issachar, Zebulun and Benjamin; ⁴Dan and Naphtali; Gad and Asher. ⁵The descendants of Jacob numbered seventy[a] in all; Joseph was already in Egypt.

⁶Now Joseph and all his brothers and all that generation died, ⁷but the Israelites were fruitful and multiplied greatly and became exceedingly numerous, so that the land was filled with them.

⁸Then a new king, who did not know about Joseph, came to power in Egypt. ⁹"Look," he said to his people, "the Israelites have become much too numerous for us. ¹⁰Come, we must deal shrewdly with them or they will become even more numerous and, if war breaks out, will join our enemies, fight against us and leave the country."

¹¹So they put slave masters over them to oppress them with forced labor, and they built Pithom and Rameses as store cities for Pharaoh. ¹²But the more they were oppressed, the more they multiplied and spread; so the Egyptians came to dread the Israelites ¹³and worked them ruthlessly. ¹⁴They made their lives bitter with hard labor in brick and mortar and with all kinds of work in the fields; in all their hard labor the Egyptians used them ruthlessly.

¹⁵The king of Egypt said to the Hebrew midwives, whose names were Shiphrah and Puah, ¹⁶"When you help the Hebrew women in childbirth and observe them on the delivery stool, if it is a boy, kill him; but if it is a girl, let her live." ¹⁷The midwives, however, feared God and did not do what the king of Egypt had told them to do; they let the boys live. ¹⁸Then the king of Egypt summoned the midwives and asked them, "Why have you done this? Why have you let the boys live?"

¹⁹The midwives answered Pharaoh, "Hebrew women are not like Egyptian women; they are vigorous and give birth before the midwives arrive."

---

a 5 Masoretic Text (see also Gen. 46:27); Dead Sea Scrolls and Septuagint (see also Acts 7:14 and note at Gen. 46:27) *seventy-five*

出埃及記

以色列人受欺壓

1 以色列的眾子,各帶家眷和雅各一同來到埃及。他們的名字記在下面:²有呂便、西緬、利未、猶大、³以薩迦、西布倫、便雅憫、⁴但、拿弗他利、迦得、亞設。⁵凡從雅各而生的,共有七十人;約瑟已經在埃及。

⁶約瑟和他的弟兄,並那一代的人都死了。⁷以色列人生養眾多,並且繁茂,極其強盛,滿了那地。

⁸有不認識約瑟的新王起來,治理埃及,⁹對他的百姓說:"看哪,這以色列民比我們還多,又比我們強盛。¹⁰來吧!我們不如用巧計待他們,恐怕他們多起來,日後若遇甚麼爭戰的事,就連合我們的仇敵攻擊我們,離開這地去了。"

¹¹於是埃及人派督工的轄制他們,加重擔苦害他們。他們為法老建造兩座積貨城,就是比東和蘭塞。¹²只是越發苦害他們,他們越發多起來,越發蔓延,埃及人就因以色列人愁煩。¹³埃及人嚴嚴地使以色列人做工,¹⁴使他們因做苦工覺得命苦;無論是和泥,是做磚,是做田間各樣的工,在一切的工上都嚴嚴地待他們。

¹⁵有希伯來的兩個收生婆,一名施弗拉,一名普阿。埃及王對她們說:¹⁶"你們為希伯來婦人收生,看她們臨盆的時候,若是男孩,就把他殺了;若是女孩,就留她存活。"¹⁷但是收生婆敬畏神,不照埃及王的吩咐行,竟存留男孩的性命。¹⁸埃及王召了收生婆來,說:"你們為甚麼做這事,存留男孩的性命呢?"

¹⁹收生婆對法老說:"因為希伯來婦人與埃及婦人不同,希伯來婦人本是健壯的(註:原文作"活潑的"),收生婆還沒有到,她們已經生產了。"

²⁰神厚待收生婆。<u>以色列人多起來</u>，極其強盛。²¹收生婆因為敬畏神，神便叫她們成立家室。

²²法老吩咐他的眾民說：「<u>以色列人所生的男孩，你們都要丟在河裏；一切的女孩，你們要存留她的性命。</u>」

摩西的出生

2 有一個利未家的人，娶了一個<u>利未女子</u>為妻。²那女人懷孕，生一個兒子，見他俊美，就藏了他三個月。³後來不能再藏，就取了一個蒲草箱，抹上石漆和石油，將孩子放在裏頭，把箱子擱在河邊的蘆荻中。⁴孩子的姐姐遠遠站着，要知道他究竟怎麼樣。

⁵法老的女兒來到河邊洗澡，她的使女們在河邊行走。她看見箱子在蘆荻中，就打發一個婢女拿來。⁶她打開箱子，看見那孩子。孩子哭了，她就可憐他，說：「這是<u>希伯來</u>人的一個孩子。」

⁷孩子的姐姐對法老的女兒說：「我去在<u>希伯來</u>婦人中，叫一個奶媽來，為你奶這孩子，可以不可以？」
⁸法老的女兒說：「可以。」童女就去叫了孩子的母親來。⁹法老的女兒對她說：「你把這孩子抱去，為我奶他，我必給你工價。」婦人就抱了孩子去奶他。¹⁰孩子漸長，婦人把他帶到法老的女兒那裏，就作了她的兒子。她給孩子起名叫<u>摩西</u>，意思說：「因我把他從水裏拉出來。」

摩西逃往米甸

¹¹後來<u>摩西</u>長大，他出去到他弟兄那裏，看他們的重擔，見一個<u>埃及</u>人打<u>希伯來</u>人的一個弟兄。¹²他左右觀看，見沒有人，就把<u>埃及</u>人打死了，藏在沙土裏。¹³第二天他出去，見有兩個<u>希伯來</u>人爭鬥，就對那欺負人的說：「你為甚麼打你同族的人呢？」

¹⁴那人說：「誰立你作我們的首領和審判官呢？難道你要殺我，像殺

²⁰So God was kind to the midwives and the people increased and became even more numerous. ²¹And because the midwives feared God, he gave them families of their own.

²²Then Pharaoh gave this order to all his people: "Every boy that is born[a] you must throw into the Nile, but let every girl live."

The Birth of Moses

2 Now a man of the house of Levi married a Levite woman, ²and she became pregnant and gave birth to a son. When she saw that he was a fine child, she hid him for three months. ³But when she could hide him no longer, she got a papyrus basket for him and coated it with tar and pitch. Then she placed the child in it and put it among the reeds along the bank of the Nile. ⁴His sister stood at a distance to see what would happen to him.

⁵Then Pharaoh's daughter went down to the Nile to bathe, and her attendants were walking along the river bank. She saw the basket among the reeds and sent her slave girl to get it. ⁶She opened it and saw the baby. He was crying, and she felt sorry for him. "This is one of the Hebrew babies," she said.

⁷Then his sister asked Pharaoh's daughter, "Shall I go and get one of the Hebrew women to nurse the baby for you?"

⁸"Yes, go," she answered. And the girl went and got the baby's mother. ⁹Pharaoh's daughter said to her, "Take this baby and nurse him for me, and I will pay you." So the woman took the baby and nursed him. ¹⁰When the child grew older, she took him to Pharaoh's daughter and he became her son. She named him Moses,[b] saying, "I drew him out of the water."

Moses Flees to Midian

¹¹One day, after Moses had grown up, he went out to where his own people were and watched them at their hard labor. He saw an Egyptian beating a Hebrew, one of his own people. ¹²Glancing this way and that and seeing no one, he killed the Egyptian and hid him in the sand. ¹³The next day he went out and saw two Hebrews fighting. He asked the one in the wrong, "Why are you hitting your fellow Hebrew?"

¹⁴The man said, "Who made you ruler and judge over us? Are you thinking of killing me as

a 22 Masoretic Text; Samaritan Pentateuch, Septuagint and Targums born to the Hebrews　　b 10 Moses sounds like the Hebrew for draw out.

you killed the Egyptian?" Then Moses was afraid and thought, "What I did must have become known."

15When Pharaoh heard of this, he tried to kill Moses, but Moses fled from Pharaoh and went to live in Midian, where he sat down by a well. 16Now a priest of Midian had seven daughters, and they came to draw water and fill the troughs to water their father's flock. 17Some shepherds came along and drove them away, but Moses got up and came to their rescue and watered their flock.

18When the girls returned to Reuel their father, he asked them, "Why have you returned so early today?"

19They answered, "An Egyptian rescued us from the shepherds. He even drew water for us and watered the flock."

20"And where is he?" he asked his daughters. "Why did you leave him? Invite him to have something to eat."

21Moses agreed to stay with the man, who gave his daughter Zipporah to Moses in marriage. 22Zipporah gave birth to a son, and Moses named him Gershom,a saying, "I have become an alien in a foreign land."

23During that long period, the king of Egypt died. The Israelites groaned in their slavery and cried out, and their cry for help because of their slavery went up to God. 24God heard their groaning and he remembered his covenant with Abraham, with Isaac and with Jacob. 25So God looked on the Israelites and was concerned about them.

Moses and the Burning Bush

3 Now Moses was tending the flock of Jethro his father-in-law, the priest of Midian, and he led the flock to the far side of the desert and came to Horeb, the mountain of God. 2There the angel of the LORD appeared to him in flames of fire from within a bush. Moses saw that though the bush was on fire it did not burn up. 3So Moses thought, "I will go over and see this strange sight—why the bush does not burn up."

4When the LORD saw that he had gone over to look, God called to him from within the bush, "Moses! Moses!"

And Moses said, "Here I am."

5"Do not come any closer," God said. "Take off your sandals, for the place where you are standing is holy ground." 6Then he said, "I am the God of your father, the God of Abraham, the

那埃及人嗎？"摩西便懼怕，說："這事必是被人知道了。"

15法老聽見這事，就想殺摩西，但摩西躲避法老，逃往米甸地居住。16一日，他在井旁坐下，米甸的祭司有七個女兒，她們來打水，打滿了槽，要飲父親的羣羊。17有牧羊的人來把她們趕走了，摩西卻起來幫助她們，又飲了她們的羣羊。

18她們來到父親流珥那裏，他說："今日你們為何來得這麼快呢？"

19她們說："有一個埃及人救我們脫離牧羊人的手，並且為我們打水飲了羣羊。"

20他對女兒們說："那個人在哪裏？你們為甚麼撇下他呢？你們去請他來吃飯。"

21摩西甘心和那人同住；那人把他的女兒西坡拉給摩西為妻。22西坡拉生了一個兒子，摩西給他起名叫革舜，意思說："因我在外邦作了寄居的。"

23過了多年，埃及王死了。以色列人因做苦工，就歎息哀求，他們的哀聲達於神。24神聽見他們的哀聲，就記念他與亞伯拉罕、以撒、雅各所立的約。25神看顧以色列人，也知道他們的苦情。

摩西與燃燒的荊棘

3 摩西牧養他岳父米甸祭司葉忒羅的羊羣。一日，領羊羣往野外去，到了神的山，就是何烈山，2耶和華的使者從荊棘裏火焰中向摩西顯現。摩西觀看，不料，荊棘被火燒着，卻沒有燒燬。3摩西說："我要過去看這大異象，這荊棘為何沒有燒壞呢？"

4耶和華神見他過去要看，就從荊棘裏呼叫說："摩西！摩西！"

他說："我在這裏。"

5神說："不要近前來，當把你腳上的鞋脫下來，因為你所站之地是聖地。"6又說："我是你父親的神，是亞伯拉罕的神，以撒的神，雅

---

a 22 Gershom sounds like the Hebrew for an alien there.

各的神。」摩西蒙上臉，因為怕看神。

7耶和華說：「我的百姓在埃及所受的困苦，我實在看見了；他們因受督工的轄制所發的哀聲，我也聽見了。我原知道他們的痛苦。8我下來是要救他們脫離埃及人的手，領他們出了那地，到美好寬闊流奶與蜜之地，就是迦南人、赫人、亞摩利人、比利洗人、希未人、耶布斯人之地。9現在以色列人的哀聲達到我耳中，我也看見埃及人怎樣欺壓他們。10故此，我要打發你去見法老，使你可以將我的百姓以色列人從埃及領出來。」

11摩西對神說：「我是甚麼人，竟能去見法老，將以色列人從埃及領出來呢？」12神說：「我必與你同在。你將百姓從埃及領出來之後，你們必在這山上侍奉我，這就是我打發你去的證據。」

13摩西對神說：「我到以色列人那裏，對他們說：『你們祖宗的神打發我到你們這裏來。』他們若問我說：『他叫甚麼名字？』我要對他們說甚麼呢？」

14神對摩西說：「我是自有永有的。」又說：「你要對以色列人這樣說：『那自有的打發我到你們這裏來。』」

15神又對摩西說：「你要對以色列人這樣說：『耶和華你們祖宗的神，就是亞伯拉罕的神，以撒的神，雅各的神，打發我到你們這裏來。』耶和華是我的名，直到永遠；這也是我的紀念，直到萬代。

16「你去招聚以色列的長老，對他們說：『耶和華你們祖宗的神，就是亞伯拉罕的神，以撒的神，雅各的神，向我顯現，說：我實在眷顧了你們，我也看見埃及人怎樣待你們。17我也說：要將你們從埃及的困苦中領出來，往迦南人、赫人、亞摩利人、比利洗人、希未人、耶布斯人的地去，就是到流奶與蜜之地。』18「他們必聽你的話。你和以色列的長老要去見埃及王，對他說：『耶和華希伯來人的神遇見了我們，現在求你容我們往曠野去，走三天的

God of Isaac and the God of Jacob." At this, Moses hid his face, because he was afraid to look at God.

7The LORD said, "I have indeed seen the misery of my people in Egypt. I have heard them crying out because of their slave drivers, and I am concerned about their suffering. 8So I have come down to rescue them from the hand of the Egyptians and to bring them up out of that land into a good and spacious land, a land flowing with milk and honey—the home of the Canaanites, Hittites, Amorites, Perizzites, Hivites and Jebusites. 9And now the cry of the Israelites has reached me, and I have seen the way the Egyptians are oppressing them. 10So now, go. I am sending you to Pharaoh to bring my people the Israelites out of Egypt."

11But Moses said to God, "Who am I, that I should go to Pharaoh and bring the Israelites out of Egypt?"

12And God said, "I will be with you. And this will be the sign to you that it is I who have sent you: When you have brought the people out of Egypt, you*a* will worship God on this mountain."

13Moses said to God, "Suppose I go to the Israelites and say to them, 'The God of your fathers has sent me to you,' and they ask me, 'What is his name?' Then what shall I tell them?"

14God said to Moses, "I AM WHO I AM.*b* This is what you are to say to the Israelites: 'I AM has sent me to you.'"

15God also said to Moses, "Say to the Israelites, 'The LORD,*c* the God of your fathers—the God of Abraham, the God of Isaac and the God of Jacob—has sent me to you.' This is my name forever, the name by which I am to be remembered from generation to generation.

16"Go, assemble the elders of Israel and say to them, 'The LORD, the God of your fathers—the God of Abraham, Isaac and Jacob—appeared to me and said: I have watched over you and have seen what has been done to you in Egypt. 17And I have promised to bring you up out of your misery in Egypt into the land of the Canaanites, Hittites, Amorites, Perizzites, Hivites and Jebusites—a land flowing with milk and honey.'

18"The elders of Israel will listen to you. Then you and the elders are to go to the king of Egypt and say to him, 'The LORD, the God of the Hebrews, has met with us. Let us take a three-

---

a 12 The Hebrew is plural.　　*b 14* Or *I WILL BE WHAT I WILL BE*
c 15 The Hebrew for LORD sounds like and may be derived from the Hebrew for *I AM* in verse 14.

day journey into the desert to offer sacrifices to the LORD our God.' ¹⁹But I know that the king of Egypt will not let you go unless a mighty hand compels him. ²⁰So I will stretch out my hand and strike the Egyptians with all the wonders that I will perform among them. After that, he will let you go.

²¹"And I will make the Egyptians favorably disposed toward this people, so that when you leave you will not go empty-handed. ²²Every woman is to ask her neighbor and any woman living in her house for articles of silver and gold and for clothing, which you will put on your sons and daughters. And so you will plunder the Egyptians."

Signs for Moses

4 Moses answered, "What if they do not believe me or listen to me and say, 'The LORD did not appear to you'?"

²Then the LORD said to him, "What is that in your hand?"

"A staff," he replied.

³The LORD said, "Throw it on the ground."

Moses threw it on the ground and it became a snake, and he ran from it. ⁴Then the LORD said to him, "Reach out your hand and take it by the tail." So Moses reached out and took hold of the snake and it turned back into a staff in his hand. ⁵"This," said the LORD, "is so that they may believe that the LORD, the God of their fathers—the God of Abraham, the God of Isaac and the God of Jacob—has appeared to you."

⁶Then the LORD said, "Put your hand inside your cloak." So Moses put his hand into his cloak, and when he took it out, it was leprous,ᵃ like snow.

⁷"Now put it back into your cloak," he said. So Moses put his hand back into his cloak, and when he took it out, it was restored, like the rest of his flesh.

⁸Then the LORD said, "If they do not believe you or pay attention to the first miraculous sign, they may believe the second. ⁹But if they do not believe these two signs or listen to you, take some water from the Nile and pour it on the dry ground. The water you take from the river will become blood on the ground."

¹⁰Moses said to the LORD, "O Lord, I have never been eloquent, neither in the past nor since you have spoken to your servant. I am slow of speech and tongue."

路程,為要祭祀耶和華我們的神。'¹⁹我知道雖用大能的手,埃及王也不容你們去。²⁰我必伸手在埃及中間施行我一切的奇事,攻擊那地,然後他才容你們去。

²¹"我必叫你們在埃及人眼前蒙恩,你們去的時候,就不至於空手而去。²²但各婦女必向她的鄰舍,並居住在她家裏的女人要金器、銀器和衣裳,好給你們的兒女穿戴,這樣你們就把埃及人的財物奪去了。"

給摩西的憑證

4 摩西回答說:"他們必不信我,也不聽我的話,必說:'耶和華並沒有向你顯現!'"

²耶和華對摩西說:"你手裏是甚麼?"

他說:"是杖。"

³耶和華說:"丟在地上。"

他一丟下去,就變作蛇,摩西便跑開。⁴耶和華對摩西說:"伸出手來拿住牠的尾巴,牠必在你手中仍變為杖。⁵如此好叫他們信耶和華他們祖宗的神,就是亞伯拉罕的神,以撒的神,雅各的神,是向你顯現了。"

⁶耶和華又對他說:"把手放在懷裏。"他就把手放在懷裏,及至抽出來,不料,手長了大痲瘋,有雪那樣白。

⁷耶和華說:"再把手放在懷裏。"他就再把手放在懷裏,及至從懷裏抽出來,不料,手已經復原,與周身的肉一樣。

⁸又說:"倘或他們不聽你的話,也不信頭一個神蹟,他們必信第二個神蹟。⁹這兩個神蹟若都不信,也不聽你的話,你就從河裏取些水,倒在旱地上,你從河裏取的水必在旱地上變作血。"

¹⁰摩西對耶和華說:"主啊,我素日不是能言的人,就是從你對僕人說話以後,也是這樣,我本是拙口笨舌的。"

ᵃ 6 The Hebrew word was used for various diseases affecting the skin—not necessarily leprosy.

11耶和華對他說：“誰造人的口呢？誰使人口啞、耳聾、目明、眼瞎呢？豈不是我耶和華嗎？12現在去吧！我必賜你口才，指教你所當說的話。”

13摩西說：“主啊，你願意打發誰，就打發誰去吧！”

14耶和華向摩西發怒說：“不是有你的哥哥利未人亞倫嗎？我知道他是能言的，現在他出來迎接你，他一見你，心裏就歡喜。15你要將當說的話傳給他；我也要賜你和他口才，又要指教你們所當行的事。16他要替你對百姓說話；你要以他當作口，他要以你當作神。17你手裏要拿這杖，好行神蹟。”

摩西回埃及

18於是摩西回到他岳父葉忒羅那裏，對他說：“求你容我回去見我在埃及的弟兄，看他們還在不在。”

葉忒羅對摩西說：“你可以平平安安地去吧！”

19耶和華在米甸對摩西說：“你要回埃及去，因為尋索你命的人都死了。”20摩西就帶着妻子和兩個兒子，叫他們都騎上驢，回埃及地去。摩西手裏拿着神的杖。

21耶和華對摩西說：“你回到埃及的時候要留意，將我所指示你的一切奇事，行在法老面前，但我要使（註：或作“任憑”。下同）他的心剛硬，他必不容百姓去。22你要對法老說：‘耶和華這樣說：以色列是我的兒子，我的長子。23我對你說過，容我的兒子去，好侍奉我，你還是不肯容他去。看哪，我要殺你的長子。’”

24摩西在路上住宿的地方，耶和華遇見他，想要殺他。25西坡拉就拿一塊火石，割下他兒子的陽皮，丟在摩西腳前，說：“你真是我的血郎了。”26這樣耶和華才放了他。西坡拉說：“你因割禮就是血郎了。”

27耶和華對亞倫說：“你往曠野去迎接摩西。”他就去，在神的山遇見摩西，和他親嘴。28摩西將耶和華打發他所說的言語和囑咐他所行的神

11The LORD said to him, "Who gave man his mouth? Who makes him deaf or mute? Who gives him sight or makes him blind? Is it not I, the LORD? 12Now go; I will help you speak and will teach you what to say."

13But Moses said, "O Lord, please send someone else to do it."

14Then the LORD's anger burned against Moses and he said, "What about your brother, Aaron the Levite? I know he can speak well. He is already on his way to meet you, and his heart will be glad when he sees you. 15You shall speak to him and put words in his mouth; I will help both of you speak and will teach you what to do. 16He will speak to the people for you, and it will be as if he were your mouth and as if you were God to him. 17But take this staff in your hand so you can perform miraculous signs with it."

Moses Returns to Egypt

18Then Moses went back to Jethro his father-in-law and said to him, "Let me go back to my own people in Egypt to see if any of them are still alive."

Jethro said, "Go, and I wish you well."

19Now the LORD had said to Moses in Midian, "Go back to Egypt, for all the men who wanted to kill you are dead." 20So Moses took his wife and sons, put them on a donkey and started back to Egypt. And he took the staff of God in his hand.

21The LORD said to Moses, "When you return to Egypt, see that you perform before Pharaoh all the wonders I have given you the power to do. But I will harden his heart so that he will not let the people go. 22Then say to Pharaoh, 'This is what the LORD says: Israel is my firstborn son, 23and I told you, "Let my son go, so he may worship me." But you refused to let him go; so I will kill your firstborn son.'"

24At a lodging place on the way, the LORD met ⌊Moses⌋ᵃ and was about to kill him. 25But Zipporah took a flint knife, cut off her son's foreskin and touched ⌊Moses'⌋ feet with it.ᵇ "Surely you are a bridegroom of blood to me," she said. 26So the LORD let him alone. (At that time she said "bridegroom of blood," referring to circumcision.)

27The LORD said to Aaron, "Go into the desert to meet Moses." So he met Moses at the mountain of God and kissed him. 28Then Moses told Aaron everything the LORD had sent him to say,

a 24 Or ⌊Moses' son⌋; Hebrew him   b 25 Or and drew near ⌊Moses'⌋ feet

and also about all the miraculous signs he had commanded him to perform.

29Moses and Aaron brought together all the elders of the Israelites, 30and Aaron told them everything the LORD had said to Moses. He also performed the signs before the people, 31and they believed. And when they heard that the LORD was concerned about them and had seen their misery, they bowed down and worshiped.

Bricks Without Straw

5 Afterward Moses and Aaron went to Pharaoh and said, "This is what the LORD, the God of Israel, says: 'Let my people go, so that they may hold a festival to me in the desert.'"

2Pharaoh said, "Who is the LORD, that I should obey him and let Israel go? I do not know the LORD and I will not let Israel go."

3Then they said, "The God of the Hebrews has met with us. Now let us take a three-day journey into the desert to offer sacrifices to the LORD our God, or he may strike us with plagues or with the sword."

4But the king of Egypt said, "Moses and Aaron, why are you taking the people away from their labor? Get back to your work!" 5Then Pharaoh said, "Look, the people of the land are now numerous, and you are stopping them from working."

6That same day Pharaoh gave this order to the slave drivers and foremen in charge of the people: 7"You are no longer to supply the people with straw for making bricks; let them go and gather their own straw. 8But require them to make the same number of bricks as before; don't reduce the quota. They are lazy; that is why they are crying out, 'Let us go and sacrifice to our God.' 9Make the work harder for the men so that they keep working and pay no attention to lies."

10Then the slave drivers and the foremen went out and said to the people, "This is what Pharaoh says: 'I will not give you any more straw. 11Go and get your own straw wherever you can find it, but your work will not be reduced at all.'" 12So the people scattered all over Egypt to gather stubble to use for straw. 13The slave drivers kept pressing them, saying, "Complete the work required of you for each day, just as when you had straw." 14The Israelite foremen appointed by Pharaoh's slave drivers were beaten and were asked, "Why didn't you meet your quota of bricks yesterday or today, as before?"

15Then the Israelite foremen went and appealed to Pharaoh: "Why have you treated

蹟，都告訴了亞倫。

29摩西、亞倫就去招聚以色列的眾長老。30亞倫將耶和華對摩西所說的一切話述說了一遍，又在百姓眼前行了那些神蹟，31百姓就信了。以色列人聽見耶和華眷顧他們，鑒察他們的困苦，就低頭下拜。

無草做磚

5 後來摩西、亞倫去對法老說："耶和華以色列的神這樣說：'容我的百姓去，在曠野向我守節。'"

2法老說："耶和華是誰，使我聽他的話，容以色列人去呢？我不認識耶和華，也不容以色列人去。"

3他們說："希伯來人的神遇見了我們，求你容我們往曠野去，走三天的路程，祭祀耶和華我們的神，免得他用瘟疫、刀兵攻擊我們。"

4埃及王對他們說："摩西、亞倫，你們為甚麼叫百姓曠工呢？你們去擔你們的擔子吧！"5又說："看哪，這地的以色列人如今眾多，你們竟叫他們歇下擔子！"

6當天，法老吩咐督工的和官長說：7"你們不可照常把草給百姓做磚，叫他們自己去撿草。8他們素常做磚的數目，你們仍舊向他們要，一點不可減少！因為他們是懶惰的，所以呼求說：'容我們去祭祀我們的神。'9你們要把更重的工夫加在這些人身上，叫他們勞碌，不聽虛謊的言語。"

10督工的和官長出來對百姓說："法老這樣說：'我不給你們草。11你們自己在哪裏能找草，就往那裏去找吧！但你們的工一點不可減少。'"12於是百姓散在埃及遍地，撿碎稭當作草。13督工的催着說："你們一天當完一天的工，與先前有草一樣。"14法老督工的責打他所派以色列人的官長，說："你們昨天、今天為甚麼沒有照向來的數目做磚、完你們的工作呢？"

15以色列人的官長就來哀求法老說："為甚麼這樣待你的僕人？

16督工的不把草給僕人，並且對我們說：「做磚吧！」看哪，你僕人挨了打，其實是你百姓的錯。」

17但法老說：「你們是懶惰的！你們是懶惰的！所以說：『容我們去祭祀耶和華。』18現在你們去做工吧！草是不給你們的，磚卻要如數交納。」

19以色列人的官長聽說「你們每天做磚的工作一點不可減少」，就知道是遭遇禍患了。20他們離了法老出來，正遇見摩西、亞倫站在對面，21就向他們說：「願耶和華鑒察你們，施行判斷，因你們使我們在法老和他臣僕面前有了臭名，把刀遞在他們手中殺我們。」

神應許拯救

22摩西回到耶和華那裏，說：「主啊，你為甚麼苦待這百姓呢？為甚麼打發我去呢？23自從我去見法老，奉你的名說話，他就苦待這百姓，你一點也沒有拯救他們。」

6 耶和華對摩西說：「現在你必看見我向法老所行的事，使他因我大能的手容以色列人去，且把他們趕出他的地。」

2神曉諭摩西說：「我是耶和華。3我從前向亞伯拉罕、以撒、雅各顯現為全能的神，至於我名耶和華，他們未曾知道。4我與他們堅定所立的約，要把他們寄居的迦南地賜給他們。5我也聽見以色列人被埃及人苦待的哀聲，我也記念我的約。

6「所以你要對以色列人說：『我是耶和華。我要用伸出來的膀臂重重地刑罰埃及人，救贖你們脫離他們的重擔，不做他們的苦工。7我要以你們為我的百姓，我也要作你們的神。你們要知道我是耶和華你們的神，是救你們脫離埃及人之重擔的。8我起誓應許給亞伯拉罕、以撒、雅各的那地，我要把你們領進去，將那地賜給你們為業。我是耶和華。』」

your servants this way? 16Your servants are given no straw, yet we are told, 'Make bricks!' Your servants are being beaten, but the fault is with your own people."

17Pharaoh said, "Lazy, that's what you are— lazy! That is why you keep saying, 'Let us go and sacrifice to the LORD.' 18Now get to work. You will not be given any straw, yet you must produce your full quota of bricks."

19The Israelite foremen realized they were in trouble when they were told, "You are not to reduce the number of bricks required of you for each day." 20When they left Pharaoh, they found Moses and Aaron waiting to meet them, 21and they said, "May the LORD look upon you and judge you! You have made us a stench to Pharaoh and his officials and have put a sword in their hand to kill us."

God Promises Deliverance

22Moses returned to the LORD and said, "O Lord, why have you brought trouble upon this people? Is this why you sent me? 23Ever since I went to Pharaoh to speak in your name, he has brought trouble upon this people, and you have not rescued your people at all."

6 Then the LORD said to Moses, "Now you will see what I will do to Pharaoh: Because of my mighty hand he will let them go; because of my mighty hand he will drive them out of his country."

2God also said to Moses, "I am the LORD. 3I appeared to Abraham, to Isaac and to Jacob as God Almighty,a but by my name the LORDb I did not make myself known to them.c 4I also established my covenant with them to give them the land of Canaan, where they lived as aliens. 5Moreover, I have heard the groaning of the Israelites, whom the Egyptians are enslaving, and I have remembered my covenant.

6"Therefore, say to the Israelites: 'I am the LORD, and I will bring you out from under the yoke of the Egyptians. I will free you from being slaves to them, and I will redeem you with an outstretched arm and with mighty acts of judgment. 7I will take you as my own people, and I will be your God. Then you will know that I am the LORD your God, who brought you out from under the yoke of the Egyptians. 8And I will bring you to the land I swore with uplifted hand to give to Abraham, to Isaac and to Jacob. I will give it to you as a possession. I am the LORD.' "

a 3 Hebrew El-Shaddai   b 3 See note at Exodus 3:15.

c 3 Or Almighty, and by my name the LORD did I not let myself be known to them?

⁹Moses reported this to the Israelites, but they did not listen to him because of their discouragement and cruel bondage.

¹⁰Then the LORD said to Moses, ¹¹"Go, tell Pharaoh king of Egypt to let the Israelites go out of his country."

¹²But Moses said to the LORD, "If the Israelites will not listen to me, why would Pharaoh listen to me, since I speak with faltering lips*ᵃ*?"

Family Record of Moses and Aaron

¹³Now the LORD spoke to Moses and Aaron about the Israelites and Pharaoh king of Egypt, and he commanded them to bring the Israelites out of Egypt.

¹⁴These were the heads of their families*ᵇ*:

The sons of Reuben the firstborn son of Israel were Hanoch and Pallu, Hezron and Carmi. These were the clans of Reuben.

¹⁵The sons of Simeon were Jemuel, Jamin, Ohad, Jakin, Zohar and Shaul the son of a Canaanite woman. These were the clans of Simeon.

¹⁶These were the names of the sons of Levi according to their records: Gershon, Kohath and Merari. Levi lived 137 years.

¹⁷The sons of Gershon, by clans, were Libni and Shimei.

¹⁸The sons of Kohath were Amram, Izhar, Hebron and Uzziel. Kohath lived 133 years.

¹⁹The sons of Merari were Mahli and Mushi.

These were the clans of Levi according to their records.

²⁰Amram married his father's sister Jochebed, who bore him Aaron and Moses. Amram lived 137 years.

²¹The sons of Izhar were Korah, Nepheg and Zicri.

²²The sons of Uzziel were Mishael, Elzaphan and Sithri.

²³Aaron married Elisheba, daughter of Amminadab and sister of Nahshon, and she bore him Nadab and Abihu, Eleazar and Ithamar.

²⁴The sons of Korah were Assir, Elkanah and Abiasaph. These were the Korahite clans.

²⁵Eleazar son of Aaron married one of the daughters of Putiel, and she bore him Phinehas.

---

a 12 Hebrew *I am uncircumcised of lips*; also in verse 30
b 14 The Hebrew for *families* here and in verse 25 refers to units larger than clans.

---

⁹摩西將這話告訴以色列人，只是他們因苦工愁煩，不肯聽他的話。

¹⁰耶和華曉諭摩西說：¹¹"你進去對埃及王法老說，要容以色列人出他的地。"

¹²摩西在耶和華面前說："以色列人尚且不聽我的話，法老怎肯聽我這拙口笨舌的人呢？"

摩西與亞倫的家譜

¹³耶和華吩咐摩西、亞倫往以色列人和埃及王法老那裏去，把以色列人從埃及地領出來。

¹⁴以色列人家長的名字記在下面：

以色列長子呂便的兒子是哈諾、法路、希斯崙、迦米，這是呂便的各家。

¹⁵西緬的兒子是耶母利、雅憫、阿轄、雅斤、瑣轄，和迦南女子的兒子掃羅，這是西緬的各家。

¹⁶利未眾子的名字，按着他們的後代記在下面：就是革順、哥轄、米拉利；利未一生的歲數是一百三十七歲。

¹⁷革順的兒子按着家室是立尼、示每。

¹⁸哥轄的兒子是暗蘭、以斯哈、希伯倫、烏薛；哥轄一生的歲數是一百三十三歲。

¹⁹米拉利的兒子是抹利和母示。這是利未的家，都按着他們的後代。

²⁰暗蘭娶了他父親的妹妹約基別為妻，她給他生了亞倫和摩西；暗蘭一生的歲數是一百三十七歲。

²¹以斯哈的兒子是可拉、尼斐、細基利。

²²烏薛的兒子是米沙利、以利撒反、西提利。

²³亞倫娶了亞米拿達的女兒拿順的妹妹以利沙巴為妻，她給他生了拿答、亞比戶、以利亞撒、以他瑪。

²⁴可拉的兒子是亞惜、以利加拿、亞比亞撒；這是可拉的各家。

²⁵亞倫的兒子以利亞撒，娶了普鐵的一個女兒為妻，她給他生了非尼哈。

這是利未人的家長，都按着他們的家。

26耶和華説：「將以色列人按着他們的軍隊從埃及地領出來。」這是對那亞倫、摩西説的。27對埃及王法老説：「要將以色列人從埃及領出來的，就是這摩西、亞倫。」

亞倫代摩西發言

28當耶和華在埃及地對摩西説話的日子，29他向摩西説：「我是耶和華，我對你説的一切話，你都要告訴埃及王法老。」30摩西在耶和華面前説：「看哪，我是拙口笨舌的人，法老怎肯聽我呢？」

7 耶和華對摩西説：「我使你在法老面前代替神，你的哥哥亞倫是替你説話的。2凡我所吩咐你的，你都要説。你的哥哥亞倫要對法老説，容以色列人出他的地。3我要使法老的心剛硬，也要在埃及地多行神蹟奇事。4但法老必不聽你們，我要伸手重重地刑罰埃及，將我的軍隊以色列民從埃及地領出來。5我伸手攻擊埃及，將以色列人從他們中間領出來的時候，埃及人就要知道我是耶和華。」

6摩西、亞倫這樣行，耶和華怎樣吩咐他們，他們就照樣行了。7摩西、亞倫與法老説話的時候，摩西八十歲，亞倫八十三歲。

亞倫的杖變為蛇

8耶和華曉諭摩西、亞倫説：9「法老若對你們説：『你們行件奇事吧！』你就吩咐亞倫説：『把杖丟在法老面前，使杖變作蛇。』」

10摩西、亞倫進去見法老，就照耶和華所吩咐的行，亞倫把杖丟在法老和臣僕面前，杖就變作蛇。11於是，法老召了博士和術士來，他們是埃及行法術的，也用邪術照樣而行。12他們各人丟下自己的杖，杖就變作蛇，但亞倫的杖吞了他們的杖。13法老心裏剛硬，不肯聽從摩西、亞倫，正如耶和華所説的。

These were the heads of the Levite families, clan by clan.

26It was this same Aaron and Moses to whom the LORD said, "Bring the Israelites out of Egypt by their divisions." 27They were the ones who spoke to Pharaoh king of Egypt about bringing the Israelites out of Egypt. It was the same Moses and Aaron.

Aaron to Speak for Moses

28Now when the LORD spoke to Moses in Egypt, 29he said to him, "I am the LORD. Tell Pharaoh king of Egypt everything I tell you."

30But Moses said to the LORD, "Since I speak with faltering lips, why would Pharaoh listen to me?"

7 Then the LORD said to Moses, "See, I have made you like God to Pharaoh, and your brother Aaron will be your prophet. 2You are to say everything I command you, and your brother Aaron is to tell Pharaoh to let the Israelites go out of his country. 3But I will harden Pharaoh's heart, and though I multiply my miraculous signs and wonders in Egypt, 4he will not listen to you. Then I will lay my hand on Egypt and with mighty acts of judgment I will bring out my divisions, my people the Israelites. 5And the Egyptians will know that I am the LORD when I stretch out my hand against Egypt and bring the Israelites out of it."

6Moses and Aaron did just as the LORD commanded them. 7Moses was eighty years old and Aaron eighty-three when they spoke to Pharaoh.

Aaron's Staff Becomes a Snake

8The LORD said to Moses and Aaron, 9"When Pharaoh says to you, 'Perform a miracle,' then say to Aaron, 'Take your staff and throw it down before Pharaoh,' and it will become a snake."

10So Moses and Aaron went to Pharaoh and did just as the LORD commanded. Aaron threw his staff down in front of Pharaoh and his officials, and it became a snake. 11Pharaoh then summoned wise men and sorcerers, and the Egyptian magicians also did the same things by their secret arts: 12Each one threw down his staff and it became a snake. But Aaron's staff swallowed up their staffs. 13Yet Pharaoh's heart became hard and he would not listen to them, just as the LORD had said.

The Plague of Blood

¹⁴Then the LORD said to Moses, "Pharaoh's heart is unyielding; he refuses to let the people go. ¹⁵Go to Pharaoh in the morning as he goes out to the water. Wait on the bank of the Nile to meet him, and take in your hand the staff that was changed into a snake. ¹⁶Then say to him, 'The LORD, the God of the Hebrews, has sent me to say to you: Let my people go, so that they may worship me in the desert. But until now you have not listened. ¹⁷This is what the LORD says: By this you will know that I am the LORD: With the staff that is in my hand I will strike the water of the Nile, and it will be changed into blood. ¹⁸The fish in the Nile will die, and the river will stink; the Egyptians will not be able to drink its water.'"

¹⁹The LORD said to Moses, "Tell Aaron, 'Take your staff and stretch out your hand over the waters of Egypt—over the streams and canals, over the ponds and all the reservoirs'—and they will turn to blood. Blood will be everywhere in Egypt, even in the wooden buckets and stone jars."

²⁰Moses and Aaron did just as the LORD had commanded. He raised his staff in the presence of Pharaoh and his officials and struck the water of the Nile, and all the water was changed into blood. ²¹The fish in the Nile died, and the river smelled so bad that the Egyptians could not drink its water. Blood was everywhere in Egypt.

²²But the Egyptian magicians did the same things by their secret arts, and Pharaoh's heart became hard; he would not listen to Moses and Aaron, just as the LORD had said. ²³Instead, he turned and went into his palace, and did not take even this to heart. ²⁴And all the Egyptians dug along the Nile to get drinking water, because they could not drink the water of the river.

The Plague of Frogs

²⁵Seven days passed after the LORD struck the Nile. **8** ¹Then the LORD said to Moses, "Go to Pharaoh and say to him, 'This is what the LORD says: Let my people go, so that they may worship me. ²If you refuse to let them go, I will plague your whole country with frogs. ³The Nile will teem with frogs. They will come up into your palace and your bedroom and onto your bed, into the houses of your officials and on your people, and into your ovens and kneading troughs. ⁴The frogs will go up on you and your people and all your officials.'"

水變血之災

¹⁴耶和華對摩西說："法老心裏固執，不肯容百姓去。¹⁵明日早晨他出來往水邊去，你要往河邊迎接他，手裏要拿那變過蛇的杖，¹⁶對他說：'耶和華希伯來人的神打發我來見你，說：容我的百姓去，好在曠野侍奉我。到如今你還是不聽。'¹⁷耶和華這樣說：'我要用我手裏的杖擊打河中的水，水就變作血，因此，你必知道我是耶和華。¹⁸河裏的魚必死，河也要腥臭，埃及人就要厭惡吃這河裏的水。'"

¹⁹耶和華曉諭摩西說："你對亞倫說：'把你的杖伸在埃及所有的水以上，就是在他們的江、河、池、塘以上，叫水都變作血。在埃及遍地，無論在木器中、石器中，都必有血。'"

²⁰摩西、亞倫就照耶和華所吩咐的行，亞倫在法老和臣僕眼前舉杖擊打河裏的水，河裏的水都變作血了。²¹河裏的魚死了，河也腥臭了，埃及人就不能吃這河裏的水，埃及遍地都有了血。

²²埃及行法術的，也用邪術照樣而行。法老心裏剛硬，不肯聽摩西、亞倫，正如耶和華所說的。²³法老轉身進宮，也不把這事放在心上。²⁴埃及人都在河的兩邊挖地，要得水喝，因為他們不能喝這河裏的水。

蛙災

²⁵耶和華擊打河以後滿了七天。**8** ¹耶和華吩咐摩西說："你進去見法老，對他說：'耶和華這樣說：容我的百姓去，好侍奉我。²你若不肯容他們去，我必使青蛙糟蹋你的四境。³河裏要滋生青蛙，這青蛙要上來進你的宮殿和你的臥房，上你的牀榻，進你臣僕的房屋，上你百姓的身上，進你的爐灶和你的摶麵盆，⁴又要上你和你百姓並你眾臣僕的身上。'"

⁵耶和華曉諭摩西說：“你對亞倫說：‘把你的杖伸在江、河、池以上，使青蛙到埃及地上來。’”

⁶亞倫便伸杖在埃及的諸水以上，青蛙就上來，遮滿了埃及地。⁷行法術的也用他們的邪術照樣而行，叫青蛙上了埃及地。

⁸法老召了摩西、亞倫來，說：“請你們求耶和華使這青蛙離開我和我的民，我就容百姓去祭祀耶和華。”

⁹摩西對法老說：“任憑你吧！我要何時為你和你的臣僕並你的百姓祈求，除滅青蛙離開你和你的宮殿，只留在河裏呢？”

¹⁰他說：“明天。”

摩西說：“可以照你的話吧！好叫你知道沒有像耶和華我們神的。¹¹青蛙要離開你和你的宮殿，並你的臣僕與你的百姓，只留在河裏。”

¹²於是摩西、亞倫離開法老出去。摩西為擾害法老的青蛙呼求耶和華。¹³耶和華就照摩西的話行，凡在房裏、院中、田間的青蛙都死了。¹⁴眾人把青蛙聚攏成堆，遍地就都腥臭。¹⁵但法老見災禍鬆緩，就硬着心不肯聽他們，正如耶和華所說的。

虱災

¹⁶耶和華吩咐摩西說：“你對亞倫說：‘伸出你的杖擊打地上的塵土，使塵土在埃及遍地變作虱子（註：或作“蚋蟲”。下同）。’”¹⁷他們就這樣行，亞倫伸杖擊打地上的塵土，就在人身上和牲畜身上有了虱子；埃及遍地的塵土都變成虱子了。¹⁸行法術的也用邪術要生出虱子來，卻是不能。於是在人身上和牲畜身上都有了虱子。

¹⁹行法術的就對法老說：“這是神的手段。”法老心裏剛硬，不肯聽摩西、亞倫，正如耶和華所說的。

蠅災

²⁰耶和華對摩西說：“你清早起來，法老來到水邊，你站在他面前，對他說：‘耶和華這樣說：容我的百

⁵Then the LORD said to Moses, "Tell Aaron, 'Stretch out your hand with your staff over the streams and canals and ponds, and make frogs come up on the land of Egypt.'"

⁶So Aaron stretched out his hand over the waters of Egypt, and the frogs came up and covered the land. ⁷But the magicians did the same things by their secret arts; they also made frogs come up on the land of Egypt.

⁸Pharaoh summoned Moses and Aaron and said, "Pray to the LORD to take the frogs away from me and my people, and I will let your people go to offer sacrifices to the LORD."

⁹Moses said to Pharaoh, "I leave to you the honor of setting the time for me to pray for you and your officials and your people that you and your houses may be rid of the frogs, except for those that remain in the Nile."

¹⁰"Tomorrow," Pharaoh said.

Moses replied, "It will be as you say, so that you may know there is no one like the LORD our God. ¹¹The frogs will leave you and your houses, your officials and your people; they will remain only in the Nile."

¹²After Moses and Aaron left Pharaoh, Moses cried out to the LORD about the frogs he had brought on Pharaoh. ¹³And the LORD did what Moses asked. The frogs died in the houses, in the courtyards and in the fields. ¹⁴They were piled into heaps, and the land reeked of them. ¹⁵But when Pharaoh saw that there was relief, he hardened his heart and would not listen to Moses and Aaron, just as the LORD had said.

The Plague of Gnats

¹⁶Then the LORD said to Moses, "Tell Aaron, 'Stretch out your staff and strike the dust of the ground,' and throughout the land of Egypt the dust will become gnats." ¹⁷They did this, and when Aaron stretched out his hand with the staff and struck the dust of the ground, gnats came upon men and animals. All the dust throughout the land of Egypt became gnats. ¹⁸But when the magicians tried to produce gnats by their secret arts, they could not. And the gnats were on men and animals.

¹⁹The magicians said to Pharaoh, "This is the finger of God." But Pharaoh's heart was hard and he would not listen, just as the LORD had said.

The Plague of Flies

²⁰Then the LORD said to Moses, "Get up early in the morning and confront Pharaoh as he goes to the water and say to him, 'This is what the LORD says: Let my people go, so that they may

worship me. ²¹If you do not let my people go, I will send swarms of flies on you and your officials, on your people and into your houses. The houses of the Egyptians will be full of flies, and even the ground where they are.

²²" 'But on that day I will deal differently with the land of Goshen, where my people live; no swarms of flies will be there, so that you will know that I, the LORD, am in this land. ²³I will make a distinction^a between my people and your people. This miraculous sign will occur tomorrow.' "

²⁴And the LORD did this. Dense swarms of flies poured into Pharaoh's palace and into the houses of his officials, and throughout Egypt the land was ruined by the flies.

²⁵Then Pharaoh summoned Moses and Aaron and said, "Go, sacrifice to your God here in the land."

²⁶But Moses said, "That would not be right. The sacrifices we offer the LORD our God would be detestable to the Egyptians. And if we offer sacrifices that are detestable in their eyes, will they not stone us? ²⁷We must take a three-day journey into the desert to offer sacrifices to the LORD our God, as he commands us."

²⁸Pharaoh said, "I will let you go to offer sacrifices to the LORD your God in the desert, but you must not go very far. Now pray for me."

²⁹Moses answered, "As soon as I leave you, I will pray to the LORD, and tomorrow the flies will leave Pharaoh and his officials and his people. Only be sure that Pharaoh does not act deceitfully again by not letting the people go to offer sacrifices to the LORD."

³⁰Then Moses left Pharaoh and prayed to the LORD, ³¹and the LORD did what Moses asked: The flies left Pharaoh and his officials and his people; not a fly remained. ³²But this time also Pharaoh hardened his heart and would not let the people go.

The Plague on Livestock

9 Then the LORD said to Moses, "Go to Pharaoh and say to him, 'This is what the LORD, the God of the Hebrews, says: "Let my people go, so that they may worship me." ²If you refuse to let them go and continue to hold them back, ³the hand of the LORD will bring a terrible plague on your livestock in the field—on your horses and donkeys and camels and on your cattle and sheep and goats. ⁴But the LORD will make a distinction between the livestock of Israel and that of Egypt, so that no ani-

姓去，好侍奉我。²¹你若不容我的百姓去，我要叫成羣的蒼蠅到你和你臣僕並你百姓的身上，進你的房屋，並且埃及人的房屋和他們所住的地，都要滿了成羣的蒼蠅。

²²" '當那日，我必分別我百姓所住的歌珊地，使那裏沒有成羣的蒼蠅，好叫你知道我是天下的耶和華。²³我要將我的百姓和你的百姓分別出來；明天必有這神蹟。' "

²⁴耶和華就這樣行，蒼蠅成了大羣，進入法老的宮殿和他臣僕的房屋；埃及遍地就因這成羣的蒼蠅敗壞了。

²⁵法老召了摩西、亞倫來，說："你們去，在這地祭祀你們的神吧！"

²⁶摩西說："這樣行本不相宜，因為我們要把埃及人所厭惡的祭祀耶和華我們的神；若把埃及人所厭惡的在他們眼前獻為祭，他們豈不拿石頭打死我們嗎？²⁷我們要往曠野去，走三天的路程，照着耶和華我們神所要吩咐我們的祭祀他。"

²⁸法老說："我容你們去，在曠野祭祀耶和華你們的神，只是不要走得很遠，求你們為我祈禱。"

²⁹摩西說："我要出去求耶和華，使成羣的蒼蠅明天離開法老和法老的臣僕並法老的百姓，法老卻不可再行詭詐，不容百姓去祭祀耶和華。"

³⁰於是摩西離開法老去求耶和華。³¹耶和華就照摩西的話行，叫成羣的蒼蠅離開法老和他的臣僕並他的百姓，一個也沒有留下。³²這一次法老又硬着心，不容百姓去。

畜疫之災

9 耶和華吩咐摩西說："你進去見法老，對他說：'耶和華希伯來人的神這樣說：容我的百姓去，好侍奉我。²你若不肯容他們去，仍舊強留他們，³耶和華的手加在你田間的牲畜上，就是在馬、驢、駱駝、牛羣、羊羣上，必有重重的瘟疫。⁴耶和華要分別以色列的牲畜和埃及的牲畜，凡屬以色列人

---

^a 23 Septuagint and Vulgate; Hebrew *will put a deliverance*

的，一樣都不死。’”

⁵耶和華就定了時候，說：“明天耶和華必在此地行這事。”⁶第二天，耶和華就行這事。<u>埃及</u>的牲畜幾乎都死了，只是<u>以色列</u>人的牲畜一個都沒有死。⁷法老打發人去看，誰知，<u>以色列</u>人的牲畜連一個都沒有死。法老的心卻是固執，不容百姓去。

瘡災

⁸耶和華吩咐<u>摩西</u>、<u>亞倫</u>說：“你們取幾捧爐灰，<u>摩西</u>要在法老面前向天揚起來。⁹這灰要在<u>埃及</u>全地變作塵土，在人身上和牲畜身上，成了起泡的瘡。”

¹⁰<u>摩西</u>、<u>亞倫</u>取了爐灰，站在法老面前。<u>摩西</u>向天揚起來，就在人身上和牲畜身上，成了起泡的瘡。¹¹行法術的在<u>摩西</u>面前站立不住，因為在他們身上和一切<u>埃及</u>人身上都有這瘡。¹²耶和華使法老的心剛硬，不聽他們，正如耶和華對<u>摩西</u>所說的。

雹災

¹³耶和華對<u>摩西</u>說：“你清早起來，站在法老面前，對他說：‘耶和華<u>希伯來</u>人的神這樣說：容我的百姓去，好侍奉我。¹⁴因為這一次我要叫一切的災殃臨到你和你臣僕並你百姓的身上，叫你知道在普天下沒有像我的。¹⁵我若伸手用瘟疫攻擊你和你的百姓，你早就從地上除滅了。¹⁶其實我叫你存立，是特要向你顯我的大能，並要使我的名傳遍天下。¹⁷你還向我的百姓自高，不容他們去嗎？¹⁸到明天約在這時候，我必叫重大的冰雹降下，自從埃及開國以來，沒有這樣的冰雹。¹⁹現在你要打發人把你的牲畜和你田間一切所有的催進來，凡在田間不收回家的，無論是人是牲畜，冰雹必降在他們身上，他們就必死。’”

mal belonging to the Israelites will die.' "

⁵The L<small>ORD</small> set a time and said, "Tomorrow the L<small>ORD</small> will do this in the land." ⁶And the next day the L<small>ORD</small> did it: All the livestock of the Egyptians died, but not one animal belonging to the Israelites died. ⁷Pharaoh sent men to investigate and found that not even one of the animals of the Israelites had died. Yet his heart was unyielding and he would not let the people go.

The Plague of Boils

⁸Then the L<small>ORD</small> said to Moses and Aaron, "Take handfuls of soot from a furnace and have Moses toss it into the air in the presence of Pharaoh. ⁹It will become fine dust over the whole land of Egypt, and festering boils will break out on men and animals throughout the land."

¹⁰So they took soot from a furnace and stood before Pharaoh. Moses tossed it into the air, and festering boils broke out on men and animals. ¹¹The magicians could not stand before Moses because of the boils that were on them and on all the Egyptians. ¹²But the L<small>ORD</small> hardened Pharaoh's heart and he would not listen to Moses and Aaron, just as the L<small>ORD</small> had said to Moses.

The Plague of Hail

¹³Then the L<small>ORD</small> said to Moses, "Get up early in the morning, confront Pharaoh and say to him, 'This is what the L<small>ORD</small>, the God of the Hebrews, says: Let my people go, so that they may worship me, ¹⁴or this time I will send the full force of my plagues against you and against your officials and your people, so you may know that there is no one like me in all the earth. ¹⁵For by now I could have stretched out my hand and struck you and your people with a plague that would have wiped you off the earth. ¹⁶But I have raised you up^a for this very purpose, that I might show you my power and that my name might be proclaimed in all the earth. ¹⁷You still set yourself against my people and will not let them go. ¹⁸Therefore, at this time tomorrow I will send the worst hailstorm that has ever fallen on Egypt, from the day it was founded till now. ¹⁹Give an order now to bring your livestock and everything you have in the field to a place of shelter, because the hail will fall on every man and animal that has not been brought in and is still out in the field, and they will die.' "

a 16 Or have spared you

20Those officials of Pharaoh who feared the word of the LORD hurried to bring their slaves and their livestock inside. 21But those who ignored the word of the LORD left their slaves and livestock in the field.

22Then the LORD said to Moses, "Stretch out your hand toward the sky so that hail will fall all over Egypt—on men and animals and on everything growing in the fields of Egypt." 23When Moses stretched out his staff toward the sky, the LORD sent thunder and hail, and lightning flashed down to the ground. So the LORD rained hail on the land of Egypt; 24hail fell and lightning flashed back and forth. It was the worst storm in all the land of Egypt since it had become a nation. 25Throughout Egypt hail struck everything in the fields—both men and animals; it beat down everything growing in the fields and stripped every tree. 26The only place it did not hail was the land of Goshen, where the Israelites were.

27Then Pharaoh summoned Moses and Aaron. "This time I have sinned," he said to them. "The LORD is in the right, and I and my people are in the wrong. 28Pray to the LORD, for we have had enough thunder and hail. I will let you go; you don't have to stay any longer."

29Moses replied, "When I have gone out of the city, I will spread out my hands in prayer to the LORD. The thunder will stop and there will be no more hail, so you may know that the earth is the LORD's. 30But I know that you and your officials still do not fear the LORD God."

31(The flax and barley were destroyed, since the barley had headed and the flax was in bloom. 32The wheat and spelt, however, were not destroyed, because they ripen later.)

33Then Moses left Pharaoh and went out of the city. He spread out his hands toward the LORD; the thunder and hail stopped, and the rain no longer poured down on the land. 34When Pharaoh saw that the rain and hail and thunder had stopped, he sinned again: He and his officials hardened their hearts. 35So Pharaoh's heart was hard and he would not let the Israelites go, just as the LORD had said through Moses.

The Plague of Locusts

10 Then the LORD said to Moses, "Go to Pharaoh, for I have hardened his heart and the hearts of his officials so that I may perform these miraculous signs of mine among them 2that you may tell your children and grandchildren how I dealt harshly with the Egyptians and how I performed my signs

20法老的臣僕中懼怕耶和華這話的，便叫他的奴僕和牲畜跑進家來；21但那不把耶和華這話放在心上的，就將他的奴僕和牲畜留在田裏。

22耶和華對摩西說："你向天伸杖，使埃及遍地的人身上和牲畜身上，並田間各樣菜蔬上，都有冰雹。"23摩西向天伸杖，耶和華就打雷、下雹，有火閃到地上，耶和華下雹在埃及地上。24那時，雹與火攙雜，甚是厲害，自從埃及成國以來，遍地沒有這樣的。25在埃及遍地，雹擊打了田間所有的人和牲畜，並一切的菜蔬，又打壞田間一切的樹木。26惟獨以色列人所住的歌珊地沒有冰雹。

27法老打發人召摩西、亞倫來，對他們說："這一次我犯了罪了，耶和華是公義的，我和我的百姓是邪惡的。28這雷轟和冰雹已經夠了。請你們求耶和華，我就容你們去，不再留住你們。"

29摩西對他說："我一出城，就要向耶和華舉手禱告，雷必止住，也不再有冰雹，叫你知道全地都是屬耶和華的。30至於你和你的臣僕，我知道你們還是不懼怕耶和華神。"

31那時，麻和大麥被雹擊打，因為大麥已經吐穗，麻也開了花。32只是小麥和粗麥沒有被擊打，因為還沒有長成。

33摩西離了法老出城，向耶和華舉手禱告，雷和雹就止住，雨也不再澆在地上了。34法老見雨和雹與雷止住，就越發犯罪，他和他的臣僕都硬着心。35法老的心剛硬，不容以色列人去，正如耶和華藉着摩西所說的。

蝗災

10 耶和華對摩西說："你進去見法老；我使他和他臣僕的心剛硬，為要在他們中間顯我這些神蹟，2並要叫你將我向埃及人所做的事，和在他們中間所行的神蹟，傳於你兒子和你孫子的耳中，好叫你們知道我是耶和華。"

3摩西、亞倫就進去見法老，對他說："耶和華希伯來人的神這樣說：'你在我面前不肯自卑要到幾時呢？容我的百姓去，好侍奉我。4你若不肯容我的百姓去，明天我要使蝗蟲進入你的境內，5遮滿地面，甚至看不見地，並且吃地所剩下冰雹所剩的和田間所長的一切樹木。6你的宮殿和你眾臣僕的房屋，並一切埃及人的房屋，都要被蝗蟲佔滿了。自從你祖宗和你祖宗的祖宗在世以來，直到今日，沒有見過這樣的災。'"摩西就轉身離開法老出去。

7法老的臣僕對法老說："這人為我們的網羅，要到幾時呢？容這些人去，侍奉耶和華他們的神吧！埃及已經敗壞了，你還不知道嗎？"

8於是摩西、亞倫被召回來見法老，法老對他們說："你們去侍奉耶和華你們的神，但那要去的是誰呢？"

9摩西說："我們要和我們的老的、少的、兒子女兒同去，且把羊群牛群一同帶去，因為我們務要向耶和華守節。"

10法老對他們說："我容你們和你們婦人孩子去的時候，耶和華與你們同在吧！你們要謹慎，因為有禍在你們眼前（註：或作"你們存着惡意"），11不可都去，你們這壯年人去侍奉耶和華吧！因為這是你們所求的。"於是，把他們從法老面前攆出去。

12耶和華對摩西說："你向埃及地伸杖，使蝗蟲到埃及地上來，吃地上一切的菜蔬，就是冰雹所剩的。"

13摩西就向埃及地伸杖，那一晝一夜，耶和華使東風颳在埃及地上。到了早晨，東風把蝗蟲颳了來。14蝗蟲上來，落在埃及的四境，甚是厲害，以前沒有這樣的，以後也必沒有。15因為這蝗蟲遮滿地面，甚至地都黑暗了，又吃地上一切的菜蔬，和冰雹所剩樹上的果子。埃及遍地，無論是樹木、是田間的菜蔬，連一點青的也沒有留下。

among them, and that you may know that I am the LORD."

3So Moses and Aaron went to Pharaoh and said to him, "This is what the LORD, the God of the Hebrews, says: 'How long will you refuse to humble yourself before me? Let my people go, so that they may worship me. 4If you refuse to let them go, I will bring locusts into your country tomorrow. 5They will cover the face of the ground so that it cannot be seen. They will devour what little you have left after the hail, including every tree that is growing in your fields. 6They will fill your houses and those of all your officials and all the Egyptians—something neither your fathers nor your forefathers have ever seen from the day they settled in this land till now.' " Then Moses turned and left Pharaoh.

7Pharaoh's officials said to him, "How long will this man be a snare to us? Let the people go, so that they may worship the LORD their God. Do you not yet realize that Egypt is ruined?"

8Then Moses and Aaron were brought back to Pharaoh. "Go, worship the LORD your God," he said. "But just who will be going?"

9Moses answered, "We will go with our young and old, with our sons and daughters, and with our flocks and herds, because we are to celebrate a festival to the LORD."

10Pharaoh said, "The LORD be with you—if I let you go, along with your women and children! Clearly you are bent on evil.*a* 11No! Have only the men go; and worship the LORD, since that's what you have been asking for." Then Moses and Aaron were driven out of Pharaoh's presence.

12And the LORD said to Moses, "Stretch out your hand over Egypt so that locusts will swarm over the land and devour everything growing in the fields, everything left by the hail."

13So Moses stretched out his staff over Egypt, and the LORD made an east wind blow across the land all that day and all that night. By morning the wind had brought the locusts; 14they invaded all Egypt and settled down in every area of the country in great numbers. Never before had there been such a plague of locusts, nor will there ever be again. 15They covered all the ground until it was black. They devoured all that was left after the hail—everything growing in the fields and the fruit on the trees. Nothing green remained on tree or plant in all the land of Egypt.

a 10 Or Be careful, trouble is in store for you!

16Pharaoh quickly summoned Moses and Aaron and said, "I have sinned against the LORD your God and against you. 17Now forgive my sin once more and pray to the LORD your God to take this deadly plague away from me."

18Moses then left Pharaoh and prayed to the LORD. 19And the LORD changed the wind to a very strong west wind, which caught up the locusts and carried them into the Red Sea.*a* Not a locust was left anywhere in Egypt. 20But the LORD hardened Pharaoh's heart, and he would not let the Israelites go.

The Plague of Darkness

21Then the LORD said to Moses, "Stretch out your hand toward the sky so that darkness will spread over Egypt—darkness that can be felt." 22So Moses stretched out his hand toward the sky, and total darkness covered all Egypt for three days. 23No one could see anyone else or leave his place for three days. Yet all the Israelites had light in the places where they lived.

24Then Pharaoh summoned Moses and said, "Go, worship the LORD. Even your women and children may go with you; only leave your flocks and herds behind."

25But Moses said, "You must allow us to have sacrifices and burnt offerings to present to the LORD our God. 26Our livestock too must go with us; not a hoof is to be left behind. We have to use some of them in worshiping the LORD our God, and until we get there we will not know what we are to use to worship the LORD."

27But the LORD hardened Pharaoh's heart, and he was not willing to let them go. 28Pharaoh said to Moses, "Get out of my sight! Make sure you do not appear before me again! The day you see my face you will die."

29"Just as you say," Moses replied, "I will never appear before you again."

The Plague on the Firstborn

11 Now the LORD had said to Moses, "I will bring one more plague on Pharaoh and on Egypt. After that, he will let you go from here, and when he does, he will drive you out completely. 2Tell the people that men and women alike are to ask their neighbors for articles of silver and gold." 3(The LORD made the Egyptians favorably disposed toward the people, and Moses himself was highly regarded in Egypt by Pharaoh's officials and by the people.)

4So Moses said, "This is what the LORD says:

16於是法老急忙召了摩西、亞倫來，說："我得罪耶和華你們的神，又得罪了你們。17現在求你，只這一次，饒恕我的罪，求耶和華你們的神，使我脫離這一次的死亡。"

18摩西就離開法老去求耶和華。19耶和華轉了極大的西風，把蝗蟲颳起，吹入紅海，在埃及的四境連一個也沒有留下。20但耶和華使法老的心剛硬，不容以色列人去。

黑暗之災

21耶和華對摩西說："你向天伸杖，使埃及地黑暗，這黑暗似乎摸得着。"22摩西向天伸杖，埃及遍地就烏黑了三天。23三天之久，人不能相見，誰也不敢起來離開本處，惟有以色列人家中都有亮光。

24法老就召摩西來，說："你們去侍奉耶和華，只是你們的羊羣牛羣要留下，你們的婦人、孩子可以和你們同去。"

25摩西說："你總要把祭物和燔祭牲交給我們，使我們可以祭祀耶和華我們的神。26我們的牲畜也要帶去，連一蹄也不留下，因為我們要從其中取出來，侍奉耶和華我們的神。我們未到那裏，還不知道用甚麼侍奉耶和華。"

27但耶和華使法老的心剛硬，不肯容他們去。28法老對摩西說："你離開我去吧！你要小心，不要再見我的面，因為你見我面的那日，你就必死！"

29摩西說："你說得好，我必不再見你的面了。"

殺長子之災

11 耶和華對摩西說："我再使一樣的災殃臨到法老和埃及，然後他必容你們離開這地。他容你們去的時候，總要催逼你們都從這地出去。2你要傳於百姓的耳中，叫他們男女各人向鄰舍要金器銀器。"3耶和華叫百姓在埃及人眼前蒙恩，並且摩西在埃及地法老臣僕和百姓的眼中，看為極大。

4摩西說："耶和華這樣說：

---

a 19 Hebrew Yam Suph; that is, Sea of Reeds

'約到半夜，我必出去巡行埃及遍地，⁵凡在埃及地，從坐寶座的法老，直到磨子後的婢女，所有的長子，以及一切頭生的牲畜，都必死。⁶埃及遍地必有大哀號，從前沒有這樣的，後來也必沒有。⁷至於以色列中，無論是人是牲畜，連狗也不敢向他們搖舌。'好叫你們知道耶和華是將我以埃及和以色列人分別出來。⁸你這一切臣僕都要俯伏來見我，說：'求你和跟從你的百姓都出去'，然後我要出去。"於是，摩西氣忿忿地離開法老出去了。

⁹耶和華對摩西說："法老必不聽你們，使我的奇事在埃及地多起來。"¹⁰摩西、亞倫在法老面前行了這一切奇事，耶和華使法老的心剛硬，不容以色列人出離他的地。

逾越節

12 耶和華在埃及地曉諭摩西、亞倫說：²"你們要以本月為正月，為一年之首。³你們吩咐以色列全會眾說：'本月初十日，各人要按着父家取羊羔，一家一隻。⁴若是一家的人太少，吃不了一隻羊羔，本人就要和他隔壁的鄰舍共取一隻。你們預備羊羔，要按着人數和飯量計算。⁵要無殘疾、一歲的公羊羔，你們或從綿羊裏取，或從山羊裏取，都可以。⁶要留到本月十四日，在黃昏的時候，以色列全會眾把羊羔宰了。⁷各家要取點血，塗在吃羊羔的房屋左右的門框上和門楣上。⁸當夜要吃羊羔的肉，用火烤了，與無酵餅和苦菜同吃。⁹不可吃生的，斷不可吃水煮的，要帶着頭、腿、五臟，用火烤了吃。¹⁰不可剩下一點留到早晨，若留到早晨，要用火燒了。¹¹你們吃羊羔當腰間束帶，腳上穿鞋，手中拿杖，趕緊地吃，這是耶和華的逾越節。

'About midnight I will go throughout Egypt. ⁵Every firstborn son in Egypt will die, from the firstborn son of Pharaoh, who sits on the throne, to the firstborn son of the slave girl, who is at her hand mill, and all the firstborn of the cattle as well. ⁶There will be loud wailing throughout Egypt—worse than there has ever been or ever will be again. ⁷But among the Israelites not a dog will bark at any man or animal.' Then you will know that the LORD makes a distinction between Egypt and Israel. ⁸All these officials of yours will come to me, bowing down before me and saying, 'Go, you and all the people who follow you!' After that I will leave." Then Moses, hot with anger, left Pharaoh.

⁹The LORD had said to Moses, "Pharaoh will refuse to listen to you—so that my wonders may be multiplied in Egypt." ¹⁰Moses and Aaron performed all these wonders before Pharaoh, but the LORD hardened Pharaoh's heart, and he would not let the Israelites go out of his country.

The Passover

12 The LORD said to Moses and Aaron in Egypt, ²"This month is to be for you the first month, the first month of your year. ³Tell the whole community of Israel that on the tenth day of this month each man is to take a lamb[a] for his family, one for each household. ⁴If any household is too small for a whole lamb, they must share one with their nearest neighbor, having taken into account the number of people there are. You are to determine the amount of lamb needed in accordance with what each person will eat. ⁵The animals you choose must be year-old males without defect, and you may take them from the sheep or the goats. ⁶Take care of them until the fourteenth day of the month, when all the people of the community of Israel must slaughter them at twilight. ⁷Then they are to take some of the blood and put it on the sides and tops of the doorframes of the houses where they eat the lambs. ⁸That same night they are to eat the meat roasted over the fire, along with bitter herbs, and bread made without yeast. ⁹Do not eat the meat raw or cooked in water, but roast it over the fire—head, legs and inner parts. ¹⁰Do not leave any of it till morning; if some is left till morning, you must burn it. ¹¹This is how you are to eat it: with your cloak tucked into your belt, your sandals on your feet and your staff in your hand. Eat it in haste; it is the LORD's Passover.

a 3 The Hebrew word can mean lamb or kid; also in verse 4.

12"On that same night I will pass through Egypt and strike down every firstborn—both men and animals—and I will bring judgment on all the gods of Egypt. I am the LORD. 13The blood will be a sign for you on the houses where you are; and when I see the blood, I will pass over you. No destructive plague will touch you when I strike Egypt.

14"This is a day you are to commemorate; for the generations to come you shall celebrate it as a festival to the LORD—a lasting ordinance. 15For seven days you are to eat bread made without yeast. On the first day remove the yeast from your houses, for whoever eats anything with yeast in it from the first day through the seventh must be cut off from Israel. 16On the first day hold a sacred assembly, and another one on the seventh day. Do no work at all on these days, except to prepare food for everyone to eat—that is all you may do.

17"Celebrate the Feast of Unleavened Bread, because it was on this very day that I brought your divisions out of Egypt. Celebrate this day as a lasting ordinance for the generations to come. 18In the first month you are to eat bread made without yeast, from the evening of the fourteenth day until the evening of the twenty-first day. 19For seven days no yeast is to be found in your houses. And whoever eats anything with yeast in it must be cut off from the community of Israel, whether he is an alien or native-born. 20Eat nothing made with yeast. Wherever you live, you must eat unleavened bread."

21Then Moses summoned all the elders of Israel and said to them, "Go at once and select the animals for your families and slaughter the Passover lamb. 22Take a bunch of hyssop, dip it into the blood in the basin and put some of the blood on the top and on both sides of the doorframe. Not one of you shall go out the door of his house until morning. 23When the LORD goes through the land to strike down the Egyptians, he will see the blood on the top and sides of the doorframe and will pass over that doorway, and he will not permit the destroyer to enter your houses and strike you down.

24"Obey these instructions as a lasting ordinance for you and your descendants. 25When you enter the land that the LORD will give you as he promised, observe this ceremony. 26And when your children ask you, 'What does this ceremony mean to you?' 27then tell them, 'It is the Passover sacrifice to the LORD, who passed over the houses of the Israelites in Egypt and spared our homes when he struck down the

12 "因為那夜我要巡行埃及地,把埃及地一切頭生的,無論是人是牲畜,都擊殺了,又要敗壞埃及一切的神。我是耶和華。13這血要在你們所住的房屋上作記號,我一見這血,就越過你們去,我擊殺埃及地頭生的時候,災殃必不臨到你們身上滅你們。

14 "你們要記念這日,守為耶和華的節,作為你們世世代代永遠的定例。15你們要吃無酵餅七日。頭一日要把酵從你們各家中除去,因為從頭一日起,到第七日為止,凡吃有酵之餅的,必從以色列中剪除。16頭一日你們當有聖會,第七日也當有聖會,這兩日之內,除了預備各人所要吃的以外,無論何工都不可做。

17 "你們要守無酵節,因為我正當這日把你們的軍隊從埃及地領出來,所以你們要守這日,作為世世代代永遠的定例。18從正月十四日晚上,直到二十一日晚上,你們要吃無酵餅。19在你們各家中,七日之內不可有酵,因為凡吃有酵之物的,無論是寄居的,是本地的,必從以色列的會中剪除。20有酵的物,你們都不可吃,在你們一切住處要吃無酵餅。"

21於是,摩西召了以色列的眾長老來,對他們說:"你們要按着家口取出羊羔,把這逾越節的羊羔宰了。22拿一把牛膝草,蘸盆裏的血,打在門楣上和左右的門框上。你們誰也不可出自己的房門,直到早晨。23因為耶和華要巡行擊殺埃及人,他看見血在門楣上和左右的門框上,就必越過那門,不容滅命的進你們的房屋,擊殺你們。

24 "這例,你們要守着,作為你們和你們子孫永遠的定例。25日後,你們到了耶和華按着所應許賜給你們的那地,就要守這禮。26你們的兒女問你們說:'行這禮是甚麼意思?'27你們就說:'這是獻給耶和華逾越節的祭。當以色列人在埃及的時候,他擊殺埃及人,越過以色列人的房屋，救了我們各家。’」於是，百姓低頭下拜。28耶和華怎樣吩咐摩西、亞倫，以色列人就怎樣行。

29到了半夜，耶和華把埃及地所有的長子，就是從坐寶座的法老，直到被擄囚在監裏之人的長子，以及一切頭生的牲畜，盡都殺了。30法老和一切臣僕，並埃及眾人，夜間都起來了，在埃及有大哀號，無一家不死一個人的。

出埃及

31夜間，法老召了摩西、亞倫來，說：「起來！連你們帶以色列人，從我民中出去，依你們所說的，去侍奉耶和華吧！32也依你們所說的，連羊羣牛羣帶着走吧！並要為我祝福。」

33埃及人催促百姓，打發他們快快出離那地，因為埃及人說：「我們都要死了。」34百姓就拿着沒有酵的生麵，把摶麵盆包在衣服中，扛在肩頭上。35以色列人照着摩西的話行，向埃及人要金器銀器和衣裳。36耶和華叫百姓在埃及人眼前蒙恩，以致埃及人給他們所要的，他們就把埃及人的財物奪去了。

37以色列人從蘭塞起行，往疏割去，除了婦人孩子，步行的男人約有六十萬。38又有許多閒雜人，並有羊羣牛羣，和他們一同上去。39他們用埃及帶出來的生麵烤成無酵餅，這生麵原沒有發起，因為他們被催逼離則埃及不能耽延，也沒有為自己預備甚麼食物。

40以色列人住在埃及共有四百三十年。41正滿了四百三十年的那一天，耶和華的軍隊都從埃及地出來了。42這夜是耶和華的夜，因耶和華領他們出了埃及地，所以當向耶和華謹守，是以色列眾人世世代代該謹守的。

逾越節的條例

43耶和華對摩西、亞倫說：「逾越節的例是這樣：

Egyptians.' " Then the people bowed down and worshiped. 28The Israelites did just what the LORD commanded Moses and Aaron.

29At midnight the LORD struck down all the firstborn in Egypt, from the firstborn of Pharaoh, who sat on the throne, to the firstborn of the prisoner, who was in the dungeon, and the firstborn of all the livestock as well. 30Pharaoh and all his officials and all the Egyptians got up during the night, and there was loud wailing in Egypt, for there was not a house without someone dead.

The Exodus

31During the night Pharaoh summoned Moses and Aaron and said, "Up! Leave my people, you and the Israelites! Go, worship the LORD as you have requested. 32Take your flocks and herds, as you have said, and go. And also bless me."

33The Egyptians urged the people to hurry and leave the country. "For otherwise," they said, "we will all die!" 34So the people took their dough before the yeast was added, and carried it on their shoulders in kneading troughs wrapped in clothing. 35The Israelites did as Moses instructed and asked the Egyptians for articles of silver and gold and for clothing. 36The LORD had made the Egyptians favorably disposed toward the people, and they gave them what they asked for; so they plundered the Egyptians.

37The Israelites journeyed from Rameses to Succoth. There were about six hundred thousand men on foot, besides women and children. 38Many other people went up with them, as well as large droves of livestock, both flocks and herds. 39With the dough they had brought from Egypt, they baked cakes of unleavened bread. The dough was without yeast because they had been driven out of Egypt and did not have time to prepare food for themselves.

40Now the length of time the Israelite people lived in Egypt*a* was 430 years. 41At the end of the 430 years, to the very day, all the LORD's divisions left Egypt. 42Because the LORD kept vigil that night to bring them out of Egypt, on this night all the Israelites are to keep vigil to honor the LORD for the generations to come.

Passover Restrictions

43The LORD said to Moses and Aaron, "These are the regulations for the Passover:

---

a 40 Masoretic Text; Samaritan Pentateuch and Septuagint Egypt and Canaan

"No foreigner is to eat of it. ⁴⁴Any slave you have bought may eat of it after you have circumcised him, ⁴⁵but a temporary resident and a hired worker may not eat of it.

⁴⁶"It must be eaten inside one house; take none of the meat outside the house. Do not break any of the bones. ⁴⁷The whole community of Israel must celebrate it.

⁴⁸"An alien living among you who wants to celebrate the LORD's Passover must have all the males in his household circumcised; then he may take part like one born in the land. No uncircumcised male may eat of it. ⁴⁹The same law applies to the native-born and to the alien living among you."

⁵⁰All the Israelites did just what the LORD had commanded Moses and Aaron. ⁵¹And on that very day the LORD brought the Israelites out of Egypt by their divisions.

Consecration of the Firstborn

13 The LORD said to Moses, ²"Consecrate to me every firstborn male. The first offspring of every womb among the Israelites belongs to me, whether man or animal."

³Then Moses said to the people, "Commemorate this day, the day you came out of Egypt, out of the land of slavery, because the LORD brought you out of it with a mighty hand. Eat nothing containing yeast. ⁴Today, in the month of Abib, you are leaving. ⁵When the LORD brings you into the land of the Canaanites, Hittites, Amorites, Hivites and Jebusites — the land he swore to your forefathers to give you, a land flowing with milk and honey — you are to observe this ceremony in this month: ⁶For seven days eat bread made without yeast and on the seventh day hold a festival to the LORD. ⁷Eat unleavened bread during those seven days; nothing with yeast in it is to be seen among you, nor shall any yeast be seen anywhere within your borders. ⁸On that day tell your son, 'I do this because of what the LORD did for me when I came out of Egypt.' ⁹This observance will be for you like a sign on your hand and a reminder on your forehead that the law of the LORD is to be on your lips. For the LORD brought you out of Egypt with his mighty hand. ¹⁰You must keep this ordinance at the appointed time year after year.

¹¹"After the LORD brings you into the land of the Canaanites and gives it to you, as he promised on oath to you and your forefathers, ¹²you are to give over to the LORD the first off-

"外邦人都不可吃這羊羔。⁴⁴但各人用銀子買的奴僕,既受了割禮,就可以吃。⁴⁵寄居的和雇工人都不可吃。

⁴⁶"應當在一個房子裏吃,不可把一點肉從房子裏帶到外頭去。羊羔的骨頭一根也不可折斷。⁴⁷以色列全會眾都要守這禮。

⁴⁸"若有外人寄居在你們中間,願向耶和華守逾越節,他所有的男子務要受割禮,然後才容他前來遵守,他也就像本地人一樣;但未受割禮的,都不可吃這羊羔。⁴⁹本地人和寄居在你們中間的外人同歸一例。"

⁵⁰耶和華怎樣吩咐摩西、亞倫,以色列眾人就怎樣行了。⁵¹正當那日,耶和華將以色列人按着他們的軍隊,從埃及地領出來。

頭生的分別為聖

13 耶和華曉諭摩西說:²"以色列中凡頭生的,無論是人是牲畜,都是我的,要分別為聖歸我。"

³摩西對百姓說:"你們要記念從埃及為奴之家出來的這日,因為耶和華用大能的手將你們從這地方領出來,有酵的餅都不可吃。⁴亞筆月間的這日是你們出來的日子。⁵將來耶和華領你進迦南人、赫人、亞摩利人、希未人、耶布斯人之地,就是他向你的祖宗起誓應許給你那流奶與蜜之地,那時你要在這月間守這禮。⁶你要吃無酵餅七日,到第七日要向耶和華守節。⁷這七日之久,要吃無酵餅,在你四境之內不可見有酵的餅,也不可見發酵的物。⁸當那日,你要告訴你的兒子說:'這是因耶和華在我出埃及的時候為我所行的事。'⁹這要在你手上作記號,在你額上作記念,使耶和華的律法常在你口中,因為耶和華曾用大能的手將你從埃及領出來。¹⁰所以你每年要按着日期守這例。

¹¹"將來,耶和華照他向你和你祖宗所起的誓,將你領進迦南人之地,把這地賜給你。¹²那時你要將一

切頭生的，並牲畜中頭生的，歸給耶和華；公的都要屬耶和華。¹³凡頭生的驢，你要用羊羔代贖，若不代贖，就要打折牠的頸項。凡你兒子中頭生的都要贖出來。

¹⁴“日後，你的兒子問你說：‘這是甚麼意思？’你就說：‘耶和華用大能的手將我們從埃及為奴之家領大能的手將我們從埃及為奴之家領出來，耶和華幾乎不容我們去，耶和華就把埃及地所有頭生的，無論是人是牲畜，都殺了，因此我把一切頭生的公牲畜獻給耶和華為祭，但將頭生的兒子都贖出來。’¹⁶這要在你手上作記號，在你額上作經文，因為耶和華用大能的手將我們從埃及領出來。”

過紅海

¹⁷法老容百姓去的時候，非利士地的道路雖近，神卻不領他們從那裏走，因為神說：“恐怕百姓遇見打仗後悔，就回埃及去。”¹⁸所以神領百姓繞道而行，走紅海曠野的路。以色列人出埃及地，都帶着兵器上去。

¹⁹摩西把約瑟的骸骨一同帶去，因為約瑟曾叫以色列人嚴嚴地起誓，對他們說：“神必眷顧你們，你們要把我的骸骨從這裏一同帶上去。”

²⁰他們從疏割起行，在曠野邊的以倘安營。²¹日間，耶和華在雲柱中領他們的路；夜間，在火柱中光照他們，使他們日夜都可以行走。²²日間雲柱，夜間火柱，總不離開百姓的面前。

14 耶和華曉諭摩西說：²“你吩咐以色列人轉回，安營在比哈希錄前、密奪和海的中間，對着巴力洗分靠近海邊安營。³法老必說：‘以色列人在地中繞迷了，曠野把他們困住了。’⁴我要使法老的心剛硬，他要追趕他們，我便在法老和他全軍身上得榮耀，埃及人就知道我是耶和華。”於是，以色列人這樣行了。

spring of every womb. All the firstborn males of your livestock belong to the LORD. ¹³Redeem with a lamb every firstborn donkey, but if you do not redeem it, break its neck. Redeem every firstborn among your sons.

¹⁴“In days to come, when your son asks you, 'What does this mean?' say to him, 'With a mighty hand the LORD brought us out of Egypt, out of the land of slavery. ¹⁵When Pharaoh stubbornly refused to let us go, the LORD killed every firstborn in Egypt, both man and animal. This is why I sacrifice to the LORD the first male offspring of every womb and redeem each of my firstborn sons.' ¹⁶And it will be like a sign on your hand and a symbol on your forehead that the LORD brought us out of Egypt with his mighty hand.”

Crossing the Sea

¹⁷When Pharaoh let the people go, God did not lead them on the road through the Philistine country, though that was shorter. For God said, “If they face war, they might change their minds and return to Egypt.” ¹⁸So God led the people around by the desert road toward the Red Sea.ᵃ The Israelites went up out of Egypt armed for battle.

¹⁹Moses took the bones of Joseph with him because Joseph had made the sons of Israel swear an oath. He had said, “God will surely come to your aid, and then you must carry my bones up with you from this place.”ᵇ

²⁰After leaving Succoth they camped at Etham on the edge of the desert. ²¹By day the LORD went ahead of them in a pillar of cloud to guide them on their way and by night in a pillar of fire to give them light, so that they could travel by day or night. ²²Neither the pillar of cloud by day nor the pillar of fire by night left its place in front of the people.

14 Then the LORD said to Moses, ²“Tell the Israelites to turn back and encamp near Pi Hahiroth, between Migdol and the sea. They are to encamp by the sea, directly opposite Baal Zephon. ³Pharaoh will think, 'The Israelites are wandering around the land in confusion, hemmed in by the desert.' ⁴And I will harden Pharaoh's heart, and he will pursue them. But I will gain glory for myself through Pharaoh and all his army, and the Egyptians will know that I am the LORD.” So the Israelites did this.

a 18 Hebrew *Yam Suph*; that is, Sea of Reeds　　b 19 See Gen. 50:25.

⁵When the king of Egypt was told that the people had fled, Pharaoh and his officials changed their minds about them and said, "What have we done? We have let the Israelites go and have lost their services!" ⁶So he had his chariot made ready and took his army with him. ⁷He took six hundred of the best chariots, along with all the other chariots of Egypt, with officers over all of them. ⁸The LORD hardened the heart of Pharaoh king of Egypt, so that he pursued the Israelites, who were marching out boldly. ⁹The Egyptians—all Pharaoh's horses and chariots, horsemen^a and troops—pursued the Israelites and overtook them as they camped by the sea near Pi Hahiroth, opposite Baal Zephon.

¹⁰As Pharaoh approached, the Israelites looked up, and there were the Egyptians, marching after them. They were terrified and cried out to the LORD. ¹¹They said to Moses, "Was it because there were no graves in Egypt that you brought us to the desert to die? What have you done to us by bringing us out of Egypt? ¹²Didn't we say to you in Egypt, 'Leave us alone; let us serve the Egyptians'? It would have been better for us to serve the Egyptians than to die in the desert!"

¹³Moses answered the people, "Do not be afraid. Stand firm and you will see the deliverance the LORD will bring you today. The Egyptians you see today you will never see again. ¹⁴The LORD will fight for you; you need only to be still."

¹⁵Then the LORD said to Moses, "Why are you crying out to me? Tell the Israelites to move on. ¹⁶Raise your staff and stretch out your hand over the sea to divide the water so that the Israelites can go through the sea on dry ground. ¹⁷I will harden the hearts of the Egyptians so that they will go in after them. And I will gain glory through Pharaoh and all his army, through his chariots and his horsemen. ¹⁸The Egyptians will know that I am the LORD when I gain glory through Pharaoh, his chariots and his horsemen."

¹⁹Then the angel of God, who had been traveling in front of Israel's army, withdrew and went behind them. The pillar of cloud also moved from in front and stood behind them, ²⁰coming between the armies of Egypt and Israel. Throughout the night the cloud brought darkness to the one side and light to the other side; so neither went near the other all night long.

⁵有人告訴埃及王說："百姓逃跑！"法老和他的臣僕就向百姓變心，說："我們容以色列人去不再服侍我們，這做的是甚麼事呢？" ⁶法老就預備他的車輛，帶領軍兵同去，⁷並帶着六百輛特選的車和埃及所有的車，每輛都有車兵長。⁸耶和華使埃及王法老的心剛硬，他就追趕以色列人，因為以色列人是昂然無懼地出埃及。⁹埃及人追趕他們，法老一切的馬匹、車輛、馬兵與軍兵，就在海邊上靠近比哈希錄對着巴力洗分，在他們安營的地方追上了。

¹⁰法老臨近的時候，以色列人舉目看見埃及人追來，就甚懼怕，向耶和華哀求。¹¹他們對摩西說："難道在埃及沒有墳地，你把我們帶來死在曠野嗎？你為甚麼這樣待我們，將我們從埃及領出來呢？¹²我們在埃及豈沒有對你說過，不要攪擾我們，容我們服侍埃及人？因為服侍埃及人比死在曠野還好。"

¹³摩西對百姓說："不要懼怕，只管站住！看耶和華今天向你們所要施行的救恩。因為，你們今天所看見的埃及人，必永遠不再看見了。¹⁴耶和華必為你們爭戰，你們只管靜默，不要做聲。"

¹⁵耶和華對摩西說："你為甚麼向我哀求呢？你吩咐以色列人往前走。¹⁶你舉手向海伸杖，把水分開，以色列人要下海中走乾地。¹⁷我要使埃及人的心剛硬，他們就跟着下去，我要在法老和他的全軍、車輛、馬兵上得榮耀。¹⁸我在法老和他的車輛、馬兵上得榮耀的時候，埃及人就知道我是耶和華了。"

¹⁹在以色列營前行走神的使者，轉到他們後邊去；雲柱也從他們前邊轉到他們後邊立。²⁰在埃及營和以色列營中間有雲柱，一邊黑暗，一邊發光，終夜兩下不得相近。

---

a 9 Or charioteers; also in verses 17, 18, 23, 26 and 28

21摩西向海伸杖，耶和華便用大東風，使海水一夜退去，水便分開，海就成了乾地。22以色列人下海中走乾地，水在他們的左右作了牆垣。

23埃及人追趕他們，法老一切的馬匹、車輛和馬兵都跟着下到海中。24到了晨更的時候，耶和華從雲火柱中向埃及的軍兵觀看，使埃及的軍兵混亂了；25又使他們的車輪脫落，難以行走，以致埃及人說：「我們從以色列人面前逃跑吧！因耶和華為他們攻擊我們了。」

26耶和華對摩西說：「你向海伸杖，叫水仍合在埃及人並他們的車輛、馬兵身上。」27摩西就向海伸杖，到了天一亮，海水仍舊復原。埃及人避水逃跑的時候，耶和華把他們推翻在海中，28水就回流，淹沒了車輛和馬兵，那些跟着以色列人下海法老的全軍，連一個也沒有剩下。

29以色列人卻在海中走乾地，水在他們的左右作了牆垣。30當日，耶和華這樣拯救以色列人脫離埃及人的手，以色列人看見埃及人的死屍都在海邊了。31以色列人看見耶和華向埃及人所行的大事，就敬畏耶和華，又信服他和他的僕人摩西。

摩西與米利暗的歌

15 那時，摩西和以色列人向耶和華唱歌說：

「我要向耶和華歌唱，
　因他大大戰勝，
將馬和騎馬的
　投在海中。
2耶和華是我的力量、我的詩歌，
　也成了我的拯救。
這是我的神，我要讚美他；
　是我父親的神，我要尊崇他。
3耶和華是戰士，
　他的名是耶和華。

21Then Moses stretched out his hand over the sea, and all that night the LORD drove the sea back with a strong east wind and turned it into dry land. The waters were divided, 22and the Israelites went through the sea on dry ground, with a wall of water on their right and on their left.

23The Egyptians pursued them, and all Pharaoh's horses and chariots and horsemen followed them into the sea. 24During the last watch of the night the LORD looked down from the pillar of fire and cloud at the Egyptian army and threw it into confusion. 25He made the wheels of their chariots come off[a] so that they had difficulty driving. And the Egyptians said, "Let's get away from the Israelites! The LORD is fighting for them against Egypt."

26Then the LORD said to Moses, "Stretch out your hand over the sea so that the waters may flow back over the Egyptians and their chariots and horsemen." 27Moses stretched out his hand over the sea, and at daybreak the sea went back to its place. The Egyptians were fleeing toward[b] it, and the LORD swept them into the sea. 28The water flowed back and covered the chariots and horsemen—the entire army of Pharaoh that had followed the Israelites into the sea. Not one of them survived.

29But the Israelites went through the sea on dry ground, with a wall of water on their right and on their left. 30That day the LORD saved Israel from the hands of the Egyptians, and Israel saw the Egyptians lying dead on the shore. 31And when the Israelites saw the great power the LORD displayed against the Egyptians, the people feared the LORD and put their trust in him and in Moses his servant.

The Song of Moses and Miriam

15 Then Moses and the Israelites sang this song to the LORD:

"I will sing to the LORD,
　for he is highly exalted.
The horse and its rider
　he has hurled into the sea.
2The LORD is my strength and my song;
　he has become my salvation.
He is my God, and I will praise him,
　my father's God, and I will exalt him.
3The LORD is a warrior;
　the LORD is his name.

a 25 Or He jammed the wheels of their chariots (see Samaritan Pentateuch, Septuagint and Syriac)　*b 27 Or from*

4Pharaoh's chariots and his army
    he has hurled into the sea.
The best of Pharaoh's officers
    are drowned in the Red Sea.*a*
5The deep waters have covered them;
    they sank to the depths like a stone.

6"Your right hand, O LORD,
    was majestic in power.
Your right hand, O LORD,
    shattered the enemy.
7In the greatness of your majesty
    you threw down those who opposed you.
You unleashed your burning anger;
    it consumed them like stubble.
8By the blast of your nostrils
    the waters piled up.
The surging waters stood firm like a wall;
    the deep waters congealed in the heart of the
       sea.

9"The enemy boasted,
    'I will pursue, I will overtake them.
I will divide the spoils;
    I will gorge myself on them.
I will draw my sword
    and my hand will destroy them.'
10But you blew with your breath,
    and the sea covered them.
They sank like lead
    in the mighty waters.

11"Who among the gods is like you, O LORD?
    Who is like you—
       majestic in holiness,
       awesome in glory,
       working wonders?
12You stretched out your right hand
    and the earth swallowed them.

13"In your unfailing love you will lead
    the people you have redeemed.
In your strength you will guide them
    to your holy dwelling.
14The nations will hear and tremble;
    anguish will grip the people of Philistia.
15The chiefs of Edom will be terrified,
    the leaders of Moab will be seized with
       trembling,
the people*b* of Canaan will melt away;
16 terror and dread will fall upon them.
By the power of your arm
    they will be as still as a stone—

4法老的車輛、軍兵,
    耶和華已拋在海中,
他特選的軍長
    都沉於紅海。
5深水淹沒他們,
    他們如同石頭墜到深處。

6 "耶和華啊,你的右手
    施展能力,顯出榮耀;
耶和華啊,你的右手
    摔碎仇敵。
7你大發威嚴,
    推翻那些起來攻擊你的;
你發出烈怒如火,
    燒滅他們像燒碎稭一樣。
8你發鼻中的氣,
    水便聚起成堆,
大水直立如壘,
    海中的深水凝結。

9 "仇敵說:
    '我要追趕,我要追上;
我要分擄物,
    我要在他們身上稱我的心願。
我要拔出刀來,
    親手殺滅他們。'
10你叫風一吹,
    海就把他們淹沒;
他們如鉛沉在大水之中。

11 "耶和華啊,
    眾神之中誰能像你?
誰能像你至聖至榮,
    可頌可畏,
    施行奇事?
12你伸出右手,
    地便吞滅他們。

13 "你憑慈愛
    領了你所贖的百姓;
你憑能力
    引他們到了你的聖所。
14外邦人聽見就發顫,
    疼痛抓住非利士的居民;
15那時,
    以東的族長驚惶,
摩押的英雄被戰兢抓住,
    迦南的居民心都消化了。
16驚駭恐懼臨到他們。
    耶和華啊,因你膀臂的大能,
他們如石頭寂然不動,

---

a 4 Hebrew *Yam Suph*; that is, Sea of Reeds; also in verse 22
b 15 Or *rulers*

等候你的百姓過去，
　　等候你所贖的百姓過去。
17你要將他們領進去，
　　栽於你產業的山上。
耶和華啊，
　　就是你為自己所造的住處；
主啊，
　　就是你手所建立的聖所。
18耶和華必作王，
　　直到永永遠遠！」

19法老的馬匹、車輛和馬兵下到海中，耶和華使海水回流淹沒他們，惟有以色列人在海中走乾地。20亞倫的姐姐女先知米利暗，手裏拿着鼓，眾婦女也跟她出去拿鼓跳舞。21米利暗應聲說：

「你們要歌頌耶和華，
　　因他大大戰勝，
將馬和騎馬的
　　投在海中。」

瑪拉與以琳的泉水

22摩西領以色列人從紅海往前行，到了書珥的曠野，在曠野走了三天，找不着水。23到了瑪拉，不能喝那裏的水，因為水苦，所以那地名叫瑪拉。24百姓就向摩西發怨言，說：「我們喝甚麼呢？」

25摩西呼求耶和華，耶和華指示他一棵樹，他把樹丟在水裏，水就變甜了。
耶和華在那裏為他們定了律例、典章，在那裏試驗他們。26又說：「你若留意聽耶和華你神的話，又行我眼中看為正的事，留心聽我的誡命，守我一切的律例，我就不將所加與埃及人的疾病加在你身上，因為我耶和華是醫治你的。」

27他們到了以琳，在那裏有十二股水泉，七十棵棕樹，他們就在那裏的水邊安營。

嗎哪與鵪鶉

16 以色列全會眾從以琳起行，在出埃及後第二個月十五日，到了以琳和西奈中間、

until your people pass by, O LORD,
until the people you bought[a] pass by.
17You will bring them in and plant them
on the mountain of your inheritance—
the place, O LORD, you made for your
dwelling,
the sanctuary, O Lord, your hands
established.
18The LORD will reign
for ever and ever."

19When Pharaoh's horses, chariots and horsemen[b] went into the sea, the LORD brought the waters of the sea back over them, but the Israelites walked through the sea on dry ground. 20Then Miriam the prophetess, Aaron's sister, took a tambourine in her hand, and all the women followed her, with tambourines and dancing. 21Miriam sang to them:

"Sing to the LORD,
for he is highly exalted.
The horse and its rider
he has hurled into the sea."

The Waters of Marah and Elim

22Then Moses led Israel from the Red Sea and they went into the Desert of Shur. For three days they traveled in the desert without finding water. 23When they came to Marah, they could not drink its water because it was bitter. (That is why the place is called Marah.[c]) 24So the people grumbled against Moses, saying, "What are we to drink?"

25Then Moses cried out to the LORD, and the LORD showed him a piece of wood. He threw it into the water, and the water became sweet.

There the LORD made a decree and a law for them, and there he tested them. 26He said, "If you listen carefully to the voice of the LORD your God and do what is right in his eyes, if you pay attention to his commands and keep all his decrees, I will not bring on you any of the diseases I brought on the Egyptians, for I am the LORD, who heals you."

27Then they came to Elim, where there were twelve springs and seventy palm trees, and they camped there near the water.

Manna and Quail

16 The whole Israelite community set out from Elim and came to the Desert of Sin, which is between Elim and Sinai, on the fifteenth day of the second month after they had

a 16 Or created　　b 19 Or charioteers　　c 23 Marah means bitter.

come out of Egypt. ²In the desert the whole community grumbled against Moses and Aaron. ³The Israelites said to them, "If only we had died by the LORD's hand in Egypt! There we sat around pots of meat and ate all the food we wanted, but you have brought us out into this desert to starve this entire assembly to death."

⁴Then the LORD said to Moses, "I will rain down bread from heaven for you. The people are to go out each day and gather enough for that day. In this way I will test them and see whether they will follow my instructions. ⁵On the sixth day they are to prepare what they bring in, and that is to be twice as much as they gather on the other days."

⁶So Moses and Aaron said to all the Israelites, "In the evening you will know that it was the LORD who brought you out of Egypt, ⁷and in the morning you will see the glory of the LORD, because he has heard your grumbling against him. Who are we, that you should grumble against us?" ⁸Moses also said, "You will know that it was the LORD when he gives you meat to eat in the evening and all the bread you want in the morning, because he has heard your grumbling against him. Who are we? You are not grumbling against us, but against the LORD."

⁹Then Moses told Aaron, "Say to the entire Israelite community, 'Come before the LORD, for he has heard your grumbling.'"

¹⁰While Aaron was speaking to the whole Israelite community, they looked toward the desert, and there was the glory of the LORD appearing in the cloud.

¹¹The LORD said to Moses, ¹²"I have heard the grumbling of the Israelites. Tell them, 'At twilight you will eat meat, and in the morning you will be filled with bread. Then you will know that I am the LORD your God.'"

¹³That evening quail came and covered the camp, and in the morning there was a layer of dew around the camp. ¹⁴When the dew was gone, thin flakes like frost on the ground appeared on the desert floor. ¹⁵When the Israelites saw it, they said to each other, "What is it?" For they did not know what it was.

Moses said to them, "It is the bread the LORD has given you to eat. ¹⁶This is what the LORD has commanded: 'Each one is to gather as much as he needs. Take an omer*a* for each person you have in your tent.'"

¹⁷The Israelites did as they were told; some gathered much, some little. ¹⁸And when they

a 16 That is, probably about 2 quarts (about 2 liters); also in verses 18, 32, 33 and 36

汛的曠野。²以色列全會眾在曠野向摩西、亞倫發怨言，³說："巴不得我們早死在埃及地耶和華的手下；那時我們坐在肉鍋旁邊，吃得飽足。你們將我們領出來，到這曠野，是要叫這全會眾都餓死啊！"

⁴耶和華對摩西說："我要將糧食從天降給你們。百姓可以出去，每天收每天的分，我好試驗他們遵不遵我的法度。⁵到第六天他們要把所收進來的預備好了，比每天所收的多一倍。"

⁶摩西、亞倫對以色列眾人說："到了晚上，你們要知道是耶和華將你們從埃及地領出來的。⁷早晨，你們要看見耶和華的榮耀，因為耶和華聽見你們向他所發的怨言了。我們算甚麼，你們竟向我們發怨言呢？"⁸摩西又說："耶和華晚上必給你們肉吃，早晨必給你們食物得飽，因為你們向耶和華發的怨言，他都聽見了。我們算甚麼？你們的怨言不是向我們發的，乃是向耶和華發的。"

⁹摩西對亞倫說："你告訴以色列全會眾說：'你們就近耶和華面前，因為他已經聽見你們的怨言了。'"

¹⁰亞倫正對以色列全會眾說話的時候，他們向曠野觀看，不料，耶和華的榮光在雲中顯現。

¹¹耶和華曉諭摩西說：¹²"我已經聽見以色列人的怨言，你告訴他們說：'到黃昏的時候，你們要吃肉，早晨必有食物得飽，你們就知道我是耶和華你們的神。'"

¹³到了晚上，有鵪鶉飛來，遮滿了營。早晨，在營四圍的地上有露水。¹⁴露水上升之後，不料，野地面上有如白霜的小圓物。¹⁵以色列人看見，不知道是甚麼，就彼此對問說："這是甚麼呢？"

摩西對他們說："這就是耶和華給你們吃的食物。¹⁶耶和華所吩咐的是這樣：你們要按着各人的飯量，為帳棚裏的人按着人數收起來，各拿一俄梅珥。"

¹⁷以色列人就這樣行；有多收的，有少收的。¹⁸及至用俄梅珥量一

量，多收的也沒有餘，少收的也沒有缺，各人按着自己的飯量收取。

19摩西對他們說："所收的，不許甚麼人留到早晨。"

20然而他們不聽摩西的話，內中有留到早晨的，就生蟲變臭了。摩西便向他們發怒。

21他們每日早晨，按着各人的飯量收取，日頭一發熱，就消化了。22到第六天，他們收了雙倍的食物，每人兩俄梅珥。會眾的官長來告訴摩西，23摩西對他們說："耶和華這樣說：'明天是聖安息日，是向耶和華守的聖安息日，你們要烤的就烤了，要煮的就煮了，所剩下的都留到早晨。'"

24他們就照摩西的吩咐留到早晨，也不臭，裏頭也沒有蟲子。25摩西說："你們今天吃這個吧！因為今天是向耶和華守的安息日，你們在田野必揀不着。26六天可以收取，第七天乃是安息日，那一天必沒有了。"

27第七天百姓中有人出去收，甚麼也找不着。28耶和華對摩西說："你們不肯守我的誡命和律法，要到幾時呢？29你們看！耶和華既將安息日賜給你們，所以第六天他賜給你們兩天的食物，第七天各人要住在自己的地方，不許甚麼人出去。"30於是，百姓第七天安息了。

31這食物，以色列家叫嗎哪，樣子像芫荽子，顏色是白的，滋味如同攙蜜的薄餅。32摩西說："耶和華所吩咐的是這樣：將一滿俄梅珥嗎哪留到世世代代，使後人可以看見我當日將你們領出埃及地，在曠野所給你們吃的食物。"

33摩西對亞倫說："你拿一個罐子，盛一滿俄梅珥嗎哪，存在耶和華面前，要留到世世代代。"

34耶和華怎麼吩咐摩西，亞倫就怎麼行，把嗎哪放在法櫃前存留。35以色列人吃嗎哪共四十年，直到進

measured it by the omer, he who gathered much did not have too much, and he who gathered little did not have too little. Each one gathered as much as he needed.

19Then Moses said to them, "No one is to keep any of it until morning."

20However, some of them paid no attention to Moses; they kept part of it until morning, but it was full of maggots and began to smell. So Moses was angry with them.

21Each morning everyone gathered as much as he needed, and when the sun grew hot, it melted away. 22On the sixth day, they gathered twice as much—two omers[a] for each person—and the leaders of the community came and reported this to Moses. 23He said to them, "This is what the LORD commanded: 'Tomorrow is to be a day of rest, a holy Sabbath to the LORD. So bake what you want to bake and boil what you want to boil. Save whatever is left and keep it until morning.'"

24So they saved it until morning, as Moses commanded, and it did not stink or get maggots in it. 25"Eat it today," Moses said, "because today is a Sabbath to the LORD. You will not find any of it on the ground today. 26Six days you are to gather it, but on the seventh day, the Sabbath, there will not be any."

27Nevertheless, some of the people went out on the seventh day to gather it, but they found none. 28Then the LORD said to Moses, "How long will you[b] refuse to keep my commands and my instructions? 29Bear in mind that the LORD has given you the Sabbath; that is why on the sixth day he gives you bread for two days. Everyone is to stay where he is on the seventh day; no one is to go out." 30So the people rested on the seventh day.

31The people of Israel called the bread manna.[c] It was white like coriander seed and tasted like wafers made with honey. 32Moses said, "This is what the LORD has commanded: 'Take an omer of manna and keep it for the generations to come, so they can see the bread I gave you to eat in the desert when I brought you out of Egypt.'"

33So Moses said to Aaron, "Take a jar and put an omer of manna in it. Then place it before the LORD to be kept for the generations to come."

34As the LORD commanded Moses, Aaron put the manna in front of the Testimony, that it might be kept. 35The Israelites ate manna forty years,

a 22 That is, probably about 4 quarts (about 4.5 liters)
b 28 The Hebrew is plural.　c 31 Manna means What is it? (see verse 15).

until they came to a land that was settled; they ate manna until they reached the border of Canaan. ³⁶(An omer is one tenth of an ephah.)

Water From the Rock

17 The whole Israelite community set out from the Desert of Sin, traveling from place to place as the LORD commanded. They camped at Rephidim, but there was no water for the people to drink. ²So they quarreled with Moses and said, "Give us water to drink."

Moses replied, "Why do you quarrel with me? Why do you put the LORD to the test?"

³But the people were thirsty for water there, and they grumbled against Moses. They said, "Why did you bring us up out of Egypt to make us and our children and livestock die of thirst?"

⁴Then Moses cried out to the LORD, "What am I to do with these people? They are almost ready to stone me."

⁵The LORD answered Moses, "Walk on ahead of the people. Take with you some of the elders of Israel and take in your hand the staff with which you struck the Nile, and go. ⁶I will stand there before you by the rock at Horeb. Strike the rock, and water will come out of it for the people to drink." So Moses did this in the sight of the elders of Israel. ⁷And he called the place Massah*ᵃ* and Meribah*ᵇ* because the Israelites quarreled and because they tested the LORD saying, "Is the LORD among us or not?"

The Amalekites Defeated

⁸The Amalekites came and attacked the Israelites at Rephidim. ⁹Moses said to Joshua, "Choose some of our men and go out to fight the Amalekites. Tomorrow I will stand on top of the hill with the staff of God in my hands."

¹⁰So Joshua fought the Amalekites as Moses had ordered, and Moses, Aaron and Hur went to the top of the hill. ¹¹As long as Moses held up his hands, the Israelites were winning, but whenever he lowered his hands, the Amalekites were winning. ¹²When Moses' hands grew tired, they took a stone and put it under him and he sat on it. Aaron and Hur held his hands up— one on one side, one on the other—so that his hands remained steady till sunset. ¹³So Joshua overcame the Amalekite army with the sword.

¹⁴Then the LORD said to Moses, "Write this on a scroll as something to be remembered and make sure that Joshua hears it, because I will completely blot out the memory of Amalek from under heaven."

了有人居住之地，就是迦南的境界。
³⁶（俄梅珥乃伊法十分之一。）

磐石出水

17 以色列全會眾都遵耶和華的吩咐，按着站口從汛的曠野往前行，在利非訂安營。百姓沒有水喝，²所以與摩西爭鬧，說：「給我們水喝吧！」

摩西對他們說：「你們為甚麼與我爭鬧，為甚麼試探耶和華呢？」

³百姓在那裏甚渴，要喝水，就向摩西發怨言，說：「你為甚麼將我們從埃及領出來，使我們和我們的兒女並牲畜都渴死呢？」

⁴摩西就呼求耶和華說：「我向這百姓怎樣行呢？他們幾乎要拿石頭打死我。」

⁵耶和華對摩西說：「你手裏拿着你先前擊打河水的杖，帶領以色列的幾個長老，從百姓面前走過去。⁶我必在何烈的磐石那裏站在你面前，你要擊打磐石，從磐石裏必有水流出來，使百姓可以喝。」摩西就在以色列的長老眼前這樣行了。⁷他給那地方起名叫瑪撒（註：就是「試探」的意思），又叫米利巴（註：就是「爭鬧」的意思），因以色列人爭鬧，又因他們試探耶和華說：「耶和華是在我們中間不是？」

打敗亞瑪力人

⁸那時，亞瑪力人來在利非訂，和以色列人爭戰。⁹摩西對約書亞說：「你為我們選出人來，出去和亞瑪力人爭戰。明天我手裏要拿着神的杖，站在山頂上。」

¹⁰於是約書亞照着摩西對他所說的話行，和亞瑪力人爭戰。摩西、亞倫與戶珥都上了山頂。¹¹摩西何時舉手，以色列人就得勝；何時垂手，亞瑪力人就得勝。¹²但摩西的手發沉，他們就搬石頭來，放在他以下，他就坐在上面。亞倫與戶珥扶着他的手，一個在這邊，一個在那邊，他的手就穩住，直到日落的時候。¹³約書亞用刀殺了亞瑪力王和他的百姓。

¹⁴耶和華對摩西說：「我要將亞瑪力的名號從天下全然塗抹了，你要將這話寫在書上作紀念，又念給約書亞聽。」

---

a 7 Massah means *testing.*　　*b 7 Meribah* means *quarreling.*

15摩西築了一座壇，起名叫耶和華尼西（註：就是"耶和華是我旌旗"的意思）；16又說："耶和華已經起了誓，必世世代代和亞瑪力人爭戰。"

葉忒羅來見摩西

18 摩西的岳父米甸祭司葉忒羅，聽見神為摩西和神的百姓以色列所行的一切事，就是耶和華將以色列從埃及領出來的事。

2便帶着摩西的妻子西坡拉，就是摩西從前打發回去的，3又帶着西坡拉的兩個兒子，一個名叫革舜，因為摩西說："我在外邦作了寄居的"；4一個名叫以利以謝，因為他說："我父親的神幫助了我，救我脫離法老的刀。"

5摩西的岳父葉忒羅，帶着摩西的妻子和兩個兒子來到神的山，就是摩西在曠野安營的地方。6他對摩西說："我是你岳父葉忒羅，帶着你的妻子和兩個兒子來到你這裏。"

7摩西迎接他的岳父，向他下拜，與他親嘴，彼此問安，都進了帳棚。8摩西將耶和華為以色列的緣故向法老和埃及人所行的一切事，以及路上所遭遇的一切艱難，並耶和華怎樣搭救他們，都述說與他岳父聽。

9葉忒羅因耶和華待以色列的一切好處，就是拯救他們脫離埃及人的手，便甚歡喜。10葉忒羅說："耶和華是應當稱頌的，他救了你們脫離埃及人和法老的手，將這百姓從埃及人的手下救出來。11我現今在埃及人向這百姓發狂傲的事上，得知耶和華比萬神都大。"12摩西的岳父葉忒羅把燔祭和平安祭獻給神。亞倫和以色列的眾長老都來了，與摩西的岳父在神面前吃飯。

13第二天，摩西坐着審判百姓，百姓從早到晚都站在摩西的左右。14摩西的岳父看見他向百姓所做的一

Jethro Visits Moses

18 Now Jethro, the priest of Midian and father-in-law of Moses, heard of everything God had done for Moses and for his people Israel, and how the LORD had brought Israel out of Egypt.

2After Moses had sent away his wife Zipporah, his father-in-law Jethro received her 3and her two sons. One son was named Gershom,[b] for Moses said, "I have become an alien in a foreign land"; 4and the other was named Eliezer,[c] for he said, "My father's God was my helper; he saved me from the sword of Pharaoh."

5Jethro, Moses' father-in-law, together with Moses' sons and wife, came to him in the desert, where he was camped near the mountain of God. 6Jethro had sent word to him, "I, your father-in-law Jethro, am coming to you with your wife and her two sons."

7So Moses went out to meet his father-in-law and bowed down and kissed him. They greeted each other and then went into the tent. 8Moses told his father-in-law about everything the LORD had done to Pharaoh and the Egyptians for Israel's sake and about all the hardships they had met along the way and how the LORD had saved them.

9Jethro was delighted to hear about all the good things the LORD had done for Israel in rescuing them from the hand of the Egyptians. 10He said, "Praise be to the LORD, who rescued you from the hand of the Egyptians and of Pharaoh, and who rescued the people from the hand of the Egyptians. 11Now I know that the LORD is greater than all other gods, for he did this to those who had treated Israel arrogantly." 12Then Jethro, Moses' father-in-law, brought a burnt offering and other sacrifices to God, and Aaron came with all the elders of Israel to eat bread with Moses' father-in-law in the presence of God.

13The next day Moses took his seat to serve as judge for the people, and they stood around him from morning till evening. 14When his father-in-

a 16 Or "Because a hand was against the throne of the LORD, the
b 3 Gershom sounds like the Hebrew for an alien there.
c 4 Eliezer means my God is helper.

law saw all that Moses was doing for the people, he said, "What is this you are doing for the people? Why do you alone sit as judge, while all these people stand around you from morning till evening?"

15Moses answered him, "Because the people come to me to seek God's will. 16Whenever they have a dispute, it is brought to me, and I decide between the parties and inform them of God's decrees and laws."

17Moses' father-in-law replied, "What you are doing is not good. 18You and these people who come to you will only wear yourselves out. The work is too heavy for you; you cannot handle it alone. 19Listen now to me and I will give you some advice, and may God be with you. You must be the people's representative before God and bring their disputes to him. 20Teach them the decrees and laws, and show them the way to live and the duties they are to perform. 21But select capable men from all the people—men who fear God, trustworthy men who hate dishonest gain—and appoint them as officials over thousands, hundreds, fifties and tens. 22Have them serve as judges for the people at all times, but have them bring every difficult case to you; the simple cases they can decide themselves. That will make your load lighter, because they will share it with you. 23If you do this and God so commands, you will be able to stand the strain, and all these people will go home satisfied."

24Moses listened to his father-in-law and did everything he said. 25He chose capable men from all Israel and made them leaders of the people, officials over thousands, hundreds, fifties and tens. 26They served as judges for the people at all times. The difficult cases they brought to Moses, but the simple ones they decided themselves.

27Then Moses sent his father-in-law on his way, and Jethro returned to his own country.

At Mount Sinai

19 In the third month after the Israelites left Egypt—on the very day—they came to the Desert of Sinai. 2After they set out from Rephidim, they entered the Desert of Sinai, and Israel camped there in the desert in front of the mountain.

3Then Moses went up to God, and the LORD called to him from the mountain and said, "This is what you are to say to the house of Jacob and what you are to tell the people of Israel: 4'You yourselves have seen what I did to Egypt, and how I carried you on eagles' wings and brought

切事，就說："你向百姓做的是甚麼事呢？你為甚麼獨自坐着，眾百姓從早到晚都站在你的左右呢？"

15摩西對岳父說："這是因百姓到我這裏來求問神。16他們有事的時候就到我這裏來，我便在兩造之間施行審判，我又叫他們知道神的律例和法度。"

17摩西的岳父說："你這做的不好。18你和這些百姓必都疲憊，因為這事太重，你獨自一人辦理不了。19現在你要聽我的話，我為你出個主意，願神與你同在。你要替百姓到神面前，將案件奏告神；20又要將律例和法度教訓他們，指示他們當行的道、當做的事；21並要從百姓中揀選有才能的人，就是敬畏神、誠實無妄、恨不義之財的人，派他們作千夫長、百夫長、五十夫長、十夫長，管理百姓。22叫他們隨時審判百姓，大事都要呈到你這裏，小事他們自己可以審判。這樣，你就輕省些，他們也可以同當此任。23你若這樣行，神也這樣吩咐你，你就能受得住，這百姓也都平平安安歸回他們的住處。"

24於是，摩西聽從他岳父的話，按着他所說的去行。25摩西從以色列人中揀選了有才能的人，立他們為百姓的首領，作千夫長、百夫長、五十夫長、十夫長。26他們隨時審判百姓，有難斷的案件就呈到摩西那裏，但各樣小事他們自己審判。

27此後，摩西讓他的岳父去，他就往本地去了。

在西奈山

19 以色列人出埃及地以後，滿了三個月的那一天，就來到西奈的曠野。2他們離了利非訂，來到西奈的曠野，就在那裏的山下安營。

3摩西到神那裏，耶和華從山上呼喚他說："你要這樣告訴雅各家，曉諭以色列人說：4'我向埃及人所行的事，你們都看見了，且看見我如鷹將你們背在翅膀上，帶來歸我。

⁵如今你們若實在聽從我的話，遵守我的約，就要在萬民中作屬我的子民，因為全地都是我的。⁶你們要歸我作祭司的國度，為聖潔的國民。'這些話你要告訴以色列人。"

⁷摩西去召了民間的長老來，將耶和華所吩咐他的話，都在他們面前陳明。⁸百姓都同聲回答說："凡耶和華所說的，我們都要遵行。"摩西就將百姓的話回覆耶和華。

⁹耶和華對摩西說："我要在密雲中臨到你那裏，叫百姓在我與你說話的時候可以聽見，也可以永遠信你了。"於是摩西將百姓的話奏告耶和華。

¹⁰耶和華又對摩西說："你往百姓那裏去，叫他們今天明天自潔，又叫他們洗衣服。¹¹到第三天要預備好了，因為第三天耶和華要在眾百姓眼前降臨在西奈山上。¹²你要在山的四圍給百姓定界限，說：'你們當謹慎，不可上山去，也不可摸山的邊界；凡摸這山的，必要治死他。¹³不可用手摸他，必用石頭打死，或用箭射透；無論是人是牲畜，都不得活。'到角聲拖長的時候，他們才可到山根來。"

¹⁴摩西下山往百姓那裏去，叫他們自潔，他們就洗衣服。¹⁵他對百姓說："到第三天要預備好了，不可親近女人。"

¹⁶到了第三天早晨，在山上有雷轟、閃電和密雲，並且角聲甚大，營中的百姓盡都發顫。¹⁷摩西率領百姓出營迎接神，都站在山下。¹⁸西奈全山冒煙，因為耶和華在火中降於此上，山的煙氣上騰，如燒窰一般，遍山大大地震動。¹⁹角聲漸漸地高而又高，摩西就說話，神有聲音答應他。

you to myself. ⁵Now if you obey me fully and keep my covenant, then out of all nations you will be my treasured possession. Although the whole earth is mine, ⁶you*ᵃ* will be for me a kingdom of priests and a holy nation.' These are the words you are to speak to the Israelites."

⁷So Moses went back and summoned the elders of the people and set before them all the words the LORD had commanded him to speak. ⁸The people all responded together, "We will do everything the LORD has said." So Moses brought their answer back to the LORD.

⁹The LORD said to Moses, "I am going to come to you in a dense cloud, so that the people will hear me speaking with you and will always put their trust in you." Then Moses told the LORD what the people had said.

¹⁰And the LORD said to Moses, "Go to the people and consecrate them today and tomorrow. Have them wash their clothes ¹¹and be ready by the third day, because on that day the LORD will come down on Mount Sinai in the sight of all the people. ¹²Put limits for the people around the mountain and tell them, 'Be careful that you do not go up the mountain or touch the foot of it. Whoever touches the mountain shall surely be put to death. ¹³He shall surely be stoned or shot with arrows; not a hand is to be laid on him. Whether man or animal, he shall not be permitted to live.' Only when the ram's horn sounds a long blast may they go up to the mountain."

¹⁴After Moses had gone down the mountain to the people, he consecrated them, and they washed their clothes. ¹⁵Then he said to the people, "Prepare yourselves for the third day. Abstain from sexual relations."

¹⁶On the morning of the third day there was thunder and lightning, with a thick cloud over the mountain, and a very loud trumpet blast. Everyone in the camp trembled. ¹⁷Then Moses led the people out of the camp to meet with God, and they stood at the foot of the mountain. ¹⁸Mount Sinai was covered with smoke, because the LORD descended on it in fire. The smoke billowed up from it like smoke from a furnace, the whole mountain*ᵇ* trembled violently, ¹⁹and the sound of the trumpet grew louder and louder. Then Moses spoke and the voice of God answered him.*ᶜ*

---

a 5,6 Or possession, for the whole earth is mine. ⁶You

b 18 Most Hebrew manuscripts; a few Hebrew manuscripts and Septuagint all the people   *c 19 Or and God answered him with thunder*

²⁰The LORD descended to the top of Mount Sinai and called Moses to the top of the mountain. So Moses went up ²¹and the LORD said to him, "Go down and warn the people so they do not force their way through to see the LORD and many of them perish. ²²Even the priests, who approach the LORD, must consecrate themselves, or the LORD will break out against them."

²³Moses said to the LORD, "The people cannot come up Mount Sinai, because you yourself warned us, 'Put limits around the mountain and set it apart as holy.' "

²⁴The LORD replied, "Go down and bring Aaron up with you. But the priests and the people must not force their way through to come up to the LORD, or he will break out against them."

²⁵So Moses went down to the people and told them.

The Ten Commandments

20 And God spoke all these words:

²"I am the LORD your God, who brought you out of Egypt, out of the land of slavery.

³"You shall have no other gods before^a me.

⁴"You shall not make for yourself an idol in the form of anything in heaven above or on the earth beneath or in the waters below. ⁵You shall not bow down to them or worship them; for I, the LORD your God, am a jealous God, punishing the children for the sin of the fathers to the third and fourth generation of those who hate me, ⁶but showing love to a thousand ⌊generations⌋ of those who love me and keep my commandments.

⁷"You shall not misuse the name of the LORD your God, for the LORD will not hold anyone guiltless who misuses his name.

⁸"Remember the Sabbath day by keeping it holy. ⁹Six days you shall labor and do all your work, ¹⁰but the seventh day is a Sabbath to the LORD your God. On it you shall not do any work, neither you, nor your son or daughter, nor your manservant or maidservant, nor your animals, nor the alien within your gates. ¹¹For in six days the LORD made the heavens and the earth, the sea, and all that is in them, but he rested on the seventh day. Therefore the LORD blessed the Sabbath day and made it holy.

²⁰耶和華降臨在西奈山頂上，耶和華召摩西上山頂，摩西就上去。
²¹耶和華對摩西說：「你下去囑咐百姓，不可闖過來到我面前觀看，恐怕他們有多人死亡；²²又叫親近我的祭司自潔，恐怕我忽然出來擊殺他們。」

²³摩西對耶和華說：「百姓不能上西奈山，因為你已經囑咐我們說：『要在山的四圍定界限，叫山成聖。』」

²⁴耶和華對他說：「下去吧！你要和亞倫一同上來，只是祭司和百姓不可闖過來上到我面前，恐怕我忽然出來擊殺他們。」

²⁵於是摩西下到百姓那裏告訴他們。

十誡

20 神吩咐這一切的話，說：

²「我是耶和華你的神，曾將你從埃及地為奴之家領出來。

³「除了我以外，你不可有別的神。

⁴「不可為自己雕刻偶像；也不可做甚麼形像彷彿上天、下地和地底下、水中的百物。⁵不可跪拜那些像；也不可侍奉它，因為我耶和華你的神，是忌邪的神。恨我的，我必追討他的罪，自父及子，直到三四代；⁶愛我、守我誡命的，我必向他們發慈愛，直到千代。

⁷「不可妄稱耶和華你神的名；因為妄稱耶和華名的，耶和華必不以他為無罪。

⁸「當記念安息日，守為聖日。⁹六日要勞碌做你一切的工，¹⁰但第七日是向耶和華你神當守的安息日。這一日你和你的兒女、僕婢、牲畜，並你城裏寄居的客旅，無論何工都不可做。¹¹因為六日之內，耶和華造天、地、海和其中的萬物，第七日便安息，所以耶和華賜福與安息日，定為聖日。

a 3 Or besides

12 “當孝敬父母，使你的日子在耶和
華你神所賜你的地上得以長
久。

13 “不可殺人。

14 “不可姦淫。

15 “不可偷盜。

16 “不可作假見證陷害人。

17 “不可貪戀人的房屋；也不可貪戀
人的妻子、僕婢、牛驢，並他
一切所有的。”

18 眾百姓見雷轟、閃電、角聲、
山上冒煙，就都發顫，遠遠地站立，
19 對摩西說：“求你和我們說話，我
們必聽，不要神和我們說話，恐怕我
們死亡。”

20 摩西對百姓說：“不要懼怕，
因為神降臨是要試驗你們，叫你們時
常敬畏他，不至犯罪。”

21 於是百姓遠遠地站立，摩西就
挨近神所在的幽暗之中。

偶像與祭壇

22 耶和華對摩西說：“你要向以
色列人這樣說：‘你們自己看見我從
天上和你們說話了。23 你們不可做甚
麼神像與我相配，不可為自己做金銀
的神像。

24 “‘你要為我築土壇，在上面
以牛羊獻為燔祭和平安祭。凡記下我
名的地方，我必到那裏賜福給你。
25 你若為我築一座石壇，不可用鑿成
的石頭，因你在上頭一動家具，就把
壇污穢了。26 你上我的壇，不可用臺
階，免得露出你的下體來。’

21 “你在百姓面前所要立的典
章是這樣：

希伯來人奴僕

2 “你若買希伯來人作奴僕，他
必服侍你六年，第七年他可以自由，
白白地出去。3 他若孤身來，就可以
孤身去；他若有妻，他的妻就可以同
他出去。4 他主人若給他妻子，妻子

12 "Honor your father and your mother, so that
you may live long in the land the LORD
your God is giving you.

13 "You shall not murder.

14 "You shall not commit adultery.

15 "You shall not steal.

16 "You shall not give false testimony against
your neighbor.

17 "You shall not covet your neighbor's house.
You shall not covet your neighbor's wife,
or his manservant or maidservant, his ox
or donkey, or anything that belongs to
your neighbor."

18 When the people saw the thunder and
lightning and heard the trumpet and saw the
mountain in smoke, they trembled with fear.
They stayed at a distance 19 and said to Moses,
"Speak to us yourself and we will listen. But do
not have God speak to us or we will die."

20 Moses said to the people, "Do not be afraid.
God has come to test you, so that the fear of God
will be with you to keep you from sinning."

21 The people remained at a distance, while
Moses approached the thick darkness where
God was.

Idols and Altars

22 Then the LORD said to Moses, "Tell the
Israelites this: 'You have seen for yourselves
that I have spoken to you from heaven: 23 Do not
make any gods to be alongside me; do not make
for yourselves gods of silver or gods of gold.

24 " 'Make an altar of earth for me and sacrifice on it your burnt offerings and fellowship
offerings,[a] your sheep and goats and your cattle.
Wherever I cause my name to be honored, I will
come to you and bless you. 25 If you make an
altar of stones for me, do not build it with
dressed stones, for you will defile it if you use a
tool on it. 26 And do not go up to my altar on
steps, lest your nakedness be exposed on it.'

21 "These are the laws you are to set before
them:

Hebrew Servants

2 "If you buy a Hebrew servant, he is to serve
you for six years. But in the seventh year, he
shall go free, without paying anything. 3 If he
comes alone, he is to go free alone; but if he has
a wife when he comes, she is to go with him. 4 If
his master gives him a wife and she bears him

a 24 Traditionally peace offerings

sons or daughters, the woman and her children shall belong to her master, and only the man shall go free.

5"But if the servant declares, 'I love my master and my wife and children and do not want to go free,' 6then his master must take him before the judges.[a] He shall take him to the door or the doorpost and pierce his ear with an awl. Then he will be his servant for life.

7"If a man sells his daughter as a servant, she is not to go free as menservants do. 8If she does not please the master who has selected her for himself,[b] he must let her be redeemed. He has no right to sell her to foreigners, because he has broken faith with her. 9If he selects her for his son, he must grant her the rights of a daughter. 10If he marries another woman, he must not deprive the first one of her food, clothing and marital rights. 11If he does not provide her with these three things, she is to go free, without any payment of money.

Personal Injuries

12"Anyone who strikes a man and kills him shall surely be put to death. 13However, if he does not do it intentionally, but God lets it happen, he is to flee to a place I will designate. 14But if a man schemes and kills another man deliberately, take him away from my altar and put him to death.

15"Anyone who attacks[c] his father or his mother must be put to death.

16"Anyone who kidnaps another and either sells him or still has him when he is caught must be put to death.

17"Anyone who curses his father or mother must be put to death.

18"If men quarrel and one hits the other with a stone or with his fist[d] and he does not die but is confined to bed, 19the one who struck the blow will not be held responsible if the other gets up and walks around outside with his staff; however, he must pay the injured man for the loss of his time and see that he is completely healed.

20"If a man beats his male or female slave with a rod and the slave dies as a direct result, he must be punished, 21but he is not to be punished if the slave gets up after a day or two, since the slave is his property.

22"If men who are fighting hit a pregnant woman and she gives birth prematurely[e] but there is no serious injury, the offender must be

給他生了兒子或女兒,妻子和兒女要歸主人,他要獨自出去。

5 "倘或奴僕明說:'我愛我的主人和我的妻子兒女,不願意自由出去。'6他的主人就要帶他到審判官那裏(註:"審判官"或作"神"。下同),又要帶他到門前,靠着門框,用錐子穿他的耳朵,他就永遠服侍主人。

7 "人若賣女兒作婢女,婢女不可像男僕那樣出去。8主人選定她歸自己,若不喜歡她,就要許她贖身;主人既然用詭詐待她,就沒有權柄賣給外邦人。9主人若選定她給自己的兒子,就當待她如同女兒。10若另娶一個,那女子的吃食、衣服並好合的事,仍不可減少。11若不向她行這三樣,她就可以不用錢贖,白白地出去。

人身傷害

12 "打人以致打死的,必要把他治死。13人若不是埋伏着殺人,乃是神交在他手中,我就設下一個地方,他可以往那裏逃跑。14人若任意用詭計殺了他的鄰舍,就是逃到我的壇那裏,也當捉去把他治死。

15 "打父母的,必要把他治死。

16 "拐帶人口,或是把人賣了,或是留在他手下,必要把他治死。

17 "咒罵父母的,必要把他治死。

18 "人若彼此相爭,這個用石頭或是拳頭打那個,尚且不至於死,不過躺臥在牀,19若再能起來扶杖而出,那打他的可算無罪;但要將他誤的工夫用錢賠補,並要將他全然醫好。

20 "人若用棍子打奴僕或婢女,立時死在他的手下,他必要受刑;21若過一兩天才死,就可以不受刑,因為是用錢買的。

22 "人若彼此爭鬥,傷害有孕的婦人,甚至墜胎,隨後卻無別害,那

傷害她的總要按婦人的丈夫所要的，照審判官所斷的受罰。²³若有別害，就要以命償命，²⁴以眼還眼，以牙還牙，以手還手，以腳還腳，²⁵以烙還烙，以傷還傷，以打還打。

²⁶"人若打壞了他奴僕或是婢女的一隻眼，就要因他的眼放他去得以自由。²⁷若打掉了他奴僕或是婢女的一個牙，就要因他的牙放他去以自由。

²⁸"牛若觸死男人或是女人，總要用石頭打死那牛，卻不可吃牠的肉；牛的主人可算無罪。²⁹倘若那牛素來是觸人的，有人報告了牛主，他竟不把牛拴着，以致把男人或是女人觸死，就要用石頭打死那牛，牛主也必治死。³⁰若罰他贖命的價銀，他必照所罰的贖他的命。³¹牛無論觸了人的兒子或是女兒，必照這例辦理。³²牛若觸了奴僕或是婢女，必將銀子三十舍客勒給他們的主人，也要用石頭把牛打死。

³³"人若敞着井口，或挖井不遮蓋，有牛或驢掉在裏頭，³⁴井主要拿錢賠還本主人，死牲畜要歸自己。

³⁵"這人的牛若傷了那人的牛，以至於死，他們要賣了活牛，平分價值，也要平分死牛。³⁶人若知道這牛素來是觸人的，主人竟不把牛拴着，他必要以牛還牛，死牛要歸自己。

保護財產

22 "人若偷牛或羊，無論是宰了，是賣了，他就要以五牛賠一牛，四羊賠一羊。

² "人若遇見賊挖窟窿，把賊打了，以至於死，就不能為他有流血的罪；³若太陽已經出來，就為他有流血的罪。

"賊若被拿，總要賠還；若他一無所有，就要被賣，頂他所偷的物。

fined whatever the woman's husband demands and the court allows. ²³But if there is serious injury, you are to take life for life, ²⁴eye for eye, tooth for tooth, hand for hand, foot for foot, ²⁵burn for burn, wound for wound, bruise for bruise.

²⁶"If a man hits a manservant or maidservant in the eye and destroys it, he must let the servant go free to compensate for the eye. ²⁷And if he knocks out the tooth of a manservant or maidservant, he must let the servant go free to compensate for the tooth.

²⁸"If a bull gores a man or a woman to death, the bull must be stoned to death, and its meat must not be eaten. But the owner of the bull will not be held responsible. ²⁹If, however, the bull has had the habit of goring and the owner has been warned but has not kept it penned up and it kills a man or woman, the bull must be stoned and the owner also must be put to death. ³⁰However, if payment is demanded of him, he may redeem his life by paying whatever is demanded. ³¹This law also applies if the bull gores a son or daughter. ³²If the bull gores a male or female slave, the owner must pay thirty shekels^a of silver to the master of the slave, and the bull must be stoned.

³³"If a man uncovers a pit or digs one and fails to cover it and an ox or a donkey falls into it, ³⁴the owner of the pit must pay for the loss; he must pay its owner, and the dead animal will be his.

³⁵"If a man's bull injures the bull of another and it dies, they are to sell the live one and divide both the money and the dead animal equally. ³⁶However, if it was known that the bull had the habit of goring, yet the owner did not keep it penned up, the owner must pay, animal for animal, and the dead animal will be his.

Protection of Property

22 "If a man steals an ox or a sheep and slaughters it or sells it, he must pay back five head of cattle for the ox and four sheep for the sheep.

²"If a thief is caught breaking in and is struck so that he dies, the defender is not guilty of bloodshed; ³but if it happens^b after sunrise, he is guilty of bloodshed.

"A thief must certainly make restitution, but if he has nothing, he must be sold to pay for his theft.

---

a 32 That is, about 12 ounces (about 0.3 kilogram)　*b 3* Or *if he strikes him*

4"If the stolen animal is found alive in his possession—whether ox or donkey or sheep—he must pay back double.

5"If a man grazes his livestock in a field or vineyard and lets them stray and they graze in another man's field, he must make restitution from the best of his own field or vineyard.

6"If a fire breaks out and spreads into thornbushes so that it burns shocks of grain or standing grain or the whole field, the one who started the fire must make restitution.

7"If a man gives his neighbor silver or goods for safekeeping and they are stolen from the neighbor's house, the thief, if he is caught, must pay back double. 8But if the thief is not found, the owner of the house must appear before the judges[a] to determine whether he has laid his hands on the other man's property. 9In all cases of illegal possession of an ox, a donkey, a sheep, a garment, or any other lost property about which somebody says, 'This is mine,' both parties are to bring their cases before the judges. The one whom the judges declare[b] guilty must pay back double to his neighbor.

10"If a man gives a donkey, an ox, a sheep or any other animal to his neighbor for safekeeping and it dies or is injured or is taken away while no one is looking, 11the issue between them will be settled by the taking of an oath before the LORD that the neighbor did not lay hands on the other person's property. The owner is to accept this, and no restitution is required. 12But if the animal was stolen from the neighbor, he must make restitution to the owner. 13If it was torn to pieces by a wild animal, he shall bring in the remains as evidence and he will not be required to pay for the torn animal.

14"If a man borrows an animal from his neighbor and it is injured or dies while the owner is not present, he must make restitution. 15But if the owner is with the animal, the borrower will not have to pay. If the animal was hired, the money paid for the hire covers the loss.

Social Responsibility

16"If a man seduces a virgin who is not pledged to be married and sleeps with her, he must pay the bride-price, and she shall be his wife. 17If her father absolutely refuses to give her to him, he must still pay the bride-price for virgins.

18"Do not allow a sorceress to live.

19"Anyone who has sexual relations with an animal must be put to death.

4 "若他所偷的,或牛,或驢,或羊,仍在他手下存活,他就要加倍賠還。

5 "人若在田間或在葡萄園裏放牲畜,任憑牲畜上別人的田裏去吃,就必拿自己田間上好的,和葡萄園上好的賠還。

6 "若點火焚燒荊棘,以致將別人堆積的禾捆,站着的禾稼,或是田園,都燒盡了,那點火的必要賠還。

7 "人若將銀錢或家具交付鄰舍看守,這物從那人的家被偷去,若把賊找到了,賊要加倍賠還;8若找不到賊,那家主就近審判官,要看看他拿了原主的物件沒有。9兩個人的案件,無論是為甚麼過犯,或是為牛,為驢,為羊,為衣裳,或是為甚麼失掉之物,有一人說:'這是我的',兩造就要將案件稟告審判官,審判官定誰有罪,誰就要加倍賠還。

10 "人若將驢,或牛,或羊,或別的牲畜,交付鄰舍看守,牲畜或死,或受傷,或被趕去,無人看見,11那看守的人,要憑着耶和華起誓。手裏未曾拿鄰舍的物,本主就要罷休,看守的人不必賠還。12牲畜若從看守的那裏被偷去,他就要賠還本主;13若被野獸撕碎,看守的要帶來當作證據,所撕的不必賠還。

14 "人若向鄰舍借甚麼,所借的或受傷,或死,本主沒有同在一處,借的人總要賠還。15若本主同在一處,他就不必賠還;若是雇的,也不必賠還,本是為雇價來的。

社會責任

16 "人若引誘沒有受聘的處女,與她行淫,他總要交出聘禮,娶她為妻。17若女子的父親決不肯將女子給他,他就要按處女的聘禮,交出錢來。

18 "行邪術的女人,不可容她存活。

19 "凡與獸淫合的,總要把他治死。

---

a 8 Or before God; also in verse 9   b 9 Or whom God declares

²⁰"祭祀別神，不單單祭祀耶和華的，那人必要滅絕。

²¹"不可虧負寄居的，也不可欺壓他，因為你們在埃及地也作過寄居的。

²²"不可苦待寡婦和孤兒。²³若是苦待他們一點，他們向我一哀求，我總要聽他們的哀聲，²⁴並要發烈怒，用刀殺你們，使你們的妻子為寡婦，兒女為孤兒。

²⁵"我民中有貧窮人與你同住，你若借錢給他，不可如放債的向他取利。²⁶你即或拿鄰舍的衣服作當頭，必在日落以先歸還他；²⁷因他只有這一件當蓋頭，是他貼身的衣服，若是沒有，他拿甚麼睡覺呢？他哀求我，我就應允，因為我是有恩惠的。

²⁸"不可毀謗神，也不可毀謗你百姓的官長。

²⁹"你要從你莊稼中的穀和酒醡中滴出來的酒拿來獻上，不可遲延。

"你要將頭生的兒子歸給我。³⁰你牛羊頭生的，也要這樣，七天當跟着母，第八天要歸給我。

³¹"你們要在我面前為聖潔的人，因此，田間被野獸撕裂牲畜的肉，你們不可吃，要丟給狗吃。

公平與憐憫的條例

23

"不可隨夥佈散謠言，不可與惡人連手妄作見證。

²"不可隨眾行惡，不可在爭訟的事上隨眾偏行，作見證屈枉正直；³也不可在爭訟的事上偏護窮人。

⁴"若遇見你仇敵的牛或驢失迷了路，總要牽回來交給他。⁵若看見恨你人的驢壓臥在重馱之下，不可走開，務要和驢主一同抬開重馱。

⁶"不可在窮人爭訟的事上屈枉正直。⁷當遠離虛假的事。不可殺無辜和有義的人，因我必不以惡人為義。

²⁰"Whoever sacrifices to any god other than the LORD must be destroyed.^a

²¹"Do not mistreat an alien or oppress him, for you were aliens in Egypt.

²²"Do not take advantage of a widow or an orphan. ²³If you do and they cry out to me, I will certainly hear their cry. ²⁴My anger will be aroused, and I will kill you with the sword; your wives will become widows and your children fatherless.

²⁵"If you lend money to one of my people among you who is needy, do not be like a moneylender; charge him no interest.^b ²⁶If you take your neighbor's cloak as a pledge, return it to him by sunset, ²⁷because his cloak is the only covering he has for his body. What else will he sleep in? When he cries out to me, I will hear, for I am compassionate.

²⁸"Do not blaspheme God^c or curse the ruler of your people.

²⁹"Do not hold back offerings from your granaries or your vats.^d

"You must give me the firstborn of your sons. ³⁰Do the same with your cattle and your sheep. Let them stay with their mothers for seven days, but give them to me on the eighth day.

³¹"You are to be my holy people. So do not eat the meat of an animal torn by wild beasts; throw it to the dogs.

Laws of Justice and Mercy

23

"Do not spread false reports. Do not help a wicked man by being a malicious witness.

²"Do not follow the crowd in doing wrong. When you give testimony in a lawsuit, do not pervert justice by siding with the crowd, ³and do not show favoritism to a poor man in his lawsuit.

⁴"If you come across your enemy's ox or donkey wandering off, be sure to take it back to him. ⁵If you see the donkey of someone who hates you fallen down under its load, do not leave it there; be sure you help him with it.

⁶"Do not deny justice to your poor people in their lawsuits. ⁷Have nothing to do with a false charge and do not put an innocent or honest person to death, for I will not acquit the guilty.

---

a 20 The Hebrew term refers to the irrevocable giving over of things or persons to the LORD, often by totally destroying them.　*b 25* Or *excessive interest*　*c 28* Or *Do not revile the judges*　*d 29* The meaning of the Hebrew for this phrase is uncertain.

8"Do not accept a bribe, for a bribe blinds those who see and twists the words of the righteous.

9"Do not oppress an alien; you yourselves know how it feels to be aliens, because you were aliens in Egypt.

Sabbath Laws

10"For six years you are to sow your fields and harvest the crops, 11but during the seventh year let the land lie unplowed and unused. Then the poor among your people may get food from it, and the wild animals may eat what they leave. Do the same with your vineyard and your olive grove.

12"Six days do your work, but on the seventh day do not work, so that your ox and your donkey may rest and the slave born in your household, and the alien as well, may be refreshed.

13"Be careful to do everything I have said to you. Do not invoke the names of other gods; do not let them be heard on your lips.

The Three Annual Festivals

14"Three times a year you are to celebrate a festival to me.

15"Celebrate the Feast of Unleavened Bread; for seven days eat bread made without yeast, as I commanded you. Do this at the appointed time in the month of Abib, for in that month you came out of Egypt.

"No one is to appear before me empty-handed.

16"Celebrate the Feast of Harvest with the firstfruits of the crops you sow in your field.

"Celebrate the Feast of Ingathering at the end of the year, when you gather in your crops from the field.

17"Three times a year all the men are to appear before the Sovereign LORD.

18"Do not offer the blood of a sacrifice to me along with anything containing yeast.

"The fat of my festival offerings must not be kept until morning.

19"Bring the best of the firstfruits of your soil to the house of the LORD your God.

"Do not cook a young goat in its mother's milk.

God's Angel to Prepare the Way

20"See, I am sending an angel ahead of you to guard you along the way and to bring you to the place I have prepared. 21Pay attention to him and listen to what he says. Do not rebel against him; he will not forgive your rebellion, since my Name is in him. 22If you listen carefully to what

8 "不可受賄賂,因為賄賂能叫明眼人變瞎了,又能顛倒義人的話。

9 "不可欺壓寄居的,因為你們在埃及地作過寄居的,知道寄居的心。

安息的條例

10 "六年你要耕種田地,收藏土產,11只是第七年要叫地歇息,不耕不種,使你民中的窮人有吃的。他們所剩下的,野獸可以吃。你的葡萄園和橄欖園,也要照樣辦理。

12 "六日你要做工,第七日要安息,使牛、驢可以歇息。並使你婢女的兒子和寄居的都可以舒暢。

13 "凡我對你們說的話,你們要謹守。別神的名你不可提,也不可從你口中傳說。

三大節期

14 "一年三次,你要向我守節。

15 "你要守除酵節,照我所吩咐你的,在亞筆月內所定的日期,吃無酵餅七天。

"誰也不可空手朝見我,因為你是這月出了埃及。

16 "又要守收割節,所收的是你田間所種、勞碌得來初熟之物。

"並在年底收藏,要守收藏節。

17 "一切的男丁要一年三次朝見主耶和華。

18 "不可將我祭牲的血和有酵的餅一同獻上。

"也不可將我節上祭牲的脂油留到早晨。

19 "地裏首先初熟之物要送到耶和華你神的殿。

"不可用山羊羔母的奶煮山羊羔。

神的使者預備道路

20 "看哪,我差遣使者在你前面,在路上保護你,領你到我所預備的地方去。21他是奉我名來的,你們要在他面前謹慎,聽從他的話,不可惹他(註:"惹"或作"違背"),因為他必不赦免你們的過犯。22你若實在聽從他的話，照着我一切所說的去行，我就向你的仇敵作仇敵，向你的敵人作敵人。²³我的使者要在你前面行，領你到亞摩利人、赫人、比利洗人、迦南人、希未人、耶布斯人那裏去，我必將他們剪除。²⁴你不可跪拜他們的神，不可侍奉他，也不可效法他們的行為，卻要把神像盡行拆毀，打碎他們的柱像。²⁵你們要侍奉耶和華你們的神，他必賜福與你的糧與你的水，也必從你們中間除去疾病。²⁶你境內必沒有墜胎的、不生產的，我要使你滿了你年日的數目。

²⁷"凡你所到的地方，我要使那裏的眾民，在你面前驚駭、擾亂，又要使你一切仇敵轉背逃跑。²⁸我要打發黃蜂飛在你前面，把希未人、迦南人、赫人攆出去。²⁹我不在一年之內將他們從你面前攆出去，恐怕地成為荒涼，野地的獸多起來害你。³⁰我要漸漸地將他們從你面前攆出去，等到你的人數加多，承受那地為業。

³¹"我要定你的境界，從紅海直到非利士海，又從曠野直到大河。我要將那地的居民交在你手中，你要將他們從你面前攆出去。³²不可和他們並他們的神立約。³³他們不可住在你的地上，恐怕他們使你得罪我。你若侍奉他們的神，這必成為你的網羅。"

立約

24 耶和華對摩西說："你和亞倫、拿答、亞比戶，並以色列長老中的七十人，都要上到我這裏來，遠遠地下拜。²惟獨你可以親近耶和華，他們卻不可親近；百姓也不可和你一同上來。"

³摩西下山，將耶和華的命令、典章都述說與百姓聽。眾百姓齊聲說："耶和華所吩咐的，我們都必遵行。"⁴摩西將耶和華的命令都寫上。

清早起來，在山下築一座壇，按以色列十二支派，立十二根柱子。⁵又打發以色列人中的少年人去獻燔

he says and do all that I say, I will be an enemy to your enemies and will oppose those who oppose you. ²³My angel will go ahead of you and bring you into the land of the Amorites, Hittites, Perizzites, Canaanites, Hivites and Jebusites, and I will wipe them out. ²⁴Do not bow down before their gods or worship them or follow their practices. You must demolish them and break their sacred stones to pieces. ²⁵Worship the LORD your God, and his blessing will be on your food and water. I will take away sickness from among you, ²⁶and none will miscarry or be barren in your land. I will give you a full life span.

²⁷"I will send my terror ahead of you and throw into confusion every nation you encounter. I will make all your enemies turn their backs and run. ²⁸I will send the hornet ahead of you to drive the Hivites, Canaanites and Hittites out of your way. ²⁹But I will not drive them out in a single year, because the land would become desolate and the wild animals too numerous for you. ³⁰Little by little I will drive them out before you, until you have increased enough to take possession of the land.

³¹"I will establish your borders from the Red Sea*ᵃ* to the Sea of the Philistines,*ᵇ* and from the desert to the River.*ᶜ* I will hand over to you the people who live in the land and you will drive them out before you. ³²Do not make a covenant with them or with their gods. ³³Do not let them live in your land, or they will cause you to sin against me, because the worship of their gods will certainly be a snare to you."

The Covenant Confirmed

24 Then he said to Moses, "Come up to the LORD, you and Aaron, Nadab and Abihu, and seventy of the elders of Israel. You are to worship at a distance, ²but Moses alone is to approach the LORD; the others must not come near. And the people may not come up with him."

³When Moses went and told the people all the LORD's words and laws, they responded with one voice, "Everything the LORD has said we will do." ⁴Moses then wrote down everything the LORD had said.

He got up early the next morning and built an altar at the foot of the mountain and set up twelve stone pillars representing the twelve tribes of Israel. ⁵Then he sent young Israelite men, and they offered burnt offerings and sacri-

a 31 Hebrew Yam Suph; that is, Sea of Reeds　*b 31 That is, the Mediterranean*　*c 31 That is, the Euphrates*

ficed young bulls as fellowship offerings[a] to the LORD. [6]Moses took half of the blood and put it in bowls, and the other half he sprinkled on the altar. [7]Then he took the Book of the Covenant and read it to the people. They responded, "We will do everything the LORD has said; we will obey."

[8]Moses then took the blood, sprinkled it on the people and said, "This is the blood of the covenant that the LORD has made with you in accordance with all these words."

[9]Moses and Aaron, Nadab and Abihu, and the seventy elders of Israel went up [10]and saw the God of Israel. Under his feet was something like a pavement made of sapphire,[b] clear as the sky itself. [11]But God did not raise his hand against these leaders of the Israelites; they saw God, and they ate and drank.

[12]The LORD said to Moses, "Come up to me on the mountain and stay here, and I will give you the tablets of stone, with the law and commands I have written for their instruction."

[13]Then Moses set out with Joshua his aide, and Moses went up on the mountain of God. [14]He said to the elders, "Wait here for us until we come back to you. Aaron and Hur are with you, and anyone involved in a dispute can go to them."

[15]When Moses went up on the mountain, the cloud covered it, [16]and the glory of the LORD settled on Mount Sinai. For six days the cloud covered the mountain, and on the seventh day the LORD called to Moses from within the cloud. [17]To the Israelites the glory of the LORD looked like a consuming fire on top of the mountain. [18]Then Moses entered the cloud as he went on up the mountain. And he stayed on the mountain forty days and forty nights.

Offerings for the Tabernacle

25 The LORD said to Moses, [2]"Tell the Israelites to bring me an offering. You are to receive the offering for me from each man whose heart prompts him to give. [3]These are the offerings you are to receive from them: gold, silver and bronze; [4]blue, purple and scarlet yarn and fine linen; goat hair; [5]ram skins dyed red and hides of sea cows[c]; acacia wood; [6]olive oil for the light; spices for the anointing oil and for the fragrant incense; [7]and onyx stones and other gems to be mounted on the ephod and breastpiece.

祭，又向耶和華獻牛為平安祭。[6]摩西將血一半盛在盆中，一半灑在壇上。[7]又將約書念給百姓聽，他們說："耶和華所吩咐的，我們都必遵行。"

[8]摩西將血灑在百姓身上，說："你看！這是立約的血，是耶和華按這一切話與你們立約的憑據。"

[9]摩西、亞倫、拿答、亞比戶、並以色列長老中的七十人，都上了山。[10]他們看見以色列的神，他腳下彷彿有平鋪的藍寶石，如同天色明淨。[11]他的手不加害在以色列的尊者身上，他們觀看神，他們又吃又喝。

[12]耶和華對摩西說："你上山到我這裏來，住在這裏，我要將石版並我所寫的律法和誡命賜給你，使你可以教訓百姓。"

[13]摩西和他的幫手約書亞起來，上了神的山。[14]摩西對長老說："你們在這裏等着，等到我們再回來，有亞倫、戶珥與你們同在。凡有爭訟的，都可以就近他們去。"

[15]摩西上山，有雲彩把山遮蓋。[16]耶和華的榮耀停於西奈山，雲彩遮蓋山六天，第七天他從雲中召摩西。[17]耶和華的榮耀在山頂上，在以色列人眼前，形狀如烈火。[18]摩西進入雲中上山，在山上四十晝夜。

為會幕奉獻

25 耶和華曉諭摩西說：[2]"你告訴以色列人當為我送禮物來，凡甘心樂意的，你們就可以收下歸我。[3]所要收的禮物就是：金、銀、銅，[4]藍色、紫色、朱紅色線，細麻，山羊毛，[5]染紅的公羊皮、海狗皮，皂莢木，[6]點燈的油，並做膏油和香的香料，[7]紅瑪瑙與別樣的寶石，可以鑲嵌在以弗得和胸牌上。

---

a 5 Traditionally peace offerings   b 10 Or lapis lazuli   c 5 That is, dugongs

8 “又當為我造聖所，使我可以住在他們中間。9 製造帳幕和其中的一切器具，都要照我所指示你的樣式。

約櫃

10 “要用皂莢木做一櫃，長二肘半，寬一肘半，高一肘半。11 要裏外包上精金，四圍鑲上金牙邊。12 也要鑄四個金環，安在櫃的四腳上，這邊兩環，那邊兩環。13 要用皂莢木做兩根杠，用金包裹。14 要把杠穿在櫃旁的環內，以便抬櫃。15 這杠要常在櫃的環內，不可抽出來。16 必將我所賜給你的法版放在櫃裏。

17 “要用精金做施恩座（註：“施恩”或作“蔽罪”。下同），長二肘半，寬一肘半。18 要用金子錘出兩個基路伯來，安在施恩座的兩頭。19 這頭做一個基路伯，那頭做一個基路伯。二基路伯要接連一塊，在施恩座的兩頭。20 二基路伯要高張翅膀，遮掩施恩座。基路伯要臉對臉，朝着施恩座。21 要將施恩座安在櫃的上邊，又將我所要賜給你的法版放在櫃裏。22 我要在那裏與你相會，又要從法櫃施恩座上二基路伯中間，和你說我所要吩咐你傳給以色列人的一切事。

桌子

23 “要用皂莢木做一張桌子，長二肘，寬一肘，高一肘半。24 要包上精金，四圍鑲上金牙邊。25 桌子的四圍各做一掌寬的橫梁，橫梁上鑲着金牙邊。26 要做四個金環，安在桌子的四角上，就是桌子四腳上的四角。27 安環子的地方要挨近橫梁，可以穿杠抬桌子。28 要用皂莢木做兩根杠，用金包裹，以便抬桌子。29 要做桌子

8"Then have them make a sanctuary for me, and I will dwell among them. 9Make this tabernacle and all its furnishings exactly like the pattern I will show you.

The Ark

10"Have them make a chest of acacia wood—two and a half cubits long, a cubit and a half wide, and a cubit and a half high.*a* 11Overlay it with pure gold, both inside and out, and make a gold molding around it. 12Cast four gold rings for it and fasten them to its four feet, with two rings on one side and two rings on the other. 13Then make poles of acacia wood and overlay them with gold. 14Insert the poles into the rings on the sides of the chest to carry it. 15The poles are to remain in the rings of this ark; they are not to be removed. 16Then put in the ark the Testimony, which I will give you.

17"Make an atonement cover*b* of pure gold—two and a half cubits long and a cubit and a half wide.*c* 18And make two cherubim out of hammered gold at the ends of the cover. 19Make one cherub on one end and the second cherub on the other; make the cherubim of one piece with the cover, at the two ends. 20The cherubim are to have their wings spread upward, overshadowing the cover with them. The cherubim are to face each other, looking toward the cover. 21Place the cover on top of the ark and put in the ark the Testimony, which I will give you. 22There, above the cover between the two cherubim that are over the ark of the Testimony, I will meet with you and give you all my commands for the Israelites.

The Table

23"Make a table of acacia wood—two cubits long, a cubit wide and a cubit and a half high.*d* 24Overlay it with pure gold and make a gold molding around it. 25Also make around it a rim a handbreadth*e* wide and put a gold molding on the rim. 26Make four gold rings for the table and fasten them to the four corners, where the four legs are. 27The rings are to be close to the rim to hold the poles used in carrying the table. 28Make the poles of acacia wood, overlay them with gold and carry the table with them. 29And make

a 10 That is, about 3 3/4 feet (about 1.1 meters) long and 2 1/4 feet (about 0.7 meter) wide and high   *b 17* Traditionally *a mercy seat*   *c 17* That is, about 3 3/4 feet (about 1.1 meters) long and 2 1/4 feet (about 0.7 meter) wide   *d 23* That is, about 3 feet (about 0.9 meter) long and 1 1/2 feet (about 0.5 meter) wide and 2 1/4 feet (about 0.7 meter) high   *e 25* That is, about 3 inches (about 8 centimeters)

its plates and dishes of pure gold, as well as its pitchers and bowls for the pouring out of offerings. ³⁰Put the bread of the Presence on this table to be before me at all times.

The Lampstand

³¹"Make a lampstand of pure gold and hammer it out, base and shaft; its flowerlike cups, buds and blossoms shall be of one piece with it. ³²Six branches are to extend from the sides of the lampstand—three on one side and three on the other. ³³Three cups shaped like almond flowers with buds and blossoms are to be on one branch, three on the next branch, and the same for all six branches extending from the lampstand. ³⁴And on the lampstand there are to be four cups shaped like almond flowers with buds and blossoms. ³⁵One bud shall be under the first pair of branches extending from the lampstand, a second bud under the second pair, and a third bud under the third pair—six branches in all. ³⁶The buds and branches shall all be of one piece with the lampstand, hammered out of pure gold.

³⁷"Then make its seven lamps and set them up on it so that they light the space in front of it. ³⁸Its wick trimmers and trays are to be of pure gold. ³⁹A talent*ᵃ* of pure gold is to be used for the lampstand and all these accessories. ⁴⁰See that you make them according to the pattern shown you on the mountain.

The Tabernacle

26 "Make the tabernacle with ten curtains of finely twisted linen and blue, purple and scarlet yarn, with cherubim worked into them by a skilled craftsman. ²All the curtains are to be the same size—twenty-eight cubits long and four cubits wide.*ᵇ* ³Join five of the curtains together, and do the same with the other five. ⁴Make loops of blue material along the edge of the end curtain in one set, and do the same with the end curtain in the other set. ⁵Make fifty loops on one curtain and fifty loops on the end curtain of the other set, with the loops opposite each other. ⁶Then make fifty gold clasps and use them to fasten the curtains together so that the tabernacle is a unit.

⁷"Make curtains of goat hair for the tent over the tabernacle—eleven altogether. ⁸All eleven curtains are to be the same size—thirty cubits

上的盤子、調羹，並奠酒的爵和瓶，這都要用精金製作。³⁰又要在桌子上，在我面前，常擺陳設餅。

燈臺

³¹"要用精金做一個燈臺。燈臺的座和幹與杯、球、花都要接連一塊錘出來。³²燈臺兩旁要杈出六個枝子，這旁三個，那旁三個。³³這旁每枝上有三個杯，形狀像杏花，有球、有花；那旁每枝上也有三個杯，形狀像杏花，有球、有花。從燈臺杈出來的六個枝子都是如此。³⁴燈臺上有四個杯，形狀像杏花，有球、有花。³⁵燈臺每兩個枝子以下，有球與枝子接連一塊，燈臺出的六個枝子都是如此。³⁶球和枝子要接連一塊，都是一塊精金錘出來的。

³⁷"要做燈臺的七個燈盞，祭司要點這燈，使燈光對照。³⁸燈臺的蠟剪和蠟花盤也是要精金的。³⁹做燈臺和這一切的器具，要用精金一他連得。⁴⁰要謹慎做這些物件，都要照着在山上指示你的樣式。

會幕

26 "你要用十幅幔子做帳幕。這些幔子要用撚的細麻和藍色、紫色、朱紅色線製造，並用巧匠的手工繡上基路伯。²每幅幔子要長二十八肘，寬四肘，幔子都要一樣的尺寸。³這五幅幔子要幅幅相連，那五幅幔子也要幅幅相連。⁴在這相連的幔子末幅邊上要做藍色的鈕扣，在那相連的幔子末幅邊上也要照樣做。⁵要在這相連的幔子上做五十個鈕扣，在那相連的幔子上也做五十個鈕扣，都要兩兩相對。⁶又要做五十個金鈎，用鈎使幔子相連，這才成了一個帳幕。

⁷"你要用山羊毛織十一幅幔子，作為帳幕以上的罩棚。⁸每幅幔子要長三十肘，寬四肘，十一幅幔子

a 39 That is, about *75 pounds* (about 34 kilograms)
b 2 That is, about *42 feet* (about 12.5 meters) long and 6 feet (about 1.8 meters) wide

都要一樣的尺寸。⁹要把五幅幔子連成一幅，又把六幅幔子連成一幅。這第六幅幔子要在罩棚的前面摺上去。¹⁰在這相連的幔子末幅邊上要做五十個鈕扣，在那相連的幔子末幅邊上也做五十個鈕扣。¹¹又要做五十個銅鉤，鉤在鈕扣中，使罩棚連成一個。¹²罩棚的幔子所餘那垂下來的半幅幔子，要垂在帳幕的後頭。¹³罩棚的幔子所餘長的，這邊一肘，那邊一肘，要垂在帳幕的兩旁，遮蓋帳幕。¹⁴又要用染紅的公羊皮做罩棚的蓋，再用海狗皮做一層罩棚上的頂蓋。

¹⁵ "你要用皂莢木做帳幕的豎板。¹⁶每塊要長十肘，寬一肘半。¹⁷每塊必有兩榫相對，帳幕一切的板都要這樣做。¹⁸帳幕的南面要做板二十塊。¹⁹在這二十塊板底下要做四十個帶卯的銀座，兩卯接這塊板上的兩榫，兩卯接那塊板上的兩榫。²⁰帳幕第二面，就是北面，也要做板二十塊，²¹和帶卯的銀座四十個。這板底下有兩卯，那板底下也有兩卯。²²帳幕的後面，就是西面，要做板六塊。²³帳幕後面的拐角要做板兩塊。²⁴板的下半截要雙的，上半截要整的，直頂到第一個環子，兩塊都要這樣做兩個拐角。²⁵必有八塊板和十六個帶卯的銀座——這板底下有兩卯，那板底下也有兩卯。

²⁶ "你要用皂莢木做閂。為帳幕這面的板做五閂，²⁷為帳幕那面的板做五閂，又為帳幕後面的板做五閂。²⁸板腰間的中閂要從這一頭通到那一頭。²⁹板要用金子包裹，又要做板上的金環套閂，閂也要用金子包裹。

³⁰ "要照着在山上指示你的樣式立起帳幕。

³¹ "你要用藍色、紫色、朱紅色線和撚的細麻織幔子，以巧匠的手工繡上基路伯。³²要把幔子掛在四根包金的皂莢木柱子上，柱子上當有金鉤，柱子安在四個帶卯的銀座上。

long and four cubits wide.ᵃ ⁹Join five of the curtains together into one set and the other six into another set. Fold the sixth curtain double at the front of the tent. ¹⁰Make fifty loops along the edge of the end curtain in one set and also along the edge of the end curtain in the other set. ¹¹Then make fifty bronze clasps and put them in the loops to fasten the tent together as a unit. ¹²As for the additional length of the tent curtains, the half curtain that is left over is to hang down at the rear of the tabernacle. ¹³The tent curtains will be a cubitᵇ longer on both sides; what is left will hang over the sides of the tabernacle so as to cover it. ¹⁴Make for the tent a covering of ram skins dyed red, and over that a covering of hides of sea cows.ᶜ

¹⁵"Make upright frames of acacia wood for the tabernacle. ¹⁶Each frame is to be ten cubits long and a cubit and a half wide,ᵈ ¹⁷with two projections set parallel to each other. Make all the frames of the tabernacle in this way. ¹⁸Make twenty frames for the south side of the tabernacle ¹⁹and make forty silver bases to go under them—two bases for each frame, one under each projection. ²⁰For the other side, the north side of the tabernacle, make twenty frames ²¹and forty silver bases—two under each frame. ²²Make six frames for the far end, that is, the west end of the tabernacle, ²³and make two frames for the corners at the far end. ²⁴At these two corners they must be double from the bottom all the way to the top, and fitted into a single ring; both shall be like that. ²⁵So there will be eight frames and sixteen silver bases—two under each frame.

²⁶"Also make crossbars of acacia wood: five for the frames on one side of the tabernacle, ²⁷five for those on the other side, and five for the frames on the west, at the far end of the tabernacle. ²⁸The center crossbar is to extend from end to end at the middle of the frames. ²⁹Overlay the frames with gold and make gold rings to hold the crossbars. Also overlay the crossbars with gold.

³⁰"Set up the tabernacle according to the plan shown you on the mountain.

³¹"Make a curtain of blue, purple and scarlet yarn and finely twisted linen, with cherubim worked into it by a skilled craftsman. ³²Hang it with gold hooks on four posts of acacia wood overlaid with gold and standing on four silver

bases. ³³Hang the curtain from the clasps and place the ark of the Testimony behind the curtain. The curtain will separate the Holy Place from the Most Holy Place. ³⁴Put the atonement cover on the ark of the Testimony in the Most Holy Place. ³⁵Place the table outside the curtain on the north side of the tabernacle and put the lampstand opposite it on the south side.

³⁶"For the entrance to the tent make a curtain of blue, purple and scarlet yarn and finely twisted linen—the work of an embroiderer. ³⁷Make gold hooks for this curtain and five posts of acacia wood overlaid with gold. And cast five bronze bases for them.

The Altar of Burnt Offering

27 "Build an altar of acacia wood, three cubits[a] high; it is to be square, five cubits long and five cubits wide.[b] ²Make a horn at each of the four corners, so that the horns and the altar are of one piece, and overlay the altar with bronze. ³Make all its utensils of bronze—its pots to remove the ashes, and its shovels, sprinkling bowls, meat forks and firepans. ⁴Make a grating for it, a bronze network, and make a bronze ring at each of the four corners of the network. ⁵Put it under the ledge of the altar so that it is halfway up the altar. ⁶Make poles of acacia wood for the altar and overlay them with bronze. ⁷The poles are to be inserted into the rings so they will be on two sides of the altar when it is carried. ⁸Make the altar hollow, out of boards. It is to be made just as you were shown on the mountain.

The Courtyard

⁹"Make a courtyard for the tabernacle. The south side shall be a hundred cubits[c] long and is to have curtains of finely twisted linen, ¹⁰with twenty posts and twenty bronze bases and with silver hooks and bands on the posts. ¹¹The north side shall also be a hundred cubits long and is to have curtains, with twenty posts and twenty bronze bases and with silver hooks and bands on the posts.

¹²"The west end of the courtyard shall be fifty cubits[d] wide and have curtains, with ten posts and ten bases. ¹³On the east end, toward the sunrise, the courtyard shall also be fifty cubits

³³要使幔子垂在鈎子下，把法櫃抬進幔子內，這幔子要將聖所和至聖所隔開。³⁴又要把施恩座安在至聖所內的法櫃上。³⁵把桌子安在幔子外帳幕的北面，把燈台安在帳幕的南面，彼此相對。

³⁶"你要拿藍色、紫色、朱紅色線和撚的細麻，用繡花的手工織帳幕的門簾。³⁷要用皂莢木為簾子做五根柱子，用金子包裹，柱子上當有金鈎，又要為柱子用銅鑄造五個帶卯的座。

燔祭壇

27 "你要用皂莢木做壇，這壇要四方的，長五肘，寬五肘，高三肘。²要在壇的四拐角上做四個角，與壇接連一塊，用銅把壇包裹。³要做盆，收去壇上的灰，又做鏟子、盤子、肉叉子、火鼎；壇上一切的器具都用銅做。⁴要為壇做一個銅網，在網的四角上做四個銅環。⁵把網安在壇四面的圍腰板以下，使網從下達到壇的半腰。⁶又要用皂莢木為壇作杠用銅包裹。⁷這杠要穿在壇兩旁的環子內，用以抬壇。⁸要用板做壇，壇是空的，都照着在山上指示你的樣式做。

院子

⁹"你要做帳幕的院子，院子的南面要用撚的細麻做帷子，長一百肘。¹⁰帷子的柱子要二十根，帶卯的銅座二十個，柱子上的鈎子和杆子都要用銀子做。¹¹北面也當有帷子，長一百肘，帷子的柱子二十根，帶卯的銅座二十個，柱子上的鈎子和杆子都要用銀子做。

¹²"院子的西面當有帷子，寬五十肘。帷子的柱子十根，帶卯的座十個。¹³院子的東面要寬五十肘。

---

^a 1 That is, about 4 1/2 feet (about 1.3 meters)

^b 1 That is, about 7 1/2 feet (about 2.3 meters) long and wide

^c 9 That is, about 150 feet (about 46 meters); also in verse 11

^d 12 That is, about 75 feet (about 23 meters); also in verse 13

¹⁴門這邊的帷子要十五肘，帷子的柱子三根，帶卯的座三個；¹⁵門那邊的帷子也要十五肘，帷子的柱子三根，帶卯的座三個。

¹⁶「院子的門當有簾子，長二十肘，要拿藍色、紫色、朱紅色線和撚的細麻，用繡花的手工織成，柱子四根，帶卯的座四個。¹⁷院子四圍一切的柱子都要用銀杆連絡，柱子上的鈎子要用銀做，帶卯的座要用銅做。¹⁸院子要長一百肘，寬五十肘，高五肘，帷子要用撚的細麻做，帶卯的座要用銅做。¹⁹帳幕各樣用處的器具，並帳幕一切的橛子，和院子裏一切的橛子都要用銅做。

點燈之油

²⁰「你要吩咐以色列人，把那為點燈搗成的清橄欖油拿來給你，使燈常常點着。²¹在會幕中法櫃前的幔外，亞倫和他的兒子，從晚上到早晨，要在耶和華面前經理這燈，這要作以色列人世世代代永遠的定例。

祭司衣服

28 「你要從以色列人中，使你的哥哥亞倫和他的兒子拿答、亞比戶、以利亞撒、以他瑪一同就近你，給我供祭司的職分。²你要給你哥哥亞倫做聖衣為榮耀，為華美。³又要吩咐一切心中有智慧的，就是我用智慧的靈所充滿的，給亞倫做衣服，使他分別為聖，可以給我供祭司的職分。⁴所要做的就是胸牌、以弗得、外袍、雜色的內袍、冠冕、腰帶，使你哥哥亞倫和他兒子穿這聖服，可以給我供祭司的職分。⁵要用金線和藍色、紫色、朱紅色線，並細麻去做。

wide. ¹⁴Curtains fifteen cubits^a long are to be on one side of the entrance, with three posts and three bases, ¹⁵and curtains fifteen cubits long are to be on the other side, with three posts and three bases.

¹⁶"For the entrance to the courtyard, provide a curtain twenty cubits^b long, of blue, purple and scarlet yarn and finely twisted linen—the work of an embroiderer—with four posts and four bases. ¹⁷All the posts around the courtyard are to have silver bands and hooks, and bronze bases. ¹⁸The courtyard shall be a hundred cubits long and fifty cubits wide,^c with curtains of finely twisted linen five cubits^d high, and with bronze bases. ¹⁹All the other articles used in the service of the tabernacle, whatever their function, including all the tent pegs for it and those for the courtyard, are to be of bronze.

Oil for the Lampstand

²⁰"Command the Israelites to bring you clear oil of pressed olives for the light so that the lamps may be kept burning. ²¹In the Tent of Meeting, outside the curtain that is in front of the Testimony, Aaron and his sons are to keep the lamps burning before the LORD from evening till morning. This is to be a lasting ordinance among the Israelites for the generations to come.

The Priestly Garments

28 "Have Aaron your brother brought to you from among the Israelites, along with his sons Nadab and Abihu, Eleazar and Ithamar, so they may serve me as priests. ²Make sacred garments for your brother Aaron, to give him dignity and honor. ³Tell all the skilled men to whom I have given wisdom in such matters that they are to make garments for Aaron, for his consecration, so he may serve me as priest. ⁴These are the garments they are to make: a breastpiece, an ephod, a robe, a woven tunic, a turban and a sash. They are to make these sacred garments for your brother Aaron and his sons, so they may serve me as priests. ⁵Have them use gold, and blue, purple and scarlet yarn, and fine linen.

---

^a 14 That is, about 22 1/2 feet (about 6.9 meters); also in verse 15　^b 16 That is, about 30 feet (about 9 meters)　^c 18 That is, about 150 feet (about 46 meters) long and 75 feet (about 23 meters) wide　^d 18 That is, about 7 1/2 feet (about 2.3 meters)

The Ephod

6"Make the ephod of gold, and of blue, purple and scarlet yarn, and of finely twisted linen—the work of a skilled craftsman. 7It is to have two shoulder pieces attached to two of its corners, so it can be fastened. 8Its skillfully woven waistband is to be like it—of one piece with the ephod and made with gold, and with blue, purple and scarlet yarn, and with finely twisted linen.

9"Take two onyx stones and engrave on them the names of the sons of Israel 10in the order of their birth—six names on one stone and the remaining six on the other. 11Engrave the names of the sons of Israel on the two stones the way a gem cutter engraves a seal. Then mount the stones in gold filigree settings 12and fasten them on the shoulder pieces of the ephod as memorial stones for the sons of Israel. Aaron is to bear the names on his shoulders as a memorial before the LORD. 13Make gold filigree settings 14and two braided chains of pure gold, like a rope, and attach the chains to the settings.

The Breastpiece

15"Fashion a breastpiece for making decisions—the work of a skilled craftsman. Make it like the ephod: of gold, and of blue, purple and scarlet yarn, and of finely twisted linen. 16It is to be square—a span^a long and a span wide—and folded double. 17Then mount four rows of precious stones on it. In the first row there shall be a ruby, a topaz and a beryl; 18in the second row a turquoise, a sapphire^b and an emerald; 19in the third row a jacinth, an agate and an amethyst; 20in the fourth row a chrysolite, an onyx and a jasper.^{c} Mount them in gold filigree settings. 21There are to be twelve stones, one for each of the names of the sons of Israel, each engraved like a seal with the name of one of the twelve tribes.

22"For the breastpiece make braided chains of pure gold, like a rope. 23Make two gold rings for it and fasten them to two corners of the breastpiece. 24Fasten the two gold chains to the rings at the corners of the breastpiece, 25and the other ends of the chains to the two settings, attaching them to the shoulder pieces of the ephod at the front. 26Make two gold rings and attach them to the other two corners of the breastpiece on the inside edge next to the ephod. 27Make two more gold rings and attach them to the bottom of the

以弗得

6 "他們要拿金線和藍色、紫色、朱紅色線，並撚的細麻，用巧匠的手工做以弗得。7以弗得當有兩條肩帶，接上兩頭，使它相連。8其上巧工織的帶子，要和以弗得一樣的做法，用以束上，與以弗得接連一塊；要用金線和藍色、紫色、朱紅色線，並撚的細麻做成。

9 "要取兩塊紅瑪瑙，在上面刻以色列兒子的名字，10六個名字在這塊寶石上，六個名字在那塊寶石上，都照他們生來的次序。11要用刻寶石的手工，彷彿刻圖書，按着以色列兒子的名字，刻這兩塊寶石，要鑲在金槽上。12要將這兩塊寶石安在以弗得的兩條肩帶上，為以色列人做紀念石。亞倫要在兩肩上擔他們的名字，在耶和華面前作為紀念。13要用金子做二槽。14又拿精金，用撚工彷彿撚繩子，做兩條鍊子，把這撚成的鍊子搭在二槽上。

胸牌

15 "你要用巧匠的手工，做一個決斷的胸牌。要和以弗得一樣的做法，用金線和藍色、紫色、朱紅色線，並撚的細麻做成。16這胸牌要四方的、疊為兩層，長一虎口，寬一虎口。17要在上面鑲寶石四行：第一行是紅寶石、紅璧璽、紅玉；18第二行是綠寶石、藍寶石、金鋼石；19第三行是紫瑪瑙、白瑪瑙、紫晶；20第四行是水蒼玉、紅瑪瑙、碧玉；這都要鑲在金槽中。21這些寶石都要按着以色列十二個兒子的名字，彷彿刻圖書，刻十二個支派的名字。

22 "要在胸牌上，用精金撚成如繩的鍊子。23在胸牌上也要做兩個金環，安在胸牌的兩頭。24要把那兩條撚成的金鍊子，穿過胸牌兩頭的環子。25又要把鍊子的那兩頭接在兩槽上，安在以弗得前面肩帶上。26要做兩個金環，安在胸牌的兩頭，在以弗得裏面的邊上。27又要做兩個金環，安在以弗得前面兩條肩帶的下邊，挨

---

a 16 That is, about 9 inches (about 22 centimeters) b 18 Or *lapis lazuli* c 20 The precise identification of some of these precious stones is uncertain.

近相接之處，在以弗得巧工織的帶子以上。28要用藍細帶子把胸牌的環子與以弗得的環子繫住，使胸牌貼在以弗得巧工織的帶子上，不可與以弗得離縫。

29 "亞倫進聖所的時候，要將決斷胸牌，就是刻着以色列兒子名字的，帶在胸前，在耶和華面前常作紀念。30又要將烏陵和土明放在決斷的胸牌裏。亞倫進到耶和華面前的時候，要帶在胸前，在耶和華面前常將以色列人的決斷牌帶在胸前。

其他祭司衣袍

31 "你要做以弗得的外袍，顏色全是藍的。32袍上要為頭留一領口，口的周圍織出領邊來，彷彿鎧甲的領口，免得破裂。33袍子周圍底邊上，要用藍色、紫色、朱紅色線做石榴，在袍子周圍的石榴中間要有金鈴鐺。34一個金鈴鐺一個石榴，一個金鈴鐺一個石榴，在袍子周圍的底邊上。35亞倫供職的時候要穿這袍子。他進聖所到耶和華面前，以及出來的時候，袍上的響聲必被聽見，使他不至於死亡。

36 "你要用精金做一面牌，在上面按刻圖書之法，刻着：歸耶和華為聖。37要用一條藍細帶子將牌繫在冠冕的前面。38這牌必在亞倫的額上，亞倫要擔當干犯聖物條例的罪孽。這聖物是以色列人在一切的聖禮物上所分別為聖的。這牌要常在他的額上，使他們可以在耶和華面前蒙悅納。

39 "要用雜色細麻線織內袍，用細麻布做冠冕，又用繡花的手工做腰帶。40要為亞倫的兒子做內袍、腰帶、裹頭巾，為榮耀，為華美。41要把這些給你的哥哥亞倫和他的兒子穿戴，又要膏他們，將他們分別為聖，好給我供祭司的職分。

42 "要給他們做細麻布褲子，遮掩下體，褲子當從腰達到大腿。43亞倫和他兒子進入會幕，或就近壇，在聖所供職的時候必穿上，免得擔罪而死。

"這要為亞倫和他的後裔作永遠的定例。

shoulder pieces on the front of the ephod, close to the seam just above the waistband of the ephod. 28The rings of the breastpiece are to be tied to the rings of the ephod with blue cord, connecting it to the waistband, so that the breastpiece will not swing out from the ephod.

29"Whenever Aaron enters the Holy Place, he will bear the names of the sons of Israel over his heart on the breastpiece of decision as a continuing memorial before the LORD. 30Also put the Urim and the Thummim in the breastpiece, so they may be over Aaron's heart whenever he enters the presence of the LORD. Thus Aaron will always bear the means of making decisions for the Israelites over his heart before the LORD.

Other Priestly Garments

31"Make the robe of the ephod entirely of blue cloth, 32with an opening for the head in its center. There shall be a woven edge like a collar*a* around this opening, so that it will not tear. 33Make pomegranates of blue, purple and scarlet yarn around the hem of the robe, with gold bells between them. 34The gold bells and the pomegranates are to alternate around the hem of the robe. 35Aaron must wear it when he ministers. The sound of the bells will be heard when he enters the Holy Place before the LORD and when he comes out, so that he will not die.

36"Make a plate of pure gold and engrave on it as on a seal: HOLY TO THE LORD. 37Fasten a blue cord to it to attach it to the turban; it is to be on the front of the turban. 38It will be on Aaron's forehead, and he will bear the guilt involved in the sacred gifts the Israelites consecrate, whatever their gifts may be. It will be on Aaron's forehead continually so that they will be acceptable to the LORD.

39"Weave the tunic of fine linen and make the turban of fine linen. The sash is to be the work of an embroiderer. 40Make tunics, sashes and headbands for Aaron's sons, to give them dignity and honor. 41After you put these clothes on your brother Aaron and his sons, anoint and ordain them. Consecrate them so they may serve me as priests.

42"Make linen undergarments as a covering for the body, reaching from the waist to the thigh. 43Aaron and his sons must wear them whenever they enter the Tent of Meeting or approach the altar to minister in the Holy Place, so that they will not incur guilt and die.

"This is to be a lasting ordinance for Aaron and his descendants.

---

a 32 The meaning of the Hebrew for this word is uncertain.

Consecration of the Priests

29 "This is what you are to do to consecrate them, so they may serve me as
priests: Take a young bull and two rams
without defect. ²And from fine wheat flour,
without yeast, make bread, and cakes mixed
with oil, and wafers spread with oil. ³Put them
in a basket and present them in it—along with
the bull and the two rams. ⁴Then bring Aaron
and his sons to the entrance to the Tent of
Meeting and wash them with water. ⁵Take the
garments and dress Aaron with the tunic, the
robe of the ephod, the ephod itself and the
breastpiece. Fasten the ephod on him by its skillfully woven waistband. ⁶Put the turban on his
head and attach the sacred diadem to the turban. ⁷Take the anointing oil and anoint him by
pouring it on his head. ⁸Bring his sons and dress
them in tunics ⁹and put headbands on them.
Then tie sashes on Aaron and his sons.ᵃ The
priesthood is theirs by a lasting ordinance. In
this way you shall ordain Aaron and his sons.

¹⁰"Bring the bull to the front of the Tent of
Meeting, and Aaron and his sons shall lay their
hands on its head. ¹¹Slaughter it in the LORD's
presence at the entrance to the Tent of Meeting.
¹²Take some of the bull's blood and put it on the
horns of the altar with your finger, and pour out
the rest of it at the base of the altar. ¹³Then take
all the fat around the inner parts, the covering of
the liver, and both kidneys with the fat on them,
and burn them on the altar. ¹⁴But burn the bull's
flesh and its hide and its offal outside the camp.
It is a sin offering.

¹⁵"Take one of the rams, and Aaron and his
sons shall lay their hands on its head.
¹⁶Slaughter it and take the blood and sprinkle it
against the altar on all sides. ¹⁷Cut the ram into
pieces and wash the inner parts and the legs,
putting them with the head and the other
pieces. ¹⁸Then burn the entire ram on the altar. It
is a burnt offering to the LORD, a pleasing
aroma, an offering made to the LORD by fire.

¹⁹"Take the other ram, and Aaron and his
sons shall lay their hands on its head. ²⁰Slaughter
it, take some of its blood and put it on the lobes
of the right ears of Aaron and his sons, on the
thumbs of their right hands, and on the big toes
of their right feet. Then sprinkle blood against
the altar on all sides. ²¹And take some of the
blood on the altar and some of the anointing oil
and sprinkle it on Aaron and his garments and
on his sons and their garments. Then he and his
sons and their garments will be consecrated.

ᵃ 9 Hebrew; Septuagint *on them*

使祭司成聖

29 "你使亞倫和他兒子成聖,
給我供祭司的職分,要如此
行:取一隻公牛犢,兩隻無
殘疾的公綿羊, ²無酵餅和調油的無
酵餅,與抹油的無酵薄餅,這都要用
細麥麵做成。 ³這餅要裝在一個筐子
裏,連筐子帶來,又把公牛和兩隻公
綿羊牽來。 ⁴要使亞倫和他兒子到會
幕門口來,用水洗身。 ⁵要給亞倫穿
上內袍和以弗得的外袍,並以弗得,
又帶上胸牌,束上以弗得巧工織的帶
子, ⁶把冠冕戴在他頭上,將聖冠加
在冠冕上。 ⁷就把膏油倒在他頭上膏
他。 ⁸要叫他的兒子來,給他們穿上
內袍。 ⁹給亞倫和他兒子束上腰帶,
包上裹頭巾,他們就憑永遠的定例得
了祭司的職任;又要將亞倫和他兒子
分別為聖。

¹⁰ "你要把公牛牽到會幕前,亞
倫和他兒子要按手在公牛的頭上。
¹¹你要在耶和華面前,在會幕門口,
宰這公牛。 ¹²要取些公牛的血,用指
頭抹在壇的四角上,把血都倒在壇腳
那裏。 ¹³要把一切蓋臟的脂油與肝上
的網子,並兩個腰子和腰子上的脂
油,都燒在壇上。 ¹⁴只是公牛的皮、
肉、糞都要用火燒在營外;這牛是贖
罪祭。

¹⁵ "你要牽一隻公綿羊來,亞倫
和他兒子要按手在這羊的頭上。 ¹⁶要
宰這羊,把血灑在壇的周圍。 ¹⁷要把
羊切成塊子,洗淨五臟和腿,連塊子
帶頭,都放在一處。 ¹⁸要把全羊燒在
壇上,是給耶和華獻的燔祭,是獻給
耶和華為馨香的火祭。

¹⁹ "你要將那一隻公綿羊牽來,
亞倫和他兒子要按手在羊的頭上。
²⁰你要宰這羊,取點血抹在亞倫的右
耳垂上和他兒子的右耳垂上,又抹在
他們右手的大拇指上和右腳的大拇指
上,並要把血灑在壇的四圍。 ²¹你要
取點膏油和壇上的血,彈在亞倫和他
的衣服上,並他兒子和他兒子的衣服
上,他們和他們的衣服就一同成聖。

²²"你要取這羊的脂油和肥尾巴，並蓋臟的脂油與肝上的網子，兩個腰子和腰子上的脂油並右腿（這是承接聖職所獻的羊）。²³再從耶和華面前裝無酵餅的筐子中取一個餅、一個調油的餅和一個薄餅，²⁴都放在亞倫的手上和他兒子的手上，作為搖祭，在耶和華面前搖一搖。²⁵要從他們手中接過來，燒在耶和華面前壇上的燔祭上，是獻給耶和華為馨香的火祭。²⁶你要取亞倫承接聖職所獻公羊的胸，作為搖祭，在耶和華面前搖一搖，這就可以作你的分。

²⁷"那搖祭的胸和舉祭的腿，就是承接聖職所搖的、所舉的，是歸亞倫和他兒子的。這些你都要成為聖，²⁸作亞倫和他子孫從以色列人中永遠所得的份，因為是舉祭。這要從以色列人的平安祭中，作為獻給耶和華的舉祭。

²⁹"亞倫的聖衣要留給他的子孫，可以穿着受膏，又穿着承接聖職。³⁰他的子孫接續他當祭司的，每逢進會幕在聖所供職的時候，要穿七天。

³¹"你要將承接聖職所獻公羊的肉煮在聖處。³²亞倫和他兒子要在會幕門口吃這羊的肉和筐內的餅。³³他們吃那些贖罪之物，好承接聖職，使他們成聖；只是外人不可吃，因為這是聖物。³⁴那承接聖職所獻的肉或餅，若有一點留到早晨，就要用火燒了，不可吃這物，因為是聖物。

³⁵"你要這樣照我一切所吩咐的，向亞倫和他兒子行承接聖職的禮七天。³⁶每天要獻公牛一隻為贖罪祭。你潔淨壇的時候，壇就潔淨了，且要用膏抹壇使壇成聖。³⁷要潔淨壇七天，使壇成聖，壇就成為至聖。凡挨着壇的都成為聖。

³⁸"你每天所要獻在壇上的，就是兩隻一歲的羊羔，³⁹早晨要獻這一隻，黃昏的時候要獻那一隻。⁴⁰和這一隻羊羔同獻的，要用細麵伊法十分

²²"Take from this ram the fat, the fat tail, the fat around the inner parts, the covering of the liver, both kidneys with the fat on them, and the right thigh. (This is the ram for the ordination.) ²³From the basket of bread made without yeast, which is before the LORD, take a loaf, and a cake made with oil, and a wafer. ²⁴Put all these in the hands of Aaron and his sons and wave them before the LORD as a wave offering. ²⁵Then take them from their hands and burn them on the altar along with the burnt offering for a pleasing aroma to the LORD, an offering made to the LORD by fire. ²⁶After you take the breast of the ram for Aaron's ordination, wave it before the LORD as a wave offering, and it will be your share.

²⁷"Consecrate those parts of the ordination ram that belong to Aaron and his sons: the breast that was waved and the thigh that was presented. ²⁸This is always to be the regular share from the Israelites for Aaron and his sons. It is the contribution the Israelites are to make to the LORD from their fellowship offerings.^a

²⁹"Aaron's sacred garments will belong to his descendants so that they can be anointed and ordained in them. ³⁰The son who succeeds him as priest and comes to the Tent of Meeting to minister in the Holy Place is to wear them seven days.

³¹"Take the ram for the ordination and cook the meat in a sacred place. ³²At the entrance to the Tent of Meeting, Aaron and his sons are to eat the meat of the ram and the bread that is in the basket. ³³They are to eat these offerings by which atonement was made for their ordination and consecration. But no one else may eat them, because they are sacred. ³⁴And if any of the meat of the ordination ram or any bread is left over till morning, burn it up. It must not be eaten, because it is sacred.

³⁵"Do for Aaron and his sons everything I have commanded you, taking seven days to ordain them. ³⁶Sacrifice a bull each day as a sin offering to make atonement. Purify the altar by making atonement for it, and anoint it to consecrate it. ³⁷For seven days make atonement for the altar and consecrate it. Then the altar will be most holy, and whatever touches it will be holy.

³⁸"This is what you are to offer on the altar regularly each day: two lambs a year old. ³⁹Offer one in the morning and the other at twilight. ⁴⁰With the first lamb offer a tenth of an ephah^b of fine flour mixed with a quarter of a

---

a 28 Traditionally *peace offerings*　　*b 40* That is, probably about 2 quarts (about 2 liters)

hin*a* of oil from pressed olives, and a quarter of a hin of wine as a drink offering. 41Sacrifice the other lamb at twilight with the same grain offering and its drink offering as in the morning—a pleasing aroma, an offering made to the LORD by fire.

42"For the generations to come this burnt offering is to be made regularly at the entrance to the Tent of Meeting before the LORD. There I will meet you and speak to you; 43there also I will meet with the Israelites, and the place will be consecrated by my glory.

44"So I will consecrate the Tent of Meeting and the altar and will consecrate Aaron and his sons to serve me as priests. 45Then I will dwell among the Israelites and be their God. 46They will know that I am the LORD their God, who brought them out of Egypt so that I might dwell among them. I am the LORD their God.

The Altar of Incense

30 "Make an altar of acacia wood for burning incense. 2It is to be square, a cubit long and a cubit wide, and two cubits high*b*—its horns of one piece with it. 3Overlay the top and all the sides and the horns with pure gold, and make a gold molding around it. 4Make two gold rings for the altar below the molding—two on opposite sides—to hold the poles used to carry it. 5Make the poles of acacia wood and overlay them with gold. 6Put the altar in front of the curtain that is before the ark of the Testimony—before the atonement cover that is over the Testimony—where I will meet with you.

7"Aaron must burn fragrant incense on the altar every morning when he tends the lamps. 8He must burn incense again when he lights the lamps at twilight so incense will burn regularly before the LORD for the generations to come. 9Do not offer on this altar any other incense or any burnt offering or grain offering, and do not pour a drink offering on it. 10Once a year Aaron shall make atonement on its horns. This annual atonement must be made with the blood of the atoning sin offering for the generations to come. It is most holy to the LORD."

Atonement Money

11Then the LORD said to Moses, 12"When you take a census of the Israelites to count them, each one must pay the LORD a ransom for his life

---

之一與搗成的油一欣四分之一調和，又用酒一欣四分之一作為奠祭。41那一隻羊羔要在黃昏的時候獻上，照着早晨的素祭和奠祭的禮辦理，作為獻給耶和華馨香的火祭。

42 "這要在耶和華面前、會幕門口，作你們世世代代常獻的燔祭。我要在那裏與你們相會，和你們說話。43我要在那裏與以色列人相會，會幕就要因我的榮耀成為聖。

44 "我要使會幕和壇成聖，也要使亞倫和他的兒子成聖，給我供祭司的職分。45我要住在以色列人中間，作他們的神。46他們必知道我是耶和華他們的神，是將他們從埃及地領出來的，為要住在他們中間。我是耶和華他們的神。

香壇

30 "你要用皂莢木做一座燒香的壇。2這壇要四方的，長一肘，寬一肘，高二肘。壇的四角要與壇接連一塊。3要用精金把壇的上面，與壇的四圍，並壇的四角包裹，又要在壇的四圍鑲上金牙邊。4要做兩個金環安在牙子邊以下，在壇的兩旁，兩根橫撐上，作為穿杠的用處，以便抬壇。5要用皂莢木做杠，用金包裹。6要把壇放在法櫃前的幔子外，對着法櫃上的施恩座，就是我要與你相會的地方。

7 "亞倫在壇上要燒馨香料做的香；每早晨他收拾燈的時候，要燒這香。8黃昏點燈的時候，他要在耶和華面前燒這香，作為世世代代常燒的香。9在這壇上不可奉上異樣的香，不可獻燔祭、素祭，也不可澆上奠祭。10亞倫一年一次要在壇的角上行贖罪之禮，他一年一次要用贖罪祭牲的血，在壇上行贖罪之禮，作為世世代代的定例。這壇在耶和華面前為至聖。"

贖罪銀

11耶和華曉諭摩西說，12 "你要按以色列人被數的計算總數。你數的時候，他們各人要為自己的生命把贖

---

a 40 That is, probably about 1 quart (about 1 liter)

b 2 That is, about 1 1/2 feet (about 0.5 meter) long and wide and about 3 feet (about 0.9 meter) high

價奉給耶和華，免得數的時候在他們中間有災殃。¹³凡過去歸那些被數之人的，每人要按聖所的平，拿銀子半舍客勒，這半舍客勒是奉給耶和華的禮物。一舍客勒是二十季拉。¹⁴凡過去歸那些被數的人，從二十歲以外的，要將這禮物奉給耶和華。¹⁵他們為贖生命將禮物奉給耶和華，富足的不可多出，貧窮的也不可少出，各人要出半舍客勒。¹⁶你要從以色列人收這贖罪銀，作為會幕的使用，可以在耶和華面前為以色列人作紀念，贖生命。”

洗濯盆

¹⁷耶和華曉諭摩西說：¹⁸ “你要用銅做洗濯盆和盆座，以便洗濯。要將盆放在會幕和壇的中間，在盆裏盛水。¹⁹亞倫和他的兒子要在這盆裏洗手洗腳。²⁰他們進會幕，或是就近壇前供職，給耶和華獻火祭的時候，必用水洗濯，免得死亡。²¹他們洗手洗腳，就免得死亡。這要作亞倫和他後裔世世代代永遠的定例。”

膏油

²²耶和華曉諭摩西說：²³ “你要取上品的香料，就是流質的沒藥五百舍客勒，香肉桂一半，就是二百五十舍客勒，菖蒲二百五十舍客勒，²⁴桂皮五百舍客勒，都按着聖所的平，又取橄欖油一欣，²⁵按做香之法，調和做成聖膏油。²⁶要用這膏油抹會幕和法櫃，²⁷桌子與桌子的一切器具，燈臺和燈臺的器具，並香壇，²⁸燔祭壇和壇的一切器具，洗濯盆和盆座。²⁹要使這些物成為聖、好成為至聖，凡挨着的都成為聖。

³⁰ “要膏亞倫和他的兒子，使他們成為聖，可以給我供祭司的職分。³¹你要對以色列人說：‘這油，我要世世代代以為聖膏油，³²不可倒在別

at the time he is counted. Then no plague will come on them when you number them. ¹³Each one who crosses over to those already counted is to give a half shekel,ᵃ according to the sanctuary shekel, which weighs twenty gerahs. This half shekel is an offering to the LORD. ¹⁴All who cross over, those twenty years old or more, are to give an offering to the LORD. ¹⁵The rich are not to give more than a half shekel and the poor are not to give less when you make the offering to the LORD to atone for your lives. ¹⁶Receive the atonement money from the Israelites and use it for the service of the Tent of Meeting. It will be a memorial for the Israelites before the LORD, making atonement for your lives."

Basin for Washing

¹⁷Then the LORD said to Moses, ¹⁸"Make a bronze basin, with its bronze stand, for washing. Place it between the Tent of Meeting and the altar, and put water in it. ¹⁹Aaron and his sons are to wash their hands and feet with water from it. ²⁰Whenever they enter the Tent of Meeting, they shall wash with water so that they will not die. Also, when they approach the altar to minister by presenting an offering made to the LORD by fire, ²¹they shall wash their hands and feet so that they will not die. This is to be a lasting ordinance for Aaron and his descendants for the generations to come."

Anointing Oil

²²Then the LORD said to Moses, ²³"Take the following fine spices: 500 shekelsᵇ of liquid myrrh, half as much (that is, 250 shekels) of fragrant cinnamon, 250 shekels of fragrant cane, ²⁴500 shekels of cassia—all according to the sanctuary shekel—and a hinᶜ of olive oil. ²⁵Make these into a sacred anointing oil, a fragrant blend, the work of a perfumer. It will be the sacred anointing oil. ²⁶Then use it to anoint the Tent of Meeting, the ark of the Testimony, ²⁷the table and all its articles, the lampstand and its accessories, the altar of incense, ²⁸the altar of burnt offering and all its utensils, and the basin with its stand. ²⁹You shall consecrate them so they will be most holy, and whatever touches them will be holy.

³⁰"Anoint Aaron and his sons and consecrate them so they may serve me as priests. ³¹Say to the Israelites, 'This is to be my sacred anointing oil for the generations to come. ³²Do not pour it

---

ᵃ 13 That is, about 1/5 ounce (about 6 grams); also in verse 15
ᵇ 23 That is, about 12 1/2 pounds (about 6 kilograms)
ᶜ 24 That is, probably about 4 quarts (about 4 liters)

on men's bodies and do not make any oil with the same formula. It is sacred, and you are to consider it sacred. [33]Whoever makes perfume like it and whoever puts it on anyone other than a priest must be cut off from his people.' "

Incense

[34]Then the LORD said to Moses, "Take fragrant spices—gum resin, onycha and galbanum—and pure frankincense, all in equal amounts, [35]and make a fragrant blend of incense, the work of a perfumer. It is to be salted and pure and sacred. [36]Grind some of it to powder and place it in front of the Testimony in the Tent of Meeting, where I will meet with you. It shall be most holy to you. [37]Do not make any incense with this formula for yourselves; consider it holy to the LORD. [38]Whoever makes any like it to enjoy its fragrance must be cut off from his people."

Bezalel and Oholiab

31 Then the LORD said to Moses, [2]"See, I have chosen Bezalel son of Uri, the son of Hur, of the tribe of Judah, [3]and I have filled him with the Spirit of God, with skill, ability and knowledge in all kinds of crafts— [4]to make artistic designs for work in gold, silver and bronze, [5]to cut and set stones, to work in wood, and to engage in all kinds of craftsmanship. [6]Moreover, I have appointed Oholiab son of Ahisamach, of the tribe of Dan, to help him. Also I have given skill to all the craftsmen to make everything I have commanded you: [7]the Tent of Meeting, the ark of the Testimony with the atonement cover on it, and all the other furnishings of the tent— [8]the table and its articles, the pure gold lampstand and all its accessories, the altar of incense, [9]the altar of burnt offering and all its utensils, the basin with its stand— [10]and also the woven garments, both the sacred garments for Aaron the priest and the garments for his sons when they serve as priests, [11]and the anointing oil and fragrant incense for the Holy Place. They are to make them just as I commanded you."

The Sabbath

[12]Then the LORD said to Moses, [13]"Say to the Israelites, 'You must observe my Sabbaths. This will be a sign between me and you for the generations to come, so you may know that I am the LORD, who makes you holy.[a]

a 13 Or who sanctifies you; or who sets you apart as holy

香

[34]耶和華吩咐摩西說："你要取馨香的香料,就是拿他弗、施喜列、喜利比拿。這馨香的香料和淨乳香,各樣要一般大的分量。[35]你要用這些加上鹽,按做香之法,做成清淨聖潔的香。[36]這香要取點搗得極細,放在會幕內、法櫃前,我要在那裏與你相會。你們要以這香為至聖。[37]你們不可按這調和之法為自己做香;要以這香為聖,歸耶和華。[38]凡做香和這香一樣,為要聞香味的,這人要從民中剪除。"

比撒列與亞何利亞伯

31 耶和華曉諭摩西說:[2]"看哪,猶大支派中戶珥的孫子、烏利的兒子比撒列,我已經提他的名召他。[3]我也以我的靈充滿了他,使他有智慧,有聰明,有知識,能做各樣的工,[4]能想出巧工,用金、銀、銅製造各物,[5]又能刻寶石,可以鑲嵌,能雕刻木頭,能做各樣的工。[6]我分派但支派中亞希撒抹的兒子亞何利亞伯與他同工。凡心裏有智慧的,我更使他們有智慧,能做我一切所吩咐的,[7]就是會幕和法櫃,並其上的施恩座,與會幕中一切的器具;[8]桌子和桌子的器具,精金的燈臺和燈臺的一切器具並香壇;[9]燔祭壇和壇的一切器具,並洗濯盆與盆座;[10]精工做的禮服,和祭司亞倫並他兒子用以供祭司職分的聖衣;[11]膏油和為聖所用馨香的香料。他們都要照我一切所吩咐的去做。"

安息日

[12]耶和華曉諭摩西說:[13]"你要吩咐以色列人說:'你們務要守我的安息日,因為這是你我之間世世代代的證據,使你們知道我耶和華是叫你們成為聖的。

14 "'所以你們要守安息日，以為聖日。凡干犯這日的，必要把他治死；凡在這日做工的，必從民中剪除。15 六日要做工，但第七日是安息聖日，是向耶和華守為聖的；凡在安息日做工的，必要把他治死。'16 故此，以色列人要世世代代守安息日為永遠的約。17 這是我和以色列人永遠的證據，因為六日之內耶和華造天地，第七日便安息舒暢。'"

18 耶和華在西奈山和摩西說完了話，就把兩塊法版交給他，是神用指頭寫的石版。

金牛犢

32 百姓見摩西遲延不下山，就大家聚集到亞倫那裏，對他說："起來！為我們做神像，可以在我們前面引路，因為領我們出埃及地的那個摩西，我們不知道他遭了甚麼事。"

2 亞倫對他們說："你們去摘下你們妻子、兒女耳上的金環，拿來給我。"3 百姓就都摘下他們耳上的金環，拿來給亞倫。4 亞倫從他們手裏接過來，鑄了一隻牛犢，用雕刻的器具做成。他們就說："以色列啊，這是領你出埃及地的神。"

5 亞倫看見，就在牛犢面前築壇，且宣告說："明日要向耶和華守節。"6 次日清早，百姓起來獻燔祭和平安祭，就坐下吃喝，起來玩耍。

7 耶和華吩咐摩西說："下去吧！因為你的百姓，就是你從埃及地領出來的，已經敗壞了。8 他們快快偏離了我所吩咐的道，為自己鑄了一隻牛犢，向它下拜獻祭，說：'以色列啊，這就是領你出埃及地的神。'"

9 耶和華對摩西說："我看這百姓真是硬着頸項的百姓。10 你且由着

14 " 'Observe the Sabbath, because it is holy to you. Anyone who desecrates it must be put to death; whoever does any work on that day must be cut off from his people. 15For six days, work is to be done, but the seventh day is a Sabbath of rest, holy to the LORD. Whoever does any work on the Sabbath day must be put to death. 16The Israelites are to observe the Sabbath, celebrating it for the generations to come as a lasting covenant. 17It will be a sign between me and the Israelites forever, for in six days the LORD made the heavens and the earth, and on the seventh day he abstained from work and rested.' "

18When the LORD finished speaking to Moses on Mount Sinai, he gave him the two tablets of the Testimony, the tablets of stone inscribed by the finger of God.

The Golden Calf

32 When the people saw that Moses was so long in coming down from the mountain, they gathered around Aaron and said, "Come, make us gods*a* who will go before us. As for this fellow Moses who brought us up out of Egypt, we don't know what has happened to him."

2Aaron answered them, "Take off the gold earrings that your wives, your sons and your daughters are wearing, and bring them to me." 3So all the people took off their earrings and brought them to Aaron. 4He took what they handed him and made it into an idol cast in the shape of a calf, fashioning it with a tool. Then they said, "These are your gods,*b* O Israel, who brought you up out of Egypt."

5When Aaron saw this, he built an altar in front of the calf and announced, "Tomorrow there will be a festival to the LORD." 6So the next day the people rose early and sacrificed burnt offerings and presented fellowship offerings.*c* Afterward they sat down to eat and drink and got up to indulge in revelry.

7Then the LORD said to Moses, "Go down, because your people, whom you brought up out of Egypt, have become corrupt. 8They have been quick to turn away from what I commanded them and have made themselves an idol cast in the shape of a calf. They have bowed down to it and sacrificed to it and have said, 'These are your gods, O Israel, who brought you up out of Egypt.'

9"I have seen these people," the LORD said to Moses, "and they are a stiff-necked people. 10Now

a 1 Or a god; also in verses 23 and 31   b 4 Or This is your god; also in verse 8   c 6 Traditionally peace offerings

leave me alone so that my anger may burn against them and that I may destroy them. Then I will make you into a great nation."

11But Moses sought the favor of the LORD his God. "O LORD," he said, "why should your anger burn against your people, whom you brought out of Egypt with great power and a mighty hand? 12Why should the Egyptians say, 'It was with evil intent that he brought them out, to kill them in the mountains and to wipe them off the face of the earth'? Turn from your fierce anger; relent and do not bring disaster on your people. 13Remember your servants Abraham, Isaac and Israel, to whom you swore by your own self: 'I will make your descendants as numerous as the stars in the sky and I will give your descendants all this land I promised them, and it will be their inheritance forever.' " 14Then the LORD relented and did not bring on his people the disaster he had threatened.

15Moses turned and went down the mountain with the two tablets of the Testimony in his hands. They were inscribed on both sides, front and back. 16The tablets were the work of God; the writing was the writing of God, engraved on the tablets.

17When Joshua heard the noise of the people shouting, he said to Moses, "There is the sound of war in the camp."

18Moses replied:

"It is not the sound of victory,
    it is not the sound of defeat;
    it is the sound of singing that I hear."

19When Moses approached the camp and saw the calf and the dancing, his anger burned and he threw the tablets out of his hands, breaking them to pieces at the foot of the mountain. 20And he took the calf they had made and burned it in the fire; then he ground it to powder, scattered it on the water and made the Israelites drink it.

21He said to Aaron, "What did these people do to you, that you led them into such great sin?"

22"Do not be angry, my lord," Aaron answered. "You know how prone these people are to evil. 23They said to me, 'Make us gods who will go before us. As for this fellow Moses who brought us up out of Egypt, we don't know what has happened to him.' 24So I told them, 'Whoever has any gold jewelry, take it off.' Then they gave me the gold, and I threw it into the fire, and out came this calf !"

我，我要向他們發烈怒，將他們滅絕，使你的後裔成為大國。"

11摩西便懇求耶和華他的神說："耶和華啊，你為甚麼向你的百姓發烈怒呢？這百姓是你用大力和大能的手從埃及地領出來的。12為甚麼使埃及人議論說：'他領他們出去，是要降禍與他們，把他們殺在山中，將他們從地上除滅。'求你轉意，不發你的烈怒；後悔，不降禍與你的百姓。13求你記念你的僕人亞伯拉罕、以撒、以色列，你曾指着自己起誓說：'我必使你們的後裔像天上的星那樣多，並且我所應許的這全地，必給你們的後裔，他們要永遠承受為業。' " 14於是耶和華後悔，不把所說的禍降與他的百姓。

15摩西轉身下山，手裏拿着兩塊法版。這版是兩面寫的，這面那面都有字。16是神的工作，字是神寫的，刻在版上。

17約書亞一聽見百姓呼喊的聲音，就對摩西說："在營裏有爭戰的聲音。"

18摩西說：

"這不是人打勝仗的聲音，
    也不是人打敗仗的聲音，
    我所聽見的，乃是人歌唱的聲音。"

19摩西挨近營前，就看見牛犢，又看見人跳舞，便發烈怒，把兩塊版扔在山下摔碎了，20又將他們所鑄的牛犢用火焚燒，磨得粉碎，撒在水面上，叫以色列人喝。

21摩西對亞倫說："這百姓向你做了甚麼？你竟使他們陷在大罪裏！"

22亞倫說："求我主不要發烈怒，這百姓專於作惡，是你知道的。23他們對我說：'你為我們做神像，可以在我們前面引路，因為領我們出埃及地的那個摩西，我們不知道他遭了甚麼事。'24我對他們說：'凡有金環的，可以摘下來'，他們就給了我，我把金環扔在火中，這牛犢便出來了。"

²⁵摩西見百姓放肆（亞倫縱容他們，使他們在仇敵中間被譏刺），²⁶就站在營門中說：「凡屬耶和華的，都要到我這裏來！」於是利未的子孫都到他那裏聚集。

²⁷他對他們說：「耶和華以色列的神這樣說：『你們各人把刀跨在腰間，在營中往來，從這門到那門，各人殺他的弟兄與同伴並鄰舍。』」²⁸利未的子孫照摩西的話行了。那一天，百姓中被殺的約有三千。²⁹摩西說：「今天你們要自潔，歸耶和華為聖，各人攻擊他的兒子和弟兄，使耶和華賜福與你們。」

³⁰到了第二天，摩西對百姓說：「你們犯了大罪，我如今要上耶和華那裏去，或者可以為你們贖罪。」

³¹摩西回到耶和華那裏說：「唉！這百姓犯了大罪，為自己做了金像。³²倘或你肯赦免他們的罪……不然，求你從你所寫的冊上塗抹我的名。」

³³耶和華對摩西說：「誰得罪我，我就從我的冊上塗抹誰的名。³⁴現在你去領這百姓，往我所告訴你的地方去，我的使者必在你前面引路，只是到我追討的日子，我必追討他們的罪。」

³⁵耶和華殺百姓的緣故是因他們同亞倫做了牛犢。

33 耶和華吩咐摩西說：「我曾起誓應許亞伯拉罕、以撒、雅各說：『要將迦南地賜給你的後裔。』現在你和你從埃及地所領出來的百姓，要從這裏往那地去。²我要差遣使者在你前面，攆出迦南人、亞摩利人、赫人、比利洗人、希未人、耶布斯人，³領你到那流奶與蜜之地。我自己不同你們上去，因為你們是硬着頸項的百姓，恐怕我在路上把你們滅絕。」

⁴百姓聽見這凶信就悲哀，也沒有人佩戴妝飾。⁵耶和華對摩西說：「你告訴以色列人說：『耶和華說：你們是硬着頸項的百姓，我若一霎時臨到你們中間，必滅絕你們。現在你們要把身上的妝飾摘下來，使我可以知道怎樣待你們。』」⁶以色列人從住何烈山以後，就把身上的妝飾摘得乾淨。

²⁵Moses saw that the people were running wild and that Aaron had let them get out of control and so become a laughingstock to their enemies. ²⁶So he stood at the entrance to the camp and said, "Whoever is for the LORD, come to me." And all the Levites rallied to him.

²⁷Then he said to them, "This is what the LORD, the God of Israel, says: 'Each man strap a sword to his side. Go back and forth through the camp from one end to the other, each killing his brother and friend and neighbor.' " ²⁸The Levites did as Moses commanded, and that day about three thousand of the people died. ²⁹Then Moses said, "You have been set apart to the LORD today, for you were against your own sons and brothers, and he has blessed you this day."

³⁰The next day Moses said to the people, "You have committed a great sin. But now I will go up to the LORD; perhaps I can make atonement for your sin."

³¹So Moses went back to the LORD and said, "Oh, what a great sin these people have committed! They have made themselves gods of gold. ³²But now, please forgive their sin—but if not, then blot me out of the book you have written."

³³The LORD replied to Moses, "Whoever has sinned against me I will blot out of my book. ³⁴Now go, lead the people to the place I spoke of, and my angel will go before you. However, when the time comes for me to punish, I will punish them for their sin."

³⁵And the LORD struck the people with a plague because of what they did with the calf Aaron had made.

33 Then the LORD said to Moses, "Leave this place, you and the people you brought up out of Egypt, and go up to the land I promised on oath to Abraham, Isaac and Jacob, saying, 'I will give it to your descendants.' ²I will send an angel before you and drive out the Canaanites, Amorites, Hittites, Perizzites, Hivites and Jebusites. ³Go up to the land flowing with milk and honey. But I will not go with you, because you are a stiff-necked people and I might destroy you on the way."

⁴When the people heard these distressing words, they began to mourn and no one put on any ornaments. ⁵For the LORD had said to Moses, "Tell the Israelites, 'You are a stiff-necked people. If I were to go with you even for a moment, I might destroy you. Now take off your ornaments and I will decide what to do with you.' " ⁶So the Israelites stripped off their ornaments at Mount Horeb.

The Tent of Meeting

7Now Moses used to take a tent and pitch it outside the camp some distance away, calling it the "tent of meeting." Anyone inquiring of the LORD would go to the tent of meeting outside the camp. 8And whenever Moses went out to the tent, all the people rose and stood at the entrances to their tents, watching Moses until he entered the tent. 9As Moses went into the tent, the pillar of cloud would come down and stay at the entrance, while the LORD spoke with Moses. 10Whenever the people saw the pillar of cloud standing at the entrance to the tent, they all stood and worshiped, each at the entrance to his tent. 11The LORD would speak to Moses face to face, as a man speaks with his friend. Then Moses would return to the camp, but his young aide Joshua son of Nun did not leave the tent.

Moses and the Glory of the LORD

12Moses said to the LORD, "You have been telling me, 'Lead these people,' but you have not let me know whom you will send with me. You have said, 'I know you by name and you have found favor with me.' 13If you are pleased with me, teach me your ways so I may know you and continue to find favor with you. Remember that this nation is your people."

14The LORD replied, "My Presence will go with you, and I will give you rest."

15Then Moses said to him, "If your Presence does not go with us, do not send us up from here. 16How will anyone know that you are pleased with me and with your people unless you go with us? What else will distinguish me and your people from all the other people on the face of the earth?"

17And the LORD said to Moses, "I will do the very thing you have asked, because I am pleased with you and I know you by name."

18Then Moses said, "Now show me your glory."

19And the LORD said, "I will cause all my goodness to pass in front of you, and I will proclaim my name, the LORD, in your presence. I will have mercy on whom I will have mercy, and I will have compassion on whom I will have compassion. 20But," he said, "you cannot see my face, for no one may see me and live."

21Then the LORD said, "There is a place near me where you may stand on a rock. 22When my glory passes by, I will put you in a cleft in the rock and cover you with my hand until I have passed by. 23Then I will remove my hand and you will see my back; but my face must not be seen."

會幕

7摩西素常將帳棚支搭在營外，離營卻遠，他稱這帳棚為會幕，凡求問耶和華的，就到營外的會幕那裏去。8當摩西出營到會幕去的時候，百姓就都起來，各人站在自己帳棚的門口，望着摩西，直等到他進了會幕。9摩西進會幕的時候，雲柱降下來，立在會幕的門前，耶和華便與摩西說話。10眾百姓看見雲柱立在會幕門前，就都起來，各人在自己帳棚的門口下拜。11耶和華與摩西面對面說話，好像人與朋友說話一般。摩西轉到營裏去，惟有他的幫手一個少年人嫩的兒子約書亞，不離開會幕。

摩西與主的榮耀

12摩西對耶和華說："你吩咐我說：'將這百姓領上去'，卻沒有叫我知道你要打發誰與我同去。只說：'我按你的名認識你，你在我眼前也蒙了恩。' 13我如今若在你眼前蒙恩，求你將你的道指示我，使我可以認識你，好在你眼前蒙恩，求你想到這民是你的民。"

14耶和華說："我必親自和你同去，使你得安息。"

15摩西說："你若不親自和我同去，就不要把我們從這裏領上去。16人在何事上得以知道我和你的百姓在你眼前蒙恩呢？豈不是因你與我們同去，使我和你的百姓與地上的萬民有分別嗎？"

17耶和華對摩西說："你這所求的我也要行，因為你在我眼前蒙了恩，並且我按你的名認識你。"

18摩西說："求你顯出你的榮耀給我看。"

19耶和華說："我要顯我一切的恩慈，在你面前經過，宣告我的名。我要恩待誰，就恩待誰；要憐憫誰，就憐憫誰。"20又說："你不能看見我的面，因為人見我的面不能存活。"

21耶和華說："看哪，在我這裏有地方，你要站在磐石上。22我的榮耀經過的時候，我必將你放在磐石穴中，用我的手遮掩你，等我過去，23然後我要將我的手收回，你就得見我的背，卻不得見我的面。"

新法版

34 耶和華吩咐摩西說：“你要鑿出兩塊石版，和先前你摔碎的那版一樣，其上的字我要寫在這版上。²明日早晨，你要預備好了，上西奈山，在山頂上站在我面前。³誰也不可和你一同上去，遍山都不可有人，在山根也不可叫羊羣牛羣吃草。”

⁴摩西就鑿出兩塊石版，和先前的一樣。清晨起來，照耶和華所吩咐的上西奈山去，手裏拿着兩塊石版。⁵耶和華在雲中降臨，和摩西一同站在那裏，宣告耶和華的名。⁶耶和華在他面前宣告說：“耶和華，耶和華，是有憐憫、有恩典的神，不輕易發怒，並有豐盛的慈愛和誠實。⁷為千萬人存留慈愛，赦免罪孽、過犯和罪惡，萬不以有罪的為無罪，必追討他的罪，自父及子，直到三四代。”

⁸摩西急忙伏地下拜，⁹說：“主啊，我若在你眼前蒙恩，求你在我們中間同行，又求你赦免我們的罪孽和罪惡，以我們為你的產業。”

¹⁰耶和華說：“我要立約，要在百姓面前行奇妙的事，是在遍地萬國中所未曾行的，在你四圍的外邦人，就要看見耶和華的作為，因我向你所行的是可畏懼的事。¹¹我今天所吩咐你的，你要謹守，我要從你面前攆出亞摩利人、迦南人、赫人、比利洗人、希未人、耶布斯人。¹²你要謹慎，不可與你所去那地的居民立約，恐怕成為你們中間的網羅；¹³卻要拆毀他們的祭壇，打碎他們的柱像，砍下他們的木偶。¹⁴不可敬拜別神，因為耶和華是忌邪的神，名為忌邪者。

¹⁵“只怕你與那地的居民立約，百姓隨從他們的神，就行邪淫，祭祀他們的神，有人叫你，你便吃他的祭物；¹⁶又為你的兒子娶他們的女兒為妻，他們的女兒隨從他們的神，行邪淫，使你的兒子也隨從他們的神

The New Stone Tablets

34 The LORD said to Moses, "Chisel out two stone tablets like the first ones, and I will write on them the words that were on the first tablets, which you broke. ²Be ready in the morning, and then come up on Mount Sinai. Present yourself to me there on top of the mountain. ³No one is to come with you or be seen anywhere on the mountain; not even the flocks and herds may graze in front of the mountain."

⁴So Moses chiseled out two stone tablets like the first ones and went up Mount Sinai early in the morning, as the LORD had commanded him; and he carried the two stone tablets in his hands. ⁵Then the LORD came down in the cloud and stood there with him and proclaimed his name, the LORD. ⁶And he passed in front of Moses, proclaiming, "The LORD, the LORD, the compassionate and gracious God, slow to anger, abounding in love and faithfulness, ⁷maintaining love to thousands, and forgiving wickedness, rebellion and sin. Yet he does not leave the guilty unpunished; he punishes the children and their children for the sin of the fathers to the third and fourth generation."

⁸Moses bowed to the ground at once and worshiped. ⁹"O Lord, if I have found favor in your eyes," he said, "then let the Lord go with us. Although this is a stiff-necked people, forgive our wickedness and our sin, and take us as your inheritance."

¹⁰Then the LORD said: "I am making a covenant with you. Before all your people I will do wonders never before done in any nation in all the world. The people you live among will see how awesome is the work that I, the LORD, will do for you. ¹¹Obey what I command you today. I will drive out before you the Amorites, Canaanites, Hittites, Perizzites, Hivites and Jebusites. ¹²Be careful not to make a treaty with those who live in the land where you are going, or they will be a snare among you. ¹³Break down their altars, smash their sacred stones and cut down their Asherah poles.ᵃ ¹⁴Do not worship any other god, for the LORD, whose name is Jealous, is a jealous God.

¹⁵"Be careful not to make a treaty with those who live in the land; for when they prostitute themselves to their gods and sacrifice to them, they will invite you and you will eat their sacrifices. ¹⁶And when you choose some of their daughters as wives for your sons and those daughters prostitute themselves to their gods,

a 13 That is, symbols of the goddess Asherah

they will lead your sons to do the same.

17"Do not make cast idols.

18"Celebrate the Feast of Unleavened Bread. For seven days eat bread made without yeast, as I commanded you. Do this at the appointed time in the month of Abib, for in that month you came out of Egypt.

19"The first offspring of every womb belongs to me, including all the firstborn males of your livestock, whether from herd or flock. 20Redeem the firstborn donkey with a lamb, but if you do not redeem it, break its neck. Redeem all your firstborn sons.

"No one is to appear before me empty-handed.

21"Six days you shall labor, but on the seventh day you shall rest; even during the plowing season and harvest you must rest.

22"Celebrate the Feast of Weeks with the firstfruits of the wheat harvest, and the Feast of Ingathering at the turn of the year.*a* 23Three times a year all your men are to appear before the Sovereign LORD, the God of Israel. 24I will drive out nations before you and enlarge your territory, and no one will covet your land when you go up three times each year to appear before the LORD your God.

25"Do not offer the blood of a sacrifice to me along with anything containing yeast, and do not let any of the sacrifice from the Passover Feast remain until morning.

26"Bring the best of the firstfruits of your soil to the house of the LORD your God.

"Do not cook a young goat in its mother's milk."

27Then the LORD said to Moses, "Write down these words, for in accordance with these words I have made a covenant with you and with Israel." 28Moses was there with the LORD forty days and forty nights without eating bread or drinking water. And he wrote on the tablets the words of the covenant—the Ten Commandments.

The Radiant Face of Moses

29When Moses came down from Mount Sinai with the two tablets of the Testimony in his hands, he was not aware that his face was radiant because he had spoken with the LORD. 30When Aaron and all the Israelites saw Moses, his face was radiant, and they were afraid to come near him. 31But Moses called to them; so Aaron and all the leaders of the community came back to him, and he spoke to them.

a 22 That is, in the fall

行邪淫。

17 "不可為自己鑄造神像。

18 "你要守除酵節,照我所吩咐你的,在亞筆月內所定的日期吃無酵餅七天,因為你是這亞筆月內出了埃及。

19 凡頭生的都是我的;一切牲畜頭生的,無論是牛是羊,公的都是我的。20頭生的驢要用羊羔代贖,若不代贖,就要打折牠的頸項。凡頭生的兒子都要贖出來。

"誰也不可空手朝見我。

21 "你六日要做工,第七日要安息;雖在耕種收割的時候,也要安息。

22 "在收割初熟麥子的時候,要守七七節。又在年底,要守收藏節。23你們一切男丁,要一年三次朝見主耶和華以色列的神。24我要從你面前趕出外邦人,擴張你的境界。你一年三次上去朝見耶和華你神的時候,必沒有人貪慕你的地土。

25 "你不可將我祭物的血和有酵的餅一同獻上。逾越節的祭物也不可留到早晨。

26 "地裏首先初熟之物,要送到耶和華你神的殿。

"不可用山羊羔母的奶煮山羊羔。"

27耶和華吩咐摩西說:"你要將這些話寫上,因為我是按這話與你和以色列人立約。"28摩西在耶和華那裏四十晝夜,也不吃飯,也不喝水。耶和華將這約的話,就是十條誡,寫在兩塊版上。

摩西臉上發光

29摩西手裏拿着兩塊法版下西奈山的時候,不知道自己的面皮因耶和華和他說話就發了光。30亞倫和以色列眾人看見摩西的面皮發光,就怕挨近他。31摩西叫他們來,於是亞倫和會眾的官長都到他那裏去,摩西就與他們説話。³²隨後，以色列眾人都近前來，他就把耶和華在西奈山與他所説的一切話都吩咐他們。

³³摩西與他們説完了話，就用帕子蒙上臉。³⁴但摩西進到耶和華面前與他説話，就揭去帕子；及至出來的時候，便將耶和華所吩咐的告訴以色列人。³⁵以色列人看見摩西的面皮發光，摩西又用帕子蒙上臉，等到他進去與耶和華説話，就揭去帕子。

安息日的條例

35 摩西招聚以色列全會眾，對他們説："這是耶和華所吩咐的話，叫你們照着行。²六日要做工，第七日乃為聖日，當向耶和華守為安息聖日；凡這日之內做工的，必把他治死。³當安息日，不可在你們一切的住處生火。"

帳幕的材料

⁴摩西對以色列全會眾説："耶和華所吩咐的是這樣：⁵你們中間要拿禮物獻給耶和華。凡樂意獻的，可以拿耶和華的禮物來，就是金、銀、銅，⁶藍色、紫色、朱紅色線，細麻，山羊毛，⁷染紅的公羊皮、海狗皮、皂莢木，⁸點燈的油，並做膏油和香的香料，⁹紅瑪瑙與別樣的寶石，可以鑲嵌在以弗得和胸牌上。

¹⁰"你們中間凡心裏有智慧的，都要來做耶和華一切所吩咐的：¹¹就是帳幕和帳幕的罩棚，並帳幕的蓋、鈎子、板、閂、柱子、帶卯的座；¹²櫃和櫃的杠，施恩座和遮掩櫃的幔子；¹³桌子和桌子的杠與桌子的一切器具，並陳設餅；¹⁴燈臺和燈臺的器具，燈盞並點燈的油；¹⁵香壇和壇的杠，膏油和馨香的香料，並帳幕門口的簾子；¹⁶燔祭壇和壇的銅網、壇的杠，並壇的一切器具，洗濯盆和盆座；¹⁷院子的帷子和帷子的柱子，帶卯的座和院子的門簾；¹⁸帳幕的橛子，並院子的橛子，和這兩處的繩子；¹⁹精工做的禮服，和祭司亞倫並

Sabbath Regulations

³²Afterward all the Israelites came near him, and he gave them all the commands the LORD had given him on Mount Sinai.

³³When Moses finished speaking to them, he put a veil over his face. ³⁴But whenever he entered the LORD's presence to speak with him, he removed the veil until he came out. And when he came out and told the Israelites what he had been commanded, ³⁵they saw that his face was radiant. Then Moses would put the veil back over his face until he went in to speak with the LORD.

Sabbath Regulations

35 Moses assembled the whole Israelite community and said to them, "These are the things the LORD has commanded you to do: ²For six days, work is to be done, but the seventh day shall be your holy day, a Sabbath of rest to the LORD. Whoever does any work on it must be put to death. ³Do not light a fire in any of your dwellings on the Sabbath day."

Materials for the Tabernacle

⁴Moses said to the whole Israelite community, "This is what the LORD has commanded: ⁵From what you have, take an offering for the LORD. Everyone who is willing is to bring to the LORD an offering of gold, silver and bronze; ⁶blue, purple and scarlet yarn and fine linen; goat hair; ⁷ram skins dyed red and hides of sea cows*ᵃ*; acacia wood; ⁸olive oil for the light; spices for the anointing oil and for the fragrant incense; ⁹and onyx stones and other gems to be mounted on the ephod and breastpiece.

¹⁰"All who are skilled among you are to come and make everything the LORD has commanded: ¹¹the tabernacle with its tent and its covering, clasps, frames, crossbars, posts and bases; ¹²the ark with its poles and the atonement cover and the curtain that shields it; ¹³the table with its poles and all its articles and the bread of the Presence; ¹⁴the lampstand that is for light with its accessories, lamps and oil for the light; ¹⁵the altar of incense with its poles, the anointing oil and the fragrant incense; the curtain for the doorway at the entrance to the tabernacle; ¹⁶the altar of burnt offering with its bronze grating, its poles and all its utensils; the bronze basin with its stand; ¹⁷the curtains of the courtyard with its posts and bases, and the curtain for the entrance to the courtyard; ¹⁸the tent pegs for the tabernacle and for the courtyard, and their ropes; ¹⁹the

a 7 That is, dugongs; also in verse 23

woven garments worn for ministering in the sanctuary—both the sacred garments for Aaron the priest and the garments for his sons when they serve as priests."

²⁰Then the whole Israelite community withdrew from Moses' presence, ²¹and everyone who was willing and whose heart moved him came and brought an offering to the LORD for the work on the Tent of Meeting, for all its service, and for the sacred garments. ²²All who were willing, men and women alike, came and brought gold jewelry of all kinds: brooches, earrings, rings and ornaments. They all presented their gold as a wave offering to the LORD. ²³Everyone who had blue, purple or scarlet yarn or fine linen, or goat hair, ram skins dyed red or hides of sea cows brought them. ²⁴Those presenting an offering of silver or bronze brought it as an offering to the LORD, and everyone who had acacia wood for any part of the work brought it. ²⁵Every skilled woman spun with her hands and brought what she had spun—blue, purple or scarlet yarn or fine linen. ²⁶And all the women who were willing and had the skill spun the goat hair. ²⁷The leaders brought onyx stones and other gems to be mounted on the ephod and breastpiece. ²⁸They also brought spices and olive oil for the light and for the anointing oil and for the fragrant incense. ²⁹All the Israelite men and women who were willing brought to the LORD freewill offerings for all the work the LORD through Moses had commanded them to do.

Bezalel and Oholiab

³⁰Then Moses said to the Israelites, "See, the LORD has chosen Bezalel son of Uri, the son of Hur, of the tribe of Judah, ³¹and he has filled him with the Spirit of God, with skill, ability and knowledge in all kinds of crafts— ³²to make artistic designs for work in gold, silver and bronze, ³³to cut and set stones, to work in wood and to engage in all kinds of artistic craftsmanship. ³⁴And he has given both him and Oholiab son of Ahisamach, of the tribe of Dan, the ability to teach others. ³⁵He has filled them with skill to do all kinds of work as craftsmen, designers, embroiderers in blue, purple and scarlet yarn and fine linen, and weavers—all of them master craftsmen and designers. ¹So Bezalel, Oholiab and every skilled person to whom the LORD has given skill and ability to know how to carry out all the work of constructing the sanctuary are to do the work just as the LORD has commanded."

36

他兒子在聖所用以供祭司職分的聖衣。"

²⁰以色列全會眾從摩西面前退去。²¹凡心裏受感和甘心樂意的都拿耶和華的禮物來,用以做會幕和其中一切的使用,又用以做聖衣。²²凡心裏樂意獻禮物的,連男帶女,各將金器,就是胸前針、耳環(註:或作"鼻環")、打印的戒指和手釧,帶來獻給耶和華。²³凡有藍色、紫色、朱紅色線,細麻,山羊毛,染紅的公羊皮、海狗皮的,都拿了來。²⁴凡獻銀子和銅給耶和華為禮物的都拿了來。凡有皂莢木可做甚麼使用的也拿了來。²⁵凡心中有智慧的婦女親手紡線,把所紡的藍色、紫色、朱紅色線和細麻都拿了來。²⁶凡有智慧心裏受感的婦女就紡山羊毛。²⁷眾官長把紅瑪瑙和別樣的寶石,可以鑲嵌在以弗得與胸牌上的,都拿了來;²⁸又拿香料做香,拿油點燈,做膏油。²⁹以色列人,無論男女,凡甘心樂意獻禮物給耶和華的,都將禮物拿來,做耶和華藉摩西所吩咐的一切工。

比撒列與亞何利亞伯

³⁰摩西對以色列人說:"猶大支派中戶珥的孫子、烏利的兒子比撒列,耶和華已經提他的名召他,³¹又以神的靈充滿了他,使他有智慧、聰明、知識,能做各樣的工;³²能想出巧工,用金、銀、銅製造各物;³³又能刻寶石,可以鑲嵌;能雕刻木頭,能做各樣的巧工。³⁴耶和華又使他和但支派中,亞希撒抹的兒子亞何利亞伯,心裏靈明,能教導人。³⁵耶和華使他們的心滿有智慧,能做各樣的工。無論是雕刻的工,巧匠的工,用藍色、紫色、朱紅色線和細麻繡花的工,並機匠的工,他們都能做,也能想出奇巧的工。¹比撒列和亞何利亞伯,並一切心裏有智慧的,就是蒙耶和華賜智慧聰明,叫他知道做聖所各樣使用之工的,都要照耶和華所吩咐的做工。"

36

²凡耶和華賜他心裏有智慧，而且受感前來做這工的，摩西把他們和比撒列並亞何利亞伯一同召來。³這些人就從摩西收了以色列人為做聖所並聖所使用之工所拿來的禮物。百姓每早晨還把甘心獻的禮物拿來。⁴凡做聖所一切工的智慧人，各都離開他所做的工，⁵來對摩西說："百姓為耶和華吩咐使用之工所拿來的，富富有餘。"

⁶摩西傳命，他們就在全營中宣告說："無論男女，不必再為聖所拿甚麼禮物來。"這樣才攔住百姓不再拿禮物來。⁷因為他們所有的材料夠做一切當做的物，而且有餘。

帳幕

⁸他們中間，凡心裏有智慧做工的，用十幅幔子做帳幕。這幔子是比撒列用撚的細麻和藍色、紫色、朱紅色線製造的，並用巧匠的手工繡上基路伯。⁹每幅幔子長二十八肘，寬四肘，都是一樣的尺寸。¹⁰他使這五幅幔子幅幅相連，又使那五幅幔子幅幅相連。¹¹在這相連的幔子末幅邊上做藍色的鈕扣，在那相連的幔子末幅邊上也照樣做。¹²在這相連的幔子上做五十個鈕扣，在那相連的幔子上也做五十個鈕扣，都是兩兩相對。¹³又做五十個金鈎，使幔子相連。這才成了一個帳幕。

¹⁴他用山羊毛織十一幅幔子，作為帳幕以上的罩棚。¹⁵每幅幔子長三十肘，寬四肘。十一幅幔子都是一樣的尺寸。¹⁶他把五幅幔子連成一幅，又把六幅幔子連成一幅。¹⁷在這相連的幔子末幅邊上做五十個鈕扣，在那相連的幔子末幅邊上也做五十個鈕扣。¹⁸又做五十個銅鈎，使罩棚連成一個，¹⁹並用染紅的公羊皮做罩棚的蓋，再用海狗皮做一層罩棚上的頂蓋。

²⁰他用皂莢木做帳幕的豎板。

²Then Moses summoned Bezalel and Oholiab and every skilled person to whom the LORD had given ability and who was willing to come and do the work. ³They received from Moses all the offerings the Israelites had brought to carry out the work of constructing the sanctuary. And the people continued to bring freewill offerings morning after morning. ⁴So all the skilled craftsmen who were doing all the work on the sanctuary left their work ⁵and said to Moses, "The people are bringing more than enough for doing the work the LORD commanded to be done."

⁶Then Moses gave an order and they sent this word throughout the camp: "No man or woman is to make anything else as an offering for the sanctuary." And so the people were restrained from bringing more, ⁷because what they already had was more than enough to do all the work.

The Tabernacle

⁸All the skilled men among the workmen made the tabernacle with ten curtains of finely twisted linen and blue, purple and scarlet yarn, with cherubim worked into them by a skilled craftsman. ⁹All the curtains were the same size—twenty-eight cubits long and four cubits wide.ᵃ ¹⁰They joined five of the curtains together and did the same with the other five. ¹¹Then they made loops of blue material along the edge of the end curtain in one set, and the same was done with the end curtain in the other set. ¹²They also made fifty loops on one curtain and fifty loops on the end curtain of the other set, with the loops opposite each other. ¹³Then they made fifty gold clasps and used them to fasten the two sets of curtains together so that the tabernacle was a unit.

¹⁴They made curtains of goat hair for the tent over the tabernacle—eleven altogether. ¹⁵All eleven curtains were the same size—thirty cubits long and four cubits wide.ᵇ ¹⁶They joined five of the curtains into one set and the other six into another set. ¹⁷Then they made fifty loops along the edge of the end curtain in one set and also along the edge of the end curtain in the other set. ¹⁸They made fifty bronze clasps to fasten the tent together as a unit. ¹⁹Then they made for the tent a covering of ram skins dyed red, and over that a covering of hides of sea cows.ᶜ

²⁰They made upright frames of acacia wood

---

a 9 That is, about 42 feet (about 12.5 meters) long and 6 feet (about 1.8 meters) wide　　b 15 That is, about 45 feet (about 13.5 meters) long and 6 feet (about 1.8 meters) wide
c 19 That is, dugongs

for the tabernacle. ²¹Each frame was ten cubits long and a cubit and a half wide,^a ²²with two projections set parallel to each other. They made all the frames of the tabernacle in this way. ²³They made twenty frames for the south side of the tabernacle ²⁴and made forty silver bases to go under them—two bases for each frame, one under each projection. ²⁵For the other side, the north side of the tabernacle, they made twenty frames ²⁶and forty silver bases—two under each frame. ²⁷They made six frames for the far end, that is, the west end of the tabernacle, ²⁸and two frames were made for the corners of the tabernacle at the far end. ²⁹At these two corners the frames were double from the bottom all the way to the top and fitted into a single ring; both were made alike. ³⁰So there were eight frames and sixteen silver bases—two under each frame.

³¹They also made crossbars of acacia wood: five for the frames on one side of the tabernacle, ³²five for those on the other side, and five for the frames on the west, at the far end of the tabernacle. ³³They made the center crossbar so that it extended from end to end at the middle of the frames. ³⁴They overlaid the frames with gold and made gold rings to hold the crossbars. They also overlaid the crossbars with gold.

³⁵They made the curtain of blue, purple and scarlet yarn and finely twisted linen, with cherubim worked into it by a skilled craftsman. ³⁶They made four posts of acacia wood for it and overlaid them with gold. They made gold hooks for them and cast their four silver bases. ³⁷For the entrance to the tent they made a curtain of blue, purple and scarlet yarn and finely twisted linen—the work of an embroiderer; ³⁸and they made five posts with hooks for them. They overlaid the tops of the posts and their bands with gold and made their five bases of bronze.

The Ark

37 Bezalel made the ark of acacia wood—two and a half cubits long, a cubit and a half wide, and a cubit and a half high.^b ²He overlaid it with pure gold, both inside and out, and made a gold molding around it. ³He cast four gold rings for it and fastened them to its four feet, with two rings on one side and two rings on the other. ⁴Then he made poles of acacia wood and overlaid them with gold. ⁵And he inserted the poles into the rings on the sides of the ark to carry it.

^a 21 That is, about 15 feet (about 4.5 meters) long and 2 1/4 feet (about 0.7 meter) wide   ^b 1 That is, about 3 3/4 feet (about 1.1 meters) long and 2 1/4 feet (about 0.7 meter) wide and high

²¹每塊長十肘，寬一肘半；²²每塊有兩榫相對，帳幕一切的板都是這樣做。²³帳幕的南面做板二十塊。²⁴在這二十塊板底下，又做四十個帶卯的銀座。兩卯接這塊板上的兩榫，兩卯接那塊板上的兩榫。²⁵帳幕的第二面，就是北面，也做板二十塊，²⁶和帶卯的銀座四十個。這板底下有兩卯，那板底下也有兩卯。²⁷帳幕的後面，就是西面，做板六塊。²⁸帳幕後面的拐角做板兩塊。²⁹板的下半截是雙的，上半截是整的，直到第一個環子；在帳幕的兩個拐角上都是這樣做。³⁰有八塊板和十六個帶卯的銀座，每塊板底下有兩卯。

³¹他用皂莢木做閂。為帳幕這面的板做五閂，³²為帳幕那面的板做五閂，又為帳幕後面的板做五閂。³³使板腰間的中閂從這一頭通到那一頭。³⁴用金子將板包裹，又做板上的金環套閂；閂也用金子包裹。

³⁵他用藍色、紫色、朱紅色線和撚的細麻織幔子，以巧匠的手工繡上基路伯。³⁶為幔子做四根皂莢木柱子，用金包裹，柱子上有金鈎，又為柱子鑄了四個帶卯的銀座。³⁷拿藍色、紫色、朱紅色線和撚的細麻，用繡花的手工織帳幕的門簾。³⁸又為簾子做五根柱子和柱子上的鈎子，用金子把柱頂和柱子上的杆子包裹。柱子有五個帶卯的座，是銅的。

約櫃

37 比撒列用皂莢木做櫃，長二肘半，寬一肘半，高一肘半。²裏外包上精金，四圍鑲上金牙邊。³又鑄四個金環，安在櫃的四腳上，這邊兩環，那邊兩環。⁴用皂莢木做兩根杠，用金包裹。⁵把杠穿在櫃旁的環內，以便抬櫃。

⁶用精金做施恩座，長二肘半，寬一肘半。⁷用金子錘出兩個基路伯來，安在施恩座的兩頭，⁸這頭做一個基路伯，那頭做一個基路伯，二基路伯接連一塊，在施恩座的兩頭。⁹二基路伯高張翅膀，遮掩施恩座，基路伯是臉對臉，朝着施恩座。

桌子

¹⁰他用皂莢木做一張桌子，長二肘，寬一肘，高一肘半。¹¹又包上精金，四圍鑲上金牙邊。¹²桌子的四圍各做一掌寬的橫梁，橫梁上鑲着金牙邊。¹³又鑄了四個金環，安在桌子四腳的四角上。¹⁴安環子的地方，是挨近橫梁，可以穿杠抬桌子。¹⁵他用皂莢木做兩根杠，用金包裹，以便抬桌子。¹⁶又用精金做桌子上的器皿，就是盤子、調羹，並奠酒的瓶和爵。

燈臺

¹⁷他用精金做一個燈臺，這燈臺的座和幹，與杯、球、花，都是接連一塊錘出來的。¹⁸燈臺兩旁杈出六個枝子，這旁三個，那旁三個。¹⁹這旁每枝上有三個杯，形狀像杏花，有球、有花，那旁每枝上也有三個杯，形狀像杏花，有球、有花。從燈臺杈出來的六個枝子都是如此。²⁰燈臺上有四個杯，形狀像杏花，有球、有花。²¹燈臺每兩個枝子以下有球，與枝子接連一塊；燈臺杈出的六個枝子都是如此。²²球和枝子是接連一塊，都是一塊精金錘出來的。

²³用精金做燈臺的七個燈盞，並燈臺的蠟剪和蠟花盤。²⁴他用精金一他連得做燈臺和燈臺的一切器具。

⁶He made the atonement cover of pure gold—two and a half cubits long and a cubit and a half wide.ᵃ ⁷Then he made two cherubim out of hammered gold at the ends of the cover. ⁸He made one cherub on one end and the second cherub on the other; at the two ends he made them of one piece with the cover. ⁹The cherubim had their wings spread upward, overshadowing the cover with them. The cherubim faced each other, looking toward the cover.

The Table

¹⁰Theyᵇ made the table of acacia wood—two cubits long, a cubit wide, and a cubit and a half high.ᶜ ¹¹Then they overlaid it with pure gold and made a gold molding around it. ¹²They also made around it a rim a handbreadthᵈ wide and put a gold molding on the rim. ¹³They cast four gold rings for the table and fastened them to the four corners, where the four legs were. ¹⁴The rings were put close to the rim to hold the poles used in carrying the table. ¹⁵The poles for carrying the table were made of acacia wood and were overlaid with gold. ¹⁶And they made from pure gold the articles for the table—its plates and dishes and bowls and its pitchers for the pouring out of drink offerings.

The Lampstand

¹⁷They made the lampstand of pure gold and hammered it out, base and shaft; its flowerlike cups, buds and blossoms were of one piece with it. ¹⁸Six branches extended from the sides of the lampstand—three on one side and three on the other. ¹⁹Three cups shaped like almond flowers with buds and blossoms were on one branch, three on the next branch and the same for all six branches extending from the lampstand. ²⁰And on the lampstand were four cups shaped like almond flowers with buds and blossoms. ²¹One bud was under the first pair of branches extending from the lampstand, a second bud under the second pair, and a third bud under the third pair—six branches in all. ²²The buds and the branches were all of one piece with the lampstand, hammered out of pure gold.

²³They made its seven lamps, as well as its wick trimmers and trays, of pure gold. ²⁴They made the lampstand and all its accessories from one talentᵃ of pure gold.

---

a 6 That is, about 3 3/4 feet (about 1.1 meters) long and 2 1/4 feet (about 0.7 meter) wide   b 10 Or *He*; also in verses 11-29
c 10 That is, about 3 feet (about 0.9 meter) long, 1 1/2 feet (about 0.5 meter) wide, and 2 1/4 feet (about 0.7 meter) high
d 12 That is, about 3 inches (about 8 centimeters)

The Altar of Incense

25They made the altar of incense out of acacia wood. It was square, a cubit long and a cubit wide, and two cubits high[b]—its horns of one piece with it. 26They overlaid the top and all the sides and the horns with pure gold, and made a gold molding around it. 27They made two gold rings below the molding—two on opposite sides—to hold the poles used to carry it. 28They made the poles of acacia wood and overlaid them with gold.

29They also made the sacred anointing oil and the pure, fragrant incense—the work of a perfumer.

The Altar of Burnt Offering

38 They[c] built the altar of burnt offering of acacia wood, three cubits[d] high; it was square, five cubits long and five cubits wide.[e] 2They made a horn at each of the four corners, so that the horns and the altar were of one piece, and they overlaid the altar with bronze. 3They made all its utensils of bronze—its pots, shovels, sprinkling bowls, meat forks and firepans. 4They made a grating for the altar, a bronze network, to be under its ledge, halfway up the altar. 5They cast bronze rings to hold the poles for the four corners of the bronze grating. 6They made the poles of acacia wood and overlaid them with bronze. 7They inserted the poles into the rings so they would be on the sides of the altar for carrying it. They made it hollow, out of boards.

Basin for Washing

8They made the bronze basin and its bronze stand from the mirrors of the women who served at the entrance to the Tent of Meeting.

The Courtyard

9Next they made the courtyard. The south side was a hundred cubits[f] long and had curtains of finely twisted linen, 10with twenty posts and twenty bronze bases, and with silver hooks and bands on the posts. 11The north side was also a hundred cubits long and had twenty posts and twenty bronze bases, with silver hooks and bands on the posts.

香壇

25他用皂莢木做香壇，是四方的，長一肘，寬一肘，高二肘。壇的四角與壇接連上一塊。26又用精金把壇的上面與壇的四面，並壇的四角包裹，又在壇的四圍鑲上金牙邊。27做兩個金環，安在牙邊以下，在壇的兩旁、兩根橫撐上，作為穿杠的用處，以便抬壇。28用皂莢木做杠，用金包裹。

29又按做香之法做聖膏油和馨香料的淨香。

燔祭壇

38 他用皂莢木做燔祭壇，是四方的，長五肘，寬五肘，高三肘。2在壇的四拐角上做四個角，與壇接連一塊，用銅把壇包裹。3他做壇上的盆、鏟子、盤子、肉叉子、火鼎；這一切器具都是用銅做的。4又為壇做一個銅網，安在壇四面的圍腰板以下，從下達到壇的半腰。5為銅網的四角鑄四個環子，作為穿杠的用處。6用皂莢木做杠，用銅包裹。7把杠穿在壇兩旁的環子內，用以抬壇。並用板做壇，壇是空的。

洗濯盆

8他用銅做洗濯盆和盆座，是用會幕門前伺候的婦人之鏡子做的。

院子

9他做帳幕的院子，院子的南面，用撚的細麻做帷子，寬一百肘。10帷子的柱子二十根，帶卯的銅座二十個，柱子上的鉤子和杆子都是用銀子做的。11北面也有帷子，寬一百肘。帷子的柱子二十根，帶卯的銅座二十個，柱子上的鉤子和杆子都是用銀子做的。

---

a 24 That is, about 75 pounds (about 34 kilograms)
b 25 That is, about 1 1/2 feet (about 0.5 meter) long and wide, and about 3 feet (about 0.9 meter) high   c 1 Or He; also in verses 2-9   d 1 That is, about 4 1/2 feet (about 1.3 meters)
e 1 That is, about 7 1/2 feet (about 2.3 meters) long and wide
f 9 That is, about 150 feet (about 46 meters)

¹²院子的西面有帷子，寬五十肘。帷子的柱子十根，帶卯的座十個，柱子的鈎子和杆子都是用銀子做的。¹³院子的東面，寬五十肘。¹⁴、¹⁵門這邊的帷子十五肘，那邊也是一樣。帷子的柱子三根，帶卯的座三個。在門的左右各有帷子十五肘，帷子的柱子三根，帶卯的座三個。¹⁶院子四面的帷子，都是用撚的細麻做的。¹⁷柱子帶卯的座是銅的，柱子上的鈎子和杆子是銀的，柱頂是用銀子包的。院子一切的柱子都是用銀杆連絡的。

¹⁸院子的門簾是以繡花的手工，用藍色、紫色、朱紅色線和撚的細麻織的，寬二十肘，高五肘，與院子的帷子相配。¹⁹帷子的柱子四根，帶卯的銅座四個，柱子上的鈎子和杆子是銀的，柱頂是用銀子包的。²⁰帳幕一切的橛子和院子四圍的橛子都是銅的。

所用的材料

²¹這是法櫃的帳幕中利未人所用物件的總數，是照摩西的吩咐，經祭司亞倫的兒子以他瑪的手數點的。²²凡耶和華所吩咐摩西的，都是猶大支派戶珥的孫子、烏利的兒子比撒列做的。²³與他同工的，有但支派中亞希撒抹的兒子亞何利亞伯；他是雕刻匠，又是巧匠，又能用藍色、紫色、朱紅色線和細麻繡花。²⁴為聖所一切工作使用所獻的金子，按聖所的平，有二十九他連得並七百三十舍客勒。

²⁵會中被數的人所出的銀子，按聖所的平，有一百他連得並一千七百七十五舍客勒。²⁶凡過去歸那些被數之人的，從二十歲以外，有六十萬零三千五百五十人，按聖所的平，每人

¹²The west end was fifty cubits*ᵃ* wide and had curtains, with ten posts and ten bases, with silver hooks and bands on the posts. ¹³The east end, toward the sunrise, was also fifty cubits wide. ¹⁴Curtains fifteen cubits*ᵇ* long were on one side of the entrance, with three posts and three bases, ¹⁵and curtains fifteen cubits long were on the other side of the entrance to the courtyard, with three posts and three bases. ¹⁶All the curtains around the courtyard were of finely twisted linen. ¹⁷The bases for the posts were bronze. The hooks and bands on the posts were silver, and their tops were overlaid with silver; so all the posts of the courtyard had silver bands.

¹⁸The curtain for the entrance to the courtyard was of blue, purple and scarlet yarn and finely twisted linen—the work of an embroiderer. It was twenty cubits*ᶜ* long and, like the curtains of the courtyard, five cubits*ᵈ* high, ¹⁹with four posts and four bronze bases. Their hooks and bands were silver, and their tops were overlaid with silver. ²⁰All the tent pegs of the tabernacle and of the surrounding courtyard were bronze.

The Materials Used

²¹These are the amounts of the materials used for the tabernacle, the tabernacle of the Testimony, which were recorded at Moses' command by the Levites under the direction of Ithamar son of Aaron, the priest. ²²(Bezalel son of Uri, the son of Hur, of the tribe of Judah, made everything the LORD commanded Moses; ²³with him was Oholiab son of Ahisamach, of the tribe of Dan—a craftsman and designer, and an embroiderer in blue, purple and scarlet yarn and fine linen.) ²⁴The total amount of the gold from the wave offering used for all the work on the sanctuary was 29 talents and 730 shekels,*ᵉ* according to the sanctuary shekel.

²⁵The silver obtained from those of the community who were counted in the census was 100 talents and 1,775 shekels,*ᶠ* according to the sanctuary shekel— ²⁶one beka per person, that is, half a shekel,*ᵍ* according to the sanctuary shekel, from everyone who had crossed over to those counted, twenty years old or more, a total of

---

a 12 That is, about 75 feet (about 23 meters)　　*b 14* That is, about 22 1/2 feet (about 6.9 meters)　　*c 18* That is, about 30 feet (about 9 meters)　　*d 18* That is, about 7 1/2 feet (about 2.3 meters)　　*e 24* The weight of the gold was a little over one ton (about 1 metric ton).　　*f 25* The weight of the silver was a little over 3 3/4 tons (about 3.4 metric tons).　　*g 26* That is, about 1/5 ounce (about 5.5 grams)

603,550 men. ²⁷The 100 talents^a of silver were used to cast the bases for the sanctuary and for the curtain—100 bases from the 100 talents, one talent for each base. ²⁸They used the 1,775 shekels^b to make the hooks for the posts, to overlay the tops of the posts, and to make their bands.

²⁹The bronze from the wave offering was 70 talents and 2,400 shekels.^c ³⁰They used it to make the bases for the entrance to the Tent of Meeting, the bronze altar with its bronze grating and all its utensils, ³¹the bases for the surrounding courtyard and those for its entrance and all the tent pegs for the tabernacle and those for the surrounding courtyard.

The Priestly Garments

39 From the blue, purple and scarlet yarn they made woven garments for ministering in the sanctuary. They also made sacred garments for Aaron, as the LORD commanded Moses.

The Ephod

²They^d made the ephod of gold, and of blue, purple and scarlet yarn, and of finely twisted linen. ³They hammered out thin sheets of gold and cut strands to be worked into the blue, purple and scarlet yarn and fine linen—the work of a skilled craftsman. ⁴They made shoulder pieces for the ephod, which were attached to two of its corners, so it could be fastened. ⁵Its skillfully woven waistband was like it—of one piece with the ephod and made with gold, and with blue, purple and scarlet yarn, and with finely twisted linen, as the LORD commanded Moses.

⁶They mounted the onyx stones in gold filigree settings and engraved them like a seal with the names of the sons of Israel. ⁷Then they fastened them on the shoulder pieces of the ephod as memorial stones for the sons of Israel, as the LORD commanded Moses.

The Breastpiece

⁸They fashioned the breastpiece—the work of a skilled craftsman. They made it like the ephod: of gold, and of blue, purple and scarlet yarn, and of finely twisted linen. ⁹It was square—a span^e long and a span wide—and folded double. ¹⁰Then they mounted four rows of precious

出銀半舍客勒，就是一比加。²⁷用那一百他連得銀子鑄造聖所帶卯的座，和幔子柱子帶卯的座，一百他連得共一百帶卯的座；每帶卯的座用一他連得。²⁸用那一千七百七十五舍客勒銀子做柱子上的鈎子，包裹柱頂並柱子上的杆子。

²⁹所獻的銅，有七十他連得並二千四百舍客勒。³⁰用這銅做會幕門帶卯的座和銅壇，並壇上的銅網和壇的一切器具，³¹並院子四圍帶卯的座和院門帶卯的座，與帳幕一切的橛子和院子四圍所有的橛子。

祭司衣服

39 比撒列用藍色、紫色、朱紅色線做精緻的衣服，在聖所用以供職，又為亞倫做聖衣，是照耶和華所吩咐摩西的。

以弗得

²他用金線和藍色、紫色、朱紅色線並撚的細麻做以弗得。³把金子錘成薄片，剪出線來，與藍色、紫色、朱紅色線，用巧匠的手工一同繡上。⁴又為以弗得做兩條相連的肩帶，接連在以弗得的兩頭。⁵其上巧工織的帶子和以弗得一樣的做法，用以束上，與以弗得接連一塊，是用金線和藍色、紫色、朱紅色線並撚的細麻做的，是照耶和華所吩咐摩西的。

⁶又琢出兩塊紅瑪瑙，鑲在金槽上，彷彿刻圖書，按着以色列兒子的名字雕刻。⁷將這兩塊寶石，安在以弗得的兩條肩帶上，為以色列人做紀念石，是照耶和華所吩咐摩西的。

胸牌

⁸他用巧匠的手工做胸牌，和以弗得一樣的做法，用金線與藍色、紫色、朱紅色線並撚的細麻做的。⁹胸牌是四方的，疊為兩層，這兩層長一虎口，寬一虎口。¹⁰上面鑲着寶石四

---

a 27 That is, about 3 3/4 tons (about 3.4 metric tons)
b 28 That is, about 45 pounds (about 20 kilograms)
c 29 The weight of the bronze was about 2 1/2 tons (about 2.4 metric tons).   *d 2 Or He; also in verses 7, 8 and 22*
e 9 That is, about 9 inches (about 22 centimeters)

行：第一行是紅寶石、紅璧璽、紅
玉；11第二行是綠寶石、藍寶石、金
鋼石；12第三行是紫瑪瑙、白瑪瑙、
紫晶；13第四行是水蒼玉、紅瑪瑙、
碧玉。這都鑲在金槽中。14這些寶石
都是按着以色列十二個兒子的名字，
彷彿刻圖書，刻十二個支派的名字。

15在胸牌上，用精金擰成如繩子
的鏈子。16又做兩個金槽和兩個金
環，安在胸牌的兩頭。17把那兩條擰
成的金鏈子，穿過胸牌兩頭的環子。
18又把鏈子的那兩頭接在兩槽上，安
在以弗得前面肩帶上。19做兩個金
環，安在胸牌的兩頭，在以弗得裏面
的邊上。20又做兩個金環，安在以弗
得前面兩條肩帶的下邊，挨近相接之
處，在以弗得巧工織的帶子以上。
21用一條藍細帶子把胸牌的環子和以
弗得的環子繫住，使胸牌貼在以弗得
巧工織的帶子上，不可與以弗得離
縫，是照耶和華所吩咐摩西的。

其他祭司衣袍

22他用織工做以弗得的外袍，顏
色全是藍的。23袍上留一領口，口的
周圍織出領邊來，彷彿鎧甲的領口，
免得破裂。24在袍子底邊上，用藍
色、紫色、朱紅色線並撚的細麻做石
榴。25又用精金做鈴鐺，把鈴鐺釘在
袍子周圍底邊上的石榴中間。26一個
鈴鐺一個石榴，一個鈴鐺一個石榴，
在袍子周圍底邊上，用以供職，是照
耶和華所吩咐摩西的。

27他用織成的細麻布為亞倫和他
的兒子做內袍。28並用細麻布做冠冕
和華美的裹頭巾，用撚的細麻布做褲
子。29又用藍色、紫色、朱紅色線並
撚的細麻，以繡花的手工做腰帶，是
照耶和華所吩咐摩西的。

stones on it. In the first row there was a ruby, a topaz and a beryl; 11in the second row a turquoise, a sapphire*a* and an emerald; 12in the third row a jacinth, an agate and an amethyst; 13in the fourth row a chrysolite, an onyx and a jasper.*b* They were mounted in gold filigree settings. 14There were twelve stones, one for each of the names of the sons of Israel, each engraved like a seal with the name of one of the twelve tribes.

15For the breastpiece they made braided chains of pure gold, like a rope. 16They made two gold filigree settings and two gold rings, and fastened the rings to two of the corners of the breastpiece. 17They fastened the two gold chains to the rings at the corners of the breastpiece, 18and the other ends of the chains to the two settings, attaching them to the shoulder pieces of the ephod at the front. 19They made two gold rings and attached them to the other two corners of the breastpiece on the inside edge next to the ephod. 20Then they made two more gold rings and attached them to the bottom of the shoulder pieces on the front of the ephod, close to the seam just above the waistband of the ephod. 21They tied the rings of the breastpiece to the rings of the ephod with blue cord, connecting it to the waistband so that the breastpiece would not swing out from the ephod—as the LORD commanded Moses.

Other Priestly Garments

22They made the robe of the ephod entirely of blue cloth—the work of a weaver— 23with an opening in the center of the robe like the opening of a collar,*c* and a band around this opening, so that it would not tear. 24They made pomegranates of blue, purple and scarlet yarn and finely twisted linen around the hem of the robe. 25And they made bells of pure gold and attached them around the hem between the pomegranates. 26The bells and pomegranates alternated around the hem of the robe to be worn for ministering, as the LORD commanded Moses.

27For Aaron and his sons, they made tunics of fine linen—the work of a weaver— 28and the turban of fine linen, the linen headbands and the undergarments of finely twisted linen. 29The sash was of finely twisted linen and blue, purple and scarlet yarn—the work of an embroiderer—as the LORD commanded Moses.

a 11 Or *lapis lazuli*　　*b 13* The precise identification of some of these precious stones is uncertain.　　*c 23* The meaning of the Hebrew for this word is uncertain.

³⁰They made the plate, the sacred diadem, out of pure gold and engraved on it, like an inscription on a seal: HOLY TO THE LORD. ³¹Then they fastened a blue cord to it to attach it to the turban, as the LORD commanded Moses.

Moses Inspects the Tabernacle

³²So all the work on the tabernacle, the Tent of Meeting, was completed. The Israelites did everything just as the LORD commanded Moses. ³³Then they brought the tabernacle to Moses: the tent and all its furnishings, its clasps, frames, crossbars, posts and bases; ³⁴the covering of ram skins dyed red, the covering of hides of sea cows*ᵃ* and the shielding curtain; ³⁵the ark of the Testimony with its poles and the atonement cover; ³⁶the table with all its articles and the bread of the Presence; ³⁷the pure gold lampstand with its row of lamps and all its accessories, and the oil for the light; ³⁸the gold altar, the anointing oil, the fragrant incense, and the curtain for the entrance to the tent; ³⁹the bronze altar with its bronze grating, its poles and all its utensils; the basin with its stand; ⁴⁰the curtains of the courtyard with its posts and bases, and the curtain for the entrance to the courtyard; the ropes and tent pegs for the courtyard; all the furnishings for the tabernacle, the Tent of Meeting; ⁴¹and the woven garments worn for ministering in the sanctuary, both the sacred garments for Aaron the priest and the garments for his sons when serving as priests.

⁴²The Israelites had done all the work just as the LORD had commanded Moses. ⁴³Moses inspected the work and saw that they had done it just as the LORD had commanded. So Moses blessed them.

Setting Up the Tabernacle

40 Then the LORD said to Moses: ²"Set up the tabernacle, the Tent of Meeting, on the first day of the first month. ³Place the ark of the Testimony in it and shield the ark with the curtain. ⁴Bring in the table and set out what belongs on it. Then bring in the lampstand and set up its lamps. ⁵Place the gold altar of incense in front of the ark of the Testimony and put the curtain at the entrance to the tabernacle.

⁶"Place the altar of burnt offering in front of the entrance to the tabernacle, the Tent of Meeting; ⁷place the basin between the Tent of Meeting and the altar and put water in it. ⁸Set up the courtyard around it and put the curtain at the entrance to the courtyard.

---

a 34 That is, dugongs

³⁰他用精金做聖冠上的牌，在上面按刻圖書之法，刻着：**歸耶和華為聖**。³¹又用一條藍細帶子，將牌繫在冠冕上，是照耶和華所吩咐摩西的。

摩西檢查會幕

³²帳幕，就是會幕，一切的工就這樣做完了。凡耶和華所吩咐摩西的，以色列人都照樣做了。³³他們送到摩西那裏，帳幕和帳幕的一切器具，就是鈎子、板、閂、柱子、帶卯的座、³⁴染紅公羊皮的蓋、海狗皮的頂蓋，和遮掩櫃的幔子、³⁵法櫃和櫃的杠並施恩座；³⁶桌子和桌子的一切器具並陳設餅；³⁷精金的燈臺和擺列的燈盞，與燈臺的一切器具，並點燈的油；³⁸金壇、膏油、馨香的香料、會幕的門簾、³⁹銅壇和壇上的銅網、壇的杠並壇的一切器具，洗濯盆和盆座；⁴⁰院子的帷子和柱子，並帶卯的座，院子的門簾、繩子、橛子，並帳幕和會幕中一切使用的器具；⁴¹精工做的禮服，和祭司亞倫並他兒子在聖所用以供祭司職分的聖衣。

⁴²這一切工作，都是以色列人照耶和華所吩咐摩西做的。⁴³耶和華怎樣吩咐的，他們就怎樣做了。摩西看見一切的工都做成了，就給他們祝福。

立起會幕

40 耶和華曉諭摩西說：²"正月初一日，你要立起帳幕，³把法櫃安放在裏面，用幔子將櫃遮掩。⁴把桌子搬進去，擺設上面的物。把燈臺搬進去，點其上的燈。⁵把燒香的金壇安在法櫃前，掛上帳幕的門簾。

⁶"把燔祭壇安在帳幕門前。⁷把洗濯盆安在會幕和壇的中間，在盆裏盛水。⁸又在四圍立院帷，把院子的門簾掛上。

9 "用膏油把帳幕和其中所有的都抹上，使帳幕和一切器具成聖，就都成聖；10 又要抹燔祭壇和一切器具使壇成聖，就都成為至聖；11 要抹洗濯盆和盆座，使盆成聖。

12 "要使亞倫和他兒子到會幕門口來，用水洗身。13 要給亞倫穿上聖衣，又膏他，使他成聖，可以給我供祭司的職分。14 又要使他兒子來，給他們穿上內袍。15 怎樣膏他們的父親，也要照樣膏他們，使他們給我供祭司的職分。他們世世代代凡受膏的，就永遠當祭司的職任。" 16 摩西這樣行，都是照耶和華所吩咐他的。

17 第二年正月初一日，帳幕就立起來。18 摩西立帳幕，安上帶卯的座，立上板，穿上閂，立起柱子。19 在帳幕以上搭罩棚，把罩棚的頂蓋，蓋在其上，是照耶和華所吩咐他的。

20 又把法版放在櫃裏，把杠穿在櫃的兩旁，把施恩座安在櫃上。21 把櫃抬進帳幕，掛上遮掩櫃的幔子，把法櫃遮掩了，是照耶和華所吩咐他的。

22 又把桌子安在會幕內，在帳幕北邊，在幔子外。23 在桌子上將餅陳設在耶和華面前，是照耶和華所吩咐他的。
24 又把燈臺安在會幕內，在帳幕南邊，與桌子相對，25 在耶和華面前點燈，是照耶和華所吩咐他的。

26 把金壇安在會幕內的幔子前，27 在壇上燒了馨香料做的香，是照耶和華所吩咐他的。28 又掛上帳幕的門簾。

29 在會幕的帳幕門前，安設燔祭壇，把燔祭和素祭獻在其上，是照耶和華所吩咐他的。

30 把洗濯盆安在會幕和壇的中間，盆中盛水，以便洗濯。31 摩西和亞倫並亞倫的兒子，在這盆裏洗手洗腳。32 他們進會幕或就近壇的時候，便都洗濯，是照耶和華所吩咐他的。

9"Take the anointing oil and anoint the tabernacle and everything in it; consecrate it and all its furnishings, and it will be holy. 10Then anoint the altar of burnt offering and all its utensils; consecrate the altar, and it will be most holy. 11Anoint the basin and its stand and consecrate them.

12"Bring Aaron and his sons to the entrance to the Tent of Meeting and wash them with water. 13Then dress Aaron in the sacred garments, anoint him and consecrate him so he may serve me as priest. 14Bring his sons and dress them in tunics. 15Anoint them just as you anointed their father, so they may serve me as priests. Their anointing will be to a priesthood that will continue for all generations to come." 16Moses did everything just as the LORD commanded him.

17So the tabernacle was set up on the first day of the first month in the second year. 18When Moses set up the tabernacle, he put the bases in place, erected the frames, inserted the crossbars and set up the posts. 19Then he spread the tent over the tabernacle and put the covering over the tent, as the LORD commanded him.

20He took the Testimony and placed it in the ark, attached the poles to the ark and put the atonement cover over it. 21Then he brought the ark into the tabernacle and hung the shielding curtain and shielded the ark of the Testimony, as the LORD commanded him.

22Moses placed the table in the Tent of Meeting on the north side of the tabernacle outside the curtain 23and set out the bread on it before the LORD, as the LORD commanded him.

24He placed the lampstand in the Tent of Meeting opposite the table on the south side of the tabernacle 25and set up the lamps before the LORD, as the LORD commanded him.

26Moses placed the gold altar in the Tent of Meeting in front of the curtain 27and burned fragrant incense on it, as the LORD commanded him. 28Then he put up the curtain at the entrance to the tabernacle.

29He set the altar of burnt offering near the entrance to the tabernacle, the Tent of Meeting, and offered on it burnt offerings and grain offerings, as the LORD commanded him.

30He placed the basin between the Tent of Meeting and the altar and put water in it for washing, 31and Moses and Aaron and his sons used it to wash their hands and feet. 32They washed whenever they entered the Tent of Meeting or approached the altar, as the LORD commanded Moses.

³³Then Moses set up the courtyard around the tabernacle and altar and put up the curtain at the entrance to the courtyard. And so Moses finished the work.

The Glory of the Lord

³⁴Then the cloud covered the Tent of Meeting, and the glory of the Lord filled the tabernacle. ³⁵Moses could not enter the Tent of Meeting because the cloud had settled upon it, and the glory of the Lord filled the tabernacle.

³⁶In all the travels of the Israelites, whenever the cloud lifted from above the tabernacle, they would set out; ³⁷but if the cloud did not lift, they did not set out—until the day it lifted. ³⁸So the cloud of the Lord was over the tabernacle by day, and fire was in the cloud by night, in the sight of all the house of Israel during all their travels.

³³在帳幕和壇的四圍，立了院帷，把院子的門簾掛上。這樣，<u>摩西</u>就完了工。

主的榮光

³⁴當時，雲彩遮蓋會幕，耶和華的榮光就充滿了帳幕。³⁵<u>摩西</u>不能進會幕，因為雲彩停在其上，並且耶和華的榮光充滿了帳幕。

³⁶每逢雲彩從帳幕收上去，<u>以色列</u>人就起程前往；³⁷雲彩若不收上去，他們就不起程，直等到雲彩收上去。³⁸日間，耶和華的雲彩是在帳幕以上；夜間，雲中有火，在<u>以色列</u>全家的眼前，在他們所行的路上都是這樣。

圖三：出埃及記中的主要地方
MAP 3 : KEY PLACES IN EXODUS

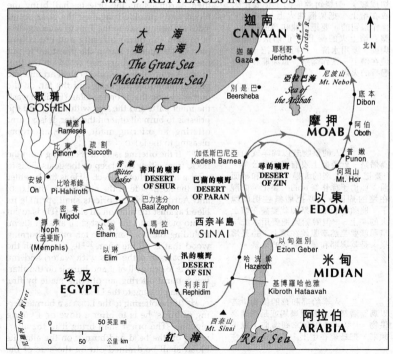

利未記

Leviticus

燔祭

1 耶和華從會幕中呼叫摩西，對他說：²「你曉諭以色列人說：『你們中間若有人獻供物給耶和華，要從牛羣羊羣中，獻牲畜為供物。

³「『他的供物若以牛為燔祭，就要在會幕門口獻一隻沒有殘疾的公牛，可以在耶和華面前蒙悅納。⁴他要按手在燔祭牲的頭上，燔祭便蒙悅納，為他贖罪。⁵他要在耶和華面前宰公牛；亞倫子孫作祭司的，要奉上血，把血灑在會幕門口壇的周圍。⁶那人要剝去燔祭牲的皮，把燔祭牲切成塊子。⁷祭司亞倫的子孫要把火放在壇上，把柴擺在火上。⁸亞倫子孫作祭司的，要把肉塊和頭並脂油，擺在壇上火的柴上。⁹但燔祭的臟腑與腿，要用水洗。祭司就要把一切全燒在壇上，當作燔祭，獻與耶和華為馨香的火祭。

¹⁰「『人的供物若以綿羊或山羊為燔祭，就要獻上沒有殘疾的公羊。¹¹要把羊宰於壇的北邊，在耶和華面前；亞倫子孫作祭司的，要把羊血灑在壇的周圍。¹²要把燔祭牲切成塊子，連頭和脂油，祭司就要擺在壇上火的柴上。¹³但臟腑與腿要用水洗，祭司就要全然奉獻燒在壇上。這是燔祭，是獻與耶和華為馨香的火祭。

¹⁴「『人奉給耶和華的供物，若以鳥為燔祭，就要獻斑鳩或是雛鴿為供物。¹⁵祭司要把鳥拿到壇前，揪下頭來，把鳥燒在壇上，鳥的血要流在

The Burnt Offering

1 The LORD called to Moses and spoke to him from the Tent of Meeting. He said, ²"Speak to the Israelites and say to them: 'When any of you brings an offering to the LORD, bring as your offering an animal from either the herd or the flock.

³"'If the offering is a burnt offering from the herd, he is to offer a male without defect. He must present it at the entrance to the Tent of Meeting so that it*ᵃ* will be acceptable to the LORD. ⁴He is to lay his hand on the head of the burnt offering, and it will be accepted on his behalf to make atonement for him. ⁵He is to slaughter the young bull before the LORD, and then Aaron's sons the priests shall bring the blood and sprinkle it against the altar on all sides at the entrance to the Tent of Meeting. ⁶He is to skin the burnt offering and cut it into pieces. ⁷The sons of Aaron the priest are to put fire on the altar and arrange wood on the fire. ⁸Then Aaron's sons the priests shall arrange the pieces, including the head and the fat, on the burning wood that is on the altar. ⁹He is to wash the inner parts and the legs with water, and the priest is to burn all of it on the altar. It is a burnt offering, an offering made by fire, an aroma pleasing to the LORD.

¹⁰"'If the offering is a burnt offering from the flock, from either the sheep or the goats, he is to offer a male without defect. ¹¹He is to slaughter it at the north side of the altar before the LORD, and Aaron's sons the priests shall sprinkle its blood against the altar on all sides. ¹²He is to cut it into pieces, and the priest shall arrange them, including the head and the fat, on the burning wood that is on the altar. ¹³He is to wash the inner parts and the legs with water, and the priest is to bring all of it and burn it on the altar. It is a burnt offering, an offering made by fire, an aroma pleasing to the LORD.

¹⁴"'If the offering to the LORD is a burnt offering of birds, he is to offer a dove or a young pigeon. ¹⁵The priest shall bring it to the altar, wring off the head and burn it on the altar; its blood shall be drained out on the side of the

a 3 Or he

altar. [16]He is to remove the crop with its contents[a] and throw it to the east side of the altar, where the ashes are. [17]He shall tear it open by the wings, not severing it completely, and then the priest shall burn it on the wood that is on the fire on the altar. It is a burnt offering, an offering made by fire, an aroma pleasing to the LORD.

The Grain Offering

2 " 'When someone brings a grain offering to the LORD, his offering is to be of fine flour. He is to pour oil on it, put incense on it [2]and take it to Aaron's sons the priests. The priest shall take a handful of the fine flour and oil, together with all the incense, and burn this as a memorial portion on the altar, an offering made by fire, an aroma pleasing to the LORD. [3]The rest of the grain offering belongs to Aaron and his sons; it is a most holy part of the offerings made to the LORD by fire.

[4]" 'If you bring a grain offering baked in an oven, it is to consist of fine flour: cakes made without yeast and mixed with oil, or[b] wafers made without yeast and spread with oil. [5]If your grain offering is prepared on a griddle, it is to be made of fine flour mixed with oil, and without yeast. [6]Crumble it and pour oil on it; it is a grain offering. [7]If your grain offering is cooked in a pan, it is to be made of fine flour and oil. [8]Bring the grain offering made of these things to the LORD; present it to the priest, who shall take it to the altar. [9]He shall take out the memorial portion from the grain offering and burn it on the altar as an offering made by fire, an aroma pleasing to the LORD. [10]The rest of the grain offering belongs to Aaron and his sons; it is a most holy part of the offerings made to the LORD by fire.

[11]" 'Every grain offering you bring to the LORD must be made without yeast, for you are not to burn any yeast or honey in an offering made to the LORD by fire. [12]You may bring them to the LORD as an offering of the firstfruits, but they are not to be offered on the altar as a pleasing aroma. [13]Season all your grain offerings with salt. Do not leave the salt of the covenant of your God out of your grain offerings; add salt to all your offerings.

[14]" 'If you bring a grain offering of firstfruits to the LORD, offer crushed heads of new grain roasted in the fire. [15]Put oil and incense on it; it is a grain offering. [16]The priest shall burn the memorial portion of the crushed grain and the

壇的旁邊。[16]又要把鳥的嗉子和髒物除掉（註：“髒物”或作“翎毛”），丟在壇的東邊倒灰的地方。[17]要拿着鳥的兩個翅膀，把鳥撕開，只是不可撕斷，祭司要在壇上、在火的柴上焚燒。這是燔祭，是獻與耶和華為馨香的火祭。

素祭

2 " '若有人獻素祭為供物給耶和華，要用細麵澆上油，加上乳香，[2]帶到亞倫子孫作祭司的那裏。祭司就要從細麵中取出一把來，並取些油和所有的乳香，然後要把所取的這些作為紀念，燒在壇上，是獻與耶和華為馨香的火祭。[3]素祭所剩的要歸給亞倫和他的子孫；這是獻與耶和華的火祭中為至聖的。

[4]" '若用爐中烤的物為素祭，就要用調油的無酵細麵餅，或是抹油的無酵薄餅。[5]若用鐵鏊上做的物為素祭，就要用調油的無酵細麵，[6]分成塊子，澆上油，這是素祭。[7]若用煎盤做的物為素祭，就要用油與細麵做成。[8]要把這些東西做的素祭帶到耶和華面前，並奉給祭司帶到壇前。[9]祭司要從素祭中取出作為紀念的，燒在壇上，是獻與耶和華為馨香的火祭。[10]素祭所剩的，要歸給亞倫和他的子孫。這是獻與耶和華的火祭中為至聖的。

[11]" '凡獻給耶和華的素祭都不可用酵，因為你們不可燒一點酵、一點蜜，當作火祭獻給耶和華。[12]這些物要獻給耶和華作為初熟的供物，只是不可在壇上獻為馨香的祭。[13]凡素祭的供物都要用鹽調和，在素祭上不可缺了你神立約的鹽；一切的供物都要配鹽而獻。

[14]" '若向耶和華獻初熟之物為素祭，要獻上烘了的禾穗子，就是軋了的新穗子，當作初熟之物的素祭，[15]並要抹上油，加上乳香，這是素祭。[16]祭司要把其中作為紀念的，就是一些軋了的禾穗子和一些油，並所

---

a 16 Or *crop and the feathers*; the meaning of the Hebrew for this word is uncertain. *b 4* Or *and*

有的乳香，都焚燒，是向耶和華獻的火祭。

平安祭

3 「『人獻供物為平安祭（註：「平安」或作「酬恩」。下同），若是從牛羣中獻，無論是公的是母的，必用沒有殘疾的獻在耶和華面前。²他要按手在供物的頭上，宰於會幕門口。亞倫子孫作祭司的，要把血灑在壇的周圍。³從平安祭中，將火祭獻給耶和華，也要把蓋臟的脂油和臟上所有的脂油，⁴並兩個腰子和腰子上的脂油，就是靠腰兩旁的脂油，與肝上的網子和腰子，一概取下。⁵亞倫的子孫要把這些燒在壇的燔祭上，就是在火的柴上，是獻與耶和華為馨香的火祭。

⁶ 「『人向耶和華獻供物為平安祭，若是從羊羣中獻，無論是公的是母的，必用沒有殘疾的。⁷若獻一隻羊羔為供物，必在耶和華面前獻上，⁸並要按手在供物的頭上，宰於會幕前。亞倫的子孫，要把血灑在壇的周圍。⁹從平安祭中，將火祭獻給耶和華，其中的脂油和整肥尾巴，都要在靠近脊骨處取下，並要把蓋臟的脂油和臟上所有的脂油，¹⁰兩個腰子和腰子上的脂油，就是靠腰兩旁的脂油，並肝上的網子和腰子，一概取下。¹¹祭司要在壇上焚燒，是獻給耶和華為食物的火祭。

¹² 「『人的供物若是山羊，必在耶和華面前獻上。¹³要按手在山羊頭上，宰於會幕前。亞倫的子孫要把血灑在壇的周圍，¹⁴、¹⁵又把蓋臟的脂油和臟上所有的脂油，兩個腰子和腰子上的脂油，就是靠腰兩旁的脂油，並肝上的網子和腰子，一概取下，獻給耶和華為火祭。¹⁶祭司要在壇上焚燒，作為馨香火祭的食物。脂油都是耶和華的。

¹⁷ 「『在你們一切的住處，脂油和血都不可吃，這要成為你們世世代代永遠的定例。』」

oil, together with all the incense, as an offering made to the LORD by fire.

The Fellowship Offering

3 " 'If someone's offering is a fellowship offering,ᵃ and he offers an animal from the herd, whether male or female, he is to present before the LORD an animal without defect. ²He is to lay his hand on the head of his offering and slaughter it at the entrance to the Tent of Meeting. Then Aaron's sons the priests shall sprinkle the blood against the altar on all sides. ³From the fellowship offering he is to bring a sacrifice made to the LORD by fire: all the fat that covers the inner parts or is connected to them, ⁴both kidneys with the fat on them near the loins, and the covering of the liver, which he will remove with the kidneys. ⁵Then Aaron's sons are to burn it on the altar on top of the burnt offering that is on the burning wood, as an offering made by fire, an aroma pleasing to the LORD.

⁶ 'If he offers an animal from the flock as a fellowship offering to the LORD, he is to offer a male or female without defect. ⁷If he offers a lamb, he is to present it before the LORD. ⁸He is to lay his hand on the head of his offering and slaughter it in front of the Tent of Meeting. Then Aaron's sons shall sprinkle its blood against the altar on all sides. ⁹From the fellowship offering he is to bring a sacrifice made to the LORD by fire: its fat, the entire fat tail cut off close to the backbone, all the fat that covers the inner parts or is connected to them, ¹⁰both kidneys with the fat on them near the loins, and the covering of the liver, which he will remove with the kidneys. ¹¹The priest shall burn them on the altar as food, an offering made to the LORD by fire.

¹² " 'If his offering is a goat, he is to present it before the LORD. ¹³He is to lay his hand on its head and slaughter it in front of the Tent of Meeting. Then Aaron's sons shall sprinkle its blood against the altar on all sides. ¹⁴From what he offers he is to make this offering to the LORD by fire: all the fat that covers the inner parts or is connected to them, ¹⁵both kidneys with the fat on them near the loins, and the covering of the liver, which he will remove with the kidneys. ¹⁶The priest shall burn them on the altar as food, an offering made by fire, a pleasing aroma. All the fat is the LORD's.

¹⁷" 'This is a lasting ordinance for the generations to come, wherever you live: You must not eat any fat or any blood.' "

a 1 Traditionally *peace offering*; also in verses 3, 6 and 9

The Sin Offering

4 The LORD said to Moses, ²"Say to the Israelites: 'When anyone sins unintentionally and does what is forbidden in any of the LORD's commands—

³" 'If the anointed priest sins, bringing guilt on the people, he must bring to the LORD a young bull without defect as a sin offering for the sin he has committed. ⁴He is to present the bull at the entrance to the Tent of Meeting before the LORD. He is to lay his hand on its head and slaughter it before the LORD. ⁵Then the anointed priest shall take some of the bull's blood and carry it into the Tent of Meeting. ⁶He is to dip his finger into the blood and sprinkle some of it seven times before the LORD, in front of the curtain of the sanctuary. ⁷The priest shall then put some of the blood on the horns of the altar of fragrant incense that is before the LORD in the Tent of Meeting. The rest of the bull's blood he shall pour out at the base of the altar of burnt offering at the entrance to the Tent of Meeting. ⁸He shall remove all the fat from the bull of the sin offering—the fat that covers the inner parts or is connected to them, ⁹both kidneys with the fat on them near the loins, and the covering of the liver, which he will remove with the kidneys— ¹⁰just as the fat is removed from the ox*a* sacrificed as a fellowship offering.*b* Then the priest shall burn them on the altar of burnt offering. ¹¹But the hide of the bull and all its flesh, as well as the head and legs, the inner parts and offal— ¹²that is, all the rest of the bull—he must take outside the camp to a place ceremonially clean, where the ashes are thrown, and burn it in a wood fire on the ash heap.

¹³" 'If the whole Israelite community sins unintentionally and does what is forbidden in any of the LORD's commands, even though the community is unaware of the matter, they are guilty. ¹⁴When they become aware of the sin they committed, the assembly must bring a young bull as a sin offering and present it before the Tent of Meeting. ¹⁵The elders of the community are to lay their hands on the bull's head before the LORD, and the bull shall be slaughtered before the LORD. ¹⁶Then the anointed priest is to take some of the bull's blood into the Tent of Meeting. ¹⁷He shall dip his finger into the blood and sprinkle it before the LORD seven times in front of the curtain. ¹⁸He is to put some of the

a 10 The Hebrew word can include both male and female.

b 10 Traditionally peace offering; also in verses 26, 31 and 35

贖罪祭

4 耶和華對摩西說：² "你曉諭以色列人說：'若有人在耶和華所吩咐不可行的甚麼事上誤犯了一件——

³ "'或是受膏的祭司犯罪，使百姓陷在罪裏，就當為他所犯的罪，把沒有殘疾的公牛犢獻給耶和華為贖罪祭。⁴他要牽公牛到會幕門口，在耶和華面前按手在牛的頭上，把牛宰於耶和華面前。⁵受膏的祭司要取些公牛的血帶到會幕，⁶把指頭蘸於血中，在耶和華面前對着聖所的幔子彈血七次。⁷又要把些血抹在會幕內耶和華面前香壇的四角上，再把公牛所有的血倒在會幕門口燔祭壇的腳那裏。⁸要把贖罪祭公牛所有的脂油，乃是蓋臟的脂油和臟上所有的脂油，⁹並兩個腰子和腰子上的脂油，就是靠腰兩旁的脂油，與肝上的網子和腰子，一概取下，¹⁰與平安祭公牛上所取的一樣。祭司要把這些燒在燔祭的壇上。¹¹公牛的皮和所有的肉並頭、腿、臟、腑、糞，¹²就是全公牛，要搬到營外潔淨之地、倒灰之所，用火燒在柴上。

¹³ "'以色列全會眾，若行了耶和華所吩咐不可行的甚麼事，誤犯了罪，是隱而未現、會眾看不出來的，¹⁴會眾一知道所犯的罪，就要獻一隻公牛犢為贖罪祭，牽到會幕前。¹⁵會中的長老就要在耶和華面前按手在牛的頭上，將牛在耶和華面前宰了。¹⁶受膏的祭司要取些公牛的血帶到會幕，¹⁷把指頭蘸於血中，在耶和華面前對着幔子彈血七次。¹⁸又要把些血

抹在會幕內耶和華面前壇的四角上，再把所有的血倒在會幕門口，燔祭壇的腳那裏。¹⁹把牛所有的脂油都取下，燒在壇上。²⁰收拾這牛，與那贖罪祭的牛一樣。祭司要為他們贖罪，他們必蒙赦免。²¹他要把牛搬到營外燒了，像燒頭一個牛一樣。這是會眾的贖罪祭。

²² "'官長若行了耶和華他神所吩咐不可行的甚麼事，誤犯了罪，²³所犯的罪自己知道了，就要牽一隻沒有殘疾的公山羊為供物，²⁴按手在羊的頭上，宰於耶和華面前，宰燔祭牲的地方。這是贖罪祭。²⁵祭司要用指頭蘸些贖罪祭牲的血，抹在燔祭壇的四角上，把血倒在燔祭壇的腳那裏。²⁶所有的脂油，祭司都要燒在壇上，正如平安祭的脂油一樣。至於他的罪，祭司要為他贖了，他必蒙赦免。

²⁷ "'民中若有人行了耶和華所吩咐不可行的甚麼事，誤犯了罪，²⁸所犯的罪自己知道了，就要為所犯的罪，牽一隻沒有殘疾的母山羊為供物，²⁹按手在贖罪祭牲的頭上，在那宰燔祭牲的地方宰了。³⁰祭司要用指頭蘸些羊的血，抹在燔祭壇的四角上，所有的血都要倒在壇的腳那裏。³¹又要把羊所有的脂油都取下，正如取平安祭牲的脂油一樣。祭司要在壇上焚燒，在耶和華面前作為馨香的祭，為他贖罪，他必蒙赦免。

³² "'人若牽一隻綿羊羔為贖罪祭的供物，必要牽一隻沒有殘疾的母羊，³³按手在贖罪祭牲的頭上，在那宰燔祭牲的地方宰了作贖罪祭。³⁴祭司要用指頭蘸些贖罪祭牲的血，抹在燔祭壇的四角上。所有的血都要倒在壇的腳那裏，³⁵又要把所有的脂油都

blood on the horns of the altar that is before the LORD in the Tent of Meeting. The rest of the blood he shall pour out at the base of the altar of burnt offering at the entrance to the Tent of Meeting. ¹⁹He shall remove all the fat from it and burn it on the altar, ²⁰and do with this bull just as he did with the bull for the sin offering. In this way the priest will make atonement for them, and they will be forgiven. ²¹Then he shall take the bull outside the camp and burn it as he burned the first bull. This is the sin offering for the community.

²²" 'When a leader sins unintentionally and does what is forbidden in any of the commands of the LORD his God, he is guilty. ²³When he is made aware of the sin he committed, he must bring as his offering a male goat without defect. ²⁴He is to lay his hand on the goat's head and slaughter it at the place where the burnt offering is slaughtered before the LORD. It is a sin offering. ²⁵Then the priest shall take some of the blood of the sin offering with his finger and put it on the horns of the altar of burnt offering and pour out the rest of the blood at the base of the altar. ²⁶He shall burn all the fat on the altar as he burned the fat of the fellowship offering. In this way the priest will make atonement for the man's sin, and he will be forgiven.

²⁷" 'If a member of the community sins unintentionally and does what is forbidden in any of the LORD's commands, he is guilty. ²⁸When he is made aware of the sin he committed, he must bring as his offering for the sin he committed a female goat without defect. ²⁹He is to lay his hand on the head of the sin offering and slaughter it at the place of the burnt offering. ³⁰Then the priest is to take some of the blood with his finger and put it on the horns of the altar of burnt offering and pour out the rest of the blood at the base of the altar. ³¹He shall remove all the fat, just as the fat is removed from the fellowship offering, and the priest shall burn it on the altar as an aroma pleasing to the LORD. In this way the priest will make atonement for him, and he will be forgiven.

³²" 'If he brings a lamb as his sin offering, he is to bring a female without defect. ³³He is to lay his hand on its head and slaughter it for a sin offering at the place where the burnt offering is slaughtered. ³⁴Then the priest shall take some of the blood of the sin offering with his finger and put it on the horns of the altar of burnt offering and pour out the rest of the blood at the base of the altar. ³⁵He shall remove all the fat, just as the

fat is removed from the lamb of the fellowship offering, and the priest shall burn it on the altar on top of the offerings made to the LORD by fire. In this way the priest will make atonement for him for the sin he has committed, and he will be forgiven.

5 " 'If a person sins because he does not speak up when he hears a public charge to testify regarding something he has seen or learned about, he will be held responsible.

2" 'Or if a person touches anything ceremonially unclean—whether the carcasses of unclean wild animals or of unclean livestock or of unclean creatures that move along the ground—even though he is unaware of it, he has become unclean and is guilty.

3" 'Or if he touches human uncleanness—anything that would make him unclean—even though he is unaware of it, when he learns of it he will be guilty.

4" 'Or if a person thoughtlessly takes an oath to do anything, whether good or evil—in any matter one might carelessly swear about—even though he is unaware of it, in any case when he learns of it he will be guilty.

5" 'When anyone is guilty in any of these ways, he must confess in what way he has sinned 6and, as a penalty for the sin he has committed, he must bring to the LORD a female lamb or goat from the flock as a sin offering; and the priest shall make atonement for him for his sin.

7" 'If he cannot afford a lamb, he is to bring two doves or two young pigeons to the LORD as a penalty for his sin—one for a sin offering and the other for a burnt offering. 8He is to bring them to the priest, who shall first offer the one for the sin offering. He is to wring its head from its neck, not severing it completely, 9and is to sprinkle some of the blood of the sin offering against the side of the altar; the rest of the blood must be drained out at the base of the altar. It is a sin offering. 10The priest shall then offer the other as a burnt offering in the prescribed way and make atonement for him for the sin he has committed, and he will be forgiven.

11" 'If, however, he cannot afford two doves or two young pigeons, he is to bring as an offering for his sin a tenth of an ephah*a* of fine flour for a sin offering. He must not put oil or incense on it, because it is a sin offering. 12He is to bring it to the priest, who shall take a handful of it as a memorial portion and burn it on the altar on top

a 11 That is, probably about 2 quarts (about 2 liters)

取下,正如取平安祭羊羔的脂油一樣。祭司要按獻給耶和華火祭的條例,燒在壇上。至於所犯的罪,祭司要為他贖了,他必蒙赦免。

5 " '若有人聽見發誓的聲音(註:或作"若有人聽見叫人發誓的聲音"),他本是見證,卻不把所看見的、所知道的說出來,這就是罪;他要擔當他的罪孽。

2 " '或是有人摸了不潔的物,無論是不潔的死獸,是不潔的死畜,是不潔的死蟲,他卻不知道,因此成了不潔,就有了罪。

3 " '或是他摸了別人的污穢,無論是染了甚麼污穢,他卻不知道;一知道了,就有了罪。

4 " '或是有人嘴裏冒失發誓,要行惡、要行善,無論人在甚麼事上冒失發誓,他卻不知道;一知道了,就要在這其中的一件上有了罪。

5 " '他有了罪的時候,就要承認所犯的罪,6並要因所犯的罪,把他的贖愆祭牲,就是羊羣中的母羊,或是一隻羊羔,或是一隻山羊,牽到耶和華面前為贖罪祭。至於他的罪,祭司要為他贖了。

7 " '他的力量若不夠獻一隻羊羔,就要因所犯的罪,把兩隻斑鳩或是兩隻雛鴿,帶到耶和華面前為贖愆祭:一隻作贖罪祭,一隻作燔祭。8把這些帶到祭司那裏,祭司就要先把那贖罪祭獻上,從鳥的頸項上揪下頭來,只是不可把鳥撕斷。9也把些贖罪祭牲的血,彈在壇的旁邊,剩下的血要流在壇的腳那裏。這是贖罪祭。10他要照例獻第二隻為燔祭。至於他所犯的罪,祭司要為他贖了,他必蒙赦免。

11 " '他的力量若不夠獻兩隻斑鳩或是兩隻雛鴿,就要因所犯的罪帶供物來,就是細麵伊法十分之一為贖罪祭;不可加上油,也不可加上乳香,因為是贖罪祭。12他要把供物帶到祭司那裏,祭司要取出自己的一把來作為紀念,按獻給耶和華火祭的條例，燒在壇上。這是贖罪祭。¹³至於他在這幾件事中所犯的罪，祭司要為他贖了，他必蒙赦免。剩下的麵都歸與祭司，和素祭一樣。’”

贖愆祭

¹⁴耶和華曉諭摩西說：¹⁵“人若在耶和華的聖物上誤犯了罪，有了過犯，就要照你所估的，按聖所的舍客勒拿銀子，將贖愆祭牲，就是羊羣中一隻沒有殘疾的公綿羊，牽到耶和華面前為贖愆祭；¹⁶並且他因在聖物上的差錯要償還，另外加五分之一，都給祭司。祭司要用贖愆祭的公綿羊為他贖罪，他必蒙赦免。

¹⁷“若有人犯罪，行了耶和華所吩咐不可行的甚麼事，他雖然不知道，還是有了罪，就要擔當他的罪孽。¹⁸也要照你所估定的價，從羊羣中牽一隻沒有殘疾的公綿羊來，給祭司作贖愆祭。至於他誤行的那錯事，祭司要為他贖罪，他必蒙赦免。¹⁹這是贖愆祭，因他在耶和華面前實在有了罪。”

6 耶和華曉諭摩西說：²“若有人犯罪，干犯耶和華，在鄰舍交付他的物上，或是在交易上行了詭詐，或是搶奪人的財物，或是欺壓鄰舍，³或是在撿了遺失的物上行了詭詐，說謊起誓，在這一切的事上犯了甚麼罪。⁴他既犯了罪，有了過犯，就要歸還他所搶奪的，或是因欺壓所得的，或是人交付他的，或是人遺失他所撿的物，⁵或是他因甚麼物起了假誓，就要如數歸還，另外加上五分之一，在查出他有罪的日子，要交還本主。⁶也要照你所估定的價，把贖愆祭牲，就是羊羣中一隻沒有殘疾的公綿羊，牽到耶和華面前，給祭司為贖愆祭。⁷祭司要在耶和華面前為他贖罪；他無論行了甚麼事，使他有了罪，都必蒙赦免。”

of the offerings made to the LORD by fire. It is a sin offering. ¹³In this way the priest will make atonement for him for any of these sins he has committed, and he will be forgiven. The rest of the offering will belong to the priest, as in the case of the grain offering.' "

The Guilt Offering

¹⁴The LORD said to Moses: ¹⁵"When a person commits a violation and sins unintentionally in regard to any of the LORD's holy things, he is to bring to the LORD as a penalty a ram from the flock, one without defect and of the proper value in silver, according to the sanctuary shekel.^a It is a guilt offering. ¹⁶He must make restitution for what he has failed to do in regard to the holy things, add a fifth of the value to that and give it all to the priest, who will make atonement for him with the ram as a guilt offering, and he will be forgiven.

¹⁷"If a person sins and does what is forbidden in any of the LORD's commands, even though he does not know it, he is guilty and will be held responsible. ¹⁸He is to bring to the priest as a guilt offering a ram from the flock, one without defect and of the proper value. In this way the priest will make atonement for him for the wrong he has committed unintentionally, and he will be forgiven. ¹⁹It is a guilt offering; he has been guilty of^b wrongdoing against the LORD."

6 The LORD said to Moses: ²"If anyone sins and is unfaithful to the LORD by deceiving his neighbor about something entrusted to him or left in his care or stolen, or if he cheats him, ³or if he finds lost property and lies about it, or if he swears falsely, or if he commits any such sin that people may do— ⁴when he thus sins and becomes guilty, he must return what he has stolen or taken by extortion, or what was entrusted to him, or the lost property he found, ⁵or whatever it was he swore falsely about. He must make restitution in full, add a fifth of the value to it and give it all to the owner on the day he presents his guilt offering. ⁶And as a penalty he must bring to the priest, that is, to the LORD, his guilt offering, a ram from the flock, one without defect and of the proper value. ⁷In this way the priest will make atonement for him before the LORD, and he will be forgiven for any of these things he did that made him guilty."

a 15 That is, about 2/5 ounce (about 11.5 grams)　　　b 19 Or has made full expiation for his

The Burnt Offering

⁸The LORD said to Moses: ⁹"Give Aaron and his sons this command: 'These are the regulations for the burnt offering: The burnt offering is to remain on the altar hearth throughout the night, till morning, and the fire must be kept burning on the altar. ¹⁰The priest shall then put on his linen clothes, with linen undergarments next to his body, and shall remove the ashes of the burnt offering that the fire has consumed on the altar and place them beside the altar. ¹¹Then he is to take off these clothes and put on others, and carry the ashes outside the camp to a place that is ceremonially clean. ¹²The fire on the altar must be kept burning; it must not go out. Every morning the priest is to add firewood and arrange the burnt offering on the fire and burn the fat of the fellowship offerings*ᵃ* on it. ¹³The fire must be kept burning on the altar continuously; it must not go out.

The Grain Offering

¹⁴" 'These are the regulations for the grain offering: Aaron's sons are to bring it before the LORD, in front of the altar. ¹⁵The priest is to take a handful of fine flour and oil, together with all the incense on the grain offering, and burn the memorial portion on the altar as an aroma pleasing to the LORD. ¹⁶Aaron and his sons shall eat the rest of it, but it is to be eaten without yeast in a holy place; they are to eat it in the courtyard of the Tent of Meeting. ¹⁷It must not be baked with yeast; I have given it as their share of the offerings made to me by fire. Like the sin offering and the guilt offering, it is most holy. ¹⁸Any male descendant of Aaron may eat it. It is his regular share of the offerings made to the LORD by fire for the generations to come. Whatever touches them will become holy.*ᵇ*' "

¹⁹The LORD also said to Moses, ²⁰"This is the offering Aaron and his sons are to bring to the LORD on the day he*ᶜ* is anointed: a tenth of an ephah*ᵈ* of fine flour as a regular grain offering, half of it in the morning and half in the evening. ²¹Prepare it with oil on a griddle; bring it well-mixed and present the grain offering broken*ᵉ* in pieces as an aroma pleasing to the LORD. ²²The son who is to succeed him as anointed priest shall prepare it. It is the LORD's regular share and is to be burned completely. ²³Every grain

燔祭

⁸耶和華曉諭摩西說：⁹"你要吩咐亞倫和他的子孫說：'燔祭的條例乃是這樣：燔祭要放在壇的柴上，從晚上到天亮，壇上的火要常常燒着。¹⁰祭司要穿上細麻布衣服，又要把細麻布褲子穿在身上，把壇上所燒的燔祭灰收起來，倒在壇的旁邊。¹¹隨後要脫去這衣服，穿上別的衣服，把灰拿到營外潔淨之處。¹²壇上的火要在其上常常燒着，不可熄滅。祭司要每日早晨在上面燒柴，並要把燔祭擺在壇上，在其上燒平安祭牲的脂油，¹³在壇上必有常常燒着的火，不可熄滅。

素祭

¹⁴" '素祭的條例乃是這樣：亞倫的子孫要在壇前，把這祭獻在耶和華面前。¹⁵祭司要從其中，就是從素祭的細麵中，取出自己的一把，又要取些油和素祭上所有的乳香，燒在壇上，奉給耶和華為馨香素祭的紀念。¹⁶所剩下的，亞倫和他子孫要吃，必在聖處不帶酵而吃，要在會幕的院子裏吃。¹⁷烤的時候，不可擦酵，這是從所獻給我的火祭中賜給他們的分，是至聖的，和贖罪祭並贖愆祭一樣。¹⁸凡獻給耶和華的火祭，亞倫子孫中的男丁都要吃這一分，直到萬代，作他們永得的分。摸這些祭物的，都要成為聖。' "

¹⁹耶和華曉諭摩西說：²⁰"當亞倫受膏的日子，他和他子孫所要獻給耶和華的供物，就是細麵伊法十分之一，為常獻的素祭，早晨一半，晚上一半。²¹要在鐵鏊上用油調和做成，調勻了，你就拿進來，烤好了，分成塊子，獻給耶和華為馨香的素祭。²²亞倫的子孫中，接續他為受膏的祭司，要把這素祭獻上，要全燒給耶和華。這是永遠的定例。²³祭司的素祭

---

a 12 Traditionally *peace offerings*   *b* 18 Or *Whoever touches them must be holy*; similarly in verse 27   *c* 20 Or *each*
d 20 That is, probably about 2 quarts (about 2 liters)
e 21 The meaning of the Hebrew for this word is uncertain.

都要燒了，卻不可吃。"

贖罪祭

24耶和華曉諭摩西說：25 "你對亞倫和他的子孫說：'贖罪祭的條例乃是這樣：要在耶和華面前宰燔祭牲的地方，宰贖罪祭牲，這是至聖的。26為贖罪獻這祭的祭司要吃，要在聖處，就是在會幕的院子裏吃。27凡摸這祭肉的，要成為聖。這祭牲的血若彈在甚麼衣服上，所彈的那一件，要在聖處洗淨。28惟有煮祭物的瓦器要打碎；若是煮在銅器裏，這銅器要擦磨，在水中涮淨。29凡祭司中的男丁都可以吃，這是至聖的。30凡贖罪祭，若將血帶進會幕在聖所贖罪，那肉都不可吃，必用火焚燒。

贖愆祭

7 "'贖愆祭的條例乃是如此，這祭是至聖的。2人在哪裏宰燔祭牲，也要在那裏宰贖愆祭牲。其血，祭司要灑在壇的周圍。3又要將肥尾巴和蓋臟的脂油，4兩個腰子和腰子上的脂油，就是靠腰兩旁的脂油，並肝上的網子和腰子，一概取下。5祭司要在壇上焚燒，為獻給耶和華的火祭，是贖愆祭。6祭司中的男丁都可以吃這祭物，要在聖處吃，是至聖的。

7 "'贖罪祭怎樣，贖愆祭也是怎樣，兩個祭是一個條例。獻贖愆祭贖罪的祭司要得這祭物。8獻燔祭的祭司，無論為誰奉獻，要親自得他所獻那燔祭牲的皮。9凡在爐中烤的素祭，和煎盤中做的，並鐵鏊上做的，都要歸那獻的祭司。10凡素祭，無論是油調和的，是乾的，都要歸亞倫的子孫，大家均分。

平安祭

11 "'人獻與耶和華平安祭的條例乃是這樣：12 "'他若為感謝獻上，就要用調油的無酵餅和抹油的無酵薄餅，並

offering of a priest shall be burned completely; it must not be eaten."

The Sin Offering

24The LORD said to Moses, 25"Say to Aaron and his sons: 'These are the regulations for the sin offering: The sin offering is to be slaughtered before the LORD in the place the burnt offering is slaughtered; it is most holy. 26The priest who offers it shall eat it; it is to be eaten in a holy place, in the courtyard of the Tent of Meeting. 27Whatever touches any of the flesh will become holy, and if any of the blood is spattered on a garment, you must wash it in a holy place. 28The clay pot the meat is cooked in must be broken; but if it is cooked in a bronze pot, the pot is to be scoured and rinsed with water. 29Any male in a priest's family may eat it; it is most holy. 30But any sin offering whose blood is brought into the Tent of Meeting to make atonement in the Holy Place must not be eaten; it must be burned.

The Guilt Offering

7 "'These are the regulations for the guilt offering, which is most holy: 2The guilt offering is to be slaughtered in the place where the burnt offering is slaughtered, and its blood is to be sprinkled against the altar on all sides. 3All its fat shall be offered: the fat tail and the fat that covers the inner parts, 4both kidneys with the fat on them near the loins, and the covering of the liver, which is to be removed with the kidneys. 5The priest shall burn them on the altar as an offering made to the LORD by fire. It is a guilt offering. 6Any male in a priest's family may eat it, but it must be eaten in a holy place; it is most holy.

7"'The same law applies to both the sin offering and the guilt offering: They belong to the priest who makes atonement with them. 8The priest who offers a burnt offering for anyone may keep its hide for himself. 9Every grain offering baked in an oven or cooked in a pan or on a griddle belongs to the priest who offers it, 10and every grain offering, whether mixed with oil or dry, belongs equally to all the sons of Aaron.

The Fellowship Offering

11" 'These are the regulations for the fellowship offering a person may present to the LORD:
12" 'If he offers it as an expression of thankfulness, then along with this thank offering he is to offer cakes of bread made without yeast and

a 11 Traditionally peace offering; also in verses 13-37

mixed with oil, wafers made without yeast and spread with oil, and cakes of fine flour well-kneaded and mixed with oil. 13Along with his fellowship offering of thanksgiving he is to present an offering with cakes of bread made with yeast. 14He is to bring one of each kind as an offering, a contribution to the LORD; it belongs to the priest who sprinkles the blood of the fellowship offerings. 15The meat of his fellowship offering of thanksgiving must be eaten on the day it is offered; he must leave none of it till morning.

16" 'If, however, his offering is the result of a vow or is a freewill offering, the sacrifice shall be eaten on the day he offers it, but anything left over may be eaten on the next day. 17Any meat of the sacrifice left over till the third day must be burned up. 18If any meat of the fellowship offering is eaten on the third day, it will not be accepted. It will not be credited to the one who offered it, for it is impure; the person who eats any of it will be held responsible.

19" 'Meat that touches anything ceremonially unclean must not be eaten; it must be burned up. As for other meat, anyone ceremonially clean may eat it. 20But if anyone who is unclean eats any meat of the fellowship offering belonging to the LORD, that person must be cut off from his people. 21If anyone touches something unclean—whether human uncleanness or an unclean animal or any unclean, detestable thing—and then eats any of the meat of the fellowship offering belonging to the LORD, that person must be cut off from his people.' "

Eating Fat and Blood Forbidden

22The LORD said to Moses, 23"Say to the Israelites: 'Do not eat any of the fat of cattle, sheep or goats. 24The fat of an animal found dead or torn by wild animals may be used for any other purpose, but you must not eat it. 25Anyone who eats the fat of an animal from which an offering by fire may be*a* made to the LORD must be cut off from his people. 26And wherever you live, you must not eat the blood of any bird or animal. 27If anyone eats blood, that person must be cut off from his people.' "

The Priests' Share

28The LORD said to Moses, 29"Say to the Israelites: 'Anyone who brings a fellowship offering to the LORD is to bring part of it as his sacrifice to the LORD. 30With his own hands he is to bring the offering made to the LORD by fire;

a 25 Or fire is

用油調勻細麵做的餅，與感謝祭一同獻上。13要用有酵的餅和為感謝獻的平安祭，與供物一同獻上。14從各樣的供物中，他要把一個餅獻給耶和華為舉祭，是要歸給灑平安祭牲血的祭司。15為感謝獻平安祭牲的肉，要在獻的日子吃，一點不可留到早晨。

16" '若所獻的是為還願，或是甘心獻的，必在獻祭的日子吃，所剩下的，第二天也可以吃。17但所剩下的祭肉，到第三天要用火焚燒。18第三天若吃了平安祭的肉，這祭必不蒙悅納；人所獻的，也不算為祭，反為可憎嫌的，吃這祭肉的，就必擔當他的罪孽。

19" '挨了污穢物的肉就不可吃，要用火焚燒。至於平安祭的肉，凡潔淨的人都要吃。20只是獻與耶和華平安祭的肉，人若不潔淨而吃了，這人必從民中剪除。21有人摸了甚麼不潔淨的物，或是人的不潔淨，或是不潔淨的牲畜，或是不潔可憎之物，吃了獻與耶和華平安祭的肉，這人必從民中剪除。' "

禁止吃脂油與血

22耶和華對摩西說：23 "你曉諭以色列人說：'牛的脂油、綿羊的脂油、山羊的脂油，你們都不可吃。24自死的和被野獸撕裂的，那脂油可以做別的使用，只是你們萬不可吃。25無論何人吃了獻給耶和華當火祭牲畜的脂油，那人必從民中剪除。26在你們一切的住處，無論是雀鳥的血、是野獸的血，你們都不可吃。27無論是誰吃血，那人必從民中剪除。' "

祭司當得之分

28耶和華對摩西說：29 "你曉諭以色列人說：'獻平安祭給耶和華的，要從平安祭中取些來奉給耶和華。30他親手獻給耶和華的火祭，就是脂油和胸，要帶來，好把胸在耶和華面前作搖祭，搖一搖。³¹祭司要把脂油在壇上焚燒，但胸要歸亞倫和他的子孫。³²你們要把平安祭中把右腿作舉祭，奉給祭司。³³亞倫子孫中，獻平安祭牲血和脂油的，要得這右腿為分。³⁴因為我從以色列人的平安祭中，取了這搖的胸和舉的腿，給祭司亞倫和他子孫，作他們從以色列人中所永得的分。'"

³⁵這是從耶和華火祭中，作亞倫受膏的分和他子孫受膏的分，正在摩西（註：原文作"他"）叫他們前來給耶和華供祭司職分的日子，³⁶就是在摩西（註：原文作"他"）膏他們的日子，耶和華吩咐以色列人給他們的。這是他們世世代代永得的分。

³⁷這就是燔祭、素祭、贖罪祭、贖愆祭和平安祭的條例，並承接聖職的禮，³⁸都是耶和華在西奈山所吩咐摩西的，就是他在西奈曠野吩咐以色列人獻供物給耶和華之日所說的。

膏立亞倫和他的兒子

8 耶和華曉諭摩西說：²"你將亞倫和他兒子一同帶來，並將聖衣、膏油，與贖罪祭的一隻公牛、兩隻公綿羊、一筐無酵餅都帶來，³又招聚會眾到會幕門口。"⁴摩西就照耶和華所吩咐的行了。於是會眾聚集在會幕門口。

⁵摩西告訴會眾說："這就是耶和華所吩咐當行的事。"⁶摩西帶了亞倫和他兒子來，用水洗了他們。⁷給亞倫穿上內袍，束上腰帶，穿上外袍，又加上以弗得，用其上巧工織的帶子，把以弗得繫在他身上；⁸又給他戴上胸牌，把烏陵和土明放在胸牌內；⁹把冠冕戴在他頭上，在冠冕的前面釘上金牌，就是聖冠。都是照耶和華所吩咐摩西的。

¹⁰摩西用膏油抹帳幕和其中所有的，使它成聖；¹¹又用膏油在壇上彈

he is to bring the fat, together with the breast, and wave the breast before the LORD as a wave offering. ³¹The priest shall burn the fat on the altar, but the breast belongs to Aaron and his sons. ³²You are to give the right thigh of your fellowship offerings to the priest as a contribution. ³³The son of Aaron who offers the blood and the fat of the fellowship offering shall have the right thigh as his share. ³⁴From the fellowship offerings of the Israelites, I have taken the breast that is waved and the thigh that is presented and have given them to Aaron the priest and his sons as their regular share from the Israelites.' "

³⁵This is the portion of the offerings made to the LORD by fire that were allotted to Aaron and his sons on the day they were presented to serve the LORD as priests. ³⁶On the day they were anointed, the LORD commanded that the Israelites give this to them as their regular share for the generations to come.

³⁷These, then, are the regulations for the burnt offering, the grain offering, the sin offering, the guilt offering, the ordination offering and the fellowship offering, ³⁸which the LORD gave Moses on Mount Sinai on the day he commanded the Israelites to bring their offerings to the LORD, in the Desert of Sinai.

The Ordination of Aaron and His Sons

8 The LORD said to Moses, ²"Bring Aaron and his sons, their garments, the anointing oil, the bull for the sin offering, the two rams and the basket containing bread made without yeast, ³and gather the entire assembly at the entrance to the Tent of Meeting." ⁴Moses did as the LORD commanded him, and the assembly gathered at the entrance to the Tent of Meeting.

⁵Moses said to the assembly, "This is what the LORD has commanded to be done." ⁶Then Moses brought Aaron and his sons forward and washed them with water. ⁷He put the tunic on Aaron, tied the sash around him, clothed him with the robe and put the ephod on him. He also tied the ephod to him by its skillfully woven waistband; so it was fastened on him. ⁸He placed the breastpiece on him and put the Urim and Thummim in the breastpiece. ⁹Then he placed the turban on Aaron's head and set the gold plate, the sacred diadem, on the front of it, as the LORD commanded Moses.

¹⁰Then Moses took the anointing oil and anointed the tabernacle and everything in it, and so consecrated them. ¹¹He sprinkled some

of the oil on the altar seven times, anointing the altar and all its utensils and the basin with its stand, to consecrate them. ¹²He poured some of the anointing oil on Aaron's head and anointed him to consecrate him. ¹³Then he brought Aaron's sons forward, put tunics on them, tied sashes around them and put headbands on them, as the LORD commanded Moses.

¹⁴He then presented the bull for the sin offering, and Aaron and his sons laid their hands on its head. ¹⁵Moses slaughtered the bull and took some of the blood, and with his finger he put it on all the horns of the altar to purify the altar. He poured out the rest of the blood at the base of the altar. So he consecrated it to make atonement for it. ¹⁶Moses also took all the fat around the inner parts, the covering of the liver, and both kidneys and their fat, and burned it on the altar. ¹⁷But the bull with its hide and its flesh and its offal he burned up outside the camp, as the LORD commanded Moses.

¹⁸He then presented the ram for the burnt offering, and Aaron and his sons laid their hands on its head. ¹⁹Then Moses slaughtered the ram and sprinkled the blood against the altar on all sides. ²⁰He cut the ram into pieces and burned the head, the pieces and the fat. ²¹He washed the inner parts and the legs with water and burned the whole ram on the altar as a burnt offering, a pleasing aroma, an offering made to the LORD by fire, as the LORD commanded Moses.

²²He then presented the other ram, the ram for the ordination, and Aaron and his sons laid their hands on its head. ²³Moses slaughtered the ram and took some of its blood and put it on the lobe of Aaron's right ear, on the thumb of his right hand and on the big toe of his right foot. ²⁴Moses also brought Aaron's sons forward and put some of the blood on the lobes of their right ears, on the thumbs of their right hands and on the big toes of their right feet. Then he sprinkled blood against the altar on all sides. ²⁵He took the fat, the fat tail, all the fat around the inner parts, the covering of the liver, both kidneys and their fat and the right thigh. ²⁶Then from the basket of bread made without yeast, which was before the LORD, he took a cake of bread, and one made with oil, and a wafer; he put these on the fat portions and on the right thigh. ²⁷He put all these in the hands of Aaron and his sons and waved them before the LORD as a wave offering. ²⁸Then Moses took them from their hands and burned them on the altar on top of the burnt offering as an ordination offering, a pleasing aroma, an offering made to the LORD by fire.

了七次，又抹了壇和壇的一切器皿，並洗濯盆和盆座，使它成聖；¹²又把膏油倒在亞倫的頭上膏他，使他成聖。¹³摩西帶了亞倫的兒子來，給他們穿上內袍，束上腰帶，包上裹頭巾，都是照耶和華所吩咐摩西的。

¹⁴他牽了贖罪祭的公牛來，亞倫和他兒子按手在贖罪祭公牛的頭上，¹⁵就宰了公牛。摩西用指頭蘸血，抹在壇上四角的周圍，使壇潔淨；把血倒在壇的腳那裏，使壇成聖，壇就潔淨了。¹⁶又取臟上所有的脂油和肝上的網子，並兩個腰子與腰子上的脂油，都燒在壇上。¹⁷惟有公牛，連皮帶肉並糞，用火燒在營外，都是照耶和華所吩咐摩西的。

¹⁸他奉上燔祭的公綿羊。亞倫和他兒子按手在羊的頭上，¹⁹就宰了公羊。摩西把血灑在壇的周圍，²⁰把羊切成塊子，把頭和肉塊並脂油都燒了；²¹用水洗了臟腑和腿，就把全羊燒在壇上，為馨香的燔祭，是獻給耶和華的火祭，都是照耶和華所吩咐摩西的。

²²他又奉上第二隻公綿羊，就是承接聖職之禮的羊。亞倫和他兒子按手在羊的頭上，²³就宰了羊。摩西把些血抹在亞倫的右耳垂上和右手的大拇指上，並右腳的大拇指上。²⁴又帶了亞倫的兒子來，把些血抹在他們的右耳垂上和右手的大拇指上，並右腳的大拇指上，又把血灑在壇的周圍。²⁵取脂油和肥尾巴，並臟上一切的脂油與肝上的網子，兩個腰子和腰子上的脂油並右腿，²⁶再從耶和華面前盛無酵餅的筐子裏，取出一個無酵餅，一個油餅，一個薄餅，都放在脂油和右腿上。²⁷把這一切放在亞倫的手上，和他兒子的手上作搖祭，在耶和華面前搖一搖。²⁸摩西從他們的手上拿下來，燒在壇上的燔祭上，都是為承接聖職獻給耶和華馨香的火祭。

29摩西拿羊的胸作為搖祭，在耶和華面前搖一搖，是承接聖職之禮，歸摩西的分，都是照耶和華所吩咐摩西的。

30摩西取點膏油和壇上的血，彈在亞倫和他的衣服上，並他兒子和他兒子的衣服上，使他和他們的衣服一同成聖。

31摩西對亞倫和他兒子說："把肉煮在會幕門口，在那裏吃；又吃承接聖職筐子裏的餅，按我所吩咐的說（註：或作"按所吩咐我的說"）：'這是亞倫和他兒子要吃的。' 32剩下的肉和餅，你們要用火焚燒。33你們七天不可出會幕的門，等到你們承接聖職的日子滿了，因為主叫你們七天承接聖職。34像今天所行的，都是耶和華吩咐行的，為你們贖罪。35七天你們要晝夜住在會幕門口，遵守耶和華的吩咐，免得你們死亡，因為所吩咐我的就是這樣。"36於是亞倫和他兒子行了耶和華藉著摩西所吩咐的一切事。

祭司開始供職

9 到了第八天，摩西召了亞倫和他兒子，並以色列的眾長老來，2對亞倫說："你當取牛犢中的一隻公牛犢作贖罪祭，一隻公綿羊作燔祭，都要沒有殘疾的，獻在耶和華面前。3你也要對以色列人說：'你們當取一隻公山羊作贖罪祭，又取一隻牛犢和一隻綿羊羔，都要一歲沒有殘疾的作燔祭。4又取一隻公牛、一隻公綿羊作平安祭，獻在耶和華面前，並取調油的素祭，因為今天耶和華要向你們顯現。'"

5於是他們把摩西所吩咐的帶到會幕前，全會眾都近前來，站在耶和華面前。6摩西說："這是耶和華吩咐你們所當行的，耶和華的榮光就要向你們顯現。"

7摩西對亞倫說："你就近壇前，獻你的贖罪祭和燔祭，為自己與百姓贖罪；又獻上百姓的供物，為他

29He also took the breast—Moses' share of the ordination ram—and waved it before the LORD as a wave offering, as the LORD commanded Moses.

30Then Moses took some of the anointing oil and some of the blood from the altar and sprinkled them on Aaron and his garments and on his sons and their garments. So he consecrated Aaron and his garments and his sons and their garments.

31Moses then said to Aaron and his sons, "Cook the meat at the entrance to the Tent of Meeting and eat it there with the bread from the basket of ordination offerings, as I commanded, saying,a 'Aaron and his sons are to eat it.' 32Then burn up the rest of the meat and the bread. 33Do not leave the entrance to the Tent of Meeting for seven days, until the days of your ordination are completed, for your ordination will last seven days. 34What has been done today was commanded by the LORD to make atonement for you. 35You must stay at the entrance to the Tent of Meeting day and night for seven days and do what the LORD requires, so you will not die; for that is what I have been commanded." 36So Aaron and his sons did everything the LORD commanded through Moses.

The Priests Begin Their Ministry

9 On the eighth day Moses summoned Aaron and his sons and the elders of Israel. 2He said to Aaron, "Take a bull calf for your sin offering and a ram for your burnt offering, both without defect, and present them before the LORD. 3Then say to the Israelites: 'Take a male goat for a sin offering, a calf and a lamb—both a year old and without defect—for a burnt offering, 4and an oxb and a ram for a fellowship offeringc to sacrifice before the LORD, together with a grain offering mixed with oil. For today the LORD will appear to you.' "

5They took the things Moses commanded to the front of the Tent of Meeting, and the entire assembly came near and stood before the LORD. 6Then Moses said, "This is what the LORD has commanded you to do, so that the glory of the LORD may appear to you."

7Moses said to Aaron, "Come to the altar and sacrifice your sin offering and your burnt offering and make atonement for yourself and the people; sacrifice the offering that is for the peo-

---

a 31 Or I was commanded:　　b 4 The Hebrew word can include both male and female; also in verses 18 and 19.

c 4 Traditionally peace offering; also in verses 18 and 22

ple and make atonement for them, as the LORD has commanded."

⁸So Aaron came to the altar and slaughtered the calf as a sin offering for himself. ⁹His sons brought the blood to him, and he dipped his finger into the blood and put it on the horns of the altar; the rest of the blood he poured out at the base of the altar. ¹⁰On the altar he burned the fat, the kidneys and the covering of the liver from the sin offering, as the LORD commanded Moses; ¹¹the flesh and the hide he burned up outside the camp.

¹²Then he slaughtered the burnt offering. His sons handed him the blood, and he sprinkled it against the altar on all sides. ¹³They handed him the burnt offering piece by piece, including the head, and he burned them on the altar. ¹⁴He washed the inner parts and the legs and burned them on top of the burnt offering on the altar.

¹⁵Aaron then brought the offering that was for the people. He took the goat for the people's sin offering and slaughtered it and offered it for a sin offering as he did with the first one.

¹⁶He brought the burnt offering and offered it in the prescribed way. ¹⁷He also brought the grain offering, took a handful of it and burned it on the altar in addition to the morning's burnt offering.

¹⁸He slaughtered the ox and the ram as the fellowship offering for the people. His sons handed him the blood, and he sprinkled it against the altar on all sides. ¹⁹But the fat portions of the ox and the ram—the fat tail, the layer of fat, the kidneys and the covering of the liver— ²⁰these they laid on the breasts, and then Aaron burned the fat on the altar. ²¹Aaron waved the breasts and the right thigh before the LORD as a wave offering, as Moses commanded.

²²Then Aaron lifted his hands toward the people and blessed them. And having sacrificed the sin offering, the burnt offering and the fellowship offering, he stepped down.

²³Moses and Aaron then went into the Tent of Meeting. When they came out, they blessed the people; and the glory of the LORD appeared to all the people. ²⁴Fire came out from the presence of the LORD and consumed the burnt offering and the fat portions on the altar. And when all the people saw it, they shouted for joy and fell facedown.

The Death of Nadab and Abihu

10 Aaron's sons Nadab and Abihu took their censers, put fire in them and added incense; and they offered unauthorized fire before the LORD, contrary to his

們贖罪，都照耶和華所吩咐的。”

⁸於是亞倫就近壇前，宰了為自己作贖罪祭的牛犢。⁹亞倫的兒子把血奉給他，他就把指頭蘸在血中，抹在壇的四角上，又把血倒在壇腳那裏。¹⁰惟有贖罪祭的脂油和腰子，並肝上取的網子，都燒在壇上，是照耶和華所吩咐摩西的。¹¹又用火將肉和皮燒在營外。

¹²亞倫宰了燔祭牲，他兒子把血遞給他，他就灑在壇的周圍。¹³又把燔祭一塊一塊地連頭遞給他，他都燒在壇上。¹⁴又洗了臟腑和腿，燒在壇上的燔祭上。

¹⁵他奉上百姓的供物，把羊給百姓作贖罪祭的公山羊宰了，為罪獻上，和先獻的一樣。

¹⁶也奉上燔祭，照例而獻。¹⁷他又奉上素祭，從其中取一滿把，燒在壇上，這是在早晨的燔祭以外。

¹⁸亞倫宰了那給百姓作平安祭的公牛和公綿羊。他兒子把血遞給他，他就灑在壇的周圍；¹⁹又把公牛和公綿羊的脂油、肥尾巴，並蓋臟的脂油與腰子，和肝上的網子，都遞給他，²⁰把脂油放在胸上，他就把脂油燒在壇上；²¹胸和右腿，亞倫當作搖祭，在耶和華面前搖一搖，都是照摩西所吩咐的。

²²亞倫向百姓舉手，為他們祝福。他獻了贖罪祭、燔祭、平安祭，就下來了。

²³摩西、亞倫進入會幕，又出來為百姓祝福，耶和華的榮光就向眾民顯現。²⁴有火從耶和華面前出來，在壇上燒盡燔祭和脂油。眾民一見，就都歡呼，俯伏在地。

拿答和亞比戶之死

10 亞倫的兒子拿答、亞比戶，各拿自己的香爐，盛上火，加上香，在耶和華面前獻上凡火，是耶和華沒有吩咐他們的，²就有火從耶和華面前出來，把他們燒滅，他們就死在耶和華面前。³於是摩西對亞倫說：「這就是耶和華所說：

" '我在親近我的人中
　要顯為聖；
　在眾民面前，
　我要得榮耀。' "

亞倫就默默不言。

⁴摩西召了亞倫叔父烏薛的兒子米沙利、以利撒反來，對他們說：「上前來，把你們的親屬從聖所前抬到營外。」⁵於是二人上前來，把他們穿着袍子抬到營外，是照摩西所吩咐的。

⁶摩西對亞倫和他兒子以利撒、以他瑪說：「不可蓬頭散髮，也不可撕裂衣裳，免得你們死亡，又免得耶和華向會眾發怒。只要你們的弟兄以色列全家為耶和華所發的火哀哭。⁷你們也不可出會幕的門，恐怕你們死亡，因為耶和華的膏油在你們的身上。」他們就照摩西的話行了。

⁸耶和華曉諭亞倫說：⁹「你和你兒子進會幕的時候，清酒、濃酒都不可喝，免得你們死亡。這要作你們世世代代永遠的定例，¹⁰使你們可以將聖的、俗的，潔淨的、不潔淨的，分別出來；¹¹又使你們可以將耶和華藉摩西曉諭以色列人的一切律例教訓他們。」

¹²摩西對亞倫和他剩下的兒子以利亞撒、以他瑪說：「你們獻給耶和華火祭中所剩的素祭，要在壇旁不帶酵而吃，因為是至聖的。¹³你們要在聖處吃，因為在獻給耶和華的火祭中，這是你的分和你兒子的分，所吩咐我的本是這樣。¹⁴所搖的胸、所舉的腿，你們要在潔淨地方吃，你和你的兒女都要同吃，因為這些是從以色列人平安祭中給你，當你的分和你兒子的分。¹⁵所舉的腿、所搖的胸，他們要與火祭的脂油一同帶來當搖祭，在耶和華面前搖一搖，這要歸你和你

command. ²So fire came out from the presence of the LORD and consumed them, and they died before the LORD. ³Moses then said to Aaron, "This is what the LORD spoke of when he said:

" 'Among those who approach me
  I will show myself holy;
  in the sight of all the people
  I will be honored.' "

Aaron remained silent.

⁴Moses summoned Mishael and Elzaphan, sons of Aaron's uncle Uzziel, and said to them, "Come here; carry your cousins outside the camp, away from the front of the sanctuary." ⁵So they came and carried them, still in their tunics, outside the camp, as Moses ordered.

⁶Then Moses said to Aaron and his sons Eleazar and Ithamar, "Do not let your hair become unkempt,[a] and do not tear your clothes, or you will die and the LORD will be angry with the whole community. But your relatives, all the house of Israel, may mourn for those the LORD has destroyed by fire. ⁷Do not leave the entrance to the Tent of Meeting or you will die, because the LORD's anointing oil is on you." So they did as Moses said.

⁸Then the LORD said to Aaron, ⁹"You and your sons are not to drink wine or other fermented drink whenever you go into the Tent of Meeting, or you will die. This is a lasting ordinance for the generations to come. ¹⁰You must distinguish between the holy and the common, between the unclean and the clean, ¹¹and you must teach the Israelites all the decrees the LORD has given them through Moses."

¹²Moses said to Aaron and his remaining sons, Eleazar and Ithamar, "Take the grain offering left over from the offerings made to the LORD by fire and eat it prepared without yeast beside the altar, for it is most holy. ¹³Eat it in a holy place, because it is your share and your sons' share of the offerings made to the LORD by fire; for so I have been commanded. ¹⁴But you and your sons and your daughters may eat the breast that was waved and the thigh that was presented. Eat them in a ceremonially clean place; they have been given to you and your children as your share of the Israelites' fellowship offerings.[b] ¹⁵The thigh that was presented and the breast that was waved must be brought with the fat portions of the offerings made by fire, to be waved before the LORD as a wave offer-

a 6 Or Do not uncover your heads   b 14 Traditionally peace offerings

ing. This will be the regular share for you and your children, as the LORD has commanded."

16When Moses inquired about the goat of the sin offering and found that it had been burned up, he was angry with Eleazar and Ithamar, Aaron's remaining sons, and asked, 17"Why didn't you eat the sin offering in the sanctuary area? It is most holy; it was given to you to take away the guilt of the community by making atonement for them before the LORD. 18Since its blood was not taken into the Holy Place, you should have eaten the goat in the sanctuary area, as I commanded."

19Aaron replied to Moses, "Today they sacrificed their sin offering and their burnt offering before the LORD, but such things as this have happened to me. Would the LORD have been pleased if I had eaten the sin offering today?" 20When Moses heard this, he was satisfied.

Clean and Unclean Food

11 The LORD said to Moses and Aaron, 2"Say to the Israelites: 'Of all the animals that live on land, these are the ones you may eat: 3You may eat any animal that has a split hoof completely divided and that chews the cud.

4" 'There are some that only chew the cud or only have a split hoof, but you must not eat them. The camel, though it chews the cud, does not have a split hoof; it is ceremonially unclean for you. 5The coney,a though it chews the cud, does not have a split hoof; it is unclean for you. 6The rabbit, though it chews the cud, does not have a split hoof; it is unclean for you. 7And the pig, though it has a split hoof completely divided, does not chew the cud; it is unclean for you. 8You must not eat their meat or touch their carcasses; they are unclean for you.

9" 'Of all the creatures living in the water of the seas and the streams, you may eat any that have fins and scales. 10But all creatures in the seas or streams that do not have fins and scales—whether among all the swarming things or among all the other living creatures in the water—you are to detest. 11And since you are to detest them, you must not eat their meat and you must detest their carcasses. 12Anything living in the water that does not have fins and scales is to be detestable to you.

13" 'These are the birds you are to detest and not eat because they are detestable: the eagle, the

兒子，當作永得的分，都是照耶和華所吩咐的。」

16當下摩西急切地尋找作贖罪祭的公山羊，誰知已經焚燒了，便向亞倫剩下的兒子以利亞撒、以他瑪發怒說：17「這贖罪祭既是至聖的，主又給了你們，為要你們擔當會眾的罪孽，在耶和華面前為他們贖罪，你們為何沒有在聖所吃呢？18看哪，這祭牲的血並沒有拿到聖所裏去。你們本當照我所吩咐的，在聖所裏吃這祭肉。」

19亞倫對摩西說：「今天他們在耶和華面前獻上贖罪祭和燔祭，我又遇見這樣的災，若今天吃了贖罪祭，耶和華豈能看為美呢？」20摩西聽見這話，便以為美。

潔淨與不潔淨的食物

11 耶和華對摩西、亞倫說：2「你們曉諭以色列人說：『在地上一切走獸中可吃的乃是這些：3凡蹄分兩瓣、倒嚼的走獸，你們都可以吃。

4「『但那倒嚼或分蹄之中不可吃的乃是：駱駝，因為倒嚼不分蹄，就與你們不潔淨；5沙番，因為倒嚼不分蹄，就與你們不潔淨；6兔子，因為倒嚼不分蹄，就與你們不潔淨；7豬，因為蹄分兩瓣，卻不倒嚼，就與你們不潔淨。8這些獸的肉，你們不可吃；死的，你們不可摸，都與你們不潔淨。

9「『水中可吃的乃是這些：凡在水裏、海裏、河裏，有翅有鱗的，都可以吃。10凡在海裏、河裏，並一切水裏游動的活物，無翅無鱗的，你們都當以為可憎。11這些無翅無鱗以為可憎的，你們不可吃牠的肉，死的也當以為可憎。12凡水裏無翅無鱗的，你們都當以為可憎。

13「『雀鳥中你們當以為可憎、不可吃的乃是：鵰、狗頭鵰、紅頭

---

a 5 That is, the hyrax or rock badger

鵰、¹⁴鷂鷹、小鷹與其類；¹⁵烏鴉與其類；¹⁶鴕鳥、夜鷹、魚鷹、鷹與其類；¹⁷鴞鳥、鸕鷀、貓頭鷹、¹⁸角鴟、鵜鶘、禿鵰、¹⁹鸛、鷺鷥與其類；戴鵀與蝙蝠。

²⁰ " '凡有翅膀用四足爬行的物，你們都當以為可憎。²¹只是有翅膀用四足爬行的物中，有足有腿，在地上蹦跳的，你們還可以吃。²²其中有蝗蟲、螞蚱、蟋蟀與其類，蚱蜢與其類，這些你們都可以吃。²³但是有翅膀、有四足的爬物，你們都當以為可憎。

²⁴ " '這些都能使你們不潔淨；凡摸了死的，必不潔淨到晚上。²⁵凡拿了死的，必不潔淨到晚上，並要洗衣服。

²⁶ " '凡走獸分蹄不成兩瓣，也不倒嚼的，是與你們不潔淨；凡摸了的就不潔淨。²⁷凡四足的走獸，用掌行走的，是與你們不潔淨；摸其屍的，必不潔淨到晚上；²⁸拿其屍的，必不潔淨到晚上，並要洗衣服。這些是與你們不潔淨的。

²⁹ " '地上爬物，與你們不潔淨的乃是這些：鼬鼠、鼫鼠、蜥蜴與其類；³⁰壁虎、龍子、守宮、蛇醫、蠑蜓。³¹這些爬物都是與你們不潔淨的。在牠死了以後，凡摸了的，必不潔淨到晚上；³²其中死了的，掉在甚麼東西上，這東西就不潔淨。無論是木器、衣服、皮子、口袋，不拘是做甚麼工用的器皿，須要放在水中，必不潔淨到晚上；到晚上才潔淨了。³³若有死了掉在瓦器裏的，其中不拘有甚麼，就不潔淨，你們要把這瓦器打破了。³⁴其中一切可吃的食物，沾水的就不潔淨，並且那樣器皿中一切可喝的，也必不潔淨。³⁵其中已死的，若有一點掉在甚麼物件上，那物件就不潔淨，不拘是爐子、是鍋臺，就要打碎，都不潔淨，也必與你們不潔淨。³⁶但是泉源，或是聚水的池子，仍是潔淨；惟挨了那死的，就不潔淨。³⁷若是死的，有一點掉在要種

vulture, the black vulture, ¹⁴the red kite, any kind of black kite, ¹⁵any kind of raven, ¹⁶the horned owl, the screech owl, the gull, any kind of hawk, ¹⁷the little owl, the cormorant, the great owl, ¹⁸the white owl, the desert owl, the osprey, ¹⁹the stork, any kind of heron, the hoopoe and the bat.ᵃ

²⁰" 'All flying insects that walk on all fours are to be detestable to you. ²¹There are, however, some winged creatures that walk on all fours that you may eat: those that have jointed legs for hopping on the ground. ²²Of these you may eat any kind of locust, katydid, cricket or grasshopper. ²³But all other winged creatures that have four legs you are to detest.

²⁴" 'You will make yourselves unclean by these; whoever touches their carcasses will be unclean till evening. ²⁵Whoever picks up one of their carcasses must wash his clothes, and he will be unclean till evening.

²⁶" 'Every animal that has a split hoof not completely divided or that does not chew the cud is unclean for you; whoever touches ⌊the carcass of⌋ any of them will be unclean. ²⁷Of all the animals that walk on all fours, those that walk on their paws are unclean for you; whoever touches their carcasses will be unclean till evening. ²⁸Anyone who picks up their carcasses must wash his clothes, and he will be unclean till evening. They are unclean for you.

²⁹" 'Of the animals that move about on the ground, these are unclean for you: the weasel, the rat, any kind of great lizard, ³⁰the gecko, the monitor lizard, the wall lizard, the skink and the chameleon. ³¹Of all those that move along the ground, these are unclean for you. Whoever touches them when they are dead will be unclean till evening. ³²When one of them dies and falls on something, that article, whatever its use, will be unclean, whether it is made of wood, cloth, hide or sackcloth. Put it in water; it will be unclean till evening, and then it will be clean. ³³If one of them falls into a clay pot, everything in it will be unclean, and you must break the pot. ³⁴Any food that could be eaten but has water on it from such a pot is unclean, and any liquid that could be drunk from it is unclean. ³⁵Anything that one of their carcasses falls on becomes unclean; an oven or cooking pot must be broken up. They are unclean, and you are to regard them as unclean. ³⁶A spring, however, or a cistern for collecting water remains clean, but anyone who touches one of these carcasses is unclean. ³⁷If a carcass falls on

a 19 The precise identification of some of the birds, insects and animals in this chapter is uncertain.

any seeds that are to be planted, they remain clean. 38But if water has been put on the seed and a carcass falls on it, it is unclean for you.

39" 'If an animal that you are allowed to eat dies, anyone who touches the carcass will be unclean till evening. 40Anyone who eats some of the carcass must wash his clothes, and he will be unclean till evening. Anyone who picks up the carcass must wash his clothes, and he will be unclean till evening.

41" 'Every creature that moves about on the ground is detestable; it is not to be eaten. 42You are not to eat any creature that moves about on the ground, whether it moves on its belly or walks on all fours or on many feet; it is detestable. 43Do not defile yourselves by any of these creatures. Do not make yourselves unclean by means of them or be made unclean by them. 44I am the LORD your God; consecrate yourselves and be holy, because I am holy. Do not make yourselves unclean by any creature that moves about on the ground. 45I am the LORD who brought you up out of Egypt to be your God; therefore be holy, because I am holy.

46" 'These are the regulations concerning animals, birds, every living thing that moves in the water and every creature that moves about on the ground. 47You must distinguish between the unclean and the clean, between living creatures that may be eaten and those that may not be eaten.' "

Purification After Childbirth

12 The LORD said to Moses, 2"Say to the Israelites: 'A woman who becomes pregnant and gives birth to a son will be ceremonially unclean for seven days, just as she is unclean during her monthly period. 3On the eighth day the boy is to be circumcised. 4Then the woman must wait thirty-three days to be purified from her bleeding. She must not touch anything sacred or go to the sanctuary until the days of her purification are over. 5If she gives birth to a daughter, for two weeks the woman will be unclean, as during her period. Then she must wait sixty-six days to be purified from her bleeding.

6" 'When the days of her purification for a son or daughter are over, she is to bring to the priest at the entrance to the Tent of Meeting a year-old lamb for a burnt offering and a young pigeon or a dove for a sin offering. 7He shall offer them before the LORD to make atonement for her, and then she will be ceremonially clean from her flow of blood.

的子粒上,子粒仍是潔淨;38若水已經澆在子粒上,那死的有一點掉在上頭,這子粒就與你們不潔淨。

39 " '你們可吃的走獸,若是死了,有人摸牠,必不潔淨到晚上; 40有人吃那死了的走獸,必不潔淨到晚上,並要洗衣服;拿了死走獸的,必不潔淨到晚上,並要洗衣服。

41 " '凡地上的爬物是可憎的都不可吃。42凡用肚子行走的和用四足行走的,或是有許多足的,就是一切爬在地上的,你們都不可吃,因為是可憎的。43你們不可因甚麼爬物使自己成為可憎的,也不可因這些使自己不潔淨,以致染了污穢。44我是耶和華你們的神,所以你們要成為聖潔,因為我是聖潔的。你們也不可在地上的爬物污穢自己。45我是把你們從埃及地領出來的耶和華,要作你們的神,所以你們要聖潔,因為我是聖潔的。

46 " '這是走獸、飛鳥,和水中游動的活物,並地上爬物的條例。47要把潔淨的和不潔淨的,可吃的與不可吃的活物,都分別出來。' "

產婦得潔淨的條例

12 耶和華對摩西說:2"你曉諭以色列人說:'若有婦人懷孕生男孩,她就不潔淨七天,像在月經污穢的日子不潔淨一樣。3第八天要給男孩行割禮。4婦人在產血不潔之中,要家居三十三天。她潔淨的日子未滿,不可摸聖物,也不可進入聖所。5她若生女孩,就不潔淨兩個七天,像污穢的時候一樣,要在產血不潔之中,家居六十六天。

6 " '滿了潔淨的日子,無論是為男孩,是為女孩,她要把一歲的羊羔為燔祭,一隻雛鴿或是一隻斑鳩為贖罪祭,帶到會幕門口交給祭司。7祭司要獻在耶和華面前,為她贖罪,她的血源就潔淨了。

" '這條例是為生育的婦人，無論是生男生女。8她的力量若不夠獻一隻羊羔，她就要取兩隻斑鳩或是兩隻雛鴿，一隻為燔祭，一隻為贖罪祭。祭司要為她贖罪，她就潔淨了。'"

關於傳染性皮膚病的條例

13 耶和華曉諭摩西、亞倫說：
2"人的肉皮上若長了癤子，或長了癬，或長了火斑，在他肉皮上成了大痲瘋的災病，就要將他帶到祭司亞倫或亞倫作祭司的一個子孫面前。3祭司要察看肉皮上的災病，若災病處的毛已經變白，災病的現象深於肉上的皮，這便是大痲瘋的災病。祭司要察看他，定他為不潔淨。4若火斑在他肉皮上是白的，現象不深於皮，其上的毛也沒有變白，祭司就要將有災病的人關鎖七天。5第七天，祭司要察看他，若看災病止住了，沒有在皮上發散，祭司還要將他關鎖七天。6第七天，祭司要再察看他，若災病發暗，而且沒有在皮上發散，祭司要定他為潔淨，原來是癬。那人就要洗衣服，得為潔淨。7但他為得潔淨，將身體給祭司察看以後，癬若在皮上發散開了，他要再將身體給祭司察看。8祭司要察看，癬若在皮上發散，就要定他為不潔淨，是大痲瘋。

9"人有了大痲瘋的災病，就要將他帶到祭司面前。10祭司要察看，皮上若長了白癤，使毛變白，在長白癤之處有了紅瘀肉，11這是肉皮上的舊大痲瘋。祭司要定他為不潔淨，不用將他關鎖，因為他是不潔淨了。

12"大痲瘋若在皮上四外發散，長滿了患災病人的皮，據祭司察看，從頭到腳無處不有，13祭司就要察看，全身的肉若長滿了大痲瘋，就要

" 'These are the regulations for the woman who gives birth to a boy or a girl. 8If she cannot afford a lamb, she is to bring two doves or two young pigeons, one for a burnt offering and the other for a sin offering. In this way the priest will make atonement for her, and she will be clean.' "

Regulations About Infectious Skin Diseases

13 The LORD said to Moses and Aaron,
2"When anyone has a swelling or a rash or a bright spot on his skin that may become an infectious skin disease,[a] he must be brought to Aaron the priest or to one of his sons[b] who is a priest. 3The priest is to examine the sore on his skin, and if the hair in the sore has turned white and the sore appears to be more than skin deep,[c] it is an infectious skin disease. When the priest examines him, he shall pronounce him ceremonially unclean. 4If the spot on his skin is white but does not appear to be more than skin deep and the hair in it has not turned white, the priest is to put the infected person in isolation for seven days. 5On the seventh day the priest is to examine him, and if he sees that the sore is unchanged and has not spread in the skin, he is to keep him in isolation another seven days. 6On the seventh day the priest is to examine him again, and if the sore has faded and has not spread in the skin, the priest shall pronounce him clean; it is only a rash. The man must wash his clothes, and he will be clean. 7But if the rash does spread in his skin after he has shown himself to the priest to be pronounced clean, he must appear before the priest again. 8The priest is to examine him, and if the rash has spread in the skin, he shall pronounce him unclean; it is an infectious disease.

9"When anyone has an infectious skin disease, he must be brought to the priest. 10The priest is to examine him, and if there is a white swelling in the skin that has turned the hair white and if there is raw flesh in the swelling, 11it is a chronic skin disease and the priest shall pronounce him unclean. He is not to put him in isolation, because he is already unclean.

12"If the disease breaks out all over his skin and, so far as the priest can see, it covers all the skin of the infected person from head to foot, 13the priest is to examine him, and if the disease has covered his whole body, he shall pronounce

---

a 2 Traditionally *leprosy;* the Hebrew word was used for various diseases affecting the skin—not necessarily leprosy; also elsewhere in this chapter.　　*b 2* Or *descendants*　　*c 3* Or *be lower than the rest of the skin;* also elsewhere in this chapter

that person clean. Since it has all turned white, he is clean. [14]But whenever raw flesh appears on him, he will be unclean. [15]When the priest sees the raw flesh, he shall pronounce him unclean. The raw flesh is unclean; he has an infectious disease. [16]Should the raw flesh change and turn white, he must go to the priest. [17]The priest is to examine him, and if the sores have turned white, the priest shall pronounce the infected person clean; then he will be clean.

[18]"When someone has a boil on his skin and it heals, [19]and in the place where the boil was, a white swelling or reddish-white spot appears, he must present himself to the priest. [20]The priest is to examine it, and if it appears to be more than skin deep and the hair in it has turned white, the priest shall pronounce him unclean. It is an infectious skin disease that has broken out where the boil was. [21]But if, when the priest examines it, there is no white hair in it and it is not more than skin deep and has faded, then the priest is to put him in isolation for seven days. [22]If it is spreading in the skin, the priest shall pronounce him unclean; it is infectious. [23]But if the spot is unchanged and has not spread, it is only a scar from the boil, and the priest shall pronounce him clean.

[24]"When someone has a burn on his skin and a reddish-white or white spot appears in the raw flesh of the burn, [25]the priest is to examine the spot, and if the hair in it has turned white, and it appears to be more than skin deep, it is an infectious disease that has broken out in the burn. The priest shall pronounce him unclean; it is an infectious skin disease. [26]But if the priest examines it and there is no white hair in the spot and if it is not more than skin deep and has faded, then the priest is to put him in isolation for seven days. [27]On the seventh day the priest is to examine him, and if it is spreading in the skin, the priest shall pronounce him unclean; it is an infectious skin disease. [28]If, however, the spot is unchanged and has not spread in the skin but has faded, it is a swelling from the burn, and the priest shall pronounce him clean; it is only a scar from the burn.

[29]"If a man or woman has a sore on the head or on the chin, [30]the priest is to examine the sore, and if it appears to be more than skin deep and the hair in it is yellow and thin, the priest shall pronounce that person unclean; it is an itch, an infectious disease of the head or chin. [31]But if, when the priest examines this kind of sore, it does not seem to be more than skin deep and there is no black hair in it, then the priest is to

定那患災病的為潔淨，全身都變為白，他乃潔淨了。[14]但紅肉幾時顯在他的身上，就幾時不潔淨。[15]祭司一看那紅肉，就要定他為不潔淨，紅肉本是不潔淨，是大痲瘋。[16]紅肉若在復原，又變白了，他就要來見祭司。[17]祭司要察看，災病處若變白了，祭司就要定那患災病的為潔淨，他乃潔淨了。

[18] "人若在皮肉上長瘡，卻治好了，[19]在長瘡之處又起了白癤，或是白中帶紅的火斑，就要給祭司察看。[20]祭司要察看，若現象窪於皮，其上的毛也變白了，就要定他為不潔淨，是大痲瘋的災病發在瘡中。[21]祭司若察看，其上沒有白毛，也沒有窪於皮，乃是發暗，就要將他關鎖七天；[22]若在皮上發散開了，祭司就要定他為不潔淨，是災病。[23]火斑若在原處止住，沒有發散，便是瘡的痕跡，祭司就要定他為潔淨。

[24] "人的皮肉上若起了火毒，火毒的瘀肉成了火斑，或是白中帶紅的，或是全白的，[25]祭司就要察看，火斑中的毛若變白了，現象又深於皮，是大痲瘋在火毒中發出，就要定他為不潔淨，是大痲瘋的災病。[26]但是祭司察看，在火斑中若沒有白毛，也沒有窪於皮，乃是發暗，就要將他關鎖七天。[27]到第七天，祭司要察看他，火斑若在皮上發散開了，就要定他為不潔淨，是大痲瘋的災病。[28]火斑若在原處止住，沒有在皮上發散，乃是發暗，是起的火毒，祭司要定他為潔淨，不過是火毒的痕跡。

[29] "無論男女，若在頭上有災病，或是男人鬍鬚上有災病，[30]祭司就要察看。這災病現象若深於皮，其間有細黃毛，就要定他為不潔淨。這是頭疥，是頭上或是鬍鬚上的大痲瘋。[31]祭司若察看頭疥的災病，現象不深於皮，其間也沒有黑毛，就要將

長頭疥災病的關鎖七天。³²第七天，祭司要察看災病，若頭疥沒有發散，其間也沒有黃毛，頭疥的現象不深於皮，³³那人就要剃去鬚髮，但他不可剃頭疥之處。祭司要將那長頭疥的，再關鎖七天。³⁴第七天，祭司要察看頭疥，頭疥若沒有在皮上發散，現象也不深於皮，就要定他為潔淨，他要洗衣服，便成為潔淨。³⁵但他得潔淨以後，頭疥若在皮上發散開了，³⁶祭司就要察看他。頭疥若在皮上發散，就不必找那黃毛，他是不潔淨了。³⁷祭司若看頭疥已經止住，其間也長了黑毛，頭疥已然痊愈，那人是潔淨了，就要定他為潔淨。

³⁸ "無論男女，皮肉上若起了火斑，就是白火斑，³⁹祭司就要察看。他們肉皮上的火斑若白中帶黑，這是皮上發出的白癬，那人是潔淨了。

⁴⁰ "人頭上的髮若掉了，他不過是頭禿，還是潔淨。⁴¹他頂前若掉了頭髮，他不過是頂門禿，還是潔淨。⁴²頭禿處或是頂門禿處，若有白中帶紅的災病，這就是大痲瘋，發在他頭禿處或是頂門禿處，⁴³祭司就要察看。他起的那災病若在頭禿處或是頂門禿處有白中帶紅的，像肉皮上大痲瘋的現象，⁴⁴那人就是長大痲瘋不潔淨的，祭司總要定他為不潔淨，他的災病是在頭上。

⁴⁵ "身上有長大痲瘋災病的，他的衣服要撕裂，也要蓬頭散髮，蒙着上唇，喊叫說：'不潔淨了！不潔淨了！'⁴⁶災病在他身上的日子，他便是不潔淨。他既是不潔淨，就要獨居營外。

關於霉菌的大痲瘋的條例

⁴⁷ "染了大痲瘋災病的衣服，無論是羊毛衣服、是麻布衣服，⁴⁸無論是在經上、在緯上，是麻布的、是羊毛的，是在皮子上，或在皮子做的甚麼物件上，⁴⁹或在衣服上、皮子上、經上、緯上，或在皮子做的甚麼物件上，這災病若是發綠，或是發紅，是大痲瘋的災病，要給祭司察看。⁵⁰祭司就要察看那災病，把染了災病的物件關鎖七天。⁵¹第七天，他要察看那災病，災病或在衣服上、經上、緯

put the infected person in isolation for seven days. ³²On the seventh day the priest is to examine the sore, and if the itch has not spread and there is no yellow hair in it and it does not appear to be more than skin deep, ³³he must be shaved except for the diseased area, and the priest is to keep him in isolation another seven days. ³⁴On the seventh day the priest is to examine the itch, and if it has not spread in the skin and appears to be no more than skin deep, the priest shall pronounce him clean. He must wash his clothes, and he will be clean. ³⁵But if the itch does spread in the skin after he is pronounced clean, ³⁶the priest is to examine him, and if the itch has spread in the skin, the priest does not need to look for yellow hair; the person is unclean. ³⁷If, however, in his judgment it is unchanged and black hair has grown in it, the itch is healed. He is clean, and the priest shall pronounce him clean.

³⁸"When a man or woman has white spots on the skin, ³⁹the priest is to examine them, and if the spots are dull white, it is a harmless rash that has broken out on the skin; that person is clean.

⁴⁰"When a man has lost his hair and is bald, he is clean. ⁴¹If he has lost his hair from the front of his scalp and has a bald forehead, he is clean. ⁴²But if he has a reddish-white sore on his bald head or forehead, it is an infectious disease breaking out on his head or forehead. ⁴³The priest is to examine him, and if the swollen sore on his head or forehead is reddish-white like an infectious skin disease, ⁴⁴the man is diseased and is unclean. The priest shall pronounce him unclean because of the sore on his head.

⁴⁵"The person with such an infectious disease must wear torn clothes, let his hair be unkempt,[a] cover the lower part of his face and cry out, 'Unclean! Unclean!' ⁴⁶As long as he has the infection he remains unclean. He must live alone; he must live outside the camp.

Regulations About Mildew

⁴⁷"If any clothing is contaminated with mildew—any woolen or linen clothing, ⁴⁸any woven or knitted material of linen or wool, any leather or anything made of leather— ⁴⁹and if the contamination in the clothing, or leather, or woven or knitted material, or any leather article, is greenish or reddish, it is a spreading mildew and must be shown to the priest. ⁵⁰The priest is to examine the mildew and isolate the affected article for seven days. ⁵¹On the seventh day he is to examine it, and if the mildew has spread in

a 45 Or clothes, uncover his head

the clothing, or the woven or knitted material, or the leather, whatever its use, it is a destructive mildew; the article is unclean. [52]He must burn up the clothing, or the woven or knitted material of wool or linen, or any leather article that has the contamination in it, because the mildew is destructive; the article must be burned up.

[53]"But if, when the priest examines it, the mildew has not spread in the clothing, or the woven or knitted material, or the leather article, [54]he shall order that the contaminated article be washed. Then he is to isolate it for another seven days. [55]After the affected article has been washed, the priest is to examine it, and if the mildew has not changed its appearance, even though it has not spread, it is unclean. Burn it with fire, whether the mildew has affected one side or the other. [56]If, when the priest examines it, the mildew has faded after the article has been washed, he is to tear the contaminated part out of the clothing, or the leather, or the woven or knitted material. [57]But if it reappears in the clothing, or in the woven or knitted material, or in the leather article, it is spreading, and whatever has the mildew must be burned with fire. [58]The clothing, or the woven or knitted material, or any leather article that has been washed and is rid of the mildew, must be washed again, and it will be clean."

[59]These are the regulations concerning contamination by mildew in woolen or linen clothing, woven or knitted material, or any leather article, for pronouncing them clean or unclean.

Cleansing From Infectious Skin Diseases

14 The LORD said to Moses, [2]"These are the regulations for the diseased person at the time of his ceremonial cleansing, when he is brought to the priest: [3]The priest is to go outside the camp and examine him. If the person has been healed of his infectious skin disease,[a] [4]the priest shall order that two live clean birds and some cedar wood, scarlet yarn and hyssop be brought for the one to be cleansed. [5]Then the priest shall order that one of the birds be killed over fresh water in a clay pot. [6]He is to take the live bird and dip it, together with the cedar wood, the scarlet yarn and the hyssop, into the blood of the bird that was killed over the fresh water. [7]Seven times he shall sprinkle the one to be cleansed of the infec-

上、皮子上,若發散,,這皮子無論當作何用,這災病是蠶食的大痲瘋,都是不潔淨了。[52]那染了災病的衣服,或是經上、緯上、羊毛上、麻衣上,或是皮子做的甚麼物件上,他都要焚燒,因為這是蠶食的大痲瘋,必在火中焚燒。

[53]"祭司要察看,若災病在衣服上、經上、緯上,或是皮子做的甚麼物件上,沒有發散,[54]祭司就要吩咐他們,把染了災病的物件洗了,再關鎖七天。[55]洗過以後,祭司要察看,那物件若沒有變色,災病也沒有消散,那物件就不潔淨,是透重的災病,無論正面反面,都要在火中焚燒。[56]洗過以後,祭司要察看,若見那災病發暗,他就要把那災病從衣服上、皮子上、經上、緯上都撕去。[57]若仍現在衣服上,或是經上、緯上、皮子做的甚麼物件上,這就是災病又發了,必用火焚燒那染災病的物件。[58]所洗的衣服,或是經,或是緯,或是皮子做的甚麼物件,若災病離開了,要再洗,就潔淨了。"

[59]這就是大痲瘋災病的條例。無論是在羊毛衣服上、麻布衣服上、經上、緯上和皮子做的甚麼物件上,可以定為潔淨或是不潔淨。

潔淨皮膚傳染病

14 耶和華曉諭摩西說:[2]"長大痲瘋得潔淨的日子,其例乃是這樣:要帶他去見祭司,[3]祭司要出到營外察看,若見他的大痲瘋痊愈了,[4]就要吩咐人為那求潔淨的,拿兩隻潔淨的活鳥和香柏木、朱紅色線並牛膝草來。[5]祭司要吩咐用瓦器盛活水,把一隻鳥宰在上面。[6]至於那隻活鳥,祭司要把牠和香柏木、朱紅色線並牛膝草,一同蘸於宰在活水上的鳥血中,[7]用以在那長大痲瘋求潔淨的人身上灑七次,就定他

---

a 3 Traditionally *leprosy*; the Hebrew word was used for various diseases affecting the skin—not necessarily leprosy; also elsewhere in this chapter.

為潔淨，又把活鳥放在田野裏。

8 "求潔淨的人當洗衣服，剃去毛髮，用水洗澡，就潔淨了。然後可以進營，只是要在自己的帳棚外居住七天。9第七天，再把頭上所有的頭髮與鬍鬚、眉毛並全身的毛都剃了；又要洗衣服，用水洗身，就潔淨了。

10 "第八天，他要取兩隻沒有殘疾的公羊羔和一隻沒有殘疾、一歲的母羊羔，又要把調油的細麵伊法十分之三為素祭，並油一羅革一同取來。11行潔淨之禮的祭司，要將那求潔淨的人和這些東西安置在會幕門口，耶和華面前。

12 "祭司要取一隻公羊羔獻為贖愆祭，和那一羅革油一同作搖祭，在耶和華面前搖一搖。13把公羊羔宰於聖地，就是宰贖罪祭牲和燔祭牲之地。贖愆祭要歸祭司，與贖罪祭一樣，是至聖的。14祭司要取些贖愆祭牲的血，抹在求潔淨人的右耳垂上和右手的大拇指上，並右腳的大拇指上。15祭司要從那一羅革油中取些倒在自己的左手掌裏，16把右手的一個指頭蘸在左手的油裏，在耶和華面前用指頭彈七次。17手裏所剩的油，抹在那求潔淨人的右耳垂上和右手的大拇指上，並右腳的大拇指上，就是抹在贖愆祭牲的血上。18祭司手裏所剩的油，要抹在那求潔淨人的頭上，在耶和華面為他贖罪。

19 "祭司要獻贖罪祭，為那本不潔淨求潔淨的人贖罪，然後要宰燔祭牲。20把燔祭和素祭獻在壇上為他贖罪，他就潔淨了。

21 "他若貧窮不能預備夠數，就要取一隻公羊羔作贖愆祭，可以搖一

tious disease and pronounce him clean. Then he is to release the live bird in the open fields.

8"The person to be cleansed must wash his clothes, shave off all his hair and bathe with water; then he will be ceremonially clean. After this he may come into the camp, but he must stay outside his tent for seven days. 9On the seventh day he must shave off all his hair; he must shave his head, his beard, his eyebrows and the rest of his hair. He must wash his clothes and bathe himself with water, and he will be clean.

10"On the eighth day he must bring two male lambs and one ewe lamb a year old, each without defect, along with three-tenths of an ephah*a* of fine flour mixed with oil for a grain offering, and one log*b* of oil. 11The priest who pronounces him clean shall present both the one to be cleansed and his offerings before the LORD at the entrance to the Tent of Meeting.

12"Then the priest is to take one of the male lambs and offer it as a guilt offering, along with the log of oil; he shall wave them before the LORD as a wave offering. 13He is to slaughter the lamb in the holy place where the sin offering and the burnt offering are slaughtered. Like the sin offering, the guilt offering belongs to the priest; it is most holy. 14The priest is to take some of the blood of the guilt offering and put it on the lobe of the right ear of the one to be cleansed, on the thumb of his right hand and on the big toe of his right foot. 15The priest shall then take some of the log of oil, pour it in the palm of his own left hand, 16dip his right forefinger into the oil in his palm, and with his finger sprinkle some of it before the LORD seven times. 17The priest is to put some of the oil remaining in his palm on the lobe of the right ear of the one to be cleansed, on the thumb of his right hand and on the big toe of his right foot, on top of the blood of the guilt offering. 18The rest of the oil in his palm the priest shall put on the head of the one to be cleansed and make atonement for him before the LORD.

19"Then the priest is to sacrifice the sin offering and make atonement for the one to be cleansed from his uncleanness. After that, the priest shall slaughter the burnt offering 20and offer it on the altar, together with the grain offering, and make atonement for him, and he will be clean.

21"If, however, he is poor and cannot afford these, he must take one male lamb as a guilt

---

a 10 That is, probably about 6 quarts (about 6.5 liters)
b 10 That is, probably about 2/3 pint (about 0.3 liter); also in verses 12, 15, 21 and 24

offering to be waved to make atonement for him, together with a tenth of an ephah*a* of fine flour mixed with oil for a grain offering, a log of oil, [22]and two doves or two young pigeons, which he can afford, one for a sin offering and the other for a burnt offering.

[23]"On the eighth day he must bring them for his cleansing to the priest at the entrance to the Tent of Meeting, before the LORD. [24]The priest is to take the lamb for the guilt offering, together with the log of oil, and wave them before the LORD as a wave offering. [25]He shall slaughter the lamb for the guilt offering and take some of its blood and put it on the lobe of the right ear of the one to be cleansed, on the thumb of his right hand and on the big toe of his right foot. [26]The priest is to pour some of the oil into the palm of his own left hand, [27]and with his right forefinger sprinkle some of the oil from his palm seven times before the LORD. [28]Some of the oil in his palm he is to put on the same places he put the blood of the guilt offering—on the lobe of the right ear of the one to be cleansed, on the thumb of his right hand and on the big toe of his right foot. [29]The rest of the oil in his palm the priest shall put on the head of the one to be cleansed, to make atonement for him before the LORD. [30]Then he shall sacrifice the doves or the young pigeons, which the person can afford, [31]one*b* as a sin offering and the other as a burnt offering, together with the grain offering. In this way the priest will make atonement before the LORD on behalf of the one to be cleansed."

[32]These are the regulations for anyone who has an infectious skin disease and who cannot afford the regular offerings for his cleansing.

Cleansing From Mildew

[33]The LORD said to Moses and Aaron, [34]"When you enter the land of Canaan, which I am giving you as your possession, and I put a spreading mildew in a house in that land, [35]the owner of the house must go and tell the priest, 'I have seen something that looks like mildew in my house.' [36]The priest is to order the house to be emptied before he goes in to examine the mildew, so that nothing in the house will be pronounced unclean. After this the priest is to go in and inspect the house. [37]He is to examine the mildew on the walls, and if it has greenish or reddish depressions that appear to be deeper than the surface of the wall, [38]the priest shall go

---

搖，為他贖罪；也要把調油的細麵伊法十分之一為素祭，和油一羅革一同取來。[22]又照他的力量取兩隻斑鳩或是兩隻雛鴿，一隻作贖罪祭，一隻作燔祭。

[23]"第八天，要為潔淨，把這些帶到會幕門口，耶和華面前，交給祭司。[24]祭司要把贖愆祭的羊羔和那一羅革油一同作搖祭，在耶和華面前搖一搖。[25]要宰了贖愆祭的羊羔，取些贖愆祭牲的血，抹在那求潔淨人的右耳垂上和右手的大拇指上，並右腳的大拇指上。[26]祭司要把些油倒在自己的左手掌裏，[27]把左手裏的油，在耶和華面前，用右手的一個指頭彈七次。[28]又把手裏的油，抹些在那求潔淨人的右耳垂上和右手的大拇指上，並右腳的大拇指上，就是抹贖愆祭之血的原處。[29]祭司手裏所剩的油，要抹在那求潔淨人的頭上，在耶和華面前為他贖罪。[30]那人又要照他的力量獻上一隻斑鳩或是一隻雛鴿，[31]就是他所能辦的，一隻為贖罪祭，一隻為燔祭，與素祭一同獻上。祭司要在耶和華面前為他贖罪。"

[32]這是那有大痲瘋災病的人，不能將關乎得潔淨之物預備夠數的條例。

潔淨感染痲瘋的房屋

[33]耶和華曉諭摩西、亞倫說：[34]"你們到了我賜給你們為業的迦南地，我若使你們所得為業之地的房屋中有大痲瘋的災病，[35]房主就要去告訴祭司說：'據我看，房屋中似乎有災病。'[36]祭司還沒有進去察看災病以前，就要吩咐人把房子騰空，免得房子裏所有的都成了不潔淨。然後祭司要進去察看房子。[37]他要察看那災病，災病若在房子的牆上有發綠或發紅的凹斑紋，現象窪於牆，[38]祭司就

---

a 21 That is, probably about 2 quarts (about 2 liters)

b 31 Septuagint and Syriac; Hebrew *31such as the person can afford, one*

要出到房門外，把房子封鎖七天。
³⁹第七天，祭司要再去察看，災病若
在房子的牆上發散，⁴⁰就要吩咐人把
那有災病的石頭挖出來，扔在城外不
潔淨之處；⁴¹也要叫人刮房內的四
圍，所刮掉的灰泥，要倒在城外不潔
淨之處；⁴²又要用別的石頭，代替那
挖出來的石頭，要另用灰泥墁房子。

⁴³ "他挖出石頭，刮了房子，墁
了以後，災病若在房子裏又發現，
⁴⁴祭司就要進去察看。災病若在房子
裏發散，這就是房內蠶食的大痲瘋，
是不潔淨。⁴⁵他就要拆毀房子，把石
頭、木頭、灰泥都搬到城外不潔淨之
處。

⁴⁶ "在房子封鎖的時候，進去的
人必不潔淨到晚上。⁴⁷在房子裏躺着
的必洗衣服；在房子裏吃飯的也必洗
衣服。

⁴⁸ "房子墁了以後，祭司若進去
察看，見災病在房內沒有發散，就要
定房子為潔淨，因為災病已經消除。
⁴⁹要為潔淨房子，取兩隻鳥和香柏
木、朱紅色線並牛膝草，⁵⁰用瓦器盛
活水，把一隻鳥宰在上面，⁵¹把香柏
木、牛膝草、朱紅色線並那活鳥，都
蘸在被宰的鳥血中與活水中，用以灑
房子七次。⁵²要用鳥血、活水、活
鳥、香柏木、牛膝草並朱紅色線，潔
淨那房子。⁵³但要把活鳥放在城外田
野裏。這樣潔淨房子 (註：原文作 "為房
子贖罪")，房子就潔淨了。"

⁵⁴這是為各類大痲瘋的災病和頭
疥，⁵⁵並衣服與房子的大痲瘋，⁵⁶以
及瘤子、癬、火斑所立的條例，⁵⁷指
明何時為潔淨，何時為不潔淨。

這是大痲瘋的條例。

漏症造成不潔

15 耶和華對摩西、亞倫說：
²"你們曉諭以色列人說：
'人若身患漏症，他因這漏
症就不潔淨了。³他患漏症，無論是
下流的，是止住的，都是不潔淨。

out the doorway of the house and close it up for
seven days. ³⁹On the seventh day the priest shall
return to inspect the house. If the mildew has
spread on the walls, ⁴⁰he is to order that the contaminated stones be torn out and thrown into an
unclean place outside the town. ⁴¹He must have
all the inside walls of the house scraped and the
material that is scraped off dumped into an
unclean place outside the town. ⁴²Then they are
to take other stones to replace these and take
new clay and plaster the house.

⁴³"If the mildew reappears in the house after
the stones have been torn out and the house
scraped and plastered, ⁴⁴the priest is to go and
examine it and, if the mildew has spread in the
house, it is a destructive mildew; the house is
unclean. ⁴⁵It must be torn down—its stones, timbers and all the plaster—and taken out of the
town to an unclean place.

⁴⁶"Anyone who goes into the house while it
is closed up will be unclean till evening.
⁴⁷Anyone who sleeps or eats in the house must
wash his clothes.

⁴⁸"But if the priest comes to examine it and
the mildew has not spread after the house has
been plastered, he shall pronounce the house
clean, because the mildew is gone. ⁴⁹To purify
the house he is to take two birds and some cedar
wood, scarlet yarn and hyssop. ⁵⁰He shall kill
one of the birds over fresh water in a clay pot.
⁵¹Then he is to take the cedar wood, the hyssop,
the scarlet yarn and the live bird, dip them into
the blood of the dead bird and the fresh water,
and sprinkle the house seven times. ⁵²He shall
purify the house with the bird's blood, the fresh
water, the live bird, the cedar wood, the hyssop
and the scarlet yarn. ⁵³Then he is to release the
live bird in the open fields outside the town. In
this way he will make atonement for the house,
and it will be clean."

⁵⁴These are the regulations for any infectious
skin disease, for an itch, ⁵⁵for mildew in clothing
or in a house, ⁵⁶and for a swelling, a rash or a
bright spot, ⁵⁷to determine when something is
clean or unclean.

These are the regulations for infectious skin
diseases and mildew.

Discharges Causing Uncleanness

15 The LORD said to Moses and Aaron,
²"Speak to the Israelites and say to them:
'When any man has a bodily discharge,
the discharge is unclean. ³Whether it continues
flowing from his body or is blocked, it will make
him unclean. This is how his discharge will bring
about uncleanness:

4" 'Any bed the man with a discharge lies on will be unclean, and anything he sits on will be unclean. 5Anyone who touches his bed must wash his clothes and bathe with water, and he will be unclean till evening. 6Whoever sits on anything that the man with a discharge sat on must wash his clothes and bathe with water, and he will be unclean till evening.

7" 'Whoever touches the man who has a discharge must wash his clothes and bathe with water, and he will be unclean till evening.

8" 'If the man with the discharge spits on someone who is clean, that person must wash his clothes and bathe with water, and he will be unclean till evening.

9" 'Everything the man sits on when riding will be unclean, 10and whoever touches any of the things that were under him will be unclean till evening; whoever picks up those things must wash his clothes and bathe with water, and he will be unclean till evening.

11" 'Anyone the man with a discharge touches without rinsing his hands with water must wash his clothes and bathe with water, and he will be unclean till evening.

12" 'A clay pot that the man touches must be broken, and any wooden article is to be rinsed with water.

13" 'When a man is cleansed from his discharge, he is to count off seven days for his ceremonial cleansing; he must wash his clothes and bathe himself with fresh water, and he will be clean. 14On the eighth day he must take two doves or two young pigeons and come before the LORD to the entrance to the Tent of Meeting and give them to the priest. 15The priest is to sacrifice them, the one for a sin offering and the other for a burnt offering. In this way he will make atonement before the LORD for the man because of his discharge.

16" 'When a man has an emission of semen, he must bathe his whole body with water, and he will be unclean till evening. 17Any clothing or leather that has semen on it must be washed with water, and it will be unclean till evening. 18When a man lies with a woman and there is an emission of semen, both must bathe with water, and they will be unclean till evening.

19" 'When a woman has her regular flow of blood, the impurity of her monthly period will last seven days, and anyone who touches her will be unclean till evening.

20" 'Anything she lies on during her period will be unclean, and anything she sits on will be unclean. 21Whoever touches her bed must wash his clothes and bathe with water, and he will be

4 " '他所躺的牀都為不潔淨，所坐的物也為不潔淨。5凡摸那牀的，必不潔淨到晚上，並要洗衣服，用水洗澡。6那坐患漏症人所坐之物的，必不潔淨到晚上，並要洗衣服，用水洗澡。

7 " '那摸患漏症人身體的，必不潔淨到晚上，並要洗衣服，用水洗澡。

8 " '若患漏症人吐在潔淨的人身上，那人必不潔淨到晚上，並要洗衣服，用水洗澡。

9 " '患漏症人所騎的鞍子也為不潔淨。10凡摸了他身下之物的，必不潔淨到晚上；拿了那物的，必不潔淨到晚上，並要洗衣服，用水洗澡。

11 " '患漏症的人沒有用水涮手，無論摸了誰，誰必不潔淨到晚上，並要洗衣服，用水洗澡。

12 " '患漏症人所摸的瓦器，就必打破；所摸的一切木器，也必用水涮洗。

13 " '患漏症的人痊愈了，就要為潔淨自己計算七天，也必洗衣服，用活水洗身，就潔淨了。14第八天，要取兩隻斑鳩或是兩隻雛鴿，來到會幕門口，耶和華面前，把鳥交給祭司。15祭司要獻上一隻為贖罪祭，一隻為燔祭，因那人患的漏症，祭司要在耶和華面前為他贖罪。

16 " '人若夢遺，他必不潔淨到晚上，並要用水洗全身。17無論是衣服、是皮子，被精所染，必不潔淨到晚上，並要用水洗。18若男女交合，兩個人必不潔淨到晚上，並要用水洗澡。

19 " '女人行經，必污穢七天，凡摸她的，必不潔淨到晚上。

20 " '女人在污穢之中，凡她所躺的物件都為不潔淨，所坐的物件也都不潔淨。21凡摸她牀的，必不潔淨到晚上，並要洗衣服，用水洗澡。

22凡摸她所坐甚麼物件的，必不潔淨到晚上，並要洗衣服，用水洗澡。23在女人的牀上，或在她坐的物上，若有別的物件，人一摸了，必不潔淨到晚上。

24 "'男人若與那女人同房，染了她的污穢，就要七天不潔淨；所躺的牀也為不潔淨。

25 "'女人若在經期以外患多日的血漏；或是經期過長，有了漏症，她就因這漏症不潔淨，與她在經期不潔淨一樣。26她在患漏症的日子所躺的牀，所坐的物都要看為不潔淨，與她月經的時候一樣。27凡摸這些物件的，就為不潔淨，必不潔淨到晚上，並要洗衣服，用水洗澡。

28 "'女人的漏症若好了，就要計算七天，然後才為潔淨。29第八天，要取兩隻斑鳩或是兩隻雛鴿，帶到會幕門口給祭司。30祭司要獻一隻為贖罪祭，一隻為燔祭，因那人血漏不潔，祭司要在耶和華面前為她贖罪。

31 "'你們要這樣使以色列人與他們的污穢隔絕，免得他們玷污我的帳幕，就因自己的污穢死亡。'"

32這是患漏症和夢遺而不潔淨的，33並有月經病的和患漏症的，無論男女，並人與不潔淨女人同房的條例。

贖罪日

16 亞倫的兩個兒子近到耶和華面前死了。死了之後，耶和華曉諭摩西說：2 "要告訴你哥哥亞倫，不可隨時進聖所的幔子內，到櫃上的施恩座前，免得他死亡，因為我要從雲中顯現在施恩座上。

3 "亞倫進聖所，要帶一隻公牛犢為贖罪祭，一隻公綿羊為燔祭。

unclean till evening. 22Whoever touches anything she sits on must wash his clothes and bathe with water, and he will be unclean till evening. 23Whether it is the bed or anything she was sitting on, when anyone touches it, he will be unclean till evening.

24 'If a man lies with her and her monthly flow touches him, he will be unclean for seven days; any bed he lies on will be unclean.

25 'When a woman has a discharge of blood for many days at a time other than her monthly period or has a discharge that continues beyond her period, she will be unclean as long as she has the discharge, just as in the days of her period. 26Any bed she lies on while her discharge continues will be unclean, as is her bed during her monthly period, and anything she sits on will be unclean, as during her period. 27Whoever touches them will be unclean; he must wash his clothes and bathe with water, and he will be unclean till evening.

28 'When she is cleansed from her discharge, she must count off seven days, and after that she will be ceremonially clean. 29On the eighth day she must take two doves or two young pigeons and bring them to the priest at the entrance to the Tent of Meeting. 30The priest is to sacrifice one for a sin offering and the other for a burnt offering. In this way he will make atonement for her before the LORD for the uncleanness of her discharge.

31 'You must keep the Israelites separate from things that make them unclean, so they will not die in their uncleanness for defiling my dwelling place,[a] which is among them.' "

32These are the regulations for a man with a discharge, for anyone made unclean by an emission of semen, 33for a woman in her monthly period, for a man or a woman with a discharge, and for a man who lies with a woman who is ceremonially unclean.

The Day of Atonement

16 The LORD spoke to Moses after the death of the two sons of Aaron who died when they approached the LORD. 2The LORD said to Moses: "Tell your brother Aaron not to come whenever he chooses into the Most Holy Place behind the curtain in front of the atonement cover on the ark, or else he will die, because I appear in the cloud over the atonement cover.

3"This is how Aaron is to enter the sanctuary area: with a young bull for a sin offering and a

a 31 Or my tabernacle

ram for a burnt offering. ⁴He is to put on the sacred linen tunic, with linen undergarments next to his body; he is to tie the linen sash around him and put on the linen turban. These are sacred garments; so he must bathe himself with water before he puts them on. ⁵From the Israelite community he is to take two male goats for a sin offering and a ram for a burnt offering.

⁶"Aaron is to offer the bull for his own sin offering to make atonement for himself and his household. ⁷Then he is to take the two goats and present them before the LORD at the entrance to the Tent of Meeting. ⁸He is to cast lots for the two goats—one lot for the LORD and the other for the scapegoat.ᵃ ⁹Aaron shall bring the goat whose lot falls to the LORD and sacrifice it for a sin offering. ¹⁰But the goat chosen by lot as the scapegoat shall be presented alive before the LORD to be used for making atonement by sending it into the desert as a scapegoat.

¹¹"Aaron shall bring the bull for his own sin offering to make atonement for himself and his household, and he is to slaughter the bull for his own sin offering. ¹²He is to take a censer full of burning coals from the altar before the LORD and two handfuls of finely ground fragrant incense and take them behind the curtain. ¹³He is to put the incense on the fire before the LORD, and the smoke of the incense will conceal the atonement cover above the Testimony, so that he will not die. ¹⁴He is to take some of the bull's blood and with his finger sprinkle it on the front of the atonement cover; then he shall sprinkle some of it with his finger seven times before the atonement cover.

¹⁵"He shall then slaughter the goat for the sin offering for the people and take its blood behind the curtain and do with it as he did with the bull's blood: He shall sprinkle it on the atonement cover and in front of it. ¹⁶In this way he will make atonement for the Most Holy Place because of the uncleanness and rebellion of the Israelites, whatever their sins have been. He is to do the same for the Tent of Meeting, which is among them in the midst of their uncleanness. ¹⁷No one is to be in the Tent of Meeting from the time Aaron goes in to make atonement in the Most Holy Place until he comes out, having made atonement for himself, his household and the whole community of Israel.

¹⁸"Then he shall come out to the altar that is before the LORD and make atonement for it. He shall take some of the bull's blood and some of

ᵃ 8 That is, the goat of removal; Hebrew azazel; also in verses 10 and 26

⁴要穿上細麻布聖內袍，把細麻布褲子穿在身上，腰束細麻布帶子，頭戴細麻布冠冕；這都是聖服。他要用水洗身，然後穿戴。⁵要從以色列會眾取兩隻公山羊為贖罪祭，一隻公綿羊為燔祭。

⁶ "亞倫要把贖罪祭的公牛奉上，為自己和本家贖罪。⁷也要把兩隻公山羊安置在會幕門口，耶和華面前，⁸為那兩隻羊拈鬮：一鬮歸與耶和華，一鬮歸與阿撒瀉勒。⁹亞倫要把那拈鬮歸與耶和華的羊，獻為贖罪祭；¹⁰但那拈鬮歸與阿撒瀉勒的羊，要活着安置在耶和華面前，用以贖罪，打發人送到曠野去，歸與阿撒瀉勒。

¹¹ "亞倫要把贖罪祭的公牛牽來宰了，為自己和本家贖罪。¹²拿香爐，從耶和華面前的壇上盛滿火炭；又拿一捧搗細的香料，都帶入幔子內。¹³在耶和華面前，把香放在火上，使香的煙雲遮掩法櫃上的施恩座，免得他死亡。¹⁴也要取些公牛的血，用指頭彈在施恩座的束面，又在施恩座的前面彈血七次。

¹⁵ "隨後他要宰那為百姓作贖罪祭的公山羊，把羊的血帶入幔子內，彈在施恩座的上面和前面，好像彈公牛的血一樣。¹⁶他因以色列人諸般的污穢、過犯，就是他們一切的罪愆，當這樣在聖所行贖罪之禮，並因會幕在他們污穢之中，也要照樣而行。¹⁷他進聖所贖罪的時候，會幕裏不可有人，直等到他為自己和本家，並以色列全會眾，贖了罪出來。

¹⁸ "他出來，要到耶和華面前的壇那裏，在壇上行贖罪之禮，又要取些公牛的血和公山羊的血，抹在壇上

四角的周圍。¹⁹也要用指頭把血彈在壇上七次，潔淨了壇，從壇上除掉以色列人諸般的污穢，使壇成聖。

²⁰"亞倫為聖所和會幕並壇獻完了贖罪祭，就要把那隻活着的公山羊奉上。²¹兩手按在羊頭上，承認以色列人諸般的罪孽、過犯，就是他們一切的罪愆，把這罪都歸在羊的頭上，藉着所派之人的手，送到曠野去。²²要把這羊放在曠野，這羊要擔當他們一切的罪孽，帶到無人之地。

²³"亞倫要進會幕，把他進聖所時所穿的細麻布衣服脫下，放在那裏；²⁴又要在聖處用水洗身，穿上衣服出來，把自己的燔祭和百姓的燔祭獻上，為自己和百姓贖罪。²⁵贖罪祭牲的脂油要在壇上焚燒。

²⁶"那放羊歸與阿撒瀉勒的人，要洗衣服，用水洗身，然後進營。²⁷作贖罪祭的公牛和公山羊的血，既帶入聖所贖罪，這牛羊就要搬到營外，將皮、肉、糞用火焚燒。²⁸焚燒的人要洗衣服，用水洗身，然後進營。

²⁹"每逢七月初十日，你們要刻苦己心，無論是本地人，是寄居在你們中間的外人，甚麼工都不可做；這要作你們永遠的定例。³⁰因在這日要為你們贖罪，使你們潔淨，你們要在耶和華面前得以潔淨，脫盡一切的罪愆。³¹這日你們要守為聖安息日，要刻苦己心；這為永遠的定例。³²那受膏接續他父親承接聖職的祭司，要穿上細麻布的聖衣，行贖罪之禮。³³他要在至聖所和會幕與壇行贖罪之禮，並要為眾祭司和會眾的百姓贖罪。

³⁴"這要作你們永遠的定例，就是因以色列人一切的罪，要一年一次為他們贖罪。"

the goat's blood and put it on all the horns of the altar. ¹⁹He shall sprinkle some of the blood on it with his finger seven times to cleanse it and to consecrate it from the uncleanness of the Israelites.

²⁰"When Aaron has finished making atonement for the Most Holy Place, the Tent of Meeting and the altar, he shall bring forward the live goat. ²¹He is to lay both hands on the head of the live goat and confess over it all the wickedness and rebellion of the Israelites—all their sins—and put them on the goat's head. He shall send the goat away into the desert in the care of a man appointed for the task. ²²The goat will carry on itself all their sins to a solitary place; and the man shall release it in the desert.

²³"Then Aaron is to go into the Tent of Meeting and take off the linen garments he put on before he entered the Most Holy Place, and he is to leave them there. ²⁴He shall bathe himself with water in a holy place and put on his regular garments. Then he shall come out and sacrifice the burnt offering for himself and the burnt offering for the people, to make atonement for himself and for the people. ²⁵He shall also burn the fat of the sin offering on the altar.

²⁶"The man who releases the goat as a scapegoat must wash his clothes and bathe himself with water; afterward he may come into the camp. ²⁷The bull and the goat for the sin offerings, whose blood was brought into the Most Holy Place to make atonement, must be taken outside the camp; their hides, flesh and offal are to be burned up. ²⁸The man who burns them must wash his clothes and bathe himself with water; afterward he may come into the camp.

²⁹"This is to be a lasting ordinance for you: On the tenth day of the seventh month you must deny yourselvesᵃ and not do any work—whether native-born or an alien living among you— ³⁰because on this day atonement will be made for you, to cleanse you. Then, before the LORD, you will be clean from all your sins. ³¹It is a sabbath of rest, and you must deny yourselves; it is a lasting ordinance. ³²The priest who is anointed and ordained to succeed his father as high priest is to make atonement. He is to put on the sacred linen garments ³³and make atonement for the Most Holy Place, for the Tent of Meeting and the altar, and for the priests and all the people of the community.

³⁴"This is to be a lasting ordinance for you: Atonement is to be made once a year for all the sins of the Israelites."

a 29 Or must fast; also in verse 31

And it was done, as the LORD commanded Moses.

Eating Blood Forbidden

17 The LORD said to Moses, 2"Speak to Aaron and his sons and to all the Israelites and say to them: 'This is what the LORD has commanded: 3Any Israelite who sacrifices an ox,*a* a lamb or a goat in the camp or outside of it 4instead of bringing it to the entrance to the Tent of Meeting to present it as an offering to the LORD in front of the tabernacle of the LORD—that man shall be considered guilty of bloodshed; he has shed blood and must be cut off from his people. 5This is so the Israelites will bring to the LORD the sacrifices they are now making in the open fields. They must bring them to the priest, that is, to the LORD, at the entrance to the Tent of Meeting and sacrifice them as fellowship offerings.*b* 6The priest is to sprinkle the blood against the altar of the LORD at the entrance to the Tent of Meeting and burn the fat as an aroma pleasing to the LORD. 7They must no longer offer any of their sacrifices to the goat idols*c* to whom they prostitute themselves. This is to be a lasting ordinance for them and for the generations to come.'

8"Say to them: 'Any Israelite or any alien living among them who offers a burnt offering or sacrifice 9and does not bring it to the entrance to the Tent of Meeting to sacrifice it to the LORD—that man must be cut off from his people.

10" 'Any Israelite or any alien living among them who eats any blood—I will set my face against that person who eats blood and will cut him off from his people. 11For the life of a creature is in the blood, and I have given it to you to make atonement for yourselves on the altar; it is the blood that makes atonement for one's life. 12Therefore I say to the Israelites, "None of you may eat blood, nor may an alien living among you eat blood."

13" 'Any Israelite or any alien living among you who hunts any animal or bird that may be eaten must drain out the blood and cover it with earth, 14because the life of every creature is its blood. That is why I have said to the Israelites, "You must not eat the blood of any creature, because the life of every creature is its blood; anyone who eats it must be cut off."

15" 'Anyone, whether native-born or alien, who eats anything found dead or torn by wild animals must wash his clothes and bathe with

於是，亞倫照耶和華所吩咐摩西的行了。

嚴禁吃血

17 耶和華對摩西說：2"你曉諭亞倫和他兒子並以色列眾人說：'耶和華所吩咐的乃是這樣：3凡以色列家中的人，宰公牛或是綿羊羔，或是山羊，不拘宰於營內營外，4若未曾牽到會幕門口，耶和華的帳幕前獻給耶和華為供物，流血的罪必歸到那人身上。他流了血，要從民中剪除。5這是為要使以色列人把他們在田野裏所獻的祭，帶到會幕門口，耶和華面前，交給祭司，獻與耶和華為平安祭。6祭司要把血灑在會幕門口，耶和華的壇上，把脂油焚燒，獻給耶和華為馨香的祭。7他們不可再獻祭給他們行邪淫所隨從的鬼魔（註：原文作"公山羊"）。這要作他們世世代代永遠的定例。'

8"你要曉諭他們說：'凡以色列家中的人，或是寄居在他們中間的外人，獻燔祭或是平安祭，9若不帶到會幕門口獻給耶和華，那人必從民中剪除。

10" '凡以色列家中的人，或是寄居在他們中間的外人，若吃甚麼血，我必向那吃血的人變臉，把他從民中剪除。11因為活物的生命是在血中，我把這血賜給你們，可以在壇上為你們的生命贖罪。因血裏有生命，所以能贖罪。12因此我對以色列人說："你們都不可吃血，寄居在你們中間的外人，也不可吃血。"

13" '凡以色列人，或是寄居在他們中間的外人，若打獵得了可吃的禽獸，必放出牠的血來，用土掩蓋。14論到一切活物的生命，所以我對以色列人說：無論甚麼活物的血，你們都不可吃，因為一切活物的血就是牠的生命。凡吃了血的，必被剪除。

15" '凡吃自死的，或是被野獸撕裂的，無論是本地人，是寄居的，必不潔淨到晚上，都要洗衣服，用水

---

a 3 The Hebrew word can include both male and female.
b 5 Traditionally *peace offerings*   *c 7* Or *demons*

洗身，到了晚上，才為潔淨。16但他若不洗衣服，也不洗身，就必擔當他的罪孽。'"

亂倫淫亂

18 耶和華對摩西說：2"你曉諭以色列人說：'我是耶和華你們的神。3你們從前住的埃及地，那裏人的行為，你們不可效法；我要領你們到的迦南地，那裏人的行為，也不可效法，也不可照他們的惡俗行。4你們要遵我的典章，守我的律例，按此而行。我是耶和華你們的神。5所以你們要守我的律例、典章。人若遵行，就必因此活着。我是耶和華。

6"'你們都不可露骨肉之親的下體，親近他們。我是耶和華。

7"'不可露你母親的下體，羞辱了你父親。她是你的母親，不可露她的下體。

8"'不可露你繼母的下體，這本是你父親的下體。

9"'你的姐妹，不拘是異母同父的，是異父同母的，無論是生在家，生在外的，都不可露她們的下體。

10"'不可露你孫女或是外孫女的下體，露了她們的下體，就是露了自己的下體。

11"'你繼母從你父親生的女兒，本是你的妹妹，不可露她的下體。

12"'不可露你姑母的下體，她是你父親的骨肉之親。

13"'不可露你姨母的下體，她是你母親的骨肉之親。

14"'不可親近你伯叔之妻，羞辱了你伯叔，她是你的伯叔母。

15"'不可露你兒婦的下體，她是你兒子的妻，不可露她的下體。

16"'不可露你弟兄妻子的下體，這本是你弟兄的下體。

17"'不可露了婦人的下體，又露她女兒的下體，也不可娶她孫女或是外孫女，露她們的下體，她們是骨肉之親，這本是大惡。

18"'你妻還在的時候，不可另娶她的姐妹作對頭，露她的下體。

water, and he will be ceremonially unclean till evening; then he will be clean. 16But if he does not wash his clothes and bathe himself, he will be held responsible.' "

Unlawful Sexual Relations

18 The LORD said to Moses, 2"Speak to the Israelites and say to them: 'I am the LORD your God. 3You must not do as they do in Egypt, where you used to live, and you must not do as they do in the land of Canaan, where I am bringing you. Do not follow their practices. 4You must obey my laws and be careful to follow my decrees. I am the LORD your God. 5Keep my decrees and laws, for the man who obeys them will live by them. I am the LORD.

6"'No one is to approach any close relative to have sexual relations. I am the LORD.

7"'Do not dishonor your father by having sexual relations with your mother. She is your mother; do not have relations with her.

8"'Do not have sexual relations with your father's wife; that would dishonor your father.

9"'Do not have sexual relations with your sister, either your father's daughter or your mother's daughter, whether she was born in the same home or elsewhere.

10"'Do not have sexual relations with your son's daughter or your daughter's daughter; that would dishonor you.

11"'Do not have sexual relations with the daughter of your father's wife, born to your father; she is your sister.

12"'Do not have sexual relations with your father's sister; she is your father's close relative.

13"'Do not have sexual relations with your mother's sister, because she is your mother's close relative.

14"'Do not dishonor your father's brother by approaching his wife to have sexual relations; she is your aunt.

15"'Do not have sexual relations with your daughter-in-law. She is your son's wife; do not have relations with her.

16"'Do not have sexual relations with your brother's wife; that would dishonor your brother.

17"'Do not have sexual relations with both a woman and her daughter. Do not have sexual relations with either her son's daughter or her daughter's daughter; they are her close relatives. That is wickedness.

18"'Do not take your wife's sister as a rival wife and have sexual relations with her while your wife is living.

19" 'Do not approach a woman to have sexual relations during the uncleanness of her monthly period.

20" 'Do not have sexual relations with your neighbor's wife and defile yourself with her.

21" 'Do not give any of your children to be sacrificed[a] to Molech, for you must not profane the name of your God. I am the LORD.

22" 'Do not lie with a man as one lies with a woman; that is detestable.

23" 'Do not have sexual relations with an animal and defile yourself with it. A woman must not present herself to an animal to have sexual relations with it; that is a perversion.

24" 'Do not defile yourselves in any of these ways, because this is how the nations that I am going to drive out before you became defiled. 25Even the land was defiled; so I punished it for its sin, and the land vomited out its inhabitants. 26But you must keep my decrees and my laws. The native-born and the aliens living among you must not do any of these detestable things, 27for all these things were done by the people who lived in the land before you, and the land became defiled. 28And if you defile the land, it will vomit you out as it vomited out the nations that were before you.

29" 'Everyone who does any of these detestable things—such persons must be cut off from their people. 30Keep my requirements and do not follow any of the detestable customs that were practiced before you came and do not defile yourselves with them. I am the LORD your God.' "

Various Laws

19 The LORD said to Moses, 2"Speak to the entire assembly of Israel and say to them: 'Be holy because I, the LORD your God, am holy.

3" 'Each of you must respect his mother and father, and you must observe my Sabbaths. I am the LORD your God.

4" 'Do not turn to idols or make gods of cast metal for yourselves. I am the LORD your God.

5" 'When you sacrifice a fellowship offering[b] to the LORD, sacrifice it in such a way that it will be accepted on your behalf. 6It shall be eaten on the day you sacrifice it or on the next day; anything left over until the third day must be burned up. 7If any of it is eaten on the third day, it is impure and will not be accepted. 8Whoever eats it will be held responsible because he has

a 21 Or to be passed through [the fire] b 5 Traditionally peace offering

19 " '女人行經不潔淨的時候，不可露她的下體，與她親近。

20 " '不可與鄰舍的妻行淫，玷污自己。

21 " '不可使你的兒女經火歸與摩洛，也不可褻瀆你神的名。我是耶和華。

22 " '不可與男人苟合，像與女人一樣，這本是可憎惡的。

23 " '不可與獸淫合，玷污自己。女人也不可站在獸前，與牠淫合，這本是逆性的事。

24 " '在這一切的事上，你們都不可玷污自己，因為我在你們面前所逐出的列邦，在這一切的事上玷污了自己。25連地也玷污了，所以我追討那地的罪孽，那地也吐出它的居民。26故此你們要守我的律例、典章。這一切可憎惡的事，無論是本地人，是寄居在你們中間的外人，都不可行。(27在你們以先居住那地的人，行了這一切可憎惡的事，地就玷污了。)28免得你們玷污那地的時候，地就把你們吐出，像吐出在你們以先的國民一樣。

29 " '無論甚麼人，行了其中可憎的一件事，必從民中剪除。30所以你們要守我所吩咐的，免得你們隨從那些可憎的惡俗，就是在你們以先的人所常行的，以致玷污了自己。我是耶和華你們的神。' "

各項法例

19 耶和華對摩西說：2"你曉諭以色列全會眾說：'你們要聖潔，因為我耶和華你們的神是聖潔的。

3 " '你們各人都當孝敬父母，也要守我的安息日。我是耶和華你們的神。

4 " '你們不可偏向虛無的神，也不可為自己鑄造神像。我是耶和華你們的神。

5 " '你們獻平安祭給耶和華的時候，要獻得可蒙悅納。6這祭物要在獻的那一天和第二天吃，若有剩到第三天的，就必用火焚燒。7第三天若再吃，這就為可憎惡的，必不蒙悅納。8凡吃的人，必擔當他的罪孽，因為他褻瀆了耶和華的聖物，那人必從民中剪除。

9 "'在你們的地收割莊稼，不可割盡田角，也不可拾取所遺落的。10不可摘盡葡萄園的果子，也不可拾取葡萄園所掉的果子，要留給窮人和寄居的。我是耶和華你們的神。

11 "'你們不可偷盜，

"'不可欺騙，

"'也不可彼此說謊。

12 "'不可指着我的名起假誓，褻瀆你神的名。我是耶和華。

13 "'不可欺壓你的鄰舍，也不可搶奪他的物。

"'雇工人的工價，不可在你那裏過夜留到早晨。

14 "'不可咒罵聾子，也不可將絆腳石放在瞎子面前，只要敬畏你的神。我是耶和華。

15 "'你們施行審判，不可行不義，不可偏護窮人，也不可重看有勢力的人，只要按着公義審判你的鄰舍。

16 "'不可在民中往來搬弄是非，也不可與鄰舍為敵，置之於死（註：原文作"流他的血"）。我是耶和華。

17 "'不可心裏恨你的弟兄；總要指摘你的鄰舍，免得因他擔罪。

18 "'不可報仇，也不可埋怨你本國的子民，卻要愛人如己。我是耶和華。

19 "'你們要守我的律例。

"'不可叫你的牲畜與異類配合。

"'不可用兩樣攙雜的種種你的地。

"'也不可用兩樣攙雜的料做衣服穿在身上。

20 "'婢女許配了丈夫，還沒有被贖得釋放，人若與她行淫，二人要受刑罰，卻不把他們治死，因為婢女還沒有得自由。21那人要把贖愆祭，就是一隻公綿羊牽到會幕門口，耶和華面前。22祭司要用贖愆祭的羊在耶和華面前贖他所犯的罪，他的罪就必蒙赦免。

23 "'你們到了迦南地，栽種各樣結果子的樹木，就要以所結的果子如未受割禮的一樣。三年之久，你們要以這些果子，如未受割禮的，是不可吃的。24但第四年所結的果子全要

desecrated what is holy to the LORD; that person must be cut off from his people.

9 'When you reap the harvest of your land, do not reap to the very edges of your field or gather the gleanings of your harvest. 10Do not go over your vineyard a second time or pick up the grapes that have fallen. Leave them for the poor and the alien. I am the LORD your God.

11" 'Do not steal.

" 'Do not lie.

" 'Do not deceive one another.

12" 'Do not swear falsely by my name and so profane the name of your God. I am the LORD.

13" 'Do not defraud your neighbor or rob him.

" 'Do not hold back the wages of a hired man overnight.

14" 'Do not curse the deaf or put a stumbling block in front of the blind, but fear your God. I am the LORD.

15" 'Do not pervert justice; do not show partiality to the poor or favoritism to the great, but judge your neighbor fairly.

16" 'Do not go about spreading slander among your people.

" 'Do not do anything that endangers your neighbor's life. I am the LORD.

17" 'Do not hate your brother in your heart. Rebuke your neighbor frankly so you will not share in his guilt.

18" 'Do not seek revenge or bear a grudge against one of your people, but love your neighbor as yourself. I am the LORD.

19" 'Keep my decrees.

" 'Do not mate different kinds of animals.

" 'Do not plant your field with two kinds of seed.

" 'Do not wear clothing woven of two kinds of material.

20" 'If a man sleeps with a woman who is a slave girl promised to another man but who has not been ransomed or given her freedom, there must be due punishment. Yet they are not to be put to death, because she had not been freed. 21The man, however, must bring a ram to the entrance to the Tent of Meeting for a guilt offering to the LORD. 22With the ram of the guilt offering the priest is to make atonement for him before the LORD for the sin he has committed, and his sin will be forgiven.

23" 'When you enter the land and plant any kind of fruit tree, regard its fruit as forbidden.*a* For three years you are to consider it forbidden*a*; it must not be eaten. 24In the fourth year

a 23 Hebrew uncircumcised

all its fruit will be holy, an offering of praise to the LORD. ²⁵But in the fifth year you may eat its fruit. In this way your harvest will be increased. I am the LORD your God.

²⁶" 'Do not eat any meat with the blood still in it.

" 'Do not practice divination or sorcery.

²⁷" 'Do not cut the hair at the sides of your head or clip off the edges of your beard.

²⁸" 'Do not cut your bodies for the dead or put tattoo marks on yourselves. I am the LORD.

²⁹" 'Do not degrade your daughter by making her a prostitute, or the land will turn to prostitution and be filled with wickedness.

³⁰" 'Observe my Sabbaths and have reverence for my sanctuary. I am the LORD.

³¹" 'Do not turn to mediums or seek out spiritists, for you will be defiled by them. I am the LORD your God.

³²" 'Rise in the presence of the aged, show respect for the elderly and revere your God. I am the LORD.

³³" 'When an alien lives with you in your land, do not mistreat him. ³⁴The alien living with you must be treated as one of your native-born. Love him as yourself, for you were aliens in Egypt. I am the LORD your God.

³⁵" 'Do not use dishonest standards when measuring length, weight or quantity. ³⁶Use honest scales and honest weights, an honest ephah[a] and an honest hin.[b] I am the LORD your God, who brought you out of Egypt.

³⁷" 'Keep all my decrees and all my laws and follow them. I am the LORD.' "

Punishments for Sin

20 The LORD said to Moses, ²"Say to the Israelites: 'Any Israelite or any alien living in Israel who gives[c] any of his children to Molech must be put to death. The people of the community are to stone him. ³I will set my face against that man and I will cut him off from his people; for by giving his children to Molech, he has defiled my sanctuary and profaned my holy name. ⁴If the people of the community close their eyes when that man gives one of his children to Molech and they fail to put him to death, ⁵I will set my face against that man and his family and will cut off from their people both him and all who follow him in prostituting themselves to Molech.

⁶" 'I will set my face against the person who turns to mediums and spiritists to prostitute

成為聖，用以讚美耶和華。²⁵第五年，你們要吃那樹上的果子，好叫樹給你們結果子更多。我是耶和華你們的神。

²⁶ " '你們不可吃帶血的物。

" '不可用法術，也不可觀兆。

²⁷ " '頭的周圍不可剃（註："周圍"或作"兩鬢"），鬍鬚的周圍也不可損壞。

²⁸ " '不可為死人用刀劃身，也不可在身上刺花紋。我是耶和華。

²⁹ " '不可辱沒你的女兒，使她為娼妓。恐怕地上的人專向淫亂，地就滿了大惡。

³⁰ " '你們要守我的安息日，敬我的聖所。我是耶和華。

³¹ " '不可偏向那些交鬼的和行巫術的；不可求問他們，以致被他們玷污了。我是耶和華你們的神。

³² " '在白髮的人面前，你要站起來；也要尊敬老人，又要敬畏你的神。我是耶和華。

³³ " '若有外人在你們國中和你同居，就不可欺負他。³⁴和你們同居的外人，你們要看他如本地人一樣，並要愛他如己，因為你們在埃及地也作過寄居的。我是耶和華你們的神。

³⁵ " '你們施行審判，不可行不義。在尺、秤、升、斗上也是如此。³⁶要用公道天平、公道法碼、公道升斗、公道秤。我是耶和華你們的神，曾把你們從埃及地領出來的。

³⁷ " '你們要謹守遵行我一切的律例、典章。我是耶和華。' "

犯罪的刑罰

20 耶和華對摩西說：²"你還要曉諭以色列人說：'凡以色列人，或是在以色列中寄居的外人，把自己的兒女獻給摩洛的，總要治死他。本地人要用石頭把他打死。³我也要向那人變臉，把他從民中剪除，因為他把兒女獻給摩洛，玷污我的聖所，褻瀆我的聖名。⁴那人把兒女獻給摩洛，本地人若佯為不見，不把他治死，⁵我就要向這人和他的家變臉，把他和一切隨他與摩洛行邪淫的人都從民中剪除。

⁶ " '人偏向交鬼的和行巫術的，隨他們行邪淫，我要向那人變

a 36 An ephah was a dry measure.　　b 36 A hin was a liquid measure.　　c 2 Or *sacrifices*; also in verses 3 and 4

臉，把他從民中剪除。

7 "'所以你們要自潔成聖，因為我是耶和華你們的神。8你們要謹守遵行我的律例，我是叫你們成聖的耶和華。

9 "'凡咒罵父母的，總要治死他；他咒罵了父母，他的罪要歸到他身上（註："罪"原文作"血"。本章同）。

10 "'與鄰舍之妻行淫的，姦夫淫婦都必治死。

11 "'與繼母行淫的，就是羞辱了他父親，總要把他們二人治死，罪要歸到他們身上。

12 "'與兒婦同房的，總要把他們二人治死，他們行了逆倫的事，罪要歸到他們身上。

13 "'人若與男人苟合，像與女人一樣，他們二人行了可憎的事，總要把他們治死，罪要歸到他們身上。

14 "'人若娶妻，並娶其母，便是大惡，要把這三人用火焚燒，使你們中間免去大惡。

15 "'人若與獸淫合，總要治死他，也要殺那獸。

16 "'女人若與獸親近，與牠淫合，你要殺那女人和那獸，總要把他們治死，罪要歸到他們身上。

17 "'人若娶他的姐妹，無論是異母同父的，是異父同母的，彼此見了下體，這是可恥的事，他們必在本民的眼前被剪除。他露了姐妹的下體，必擔當自己的罪孽。

18 "'婦人有月經，若與她同房，露了她的下體，就是露了婦人的血源，婦人也露了自己的血源，二人必從民中剪除。

19 "'不可露姨母或是姑母的下體，這是露了骨肉之親的下體，二人必擔當自己的罪孽。

20 "'人若與伯叔之妻同房，就羞辱了他的伯叔，二人要擔當自己的

himself by following them, and I will cut him off from his people.

7 "'Consecrate yourselves and be holy, because I am the LORD your God. 8Keep my decrees and follow them. I am the LORD, who makes you holy.*a*

9 "'If anyone curses his father or mother, he must be put to death. He has cursed his father or his mother, and his blood will be on his own head.

10 "'If a man commits adultery with another man's wife—with the wife of his neighbor—both the adulterer and the adulteress must be put to death.

11 "'If a man sleeps with his father's wife, he has dishonored his father. Both the man and the woman must be put to death; their blood will be on their own heads.

12 "'If a man sleeps with his daughter-in-law, both of them must be put to death. What they have done is a perversion; their blood will be on their own heads.

13 "'If a man lies with a man as one lies with a woman, both of them have done what is detestable. They must be put to death; their blood will be on their own heads.

14 "'If a man marries both a woman and her mother, it is wicked. Both he and they must be burned in the fire, so that no wickedness will be among you.

15 "'If a man has sexual relations with an animal, he must be put to death, and you must kill the animal.

16 "'If a woman approaches an animal to have sexual relations with it, kill both the woman and the animal. They must be put to death; their blood will be on their own heads.

17 "'If a man marries his sister, the daughter of either his father or his mother, and they have sexual relations, it is a disgrace. They must be cut off before the eyes of their people. He has dishonored his sister and will be held responsible.

18 "'If a man lies with a woman during her monthly period and has sexual relations with her, he has exposed the source of her flow, and she has also uncovered it. Both of them must be cut off from their people.

19 "'Do not have sexual relations with the sister of either your mother or your father, for that would dishonor a close relative; both of you would be held responsible.

20 "'If a man sleeps with his aunt, he has dishonored his uncle. They will be held responsi-

a 8 Or who sanctifies you; or who sets you apart as holy

ble; they will die childless.

21" 'If a man marries his brother's wife, it is an act of impurity; he has dishonored his brother. They will be childless.

22" 'Keep all my decrees and laws and follow them, so that the land where I am bringing you to live may not vomit you out. 23You must not live according to the customs of the nations I am going to drive out before you. Because they did all these things, I abhorred them. 24But I said to you, "You will possess their land; I will give it to you as an inheritance, a land flowing with milk and honey." I am the LORD your God, who has set you apart from the nations.

25" 'You must therefore make a distinction between clean and unclean animals and between unclean and clean birds. Do not defile yourselves by any animal or bird or anything that moves along the ground—those which I have set apart as unclean for you. 26You are to be holy to me[a] because I, the LORD, am holy, and I have set you apart from the nations to be my own.

27" 'A man or woman who is a medium or spiritist among you must be put to death. You are to stone them; their blood will be on their own heads.' "

Rules for Priests

21 The LORD said to Moses, "Speak to the priests, the sons of Aaron, and say to them: 'A priest must not make himself ceremonially unclean for any of his people who die, 2except for a close relative, such as his mother or father, his son or daughter, his brother, 3or an unmarried sister who is dependent on him since she has no husband—for her he may make himself unclean. 4He must not make himself unclean for people related to him by marriage,[b] and so defile himself.

5" 'Priests must not shave their heads or shave off the edges of their beards or cut their bodies. 6They must be holy to their God and must not profane the name of their God. Because they present the offerings made to the LORD by fire, the food of their God, they are to be holy.

7" 'They must not marry women defiled by prostitution or divorced from their husbands, because priests are holy to their God. 8Regard them as holy, because they offer up the food of your God. Consider them holy, because I the LORD am holy—I who make you holy.[c]

罪,必無子女而死。

21 "'人若娶弟兄之妻,這本是污穢的事,羞辱了他的弟兄,二人必無子女。

22 "'所以,你們要謹守遵行我一切的律例、典章,免得我領你們去住的那地把你們吐出。23我在你們面前所逐出的國民,你們不可隨從他們的風俗,因為他們行了這一切的事,所以我厭惡他們。24但我對你們說過:你們要承受他們的地,就是我要賜給你們為業流奶與蜜之地。我是耶和華你們的神,使你們與萬民有分別的。

25 "'所以,你們要把潔淨和不潔淨的禽獸分別出來,不可因我給你們分為不潔淨的禽獸,或是滋生在地上的活物,使自己成為可憎惡的。26你們要歸我為聖,因為我耶和華是聖的,並叫你們與萬民有分別,使你們作我的民。

27 "'無論男女,是交鬼的或行巫術的,總要治死他們,人必用石頭把他們打死,罪要歸到他們身上。'"

祭司條例

21 耶和華對摩西說:"你告訴亞倫子孫作祭司的說:'祭司不可為民中的死人沾染自己。2除非為他骨肉之親的父母、兒女、弟兄,3和未曾出嫁作處女的姐妹,才可以沾染自己。4祭司既在民中為首,就不可從俗沾染自己。

5 "'不可使頭光禿,不可剃除鬍鬚的周圍,也不可用刀割身。6要歸神為聖,不可褻瀆神的名,因為耶和華的火祭,就是神的食物,是他們獻的,所以他們要成為聖。

7 "'不可娶妓女或被污的女人為妻,也不可娶被休的婦人為妻,因為祭司是歸神為聖。8所以你要使他成聖,因為他奉獻你神的食物。你要以他為聖,因為我使你們成聖的耶和華是聖的。

---

a 26 Or *be my holy ones*   b 4 Or *unclean as a leader among his people*   c 8 Or *who sanctify you; or who set you apart as holy*

9 " '祭司的女兒若行淫，辱沒自己，就辱沒了父親，必用火將她焚燒。

10 " '在弟兄中作大祭司，頭上倒了膏油，又承接聖職，穿了聖衣的，不可蓬頭散髮，也不可撕裂衣服；11不可挨近死屍，也不可為父母沾染自己；12不可出聖所，也不可褻瀆神的聖所，因為神膏油的冠冕在他頭上。我是耶和華。

13 " '他要娶處女為妻。14寡婦或是被休的婦人，或是被污為妓的女人，都不可娶，只可娶本民中的處女為妻。15不可在民中辱沒他的兒女，因為我是叫他成聖的耶和華。' "

16耶和華對摩西說：17 "你告訴亞倫說：'你世世代代的後裔，凡有殘疾的，都不可近前來獻他神的食物。18因為凡有殘疾的，無論是瞎眼的、瘸腿的、塌鼻子的、肢體有餘的、19折腳折手的、20駝背的、矮矬的、眼睛有毛病的、長癬的、長疥的，或是損壞腎子的，都不可近前來。21祭司亞倫的後裔，凡有殘疾的，都不可近前來，將火祭獻給耶和華。他有殘疾，不可近前來獻神的食物。22神的食物，無論是聖的、至聖的，他都可以吃。23但不可進到幔子前，也不可就近壇前，因為他有殘疾，免得褻瀆我的聖所。我是叫他成聖的耶和華。' "

24於是，摩西曉諭亞倫和亞倫的子孫，並以色列眾人。

22 耶和華對摩西說：2 "你吩咐亞倫和他子孫說：要遠離以色列人所分別為聖歸給我的聖物，免得褻瀆我的聖名。我是耶和華。

3 "你要對他們說：'你們世世代代的後裔，凡身上有污穢，親近以色列人所分別為聖歸耶和華聖物的，那人必在我面前剪除。我是耶和華。

9" 'If a priest's daughter defiles herself by becoming a prostitute, she disgraces her father; she must be burned in the fire.

10" 'The high priest, the one among his brothers who has had the anointing oil poured on his head and who has been ordained to wear the priestly garments, must not let his hair become unkempt[a] or tear his clothes. 11He must not enter a place where there is a dead body. He must not make himself unclean, even for his father or mother, 12nor leave the sanctuary of his God or desecrate it, because he has been dedicated by the anointing oil of his God. I am the LORD.

13" 'The woman he marries must be a virgin. 14He must not marry a widow, a divorced woman, or a woman defiled by prostitution, but only a virgin from his own people, 15so he will not defile his offspring among his people. I am the LORD, who makes him holy.[b] '

16The LORD said to Moses, 17"Say to Aaron: 'For the generations to come none of your descendants who has a defect may come near to offer the food of his God. 18No man who has any defect may come near: no man who is blind or lame, disfigured or deformed; 19no man with a crippled foot or hand, 20or who is hunchbacked or dwarfed, or who has any eye defect, or who has festering or running sores or damaged testicles. 21No descendant of Aaron the priest who has any defect is to come near to present the offerings made to the LORD by fire. He has a defect; he must not come near to offer the food of his God. 22He may eat the most holy food of his God, as well as the holy food; 23yet because of his defect, he must not go near the curtain or approach the altar, and so desecrate my sanctuary. I am the LORD, who makes them holy.[c] '

24So Moses told this to Aaron and his sons and to all the Israelites.

22 The LORD said to Moses, 2"Tell Aaron and his sons to treat with respect the sacred offerings the Israelites consecrate to me, so they will not profane my holy name. I am the LORD.

3"Say to them: 'For the generations to come, if any of your descendants is ceremonially unclean and yet comes near the sacred offerings that the Israelites consecrate to the LORD, that person must be cut off from my presence. I am the LORD.

a 10 Or not uncover his head　b 15 Or who sanctifies him; or who sets him apart as holy　c 23 Or who sanctifies them; or who sets them apart as holy

4" 'If a descendant of Aaron has an infectious skin disease*a* or a bodily discharge, he may not eat the sacred offerings until he is cleansed. He will also be unclean if he touches something defiled by a corpse or by anyone who has an emission of semen, 5or if he touches any crawling thing that makes him unclean, or any person who makes him unclean, whatever the uncleanness may be. 6The one who touches any such thing will be unclean till evening. He must not eat any of the sacred offerings unless he has bathed himself with water. 7When the sun goes down, he will be clean, and after that he may eat the sacred offerings, for they are his food. 8He must not eat anything found dead or torn by wild animals, and so become unclean through it. I am the LORD.

9" 'The priests are to keep my requirements so that they do not become guilty and die for treating them with contempt. I am the LORD, who makes them holy.*b*

10" 'No one outside a priest's family may eat the sacred offering, nor may the guest of a priest or his hired worker eat it. 11But if a priest buys a slave with money, or if a slave is born in his household, that slave may eat his food. 12If a priest's daughter marries anyone other than a priest, she may not eat any of the sacred contributions. 13But if a priest's daughter becomes a widow or is divorced, yet has no children, and she returns to live in her father's house as in her youth, she may eat of her father's food. No unauthorized person, however, may eat any of it.

14" 'If anyone eats a sacred offering by mistake, he must make restitution to the priest for the offering and add a fifth of the value to it. 15The priests must not desecrate the sacred offerings the Israelites present to the LORD 16by allowing them to eat the sacred offerings and so bring upon them guilt requiring payment. I am the LORD, who makes them holy.' "

Unacceptable Sacrifices

17The LORD said to Moses, 18"Speak to Aaron and his sons and to all the Israelites and say to them: 'If any of you—either an Israelite or an alien living in Israel—presents a gift for a burnt offering to the LORD, either to fulfill a vow or as a freewill offering, 19you must present a male without defect from the cattle, sheep or goats in

---

a 4 Traditionally *leprosy*; the Hebrew word was used for various diseases affecting the skin—not necessarily leprosy.
b 9 Or *who sanctifies them*; or *who sets them apart as holy*; also in verse 16

---

4 " '亞倫的後裔，凡長大痲瘋的，或是有漏症的，不可吃聖物，直等他潔淨了。無論誰摸那死屍不潔淨的物（註："物"或作"人"），或是遺精的人，5或是摸甚麼使他不潔淨的爬物，或是摸那使他不潔淨的人（不拘那人有甚麼不潔淨），6摸了這些人、物的，必不潔淨到晚上。若不用水洗身，就不可吃聖物。7日落的時候，他就潔淨了，然後可以吃聖物，因為這是他的食物。8自死的，或是被野獸撕裂的，他不可吃，因此污穢自己。我是耶和華。

9 " '所以他們要守我所吩咐的，免得輕忽了，因此擔罪而死。我是叫他們成聖的耶和華。

10 " '凡外人不可吃聖物，寄居在祭司家的，或是雇工人，都不可吃聖物。11倘若祭司買人，是他的錢買的，那人就可以吃聖物；生在他家的人也可以吃。12祭司的女兒若嫁外人，就不可吃舉祭的聖物。13但祭司的女兒若是寡婦，或是被休的，沒有孩子，又歸回父家，與她青年一樣，就可以吃她父親的食物；只是外人不可吃。

14 " '若有人誤吃了聖物，要照聖物的原數加上五分之一，交給祭司。15祭司不可褻瀆以色列人所獻給耶和華的聖物，16免得他們在吃聖物上自取罪孽，因為我是叫他們成聖的耶和華。' "

不蒙悅納的祭物

17耶和華對摩西說：18"你曉諭亞倫和他子孫，並以色列眾人說：'以色列家的人，或在以色列中寄居的，凡獻供物，無論是所許的願，是甘心獻的，就是獻給耶和華作燔祭的，19要將沒有殘疾的公牛，或是綿羊，或是山羊獻上，如此方蒙悅納。
20凡有殘疾的，你們不可獻上，因為
這不蒙悅納。21凡從牛羣或是羊羣
中，將平安祭獻給耶和華，為要還特
許的願，或是作甘心獻的，所獻的必
純全無殘疾的，才蒙悅納。22瞎眼
的、折傷的、殘廢的、有瘤子的、長
癬的、長疥的都不可獻給耶和華，也
不可有壇上作為火祭獻給耶和華。
23無論是公牛、是綿羊羔，若肢體有
餘的，或是缺少的，只可作甘心祭獻
上；用以還願，卻不蒙悅納。24腎子
損傷的，或是壓碎的，或是破裂的，
或是騸了的，不可獻給耶和華，在你
們的地上也不可這樣行。25這類的
物，你們從外人的手，一樣也不可接
受作你們神的食物獻上，因為這些都
有損壞，有殘疾，不蒙悅納。'"

26耶和華曉諭摩西說：27"才生
的公牛，或是綿羊，或是山羊，七天
當跟着母；從第八天以後，可以當供
物蒙悅納，作為耶和華的火祭。28無
論是母牛、是母羊，不可同日宰母和
子。

29"你們獻感謝祭給耶和華，要
獻得可蒙悅納。30要當天吃，一點不
可留到早晨。我是耶和華。

31"你們要謹守遵行我的誡命。
我是耶和華。32你們不可褻瀆我的聖
名，我在以色列人中，卻要被尊為
聖。我是叫你們成聖的耶和華。33把
你們從埃及地領出來，作你們的神。
我是耶和華。"

23 耶和華對摩西說：2"你曉諭
以色列人說：'耶和華的節
期，你們要宣告為聖會的節
期。

安息日

3"'六日要做工，第七日是聖
安息日；當有聖會，你們甚麼工都不
可做。這是在你們一切的住處向耶和
華守的安息日。

order that it may be accepted on your behalf.
20Do not bring anything with a defect, because it
will not be accepted on your behalf. 21When
anyone brings from the herd or flock a fellowship offering*a* to the LORD to fulfill a special vow
or as a freewill offering, it must be without
defect or blemish to be acceptable. 22Do not offer
to the LORD the blind, the injured or the
maimed, or anything with warts or festering or
running sores. Do not place any of these on the
altar as an offering made to the LORD by fire.
23You may, however, present as a freewill offering an ox*b* or a sheep that is deformed or stunt-
ed, but it will not be accepted in fulfillment of a
vow. 24You must not offer to the LORD an animal
whose testicles are bruised, crushed, torn or cut.
You must not do this in your own land, 25and
you must not accept such animals from the
hand of a foreigner and offer them as the food of
your God. They will not be accepted on your
behalf, because they are deformed and have
defects.' "

26The LORD said to Moses, 27"When a calf, a
lamb or a goat is born, it is to remain with its
mother for seven days. From the eighth day on,
it will be acceptable as an offering made to the
LORD by fire. 28Do not slaughter a cow or a
sheep and its young on the same day.

29"When you sacrifice a thank offering to the
LORD, sacrifice it in such a way that it will be
accepted on your behalf. 30It must be eaten that
same day; leave none of it till morning. I am the
LORD.

31"Keep my commands and follow them. I
am the LORD. 32Do not profane my holy name. I
must be acknowledged as holy by the Israelites.
I am the LORD, who makes*c* you holy*d* 33and
who brought you out of Egypt to be your God. I
am the LORD."

23 The LORD said to Moses, 2"Speak to the
Israelites and say to them: 'These are
my appointed feasts, the appointed
feasts of the LORD, which you are to proclaim as
sacred assemblies.

The Sabbath

3"'There are six days when you may work,
but the seventh day is a Sabbath of rest, a day of
sacred assembly. You are not to do any work;
wherever you live, it is a Sabbath to the LORD.

---

a 21 Traditionally peace offering　*b 23 The Hebrew word can
include both male and female.*　*c 32 Or made*
d 32 Or who sanctifies you; or who sets you apart as holy

The Passover and Unleavened Bread

4" 'These are the LORD's appointed feasts, the sacred assemblies you are to proclaim at their appointed times: 5The LORD's Passover begins at twilight on the fourteenth day of the first month. 6On the fifteenth day of that month the LORD's Feast of Unleavened Bread begins; for seven days you must eat bread made without yeast. 7On the first day hold a sacred assembly and do no regular work. 8For seven days present an offering made to the LORD by fire. And on the seventh day hold a sacred assembly and do no regular work.' "

Firstfruits

9The LORD said to Moses, 10"Speak to the Israelites and say to them: 'When you enter the land I am going to give you and you reap its harvest, bring to the priest a sheaf of the first grain you harvest. 11He is to wave the sheaf before the LORD so it will be accepted on your behalf; the priest is to wave it on the day after the Sabbath. 12On the day you wave the sheaf, you must sacrifice as a burnt offering to the LORD a lamb a year old without defect, 13together with its grain offering of two-tenths of an ephah^a of fine flour mixed with oil—an offering made to the LORD by fire, a pleasing aroma— and its drink offering of a quarter of a hin^b of wine. 14You must not eat any bread, or roasted or new grain, until the very day you bring this offering to your God. This is to be a lasting ordinance for the generations to come, wherever you live.

Feast of Weeks

15" 'From the day after the Sabbath, the day you brought the sheaf of the wave offering, count off seven full weeks. 16Count off fifty days up to the day after the seventh Sabbath, and then present an offering of new grain to the LORD. 17From wherever you live, bring two loaves made of two-tenths of an ephah of fine flour, baked with yeast, as a wave offering of firstfruits to the LORD. 18Present with this bread seven male lambs, each a year old and without defect, one young bull and two rams. They will be a burnt offering to the LORD, together with their grain offerings and drink offerings—an offering made by fire, an aroma pleasing to the LORD. 19Then sacrifice one male goat for a sin offering and two lambs, each a year old, for a

逾越節與無酵餅

4 "'耶和華的節期，就是你們到了日期要宣告為聖會的，乃是這些：5正月十四日黃昏的時候，是耶和華的逾越節。6這月十五日是向耶和華守的無酵節，你們要吃無酵餅七日。7第一日當有聖會，甚麼勞碌的工都不可做。8要將火祭獻給耶和華七日。第七日是聖會，甚麼勞碌的工都不可做。'"

初熟的莊稼

9耶和華對摩西說：10 "你曉諭以色列人說：'你們到了我賜給你們的地，收割莊稼的時候，要將初熟的莊稼一捆帶給祭司。11他要把這一捆在耶和華面前搖一搖，使你們得蒙悅納。祭司要在安息日的次日，把這捆搖一搖。12搖這捆的日子，你們要把一歲、沒有殘疾的公綿羊羔獻給耶和華為燔祭。13同獻的素祭，就是調油的細麵伊法十分之二，作為馨香的火祭獻給耶和華；同獻的奠祭，要酒一欣四分之一。14無論是餅，是烘的子粒，是新穗子，你們都不可吃，直等到把你們獻給神的供物帶來的那一天才可以吃。這在你們一切的住處，作為世世代代永遠的定例。

五旬節

15 "'你們要從安息日的次日，獻禾捆為搖祭的那日算起，要滿了七個安息日。16到第七個安息日的次日，共計五十天，又要將新素祭獻給耶和華。17要從你們的住處取出細麵伊法十分之二，加酵，烤成兩個搖祭的餅，當作初熟之物獻給耶和華。18又要將一歲、沒有殘疾的羊羔七隻，公牛犢一隻，公綿羊兩隻和餅一同奉上。這些與同獻的素祭和奠祭，要作為燔祭獻給耶和華，就是作馨香的火祭獻給耶和華。19你們要獻一隻公山羊為贖罪祭，兩隻一歲的公綿羊

---

a 13 That is, probably about 4 quarts (about 4.5 liters); also in verse 17 b 13 That is, probably about 1 quart (about 1 liter)

羔為平安祭。20祭司要把這些和初熟麥子做的餅，一同作搖祭，在耶和華面前搖一搖；這是獻與耶和華為聖物歸給祭司的。21當這日，你們要宣告聖會；甚麼勞碌的工都不可做。這在你們一切的住處，作為世世代代永遠的定例。

22 " '在你們的地收割莊稼，不可割盡田角，也不可拾取所遺落的，要留給窮人和寄居的。我是耶和華你們的神。' "

吹角節

23耶和華對摩西說：24 "你曉諭以色列人說：'七月初一，你們要守為聖安息日，要吹角作紀念，當有聖會，25甚麼勞碌的工都不可做。要將火祭獻給耶和華。' "

贖罪日

26耶和華曉諭摩西說：27 "七月初十是贖罪日，你們要守為聖會，並要刻苦己心，也要將火祭獻給耶和華。28當這日，甚麼工都不可做，因為是贖罪日，要在耶和華你們的神面前贖罪。29當這日，凡不刻苦己心的，必從民中剪除。30凡這日做甚麼工的，我必將他從民中除滅。31你們甚麼工都不可做。這在你們一切的住處，作為世世代代永遠的定例。32你們要守這日為聖安息日，並要刻苦己心，從這月初九日晚上到次日晚上，要守為安息日。"

住棚節

33耶和華對摩西說：34 "你曉諭以色列人說：'這七月十五日是住棚節，要在耶和華面前守這節七日。35第一日當有聖會，甚麼勞碌的工都不可做。36七日內要將火祭獻給耶和華。第八日當守聖會，要將火祭獻給耶和華。這是嚴肅會，甚麼勞碌的工都不可做。

fellowship offering.[a] 20The priest is to wave the two lambs before the LORD as a wave offering, together with the bread of the firstfruits. They are a sacred offering to the LORD for the priest. 21On that same day you are to proclaim a sacred assembly and do no regular work. This is to be a lasting ordinance for the generations to come, wherever you live.

22" 'When you reap the harvest of your land, do not reap to the very edges of your field or gather the gleanings of your harvest. Leave them for the poor and the alien. I am the LORD your God.' "

Feast of Trumpets

23The LORD said to Moses, 24"Say to the Israelites: 'On the first day of the seventh month you are to have a day of rest, a sacred assembly commemorated with trumpet blasts. 25Do no regular work, but present an offering made to the LORD by fire.' "

Day of Atonement

26The LORD said to Moses, 27"The tenth day of this seventh month is the Day of Atonement. Hold a sacred assembly and deny yourselves,[b] and present an offering made to the LORD by fire. 28Do no work on that day, because it is the Day of Atonement, when atonement is made for you before the LORD your God. 29Anyone who does not deny himself on that day must be cut off from his people. 30I will destroy from among his people anyone who does any work on that day. 31You shall do no work at all. This is to be a lasting ordinance for the generations to come, wherever you live. 32It is a sabbath of rest for you, and you must deny yourselves. From the evening of the ninth day of the month until the following evening you are to observe your sabbath."

Feast of Tabernacles

33The LORD said to Moses, 34"Say to the Israelites: 'On the fifteenth day of the seventh month the LORD's Feast of Tabernacles begins, and it lasts for seven days. 35The first day is a sacred assembly; do no regular work. 36For seven days present offerings made to the LORD by fire, and on the eighth day hold a sacred assembly and present an offering made to the LORD by fire. It is the closing assembly; do no regular work.

---

a 19 Traditionally *peace offering*   *b 27* Or *and fast*; also in verses 29 and 32

37(" 'These are the LORD's appointed feasts, which you are to proclaim as sacred assemblies for bringing offerings made to the LORD by fire—the burnt offerings and grain offerings, sacrifices and drink offerings required for each day. 38These offerings are in addition to those for the LORD's Sabbaths and*a* in addition to your gifts and whatever you have vowed and all the freewill offerings you give to the LORD.)

39" 'So beginning with the fifteenth day of the seventh month, after you have gathered the crops of the land, celebrate the festival to the LORD for seven days; the first day is a day of rest, and the eighth day also is a day of rest. 40On the first day you are to take choice fruit from the trees, and palm fronds, leafy branches and poplars, and rejoice before the LORD your God for seven days. 41Celebrate this as a festival to the LORD for seven days each year. This is to be a lasting ordinance for the generations to come; celebrate it in the seventh month. 42Live in booths for seven days: All native-born Israelites are to live in booths 43so your descendants will know that I had the Israelites live in booths when I brought them out of Egypt. I am the LORD your God.' "

44So Moses announced to the Israelites the appointed feasts of the LORD.

Oil and Bread Set Before the LORD

24 The LORD said to Moses, 2"Command the Israelites to bring you clear oil of pressed olives for the light so that the lamps may be kept burning continually. 3Outside the curtain of the Testimony in the Tent of Meeting, Aaron is to tend the lamps before the LORD from evening till morning, continually. This is to be a lasting ordinance for the generations to come. 4The lamps on the pure gold lampstand before the LORD must be tended continually.

5"Take fine flour and bake twelve loaves of bread, using two-tenths of an ephah*b* for each loaf. 6Set them in two rows, six in each row, on the table of pure gold before the LORD. 7Along each row put some pure incense as a memorial portion to represent the bread and to be an offering made to the LORD by fire. 8This bread is to be set out before the LORD regularly, Sabbath after Sabbath, on behalf of the Israelites, as a lasting covenant. 9It belongs to Aaron and his sons, who are to eat it in a holy place, because it

a 38 Or These feasts are in addition to the LORD's Sabbaths, and these offerings are   b 5 That is, probably about 4 quarts (about 4.5 liters)

37 " '這是耶和華的節期，就是你們要宣告為聖會的節期。要將火祭、燔祭、素祭、祭物並奠祭，各日，獻給耶和華。38這是在耶和華的安息日以外，又在你們的供物和所許的願，並甘心獻給耶和華的以外。

39 " '你們收藏了地的出產，就從七月十五日起，要守耶和華的節七日。第一日為聖安息，第八日也為聖安息。40第一日，要拿美好樹上的果子和棕樹上的枝子，與茂密樹的枝條，並河旁的柳枝，在耶和華你們的神面前歡樂七日。41每年七月間，要向耶和華守這節七日，這為你們世世代代永遠的定例。42你們要住在棚裏，凡以色列家的人，都要住在棚裏，43好叫你們世世代代知道我領以色列人出埃及地的時候，曾使他們住在棚裏。我是耶和華你們的神。' "

44於是，摩西將耶和華的節期傳給以色列人。

油與陳設餅擺列在主面前

24 耶和華曉諭摩西說：2 "要吩咐以色列人，把那為點燈搗成的清橄欖油拿來給你，使燈常常點着。3在會幕中法櫃的幔子外，亞倫從晚上到早晨，必在耶和華面前經理這燈。這要作你們世世代代永遠的定例。4他要在耶和華面前常收拾精金燈臺上的燈。

5 "你要取細麵，烤成十二個餅，每餅用麵伊法十分之二。6要把餅擺列兩行（註："行"或作"摞"。下同），每行六個，在耶和華面前精金的桌子上。7又要把淨乳香放在每行餅上，作為紀念，就是作為火祭獻給耶和華。8每安息日要常擺在耶和華面前，這為以色列人作永遠的約。9這餅是要給亞倫和他子孫的，他們要在聖處吃，為永遠的定例，因為在獻給耶和華的火祭中是至聖的。"

用石頭打死褻瀆的人

10有一個以色列婦人的兒子,他父親是埃及人,一日間遊在以色列人中,這以色列婦人的兒子和一個以色列人在營裏爭鬥。11這以色列婦人的兒子褻瀆了聖名,並且咒詛,就有人把他送到摩西那裏。(他母親名叫示羅密,是但支派底伯利的女兒。)12他們把那人收在監裏,要得耶和華所指示的話。

13耶和華曉諭摩西說:14"把那咒詛聖名的人帶到營外,叫聽見的人都放手在他頭上,全會眾就要用石頭打死他。15你要曉諭以色列人說:'凡咒詛神的,必擔當他的罪。16那褻瀆耶和華名的,必被治死,全會眾總要用石頭打死他。不管是寄居的,是本地人,他褻瀆耶和華名的時候,必被治死。

17"'打死人的,必被治死;18打死牲畜的,必賠上牲畜,以命償命。19人若使他鄰舍的身體有殘疾,他怎樣行,也要照樣向他行:20以傷還傷,以眼還眼,以牙還牙。他怎樣叫人的身體有殘疾,也要照樣向他行。21打死牲畜的,必賠上牲畜;打死人的,必被治死。22不管是寄居的,是本地人,同歸一例。我是耶和華你們的神。'"

23於是,摩西曉諭以色列人,他們就把那咒詛聖名的人帶到營外,用石頭打死。以色列人就照耶和華所吩咐摩西的行了。

安息年

25 耶和華在西奈山對摩西說:2"你曉諭以色列人說:'你們到了我所賜你們那地的時候,地就要向耶和華守安息。3六年要耕種田地,也要修理葡萄園,收藏地的出產。4第七年,地要守聖安息,就是向耶和華守的安息,不可耕種田地,也不可修理葡萄園。5遺落自長的莊稼,不可收割;沒有修理的葡萄樹也不可摘取葡萄。這年,地要守聖安息。6地在安息年所出的,要給你和你的僕人、婢女、雇工人,並

is a most holy part of their regular share of the offerings made to the LORD by fire."

A Blasphemer Stoned

10Now the son of an Israelite mother and an Egyptian father went out among the Israelites, and a fight broke out in the camp between him and an Israelite. 11The son of the Israelite woman blasphemed the Name with a curse; so they brought him to Moses. (His mother's name was Shelomith, the daughter of Dibri the Danite.) 12They put him in custody until the will of the LORD should be made clear to them.

13Then the LORD said to Moses: 14"Take the blasphemer outside the camp. All those who heard him are to lay their hands on his head, and the entire assembly is to stone him. 15Say to the Israelites: 'If anyone curses his God, he will be held responsible; 16anyone who blasphemes the name of the LORD must be put to death. The entire assembly must stone him. Whether an alien or native-born, when he blasphemes the Name, he must be put to death.

17"'If anyone takes the life of a human being, he must be put to death. 18Anyone who takes the life of someone's animal must make restitution—life for life. 19If anyone injures his neighbor, whatever he has done must be done to him: 20fracture for fracture, eye for eye, tooth for tooth. As he has injured the other, so he is to be injured. 21Whoever kills an animal must make restitution, but whoever kills a man must be put to death. 22You are to have the same law for the alien and the native-born. I am the LORD your God.'"

23Then Moses spoke to the Israelites, and they took the blasphemer outside the camp and stoned him. The Israelites did as the LORD commanded Moses.

The Sabbath Year

25 The LORD said to Moses on Mount Sinai, 2"Speak to the Israelites and say to them: 'When you enter the land I am going to give you, the land itself must observe a sabbath to the LORD. 3For six years sow your fields, and for six years prune your vineyards and gather their crops. 4But in the seventh year the land is to have a sabbath of rest, a sabbath to the LORD. Do not sow your fields or prune your vineyards. 5Do not reap what grows of itself or harvest the grapes of your untended vines. The land is to have a year of rest. 6Whatever the land yields during the sabbath year will be food for you—for yourself, your manservant and maidservant, and the hired worker and temporary resident who live among you, [7]as well as for your livestock and the wild animals in your land. Whatever the land produces may be eaten.

The Year of Jubilee

[8] 'Count off seven sabbaths of years—seven times seven years—so that the seven sabbaths of years amount to a period of forty-nine years. [9]Then have the trumpet sounded everywhere on the tenth day of the seventh month; on the Day of Atonement sound the trumpet throughout your land. [10]Consecrate the fiftieth year and proclaim liberty throughout the land to all its inhabitants. It shall be a jubilee for you; each one of you is to return to his family property and each to his own clan. [11]The fiftieth year shall be a jubilee for you; do not sow and do not reap what grows of itself or harvest the untended vines. [12]For it is a jubilee and is to be holy for you; eat only what is taken directly from the fields.

[13]' In this Year of Jubilee everyone is to return to his own property.

[14]' If you sell land to one of your countrymen or buy any from him, do not take advantage of each other. [15]You are to buy from your countryman on the basis of the number of years since the Jubilee. And he is to sell to you on the basis of the number of years left for harvesting crops. [16]When the years are many, you are to increase the price, and when the years are few, you are to decrease the price, because what he is really selling you is the number of crops. [17]Do not take advantage of each other, but fear your God. I am the LORD your God.

[18]' Follow my decrees and be careful to obey my laws, and you will live safely in the land. [19]Then the land will yield its fruit, and you will eat your fill and live there in safety. [20]You may ask, "What will we eat in the seventh year if we do not plant or harvest our crops?" [21]I will send you such a blessing in the sixth year that the land will yield enough for three years. [22]While you plant during the eighth year, you will eat from the old crop and will continue to eat from it until the harvest of the ninth year comes in.

[23]' The land must not be sold permanently, because the land is mine and you are but aliens and my tenants. [24]Throughout the country that you hold as a possession, you must provide for the redemption of the land.

[25]' If one of your countrymen becomes poor and sells some of his property, his nearest relative is to come and redeem what his countryman has sold. [26]If, however, a man has no one to redeem it for him but he himself prospers and

寄居的外人當食物。[7]這年的土產，也要給你的牲畜和你地上的走獸當食物。

禧年

[8] "'你要算計七個安息年，就是七七年。這便為你成了七個安息年，共是四十九年。[9]當年七月初十日，你要大發角聲，這日就是贖罪日，要在遍地發出角聲。[10]第五十年你們要當作聖年，在遍地給一切的居民宣告自由。這年必為你們的禧年，各人要歸自己的產業，各歸本家。[11]第五十年要作為你們的禧年。這年不可耕種，地中自長的，不可收割；沒有修理的葡萄樹，也不可摘取葡萄。[12]因為這是禧年，你們要當作聖年，吃地中自出的土產。

[13] "'這禧年，你們各人要歸自己的地業。

[14] "'你若賣甚麼給鄰舍，或是從鄰舍的手中買甚麼，彼此不可虧負。[15]你要按禧年以後的年數向鄰舍買；他也要按年數的收成賣給你。[16]年歲若多，要照數加添價值；年歲若少，要照數減去價值，因為他照收成的數目賣給你。[17]你們彼此不可虧負，只要敬畏你們的神，因為我是耶和華你們的神。

[18] "'我的律例，你們要遵行，我的典章，你們要謹守，就可以在那地上安然居住。[19]地必出土產，你們就要吃飽，在那地上安然居住。[20]你們若說："這第七年我們不耕種，也不收藏土產，吃甚麼呢？"[21]我必在第六年將我所命的福賜給你們，地便生三年的土產。[22]第八年，你們要耕種，也要吃陳糧；等到第九年出產收來的時候，你們還吃陳糧。

[23] "'地不可永賣，因為地是我的；你們在我面前是客旅、是寄居的。[24]在你們所得為業的全地，也要准人將地贖回。

[25] "'你的弟兄（註："弟兄"指本國人說。下同），若漸漸窮乏，賣了幾分地業，他至近的親屬就要來把弟兄所賣的贖回。[26]若沒有能給他贖回的，

他自己漸漸富足，能夠贖回，27就要算出賣地的年數，把餘剩年數的價值還那買主，自己便歸回自己的地業。28倘若不能為自己得回所賣的，仍要存在買主的手裏，直到禧年。到了禧年，地業要出買主的手，自己便歸回自己的地業。

29 "'人若賣城內的住宅，賣了以後，一年之內可以贖回。在一整年，必有贖回的權柄。30若在一整年之內不贖回，這城內的房屋，就定準永歸買主，世世代代為業。在禧年也不得出買主的手。31但房屋在無城牆的村莊裏，要看如鄉下的田地一樣，可以贖回。到了禧年，都要出買主的手。

32 "'然而利未人所得為業的城邑，其中的房屋，利未人可以隨時贖回。33若是一個利未人不將所賣的房屋贖回，是在所得為業的城內，到了禧年，就要出買主的手，因為利未人城邑的房屋，是他們在以色列人中的產業。34只是他們各城郊野之地不可賣，因為是他們永遠的產業。

35 "'你的弟兄在你那裏若漸漸貧窮，手中缺乏，你就要幫補他，使他與你同住，像外人和寄居的一樣。36不可向他取利，也不可向他多要，只要敬畏你的神，使你的弟兄與你同住。37你借錢給他，不可向他取利；借糧給他，也不可向他多要。38我是耶和華你們的神，曾領你們從埃及地出來，為要把迦南地賜給你們，要作你們的神。

39 "'你的弟兄若在你那裏漸漸窮乏，將自己賣給你，你不可叫他像奴僕服侍你。40他要在你那裏像雇工人和寄居的一樣，要服侍你直到禧年。41到了禧年，他和他兒女要離開你，一同出去歸回本家，到他祖宗的地業那裏去。42因為他們是我的僕人，是我從埃及地領出來的，不可賣為奴僕。43不可嚴嚴地轄管他，只要敬畏你的神。

44 "'至於你的奴僕、婢女，可

acquires sufficient means to redeem it, [27]he is to determine the value for the years since he sold it and refund the balance to the man to whom he sold it; he can then go back to his own property. [28]But if he does not acquire the means to repay him, what he sold will remain in the possession of the buyer until the Year of Jubilee. It will be returned in the Jubilee, and he can then go back to his property.

[29]" 'If a man sells a house in a walled city, he retains the right of redemption a full year after its sale. During that time he may redeem it. [30]If it is not redeemed before a full year has passed, the house in the walled city shall belong permanently to the buyer and his descendants. It is not to be returned in the Jubilee. [31]But houses in villages without walls around them are to be considered as open country. They can be redeemed, and they are to be returned in the Jubilee.

[32]" 'The Levites always have the right to redeem their houses in the Levitical towns, which they possess. [33]So the property of the Levites is redeemable—that is, a house sold in any town they hold—and is to be returned in the Jubilee, because the houses in the towns of the Levites are their property among the Israelites. [34]But the pastureland belonging to their towns must not be sold; it is their permanent possession.

[35]" 'If one of your countrymen becomes poor and is unable to support himself among you, help him as you would an alien or a temporary resident, so he can continue to live among you. [36]Do not take interest of any kind[a] from him, but fear your God, so that your countryman may continue to live among you. [37]You must not lend him money at interest or sell him food at a profit. [38]I am the LORD your God, who brought you out of Egypt to give you the land of Canaan and to be your God.

[39]" 'If one of your countrymen becomes poor among you and sells himself to you, do not make him work as a slave. [40]He is to be treated as a hired worker or a temporary resident among you; he is to work for you until the Year of Jubilee. [41]Then he and his children are to be released, and he will go back to his own clan and to the property of his forefathers. [42]Because the Israelites are my servants, whom I brought out of Egypt, they must not be sold as slaves. [43]Do not rule over them ruthlessly, but fear your God.

[44]" 'Your male and female slaves are to come from the nations around you; from them you

a 36 Or take excessive interest; similarly in verse 37

may buy slaves. ⁴⁵You may also buy some of the temporary residents living among you and members of their clans born in your country, and they will become your property. ⁴⁶You can will them to your children as inherited property and can make them slaves for life, but you must not rule over your fellow Israelites ruthlessly.

⁴⁷'If an alien or a temporary resident among you becomes rich and one of your countrymen becomes poor and sells himself to the alien living among you or to a member of the alien's clan, ⁴⁸he retains the right of redemption after he has sold himself. One of his relatives may redeem him: ⁴⁹An uncle or a cousin or any blood relative in his clan may redeem him. Or if he prospers, he may redeem himself. ⁵⁰He and his buyer are to count the time from the year he sold himself up to the Year of Jubilee. The price for his release is to be based on the rate paid to a hired man for that number of years. ⁵¹If many years remain, he must pay for his redemption a larger share of the price paid for him. ⁵²If only a few years remain until the Year of Jubilee, he is to compute that and pay for his redemption accordingly. ⁵³He is to be treated as a man hired from year to year; you must see to it that his owner does not rule over him ruthlessly.

⁵⁴'Even if he is not redeemed in any of these ways, he and his children are to be released in the Year of Jubilee, ⁵⁵for the Israelites belong to me as servants. They are my servants, whom I brought out of Egypt. I am the LORD your God.

Reward for Obedience

26 " 'Do not make idols or set up an image or a sacred stone for yourselves, and do not place a carved stone in your land to bow down before it. I am the LORD your God.

²" 'Observe my Sabbaths and have reverence for my sanctuary. I am the LORD.

³" 'If you follow my decrees and are careful to obey my commands, ⁴I will send you rain in its season, and the ground will yield its crops and the trees of the field their fruit. ⁵Your threshing will continue until grape harvest and the grape harvest will continue until planting, and you will eat all the food you want and live in safety in your land.

⁶" 'I will grant peace in the land, and you will lie down and no one will make you afraid. I will remove savage beasts from the land, and the sword will not pass through your country. ⁷You will pursue your enemies, and they will fall by the sword before you. ⁸Five of you will chase a hundred, and a hundred of you will chase ten

以從你四圍的國中買。⁴⁵並且那寄居在你們中間的外人和他們的家屬，在你們地上所生的，你們也可以從其中買人，他們要作你們的產業。⁴⁶你們要將他們遺留給你們的子孫為產業，要永遠從他們中間揀出奴僕，只是你們的弟兄以色列人，你們不可嚴嚴地轄管。

⁴⁷" '住在你那裏的外人，或是寄居的，若漸漸富足，你的弟兄卻漸漸窮乏，將自己賣給那外人、或是寄居的、或是外人的宗族，⁴⁸賣了以後，可以將他贖回。無論是他的弟兄、⁴⁹或伯叔、伯叔的兒子、本家的近支，都可以贖他。他自己若漸漸富足，也可以自贖。⁵⁰他要和買主計算，從賣自己的那年起，算到禧年，所賣的價值照着年數多少，好像工人每年的工價。⁵¹若缺少的年數多，就要按着年數，從買價中償還他的贖價。⁵²若到禧年只缺少幾年，就要按着年數和買主計算，償還他的贖價。⁵³他和買主同住，要像每年雇的工人，買主不可嚴嚴地轄管他。

⁵⁴" '他若不這樣被贖，到了禧年，要和他的兒女一同出去。⁵⁵因為以色列人都是我的僕人，是我從埃及地領出來的。我是耶和華你們的神。

順從的人蒙福

26 " '你們不可做甚麼虛無的神像，不可立雕刻的偶像或是柱像；也不可在你們的地上安甚麼鏨成的石像，向它跪拜，因為我是耶和華你們的神。

² " '你們要守我的安息日，敬我的聖所。我是耶和華。

³ " '你們若遵行我的律例，謹守我的誡命，⁴我就給你們降下時雨，叫地生出土產，田野的樹木結果子。⁵你們打糧食要打到摘葡萄的時候，摘葡萄要摘到撒種的時候，並且要吃得飽足，在你們的地上安然居住。

⁶ " '我要賜平安在你們的地上，你們躺臥，無人驚嚇。我要叫惡獸從你們的地上息滅；刀劍也必不經過你們的地。⁷你們要追趕仇敵，他們必倒在你們刀下。⁸你們五個人要追趕一百人，一百人要追趕一萬人，

仇敵必倒在你們刀下。

9 "'我要眷顧你們,使你們生養眾多,也要與你們堅定所立的約。10你們要吃陳糧,又因新糧挪開陳糧。11我要在你們中間立我的帳幕,我的心也不厭惡你們。12我要在你們中間行走,我要作你們的神,你們要作我的子民。13我是耶和華你們的神,曾將你們從埃及地領出來,使你們不作埃及人的奴僕;我也折斷你們所負的軛,叫你們挺身而走。

悖逆的人受懲

14 "'你們若不聽從我,不遵行我的誡命,15厭棄我的律例,厭惡我的典章,不遵行我一切的誡命,背棄我的約,16我待你們就要這樣:我必命定驚惶,叫眼目乾癟、精神消耗的癆病、熱病轄制你們。你們也要白白地撒種,因為仇敵要吃你們所種的。17我要向你們變臉,你們就要敗在仇敵面前。恨惡你們的,必轄管你們。無人追趕,你們卻要逃跑。

18 "'你們因這些事若還不聽從我,我就要為你們的罪加七倍懲罰你們。19我必斷絕你們因勢力而有的驕傲,又要使覆你們的天如鐵,載你們的地如銅。20你們要白白地勞力,因為你們的地不出土產,其上的樹木也不結果子。

21 "'你們行事若與我反對,不肯聽從我,我就要按你們的罪加七倍降災與你們。22我也要打發野地的走獸到你們中間,搶吃你們的兒女,吞滅你們的牲畜,使你們的人數減少,道路荒涼。

23 "'你們因這些事若仍不改正歸我,行事與我反對,24我就要行事與你們反對,因你們的罪擊打你們七次。25我又要使刀劍臨到你們,報復你們背約的仇。聚集你們在各城內,降瘟疫在你們中間,也必將你們交在仇敵的手中。26我要折斷你們的杖,就是斷絕你們的糧。那時,必有十個女人在一個爐子給你們烤餅,按分量

thousand, and your enemies will fall by the sword before you.

9" 'I will look on you with favor and make you fruitful and increase your numbers, and I will keep my covenant with you. 10You will still be eating last year's harvest when you will have to move it out to make room for the new. 11I will put my dwelling place[a] among you, and I will not abhor you. 12I will walk among you and be your God, and you will be my people. 13I am the LORD your God, who brought you out of Egypt so that you would no longer be slaves to the Egyptians; I broke the bars of your yoke and enabled you to walk with heads held high.

Punishment for Disobedience

14" 'But if you will not listen to me and carry out all these commands, 15and if you reject my decrees and abhor my laws and fail to carry out all my commands and so violate my covenant, 16then I will do this to you: I will bring upon you sudden terror, wasting diseases and fever that will destroy your sight and drain away your life. You will plant seed in vain, because your enemies will eat it. 17I will set my face against you so that you will be defeated by your enemies; those who hate you will rule over you, and you will flee even when no one is pursuing you.

18" 'If after all this you will not listen to me, I will punish you for your sins seven times over. 19I will break down your stubborn pride and make the sky above you like iron and the ground beneath you like bronze. 20Your strength will be spent in vain, because your soil will not yield its crops, nor will the trees of the land yield their fruit.

21" 'If you remain hostile toward me and refuse to listen to me, I will multiply your afflictions seven times over, as your sins deserve. 22I will send wild animals against you, and they will rob you of your children, destroy your cattle and make you so few in number that your roads will be deserted.

23" 'If in spite of these things you do not accept my correction but continue to be hostile toward me, 24I myself will be hostile toward you and will afflict you for your sins seven times over. 25And I will bring the sword upon you to avenge the breaking of the covenant. When you withdraw into your cities, I will send a plague among you, and you will be given into enemy hands. 26When I cut off your supply of bread, ten women will be able to bake your bread in

a 11 Or my tabernacle

one oven, and they will dole out the bread by weight. You will eat, but you will not be satisfied.

27" 'If in spite of this you still do not listen to me but continue to be hostile toward me, 28then in my anger I will be hostile toward you, and I myself will punish you for your sins seven times over. 29You will eat the flesh of your sons and the flesh of your daughters. 30I will destroy your high places, cut down your incense altars and pile your dead bodies on the lifeless forms of your idols, and I will abhor you. 31I will turn your cities into ruins and lay waste your sanctuaries, and I will take no delight in the pleasing aroma of your offerings. 32I will lay waste the land, so that your enemies who live there will be appalled. 33I will scatter you among the nations and will draw out my sword and pursue you. Your land will be laid waste, and your cities will lie in ruins. 34Then the land will enjoy its sabbath years all the time that it lies desolate and you are in the country of your enemies; then the land will rest and enjoy its sabbaths. 35All the time that it lies desolate, the land will have the rest it did not have during the sabbaths you lived in it.

36" 'As for those of you who are left, I will make their hearts so fearful in the lands of their enemies that the sound of a windblown leaf will put them to flight. They will run as though fleeing from the sword, and they will fall, even though no one is pursuing them. 37They will stumble over one another as though fleeing from the sword, even though no one is pursuing them. So you will not be able to stand before your enemies. 38You will perish among the nations; the land of your enemies will devour you. 39Those of you who are left will waste away in the lands of their enemies because of their sins; also because of their fathers' sins they will waste away.

40" 'But if they will confess their sins and the sins of their fathers—their treachery against me and their hostility toward me, 41which made me hostile toward them so that I sent them into the land of their enemies—then when their uncircumcised hearts are humbled and they pay for their sin, 42I will remember my covenant with Jacob and my covenant with Isaac and my covenant with Abraham, and I will remember the land. 43For the land will be deserted by them and will enjoy its sabbaths while it lies desolate without them. They will pay for their sins because they rejected my laws and abhorred my decrees. 44Yet in spite of this, when they are in the land of their enemies, I will not reject them

秤給你們；你們要吃，也吃不飽。

27 " '你們因這一切的事若不聽從我，卻行事與我反對，28我就要發烈怒，行事與你們反對。又因你們的罪懲罰你們七次。29並且你們要吃兒子的肉，也要吃女兒的肉。30我又要毀壞你們的邱壇，砍下你們的日像，把你們的屍首扔在你們偶像的身上。我的心也必厭惡你們。31我要使你們的城邑變為荒涼，使你們的眾聖所成為荒場。我也不聞你們馨香的香氣。32我要使地成為荒場，住在其上的仇敵就因此詫異。33我要把你們散在列邦中，我也要拔刀追趕你們。你們的地要成為荒場，你們的城邑要變為荒涼。34你們在仇敵之地居住的時候，你們的地荒涼，要享受眾安息；正在那時候，地要歇息，享受安息。35地多時為荒場，就要多時歇息。地這樣歇息，是你們住在其上的安息年所不能得的。

36 " '至於你們剩下的人，我要使他們在仇敵之地心驚膽怯。葉子被風吹的響聲，要追趕他們；他們要逃避，像人逃避刀劍。無人追趕，卻要跌倒；37無人追趕，他們要彼此撞跌，像在刀劍之前。你們在仇敵面前，也必站立不住。38你們要在列邦中滅亡，仇敵之地要吞吃你們。39你們剩下的人，必因自己的罪孽和祖宗的罪孽，在仇敵之地消滅。

40 " '他們要承認自己的罪和他們祖宗的罪，就是干犯我的那罪；並且承認自己行事與我反對，41我所以行事與他們反對，把他們帶到仇敵之地。那時，他們未受割禮的心若謙卑了，他們也服了罪孽的刑罰，42我就要記念我與雅各所立的約，與以撒所立的約，與亞伯拉罕所立的約，並要記念這地。43他們離開這地，地在荒廢無人的時候，就要享受安息。並且他們要服罪孽的刑罰，因為他們厭棄了我的典章，心中厭惡了我的律例。44雖是這樣，他們在仇敵之地，我卻不厭棄他們，也不厭惡他們，將他們盡行滅絕，也不背棄我與他們所立的約，因為我是耶和華他們的神。45我卻要為他們的緣故記念我與他們先祖所立的約。他們的先祖是我在列邦人眼前、從埃及地領出來的，為要作他們的神。我是耶和華。'"

46這些律例、典章和法度，是耶和華與以色列人在西奈山藉着摩西立的。

贖回獻主之物

27 耶和華對摩西說：2 "你曉諭以色列人說：'人還特許的願，被許的人要按你所估的價值歸給耶和華。3你估定的從二十歲到六十歲的男人，要按聖所的平，估定價銀五十舍客勒；4若是女人，你要估定三十舍客勒；5若是從五歲到二十歲，男子你要估定二十舍客勒，女子估定十舍客勒；6若是從一月到五歲，男子你要估定五舍客勒，女子估定三舍客勒；7若是從六十歲以上，男人你要估定十五舍客勒，女人估定十舍客勒。8他若貧窮不能照你所估定的價，就要把他帶到祭司面前，祭司要按許願人的力量估定他的價。

9 "'所許的若是牲畜，就是人獻給耶和華為供物的，凡這一類獻給耶和華的，都要成為聖。10人不可改換，也不可更換；或是好的換壞的，或是壞的換好的。若以牲畜更換牲畜，所許的與所換的都要成為聖。11若牲畜不潔淨，是不可獻給耶和華為供物的，就要把牲畜安置在祭司面前。12祭司就要估定價值，牲畜是好是壞，祭司怎樣估定，就要以怎樣為是。13他若一定要贖回，就要在你所估定的價值以外加上五分之一。

or abhor them so as to destroy them completely, breaking my covenant with them. I am the LORD their God. 45But for their sake I will remember the covenant with their ancestors whom I brought out of Egypt in the sight of the nations to be their God. I am the LORD.' "

46These are the decrees, the laws and the regulations that the LORD established on Mount Sinai between himself and the Israelites through Moses.

Redeeming What Is the LORD's

27 The LORD said to Moses, 2"Speak to the Israelites and say to them: 'If anyone makes a special vow to dedicate persons to the LORD by giving equivalent values, 3set the value of a male between the ages of twenty and sixty at fifty shekels*a* of silver, according to the sanctuary shekel*b*; 4and if it is a female, set her value at thirty shekels.*c* 5If it is a person between the ages of five and twenty, set the value of a male at twenty shekels*d* and of a female at ten shekels.*e* 6If it is a person between one month and five years, set the value of a male at five shekels*f* of silver and that of a female at three shekels*g* of silver. 7If it is a person sixty years old or more, set the value of a male at fifteen shekels*h* and of a female at ten shekels. 8If anyone making the vow is too poor to pay the specified amount, he is to present the person to the priest, who will set the value for him according to what the man making the vow can afford.

9 'If what he vowed is an animal that is acceptable as an offering to the LORD, such an animal given to the LORD becomes holy. 10He must not exchange it or substitute a good one for a bad one, or a bad one for a good one; if he should substitute one animal for another, both it and the substitute become holy. 11If what he vowed is a ceremonially unclean animal—one that is not acceptable as an offering to the LORD—the animal must be presented to the priest, 12who will judge its quality as good or bad. Whatever value the priest then sets, that is what it will be. 13If the owner wishes to redeem the animal, he must add a fifth to its value.

---

a 3 That is, about 1 1/4 pounds (about 0.6 kilogram); also in verse 16   *b* 3 That is, about 2/5 ounce (about 11.5 grams); also in verse 25   *c* 4 That is, about 12 ounces (about 0.3 kilogram)   *d* 5 That is, about 8 ounces (about 0.2 kilogram)   *e* 5 That is, about 4 ounces (about 110 grams); also in verse 7   *f* 6 That is, about 2 ounces (about 55 grams);   *g* 6 That is, about 1 1/4 ounces (about 35 grams);   *h* 7 That is, about 6 ounces (about 170 grams)

14" 'If a man dedicates his house as something holy to the LORD, the priest will judge its quality as good or bad. Whatever value the priest then sets, so it will remain. 15If the man who dedicates his house redeems it, he must add a fifth to its value, and the house will again become his.

16" 'If a man dedicates to the LORD part of his family land, its value is to be set according to the amount of seed required for it—fifty shekels of silver to a homer*a* of barley seed. 17If he dedicates his field during the Year of Jubilee, the value that has been set remains. 18But if he dedicates his field after the Jubilee, the priest will determine the value according to the number of years that remain until the next Year of Jubilee, and its set value will be reduced. 19If the man who dedicates the field wishes to redeem it, he must add a fifth to its value, and the field will again become his. 20If, however, he does not redeem the field, or if he has sold it to someone else, it can never be redeemed. 21When the field is released in the Jubilee, it will become holy, like a field devoted to the LORD; it will become the property of the priests.*b*

22" 'If a man dedicates to the LORD a field he has bought, which is not part of his family land, 23the priest will determine its value up to the Year of Jubilee, and the man must pay its value on that day as something holy to the LORD. 24In the Year of Jubilee the field will revert to the person from whom the man bought it, the one whose land it was. 25Every value is to be set according to the sanctuary shekel, twenty gerahs to the shekel.

26" 'No one, however, may dedicate the firstborn of an animal, since the firstborn already belongs to the LORD; whether an ox*c* or a sheep, it is the LORD's. 27If it is one of the unclean animals, he may buy it back at its set value, adding a fifth of the value to it. If he does not redeem it, it is to be sold at its set value.

28" 'But nothing that a man owns and devotes*d* to the LORD—whether man or animal or family land— may be sold or redeemed; everything so devoted is most holy to the LORD. 29" 'No person devoted to destruction*e* may be ransomed; he must be put to death.

14 " '人將房屋分別為聖，歸給耶和華，祭司就要估定價值。房屋是好是壞，祭司怎樣估定，就要以怎樣為定。15將房屋分別為聖的人，若要贖回房屋，就必在你所估定的價值以外加上五分之一，房屋仍舊歸他。

16 " '人若將承受為業的幾分地分別為聖，歸給耶和華，你要按這地撒種多少估定價值。若撒大麥一賀梅珥，要估價五十舍客勒。17他若從禧年將地分別為聖，就要以你所估定的價為定。18倘若他在禧年以後將地分別為聖，祭司就要按着至到禧年所剩的年數，推算價值，也要從你所估的減去價值。19將地分別為聖的人，若定要把地贖回，他便要在你所估的價值以外加上五分之一，地就准定歸他。20他若不贖回那地，或是將地賣給別人，就再不能贖了。21但到了禧年，那地從買主手下出來的時候，就要歸耶和華為聖，和永獻的地一樣，要歸祭司為業。

22 " '他若將所買的一塊地，不是承受為業的，分別為聖歸耶和華，23祭司就要將你所估的價值給他推算到禧年。當日他要以你所估的價銀為聖，歸給耶和華。24到了禧年，那地要歸賣主，就是那承受為業的原主。25凡你所估定的價銀，都要按着聖所的平，二十季拉為一舍客勒。

26 " '惟獨牲畜中頭生的，無論是牛是羊，既歸耶和華，誰也不可再分別為聖，因為這是耶和華的。27若是不潔淨的牲畜生的，就要按你所估定的價值，加上五分之一贖回；若不贖回，就要按你所估定的價值賣了。

28 " '但一切永獻的，就是人從他所有永獻給耶和華的，無論是人，是牲畜，是他承受為業的地，都不可賣，也不可贖。凡永獻的是歸耶和華為至聖。
29 " '凡從人中當滅的都不可贖，必被治死。

*a 16 That is, probably about 6 bushels (about 220 liters)
b 21 Or priest   c 26 The Hebrew word can include both male and female.   d 28 The Hebrew term refers to the irrevocable giving over of things or persons to the LORD.   e 29 The Hebrew term refers to the irrevocable giving over of things or persons to the LORD, often by totally destroying them.*

30 "'地上所有的，無論是地上的種子是樹上的果子，十分之一是耶和華的，是歸給耶和華為聖的。31人若要贖這十分之一的甚麼物，就要加上五分之一。32凡牛羣羊羣中，一切從杖下經過的，每第十隻要歸給耶和華為聖。33不可問是好是壞，也不可更換；若定要更換，所更換的與本來的牲畜都要成為聖，不可贖回。'"

34這就是耶和華在西奈山為以色列人所吩咐摩西的命令。

30" 'A tithe of everything from the land, whether grain from the soil or fruit from the trees, belongs to the LORD; it is holy to the LORD. 31If a man redeems any of his tithe, he must add a fifth of the value to it. 32The entire tithe of the herd and flock—every tenth animal that passes under the shepherd's rod—will be holy to the LORD. 33He must not pick out the good from the bad or make any substitution. If he does make a substitution, both the animal and its substitute become holy and cannot be redeemed.'"

34These are the commands the LORD gave Moses on Mount Sinai for the Israelites.

表五：猶太人的七節期
TABLE 5 : 7 FEASTS OF THE JEWS

節期 Feast	日期 Date		慶祝原因 Celebrated for	意義 Meaning
逾越節 Passover (23:5)	猶曆正月十四晚 陽曆三/四月 Jewish : Jan 14 Solar : Mar/Apr	（一天） (1 day)	天使越過門楣塗羊血的家庭，不殺其長子及全族脫離奴隸的生活 Firstborn spared and freedom from Egyptian slavery	記念神的拯救 Reminding of God's deliverance
無酵節 Unleavened Bread (23:15-22)	猶曆正月十五至廿一日 陽曆三/四月 Jewish : Jan 15-21 Solar : Mar/Apr	（七天） (7 days)	記念出埃及時吃無酵餅 Exodus from Egypt, eating unleavened bread	離舊入新，過聖潔的生活 Leaving the old life behind and entering a new way of living
初熟節 Firstfruits (23:9-14)	猶曆正月十六日 陽曆三/四月 Jewish : Jan 16 Solar : Mar/Apr	（一天） (1 day)	大麥初熟，可以收割了 The first crops of the barley harvest	記念神的供應 Reminding of God's providence
五旬節/收割節/七七節 Pentecost/ Weeks (23:15-22)	猶曆三月初六日 陽曆五/六月 Jewish : Mar 6 Solar : May/Jun	（一天） (1 day)	大麥收割完畢，開始收割小麥 End of barley harvest and beginning of wheat harvest	為豐收而表示喜樂和感恩 Rejoicing and thanks-giving for bountiful harvest
吹角節 Trumpets (23:23-25)	猶曆七月初一日 陽曆九/十月 Jewish : Jul 1 Solar : Sep/Oct	（一天） (1 day)	民事曆元旦及新年 Civil New Year's day	宣告神的勝利 Proclaiming God's victory
贖罪日 Day of Atonement (23:26-35)	猶曆七月初十日 陽曆九/十月 Jewish : Jul 10 Solar : Sep/Oct	（一天） (1 day)	神的救贖，個人與全國的罪都得赦免 God's salvation, the removal of sin from individual and the nation	除罪與神恢復相交 Restoring fellowship with God
住棚節/收藏節 Tabernacles (23:33-43)	猶曆七月十五日 陽曆九/十月 Jewish : Jul 15 Solar : Sep/Oct	（七天） (7 days)	秋收冬藏，記念神在曠野中的保護和引領 End of harvest, God's protection and guidance in the desert	重新向神委身、信靠祂引領和保護，得享安息 Renewing committment to God, trust in his guidance, protection and enjoying rest

Numbers

民數記

The Census

1 The LORD spoke to Moses in the Tent of Meeting in the Desert of Sinai on the first day of the second month of the second year after the Israelites came out of Egypt. He said: ²"Take a census of the whole Israelite community by their clans and families, listing every man by name, one by one. ³You and Aaron are to number by their divisions all the men in Israel twenty years old or more who are able to serve in the army. ⁴One man from each tribe, each the head of his family, is to help you. ⁵These are the names of the men who are to assist you:

from Reuben, Elizur son of Shedeur;
⁶from Simeon, Shelumiel son of Zurishaddai;
⁷from Judah, Nahshon son of Amminadab;
⁸from Issachar, Nethanel son of Zuar;
⁹from Zebulun, Eliab son of Helon;
¹⁰from the sons of Joseph:
from Ephraim, Elishama son of Ammihud;
from Manasseh, Gamaliel son of Pedahzur;
¹¹from Benjamin, Abidan son of Gideoni;
¹²from Dan, Ahiezer son of Ammishaddai;
¹³from Asher, Pagiel son of Ocran;
¹⁴from Gad, Eliasaph son of Deuel;
¹⁵from Naphtali, Ahira son of Enan."

¹⁶These were the men appointed from the community, the leaders of their ancestral tribes. They were the heads of the clans of Israel.

¹⁷Moses and Aaron took these men whose names had been given, ¹⁸and they called the whole community together on the first day of the second month. The people indicated their ancestry by their clans and families, and the men twenty years old or more were listed by name, one by one, ¹⁹as the LORD commanded Moses. And so he counted them in the Desert of Sinai:

統計人口

1 以色列人出埃及地後，第二年二月初一日，耶和華在西奈的曠野、會幕中曉諭摩西說：²"你要按以色列全會眾的家室、宗族、人名的數目，計算所有的男丁。³凡以色列中，從二十歲以外能出去打仗的，你和亞倫要照他們的軍隊數點。⁴每支派中，必有一人作本支派的族長，幫助你們。⁵他們的名字：

屬呂便的，有示丟珥的兒子以利蓿；
⁶屬西緬的，有蘇利沙代的兒子示路蔑；
⁷屬猶大的，有亞米拿達的兒子拿順；
⁸屬以薩迦的，有蘇押的兒子拿坦業；
⁹屬西布倫的，有希倫的兒子以利押；
¹⁰約瑟子孫屬以法蓮的，
有亞米忽的兒子以利沙瑪；
屬瑪拿西的，
有比大蓿的兒子迦瑪列；

¹¹屬便雅憫的，有基多尼的兒子亞比但；
¹²屬但的，有亞米沙代的兒子亞希以謝；
¹³屬亞設的，有俄蘭的兒子帕結；
¹⁴屬迦得的，有丟珥的兒子以利雅薩；
¹⁵屬拿弗他利的，有以南的兒子亞希拉。

¹⁶這都是從會中選召的，各作本支派的首領，都是以色列軍中的統領。

¹⁷於是，摩西、亞倫帶着這些按名指定的人，¹⁸當二月初一日招聚全會眾。會眾就照他們的家室、宗族、人名的數目，從二十歲以外的，都述說自己的家譜。¹⁹耶和華怎樣吩咐摩西，他就怎樣在西奈的曠野數點他們。

20、21以色列的長子，呂便子孫的後代：

照着家室、宗族、人名的數目，從二十歲以外，凡能出去打仗、被數的男丁，共有四萬六千五百名。

22、23西緬子孫的後代：

照着家室、宗族、人名的數目，從二十歲以外，凡能出去打仗、被數的男丁，共有五萬九千三百名。

24、25迦得子孫的後代：

照着家室、宗族、人名的數目，從二十歲以外，凡能出去打仗、被數的，共有四萬五千六百五十名。

26、27猶大子孫的後代：

照着家室、宗族、人名的數目，從二十歲以外，凡能出去打仗、被數的，共有七萬四千六百名。

28、29以薩迦子孫的後代：

照着家室、宗族、人名的數目，從二十歲以外，凡能出去打仗、被數的，共有五萬四千四百名。

30、31西布倫子孫的後代：

照着家室、宗族、人名的數目，從二十歲以外，凡能出去打仗、被數的，共有五萬七千四百名。

32、33約瑟子孫：

屬以法蓮子孫的後代，

照着家室、宗族、人名的數目，從二十歲以外，凡能出去打仗、被數的，共有四萬零五百名。

34、35瑪拿西子孫的後代：

照着家室、宗族、人名的數目，從二十歲以外，凡能出去

20From the descendants of Reuben the firstborn son of Israel:

All the men twenty years old or more who were able to serve in the army were listed by name, one by one, according to the records of their clans and families. 21The number from the tribe of Reuben was 46,500.

22From the descendants of Simeon:

All the men twenty years old or more who were able to serve in the army were counted and listed by name, one by one, according to the records of their clans and families. 23The number from the tribe of Simeon was 59,300.

24From the descendants of Gad:

All the men twenty years old or more who were able to serve in the army were listed by name, according to the records of their clans and families. 25The number from the tribe of Gad was 45,650.

26From the descendants of Judah:

All the men twenty years old or more who were able to serve in the army were listed by name, according to the records of their clans and families. 27The number from the tribe of Judah was 74,600.

28From the descendants of Issachar:

All the men twenty years old or more who were able to serve in the army were listed by name, according to the records of their clans and families. 29The number from the tribe of Issachar was 54,400.

30From the descendants of Zebulun:

All the men twenty years old or more who were able to serve in the army were listed by name, according to the records of their clans and families. 31The number from the tribe of Zebulun was 57,400.

32From the sons of Joseph:

From the descendants of Ephraim:

All the men twenty years old or more who were able to serve in the army were listed by name, according to the records of their clans and families. 33The number from the tribe of Ephraim was 40,500.

34From the descendants of Manasseh:

All the men twenty years old or more who were able to serve in the army were listed by name, according to the records of their clans and families. 35The number from the tribe of Manasseh was 32,200.

36From the descendants of Benjamin:
All the men twenty years old or more who were able to serve in the army were listed by name, according to the records of their clans and families. 37The number from the tribe of Benjamin was 35,400.

38From the descendants of Dan:
All the men twenty years old or more who were able to serve in the army were listed by name, according to the records of their clans and families. 39The number from the tribe of Dan was 62,700.

40From the descendants of Asher:
All the men twenty years old or more who were able to serve in the army were listed by name, according to the records of their clans and families. 41The number from the tribe of Asher was 41,500.

42From the descendants of Naphtali:
All the men twenty years old or more who were able to serve in the army were listed by name, according to the records of their clans and families. 43The number from the tribe of Naphtali was 53,400.

44These were the men counted by Moses and Aaron and the twelve leaders of Israel, each one representing his family. 45All the Israelites twenty years old or more who were able to serve in Israel's army were counted according to their families. 46The total number was 603,550.

47The families of the tribe of Levi, however, were not counted along with the others. 48The LORD had said to Moses: 49"You must not count the tribe of Levi or include them in the census of the other Israelites. 50Instead, appoint the Levites to be in charge of the tabernacle of the Testimony—over all its furnishings and everything belonging to it. They are to carry the tabernacle and all its furnishings; they are to take care of it and encamp around it. 51Whenever the tabernacle is to move, the Levites are to take it down, and whenever the tabernacle is to be set up, the Levites shall do it. Anyone else who goes near it shall be put to death. 52The Israelites are to set up their tents by divisions, each man in his own camp under his own standard. 53The Levites, however, are to set up their tents

打仗、被數的，共有三萬二千二百名。

36、37便雅憫子孫的後代：
照着家室、宗族、人名的數目，從二十歲以外，凡能出去打仗、被數的，共有三萬五千四百名。

38、39但子孫的後代：
照着家室、宗族、人名的數目，從二十歲以外，凡能出去打仗、被數的，共有六萬二千七百名。

40、41亞設子孫的後代：
照着家室、宗族、人名的數目，從二十歲以外，凡能出去打仗、被數的，共有四萬一千五百名。

42、43拿弗他利子孫的後代：
照着家室、宗族、人名的數目，從二十歲以外，凡能出去打仗、被數的，共有五萬三千四百名。

44這些就是被數點的，是摩西、亞倫和以色列中十二個首領所數點的，這十二個人各作各宗族的代表。45、46這樣，凡以色列人中被數的，照着宗族，從二十歲以外，能出去打仗、被數的，共有六十萬零三千五百五十名。47利未人卻沒有按着支派數在其中，48因為耶和華曉諭摩西說：49"惟獨利未支派你不可數點，也不可在以色列人中計算他們的總數。50只要派利未人管法櫃的帳幕和其中的器具，並屬乎帳幕的，他們要抬帳幕和其中的器具（註："抬"或作"搬運"），並要辦理帳幕的事，在帳幕的四圍安營。51帳幕將往前行的時候，利未人要拆卸；將支搭的時候，利未人要豎起。近前來的外人必被治死。52以色列人支搭帳棚，要照他們的軍隊，各歸本營，各歸本纛。53但利未人要在法櫃帳幕的四圍安營，免得忿怒臨到以色列會眾；利未人並要謹守法櫃的帳幕。"

⁵⁴以色列人就這樣行。凡耶和華所吩咐摩西的，他們就照樣行了。

各支派安營的位置

2 耶和華曉諭摩西、亞倫說：
²"以色列人要各歸自己的纛下，在本族的旗號那裏，對着會幕的四圍安營。"

³在東邊，向日出之地，照着軍隊安營的，是猶大營的纛。有亞米拿達的兒子拿順作猶大人的首領。⁴他軍隊被數的，共有七萬四千六百名。
⁵挨着他安營的，是以薩迦支派，有蘇押的兒子拿坦業作以薩迦人的首領。⁶他軍隊被數的，共有五萬四千四百名。
⁷又有西布倫支派。希倫的兒子以利押作西布倫人的首領。⁸他軍隊被數的，共有五萬七千四百名。
⁹凡屬猶大營按着軍隊被數的，共有十八萬六千四百名，要作第一隊往前行。

¹⁰在南邊，按着軍隊是呂便營的纛。有示丟珥的兒子以利蒥作呂便人的首領。¹¹他軍隊被數的，共有四萬六千五百名。
¹²挨着他安營的是西緬支派。蘇利沙代的兒子示路蔑作西緬人的首領。¹³他軍隊被數的，共有五萬九千三百名。
¹⁴又有迦得支派。丟珥的兒子以利雅薩作迦得人的首領。¹⁵他軍隊被數的，共有四萬五千六百五十名。
¹⁶凡屬呂便營按着軍隊被數的，共有十五萬一千四百五十名，要作第二隊往前行。

¹⁷隨後，會幕要往前行，有利未營在諸營中間。他們怎樣安營，就怎樣往前行，各按本位，各歸本纛。

---

around the tabernacle of the Testimony so that wrath will not fall on the Israelite community. The Levites are to be responsible for the care of the tabernacle of the Testimony."

⁵⁴The Israelites did all this just as the LORD commanded Moses.

The Arrangement of the Tribal Camps

2 The LORD said to Moses and Aaron:
²"The Israelites are to camp around the Tent of Meeting some distance from it, each man under his standard with the banners of his family."

³On the east, toward the sunrise, the divisions of the camp of Judah are to encamp under their standard. The leader of the people of Judah is Nahshon son of Amminadab. ⁴His division numbers 74,600.
⁵The tribe of Issachar will camp next to them. The leader of the people of Issachar is Nethanel son of Zuar. ⁶His division numbers 54,400.
⁷The tribe of Zebulun will be next. The leader of the people of Zebulun is Eliab son of Helon. ⁸His division numbers 57,400.
⁹All the men assigned to the camp of Judah, according to their divisions, number 186,400. They will set out first.

¹⁰On the south will be the divisions of the camp of Reuben under their standard. The leader of the people of Reuben is Elizur son of Shedeur. ¹¹His division numbers 46,500.
¹²The tribe of Simeon will camp next to them. The leader of the people of Simeon is Shelumiel son of Zurishaddai. ¹³His division numbers 59,300.
¹⁴The tribe of Gad will be next. The leader of the people of Gad is Eliasaph son of Deuel.^a ¹⁵His division numbers 45,650.
¹⁶All the men assigned to the camp of Reuben, according to their divisions, number 151,450. They will set out second.

¹⁷Then the Tent of Meeting and the camp of the Levites will set out in the middle of the camps. They will set out in the same order as they encamp, each in his own place under his standard.

---

a 14 Many manuscripts of the Masoretic Text, Samaritan Pentateuch and Vulgate (see also Num. 1:14); most manuscripts of the Masoretic Text *Reuel*

18On the west will be the divisions of the camp of Ephraim under their standard. The leader of the people of Ephraim is Elishama son of Ammihud. 19His division numbers 40,500.

20The tribe of Manasseh will be next to them. The leader of the people of Manasseh is Gamaliel son of Pedahzur. 21His division numbers 32,200.

22The tribe of Benjamin will be next. The leader of the people of Benjamin is Abidan son of Gideoni. 23His division numbers 35,400.

24All the men assigned to the camp of Ephraim, according to their divisions, number 108,100. They will set out third.

25On the north will be the divisions of the camp of Dan, under their standard. The leader of the people of Dan is Ahiezer son of Ammishaddai. 26His division numbers 62,700.

27The tribe of Asher will camp next to them. The leader of the people of Asher is Pagiel son of Ocran. 28His division numbers 41,500.

29The tribe of Naphtali will be next. The leader of the people of Naphtali is Ahira son of Enan. 30His division numbers 53,400.

31All the men assigned to the camp of Dan number 157,600. They will set out last, under their standards.

32These are the Israelites, counted according to their families. All those in the camps, by their divisions, number 603,550. 33The Levites, however, were not counted along with the other Israelites, as the LORD commanded Moses.

34So the Israelites did everything the LORD commanded Moses; that is the way they encamped under their standards, and that is the way they set out, each with his clan and family.

The Levites

3 This is the account of the family of Aaron and Moses at the time the LORD talked with Moses on Mount Sinai.

2The names of the sons of Aaron were Nadab the firstborn and Abihu, Eleazar and Ithamar. 3Those were the names of Aaron's sons, the anointed priests, who were ordained to serve as priests. 4Nadab and Abihu, however, fell dead before the LORD when they made an offering with unauthorized fire before him in the Desert of Sinai. They had no sons; so only Eleazar and

18在西邊，按着軍隊是以法蓮營的纛。亞米忽的兒子以利沙瑪作以法蓮人的首領。19他軍隊被數的，共有四萬零五百名。

20挨着他的是瑪拿西支派。比大薛的兒子迦瑪列作瑪拿西人的首領。21他軍隊被數的，共有三萬二千二百名。

22又有便雅憫支派。基多尼的兒子亞比但作便雅憫人的首領。23他軍隊被數的，共有三萬五千四百名。

24凡屬以法蓮營按着軍隊被數的，共有十萬零八千一百名，要作第三隊往前行。

25在北邊，按着軍隊是但營的纛。亞米沙代的兒子亞希以謝作但人的首領。26他軍隊被數的，共有六萬二千七百名。

27挨着他安營的，是亞設支派。俄蘭的兒子帕結作亞設人的首領。28他軍隊被數的，共有四萬一千五百名。

29又有拿弗他利支派。以南的兒子亞希拉作拿弗他利人的首領。30他軍隊被數的，共有五萬三千四百名。

31凡但營被數的，共有十五萬七千六百名，要歸本纛作末隊往前行。

32這些以色列人，照他們的宗族，按他們的軍隊，在諸營中被數的，共有六十萬零三千五百五十名。33惟獨利未人沒有數在以色列人中，是照耶和華所吩咐摩西的。

34以色列人就這樣行，各人照他們的家室、宗族，歸於本纛，安營起行，都是照耶和華所吩咐摩西的。

利未人

3 耶和華在西奈山曉諭摩西的日子，亞倫和摩西的後代如下：

2亞倫的兒子，長子名叫拿答，還有亞比戶、以利亞撒、以他瑪。3這是亞倫兒子的名字，都是受膏的祭司，是摩西叫他們承接聖職供祭司職分的。4拿答、亞比戶在西奈的曠野向耶和華獻凡火的時候，就死在耶和華面前了，他們也沒有兒子。以利亞撒、以他瑪在他們的父親亞倫面前供祭司的職分。

5耶和華曉諭摩西說：6"你使利未支派近前來，站在祭司亞倫面前，好服侍他，7替他和會眾在會幕前守所吩咐的，辦理帳幕的事。8又要看守會幕的器具，並守所吩咐以色列人的，辦理帳幕的事。9你要將利未人給亞倫和他的兒子，因為他們是從以色列人中選出來給他的。10你要囑咐亞倫和他兒子，謹守自己祭司的職任。近前來的外人必被治死。"

11耶和華曉諭摩西說：12"我從以色列人中揀選了利未人，代替以色列人一切頭生的，利未人要歸我。13因為凡頭生的是我的，我在埃及地擊殺一切頭生的那日，就把以色列中一切頭生的，連人帶牲畜都分別為聖歸我，他們定要屬我。我是耶和華。"

14耶和華在西奈的曠野曉諭摩西說：15"你要照利未人的宗族、家室數點他們。凡一個月以外的男子都要數點。"16於是，摩西照耶和華所吩咐的數點他們。

17利未眾子的名字是：
　　革順、哥轄、米拉利。
18革順的兒子，按着家室是：
　　立尼、示每。
19哥轄的兒子，按着家室是：
　　暗蘭、以斯哈、希伯倫、烏薛；
20米拉利的兒子，按着家室是：
　　抹利、母示。
這些按着宗族是利未人的家室。

21屬革順的，有立尼族、示每族，這是革順的二族。22其中被數、從一個月以外所有的男子，共有七千五百名。23這革順的二族，要在帳幕後西邊安營。24拉伊勒的兒子以利雅薩作革順人宗族的首領。25革順的子孫在會幕中所要看守的，就是帳幕和罩棚，並罩棚的蓋與會幕的門簾，26院子的帷子和門簾（院子是圍帳幕

Ithamar served as priests during the lifetime of their father Aaron.

5The LORD said to Moses, 6"Bring the tribe of Levi and present them to Aaron the priest to assist him. 7They are to perform duties for him and for the whole community at the Tent of Meeting by doing the work of the tabernacle. 8They are to take care of all the furnishings of the Tent of Meeting, fulfilling the obligations of the Israelites by doing the work of the tabernacle. 9Give the Levites to Aaron and his sons; they are the Israelites who are to be given wholly to him.a 10Appoint Aaron and his sons to serve as priests; anyone else who approaches the sanctuary must be put to death."

11The LORD also said to Moses, 12"I have taken the Levites from among the Israelites in place of the first male offspring of every Israelite woman. The Levites are mine, 13for all the first-born are mine. When I struck down all the first-born in Egypt, I set apart for myself every first-born in Israel, whether man or animal. They are to be mine. I am the LORD."

14The LORD said to Moses in the Desert of Sinai, 15"Count the Levites by their families and clans. Count every male a month old or more." 16So Moses counted them, as he was commanded by the word of the LORD.

17These were the names of the sons of Levi:
　　Gershon, Kohath and Merari.
18These were the names of the Gershonite clans:
　　Libni and Shimei.
19The Kohathite clans:
　　Amram, Izhar, Hebron and Uzziel.
20The Merarite clans:
　　Mahli and Mushi.
These were the Levite clans, according to their families.

21To Gershon belonged the clans of the Libnites and Shimeites; these were the Gershonite clans. 22The number of all the males a month old or more who were counted was 7,500. 23The Gershonite clans were to camp on the west, behind the tabernacle. 24The leader of the families of the Gershonites was Eliasaph son of Lael. 25At the Tent of Meeting the Gershonites were responsible for the care of the tabernacle and tent, its coverings, the curtain at the entrance to the Tent of Meeting, 26the curtains of the courtyard, the curtain at the entrance to the courtyard surrounding the tabernacle and altar,

a 9 Most manuscripts of the Masoretic Text; some manuscripts of the Masoretic Text, Samaritan Pentateuch and Septuagint (see also Num. 8:16) to me

and the ropes—and everything related to their use.

²⁷To Kohath belonged the clans of the Amramites, Izharites, Hebronites and Uzzielites; these were the Kohathite clans. ²⁸The number of all the males a month old or more was 8,600.^a The Kohathites were responsible for the care of the sanctuary. ²⁹The Kohathite clans were to camp on the south side of the tabernacle. ³⁰The leader of the families of the Kohathite clans was Elizaphan son of Uzziel. ³¹They were responsible for the care of the ark, the table, the lampstand, the altars, the articles of the sanctuary used in ministering, the curtain, and everything related to their use. ³²The chief leader of the Levites was Eleazar son of Aaron, the priest. He was appointed over those who were responsible for the care of the sanctuary.

³³To Merari belonged the clans of the Mahlites and the Mushites; these were the Merarite clans. ³⁴The number of all the males a month old or more who were counted was 6,200. ³⁵The leader of the families of the Merarite clans was Zuriel son of Abihail; they were to camp on the north side of the tabernacle. ³⁶The Merarites were appointed to take care of the frames of the tabernacle, its crossbars, posts, bases, all its equipment, and everything related to their use, ³⁷as well as the posts of the surrounding courtyard with their bases, tent pegs and ropes.

³⁸Moses and Aaron and his sons were to camp to the east of the tabernacle, toward the sunrise, in front of the Tent of Meeting. They were responsible for the care of the sanctuary on behalf of the Israelites. Anyone else who approached the sanctuary was to be put to death.

³⁹The total number of Levites counted at the LORD's command by Moses and Aaron according to their clans, including every male a month old or more, was 22,000.

⁴⁰The LORD said to Moses, "Count all the firstborn Israelite males who are a month old or more and make a list of their names. ⁴¹Take the Levites for me in place of all the firstborn of the Israelites, and the livestock of the Levites in place of all the firstborn of the livestock of the Israelites. I am the LORD."

a 28 Hebrew; some Septuagint manuscripts 8,300

和壇的），並一切使用的繩子。

²⁷屬哥轄的，有暗蘭族、以斯哈族、希伯倫族、烏薛族，這是哥轄的諸族。²⁸按所有男子的數目，從一個月以外看守聖所的，共有八千六百名。²⁹哥轄兒子的諸族要在帳幕的南邊安營。³⁰烏薛的兒子以利亞反作哥轄宗族家室的首領。³¹他們所要看守的是約櫃、桌子、燈臺、兩座壇與聖所內使用的器皿，並簾子和一切使用之物。³²祭司亞倫的兒子以利亞撒作利未人眾首領的領袖，要監察那些看守聖所的人。

³³屬米拉利的，有抹利族、母示族，這是米拉利的二族。³⁴他們被數的，按所有男子的數目，從一個月以外的，共有六千二百名。³⁵亞比亥的兒子蘇列作米拉利二宗族的首領。他們要在帳幕的北邊安營。³⁶米拉利子孫的職分是看守帳幕的板、閂、柱子、帶卯的座和帳幕一切所使用的器具，³⁷院子四圍的柱子，帶卯的座，橛子和繩子。

³⁸在帳幕前東邊，向日出之地安營的是摩西、亞倫和亞倫的兒子。他們看守聖所，替以色列人守耶和華所吩咐的。近前來的外人必被治死。

³⁹凡被數的利未人，就是摩西、亞倫照耶和華吩咐所數的，按着家室，從一個月以外的男子，共有二萬二千名。

⁴⁰耶和華對摩西說："你要從以色列人中數點一個月以外凡頭生的男子，把他們的名字記下。⁴¹我是耶和華，你要揀選利未人歸我，代替以色列人所有頭生的；也取利未人的牲畜代替以色列所有頭生的牲畜。"

⁴²摩西就照耶和華所吩咐的，把以色列人頭生的都數點了。⁴³按人名的數目，從一個月以外，凡頭生的男子，共有二萬二千二百七十三名。

⁴⁴耶和華曉諭摩西說：⁴⁵“你揀選利未人代替以色列人所有頭生的；也取利未人的牲畜代替以色列人的牲畜。利未人要歸我，我是耶和華。⁴⁶以色列人中頭生的男子，比利未人多二百七十三個，必當將他們贖出來。⁴⁷你要按人丁，照聖所的平，每人取贖銀五舍客勒（一舍客勒是二十季拉），⁴⁸把那多餘之人的贖銀，交給亞倫和他的兒子。”

⁴⁹於是摩西從那被利未人所贖以外的人取了贖銀。⁵⁰從以色列人頭生的所取之銀，按聖所的平，有一千三百六十五舍客勒。⁵¹摩西照耶和華的話，把這贖銀給亞倫和他的兒子，正如耶和華所吩咐的。

哥轄子孫

4 耶和華曉諭摩西、亞倫說：²“你從利未人中，將哥轄子孫的總數，照他們的家室、宗族，³從三十歲直到五十歲，凡前來任職在會幕裏辦事的，全都計算。

⁴“哥轄子孫在會幕搬運至聖之物，所辦的事乃是這樣：⁵起營的時候，亞倫和他兒子要進去摘下遮掩櫃的幔子，用以蒙蓋法櫃。⁶又用海狗皮蓋在上頭，再蒙上純藍色的毯子，把杠穿上。

⁷“又用藍色毯子鋪在陳設餅的桌子上，將盤子、調羹、奠酒的爵和杯擺在上頭。桌子上也必有常設的餅。⁸在其上又要蒙朱紅色的毯子，再蒙上海狗皮，把杠穿上。

⁹“要拿藍色毯子，把燈臺和燈臺上所用的燈盞、剪子、蠟花盤，並一切盛油的器皿，全都遮蓋。¹⁰又要把燈臺和燈臺的一切器具包在海狗皮裏，放在抬架上。

⁴²So Moses counted all the firstborn of the Israelites, as the LORD commanded him. ⁴³The total number of firstborn males a month old or more, listed by name, was 22,273.

⁴⁴The LORD also said to Moses, ⁴⁵"Take the Levites in place of all the firstborn of Israel, and the livestock of the Levites in place of their livestock. The Levites are to be mine. I am the LORD. ⁴⁶To redeem the 273 firstborn Israelites who exceed the number of the Levites, ⁴⁷collect five shekels[a] for each one, according to the sanctuary shekel, which weighs twenty gerahs. ⁴⁸Give the money for the redemption of the additional Israelites to Aaron and his sons."

⁴⁹So Moses collected the redemption money from those who exceeded the number redeemed by the Levites. ⁵⁰From the firstborn of the Israelites he collected silver weighing 1,365 shekels,[b] according to the sanctuary shekel. ⁵¹Moses gave the redemption money to Aaron and his sons, as he was commanded by the word of the LORD.

The Kohathites

4 The LORD said to Moses and Aaron: ²"Take a census of the Kohathite branch of the Levites by their clans and families. ³Count all the men from thirty to fifty years of age who come to serve in the work in the Tent of Meeting.

⁴"This is the work of the Kohathites in the Tent of Meeting: the care of the most holy things. ⁵When the camp is to move, Aaron and his sons are to go in and take down the shielding curtain and cover the ark of the Testimony with it. ⁶Then they are to cover this with hides of sea cows,[c] spread a cloth of solid blue over that and put the poles in place.

⁷"Over the table of the Presence they are to spread a blue cloth and put on it the plates, dishes and bowls, and the jars for drink offerings; the bread that is continually there is to remain on it. ⁸Over these they are to spread a scarlet cloth, cover that with hides of sea cows and put its poles in place.

⁹"They are to take a blue cloth and cover the lampstand that is for light, together with its lamps, its wick trimmers and trays, and all its jars for the oil used to supply it. ¹⁰Then they are to wrap it and all its accessories in a covering of hides of sea cows and put it on a carrying frame.

---

a 47 That is, about 2 ounces (about 55 grams)

b 50 That is, about 35 pounds (about 15.5 kilograms)

c 6 That is, dugongs; also in verses 8, 10, 11, 12, 14 and 25

11"Over the gold altar they are to spread a blue cloth and cover that with hides of sea cows and put its poles in place.

12"They are to take all the articles used for ministering in the sanctuary, wrap them in a blue cloth, cover that with hides of sea cows and put them on a carrying frame.

13"They are to remove the ashes from the bronze altar and spread a purple cloth over it. 14Then they are to place on it all the utensils used for ministering at the altar, including the firepans, meat forks, shovels and sprinkling bowls. Over it they are to spread a covering of hides of sea cows and put its poles in place.

15"After Aaron and his sons have finished covering the holy furnishings and all the holy articles, and when the camp is ready to move, the Kohathites are to come to do the carrying. But they must not touch the holy things or they will die. The Kohathites are to carry those things that are in the Tent of Meeting.

16"Eleazar son of Aaron, the priest, is to have charge of the oil for the light, the fragrant incense, the regular grain offering and the anointing oil. He is to be in charge of the entire tabernacle and everything in it, including its holy furnishings and articles."

17The LORD said to Moses and Aaron, 18"See that the Kohathite tribal clans are not cut off from the Levites. 19So that they may live and not die when they come near the most holy things, do this for them: Aaron and his sons are to go into the sanctuary and assign to each man his work and what he is to carry. 20But the Kohathites must not go in to look at the holy things, even for a moment, or they will die."

The Gershonites

21The LORD said to Moses, 22"Take a census also of the Gershonites by their families and clans. 23Count all the men from thirty to fifty years of age who come to serve in the work at the Tent of Meeting.

24"This is the service of the Gershonite clans as they work and carry burdens: 25They are to carry the curtains of the tabernacle, the Tent of Meeting, its covering and the outer covering of hides of sea cows, the curtains for the entrance to the Tent of Meeting, 26the curtains of the courtyard surrounding the tabernacle and altar, the curtain for the entrance, the ropes and all the equipment used in its service. The Gershonites are to do all that needs to be done with these things. 27All their service, whether carrying or doing other work, is to be done under the direction of Aaron and his sons. You shall assign to

11 "在金壇上要鋪藍色毯子，蒙上海狗皮，把杠穿上。

12 "又要把聖所用的一切器具，包在藍色毯子裏，用海狗皮蒙上，放在抬架上。

13 "要收去壇上的灰，把紫色毯子鋪在壇上。14又要把所用的一切器具，就是火鼎、肉叉子、鏟子、盤子，一切屬壇的器具都擺在壇上，又蒙上海狗皮，把杠穿上。

15 "將要起營的時候，亞倫和他兒子把聖所和聖所的一切器具遮蓋完了，哥轄的子孫就要來抬，只是不可摸聖物，免得他們死亡。會幕裏這些物件是哥轄子孫所當抬的。

16 "祭司亞倫的兒子以利亞撒所要看守的是點燈的油與香料，並當獻的素祭和膏油，也要看守全帳幕與其中所有的，並聖所和聖所的器具。"

17耶和華曉諭摩西、亞倫說：18 "你們不可將哥轄人的支派從利未人中剪除。19他們挨近至聖物的時候，亞倫和他兒子要進去派他們各人所當辦的、所當抬的，這樣待他們，好使他們活着，不至死亡。20只是他們連片時不可進去觀看聖所，免得他們死亡。"

革順子孫

21耶和華曉諭摩西說：22 "你要將革順子孫的總數，照着宗族、家室，23從三十歲直到五十歲，凡前來任職在會幕裏辦事的，全都數點。

24 "革順人各族所辦的事、所抬的物乃是這樣：25他們要抬帳幕的幔子和會幕、並會幕的蓋、與其上的海狗皮和會幕的門簾，26院子的帷子和門簾（院子是圍帳幕和壇的）、繩子，並所用的器具，不論是做甚麼用的，他們都要經理。27革順的子孫在一切抬物辦事之上，都要憑亞倫和他兒子的吩咐，他們所當抬的，要派他們看守。²⁸這是<u>革順</u>子孫的各族在會幕裏所辦的事，他們所看守的，必在祭司<u>亞倫</u>兒子<u>以他瑪</u>的手下。

米拉利子孫

²⁹「至於<u>米拉利</u>的子孫，你要照着家室、宗族，把他們數點。³⁰從三十歲直到五十歲，凡前來任職、在會幕裏辦事的，你都要數點。³¹他們辦理會幕的事，就是抬帳幕的板、閂、柱子，和帶卯的座，³²院子四圍的柱子和其上帶卯的座、橛子、繩子，並一切使用的器具。他們所抬的器具，你們要按名指定。³³這是<u>米拉利</u>子孫各族在會幕裏所辦的事，都在祭司<u>亞倫</u>兒子<u>以他瑪</u>的手下。」

數點利未各宗族

³⁴<u>摩西</u>、<u>亞倫</u>與會眾的諸首領將<u>哥轄</u>的子孫照着家室、宗族，³⁵從三十歲直到五十歲，凡前來任職、在會幕裏辦事的，都數點了。³⁶被數的共有二千七百五十名。³⁷這是<u>哥轄</u>各族中被數的，是在會幕裏辦事的，就是<u>摩西</u>、<u>亞倫</u>照耶和華藉<u>摩西</u>所吩咐數點的。

³⁸<u>革順</u>子孫中被數的，照着家室、宗族，³⁹、⁴⁰從三十歲直到五十歲，凡前來任職、在會幕裏辦事的，共有二千六百三十名。⁴¹這是<u>革順</u>子孫各族中被數的，是在會幕裏辦事的，就是<u>摩西</u>、<u>亞倫</u>照耶和華藉<u>摩西</u>所吩咐數點的。

⁴²<u>米拉利</u>子孫中各族被數的，照着家室、宗族，⁴³、⁴⁴從三十歲直到五十歲，凡前來任職、在會幕裏辦事的，共有三千二百名。⁴⁵這是<u>米拉利</u>子孫各族中被數的，就是<u>摩西</u>、<u>亞倫</u>照耶和華藉<u>摩西</u>所吩咐數點的。

⁴⁶凡被數的<u>利未</u>人，就是<u>摩西</u>、<u>亞倫</u>並<u>以色列</u>眾首領，照着家室、宗族所數點的，⁴⁷、⁴⁸從三十歲直到五十歲，凡前來任職、在會幕裏做抬物之工的，共有八千五百八十名。⁴⁹<u>摩西</u>按他們所辦的事、所抬的物，憑耶和華的吩咐數點他們。

them as their responsibility all they are to carry. ²⁸This is the service of the Gershonite clans at the Tent of Meeting. Their duties are to be under the direction of Ithamar son of Aaron, the priest.

The Merarites

²⁹"Count the Merarites by their clans and families. ³⁰Count all the men from thirty to fifty years of age who come to serve in the work at the Tent of Meeting. ³¹This is their duty as they perform service at the Tent of Meeting: to carry the frames of the tabernacle, its crossbars, posts and bases, ³²as well as the posts of the surrounding courtyard with their bases, tent pegs, ropes, all their equipment and everything related to their use. Assign to each man the specific things he is to carry. ³³This is the service of the Merarite clans as they work at the Tent of Meeting under the direction of Ithamar son of Aaron, the priest."

The Numbering of the Levite Clans

³⁴Moses, Aaron and the leaders of the community counted the Kohathites by their clans and families. ³⁵All the men from thirty to fifty years of age who came to serve in the work in the Tent of Meeting, ³⁶counted by clans, were 2,750. ³⁷This was the total of all those in the Kohathite clans who served in the Tent of Meeting. Moses and Aaron counted them according to the LORD's command through Moses.

³⁸The Gershonites were counted by their clans and families. ³⁹All the men from thirty to fifty years of age who came to serve in the work at the Tent of Meeting, ⁴⁰counted by their clans and families, were 2,630. ⁴¹This was the total of those in the Gershonite clans who served in the Tent of Meeting. Moses and Aaron counted them according to the LORD's command.

⁴²The Merarites were counted by their clans and families. ⁴³All the men from thirty to fifty years of age who came to serve in the work at the Tent of Meeting, ⁴⁴counted by their clans, were 3,200. ⁴⁵This was the total of those in the Merarite clans. Moses and Aaron counted them according to the LORD's command through Moses.

⁴⁶So Moses, Aaron and the leaders of Israel counted all the Levites by their clans and families. ⁴⁷All the men from thirty to fifty years of age who came to do the work of serving and carrying the Tent of Meeting ⁴⁸numbered 8,580. ⁴⁹At the LORD's command through Moses, each was assigned his work and told what to carry.

Thus they were counted, as the LORD commanded Moses.

The Purity of the Camp

5 The LORD said to Moses, 2"Command the Israelites to send away from the camp anyone who has an infectious skin disease*a* or a discharge of any kind, or who is ceremonially unclean because of a dead body. 3Send away male and female alike; send them outside the camp so they will not defile their camp, where I dwell among them." 4The Israelites did this; they sent them outside the camp. They did just as the LORD had instructed Moses.

Restitution for Wrongs

5The LORD said to Moses, 6"Say to the Israelites: 'When a man or woman wrongs another in any way*b* and so is unfaithful to the LORD, that person is guilty 7and must confess the sin he has committed. He must make full restitution for his wrong, add one fifth to it and give it all to the person he has wronged. 8But if that person has no close relative to whom restitution can be made for the wrong, the restitution belongs to the LORD and must be given to the priest, along with the ram with which atonement is made for him. 9All the sacred contributions the Israelites bring to a priest will belong to him. 10Each man's sacred gifts are his own, but what he gives to the priest will belong to the priest.' "

The Test for an Unfaithful Wife

11Then the LORD said to Moses, 12"Speak to the Israelites and say to them: 'If a man's wife goes astray and is unfaithful to him 13by sleeping with another man, and this is hidden from her husband and her impurity is undetected (since there is no witness against her and she has not been caught in the act), 14and if feelings of jealousy come over her husband and he suspects his wife and she is impure—or if he is jealous and suspects her even though she is not impure— 15then he is to take his wife to the priest. He must also take an offering of a tenth of an ephah*c* of barley flour on her behalf. He must not pour oil on it or put incense on it, because it is a grain offering for jealousy, a reminder offering to draw attention to guilt.

---

a 2 Traditionally leprosy; *the Hebrew word was used for various diseases affecting the skin—not necessarily leprosy.*

b 6 Or woman commits any wrong common to mankind

c 15 That is, probably about 2 quarts (about 2 liters)

他們這樣被摩西數點，正如耶和華所吩咐他的。

潔淨營地

5 耶和華曉諭摩西說：2 "你吩咐以色列人，使一切長大痲瘋的，患漏症的，並因死屍不潔淨的，都出營外去。3 無論男女，都要使他們出到營外，免得污穢他們的營。這營是我所住的。"4 以色列人就這樣行，使他們出到營外。耶和華怎樣吩咐摩西，以色列人就怎樣行了。

因罪賠償

5 耶和華對摩西說：6 "你曉諭以色列人說：'無論男女，若犯了人所常犯的罪，以致干犯耶和華，那人就有了罪。7 他要承認所犯的罪，將所虧負人的，如數賠還；另外加上五分之一，也歸與所虧負的人。8 那人若沒有親屬可受所賠還的，那所賠還的就要歸與服事耶和華的祭司，至於那為他贖罪的公羊是在外。9 以色列人一切的聖物中，所奉給祭司的舉祭，都要歸與祭司。10 各人所分別為聖的物，無論是甚麼，都要歸給祭司。'"

試驗妻子不貞之法

11 耶和華對摩西說：12 "你曉諭以色列人說：'人的妻若有邪行，得罪她丈夫，13 有人與她行淫，事情嚴密瞞過她丈夫，而且她被玷污，沒有作見證的人，當她行淫的時候也沒有被捉住，14 她丈夫生了疑恨的心，疑恨她，她是被玷污；或是她丈夫生了疑恨的心，疑恨她，她並沒有被玷污。15 這人就要將妻送到祭司那裏，又為她帶着大麥麵伊法十分之一作供物，不可澆上油，也不可加上乳香，因為這是疑恨的素祭，是思念的素祭，使人思念罪孽。

16 "'祭司要使那婦人近前來，站在耶和華面前。17祭司要把聖水盛在瓦器裏，又從帳幕的地上取點塵土放在水中。18祭司要叫那婦人蓬頭散髮，站在耶和華面前，把思念的素祭，就是疑恨的素祭，放在她手中。祭司手裏拿着致咒詛的苦水，19要叫婦人起誓，對她說：若沒有人與你行淫，也未曾背着丈夫做污穢的事，你就免受這致咒詛苦水的災。20你若背着丈夫，行了污穢的事，在你丈夫以外有人與你行淫，21（祭司叫婦人發咒起誓）願耶和華叫你大腿消瘦，肚腹發脹，使你在你民中被人咒詛，成了誓語。22並且這致咒詛的水入你的腸中，要叫你的肚腹發脹，大腿消瘦。

"'婦人要回答說：阿們！阿們！

23 "'祭司要寫這咒詛的話，將所寫的字抹在苦水裏，24又叫婦人喝這致咒詛的苦水，這水要進入她裏面變苦了。25祭司要從婦人的手中取那疑恨的素祭，在耶和華面前搖一搖，拿到壇前。26又要從素祭中取出一把，作為這事的記念，燒在壇上，然後叫婦人喝這水。27叫她喝了以後，她若被玷污得罪了丈夫，這致咒詛的水必進入她裏面變苦了，她的肚腹就要發脹，大腿就要消瘦，那婦人便要在她民中被人咒詛。28若婦人沒有被玷污，卻是清潔的，就要免受這災，且要懷孕。

29 "'妻子背着丈夫行了污穢的事，30或是人生了疑恨的心，疑恨他的妻，就有這疑恨的條例。那時他要叫婦人站在耶和華面前，祭司要在她

16" 'The priest shall bring her and have her stand before the LORD. 17Then he shall take some holy water in a clay jar and put some dust from the tabernacle floor into the water. 18After the priest has had the woman stand before the LORD, he shall loosen her hair and place in her hands the reminder offering, the grain offering for jealousy, while he himself holds the bitter water that brings a curse. 19Then the priest shall put the woman under oath and say to her, "If no other man has slept with you and you have not gone astray and become impure while married to your husband, may this bitter water that brings a curse not harm you. 20But if you have gone astray while married to your husband and you have defiled yourself by sleeping with a man other than your husband"— 21here the priest is to put the woman under this curse of the oath—"may the LORD cause your people to curse and denounce you when he causes your thigh to waste away and your abdomen to swell.*a* 22May this water that brings a curse enter your body so that your abdomen swells and your thigh wastes away.*b*"

" 'Then the woman is to say, "Amen. So be it."

23" 'The priest is to write these curses on a scroll and then wash them off into the bitter water. 24He shall have the woman drink the bitter water that brings a curse, and this water will enter her and cause bitter suffering. 25The priest is to take from her hands the grain offering for jealousy, wave it before the LORD and bring it to the altar. 26The priest is then to take a handful of the grain offering as a memorial offering and burn it on the altar; after that, he is to have the woman drink the water. 27If she has defiled herself and been unfaithful to her husband, then when she is made to drink the water that brings a curse, it will go into her and cause bitter suffering; her abdomen will swell and her thigh waste away,*c* and she will become accursed among her people. 28If, however, the woman has not defiled herself and is free from impurity, she will be cleared of guilt and will be able to have children.

29" 'This, then, is the law of jealousy when a woman goes astray and defiles herself while married to her husband, 30or when feelings of jealousy come over a man because he suspects his wife. The priest is to have her stand before

a 21 Or causes you to have a miscarrying womb and barrenness
b 22 Or body and cause you to be barren and have a miscarrying womb　c 27 Or suffering; she will have barrenness and a miscarrying womb

the LORD and is to apply this entire law to her. [31]The husband will be innocent of any wrongdoing, but the woman will bear the consequences of her sin.'"

The Nazirite

6 The LORD said to Moses, [2]"Speak to the Israelites and say to them: 'If a man or woman wants to make a special vow, a vow of separation to the LORD as a Nazirite, [3]he must abstain from wine and other fermented drink and must not drink vinegar made from wine or from other fermented drink. He must not drink grape juice or eat grapes or raisins. [4]As long as he is a Nazirite, he must not eat anything that comes from the grapevine, not even the seeds or skins.

[5]'During the entire period of his vow of separation no razor may be used on his head. He must be holy until the period of his separation to the LORD is over; he must let the hair of his head grow long. [6]Throughout the period of his separation to the LORD he must not go near a dead body. [7]Even if his own father or mother or brother or sister dies, he must not make himself ceremonially unclean on account of them, because the symbol of his separation to God is on his head. [8]Throughout the period of his separation he is consecrated to the LORD.

[9]'If someone dies suddenly in his presence, thus defiling the hair he has dedicated, he must shave his head on the day of his cleansing—the seventh day. [10]Then on the eighth day he must bring two doves or two young pigeons to the priest at the entrance to the Tent of Meeting. [11]The priest is to offer one as a sin offering and the other as a burnt offering to make atonement for him because he sinned by being in the presence of the dead body. That same day he is to consecrate his head. [12]He must dedicate himself to the LORD for the period of his separation and must bring a year-old male lamb as a guilt offering. The previous days do not count, because he became defiled during his separation.

[13]'Now this is the law for the Nazirite when the period of his separation is over. He is to be brought to the entrance to the Tent of Meeting. [14]There he is to present his offerings to the LORD: a year-old male lamb without defect for a burnt offering, a year-old ewe lamb without defect for a sin offering, a ram without defect for a fellowship offering,[a] [15]together with their grain offerings and drink offerings, and a basket

a 14 Traditionally peace offering; also in verses 17 and 18

身上照這條例而行，[31]男人就為無罪，婦人必擔當自己的罪孽。'"

拿細耳人

6 耶和華對摩西說：[2]"你曉諭以色列人說：'無論男女許了特別的願，就是拿細耳人的願（註："拿細耳"就是"歸主"的意思。下同），要離俗歸耶和華。[3]他就要遠離清酒、濃酒，也不可喝甚麼清酒、濃酒做的醋，不可喝甚麼葡萄汁，也不可吃鮮葡萄和乾葡萄。[4]在一切離俗的日子，凡葡萄樹上結的，自核至皮所做的物，都不可吃。

[5]"'在他一切許願離俗的日子，不可用剃頭刀剃頭，要由髮綹長長了，他要聖潔，直到離俗歸耶和華的日子滿了。[6]在他離俗歸耶和華的一切日子，不可挨近死屍。[7]他的父母或是他弟兄姐妹死了的時候，他不可因他們使自己不潔淨，因為那離俗歸神的憑據是在他頭上。[8]在他一切離俗的日子是歸耶和華為聖。

[9]"'若在他旁邊忽然有人死了，以致沾染了他離俗的頭，他要在第七日得潔淨的時候剃頭。[10]第八日，他要把兩隻斑鳩或兩隻雛鴿，帶到會幕門口交給祭司。[11]祭司要獻一隻作贖罪祭，一隻作燔祭，為他贖那因死屍而有的罪，並要當日使他的頭成為聖潔。[12]他要另選離俗歸耶和華的日子，又要牽一隻一歲的公羊羔來作贖愆祭；但先前的日子要歸徒然，因為他在離俗之間被玷污了。

[13]"'拿細耳人滿了離俗的日子乃有這條例：人要領他到會幕門口，[14]他要將供物奉給耶和華，就是一隻沒有殘疾、一歲的公羊羔作燔祭，一隻沒有殘疾、一歲的母羊羔作贖罪祭，和一隻沒有殘疾的公綿羊作平安祭，[15]並一筐子無酵調油的細麵餅與

抹油的無酵薄餅，並同獻的素祭和奠祭。

16 「『祭司要在耶和華面前獻那人的贖罪祭和燔祭，17也要把那隻公羊和那筐無酵餅，獻給耶和華作平安祭，又要將同獻的素祭和奠祭獻上。

18 「『拿細耳人要在會幕門口剃離俗的頭，把離俗頭上的髮，放在平安祭下的火上。

19 「『他剃了以後，祭司就要取那已煮的公羊一條前腿，又從筐子裏取一個無酵餅和一個無酵薄餅，都放在他手上。20祭司要拿這些作為搖祭，在耶和華面前搖一搖；這與所搖的胸，所舉的腿，同為聖物歸給祭司，然後拿細耳人可以喝酒。

21 「『許願的拿細耳人為離俗所獻的供物，和他以外所能得的獻給耶和華，就有這條例。他怎樣許願，就當照離俗的條例行。』」

祭司的祝福

22耶和華曉諭摩西說：23 「你告訴亞倫和他兒子說：『你們要這樣為以色列人祝福，說：

24 「『願耶和華賜福給你，
　保護你。
25願耶和華使他的臉光照你，
　賜恩給你。
26願耶和華向你仰臉，
　賜你平安。』

27 「他們要如此奉我的名為以色列人祝福，我也要賜福給他們。」

會幕建成所獻之供物

7 摩西立完了帳幕，就把帳幕用膏抹了，使它成聖。又把其中的器具和壇，並壇上的器具都抹了，使它成聖。2當天，以色列的眾首領，就是各族的族長，都來奉獻。他們是各支派的首領，管理那些被數的人。3他們把自己的供物送到耶和華面前，就是六輛篷子車和十二隻公牛。每兩個首領奉獻一輛車，每首領奉獻一隻牛。他們把這些都奉到帳幕前。

of bread made without yeast—cakes made of fine flour mixed with oil, and wafers spread with oil.

16"The priest is to present them before the LORD and make the sin offering and the burnt offering. 17He is to present the basket of unleavened bread and is to sacrifice the ram as a fellowship offering to the LORD, together with its grain offering and drink offering.

18"'Then at the entrance to the Tent of Meeting, the Nazirite must shave off the hair that he dedicated. He is to take the hair and put it in the fire that is under the sacrifice of the fellowship offering.

19"'After the Nazirite has shaved off the hair of his dedication, the priest is to place in his hands a boiled shoulder of the ram, and a cake and a wafer from the basket, both made without yeast. 20The priest shall then wave them before the LORD as a wave offering; they are holy and belong to the priest, together with the breast that was waved and the thigh that was presented. After that, the Nazirite may drink wine.

21"'This is the law of the Nazirite who vows his offering to the LORD in accordance with his separation, in addition to whatever else he can afford. He must fulfill the vow he has made, according to the law of the Nazirite.'"

The Priestly Blessing

22The LORD said to Moses, 23"Tell Aaron and his sons, 'This is how you are to bless the Israelites. Say to them:

24" ' "The LORD bless you
　and keep you;
25the LORD make his face shine upon you
　and be gracious to you;
26the LORD turn his face toward you
　and give you peace." '

27"So they will put my name on the Israelites, and I will bless them."

Offerings at the Dedication of the Tabernacle

7 When Moses finished setting up the tabernacle, he anointed it and consecrated it and all its furnishings. He also anointed and consecrated the altar and all its utensils. 2Then the leaders of Israel, the heads of families who were the tribal leaders in charge of those who were counted, made offerings. 3They brought as their gifts before the LORD six covered carts and twelve oxen—an ox from each leader and a cart from every two. These they presented before the tabernacle.

⁴The LORD said to Moses, ⁵"Accept these from them, that they may be used in the work at the Tent of Meeting. Give them to the Levites as each man's work requires."

⁶So Moses took the carts and oxen and gave them to the Levites. ⁷He gave two carts and four oxen to the Gershonites, as their work required, ⁸and he gave four carts and eight oxen to the Merarites, as their work required. They were all under the direction of Ithamar son of Aaron, the priest. ⁹But Moses did not give any to the Kohathites, because they were to carry on their shoulders the holy things, for which they were responsible.

¹⁰When the altar was anointed, the leaders brought their offerings for its dedication and presented them before the altar. ¹¹For the LORD had said to Moses, "Each day one leader is to bring his offering for the dedication of the altar."

¹²The one who brought his offering on the first day was Nahshon son of Amminadab of the tribe of Judah.

¹³His offering was one silver plate weighing a hundred and thirty shekels,ᵃ and one silver sprinkling bowl weighing seventy shekels,ᵇ both according to the sanctuary shekel, each filled with fine flour mixed with oil as a grain offering; ¹⁴one gold dish weighing ten shekels,ᶜ filled with incense; ¹⁵one young bull, one ram and one male lamb a year old, for a burnt offering; ¹⁶one male goat for a sin offering; ¹⁷and two oxen, five rams, five male goats and five male lambs a year old, to be sacrificed as a fellowship offering.ᵈ This was the offering of Nahshon son of Amminadab.

¹⁸On the second day Nethanel son of Zuar, the leader of Issachar, brought his offering.

¹⁹The offering he brought was one silver plate weighing a hundred and thirty shekels, and one silver sprinkling bowl weighing seventy shekels, both according to the sanctuary shekel, each filled with fine flour mixed with oil as a grain offering; ²⁰one gold dish weighing ten shekels, filled with incense; ²¹one young bull, one ram and one male lamb a year old, for a burnt offering; ²²one male goat

---

⁴耶和華曉諭摩西說：⁵"你要收下這些，好作會幕的使用，都要照利未人所辦的事交給他們。"

⁶於是，摩西收了車和牛，交給利未人。⁷把兩輛車，四隻牛，照革順子孫所辦的事交給他們；⁸又把四輛車，八隻牛，照米拉利子孫所辦的事交給他們，他們都在祭司亞倫的兒子以他瑪手下。⁹但車與牛都沒有交給哥轄子孫，因為他們辦的是聖所的事，在肩頭上抬聖物。

¹⁰用膏抹壇的日子，首領都來行奉獻壇的禮，眾首領就在壇前獻供物。¹¹耶和華對摩西說："眾首領為行奉獻壇的禮，要每天一個首領來獻供物。"

¹²頭一日獻供物的，是猶大支派的亞米拿達的兒子拿順。

¹³他的供物是：一個銀盤子，重一百三十舍客勒，一個銀碗，重七十舍客勒，都是按聖所的平，也都盛滿了調油的細麵作素祭；¹⁴一個金盂，重十舍客勒，盛滿了香；¹⁵一隻公牛犢，一隻公綿羊，一隻一歲的公羊羔作燔祭；¹⁶一隻公山羊作贖罪祭；¹⁷兩隻公牛，五隻公綿羊，五隻公山羊，五隻一歲的公羊羔作平安祭。這是亞米拿達兒子拿順的供物。

¹⁸第二日來獻的，是以薩迦子孫的首領、蘇押的兒子拿坦業。

¹⁹他獻為供物的是：一個銀盤子，重一百三十舍客勒，一個銀碗，重七十舍客勒，都是按聖所的平，也都盛滿了調油的細麵作素祭；²⁰一個金盂，重十舍客勒，盛滿了香；²¹一隻公牛犢，一隻公綿羊，一隻一歲的公羊羔作燔祭；²²一隻公山

---

a 13 That is, about 3 1/4 pounds (about 1.5 kilograms); also elsewhere in this chapter   *b 13* That is, about 1 3/4 pounds (about 0.8 kilogram); also elsewhere in this chapter   *c 14* That is, about 4 ounces (about 110 grams); also elsewhere in this chapter   *d 17* Traditionally *peace offering*; also elsewhere in this chapter

羊作贖罪祭；²³兩隻公牛，五隻公綿羊，五隻公山羊，五隻一歲的公羊羔作平安祭。這是蘇押兒子拿坦業的供物。

²⁴第三日來獻的，是西布倫子孫的首領、希倫的兒子以利押。

²⁵他的供物是：一個銀盤子，重一百三十舍客勒，一個銀碗，重七十舍客勒，都是按聖所的平，也都盛滿了調油的細麵作素祭；²⁶一個金盂，重十舍客勒，盛滿了香；²⁷一隻公牛犢，一隻公綿羊，一隻一歲的公羊羔作燔祭；²⁸一隻公山羊作贖罪祭；²⁹兩隻公牛，五隻公綿羊，五隻公山羊，五隻一歲的公羊羔作平安祭。這是希倫兒子以利押的供物。

³⁰第四日來獻的，是呂便子孫的首領、示丟珥的兒子以利蓿。

³¹他的供物是：一個銀盤子，重一百三十舍客勒，一個銀碗，重七十舍客勒，都是按聖所的平，也都盛滿了調油的細麵作素祭；³²一個金盂，重十舍客勒，盛滿了香；³³一隻公牛犢，一隻公綿羊，一隻一歲的公羊羔作燔祭；³⁴一隻公山羊作贖罪祭；³⁵兩隻公牛，五隻公綿羊，五隻公山羊，五隻一歲的公羊羔作平安祭。這是示丟珥的兒子以利蓿的供物。

³⁶第五日來獻的，是西緬子孫的首領、蘇利沙代的兒子示路蔑。

³⁷他的供物是：一個銀盤子，重一百三十舍客勒，一個銀碗，重七十舍客勒，都是按聖所的平，也都盛滿了調油的細麵作素祭；³⁸一個金盂，重十舍客勒，盛滿了香；³⁹一隻公牛犢，一隻公綿羊，一隻一歲的公羊羔作燔祭；⁴⁰一隻公山羊作贖罪祭；⁴¹兩隻公牛，五隻公綿羊，五隻公山羊，五隻一歲的公羊羔作平安祭。這是蘇利沙代兒子示路蔑的供物。

for a sin offering; ²³and two oxen, five rams, five male goats and five male lambs a year old, to be sacrificed as a fellowship offering. This was the offering of Nethanel son of Zuar.

²⁴On the third day, Eliab son of Helon, the leader of the people of Zebulun, brought his offering.
²⁵His offering was one silver plate weighing a hundred and thirty shekels, and one silver sprinkling bowl weighing seventy shekels, both according to the sanctuary shekel, each filled with fine flour mixed with oil as a grain offering; ²⁶one gold dish weighing ten shekels, filled with incense; ²⁷one young bull, one ram and one male lamb a year old, for a burnt offering; ²⁸one male goat for a sin offering; ²⁹and two oxen, five rams, five male goats and five male lambs a year old, to be sacrificed as a fellowship offering. This was the offering of Eliab son of Helon.

³⁰On the fourth day Elizur son of Shedeur, the leader of the people of Reuben, brought his offering.
³¹His offering was one silver plate weighing a hundred and thirty shekels, and one silver sprinkling bowl weighing seventy shekels, both according to the sanctuary shekel, each filled with fine flour mixed with oil as a grain offering; ³²one gold dish weighing ten shekels, filled with incense; ³³one young bull, one ram and one male lamb a year old, for a burnt offering; ³⁴one male goat for a sin offering; ³⁵and two oxen, five rams, five male goats and five male lambs a year old, to be sacrificed as a fellowship offering. This was the offering of Elizur son of Shedeur.

³⁶On the fifth day Shelumiel son of Zurishaddai, the leader of the people of Simeon, brought his offering.
³⁷His offering was one silver plate weighing a hundred and thirty shekels, and one silver sprinkling bowl weighing seventy shekels, both according to the sanctuary shekel, each filled with fine flour mixed with oil as a grain offering; ³⁸one gold dish weighing ten shekels, filled with incense; ³⁹one young bull, one ram and one male lamb a year old, for a burnt offering; ⁴⁰one male goat for a sin offering; ⁴¹and two oxen, five rams, five male goats and five male lambs a year old, to be sacrificed as a fellowship offering. This was the offering of Shelumiel son of Zurishaddai.

42On the sixth day Eliasaph son of Deuel, the leader of the people of Gad, brought his offering.

43His offering was one silver plate weighing a hundred and thirty shekels, and one silver sprinkling bowl weighing seventy shekels, both according to the sanctuary shekel, each filled with fine flour mixed with oil as a grain offering; 44one gold dish weighing ten shekels, filled with incense; 45one young bull, one ram and one male lamb a year old, for a burnt offering; 46one male goat for a sin offering; 47and two oxen, five rams, five male goats and five male lambs a year old, to be sacrificed as a fellowship offering. This was the offering of Eliasaph son of Deuel.

48On the seventh day Elishama son of Ammihud, the leader of the people of Ephraim, brought his offering.

49His offering was one silver plate weighing a hundred and thirty shekels, and one silver sprinkling bowl weighing seventy shekels, both according to the sanctuary shekel, each filled with fine flour mixed with oil as a grain offering; 50one gold dish weighing ten shekels, filled with incense; 51one young bull, one ram and one male lamb a year old, for a burnt offering; 52one male goat for a sin offering; 53and two oxen, five rams, five male goats and five male lambs a year old, to be sacrificed as a fellowship offering. This was the offering of Elishama son of Ammihud.

54On the eighth day Gamaliel son of Pedahzur, the leader of the people of Manasseh, brought his offering.

55His offering was one silver plate weighing a hundred and thirty shekels, and one silver sprinkling bowl weighing seventy shekels, both according to the sanctuary shekel, each filled with fine flour mixed with oil as a grain offering; 56one gold dish weighing ten shekels, filled with incense; 57one young bull, one ram and one male lamb a year old, for a burnt offering; 58one male goat for a sin offering; 59and two oxen, five rams, five male goats and five male lambs a year old, to be sacrificed as a fellowship offering. This was the offering of Gamaliel son of Pedahzur.

60On the ninth day Abidan son of Gideoni, the leader of the people of Benjamin, brought his offering.

61His offering was one silver plate weighing a hundred and thirty shekels, and one silver

42第六日來獻的，是迦得子孫的首領、丟珥的兒子以利雅薩。

43他的供物是：一個銀盤子，重一百三十舍客勒，一個銀碗，重七十舍客勒，都是按聖所的平，也都盛滿了調油的細麵作素祭；44一個金盂，重十舍客勒，盛滿了香；45一隻公牛犢，一隻公綿羊，一隻一歲的公羊羔作燔祭；46一隻公山羊作贖罪祭；47兩隻公牛，五隻公綿羊，五隻公山羊，五隻一歲的公羊羔作平安祭。這是丟珥的兒子以利雅薩的供物。

48第七日來獻的，是以法蓮子孫的首領、亞米忽的兒子以利沙瑪。

49他的供物是：一個銀盤子，重一百三十舍客勒，一個銀碗，重七十舍客勒，都是按聖所的平，也都盛滿了調油的細麵作素祭；50一個金盂，重十舍客勒，盛滿了香；51一隻公牛犢，一隻公綿羊，一隻一歲的公羊羔作燔祭；52一隻公山羊作贖罪祭；53兩隻公牛，五隻公綿羊，五隻公山羊，五隻一歲的公羊羔作平安祭。這是亞米忽兒子以利沙瑪的供物。

54第八日來獻的，是瑪拿西子孫的首領、比大薛的兒子迦瑪列。

55他的供物是：一個銀盤子，重一百三十舍客勒，一個銀碗，重七十舍客勒，都是按聖所的平，也都盛滿了調油的細麵作素祭；56一個金盂，重十舍客勒，盛滿了香；57一隻公牛犢，一隻公綿羊，一隻一歲的公羊羔作燔祭；58一隻公山羊作贖罪祭；59兩隻公牛，五隻公綿羊，五隻公山羊，五隻一歲的公羊羔作平安祭。這是比大薛兒子迦瑪列的供物。

60第九日來獻的，是便雅憫子孫的首領、基多尼的兒子亞比但。

61他的供物是：一個銀盤子，重一百三十舍客勒，一個銀碗，重七十舍客勒，都是按聖所的平，也都盛滿了調油的細麵作素祭；62一個金盂，重十舍客勒，盛滿了香；63一隻公牛犢，一隻公綿羊，一隻一歲的公羊羔作燔祭；64一隻公山羊作贖罪祭；65兩隻公牛，五隻公綿羊，五隻公山羊，五隻一歲的公羊羔作平安祭。這是基多尼兒子亞比但的供物。

66第十日來獻的，是但子孫的首領、亞米沙代的兒子亞希以謝。

67他的供物是：一個銀盤子，重一百三十舍客勒，一個銀碗，重七十舍客勒，都是按聖所的平，也都盛滿了調油的細麵作素祭；68一個金盂，重十舍客勒，盛滿了香；69一隻公牛犢，一隻公綿羊，一隻一歲的公羊羔作燔祭；70一隻公山羊作贖罪祭；71兩隻公牛，五隻公綿羊，五隻公山羊，五隻一歲的公羊羔作平安祭。這是亞米沙代兒子亞希以謝的供物。

72第十一日來獻的，是亞設子孫的首領、俄蘭的兒子帕結。

73他的供物是：一個銀盤子，重一百三十舍客勒，一個銀碗，重七十舍客勒，都是按聖所的平，也都盛滿了調油的細麵作素祭；74一個金盂，重十舍客勒，盛滿了香；75一隻公牛犢，一隻公綿羊，一隻一歲的公羊羔作燔祭；76一隻公山羊作贖罪祭；77兩隻公牛，五隻公綿羊，五隻公山羊，五隻一歲的公羊羔作平安祭。這是俄蘭兒子帕結的供物。

78第十二日來獻的，是拿弗他利子孫的首領、以南的兒子亞希拉。

79他的供物是：一個銀盤子，重一百三十舍客勒，一個銀碗，重七十舍客勒，都是按聖所的平，也都盛滿了調油的細麵作素祭；80一個金盂，重十舍客勒，盛滿了香；81一隻公牛犢，一隻公綿羊，一隻

sprinkling bowl weighing seventy shekels, both according to the sanctuary shekel, each filled with fine flour mixed with oil as a grain offering; 62one gold dish weighing ten shekels, filled with incense; 63one young bull, one ram and one male lamb a year old, for a burnt offering; 64one male goat for a sin offering; 65and two oxen, five rams, five male goats and five male lambs a year old, to be sacrificed as a fellowship offering. This was the offering of Abidan son of Gideoni.

66On the tenth day Ahiezer son of Ammishaddai, the leader of the people of Dan, brought his offering.

67His offering was one silver plate weighing a hundred and thirty shekels, and one silver sprinkling bowl weighing seventy shekels, both according to the sanctuary shekel, each filled with fine flour mixed with oil as a grain offering; 68one gold dish weighing ten shekels, filled with incense; 69one young bull, one ram and one male lamb a year old, for a burnt offering; 70one male goat for a sin offering; 71and two oxen, five rams, five male goats and five male lambs a year old, to be sacrificed as a fellowship offering. This was the offering of Ahiezer son of Ammishaddai.

72On the eleventh day Pagiel son of Ocran, the leader of the people of Asher, brought his offering.

73His offering was one silver plate weighing a hundred and thirty shekels, and one silver sprinkling bowl weighing seventy shekels, both according to the sanctuary shekel, each filled with fine flour mixed with oil as a grain offering; 74one gold dish weighing ten shekels, filled with incense; 75one young bull, one ram and one male lamb a year old, for a burnt offering; 76one male goat for a sin offering; 77and two oxen, five rams, five male goats and five male lambs a year old, to be sacrificed as a fellowship offering. This was the offering of Pagiel son of Ocran.

78On the twelfth day Ahira son of Enan, the leader of the people of Naphtali, brought his offering.

79His offering was one silver plate weighing a hundred and thirty shekels, and one silver sprinkling bowl weighing seventy shekels, both according to the sanctuary shekel, each filled with fine flour mixed with oil as a grain offering; 80one gold dish weighing ten shekels, filled with incense; 81one young bull, one ram and one male lamb a year old, for a burnt offering; [82]one male goat for a sin offering; [83]and two oxen, five rams, five male goats and five male lambs a year old, to be sacrificed as a fellowship offering. This was the offering of Ahira son of Enan.

[84]These were the offerings of the Israelite leaders for the dedication of the altar when it was anointed: twelve silver plates, twelve silver sprinkling bowls and twelve gold dishes. [85]Each silver plate weighed a hundred and thirty shekels, and each sprinkling bowl seventy shekels. Altogether, the silver dishes weighed two thousand four hundred shekels,[a] according to the sanctuary shekel. [86]The twelve gold dishes filled with incense weighed ten shekels each, according to the sanctuary shekel. Altogether, the gold dishes weighed a hundred and twenty shekels.[b] [87]The total number of animals for the burnt offering came to twelve young bulls, twelve rams and twelve male lambs a year old, together with their grain offering. Twelve male goats were used for the sin offering. [88]The total number of animals for the sacrifice of the fellowship offering came to twenty-four oxen, sixty rams, sixty male goats and sixty male lambs a year old. These were the offerings for the dedication of the altar after it was anointed.

[89]When Moses entered the Tent of Meeting to speak with the LORD, he heard the voice speaking to him from between the two cherubim above the atonement cover on the ark of the Testimony. And he spoke with him.

Setting Up the Lamps

8 The LORD said to Moses, [2]"Speak to Aaron and say to him, 'When you set up the seven lamps, they are to light the area in front of the lampstand.' "

[3]Aaron did so; he set up the lamps so that they faced forward on the lampstand, just as the LORD commanded Moses. [4]This is how the lampstand was made: It was made of hammered gold—from its base to its blossoms. The lampstand was made exactly like the pattern the LORD had shown Moses.

The Setting Apart of the Levites

[5]The LORD said to Moses: [6]"Take the Levites from among the other Israelites and make them ceremonially clean. [7]To purify them, do this: Sprinkle the water of cleansing on them; then

一歲的公羊羔作燔祭；[82]一隻公山羊作贖罪祭；[83]兩隻公牛，五隻公綿羊，五隻公山羊，五隻一歲的公羊羔作平安祭。這是<u>以南</u>兒子<u>亞希拉</u>的供物。

[84]用膏抹壇的日子，<u>以色列</u>的眾首領為行獻壇之禮所獻的是：銀盤子十二個，銀碗十二個，金盂十二個。[85]每盤子重一百三十舍客勒，每碗重七十舍客勒，一切器皿的銀子，按聖所的平，共有二千四百舍客勒。[86]十二個金盂盛滿了香，按聖所的平，每盂重十舍客勒，所有的金子共一百二十舍客勒。[87]作燔祭的，共有公牛十二隻，公羊十二隻，一歲的公羊羔十二隻，並同獻的素祭作贖罪祭的公山羊十二隻。[88]作平安祭的，共有公牛二十四隻，公綿羊六十隻，公山羊六十隻，一歲的公羊羔六十隻。這就是用膏抹壇之後，為行奉獻壇之禮所獻的。

[89]<u>摩西</u>進會幕要與耶和華說話的時候，聽見法櫃的施恩座以上、二基路伯中間，有與他說話的聲音，就是耶和華與他說話。

點燈之例

8 耶和華曉諭<u>摩西</u>說：[2]"你告訴<u>亞倫</u>說：'點燈的時候，七盞燈都要向燈臺前面發光。'"

[3]<u>亞倫</u>便這樣行；他點燈臺上的燈，使燈向前發光，是照耶和華所吩咐<u>摩西</u>的。[4]這燈臺的做法，是用金子錘出來的，連座帶花都是錘出來的。<u>摩西</u>製造燈臺，是照耶和華所指示的樣式。

利未人分別為聖

[5]耶和華曉諭<u>摩西</u>說：[6]"你從<u>以色列</u>人中選出<u>利未</u>人來，潔淨他們。[7]潔淨他們當這樣行：用除罪水彈在他們身上，又叫他們用剃頭刀刮全

---

a 85 That is, about 60 pounds (about 28 kilograms)

b 86 That is, about 3 pounds (about 1.4 kilograms)

身，洗衣服，潔淨自己。⁸然後叫他們取一隻公牛犢，並同獻的素祭，就是調油的細麵；你要另取一隻公牛犢作贖罪祭。⁹將利未人奉到會幕前，招聚以色列全會眾。¹⁰將利未人奉到耶和華面前，以色列人要按手在他們頭上。¹¹亞倫也將他們奉到耶和華面前，為以色列人當作搖祭，使他們好辦耶和華的事。

¹²「利未人要按手在那兩隻牛的頭上。你要將一隻作贖罪祭，一隻作燔祭，獻給耶和華，為利未人贖罪。¹³你也要使利未人站在亞倫和他兒子面前，將他們當作搖祭奉給耶和華。¹⁴這樣，你從以色列人中將利未人分別出來，利未人便要歸我。

¹⁵「此後利未人要進去辦會幕的事；你要潔淨他們，將他們當作搖祭奉上。¹⁶因為他們是從以色列人中全然給我的，我揀選他們歸我，是代替以色列人中一切頭生的。¹⁷以色列人中一切頭生的，連人帶牲畜，都是我的。我在埃及地擊殺一切頭生的那天，將他們分別為聖歸我。¹⁸我揀選利未人代替以色列人中一切頭生的。¹⁹我從以色列人中，將利未人當作賞賜給亞倫和他的兒子，在會幕中辦以色列人的事，又為以色列人贖罪，免得他們挨近聖所，有災殃臨到他們中間。」

²⁰摩西、亞倫並以色列全會眾，便向利未人如此行。凡耶和華指着利未人所吩咐摩西的，以色列人就向他們這樣行。²¹於是利未人潔淨自己，除了罪，洗了衣服，亞倫將他們當作搖祭奉到耶和華面前，又為他們贖罪，潔淨他們。²²然後利未人進去，在亞倫和他兒子面前，在會幕中辦事。耶和華指着利未人怎樣吩咐摩西，以色列人就這樣向他們行了。

²³耶和華曉諭摩西說：²⁴「利未人是這樣：從二十五歲以外，他們要前來任職，辦會幕的事。²⁵到了五十歲要停工退任，不再辦事。²⁶只要在會幕裏和他們的弟兄一同伺候，謹守

have them shave their whole bodies and wash their clothes, and so purify themselves. ⁸Have them take a young bull with its grain offering of fine flour mixed with oil; then you are to take a second young bull for a sin offering. ⁹Bring the Levites to the front of the Tent of Meeting and assemble the whole Israelite community. ¹⁰You are to bring the Levites before the LORD, and the Israelites are to lay their hands on them. ¹¹Aaron is to present the Levites before the LORD as a wave offering from the Israelites, so that they may be ready to do the work of the LORD.

¹²"After the Levites lay their hands on the heads of the bulls, use the one for a sin offering to the LORD and the other for a burnt offering, to make atonement for the Levites. ¹³Have the Levites stand in front of Aaron and his sons and then present them as a wave offering to the LORD. ¹⁴In this way you are to set the Levites apart from the other Israelites, and the Levites will be mine.

¹⁵"After you have purified the Levites and presented them as a wave offering, they are to come to do their work at the Tent of Meeting. ¹⁶They are the Israelites who are to be given wholly to me. I have taken them as my own in place of the firstborn, the first male offspring from every Israelite woman. ¹⁷Every firstborn male in Israel, whether man or animal, is mine. When I struck down all the firstborn in Egypt, I set them apart for myself. ¹⁸And I have taken the Levites in place of all the firstborn sons in Israel. ¹⁹Of all the Israelites, I have given the Levites as gifts to Aaron and his sons to do the work at the Tent of Meeting on behalf of the Israelites and to make atonement for them so that no plague will strike the Israelites when they go near the sanctuary."

²⁰Moses, Aaron and the whole Israelite community did with the Levites just as the LORD commanded Moses. ²¹The Levites purified themselves and washed their clothes. Then Aaron presented them as a wave offering before the LORD and made atonement for them to purify them. ²²After that, the Levites came to do their work at the Tent of Meeting under the supervision of Aaron and his sons. They did with the Levites just as the LORD commanded Moses.

²³The LORD said to Moses, ²⁴"This applies to the Levites: Men twenty-five years old or more shall come to take part in the work at the Tent of Meeting, ²⁵but at the age of fifty, they must retire from their regular service and work no longer. ²⁶They may assist their brothers in performing their duties at the Tent of Meeting, but

they themselves must not do the work. This, then, is how you are to assign the responsibilities of the Levites."

The Passover

9 The LORD spoke to Moses in the Desert of Sinai in the first month of the second year after they came out of Egypt. He said, ²"Have the Israelites celebrate the Passover at the appointed time. ³Celebrate it at the appointed time, at twilight on the fourteenth day of this month, in accordance with all its rules and regulations."

⁴So Moses told the Israelites to celebrate the Passover, ⁵and they did so in the Desert of Sinai at twilight on the fourteenth day of the first month. The Israelites did everything just as the LORD commanded Moses.

⁶But some of them could not celebrate the Passover on that day because they were ceremonially unclean on account of a dead body. So they came to Moses and Aaron that same day ⁷and said to Moses, "We have become unclean because of a dead body, but why should we be kept from presenting the LORD's offering with the other Israelites at the appointed time?"

⁸Moses answered them, "Wait until I find out what the LORD commands concerning you."

⁹Then the LORD said to Moses, ¹⁰"Tell the Israelites: 'When any of you or your descendants are unclean because of a dead body or are away on a journey, they may still celebrate the LORD's Passover. ¹¹They are to celebrate it on the fourteenth day of the second month at twilight. They are to eat the lamb, together with unleavened bread and bitter herbs. ¹²They must not leave any of it till morning or break any of its bones. When they celebrate the Passover, they must follow all the regulations. ¹³But if a man who is ceremonially clean and not on a journey fails to celebrate the Passover, that person must be cut off from his people because he did not present the LORD's offering at the appointed time. That man will bear the consequences of his sin.

¹⁴" 'An alien living among you who wants to celebrate the LORD's Passover must do so in accordance with its rules and regulations. You must have the same regulations for the alien and the native-born.' "

The Cloud Above the Tabernacle

¹⁵On the day the tabernacle, the Tent of the Testimony, was set up, the cloud covered it. From evening till morning the cloud above the tabernacle looked like fire. ¹⁶That is how it con-

所吩咐的，不再辦事了。至於所吩咐利未人的，你要這樣向他們行。"

逾越節

9 以色列人出埃及地以後，第二年正月，耶和華在西奈的曠野吩咐摩西說：² "以色列人應當在所定的日期守逾越節，³就是本月十四日黃昏的時候，你們要在所定的日期守這節，要按這節的律例、典章而守。"

⁴於是摩西吩咐以色列人守逾越節。⁵他們就在西奈的曠野，正月十四日黃昏的時候守逾越節。凡耶和華所吩咐摩西的，以色列人都照樣行了。

⁶有幾個人因死屍而不潔淨，不能在那日守逾越節。當日他們到摩西、亞倫面前，⁷說："我們雖因死屍而不潔淨，為何被阻止不得同以色列人在所定的日期獻耶和華的供物呢？"

⁸摩西對他們說："你們暫且等候，我可以去聽耶和華指著你們是怎樣吩咐的。"

⁹耶和華對摩西說：¹⁰ "你曉諭以色列人說：'你們和你們後代中，若有人因死屍而不潔淨，或在遠方行路，還要向耶和華守逾越節。¹¹他們要在二月十四日黃昏的時候守逾越節。要用無酵餅與苦菜，和逾越節的羊羔同吃。¹²一點不可留到早晨，羊羔的骨頭一根也不可折斷。他們要照逾越節的一切律例而守。¹³但潔淨而不行路的人，若推辭不守逾越節，那人要從民中剪除，因為他在所定的日期不獻耶和華的供物，應該擔當他的罪。

¹⁴ " '若有外人寄居在你們中間，願意向耶和華守逾越節，他要照逾越節的律例、典章行，不管是寄居的，是本地人，同歸一例。' "

雲彩遮蓋會幕

¹⁵立起帳幕的那日，有雲彩遮蓋帳幕，就是法櫃的帳幕。從晚上到早晨，雲彩在其上，形狀如火。¹⁶常是

這樣，雲彩遮蓋帳幕，夜間形狀如火。¹⁷雲彩幾時從帳幕收上去，<u>以色列人就幾時起行</u>；雲彩在哪裏停住，<u>以色列人就在那裏安營</u>。¹⁸<u>以色列人遵耶和華的吩咐起行</u>；也遵耶和華的吩咐安營。雲彩在帳幕上停住幾時，他們就住營幾時。¹⁹雲彩在帳幕上停留許多日子，<u>以色列人就守耶和華所吩咐的不起行</u>。²⁰有時雲彩在帳幕上幾天，他們就照耶和華的吩咐住營，也照耶和華的吩咐起行。²¹有時從晚上到早晨，有這雲彩在帳幕上，早晨雲彩收上去，他們就起行。有時晝夜雲彩停在帳幕上，收上去的時候，他們就起行。²²雲彩停留在帳幕上，無論是兩天，是一月，是一年，<u>以色列人就住營不起行</u>；但雲彩收上去，他們就起行。²³他們遵耶和華的吩咐安營，也遵耶和華的吩咐起行。他們守耶和華所吩咐的，都是憑耶和華吩咐<u>摩西</u>的。

銀號

10 耶和華曉諭<u>摩西</u>說：²"你要用銀子做兩枝號，都要錘出來的，用以招聚會眾，並叫眾營起行。³吹這號的時候，全會眾要到你那裏，聚集在會幕門口。⁴若單吹一枝，眾首領，就是<u>以色列</u>軍中的統領，要聚集到你那裏。⁵吹出大聲的時候，東邊安的營都要起行。⁶二次吹出大聲的時候，南邊安的營都要起行，他們將起行必吹出大聲。⁷但招聚會眾的時候，你們要吹號，卻不要吹出大聲。

⁸"<u>亞倫</u>子孫作祭司的要吹這號，這要作你們世世代代永遠的定例。⁹你們在自己的地，與欺壓你們的敵人打仗，就要用號吹出大聲，便在耶和華你們的神面前得蒙記念，也蒙拯救脫離仇敵。¹⁰在你們快樂的日子和節期，並月朔，獻燔祭和平安祭，也要吹號，這都要在你們的神面前作為記念。我是耶和華你們的神。"

tinued to be; the cloud covered it, and at night it looked like fire. ¹⁷Whenever the cloud lifted from above the Tent, the Israelites set out; wherever the cloud settled, the Israelites encamped. ¹⁸At the LORD's command the Israelites set out, and at his command they encamped. As long as the cloud stayed over the tabernacle, they remained in camp. ¹⁹When the cloud remained over the tabernacle a long time, the Israelites obeyed the LORD's order and did not set out. ²⁰Sometimes the cloud was over the tabernacle only a few days; at the LORD's command they would encamp, and then at his command they would set out. ²¹Sometimes the cloud stayed only from evening till morning, and when it lifted in the morning, they set out. Whether by day or by night, whenever the cloud lifted, they set out. ²²Whether the cloud stayed over the tabernacle for two days or a month or a year, the Israelites would remain in camp and not set out; but when it lifted, they would set out. ²³At the LORD's command they encamped, and at the LORD's command they set out. They obeyed the LORD's order, in accordance with his command through Moses.

The Silver Trumpets

10 The LORD said to Moses: ²"Make two trumpets of hammered silver, and use them for calling the community together and for having the camps set out. ³When both are sounded, the whole community is to assemble before you at the entrance to the Tent of Meeting. ⁴If only one is sounded, the leaders—the heads of the clans of Israel—are to assemble before you. ⁵When a trumpet blast is sounded, the tribes camping on the east are to set out. ⁶At the sounding of a second blast, the camps on the south are to set out. The blast will be the signal for setting out. ⁷To gather the assembly, blow the trumpets, but not with the same signal.

⁸"The sons of Aaron, the priests, are to blow the trumpets. This is to be a lasting ordinance for you and the generations to come. ⁹When you go into battle in your own land against an enemy who is oppressing you, sound a blast on the trumpets. Then you will be remembered by the LORD your God and rescued from your enemies. ¹⁰Also at your times of rejoicing—your appointed feasts and New Moon festivals—you are to sound the trumpets over your burnt offerings and fellowship offerings,^a and they will be a memorial for you before your God. I am the LORD your God."

a 10 Traditionally peace offerings

The Israelites Leave Sinai

[11]On the twentieth day of the second month of the second year, the cloud lifted from above the tabernacle of the Testimony. [12]Then the Israelites set out from the Desert of Sinai and traveled from place to place until the cloud came to rest in the Desert of Paran. [13]They set out, this first time, at the LORD's command through Moses.

[14]The divisions of the camp of Judah went first, under their standard. Nahshon son of Amminadab was in command. [15]Nethanel son of Zuar was over the division of the tribe of Issachar, [16]and Eliab son of Helon was over the division of the tribe of Zebulun. [17]Then the tabernacle was taken down, and the Gershonites and Merarites, who carried it, set out.

[18]The divisions of the camp of Reuben went next, under their standard. Elizur son of Shedeur was in command. [19]Shelumiel son of Zurishaddai was over the division of the tribe of Simeon, [20]and Eliasaph son of Deuel was over the division of the tribe of Gad. [21]Then the Kohathites set out, carrying the holy things. The tabernacle was to be set up before they arrived.

[22]The divisions of the camp of Ephraim went next, under their standard. Elishama son of Ammihud was in command. [23]Gamaliel son of Pedahzur was over the division of the tribe of Manasseh, [24]and Abidan son of Gideoni was over the division of the tribe of Benjamin.

[25]Finally, as the rear guard for all the units, the divisions of the camp of Dan set out, under their standard. Ahiezer son of Ammishaddai was in command. [26]Pagiel son of Ocran was over the division of the tribe of Asher, [27]and Ahira son of Enan was over the division of the tribe of Naphtali. [28]This was the order of march for the Israelite divisions as they set out.

[29]Now Moses said to Hobab son of Reuel the Midianite, Moses' father-in-law, "We are setting out for the place about which the LORD said, 'I will give it to you.' Come with us and we will treat you well, for the LORD has promised good things to Israel."

[30]He answered, "No, I will not go; I am going back to my own land and my own people."

[31]But Moses said, "Please do not leave us. You know where we should camp in the desert, and you can be our eyes. [32]If you come with us, we will share with you whatever good things the LORD gives us."

[33]So they set out from the mountain of the LORD and traveled for three days. The ark of the covenant of the LORD went before them during those three days to find them a place to rest.

以色列人離開西奈

[11]第二年二月二十日，雲彩從法櫃的帳幕收上去。[12]以色列人就按站往前行，離開西奈的曠野，雲彩停住在巴蘭的曠野。[13]這是他們照耶和華藉摩西所吩咐的，初次往前行。

[14]按着軍隊首先往前行的是猶大營的纛。統領軍隊的是亞米拿達的兒子拿順；[15]統領以薩迦支派軍隊的是蘇押的兒子拿坦業；[16]統領西布倫支派軍隊的是希倫的兒子以利押。[17]帳幕拆卸，革順的子孫和米拉利的子孫，就抬着帳幕先往前行。

[18]按着軍隊往前行的是呂便營的纛。統領軍隊的是示丟珥的兒子以利蓿；[19]統領西緬支派軍隊的是蘇利沙代的兒子示路蔑；[20]統領迦得支派軍隊的是丟珥的兒子以利雅薩。[21]哥轄人抬着聖物先往前行，他們未到以前，抬帳幕的已經把帳幕支好。

[22]按着軍隊往前行的是以法蓮營的纛。統領軍隊的是亞米忽的兒子以利沙瑪；[23]統領瑪拿西支派軍隊的是比大蓿的兒子迦瑪列；[24]統領便雅憫支派軍隊的是基多尼的兒子亞比但。

[25]在諸營末後的是但營的纛，按着軍隊往前行。統領軍隊的是亞米沙代的兒子亞希以謝；[26]統領亞設支派軍隊的是俄蘭的兒子帕結；[27]統領拿弗他利支派軍隊的是以南的兒子亞希拉。[28]以色列人按着軍隊往前行，就是這樣。

[29]摩西對他岳父（註：或作"內兄"）米甸人流珥的兒子何巴說："我們要行路往耶和華所應許之地去，他曾說：'我要將這地賜給你們。'現在求你和我們同去，我們必厚待你，因為耶和華指着以色列人已經應許給好處。"

[30]何巴回答說："我不去，我要回本地本族那裏去。"

[31]摩西說："求你不要離開我們，因為你知道我們要在曠野安營，你可以當作我們的眼目。[32]你若和我們同去，將來耶和華有甚麼好處待我們，我們也必以甚麼好處待你。"

[33]以色列人離開耶和華的山，往前行了三天的路程；耶和華的約櫃在前頭行了三天的路程，為他們尋找安

歇的地方。³⁴他們拔營往前行，日間有耶和華的雲彩在他們以上。

³⁵約櫃往前行的時候，摩西就説：

"耶和華啊，求你興起！
願你的仇敵四散，
願恨你的人從你面前逃跑。"

³⁶約櫃停住的時候，他就説：

"耶和華啊，
求你回到以色列的千萬人中！"

主使火焚燒

11 眾百姓發怨言，他們的惡語達到耶和華的耳中。耶和華聽見了就怒氣發作，使火在他們中間焚燒，直燒到營的邊界。²百姓向摩西哀求，摩西祈求耶和華，火就熄了。³那地方便叫作他備拉，因為耶和華的火燒在他們中間。

主賜鵪鶉

⁴他們中間的閒雜人大起貪慾的心，以色列人又哭號説："誰給我們肉吃呢？⁵我們記得在埃及的時候，不花錢就吃魚，也記得有黃瓜、西瓜、韭菜、葱、蒜。⁶現在我們的心血枯竭了，除這嗎哪以外，在我們眼前並沒有別的東西！"

⁷這嗎哪彷彿芫荽子，又好像珍珠。⁸百姓周圍行走，把嗎哪收起來，或用磨推，或用臼搗，煮在鍋中，又做成餅，滋味好像新油。⁹夜間露水降在營中，嗎哪也隨着降下。

¹⁰摩西聽見百姓各在各家的帳棚門口哭號，耶和華的怒氣便大發作，摩西就不喜悦。¹¹摩西對耶和華説："你為何苦待僕人？我為何不在你眼前蒙恩，竟把這管理百姓的重任加在我身上呢？¹²這百姓豈是我懷的胎，豈是我生下來的呢？你竟對我説：'把他們抱在懷裏，如養育之父抱吃奶的孩子，直抱到你起誓應許給他們祖宗的地去。'¹³我從哪裏得肉給這百姓吃呢？他們都向我哭號説：'你給我們肉吧！'¹⁴管理這百姓的責任太重了，我獨自擔當不起。¹⁵你這樣待我，我若在你眼前蒙恩，求你立

³⁴The cloud of the LORD was over them by day when they set out from the camp.

³⁵Whenever the ark set out, Moses said,

"Rise up, O LORD!
May your enemies be scattered;
may your foes flee before you."

³⁶Whenever it came to rest, he said,

"Return, O LORD,
to the countless thousands of Israel."

Fire From the LORD

11 Now the people complained about their hardships in the hearing of the LORD, and when he heard them his anger was aroused. Then fire from the LORD burned among them and consumed some of the outskirts of the camp. ²When the people cried out to Moses, he prayed to the LORD and the fire died down. ³So that place was called Taberah,ᵃ because fire from the LORD had burned among them.

Quail From the LORD

⁴The rabble with them began to crave other food, and again the Israelites started wailing and said, "If only we had meat to eat! ⁵We remember the fish we ate in Egypt at no cost— also the cucumbers, melons, leeks, onions and garlic. ⁶But now we have lost our appetite; we never see anything but this manna!"

⁷The manna was like coriander seed and looked like resin. ⁸The people went around gathering it, and then ground it in a handmill or crushed it in a mortar. They cooked it in a pot or made it into cakes. And it tasted like something made with olive oil. ⁹When the dew settled on the camp at night, the manna also came down.

¹⁰Moses heard the people of every family wailing, each at the entrance to his tent. The LORD became exceedingly angry, and Moses was troubled. ¹¹He asked the LORD, "Why have you brought this trouble on your servant? What have I done to displease you that you put the burden of all these people on me? ¹²Did I conceive all these people? Did I give them birth? Why do you tell me to carry them in my arms, as a nurse carries an infant, to the land you promised on oath to their forefathers? ¹³Where can I get meat for all these people? They keep wailing to me, 'Give us meat to eat!' ¹⁴I cannot carry all these people by myself; the burden is too heavy for me. ¹⁵If this is how you are going

a 3 Taberah means burning.

to treat me, put me to death right now—if I have found favor in your eyes—and do not let me face my own ruin."

¹⁶The LORD said to Moses: "Bring me seventy of Israel's elders who are known to you as leaders and officials among the people. Have them come to the Tent of Meeting, that they may stand there with you. ¹⁷I will come down and speak with you there, and I will take of the Spirit that is on you and put the Spirit on them. They will help you carry the burden of the people so that you will not have to carry it alone.

¹⁸"Tell the people: 'Consecrate yourselves in preparation for tomorrow, when you will eat meat. The LORD heard you when you wailed, "If only we had meat to eat! We were better off in Egypt!" Now the LORD will give you meat, and you will eat it. ¹⁹You will not eat it for just one day, or two days, or five, ten or twenty days, ²⁰but for a whole month—until it comes out of your nostrils and you loathe it—because you have rejected the LORD, who is among you, and have wailed before him, saying, "Why did we ever leave Egypt?" ' "

²¹But Moses said, "Here I am among six hundred thousand men on foot, and you say, 'I will give them meat to eat for a whole month!' ²²Would they have enough if flocks and herds were slaughtered for them? Would they have enough if all the fish in the sea were caught for them?"

²³The LORD answered Moses, "Is the LORD's arm too short? You will now see whether or not what I say will come true for you."

²⁴So Moses went out and told the people what the LORD had said. He brought together seventy of their elders and had them stand around the Tent. ²⁵Then the LORD came down in the cloud and spoke with him, and he took of the Spirit that was on him and put the Spirit on the seventy elders. When the Spirit rested on them, they prophesied, but they did not do so again.^a

²⁶However, two men, whose names were Eldad and Medad, had remained in the camp. They were listed among the elders, but did not go out to the Tent. Yet the Spirit also rested on them, and they prophesied in the camp. ²⁷A young man ran and told Moses, "Eldad and Medad are prophesying in the camp."

²⁸Joshua son of Nun, who had been Moses' aide since youth, spoke up and said, "Moses, my lord, stop them!"

²⁹But Moses replied, "Are you jealous for my

時將我殺了,不叫我見自己的苦情。"

¹⁶耶和華對摩西說:"你從以色列的長老中招聚七十個人,就是你所知道作百姓的長老和官長的,到我這裏來,領他們到會幕前,使他們和你一同站立。¹⁷我要在那裏降臨與你說話,也要把降於你身上的靈分賜他們,他們就和你同當這管百姓的重任,免得你獨自擔當。

¹⁸又要對百姓說:'你們應當自潔,預備明天吃肉,因為你們哭號說:誰給我們肉吃!我們在埃及很好。這聲音達到了耶和華的耳中,所以他必給你們肉吃。¹⁹你們不止吃一天、兩天、五天、十天、二十天,²⁰要吃一個整月,甚至肉從你們鼻孔裏噴出來,使你們厭惡了,因為你們厭棄住在你們中間的耶和華,在他面前哭號說:我們為何出了埃及呢?'"

²¹摩西對耶和華說:"這與我同住的百姓,步行的男人有六十萬,你還說:'我要把肉給他們,使他們可以吃一個整月。'²²難道給他們宰了羊羣牛羣,或是把海中所有的魚都聚了來,就夠他們吃嗎?"

²³耶和華對摩西說:"耶和華的膀臂豈是縮短了嗎?現在要看我的話向你應驗不應驗!"

²⁴摩西出去,將耶和華的話告訴百姓,又招聚百姓的長老中七十個人來,使他們站在會幕的四圍。²⁵耶和華在雲中降臨,對摩西說話,把降與他身上的靈分賜那七十個長老,靈停在他們身上的時候,他們就受感說話,以後卻沒有再說。

²⁶但有兩個人仍在營裏,一個名叫伊利達,一個名叫米達。他們本是在那些被錄的人中,卻沒有到會幕那裏去。靈停在他們身上,他們就在營裏說預言。²⁷有個少年人跑來告訴摩西說:"伊利達、米達在營裏說預言。"

²⁸摩西的幫手,嫩的兒子約書亞,就是摩西所揀選的一個人,說:"請我主摩西禁止他們!"

²⁹摩西對他說:"你為我的緣故

^a 25 Or *prophesied and continued to do so*

嫉妒人嗎？惟願耶和華的百姓都受感說話，願耶和華把他的靈降在他們身上！」30於是，摩西和以色列的長老都回到營裏去了。

31有風從耶和華那裏颳起，把鵪鶉由海面颳來，飛散在營邊和營的四圍；這邊約有一天的路程，那邊約有一天的路程，離地面約有二肘。32百姓起來，終日終夜，並次日一整天，捕取鵪鶉，至少的也取了十賀梅珥，為自己擺列在營的四圍。33肉在他們牙齒之間，尚未嚼爛，耶和華的怒氣就向他們發作，用最重的災殃擊殺了他們。34那地方便叫作基博羅哈他瓦（註：就是"貪慾之人的墳墓"），因為他們在那裏埋那起貪慾之心的人。

35百姓從基博羅哈他瓦走到哈洗錄，就住在哈洗錄。

米利暗與亞倫反對摩西

12 摩西娶了古實女子為妻。米利暗和亞倫因他所娶的古實女子，就毀謗他，說：2「難道耶和華單與摩西說話，不也與我們說話嗎？」這話耶和華聽見了。

3摩西為人極其謙和，勝過世上的眾人。

4耶和華忽然對摩西、亞倫、米利暗說：「你們三個人都出來到會幕這裏。」他們三個人就出來了。5耶和華在雲柱中降臨，站在會幕門口，召亞倫和米利暗，二人就出來了。6耶和華說：「你們且聽我的話：

"你們中間若有先知，
　我耶和華必在異象中向他顯現，
　在夢中與他說話。
7我的僕人摩西不是這樣，
　他是在我全家盡忠的。
8我要與他面對面說話，
　乃是明說，不用謎語，
　並且他必見我的形像。
　你們毀謗我的僕人摩西，
　為何不懼怕呢？"

sake? I wish that all the LORD's people were prophets and that the LORD would put his Spirit on them!" 30Then Moses and the elders of Israel returned to the camp.

31Now a wind went out from the LORD and drove quail in from the sea. It brought them[a] down all around the camp to about three feet[b] above the ground, as far as a day's walk in any direction. 32All that day and night and all the next day the people went out and gathered quail. No one gathered less than ten homers.[c] Then they spread them out all around the camp. 33But while the meat was still between their teeth and before it could be consumed, the anger of the LORD burned against the people, and he struck them with a severe plague. 34Therefore the place was named Kibroth Hattaavah,[d] because there they buried the people who had craved other food.

35From Kibroth Hattaavah the people traveled to Hazeroth and stayed there.

Miriam and Aaron Oppose Moses

12 Miriam and Aaron began to talk against Moses because of his Cushite wife, for he had married a Cushite. 2"Has the LORD spoken only through Moses?" they asked. "Hasn't he also spoken through us?" And the LORD heard this.

3(Now Moses was a very humble man, more humble than anyone else on the face of the earth.)

4At once the LORD said to Moses, Aaron and Miriam, "Come out to the Tent of Meeting, all three of you." So the three of them came out. 5Then the LORD came down in a pillar of cloud; he stood at the entrance to the Tent and summoned Aaron and Miriam. When both of them stepped forward, 6he said, "Listen to my words:

"When a prophet of the LORD is among you,
　I reveal myself to him in visions,
　I speak to him in dreams.
7But this is not true of my servant Moses;
　he is faithful in all my house.
8With him I speak face to face,
　clearly and not in riddles;
　he sees the form of the LORD.
　Why then were you not afraid
　to speak against my servant Moses?"

a 31 Or They flew　b 31 Hebrew two cubits (about 1 meter)
c 32 That is, probably about 60 bushels (about 2.2 kiloliters)
d 34 Kibroth Hattaavah means graves of craving.

⁹The anger of the LORD burned against them, and he left them.

¹⁰When the cloud lifted from above the Tent, there stood Miriam—leprous,ᵃ like snow. Aaron turned toward her and saw that she had leprosy; ¹¹and he said to Moses, "Please, my lord, do not hold against us the sin we have so foolishly committed. ¹²Do not let her be like a stillborn infant coming from its mother's womb with its flesh half eaten away."

¹³So Moses cried out to the LORD, "O God, please heal her!"

¹⁴The LORD replied to Moses, "If her father had spit in her face, would she not have been in disgrace for seven days? Confine her outside the camp for seven days; after that she can be brought back." ¹⁵So Miriam was confined outside the camp for seven days, and the people did not move on till she was brought back.

¹⁶After that, the people left Hazeroth and encamped in the Desert of Paran.

Exploring Canaan

13 The LORD said to Moses, ²"Send some men to explore the land of Canaan, which I am giving to the Israelites. From each ancestral tribe send one of its leaders."

³So at the LORD's command Moses sent them out from the Desert of Paran. All of them were leaders of the Israelites. ⁴These are their names:

from the tribe of Reuben, Shammua son of Zaccur;
⁵from the tribe of Simeon, Shaphat son of Hori;
⁶from the tribe of Judah, Caleb son of Jephunneh;
⁷from the tribe of Issachar, Igal son of Joseph;
⁸from the tribe of Ephraim, Hoshea son of Nun;
⁹from the tribe of Benjamin, Palti son of Raphu;
¹⁰from the tribe of Zebulun, Gaddiel son of Sodi;
¹¹from the tribe of Manasseh (a tribe of Joseph), Gaddi son of Susi;
¹²from the tribe of Dan, Ammiel son of Gemalli;
¹³from the tribe of Asher, Sethur son of Michael;
¹⁴from the tribe of Naphtali, Nahbi son of Vophsi;
¹⁵from the tribe of Gad, Geuel son of Maki.

ᵃ 10 The Hebrew word was used for various diseases affecting the skin—not necessarily leprosy.

⁹耶和華就向他們二人發怒而去。

¹⁰雲彩從會幕上挪開了。不料，米利暗長了大痲瘋，有雪那樣白。亞倫一看米利暗長了大痲瘋，¹¹就對摩西說：「我主啊，求你不要因我們愚昧犯罪，便將這罪加在我們身上。¹²求你不要使她像那出母腹、肉已半爛的死胎。」

¹³於是摩西哀求耶和華說：「神啊，求你醫治她！」

¹⁴耶和華對摩西說：「她父親若吐唾沫在她臉上，她豈不蒙羞七天嗎？現在要把她在營外關鎖七天，然後才可以領她進來。」¹⁵於是米利暗關鎖在營外七天。百姓沒有行路，直等到把米利暗領進來。

¹⁶以後百姓從哈洗錄起行，在巴蘭的曠野安營。

窺探迦南地

13 耶和華曉諭摩西說：²"你打發人去窺探我所賜給以色列人的迦南地，他們每支派中要打發一個人，都要作首領的。"

³摩西就照耶和華的吩咐，從巴蘭的曠野打發他們去，他們都是以色列人的族長。⁴他們的名字：

屬呂便支派的有撒刻的兒子沙母亞；
⁵屬西緬支派的有何利的兒子沙法；
⁶屬猶大支派的有耶孚尼的兒子迦勒；
⁷屬以薩迦支派的有約色的兒子以迦；
⁸屬以法蓮支派的有嫩的兒子何西阿；
⁹屬便雅憫支派的有拉孚的兒子帕提；
¹⁰屬西布倫支派的有梭底的兒子迦疊；
¹¹約瑟的子孫屬瑪拿西支派的有穌西的兒子迦底；
¹²屬但支派的有基瑪利的兒子亞米利；
¹³屬亞設支派的有米迦勒的兒子西帖；
¹⁴屬拿弗他利支派的有縛西的兒子拿比；
¹⁵屬迦得支派的有瑪基的兒子臼利。

¹⁶這就是<u>摩西</u>所打發窺探那地之人的名字。<u>摩西</u>就稱<u>嫩</u>的兒子<u>何西阿</u>為<u>約書亞</u>。

¹⁷<u>摩西</u>打發他們去窺探<u>迦南</u>地，說："你們從南地上山地去，¹⁸看那地如何，其中所住的民是強是弱，是多是少，¹⁹所住之地是好是歹，所住之處是營盤是堅城？²⁰又看那地土是肥美是瘠薄，其中有樹木沒有？你們要放開膽量，把那地的果子帶些來。"那時正是葡萄初熟的時候。

²¹他們上去窺探那地，從<u>尋</u>的曠野到<u>利合</u>，直到<u>哈馬口</u>。²²他們從南地上去，到了<u>希伯崙</u>，在那裏有<u>亞衲</u>族人<u>亞希幔</u>、<u>示篩</u>、<u>撻買</u>。原來<u>希伯崙</u>城被建造比<u>埃及</u>的<u>鎖安</u>城早七年。²³他們到了<u>以實各谷</u>，從那裏砍了葡萄樹的一枝，上頭有一掛葡萄，兩個人用杠抬着，又帶了些石榴和無花果來。²⁴因為<u>以色列</u>人從那裏砍來的那掛葡萄，所以那地方叫做<u>以實各谷</u>。²⁵過了四十天，他們窺探那地才回來。

報告窺探結果

²⁶到了<u>巴蘭</u>曠野的<u>加低斯</u>，見<u>摩西</u>、<u>亞倫</u>並<u>以色列</u>的全會眾，回報<u>摩西</u>、<u>亞倫</u>並全會眾，又把那地的果子給他們看。²⁷又告訴<u>摩西</u>說："我們到了你所打發我們去的那地，果然是流奶與蜜之地，這就是那地的果子。²⁸然而住那地的民強壯，城邑也堅固寬大，並且我們在那裏看見了<u>亞衲</u>族的人。²⁹<u>亞瑪力</u>人住在南地；<u>赫</u>人、<u>耶布斯</u>人、<u>亞摩利</u>人住在山地；<u>迦南</u>人住在海邊，並<u>約旦河</u>旁。"

³⁰<u>迦勒</u>在<u>摩西</u>面前安撫百姓，說："我們立刻上去得那地吧！我們足能得勝。"

³¹但那些和他同去的人說："我們不能上去攻擊那民，因為他們比我們強壯。"³²探子中有人論到所窺探之地，向<u>以色列</u>人報惡信，說："我

¹⁶These are the names of the men Moses sent to explore the land. (Moses gave Hoshea son of Nun the name Joshua.)

¹⁷When Moses sent them to explore Canaan, he said, "Go up through the Negev and on into the hill country. ¹⁸See what the land is like and whether the people who live there are strong or weak, few or many. ¹⁹What kind of land do they live in? Is it good or bad? What kind of towns do they live in? Are they unwalled or fortified? ²⁰How is the soil? Is it fertile or poor? Are there trees on it or not? Do your best to bring back some of the fruit of the land." (It was the season for the first ripe grapes.)

²¹So they went up and explored the land from the Desert of Zin as far as Rehob, toward Lebo[a] Hamath. ²²They went up through the Negev and came to Hebron, where Ahiman, Sheshai and Talmai, the descendants of Anak, lived. (Hebron had been built seven years before Zoan in Egypt.) ²³When they reached the Valley of Eshcol,[b] they cut off a branch bearing a single cluster of grapes. Two of them carried it on a pole between them, along with some pomegranates and figs. ²⁴That place was called the Valley of Eshcol because of the cluster of grapes the Israelites cut off there. ²⁵At the end of forty days they returned from exploring the land.

Report on the Exploration

²⁶They came back to Moses and Aaron and the whole Israelite community at Kadesh in the Desert of Paran. There they reported to them and to the whole assembly and showed them the fruit of the land. ²⁷They gave Moses this account: "We went into the land to which you sent us, and it does flow with milk and honey! Here is its fruit. ²⁸But the people who live there are powerful, and the cities are fortified and very large. We even saw descendants of Anak there. ²⁹The Amalekites live in the Negev; the Hittites, Jebusites and Amorites live in the hill country; and the Canaanites live near the sea and along the Jordan."

³⁰Then Caleb silenced the people before Moses and said, "We should go up and take possession of the land, for we can certainly do it."

³¹But the men who had gone up with him said, "We can't attack those people; they are stronger than we are." ³²And they spread among the Israelites a bad report about the land

a 21 Or toward the entrance to　b 23 Eshcol means cluster; also in verse 24.

they had explored. They said, "The land we explored devours those living in it. All the people we saw there are of great size. ³³We saw the Nephilim there (the descendants of Anak come from the Nephilim). We seemed like grasshoppers in our own eyes, and we looked the same to them."

The People Rebel

14 That night all the people of the community raised their voices and wept aloud. ²All the Israelites grumbled against Moses and Aaron, and the whole assembly said to them, "If only we had died in Egypt! Or in this desert! ³Why is the LORD bringing us to this land only to let us fall by the sword? Our wives and children will be taken as plunder. Wouldn't it be better for us to go back to Egypt?" ⁴And they said to each other, "We should choose a leader and go back to Egypt."

⁵Then Moses and Aaron fell facedown in front of the whole Israelite assembly gathered there. ⁶Joshua son of Nun and Caleb son of Jephunneh, who were among those who had explored the land, tore their clothes ⁷and said to the entire Israelite assembly, "The land we passed through and explored is exceedingly good. ⁸If the LORD is pleased with us, he will lead us into that land, a land flowing with milk and honey, and will give it to us. ⁹Only do not rebel against the LORD. And do not be afraid of the people of the land, because we will swallow them up. Their protection is gone, but the LORD is with us. Do not be afraid of them."

¹⁰But the whole assembly talked about stoning them. Then the glory of the LORD appeared at the Tent of Meeting to all the Israelites. ¹¹The LORD said to Moses, "How long will these people treat me with contempt? How long will they refuse to believe in me, in spite of all the miraculous signs I have performed among them? ¹²I will strike them down with a plague and destroy them, but I will make you into a nation greater and stronger than they."

¹³Moses said to the LORD, "Then the Egyptians will hear about it! By your power you brought these people up from among them. ¹⁴And they will tell the inhabitants of this land about it. They have already heard that you, O LORD, are with these people and that you, O LORD, have been seen face to face, that your cloud stays over them, and that you go before them in a pillar of cloud by day and a pillar of fire by night. ¹⁵If you put these people to death all at one time, the nations who have heard this report about you will say, ¹⁶'The LORD was not

們所窺探經過之地，是吞吃居民之地，我們在那裏所看見的人民都身量高大。³³我們在那裏看見亞衲族人，就是偉人，他們是偉人的後裔。據我們看自己就如蚱蜢一樣，據他們看我們也是如此。"

百姓悖逆

14 當下全會眾大聲喧嚷，那夜百姓都哭號。²以色列眾人向摩西、亞倫發怨言，全會眾對他們說："巴不得我們早死在埃及地，或是死在這曠野。³耶和華為甚麼把我們領到那地，使我們倒在刀下呢？我們的妻子和孩子必被擄掠，我們回埃及去豈不好嗎？"⁴眾人彼此說："我們不如立一個首領，回埃及去吧！"

⁵摩西、亞倫就俯伏在以色列全會眾面前。⁶窺探地的人中，嫩的兒子約書亞和耶孚尼的兒子迦勒，撕裂衣服，⁷對以色列全會眾說："我們所窺探經過之地是極美之地。⁸耶和華若喜悅我們，就必將我們領進那地，把地賜給我們，那地原是流奶與蜜之地。⁹但你們不可背叛耶和華，也不要怕那地的居民，因為他們是我們的食物，並且蔭庇他們的已經離開他們。有耶和華與我們同在，不要怕他們！"

¹⁰但全會眾說："拿石頭打死他們二人！"忽然，耶和華的榮光在會幕中向以色列眾人顯現。¹¹耶和華對摩西說："這百姓藐視我要到幾時呢？我在他們中間行了這一切神蹟，他們還不信我要到幾時呢？¹²我要用瘟疫擊殺他們，使他們不得承受那地，叫你的後裔成為大國，比他們強勝。"

¹³摩西對耶和華說："埃及人必聽見這事，因為你曾施展大能，將這百姓從他們中間領上來。¹⁴埃及人要將這事傳給迦南地的居民，那民已經聽見你耶和華是在這百姓中間，因為你面對面被人看見，有你的雲彩停在他們以上。你日間在雲柱中，夜間在火柱中，在他們前面行。¹⁵如今你若把這百姓殺了，如殺一人，那些聽見你名聲的列邦必議論說：¹⁶'耶和華

因為不能把這百姓領進他向他們起誓應許之地，所以在曠野把他們殺了。'

17 "現在求主大顯能力，照你所說過的話說：18 '耶和華不輕易發怒，並有豐盛的慈愛，赦免罪孽和過犯，萬不以有罪的為無罪，必追討他的罪，自父及子，直到三四代。' 19求你照你的大慈愛赦免這百姓的罪孽，好像你從埃及到如今常赦免他們一樣。"

20耶和華說："我照着你的話赦免了他們。21然我指着我的永生起誓，遍地要被我的榮耀充滿。22這些人雖看見我的榮耀和我在埃及與曠野所行的神蹟，仍然試探我這十次，不聽從我的話，23他們斷不得看見我向他們的祖宗所起誓應許之地。凡藐視我的，一個也不得看見；24惟獨我的僕人迦勒，因他另有一個心志，專一跟從我，我就把他領進他所去過的那地；他的後裔也必得那地為業。25亞瑪力人和迦南人住在谷中，明天你們要轉回，從紅海的路往曠野去。"

26耶和華對摩西、亞倫說：27 "這惡會眾向我發怨言，我忍耐他們要到幾時呢？以色列人向我所發的怨言，我都聽見了。28你們告訴他們，耶和華說：'我指着我的永生起誓：我必要照你們達到我耳中的話待你們。29你們的屍首必倒在這曠野，並且你們中間凡被數點、從二十歲以外向我發怨言的，30必不得進我起誓應許叫你們住的那地；惟有耶孚尼的兒子迦勒和嫩的兒子約書亞才能進去。31但你們的婦人孩子，就是你們所說要被擄掠的，我必把他們領進去，他們就得知你們所厭棄的那地。32至於你們，你們的屍首必倒在這曠野；33你們的兒女必在曠野飄流四十年，擔當你們淫行的罪，直到你們的屍首在曠野消滅。34按你們窺探那地的四十日，一年頂一日，你們要擔當罪孽四十年，就知道我與你們疏遠了。'35我耶和華說過，我總要這樣待這一

able to bring these people into the land he promised them on oath; so he slaughtered them in the desert.'

17"Now may the Lord's strength be displayed, just as you have declared: 18The LORD is slow to anger, abounding in love and forgiving sin and rebellion. Yet he does not leave the guilty unpunished; he punishes the children for the sin of the fathers to the third and fourth generation.' 19In accordance with your great love, forgive the sin of these people, just as you have pardoned them from the time they left Egypt until now."

20The LORD replied, "I have forgiven them, as you asked. 21Nevertheless, as surely as I live and as surely as the glory of the LORD fills the whole earth, 22not one of the men who saw my glory and the miraculous signs I performed in Egypt and in the desert but who disobeyed me and tested me ten times— 23not one of them will ever see the land I promised on oath to their forefathers. No one who has treated me with contempt will ever see it. 24But because my servant Caleb has a different spirit and follows me wholeheartedly, I will bring him into the land he went to, and his descendants will inherit it. 25Since the Amalekites and Canaanites are living in the valleys, turn back tomorrow and set out toward the desert along the route to the Red Sea.a"

26The LORD said to Moses and Aaron: 27"How long will this wicked community grumble against me? I have heard the complaints of these grumbling Israelites. 28So tell them, 'As surely as I live, declares the LORD, I will do to you the very things I heard you say: 29In this desert your bodies will fall—every one of you twenty years old or more who was counted in the census and who has grumbled against me. 30Not one of you will enter the land I swore with uplifted hand to make your home, except Caleb son of Jephunneh and Joshua son of Nun. 31As for your children that you said would be taken as plunder, I will bring them in to enjoy the land you have rejected. 32But you—your bodies will fall in this desert. 33Your children will be shepherds here for forty years, suffering for your unfaithfulness, until the last of your bodies lies in the desert. 34For forty years—one year for each of the forty days you explored the land—you will suffer for your sins and know what it is like to have me against you.' 35I, the LORD, have spoken, and I will surely do these things to this whole wicked community, which has banded

a 25 Hebrew Yam Suph; that is, Sea of Reeds

together against me. They will meet their end in this desert; here they will die."

³⁶So the men Moses had sent to explore the land, who returned and made the whole community grumble against him by spreading a bad report about it— ³⁷these men responsible for spreading the bad report about the land were struck down and died of a plague before the LORD. ³⁸Of the men who went to explore the land, only Joshua son of Nun and Caleb son of Jephunneh survived.

³⁹When Moses reported this to all the Israelites, they mourned bitterly. ⁴⁰Early the next morning they went up toward the high hill country. "We have sinned," they said. "We will go up to the place the LORD promised."

⁴¹But Moses said, "Why are you disobeying the LORD's command? This will not succeed! ⁴²Do not go up, because the LORD is not with you. You will be defeated by your enemies, ⁴³for the Amalekites and Canaanites will face you there. Because you have turned away from the LORD, he will not be with you and you will fall by the sword."

⁴⁴Nevertheless, in their presumption they went up toward the high hill country, though neither Moses nor the ark of the LORD's covenant moved from the camp. ⁴⁵Then the Amalekites and Canaanites who lived in that hill country came down and attacked them and beat them down all the way to Hormah.

Supplementary Offerings

15 The LORD said to Moses, ²"Speak to the Israelites and say to them: 'After you enter the land I am giving you as a home ³and you present to the LORD offerings made by fire, from the herd or the flock, as an aroma pleasing to the LORD—whether burnt offerings or sacrifices, for special vows or freewill offerings or festival offerings— ⁴then the one who brings his offering shall present to the LORD a grain offering of a tenth of an ephah^a of fine flour mixed with a quarter of a hin^b of oil. ⁵With each lamb for the burnt offering or the sacrifice, prepare a quarter of a hin of wine as a drink offering.

⁶" 'With a ram prepare a grain offering of two-tenths of an ephah^c of fine flour mixed with a third of a hin^d of oil, ⁷and a third of a hin of

切聚集敵我的惡會眾，他們必在這曠野消滅，在這裏死亡。"

³⁶摩西所打發窺探那地的人回來，報那地的惡信，叫全會眾向摩西發怨言，³⁷這些報惡信的人都遭瘟疫，死在耶和華面前。³⁸其中惟有嫩的兒子約書亞和耶孚尼的兒子迦勒仍然存活。

³⁹摩西將這些話告訴以色列眾人，他們就甚悲哀。⁴⁰清早起來上山頂去，說："我們在這裏，我們有罪了，情願上耶和華所應許的地方去。"

⁴¹摩西說："你們為何違背耶和華的命令呢？這事不能順利了。⁴²不要上去，因為耶和華不在你們中間，恐怕你們被仇敵殺敗了。⁴³亞瑪力人和迦南人都在你們面前，你們必倒在刀下，因你們退回不跟從耶和華，所以他必不與你們同在。"

⁴⁴他們卻擅敢上山頂去，然而耶和華的約櫃和摩西沒有出營。⁴⁵於是亞瑪力人和住在那山上的迦南人都下來擊打他們，把他們殺退了，直到何珥瑪。

獻祭的條例

15 耶和華對摩西說：²"你曉諭以色列人說："你們到了我所賜給你們居住的地，³若願意從牛羣羊羣中取牛羊作火祭，獻給耶和華，無論是燔祭是平安祭，為要還特許的願，或是作甘心祭，或是逢你們節期獻的，都要奉給耶和華為馨香之祭。⁴那獻供物的，就要將細麵伊法十分之一，並油一欣四分之一，調和作素祭，獻給耶和華。⁵無論是燔祭是平安祭，你要為每隻綿羊羔，一同預備奠祭的酒一欣四分之一。

⁶"'為公綿羊預備細麵伊法十分之二，並油一欣三分之一，調和作素祭。⁷又用酒一欣三分之一作奠

---

^a 4 That is, probably about 2 quarts (about 2 liters)   ^b 4 That is, probably about 1 quart (about 1 liter); also in verse 5
^c 6 That is, probably about 4 quarts (about 4.5 liters)
^d 6 That is, probably about 1 1/4 quarts (about 1.2 liters); also in verse 7

祭，獻給耶和華為馨香之祭。

8 「『你預備公牛作燔祭，或是作平安祭，為要還特許的願，或是作平安祭，獻給耶和華，9就要把細麵伊法十分之三，並油半欣，調和作素祭，和公牛一獻上。10又用酒半欣作奠祭，獻給耶和華為馨香的火祭。11獻公牛、公綿羊、綿羊羔、山羊羔，每隻都要這樣辦理。12照你們所預備的數目，按着隻數都要這樣辦理。

13 「『凡本地人將馨香的火祭獻給耶和華，都要這樣辦理。14若有外人和你們同居，或有人世世代代住在你們中間，願意將馨香的火祭獻給耶和華，你們怎樣辦理，他也要照樣辦理。15至於會眾，你們和同居的外人都歸一例，作為你們世世代代永遠的定例。在耶和華面前你們怎樣，寄居的也要怎樣。16你們並與你們同居的外人，當有一樣的條例，一樣的典章。』」

17耶和華對摩西說：18 「你曉諭以色列人說：『你們到了我所領你們進去的那地，19吃那地的糧食，就要把舉祭獻給耶和華。20你們要用初熟的麥子磨麵，做餅當舉祭奉獻；你們舉上，好像舉禾場的舉祭一樣。21你們世世代代要用初熟的麥子磨麵，當舉祭獻給耶和華。

為誤犯獻祭之例

22 「『你們有錯誤的時候，不守耶和華所曉諭摩西的這一切命令，23就是耶和華藉摩西一切所吩咐你們的，自那日以至你們的世世代代，24若有誤行，是會眾所不知道的，後來全會眾就要將一隻公牛犢作燔祭，並照典章把素祭和奠祭，一同獻給耶和華為馨香之祭，又獻一隻公山羊作贖罪祭。25祭司要為以色列全會眾贖罪，他們就必蒙赦免，因為這是錯誤。他們又因自己的錯誤，把供物，

wine as a drink offering. Offer it as an aroma pleasing to the LORD.

8" 'When you prepare a young bull as a burnt offering or sacrifice, for a special vow or a fellowship offering[a] to the LORD, 9bring with the bull a grain offering of three-tenths of an ephah[b] of fine flour mixed with half a hin[c] of oil. 10Also bring half a hin of wine as a drink offering. It will be an offering made by fire, an aroma pleasing to the LORD. 11Each bull or ram, each lamb or young goat, is to be prepared in this manner. 12Do this for each one, for as many as you prepare.

13" 'Everyone who is native-born must do these things in this way when he brings an offering made by fire as an aroma pleasing to the LORD. 14For the generations to come, whenever an alien or anyone else living among you presents an offering made by fire as an aroma pleasing to the LORD, he must do exactly as you do. 15The community is to have the same rules for you and for the alien living among you; this is a lasting ordinance for the generations to come. You and the alien shall be the same before the LORD: 16The same laws and regulations will apply both to you and to the alien living among you.' "

17The LORD said to Moses, 18"Speak to the Israelites and say to them: 'When you enter the land to which I am taking you 19and you eat the food of the land, present a portion as an offering to the LORD. 20Present a cake from the first of your ground meal and present it as an offering from the threshing floor. 21Throughout the generations to come you are to give this offering to the LORD from the first of your ground meal.

Offerings for Unintentional Sins

22" 'Now if you unintentionally fail to keep any of these commands the LORD gave Moses— 23any of the LORD's commands to you through him, from the day the LORD gave them and continuing through the generations to come— 24and if this is done unintentionally without the community being aware of it, then the whole community is to offer a young bull for a burnt offering as an aroma pleasing to the LORD, along with its prescribed grain offering and drink offering, and a male goat for a sin offering. 25The priest is to make atonement for the whole Israelite community, and they will be forgiven, for it was not intentional and they have brought

a 8 Traditionally *peace offering*　　*b 9* That is, probably about 6 quarts (about 6.5 liters)　　*c 9* That is, probably about 2 quarts (about 2 liters); also in verse 10

to the LORD for their wrong an offering made by fire and a sin offering. 26The whole Israelite community and the aliens living among them will be forgiven, because all the people were involved in the unintentional wrong.

27" 'But if just one person sins unintentionally, he must bring a year-old female goat for a sin offering. 28The priest is to make atonement before the LORD for the one who erred by sinning unintentionally, and when atonement has been made for him, he will be forgiven. 29One and the same law applies to everyone who sins unintentionally, whether he is a native-born Israelite or an alien.

30" 'But anyone who sins defiantly, whether native-born or alien, blasphemes the LORD, and that person must be cut off from his people. 31Because he has despised the LORD's word and broken his commands, that person must surely be cut off; his guilt remains on him.' "

The Sabbath-Breaker Put to Death

32While the Israelites were in the desert, a man was found gathering wood on the Sabbath day. 33Those who found him gathering wood brought him to Moses and Aaron and the whole assembly, 34and they kept him in custody, because it was not clear what should be done to him. 35Then the LORD said to Moses, "The man must die. The whole assembly must stone him outside the camp. 36So the assembly took him outside the camp and stoned him to death, as the LORD commanded Moses.

Tassels on Garments

37The LORD said to Moses, 38"Speak to the Israelites and say to them: 'Throughout the generations to come you are to make tassels on the corners of your garments, with a blue cord on each tassel. 39You will have these tassels to look at and so you will remember all the commands of the LORD, that you may obey them and not prostitute yourselves by going after the lusts of your own hearts and eyes. 40Then you will remember to obey all my commands and will be consecrated to your God. 41I am the LORD your God, who brought you out of Egypt to be your God. I am the LORD your God.' "

Korah, Dathan and Abiram

16 Korah son of Izhar, the son of Kohath, the son of Levi, and certain Reubenites—Dathan and Abiram, sons of Eliab, and On son of Peleth—became

就是向耶和華獻的火祭和贖罪祭,一並奉到耶和華面前。26以色列全會眾和寄居在他們中間的外人,就必蒙赦免,因為這罪是百姓誤犯的。

27 " '若有一個人誤犯了罪,他就要獻一歲的母山羊作贖罪祭。28那誤行的人犯罪的時候,祭司要在耶和華面前為他贖罪,他就必蒙赦免。29以色列中的本地人和寄居在他們中間的外人,若誤行了甚麼事,必歸一樣的條例。

30 " '但那擅敢行事的,無論是本地人,是寄居的,他褻瀆了耶和華,必從民中剪除。31因他藐視耶和華的言語,違背耶和華的命令,那人總要剪除;他的罪孽要歸到他身上。' "

違反安息日者處死

32以色列人在曠野的時候,遇見一個人在安息日撿柴。33遇見他撿柴的人,就把他帶到摩西、亞倫並全會眾那裏,34將他收在監內,因為當怎樣辦他,還沒有指明。35耶和華吩咐摩西說:"總要把那人治死,全會眾要在營外用石頭把他打死。" 36於是全會眾將他帶到營外,用石頭打死他,是照耶和華所吩咐摩西的。

衣服上做繸子

37耶和華曉諭摩西說:38 "你吩咐以色列人,叫他們世世代代在衣服邊上做繸子,又在底邊的繸子上,釘一根藍細帶子。39你們佩帶這繸子,好叫你們看見就記念遵行耶和華一切的命令,不隨從自己的心意、眼目行邪淫,像你們素常一樣,40使你們記念遵行我一切的命令,成為聖潔,歸與你們的神。41我是耶和華你們的神,曾把你們從埃及地領出來,要作你們的神。我是耶和華你們的神。"

可拉、大坍與亞比蘭

16 利未的曾孫、哥轄的孫子、以斯哈的兒子可拉,和呂便子孫中以利押的兒子大坍、亞比蘭,與比勒的兒子安,

²並以色列會中的二百五十個首領，就是有名望選入會中的人，在摩西面前一同起來，³聚集攻擊摩西、亞倫，說：「你們擅自專權！全會眾既是聖潔，耶和華也在他們中間，你們為甚麼自高，超過耶和華的會眾呢？」

⁴摩西聽見這話就俯伏在地，⁵對可拉和他一黨的人說：「到了早晨，耶和華必指示誰是屬他的，誰是聖潔的，就叫誰親近他；他所揀選的是誰，必叫誰親近他。⁶可拉啊，你們要這樣行：你和你的一黨要拿香爐來。⁷明日在耶和華面前，把火盛在爐中，把香放在其上。耶和華揀選誰，誰就為聖潔。你們這利未的子孫擅自專權了！」

⁸摩西又對可拉說：「利未的子孫哪，你們聽我說：⁹以色列的神從以色列會中將你們分別出來，使你們親近他，辦耶和華帳幕的事，並站在會眾面前替他們當差。¹⁰耶和華又使你和你一切弟兄，利未的子孫，一同親近他，這豈為小事？你們還要求祭司的職任嗎？¹¹你和你一黨的人聚集，是要攻擊耶和華。亞倫算甚麼，你們竟向他發怨言呢？」

¹²摩西打發人去召以利押的兒子大坍、亞比蘭。他們說：「我們不上去！¹³你將我們從流奶與蜜之地領上來，要在曠野殺我們，這豈為小事？你還要自立為王轄管我們嗎？¹⁴並且你沒有將我們領到流奶與蜜之地，也沒有把田地和葡萄園給我們為業。難道你要剜這些人的眼睛嗎？我們不上去！」

¹⁵摩西就甚發怒，對耶和華說：「求你不要享受他們的供物，我並沒有奪過他們一匹驢，也沒有害過他們一個人。」

¹⁶摩西對可拉說：「明天你和你一黨的人並亞倫，都要站在耶和華面前。¹⁷各人要拿一個香爐，共二百五十個，把香放在上面，到耶和華面前。你和亞倫也各拿自己的香爐。」¹⁸於是他們各人拿一個香爐，盛上火，加上香，同摩西、亞倫站在會幕

insolent*a* ²and rose up against Moses. With them were 250 Israelite men, well-known community leaders who had been appointed members of the council. ³They came as a group to oppose Moses and Aaron and said to them, "You have gone too far! The whole community is holy, every one of them, and the LORD is with them. Why then do you set yourselves above the LORD's assembly?"

⁴When Moses heard this, he fell facedown. ⁵Then he said to Korah and all his followers: "In the morning the LORD will show who belongs to him and who is holy, and he will have that person come near him. The man he chooses he will cause to come near him. ⁶You, Korah, and all your followers are to do this: Take censers ⁷and tomorrow put fire and incense in them before the LORD. The man the LORD chooses will be the one who is holy. You Levites have gone too far!"

⁸Moses also said to Korah, "Now listen, you Levites! ⁹Isn't it enough for you that the God of Israel has separated you from the rest of the Israelite community and brought you near himself to do the work at the LORD's tabernacle and to stand before the community and minister to them? ¹⁰He has brought you and all your fellow Levites near himself, but now you are trying to get the priesthood too. ¹¹It is against the LORD that you and all your followers have banded together. Who is Aaron that you should grumble against him?"

¹²Then Moses summoned Dathan and Abiram, the sons of Eliab. But they said, "We will not come! ¹³Isn't it enough that you have brought us up out of a land flowing with milk and honey to kill us in the desert? And now you also want to lord it over us? ¹⁴Moreover, you haven't brought us into a land flowing with milk and honey or given us an inheritance of fields and vineyards. Will you gouge out the eyes of*b* these men? No, we will not come!"

¹⁵Then Moses became very angry and said to the LORD, "Do not accept their offering. I have not taken so much as a donkey from them, nor have I wronged any of them."

¹⁶Moses said to Korah, "You and all your followers are to appear before the LORD tomorrow—you and they and Aaron. ¹⁷Each man is to take his censer and put incense in it—250 censers in all—and present it before the LORD. You and Aaron are to present your censers also." ¹⁸So each man took his censer, put fire and incense in it, and stood with Moses and

a 1 Or Peleth—took [men]　b 14 Or you make slaves of; or you deceive

Aaron at the entrance to the Tent of Meeting. [19]When Korah had gathered all his followers in opposition to them at the entrance to the Tent of Meeting, the glory of the LORD appeared to the entire assembly. [20]The LORD said to Moses and Aaron, [21]"Separate yourselves from this assembly so I can put an end to them at once."

[22]But Moses and Aaron fell facedown and cried out, "O God, God of the spirits of all mankind, will you be angry with the entire assembly when only one man sins?"

[23]Then the LORD said to Moses, [24]"Say to the assembly, 'Move away from the tents of Korah, Dathan and Abiram.'"

[25]Moses got up and went to Dathan and Abiram, and the elders of Israel followed him. [26]He warned the assembly, "Move back from the tents of these wicked men! Do not touch anything belonging to them, or you will be swept away because of all their sins." [27]So they moved away from the tents of Korah, Dathan and Abiram. Dathan and Abiram had come out and were standing with their wives, children and little ones at the entrances to their tents.

[28]Then Moses said, "This is how you will know that the LORD has sent me to do all these things and that it was not my idea: [29]If these men die a natural death and experience only what usually happens to men, then the LORD has not sent me. [30]But if the LORD brings about something totally new, and the earth opens its mouth and swallows them, with everything that belongs to them, and they go down alive into the grave,[a] then you will know that these men have treated the LORD with contempt."

[31]As soon as he finished saying all this, the ground under them split apart [32]and the earth opened its mouth and swallowed them, with their households and all Korah's men and all their possessions. [33]They went down alive into the grave, with everything they owned; the earth closed over them, and they perished and were gone from the community. [34]At their cries, all the Israelites around them fled, shouting, "The earth is going to swallow us too!"

[35]And fire came out from the LORD and consumed the 250 men who were offering the incense.

[36]The LORD said to Moses, [37]"Tell Eleazar son of Aaron, the priest, to take the censers out of the smoldering remains and scatter the coals some distance away, for the censers are holy— [38]the censers of the men who sinned at the cost of their lives. Hammer the censers into sheets to

a 30 Hebrew Sheol; also in verse 33

門前。[19]可拉招聚全會眾到會幕門前，要攻擊摩西、亞倫；耶和華的榮光就向全會眾顯現。[20]耶和華曉諭摩西、亞倫說：[21]"你們離開這會眾，我好在轉眼之間把他們滅絕。"

[22]摩西、亞倫就俯伏在地說："神，萬人之靈的神啊！一人犯罪，你就要向全會眾發怒嗎？"

[23]耶和華曉諭摩西說：[24]"你吩咐會眾說：'你們離開可拉、大坍、亞比蘭帳棚的四圍。'"

[25]摩西起來，往大坍、亞比蘭那裏去，以色列的長老也隨着他去。[26]他吩咐會眾說："你們離開這惡人的帳棚吧！他們的物件，甚麼都不可摸，恐怕你們陷在他們的罪中，與他們一同消滅。"[27]於是眾人離開可拉、大坍、亞比蘭帳棚的四圍。大坍、亞比蘭帶着妻子、兒女、小孩子，都出來，站在自己的帳棚門口。

[28]摩西說："我行的這一切事，本不是憑我自己心意行的，乃是耶和華打發我行的，必有證據使你們知道。[29]這些人死若與世人無異，或是他們所遭的與世人相同，就不是耶和華打發我來的。[30]倘若耶和華創作一件新事，使地開口，把他們和一切屬他們的都吞下去，叫他們活活地墜落陰間，你們就明白這些人是藐視耶和華了。"

[31]摩西剛說完了這一切話，他們腳下的地就開了口，[32]把他們和他們的家眷，並一切屬可拉的人丁、財物都吞下去。[33]這樣，他們和一切屬他們的，都活活地墜落陰間，地口在他們上頭照舊合閉，他們就從會中滅亡。[34]在他們四圍的以色列眾人聽他們呼號，就都逃跑，說："恐怕地也把我們吞下去！"

[35]又有火從耶和華那裏出來，燒滅了那獻香的二百五十個人。

[36]耶和華曉諭摩西說：[37]"你吩咐祭司亞倫的兒子以利亞撒，從火中撿起那些香爐來，把火撒在別處，因為那些香爐是聖的。[38]把那些犯罪自害己命之人的香爐，叫人錘成片子，

用以包壇，那些香爐本是他們在耶和華面前獻過的，所以是聖的，並且可以給以色列人作記號。"

³⁹於是祭司以利亞撒將被燒之人所獻的銅香爐拿來，人就錘出來用以包壇，⁴⁰給以色列人作紀念，使亞倫後裔之外的人，不得近前來，在耶和華面前燒香，免得他遭可拉和他一黨所遭的。這乃是照耶和華藉着摩西所吩咐的。

⁴¹第二天，以色列全會眾都向摩西、亞倫發怨言，說："你們殺了耶和華的百姓了。"

⁴²會眾聚集攻擊摩西、亞倫的時候，向會幕觀看，不料，有雲彩遮蓋了，耶和華的榮光顯現。⁴³摩西、亞倫就來到會幕前。⁴⁴耶和華吩咐摩西說：⁴⁵"你們離開這會眾，我好在轉眼之間把他們滅絕。"他們二人就俯伏於地。

⁴⁶摩西對亞倫說："拿你的香爐，把壇上的火盛在其中，又加上香，快快帶到會眾那裏，為他們贖罪，因為有忿怒從耶和華那裏出來，瘟疫已經發作了。"⁴⁷亞倫照着摩西所說的拿來，跑到會中，不料，瘟疫在百姓中已經發作了。他就加上香，為百姓贖罪，⁴⁸他站在活人死人中間，瘟疫就止住了。⁴⁹除了因可拉事情死的以外，遭瘟疫死的，共有一萬四千七百人。⁵⁰亞倫回到會幕門口，到摩西那裏，瘟疫已經止住了。

亞倫之杖發芽

17 耶和華對摩西說：²"你曉諭以色列人，從他們手下取杖，每支派一根。從他們所有的首領，按着支派，共取十二根；你要將各人的名字寫在各人的杖上，³並要將亞倫的名字寫在利未的杖上，因為各族長必有一根杖。⁴你要把這些杖存在會幕內法櫃前，就是我與你們相會之處。⁵後來我所揀選的那人，他的杖必發芽。這樣，我必使以色列人向你們所發的怨言止息，不再達到我耳中。"

⁶於是摩西曉諭以色列人，他們的首領就把杖交給他，按着支派每首領一根，共有十二根；亞倫的杖也在其中。⁷摩西就把杖存在法櫃的帳幕內，在耶和華面前。

overlay the altar, for they were presented before the LORD and have become holy. Let them be a sign to the Israelites."

³⁹So Eleazar the priest collected the bronze censers brought by those who had been burned up, and he had them hammered out to overlay the altar, ⁴⁰as the LORD directed him through Moses. This was to remind the Israelites that no one except a descendant of Aaron should come to burn incense before the LORD, or he would become like Korah and his followers.

⁴¹The next day the whole Israelite community grumbled against Moses and Aaron. "You have killed the LORD's people," they said.

⁴²But when the assembly gathered in opposition to Moses and Aaron and turned toward the Tent of Meeting, suddenly the cloud covered it and the glory of the LORD appeared. ⁴³Then Moses and Aaron went to the front of the Tent of Meeting, ⁴⁴and the LORD said to Moses, ⁴⁵"Get away from this assembly so I can put an end to them at once." And they fell facedown.

⁴⁶Then Moses said to Aaron, "Take your censer and put incense in it, along with fire from the altar, and hurry to the assembly to make atonement for them. Wrath has come out from the LORD; the plague has started." ⁴⁷So Aaron did as Moses said, and ran into the midst of the assembly. The plague had already started among the people, but Aaron offered the incense and made atonement for them. ⁴⁸He stood between the living and the dead, and the plague stopped. ⁴⁹But 14,700 people died from the plague, in addition to those who had died because of Korah. ⁵⁰Then Aaron returned to Moses at the entrance to the Tent of Meeting, for the plague had stopped.

The Budding of Aaron's Staff

17 The LORD said to Moses, ²"Speak to the Israelites and get twelve staffs from them, one from the leader of each of their ancestral tribes. Write the name of each man on his staff. ³On the staff of Levi write Aaron's name, for there must be one staff for the head of each ancestral tribe. ⁴Place them in the Tent of Meeting in front of the Testimony, where I meet with you. ⁵The staff belonging to the man I choose will sprout, and I will rid myself of this constant grumbling against you by the Israelites."

⁶So Moses spoke to the Israelites, and their leaders gave him twelve staffs, one for the leader of each of their ancestral tribes, and Aaron's staff was among them. ⁷Moses placed the staffs before the LORD in the Tent of the Testimony.

⁸The next day Moses entered the Tent of the Testimony and saw that Aaron's staff, which represented the house of Levi, had not only sprouted but had budded, blossomed and produced almonds. ⁹Then Moses brought out all the staffs from the LORD's presence to all the Israelites. They looked at them, and each man took his own staff.

¹⁰The LORD said to Moses, "Put back Aaron's staff in front of the Testimony, to be kept as a sign to the rebellious. This will put an end to their grumbling against me, so that they will not die." ¹¹Moses did just as the LORD commanded him.

¹²The Israelites said to Moses, "We will die! We are lost, we are all lost! ¹³Anyone who even comes near the tabernacle of the LORD will die. Are we all going to die?"

Duties of Priests and Levites

18 The LORD said to Aaron, "You, your sons and your father's family are to bear the responsibility for offenses against the sanctuary, and you and your sons alone are to bear the responsibility for offenses against the priesthood. ²Bring your fellow Levites from your ancestral tribe to join you and assist you when you and your sons minister before the Tent of the Testimony. ³They are to be responsible to you and are to perform all the duties of the Tent, but they must not go near the furnishings of the sanctuary or the altar, or both they and you will die. ⁴They are to join you and be responsible for the care of the Tent of Meeting—all the work at the Tent—and no one else may come near where you are.

⁵"You are to be responsible for the care of the sanctuary and the altar, so that wrath will not fall on the Israelites again. ⁶I myself have selected your fellow Levites from among the Israelites as a gift to you, dedicated to the LORD to do the work at the Tent of Meeting. ⁷But only you and your sons may serve as priests in connection with everything at the altar and inside the curtain. I am giving you the service of the priesthood as a gift. Anyone else who comes near the sanctuary must be put to death."

Offerings for Priests and Levites

⁸Then the LORD said to Aaron, "I myself have put you in charge of the offerings presented to me; all the holy offerings the Israelites give me I give to you and your sons as your portion and regular share. ⁹You are to have the part of the most holy offerings that is kept from the fire. From all the gifts they bring me as most holy

⁸第二天，摩西進法櫃的帳幕去。誰知，利未族亞倫的杖已經發了芽，生了花苞，開了花，結了熟杏。⁹摩西就把所有的杖從耶和華面前拿出來，給以色列眾人看，他們看見了，各首領就把自己的杖拿去。

¹⁰耶和華吩咐摩西說："把亞倫的杖還放在法櫃前，給這些背叛之子留作記號。這樣，你就使他們向我發的怨言止息，免得他們死亡。"¹¹摩西就這樣行。耶和華怎樣吩咐他，他就怎樣行了。

¹²以色列人對摩西說："我們死啦！我們滅亡啦！都滅亡啦！¹³凡挨近耶和華帳幕的是必死的，我們都要死亡嗎？"

祭司與利未人的職責

18 耶和華對亞倫說："你和你的兒子，並你本族的人，要一同擔當干犯聖所的罪孽；你和你的兒子，也要一同擔當干犯祭司職任的罪孽。²你要帶你弟兄利未人，就是你祖宗支派的人前來，使他們與你聯合，服侍你，只是你和你的兒子，要一同在法櫃的帳幕前供職。³他們要守所吩咐你的，並守全帳幕，只是不可挨近聖所的器具和壇，免得他們和你們都死亡。⁴他們要與你聯合，也要看守會幕，辦理帳幕一切的事，只是外人不可挨近你們。

⁵"你們要看守聖所和壇，免得忿怒再臨到以色列人。⁶我已將你們的弟兄利未人，從以色列人中揀選出來歸耶和華，是給你們為賞賜的，為要辦理會幕的事。⁷你和你的兒子要為一切屬壇和幔子內的事，一同守祭司的職任。你們要這樣供職，我將祭司的職任給你們當作賞賜侍奉我。凡挨近的外人必被治死。"

祭司與利未人當得的分

⁸耶和華曉諭亞倫說："我已將歸我的舉祭，就是以色列人一切分別為聖的物，交給你經管，因你受過膏，把這些都賜給你和你的子孫，當作永得的分。⁹以色列人歸給我至聖的供物，就是一切的素祭、贖罪

祭、贖愆祭，其中所有存留不經火的，都為至聖之物，要歸給你和你的子孫。¹⁰你要拿這些當至聖物吃，凡男丁都可以吃，你當以此物為聖。

¹¹ "以色列人所獻的舉祭並搖祭，都是你的，我已賜給你和你的兒女，當作永得的分，凡在你家中的潔淨人都可以吃。

¹² "凡油中、新酒中、五穀中至好的，就是以色列人所獻給耶和華初熟之物，我都賜給你。¹³凡從他們地上所帶來給耶和華初熟之物，也都要歸與你。你家中的潔淨人都可以吃。

¹⁴ "以色列中一切永獻的都必歸與你。¹⁵他們所有奉給耶和華的，連人帶牲畜，凡頭生的都要歸給你；只是人頭生的，總要贖出來；不潔淨牲畜頭生的，也要贖出來。¹⁶其中在一月之外所當贖的，要照你所估定的價，按聖所的平，用銀子五舍客勒贖出來（一舍客勒是二十季拉）。

¹⁷ "只是頭生的牛，或是頭生的綿羊和山羊，必不可贖，都是聖的，要把牠的血灑在壇上，把牠的脂油焚燒，當作馨香的火祭獻給耶和華。¹⁸牠的肉必歸你，像被搖的胸、被舉的右腿歸你一樣。¹⁹凡以色列人所獻給耶和華聖物中的舉祭，我都賜給你和你的兒女，當作永得的分。這是給你和你的後裔，在耶和華面前作為永遠的鹽約（註："鹽"即"不廢壞"的意思）。"

²⁰耶和華對亞倫說："你在以色列人的境內不可有產業，在他們中間也不可有分。我就是你的分，是你的產業。

²¹ "凡以色列中出產的十分之一，我已賜給利未的子孫為業，因他們所辦的是會幕的事，所以賜給他們為酬他們的勞。²²從今以後，以色列人不可挨近會幕，免得他們擔罪而死。²³惟獨利未人要辦會幕的事，擔當罪孽，這要作你們世世代代永遠的定例。他們在以色列人中不可有產業，²⁴因為以色列人中出產的十分之

offerings, whether grain or sin or guilt offerings, that part belongs to you and your sons. ¹⁰Eat it as something most holy; every male shall eat it. You must regard it as holy.

¹¹"This also is yours: whatever is set aside from the gifts of all the wave offerings of the Israelites. I give this to you and your sons and daughters as your regular share. Everyone in your household who is ceremonially clean may eat it.

¹²"I give you all the finest olive oil and all the finest new wine and grain they give the LORD as the firstfruits of their harvest. ¹³All the land's firstfruits that they bring to the LORD will be yours. Everyone in your household who is ceremonially clean may eat it.

¹⁴"Everything in Israel that is devoted*ᵃ* to the LORD is yours. ¹⁵The first offspring of every womb, both man and animal, that is offered to the LORD is yours. But you must redeem every firstborn son and every firstborn male of unclean animals. ¹⁶When they are a month old, you must redeem them at the redemption price set at five shekels*ᵇ* of silver, according to the sanctuary shekel, which weighs twenty gerahs.

¹⁷"But you must not redeem the firstborn of an ox, a sheep or a goat; they are holy. Sprinkle their blood on the altar and burn their fat as an offering made by fire, an aroma pleasing to the LORD. ¹⁸Their meat is to be yours, just as the breast of the wave offering and the right thigh are yours. ¹⁹Whatever is set aside from the holy offerings the Israelites present to the LORD I give to you and your sons and daughters as your regular share. It is an everlasting covenant of salt before the LORD for both you and your offspring."

²⁰The LORD said to Aaron, "You will have no inheritance in their land, nor will you have any share among them; I am your share and your inheritance among the Israelites.

²¹"I give to the Levites all the tithes in Israel as their inheritance in return for the work they do while serving at the Tent of Meeting. ²²From now on the Israelites must not go near the Tent of Meeting, or they will bear the consequences of their sin and will die. ²³It is the Levites who are to do the work at the Tent of Meeting and bear the responsibility for offenses against it. This is a lasting ordinance for the generations to come. They will receive no inheritance among the Israelites. ²⁴Instead, I give to the Levites as

---

a 14 The Hebrew term refers to the irrevocable giving over of things or persons to the LORD.　　*b 16* That is, about 2 ounces (about 55 grams)

their inheritance the tithes that the Israelites present as an offering to the LORD. That is why I said concerning them: 'They will have no inheritance among the Israelites.'"

25The LORD said to Moses, 26"Speak to the Levites and say to them: 'When you receive from the Israelites the tithe I give you as your inheritance, you must present a tenth of that tithe as the LORD's offering. 27Your offering will be reckoned to you as grain from the threshing floor or juice from the winepress. 28In this way you also will present an offering to the LORD from all the tithes you receive from the Israelites. From these tithes you must give the LORD's portion to Aaron the priest. 29You must present as the LORD's portion the best and holiest part of everything given to you.'

30"Say to the Levites: 'When you present the best part, it will be reckoned to you as the product of the threshing floor or the winepress. 31You and your households may eat the rest of it anywhere, for it is your wages for your work at the Tent of Meeting. 32By presenting the best part of it you will not be guilty in this matter; then you will not defile the holy offerings of the Israelites, and you will not die.'"

The Water of Cleansing

19 The LORD said to Moses and Aaron: 2"This is a requirement of the law that the LORD has commanded: Tell the Israelites to bring you a red heifer without defect or blemish and that has never been under a yoke. 3Give it to Eleazar the priest; it is to be taken outside the camp and slaughtered in his presence. 4Then Eleazar the priest is to take some of its blood on his finger and sprinkle it seven times toward the front of the Tent of Meeting. 5While he watches, the heifer is to be burned—its hide, flesh, blood and offal. 6The priest is to take some cedar wood, hyssop and scarlet wool and throw them onto the burning heifer. 7After that, the priest must wash his clothes and bathe himself with water. He may then come into the camp, but he will be ceremonially unclean till evening. 8The man who burns it must also wash his clothes and bathe with water, and he too will be unclean till evening.

9"A man who is clean shall gather up the ashes of the heifer and put them in a ceremonially clean place outside the camp. They shall be kept by the Israelite community for use in the water of cleansing; it is for purification from sin. 10The man who gathers up the ashes of the heifer must also wash his clothes, and he too will be unclean till evening. This will be a last-

一，就是獻給耶和華為舉祭的，我已賜給利未人為業。所以我對他們說：'在以色列人中不可有產業。'"

25耶和華吩咐摩西說：26"你曉諭利未人說：'你們從以色列人中所取的十分之一，就是我給你們為業的，要再從那十分之一中取十分之一，作為舉祭獻給耶和華。27這舉祭要算為你們場上的穀，又如滿酒醡的酒。28這樣，你們從以色列人中所得的十分之一，也要作舉祭獻給耶和華；從這十分之一中，將所獻給耶和華的舉祭歸給祭司亞倫。29奉給你們的一切禮物，要從其中將至好的，就是分別為聖的，獻給耶和華為舉祭。'

30"所以你要對利未人說：'你們從其中將至好的舉起，這就算為你們場上的糧，又如酒醡的酒。31你們和你們家屬隨處可以吃，這原是你們的賞賜，是酬你們在會幕裏辦事的勞。32你們從其中將至好的舉起，就不至因這物擔罪。你們不可褻瀆以色列人的聖物，免得死亡。'"

除污穢的水

19 耶和華曉諭摩西、亞倫說：2"耶和華命定律法中的一條律例乃是這樣說：你要吩咐以色列人，把一隻沒有殘疾、未曾負軛、純紅的母牛牽到你這裏來，3交給祭司以利亞撒，他必牽到營外，人就把牛宰在他面前。4祭司以利亞撒要用指頭蘸這牛的血，向會幕前面彈七次。5人要在他眼前把這母牛焚燒，牛的皮、肉、血、糞都要焚燒。6祭司要把香柏木、牛膝草、朱紅色線都丟在燒牛的火中。7祭司必不潔淨到晚上，要洗衣服，用水洗身，然後可以進營；8燒牛的人必不潔淨到晚上，也要洗衣服，用水洗身。

9"必有一個潔淨的人，收起母牛的灰，存在營外潔淨的地方，為以色列人會眾調做除污穢的水。這本是除罪的。10收起母牛灰的人，必不潔淨到晚上，要洗衣服。這要給以色列人和寄居在他們中間的外人，作為永遠的定例。

11 「摸了人死屍的，就必七天不潔淨。12那人到第三天，要用這除污穢的水潔淨自己，第七天就潔淨了。他若在第三天不潔淨自己，第七天就不潔淨了。13凡摸了人死屍，不潔淨自己的，就玷污了耶和華的帳幕，這人必從以色列中剪除，因為那除污穢的水沒有灑在他身上，他就為不潔淨，污穢還在他身上。

14 「人死在帳棚裏的條例乃是這樣：凡進那帳棚的，和一切在帳棚裏的，都必七天不潔淨。15凡敞口的器皿，就是沒有紮上蓋的，也是不潔淨。

16 「無論何人在田野裏摸了被刀殺的，或屍首，或是人的骨頭，或是墳墓，就要七天不潔淨。

17 「要為這不潔淨的人拿些燒成的除罪灰放在器皿裏，倒上活水。18必當有一個潔淨的人拿牛膝草蘸於這水中，把水灑在帳棚上，和一切器皿並帳棚內的眾人身上，又灑在摸了骨頭，或摸了被殺的，或摸了自死的，或摸了墳墓的那人身上。19第三天和第七天，潔淨的人要灑水在不潔淨的人身上，第七天就使他成為潔淨。那人要洗衣服，用水洗澡，到晚上就潔淨了。20但那污穢而不潔淨自己的，要將他從會中剪除，因為他玷污了耶和華的聖所。除污穢的水沒有灑在他身上，他是不潔淨的。21這要給你們作為永遠的定例。

「並且那灑除污穢水的人要洗衣服。凡摸除污穢水的，必不潔淨到晚上。22不潔淨人所摸的一切物，就不潔淨；摸了這物的人必不潔淨到晚上。」

磐石出水

20 正月間，以色列全會眾到了尋的曠野，就住在加低斯。米利暗死在那裏，就葬在那裏。

ing ordinance both for the Israelites and for the aliens living among them.

11"Whoever touches the dead body of anyone will be unclean for seven days. 12He must purify himself with the water on the third day and on the seventh day; then he will be clean. But if he does not purify himself on the third and seventh days, he will not be clean. 13Whoever touches the dead body of anyone and fails to purify himself defiles the LORD's tabernacle. That person must be cut off from Israel. Because the water of cleansing has not been sprinkled on him, he is unclean; his uncleanness remains on him.

14"This is the law that applies when a person dies in a tent: Anyone who enters the tent and anyone who is in it will be unclean for seven days, 15and every open container without a lid fastened on it will be unclean.

16"Anyone out in the open who touches someone who has been killed with a sword or someone who has died a natural death, or anyone who touches a human bone or a grave, will be unclean for seven days.

17"For the unclean person, put some ashes from the burned purification offering into a jar and pour fresh water over them. 18Then a man who is ceremonially clean is to take some hyssop, dip it in the water and sprinkle the tent and all the furnishings and the people who were there. He must also sprinkle anyone who has touched a human bone or a grave or someone who has been killed or someone who has died a natural death. 19The man who is clean is to sprinkle the unclean person on the third and seventh days, and on the seventh day he is to purify him. The person being cleansed must wash his clothes and bathe with water, and that evening he will be clean. 20But if a person who is unclean does not purify himself, he must be cut off from the community, because he has defiled the sanctuary of the LORD. The water of cleansing has not been sprinkled on him, and he is unclean. 21This is a lasting ordinance for them.

"The man who sprinkles the water of cleansing must also wash his clothes, and anyone who touches the water of cleansing will be unclean till evening. 22Anything that an unclean person touches becomes unclean, and anyone who touches it becomes unclean till evening."

Water From the Rock

20 In the first month the whole Israelite community arrived at the Desert of Zin, and they stayed at Kadesh. There Miriam died and was buried.

²Now there was no water for the community, and the people gathered in opposition to Moses and Aaron. ³They quarreled with Moses and said, "If only we had died when our brothers fell dead before the LORD! ⁴Why did you bring the LORD's community into this desert, that we and our livestock should die here? ⁵Why did you bring us up out of Egypt to this terrible place? It has no grain or figs, grapevines or pomegranates. And there is no water to drink!"

⁶Moses and Aaron went from the assembly to the entrance to the Tent of Meeting and fell facedown, and the glory of the LORD appeared to them. ⁷The LORD said to Moses, ⁸"Take the staff, and you and your brother Aaron gather the assembly together. Speak to that rock before their eyes and it will pour out its water. You will bring water out of the rock for the community so they and their livestock can drink."

⁹So Moses took the staff from the LORD's presence, just as he commanded him. ¹⁰He and Aaron gathered the assembly together in front of the rock and Moses said to them, "Listen, you rebels, must we bring you water out of this rock?" ¹¹Then Moses raised his arm and struck the rock twice with his staff. Water gushed out, and the community and their livestock drank.

¹²But the LORD said to Moses and Aaron, "Because you did not trust in me enough to honor me as holy in the sight of the Israelites, you will not bring this community into the land I give them."

¹³These were the waters of Meribah,ᵃ where the Israelites quarreled with the LORD and where he showed himself holy among them.

Edom Denies Israel Passage

¹⁴Moses sent messengers from Kadesh to the king of Edom, saying:

"This is what your brother Israel says: You know about all the hardships that have come upon us. ¹⁵Our forefathers went down into Egypt, and we lived there many years. The Egyptians mistreated us and our fathers, ¹⁶but when we cried out to the LORD, he heard our cry and sent an angel and brought us out of Egypt.

"Now we are here at Kadesh, a town on the edge of your territory. ¹⁷Please let us pass through your country. We will not go through any field or vineyard, or drink water from any well. We will travel along the king's high-

---

²會眾沒有水喝，就聚集攻擊摩西、亞倫。³百姓向摩西爭鬧說："我們的弟兄曾死在耶和華面前，我們恨不得與他們同死！⁴你們為何把耶和華的會眾領到這曠野，使我們和牲畜都死在這裏呢？⁵你們為何逼着我們出埃及，領我們到這壞地方呢？這地方不好撒種，也沒有無花果樹、葡萄樹、石榴樹，又沒有水喝！"

⁶摩西、亞倫離開會眾到會幕門口，俯伏在地，耶和華的榮光向他們顯現。⁷耶和華曉諭摩西說：⁸"你拿着杖去，和你的哥哥亞倫招聚會眾，在他們眼前吩咐磐石發出水來，水就從磐石流出，給會眾和他們的牲畜喝。"

⁹於是，摩西照耶和華所吩咐的，從耶和華面前取了杖去。¹⁰摩西、亞倫就招聚會眾到磐石前。摩西說："你們這些背叛的人聽我說：我為你們使水從這磐石中流出來嗎？"¹¹摩西舉手，用杖擊打磐石兩下，就有許多水流出來，會眾和他們的牲畜都喝了。

¹²耶和華對摩西、亞倫說："因為你們不信我，不在以色列人眼前尊我為聖，所以你們必不得領這會眾進我所賜給他們的地去。"

¹³這水名叫米利巴水，是因以色列人向耶和華爭鬧，耶和華就在他們面前顯為聖（註："米利巴"就是"爭鬧"的意思）。

以東不容以色列人通過

¹⁴摩西從加低斯差遣使者去見以東王，說：

"你的弟兄以色列人這樣說：我們所遭遇的一切艱難，¹⁵就是我們的列祖下到埃及，我們在埃及久住，埃及人惡待我們的列祖和我們。¹⁶我們哀求耶和華的時候，他聽了我們的聲音，差遣使者把我們從埃及領出來。這事你都知道。

"如今，我們在你邊界上的城加低斯，¹⁷求你容我們從你的地經過，我們不走田間和葡萄園，也不喝井裏的水，只走大道（註：原文作

ᵃ 13 Meribah means quarreling.

"王道"），不偏左右，直到過了你的境界。"

18以東王說：

"你不可從我的地經過，免得我帶刀出去攻擊你。"

19以色列人說：

"我們要走大道上去，我們和牲畜若喝你的水，必給你價值。不求別的，只求你容我們步行過去。"

20以東王說：

"你們不可經過！"

就率領許多人出來，要用強硬的手攻擊以色列人。21這樣，以東王不肯容以色列人從他的境界過去。於是他們轉去離開他。

亞倫逝世

22以色列全會眾從加低斯起行，到了何珥山。23耶和華在附近以東邊界的何珥山上曉諭摩西、亞倫，說：24"亞倫要歸到他列祖（註：原文作"本民"）那裏，他必不得入我所賜給以色列人的地，因為在米利巴水你們違背了我的命。25你帶亞倫和他的兒子以利亞撒上何珥山，26把亞倫的聖衣脫下來，給他的兒子以利亞撒穿上，亞倫必死在那裏歸他列祖。"

27摩西就照耶和華所吩咐的行。三人當着會眾的眼前上了何珥山。28摩西把亞倫的聖衣脫下來，給他的兒子以利亞撒穿上，亞倫就死在山頂那裏，於是摩西和以利亞撒下了山。29全會眾，就是以色列全家，見亞倫已經死了，便都為亞倫哀哭了三十天。

毀滅亞拉得

21 住南地的迦南人亞拉得王，聽說以色列人從亞他林路來，就和以色列人爭戰，擄了他們幾個人。2以色列人向耶和華發願說："你若將這民交付我手，我就把他們的城邑盡行毀滅。"

way and not turn to the right or to the left until we have passed through your territory."

18But Edom answered:

"You may not pass through here; if you try, we will march out and attack you with the sword."

19The Israelites replied:

"We will go along the main road, and if we or our livestock drink any of your water, we will pay for it. We only want to pass through on foot—nothing else."

20Again they answered:

"You may not pass through."

Then Edom came out against them with a large and powerful army. 21Since Edom refused to let them go through their territory, Israel turned away from them.

The Death of Aaron

22The whole Israelite community set out from Kadesh and came to Mount Hor. 23At Mount Hor, near the border of Edom, the LORD said to Moses and Aaron, 24"Aaron will be gathered to his people. He will not enter the land I give the Israelites, because both of you rebelled against my command at the waters of Meribah. 25Get Aaron and his son Eleazar and take them up Mount Hor. 26Remove Aaron's garments and put them on his son Eleazar, for Aaron will be gathered to his people; he will die there."

27Moses did as the LORD commanded: They went up Mount Hor in the sight of the whole community. 28Moses removed Aaron's garments and put them on his son Eleazar. And Aaron died there on top of the mountain. Then Moses and Eleazar came down from the mountain, 29and when the whole community learned that Aaron had died, the entire house of Israel mourned for him thirty days.

Arad Destroyed

21 When the Canaanite king of Arad, who lived in the Negev, heard that Israel was coming along the road to Atharim, he attacked the Israelites and captured some of them. 2Then Israel made this vow to the LORD: "If you will deliver these people into our hands, we will totally destroy[a] their cities." [3]The LORD listened to Israel's plea and gave the Canaanites over to them. They completely destroyed them and their towns; so the place was named Hormah.[b]

The Bronze Snake

[4]They traveled from Mount Hor along the route to the Red Sea,[c] to go around Edom. But the people grew impatient on the way; [5]they spoke against God and against Moses, and said, "Why have you brought us up out of Egypt to die in the desert? There is no bread! There is no water! And we detest this miserable food!"

[6]Then the LORD sent venomous snakes among them; they bit the people and many Israelites died. [7]The people came to Moses and said, "We sinned when we spoke against the LORD and against you. Pray that the LORD will take the snakes away from us." So Moses prayed for the people.

[8]The LORD said to Moses, "Make a snake and put it up on a pole; anyone who is bitten can look at it and live." [9]So Moses made a bronze snake and put it up on a pole. Then when anyone was bitten by a snake and looked at the bronze snake, he lived.

The Journey to Moab

[10]The Israelites moved on and camped at Oboth. [11]Then they set out from Oboth and camped in Iye Abarim, in the desert that faces Moab toward the sunrise. [12]From there they moved on and camped in the Zered Valley. [13]They set out from there and camped alongside the Arnon, which is in the desert extending into Amorite territory. The Arnon is the border of Moab, between Moab and the Amorites. [14]That is why the Book of the Wars of the LORD says:

". . . Waheb in Suphah[d] and the ravines,
    the Arnon[15]and[e] the slopes of the ravines
    that lead to the site of Ar
    and lie along the border of Moab."

[16]From there they continued on to Beer, the well where the LORD said to Moses, "Gather the people together and I will give them water."

a 2 The Hebrew term refers to the irrevocable giving over of things or persons to the LORD, often by totally destroying them; also in verse 3.   b 3 Hormah means destruction.
c 4 Hebrew Yam Suph; that is, Sea of Reeds   d 14 The meaning of the Hebrew for this phrase is uncertain.
e 14,15 Or "I have been given from Suphah and the ravines / of the Arnon 15to

[3]耶和華應允了以色列人,把迦南人交付他們,他們就把迦南人和迦南人的城邑盡行毀滅。那地方的名便叫何珥瑪(註:"何珥瑪"就是"毀滅"的意思)。

銅蛇

[4]他們從何珥山起行,往紅海那條路走,要繞過以東地。百姓因這路難行,心中甚是煩躁,[5]就怨讟神和摩西,說:"你們為甚麼把我們從埃及領出來,使我們死在曠野呢?這裏沒有糧,沒有水,我們的心厭惡這淡薄的食物!"

[6]於是耶和華使火蛇進入百姓中間,蛇就咬他們,以色列人中死了許多。[7]百姓到摩西那裏說:"我們怨讟耶和華和你,有罪了,求你禱告耶和華,叫這些蛇離開我們。"於是,摩西為百姓禱告。

[8]耶和華對摩西說:"你製造一條火蛇,掛在杆子上,凡被咬的,一望這蛇,就必得活。"[9]摩西便製造一條銅蛇,掛在杆子上,凡被蛇咬的,一望這銅蛇,就活了。

往摩押的路程

[10]以色列人起行,安營在阿伯。[11]又從阿伯起行,安營在以耶亞巴琳,與摩押相對的曠野,向日出之地。[12]從那裏起行,安營在撒烈谷。[13]從那裏起行,安營在亞嫩河那邊;這亞嫩河是在曠野,從亞摩利的境界流出來的。原來亞嫩河是摩押的邊界,在摩押和亞摩利人搭界的地方。[14]所以耶和華的戰記上說:

"蘇法的哇哈伯與亞嫩河的谷,
[15]並向亞珥城眾谷的下坡,
是靠近摩押的境界。"

[16]以色列人從那裏起行,到了比珥(註:"比珥"就是"井"的意思)。從前耶和華吩咐摩西說:"招聚百姓,我好給他們水喝。",說的就是這井。

17當時，以色列人唱歌説：

"井啊，湧上水來！
　你們要向這井歌唱。
18這井是首領和民中的尊貴人，
　用圭、用杖所挖所掘的。"

以色列人從曠野往瑪他拿去，19從瑪他拿到拿哈列，從拿哈列到巴末，20從巴末到了摩押地的谷，又到那下望曠野之毘斯迦的山頂。

戰敗西宏與噩

21以色列人差遣使者去見亞摩利人的王西宏，説：

22 "求你容我們從你的地經過，我們不偏入田間和葡萄園，也不喝井裏的水，只走大道（註：原文作"王道"），直到過了你的境界。"

23西宏不容以色列人從他的境界經過，就招聚他的眾民出到曠野，要攻擊以色列人，到了雅雜，與以色列人爭戰。24以色列人用刀殺了他，得了他的地，從亞嫩河到雅博河，直到亞捫人的境界，因為亞捫人的境界多有堅壘。25以色列人奪取這一切的城邑，也住亞摩利人的城邑，就是希實本與希實本的一切鄉村。26這希實本是亞摩利王西宏的京城，西宏曾與摩押的先王爭戰，從他手中奪取了全地，直到亞嫩河。

27所以那些作詩歌的説：

"你們來到希實本，
　願西宏的城被修造，被建立。

28 "因為有火從希實本發出，
　有火焰出於西宏的城，
　燒盡摩押的亞珥和亞嫩河邱壇的
　　祭司（註："祭司"原文作"主"）。
29摩押啊，你有禍了！
　基抹的民哪，你們滅亡了！
　基抹的男子逃奔，
　女子被擄，
　交付亞摩利的王西宏。

30 "我們射了他們，
　希實本直到底本盡皆毀滅。

17Then Israel sang this song:

"Spring up, O well!
　Sing about it,
18about the well that the princes dug,
　that the nobles of the people sank—
　the nobles with scepters and staffs."

Then they went from the desert to Mattanah, 19from Mattanah to Nahaliel, from Nahaliel to Bamoth, 20and from Bamoth to the valley in Moab where the top of Pisgah overlooks the wasteland.

Defeat of Sihon and Og

21Israel sent messengers to say to Sihon king of the Amorites:

22"Let us pass through your country. We will not turn aside into any field or vineyard, or drink water from any well. We will travel along the king's highway until we have passed through your territory."

23But Sihon would not let Israel pass through his territory. He mustered his entire army and marched out into the desert against Israel. When he reached Jahaz, he fought with Israel. 24Israel, however, put him to the sword and took over his land from the Arnon to the Jabbok, but only as far as the Ammonites, because their border was fortified. 25Israel captured all the cities of the Amorites and occupied them, including Heshbon and all its surrounding settlements. 26Heshbon was the city of Sihon king of the Amorites, who had fought against the former king of Moab and had taken from him all his land as far as the Arnon.

27That is why the poets say:

"Come to Heshbon and let it be rebuilt;
　let Sihon's city be restored.

28"Fire went out from Heshbon,
　a blaze from the city of Sihon.
　It consumed Ar of Moab,
　the citizens of Arnon's heights.
29Woe to you, O Moab!
　You are destroyed, O people of Chemosh!
　He has given up his sons as fugitives
　and his daughters as captives
　to Sihon king of the Amorites.

30"But we have overthrown them;
　Heshbon is destroyed all the way to Dibon.

We have demolished them as far as Nophah,
which extends to Medeba."

31So Israel settled in the land of the Amorites.
32After Moses had sent spies to Jazer, the
Israelites captured its surrounding settlements
and drove out the Amorites who were there.
33Then they turned and went up along the road
toward Bashan, and Og king of Bashan and his
whole army marched out to meet them in battle
at Edrei.

34The LORD said to Moses, "Do not be afraid
of him, for I have handed him over to you, with
his whole army and his land. Do to him what
you did to Sihon king of the Amorites, who
reigned in Heshbon."

35So they struck him down, together with his
sons and his whole army, leaving them no survivors. And they took possession of his land.

Balak Summons Balaam

22 Then the Israelites traveled to the plains
of Moab and camped along the Jordan
across from Jericho.[a]
2Now Balak son of Zippor saw all that Israel
had done to the Amorites, 3and Moab was terrified because there were so many people. Indeed,
Moab was filled with dread because of the
Israelites.

4The Moabites said to the elders of Midian,
"This horde is going to lick up everything
around us, as an ox licks up the grass of the
field."

So Balak son of Zippor, who was king of
Moab at that time, 5sent messengers to summon
Balaam son of Beor, who was at Pethor, near the
River,[b] in his native land. Balak said:

"A people has come out of Egypt; they
cover the face of the land and have settled
next to me. 6Now come and put a curse on
these people, because they are too powerful
for me. Perhaps then I will be able to defeat
them and drive them out of the country. For I
know that those you bless are blessed, and
those you curse are cursed."

7The elders of Moab and Midian left, taking
with them the fee for divination. When they
came to Balaam, they told him what Balak had
said.

8"Spend the night here," Balaam said to
them, "and I will bring you back the answer the

我們使地變為荒場,直到挪法,
這挪法直延到米底巴。"

31這樣,以色列人就住在亞摩利人
之地。

32摩西打發人去窺探雅謝,以色
列人就佔了雅謝的鎮市,趕出那裏的
亞摩利人。33以色列人轉回,向巴珊
去。巴珊王噩和他的眾民都出來,在
以得來與他們交戰。

34耶和華對摩西說:"不要怕
他,因我已將他和他的眾民,並他的
地,都交在你手中,你要待他像從前
待住希實本的亞摩利王西宏一般。"

35於是,他們殺了他和他的眾
子,並他的眾民,沒有留下一個,就
得住他的地。

巴勒召巴蘭

22 以色列人起行,在摩押平
原、約旦河東,對着耶利哥
安營。
2以色列人向亞摩利人所行的一
切事,西撥的兒子巴勒都看見了。
3摩押人因以色列民甚多,就大大懼
怕,心內憂急。

4對米甸的長老說:"現在這眾
人要把我們四圍所有的一概餂盡,就
如牛餂盡田間的草一般。"

那時西撥的兒子巴勒作摩押王。
5他差遣使者往大河邊的毗奪去,到
比珥的兒子巴蘭本鄉那裏,召巴蘭
來,說:

"有一宗民從埃及出來,遮滿地
面,與我對住。6這民比我強盛,
現在求你來為我咒詛他們,或者我
能得勝,攻打他們,趕出此地。因
為我知道你為誰祝福,誰就得福;
你咒詛誰,誰就受咒詛。"

7摩押的長老和米甸的長老手裏
拿着卦金到了巴蘭那裏,將巴勒的話
都告訴了他。

8巴蘭說:"你們今夜在這裏住
宿,我必照耶和華所曉諭我的,回報

a 1 Hebrew Jordan of Jericho; possibly an ancient name for the
Jordan River   b 5 That is, the Euphrates

你們。」摩押的使臣就在巴蘭那裏住下了。

9 神臨到巴蘭那裏說：「在你這裏的人都是誰？」

10 巴蘭回答說：「是摩押王西撥的兒子巴勒，打發人到我這裏來，說：11『從埃及出來的民遮滿地面，你來為我咒詛他們，或者我能與他們爭戰，把他們趕出去。』」

12 神對巴蘭說：「你不可同他們去，也不可咒詛那民，因為那民是蒙福的。」

13 巴蘭早晨起來，對巴勒的使臣說：「你們回本地去吧，因為耶和華不容我和你們同去。」

14 摩押的使臣就起來，回巴勒那裏去，說：「巴蘭不肯和我們同來。」

15 巴勒又差遣使臣，比先前的又多又尊貴。16 他們到了巴蘭那裏，對他說：

「西撥的兒子巴勒這樣說：求你不容甚麼事攔阻你不到我這裏來，17 因為我必使你得極大的尊榮，你向我要甚麼，我就給你甚麼，只求你來為我咒詛這民。」

18 巴蘭回答巴勒的臣僕說：「巴勒是將他滿屋的金銀給我，我行大事小事也不得越過耶和華我神的命。19 現在我請你們今夜在這裏住宿，等我得知耶和華還要對我說甚麼。」

20 當夜神臨到巴蘭那裏說：「這些人若來召你，你就起來同他們去，你只要遵行我對你所說的話。」

巴蘭的驢

21 巴蘭早晨起來，備上驢，和摩押的使臣一同去了。22 神因他去就發了怒，耶和華的使者站在路上敵擋他。他騎着驢，有兩個僕人跟隨他。23 驢看見耶和華的使者站在路上，手裏有拔出來的刀，就從路上跨進田間，巴蘭便打驢要叫牠回轉上路。

24 耶和華的使者就站在葡萄園的窄路上，這邊有牆，那邊也有牆。25 驢看見耶和華的使者就貼靠牆，將巴蘭的腳擠傷了，巴蘭又打牠。

LORD gives me." So the Moabite princes stayed with him.

9God came to Balaam and asked, "Who are these men with you?"

10Balaam said to God, "Balak son of Zippor, king of Moab, sent me this message: 11'A people that has come out of Egypt covers the face of the land. Now come and put a curse on them for me. Perhaps then I will be able to fight them and drive them away.'"

12But God said to Balaam, "Do not go with them. You must not put a curse on those people, because they are blessed."

13The next morning Balaam got up and said to Balak's princes, "Go back to your own country, for the LORD has refused to let me go with you."

14So the Moabite princes returned to Balak and said, "Balaam refused to come with us."

15Then Balak sent other princes, more numerous and more distinguished than the first. 16They came to Balaam and said:

"This is what Balak son of Zippor says: Do not let anything keep you from coming to me, 17because I will reward you handsomely and do whatever you say. Come and put a curse on these people for me."

18But Balaam answered them, "Even if Balak gave me his palace filled with silver and gold, I could not do anything great or small to go beyond the command of the LORD my God. 19Now stay here tonight as the others did, and I will find out what else the LORD will tell me."

20That night God came to Balaam and said, "Since these men have come to summon you, go with them, but do only what I tell you."

Balaam's Donkey

21Balaam got up in the morning, saddled his donkey and went with the princes of Moab. 22But God was very angry when he went, and the angel of the LORD stood in the road to oppose him. Balaam was riding on his donkey, and his two servants were with him. 23When the donkey saw the angel of the LORD standing in the road with a drawn sword in his hand, she turned off the road into a field. Balaam beat her to get her back on the road.

24Then the angel of the LORD stood in a narrow path between two vineyards, with walls on both sides. 25When the donkey saw the angel of the LORD, she pressed close to the wall, crushing Balaam's foot against it. So he beat her again.

26Then the angel of the LORD moved on ahead and stood in a narrow place where there was no room to turn, either to the right or to the left. 27When the donkey saw the angel of the LORD, she lay down under Balaam, and he was angry and beat her with his staff. 28Then the LORD opened the donkey's mouth, and she said to Balaam, "What have I done to you to make you beat me these three times?"

29Balaam answered the donkey, "You have made a fool of me! If I had a sword in my hand, I would kill you right now."

30The donkey said to Balaam, "Am I not your own donkey, which you have always ridden, to this day? Have I been in the habit of doing this to you?"

"No," he said.

31Then the LORD opened Balaam's eyes, and he saw the angel of the LORD standing in the road with his sword drawn. So he bowed low and fell facedown.

32The angel of the LORD asked him, "Why have you beaten your donkey these three times? I have come here to oppose you because your path is a reckless one before me.a 33The donkey saw me and turned away from me these three times. If she had not turned away, I would certainly have killed you by now, but I would have spared her."

34Balaam said to the angel of the LORD, "I have sinned. I did not realize you were standing in the road to oppose me. Now if you are displeased, I will go back."

35The angel of the LORD said to Balaam, "Go with the men, but speak only what I tell you." So Balaam went with the princes of Balak.

36When Balak heard that Balaam was coming, he went out to meet him at the Moabite town on the Arnon border, at the edge of his territory. 37Balak said to Balaam, "Did I not send you an urgent summons? Why didn't you come to me? Am I really not able to reward you?"

38"Well, I have come to you now," Balaam replied. "But can I say just anything? I must speak only what God puts in my mouth."

39Then Balaam went with Balak to Kiriath Huzoth. 40Balak sacrificed cattle and sheep, and gave some to Balaam and the princes who were with him. 41The next morning Balak took Balaam up to Bamoth Baal, and from there he saw part of the people.

26耶和華的使者又往前去，站在狹窄之處，左右都沒有轉折的地方。27驢看見耶和華的使者，就臥在巴蘭底下，巴蘭發怒用杖打驢。28耶和華叫驢開口，對巴蘭說："我向你行了甚麼，你竟打我這三次呢？"

29巴蘭對驢說："因為你戲弄我，我恨不能手中有刀，把你殺了。"

30驢對巴蘭說："我不是你從小時直到今日所騎的驢嗎？我素常向你這樣行過嗎？"

巴蘭說："沒有。"

31當時，耶和華使巴蘭的眼目明亮，他就看見耶和華的使者站在路上，手裏有拔出來的刀，巴蘭便低頭俯伏在地。

32耶和華的使者對他說："你為何這三次打你的驢呢？我出來敵擋你，因你所行的在我面前偏僻。33驢看見我就三次從我面前偏過去；驢若沒有偏過去，我早把你殺了，留牠存活。"

34巴蘭對耶和華的使者說："我有罪了，我不知道你站在路上阻擋我。你若不喜歡我去，我就轉回。"

35耶和華的使者對巴蘭說："你同這些人去吧！你只要說我對你說的話。"於是巴蘭同着巴勒的使臣去了。

36巴勒聽見巴蘭來了，就往摩押京城去迎接他，這城是在邊界上，在亞嫩河旁。37巴勒對巴蘭說："我不是急急地打發人到你那裏去召你嗎？你為何不到我這裏來呢？我豈不能使你得尊榮嗎？"

38巴蘭說："我已經到你這裏來了，現在我豈能擅自說甚麼呢？神將甚麼話傳給我，我就說甚麼。"

39巴蘭和巴勒同行，來到基列胡瑣。40巴勒宰了（註：原文作"獻"）牛羊，送給巴蘭和陪伴的使臣。41到了早晨，巴勒領巴蘭到巴力的高處，巴蘭從那裏觀看以色列營的邊界。

---

a 32 The meaning of the Hebrew for this clause is uncertain.

巴蘭第一次傳諭

23 巴蘭對巴勒說：“你在這裏給我築七座壇，為我預備七隻公牛，七隻公羊。” ²巴勒照巴蘭的話行了。巴勒和巴蘭在每座壇上獻一隻公牛，一隻公羊。

³巴蘭對巴勒說：“你站在你的燔祭旁邊，我且往前去，或者耶和華來迎見我，他指示我甚麼，我必告訴你。”於是巴蘭上一淨光的高處。

⁴神迎見巴蘭。巴蘭說：“我預備了七座壇，在每座壇上獻了一隻公牛，一隻公羊。”

⁵耶和華將話傳給巴蘭，又說：“你回到巴勒那裏，要如此如此說。”

⁶他就回到巴勒那裏，見他同摩押的使臣都站在燔祭旁邊。⁷巴蘭便題起詩歌說：

“巴勒引我出亞蘭；
　摩押王引我出東山，
說：
‘來啊，為我咒詛雅各；
　來啊，怒罵以色列。’
⁸神沒有咒詛的，
　我焉能咒詛？
耶和華沒有怒罵的，
　我焉能怒罵？
⁹我從高峯看他，
　從小山望他。
這是獨居的民，
　不列在萬民中。
¹⁰誰能數點雅各的塵土？
　誰能計算以色列的四分之一？
我願如義人之死而死，
　我願如義人之終而終。”

¹¹巴勒對巴蘭說：“你向我做的是甚麼事呢？我領你來咒詛我的仇敵，不料你竟為他們祝福！”

¹²他回答說：“耶和華傳給我的話，我能不謹慎傳說嗎？”

巴蘭第二次傳諭

¹³巴勒說：“求你同我往別處去，在那裏可以看見他們；你不能全看見，只能看見他們邊界上的人，在那裏要為我咒詛他們。”¹⁴於是領巴蘭到了瑣腓田，上了毘斯迦山頂，築七座壇，每座壇上獻一隻公牛，一隻公羊。

¹⁵巴蘭對巴勒說：“你站在這燔祭旁邊，等我往那邊去迎見耶和華。”

Balaam's First Oracle

23 Balaam said, "Build me seven altars here, and prepare seven bulls and seven rams for me." ²Balak did as Balaam said, and the two of them offered a bull and a ram on each altar.

³Then Balaam said to Balak, "Stay here beside your offering while I go aside. Perhaps the LORD will come to meet with me. Whatever he reveals to me I will tell you." Then he went off to a barren height.

⁴God met with him, and Balaam said, "I have prepared seven altars, and on each altar I have offered a bull and a ram."

⁵The LORD put a message in Balaam's mouth and said, "Go back to Balak and give him this message."

⁶So he went back to him and found him standing beside his offering, with all the princes of Moab. ⁷Then Balaam uttered his oracle:

"Balak brought me from Aram,
　the king of Moab from the eastern
　　mountains.
'Come,' he said, 'curse Jacob for me;
　come, denounce Israel.'
⁸How can I curse
　those whom God has not cursed?
How can I denounce
　those whom the LORD has not denounced?
⁹From the rocky peaks I see them,
　from the heights I view them.
I see a people who live apart
　and do not consider themselves one of the
　　nations.
¹⁰Who can count the dust of Jacob
　or number the fourth part of Israel?
Let me die the death of the righteous,
　and may my end be like theirs!"

¹¹Balak said to Balaam, "What have you done to me? I brought you to curse my enemies, but you have done nothing but bless them!"

¹²He answered, "Must I not speak what the LORD puts in my mouth?"

Balaam's Second Oracle

¹³Then Balak said to him, "Come with me to another place where you can see them; you will see only a part but not all of them. And from there, curse them for me." ¹⁴So he took him to the field of Zophim on the top of Pisgah, and there he built seven altars and offered a bull and a ram on each altar.

¹⁵Balaam said to Balak, "Stay here beside your offering while I meet with him over there."

16The LORD met with Balaam and put a message in his mouth and said, "Go back to Balak and give him this message."

17So he went to him and found him standing beside his offering, with the princes of Moab. Balak asked him, "What did the LORD say?"

18Then he uttered his oracle:

"Arise, Balak, and listen;
    hear me, son of Zippor.
19God is not a man, that he should lie,
    nor a son of man, that he should change his
        mind.
Does he speak and then not act?
    Does he promise and not fulfill?
20I have received a command to bless;
    he has blessed, and I cannot change it.
21"No misfortune is seen in Jacob,
    no misery observed in Israel.*
The LORD their God is with them;
    the shout of the King is among them.
22God brought them out of Egypt;
    they have the strength of a wild ox.
23There is no sorcery against Jacob,
    no divination against Israel.
It will now be said of Jacob
    and of Israel, 'See what God has done!'
24The people rise like a lioness;
    they rouse themselves like a lion
that does not rest till he devours his prey
    and drinks the blood of his victims."

25Then Balak said to Balaam, "Neither curse them at all nor bless them at all!"

26Balaam answered, "Did I not tell you I must do whatever the LORD says?"

Balaam's Third Oracle

27Then Balak said to Balaam, "Come, let me take you to another place. Perhaps it will please God to let you curse them for me from there." 28And Balak took Balaam to the top of Peor, overlooking the wasteland.

29Balaam said, "Build me seven altars here, and prepare seven bulls and seven rams for me." 30Balak did as Balaam had said, and offered a bull and a ram on each altar.

24 Now when Balaam saw that it pleased the LORD to bless Israel, he did not resort to sorcery as at other times, but turned his face toward the desert. 2When Balaam looked out and saw Israel encamped tribe by tribe, the Spirit of God came upon him

a 21 Or He has not looked on Jacob's offenses / or on the wrongs found in Israel.

16耶和華臨到巴蘭那裏，將話傳給他，又說：「你回到巴勒那裏，要如此如此說。」

17他就回到巴勒那裏，見他站在燔祭旁邊，摩押的使臣也和他在一處。巴勒問他說：「耶和華說了甚麼話呢？」

18巴蘭就題詩歌說：

「巴勒，你起來聽；
    西撥的兒子，你聽我言。
19神非人，必不致說謊；
    也非人子，必不致後悔。
他說話豈不照著行呢？
    他發言豈不要成就呢？
20我奉命祝福，
    神也曾賜福，此事我不能翻轉。
21「他未見雅各中有罪孽，
    也未見以色列中有奸惡。
耶和華他的神和他同在，
    有歡呼王的聲音在他們中間。
22神領他們出埃及，
    他們似乎有野牛之力。
23斷沒有法術可以害雅各，
    也沒有占卜可以害以色列。
現在必有人論及雅各，
    就是論及以色列說：
    『神為他行了何等的大事！』
24這民起來彷彿母獅，
    挺身好像公獅，
未曾吃野食，未曾喝被傷者之血，
    決不躺臥。」

25巴勒對巴蘭說：「你一點不要咒詛他們，也不要為他們祝福。」

26巴蘭回答巴勒說：「我豈不是告訴你說：凡耶和華所說的，我必須遵行嗎？」

巴蘭第三次傳諭

27巴勒對巴蘭說：「來吧，我領你往別處去，或者神喜歡你在那裏為我咒詛他們。」28巴勒就領巴蘭到那下望曠野的毗珥山頂上。

29巴蘭對巴勒說：「你在這裏為我築七座壇，又在這裏為我預備七隻公牛、七隻公羊。」30巴勒就照巴蘭的話行，在每座壇上獻一隻公牛、一隻公羊。

24 巴蘭見耶和華喜歡賜福與以色列，就不像前兩次去求法術，卻面向曠野。2巴蘭舉目，看見以色列人照著支派居住，神的靈就臨到他身上。

³他便題起詩歌說：

　　“比珥的兒子巴蘭說：
　　　　眼目閉住的人說（註：“閉住”或作
　　　　“睜開”），
⁴得聽神的言語，
　　　得見全能者的異象，
　　　眼目睜開而仆倒的人說：

⁵　“雅各啊，你的帳棚何等華美！
　　　以色列啊，你的帳幕何其華麗！

⁶　“如接連的山谷，
　　　如河旁的園子，
　　　如耶和華所栽的沉香樹，
　　　如水邊的香柏木，
⁷水要從他的桶裏流出，
　　　種子要撒在多水之處。

　　“他的王必超過亞甲，
　　　他的國必要振興。

⁸　“神領他出埃及，
　　　他似乎有野牛之力。
　　　他要吞吃敵國，
　　　折斷他們的骨頭，
　　　用箭射透他們。
⁹他蹲如公獅，
　　　臥如母獅，誰敢惹他？

　　“凡給你祝福的，願他蒙福；
　　　凡咒詛你的，願他受咒詛。”

　　¹⁰巴勒向巴蘭生氣，就拍起手
來，對巴蘭說：“我召你來為我咒詛
仇敵，不料，你這三次竟為他們祝
福。¹¹如今你快回本地去吧！我想使
你得大尊榮，耶和華卻阻止你不得尊
榮。”

　　¹²巴蘭對巴勒說：“我豈不是對
你所差遣到我那裏的使者說：¹³‘巴
勒就是將他滿屋的金銀給我，我也不
得越過耶和華的命，憑自己的心意行
好行歹，耶和華說甚麼，我就要說甚
麼’？¹⁴現在我要回本族去，你來，
我告訴你這民日後要怎樣待你的
民。”

巴蘭第四次傳諭
　　¹⁵他就題起詩歌說：

　　“比珥的兒子巴蘭說：

³and he uttered his oracle:

　　"The oracle of Balaam son of Beor,
　　　the oracle of one whose eye sees clearly,
⁴the oracle of one who hears the words of God,
　　who sees a vision from the Almighty,ᵃ
　　who falls prostrate, and whose eyes are
　　　opened:

⁵"How beautiful are your tents, O Jacob,
　　your dwelling places, O Israel!

⁶"Like valleys they spread out,
　　like gardens beside a river,
　　like aloes planted by the LORD,
　　like cedars beside the waters.
⁷Water will flow from their buckets;
　　their seed will have abundant water.

　　"Their king will be greater than Agag;
　　　their kingdom will be exalted.

⁸"God brought them out of Egypt;
　　they have the strength of a wild ox.
　　They devour hostile nations
　　and break their bones in pieces;
　　　with their arrows they pierce them.
⁹Like a lion they crouch and lie down,
　　like a lioness—who dares to rouse them?

　　"May those who bless you be blessed
　　and those who curse you be cursed!"

¹⁰Then Balak's anger burned against Balaam.
He struck his hands together and said to him, "I
summoned you to curse my enemies, but you
have blessed them these three times. ¹¹Now
leave at once and go home! I said I would
reward you handsomely, but the LORD has kept
you from being rewarded."

　　¹²Balaam answered Balak, "Did I not tell the
messengers you sent me, ¹³'Even if Balak gave
me his palace filled with silver and gold, I could
not do anything of my own accord, good or bad,
to go beyond the command of the LORD—and I
must say only what the LORD says'? ¹⁴Now I am
going back to my people, but come, let me warn
you of what this people will do to your people
in days to come."

Balaam's Fourth Oracle
　　¹⁵Then he uttered his oracle:

　　"The oracle of Balaam son of Beor,

---

a 4 Hebrew Shaddai; also in verse 16

the oracle of one whose eye sees clearly,
¹⁶the oracle of one who hears the words of God,
who has knowledge from the Most High,
who sees a vision from the Almighty,
who falls prostrate, and whose eyes are
opened:

¹⁷"I see him, but not now;
I behold him, but not near.
A star will come out of Jacob;
a scepter will rise out of Israel.
He will crush the foreheads of Moab,
the skulls^a of^b all the sons of Sheth.^c
¹⁸Edom will be conquered;
Seir, his enemy, will be conquered,
but Israel will grow strong.
¹⁹A ruler will come out of Jacob
and destroy the survivors of the city."

Balaam's Final Oracles

²⁰Then Balaam saw Amalek and uttered his
oracle:

"Amalek was first among the nations,
but he will come to ruin at last."

²¹Then he saw the Kenites and uttered his
oracle:

"Your dwelling place is secure,
your nest is set in a rock;
²²yet you Kenites will be destroyed
when Asshur takes you captive."

²³Then he uttered his oracle:

"Ah, who can live when God does this?^d
²⁴ Ships will come from the shores of Kittim;
they will subdue Asshur and Eber,
but they too will come to ruin."

²⁵Then Balaam got up and returned home
and Balak went his own way.

Moab Seduces Israel

25 While Israel was staying in Shittim, the
men began to indulge in sexual immorality with Moabite women, ²who invited them to the sacrifices to their gods. The people ate and bowed down before these gods. ³So

眼目閉住的人說（註：「閉住」或作
「睜開」）：
¹⁶得聽神的言語，
明白至高者的意旨，
看見全能者的異象，
眼目睜開而仆倒的人說：

¹⁷"我看他卻不在現時，
我望他卻不在近日。
有星要出於雅各，
有杖要興於以色列，
必打破摩押的四角，
毀壞擾亂之子。
¹⁸他必得以東為基業，
又得仇敵之地西珥為產業。
以色列必行事勇敢。
¹⁹有一位出於雅各的，必掌大權，
他要除滅城中的餘民。"

巴蘭最後傳諭

²⁰巴蘭觀看亞瑪力，就題起詩歌
說：

"亞瑪力原為諸國之首，
但他終必沉淪。"

²¹巴蘭觀看基尼人，就題起詩歌
說：

"你的住處本是堅固，
你的窩巢做在巖石中；
²²然而基尼必至衰微，
直到亞述把你擄去。"

²³巴蘭又題起詩歌說：

"哀哉！神行這事，誰能得活？
²⁴必有人乘船從基提界而來，
苦害亞述，苦害希伯，
他也必至沉淪。"

²⁵於是巴蘭起來回他本地去，巴
勒也回去了。

摩押引誘以色列犯罪

25 以色列人住在什亭，百姓與
摩押女子行起淫亂。²因為這
女子叫百姓來，一同給她們
的神獻祭，百姓就吃她們的祭物，跪
拜她們的神。³以色列人與巴力毗珥

---

a 17 Samaritan Pentateuch (see also Jer. 48:45); the meaning of
the word in the Masoretic Text is uncertain.   *b 17* Or possibly
Moab, / batter   *c 17* Or *all the noisy boasters*   *d 23* Masoretic
Text; with a different word division of the Hebrew *A people
will gather from the north.*

連合，耶和華的怒氣就向以色列人發作。

⁴耶和華吩咐摩西說："將百姓中所有的族長在我面前對着日頭懸掛，使我向以色列人所發的怒氣可以消了。"

⁵於是摩西吩咐以色列的審判官說："凡屬你們的人，有與巴力毘珥連合的，你們各人要把他們殺了。"

⁶摩西和以色列全會眾正在會幕門前哭泣的時候，誰知，有以色列中的一個人，當他們眼前，帶着一個米甸女人到他弟兄那裏去。⁷祭司亞倫的孫子、以利亞撒的兒子非尼哈看見了，就從會中起來，手裏拿着槍，⁸跟隨那以色列人進亭子裏去，便將以色列人和那女人由腹中刺透。這樣，在以色列人中瘟疫就止息了。⁹那時遭瘟疫死的，有二萬四千人。

¹⁰耶和華曉諭摩西說："¹¹"祭司亞倫的孫子、以利亞撒的兒子非尼哈，使我向以色列人所發的怒消了，因他在他們中間，以我的忌邪為心，使我不在忌邪中把他們除滅。¹²因此，你要說：'我將我平安的約賜給他。¹³這約要給他和他的後裔，作為永遠當祭司職任的約，因他為神有忌邪的心，為以色列人贖罪。'"

¹⁴那與米甸女人一同被殺的以色列人，名叫心利，是撒路的兒子，是西緬一個宗族的首領。¹⁵那被殺的米甸女人，名叫哥斯比，是蘇珥的女兒，這蘇珥是米甸一個宗族的首領。

¹⁶耶和華曉諭摩西說："¹⁷"你要擾害米甸人，擊殺他們，¹⁸因為他們用詭計擾害你們，在毘珥的事上，和他們的姊妹米甸首領的女兒哥斯比的事上，用這詭計誘惑了你們。這哥斯比當瘟疫流行的日子，因毘珥的事被殺了。"

第二次統計人口

26 瘟疫之後，耶和華曉諭摩西和祭司亞倫的兒子以利亞撒說：²"你們要將以色列全會眾，按他們的宗族，凡以色列中從二十歲以外、能出去打仗的，計算總數。"³摩西和祭司以利亞撒在摩押平原與耶利哥相對的約旦河邊，向以

Israel joined in worshiping the Baal of Peor. And the LORD's anger burned against them.

⁴The LORD said to Moses, "Take all the leaders of these people, kill them and expose them in broad daylight before the LORD, so that the LORD's fierce anger may turn away from Israel."

⁵So Moses said to Israel's judges, "Each of you must put to death those of your men who have joined in worshiping the Baal of Peor."

⁶Then an Israelite man brought to his family a Midianite woman right before the eyes of Moses and the whole assembly of Israel while they were weeping at the entrance to the Tent of Meeting. ⁷When Phinehas son of Eleazar, the son of Aaron, the priest, saw this, he left the assembly, took a spear in his hand ⁸and followed the Israelite into the tent. He drove the spear through both of them—through the Israelite and into the woman's body. Then the plague against the Israelites was stopped; ⁹but those who died in the plague numbered 24,000.

¹⁰The LORD said to Moses, ¹¹"Phinehas son of Eleazar, the son of Aaron, the priest, has turned my anger away from the Israelites; for he was as zealous as I am for my honor among them, so that in my zeal I did not put an end to them. ¹²Therefore tell him I am making my covenant of peace with him. ¹³He and his descendants will have a covenant of a lasting priesthood, because he was zealous for the honor of his God and made atonement for the Israelites."

¹⁴The name of the Israelite who was killed with the Midianite woman was Zimri son of Salu, the leader of a Simeonite family. ¹⁵And the name of the Midianite woman who was put to death was Cozbi daughter of Zur, a tribal chief of a Midianite family.

¹⁶The LORD said to Moses, ¹⁷"Treat the Midianites as enemies and kill them, ¹⁸because they treated you as enemies when they deceived you in the affair of Peor and their sister Cozbi, the daughter of a Midianite leader, the woman who was killed when the plague came as a result of Peor."

The Second Census

26 After the plague the LORD said to Moses and Eleazar son of Aaron, the priest, ²"Take a census of the whole Israelite community by families—all those twenty years old or more who are able to serve in the army of Israel." ³So on the plains of Moab by the Jordan across from Jericho,ᵃ Moses and Eleazar the

a 3 Hebrew Jordan of Jericho; possibly an ancient name for the Jordan River; also in verse 63

priest spoke with them and said, [4]"Take a census of the men twenty years old or more, as the LORD commanded Moses."

These were the Israelites who came out of Egypt:

[5]The descendants of Reuben, the firstborn son of Israel, were:

through Hanoch, the Hanochite clan;
through Pallu, the Palluite clan;
[6]through Hezron, the Hezronite clan;
through Carmi, the Carmite clan.

[7]These were the clans of Reuben; those numbered were 43,730.

[8]The son of Pallu was Eliab, [9]and the sons of Eliab were Nemuel, Dathan and Abiram. The same Dathan and Abiram were the community officials who rebelled against Moses and Aaron and were among Korah's followers when they rebelled against the LORD. [10]The earth opened its mouth and swallowed them along with Korah, whose followers died when the fire devoured the 250 men. And they served as a warning sign. [11]The line of Korah, however, did not die out.

[12]The descendants of Simeon by their clans were:

through Nemuel, the Nemuelite clan;
through Jamin, the Jaminite clan;
through Jakin, the Jakinite clan;
[13]through Zerah, the Zerahite clan;
through Shaul, the Shaulite clan.

[14]These were the clans of Simeon; there were 22,200 men.

[15]The descendants of Gad by their clans were:
through Zephon, the Zephonite clan;
through Haggi, the Haggite clan;
through Shuni, the Shunite clan;
[16]through Ozni, the Oznite clan;
through Eri, the Erite clan;
[17]through Arodi,[a] the Arodite clan;
through Areli, the Arelite clan.

[18]These were the clans of Gad; those numbered were 40,500.

[19]Er and Onan were sons of Judah, but they died in Canaan.

[20]The descendants of Judah by their clans were:
through Shelah, the Shelanite clan;
through Perez, the Perezite clan;
through Zerah, the Zerahite clan.

---

a 17 Samaritan Pentateuch and Syriac (see also Gen. 46:16); Masoretic Text *Arod*

色列人說：[4]"將你們中間從二十歲以外的計算總數。"

是照耶和華吩咐出埃及地的摩西和以色列人的話。

[5]以色列的長子是呂便。呂便的眾子：
屬哈諾的，有哈諾族；
屬法路的，有法路族；
[6]屬希斯倫的，有希斯倫族；
屬迦米的，有迦米族。

[7]這就是呂便的各族，其中被數的，共有四萬三千七百三十名。

[8]法路的兒子是以利押。[9]以利押的眾子是尼母利、大坍、亞比蘭。這大坍、亞比蘭，就是從會中選召的，與可拉一黨同向耶和華爭鬧的時候，也向摩西、亞倫爭鬧，[10]地便開口吞了他們，和可拉、可拉的黨類一同死亡。那時火燒滅了二百五十個人，他們就作了警戒。[11]然而可拉的眾子沒有死亡。

[12]按着家族，西緬的眾子：
屬尼母利的，有尼母利族；
屬雅憫的，有雅憫族；
屬雅斤的，有雅斤族；
[13]屬謝拉的，有謝拉族；
屬掃羅的，有掃羅族。

[14]這就是西緬的各族，共有二萬二千二百名。

[15]按着家族，迦得的眾子：
屬洗分的，有洗分族；
屬哈基的，有哈基族；
屬書尼的，有書尼族；
[16]屬阿斯尼的，有阿斯尼族；
屬以利的，有以利族；
[17]屬亞律的，有亞律族；
屬亞列利的，有亞列利族。

[18]這就是迦得子孫的各族，照他們中間被數的，共有四萬零五百名。

[19]猶大的兒子是珥和俄南。這珥和俄南死在迦南地。

[20]按着家族，猶大其餘的眾子：
屬示拉的，有示拉族；
屬法勒斯的，有法勒斯族；
屬謝拉的，有謝拉族。

²¹法勒斯的兒子：
　　屬希斯倫的，有希斯倫族；
　　屬哈母勒的，有哈母勒族。
²²這就是猶大的各族，照他們中間被
數的，共有七萬六千五百名。

²³按着家族，以薩迦的眾子：

　　屬陀拉的，有陀拉族；
　　屬普瓦的，有普瓦族；
　²⁴屬雅述的，有雅述族；
　　屬伸崙的，有伸崙族。
²⁵這就是以薩迦的各族，照他們中間
被數的，共有六萬四千三百名。

²⁶按着家族，西布倫的眾子：

　　屬西烈的，有西烈族；
　　屬以倫的，有以倫族；
　　屬雅利的，有雅利族。
²⁷這就是西布倫的各族，照他們中間
被數的，共有六萬零五百名。

²⁸按着家族，約瑟的兒子有瑪拿西、
以法蓮。

²⁹瑪拿西的眾子：
　　屬瑪吉的，有瑪吉族；
　　瑪吉生基列；
　　屬基列的，有基列族。
³⁰基列的眾子：
　　屬伊以謝的，有伊以謝族；
　　屬希勒的，有希勒族；
　³¹屬亞斯烈的，有亞斯烈族；
　　屬示劍的，有示劍族；
　³²屬示米大的，有示米大族；
　　屬希弗的，有希弗族。
³³希弗的兒子西羅非哈沒兒子，只有
女兒。西羅非哈女兒的名字，就是
瑪拉、挪阿、曷拉、密迦、得撒。

³⁴這就是瑪拿西的各族，他們中間被
數的，共有五萬二千七百名。

³⁵按着家族，以法蓮的眾子：

　　屬書提拉的，有書提拉族；
　　屬比結的，有比結族；
　　屬他罕的，有他罕族。
³⁶書提拉的眾子：
　　屬以蘭的，有以蘭族。
³⁷這就是以法蓮子孫的各族，照他們
中間被數的，共有三萬二千五百名。

²¹The descendants of Perez were:
　　through Hezron, the Hezronite clan;
　　through Hamul, the Hamulite clan.
²²These were the clans of Judah; those numbered were 76,500.

²³The descendants of Issachar by their clans
were:
　　through Tola, the Tolaite clan;
　　through Puah, the Puite*a* clan;
　²⁴through Jashub, the Jashubite clan;
　　through Shimron, the Shimronite clan.
²⁵These were the clans of Issachar; those numbered were 64,300.

²⁶The descendants of Zebulun by their clans
were:
　　through Sered, the Seredite clan;
　　through Elon, the Elonite clan;
　　through Jahleel, the Jahleelite clan.
²⁷These were the clans of Zebulun; those numbered were 60,500.

²⁸The descendants of Joseph by their clans
through Manasseh and Ephraim were:

²⁹The descendants of Manasseh:
　　through Makir, the Makirite clan (Makir was
　　　the father of Gilead);
　　through Gilead, the Gileadite clan.
³⁰These were the descendants of Gilead:
　　through Iezer, the Iezerite clan;
　　through Helek, the Helekite clan;
　³¹through Asriel, the Asrielite clan;
　　through Shechem, the Shechemite clan;
　³²through Shemida, the Shemidaite clan;
　　through Hepher, the Hepherite clan.
　³³(Zelophehad son of Hepher had no sons;
　　he had only daughters, whose names
　　were Mahlah, Noah, Hoglah, Milcah and
　　Tirzah.)
³⁴These were the clans of Manasseh; those numbered were 52,700.

³⁵These were the descendants of Ephraim by
their clans:
　　through Shuthelah, the Shuthelahite clan;
　　through Beker, the Bekerite clan;
　　through Tahan, the Tahanite clan.
³⁶These were the descendants of Shuthelah:
　　through Eran, the Eranite clan.
³⁷These were the clans of Ephraim; those numbered were 32,500.

a 23 Samaritan Pentateuch, Septuagint, Vulgate and Syriac
(see also 1 Chron. 7:1); Masoretic Text *through Puvah, the Punite*

These were the descendants of Joseph by their clans.

38The descendants of Benjamin by their clans were:

through Bela, the Belaite clan;
through Ashbel, the Ashbelite clan;
through Ahiram, the Ahiramite clan;
39through Shupham,*a* the Shuphamite clan;
through Hupham, the Huphamite clan.
40The descendants of Bela through Ard and Naaman were:
through Ard,*b* the Ardite clan;
through Naaman, the Naamite clan.
41These were the clans of Benjamin; those numbered were 45,600.

42These were the descendants of Dan by their clans:
through Shuham, the Shuhamite clan.
These were the clans of Dan: 43All of them were Shuhamite clans; and those numbered were 64,400.

44The descendants of Asher by their clans were:
through Imnah, the Imnite clan;
through Ishvi, the Ishvite clan;
through Beriah, the Beriite clan;
45and through the descendants of Beriah:
through Heber, the Heberite clan;
through Malkiel, the Malkielite clan.
46(Asher had a daughter named Serah.)
47These were the clans of Asher; those numbered were 53,400.

48The descendants of Naphtali by their clans were:
through Jahzeel, the Jahzeelite clan;
through Guni, the Gunite clan;
49through Jezer, the Jezerite clan;
through Shillem, the Shillemite clan.
50These were the clans of Naphtali; those numbered were 45,400.

51The total number of the men of Israel was 601,730.

52The LORD said to Moses, 53"The land is to be allotted to them as an inheritance based on the number of names. 54To a larger group give a

按着家族，這都是約瑟的子孫。

38按着家族，便雅憫的眾子：

屬比拉的，有比拉族；
屬亞實別的，有亞實別族；
屬亞希蘭的，有亞希蘭族；
39屬書反的，有書反族；
屬戶反的，有戶反族。
40比拉的眾子是亞勒、乃幔：
屬亞勒的，有亞勒族；
屬乃幔的，有乃幔族。

41按着家族，這就是便雅憫的子孫，其中被數的，共有四萬五千六百名。

42按着家族，但的眾子：

屬書含的，有書含族。
按着家族，這就是但的各族。43照其中被數的，書含所有的各族，共有六萬四千四百名。

44按着家族，亞設的眾子：
屬音拿的，有音拿族；
屬亦施韋的，有亦施韋族；
屬比利亞的，有比利亞族。
45比利亞的眾子：
屬希別的，有希別族；
屬瑪結的，有瑪結族。
46亞設的女兒名叫西拉。
47這就是亞設子孫的各族，照他們中間被數的，共有五萬三千四百名。

48按着家族，拿弗他利的眾子：

屬雅薛的，有雅薛族；
屬沽尼的，有沽尼族；
49屬耶色的，有耶色族；
屬示冷的，有示冷族。
50按着家族，這就是拿弗他利的各族，他們中間被數的，共有四萬五千四百名。

51以色列人中被數的，共有六十萬零一千七百三十名。

52耶和華曉諭摩西說：53"你要按着人名的數目，將地分給這些人為業。54人多的，你要把產業多分給

a 39 A few manuscripts of the Masoretic Text, Samaritan Pentateuch, Vulgate and Syriac (see also Septuagint); most manuscripts of the Masoretic Text *Shephupham*
b 40 Samaritan Pentateuch and Vulgate (see also Septuagint); Masoretic Text does not have *through Ard.*

他們；人少的，你要把產業少分給他們；要照被數的人數，把產業分給各人。55雖是這樣，還要拈鬮分地。他們要按着祖宗各支派的名字承受為業。56要按着所拈的鬮，看人數多，人數少，把產業分給他們。"

57利未人，按着他們的各族被數的：

屬革順的，有革順族；
屬哥轄的，有哥轄族；
屬米拉利的，有米拉利族。
58利未的各族：
有立尼族、
希伯倫族、
瑪利族、
母示族、
可拉族。
哥轄生暗蘭。59暗蘭的妻，名叫約基別，是利未女子，生在埃及。她給暗蘭生了亞倫、摩西，並他們的姐姐米利暗。60亞倫生拿答、亞比戶、以利亞撒、以他瑪。61拿答、亞比戶在耶和華面前獻凡火的時候，就死了。

62利未人中，凡一個月以外被數的男丁，共有二萬三千。他們本來沒有數在以色列人中，因為在以色列人中，沒有分給他們產業。

63這些就是被摩西和祭司以利亞撒所數的，他們在摩押平原與耶利哥相對的約旦河邊數點以色列人。64但被數的人中，沒有一個是摩西和祭司亞倫從前在西奈的曠野所數的以色列人，65因為耶和華論到他們說："他們必要死在曠野。"所以，除了耶孚尼的兒子迦勒和嫩的兒子約書亞以外，連一個人也沒有存留。

西羅非哈的女兒

27 屬約瑟的兒子瑪拿西的各族，有瑪拿西的玄孫、瑪吉的曾孫、基列的孫子、希弗的兒子西羅非哈的女兒，名叫瑪拉、挪阿、曷拉、密迦、得撒。她們前來，2站在會幕門口，在摩西和祭司以

larger inheritance, and to a smaller group a smaller one; each is to receive its inheritance according to the number of those listed. 55Be sure that the land is distributed by lot. What each group inherits will be according to the names for its ancestral tribe. 56Each inheritance is to be distributed by lot among the larger and smaller groups."

57These were the Levites who were counted by their clans:
through Gershon, the Gershonite clan;
through Kohath, the Kohathite clan;
through Merari, the Merarite clan.
58These also were Levite clans:
the Libnite clan,
the Hebronite clan,
the Mahlite clan,
the Mushite clan,
the Korahite clan.
(Kohath was the forefather of Amram; 59the name of Amram's wife was Jochebed, a descendant of Levi, who was born to the Levites[a] in Egypt. To Amram she bore Aaron, Moses and their sister Miriam. 60Aaron was the father of Nadab and Abihu, Eleazar and Ithamar. 61But Nadab and Abihu died when they made an offering before the LORD with unauthorized fire.)

62All the male Levites a month old or more numbered 23,000. They were not counted along with the other Israelites because they received no inheritance among them.

63These are the ones counted by Moses and Eleazar the priest when they counted the Israelites on the plains of Moab by the Jordan across from Jericho. 64Not one of them was among those counted by Moses and Aaron the priest when they counted the Israelites in the Desert of Sinai. 65For the LORD had told those Israelites they would surely die in the desert, and not one of them was left except Caleb son of Jephunneh and Joshua son of Nun.

Zelophehad's Daughters

27 The daughters of Zelophehad son of Hepher, the son of Gilead, the son of Makir, the son of Manasseh, belonged to the clans of Manasseh son of Joseph. The names of the daughters were Mahlah, Noah, Hoglah, Milcah and Tirzah. They approached 2the entrance to the Tent of Meeting and stood

a 59 Or Jochebed, a daughter of Levi, who was born to Levi

before Moses, Eleazar the priest, the leaders and the whole assembly, and said, [3]"Our father died in the desert. He was not among Korah's followers, who banded together against the LORD, but he died for his own sin and left no sons. [4]Why should our father's name disappear from his clan because he had no son? Give us property among our father's relatives."

[5]So Moses brought their case before the LORD [6]and the LORD said to him, [7]"What Zelophehad's daughters are saying is right. You must certainly give them property as an inheritance among their father's relatives and turn their father's inheritance over to them.

[8]"Say to the Israelites, 'If a man dies and leaves no son, turn his inheritance over to his daughter. [9]If he has no daughter, give his inheritance to his brothers. [10]If he has no brothers, give his inheritance to his father's brothers. [11]If his father had no brothers, give his inheritance to the nearest relative in his clan, that he may possess it. This is to be a legal requirement for the Israelites, as the LORD commanded Moses.' "

Joshua to Succeed Moses

[12]Then the LORD said to Moses, "Go up this mountain in the Abarim range and see the land I have given the Israelites. [13]After you have seen it, you too will be gathered to your people, as your brother Aaron was, [14]for when the community rebelled at the waters in the Desert of Zin, both of you disobeyed my command to honor me as holy before their eyes." (These were the waters of Meribah Kadesh, in the Desert of Zin.)

[15]Moses said to the LORD, [16]"May the LORD, the God of the spirits of all mankind, appoint a man over this community [17]to go out and come in before them, one who will lead them out and bring them in, so the LORD's people will not be like sheep without a shepherd."

[18]So the LORD said to Moses, "Take Joshua son of Nun, a man in whom is the spirit,[a] and lay your hand on him. [19]Have him stand before Eleazar the priest and the entire assembly and commission him in their presence. [20]Give him some of your authority so the whole Israelite community will obey him. [21]He is to stand before Eleazar the priest, who will obtain decisions for him by inquiring of the Urim before the LORD. At his command he and the entire community of the Israelites will go out, and at his command they will come in."

[22]Moses did as the LORD commanded him. He took Joshua and had him stand before Eleazar

a 18 Or Spirit

利亞撒，並眾首領與全會眾面前，說：[3]"我們的父親死在曠野，他不與可拉同黨聚集攻擊耶和華，是在自己罪中死的，他也沒有兒子。[4]為甚麼因我們的父親沒有兒子，就把他的名從他族中除掉呢？求你們在我們父親的弟兄中分給我們產業。"

[5]於是摩西將她們的案件，呈到耶和華面前。[6]耶和華曉諭摩西說：[7]"西羅非哈的女兒說得有理，你定要在她們父親的弟兄中，把地分給她們為業，要將她們父親的產業歸給她們。

[8]"你也要曉諭以色列人說：'人若死了沒有兒子，就要把他的產業歸給他的女兒；[9]他若沒有女兒，就要把他的產業給他的弟兄；[10]他若沒有弟兄，就要把他的產業給他父親的弟兄；[11]他父親若沒有弟兄，就要把他的產業給他族中最近的親屬，他便要得為業。這要作以色列人的律例、典章，是照耶和華所吩咐摩西的。'"

約書亞繼承摩西

[12]耶和華對摩西說："你上這亞巴琳山，觀看我所賜給以色列人的地，[13]看了以後，你也必歸到你列祖，（註：原文作"本民"）那裏，像你哥哥亞倫一樣。[14]因為你們在尋的曠野，當會眾爭鬧的時候，違背了我的命，沒有在湧水之地、會眾眼前尊我為聖。"（這水，就是尋的曠野加低斯米利巴水。）

[15]摩西對耶和華說：[16]"願耶和華萬人之靈的神，立一個人治理會眾，[17]可以在他們面前出入，也可以引導他們，免得耶和華的會眾如同沒有牧人的羊羣一般。"

[18]耶和華對摩西說："嫩的兒子約書亞是心中有聖靈的，你將他領來，按手在他頭上，[19]使他站在祭司以利亞撒和全會眾面前，囑咐他，[20]又將你的尊榮給他幾分，使以色列全會眾都聽從他。[21]他要站在祭司以利亞撒面前，以利亞撒要憑烏陵的判斷，在耶和華面前為他求問。他和以色列全會眾，都要遵以利亞撒的命出入。"

[22]於是摩西照耶和華所吩咐的，將約書亞領來，使他站在祭司以利亞

撒和全會眾面前，²³按手在他頭上，囑咐他，是照耶和華藉摩西所說的話。

每日獻的祭

28 耶和華曉諭摩西說：² "你要吩咐以色列人說：'獻給我的供物，就是獻給我作馨香火祭的食物，你們要按日期獻給我。' ³又要對他們說：'你們要獻給耶和華的火祭，就是沒有殘疾、一歲的公羊羔，每日兩隻，作為常獻的燔祭。⁴早晨要獻一隻，黃昏的時候要獻一隻。⁵又用細麵伊法十分之一，並搗成的油一欣四分之一，調和作為素祭。⁶這是在西奈山所命定為常獻的燔祭，是獻給耶和華為馨香的火祭。⁷為這一隻羊羔，要同獻奠祭的酒一欣四分之一。在聖所中，你要將醇酒奉給耶和華為奠祭。⁸晚上，你要獻那一隻羊羔，必照早晨的素祭和同獻的奠祭獻上，作為馨香的火祭，獻給耶和華。

安息日獻的祭

⁹ "'當安息日，要獻兩隻沒有殘疾、一歲的公羊羔，並用調油的細麵伊法十分之二為素祭，又將同獻的奠祭獻上。¹⁰這是每安息日獻的燔祭，那常獻的燔祭和同獻的奠祭在外。

每月獻的祭

¹¹ "'每月朔，你們要將兩隻公牛犢，一隻公綿羊，七隻沒有殘疾、一歲的公羊羔，獻給耶和華為燔祭。¹²每隻公牛要用調油的細麵伊法十分之三作為素祭；那隻公羊也用調油的細麵伊法十分之二作為素祭。¹³每隻羊羔要用調油的細麵伊法十分之一作為素祭和馨香的燔祭，是獻給耶和

the priest and the whole assembly. ²³Then he laid his hands on him and commissioned him, as the LORD instructed through Moses.

Daily Offerings

28 The LORD said to Moses, ²"Give this command to the Israelites and say to them: 'See that you present to me at the appointed time the food for my offerings made by fire, as an aroma pleasing to me.' ³Say to them: 'This is the offering made by fire that you are to present to the LORD: two lambs a year old without defect, as a regular burnt offering each day. ⁴Prepare one lamb in the morning and the other at twilight, ⁵together with a grain offering of a tenth of an ephah*a* of fine flour mixed with a quarter of a hin*b* of oil from pressed olives. ⁶This is the regular burnt offering instituted at Mount Sinai as a pleasing aroma, an offering made to the LORD by fire. ⁷The accompanying drink offering is to be a quarter of a hin of fermented drink with each lamb. Pour out the drink offering to the LORD at the sanctuary. ⁸Prepare the second lamb at twilight, along with the same kind of grain offering and drink offering that you prepare in the morning. This is an offering made by fire, an aroma pleasing to the LORD.

Sabbath Offerings

⁹" 'On the Sabbath day, make an offering of two lambs a year old without defect, together with its drink offering and a grain offering of two-tenths of an ephah*c* of fine flour mixed with oil. ¹⁰This is the burnt offering for every Sabbath, in addition to the regular burnt offering and its drink offering.

Monthly Offerings

¹¹ 'On the first of every month, present to the LORD a burnt offering of two young bulls, one ram and seven male lambs a year old, all without defect. ¹²With each bull there is to be a grain offering of three-tenths of an ephah*d* of fine flour mixed with oil; with the ram, a grain offering of two-tenths of an ephah of fine flour mixed with oil; ¹³and with each lamb, a grain offering of a tenth of an ephah of fine flour mixed with oil. This is for a burnt offering, a pleasing aroma, an offering made to the LORD

a 5 That is, probably about 2 quarts (about 2 liters); also in verses 13, 21 and 29　　*b 5* That is, probably about 1 quart (about 1 liter); also in verses 7 and 14　　*c 9* That is, probably about 4 quarts (about 4.5 liters); also in verses 12, 20 and 28　　*d 12* That is, probably about 6 quarts (about 6.5 liters); also in verses 20 and 28

by fire. 14With each bull there is to be a drink offering of half a hin*a* of wine; with the ram, a third of a hin*b*; and with each lamb, a quarter of a hin. This is the monthly burnt offering to be made at each new moon during the year. 15Besides the regular burnt offering with its drink offering, one male goat is to be presented to the LORD as a sin offering.

The Passover

16" 'On the fourteenth day of the first month the LORD's Passover is to be held. 17On the fifteenth day of this month there is to be a festival; for seven days eat bread made without yeast. 18On the first day hold a sacred assembly and do no regular work. 19Present to the LORD an offering made by fire, a burnt offering of two young bulls, one ram and seven male lambs a year old, all without defect. 20With each bull prepare a grain offering of three-tenths of an ephah of fine flour mixed with oil; with the ram, two-tenths; 21and with each of the seven lambs, one-tenth. 22Include one male goat as a sin offering to make atonement for you. 23Prepare these in addition to the regular morning burnt offering. 24In this way prepare the food for the offering made by fire every day for seven days as an aroma pleasing to the LORD; it is to be prepared in addition to the regular burnt offering and its drink offering. 25On the seventh day hold a sacred assembly and do no regular work.

Feast of Weeks

26" 'On the day of firstfruits, when you present to the LORD an offering of new grain during the Feast of Weeks, hold a sacred assembly and do no regular work. 27Present a burnt offering of two young bulls, one ram and seven male lambs a year old as an aroma pleasing to the LORD. 28With each bull there is to be a grain offering of three-tenths of an ephah of fine flour mixed with oil; with the ram, two-tenths; 29and with each of the seven lambs, one-tenth. 30Include one male goat to make atonement for you. 31Prepare these together with their drink offerings, in addition to the regular burnt offering and its grain offering. Be sure the animals are without defect.

Feast of Trumpets

29 " 'On the first day of the seventh month hold a sacred assembly and do no regular work. It is a day for you to sound the

a 14 That is, probably about 2 quarts (about 2 liters)
b 14 That is, probably about 1 1/4 quarts (about 1.2 liters)

華的火祭。14一隻公牛要奠酒半欣；一隻公羊要奠酒一欣三分之一；一隻羊羔也奠酒一欣四分之一。這是每月的燔祭，一年之中要月月如此。15又要將一隻公山羊為贖罪祭，獻給耶和華，要獻在常獻的燔祭和同獻的奠祭以外。

逾越節

16" '正月十四日，是耶和華的逾越節。17這月十五日是節期，要吃無酵餅七日。18第一日當有聖會，甚麼勞碌的工都不可做。19當將公牛犢兩隻，公綿羊一隻，一歲的公羊羔七隻，都要沒有殘疾的，用火獻給耶和華為燔祭。20同獻的素祭用調油的細麵，為一隻公牛要獻伊法十分之三；為一隻公羊要獻伊法十分之二；21為那七隻羊羔，每隻要獻伊法十分之一；22並獻一隻公山羊作贖罪祭，為你們贖罪。23你們獻這些，要在早晨常獻的燔祭以外。24一連七日，每日要照這例，把馨香火祭的食物獻給耶和華，是在常獻的燔祭和同獻的奠祭以外。25第七日當有聖會，甚麼勞碌的工都不可做。

七七節

26" '七七節莊稼初熟，你們獻新素祭給耶和華的日子，當有聖會，甚麼勞碌的工都不可做。27只要將公牛犢兩隻，公綿羊一隻，一歲的公羊羔七隻，作為馨香的燔祭，獻給耶和華。28同獻的素祭用調油的細麵，為每隻公牛要獻伊法十分之三；為一隻公羊要獻伊法十分之二；29為那七隻羊羔，每隻要獻伊法十分之一；30並獻一隻公山羊為你們贖罪。31這些，你們要獻在常獻的燔祭和同獻的素祭並同獻的奠祭以外，都要沒有殘疾的。

吹角節

29 " '七月初一日，你們當有聖會，甚麼勞碌的工都不可做，是你們當守為吹角的日子。2你們要將公牛犢一隻，公綿羊一隻，沒有殘疾一歲的公羊羔七隻，作為馨香的燔祭獻給耶和華。3同獻的素祭用調油的細麵，為一隻公牛要獻伊法十分之三；為一隻公羊要獻伊法十分之二；4為那七隻羊羔，每隻要獻伊法十分之一；5又獻一隻公山羊作贖罪祭，為你們贖罪。6這些是在月朔的燔祭和同獻的素祭，並常獻的燔祭與同獻的素祭，以及照例同獻的奠祭以外，都作為馨香的火祭獻給耶和華。

贖罪日

7　　'七月初十日，你們當有聖會，要刻苦己心，甚麼工都不可做。8只要將公牛犢一隻，公綿羊一隻，一歲的公羊羔七隻，都要沒有殘疾的，作為馨香的燔祭獻給耶和華。9同獻的素祭用調油的細麵，為一隻公牛要獻伊法十分之三；為一隻公羊要獻伊法十分之二；10為那七隻羊羔每隻要獻伊法十分之一；11又獻一隻公山羊為贖罪祭。這是在贖罪祭和常獻的燔祭，與同獻的素祭並同獻的奠祭以外。

住棚節

12　　'七月十五日，你們當有聖會，甚麼勞碌的工都不可做，要向耶和華守節七日。13又要將公牛犢十三隻，公綿羊兩隻，一歲的公羊羔十四隻，都要沒有殘疾的，用火獻給耶和華為馨香的燔祭。14同獻的素祭用調油的細麵，為那十三隻公牛，每隻要獻伊法十分之三；為那兩隻公羊，每隻要獻伊法十分之二；15為那十四隻羊羔，每隻要獻伊法十分之一；16並獻一隻公山羊為贖罪祭。這是在常獻的燔祭和同獻的素祭並同獻的奠祭以外。

17　　'第二日要獻公牛犢十二隻，公綿羊兩隻，沒有殘疾、一歲的公羊羔十四隻，18並為公牛、公羊和羊羔，按數照例，獻同獻的素祭和同獻的奠祭；19又要獻一隻公山羊為贖

trumpets. 2As an aroma pleasing to the LORD, prepare a burnt offering of one young bull, one ram and seven male lambs a year old, all without defect. 3With the bull prepare a grain offering of three-tenths of an ephah*a* of fine flour mixed with oil; with the ram, two-tenths*b*; 4and with each of the seven lambs, one-tenth.*c* 5Include one male goat as a sin offering to make atonement for you. 6These are in addition to the monthly and daily burnt offerings with their grain offerings and drink offerings as specified. They are offerings made to the LORD by fire—a pleasing aroma.

Day of Atonement

7" 'On the tenth day of this seventh month hold a sacred assembly. You must deny yourselves*d* and do no work. 8Present as an aroma pleasing to the LORD a burnt offering of one young bull, one ram and seven male lambs a year old, all without defect. 9With the bull prepare a grain offering of three-tenths of an ephah of fine flour mixed with oil; with the ram, two-tenths; 10and with each of the seven lambs, one-tenth. 11Include one male goat as a sin offering, in addition to the sin offering for atonement and the regular burnt offering with its grain offering, and their drink offerings.

Feast of Tabernacles

12" 'On the fifteenth day of the seventh month, hold a sacred assembly and do no regular work. Celebrate a festival to the LORD for seven days. 13Present an offering made by fire as an aroma pleasing to the LORD, a burnt offering of thirteen young bulls, two rams and fourteen male lambs a year old, all without defect. 14With each of the thirteen bulls prepare a grain offering of three-tenths of an ephah of fine flour mixed with oil; with each of the two rams, two-tenths; 15and with each of the fourteen lambs, one-tenth. 16Include one male goat as a sin offering, in addition to the regular burnt offering with its grain offering and drink offering.

17" 'On the second day prepare twelve young bulls, two rams and fourteen male lambs a year old, all without defect. 18With the bulls, rams and lambs, prepare their grain offerings and drink offerings according to the number specified. 19Include one male goat as a sin offering, in

a 3 That is, probably about 6 quarts (about 6.5 liters); also in verses 9 and 14　　*b 3* That is, probably about 4 quarts (about 4.5 liters); also in verses 9 and 14　　*c 4* That is, probably about 2 quarts (about 2 liters); also in verses 10 and 15　　*d 7* Or *must fast*

addition to the regular burnt offering with its grain offering, and their drink offerings.

20" 'On the third day prepare eleven bulls, two rams and fourteen male lambs a year old, all without defect. 21With the bulls, rams and lambs, prepare their grain offerings and drink offerings according to the number specified. 22Include one male goat as a sin offering, in addition to the regular burnt offering with its grain offering and drink offering.

23" 'On the fourth day prepare ten bulls, two rams and fourteen male lambs a year old, all without defect. 24With the bulls, rams and lambs, prepare their grain offerings and drink offerings according to the number specified. 25Include one male goat as a sin offering, in addition to the regular burnt offering with its grain offering and drink offering.

26" 'On the fifth day prepare nine bulls, two rams and fourteen male lambs a year old, all without defect. 27With the bulls, rams and lambs, prepare their grain offerings and drink offerings according to the number specified. 28Include one male goat as a sin offering, in addition to the regular burnt offering with its grain offering and drink offering.

29" 'On the sixth day prepare eight bulls, two rams and fourteen male lambs a year old, all without defect. 30With the bulls, rams and lambs, prepare their grain offerings and drink offerings according to the number specified. 31Include one male goat as a sin offering, in addition to the regular burnt offering with its grain offering and drink offering.

32" 'On the seventh day prepare seven bulls, two rams and fourteen male lambs a year old, all without defect. 33With the bulls, rams and lambs, prepare their grain offerings and drink offerings according to the number specified. 34Include one male goat as a sin offering, in addition to the regular burnt offering with its grain offering and drink offering.

35" 'On the eighth day hold an assembly and do no regular work. 36Present an offering made by fire as an aroma pleasing to the LORD, a burnt offering of one bull, one ram and seven male lambs a year old, all without defect. 37With the bull, the ram and the lambs, prepare their grain offerings and drink offerings according to the number specified. 38Include one male goat as a sin offering, in addition to the regular burnt offering with its grain offering and drink offering.

39" 'In addition to what you vow and your freewill offerings, prepare these for the LORD at your appointed feasts: your burnt offerings,

罪祭。這是在常獻的燔祭和同獻的素祭並同獻的奠祭以外。

20 "「第三日要獻公牛十一隻，公羊兩隻，沒有殘疾、一歲的公羊羔十四隻，21並為公牛、公羊和羊羔，按數照例，獻同獻的素祭和同獻的奠祭；22又要獻一隻公山羊為贖罪祭。這是在常獻的燔祭和同獻的素祭並同獻的奠祭以外。

23 "「第四日要獻公牛十隻，公羊兩隻，沒有殘疾、一歲的公羊羔十四隻，24並為公牛、公羊和羊羔，按數照例，獻同獻的素祭和同獻的奠祭；25又要獻一隻公山羊為贖罪祭。這是在常獻的燔祭和同獻的素祭並同獻的奠祭以外。

26 "「第五日要獻公牛九隻，公羊兩隻，沒有殘疾、一歲的公羊羔十四隻，27並為公牛、公羊和羊羔，按數照例，獻同獻的素祭和同獻的奠祭；28又要獻一隻公山羊為贖罪祭。這是在常獻的燔祭和同獻的素祭並同獻的奠祭以外。

29 "「第六日要獻公牛八隻，公羊兩隻，沒有殘疾、一歲的公羊羔十四隻，30並為公牛、公羊和羊羔，按數照例，獻同獻的素祭和同獻的奠祭；31又要獻一隻公山羊為贖罪祭。這是在常獻的燔祭和同獻的素祭並同獻的奠祭以外。

32 "「第七日要獻公牛七隻，公羊兩隻，沒有殘疾、一歲的公羊羔十四隻，33並為公牛、公羊和羊羔，按數照例，獻同獻的素祭和同獻的奠祭；34又要獻一隻公山羊為贖罪祭。這是在常獻的燔祭和同獻的素祭並同獻的奠祭以外。

35 "「第八日你們當有嚴肅會，甚麼勞碌的工都不可做。36只要將公牛一隻，公羊一隻，沒有殘疾、一歲的公羊羔七隻，作火祭獻給耶和華為馨香的燔祭；37並為公牛、公羊和羊羔，按數照例，獻同獻的素祭和同獻的奠祭；38又要獻一隻公山羊為贖罪祭。這是在常獻的燔祭和同獻的素祭並同獻的奠祭以外。

39 "「這些祭要在你們的節期獻給耶和華，都在所許的願並甘心所獻的以外，作為你們的燔祭、素祭、奠祭和平安祭。’”

40於是摩西照耶和華所吩咐他的一切話，告訴以色列人。

許願

30 摩西曉諭以色列各支派的首領說："耶和華所吩咐的乃是這樣：2人若向耶和華許願或起誓，要約束自己，就不可食言，必要按口中所出的一切話行。

3 "女子年幼還在父家的時候，若向耶和華許願要約束自己，4她父親也聽見她所許的願，並約束自己的話，卻向她默默不言，她所許的願並約束自己的話，就都要為定。5但她父親聽見的日子，若不應承，她所許的願和約束自己的話，就都不得為定；耶和華也必赦免她，因為她父親不應承。

6 "她若出了嫁，有願在身，或是口中出了約束自己的冒失話，7她丈夫聽見的日子，卻向她默默不言，她所許的願並約束自己的話，就都要為定。8但她丈夫聽見的日子，若不應承，就算廢了她所許的願和她出口約束自己的冒失話，耶和華也必赦免她。

9 "寡婦或是被休的婦人所許的願，就是她約束自己的話，都要為定。

10 "她若在丈夫家裏許了願或起了誓約束自己，11丈夫聽見卻向她默默不言，也沒有不應承，她所許的願並約束自己的話，就都要為定。12丈夫聽見的日子，若把這兩樣全廢了，婦人口中所許的願或是約束自己的話，就都不得為定，因她丈夫已經把這兩樣廢了；耶和華也必赦免她。13凡她所許的願和刻苦約束自己所起的誓，她丈夫可以堅定，也可以廢去。14倘若她丈夫天天向她默默不言，就算是堅定她所許的願和約束自己的話，因丈夫聽見的日子向她默默不言，就使這兩樣堅定。15但她丈夫聽見以後，若使這兩樣全廢了，就要擔當婦人的罪孽。"

16這是丈夫待妻子，父親待女兒，女兒年幼還在父家，耶和華所吩

grain offerings, drink offerings and fellowship offerings.ᵃ"

40Moses told the Israelites all that the LORD commanded him.

Vows

30 Moses said to the heads of the tribes of Israel: "This is what the LORD commands: 2When a man makes a vow to the LORD or takes an oath to obligate himself by a pledge, he must not break his word but must do everything he said.

3"When a young woman still living in her father's house makes a vow to the LORD or obligates herself by a pledge 4and her father hears about her vow or pledge but says nothing to her, then all her vows and every pledge by which she obligated herself will stand. 5But if her father forbids her when he hears about it, none of her vows or the pledges by which she obligated herself will stand; the LORD will release her because her father has forbidden her.

6"If she marries after she makes a vow or after her lips utter a rash promise by which she obligates herself 7and her husband hears about it but says nothing to her, then her vows or the pledges by which she obligated herself will stand. 8But if her husband forbids her when he hears about it, he nullifies the vow that obligates her or the rash promise by which she obligates herself, and the LORD will release her.

9"Any vow or obligation taken by a widow or divorced woman will be binding on her.

10"If a woman living with her husband makes a vow or obligates herself by a pledge under oath 11and her husband hears about it but says nothing to her and does not forbid her, then all her vows or the pledges by which she obligated herself will stand. 12But if her husband nullifies them when he hears about them, then none of the vows or pledges that came from her lips will stand. Her husband has nullified them, and the LORD will release her. 13Her husband may confirm or nullify any vow she makes or any sworn pledge to deny herself. 14But if her husband says nothing to her about it from day to day, then he confirms all her vows or the pledges binding on her. He confirms them by saying nothing to her when he hears about them. 15If, however, he nullifies them some time after he hears about them, then he is responsible for her guilt."

16These are the regulations the LORD gave Moses concerning relationships between a man

a 39 Traditionally peace offerings

and his wife, and between a father and his young daughter still living in his house.

Vengeance on the Midianites

31 The LORD said to Moses, 2"Take vengeance on the Midianites for the Israelites. After that, you will be gathered to your people."

3So Moses said to the people, "Arm some of your men to go to war against the Midianites and to carry out the LORD's vengeance on them. 4Send into battle a thousand men from each of the tribes of Israel." 5So twelve thousand men armed for battle, a thousand from each tribe, were supplied from the clans of Israel. 6Moses sent them into battle, a thousand from each tribe, along with Phinehas son of Eleazar, the priest, who took with him articles from the sanctuary and the trumpets for signaling.

7They fought against Midian, as the LORD commanded Moses, and killed every man. 8Among their victims were Evi, Rekem, Zur, Hur and Reba—the five kings of Midian. They also killed Balaam son of Beor with the sword. 9The Israelites captured the Midianite women and children and took all the Midianite herds, flocks and goods as plunder. 10They burned all the towns where the Midianites had settled, as well as all their camps. 11They took all the plunder and spoils, including the people and animals, 12and brought the captives, spoils and plunder to Moses and Eleazar the priest and the Israelite assembly at their camp on the plains of Moab, by the Jordan across from Jericho.*a*

13Moses, Eleazar the priest and all the leaders of the community went to meet them outside the camp. 14Moses was angry with the officers of the army—the commanders of thousands and commanders of hundreds—who returned from the battle.

15"Have you allowed all the women to live?" he asked them. 16"They were the ones who followed Balaam's advice and were the means of turning the Israelites away from the LORD in what happened at Peor, so that a plague struck the LORD's people. 17Now kill all the boys. And kill every woman who has slept with a man, 18but save for yourselves every girl who has never slept with a man.

19"All of you who have killed anyone or touched anyone who was killed must stay outside the camp seven days. On the third and seventh days you must purify yourselves and your

a 12 Hebrew Jordan of Jericho; possibly an ancient name for the Jordan River

附<u>摩西</u>的律例。

報復米甸人

31 耶和華吩咐<u>摩西</u>說：2"你要在米甸人身上報<u>以色列</u>人的仇，後來要歸到你列祖（註：原文作"本民"）那裏。"

3<u>摩西</u>吩咐百姓說："要從你們中間叫人帶兵器出去攻擊<u>米甸</u>，好在<u>米甸</u>人身上為耶和華報仇。4從<u>以色列</u>眾支派中，每支派要打發一千人去打仗。"5於是從<u>以色列</u>千萬人中，每支派交出一千人，共一萬二千人，帶着兵器預備打仗。6<u>摩西</u>就打發每支派的一千人去打仗，並打發祭司<u>以利亞撒</u>的兒子<u>非尼哈</u>同去，<u>非尼哈</u>手裏拿着聖所的器皿和吹大聲的號筒。

7他們就照耶和華所吩咐<u>摩西</u>的，與<u>米甸</u>人打仗，殺了所有的男丁。8在所殺的人中，殺了<u>米甸</u>的五王：就是<u>以未</u>、<u>利金</u>、<u>蘇珥</u>、<u>戶珥</u>、<u>利巴</u>，又用刀殺了<u>比珥</u>的兒子<u>巴蘭</u>。9<u>以色列</u>人擄了<u>米甸</u>人的婦女孩子，並將他們的牲畜、羊羣和所有的財物都奪了來，當作擄物。10又用火焚燒他們所住的城邑和所有的營寨。11把一切所奪的、所擄的，連人帶牲畜都帶了去，12將所擄的人，所奪的牲畜、財物，都帶到<u>摩押</u>平原，在<u>約旦</u>河邊與<u>耶利哥</u>相對的營盤，交給<u>摩西</u>和祭司<u>以利亞撒</u>，並<u>以色列</u>的會眾。

13<u>摩西</u>和祭司<u>以利亞撒</u>，並會眾一切的首領，都出到營外迎接他們。14<u>摩西</u>向打仗回來的軍長，就是千夫長、百夫長發怒。

15對他們說："你們要存留這一切婦女的活命嗎？16這些婦女，因<u>巴蘭</u>的計謀，叫<u>以色列</u>人在<u>毘珥</u>的事上得罪耶和華，以致耶和華的會眾遭遇瘟疫。17所以，你們要把一切的男孩和所有已嫁的女子都殺了。18但女孩子中，凡沒有出嫁的，你們都可以存留她的活命。

19"你們要在營外駐紮七日，凡殺了人的，和一切摸了被殺的，並你們所擄來的人口，第三日，第七日，都要潔淨自己，²⁰也要因一切的衣服、皮物、山羊毛織的物和各樣的木器，潔淨自己。”

²¹祭司以利亞撒對打仗回來的兵丁說：“耶和華所吩咐摩西律法中的條例乃是這樣：²²金、銀、銅、鐵、錫、鉛，²³凡能見火的，你們要叫它經火，就為潔淨，然而還要用除污穢的水潔淨它；凡不能見火的，你們要叫它過水。²⁴第七日，你們要洗衣服，就為潔淨，然後可以進營。”

分所擄之物

²⁵耶和華曉諭摩西說：²⁶“你和祭司以利亞撒，並會眾的各族長，要計算所擄來的人口和牲畜的總數。²⁷把所擄來的分作兩半：一半歸與出去打仗的精兵；一半歸與全會眾。²⁸又要從出去打仗所得的人口、牛、驢、羊羣中，每五百取一，作為貢物奉給耶和華。²⁹從他們一半之中，要取出來交給祭司以利亞撒，作為耶和華的舉祭。³⁰從以色列人的一半之中，就是從人口、牛、驢、羊羣、各樣牲畜中，每五十取一，交給看守耶和華帳幕的利未人。”³¹於是，摩西和祭司以利亞撒照耶和華所吩咐摩西的行了。

³²除了兵丁所奪的財物以外，所擄來的：羊六十七萬五千隻，³³牛七萬二千隻，³⁴驢六萬一千匹，³⁵女人共三萬二千口，都是沒有出嫁的。

³⁶出去打仗之人的分，就是他們所得的那一半，共計

羊三十三萬七千五百隻，³⁷從其中歸耶和華為貢物的，有六百七十五隻；
³⁸牛三萬六千隻，從其中歸耶和華為貢物的，有七十二隻；
³⁹驢三萬零五百匹，從其中歸耶和華為貢物的，有六十一匹；
⁴⁰人一萬六千口，從其中歸耶和華的，有三十二口。

⁴¹摩西把貢物，就是歸與耶和華的舉祭，交給祭司以利亞撒，是照耶和華所吩咐摩西的。

⁴²以色列人所得的那一半，就是摩西從打仗的人取來分給他們的。

（⁴³會眾的那一半有：羊三十三萬七千五百隻，⁴⁴牛三萬六千隻，⁴⁵驢三萬零五百匹，⁴⁶人一萬六千口。）⁴⁷無論

captives. ²⁰Purify every garment as well as everything made of leather, goat hair or wood."

²¹Then Eleazar the priest said to the soldiers who had gone into battle, "This is the requirement of the law that the LORD gave Moses: ²²Gold, silver, bronze, iron, tin, lead ²³and anything else that can withstand fire must be put through the fire, and then it will be clean. But it must also be purified with the water of cleansing. And whatever cannot withstand fire must be put through that water. ²⁴On the seventh day wash your clothes and you will be clean. Then you may come into the camp."

Dividing the Spoils

²⁵The LORD said to Moses, ²⁶"You and Eleazar the priest and the family heads of the community are to count all the people and animals that were captured. ²⁷Divide the spoils between the soldiers who took part in the battle and the rest of the community. ²⁸From the soldiers who fought in the battle, set apart as tribute for the LORD one out of every five hundred, whether persons, cattle, donkeys, sheep or goats. ²⁹Take this tribute from their half share and give it to Eleazar the priest as the LORD's part. ³⁰From the Israelites' half, select one out of every fifty, whether persons, cattle, donkeys, sheep, goats or other animals. Give them to the Levites, who are responsible for the care of the LORD's tabernacle." ³¹So Moses and Eleazar the priest did as the LORD commanded Moses.

³²The plunder remaining from the spoils that the soldiers took was 675,000 sheep, ³³72,000 cattle, ³⁴61,000 donkeys ³⁵and 32,000 women who had never slept with a man.

³⁶The half share of those who fought in the battle was:

337,500 sheep, ³⁷of which the tribute for the LORD was 675;
³⁸36,000 cattle, of which the tribute for the LORD was 72;
³⁹30,500 donkeys, of which the tribute for the LORD was 61;
⁴⁰16,000 people, of which the tribute for the LORD was 32.

⁴¹Moses gave the tribute to Eleazar the priest as the LORD's part, as the LORD commanded Moses.

⁴²The half belonging to the Israelites, which Moses set apart from that of the fighting men—⁴³the community's half—was 337,500 sheep, ⁴⁴36,000 cattle, ⁴⁵30,500 donkeys ⁴⁶and 16,000 people. ⁴⁷From the Israelites' half, Moses select-

ed one out of every fifty persons and animals, as the LORD commanded him, and gave them to the Levites, who were responsible for the care of the LORD's tabernacle.

48Then the officers who were over the units of the army—the commanders of thousands and commanders of hundreds—went to Moses 49and said to him, "Your servants have counted the soldiers under our command, and not one is missing. 50So we have brought as an offering to the LORD the gold articles each of us acquired—armlets, bracelets, signet rings, earrings and necklaces—to make atonement for ourselves before the LORD."

51Moses and Eleazar the priest accepted from them the gold—all the crafted articles. 52All the gold from the commanders of thousands and commanders of hundreds that Moses and Eleazar presented as a gift to the LORD weighed 16,750 shekels.a 53Each soldier had taken plunder for himself. 54Moses and Eleazar the priest accepted the gold from the commanders of thousands and commanders of hundreds and brought it into the Tent of Meeting as a memorial for the Israelites before the LORD.

The Transjordan Tribes

32 The Reubenites and Gadites, who had very large herds and flocks, saw that the lands of Jazer and Gilead were suitable for livestock. 2So they came to Moses and Eleazar the priest and to the leaders of the community, and said, 3"Ataroth, Dibon, Jazer, Nimrah, Heshbon, Elealeh, Sebam, Nebo and Beon— 4the land the LORD subdued before the people of Israel—are suitable for livestock, and your servants have livestock. 5If we have found favor in your eyes," they said, "let this land be given to your servants as our possession. Do not make us cross the Jordan."

6Moses said to the Gadites and Reubenites, "Shall your countrymen go to war while you sit here? 7Why do you discourage the Israelites from going over into the land the LORD has given them? 8This is what your fathers did when I sent them from Kadesh Barnea to look over the land. 9After they went up to the Valley of Eshcol and viewed the land, they discouraged the Israelites from entering the land the LORD had given them. 10The LORD's anger was aroused that day and he swore this oath: 11'Because they have not followed me wholeheartedly, not one of the men twenty years old or more who came up out of Egypt will see the

a 52 That is, about 420 pounds (about 190 kilograms)

是人口,是牲畜,摩西每五十取一,交給看守耶和華帳幕的利未人,是照耶和華所吩咐摩西的。

48帶領千軍的各軍長,就是千夫長、百夫長,都近前來見摩西,49對他說:"僕人權下的兵,已經計算總數,並不短少一人。50如今我們將各人所得的金器,就是腳鍊子、鐲子、打印的戒指、耳環、手釧,都送來為耶和華的供物,好在耶和華面前為我們的生命贖罪。"

51摩西和祭司以利亞撒就收了他們的金子,都是打成的器皿。52千夫長、百夫長所獻給耶和華為舉祭的金子,共有一萬六千七百五十舍客勒。53各兵丁都為自己奪了財物。54摩西和祭司以利亞撒,收了千夫長、百夫長的金子,就帶進會幕,在耶和華面前作為以色列人的紀念。

約旦河東的支派

32 呂便子孫和迦得子孫的牲畜極其眾多,他們看見雅謝地和基列地是可牧放牲畜之地,2就來見摩西和祭司以利亞撒,並會眾的首領,說:3"亞大錄、底本、雅謝、寧拉、希實本、以利亞利、示班、尼波、比穩,4就是耶和華在以色列會眾前面所攻取之地,是可牧放牲畜之地,你僕人也有牲畜。"5又說:"我們若在你眼前蒙恩,求你把這地給我們為業,不要領我們過約旦河。"

6摩西對迦得子孫和呂便子孫說:"難道你們的弟兄去打仗,你們竟坐在這裏嗎?7你們為何使以色列人灰心喪膽,不過去進入耶和華所賜給他們的那地呢?8我先前從加低斯巴尼亞打發你們先祖去窺探那地,他們也是這樣行。9他們上以實各谷,去窺探那地回來的時候,使以色列人灰心喪膽,不進入耶和華所賜給他們的地。10當日,耶和華的怒氣發作,就起誓說:11'凡從埃及上來二十歲以外的人,斷不得看見我對亞伯拉

罕、以撒、雅各起誓應許之地，因為
他們沒有專心跟從我，12惟有基尼洗
族耶孚尼的兒子迦勒和嫩的兒子約書
亞可以看見，因為他們專心跟從
我。' 13耶和華的怒氣向以色列人發
作，使他們在曠野飄流四十年，等到
在耶和華眼前行惡的那一代人都消滅
了。

14 "誰知，你們起來接續先祖，
增添罪人的數目，使耶和華向以色列
大發烈怒。15你們若退後不跟從他，
他還要把以色列人撇在曠野，便是你
們使這眾民滅亡。"

16兩支派的人挨近摩西說："我
們要在這裏為牲畜壘圈，為婦人孩子
造城；17我們自己要帶兵器，行在以
色列人的前頭，好把他們領到他們的
地方；但我們的婦人孩子，因這地居
民的緣故，要住在堅固的城內。18我
們不回家，直等到以色列人各承受自
己的產業。19我們不和他們在約旦河
那邊一帶之地同受產業，因為我們的
產業是坐落在約旦河東邊這裏。"

20摩西對他們說："你們若這樣
行，在耶和華面前帶着兵器出去打
仗，21所有帶兵器的人都要在耶和華
面前過約旦河，等他趕出他的仇敵，
22那地被耶和華制伏了，然後你們可
以回來，向耶和華和以色列才為無
罪，這地也必在耶和華面前歸你們為
業。

23 "倘若你們不這樣行，就得罪
耶和華，要知道你們的罪必追上你
們。24如今你們口中所出的，只管去
行，為你們的婦人孩子造城，為你們
的羊羣壘圈。"

25迦得子孫和呂便子孫對摩西
說："僕人要照我主所吩咐的去行。
26我們的妻子、孩子、羊羣和所有的
牲畜，都要留在基列的各城。27但你
的僕人，凡帶兵器的，都要照我主所
說的話，在耶和華面前過去打仗。"

28於是，摩西為他們囑咐祭司以
利亞撒和嫩的兒子約書亞，並以色列
眾支派的族長，29說："迦得子孫和
呂便子孫，凡帶兵器在耶和華面前去
打仗的，若與你們一同過約旦河，那
地被你們制伏了，你們就要把基列地
給他們為業；30倘若他們不帶兵器和

land I promised on oath to Abraham, Isaac and Jacob— 12not one except Caleb son of Jephunneh the Kenizzite and Joshua son of Nun, for they followed the LORD wholeheartedly.' 13The LORD's anger burned against Israel and he made them wander in the desert forty years, until the whole generation of those who had done evil in his sight was gone.

14"And here you are, a brood of sinners, standing in the place of your fathers and making the LORD even more angry with Israel. 15If you turn away from following him, he will again leave all this people in the desert, and you will be the cause of their destruction."

16Then they came up to him and said, "We would like to build pens here for our livestock and cities for our women and children. 17But we are ready to arm ourselves and go ahead of the Israelites until we have brought them to their place. Meanwhile our women and children will live in fortified cities, for protection from the inhabitants of the land. 18We will not return to our homes until every Israelite has received his inheritance. 19We will not receive any inheritance with them on the other side of the Jordan, because our inheritance has come to us on the east side of the Jordan."

20Then Moses said to them, "If you will do this—if you will arm yourselves before the LORD for battle, 21and if all of you will go armed over the Jordan before the LORD until he has driven his enemies out before him— 22then when the land is subdued before the LORD, you may return and be free from your obligation to the LORD and to Israel. And this land will be your possession before the LORD.

23"But if you fail to do this, you will be sinning against the LORD; and you may be sure that your sin will find you out. 24Build cities for your women and children, and pens for your flocks, but do what you have promised."

25The Gadites and Reubenites said to Moses, "We your servants will do as our lord commands. 26Our children and wives, our flocks and herds will remain here in the cities of Gilead. 27But your servants, every man armed for battle, will cross over to fight before the LORD, just as our lord says."

28Then Moses gave orders about them to Eleazar the priest and Joshua son of Nun and to the family heads of the Israelite tribes. 29He said to them, "If the Gadites and Reubenites, every man armed for battle, cross over the Jordan with you before the LORD, then when the land is subdued before you, give them the land of Gilead as their possession. 30But if they do not cross over with you armed, they must accept their possession with you in Canaan."

³¹The Gadites and Reubenites answered, "Your servants will do what the LORD has said. ³²We will cross over before the LORD into Canaan armed, but the property we inherit will be on this side of the Jordan."

³³Then Moses gave to the Gadites, the Reubenites and the half-tribe of Manasseh son of Joseph the kingdom of Sihon king of the Amorites and the kingdom of Og king of Bashan—the whole land with its cities and the territory around them.

³⁴The Gadites built up Dibon, Ataroth, Aroer, ³⁵Atroth Shophan, Jazer, Jogbehah, ³⁶Beth Nimrah and Beth Haran as fortified cities, and built pens for their flocks. ³⁷And the Reubenites rebuilt Heshbon, Elealeh and Kiriathaim, ³⁸as well as Nebo and Baal Meon (these names were changed) and Sibmah. They gave names to the cities they rebuilt.

³⁹The descendants of Makir son of Manasseh went to Gilead, captured it and drove out the Amorites who were there. ⁴⁰So Moses gave Gilead to the Makirites, the descendants of Manasseh, and they settled there. ⁴¹Jair, a descendant of Manasseh, captured their settlements and called them Havvoth Jair.ᵃ ⁴²And Nobah captured Kenath and its surrounding settlements and called it Nobah after himself.

Stages in Israel's Journey

33 Here are the stages in the journey of the Israelites when they came out of Egypt by divisions under the leadership of Moses and Aaron. ²At the LORD's command Moses recorded the stages in their journey. This is their journey by stages:

³The Israelites set out from Rameses on the fifteenth day of the first month, the day after the Passover. They marched out boldly in full view of all the Egyptians, ⁴who were burying all their firstborn, whom the LORD had struck down among them; for the LORD had brought judgment on their gods.

⁵The Israelites left Rameses and camped at Succoth.

⁶They left Succoth and camped at Etham, on the edge of the desert.

⁷They left Etham, turned back to Pi Hahiroth, to the east of Baal Zephon, and camped near Migdol.

你們一同過去，就要在迦南地你們中間得產業。"

³¹迦得子孫和呂便子孫回答說："耶和華怎樣吩咐僕人，僕人就怎樣行。³²我們要帶兵器，在耶和華面前過去，進入迦南地，只是約旦河這邊我們所得為業之地，仍歸我們。"

³³摩西將亞摩利王西宏的國和巴珊王噩的國，連那地和周圍的城邑，都給了迦得子孫和呂便子孫，並約瑟的兒子瑪拿西半個支派。

³⁴迦得子孫建造底本、亞他錄、亞羅珥、³⁵亞他錄朔反、雅謝、約比哈、³⁶伯寧拉、伯哈蘭，都是堅固城，他們又壘羊圈。³⁷呂便子孫建造希實本、以利亞利、基列亭、³⁸尼波、巴力免、西比瑪（尼波、巴力免，名字是改了的），又給他們所建造的城另起別名。

³⁹瑪拿西的兒子瑪吉，他的子孫往基列去，佔了那地，趕出那裏的亞摩利人。⁴⁰摩西將基列賜給瑪拿西的兒子瑪吉，他子孫就住在那裏。⁴¹瑪拿西的子孫睚珥，去佔了基列的村莊，就稱這些村莊為哈倭特睚珥；⁴²挪巴去佔了基納和基納的鄉村，就按自己的名稱基納為挪巴。

以色列人的行程

33 以色列人按着軍隊，在摩西、亞倫的手下出埃及地所行的路程（註：或作"站口"。下同）記在下面。²摩西遵着耶和華的吩咐，記載他們所行的路程，其路程乃是這樣：

³正月十五日，就是逾越節的次日，以色列人從蘭塞起行，在一切埃及人眼前昂然無懼地出去。⁴那時，埃及人正葬埋他們的長子，就是耶和華在他們中間所擊殺的，耶和華也敗壞他們的神。

⁵以色列人從蘭塞起行，安營在疏割。

⁶從疏割起行，安營在曠野邊的以倘。

⁷從以倘起行，轉到比哈希錄，是在巴力洗分對面，就在密奪安營。

---

a 41 Or them the settlements of Jair

⁸從比哈希錄對面起行，經過海中到了書珥曠野，又在伊坦的曠野走了三天的路程，就安營在瑪拉。

⁹從瑪拉起行，來到以琳，以琳有十二股水泉，七十棵棕樹，就在那裏安營。

¹⁰從以琳起行，安營在紅海邊。

¹¹從紅海邊起行，安營在汛的曠野。

¹²從汛的曠野起行，安營在脫加。

¹³從脫加起行，安營在亞錄。

¹⁴從亞錄起行，安營在利非訂，在那裏百姓沒有水喝。

¹⁵從利非訂起行，安營在西奈的曠野。

¹⁶從西奈的曠野起行，安營在基博羅哈他瓦。

¹⁷從基博羅哈他瓦起行，安營在哈洗錄。

¹⁸從哈洗錄起行，安營在利提瑪。

¹⁹從利提瑪起行，安營在臨門帕烈。

²⁰從臨門帕烈起行，安營在立拿。

²¹從立拿起行，安營在勒撒。

²²從勒撒起行，安營在基希拉他。

²³從基希拉他起行，安營在沙斐山。

²⁴從沙斐山起行，安營在哈拉大。

²⁵從哈拉大起行，安營在瑪吉希錄。

²⁶從瑪吉希錄起行，安營在他哈。

²⁷從他哈起行，安營在他拉。

²⁸從他拉起行，安營在密加。

²⁹從密加起行，安營在哈摩拿。

³⁰從哈摩拿起行，安營在摩西錄。

³¹從摩西錄起行，安營在比尼亞干。

³²從比尼亞干起行，安營在曷哈及甲。

⁸They left Pi Hahiroth[a] and passed through the sea into the desert, and when they had traveled for three days in the Desert of Etham, they camped at Marah.

⁹They left Marah and went to Elim, where there were twelve springs and seventy palm trees, and they camped there.

¹⁰They left Elim and camped by the Red Sea.[b]

¹¹They left the Red Sea and camped in the Desert of Sin.

¹²They left the Desert of Sin and camped at Dophkah.

¹³They left Dophkah and camped at Alush.

¹⁴They left Alush and camped at Rephidim, where there was no water for the people to drink.

¹⁵They left Rephidim and camped in the Desert of Sinai.

¹⁶They left the Desert of Sinai and camped at Kibroth Hattaavah.

¹⁷They left Kibroth Hattaavah and camped at Hazeroth.

¹⁸They left Hazeroth and camped at Rithmah.

¹⁹They left Rithmah and camped at Rimmon Perez.

²⁰They left Rimmon Perez and camped at Libnah.

²¹They left Libnah and camped at Rissah.

²²They left Rissah and camped at Kehelathah.

²³They left Kehelathah and camped at Mount Shepher.

²⁴They left Mount Shepher and camped at Haradah.

²⁵They left Haradah and camped at Makheloth.

²⁶They left Makheloth and camped at Tahath.

²⁷They left Tahath and camped at Terah.

²⁸They left Terah and camped at Mithcah.

²⁹They left Mithcah and camped at Hashmonah.

³⁰They left Hashmonah and camped at Moseroth.

³¹They left Moseroth and camped at Bene Jaakan.

³²They left Bene Jaakan and camped at Hor Haggidgad.

a 8 Many manuscripts of the Masoretic Text, Samaritan Pentateuch and Vulgate; most manuscripts of the Masoretic Text *left from before Hahiroth*　　*b 10* Hebrew *Yam Suph*; that is, Sea of Reeds; also in verse 11

³³They left Hor Haggidgad and camped at Jotbathah.

³⁴They left Jotbathah and camped at Abronah.

³⁵They left Abronah and camped at Ezion Geber.

³⁶They left Ezion Geber and camped at Kadesh, in the Desert of Zin.

³⁷They left Kadesh and camped at Mount Hor, on the border of Edom. ³⁸At the LORD's command Aaron the priest went up Mount Hor, where he died on the first day of the fifth month of the fortieth year after the Israelites came out of Egypt. ³⁹Aaron was a hundred and twenty-three years old when he died on Mount Hor.

⁴⁰The Canaanite king of Arad, who lived in the Negev of Canaan, heard that the Israelites were coming.

⁴¹They left Mount Hor and camped at Zalmonah.

⁴²They left Zalmonah and camped at Punon.

⁴³They left Punon and camped at Oboth.

⁴⁴They left Oboth and camped at Iye Abarim, on the border of Moab.

⁴⁵They left Iyim^a and camped at Dibon Gad.

⁴⁶They left Dibon Gad and camped at Almon Diblathaim.

⁴⁷They left Almon Diblathaim and camped in the mountains of Abarim, near Nebo.

⁴⁸They left the mountains of Abarim and camped on the plains of Moab by the Jordan across from Jericho.^b ⁴⁹There on the plains of Moab they camped along the Jordan from Beth Jeshimoth to Abel Shittim.

⁵⁰On the plains of Moab by the Jordan across from Jericho the LORD said to Moses, ⁵¹"Speak to the Israelites and say to them: 'When you cross the Jordan into Canaan, ⁵²drive out all the inhabitants of the land before you. Destroy all their carved images and their cast idols, and demolish all their high places. ⁵³Take possession of the land and settle in it, for I have given you the land to possess. ⁵⁴Distribute the land by lot, according to your clans. To a larger group give a larger inheritance, and to a smaller group a smaller one. Whatever falls to them by lot will be theirs. Distribute it according to your ancestral tribes.

⁵⁵"'But if you do not drive out the inhabitants of the land, those you allow to remain will

³³從曷哈及甲起行，安營在約巴他。

³⁴從約巴他起行，安營在阿博拿。

³⁵從阿博拿起行，安營在以旬迦別。

³⁶從以旬迦別起行，安營在尋的曠野，就是加低斯。

³⁷從加低斯起行，安營在何珥山以東地的邊界。³⁸以色列人出了埃及地後四十年，五月初一日，祭司亞倫遵着耶和華的吩咐上何珥山，就死在那裏。³⁹亞倫死在何珥山的時候，年一百二十三歲。

⁴⁰住在迦南南地的迦南人亞拉得王，聽說以色列人來了。

⁴¹以色列人從何珥山起行，安營在撒摩拿。

⁴²從撒摩拿起行，安營在普嫩。

⁴³從普嫩起行，安營在阿伯。

⁴⁴從阿伯起行，安營在以耶亞巴琳、摩押的邊界。

⁴⁵從以耶亞巴琳起行，安營在底本迦得。

⁴⁶從底本迦得起行，安營在亞門低比拉太音。

⁴⁷從亞門低比拉太音起行，安營在尼波對面的亞巴琳山裏。

⁴⁸從亞巴琳山起行，安營在摩押平原、約旦河邊、耶利哥對面。⁴⁹他們在摩押平原沿約旦河邊安營，從伯施末直到亞伯什亭。

⁵⁰耶和華在摩押平原、約旦河邊、耶利哥對面曉諭摩西說：⁵¹"你吩咐以色列人說：'你們過約旦河進迦南地的時候，⁵²就要從你們面前趕出那裏所有的居民，毀滅他們一切鑿成的石像，和他們一切鑄成的偶像，又拆毀他們一切的邱壇。⁵³你們要奪那地，住在其中，因我把那地賜給你們為業。⁵⁴你們要按家室拈鬮，承受那地。人多的，要把產業多分給他們；人少的，要把產業少分給他們。拈出何地給何人，就要歸何人。你們要按宗族的支派承受。

⁵⁵"'倘若你們不趕出那地的居民，所容留的居民，就必作你們眼中

^a 45 That is, Iye Abarim　　^b 48 Hebrew *Jordan of Jericho;* possibly an ancient name for the Jordan River; also in verse 50

的刺，肋下的荊棘，也必在你們所住的地上擾害你們。⁵⁶而且我素常有意怎樣待他們，也必照樣待你們。'"

迦南的地界

34 耶和華曉諭摩西說：²"你吩咐以色列人說：'你們到了迦南地，就是歸你們為業的迦南四境之地：

³"'南角要從尋的曠野，貼着以東的邊界；南界要從鹽海東頭起，⁴繞到亞克拉濱坡的南邊，接連到尋，直通到加低斯巴尼亞的南邊，又通到哈薩亞達，接連到押們，⁵從押們轉到埃及小河，直通到海為止。

⁶"'西邊要以大海為界，這就是你們的西界。

⁷"'北界要從大海起，劃到何珥山；⁸從何珥山劃到哈馬口，通到西達達，⁹又通到西斐崙，直到哈薩以難。這要作你們的北界。

¹⁰"'你們要從哈薩以難劃到示番為東界。¹¹這界要從示番下到亞延東邊的利比拉，又要達到基尼烈湖的東邊；¹²這界要下到約旦河，通到鹽海為止。

"'這四圍的邊界以內，要作你們的地。'"

¹³摩西吩咐以色列人說："這地就是耶和華吩咐拈鬮給九個半支派承受為業的。¹⁴因為呂便支派和迦得支派按着宗族受了產業，瑪拿西半個支派也受了產業。¹⁵這兩個半支派已經在耶利哥對面、約旦河東向日出之地受了產業。"

¹⁶耶和華曉諭摩西說：¹⁷"要給你們分地為業之人的名字，是祭司以利亞撒和嫩的兒子約書亞。¹⁸又要從

become barbs in your eyes and thorns in your sides. They will give you trouble in the land where you will live. ⁵⁶And then I will do to you what I plan to do to them.'"

Boundaries of Canaan

34 The LORD said to Moses, ²"Command the Israelites and say to them: 'When you enter Canaan, the land that will be allotted to you as an inheritance will have these boundaries:

³"'Your southern side will include some of the Desert of Zin along the border of Edom. On the east, your southern boundary will start from the end of the Salt Sea,ᵃ ⁴cross south of Scorpionᵇ Pass, continue on to Zin and go south of Kadesh Barnea. Then it will go to Hazar Addar and over to Azmon, ⁵where it will turn, join the Wadi of Egypt and end at the Sea.ᶜ

⁶"'Your western boundary will be the coast of the Great Sea. This will be your boundary on the west.

⁷"'For your northern boundary, run a line from the Great Sea to Mount Hor ⁸and from Mount Hor to Leboᵈ Hamath. Then the boundary will go to Zedad, ⁹continue to Ziphron and end at Hazar Enan. This will be your boundary on the north.

¹⁰"'For your eastern boundary, run a line from Hazar Enan to Shepham. ¹¹The boundary will go down from Shepham to Riblah on the east side of Ain and continue along the slopes east of the Sea of Kinnereth.ᵉ ¹²Then the boundary will go down along the Jordan and end at the Salt Sea.

"'This will be your land, with its boundaries on every side.'"

¹³Moses commanded the Israelites: "Assign this land by lot as an inheritance. The LORD has ordered that it be given to the nine and a half tribes, ¹⁴because the families of the tribe of Reuben, the tribe of Gad and the half-tribe of Manasseh have received their inheritance. ¹⁵These two and a half tribes have received their inheritance on the east side of the Jordan of Jericho,ᶠ toward the sunrise."

¹⁶The LORD said to Moses, ¹⁷"These are the names of the men who are to assign the land for you as an inheritance: Eleazar the priest and Joshua son of Nun. ¹⁸And appoint one leader

a 3 That is, the Dead Sea; also in verse 12　　b 4 Hebrew Akrabbim　　c 5 That is, the Mediterranean; also in verses 6 and 7　　d 8 Or to the entrance to　　e 11 That is, Galilee　　f 15 Jordan of Jericho was possibly an ancient name for the Jordan River.

from each tribe to help assign the land. [19]These are their names:

Caleb son of Jephunneh,
　　from the tribe of Judah;
[20]Shemuel son of Ammihud,
　　from the tribe of Simeon;
[21]Elidad son of Kislon,
　　from the tribe of Benjamin;
[22]Bukki son of Jogli,
　　the leader from the tribe of Dan;
[23]Hanniel son of Ephod,
　　the leader from the tribe of Manasseh son of Joseph;
[24]Kemuel son of Shiphtan,
　　the leader from the tribe of Ephraim son of Joseph;
[25]Elizaphan son of Parnach,
　　the leader from the tribe of Zebulun;
[26]Paltiel son of Azzan,
　　the leader from the tribe of Issachar;
[27]Ahihud son of Shelomi,
　　the leader from the tribe of Asher;
[28]Pedahel son of Ammihud,
　　the leader from the tribe of Naphtali."

[29]These are the men the LORD commanded to assign the inheritance to the Israelites in the land of Canaan.

Towns for the Levites

35 On the plains of Moab by the Jordan across from Jericho,[a] the LORD said to Moses, [2]"Command the Israelites to give the Levites towns to live in from the inheritance the Israelites will possess. And give them pasturelands around the towns. [3]Then they will have towns to live in and pasturelands for their cattle, flocks and all their other livestock.

[4]"The pasturelands around the towns that you give the Levites will extend out fifteen hundred feet[b] from the town wall. [5]Outside the town, measure three thousand feet[c] on the east side, three thousand on the south side, three thousand on the west and three thousand on the north, with the town in the center. They will have this area as pastureland for the towns.

Cities of Refuge

[6]"Six of the towns you give the Levites will be cities of refuge, to which a person who has killed someone may flee. In addition, give them forty-two other towns. [7]In all you must give the

a 1 Hebrew *Jordan of Jericho*; possibly an ancient name for the Jordan River　b 4 Hebrew *a thousand cubits* (about 450 meters)　c 5 Hebrew *two thousand cubits* (about 900 meters)

每支派中選一個首領幫助他們。[19]這些人的名字：

　　猶大支派有耶孚尼的兒子迦勒；

[20]西緬支派有亞米忽的兒子
　　示母利；
[21]便雅憫支派有基斯倫的兒子
　　以利達；
[22]但支派有一個首領，
　　約利的兒子布基；
[23]約瑟的子孫瑪拿西支派有一個首
　　領，以弗的兒子漢聶；

[24]以法蓮支派有一個首領，
　　拾弗但的兒子基母利；

[25]西布倫支派有一個首領，
　　帕納的兒子以利撒番；
[26]以薩迦支派有一個首領，
　　阿散的兒子帕鐵；
[27]亞設支派有一個首領，
　　示羅米的兒子亞希忽；
[28]拿弗他利支派有一個首領，
　　亞米忽的兒子比大黑。"

[29]這些人就是耶和華所吩咐、在迦南地把產業分給以色列人的。

給利未人的城邑

35 耶和華在摩押平原、約旦河邊、耶利哥對面曉諭摩西說：[2]"你吩咐以色列人，要從所得為業的地中把些城給利未人居住，也要把這城四圍的郊野給利未人。[3]這城邑要歸他們居住，城邑的郊野可以牧養他們的牛羊和各樣的牲畜，又可以安置他們的財物。

[4]"你們給利未人的郊野，要從城根起，四圍往外量一千肘。[5]另外，東量二千肘，南量二千肘，西量二千肘，北量二千肘為邊界，城在當中，這要歸他們作城邑的郊野。

逃城

[6]"你們給利未人的邑舍，其中當有六座逃城，使誤殺人的可以逃到那裏。此外還要給他們四十二座城。[7]你們要給利未人的城共有四十八

座,連城帶郊野都要給他們。⁸以色列人所得的地業,從中要把些城邑給利未人。人多的就多給,人少的就少給。各支派要按所承受為業之地把城邑給利未人。"

⁹耶和華曉諭摩西說:¹⁰"你吩咐以色列人說:'你們過約旦河,進了迦南地,¹¹就要分出幾座城,為你們作逃城,使誤殺人的可以逃到那裏。¹²這些城可以作逃避報仇人的城,使誤殺人的不至於死,等他站在會眾面前聽審判。¹³你們所分出來的城,要作六座逃城。¹⁴在約旦河東要分出三座城;在迦南地也要分出三座城,都作逃城。¹⁵這六座城要給以色列人和他們中間的外人,並寄居的,作為逃城,使誤殺人的都可以逃到那裏。

¹⁶"'倘若人用鐵器打人,以致打死,他就是故殺人的,故殺人的必被治死。¹⁷若用可以打死人的石頭打死了人,他就是故殺人的,故殺人的必被治死。¹⁸若用可以打死人的木器打死了人,他就是故殺人的,故殺人的必被治死。¹⁹報血仇的必親自殺那故殺人的,一遇見就殺他。²⁰人若因怨恨把人推倒,或是埋伏往人身上扔物,以至於死;²¹或是因仇恨用手打人,以至於死,那打人的必被治死。他是故殺人的,報血仇的一遇見就殺他。

²²"'倘若人沒有仇恨,忽然將人推倒;或是沒有埋伏,把物扔在人身上;²³或是沒有看見的時候,用可以打死人的石頭,扔在人身上,以至於死,本來與他無仇,也無意害他。²⁴會眾就要照典章,在打死人的和報血仇的中間審判。²⁵會眾要救這誤殺人的脫離報血仇人的手,也要使他歸入逃城。他要住在其中,直等到受聖膏的大祭司死了。

²⁶"'但誤殺人的,無論甚麼時候,若出了逃城的境外,²⁷報血仇的在逃城境外遇見他,將他殺了,報血

Levites forty-eight towns, together with their pasturelands. ⁸The towns you give the Levites from the land the Israelites possess are to be given in proportion to the inheritance of each tribe: Take many towns from a tribe that has many, but few from one that has few."

⁹Then the LORD said to Moses: ¹⁰"Speak to the Israelites and say to them: 'When you cross the Jordan into Canaan, ¹¹select some towns to be your cities of refuge, to which a person who has killed someone accidentally may flee. ¹²They will be places of refuge from the avenger, so that a person accused of murder may not die before he stands trial before the assembly. ¹³These six towns you give will be your cities of refuge. ¹⁴Give three on this side of the Jordan and three in Canaan as cities of refuge. ¹⁵These six towns will be a place of refuge for Israelites, aliens and any other people living among them, so that anyone who has killed another accidentally can flee there.

¹⁶"'If a man strikes someone with an iron object so that he dies, he is a murderer; the murderer shall be put to death. ¹⁷Or if anyone has a stone in his hand that could kill, and he strikes someone so that he dies, he is a murderer; the murderer shall be put to death. ¹⁸Or if anyone has a wooden object in his hand that could kill, and he hits someone so that he dies, he is a murderer; the murderer shall be put to death. ¹⁹The avenger of blood shall put the murderer to death; when he meets him, he shall put him to death. ²⁰If anyone with malice aforethought shoves another or throws something at him intentionally so that he dies ²¹or if in hostility he hits him with his fist so that he dies, that person shall be put to death; he is a murderer. The avenger of blood shall put the murderer to death when he meets him.

²²"'But if without hostility someone suddenly shoves another or throws something at him unintentionally ²³or, without seeing him, drops a stone on him that could kill him, and he dies, then since he was not his enemy and he did not intend to harm him, ²⁴the assembly must judge between him and the avenger of blood according to these regulations. ²⁵The assembly must protect the one accused of murder from the avenger of blood and send him back to the city of refuge to which he fled. He must stay there until the death of the high priest, who was anointed with the holy oil.

²⁶"'But if the accused ever goes outside the limits of the city of refuge to which he has fled ²⁷and the avenger of blood finds him outside the city, the avenger of blood may kill the accused

without being guilty of murder. 28The accused must stay in his city of refuge until the death of the high priest; only after the death of the high priest may he return to his own property.

29" 'These are to be legal requirements for you throughout the generations to come, wherever you live.

30" 'Anyone who kills a person is to be put to death as a murderer only on the testimony of witnesses. But no one is to be put to death on the testimony of only one witness.

31" 'Do not accept a ransom for the life of a murderer, who deserves to die. He must surely be put to death.

32" 'Do not accept a ransom for anyone who has fled to a city of refuge and so allow him to go back and live on his own land before the death of the high priest.

33" 'Do not pollute the land where you are. Bloodshed pollutes the land, and atonement cannot be made for the land on which blood has been shed, except by the blood of the one who shed it. 34Do not defile the land where you live and where I dwell, for I, the LORD, dwell among the Israelites.' "

Inheritance of Zelophehad's Daughters

36 The family heads of the clan of Gilead son of Makir, the son of Manasseh, who were from the clans of the descendants of Joseph, came and spoke before Moses and the leaders, the heads of the Israelite families. 2They said, "When the LORD commanded my lord to give the land as an inheritance to the Israelites by lot, he ordered you to give the inheritance of our brother Zelophehad to his daughters. 3Now suppose they marry men from other Israelite tribes; then their inheritance will be taken from our ancestral inheritance and added to that of the tribe they marry into. And so part of the inheritance allotted to us will be taken away. 4When the Year of Jubilee for the Israelites comes, their inheritance will be added to that of the tribe into which they marry, and their property will be taken from the tribal inheritance of our forefathers."

5Then at the LORD's command Moses gave this order to the Israelites: "What the tribe of the descendants of Joseph is saying is right. 6This is what the LORD commands for Zelophehad's daughters: They may marry anyone they please as long as they marry within the tribal clan of their father. 7No inheritance in Israel is to pass from tribe to tribe, for every Israelite shall keep the tribal land inherited from his forefathers. 8Every daughter who inherits land in any

仇的就沒有流血之罪。28因為誤殺人的該住在逃城裏，等到大祭司死了。大祭司死了以後，誤殺人的才可以回到他所得為業之地。

29 "'這在你們一切的住處，要作你們世世代代的律例、典章。

30 "'無論誰故殺人，要憑幾個見證人的口，把那故殺人的殺了，只是不可憑一個見證的口叫人死。

31 "'故殺人犯死罪的，你們不可收贖價代替他的命，他必被治死。

32 "'那逃到逃城的人，你們不可為他收贖價，使他在大祭司未死以先，再來住在本地。

33 "'這樣，你們就不污穢所住之地，因為血是污穢地的。若有在地上流人血的，非流那殺人者的血，那地就不得潔淨（註："潔淨"原文作"贖"）。34你們不可玷污所住之地，就是我住在其中之地，因為我耶和華住在以色列人中間。'"

西羅非哈的女兒承受產業

36 約瑟的後裔、瑪拿西的孫子、瑪吉的兒子基列，他子孫中的諸族長來到摩西和作首領的以色列人族長面前，2說："耶和華曾吩咐我主，拈鬮分地給以色列人為業，我主也受了耶和華的吩咐，將我們弟兄西羅非哈的產業分給他的眾女兒。3她們若嫁以色列別支派的人，就必將我們祖宗所遺留的產業加在她們丈夫支派的產業中。這樣，我們拈鬮所得的產業就要減少了。4到了以色列人的禧年，這女兒的產業就必加在她們丈夫支派的產業上。這樣，我們祖宗支派的產業就減少了。"

5摩西照耶和華的話吩咐以色列人說："約瑟支派的人說得有理。6論到西羅非哈的眾女兒，耶和華這樣吩咐說：她們可以隨意嫁人，只是要嫁同宗支派的人。7這樣，以色列人的產業就不從這支派歸到那支派，因為以色列人要各守各祖宗支派的產業。8凡在以色列支派中得了產業的女子，必作同宗支派人的妻，好叫以色列人各自承受他祖宗的產業。⁹這樣，他們的產業就不從這支派歸到那支派，因為以色列支派的人，要各守各的產業。”

¹⁰耶和華怎樣吩咐摩西，西羅非哈女兒就怎樣行。¹¹西羅非哈的女兒瑪拉、得撒、曷拉、密迦、挪阿，都嫁了她們伯叔的兒子。¹²她們嫁入約瑟兒子、瑪拿西子孫的族中，她們的產業仍留在同宗支派中。

¹³這是耶和華在摩押平原、約旦河邊、耶利哥對面，藉着摩西所吩咐以色列人的命令、典章。

Israelite tribe must marry someone in her father's tribal clan, so that every Israelite will possess the inheritance of his fathers. ⁹No inheritance may pass from tribe to tribe, for each Israelite tribe is to keep the land it inherits."

¹⁰So Zelophehad's daughters did as the LORD commanded Moses. ¹¹Zelophehad's daughters—Mahlah, Tirzah, Hoglah, Milcah and Noah—married their cousins on their father's side. ¹²They married within the clans of the descendants of Manasseh son of Joseph, and their inheritance remained in their father's clan and tribe.

¹³These are the commands and regulations the LORD gave through Moses to the Israelites on the plains of Moab by the Jordan across from Jericho.ᵃ

表六：曠野中各支派在會幕前安營的位置
TABLE 6 : THE ARRANGEMENT OF THE TRIBAL CAMPS

	*41,500 ▲53,400 亞設 Asher	*62,700 ▲64,400 但 Dan	*53,400 ▲45,400 拿弗他利 Naphtali	北 N	
*35,400 ▲45,600 便雅憫 Benjamin		米拉利 （利未之子） Merari (Son of Levi)		以薩迦 Issachar	*54,400 ▲64,300
*40,500 ▲32,500 以法蓮 Ephraim	革順 （利未之子） Gershon (Son of Levi)	會　幕 TABERNACLE	摩西 Moses 亞倫 Aaron	猶大 Judah	*74,600 ▲76,500
*32,200 ▲52,700 瑪拿西 Manasseh		哥轄 （利未之子） Kohath (Son of Levi)	亞倫兒子 Sons of Aaron	西布倫 Zebulun	*57,400 ▲60,500
	迦得 Gad *45,650 ▲40,500	呂便 Reuben *46,500 ▲43,730	西緬 Simeon *22,200 ▲59,300		

*1章 ：出埃及時二十歲以上男丁人數，共603,550人。
▲26章 ：入迦南前二十歲以上男丁人數，共601,730人。

*Ch.1 : population of men above 20 during leaving Egypt, 603,550 in total.
▲Ch.26 : population of men above 20 before entering Canaan, 601,730 in total.

a 13 Hebrew Jordan of Jericho; possibly an ancient name for the Jordan River

Deuteronomy

申命記

The Command to Leave Horeb

1 These are the words Moses spoke to all Israel in the desert east of the Jordan—that is, in the Arabah—opposite Suph, between Paran and Tophel, Laban, Hazeroth and Dizahab. ²(It takes eleven days to go from Horeb to Kadesh Barnea by the Mount Seir road.)

³In the fortieth year, on the first day of the eleventh month, Moses proclaimed to the Israelites all that the LORD had commanded him concerning them. ⁴This was after he had defeated Sihon king of the Amorites, who reigned in Heshbon, and at Edrei had defeated Og king of Bashan, who reigned in Ashtaroth.

⁵East of the Jordan in the territory of Moab, Moses began to expound this law, saying:

⁶The LORD our God said to us at Horeb, "You have stayed long enough at this mountain. ⁷Break camp and advance into the hill country of the Amorites; go to all the neighboring peoples in the Arabah, in the mountains, in the western foothills, in the Negev and along the coast, to the land of the Canaanites and to Lebanon, as far as the great river, the Euphrates. ⁸See, I have given you this land. Go in and take possession of the land that the LORD swore he would give to your fathers—to Abraham, Isaac and Jacob—and to their descendants after them."

The Appointment of Leaders

⁹At that time I said to you, "You are too heavy a burden for me to carry alone. ¹⁰The LORD your God has increased your numbers so that today you are as many as the stars in the sky. ¹¹May the LORD, the God of your fathers, increase you a thousand times and bless you as he has promised! ¹²But how can I bear your problems and your burdens and your disputes all by myself? ¹³Choose some wise, understanding and respected men from each of your tribes, and I will set them over you."

¹⁴You answered me, "What you propose to do is good."

¹⁵So I took the leading men of your tribes, wise and respected men, and appointed them to

命令離何烈山

1 以下所記的是摩西在約旦河東的曠野、疏弗對面的亞拉巴，就是巴蘭、陀弗、拉班、哈洗錄、底撒哈中間，向以色列眾人所說的話。²從何烈山經過西珥山，到加低斯巴尼亞，有十一天的路程。

³出埃及第四十年十一月初一日，摩西照耶和華藉着他所吩咐以色列人的話都曉諭他們。⁴那時，他已經擊殺了住希實本的亞摩利王西宏，和住以得來、亞斯他錄的巴珊王噩。

⁵摩西在約旦河東的摩押地講律法說：

⁶耶和華我們的神在何烈山曉諭我們說："你們在這山上住的日子夠了，⁷要起行轉到亞摩利人的山地和靠近這山地的各處，就是亞拉巴、山地、高原、南地、沿海一帶迦南人的地，並黎巴嫩山又到幼發拉底大河。⁸如今我將這地擺在你們面前，你們要進去得這地，就是耶和華向你們列祖亞伯拉罕、以撒、雅各起誓應許賜給他們和他們後裔為業之地。"

立首領

⁹那時我對你們說："管理你們的重任，我獨自擔當不起。¹⁰耶和華你們的神使你們多起來。看哪，你們今日像天上的星那樣多。¹¹惟願耶和華你們列祖的神使你們比如今更多千倍，照他所應許你們的話賜福與你們。¹²但你們的麻煩，和管理你們的重任，並你們的爭訟，我獨自一人怎能擔當得起呢？¹³你們要按着各支派選舉有智慧、有見識、為眾人所認識的，我立他們為你們的首領。"

¹⁴你們回答我說："照你所說的行了為妙。"

¹⁵我便將你們各支派的首領，有智慧、為眾人所認識的，照你們的

支派，立他們為官長、千夫長、百夫長、五十夫長、十夫長，管理你們。16當時，我囑咐你們的審判官說：你們聽訟，無論是弟兄彼此爭訟，是與同居的外人爭訟，都要按公義判斷。17審判的時候，不可看人的外貌；聽訟不可分貴賤，不可懼怕人，因為審判是屬乎神的。若有難斷的案件，可以呈到我這裏，我就判斷。18那時，我將你們所當行的事都吩咐你們了。

派出探子

19我們照着耶和華我們神所吩咐的，從何烈山起行，經過你們所看見那大而可怕的曠野，往亞摩利人的山地去，到了加低斯巴尼亞。20我對你們說：「你們已經到了耶和華我們神所賜給我們的亞摩利人之山地。21看哪，耶和華你的神已將那地擺在你面前，你要照耶和華你列祖的神所說的上去得那地為業，不要懼怕，也不要驚惶。」

22你們都就近我來，說：「我們要先打發人去，為我們窺探那地，將我們上去該走何道，必進何城，都回報我們。」

23這話我以為美，就從你們中間選了十二個人，每支派一人。24於是他們起身上山地去，到以實各谷，窺探那地。25他們手裏拿着那地的果子下來，到我們那裏，回報說：「耶和華我們的神所賜給我們的是美地。」

違背主

26你們卻不肯上去，竟違背了耶和華你們神的命令，27在帳棚內發怨言說：「耶和華因為恨我們，所以將我們從埃及地領出來，要交在亞摩利人手中，除滅我們。28我們上哪裏去呢？我們的弟兄使我們的心消化，說：『那地的民比我們又大又高，城邑又廣大又堅固，高得頂天，並且我們在那裏看見亞衲族的人。』」

29我就對你們說：「不要驚恐，也不要怕他們。30在你們前面行的耶和華你們的神必為你們爭戰，正如他在埃及和曠野，在你們眼前所行的一樣。31你們在曠野所行的路上，也曾見耶和華你們的神撫養你們，如同人撫養兒子一般，直等你們來到這地方。」

have authority over you—as commanders of thousands, of hundreds, of fifties and of tens and as tribal officials. 16And I charged your judges at that time: Hear the disputes between your brothers and judge fairly, whether the case is between brother Israelites or between one of them and an alien. 17Do not show partiality in judging; hear both small and great alike. Do not be afraid of any man, for judgment belongs to God. Bring me any case too hard for you, and I will hear it. 18And at that time I told you everything you were to do.

Spies Sent Out

19Then, as the LORD our God commanded us, we set out from Horeb and went toward the hill country of the Amorites through all that vast and dreadful desert that you have seen, and so we reached Kadesh Barnea. 20Then I said to you, "You have reached the hill country of the Amorites, which the LORD our God is giving us. 21See, the LORD your God has given you the land. Go up and take possession of it as the LORD, the God of your fathers, told you. Do not be afraid; do not be discouraged."

22Then all of you came to me and said, "Let us send men ahead to spy out the land for us and bring back a report about the route we are to take and the towns we will come to."

23The idea seemed good to me; so I selected twelve of you, one man from each tribe. 24They left and went up into the hill country, and came to the Valley of Eshcol and explored it. 25Taking with them some of the fruit of the land, they brought it down to us and reported, "It is a good land that the LORD our God is giving us."

Rebellion Against the LORD

26But you were unwilling to go up; you rebelled against the command of the LORD your God. 27You grumbled in your tents and said, "The LORD hates us; so he brought us out of Egypt to deliver us into the hands of the Amorites to destroy us. 28Where can we go? Our brothers have made us lose heart. They say, 'The people are stronger and taller than we are; the cities are large, with walls up to the sky. We even saw the Anakites there.' "

29Then I said to you, "Do not be terrified; do not be afraid of them. 30The LORD your God, who is going before you, will fight for you, as he did for you in Egypt, before your very eyes, 31and in the desert. There you saw how the LORD your God carried you, as a father carries his son, all the way you went until you reached this place."

³²In spite of this, you did not trust in the LORD your God, ³³who went ahead of you on your journey, in fire by night and in a cloud by day, to search out places for you to camp and to show you the way you should go.

³⁴When the LORD heard what you said, he was angry and solemnly swore: ³⁵"Not a man of this evil generation shall see the good land I swore to give your forefathers, ³⁶except Caleb son of Jephunneh. He will see it, and I will give him and his descendants the land he set his feet on, because he followed the LORD wholeheartedly."

³⁷Because of you the LORD became angry with me also and said, "You shall not enter it, either. ³⁸But your assistant, Joshua son of Nun, will enter it. Encourage him, because he will lead Israel to inherit it. ³⁹And the little ones that you said would be taken captive, your children who do not yet know good from bad—they will enter the land. I will give it to them and they will take possession of it. ⁴⁰But as for you, turn around and set out toward the desert along the route to the Red Sea.ª"

⁴¹Then you replied, "We have sinned against the LORD. We will go up and fight, as the LORD our God commanded us." So every one of you put on his weapons, thinking it easy to go up into the hill country.

⁴²But the LORD said to me, "Tell them, 'Do not go up and fight, because I will not be with you. You will be defeated by your enemies.'"

⁴³So I told you, but you would not listen. You rebelled against the LORD's command and in your arrogance you marched up into the hill country. ⁴⁴The Amorites who lived in those hills came out against you; they chased you like a swarm of bees and beat you down from Seir all the way to Hormah. ⁴⁵You came back and wept before the LORD, but he paid no attention to your weeping and turned a deaf ear to you. ⁴⁶And so you stayed in Kadesh many days—all the time you spent there.

Wanderings in the Desert

2 Then we turned back and set out toward the desert along the route to the Red Sea,ª as the LORD had directed me. For a long time we made our way around the hill country of Seir.

²Then the LORD said to me, ³"You have made your way around this hill country long enough; now turn north. ⁴Give the people these orders:

³²你們在這事上卻不信耶和華你們的神。³³他在路上,在你們前面行,為你們找安營的地方。夜間在火柱裏,日間在雲柱裏,指示你們所當行的路。

³⁴耶和華聽見你們這話,就發怒起誓說:³⁵"這惡世代的人,連一個也不得見我起誓應許賜給你們列祖的美地;³⁶惟有耶孚尼的兒子迦勒必得看見,並且我要將他所踏過的地賜給他和他的子孫,因為他專心跟從我。"

³⁷耶和華為你的緣故也向我發怒,說:"你必不得進入那地。³⁸伺候你、嫩的兒子約書亞,他必得進入那地,你要勉勵他,因為他要使以色列人承受那地為業。³⁹並且你們的婦人孩子,就是你們所說必被擄掠的,和今日不知善惡的兒女,必進入那地。我要將那地賜給他們,他們必得為業。⁴⁰至於你們,要轉回,從紅海的路往曠野去。"

⁴¹那時,你們回答我說:"我們得罪了耶和華,情願照耶和華我們神一切所吩咐的上去爭戰。"於是你們各人帶着兵器,爭先上山地去了。

⁴²耶和華吩咐我說:"你對他們說:'不要上去,也不要爭戰,因我不在你們中間,恐怕你們被仇敵殺敗了。'"

⁴³我就告訴了你們,你們卻不聽從,竟違背耶和華的命令,擅自上山地去了。⁴⁴住那山地的亞摩利人就出來攻擊你們,追趕你們如蜂擁一般,在西珥殺退你們,直到何珥瑪。⁴⁵你們便回來,在耶和華面前哭號;耶和華卻不聽你們的聲音,也不向你們側耳。⁴⁶於是你們在加低斯住了許多日子。

飄流曠野

2 此後,我們轉回,從紅海的路往曠野去,是照耶和華所吩咐我的;我們在西珥山繞行了許多日子。

²耶和華對我說:³"你們繞行這山的日子夠了,要轉向北去。⁴你吩

ª 40,1 Hebrew Yam Suph; that is, Sea of Reeds

咐百姓说：「你们弟兄以扫的子孙住在西珥，你们要经过他们的境界，他们必惧怕你们，所以你们要分外谨慎。5不可与他们争战，他们的地，连脚掌可踏之处，我都不给你们，因我已将西珥山赐给以扫为业。6你们要用钱向他们买粮吃，也要用钱向他们买水喝。』」

7因为耶和华你的神，在你手里所办的一切事上，已赐福与你。你走这大旷野，他都知道了。这四十年，耶和华你的神常与你同在，故此你一无所缺。

8于是，我们离了我们弟兄以扫子孙所住的西珥，从亚拉巴的路，经过以拉他、以旬迦别，转向摩押旷野的路去。

9耶和华吩咐我说：「不可扰害摩押人，也不可与他们争战。他们的地，我不赐给你为业，因我已将亚珥赐给罗得的子孙为业。」

(10先前，有以米人住在那里，民数众多，身体高大，像亚衲人一样。11这以米人像亚衲人，也算为利乏音人，摩押人称他们为以米人。12先前，何利人也住在西珥，但以扫的子孙将他们除灭，得了他们的地，接着居住，就如以色列在耶和华赐给他为业之地所行的一样。)

13「现在，起来过撒烈溪！」于是我们过了撒烈溪。

14自从离开加低斯巴尼亚，到过了撒烈溪的时候，共有三十八年，等那世代的兵丁都从营中灭尽，正如耶和华向他们所起的誓。15耶和华的手也攻击他们，将他们从营中除灭，直到灭尽。

16兵丁从民中都灭尽死亡以后，17耶和华吩咐我说：18「你今天要从摩押的境界亚珥经过，19走近亚扪人之地，不可扰害他们，也不可与他们争战。亚扪人的地，我不赐给你们为业，因我已将那地赐给罗得的子孙为业。」

(20那地也算为利乏音人之地，先前利乏音人住在那里，亚扪人称他们为散送冥。21那民众多，身体高大，像亚衲人一样，但耶和华从亚扪人面前除灭他们，亚扪人就得了他们

'You are about to pass through the territory of your brothers the descendants of Esau, who live in Seir. They will be afraid of you, but be very careful. 5Do not provoke them to war, for I will not give you any of their land, not even enough to put your foot on. I have given Esau the hill country of Seir as his own. 6You are to pay them in silver for the food you eat and the water you drink.' "

7The LORD your God has blessed you in all the work of your hands. He has watched over your journey through this vast desert. These forty years the LORD your God has been with you, and you have not lacked anything.

8So we went on past our brothers the descendants of Esau, who live in Seir. We turned from the Arabah road, which comes up from Elath and Ezion Geber, and traveled along the desert road of Moab.

9Then the LORD said to me, "Do not harass the Moabites or provoke them to war, for I will not give you any part of their land. I have given Ar to the descendants of Lot as a possession."

10(The Emites used to live there—a people strong and numerous, and as tall as the Anakites. 11Like the Anakites, they too were considered Rephaites, but the Moabites called them Emites. 12Horites used to live in Seir, but the descendants of Esau drove them out. They destroyed the Horites from before them and settled in their place, just as Israel did in the land the LORD gave them as their possession.)

13And the LORD said, "Now get up and cross the Zered Valley." So we crossed the valley.

14Thirty-eight years passed from the time we left Kadesh Barnea until we crossed the Zered Valley. By then, that entire generation of fighting men had perished from the camp, as the LORD had sworn to them. 15The LORD's hand was against them until he had completely eliminated them from the camp.

16Now when the last of these fighting men among the people had died, 17the LORD said to me, 18"Today you are to pass by the region of Moab at Ar. 19When you come to the Ammonites, do not harass them or provoke them to war, for I will not give you possession of any land belonging to the Ammonites. I have given it as a possession to the descendants of Lot."

20(That too was considered a land of the Rephaites, who used to live there; but the Ammonites called them Zamzummites. 21They were a people strong and numerous, and as tall as the Anakites. The LORD destroyed them from before the Ammonites, who drove them out and settled in their place. ²²The LORD had done the same for the descendants of Esau, who lived in Seir, when he destroyed the Horites from before them. They drove them out and have lived in their place to this day. ²³And as for the Avvites who lived in villages as far as Gaza, the Caphtorites coming out from Caphtor*a* destroyed them and settled in their place.)

Defeat of Sihon King of Heshbon

²⁴"Set out now and cross the Arnon Gorge. See, I have given into your hand Sihon the Amorite, king of Heshbon, and his country. Begin to take possession of it and engage him in battle. ²⁵This very day I will begin to put the terror and fear of you on all the nations under heaven. They will hear reports of you and will tremble and be in anguish because of you."

²⁶From the desert of Kedemoth I sent messengers to Sihon king of Heshbon offering peace and saying, ²⁷"Let us pass through your country. We will stay on the main road; we will not turn aside to the right or to the left. ²⁸Sell us food to eat and water to drink for their price in silver. Only let us pass through on foot— ²⁹as the descendants of Esau, who live in Seir, and the Moabites, who live in Ar, did for us—until we cross the Jordan into the land the LORD our God is giving us." ³⁰But Sihon king of Heshbon refused to let us pass through. For the LORD your God had made his spirit stubborn and his heart obstinate in order to give him into your hands, as he has now done.

³¹The LORD said to me, "See, I have begun to deliver Sihon and his country over to you. Now begin to conquer and possess his land."

³²When Sihon and all his army came out to meet us in battle at Jahaz, ³³the LORD our God delivered him over to us and we struck him down, together with his sons and his whole army. ³⁴At that time we took all his towns and completely destroyed*b* them—men, women and children. We left no survivors. ³⁵But the livestock and the plunder from the towns we had captured we carried off for ourselves. ³⁶From Aroer on the rim of the Arnon Gorge, and from the town in the gorge, even as far as Gilead, not one town was too strong for us. The LORD our God gave us all of them. ³⁷But in accordance with the command of the LORD our God, you did not encroach on any of the land of the Ammonites, neither the land along the course of

a 23 That is, Crete   b 34 The Hebrew term refers to the irrevocable giving over of things or persons to the LORD, often by totally destroying them.

的地，接着居住。²²正如耶和華從前為住西珥的以掃子孫，將何利人從他們面前除滅，他們得了何利人的地，接着居住一樣，直到今日。²³從迦斐託出來的迦斐託人，將先前住在鄉村直到迦薩的亞衛人除滅，接着居住。）

打敗希實本王西宏

²⁴ "你們起來前往，過亞嫩谷，我已將亞摩利人希實本王西宏和他的地交在你手中，你要與他爭戰奪得他的地為業。²⁵從今日起，我要使天下萬民聽見你的名聲都驚恐、懼怕，且因你發顫傷慟。"

²⁶我從基底莫的曠野，差遣使者去見希實本王西宏，用和睦的話說：²⁷ "求你容我從你的地經過，只走大道，不偏左右。²⁸你可以賣糧給我吃，也可以賣水給我喝。只要容我步行通過，²⁹就如住西珥的以掃子孫，和住亞珥的摩押人待我一樣，等我過了約旦河，好進入耶和華我們神所賜給我們的地。"³⁰但希實本王西宏不容我們從他那裏經過，因為耶和華你的神使他心中剛硬，性情頑梗，為要將他交在你手中，像今日一樣。

³¹耶和華對我說："從此起首，我要將西宏和他的地交給你，你要得他的地為業。"

³²那時，西宏和他的眾民出來攻擊我們，在雅雜與我們交戰。³³耶和華我們的神將他交給我們，我們就把他和他的兒子，並他的眾民都擊殺了。³⁴我們奪了他的一切城邑，將有人煙的各城，連女人帶孩子，盡都毀滅，沒有留下一個。³⁵惟有牲畜和所奪的各城，並其中的財物，都取為自己的掠物。³⁶從亞嫩谷邊的亞羅珥和谷中的城，直到基列，耶和華我們的神都交給我們了，沒有一座城高得使我們不能攻取的。³⁷惟有亞捫人之地，凡靠近雅博河的地，並山地的城邑，與耶和華我們神所

禁止我們去的地方，都沒有挨近。

打敗巴珊王噩

3 以後，我們轉回向巴珊去。巴珊王噩和他的眾民都出來，在以得來與我們交戰。²耶和華對我說："不要怕他！因我已將他和他的眾民，並他的地都交在你手中，你要待他像從前待住希實本的亞摩利王西宏一樣。"

³於是耶和華我們的神也將巴珊王噩和他的眾民都交在我們手中，我們殺了他們，沒有留下一個。⁴那時，我們奪了他所有的城，共有六十座，沒有一座城不被我們所奪。這為亞珥歌伯的全境，就是巴珊地噩王的國。⁵這些城都有堅固的高牆，有門、有閂；此外還有許多無城牆的鄉村。⁶我們將這些都毀滅了，像從前待希實本王西宏一樣，把有人煙的各城，連女人帶孩子，盡都毀滅。⁷惟有一切牲畜和城中的財物，都取為自己的掠物。

⁸那時我們從約旦河東兩個亞摩利王的手，將亞嫩谷直到黑門山之地奪過來。⁹（這黑門山，西頓人稱為西連，亞摩利人稱為示尼珥。）¹⁰就是奪了平原的各城，基列全地、巴珊全地，直到撒迦和以得來，都是巴珊王噩國內的城邑。¹¹（利乏音人所剩下的，只有巴珊王噩。他的床是鐵的，長九肘、寬四肘，都是以人肘為度。現今豈不是在亞捫人的拉巴嗎？）

分配土地

¹²那時，我們得了這地。從亞嫩谷邊的亞羅珥起，我將基列山地的一半，並其中的城邑，都給了呂便人和迦得人。¹³其餘的基列地和巴珊全地，就是噩王的國，我給了瑪拿西半支派。亞珥歌伯全地乃是巴珊全地，這叫作利乏音人之地。¹⁴瑪拿西的子孫睚珥佔了亞珥歌伯全境，直到基述人和瑪迦人的交界，就按自己的名稱

the Jabbok nor that around the towns in the hills.

Defeat of Og King of Bashan

3 Next we turned and went up along the road toward Bashan, and Og king of Bashan with his whole army marched out to meet us in battle at Edrei. ²The LORD said to me, "Do not be afraid of him, for I have handed him over to you with his whole army and his land. Do to him what you did to Sihon king of the Amorites, who reigned in Heshbon."

³So the LORD our God also gave into our hands Og king of Bashan and all his army. We struck them down, leaving no survivors. ⁴At that time we took all his cities. There was not one of the sixty cities that we did not take from them—the whole region of Argob, Og's kingdom in Bashan. ⁵All these cities were fortified with high walls and with gates and bars, and there were also a great many unwalled villages. ⁶We completely destroyed[a] them, as we had done with Sihon king of Heshbon, destroying[a] every city—men, women and children. ⁷But all the livestock and the plunder from their cities we carried off for ourselves.

⁸So at that time we took from these two kings of the Amorites the territory east of the Jordan, from the Arnon Gorge as far as Mount Hermon. ⁹(Hermon is called Sirion by the Sidonians; the Amorites call it Senir.) ¹⁰We took all the towns on the plateau, and all Gilead, and all Bashan as far as Salecah and Edrei, towns of Og's kingdom in Bashan. ¹¹(Only Og king of Bashan was left of the remnant of the Rephaites. His bed[b] was made of iron and was more than thirteen feet long and six feet wide.[c] It is still in Rabbah of the Ammonites.)

Division of the Land

¹²Of the land that we took over at that time, I gave the Reubenites and the Gadites the territory north of Aroer by the Arnon Gorge, including half the hill country of Gilead, together with its towns. ¹³The rest of Gilead and also all of Bashan, the kingdom of Og, I gave to the half tribe of Manasseh. (The whole region of Argob in Bashan used to be known as a land of the Rephaites. ¹⁴Jair, a descendant of Manasseh, took the whole region of Argob as far as the border of the Geshurites and the Maacathites; it

---

a 6 The Hebrew term refers to the irrevocable giving over of things or persons to the LORD. often by totally destroying them. b 11 Or sarcophagus c 11 Hebrew nine cubits long and four cubits wide (about 4 meters long and 1.8 meters wide)

was named after him, so that to this day Bashan is called Havvoth Jair.[a] [15]And I gave Gilead to Makir. [16]But to the Reubenites and the Gadites I gave the territory extending from Gilead down to the Arnon Gorge (the middle of the gorge being the border) and out to the Jabbok River, which is the border of the Ammonites. [17]Its western border was the Jordan in the Arabah, from Kinnereth to the Sea of the Arabah (the Salt Sea[b]), below the slopes of Pisgah.

[18]I commanded you at that time: "The LORD your God has given you this land to take possession of it. But all your able-bodied men, armed for battle, must cross over ahead of your brother Israelites. [19]However, your wives, your children and your livestock (I know you have much livestock) may stay in the towns I have given you, [20]until the LORD gives rest to your brothers as he has to you, and they too have taken over the land that the LORD your God is giving them, across the Jordan. After that, each of you may go back to the possession I have given you."

Moses Forbidden to Cross the Jordan

[21]At that time I commanded Joshua: "You have seen with your own eyes all that the LORD your God has done to these two kings. The LORD will do the same to all the kingdoms over there where you are going. [22]Do not be afraid of them; the LORD your God himself will fight for you."

[23]At that time I pleaded with the LORD: [24]"O Sovereign LORD, you have begun to show to your servant your greatness and your strong hand. For what god is there in heaven or on earth who can do the deeds and mighty works you do? [25]Let me go over and see the good land beyond the Jordan—that fine hill country and Lebanon." [26]But because of you the LORD was angry with me and would not listen to me. "That is enough," the LORD said. "Do not speak to me anymore about this matter. [27]Go up to the top of Pisgah and look west and north and south and east. Look at the land with your own eyes, since you are not going to cross this Jordan. [28]But commission Joshua, and encourage and strengthen him, for he will lead this people across and will cause them to inherit the land that you will see." [29]So we stayed in the valley near Beth Peor.

這巴珊地為哈倭特睚珥,直到今日。[15]我又將基列給了瑪吉。[16]從基列到亞嫩谷,以谷中為界,直到亞捫人交界的雅博河,我給了呂便人和迦得人,[17]又將亞拉巴和靠近約旦河之地,從基尼烈直到亞拉巴海,就是鹽海,並毘斯迦山根東邊之地,都給了他們。

[18]那時,我吩咐你們說:"耶和華你們的神已將這地賜給你們為業。你們所有的勇士都要帶着兵器,在你們的弟兄以色列人前面過去。[19]但你們的妻子、孩子、牲畜(我知道你們有許多的牲畜),可以住在我所賜給你們的各城裏。[20]等到你們弟兄在約旦河那邊,也得耶和華你們神所賜給他們的地,又使他們得享平安,與你們一樣,你們才可以回到我所賜給你們為業之地。"

摩西不得渡約旦河

[21]那時我吩咐約書亞說:"你親眼看見了耶和華你神向這二王所行的;耶和華也必向你所要去的各國照樣行。[22]你不要怕他們,因那為你爭戰的是耶和華你的神。"

[23]那時,我懇求耶和華說;[24]"主耶和華啊,你已將你的大力大能顯給僕人看,在天上,在地下,有甚麼神能像你行事,像你有大能的作為呢?[25]求你容我過去,看約旦河那邊的美地,就是那佳美的山地和黎巴嫩。"

[26]但耶和華因你們的緣故向我發怒,不應允我,對我說:"罷了!你不要向我再提這事。[27]你且上毘斯迦山頂去,向東、西、南、北舉目觀望,因為你必不能過這約旦河。[28]你卻要囑咐約書亞,勉勵他,使他膽壯,因為他必在這百姓前面過去,使他們承受你所要觀看之地。"[29]於是,我們住在伯毘珥對面的谷中。

a 14 Or called the settlements of Jair   b 17 That is, the Dead Sea

命令守律法

4 以色列人哪，現在我所教訓你們的律例、典章，你們要聽從遵行，好叫你們存活，得以進入耶和華你們列祖之神所賜給你們的地，承受為業。²所吩咐你們的話，你們不可加添，也不可刪減，好叫你們遵守我所吩咐的，就是耶和華你們神的命令。

³耶和華因巴力毘珥的事所行的，你們親眼看見了。凡隨從巴力毘珥的人，耶和華你們的神都從你們中間除滅了。⁴惟有你們專靠耶和華你們神的人，今日全都存活。

⁵我照着耶和華我神所吩咐的，將律例、典章教訓你們，使你們在所要進去得為業的地上遵行。⁶所以你們要謹守遵行，這就是你們在萬民眼前的智慧、聰明。他們聽見這一切律例，必說：「這大國的人真是有智慧、有聰明。」⁷哪一大國的人有神與他們相近，像耶和華我們的神，在我們求告他的時候與我們相近呢？⁸又哪一大國有這樣公義的律例、典章，像我今日在你們面前所陳明的這一切律法呢？

⁹你只要謹慎，殷勤保守你的心靈，免得忘記你親眼所看見的事，又免得你一生這事離開你的心，總要傳給你的子子孫孫。¹⁰你在何烈山站在耶和華你神面前的那日，耶和華對我說：「你為我招聚百姓，我要叫他們聽見我的話，使他們存活在世的日子，可以學習敬畏我，又可以教訓兒女這樣行。」¹¹那時你們近前來，站在山下，山上有火焰沖天，並有昏黑、密雲、幽暗。¹²耶和華從火焰中對你們說話，你們只聽見聲音，卻沒有看見形像。¹³他將所吩咐你們當守的約指示你們，就是十條誡，並將這誡寫在兩塊石版上。¹⁴那時耶和華又吩咐我將律例、典章教訓你們，使你們在所要過去得為業的地上遵行。

禁拜偶像

¹⁵所以你們要分外謹慎，因為耶和華在何烈山從火中對你們說話的那日，你們沒有看見甚麼形像。¹⁶惟恐你們敗壞自己，雕刻偶像，彷彿甚麼

Obedience Commanded

4 Hear now, O Israel, the decrees and laws I am about to teach you. Follow them so that you may live and may go in and take possession of the land that the LORD, the God of your fathers, is giving you. ²Do not add to what I command you and do not subtract from it, but keep the commands of the LORD your God that I give you.

³You saw with your own eyes what the LORD did at Baal Peor. The LORD your God destroyed from among you everyone who followed the Baal of Peor, ⁴but all of you who held fast to the LORD your God are still alive today.

⁵See, I have taught you decrees and laws as the LORD my God commanded me, so that you may follow them in the land you are entering to take possession of it. ⁶Observe them carefully, for this will show your wisdom and understanding to the nations, who will hear about all these decrees and say, "Surely this great nation is a wise and understanding people." ⁷What other nation is so great as to have their gods near them the way the LORD our God is near us whenever we pray to him? ⁸And what other nation is so great as to have such righteous decrees and laws as this body of laws I am setting before you today?

⁹Only be careful, and watch yourselves closely so that you do not forget the things your eyes have seen or let them slip from your heart as long as you live. Teach them to your children and to their children after them. ¹⁰Remember the day you stood before the LORD your God at Horeb, when he said to me, "Assemble the people before me to hear my words so that they may learn to revere me as long as they live in the land and may teach them to their children." ¹¹You came near and stood at the foot of the mountain while it blazed with fire to the very heavens, with black clouds and deep darkness. ¹²Then the LORD spoke to you out of the fire. You heard the sound of words but saw no form; there was only a voice. ¹³He declared to you his covenant, the Ten Commandments, which he commanded you to follow and then wrote them on two stone tablets. ¹⁴And the LORD directed me at that time to teach you the decrees and laws you are to follow in the land that you are crossing the Jordan to possess.

Idolatry Forbidden

¹⁵You saw no form of any kind the day the LORD spoke to you at Horeb out of the fire. Therefore watch yourselves very carefully, ¹⁶so that you do not become corrupt and make for

yourselves an idol, an image of any shape, whether formed like a man or a woman, [17]or like any animal on earth or any bird that flies in the air, [18]or like any creature that moves along the ground or any fish in the waters below. [19]And when you look up to the sky and see the sun, the moon and the stars—all the heavenly array—do not be enticed into bowing down to them and worshiping things the LORD your God has apportioned to all the nations under heaven. [20]But as for you, the LORD took you and brought you out of the iron-smelting furnace, out of Egypt, to be the people of his inheritance, as you now are.

[21]The LORD was angry with me because of you, and he solemnly swore that I would not cross the Jordan and enter the good land the LORD your God is giving you as your inheritance. [22]I will die in this land; I will not cross the Jordan; but you are about to cross over and take possession of that good land. [23]Be careful not to forget the covenant of the LORD your God that he made with you; do not make for yourselves an idol in the form of anything the LORD your God has forbidden. [24]For the LORD your God is a consuming fire, a jealous God.

[25]After you have had children and grandchildren and have lived in the land a long time—if you then become corrupt and make any kind of idol, doing evil in the eyes of the LORD your God and provoking him to anger, [26]I call heaven and earth as witnesses against you this day that you will quickly perish from the land that you are crossing the Jordan to possess. You will not live there long but will certainly be destroyed. [27]The LORD will scatter you among the peoples, and only a few of you will survive among the nations to which the LORD will drive you. [28]There you will worship man-made gods of wood and stone, which cannot see or hear or eat or smell. [29]But if from there you seek the LORD your God, you will find him if you look for him with all your heart and with all your soul. [30]When you are in distress and all these things have happened to you, then in later days you will return to the LORD your God and obey him. [31]For the LORD your God is a merciful God; he will not abandon or destroy you or forget the covenant with your forefathers, which he confirmed to them by oath.

The LORD Is God

[32]Ask now about the former days, long before your time, from the day God created man on the earth; ask from one end of the heavens to the other. Has anything so great as this ever hap-

男像女像，[17]或地上走獸的像，或空中飛鳥的像，[18]或地上爬物的像，或地底下水中魚的像。[19]又恐怕你向天舉目觀看，見耶和華你的神為天下萬民所擺列的日、月、星，就是天上的萬象，自己便被勾引敬拜事奉它。[20]耶和華將你們從埃及領出來脫離鐵爐，要特作自己產業的子民，像今日一樣。

[21]耶和華又因你們的緣故，向我發怒起誓，必不容我過約旦河，也不容我進入耶和華你神所賜你為業的那美地。[22]我只得死在這地，不能過約旦河；但你們必過去得那美地。[23]你們要謹慎，免得忘記耶和華你們神與你們所立的約，為自己雕刻偶像，就是耶和華你神所禁止你做的偶像，[24]因為耶和華你的神乃是烈火，是忌邪的神。

[25]你們在那地住久了，生子生孫，就雕刻偶像，彷彿甚麼形像，敗壞自己，行耶和華你神眼中看為惡的事，惹他發怒。[26]我今日呼天喚地向你們作見證，你們必在過約旦河得為業的地上速速滅盡！你們不能在那地上長久，必盡行除滅。[27]耶和華必使你們分散在萬民中，在他所領你們到的萬國裏，你們剩下的人數稀少。[28]在那裏你們必侍奉人手所造的神，就是用木石造成，不能看、不能聽、不能吃、不能聞的神。[29]但你們在那裏必尋求耶和華你的神。你盡心盡性尋求他的時候，就必尋見。[30]日後你遭遇一切患難的時候，你必歸回耶和華你的神，聽從他的話。[31]耶和華你神原是有憐憫的神，他總不撇下你、不滅絕你，也不忘記他起誓與你列祖所立的約。

惟有主是神

[32]、[33]你且考察在你以前的世代，自神造人在世以來，從天這邊到天那邊，曾有何民聽見神在火中

說話的聲音，像你聽見還能存活呢？
這樣的大事何曾有、何曾聽見呢？
34神何曾從別的國中將一國的人民領
出來，用試驗、神蹟、奇事、爭戰、
大能的手，和伸出來的膀臂，並大可
畏的事，像耶和華你們的神在埃及，
在你們眼前為你們所行的一切事呢？

35這是顯給你看，要使你知道，
惟有耶和華他是神，除他以外，再無
別神。36他從天上使你聽見他的聲
音，為要教訓你；又在地上使你看見
他的烈火，並且聽見他從火中所說的
話。37因他愛你的列祖，所以揀選他
們的後裔，用大能親自領你出了埃
及，38要將比你強大的國民從你面前
趕出，領你進去，將他們的地賜你為
業，像今日一樣。

39所以今日你要知道，也要記在
心上，天上地下惟有耶和華他是神，
除他以外，再無別神。40我今日將他
的律例、誡命曉諭你，你要遵守，使
你和你的子孫可以得福，並使你的日
子在耶和華你神所賜的地上得以長
久。

逃城

41那時摩西在約旦河東，向日出
之地，分定三座城，42使那素無仇
恨、無心殺了人的，可以逃到這三城
之中的一座城，就得存活。43為便
人分定曠野平原的比悉；為迦得人分
定基列的拉末；為瑪拿西人分定巴珊
的哥蘭。

陳明律法

44摩西在以色列人面前所陳明的
律法，45就是摩西在以色列人出埃及
後所傳給他們的法度、律例、典章。
46在約旦河東伯毘珥對面的谷中，在
住希實本亞摩利王西宏之地，這西
宏是摩西和以色列人出埃及後所擊殺
的。47他們得了他的地，又得了巴珊
王噩的地，就是兩個亞摩利王，在約
旦河東向日出之地。48從亞嫩谷邊的
亞羅珥，直到西雲山，就是黑門山。

pened, or has anything like it ever been heard
of? 33Has any other people heard the voice of
God[a] speaking out of fire, as you have, and
lived? 34Has any god ever tried to take for himself one nation out of another nation, by test-
ings, by miraculous signs and wonders, by war,
by a mighty hand and an outstretched arm, or
by great and awesome deeds, like all the things
the LORD your God did for you in Egypt before
your very eyes?

35You were shown these things so that you
might know that the LORD is God; besides him
there is no other. 36From heaven he made you
hear his voice to discipline you. On earth he
showed you his great fire, and you heard his
words from out of the fire. 37Because he loved
your forefathers and chose their descendants
after them, he brought you out of Egypt by his
Presence and his great strength, 38to drive out
before you nations greater and stronger than
you and to bring you into their land to give it to
you for your inheritance, as it is today.

39Acknowledge and take to heart this day
that the LORD is God in heaven above and on the
earth below. There is no other. 40Keep his
decrees and commands, which I am giving you
today, so that it may go well with you and your
children after you and that you may live long in
the land the LORD your God gives you for all
time.

Cities of Refuge

41Then Moses set aside three cities east of the
Jordan, 42to which anyone who had killed a person could flee if he had unintentionally killed
his neighbor without malice aforethought. He
could flee into one of these cities and save his
life. 43The cities were these: Bezer in the desert
plateau, for the Reubenites; Ramoth in Gilead,
for the Gadites; and Golan in Bashan, for the
Manassites.

Introduction to the Law

44This is the law Moses set before the Israelites. 45These are the stipulations, decrees and
laws Moses gave them when they came out of
Egypt 46and were in the valley near Beth Peor
east of the Jordan, in the land of Sihon king of
the Amorites, who reigned in Heshbon and was
defeated by Moses and the Israelites as they
came out of Egypt. 47They took possession of his
land and the land of Og king of Bashan, the two
Amorite kings east of the Jordan. 48This land
extended from Aroer on the rim of the Arnon

a 33 Or of a god

Gorge to Mount Siyon[a] (that is, Hermon), [49]and included all the Arabah east of the Jordan, as far as the Sea of the Arabah,[b] below the slopes of Pisgah.

The Ten Commandments

5 Moses summoned all Israel and said:
Hear, O Israel, the decrees and laws I declare in your hearing today. Learn them and be sure to follow them. [2]The LORD our God made a covenant with us at Horeb. [3]It was not with our fathers that the LORD made this covenant, but with us, with all of us who are alive here today. [4]The LORD spoke to you face to face out of the fire on the mountain. [5](At that time I stood between the LORD and you to declare to you the word of the LORD, because you were afraid of the fire and did not go up the mountain.) And he said:

[6]"I am the LORD your God, who brought you out of Egypt, out of the land of slavery.

[7]"You shall have no other gods before[c] me.

[8]"You shall not make for yourself an idol in the form of anything in heaven above or on the earth beneath or in the waters below. [9]You shall not bow down to them or worship them; for I, the LORD your God, am a jealous God, punishing the children for the sin of the fathers to the third and fourth generation of those who hate me, [10]but showing love to a thousand generations of those who love me and keep my commandments.

[11]"You shall not misuse the name of the LORD your God, for the LORD will not hold anyone guiltless who misuses his name.

[12]"Observe the Sabbath day by keeping it holy, as the LORD your God has commanded you. [13]Six days you shall labor and do all your work, [14]but the seventh day is a Sabbath to the LORD your God. On it you shall not do any work, neither you, nor your son or daughter, nor your manservant or maidservant, nor your ox, your donkey or any of your animals, nor the alien within your gates, so that your manservant and maidservant may rest, as you do. [15]Remember that you were slaves in Egypt and that the LORD your God brought you out of there with a mighty hand and an outstretched arm.

---

[49]還有約旦河東的全亞拉巴，直到亞拉巴海，靠近毗斯迦山根。

十誡

5 摩西將以色列眾人召了來，對他們說：以色列人哪，我今日曉諭你們的律例、典章，你們要聽，可以學習，謹守遵行。[2]耶和華我們的神在何烈山與我們立約。[3]這約不是與我們列祖立的，乃是與我們今日在這裏存活之人立的。[4]耶和華在山上，從火中，面對面與你們說話，[5]（那時我站在耶和華和你們中間，要將耶和華的話傳給你們，因為你們懼怕那火，沒有上山。）

[6]說：「我是耶和華你的神，曾將你從埃及地為奴之家領出來。

[7]「除了我以外，你不可有別的神。

[8]「不可為自己雕刻偶像，也不可做甚麼形像，彷彿上天、下地和地底下水中的百物。[9]不可跪拜那些像，也不可侍奉它，因為我耶和華你的神是忌邪的神。恨我的，我必追討他的罪，自父及子，直到三四代；[10]愛我、守我誡命的，我必向他們發慈愛，直到千代。

[11]「不可妄稱耶和華你神的名，因為妄稱耶和華名的，耶和華必不以他為無罪。

[12]「當照耶和華你神所吩咐的，守安息日為聖日。[13]六日要勞碌做你一切的工，[14]但第七日是向耶和華你神當守的安息日。這一日你和你的兒女、僕婢、牛、驢、牲畜，並在你城裏寄居的客旅，無論何工都不可做，使你的僕婢可以和你一樣安息。[15]你也要記念你在埃及地作過奴僕，耶和華你神用大能的手和伸出來的膀臂，將你從那裏領

---

a 48 Hebrew; Syriac (see also Deut. 3:9) Sirion   b 49 That is, the Dead Sea   c 7 Or besides

出來。因此，耶和華你的神吩咐你守安息日。

16 "當照耶和華你神所吩咐的孝敬父母，使你得福，並使你的日子，在耶和華你神所賜你的地上得以長久。

17 "不可殺人。

18 "不可姦淫。

19 "不可偷盜。

20 "不可作假見證陷害人。

21 "不可貪戀人的妻子；也不可貪圖人的房屋、田地、僕婢、牛、驢，並他一切所有的。"

22 這些話是耶和華在山上，從火中、雲中、幽暗中，大聲曉諭你們全會眾的，此外並沒有添別的話。他就把這話寫在兩塊石版上，交給我了。

23 那時，火焰燒山，你們聽見從黑暗中出來的聲音，你們支派中所有的首領和長老都來就近我，24 說："看哪，耶和華我們神將他的榮光和他的大能顯給我們看，我們又聽見他的聲音從火中出來。今日我們得見神與人說話，人還存活。25 現在這大火將要燒滅我們，我們何必冒死呢？若再聽見耶和華我們神的聲音，就必死亡。26 凡屬血氣的，曾有何人聽見永生神的聲音從火中出來，像我們聽見還能存活呢？27 求你近前去，聽耶和華我們神所要說的一切話，將他對你說的話都傳給我們，我們就聽從遵行。"

28 你們對我說的話，耶和華都聽見了。耶和華對我說："這百姓的話我聽見了，他們所說的都是。29 惟願他們存這樣的心敬畏我，常遵守我的一切誡命，使他們和他們的子孫永遠得福。

30 "你去對他們說：你們回帳棚去吧！31 至於你，可以站在我這裏，我要將一切誡命、律例、典章傳給你，你要教訓他們，使他們在我賜他們為業的地上遵行。"

32 所以，你們要照耶和華你們神所吩咐的謹守遵行，不可偏離左右。33 耶和華你們神所吩咐你們行的，你們都要去行，使你們可以存活得福，

Therefore the LORD your God has commanded you to observe the Sabbath day.

16"Honor your father and your mother, as the LORD your God has commanded you, so that you may live long and that it may go well with you in the land the LORD your God is giving you.

17"You shall not murder.

18"You shall not commit adultery.

19"You shall not steal.

20"You shall not give false testimony against your neighbor.

21"You shall not covet your neighbor's wife. You shall not set your desire on your neighbor's house or land, his manservant or maidservant, his ox or donkey, or anything that belongs to your neighbor."

22These are the commandments the LORD proclaimed in a loud voice to your whole assembly there on the mountain from out of the fire, the cloud and the deep darkness; and he added nothing more. Then he wrote them on two stone tablets and gave them to me.

23When you heard the voice out of the darkness, while the mountain was ablaze with fire, all the leading men of your tribes and your elders came to me. 24And you said, "The LORD our God has shown us his glory and his majesty, and we have heard his voice from the fire. Today we have seen that a man can live even if God speaks with him. 25But now, why should we die? This great fire will consume us, and we will die if we hear the voice of the LORD our God any longer. 26For what mortal man has ever heard the voice of the living God speaking out of fire, as we have, and survived? 27Go near and listen to all that the LORD our God says. Then tell us whatever the LORD our God tells you. We will listen and obey."

28The LORD heard you when you spoke to me and the LORD said to me, "I have heard what this people said to you. Everything they said was good. 29Oh, that their hearts would be inclined to fear me and keep all my commands always, so that it might go well with them and their children forever!

30"Go, tell them to return to their tents. 31But you stay here with me so that I may give you all the commands, decrees and laws you are to teach them to follow in the land I am giving them to possess."

32So be careful to do what the LORD your God has commanded you; do not turn aside to the right or to the left. 33Walk in all the way that the LORD your God has commanded you, so that you may live and prosper and prolong your days in the land that you will possess.

Love the LORD Your God

6 These are the commands, decrees and laws the LORD your God directed me to teach you to observe in the land that you are crossing the Jordan to possess, ²so that you, your children and their children after them may fear the LORD your God as long as you live by keeping all his decrees and commands that I give you, and so that you may enjoy long life. ³Hear, O Israel, and be careful to obey so that it may go well with you and that you may increase greatly in a land flowing with milk and honey, just as the LORD, the God of your fathers, promised you.

⁴Hear, O Israel: The LORD our God, the LORD is one.ᵃ ⁵Love the LORD your God with all your heart and with all your soul and with all your strength. ⁶These commandments that I give you today are to be upon your hearts. ⁷Impress them on your children. Talk about them when you sit at home and when you walk along the road, when you lie down and when you get up. ⁸Tie them as symbols on your hands and bind them on your foreheads. ⁹Write them on the doorframes of your houses and on your gates.

¹⁰When the LORD your God brings you into the land he swore to your fathers, to Abraham, Isaac and Jacob, to give you—a land with large, flourishing cities you did not build, ¹¹houses filled with all kinds of good things you did not provide, wells you did not dig, and vineyards and olive groves you did not plant—then when you eat and are satisfied, ¹²be careful that you do not forget the LORD, who brought you out of Egypt, out of the land of slavery.

¹³Fear the LORD your God, serve him only and take your oaths in his name. ¹⁴Do not follow other gods, the gods of the peoples around you; ¹⁵for the LORD your God, who is among you, is a jealous God and his anger will burn against you, and he will destroy you from the face of the land. ¹⁶Do not test the LORD your God as you did at Massah. ¹⁷Be sure to keep the commands of the LORD your God and the stipulations and decrees he has given you. ¹⁸Do what is right and good in the LORD's sight, so that it may go well with you and you may go in and take over the good land that the LORD promised on oath to your forefathers, ¹⁹thrusting out all your enemies before you, as the LORD said.

a 4 Or *The LORD our God is one LORD;* or *The LORD is our God, the LORD is one;* or *The LORD is our God, the LORD alone*

並使你們的日子在所要承受的地上得以長久。

愛主你的神

6 這是耶和華你們神所吩咐教訓你們的誡命、律例、典章,使你們在所要過去得為業的地上遵行,²好叫你和你子子孫孫一生敬畏耶和華你的神,謹守他的一切律例、誡命,就是我所吩咐你的,使你的日子得以長久。³以色列啊!你要聽,要謹守遵行,使你可以在那流奶與蜜之地得以享福,人數極其增多,正如耶和華你列祖的神所應許你的。

⁴以色列啊!你要聽:耶和華我們神是獨一的主。⁵你要盡心、盡性、盡力愛耶和華你的神。⁶我今日所吩咐你的話都要記在心上,⁷也要殷勤教訓你的兒女,無論你坐在家裏,行在路上,躺下,起來,都要談論;⁸也要繫在手上為記號,戴在額上為經文;⁹又要寫在你房屋的門框上,並你的城門上。

¹⁰耶和華你的神,領你進他向你列祖亞伯拉罕、以撒、雅各起誓應許給你的地。那裏有城邑,又大又美,非你所建造的;¹¹有房屋,裝滿各樣美物,非你所裝滿的;有鑿成的水井,非你所鑿成的;還有葡萄園、橄欖園,非你所栽種的,你吃了而且飽足。¹²那時你要謹慎,免得你忘記將你從埃及地為奴之家領出來的耶和華。

¹³你要敬畏耶和華你的神,侍奉他,指着他的名起誓。¹⁴不可隨從別神,就是你們四圍國民的神,¹⁵因為在你們中間的耶和華你神,是忌邪的神。惟恐耶和華你神的怒氣向你發作,就把你從地上除滅。¹⁶你們不可試探耶和華你們的神,像你們在瑪撒那樣試探他。¹⁷要留意遵守耶和華你們神所吩咐的誡命、法度、律例。¹⁸耶和華眼中看為正、看為善的,你都要遵行,使你可以享福,並可以進去得耶和華向你列祖起誓應許的那美地,¹⁹照耶和華所說的,從你面前攆出你的一切仇敵。

20日後，你的兒子問你說：“耶和華我們神吩咐你們的這些法度、律例、典章是甚麼意思呢？” 21你就告訴你的兒子說：“我們在埃及作過法老的奴僕，耶和華用大能的手將我們從埃及領出來，22在我們眼前，將重大可怕的神蹟奇事，施行在埃及地和法老並他全家的身上，23將我們從那裏領出來，要領我們進入他向我們列祖起誓應許之地，把這地賜給我們。24耶和華又吩咐我們遵行這一切律例，要敬畏耶和華我們的神，使我們常得好處，蒙他保全我們的生命，像今日一樣。25我們若照耶和華我們神所吩咐的一切誡命，謹守遵行，這就是我們的義了。”

趕出異族

7 耶和華你神領你進入要得為業之地，從你面前趕出許多國民，就是赫人、革迦撒人、亞摩利人、迦南人、比利洗人、希未人、耶布斯人，共七國的民，都比你強大。2耶和華你神將他們交給你擊殺，那時你要把他們滅絕淨盡，不可與他們立約，也不可憐恤他們；3不可與他們結親，不可將你的女兒嫁他們的兒子；也不可叫你的兒子娶他們的女兒，4因為他必使你兒子轉離不跟從主，去侍奉別神，以致耶和華的怒氣向你們發作，就速速地將你們滅絕。5你們卻要這樣待他們：拆毀他們的祭壇，打碎他們的柱像，砍下他們的木偶，用火焚燒他們雕刻的偶像。6因為你歸耶和華你神為聖潔的民，耶和華你神從地上的萬民中揀選你，特作自己的子民。

7耶和華專愛你們，揀選你們，並非因你們的人數多於別民，原來你們的人數在萬民中是最少的。8只因耶和華愛你們，又因要守他向你們列祖所起的誓，就用大能的手領你們出來，從為奴之家救贖你們脫離埃及王

20In the future, when your son asks you, "What is the meaning of the stipulations, decrees and laws the LORD our God has commanded you?" 21tell him: "We were slaves of Pharaoh in Egypt, but the LORD brought us out of Egypt with a mighty hand. 22Before our eyes the LORD sent miraculous signs and wonders—great and terrible—upon Egypt and Pharaoh and his whole household. 23But he brought us out from there to bring us in and give us the land that he promised on oath to our forefathers. 24The LORD commanded us to obey all these decrees and to fear the LORD our God, so that we might always prosper and be kept alive, as is the case today. 25And if we are careful to obey all this law before the LORD our God, as he has commanded us, that will be our righteousness."

Driving Out the Nations

7 When the LORD your God brings you into the land you are entering to possess and drives out before you many nations—the Hittites, Girgashites, Amorites, Canaanites, Perizzites, Hivites and Jebusites, seven nations larger and stronger than you— 2and when the LORD your God has delivered them over to you and you have defeated them, then you must destroy them totally.[a] Make no treaty with them, and show them no mercy. 3Do not intermarry with them. Do not give your daughters to their sons or take their daughters for your sons, 4for they will turn your sons away from following me to serve other gods, and the LORD's anger will burn against you and will quickly destroy you. 5This is what you are to do to them: Break down their altars, smash their sacred stones, cut down their Asherah poles[b] and burn their idols in the fire. 6For you are a people holy to the LORD your God. The LORD your God has chosen you out of all the peoples on the face of the earth to be his people, his treasured possession.

7The LORD did not set his affection on you and choose you because you were more numerous than other peoples, for you were the fewest of all peoples. 8But it was because the LORD loved you and kept the oath he swore to your forefathers that he brought you out with a mighty hand and redeemed you from the land of slavery, from the power of Pharaoh king of

---

a 2 The Hebrew term refers to the irrevocable giving over of things or persons to the LORD, often by totally destroying them; also in verse 26.　　b 5 That is, symbols of the goddess Asherah; here and elsewhere in Deuteronomy

Egypt. [9]Know therefore that the LORD your God is God; he is the faithful God, keeping his covenant of love to a thousand generations of those who love him and keep his commands. [10]But

those who hate him he will repay to their face
　　by destruction;
he will not be slow to repay to their face
　　those who hate him.

[11]Therefore, take care to follow the commands, decrees and laws I give you today.

[12]If you pay attention to these laws and are careful to follow them, then the LORD your God will keep his covenant of love with you, as he swore to your forefathers. [13]He will love you and bless you and increase your numbers. He will bless the fruit of your womb, the crops of your land—your grain, new wine and oil—the calves of your herds and the lambs of your flocks in the land that he swore to your forefathers to give you. [14]You will be blessed more than any other people; none of your men or women will be childless, nor any of your livestock without young. [15]The LORD will keep you free from every disease. He will not inflict on you the horrible diseases you knew in Egypt, but he will inflict them on all who hate you. [16]You must destroy all the peoples the LORD your God gives over to you. Do not look on them with pity and do not serve their gods, for that will be a snare to you.

[17]You may say to yourselves, "These nations are stronger than we are. How can we drive them out?" [18]But do not be afraid of them; remember well what the LORD your God did to Pharaoh and to all Egypt. [19]You saw with your own eyes the great trials, the miraculous signs and wonders, the mighty hand and outstretched arm, with which the LORD your God brought you out. The LORD your God will do the same to all the peoples you now fear. [20]Moreover, the LORD your God will send the hornet among them until even the survivors who hide from you have perished. [21]Do not be terrified by them, for the LORD your God, who is among you, is a great and awesome God. [22]The LORD your God will drive out those nations before you, little by little. You will not be allowed to eliminate them all at once, or the wild animals will multiply around you. [23]But the LORD your God will deliver them over to you, throwing them into great confusion until they are destroyed. [24]He will give their kings into your hand, and you will wipe out their names from

法老的手。[9]所以你要知道耶和華你的神,他是神,是信實的神,向愛他、守他誡命的人守約,施慈愛直到千代。

[10]向恨他的人當面報應他們,
　　將他們滅絕;
凡恨他的人,必報應他們,
　　決不遲延。

[11]所以你要謹守遵行我今日所吩咐你的誡命、律例、典章。

[12]你們果然聽從這些典章,謹守遵行,耶和華你神就必照他向你列祖所起的誓守約,施慈愛。[13]他必愛你,賜福與你,使你人數增多;也必在他向你列祖起誓應許給你的地上,賜福與你身所生的、地所產的,並你的五穀、新酒和油,以及牛犢、羊羔。[14]你必蒙福勝過萬民,你們的男女沒有不能生養的,牲畜也沒有不能生育的。[15]耶和華必使一切的病症離開你。你所知道埃及各樣的惡疾,他不加在你身上,只加在一切恨你的人身上。[16]耶和華你神所要交給你的一切人民,你要將他們除滅,你眼不可顧惜他們。你也不可侍奉他們的神,因這必成為你的網羅。

[17]你若心裏說:「這些國的民比我更多,我怎能趕出他們呢?」[18]你不要懼怕他們,要牢牢記念耶和華你神向法老和埃及全地所行的事,[19]就是你親眼所看見的大試驗、神蹟、奇事,和大能的手,並伸出來的膀臂,都是耶和華你神領你出來所用的。耶和華你神必照樣待你所懼怕的一切人民。[20]並且耶和華你神必打發黃蜂飛到他們中間,直到那剩下而藏躲的人從你面前滅亡。[21]你不要因他們驚恐,因為耶和華你神在你們中間是大而可畏的神。[22]耶和華你神必將這些國的民,從你面前漸漸趕出,你不可把他們速速滅盡,恐怕野地的獸多起來害你。[23]耶和華你神必將他們交給你,大大地擾亂他們,直到他們滅絕了;[24]又要將他們的君王交在你手中,你就使他們的名從天下消滅。必無一人

能在你面前站立得住，直到你將他們滅絕了。²⁵他們雕刻的神像，你們要用火焚燒，其上的金銀你不可貪圖，也不可收取，免得你因此陷入網羅，這原是耶和華你神所憎惡的。²⁶可憎的物，你不可帶進家去，不然，你就成了當毀滅的，與那物一樣。你要十分厭惡、十分憎嫌，因為這是當毀滅的物。

不可忘記主

8 我今日所吩咐的一切誡命，你們要謹守遵行，好叫你們存活，人數增多，且進去得耶和華向你們列祖起誓應許的那地。²你也要記念耶和華你的神在曠野引導你這四十年，是要苦煉你、試驗你，要知道你心內如何，肯守他的誡命不肯。³他苦煉你，任你飢餓，將你和你列祖所不認識的嗎哪賜給你吃，使你知道人活著不是單靠食物，乃是靠耶和華口裏所出的一切話。⁴這四十年，你的衣服沒有穿破，你的腳也沒有腫。⁵你當心裏思想，耶和華你神管教你，好像人管教兒子一樣。

⁶你要謹守耶和華你神的誡命，遵行他的道，敬畏他，⁷因為耶和華你神領你進入美地，那地有河、有泉、有源，從山谷中流出水來；⁸那地有小麥、大麥、葡萄樹、無花果樹、石榴樹、橄欖樹和蜜。⁹你在那地不缺食物，一無所缺。那地的石頭是鐵，山內可以挖銅。

¹⁰你吃得飽足，就要稱頌耶和華你的神，因他將那美地賜給你了。¹¹你要謹慎，免得忘記耶和華你的神，不守他的誡命、典章、律例，就是我今日所吩咐你的。¹²恐怕你吃得飽足，建造美好的房屋居住，¹³你的牛羊加多，你的金銀增添，並你所有的全都加增，¹⁴你就心高氣傲，忘記耶和華你的神，就是將你從埃及地為奴之家領出來的，¹⁵引你經過那大而可怕的曠野，那裏有火蛇、蠍子、乾旱無水之地。他曾為你使水從堅硬的

under heaven. No one will be able to stand up against you; you will destroy them. ²⁵The images of their gods are to burn in the fire. Do not covet the silver and gold on them, and do not take it for yourselves, or you will be ensnared by it, for it is detestable to the LORD your God. ²⁶Do not bring a detestable thing into your house or you, like it, will be set apart for destruction. Utterly abhor and detest it, for it is set apart for destruction.

Do Not Forget the LORD

8 Be careful to follow every command I am giving you today, so that you may live and increase and may enter and possess the land that the LORD promised on oath to your forefathers. ²Remember how the LORD your God led you all the way in the desert these forty years, to humble you and to test you in order to know what was in your heart, whether or not you would keep his commands. ³He humbled you, causing you to hunger and then feeding you with manna, which neither you nor your fathers had known, to teach you that man does not live on bread alone but on every word that comes from the mouth of the LORD. ⁴Your clothes did not wear out and your feet did not swell during these forty years. ⁵Know then in your heart that as a man disciplines his son, so the LORD your God disciplines you.

⁶Observe the commands of the LORD your God, walking in his ways and revering him. ⁷For the LORD your God is bringing you into a good land—a land with streams and pools of water, with springs flowing in the valleys and hills; ⁸a land with wheat and barley, vines and fig trees, pomegranates, olive oil and honey; ⁹a land where bread will not be scarce and you will lack nothing; a land where the rocks are iron and you can dig copper out of the hills.

¹⁰When you have eaten and are satisfied, praise the LORD your God for the good land he has given you. ¹¹Be careful that you do not forget the LORD your God, failing to observe his commands, his laws and his decrees that I am giving you this day. ¹²Otherwise, when you eat and are satisfied, when you build fine houses and settle down, ¹³and when your herds and flocks grow large and your silver and gold increase and all you have is multiplied, ¹⁴then your heart will become proud and you will forget the LORD your God, who brought you out of Egypt, out of the land of slavery. ¹⁵He led you through the vast and dreadful desert, that thirsty and waterless land, with its venomous snakes and scorpions. He brought you water out

of hard rock. [16]He gave you manna to eat in the desert, something your fathers had never known, to humble and to test you so that in the end it might go well with you. [17]You may say to yourself, "My power and the strength of my hands have produced this wealth for me." [18]But remember the LORD your God, for it is he who gives you the ability to produce wealth, and so confirms his covenant, which he swore to your forefathers, as it is today.

[19]If you ever forget the LORD your God and follow other gods and worship and bow down to them, I testify against you today that you will surely be destroyed. [20]Like the nations the LORD destroyed before you, so you will be destroyed for not obeying the LORD your God.

Not Because of Israel's Righteousness

9 Hear, O Israel. You are now about to cross the Jordan to go in and dispossess nations greater and stronger than you, with large cities that have walls up to the sky. [2]The people are strong and tall—Anakites! You know about them and have heard it said: "Who can stand up against the Anakites?" [3]But be assured today that the LORD your God is the one who goes across ahead of you like a devouring fire. He will destroy them; he will subdue them before you. And you will drive them out and annihilate them quickly, as the LORD has promised you.

[4]After the LORD your God has driven them out before you, do not say to yourself, "The LORD has brought me here to take possession of this land because of my righteousness." No, it is on account of the wickedness of these nations that the LORD is going to drive them out before you. [5]It is not because of your righteousness or your integrity that you are going in to take possession of their land; but on account of the wickedness of these nations, the LORD your God will drive them out before you, to accomplish what he swore to your fathers, to Abraham, Isaac and Jacob. [6]Understand, then, that it is not because of your righteousness that the LORD your God is giving you this good land to possess, for you are a stiff-necked people.

The Golden Calf

[7]Remember this and never forget how you provoked the LORD your God to anger in the desert. From the day you left Egypt until you arrived here, you have been rebellious against the LORD. [8]At Horeb you aroused the LORD's wrath so that he was angry enough to destroy you. [9]When I went up on the mountain to

磐石中流出來；[16]又在曠野將你列祖所不認識的嗎哪賜給你吃，是要苦煉你、試驗你，叫你終久享福。[17]恐怕你心裏說："這貨財是我力量、我能力得來的。"[18]你要記念耶和華你的神，因為得貨財的力量是他給你的，為要堅定他向你列祖起誓所立的約，像今日一樣。

[19]你若忘記耶和華你的神，隨從別神，侍奉敬拜，你們必定滅亡。這是我今日警戒你們的。[20]耶和華在你們面前怎樣使列國的民滅亡，你們也必照樣滅亡，因為你們不聽從耶和華你們神的話。

不是因以色列人的義

9 以色列啊，你當聽！你今日要過約旦河，進去趕出比你強大的國民，得着廣大堅固、高得頂天的城邑。[2]那民是亞衲族的人，又大又高，是你所知道的；也曾聽見有人指着他們說："誰能在亞衲族人面前站立得住呢？"[3]你今日當知道，耶和華你的神在你前面過去，如同烈火，要滅絕他們，將他們制伏在你面前。這樣，你就要照耶和華所說的趕出他們，使他們速速滅亡。

[4]耶和華你的神將這些國民從你面前攆出以後，你心裏不可說："耶和華將我領進來得這地，是因我的義。"其實，耶和華將他們從你面前趕出去，是因他們的惡。[5]你進去得他們的地，並不是因你的義，也不是因你心裏正直，乃是因這些國民的惡，耶和華你的神將他們從你面前趕出去，又因耶和華要堅定他向你列祖亞伯拉罕、以撒、雅各起誓所應許的話。[6]你當知道，耶和華你神將這美地賜你為業，並不是因你的義，你本是硬着頸項的百姓。

金牛犢

[7]你當記念不忘，你在曠野怎樣惹耶和華你神發怒。自從你出了埃及地的那日，直到你們來到這地方，你們時常悖逆耶和華。[8]你們在何烈山又惹耶和華發怒，他惱怒你們，要滅絕你們。[9]我上了山，要領

受兩塊石版，就是耶和華與你們立約的版。那時我在山上住了四十晝夜，沒有吃飯，也沒有喝水。¹⁰耶和華把那兩塊石版交給我，是神用指頭寫的。版上所寫的，是照耶和華在大會的日子，在山上從火中對你們所說的一切話。

¹¹過了四十晝夜，耶和華把那兩塊石版，就是約版，交給我。¹²對我說："你起來，趕快下去！因為你從埃及領出來的百姓已經敗壞了自己。他們快快地偏離了我所吩咐的道，為自己鑄成了偶像。"

¹³耶和華又對我說："我看這百姓是硬着頸項的百姓。¹⁴你且由着我，我要滅絕他們，將他們的名從天下塗抹，使你的後裔比他們成為更大更強的國。"

¹⁵於是我轉身下山，山被火燒着，兩塊約版在我兩手之中。¹⁶我一看見你們得罪了耶和華你們的神，鑄成了牛犢，快快地偏離了耶和華所吩咐你們的道，¹⁷我就把那兩塊版從我手中扔下去，在你們眼前摔碎了。

¹⁸因你們所犯的一切罪，行了耶和華眼中看為惡的事，惹他發怒，我就像從前俯伏在耶和華面前四十晝夜，沒有吃飯，也沒有喝水。¹⁹我因耶和華向你們大發烈怒，要滅絕你們，就甚害怕，但那次耶和華又應允了我。²⁰耶和華也向亞倫甚是發怒，要滅絕他，那時我又為亞倫祈禱。²¹我把你們叫你們犯罪所鑄的牛犢用火焚燒，又搗碎磨得很細，以致細如灰塵，我就把這灰塵撒在從山上流下來的溪水中。

²²你們在他備拉、瑪撒、基博羅哈他瓦又惹耶和華發怒。

²³耶和華打發你們離開加低斯巴尼亞，說："你們上去，得我所賜給你們的地。"那時你們違背了耶和華

receive the tablets of stone, the tablets of the covenant that the LORD had made with you, I stayed on the mountain forty days and forty nights; I ate no bread and drank no water. ¹⁰The LORD gave me two stone tablets inscribed by the finger of God. On them were all the commandments the LORD proclaimed to you on the mountain out of the fire, on the day of the assembly.

¹¹At the end of the forty days and forty nights, the LORD gave me the two stone tablets, the tablets of the covenant. ¹²Then the LORD told me, "Go down from here at once, because your people whom you brought out of Egypt have become corrupt. They have turned away quickly from what I commanded them and have made a cast idol for themselves."

¹³And the LORD said to me, "I have seen this people, and they are a stiff-necked people indeed! ¹⁴Let me alone, so that I may destroy them and blot out their name from under heaven. And I will make you into a nation stronger and more numerous than they."

¹⁵So I turned and went down from the mountain while it was ablaze with fire. And the two tablets of the covenant were in my hands.ᵃ ¹⁶When I looked, I saw that you had sinned against the LORD your God; you had made for yourselves an idol cast in the shape of a calf. You had turned aside quickly from the way that the LORD had commanded you. ¹⁷So I took the two tablets and threw them out of my hands, breaking them to pieces before your eyes.

¹⁸Then once again I fell prostrate before the LORD for forty days and forty nights; I ate no bread and drank no water, because of all the sin you had committed, doing what was evil in the LORD's sight and so provoking him to anger. ¹⁹I feared the anger and wrath of the LORD, for he was angry enough with you to destroy you. But again the LORD listened to me. ²⁰And the LORD was angry enough with Aaron to destroy him, but at that time I prayed for Aaron too. ²¹Also I took that sinful thing of yours, the calf you had made, and burned it in the fire. Then I crushed it and ground it to powder as fine as dust and threw the dust into a stream that flowed down the mountain.

²²You also made the LORD angry at Taberah, at Massah and at Kibroth Hattaavah.

²³And when the LORD sent you out from Kadesh Barnea, he said, "Go up and take possession of the land I have given you." But you rebelled against the command of the LORD your

---

a 15 Or And I had the two tablets of the covenant with me, one in each hand

God. You did not trust him or obey him. 24You have been rebellious against the LORD ever since I have known you.

25I lay prostrate before the LORD those forty days and forty nights because the LORD had said he would destroy you. 26I prayed to the LORD and said, "O Sovereign LORD, do not destroy your people, your own inheritance that you redeemed by your great power and brought out of Egypt with a mighty hand. 27Remember your servants Abraham, Isaac and Jacob. Overlook the stubbornness of this people, their wickedness and their sin. 28Otherwise, the country from which you brought us will say, 'Because the LORD was not able to take them into the land he had promised them, and because he hated them, he brought them out to put them to death in the desert.' 29But they are your people, your inheritance that you brought out by your great power and your outstretched arm."

Tablets Like the First Ones

10 At that time the LORD said to me, "Chisel out two stone tablets like the first ones and come up to me on the mountain. Also make a wooden chest.*a* 2I will write on the tablets the words that were on the first tablets, which you broke. Then you are to put them in the chest."

3So I made the ark out of acacia wood and chiseled out two stone tablets like the first ones, and I went up on the mountain with the two tablets in my hands. 4The LORD wrote on these tablets what he had written before, the Ten Commandments he had proclaimed to you on the mountain, out of the fire, on the day of the assembly. And the LORD gave them to me. 5Then I came back down the mountain and put the tablets in the ark I had made, as the LORD commanded me, and they are there now.

6(The Israelites traveled from the wells of the Jaakanites to Moserah. There Aaron died and was buried, and Eleazar his son succeeded him as priest. 7From there they traveled to Gudgodah and on to Jotbathah, a land with streams of water. 8At that time the LORD set apart the tribe of Levi to carry the ark of the covenant of the LORD, to stand before the LORD to minister and to pronounce blessings in his name, as they still do today. 9That is why the Levites have no share or inheritance among their brothers; the LORD is their inheritance, as the LORD your God told them.)

10Now I had stayed on the mountain forty

你們神的命令，不信服他，不聽從他的話。24自從我認識你們以來，你們常常悖逆耶和華。

25我因耶和華說要滅絕你們，就在耶和華面前照舊俯伏四十晝夜。26我祈禱耶和華說："主耶和華啊，求你不要滅絕你的百姓。他們是你的產業，是你用大力救贖的，用大能從埃及領出來的。27求你記念你的僕人亞伯拉罕、以撒、雅各，不要想念這百姓的頑梗、邪惡、罪過，28免得你領我們出來的那地之人說：'耶和華因為不能將這百姓領進他所應許之地，又因恨他們，所以領他們出去，要在曠野殺他們。' 29其實他們是你的百姓、你的產業，是你用大能和伸出來的膀臂領出來的。"

重造法版

10 那時，耶和華吩咐我說："你要鑿出兩塊石版，和先前的一樣，上山到我這裏來，又要做一木櫃。2你先前摔碎的那版，其上的字我要寫在這版上，你要將這版放在櫃中。"

3於是，我用皂莢木做了一櫃，又鑿出兩塊石版，和先前的一樣，手裏拿這兩塊版上山去了。4耶和華將那大會之日、在山上從火中所傳與你們的十條誡，照先前所寫的，寫在這版上，將版交給我了。5我轉身下山，將這版放在我所做的櫃中，現今還在那裏，正如耶和華所吩咐我的。

（6以色列人從比羅比尼亞干（註：或作"亞干井"）起行，到了摩西拉。亞倫死在那裏，就葬在那裏。他兒子以利亞撒接續他供祭司的職分。7他們從那裏起行，到了谷歌大，又從谷歌大到了有溪水之地的約巴他。8那時，耶和華將利未支派分別出來，抬耶和華的約櫃，又侍立在耶和華面前侍奉他，奉他的名祝福，直到今日。9所以利未人在他弟兄中無分無業，耶和華是他的產業，正如耶和華你神所應許他的。）

10我又像從前在山上住了四十晝

---

a 1 That is, an ark

夜。那次耶和華也應允我，不忍將你滅絕。11耶和華吩咐我說：“你起來引導這百姓，使他們進去得我向他們列祖起誓應許所賜之地。”

敬畏主

12以色列啊，現在耶和華你神向你所要的是甚麼呢？只要你敬畏耶和華你的神，遵行他的道，愛他，盡心盡性侍奉他。13遵守他的誡命、律例，就是我今日所吩咐你的，為要叫你得福。

14看哪，天和天上的天，地和地上所有的，都屬耶和華你的神。15耶和華但喜悅你的列祖，愛他們，從萬民中揀選他們的後裔，就是你們，像今日一樣。16所以你們要將心裏的污穢除掉，不可再硬着頸項。17因為耶和華你們的神，他是萬神之神，萬主之主，至大的神，大有能力，大而可畏，不以貌取人，也不受賄賂。18他為孤兒寡婦伸冤，又憐愛寄居的，賜給他衣食。19所以你們要憐愛寄居的，因為你們在埃及地也作過寄居的。20你要敬畏耶和華你的神，侍奉他，專靠他，也要指着他的名起誓。21他是你所讚美的，是你的神，為你做了那大而可畏的事，是你親眼所看見的。22你的列祖七十人下埃及，現在耶和華你的神使你如同天上的星那樣多。

愛和順服主

11 你要愛耶和華你的神，常守他的吩咐、律例、典章、誡命。2你們今日當知道，我本不是和你們的兒女說話，因為他們不知道，也沒有看見耶和華你們神的管教、威嚴、大能的手和伸出來的膀臂，3並他在埃及中向埃及王法老和其全地所行的神蹟奇事；4也沒有看見他怎樣待埃及的軍兵、車馬，他們追趕你們的時候，耶和華怎樣使紅海的水淹沒他們，將他們滅絕，直到今日，5並他在曠野怎樣待你們，以至

days and nights, as I did the first time, and the LORD listened to me at this time also. It was not his will to destroy you. 11"Go," the LORD said to me, "and lead the people on their way, so that they may enter and possess the land that I swore to their fathers to give them."

Fear the LORD

12And now, O Israel, what does the LORD your God ask of you but to fear the LORD your God, to walk in all his ways, to love him, to serve the LORD your God with all your heart and with all your soul, 13and to observe the LORD's commands and decrees that I am giving you today for your own good?

14To the LORD your God belong the heavens, even the highest heavens, the earth and everything in it. 15Yet the LORD set his affection on your forefathers and loved them, and he chose you, their descendants, above all the nations, as it is today. 16Circumcise your hearts, therefore, and do not be stiff-necked any longer. 17For the LORD your God is God of gods and Lord of lords, the great God, mighty and awesome, who shows no partiality and accepts no bribes. 18He defends the cause of the fatherless and the widow, and loves the alien, giving him food and clothing. 19And you are to love those who are aliens, for you yourselves were aliens in Egypt. 20Fear the LORD your God and serve him. Hold fast to him and take your oaths in his name. 21He is your praise; he is your God, who performed for you those great and awesome wonders you saw with your own eyes. 22Your forefathers who went down into Egypt were seventy in all, and now the LORD your God has made you as numerous as the stars in the sky.

Love and Obey the LORD

11 Love the LORD your God and keep his requirements, his decrees, his laws and his commands always. 2Remember today that your children were not the ones who saw and experienced the discipline of the LORD your God: his majesty, his mighty hand, his outstretched arm; 3the signs he performed and the things he did in the heart of Egypt, both to Pharaoh king of Egypt and to his whole country; 4what he did to the Egyptian army, to its horses and chariots, how he overwhelmed them with the waters of the Red Sea*a* as they were pursuing you, and how the LORD brought lasting ruin on them. 5It was not your children who saw what he did for you in the desert until you

a 4 Hebrew Yam Suph; that is, Sea of Reeds

arrived at this place, 6and what he did to Dathan and Abiram, sons of Eliab the Reubenite, when the earth opened its mouth right in the middle of all Israel and swallowed them up with their households, their tents and every living thing that belonged to them. 7But it was your own eyes that saw all these great things the LORD has done.

8Observe therefore all the commands I am giving you today, so that you may have the strength to go in and take over the land that you are crossing the Jordan to possess, 9and so that you may live long in the land that the LORD swore to your forefathers to give to them and their descendants, a land flowing with milk and honey. 10The land you are entering to take over is not like the land of Egypt, from which you have come, where you planted your seed and irrigated it by foot as in a vegetable garden. 11But the land you are crossing the Jordan to take possession of is a land of mountains and valleys that drinks rain from heaven. 12It is a land the LORD your God cares for; the eyes of the LORD your God are continually on it from the beginning of the year to its end.

13So if you faithfully obey the commands I am giving you today—to love the LORD your God and to serve him with all your heart and with all your soul— 14then I will send rain on your land in its season, both autumn and spring rains, so that you may gather in your grain, new wine and oil. 15I will provide grass in the fields for your cattle, and you will eat and be satisfied.

16Be careful, or you will be enticed to turn away and worship other gods and bow down to them. 17Then the LORD's anger will burn against you, and he will shut the heavens so that it will not rain and the ground will yield no produce, and you will soon perish from the good land the LORD is giving you. 18Fix these words of mine in your hearts and minds; tie them as symbols on your hands and bind them on your foreheads. 19Teach them to your children, talking about them when you sit at home and when you walk along the road, when you lie down and when you get up. 20Write them on the doorframes of your houses and on your gates, 21so that your days and the days of your children may be many in the land that the LORD swore to give your forefathers, as many as the days that the heavens are above the earth.

22If you carefully observe all these commands I am giving you to follow—to love the LORD your God, to walk in all his ways and to hold fast to him— 23then the LORD will drive out all these nations before you, and you will dispos-

你們來到這地方；6也沒有看見他怎樣待呂便子孫以利押的兒子大坍、亞比蘭，地怎樣在以色列人中間開口吞了他們和他們的家眷，並帳棚與跟他們的一切活物；7惟有你們親眼看見耶和華所做的一切大事。

8所以，你們要守我今日所吩咐的一切誡命，使你們膽壯，能以進去，得你們所要得的那地，9並使你們的日子，在耶和華向你們列祖起誓應許給他們和他們後裔的地上得以長久，那是流奶與蜜之地。10你們要進去得為業的那地，本不像你出來的埃及地，你在那裏撒種，用腳澆灌，像澆灌菜園一樣。11你們要過去得為業的那地，乃是有山、有谷、雨水滋潤之地。12是耶和華你神所眷顧的，從歲首到年終，耶和華你神的眼目時常看顧那地。

13你們若留意聽從我今日所吩咐的誡命，愛耶和華你們的神，盡心盡性侍奉他，14他（註：原文作「我」）必按時降秋雨春雨在你們的地上，使你們可以收藏五穀、新酒和油。15也必使你吃得飽足，並使田野為你的牲畜長草。

16你們要謹慎，免得心中受迷惑，就偏離正路，去侍奉敬拜別神。17耶和華的怒氣向你們發作，就使天閉塞不下雨，地也不出產，使你們在耶和華所賜給你們的美地上速速滅亡。18你們要將我這話存在心內，留在意中，繫在手上為記號，戴在額上為經文；19也要教訓你們的兒女，無論坐在家裏，行在路上，躺下，起來，都要談論；20又要寫在房屋的門框上，並城門上，21使你們和你們子孫的日子，在耶和華向你們列祖起誓應許給他們的地上得以增多，如天覆地的日子那樣多。

22你們若留意謹守遵行我所吩咐這一切的誡命，愛耶和華你們的神，行他的道，專靠他，23他必從你們面前趕出這一切國民，就是比你們更大更強的國民，你們也要得他們的地。24凡你們腳掌所踏之地都必歸你們，從曠野和黎巴嫩，並幼發拉底大河，直到西海，都要作你們的境界。25必無一人能在你們面前站立得住；耶和華你們的神，必照他所說的，使懼怕驚恐臨到你們所踏之地的居民。

26看哪，我今日將祝福與咒詛的話都陳明在你們面前。27你們若聽從耶和華你們神的誡命，就是我今日吩咐你們的，就必蒙福；28你們若不聽從耶和華你們神的誡命，偏離我今日吩咐你們的道，去侍奉你們素來所不認識的別神，就必受禍。29及至耶和華你的神領你進入要去得為業的那地，你就要將祝福的話陳明在基利心山上，將咒詛的話陳明在以巴路山上。30這二山豈不是在約旦河那邊、日落之處，在住亞拉巴的迦南人之地，與吉甲相對，靠近摩利橡樹嗎？31你們要過約旦河，進去得耶和華你們神所賜你們為業之地，在那地居住。32你們要謹守遵行我今日在你們面前所陳明的一切律例、典章。

唯一敬拜之處

12 你們存活於世的日子，在耶和華你們列祖的神所賜你們為業的地上，要謹守遵行的律例、典章乃是這些：2你們要將所趕出的國民侍奉神的各地方，無論是在高山、在小山、在各青翠樹下，都毀壞了。3也要拆毀他們的祭壇，打碎他們的柱像，用火焚燒他們的木偶，砍下他們雕刻的神像，並將其名從那地方除滅。

4你們不可照他們那樣侍奉耶和華你們的神。5但耶和華你們的神從你們各支派中，選擇何處為立他名的居所，你們就當往那裏去求問，6將你們的燔祭、平安祭，十分取一之物，和手中的舉祭，並還願祭、甘心祭，以及牛羣羊羣中頭生的，都奉到那裏。7在那裏，耶和華你們神的面前，你們和你們的家屬都可以吃，並且因你所辦的一切事蒙耶和華你的

sess nations larger and stronger than you. 24Every place where you set your foot will be yours: Your territory will extend from the desert to Lebanon, and from the Euphrates River to the western sea.ᵃ 25No man will be able to stand against you. The LORD your God, as he promised you, will put the terror and fear of you on the whole land, wherever you go.

26See, I am setting before you today a blessing and a curse— 27the blessing if you obey the commands of the LORD your God that I am giving you today; 28the curse if you disobey the commands of the LORD your God and turn from the way that I command you today by following other gods, which you have not known. 29When the LORD your God has brought you into the land you are entering to possess, you are to proclaim on Mount Gerizim the blessings, and on Mount Ebal the curses. 30As you know, these mountains are across the Jordan, west of the road,ᵇ toward the setting sun, near the great trees of Moreh, in the territory of those Canaanites living in the Arabah in the vicinity of Gilgal. 31You are about to cross the Jordan to enter and take possession of the land the LORD your God is giving you. When you have taken it over and are living there, 32be sure that you obey all the decrees and laws I am setting before you today.

The One Place of Worship

12 These are the decrees and laws you must be careful to follow in the land that the LORD, the God of your fathers, has given you to possess—as long as you live in the land. 2Destroy completely all the places on the high mountains and on the hills and under every spreading tree where the nations you are dispossessing worship their gods. 3Break down their altars, smash their sacred stones and burn their Asherah poles in the fire; cut down the idols of their gods and wipe out their names from those places.

4You must not worship the LORD your God in their way. 5But you are to seek the place the LORD your God will choose from among all your tribes to put his Name there for his dwelling. To that place you must go; 6there bring your burnt offerings and sacrifices, your tithes and special gifts, what you have vowed to give and your freewill offerings, and the firstborn of your herds and flocks. 7There, in the presence of the LORD your God, you and your families shall eat and shall rejoice in everything you have put

a 24 That is, the Mediterranean   b 30 Or Jordan, westward your hand to, because the LORD your God has blessed you.

[8]You are not to do as we do here today, everyone as he sees fit, [9]since you have not yet reached the resting place and the inheritance the LORD your God is giving you. [10]But you will cross the Jordan and settle in the land the LORD your God is giving you as an inheritance, and he will give you rest from all your enemies around you so that you will live in safety. [11]Then to the place the LORD your God will choose as a dwelling for his Name—there you are to bring everything I command you: your burnt offerings and sacrifices, your tithes and special gifts, and all the choice possessions you have vowed to the LORD. [12]And there rejoice before the LORD your God, you, your sons and daughters, your menservants and maidservants, and the Levites from your towns, who have no allotment or inheritance of their own. [13]Be careful not to sacrifice your burnt offerings anywhere you please. [14]Offer them only at the place the LORD will choose in one of your tribes, and there observe everything I command you.

[15]Nevertheless, you may slaughter your animals in any of your towns and eat as much of the meat as you want, as if it were gazelle or deer, according to the blessing the LORD your God gives you. Both the ceremonially unclean and the clean may eat it. [16]But you must not eat the blood; pour it out on the ground like water. [17]You must not eat in your own towns the tithe of your grain and new wine and oil, or the firstborn of your herds and flocks, or whatever you have vowed to give, or your freewill offerings or special gifts. [18]Instead, you are to eat them in the presence of the LORD your God at the place the LORD your God will choose—you, your sons and daughters, your menservants and maidservants, and the Levites from your towns—and you are to rejoice before the LORD your God in everything you put your hand to. [19]Be careful not to neglect the Levites as long as you live in your land.

[20]When the LORD your God has enlarged your territory as he promised you, and you crave meat and say, "I would like some meat," then you may eat as much of it as you want. [21]If the place where the LORD your God chooses to put his Name is too far away from you, you may slaughter animals from the herds and flocks the LORD has given you, as I have commanded you, and in your own towns you may eat as much of them as you want. [22]Eat them as you would gazelle or deer. Both the ceremonially unclean and the clean may eat. [23]But be sure

神賜福，就都歡樂。

[8]我們今日在這裏所行的，是各人行自己眼中看為正的事，你們將來不可這樣行，[9]因為你們還沒有到耶和華你神所賜你的安息地，所給你的產業。[10]但你們過了約旦河，得以住在耶和華你們神使你們承受為業之地，又使你們太平，不被四圍的一切仇敵擾亂，安然居住。[11]那時要將我所吩咐你們的燔祭、平安祭，十分取一之物，和手中的舉祭，並向耶和華許願獻的一切美祭，都奉到耶和華你們神所選擇要立為他名的居所。[12]你們和兒女、僕婢，並住在你們城裏無分無業的利未人，都要在耶和華你們的神面前歡樂。[13]你要謹慎，不可在你所看中的各處獻燔祭。[14]惟獨耶和華從你那一支派中所選擇的地方，你就要在那裏獻燔祭，行我一切所吩咐你的。

[15]然而，在你各城裏都可以照耶和華你神所賜你的福分，隨心所欲宰牲吃肉，無論潔淨人、不潔淨人都可以吃，就如吃羚羊與鹿一般。[16]只是不可吃血，要倒在地上，如同倒水一樣。[17]你的五穀、新酒，和油的十分之一，或是牛羣羊羣中頭生的，或是你許願獻的、甘心獻的，或是手中的舉祭，都不可在你城裏吃，[18]但要在耶和華你的神面前吃，在耶和華你神所要選擇的地方，你和兒女、僕婢，並住在你城裏的利未人，都可以吃。也要因你手所辦的，在耶和華你神面前歡樂。[19]你要謹慎，在你所住的地方，永不可丟棄利未人。

[20]耶和華你的神照他所應許，擴張你境界的時候，你心裏想要吃肉，說："我要吃肉"，就可以隨心所欲地吃肉。[21]耶和華你神所選擇要立他名的地方若離你太遠，就可以照我所吩咐的，將耶和華賜給你的牛羊取些宰了，可以隨心所欲在你城裏吃。[22]你吃那肉，要像吃羚羊與鹿一般，無論潔淨人、不潔淨人都可以吃。[23]只是你要心意堅定，不

可吃血，因為血是生命，不可將血（註：原文作「生命」）與肉同吃。24不可吃血，要倒在地上，如同倒水一樣。25不可吃血。這樣，你行耶和華眼中看為正的事，你和你的子孫就可以得福。

26只是你分別為聖的物和你的還願祭，要奉到耶和華所選擇的地方去。27你的燔祭，連肉帶血，都要獻在耶和華你神的壇上。平安祭的血要倒在耶和華你神的壇上；平安祭的肉，你自己可以吃。28你要謹守聽從我所吩咐的話，行耶和華你神眼中看為善、看為正的事，這樣，你和你的子孫就可以永遠享福。

29耶和華你神將你要去趕出的國民從你面前剪除，你得了他們的地居住，30那時就要謹慎，不可在他們除滅之後，隨從他們的惡俗，陷入網羅，也不可訪問他們的神，說：「這些國民怎樣侍奉他們的神，我也要照樣行。」31你不可向耶和華你神這樣行，因為他們向他們的神行了耶和華所憎嫌、所恨惡的一切事，甚至將自己的兒女用火焚燒，獻與他們的神。

32凡我所吩咐的，你們都要謹守遵行，不可加添，也不可刪減。

不可敬拜別的神

13 你們中間若有先知或是做夢的起來，向你顯個神蹟奇事，2對你說：「我們去隨從你素來所不認識的別神，侍奉他吧！」他所顯的神蹟奇事，雖有應驗，3你也不可聽那先知或是那做夢之人的話。因為這是耶和華你們的神試驗你們，要知道你們是盡心盡性愛耶和華你們的神不是。4你們要順從耶和華你們的神，敬畏他，謹守他的誡命，聽從他的話，侍奉他，專靠他。5那先知或是那做夢的，既用言語叛逆那領你們出埃及地、救贖你脫離為奴之家的耶和華你們的神，要勾引你離開耶和華你神所吩咐你行的道，你便要將他治死，這樣就把那惡從你們中間除掉。

you do not eat the blood, because the blood is the life, and you must not eat the life with the meat. 24You must not eat the blood; pour it out on the ground like water. 25Do not eat it, so that it may go well with you and your children after you, because you will be doing what is right in the eyes of the LORD.

26But take your consecrated things and whatever you have vowed to give, and go to the place the LORD will choose. 27Present your burnt offerings on the altar of the LORD your God, both the meat and the blood. The blood of your sacrifices must be poured beside the altar of the LORD your God, but you may eat the meat. 28Be careful to obey all these regulations I am giving you, so that it may always go well with you and your children after you, because you will be doing what is good and right in the eyes of the LORD your God.

29The LORD your God will cut off before you the nations you are about to invade and dispossess. But when you have driven them out and settled in their land, 30and after they have been destroyed before you, be careful not to be ensnared by inquiring about their gods, saying, "How do these nations serve their gods? We will do the same." 31You must not worship the LORD your God in their way, because in worshiping their gods, they do all kinds of detestable things the LORD hates. They even burn their sons and daughters in the fire as sacrifices to their gods.

32See that you do all I command you; do not add to it or take away from it.

Worshiping Other Gods

13 If a prophet, or one who foretells by dreams, appears among you and announces to you a miraculous sign or wonder, 2and if the sign or wonder of which he has spoken takes place, and he says, "Let us follow other gods" (gods you have not known) "and let us worship them," 3you must not listen to the words of that prophet or dreamer. The LORD your God is testing you to find out whether you love him with all your heart and with all your soul. 4It is the LORD your God you must follow, and him you must revere. Keep his commands and obey him; serve him and hold fast to him. 5That prophet or dreamer must be put to death, because he preached rebellion against the LORD your God, who brought you out of Egypt and redeemed you from the land of slavery; he has tried to turn you from the way the LORD your God commanded you to follow. You must purge the evil from among you.

⁶If your very own brother, or your son or daughter, or the wife you love, or your closest friend secretly entices you, saying, "Let us go and worship other gods" (gods that neither you nor your fathers have known, ⁷gods of the peoples around you, whether near or far, from one end of the land to the other), ⁸do not yield to him or listen to him. Show him no pity. Do not spare him or shield him. ⁹You must certainly put him to death. Your hand must be the first in putting him to death, and then the hands of all the people. ¹⁰Stone him to death, because he tried to turn you away from the LORD your God, who brought you out of Egypt, out of the land of slavery. ¹¹Then all Israel will hear and be afraid, and no one among you will do such an evil thing again.

¹²If you hear it said about one of the towns the LORD your God is giving you to live in ¹³that wicked men have arisen among you and have led the people of their town astray, saying, "Let us go and worship other gods" (gods you have not known), ¹⁴then you must inquire, probe and investigate it thoroughly. And if it is true and it has been proved that this detestable thing has been done among you, ¹⁵you must certainly put to the sword all who live in that town. Destroy it completely,*a* both its people and its livestock. ¹⁶Gather all the plunder of the town into the middle of the public square and completely burn the town and all its plunder as a whole burnt offering to the LORD your God. It is to remain a ruin forever, never to be rebuilt. ¹⁷None of those condemned things*a* shall be found in your hands, so that the LORD will turn from his fierce anger; he will show you mercy, have compassion on you, and increase your numbers, as he promised on oath to your forefathers, ¹⁸because you obey the LORD your God, keeping all his commands that I am giving you today and doing what is right in his eyes.

Clean and Unclean Food

14 You are the children of the LORD your God. Do not cut yourselves or shave the front of your heads for the dead, ²for you are a people holy to the LORD your God. Out of all the peoples on the face of the earth, the LORD has chosen you to be his treasured possession.

³Do not eat any detestable thing. ⁴These are

a 15,17 The Hebrew term refers to the irrevocable giving over of things or persons to the LORD, often by totally destroying them.

⁶你的同胞弟兄，或是你的兒女，或是你懷中的妻，或是如同你性命的朋友，若暗中引誘你，說："我們不如去侍奉你和你列祖素來所不認識的別神，⁷是你四圍列國的神。"無論是離你近、離你遠，從地這邊到地那邊的神，⁸你不可依從他，也不可聽從他，眼不可顧惜他；你不可憐恤他，也不可遮庇他。⁹總要殺他，你先下手，然後眾民也下手，將他治死。¹⁰要用石頭打死他，因為他想要勾引你離開那領你出埃及地為奴之家的耶和華你的神。¹¹以色列眾人都要聽見害怕，就不敢在你們中間再行這樣的惡了。

¹²、¹³在耶和華你神所賜你居住的各城中，你若聽人說，有些匪類從你們中間的一座城出來勾引本城的居民，說："我們不如去侍奉你們素來所不認識的別神。"¹⁴你就要探聽、查究，細細地訪問，果然是真，準有這可憎惡的事行在你們中間，¹⁵你必要用刀殺那城裏的居民，把城裏所有的，連牲畜都用刀殺盡。¹⁶你從那城裏所奪的財物都要堆積在街市上，用火將城和其內所奪的財物都在耶和華你神面前燒盡，那城就永為荒堆，不可再建造。¹⁷、¹⁸那當毀滅的物，連一點都不可粘你的手。你要聽從耶和華你神的話，遵守我今日所吩咐你的一切誡命，行耶和華你神眼中看為正的事，耶和華就必轉意，不發烈怒，恩待你、憐恤你，照他向你列祖所起的誓使你人數增多。

潔淨與不潔淨的食物

14 你們是耶和華你們神的兒女。不可為死人用刀劃身，也不可將額上剃光，²因為你歸耶和華你神為聖潔的民，耶和華從地上的萬民中，揀選你特作自己的子民。

³凡可憎的物都不可吃。⁴可吃的

牲畜就是牛、綿羊、山羊、⁵鹿、羚羊、麃子、野山羊、麋鹿、黃羊、青羊，你們都可以吃。⁶凡分蹄成為兩瓣又倒嚼的走獸，你們都可以吃。⁷但那些倒嚼，或是分蹄之中不可吃的，乃是駱駝、兔子、沙番，因為是倒嚼不分蹄，就與你們不潔淨；⁸豬，因為是分蹄卻不倒嚼，就與你們不潔淨。這些獸的肉你們不可吃，死的也不可摸。

⁹水中可吃的乃是這些：凡有翅有鱗的都可以吃；¹⁰凡無翅無鱗的都不可吃，是與你們不潔淨。

¹¹凡潔淨的鳥，你們都可以吃；¹²不可吃的乃是鵰、狗頭鵰、紅頭鵰、¹³鷂鷹、小鷹、鷂鷹與其類、¹⁴烏鴉與其類、¹⁵鴕鳥、夜鷹、魚鷹、鷹與其類、¹⁶鴞鳥、貓頭鷹、角鴟、¹⁷鵜鶘、禿鵰、鸕鶿、¹⁸鸛、鷺鷥與其類，戴鵀與蝙蝠。

¹⁹凡有翅膀爬行的物，是與你們不潔淨，都不可吃。²⁰凡潔淨的鳥，你們都可以吃。

²¹凡自死的，你們都不可吃，可以給你城裏寄居的吃，或賣與外人吃，因為你是歸耶和華你神為聖潔的民。

不可用山羊羔母的奶煮山羊羔。

十分之一奉獻

²²你要把你撒種所產的，就是你田地每年所出的，十分取一分。²³又要把你的五穀、新酒和油的十分之一，並牛羣羊羣中頭生的，吃在耶和華你神面前，就是他所選擇要立為他名的居所。這樣，你可以學習時常敬畏耶和華你的神。²⁴當耶和華你神賜福與你的時候，耶和華你神所選擇要立為他名的地方，若離你太遠，那路也太長，使你不能把這物帶到那裏去，²⁵你就可以換成銀子，將銀子包起來拿在手中，往耶和華你神所要選擇的地方去。²⁶你用這銀子，隨心所欲，或買牛羊，或買清酒濃酒，凡你

the animals you may eat: the ox, the sheep, the goat, ⁵the deer, the gazelle, the roe deer, the wild goat, the ibex, the antelope and the mountain sheep.*ᵃ* ⁶You may eat any animal that has a split hoof divided in two and that chews the cud. ⁷However, of those that chew the cud or that have a split hoof completely divided you may not eat the camel, the rabbit or the coney.*ᵇ* Although they chew the cud, they do not have a split hoof; they are ceremonially unclean for you. ⁸The pig is also unclean; although it has a split hoof, it does not chew the cud. You are not to eat their meat or touch their carcasses.

⁹Of all the creatures living in the water, you may eat any that has fins and scales. ¹⁰But anything that does not have fins and scales you may not eat; for you it is unclean.

¹¹You may eat any clean bird. ¹²But these you may not eat: the eagle, the vulture, the black vulture, ¹³the red kite, the black kite, any kind of falcon, ¹⁴any kind of raven, ¹⁵the horned owl, the screech owl, the gull, any kind of hawk, ¹⁶the little owl, the great owl, the white owl, ¹⁷the desert owl, the osprey, the cormorant, ¹⁸the stork, any kind of heron, the hoopoe and the bat.

¹⁹All flying insects that swarm are unclean to you; do not eat them. ²⁰But any winged creature that is clean you may eat.

²¹Do not eat anything you find already dead. You may give it to an alien living in any of your towns, and he may eat it, or you may sell it to a foreigner. But you are a people holy to the LORD your God.

Do not cook a young goat in its mother's milk.

Tithes

²²Be sure to set aside a tenth of all that your fields produce each year. ²³Eat the tithe of your grain, new wine and oil, and the firstborn of your herds and flocks in the presence of the LORD your God at the place he will choose as a dwelling for his Name, so that you may learn to revere the LORD your God always. ²⁴But if that place is too distant and you have been blessed by the LORD your God and cannot carry your tithe (because the place where the LORD will choose to put his Name is so far away), ²⁵then exchange your tithe for silver, and take the silver with you and go to the place the LORD your God will choose. ²⁶Use the silver to buy whatever you like: cattle, sheep, wine or other ferment-

a 5 The precise identification of some of the birds and animals in this chapter is uncertain.　　*b 7* That is, the hyrax or rock badger

ed drink, or anything you wish. Then you and your household shall eat there in the presence of the LORD your God and rejoice. 27And do not neglect the Levites living in your towns, for they have no allotment or inheritance of their own.

28At the end of every three years, bring all the tithes of that year's produce and store it in your towns, 29so that the Levites (who have no allotment or inheritance of their own) and the aliens, the fatherless and the widows who live in your towns may come and eat and be satisfied, and so that the LORD your God may bless you in all the work of your hands.

The Year for Canceling Debts

15 At the end of every seven years you must cancel debts. 2This is how it is to be done: Every creditor shall cancel the loan he has made to his fellow Israelite. He shall not require payment from his fellow Israelite or brother, because the LORD's time for canceling debts has been proclaimed. 3You may require payment from a foreigner, but you must cancel any debt your brother owes you. 4However, there should be no poor among you, for in the land the LORD your God is giving you to possess as your inheritance, he will richly bless you, 5if only you fully obey the LORD your God and are careful to follow all these commands I am giving you today. 6For the LORD your God will bless you as he has promised, and you will lend to many nations but will borrow from none. You will rule over many nations but none will rule over you.

7If there is a poor man among your brothers in any of the towns of the land that the LORD your God is giving you, do not be hardhearted or tightfisted toward your poor brother. 8Rather be openhanded and freely lend him whatever he needs. 9Be careful not to harbor this wicked thought: "The seventh year, the year for canceling debts, is near," so that you do not show ill will toward your needy brother and give him nothing. He may then appeal to the LORD against you, and you will be found guilty of sin. 10Give generously to him and do so without a grudging heart; then because of this the LORD your God will bless you in all your work and in everything you put your hand to. 11There will always be poor people in the land. Therefore I command you to be openhanded toward your brothers and toward the poor and needy in your land.

Freeing Servants

12If a fellow Hebrew, a man or a woman, sells himself to you and serves you six years, in the seventh year you must let him go free.

心所想的都可以買。你和你的家屬,在耶和華你神的面前吃喝快樂。27住在你城裏的利未人,你不可丟棄他,因為他在你們中間無分無業。

28每逢三年的末一年,你要將本年的土產十分之一都取出來,積存在你的城中。29在你城裏無分無業的利未人,和你城裏寄居的,並孤兒寡婦,都可以來,吃得飽足。這樣,耶和華你的神必在你手裏所辦的一切事上,賜福與你。

豁免年

15 每逢七年末一年,你要施行豁免。2豁免的定例乃是這樣:凡債主要把所借給鄰舍的豁免了,不可向鄰舍和弟兄追討,因為耶和華的豁免年已經宣告了。3若借給外邦人,你可以向他追討;但借給你弟兄,無論是甚麼,你要鬆手豁免了。4、5你若留意聽從耶和華你神的話,謹守遵行我今日所吩咐你這一切的命令,就必在你們中間沒有窮人了。(在耶和華你神所賜你為業的地上,耶和華必大大賜福與你。)6因為耶和華你的神,必照他所應許你的賜福與你。你必借給許多國民,卻不至向他們借貸;你必管轄許多國民,他們卻不能管轄你。

7在耶和華你神所賜你的地上,無論哪一座城裏,你弟兄中若有一個窮人,你不可忍著心、揸著手,不幫補你窮乏的弟兄;8總要向他鬆開手,照他所缺乏的借給他,補他的不足。9你要謹慎,不可心裏起惡念,說:"第七年的豁免年快到了",你便惡眼看你窮乏的弟兄,甚麼都不給他,以致他因你求告耶和華,罪便歸於你了。10你總要給他,給他的時候,心裏不可愁煩,因耶和華你的神必在你這一切所行的,並你手裏所辦的事上,賜福與你。11原來地上的窮人永不斷絕,所以我吩咐你說:"總要向你地上困苦窮乏的弟兄鬆開手。"

釋放奴僕

12你弟兄中,若有一個希伯來男人,或希伯來女人被賣給你,服侍你六年,到第七年就要任他自由出去。¹³你任他自由的時候，不可使他空手而去。¹⁴要從你羊羣、禾場、酒醡之中，多多地給他，耶和華你的神怎樣賜福與你，你也要照樣給他。¹⁵要記念你在埃及地作過奴僕，耶和華你的神將你救贖。因此，我今日吩咐你這件事。

¹⁶他若對你說："我不願意離開你"，是因他愛你和你的家，且因在你那裏很好，¹⁷你就要拿錐子將他的耳朵在門上刺透，他便永為你的奴僕了。你待婢女也要這樣。

¹⁸你任他自由的時候，不可以為難事，因他服侍你六年，較比雇工的工價多加一倍了。耶和華你的神，就必在你所做的一切事上賜福與你。

頭生的牲畜

¹⁹你牛羣羊羣中頭生的，凡是公的都要分別為聖，歸耶和華你的神。牛羣中頭生的不可用牠耕地；羊羣中頭生的不可剪毛。²⁰這頭生的，你和你的家屬，每年要在耶和華所選擇的地方，在耶和華你神面前吃。²¹這頭生的若有甚麼殘疾，就如瘸腿的、瞎眼的，無論有甚麼惡殘疾，都不可獻給耶和華你的神。²²可以在你城裏吃，潔淨人與不潔淨人都可以吃，就如吃羚羊與鹿一般。²³只是不可吃牠的血，要倒在地上，如同倒水一樣。

逾越節

16 你要注意亞筆月，向耶和華你的神守逾越節，因為耶和華你的神在亞筆月夜間，領你出埃及。²你當在耶和華所選擇要立為他名的居所，從牛羣羊羣中，將逾越節的祭牲獻給耶和華你的神。³你吃這祭牲，不可吃有酵的餅，七日之內要吃無酵餅，就是困苦餅，（你本是急忙出了埃及地，）要叫你一生一世記念你從埃及地出來的日子。⁴在你四境之內，七日不可見麵酵，頭一日晚上所獻的肉，一點不可留到早晨。

⁵在耶和華你神所賜的各城中，你不可獻逾越節的祭；⁶只當在耶和華你神所選擇要立為他名的居所，晚上日落的時候，乃是你出埃及的時

¹³And when you release him, do not send him away empty-handed. ¹⁴Supply him liberally from your flock, your threshing floor and your winepress. Give to him as the LORD your God has blessed you. ¹⁵Remember that you were slaves in Egypt and the LORD your God redeemed you. That is why I give you this command today.

¹⁶But if your servant says to you, "I do not want to leave you," because he loves you and your family and is well off with you, ¹⁷then take an awl and push it through his ear lobe into the door, and he will become your servant for life. Do the same for your maidservant.

¹⁸Do not consider it a hardship to set your servant free, because his service to you these six years has been worth twice as much as that of a hired hand. And the LORD your God will bless you in everything you do.

The Firstborn Animals

¹⁹Set apart for the LORD your God every firstborn male of your herds and flocks. Do not put the firstborn of your oxen to work, and do not shear the firstborn of your sheep. ²⁰Each year you and your family are to eat them in the presence of the LORD your God at the place he will choose. ²¹If an animal has a defect, is lame or blind, or has any serious flaw, you must not sacrifice it to the LORD your God. ²²You are to eat it in your own towns. Both the ceremonially unclean and the clean may eat it, as if it were gazelle or deer. ²³But you must not eat the blood; pour it out on the ground like water.

Passover

16 Observe the month of Abib and celebrate the Passover of the LORD your God, because in the month of Abib he brought you out of Egypt by night. ²Sacrifice as the Passover to the LORD your God an animal from your flock or herd at the place the LORD will choose as a dwelling for his Name. ³Do not eat it with bread made with yeast, but for seven days eat unleavened bread, the bread of affliction, because you left Egypt in haste—so that all the days of your life you may remember the time of your departure from Egypt. ⁴Let no yeast be found in your possession in all your land for seven days. Do not let any of the meat you sacrifice on the evening of the first day remain until morning.

⁵You must not sacrifice the Passover in any town the LORD your God gives you ⁶except in the place he will choose as a dwelling for his Name. There you must sacrifice the Passover in the evening, when the sun goes down, on the

anniversary*a* of your departure from Egypt. [7]Roast it and eat it at the place the LORD your God will choose. Then in the morning return to your tents. [8]For six days eat unleavened bread and on the seventh day hold an assembly to the LORD your God and do no work.

Feast of Weeks

[9]Count off seven weeks from the time you begin to put the sickle to the standing grain. [10]Then celebrate the Feast of Weeks to the LORD your God by giving a freewill offering in proportion to the blessings the LORD your God has given you. [11]And rejoice before the LORD your God at the place he will choose as a dwelling for his Name—you, your sons and daughters, your menservants and maidservants, the Levites in your towns, and the aliens, the fatherless and the widows living among you. [12]Remember that you were slaves in Egypt, and follow carefully these decrees.

Feast of Tabernacles

[13]Celebrate the Feast of Tabernacles for seven days after you have gathered the produce of your threshing floor and your winepress. [14]Be joyful at your Feast—you, your sons and daughters, your menservants and maidservants, and the Levites, the aliens, the fatherless and the widows who live in your towns. [15]For seven days celebrate the Feast to the LORD your God at the place the LORD will choose. For the LORD your God will bless you in all your harvest and in all the work of your hands, and your joy will be complete.

[16]Three times a year all your men must appear before the LORD your God at the place he will choose: at the Feast of Unleavened Bread, the Feast of Weeks and the Feast of Tabernacles. No man should appear before the LORD empty-handed: [17]Each of you must bring a gift in proportion to the way the LORD your God has blessed you.

Judges

[18]Appoint judges and officials for each of your tribes in every town the LORD your God is giving you, and they shall judge the people fairly. [19]Do not pervert justice or show partiality. Do not accept a bribe, for a bribe blinds the eyes of the wise and twists the words of the righteous. [20]Follow justice and justice alone, so that you may live and possess the land the LORD your God is giving you.

a 6 Or down, at the time of day

候，獻逾越節的祭。[7]當在耶和華你神所選擇的地方把肉烤了吃（註：「烤」或作「煮」），次日早晨就回到你的帳棚去。[8]你要吃無酵餅六日，第七日要向耶和華你的神守嚴肅會，不可做工。

七七節

[9]你要計算七七日：從你開鐮收割禾稼時算起，共計七七日。[10]你要照耶和華你神所賜你的福，手裏拿着甘心祭，獻在耶和華你的神面前，守七七節。[11]你和你兒女、僕婢，並住在你城裏的利未人，以及在你們中間寄居的與孤兒寡婦，都要在耶和華你神所選擇立為他名的居所，在耶和華你的神面前歡樂。[12]你也要記念你在埃及作過奴僕，你要謹守遵行這些律例。

住棚節

[13]你把禾場的穀、酒醡的酒收藏以後，就要守住棚節七日。[14]守節的時候，你和你兒女、僕婢，並住在你城裏的利未人，以及寄居的與孤兒寡婦，都要歡樂。[15]在耶和華所選擇的地方，你當向耶和華你的神守節七日，因為耶和華你神在你一切的土產上，和你手裏所辦的事上要賜福與你，你就非常的歡樂。

[16]你一切的男丁要在除酵節、七七節、住棚節，一年三次，在耶和華你神所選擇的地方朝見他，卻不可空手朝見。[17]各人要按自己的力量，照耶和華你神所賜的福分，奉獻禮物。

審判官

[18]你要在耶和華你神所賜的各城裏，按着各支派設立審判官和官長。他們必按公義的審判判斷百姓。[19]不可屈枉正直，不可看人的外貌，也不可受賄賂，因為賄賂能叫智慧人的眼變瞎了，又能顛倒義人的話。[20]你要追求至公、至義，好叫你存活，承受耶和華你神所賜你的地。

不可敬拜別的神

21你要為耶和華你的神築壇，不可在壇旁栽甚麼樹木作為木偶。22也不可為自己設立柱像，這是耶和華你神所恨惡的。

17 凡有殘疾，或有甚麼惡病的牛羊，你都不可獻給耶和華你的神，因為這是耶和華你神所憎惡的。

2在你們中間，在耶和華你神所賜你的諸城中，無論哪座城裏，若有人，或男或女，行耶和華你神眼中看為惡的事，違背了他的約，3去侍奉敬拜別神，或拜日頭，或拜月亮，或拜天象，是主不曾吩咐的，4有人告訴你，你也聽見了，就要細細地探聽。果然是真，準有這可憎惡的事行在以色列中，5你就要將行這惡事的男人或女人拉到城門外，用石頭將他打死。6要憑兩三個人的口作見證，將那當死的人治死；不可憑一個人的口作見證將他治死。7見證人要先下手，然後眾民也下手將他治死。這樣，就把那惡從你們中間除掉。

審理案件

8你城中若起了爭訟的事，或因流血，或因爭競，或因毆打，是你難斷的案件，你就當起來，往耶和華你神所選擇的地方，9去見祭司利未人，並當時的審判官，求問他們，他們必將判語指示你。10他們在耶和華所選擇的地方指示你的判語，你必照着他們所指教你的一切話謹守遵行。11要按他們所指教你的律法，照他們所斷定的去行，他們所指示你的判語，你不可偏離左右。12若有人擅敢不聽從那侍立在耶和華你神面前的祭司，或不聽從審判官，那人就必治死。這樣，便將那惡從以色列中除掉。13眾百姓都要聽見害怕，不再擅敢行事。

君王

14到了耶和華你神所賜你的地，得了那地居住的時候，若説："我要立王治理我，像四圍的國一樣。"

Worshiping Other Gods

21Do not set up any wooden Asherah pole[a] beside the altar you build to the LORD your God, 22and do not erect a sacred stone, for these the LORD your God hates.

17 Do not sacrifice to the LORD your God an ox or a sheep that has any defect or flaw in it, for that would be detestable to him.

2If a man or woman living among you in one of the towns the LORD gives you is found doing evil in the eyes of the LORD your God in violation of his covenant, 3and contrary to my command has worshiped other gods, bowing down to them or to the sun or the moon or the stars of the sky, 4and this has been brought to your attention, then you must investigate it thoroughly. If it is true and it has been proved that this detestable thing has been done in Israel, 5take the man or woman who has done this evil deed to your city gate and stone that person to death. 6On the testimony of two or three witnesses a man shall be put to death, but no one shall be put to death on the testimony of only one witness. 7The hands of the witnesses must be the first in putting him to death, and then the hands of all the people. You must purge the evil from among you.

Law Courts

8If cases come before your courts that are too difficult for you to judge—whether bloodshed, lawsuits or assaults—take them to the place the LORD your God will choose. 9Go to the priests, who are Levites, and to the judge who is in office at that time. Inquire of them and they will give you the verdict. 10You must act according to the decisions they give you at the place the LORD will choose. Be careful to do everything they direct you to do. 11Act according to the law they teach you and the decisions they give you. Do not turn aside from what they tell you, to the right or to the left. 12The man who shows contempt for the judge or for the priest who stands ministering there to the LORD your God must be put to death. You must purge the evil from Israel. 13All the people will hear and be afraid, and will not be contemptuous again.

The King

14When you enter the land the LORD your God is giving you and have taken possession of it and settled in it, and you say, "Let us set a king over us like all the nations around us,"

---

a 21 Or Do not plant any tree dedicated to Asherah

15be sure to appoint over you the king the LORD your God chooses. He must be from among your own brothers. Do not place a foreigner over you, one who is not a brother Israelite. 16The king, moreover, must not acquire great numbers of horses for himself or make the people return to Egypt to get more of them, for the LORD has told you, "You are not to go back that way again." 17He must not take many wives, or his heart will be led astray. He must not accumulate large amounts of silver and gold.

18When he takes the throne of his kingdom, he is to write for himself on a scroll a copy of this law, taken from that of the priests, who are Levites. 19It is to be with him, and he is to read it all the days of his life so that he may learn to revere the LORD his God and follow carefully all the words of this law and these decrees 20and not consider himself better than his brothers and turn from the law to the right or to the left. Then he and his descendants will reign a long time over his kingdom in Israel.

Offerings for Priests and Levites

18 The priests, who are Levites—indeed the whole tribe of Levi—are to have no allotment or inheritance with Israel. They shall live on the offerings made to the LORD by fire, for that is their inheritance. 2They shall have no inheritance among their brothers; the LORD is their inheritance, as he promised them.

3This is the share due the priests from the people who sacrifice a bull or a sheep: the shoulder, the jowls and the inner parts. 4You are to give them the firstfruits of your grain, new wine and oil, and the first wool from the shearing of your sheep, 5for the LORD your God has chosen them and their descendants out of all your tribes to stand and minister in the LORD's name always.

6If a Levite moves from one of your towns anywhere in Israel where he is living, and comes in all earnestness to the place the LORD will choose, 7he may minister in the name of the LORD his God like all his fellow Levites who serve there in the presence of the LORD. 8He is to share equally in their benefits, even though he has received money from the sale of family possessions.

Detestable Practices

9When you enter the land the LORD your God is giving you, do not learn to imitate the detestable ways of the nations there. 10Let no one be found among you who sacrifices his son or

15你總要立耶和華你神所揀選的人為王，必從你弟兄中立一人，不可立你弟兄以外的人為王。16只是王不可為自己加添馬匹，也不可使百姓回埃及去，為要加添他的馬匹，因耶和華曾吩咐你們說：「不可再回那條路去。」17他也不可為自己多立妃嬪，恐怕他的心偏邪；也不可為自己多積金銀。

18他登了國位，就要將祭司利未人面前的這律法書，為自己抄錄一本，19存在他那裏；要平生誦讀，好學習敬畏耶和華他的神，謹守遵行這律法書上的一切言語和這些律例，20免得他向弟兄心高氣傲，偏左偏右，離了這誡命。這樣，他和他的子孫，便可在以色列中，在國位上年長日久。

祭司與利未人當得之分

18 祭司利未人和利未全支派，必在以色列中無分無業，他們所吃用的，就是獻給耶和華的火祭和一切所捐的。2他們在弟兄中必沒有產業，耶和華是他們的產業，正如耶和華所應許他們的。

3祭司從百姓所當得的分乃是這樣：凡獻牛或羊為祭的，要把前腿和兩腮並脾胃給祭司。4初收的五穀、新酒和油，並初剪的羊毛，也要給他。5因為耶和華你的神，從你各支派中將他揀選出來，使他和他子孫永遠奉耶和華的名侍立侍奉。

6利未人，無論寄居在以色列中的哪一座城，若從那裏出來，一心願意到耶和華所選擇的地方，7就要奉耶和華他神的名侍奉，像他眾弟兄利未人侍立在耶和華面前侍奉一樣。8除了他賣祖父產業所得的以外，還要得一分祭物與他們同吃。

不可隨從惡俗

9你到了耶和華你神所賜之地，那些國民所行可憎惡的事，你不可學着行。10你們中間不可有人使兒女經火，也不可有占卜的、觀兆的、用法術的、行邪術的、11用迷術的、交鬼的、行巫術的、過陰的。12凡行這些事的，都為耶和華所憎惡，因那些國民行這可憎惡的事，所以耶和華你的神將他們從你面前趕出。13你要在耶和華你的神面前作完全人。

先知

14因你所要趕出的那些國民，都聽信觀兆的和占卜的；至於你，耶和華你的神從來不許你這樣行。15耶和華你的神要從你們弟兄中間給你興起一位先知像我，你們要聽從他。16正如你在何烈山大會的日子求耶和華你神一切的話，說：「求你不再叫我聽見耶和華我神的聲音，也不再叫我看見這大火，免得我死亡。」

17耶和華就對我說：「他們所說的是。18我必在他們弟兄中間，給他們興起一位先知像你。我要將當說的話傳給他；他要將我一切所吩咐的都傳給他們。19誰不聽他奉我名所說的話，我必討誰的罪。20若有先知擅敢託我的名說我所未曾吩咐他說的話，或是奉別神的名說話，那先知就必治死。」

21你心裏若說：「耶和華所未曾吩咐的話，我們怎能知道呢？」22先知託耶和華的名說話，所說的若不成就，也無效驗，這就是耶和華所未曾吩咐的，是那先知擅自說的，你不要怕他。

逃城

19 耶和華你神將列國之民剪除的時候，耶和華你神也將他們的地賜給你，你接着住他們的城邑並他們的房屋，2就要在耶和華你神所賜你為業的地上分定三座城。3要將耶和華你神使你承受為業的地分為三段，又要預備道路，使誤殺人的，都可以逃到那裏去。

daughter in[a] the fire, who practices divination or sorcery, interprets omens, engages in witchcraft, 11or casts spells, or who is a medium or spiritist or who consults the dead. 12Anyone who does these things is detestable to the LORD, and because of these detestable practices the LORD your God will drive out those nations before you. 13You must be blameless before the LORD your God.

The Prophet

14The nations you will dispossess listen to those who practice sorcery or divination. But as for you, the LORD your God has not permitted you to do so. 15The LORD your God will raise up for you a prophet like me from among your own brothers. You must listen to him. 16For this is what you asked of the LORD your God at Horeb on the day of the assembly when you said, "Let us not hear the voice of the LORD our God nor see this great fire anymore, or we will die."

17The LORD said to me: "What they say is good. 18I will raise up for them a prophet like you from among their brothers; I will put my words in his mouth, and he will tell them everything I command him. 19If anyone does not listen to my words that the prophet speaks in my name, I myself will call him to account. 20But a prophet who presumes to speak in my name anything I have not commanded him to say, or a prophet who speaks in the name of other gods, must be put to death."

21You may say to yourselves, "How can we know when a message has not been spoken by the LORD?" 22If what a prophet proclaims in the name of the LORD does not take place or come true, that is a message the LORD has not spoken. That prophet has spoken presumptuously. Do not be afraid of him.

Cities of Refuge

19 When the LORD your God has destroyed the nations whose land he is giving you, and when you have driven them out and settled in their towns and houses, 2then set aside for yourselves three cities centrally located in the land the LORD your God is giving you to possess. 3Build roads to them and divide into three parts the land the LORD your God is giving you as an inheritance, so that anyone who kills a man may flee there.

a 10 Or who makes his son or daughter pass through

⁴This is the rule concerning the man who kills another and flees there to save his life—one who kills his neighbor unintentionally, without malice aforethought. ⁵For instance, a man may go into the forest with his neighbor to cut wood, and as he swings his ax to fell a tree, the head may fly off and hit his neighbor and kill him. That man may flee to one of these cities and save his life. ⁶Otherwise, the avenger of blood might pursue him in a rage, overtake him if the distance is too great, and kill him even though he is not deserving of death, since he did it to his neighbor without malice aforethought. ⁷This is why I command you to set aside for yourselves three cities.

⁸If the LORD your God enlarges your territory, as he promised on oath to your forefathers, and gives you the whole land he promised them, ⁹because you carefully follow all these laws I command you today—to love the LORD your God and to walk always in his ways—then you are to set aside three more cities. ¹⁰Do this so that innocent blood will not be shed in your land, which the LORD your God is giving you as your inheritance, and so that you will not be guilty of bloodshed.

¹¹But if a man hates his neighbor and lies in wait for him, assaults and kills him, and then flees to one of these cities, ¹²the elders of his town shall send for him, bring him back from the city, and hand him over to the avenger of blood to die. ¹³Show him no pity. You must purge from Israel the guilt of shedding innocent blood, so that it may go well with you.

¹⁴Do not move your neighbor's boundary stone set up by your predecessors in the inheritance you receive in the land the LORD your God is giving you to possess.

Witnesses

¹⁵One witness is not enough to convict a man accused of any crime or offense he may have committed. A matter must be established by the testimony of two or three witnesses.

¹⁶If a malicious witness takes the stand to accuse a man of a crime, ¹⁷the two men involved in the dispute must stand in the presence of the LORD before the priests and the judges who are in office at the time. ¹⁸The judges must make a thorough investigation, and if the witness proves to be a liar, giving false testimony against his brother, ¹⁹then do to him as he intended to do to his brother. You must purge the evil from among you. ²⁰The rest of the people will hear of this and be afraid, and never again will such an evil thing be done among

⁴誤殺人的逃到那裏可以存活，定例乃是這樣：凡素無仇恨、無心殺了人的，⁵就如人與鄰舍同入樹林砍伐樹木，手拿斧子一砍，本想砍下樹木，不料，斧頭脫了把，飛落在鄰舍身上，以致於死，這人逃到那些城的一座城，就可以存活，⁶免得報血仇的，心中火熱追趕他，因路遠就追上將他殺死，其實他不該死，因為他與被殺的素無仇恨。⁷所以我吩咐你說：要分定三座城。

⁸耶和華你神若照他向你列祖所起的誓，擴張你的境界，將所應許賜你列祖的地全然給你。⁹你若謹守遵行我今日所吩咐的這一切誡命，愛耶和華你的神，常常遵行他的道，就要在這三座城之外，再添三座城，¹⁰免得無辜之人的血流在耶和華你神所賜你為業的地上，流血的罪就歸於你。

¹¹若有人恨他的鄰舍，埋伏着起來擊殺他，以致於死，便逃到這些城的一座城，¹²本城的長老就要打發人去，從那裏帶出他來，交在報血仇的手中，將他治死。¹³你眼不可顧惜他，卻要從以色列中除掉流無辜血的罪，使你可以得福。

¹⁴在耶和華你神所賜你承受為業之地，不可挪移你鄰舍的地界，那是先人所定的。

見證人

¹⁵人無論犯甚麼罪，作甚麼惡，不可憑一個人的口作見證，總要憑兩三個人的口作見證才可定案。

¹⁶若有兇惡的見證人起來，見證某人作惡，¹⁷這兩個爭訟的人就要站在耶和華面前，和當時的祭司，並審判官面前，¹⁸審判官要細細地查究，若見證人果然是作假見證的，以假見證陷害弟兄，¹⁹你們就要待他如同他想要待的弟兄。這樣，就把那惡從你們中間除掉。²⁰別人聽見都要害怕，就不敢在你們中間再行這

樣的惡了。²¹你眼不可顧惜，要以命償命，以眼還眼，以牙還牙，以手還手，以腳還腳。

赴戰

20 你出去與仇敵爭戰的時候，看見馬匹、車輛，並有比你多的人民，不要怕他們，因為領你出埃及地的耶和華你神與你同在。²你們將要上陣的時候，祭司要到百姓面前宣告說：³"以色列人哪，你們當聽：你們今日將要與仇敵爭戰，不要膽怯，不要懼怕戰兢，也不要因他們驚恐，⁴因為耶和華你們的神與你們同去，要為你們與仇敵爭戰，拯救你們。"

⁵官長也要對百姓宣告說："誰建造房屋，尚未奉獻，他可以回家去，恐怕他陣亡，別人去奉獻；⁶誰種葡萄園，尚未用所結的果子，他可以回家去，恐怕他陣亡，別人去用；⁷誰聘定了妻，尚未迎娶，他可以回家去，恐怕他陣亡，別人去娶。"⁸官長又要對百姓宣告說："誰懼怕膽怯，他可以回家去，恐怕他弟兄的心消化，和他一樣。"⁹官長對百姓宣告完了，就當派軍長率領他們。

¹⁰你臨近一座城要攻打的時候，先要對城裏的民宣告和睦的話。¹¹他們若以和睦的話回答你，給你開了城，城裏所有的人都要給你效勞，服侍你；¹²若不肯與你和好，反要與你打仗，你就要圍困那城。¹³耶和華你的神把城交付你手，你就要用刀殺盡這城的男丁。¹⁴惟有婦女、孩子、牲畜，和城內一切的財物，你可以取為自己的掠物。耶和華你神把你仇敵的財物賜給你，你可以吃用。¹⁵離你甚遠的各城，不是這些國民的城，你都要這樣待他。

¹⁶但這些國民的城，耶和華你神既賜你為業，其中凡有氣息的，一個不可存留。¹⁷只要照耶和華你神所吩咐的，將這赫人、亞摩利人、迦南人、比利洗人、希未人、耶布斯人都

you. ²¹Show no pity: life for life, eye for eye, tooth for tooth, hand for hand, foot for foot.

Going to War

20 When you go to war against your enemies and see horses and chariots and an army greater than yours, do not be afraid of them, because the LORD your God, who brought you up out of Egypt, will be with you. ²When you are about to go into battle, the priest shall come forward and address the army. ³He shall say: "Hear, O Israel, today you are going into battle against your enemies. Do not be fainthearted or afraid; do not be terrified or give way to panic before them. ⁴For the LORD your God is the one who goes with you to fight for you against your enemies to give you victory."

⁵The officers shall say to the army: "Has anyone built a new house and not dedicated it? Let him go home, or he may die in battle and someone else may dedicate it. ⁶Has anyone planted a vineyard and not begun to enjoy it? Let him go home, or he may die in battle and someone else enjoy it. ⁷Has anyone become pledged to a woman and not married her? Let him go home, or he may die in battle and someone else marry her." ⁸Then the officers shall add, "Is any man afraid or fainthearted? Let him go home so that his brothers will not become disheartened too." ⁹When the officers have finished speaking to the army, they shall appoint commanders over it.

¹⁰When you march up to attack a city, make its people an offer of peace. ¹¹If they accept and open their gates, all the people in it shall be subject to forced labor and shall work for you. ¹²If they refuse to make peace and they engage you in battle, lay siege to that city. ¹³When the LORD your God delivers it into your hand, put to the sword all the men in it. ¹⁴As for the women, the children, the livestock and everything else in the city, you may take these as plunder for yourselves. And you may use the plunder the LORD your God gives you from your enemies. ¹⁵This is how you are to treat all the cities that are at a distance from you and do not belong to the nations nearby.

¹⁶However, in the cities of the nations the LORD your God is giving you as an inheritance, do not leave alive anything that breathes. ¹⁷Completely destroy[a] them — the Hittites, Amorites, Canaanites, Perizzites, Hivites and Jebusites—as the LORD your God has command-

---

a 17 The Hebrew term refers to the irrevocable giving over of things or persons to the LORD, often by totally destroying them.

ed you. [18]Otherwise, they will teach you to follow all the detestable things they do in worshiping their gods, and you will sin against the LORD your God.

[19]When you lay siege to a city for a long time, fighting against it to capture it, do not destroy its trees by putting an ax to them, because you can eat their fruit. Do not cut them down. Are the trees of the field people, that you should besiege them?[a] [20]However, you may cut down trees that you know are not fruit trees and use them to build siege works until the city at war with you falls.

Atonement for an Unsolved Murder

21 If a man is found slain, lying in a field in the land the LORD your God is giving you to possess, and it is not known who killed him, [2]your elders and judges shall go out and measure the distance from the body to the neighboring towns. [3]Then the elders of the town nearest the body shall take a heifer that has never been worked and has never worn a yoke [4]and lead her down to a valley that has not been plowed or planted and where there is a flowing stream. There in the valley they are to break the heifer's neck. [5]The priests, the sons of Levi, shall step forward, for the LORD your God has chosen them to minister and to pronounce blessings in the name of the LORD and to decide all cases of dispute and assault. [6]Then all the elders of the town nearest the body shall wash their hands over the heifer whose neck was broken in the valley, [7]and they shall declare: "Our hands did not shed this blood, nor did our eyes see it done. [8]Accept this atonement for your people Israel, whom you have redeemed, O LORD, and do not hold your people guilty of the blood of an innocent man." And the bloodshed will be atoned for. [9]So you will purge from yourselves the guilt of shedding innocent blood, since you have done what is right in the eyes of the LORD.

Marrying a Captive Woman

[10]When you go to war against your enemies and the LORD your God delivers them into your hands and you take captives, [11]if you notice among the captives a beautiful woman and are attracted to her, you may take her as your wife. [12]Bring her into your home and have her shave her head, trim her nails [13]and put aside the clothes she was wearing when captured. After she has lived in your house and mourned her

---

a 19 Or *down to use in the siege, for the fruit trees are for the benefit of man.*

滅絕淨盡，[18]免得他們教導你們學習一切可憎惡的事，就是他們向自己神所行的，以致你們得罪耶和華你們的神。

[19]你若許久圍困攻打所要取的一座城，就不可舉斧子砍壞樹木，因為你可以吃那樹上的果子，不可砍伐，田間的樹木豈是人，叫你糟蹋嗎？[20]惟獨你所知道不是結果子的樹木可以毀壞、砍伐，用以修築營壘，攻擊那與你打仗的城，直到攻塌了。

為不能斷定之殺人案贖罪

21 在耶和華你神所賜你為業的地上，若遇見被殺的人倒在田野，不知道是誰殺的，[2]長老和審判官就要出去，從被殺的人那裏量起，直量到四圍的城邑。[3]看哪城離被殺的人最近，那城的長老就要從牛羣中取一隻未曾耕地、未曾負軛的母牛犢，[4]把母牛犢牽到流水、未曾耕種的山谷去，在谷中打折母牛犢的頸項。[5]祭司利未的子孫要近前來，因為耶和華你的神揀選了他們侍奉他，奉耶和華的名祝福，所有爭訟毆打的事都要憑他們判斷。[6]那城的眾長老，就是離被殺的人最近的，要在那山谷中，在所打折頸項的母牛犢以上洗手，[7]禱告（註：原文作“回答”）說：“我們的手未曾流這人的血，我們的眼也未曾看見這事。[8]耶和華啊，求你赦免你所救贖的以色列民，不要使流無辜血的罪歸在你的百姓以色列中間。”這樣，流血的罪必得赦免。[9]你行耶和華眼中看為正的事，就可以從你們中間除掉流無辜血的罪。

娶被擄女子之例

[10]你出去與仇敵爭戰的時候，耶和華你的神將他們交在你手中，你就擄了他們去。[11]若在被擄的人中見有美貌的女子，戀慕她，要娶她為妻，[12]就可以領她到你家裏去，她便要剃頭髮，修指甲，[13]脫去被擄時所穿的衣服，住在你家裏哀哭父母一

個整月，然後可以與她同房。你作她的丈夫，她作你的妻子。14後來你若不喜悅她，就要由她隨意出去，決不可為錢賣她，也不可當婢女待她，因為你玷污了她。

長子的權利

15人若有二妻，一為所愛，一為所惡，所愛的、所惡的都給他生了兒子，但長子是所惡之妻生的，16到了把產業分給兒子承受的時候，不可將所愛之妻生的兒子立為長子，在所惡之妻生的兒子以上；17卻要認所惡之妻生的兒子為長子，將產業多加一分給他，因這兒子是他力量強壯的時候生的，長子的名分本當歸他。

悖逆的兒子

18人若有頑梗悖逆的兒子，不聽從父母的話，他們雖懲治他，他仍不聽從，19父母就要抓住他，將他帶到本地的城門、本城的長老那裏，20對長老說："我們這兒子頑梗悖逆，不聽從我們的話，是貪食好酒的人。"21本城的眾人就要用石頭將他打死。這樣，就把那惡從你們中間除掉，以色列眾人都要聽見害怕。

各樣條例

22人若犯該死的罪，被治死了，你將他掛在木頭上。23他的屍首不可留在木頭上過夜，必要當日將他葬埋，免得玷污了耶和華你神所賜你為業之地。因為被掛的人是在神面前受咒詛的。

22 你若看見弟兄的牛或羊失迷了路，不可佯為不見，總要把牠牽回來交給你的弟兄。2你弟兄若離你遠，或是你不認識他，就要牽到你家去，留在你那裏，等你弟兄來尋找，就還給他。3你的弟兄無論失落甚麼，或是驢，或是衣服，你若遇見，都要這樣行，不可佯為不見。

4你若看見弟兄的牛或驢跌倒在路上，不可佯為不見，總要幫助他拉起來。

father and mother for a full month, then you may go to her and be her husband and she shall be your wife. 14If you are not pleased with her, let her go wherever she wishes. You must not sell her or treat her as a slave, since you have dishonored her.

The Right of the Firstborn

15If a man has two wives, and he loves one but not the other, and both bear him sons but the firstborn is the son of the wife he does not love, 16when he wills his property to his sons, he must not give the rights of the firstborn to the son of the wife he loves in preference to his actual firstborn, the son of the wife he does not love. 17He must acknowledge the son of his unloved wife as the firstborn by giving him a double share of all he has. That son is the first sign of his father's strength. The right of the firstborn belongs to him.

A Rebellious Son

18If a man has a stubborn and rebellious son who does not obey his father and mother and will not listen to them when they discipline him, 19his father and mother shall take hold of him and bring him to the elders at the gate of his town. 20They shall say to the elders, "This son of ours is stubborn and rebellious. He will not obey us. He is a profligate and a drunkard." 21Then all the men of his town shall stone him to death. You must purge the evil from among you. All Israel will hear of it and be afraid.

Various Laws

22If a man guilty of a capital offense is put to death and his body is hung on a tree, 23you must not leave his body on the tree overnight. Be sure to bury him that same day, because anyone who is hung on a tree is under God's curse. You must not desecrate the land the LORD your God is giving you as an inheritance.

22 If you see your brother's ox or sheep straying, do not ignore it but be sure to take it back to him. 2If the brother does not live near you or if you do not know who he is, take it home with you and keep it until he comes looking for it. Then give it back to him. 3Do the same if you find your brother's donkey or his cloak or anything he loses. Do not ignore it.

4If you see your brother's donkey or his ox fallen on the road, do not ignore it. Help him get it to its feet.

⁵A woman must not wear men's clothing, nor a man wear women's clothing, for the LORD your God detests anyone who does this.

⁶If you come across a bird's nest beside the road, either in a tree or on the ground, and the mother is sitting on the young or on the eggs, do not take the mother with the young. ⁷You may take the young, but be sure to let the mother go, so that it may go well with you and you may have a long life.

⁸When you build a new house, make a parapet around your roof so that you may not bring the guilt of bloodshed on your house if someone falls from the roof.

⁹Do not plant two kinds of seed in your vineyard; if you do, not only the crops you plant but also the fruit of the vineyard will be defiled.ᵃ

¹⁰Do not plow with an ox and a donkey yoked together.

¹¹Do not wear clothes of wool and linen woven together.

¹²Make tassels on the four corners of the cloak you wear.

Marriage Violations

¹³If a man takes a wife and, after lying with her, dislikes her ¹⁴and slanders her and gives her a bad name, saying, "I married this woman, but when I approached her, I did not find proof of her virginity," ¹⁵then the girl's father and mother shall bring proof that she was a virgin to the town elders at the gate. ¹⁶The girl's father will say to the elders, "I gave my daughter in marriage to this man, but he dislikes her. ¹⁷Now he has slandered her and said, 'I did not find your daughter to be a virgin.' But here is the proof of my daughter's virginity." Then her parents shall display the cloth before the elders of the town, ¹⁸and the elders shall take the man and punish him. ¹⁹They shall fine him a hundred shekels of silverᵇ and give them to the girl's father, because this man has given an Israelite virgin a bad name. She shall continue to be his wife; he must not divorce her as long as he lives.

²⁰If, however, the charge is true and no proof of the girl's virginity can be found, ²¹she shall be brought to the door of her father's house and there the men of her town shall stone her to death. She has done a disgraceful thing in Israel by being promiscuous while still in her father's house. You must purge the evil from among you.

⁵婦女不可穿戴男子所穿戴的；男子也不可穿婦女的衣服，因為這樣行都是耶和華你神所憎惡的。

⁶你若路上遇見鳥窩，或在樹上，或在地上，裏頭有雛或有蛋，母鳥伏在雛上或在蛋上，你不可連母帶雛一併取去。⁷總要放母，只可取雛，這樣你就可以享福，日子得以長久。

⁸你若建造房屋，要在房上的四圍安欄杆，免得有人從房上掉下來，流血的罪就歸於你家。

⁹不可把兩樣種子種在你的葡萄園裏，免得你撒種所結的和葡萄園的果子都要充公。

¹⁰不可並用牛、驢耕地。

¹¹不可穿羊毛、細麻兩樣攙雜料做的衣服。

¹²你要在所披的外衣上四圍做繸子。

違犯婚姻條例

¹³人若娶妻，與她同房之後恨惡她，¹⁴信口說她，將醜名加在她身上，說："我娶了這女子與她同房，見她沒有貞潔的憑據。"¹⁵女子的父母就要把女子貞潔的憑據拿出來，帶到本城門長老那裏。¹⁶女子的父親要對長老說："我將我的女兒給這人為妻，他恨惡她，¹⁷信口說她，說：'我見你的女兒沒有貞潔的憑據。'其實這就是我女兒貞潔的憑據。"父母就把那布鋪在本城的長老面前。¹⁸本城的長老要拿住那人，懲治他，¹⁹並要罰他一百舍客勒銀子，給女子的父親，因為他將醜名加在以色列的一個處女身上。女子仍作他的妻，終身不可休她。

²⁰但這事若是真的，女子沒有貞潔的憑據，²¹就要將女子帶到她父家的門口，本城的人要用石頭將她打死，因為她在父家行了淫亂，在以色列中做了醜事。這樣，就把那惡從你們中間除掉。

ᵃ 9 Or be forfeited to the sanctuary   ᵇ 19 That is, about 2 1/2 pounds (about 1 kilogram)

22若遇見人與有丈夫的婦人行淫，就要將姦夫、淫婦一併治死。這樣，就把那惡從以色列中除掉。

23若有處女已經許配丈夫，有人在城裏遇見她，與她行淫，24你們就要把這二人帶到本城門，用石頭打死，女子是因為雖在城裏卻沒有喊叫；男子是因為玷污別人的妻。這樣，就把那惡從你們中間除掉。

25若有男子在田野遇見已經許配人的女子，強與她行淫，只要將那男子治死，26但不可辦女子，她本沒有該死的罪，這事就類乎人起來攻擊鄰舍，將他殺了一樣。27因為男子是在田野遇見那已經許配人的女子，女子喊叫並無人救她。

28若有男子遇見沒有許配人的處女，抓住她與她行淫，被人看見，29這男子就要拿五十舍客勒銀子給女子的父親，因他玷污了這女子，就要娶她為妻，終身不可休她。

30人不可娶繼母為妻，不可掀開他父親的衣襟。

排除會外

23 凡外腎受傷的，或被閹割的，不可入耶和華的會。

2私生子不可入耶和華的會；他的子孫直到十代，也不可入耶和華的會。

3亞捫人或是摩押人不可入耶和華的會；他們的子孫雖過十代，也永不可入耶和華的會。4因為你們出埃及的時候，他們沒有拿食物和水在路上迎接你們，又因他們雇了美索不達米亞的毘奪人比珥的兒子巴蘭來咒詛你們。5然而耶和華你的神不肯聽從巴蘭，卻使那咒詛的言語變為祝福的話，因為耶和華你的神愛你。6你一生一世永不可求他們的平安和他們的利益。

7不可憎惡以東人，因為他是你的弟兄；不可憎惡埃及人，因為你在他的地上作過寄居的。8他們第三代

22If a man is found sleeping with another man's wife, both the man who slept with her and the woman must die. You must purge the evil from Israel.

23If a man happens to meet in a town a virgin pledged to be married and he sleeps with her, 24you shall take both of them to the gate of that town and stone them to death—the girl because she was in a town and did not scream for help, and the man because he violated another man's wife. You must purge the evil from among you.

25But if out in the country a man happens to meet a girl pledged to be married and rapes her, only the man who has done this shall die. 26Do nothing to the girl; she has committed no sin deserving death. This case is like that of someone who attacks and murders his neighbor, 27for the man found the girl out in the country, and though the betrothed girl screamed, there was no one to rescue her.

28If a man happens to meet a virgin who is not pledged to be married and rapes her and they are discovered, 29he shall pay the girl's father fifty shekels of silver.[a] He must marry the girl, for he has violated her. He can never divorce her as long as he lives.

30A man is not to marry his father's wife; he must not dishonor his father's bed.

Exclusion From the Assembly

23 No one who has been emasculated by crushing or cutting may enter the assembly of the LORD.

2No one born of a forbidden marriage[b] nor any of his descendants may enter the assembly of the LORD, even down to the tenth generation.

3No Ammonite or Moabite or any of his descendants may enter the assembly of the LORD, even down to the tenth generation. 4For they did not come to meet you with bread and water on your way when you came out of Egypt, and they hired Balaam son of Beor from Pethor in Aram Naharaim[c] to pronounce a curse on you. 5However, the LORD your God would not listen to Balaam but turned the curse into a blessing for you, because the LORD your God loves you. 6Do not seek a treaty of friendship with them as long as you live.

7Do not abhor an Edomite, for he is your brother. Do not abhor an Egyptian, because you lived as an alien in his country. 8The third gen-

a 29 That is, about 1 1/4 pounds (about 0.6 kilogram)
b 2 Or one of illegitimate birth　　c 4 That is, Northwest Mesopotamia

eration of children born to them may enter the assembly of the LORD.

Uncleanness in the Camp

[9]When you are encamped against your enemies, keep away from everything impure. [10]If one of your men is unclean because of a nocturnal emission, he is to go outside the camp and stay there. [11]But as evening approaches he is to wash himself, and at sunset he may return to the camp.

[12]Designate a place outside the camp where you can go to relieve yourself. [13]As part of your equipment have something to dig with, and when you relieve yourself, dig a hole and cover up your excrement. [14]For the LORD your God moves about in your camp to protect you and to deliver your enemies to you. Your camp must be holy, so that he will not see among you anything indecent and turn away from you.

Miscellaneous Laws

[15]If a slave has taken refuge with you, do not hand him over to his master. [16]Let him live among you wherever he likes and in whatever town he chooses. Do not oppress him.

[17]No Israelite man or woman is to become a shrine prostitute. [18]You must not bring the earnings of a female prostitute or of a male prostitute[a] into the house of the LORD your God to pay any vow, because the LORD your God detests them both.

[19]Do not charge your brother interest, whether on money or food or anything else that may earn interest. [20]You may charge a foreigner interest, but not a brother Israelite, so that the LORD your God may bless you in everything you put your hand to in the land you are entering to possess.

[21]If you make a vow to the LORD your God, do not be slow to pay it, for the LORD your God will certainly demand it of you and you will be guilty of sin. [22]But if you refrain from making a vow, you will not be guilty. [23]Whatever your lips utter you must be sure to do, because you made your vow freely to the LORD your God with your own mouth.

[24]If you enter your neighbor's vineyard, you may eat all the grapes you want, but do not put any in your basket. [25]If you enter your neighbor's grainfield, you may pick kernels with your hands, but you must not put a sickle to his standing grain.

a 18 Hebrew of a dog

子孫可以入耶和華的會。

保持營內潔淨

[9]你出兵攻打仇敵，就要遠避諸惡。[10]你們中間若有人夜間偶然夢遺不潔淨，就要出到營外，不可入營。[11]到傍晚的時候，他要用水洗澡，及至日落了才可以入營。

[12]你在營外也該定出一個地方作為便所。[13]在你器械之中當預備一把鍬，你出營外便溺以後，用以鏟土，轉身掩蓋。[14]因為耶和華你的神常在你營中行走，要救護你，將仇敵交給你，所以你的營盤當聖潔，免得他見你那裏有污穢，就離開你。

其他條例

[15]若有奴僕脫了主人的手，逃到你那裏，你不可將他交付他的主人。[16]他必在你那裏與你同住，在你的城邑中，要由他選擇一個所喜悅的地方居住，你不可欺負他。

[17]以色列的女子中不可有妓女；以色列的男子中不可有孌童。[18]娼妓所得的錢，或孌童（註：原文作“狗”）所得的價，你不可帶入耶和華你神的殿還願，因為這兩樣都是耶和華你神所憎惡的。

[19]你借給你弟兄的，或是錢財或是糧食，無論甚麼可生利的物，都不可取利。[20]借給外邦人可以取利，只是借給你弟兄不可取利。這樣，耶和華你神必在你所去得為業的地上，和你手裏所辦的一切事上賜福與你。

[21]你向耶和華你的神許願，償還不可遲延，因為耶和華你的神必定向你追討，你不償還就有罪。[22]你若不許願，倒無罪。[23]你嘴裏所出的，就是你口中應許甘心所獻的，要照你向耶和華你神所許的願謹守遵行。

[24]你進了鄰舍的葡萄園，可以隨意吃飽了葡萄，只是不可裝在器皿中。[25]你進了鄰舍站着的禾稼，可以用手摘穗子，只是不可用鐮刀割取禾稼。

24

人若娶妻以後，見她有甚麼不合理的事，不喜悅她，就可以寫休書交在她手中，打發她離開夫家。²婦人離開夫家以後，可以去嫁別人。³後夫若恨惡她，寫休書交在她手中，打發她離開夫家，或是娶她為妻的後夫死了，⁴打發她去的前夫不可在婦人玷污之後再娶她為妻，因為這是耶和華所憎惡的。不可使耶和華你神所賜為業之地被玷污了。

⁵新娶妻之人，不可從軍出征，也不可託他辦理甚麼公事，可以在家清閒一年，使他所娶的妻快活。

⁶不可拿人的全盤磨石或是上磨石作當頭，因為這是拿人的命作當頭。

⁷若遇見人拐帶以色列中的一個弟兄，當奴才待他，或是賣了他。那拐帶人的就必治死。這樣，便將那惡從你們中間除掉。

⁸在大痲瘋的災病上，你們要謹慎，照祭司利未人一切所指教你們的留意遵行。我怎樣吩咐他們，你們要怎樣遵行。⁹當記念出埃及後，在路上耶和華你神向米利暗所行的事。

¹⁰你借給鄰舍，不拘是甚麼，不可進他家拿他的當頭。¹¹要站在外面，等那向你借貸的人把當頭拿出來交給你。¹²他若是窮人，你不可留他的當頭過夜。¹³日落的時候，總要把當頭還他，使他用那件衣服蓋着睡覺，他就為你祝福，這在耶和華你神面前就是你的義了。

¹⁴困苦窮乏的雇工，無論是你的弟兄或是在你城裏寄居的，你不可欺負他。¹⁵要當日給他工價，不可等到日落，因為他窮苦，把心放在工價上，恐怕他因你喊告耶和華，罪便歸你了。

¹⁶不可因子殺父，也不可因父殺子；凡被殺的都為本身的罪。

¹⁷你不可向寄居的和孤兒屈枉正

24

If a man marries a woman who becomes displeasing to him because he finds something indecent about her, and he writes her a certificate of divorce, gives it to her and sends her from his house, ²and if after she leaves his house she becomes the wife of another man, ³and her second husband dislikes her and writes her a certificate of divorce, gives it to her and sends her from his house, or if he dies, ⁴then her first husband, who divorced her, is not allowed to marry her again after she has been defiled. That would be detestable in the eyes of the LORD. Do not bring sin upon the land the LORD your God is giving you as an inheritance.

⁵If a man has recently married, he must not be sent to war or have any other duty laid on him. For one year he is to be free to stay at home and bring happiness to the wife he has married.

⁶Do not take a pair of millstones—not even the upper one—as security for a debt, because that would be taking a man's livelihood as security.

⁷If a man is caught kidnapping one of his brother Israelites and treats him as a slave or sells him, the kidnapper must die. You must purge the evil from among you.

⁸In cases of leprous[a] diseases be very careful to do exactly as the priests, who are Levites, instruct you. You must follow carefully what I have commanded them. ⁹Remember what the LORD your God did to Miriam along the way after you came out of Egypt.

¹⁰When you make a loan of any kind to your neighbor, do not go into his house to get what he is offering as a pledge. ¹¹Stay outside and let the man to whom you are making the loan bring the pledge out to you. ¹²If the man is poor, do not go to sleep with his pledge in your possession. ¹³Return his cloak to him by sunset so that he may sleep in it. Then he will thank you, and it will be regarded as a righteous act in the sight of the LORD your God.

¹⁴Do not take advantage of a hired man who is poor and needy, whether he is a brother Israelite or an alien living in one of your towns. ¹⁵Pay him his wages each day before sunset, because he is poor and is counting on it. Otherwise he may cry to the LORD against you, and you will be guilty of sin.

¹⁶Fathers shall not be put to death for their children, nor children put to death for their fathers; each is to die for his own sin.

¹⁷Do not deprive the alien or the fatherless of

---

a 8 The Hebrew word was used for various diseases affecting the skin—not necessarily leprosy.

justice, or take the cloak of the widow as a pledge. [18]Remember that you were slaves in Egypt and the LORD your God redeemed you from there. That is why I command you to do this.

[19]When you are harvesting in your field and you overlook a sheaf, do not go back to get it. Leave it for the alien, the fatherless and the widow, so that the LORD your God may bless you in all the work of your hands. [20]When you beat the olives from your trees, do not go over the branches a second time. Leave what remains for the alien, the fatherless and the widow. [21]When you harvest the grapes in your vineyard, do not go over the vines again. Leave what remains for the alien, the fatherless and the widow. [22]Remember that you were slaves in Egypt. That is why I command you to do this.

25 When men have a dispute, they are to take it to court and the judges will decide the case, acquitting the innocent and condemning the guilty. [2]If the guilty man deserves to be beaten, the judge shall make him lie down and have him flogged in his presence with the number of lashes his crime deserves, [3]but he must not give him more than forty lashes. If he is flogged more than that, your brother will be degraded in your eyes.

[4]Do not muzzle an ox while it is treading out the grain.

[5]If brothers are living together and one of them dies without a son, his widow must not marry outside the family. Her husband's brother shall take her and marry her and fulfill the duty of a brother-in-law to her. [6]The first son she bears shall carry on the name of the dead brother so that his name will not be blotted out from Israel.

[7]However, if a man does not want to marry his brother's wife, she shall go to the elders at the town gate and say, "My husband's brother refuses to carry on his brother's name in Israel. He will not fulfill the duty of a brother-in-law to me." [8]Then the elders of his town shall summon him and talk to him. If he persists in saying, "I do not want to marry her," [9]his brother's widow shall go up to him in the presence of the elders, take off one of his sandals, spit in his face and say, "This is what is done to the man who will not build up his brother's family line." [10]That man's line shall be known in Israel as The Family of the Unsandaled.

[11]If two men are fighting and the wife of one of them comes to rescue her husband from his assailant, and she reaches out and seizes him by

直，也不可拿寡婦的衣裳作當頭。[18]要記念你在埃及作過奴僕，耶和華你的神從那裏將你救贖，所以我吩咐你這樣行。

[19]你在田間收割莊稼，若忘下一捆，不可回去再取，要留給寄居的與孤兒寡婦。這樣，耶和華你神必在你手裏所辦的一切事上賜福與你。[20]你打橄欖樹，枝上剩下的，不可再打，要留給寄居的與孤兒寡婦。[21]你摘葡萄園的葡萄，所剩下的，不可再摘，要留給寄居的與孤兒寡婦。[22]你也要記念你在埃及地作過奴僕，所以我吩咐你這樣行。

25 人若有爭訟，來聽審判，審判官就要定義人有理，定惡人有罪。[2]惡人若該受責打，審判官就要叫他當面伏在地上，按着他的罪照數責打。[3]只可打他四十下，不可過數；若過數，便是輕賤你的弟兄了。

[4]牛在場上踹穀的時候，不可籠住牠的嘴。

[5]弟兄同居，若死了一個，沒有兒子，死人的妻不可出嫁外人，她丈夫的兄弟當盡弟兄的本分，娶她為妻，與她同房。[6]婦人生的長子必歸死兄的名下，免得他的名在以色列中塗抹了。

[7]那人若不願意娶他哥哥的妻，他哥哥的妻就要到城門長老那裏，說："我丈夫的兄弟不肯在以色列中興起他哥哥的名字，不給我盡弟兄的本分。"[8]本城的長老就要召那人來問他，他若執意說："我不願意娶她。"[9]他哥哥的妻就要當着長老到那人的跟前，脫了他的鞋，吐唾沫在他臉上，說："凡不為哥哥建立家室的，都要這樣待他。"[10]在以色列中，他的名必稱為脫鞋之家。

[11]若有二人爭鬥，這人的妻近前來，要救她丈夫脫離那打她丈夫之

人的手，抓住那人的下體，12就要砍斷婦人的手，眼不可顧惜她。

13你囊中不可有一大一小兩樣的法碼；14你家裏不可有一大一小兩樣的升斗。15當用對準公平的法碼、公平的升斗。這樣，在耶和華你神所賜你的地上，你的日子就可以長久。16因為行非義之事的人，都是耶和華你神所憎惡的。

17你要記念你們出埃及的時候，亞瑪力人在路上怎樣待你。18他們在路上遇見你，趁你疲乏困倦，擊殺你儘後邊軟弱的人，並不敬畏神。19所以耶和華你神使你不被四圍一切的仇敵擾亂，在耶和華你神賜你為業的地上得享平安。那時，你要將亞瑪力的名號從天下塗抹了，不可忘記。

初熟土產與十分之一奉獻

26 你進去得了耶和華你神所賜你為業之地居住，2就要從耶和華你神賜你的地上，將所收的各種初熟的土產取些來，盛在筐子裏，往耶和華你神所選擇要立為他名的居所去，3見當時作祭司的，對他說：「我今日向耶和華你神明認，我已來到耶和華向我們列祖起誓應許賜給我們的地。」4祭司就從你手裏取過筐子來，放在耶和華你神的壇前。5你要在耶和華你神面前說：「我祖原是一個將亡的亞蘭人，下到埃及寄居。他人口稀少，在那裏卻成了又大又強、人數很多的國民。6埃及人惡待我們，苦害我們，將苦工加在我們身上。7於是我們哀求耶和華我們列祖的神，耶和華聽見我們的聲音，看見我們所受的困苦、勞碌、欺壓，8他就用大能的手和伸出來的膀臂，並大可畏的事與神蹟奇事，領我們出了埃及，9將我們領進這地方，把這流奶與蜜之地賜給我們。10耶和華啊，現在我把你所賜給我地上初熟的土產奉了來。」隨後你要把筐子放在耶和華你神面前，向耶和華你神的神下拜。11你和利未人，並在你們中間寄居的，要因耶和華你神所賜你和你家的一切福分歡樂。

his private parts, 12you shall cut off her hand. Show her no pity.

13Do not have two differing weights in your bag—one heavy, one light. 14Do not have two differing measures in your house—one large, one small. 15You must have accurate and honest weights and measures, so that you may live long in the land the LORD your God is giving you. 16For the LORD your God detests anyone who does these things, anyone who deals dishonestly.

17Remember what the Amalekites did to you along the way when you came out of Egypt. 18When you were weary and worn out, they met you on your journey and cut off all who were lagging behind; they had no fear of God. 19When the LORD your God gives you rest from all the enemies around you in the land he is giving you to possess as an inheritance, you shall blot out the memory of Amalek from under heaven. Do not forget!

Firstfruits and Tithes

26 When you have entered the land the LORD your God is giving you as an inheritance and have taken possession of it and settled in it, 2take some of the firstfruits of all that you produce from the soil of the land the LORD your God is giving you and put them in a basket. Then go to the place the LORD your God will choose as a dwelling for his Name 3and say to the priest in office at the time, "I declare today to the LORD your God that I have come to the land the LORD swore to our forefathers to give us." 4The priest shall take the basket from your hands and set it down in front of the altar of the LORD your God. 5Then you shall declare before the LORD your God: "My father was a wandering Aramean, and he went down into Egypt with a few people and lived there and became a great nation, powerful and numerous. 6But the Egyptians mistreated us and made us suffer, putting us to hard labor. 7Then we cried out to the LORD, the God of our fathers, and the LORD heard our voice and saw our misery, toil and oppression. 8So the LORD brought us out of Egypt with a mighty hand and an outstretched arm, with great terror and with miraculous signs and wonders. 9He brought us to this place and gave us this land, a land flowing with milk and honey; 10and now I bring the firstfruits of the soil that you, O LORD, have given me." Place the basket before the LORD your God and bow down before him. 11And you and the Levites and the aliens among you shall rejoice in all the good things the LORD your God has given to you and your household.

12When you have finished setting aside a tenth of all your produce in the third year, the year of the tithe, you shall give it to the Levite, the alien, the fatherless and the widow, so that they may eat in your towns and be satisfied. 13Then say to the LORD your God: "I have removed from my house the sacred portion and have given it to the Levite, the alien, the fatherless and the widow, according to all you commanded. I have not turned aside from your commands nor have I forgotten any of them. 14I have not eaten any of the sacred portion while I was in mourning, nor have I removed any of it while I was unclean, nor have I offered any of it to the dead. I have obeyed the LORD my God; I have done everything you commanded me. 15Look down from heaven, your holy dwelling place, and bless your people Israel and the land you have given us as you promised on oath to our forefathers, a land flowing with milk and honey."

Follow the LORD's Commands

16The LORD your God commands you this day to follow these decrees and laws; carefully observe them with all your heart and with all your soul. 17You have declared this day that the LORD is your God and that you will walk in his ways, that you will keep his decrees, commands and laws, and that you will obey him. 18And the LORD has declared this day that you are his people, his treasured possession as he promised, and that you are to keep all his commands. 19He has declared that he will set you in praise, fame and honor high above all the nations he has made and that you will be a people holy to the LORD your God, as he promised.

The Altar on Mount Ebal

27 Moses and the elders of Israel commanded the people: "Keep all these commands that I give you today. 2When you have crossed the Jordan into the land the LORD your God is giving you, set up some large stones and coat them with plaster. 3Write on them all the words of this law when you have crossed over to enter the land the LORD your God is giving you, a land flowing with milk and honey, just as the LORD, the God of your fathers, promised you. 4And when you have crossed the Jordan, set up these stones on Mount Ebal, as I command you today, and coat them with plaster. 5Build there an altar to the LORD your God, an altar of stones. Do not use any iron tool upon them. 6Build the altar of the LORD your God with

12每逢三年，就是十分取一之年，你取完了一切土產的十分之一，要分給利未人和寄居的，與孤兒寡婦，使他們在你城中可以吃得飽足。13你又要在耶和華你神面前說："我已將聖物從我家裏拿出來，給了利未人和寄居的，與孤兒寡婦，是照你所吩咐我的一切命令。你的命令我都沒有違背，也沒有忘記。14我守喪的時候，沒有吃這聖物；不潔淨的時候，也沒有拿出來；又沒有為死人送去。我聽從了耶和華我神的話，都照你所吩咐的行了。15求你從天上你的聖所垂看，賜福給你的百姓以色列與你所賜給我們的地，就是你向我們列祖起誓賜我們流奶與蜜之地。"

謹守主的誡命

16耶和華你的神今日吩咐你行這些律例、典章，所以你要盡心、盡性謹守遵行。17你今日認耶和華為你的神，應許遵行他的道，謹守他的律例、誡命、典章，聽從他的話。18耶和華今日照他所應許你的，也認你為他的子民，使你謹守他的一切誡命，19又使你得稱讚、美名、尊榮，超乎他所造的萬民之上，並照他所應許的，使你歸耶和華你神為聖潔的民。

以巴路山上築祭壇

27 摩西和以色列的眾長老吩咐百姓說："你們要遵守我今日所吩咐的一切誡命。2你們過約旦河，到了耶和華你神所賜給你的地，當天要立起幾塊大石頭，墁上石灰，3把這律法的一切話寫在石頭上。你過了河，可以進入耶和華你神所賜你流奶與蜜之地，正如耶和華你列祖之神所應許你的。4你們過了約旦河，就要在以巴路山上照我今日所吩咐的，將這些石頭立起來，墁上石灰。5在那裏要為耶和華你的神築一座石壇，在石頭上不可動鐵器，6要用沒有鑿過的石頭築耶和華你神的壇。在壇上要將燔祭獻給耶和華你的神；7又要獻平安祭，且在那裏吃；在耶和華你的神面前歡樂。8你要將這律法的一切話，明明地寫在石頭上。」

以巴路山上宣告咒詛

9摩西和祭司利未人曉諭以色列眾人說：「以色列阿，要默默靜聽。你今日成為耶和華你神的百姓了，10所以要聽從耶和華你神的話，遵行他的誡命、律例，就是我今日所吩咐你的。」

11當日，摩西囑咐百姓說：

12你們過了約旦河，西緬、利未、猶大、以薩迦、約瑟、便雅憫六個支派的人，都要站在基利心山上為百姓祝福。13呂便、迦得、亞設、西布倫、但、拿弗他利六個支派的人，都要站在以巴路山上宣布咒詛。

14利未人要向以色列眾人高聲說：

15「有人製造耶和華所憎惡的偶像，或雕刻，或鑄造，就是工匠手所做的，在暗中設立，那人必受咒詛！」

百姓都要答應說：
「阿們！」
16「輕慢父母的，必受咒詛！」

百姓都要說：
「阿們！」
17「挪移鄰舍地界的，必受咒詛！」

百姓都要說：
「阿們！」
18「使瞎子走差路的，必受咒詛！」

百姓都要說：
「阿們！」
19「向寄居的和孤兒寡婦屈枉正直的，必受咒詛！」

百姓都要說：
「阿們！」
20「與繼母行淫的，必受咒詛！因為掀開他父親的衣襟。」

百姓都要說：
「阿們！」

fieldstones and offer burnt offerings on it to the LORD your God. 7Sacrifice fellowship offerings*a* there, eating them and rejoicing in the presence of the LORD your God. 8And you shall write very clearly all the words of this law on these stones you have set up."

Curses From Mount Ebal

9Then Moses and the priests, who are Levites, said to all Israel, "Be silent, O Israel, and listen! You have now become the people of the LORD your God. 10Obey the LORD your God and follow his commands and decrees that I give you today."

11On the same day Moses commanded the people:

12When you have crossed the Jordan, these tribes shall stand on Mount Gerizim to bless the people: Simeon, Levi, Judah, Issachar, Joseph and Benjamin. 13And these tribes shall stand on Mount Ebal to pronounce curses: Reuben, Gad, Asher, Zebulun, Dan and Naphtali.

14The Levites shall recite to all the people of Israel in a loud voice:

15"Cursed is the man who carves an image or casts an idol—a thing detestable to the LORD, the work of the craftsman's hands—and sets it up in secret."

Then all the people shall say,
"Amen!"
16"Cursed is the man who dishonors his father or his mother."

Then all the people shall say,
"Amen!"
17"Cursed is the man who moves his neighbor's boundary stone."

Then all the people shall say,
"Amen!"
18"Cursed is the man who leads the blind astray on the road."

Then all the people shall say,
"Amen!"
19"Cursed is the man who withholds justice from the alien, the fatherless or the widow."

Then all the people shall say,
"Amen!"
20"Cursed is the man who sleeps with his father's wife, for he dishonors his father's bed."

Then all the people shall say,
"Amen!"

a 7 Traditionally peace offerings

21"Cursed is the man who has sexual relations with any animal."

Then all the people shall say,

"Amen!"

22"Cursed is the man who sleeps with his sister, the daughter of his father or the daughter of his mother."

Then all the people shall say,

"Amen!"

23"Cursed is the man who sleeps with his mother-in-law."

Then all the people shall say,

"Amen!"

24"Cursed is the man who kills his neighbor secretly."

Then all the people shall say,

"Amen!"

25"Cursed is the man who accepts a bribe to kill an innocent person."

Then all the people shall say,

"Amen!"

26"Cursed is the man who does not uphold the words of this law by carrying them out."

Then all the people shall say,

"Amen!"

Blessings for Obedience

28 If you fully obey the LORD your God and carefully follow all his commands I give you today, the LORD your God will set you high above all the nations on earth. 2All these blessings will come upon you and accompany you if you obey the LORD your God:

3You will be blessed in the city and blessed in the country.

4The fruit of your womb will be blessed, and the crops of your land and the young of your livestock—the calves of your herds and the lambs of your flocks.

5Your basket and your kneading trough will be blessed.

6You will be blessed when you come in and blessed when you go out.

7The LORD will grant that the enemies who rise up against you will be defeated before you. They will come at you from one direction but flee from you in seven.

8The LORD will send a blessing on your barns and on everything you put your hand to. The LORD your God will bless you in the land he is giving you.

9The LORD will establish you as his holy people, as he promised you on oath, if you keep the

21 "與獸淫合的，必受咒詛！"

百姓都要説：

"阿們！"

22 "與異母同父或異父同母的姐妹行淫的，必受咒詛！"

百姓都要説：

"阿們！"

23 "與岳母行淫的，必受咒詛！"

百姓都要説：

"阿們！"

24 "暗中殺人的，必受咒詛！"

百姓都要説：

"阿們！"

25 "受賄賂害死無辜之人的，必受咒詛！"

百姓都要説：

"阿們！"

26 "不堅守遵行這律法言語的，必受咒詛！"

百姓都要説：

"阿們！"

遵命蒙福

28 你若留意聽從耶和華你神的話，謹守遵行他的一切誡命，就是我今日所吩咐你的，他必使你超乎天下萬民之上。 2你若聽從耶和華你神的話，這以下的福必追隨你，臨到你身上：

3你在城裏必蒙福，在田間也必蒙福。

4你身所生的，地所產的，牲畜所下的，以及牛犢、羊羔都必蒙福。

5你的筐子和你的搏麵盆都必蒙福。

6你出也蒙福，入也蒙福。

7仇敵起來攻擊你，耶和華必使他們在你面前被你殺敗，他們從一條路來攻擊你，必從七條路逃跑。

8在你倉房裏，並你手所辦的一切事上，耶和華所命的福必臨到你。耶和華你神也要在所給你的地上賜福與你。

9你若謹守耶和華你神的誡命，遵行他的道，他必照着向你所起的誓，立你作為自己的聖民。10天下萬民見你歸在耶和華的名下，就要懼怕你。11你在耶和華向你列祖起誓應許賜your的地上，他必使你身所生的，牲畜所下的，地所產的，都綽綽有餘。

12耶和華必為你開天上的府庫，按時降雨在你的地上。在你手裏所辦的一切事上賜福與你。你必借給許多國民，卻不至向他們借貸。13、14你若聽從耶和華你神的誡命，就是我今日所吩咐你的，謹守遵行，不偏左右，也不隨從侍奉別神，耶和華就必使你作首不作尾，但居上不居下。

悖逆受咒詛

15你若不聽從耶和華你神的話，不謹守遵行他的一切誡命律例，就是我今日所吩咐你的，這以下的咒詛都必追隨你，臨到你身上：

16你在城裏必受咒詛，在田間也必受咒詛；

17你的筐子和你的摶麵盆都必受咒詛；

18你身所生的、地所產的，以及牛犢、羊羔都必受咒詛。

19你出也受咒詛，入也受咒詛。

20耶和華因你行惡離棄他，必在你手裏所辦的一切事上，使咒詛、擾亂、責罰臨到你，直到你被毀滅，速速地滅亡。21耶和華必使瘟疫貼在你身上，直到他將你從所進去得為業的地上滅絕。22耶和華要用癆病、熱病、火症、瘧疾、刀劍、旱風（註：或作"乾旱"）、霉爛攻擊你，這都要追趕你，直到你滅亡。23你頭上的天要變為銅，腳下的地要變為鐵。24耶和華要使那降在你地上的雨變為塵沙，從天臨在你身上，直到你滅亡。

25耶和華必使你敗在仇敵面前，

commands of the LORD your God and walk in his ways. [10]Then all the peoples on earth will see that you are called by the name of the LORD, and they will fear you. [11]The LORD will grant you abundant prosperity—in the fruit of your womb, the young of your livestock and the crops of your ground—in the land he swore to your forefathers to give you.

[12]The LORD will open the heavens, the storehouse of his bounty, to send rain on your land in season and to bless all the work of your hands. You will lend to many nations but will borrow from none. [13]The LORD will make you the head, not the tail. If you pay attention to the commands of the LORD your God that I give you this day and carefully follow them, you will always be at the top, never at the bottom. [14]Do not turn aside from any of the commands I give you today, to the right or to the left, following other gods and serving them.

Curses for Disobedience

[15]However, if you do not obey the LORD your God and do not carefully follow all his commands and decrees I am giving you today, all these curses will come upon you and overtake you:

[16]You will be cursed in the city and cursed in the country.

[17]Your basket and your kneading trough will be cursed.

[18]The fruit of your womb will be cursed, and the crops of your land, and the calves of your herds and the lambs of your flocks.

[19]You will be cursed when you come in and cursed when you go out.

[20]The LORD will send on you curses, confusion and rebuke in everything you put your hand to, until you are destroyed and come to sudden ruin because of the evil you have done in forsaking him.[a] [21]The LORD will plague you with diseases until he has destroyed you from the land you are entering to possess. [22]The LORD will strike you with wasting disease, with fever and inflammation, with scorching heat and drought, with blight and mildew, which will plague you until you perish. [23]The sky over your head will be bronze, the ground beneath you iron. [24]The LORD will turn the rain of your country into dust and powder; it will come down from the skies until you are destroyed.

[25]The LORD will cause you to be defeated

a 20 Hebrew *me*

before your enemies. You will come at them from one direction but flee from them in seven, and you will become a thing of horror to all the kingdoms on earth. 26Your carcasses will be food for all the birds of the air and the beasts of the earth, and there will be no one to frighten them away. 27The LORD will afflict you with the boils of Egypt and with tumors, festering sores and the itch, from which you cannot be cured. 28The LORD will afflict you with madness, blindness and confusion of mind. 29At midday you will grope about like a blind man in the dark. You will be unsuccessful in everything you do; day after day you will be oppressed and robbed, with no one to rescue you.

30You will be pledged to be married to a woman, but another will take her and ravish her. You will build a house, but you will not live in it. You will plant a vineyard, but you will not even begin to enjoy its fruit. 31Your ox will be slaughtered before your eyes, but you will eat none of it. Your donkey will be forcibly taken from you and will not be returned. Your sheep will be given to your enemies, and no one will rescue them. 32Your sons and daughters will be given to another nation, and you will wear out your eyes watching for them day after day, powerless to lift a hand. 33A people that you do not know will eat what your land and labor produce, and you will have nothing but cruel oppression all your days. 34The sights you see will drive you mad. 35The LORD will afflict your knees and legs with painful boils that cannot be cured, spreading from the soles of your feet to the top of your head.

36The LORD will drive you and the king you set over you to a nation unknown to you or your fathers. There you will worship other gods, gods of wood and stone. 37You will become a thing of horror and an object of scorn and ridicule to all the nations where the LORD will drive you.

38You will sow much seed in the field but you will harvest little, because locusts will devour it. 39You will plant vineyards and cultivate them but you will not drink the wine or gather the grapes, because worms will eat them. 40You will have olive trees throughout your country but you will not use the oil, because the olives will drop off. 41You will have sons and daughters but you will not keep them, because they will go into captivity. 42Swarms of locusts will take over all your trees and the crops of your land.

43The alien who lives among you will rise above you higher and higher, but you will sink lower and lower. 44He will lend to you, but you

你從一條路去攻擊他們，必從七條路逃跑。你必在天下萬國中拋來拋去。26你的屍首必給空中的飛鳥和地上的走獸作食物，並無人鬨趕。27耶和華必用埃及人的瘡並痔瘡、牛皮癬與疥攻擊你，使你不能醫治。28耶和華必用癲狂、眼瞎、心驚攻擊你。29你必在午間摸索，好像瞎子在暗中摸索一樣。你所行的必不亨通，時常遭遇欺壓、搶奪，無人搭救。

30你聘定了妻，別人必與她同房；你建造房屋，不得住在其內；你栽種葡萄園，也不得用其中的果子。31你的牛在你眼前宰了，你必不得吃牠的肉；你的驢在你眼前被搶奪，不得歸還；你的羊歸了仇敵，無人搭救。32你的兒女必歸與別國的民，你的眼目終日切望，甚至失明，你手中無力拯救。33你的土產和你勞碌得來的，必被你所不認識的國民吃盡。你時常被欺負，受壓制，34甚至你因眼中所看見的，必致瘋狂。35耶和華必攻擊你，使你膝上腿上，從腳掌到頭頂，長毒瘡無法醫治。

36耶和華必將你和你所立的王領到你和你列祖素不認識的國去，在那裏你必侍奉木頭石頭的神。37你在耶和華領你到的各國中，要令人驚駭、笑談、譏誚。

38你帶到田間的種子雖多，收進來的卻少，因為被蝗蟲吃了。39你栽種修理葡萄園，卻不得收葡萄，也不得喝葡萄酒，因為被蟲子吃了。40你全境有橄欖樹，卻不得其油抹身，因為樹上的橄欖不熟自落了。41你生兒養女，卻不算是你的，因為必被擄去。42你所有的樹木和你地裏的出產必被蝗蟲所吃。

43在你中間寄居的，必漸漸上升，比你高而又高；你必漸漸下降，低而又低。44他必借給你，你卻不能借給他；他必作首，你必作尾。

⁴⁵這一切咒詛必追隨你，趕上你，直到你滅亡，因為你不聽從耶和華你神的話，不遵守他所吩咐的誡命律例。⁴⁶這些咒詛，必在你和你後裔的身上成為異蹟、奇事，直到永遠。⁴⁷因為你富有的時候，不歡心樂意地侍奉耶和華你的神，⁴⁸所以你必在飢餓、乾渴、赤露、缺乏之中，侍奉耶和華所打發來攻擊你的仇敵。他必把鐵軛加在你的頸項上，直到將你滅絕。

⁴⁹耶和華要從遠方地極帶一國的民，如鷹飛來攻擊你。這民的言語，你不懂得；⁵⁰這民的面貌兇惡，不顧恤年老的，也不恩待年少的。⁵¹他們必吃你牲畜所下的和你地土所產的，直到你滅亡。你的五穀、新酒和油，以及牛犢、羊羔都不給你留下，直到將你滅絕。⁵²他們必將你困在你各城裏，直到你所倚靠高大堅固的城牆都被攻塌。他們必將你困在耶和華你神所賜你遍地的各城裏。

⁵³你在仇敵圍困窘迫之中，必吃你本身所生的，就是耶和華你神所賜給你的兒女之肉。⁵⁴你們中間柔弱嬌嫩的人必惡眼看他弟兄和他懷中的妻，並他餘剩的兒女，⁵⁵甚至在你受仇敵圍困窘迫的城中，他要吃兒女的肉，不肯分一點給他的親人，因為他一無所剩。⁵⁶你們中間柔弱嬌嫩的婦人，是因嬌嫩柔弱不肯把腳踏地的，必惡眼看她懷中的丈夫和她的兒女。⁵⁷她兩腿中間出來的嬰孩與她所要生的兒女，她因缺乏一切，就要在你受仇敵圍困窘迫的城中，將他們暗暗地吃了。

⁵⁸、⁵⁹這書上所寫律法的一切話，是叫你敬畏耶和華你神可榮可畏的名。你若不謹守遵行，耶和華就必將奇災，就是至大至長的災，至重至久的病，加在你和你後裔的身上。

will not lend to him. He will be the head, but you will be the tail.

⁴⁵All these curses will come upon you. They will pursue you and overtake you until you are destroyed, because you did not obey the LORD your God and observe the commands and decrees he gave you. ⁴⁶They will be a sign and a wonder to you and your descendants forever. ⁴⁷Because you did not serve the LORD your God joyfully and gladly in the time of prosperity, ⁴⁸therefore in hunger and thirst, in nakedness and dire poverty, you will serve the enemies the LORD sends against you. He will put an iron yoke on your neck until he has destroyed you.

⁴⁹The LORD will bring a nation against you from far away, from the ends of the earth, like an eagle swooping down, a nation whose language you will not understand, ⁵⁰a fierce-looking nation without respect for the old or pity for the young. ⁵¹They will devour the young of your livestock and the crops of your land until you are destroyed. They will leave you no grain, new wine or oil, nor any calves of your herds or lambs of your flocks until you are ruined. ⁵²They will lay siege to all the cities throughout your land until the high fortified walls in which you trust fall down. They will besiege all the cities throughout the land the LORD your God is giving you.

⁵³Because of the suffering that your enemy will inflict on you during the siege, you will eat the fruit of the womb, the flesh of the sons and daughters the LORD your God has given you. ⁵⁴Even the most gentle and sensitive man among you will have no compassion on his own brother or the wife he loves or his surviving children, ⁵⁵and he will not give to one of them any of the flesh of his children that he is eating. It will be all he has left because of the suffering your enemy will inflict on you during the siege of all your cities. ⁵⁶The most gentle and sensitive woman among you—so sensitive and gentle that she would not venture to touch the ground with the sole of her foot—will begrudge the husband she loves and her own son or daughter ⁵⁷the afterbirth from her womb and the children she bears. For she intends to eat them secretly during the siege and in the distress that your enemy will inflict on you in your cities.

⁵⁸If you do not carefully follow all the words of this law, which are written in this book, and do not revere this glorious and awesome name —the LORD your God— ⁵⁹the LORD will send fearful plagues on you and your descendants, harsh and prolonged disasters, and severe and

lingering illnesses. [60]He will bring upon you all the diseases of Egypt that you dreaded, and they will cling to you. [61]The LORD will also bring on you every kind of sickness and disaster not recorded in this Book of the Law, until you are destroyed. [62]You who were as numerous as the stars in the sky will be left but few in number, because you did not obey the LORD your God. [63]Just as it pleased the LORD to make you prosper and increase in number, so it will please him to ruin and destroy you. You will be uprooted from the land you are entering to possess.

[64]Then the LORD will scatter you among all nations, from one end of the earth to the other. There you will worship other gods—gods of wood and stone, which neither you nor your fathers have known. [65]Among those nations you will find no repose, no resting place for the sole of your foot. There the LORD will give you an anxious mind, eyes weary with longing, and a despairing heart. [66]You will live in constant suspense, filled with dread both night and day, never sure of your life. [67]In the morning you will say, "If only it were evening!" and in the evening, "If only it were morning!"—because of the terror that will fill your hearts and the sights that your eyes will see. [68]The LORD will send you back in ships to Egypt on a journey I said you should never make again. There you will offer yourselves for sale to your enemies as male and female slaves, but no one will buy you.

Renewal of the Covenant

29 These are the terms of the covenant the LORD commanded Moses to make with the Israelites in Moab, in addition to the covenant he had made with them at Horeb.

[2]Moses summoned all the Israelites and said to them:

Your eyes have seen all that the LORD did in Egypt to Pharaoh, to all his officials and to all his land. [3]With your own eyes you saw those great trials, those miraculous signs and great wonders. [4]But to this day the LORD has not given you a mind that understands or eyes that see or ears that hear. [5]During the forty years that I led you through the desert, your clothes did not wear out, nor did the sandals on your feet. [6]You ate no bread and drank no wine or other fermented drink. I did this so that you might know that I am the LORD your God.

[7]When you reached this place, Sihon king of Heshbon and Og king of Bashan came out to fight against us, but we defeated them. [8]We took

[60]也必使你所懼怕埃及人的病都臨到你，貼在你身上。[61]又必將沒有寫在這律法書上的各樣疾病、災殃降在你身上，直到你滅亡。[62]你們先前雖然像天上的星那樣多，卻因不聽從耶和華你神的話，所剩的人數就稀少了。[63]先前耶和華怎樣喜悅善待你們，使你們眾多，也要照樣喜悅毀滅你們，使你們滅亡，並且你們從所要進去得的地上必被拔除。

[64]耶和華必使你們分散在萬民中，從地這邊到地那邊，你必在那裏侍奉你和你列祖素不認識木頭石頭的神。[65]在那些國中，你必不得安逸，也不得落腳之地，耶和華卻使你在那裏心中跳動，眼目失明，精神消耗。[66]你的性命必懸懸無定，你晝夜恐懼，自料性命難保。[67]你因心裏所恐懼的，眼中所看見的，早晨必說：「巴不得到晚上才好！」晚上必說：「巴不得到早晨才好！」[68]耶和華必使你坐船回埃及去，走我曾告訴你不得再見的路，在那裏你必賣己身與仇敵作奴婢，卻無人買。

重新立約

29 這是耶和華在摩押地吩咐摩西與以色列人立約的話，是在他和他們於何烈山所立的約之外。

[2]摩西召了以色列眾人來，對他們說：

耶和華在埃及地，在你們眼前向法老和他眾臣僕，並他全地所行的一切事，你們都看見了，[3]就是你親眼看見的大試驗和神蹟，並那些大奇事。[4]但耶和華到今日沒有使你們心能明白、眼能看見、耳能聽見。[5]我領你們在曠野四十年，你們身上的衣服並沒有穿破，腳上的鞋也沒有穿壞。[6]你們沒有吃餅，也沒有喝清酒、濃酒，這要使你們知道，耶和華是你們的神。

[7]你們來到這地方，希實本王西宏、巴珊王噩都出來與我們交戰，我們就擊殺了他們。[8]取了他們的地

給呂便支派、迦得支派和瑪拿西半支派為業。

9所以你們要謹守遵行這約的話，好叫你們在一切所行的事上亨通。10、11今日你們的首領、族長（註：原文作"支派"）、長老、官長、以色列的男丁、你們的妻子兒女，和營中寄居的，以及為你們劈柴挑水的人，都站在耶和華你們的神面前，12為要你順從耶和華你神今日與你所立的約，向你所起的誓。13這樣，他要照他向你所應許的話，又向你列祖亞伯拉罕、以撒、雅各所起的誓，今日立你作他的子民，他作你的神。14我不但與你們立這約，起這誓，15凡與我們一同站在耶和華我們神面前的，並今日不在我們這裏的人，我也與他們立這約，起這誓。

（16我們曾住過埃及地，也從列國經過，這是你們知道的。17你們也看見他們中間可憎之物，並他們木、石、金、銀的偶像。）18惟恐你們中間，或男或女，或族長或支派長，今日心裏偏離耶和華我們的神，去侍奉那些國的神。又怕你們中間有惡根生出苦菜和茵蔯來。

19聽見這咒詛的話，心裏仍是自誇說："我雖然行事心裏頑梗，連累眾人，卻還是平安。"20耶和華必不饒恕他，耶和華的怒氣與憤恨要向他發作，如煙冒出，將這書上所寫的一切咒詛都加在他身上。耶和華又要從天下塗抹他的名，21也必照着寫在律法書上約中的一切咒詛，將他從以色列眾支派中分別出來，使他受禍。

22你們的後代，就是以後興起來的子孫，和遠方來的外人，看見這地的災殃，並耶和華所降與這地的疾病，23又看見遍地有硫磺，有鹽鹵，有火跡，沒有耕種，沒有出產，連草都不生長，好像耶和華在忿怒中所傾覆的所多瑪、蛾摩拉、押瑪、洗扁一

their land and gave it as an inheritance to the Reubenites, the Gadites and the half-tribe of Manasseh.

9Carefully follow the terms of this covenant, so that you may prosper in everything you do. 10All of you are standing today in the presence of the LORD your God—your leaders and chief men, your elders and officials, and all the other men of Israel, 11together with your children and your wives, and the aliens living in your camps who chop your wood and carry your water. 12You are standing here in order to enter into a covenant with the LORD your God, a covenant the LORD is making with you this day and sealing with an oath, 13to confirm you this day as his people, that he may be your God as he promised you and as he swore to your fathers, Abraham, Isaac and Jacob. 14I am making this covenant, with its oath, not only with you 15who are standing here with us today in the presence of the LORD our God but also with those who are not here today.

16You yourselves know how we lived in Egypt and how we passed through the countries on the way here. 17You saw among them their detestable images and idols of wood and stone, of silver and gold. 18Make sure there is no man or woman, clan or tribe among you today whose heart turns away from the LORD our God to go and worship the gods of those nations; make sure there is no root among you that produces such bitter poison.

19When such a person hears the words of this oath, he invokes a blessing on himself and therefore thinks, "I will be safe, even though I persist in going my own way." This will bring disaster on the watered land as well as the dry.[a] 20The LORD will never be willing to forgive him; his wrath and zeal will burn against that man. All the curses written in this book will fall upon him, and the LORD will blot out his name from under heaven. 21The LORD will single him out from all the tribes of Israel for disaster, according to all the curses of the covenant written in this Book of the Law.

22Your children who follow you in later generations and foreigners who come from distant lands will see the calamities that have fallen on the land and the diseases with which the LORD has afflicted it. 23The whole land will be a burning waste of salt and sulfur—nothing planted, nothing sprouting, no vegetation growing on it. It will be like the destruction of Sodom and Gomorrah, Admah and Zeboiim, which the

a 19 Or way, in order to add drunkenness to thirst."

LORD overthrew in fierce anger. [24]All the nations will ask: "Why has the LORD done this to this land? Why this fierce, burning anger?"

[25]And the answer will be: "It is because this people abandoned the covenant of the LORD, the God of their fathers, the covenant he made with them when he brought them out of Egypt. [26]They went off and worshiped other gods and bowed down to them, gods they did not know, gods he had not given them. [27]Therefore the LORD's anger burned against this land, so that he brought on it all the curses written in this book. [28]In furious anger and in great wrath the LORD uprooted them from their land and thrust them into another land, as it is now."

[29]The secret things belong to the LORD our God, but the things revealed belong to us and to our children forever, that we may follow all the words of this law.

Prosperity After Turning to the LORD

30 When all these blessings and curses I have set before you come upon you and you take them to heart wherever the LORD your God disperses you among the nations, [2]and when you and your children return to the LORD your God and obey him with all your heart and with all your soul according to everything I command you today, [3]then the LORD your God will restore your fortunes[a] and have compassion on you and gather you again from all the nations where he scattered you. [4]Even if you have been banished to the most distant land under the heavens, from there the LORD your God will gather you and bring you back. [5]He will bring you to the land that belonged to your fathers, and you will take possession of it. He will make you more prosperous and numerous than your fathers. [6]The LORD your God will circumcise your hearts and the hearts of your descendants, so that you may love him with all your heart and with all your soul, and live. [7]The LORD your God will put all these curses on your enemies who hate and persecute you. [8]You will again obey the LORD and follow all his commands I am giving you today. [9]Then the LORD your God will make you most prosperous in all the work of your hands and in the fruit of your womb, the young of your livestock and the crops of your land. The LORD will again delight in you and make you prosperous, just as he delighted in your fathers, [10]if you obey the LORD your God and keep his commands and decrees that are written in this Book of the Law

a 3 Or will bring you back from captivity

樣。[24]所看見的人,連萬國人,都必問說:"耶和華為何向此地這樣行呢?這樣大發烈怒是甚麼意思呢?"

[25]人必回答說:"是因這地的人離棄了耶和華他們列祖的神,領他們出埃及地的時候與他們所立的約,[26]去侍奉敬拜素不認識的別神,是耶和華所未曾給他們安排的。[27]所以耶和華的怒氣向這地發作,將這書上所寫的一切咒詛,都降在這地上。[28]耶和華在怒氣、忿怒、大惱恨中,將他們從本地拔出來,扔在別的地上,像今日一樣。"

[29]隱秘的事是屬耶和華我們神的;惟有明顯的事是永遠屬我們和我們子孫的,好叫我們遵行這律法上的一切話。

歸向主得福氣

30 我所陳明在你面前的這一切咒詛都臨到你身上,你在耶和華你神追趕你到的萬國中,必心裏追念祝福的話。[2]你和你的子孫,若盡心、盡性歸向耶和華你的神,照着我今日一切所吩咐的聽從他的話,[3]那時,耶和華你的神必憐恤你,救回你這被擄的子民,耶和華你的神要回轉過來,從分散你到的萬民中將你招聚回來。[4]你被趕散的人,就是在天涯的,耶和華你的神也必從那裏將你招聚回來。[5]耶和華你的神必領你進入你列祖所得的地,使你可以得着;又必善待你,使你的人數比你列祖眾多。[6]耶和華你神必將你心裏和你後裔心裏的污穢除掉,好叫你盡心、盡性愛耶和華你的神,使你可以存活。[7]耶和華你的神必將這一切咒詛加在你仇敵和恨惡你、逼迫你的人身上。[8]你必歸回聽從耶和華的話,遵行他的一切誡命,就是我今日所吩咐你的。[9]、[10]你若聽從耶和華你神的話,謹守這律法書上所寫的誡命、律例,又盡心、盡性歸向耶和華你的神,他必使你手裏所辦的一切事,並你身所生的,牲畜所下的,地土所產的,都綽綽有餘,因為耶和華必再喜悅你，降福與你，像從前喜悅你列祖一樣。

生與死的抉擇

11我今日所吩咐你的誡命，不是你難行的，也不是離你遠的。12不是在天上，使你說：「誰替我們上天取下來，使我們聽見可以遵行呢？」13也不是在海外，使你說：「誰替我們過海取了來，使我們聽見可以遵行呢？」14這話卻離你甚近，就在你口中，在你心裏，使你可以遵行。

15看哪，我今日將生與福，死與禍，陳明在你面前。16吩咐你愛耶和華你的神，遵行他的道，謹守他的誡命、律例、典章，使你可以存活，人數增多，耶和華你神就必在你所要進去得為業的地上賜福與你。

17倘若你心裏偏離，不肯聽從，卻被勾引去敬拜侍奉別神，18我今日明明告訴你們：你們必要滅亡，在你過約旦河進去得為業的地上，你的日子必不長久。

19我今日呼天喚地向你作見證，我將生死禍福陳明在你面前，所以你要揀選生命，使你和你的後裔都得存活，20且愛耶和華你的神，聽從他的話，專靠他，因為他是你的生命，你的日子長久也在乎他。這樣，你就可以在耶和華向你列祖亞伯拉罕、以撒、雅各起誓應許所賜的地上居住。

約書亞繼承摩西

31 摩西去告訴以色列眾人，2說：「我現在一百二十歲了，不能照常出入，耶和華也曾對我說：『你必不得過這約旦河。』3耶和華你們的神必引導你們過去，將這些國民在你們面前滅絕，你們就得他們的地。約書亞必引導你們過去，正如耶和華所說的。4耶和華必待他們，如同從前待他所滅絕的亞摩利二王西宏與噩以及他們的國一樣。5耶和華必將他們交給你們，你們要照我所吩咐的一切命令待他們。6你們當剛強壯膽，不要害怕，也不要畏懼他們，因為耶和華你的神和你同去。他必不撇下你，也不丟棄你。」

and turn to the LORD your God with all your heart and with all your soul.

The Offer of Life or Death

11Now what I am commanding you today is not too difficult for you or beyond your reach. 12It is not up in heaven, so that you have to ask, "Who will ascend into heaven to get it and proclaim it to us so we may obey it?" 13Nor is it beyond the sea, so that you have to ask, "Who will cross the sea to get it and proclaim it to us so we may obey it?" 14No, the word is very near you; it is in your mouth and in your heart so you may obey it.

15See, I set before you today life and prosperity, death and destruction. 16For I command you today to love the LORD your God, to walk in his ways, and to keep his commands, decrees and laws; then you will live and increase, and the LORD your God will bless you in the land you are entering to possess.

17But if your heart turns away and you are not obedient, and if you are drawn away to bow down to other gods and worship them, 18I declare to you this day that you will certainly be destroyed. You will not live long in the land you are crossing the Jordan to enter and possess.

19This day I call heaven and earth as witnesses against you that I have set before you life and death, blessings and curses. Now choose life, so that you and your children may live 20and that you may love the LORD your God, listen to his voice, and hold fast to him. For the LORD is your life, and he will give you many years in the land he swore to give to your fathers, Abraham, Isaac and Jacob.

Joshua to Succeed Moses

31 Then Moses went out and spoke these words to all Israel: 2"I am now a hundred and twenty years old and I am no longer able to lead you. The LORD has said to me, 'You shall not cross the Jordan.' 3The LORD your God himself will cross over ahead of you. He will destroy these nations before you, and you will take possession of their land. Joshua also will cross over ahead of you, as the LORD said. 4And the LORD will do to them what he did to Sihon and Og, the kings of the Amorites, whom he destroyed along with their land. 5The LORD will deliver them to you, and you must do to them all that I have commanded you. 6Be strong and courageous. Do not be afraid or terrified because of them, for the LORD your God goes with you; he will never leave you nor forsake you."

7Then Moses summoned Joshua and said to him in the presence of all Israel, "Be strong and courageous, for you must go with this people into the land that the LORD swore to their forefathers to give them, and you must divide it among them as their inheritance. 8The LORD himself goes before you and will be with you; he will never leave you nor forsake you. Do not be afraid; do not be discouraged."

The Reading of the Law

9So Moses wrote down this law and gave it to the priests, the sons of Levi, who carried the ark of the covenant of the LORD, and to all the elders of Israel. 10Then Moses commanded them: "At the end of every seven years, in the year for canceling debts, during the Feast of Tabernacles, 11when all Israel comes to appear before the LORD your God at the place he will choose, you shall read this law before them in their hearing. 12Assemble the people—men, women and children, and the aliens living in your towns—so they can listen and learn to fear the LORD your God and follow carefully all the words of this law. 13Their children, who do not know this law, must hear it and learn to fear the LORD your God as long as you live in the land you are crossing the Jordan to possess."

Israel's Rebellion Predicted

14The LORD said to Moses, "Now the day of your death is near. Call Joshua and present yourselves at the Tent of Meeting, where I will commission him." So Moses and Joshua came and presented themselves at the Tent of Meeting.

15Then the LORD appeared at the Tent in a pillar of cloud, and the cloud stood over the entrance to the Tent. 16And the LORD said to Moses: "You are going to rest with your fathers, and these people will soon prostitute themselves to the foreign gods of the land they are entering. They will forsake me and break the covenant I made with them. 17On that day I will become angry with them and forsake them; I will hide my face from them, and they will be destroyed. Many disasters and difficulties will come upon them, and on that day they will ask, 'Have not these disasters come upon us because our God is not with us?' 18And I will certainly hide my face on that day because of all their wickedness in turning to other gods.

19"Now write down for yourselves this song and teach it to the Israelites and have them sing it, so that it may be a witness for me against them. 20When I have brought them into the land

7摩西召了約書亞來，在以色列眾人眼前對他說："你當剛強壯膽，因為你要和這百姓一同進入耶和華向他們列祖起誓應許所賜之地，你也要使他們承受那地為業。8耶和華必在你前面行，他必與你同在，必不撇下你，也不丟棄你。不要懼怕，也不要驚惶。"

誦讀律法

9摩西將這律法寫出來，交給抬耶和華約櫃的祭司利未子孫和以色列的眾長老。10摩西吩咐他們說："每逢七年的末一年，就在豁免年的定期住棚節的時候，11以色列眾人來到耶和華你神所選擇的地方朝見他。那時，你要在以色列眾人面前將這律法念給他們聽。12要招聚他們男、女、孩子，並城裏寄居的，使他們聽、使他們學習，好敬畏耶和華你們的神，謹守遵行這律法的一切話。13也使他們未曾曉得這律法的兒女得以聽見，學習敬畏耶和華你們的神，在你們過約旦河要得為業之地，存活的日子，常常這樣行。"

預言以色列悖逆

14耶和華對摩西說："你的死期臨近了，要召約書亞來，你們二人站在會幕裏，我好囑咐他。"於是摩西和約書亞去站在會幕裏。

15耶和華在會幕裏雲柱中顯現，雲柱停在會幕門以上。16耶和華又對摩西說："你必和你列祖同睡。這百姓要起來，在他們所要去的地上，在那地的人中，隨從外邦神行邪淫離棄我，違背我與他們所立的約。17那時，我的怒氣必向他們發作，我也必離棄他們，掩面不顧他們，以致他們被吞滅，並有許多的禍患災難臨到他們。那日他們必說：'這些禍患臨到我們，豈不是因我們的神不在我們中間嗎？'18那時，因他們偏向別神所行的一切惡，我必定掩面不顧他們。

19"現在你要寫一篇歌，教導以色列人，傳給他們，使這歌見證他們的不是，20因為我將他們領進我向他們列祖起誓應許那流奶與蜜之地，他們在那裏吃得飽足，身體肥胖，就必偏向別神，侍奉他們，藐視我，背棄我的約。21那時，有許多禍患災難臨到他們，這歌必在他們面前作見證，他們後裔的口中必念誦不忘。我未領他們到我所起誓應許之地以先，他們所懷的意念我都知道了。」22當日摩西就寫了一篇歌，教導以色列人。

23耶和華囑咐嫩的兒子約書亞說：「你當剛強壯膽，因為你必領以色列人進我所起誓應許他們的地，我必與你同在。」

24摩西將這律法的話寫在書上，及至寫完了，25就吩咐抬耶和華約櫃的利未人說：26「將這律法書放在耶和華你們神的約櫃旁，可以在那裏見證以色列人的不是，27因為我知道你們是悖逆的，是硬着頸項的。我今日還活着與你們同在，你們尚且悖逆耶和華，何況我死後呢？28你們要將你們支派的眾長老和官長都招聚了來，我好將這些話說與他們聽，並呼天喚地見證他們的不是。29我知道我死後，你們必全然敗壞，偏離我所吩咐你們的道，行耶和華眼中看為惡的事，以手所做的惹他發怒，日後必有禍患臨到你們。」

摩西的歌

30摩西將這一篇歌的話都說與以色列全會眾聽：

32 諸天哪，側耳！我要說話；願地也聽我口中的言語。
2我的教訓要淋滴如雨，
　我的言語要滴落如露，
如細雨降在嫩草上，
　如甘霖降在菜蔬中。

3我要宣告耶和華的名；
　你們要將大德歸與我們的神。
4他是磐石，他的作為完全，
　他所行的無不公平，
是誠實無偽的神，
　又公義，又正直。

flowing with milk and honey, the land I promised on oath to their forefathers, and when they eat their fill and thrive, they will turn to other gods and worship them, rejecting me and breaking my covenant. 21And when many disasters and difficulties come upon them, this song will testify against them, because it will not be forgotten by their descendants. I know what they are disposed to do, even before I bring them into the land I promised them on oath." 22So Moses wrote down this song that day and taught it to the Israelites.

23The LORD gave this command to Joshua son of Nun: "Be strong and courageous, for you will bring the Israelites into the land I promised them on oath, and I myself will be with you."

24After Moses finished writing in a book the words of this law from beginning to end, 25he gave this command to the Levites who carried the ark of the covenant of the LORD: 26"Take this Book of the Law and place it beside the ark of the covenant of the LORD your God. There it will remain as a witness against you. 27For I know how rebellious and stiff-necked you are. If you have been rebellious against the LORD while I am still alive and with you, how much more will you rebel after I die! 28Assemble before me all the elders of your tribes and all your officials, so that I can speak these words in their hearing and call heaven and earth to testify against them. 29For I know that after my death you are sure to become utterly corrupt and to turn from the way I have commanded you. In days to come, disaster will fall upon you because you will do evil in the sight of the LORD and provoke him to anger by what your hands have made."

The Song of Moses

30And Moses recited the words of this song from beginning to end in the hearing of the whole assembly of Israel:

32 Listen, O heavens, and I will speak;
hear, O earth, the words of my mouth.
2Let my teaching fall like rain
and my words descend like dew,
like showers on new grass,
like abundant rain on tender plants.

3I will proclaim the name of the LORD.
Oh, praise the greatness of our God!
4He is the Rock, his works are perfect,
and all his ways are just.
A faithful God who does no wrong,
upright and just is he.

⁵They have acted corruptly toward him;
    to their shame they are no longer his
        children,
    but a warped and crooked generation.ᵃ
⁶Is this the way you repay the LORD,
    O foolish and unwise people?
Is he not your Father, your Creator,ᵇ
    who made you and formed you?

⁷Remember the days of old;
    consider the generations long past.
Ask your father and he will tell you,
    your elders, and they will explain to you.
⁸When the Most High gave the nations their
        inheritance,
    when he divided all mankind,
he set up boundaries for the peoples
    according to the number of the sons of
        Israel.ᶜ
⁹For the LORD's portion is his people,
    Jacob his allotted inheritance.

¹⁰In a desert land he found him,
    in a barren and howling waste.
He shielded him and cared for him;
    he guarded him as the apple of his eye,
¹¹like an eagle that stirs up its nest
    and hovers over its young,
that spreads its wings to catch them
    and carries them on its pinions.
¹²The LORD alone led him;
    no foreign god was with him.

¹³He made him ride on the heights of the land
    and fed him with the fruit of the fields.
He nourished him with honey from the rock,
    and with oil from the flinty crag,
¹⁴with curds and milk from herd and flock
    and with fattened lambs and goats,
with choice rams of Bashan
    and the finest kernels of wheat.
You drank the foaming blood of the grape.

¹⁵Jeshurunᵈ grew fat and kicked;
    filled with food, he became heavy and sleek.
He abandoned the God who made him
    and rejected the Rock his Savior.
¹⁶They made him jealous with their foreign
        gods
    and angered him with their detestable idols.

⁵這乖僻彎曲的世代,
    向他行事邪僻,
有這弊病,
    就不是他的兒女。
⁶愚昧無知的民哪,
    你們這樣報答耶和華嗎?
他豈不是你的父,將你買來的嗎?
    他是製造你、建立你的。

⁷你當追想上古之日,
    思念歷代之年。
問你的父親,他必指示你;
    問你的長者,他必告訴你。
⁸至高者
    將地業賜給列邦,
    將世人分開,
就照以色列人的數目,
    立定萬民的疆界。
⁹耶和華的分,本是他的百姓;
    他的產業,本是雅各。

¹⁰耶和華遇見他在曠野、
    荒涼野獸吼叫之地,
就環繞他、看顧他,
    保護他,如同保護眼中的瞳人。
¹¹又如鷹攪動巢窩,
    在雛鷹以上兩翅搧展,
    接取雛鷹,
    背在兩翼之上。
¹²這樣,耶和華獨自引導他,
    並無外邦神與他同在。

¹³耶和華使他乘駕地的高處,
    得吃田間的土產;
又使他從磐石中咂蜜,
    從堅石中吸油;
¹⁴也吃牛的奶油,
    羊的奶,羊羔的脂油,
巴珊所出的公綿羊和山羊,
    與上好的麥子,
    也喝葡萄汁釀的酒。

¹⁵但耶書崙漸漸肥胖、粗壯、光潤,
    踢跳奔跑,
便離棄造他的神,
    輕看救他的磐石,
¹⁶敬拜別神,觸動神的憤恨,
    行可憎惡的事,
    惹了他的怒氣。

ᵃ 5 Or Corrupt are they and not his children, / a generation warped
and twisted to their shame   ᵇ 6 Or Father, who bought you
ᶜ 8 Masoretic Text; Dead Sea Scrolls (see also Septuagint) *sons
of God*   ᵈ 15 *Jeshurun* means *the upright one,* that is, Israel.

¹⁷所祭祀的鬼魔並非真神，
　　乃是素不認識的神，
　　是近來新興的，
　　是你列祖所不畏懼的。
¹⁸你輕忽生你的磐石，
　　忘記產你的神。

¹⁹耶和華看見他的兒女惹動他，
　　就厭惡他們，說：

²⁰ "我要向他們掩面，
　　看他們的結局如何。
　　他們本是極乖僻的族類，
　　心中無誠實的兒女。
²¹他們以那不算真神的，
　　觸動我的憤恨；
　　以虛無的神惹了我的怒氣。
　　我也要以那不成子民的，
　　觸動他們的憤恨；
　　以愚昧的國民惹了他們的怒氣。
²²因為在我怒中有火燒起，
　　直燒到極深的陰間，
　　把地和地的出產，
　　盡都焚燒，
　　山的根基也燒着了。

²³ "我要將禍患堆在他們身上，
　　把我的箭向他們射盡。
²⁴他們必因飢餓消瘦，
　　被炎熱苦毒吞滅。
　　我要打發野獸用牙齒咬他們，
　　並土中腹行的，
　　用毒氣害他們。
²⁵外頭有刀劍，內室有驚恐，
　　使人喪亡，
　　使少男、童女、
　　吃奶的、白髮的，
　　盡都滅絕。
²⁶我說：我必將他們分散遠方，
　　使他們的名號從人間除滅。
²⁷惟恐仇敵惹動我，
　　只怕敵人錯看，說：
　　'是我們手的能力，
　　並非耶和華所行的。' "

²⁸因為以色列民毫無計謀，
　　心中沒有聰明。
²⁹惟願他們有智慧，
　　能明白這事，
　　肯思念他們的結局。
³⁰若不是他們的磐石賣了他們，
　　若不是耶和華交出他們，
　　一人焉能追趕他們千人，
　　　　二人焉能使萬人逃跑呢？

¹⁷They sacrificed to demons, which are not God—
　　gods they had not known,
　　gods that recently appeared,
　　gods your fathers did not fear.
¹⁸You deserted the Rock, who fathered you;
　　you forgot the God who gave you birth.

¹⁹The LORD saw this and rejected them
　　because he was angered by his sons and
　　　　daughters.
²⁰"I will hide my face from them," he said,
　　"and see what their end will be;
　for they are a perverse generation,
　　children who are unfaithful.
²¹They made me jealous by what is no god
　　and angered me with their worthless idols.
　I will make them envious by those who are
　　　　not a people;
　I will make them angry by a nation that has
　　no understanding.
²²For a fire has been kindled by my wrath,
　　one that burns to the realm of death*a* below.
　It will devour the earth and its harvests
　　and set afire the foundations of the
　　　　mountains.

²³"I will heap calamities upon them
　　and spend my arrows against them.
²⁴I will send wasting famine against them,
　　consuming pestilence and deadly plague;
　I will send against them the fangs of wild
　　　　beasts,
　　the venom of vipers that glide in the dust.
²⁵In the street the sword will make them
　　　　childless;
　　in their homes terror will reign.
　Young men and young women will perish,
　　infants and gray-haired men.
²⁶I said I would scatter them
　　and blot out their memory from mankind,
²⁷but I dreaded the taunt of the enemy,
　　lest the adversary misunderstand
　and say, 'Our hand has triumphed;
　　the LORD has not done all this.' "

²⁸They are a nation without sense,
　　there is no discernment in them.
²⁹If only they were wise and would understand
　　　　this
　　and discern what their end will be!
³⁰How could one man chase a thousand,
　　or two put ten thousand to flight,
　　unless their Rock had sold them,
　　unless the LORD had given them up?

a 22 Hebrew to Sheol

31For their rock is not like our Rock,
   as even our enemies concede.
32Their vine comes from the vine of Sodom
   and from the fields of Gomorrah.
  Their grapes are filled with poison,
   and their clusters with bitterness.
33Their wine is the venom of serpents,
   the deadly poison of cobras.

34"Have I not kept this in reserve
   and sealed it in my vaults?
35It is mine to avenge; I will repay.
  In due time their foot will slip;
  their day of disaster is near
   and their doom rushes upon them."

36The LORD will judge his people
   and have compassion on his servants
  when he sees their strength is gone
   and no one is left, slave or free.
37He will say: "Now where are their gods,
   the rock they took refuge in,
38the gods who ate the fat of their sacrifices
   and drank the wine of their drink offerings?
  Let them rise up to help you!
  Let them give you shelter!

39"See now that I myself am He!
   There is no god besides me.
 I put to death and I bring to life,
  I have wounded and I will heal,
  and no one can deliver out of my hand.
40I lift my hand to heaven and declare:
  As surely as I live forever,
41when I sharpen my flashing sword
   and my hand grasps it in judgment,
  I will take vengeance on my adversaries
   and repay those who hate me.
42I will make my arrows drunk with blood,
   while my sword devours flesh:
  the blood of the slain and the captives,
  the heads of the enemy leaders."

43Rejoice, O nations, with his people,[a,b]
  for he will avenge the blood of his servants;
  he will take vengeance on his enemies
   and make atonement for his land and
   people.

44Moses came with Joshua[c] son of Nun and spoke all the words of this song in the hearing of the people. 45When Moses finished reciting all

a 43 Or Make his people rejoice, O nations   *b 43 Masoretic Text; Dead Sea Scrolls (see also Septuagint) people, / and let all the angels worship him /*   *c 44 Hebrew Hoshea, a variant of Joshua*

31據我們的仇敵自己斷定，
  他們的磐石不如我們的磐石。
32他們的葡萄樹是所多瑪的葡萄樹，
  蛾摩拉田園所生的。
 他們的葡萄是毒葡萄，
  全挂都是苦的。
33他們的酒是大蛇的毒氣，
  是虺蛇殘害的惡毒。

34"這不都是積蓄在我這裏，
  封鎖在我府庫中嗎？
35他們失腳的時候，伸冤報應在我；
  因他們遭災的日子近了，
  那要臨在他們身上的，
  必速速來到。"

36耶和華見他百姓毫無能力，
  無論困住的、自由的都沒有剩下，
  就必為他們伸冤，
  為他的僕人後悔。
37他必說："他們的神，
  他們所投靠的磐石，
38就是向來吃他們祭牲的脂油，
  喝他們奠祭之酒的，在哪裏呢？
 他可以興起幫助你們，
  護衛你們！

39"你們如今要知道：
  我，惟有我是神，
  在我以外並無別神。
 我使人死，我使人活；
  我損傷，我也醫治，
  並無人能從我手中救出來。
40我向天舉手說，我憑我的永生起誓：
41我若磨我閃亮的刀，
  手掌審判之權，
  就必報復我的敵人，
  報應恨我的人。
42我要使我的箭飲血飲醉，
  就是被殺被擄之人的血。
 我的刀要吃肉，
  乃是仇敵中首領之頭的肉。"

43你們外邦人，
  當與主的百姓一同歡呼，
  因他要伸他僕人流血的冤，
  報應他的敵人，潔淨他的地，
  救贖他的百姓。

44摩西和嫩的兒子約書亞，去將這歌的一切話說給百姓聽。45摩西向以色列眾人說完了這一切的話，

46又說：「我今日所警教你們的，你們都要放在心上，要吩咐你們的子孫謹守遵行這律法上的話。47因為這不是虛空與你們無關的事，乃是你們的生命，在你們過約旦河要得為業的地上，必因這事日子得以長久。」

摩西將死於尼波山

48當日，耶和華吩咐摩西說：49「你上這亞巴琳山中的尼波山去，在摩押地與耶利哥相對，觀看我所要賜給以色列人為業的迦南地。50你必死在你所登的山上，歸你列祖（註：原文作「本民」）去，像你哥哥亞倫死在何珥山上，歸他的列祖一樣。51因為你們在尋的曠野，加低斯的米利巴水，在以色列人中沒有尊我為聖，得罪了我。52我所賜給以色列人的地，你可以遠遠地觀看，卻不得進去。」

摩西祝福各支派

33 以下是神人摩西在未死之先，為以色列人所祝的福。2他說：

"耶和華從西奈而來，
　從西珥向他們顯現，
　從巴蘭山發出光輝，
從萬萬聖者中來臨，
　從他右手為百姓傳出烈火的律法。
3他疼愛百姓，
　眾聖徒都在他手中。
他們坐在他的腳下，
　領受他的言語。
4摩西將律法傳給我們，
　作為雅各會眾的產業。
5百姓的眾首領，以色列的各支派，
　一同聚會的時候，
耶和華（註：原文作「他」）在耶書崙中
　為王。

6 "願呂便存活不至死亡，
　願他人數不至稀少。"

7為猶大祝福說：

these words to all Israel, 46he said to them, "Take to heart all the words I have solemnly declared to you this day, so that you may command your children to obey carefully all the words of this law. 47They are not just idle words for you—they are your life. By them you will live long in the land you are crossing the Jordan to possess."

Moses to Die on Mount Nebo

48On that same day the LORD told Moses, 49"Go up into the Abarim Range to Mount Nebo in Moab, across from Jericho, and view Canaan, the land I am giving the Israelites as their own possession. 50There on the mountain that you have climbed you will die and be gathered to your people, just as your brother Aaron died on Mount Hor and was gathered to his people. 51This is because both of you broke faith with me in the presence of the Israelites at the waters of Meribah Kadesh in the Desert of Zin and because you did not uphold my holiness among the Israelites. 52Therefore, you will see the land only from a distance; you will not enter the land I am giving to the people of Israel."

Moses Blesses the Tribes

33 This is the blessing that Moses the man of God pronounced on the Israelites before his death. 2He said:

"The LORD came from Sinai
　and dawned over them from Seir;
　he shone forth from Mount Paran.
He came with^d myriads of holy ones
　from the south, from his mountain slopes.^{b}
3Surely it is you who love the people;
　all the holy ones are in your hand.
At your feet they all bow down,
　and from you receive instruction,
4the law that Moses gave us,
　the possession of the assembly of Jacob.
5He was king over Jeshurun^c
　when the leaders of the people assembled,
　along with the tribes of Israel.

6"Let Reuben live and not die,
　nor^d his men be few."

7And this he said about Judah:

---

a 2 Or *from*　　*b* 2 The meaning of the Hebrew for this phrase is uncertain.　　*c* 5 *Jeshurun* means *the upright one,* that is, Israel; also in verse 26.　　*d* 6 Or *but let*

"Hear, O LORD, the cry of Judah;
  bring him to his people.
With his own hands he defends his cause.
  Oh, be his help against his foes!"

8About Levi he said:

"Your Thummim and Urim belong
  to the man you favored.
You tested him at Massah;
  you contended with him at the waters of
  Meribah.
9He said of his father and mother,
  'I have no regard for them.'
He did not recognize his brothers
  or acknowledge his own children,
but he watched over your word
  and guarded your covenant.
10He teaches your precepts to Jacob
  and your law to Israel.
He offers incense before you
  and whole burnt offerings on your altar.
11Bless all his skills, O LORD,
  and be pleased with the work of his hands.
Smite the loins of those who rise up against
  him;
  strike his foes till they rise no more."

12About Benjamin he said:

"Let the beloved of the LORD rest secure in
  him,
for he shields him all day long,
  and the one the Lord loves rests between his
  shoulders."

13About Joseph he said:

"May the LORD bless his land
  with the precious dew from heaven above
  and with the deep waters that lie below;
14with the best the sun brings forth
  and the finest the moon can yield;
15with the choicest gifts of the ancient
  mountains
  and the fruitfulness of the everlasting hills;
16with the best gifts of the earth and its fullness
  and the favor of him who dwelt in the
  burning bush.
Let all these rest on the head of Joseph,
  on the brow of the prince among[a] his
  brothers.
17In majesty he is like a firstborn bull;
  his horns are the horns of a wild ox.

a 16 Or of the one separated from

求耶和華俯聽猶大的聲音,
  引導他歸於本族,
他曾用手為自己爭戰,
  你必幫助他攻擊敵人。"

8論利未說:

"耶和華啊,
  你的土明和烏陵
  都在你的虔誠人那裏。
你在瑪撒曾試驗他,
  在米利巴水與他爭論。
9他論自己的父母說:
  '我未曾看見。'
他也不承認弟兄,
  也不認識自己的兒女。
這是因利未人遵行你的話,
  謹守你的約。
10他們要將你的典章教訓雅各,
  將你的律法教訓以色列。
他們要把香焚在你面前,
  把全牲的燔祭獻在你的壇上。
11求耶和華降福在他的財物上,
  悅納他手裏所辦的事。
那些起來攻擊他和恨惡他的人,
  願你刺透他們的腰,
  使他們不得再起來。"

12論便雅憫說:

"耶和華所親愛的,
  必同耶和華安然居住;
耶和華終日遮蔽他,
  也住在他兩肩之中。"

13論約瑟說:

"願他的地蒙耶和華賜福,
  得天上的寶物、甘露,
  以及地裏所藏的泉水;
14得太陽所曬熟的美果,
  月亮所養成的寶物;
15得上古之山的至寶,
  永世之嶺的寶物;

16得地和其中所充滿的寶物,
  並住荊棘中上主的喜悅。
願這些福都歸於約瑟的頭上,
  歸於那與弟兄迥別之人的頂上。

17他為牛羣中頭生的,有威嚴;
  他的角是野牛的角,

用以牴觸萬邦，直到地極。
這角，是以法蓮的萬萬，
瑪拿西的千千。"

With them he will gore the nations,
even those at the ends of the earth.
Such are the ten thousands of Ephraim;
such are the thousands of Manasseh."

18論西布倫說：

"西布倫哪，你出外可以歡喜。
以薩迦啊，在你帳棚裏可以快樂。
19他們要將列邦召到山上，
在那裏獻公義的祭，
因為他們要吸取海裏的豐富，
並沙中所藏的珍寶。"

18About Zebulun he said:

"Rejoice, Zebulun, in your going out,
and you, Issachar, in your tents.
19They will summon peoples to the mountain
and there offer sacrifices of righteousness;
they will feast on the abundance of the seas,
on the treasures hidden in the sand."

20論迦得說：

"使迦得擴張的應當稱頌！
迦得住如母獅，他撕裂膀臂，
連頭頂也撕裂。
21他為自己選擇頭一段地，
因在那裏有設立律法者的分存留。
他與百姓的首領同來，
他施行耶和華的公義，
和耶和華與以色列所立的典章。"

20About Gad he said:

"Blessed is he who enlarges Gad's domain!
Gad lives there like a lion,
tearing at arm or head.
21He chose the best land for himself;
the leader's portion was kept for him.
When the heads of the people assembled,
he carried out the LORD's righteous will,
and his judgments concerning Israel."

22論但說：

"但為小獅子，
從巴珊跳出來。"

22About Dan he said:

"Dan is a lion's cub,
springing out of Bashan."

23論拿弗他利說：

"拿弗他利啊，
你足沾恩惠，
滿得耶和華的福，
可以得西方和南方為業。"

23About Naphtali he said:

"Naphtali is abounding with the favor of the
LORD
and is full of his blessing;
he will inherit southward to the lake."

24論亞設說：

"願亞設享受多子的福樂，
得他弟兄的喜悅，
可以把腳蘸在油中。
25你的門閂（註："門閂"或作"鞋"）
是銅的、鐵的。
你的日子如何，你的力量也必如何。

24About Asher he said:

"Most blessed of sons is Asher;
let him be favored by his brothers,
and let him bathe his feet in oil.
25The bolts of your gates will be iron and
bronze,
and your strength will equal your days.

26"耶書崙哪，沒有能比神的。
他為幫助你，乘在天空，
顯其威榮，駕行穹蒼。
27永生的神是你的居所，
他永久的膀臂在你以下。
他在你前面攆出仇敵，
說：'毀滅吧！'
28以色列安然居住，
雅各的本源獨居五穀新酒之地，

26"There is no one like the God of Jeshurun,
who rides on the heavens to help you
and on the clouds in his majesty.
27The eternal God is your refuge,
and underneath are the everlasting arms.
He will drive out your enemy before you,
saying, 'Destroy him!'
28So Israel will live in safety alone;
Jacob's spring is secure

in a land of grain and new wine,
  where the heavens drop dew.
[29]Blessed are you, O Israel!
  Who is like you,
  a people saved by the LORD?
He is your shield and helper
  and your glorious sword.
Your enemies will cower before you,
  and you will trample down their high
  places.[a] "

The Death of Moses

34 Then Moses climbed Mount Nebo from the plains of Moab to the top of Pisgah, across from Jericho. There the LORD showed him the whole land—from Gilead to Dan, [2]all of Naphtali, the territory of Ephraim and Manasseh, all the land of Judah as far as the western sea,[b] [3]the Negev and the whole region from the Valley of Jericho, the City of Palms, as far as Zoar. [4]Then the LORD said to him, "This is the land I promised on oath to Abraham, Isaac and Jacob when I said, 'I will give it to your descendants.' I have let you see it with your eyes, but you will not cross over into it."

[5]And Moses the servant of the LORD died there in Moab, as the LORD had said. [6]He buried him[c] in Moab, in the valley opposite Beth Peor, but to this day no one knows where his grave is. [7]Moses was a hundred and twenty years old when he died, yet his eyes were not weak nor his strength gone. [8]The Israelites grieved for Moses in the plains of Moab thirty days, until the time of weeping and mourning was over.

[9]Now Joshua son of Nun was filled with the spirit[d] of wisdom because Moses had laid his hands on him. So the Israelites listened to him and did what the LORD had commanded Moses.

[10]Since then, no prophet has risen in Israel like Moses, whom the LORD knew face to face, [11]who did all those miraculous signs and wonders the LORD sent him to do in Egypt — to Pharaoh and to all his officials and to his whole land. [12]For no one has ever shown the mighty power or performed the awesome deeds that Moses did in the sight of all Israel.

---

a 29 Or *will tread upon their bodies*   b 2 That is, the
Mediterranean   c 6 Or *He was buried*   d 9 Or *Spirit*

他的天也滴甘露。

[29]以色列啊，你是有福的！
  誰像你這蒙耶和華
  所拯救的百姓呢？
他是你的盾牌，幫助你，
  是你威榮的刀劍；
你的仇敵必投降你，
  你必踏在他們的高處。"

摩西的死

34 摩西從摩押平原登尼波山，上了那與耶利哥相對的毗斯迦山頂。耶和華把以色列全地直到但，[2]拿弗他利全地，以法蓮、瑪拿西的地，猶大全地直到西海，[3]南地和棕樹城耶利哥的平原，直到瑣珥，都指給他看。[4]耶和華對他說："這는是我向亞伯拉罕、以撒、雅各起誓應許之地，說：'我必將這地賜給你的後裔。' 現在我使你眼睛看見了，你卻不得過到那裏去。"

[5]於是，耶和華的僕人摩西死在摩押地，正如耶和華所說的。[6]耶和華將他埋葬在摩押地，伯毗珥對面的谷中，只是到今日沒有人知道他的墳墓。[7]摩西死的時候年一百二十歲。眼目沒有昏花，精神沒有衰敗。[8]以色列人在摩押平原為摩西哀哭了三十日，為摩西居喪哀哭的日子就滿了。

[9]嫩的兒子約書亞，因為摩西曾按手在他頭上，就被智慧的靈充滿，以色列人便聽從他，照着耶和華吩咐摩西的行了。

[10]以後以色列中再沒有興起先知像摩西的；他是耶和華面對面所認識的。[11]耶和華打發他在埃及地向法老和他的一切臣僕，並他的全地，行各樣神蹟奇事，[12]又在以色列眾人眼前顯大能的手，行一切大而可畏的事。

約書亞記

Joshua

主對約書亞的囑咐

1 耶和華的僕人摩西死了以後，耶和華曉諭摩西的幫手、嫩的兒子約書亞說：²"我的僕人摩西死了。現在你要起來，和眾百姓過這約旦河，往我所要賜給以色列人的地去。³凡你們腳掌所踏之地，我都照着我所應許摩西的話賜給你們了。⁴從曠野和這黎巴嫩，直到幼發拉底大河，赫人的全地，又到大海日落之處，都要作你們的境界。⁵你平生的日子，必無一人能在你面前站立得住。我怎樣與摩西同在，也必照樣與你同在；我必不撇下你，也不丟棄你。

⁶"你當剛強壯膽！因為你必使這百姓承受那地為業，就是我向他們列祖起誓應許賜給他們的地。⁷只要剛強，大大壯膽，謹守遵行我僕人摩西所吩咐你的一切律法，不可偏離左右，使你無論往哪裏去，都可以順利。⁸這律法書不可離開你的口，總要晝夜思想，好使你謹守遵行這書上所寫的一切話。如此，你的道路就可以亨通，凡事順利。⁹我豈沒有吩咐你嗎？你當剛強壯膽！不要懼怕，也不要驚惶，因為你無論往哪裏去，耶和華你的神必與你同在。"

¹⁰於是，約書亞吩咐百姓的官長說：¹¹"你們要走遍營中，吩咐百姓說：'當預備食物。因為三日之內，你們要過這約旦河，進去得那耶和華你們神賜你們為業之地。'"

¹²約書亞對呂便人、迦得人和瑪拿西半支派的人說：¹³"你們要追念耶和華的僕人摩西所吩咐你們的話說：'耶和華你們的神使你們得享平安，也必將這地賜給你們。'¹⁴你們的妻子、孩子和牲畜都可以留在約旦河東摩西所給你們的地；但你們中間一切大能的勇士都要帶着兵器，在你們的弟兄前面過去，幫助他們。¹⁵等到耶和華使你們的弟兄像你們一樣得享平安，並且得着耶和

The LORD Commands Joshua

1 After the death of Moses the servant of the LORD, the LORD said to Joshua son of Nun, Moses' aide: ²"Moses my servant is dead. Now then, you and all these people, get ready to cross the Jordan River into the land I am about to give to them—to the Israelites. ³I will give you every place where you set your foot, as I promised Moses. ⁴Your territory will extend from the desert to Lebanon, and from the great river, the Euphrates—all the Hittite country—to the Great Sea*a* on the west. ⁵No one will be able to stand up against you all the days of your life. As I was with Moses, so I will be with you; I will never leave you nor forsake you.

⁶"Be strong and courageous, because you will lead these people to inherit the land I swore to their forefathers to give them. ⁷Be strong and very courageous. Be careful to obey all the law my servant Moses gave you; do not turn from it to the right or to the left, that you may be successful wherever you go. ⁸Do not let this Book of the Law depart from your mouth; meditate on it day and night, so that you may be careful to do everything written in it. Then you will be prosperous and successful. ⁹Have I not commanded you? Be strong and courageous. Do not be terrified; do not be discouraged, for the LORD your God will be with you wherever you go."

¹⁰So Joshua ordered the officers of the people: ¹¹"Go through the camp and tell the people, 'Get your supplies ready. Three days from now you will cross the Jordan here to go in and take possession of the land the LORD your God is giving you for your own.'"

¹²But to the Reubenites, the Gadites and the half-tribe of Manasseh, Joshua said, ¹³"Remember the command that Moses the servant of the LORD gave you: 'The LORD your God is giving you rest and has granted you this land.' ¹⁴Your wives, your children and your livestock may stay in the land that Moses gave you east of the Jordan, but all your fighting men, fully armed, must cross over ahead of your brothers. You are to help your brothers ¹⁵until the LORD gives them rest, as he has done for you, and until they

---

a 4 That is, the Mediterranean

too have taken possession of the land that the LORD your God is giving them. After that, you may go back and occupy your own land, which Moses the servant of the LORD gave you east of the Jordan toward the sunrise."

16Then they answered Joshua, "Whatever you have commanded us we will do, and wherever you send us we will go. 17Just as we fully obeyed Moses, so we will obey you. Only may the LORD your God be with you as he was with Moses. 18Whoever rebels against your word and does not obey your words, whatever you may command them, will be put to death. Only be strong and courageous!"

Rahab and the Spies

2 Then Joshua son of Nun secretly sent two spies from Shittim. "Go, look over the land," he said, "especially Jericho." So they went and entered the house of a prostitute[a] named Rahab and stayed there.

2The king of Jericho was told, "Look! Some of the Israelites have come here tonight to spy out the land. 3So the king of Jericho sent this message to Rahab: "Bring out the men who came to you and entered your house, because they have come to spy out the whole land."

4But the woman had taken the two men and hidden them. She said, "Yes, the men came to me, but I did not know where they had come from. 5At dusk, when it was time to close the city gate, the men left. I don't know which way they went. Go after them quickly. You may catch up with them." 6(But she had taken them up to the roof and hidden them under the stalks of flax she had laid out on the roof.) 7So the men set out in pursuit of the spies on the road that leads to the fords of the Jordan, and as soon as the pursuers had gone out, the gate was shut.

8Before the spies lay down for the night, she went up on the roof 9and said to them, "I know that the LORD has given this land to you and that a great fear of you has fallen on us, so that all who live in this country are melting in fear because of you. 10We have heard how the LORD dried up the water of the Red Sea[b] for you when you came out of Egypt, and what you did to Sihon and Og, the two kings of the Amorites east of the Jordan, whom you completely destroyed.[c] 11When we heard of it, our hearts melted and everyone's courage failed because of you, for the LORD your

華你們神所賜他們為業之地,那時才可以回你們所得之地,承受為業,就是耶和華的僕人<u>摩西</u>在<u>約旦河</u>東、向日出之地所給你們的。"

16他們回答<u>約書亞</u>說:"你所吩咐我們行的,我們都必行;你所差遣我們去的,我們都必去。17我們從前在一切事上怎樣聽從<u>摩西</u>,現在也必照樣聽從你;惟願耶和華你的神與你同在,像與<u>摩西</u>同在一樣。18無論甚麼人違背你的命令,不聽從你所吩咐他的一切話,就必治死他。你只要剛強壯膽!"

喇合與探子

2 當下,<u>嫩</u>的兒子<u>約書亞</u>從<u>什亭</u>暗暗打發兩個人作探子,吩咐說:"你們去窺探那地和<u>耶利哥</u>。"於是二人去了,來到一個妓女名叫<u>喇合</u>的家裏,就在那裏躺臥。

2有人告訴<u>耶利哥</u>王說:"今夜有<u>以色列</u>人來到這裏窺探此地。" 3<u>耶利哥</u>王打發人去見<u>喇合</u>說:"那來到你這裏、進了你家的人要交出來,因為他們來窺探全地。"

4女人將二人隱藏,就回答說:"那人果然到我這裏來,他們是哪裏來的我卻不知道。5天黑、要關城門的時候,他們出去了,往哪裏去我卻不知道。你們快快地去追趕,就必追上。" 6(先是女人領二人上了房頂,將他們藏在那裏所擺的麻稭中。) 7那些人就往<u>約旦河</u>的渡口追趕他們去了。追趕他們的人一出去,城門就關了。

8二人還沒有躺臥,女人就上房頂,到他們那裏,9對他們說:"我知道耶和華已經把這地賜給你們,並且因你們的緣故我們都驚慌了。這地的一切居民在你們面前心都消化了。10因為我們聽見你們出<u>埃及</u>的時候,耶和華怎樣在你們面前使<u>紅海</u>的水乾了,並且你們怎樣待<u>約旦河</u>東的兩個<u>亞摩利王西宏和噩</u>,將他們盡行毀滅。11我們一聽見這些事,心就消化了。因你們的緣故,並無一人有膽氣。耶和華你們的神,本是上天下地

a 1 Or possibly an innkeeper   b 10 Hebrew Yam Suph; that is, Sea of Reeds   c 10 The Hebrew term refers to the irrevocable giving over of things or persons to the LORD, often by totally destroying them.

的神。12現在我既是恩待你們，求你們指着耶和華向我起誓，也要恩待我父家，並給我一個實在的證據，13救活我的父母、弟兄、姐妹和一切屬他們的，拯救我們性命不死。"

14二人對她說："你若不洩漏我們這件事，我們情願替你們死。耶和華將這地賜給我們的時候，我們必以慈愛誠實待你。"

15於是女人用繩子將二人從窗戶裏縋下去，因她的房子是在城牆邊上，她也住在城牆上。16她對他們說："你們且往山上去，恐怕追趕的人碰見你們。要在那裏隱藏三天，等追趕的人回來，然後才可以走你們的路。"

17二人對她說："你要這樣行。不然，你叫我們所起的誓就與我們無干了。18我們來到這地的時候，你要把這條朱紅線繩繫在縋我們下去的窗戶上。並要使你的父母、弟兄和你父的全家都聚集在你家中。19凡出了你家門往街上去的，他的罪（註："罪"原文作"血"）必歸到自己的頭上，與我們無干了。凡在你家裏的，若有人下手害他，流他血的罪就歸到我們的頭上。20你若洩漏我們這件事，你叫我們所起的誓就與我們無干了。"

21女人說："照你們的話行吧！"於是打發他們去了，又把朱紅線繩繫在窗戶上。

22二人到山上，在那裏住了三天，等着追趕的人回去了。追趕的人一路找他們，卻找不着。23二人就下山回來，過了河，到嫩的兒子約書亞那裏，向他述說所遭遇的一切事。24又對約書亞說："耶和華果然將那全地交在我們手中，那地的一切居民在我們面前心都消化了。"

過約旦河

3 約書亞清早起來，和以色列眾人都離開什亭，來到約旦河，就住在那裏，等候過河。2過了三天，官長走遍營中，3吩咐百姓說："你們看見耶和華你們神的約櫃，又見祭司利未人抬着，就要離開所住的地方，跟着約櫃去。4只是你們和約櫃相離，要量二

God is God in heaven above and on the earth below. 12Now then, please swear to me by the LORD that you will show kindness to my family, because I have shown kindness to you. Give me a sure sign 13that you will spare the lives of my father and mother, my brothers and sisters, and all who belong to them, and that you will save us from death."

14"Our lives for your lives!" the men assured her. "If you don't tell what we are doing, we will treat you kindly and faithfully when the LORD gives us the land."

15So she let them down by a rope through the window, for the house she lived in was part of the city wall. 16Now she had said to them, "Go to the hills so the pursuers will not find you. Hide yourselves there three days until they return, and then go on your way."

17The men said to her, "This oath you made us swear will not be binding on us 18unless, when we enter the land, you have tied this scarlet cord in the window through which you let us down, and unless you have brought your father and mother, your brothers and all your family into your house. 19If anyone goes outside your house into the street, his blood will be on his own head; we will not be responsible. As for anyone who is in the house with you, his blood will be on our head if a hand is laid on him. 20But if you tell what we are doing, we will be released from the oath you made us swear."

21"Agreed," she replied. "Let it be as you say." So she sent them away and they departed. And she tied the scarlet cord in the window.

22When they left, they went into the hills and stayed there three days, until the pursuers had searched all along the road and returned without finding them. 23Then the two men started back. They went down out of the hills, forded the river and came to Joshua son of Nun and told him everything that had happened to them. 24They said to Joshua, "The LORD has surely given the whole land into our hands; all the people are melting in fear because of us."

Crossing the Jordan

3 Early in the morning Joshua and all the Israelites set out from Shittim and went to the Jordan, where they camped before crossing over. 2After three days the officers went throughout the camp, 3giving orders to the people: "When you see the ark of the covenant of the LORD your God, and the priests, who are Levites, carrying it, you are to move out from your positions and follow it. 4Then you will know which

way to go, since you have never been this way before. But keep a distance of about a thousand yards[a] between you and the ark; do not go near it."

[5]Joshua told the people, "Consecrate yourselves, for tomorrow the LORD will do amazing things among you."

[6]Joshua said to the priests, "Take up the ark of the covenant and pass on ahead of the people." So they took it up and went ahead of the people.

[7]And the LORD said to Joshua, "Today I will begin to exalt you in the eyes of all Israel, so they may know that I am with you as I was with Moses. [8]Tell the priests who carry the ark of the covenant: 'When you reach the edge of the Jordan's waters, go and stand in the river.' "

[9]Joshua said to the Israelites, "Come here and listen to the words of the LORD your God. [10]This is how you will know that the living God is among you and that he will certainly drive out before you the Canaanites, Hittites, Hivites, Perizzites, Girgashites, Amorites and Jebusites. [11]See, the ark of the covenant of the Lord of all the earth will go into the Jordan ahead of you. [12]Now then, choose twelve men from the tribes of Israel, one from each tribe. [13]And as soon as the priests who carry the ark of the LORD—the Lord of all the earth—set foot in the Jordan, its waters flowing downstream will be cut off and stand up in a heap."

[14]So when the people broke camp to cross the Jordan, the priests carrying the ark of the covenant went ahead of them. [15]Now the Jordan is at flood stage all during harvest. Yet as soon as the priests who carried the ark reached the Jordan and their feet touched the water's edge, [16]the water from upstream stopped flowing. It piled up in a heap a great distance away, at a town called Adam in the vicinity of Zarethan, while the water flowing down to the Sea of the Arabah (the Salt Sea[b]) was completely cut off. So the people crossed over opposite Jericho. [17]The priests who carried the ark of the covenant of the LORD stood firm on dry ground in the middle of the Jordan, while all Israel passed by until the whole nation had completed the crossing on dry ground.

4 When the whole nation had finished crossing the Jordan, the LORD said to Joshua, [2]"Choose twelve men from among the people, one from each tribe, [3]and tell them to take up twelve stones from the middle of the Jordan from right where the priests stood

千肘，不可與約櫃相近，使你們知道所當走的路，因為這條路你們向來沒有走過。”

[5]約書亞吩咐百姓說：“你們要自潔，因為明天耶和華必在你們中間行奇事。”

[6]約書亞又吩咐祭司說：“你們抬起約櫃，在百姓前頭過去。”於是他們抬起約櫃，在百姓前頭走。

[7]耶和華對約書亞說：“從今日起，我必使你在以色列眾人眼前尊大，使他們知道我怎樣與摩西同在，也必照樣與你同在。[8]你要吩咐抬約櫃的祭司說：‘你們到了約旦河的水邊上，就要在約旦河水裏站住。’”

[9]約書亞對以色列人說：“你們近前來，聽耶和華你們神的話。”[10][11]約書亞說：“看哪！普天下主的約櫃必在你們前頭過去，到約旦河裏，因此你們就知道在你們中間有永生神。並且他必在你們面前趕出迦南人、赫人、希未人、比利洗人、革迦撒人、亞摩利人、耶布斯人。[12]你們現在要從以色列支派中揀選十二個人，每支派一人，[13]等到抬普天下主耶和華約櫃的祭司把腳站在約旦河水裏，約旦河的水，就是從上往下流的水，必然斷絕，立起成壘。”

[14]百姓離開帳棚，要過約旦河的時候，抬約櫃的祭司乃在百姓的前頭。[15]他們到了約旦河，腳一入水（原來約旦河水在收割的日子漲過兩岸），[16]那從上往下流的水，便在極遠之地、撒拉但旁的亞當城那裏停住，立起成壘；那往亞拉巴的海，就是鹽海，下流的水全然斷絕。於是百姓在耶利哥的對面過去了。[17]抬耶和華約櫃的祭司在約旦河中的乾地上站定，以色列眾人都從乾地上過去，直到國民盡都過了約旦河。

4 國民盡都過了約旦河，耶和華就對約書亞說：[2]“你從民中要揀選十二個人，每支派一人，[3]吩咐他們說：‘你們從這裏，從約旦河中，祭司腳站定的地方，取十二塊石頭帶過去，放在

---

a 4 Hebrew *about two thousand cubits* (about 900 meters)

b 16 That is, the Dead Sea

你們今夜要住宿的地方。'"

4於是約書亞將他從以色列人中所預備的那十二個人，每支派一人，都召了來。5對他們說："你們下約旦河中，過到耶和華你們神的約櫃前頭，按着以色列人十二支派的數目，每人取一塊石頭扛在肩上。6這些石頭在你們中間可以作為證據。日後你們的子孫問你們說：'這些石頭是甚麼意思？'7你們就對他們說：'這是因為約旦河的水在耶和華的約櫃前斷絕；約櫃過約旦河的時候，約旦河的水就斷絕了。這些石頭要使以色列人永遠的記念。'"

8以色列人就照約書亞所吩咐的，按着以色列人支派的數目，從約旦河中取了十二塊石頭，都遵耶和華所吩咐約書亞的行了。他們把石頭帶過去，到他們所住宿的地方，就放在那裏。9約書亞另把十二塊石頭立在約旦河中，在抬約櫃的祭司腳站立的地方；直到今日，那石頭還在那裏。

10抬約櫃的祭司站在約旦河中，等到耶和華曉諭約書亞吩咐百姓的事辦完了，是照摩西所吩咐約書亞的一切話。於是百姓急速過去了。11眾百姓盡乾的過了河，耶和華的約櫃和祭司就在百姓面前過去。12呂便人、迦得人、瑪拿西半支派的人，都照摩西所吩咐他們的，帶着兵器在以色列人前頭過去。13約有四萬人都準備打仗，在耶和華面前過去，到耶利哥的平原，等候上陣。

14當那日，耶和華使約書亞在以色列眾人眼前尊大。在他平生的日子，百姓敬畏他，像從前敬畏摩西一樣。

15耶和華曉諭約書亞說：16"你吩咐抬法櫃的祭司從約旦河裏上來。"

17約書亞就吩咐祭司說："你們從約旦河裏上來。"

18抬耶和華約櫃的祭司從約旦河裏上來，腳掌剛落旱地，約旦河的水就流到原處，仍舊漲過兩岸。

19正月初十日，百姓從約旦河裏上來，就在吉甲，在耶利哥的東邊

and to carry them over with you and put them down at the place where you stay tonight."

4So Joshua called together the twelve men he had appointed from the Israelites, one from each tribe, 5and said to them, "Go over before the ark of the LORD your God into the middle of the Jordan. Each of you is to take up a stone on his shoulder, according to the number of the tribes of the Israelites, 6to serve as a sign among you. In the future, when your children ask you, 'What do these stones mean?' 7tell them that the flow of the Jordan was cut off before the ark of the covenant of the LORD. When it crossed the Jordan, the waters of the Jordan were cut off. These stones are to be a memorial to the people of Israel forever."

8So the Israelites did as Joshua commanded them. They took twelve stones from the middle of the Jordan, according to the number of the tribes of the Israelites, as the LORD had told Joshua; and they carried them over with them to their camp, where they put them down. 9Joshua set up the twelve stones that had been[a] in the middle of the Jordan at the spot where the priests who carried the ark of the covenant had stood. And they are there to this day.

10Now the priests who carried the ark remained standing in the middle of the Jordan until everything the LORD had commanded Joshua was done by the people, just as Moses had directed Joshua. The people hurried over, 11and as soon as all of them had crossed, the ark of the LORD and the priests came to the other side while the people watched. 12The men of Reuben, Gad and the half-tribe of Manasseh crossed over, armed, in front of the Israelites, as Moses had directed them. 13About forty thousand armed for battle crossed over before the LORD to the plains of Jericho for war.

14That day the LORD exalted Joshua in the sight of all Israel; and they revered him all the days of his life, just as they revered Moses.

15Then the LORD said to Joshua, 16"Command the priests carrying the ark of the Testimony to come up out of the Jordan."

17So Joshua commanded the priests, "Come up out of the Jordan."

18And the priests came up out of the river carrying the ark of the covenant of the LORD. No sooner had they set their feet on the dry ground than the waters of the Jordan returned to their place and ran at flood stage as before.

19On the tenth day of the first month the people went up from the Jordan and camped at

a 9 Or Joshua also set up twelve stones

Gilgal on the eastern border of Jericho. [20]And Joshua set up at Gilgal the twelve stones they had taken out of the Jordan. [21]He said to the Israelites, "In the future when your descendants ask their fathers, 'What do these stones mean?' [22]tell them, 'Israel crossed the Jordan on dry ground.' [23]For the LORD your God dried up the Jordan before you until you had crossed over. The LORD your God did to the Jordan just what he had done to the Red Sea[a] when he dried it up before us until we had crossed over. [24]He did this so that all the peoples of the earth might know that the hand of the LORD is powerful and so that you might always fear the LORD your God."

Circumcision at Gilgal

5 Now when all the Amorite kings west of the Jordan and all the Canaanite kings along the coast heard how the LORD had dried up the Jordan before the Israelites until we had crossed over, their hearts melted and they no longer had the courage to face the Israelites.

[2]At that time the LORD said to Joshua, "Make flint knives and circumcise the Israelites again." [3]So Joshua made flint knives and circumcised the Israelites at Gibeath Haaraloth.[b]

[4]Now this is why he did so: All those who came out of Egypt—all the men of military age—died in the desert on the way after leaving Egypt. [5]All the people that came out had been circumcised, but all the people born in the desert during the journey from Egypt had not. [6]The Israelites had moved about in the desert forty years until all the men who were of military age when they left Egypt had died, since they had not obeyed the LORD. For the LORD had sworn to them that they would not see the land that he had solemnly promised their fathers to give us, a land flowing with milk and honey. [7]So he raised up their sons in their place, and these were the ones Joshua circumcised. They were still uncircumcised because they had not been circumcised on the way. [8]And after the whole nation had been circumcised, they remained where they were in camp until they were healed.

[9]Then the LORD said to Joshua, "Today I have rolled away the reproach of Egypt from you." So the place has been called Gilgal[c] to this day.

安營。[20]他們從約旦河中取來的那十二塊石頭,約書亞就立在吉甲。[21]對以色列人説:"日後你們的子孫問他們的父親説:'這些石頭是甚麼意思?'[22]你們就告訴他們説:'以色列人曾走乾地過這約旦河。'[23]因為耶和華你們的神在你們前面使約旦河的水乾了,等着你們過來,就如耶和華你們的神從前在我們前面使紅海乾了,等着我們過來一樣,[24]要使地上萬民都知道,耶和華的手大有能力,也要使你們永遠敬畏耶和華你們的神。"

在吉甲行割禮

5 約旦河西亞摩利人的諸王和靠海迦南人的諸王,聽見耶和華在以色列人前面使約旦河的水乾了,等到我們過去,他們的心因以色列人的緣故就消化了,不再有膽氣。

[2]那時,耶和華吩咐約書亞説:"你製造火石刀,第二次給以色列人行割禮。"[3]約書亞就製造了火石刀,在除皮山那裏給以色列人行割禮。

[4]約書亞行割禮的緣故,是因為從埃及出來的眾民,就是一切能打仗的男丁,出了埃及以後,都死在曠野的路上。[5]因為出來的眾民都受過割禮,惟獨出埃及以後,在曠野的路上所生的眾民,都沒有受過割禮。[6]以色列人在曠野走了四十年,等到國民,就是出埃及的兵丁,都消滅了,因為他們沒有聽從耶和華的話。耶和華曾向他們起誓,必不容他們看見耶和華向他們列祖起誓應許賜給我們的地,就是流奶與蜜之地。[7]他們的子孫,就是耶和華所興起來接續他們的,都沒有受過割禮;因為在路上沒有給他們行割禮,約書亞這才給他們行了。[8]國民都受完了割禮,就住在營中自己的地方,等到痊愈了。

[9]耶和華對約書亞説:"我今日將埃及的羞辱從你們身上滾去了。"因此,那地方名叫吉甲(註:"吉甲"就是"滾"的意思),直到今日。

---

a 23 Hebrew *Yam Suph*; that is, Sea of Reeds   b 3 *Gibeath Haaraloth* means *hill of foreskins.*   c 9 *Gilgal* sounds like the Hebrew for *roll.*

10以色列人在吉甲安營。正月十四日晚上，在耶利哥的平原守逾越節。11逾越節的次日，他們就吃了那地的出產；正當那日，吃無酵餅和烘的穀。12他們吃了那地的出產，第二日嗎哪就止住了，以色列人也不再有嗎哪了。那一年，他們卻吃迦南地的出產。

耶利哥城塌陷

13約書亞靠近耶利哥的時候，舉目觀看，不料，有一個人手裏有拔出來的刀，對面站立。約書亞到他那裏，問他說："你是幫助我們呢？是幫助我們敵人呢？"

14他回答說："不是的，我來是要作耶和華軍隊的元帥。"約書亞就俯伏在地下拜，說："我主有甚麼話吩咐僕人？"

15耶和華軍隊的元帥對約書亞說："把你腳上的鞋脫下來，因為你所站的地方是聖的。"約書亞就照着行了。

6 耶利哥的城門因以色列人就關得嚴緊，無人出入。

2耶和華曉諭約書亞說："看哪，我已經把耶利哥和耶利哥的王，並大能的勇士，都交在你手中。3你們的一切兵丁要圍繞這城，一日圍繞一次，六日都要這樣行。4七個祭司要拿七個羊角走在約櫃前。到第七日，你們要繞城七次，祭司也要吹角。5他們吹的角聲拖長，你們聽見角聲，眾百姓要大聲呼喊，城牆就必塌陷，各人都要往前直上。"

6嫩的兒子約書亞召了祭司來，吩咐他們說："你們抬起約櫃來，要有七個祭司拿七個羊角走在耶和華的約櫃前。"7又對百姓說："你們前去繞城，帶兵器的要走在耶和華的約櫃前。"

8約書亞對百姓說完了話，七個祭司拿七個羊角走在耶和華的約櫃前吹角，耶和華的約櫃在他們後面跟隨。9帶兵器的走在吹角的祭司前面，後隊隨着約櫃行。祭司一面走一面吹。10約書亞吩咐百姓說："你

10On the evening of the fourteenth day of the month, while camped at Gilgal on the plains of Jericho, the Israelites celebrated the Passover. 11The day after the Passover, that very day, they ate some of the produce of the land: unleavened bread and roasted grain. 12The manna stopped the day after*a* they ate this food from the land; there was no longer any manna for the Israelites, but that year they ate of the produce of Canaan.

The Fall of Jericho

13Now when Joshua was near Jericho, he looked up and saw a man standing in front of him with a drawn sword in his hand. Joshua went up to him and asked, "Are you for us or for our enemies?"

14"Neither," he replied, "but as commander of the army of the LORD I have now come." Then Joshua fell facedown to the ground in reverence, and asked him, "What message does my Lord*b* have for his servant?"

15The commander of the LORD's army replied, "Take off your sandals, for the place where you are standing is holy." And Joshua did so.

6 Now Jericho was tightly shut up because of the Israelites. No one went out and no one came in.

2Then the LORD said to Joshua, "See, I have delivered Jericho into your hands, along with its king and its fighting men. 3March around the city once with all the armed men. Do this for six days. 4Have seven priests carry trumpets of rams' horns in front of the ark. On the seventh day, march around the city seven times, with the priests blowing the trumpets. 5When you hear them sound a long blast on the trumpets, have all the people give a loud shout; then the wall of the city will collapse and the people will go up, every man straight in."

6So Joshua son of Nun called the priests and said to them, "Take up the ark of the covenant of the LORD and have seven priests carry trumpets in front of it." 7And he ordered the people, "Advance! March around the city, with the armed guard going ahead of the ark of the LORD."

8When Joshua had spoken to the people, the seven priests carrying the seven trumpets before the LORD went forward, blowing their trumpets, and the ark of the LORD's covenant followed them. 9The armed guard marched ahead of the priests who blew the trumpets, and the rear guard followed the ark. All this time the trumpets were sounding. 10But Joshua had com-

a 12 Or the day　　b 14 Or lord

manded the people, "Do not give a war cry, do not raise your voices, do not say a word until the day I tell you to shout. Then shout!" [11]So he had the ark of the LORD carried around the city, circling it once. Then the people returned to camp and spent the night there.

[12]Joshua got up early the next morning and the priests took up the ark of the LORD. [13]The seven priests carrying the seven trumpets went forward, marching before the ark of the LORD and blowing the trumpets. The armed men went ahead of them and the rear guard followed the ark of the LORD, while the trumpets kept sounding. [14]So on the second day they marched around the city once and returned to the camp. They did this for six days.

[15]On the seventh day, they got up at daybreak and marched around the city seven times in the same manner, except that on that day they circled the city seven times. [16]The seventh time around, when the priests sounded the trumpet blast, Joshua commanded the people, "Shout! For the LORD has given you the city! [17]The city and all that is in it are to be devoted[a] to the LORD. Only Rahab the prostitute[b] and all who are with her in her house shall be spared, because she hid the spies we sent. [18]But keep away from the devoted things, so that you will not bring about your own destruction by taking any of them. Otherwise you will make the camp of Israel liable to destruction and bring trouble on it. [19]All the silver and gold and the articles of bronze and iron are sacred to the LORD and must go into his treasury."

[20]When the trumpets sounded, the people shouted, and at the sound of the trumpet, when the people gave a loud shout, the wall collapsed; so every man charged straight in, and they took the city. [21]They devoted the city to the LORD and destroyed with the sword every living thing in it—men and women, young and old, cattle, sheep and donkeys.

[22]Joshua said to the two men who had spied out the land, "Go into the prostitute's house and bring her out and all who belong to her, in accordance with your oath to her." [23]So the young men who had done the spying went in and brought out Rahab, her father and mother and brothers and all who belonged to her. They brought out her entire family and put them in a place outside the camp of Israel.

a 17 The Hebrew term refers to the irrevocable giving over of things or persons to the LORD, often by totally destroying them; also in verses 18 and 21. *b 17* Or possibly *innkeeper*; also in verses 22 and 25

們不可呼喊,不可出聲,連一句話也不可出你們的口,等到我吩咐你們呼喊的日子,那時才可以呼喊。"[11]這樣,他使耶和華的約櫃繞城,把城繞了一次,眾人回到營裏,就在營裏住宿。

[12]約書亞清早起來,祭司又抬起耶和華的約櫃。[13]七個祭司拿七個羊角,在耶和華的約櫃前,時常行走吹角,帶兵器的在他們前面走,後隊隨着耶和華的約櫃行。祭司一面走一面吹。[14]第二日,眾人把城繞了一次,就回營裏去。六日都是這樣行。

[15]第七日清早,黎明的時候,他們起來,照樣繞城七次;惟獨這日把城繞了七次。[16]到了第七次,祭司吹角的時候,約書亞吩咐百姓說:"呼喊吧!因為耶和華已經把城交給你們了![17]這城和其中所有的都要在耶和華面前毀滅;只有妓女喇合與她家中所有的可以存活,因為她隱藏了我們所打發的使者。[18]至於你們,務要謹慎,不可取那當滅的物,恐怕你們取了那當滅的物,就連累以色列的全營,使全營受咒詛。[19]惟有金子、銀子和銅鐵的器皿都要歸耶和華為聖,必入耶和華的庫中。"

[20]於是百姓呼喊,祭司也吹角。百姓聽見角聲,便大聲呼喊,城牆就塌陷,百姓便上去進城,各人往前直上,將城奪取。[21]又將城中所有的,不拘男女老少、牛羊和驢,都用刀殺盡。

[22]約書亞吩咐窺探地的兩個人說:"你們進那妓女的家,照着你們向她所起的誓,將那女人和她所有的都從那裏帶出來。"[23]當探子的兩個少年人就進去,將喇合與她的父母、弟兄和她所有的,並她一切的親眷,都帶出來,安置在以色列的營外。

24眾人就用火將城和其中所有的焚燒了。惟有金子、銀子和銅鐵的器皿，都放在耶和華殿的庫中。25約書亞卻把妓女喇合與她父家，並她所有的，都救活了，因為她隱藏了約書亞所打發窺探耶利哥的使者，她就住在以色列中，直到今日。

26當時約書亞叫眾人起誓說："有興起重修這耶利哥城的人，當在耶和華面前受咒詛：

"他立根基的時候，
　　必喪長子；
安門的時候，
　　必喪幼子。"

27耶和華與約書亞同在，約書亞的聲名傳揚遍地。

亞干犯罪

7 以色列人在當滅的物上犯了罪，因為猶大支派中，謝拉的曾孫、撒底的孫子、迦米的兒子亞干取了當滅的物，耶和華的怒氣就向以色列人發作。

2當下，約書亞從耶利哥打發人往伯特利東邊靠近伯亞文的艾城去，吩咐他們說："你們上去窺探那地。"他們就上去窺探艾城。

3他們回到約書亞那裏，對他說："眾民不必都上去，只要二三千人上去，就能攻取艾城；不必勞累眾民都去，因為那裏的人少。"

4於是民中約有三千人上那裏去，竟在艾城人面前逃跑了。5艾城的人擊殺了他們三十六人，從城門前追趕他們，直到示巴琳，在下坡殺敗他們。眾民的心就消化如水。

6約書亞便撕裂衣服，他和以色列的長老把灰撒在頭上，在耶和華的約櫃前，俯伏在地，直到晚上。7約書亞說："哀哉！主耶和華啊，你為甚麼領這百姓過約旦河，將我們交在亞摩利人的手中，使我們滅亡呢？我們不如住在約旦河那邊倒好。8主啊，以色列人既在仇敵面

24Then they burned the whole city and everything in it, but they put the silver and gold and the articles of bronze and iron into the treasury of the LORD's house. 25But Joshua spared Rahab the prostitute, with her family and all who belonged to her, because she hid the men Joshua had sent as spies to Jericho — and she lives among the Israelites to this day.

26At that time Joshua pronounced this solemn oath: "Cursed before the LORD is the man who undertakes to rebuild this city, Jericho:

"At the cost of his firstborn son
　　will he lay its foundations;
at the cost of his youngest
　　will he set up its gates."

27So the LORD was with Joshua, and his fame spread throughout the land.

Achan's Sin

7 But the Israelites acted unfaithfully in regard to the devoted things[a]; Achan son of Carmi, the son of Zimri,[b] the son of Zerah, of the tribe of Judah, took some of them. So the LORD's anger burned against Israel.

2Now Joshua sent men from Jericho to Ai, which is near Beth Aven to the east of Bethel, and told them, "Go up and spy out the region." So the men went up and spied out Ai.

3When they returned to Joshua, they said, "Not all the people will have to go up against Ai. Send two or three thousand men to take it and do not weary all the people, for only a few men are there." 4So about three thousand men went up; but they were routed by the men of Ai, 5who killed about thirty-six of them. They chased the Israelites from the city gate as far as the stone quarries[c] and struck them down on the slopes. At this the hearts of the people melted and became like water.

6Then Joshua tore his clothes and fell face-down to the ground before the ark of the LORD, remaining there till evening. The elders of Israel did the same, and sprinkled dust on their heads. 7And Joshua said, "Ah, Sovereign LORD, why did you ever bring this people across the Jordan to deliver us into the hands of the Amorites to destroy us? If only we had been content to stay on the other side of the Jordan! 8O Lord, what

---

a 1 The Hebrew term refers to the irrevocable giving over of things or persons to the LORD, often by totally destroying them; also in verses 11, 12, 13 and 15.　b 1 See Septuagint and 1 Chron. 2:6; Hebrew Zabdi; also in verses 17 and 18.
c 5 Or as far as Shebarim

can I say, now that Israel has been routed by its enemies? [9]The Canaanites and the other people of the country will hear about this and they will surround us and wipe out our name from the earth. What then will you do for your own great name?"

[10]The LORD said to Joshua, "Stand up! What are you doing down on your face? [11]Israel has sinned; they have violated my covenant, which I commanded them to keep. They have taken some of the devoted things; they have stolen, they have lied, they have put them with their own possessions. [12]That is why the Israelites cannot stand against their enemies; they turn their backs and run because they have been made liable to destruction. I will not be with you anymore unless you destroy whatever among you is devoted to destruction.

[13]"Go, consecrate the people. Tell them, 'Consecrate yourselves in preparation for tomorrow; for this is what the LORD, the God of Israel, says: That which is devoted is among you, O Israel. You cannot stand against your enemies until you remove it.

[14]" 'In the morning, present yourselves tribe by tribe. The tribe that the LORD takes shall come forward clan by clan; the clan that the LORD takes shall come forward family by family; and the family that the LORD takes shall come forward man by man. [15]He who is caught with the devoted things shall be destroyed by fire, along with all that belongs to him. He has violated the covenant of the LORD and has done a disgraceful thing in Israel!' "

[16]Early the next morning Joshua had Israel come forward by tribes, and Judah was taken. [17]The clans of Judah came forward, and he took the Zerahites. He had the clan of the Zerahites come forward by families, and Zimri was taken. [18]Joshua had his family come forward man by man, and Achan son of Carmi, the son of Zimri, the son of Zerah, of the tribe of Judah, was taken.

[19]Then Joshua said to Achan, "My son, give glory to the LORD,[a] the God of Israel, and give him the praise.[b] Tell me what you have done; do not hide it from me."

[20]Achan replied, "It is true! I have sinned against the LORD, the God of Israel. This is what I have done: [21]When I saw in the plunder a beautiful robe from Babylonia,[c] two hundred shekels[d] of silver and a wedge of gold weighing

---

前轉背逃跑，我還有甚麼可說的呢？[9]迦南人和這地一切的居民聽見了，就必圍困我們，將我們的名從地上除滅。那時你為你的大名要怎樣行呢？"

[10]耶和華吩咐約書亞說："起來！你為何這樣俯伏在地呢？[11]以色列人犯了罪，違背了我所吩咐他們的約，取了當滅的物，又偷竊，又行詭詐，又把那當滅的放在他們的家具裏。[12]因此，以色列人在仇敵面前站立不住。他們在仇敵面前轉背逃跑，是因成了被咒詛的，你們若不把當滅的物從你們中間除掉，我就不再與你們同在了。

[13]"你起來，叫百姓自潔，對他們說：'你們要自潔，預備明天，因為耶和華以色列的神這樣說：以色列啊，你們中間有當滅的物。你們若不除掉，在仇敵面前必站立不住。

[14]" '到了早晨，你們要按着支派近前來；耶和華所取的支派，要按着宗族近前來；耶和華所取的宗族，要按着家室近前來；耶和華所取的家室，要按着人丁，一個一個地近前來。[15]被取的人，有當滅的物在他那裏，他和他所有的必被火焚燒，因他違背了耶和華的約，又因他在以色列中行了愚妄的事。' "

[16]於是約書亞清早起來，使以色列人按着支派近前來，取出來的是猶大支派；[17]使猶大支派（註：原文作"宗族"）近前來，就取了謝拉的宗族；使謝拉的宗族，按着家室人丁，一個一個地近前來，取出來的是撒底；[18]使撒底的家室，按着人丁，一個一個地近前來，就取出猶大支派的人謝拉的曾孫、撒底的孫子、迦米的兒子亞干。

[19]約書亞對亞干說："我兒，我勸你將榮耀歸給耶和華以色列的神，在他面前認罪，將你所做的事告訴我，不要向我隱瞞。"

[20]亞干回答約書亞說："我實在得罪了耶和華以色列的神。我所做的事如此如此；[21]我在所奪的財物中，看見一件美好的示拿衣服、二百舍客勒銀子、一條金子重五十舍客勒，

---

a 19 A solemn charge to tell the truth　　*b 19* Or *and confess to him*　　*c 21* Hebrew *Shinar*　　*d 21* That is, about 5 pounds (about 2.3 kilograms)

我就貪愛這些物件，便拿去了。現今藏在我帳棚內的地裏，銀子在衣服底下。」

²²約書亞就打發人跑到亞干的帳棚裏。那件衣服果然藏在他帳棚內，銀子在底下。²³他們就從帳棚裏取出來，拿到約書亞和以色列眾人那裏，放在耶和華面前。

²⁴約書亞和以色列眾人把謝拉的曾孫亞干和那銀子、那件衣服、那條金子，並亞干的兒女、牛、驢、羊、帳棚，以及他所有的，都帶到亞割谷去。²⁵約書亞說：「你為甚麼連累我們呢？今日耶和華必叫你受連累。」

於是以色列眾人用石頭打死他，將石頭扔在其上，又用火焚燒他所有的（註：「他所有的」原文作「他們」）。²⁶眾人在亞干身上堆起一大堆石頭，直存到今日。於是耶和華轉意，不發他的烈怒。因此那地方名叫亞割谷（註：「亞割」就是「連累」的意思），直到今日。

艾城被毀

8 耶和華對約書亞說：「不要懼怕，也不要驚惶。你起來率領一切兵丁上艾城去，我已經把艾城的王和他的民、他的城並他的地，都交在你手裏。²你怎樣待耶利哥和耶利哥的王，也當照樣待艾城和艾城的王。只是城內所奪的財物和牲畜，你們可以取為自己的掠物。你要在城後設下伏兵。」

³於是，約書亞和一切兵丁都起來，要上艾城去。約書亞選了三萬大能的勇士，夜間打發他們前往，⁴吩咐他們說：「你們要在城後埋伏，不可離城太遠，都要各自準備。⁵我與我所帶領的眾民要向城前往。城裏的人像初次出來攻擊我們的時候，我們就在他們面前逃跑。⁶他們必出來追趕我們，直到我們引誘他們離開城，因為他們必說：『這些人像初次在我們面前逃跑。』所以我們要在他們面前逃跑，⁷你們就從埋伏的地方起來，奪取那城，因為耶和華你們的神必把城交在你們手裏。⁸你們奪了城以後，就放火燒城，要照耶和華的話行。這是我吩咐你們的。」

⁹約書亞打發他們前往，他們就上埋伏的地方去，住在伯特利和艾

fifty shekels,^a I coveted them and took them. They are hidden in the ground inside my tent, with the silver underneath."

²²So Joshua sent messengers, and they ran to the tent, and there it was, hidden in his tent, with the silver underneath. ²³They took the things from the tent, brought them to Joshua and all the Israelites and spread them out before the LORD.

²⁴Then Joshua, together with all Israel, took Achan son of Zerah, the silver, the robe, the gold wedge, his sons and daughters, his cattle, donkeys and sheep, his tent and all that he had, to the Valley of Achor. ²⁵Joshua said, "Why have you brought this trouble on us? The LORD will bring trouble on you today."

Then all Israel stoned him, and after they had stoned the rest, they burned them. ²⁶Over Achan they heaped up a large pile of rocks, which remains to this day. Then the LORD turned from his fierce anger. Therefore that place has been called the Valley of Achor^b ever since.

Ai Destroyed

8 Then the LORD said to Joshua, "Do not be afraid; do not be discouraged. Take the whole army with you, and go up and attack Ai. For I have delivered into your hands the king of Ai, his people, his city and his land. ²You shall do to Ai and its king as you did to Jericho and its king, except that you may carry off their plunder and livestock for yourselves. Set an ambush behind the city."

³So Joshua and the whole army moved out to attack Ai. He chose thirty thousand of his best fighting men and sent them out at night ⁴with these orders: "Listen carefully. You are to set an ambush behind the city. Don't go very far from it. All of you be on the alert. ⁵I and all those with me will advance on the city, and when the men come out against us, as they did before, we will flee from them. ⁶They will pursue us until we have lured them away from the city, for they will say, 'They are running away from us as they did before.' So when we flee from them, ⁷you are to rise up from ambush and take the city. The LORD your God will give it into your hand. ⁸When you have taken the city, set it on fire. Do what the LORD has commanded. See to it; you have my orders."

⁹Then Joshua sent them off, and they went to the place of ambush and lay in wait between

^a 21 That is, about 1 1/4 pounds (about 0.6 kilogram)
^b 26 Achor means trouble.

Bethel and Ai, to the west of Ai—but Joshua spent that night with the people.

¹⁰Early the next morning Joshua mustered his men, and he and the leaders of Israel marched before them to Ai. ¹¹The entire force that was with him marched up and approached the city and arrived in front of it. They set up camp north of Ai, with the valley between them and the city. ¹²Joshua had taken about five thousand men and set them in ambush between Bethel and Ai, to the west of the city. ¹³They had the soldiers take up their positions—all those in the camp to the north of the city and the ambush to the west of it. That night Joshua went into the valley.

¹⁴When the king of Ai saw this, he and all the men of the city hurried out early in the morning to meet Israel in battle at a certain place overlooking the Arabah. But he did not know that an ambush had been set against him behind the city. ¹⁵Joshua and all Israel let themselves be driven back before them, and they fled toward the desert. ¹⁶All the men of Ai were called to pursue them, and they pursued Joshua and were lured away from the city. ¹⁷Not a man remained in Ai or Bethel who did not go after Israel. They left the city open and went in pursuit of Israel.

¹⁸Then the LORD said to Joshua, "Hold out toward Ai the javelin that is in your hand, for into your hand I will deliver the city." So Joshua held out his javelin toward Ai. ¹⁹As soon as he did this, the men in the ambush rose quickly from their position and rushed forward. They entered the city and captured it and quickly set it on fire.

²⁰The men of Ai looked back and saw the smoke of the city rising against the sky, but they had no chance to escape in any direction, for the Israelites who had been fleeing toward the desert had turned back against their pursuers. ²¹For when Joshua and all Israel saw that the ambush had taken the city and that smoke was going up from the city, they turned around and attacked the men of Ai. ²²The men of the ambush also came out of the city against them, so that they were caught in the middle, with Israelites on both sides. Israel cut them down, leaving them neither survivors nor fugitives. ²³But they took the king of Ai alive and brought him to Joshua.

²⁴When Israel had finished killing all the men of Ai in the fields and in the desert where they had chased them, and when every one of them had been put to the sword, all the Israelites returned to Ai and killed those who were in it. ²⁵Twelve thousand men and women fell that day—all the people of Ai. ²⁶For Joshua did not

城的中間，就是在艾城的西邊。這夜約書亞卻在民中住宿。

¹⁰約書亞清早起來，點齊百姓，他和以色列的長老在百姓前面上艾城去。¹¹眾民，就是他所帶領的兵丁，都上去向前直往，來到城前，在艾城北邊安營。在約書亞和艾城中間有一山谷。¹²他挑了約有五千人，使他們埋伏在伯特利和艾城的中間，就是在艾城的西邊。¹³於是安置了百姓，就是城北的全軍和城西的伏兵。這夜約書亞進入山谷之中。

¹⁴艾城的王看見這景況，就和全城的人，清早急忙起來，按所定的時候，出到亞拉巴前，要與以色列人交戰，王卻不知道在城後有伏兵。¹⁵約書亞和以色列眾人在他們面前裝敗，往那通曠野的路逃跑。¹⁶城內的眾民都被招聚，追趕他們。艾城人追趕的時候，就被引誘離開城。¹⁷艾城和伯特利城沒有一人不出來追趕以色列人的，撇了敞開的城門，去追趕以色列人。

¹⁸耶和華吩咐約書亞說："你向艾城伸出手裏的短槍，因為我要將城交在你手裏。"約書亞就向城伸出手裏的短槍。¹⁹他一伸手，伏兵就從埋伏的地方急忙起來，奪了城，跑進城去，放火焚燒。

²⁰艾城的人回頭一看，不料，城中煙氣沖天，他們就無力向左向右逃跑。那往曠野逃跑的百姓，便轉身攻擊追趕他們的人。²¹約書亞和以色列眾人見伏兵已經奪了城，城中煙氣飛騰，就轉身回去，擊殺艾城的人。²²伏兵也出城迎擊艾城人，艾城人就困在以色列人中間，前後都是以色列人。於是以色列人擊殺他們，沒有留下一個，也沒有一個逃脫的。²³生擒了艾城的王，將他解到約書亞那裏。

²⁴以色列人在田間和曠野，殺盡所追趕一切艾城的居民。艾城人倒在刀下，直到滅盡，以色列眾人就回到艾城，用刀殺了城中的人。²⁵當日殺斃的人，連男帶女共有一萬二千，就是艾城所有的人。²⁶約書亞沒有收回

手裏所伸出來的短槍，直到把艾城的一切居民盡行殺滅。27惟獨城中的牲畜和財物，以色列人都取為自己的掠物，是照耶和華所吩咐約書亞的話。

28約書亞將艾城焚燒，使城永為高堆、荒場，直到今日；29又將艾城王掛在樹上，直到晚上。日落的時候，約書亞吩咐人把屍首從樹上取下來，丟在城門口。在屍首上堆成一大堆石頭，直存到今日。

在以巴路山上重申聖約

30那時，約書亞在以巴路山上為耶和華以色列的神築一座壇，31是用沒有動過鐵器的整石頭築的，照着耶和華僕人摩西所吩咐以色列人的話，正如摩西律法書上所寫的。眾人在這壇上給耶和華奉獻燔祭和平安祭。32約書亞在那裏，當着以色列人面前，將摩西所寫的律法抄寫在石頭上。33以色列眾人，無論是本地人，是寄居的，和長老、官長，並審判官，都站在約櫃兩旁，在抬耶和華約櫃的祭司利未人面前，一半對着基利心山，一半對着以巴路山，為以色列民祝福，正如耶和華僕人摩西先前所吩咐的。

34隨後約書亞將律法上祝福、咒詛的話，照着律法書上一切所寫的，都宣讀了一遍。35摩西所吩咐的一切話，約書亞在以色列全會眾和婦女、孩子，並他們中間寄居的外人面前，沒有一句不宣讀的。

基遍人的欺詐

9 約旦河西，住山地、高原，並對着黎巴嫩山沿大海一帶的諸王，就是赫人、亞摩利人、迦南人、比利洗人、希未人、耶布斯人的諸王，2就都聚集，同心合意地要與約書亞和以色列人爭戰。

draw back the hand that held out his javelin until he had destroyed[a] all who lived in Ai. 27But Israel did carry off for themselves the livestock and plunder of this city, as the LORD had instructed Joshua.

28So Joshua burned Ai and made it a permanent heap of ruins, a desolate place to this day. 29He hung the king of Ai on a tree and left him there until evening. At sunset, Joshua ordered them to take his body from the tree and throw it down at the entrance of the city gate. And they raised a large pile of rocks over it, which remains to this day.

The Covenant Renewed at Mount Ebal

30Then Joshua built on Mount Ebal an altar to the LORD, the God of Israel, 31as Moses the servant of the LORD had commanded the Israelites. He built it according to what is written in the Book of the Law of Moses—an altar of uncut stones, on which no iron tool had been used. On it they offered to the LORD burnt offerings and sacrificed fellowship offerings.[b] 32There, in the presence of the Israelites, Joshua copied on stones the law of Moses, which he had written. 33All Israel, aliens and citizens alike, with their elders, officials and judges, were standing on both sides of the ark of the covenant of the LORD, facing those who carried it—the priests, who were Levites. Half of the people stood in front of Mount Gerizim and half of them in front of Mount Ebal, as Moses the servant of the LORD had formerly commanded when he gave instructions to bless the people of Israel.

34Afterward, Joshua read all the words of the law—the blessings and the curses—just as it is written in the Book of the Law. 35There was not a word of all that Moses had commanded that Joshua did not read to the whole assembly of Israel, including the women and children, and the aliens who lived among them.

The Gibeonite Deception

9 Now when all the kings west of the Jordan heard about these things—those in the hill country, in the western foothills, and along the entire coast of the Great Sea[c] as far as Lebanon (the kings of the Hittites, Amorites, Canaanites, Perizzites, Hivites and Jebusites)— 2they came together to make war against Joshua and Israel.

---

a 26 The Hebrew term refers to the irrevocable giving over of things or persons to the LORD, often by totally destroying them.　*b 31* Traditionally *peace offerings*　*c 1* That is, the Mediterranean

³However, when the people of Gibeon heard what Joshua had done to Jericho and Ai, ⁴they resorted to a ruse: They went as a delegation whose donkeys were loaded*ᵃ* with worn-out sacks and old wineskins, cracked and mended. ⁵The men put worn and patched sandals on their feet and wore old clothes. All the bread of their food supply was dry and moldy. ⁶Then they went to Joshua in the camp at Gilgal and said to him and the men of Israel, "We have come from a distant country; make a treaty with us."

⁷The men of Israel said to the Hivites, "But perhaps you live near us. How then can we make a treaty with you?"

⁸"We are your servants," they said to Joshua.

But Joshua asked, "Who are you and where do you come from?"

⁹They answered: "Your servants have come from a very distant country because of the fame of the LORD your God. For we have heard reports of him: all that he did in Egypt, ¹⁰and all that he did to the two kings of the Amorites east of the Jordan—Sihon king of Heshbon, and Og king of Bashan, who reigned in Ashtaroth. ¹¹And our elders and all those living in our country said to us, 'Take provisions for your journey; go and meet them and say to them, "We are your servants; make a treaty with us." ' ¹²This bread of ours was warm when we packed it at home on the day we left to come to you. But now see how dry and moldy it is. ¹³And these wineskins that we filled were new, but see how cracked they are. And our clothes and sandals are worn out by the very long journey."

¹⁴The men of Israel sampled their provisions but did not inquire of the LORD. ¹⁵Then Joshua made a treaty of peace with them to let them live, and the leaders of the assembly ratified it by oath.

¹⁶Three days after they made the treaty with the Gibeonites, the Israelites heard that they were neighbors, livin near them. ¹⁷So the Israelites set out and on the third day came to their cities: Gibeon, Kephirah, Beeroth and Kiriath Jearim. ¹⁸But the Israelites did not attack them, because the leaders of the assembly had sworn an oath to them by the LORD, the God of Israel. The whole assembly grumbled against the leaders, ¹⁹but all the leaders answered, "We have given them our oath by the LORD, the God of Israel, and we cannot touch them now. ²⁰This

a 4 Most Hebrew manuscripts; some Hebrew manuscripts, Vulgate and Syriac (see also Septuagint) *They prepared provisions and loaded their donkeys*

³基遍的居民聽見約書亞向耶利哥和艾城所行的事，⁴就設詭計，假充使者，拿舊口袋和破裂縫補的舊皮酒袋馱在驢上；⁵將補過的舊鞋穿在腳上，把舊衣服穿在身上。他們所帶的餅都是乾的，長了霉了。⁶他們到吉甲營中見約書亞，對他和以色列人說："我們是從遠方來的，現在求你與我們立約。"

⁷以色列人對這些希未人說："只怕你們是住在我們中間的，若是這樣，怎能和你們立約呢？"

⁸他們對約書亞說："我們是你的僕人。"

約書亞問他們說："你們是甚麼人？是從哪裏來的？"

⁹他們回答說："僕人從極遠之地而來，是因聽見耶和華你神的名聲和他在埃及所行的一切事，¹⁰並他向約旦河東的兩個亞摩利王，就是希實本王西宏和在亞斯他錄的巴珊王噩一切所行的事。¹¹我們的長老和我們那地的一切居民對我們說：'你們手裏要帶着路上用的食物，去迎接以色列人，對他們說：我們是你們的僕人，現在求你們與我們立約。'¹²我們出來要往你們這裏來的日子，從家裏帶出來的這餅還是熱的；看哪，現在都乾了，長了霉了。¹³這皮酒袋，我們盛酒的時候還是新的；看哪，現在已經破裂。我們這衣服和鞋，因為道路甚遠，也都穿舊了。"

¹⁴以色列人受了他們些食物，並沒有求問耶和華。¹⁵於是約書亞與他們講和，與他們立約，容他們活着，會眾的首領也向他們起誓。

¹⁶以色列人與他們立約之後，過了三天，才聽見他們是近鄰，住在以色列人中間的。¹⁷以色列人起行，第三天到了他們的城邑，就是基遍、基非拉、比錄、基列耶琳。¹⁸因為會眾的首領已經指着耶和華以色列的神向他們起誓，所以以色列人不擊殺他們。

全會眾就向首領發怨言。¹⁹眾首領對全會眾說："我們已經指着耶和華以色列的神向他們起誓，現在我們不能害他們。²⁰我們要如此待他們，容他們活着，免得有忿怒因我們所起的誓臨到我們身上。」²¹首領又對會眾說：「要容他們活着。」於是他們為全會眾作了劈柴挑水的人，正如首領對他們所說的話。

²²約書亞召了他們來，對他們說：「為甚麼欺哄我們說『我們離你們甚遠』呢？其實你們是住在我們中間。²³現在你們是被咒詛的！你們中間的人必斷不了作奴僕，為我神的殿作劈柴挑水的人。」

²⁴他們回答約書亞說：「因為有人實在告訴你的僕人，耶和華你的神曾吩咐他的僕人摩西，把這全地賜給你們，並在你們面前滅絕這地的一切居民；所以我們為你們的緣故甚怕喪命，就行了這事。²⁵現在我們在你手中，你以怎樣待我們為善為正，就怎樣做吧！」

²⁶於是約書亞這樣待他們，救他們脫離以色列人的手，以色列人就沒有殺他們。²⁷當日約書亞使他們在耶和華所要選擇的地方，為會眾和耶和華的壇作劈柴挑水的人，直到今日。

日頭停住

10 耶路撒冷王亞多尼洗德聽見約書亞奪了艾城，盡行毀滅，怎樣待耶利哥和耶利哥的王，也照樣待艾城和艾城的王。又聽見基遍的居民與以色列人立了和約，住在他們中間，²就甚懼怕，因為基遍是一座大城，如都城一般，比艾城更大，並且城內的人都是勇士。³所以耶路撒冷王亞多尼洗德打發人去見希伯崙王何咸、耶末王毘蘭、拉吉王雅非亞和伊磯倫王底璧，說：⁴「求你們上來幫助我，我們好攻打基遍，因為他們與約書亞和以色列人立了和約。」

⁵於是五個亞摩利王，就是耶路撒冷王、希伯崙王、耶末王、拉吉王、伊磯倫王，大家聚集，率領他們的眾軍上去，對着基遍安營，攻打基遍。

⁶基遍人就打發人往吉甲的營中去見約書亞，說：「你不要袖手不顧你的僕人，求你速速上來拯救我

is what we will do to them: We will let them live, so that wrath will not fall on us for breaking the oath we swore to them." ²¹They continued, "Let them live, but let them be woodcutters and water carriers for the entire community." So the leaders' promise to them was kept.

²²Then Joshua summoned the Gibeonites and said, "Why did you deceive us by saying, 'We live a long way from you,' while actually you live near us? ²³You are now under a curse: You will never cease to serve as woodcutters and water carriers for the house of my God."

²⁴They answered Joshua, "Your servants were clearly told how the LORD your God had commanded his servant Moses to give you the whole land and to wipe out all its inhabitants from before you. So we feared for our lives because of you, and that is why we did this. ²⁵We are now in your hands. Do to us whatever seems good and right to you."

²⁶So Joshua saved them from the Israelites, and they did not kill them. ²⁷That day he made the Gibeonites woodcutters and water carriers for the community and for the altar of the LORD at the place the LORD would choose. And that is what they are to this day.

The Sun Stands Still

10 Now Adoni-Zedek king of Jerusalem heard that Joshua had taken Ai and totally destroyed[a] it, doing to Ai and its king as he had done to Jericho and its king, and that the people of Gibeon had made a treaty of peace with Israel and were living near them. ²He and his people were very much alarmed at this, because Gibeon was an important city, like one of the royal cities; it was larger than Ai, and all its men were good fighters. ³So Adoni-Zedek king of Jerusalem appealed to Hoham king of Hebron, Piram king of Jarmuth, Japhia king of Lachish and Debir king of Eglon. ⁴"Come up and help me attack Gibeon," he said, "because it has made peace with Joshua and the Israelites."

⁵Then the five kings of the Amorites—the kings of Jerusalem, Hebron, Jarmuth, Lachish and Eglon—joined forces. They moved up with all their troops and took up positions against Gibeon and attacked it.

⁶The Gibeonites then sent word to Joshua in the camp at Gilgal: "Do not abandon your servants. Come up to us quickly and save us! Help

---

a 1 The Hebrew term refers to the irrevocable giving over of things or persons to the LORD, often by totally destroying them; also in verses 28, 35, 37, 39 and 40.

us, because all the Amorite kings from the hill country have joined forces against us."

7So Joshua marched up from Gilgal with his entire army, including all the best fighting men. 8The LORD said to Joshua, "Do not be afraid of them; I have given them into your hand. Not one of them will be able to withstand you."

9After an all-night march from Gilgal, Joshua took them by surprise. 10The LORD threw them into confusion before Israel, who defeated them in a great victory at Gibeon. Israel pursued them along the road going up to Beth Horon and cut them down all the way to Azekah and Makkedah. 11As they fled before Israel on the road down from Beth Horon to Azekah, the LORD hurled large hailstones down on them from the sky, and more of them died from the hailstones than were killed by the swords of the Israelites.

12On the day the LORD gave the Amorites over to Israel, Joshua said to the LORD in the presence of Israel:

"O sun, stand still over Gibeon,
   O moon, over the Valley of Aijalon."
13So the sun stood still,
   and the moon stopped,
   till the nation avenged itself on[a] its enemies,

as it is written in the Book of Jashar.

The sun stopped in the middle of the sky and delayed going down about a full day. 14There has never been a day like it before or since, a day when the LORD listened to a man. Surely the LORD was fighting for Israel!

15Then Joshua returned with all Israel to the camp at Gilgal.

Five Amorite Kings Killed

16Now the five kings had fled and hidden in the cave at Makkedah. 17When Joshua was told that the five kings had been found hiding in the cave at Makkedah, 18he said, "Roll large rocks up to the mouth of the cave, and post some men there to guard it. 19But don't stop! Pursue your enemies, attack them from the rear and don't let them reach their cities, for the LORD your God has given them into your hand."

20So Joshua and the Israelites destroyed them completely—almost to a man—but the few who were left reached their fortified cities. 21The whole army then returned safely to Joshua in the camp at Makkedah, and no one uttered a word against the Israelites.

a 13 Or nation triumphed over

們，幫助我們，因為住山地亞摩利人的諸王都聚集攻擊我們。"

7於是約書亞和一切兵丁，並大能的勇士，都從吉甲上去。8耶和華對約書亞說："不要怕他們，因為我已將他們交在你手裏，他們無一人能在你面前站立得住。"

9約書亞就終夜從吉甲上去，猛然臨到他們那裏。10耶和華使他們在以色列人面前潰亂。約書亞在基遍大大地殺敗他們，追趕他們在伯和崙的上坡路，擊殺他們直到亞西加和瑪基大。11他們在以色列人面前逃跑，正在伯和崙下坡的時候，耶和華從天上降大冰雹在他們身上（註："冰雹"原文作"石頭"），直降到亞西加，打死他們。被冰雹打死的，比以色列人用刀殺死的還多。

12當耶和華將亞摩利人交付以色列人的日子，約書亞就禱告耶和華，在以色列人眼前說：

"日頭啊，你要停在基遍；
   月亮啊，你要止在亞雅崙谷。"
13於是日頭停留，
   月亮止住，
   直等國民向敵人報仇。

這事豈不是寫在雅煞珥書上嗎？

日頭在天當中停住，不急速下落，約有一日之久。14在這日以前，這日以後，耶和華聽人的禱告，沒有像這日的，是因耶和華為以色列爭戰。

15約書亞和以色列眾人回到吉甲的營中。

殺死亞摩利五王

16那五王逃跑，藏在瑪基大洞裏。17有人告訴約書亞說："那五王已經找到了，都藏在瑪基大洞裏。"18約書亞說："你們把幾塊大石頭滾到洞口，派人看守。19你們卻不可躭延，要追趕你們的仇敵，擊殺他們儘後邊的人，不容他們進自己的城邑，因為耶和華你們的神已經把他們交在你們手裏。"

20約書亞和以色列人大大殺敗他們，直到將他們滅盡，其中剩下的人都進了堅固的城。21眾百姓就安然回瑪基大營中，到約書亞那裏。沒有一人敢向以色列人饒舌。

²²約書亞說：「打開洞口，將那五王從洞裏帶出來，領到我面前。」²³眾人就這樣行，將那五王，就是耶路撒冷王、希伯崙王、耶末王、拉吉王、伊磯倫王，從洞裏帶出來，領到約書亞面前。²⁴帶出那五王到約書亞面前的時候，約書亞就召了以色列眾人來，對那些和他同去的軍長說：「你們近前來，把腳踏在這些王的頸項上。」他們就近前來，把腳踏在這些王的頸項上。

²⁵約書亞對他們說：「你們不要懼怕，也不要驚惶，應當剛強壯膽。因為耶和華必這樣待你們所要攻打的一切仇敵。」²⁶隨後約書亞將這五王殺死，掛在五棵樹上。他們就在樹上直掛到晚上。

²⁷日頭要落的時候，約書亞一吩咐，人就把屍首從樹上取下來，丟在他們藏過的洞裏，把幾塊大石頭放在洞口，直存到今日。

²⁸當日約書亞奪了瑪基大，用刀擊殺城中的人和王，將其中一切人口盡行殺滅，沒有留下一個。他待瑪基大王像從前待耶利哥王一樣。

攻取南部諸城

²⁹約書亞和以色列眾人從瑪基大往立拿去，攻打立拿。³⁰耶和華將立拿和立拿的王也交在以色列人手裏。約書亞攻打這城，用刀擊殺了城中的一切人口，沒有留下一個。他待立拿王像從前待耶利哥王一樣。

³¹約書亞和以色列眾人從立拿往拉吉去，對着拉吉安營，攻打這城。³²耶和華將拉吉交在以色列人的手裏。第二天約書亞就奪了拉吉，用刀擊殺了城中的一切人口，是照他向立拿一切所行的。³³那時基色王荷蘭上來幫助拉吉，約書亞就把他和他的民都擊殺了，沒有留下一個。

³⁴約書亞和以色列眾人從拉吉往伊磯倫去，對着伊磯倫安營，攻打這城。³⁵當日就奪了城，用刀擊殺了城中的人。那日約書亞將城中的一切人口盡行殺滅，是照他向拉吉一切所行的。

³⁶約書亞和以色列眾人從伊磯倫上希伯崙去，攻打這城，³⁷就奪了希伯崙和屬希伯崙的諸城邑，用刀將城中的人與王，並那些城邑中的人口，都擊殺了，沒有留下一個，是

²²Joshua said, "Open the mouth of the cave and bring those five kings out to me." ²³So they brought the five kings out of the cave—the kings of Jerusalem, Hebron, Jarmuth, Lachish and Eglon. ²⁴When they had brought these kings to Joshua, he summoned all the men of Israel and said to the army commanders who had come with him, "Come here and put your feet on the necks of these kings." So they came forward and placed their feet on their necks.

²⁵Joshua said to them, "Do not be afraid; do not be discouraged. Be strong and courageous. This is what the LORD will do to all the enemies you are going to fight." ²⁶Then Joshua struck and killed the kings and hung them on five trees, and they were left hanging on the trees until evening.

²⁷At sunset Joshua gave the order and they took them down from the trees and threw them into the cave where they had been hiding. At the mouth of the cave they placed large rocks, which are there to this day.

²⁸That day Joshua took Makkedah. He put the city and its king to the sword and totally destroyed everyone in it. He left no survivors. And he did to the king of Makkedah as he had done to the king of Jericho.

Southern Cities Conquered

²⁹Then Joshua and all Israel with him moved on from Makkedah to Libnah and attacked it. ³⁰The LORD also gave that city and its king into Israel's hand. The city and everyone in it Joshua put to the sword. He left no survivors there. And he did to its king as he had done to the king of Jericho.

³¹Then Joshua and all Israel with him moved on from Libnah to Lachish; he took up positions against it and attacked it. ³²The LORD handed Lachish over to Israel, and Joshua took it on the second day. The city and everyone in it he put to the sword, just as he had done to Libnah. ³³Meanwhile, Horam king of Gezer had come up to help Lachish, but Joshua defeated him and his army—until no survivors were left.

³⁴Then Joshua and all Israel with him moved on from Lachish to Eglon; they took up positions against it and attacked it. ³⁵They captured it that same day and put it to the sword and totally destroyed everyone in it, just as they had done to Lachish.

³⁶Then Joshua and all Israel with him went up from Eglon to Hebron and attacked it. ³⁷They took the city and put it to the sword, together with its king, its villages and everyone in it.

Hermon, including all the eastern side of the Arabah:

²Sihon king of the Amorites,

who reigned in Heshbon. He ruled from Aroer on the rim of the Arnon Gorge—from the middle of the gorge—to the Jabbok River, which is the border of the Ammonites. This included half of Gilead. ³He also ruled over the eastern Arabah from the Sea of Kinnereth[a] to the Sea of the Arabah (the Salt Sea[b]), to Beth Jeshimoth, and then southward below the slopes of Pisgah.

⁴And the territory of Og king of Bashan,

one of the last of the Rephaites, who reigned in Ashtaroth and Edrei. ⁵He ruled over Mount Hermon, Salecah, all of Bashan to the border of the people of Geshur and Maacah, and half of Gilead to the border of Sihon king of Heshbon.

⁶Moses, the servant of the LORD, and the Israelites conquered them. And Moses the servant of the LORD gave their land to the Reubenites, the Gadites and the half-tribe of Manasseh to be their possession.

⁷These are the kings of the land that Joshua and the Israelites conquered on the west side of the Jordan, from Baal Gad in the Valley of Lebanon to Mount Halak, which rises toward Seir (their lands Joshua gave as an inheritance to the tribes of Israel according to their tribal divisions— ⁸the hill country, the western foothills, the Arabah, the mountain slopes, the desert and the Negev—the lands of the Hittites, Amorites, Canaanites, Perizzites, Hivites and Jebusites):

⁹ the king of Jericho	one
the king of Ai (near Bethel)	one
¹⁰ the king of Jerusalem	one
the king of Hebron	one
¹¹ the king of Jarmuth	one
the king of Lachish	one
¹² the king of Eglon	one
the king of Gezer	one
¹³ the king of Debir	one
the king of Geder	one
¹⁴ the king of Hormah	one
the king of Arad	one
¹⁵ the king of Libnah	one
the king of Adullam	one
¹⁶ the king of Makkedah	one
the king of Bethel	one
¹⁷ the king of Tappuah	one

a 3 That is, Galilee   b 3 That is, the Dead Sea

山，並東邊的全亞拉巴之地。

²這二王，有住希實本、亞摩利人的王西宏。他所管之地是從嫩谷邊的亞羅珥和谷中的城，並基列一半，直到亞捫人的境界，雅博河，³與約旦河東邊的亞拉巴，直到基尼烈海，又到亞拉巴的海，就是鹽海，通伯耶西末的路以及南方，直到毘斯迦的山根。

⁴又有巴珊王噩，他是利乏音人所剩下的，住在亞斯他錄和以得來。⁵他所管之地是黑門山、撒迦、巴珊全地，直到基述人和瑪迦人的境界，並基列一半，直到希實本王西宏的境界。

⁶這二王是耶和華僕人摩西和以色列人所擊殺的，耶和華僕人摩西將他們的地賜給呂便人、迦得人和瑪拿西半支派的人為業。

⁷約書亞和以色列人在約旦河西擊殺了諸王。他們的地是從黎巴嫩平原的巴力迦得，直到上西珥的哈拉山。約書亞就將那地按着以色列支派的宗族分給他們為業，⁸就是赫人、亞摩利人、迦南人、比利洗人、希未人、耶布斯人的山地、高原亞拉巴、山坡、曠野和南地。

⁹他們的王：一個是耶利哥王，	
一個是靠近伯特利的艾城王，	
¹⁰一個是耶路撒冷王，	
一個是希伯崙王，	
¹¹一個是耶末王，	
一個是拉吉王，	
¹²一個是伊磯倫王，	
一個是基色王，	
¹³一個是底璧王，	
一個是基德王，	
¹⁴一個是何珥瑪王，	
一個是亞拉得王，	
¹⁵一個是立拿王，	
一個是亞杜蘭王，	
¹⁶一個是瑪基大王，	
一個是伯特利王，	
¹⁷一個是他普亞王，	

一個是希弗王，
18 一個是亞弗王，
一個是拉沙崙王，
19 一個是瑪頓王，
一個是夏瑣王，
20 一個是伸崙米崙王，
一個是押煞王，
21 一個是他納王，
一個是米吉多王，
22 一個是基低斯王，
一個是靠近迦密的約念王，
23 一個是多珥山岡的多珥王，
一個是吉甲的戈印王，
24 一個是得撒王。
共計三十一個王。

尚未攻取之地

13 約書亞年紀老邁，耶和華對他說："你年紀老邁了，還有許多未得之地。

2 "就是非利士人的全境和基述人的全地。3 從埃及前的西曷河往北，直到以革倫的境界，就算屬迦南人之地。有非利士人五個首領所管的迦薩人、亞實突人、亞實基倫人、迦特人、以革倫人之地，並有南方亞衛人之地。4 又有迦南人的全地，並屬西頓人的米亞拉到亞弗，直到亞摩利人的境界。5 還有迦巴勒人之地，並向日出的全黎巴嫩，就是從黑門山根的巴力迦得，直到哈馬口。

6 "山地的一切居民，從黎巴嫩直到米斯利弗瑪音，就是所有的西頓人，我必在以色列人面前趕出他們去。你只管照我所吩咐的，將這地拈鬮分給以色列人為業。7 現在你要把這地分給九個支派和瑪拿西半個支派為業。"

分約旦河東之地

8 瑪拿西那半支派和呂便、迦得二支派已經受了產業，就是耶和華的僕人摩西在約旦河東所賜給他們的。

the king of Hepher	one
18 the king of Aphek	one
the king of Lasharon	one
19 the king of Madon	one
the king of Hazor	one
20 the king of Shimron Meron	one
the king of Acshaph	one
21 the king of Taanach	one
the king of Megiddo	one
22 the king of Kedesh	one
the king of Jokneam in Carmel	one
23 the king of Dor (in Naphoth Dor*a*)	one
the king of Goyim in Gilgal	one
24 the king of Tirzah	one
thirty-one kings in all.	

Land Still to Be Taken

13 When Joshua was old and well advanced in years, the LORD said to him, "You are very old, and there are still very large areas of land to be taken over.

2"This is the land that remains: all the regions of the Philistines and Geshurites: 3from the Shihor River on the east of Egypt to the territory of Ekron on the north, all of it counted as Canaanite (the territory of the five Philistine rulers in Gaza, Ashdod, Ashkelon, Gath and Ekron—that of the Avvites); 4from the south, all the land of the Canaanites, from Arah of the Sidonians as far as Aphek, the region of the Amorites, 5the area of the Gebalites*b*; and all Lebanon to the east, from Baal Gad below Mount Hermon to Lebo*c* Hamath.

6"As for all the inhabitants of the mountain regions from Lebanon to Misrephoth Maim, that is, all the Sidonians, I myself will drive them out before the Israelites. Be sure to allocate this land to Israel for an inheritance, as I have instructed you, 7and divide it as an inheritance among the nine tribes and half of the tribe of Manasseh."

Division of the Land East of the Jordan

8The other half of Manasseh,*d* the Reubenites and the Gadites had received the inheritance that Moses had given them east of the Jordan, as he, the servant of the LORD, had assigned it to them.

a 23 Or in the heights of Dor　　*b 5 That is, the area of Byblos*
c 5 Or to the entrance to　　*d 8 Hebrew With it (that is, with the other half of Manasseh)*

9It extended from Aroer on the rim of the Arnon Gorge, and from the town in the middle of the gorge, and included the whole plateau of Medeba as far as Dibon, 10and all the towns of Sihon king of the Amorites, who ruled in Heshbon, out to the border of the Ammonites. 11It also included Gilead, the territory of the people of Geshur and Maacah, all of Mount Hermon and all Bashan as far as Salecah— 12that is, the whole kingdom of Og in Bashan, who had reigned in Ashtaroth and Edrei and had survived as one of the last of the Rephaites. Moses had defeated them and taken over their land. 13But the Israelites did not drive out the people of Geshur and Maacah, so they continue to live among the Israelites to this day.

14But to the tribe of Levi he gave no inheritance, since the offerings made by fire to the LORD, the God of Israel, are their inheritance, as he promised them.

15This is what Moses had given to the tribe of Reuben, clan by clan:

16The territory from Aroer on the rim of the Arnon Gorge, and from the town in the middle of the gorge, and the whole plateau past Medeba 17to Heshbon and all its towns on the plateau, including Dibon, Bamoth Baal, Beth Baal Meon, 18Jahaz, Kedemoth, Mephaath, 19Kiriathaim, Sibmah, Zereth Shahar on the hill in the valley, 20Beth Peor, the slopes of Pisgah, and Beth Jeshimoth 21—all the towns on the plateau and the entire realm of Sihon king of the Amorites, who ruled at Heshbon. Moses had defeated him and the Midianite chiefs, Evi, Rekem, Zur, Hur and Reba—princes allied with Sihon—who lived in that country. 22In addition to those slain in battle, the Israelites had put to the sword Balaam son of Beor, who practiced divination. 23The boundary of the Reubenites was the bank of the Jordan. These towns and their villages were the inheritance of the Reubenites, clan by clan.

24This is what Moses had given to the tribe of Gad, clan by clan:

25The territory of Jazer, all the towns of Gilead and half the Ammonite country as far as Aroer, near Rabbah; 26and from Heshbon to Ramath Mizpah and Betonim, and from

9是從亞嫩谷邊的亞羅珥和谷中的城，並米底巴的全平原，直到底本，10和在希實本作王亞摩利王西宏的諸城，直到亞捫人的境界。11又有基列地、基述人、瑪迦人的地界並黑門全山、巴珊全地，直到撒迦。12又有巴珊王噩的全國，他在亞斯他錄和以得來作王，利乏音人所存留的只剩下他。這些地的人，都是摩西所擊殺所趕逐的。13以色列人卻沒有趕逐基述人、瑪迦人，這些人仍住在以色列中，直到今日。

14只是利未支派，摩西（註：原文作"他"）沒有把產業分給他們。他們的產業乃是獻與耶和華以色列神的火祭，正如耶和華所應許他們的。

15摩西按着呂便支派的宗族分給他們產業：

16他們的境界是亞嫩谷邊的亞羅珥和谷中的城，靠近米底巴的全平原；17希實本並屬希實本平原的各城，底本、巴末巴力、伯巴力勉、18雅雜、基底莫、米法押、19基列亭、西比瑪、谷中山的細列哈沙轄、20伯昆珥、昆斯迦山坡、伯耶西末、21平原的各城，並亞摩利王西宏的全國。這西宏曾在希實本作王，摩西把他和米甸的族長以未、利金、蘇珥、戶珥、利巴擊殺了。這都是住那地屬西宏為首領的。22那時以色列人在所殺的人中，也用刀殺了比珥的兒子術士巴蘭。23呂便人的境界就是約旦河與靠近約旦河的地。以上是呂便人按着宗族所得為業的諸城，並屬城的村莊。

24摩西按着迦得支派的宗族分給他們產業：

25他們的境界是雅謝和基列的各城，並亞捫人的一半地，直到拉巴前的亞羅珥。26從希實本到拉抹米斯巴和比多寧，又從瑪哈念到底璧的境界，27並谷中的<u>伯亞蘭</u>、<u>伯寧拉</u>、<u>疏割</u>、<u>撒分</u>，就是<u>希實本王西宏</u>國中的餘地，以及<u>約旦河</u>與靠近<u>約旦河</u>的地，直到<u>基尼烈海</u>的極邊，都在<u>約旦河</u>東。28以上是<u>迦得</u>人按着宗族所得為業的諸城，並屬城的村莊。

29<u>摩西</u>把產業分給<u>瑪拿西</u>半支派，是按着<u>瑪拿西</u>半支派的宗族所分的：

30他們的境界是從<u>瑪哈念</u>起，包括<u>巴珊</u>全地，就是<u>巴珊</u>王<u>噩</u>的全國，並在<u>巴珊</u>、<u>睚珥</u>的一切城邑，共六十個。31<u>基列</u>的一半，並<u>亞斯他錄</u>、<u>以得來</u>，就是屬<u>巴珊</u>王<u>噩</u>國的二城，是按着宗族給<u>瑪拿西</u>的兒子<u>瑪吉</u>的一半子孫。

32以上是<u>摩西</u>在<u>約旦河</u>東對着<u>耶利哥</u>的<u>摩押平原</u>所分給他們的產業。33只是<u>利未</u>支派，<u>摩西</u>沒有把產業分給他們。耶和華<u>以色列</u>的神是他們的產業，正如耶和華所應許他們的。

分約旦河西之地

14 <u>以色列</u>人在<u>迦南</u>地所得的產業，就是祭司<u>以利亞撒</u>和<u>嫩</u>的兒子<u>約書亞</u>，並<u>以色列</u>各支派的族長所分給他們的，都記在下面，2是照耶和華藉<u>摩西</u>所吩咐的，把產業拈鬮分給九個半支派。3原來，<u>摩西</u>在<u>約旦河</u>東，已經把產業分給那兩個半支派，只是在他們中間沒有把產業分給<u>利未</u>人。4因為<u>約瑟</u>的子孫是兩個支派，就是<u>瑪拿西</u>和<u>以法蓮</u>，所以沒有把地分給<u>利未</u>人。但給他們城邑居住，並城邑的郊野，可以牧養他們的牲畜，安置他們的財物。5耶和華怎樣吩咐<u>摩西</u>，<u>以色列</u>人就照樣行，把地分了。

迦勒分得希伯崙

6那時<u>猶大</u>人來到<u>吉甲</u>見<u>約書亞</u>，有<u>基尼洗</u>族<u>耶孚尼</u>的兒子<u>迦勒</u>對<u>約書亞</u>說：「耶和華在<u>加低斯巴尼亞</u>指着我與你對神人<u>摩西</u>所說的話，你都知道了。7耶和華的僕人<u>摩</u>

Mahanaim to the territory of Debir; 27and in the valley, Beth Haram, Beth Nimrah, Succoth and Zaphon with the rest of the realm of Sihon king of Heshbon (the east side of the Jordan, the territory up to the end of the Sea of Kinnereth[a]). 28These towns and their villages were the inheritance of the Gadites, clan by clan.

29This is what Moses had given to the half-tribe of Manasseh, that is, to half the family of the descendants of Manasseh, clan by clan:

30The territory extending from Mahanaim and including all of Bashan, the entire realm of Og king of Bashan—all the settlements of Jair in Bashan, sixty towns, 31half of Gilead, and Ashtaroth and Edrei (the royal cities of Og in Bashan). This was for the descendants of Makir son of Manasseh—for half of the sons of Makir, clan by clan.

32This is the inheritance Moses had given when he was in the plains of Moab across the Jordan east of Jericho. 33But to the tribe of Levi, Moses had given no inheritance; the LORD, the God of Israel, is their inheritance, as he promised them.

Division of the Land West of the Jordan

14 Now these are the areas the Israelites received as an inheritance in the land of Canaan, which Eleazar the priest, Joshua son of Nun and the heads of the tribal clans of Israel allotted to them. 2Their inheritances were assigned by lot to the nine-and-a-half tribes, as the LORD had commanded through Moses. 3Moses had granted the two-and-a-half tribes their inheritance east of the Jordan but had not granted the Levites an inheritance among the rest, 4for the sons of Joseph had become two tribes—Manasseh and Ephraim. The Levites received no share of the land but only towns to live in, with pasturelands for their flocks and herds. 5So the Israelites divided the land, just as the LORD had commanded Moses.

Hebron Given to Caleb

6Now the men of Judah approached Joshua at Gilgal, and Caleb son of Jephunneh the Kenizzite said to him, "You know what the LORD said to Moses the man of God at Kadesh Barnea about you and me. 7I was forty years old

---

a 27 That is, Galilee

when Moses the servant of the LORD sent me from Kadesh Barnea to explore the land. And I brought him back a report according to my convictions, [8]but my brothers who went up with me made the hearts of the people melt with fear. I, however, followed the LORD my God wholeheartedly. [9]So on that day Moses swore to me, 'The land on which your feet have walked will be your inheritance and that of your children forever, because you have followed the LORD my God wholeheartedly.'[a]

[10]"Now then, just as the LORD promised, he has kept me alive for forty-five years since the time he said this to Moses, while Israel moved about in the desert. So here I am today, eighty-five years old! [11]I am still as strong today as the day Moses sent me out; I'm just as vigorous to go out to battle now as I was then. [12]Now give me this hill country that the LORD promised me that day. You yourself heard then that the Anakites were there and their cities were large and fortified, but, the LORD helping me, I will drive them out just as he said."

[13]Then Joshua blessed Caleb son of Jephunneh and gave him Hebron as his inheritance. [14]So Hebron has belonged to Caleb son of Jephunneh the Kenizzite ever since, because he followed the LORD, the God of Israel, wholeheartedly. [15](Hebron used to be called Kiriath Arba after Arba, who was the greatest man among the Anakites.)

Then the land had rest from war.

Allotment for Judah

15 The allotment for the tribe of Judah, clan by clan, extended down to the territory of Edom, to the Desert of Zin in the extreme south.

[2]Their southern boundary started from the bay at the southern end of the Salt Sea,[b] [3]crossed south of Scorpion[c] Pass, continued on to Zin and went over to the south of Kadesh Barnea. Then it ran past Hezron up to Addar and curved around to Karka. [4]It then passed along to Azmon and joined the Wadi of Egypt, ending at the sea. This is their[d] southern boundary.

[5]The eastern boundary is the Salt Sea as far as the mouth of the Jordan.

The northern boundary started from the bay of the sea at the mouth of the Jordan, [6]went up to Beth Hoglah and continued north of Beth Arabah to the Stone of Bohan son of

西，從加低斯巴尼亞打發我窺探這地，那時我正四十歲，我按着心意回報他。[8]然而同我上去的眾弟兄，使百姓的心消化，但我專心跟從耶和華我的神。[9]當日摩西起誓說：'你腳所踏之地，定要歸你和你的子孫永遠為業，因為你專心跟從耶和華我的神。'

[10]"自從耶和華對摩西說這話的時候，耶和華照他所應許的，使我存活這四十五年，那時以色列人在曠野行走。看哪！現今我八十五歲了，[11]我還是強壯，像摩西打發我去的那天一樣。無論是爭戰、是出入，我的力量那時如何，現在還是如何。[12]求你將耶和華那日應許的這山地給我，那裏有亞衲族人，並寬大堅固的城，你也曾聽見了。或者耶和華照他所應許的與我同在，我就把他們趕出去。"

[13]於是約書亞為耶孚尼的兒子迦勒祝福，將希伯崙給他為業。[14]所以希伯崙作了基尼洗族耶孚尼的兒子迦勒的產業，直到今日，因為他專心跟從耶和華以色列的神。[15]希伯崙從前名叫基列亞巴。亞巴是亞衲族中最尊大的人。

於是國中太平，沒有爭戰了。

猶大分得之地

15 猶大支派按着宗族拈鬮所得之地是在儘南邊，到以東的交界，向南直到尋的曠野。

[2]他們的南界，是從鹽海的儘邊，就是從朝南的海汊起，[3]通到亞克拉濱坡的南邊，接連到尋，上到加低斯巴尼亞的南邊，又過希斯崙，上到亞達珥，繞到甲加，[4]接連到押們，通到埃及小河，直通到海為止。這就是他們的南界。

[5]東界是從鹽海南邊到約旦河口。

北界，是從約旦河口的海汊起，[6]上到伯曷拉，過伯亞拉巴的北邊，上到呂便之子波罕的磐石。

---

[a] 9 Deut. 1:36   [b] 2 That is, the Dead Sea; also in verse 5
[c] 3 Hebrew *Akrabbim*   [d] 4 Hebrew *your*

7從亞割谷往北，上到底璧，直向河南亞都冥坡對面的吉甲。又接連到隱示麥泉，直通到隱羅結，8上到欣嫩子谷，貼近耶布斯的南界（耶布斯就是耶路撒冷）。又上到欣嫩谷西邊的山頂，就是在利乏音谷極北的邊界。9又從山頂延到尼弗多亞的水源，通到以弗崙山的城邑，又延到巴拉（巴拉就是基列耶琳）。10又從巴拉往西繞到西珥山，接連到耶琳山的北邊（耶琳就是基撒崙）。又下到伯示麥過亭納，11通到以革倫北邊，延到施基崙，接連到巴拉山，又通到雅比聶，直通到海為止。

12西界就是大海和靠近大海之地。
這是猶大人按着宗族所得之地四圍的交界。

13約書亞照耶和華所吩咐的，將猶大人中的一段地，就是基列亞巴，分給耶孚尼的兒子迦勒。亞巴是亞衲族的始祖（基列亞巴就是希伯崙）。14迦勒就從那裏趕出亞衲族的三個族長，就是示篩、亞希幔、撻買。15又從那裏上去，攻擊底璧的居民，這底璧從前名叫基列西弗。16迦勒說："誰能攻打基列西弗，將城奪取，我就把我女兒押撒給他為妻。"17迦勒兄弟基納斯的兒子俄陀聶奪取了那城，迦勒就把女兒押撒給他為妻。

18押撒過門的時候，勸丈夫向她父親求一塊田。押撒一下驢，迦勒問她說："你要甚麼？"

19她說："求你賜福給我，你既將我安置在南地，求你也給我水泉。"她父親就把上泉下泉賜給她。

20以下是猶大支派按着宗族所得的產業：

Reuben. 7The boundary then went up to Debir from the Valley of Achor and turned north to Gilgal, which faces the Pass of Adummim south of the gorge. It continued along to the waters of En Shemesh and came out at En Rogel. 8Then it ran up the Valley of Ben Hinnom along the southern slope of the Jebusite city (that is, Jerusalem). From there it climbed to the top of the hill west of the Hinnom Valley at the northern end of the Valley of Rephaim. 9From the hilltop the boundary headed toward the spring of the waters of Nephtoah, came out at the towns of Mount Ephron and went down toward Baalah (that is, Kiriath Jearim). 10Then it curved westward from Baalah to Mount Seir, ran along the northern slope of Mount Jearim (that is, Kesalon), continued down to Beth Shemesh and crossed to Timnah. 11It went to the northern slope of Ekron, turned toward Shikkeron, passed along to Mount Baalah and reached Jabneel. The boundary ended at the sea.

12The western boundary is the coastline of the Great Sea.*a*
These are the boundaries around the people of Judah by their clans.

13In accordance with the LORD's command to him, Joshua gave to Caleb son of Jephunneh a portion in Judah—Kiriath Arba, that is, Hebron. (Arba was the forefather of Anak.) 14From Hebron Caleb drove out the three Anakites—Sheshai, Ahiman and Talmai—descendants of Anak. 15From there he marched against the people living in Debir (formerly called Kiriath Sepher). 16And Caleb said, "I will give my daughter Acsah in marriage to the man who attacks and captures Kiriath Sepher." 17Othniel son of Kenaz, Caleb's brother, took it; so Caleb gave his daughter Acsah to him in marriage.

18One day when she came to Othniel, she urged him*b* to ask her father for a field. When she got off her donkey, Caleb asked her, "What can I do for you?"

19She replied, "Do me a special favor. Since you have given me land in the Negev, give me also springs of water." So Caleb gave her the upper and lower springs.

20This is the inheritance of the tribe of Judah, clan by clan:

a 12 That is, the Mediterranean; also in verse 47
b 18 Hebrew and some Septuagint manuscripts; other Septuagint manuscripts (see also note at Judges 1:14) *Othniel, he urged her*

21The southernmost towns of the tribe of Judah in the Negev toward the boundary of Edom were:

Kabzeel, Eder, Jagur, 22Kinah, Dimonah, Adadah, 23Kedesh, Hazor, Ithnan, 24Ziph, Telem, Bealoth, 25Hazor Hadattah, Kerioth Hezron (that is, Hazor), 26Amam, Shema, Moladah, 27Hazar Gaddah, Heshmon, Beth Pelet, 28Hazar Shual, Beersheba, Biziothiah, 29Baalah, Iim, Ezem, 30Eltolad, Kesil, Hormah, 31Ziklag, Madmannah, Sansannah, 32Lebaoth, Shilhim, Ain and Rimmon—a total of twenty-nine towns and their villages.

33In the western foothills:

Eshtaol, Zorah, Ashnah, 34Zanoah, En Gannim, Tappuah, Enam, 35Jarmuth, Adullam, Socoh, Azekah, 36Shaaraim, Adithaim and Gederah (or Gederothaim)a — fourteen towns and their villages.

37Zenan, Hadashah, Migdal Gad, 38Dilean, Mizpah, Joktheel, 39Lachish, Bozkath, Eglon, 40Cabbon, Lahmas, Kitlish, 41Gederoth, Beth Dagon, Naamah and Makkedah—sixteen towns and their villages.

42Libnah, Ether, Ashan, 43Iphtah, Ashnah, Nezib, 44Keilah, Aczib and Mareshah—nine towns and their villages.

45Ekron, with its surrounding settlements and villages; 46west of Ekron, all that were in the vicinity of Ashdod, together with their villages; 47Ashdod, its surrounding settlements and villages; and Gaza, its settlements and villages, as far as the Wadi of Egypt and the coastline of the Great Sea.

48In the hill country:

Shamir, Jattir, Socoh, 49Dannah, Kiriath Sannah (that is, Debir), 50Anab, Eshtemoh, Anim, 51Goshen, Holon and Giloh—eleven towns and their villages.

52Arab, Dumah, Eshan, 53Janim, Beth Tappuah, Aphekah, 54Humtah, Kiriath Arba (that is, Hebron) and Zior—nine towns and their villages.

55Maon, Carmel, Ziph, Juttah, 56Jezreel, Jokdeam, Zanoah, 57Kain, Gibeah and Timnah—ten towns and their villages.

a 36 Or Gederah and Gederothaim

21猶大支派儘南邊的城邑，與以東交界相近的，就是：

甲薛、以得、雅姑珥、22基拿、底摩拿、亞大達、23基低斯、夏瑣、以提楠、24西弗、提鍊、比亞綠、25夏瑣哈大他、加略希斯崙（加略希斯崙就是夏瑣）、26亞曼、示瑪、摩拉大、27哈薩迦大、黑實門、伯帕列、28哈薩書亞、別是巴、比斯約他、29巴拉、以因、以森、30伊勒多臘、基失、何珥瑪、31洗革拉、麥瑪拿、三撒拿、32利巴勿、實忻、亞因、臨門，共二十九座城，還有屬城的村莊。

33在高原有：

以實陶、瑣拉、亞實拿、34撒挪亞、隱干寧、他普亞、以楠、35耶末、亞杜蘭、梭哥、亞西加、36沙拉音、亞底他音，基底拉、基底羅他音，共十四座城，還有屬城的村莊。

37又有洗楠、哈大沙、麥大迦得、38底連、米斯巴、約帖、39拉吉、波斯加、伊磯倫、40迦本、拉幔、基提利、41基低羅、伯大袞、拿瑪、瑪基大，共十六座城，還有屬城的村莊。

42又有立拿、以帖、亞珊、43益弗他、亞實拿、尼悉、44基伊拉、亞革悉、瑪利沙，共九座城，還有屬城的村莊。

45又有以革倫和屬以革倫的鎮市村莊。46從以革倫直到海，一切靠近亞實突之地，並屬其地的村莊。47亞實突和屬亞實突的鎮市村莊，迦薩和屬迦薩的鎮市村莊，直到埃及小河，並大海和靠近大海之地。

48在山地有：

沙密、雅提珥、梭哥、49大拿、基列薩拿（基列薩拿就是底璧）、50亞拿伯、以實提莫、亞念、51歌珊、何倫、基羅，共十一座城，還有屬城的村莊。

52又有亞拉、度瑪、以珊、53雅農、伯他普亞、亞非加、54宏他、基列亞巴（基列亞巴就是希伯崙）、洗珥，共九座城，還有屬城的村莊。

55又有瑪雲、迦密、西弗、淤他、56耶斯列、約甸、撒挪亞、57該隱、基比亞、亭納，共十座城，還有屬城的村莊。

58又有哈忽、伯夙、基突、59瑪臘、伯亞諾、伊勒提君，共六座城，還有屬城的村莊。

60又有基列巴力（基列巴力就是基列耶琳）、拉巴，共兩座城，還有屬城的村莊。

61在曠野有：

伯亞拉巴、密丁、西迦迦、62匿珊、鹽城、隱基底，共六座城，還有屬城的村莊。

63至於住耶路撒冷的耶布斯人，猶大人不能把他們趕出去，耶布斯人卻在耶路撒冷與猶大人同住，直到今日。

以法蓮與瑪拿西分得之地

16 約瑟的子孫拈鬮所得之地，是從靠近耶利哥的約旦河起，以耶利哥東邊的水為界，從耶利哥上去，通過山地的曠野，到伯特利。2又從伯特利到路斯，接連到亞基人的境界，至亞他綠。3又往西下到押利提人的境界，到下伯和崙的境界，直到基色，通到海為止。

4約瑟的兒子瑪拿西、以法蓮就得了他們的地業。

5以法蓮子孫的境界，按着宗族所得的，記在下面：他們地業的東界，是亞他綠亞達到上伯和崙；6往西通到北邊的密米他，又向東繞到他納約拿，又接連到雅挪哈的東邊；7從雅挪哈下到亞他綠，又到拿拉，達到耶利哥，通到約旦河為止。8從他普亞往西，到加拿河，直通到海為止。這就是以法蓮支派按着宗族所得的地業。9另外在瑪拿西人地業中，得了些城邑和屬城的村莊。這都是分給以法蓮子孫的。

10他們沒有趕出住基色的迦南人；迦南人卻住在以法蓮人中間，成為做苦工的僕人，直到今日。

17 瑪拿西是約瑟的長子，他的支派拈鬮所得之地，記在下面。至於瑪拿西的長子基列之父（註：“父”或作“主”）瑪吉，因

58Halhul, Beth Zur, Gedor, 59Maarath, Beth Anoth and Eltekon—six towns and their villages.

60Kiriath Baal (that is, Kiriath Jearim) and Rabbah—two towns and their villages.

61In the desert:

Beth Arabah, Middin, Secacah, 62Nibshan, the City of Salt and En Gedi—six towns and their villages.

63Judah could not dislodge the Jebusites, who were living in Jerusalem; to this day the Jebusites live there with the people of Judah.

Allotment for Ephraim and Manasseh

16 The allotment for Joseph began at the Jordan of Jericho,[a] east of the waters of Jericho, and went up from there through the desert into the hill country of Bethel. 2It went on from Bethel (that is, Luz),[b] crossed over to the territory of the Arkites in Ataroth, 3descended westward to the territory of the Japhletites as far as the region of Lower Beth Horon and on to Gezer, ending at the sea.

4So Manasseh and Ephraim, the descendants of Joseph, received their inheritance.

5This was the territory of Ephraim, clan by clan:

The boundary of their inheritance went from Ataroth Addar in the east to Upper Beth Horon 6and continued to the sea. From Micmethath on the north it curved eastward to Taanath Shiloh, passing by it to Janoah on the east. 7Then it went down from Janoah to Ataroth and Naarah, touched Jericho and came out at the Jordan. 8From Tappuah the border went west to the Kanah Ravine and ended at the sea. This was the inheritance of the tribe of the Ephraimites, clan by clan. 9It also included all the towns and their villages that were set aside for the Ephraimites within the inheritance of the Manassites.

10They did not dislodge the Canaanites living in Gezer; to this day the Canaanites live among the people of Ephraim but are required to do forced labor.

17 This was the allotment for the tribe of Manasseh as Joseph's firstborn, that is, for Makir, Manasseh's firstborn. Makir was the ancestor of the Gileadites, who had received Gilead and Bashan because the

---

a 1 Jordan of Jericho was possibly an ancient name for the Jordan River b 2 Septuagint; Hebrew Bethel to Luz

Makirites were great soldiers. ²So this allotment was for the rest of the people of Manasseh—the clans of Abiezer, Helek, Asriel, Shechem, Hepher and Shemida. These are the other male descendants of Manasseh son of Joseph by their clans.

³Now Zelophehad son of Hepher, the son of Gilead, the son of Makir, the son of Manasseh, had no sons but only daughters, whose names were Mahlah, Noah, Hoglah, Milcah and Tirzah. ⁴They went to Eleazar the priest, Joshua son of Nun, and the leaders and said, "The LORD commanded Moses to give us an inheritance among our brothers." So Joshua gave them an inheritance along with the brothers of their father, according to the LORD's command. ⁵Manasseh's share consisted of ten tracts of land besides Gilead and Bashan east of the Jordan, ⁶because the daughters of the tribe of Manasseh received an inheritance among the sons. The land of Gilead belonged to the rest of the descendants of Manasseh.

⁷The territory of Manasseh extended from Asher to Micmethath east of Shechem. The boundary ran southward from there to include the people living at En Tappuah. ⁸(Manasseh had the land of Tappuah, but Tappuah itself, on the boundary of Manasseh, belonged to the Ephraimites.) ⁹Then the boundary continued south to the Kanah Ravine. There were towns belonging to Ephraim lying among the towns of Manasseh, but the boundary of Manasseh was the northern side of the ravine and ended at the sea. ¹⁰On the south the land belonged to Ephraim, on the north to Manasseh. The territory of Manasseh reached the sea and bordered Asher on the north and Issachar on the east. ¹¹Within Issachar and Asher, Manasseh also had Beth Shan, Ibleam and the people of Dor, Endor, Taanach and Megiddo, together with their surrounding settlements (the third in the list is Naphoth[a]).

¹²Yet the Manassites were not able to occupy these towns, for the Canaanites were determined to live in that region. ¹³However, when the Israelites grew stronger, they subjected the Canaanites to forced labor but did not drive them out completely.

¹⁴The people of Joseph said to Joshua, "Why have you given us only one allotment and one portion for an inheritance? We are a numerous people and the LORD has blessed us abundantly."

為是勇士，就得了基列和巴珊。²瑪拿西其餘的子孫按着宗族拈鬮分地，就是亞比以謝子孫、希勒子孫、亞斯列子孫、示劍子孫、希弗子孫、示米大子孫；這些按着宗族，都是約瑟兒子瑪拿西子孫的男丁。

³瑪拿西的玄孫、瑪吉的曾孫、基列的孫子、希弗的兒子西羅非哈沒有兒子，只有女兒。他的女兒名叫瑪拉、挪阿、曷拉、密迦、得撒，⁴她們來到祭司以利亞撒和嫩的兒子約書亞並眾首領面前，說："耶和華曾吩咐摩西在我們弟兄中分給我們產業。"於是約書亞照耶和華所吩咐的，在他們伯叔中，把產業分給她們。⁵除了約旦河東的基列和巴珊地之外，還有十分地歸瑪拿西，⁶因為瑪拿西的孫女們在瑪拿西的孫子中得了產業。基列地是屬瑪拿西其餘的子孫。

⁷瑪拿西的境界：從亞設起，到示劍前的密米他，往北到隱他普亞居民之地。⁸他普亞地歸瑪拿西，只是瑪拿西境界上的他普亞城歸以法蓮子孫。⁹其界下到加拿河的南邊，在瑪拿西城邑中的這些城邑都歸以法蓮。瑪拿西的地界，是在河北直通到海為止。¹⁰南歸以法蓮，北歸瑪拿西，以海為界。北邊到亞設，東邊到以薩迦。

¹¹瑪拿西在以薩迦和亞設境內，有伯善和屬伯善的鎮市，以伯蓮和屬以伯蓮的鎮市，多珥的居民和屬多珥的鎮市。又有三處山岡，就是隱多珥和屬隱多珥的鎮市，他納的居民和屬他納的鎮市，米吉多的居民和屬米吉多的鎮市。¹²只是瑪拿西子孫不能趕出這些城的居民，迦南人偏要住在那地。¹³及至以色列人強盛了，就使迦南人做苦工，沒有把他們全然趕出。

¹⁴約瑟的子孫對約書亞說："耶和華對如今既然賜福與我們，我們也族大人多，你為甚麼但將一鬮一段之地分給我們為業呢？"

a 11 That is, Naphoth Dor

15約書亞說：「你們如果族大人多，嫌以法蓮山地窄小，就可以上比利洗人、利乏音人之地，在樹林中砍伐樹木。」

16約瑟的子孫說：「那山地容不下我們，並且住平原的迦南人，就是住伯善和屬伯善的鎮市，並住耶斯列平原的人，都有鐵車。」

17約書亞對約瑟家，就是以法蓮和瑪拿西人，說：「你是族大人多並且強盛，不可僅有一鬮之地。18山地也要歸你，雖是樹林你也可以砍伐，靠近之地必歸你。迦南人雖有鐵車，雖是強盛，你也能把他們趕出去。」

分其餘之地

18 以色列的全會眾都聚集在示羅，把會幕設立在那裏，那地已經被他們制伏了。2以色列人中其餘的七個支派，還沒有分給他們地業。

3約書亞對以色列人說：「耶和華你們列祖的神所賜給你們的地，你們就延不去得，要到幾時呢？4你們每支派當選舉三個人，我要打發他們去，他們就要起身走遍那地，按着各支派應得的地業寫明（註：或作「畫圖」），就回到我這裏來。5他們要將地分做七分。猶大仍在南方，住在他的境內；約瑟家仍在北方，住在他的境內。6你們要將地分做七分，寫明了拿到我這裏來。我要在耶和華我們神面前為你們拈鬮。7利未人在你們中間沒有分，因為供耶和華祭司的職任，就是他們的產業。迦得支派、呂便支派和瑪拿西半支派，已經在約旦河東得了地業，就是耶和華僕人摩西所給他們的。」

8劃地勢的人起身去的時候，約書亞囑咐他們說：「你們去走遍那地，劃明地勢，就回到我這裏來，我要在示羅這裏耶和華面前，為你們拈鬮。」9他們就去了，走遍那地，按着城邑分做七分，寫在冊子上，回到示羅營中見約書亞。10約書亞就在示羅耶和華面前，為他們拈

15"If you are so numerous," Joshua answered, "and if the hill country of Ephraim is too small for you, go up into the forest and clear land for yourselves there in the land of the Perizzites and Rephaites."

16The people of Joseph replied, "The hill country is not enough for us, and all the Canaanites who live in the plain have iron chariots, both those in Beth Shan and its settlements and those in the Valley of Jezreel."

17But Joshua said to the house of Joseph—to Ephraim and Manasseh—"You are numerous and very powerful. You will have not only one allotment 18but the forested hill country as well. Clear it, and its farthest limits will be yours; though the Canaanites have iron chariots and though they are strong, you can drive them out."

Division of the Rest of the Land

18 The whole assembly of the Israelites gathered at Shiloh and set up the Tent of Meeting there. The country was brought under their control, 2but there were still seven Israelite tribes who had not yet received their inheritance.

3So Joshua said to the Israelites: "How long will you wait before you begin to take possession of the land that the LORD, the God of your fathers, has given you? 4Appoint three men from each tribe. I will send them out to make a survey of the land and to write a description of it, according to the inheritance of each. Then they will return to me. 5You are to divide the land into seven parts. Judah is to remain in its territory on the south and the house of Joseph in its territory on the north. 6After you have written descriptions of the seven parts of the land, bring them here to me and I will cast lots for you in the presence of the LORD our God. 7The Levites, however, do not get a portion among you, because the priestly service of the LORD is their inheritance. And Gad, Reuben and the half-tribe of Manasseh have already received their inheritance on the east side of the Jordan. Moses the servant of the LORD gave it to them."

8As the men started on their way to map out the land, Joshua instructed them, "Go and make a survey of the land and write a description of it. Then return to me, and I will cast lots for you here at Shiloh in the presence of the LORD." 9So the men left and went through the land. They wrote its description on a scroll, town by town, in seven parts, and returned to Joshua in the camp at Shiloh. 10Joshua then cast lots for them in Shiloh in the presence of the LORD, and there he distributed the land to the Israelites according to their tribal divisions.

Allotment for Benjamin

¹¹The lot came up for the tribe of Benjamin, clan by clan. Their allotted territory lay between the tribes of Judah and Joseph:

¹²On the north side their boundary began at the Jordan, passed the northern slope of Jericho and headed west into the hill country, coming out at the desert of Beth Aven. ¹³From there it crossed to the south slope of Luz (that is, Bethel) and went down to Ataroth Addar on the hill south of Lower Beth Horon.

¹⁴From the hill facing Beth Horon on the south the boundary turned south along the western side and came out at Kiriath Baal (that is, Kiriath Jearim), a town of the people of Judah. This was the western side.

¹⁵The southern side began at the outskirts of Kiriath Jearim on the west, and the boundary came out at the spring of the waters of Nephtoah. ¹⁶The boundary went down to the foot of the hill facing the Valley of Ben Hinnom, north of the Valley of Rephaim. It continued down the Hinnom Valley along the southern slope of the Jebusite city and so to En Rogel. ¹⁷It then curved north, went to En Shemesh, continued to Geliloth, which faces the Pass of Adummim, and ran down to the Stone of Bohan son of Reuben. ¹⁸It continued to the northern slope of Beth Arabah*a* and on down into the Arabah. ¹⁹It then went to the northern slope of Beth Hoglah and came out at the northern bay of the Salt Sea,*b* at the mouth of the Jordan in the south. This was the southern boundary.

²⁰The Jordan formed the boundary on the eastern side.

These were the boundaries that marked out the inheritance of the clans of Benjamin on all sides.

²¹The tribe of Benjamin, clan by clan, had the following cities:

Jericho, Beth Hoglah, Emek Keziz, ²²Beth Arabah, Zemaraim, Bethel, ²³Avvim, Parah, Ophrah, ²⁴Kephar Ammoni, Ophni and Geba—twelve towns and their villages.

²⁵Gibeon, Ramah, Beeroth, ²⁶Mizpah, Kephirah, Mozah, ²⁷Rekem, Irpeel, Taralah,

---

圍。約書亞在那裏按着以色列人的支派，將地分給他們。

便雅憫分得之地

¹¹便雅憫支派，按着宗族拈鬮所得之地，是在猶大、約瑟子孫中間：

¹²他們的北界是從約旦河起，往上貼近耶利哥的北邊，又往西通過山地，直到伯亞文的曠野。¹³從那裏往南接連到路斯，貼近路斯（路斯就是伯特利），又下到亞他綠亞達，靠近下伯和崙南邊的山。

¹⁴從那裏往西，又轉向南，從伯和崙南對面的山，直達到猶大人的城基列巴力（基列巴力就是基列耶琳），這是西界。

¹⁵南界，是從基列耶琳的儘邊起，往西達到尼弗多亞的水源。¹⁶又下到欣嫩子谷對面山的儘邊，就是利乏音谷北邊的山。又下到欣嫩谷，貼近耶布斯的南邊，又下到隱羅結。¹⁷又往北通到隱示麥，達到亞都冥坡對面的基利綠。又下到呂便之子波罕的磐石。¹⁸又接連到亞拉巴對面，往北下到亞拉巴。¹⁹又接連到伯曷拉的北邊，直通到鹽海的北汊，就是約旦河的南頭，這是南界。

²⁰東界是約旦河。

這是便雅憫人按着宗族，照他們四圍的交界所得的地業。

²¹便雅憫支派按着宗族所得的城邑，就是：

耶利哥、伯曷拉、伊麥基悉、²²伯亞拉巴、洗瑪臉、伯特利、²³亞文、巴拉、俄弗拉、²⁴基法阿摩尼、俄弗尼、迦巴，共十二座城，還有屬城的村莊。

²⁵又有基遍、拉瑪、比錄、²⁶米斯巴、基非拉、摩撒、²⁷利堅、伊

---

a 18 Septuagint; Hebrew *slope facing the Arabah*   *b 19* That is, the Dead Sea

利毘勒、他拉拉、28洗拉、以利
弗、耶布斯（耶布斯就是耶路撒
冷）、基比亞、基列，共十四座
城，還有屬城的村莊。

這是便雅憫人按着宗族所得的地
業。

西緬分得之地

19 為西緬支派的人，按着宗
族，拈出第二圖。他們所得
的地業是在猶大人地業中
間。2他們所得為業之地，就是：

　　別是巴（或名示巴）、摩拉
大、3哈薩書亞、巴拉、以森、4伊
利多拉、比土力、何珥瑪、5洗革
拉、伯瑪加博、哈薩蘇撒、6伯利巴
勿、沙魯險，共十三座城，還有屬
城的村莊。

　　7又有亞因、利門、以帖、亞
珊，共四座城，還有屬城的村莊。
8並有這些城邑四圍一切的村莊，直
到巴拉比珥，就是南地的拉瑪。

這是西緬支派按着宗族所得的地
業。9西緬人的地業是從猶大人地業
中得來的，因為猶大人的分過多，
所以西緬人在他們的地業中得了地
業。

西布倫分得之地

10為西布倫人，按着宗族，拈出第三
圖：

　　他們地業的境界是到撒立。
11往西上到瑪拉拉，達到大巴設，
又達到約念前的河。12又從撒立往
東轉向日出之地，到吉斯綠他泊
的境界，又通到大比拉，上到雅
非亞。13從那裏往東，接連到迦特
希弗，至以特加汛，通到臨門，
臨門延到尼亞。14又繞過尼亞的北
邊，轉到哈拿頓，通到伊弗他伊
勒谷。15還有加他、拿哈拉、伸
崙、以大拉、伯利恆，共有十二
座城，還有屬城的村莊。

16這些城並屬城的村莊，就是西布倫
人按着宗族所得的地業。

以薩迦分得之地

17為以薩迦人，按着宗族，拈出第四
圖。18他們的境界是：

　　耶斯列、基蘇律、書念、19哈
弗連、示按、亞拿哈拉、20拉壁、

28Zelah, Haeleph, the Jebusite city (that is, Jerusalem), Gibeah and Kiriath—fourteen towns and their villages.

This was the inheritance of Benjamin for its clans.

Allotment for Simeon

19 The second lot came out for the tribe of Simeon, clan by clan. Their inheritance lay within the territory of Judah. 2It included:

Beersheba (or Sheba),[a] Moladah, 3Hazar Shual, Balah, Ezem, 4Eltolad, Bethul, Hormah, 5Ziklag, Beth Marcaboth, Hazar Susah, 6Beth Lebaoth and Sharuhen—thirteen towns and their villages;

7Ain, Rimmon, Ether and Ashan—four towns and their villages— 8and all the villages around these towns as far as Baalath Beer (Ramah in the Negev).

This was the inheritance of the tribe of the Simeonites, clan by clan. 9The inheritance of the Simeonites was taken from the share of Judah, because Judah's portion was more than they needed. So the Simeonites received their inheritance within the territory of Judah.

Allotment for Zebulun

10The third lot came up for Zebulun, clan by clan:

The boundary of their inheritance went as far as Sarid. 11Going west it ran to Maralah, touched Dabbesheth, and extended to the ravine near Jokneam. 12It turned east from Sarid toward the sunrise to the territory of Kisloth Tabor and went on to Daberath and up to Japhia. 13Then it continued eastward to Gath Hepher and Eth Kazin; it came out at Rimmon and turned toward Neah. 14There the boundary went around on the north to Hannathon and ended at the Valley of Iphtah El. 15Included were Kattath, Nahalal, Shimron, Idalah and Bethlehem. There were twelve towns and their villages.

16These towns and their villages were the inheritance of Zebulun, clan by clan.

Allotment for Issachar

17The fourth lot came out for Issachar, clan by clan. 18Their territory included:

Jezreel, Kesulloth, Shunem, 19Hapharaim, Shion, Anaharath, 20Rabbith, Kishion, Ebez,

---

a 2 Or Beersheba, Sheba; 1 Chron. 4:28 does not have Sheba.

21Remeth, En Gannim, En Haddah and Beth Pazzez. 22The boundary touched Tabor, Shahazumah and Beth Shemesh, and ended at the Jordan. There were sixteen towns and their villages.

23These towns and their villages were the inheritance of the tribe of Issachar, clan by clan.

Allotment for Asher

24The fifth lot came out for the tribe of Asher, clan by clan. 25Their territory included:

Helkath, Hali, Beten, Acshaph, 26Allammelech, Amad and Mishal. On the west the boundary touched Carmel and Shihor Libnath. 27It then turned east toward Beth Dagon, touched Zebulun and the Valley of Iphtah El, and went north to Beth Emek and Neiel, passing Cabul on the left. 28It went to Abdon,a Rehob, Hammon and Kanah, as far as Greater Sidon. 29The boundary then turned back toward Ramah and went to the fortified city of Tyre, turned toward Hosah and came out at the sea in the region of Aczib, 30Ummah, Aphek and Rehob. There were twenty-two towns and their villages.

31These towns and their villages were the inheritance of the tribe of Asher, clan by clan.

Allotment for Naphtali

32The sixth lot came out for Naphtali, clan by clan:

33Their boundary went from Heleph and the large tree in Zaanannim, passing Adami Nekeb and Jabneel to Lakkum and ending at the Jordan. 34The boundary ran west through Aznoth Tabor and came out at Hukkok. It touched Zebulun on the south, Asher on the west and the Jordanb on the east. 35The fortified cities were Ziddim, Zer, Hammath, Rakkath, Kinnereth, 36Adamah, Ramah, Hazor, 37Kedesh, Edrei, En Hazor, 38Iron, Migdal El, Horem, Beth Anath and Beth Shemesh. There were nineteen towns and their villages.

39These towns and their villages were the inheritance of the tribe of Naphtali, clan by clan.

Allotment for Dan

40The seventh lot came out for the tribe of Dan, clan by clan. 41The territory of their inheritance included:

a 28 Some Hebrew manuscripts (see also Joshua 21:30); most Hebrew manuscripts Ebron　　b 34 Septuagint; Hebrew west, and Judah, the Jordan,

基善、亞別、21利篾、隱干寧、隱哈大、伯哈薛，22又達到他泊、沙哈洗瑪、伯示麥，直通到約旦河為止，共十六座城，還有屬城的村莊。

23這些城並屬城的村莊，就是以薩迦支派按着宗族所得的地業。

亞設分得之地

24為亞設支派，按着宗族，拈出第五圖。25他們的境界是：

黑甲、哈利、比田、押煞、26亞拉米勒、亞末、米沙勒，往西達到迦密，又到希曷立納，27轉向日出之地，到伯大袞，達到細步倫，往北到伊弗他伊勒谷，到伯以墨和尼業，也通到迦步勒的左邊。28又到義伯崙、利合、哈們、加拿，直到西頓大城，29轉到拉瑪和堅固城推羅，又轉到何薩，靠近亞革悉一帶地方，直通到海。30又有烏瑪、亞弗、利合，共二十二座城，還有屬城的村莊。

31這些城並屬城的村莊，就是亞設支派按着宗族所得的地業。

拿弗他利分得之地

32為拿弗他利人，按着宗族，拈出第六圖：

33他們的境界是從希利弗，從撒拿音的橡樹，從亞大米尼吉和雅比聶，直到拉共，通到約旦河。34又轉向西到亞斯納他泊，從那裏通到戶割，南邊到西布倫，西邊到亞設，又向日出之地，達到約旦河那裏的猶大。35堅固的城，就是西丁、側耳、哈末、拉甲、基尼烈、36亞大瑪、拉瑪、夏瑣、37基低斯、以得來、隱夏瑣、38以利穩、密大伊勒、和璉、伯亞納、伯示麥，共十九座城，還有屬城的村莊。

39這些城並屬城的村莊，就是拿弗他利支派按着宗族所得的地業。

但分得之地

40為但支派，按着宗族，拈出第七圖。41他們地業的境界是：

瑣拉、以實陶、伊珥示麥、 ⁴²沙拉賓、亞雅崙、伊提拉、 ⁴³以倫、亭拿他、以革倫、 ⁴⁴伊利提基、基比頓、巴拉、 ⁴⁵伊胡得、比尼比拉、迦特臨門、 ⁴⁶美耶昆、拉昆、並約帕對面的地界。

⁴⁷但人的地界，越過原得的地界，因為但人上去攻取利善，用刀擊殺城中的人，得了那城，住在其中，以他們先祖但的名，將利善改名為但。

⁴⁸這些城並屬城的村莊，就是但支派按着宗族所得的地業。

約書亞得之地

⁴⁹以色列人按着境界分完了地業，就在他們中間將地給嫩的兒子約書亞為業，⁵⁰是照耶和華的吩咐，將約書亞所求的城，就是以法蓮山地的亭拿西拉城，給了他。他就修那城，住在其中。

⁵¹這就是祭司以利亞撒和嫩的兒子約書亞，並以色列各支派的族長，在示羅會幕門口，耶和華面前，拈鬮所分的地業。這樣，他們把地分完了。

逃城

20 耶和華曉諭約書亞說：² "你吩咐以色列人說：你們要照着我藉摩西所曉諭你們的，為自己設立逃城。³使那無心而誤殺人的，可以逃到那裏。這些城可以作你們逃避報血仇人的地方。

⁴ "那殺人的要逃到這些城中的一座，站在城門口，將他的事情說給城內的長老們聽。他們就把他收進城裏，給他地方，使他住在他們中間。⁵若是報血仇的追了他來，長老不可將他交在報血仇的手裏，因為他是素無仇恨、無心殺了人的。⁶他要住在那城裏，站在會眾面前聽審判，等到那時的大祭司死了，殺人的才可以回到本城本家，就是他所逃出來的那城。"

⁷於是，以色列人在拿弗他利山地，分定加利利的基低斯；在以法蓮山地，分定示劍；在猶大山地，分定基列亞巴（基列亞巴就是希伯崙）。⁸又在約旦河外耶利哥東，從

Zorah, Eshtaol, Ir Shemesh, ⁴²Shaalabbin, Aijalon, Ithlah, ⁴³Elon, Timnah, Ekron, ⁴⁴Eltekeh, Gibbethon, Baalath, ⁴⁵Jehud, Bene Berak, Gath Rimmon, ⁴⁶Me Jarkon and Rakkon, with the area facing Joppa.

⁴⁷(But the Danites had difficulty taking possession of their territory, so they went up and attacked Leshem, took it, put it to the sword and occupied it. They settled in Leshem and named it Dan after their forefather.)

⁴⁸These towns and their villages were the inheritance of the tribe of Dan, clan by clan.

Allotment for Joshua

⁴⁹When they had finished dividing the land into its allotted portions, the Israelites gave Joshua son of Nun an inheritance among them, ⁵⁰as the LORD had commanded. They gave him the town he asked for—Timnath Serah^a in the hill country of Ephraim. And he built up the town and settled there.

⁵¹These are the territories that Eleazar the priest, Joshua son of Nun and the heads of the tribal clans of Israel assigned by lot at Shiloh in the presence of the LORD at the entrance to the Tent of Meeting. And so they finished dividing the land.

Cities of Refuge

20 Then the LORD said to Joshua: ²"Tell the Israelites to designate the cities of refuge, as I instructed you through Moses, ³so that anyone who kills a person accidentally and unintentionally may flee there and find protection from the avenger of blood.

⁴"When he flees to one of these cities, he is to stand in the entrance of the city gate and state his case before the elders of that city. Then they are to admit him into their city and give him a place to live with them. ⁵If the avenger of blood pursues him, they must not surrender the one accused, because he killed his neighbor unintentionally and without malice aforethought. ⁶He is to stay in that city until he has stood trial before the assembly and until the death of the high priest who is serving at that time. Then he may go back to his own home in the town from which he fled."

⁷So they set apart Kedesh in Galilee in the hill country of Naphtali, Shechem in the hill country of Ephraim, and Kiriath Arba (that is, Hebron) in the hill country of Judah. ⁸On the east side of

a 50 Also known as Timnath Heres (see Judges 2:9)

the Jordan of Jericho^a they designated Bezer in the desert on the plateau in the tribe of Reuben, Ramoth in Gilead in the tribe of Gad, and Golan in Bashan in the tribe of Manasseh. ⁹Any of the Israelites or any alien living among them who killed someone accidentally could flee to these designated cities and not be killed by the avenger of blood prior to standing trial before the assembly.

Towns for the Levites

21 Now the family heads of the Levites approached Eleazar the priest, Joshua son of Nun, and the heads of the other tribal families of Israel ²at Shiloh in Canaan and said to them, "The LORD commanded through Moses that you give us towns to live in, with pasturelands for our livestock." ³So, as the LORD had commanded, the Israelites gave the Levites the following towns and pasturelands out of their own inheritance:

⁴The first lot came out for the Kohathites, clan by clan. The Levites who were descendants of Aaron the priest were allotted thirteen towns from the tribes of Judah, Simeon and Benjamin. ⁵The rest of Kohath's descendants were allotted ten towns from the clans of the tribes of Ephraim, Dan and half of Manasseh.

⁶The descendants of Gershon were allotted thirteen towns from the clans of the tribes of Issachar, Asher, Naphtali and the half-tribe of Manasseh in Bashan.

⁷The descendants of Merari, clan by clan, received twelve towns from the tribes of Reuben, Gad and Zebulun.

⁸So the Israelites allotted to the Levites these towns and their pasturelands, as the LORD had commanded through Moses.

⁹From the tribes of Judah and Simeon they allotted the following towns by name ¹⁰(these towns were assigned to the descendants of Aaron who were from the Kohathite clans of the Levites, because the first lot fell to them):

¹¹They gave them Kiriath Arba (that is, Hebron), with its surrounding pastureland, in the hill country of Judah. (Arba was the forefather of Anak.) ¹²But the fields and villages around the city they had given to Caleb son of Jephunneh as his possession.

¹³So to the descendants of Aaron the priest they gave Hebron (a city of refuge for one accused of murder), Libnah, ¹⁴Jattir,

---

a 8 Jordan of Jericho was possibly an ancient name for the Jordan River.

呂便支派中，在曠野的平原，設立比悉；從迦得支派中，設立基列的拉末；從瑪拿西支派中，設立巴珊的哥蘭。⁹這都是為以色列眾人和在他們中間寄居的外人所分定的地邑，使誤殺人的都可以逃到那裏，不死在報血仇人的手中，等他站在會眾面前聽審判。

給利未人的城邑

21 那時，利未人的眾族長來到祭司以利亞撒和嫩的兒子約書亞，並以色列各支派的族長面前。²在迦南地的示羅對他們說："從前耶和華藉着摩西吩咐給我們城邑居住，並城邑的郊野可以牧養我們的牲畜。"³於是以色列人照耶和華所吩咐的，從自己的地業中，將以下所記的城邑和城邑的郊野給了利未人：

⁴為哥轄族拈鬮，利未人的祭司亞倫的子孫，從猶大支派、西緬支派、便雅憫支派的地業中，按鬮得了十三座城。⁵哥轄其餘的子孫，從以法蓮支派、但支派、瑪拿西半支派的地業中，按鬮得了十座城。

⁶革順的子孫，從以薩迦支派、亞設支派、拿弗他利支派、住巴珊的瑪拿西半支派的地業中，按鬮得了十三座城。

⁷米拉利的子孫，按着宗族，從呂便支派、迦得支派、西布倫支派的地業中，按鬮得了十二座城。

⁸以色列人照耶和華藉摩西所吩咐的，將這些城邑和城邑的郊野，按鬮分給利未人。

^{9、10}從猶大支派、西緬支派的地業中，將以下所記的城給了利未支派哥轄宗族亞倫的子孫，因為給他們拈出頭一鬮：

¹¹將猶大山地的基列亞巴和四圍的郊野給了他們。亞巴是亞衲族的始祖（基列亞巴就是希伯崙）。¹²惟將屬城的田地和村莊，給了耶孚尼的兒子迦勒為業。

¹³以色列人將希伯崙，就是誤殺人的逃城和屬城的郊野，給了祭司亞倫的子孫。又給他們立拿和屬城的郊野，¹⁴雅提珥和屬城的郊野，以

實提莫和屬城的郊野，¹⁵何崙和屬城的郊野，底璧和屬城的郊野，¹⁶亞因和屬城的郊野，淤他和屬城的郊野，伯示麥和屬城的郊野，共九座城，都是從這二支派中分出來的。

¹⁷又從便雅憫支派的地業中給了他們基遍和屬城的郊野，迦巴和屬城的郊野，¹⁸亞拿突和屬城的郊野，亞勒們和屬城的郊野，共四座城。

¹⁹亞倫子孫作祭司的共有十三座城，還有屬城的郊野。

²⁰利未支派中哥轄的宗族，就是哥轄其餘的子孫，拈鬮所得的城有從以法蓮支派中分出來的：

²¹以色列人將以法蓮山地的示劍，就是誤殺人的逃城和屬城的郊野，給了他們。又給他們基色和屬城的郊野，²²基伯先和屬城的郊野、伯和崙和屬城的郊野，共四座城。

²³又從但支派的地業中給了他們伊利提基和屬城的郊野、基比頓和屬城的郊野，²⁴亞雅崙和屬城的郊野，迦特臨門和屬城的郊野，共四座城。

²⁵又從瑪拿西半支派的地業中給了他們他納和屬城的郊野，迦特臨門和屬城的郊野，共兩座城。

²⁶哥轄其餘的子孫共有十座城，還有屬城的郊野。

²⁷以色列人又從瑪拿西半支派的地業中將巴珊的哥蘭，就是誤殺人的逃城和屬城的郊野，給了利未支派革順的子孫。又給他們比施提拉和屬城的郊野，共兩座城。

²⁸又從以薩迦支派的地業中，給了他們基善和屬城的郊野，大比拉和屬城的郊野，²⁹耶末和屬城的郊野，隱干寧和屬城的郊野，共四座城。

³⁰又從亞設支派的地業中給了他們米沙勒和屬城的郊野，押頓和屬城的郊野，³¹黑甲和屬城的郊野，利合和屬城的郊野，共四座城。

³²又從拿弗他利支派中將加利利的基低斯，就是誤殺人的逃城和屬城的郊野，給了他們。又給他們哈末多珥和屬城的郊野，加珥坦和屬城的郊野，共三座城。

³³革順人按著宗族所得的城，共十三座，還有屬城的郊野。

Eshtemoa, ¹⁵Holon, Debir, ¹⁶Ain, Juttah and Beth Shemesh, together with their pasturelands—nine towns from these two tribes.

¹⁷And from the tribe of Benjamin they gave them Gibeon, Geba, ¹⁸Anathoth and Almon, together with their pasturelands—four towns.

¹⁹All the towns for the priests, the descendants of Aaron, were thirteen, together with their pasturelands.

²⁰The rest of the Kohathite clans of the Levites were allotted towns from the tribe of Ephraim:

²¹In the hill country of Ephraim they were given Shechem (a city of refuge for one accused of murder) and Gezer, ²²Kibzaim and Beth Horon, together with their pasturelands—four towns.

²³Also from the tribe of Dan they received Eltekeh, Gibbethon, ²⁴Aijalon and Gath Rimmon, together with their pasturelands—four towns.

²⁵From half the tribe of Manasseh they received Taanach and Gath Rimmon, together with their pasturelands—two towns.

²⁶All these ten towns and their pasturelands were given to the rest of the Kohathite clans.

²⁷The Levite clans of the Gershonites were given:
from the half-tribe of Manasseh,
Golan in Bashan (a city of refuge for one accused of murder) and Be Eshtarah, together with their pasturelands—two towns;
²⁸from the tribe of Issachar,
Kishion, Daberath, ²⁹Jarmuth and En Gannim, together with their pasturelands—four towns;
³⁰from the tribe of Asher,
Mishal, Abdon, ³¹Helkath and Rehob, together with their pasturelands—four towns;
³²from the tribe of Naphtali,
Kedesh in Galilee (a city of refuge for one accused of murder), Hammoth Dor and Kartan, together with their pasturelands—three towns.
³³All the towns of the Gershonite clans were thirteen, together with their pasturelands.

³⁴The Merarite clans (the rest of the Levites) were given:

from the tribe of Zebulun,

Jokneam, Kartah, ³⁵Dimnah and Nahalal, together with their pasturelands—four towns;

³⁶ from the tribe of Reuben,

Bezer, Jahaz, ³⁷Kedemoth and Mephaath, together with their pasturelands—four towns;

³⁸ from the tribe of Gad,

Ramoth in Gilead (a city of refuge for one accused of murder), Mahanaim, ³⁹Heshbon and Jazer, together with their pasturelands—four towns in all.

⁴⁰All the towns allotted to the Merarite clans, who were the rest of the Levites, were twelve.

⁴¹The towns of the Levites in the territory held by the Israelites were forty-eight in all, together with their pasturelands. ⁴²Each of these towns had pasturelands surrounding it; this was true for all these towns.

⁴³So the LORD gave Israel all the land he had sworn to give their forefathers, and they took possession of it and settled there. ⁴⁴The LORD gave them rest on every side, just as he had sworn to their forefathers. Not one of their enemies withstood them; the LORD handed all their enemies over to them. ⁴⁵Not one of all the LORD's good promises to the house of Israel failed; every one was fulfilled.

Eastern Tribes Return Home

22 Then Joshua summoned the Reubenites, the Gadites and the half-tribe of Manasseh ²and said to them, "You have done all that Moses the servant of the LORD commanded, and you have obeyed me in everything I commanded. ³For a long time now—to this very day—you have not deserted your brothers but have carried out the mission the LORD your God gave you. ⁴Now that the LORD your God has given your brothers rest as he promised, return to your homes in the land that Moses the servant of the LORD gave you on the other side of the Jordan. ⁵But be very careful to keep the commandment and the law that Moses the servant of the LORD gave you: to love the LORD your God, to walk in all his ways, to obey his commands, to hold fast to him and to serve him with all your heart and all your soul."

⁶Then Joshua blessed them and sent them away, and they went to their homes. ⁷(To the half-tribe of Manasseh Moses had given land in Bashan, and to the other half of the tribe Joshua

³⁴其餘利未支派米拉利子孫，從西布倫支派的地業中所得的就是：約念和屬城的郊野，加珥他和屬城的郊野，³⁵丁拿和屬城的郊野，拿哈拉和屬城的郊野，共四座城。

³⁶又從呂便支派的地業中給了他們比悉和屬城的郊野，雅雜和屬城的郊野，³⁷基底莫和屬城的郊野，米法押和屬城的郊野，共四座城。

³⁸又從迦得支派的地業中，將基列的拉末，就是誤殺人的逃城和屬城的郊野，給了他們。又給他們瑪哈念和屬城的郊野，³⁹希實本和屬城的郊野，雅謝和屬城的郊野，共四座城。

⁴⁰其餘利未支派的人，就是米拉利的子孫，按着宗族拈鬮所得的，共十二座城。

⁴¹利未人在以色列人的地業中所得的城，共四十八座，並有屬城的郊野。⁴²這些城四圍都有屬城的郊野，城城都是如此。

⁴³這樣，耶和華將從前向他們列祖起誓所應許的全地，賜給以色列人，他們就得了為業，住在其中。⁴⁴耶和華照着向他們列祖起誓所應許的一切話，使他們四境平安，他們一切仇敵中，沒有一人在他們面前站立得住，耶和華把一切仇敵都交在他們手中。⁴⁵耶和華應許賜福給以色列家的話，一句也沒有落空，都應驗了。

約旦河東支派歸回原居地

22 當時，約書亞召了呂便人、迦得人和瑪拿西半支派的人來，²對他們說："耶和華僕人摩西所吩咐你們的，你們都遵守了；我所吩咐你們的，你們也都聽從了。³你們這許多日子，總沒有撇離你們的弟兄，直到今日，並守了耶和華你們神所吩咐你們當守的。⁴如今耶和華你們神照着他所應許的，使你們弟兄得享平安，現在可以轉回你們的帳棚，到耶和華的僕人摩西在約旦河東所賜你們為業之地。⁵只要切切地謹慎遵行耶和華僕人摩西所吩咐你們的誡命律法，愛耶和華你們的神，行他一切的道，守他的誡命，專靠他，盡心盡性侍奉他。"

⁶於是約書亞為他們祝福，打發他們去，他們就回自己的帳棚去了。⁷瑪拿西那半支派，摩西早已在巴珊分給他們地業。這半支派，約書亞在

約旦河西，在他們弟兄中，分給他們地業。約書亞打發他們回帳棚的時候為他們祝福，8對他們說："你們帶許多財物，許多牲畜和金、銀、銅、鐵、並許多衣服，回你們的帳棚去，要將你們從仇敵奪來的物，與你們眾弟兄同分。"

9於是呂便人、迦得人、瑪拿西半支派的人，從迦南地的示羅起行，離開以色列人，回往他們得為業的基列地，就是照耶和華藉摩西所吩咐的得了為業之地。

10呂便人、迦得人和瑪拿西半支派的人，到了靠近約旦河的一帶迦南地，就在約旦河那裏築了一座壇，那壇看着高大。11以色列人聽說呂便人、迦得人、瑪拿西半支派的人靠近約旦河邊，在迦南地屬以色列人的那邊築了一座壇。12全會眾一聽見，就聚集在示羅，要上去攻打他們。

13以色列人打發祭司以利亞撒的兒子非尼哈，往基列地去見呂便人、迦得人、瑪拿西半支派的人。14又打發十個首領與非尼哈同去，就是以色列每支派的一個首領，都是以色列軍中的統領。

15他們到了基列地，見呂便人、迦得人和瑪拿西半支派的人，對他們說：16"耶和華全會眾這樣說：'你們今日轉去不跟從耶和華，干犯以色列的神，為自己築一座壇，悖逆了耶和華，這犯的是甚麼罪呢？17從前拜毘珥的罪孽還算小嗎？雖然瘟疫臨到耶和華的會眾，到今日我們還沒有洗淨這罪。18你們今日竟轉去不跟從耶和華嗎？

"'你們今日既悖逆耶和華，明日他必向以色列全會眾發怒。19你們所得為業之地，若嫌不潔淨，就可以過到耶和華之地，就是耶和華的帳幕所住之地，在我們中間得地業；只是不可悖逆耶和華，也不可得罪我們，在耶和華我們神的壇以外為自己築壇。20當前謝拉的曾孫亞干，豈不是在那當滅的物上犯了罪，就有忿怒臨到以色列全會眾嗎？那人在所犯的罪中，不獨一人死亡。'"

gave land on the west side of the Jordan with their brothers.) When Joshua sent them home, he blessed them, [8]saying, "Return to your homes with your great wealth—with large herds of livestock, with silver, gold, bronze and iron, and a great quantity of clothing—and divide with your brothers the plunder from your enemies."

[9]So the Reubenites, the Gadites and the half-tribe of Manasseh left the Israelites at Shiloh in Canaan to return to Gilead, their own land, which they had acquired in accordance with the command of the LORD through Moses.

[10]When they came to Geliloth near the Jordan in the land of Canaan, the Reubenites, the Gadites and the half-tribe of Manasseh built an imposing altar there by the Jordan. [11]And when the Israelites heard that they had built the altar on the border of Canaan at Geliloth near the Jordan on the Israelite side, [12]the whole assembly of Israel gathered at Shiloh to go to war against them.

[13]So the Israelites sent Phinehas son of Eleazar, the priest, to the land of Gilead—to Reuben, Gad and the half-tribe of Manasseh. [14]With him they sent ten of the chief men, one for each of the tribes of Israel, each the head of a family division among the Israelite clans.

[15]When they went to Gilead—to Reuben, Gad and the half-tribe of Manasseh—they said to them: [16]"The whole assembly of the LORD says: 'How could you break faith with the God of Israel like this? How could you turn away from the LORD and build yourselves an altar in rebellion against him now? [17]Was not the sin of Peor enough for us? Up to this very day we have not cleansed ourselves from that sin, even though a plague fell on the community of the LORD! [18]And are you now turning away from the LORD?

"'If you rebel against the LORD today, tomorrow he will be angry with the whole community of Israel. [19]If the land you possess is defiled, come over to the LORD's land, where the LORD's tabernacle stands, and share the land with us. But do not rebel against the LORD or against us by building an altar for yourselves, other than the altar of the LORD our God. [20]When Achan son of Zerah acted unfaithfully regarding the devoted things,[a] did not wrath come upon the whole community of Israel? He was not the only one who died for his sin.'"

---

a 20 The Hebrew term refers to the irrevocable giving over of things or persons to the LORD, often by totally destroying them.

²¹Then Reuben, Gad and the half-tribe of Manasseh replied to the heads of the clans of Israel: ²²"The Mighty One, God, the LORD! The Mighty One, God, the LORD! He knows! And let Israel know! If this has been in rebellion or disobedience to the LORD, do not spare us this day. ²³If we have built our own altar to turn away from the LORD and to offer burnt offerings and grain offerings, or to sacrifice fellowship offerings*d* on it, may the LORD himself call us to account.

²⁴"No! We did it for fear that some day your descendants might say to ours, 'What do you have to do with the LORD, the God of Israel? ²⁵The LORD has made the Jordan a boundary between us and you—you Reubenites and Gadites! You have no share in the LORD.' So your descendants might cause ours to stop fearing the LORD.

²⁶"That is why we said, 'Let us get ready and build an altar—but not for burnt offerings or sacrifices.' ²⁷On the contrary, it is to be a witness between us and you and the generations that follow, that we will worship the LORD at his sanctuary with our burnt offerings, sacrifices and fellowship offerings. Then in the future your descendants will not be able to say to ours, 'You have no share in the LORD.'

²⁸"And we said, 'If they ever say this to us, or to our descendants, we will answer: Look at the replica of the LORD's altar, which our fathers built, not for burnt offerings and sacrifices, but as a witness between us and you.'

²⁹"Far be it from us to rebel against the LORD and turn away from him today by building an altar for burnt offerings, grain offerings and sacrifices, other than the altar of the LORD our God that stands before his tabernacle."

³⁰When Phinehas the priest and the leaders of the community—the heads of the clans of the Israelites—heard what Reuben, Gad and Manasseh had to say, they were pleased. ³¹And Phinehas son of Eleazar, the priest, said to Reuben, Gad and Manasseh, "Today we know that the LORD is with us, because you have not acted unfaithfully toward the LORD in this matter. Now you have rescued the Israelites from the LORD's hand."

³²Then Phinehas son of Eleazar, the priest, and the leaders returned to Canaan from their meeting with the Reubenites and Gadites in Gilead and reported to the Israelites. ³³They were glad to hear the report and praised God. And they talked no more about going to war against them to devastate the country where the Reubenites and the Gadites lived.

²¹於是呂便人、迦得人、瑪拿西半支派的人回答以色列軍中的統領說：²²"大能者神耶和華！大能者神耶和華！他是知道的。以色列人也必知道。我們若有悖逆的意思，或是干犯耶和華（願你今日不保佑我們）²³為自己築壇，要轉去不跟從耶和華，或是要將燔祭、素祭、平安祭獻在壇上，願耶和華親自討我們的罪。

²⁴"我們行這事並非無故，是特意做的，說：恐怕日後你們的子孫對我們的子孫說：'你們與耶和華以色列的神有何關涉呢？²⁵因為耶和華把約旦河定為我們和你們這呂便人、迦得人的交界，你們與耶和華無分了。'這樣，你們的子孫就使我們的子孫不再敬畏耶和華了。

²⁶"因此我們說：'不如為自己築一座壇，不是為獻祭，也不是為獻別的祭，²⁷乃是為你我中間和你我後人中間作證據，好叫我們也在耶和華面前獻燔祭、平安祭，和別的祭侍奉他，免得你們的子孫日後對我們的子孫說：你們與耶和華無分了。'

²⁸"所以我們說：'日後你們對我們，或對我們的後人這樣說，我們就可以回答說：你們看我們列祖所築的壇，是耶和華壇的樣式，這並不是為獻燔祭，也不是為獻別的祭，乃是為作你我中間的證據。'

²⁹"我們在耶和華我們神帳幕前的壇以外，另築一座壇，為獻燔祭、素祭和別的祭，悖逆耶和華，今日轉去不跟從他，我們斷沒有這個意思！"

³⁰祭司非尼哈與會中的首領，就是與他同來以色列軍中的統領，聽見呂便人、迦得人、瑪拿西人所說的話，就都以為美。³¹祭司以利亞撒的兒子非尼哈對呂便人、迦得人、瑪拿西人說："今日我們知道耶和華在我們中間，因為你們沒有向他犯了這罪。現在你們救以色列人脫離耶和華的手了。"

³²祭司以利亞撒的兒子非尼哈與眾首領離了呂便人、迦得人，從基列地回往迦南地，到了以色列人那裏，便將這事回報他們。³³以色列人以這事為美，就稱頌神，不再提上去攻打呂便人、迦得人，毀壞他們所住的地了。

a 23 Traditionally *peace offerings*; also in verse 27

³⁴呂便人、迦得人給壇起名叫證壇。意思說：這壇在我們中間證明耶和華是神。

約書亞對首領臨別贈言

23 耶和華使以色列人安靜，不與四圍的一切仇敵爭戰，已經多日。約書亞年紀老邁，²就把以色列眾人的長老、族長、審判官並官長都召了來，對他們說："我年紀已經老邁。³耶和華你們的神，因你們的緣故，向那些國所行的一切事，你們親眼看見了，因那為你們爭戰的是耶和華你們的神。⁴我所剪除和所剩下的各國，從約旦河起，到日落之處的大海，我已經拈鬮分給你們各支派為業。⁵耶和華你們的神必將他們從你們面前趕出去，使他們離開你們，你們就必得他們的地為業，正如耶和華你們的神所應許的。

⁶ "所以你們要大大壯膽，謹守遵行寫在摩西律法書上的一切話，不可偏離左右。⁷不可與你們中間所剩下的這些國民攙雜。他們的神，你們不可提他的名，不可指着他起誓，也不可侍奉、叩拜；⁸只要照着你們到今日所行的，專靠耶和華你們的神。

⁹ "因為耶和華已經把那又大又強的國民從你們面前趕出，直到今日，沒有一人在你們面前站立得住。¹⁰你們一人必追趕千人，因耶和華你們的神照他所應許的，為你們爭戰。¹¹你們要分外謹慎，愛耶和華你們的神。

¹² "你們若稍微轉去，與你們中間所剩下的這些國民聯絡，彼此結親，互相往來，¹³你們要確實知道，耶和華你們的神必不再將他們從你們眼前趕出；他們卻要成為你們的網羅、機檻、肋上的鞭、眼中的刺，直到你們在耶和華你們神所賜的這美地上滅亡。

¹⁴ "我現在要走世人必走的路。你們是一心一意地知道，耶和華你們神所應許賜福與你們的話沒有一句落空，都應驗在你們身上了。¹⁵耶和華你們神所應許的一切福氣，怎樣臨到你們身上，耶和華也必照樣

³⁴And the Reubenites and the Gadites gave the altar this name: A Witness Between Us that the LORD is God.

Joshua's Farewell to the Leaders

23 After a long time had passed and the LORD had given Israel rest from all their enemies around them, Joshua, by then old and well advanced in years, ²summoned all Israel—their elders, leaders, judges and officials—and said to them: "I am old and well advanced in years. ³You yourselves have seen everything the LORD your God has done to all these nations for your sake; it was the LORD your God who fought for you. ⁴Remember how I have allotted as an inheritance for your tribes all the land of the nations that remain—the nations I conquered—between the Jordan and the Great Sea*a* in the west. ⁵The LORD your God himself will drive them out of your way. He will push them out before you, and you will take possession of their land, as the LORD your God promised you.

⁶ "Be very strong; be careful to obey all that is written in the Book of the Law of Moses, without turning aside to the right or to the left. ⁷Do not associate with these nations that remain among you; do not invoke the names of their gods or swear by them. You must not serve them or bow down to them. ⁸But you are to hold fast to the LORD your God, as you have until now.

⁹ "The LORD has driven out before you great and powerful nations; to this day no one has been able to withstand you. ¹⁰One of you routs a thousand, because the LORD your God fights for you, just as he promised. ¹¹So be very careful to love the LORD your God.

¹² "But if you turn away and ally yourselves with the survivors of these nations that remain among you and if you intermarry with them and associate with them, ¹³then you may be sure that the LORD your God will no longer drive out these nations before you. Instead, they will become snares and traps for you, whips on your backs and thorns in your eyes, until you perish from this good land, which the LORD your God has given you.

¹⁴ "Now I am about to go the way of all the earth. You know with all your heart and soul that not one of all the good promises the LORD your God gave you has failed. Every promise has been fulfilled; not one has failed. ¹⁵But just as every good promise of the LORD your God has come true, so the LORD will bring on you all the

a 4 That is, the Mediterranean

evil he has threatened, until he has destroyed you from this good land he has given you. [16]If you violate the covenant of the LORD your God, which he commanded you, and go and serve other gods and bow down to them, the LORD's anger will burn against you, and you will quickly perish from the good land he has given you."

The Covenant Renewed at Shechem

24 Then Joshua assembled all the tribes of Israel at Shechem. He summoned the elders, leaders, judges and officials of Israel, and they presented themselves before God.

[2]Joshua said to all the people, "This is what the LORD, the God of Israel, says: 'Long ago your forefathers, including Terah the father of Abraham and Nahor, lived beyond the River[a] and worshiped other gods. [3]But I took your father Abraham from the land beyond the River and led him throughout Canaan and gave him many descendants. I gave him Isaac, [4]and to Isaac I gave Jacob and Esau. I assigned the hill country of Seir to Esau, but Jacob and his sons went down to Egypt.

[5]" 'Then I sent Moses and Aaron, and I afflicted the Egyptians by what I did there, and I brought you out. [6]When I brought your fathers out of Egypt, you came to the sea, and the Egyptians pursued them with chariots and horsemen[b] as far as the Red Sea.[c] [7]But they cried to the LORD for help, and he put darkness between you and the Egyptians; he brought the sea over them and covered them. You saw with your own eyes what I did to the Egyptians. Then you lived in the desert for a long time.

[8]" 'I brought you to the land of the Amorites who lived east of the Jordan. They fought against you, but I gave them into your hands. I destroyed them from before you, and you took possession of their land. [9]When Balak son of Zippor, the king of Moab, prepared to fight against Israel, he sent for Balaam son of Beor to put a curse on you. [10]But I would not listen to Balaam, so he blessed you again and again, and I delivered you out of his hand.

[11]" 'Then you crossed the Jordan and came to Jericho. The citizens of Jericho fought against you, as did also the Amorites, Perizzites, Canaanites, Hittites, Girgashites, Hivites and Jebusites, but I gave them into your hands. [12]I sent the hornet ahead of you, which drove them out before you—also the two Amorite kings. You did not do it with your own sword and

使各樣禍患臨到你們身上，直到把你們從耶和華你們神所賜的這美地上除滅。[16]你們若違背耶和華你們神吩咐你們所守的約，去侍奉別神，叩拜他，耶和華的怒氣必向你們發作，使你們在他所賜的美地上速速滅亡。'"

在示劍重申聖約

24 約書亞將以色列的眾支派聚集在示劍，召了以色列的長老、族長、審判官並官長來，他們就站在神面前。

[2]約書亞對眾民說："耶和華以色列的神如此說：'古時你們的列祖，就是亞伯拉罕和拿鶴的父親他拉，住在大河那邊侍奉別神，[3]我將你們的祖宗亞伯拉罕從大河那邊帶來，領他走遍迦南全地，又使他的子孫眾多，把以撒賜給他。[4]又把雅各和以掃賜給以撒，將西珥山賜給以掃為業。後來雅各和他的子孫下到埃及去了。

[5]" '我差遣摩西、亞倫，並照我在埃及中所行的降災與埃及，然後把你們領出來。[6]我領你們列祖出埃及，他們就到了紅海，埃及人帶領車輛馬兵追趕你們列祖到紅海。[7]你們列祖哀求耶和華，他就使你們和埃及人中間黑暗了，又使海水淹沒埃及人。我在埃及所行的事，你們親眼見過；你們在曠野也住了許多年日。

[8]" '我領你們到約旦河東亞摩利人所住之地。他們與你們爭戰，我將他們交在你們手中，你們便得了他們的地為業；我也在你們面前將他們滅絕。[9]那時摩押王西撥的兒子巴勒起來攻擊耶和華，他發人召了比珥的兒子巴蘭來咒詛你們。[10]我不肯聽巴蘭的話，所以他倒為你們連連祝福。這樣，我便救你們脫離巴勒的手。

[11]" '你們過了約旦河，到了耶利哥。耶利哥人、亞摩利人、比利洗人、迦南人、赫人、革迦撒人、希未人、耶布斯人都與你們爭戰，我把他們交在你們手裏。[12]我打發黃蜂飛在你們前面，將亞摩利人的二王從你們面前攆出，並不是用你的刀，也不是

---

a 2 That is, the Euphrates; also in verses 3, 14 and 15
b 6 Or *charioteers*   c 6 Hebrew *Yam Suph*; that is, Sea of Reeds

用你的弓。13我賜給你們地土，非你們所修治的；我賜給你們城邑，非你們所建造的。你們就住在其中，又得吃非你們所栽種的葡萄園、橄欖園的果子。」

14「現在你們要敬畏耶和華，誠心實意地侍奉他，將你們列祖在大河那邊和在埃及所侍奉的神除掉，去侍奉耶和華。15若是你們以侍奉耶和華為不好，今日就可以選擇所要侍奉的；是你們列祖在大河那邊所侍奉的神呢？是你們所住這地的亞摩利人的神呢？至於我和我家，我們必定侍奉耶和華。」

16百姓回答說：「我們斷不敢離棄耶和華去侍奉別神，17因耶和華我們的神曾將我們和我們列祖從埃及地為奴之家領出來，在我們眼前行了那些大神蹟，在我們所行的道上，所經過的諸國，都保護了我們。18耶和華又把住此地的亞摩利人都從我們面前趕出去。所以，我們必侍奉耶和華，因為他是我們的神。」

19約書亞對百姓說：「你們不能侍奉耶和華，因為他是聖潔的神，是忌邪的神，必不赦免你們的過犯罪惡。20你們若離棄耶和華去侍奉外邦神，耶和華在降福之後，必轉而降禍與你們，把你們滅絕。」

21百姓回答約書亞說：「不然，我們定要侍奉耶和華！」

22約書亞對百姓說：「你們選定耶和華，要侍奉他，你們自己作見證吧！」

他們說：「我們願意作見證。」

23約書亞說：「你們現在要除掉你們中間的外邦神，專心歸向耶和華以色列的神。」

24百姓回答約書亞說：「我們必侍奉耶和華我們的神，聽從他的話。」

25當日，約書亞就與百姓立約，在示劍為他們立定律例典章。26約書亞將這些話都寫在神的律法書上，又將一塊大石頭立在橡樹下耶和華的聖所旁邊。

27約書亞對百姓說：「看哪！這石頭可以向我們作見證，因為是聽見了耶和華所吩咐我們的一切話，倘或你們背棄你們的神，這石頭就可以向你們作見證（註：「倘或云云」或作「所以要向你們作見證，免得你們背棄耶和華你們的神」）。」

bow. 13So I gave you a land on which you did not toil and cities you did not build; and you live in them and eat from vineyards and olive groves that you did not plant.'

14"Now fear the LORD and serve him with all faithfulness. Throw away the gods your forefathers worshiped beyond the River and in Egypt, and serve the LORD. 15But if serving the LORD seems undesirable to you, then choose for yourselves this day whom you will serve, whether the gods your forefathers served beyond the River, or the gods of the Amorites, in whose land you are living. But as for me and my household, we will serve the LORD."

16Then the people answered, "Far be it from us to forsake the LORD to serve other gods! 17It was the LORD our God himself who brought us and our fathers up out of Egypt, from that land of slavery, and performed those great signs before our eyes. He protected us on our entire journey and among all the nations through which we traveled. 18And the LORD drove out before us all the nations, including the Amorites, who lived in the land. We too will serve the LORD, because he is our God."

19Joshua said to the people, "You are not able to serve the LORD. He is a holy God; he is a jealous God. He will not forgive your rebellion and your sins. 20If you forsake the LORD and serve foreign gods, he will turn and bring disaster on you and make an end of you, after he has been good to you."

21But the people said to Joshua, "No! We will serve the LORD."

22Then Joshua said, "You are witnesses against yourselves that you have chosen to serve the LORD."

"Yes, we are witnesses," they replied.

23"Now then," said Joshua, "throw away the foreign gods that are among you and yield your hearts to the LORD, the God of Israel."

24And the people said to Joshua, "We will serve the LORD our God and obey him."

25On that day Joshua made a covenant for the people, and there at Shechem he drew up for them decrees and laws. 26And Joshua recorded these things in the Book of the Law of God. Then he took a large stone and set it up there under the oak near the holy place of the LORD.

27"See!" he said to all the people. "This stone will be a witness against us. It has heard all the words the LORD has said to us. It will be a witness against you if you are untrue to your God."

Buried in the Promised Land

²⁸Then Joshua sent the people away, each to his own inheritance.

²⁹After these things, Joshua son of Nun, the servant of the LORD, died at the age of a hundred and ten. ³⁰And they buried him in the land of his inheritance, at Timnath Serah^a in the hill country of Ephraim, north of Mount Gaash.

³¹Israel served the LORD throughout the lifetime of Joshua and of the elders who outlived him and who had experienced everything the LORD had done for Israel.

³²And Joseph's bones, which the Israelites had brought up from Egypt, were buried at Shechem in the tract of land that Jacob bought for a hundred pieces of silver^b from the sons of Hamor, the father of Shechem. This became the inheritance of Joseph's descendants.

³³And Eleazar son of Aaron died and was buried at Gibeah, which had been allotted to his son Phinehas in the hill country of Ephraim.

葬於應許之地

²⁸於是約書亞打發百姓各歸自己的地業去了。

²⁹這些事以後，耶和華的僕人嫩的兒子約書亞，正一百一十歲就死了。³⁰以色列人將他葬在他地業的境內，就是在以法蓮山地的亭拿西拉，在迦實山的北邊。

³¹約書亞在世和約書亞死後，那些知道耶和華為以色列人所行諸事的長老還在的時候，以色列人侍奉耶和華。

³²以色列人從埃及所帶來約瑟的骸骨，葬埋在示劍，就是在雅各從前用一百塊銀子向示劍的父親哈抹的子孫所買的那塊地裏，這就作了約瑟子孫的產業。

³³亞倫的兒子以利亞撒也死了，就把他葬在他兒子非尼哈以法蓮山地所得的小山上。

圖四：約書亞記中的主要地方
MAP 4 : KEY PLACES IN JOSHUA

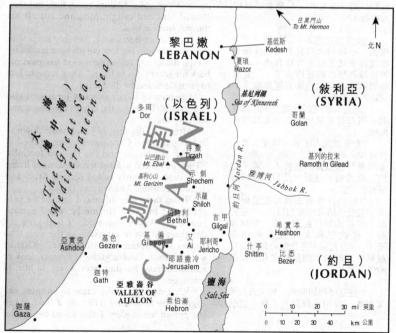

---

a 30 Also known as Timnath Heres (see Judges 2:9)

士師記

JUDGES

以色列人攻擊迦南殘餘

1 約書亞死後，以色列人求問耶和華說："我們中間誰當首先上去攻擊迦南人，與他們爭戰？"

² 耶和華說："猶大當先上去，我已將那地交在他手中。"

³ 猶大對他哥哥西緬說："請你同我到拈鬮所得之地去，好與迦南人爭戰；以後我也同你到你拈鬮所得之地去。"於是西緬與他同去。

⁴ 猶大就上去。耶和華將迦南人和比利洗人交在他們手中，他們在比色擊殺了一萬人。⁵ 又在那裏遇見亞多尼比色，與他爭戰，殺敗迦南人和比利洗人。⁶ 亞多尼比色逃跑，他們追趕，拿住他，砍斷他手腳的大拇指。

⁷ 亞多尼比色說："從前有七十個王，手腳的大拇指都被我砍斷，在我桌子底下拾取零碎食物。現在神按着我所行的報應我了。"於是他們將亞多尼比色帶到耶路撒冷，他就死在那裏。

⁸ 猶大人攻打耶路撒冷，將城攻取，用刀殺了城內的人，並且放火燒城。

⁹ 後來猶大人下去，與住山地、南地和高原的迦南人爭戰。¹⁰ 猶大人去攻擊住希伯崙的迦南人，殺了示篩、亞希幔、撻買。希伯崙從前名叫基列亞巴。

¹¹ 他們從那裏去攻擊底璧的居民。底璧從前名叫基列西弗。¹² 迦勒說："誰能攻打基列西弗，將城奪取，我就把我女兒押撒給他為妻。"¹³ 迦勒兄弟基納斯的兒子俄陀聶奪取了那城，迦勒就把女兒押撒給他為妻。

¹⁴ 押撒過門的時候，勸丈夫向她父親求一塊田。押撒一下驢，迦勒

Israel Fights the Remaining Canaanites

1 After the death of Joshua, the Israelites asked the LORD, "Who will be the first to go up and fight for us against the Canaanites?"

²The LORD answered, "Judah is to go; I have given the land into their hands."

³Then the men of Judah said to the Simeonites their brothers, "Come up with us into the territory allotted to us, to fight against the Canaanites. We in turn will go with you into yours." So the Simeonites went with them.

⁴When Judah attacked, the LORD gave the Canaanites and Perizzites into their hands and they struck down ten thousand men at Bezek. ⁵It was there that they found Adoni-Bezek and fought against him, putting to rout the Canaanites and Perizzites. ⁶Adoni-Bezek fled, but they chased him and caught him, and cut off his thumbs and big toes.

⁷Then Adoni-Bezek said, "Seventy kings with their thumbs and big toes cut off have picked up scraps under my table. Now God has paid me back for what I did to them." They brought him to Jerusalem, and he died there.

⁸The men of Judah attacked Jerusalem also and took it. They put the city to the sword and set it on fire.

⁹After that, the men of Judah went down to fight against the Canaanites living in the hill country, the Negev and the western foothills. ¹⁰They advanced against the Canaanites living in Hebron (formerly called Kiriath Arba) and defeated Sheshai, Ahiman and Talmai.

¹¹From there they advanced against the people living in Debir (formerly called Kiriath Sepher). ¹²And Caleb said, "I will give my daughter Acsah in marriage to the man who attacks and captures Kiriath Sepher." ¹³Othniel son of Kenaz, Caleb's younger brother, took it; so Caleb gave his daughter Acsah to him in marriage.

¹⁴One day when she came to Othniel, she urged him*a* to ask her father for a field. When she got off her donkey, Caleb asked her, "What

---

a 14 Hebrew; Septuagint and Vulgate Othniel, he urged her

can I do for you?"

15She replied, "Do me a special favor. Since you have given me land in the Negev, give me also springs of water." Then Caleb gave her the upper and lower springs.

16The descendants of Moses' father-in-law, the Kenite, went up from the City of Palms*a* with the men of Judah to live among the people of the Desert of Judah in the Negev near Arad.

17Then the men of Judah went with the Simeonites their brothers and attacked the Canaanites living in Zephath, and they totally destroyed*b* the city. Therefore it was called Hormah.*c* 18The men of Judah also took*d* Gaza, Ashkelon and Ekron—each city with its territory.

19The LORD was with the men of Judah. They took possession of the hill country, but they were unable to drive the people from the plains, because they had iron chariots. 20As Moses had promised, Hebron was given to Caleb, who drove from it the three sons of Anak. 21The Benjamites, however, failed to dislodge the Jebusites, who were living in Jerusalem; to this day the Jebusites live there with the Benjamites.

22Now the house of Joseph attacked Bethel, and the LORD was with them. 23When they sent men to spy out Bethel (formerly called Luz), 24the spies saw a man coming out of the city and they said to him, "Show us how to get into the city and we will see that you are treated well." 25So he showed them, and they put the city to the sword but spared the man and his whole family. 26He then went to the land of the Hittites, where he built a city and called it Luz, which is its name to this day.

27But Manasseh did not drive out the people of Beth Shan or Taanach or Dor or Ibleam or Megiddo and their surrounding settlements, for the Canaanites were determined to live in that land. 28When Israel became strong, they pressed the Canaanites into forced labor but never drove them out completely. 29Nor did Ephraim drive out the Canaanites living in Gezer, but the Canaanites continued to live there among them. 30Neither did Zebulun drive out the Canaanites living in Kitron or Nahalol, who remained among them; but they did subject them to forced labor. 31Nor did Asher drive out those living in Acco or Sidon or Ahlab or Aczib or Helbah or Aphek or Rehob, 32and because of

a 16 That is, Jericho　b 17 The Hebrew term refers to the irrevocable giving over of things or persons to the LORD, often by totally destroying them.　c 17 Hormah means *destruction*.
d 18 Hebrew; Septuagint *Judah did not take*

問她説："你要甚麼？"

15她説："求你賜福給我。你既將我安置在南地，求你也給我水泉。"迦勒就把上泉下泉賜給她。

16摩西的內兄（註：或作"岳父"）是基尼人，他的子孫與猶大人一同離了棕樹城，往亞拉得以南的猶大曠野去，就住在民中。

17猶大和他哥哥西緬同去，擊殺了住洗法的迦南人，將城盡行毀滅，那城的名便叫何珥瑪。18猶大又取了迦薩和迦薩的四境，亞實基倫和亞實基倫的四境，以革倫和以革倫的四境。

19耶和華與猶大同在，猶大就趕出山地的居民，只是不能趕出平原的居民，因為他們有鐵車。20以色列人照摩西所説的，將希伯崙給了迦勒，迦勒就從那裏趕出亞衲族的三個族長。21便雅憫人沒有趕出住耶路撒冷的耶布斯人。耶布斯人仍在耶路撒冷與便雅憫人同住，直到今日。

22約瑟家也上去攻打伯特利，耶和華與他們同在。23約瑟家打發人去窺探伯特利。那城起先名叫路斯。24窺探的人看見一個人從城裏出來，就對他説："求你將進城的路指示我們，我們必恩待你。"25那人將進城的路指示他們，他們就用刀擊殺了城中的居民，但將那人和他全家放去。26那人往赫人之地去，築了一座城，起名叫路斯。那城到如今還叫這名。

27瑪拿西沒有趕出伯善和屬伯善鄉村的居民，他納和屬他納鄉村的居民，多珥和屬多珥鄉村的居民，以伯蓮和屬以伯蓮鄉村的居民，米吉多和屬米吉多鄉村的居民。迦南人卻執意住在那些地方。28及至以色列強盛了，就使迦南人做苦工，沒有把他們全然趕出。29以法蓮沒有趕出住基色的迦南人。於是迦南人仍住在基色，在以法蓮中間。30西布倫沒有趕出基倫的居民和拿哈拉的居民。於是迦南人仍住在西布倫中間，成了服苦的人。31亞設沒有趕出亞柯和西頓的居民，亞黑拉和亞革悉的居民，黑巴、亞弗革與利合的居民。32於是亞設因為沒有趕出那地的迦南人，就住在他們中間。³³拿弗他利沒有趕出伯示麥和伯亞納的居民。於是拿弗他利就住在那地的迦南人中間，然而伯示麥和伯亞納的居民，成了服苦的人。³⁴亞摩利人強逼但人住在山地，不容他們下到平原。³⁵亞摩利人卻執意住在希烈山和亞雅倫並沙賓。然而約瑟家勝了他們，使他們成了服苦的人。³⁶亞摩利人的境界，是從亞克拉濱坡，從西拉而上。

主的使者在波金顯現

2 耶和華的使者從吉甲上到波金，對以色列人說：「我使你們從埃及上來，領你們到我向你們列祖起誓應許之地。我又說：『我永不廢棄與你們所立的約。²你們也不可與這地的居民立約，要拆毀他們的祭壇。』你們竟沒有聽從我的話！為何這樣行呢？³因此我又說：『我必不將他們從你們面前趕出；他們必作你們肋下的荊棘，他們的神必作你們的網羅。』」

⁴耶和華的使者向以色列眾人說這話的時候，百姓就放聲而哭。⁵於是給那地方起名叫波金（註：就是「哭」的意思），眾人在那裏向耶和華獻祭。

違命與失敗

⁶從前約書亞打發以色列百姓去的時候，他們各歸自己的地業，佔據地土。⁷約書亞在世和約書亞死後，那些見耶和華為以色列人所行大事的長老還在的時候，百姓都侍奉耶和華。

⁸耶和華的僕人、嫩的兒子約書亞，正一百一十歲就死了。⁹以色列人將他葬在他地業的境內，就是在以法蓮山地的亭拿希烈，在迦實山的北邊。

¹⁰那世代的人也都歸了自己的列祖。後來有別的世代興起，不知道耶和華，也不知道耶和華為以色列人所行的事。¹¹以色列人行耶和華眼中看為惡的事，去侍奉諸巴力，¹²離棄了領他們出埃及地的耶和華——他們列祖的神，去叩拜別神，就是

this the people of Asher lived among the Canaanite inhabitants of the land. ³³Neither did Naphtali drive out those living in Beth Shemesh or Beth Anath; but the Naphtalites too lived among the Canaanite inhabitants of the land, and those living in Beth Shemesh and Beth Anath became forced laborers for them. ³⁴The Amorites confined the Danites to the hill country, not allowing them to come down into the plain. ³⁵And the Amorites were determined also to hold out in Mount Heres, Aijalon and Shaalbim, but when the power of the house of Joseph increased, they too were pressed into forced labor. ³⁶The boundary of the Amorites was from Scorpion^a Pass to Sela and beyond.

The Angel of the LORD at Bokim

2 The angel of the LORD went up from Gilgal to Bokim and said, "I brought you up out of Egypt and led you into the land that I swore to give to your forefathers. I said, 'I will never break my covenant with you, ²and you shall not make a covenant with the people of this land, but you shall break down their altars.' Yet you have disobeyed me. Why have you done this? ³Now therefore I tell you that I will not drive them out before you; they will be ⌊thorns⌋ in your sides and their gods will be a snare to you."

⁴When the angel of the LORD had spoken these things to all the Israelites, the people wept aloud, ⁵and they called that place Bokim.^{b} There they offered sacrifices to the LORD.

Disobedience and Defeat

⁶After Joshua had dismissed the Israelites, they went to take possession of the land, each to his own inheritance. ⁷The people served the LORD throughout the lifetime of Joshua and of the elders who outlived him and who had seen all the great things the LORD had done for Israel.

⁸Joshua son of Nun, the servant of the LORD, died at the age of a hundred and ten. ⁹And they buried him in the land of his inheritance, at Timnath Heres^c in the hill country of Ephraim, north of Mount Gaash.

¹⁰After that whole generation had been gathered to their fathers, another generation grew up, who knew neither the LORD nor what he had done for Israel. ¹¹Then the Israelites did evil in the eyes of the LORD and served the Baals. ¹²They forsook the LORD, the God of their fathers, who had brought them out of Egypt.

---

a 36 Hebrew *Akrabbim*   *b 5 Bokim* means *weepers.*

c 9 Also known as *Timnath Serah* (see Joshua 19:50 and 24:30)

They followed and worshiped various gods of the peoples around them. They provoked the LORD to anger [13]because they forsook him and served Baal and the Ashtoreths. [14]In his anger against Israel the LORD handed them over to raiders who plundered them. He sold them to their enemies all around, whom they were no longer able to resist. [15]Whenever Israel went out to fight, the hand of the LORD was against them to defeat them, just as he had sworn to them. They were in great distress.

[16]Then the LORD raised up judges,[a] who saved them out of the hands of these raiders. [17]Yet they would not listen to their judges but prostituted themselves to other gods and worshiped them. Unlike their fathers, they quickly turned from the way in which their fathers had walked, the way of obedience to the LORD's commands. [18]Whenever the LORD raised up a judge for them, he was with the judge and saved them out of the hands of their enemies as long as the judge lived; for the LORD had compassion on them as they groaned under those who oppressed and afflicted them. [19]But when the judge died, the people returned to ways even more corrupt than those of their fathers, following other gods and serving and worshiping them. They refused to give up their evil practices and stubborn ways.

[20]Therefore the LORD was very angry with Israel and said, "Because this nation has violated the covenant that I laid down for their forefathers and has not listened to me, [21]I will no longer drive out before them any of the nations Joshua left when he died. [22]I will use them to test Israel and see whether they will keep the way of the LORD and walk in it as their forefathers did." [23]The LORD had allowed those nations to remain; he did not drive them out at once by giving them into the hands of Joshua.

3 These are the nations the LORD left to test all those Israelites who had not experienced any of the wars in Canaan [2](he did this only to teach warfare to the descendants of the Israelites who had not had previous battle experience): [3]the five rulers of the Philistines, all the Canaanites, the Sidonians, and the Hivites living in the Lebanon mountains from Mount Baal Hermon to Lebo[b] Hamath. [4]They were left to test the Israelites to see whether they would obey the LORD's commands, which he had given their forefathers through Moses.

a 16 Or leaders; similarly in verses 17-19　　*b 3 Or to the entrance to*

四圍列國的神，惹耶和華發怒。[13]並離棄耶和華，去侍奉巴力和亞斯她錄。[14]耶和華的怒氣向以色列人發作，就把他們交在搶奪他們的人手中。又將他們付與四圍仇敵的手中，甚至他們在仇敵面前再不能站立得住。[15]他們無論往何處去，耶和華都以災禍攻擊他們，正如耶和華所說的話，又如耶和華向他們所起的誓。他們便極其困苦。

[16]耶和華興起士師，士師就拯救他們脫離搶奪他們人的手。[17]他們卻不聽從士師，竟隨從叩拜別神，行了邪淫，速速地偏離他們列祖所行的道，不如他們列祖順從耶和華的命令。[18]耶和華為他們興起士師，就與那士師同在。士師在世的一切日子，耶和華拯救他們脫離仇敵的手。他們因受欺壓擾害，就哀聲歎氣，所以耶和華後悔了。[19]及至士師死後，他們就轉去行惡，比他們列祖更甚，去侍奉叩拜別神，總不斷絕頑梗的惡行。

[20]於是耶和華的怒氣向以色列人發作。他說："因這民違背我吩咐他們列祖所守的約，不聽從我的話，[21]所以約書亞死的時候所剩下的各族，我必不再從他們面前趕出。[22]為要藉此試驗以色列人，看他們肯照他們列祖謹守遵行我的道不肯。"[23]這樣耶和華留下各族，不將他們速速趕出，也沒有交付約書亞的手。

3 耶和華留下這幾族，為要試驗那不曾知道與迦南爭戰之事的以色列人，[2]好叫以色列的後代又知道又學習未曾曉得的戰事。[3]所留下的，就是非利士的五個首領和一切迦南人、西頓人，並住黎巴嫩山的希未人，從巴力黑們山直到哈馬口。[4]留下這幾族，為要試驗以色列人，知道他們肯聽從耶和華藉摩西吩咐他們列祖的誡命不肯。

5以色列人竟住在迦南人、赫人、亞摩利人、比利洗人、希未人、耶布斯人中間，6娶他們的女兒為妻，將自己的女兒嫁給他們的兒子，並侍奉他們的神。

俄陀聶

7以色列人行耶和華眼中看為惡的事，忘記耶和華他們的神，去侍奉諸巴力和亞舍拉。8所以，耶和華的怒氣向以色列人發作，就把他們交在美索不達米亞王古珊利薩田的手中。以色列人服侍古珊利薩田八年。9以色列人呼求耶和華的時候，耶和華就為他們興起一位拯救者救他們，就是迦勒兄弟，基納斯的兒子俄陀聶。10耶和華的靈降在他身上，他就作了以色列的士師，出去爭戰。耶和華將美索不達米亞王古珊利薩田交在他手中，他便勝了古珊利薩田。11於是國中太平四十年。基納斯的兒子俄陀聶死了。

以笏

12以色列人又行耶和華眼中看為惡的事，耶和華就使摩押王伊磯倫強盛，攻擊以色列人。13伊磯倫招聚亞捫人和亞瑪力人，去攻打以色列人，佔據棕樹城。14於是以色列人服侍摩押王伊磯倫十八年。

15以色列人呼求耶和華的時候，耶和華就為他們興起一位拯救者，就是便雅憫人基拉的兒子以笏，他是左手便利的。以色列人託他送禮物給摩押王伊磯倫。16以笏打了一把兩刃的劍，長一肘，帶在右腿上衣服裏面。17他將禮物獻給摩押王伊磯倫，原來伊磯倫極其肥胖。18以笏獻完禮物，便將抬禮物的人打發走了。19自己卻從靠近吉甲鑿石之地回來，說：「王啊，我有一件機密事奏告你。」

王說：「迴避吧！」於是左右侍立的人都退去了。

20以笏來到王面前，王獨自一人坐在涼樓上。以笏說：「我奉神的命報告你一件事。」王就從座位上

5The Israelites lived among the Canaanites, Hittites, Amorites, Perizzites, Hivites and Jebusites. 6They took their daughters in marriage and gave their own daughters to their sons, and served their gods.

Othniel

7The Israelites did evil in the eyes of the LORD; they forgot the LORD their God and served the Baals and the Asherahs. 8The anger of the LORD burned against Israel so that he sold them into the hands of Cushan-Rishathaim king of Aram Naharaim,a to whom the Israelites were subject for eight years. 9But when they cried out to the LORD, he raised up for them a deliverer, Othniel son of Kenaz, Caleb's younger brother, who saved them. 10The Spirit of the LORD came upon him, so that he became Israel's judgeb and went to war. The LORD gave Cushan-Rishathaim king of Aram into the hands of Othniel, who overpowered him. 11So the land had peace for forty years, until Othniel son of Kenaz died.

Ehud

12Once again the Israelites did evil in the eyes of the LORD, and because they did this evil the LORD gave Eglon king of Moab power over Israel. 13Getting the Ammonites and Amalekites to join him, Eglon came and attacked Israel, and they took possession of the City of Palms.c 14The Israelites were subject to Eglon king of Moab for eighteen years.

15Again the Israelites cried out to the LORD, and he gave them a deliverer—Ehud, a left-handed man, the son of Gera the Benjamite. The Israelites sent him with tribute to Eglon king of Moab. 16Now Ehud had made a double-edged sword about a foot and a halfd long, which he strapped to his right thigh under his clothing. 17He presented the tribute to Eglon king of Moab, who was a very fat man. 18After Ehud had presented the tribute, he sent on their way the men who had carried it. 19At the idolse near Gilgal he himself turned back and said, "I have a secret message for you, O king."

The king said, "Quiet!" And all his attendants left him.

20Ehud then approached him while he was sitting alone in the upper room of his summer palacef and said, "I have a message from God

---

a 8 That is, Northwest Mesopotamia　　b 10 Or leader
c 13 That is, Jericho　　d 16 Hebrew a cubit (about 0.5 meter)
e 19 Or the stone quarries; also in verse 26　　f 20 The meaning of the Hebrew for this phrase is uncertain.

for you." As the king rose from his seat, 21Ehud reached with his left hand, drew the sword from his right thigh and plunged it into the king's belly. 22Even the handle sank in after the blade, which came out his back. Ehud did not pull the sword out, and the fat closed in over it. 23Then Ehud went out to the porch*a*; he shut the doors of the upper room behind him and locked them.

24After he had gone, the servants came and found the doors of the upper room locked. They said, "He must be relieving himself in the inner room of the house." 25They waited to the point of embarrassment, but when he did not open the doors of the room, they took a key and unlocked them. There they saw their lord fallen to the floor, dead.

26While they waited, Ehud got away. He passed by the idols and escaped to Seirah. 27When he arrived there, he blew a trumpet in the hill country of Ephraim, and the Israelites went down with him from the hills, with him leading them.

28"Follow me," he ordered, "for the LORD has given Moab, your enemy, into your hands." So they followed him down and, taking possession of the fords of the Jordan that led to Moab, they allowed no one to cross over. 29At that time they struck down about ten thousand Moabites, all vigorous and strong; not a man escaped. 30That day Moab was made subject to Israel, and the land had peace for eighty years.

Shamgar

31After Ehud came Shamgar son of Anath, who struck down six hundred Philistines with an oxgoad. He too saved Israel.

Deborah

4 After Ehud died, the Israelites once again did evil in the eyes of the LORD. 2So the LORD sold them into the hands of Jabin, a king of Canaan, who reigned in Hazor. The commander of his army was Sisera, who lived in Harosheth Haggoyim. 3Because he had nine hundred iron chariots and had cruelly oppressed the Israelites for twenty years, they cried to the LORD for help.

4Deborah, a prophetess, the wife of Lappidoth, was leading*b* Israel at that time. 5She held court under the Palm of Deborah between Ramah and Bethel in the hill country of Ephraim, and the Israelites came to her to have their disputes decided. 6She sent for Barak son

---

a 23 The meaning of the Hebrew for this word is uncertain.

b 4 Traditionally *judging*

站起來。21以笏便伸左手,從右腿上拔出劍來,刺入王的肚腹,22連劍把都刺進去了。劍被肥肉夾住,他沒有從王的肚腹拔出來,且穿通了後身。23以笏就出到遊廊,將樓門盡都關鎖。

24以笏出來之後,王的僕人到了,看見樓門關鎖,就說:"他必是在樓上大解。"25他們等煩了,見仍不開樓門,就拿鑰匙開了。不料,他們的主人已死,倒在地上。

26他們躭延的時候,以笏就逃跑了,經過鑿石之地,逃到西伊拉。27到了,就在以法蓮山地吹角。以色列人隨着他下了山地,他在前頭引路。

28對他們說:"你們隨我來,因為耶和華已經把你們的仇敵摩押人交在你們手中。"於是他們跟着他下去,把守約旦河的渡口,不容摩押一人過去。29那時擊殺了摩押人約有一萬,都是強壯的勇士,沒有一人逃脫。30這樣摩押就被以色列人制伏了。國中太平八十年。

珊迦

31以笏之後,有亞拿的兒子珊迦,他用趕牛的棍子打死六百非利士人。他也救了以色列人。

底波拉

4 以笏死後,以色列人又行耶和華眼中看為惡的事,2耶和華就把他們付與在夏瑣作王的迦南王耶賓手中。他的將軍是西西拉,住在外邦人的夏羅設。3耶賓王有鐵車九百輛。他大大欺壓以色列人二十年,以色列人就呼求耶和華。

4有一位女先知名叫底波拉,是拉比多的妻,當時作以色列的士師。5她住在以法蓮山地拉瑪和伯特利中間,在底波拉的棕樹下。以色列人都上她那裏去聽判斷。6她打發人從拿弗他利的基低斯，將亞比挪菴的兒子巴拉召了來，對他說：“耶和華以色列的神吩咐你說：‘你率領一萬拿弗他利和西布倫人上他泊山去。7我必使耶賓的將軍西西拉率領他的車輛和全軍往基順河，到你那裏去，我必將他交在你手中。’”

8巴拉說：“你若同我去，我就去；你若不同我去，我就不去。”

9底波拉說：“我必與你同去，只是你在所行的路上得不着榮耀，因為耶和華要將西西拉交在一個婦人手裏。”於是底波拉起來，與巴拉一同往基低斯去了。10巴拉就招聚西布倫人和拿弗他利人到基低斯，跟他上去的有一萬人。底波拉也同他上去。

11摩西岳父（註：或作“內兄”）何巴的後裔基尼人希百，曾離開基尼族，到靠近基低斯、撒拿音的橡樹旁支搭帳棚。

12有人告訴西西拉：“亞比挪菴的兒子巴拉已經上他泊山了。”13西西拉就聚集所有的鐵車九百輛和跟隨他的全軍，從外邦人的夏羅設出來，到了基順河。

14底波拉對巴拉說：“你起來，今日就是耶和華將西西拉交在你手的日子。耶和華豈不在你前頭行嗎？”於是巴拉下了他泊山，跟隨他有一萬人。15耶和華使西西拉和他一切車輛全軍潰亂，在巴拉面前被刀殺敗。西西拉下車步行逃跑。16巴拉追趕車輛、軍隊，直到外邦人的夏羅設。西西拉的全軍都倒在刀下，沒有留下一人。

17只有西西拉步行逃跑，到了基尼人希百之妻雅億的帳棚，因為夏瑣王耶賓和基尼人希百家和好。

18雅億出來迎接西西拉，對他說：“請我主進來，不要懼怕。”西西拉就進了她的帳棚，雅億用被將他遮蓋。

19西西拉對雅億說：“我渴了，求你給我一點水喝。”雅億就打開皮袋，給他奶子喝，仍舊把他遮蓋。

20西西拉又對雅億說：“請你站在帳棚門口，若有人來問你說：‘有人在這裏沒有？’你就說：‘沒有。’”

of Abinoam from Kedesh in Naphtali and said to him, "The LORD, the God of Israel, commands you: 'Go, take with you ten thousand men of Naphtali and Zebulun and lead the way to Mount Tabor. 7I will lure Sisera, the commander of Jabin's army, with his chariots and his troops to the Kishon River and give him into your hands.' "

8Barak said to her, "If you go with me, I will go; but if you don't go with me, I won't go."

9"Very well," Deborah said, "I will go with you. But because of the way you are going about this,ᵃ the honor will not be yours, for the LORD will hand Sisera over to a woman." So Deborah went with Barak to Kedesh, 10where he summoned Zebulun and Naphtali. Ten thousand men followed him, and Deborah also went with him.

11Now Heber the Kenite had left the other Kenites, the descendants of Hobab, Moses' brother-in-law,ᵇ and pitched his tent by the great tree in Zaanannim near Kedesh.

12When they told Sisera that Barak son of Abinoam had gone up to Mount Tabor, 13Sisera gathered together his nine hundred iron chariots and all the men with him, from Harosheth Haggoyim to the Kishon River.

14Then Deborah said to Barak, "Go! This is the day the LORD has given Sisera into your hands. Has not the LORD gone ahead of you?" So Barak went down Mount Tabor, followed by ten thousand men. 15At Barak's advance, the LORD routed Sisera and all his chariots and army by the sword, and Sisera abandoned his chariot and fled on foot. 16But Barak pursued the chariots and army as far as Harosheth Haggoyim. All the troops of Sisera fell by the sword; not a man was left.

17Sisera, however, fled on foot to the tent of Jael, the wife of Heber the Kenite, because there were friendly relations between Jabin king of Hazor and the clan of Heber the Kenite.

18Jael went out to meet Sisera and said to him, "Come, my lord, come right in. Don't be afraid." So he entered her tent, and she put a covering over him.

19"I'm thirsty," he said. "Please give me some water." She opened a skin of milk, gave him a drink, and covered him up.

20"Stand in the doorway of the tent," he told her. "If someone comes by and asks you, 'Is anyone here?' say 'No.' "

a 9 Or But on the expedition you are undertaking　b 11 Or father-in-law

²¹But Jael, Heber's wife, picked up a tent peg and a hammer and went quietly to him while he lay fast asleep, exhausted. She drove the peg through his temple into the ground, and he died.

²²Barak came by in pursuit of Sisera, and Jael went out to meet him. "Come," she said, "I will show you the man you're looking for." So he went in with her, and there lay Sisera with the tent peg through his temple—dead.

²³On that day God subdued Jabin, the Canaanite king, before the Israelites. ²⁴And the hand of the Israelites grew stronger and stronger against Jabin, the Canaanite king, until they destroyed him.

The Song of Deborah

5 On that day Deborah and Barak son of Abinoam sang this song:

²"When the princes in Israel take the lead,
   when the people willingly offer
         themselves—
       praise the LORD!

³"Hear this, you kings! Listen, you rulers!
   I will sing to*ᵃ* the LORD, I will sing;
   I will make music to*ᵇ* the LORD, the God of
      Israel.

⁴"O LORD, when you went out from Seir,
   when you marched from the land of Edom,
  the earth shook, the heavens poured,
   the clouds poured down water.
⁵The mountains quaked before the LORD, the
     One of Sinai,
  before the LORD, the God of Israel.

⁶"In the days of Shamgar son of Anath,
   in the days of Jael, the roads were
     abandoned;
  travelers took to winding paths.
⁷Village life*ᶜ* in Israel ceased,
   ceased until I,*ᵈ* Deborah, arose,
   arose a mother in Israel.
⁸When they chose new gods,
   war came to the city gates,
  and not a shield or spear was seen
   among forty thousand in Israel.
⁹My heart is with Israel's princes,
   with the willing volunteers among the
     people.
   Praise the Lord!

²¹西西拉疲乏沉睡。希百的妻雅億取了帳棚的橛子,手裏拿着錘子,輕悄悄地到他旁邊,將橛子從他鬢邊釘進去,釘入地裏。西西拉就死了。

²²巴拉追趕西西拉的時候,雅億出來迎接他說:「來吧,我將你所尋找的人給你看。」他就進入帳棚,看見西西拉已經死了,倒在地上,橛子還在他鬢中。

²³這樣,神使迦南王耶賓被以色列人制伏了。²⁴從此以色列人的手越發有力,勝了迦南王耶賓,直到將他滅絕了。

底波拉之歌

5 那時底波拉和亞比挪菴的兒子巴拉作歌,說:

² 「因為以色列中有軍長率領,
   百姓也甘心犧牲自己,
   你們應當頌讚耶和華!

³ 「君王啊,要聽!
   王子啊,要側耳而聽!
  我要向耶和華歌唱,
   我要歌頌耶和華以色列的神。

⁴ 「耶和華啊,你從西珥出來,
   由以東地行走,
  那時地震天漏,
   雲也落雨。
⁵山見耶和華的面就震動;
   西奈山見耶和華以色列神的面,
   也是如此。

⁶ 「在亞拿之子珊迦的時候,
   又在雅億的日子,
  大道無人行走,
   都是繞道而行。
⁷以色列中的官長停職,
   直到我底波拉興起,
   等我興起作以色列的母。
⁸以色列人選擇新神,
   爭戰的事就臨到城門。
  那時,以色列四萬人中,
   豈能見籐牌槍矛呢?
⁹我心傾向以色列的首領,
   他們在民中
     甘心犧牲自己。
   你們應當頌讚耶和華!

*a 3 Or of   b 3 Or / with song I will praise   c 7 Or Warriors
d 7 Or you*

¹⁰ "騎白驢的、
　　坐繡花毯子的、
　　行路的，
　　你們都當傳揚！
¹¹ 在遠離弓箭響聲打水之處，
　　人必述說耶和華公義的作為，
　　就是他治理以色列公義的作為。

　 "那時耶和華的民
　　下到城門。
¹² '底波拉啊，興起！興起！
　　你當興起，興起，唱歌。
　　亞比挪菴的兒子巴拉啊，
　　你當奮興，
　　擄掠你的敵人。'

¹³ "那時有餘剩的貴冑
　　和百姓一同下來；
　　耶和華降臨，
　　為我攻擊勇士。
¹⁴ 有根本在亞瑪力人的地，
　　從以法蓮下來的，
　　便雅憫在民中跟隨你；
　　有掌權的
　　從瑪吉下來。
　　有持杖檢點民數的
　　從西布倫下來。
¹⁵ 以薩迦的首領與底波拉同來，
　　以薩迦怎樣，巴拉也怎樣。
　　眾人都跟隨巴拉，衝下平原。
　　在呂便的溪水旁
　　有心中定大志的。
¹⁶ 你為何坐在羊圈內，
　　聽羣中吹笛的聲音呢？
　　在呂便的溪水旁
　　有心中設大謀的。
¹⁷ 基列人安居在約旦河外。
　　但人為何等在船上？
　　亞設人在海口靜坐，
　　在港口安居。
¹⁸ 西布倫人是拚命敢死的，
　　拿弗他利人在田野的高處，
　　也是如此。
¹⁹ "君王都來爭戰。
　　那時迦南諸王
　　在米吉多水旁的他納爭戰，
　　卻未得擄掠銀錢。
²⁰ 星宿從天上爭戰，
　　從其軌道攻擊西西拉。
²¹ 基順古河把敵人沖沒。
　　我的靈啊，
　　應當努力前行。

¹⁰"You who ride on white donkeys,
　　sitting on your saddle blankets,
　　and you who walk along the road,
　consider ¹¹the voice of the singers^a at the
　　watering places.
　They recite the righteous acts of the LORD,
　　the righteous acts of his warriors^b in Israel.

　"Then the people of the LORD
　　went down to the city gates.
¹²'Wake up, wake up, Deborah!
　Wake up, wake up, break out in song!
　Arise, O Barak!
　　Take captive your captives, O son of
　　Abinoam.'

¹³"Then the men who were left
　　came down to the nobles;
　the people of the LORD
　　came to me with the mighty.
¹⁴Some came from Ephraim, whose roots were
　　in Amalek;
　Benjamin was with the people who followed
　　you.
　From Makir captains came down,
　　from Zebulun those who bear a
　　commander's staff.
¹⁵The princes of Issachar were with Deborah;
　　yes, Issachar was with Barak,
　　rushing after him into the valley.
　In the districts of Reuben
　　there was much searching of heart.
¹⁶Why did you stay among the campfires^c
　　to hear the whistling for the flocks?
　In the districts of Reuben
　　there was much searching of heart.
¹⁷Gilead stayed beyond the Jordan.
　　And Dan, why did he linger by the ships?
　Asher remained on the coast
　　and stayed in his coves.
¹⁸The people of Zebulun risked their very lives;
　　so did Naphtali on the heights of the field.

¹⁹"Kings came, they fought;
　　the kings of Canaan fought
　at Taanach by the waters of Megiddo,
　　but they carried off no silver, no plunder.
²⁰From the heavens the stars fought,
　　from their courses they fought against Sisera.
²¹The river Kishon swept them away,
　　the age-old river, the river Kishon.
　　March on, my soul; be strong!

*a 11 Or archers; the meaning of the Hebrew for this word is
uncertain.　b 11 Or villagers　c 16 Or saddlebags*

²²Then thundered the horses' hoofs—
　　galloping, galloping go his mighty steeds.
²³'Curse Meroz,' said the angel of the LORD.
　　'Curse its people bitterly,
　　because they did not come to help the LORD,
　　to help the LORD against the mighty.'

²⁴"Most blessed of women be Jael,
　　the wife of Heber the Kenite,
　　most blessed of tent-dwelling women.
²⁵He asked for water, and she gave him milk;
　　in a bowl fit for nobles she brought him
　　curdled milk.
²⁶Her hand reached for the tent peg,
　　her right hand for the workman's hammer.
　　She struck Sisera, she crushed his head,
　　she shattered and pierced his temple.
²⁷At her feet he sank,
　　he fell; there he lay.
　　At her feet he sank, he fell;
　　where he sank, there he fell—dead.

²⁸"Through the window peered Sisera's mother;
　　behind the lattice she cried out,
　　'Why is his chariot so long in coming?
　　Why is the clatter of his chariots delayed?'
²⁹The wisest of her ladies answer her;
　　indeed, she keeps saying to herself,
³⁰'Are they not finding and dividing the spoils:
　　a girl or two for each man,
　　colorful garments as plunder for Sisera,
　　colorful garments embroidered,
　　highly embroidered garments for my neck—
　　all this as plunder?'

³¹"So may all your enemies perish, O Lord!
　　But may they who love you be like the sun
　　when it rises in its strength."

Then the land had peace forty years.

Gideon

6 Again the Israelites did evil in the eyes
of the LORD, and for seven years he gave
them into the hands of the Midianites.
²Because the power of Midian was so oppres-
sive, the Israelites prepared shelters for themselves in mountain clefts, caves and strongholds.
³Whenever the Israelites planted their crops, the
Midianites, Amalekites and other eastern peoples invaded the country. ⁴They camped on the
land and ruined the crops all the way to Gaza
and did not spare a living thing for Israel, neither sheep nor cattle nor donkeys. ⁵They came
up with their livestock and their tents like
swarms of locusts. It was impossible to count

---

²²那時壯馬馳驅、
　　踢跳、奔騰。
²³耶和華的使者說：'應當咒詛米羅斯，
　　大大咒詛其中的居民，
　　因為他們不來幫助耶和華，
　　不來幫助耶和華攻擊勇士。'

²⁴"願基尼人希百的妻雅億
　　比眾婦人多得福氣，
　　比住帳棚的婦人更蒙福祉。
²⁵西西拉求水，
　　雅億給他奶子，
　　用寶貴的盤子，給他奶油。
²⁶雅億左手拿着帳棚的橛子，
　　右手拿着匠人的錘子，
　　擊打西西拉，打傷他的頭，
　　把他的鬢角打破穿通。
²⁷西西拉在她腳前曲身仆倒，
　　在她腳前曲身倒臥。
　　在那裏曲身，
　　就在那裏死亡。

²⁸"西西拉的母親從窗戶裏往外觀看，
　　從窗櫺中呼叫說：
　　'他的戰車為何躭延不來呢？
　　他的車輪為何行得慢呢？'
²⁹聰明的宮女安慰她（註：原文作"回答
　　她"），她也自言自語地說：
³⁰'他們莫非得財而分，
　　每人得了一兩個女子，
　　西西拉得了彩衣為擄物，
　　得繡花的彩衣為掠物，
　　這彩衣兩面繡花，
　　乃是披在被擄之人頸項上的？'

³¹"耶和華啊，願你的仇敵都這樣滅亡！
　　願愛你的人如日頭出現，
　　光輝烈烈！"

這樣，國中太平四十年。

基甸

6 以色列人又行耶和華眼中看
為惡的事，耶和華就把他們
交在米甸人手裏七年。²米甸
人壓制以色列人，以色列人因為米甸
人，就在山中挖穴、挖洞、建造營
寨。³以色列人每逢撒種之後，米甸
人、亞瑪力人和東方人都上來攻打他
們，⁴對着他們安營，毀壞土產，直
到迦薩，沒有給以色列人留下食物，
牛、羊、驢也沒有留下。⁵因為那些
人帶着牲畜帳棚來，像蝗蟲那樣多，

人和駱駝無數，都進入國內，毀壞全地。6以色列人因米甸人的緣故，極其窮乏，就呼求耶和華。

7以色列人因米甸人的緣故，呼求耶和華，8耶和華就差遣先知到以色列人那裏，對他們說："耶和華以色列的神如此說：'我曾領你們從埃及上來，出了為奴之家，9救你們脫離埃及人的手，並脫離一切欺壓你們之人的手，把他們從你們面前趕出，將他們的地賜給你們。10又對你們說：我是耶和華你們的神。你們住在亞摩利人的地，不可敬畏他們的神。你們竟不聽從我的話。'"

11耶和華的使者到了俄弗拉，坐在亞比以謝族人約阿施的橡樹下。約阿施的兒子基甸正在酒醡那裏打麥子，為要防備米甸人。12耶和華的使者向基甸顯現，對他說："大能的勇士啊，耶和華與你同在！"

13基甸說："主啊，耶和華若與我們同在，我們何至遭遇這一切事呢？我們的列祖不是向我們說，耶和華領我們從埃及上來嗎？他那樣奇妙的作為在哪裏呢？現在他卻丟棄我們，將我們交在米甸人手裏。"

14耶和華觀看基甸，說："你靠着你這能力去從米甸人手裏拯救以色列人，不是我差遣你去的嗎？"

15基甸說："主啊，我有何能拯救以色列人呢？我家在瑪拿西支派中是至貧窮的，我在我父家是至微小的。"

16耶和華對他說："我與你同在，你就必擊打米甸人，如擊打一人一樣。"

17基甸說："我若在你眼前蒙恩，求你給我一個證據，使我知道與我說話的就是主。18求你不要離開這裏，等我歸回，將禮物帶來供在你面前。"

主說："我必等你回來。"

19基甸去預備了一隻山羊羔，用一伊法細麵做了無酵餅，將肉放在筐內，把湯盛在壺中，帶到橡樹下，獻在使者面前。

20神的使者吩咐基甸說："將肉和無酵餅放在這磐石上，把湯倒出來。"他就這樣行了。21耶和華的使者伸出手內的杖，杖頭挨了肉和無酵餅，就有火從磐石中出來，燒盡

the men and their camels; they invaded the land to ravage it. 6Midian so impoverished the Israelites that they cried out to the LORD for help.

7When the Israelites cried to the LORD because of Midian, 8he sent them a prophet, who said, "This is what the LORD, the God of Israel, says: I brought you up out of Egypt, out of the land of slavery. 9I snatched you from the power of Egypt and from the hand of all your oppressors. I drove them from before you and gave you their land. 10I said to you, 'I am the LORD your God; do not worship the gods of the Amorites, in whose land you live.' But you have not listened to me."

11The angel of the LORD came and sat down under the oak in Ophrah that belonged to Joash the Abiezrite, where his son Gideon was threshing wheat in a winepress to keep it from the Midianites. 12When the angel of the LORD appeared to Gideon, he said, "The LORD is with you, mighty warrior."

13"But sir," Gideon replied, "if the LORD is with us, why has all this happened to us? Where are all his wonders that our fathers told us about when they said, 'Did not the LORD bring us up out of Egypt?' But now the LORD has abandoned us and put us into the hand of Midian."

14The LORD turned to him and said, "Go in the strength you have and save Israel out of Midian's hand. Am I not sending you?"

15"But Lord,a" Gideon asked, "how can I save Israel? My clan is the weakest in Manasseh, and I am the least in my family."

16The LORD answered, "I will be with you, and you will strike down all the Midianites together."

17Gideon replied, "If now I have found favor in your eyes, give me a sign that it is really you talking to me. 18Please do not go away until I come back and bring my offering and set it before you."

And the LORD said, "I will wait until you return."

19Gideon went in, prepared a young goat, and from an ephahb of flour he made bread without yeast. Putting the meat in a basket and its broth in a pot, he brought them out and offered them to him under the oak.

20The angel of God said to him, "Take the meat and the unleavened bread, place them on this rock, and pour out the broth." And Gideon did so. 21With the tip of the staff that was in his hand, the angel of the LORD touched the meat

---

a 15 Or sir　b 19 That is, probably about 3/5 bushel (about 22 liters)

and the unleavened bread. Fire flared from the rock, consuming the meat and the bread. And the angel of the LORD disappeared. ²²When Gideon realized that it was the angel of the LORD, he exclaimed, "Ah, Sovereign LORD! I have seen the angel of the LORD face to face!"

²³But the LORD said to him, "Peace! Do not be afraid. You are not going to die."

²⁴So Gideon built an altar to the LORD there and called it The LORD is Peace. To this day it stands in Ophrah of the Abiezrites.

²⁵That same night the LORD said to him, "Take the second bull from your father's herd, the one seven years old.ᵃ Tear down your father's altar to Baal and cut down the Asherah poleᵇ beside it. ²⁶Then build a proper kind ofᶜ altar to the LORD your God on the top of this height. Using the wood of the Asherah pole that you cut down, offer the secondᵈ bull as a burnt offering."

²⁷So Gideon took ten of his servants and did as the LORD told him. But because he was afraid of his family and the men of the town, he did it at night rather than in the daytime.

²⁸In the morning when the men of the town got up, there was Baal's altar, demolished, with the Asherah pole beside it cut down and the second bull sacrificed on the newly built altar!

²⁹They asked each other, "Who did this?"

When they carefully investigated, they were told, "Gideon son of Joash did it."

³⁰The men of the town demanded of Joash, "Bring out your son. He must die, because he has broken down Baal's altar and cut down the Asherah pole beside it."

³¹But Joash replied to the hostile crowd around him, "Are you going to plead Baal's cause? Are you trying to save him? Whoever fights for him shall be put to death by morning! If Baal really is a god, he can defend himself when someone breaks down his altar." ³²So that day they called Gideon "Jerub-Baal,"ᵉ saying, "Let Baal contend with him," because he broke down Baal's altar.

³³Now all the Midianites, Amalekites and other eastern peoples joined forces and crossed over the Jordan and camped in the Valley of Jezreel. ³⁴Then the Spirit of the LORD came upon Gideon, and he blew a trumpet, summoning the

---

了肉和無酵餅。耶和華的使者也就不見了。²²基甸見他是耶和華的使者，就說："哀哉！主耶和華啊，我不好了，因為我覿面看見耶和華的使者。"

²³耶和華對他說："你放心，不要懼怕，你必不至死！"

²⁴於是基甸在那裏為耶和華築了一座壇，起名叫"耶和華沙龍"（註：就是"耶和華賜平安"的意思）。這壇在亞比以謝族的俄弗拉，直到如今。

²⁵當那夜，耶和華吩咐基甸說："你取你父親的牛來，就是（註：或作"和"）那七歲的第二隻牛犢，並拆毀你父親為巴力所築的壇，砍下壇旁的木偶。²⁶在這磐石（註：原文作"保障"）上，整整齊齊地為耶和華你的神築一座壇，將第二隻牛獻為燔祭，用你所砍下的木偶作柴。"

²⁷基甸就從他僕人中挑了十個人，照着耶和華吩咐他的行了。他因怕父家和本城的人，不敢在白晝行這事，就在夜間行了。

²⁸城裏的人清早起來，見巴力的壇拆毀，壇旁的木偶砍下，第二隻牛獻在新築的壇上。

²⁹就彼此說："這事是誰做的呢？"他們訪查之後，就說："這是約阿施的兒子基甸做的。"

³⁰城裏的人對約阿施說："將你兒子交出來，好治死他，因為他拆毀了巴力的壇，砍下壇旁的木偶。"

³¹約阿施回答站着攻擊他的眾人說："你們是為巴力爭論嗎？你們要救他嗎？誰為他爭論，趁早將誰治死！巴力若果是神，有人拆毀他的壇，讓他為自己爭論吧！"³²所以當日人稱基甸為耶路巴力，意思說："他拆毀巴力的壇，讓巴力與他爭論。"

³³那時，米甸人、亞瑪力人和東方人都聚集過河，在耶斯列平原安營。³⁴耶和華的靈降在基甸身上，他就吹角，亞比以謝族都聚集跟隨他；

ᵃ 25 Or *Take a full-grown, mature bull from your father's herd*
ᵇ 25 *That is, a symbol of the goddess Asherah; here and elsewhere in Judges*   ᶜ 26 Or *build with layers of stone an*   ᵈ 26 Or *full-grown; also in verse 28*   ᵉ 32 Jerub-Baal *means let Baal contend.*

35他打發人走遍瑪拿西地，瑪拿西人也聚集跟隨他；又打發人去見亞設人、西布倫人、拿弗他利人，他們也都出來與他們會合。

36基甸對神說：「你若果照着所說的話，藉我手拯救以色列人，37我就把一團羊毛放在禾場上。若單是羊毛上有露水，別的地方都是乾的，我就知道你必照着所說的話，藉我手拯救以色列人。」38次日早晨，基甸起來，見果然是這樣：將羊毛擠一擠，從羊毛中擰出滿盆的露水來。

39基甸又對神說：「求你不要向我發怒，我再說這一次：讓我將羊毛再試一次。但願羊毛是乾的，別的地方都有露水。」40這夜神也如此行：獨羊毛上是乾的，別的地方都有露水。

基甸打敗米甸人

7 耶路巴力就是基甸，他和一切跟隨的人早晨起來，在哈律泉旁安營。米甸營在他們北邊的平原，靠近摩利岡。2耶和華對基甸說：「跟隨你的人過多，我不能將米甸人交在他們手中，免得以色列人向我誇大，說：『是我們自己的手救了我們。』3現在你要向這些人宣告說：『凡懼怕膽怯的，可以離開基列山回去。』」於是有二萬二千人回去，只剩下一萬。

4耶和華對基甸說：「人還是過多。你要帶他們下到水旁，我好在那裏為你試試他們。我指點誰說：『這人可以同你去。』他就可以同你去；我指點誰說：『這人不可同你去。』他就不可同你去。」

5基甸就帶他們下到水旁。耶和華對基甸說：「凡用舌頭舔水，像狗舔的，要使他單站在一處；凡跪下喝水的，也要使他單站在一處。」6於是用手捧着舔水的有三百人，其餘的都跪下喝水。

7耶和華對基甸說：「我要用這舔水的三百人拯救你們，將米甸人交在你手中；其餘的人，都可以各歸各處去。」8這三百人就帶着食物和角，其餘的以色列人，基甸都打發他們各歸各的帳棚，只留下這三百人。

米甸營在他下邊的平原裏。9當那夜，耶和華吩咐基甸說：「起

Abiezrites to follow him. 35He sent messengers throughout Manasseh, calling them to arms, and also into Asher, Zebulun and Naphtali, so that they too went up to meet them.

36Gideon said to God, "If you will save Israel by my hand as you have promised— 37look, I will place a wool fleece on the threshing floor. If there is dew only on the fleece and all the ground is dry, then I will know that you will save Israel by my hand, as you said." 38And that is what happened. Gideon rose early the next day; he squeezed the fleece and wrung out the dew—a bowlful of water.

39Then Gideon said to God, "Do not be angry with me. Let me make just one more request. Allow me one more test with the fleece. This time make the fleece dry and the ground covered with dew." 40That night God did so. Only the fleece was dry; all the ground was covered with dew.

Gideon Defeats the Midianites

7 Early in the morning, Jerub-Baal (that is, Gideon) and all his men camped at the spring of Harod. The camp of Midian was north of them in the valley near the hill of Moreh. 2The LORD said to Gideon, "You have too many men for me to deliver Midian into their hands. In order that Israel may not boast against me that her own strength has saved her, 3announce now to the people, 'Anyone who trembles with fear may turn back and leave Mount Gilead.' " So twenty-two thousand men left, while ten thousand remained.

4But the LORD said to Gideon, "There are still too many men. Take them down to the water, and I will sift them for you there. If I say, 'This one shall go with you,' he shall go; but if I say, 'This one shall not go with you,' he shall not go."

5So Gideon took the men down to the water. There the LORD told him, "Separate those who lap the water with their tongues like a dog from those who kneel down to drink." 6Three hundred men lapped with their hands to their mouths. All the rest got down on their knees to drink.

7The LORD said to Gideon, "With the three hundred men that lapped I will save you and give the Midianites into your hands. Let all the other men go, each to his own place." 8So Gideon sent the rest of the Israelites to their tents but kept the three hundred, who took over the provisions and trumpets of the others.

Now the camp of Midian lay below him in the valley. 9During that night the LORD said to

Gideon, "Get up, go down against the camp, because I am going to give it into your hands. 10If you are afraid to attack, go down to the camp with your servant Purah 11and listen to what they are saying. Afterward, you will be encouraged to attack the camp." So he and Purah his servant went down to the outposts of the camp. 12The Midianites, the Amalekites and all the other eastern peoples had settled in the valley, thick as locusts. Their camels could no more be counted than the sand on the seashore.

13Gideon arrived just as a man was telling a friend his dream. "I had a dream," he was saying. "A round loaf of barley bread came tumbling into the Midianite camp. It struck the tent with such force that the tent overturned and collapsed."

14His friend responded, "This can be nothing other than the sword of Gideon son of Joash, the Israelite. God has given the Midianites and the whole camp into his hands."

15When Gideon heard the dream and its interpretation, he worshiped God. He returned to the camp of Israel and called out, "Get up! The LORD has given the Midianite camp into your hands." 16Dividing the three hundred men into three companies, he placed trumpets and empty jars in the hands of all of them, with torches inside.

17"Watch me," he told them. "Follow my lead. When I get to the edge of the camp, do exactly as I do. 18When I and all who are with me blow our trumpets, then from all around the camp blow yours and shout, 'For the LORD and for Gideon.'"

19Gideon and the hundred men with him reached the edge of the camp at the beginning of the middle watch, just after they had changed the guard. They blew their trumpets and broke the jars that were in their hands. 20The three companies blew the trumpets and smashed the jars. Grasping the torches in their left hands and holding in their right hands the trumpets they were to blow, they shouted, "A sword for the LORD and for Gideon!" 21While each man held his position around the camp, all the Midianites ran, crying out as they fled.

22When the three hundred trumpets sounded, the LORD caused the men throughout the camp to turn on each other with their swords. The army fled to Beth Shittah toward Zererah as far as the border of Abel Meholah near Tabbath. 23Israelites from Naphtali, Asher and all Manasseh were called out, and they pursued the Midianites. 24Gideon sent messengers throughout the hill country of Ephraim, saying, "Come

來，下到米甸營裏去，因我已將他們交在你手中。10倘若你怕下去，就帶你的僕人普拉下到那營裏去。11你必聽見他們所說的，然後你就有膽量下去攻營。”於是基甸帶着僕人普拉下到營旁。12米甸人、亞瑪力人和一切東方人都布散在平原，如同蝗蟲那樣多。他們的駱駝無數，多如海邊的沙。

13基甸到了，就聽見一人將夢告訴同伴說：“我做了一夢，夢見一個大麥餅滾入米甸營中，到了帳幕，將帳幕撞倒，帳幕就翻轉傾覆了。”

14那同伴說：“這不是別的，乃是以色列人約阿施的兒子基甸的刀。神已將米甸和全軍都交在他的手中。”

15基甸聽見這夢和夢的講解，就敬拜神，回到以色列營中，說：“起來吧！耶和華已將米甸的軍隊交在你們手中了。”16於是基甸將三百人分作三隊，把角和空瓶交在各人手裏，瓶內都藏着火把。

17吩咐他們說：“你們要看看我行事，我到了營的旁邊怎樣行，你們也要怎樣行。18我和一切跟隨我的人吹角的時候，你們也要在營的四圍吹角，喊叫說：‘耶和華和基甸的刀！’”

19基甸和跟隨他的一百人，在三更之初才換更的時候，來到營旁，就吹角，打破手中的瓶。20三隊的人就都吹角，打破瓶子，左手拿着火把，右手拿着角，喊叫說：“耶和華和基甸的刀！”21他們在營的四圍各站各的地方。全營的人都亂竄；三百人吶喊，使他們逃跑。

22三百人就吹角，耶和華使全營的人用刀互相擊殺，逃到西利拉的伯哈示他，直逃到靠近他巴的亞伯米何拉。23以色列人就從拿弗他利、亞設和瑪拿西全地聚集來追趕米甸人。24基甸打發人走遍以法蓮山地，說：

"你們下來攻擊米甸人，爭先把守<u>約旦河</u>的渡口，<u>直到伯巴拉</u>。"

於是<u>以法蓮</u>的眾人聚集，把守<u>約旦河</u>的渡口，<u>直到伯巴拉</u>。²⁵捉住了米甸人的兩個首領：一名<u>俄立</u>，一名<u>西伊伯</u>。將<u>俄立</u>殺在<u>俄立</u>磐石上，將<u>西伊伯</u>殺在<u>西伊伯</u>酒醡那裏。又追趕米甸人，將<u>俄立</u>和<u>西伊伯</u>的首級，帶過<u>約旦河</u>，到<u>基甸</u>那裏。

西巴與撒慕拿

8 <u>以法蓮</u>人對<u>基甸</u>説："你去與米甸人爭戰，沒有招呼我們同去，為甚麼這樣待我們呢？"他們就與<u>基甸</u>大大地爭吵。

²<u>基甸</u>對他們説："我所行的豈能比你們所行的呢？<u>以法蓮</u>拾取剩下的葡萄，不強過<u>亞比以謝</u>所摘的葡萄嗎？³神已將米甸人的兩個首領<u>俄立</u>和<u>西伊伯</u>交在你們手中；我所行的，豈能比你們所行的呢？"<u>基甸</u>説了這話，<u>以法蓮</u>人的怒氣就消了。

⁴<u>基甸</u>和跟隨他的三百人到<u>約旦河</u>過渡，雖然疲乏，還是追趕。⁵<u>基甸</u>對<u>疏割</u>人説："求你們拿餅來給跟隨我的人吃，因為他們疲乏了。我們追趕米甸人的兩個王<u>西巴</u>和<u>撒慕拿</u>。"

<u>疏割</u>人的首領回答説："<u>西巴</u>和<u>撒慕拿</u>已經在你手裏，你使我們將餅給你的軍兵嗎？"

⁷<u>基甸</u>説："耶和華將<u>西巴</u>和<u>撒慕拿</u>交在我手之後，我就用野地的荊條和枳棘打傷你們。"

⁸<u>基甸</u>從那裏上到<u>毘努伊勒</u>，對那裏的人也是這樣説；<u>毘努伊勒</u>人也與<u>疏割</u>人回答他的話一樣。⁹他向<u>毘努伊勒</u>人説："我平平安安回來的時候，我必拆毀這樓。"

¹⁰那時，<u>西巴</u>和<u>撒慕拿</u>並跟隨他們的軍隊，都在<u>加各</u>，約有一萬五千人，就是東方人全軍所剩下的；已經被殺約有十二萬拿刀的。¹¹<u>基甸</u>就由<u>挪巴</u>和<u>約比哈</u>東邊，從住帳棚人的路上去，殺敗了米甸人的軍兵，因為他們坦然無懼。¹²<u>西巴</u>和<u>撒慕拿</u>逃跑，<u>基甸</u>追趕他們，捉住米甸的二王<u>西巴</u>和<u>撒慕拿</u>，驚散全軍。

down against the Midianites and seize the waters of the Jordan ahead of them as far as Beth Barah."

So all the men of Ephraim were called out and they took the waters of the Jordan as far as Beth Barah. ²⁵They also captured two of the Midianite leaders, Oreb and Zeeb. They killed Oreb at the rock of Oreb, and Zeeb at the winepress of Zeeb. They pursued the Midianites and brought the heads of Oreb and Zeeb to Gideon, who was by the Jordan.

Zebah and Zalmunna

8 Now the Ephraimites asked Gideon, "Why have you treated us like this? Why didn't you call us when you went to fight Midian?" And they criticized him sharply.

²But he answered them, "What have I accomplished compared to you? Aren't the gleanings of Ephraim's grapes better than the full grape harvest of Abiezer? ³God gave Oreb and Zeeb, the Midianite leaders, into your hands. What was I able to do compared to you?" At this, their resentment against him subsided.

⁴Gideon and his three hundred men, exhausted yet keeping up the pursuit, came to the Jordan and crossed it. ⁵He said to the men of Succoth, "Give my troops some bread; they are worn out, and I am still pursuing Zebah and Zalmunna, the kings of Midian."

⁶But the officials of Succoth said, "Do you already have the hands of Zebah and Zalmunna in your possession? Why should we give bread to your troops?"

⁷Then Gideon replied, "Just for that, when the Lord has given Zebah and Zalmunna into my hand, I will tear your flesh with desert thorns and briers."

⁸From there he went up to Peniel[a] and made the same request of them, but they answered as the men of Succoth had. ⁹So he said to the men of Peniel, "When I return in triumph, I will tear down this tower."

¹⁰Now Zebah and Zalmunna were in Karkor with a force of about fifteen thousand men, all that were left of the armies of the eastern peoples; a hundred and twenty thousand swordsmen had fallen. ¹¹Gideon went up by the route of the nomads east of Nobah and Jogbehah and fell upon the unsuspecting army. ¹²Zebah and Zalmunna, the two kings of Midian, fled, but he pursued them and captured them, routing their entire army.

---

a 8 Hebrew Penuel, a variant of Peniel; also in verses 9 and 17

13Gideon son of Joash then returned from the battle by the Pass of Heres. 14He caught a young man of Succoth and questioned him, and the young man wrote down for him the names of the seventy-seven officials of Succoth, the elders of the town. 15Then Gideon came and said to the men of Succoth, "Here are Zebah and Zalmunna, about whom you taunted me by saying, 'Do you already have the hands of Zebah and Zalmunna in your possession? Why should we give bread to your exhausted men?' " 16He took the elders of the town and taught the men of Succoth a lesson by punishing them with desert thorns and briers. 17He also pulled down the tower of Peniel and killed the men of the town.

18Then he asked Zebah and Zalmunna, "What kind of men did you kill at Tabor?"

"Men like you," they answered, "each one with the bearing of a prince."

19Gideon replied, "Those were my brothers, the sons of my own mother. As surely as the LORD lives, if you had spared their lives, I would not kill you." 20Turning to Jether, his oldest son, he said, "Kill them!" But Jether did not draw his sword, because he was only a boy and was afraid.

21Zebah and Zalmunna said, "Come, do it yourself. 'As is the man, so is his strength.' " So Gideon stepped forward and killed them, and took the ornaments off their camels' necks.

Gideon's Ephod

22The Israelites said to Gideon, "Rule over us—you, your son and your grandson—because you have saved us out of the hand of Midian."

23But Gideon told them, "I will not rule over you, nor will my son rule over you. The LORD will rule over you." 24And he said, "I do have one request, that each of you give me an earring from your share of the plunder." (It was the custom of the Ishmaelites to wear gold earrings.)

25They answered, "We'll be glad to give them." So they spread out a garment, and each man threw a ring from his plunder onto it. 26The weight of the gold rings he asked for came to seventeen hundred shekels,*a* not counting the ornaments, the pendants and the purple garments worn by the kings of Midian or the chains that were on their camels' necks. 27Gideon made the gold into an ephod, which he placed in Ophrah, his town. All Israel prostituted themselves by worshiping it there, and it became a snare to Gideon and his family.

13約阿施的兒子基甸,由希列斯坡從陣上回來,14捉住疏割的一個少年人,問他:"疏割的首領長老是誰?"他就將首領長老七十七個人的名字寫出來。15基甸到了疏割,對那裏的人說:"你們從前譏誚我說:'西巴和撒慕拿已經在你手裏,你使我們將餅給跟隨你的疲乏人嗎?'現在西巴和撒慕拿在這裏。"16於是捉住那城內的長老,用野地的荊條和枳棘責打(註:原文作"指教")疏割人;17又拆了毗努伊勒的樓,殺了那城裏的人。

18基甸問西巴和撒慕拿說:"你們在他泊山所殺的人是甚麼樣式?"

回答說:"他們好像你,各人都有王子的樣式。"

19基甸說:"他們是我同母的弟兄。我指著永生的耶和華起誓,你們從前若存留他們的性命,我如今就不殺你們了。"20於是對他的長子益帖說:"你起來殺他們。"但益帖因為是童子,害怕不敢拔刀。

21西巴和撒慕拿說:"你自己起來殺我們吧!因為人如何,力量也是如何。"基甸就起來,殺了西巴和撒慕拿,奪獲他們駱駝項上戴的月牙圈。

基甸的以弗得

22以色列人對基甸說:"你既救我們脫離米甸人的手,願你和你的兒孫管理我們。"

23基甸說:"我不管理你們,我的兒子也不管理你們,惟有耶和華管理你們。"24基甸又對他們說:"我有一件事求你們:請你們各人將所奪的耳環給我。"(原來仇敵是以實瑪利人,都是戴金耳環的。)

25他們說:"我們情願給你。"就鋪開一件外衣,各人將所奪的耳環丟在其上。26基甸所要出來的金耳環,重一千七百舍客勒金子。此外還有米甸王所戴的月環、耳墜和所穿的紫色衣服,並駱駝項上的金鍊子。27基甸以此製造了一個以弗得,設立在本城俄弗拉,後來以色列人拜那以弗得行了邪淫。這就作了基甸和他全家的網羅。

---

a 26 That is, about 43 pounds (about 19.5 kilograms)

基甸逝世

28這樣，米甸人被以色列人制伏了，不敢再抬頭。基甸還在的日子，國中太平四十年。

29約阿施的兒子耶路巴力回去，住在自己家裏。30基甸有七十個親生的兒子，因為他有許多的妻。31他的妾住在示劍，也給他生了一個兒子。基甸與他起名叫亞比米勒。32約阿施的兒子基甸，年紀老邁而死，葬在亞比以謝族的俄弗拉，在他父親約阿施的墳墓裏。

33基甸死後，以色列人又去隨從諸巴力行邪淫，以巴力比利土為他們的神。34以色列人不記念耶和華他們的神，就是拯救他們脫離四圍仇敵之手的，35也不照着耶路巴力，就是基甸向他們所施的恩惠，厚待他的家。

亞比米勒

9 耶路巴力的兒子亞比米勒到了示劍見他的眾母舅，對他們和他外祖全家的人說：2 "請你們問示劍的眾人說，是耶路巴力的眾子七十人都管理你們好呢？還是一人管理你們好呢？你們又要記念我是你們的骨肉。"

3他的眾母舅便將這一切話，為他說給示劍人聽。示劍人的心就歸向亞比米勒。他們說："他原是我們的弟兄。"4就從巴力比利土的廟中取了七十舍客勒銀子給亞比米勒，亞比米勒用以雇了些匪徒跟隨他。5他往俄弗拉到他父親的家，將他弟兄——耶路巴力的眾子七十人，都殺在一塊磐石上，只剩下耶路巴力的小兒子約坦，因為他躲藏了。6示劍人和米羅人都一同聚集，往示劍橡樹旁的柱子那裏，立亞比米勒為王。

7有人將這事告訴約坦，他就去站在基利心山頂上，向眾人大聲喊叫說："示劍人哪，你們要聽我的話，神也就聽你們的話。8有一時樹木要膏一樹為王，管理他們，就去對橄欖樹說：'請你作我們的王。'

9"橄欖樹回答說：'我豈肯止住供奉神明和尊重人的油，飄颻在眾樹之上呢？'

10"樹木對無花果樹說：'請你來作我們的王。'

Gideon's Death

28Thus Midian was subdued before the Israelites and did not raise its head again. During Gideon's lifetime, the land enjoyed peace forty years.

29Jerub-Baal son of Joash went back home to live. 30He had seventy sons of his own, for he had many wives. 31His concubine, who lived in Shechem, also bore him a son, whom he named Abimelech. 32Gideon son of Joash died at a good old age and was buried in the tomb of his father Joash in Ophrah of the Abiezrites.

33No sooner had Gideon died than the Israelites again prostituted themselves to the Baals. They set up Baal-Berith as their god and 34did not remember the LORD their God, who had rescued them from the hands of all their enemies on every side. 35They also failed to show kindness to the family of Jerub-Baal (that is, Gideon) for all the good things he had done for them.

Abimelech

9 Abimelech son of Jerub-Baal went to his mother's brothers in Shechem and said to them and to all his mother's clan, 2"Ask all the citizens of Shechem, 'Which is better for you: to have all seventy of Jerub-Baal's sons rule over you, or just one man?' Remember, I am your flesh and blood."

3When the brothers repeated all this to the citizens of Shechem, they were inclined to follow Abimelech, for they said, "He is our brother." 4They gave him seventy shekels*a* of silver from the temple of Baal-Berith, and Abimelech used it to hire reckless adventurers, who became his followers. 5He went to his father's home in Ophrah and on one stone murdered his seventy brothers, the sons of Jerub-Baal. But Jotham, the youngest son of Jerub-Baal, escaped by hiding. 6Then all the citizens of Shechem and Beth Millo gathered beside the great tree at the pillar in Shechem to crown Abimelech king.

7When Jotham was told about this, he climbed up on the top of Mount Gerizim and shouted to them, "Listen to me, citizens of Shechem, so that God may listen to you. 8One day the trees went out to anoint a king for themselves. They said to the olive tree, 'Be our king.'

9"But the olive tree answered, 'Should I give up my oil, by which both gods and men are honored, to hold sway over the trees?'

10"Next, the trees said to the fig tree, 'Come and be our king.'

a 4 That is, about 1 3/4 pounds (about 0.8 kilogram)

¹¹"But the fig tree replied, 'Should I give up my fruit, so good and sweet, to hold sway over the trees?'

¹²"Then the trees said to the vine, 'Come and be our king.'

¹³"But the vine answered, 'Should I give up my wine, which cheers both gods and men, to hold sway over the trees?'

¹⁴"Finally all the trees said to the thornbush, 'Come and be our king.'

¹⁵"The thornbush said to the trees, 'If you really want to anoint me king over you, come and take refuge in my shade; but if not, then let fire come out of the thornbush and consume the cedars of Lebanon!'

¹⁶"Now if you have acted honorably and in good faith when you made Abimelech king, and if you have been fair to Jerub-Baal and his family, and if you have treated him as he deserves— ¹⁷and to think that my father fought for you, risked his life to rescue you from the hand of Midian ¹⁸(but today you have revolted against my father's family, murdered his seventy sons on a single stone, and made Abimelech, the son of his slave girl, king over the citizens of Shechem because he is your brother)— ¹⁹if then you have acted honorably and in good faith toward Jerub-Baal and his family today, may Abimelech be your joy, and may you be his, too! ²⁰But if you have not, let fire come out from Abimelech and consume you, citizens of Shechem and Beth Millo, and let fire come out from you, citizens of Shechem and Beth Millo, and consume Abimelech!"

²¹Then Jotham fled, escaping to Beer, and he lived there because he was afraid of his brother Abimelech.

²²After Abimelech had governed Israel three years, ²³God sent an evil spirit between Abimelech and the citizens of Shechem, who acted treacherously against Abimelech. ²⁴God did this in order that the crime against Jerub-Baal's seventy sons, the shedding of their blood, might be avenged on their brother Abimelech and on the citizens of Shechem, who had helped him murder his brothers. ²⁵In opposition to him these citizens of Shechem set men on the hilltops to ambush and rob everyone who passed by, and this was reported to Abimelech.

²⁶Now Gaal son of Ebed moved with his brothers into Shechem, and its citizens put their confidence in him. ²⁷After they had gone out into the fields and gathered the grapes and trodden them, they held a festival in the temple of their god. While they were eating and drinking,

¹¹ "無花果樹回答說：'我豈肯止住所結甜美的果子，飄颻在眾樹之上呢？'

¹² "樹木對葡萄樹說：'請你來作我們的王。'

¹³ "葡萄樹回答說：'我豈肯止住使神明和人喜樂的新酒，飄颻在眾樹之上呢？'

¹⁴ "眾樹對荊棘說：'請你來作我們的王。'

¹⁵ "荊棘回答說：'你們若誠誠實實地膏我為王，就要投在我的蔭下，不然願火從荊棘裏出來，燒滅黎巴嫩的香柏樹！'

¹⁶ "現在你們立亞比米勒為王，若按誠實正直善待耶路巴力和他的全家，這就是酬他的勞。¹⁷從前我父冒死為你們爭戰，救了你們脫離米甸人的手。¹⁸你們如今起來攻擊我的父家，將他眾子七十人殺在一塊磐石上，又立他婢女所生的兒子亞比米勒為示劍人的王；他原是你們的弟兄。¹⁹你們如今若按誠實正直待耶路巴力和他的家，就可因亞比米勒得歡樂，他也可因你們得歡樂。²⁰不然，願火從亞比米勒發出，燒滅示劍人和米羅眾人。又願火從示劍人和米羅人中出來，燒滅亞比米勒。"

²¹約坦因怕他弟兄亞比米勒，就逃跑，來到比珥住在那裏。

²²亞比米勒管理以色列人三年。²³神使惡魔降在亞比米勒和示劍人中間，示劍人就以詭詐待亞比米勒。²⁴這是要叫耶路巴力七十個兒子所受的殘害，歸與他們的哥哥亞比米勒。又叫那流他們血的罪，歸與幫助他殺弟兄的示劍人。²⁵示劍人在山頂上設埋伏，等候亞比米勒。凡從他們那裏經過的人，他們就搶奪。有人將這事告訴亞比米勒。

²⁶以別的兒子迦勒和他的弟兄來到示劍，示劍人都信靠他。²⁷示劍人出城到田間去，摘下葡萄，踹酒，設擺筵宴，進他們神的廟中吃喝，咒詛

亞比米勒。²⁸以別的兒子迦勒說：
"亞比米勒是誰？示劍是誰？使我
們服侍他呢？他不是耶路巴力的兒
子嗎？他的幫手不是西布勒嗎？你
們可以服侍示劍的父親哈抹的後
裔。我們為何服侍亞比米勒呢？²⁹惟
願這民歸我的手下，我就除掉亞比
米勒。"迦勒又對亞比米勒說：
"增添你的軍兵出來吧！"

³⁰邑宰西布勒聽見以別的兒子迦
勒的話，就發怒，³¹悄悄地打發人去
見亞比米勒，說："以別的兒子迦
勒和他的弟兄到了示劍，煽惑城中
的民攻擊你。³²現在你和跟隨你的人
今夜起來，在田間埋伏。³³到早晨太
陽一出，你就起來闖城。迦勒和跟
隨他的人出來攻擊你的時候，你便
向他們見機而作。"

³⁴於是亞比米勒和跟隨他的眾人
夜間起來，分作四隊，埋伏等候示
劍人。³⁵以別的兒子迦勒出去，站在
城門口。亞比米勒和跟隨他的人，
從埋伏之處起來。

³⁶迦勒看見那些人，就對西布勒
說："看哪，有人從山頂上下來
了。"
西布勒說："你看見山的影
子，以為是人。"
³⁷迦勒又說："看哪，有人從高
處下來，又有一隊從米惡尼尼橡樹
的路上而來。"
³⁸西布勒對他說："你曾說，亞
比米勒是誰，叫我們服侍他？你所誇
的口在哪裏呢？這不是你所藐視的民
嗎？你現在出去，與他們交戰吧！"
³⁹於是迦勒率領示劍人出去，與
亞比米勒交戰。⁴⁰亞比米勒追趕迦
勒，迦勒在他面前逃跑，有許多受
傷仆倒的，直到城門。⁴¹亞比米勒住
在亞魯瑪。西布勒趕出迦勒和他弟
兄，不准他們住在示劍。
⁴²次日，民出到田間，有人告訴
亞比米勒。⁴³他就把他的人分作三
隊，埋伏在田間，看見示劍人從城
裏出來，就起來擊殺他們。⁴⁴亞比米
勒和跟隨他的一隊向前闖去，站在

they cursed Abimelech. ²⁸Then Gaal son of Ebed said, "Who is Abimelech, and who is Shechem, that we should be subject to him? Isn't he Jerub-Baal's son, and isn't Zebul his deputy? Serve the men of Hamor, Shechem's father! Why should we serve Abimelech? ²⁹If only this people were under my command! Then I would get rid of him. I would say to Abimelech, 'Call out your whole army!' "^a

³⁰When Zebul the governor of the city heard what Gaal son of Ebed said, he was very angry. ³¹Under cover he sent messengers to Abimelech, saying, "Gaal son of Ebed and his brothers have come to Shechem and are stirring up the city against you. ³²Now then, during the night you and your men should come and lie in wait in the fields. ³³In the morning at sunrise, advance against the city. When Gaal and his men come out against you, do whatever your hand finds to do."

³⁴So Abimelech and all his troops set out by night and took up concealed positions near Shechem in four companies. ³⁵Now Gaal son of Ebed had gone out and was standing at the entrance to the city gate just as Abimelech and his soldiers came out from their hiding place.

³⁶When Gaal saw them, he said to Zebul, "Look, people are coming down from the tops of the mountains!"

Zebul replied, "You mistake the shadows of the mountains for men."

³⁷But Gaal spoke up again: "Look, people are coming down from the center of the land, and a company is coming from the direction of the soothsayers' tree."

³⁸Then Zebul said to him, "Where is your big talk now, you who said, 'Who is Abimelech that we should be subject to him?' Aren't these the men you ridiculed? Go out and fight them!"

³⁹So Gaal led out^b the citizens of Shechem and fought Abimelech. ⁴⁰Abimelech chased him, and many fell wounded in the flight—all the way to the entrance to the gate. ⁴¹Abimelech stayed in Arumah, and Zebul drove Gaal and his brothers out of Shechem.

⁴²The next day the people of Shechem went out to the fields, and this was reported to Abimelech. ⁴³So he took his men, divided them into three companies and set an ambush in the fields. When he saw the people coming out of the city, he rose to attack them. ⁴⁴Abimelech and the companies with him rushed forward to a

---

a 29 Septuagint; Hebrew him." Then he said to Abimelech, "Call out your whole army!"   *b 39 Or Gaal went out in the sight of*

position at the entrance to the city gate. Then two companies rushed upon those in the fields and struck them down. ⁴⁵All that day Abimelech pressed his attack against the city until he had captured it and killed its people. Then he destroyed the city and scattered salt over it.

⁴⁶On hearing this, the citizens in the tower of Shechem went into the stronghold of the temple of El-Berith. ⁴⁷When Abimelech heard that they had assembled there, ⁴⁸he and all his men went up Mount Zalmon. He took an ax and cut off some branches, which he lifted to his shoulders. He ordered the men with him, "Quick! Do what you have seen me do!" ⁴⁹So all the men cut branches and followed Abimelech. They piled them against the stronghold and set it on fire over the people inside. So all the people in the tower of Shechem, about a thousand men and women, also died.

⁵⁰Next Abimelech went to Thebez and besieged it and captured it. ⁵¹Inside the city, however, was a strong tower, to which all the men and women—all the people of the city—fled. They locked themselves in and climbed up on the tower roof. ⁵²Abimelech went to the tower and stormed it. But as he approached the entrance to the tower to set it on fire, ⁵³a woman dropped an upper millstone on his head and cracked his skull.

⁵⁴Hurriedly he called to his armor-bearer, "Draw your sword and kill me, so that they can't say, 'A woman killed him.' " So his servant ran him through, and he died. ⁵⁵When the Israelites saw that Abimelech was dead, they went home.

⁵⁶Thus God repaid the wickedness that Abimelech had done to his father by murdering his seventy brothers. ⁵⁷God also made the men of Shechem pay for all their wickedness. The curse of Jotham son of Jerub-Baal came on them.

Tola

10 After the time of Abimelech a man of Issachar, Tola son of Puah, the son of Dodo, rose to save Israel. He lived in Shamir, in the hill country of Ephraim. ²He led[a] Israel twenty-three years; then he died, and was buried in Shamir.

Jair

³He was followed by Jair of Gilead, who led Israel twenty-two years. ⁴He had thirty sons, who rode thirty donkeys. They controlled thirty towns in Gilead, which to this day are called

a 2 Traditionally judged; also in verse 3

城門口，那兩隊直闖到田間，擊殺了眾人。⁴⁵亞比米勒整天攻打城，將城奪取，殺了其中的居民；將城拆毀，撒上了鹽。

⁴⁶示劍樓的人聽見了，就躲入巴力比利土廟的衛所。⁴⁷有人告訴亞比米勒說：「示劍樓的人都聚在一處。」⁴⁸亞比米勒和跟隨他的人就都上撒們山。亞比米勒手拿斧子，砍下一根樹枝，扛在肩上，對跟隨他的人說：「你們看我所行的，也當趕緊照樣行。」⁴⁹眾人就各砍一枝，跟隨亞比米勒，把樹枝堆在衛所的四圍，放火燒了衛所。以致示劍樓的人都死了，男女約有一千。

⁵⁰亞比米勒到提備斯，向提備斯安營，就攻取了那城。⁵¹城中有一座堅固的樓。城裏的眾人，無論男女，都逃進樓去，關上門，上了樓頂。⁵²亞比米勒到了樓前攻打，挨近樓門，要用火焚燒。⁵³有一個婦人把一塊上磨石拋在亞比米勒的頭上，打破了他的腦骨。

⁵⁴他就急忙喊叫拿他兵器的少年人，對他說：「拔出你的刀來，殺了我吧！免得人議論我說，他為一個婦人所殺。」於是少年人把他刺透，他就死了。⁵⁵以色列人見亞比米勒死了，便各回自己的地方去了。

⁵⁶這樣，神報應亞比米勒向他父親所行的惡，就是殺了弟兄七十個人的惡。⁵⁷示劍人的一切惡，神也都報應在他們頭上；耶路巴力的兒子約坦的咒詛歸到他們身上了。

陀拉

10 亞比米勒以後，有以薩迦人朵多的孫子，普瓦的兒子陀拉興起，拯救以色列人。他住在以法蓮山地的沙密。²陀拉作以色列的士師二十三年，就死了，葬在沙密。

睚珥

³在他以後有基列人睚珥興起，作以色列的士師二十二年。⁴他有三十個兒子，騎着三十匹驢駒。他們有三十座城邑，叫作哈倭特睚珥，直到

如今，都是在基列地。5睚珥死了，就葬在加們。

耶弗他

6以色列人又行耶和華眼中看為惡的事，去侍奉諸巴力和亞斯她錄，並亞蘭的神、西頓的神、摩押的神、亞捫人的神、非利士人的神，離棄耶和華，不侍奉他。7耶和華的怒氣向以色列人發作，就把他們交在非利士人和亞捫人的手中。8從那年起，他們擾害欺壓約旦河那邊、住亞摩利人之基列地的以色列人，共有十八年。9亞捫人又渡過約旦河去攻打猶大和便雅憫，並以法蓮族。以色列人就甚覺窘迫。10以色列人哀求耶和華說："我們得罪了你，因為離棄了我們神，去侍奉諸巴力。"

11耶和華對以色列人說："我豈沒有救過你們脫離埃及人、亞摩利人、亞捫人和非利士人嗎？12西頓人、亞瑪力人、馬雲人也都欺壓你們。你們哀求我，我就拯救你們脫離他們的手。13你們竟離棄我，侍奉別神！所以我不再救你們了。14你們去哀求所選擇的神，你們遭遇急難的時候，讓他救你們吧！"

15以色列人對耶和華說："我們犯罪了，任憑你隨意待我們吧！只求你今日拯救我們。"16以色列人就除掉他們中間的外邦神，侍奉耶和華。耶和華因以色列人受的苦難，就心中擔憂。

17當時亞捫人聚集，安營在基列。以色列人也聚集，安營在米斯巴。18基列的民和眾首領彼此商議，說："誰能先去攻打亞捫人，誰必作基列一切居民的領袖。"

11 基列人耶弗他是個大能的勇士，是妓女的兒子。耶弗他是基列所生的。2基列的妻也生了幾個兒子。他妻所生的兒子長大了，就趕逐耶弗他，說："你不可在我們父家承受產業，因為你是妓女的兒子。"3耶弗他就逃避他的弟兄，去住在陀伯地，有些匪徒到他那裏聚集，與他一同出入。

Havvoth Jair.[a] 5When Jair died, he was buried in Kamon.

Jephthah

6Again the Israelites did evil in the eyes of the LORD. They served the Baals and the Ashtoreths, and the gods of Aram, the gods of Sidon, the gods of Moab, the gods of the Ammonites and the gods of the Philistines. And because the Israelites forsook the LORD and no longer served him, 7he became angry with them. He sold them into the hands of the Philistines and the Ammonites, 8who that year shattered and crushed them. For eighteen years they oppressed all the Israelites on the east side of the Jordan in Gilead, the land of the Amorites. 9The Ammonites also crossed the Jordan to fight against Judah, Benjamin and the house of Ephraim; and Israel was in great distress. 10Then the Israelites cried out to the LORD, "We have sinned against you, forsaking our God and serving the Baals."

11The LORD replied, "When the Egyptians, the Amorites, the Ammonites, the Philistines, 12the Sidonians, the Amalekites and the Maonites[b] oppressed you and you cried to me for help, did I not save you from their hands? 13But you have forsaken me and served other gods, so I will no longer save you. 14Go and cry out to the gods you have chosen. Let them save you when you are in trouble!"

15But the Israelites said to the LORD, "We have sinned. Do with us whatever you think best, but please rescue us now." 16Then they got rid of the foreign gods among them and served the LORD. And he could bear Israel's misery no longer.

17When the Ammonites were called to arms and camped in Gilead, the Israelites assembled and camped at Mizpah. 18The leaders of the people of Gilead said to each other, "Whoever will launch the attack against the Ammonites will be the head of all those living in Gilead."

11 Jephthah the Gileadite was a mighty warrior. His father was Gilead; his mother was a prostitute. 2Gilead's wife also bore him sons, and when they were grown up, they drove Jephthah away. "You are not going to get any inheritance in our family," they said, "because you are the son of another woman." 3So Jephthah fled from his brothers and settled in the land of Tob, where a group of adventurers gathered around him and followed him.

a 4 Or called the settlements of Jair   b 12 Hebrew; some Septuagint manuscripts Midianites

4Some time later, when the Ammonites made war on Israel, 5the elders of Gilead went to get Jephthah from the land of Tob. 6"Come," they said, "be our commander, so we can fight the Ammonites."

7Jephthah said to them, "Didn't you hate me and drive me from my father's house? Why do you come to me now, when you're in trouble?"

8The elders of Gilead said to him, "Nevertheless, we are turning to you now; come with us to fight the Ammonites, and you will be our head over all who live in Gilead."

9Jephthah answered, "Suppose you take me back to fight the Ammonites and the LORD gives them to me—will I really be your head?"

10The elders of Gilead replied, "The LORD is our witness; we will certainly do as you say." 11So Jephthah went with the elders of Gilead, and the people made him head and commander over them. And he repeated all his words before the LORD in Mizpah.

12Then Jephthah sent messengers to the Ammonite king with the question: "What do you have against us that you have attacked our country?"

13The king of the Ammonites answered Jephthah's messengers, "When Israel came up out of Egypt, they took away my land from the Arnon to the Jabbok, all the way to the Jordan. Now give it back peaceably."

14Jephthah sent back messengers to the Ammonite king, 15saying:

"This is what Jephthah says: Israel did not take the land of Moab or the land of the Ammonites. 16But when they came up out of Egypt, Israel went through the desert to the Red Sea*a* and on to Kadesh. 17Then Israel sent messengers to the king of Edom, saying, 'Give us permission to go through your country,' but the king of Edom would not listen. They sent also to the king of Moab, and he refused. So Israel stayed at Kadesh.

18"Next they traveled through the desert, skirted the lands of Edom and Moab, passed along the eastern side of the country of Moab, and camped on the other side of the Arnon. They did not enter the territory of Moab, for the Arnon was its border.

19"Then Israel sent messengers to Sihon king of the Amorites, who ruled in Heshbon,

---

4過了些日子，亞捫人攻打以色列。5亞捫人攻打以色列的時候，基列的長老到陀伯地去，要叫耶弗他回來。6對耶弗他說："請你來作我們的元帥，我們好與亞捫人爭戰。"

7耶弗他回答基列的長老說："從前你們不是恨我、趕逐我出離父家嗎？現在你們遭遇急難為何到我這裏來呢？"

8基列的長老回答耶弗他說："現在我們到你這裏來，是要你同我們去，與亞捫人爭戰，你可以作基列一切居民的領袖。"

9耶弗他對基列的長老說："你們叫我回去，與亞捫人爭戰，耶和華把他交給我，我可以作你們的領袖嗎？"

10基列的長老回答耶弗他說："有耶和華在你我中間作見證，我們必定照你的話行。"11於是耶弗他同基列的長老回去，百姓就立耶弗他作領袖、作元帥。耶弗他在米斯巴將自己的一切話，陳明在耶和華面前。

12耶弗他打發使者去見亞捫人的王，說："你與我有甚麼相干，竟來到我國中攻打我呢？"

13亞捫人的王回答耶弗他的使者說："因為以色列人從埃及上來的時候，佔據我的地，從亞嫩河到雅博河，直到約旦河。現在你要好好地將這地歸還吧！"

14耶弗他又打發使者去見亞捫人的王，15對他說：

"耶弗他如此說：以色列人並沒有佔據摩押地和亞捫人的地。16以色列人從埃及上來，乃是經過曠野到紅海，來到加低斯，17就打發使者去見以東王，說：'求你容我從你的地經過。'以東王卻不應允。又照樣打發使者去見摩押王，他也不允准，以色列人就住在加低斯。

18"他們又經過曠野，繞着以東和摩押地，從摩押地的東邊過來，在亞嫩河邊安營，並沒有入摩押的境內，因為亞嫩河是摩押的邊界。

19"以色列人打發使者去見亞摩利王西宏，就是希實本的

---

a 16 Hebrew *Yam Suph;* that is, Sea of Reeds

王，對他說：'求你容我們從你的地經過，往我們自己的地方去。'²⁰西宏卻不信服以色列人，不容他們經過他的境界，乃招聚他的眾民在雅雜安營，與以色列人爭戰。

²¹ "耶和華以色列的神，將西宏和他的眾民都交在以色列人手中，以色列人就擊殺他們，得了亞摩利人的全地：²²從亞嫩河到雅博河，從曠野直到約旦河。

²³ "耶和華以色列的神，在他百姓以色列面前趕出亞摩利人，你竟要得他們的地嗎？²⁴你的神基抹所賜你的地，你不是得為業嗎？耶和華我們的神在我們面前所趕出的人，我們就得他的地。²⁵難道你比摩押王西撥的兒子巴勒還強嗎？他曾與以色列人爭競，或是與他們爭戰嗎？²⁶以色列人住希實本和屬希實本的鄉村，亞羅珥和屬亞羅珥的鄉村，並沿亞嫩河的一切城邑，已經有三百年了。在這三百年之內，你們為甚麼沒有取回這些地方呢？²⁷原來我沒有得罪你，你卻攻打我，惡待我。願審判人的耶和華，今日在以色列人和亞捫人中間判斷是非。"

²⁸但亞捫人的王不肯聽耶弗他打發人說的話。

²⁹耶和華的靈降在耶弗他身上，他就經過基列和瑪拿西，來到基列的米斯巴，又從米斯巴來到亞捫人那裏。³⁰耶弗他就向耶和華許願，說："你若將亞捫人交在我手中，³¹我從亞捫人那裏平平安安回來的時候，無論甚麼人，先從我家門出來迎接我，就必歸你，我也必將他獻上為燔祭。"

³²於是耶弗他往亞捫人那裏去，與他們爭戰；耶和華將他們交在他手中，³³他就大大殺敗他們，從亞羅珥到米匿，直到亞備勒基拉明，攻取了二十座城。這樣，亞捫人就被以色列人制伏了。

³⁴耶弗他回米斯巴到了自己的家。不料，他女兒拿着鼓跳舞出來迎接他，是他獨生的，此外無兒無女。³⁵耶弗他看見她，就撕裂衣服，說："哀哉！我的女兒啊，你使我

and said to him, 'Let us pass through your country to our own place.' ²⁰Sihon, however, did not trust Israel^a to pass through his territory. He mustered all his men and encamped at Jahaz and fought with Israel.

²¹"Then the LORD, the God of Israel, gave Sihon and all his men into Israel's hands, and they defeated them. Israel took over all the land of the Amorites who lived in that country, ²²capturing all of it from the Arnon to the Jabbok and from the desert to the Jordan.

²³"Now since the LORD, the God of Israel, has driven the Amorites out before his people Israel, what right have you to take it over? ²⁴Will you not take what your god Chemosh gives you? Likewise, whatever the LORD our God has given us, we will possess. ²⁵Are you better than Balak son of Zippor, king of Moab? Did he ever quarrel with Israel or fight with them? ²⁶For three hundred years Israel occupied Heshbon, Aroer, the surrounding settlements and all the towns along the Arnon. Why didn't you retake them during that time? ²⁷I have not wronged you, but you are doing me wrong by waging war against me. Let the LORD, the Judge,^{b} decide the dispute this day between the Israelites and the Ammonites."

²⁸The king of Ammon, however, paid no attention to the message Jephthah sent him.

²⁹Then the Spirit of the LORD came upon Jephthah. He crossed Gilead and Manasseh, passed through Mizpah of Gilead, and from there he advanced against the Ammonites. ³⁰And Jephthah made a vow to the LORD: "If you give the Ammonites into my hands, ³¹whatever comes out of the door of my house to meet me when I return in triumph from the Ammonites will be the LORD's, and I will sacrifice it as a burnt offering."

³²Then Jephthah went over to fight the Ammonites, and the LORD gave them into his hands. ³³He devastated twenty towns from Aroer to the vicinity of Minnith, as far as Abel Keramim. Thus Israel subdued Ammon.

³⁴When Jephthah returned to his home in Mizpah, who should come out to meet him but his daughter, dancing to the sound of tambourines! She was an only child. Except for her he had neither son nor daughter. ³⁵When he saw her, he tore his clothes and cried, "Oh! My

a 20 Or however, would not make an agreement for Israel
b 27 Or Ruler

daughter! You have made me miserable and wretched, because I have made a vow to the LORD that I cannot break."

[36]"My father," she replied, "you have given your word to the LORD. Do to me just as you promised, now that the LORD has avenged you of your enemies, the Ammonites. [37]But grant me this one request," she said. "Give me two months to roam the hills and weep with my friends, because I will never marry."

[38]"You may go," he said. And he let her go for two months. She and the girls went into the hills and wept because she would never marry. [39]After the two months, she returned to her father and he did to her as he had vowed. And she was a virgin.

From this comes the Israelite custom [40]that each year the young women of Israel go out for four days to commemorate the daughter of Jephthah the Gileadite.

Jephthah and Ephraim

12 The men of Ephraim called out their forces, crossed over to Zaphon and said to Jephthah, "Why did you go to fight the Ammonites without calling us to go with you? We're going to burn down your house over your head."

[2]Jephthah answered, "I and my people were engaged in a great struggle with the Ammonites, and although I called, you didn't save me out of their hands. [3]When I saw that you wouldn't help, I took my life in my hands and crossed over to fight the Ammonites, and the LORD gave me the victory over them. Now why have you come up today to fight me?"

[4]Jephthah then called together the men of Gilead and fought against Ephraim. The Gileadites struck them down because the Ephraimites had said, "You Gileadites are renegades from Ephraim and Manasseh." [5]The Gileadites captured the fords of the Jordan leading to Ephraim, and whenever a survivor of Ephraim said, "Let me cross over," the men of Gilead asked him, "Are you an Ephraimite?" If he replied, "No," [6]they said, "All right, say 'Shibboleth.' " If he said, "Sibboleth," because he could not pronounce the word correctly, they seized him and killed him at the fords of the Jordan. Forty-two thousand Ephraimites were killed at that time.

[7]Jephthah led[a] Israel six years. Then Jephthah the Gileadite died, and was buried in a town in Gilead.

甚是愁苦,叫我作難了,因為我已經向耶和華開口許願,不能挽回。"

[36]他女兒回答說:"父啊,你既向耶和華開口,就當照你口中所說的向我行,因耶和華已經在仇敵亞捫人身上為你報仇。"[37]又對父親說:"有一件事求你允准:容我去兩個月,與同伴在山上,好哀哭我終為處女。"

[38]耶弗他說:"你去吧!"就容她去兩個月。她便和同伴去了,在山上為她終為處女哀哭。[39]兩月已滿,她回到父親那裏,父親就照所許的願向她行了。女兒終身沒有親近男子。

[40]此後以色列中有個規矩,每年以色列的女子去為基列人耶弗他的女兒哀哭四天。

耶弗他與以法蓮

12 以法蓮人聚集,到了北方,對耶弗他說:"你去與亞捫人爭戰,為甚麼沒有招我們同去呢?我們必用火燒你和你的房屋。"

[2]耶弗他對他們說:"我和我的民與亞捫人大大爭戰;我招你們來,你們竟沒有來救我脫離他們的手。[3]我見你們不來救我,我就拚命前去攻擊亞捫人,耶和華將他們交在我手中。你們今日為甚麼上我這裏來攻打我呢?"

[4]於是耶弗他招聚基列人,與以法蓮人爭戰。基列人擊殺以法蓮人,是因他們說:"你們基列人在以法蓮、瑪拿西中間,不過是以法蓮逃亡的人。"[5]基列人把守約旦河的渡口,不容以法蓮人過去。以法蓮逃走的人若說:"容我過去。"基列人就問他說:"你是以法蓮人不是?"他若說:"不是。"[6]就對他說:"你說示播列。"以法蓮人因咬不真字音,便說西播列。基列人就將他拿住,殺在約旦河的渡口。那時以法蓮人被殺的有四萬二千人。

[7]耶弗他作以色列的士師六年。基列人耶弗他死了,葬在基列的一座城裏。

---

a 7 Traditionally judged; also in verses 8-14

以比讚、以倫、押頓

⁸耶弗他以後，有伯利恆人以比讚作以色列的士師。⁹他有三十個兒子，三十個女兒，女兒都嫁出去了。他給眾子從外鄉娶了三十個媳婦。他作以色列的士師七年。¹⁰以比讚死了，葬在伯利恆。

¹¹以比讚之後，有西布倫人以倫作以色列的士師十年。¹²西布倫人以倫死了，葬在西布倫地的亞雅崙。

¹³以倫之後，有比拉頓人希列的兒子押頓作以色列的士師。¹⁴他有四十個兒子，三十個孫子，騎著七十匹驢駒。押頓作以色列的士師八年。¹⁵比拉頓人希列的兒子押頓死了，葬在以法蓮地的比拉頓，在亞瑪力人的山地。

參孫生

13 以色列人又行耶和華眼中看為惡的事，耶和華將他們交在非利士人手中四十年。

²那時有一個瑣拉人，是屬但族的，名叫瑪挪亞。他的妻不懷孕，不生育。³耶和華的使者向那婦人顯現，對她說：“向來你不懷孕，不生育，如今你必懷孕生一個兒子。⁴所以你當謹慎，清酒濃酒都不可喝，一切不潔之物也不可吃。⁵你必懷孕生一個兒子，不可用剃頭刀剃他的頭，因為這孩子一出胎就歸神作拿細耳人。他必起首拯救以色列人脫離非利士人的手。”

⁶婦人就回去對丈夫說：“有一個神人到我面前來，他的相貌如神使者的相貌，甚是可畏。我沒有問他從哪裏來，他也沒有將他的名告訴我，⁷卻對我說：‘你要懷孕生一個兒子，所以清酒濃酒都不可喝，一切不潔之物也不可吃，因為這孩子從出胎一直到死，必歸神作拿細耳人。’”

⁸瑪挪亞就祈求耶和華說：“主啊，求你再差遣神人到我們這裏來，好指教我們怎樣待這將要生的孩子。”

⁹神應允瑪挪亞的話。婦人正坐在田間的時候，神的使者又到她那裏，她丈夫瑪挪亞卻沒有同她在一處。¹⁰婦人急忙跑去告訴丈夫說：“那日到我面前來的人，又向我顯現！”

Ibzan, Elon and Abdon

⁸After him, Ibzan of Bethlehem led Israel. ⁹He had thirty sons and thirty daughters. He gave his daughters away in marriage to those outside his clan, and for his sons he brought in thirty young women as wives from outside his clan. Ibzan led Israel seven years. ¹⁰Then Ibzan died, and was buried in Bethlehem.

¹¹After him, Elon the Zebulunite led Israel ten years. ¹²Then Elon died, and was buried in Aijalon in the land of Zebulun.

¹³After him, Abdon son of Hillel, from Pirathon, led Israel. ¹⁴He had forty sons and thirty grandsons, who rode on seventy donkeys. He led Israel eight years. ¹⁵Then Abdon son of Hillel died, and was buried at Pirathon in Ephraim, in the hill country of the Amalekites.

The Birth of Samson

13 Again the Israelites did evil in the eyes of the LORD, so the LORD delivered them into the hands of the Philistines for forty years.

²A certain man of Zorah, named Manoah, from the clan of the Danites, had a wife who was sterile and remained childless. ³The angel of the LORD appeared to her and said, "You are sterile and childless, but you are going to conceive and have a son. ⁴Now see to it that you drink no wine or other fermented drink and that you do not eat anything unclean, ⁵because you will conceive and give birth to a son. No razor may be used on his head, because the boy is to be a Nazirite, set apart to God from birth, and he will begin the deliverance of Israel from the hands of the Philistines."

⁶Then the woman went to her husband and told him, "A man of God came to me. He looked like an angel of God, very awesome. I didn't ask him where he came from, and he didn't tell me his name. ⁷But he said to me, 'You will conceive and give birth to a son. Now then, drink no wine or other fermented drink and do not eat anything unclean, because the boy will be a Nazirite of God from birth until the day of his death.'"

⁸Then Manoah prayed to the LORD: "O Lord, I beg you, let the man of God you sent to us come again to teach us how to bring up the boy who is to be born."

⁹God heard Manoah, and the angel of God came again to the woman while she was out in the field; but her husband Manoah was not with her. ¹⁰The woman hurried to tell her husband, "He's here! The man who appeared to me the other day!"

¹¹Manoah got up and followed his wife. When he came to the man, he said, "Are you the one who talked to my wife?"

"I am," he said.

¹²So Manoah asked him, "When your words are fulfilled, what is to be the rule for the boy's life and work?"

¹³The angel of the LORD answered, "Your wife must do all that I have told her. ¹⁴She must not eat anything that comes from the grapevine, nor drink any wine or other fermented drink nor eat anything unclean. She must do everything I have commanded her."

¹⁵Manoah said to the angel of the LORD, "We would like you to stay until we prepare a young goat for you."

¹⁶The angel of the LORD replied, "Even though you detain me, I will not eat any of your food. But if you prepare a burnt offering, offer it to the LORD." (Manoah did not realize that it was the angel of the LORD.)

¹⁷Then Manoah inquired of the angel of the LORD, "What is your name, so that we may honor you when your word comes true?"

¹⁸He replied, "Why do you ask my name? It is beyond understanding.ᵃ" ¹⁹Then Manoah took a young goat, together with the grain offering, and sacrificed it on a rock to the LORD. And the LORD did an amazing thing while Manoah and his wife watched: ²⁰As the flame blazed up from the altar toward heaven, the angel of the LORD ascended in the flame. Seeing this, Manoah and his wife fell with their faces to the ground. ²¹When the angel of the LORD did not show himself again to Manoah and his wife, Manoah realized that it was the angel of the LORD.

²²"We are doomed to die!" he said to his wife. "We have seen God!"

²³But his wife answered, "If the LORD had meant to kill us, he would not have accepted a burnt offering and grain offering from our hands, nor shown us all these things or now told us this."

²⁴The woman gave birth to a boy and named him Samson. He grew and the LORD blessed him, ²⁵and the Spirit of the LORD began to stir him while he was in Mahaneh Dan, between Zorah and Eshtaol.

Samson's Marriage

14 Samson went down to Timnah and saw there a young Philistine woman. ²When he returned, he said to his father and mother, "I have seen a Philistine woman in Timnah; now get her for me as my wife."

¹¹瑪挪亞起來跟隨他的妻來到那人面前,對他說:"與這婦人說話的就是你嗎?"

他說:"是我。"

¹²瑪挪亞說:"願你的話應驗,我們當怎樣待這孩子,他後來當怎樣呢?"

¹³耶和華的使者對瑪挪亞說:"我告訴婦人的一切事,她都當謹慎。¹⁴葡萄樹所結的都不可吃,清酒濃酒都不可喝,一切不潔之物也不可吃。凡我所吩咐的,她都當遵守。"

¹⁵瑪挪亞對耶和華的使者說:"求你容我們款留你,好為你預備一隻山羊羔。"

¹⁶耶和華的使者對瑪挪亞說:"你雖然款留我,我卻不吃你的食物,你若預備燔祭,就當獻與耶和華。"原來瑪挪亞不知道他是耶和華的使者。

¹⁷瑪挪亞對耶和華的使者說:"請將你的名告訴我,到你話應驗的時候,我們好尊敬你。"

¹⁸耶和華的使者對他說:"你何必問我的名?我名是奇妙的。"¹⁹瑪挪亞將一隻山羊羔和素祭,在磐石上獻與耶和華。使者行奇妙的事,瑪挪亞和他的妻觀看:²⁰見火焰從壇上往上升,耶和華的使者在壇上的火焰中也升上去了。瑪挪亞和他的妻看見,就俯伏於地。²¹耶和華的使者不再向瑪挪亞和他的妻顯現,瑪挪亞才知道他是耶和華的使者。

²²瑪挪亞對他的妻說:"我們必要死,因為看見了神。"

²³他的妻卻對他說:"耶和華若要殺我們,必不從我們手裏收納燔祭和素祭,並不將這一切事指示我們,今日也不將這些話告訴我們。"

²⁴後來婦人生了一個兒子,給他起名叫參孫。孩子長大,耶和華賜福與他。²⁵在瑪哈尼但,就是瑣拉和以實陶中間,耶和華的靈才感動他。

參孫的婚姻

14 參孫下到亭拿,在那裏看見一個女子,是非利士人的女兒。²參孫上來稟告他父母說:"我在亭拿看見一個女子,是非利士人的女兒,願你們給我娶來為妻。"

---

a 18 Or is wonderful

³他父母說："在你弟兄的女兒中，或在本國的民中，豈沒有一個女子，何至你去在未受割禮的非利士人中娶妻呢？"

參孫對他父親說："願你給我娶那女子，因我喜悅她。"⁴他的父母卻不知道這事是出於耶和華，因為他想機會攻擊非利士人。那時非利士人轄制以色列人。⁵參孫跟他父母下亭拿去。到了亭拿的葡萄園，見有一隻少壯獅子向他吼叫。⁶耶和華的靈大大感動參孫，他雖然手無器械，卻將獅子撕裂，如同撕裂山羊羔一樣。他行這事並沒有告訴父母。⁷參孫下去與女子說話，就喜悅她。

⁸過了些日子，再下去要娶那女子，轉向道旁要看死獅，見有一羣蜂子和蜜在死獅之內，⁹就用手取蜜，且吃且走；到了父母那裏，給他父母，他們也吃了，只是沒有告訴這蜜是從死獅之內取來的。

¹⁰他父親下去見女子。參孫在那裏設擺筵宴，因為向來少年人都有這個規矩。¹¹眾人看見參孫，就請了三十個人陪伴他。

¹²參孫對他們說："我給你們出一個謎語，你們在七日筵宴之內，若能猜出意思告訴我，我就給你們三十件裏衣，三十套衣裳；¹³你們若不能猜出意思告訴我，你們就給我三十件裏衣，三十套衣裳。"

他們說："請將謎語說給我們聽"

¹⁴參孫對他們說：

"吃的從吃者出來，
甜的從強者出來。"

他們三日不能猜出謎語的意思。
¹⁵到第七天，他們對參孫的妻說："你誆哄你丈夫，探出謎語的意思告訴我們，免得我們用火燒你和你父家。你們請了我們來，是要奪我們所有的嗎？"

¹⁶參孫的妻在丈夫面前啼哭說："你是恨我，不是愛我，你給我本國的人出謎語，卻沒有將意思告訴我。"

³His father and mother replied, "Isn't there an acceptable woman among your relatives or among all our people? Must you go to the uncircumcised Philistines to get a wife?"

But Samson said to his father, "Get her for me. She's the right one for me." ⁴(His parents did not know that this was from the LORD, who was seeking an occasion to confront the Philistines; for at that time they were ruling over Israel.) ⁵Samson went down to Timnah together with his father and mother. As they approached the vineyards of Timnah, suddenly a young lion came roaring toward him. ⁶The Spirit of the LORD came upon him in power so that he tore the lion apart with his bare hands as he might have torn a young goat. But he told neither his father nor his mother what he had done. ⁷Then he went down and talked with the woman, and he liked her.

⁸Some time later, when he went back to marry her, he turned aside to look at the lion's carcass. In it was a swarm of bees and some honey, ⁹which he scooped out with his hands and ate as he went along. When he rejoined his parents, he gave them some, and they too ate it. But he did not tell them that he had taken the honey from the lion's carcass.

¹⁰Now his father went down to see the woman. And Samson made a feast there, as was customary for bridegrooms. ¹¹When he appeared, he was given thirty companions.

¹²"Let me tell you a riddle," Samson said to them. "If you can give me the answer within the seven days of the feast, I will give you thirty linen garments and thirty sets of clothes. ¹³If you can't tell me the answer, you must give me thirty linen garments and thirty sets of clothes."

"Tell us your riddle," they said. "Let's hear it."

¹⁴He replied,

"Out of the eater, something to eat;
out of the strong, something sweet."

For three days they could not give the answer.

¹⁵On the fourthᵃ day, they said to Samson's wife, "Coax your husband into explaining the riddle for us, or we will burn you and your father's household to death. Did you invite us here to rob us?"

¹⁶Then Samson's wife threw herself on him, sobbing, "You hate me! You don't really love me. You've given my people a riddle, but you haven't told me the answer."

"I haven't even explained it to my father or mother," he replied, "so why should I explain it to you?" 17She cried the whole seven days of the feast. So on the seventh day he finally told her, because she continued to press him. She in turn explained the riddle to her people.

18Before sunset on the seventh day the men of the town said to him,

"What is sweeter than honey?
 What is stronger than a lion?"

Samson said to them,

"If you had not plowed with my heifer,
 you would not have solved my riddle."

19Then the Spirit of the LORD came upon him in power. He went down to Ashkelon, struck down thirty of their men, stripped them of their belongings and gave their clothes to those who had explained the riddle. Burning with anger, he went up to his father's house. 20And Samson's wife was given to the friend who had attended him at his wedding.

Samson's Vengeance on the Philistines

15 Later on, at the time of wheat harvest, Samson took a young goat and went to visit his wife. He said, "I'm going to my wife's room." But her father would not let him go in.

2"I was so sure you thoroughly hated her," he said, "that I gave her to your friend. Isn't her younger sister more attractive? Take her instead."

3Samson said to them, "This time I have a right to get even with the Philistines; I will really harm them." 4So he went out and caught three hundred foxes and tied them tail to tail in pairs. He then fastened a torch to every pair of tails, 5lit the torches and let the foxes loose in the standing grain of the Philistines. He burned up the shocks and standing grain, together with the vineyards and olive groves.

6When the Philistines asked, "Who did this?" they were told, "Samson, the Timnite's son-in-law, because his wife was given to his friend."

So the Philistines went up and burned her and her father to death. 7Samson said to them, "Since you've acted like this, I won't stop until I get my revenge on you." 8He attacked them viciously and slaughtered many of them. Then he went down and stayed in a cave in the rock of Etam.

參孫回答說："連我父母我都沒有告訴，豈可告訴你呢？"17七日筵宴之內，她在丈夫面前啼哭，到第七天逼着他，他才將謎語的意思告訴他妻，他妻就告訴本國的人。

18到第七天，日頭未落以前，那城裏的人對參孫說：

"有甚麼比蜜還甜呢？
 有甚麼比獅子還強呢？"

參孫對他們說：

"你們若非用我的母牛犢耕地，
 就猜不出我謎語的意思來。"

19耶和華的靈大大感動參孫，他就下到亞實基倫擊殺了三十個人，奪了他們的衣裳，將衣裳給了猜出謎語的人。參孫發怒，就上父家去了。20參孫的妻便歸了參孫的陪伴，就是作過他朋友的。

參孫報復非利士人

15 過了些日子，到割麥子的時候，參孫帶着一隻山羊羔去看他的妻，說："我要進內室見我的妻。"他岳父不容他進去。

2說："我估定你是極其恨她，因此我將她給了你的陪伴。她的妹子不是比她還美麗嗎？你可以娶來代替她吧！"

3參孫說："這回我加害於非利士人不算有罪。"4於是參孫去捉了三百隻狐狸（註：或作"野狗"），將狐狸尾巴一對一對地捆上，將火把捆在兩條尾巴中間。5點着火把，就放狐狸進入非利士人站着的禾稼，將堆集的禾捆和未割的禾稼，並橄欖園盡都燒了。

6非利士人說："這事是誰做的呢？"有人說："是亭拿人的女婿參孫，因為他岳父將他的妻給了他的陪伴。"

於是非利士人上去，用火燒了婦人和她的父親。7參孫對非利士人說："你們既然這樣行，我必向你們報仇才肯罷休。"8參孫就大大擊殺他們，連腿帶腰都砍斷了。他便下去，住在以坦磐的穴內。

9非利士人上去安營在<u>猶大</u>，布散在<u>利希</u>。10<u>猶大</u>人説：「你們為何上來攻擊我們呢？」

他們説：「我們上來是要捆綁<u>參孫</u>，他向我們怎樣行，我們也要向他怎樣行！」

11於是有三千<u>猶大</u>人下到<u>以坦磐</u>的穴內，對<u>參孫</u>説：「<u>非利士人</u>轄制我們，你不知道嗎？你向我們行的是甚麼事呢？」

他回答説：「他們向我怎樣行，我也要向他們怎樣行！」

12<u>猶大</u>人對他説：「我們下來是要捆綁你，將你交在<u>非利士人</u>手中。」

<u>參孫</u>説：「你們要向我起誓，應承你們自己不害死我。」

13他們説：「我們斷不殺你，只要將你捆綁，將你交在<u>非利士人</u>手中。」於是用兩條新繩捆綁<u>參孫</u>，將他從<u>以坦磐</u>帶上去。14<u>參孫</u>到了<u>利希</u>，非利士人都迎着喧嚷。耶和華的靈大大感動<u>參孫</u>，他臂上的繩就像火燒的麻一樣，他的綁繩都從他手上脱落下來。15他見一塊未乾的驢腮骨，就伸手拾起來，用以擊殺一千人。

16<u>參孫</u>説：

「我用驢腮骨殺人成堆，
　用驢腮骨殺了一千人。」

17説完這話，就把那腮骨從手裏拋出去了。那地便叫<u>拉末利希</u>。

18<u>參孫</u>甚覺口渴，就求告耶和華説：「你既藉僕人的手施行這麼大的拯救，豈可任我渴死，落在未受割禮的人手中呢？」19神就使<u>利希</u>的窪處裂開，有水從其中湧出來。<u>參孫</u>喝了，精神復原，因此那泉名叫<u>隱哈歌利</u>，那泉直到今日還在<u>利希</u>。

20當<u>非利士人</u>轄制<u>以色列</u>人的時候，<u>參孫</u>作<u>以色列</u>的士師二十年。

9The Philistines went up and camped in Judah, spreading out near Lehi. 10The men of Judah asked, "Why have you come to fight us?"

"We have come to take Samson prisoner," they answered, "to do to him as he did to us."

11Then three thousand men from Judah went down to the cave in the rock of Etam and said to Samson, "Don't you realize that the Philistines are rulers over us? What have you done to us?"

He answered, "I merely did to them what they did to me."

12They said to him, "We've come to tie you up and hand you over to the Philistines."

Samson said, "Swear to me that you won't kill me yourselves."

13"Agreed," they answered. "We will only tie you up and hand you over to them. We will not kill you." So they bound him with two new ropes and led him up from the rock. 14As he approached Lehi, the Philistines came toward him shouting. The Spirit of the LORD came upon him in power. The ropes on his arms became like charred flax, and the bindings dropped from his hands. 15Finding a fresh jawbone of a donkey, he grabbed it and struck down a thousand men.

16Then Samson said,

"With a donkey's jawbone
　I have made donkeys of them.*a*
With a donkey's jawbone
　I have killed a thousand men."

17When he finished speaking, he threw away the jawbone; and the place was called Ramath Lehi.*b*

18Because he was very thirsty, he cried out to the LORD, "You have given your servant this great victory. Must I now die of thirst and fall into the hands of the uncircumcised?" 19Then God opened up the hollow place in Lehi, and water came out of it. When Samson drank, his strength returned and he revived. So the spring was called En Hakkore,*c* and it is still there in Lehi.

20Samson led*d* Israel for twenty years in the days of the Philistines.

---

a 16 Or *made a heap or two;* the Hebrew for *donkey* sounds like the Hebrew for *heap.*　*b 17 Ramath Lehi* means *jawbone hill.* *c 19 En Hakkore* means *caller's spring.*　*d 20* Traditionally *judged*

Samson and Delilah

16 One day Samson went to Gaza, where he saw a prostitute. He went in to spend the night with her. ²The people of Gaza were told, "Samson is here!" So they surrounded the place and lay in wait for him all night at the city gate. They made no move during the night, saying, "At dawn we'll kill him."

³But Samson lay there only until the middle of the night. Then he got up and took hold of the doors of the city gate, together with the two posts, and tore them loose, bar and all. He lifted them to his shoulders and carried them to the top of the hill that faces Hebron.

⁴Some time later, he fell in love with a woman in the Valley of Sorek whose name was Delilah. ⁵The rulers of the Philistines went to her and said, "See if you can lure him into showing you the secret of his great strength and how we can overpower him so we may tie him up and subdue him. Each one of us will give you eleven hundred shekels^a of silver."

⁶So Delilah said to Samson, "Tell me the secret of your great strength and how you can be tied up and subdued."

⁷Samson answered her, "If anyone ties me with seven fresh thongs^b that have not been dried, I'll become as weak as any other man."

⁸Then the rulers of the Philistines brought her seven fresh thongs that had not been dried, and she tied him with them. ⁹With men hidden in the room, she called to him, "Samson, the Philistines are upon you!" But he snapped the thongs as easily as a piece of string snaps when it comes close to a flame. So the secret of his strength was not discovered.

¹⁰Then Delilah said to Samson, "You have made a fool of me; you lied to me. Come now, tell me how you can be tied."

¹¹He said, "If anyone ties me securely with new ropes that have never been used, I'll become as weak as any other man."

¹²So Delilah took new ropes and tied him with them. Then, with men hidden in the room, she called to him, "Samson, the Philistines are upon you!" But he snapped the ropes off his arms as if they were threads.

¹³Delilah then said to Samson, "Until now, you have been making a fool of me and lying to me. Tell me how you can be tied."

He replied, "If you weave the seven braids of my head into the fabric ⌊on the loom⌋ and tighten it with the pin, I'll become as weak as any

a 5 That is, about 28 pounds (about 13 kilograms)   b 7 Or bowstrings; also in verses 8 and 9

參孫與大利拉

16 參孫到了迦薩，在那裏看見一個妓女，就與她親近。²有人告訴迦薩人說："參孫到這裏來了！"他們就把他團團圍住，終夜在城門悄悄埋伏，說"等到天亮我們便殺他。"

³參孫睡到半夜，起來，將城門的門扇、門框、門閂一齊拆下來，扛在肩上，扛到希伯崙前的山頂上。

⁴後來參孫在梭烈谷喜愛一個婦人，名叫大利拉。⁵非利士人的首領上去見那婦人，對她說："求你誆哄參孫，探探他因何有這麼大的力氣，我們用何法能勝他，捆綁剋制他，我們就每人給你一千一百舍客勒銀子。"

⁶大利拉對參孫說："求你告訴我，你因何有這麼大的力氣，當用何法捆綁剋制你？"

⁷參孫回答說："人若用七條未乾的青繩子捆綁我，我就軟弱像別人一樣。"

⁸於是，非利士人的首領拿了七條未乾的青繩子來交給婦人，她就用繩子捆綁參孫。⁹有人預先埋伏在婦人的內室裏。婦人說："參孫哪，非利士人拿你來了！"參孫就掙斷繩子，如掙斷經火的麻線一般。這樣，他力氣的根由人還是不知道。

¹⁰大利拉對參孫說："你欺哄我，向我說謊言。現在求你告訴我當用何法捆綁你。"

¹¹參孫回答說："人若用沒有使過的新繩捆綁我，我就軟弱像別人一樣。"

¹²大利拉就用新繩捆綁他。對他說："參孫哪，非利士人拿你來了！"有人預先埋伏在內室裏。參孫將臂上的繩掙斷了，如掙斷一條線一樣。

¹³大利拉對參孫說："你到如今還是欺哄我，向我說謊言。求你告訴我，當用何法捆綁你。"

參孫回答說："你若將我頭上的

七條髮綹與緯線同織就可以了。」
14於是大利拉將他的髮綹與緯線同
織，用橛子釘住。

對他說：「參孫哪，非利士人
拿你來了！」參孫從睡中醒來，將
機上的橛子和緯線，一齊都拔出來
了。

15大利拉對參孫說：「你既不與
我同心，怎麼說你愛我呢？你這三
次欺哄我，沒有告訴我，你因何有
這麼大的力氣。」16大利拉天天用話
催逼他，甚至他心裏煩悶要死。

17參孫就把心中所藏的都告訴了
她，對她說：「向來人沒有用剃頭
刀剃我的頭，因為我自出母胎就歸
神作拿細耳人；若剃了我的頭髮，
我的力氣就離開我，我便軟弱像別
人一樣。」

18大利拉見他把心中所藏的都告
訴了她，就打發人到非利士人的首領
那裏，對他們說：「他已經把心中所
藏的都告訴了我，請你們再上來一
次。」於是非利士人的首領手裏拿着
銀子，上到婦人那裏。19大利拉使參
孫枕着她的膝睡覺，叫了一個人來剃
除他頭上的七條髮綹。於是大利拉剋
制他，他的力氣就離開他了。

20大利拉說：「參孫哪，非利士
人拿你來了！」

參孫從睡中醒來，心裏說，我
要像前幾次出去活動身體，他卻不
知道耶和華已經離開他了。

21非利士人將他拿住，剜了他的
眼睛，帶他下到迦薩，用銅鏈拘索
他，他就在監裏推磨。22然而他的頭
髮被剃之後，又漸漸長起來了。

參孫之死

23非利士人的首領聚集，要給他
們的神大袞獻大祭，並且歡樂。因
為他們說：「我們的神將我們的仇
敵參孫交在我們手中了。」

24眾人看見參孫，就讚美他們的
神，說：

「我們的神
　將毀壞我們地，
殺害我們許多人的仇敵，
　交在我們手中了。」

other man." So while he was sleeping, Delilah
took the seven braids of his head, wove them
into the fabric 14and*a* tightened it with the pin.

Again she called to him, "Samson, the Philistines are upon you!" He awoke from his sleep
and pulled up the pin and the loom, with the
fabric.

15Then she said to him, "How can you say, 'I
love you,' when you won't confide in me? This
is the third time you have made a fool of me and
haven't told me the secret of your great strength."
16With such nagging she prodded him day after
day until he was tired to death.

17So he told her everything. "No razor has
ever been used on my head," he said, "because I
have been a Nazirite set apart to God since birth.
If my head were shaved, my strength would
leave me, and I would become as weak as any
other man."

18When Delilah saw that he had told her
everything, she sent word to the rulers of the
Philistines, "Come back once more; he has told
me everything." So the rulers of the Philistines
returned with the silver in their hands. 19Having
put him to sleep on her lap, she called a man to
shave off the seven braids of his hair, and so
began to subdue him.*b* And his strength left
him.

20Then she called, "Samson, the Philistines
are upon you!"

He awoke from his sleep and thought, "I'll go
out as before and shake myself free." But he did
not know that the LORD had left him.

21Then the Philistines seized him, gouged out
his eyes and took him down to Gaza. Binding
him with bronze shackles, they set him to grinding in the prison. 22But the hair on his head
began to grow again after it had been shaved.

The Death of Samson

23Now the rulers of the Philistines assembled
to offer a great sacrifice to Dagon their god and
to celebrate, saying, "Our god has delivered
Samson, our enemy, into our hands."

24When the people saw him, they praised
their god, saying,

"Our god has delivered our enemy
　into our hands,
the one who laid waste our land
　and multiplied our slain."

---

a 13,14 Some Septuagint manuscripts; Hebrew *"I can, if you
weave the seven braids of my head into the fabric [on the loom]."
14 So she* 　*b 19* Hebrew; some Septuagint manuscripts *and he
began to weaken*

²⁵While they were in high spirits, they shouted, "Bring out Samson to entertain us." So they called Samson out of the prison, and he performed for them.

When they stood him among the pillars, ²⁶Samson said to the servant who held his hand, "Put me where I can feel the pillars that support the temple, so that I may lean against them." ²⁷Now the temple was crowded with men and women; all the rulers of the Philistines were there, and on the roof were about three thousand men and women watching Samson perform. ²⁸Then Samson prayed to the LORD, "O Sovereign LORD, remember me. O God, please strengthen me just once more, and let me with one blow get revenge on the Philistines for my two eyes." ²⁹Then Samson reached toward the two central pillars on which the temple stood. Bracing himself against them, his right hand on the one and his left hand on the other, ³⁰Samson said, "Let me die with the Philistines!" Then he pushed with all his might, and down came the temple on the rulers and all the people in it. Thus he killed many more when he died than while he lived.

³¹Then his brothers and his father's whole family went down to get him. They brought him back and buried him between Zorah and Eshtaol in the tomb of Manoah his father. He had led*ᵃ* Israel twenty years.

Micah's Idols

17 Now a man named Micah from the hill country of Ephraim ²said to his mother, "The eleven hundred shekels*ᵇ* of silver that were taken from you and about which I heard you utter a curse—I have that silver with me; I took it."

Then his mother said, "The LORD bless you, my son!"

³When he returned the eleven hundred shekels of silver to his mother, she said, "I solemnly consecrate my silver to the LORD for my son to make a carved image and a cast idol. I will give it back to you."

⁴So he returned the silver to his mother, and she took two hundred shekels*ᶜ* of silver and gave them to a silversmith, who made them into the image and the idol. And they were put in Micah's house.

²⁵他們正宴樂的時候，就說："叫參孫來，在我們面前戲耍戲耍。"於是將參孫從監裏提出來，他就在眾人面前戲耍。

他們使他站在兩柱中間。²⁶參孫向拉他手的童子說："求你讓我摸着托房的柱子，我要靠一靠。"²⁷那時房內充滿男女，非利士人的眾首領也都在那裏。房的平頂上約有三千男女，觀看參孫戲耍。²⁸參孫求告耶和華說："主耶和華啊，求你眷念我。神啊，求你賜我這一次的力量，使我在非利士人身上報那剜我雙眼的仇。"²⁹參孫就抱住托房的那兩根柱子，左手抱一根，右手抱一根，³⁰說："我情願與非利士人同死！"就盡力屈身，房子倒塌，壓住首領和房內的眾人。這樣，參孫死時所殺的人，比活着所殺的還多。

³¹參孫的弟兄和他父的全家，都下去取他的屍首，抬上來葬在瑣拉和以實陶中間，在他父瑪挪亞的墳墓裏。參孫作以色列的士師二十年。

米迦的偶像

17 以法蓮山地有一個人名叫米迦。²他對母親說："你那一千一百舍客勒銀子被人拿去，你因此咒詛，並且告訴了我。看哪，這銀子在我這裏，是我拿去了。"

他母親說："我兒啊，願耶和華賜福與你！"

³米迦就把這一千一百舍客勒銀子還他母親。他母親說："我分出這銀子來為你獻給耶和華，好雕刻一個像，鑄成一個像。現在我還是交給你。"

⁴米迦將銀子還他母親，他母親將二百舍客勒銀子交給銀匠，雕刻一個像，鑄成一個像，安置在米迦的屋內。

---

a 31 Traditionally *judged*   *b 2* That is, about 28 pounds (about 13 kilograms)   *c 4* That is, about 5 pounds (about 2.3 kilograms)

⁵這米迦有了神堂，又製造以弗得和家中的神像，分派他一個兒子作祭司。⁶那時以色列中沒有王，各人任意而行。

⁷猶大 伯利恆有一個少年人，是猶大族的利未人，他在那裏寄居。⁸這人離開猶大 伯利恆城，要找一個可住的地方。行路的時候，到了以法蓮山地，走到米迦的家。

⁹米迦問他說："你從哪裏來？"

他回答說："從猶大 伯利恆來。我是利未人，要找一個可住的地方。"

¹⁰米迦說："你可以住在我這裏，我以你為父、為祭司。我每年給你十舍客勒銀子，一套衣服和度日的食物。"利未人就進了他的家。¹¹利未人情願與那人同住，那人看這少年人如自己的兒子一樣。¹²米迦分派這少年者的利未人作祭司，他就住在米迦的家裏。¹³米迦說："現在我知道耶和華必賜福與我，因我有一個利未人作祭司。"

但人在拉億居住

18 那時以色列中沒有王。但支派的人仍是尋地居住，因為到那日子，他們還沒有在以色列支派中得地為業。²但人從瑣拉和以實陶打發本族中的五個勇士，去仔細窺探那地。吩咐他們說："你們去窺探那地。"

他們來到以法蓮山地，進了米迦的住宅，就在那裏住宿。³他們臨近米迦的住宅，聽出那少年利未人的口音來，就進去問他說："誰領你到這裏來？你在這裏做甚麼？你在這裏得甚麼？"

⁴他回答說："米迦待我如此如此，請我作祭司。"

⁵他們對他說："請你求問神，使我們知道所行的道路，通達不通達。"

⁶祭司對他們說："你們可以平平安安地去，你們所行的道路是在耶和華面前的。"

⁷五人就走了，來到拉億，見那裏的民安居無慮，如同西頓人安居一樣。在那地沒有人掌權擾亂他

⁵Now this man Micah had a shrine, and he made an ephod and some idols and installed one of his sons as his priest. ⁶In those days Israel had no king; everyone did as he saw fit.

⁷A young Levite from Bethlehem in Judah, who had been living within the clan of Judah, ⁸left that town in search of some other place to stay. On his way^a he came to Micah's house in the hill country of Ephraim. ⁹Micah asked him, "Where are you from?"

"I'm a Levite from Bethlehem in Judah," he said, "and I'm looking for a place to stay."

¹⁰Then Micah said to him, "Live with me and be my father and priest, and I'll give you ten shekels^b of silver a year, your clothes and your food." ¹¹So the Levite agreed to live with him, and the young man was to him like one of his sons. ¹²Then Micah installed the Levite, and the young man became his priest and lived in his house. ¹³And Micah said, "Now I know that the LORD will be good to me, since this Levite has become my priest."

Danites Settle in Laish

18 In those days Israel had no king. And in those days the tribe of the Danites was seeking a place of their own where they might settle, because they had not yet come into an inheritance among the tribes of Israel. ²So the Danites sent five warriors from Zorah and Eshtaol to spy out the land and explore it. These men represented all their clans. They told them, "Go, explore the land."

The men entered the hill country of Ephraim and came to the house of Micah, where they spent the night. ³When they were near Micah's house, they recognized the voice of the young Levite; so they turned in there and asked him, "Who brought you here? What are you doing in this place? Why are you here?"

⁴He told them what Micah had done for him, and said, "He has hired me and I am his priest."

⁵Then they said to him, "Please inquire of God to learn whether our journey will be successful."

⁶The priest answered them, "Go in peace. Your journey has the LORD's approval."

⁷So the five men left and came to Laish, where they saw that the people were living in safety, like the Sidonians, unsuspecting and secure. And since their land lacked nothing,

a 8 Or *To carry on his profession*　　*b 10* That is, about 4 ounces (about 110 grams)

they were prosperous.[a] Also, they lived a long way from the Sidonians and had no relationship with anyone else.[b]

8When they returned to Zorah and Eshtaol, their brothers asked them, "How did you find things?"

9They answered, "Come on, let's attack them! We have seen that the land is very good. Aren't you going to do something? Don't hesitate to go there and take it over. 10When you get there, you will find an unsuspecting people and a spacious land that God has put into your hands, a land that lacks nothing whatever."

11Then six hundred men from the clan of the Danites, armed for battle, set out from Zorah and Eshtaol. 12On their way they set up camp near Kiriath Jearim in Judah. This is why the place west of Kiriath Jearim is called Mahaneh Dan[c] to this day. 13From there they went on to the hill country of Ephraim and came to Micah's house.

14Then the five men who had spied out the land of Laish said to their brothers, "Do you know that one of these houses has an ephod, other household gods, a carved image and a cast idol? Now you know what to do." 15So they turned in there and went to the house of the young Levite at Micah's place and greeted him. 16The six hundred Danites, armed for battle, stood at the entrance to the gate. 17The five men who had spied out the land went inside and took the carved image, the ephod, the other household gods and the cast idol while the priest and the six hundred armed men stood at the entrance to the gate.

18When these men went into Micah's house and took the carved image, the ephod, the other household gods and the cast idol, the priest said to them, "What are you doing?"

19They answered him, "Be quiet! Don't say a word. Come with us, and be our father and priest. Isn't it better that you serve a tribe and clan in Israel as priest rather than just one man's household?" 20Then the priest was glad. He took the ephod, the other household gods and the carved image and went along with the people. 21Putting their little children, their livestock and their possessions in front of them, they turned away and left.

22When they had gone some distance from Micah's house, the men who lived near Micah were called together and overtook the Danites. 23As they shouted after them, the Danites turned

a 7 The meaning of the Hebrew for this clause is uncertain.

b 7 Hebrew; some Septuagint manuscripts with the Arameans

c 12 Mahaneh Dan means Dan's camp.

們，他們離西頓人也遠，與別人沒有來往。

8五人回到瑣拉和以實陶，見他們的弟兄。弟兄問他們說："你們有甚麼話？"

9他們回答說："起來，我們上去攻擊他們吧！我們已經窺探那地，見那地甚好。你們為何靜坐不動呢？要急速前往得那地為業，不可遲延。10你們到了那裏，必看見安居無慮的民，地也寬闊。神已將那地交在你們手中，那地百物俱全，一無所缺。"

11於是但族中的六百人，各帶兵器，從瑣拉和以實陶前往。12上到猶大的基列耶琳，在基列耶琳後邊安營。因此那地方名叫瑪哈尼但，直到今日。13他們從那裏往以法蓮山地去，來到米迦的住宅。

14從前窺探拉億地的五個人對他們的弟兄說："這宅子裏有以弗得和家中的神像，並雕刻的像與鑄成的像，你們知道嗎？現在你們要想一想當怎樣行。"15五人就進入米迦的住宅，到了那少年利未人的房內問他好。16那六百但人各帶兵器，站在門口。17窺探地的五個人走進去，將雕刻的像、以弗得、家中的神像，並鑄成的像，都拿了去。祭司和帶兵器的六百人，一同站在門口。

18那五個人進入米迦的住宅，拿出雕刻的像、以弗得、家中的神像，並鑄成的像，祭司就問他們說："你們做甚麼呢？"

19他們回答說："不要做聲，用手摀口，跟我們去吧！我們必以你為父、為祭司。你作一家的祭司好呢？還是作以色列一族一支派的祭司好呢？"20祭司心裏喜悅，便拿着以弗得和家中的神像，並雕刻的像，進入他們中間。21他們就轉身離開那裏，妻子、兒女、牲畜、財物，都在前頭。

22離米迦的住宅已遠，米迦的近鄰都聚集來，追趕但人。23呼叫但人。但人回頭問米迦說："你聚集這許多人來做甚麼呢？"

24米迦說："你們將我所做的神像和祭司都帶了去，我還有所剩的嗎？怎麼還問我說'做甚麼'呢？"

25但人對米迦說："你不要使我們聽見你的聲音，恐怕有性暴的人攻擊你，以致你和你的全家盡都喪命。"26但人還是走他們的路。米迦見他們的勢力比自己強盛，就轉身回家去了。

27但人將米迦所做的神像和他的祭司都帶到拉億，見安居無慮的民，就用刀殺了那民，又放火燒了那城。28並無人搭救，因為離西頓遠，他們又與別人沒有來往。城在平原，那平原靠近伯利合。

但人又在那裏修城居住，29照着他們始祖以色列之子但的名字，給那城起名叫但；原先那城名叫拉億。30但人就為自己設立那雕刻的像。摩西的孫子、革舜的兒子約拿單和他的子孫，作且支派的祭司，直到那地遭擄掠的日子。31神的殿在示羅多少日子，但人為自己設立米迦所雕刻的像，也在但多少日子。

利未人與他的妾侍

19 當以色列中沒有王的時候，有住以法蓮山地那邊的一個利未人，娶了一個猶大伯利恆的女子為妾。2妾行淫離開丈夫，回猶大伯利恆，到了父家，在那裏住了四個月。3她丈夫起來，帶着一個僕人、兩匹驢去見她，用好話勸她回來。女子就引丈夫進入父家。她父見了那人，便歡歡喜喜地迎接。4那人的岳父，就是女子的父親，將那人留下住了三天。於是二人一同吃喝、住宿。

5到第四天，利未人清早起來要走，女子的父親對女婿說："請你吃點飯，加添心力，然後可以行路。"6於是二人坐下一同吃喝。女子的父親對那人說："請你再住一夜，暢快你的心。"7那人起來要走，他岳父強留他，他又住了一

and said to Micah, "What's the matter with you that you called out your men to fight?"

24He replied, "You took the gods I made, and my priest, and went away. What else do I have? How can you ask, 'What's the matter with you?'"

25The Danites answered, "Don't argue with us, or some hot-tempered men will attack you, and you and your family will lose your lives." 26So the Danites went their way, and Micah, seeing that they were too strong for him, turned around and went back home.

27Then they took what Micah had made, and his priest, and went on to Laish, against a peaceful and unsuspecting people. They attacked them with the sword and burned down their city. 28There was no one to rescue them because they lived a long way from Sidon and had no relationship with anyone else. The city was in a valley near Beth Rehob.

The Danites rebuilt the city and settled there. 29They named it Dan after their forefather Dan, who was born to Israel—though the city used to be called Laish. 30There the Danites set up for themselves the idols, and Jonathan son of Gershom, the son of Moses,[a] and his sons were priests for the tribe of Dan until the time of the captivity of the land. 31They continued to use the idols Micah had made, all the time the house of God was in Shiloh.

A Levite and His Concubine

19 In those days Israel had no king.

Now a Levite who lived in a remote area in the hill country of Ephraim took a concubine from Bethlehem in Judah. 2But she was unfaithful to him. She left him and went back to her father's house in Bethlehem, Judah. After she had been there four months, 3her husband went to her to persuade her to return. He had with him his servant and two donkeys. She took him into her father's house, and when her father saw him, he gladly welcomed him. 4His father-in-law, the girl's father, prevailed upon him to stay; so he remained with him three days, eating and drinking, and sleeping there.

5On the fourth day they got up early and he prepared to leave, but the girl's father said to his son-in-law, "Refresh yourself with something to eat; then you can go." 6So the two of them sat down to eat and drink together. Afterward the girl's father said, "Please stay tonight and enjoy yourself." 7And when the man got up to go, his father-in-law persuaded him, so he stayed there

a 30 An ancient Hebrew scribal tradition, some Septuagint manuscripts and Vulgate; Masoretic Text Manasseh

that night. 8On the morning of the fifth day, when he rose to go, the girl's father said, "Refresh yourself. Wait till afternoon!" So the two of them ate together.

9Then when the man, with his concubine and his servant, got up to leave, his father-in-law, the girl's father, said, "Now look, it's almost evening. Spend the night here; the day is nearly over. Stay and enjoy yourself. Early tomorrow morning you can get up and be on your way home." 10But, unwilling to stay another night, the man left and went toward Jebus (that is, Jerusalem), with his two saddled donkeys and his concubine.

11When they were near Jebus and the day was almost gone, the servant said to his master, "Come, let's stop at this city of the Jebusites and spend the night."

12His master replied, "No. We won't go into an alien city, whose people are not Israelites. We will go on to Gibeah." 13He added, "Come, let's try to reach Gibeah or Ramah and spend the night in one of those places." 14So they went on, and the sun set as they neared Gibeah in Benjamin. 15There they stopped to spend the night. They went and sat in the city square, but no one took them into his home for the night.

16That evening an old man from the hill country of Ephraim, who was living in Gibeah (the men of the place were Benjamites), came in from his work in the fields. 17When he looked and saw the traveler in the city square, the old man asked, "Where are you going? Where did you come from?"

18He answered, "We are on our way from Bethlehem in Judah to a remote area in the hill country of Ephraim where I live. I have been to Bethlehem in Judah and now I am going to the house of the LORD. No one has taken me into his house. 19We have both straw and fodder for our donkeys and bread and wine for ourselves your servants—me, your maidservant, and the young man with us. We don't need anything."

20"You are welcome at my house," the old man said. "Let me supply whatever you need. Only don't spend the night in the square." 21So he took him into his house and fed his donkeys. After they had washed their feet, they had something to eat and drink.

22While they were enjoying themselves, some of the wicked men of the city surrounded the house. Pounding on the door, they shouted to the old man who owned the house, "Bring out the man who came to your house so we can have sex with him."

宿。8到第五天，他清早起來要走。女子的父親說：「請你吃點飯，加添心力，等到日頭偏西再走。」於是二人一同吃飯。

9那人同他的妾和僕人起來要走，他岳父，就是女子的父親，對他說：「看哪，日頭偏西了，請你再住一夜，天快晚了，可以在這裏住宿，暢快你的心。明天早早起行回家去。」10那人不願再住一夜，就備上那兩匹驢，帶着妾起身走了，來到耶布斯的對面。耶布斯就是耶路撒冷。

11臨近耶布斯的時候，日頭快要落了。僕人對主人說：「我們不如進這耶布斯人的城裏住宿。」

12主人回答說：「我們不可進不是以色列人住的外邦城，不如過到基比亞去。」13又對僕人說：「我們可以到一個地方，或住在基比亞，或住在拉瑪。」14他們就往前走。將到便雅憫的基比亞，日頭已經落了。15他們進入基比亞，要在那裏住宿，就坐在城裏的街上，因為無人接他們進家住宿。

16晚上，有一個老年人，從田間做工回來，他原是以法蓮山地的人，住在基比亞，那地方的人卻是便雅憫人。17老年人舉目看見客人坐在城裏的街上，就問他說：「你從哪裏來？要往哪裏去？」

18他回答說：「我們從猶大伯利恆來，要往以法蓮山地那邊去。我原是那裏的人，到過猶大伯利恆，現在我往耶和華的殿去，在這裏無人接我進他的家。19其實我有糧草可以餵驢，我與我的妾，並我的僕人，有餅有酒，並不缺少甚麼。」

20老年人說：「願你平安！你所需用的我都給你，只是不可在街上過夜。」21於是領他們到家裏，餵上驢，他們就洗腳吃喝。

22他們心裏正歡暢的時候，城中的匪徒圍住房子，連連叩門，對房主老人說：「你把那進你家的人帶出來，我們要與他交合。」

²³那房主出來對他們說：“弟兄們哪，不要這樣作惡。這人既然進了我的家，你們就不要行這醜事。²⁴我有個女兒，還是處女，並有這人的妾，我將她們領出來任憑你們玷辱她們，只是向這人不可行這樣的醜事。”

²⁵那些人卻不聽從他的話。那人就把他的妾拉出去給他們，他們便與她交合，終夜凌辱她，直到天色快亮才放她去。²⁶天快亮的時候，婦人回到她主人住宿的房門前，就仆倒在地，直到天亮。

²⁷早晨，她的主人起來開了房門，出去要行路。不料那婦人仆倒在房門前，兩手搭在門檻上。²⁸就對婦人說：“起來，我們走吧！”婦人卻不回答。那人便將她馱在驢上，起身回本處去了。

²⁹到了家裏，用刀將妾的屍身切成十二塊，使人拿着傳送以色列的四境。³⁰凡看見的人都說：“從以色列人出埃及地，直到今日，這樣的事沒有行過，也沒有見過。現在應當思想，大家商議當怎樣辦理。”

以色列人討伐便雅憫人

20 於是以色列從但到別是巴，以及住基列地的眾人都出來如同一人，聚集在米斯巴耶和華面前。²以色列民的首領，就是各支派的軍長，都站在神百姓的會中；拿刀的步兵共有四十萬。³以色列人上到米斯巴，便雅憫人都聽見了。以色列人說：“請你將這件惡事的情由對我們說明。”

⁴那利未人，就是被害之婦人的丈夫，回答說：“我和我的妾到了便雅憫的基比亞住宿。⁵基比亞人夜間起來，圍了我住的房子，想要殺我，又將我的妾強姦致死。⁶我就把我妾的屍身切成塊子，使人拿着傳送以色列得為業的全地，因為基比亞人在以色列中行了兇淫醜惡的事。⁷你們以色列人都當籌劃商議。”

⁸眾民都起來如同一人，說：“我們連一人都不回自己帳棚、自己房屋去。⁹我們向基比亞人必這樣

²³The owner of the house went outside and said to them, "No, my friends, don't be so vile. Since this man is my guest, don't do this disgraceful thing. ²⁴Look, here is my virgin daughter, and his concubine. I will bring them out to you now, and you can use them and do to them whatever you wish. But to this man, don't do such a disgraceful thing."

²⁵But the men would not listen to him. So the man took his concubine and sent her outside to them, and they raped her and abused her throughout the night, and at dawn they let her go. ²⁶At daybreak the woman went back to the house where her master was staying, fell down at the door and lay there until daylight.

²⁷When her master got up in the morning and opened the door of the house and stepped out to continue on his way, there lay his concubine, fallen in the doorway of the house, with her hands on the threshold. ²⁸He said to her, "Get up; let's go." But there was no answer. Then the man put her on his donkey and set out for home.

²⁹When he reached home, he took a knife and cut up his concubine, limb by limb, into twelve parts and sent them into all the areas of Israel. ³⁰Everyone who saw it said, "Such a thing has never been seen or done, not since the day the Israelites came up out of Egypt. Think about it! Consider it! Tell us what to do!"

Israelites Fight the Benjamites

20 Then all the Israelites from Dan to Beersheba and from the land of Gilead came out as one man and assembled before the LORD in Mizpah. ²The leaders of all the people of the tribes of Israel took their places in the assembly of the people of God, four hundred thousand soldiers armed with swords. ³(The Benjamites heard that the Israelites had gone up to Mizpah.) Then the Israelites said, "Tell us how this awful thing happened."

⁴So the Levite, the husband of the murdered woman, said, "I and my concubine came to Gibeah in Benjamin to spend the night. ⁵During the night the men of Gibeah came after me and surrounded the house, intending to kill me. They raped my concubine, and she died. ⁶I took my concubine, cut her into pieces and sent one piece to each region of Israel's inheritance, because they committed this lewd and disgraceful act in Israel. ⁷Now, all you Israelites, speak up and give your verdict."

⁸All the people rose as one man, saying, "None of us will go home. No, not one of us will return to his house. ⁹But now this is what we'll

do to Gibeah: We'll go up against it as the lot directs. [10]We'll take ten men out of every hundred from all the tribes of Israel, and a hundred from a thousand, and a thousand from ten thousand, to get provisions for the army. Then, when the army arrives at Gibeah[a] in Benjamin, it can give them what they deserve for all this vileness done in Israel." [11]So all the men of Israel got together and united as one man against the city.

[12]The tribes of Israel sent men throughout the tribe of Benjamin, saying, "What about this awful crime that was committed among you? [13]Now surrender those wicked men of Gibeah so that we may put them to death and purge the evil from Israel."

But the Benjamites would not listen to their fellow Israelites. [14]From their towns they came together at Gibeah to fight against the Israelites. [15]At once the Benjamites mobilized twenty-six thousand swordsmen from their towns, in addition to seven hundred chosen men from those living in Gibeah. [16]Among all these soldiers there were seven hundred chosen men who were left-handed, each of whom could sling a stone at a hair and not miss.

[17]Israel, apart from Benjamin, mustered four hundred thousand swordsmen, all of them fighting men.

[18]The Israelites went up to Bethel[b] and inquired of God. They said, "Who of us shall go first to fight against the Benjamites?"

The LORD replied, "Judah shall go first."

[19]The next morning the Israelites got up and pitched camp near Gibeah. [20]The men of Israel went out to fight the Benjamites and took up battle positions against them at Gibeah. [21]The Benjamites came out of Gibeah and cut down twenty-two thousand Israelites on the battlefield that day. [22]But the men of Israel encouraged one another and again took up their positions where they had stationed themselves the first day. [23]The Israelites went up and wept before the LORD until evening, and they inquired of the LORD. They said, "Shall we go up again to battle against the Benjamites, our brothers?"

The LORD answered, "Go up against them."

[24]Then the Israelites drew near to Benjamin the second day. [25]This time, when the Benjamites came out from Gibeah to oppose them, they cut down another eighteen thousand Israelites, all of them armed with swords.

行,照所掣的籤去攻擊他們。[10]我們要在以色列各支派中,一百人挑取十人、一千人挑取百人、一萬人挑取千人,為民運糧。等大眾到了便雅憫的基比亞,就照基比亞人在以色列中所行的醜事征伐他們。" [11]於是以色列眾人彼此連合如同一人,聚集攻擊那城。

[12]以色列眾支派打發人去,問便雅憫支派的各家說:"你們中間怎麼做了這樣的惡事呢?[13]現在你們要將基比亞的那些匪徒交出來,我們好治死他們,從以色列中除掉這惡。"

便雅憫人卻不肯聽從他們弟兄以色列人的話。[14]便雅憫人從他們的各城裏出來,聚集到了基比亞,要與以色列人打仗。[15]那時便雅憫人,從各城裏點出拿刀的,共有二萬六千。另外還有基比亞人點出七百精兵。[16]在眾軍之中有揀選的七百精兵,都是左手便利的,能用機弦甩石打人,毫髮不差。

[17]便雅憫人之外,點出以色列人拿刀的,共有四十萬,都是戰士。

[18]以色列人就起來,到伯特利去求問神說:"我們中間誰當首先上去與便雅憫人爭戰呢?"

耶和華說:"猶大當先上去。"

[19]以色列人早晨起來,對着基比亞安營。[20]以色列人出來,要與便雅憫人打仗,就在基比亞前擺陣。[21]便雅憫人就從基比亞出來,當日殺死以色列人二萬二千。[22]以色列人彼此奮勇,仍在頭一日擺陣的地方又擺陣。[23]未擺陣之先,以色列人上去,在耶和華面前哭號,直到晚上,求問耶和華說:"我們再去與我們弟兄便雅憫人打仗,可以不可以?"

耶和華說:"可以上去攻擊他們。"

[24]第二日,以色列人就上前攻擊便雅憫人。[25]便雅憫人也在這日從基比亞出來,與以色列人接戰,又殺死他們一萬八千,都是拿刀的。

a 10 One Hebrew manuscript; most Hebrew manuscripts Geba, a variant of Gibeah   b 18 Or to the house of God; also in verse 26

26以色列眾人就上到伯特利，坐在耶和華面前哭號，當日禁食直到晚上。又在耶和華面前獻燔祭和平安祭。27、28那時神的約櫃在那裏。亞倫的孫子、以利亞撒的兒子非尼哈侍立在約櫃前。以色列人問耶和華說：「我們當再出去與我們弟兄便雅憫人打仗呢？還是罷兵呢？」

耶和華說：「你們當上去，因為明日我必將他們交在你們手中。」

29以色列人在基比亞的四圍設下伏兵。30第三日，以色列人又上去攻擊便雅憫人，在基比亞前擺陣，與前兩次一樣。31便雅憫人也出來迎敵，就被引誘離城。在田間兩條路上，一通伯特利，一通基比亞，像前兩次，動手殺死以色列人約有三十個。

32便雅憫人說：「他們仍舊敗在我們面前。」但以色列人說：「我們不如逃跑引誘他們離開城到路上來。」

33以色列眾人都起來，在巴力他瑪擺陣，以色列的伏兵從馬利迦巴埋伏的地方衝上前去。34有以色列人中的一萬精兵，來到基比亞前接戰，勢派甚是兇猛，便雅憫人卻不知道災禍臨近了。35耶和華使以色列人殺敗便雅憫人。那日以色列人殺死便雅憫人二萬五千一百，都是拿刀的。36於是便雅憫人知道自己敗了。

先是以色列人，因為靠着在基比亞前所設的伏兵，就在便雅憫人面前詐敗。37伏兵急忙闖進基比亞，用刀殺死全城的人。38以色列人預先同伏兵約定在城內放火，以煙氣上騰為號。

39以色列人臨退陣的時候，便雅憫人動手殺死以色列人，約有三十個，就說：「他們仍像前次被我們殺敗了。」40當煙氣如柱從城中上騰的時候，便雅憫人回頭觀看，見全城的煙氣沖天。41以色列人又轉身回

26Then the Israelites, all the people, went up to Bethel, and there they sat weeping before the LORD. They fasted that day until evening and presented burnt offerings and fellowship offerings[a] to the LORD. 27And the Israelites inquired of the LORD. (In those days the ark of the covenant of God was there, 28with Phinehas son of Eleazar, the son of Aaron, ministering before it.) They asked, "Shall we go up again to battle with Benjamin our brother, or not?"

The LORD responded, "Go, for tomorrow I will give them into your hands."

29Then Israel set an ambush around Gibeah. 30They went up against the Benjamites on the third day and took up positions against Gibeah as they had done before. 31The Benjamites came out to meet them and were drawn away from the city. They began to inflict casualties on the Israelites as before, so that about thirty men fell in the open field and on the roads—the one leading to Bethel and the other to Gibeah.

32While the Benjamites were saying, "We are defeating them as before," the Israelites were saying, "Let's retreat and draw them away from the city to the roads."

33All the men of Israel moved from their places and took up positions at Baal Tamar, and the Israelite ambush charged out of its place on the west[b] of Gibeah.[c] 34Then ten thousand of Israel's finest men made a frontal attack on Gibeah. The fighting was so heavy that the Benjamites did not realize how near disaster was. 35The LORD defeated Benjamin before Israel, and on that day the Israelites struck down 25,100 Benjamites, all armed with swords. 36Then the Benjamites saw that they were beaten.

Now the men of Israel had given way before Benjamin, because they relied on the ambush they had set near Gibeah. 37The men who had been in ambush made a sudden dash into Gibeah, spread out and put the whole city to the sword. 38The men of Israel had arranged with the ambush that they should send up a great cloud of smoke from the city, 39and then the men of Israel would turn in the battle.

The Benjamites had begun to inflict casualties on the men of Israel (about thirty), and they said, "We are defeating them as in the first battle." 40But when the column of smoke began to rise from the city, the Benjamites turned and saw the smoke of the whole city going up into the sky. 41Then the men of Israel turned on

a 26 Traditionally *peace offerings*   b 33 Some Septuagint manuscripts and Vulgate; the meaning of the Hebrew for this word is uncertain.   c 33 Hebrew *Geba*, a variant of *Gibeah*

them, and the men of Benjamin were terrified, because they realized that disaster had come upon them. [42]So they fled before the Israelites in the direction of the desert, but they could not escape the battle. And the men of Israel who came out of the towns cut them down there. [43]They surrounded the Benjamites, chased them and easily[d] overran them in the vicinity of Gibeah on the east. [44]Eighteen thousand Benjamites fell, all of them valiant fighters. [45]As they turned and fled toward the desert to the rock of Rimmon, the Israelites cut down five thousand men along the roads. They kept pressing after the Benjamites as far as Gidom and struck down two thousand more.

[46]On that day twenty-five thousand Benjamite swordsmen fell, all of them valiant fighters. [47]But six hundred men turned and fled into the desert to the rock of Rimmon, where they stayed four months. [48]The men of Israel went back to Benjamin and put all the towns to the sword, including the animals and everything else they found. All the towns they came across they set on fire.

Wives for the Benjamites

21 The men of Israel had taken an oath at Mizpah: "Not one of us will give his daughter in marriage to a Benjamite."

[2]The people went to Bethel,[b] where they sat before God until evening, raising their voices and weeping bitterly. [3]"O LORD, the God of Israel," they cried, "why has this happened to Israel? Why should one tribe be missing from Israel today?"

[4]Early the next day the people built an altar and presented burnt offerings and fellowship offerings.[c]

[5]Then the Israelites asked, "Who from all the tribes of Israel has failed to assemble before the LORD?" For they had taken a solemn oath that anyone who failed to assemble before the LORD at Mizpah should certainly be put to death. [6]Now the Israelites grieved for their brothers, the Benjamites. "Today one tribe is cut off from Israel," they said. [7]"How can we provide wives for those who are left, since we have taken an oath by the LORD not to give them any of our daughters in marriage?" [8]Then they asked, "Which one of the tribes of Israel failed to assemble before the LORD at Mizpah?" They discovered that no one from Jabesh Gilead had come to the camp for the assembly. [9]For when

來，便雅憫人就甚驚惶，因為看見災禍臨到自己了。[42]他們在以色列人面前轉身往曠野逃跑；以色列人在後面追殺。那從各城裏出來的，也都夾攻殺滅他們。[43]以色列人圍繞便雅憫人，追趕他們，在他們歇腳之處，對着日出之地的基比亞踐踏他們。[44]便雅憫人死了的有一萬八千，都是勇士。[45]其餘的人轉身向曠野逃跑，往臨門磐去。以色列人在道路上殺了他們五千人，如拾取遺穗一樣，追到基頓又殺了他們二千人。

[46]那日便雅憫死了的，共有二萬五千人，都是拿刀的勇士。[47]只剩下六百人，轉身向曠野逃跑，到了臨門磐，就在那裏住了四個月。[48]以色列人又轉到便雅憫地，將各城的人和牲畜，並一切所遇見的，都用刀殺盡，又放火燒了一切城邑。

為便雅憫人安排妻室

21 以色列人在米斯巴曾起誓說："我們都不將女兒給便雅憫人為妻。"

[2]以色列人來到伯特利，坐在神面前直到晚上，放聲痛哭，[3]說："耶和華以色列的神啊，為何以色列中有這樣缺了一支派的事呢？"

[4]次日清早百姓起來，在那裏築了一座壇，獻燔祭和平安祭。

[5]以色列人彼此問說："以色列各支派中，誰沒有同會眾上到耶和華面前來呢？"先是以色列人起過大誓說，凡不上米斯巴到耶和華面前來的，必將他治死。

[6]以色列人為他們的弟兄便雅憫後悔，說："如今以色列中絕了一個支派了。"[7]我們既在耶和華面前起誓說，必不將我們的女兒給便雅憫人為妻，現在我們當怎樣辦理，使他們剩下的人有妻呢？"[8]又彼此問說："以色列支派中誰沒有上米斯巴到耶和華面前來呢？"他們就查出基列雅比沒有一人進營到會眾那裏，[9]因為

a 43 The meaning of the Hebrew for this word is uncertain.
b 2 Or to the house of God   c 4 Traditionally peace offerings

百姓被數的時候，沒有一個基列雅比人在那裏。

10會眾就打發一萬二千大勇士，吩咐他們說：「你們去用刀將基列雅比人連婦女帶孩子都擊殺了。11所當行的就是這樣：要將一切男子和已嫁的女子盡行殺戮。」12他們在基列雅比人中，遇見了四百個未嫁的處女，就帶到迦南地的示羅營裏。

13全會眾打發人到臨門磐的便雅憫人那裏，向他們說和睦的話。14當時便雅憫人回來了，以色列人就把所存活基列雅比的女子給他們為妻，還是不夠。

15百姓為便雅憫人後悔，因為耶和華使以色列人缺了一個支派（註：原文作「使以色列中有了破口」）。16會中的長老說：「便雅憫中的女子既然除滅了，我們當怎樣辦理，使那餘剩的人有妻呢？」17又說：「便雅憫逃脫的人當有地業，免得以色列中塗抹了一個支派。18只是我們不能將自己的女兒給他們為妻，因為以色列人曾起誓說，有將女兒給便雅憫人為妻的，必受咒詛。」19他們又說：「在利波拿以南，伯特利以北，在示劍大路以東的示羅，年年有耶和華的節期。」

20就吩咐便雅憫人說：「你們去，在葡萄園中埋伏。21若看見示羅的女子出來跳舞，就從葡萄園出來，在示羅的女子中各搶一個為妻，回便雅憫地去。22他們的父親或是弟兄若來與我們爭競，我們就說：『求你們看我們的情面，施恩給這些人，因我們在爭戰的時候沒有給他們留下女子為妻。這也不是你們將女子給他們的，若是你們給的，就算有罪。』」

23於是便雅憫人照樣而行，按着他們的數目從跳舞的女子中搶去為妻，就回自己的地業去，又重修城邑居住。

24當時以色列人離開那裏，各歸本支派、本宗族、本地業去了。

25那時以色列中沒有王，各人任意而行。

---

they counted the people, they found that none of the people of Jabesh Gilead were there.

10So the assembly sent twelve thousand fighting men with instructions to go to Jabesh Gilead and put to the sword those living there, including the women and children. 11"This is what you are to do," they said. "Kill every male and every woman who is not a virgin." 12They found among the people living in Jabesh Gilead four hundred young women who had never slept with a man, and they took them to the camp at Shiloh in Canaan.

13Then the whole assembly sent an offer of peace to the Benjamites at the rock of Rimmon. 14So the Benjamites returned at that time and were given the women of Jabesh Gilead who had been spared. But there were not enough for all of them.

15The people grieved for Benjamin, because the LORD had made a gap in the tribes of Israel. 16And the elders of the assembly said, "With the women of Benjamin destroyed, how shall we provide wives for the men who are left? 17The Benjamite survivors must have heirs," they said, "so that a tribe of Israel will not be wiped out. 18We can't give them our daughters as wives, since we Israelites have taken this oath: 'Cursed be anyone who gives a wife to a Benjamite.' 19But look, there is the annual festival of the LORD in Shiloh, to the north of Bethel, and east of the road that goes from Bethel to Shechem, and to the south of Lebonah."

20So they instructed the Benjamites, saying, 'Go and hide in the vineyards 21and watch. When the girls of Shiloh come out to join in the dancing, then rush from the vineyards and each of you seize a wife from the girls of Shiloh and go to the land of Benjamin. 22When their fathers or brothers complain to us, we will say to them, 'Do us a kindness by helping them, because we did not get wives for them during the war, and you are innocent, since you did not give your daughters to them.' "

23So that is what the Benjamites did. While the girls were dancing, each man caught one and carried her off to be his wife. Then they returned to their inheritance and rebuilt the towns and settled in them.

24At that time the Israelites left that place and went home to their tribes and clans, each to his own inheritance.

25In those days Israel had no king; everyone did as he saw fit.

Ruth

路得記

Naomi and Ruth

1 In the days when the judges ruled,[a] there was a famine in the land, and a man from Bethlehem in Judah, together with his wife and two sons, went to live for a while in the country of Moab. ²The man's name was Elimelech, his wife's name Naomi, and the names of his two sons were Mahlon and Kilion. They were Ephrathites from Bethlehem, Judah. And they went to Moab and lived there.

³Now Elimelech, Naomi's husband, died, and she was left with her two sons. ⁴They married Moabite women, one named Orpah and the other Ruth. After they had lived there about ten years, ⁵both Mahlon and Kilion also died, and Naomi was left without her two sons and her husband.

⁶When she heard in Moab that the LORD had come to the aid of his people by providing food for them, Naomi and her daughters-in-law prepared to return home from there. ⁷With her two daughters-in-law she left the place where she had been living and set out on the road that would take them back to the land of Judah.

⁸Then Naomi said to her two daughters-in-law, "Go back, each of you, to your mother's home. May the LORD show kindness to you, as you have shown to your dead and to me. ⁹May the LORD grant that each of you will find rest in the home of another husband."

Then she kissed them and they wept aloud ¹⁰and said to her, "We will go back with you to your people."

¹¹But Naomi said, "Return home, my daughters. Why would you come with me? Am I going to have any more sons, who could become your husbands? ¹²Return home, my daughters; I am too old to have another husband. Even if I thought there was still hope for me—even if I had a husband tonight and then gave birth to sons— ¹³would you wait until they grew up? Would you remain unmarried for them? No, my daughters. It is more bitter for me than for you, because the LORD's hand has gone out against me!"

拿俄米與路得

1 當士師秉政的時候,國中遭遇饑荒。在猶大伯利恆,有一個人帶着妻子和兩個兒子往摩押地去寄居。²這人名叫以利米勒,他的妻名叫拿俄米。他兩個兒子,一個名叫瑪倫,一個名叫基連,都是猶大伯利恆的以法他人。他們到了摩押地,就住在那裏。

³後來拿俄米的丈夫以利米勒死了,剩下婦人和她兩個兒子。⁴這兩個兒子娶了摩押女子為妻,一個名叫俄珥巴,一個名叫路得,在那裏住了約有十年。⁵瑪倫和基連二人也死了,剩下拿俄米,沒有丈夫,也沒有兒子。

⁶她就與兩個兒婦起身,要從摩押地歸回,因為她在摩押地聽見耶和華眷顧自己的百姓,賜糧食與他們。⁷於是她和兩個兒婦起行離開所住的地方,要回猶大地去。

⁸拿俄米對兩個兒婦說:"你們各人回娘家去吧!願耶和華恩待你們,像你們恩待已死的人與我一樣。⁹願耶和華使你們各在新夫家中得平安!"

於是,拿俄米與她們親嘴。她們就放聲而哭,¹⁰說:"不然,我們必與你一同回你本國去。"

¹¹拿俄米說:"我女兒們哪,回去吧!為何要跟我去呢?我還能生子作你們的丈夫嗎?¹²我女兒們哪,回去吧!我年紀老邁,不能再有丈夫;即或說,我還有指望,今夜有丈夫可以生子,¹³你們豈能等着他們長大呢?你們豈能等着他們不嫁別人呢?我女兒們哪,不要這樣!我為你們的緣故甚是愁苦,因為耶和華伸手攻擊我。"

¹⁴兩個兒婦又放聲而哭，俄珥巴與婆婆親嘴而別，只是路得捨不得拿俄米。

¹⁵拿俄米說：「看哪，你嫂子已經回她本國和她所拜的神那裏去了，你也跟着你嫂子回去吧！」

¹⁶路得說：「不要催我回去不跟隨你。你往哪裏去，我也往那裏去；你在哪裏住宿，我也在那裏住宿；你的國就是我的國，你的神就是我的神。¹⁷你在哪裏死，我也在那裏死，也葬在那裏。除非死能使你我相離，不然，願耶和華重重地降罰與我！」¹⁸拿俄米見路得定意要跟隨自己去，就不再勸她了。

¹⁹於是二人同行，來到伯利恆。她們到了伯利恆，合城的人就都驚訝。婦女們說：「這是拿俄米嗎？」

²⁰拿俄米對他們說：「不要叫我拿俄米（註：「拿俄米」就是「甜」的意思），要叫我瑪拉（註：「瑪拉」就是「苦」的意思），因為全能者使我受了大苦。²¹我滿滿地出去，耶和華使我空空地回來。耶和華降禍與我，全能者使我受苦。既是這樣，你們為何還叫我拿俄米呢？」

²²拿俄米和她兒婦摩押女子路得，從摩押地回來到伯利恆，正是動手割大麥的時候。

路得遇波阿斯

2 拿俄米的丈夫以利米勒的親族中，有一個人名叫波阿斯，是個大財主。

²摩押女子路得對拿俄米說：「容我往田間去，我蒙誰的恩，就在誰的身後拾取麥穗。」

拿俄米說：「女兒啊，你只管去。」³路得就去了，來到田間，在收割的人身後拾取麥穗。她恰巧到了以利米勒本族的人波阿斯那塊田裏。

⁴波阿斯正從伯利恆來，對收割的人說：「願耶和華與你們同在！」

他們回答說：「願耶和華賜福與你！」

⁵波阿斯問監管收割的僕人說：「那是誰家的女子？」

¹⁴At this they wept again. Then Orpah kissed her mother-in-law good-by, but Ruth clung to her.

¹⁵"Look," said Naomi, "your sister-in-law is going back to her people and her gods. Go back with her."

¹⁶But Ruth replied, "Don't urge me to leave you or to turn back from you. Where you go I will go, and where you stay I will stay. Your people will be my people and your God my God. ¹⁷Where you die I will die, and there I will be buried. May the LORD deal with me, be it ever so severely, if anything but death separates you and me." ¹⁸When Naomi realized that Ruth was determined to go with her, she stopped urging her.

¹⁹So the two women went on until they came to Bethlehem. When they arrived in Bethlehem, the whole town was stirred because of them, and the women exclaimed, "Can this be Naomi?"

²⁰"Don't call me Naomi,ᵃ" she told them. "Call me Mara,ᵇ because the Almightyᶜ has made my life very bitter. ²¹I went away full, but the LORD has brought me back empty. Why call me Naomi? The LORD has afflictedᵈ me; the Almighty has brought misfortune upon me."

²²So Naomi returned from Moab accompanied by Ruth the Moabitess, her daughter-in-law, arriving in Bethlehem as the barley harvest was beginning.

Ruth Meets Boaz

2 Now Naomi had a relative on her husband's side, from the clan of Elimelech, a man of standing, whose name was Boaz.

²And Ruth the Moabitess said to Naomi, "Let me go to the fields and pick up the leftover grain behind anyone in whose eyes I find favor."

Naomi said to her, "Go ahead, my daughter." ³So she went out and began to glean in the fields behind the harvesters. As it turned out, she found herself working in a field belonging to Boaz, who was from the clan of Elimelech.

⁴Just then Boaz arrived from Bethlehem and greeted the harvesters, "The LORD be with you!"

"The LORD bless you!" they called back.

⁵Boaz asked the foreman of his harvesters, "Whose young woman is that?"

a 20 Naomi means *pleasant*; also in verse 21.　*b 20 Mara* means *bitter.*　*c 20* Hebrew *Shaddai*; also in verse 21　*d 21* Or *has testified against*

⁶The foreman replied, "She is the Moabitess who came back from Moab with Naomi. ⁷She said, 'Please let me glean and gather among the sheaves behind the harvesters.' She went into the field and has worked steadily from morning till now, except for a short rest in the shelter."

⁸So Boaz said to Ruth, "My daughter, listen to me. Don't go and glean in another field and don't go away from here. Stay here with my servant girls. ⁹Watch the field where the men are harvesting, and follow along after the girls. I have told the men not to touch you. And whenever you are thirsty, go and get a drink from the water jars the men have filled."

¹⁰At this, she bowed down with her face to the ground. She exclaimed, "Why have I found such favor in your eyes that you notice me—a foreigner?"

¹¹Boaz replied, "I've been told all about what you have done for your mother-in-law since the death of your husband—how you left your father and mother and your homeland and came to live with a people you did not know before. ¹²May the LORD repay you for what you have done. May you be richly rewarded by the LORD, the God of Israel, under whose wings you have come to take refuge."

¹³"May I continue to find favor in your eyes, my lord," she said. "You have given me comfort and have spoken kindly to your servant—though I do not have the standing of one of your servant girls."

¹⁴At mealtime Boaz said to her, "Come over here. Have some bread and dip it in the wine vinegar."

When she sat down with the harvesters, he offered her some roasted grain. She ate all she wanted and had some left over. ¹⁵As she got up to glean, Boaz gave orders to his men, "Even if she gathers among the sheaves, don't embarrass her. ¹⁶Rather, pull out some stalks for her from the bundles and leave them for her to pick up, and don't rebuke her."

¹⁷So Ruth gleaned in the field until evening. Then she threshed the barley she had gathered, and it amounted to about an ephah.ᵃ ¹⁸She carried it back to town, and her mother-in-law saw how much she had gathered. Ruth also brought out and gave her what she had left over after she had eaten enough.

¹⁹Her mother-in-law asked her, "Where did you glean today? Where did you work? Blessed be the man who took notice of you!"

⁶監管收割的僕人回答說："是那摩押女子，跟隨拿俄米從摩押地回來的。⁷她說：'請你容我跟着收割的人拾取打捆剩下的麥穗。'她從早晨直到如今，除了在屋子裏坐一會兒，常在這裏。"

⁸波阿斯對路得說："女兒啊，聽我說，不要往別人田裏拾取麥穗，也不要離開這裏，要常與我使女們在一處。⁹我的僕人在那塊田收割，你就跟着他們去。我已經吩咐僕人不可欺負你。你若渴了，就可以到器皿那裏喝僕人打來的水。"

¹⁰路得就俯伏在地叩拜，對他說："我既是外邦人，怎麼蒙你的恩，這樣顧恤我呢？"

¹¹波阿斯回答說："自從你丈夫死後，凡你向婆婆所行的、並你離開父母和本地，到素不認識的民中，這些事人全都告訴我了。¹²願耶和華照你所行的賞賜你。你來投靠耶和華以色列神的翅膀下，願你滿得他的賞賜。"

¹³路得說："我主啊，願在你眼前蒙恩！我雖然不及你的一個使女，你還用慈愛的話安慰我的心。"

¹⁴到了吃飯的時候，波阿斯對路得說："你到這裏來吃餅，將餅蘸在醋裏。"

路得就在收割的人旁邊坐下，他們把烘了的穗子遞給她，她吃飽了，還有餘剩的。¹⁵她起來又拾取麥穗，波阿斯吩咐僕人說："她就是在捆中拾取麥穗，也可以容她，不可羞辱她。¹⁶並要從捆裏抽出些來，留在地下任她拾取，不可叱嚇她。"

¹⁷這樣，路得在田間拾取麥穗，直到晚上，將所拾取的打了，約有一伊法大麥。¹⁸她就把所拾取的帶進城去給婆婆看，又把她吃飽了所剩的給了婆婆。

¹⁹婆婆問她說："你今日在哪裏拾取麥穗，在哪裏做工呢？願那顧恤你的得福。"

ᵃ 17 That is, probably about 3/5 bushel (about 22 liters)

路得就告訴婆婆説："我今日在一個名叫波阿斯的人那裏做工。"

20拿俄米對兒婦説："願那人蒙耶和華賜福，因為他不斷地恩待活人死人。"拿俄米又説："那是我們本族的人，是一個至近的親屬。"

21摩押女子路得説："他對我説：'你要緊隨我的僕人拾取麥穗，直等他們收完了我的莊稼。'"

22拿俄米對兒婦路得説："女兒啊，你跟着他的使女出去，不叫人遇見你在別人田間，這才為好。"

23於是，路得與波阿斯的使女常在一處拾取麥穗，直到收完了大麥和小麥。路得仍與婆婆同住。

路得與波阿斯在簸麥場上

3 路得的婆婆拿俄米對她説："女兒啊，我不當為你找個安身之處，使你享福嗎？2你與波阿斯的使女常在一處，波阿斯不是我們的親族嗎？他今夜在場上簸大麥，3你要沐浴抹膏，換上衣服，下到場上，卻不要使那人認出你來。你等他吃喝完了，4到他睡的時候，你看準他睡的地方，就進去掀開他腳上的被，躺臥在那裏，他必告訴你所當做的事。"

5路得説："凡你所吩咐的，我必遵行。"6路得就下到場上，照她婆婆所吩咐她的而行。

7波阿斯吃喝完了，心裏歡暢，就去睡在麥堆旁邊。路得便悄悄地來掀開他腳上的被，躺臥在那裏。8到了夜半，那人忽然驚醒，翻過身來，不料，有女子躺在他的腳下。

9他就説："你是誰？"
回答説："我是你的婢女路得。求你用你的衣襟遮蓋我，因為你是我一個至近的親屬。"

10波阿斯説："女兒啊，願你蒙耶和華賜福！你末後的恩，比先前更大，因為少年人無論貧富，你都

Then Ruth told her mother-in-law about the one at whose place she had been working. "The name of the man I worked with today is Boaz," she said.

20"The LORD bless him!" Naomi said to her daughter-in-law. "He has not stopped showing his kindness to the living and the dead." She added, "That man is our close relative; he is one of our kinsman-redeemers."

21Then Ruth the Moabitess said, "He even said to me, 'Stay with my workers until they finish harvesting all my grain.'"

22Naomi said to Ruth her daughter-in-law, "It will be good for you, my daughter, to go with his girls, because in someone else's field you might be harmed."

23So Ruth stayed close to the servant girls of Boaz to glean until the barley and wheat harvests were finished. And she lived with her mother-in-law.

Ruth and Boaz at the Threshing Floor

3 One day Naomi her mother-in-law said to her, "My daughter, should I not try to find a home*a* for you, where you will be well provided for? 2Is not Boaz, with whose servant girls you have been, a kinsman of ours? Tonight he will be winnowing barley on the threshing floor. 3Wash and perfume yourself, and put on your best clothes. Then go down to the threshing floor, but don't let him know you are there until he has finished eating and drinking. 4When he lies down, note the place where he is lying. Then go and uncover his feet and lie down. He will tell you what to do."

5"I will do whatever you say," Ruth answered. 6So she went down to the threshing floor and did everything her mother-in-law told her to do.

7When Boaz had finished eating and drinking and was in good spirits, he went over to lie down at the far end of the grain pile. Ruth approached quietly, uncovered his feet and lay down. 8In the middle of the night something startled the man, and he turned and discovered a woman lying at his feet.

9"Who are you?" he asked.

"I am your servant Ruth," she said. "Spread the corner of your garment over me, since you are a kinsman-redeemer."

10"The LORD bless you, my daughter," he replied. "This kindness is greater than that which you showed earlier: You have not run

a 1 Hebrew find rest (see Ruth 1:9)

after the younger men, whether rich or poor.
[11]And now, my daughter, don't be afraid. I will
do for you all you ask. All my fellow townsmen
know that you are a woman of noble character.
[12]Although it is true that I am near of kin, there
is a kinsman-redeemer nearer than I. [13]Stay here
for the night, and in the morning if he wants to
redeem, good; let him redeem. But if he is not
willing, as surely as the LORD lives I will do it.
Lie here until morning."

[14]So she lay at his feet until morning, but got
up before anyone could be recognized; and he
said, "Don't let it be known that a woman came
to the threshing floor."

[15]He also said, "Bring me the shawl you are
wearing and hold it out." When she did so, he
poured into it six measures of barley and put it
on her. Then he[a] went back to town.

[16]When Ruth came to her mother-in-law,
Naomi asked, "How did it go, my daughter?"

Then she told her everything Boaz had done
for her [17]and added, "He gave me these six measures of barley, saying, 'Don't go back to your
mother-in-law empty-handed.' "

[18]Then Naomi said, "Wait, my daughter,
until you find out what happens. For the man
will not rest until the matter is settled today."

Boaz Marries Ruth

4 Meanwhile Boaz went up to the town
gate and sat there. When the kinsman-
redeemer he had mentioned came
along, Boaz said, "Come over here, my friend,
and sit down." So he went over and sat down.

[2]Boaz took ten of the elders of the town and
said, "Sit here," and they did so. [3]Then he said
to the kinsman-redeemer, "Naomi, who has
come back from Moab, is selling the piece of
land that belonged to our brother Elimelech. [4]I
thought I should bring the matter to your attention and suggest that you buy it in the presence
of these seated here and in the presence of the
elders of my people. If you will redeem it, do so.
But if you[b] will not, tell me, so I will know. For
no one has the right to do it except you, and I
am next in line."

"I will redeem it," he said.

[5]Then Boaz said, "On the day you buy the
land from Naomi and from Ruth the Moabitess,

沒有跟從。[11]女兒啊，現在不要懼
怕。凡你所說的，我必照着行，我本
城的人都知道你是個賢德的女子。
[12]我實在是你一個至近的親屬，只是
還有一個人比我更近。[13]你今夜在這
裏住宿，明早他若肯為你盡親屬的本
分，就由他吧；倘若不肯，我指着永
生的耶和華起誓，我必為你盡了本
分，你只管躺到天亮。"

[14]路得便在他腳下躺到天快亮，
人彼此不能辨認的時候就起來了。波
阿斯說："不可使人知道有女子到場
上來。"

[15]又對路得說："打開你所披的
外衣。"她打開了，波阿斯就撮了六
簸箕大麥，幫她扛在肩上，她便進城
去了。

[16]路得回到婆婆那裏，婆婆說：
"女兒啊，怎麼樣了？"

路得就將那人向她所行的述說了
一遍。[17]又說："那人給了我六簸箕
大麥，對我說：'你不可空手回去見
你的婆婆。'"

[18]婆婆說："女兒啊，你只管安
坐等候，看這事怎樣成就，因為那人
今日不辦成這事必不休息。"

波阿斯娶路得

4 波阿斯到了城門，坐在那
裏，恰巧波阿斯所說的那至
近的親屬經過。波阿斯說：
"某人哪，你來坐在這裏。"他就來
坐下。

[2]波阿斯又從本城的長老中揀選
了十人，對他們說："請你們坐在這
裏。"他們就都坐下。[3]波阿斯對那
至近的親屬說："從摩押地回來的拿
俄米，現在要賣我們族兄以利米勒的
那塊地。[4]我想當贖那塊地的是你，
其次是我，以外再沒有別人了。你可
以在這裏的人面前和我本國的長老面
前說明，你若肯贖就贖，若不肯贖就
告訴我。"

那人回答說："我肯贖。"

[5]波阿斯說："你從拿俄米手中
買這地的時候，也當要（註：原文作

---

a 15 Most Hebrew manuscripts; many Hebrew manuscripts,
Vulgate and Syriac *she*   b 4 Many Hebrew manuscripts,
Septuagint, Vulgate and Syriac; most Hebrew manuscripts *he*
c 5 Hebrew; Vulgate and Syriac *Naomi, you acquire Ruth the
Moabitess,*

"買"，10節同）死人的妻摩押女子路得，使死人在產業上存留他的名。"

6那人說："這樣我就不能贖了，恐怕於我的產業有礙。你可以贖我所當贖的，我不能贖了。"

7從前，在以色列中要定奪甚麼事，或贖回，或交易，這人就脫鞋給那人。以色列人都以此為證據。

8那人對波阿斯說："你自己買吧！"於是將鞋脫下來了。

9波阿斯對長老和眾民說："你們今日作見證，凡屬以利米勒和基連、瑪倫的，我都從拿俄米手中置買了，10又娶了瑪倫的妻摩押女子路得為妻，好在死人的產業上存留他的名，免得他的名在本族本鄉滅沒。你們今日可以作見證。"

11在城門坐着的眾民和長老都說："我們作見證。願耶和華使進你家的這女子，像建立以色列家的拉結、利亞二人一樣。又願你在以法他得亨通，在伯利恆得名聲。12願耶和華從這少年女子賜你後裔，使你的家像她瑪從猶大所生法勒斯的家一般。"

大衛的族譜

13於是波阿斯娶了路得為妻，與她同房，耶和華使她懷孕生了一個兒子。14婦人們對拿俄米說："耶和華是應當稱頌的！因為今日沒有撇下你，使你無至近的親屬。願這孩子在以色列中得名聲。15他必提起你的精神，奉養你的老，因為是愛慕你的那兒婦所生的。有這兒婦比有七個兒子還好！"

16拿俄米就把孩子抱在懷中，作他的養母。17鄰舍的婦人說："拿俄米得孩子了。"就給孩子起名叫俄備得。這俄備得是耶西的父，耶西是大衛的父。

18法勒斯的後代記在下面：

法勒斯生希斯崙；
19希斯崙生蘭；
蘭生亞米拿達；

you acquire^c the dead man's widow, in order to maintain the name of the dead with his property."

6At this, the kinsman-redeemer said, "Then I cannot redeem it because I might endanger my own estate. You redeem it yourself. I cannot do it."

7(Now in earlier times in Israel, for the redemption and transfer of property to become final, one party took off his sandal and gave it to the other. This was the method of legalizing transactions in Israel.)

8So the kinsman-redeemer said to Boaz, "Buy it yourself." And he removed his sandal.

9Then Boaz announced to the elders and all the people, "Today you are witnesses that I have bought from Naomi all the property of Elimelech, Kilion and Mahlon. 10I have also acquired Ruth the Moabitess, Mahlon's widow, as my wife, in order to maintain the name of the dead with his property, so that his name will not disappear from among his family or from the town records. Today you are witnesses!"

11Then the elders and all those at the gate said, "We are witnesses. May the LORD make the woman who is coming into your home like Rachel and Leah, who together built up the house of Israel. May you have standing in Ephrathah and be famous in Bethlehem. 12Through the offspring the LORD gives you by this young woman, may your family be like that of Perez, whom Tamar bore to Judah."

The Genealogy of David

13So Boaz took Ruth and she became his wife. Then he went to her, and the LORD enabled her to conceive, and she gave birth to a son. 14The women said to Naomi: "Praise be to the LORD, who this day has not left you without a kinsman-redeemer. May he become famous throughout Israel! 15He will renew your life and sustain you in your old age. For your daughter-in-law, who loves you and who is better to you than seven sons, has given him birth."

16Then Naomi took the child, laid him in her lap and cared for him. 17The women living there said, "Naomi has a son." And they named him Obed. He was the father of Jesse, the father of David.

18This, then, is the family line of Perez:

Perez was the father of Hezron,
19Hezron the father of Ram,
Ram the father of Amminadab,

20Amminadab the father of Nahshon,
  Nahshon the father of Salmon,[a]
21Salmon the father of Boaz,
  Boaz the father of Obed,
22Obed the father of Jesse,
  and Jesse the father of David.

20亞米拿達生拿順；
  拿順生撒門；
21撒門生波阿斯；
  波阿斯生俄備得；
22俄備得生耶西；
  耶西生大衛。

表七：波阿斯與路得的子孫
TABLE 7 : DESCENDANTS OF BOAZ AND RUTH

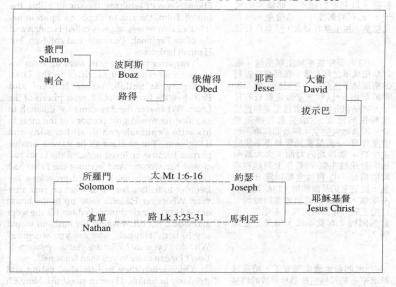

a 20 A few Hebrew manuscripts, some Septuagint
manuscripts and Vulgate (see also verse 21 and Septuagint of
1 Chron. 2:11); most Hebrew manuscripts *Salma*

撒母耳記上

1 Samuel

撒母耳的出生

1 以法蓮山地的拉瑪瑣非有一個以法蓮人，名叫以利加拿，是蘇弗的玄孫、託戶的曾孫、以利戶的孫子、耶羅罕的兒子。²他有兩個妻：一名哈拿，一名毘尼拿。毘尼拿有兒女，哈拿沒有兒女。

³這人每年從本城上到示羅，敬拜祭祀萬軍之耶和華。在那裏有以利的兩個兒子何弗尼、非尼哈，當耶和華的祭司。⁴以利加拿每逢獻祭的日子，將祭肉分給他的妻毘尼拿和毘尼拿所生的兒女。⁵給哈拿的卻是雙分，因為他愛哈拿。無奈耶和華不使哈拿生育。⁶毘尼拿見耶和華不使哈拿生育，就作她的對頭，大大激動她，要使她生氣。⁷每年上到耶和華殿的時候，以利加拿都以雙分給哈拿。毘尼拿仍是激動她，以致她哭泣不吃飯。⁸她丈夫以利加拿對她說："哈拿啊，你為何哭泣，不吃飯，心裏愁悶呢？有我不比十個兒子還好嗎？"

⁹他們在示羅吃喝完了，哈拿就站起來。祭司以利在耶和華殿的門框旁邊，坐在自己的位上。¹⁰哈拿心裏愁苦，就痛痛哭泣，祈禱耶和華，¹¹許願說："萬軍之耶和華啊，你若垂顧婢女的苦情，眷念不忘婢女，賜我一個兒子，我必使他終身歸與耶和華，不用剃頭刀剃他的頭。"

¹²哈拿在耶和華面前不住地祈禱，以利定睛看她的嘴。¹³原來哈拿心中默禱，只動嘴唇，不出聲音，因此以利以為她喝醉了。¹⁴以利對她說："你要醉到幾時呢？你不應該喝酒。"

¹⁵哈拿回答說："主啊，不是這樣。我是心裏愁苦的婦人，清酒濃酒

The Birth of Samuel

1 There was a certain man from Ramathaim, a Zuphite[a] from the hill country of Ephraim, whose name was Elkanah son of Jeroham, the son of Elihu, the son of Tohu, the son of Zuph, an Ephraimite. ²He had two wives; one was called Hannah and the other Peninnah. Peninnah had children, but Hannah had none.

³Year after year this man went up from his town to worship and sacrifice to the LORD Almighty at Shiloh, where Hophni and Phinehas, the two sons of Eli, were priests of the LORD. ⁴Whenever the day came for Elkanah to sacrifice, he would give portions of the meat to his wife Peninnah and to all her sons and daughters. ⁵But to Hannah he gave a double portion because he loved her, and the LORD had closed her womb. ⁶And because the LORD had closed her womb, her rival kept provoking her in order to irritate her. ⁷This went on year after year. Whenever Hannah went up to the house of the LORD, her rival provoked her till she wept and would not eat. ⁸Elkanah her husband would say to her, "Hannah, why are you weeping? Why don't you eat? Why are you downhearted? Don't I mean more to you than ten sons?"

⁹Once when they had finished eating and drinking in Shiloh, Hannah stood up. Now Eli the priest was sitting on a chair by the doorpost of the LORD's temple.[b] ¹⁰In bitterness of soul Hannah wept much and prayed to the LORD. ¹¹And she made a vow, saying, "O LORD Almighty, if you will only look upon your servant's misery and remember me, and not forget your servant but give her a son, then I will give him to the LORD for all the days of his life, and no razor will ever be used on his head."

¹²As she kept on praying to the LORD, Eli observed her mouth. ¹³Hannah was praying in her heart, and her lips were moving but her voice was not heard. Eli thought she was drunk ¹⁴and said to her, "How long will you keep on getting drunk? Get rid of your wine."

¹⁵"Not so, my lord," Hannah replied, "I am a woman who is deeply troubled. I have not been

---

a 1 Or from Ramathaim Zuphim   b 9 That is, tabernacle

drinking wine or beer; I was pouring out my soul to the LORD. [16]Do not take your servant for a wicked woman; I have been praying here out of my great anguish and grief."

[17]Eli answered, "Go in peace, and may the God of Israel grant you what you have asked of him."

[18]She said, "May your servant find favor in your eyes." Then she went her way and ate something, and her face was no longer downcast.

[19]Early the next morning they arose and worshiped before the LORD and then went back to their home at Ramah. Elkanah lay with Hannah his wife, and the LORD remembered her. [20]So in the course of time Hannah conceived and gave birth to a son. She named him Samuel,[a] saying, "Because I asked the LORD for him."

Hannah Dedicates Samuel

[21]When the man Elkanah went up with all his family to offer the annual sacrifice to the LORD and to fulfill his vow, [22]Hannah did not go. She said to her husband, "After the boy is weaned, I will take him and present him before the LORD, and he will live there always."

[23]"Do what seems best to you," Elkanah her husband told her. "Stay here until you have weaned him; only may the LORD make good his[b] word." So the woman stayed at home and nursed her son until she had weaned him.

[24]After he was weaned, she took the boy with her, young as he was, along with a three-year-old bull,[c] an ephah[d] of flour and a skin of wine, and brought him to the house of the LORD at Shiloh. [25]When they had slaughtered the bull, they brought the boy to Eli, [26]and she said to him, "As surely as you live, my lord, I am the woman who stood here beside you praying to the LORD. [27]I prayed for this child, and the LORD has granted me what I asked of him. [28]So now I give him to the LORD. For his whole life he will be given over to the LORD." And he worshiped the LORD there.

Hannah's Prayer

2 Then Hannah prayed and said:

"My heart rejoices in the LORD;

都沒有喝，但在耶和華面前傾心吐意。[16]不要將婢女看作不正經的女子。我因被人激動，愁苦太多，所以祈求到如今。"

[17]以利說："你可以平平安安地回去，願以色列的神允准你向他所求的！"

[18]哈拿說："願婢女在你眼前蒙恩。"於是婦人走去吃飯，面上再不帶愁容了。

[19]次日清早，他們起來，在耶和華面前敬拜，就回拉瑪。到了家裏，以利加拿和妻哈拿同房，耶和華顧念哈拿，[20]哈拿就懷孕。日期滿足，生了一個兒子，給他起名叫撒母耳，說："這是我從耶和華那裏求來的。"

哈拿獻撒母耳

[21]以利加拿和他全家都上示羅去，要向耶和華獻年祭，並還所許的願。[22]哈拿卻沒有上去，對丈夫說："等孩子斷了奶，我便帶他上去朝見耶和華，使他永遠住在那裏。"

[23]她丈夫以利加拿說："就隨你的意行吧！可以等兒子斷了奶，但願耶和華應驗他的話。"於是婦人在家裏乳養兒子，直到斷了奶。

[24]既斷了奶，就把孩子帶上示羅，到了耶和華的殿，又帶了三隻公牛，一伊法細麵，一皮袋酒。那時孩子還小。[25]宰了一隻公牛，就領孩子到以利面前。[26]婦人說："主啊，我敢在你面前起誓，從前在你這裏站着祈求耶和華的那婦人，就是我。[27]我祈求為要得這孩子，耶和華已將我所求的賜給我了。[28]所以我將這孩子歸與耶和華，使他終身歸與耶和華。"於是在那裏敬拜耶和華。

哈拿的禱告

2 哈拿禱告說：

"我的心因耶和華快樂，

---

a 20 Samuel sounds like the Hebrew for heard of God.
b 23 Masoretic Text; Dead Sea Scrolls, Septuagint and Syriac your　c 24 Dead Sea Scrolls, Septuagint and Syriac; Masoretic Text with three bulls　d 24 That is, probably about 3/5 bushel (about 22 liters)

我的角因耶和華高舉。
我的口向仇敵張開，
　我因耶和華的救恩歡欣。

2 "只有耶和華為聖，
　除他以外沒有可比的，
　也沒有磐石像我們的神。

3 "人不要誇口說驕傲的話，
　也不要出狂妄的言語，
　因耶和華是大有智識的神，
　人的行為被他衡量。

4 "勇士的弓都已折斷，
　跌倒的人以力量束腰。

5 素來飽足的，反作傭人求食；
　飢餓的，再不飢餓。
　不生育的，生了七個兒子；
　多有兒女的，反倒衰微。

6 "耶和華使人死，也使人活；
　使人下陰間，也使人往上升。
7 他使人貧窮，也使人富足；
　使人卑微，也使人高貴。
8 他從灰堆裏抬舉貧寒人，
　從糞堆中提拔窮乏人；
　使他們與王子同坐，
　得着榮耀的座位。

"地的柱子屬於耶和華，
　他將世界立在其上。

9 他必保護聖民的腳步；
　使惡人在黑暗中寂然不動。

"人都不能靠力量得勝；
10 與耶和華爭競的，必被打碎。
　耶和華必從天上以雷攻擊他；
　必審判地極的人。

"將力量賜與所立的王，
　高舉受膏者的角。"

11 以利加拿往拉瑪回家去了。那孩子在祭司以利面前侍奉耶和華。

以利的劣子

12 以利的兩個兒子是惡人，不認識耶和華。13 這二祭司待百姓是這樣的規矩：凡有人獻祭，正煮肉的時

in the LORD my horn[a] is lifted high.
My mouth boasts over my enemies,
　for I delight in your deliverance.

2 "There is no one holy[b] like the LORD;
　there is no one besides you;
　there is no Rock like our God.

3 "Do not keep talking so proudly
　or let your mouth speak such arrogance,
　for the LORD is a God who knows,
　and by him deeds are weighed.

4 "The bows of the warriors are broken,
　but those who stumbled are armed with
　　strength.
5 Those who were full hire themselves out for
　　food,
　but those who were hungry hunger no more.
　She who was barren has borne seven children,
　but she who has had many sons pines away.

6 "The LORD brings death and makes alive;
　he brings down to the grave[c] and raises up.
7 The LORD sends poverty and wealth;
　he humbles and he exalts.
8 He raises the poor from the dust
　and lifts the needy from the ash heap;
　he seats them with princes
　and has them inherit a throne of honor.

"For the foundations of the earth are the
　　LORD's;
　upon them he has set the world.
9 He will guard the feet of his saints,
　but the wicked will be silenced in darkness.

"It is not by strength that one prevails;
10 those who oppose the LORD will be shattered.
　He will thunder against them from heaven;
　the LORD will judge the ends of the earth.

"He will give strength to his king
　and exalt the horn of his anointed."

11 Then Elkanah went home to Ramah, but the boy ministered before the LORD under Eli the priest.

Eli's Wicked Sons

12 Eli's sons were wicked men; they had no regard for the LORD. 13 Now it was the practice of the priests with the people that whenever any-

---

a 1 Horn here symbolizes strength; also in verse 10.　b 2 Or no Holy One　c 6 Hebrew Sheol one offered a sacrifice and while the meat was being boiled, the servant of the priest would come with a three-pronged fork in his hand. [14]He would plunge it into the pan or kettle or caldron or pot, and the priest would take for himself whatever the fork brought up. This is how they treated all the Israelites who came to Shiloh. [15]But even before the fat was burned, the servant of the priest would come and say to the man who was sacrificing, "Give the priest some meat to roast; he won't accept boiled meat from you, but only raw."

[16]If the man said to him, "Let the fat be burned up first, and then take whatever you want," the servant would then answer, "No, hand it over now; if you don't, I'll take it by force."

[17]This sin of the young men was very great in the LORD's sight, for they[a] were treating the LORD's offering with contempt.

[18]But Samuel was ministering before the LORD—a boy wearing a linen ephod. [19]Each year his mother made him a little robe and took it to him when she went up with her husband to offer the annual sacrifice. [20]Eli would bless Elkanah and his wife, saying, "May the LORD give you children by this woman to take the place of the one she prayed for and gave to the LORD." Then they would go home. [21]And the LORD was gracious to Hannah; she conceived and gave birth to three sons and two daughters. Meanwhile, the boy Samuel grew up in the presence of the LORD.

[22]Now Eli, who was very old, heard about everything his sons were doing to all Israel and how they slept with the women who served at the entrance to the Tent of Meeting. [23]So he said to them, "Why do you do such things? I hear from all the people about these wicked deeds of yours. [24]No, my sons; it is not a good report that I hear spreading among the LORD's people. [25]If a man sins against another man, God[b] may mediate for him; but if a man sins against the LORD, who will intercede for him?" His sons, however, did not listen to their father's rebuke, for it was the LORD's will to put them to death.

[26]And the boy Samuel continued to grow in stature and in favor with the LORD and with men.

Prophecy Against the House of Eli

[27]Now a man of God came to Eli and said to him, "This is what the LORD says: 'Did I not clearly reveal myself to your father's house

候,祭司的僕人就來,手拿三齒的叉子,[14]將叉子往罐裏,或鼎裏,或釜裏,或鍋裏一插,插上來的肉,祭司都取了去。凡上到示羅的以色列人,他們都是這樣看待。[15]又在未燒脂油以前,祭司的僕人就來對獻祭的人說:"將肉給祭司,叫他烤吧!他不要煮過的,要生的。"

[16]獻祭的人若說:"必須先燒脂油,然後你可以隨意取肉。"僕人就說:"你立時給我!不然我便搶去。"

[17]如此,這二少年人的罪在耶和華面前甚重了,因為他們藐視耶和華的祭物(註:或作"他們使人厭棄給耶和華獻祭")。

[18]那時撒母耳還是孩子,穿着細麻布的以弗得,侍立在耶和華面前。[19]他母親每年為他做一件小外袍,同着丈夫上來獻年祭的時候帶來給他。[20]以利為以利加拿和他的妻祝福說:"願耶和華由這婦人再賜你後裔,代替你從耶和華求來的孩子。"他們就回本鄉去了。[21]耶和華眷顧哈拿,她就懷孕生了三個兒子,兩個女兒。那孩子撒母耳,在耶和華面前漸漸長大。

[22]以利年甚老邁,聽見他兩個兒子待以色列眾人的事,又聽見他們與會幕門前伺候的婦人苟合。[23]他就對他們說:"你們為何行這樣的事呢?我從這眾百姓聽見你們的惡行。[24]我兒啊,不可這樣!我聽見你們的風聲不好,你們使耶和華的百姓犯了罪。[25]人若得罪人,有士師審判他;人若得罪耶和華,誰能為他祈求呢?"然而他們還是不聽父親的話,因為耶和華想要殺他們。

[26]孩子撒母耳漸漸長大,耶和華與人越發喜愛他。

論以利家的預言

[27]有神人來見以利,對他說:"耶和華如此說:'你祖父在埃及法老家作奴僕的時候,我不是向他們顯

a 17 Or men   b 25 Or the judges

現嗎？²⁸在以色列眾支派中，我不是揀選人作我的祭司，使他燒香，在我壇上獻祭，在我面前穿以弗得，又將以色列人所獻的火祭都賜給你父家嗎？²⁹我所吩咐獻在我居所的祭物，你們為何踐踏？尊重你的兒子過於尊重我，將我民以色列所獻美好的祭物肥己呢？'

³⁰"因此，耶和華以色列的神說：'我曾說，你和你父家必永遠行在我面前；現在我卻說，決不容你們這樣行！因為尊重我的，我必重看他；藐視我的，他必被輕視。³¹日子必到，我要折斷你的膀臂和你父家的膀臂，使你家中沒有一個老年人。³²在神使以色列人享福的時候，你必看見我居所的敗落。在你家中必永遠沒有一個老年人。³³我必不從我壇前滅盡你家中的人，那未滅的必使你眼目乾癟，心中憂傷。你家中所生的人都必死在中年。

³⁴"'你的兩個兒子何弗尼、非尼哈所遭遇的事可作你的證據：他們二人必一日同死。³⁵我要為自己立一個忠心的祭司，他必照我的心意而行。我要為他建立堅固的家，他必永遠行在我的受膏者面前。³⁶你家所剩下的人都必來叩拜他，求塊銀子，求個餅，說：求你賜我祭司的職分，好叫我得點餅吃。'"

主呼召撒母耳

3 童子撒母耳在以利面前侍奉耶和華。當那些日子，耶和華的言語稀少，不常有默示。

²一日，以利睡臥在自己的地方。他眼目昏花，看不分明。³神的燈在神耶和華殿內約櫃那裏，還沒有熄滅，撒母耳已經睡了。⁴耶和華呼喚撒母耳。

撒母耳說："我在這裏！"⁵就跑到以利那裏，說："你呼喚我，我在這裏。"

以利回答說："我沒有呼喚你，你去睡吧！"他就去睡了。

when they were in Egypt under Pharaoh? ²⁸I chose your father out of all the tribes of Israel to be my priest, to go up to my altar, to burn incense, and to wear an ephod in my presence. I also gave your father's house all the offerings made with fire by the Israelites. ²⁹Why do you[a] scorn my sacrifice and offering that I prescribed for my dwelling? Why do you honor your sons more than me by fattening yourselves on the choice parts of every offering made by my people Israel?'

³⁰"Therefore the LORD, the God of Israel, declares: 'I promised that your house and your father's house would minister before me forever.' But now the LORD declares: 'Far be it from me! Those who honor me I will honor, but those who despise me will be disdained. ³¹The time is coming when I will cut short your strength and the strength of your father's house, so that there will not be an old man in your family line ³²and you will see distress in my dwelling. Although good will be done to Israel, in your family line there will never be an old man. ³³Every one of you that I do not cut off from my altar will be spared only to blind your eyes with tears and to grieve your heart, and all your descendants will die in the prime of life.

³⁴"'And what happens to your two sons, Hophni and Phinehas, will be a sign to you— they will both die on the same day. ³⁵I will raise up for myself a faithful priest, who will do according to what is in my heart and mind. I will firmly establish his house, and he will minister before my anointed one always. ³⁶Then everyone left in your family line will come and bow down before him for a piece of silver and a crust of bread and plead, "Appoint me to some priestly office so I can have food to eat." '"

The LORD Calls Samuel

3 The boy Samuel ministered before the LORD under Eli. In those days the word of the LORD was rare; there were not many visions.

²One night Eli, whose eyes were becoming so weak that he could barely see, was lying down in his usual place. ³The lamp of God had not yet gone out, and Samuel was lying down in the temple[b] of the LORD, where the ark of God was. ⁴Then the LORD called Samuel.

Samuel answered, "Here I am." ⁵And he ran to Eli and said, "Here I am; you called me."

But Eli said, "I did not call; go back and lie down." So he went and lay down.

a 29 The Hebrew is plural.　　b 3 That is, tabernacle

⁶Again the LORD called, "Samuel!" And Samuel got up and went to Eli and said, "Here I am; you called me."

"My son," Eli said, "I did not call; go back and lie down."

⁷Now Samuel did not yet know the LORD: The word of the LORD had not yet been revealed to him.

⁸The LORD called Samuel a third time, and Samuel got up and went to Eli and said, "Here I am; you called me."

Then Eli realized that the LORD was calling the boy. ⁹So Eli told Samuel, "Go and lie down, and if he calls you, say, 'Speak, LORD, for your servant is listening.' " So Samuel went and lay down in his place.

¹⁰The LORD came and stood there, calling as at the other times, "Samuel! Samuel!"

Then Samuel said, "Speak, for your servant is listening."

¹¹And the LORD said to Samuel: "See, I am about to do something in Israel that will make the ears of everyone who hears of it tingle. ¹²At that time I will carry out against Eli everything I spoke against his family—from beginning to end. ¹³For I told him that I would judge his family forever because of the sin he knew about; his sons made themselves contemptible,^a and he failed to restrain them. ¹⁴Therefore, I swore to the house of Eli, 'The guilt of Eli's house will never be atoned for by sacrifice or offering.' "

¹⁵Samuel lay down until morning and then opened the doors of the house of the LORD. He was afraid to tell Eli the vision, ¹⁶but Eli called him and said, "Samuel, my son."

Samuel answered, "Here I am."

¹⁷"What was it he said to you?" Eli asked. "Do not hide it from me. May God deal with you, be it ever so severely, if you hide from me anything he told you." ¹⁸So Samuel told him everything, hiding nothing from him. Then Eli said, "He is the LORD; let him do what is good in his eyes."

¹⁹The LORD was with Samuel as he grew up, and he let none of his words fall to the ground. ²⁰And all Israel from Dan to Beersheba recognized that Samuel was attested as a prophet of the LORD. ²¹The LORD continued to appear at Shiloh, and there he revealed himself to Samuel through his word.

4 And Samuel's word came to all Israel.

---

⁶耶和華又呼喚撒母耳。撒母耳起來，到以利那裏，說："你呼喚我，我在這裏。"

以利回答說："我的兒，我沒有呼喚你，你去睡吧！"

⁷那時撒母耳還未認識耶和華，也未得耶和華的默示。

⁸耶和華第三次呼喚撒母耳。撒母耳起來，到以利那裏，說："你又呼喚我，我在這裏。"

以利才明白是耶和華呼喚童子。⁹因此，以利對撒母耳說："你仍去睡吧！若再呼喚你，你就說：'耶和華啊，請說，僕人敬聽！'"撒母耳就去仍睡在原處。

¹⁰耶和華又來站着，像前三次呼喚說："撒母耳啊！撒母耳啊！"

撒母耳回答說："請說，僕人敬聽！"

¹¹耶和華對撒母耳說："我在以色列中必行一件事，叫聽見的人都必耳鳴。¹²我指着以利家所說的話，到了時候，我必始終應驗在以利身上。¹³我曾告訴他必永遠降罰與他的家，因他知道兒子作孽，自招咒詛，卻不禁止他們。¹⁴所以我向以利家起誓說：'以利家的罪孽，雖獻祭奉禮物，永不能得贖去。'"

¹⁵撒母耳睡到天亮，就開了耶和華的殿門，不敢將默示告訴以利。¹⁶以利呼喚撒母耳說："我兒撒母耳啊！"

撒母耳回答說："我在這裏！"

¹⁷以利說："耶和華對你說甚麼，你不要向我隱瞞；你若將神對你所說的隱瞞一句，願他重重地降罰與你。"¹⁸撒母耳就把一切話都告訴了以利，並沒有隱瞞。以利說："這是出於耶和華，願他憑自己的意旨而行。"

¹⁹撒母耳長大了，耶和華與他同在，使他所說的話，一句都不落空。²⁰從但到別是巴所有的以色列人，都知道耶和華立撒母耳為先知。²¹耶和華又在示羅顯現，因為耶和華將自己的話默示撒母耳。

4 撒母耳就把這話傳遍以色列地。

---

^a 13 Masoretic Text; an ancient Hebrew scribal tradition and Septuagint *sons blasphemed God*

非利士人擄走約櫃

¹以色列人出去與非利士人打仗，安營在以便以謝；非利士人安營在亞弗。²非利士人向以色列人擺陣。兩軍交戰的時候，以色列人敗在非利士人面前。非利士人在戰場上殺了他們的軍兵約有四千人。³百姓回到營裏，以色列的長老說：「耶和華今日為何使我們敗在非利士人面前呢？我們不如將耶和華的約櫃，從示羅抬到我們這裏來，好在我們中間救我們脫離敵人的手。」

⁴於是百姓打發人到示羅，從那裏將坐在二基路伯上萬軍之耶和華的約櫃抬來。以利的兩個兒子何弗尼、非尼哈與神的約櫃同來。

⁵耶和華的約櫃到了營中，以色列眾人就大聲歡呼，地便震動。⁶非利士人聽見歡呼的聲音，就說：「在希伯來人營裏大聲歡呼，是甚麼緣故呢？」

隨後就知道耶和華的約櫃到了營中。⁷非利士人就懼怕起來，說：「有神到了他們營中。」又說：「我們有禍了！向來不曾有這樣的事。⁸我們有禍了！誰能救我們脫離這些大能之神的手呢？從前在曠野用各樣災殃擊打埃及人的，就是這些神。⁹非利士人哪，你們要剛強，要作大丈夫，免得作希伯來人的奴僕，如同他們作你們的奴僕一樣。你們要作大丈夫，與他們爭戰。」

¹⁰非利士人和以色列人打仗，以色列人敗了，各向各家奔逃。被殺的人甚多，以色列的步兵仆倒了三萬。¹¹神的約櫃被擄去，以利的兩個兒子何弗尼、非尼哈也都被殺了。

以利的死

¹²當日有一個便雅憫人從陣上逃跑，衣服撕裂，頭蒙灰塵，來到示羅。¹³到了的時候，以利正在道旁坐在自己的位上觀望，為神的約櫃心裏擔憂。那人進城報信，合城的人就都呼喊起來。

¹⁴以利聽見呼喊的聲音就問說：「這喧嚷是甚麼緣故呢？」

The Philistines Capture the Ark

Now the Israelites went out to fight against the Philistines. The Israelites camped at Ebenezer, and the Philistines at Aphek. ²The Philistines deployed their forces to meet Israel, and as the battle spread, Israel was defeated by the Philistines, who killed about four thousand of them on the battlefield. ³When the soldiers returned to camp, the elders of Israel asked, "Why did the LORD bring defeat upon us today before the Philistines? Let us bring the ark of the LORD's covenant from Shiloh, so that it*a* may go with us and save us from the hand of our enemies."

⁴So the people sent men to Shiloh, and they brought back the ark of the covenant of the LORD Almighty, who is enthroned between the cherubim. And Eli's two sons, Hophni and Phinehas, were there with the ark of the covenant of God.

⁵When the ark of the LORD's covenant came into the camp, all Israel raised such a great shout that the ground shook. ⁶Hearing the uproar, the Philistines asked, "What's all this shouting in the Hebrew camp?"

When they learned that the ark of the LORD had come into the camp, ⁷the Philistines were afraid. "A god has come into the camp," they said. "We're in trouble! Nothing like this has happened before. ⁸Woe to us! Who will deliver us from the hand of these mighty gods? They are the gods who struck the Egyptians with all kinds of plagues in the desert. ⁹Be strong, Philistines! Be men, or you will be subject to the Hebrews, as they have been to you. Be men, and fight!"

¹⁰So the Philistines fought, and the Israelites were defeated and every man fled to his tent. The slaughter was very great; Israel lost thirty thousand foot soldiers. ¹¹The ark of God was captured, and Eli's two sons, Hophni and Phinehas, died.

Death of Eli

¹²That same day a Benjamite ran from the battle line and went to Shiloh, his clothes torn and dust on his head. ¹³When he arrived, there was Eli sitting on his chair by the side of the road, watching, because his heart feared for the ark of God. When the man entered the town and told what had happened, the whole town sent up a cry.

¹⁴Eli heard the outcry and asked, "What is the meaning of this uproar?"

a 3 Or he

The man hurried over to Eli, [15]who was ninety-eight years old and whose eyes were set so that he could not see. [16]He told Eli, "I have just come from the battle line; I fled from it this very day."

Eli asked, "What happened, my son?"

[17]The man who brought the news replied, "Israel fled before the Philistines, and the army has suffered heavy losses. Also your two sons, Hophni and Phinehas, are dead, and the ark of God has been captured."

[18]When he mentioned the ark of God, Eli fell backward off his chair by the side of the gate. His neck was broken and he died, for he was an old man and heavy. He had led[a] Israel forty years.

[19]His daughter-in-law, the wife of Phinehas, was pregnant and near the time of delivery. When she heard the news that the ark of God had been captured and that her father-in-law and her husband were dead, she went into labor and gave birth, but was overcome by her labor pains. [20]As she was dying, the women attending her said, "Don't despair; you have given birth to a son." But she did not respond or pay any attention.

[21]She named the boy Ichabod,[b] saying, "The glory has departed from Israel"—because of the capture of the ark of God and the deaths of her father-in-law and her husband. [22]She said, "The glory has departed from Israel, for the ark of God has been captured."

The Ark in Ashdod and Ekron

5 After the Philistines had captured the ark of God, they took it from Ebenezer to Ashdod. [2]Then they carried the ark into Dagon's temple and set it beside Dagon. [3]When the people of Ashdod rose early the next day, there was Dagon, fallen on his face on the ground before the ark of the LORD! They took Dagon and put him back in his place. [4]But the following morning when they rose, there was Dagon, fallen on his face on the ground before the ark of the LORD! His head and hands had been broken off and were lying on the threshold; only his body remained. [5]That is why to this day neither the priests of Dagon nor any others who enter Dagon's temple at Ashdod step on the threshold.

[6]The LORD's hand was heavy upon the people of Ashdod and its vicinity; he brought devasta-

那人急忙來報信給以利。[15]那時以利九十八歲了，眼目發直，不能看見。[16]那人對以利說："我是從陣上來的，今日我從陣上逃回。"

以利說："我兒，事情怎樣？"

[17]報信的回答說："以色列人在非利士人面前逃跑，民中被殺的甚多！你的兩個兒子何弗尼、非尼哈也都死了，並且神的約櫃被擄去。"

[18]他一提神的約櫃，以利就從他的位上往後跌倒，在門旁折斷頸項而死，因為他年紀老邁，身體沉重。以利作以色列的士師四十年。

[19]以利的兒婦、非尼哈的妻懷孕將到產期，她聽見神的約櫃被擄去，公公和丈夫都死了，就猛然疼痛，曲身生產。[20]將要死的時候，旁邊站着的婦人們對她說："不要怕！你生了男孩子了。"她卻不回答，也不放在心上。

[21]她給孩子起名叫以迦博，說："榮耀離開以色列了！"這是因神的約櫃被擄去，又因她公公和丈夫都死了。[22]她又說："榮耀離開以色列，因為神的約櫃被擄去了。"

約櫃在亞實突和以革倫

5 非利士人將神的約櫃從以便以謝抬到亞實突。[2]非利士人將神的約櫃抬進大袞廟，放在大袞的旁邊。[3]次日清早，亞實突人起來，見大袞仆倒在耶和華的約櫃前，臉伏於地，就把大袞仍立在原處。[4]又次日清早起來，見大袞仆倒在耶和華的約櫃前，臉伏於地，並且大袞的頭和兩手都在門檻上折斷，只剩下大袞的殘體。[5]因此，大袞的祭司和一切進亞實突大袞廟的人，都不踏大袞廟的門檻，直到今日。

[6]耶和華的手重加在亞實突人身上，敗壞他們，使他們生痔瘡。亞

---

a 18 Traditionally *judged*　　*b 21 Ichabod* means *no glory.*

實突和亞實突的四境都是如此。7亞實突人見這光景，就說：「以色列神的約櫃不可留在我們這裏，因為他的手重重加在我們和我們神大袞的身上。」8就打發人去請非利士的眾首領來聚集，問他們說：「我們向以色列神的約櫃應當怎樣行呢？」

他們回答說：「可以將以色列神的約櫃運到迦特去。」於是將以色列神的約櫃運到那裏去。

9運到之後，耶和華的手攻擊那城，使那城的人大大驚慌，無論大小都生痔瘡。10他們就把神的約櫃送到以革倫。

神的約櫃到了，以革倫人就喊嚷起來說：「他們將以色列神的約櫃運到我們這裏，要害我們和我們的眾民。」11於是打發人去請非利士的眾首領來，說：「願你們將以色列神的約櫃送回原處，免得害了我們和我們的眾民。」原來神的手重重攻擊那城，城中的人有因驚慌而死的；12未曾死的人都生了痔瘡。合城呼號，聲音上達於天。

約櫃被送還以色列

6 耶和華的約櫃在非利士人之地七個月。2非利士人將祭司和占卜的聚了來，問他們說：「我們向耶和華的約櫃應當怎樣行？請指示我們用何法將約櫃送回原處。」

3他們說：「若要將以色列神的約櫃送回去，不可空空地送去，必要給他獻賠罪的禮物，然後你們可得痊愈，並知道他的手為何不離開你們。」

4非利士人說：「應當用甚麼獻為賠罪的禮物呢？」

他們回答說：「當照非利士首領的數目，用五個金痔瘡，五個金老鼠，因為在你們眾人和你們首領的身上都是一樣的災。5所以，當製造你們痔瘡的像和毀壞你們田地老鼠的像，並要歸榮耀給以色列的神。或者他向你們和你們的神，並你們的田地，把手放輕些。6你們為何硬着心像埃及人和法老一樣呢？神在埃及人

tion upon them and afflicted them with tumors.[a]
7When the men of Ashdod saw what was happening, they said, "The ark of the god of Israel must not stay here with us, because his hand is heavy upon us and upon Dagon our god." 8So they called together all the rulers of the Philistines and asked them, "What shall we do with the ark of the god of Israel?"

They answered, "Have the ark of the god of Israel moved to Gath." So they moved the ark of the God of Israel.

9But after they had moved it, the LORD's hand was against that city, throwing it into a great panic. He afflicted the people of the city, both young and old, with an outbreak of tumors.[b] 10So they sent the ark of God to Ekron.

As the ark of God was entering Ekron, the people of Ekron cried out, "They have brought the ark of the god of Israel around to us to kill us and our people." 11So they called together all the rulers of the Philistines and said, "Send the ark of the god of Israel away; let it go back to its own place, or it[c] will kill us and our people." For death had filled the city with panic; God's hand was very heavy upon it. 12Those who did not die were afflicted with tumors, and the outcry of the city went up to heaven.

The Ark Returned to Israel

6 When the ark of the LORD had been in Philistine territory seven months, 2the Philistines called for the priests and the diviners and said, "What shall we do with the ark of the LORD? Tell us how we should send it back to its place."

3They answered, "If you return the ark of the god of Israel, do not send it away empty, but by all means send a guilt offering to him. Then you will be healed, and you will know why his hand has not been lifted from you."

4The Philistines asked, "What guilt offering should we send to him?"

They replied, "Five gold tumors and five gold rats, according to the number of the Philistine rulers, because the same plague has struck both you and your rulers. 5Make models of the tumors and of the rats that are destroying the country, and pay honor to Israel's god. Perhaps he will lift his hand from you and your gods and your land. 6Why do you harden your hearts as the Egyptians and Pharaoh did? When he[d]

a 6 Hebrew; Septuagint and Vulgate tumors. And rats appeared in their land, and death and destruction were throughout the city
b 9 Or with tumors in the groin (see Septuagint)　　c 11 Or he
d 6 That is, God

treated them harshly, did they not send the Israelites out so they could go on their way?

7"Now then, get a new cart ready, with two cows that have calved and have never been yoked. Hitch the cows to the cart, but take their calves away and pen them up. 8Take the ark of the LORD and put it on the cart, and in a chest beside it put the gold objects you are sending back to him as a guilt offering. Send it on its way, 9but keep watching it. If it goes up to its own territory, toward Beth Shemesh, then the LORD has brought this great disaster on us. But if it does not, then we will know that it was not his hand that struck us and that it happened to us by chance."

10So they did this. They took two such cows and hitched them to the cart and penned up their calves. 11They placed the ark of the LORD on the cart and along with it the chest containing the gold rats and the models of the tumors. 12Then the cows went straight up toward Beth Shemesh, keeping on the road and lowing all the way; they did not turn to the right or to the left. The rulers of the Philistines followed them as far as the border of Beth Shemesh.

13Now the people of Beth Shemesh were harvesting their wheat in the valley, and when they looked up and saw the ark, they rejoiced at the sight. 14The cart came to the field of Joshua of Beth Shemesh, and there it stopped beside a large rock. The people chopped up the wood of the cart and sacrificed the cows as a burnt offering to the LORD. 15The Levites took down the ark of the LORD, together with the chest containing the gold objects, and placed them on the large rock. On that day the people of Beth Shemesh offered burnt offerings and made sacrifices to the LORD. 16The five rulers of the Philistines saw all this and then returned that same day to Ekron.

17These are the gold tumors the Philistines sent as a guilt offering to the LORD—one each for Ashdod, Gaza, Ashkelon, Gath and Ekron. 18And the number of the gold rats was according to the number of Philistine towns belonging to the five rulers—the fortified towns with their country villages. The large rock, on which*a* they set the ark of the LORD, is a witness to this day in the field of Joshua of Beth Shemesh.

19But God struck down some of the men of Beth Shemesh, putting seventy*b* of them to death

a 18 A few Hebrew manuscripts (see also Septuagint); most Hebrew manuscripts villages as far as Greater Abel, where

b 19 A few Hebrew manuscripts; most Hebrew manuscripts and Septuagint 50,070

中間行奇事，埃及人豈不釋放以色列人，他們就去了嗎？

7 "現在你們應當造一輛新車，將兩隻未曾負軛、有乳的母牛套在車上，使牛犢回家去，離開母牛。8把耶和華的約櫃放在車上，將所獻賠罪的金物裝在匣子裏放在櫃旁，將櫃送去。9你們要看看：車若直行到以色列的境界到伯示麥去，這大災就是耶和華降在我們身上的；若不然，便可以知道不是他的手擊打我們，是我們偶然遇見的。"

10非利士人就這樣行，將兩隻有乳的母牛套在車上，將牛犢關在家裏，11把耶和華的約櫃和裝金老鼠並金痔瘡像的匣子都放在車上。12牛直行大道，往伯示麥去，一面走一面叫，不偏左右。非利士的首領跟在後面，直到伯示麥的境界。

13伯示麥人正在平原收割麥子，舉目看見約櫃，就歡喜了。14車到了伯示麥人約書亞的田間，就站住了。在那裏有一塊大磐石，他們把車劈了，將兩隻母牛獻與耶和華為燔祭。15利未人將耶和華的約櫃和裝金物的匣子拿下來，放在大磐石上。當日伯示麥人將燔祭和平安祭獻給耶和華。16非利士人的五個首領看見，當日就回以革倫去了。

17非利士人獻給耶和華作賠罪的金痔瘡像就是這些：一個是為亞實突，一個是為迦薩，一個是為亞實基倫，一個是為迦特，一個是為以革倫。18金老鼠的數目是照非利士五個首領的城邑，就是堅固的城邑和鄉村，以及大磐石。這磐石是放耶和華約櫃的，到今日還在伯示麥人約書亞的田間。

19耶和華因伯示麥人擅觀他的約櫃，就擊殺了他們七十人，那時有五萬人在那裏（註：原文作 "七十人若五萬人"）。百姓因耶和華大大擊殺他們，就哀哭了。20伯示麥人說："誰能在耶和華這聖潔的神面前侍立呢？這約櫃可以從我們這裏送到誰那裏去呢？"

21於是打發人去見基列耶琳的居民，說："非利士人將耶和華的約櫃送回來了，你們下來將約櫃接到你們那裏去吧！"

7 1基列耶琳人就下來，將耶和華的約櫃接上去，放在山上亞比拿達的家中，分派他兒子以利亞撒看守耶和華的約櫃。

撒母耳在米斯巴制伏非利士人

2約櫃在基列耶琳許久。過了二十年，以色列全家都傾向耶和華。3撒母耳對以色列全家說："你們若一心歸順耶和華，就要把外邦的神和亞斯她錄從你們中間除掉，專心歸向耶和華，單單地侍奉他。他必救你們脫離非利士人的手。"4以色列人就除掉諸巴力和亞斯她錄，單單地侍奉耶和華。

5撒母耳說："要使以色列眾人聚集在米斯巴，我好為你們禱告耶和華。"6他們就聚集在米斯巴，打水澆在耶和華面前，當日禁食，說："我們得罪了耶和華。"於是撒母耳在米斯巴審判以色列人。

7非利士人聽見以色列人聚集在米斯巴，非利士的首領就上來要攻擊以色列人。以色列人聽見，就懼怕非利士人。8以色列人對撒母耳說："願你不住地為我們呼求耶和華我們的神，救我們脫離非利士人的手。"9撒母耳就把一隻吃奶的羊羔獻與耶和華作全牲的燔祭，為以色列人呼求耶和華，耶和華就應允他。

10撒母耳正獻燔祭的時候，非利士人前來要與以色列人爭戰。當日，耶和華大發雷聲，驚亂非利士人，他們就敗在以色列人面前。11以色列人從米斯巴出來，追趕非利士人，擊殺他們，直到伯甲的下邊。

because they had looked into the ark of the LORD. The people mourned because of the heavy blow the LORD had dealt them, 20and the men of Beth Shemesh asked, "Who can stand in the presence of the LORD, this holy God? To whom will the ark go up from here?"

21Then they sent messengers to the people of Kiriath Jearim, saying, "The Philistines have returned the ark of the LORD. Come down and take it up to your place." 1So the men of Kiriath Jearim came and took up the ark of the LORD. They took it to Abinadab's house on the hill and consecrated Eleazar his son to guard the ark of the LORD.

Samuel Subdues the Philistines at Mizpah

2It was a long time, twenty years in all, that the ark remained at Kiriath Jearim, and all the people of Israel mourned and sought after the LORD. 3And Samuel said to the whole house of Israel, "If you are returning to the LORD with all your hearts, then rid yourselves of the foreign gods and the Ashtoreths and commit yourselves to the LORD and serve him only, and he will deliver you out of the hand of the Philistines." 4So the Israelites put away their Baals and Ashtoreths, and served the LORD only.

5Then Samuel said, "Assemble all Israel at Mizpah and I will intercede with the LORD for you." 6When they had assembled at Mizpah, they drew water and poured it out before the LORD. On that day they fasted and there they confessed, "We have sinned against the LORD." And Samuel was leader[a] of Israel at Mizpah.

7When the Philistines heard that Israel had assembled at Mizpah, the rulers of the Philistines came up to attack them. And when the Israelites heard of it, they were afraid because of the Philistines. 8They said to Samuel, "Do not stop crying out to the LORD our God for us, that he may rescue us from the hand of the Philistines." 9Then Samuel took a suckling lamb and offered it up as a whole burnt offering to the LORD. He cried out to the LORD on Israel's behalf, and the LORD answered him.

10While Samuel was sacrificing the burnt offering, the Philistines drew near to engage Israel in battle. But that day the LORD thundered with loud thunder against the Philistines and threw them into such a panic that they were routed before the Israelites. 11The men of Israel rushed out of Mizpah and pursued the Philistines, slaughtering them along the way to a point below Beth Car.

a 6 Traditionally judge

[12]Then Samuel took a stone and set it up between Mizpah and Shen. He named it Ebenezer,[a] saying, "Thus far has the LORD helped us." [13]So the Philistines were subdued and did not invade Israelite territory again.

Throughout Samuel's lifetime, the hand of the LORD was against the Philistines. [14]The towns from Ekron to Gath that the Philistines had captured from Israel were restored to her, and Israel delivered the neighboring territory from the power of the Philistines. And there was peace between Israel and the Amorites.

[15]Samuel continued as judge over Israel all the days of his life. [16]From year to year he went on a circuit from Bethel to Gilgal to Mizpah, judging Israel in all those places. [17]But he always went back to Ramah, where his home was, and there he also judged Israel. And he built an altar there to the LORD.

Israel Asks for a King

8 When Samuel grew old, he appointed his sons as judges for Israel. [2]The name of his firstborn was Joel and the name of his second was Abijah, and they served at Beersheba. [3]But his sons did not walk in his ways. They turned aside after dishonest gain and accepted bribes and perverted justice.

[4]So all the elders of Israel gathered together and came to Samuel at Ramah. [5]They said to him, "You are old, and your sons do not walk in your ways; now appoint a king to lead[b] us, such as all the other nations have."

[6]But when they said, "Give us a king to lead us," this displeased Samuel; so he prayed to the LORD. [7]And the LORD told him: "Listen to all that the people are saying to you; it is not you they have rejected, but they have rejected me as their king. [8]As they have done from the day I brought them up out of Egypt until this day, forsaking me and serving other gods, so they are doing to you. [9]Now listen to them; but warn them solemnly and let them know what the king who will reign over them will do."

[10]Samuel told all the words of the LORD to the people who were asking him for a king. [11]He said, "This is what the king who will reign over you will do: He will take your sons and make them serve with his chariots and horses, and they will run in front of his chariots. [12]Some he will assign to be commanders of thousands and commanders of fifties, and others to plow his ground and reap his harvest, and still others to

[12]撒母耳將一塊石頭立在米斯巴和善的中間，給石頭起名叫以便以謝，說：「到如今耶和華都幫助我們。」[13]從此，非利士人就被制伏，不敢再入以色列人的境內。

撒母耳作士師的時候，耶和華的手攻擊非利士人。[14]非利士人所取以色列人的城邑，從以革倫直到迦特，都歸以色列人了。屬這些城的四境，以色列人也從非利士人手下收回。那時以色列人與亞摩利人和好。

[15]撒母耳平生作以色列的士師。[16]他每年巡行到伯特利、吉甲、米斯巴，在這幾處審判以色列人。[17]隨後回到拉瑪，因為他的家在那裏；也在那裏審判以色列人，且為耶和華築了一座壇。

以色列人求立王

8 撒母耳年紀老邁，就立他兒子作以色列的士師。[2]長子名叫約珥，次子名叫亞比亞，他們在別是巴作士師。[3]他兒子不行他的道，貪圖財利，收受賄賂，屈枉正直。

[4]以色列的長老都聚集，來到拉瑪見撒母耳，[5]對他說：「你年紀老邁了，你兒子不行你的道。現在求你為我們立一個王治理我們，像列國一樣。」

[6]撒母耳不喜悅他們說「立一個王治理我們」，他就禱告耶和華。[7]耶和華對撒母耳說：「百姓向你說的一切話，你只管依從。因為他們不是厭棄你，乃是厭棄我，不要我作他們的王。[8]自從我領他們出埃及到如今，他們常常離棄我，侍奉別神。現在他們向你所行的，是照他們素來所行的。[9]故此你要依從他們的話，只是當警戒他們，告訴他們將來那王怎樣管轄他們。」

[10]撒母耳將耶和華的話都傳給求他立王的百姓，說：[11]「管轄你們的王必這樣行：他必派你們的兒子為他趕車、跟馬、奔走在車前；[12]又派他們作千夫長、五十夫長，為他耕種田

---

a 12 Ebenezer means stone of help.　　*b 5 Traditionally judge;*
also in verses 6 and 20

地，收割莊稼，打造軍器和車上的器械；¹³必取你們的女兒為他製造香膏，做飯烤餅；¹⁴也必取你們最好的田地、葡萄園、橄欖園，賜給他的臣僕。¹⁵你們的糧食和葡萄園所出的，他必取十分之一給他的太監和臣僕；¹⁶又必取你們的僕人婢女、健壯的少年人和你們的驢，供他的差役。¹⁷你們的羊羣，他必取十分之一，你們也必作他的僕人。¹⁸那時你們必因所揀選的王哀求耶和華，耶和華卻不應允你們。"

¹⁹百姓竟不肯聽撒母耳的話，說："不然，我們定要一個王治理我們，²⁰使我們像列國一樣，有王治理我們，統領我們，為我們爭戰。"

²¹撒母耳聽見百姓這一切話，就將這話陳明在耶和華面前。²²耶和華對撒母耳說："你只管依從他們的話，為他們立王。"

撒母耳對以色列人說："你們各歸各城去吧！"

撒母耳膏掃羅

9 有一個便雅憫人，名叫基士，是便雅憫人亞斐亞的玄孫、比歌拉的曾孫、洗羅的孫子、亞別的兒子，是個大能的勇士（註：或作"大財主"）。²他有一個兒子，名叫掃羅，又健壯、又俊美，在以色列人中沒有一個能比他的；身體比眾民高過一頭。

³掃羅的父親基士丟了幾頭驢，他就吩咐兒子掃羅說："你帶一個僕人去尋找驢。"⁴掃羅就走過以法蓮山地，又過沙利沙地，都沒有找着；又過沙琳地，驢也不在那裏；又過便雅憫地，還沒有找着。

⁵到了蘇弗地，掃羅對跟隨他的僕人說："我們不如回去，恐怕我父親不為驢掛心，反為我們擔憂。"

⁶僕人說："這城裏有一位神人，是眾人所尊重的，凡他所說的全都應驗。我們不如往他那裏去，或者他能將我們當走的路指示我們。"

make weapons of war and equipment for his chariots. ¹³He will take your daughters to be perfumers and cooks and bakers. ¹⁴He will take the best of your fields and vineyards and olive groves and give them to his attendants. ¹⁵He will take a tenth of your grain and of your vintage and give it to his officials and attendants. ¹⁶Your menservants and maidservants and the best of your cattle[a] and donkeys he will take for his own use. ¹⁷He will take a tenth of your flocks, and you yourselves will become his slaves. ¹⁸When that day comes, you will cry out for relief from the king you have chosen, and the LORD will not answer you in that day."

¹⁹But the people refused to listen to Samuel. "No!" they said. "We want a king over us. ²⁰Then we will be like all the other nations, with a king to lead us and to go out before us and fight our battles."

²¹When Samuel heard all that the people said, he repeated it before the LORD. ²²The LORD answered, "Listen to them and give them a king."

Then Samuel said to the men of Israel, "Everyone go back to his town."

Samuel Anoints Saul

9 There was a Benjamite, a man of standing, whose name was Kish son of Abiel, the son of Zeror, the son of Becorath, the son of Aphiah of Benjamin. ²He had a son named Saul, an impressive young man without equal among the Israelites—a head taller than any of the others.

³Now the donkeys belonging to Saul's father Kish were lost, and Kish said to his son Saul, "Take one of the servants with you and go and look for the donkeys." ⁴So he passed through the hill country of Ephraim and through the area around Shalisha, but they did not find them. They went on into the district of Shaalim, but the donkeys were not there. Then he passed through the territory of Benjamin, but they did not find them.

⁵When they reached the district of Zuph, Saul said to the servant who was with him, "Come, let's go back, or my father will stop thinking about the donkeys and start worrying about us."

⁶But the servant replied, "Look, in this town there is a man of God; he is highly respected, and everything he says comes true. Let's go there now. Perhaps he will tell us what way to take."

a 16 Septuagint; Hebrew young men

7Saul said to his servant, "If we go, what can we give the man? The food in our sacks is gone. We have no gift to take to the man of God. What do we have?"

8The servant answered him again. "Look," he said, "I have a quarter of a shekel[a] of silver. I will give it to the man of God so that he will tell us what way to take." 9(Formerly in Israel, if a man went to inquire of God, he would say, "Come, let us go to the seer," because the prophet of today used to be called a seer.)

10"Good," Saul said to his servant. "Come, let's go." So they set out for the town where the man of God was.

11As they were going up the hill to the town, they met some girls coming out to draw water, and they asked them, "Is the seer here?"

12"He is," they answered. "He's ahead of you. Hurry now; he has just come to our town today, for the people have a sacrifice at the high place. 13As soon as you enter the town, you will find him before he goes up to the high place to eat. The people will not begin eating until he comes, because he must bless the sacrifice; afterward, those who are invited will eat. Go up now; you should find him about this time."

14They went up to the town, and as they were entering it, there was Samuel, coming toward them on his way up to the high place.

15Now the day before Saul came, the LORD had revealed this to Samuel: 16"About this time tomorrow I will send you a man from the land of Benjamin. Anoint him leader over my people Israel; he will deliver my people from the hand of the Philistines. I have looked upon my people, for their cry has reached me."

17When Samuel caught sight of Saul, the LORD said to him, "This is the man I spoke to you about; he will govern my people."

18Saul approached Samuel in the gateway and asked, "Would you please tell me where the seer's house is?"

19"I am the seer," Samuel replied. "Go up ahead of me to the high place, for today you are to eat with me, and in the morning I will let you go and will tell you all that is in your heart. 20As for the donkeys you lost three days ago, do not worry about them; they have been found. And to whom is all the desire of Israel turned, if not to you and all your father's family?"

21Saul answered, "But am I not a Benjamite, from the smallest tribe of Israel, and is not my clan the least of all the clans of the tribe of Benjamin? Why do you say such a thing to me?"

a 8 That is, about 1/10 ounce (about 3 grams)

7掃羅對僕人說：「我們若去，有甚麼可以送那人呢？我們囊中的食物都吃盡了，也沒有禮物可以送那神人，我們還有甚麼沒有？」

8僕人回答掃羅說：「我手裏有銀子一舍客勒的四分之一，可以送那神人，請他指示我們當走的路。」9（從前以色列中，有人去問神，就說：「我們問先見去吧！」現在稱為先知的，從前稱為先見。）

10掃羅對僕人說：「你說的是，我們可以去。」於是他們往神人所住的城裏去了。

11他們上坡要進城，就遇見幾個少年女子出來打水，問她們說：「先見在這裏沒有？」

12女子回答說：「在這裏。他在你們前面，快去吧！他今日正到城裏，因為今日百姓要在邱壇獻祭。13在他還沒有上邱壇吃祭物之先，你們一進城必遇見他，因他未到，百姓不能吃，必等他先祝祭，然後請的客才吃。現在你們上去，這時候必遇見他。」

14二人就上去。將進城的時候，撒母耳正迎着他們來，要上邱壇去。

15掃羅未到的前一日，耶和華已經指示撒母耳說：16「明日這時候，我必使一個人從便雅憫地到你這裏來，你要膏他作我民以色列的君。他必救我民脫離非利士人的手；因我民的哀聲上達於我，我就眷顧他們。」

17撒母耳看見掃羅的時候，耶和華對他說：「看哪，這人就是我對你所說的，他必治理我的民。」

18掃羅在城門裏走到撒母耳跟前，說：「請告訴我，先見的寓所在哪裏？」

19撒母耳回答說：「我就是先見。你在我前面上邱壇去，因為你們今日必與我同席，明日早晨我送你去，將你心裏的事都告訴你。20至於你前三日所丟的那幾頭驢，你心裏不必掛念，已經找着了。以色列眾人所仰慕的是誰呢？不是仰慕你和你父的全家嗎？」

21掃羅說：「我不是以色列支派中至小的便雅憫人嗎？我家不是便雅憫支派中至小的家嗎？你為何對我說這樣的話呢？」

22撒母耳領掃羅和他僕人進了客堂，使他們在請來的客中坐首位，客約有三十個人。23撒母耳對廚役說：「我交給你收存的那一分祭肉，現在可以拿來。」

24廚役就把收存的腿拿來，擺在掃羅面前。撒母耳說：「這是所留下的，放在你面前可吃吧！因我請百姓的時候，特意為你存留這肉到此時。」當日掃羅就與撒母耳同席。

25眾人從邱壇下來進城，撒母耳和掃羅在房頂上說話。26次日清早起來，黎明的時候，掃羅在房頂上。撒母耳呼叫他說：「起來吧！我好送你回去。」掃羅就起來，和撒母耳一同出去。27二人下到城角，撒母耳對掃羅說：「要吩咐僕人先走（僕人就先走了）；你且站在這裏，等我將神的話傳與你聽。」

10 撒母耳拿瓶膏油倒在掃羅的頭上，與他親嘴，說：「這不是耶和華膏你作他產業的君嗎？2你今日與我離別之後，在便雅憫境內的泄撒，靠近拉結的墳墓，要遇見兩個人。他們必對你說：『你去找的那幾頭驢已經找着了。現在你父親不為驢掛心，反為你擔憂，說：我為兒子怎麼好好呢？』

3「你從那裏往前行，到了他泊的橡樹那裏，必遇見三個往伯特利去拜神的人：一個帶着三隻山羊羔，一個帶着三個餅，一個帶着一皮袋酒。4他們必問你安，給你兩個餅，你就從他們手中接過來。

5「此後你到神的山，在那裏有非利士人的防兵。你到了城的時候，必遇見一班先知從邱壇下來，前面有鼓瑟的、擊鼓的、吹笛的、彈琴的，他們都受感說話。6耶和華的靈必大大感動你，你就與他們一同受感說話，你要變為新人。

22Then Samuel brought Saul and his servant into the hall and seated them at the head of those who were invited—about thirty in number. 23Samuel said to the cook, "Bring the piece of meat I gave you, the one I told you to lay aside."

24So the cook took up the leg with what was on it and set it in front of Saul. Samuel said, "Here is what has been kept for you. Eat, because it was set aside for you for this occasion, from the time I said, 'I have invited guests.'" And Saul dined with Samuel that day.

25After they came down from the high place to the town, Samuel talked with Saul on the roof of his house. 26They rose about daybreak and Samuel called to Saul on the roof, "Get ready, and I will send you on your way." When Saul got ready, he and Samuel went outside together. 27As they were going down to the edge of the town, Samuel said to Saul, "Tell the servant to go on ahead of us"—and the servant did so— "but you stay here awhile, so that I may give you a message from God."

10 Then Samuel took a flask of oil and poured it on Saul's head and kissed him, saying, "Has not the LORD anointed you leader over his inheritance?[a] 2When you leave me today, you will meet two men near Rachel's tomb, at Zelzah on the border of Benjamin. They will say to you, 'The donkeys you set out to look for have been found. And now your father has stopped thinking about them and is worried about you. He is asking, "What shall I do about my son?" '

3"Then you will go on from there until you reach the great tree of Tabor. Three men going up to God at Bethel will meet you there. One will be carrying three young goats, another three loaves of bread, and another a skin of wine. 4They will greet you and offer you two loaves of bread, which you will accept from them.

5"After that you will go to Gibeah of God, where there is a Philistine outpost. As you approach the town, you will meet a procession of prophets coming down from the high place with lyres, tambourines, flutes and harps being played before them, and they will be prophesying. 6The Spirit of the LORD will come upon you in power, and you will prophesy with them; and you will be changed into a different person.

a 1 Hebrew; Septuagint and Vulgate over his people Israel? You will reign over the LORD's people and save them from the power of their enemies round about. And this will be a sign to you that the LORD has anointed you leader over his inheritance:

7Once these signs are fulfilled, do whatever your hand finds to do, for God is with you.

8"Go down ahead of me to Gilgal. I will surely come down to you to sacrifice burnt offerings and fellowship offerings,*a* but you must wait seven days until I come to you and tell you what you are to do."

Saul Made King

9As Saul turned to leave Samuel, God changed Saul's heart, and all these signs were fulfilled that day. 10When they arrived at Gibeah, a procession of prophets met him; the Spirit of God came upon him in power, and he joined in their prophesying. 11When all those who had formerly known him saw him prophesying with the prophets, they asked each other, "What is this that has happened to the son of Kish? Is Saul also among the prophets?"

12A man who lived there answered, "And who is their father?" So it became a saying: "Is Saul also among the prophets?" 13After Saul stopped prophesying, he went to the high place.

14Now Saul's uncle asked him and his servant, "Where have you been?"

"Looking for the donkeys," he said. "But when we saw they were not to be found, we went to Samuel."

15Saul's uncle said, "Tell me what Samuel said to you."

16Saul replied, "He assured us that the donkeys had been found." But he did not tell his uncle what Samuel had said about the kingship.

17Samuel summoned the people of Israel to the LORD at Mizpah 18and said to them, "This is what the LORD, the God of Israel, says: 'I brought Israel up out of Egypt, and I delivered you from the power of Egypt and all the kingdoms that oppressed you.' 19But you have now rejected your God, who saves you out of all your calamities and distresses. And you have said, 'No, set a king over us.' So now present yourselves before the LORD by your tribes and clans."

20When Samuel brought all the tribes of Israel near, the tribe of Benjamin was chosen. 21Then he brought forward the tribe of Benjamin, clan by clan, and Matri's clan was chosen. Finally Saul son of Kish was chosen. But when they looked for him, he was not to be found. 22So they inquired further of the LORD, "Has the man come here yet?"

And the LORD said, "Yes, he has hidden himself among the baggage."

a 8 Traditionally peace offerings

7這兆頭臨到你，你就可以趁時而做，因為神與你同在。

8 "你當在我以先下到吉甲，我也必下到那裏獻燔祭和平安祭。你要等候七日，等我到了那裏，指示你當行的事。"

掃羅被立為王

9掃羅轉身離別撒母耳，神就賜他一個新心。當日這一切兆頭都應驗了。10掃羅到了那山，有一班先知遇見他，神的靈大大感動他，他就在先知中受感說話。11素來認識掃羅的，看見他和先知一同受感說話，就彼此說："基士的兒子遇見甚麼了？掃羅也列在先知中嗎？"

12那地方有一個人說："這些人的父親是誰呢？"此後遂有句俗語說："掃羅也列在先知中嗎？"13掃羅受感說話已畢，就上邱壇去了。

14掃羅的叔叔問掃羅和他僕人說："你們往哪裏去了？"

回答說："找驢去了。我們見沒有驢，就到了撒母耳那裏。"

15掃羅的叔叔說："請將撒母耳向你們所說的話告訴我。"

16掃羅對他叔叔說："他明明地告訴我們驢已經找着了。"至於撒母耳所說的國事，掃羅卻沒有告訴叔叔。

17撒母耳將百姓招聚到米斯巴耶和華那裏，18對他們說："耶和華以色列的神如此說：'我領你們以色列人出埃及，救你們脫離埃及人的手，又救你們脫離欺壓你們各國之人的手。'19你們今日卻厭棄了救你們脫離一切災難的神，說：'求你立一個王治理我們。'現在你們應當按着支派宗族，都站在耶和華面前。"

20於是撒母耳使以色列眾支派近前來掣籤，就掣出便雅憫支派來；21又使便雅憫支派按着宗族近前來，就掣出瑪特利族；從其中又掣出基士的兒子掃羅。眾人尋找他卻尋不着，22就問耶和華說："那人到這裏來了沒有？"

耶和華說："他藏在器具中了。"

23眾人就跑去從那裏領出他來。他站在百姓中間，身體比眾民高過一頭。24撒母耳對眾民說："你們看耶和華所揀選的人，眾民中有可比他的嗎？"

眾民就大聲歡呼說："願王萬歲！"

25撒母耳將國法對百姓說明，又記在書上，放在耶和華面前。然後遣散眾民，各回各家去了。

26掃羅往基比亞回家去，有神感動的一羣人跟隨他。27但有些匪徒說："這人怎能救我們呢？"就藐視他，沒有送他禮物；掃羅卻不理會。

掃羅援救雅比城

11 亞捫人的王拿轄上來，對着基列雅比安營。雅比眾人對拿轄說："你與我們立約，我們就服侍你。"

2亞捫人拿轄說："你們若由我剜出你們各人的右眼，以此凌辱以色列眾人，我就與你們立約。"

3雅比的長老對他說："求你寬容我們七日，等我們打發人往以色列的全境去，若沒有人救我們，我們就出來歸順你。"

4使者到了掃羅住的基比亞，將這話說給百姓聽，百姓就都放聲而哭。5掃羅正從田間趕牛回來，問說："百姓為甚麼哭呢？"眾人將雅比人的話告訴他。

6掃羅聽見這話，就被神的靈大大感動，甚是發怒。7他將一對牛切成塊子，託付使者傳送以色列的全境，說："凡不出來跟隨掃羅和撒母耳的，也必這樣切開他的牛。"於是耶和華使百姓懼怕，他們就都出來如同一人。8掃羅在比色數點他們：以色列人有三十萬，猶大人有三萬。

9眾人對那使者說："你們要回覆基列雅比人說，明日太陽近午的時候，你們必得解救。"使者回去告訴雅比人，他們就歡喜了。10於是雅比

23They ran and brought him out, and as he stood among the people he was a head taller than any of the others. 24Samuel said to all the people, "Do you see the man the LORD has chosen? There is no one like him among all the people."

Then the people shouted, "Long live the king!"

25Samuel explained to the people the regulations of the kingship. He wrote them down on a scroll and deposited it before the LORD. Then Samuel dismissed the people, each to his own home.

26Saul also went to his home in Gibeah, accompanied by valiant men whose hearts God had touched. 27But some troublemakers said, "How can this fellow save us?" They despised him and brought him no gifts. But Saul kept silent.

Saul Rescues the City of Jabesh

11 Nahash the Ammonite went up and besieged Jabesh Gilead. And all the men of Jabesh said to him, "Make a treaty with us, and we will be subject to you."

2But Nahash the Ammonite replied, "I will make a treaty with you only on the condition that I gouge out the right eye of every one of you and so bring disgrace on all Israel."

3The elders of Jabesh said to him, "Give us seven days so we can send messengers throughout Israel; if no one comes to rescue us, we will surrender to you."

4When the messengers came to Gibeah of Saul and reported these terms to the people, they all wept aloud. 5Just then Saul was returning from the fields, behind his oxen, and he asked, "What is wrong with the people? Why are they weeping?" Then they repeated to him what the men of Jabesh had said.

6When Saul heard their words, the Spirit of God came upon him in power, and he burned with anger. 7He took a pair of oxen, cut them into pieces, and sent the pieces by messengers throughout Israel, proclaiming, "This is what will be done to the oxen of anyone who does not follow Saul and Samuel." Then the terror of the LORD fell on the people, and they turned out as one man. 8When Saul mustered them at Bezek, the men of Israel numbered three hundred thousand and the men of Judah thirty thousand.

9They told the messengers who had come, "Say to the men of Jabesh Gilead, 'By the time the sun is hot tomorrow, you will be delivered.'" When the messengers went and reported this to the men of Jabesh, they were elated. 10They said to the Ammonites, "Tomorrow we will surrender to you, and you can do to us whatever seems good to you."

11The next day Saul separated his men into three divisions; during the last watch of the night they broke into the camp of the Ammonites and slaughtered them until the heat of the day. Those who survived were scattered, so that no two of them were left together.

Saul Confirmed as King

12The people then said to Samuel, "Who was it that asked, 'Shall Saul reign over us?' Bring these men to us and we will put them to death."

13But Saul said, "No one shall be put to death today, for this day the LORD has rescued Israel."

14Then Samuel said to the people, "Come, let us go to Gilgal and there reaffirm the kingship." 15So all the people went to Gilgal and confirmed Saul as king in the presence of the LORD. There they sacrificed fellowship offerings[a] before the LORD, and Saul and all the Israelites held a great celebration.

Samuel's Farewell Speech

12 Samuel said to all Israel, "I have listened to everything you said to me and have set a king over you. 2Now you have a king as your leader. As for me, I am old and gray, and my sons are here with you. I have been your leader from my youth until this day. 3Here I stand. Testify against me in the presence of the LORD and his anointed. Whose ox have I taken? Whose donkey have I taken? Whom have I cheated? Whom have I oppressed? From whose hand have I accepted a bribe to make me shut my eyes? If I have done any of these, I will make it right."

4"You have not cheated or oppressed us," they replied. "You have not taken anything from anyone's hand."

5Samuel said to them, "The LORD is witness against you, and also his anointed is witness this day, that you have not found anything in my hand."

"He is witness," they said.

6Then Samuel said to the people, "It is the LORD who appointed Moses and Aaron and brought your forefathers up out of Egypt. 7Now then, stand here, because I am going to confront you with evidence before the LORD as to all the righteous acts performed by the LORD for you and your fathers.

人對亞捫人説：“明日我們出來歸順你們，你們可以隨意待我們。”

11第二日，掃羅將百姓分為三隊，在晨更的時候入了亞捫人的營，擊殺他們直到太陽近午，剩下的人都逃散，沒有二人同在一處的。

擁護掃羅為王

12百姓對撒母耳説：“那説‘掃羅豈能管理我們’的是誰呢？可以將他交出來，我們好殺死他。”

13掃羅説：“今日耶和華在以色列中施行拯救，所以不可殺人。”

14撒母耳對百姓説：“我們要往吉甲去，在那裏立國。”15眾百姓就到了吉甲那裏，在耶和華面前立掃羅為王，又在耶和華面前獻平安祭。掃羅和以色列眾人大大歡喜。

撒母耳的告別詞

12 撒母耳對以色列眾人説：“你們向我所求的，我已應允了，為你們立了一個王。2現在有這王在你們面前行。我已年老髮白，我的兒子都在你們這裏。我從幼年直到今日，都在你們前面行。3我在這裏，你們要在耶和華和他的受膏者面前給我作見證。我奪過誰的牛，搶過誰的驢，欺負過誰，虐待過誰，從誰手裏受過賄賂因而眼瞎呢？若有，我必償還。”

4眾人説：“你未曾欺負我們，虐待我們，也未曾從誰手裏受過甚麼。”

5撒母耳對他們説：“你們在我手裏沒有找着甚麼，有耶和華和他的受膏者今日為證。”

他們説：“願他為證。”

6撒母耳對百姓説：“從前立摩西、亞倫，又領你們列祖出埃及地的是耶和華。7現在你們要站住，等我在耶和華面前對你們講論耶和華向你們和你們列祖所行一切公義的事。

---

a 15 Traditionally *peace offerings*

8 "從前雅各到了埃及，後來你們列祖呼求耶和華，耶和華就差遣摩西、亞倫領你們列祖出埃及，使他們在這地方居住。

9 "他們卻忘記耶和華他們的神，他就把他們付與夏瑣將軍西西拉的手裏，和非利士人並摩押王的手裏，於是這些人常來攻擊他們。10他們就呼求耶和華說：'我們離棄耶和華，侍奉巴力和亞斯她錄，是有罪了。現在求你救我們脫離仇敵的手，我們必侍奉你。'11耶和華就差遣耶路巴力、比但、耶弗他、撒母耳，救你們脫離四圍仇敵的手，你們才安然居住。

12 "你們見亞捫人的王拿轄來攻擊你們，就對我說：'我們定要一個王治理我們。'其實耶和華你們的神是你們的王。13現在你們所求所選的王在這裏。看哪！耶和華已經為你們立王了。14你們若敬畏耶和華，侍奉他，聽從他的話，不違背他的命令，你們和治理你們的王，也都順從耶和華你們的神就好了。15倘若不聽從耶和華的話，違背他的命令，耶和華的手必攻擊你們，像從前攻擊你們列祖一樣。

16 "現在你們要站住，看耶和華在你們眼前要行一件大事。17這不是割麥子的時候嗎？我求告耶和華，他必打雷降雨，使你們又知道又看出，你們求立王的事，是在耶和華面前犯大罪了。"

18於是撒母耳求告耶和華，耶和華就在這日打雷降雨，眾民便甚懼怕耶和華和撒母耳。

19眾民對撒母耳說："求你為僕人們禱告耶和華你的神，免得我們死亡，因為我們求立王的事，正是罪上加罪了。"

20撒母耳對百姓說："不要懼怕！你們雖然行了這惡，卻不要偏離耶和華，只要盡心侍奉他。21若偏離耶和華去順從那不能救人的虛神是無益的。22耶和華既喜悅選你們作他的子民，就必因他的大名不撇棄你們。

8"After Jacob entered Egypt, they cried to the LORD for help, and the LORD sent Moses and Aaron, who brought your forefathers out of Egypt and settled them in this place.

9"But they forgot the LORD their God; so he sold them into the hand of Sisera, the commander of the army of Hazor, and into the hands of the Philistines and the king of Moab, who fought against them. 10They cried out to the LORD and said, 'We have sinned; we have forsaken the LORD and served the Baals and the Ashtoreths. But now deliver us from the hands of our enemies, and we will serve you.' 11Then the LORD sent Jerub-Baal,*a* Barak,*b* Jephthah and Samuel,*c* and he delivered you from the hands of your enemies on every side, so that you lived securely.

12"But when you saw that Nahash king of the Ammonites was moving against you, you said to me, 'No, we want a king to rule over us'—even though the LORD your God was your king. 13Now here is the king you have chosen, the one you asked for; see, the LORD has set a king over you. 14If you fear the LORD and serve and obey him and do not rebel against his commands, and if both you and the king who reigns over you follow the LORD your God—good! 15But if you do not obey the LORD, and if you rebel against his commands, his hand will be against you, as it was against your fathers.

16"Now then, stand still and see this great thing the LORD is about to do before your eyes! 17Is it not wheat harvest now? I will call upon the LORD to send thunder and rain. And you will realize what an evil thing you did in the eyes of the LORD when you asked for a king."

18Then Samuel called upon the LORD, and that same day the LORD sent thunder and rain. So all the people stood in awe of the LORD and of Samuel.

19The people all said to Samuel, "Pray to the LORD your God for your servants so that we will not die, for we have added to all our other sins the evil of asking for a king."

20"Do not be afraid," Samuel replied. "You have done all this evil; yet do not turn away from the LORD, but serve the LORD with all your heart. 21Do not turn away after useless idols. They can do you no good, nor can they rescue you, because they are useless. 22For the sake of his great name the LORD will not reject his people, because the LORD was pleased to make you

---

a 11 Also called *Gideon*　*b 11* Some Septuagint manuscripts and Syriac; Hebrew *Bedan*　*c 11* Hebrew; some Septuagint manuscripts and Syriac *Samson*

his own. ²³As for me, far be it from me that I should sin against the LORD by failing to pray for you. And I will teach you the way that is good and right. ²⁴But be sure to fear the LORD and serve him faithfully with all your heart; consider what great things he has done for you. ²⁵Yet if you persist in doing evil, both you and your king will be swept away."

Samuel Rebukes Saul

13 Saul was ⌊thirty,⌋[a] years old when he became king, and he reigned over Israel ⌊forty-⌋[b] two years.

²Saul[c] chose three thousand men from Israel; two thousand were with him at Micmash and in the hill country of Bethel, and a thousand were with Jonathan at Gibeah in Benjamin. The rest of the men he sent back to their homes.

³Jonathan attacked the Philistine outpost at Geba, and the Philistines heard about it. Then Saul had the trumpet blown throughout the land and said, "Let the Hebrews hear!" ⁴So all Israel heard the news: "Saul has attacked the Philistine outpost, and now Israel has become a stench to the Philistines." And the people were summoned to join Saul at Gilgal.

⁵The Philistines assembled to fight Israel, with three thousand[d] chariots, six thousand charioteers, and soldiers as numerous as the sand on the seashore. They went up and camped at Micmash, east of Beth Aven. ⁶When the men of Israel saw that their situation was critical and that their army was hard pressed, they hid in caves and thickets, among the rocks, and in pits and cisterns. ⁷Some Hebrews even crossed the Jordan to the land of Gad and Gilead.

Saul remained at Gilgal, and all the troops with him were quaking with fear. ⁸He waited seven days, the time set by Samuel; but Samuel did not come to Gilgal, and Saul's men began to scatter. ⁹So he said, "Bring me the burnt offering and the fellowship offerings.[e]" And Saul offered up the burnt offering. ¹⁰Just as he finished making the offering, Samuel arrived, and Saul went out to greet him.

¹¹"What have you done?" asked Samuel.

Saul replied, "When I saw that the men were scattering, and that you did not come at the set

²³至於我，斷不停止為你們禱告，以致得罪耶和華。我必以善道正路指教你們。²⁴只要你們敬畏耶和華，誠誠實實地盡心侍奉他，想念他向你們所行的事何等大。²⁵你們若仍然作惡，你們和你們的王必一同滅亡。"

撒母耳斥責掃羅

13 掃羅登基年四十歲，作以色列王二年的時候，

²就從以色列中揀選了三千人：二千跟隨掃羅在密抹和伯特利山，一千跟隨約拿單在便雅憫的基比亞；其餘的人，掃羅都打發各回各家去了。

³約拿單攻擊迦巴 非利士人的防營，非利士人聽見了。掃羅就在遍地吹角，意思說，要使希伯來人聽見。⁴以色列眾人聽見掃羅攻擊非利士人的防營，又聽見以色列人為非利士人所憎惡，就跟隨掃羅聚集在吉甲。

⁵非利士人聚集要與以色列人爭戰，有車三萬輛，馬兵六千，步兵像海邊的沙那樣多，就上來在伯亞文東邊的密抹安營。⁶以色列百姓見自己危急窘迫，就藏在山洞、叢林、石穴、隱密處和坑中。⁷有些希伯來人過了約旦河，逃到迦得和基列地。

掃羅還是在吉甲，百姓都戰戰兢兢地跟隨他。⁸掃羅照着撒母耳所定的日期等了七日。撒母耳還沒有來到吉甲，百姓也離開掃羅散去了。⁹掃羅說："把燔祭和平安祭帶到我這裏來。"掃羅就獻上燔祭。¹⁰剛獻完燔祭，撒母耳就到了。掃羅出去迎接他，要問他好。

¹¹撒母耳說："你做的是甚麼事呢？"

掃羅說："因為我見百姓離開

---

a 1 A few late manuscripts of the Septuagint; Hebrew does not have *thirty*.   *b 1* See the round number in Acts 13:21; Hebrew does not have *forty-*.   *c 1,2* Or *and when he had reigned over Israel two years,* ²*he*   *d 5* Some Septuagint manuscripts and Syriac; Hebrew *thirty thousand*   *e 9* Traditionally *peace offerings*

我散去，你也不照所定的日期來到，而且非利士人聚集在密抹。12所以我心裏說：'恐怕我沒有禱告耶和華，非利士人下到吉甲攻擊我。'我就勉強獻上燔祭。"

13撒母耳對掃羅說："你做了糊塗事了！沒有遵守耶和華你神所吩咐你的命令。若遵守，耶和華必在以色列中堅立你的王位，直到永遠。14現在你的王位必不長久。耶和華已經尋着一個合他心意的人，立他作百姓的君，因為你沒有遵守耶和華所吩咐你的。"

15撒母耳就起來，從吉甲上到便雅憫的基比亞。掃羅數點跟隨他的，約有六百人。

以色列人缺乏武器

16掃羅和他兒子約拿單並跟隨他們的人，都住在便雅憫的迦巴，但非利士人安營在密抹。17有掠兵從非利士營中出來，分為三隊：一隊往俄弗拉向書亞地去，18一隊往伯和崙去，一隊往洗波音谷對面的地境向曠野去。

19那時，以色列全地沒有一個鐵匠，因為非利士人說恐怕希伯來人製造刀槍。20以色列人要磨鋤、犁、斧、鏟，就下到非利士人那裏去磨。21但有銼可以銼鏟、犁、三齒叉、斧子並趕牛錐。

22所以到了爭戰的日子，跟隨掃羅和約拿單的人，沒有一個手裏有刀有槍的，惟獨掃羅和他兒子約拿單有。

約拿單攻擊非利士人

23非利士人的一隊防兵到了密抹的隘口。14:1有一日，掃羅的兒子約拿單對拿他兵器的少年人說："我們不如過到那邊，到非利士人的防營那裏去。"但他沒有告訴父親。

time, and that the Philistines were assembling at Micmash, 12I thought, 'Now the Philistines will come down against me at Gilgal, and I have not sought the LORD's favor.' So I felt compelled to offer the burnt offering."

13"You acted foolishly," Samuel said. "You have not kept the command the LORD your God gave you; if you had, he would have established your kingdom over Israel for all time. 14But now your kingdom will not endure; the LORD has sought out a man after his own heart and appointed him leader of his people, because you have not kept the LORD's command."

15Then Samuel left Gilgal[a] and went up to Gibeah in Benjamin, and Saul counted the men who were with him. They numbered about six hundred.

Israel Without Weapons

16Saul and his son Jonathan and the men with them were staying in Gibeah[b] in Benjamin, while the Philistines camped at Micmash. 17Raiding parties went out from the Philistine camp in three detachments. One turned toward Ophrah in the vicinity of Shual, 18another toward Beth Horon, and the third toward the borderland overlooking the Valley of Zeboim facing the desert.

19Not a blacksmith could be found in the whole land of Israel, because the Philistines had said, "Otherwise the Hebrews will make swords or spears!" 20So all Israel went down to the Philistines to have their plowshares, mattocks, axes and sickles[c] sharpened. 21The price was two thirds of a shekel[d] for sharpening plowshares and mattocks, and a third of a shekel[e] for sharpening forks and axes and for repointing goads.

22So on the day of the battle not a soldier with Saul and Jonathan had a sword or spear in his hand; only Saul and his son Jonathan had them.

Jonathan Attacks the Philistines

23Now a detachment of Philistines had gone out to the pass at Micmash. 14:1One day Jonathan son of Saul said to the young man bearing his armor, "Come, let's go over to the Philistine outpost on the other side." But he did not tell his father.

---

a 15 Hebrew; Septuagint Gilgal and went his way; the rest of the people went after Saul to meet the army, and they went out of Gilgal   b 16 Two Hebrew manuscripts; most Hebrew manuscripts Geba, a variant of Gibeah   c 20 Septuagint; Hebrew plowshares   d 21 Hebrew pim; that is, about 1/4 ounce (about 8 grams)   e 21 That is, about 1/8 ounce (about 4 grams)

²Saul was staying on the outskirts of Gibeah under a pomegranate tree in Migron. With him were about six hundred men, ³among whom was Ahijah, who was wearing an ephod. He was a son of Ichabod's brother Ahitub son of Phinehas, the son of Eli, the LORD's priest in Shiloh. No one was aware that Jonathan had left.

⁴On each side of the pass that Jonathan intended to cross to reach the Philistine outpost was a cliff; one was called Bozez, and the other Seneh. ⁵One cliff stood to the north toward Micmash, the other to the south toward Geba.

⁶Jonathan said to his young armor-bearer, "Come, let's go over to the outpost of those uncircumcised fellows. Perhaps the LORD will act in our behalf. Nothing can hinder the LORD from saving, whether by many or by few."

⁷"Do all that you have in mind," his armor-bearer said. "Go ahead; I am with you heart and soul."

⁸Jonathan said, "Come, then; we will cross over toward the men and let them see us. ⁹If they say to us, 'Wait there until we come to you,' we will stay where we are and not go up to them. ¹⁰But if they say, 'Come up to us,' we will climb up, because that will be our sign that the LORD has given them into our hands."

¹¹So both of them showed themselves to the Philistine outpost. "Look!" said the Philistines. "The Hebrews are crawling out of the holes they were hiding in." ¹²The men of the outpost shouted to Jonathan and his armor-bearer, "Come up to us and we'll teach you a lesson."

So Jonathan said to his armor-bearer, "Climb up after me; the LORD has given them into the hand of Israel."

¹³Jonathan climbed up, using his hands and feet, with his armor-bearer right behind him. The Philistines fell before Jonathan, and his armor-bearer followed and killed behind him. ¹⁴In that first attack Jonathan and his armor-bearer killed some twenty men in an area of about half an acre.ᵃ

Israel Routs the Philistines

¹⁵Then panic struck the whole army—those in the camp and field, and those in the outposts and raiding parties—and the ground shook. It was a panic sent by God.ᵇ

¹⁶Saul's lookouts at Gibeah in Benjamin saw the army melting away in all directions. ¹⁷Then Saul said to the men who were with him,

²掃羅在基比亞的儘邊，坐在米磯崙的石榴樹下，跟隨他的約有六百人。³在那裏有亞希突的兒子亞希亞，穿着以弗得。亞希突是以迦博的哥哥，非尼哈的兒子，以利的孫子。以利從前在示羅作耶和華的祭司。約拿單去了，百姓卻不知道。

⁴約拿單要從隘口過到非利士防營那裏去。這隘口兩邊各有一個山峯：一名播薛，一名西尼；⁵一峯向北，與密抹相對，一峯向南，與迦巴相對。

⁶約拿單對拿兵器的少年人說："我們不如過到未受割禮人的防營那裏去，或者耶和華為我們施展能力，因為耶和華使人得勝，不在乎人多人少。"

⁷拿兵器的對他說："隨你的心意行吧！你可以上去，我必跟隨你，與你同心。"

⁸約拿單說："我們要過到那些人那裏去，使他們看見我們。⁹他們若對我們說：'你們站住，等我們到你們那裏去'，我們就站住，不上他們那裏去。¹⁰他們若說：'你們上到我們這裏來'，這話就是我們的證據，我們便上去，因為耶和華將他們交在我們手裏了。"

¹¹二人就使非利士的防兵看見。非利士人說："希伯來人從所藏的洞穴裏出來了。"¹²防兵對約拿單和拿兵器的人說："你們上到這裏來，我們有一件事指示你們。"

約拿單就對拿兵器的人說："你跟隨我上去，因為耶和華將他們交在以色列人手裏了。"

¹³約拿單就爬上去，拿兵器的人跟隨他。約拿單殺倒非利士人，拿兵器的人也隨着殺他們。¹⁴約拿單和拿兵器的人起頭所殺的，約有二十人，都在一畝地的半犁溝之內。

以色列人打敗非利士人

¹⁵於是在營中、在田野、在眾民內，都有戰兢，防兵和掠兵也都戰兢，地也震動，戰兢之勢甚大。

¹⁶在便雅憫的基比亞，掃羅的守望兵看見非利士的軍眾潰散，四圍亂竄。¹⁷掃羅就對跟隨他的民說："你

ᵃ 14 Hebrew *half a yoke*; a "yoke" was the land plowed by a yoke of oxen in one day.   ᵇ 15 Or *a terrible panic*

們查點查點，看從我們這裏出去的是誰？"他們一查點，就知道約拿單和拿兵器的人沒有在這裏。

18 那時神的約櫃在以色列人那裏。掃羅對亞希亞說："你將神的約櫃運了來。" 19 掃羅正與祭司說話的時候，非利士營中的喧嚷越發大了。掃羅就對祭司說："停手吧！"

20 掃羅和跟隨他的人都聚集，來到戰場，看見非利士人用刀互相擊殺，大大惶亂。21 從前由四方來跟隨非利士軍的希伯來人，現在也轉過來幫助跟隨掃羅和約拿單的以色列人了。22 那藏在以法蓮山地的以色列人，聽說非利士人逃跑，就出來緊緊地追殺他們。23 這日，耶和華使以色列人得勝，一直戰到伯亞文。

約拿單吃蜜

24 掃羅叫百姓起誓說，凡不等到晚上向敵人報完了仇吃甚麼的，必受咒詛。因此這日百姓沒有吃甚麼，就極其困憊。

25 眾民進入樹林，見有蜜在地上。26 他們進了樹林，見有蜜流下來，卻沒有人敢用手取蜜入口，因為他們怕那誓言。27 約拿單沒有聽見他父親叫百姓起誓，所以伸手中的杖，用杖頭蘸在蜂房裏，轉手送入口內，眼睛就明亮了。28 百姓中有一人對他說："你父親曾叫百姓嚴嚴地起誓說，'今日吃甚麼的，必受咒詛。'因此百姓就疲乏了。"

29 約拿單說："我父親連累你們了。你看，我嘗了這一點蜜，眼睛就明亮了。30 今日百姓若任意吃了從仇敵所奪的物，擊殺的非利士人豈不更多嗎？"

31 這日，以色列人擊殺非利士人，從密抹直到亞雅崙。百姓甚是疲

"Muster the forces and see who has left us." When they did, it was Jonathan and his armorbearer who were not there.

18 Saul said to Ahijah, "Bring the ark of God." (At that time it was with the Israelites.)[a] 19 While Saul was talking to the priest, the tumult in the Philistine camp increased more and more. So Saul said to the priest, "Withdraw your hand."

20 Then Saul and all his men assembled and went to the battle. They found the Philistines in total confusion, striking each other with their swords. 21 Those Hebrews who had previously been with the Philistines and had gone up with them to their camp went over to the Israelites who were with Saul and Jonathan. 22 When all the Israelites who had hidden in the hill country of Ephraim heard that the Philistines were on the run, they joined the battle in hot pursuit. 23 So the LORD rescued Israel that day, and the battle moved on beyond Beth Aven.

Jonathan Eats Honey

24 Now the men of Israel were in distress that day, because Saul had bound the people under an oath, saying, "Cursed be any man who eats food before evening comes, before I have avenged myself on my enemies!" So none of the troops tasted food.

25 The entire army[b] entered the woods, and there was honey on the ground. 26 When they went into the woods, they saw the honey oozing out, yet no one put his hand to his mouth, because they feared the oath. 27 But Jonathan had not heard that his father had bound the people with the oath, so he reached out the end of the staff that was in his hand and dipped it into the honeycomb. He raised his hand to his mouth, and his eyes brightened.[c] 28 Then one of the soldiers told him, "Your father bound the army under a strict oath, saying, 'Cursed be any man who eats food today!' That is why the men are faint."

29 Jonathan said, "My father has made trouble for the country. See how my eyes brightened[d] when I tasted a little of this honey. 30 How much better it would have been if the men had eaten today some of the plunder they took from their enemies. Would not the slaughter of the Philistines have been even greater?"

31 That day, after the Israelites had struck down the Philistines from Micmash to Aijalon,

a 18 Hebrew; Septuagint "Bring the ephod." (At that time he wore the ephod before the Israelites.)　b 25 Or Now all the people of the land　c 27 Or his strength was renewed　d 29 Or my strength was renewed

they were exhausted. ³²They pounced on the plunder and, taking sheep, cattle and calves, they butchered them on the ground and ate them, together with the blood. ³³Then someone said to Saul, "Look, the men are sinning against the LORD by eating meat that has blood in it."

"You have broken faith," he said. "Roll a large stone over here at once." ³⁴Then he said, "Go out among the men and tell them, 'Each of you bring me your cattle and sheep, and slaughter them here and eat them. Do not sin against the LORD by eating meat with blood still in it.'"

So everyone brought his ox that night and slaughtered it there. ³⁵Then Saul built an altar to the LORD; it was the first time he had done this.

³⁶Saul said, "Let us go down after the Philistines by night and plunder them till dawn, and let us not leave one of them alive."

"Do whatever seems best to you," they replied.

But the priest said, "Let us inquire of God here."

³⁷So Saul asked God, "Shall I go down after the Philistines? Will you give them into Israel's hand?" But God did not answer him that day.

³⁸Saul therefore said, "Come here, all you who are leaders of the army, and let us find out what sin has been committed today. ³⁹As surely as the LORD who rescues Israel lives, even if it lies with my son Jonathan, he must die." But not one of the men said a word.

⁴⁰Saul then said to all the Israelites, "You stand over there; I and Jonathan my son will stand over here."

"Do what seems best to you," the men replied.

⁴¹Then Saul prayed to the LORD, the God of Israel, "Give me the right answer."ᵃ And Jonathan and Saul were taken by lot, and the men were cleared. ⁴²Saul said, "Cast the lot between me and Jonathan my son." And Jonathan was taken.

⁴³Then Saul said to Jonathan, "Tell me what you have done."

So Jonathan told him, "I merely tasted a little honey with the end of my staff. And now must I die?"

⁴⁴Saul said, "May God deal with me, be it ever so severely, if you do not die, Jonathan."

⁴⁵But the men said to Saul, "Should Jonathan die—he who has brought about this great deliv-

a 41 Hebrew; Septuagint "Why have you not answered your servant today? If the fault is in me or my son Jonathan, respond with Urim, but if the men of Israel are at fault, respond with Thummim."

乏，³²就急忙將所奪的牛羊和牛犢宰於地上，肉還帶血就吃了。³³有人告訴掃羅說："百姓吃帶血的肉，得罪耶和華了。"

掃羅說："你們有罪了，今日要將大石頭滾到我這裏來。"³⁴掃羅又說："你們散在百姓中，對他們說：'你們各人將牛羊牽到我這裏來宰了吃，不可吃帶血的肉得罪耶和華。'"

這夜，百姓就把牛羊牽到那裏宰了。³⁵掃羅為耶和華築了一座壇，這是他初次為耶和華築的壇。

³⁶掃羅說："我們不如夜裏下去追趕非利士人，搶掠他們，直到天亮，不留他們一人。"

眾民說："你看怎樣好就去行吧！"

祭司說："我們先當親近神。"

³⁷掃羅求問神說："我下去追趕非利士人可以不可以？你將他們交在以色列人手裏不交？"這日神沒有回答他。

³⁸掃羅說："你們百姓中的長老都上這裏來，查明今日是誰犯了罪。³⁹我指着救以色列永生的耶和華起誓，就是我兒子約拿單犯了罪，他也必死。"但百姓中無一人回答他。

⁴⁰掃羅就對以色列眾人說："你們站在一邊，我與我兒子約拿單也站在一邊。"

百姓對掃羅說："你看怎樣好就去行吧！"

⁴¹掃羅禱告耶和華以色列的神說："求你指示實情。"於是掣籤掣出掃羅和約拿單來，百姓盡都無事。⁴²掃羅說："你們再掣籤，看是我、是我兒子約拿單？"就掣出約拿單來。

⁴³掃羅對約拿單說："你告訴我，你做了甚麼事？"

約拿單說："我實在以手裏的杖，用杖頭蘸了一點蜜嘗了一嘗。這樣我就死嗎（註："嗎"或作"吧"）？"

⁴⁴掃羅說："約拿單哪，你定要死！若不然，願神重重地降罰與我。"

⁴⁵百姓對掃羅說："約拿單在以色列人中這樣大行拯救，豈可使他死

呢？斷乎不可！我們指着永生的耶和華起誓，連他的一根頭髮也不可落地，因為他今日與神一同做事。」於是百姓救約拿單免了死亡。

46撒羅回去，不追趕非利士人，非利士人也回本地去了。

47撒羅執掌以色列的國權，常常攻擊他四圍的一切仇敵，就是摩押人、亞捫人、以東人和瑣巴諸王，並非利士人。他無論往何處去，都打敗仇敵。48撒羅奮勇攻擊亞瑪力人，救了以色列人脫離搶掠他們之人的手。

掃羅的家族

49撒羅的兒子是約拿單、亦施韋、麥基舒亞；他的兩個女兒：長女名米拉，次女名米甲。50撒羅的妻，名叫亞希暖，是亞希瑪斯的女兒。撒羅的元帥，名叫押尼珥，是尼珥的兒子；尼珥是撒羅的叔叔。51撒羅的父親基士，押尼珥的父親尼珥，都是亞別的兒子。

52撒羅平生常與非利士人大大爭戰。撒羅遇見有能力的人或勇士，都招募了來跟隨他。

主棄絕掃羅為王

15 撒母耳對撒羅說：「耶和華差遣我膏你為王，治理他的百姓以色列，所以你當聽從耶和華的話。2萬軍之耶和華如此說：『以色列人出埃及的時候，在路上亞瑪力人怎樣待他們，怎樣抵擋他們，我都沒忘。3現在你要去擊打亞瑪力人，滅盡他們所有的，不可憐惜他們，將男女、孩童、吃奶的，並牛、羊、駱駝和驢盡行殺死。』」

4於是撒羅招聚百姓在提拉因，數點他們，共有步兵二十萬，另有猶大人一萬。5撒羅到了亞瑪力的京城，在谷中設下埋伏。6撒羅對基尼人說：「你們離開亞瑪力人下去吧！恐怕我將你們和亞瑪力人一同殺滅，因為以色列人出埃及的時候，你們曾

erance in Israel? Never! As surely as the LORD lives, not a hair of his head will fall to the ground, for he did this today with God's help." So the men rescued Jonathan, and he was not put to death.

46Then Saul stopped pursuing the Philistines, and they withdrew to their own land.

47After Saul had assumed rule over Israel, he fought against their enemies on every side: Moab, the Ammonites, Edom, the kings*a* of Zobah, and the Philistines. Wherever he turned, he inflicted punishment on them.*b* 48He fought valiantly and defeated the Amalekites, delivering Israel from the hands of those who had plundered them.

Saul's Family

49Saul's sons were Jonathan, Ishvi and Malki-Shua. The name of his older daughter was Merab, and that of the younger was Michal. 50His wife's name was Ahinoam daughter of Ahimaaz. The name of the commander of Saul's army was Abner son of Ner, and Ner was Saul's uncle. 51Saul's father Kish and Abner's father Ner were sons of Abiel.

52All the days of Saul there was bitter war with the Philistines, and whenever Saul saw a mighty or brave man, he took him into his service.

The LORD Rejects Saul as King

15 Samuel said to Saul, "I am the one the LORD sent to anoint you king over his people Israel; so listen now to the message from the LORD. 2This is what the LORD Almighty says: 'I will punish the Amalekites for what they did to Israel when they waylaid them as they came up from Egypt. 3Now go, attack the Amalekites and totally destroy*c* everything that belongs to them. Do not spare them; put to death men and women, children and infants, cattle and sheep, camels and donkeys.'"

4So Saul summoned the men and mustered them at Telaim—two hundred thousand foot soldiers and ten thousand men from Judah. 5Saul went to the city of Amalek and set an ambush in the ravine. 6Then he said to the Kenites, "Go away, leave the Amalekites so that I do not destroy you along with them; for you showed kindness to all the Israelites when they

a 47 Masoretic Text; Dead Sea Scrolls and Septuagint *king*
b 47 Hebrew; Septuagint *he was victorious*　　*c 3* The Hebrew term refers to the irrevocable giving over of things or persons to the LORD, often by totally destroying them; also in verses 8, 9, 15, 18, 20 and 21.

came up out of Egypt." So the Kenites moved away from the Amalekites.

⁷Then Saul attacked the Amalekites all the way from Havilah to Shur, to the east of Egypt. ⁸He took Agag king of the Amalekites alive, and all his people he totally destroyed with the sword. ⁹But Saul and the army spared Agag and the best of the sheep and cattle, the fat calves*a* and lambs—everything that was good. These they were unwilling to destroy completely, but everything that was despised and weak they totally destroyed.

¹⁰Then the word of the LORD came to Samuel: ¹¹"I am grieved that I have made Saul king, because he has turned away from me and has not carried out my instructions." Samuel was troubled, and he cried out to the LORD all that night.

¹²Early in the morning Samuel got up and went to meet Saul, but he was told, "Saul has gone to Carmel. There he has set up a monument in his own honor and has turned and gone on down to Gilgal."

¹³When Samuel reached him, Saul said, "The LORD bless you! I have carried out the LORD's instructions."

¹⁴But Samuel said, "What then is this bleating of sheep in my ears? What is this lowing of cattle that I hear?"

¹⁵Saul answered, "The soldiers brought them from the Amalekites; they spared the best of the sheep and cattle to sacrifice to the LORD your God, but we totally destroyed the rest."

¹⁶"Stop!" Samuel said to Saul. "Let me tell you what the LORD said to me last night."

"Tell me," Saul replied.

¹⁷Samuel said, "Although you were once small in your own eyes, did you not become the head of the tribes of Israel? The LORD anointed you king over Israel. ¹⁸And he sent you on a mission, saying, 'Go and completely destroy those wicked people, the Amalekites; make war on them until you have wiped them out.' ¹⁹Why did you not obey the LORD? Why did you pounce on the plunder and do evil in the eyes of the LORD?"

²⁰"But I did obey the LORD," Saul said. "I went on the mission the LORD assigned me. I completely destroyed the Amalekites and brought back Agag their king. ²¹The soldiers took sheep and cattle from the plunder, the best of what was devoted to God, in order to sacrifice them to the LORD your God at Gilgal."

恩待他們。"於是基尼人離開亞瑪力人去了。

⁷掃羅擊打亞瑪力人,從哈腓拉直到埃及前的書珥,⁸生擒了亞瑪力王亞甲,用刀殺盡亞瑪力的眾民。⁹掃羅和百姓卻憐惜亞甲,也愛惜上好的牛、羊、牛犢、羊羔,並一切美物,不肯滅絕;凡下賤瘦弱的,盡都殺了。

¹⁰耶和華的話臨到撒母耳說:¹¹"我立掃羅為王,我後悔了,因為他轉去不跟從我,不遵守我的命令。"撒母耳便甚憂愁,終夜哀求耶和華。

¹²撒母耳清早起來,迎接掃羅。有人告訴撒母耳說:"掃羅到了迦密,在那裏立了紀念碑,又轉身下到吉甲。"

¹³撒母耳到了掃羅那裏,掃羅對他說:"願耶和華賜福與你,耶和華的命令我已遵守了。"

¹⁴撒母耳說:"我耳中聽見有羊叫、牛鳴,是從哪裏來的呢?"

¹⁵掃羅說:"這是百姓從亞瑪力人那裏帶來的,因為他們愛惜上好的牛羊,要獻與耶和華你的神。其餘的,我們都滅盡了。"

¹⁶撒母耳對掃羅說:"你住口吧!等我將耶和華昨夜向我所說的話告訴你。"掃羅說:"請講。"

¹⁷撒母耳對掃羅說:"從前你雖然以自己為小,豈不是被立為以色列支派的元首嗎?耶和華膏你作以色列的王。¹⁸耶和華差遣你、吩咐你說:'你去擊打那些犯罪的亞瑪力人,將他們滅絕淨盡。'¹⁹你為何沒有聽從耶和華的命令,急忙擄掠財物,行耶和華眼中看為惡的事呢?"

²⁰掃羅對撒母耳說:"我實在聽從了耶和華的命令,行了耶和華所差遣我行的路,擒了亞瑪力王亞甲來,滅盡了亞瑪力人。²¹百姓卻在所當滅的物中取了最好的牛羊,要在吉甲獻與耶和華你的神。"

---

a 9 Or the grown bulls; the meaning of the Hebrew for this phrase is uncertain.

22撒母耳說：

"耶和華喜悅燔祭和平安祭，
  豈如喜悅人聽從他的話呢？
聽命勝於獻祭；
  順從勝於公羊的脂油。

23悖逆的罪與行邪術的罪相等；
  頑梗的罪與拜虛神
  和偶像的罪相同。
你既厭棄耶和華的命令，
  耶和華也厭棄你作王。"

24掃羅對撒母耳說："我有罪了！我因懼怕百姓，聽從他們的話，就違背了耶和華的命令和你的言語。25現在求你赦免我的罪，同我回去，我好敬拜耶和華。"

26撒母耳對掃羅說："我不同你回去，因為你厭棄耶和華的命令，耶和華也厭棄你作以色列的王。"

27撒母耳轉身要走，掃羅就扯住他外袍的衣襟，衣襟就撕斷了。28撒母耳對他說："如此，今日耶和華使以色列國與你斷絕，將這國賜與比你更好的人。29以色列的大能者必不至說謊，也不至後悔。因為他迥非世人，決不後悔。"

30掃羅說："我有罪了，雖然如此，求你在我百姓的長老和以色列人面前抬舉我，同我回去，我好敬拜耶和華你的神。"31於是撒母耳轉身跟隨掃羅回去，掃羅就敬拜耶和華。

32撒母耳說："要把亞瑪力王亞甲帶到我這裏來。"

亞甲就歡歡喜喜地來到他面前，心裏說，死亡的苦難必定過去了。

33撒母耳說：

"你既用刀使婦人喪子，
  這樣，你母親在婦人中
  也必喪子。"

於是，撒母耳在吉甲耶和華面前將亞甲殺死。

34撒母耳回了拉瑪。掃羅上他所住的基比亞，回自己的家去了。35撒母耳直到死的日子，再沒有見掃羅，但撒母耳為掃羅悲傷，是因耶和華後悔立他為以色列的王。

22But Samuel replied:

"Does the LORD delight in burnt offerings and
  sacrifices
  as much as in obeying the voice of the LORD?
To obey is better than sacrifice,
  and to heed is better than the fat of rams.
23For rebellion is like the sin of divination,
  and arrogance like the evil of idolatry.
Because you have rejected the word of the
    LORD,
  he has rejected you as king."

24Then Saul said to Samuel, "I have sinned. I violated the LORD's command and your instructions. I was afraid of the people and so I gave in to them. 25Now I beg you, forgive my sin and come back with me, so that I may worship the LORD."

26But Samuel said to him, "I will not go back with you. You have rejected the word of the LORD, and the LORD has rejected you as king over Israel!"

27As Samuel turned to leave, Saul caught hold of the hem of his robe, and it tore. 28Samuel said to him, "The LORD has torn the kingdom of Israel from you today and has given it to one of your neighbors—to one better than you. 29He who is the Glory of Israel does not lie or change his mind; for he is not a man, that he should change his mind."

30Saul replied, "I have sinned. But please honor me before the elders of my people and before Israel; come back with me, so that I may worship the LORD your God." 31So Samuel went back with Saul, and Saul worshiped the LORD.

32Then Samuel said, "Bring me Agag king of the Amalekites."

Agag came to him confidently,[a] thinking, "Surely the bitterness of death is past."

33But Samuel said,

"As your sword has made women childless,
  so will your mother be childless among
    women."

And Samuel put Agag to death before the LORD at Gilgal.

34Then Samuel left for Ramah, but Saul went up to his home in Gibeah of Saul. 35Until the day Samuel died, he did not go to see Saul again, though Samuel mourned for him. And the LORD was grieved that he had made Saul king over Israel.

a 32 Or him trembling, yet

Samuel Anoints David

16 The LORD said to Samuel, "How long will you mourn for Saul, since I have rejected him as king over Israel? Fill your horn with oil and be on your way; I am sending you to Jesse of Bethlehem. I have chosen one of his sons to be king."

²But Samuel said, "How can I go? Saul will hear about it and kill me."

The LORD said, "Take a heifer with you and say, 'I have come to sacrifice to the LORD.' ³Invite Jesse to the sacrifice, and I will show you what to do. You are to anoint for me the one I indicate."

⁴Samuel did what the LORD said. When he arrived at Bethlehem, the elders of the town trembled when they met him. They asked, "Do you come in peace?"

⁵Samuel replied, "Yes, in peace; I have come to sacrifice to the LORD. Consecrate yourselves and come to the sacrifice with me." Then he consecrated Jesse and his sons and invited them to the sacrifice.

⁶When they arrived, Samuel saw Eliab and thought, "Surely the LORD's anointed stands here before the LORD."

⁷But the LORD said to Samuel, "Do not consider his appearance or his height, for I have rejected him. The LORD does not look at the things man looks at. Man looks at the outward appearance, but the LORD looks at the heart."

⁸Then Jesse called Abinadab and had him pass in front of Samuel. But Samuel said, "The LORD has not chosen this one either." ⁹Jesse then had Shammah pass by, but Samuel said, "Nor has the LORD chosen this one." ¹⁰Jesse had seven of his sons pass before Samuel, but Samuel said to him, "The LORD has not chosen these." ¹¹So he asked Jesse, "Are these all the sons you have?"

"There is still the youngest," Jesse answered, "but he is tending the sheep."

Samuel said, "Send for him; we will not sit down[a] until he arrives."

¹²So he sent and had him brought in. He was ruddy, with a fine appearance and handsome features.

Then the LORD said, "Rise and anoint him; he is the one."

¹³So Samuel took the horn of oil and anointed him in the presence of his brothers, and from that day on the Spirit of the LORD came upon David in power. Samuel then went to Ramah.

撒母耳膏大衞

16 耶和華對撒母耳說："我既厭棄掃羅作以色列的王，你為他悲傷要到幾時呢？你將膏油盛滿了角，我差遣你往伯利恆人耶西那裏去，因為我在他眾子之內預定一個作王的。"

²撒母耳說："我怎能去呢？掃羅若聽見，必要殺我。"

耶和華說："你可以帶一隻牛犢去，就說：'我來是要向耶和華獻祭。'³你要請耶西來吃祭肉，我就指示你所當行的事。我所指給你的人，你要膏他。"

⁴撒母耳就照耶和華的話去行。到了伯利恆，那城裏的長老都戰戰兢兢地出來迎接他，問他說："你是為平安來的嗎？"

⁵他說："為平安來的，我是給耶和華獻祭。你們當自潔，來與我同吃祭肉。"撒母耳就使耶西和他眾子自潔，請他們來吃祭肉。

⁶他們來的時候，撒母耳看見以利押，就心裏說，耶和華的受膏者必定在他面前。

⁷耶和華卻對撒母耳說："不要看他的外貌和他身材高大，我不揀選他。因為耶和華不像人看人：人是看外貌，耶和華是看內心。"

⁸耶西叫亞比拿達從撒母耳面前經過，撒母耳說："耶和華也不揀選他。"⁹耶西又叫沙瑪從撒母耳面前經過，撒母耳說："耶和華也不揀選他。"¹⁰耶西叫他七個兒子都從撒母耳面前經過，撒母耳說："這都不是耶和華所揀選的。"¹¹撒母耳對耶西說："你的兒子都在這裏嗎？"

他回答說："還有個小的，現在放羊。"

撒母耳對耶西說："你打發人去叫他來；他若不來，我們必不坐席。"

¹²耶西就打發人去叫了他來。他面色光紅，雙目清秀，容貌俊美。

耶和華說："這就是他，你起來膏他。"

¹³撒母耳就用角裏的膏油，在他諸兄中膏了他。從這日起，耶和華的靈就大大感動大衞。撒母耳起身回拉瑪去了。

---

a 11 Some Septuagint manuscripts; Hebrew not gather around

大衛服侍掃羅

14耶和華的靈離開掃羅，有惡魔從耶和華那裏來擾亂他。

15掃羅的臣僕對他說：「現在有惡魔從神那裏來擾亂你。16我們的主可以吩咐面前的臣僕，找一個善於彈琴的來，等神那裏來的惡魔臨到你身上的時候，使他用手彈琴，你就好了。」

17掃羅對臣僕說：「你們可以為我找一個善於彈琴的，帶到我這裏來。」

18其中有一個少年人說：「我曾見伯利恆人耶西的一個兒子善於彈琴，是大有勇敢的戰士，說話合宜，容貌俊美，耶和華也與他同在。」

19於是掃羅差遣使者去見耶西，說：「請你打發你放羊的兒子大衛到我這裏來。」20耶西就把幾個餅和一皮袋酒，並一隻山羊羔，都馱在驢上，交給他兒子大衛，送與掃羅。

21大衛到了掃羅那裏，就侍立在掃羅面前。掃羅甚喜愛他，他就作了掃羅拿兵器的人。22掃羅差遣人去見耶西，說：「求你容大衛侍立在我面前，因為他在我眼前蒙了恩。」

23從神那裏來的惡魔臨到掃羅身上的時候，大衛就拿琴用手而彈，掃羅便舒暢爽快，惡魔離了他。

大衛與歌利亞

17非利士人招聚他們的軍旅，要來爭戰，聚集在屬猶大的梭哥，安營在梭哥和亞西加中間的以弗大憫。2掃羅和以色列人也聚集，在以拉谷安營，擺列隊伍要與非利士人打仗。3非利士人站在這邊山上，以色列人站在那邊山上，當中有谷。

4從非利士營中出來一個討戰的人，名叫歌利亞，是迦特人，身高六肘零一虎口；5頭戴銅盔，身穿鎧甲，甲重五千舍客勒；6腿上有銅護膝，兩肩之中背負銅戟；7槍桿粗如織布的機軸，鐵槍頭重六百舍客勒。

David in Saul's Service

14Now the Spirit of the LORD had departed from Saul, and an evil[a] spirit from the LORD tormented him.

15Saul's attendants said to him, "See, an evil spirit from God is tormenting you. 16Let our lord command his servants here to search for someone who can play the harp. He will play when the evil spirit from God comes upon you, and you will feel better."

17So Saul said to his attendants, "Find someone who plays well and bring him to me."

18One of the servants answered, "I have seen a son of Jesse of Bethlehem who knows how to play the harp. He is a brave man and a warrior. He speaks well and is a fine-looking man. And the LORD is with him."

19Then Saul sent messengers to Jesse and said, "Send me your son David, who is with the sheep." 20So Jesse took a donkey loaded with bread, a skin of wine and a young goat and sent them with his son David to Saul.

21David came to Saul and entered his service. Saul liked him very much, and David became one of his armor-bearers. 22Then Saul sent word to Jesse, saying, "Allow David to remain in my service, for I am pleased with him."

23Whenever the spirit from God came upon Saul, David would take his harp and play. Then relief would come to Saul; he would feel better, and the evil spirit would leave him.

David and Goliath

17Now the Philistines gathered their forces for war and assembled at Socoh in Judah. They pitched camp at Ephes Dammim, between Socoh and Azekah. 2Saul and the Israelites assembled and camped in the Valley of Elah and drew up their battle line to meet the Philistines. 3The Philistines occupied one hill and the Israelites another, with the valley between them.

4A champion named Goliath, who was from Gath, came out of the Philistine camp. He was over nine feet[b] tall. 5He had a bronze helmet on his head and wore a coat of scale armor of bronze weighing five thousand shekels[c]; 6on his legs he wore bronze greaves, and a bronze javelin was slung on his back. 7His spear shaft was like a weaver's rod, and its iron point weighed six hundred shekels.[d] His shield bearer

---

a 14 Or injurious; also in verses 15, 16 and 23　　b 4 Hebrew was six cubits and a span (about 3 meters)　　c 5 That is, about 125 pounds (about 57 kilograms)　　d 7 That is, about 15 pounds (about 7 kilograms)

went ahead of him.

⁸Goliath stood and shouted to the ranks of Israel, "Why do you come out and line up for battle? Am I not a Philistine, and are you not the servants of Saul? Choose a man and have him come down to me. ⁹If he is able to fight and kill me, we will become your subjects; but if I overcome him and kill him, you will become our subjects and serve us." ¹⁰Then the Philistine said, "This day I defy the ranks of Israel! Give me a man and let us fight each other." ¹¹On hearing the Philistine's words, Saul and all the Israelites were dismayed and terrified.

¹²Now David was the son of an Ephrathite named Jesse, who was from Bethlehem in Judah. Jesse had eight sons, and in Saul's time he was old and well advanced in years. ¹³Jesse's three oldest sons had followed Saul to the war: The firstborn was Eliab; the second, Abinadab; and the third, Shammah. ¹⁴David was the youngest. The three oldest followed Saul, ¹⁵but David went back and forth from Saul to tend his father's sheep at Bethlehem.

¹⁶For forty days the Philistine came forward every morning and evening and took his stand.

¹⁷Now Jesse said to his son David, "Take this ephah*ᵃ* of roasted grain and these ten loaves of bread for your brothers and hurry to their camp. ¹⁸Take along these ten cheeses to the commander of their unit.*ᵇ* See how your brothers are and bring back some assurance*ᶜ* from them. ¹⁹They are with Saul and all the men of Israel in the Valley of Elah, fighting against the Philistines."

²⁰Early in the morning David left the flock with a shepherd, loaded up and set out, as Jesse had directed. He reached the camp as the army was going out to its battle positions, shouting the war cry. ²¹Israel and the Philistines were drawing up their lines facing each other. ²²David left his things with the keeper of supplies, ran to the battle lines and greeted his brothers. ²³As he was talking with them, Goliath, the Philistine champion from Gath, stepped out from his lines and shouted his usual defiance, and David heard it. ²⁴When the Israelites saw the man, they all ran from him in great fear.

²⁵Now the Israelites had been saying, "Do you see how this man keeps coming out? He comes out to defy Israel. The king will give great wealth to the man who kills him. He will also give him his daughter in marriage and will

有一個拿盾牌的人在他前面走。

⁸歌利亞對着以色列的軍隊站立，呼叫說：「你們出來擺列隊伍做甚麼呢？我不是非利士人嗎？你們不是掃羅的僕人嗎？可以從你們中間揀選一人，使他下到我這裏來。⁹他若能與我戰鬥，將我殺死，我們就作你們的僕人；我若勝了他，將他殺死，你們就作我們的僕人，服侍我們。」¹⁰那非利士人又說：「我今日向以色列人的軍隊罵陣。你們叫一個人出來，與我戰鬥。」¹¹掃羅和以色列眾人聽見非利士人的這些話，就驚惶，極其害怕。

¹²大衛是猶大 伯利恆的以法他人耶西的兒子。耶西有八個兒子。當掃羅的時候，耶西已經老邁。¹³耶西的三個大兒子跟隨掃羅出征。這出征的三個兒子：長子名叫以利押，次子名叫亞比拿達，三子名叫沙瑪。¹⁴大衛是最小的；那三個大兒子跟隨掃羅。¹⁵大衛有時離開掃羅回伯利恆，放他父親的羊。

¹⁶那非利士人早晚都出來站着，如此四十日。

¹⁷一日，耶西對他兒子大衛說："你拿一伊法烘了的穗子和十個餅，速速地送到營裏去，交給你哥哥們；¹⁸再拿這十塊奶餅，送給他們的千夫長，且問你哥哥們好，向他們要一封信來。"¹⁹掃羅與大衛的三個哥哥和以色列眾人，在以拉谷與非利士人打仗。

²⁰大衛早晨起來，將羊交託一個看守的人，照着他父親所吩咐的話，帶着食物去了。到了輜重營，軍兵剛出到戰場，吶喊要戰。²¹以色列人和非利士人都擺列隊伍，彼此相對。²²大衛把他帶來的食物留在看守物件人的手下，跑到戰場，問他哥哥們安。²³與他們說話的時候，那討戰的，就是屬迦特的非利士人歌利亞，從非利士隊中出來，說從前所說的話，大衛都聽見了。²⁴以色列眾人看見那人就逃跑，極其害怕。

²⁵以色列人彼此說："這上來的人你看見了嗎？他上來是要向以色列人罵陣。若有能殺他的，王必賞賜他大財，將自己的女兒給他為妻，並在

a 17 That is, probably about 3/5 bushel (about 22 liters)
b 18 Hebrew *thousand*   *c* 18 Or *some token;* or *some pledge of spoils*

以色列人中免他父家納糧當差。"

26大衛問站在旁邊的人說："有人殺這非利士人，除掉以色列人的恥辱，怎樣待他呢？這未受割禮的非利士人是誰呢？竟敢向永生神的軍隊罵陣嗎？"

27百姓照先前的話回答他說："有人能殺這非利士人，必如此如此待他。"

28大衛的長兄以利押聽見大衛與他們所說的話，就向他發怒，說："你下來做甚麼呢？在曠野的那幾隻羊，你交託了誰呢？我知道你的驕傲和你心裏的惡意，你下來特為要看爭戰。"

29大衛說："我做了甚麼呢？我來豈沒有緣故嗎？"30大衛就離開他轉向別人，照先前的話而問，百姓仍照先前的話回答他。31有人聽見大衛所說的話，就告訴了掃羅，掃羅便打發人叫他來。

32大衛對掃羅說："人都不必因那非利士人膽怯。你的僕人要去與那非利士人戰鬥。"

33掃羅說："你不能去與那非利士人戰鬥，因為你年紀太輕，他自幼就作戰士。"

34大衛對掃羅說："你僕人為父親放羊，有時來了獅子，有時來了熊，從羣中啣一隻羊羔去。35我就追趕牠，擊打牠，將羊羔從牠口中救出來。牠起來要害我，我就揪着牠的鬍子，將牠打死。36你僕人曾打死獅子和熊，這未受割禮的非利士人向永生神的軍隊罵陣，也必像獅子和熊一般。"37大衛又說："耶和華救我脫離獅子和熊的爪，也必救我脫離這非利士人的手。"

掃羅對大衛說："你可以去吧！耶和華必與你同在。"

38掃羅就把自己的戰衣給大衛穿上，將銅盔給他戴上，又給他穿上鎧甲。39大衛把刀跨在戰衣外，試試能走不能走。因為素來沒有穿慣，就對掃羅說：

"我穿戴這些不能走，因為素來沒有穿慣。"於是摘脫了。40他手中拿杖，又在溪中挑選了五塊光滑石子，放在袋裏，就是牧人帶的囊裏；手中拿着甩石的機弦，就去迎那非利士人。

41非利士人也漸漸地迎着大衛

exempt his father's family from taxes in Israel."

26David asked the men standing near him, "What will be done for the man who kills this Philistine and removes this disgrace from Israel? Who is this uncircumcised Philistine that he should defy the armies of the living God?"

27They repeated to him what they had been saying and told him, "This is what will be done for the man who kills him."

28When Eliab, David's oldest brother, heard him speaking with the men, he burned with anger at him and asked, "Why have you come down here? And with whom did you leave those few sheep in the desert? I know how conceited you are and how wicked your heart is; you came down only to watch the battle."

29"Now what have I done?" said David. "Can't I even speak?" 30He then turned away to someone else and brought up the same matter, and the men answered him as before. 31What David said was overheard and reported to Saul, and Saul sent for him.

32David said to Saul, "Let no one lose heart on account of this Philistine; your servant will go and fight him."

33Saul replied, "You are not able to go out against this Philistine and fight him; you are only a boy, and he has been a fighting man from his youth."

34But David said to Saul, "Your servant has been keeping his father's sheep. When a lion or a bear came and carried off a sheep from the flock, 35I went after it, struck it and rescued the sheep from its mouth. When it turned on me, I seized it by its hair, struck it and killed it. 36Your servant has killed both the lion and the bear; this uncircumcised Philistine will be like one of them, because he has defied the armies of the living God. 37The LORD who delivered me from the paw of the lion and the paw of the bear will deliver me from the hand of this Philistine."

Saul said to David, "Go, and the LORD be with you."

38Then Saul dressed David in his own tunic. He put a coat of armor on him and a bronze helmet on his head. 39David fastened on his sword over the tunic and tried walking around, because he was not used to them.

"I cannot go in these," he said to Saul, "because I am not used to them." So he took them off. 40Then he took his staff in his hand, chose five smooth stones from the stream, put them in the pouch of his shepherd's bag and, with his sling in his hand, approached the Philistine.

41Meanwhile, the Philistine, with his shield

bearer in front of him, kept coming closer to David. [42]He looked David over and saw that he was only a boy, ruddy and handsome, and he despised him. [43]He said to David, "Am I a dog, that you come at me with sticks?" And the Philistine cursed David by his gods. [44]"Come here," he said, "and I'll give your flesh to the birds of the air and the beasts of the field!"

[45]David said to the Philistine, "You come against me with sword and spear and javelin, but I come against you in the name of the LORD Almighty, the God of the armies of Israel, whom you have defied. [46]This day the LORD will hand you over to me, and I'll strike you down and cut off your head. Today I will give the carcasses of the Philistine army to the birds of the air and the beasts of the earth, and the whole world will know that there is a God in Israel. [47]All those gathered here will know that it is not by sword or spear that the LORD saves; for the battle is the LORD's, and he will give all of you into our hands."

[48]As the Philistine moved closer to attack him, David ran quickly toward the battle line to meet him. [49]Reaching into his bag and taking out a stone, he slung it and struck the Philistine on the forehead. The stone sank into his forehead, and he fell facedown on the ground.

[50]So David triumphed over the Philistine with a sling and a stone; without a sword in his hand he struck down the Philistine and killed him.

[51]David ran and stood over him. He took hold of the Philistine's sword and drew it from the scabbard. After he killed him, he cut off his head with the sword.

When the Philistines saw that their hero was dead, they turned and ran. [52]Then the men of Israel and Judah surged forward with a shout and pursued the Philistines to the entrance of Gath[a] and to the gates of Ekron. Their dead were strewn along the Shaaraim road to Gath and Ekron. [53]When the Israelites returned from chasing the Philistines, they plundered their camp. [54]David took the Philistine's head and brought it to Jerusalem, and he put the Philistine's weapons in his own tent.

[55]As Saul watched David going out to meet the Philistine, he said to Abner, commander of the army, "Abner, whose son is that young man?"

Abner replied, "As surely as you live, O king, I don't know."

[56]The king said, "Find out whose son this

來，拿盾牌的走在前頭。[42]非利士人觀看，見了大衛，就藐視他，因為他年輕，面色光紅，容貌俊美。[43]非利士人對大衛說：「你拿杖到我這裏來，我豈是狗呢？」非利士人就指着自己的神咒詛大衛。[44]非利士人又對大衛說：「來吧！我將你的肉給空中的飛鳥、田野的走獸吃。」

[45]大衛對非利士人說：「你來攻擊我，是靠着刀槍和銅戟；我來攻擊你，是靠着萬軍之耶和華的名，就是你所怒罵帶領以色列軍隊的神。[46]今日耶和華必將你交在我手裏。我必殺你，斬你的頭；又將非利士軍兵的屍首給空中的飛鳥、地上的野獸吃，使普天下的人都知道以色列中有神；[47]又使這眾人知道耶和華使人得勝，不是用刀用槍，因為爭戰的勝敗全在乎耶和華。他必將你們交在我們手裏。」

[48]非利士人起身，迎着大衛前來。大衛急忙迎着非利士人，往戰場跑去。[49]大衛用手從囊中掏出一塊石子來，用機弦甩去，打中非利士人的額，石子進入額內，他就仆倒，面伏於地。

[50]這樣，大衛用機弦甩石，勝了那非利士人，打死他；大衛手中卻沒有刀。

[51]大衛跑去，站在非利士人身旁，將他的刀從鞘中拔出來，殺死他，割了他的頭。

非利士眾人看見他們討戰的勇士死了，就都逃跑。[52]以色列人和猶大人便起身吶喊，追趕非利士人，直到迦特（註：或作「該」）和以革倫的城門。被殺的非利士人倒在沙拉音的路上，直到迦特和以革倫。[53]以色列人追趕非利士人回來，奪了他們的營盤。[54]大衛將那非利士人的頭拿到耶路撒冷，卻將他軍裝放在自己的帳棚裏。

[55]掃羅看見大衛去攻擊非利士人，就問元帥押尼珥說：「押尼珥啊，那少年人是誰的兒子？」

押尼珥說：「我敢在王面前起誓，我不知道。」

[56]王說：「你可以問問那幼年人

是誰的兒子。"

57大衛打死非利士人回來，押尼珥領他到掃羅面前，他手中拿着非利士人的頭。

58掃羅問他說："少年人哪，你是誰的兒子？"

大衛說："我是你僕人伯利恆人耶西的兒子。"

掃羅嫉妒大衛

18 大衛對掃羅說完了話，約拿單的心與大衛的心深相契合。約拿單愛大衛，如同愛自己的性命。2那日掃羅留住大衛，不容他再回父家。3約拿單愛大衛如同愛自己的性命，就與他結盟。4約拿單從身上脫下外袍，給了大衛，又將戰衣、刀、弓、腰帶都給了他。

5掃羅無論差遣大衛往何處去，他都做事精明。掃羅就立他作戰士長，眾百姓和掃羅的臣僕無不喜悅。

6大衛打死了那非利士人，同眾人回來的時候，婦女們從以色列各城裏出來，歡歡喜喜，打鼓擊磬，歌唱跳舞，迎接掃羅王。7眾婦女舞蹈唱和，說：

　"掃羅殺死千千，
　　大衛殺死萬萬。"

8掃羅甚發怒，不喜悅這話，就說："將萬萬歸大衛，千千歸我，只剩下王位沒有給他了。"9從這日起，掃羅就怒視大衛。

10次日，從神那裏來的惡魔大大降在掃羅身上，他就在家中胡言亂語。大衛照常彈琴，掃羅手裏拿着槍。11掃羅把槍一掄，心裏說："我要將大衛刺透，釘在牆上。"大衛躲避他兩次。

12掃羅懼怕大衛，因為耶和華離開自己，與大衛同在。13所以掃羅使大衛離開自己，立他為千夫長，他就領兵出入。14大衛做事無不精明，耶

young man is."

57As soon as David returned from killing the Philistine, Abner took him and brought him before Saul, with David still holding the Philistine's head.

58"Whose son are you, young man?" Saul asked him.

David said, "I am the son of your servant Jesse of Bethlehem."

Saul's Jealousy of David

18 After David had finished talking with Saul, Jonathan became one in spirit with David, and he loved him as himself. 2From that day Saul kept David with him and did not let him return to his father's house. 3And Jonathan made a covenant with David because he loved him as himself. 4Jonathan took off the robe he was wearing and gave it to David, along with his tunic, and even his sword, his bow and his belt.

5Whatever Saul sent him to do, David did it so successfully[a] that Saul gave him a high rank in the army. This pleased all the people, and Saul's officers as well.

6When the men were returning home after David had killed the Philistine, the women came out from all the towns of Israel to meet King Saul with singing and dancing, with joyful songs and with tambourines and lutes. 7As they danced, they sang:

　"Saul has slain his thousands,
　　and David his tens of thousands."

8Saul was very angry; this refrain galled him. "They have credited David with tens of thousands," he thought, "but me with only thousands. What more can he get but the kingdom?" 9And from that time on Saul kept a jealous eye on David.

10The next day an evil[b] spirit from God came forcefully upon Saul. He was prophesying in his house, while David was playing the harp, as he usually did. Saul had a spear in his hand 11and he hurled it, saying to himself, "I'll pin David to the wall." But David eluded him twice.

12Saul was afraid of David, because the LORD was with David but had left Saul. 13So he sent David away from him and gave him command over a thousand men, and David led the troops in their campaigns. 14In everything he did he had great success,[c] because the LORD was with

a 5 Or wisely　　b 10 Or injurious　　c 14 Or he was very wise him. [15]When Saul saw how successful[a] he was, he was afraid of him. [16]But all Israel and Judah loved David, because he led them in their campaigns.

[17]Saul said to David, "Here is my older daughter Merab. I will give her to you in marriage; only serve me bravely and fight the battles of the LORD." For Saul said to himself, "I will not raise a hand against him. Let the Philistines do that!"

[18]But David said to Saul, "Who am I, and what is my family or my father's clan in Israel, that I should become the king's son-in-law?" [19]So[b] when the time came for Merab, Saul's daughter, to be given to David, she was given in marriage to Adriel of Meholah.

[20]Now Saul's daughter Michal was in love with David, and when they told Saul about it, he was pleased. [21]"I will give her to him," he thought, "so that she may be a snare to him and so that the hand of the Philistines may be against him." So Saul said to David, "Now you have a second opportunity to become my son-in-law."

[22]Then Saul ordered his attendants: "Speak to David privately and say, 'Look, the king is pleased with you, and his attendants all like you; now become his son-in-law.' "

[23]They repeated these words to David. But David said, "Do you think it is a small matter to become the king's son-in-law? I'm only a poor man and little known."

[24]When Saul's servants told him what David had said, [25]Saul replied, "Say to David, 'The king wants no other price for the bride than a hundred Philistine foreskins, to take revenge on his enemies.' " Saul's plan was to have David fall by the hands of the Philistines.

[26]When the attendants told David these things, he was pleased to become the king's son-in-law. So before the allotted time elapsed, [27]David and his men went out and killed two hundred Philistines. He brought their foreskins and presented the full number to the king so that he might become the king's son-in-law. Then Saul gave him his daughter Michal in marriage.

[28]When Saul realized that the LORD was with David and that his daughter Michal loved David, [29]Saul became still more afraid of him, and he remained his enemy the rest of his days.

[30]The Philistine commanders continued to go out to battle, and as often as they did, David met with more success[c] than the rest of Saul's officers, and his name became well known.

和華也與他同在。[15]掃羅見大衛做事精明，就甚怕他。[16]但以色列和猶大眾人都愛大衛，因為他領他們出入。

[17]掃羅對大衛說："我將大女兒米拉給你為妻，只要你為我奮勇，為耶和華爭戰。"掃羅心裏說："我不好親手害他，要藉非利士人的手害他。"

[18]大衛對掃羅說："我是誰，我是甚麼出身，我父家在以色列中是何等的家，豈敢作王的女婿呢？"[19]掃羅的女兒米拉到了當給大衛的時候，掃羅卻給了米何拉人亞得列為妻。

[20]掃羅的次女米甲愛大衛。有人告訴掃羅，掃羅就喜悅。[21]掃羅心裏說："我將這女兒給大衛，作他的網羅，好藉非利士人的手害他。"所以掃羅對大衛說："你今日可以第二次作我的女婿。"

[22]掃羅吩咐臣僕說："你們暗中對大衛說：'王喜悅你，王的臣僕也都喜愛你，所以你當作王的女婿。'"

[23]掃羅的臣僕就照這話說給大衛聽。大衛說："你們以為作王的女婿是一件小事嗎？我是貧窮卑微的人。"

[24]掃羅的臣僕回奏說，大衛所說的如此如此。[25]掃羅說："你們要對大衛這樣說：'王不要甚麼聘禮，只要一百非利士人的陽皮，好在王的仇敵身上報仇。'"掃羅的意思要使大衛喪在非利士人的手裏。

[26]掃羅的臣僕將這話告訴大衛，大衛就歡喜作王的女婿。日期還沒有到，[27]大衛和跟隨他的人起身前往，殺了二百非利士人，將陽皮滿數交給王，為要作王的女婿。於是掃羅將女兒米甲給大衛為妻。

[28]掃羅見耶和華與大衛同在，又知道女兒米甲愛大衛，[29]就更怕大衛，常作大衛的仇敵。

[30]每逢非利士軍長出來打仗，大衛比掃羅的臣僕做事精明，因此他的名被人尊重。

---

a 15 Or wise   b 19 Or However,   c 30 Or David acted more wisely

掃羅圖謀殺大衛

19 掃羅對他兒子約拿單和眾臣僕說，要殺大衛；掃羅的兒子約拿單卻甚喜愛大衛。²約拿單告訴大衛說：「我父掃羅想要殺你，所以明日早晨你要小心，到一個僻靜地方藏身。³我就出到你所藏的田裏，站在我父親旁邊，與他談論。我看他情形怎樣，我必告訴你。」

⁴約拿單向他父親掃羅替大衛說好話，說：「王不可得罪王的僕人大衛，因為他未曾得罪你，他所行的都與你大有益處。⁵他拚命殺那非利士人，耶和華為以色列眾人大行拯救。那時你看見，甚是歡喜；現在為何無故要殺大衛，流無辜人的血，自己取罪呢？」

⁶掃羅聽了約拿單的話，就指着永生的耶和華起誓說：「我必不殺他。」

⁷約拿單叫大衛來，把這一切事告訴他，帶他去見掃羅。他就仍然侍立在掃羅面前。

⁸此後又有爭戰的事。大衛出去與非利士人打仗，大大殺敗他們，他們就在他面前逃跑。

⁹從耶和華那裏來的惡魔又降在掃羅身上（掃羅手裏拿槍坐在屋裏），大衛就用手彈琴。¹⁰掃羅想要刺透大衛，釘在牆上，他卻躲開，掃羅的槍刺入牆內。當夜大衛逃走，躲避了。

¹¹掃羅打發人到大衛的房屋那裏窺探他，要等到天亮殺他。大衛的妻米甲對他說：「你今夜若不逃命，明日你要被殺。」¹²於是米甲將大衛從窗戶裏縋下去，大衛就逃走，躲避了。¹³米甲把家中的神像放在牀上，頭枕在山羊毛裝的枕頭上，用被遮蓋。

¹⁴掃羅打發人去捉拿大衛，米甲說：「他病了。」

¹⁵掃羅又打發人去看大衛，說：「當連牀將他抬來，我好殺他。」¹⁶使者進去，看見牀上有神像，頭枕在山羊毛裝的枕頭上。

¹⁷掃羅對米甲說：「你為甚麼這樣欺哄我，放我仇敵逃走呢？」

Saul Tries to Kill David

19 Saul told his son Jonathan and all the attendants to kill David. But Jonathan was very fond of David ²and warned him, "My father Saul is looking for a chance to kill you. Be on your guard tomorrow morning; go into hiding and stay there. ³I will go out and stand with my father in the field where you are. I'll speak to him about you and will tell you what I find out."

⁴Jonathan spoke well of David to Saul his father and said to him, "Let not the king do wrong to his servant David; he has not wronged you, and what he has done has benefited you greatly. ⁵He took his life in his hands when he killed the Philistine. The LORD won a great victory for all Israel, and you saw it and were glad. Why then would you do wrong to an innocent man like David by killing him for no reason?"

⁶Saul listened to Jonathan and took this oath: "As surely as the LORD lives, David will not be put to death."

⁷So Jonathan called David and told him the whole conversation. He brought him to Saul, and David was with Saul as before.

⁸Once more war broke out, and David went out and fought the Philistines. He struck them with such force that they fled before him.

⁹But an evil*ᵃ* spirit from the LORD came upon Saul as he was sitting in his house with his spear in his hand. While David was playing the harp, ¹⁰Saul tried to pin him to the wall with his spear, but David eluded him as Saul drove the spear into the wall. That night David made good his escape.

¹¹Saul sent men to David's house to watch it and to kill him in the morning. But Michal, David's wife, warned him, "If you don't run for your life tonight, tomorrow you'll be killed." ¹²So Michal let David down through a window, and he fled and escaped. ¹³Then Michal took an idol*ᵇ* and laid it on the bed, covering it with a garment and putting some goats' hair at the head.

¹⁴When Saul sent the men to capture David, Michal said, "He is ill."

¹⁵Then Saul sent the men back to see David and told them, "Bring him up to me in his bed so that I may kill him." ¹⁶But when the men entered, there was the idol in the bed, and at the head was some goats' hair.

¹⁷Saul said to Michal, "Why did you deceive me like this and send my enemy away so that he escaped?"

---

a 9 Or injurious　　b 13 Hebrew teraphim; also in verse 16

Michal told him, "He said to me, 'Let me get away. Why should I kill you?'"

18When David had fled and made his escape, he went to Samuel at Ramah and told him all that Saul had done to him. Then he and Samuel went to Naioth and stayed there. 19Word came to Saul: "David is in Naioth at Ramah"; 20so he sent men to capture him. But when they saw a group of prophets prophesying, with Samuel standing there as their leader, the Spirit of God came upon Saul's men and they also prophesied. 21Saul was told about it, and he sent more men, and they prophesied too. Saul sent men a third time, and they also prophesied. 22Finally, he himself left for Ramah and went to the great cistern at Secu. And he asked, "Where are Samuel and David?"

"Over in Naioth at Ramah," they said.

23So Saul went to Naioth at Ramah. But the Spirit of God came even upon him, and he walked along prophesying until he came to Naioth. 24He stripped off his robes and also prophesied in Samuel's presence. He lay that way all that day and night. This is why people say, "Is Saul also among the prophets?"

David and Jonathan

20 Then David fled from Naioth at Ramah and went to Jonathan and asked, "What have I done? What is my crime? How have I wronged your father, that he is trying to take my life?"

2"Never!" Jonathan replied. "You are not going to die! Look, my father doesn't do anything, great or small, without confiding in me. Why would he hide this from me? It's not so!"

3But David took an oath and said, "Your father knows very well that I have found favor in your eyes, and he has said to himself, 'Jonathan must not know this or he will be grieved.' Yet as surely as the LORD lives and as you live, there is only a step between me and death."

4Jonathan said to David, "Whatever you want me to do, I'll do for you."

5So David said, "Look, tomorrow is the New Moon festival, and I am supposed to dine with the king; but let me go and hide in the field until the evening of the day after tomorrow. 6If your father misses me at all, tell him, 'David earnestly asked my permission to hurry to Bethlehem, his hometown, because an annual sacrifice is being made there for his whole clan.' 7If he says, 'Very well,' then your servant is safe. But if he loses

米甲回答說："他對我說：'你放我走，不然，我要殺你。'"

18大衛逃避，來到拉瑪見撒母耳，將掃羅向他所行的事述說了一遍。他和撒母耳就往拿約去居住。19有人告訴掃羅說："大衛在拉瑪的拿約。"20掃羅打發人去捉拿大衛。去的人見有一班先知都受感說話，撒母耳站在其中監管他們。打發去的人也受神的靈感動說話。21有人將這事告訴掃羅，他又打發人去，他們也受感說話。掃羅第三次打發人去，他們也受感說話。22然後掃羅自己往拉瑪去，到了西沽的大井，問人說："撒母耳和大衛在哪裏呢？"

有人說："在拉瑪的拿約。"

23他就往拉瑪的拿約去。神的靈也感動他，一面走一面說話，直到拉瑪的拿約。24他就脫了衣服，在撒母耳面前受感說話，一晝一夜露體躺臥。因此有句俗語說："掃羅也列在先知中嗎？"

大衛與約拿單

20 大衛從拉瑪的拿約逃跑，來到約拿單那裏，對他說："我做了甚麼，有甚麼罪孽呢？在你父親面前犯了甚麼罪，他竟尋索我的性命呢？"

2約拿單回答說："斷然不是！你必不至死。我父做事，無論大小，沒有不叫我知道的。怎麼獨有這事隱瞞我呢？決不如此。"

3大衛又起誓說："你父親準知我在你眼前蒙恩。他心裏說，不如不叫約拿單知道，恐怕他愁煩。我指着永生的耶和華，又敢在你面前起誓，我離死不過一步。"

4約拿單對大衛："你心裏所求的，我必為你成就。"

5大衛對約拿單說："明日是初一，我當與王同席，求你容我去藏在田野，直到第三日晚上。6你父親若見我不在席上，你就說：'大衛切求我許他回本城伯利恆去，因為他全家在那裏獻年祭。'7你父親若說好，僕人就平安了；他若發怒，你就知道他決意要害我。8求你施恩與僕人，因為你在耶和華面前曾與僕人結盟。我若有罪，不如你自己殺我，何必將我交給我父親呢？」

9約拿單說：「斷無此事！我若知道我父親決意害你，我豈不告訴你呢？」

10大衛對約拿單說：「你父親若用厲言回答你，誰來告訴我呢？」

11約拿單對大衛說：「你我且往田野去。」二人就往田野去了。

12約拿單對大衛說：「願耶和華以色列的神為證。明日約在這時候，或第三日，我探我父親的意思，若向你有好意，我豈不打發人告訴你嗎？13我父親若有意害你，我不告訴你，使你平平安安地走，願耶和華重重地降罰與我。願耶和華與你同在，如同從前與我父親同在一樣。14你要照耶和華的慈愛恩待我，不但我活着的時候免我死亡，15就是我死後，耶和華從地上剪除你仇敵的時候，你也永不可向我家絕了恩惠。」

16於是約拿單與大衛家結盟，說：「願耶和華藉大衛的仇敵追討背約的罪。」17約拿單因愛大衛如同愛自己的性命，就使他再起誓。

18約拿單對他說：「明日是初一，你的座位空設，人必理會你不在那裏。19你等三日，就要速速下去，到你從前遇事所藏的地方，在以色磐石那裏等候。20我要向磐石旁邊射三箭，如同射箭靶一樣。21我要打發童子，說：『去把箭找來。』我若對童子說：『箭在後頭，把箭拿來』，你就可以回來，我指着永生的耶和華起誓，你必平安無事。22我若對童子說：『箭在前頭』，你就要去，因為是耶和華打發你去的。23至於你我今日所說的話，有耶和華在你我中間為證，直到永遠。」

24大衛就去藏在田野。到了初一日，王坐席要吃飯。25王照常坐在靠

his temper, you can be sure that he is determined to harm me. 8As for you, show kindness to your servant, for you have brought him into a covenant with you before the LORD. If I am guilty, then kill me yourself! Why hand me over to your father?"

9"Never!" Jonathan said. "If I had the least inkling that my father was determined to harm you, wouldn't I tell you?"

10David asked, "Who will tell me if your father answers you harshly?"

11"Come," Jonathan said, "let's go out into the field." So they went there together.

12Then Jonathan said to David: "By the LORD, the God of Israel, I will surely sound out my father by this time the day after tomorrow! If he is favorably disposed toward you, will I not send you word and let you know? 13But if my father is inclined to harm you, may the LORD deal with me, be it ever so severely, if I do not let you know and send you away safely. May the LORD be with you as he has been with my father. 14But show me unfailing kindness like that of the LORD as long as I live, so that I may not be killed, 15and do not ever cut off your kindness from my family—not even when the LORD has cut off every one of David's enemies from the face of the earth."

16So Jonathan made a covenant with the house of David, saying, "May the LORD call David's enemies to account." 17And Jonathan had David reaffirm his oath out of love for him, because he loved him as he loved himself.

18Then Jonathan said to David: "Tomorrow is the New Moon festival. You will be missed, because your seat will be empty. 19The day after tomorrow, toward evening, go to the place where you hid when this trouble began, and wait by the stone Ezel. 20I will shoot three arrows to the side of it, as though I were shooting at a target. 21Then I will send a boy and say, 'Go, find the arrows.' If I say to him, 'Look, the arrows are on this side of you; bring them here,' then come, because, as surely as the LORD lives, you are safe; there is no danger. 22But if I say to the boy, 'Look, the arrows are beyond you,' then you must go, because the LORD has sent you away. 23And about the matter you and I discussed—remember, the LORD is witness between you and me forever."

24So David hid in the field, and when the New Moon festival came, the king sat down to eat. 25He sat in his customary place by the wall, opposite Jonathan,[a] and Abner sat next to Saul, but David's place was empty. 26Saul said nothing that day, for he thought, "Something must have happened to David to make him ceremonially unclean—surely he is unclean." 27But the next day, the second day of the month, David's place was empty again. Then Saul said to his son Jonathan, "Why hasn't the son of Jesse come to the meal, either yesterday or today?"

28Jonathan answered, "David earnestly asked me for permission to go to Bethlehem. 29He said, 'Let me go, because our family is observing a sacrifice in the town and my brother has ordered me to be there. If I have found favor in your eyes, let me get away to see my brothers.' That is why he has not come to the king's table."

30Saul's anger flared up at Jonathan and he said to him, "You son of a perverse and rebellious woman! Don't I know that you have sided with the son of Jesse to your own shame and to the shame of the mother who bore you? 31As long as the son of Jesse lives on this earth, neither you nor your kingdom will be established. Now send and bring him to me, for he must die!"

32"Why should he be put to death? What has he done?" Jonathan asked his father. 33But Saul hurled his spear at him to kill him. Then Jonathan knew that his father intended to kill David.

34Jonathan got up from the table in fierce anger; on that second day of the month he did not eat, because he was grieved at his father's shameful treatment of David.

35In the morning Jonathan went out to the field for his meeting with David. He had a small boy with him, 36and he said to the boy, "Run and find the arrows I shoot." As the boy ran, he shot an arrow beyond him. 37When the boy came to the place where Jonathan's arrow had fallen, Jonathan called out after him, "Isn't the arrow beyond you?" 38Then he shouted, "Hurry! Go quickly! Don't stop!" The boy picked up the arrow and returned to his master. 39(The boy knew nothing of all this; only Jonathan and David knew.) 40Then Jonathan gave his weapons to the boy and said, "Go, carry them back to town."

41After the boy had gone, David got up from the south side [of the stone] and bowed down before Jonathan three times, with his face to the ground. Then they kissed each other and wept together—but David wept the most.

42Jonathan said to David, "Go in peace, for

a 25 Septuagint; Hebrew *wall. Jonathan arose*

牆的位上，約拿單侍立，押尼珥坐在掃羅旁邊，大衛的座位空設。26然而這日掃羅沒有說甚麼，他想大衛遇事，偶染不潔，他必定是不潔。27初二日大衛的座位還空設。掃羅問他兒子約拿單說："耶西的兒子為何昨日今日沒有來吃飯呢？"

28約拿單回答掃羅說："大衛切求我容他往伯利恆去。29他說：'求你容我去，因為我家在城裏有獻祭的事，我長兄吩咐我去。如今我若在你眼前蒙恩，求你容我去見我的弟兄。'所以大衛沒有赴王的席。"

30掃羅向約拿單發怒，對他說："你這頑梗背逆之婦人所生的，我豈不知道你喜悅耶西的兒子，自取羞辱，以致你母親露體蒙羞嗎？31耶西的兒子若在世間活著，你和你的國位必站立不住。現在你要打發人去，將他捉拿交給我。他是該死的！"

32約拿單對父親掃羅說："他為甚麼該死呢？他做了甚麼呢？"33掃羅向約拿單掄槍要刺他，約拿單就知道他父親決意要殺大衛。

34於是約拿單氣忿忿地從席上起來，在這初二日沒有吃飯。他因見父親羞辱大衛，就為大衛愁煩。

35次日早晨，約拿單按着與大衛約會的時候出到田野，有一個童子跟隨。36約拿單對童子說："你跑去，把我所射的箭找來。"童子跑去，約拿單就把箭射在童子前頭。37童子到了約拿單落箭之地，約拿單呼叫童子說："箭不是在你前頭嗎？"38約拿單又呼叫童子說："速速地去，不要遲延！"童子就拾起箭來，回到主人那裏。39童子卻不知道這是甚麼意思，只有約拿單和大衛知道。40約拿單將弓箭交給童子，吩咐說："你拿到城裏去。"

41童子一去，大衛就從磐石的南邊出來，俯伏在地，拜了三拜。二人親嘴，彼此哭泣，大衛哭得更慟。

42約拿單對大衛說："我們二人

曾指着耶和華的名起誓說：'願耶和
華在你我中間，並你我後裔中間為
證，直到永遠。'如今你平平安安地
去吧！"大衛就起身走了；約拿單也
回城裏去了。

大衛在挪伯

21 大衛到了挪伯祭司亞希米勒
那裏。亞希米勒戰戰兢兢地
出來迎接他，問他說："你
為甚麼獨自來，沒有人跟隨呢？"

²大衛回答祭司亞希米勒說：
"王吩咐我一件事說：'我差遣你委
託你的這件事，不要使人知道。'故
此我已派定少年人在某處等候我。
³現在你手下有甚麼？求你給我五個
餅，或是別樣的食物。"

⁴祭司對大衛說："我手下沒有
尋常的餅，只有聖餅，若少年人沒有
親近婦人才可以給。"

⁵大衛對祭司說："實在約有三
日我們沒有親近婦人。我出來的時
候，雖是尋常行路，少年人的器皿還
是潔淨的；何況今日不更是潔淨
嗎？"⁶祭司就拿聖餅給他，因為在
那裏沒有別樣餅，只有更換新餅，從
耶和華面前撤下來的陳設餅。

⁷當日有掃羅的一個臣子留在耶
和華面前。他名叫多益，是以東人，
作掃羅的司牧長。

⁸大衛問亞希米勒說："你手下
有槍有刀沒有？因為王的事甚急，連
刀劍器械我都沒有帶。"

⁹祭司說："你在以拉谷殺非利
士人歌利亞的那刀在這裏，裹在布
中，放在以弗得後邊，你要就可以拿
去。除此以外，再沒有別的。"

大衛說："這刀沒有可比的！
求你給我。"

大衛在迦特

¹⁰那日大衛起來，躲避掃羅，逃
到迦特王亞吉那裏。¹¹亞吉的臣僕對
亞吉說："這不是以色列國王大衛
嗎？那裏的婦女跳舞唱和，不是指着
他說：

we have sworn friendship with each other in the name of the LORD, saying, 'The LORD is witness between you and me, and between your descendants and my descendants forever.' " Then David left, and Jonathan went back to the town.

David at Nob

21 David went to Nob, to Ahimelech the priest. Ahimelech trembled when he met him, and asked, "Why are you alone? Why is no one with you?"

²David answered Ahimelech the priest, "The king charged me with a certain matter and said to me, 'No one is to know anything about your mission and your instructions.' As for my men, I have told them to meet me at a certain place. ³Now then, what do you have on hand? Give me five loaves of bread, or whatever you can find."

⁴But the priest answered David, "I don't have any ordinary bread on hand; however, there is some consecrated bread here—provided the men have kept themselves from women."

⁵David replied, "Indeed women have been kept from us, as usual whenever*ᵃ* I set out. The men's things*ᵇ* are holy even on missions that are not holy. How much more so today!" ⁶So the priest gave him the consecrated bread, since there was no bread there except the bread of the Presence that had been removed from before the LORD and replaced by hot bread on the day it was taken away.

⁷Now one of Saul's servants was there that day, detained before the LORD; he was Doeg the Edomite, Saul's head shepherd.

⁸David asked Ahimelech, "Don't you have a spear or a sword here? I haven't brought my sword or any other weapon, because the king's business was urgent."

⁹The priest replied, "The sword of Goliath the Philistine, whom you killed in the Valley of Elah, is here; it is wrapped in a cloth behind the ephod. If you want it, take it; there is no sword here but that one."

David said, "There is none like it; give it to me."

David at Gath

¹⁰That day David fled from Saul and went to Achish king of Gath. ¹¹But the servants of Achish said to him, "Isn't this David, the king of the land? Isn't he the one they sing about in their dances:

a 5 Or from us in the past few days since   b 5 Or bodies

" 'Saul has slain his thousands,
and David his tens of thousands'?"

¹²David took these words to heart and was very much afraid of Achish king of Gath. ¹³So he pretended to be insane in their presence; and while he was in their hands he acted like a madman, making marks on the doors of the gate and letting saliva run down his beard.

¹⁴Achish said to his servants, "Look at the man! He is insane! Why bring him to me? ¹⁵Am I so short of madmen that you have to bring this fellow here to carry on like this in front of me? Must this man come into my house?"

David at Adullam and Mizpah

22 David left Gath and escaped to the cave of Adullam. When his brothers and his father's household heard about it, they went down to him there. ²All those who were in distress or in debt or discontented gathered around him, and he became their leader. About four hundred men were with him.

³From there David went to Mizpah in Moab and said to the king of Moab, "Would you let my father and mother come and stay with you until I learn what God will do for me?" ⁴So he left them with the king of Moab, and they stayed with him as long as David was in the stronghold.

⁵But the prophet Gad said to David, "Do not stay in the stronghold. Go into the land of Judah." So David left and went to the forest of Hereth.

Saul Kills the Priests of Nob

⁶Now Saul heard that David and his men had been discovered. And Saul, spear in hand, was seated under the tamarisk tree on the hill at Gibeah, with all his officials standing around him. ⁷Saul said to them, "Listen, men of Benjamin! Will the son of Jesse give all of you fields and vineyards? Will he make all of you commanders of thousands and commanders of hundreds? ⁸Is that why you have all conspired against me? No one tells me when my son makes a covenant with the son of Jesse. None of you is concerned about me or tells me that my son has incited my servant to lie in wait for me, as he does today."

⁹But Doeg the Edomite, who was standing with Saul's officials, said, "I saw the son of Jesse come to Ahimelech son of Ahitub at Nob. ¹⁰Ahimelech inquired of the LORD for him; he also gave him provisions and the sword of Goliath the Philistine."

" '掃羅殺死千千，
大衛殺死萬萬' 嗎？"

¹²大衛將這話放在心裏，甚懼怕迦特王亞吉，¹³就在眾人面前改變了尋常的舉動，在他們手下假裝瘋癲，在城門的門扇上胡寫亂畫，使唾沫流在鬍子上。

¹⁴亞吉對臣僕說："你們看，這人是瘋子。為甚麼帶他到我這裏來呢？¹⁵我豈缺少瘋子，你們帶這人來在我面前瘋癲嗎？這人豈可進我的家呢？"

大衛在亞杜蘭洞與米斯巴

22 大衛就離開那裏，逃到亞杜蘭洞。他的弟兄和他父親的全家聽見了，就都下到他那裏。²凡受窘迫的、欠債的、心裏苦惱的，都聚集到大衛那裏。大衛就作他們的頭目，跟隨他的約有四百人。

³大衛從那裏往摩押的米斯巴去，對摩押王說："求你容我父母搬來，住在你們這裏，等我知道神要為我怎樣行。"⁴大衛領他父母到摩押王面前。大衛住山寨多少日子，他父母也住摩押王那裏多少日子。

⁵先知迦得對大衛說："你不要住在山寨，要往猶大地去。"大衛就離開那裏，進入哈列的樹林。

掃羅殺挪伯祭司

⁶掃羅在基比亞的拉瑪，坐在垂絲柳樹下，手裏拿著槍，眾臣僕侍立在左右。掃羅聽見大衛和跟隨他的人在何處，⁷就對左右侍立的臣僕說："便雅憫人哪，你們要聽我的話！耶西的兒子能將田地和葡萄園賜給你們各人嗎？能立你們各人作千夫長、百夫長嗎？⁸你們竟都結黨害我！我的兒子與耶西的兒子結盟的時候，無人告訴我；我的兒子挑唆我的臣子謀害我，就如今日的光景，也無人告訴我，為我憂慮。"

⁹那時以東人多益站在掃羅的臣僕中，對他說："我曾看見耶西的兒子到了挪伯亞希突的兒子亞希米勒那裏。¹⁰亞希米勒為他求問耶和華，又給他食物，並給他殺非利士人歌利亞的刀。"

11王就打發人將祭司亞希突的兒子亞希米勒和他父親的全家，就是住挪伯的祭司都召了來。他們就來見王。12掃羅說："亞希突的兒子，要聽我的話！"

他回答說："主啊，我在這裏。"

13掃羅對他說："你為甚麼與耶西的兒子結黨害我，將食物和刀給他，又為他求問神，使他起來謀害我，就如今日的光景？"

14亞希米勒回答王說："王的臣僕中有誰比大衛忠心呢？他是王的女婿，又是王的參謀，並且在王家中是尊貴的。15我豈是從今日才為他求問神呢？斷不是這樣！王不要將罪歸我和我父的全家；因為這事，無論大小，僕人都不知道。"

16王說："亞希米勒啊，你和你父的全家都是該死的！"

17王就吩咐左右的侍衛說："你們去殺耶和華的祭司，因為他們幫助大衛，又知道大衛逃跑，竟沒有告訴我。"

掃羅的臣子卻不肯伸手殺耶和華的祭司。

18王吩咐多益說："你去殺祭司吧！"以東人多益就去殺祭司，那日殺了穿細麻布以弗得的八十五人。19又用刀將祭司城挪伯的男女、孩童、吃奶的，和牛、羊、驢盡都殺滅。

20亞希突的兒子亞希米勒有一個兒子，名叫亞比亞他，逃到大衛那裏。21亞比亞他將掃羅殺耶和華祭司的事告訴大衛。22大衛對亞比亞他說："那日我見以東人多益在那裏，就知道他必告訴掃羅。你父的全家喪命，都是因我的緣故。23你可以住在我這裏，不要懼怕，因為尋索你命的，就是尋索我的命。你在我這裏可得保全。"

大衛拯救基伊拉

23有人告訴大衛說："非利士人攻擊基伊拉，搶奪禾場。"2所以大衛求問耶和華說："我去攻打那些非利士人可以不可以？"

耶和華對大衛說："你可以去攻打非利士人，拯救基伊拉。"

3跟隨大衛的人對他說："我們

11Then the king sent for the priest Ahimelech son of Ahitub and his father's whole family, who were the priests at Nob, and they all came to the king. 12Saul said, "Listen now, son of Ahitub."

"Yes, my lord," he answered.

13Saul said to him, "Why have you conspired against me, you and the son of Jesse, giving him bread and a sword and inquiring of God for him, so that he has rebelled against me and lies in wait for me, as he does today?"

14Ahimelech answered the king, "Who of all your servants is as loyal as David, the king's son-in-law, captain of your bodyguard and highly respected in your household? 15Was that day the first time I inquired of God for him? Of course not! Let not the king accuse your servant or any of his father's family, for your servant knows nothing at all about this whole affair."

16But the king said, "You will surely die, Ahimelech, you and your father's whole family."

17Then the king ordered the guards at his side: "Turn and kill the priests of the LORD, because they too have sided with David. They knew he was fleeing, yet they did not tell me."

But the king's officials were not willing to raise a hand to strike the priests of the LORD.

18The king then ordered Doeg, "You turn and strike down the priests." So Doeg the Edomite turned and struck them down. That day he killed eighty-five men who wore the linen ephod. 19He also put to the sword Nob, the town of the priests, with its men and women, its children and infants, and its cattle, donkeys and sheep.

20But Abiathar, a son of Ahimelech son of Ahitub, escaped and fled to join David. 21He told David that Saul had killed the priests of the LORD. 22Then David said to Abiathar: "That day, when Doeg the Edomite was there, I knew he would be sure to tell Saul. I am responsible for the death of your father's whole family. 23Stay with me; don't be afraid; the man who is seeking your life is seeking mine also. You will be safe with me."

David Saves Keilah

23When David was told, "Look, the Philistines are fighting against Keilah and are looting the threshing floors," 2he inquired of the LORD, saying, "Shall I go and attack these Philistines?"

The LORD answered him, "Go, attack the Philistines and save Keilah."

3But David's men said to him, "Here in Judah

we are afraid. How much more, then, if we go to Keilah against the Philistine forces!"

⁴Once again David inquired of the LORD, and the LORD answered him, "Go down to Keilah, for I am going to give the Philistines into your hand." ⁵So David and his men went to Keilah, fought the Philistines and carried off their livestock. He inflicted heavy losses on the Philistines and saved the people of Keilah. ⁶(Now Abiathar son of Ahimelech had brought the ephod down with him when he fled to David at Keilah.)

Saul Pursues David

⁷Saul was told that David had gone to Keilah, and he said, "God has handed him over to me, for David has imprisoned himself by entering a town with gates and bars." ⁸And Saul called up all his forces for battle, to go down to Keilah to besiege David and his men.

⁹When David learned that Saul was plotting against him, he said to Abiathar the priest, "Bring the ephod." ¹⁰David said, "O LORD, God of Israel, your servant has heard definitely that Saul plans to come to Keilah and destroy the town on account of me. ¹¹Will the citizens of Keilah surrender me to him? Will Saul come down, as your servant has heard? O LORD, God of Israel, tell your servant."

And the LORD said, "He will."

¹²Again David asked, "Will the citizens of Keilah surrender me and my men to Saul?"

And the LORD said, "They will."

¹³So David and his men, about six hundred in number, left Keilah and kept moving from place to place. When Saul was told that David had escaped from Keilah, he did not go there.

¹⁴David stayed in the desert strongholds and in the hills of the Desert of Ziph. Day after day Saul searched for him, but God did not give David into his hands.

¹⁵While David was at Horesh in the Desert of Ziph, he learned that Saul had come out to take his life. ¹⁶And Saul's son Jonathan went to David at Horesh and helped him find strength in God. ¹⁷"Don't be afraid," he said. "My father Saul will not lay a hand on you. You will be king over Israel, and I will be second to you. Even my father Saul knows this." ¹⁸The two of them made a covenant before the LORD. Then Jonathan went home, but David remained at Horesh.

¹⁹The Ziphites went up to Saul at Gibeah and said, "Is not David hiding among us in the strongholds at Horesh, on the hill of Hakilah, south of Jeshimon? ²⁰Now, O king, come down

在猶大地這裏尚且懼怕,何況往基伊拉去攻打非利士人的軍旅呢?"⁴大衛又求問耶和華。耶和華回答說:"你起身下基伊拉去,我必將非利士人交在你手裏。"⁵大衛和跟隨他的人往基伊拉去,與非利士人打仗,大大殺敗他們,又奪獲他們的牲畜。這樣,大衛救了基伊拉的居民。⁶亞希米勒的兒子亞比亞他逃到基伊拉見大衛的時候,手裏拿着以弗得。

掃羅追捕大衛

⁷有人告訴掃羅說:"大衛到了基伊拉。"掃羅說:"他進了有門有閂的城,困閉在裏頭,這是神將他交在我手裏了。"⁸於是掃羅招聚眾民,要下去攻打基伊拉城,圍困大衛和跟隨他的人。

⁹大衛知道掃羅設計謀害他,就對祭司亞比亞他說:"將以弗得拿過來。"¹⁰大衛禱告說:"耶和華以色列的神啊,你僕人聽真了掃羅要往基伊拉來,為我的緣故滅城。¹¹基伊拉人將我交在掃羅手裏不交?掃羅照着你僕人所聽的話下來不下來?耶和華以色列的神啊!求你指示僕人。"

耶和華說:"掃羅必下來。"

¹²大衛又說:"基伊拉人將我和跟隨我的人交在掃羅手裏不交?"

耶和華說:"必交出來。"

¹³大衛和跟隨他的約有六百人,就起身出了基伊拉,往他們所能往的地方去。有人告訴掃羅,大衛離開基伊拉逃走,於是掃羅不出來了。

¹⁴大衛住在曠野的山寨裏,常在西弗曠野的山地。掃羅天天尋索大衛,神卻不將大衛交在他手裏。

¹⁵大衛知道掃羅出來尋索他的命。那時他住在西弗曠野的樹林裏。¹⁶掃羅的兒子約拿單起身,往那樹林裏去見大衛,使他倚靠神得以堅固。¹⁷對他說:"不要懼怕,我父掃羅的手必不加害於你。你必作以色列的王,我也作你的宰相。這事我父掃羅知道了。"¹⁸於是二人在耶和華面前立約。大衛仍住在樹林裏,約拿單回家去了。

¹⁹西弗人上到基比亞見掃羅,說:"大衛不是在我們那裏的樹林裏山寨中,曠野南邊的哈基拉山藏着嗎?²⁰王啊,請你隨你的心願下來,

我們必親自將他交在王的手裏。"

²¹掃羅說："願耶和華賜福與你們，因你們顧恤我。²²請你們回去，再確實查明他的住處和行蹤，是誰看見他在那裏。因為我聽見人說他甚狡猾，²³所以要看準他藏匿的地方，回來據實地告訴我，我就與你們同去。他若在猶大的境內，我必從千門萬戶中搜出他來。"

²⁴西弗人就起身，在掃羅以先往西弗去。大衛和跟隨他的人卻在瑪雲曠野南邊的亞拉巴。²⁵掃羅和跟隨他的人去尋找大衛。有人告訴大衛，他就下到磐石，住在瑪雲的曠野。掃羅聽見，便在瑪雲的曠野追趕大衛。

²⁶掃羅在山這邊走，大衛和跟隨他的人在山那邊走。大衛急忙躲避掃羅，因為掃羅和跟隨他的人，四面圍住大衛和跟隨他的人，要拿獲他們。²⁷忽有使者來報告掃羅說："非利士人犯境搶掠，請王快快回去！"²⁸於是掃羅不追趕大衛，回去攻打非利士人。因此那地方名叫西拉哈瑪希羅結。²⁹大衛從那裏上去，住在隱基底的山寨裏。

大衛不殺掃羅

24 掃羅追趕非利士人回來，有人告訴他說："大衛在隱基底的曠野。"²掃羅就從以色列人中挑選三千精兵，率領他們往野羊的磐石去，尋索大衛和跟隨他的人。

³到了路旁的羊圈，在那裏有洞，掃羅進去大解。大衛和跟隨他的人正藏在洞裏的深處。⁴跟隨的人對大衛說："耶和華曾應許你說：'我要將你的仇敵交在你手裏，你可以任意待他。'如今時候到了。"大衛就起來，悄悄地割下掃羅外袍的衣襟。

⁵隨後大衛心中自責，因為割下掃羅的衣襟。⁶對跟隨他的人說："我的主乃是耶和華的受膏者，我在耶和華面前萬不敢伸手害他，因他是耶和華的受膏者。"⁷大衛用這話攔住跟隨他的人，不容他們起來害

whenever it pleases you to do so, and we will be responsible for handing him over to the king."

²¹Saul replied, "The LORD bless you for your concern for me. ²²Go and make further preparation. Find out where David usually goes and who has seen him there. They tell me he is very crafty. ²³Find out about all the hiding places he uses and come back to me with definite information.*ᵃ* Then I will go with you; if he is in the area, I will track him down among all the clans of Judah."

²⁴So they set out and went to Ziph ahead of Saul. Now David and his men were in the Desert of Maon, in the Arabah south of Jeshimon. ²⁵Saul and his men began the search, and when David was told about it, he went down to the rock and stayed in the Desert of Maon. When Saul heard this, he went into the Desert of Maon in pursuit of David.

²⁶Saul was going along one side of the mountain, and David and his men were on the other side, hurrying to get away from Saul. As Saul and his forces were closing in on David and his men to capture them, ²⁷a messenger came to Saul, saying, "Come quickly! The Philistines are raiding the land." ²⁸Then Saul broke off his pursuit of David and went to meet the Philistines. That is why they call this place Sela Hammahlekoth.*ᵇ* ²⁹And David went up from there and lived in the strongholds of En Gedi.

David Spares Saul's Life

24 After Saul returned from pursuing the Philistines, he was told, "David is in the Desert of En Gedi." ²So Saul took three thousand chosen men from all Israel and set out to look for David and his men near the Crags of the Wild Goats.

³He came to the sheep pens along the way; a cave was there, and Saul went in to relieve himself. David and his men were far back in the cave. ⁴The men said, "This is the day the LORD spoke of when he said*ᶜ* to you, 'I will give your enemy into your hands for you to deal with as you wish.'" Then David crept up unnoticed and cut off a corner of Saul's robe.

⁵Afterward, David was conscience-stricken for having cut off a corner of his robe. ⁶He said to his men, "The LORD forbid that I should do such a thing to my master, the LORD's anointed, or lift my hand against him; for he is the anointed of the LORD." ⁷With these words David rebuked his men and did not allow them to

a 23 Or me at Nacon   b 28 Sela Hammahlekoth means rock of parting.   c 4 Or "Today the LORD is saying

attack Saul. And Saul left the cave and went his way.

8Then David went out of the cave and called out to Saul, "My lord the king!" When Saul looked behind him, David bowed down and prostrated himself with his face to the ground. 9He said to Saul, "Why do you listen when men say, 'David is bent on harming you'? 10This day you have seen with your own eyes how the LORD delivered you into my hands in the cave. Some urged me to kill you, but I spared you; I said, 'I will not lift my hand against my master, because he is the LORD's anointed.' 11See, my father, look at this piece of your robe in my hand! I cut off the corner of your robe but did not kill you. Now understand and recognize that I am not guilty of wrongdoing or rebellion. I have not wronged you, but you are hunting me down to take my life. 12May the LORD judge between you and me. And may the LORD avenge the wrongs you have done to me, but my hand will not touch you. 13As the old saying goes, 'From evildoers come evil deeds,' so my hand will not touch you.

14"Against whom has the king of Israel come out? Whom are you pursuing? A dead dog? A flea? 15May the LORD be our judge and decide between us. May he consider my cause and uphold it; may he vindicate me by delivering me from your hand."

16When David finished saying this, Saul asked, "Is that your voice, David my son?" And he wept aloud. 17"You are more righteous than I," he said. "You have treated me well, but I have treated you badly. 18You have just now told me of the good you did to me; the LORD delivered me into your hands, but you did not kill me. 19When a man finds his enemy, does he let him get away unharmed? May the LORD reward you well for the way you treated me today. 20I know that you will surely be king and that the kingdom of Israel will be established in your hands. 21Now swear to me by the LORD that you will not cut off my descendants or wipe out my name from my father's family."

22So David gave his oath to Saul. Then Saul returned home, but David and his men went up to the stronghold.

David, Nabal and Abigail

25 Now Samuel died, and all Israel assembled and mourned for him; and they buried him at his home in Ramah.

Then David moved down into the Desert of

掃羅。掃羅起來，從洞裏出去行路。

8隨後大衛也起來，從洞裏出去，呼叫掃羅說："我主，我王！"掃羅回頭觀看，大衛就屈身臉伏於地下拜。9大衛對掃羅說："你為何聽信人的讒言，說：'大衛想要害你'呢？10今日你親眼看見在洞中耶和華將你交在我手裏，有人叫我殺你，我卻愛惜你，說：'我不敢伸手害我的主，因為他是耶和華的受膏者。'11我父啊！看看你外袍的衣襟在我手中。我割下你的衣襟，沒有殺你，你由此可以知道我沒有惡意叛逆你。你雖然獵取我的命，我卻沒有得罪你。12願耶和華在你我中間判斷是非，在你身上為我伸冤，我卻不親手加害於你。13古人有句俗語說：'惡事出於惡人。'我卻不親手加害於你。

14"以色列王出來要尋找誰呢？追趕誰呢？不過追趕一條死狗，一個虼蚤就是了。15願耶和華在你我中間施行審判，斷定是非，並且鑒察，為我伸冤，救我脫離你的手。"

16大衛向掃羅說完這話，掃羅說："我兒大衛，這是你的聲音嗎？"就放聲大哭。17對大衛說："你比我公義，因為你以善待我，我卻以惡待你。18你今日顯明是以善待我，因為耶和華將我交在你手裏，你卻沒有殺我。19人若遇見仇敵，豈肯放他平安無事地去呢？願耶和華因你今日向我所行的，以善報你。20我也知道你必要作王，以色列的國必堅立在你手裏。21現在你要指着耶和華向我起誓，不剪除我的後裔，在我父家不滅沒我的名。"

22於是大衛向掃羅起誓，掃羅就回家去；大衛和跟隨他的人上山寨去了。

大衛、拿八與亞比該

25 撒母耳死了，以色列眾人聚集，為他哀哭，將他葬在拉瑪他自己的墳墓裏（註："墳墓"原文作"房屋"）。

大衛起身下到巴蘭的曠野。

²在瑪雲有一個人，他的產業在迦密，是一個大富戶，有三千綿羊，一千山羊。他正在迦密剪羊毛。³那人名叫拿八，是迦勒族的人；他的妻名叫亞比該，是聰明俊美的婦人。拿八為人剛愎兇惡。

⁴大衛在曠野聽見說拿八剪羊毛，⁵大衛就打發十個僕人，吩咐他們說："你們上迦密去見拿八，提我的名問他安。⁶要對那富戶如此說：'願你平安，願你家平安，願你一切所有的都平安！

⁷ "'現在我聽說有人為你剪羊毛。你的牧人在迦密的時候，和我們在一處，我們沒有欺負他們，他們也未曾失落甚麼。⁸可以問你的僕人，他們必告訴你。所以願我的僕人在你眼前蒙恩，因為是在好日子來的。求你隨手取點賜與僕人和你兒子大衛。'"

⁹大衛的僕人到了，將這話提大衛的名都告訴了拿八，就住了口。

¹⁰拿八回答大衛的僕人說："大衛是誰？耶西的兒子是誰？近來悖逆主人奔逃的僕人甚多。¹¹我豈可將飲食和為我剪羊毛人所宰的肉，給我不知道從哪裏來的人呢？"

¹²大衛的僕人就轉身從原路回去，照這話告訴大衛。¹³大衛向跟隨他的人說："你們各人都要帶上刀。"眾人就都帶上刀，大衛也帶上刀。跟隨大衛上去的約有四百人，留下二百人看守器具。

¹⁴有拿八的一個僕人告訴拿八的妻亞比該說："大衛從曠野打發使者來問我主人的安，主人卻辱罵他們。¹⁵但是那些人待我們甚好。我們在田野與他們來往的時候，沒有受他們的欺負，也未曾失落甚麼。¹⁶我們在他們那裏牧羊的時候，他們晝夜作我們的保障。¹⁷所以你當籌劃，看怎樣行才好。不然，禍患定要臨到我主人和他全家。他性情兇暴，無人敢與他說話。"

¹⁸亞比該急忙將二百餅，兩皮袋

Maon.ᵃ ²A certain man in Maon, who had property there at Carmel, was very wealthy. He had a thousand goats and three thousand sheep, which he was shearing in Carmel. ³His name was Nabal and his wife's name was Abigail. She was an intelligent and beautiful woman, but her husband, a Calebite, was surly and mean in his dealings.

⁴While David was in the desert, he heard that Nabal was shearing sheep. ⁵So he sent ten young men and said to them, "Go up to Nabal at Carmel and greet him in my name. ⁶Say to him: 'Long life to you! Good health to you and your household! And good health to all that is yours!

⁷ "'Now I hear that it is sheep-shearing time. When your shepherds were with us, we did not mistreat them, and the whole time they were at Carmel nothing of theirs was missing. ⁸Ask your own servants and they will tell you. Therefore be favorable toward my young men, since we come at a festive time. Please give your servants and your son David whatever you can find for them.' "

⁹When David's men arrived, they gave Nabal this message in David's name. Then they waited.

¹⁰Nabal answered David's servants, "Who is this David? Who is this son of Jesse? Many servants are breaking away from their masters these days. ¹¹Why should I take my bread and water, and the meat I have slaughtered for my shearers, and give it to men coming from who knows where?"

¹²David's men turned around and went back. When they arrived, they reported every word. ¹³David said to his men, "Put on your swords!" So they put on their swords, and David put on his. About four hundred men went up with David, while two hundred stayed with the supplies.

¹⁴One of the servants told Nabal's wife Abigail: "David sent messengers from the desert to give our master his greetings, but he hurled insults at them. ¹⁵Yet these men were very good to us. They did not mistreat us, and the whole time we were out in the fields near them nothing was missing. ¹⁶Night and day they were a wall around us all the time we were herding our sheep near them. ¹⁷Now think it over and see what you can do, because disaster is hanging over our master and his whole household. He is such a wicked man that no one can talk to him."

¹⁸Abigail lost no time. She took two hundred

a 1 Some Septuagint manuscripts; Hebrew *Paran*

loaves of bread, two skins of wine, five dressed sheep, five seahs[a] of roasted grain, a hundred cakes of raisins and two hundred cakes of pressed figs, and loaded them on donkeys. [19]Then she told her servants, "Go on ahead; I'll follow you." But she did not tell her husband Nabal.

[20]As she came riding her donkey into a mountain ravine, there were David and his men descending toward her, and she met them. [21]David had just said, "It's been useless—all my watching over this fellow's property in the desert so that nothing of his was missing. He has paid me back evil for good. [22]May God deal with David,[b] be it ever so severely, if by morning I leave alive one male of all who belong to him!"

[23]When Abigail saw David, she quickly got off her donkey and bowed down before David with her face to the ground. [24]She fell at his feet and said: "My lord, let the blame be on me alone. Please let your servant speak to you; hear what your servant has to say. [25]May my lord pay no attention to that wicked man Nabal. He is just like his name—his name is Fool, and folly goes with him. But as for me, your servant, I did not see the men my master sent.

[26]"Now since the LORD has kept you, my master, from bloodshed and from avenging yourself with your own hands, as surely as the LORD lives and as you live, may your enemies and all who intend to harm your master be like Nabal. [27]And let this gift, which your servant has brought to my master, be given to the men who follow you. [28]Please forgive your servant's offense, for the LORD will certainly make a lasting dynasty for my master, because he fights the LORD's battles. Let no wrongdoing be found in you as long as you live. [29]Even though someone is pursuing you to take your life, the life of my master will be bound securely in the bundle of the living by the LORD your God. But the lives of your enemies he will hurl away as from the pocket of a sling. [30]When the LORD has done for my master every good thing he promised concerning him and has appointed him leader over Israel, [31]my master will not have on his conscience the staggering burden of needless bloodshed or of having avenged himself. And when the LORD has brought my master success, remember your servant."

[32]David said to Abigail, "Praise be to the

酒,五隻收拾好了的羊,五細亞烘好了的穗子,一百葡萄餅,二百無花果餅,都馱在驢上,[19]對僕人說:"你們前頭走,我隨着你們去。"這事她卻沒有告訴丈夫拿八。

[20]亞比該騎着驢,正下山坡,見大衛和跟隨他的人從對面下來,亞比該就迎接他們。[21]大衛曾說:"我在曠野為那人看守所有的,以致他一樣不失落,實在是徒然了!他向我以惡報善。[22]凡屬拿八的男丁,我若留一個到明日早晨,願神重重降罰與我!"

[23]亞比該見大衛,便急忙下驢,在大衛面前臉伏於地叩拜,[24]俯伏在大衛的腳前,說:"我主啊,願這罪歸我!求你容婢女向你進言,更求你聽婢女的話:[25]我主不要理這壞人拿八,他的性情與他的名相稱,他名叫拿八(註:就是"愚頑"的意思),他為人果然愚頑。但我主所打發的僕人,婢女並沒有看見。

[26]"我主啊!耶和華既然阻止你親手報仇,取流血的罪,所以我指着永生的耶和華,又敢在你面前起誓說,願你的仇敵和謀害你的人都像拿八一樣。[27]如今求你將婢女送來的禮物給跟隨你的僕人。[28]求你饒恕婢女的罪過。耶和華必為我主建立堅固的家,因我主為耶和華爭戰,並且在你平生的日子查不出有甚麼過來。[29]雖有人起來追逼你,尋索你的性命,你的性命卻在耶和華你的神那裏蒙保護,如包裹寶器一樣;你仇敵的性命,耶和華必拋去,如用機弦甩石一樣。[30]、[31]我主現在若不親手報仇,流無辜人的血,到了耶和華照所應許你的話賜福與你,立你作以色列的王,那時我主必不至心裏不安,覺得良心有虧。耶和華賜福與我主的時候,求你記念婢女。"

[32]大衛對亞比該說:"耶和華以

a 18 That is, probably about a bushel (about 37 liters)
b 22 Some Septuagint manuscripts; Hebrew with David's enemies

色列的神是應當稱頌的！因為他今日使你來迎接我。33你和你的見識也當稱讚，因為你今日攔阻我親手報仇，流人的血。34我指着阻止我加害於你的耶和華以色列永生的神起誓，你若不速速地來迎接我，到明日早晨，凡屬拿八的男丁必定不留一個。"

35大衛受了亞比該送來的禮物，就對她說："我聽了你的話，准了你的情面，你可以平平安安地回家吧！"

36亞比該到拿八那裏，見他在家裏設擺筵席，如同王的筵席。拿八快樂大醉。亞比該無論大小事都沒有告訴他，就等到次日早晨。37到了早晨，拿八醒了酒，他的妻將這些事都告訴他，他就魂不附體，身僵如石頭一般。38過了十天，耶和華擊打拿八，他就死了。

39大衛聽見拿八死了，就說："應當稱頌耶和華，因他伸了拿八羞辱我的冤，又阻止僕人行惡；也使拿八的惡歸到拿八的頭上。"

於是大衛打發人去與亞比該說，要娶她為妻。40大衛的僕人到了迦密見亞比該，對她說："大衛打發我們來見你，想要娶你為妻。"

41亞比該就起來，俯伏在地，說："我情願作婢女，洗我主僕人的腳。"42亞比該立刻起身，騎上驢，帶着五個使女，跟從大衛的使者去了，就作了大衛的妻。43大衛先娶了耶斯列人亞希暖，她們二人都作了他的妻。44掃羅已將他的女兒米甲，就是大衛的妻，給了迦琳人拉億的兒子帕提為妻。

大衛再次不殺掃羅

26 西弗人到基比亞見掃羅，說："大衛不是在曠野前的哈基拉山藏着嗎？"

2掃羅就起身，帶領以色列人中挑選的三千精兵，下到西弗的曠野，要在那裏尋索大衛。3掃羅在曠野前的哈基拉山，在道路上安營。大衛住在曠野，聽說掃羅到曠野來追尋他，4就打發人去探聽，便知道掃羅果然來到。

LORD, the God of Israel, who has sent you today to meet me. 33May you be blessed for your good judgment and for keeping me from bloodshed this day and from avenging myself with my own hands. 34Otherwise, as surely as the LORD, the God of Israel, lives, who has kept me from harming you, if you had not come quickly to meet me, not one male belonging to Nabal would have been left alive by daybreak."

35Then David accepted from her hand what she had brought him and said, "Go home in peace. I have heard your words and granted your request."

36When Abigail went to Nabal, he was in the house holding a banquet like that of a king. He was in high spirits and very drunk. So she told him nothing until daybreak. 37Then in the morning, when Nabal was sober, his wife told him all these things, and his heart failed him and he became like a stone. 38About ten days later, the LORD struck Nabal and he died.

39When David heard that Nabal was dead, he said, "Praise be to the LORD, who has upheld my cause against Nabal for treating me with contempt. He has kept his servant from doing wrong and has brought Nabal's wrongdoing down on his own head."

Then David sent word to Abigail, asking her to become his wife. 40His servants went to Carmel and said to Abigail, "David has sent us to you to take you to become his wife."

41She bowed down with her face to the ground and said, "Here is your maidservant, ready to serve you and wash the feet of my master's servants." 42Abigail quickly got on a donkey and, attended by her five maids, went with David's messengers and became his wife. 43David had also married Ahinoam of Jezreel, and they both were his wives. 44But Saul had given his daughter Michal, David's wife, to Paltiel[a] son of Laish, who was from Gallim.

David Again Spares Saul's Life

26 The Ziphites went to Saul at Gibeah and said, "Is not David hiding on the hill of Hakilah, which faces Jeshimon?"

2So Saul went down to the Desert of Ziph, with his three thousand chosen men of Israel, to search there for David. 3Saul made his camp beside the road on the hill of Hakilah facing Jeshimon, but David stayed in the desert. When he saw that Saul had followed him there, 4he sent out scouts and learned that Saul had definitely arrived.[b]

---

a 44 Hebrew Palti, a variant of Paltiel　b 4 Or had come to Nacon

⁵Then David set out and went to the place where Saul had camped. He saw where Saul and Abner son of Ner, the commander of the army, had lain down. Saul was lying inside the camp, with the army encamped around him.

⁶David then asked Ahimelech the Hittite and Abishai son of Zeruiah, Joab's brother, "Who will go down into the camp with me to Saul?"

"I'll go with you," said Abishai.

⁷So David and Abishai went to the army by night, and there was Saul, lying asleep inside the camp with his spear stuck in the ground near his head. Abner and the soldiers were lying around him.

⁸Abishai said to David, "Today God has delivered your enemy into your hands. Now let me pin him to the ground with one thrust of my spear; I won't strike him twice."

⁹But David said to Abishai, "Don't destroy him! Who can lay a hand on the LORD's anointed and be guiltless? ¹⁰As surely as the LORD lives," he said, "the LORD himself will strike him; either his time will come and he will die, or he will go into battle and perish. ¹¹But the LORD forbid that I should lay a hand on the LORD's anointed. Now get the spear and water jug that are near his head, and let's go."

¹²So David took the spear and water jug near Saul's head, and they left. No one saw or knew about it, nor did anyone wake up. They were all sleeping, because the LORD had put them into a deep sleep.

¹³Then David crossed over to the other side and stood on top of the hill some distance away; there was a wide space between them. ¹⁴He called out to the army and to Abner son of Ner, "Aren't you going to answer me, Abner?"

Abner replied, "Who are you who calls to the king?"

¹⁵David said, "You're a man, aren't you? And who is like you in Israel? Why didn't you guard your lord the king? Someone came to destroy your lord the king. ¹⁶What you have done is not good. As surely as the LORD lives, you and your men deserve to die, because you did not guard your master, the LORD's anointed. Look around you. Where are the king's spear and water jug that were near his head?"

¹⁷Saul recognized David's voice and said, "Is that your voice, David my son?"

David replied, "Yes it is, my lord the king." ¹⁸And he added, "Why is my lord pursuing his servant? What have I done, and what wrong am I guilty of? ¹⁹Now let my lord the king listen to his servant's words. If the LORD has incited you against me, then may he accept an offering. If,

⁵大衛起來，到掃羅安營的地方，看見掃羅和他的元帥尼珥的兒子押尼珥睡臥之處。掃羅睡在輜重營裏，百姓安營在他周圍。

⁶大衛對赫人亞希米勒和洗魯雅的兒子約押的兄弟亞比篩說："誰同我下到掃羅營裏去？"

亞比篩說："我同你下去！"

⁷於是大衛和亞比篩夜間到了百姓那裏，見掃羅睡在輜重營裏，他的槍在頭旁，插在地上。押尼珥和百姓睡在他周圍。

⁸亞比篩對大衛說："現在，神將你的仇敵交在你手裏，求你容我拿槍將他刺透在地，一刺就成，不用再刺。"

⁹大衛對亞比篩說："不可害死他。有誰伸手害耶和華的受膏者而無罪呢？"¹⁰大衛又說："我指着永生的耶和華起誓，他或被耶和華擊打，或是死期到了，或是出戰陣亡；¹¹我在耶和華面前萬不敢伸手害耶和華的受膏者。現在你可以將他頭旁的槍和水瓶拿來，我們就走。"

¹²大衛從掃羅的頭旁拿了槍和水瓶，二人就走了，沒有人看見，沒有人知道，也沒有人醒起，都睡着了。因為耶和華使他們沉沉地睡了。

¹³大衛過到那邊去，遠遠地站在山頂上，與他們相離甚遠。¹⁴大衛呼叫百姓和尼珥的兒子押尼珥說："押尼珥啊，你為何不答應呢？"

押尼珥說："你是誰？竟敢呼叫王呢？"

¹⁵大衛對押尼珥說："你不是個勇士嗎？以色列中誰能比你呢？民何有人進來要害死王、你的主，你為何沒有保護王、你的主呢？¹⁶你這樣是不好的。我指着永生的耶和華起誓，你們都是該死的！因為沒有保護你們的主，就是耶和華的受膏者。現在你看看王頭旁的槍和水瓶在哪裏？"

¹⁷掃羅聽出是大衛的聲音，就說："我兒大衛，這是你的聲音嗎？"

大衛說："主、我的王啊！是我的聲音。"¹⁸又說："我做了甚麼？我手裏有甚麼惡事？我主竟追趕僕人呢？¹⁹求我主我王聽僕人的話：若是耶和華激發你攻擊我，願耶和華收納祭物；若是人激發你，願他在耶和華面前受咒詛，因為他現今趕逐我，不容我在耶和華的產業上有分，說：「你去侍奉別神吧！」²⁰現在求王不要使我的血流在離耶和華遠的地方。以色列王出來是尋找一個虼蚤，如同人在山上獵取一個鷓鴣一般。」

²¹掃羅說：「我有罪了！我兒大衛，你可以回來。因你今日看我的性命為寶貴，我必不再加害於你。我是糊塗人，大大錯了！」

²²大衛說：「王的槍在這裏，可以吩咐一個僕人過來拿去。²³今日耶和華將王交在我手裏，我卻不肯伸手害耶和華的受膏者。耶和華必照各人的公義誠實報應他。²⁴我今日重看你的性命，願耶和華也重看我的性命，並且拯救我脫離一切患難。」

²⁵掃羅對大衛說：「我兒大衛，願你得福！你必做大事，也必得勝。」

於是大衛起行，掃羅回他的本處去了。

大衛在非利士人中

27 大衛心裏說：「必有一日我死在掃羅手裏，不如逃奔非利士地去。掃羅見我不在以色列的境內，就必絕望，不再尋索我，這樣我可以脫離他的手。」

²於是大衛起身，和跟隨他的六百人投奔迦特王瑪俄的兒子亞吉去了。³大衛和他的兩個妻，就是耶斯列人亞希暖和作過拿八妻的迦密人亞比該，並跟隨他的人，連各人的眷屬，都住在迦特亞吉那裏。⁴有人告訴掃羅說：「大衛逃到迦特。」掃羅就不再尋索他了。

⁵大衛對亞吉說：「我若在你眼前蒙恩，求你在京外的城邑中賜我一個地方居住。僕人何必與王同住京都呢？」

⁶當日亞吉將洗革拉賜給他，因此洗革拉屬猶大王，直到今日。⁷大衛在非利士地住了一年零四個月。

⁸大衛和跟隨他的人上去，侵奪基述人、基色人、亞瑪力人之地。這幾族歷來住在那地，從書珥直到埃及。⁹大衛擊殺那地的人，無論男女

however, men have done it, may they be cursed before the LORD! They have now driven me from my share in the LORD's inheritance and have said, 'Go, serve other gods.' ²⁰Now do not let my blood fall to the ground far from the presence of the LORD. The king of Israel has come out to look for a flea—as one hunts a partridge in the mountains."

²¹Then Saul said, "I have sinned. Come back, David my son. Because you considered my life precious today, I will not try to harm you again. Surely I have acted like a fool and have erred greatly."

²²"Here is the king's spear," David answered. "Let one of your young men come over and get it. ²³The LORD rewards every man for his righteousness and faithfulness. The LORD delivered you into my hands today, but I would not lay a hand on the LORD's anointed. ²⁴As surely as I valued your life today, so may the LORD value my life and deliver me from all trouble."

²⁵Then Saul said to David, "May you be blessed, my son David; you will do great things and surely triumph."

So David went on his way, and Saul returned home.

David Among the Philistines

27 But David thought to himself, "One of these days I will be destroyed by the hand of Saul. The best thing I can do is to escape to the land of the Philistines. Then Saul will give up searching for me anywhere in Israel, and I will slip out of his hand."

²So David and the six hundred men with him left and went over to Achish son of Maoch king of Gath. ³David and his men settled in Gath with Achish. Each man had his family with him, and David had his two wives: Ahinoam of Jezreel and Abigail of Carmel, the widow of Nabal. ⁴When Saul was told that David had fled to Gath, he no longer searched for him.

⁵Then David said to Achish, "If I have found favor in your eyes, let a place be assigned to me in one of the country towns, that I may live there. Why should your servant live in the royal city with you?"

⁶So on that day Achish gave him Ziklag, and it has belonged to the kings of Judah ever since. ⁷David lived in Philistine territory a year and four months.

⁸Now David and his men went up and raided the Geshurites, the Girzites and the Amalekites. (From ancient times these peoples had lived in the land extending to Shur and Egypt.) ⁹Whenever David attacked an area, he did not

leave a man or woman alive, but took sheep and cattle, donkeys and camels, and clothes. Then he returned to Achish.

¹⁰When Achish asked, "Where did you go raiding today?" David would say, "Against the Negev of Judah" or "Against the Negev of Jerahmeel" or "Against the Negev of the Kenites." ¹¹He did not leave a man or woman alive to be brought to Gath, for he thought, "They might inform on us and say, 'This is what David did.'" And such was his practice as long as he lived in Philistine territory. ¹²Achish trusted David and said to himself, "He has become so odious to his people, the Israelites, that he will be my servant forever."

Saul and the Witch of Endor

28 In those days the Philistines gathered their forces to fight against Israel. Achish said to David, "You must understand that you and your men will accompany me in the army."

²David said, "Then you will see for yourself what your servant can do."

Achish replied, "Very well, I will make you my bodyguard for life."

³Now Samuel was dead, and all Israel had mourned for him and buried him in his own town of Ramah. Saul had expelled the mediums and spiritists from the land.

⁴The Philistines assembled and came and set up camp at Shunem, while Saul gathered all the Israelites and set up camp at Gilboa. ⁵When Saul saw the Philistine army, he was afraid; terror filled his heart. ⁶He inquired of the LORD, but the LORD did not answer him by dreams or Urim or prophets. ⁷Saul then said to his attendants, "Find me a woman who is a medium, so I may go and inquire of her."

"There is one in Endor," they said.

⁸So Saul disguised himself, putting on other clothes, and at night he and two men went to the woman. "Consult a spirit for me," he said, "and bring up for me the one I name."

⁹But the woman said to him, "Surely you know what Saul has done. He has cut off the mediums and spiritists from the land. Why have you set a trap for my life to bring about my death?"

¹⁰Saul swore to her by the LORD, "As surely as the LORD lives, you will not be punished for this."

¹¹Then the woman asked, "Whom shall I bring up for you?"

"Bring up Samuel," he said.

¹²When the woman saw Samuel, she cried

都沒有留下一個；又奪獲牛、羊、駱駝、驢並衣服，回來見亞吉。

¹⁰亞吉說："你們今日侵奪了甚麼地方呢？"大衛說："侵奪了猶大的南方，耶拉篾的南方，基尼的南方。"¹¹無論男女，大衛沒有留下一個帶到迦特來。他說："恐怕他們將我們的事告訴人，說：'大衛住在非利士地的時候，常常這樣行。'"¹²亞吉信了大衛，心裏說："大衛使本族以色列人憎惡他，所以他必永遠作我的僕人了。"

掃羅與隱多珥的女巫

28 那時，非利士人聚集軍旅，要與以色列人打仗。亞吉對大衛說："你當知道，你和跟隨你的人都要隨我出戰。"

²大衛對亞吉說："僕人所能做的事，王必知道。"

亞吉對大衛說："這樣，我立你永遠作我的護衛長。"

³那時撒母耳已經死了，以色列眾人為他哀哭，葬他在拉瑪，就是在他本城裏。掃羅曾在國內不容有交鬼的和行巫術的人。

⁴非利士人聚集，來到書念安營；掃羅聚集以色列眾人，在基利波安營。⁵掃羅看見非利士的軍旅就懼怕，心中發顫。⁶掃羅求問耶和華，耶和華卻不藉夢，或烏陵，或先知回答他。⁷掃羅吩咐臣僕說："當為我找一個交鬼的婦人，我好去問她。"

臣僕說："在隱多珥有一個交鬼的婦人。"

⁸於是掃羅改了裝，穿上別的衣服，帶着兩個人，夜裏去見那婦人。掃羅說："求你用交鬼的法術，將我所告訴你的死人，為我招上來。"

⁹婦人對他說："你知道掃羅從國中剪除交鬼的和行巫術的。你為何陷害我的性命，使我死呢？"

¹⁰掃羅向婦人指着耶和華起誓說："我指着永生的耶和華起誓：你必不因這事受刑。"

¹¹婦人說："我為你招誰上來呢？"

回答說："為我招撒母耳上來。"

¹²婦人看見撒母耳，就大聲呼

叫，對掃羅說：“你是掃羅，為甚麼欺哄我呢？”

13王對婦人說：“不要懼怕，你看見了甚麼呢？”

婦人對掃羅說：“我看見有神從地裏上來。”

14掃羅說：“他是怎樣的形狀？”

婦人說：“有一個老人上來，身穿長衣。”

掃羅知道是撒母耳，就屈身，臉伏於地下拜。

15撒母耳對掃羅說：“你為甚麼攪擾我，招我上來呢？”

掃羅回答說：“我甚窘急，因為非利士人攻擊我，神也離開我，不再藉先知或夢回答我。因此請你上來，好指示我應當怎樣行。”

16撒母耳說：“耶和華已經離開你，且與你為敵，你何必問我呢？17耶和華照他藉我說的話，已經從你手裏奪去國權，賜與別人，就是大衛。18因你沒有聽從耶和華的命令，他惱怒亞瑪力人，你沒有滅絕他們，所以今日耶和華向你這樣行，19並且耶和華必將你和以色列人交在非利士人的手裏。明日你和你眾子必與我在一處了；耶和華必將以色列的軍兵交在非利士人手裏。”

20掃羅猛然仆倒，挺身在地，因撒母耳的話甚是懼怕。那一晝一夜沒有吃甚麼，就毫無氣力。

21婦人到掃羅面前，見他極其驚恐，對他說：“婢女聽從你的話，不顧惜自己的性命，遵從你所吩咐的。22現在求你聽婢女的話，容我在你面前擺上一點食物，你吃了可以有氣力行路。”

23掃羅不肯，說：“我不吃。”

但他的僕人和婦人再三勸他，他才聽了他們的話，從地上起來，坐在牀上。

24婦人急忙將家裏的一隻肥牛犢宰了，又拿麵摶成無酵餅烤了，25擺在掃羅和他僕人面前，他們吃完，當夜就起身走了。

out at the top of her voice and said to Saul, "Why have you deceived me? You are Saul!"

13The king said to her, "Don't be afraid. What do you see?"

The woman said, "I see a spirit*a* coming up out of the ground."

14"What does he look like?" he asked.

"An old man wearing a robe is coming up," she said.

Then Saul knew it was Samuel, and he bowed down and prostrated himself with his face to the ground.

15Samuel said to Saul, "Why have you disturbed me by bringing me up?"

"I am in great distress," Saul said. "The Philistines are fighting against me, and God has turned away from me. He no longer answers me, either by prophets or by dreams. So I have called on you to tell me what to do."

16Samuel said, "Why do you consult me, now that the LORD has turned away from you and become your enemy? 17The LORD has done what he predicted through me. The LORD has torn the kingdom out of your hands and given it to one of your neighbors—to David. 18Because you did not obey the LORD or carry out his fierce wrath against the Amalekites, the LORD has done this to you today. 19The LORD will hand over both Israel and you to the Philistines, and tomorrow you and your sons will be with me. The LORD will also hand over the army of Israel to the Philistines."

20Immediately Saul fell full length on the ground, filled with fear because of Samuel's words. His strength was gone, for he had eaten nothing all that day and night.

21When the woman came to Saul and saw that he was greatly shaken, she said, "Look, your maidservant has obeyed you. I took my life in my hands and did what you told me to do. 22Now please listen to your servant and let me give you some food so you may eat and have the strength to go on your way."

23He refused and said, "I will not eat."

But his men joined the woman in urging him, and he listened to them. He got up from the ground and sat on the couch.

24The woman had a fattened calf at the house, which she butchered at once. She took some flour, kneaded it and baked bread without yeast. 25Then she set it before Saul and his men, and they ate. That same night they got up and left.

a 13 Or see spirits; or see gods

Achish Sends David Back to Ziklag

29 The Philistines gathered all their forces at Aphek, and Israel camped by the spring in Jezreel. ²As the Philistine rulers marched with their units of hundreds and thousands, David and his men were marching at the rear with Achish. ³The commanders of the Philistines asked, "What about these Hebrews?"

Achish replied, "Is this not David, who was an officer of Saul king of Israel? He has already been with me for over a year, and from the day he left Saul until now, I have found no fault in him."

⁴But the Philistine commanders were angry with him and said, "Send the man back, that he may return to the place you assigned him. He must not go with us into battle, or he will turn against us during the fighting. How better could he regain his master's favor than by taking the heads of our own men? ⁵Isn't this the David they sang about in their dances:

" 'Saul has slain his thousands,
and David his tens of thousands'?"

⁶So Achish called David and said to him, "As surely as the LORD lives, you have been reliable, and I would be pleased to have you serve with me in the army. From the day you came to me until now, I have found no fault in you, but the rulers don't approve of you. ⁷Turn back and go in peace; do nothing to displease the Philistine rulers."

⁸"But what have I done?" asked David. "What have you found against your servant from the day I came to you until now? Why can't I go and fight against the enemies of my lord the king?"

⁹Achish answered, "I know that you have been as pleasing in my eyes as an angel of God; nevertheless, the Philistine commanders have said, 'He must not go up with us into battle.' ¹⁰Now get up early, along with your master's servants who have come with you, and leave in the morning as soon as it is light."

¹¹So David and his men got up early in the morning to go back to the land of the Philistines, and the Philistines went up to Jezreel.

David Destroys the Amalekites

30 David and his men reached Ziklag on the third day. Now the Amalekites had raided the Negev and Ziklag. They had attacked Ziklag and burned it, ²and had taken captive the women and all who were in it, both young and old. They killed none of them, but carried them off as they went on their way.

亞吉遣大衛回洗革拉

29 非利士人將他們的軍旅聚到亞弗；以色列人在耶斯列的泉旁安營。²非利士人的首領各率軍隊，或百或千，挨次前進。大衛和跟隨他的人同著亞吉跟在後邊。³非利士人的首領說："這些希伯來人在這裏做甚麼呢？"

亞吉對他們說："這不是以色列王掃羅的臣子大衛嗎？他在我這裏有些年日了。自從他投降我，直到今日，我未曾見他有過錯。"

⁴非利士人的首領向亞吉發怒，對他說："你要叫這人回你所安置他的地方，不可叫他同我們出戰，恐怕他在陣上反為我們的敵人。他用甚麼與他主人復和呢？豈不是用我們這些人的首級嗎？⁵從前以色列的婦女跳舞唱和說：

" '掃羅殺死千千，
大衛殺死萬萬' ，
所說的不是這個大衛嗎？"

⁶亞吉叫大衛來，對他說："我指著永生的耶和華起誓，你是正直人。你隨我在軍中出入，我看你甚好。自從你投奔我到如今，我未曾見你有甚麼過失，只是眾首領不喜悅你。⁷現在你可以平平安安地回去，免得非利士人的首領不歡喜你。"

⁸大衛對亞吉說："我做了甚麼呢？自從僕人到你面前，直到今日，你查出我有甚麼過錯，使我不去攻擊主我王的仇敵呢？"

⁹亞吉說："我知道你在我眼前是好人，如同神的使者一般。只是非利士人的首領說：'這人不可同我們出戰。'故此你和你跟隨你的人，就是你本主的僕人，要明日早晨起來，等到天亮回去吧！"

¹¹於是大衛和跟隨他的人早晨起來，回往非利士地去。非利士人也上耶斯列去了。

大衛擊敗亞瑪力人

30 第三日，大衛和跟隨他的人到了洗革拉。亞瑪力人已經侵奪南地，攻破洗革拉，用火焚燒，²擄了城內的婦女和其中的大小人口，卻沒有殺一個，都帶著走了。

³大衛和跟隨他的人到了那城，不料，城已燒燬，他們的妻子兒女都被擄去了。⁴大衛和跟隨他的人就放聲大哭，直哭得沒有氣力。⁵大衛的兩個妻、耶斯列人亞希暖和作過拿八妻的迦密人亞比該，也被擄去了。⁶大衛甚是焦急，因眾人為自己的兒女苦惱，說：「要用石頭打死他。」大衛卻倚靠耶和華他的神，心裏堅固。

⁷大衛對亞希米勒的兒子祭司亞比亞他說：「請你將以弗得拿過來。」亞比亞他就將以弗得拿到大衛面前。⁸大衛求問耶和華說：「我追趕敵軍，追得上追不上呢？」

耶和華說：「你可以追，必追得上，都救得回來。」

⁹於是大衛和跟隨他的六百人來到比梭溪；有不能前去的，就留在那裏。¹⁰大衛卻帶着四百人往前追趕；有二百人疲乏，不能過比梭溪，所以留在那裏。

¹¹這四百人在田野遇見一個埃及人，就帶他到大衛面前，給他餅吃，給他水喝，¹²又給他一塊無花果餅，兩個葡萄餅。他吃了，就精神復原，因為他三日三夜沒有吃餅，沒有喝水。

¹³大衛問他說：「你是屬誰的？你是哪裏的人？」

他回答說：「我是埃及的少年人，是亞瑪力人的奴僕。因我三日前患病，我主人就把我撇棄了。¹⁴我們侵奪了基利提的南方和屬猶大的地，並迦勒地的南方，又用火燒了洗革拉。」

¹⁵大衛問他說：「你肯領我們到敵軍那裏不肯？」

他回答說：「你要向我指着神起誓，不殺我，也不將我交在我主人手裏，我就領你下到敵軍那裏。」

¹⁶那人領大衛下去，見他們散在地上，吃喝跳舞，因為從非利士地和猶大地所擄來的財物甚多。¹⁷大衛從黎明直到次日晚上，擊殺他們，除了四百騎駱駝的少年人之外，沒有一個逃脫的。¹⁸亞瑪力人所擄去的財物，大衛全都奪回，並救回他的兩個妻來。¹⁹凡亞瑪力人所擄去的，無論大小、兒女、財物，大衛都奪回來，沒有失落一個。²⁰大衛所奪來的牛羣羊羣，跟隨他的人趕在原有的羣畜前

³When David and his men came to Ziklag, they found it destroyed by fire and their wives and sons and daughters taken captive. ⁴So David and his men wept aloud until they had no strength left to weep. ⁵David's two wives had been captured—Ahinoam of Jezreel and Abigail, the widow of Nabal of Carmel. ⁶David was greatly distressed because the men were talking of stoning him; each one was bitter in spirit because of his sons and daughters. But David found strength in the LORD his God.

⁷Then David said to Abiathar the priest, the son of Ahimelech, "Bring me the ephod." Abiathar brought it to him, ⁸and David inquired of the LORD, "Shall I pursue this raiding party? Will I overtake them?"

"Pursue them," he answered. "You will certainly overtake them and succeed in the rescue."

⁹David and the six hundred men with him came to the Besor Ravine, where some stayed behind, ¹⁰for two hundred men were too exhausted to cross the ravine. But David and four hundred men continued the pursuit.

¹¹They found an Egyptian in a field and brought him to David. They gave him water to drink and food to eat— ¹²part of a cake of pressed figs and two cakes of raisins. He ate and was revived, for he had not eaten any food or drunk any water for three days and three nights.

¹³David asked him, "To whom do you belong, and where do you come from?"

He said, "I am an Egyptian, the slave of an Amalekite. My master abandoned me when I became ill three days ago. ¹⁴We raided the Negev of the Kerethites and the territory belonging to Judah and the Negev of Caleb. And we burned Ziklag."

¹⁵David asked him, "Can you lead me down to this raiding party?"

He answered, "Swear to me before God that you will not kill me or hand me over to my master, and I will take you down to them."

¹⁶He led David down, and there they were, scattered over the countryside, eating, drinking and reveling because of the great amount of plunder they had taken from the land of the Philistines and from Judah. ¹⁷David fought them from dusk until the evening of the next day, and none of them got away, except four hundred young men who rode off on camels and fled. ¹⁸David recovered everything the Amalekites had taken, including his two wives. ¹⁹Nothing was missing: young or old, boy or girl, plunder or anything else they had taken. David brought everything back. ²⁰He took all the flocks and herds, and his men drove them ahead of the

other livestock, saying, "This is David's plunder."

21Then David came to the two hundred men who had been too exhausted to follow him and who were left behind at the Besor Ravine. They came out to meet David and the people with him. As David and his men approached, he greeted them. 22But all the evil men and troublemakers among David's followers said, "Because they did not go out with us, we will not share with them the plunder we recovered. However, each man may take his wife and children and go."

23David replied, "No, my brothers, you must not do that with what the LORD has given us. He has protected us and handed over to us the forces that came against us. 24Who will listen to what you say? The share of the man who stayed with the supplies is to be the same as that of him who went down to the battle. All will share alike." 25David made this a statute and ordinance for Israel from that day to this.

26When David arrived in Ziklag, he sent some of the plunder to the elders of Judah, who were his friends, saying, "Here is a present for you from the plunder of the LORD's enemies."

27He sent it to those who were in Bethel, Ramoth Negev and Jattir; 28to those in Aroer, Siphmoth, Eshtemoa 29and Racal; to those in the towns of the Jerahmeelites and the Kenites; 30to those in Hormah, Bor Ashan, Athach 31and Hebron; and to those in all the other places where David and his men had roamed.

Saul Takes His Life

31 Now the Philistines fought against Israel; the Israelites fled before them, and many fell slain on Mount Gilboa. 2The Philistines pressed hard after Saul and his sons, and they killed his sons Jonathan, Abinadab and Malki-Shua. 3The fighting grew fierce around Saul, and when the archers overtook him, they wounded him critically.

4Saul said to his armor-bearer, "Draw your sword and run me through, or these uncircumcised fellows will come and run me through and abuse me."

But his armor-bearer was terrified and would not do it; so Saul took his own sword and fell on it. 5When the armor-bearer saw that Saul was dead, he too fell on his sword and died with him. 6So Saul and his three sons and his armor-bearer and all his men died together that same day.

7When the Israelites along the valley and those across the Jordan saw that the Israelite

邊，說：「這是大衛的掠物。」

21大衛到了那疲乏不能跟隨、留在比梭溪的二百人那裏。他們出來迎接大衛並跟隨的人。大衛前來問他們安。22跟隨大衛人中的惡人和匪類說：「這些人既然沒有和我們同去，我們所奪的財物就不分給他們，只將他們各人的妻子兒女給他們，使他們帶去就是了。」

23大衛說：「弟兄們，耶和華所賜給我們的，不可不分給他們，因為他保佑我們，將那攻擊我們的敵軍交在我們手裏。24這事誰肯依從你們呢？上陣的得多少，看守器具的也得多少，應當大家平分。」25大衛定此為以色列的律例、典章，從那日直到今日。

26大衛到了洗革拉，從掠物中取些送給他朋友猶大的長老，說：「這是從耶和華仇敵那裏奪來的，送你們為禮物。」

27他送禮物給住伯特利的，南地拉末的，雅提珥的；28住亞羅珥的，息末的，以實提莫的；29住拉哈勒的，基尼篾各城的，基尼各城的；30住何珥瑪的，歌拉珊的，亞撻的；31住希伯崙的，並大衛和跟隨他的人素來所到之處的人。

掃羅自殺

31 非利士人與以色列人爭戰。以色列人在非利士人面前逃跑，在基利波有被殺仆倒的。2非利士人緊追掃羅和他兒子們，就殺了掃羅的兒子約拿單、亞比拿達、麥基舒亞。3勢派甚大，掃羅被弓箭手追上，射傷甚重。

4就吩咐拿他兵器的人說：「你拔出刀來將我刺死，免得那些未受割禮的人來刺我、凌辱我。」

但拿兵器的人甚懼怕，不肯刺他，掃羅就自己伏在刀上死了。5拿兵器的人見掃羅已死，也伏在刀上死了。6這樣，掃羅和他三個兒子，與拿他兵器的人，以及跟隨他的人，都一同死亡。

7住平原那邊並約旦河西的以色列人，見以色列軍兵逃跑，掃羅和他兒子都死了，也就棄城逃跑。非利士人便來住在其中。

⁸次日，非利士人來剝那被殺之人的衣服，看見掃羅和他三個兒子仆倒在基利波山，⁹就割下他的首級，剝了他的軍裝，打發人到非利士地的四境（註：「到」或作「送到」），報信與他們廟裏的偶像和眾民；¹⁰又將掃羅的軍裝放在亞斯她錄廟裏，將他的屍身釘在伯珊的城牆上。

¹¹基列雅比的居民聽見非利士人向掃羅所行的事，¹²他們中間所有的勇士就起身，走了一夜，將掃羅和他兒子的屍身從伯珊城牆上取下來，送到雅比那裏用火燒了；¹³將他們骸骨葬在雅比的垂絲柳樹下，就禁食七日。

army had fled and that Saul and his sons had died, they abandoned their towns and fled. And the Philistines came and occupied them.

⁸The next day, when the Philistines came to strip the dead, they found Saul and his three sons fallen on Mount Gilboa. ⁹They cut off his head and stripped off his armor, and they sent messengers throughout the land of the Philistines to proclaim the news in the temple of their idols and among their people. ¹⁰They put his armor in the temple of the Ashtoreths and fastened his body to the wall of Beth Shan.

¹¹When the people of Jabesh Gilead heard of what the Philistines had done to Saul, ¹²all their valiant men journeyed through the night to Beth Shan. They took down the bodies of Saul and his sons from the wall of Beth Shan and went to Jabesh, where they burned them. ¹³Then they took their bones and buried them under a tamarisk tree at Jabesh, and they fasted seven days.

圖五：撒母耳記中的主要地方
MAP 5 : KEY PLACES IN 1 & 2 SAMUEL

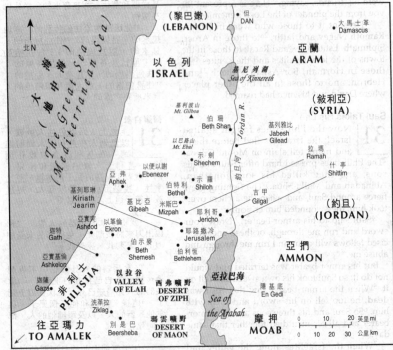

2 Samuel

撒母耳記下

David Hears of Saul's Death

1 After the death of Saul, David returned from defeating the Amalekites and stayed in Ziklag two days. ²On the third day a man arrived from Saul's camp, with his clothes torn and with dust on his head. When he came to David, he fell to the ground to pay him honor.

³"Where have you come from?" David asked him.

He answered, "I have escaped from the Israelite camp."

⁴"What happened?" David asked. "Tell me."

He said, "The men fled from the battle. Many of them fell and died. And Saul and his son Jonathan are dead."

⁵Then David said to the young man who brought him the report, "How do you know that Saul and his son Jonathan are dead?"

⁶"I happened to be on Mount Gilboa," the young man said, "and there was Saul, leaning on his spear, with the chariots and riders almost upon him. ⁷When he turned around and saw me, he called out to me, and I said, 'What can I do?'

⁸"He asked me, 'Who are you?'

" 'An Amalekite,' I answered.

⁹"Then he said to me, 'Stand over me and kill me! I am in the throes of death, but I'm still alive.'

¹⁰"So I stood over him and killed him, because I knew that after he had fallen he could not survive. And I took the crown that was on his head and the band on his arm and have brought them here to my lord."

¹¹Then David and all the men with him took hold of their clothes and tore them. ¹²They mourned and wept and fasted till evening for Saul and his son Jonathan, and for the army of the LORD and the house of Israel, because they had fallen by the sword.

¹³David said to the young man who brought him the report, "Where are you from?"

"I am the son of an alien, an Amalekite," he answered.

¹⁴David asked him, "Why were you not afraid to lift your hand to destroy the LORD's anointed?"

大衛聞掃羅死訊

1 掃羅死後，大衛擊殺亞瑪力人回來，在洗革拉住了兩天。²第三天，有一人從掃羅的營裏出來，衣服撕裂，頭蒙灰塵，到大衛面前伏地叩拜。

³大衛問他說："你從哪裏來？"

他說："我從以色列的營裏逃來。"

⁴大衛又問他說："事情怎樣？請你告訴我。"

他回答說："百姓從陣上逃跑，也有許多人仆倒死亡，掃羅和他兒子約拿單也死了。"

⁵大衛問報信的少年人說："你怎麼知道掃羅和他兒子約拿單死了呢？"

⁶報信的少年人說："我偶然到基利波山，看見掃羅伏在自己槍上，有戰車、馬兵緊緊地追他。⁷他回頭看見我，就呼叫我。我說：'我在這裏。'

⁸"他問我說：'你是甚麼人？'我說：'我是亞瑪力人。'

⁹"他說：'請你來將我殺死，因為痛苦抓住我，我的生命尚存。'

¹⁰"我準知他仆倒必不能活，就去將他殺死，把他頭上的冠冕、臂上的鐲子拿到我主這裏。"

¹¹大衛就撕裂衣服，跟隨他的人也是如此。¹²而且悲哀、哭號、禁食到晚上，是因掃羅和他兒子約拿單，並耶和華的民以色列家的人倒在刀下。

¹³大衛問報信的少年人說："你是哪裏的人？"

他說："我是亞瑪力客人的兒子。"

¹⁴大衛說："你伸手殺害耶和華的受膏者，怎麼不畏懼呢？"

15大衛叫了一個少年人來，說：
"你去殺他吧！" 16大衛對他說：
"你流人血的罪歸到自己的頭上，因
為你親口作見證說：'我殺了耶和華
的受膏者。'"少年人就把他殺了。

大衛哀悼掃羅與約拿單

17大衛作哀歌，弔掃羅和他兒子
約拿單，18且吩咐將這歌教導猶大
人。這歌名叫弓歌，寫在雅煞珥書
上。

19歌中說："以色列啊，
　　你尊榮者在山上被殺。
　　大英雄何竟死亡！

20 "不要在迦特報告，
　　不要在亞實基倫街上傳揚；
　　免得非利士的女子歡樂，
　　免得未受割禮之人的女子矜誇。

21 "基利波山哪，
　　願你那裏沒有雨露，
　　願你田地無土產可作供物！
　　因為英雄的盾牌，
　　在那裏被污丟棄。
　　掃羅的盾牌，彷彿未曾抹油。
22約拿單的弓箭，
　　非流敵人的血不退縮；
　　掃羅的刀劍，
　　非剖勇士的油不收回。

23 "掃羅和約拿單，
　　活時相悅相愛，
　　死時也不分離。
　　他們比鷹更快，
　　比獅子還強。

24 "以色列的女子啊，
　　當為掃羅哭號！
　　他曾使你們
　　穿朱紅色的美衣，
　　使你們衣服有黃金的妝飾。

25 "英雄何竟在陣上仆倒！
　　約拿單何竟在山上被殺！
26我兄約拿單哪，我為你悲傷！
　　我甚喜悅你！
　　你向我發的愛情奇妙非常，
　　過於婦女的愛情。

27 "英雄何竟仆倒！
　　戰具何竟滅沒！"

15Then David called one of his men and said,
"Go, strike him down!" So he struck him down,
and he died. 16For David had said to him, "Your
blood be on your own head. Your own mouth
testified against you when you said, 'I killed the
LORD's anointed.' "

David's Lament for Saul and Jonathan

17David took up this lament concerning Saul
and his son Jonathan, 18and ordered that the
men of Judah be taught this lament of the bow
(it is written in the Book of Jashar):

19"Your glory, O Israel, lies slain on your
　　heights.
　How the mighty have fallen!

20"Tell it not in Gath,
　　proclaim it not in the streets of Ashkelon,
　lest the daughters of the Philistines be glad,
　　lest the daughters of the uncircumcised
　　　rejoice.

21"O mountains of Gilboa,
　　may you have neither dew nor rain,
　　nor fields that yield offerings of grain.
　For there the shield of the mighty was defiled,
　　the shield of Saul—no longer rubbed with
　　　oil.
22From the blood of the slain,
　　from the flesh of the mighty,
　the bow of Jonathan did not turn back,
　　the sword of Saul did not return unsatisfied.

23"Saul and Jonathan—
　　in life they were loved and gracious,
　　and in death they were not parted.
　They were swifter than eagles,
　　they were stronger than lions.

24"O daughters of Israel,
　　weep for Saul,
　who clothed you in scarlet and finery,
　　who adorned your garments with ornaments
　　　of gold.

25"How the mighty have fallen in battle!
　　Jonathan lies slain on your heights.
26I grieve for you, Jonathan my brother;
　　you were very dear to me.
　Your love for me was wonderful,
　　more wonderful than that of women.

27"How the mighty have fallen!
　　The weapons of war have perished!"

David Anointed King Over Judah

2 In the course of time, David inquired of the LORD. "Shall I go up to one of the towns of Judah?" he asked.

The LORD said, "Go up."

David asked, "Where shall I go?"

"To Hebron," the LORD answered.

²So David went up there with his two wives, Ahinoam of Jezreel and Abigail, the widow of Nabal of Carmel. ³David also took the men who were with him, each with his family, and they settled in Hebron and its towns. ⁴Then the men of Judah came to Hebron and there they anointed David king over the house of Judah.

When David was told that it was the men of Jabesh Gilead who had buried Saul, ⁵he sent messengers to the men of Jabesh Gilead to say to them, "The LORD bless you for showing this kindness to Saul your master by burying him. ⁶May the LORD now show you kindness and faithfulness, and I too will show you the same favor because you have done this. ⁷Now then, be strong and brave, for Saul your master is dead, and the house of Judah has anointed me king over them."

War Between the Houses of David and Saul

⁸Meanwhile, Abner son of Ner, the commander of Saul's army, had taken Ish-Bosheth son of Saul and brought him over to Mahanaim. ⁹He made him king over Gilead, Ashuri[a] and Jezreel, and also over Ephraim, Benjamin and all Israel.

¹⁰Ish-Bosheth son of Saul was forty years old when he became king over Israel, and he reigned two years. The house of Judah, however, followed David. ¹¹The length of time David was king in Hebron over the house of Judah was seven years and six months.

¹²Abner son of Ner, together with the men of Ish-Bosheth son of Saul, left Mahanaim and went to Gibeon. ¹³Joab son of Zeruiah and David's men went out and met them at the pool of Gibeon. One group sat down on one side of the pool and one group on the other side.

¹⁴Then Abner said to Joab, "Let's have some of the young men get up and fight hand to hand in front of us."

"All right, let them do it," Joab said.

¹⁵So they stood up and were counted off— twelve men for Benjamin and Ish-Bosheth son of Saul, and twelve for David. ¹⁶Then each man grabbed his opponent by the head and thrust his dagger into his opponent's side, and they fell

大衞受膏作猶大王

2 此後，<u>大衞</u>問耶和華說：「我上<u>猶大</u>的一個城去可以嗎？」

耶和華說：「可以。」

<u>大衞</u>說：「我上哪一個城去呢？」耶和華說：「上<u>希伯崙</u>去。」

²於是<u>大衞</u>和他的兩個妻—一個是<u>耶斯列</u>人<u>亞希暖</u>，一個是作過<u>迦密</u>人<u>拿八</u>妻的<u>亞比該</u>，都上那裏去了。³<u>大衞</u>也將跟隨他的人和他們各人的眷屬一同帶上去，住在<u>希伯崙</u>的城邑中。⁴<u>猶大</u>人來到<u>希伯崙</u>，在那裏膏<u>大衞</u>作<u>猶大</u>家的王。

有人告訴<u>大衞</u>說：「葬埋<u>掃羅</u>的是<u>基列雅比</u>人。」⁵<u>大衞</u>就差人去見<u>基列雅比</u>人，對他們說：「你們厚待你們的主<u>掃羅</u>，將他葬埋。願耶和華賜福與你們。⁶你們既行了這事，願耶和華以慈愛誠實待你們，我也要為此厚待你們。⁷現在你們的主<u>掃羅</u>死了，<u>猶大</u>家已經膏我作他們的王，所以你們要剛強奮勇。」

大衞家與掃羅家爭戰

⁸<u>掃羅</u>的元帥<u>尼珥</u>的兒子<u>押尼珥</u>，曾將<u>掃羅</u>的兒子<u>伊施波設</u>帶過河到<u>瑪哈念</u>，⁹立他作王，治理<u>基列</u>、<u>亞書利</u>、<u>耶斯列</u>、<u>以法蓮</u>、<u>便雅憫</u>和<u>以色列</u>眾人。

¹⁰<u>掃羅</u>的兒子<u>伊施波設</u>登基的時候，年四十歲，作<u>以色列</u>王二年；惟獨<u>猶大</u>家歸從<u>大衞</u>。¹¹<u>大衞</u>在<u>希伯崙</u>作<u>猶大</u>家的王，共七年零六個月。

¹²<u>尼珥</u>的兒子<u>押尼珥</u>和<u>掃羅</u>的兒子<u>伊施波設</u>的僕人，從<u>瑪哈念</u>出來，往<u>基遍</u>去。¹³<u>洗魯雅</u>的兒子<u>約押</u>和<u>大衞</u>的僕人也出來，在<u>基遍</u>池旁與他們相遇。一班坐在池這邊，一班坐在池那邊。

¹⁴<u>押尼珥</u>對<u>約押</u>說：「讓少年人起來，在我們面前戲耍吧！」

<u>約押</u>說：「可以。」

¹⁵就按着定數起來：屬<u>掃羅</u>兒子<u>伊施波設</u>的<u>便雅憫</u>人過去十二名，<u>大衞</u>的僕人也過去十二名。¹⁶彼此揪頭，用刀刺肋，一同仆倒。所以那地

叫作希利甲哈素林，就在基遍。

17 那日的戰事兇猛，押尼珥和以色列人敗在大衛的僕人面前。

18 在那裏有洗魯雅的三個兒子：約押、亞比篩、亞撒黑。亞撒黑腳快如野鹿一般。19 亞撒黑追趕押尼珥，直追趕他不偏左右。20 押尼珥回頭說：「你是亞撒黑嗎？」

回答說：「是。」

21 押尼珥對他說：「你或轉向左，轉向右，拿住一個少年人，剝去他的戰衣。」亞撒黑卻不肯轉開不追趕他。

22 押尼珥又對亞撒黑說：「你轉開不追趕我吧！我何必殺你呢？若殺你，有甚麼臉見你哥哥約押呢？」

23 亞撒黑仍不肯轉開，故此押尼珥就用槍鐏刺入他的肚腹，甚至槍從背後透出。亞撒黑就在那裏仆倒而死。眾人趕到亞撒黑仆倒而死的地方，就都站住。

24 約押和亞比篩追趕押尼珥，日落的時候，到了通基遍曠野的路旁，基亞對面的亞瑪山。25 便雅憫人聚集，跟隨押尼珥站在一個山頂上。

26 押尼珥呼叫約押說：「刀劍豈可永遠殺人嗎？你豈不知終久必有苦楚嗎？你要等何時才叫百姓回去，不追趕弟兄呢？」

27 約押說：「我指着永生的神起誓，你若不說戲耍的那句話，今日早晨百姓就回去，不追趕弟兄了。」

28 於是約押吹角，眾民就站住，不再追趕以色列人，也不再打仗了。

29 押尼珥和跟隨他的人整夜經過亞拉巴，過約旦河走過畢倫，到了瑪哈念。

30 約押追趕押尼珥回來，聚集眾民，見大衛的僕人中缺少了十九個人和亞撒黑。31 但大衛的僕人殺了便雅憫人和跟隨押尼珥的人，共三百六十

down together. So that place in Gibeon was called Helkath Hazzurim.[a]

17 The battle that day was very fierce, and Abner and the men of Israel were defeated by David's men.

18 The three sons of Zeruiah were there: Joab, Abishai and Asahel. Now Asahel was as fleet-footed as a wild gazelle. 19 He chased Abner, turning neither to the right nor to the left as he pursued him. 20 Abner looked behind him and asked, "Is that you, Asahel?"

"It is," he answered.

21 Then Abner said to him, "Turn aside to the right or to the left; take on one of the young men and strip him of his weapons." But Asahel would not stop chasing him.

22 Again Abner warned Asahel, "Stop chasing me! Why should I strike you down? How could I look your brother Joab in the face?"

23 But Asahel refused to give up the pursuit; so Abner thrust the butt of his spear into Asahel's stomach, and the spear came out through his back. He fell there and died on the spot. And every man stopped when he came to the place where Asahel had fallen and died.

24 But Joab and Abishai pursued Abner, and as the sun was setting, they came to the hill of Ammah, near Giah on the way to the wasteland of Gibeon. 25 Then the men of Benjamin rallied behind Abner. They formed themselves into a group and took their stand on top of a hill.

26 Abner called out to Joab, "Must the sword devour forever? Don't you realize that this will end in bitterness? How long before you order your men to stop pursuing their brothers?"

27 Joab answered, "As surely as God lives, if you had not spoken, the men would have continued the pursuit of their brothers until morning.[b]"

28 So Joab blew the trumpet, and all the men came to a halt; they no longer pursued Israel, nor did they fight anymore.

29 All that night Abner and his men marched through the Arabah. They crossed the Jordan, continued through the whole Bithron[c] and came to Mahanaim.

30 Then Joab returned from pursuing Abner and assembled all his men. Besides Asahel, nineteen of David's men were found missing. 31 But David's men had killed three hundred and

a 16 Helkath Hazzurim means field of daggers or field of hostilities.
b 27 Or spoken this morning, the men would not have taken up the pursuit of their brothers; or spoken, the men would have given up the pursuit of their brothers by morning　　c 29 Or morning; or ravine; the meaning of the Hebrew for this word is uncertain.

sixty Benjamites who were with Abner. [32]They took Asahel and buried him in his father's tomb at Bethlehem. Then Joab and his men marched all night and arrived at Hebron by daybreak.

3

The war between the house of Saul and the house of David lasted a long time. David grew stronger and stronger, while the house of Saul grew weaker and weaker.

[2]Sons were born to David in Hebron:

His firstborn was Amnon the son of Ahinoam of Jezreel;

[3]his second, Kileab the son of Abigail the widow of Nabal of Carmel;

the third, Absalom the son of Maacah daughter of Talmai king of Geshur;

[4]the fourth, Adonijah the son of Haggith;

the fifth, Shephatiah the son of Abital;

[5]and the sixth, Ithream the son of David's wife Eglah.

These were born to David in Hebron.

Abner Goes Over to David

[6]During the war between the house of Saul and the house of David, Abner had been strengthening his own position in the house of Saul. [7]Now Saul had had a concubine named Rizpah daughter of Aiah. And Ish-Bosheth said to Abner, "Why did you sleep with my father's concubine?"

[8]Abner was very angry because of what Ish-Bosheth said and he answered, "Am I a dog's head—on Judah's side? This very day I am loyal to the house of your father Saul and to his family and friends. I haven't handed you over to David. Yet now you accuse me of an offense involving this woman! [9]May God deal with Abner, be it ever so severely, if I do not do for David what the LORD promised him on oath [10]and transfer the kingdom from the house of Saul and establish David's throne over Israel and Judah from Dan to Beersheba." [11]Ish-Bosheth did not dare to say another word to Abner, because he was afraid of him.

[12]Then Abner sent messengers on his behalf to say to David, "Whose land is it? Make an agreement with me, and I will help you bring all Israel over to you."

[13]"Good," said David. "I will make an agreement with you. But I demand one thing of you: Do not come into my presence unless you bring Michal daughter of Saul when you come to see me." [14]Then David sent messengers to Ish-Bosheth son of Saul, demanding, "Give me my wife Michal, whom I betrothed to myself for the price of a hundred Philistine foreskins."

[15]So Ish-Bosheth gave orders and had her

名。[32]眾人將亞撒黑送到伯利恆，葬在他父親的墳墓裏。約押和跟隨他的人走了一夜，天亮的時候到了希伯崙。

3

掃羅家和大衞家爭戰許久，大衞家日見強盛，掃羅家日見衰弱。

[2]大衞在希伯崙得了幾個兒子：

長子暗嫩，是耶斯列人亞希暖所生的；

[3]次子基利押（註："基利押"歷代上3章1節作"但以利"），是作過迦密人拿八的妻亞比該所生的；三子押沙龍，是基述王達買的女兒瑪迦所生的；

[4]四子亞多尼雅，是哈及所生的；五子示法提雅，是亞比她所生的；

[5]六子以特念，是大衞的妻以格拉所生的。

大衞這六個兒子，都是在希伯崙生的。

押尼珥歸服大衞

[6]掃羅家和大衞家爭戰的時候，押尼珥在掃羅家大有權勢。[7]掃羅有一妃嬪，名叫利斯巴，是愛亞的女兒。一日，伊施波設對押尼珥說："你為甚麼與我父的妃嬪同房呢？"

[8]押尼珥因伊施波設的話，就甚發怒，說："我豈是猶大的狗頭呢？我恩待你父掃羅的家和他的弟兄、朋友，不將你交在大衞手裏，今日你竟為這婦人責備我嗎？[9][10]我若不照着耶和華起誓應許大衞的話行，廢去掃羅的位，建立大衞的位，使他治理以色列和猶大，從但直到別是巴，願神重重地降罰與我！"[11]伊施波設懼怕押尼珥，不敢回答一句。

[12]押尼珥打發人去見大衞，替他說："這國歸誰呢？"又說："你與我立約，我必幫助你，使以色列人都歸服你。"

[13]大衞說："好！我與你立約。但有一件，你來見我面的時候，若不將掃羅的女兒米甲帶來，必不得見我的面。"[14]大衞就打發人去見掃羅的兒子伊施波設，說："你要將我的妻米甲歸還我，她是我從前用一百非利士人的陽皮所聘定的。"

[15]伊施波設就打發人去，將米甲

從拉億的兒子、她丈夫帕鐵那裏接回來。¹⁶米甲的丈夫跟著她，一面走、一面哭，直跟到巴戶琳。押尼珥說："你回去吧！"帕鐵就回去了。

¹⁷押尼珥對以色列長老說："從前你們願意大衛作王治理你們，¹⁸現在你們可以照心願而行。因為耶和華曾論到大衛說：'我必藉我僕人大衛的手，救我民以色列脫離非利士人和眾仇敵的手。'"

¹⁹押尼珥也用這話說給便雅憫人聽。又到希伯崙，將以色列人和便雅憫全家一切所喜悅的事說給大衛聽。²⁰押尼珥帶著二十個人，來到希伯崙見大衛，大衛就為押尼珥和他帶來的人設擺筵席。²¹押尼珥對大衛說："我要起身去招聚以色列眾人來見我主我王，與你立約，你就可以照著心願作王。"於是大衛送押尼珥去，押尼珥就平平安安地去了。

約押謀殺押尼珥

²²約押和大衛的僕人攻擊敵軍，帶回許多的掠物。那時押尼珥不在希伯崙大衛那裏，因大衛已經送他去，他也平平安安地去了。²³約押和跟隨他的全軍到了，就有人告訴約押說："尼珥的兒子押尼珥來見王，王送他去，他也平平安安地去了。"

²⁴約押去見王說："你這是做甚麼呢？押尼珥來見你，你為何送他去，他就蹤影不見了呢？²⁵你當曉得尼珥的兒子押尼珥來是要誆哄你，要知道你的出入和你一切所行的事。"

²⁶約押從大衛那裏出來，就打發人去追趕押尼珥，在西拉井追上他，將他帶回來。大衛卻不知道。²⁷押尼珥回到希伯崙，約押領他到城門的甕洞，假作要與他說機密話，就在那裏刺透他的肚腹，他便死了。這是報殺他兄弟亞撒黑的仇。

²⁸大衛聽見了就說："流尼珥的兒子押尼珥的血，這罪在耶和華面前必永不歸我和我的國。²⁹願流他血的罪歸到約押頭上和他父的全家；又願約押家不斷有患漏症的，長大痲瘋

taken away from her husband Paltiel son of Laish. ¹⁶Her husband, however, went with her, weeping behind her all the way to Bahurim. Then Abner said to him, "Go back home!" So he went back.

¹⁷Abner conferred with the elders of Israel and said, "For some time you have wanted to make David your king. ¹⁸Now do it! For the LORD promised David, 'By my servant David I will rescue my people Israel from the hand of the Philistines and from the hand of all their enemies.'"

¹⁹Abner also spoke to the Benjamites in person. Then he went to Hebron to tell David everything that Israel and the whole house of Benjamin wanted to do. ²⁰When Abner, who had twenty men with him, came to David at Hebron, David prepared a feast for him and his men. ²¹Then Abner said to David, "Let me go at once and assemble all Israel for my lord the king, so that they may make a compact with you, and that you may rule over all that your heart desires." So David sent Abner away, and he went in peace.

Joab Murders Abner

²²Just then David's men and Joab returned from a raid and brought with them a great deal of plunder. But Abner was no longer with David in Hebron, because David had sent him away, and he had gone in peace. ²³When Joab and all the soldiers with him arrived, he was told that Abner son of Ner had come to the king and that the king had sent him away and that he had gone in peace.

²⁴So Joab went to the king and said, "What have you done? Look, Abner came to you. Why did you let him go? Now he is gone! ²⁵You know Abner son of Ner; he came to deceive you and observe your movements and find out everything you are doing."

²⁶Joab then left David and sent messengers after Abner, and they brought him back from the well of Sirah. But David did not know it. ²⁷Now when Abner returned to Hebron, Joab took him aside into the gateway, as though to speak with him privately. And there, to avenge the blood of his brother Asahel, Joab stabbed him in the stomach, and he died.

²⁸Later, when David heard about this, he said, "I and my kingdom are forever innocent before the LORD concerning the blood of Abner son of Ner. ²⁹May his blood fall upon the head of Joab and upon all his father's house! May Joab's house never be without someone who has a run-

ning sore or leprosy[a] or who leans on a crutch or who falls by the sword or who lacks food."

30(Joab and his brother Abishai murdered Abner because he had killed their brother Asahel in the battle at Gibeon.)

31Then David said to Joab and all the people with him, "Tear your clothes and put on sackcloth and walk in mourning in front of Abner." King David himself walked behind the bier. 32They buried Abner in Hebron, and the king wept aloud at Abner's tomb. All the people wept also.

33The king sang this lament for Abner:

"Should Abner have died as the lawless die?
34 　Your hands were not bound,
　your feet were not fettered.
You fell as one falls before wicked men."

And all the people wept over him again.

35Then they all came and urged David to eat something while it was still day; but David took an oath, saying, "May God deal with me, be it ever so severely, if I taste bread or anything else before the sun sets!"

36All the people took note and were pleased; indeed, everything the king did pleased them. 37So on that day all the people and all Israel knew that the king had no part in the murder of Abner son of Ner.

38Then the king said to his men, "Do you not realize that a prince and a great man has fallen in Israel this day? 39And today, though I am the anointed king, I am weak, and these sons of Zeruiah are too strong for me. May the LORD repay the evildoer according to his evil deeds!"

Ish-Bosheth Murdered

4 When Ish-Bosheth son of Saul heard that Abner had died in Hebron, he lost courage, and all Israel became alarmed. 2Now Saul's son had two men who were leaders of raiding bands. One was named Baanah and the other Recab; they were sons of Rimmon the Beerothite from the tribe of Benjamin—Beeroth is considered part of Benjamin, 3because the people of Beeroth fled to Gittaim and have lived there as aliens to this day.

4(Jonathan son of Saul had a son who was lame in both feet. He was five years old when the news about Saul and Jonathan came from Jezreel. His nurse picked him up and fled, but as she hurried to leave, he fell and became crippled. His name was Mephibosheth.)

的，架拐而行的，被刀殺死的，缺乏飲食的。"

30約押和他兄弟亞比篩殺了押尼珥，是因押尼珥在基遍爭戰的時候，殺了他們的兄弟亞撒黑。

31大衛吩咐約押和跟隨他的眾人說："你們當撕裂衣服，腰束麻布，在押尼珥棺前哀哭。"大衛王也跟在棺後。32他們將押尼珥葬在希伯崙。王在押尼珥的墓旁放聲而哭，眾民也都哭了。

33王為押尼珥舉哀說：

"押尼珥何竟像愚頑人死呢？
34你手未曾捆綁，
　腳未曾鎖住，
你死如人死在罪孽之輩手下一樣。"

於是眾民又為押尼珥哀哭。

35日頭未落的時候，眾民來勸大衛吃飯，但大衛起誓說："我若在日頭未落以前吃飯，或吃別物，願神重重地降罰與我！"

36眾民知道了，就都喜悅。凡王所行的，眾民無不喜悅。37那日以色列眾民才知道殺尼珥的兒子押尼珥，並非出於王意。

38王對臣僕說："你們豈不知今日以色列人中，死了一個作元帥的大丈夫嗎？39我雖然受膏為王，今日還是軟弱。這洗魯雅的兩個兒子比我剛強，願耶和華照着惡人所行的惡報應他。"

伊施波設被殺

4 掃羅的兒子伊施波設聽見押尼珥死在希伯崙，手就發軟，以色列眾人也都驚惶。2掃羅的兒子伊施波設有兩個軍長：一名巴拿，一名利甲，是便雅憫支派、比錄人臨門的兒子。比錄也屬便雅憫。3比錄人早先逃到基他音，在那裏寄居，直到今日。

4掃羅的兒子約拿單有一個兒子，名叫米非波設，是瘸腿的。掃羅和約拿單死亡的消息從耶斯列傳到的時候，他才五歲。他乳母抱着他逃跑，因為跑得太急，孩子掉在地上，腿就瘸了。

---

a 29 The Hebrew word was used for various diseases affecting the skin—not necessarily leprosy.

⁵一日，比錄人臨門的兩個兒子利甲和巴拿出去，約在午熱的時候，到了伊施波設的家，伊施波設正睡午覺。⁶他們進了房子，假作要取麥子，就刺透伊施波設的肚腹逃跑了。

⁷他們進房子的時候，伊施波設正在臥房裏躺在牀上。他們將他殺死，割了他的首級，拿着首級在亞拉巴走了一夜。⁸將伊施波設的首級拿到希伯崙見大衛王，說："王的仇敵掃羅，曾尋索王的性命。看哪，這是他兒子伊施波設的首級，耶和華今日為我主我王，在掃羅和他後裔的身上報了仇。"

⁹大衛對比錄人臨門的兒子利甲和他兄弟巴拿說："我指着救我性命脫離一切苦難、永生的耶和華起誓：¹⁰從前有人報告我說'掃羅死了'，他自以為報好消息，我就拿住他，將他殺在洗革拉，這就作了他報消息的賞賜。¹¹何況惡人將義人殺在他的牀上，我豈不向你們討流他血的罪，從世上除滅你們呢？"

¹²於是大衛吩咐少年人將他們殺了，砍斷他們的手腳，掛在希伯崙的池旁；卻將伊施波設的首級，葬在希伯崙押尼珥的墳墓裏。

大衛作全以色列王

5 以色列眾支派來到希伯崙見大衛，說："我們原是你的骨肉。²從前掃羅作我們王的時候，率領以色列人出入的是你。耶和華也曾應許你說：'你必牧養我的民以色列，作以色列的君。'"

³於是以色列的長老都來到希伯崙見大衛王，大衛在希伯崙耶和華面前與他們立約，他們就膏大衛作以色列的王。

⁴大衛登基的時候年三十歲，在位四十年。⁵在希伯崙作猶大王七年零六個月，在耶路撒冷作以色列和猶大王三十三年。

⁵Now Recab and Baanah, the sons of Rimmon the Beerothite, set out for the house of Ish-Bosheth, and they arrived there in the heat of the day while he was taking his noonday rest. ⁶They went into the inner part of the house as if to get some wheat, and they stabbed him in the stomach. Then Recab and his brother Baanah slipped away.

⁷They had gone into the house while he was lying on the bed in his bedroom. After they stabbed and killed him, they cut off his head. Taking it with them, they traveled all night by way of the Arabah. ⁸They brought the head of Ish-Bosheth to David at Hebron and said to the king, "Here is the head of Ish-Bosheth son of Saul, your enemy, who tried to take your life. This day the LORD has avenged my lord the king against Saul and his offspring."

⁹David answered Recab and his brother Baanah, the sons of Rimmon the Beerothite, "As surely as the LORD lives, who has delivered me out of all trouble, ¹⁰when a man told me, 'Saul is dead,' and thought he was bringing good news, I seized him and put him to death in Ziklag. That was the reward I gave him for his news! ¹¹How much more—when wicked men have killed an innocent man in his own house and on his own bed—should I not now demand his blood from your hand and rid the earth of you!"

¹²So David gave an order to his men, and they killed them. They cut off their hands and feet and hung the bodies by the pool in Hebron. But they took the head of Ish-Bosheth and buried it in Abner's tomb at Hebron.

David Becomes King Over Israel

5 All the tribes of Israel came to David at Hebron and said, "We are your own flesh and blood. ²In the past, while Saul was king over us, you were the one who led Israel on their military campaigns. And the LORD said to you, 'You will shepherd my people Israel, and you will become their ruler.'"

³When all the elders of Israel had come to King David at Hebron, the king made a compact with them at Hebron before the LORD, and they anointed David king over Israel.

⁴David was thirty years old when he became king, and he reigned forty years. ⁵In Hebron he reigned over Judah seven years and six months, and in Jerusalem he reigned over all Israel and Judah thirty-three years.

David Conquers Jerusalem

⁶The king and his men marched to Jerusalem to attack the Jebusites, who lived there. The Jebusites said to David, "You will not get in here; even the blind and the lame can ward you off." They thought, "David cannot get in here." ⁷Nevertheless, David captured the fortress of Zion, the City of David.

⁸On that day, David said, "Anyone who conquers the Jebusites will have to use the water shaft[a] to reach those 'lame and blind' who are David's enemies.[b]" That is why they say, "The 'blind and lame' will not enter the palace."

⁹David then took up residence in the fortress and called it the City of David. He built up the area around it, from the supporting terraces[c] inward. ¹⁰And he became more and more powerful, because the LORD God Almighty was with him.

¹¹Now Hiram king of Tyre sent messengers to David, along with cedar logs and carpenters and stonemasons, and they built a palace for David. ¹²And David knew that the LORD had established him as king over Israel and had exalted his kingdom for the sake of his people Israel.

¹³After he left Hebron, David took more concubines and wives in Jerusalem, and more sons and daughters were born to him. ¹⁴These are the names of the children born to him there: Shammua, Shobab, Nathan, Solomon, ¹⁵Ibhar, Elishua, Nepheg, Japhia, ¹⁶Elishama, Eliada and Eliphelet.

David Defeats the Philistines

¹⁷When the Philistines heard that David had been anointed king over Israel, they went up in full force to search for him, but David heard about it and went down to the stronghold. ¹⁸Now the Philistines had come and spread out in the Valley of Rephaim; ¹⁹so David inquired of the LORD, "Shall I go and attack the Philistines? Will you hand them over to me?"

The LORD answered him, "Go, for I will surely hand the Philistines over to you."

²⁰So David went to Baal Perazim, and there he defeated them. He said, "As waters break out, the LORD has broken out against my enemies before me." So that place was called Baal Perazim.[d] ²¹The Philistines abandoned their idols there, and David and his men carried them off.

²²Once more the Philistines came up and

大衛攻佔耶路撒冷

⁶大衛和跟隨他的人到了耶路撒冷，要攻打住那地方的耶布斯人。耶布斯人對大衛說：「你若不趕出瞎子、瘸子，必不能進這地方。」心裏想大衛決不能進去。⁷然而大衛攻取錫安的保障，就是大衛的城。

⁸當日大衛說：「誰攻打耶布斯人，當上水溝攻打我心裏所恨惡的瘸子、瞎子。」從此有俗語說：「在那裏有瞎子、瘸子，他不能進屋去。」

⁹大衛住在保障裏，給保障起名叫大衛城。大衛又從米羅以裏，周圍築牆。¹⁰大衛日見強盛，因為耶和華萬軍之神與他同在。

¹¹推羅王希蘭將香柏木運到大衛那裏，又差遣使者和木匠、石匠給大衛建造宮殿。¹²大衛就知道耶和華堅立他作以色列王，又為自己的民以色列使他的國興旺。

¹³大衛離開希伯崙之後，在耶路撒冷又立后妃，又生兒女。¹⁴在耶路撒冷所生的兒子是：沙母亞、朔罷、拿單、所羅門、¹⁵益轄、以利書亞、尼斐、雅非亞、¹⁶以利沙瑪、以利雅大、以利法列。

大衛打敗非利士人

¹⁷非利士人聽見人膏大衛作以色列王，非利士眾人就上來尋索大衛。大衛聽見，就下到保障。¹⁸非利士人來了，布散在利乏音谷。¹⁹大衛求問耶和華說：「我可以上去攻打非利士人嗎？你將他們交在我手裏嗎？」

耶和華說：「你可以上去，我必將非利士人交在你手裏。」

²⁰大衛來到巴力毘拉心，在那裏擊殺非利士人，說：「耶和華在我面前沖破敵人，如同水沖去一般。」因此稱那地方為巴力毘拉心。²¹非利士人將偶像撇在那裏，大衛和跟隨他的人拿去了。

²²非利士人又上來，布散在利乏

---

a 8 Or use scaling hooks   b 8 Or are hated by David   c 9 Or the Millo   d 20 Baal Perazim means the lord who breaks out.

音谷。23大衛求問耶和華。耶和華說：「不要一直地上去，要轉到他們後頭，從桑樹對面攻打他們。24你聽見桑樹梢上有腳步的聲音，就要急速前去，因為那時耶和華已經在你前頭去攻打非利士人的軍隊。」25大衛就遵着耶和華所吩咐的去行，攻打非利士人，從迦巴直到基色。

運約櫃往耶路撒冷

6 大衛又聚集以色列中所有挑選的人三萬。2大衛起身率領跟隨他的眾人前往，要從巴拉猶大將神的約櫃運來。這約櫃就是坐在二基路伯上萬軍之耶和華留名的約櫃。3他們將神的約櫃從岡上亞比拿達的家裏抬出來，放在新車上。亞比拿達的兩個兒子烏撒和亞希約趕這新車。4他們將神的約櫃從岡上亞比拿達家裏抬出來的時候，亞希約在櫃前行走。5大衛和以色列的全家在耶和華面前，用松木製造的各樣樂器和琴、瑟、鼓、鈸、鑼，作樂跳舞。

6到了拿艮的禾場，因為牛失前蹄（註：或作「驚跳」），烏撒就伸手扶住神的約櫃。7神耶和華向烏撒發怒，因這錯誤擊殺他，他就死在神的約櫃旁。

8大衛因耶和華擊殺（註：原文作「闖殺」）烏撒，心裏愁煩，就稱那地方為毘列斯烏撒，直到今日。
9那日，大衛懼怕耶和華，說：「耶和華的約櫃怎可運到我這裏來？」10於是大衛不肯將耶和華的約櫃運進大衛的城，卻運到迦特人俄別以東的家中。11耶和華的約櫃在迦特人俄別以東家中三個月。耶和華賜福

spread out in the Valley of Rephaim; 23so David inquired of the LORD, and he answered, "Do not go straight up, but circle around behind them and attack them in front of the balsam trees. 24As soon as you hear the sound of marching in the tops of the balsam trees, move quickly, because that will mean the LORD has gone out in front of you to strike the Philistine army." 25So David did as the LORD commanded him, and he struck down the Philistines all the way from Gibeon[a] to Gezer.

The Ark Brought to Jerusalem

6 David again brought together out of Israel chosen men, thirty thousand in all. 2He and all his men set out from Baalah of Judah[b] to bring up from there the ark of God, which is called by the Name,[c] the name of the LORD Almighty, who is enthroned between the cherubim that are on the ark. 3They set the ark of God on a new cart and brought it from the house of Abinadab, which was on the hill. Uzzah and Ahio, sons of Abinadab, were guiding the new cart 4with the ark of God on it,[d] and Ahio was walking in front of it. 5David and the whole house of Israel were celebrating with all their might before the LORD, with songs[e] and with harps, lyres, tambourines, sistrums and cymbals.

6When they came to the threshing floor of Nacon, Uzzah reached out and took hold of the ark of God, because the oxen stumbled. 7The LORD's anger burned against Uzzah because of his irreverent act; therefore God struck him down and he died there beside the ark of God.

8Then David was angry because the LORD's wrath had broken out against Uzzah, and to this day that place is called Perez Uzzah.[f]

9David was afraid of the LORD that day and said, "How can the ark of the LORD ever come to me?" 10He was not willing to take the ark of the LORD to be with him in the City of David. Instead, he took it aside to the house of Obed-Edom the Gittite. 11The ark of the LORD remained in the house of Obed-Edom the Gittite

a 25 Septuagint (see also 1 Chron. 14:16); Hebrew *Geba*
b 2 That is, Kiriath Jearim; Hebrew *Baale Judah*, a variant of *Baalah of Judah*　c 2 Hebrew; Septuagint and Vulgate do not have *the Name*.　d 3,4 Dead Sea Scrolls and some Septuagint manuscripts; Masoretic Text *cart* 4*and they brought it with the ark of God from the house of Abinadab, which was on the hill*
e 5 See Dead Sea Scrolls, Septuagint and 1 Chronicles 13:8; Masoretic Text *celebrating before the LORD with all kinds of instruments made of pine.*　f 8 *Perez Uzzah* means *outbreak against Uzzah.*

for three months, and the LORD blessed him and his entire household.

12Now King David was told, "The LORD has blessed the household of Obed-Edom and everything he has, because of the ark of God." So David went down and brought up the ark of God from the house of Obed-Edom to the City of David with rejoicing. 13When those who were carrying the ark of the LORD had taken six steps, he sacrificed a bull and a fattened calf. 14David, wearing a linen ephod, danced before the LORD with all his might, 15while he and the entire house of Israel brought up the ark of the LORD with shouts and the sound of trumpets.

16As the ark of the LORD was entering the City of David, Michal daughter of Saul watched from a window. And when she saw King David leaping and dancing before the LORD, she despised him in her heart.

17They brought the ark of the LORD and set it in its place inside the tent that David had pitched for it, and David sacrificed burnt offerings and fellowship offerings^a before the LORD. 18After he had finished sacrificing the burnt offerings and fellowship offerings, he blessed the people in the name of the LORD Almighty. 19Then he gave a loaf of bread, a cake of dates and a cake of raisins to each person in the whole crowd of Israelites, both men and women. And all the people went to their homes.

20When David returned home to bless his household, Michal daughter of Saul came out to meet him and said, "How the king of Israel has distinguished himself today, disrobing in the sight of the slave girls of his servants as any vulgar fellow would!"

21David said to Michal, "It was before the LORD, who chose me rather than your father or anyone from his house when he appointed me ruler over the LORD's people Israel—I will celebrate before the LORD. 22I will become even more undignified than this, and I will be humiliated in my own eyes. But by these slave girls you spoke of, I will be held in honor."

23And Michal daughter of Saul had no children to the day of her death.

God's Promise to David

7 After the king was settled in his palace and the LORD had given him rest from all his enemies around him, 2he said to Nathan the prophet, "Here I am, living in a palace of cedar, while the ark of God remains in a tent."

a 17 Traditionally peace offerings; also in verse 18

給俄別以東和他的全家。

12有人告訴大衞王說：“耶和華因為約櫃賜福給俄別以東的家和一切屬他的。”大衞就去，歡歡喜喜地將神的約櫃從俄別以東家中抬到大衞的城裏。13抬耶和華約櫃的人走了六步，大衞就獻牛與肥羊為祭。14大衞穿着細麻布的以弗得，在耶和華面前極力跳舞。15這樣，大衞和以色列的全家歡呼吹角，將耶和華的約櫃抬上來。

16耶和華的約櫃進了大衞城的時候，掃羅的女兒米甲從窗戶裏觀看，見大衞王在耶和華面前踴躍跳舞，心裏就輕視他。

17眾人將耶和華的約櫃請進去，安放在所預備的地方，就是在大衞所搭的帳幕裏。大衞在耶和華面前獻燔祭和平安祭。18大衞獻完了燔祭和平安祭，就奉萬軍之耶和華的名給民祝福，19並且分給以色列眾人，無論男女，每人一個餅，一塊肉，一個葡萄餅。眾人就各回各家去了。

20大衞回家要給眷屬祝福，掃羅的女兒米甲出來迎接他，說：“以色列王今日在臣僕的婢女眼前露體，如同一個輕賤人無恥露體一樣，有好大的榮耀啊！”

21大衞對米甲說：“這是在耶和華面前；耶和華已揀選我，廢了你父和你父的全家，立我作耶和華民以色列的君，所以我必在耶和華面前跳舞。22我也必更加卑微，自己看為輕賤。你所說的那些婢女，她們倒要尊敬我。”

23掃羅的女兒米甲，直到死日，沒有生養兒女。

神對大衞的應許

7 王住在自己宮中，耶和華使他安靖，不被四圍的仇敵擾亂。2那時，王對先知拿單說：“看哪，我住在香柏木的宮中，神的約櫃反在幔子裏。”

³拿單對王說："你可以照你的心意而行，因為耶和華與你同在。"

⁴當夜耶和華的話臨到拿單說：

⁵ "你去告訴我僕人大衛，說耶和華如此說：'你豈可建造殿宇給我居住呢？⁶自從我領以色列人出埃及直到今日，我未曾住過殿宇，常在會幕和帳幕中行走。⁷凡我同以色列人所走的地方，我何曾向以色列一支派的士師，就是我吩咐牧養我民以色列的說：你們為何不給我建造香柏木的殿宇呢？'

⁸ "現在你要告訴我僕人大衛說，萬軍之耶和華如此說：'我從羊圈中將你召來，叫你不再跟從羊羣，立你作我民以色列的君。⁹你無論往哪裏去，我常與你同在，剪除你的一切仇敵。我必使你得大名，好像世上大大有名的人一樣。¹⁰我必為我民以色列選定一個地方，栽培他們，使他們住自己的地方，不再遷移；兇惡之子也不像從前擾害他們，¹¹並不像我命士師治理我民以色列的時候一樣。我必使你安靖，不被一切仇敵擾亂。

" '並且我耶和華應許你，必為你建立家室。¹²你壽數滿足、與你列祖同睡的時候，我必使你的後裔接續你的位，我也必堅定他的國。¹³他必為我的名建造殿宇，我必堅定他的國位，直到永遠。¹⁴我要作他的父，他要作我的子；他若犯了罪，我必用人的杖責打他，用人的鞭責罰他。¹⁵但我的慈愛仍不離開他，像離開在你面前所廢棄的掃羅一樣。¹⁶你的家和你的國，必在我（註：原文作"你"）面前永遠堅立。你的國位也必堅定，直到永遠。' "

¹⁷拿單就按這一切話，照這默示，告訴大衛。

³Nathan replied to the king, "Whatever you have in mind, go ahead and do it, for the LORD is with you."

⁴That night the word of the LORD came to Nathan, saying:

⁵"Go and tell my servant David, 'This is what the LORD says: Are you the one to build me a house to dwell in? ⁶I have not dwelt in a house from the day I brought the Israelites up out of Egypt to this day. I have been moving from place to place with a tent as my dwelling. ⁷Wherever I have moved with all the Israelites, did I ever say to any of their rulers whom I commanded to shepherd my people Israel, "Why have you not built me a house of cedar?" '

⁸"Now then, tell my servant David, 'This is what the LORD Almighty says: I took you from the pasture and from following the flock to be ruler over my people Israel. ⁹I have been with you wherever you have gone, and I have cut off all your enemies from before you. Now I will make your name great, like the names of the greatest men of the earth. ¹⁰And I will provide a place for my people Israel and will plant them so that they can have a home of their own and no longer be disturbed. Wicked people will not oppress them anymore, as they did at the beginning ¹¹and have done ever since the time I appointed leaders[a] over my people Israel. I will also give you rest from all your enemies.

" 'The LORD declares to you that the LORD himself will establish a house for you: ¹²When your days are over and you rest with your fathers, I will raise up your offspring to succeed you, who will come from your own body, and I will establish his kingdom. ¹³He is the one who will build a house for my Name, and I will establish the throne of his kingdom forever. ¹⁴I will be his father, and he will be my son. When he does wrong, I will punish him with the rod of men, with floggings inflicted by men. ¹⁵But my love will never be taken away from him, as I took it away from Saul, whom I removed from before you. ¹⁶Your house and your kingdom will endure forever before me[b]; your throne will be established forever.' "

¹⁷Nathan reported to David all the words of this entire revelation.

a 11 Traditionally judges　b 16 Some Hebrew manuscripts and Septuagint; most Hebrew manuscripts you

David's Prayer

¹⁸Then King David went in and sat before the LORD, and he said:

"Who am I, O Sovereign LORD, and what is my family, that you have brought me this far? ¹⁹And as if this were not enough in your sight, O Sovereign LORD, you have also spoken about the future of the house of your servant. Is this your usual way of dealing with man, O Sovereign LORD?

²⁰"What more can David say to you? For you know your servant, O Sovereign LORD. ²¹For the sake of your word and according to your will, you have done this great thing and made it known to your servant.

²²"How great you are, O Sovereign LORD! There is no one like you, and there is no God but you, as we have heard with our own ears. ²³And who is like your people Israel—the one nation on earth that God went out to redeem as a people for himself, and to make a name for himself, and to perform great and awesome wonders by driving out nations and their gods from before your people, whom you redeemed from Egypt?^a ²⁴You have established your people Israel as your very own forever, and you, O LORD, have become their God.

²⁵"And now, LORD God, keep forever the promise you have made concerning your servant and his house. Do as you promised, ²⁶so that your name will be great forever. Then men will say, 'The LORD Almighty is God over Israel!' And the house of your servant David will be established before you.

²⁷"O LORD Almighty, God of Israel, you have revealed this to your servant, saying, 'I will build a house for you.' So your servant has found courage to offer you this prayer. ²⁸O Sovereign LORD, you are God! Your words are trustworthy, and you have promised these good things to your servant. ²⁹Now be pleased to bless the house of your servant, that it may continue forever in your sight; for you, O Sovereign LORD, have spoken, and with your blessing the house of your servant will be blessed forever."

大衛的祈禱

¹⁸於是大衛王進去，坐在耶和華面前，說：

"主耶和華啊！我是誰？我的家算甚麼，你竟使我到這地步呢？¹⁹主耶和華啊！這在你眼中還看為小，又應許你僕人的家至於久遠。主耶和華啊！這豈是人所常遇的事嗎？

²⁰"主耶和華啊！我還有何言可以對你說呢？因為你知道你的僕人。²¹你行這大事使僕人知道，是因你所應許的話，也是照你的心意。

²²"主耶和華啊！你本為大。照我們耳中聽見沒有可比你的，除你以外再無神。²³世上有何民能比你的民以色列呢？你從埃及救贖他們作自己的子民，又在你贖出來的民面前行大而可畏的事，驅逐列邦人和他們的神，顯出你的大名。²⁴你曾堅立你的民以色列作你的子民，直到永遠。你耶和華也作了他們的神。

²⁵"耶和華神啊！你所應許僕人和僕人家的話，求你堅定，直到永遠，照你所說的而行。²⁶願人永遠尊你的名為大，說：‘萬軍之耶和華是治理以色列的神’。這樣，你僕人大衛的家必在你面前堅立。

²⁷"萬軍之耶和華以色列的神啊！因你啓示你的僕人說：‘我必為你建立家室’，所以僕人大膽向你如此祈禱。²⁸主耶和華啊！惟有你是神。你的話是真實的，你也應許將這福氣賜給僕人。²⁹現在求你賜福與僕人的家，可以永存在你面前。主耶和華啊！這是你所應許的，願你永遠賜福與僕人的家。"

^a 23 See Septuagint and 1 Chron. 17:21; Hebrew *wonders for your land and before your people, whom you redeemed from Egypt, from the nations and their gods.*

大衛的勝利

8 此後，<u>大衛</u>攻打<u>非利士人</u>，把他們治服，從他們手下奪取了京城的權柄（註：原文作"母城的嚼環"）。

²又攻打<u>摩押</u>人，使他們躺臥在地上，用繩量一量，量二繩的殺了，量一繩的存留。<u>摩押</u>人就歸服<u>大衛</u>，給他進貢。

³<u>瑣巴</u>王<u>利合</u>的兒子<u>哈大底謝</u>往大河去，要奪回他的國權。<u>大衛</u>就攻打他，⁴擒拿了他的馬兵一千七百，步兵二萬；將拉戰車的馬砍斷蹄筋，但留下一百輛車的馬。

⁵<u>大馬士革</u>的<u>亞蘭</u>人來幫助<u>瑣巴</u>王<u>哈大底謝</u>，<u>大衛</u>就殺了<u>亞蘭</u>人二萬二千。⁶於是<u>大衛</u>在<u>大馬士革</u>的<u>亞蘭</u>地設立防營，<u>亞蘭</u>人就歸服他，給他進貢。<u>大衛</u>無論往哪裏去，耶和華都使他得勝。

⁷他奪了<u>哈大底謝</u>臣僕所拿的金盾牌，帶到<u>耶路撒冷</u>。⁸<u>大衛</u>王又從屬<u>哈大底謝</u>的<u>比他</u>和<u>比羅他</u>城中奪取了許多的銅。

⁹<u>哈馬</u>王<u>陀以</u>聽見<u>大衛</u>殺敗<u>哈大底謝</u>的全軍，¹⁰就打發他兒子<u>約蘭</u>去見<u>大衛</u>王，問他的安，為他祝福，因為他殺敗了<u>哈大底謝</u>。原來<u>陀以</u>與<u>哈大底謝</u>常常爭戰。<u>約蘭</u>帶了金銀銅的器皿來。

¹¹<u>大衛</u>王將這些器皿，和他治服各國所得來的金銀都分別為聖，獻給耶和華。¹²就是從<u>亞蘭</u>、<u>摩押</u>、<u>亞捫</u>、<u>非利士</u>、<u>亞瑪力</u>人所得來的，以及從<u>瑣巴</u>王<u>利合</u>的兒子<u>哈大底謝</u>所掠之物。

¹³<u>大衛</u>在<u>鹽谷</u>擊殺了<u>亞蘭</u>（註：或作"以東"見詩篇60篇詩題）一萬八千人回

David's Victories

8 In the course of time, David defeated the Philistines and subdued them, and he took Metheg Ammah from the control of the Philistines.

²David also defeated the Moabites. He made them lie down on the ground and measured them off with a length of cord. Every two lengths of them were put to death, and the third length was allowed to live. So the Moabites became subject to David and brought tribute.

³Moreover, David fought Hadadezer son of Rehob, king of Zobah, when he went to restore his control along the Euphrates River. ⁴David captured a thousand of his chariots, seven thousand charioteers[a] and twenty thousand foot soldiers. He hamstrung all but a hundred of the chariot horses.

⁵When the Arameans of Damascus came to help Hadadezer king of Zobah, David struck down twenty-two thousand of them. ⁶He put garrisons in the Aramean kingdom of Damascus, and the Arameans became subject to him and brought tribute. The LORD gave David victory wherever he went.

⁷David took the gold shields that belonged to the officers of Hadadezer and brought them to Jerusalem. ⁸From Tebah[b] and Berothai, towns that belonged to Hadadezer, King David took a great quantity of bronze.

⁹When Tou[c] king of Hamath heard that David had defeated the entire army of Hadadezer, ¹⁰he sent his son Joram[d] to King David to greet him and congratulate him on his victory in battle over Hadadezer, who had been at war with Tou. Joram brought with him articles of silver and gold and bronze.

¹¹King David dedicated these articles to the LORD, as he had done with the silver and gold from all the nations he had subdued: ¹²Edom[e] and Moab, the Ammonites and the Philistines, and Amalek. He also dedicated the plunder taken from Hadadezer son of Rehob, king of Zobah.

¹³And David became famous after he returned from striking down eighteen thousand

---

a 4 Septuagint (see also Dead Sea Scrolls and 1 Chron. 18:4);
Masoretic Text *captured seventeen hundred of his charioteers*
b 8 See some Septuagint manuscripts (see also 1 Chron. 18:8);
Hebrew *Betah.*　　*c 9* Hebrew *Toi,* a variant of *Tou;* also in
verse 10　　*d 10* A variant of *Hadoram*　　*e 12* Some Hebrew
manuscripts, Septuagint and Syriac (see also 1 Chron. 18:11);
most Hebrew manuscripts *Aram*

Edomites[a] in the Valley of Salt.

¹⁴He put garrisons throughout Edom, and all the Edomites became subject to David. The LORD gave David victory wherever he went.

David's Officials

¹⁵David reigned over all Israel, doing what was just and right for all his people. ¹⁶Joab son of Zeruiah was over the army; Jehoshaphat son of Ahilud was recorder; ¹⁷Zadok son of Ahitub and Ahimelech son of Abiathar were priests; Seraiah was secretary; ¹⁸Benaiah son of Jehoiada was over the Kerethites and Pelethites; and David's sons were royal advisers.[b]

David and Mephibosheth

9 David asked, "Is there anyone still left of the house of Saul to whom I can show kindness for Jonathan's sake?"

²Now there was a servant of Saul's household named Ziba. They called him to appear before David, and the king said to him, "Are you Ziba?"

"Your servant," he replied.

³The king asked, "Is there no one still left of the house of Saul to whom I can show God's kindness?"

Ziba answered the king, "There is still a son of Jonathan; he is crippled in both feet."

⁴"Where is he?" the king asked.

Ziba answered, "He is at the house of Makir son of Ammiel in Lo Debar."

⁵So King David had him brought from Lo Debar, from the house of Makir son of Ammiel.

⁶When Mephibosheth son of Jonathan, the son of Saul, came to David, he bowed down to pay him honor.

David said, "Mephibosheth!"

"Your servant," he replied.

⁷"Don't be afraid," David said to him, "for I will surely show you kindness for the sake of your father Jonathan. I will restore to you all the land that belonged to your grandfather Saul, and you will always eat at my table."

⁸Mephibosheth bowed down and said, "What is your servant, that you should notice a dead dog like me?"

⁹Then the king summoned Ziba, Saul's servant, and said to him, "I have given your master's grandson everything that belonged to Saul and his family. ¹⁰You and your sons and your servants are to farm the land for him and bring

來，就得了大名。

¹⁴又在以東全地設立防營，以東人就都歸服大衛。大衛無論往哪裏去，耶和華都使他得勝。

大衛的官員

¹⁵大衛作以色列眾人的王，又向眾民秉公行義。¹⁶洗魯雅的兒子約押作元帥；亞希律的兒子約沙法作史官；¹⁷亞希突的兒子撒督和亞比亞他的兒子亞希米勒作祭司長；西萊雅作書記；¹⁸耶何耶大的兒子比拿雅統轄基利提人和比利提人。大衛的眾子都作領袖。

大衛與米非波設

9 大衛問說："掃羅家還有剩下的人沒有？我要因約拿單的緣故向他施恩。"

²掃羅家有一個僕人，名叫洗巴，有人叫他來見大衛，王問他說："你是洗巴嗎？"

回答說："僕人是。"

³王說："掃羅家還有人沒有？我要照神的慈愛恩待他。"

洗巴對王說："還有約拿單的一個兒子，是瘸腿的。"

⁴王說："他在哪裏？"

洗巴對王說："他在羅底巴亞米利的兒子瑪吉家裏。"

⁵於是大衛王打發人去，從羅底巴亞米利的兒子瑪吉家裏召了他來。

⁶掃羅的孫子、約拿單的兒子米非波設來見大衛，伏地叩拜。

大衛說："米非波設！"

米非波設說："僕人在此。"

⁷大衛說："你不要懼怕，我必因你父親約拿單的緣故施恩與你，將你祖父掃羅的一切田地都歸還你，你也可以常與我同席吃飯。"

⁸米非波設又叩拜說："僕人算甚麼？不過如死狗一般，竟蒙王這樣眷顧！"

⁹王召了掃羅的僕人洗巴來，對他說："我已將屬掃羅和他的一切家產都賜給你主人的兒子了。¹⁰你和你的眾子、僕人要為你主人的兒子米非

---

a 13 A few Hebrew manuscripts, Septuagint and Syriac (see also 1 Chron. 18:12); most Hebrew manuscripts *Aram* (that is, Arameans)   *b 18* Or *were priests*

波設耕種田地，把所產的拿來供他食
用；他卻要常與我同席吃飯。"洗巴
有十五個兒子，二十個僕人。

11洗巴對王說："凡我主我王吩
咐僕人的，僕人都必遵行。"王又
說："米非波設必與我同席吃飯，如
王的兒子一樣。"

12米非波設有一個小兒子，名叫
米迦。凡住在洗巴家裏的人，都作了
米非波設的僕人。13於是米非波設住
在耶路撒冷，常與王同席吃飯。他兩
腿都是瘸的。

大衛戰敗亞捫人

10 此後，亞捫人的王死了，他
兒子哈嫩接續他作王。2大
衛說："我要照哈嫩的父親拿
轄厚待我的恩典厚待哈嫩。"於是大
衛差遣臣僕，為他喪父安慰他。

大衛的臣僕到了亞捫人的境
內，3但亞捫人的首領對他們的主哈
嫩說："大衛差人來安慰你，你想他
是尊敬你父親嗎？他差臣僕來不是詳
察窺探，要傾覆這城嗎？"4哈嫩便
將大衛臣僕的鬍鬚剃去一半，又割斷
他們下半截的衣服，使他們露出下
體，打發他們回去。

5有人告訴大衛，他就差人去迎
接他們，因為他們甚覺羞恥；告訴他
們說："可以住在耶利哥，等到鬍鬚
長起再回來。"

6亞捫人知道大衛憎惡他們，就
打發人去，招募伯利合的亞蘭人和瑣
巴的亞蘭人，步兵二萬，與瑪迦王的
人一千，陀伯人一萬二千。

7大衛聽見了，就差派約押統帶
勇猛的全軍出去。8亞捫人出來在城
門前擺陣；瑣巴與利合的亞蘭人、陀
伯人並瑪迦人，另在郊野擺陣。

9約押看見敵人在他前後擺陣，
就從以色列軍中挑選精兵，使他們對

in the crops, so that your master's grandson
may be provided for. And Mephibosheth,
grandson of your master, will always eat at my
table." (Now Ziba had fifteen sons and twenty
servants.)

11Then Ziba said to the king, "Your servant
will do whatever my lord the king commands
his servant to do." So Mephibosheth ate at David's[a] table like one of the king's sons.

12Mephibosheth had a young son named
Mica, and all the members of Ziba's household
were servants of Mephibosheth. 13And Mephibosheth lived in Jerusalem, because he always
ate at the king's table, and he was crippled in
both feet.

David Defeats the Ammonites

10 In the course of time, the king of the
Ammonites died, and his son Hanun
succeeded him as king. 2David thought,
"I will show kindness to Hanun son of Nahash,
just as his father showed kindness to me." So
David sent a delegation to express his sympathy
to Hanun concerning his father.

When David's men came to the land of the
Ammonites, 3the Ammonite nobles said to
Hanun their lord, "Do you think David is honoring your father by sending men to you to
express sympathy? Hasn't David sent them to
you to explore the city and spy it out and overthrow it?" 4So Hanun seized David's men,
shaved off half of each man's beard, cut off their
garments in the middle at the buttocks, and sent
them away.

5When David was told about this, he sent
messengers to meet the men, for they were
greatly humiliated. The king said, "Stay at
Jericho till your beards have grown, and then
come back."

6When the Ammonites realized that they had
become a stench in David's nostrils, they hired
twenty thousand Aramean foot soldiers from
Beth Rehob and Zobah, as well as the king of
Maacah with a thousand men, and also twelve
thousand men from Tob.

7On hearing this, David sent Joab out with
the entire army of fighting men. 8The
Ammonites came out and drew up in battle formation at the entrance to their city gate, while
the Arameans of Zobah and Rehob and the men
of Tob and Maacah were by themselves in the
open country.

9Joab saw that there were battle lines in front
of him and behind him; so he selected some of

a 11 Septuagint; Hebrew my

the best troops in Israel and deployed them against the Arameans. [10]He put the rest of the men under the command of Abishai his brother and deployed them against the Ammonites. [11]Joab said, "If the Arameans are too strong for me, then you are to come to my rescue; but if the Ammonites are too strong for you, then I will come to rescue you. [12]Be strong and let us fight bravely for our people and the cities of our God. The LORD will do what is good in his sight."

[13]Then Joab and the troops with him advanced to fight the Arameans, and they fled before him. [14]When the Ammonites saw that the Arameans were fleeing, they fled before Abishai and went inside the city. So Joab returned from fighting the Ammonites and came to Jerusalem.

[15]After the Arameans saw that they had been routed by Israel, they regrouped. [16]Hadadezer had Arameans brought from beyond the River[a]; they went to Helam, with Shobach the commander of Hadadezer's army leading them.

[17]When David was told of this, he gathered all Israel, crossed the Jordan and went to Helam. The Arameans formed their battle lines to meet David and fought against him. [18]But they fled before Israel, and David killed seven hundred of their charioteers and forty thousand of their foot soldiers.[b] He also struck down Shobach the commander of their army, and he died there. [19]When all the kings who were vassals of Hadadezer saw that they had been defeated by Israel, they made peace with the Israelites and became subject to them.

So the Arameans were afraid to help the Ammonites anymore.

David and Bathsheba

11 In the spring, at the time when kings go off to war, David sent Joab out with the king's men and the whole Israelite army. They destroyed the Ammonites and besieged Rabbah. But David remained in Jerusalem.

[2]One evening David got up from his bed and walked around on the roof of the palace. From the roof he saw a woman bathing. The woman was very beautiful, [3]and David sent someone to find out about her. The man said, "Isn't this Bathsheba, the daughter of Eliam and the wife of Uriah the Hittite?" [4]Then David sent messengers to get her. She came to him, and he slept with her. (She had purified herself from her

着<u>亞蘭</u>人擺陣。[10]其餘的兵交與他兄弟<u>亞比篩</u>，對着<u>亞捫</u>人擺陣。[11]<u>約押</u>對<u>亞比篩</u>說："<u>亞蘭</u>人若強過我，你就來幫助我；<u>亞捫</u>人若強過你，我就去幫助你。[12]我們都當剛強，為本國的民和神的城邑作大丈夫。願耶和華憑他的意旨而行。"

[13]於是，<u>約押</u>和跟隨他的人，前進攻打<u>亞蘭</u>人，<u>亞蘭</u>人在<u>約押</u>面前逃跑。[14]<u>亞捫</u>人見<u>亞蘭</u>人逃跑，他們也在<u>亞比篩</u>面前逃跑進城。<u>約押</u>就離開<u>亞捫</u>人那裏，回<u>耶路撒冷</u>去了。

[15]<u>亞蘭</u>人見自己被<u>以色列</u>人打敗，就又聚集。[16]<u>哈大底謝</u>差遣人，將大河那邊的<u>亞蘭</u>人調來。他們到了<u>希蘭</u>，<u>哈大底謝</u>的將軍<u>朔法</u>率領他們。

[17]有人告訴<u>大衛</u>，他就聚集<u>以色列</u>眾人，過<u>約旦河</u>，來到<u>希蘭</u>。<u>亞蘭</u>人迎着<u>大衛</u>擺陣，與他打仗。[18]<u>亞蘭</u>人在<u>以色列</u>人面前逃跑。<u>大衛</u>殺了<u>亞蘭</u>七百輛戰車的人，四萬馬兵，又殺了<u>亞蘭</u>的將軍<u>朔法</u>。[19]屬<u>哈大底謝</u>的諸王，見自己被<u>以色列</u>人打敗，就與<u>以色列</u>人和好，歸服他們。

於是<u>亞蘭</u>人不敢再幫助<u>亞捫</u>人了。

大衛與拔示巴

11 過了一年，到列王出戰的時候，<u>大衛</u>又差派<u>約押</u>率領臣僕和<u>以色列</u>眾人出戰。他們就打敗<u>亞捫</u>人，圍攻<u>拉巴</u>。<u>大衛</u>仍住在<u>耶路撒冷</u>。

[2]一日，太陽平西，<u>大衛</u>從牀上起來，在王宮的平頂上遊行，看見一個婦人沐浴，容貌甚美。[3]<u>大衛</u>就差人打聽那婦人是誰。有人說："她是<u>以連</u>的女兒，<u>赫</u>人<u>烏利亞</u>的妻<u>拔示巴</u>。"[4]<u>大衛</u>差人去，將婦人接來。那時她的月經才得潔淨。她來了，<u>大</u>

a 16 That is, the Euphrates   b 18 Some Septuagint manuscripts (see also 1 Chron. 19:18); Hebrew horsemen

衛與她同房，她就回家去了。⁵於是她懷了孕，打發人去告訴大衛說：「我懷了孕。」

⁶大衛差人到約押那裏，說：「你打發赫人烏利亞到我這裏來。」約押就打發烏利亞去見大衛。⁷烏利亞來了，大衛問約押好，也問兵好，又問爭戰的事怎樣。⁸大衛對烏利亞說：「你回家去，洗洗腳吧！」烏利亞出了王宮，隨後王送他一分食物。⁹烏利亞卻和他主人的僕人一同睡在宮門外，沒有回家去。

¹⁰有人告訴大衛說：「烏利亞沒有回家去。」大衛就問烏利亞說：「你從遠路上來，為甚麼不回家去呢？」

¹¹烏利亞對大衛說：「約櫃和以色列與猶大兵都住在棚裏，我主約押和我主（註：或作「王」）的僕人都在田野安營。我豈可回家吃喝，與妻子同寢呢？我敢在王面前起誓（註：原文作「我指着王和王的性命起誓」），我決不行這事！」

¹²大衛吩咐烏利亞說：「你今日仍住在這裏，明日我打發你去。」於是烏利亞那日和次日住在耶路撒冷。¹³大衛召了烏利亞來，叫他在自己面前吃喝，使他喝醉。到了晚上，烏利亞出去與他主的僕人一同住宿，還沒有回到家裏去。

¹⁴次日早晨，大衛寫信與約押，交烏利亞隨手帶去。¹⁵信內寫着說：「要派烏利亞前進，到陣勢極險之處，你們便退後，使他被殺。」

¹⁶約押圍城的時候，知道敵人那裏有勇士，便將烏利亞派在那裏。¹⁷城裏的人出來和約押打仗。大衛的僕人中有幾個被殺的，赫人烏利亞也死了。

¹⁸於是約押差人去將爭戰的一切事告訴大衛，¹⁹又囑咐使者說：「你把爭戰的一切事對王說完了，²⁰王若發怒，問你說：『你們打仗為甚麼挨近城牆呢？豈不知敵人必從城上射箭嗎？²¹從前打死耶路比設（註：就是「耶路巴力」見士師記9章1節）兒子亞比米勒的是誰？豈不是一個婦人從城上拋下一塊上磨石來，打在他身上，他就死在提備斯麼？你們為甚麼挨近城牆呢？』你就說：『王的僕人赫人烏利亞也死了。』」

uncleanness.) Then*ᵃ* she went back home. ⁵The woman conceived and sent word to David, saying, "I am pregnant."

⁶So David sent this word to Joab: "Send me Uriah the Hittite." And Joab sent him to David. ⁷When Uriah came to him, David asked him how Joab was, how the soldiers were and how the war was going. ⁸Then David said to Uriah, "Go down to your house and wash your feet." So Uriah left the palace, and a gift from the king was sent after him. ⁹But Uriah slept at the entrance to the palace with all his master's servants and did not go down to his house.

¹⁰When David was told, "Uriah did not go home," he asked him, "Haven't you just come from a distance? Why didn't you go home?"

¹¹Uriah said to David, "The ark and Israel and Judah are staying in tents, and my master Joab and my lord's men are camped in the open fields. How could I go to my house to eat and drink and lie with my wife? As surely as you live, I will not do such a thing!"

¹²Then David said to him, "Stay here one more day, and tomorrow I will send you back." So Uriah remained in Jerusalem that day and the next. ¹³At David's invitation, he ate and drank with him, and David made him drunk. But in the evening Uriah went out to sleep on his mat among his master's servants; he did not go home.

¹⁴In the morning David wrote a letter to Joab and sent it with Uriah. ¹⁵In it he wrote, "Put Uriah in the front line where the fighting is fiercest. Then withdraw from him so he will be struck down and die."

¹⁶So while Joab had the city under siege, he put Uriah at a place where he knew the strongest defenders were. ¹⁷When the men of the city came out and fought against Joab, some of the men in David's army fell; moreover, Uriah the Hittite died.

¹⁸Joab sent David a full account of the battle. ¹⁹He instructed the messenger: "When you have finished giving the king this account of the battle, ²⁰the king's anger may flare up, and he may ask you, 'Why did you get so close to the city to fight? Didn't you know they would shoot arrows from the wall? ²¹Who killed Abimelech son of Jerub-Besheth*ᵇ*? Didn't a woman throw an upper millstone on him from the wall, so that he died in Thebez? Why did you get so close to the wall?' If he asks you this, then say to him, 'Also, your servant Uriah the Hittite is dead.' "

a 4 Or with her. When she purified herself from her uncleanness,
b 21 Also known as Jerub-Baal (that is, Gideon)

²²The messenger set out, and when he arrived he told David everything Joab had sent him to say. ²³The messenger said to David, "The men overpowered us and came out against us in the open, but we drove them back to the entrance to the city gate. ²⁴Then the archers shot arrows at your servants from the wall, and some of the king's men died. Moreover, your servant Uriah the Hittite is dead."

²⁵David told the messenger, "Say this to Joab: 'Don't let this upset you; the sword devours one as well as another. Press the attack against the city and destroy it.' Say this to encourage Joab."

²⁶When Uriah's wife heard that her husband was dead, she mourned for him. ²⁷After the time of mourning was over, David had her brought to his house, and she became his wife and bore him a son. But the thing David had done displeased the LORD.

Nathan Rebukes David

12 The LORD sent Nathan to David. When he came to him, he said, "There were two men in a certain town, one rich and the other poor. ²The rich man had a very large number of sheep and cattle, ³but the poor man had nothing except one little ewe lamb he had bought. He raised it, and it grew up with him and his children. It shared his food, drank from his cup and even slept in his arms. It was like a daughter to him.

⁴"Now a traveler came to the rich man, but the rich man refrained from taking one of his own sheep or cattle to prepare a meal for the traveler who had come to him. Instead, he took the ewe lamb that belonged to the poor man and prepared it for the one who had come to him."

⁵David burned with anger against the man and said to Nathan, "As surely as the LORD lives, the man who did this deserves to die! ⁶He must pay for that lamb four times over, because he did such a thing and had no pity."

⁷Then Nathan said to David, "You are the man! This is what the LORD, the God of Israel, says: 'I anointed you king over Israel, and I delivered you from the hand of Saul. ⁸I gave your master's house to you, and your master's wives into your arms. I gave you the house of Israel and Judah. And if all this had been too little, I would have given you even more. ⁹Why did you despise the word of the LORD by doing what is evil in his eyes? You struck down Uriah the Hittite with the sword and took his wife to be your own. You killed him with the sword of the Ammonites. ¹⁰Now, therefore, the sword will never depart from your house, because you

²²使者起身，來見<u>大衛</u>，照着<u>約押</u>所吩咐他的話奏告<u>大衛</u>。²³使者對<u>大衛</u>說："敵人強過我們，出到郊野與我們打仗，我們追殺他們，直到城門口。²⁴射箭的從城上射王的僕人，射死幾個，<u>赫人烏利亞</u>也死了。"

²⁵王向使者說："你告訴<u>約押</u>說：'不要因這事愁悶，刀劍或吞滅這人或吞滅那人，沒有一定的，你只管竭力攻城，將城傾覆。'可以用這話勉勵<u>約押</u>。"

²⁶<u>烏利亞</u>的妻聽見丈夫<u>烏利亞</u>死了，就為他哀哭。²⁷哀哭的日子過了，<u>大衛</u>差人將她接到宮裏，她就作了<u>大衛</u>的妻，給<u>大衛</u>生了一個兒子。但<u>大衛</u>所行的這事，耶和華甚不喜悅。

拿單斥責大衛

12 耶和華差遣<u>拿單</u>去見<u>大衛</u>。<u>拿單</u>到了<u>大衛</u>那裏，對他說："在一座城裏有兩個人：一個是富戶，一個是窮人。²富戶有許多牛羣羊羣；³窮人除了所買來養活的一隻小母羊羔之外，別無所有。羊羔在他家裏和他兒女一同長大，吃他所吃的，喝他所喝的，睡在他懷中，在他看來如同女兒一樣。

⁴"有一客人來到這富戶家裏，富戶捨不得從自己的牛羣羊羣中取一隻預備給客人吃，卻取了那窮人的羊羔，預備給客人吃。"

⁵<u>大衛</u>就甚惱怒那人，對<u>拿單</u>說："我指着永生的耶和華起誓，行這事的人該死！⁶他必償還羊羔四倍，因為他行這事，沒有憐恤的心。"

⁷<u>拿單</u>對<u>大衛</u>說："你就是那人！耶和華<u>以色列</u>的神如此說：'我膏你作<u>以色列</u>的王，救你脫離<u>掃羅</u>的手，⁸我將你主人的家業賜給你，將你主人的妻交在你懷裏，又將<u>以色列</u>和<u>猶大</u>家賜給你；你若還以為不足，我早就加倍地賜給你。⁹你為甚麼藐視耶和華的命令，行他眼中看為惡的事呢？你借<u>亞捫</u>人的刀殺害<u>赫人烏利亞</u>，又娶了他的妻為妻。¹⁰你既藐視我，娶了<u>赫人烏利亞</u>的妻為妻，所以

刀劍必永不離開你的家。'

11 "耶和華如此說：'我必從你家中興起禍患攻擊你，我必在你眼前把你的妃嬪賜給別人，他在日光之下就與她們同寢。12你在暗中行這事，我卻要在以色列眾人面前、日光之下報應你。'"

13大衛對拿單說："我得罪耶和華了！"

拿單說："耶和華已經除掉你的罪，你必不至於死。14只是你行這事，叫耶和華的仇敵大得褻瀆的機會，故此，你所得的孩子必定要死。"

15拿單就回家去了。耶和華擊打烏利亞妻給大衛所生的孩子，使他得重病。16所以大衛為這孩子懇求神，而且禁食，進入內室，終夜躺在地上。17他家中的老臣來到他旁邊，要把他從地上扶起來，他卻不肯起來，也不同他們吃飯。

18到第七日孩子死了。大衛的臣僕不敢告訴他孩子死了。因他們說："孩子還活着的時候，我們勸他，他尚且不肯聽我們的話，若告訴他孩子死了，豈不更加憂傷嗎？"

19大衛見臣僕彼此低聲說話，就知道孩子死了，問臣僕說："孩子死了嗎？"

他們說："死了。"

20大衛就從地上起來，沐浴、抹膏、換了衣裳，進耶和華的殿敬拜，然後回宮，吩咐人擺飯，他便吃了。

21臣僕問他說："你所行的是甚麼意思？孩子活着的時候，你禁食哭泣；孩子死了，你倒起來吃飯。"

22大衛說："孩子還活着，我禁食哭泣，因為我想，或者耶和華憐恤我，使孩子不死也未可知，23孩子死了，我何必禁食？我豈能使他返回呢？我必往他那裏去，他卻不能回我這裏來。"

24大衛安慰他的妻拔示巴，與她同寢。她就生了兒子，給他起名叫所羅門。耶和華也喜愛他，25就藉先知

despised me and took the wife of Uriah the Hittite to be your own.'

11"This is what the LORD says: 'Out of your own household I am going to bring calamity upon you. Before your very eyes I will take your wives and give them to one who is close to you, and he will lie with your wives in broad daylight. 12You did it in secret, but I will do this thing in broad daylight before all Israel.' "

13Then David said to Nathan, "I have sinned against the LORD."

Nathan replied, "The LORD has taken away your sin. You are not going to die. 14But because by doing this you have made the enemies of the LORD show utter contempt,[a] the son born to you will die."

15After Nathan had gone home, the LORD struck the child that Uriah's wife had borne to David, and he became ill. 16David pleaded with God for the child. He fasted and went into his house and spent the nights lying on the ground. 17The elders of his household stood beside him to get him up from the ground, but he refused, and he would not eat any food with them.

18On the seventh day the child died. David's servants were afraid to tell him that the child was dead, for they thought, "While the child was still living, we spoke to David but he would not listen to us. How can we tell him the child is dead? He may do something desperate."

19David noticed that his servants were whispering among themselves and he realized the child was dead. "Is the child dead?" he asked.

"Yes," they replied, "he is dead."

20Then David got up from the ground. After he had washed, put on lotions and changed his clothes, he went into the house of the LORD and worshiped. Then he went to his own house, and at his request they served him food, and he ate.

21His servants asked him, "Why are you acting this way? While the child was alive, you fasted and wept, but now that the child is dead, you get up and eat!"

22He answered, "While the child was still alive, I fasted and wept. I thought, 'Who knows? The LORD may be gracious to me and let the child live.' 23But now that he is dead, why should I fast? Can I bring him back again? I will go to him, but he will not return to me."

24Then David comforted his wife Bathsheba, and he went to her and lay with her. She gave birth to a son, and they named him Solomon. The LORD loved him; 25and because the LORD

a 14 Masoretic Text; an ancient Hebrew scribal tradition *this you have shown utter contempt for the LORD*

loved him, he sent word through Nathan the prophet to name him Jediah.[a]

26Meanwhile Joab fought against Rabbah of the Ammonites and captured the royal citadel. 27Joab then sent messengers to David, saying, "I have fought against Rabbah and taken its water supply. 28Now muster the rest of the troops and besiege the city and capture it. Otherwise I will take the city, and it will be named after me."

29So David mustered the entire army and went to Rabbah, and attacked and captured it. 30He took the crown from the head of their king[b] —its weight was a talent[c] of gold, and it was set with precious stones—and it was placed on David's head. He took a great quantity of plunder from the city 31and brought out the people who were there, consigning them to labor with saws and with iron picks and axes, and he made them work at brickmaking.[d] He did this to all the Ammonite towns. Then David and his entire army returned to Jerusalem.

Amnon and Tamar

13 In the course of time, Amnon son of David fell in love with Tamar, the beautiful sister of Absalom son of David.

2Amnon became frustrated to the point of illness on account of his sister Tamar, for she was a virgin, and it seemed impossible for him to do anything to her.

3Now Amnon had a friend named Jonadab son of Shimeah, David's brother. Jonadab was a very shrewd man. 4He asked Amnon, "Why do you, the king's son, look so haggard morning after morning? Won't you tell me?"

Amnon said to him, "I'm in love with Tamar, my brother Absalom's sister."

5"Go to bed and pretend to be ill," Jonadab said. "When your father comes to see you, say to him, 'I would like my sister Tamar to come and give me something to eat. Let her prepare the food in my sight so I may watch her and then eat it from her hand.'"

6So Amnon lay down and pretended to be ill. When the king came to see him, Amnon said to him, "I would like my sister Tamar to come and make some special bread in my sight, so I may eat from her hand."

7David sent word to Tamar at the palace: "Go to the house of your brother Amnon and prepare some food for him." 8So Tamar went to the

拿單賜他一個名字叫耶底底亞，因為耶和華愛他。

26約押攻取亞捫人的京城拉巴。 27約押打發使者去見大衛，說：「我攻打拉巴，取其水城。 28現在你要聚集其餘的軍兵來，安營圍攻這城。恐怕我取了這城，人就以我的名叫這城。」

29於是大衛聚集眾軍，往拉巴去攻城，就取了這城。 30奪了亞捫人之王所戴的金冠冕（註：「王」或作「瑪勒堪」；瑪勒堪即米勒公，又名摩洛，亞捫族之神名），其上的金子，重一他連得，又嵌着寶石。人將這冠冕戴在大衛頭上。大衛從城裏奪了許多財物， 31將城裏的人，拉出來放在鋸下，或鐵耙下，或鐵斧下，或叫他經過磚窰（註：或作「強他們用鋸，或用打糧食的鐵器，或用鐵斧做工，或使在磚窰裏服役」）。大衛待亞捫各城的居民都是如此。其後，大衛和眾軍都回耶路撒冷去了。

暗嫩與她瑪

13 大衛的兒子押沙龍有一個美貌的妹子，名叫她瑪，大衛的兒子暗嫩愛她。

2暗嫩為他妹子她瑪憂急成病。她瑪還是處女，暗嫩以為難向她行事。

3暗嫩有一個朋友，名叫約拿達，是大衛長兄示米亞的兒子，這約拿達為人極其狡猾。 4他問暗嫩說：「王的兒子啊，為何一天比一天瘦弱呢？請你告訴我。」

暗嫩回答說：「我愛我兄弟押沙龍的妹子她瑪。」

5約拿達說：「你不如躺在牀上裝病，你父親來看你，就對他說：『求父叫我妹子她瑪來，在我眼前預備食物，遞給我吃，使我看見，好從她手裏接過來吃。』」

6於是暗嫩躺臥裝病。王來看他，他對王說：「求父叫我妹子她瑪來，在我眼前為我做兩個餅，我好從她手裏接過來吃。」

7大衛就打發人到宮裏，對她瑪說：「你往你哥哥暗嫩的屋裏去，為他預備食物。」 8她瑪就到她哥哥暗

---

a 25 Jediah means loved by the LORD.   b 30 Or of Milcom (that is, Molech)   c 30 That is, about 75 pounds (about 34 kilograms)   d 31 The meaning of the Hebrew for this clause is uncertain.

嫩的屋裏，暗嫩正躺臥。她瑪摶麵，在他眼前做餅，且烤熟了，⁹在他面前，將餅從鍋裏倒出來。他卻不肯吃，便說：

"眾人離開我出去吧！"眾人就都離開他出去了。¹⁰暗嫩對她瑪說："你把食物拿進臥房，我好從你手裏接過來吃。"她瑪就把所做的餅拿進臥房，到她哥哥暗嫩那裏，¹¹拿着餅上前給他吃。他便拉住她瑪，說："我妹妹，你來與我同寢。"

¹²她瑪說："我哥哥，不要玷辱我。以色列人中不當這樣行，你不要做這醜事。¹³我玷辱了我，我何以掩蓋我的羞恥呢？你在以色列中也成了愚妄人。你可以求王，他必不禁止我歸你。"¹⁴但暗嫩不肯聽她的話，因比她力大，就玷辱她，與她同寢。

¹⁵隨後，暗嫩極其恨她。那恨她的心，比先前愛她的心更甚。對她說："你起來，去吧！"

¹⁶她瑪說："不要這樣！你趕出我去的這罪，比你才行的更重。"

但暗嫩不肯聽她的話。¹⁷就叫伺候自己的僕人來，說："將這個女子趕出去！她一出去，你就關門上閂。"¹⁸那時她瑪穿着彩衣，因為沒有出嫁的公主都是這樣穿。暗嫩的僕人就把她趕出去，關門上閂。¹⁹她瑪把灰塵撒在頭上，撕裂所穿的彩衣，以手抱頭，一面行走，一面哭喊。

²⁰他胞兄押沙龍問她說："莫非你哥哥暗嫩與你親近了嗎？我妹妹，暫且不要做聲；他是你的哥哥，不要將這事放在心上。"她瑪就孤孤單單地住在她胞兄押沙龍家裏。

²¹大衛王聽見這事，就甚發怒。²²押沙龍並不和他哥哥暗嫩說好說歹，因為暗嫩玷辱他妹妹她瑪，所以押沙龍恨惡他。

押沙龍殺暗嫩

²³過了二年，在靠近以法蓮的巴力夏瑣，有人為押沙龍剪羊毛，押沙

house of her brother Amnon, who was lying down. She took some dough, kneaded it, made the bread in his sight and baked it. ⁹Then she took the pan and served him the bread, but he refused to eat.

"Send everyone out of here," Amnon said. So everyone left him. ¹⁰Then Amnon said to Tamar, "Bring the food here into my bedroom so I may eat from your hand." And Tamar took the bread she had prepared and brought it to her brother Amnon in his bedroom. ¹¹But when she took it to him to eat, he grabbed her and said, "Come to bed with me, my sister."

¹²"Don't, my brother!" she said to him. "Don't force me. Such a thing should not be done in Israel! Don't do this wicked thing. ¹³What about me? Where could I get rid of my disgrace? And what about you? You would be like one of the wicked fools in Israel. Please speak to the king; he will not keep me from being married to you." ¹⁴But he refused to listen to her, and since he was stronger than she, he raped her.

¹⁵Then Amnon hated her with intense hatred. In fact, he hated her more than he had loved her. Amnon said to her, "Get up and get out!"

¹⁶"No!" she said to him. "Sending me away would be a greater wrong than what you have already done to me."

But he refused to listen to her. ¹⁷He called his personal servant and said, "Get this woman out of here and bolt the door after her." ¹⁸So his servant put her out and bolted the door after her. She was wearing a richly ornamented*[a]* robe, for this was the kind of garment the virgin daughters of the king wore. ¹⁹Tamar put ashes on her head and tore the ornamented*[b]* robe she was wearing. She put her hand on her head and went away, weeping aloud as she went.

²⁰Her brother Absalom said to her, "Has that Amnon, your brother, been with you? Be quiet now, my sister; he is your brother. Don't take this thing to heart." And Tamar lived in her brother Absalom's house, a desolate woman.

²¹When King David heard all this, he was furious. ²²Absalom never said a word to Amnon, either good or bad; he hated Amnon because he had disgraced his sister Tamar.

Absalom Kills Amnon

²³Two years later, when Absalom's sheepshearers were at Baal Hazor near the border of Ephraim, he invited all the king's sons to come

a 18 The meaning of the Hebrew for this phrase is uncertain.
b 19 The meaning of the Hebrew for this word is uncertain.

there. 24Absalom went to the king and said, "Your servant has had shearers come. Will the king and his officials please join me?"

25"No, my son," the king replied. "All of us should not go; we would only be a burden to you." Although Absalom urged him, he still refused to go, but gave him his blessing.

26Then Absalom said, "If not, please let my brother Amnon come with us."

The king asked him, "Why should he go with you?" 27But Absalom urged him, so he sent with him Amnon and the rest of the king's sons.

28Absalom ordered his men, "Listen! When Amnon is in high spirits from drinking wine and I say to you, 'Strike Amnon down,' then kill him. Don't be afraid. Have not I given you this order? Be strong and brave." 29So Absalom's men did to Amnon what Absalom had ordered. Then all the king's sons got up, mounted their mules and fled.

30While they were on their way, the report came to David: "Absalom has struck down all the king's sons; not one of them is left." 31The king stood up, tore his clothes and lay down on the ground; and all his servants stood by with their clothes torn.

32But Jonadab son of Shimeah, David's brother, said, "My lord should not think that they killed all the princes; only Amnon is dead. This has been Absalom's expressed intention ever since the day Amnon raped his sister Tamar. 33My lord the king should not be concerned about the report that all the king's sons are dead. Only Amnon is dead."

34Meanwhile, Absalom had fled.

Now the man standing watch looked up and saw many people on the road west of him, coming down the side of the hill. The watchman went and told the king, "I see men in the direction of Horonaim, on the side of the hill."[a]

35Jonadab said to the king, "See, the king's sons are here; it has happened just as your servant said."

36As he finished speaking, the king's sons came in, wailing loudly. The king, too, and all his servants wept very bitterly.

37Absalom fled and went to Talmai son of Ammihud, the king of Geshur. But King David mourned for his son every day.

38After Absalom fled and went to Geshur, he stayed there three years. 39And the spirit of the

龍請王的眾子與他同去。24押沙龍來見王說："現在有人為僕人剪羊毛，請王和王的臣僕與僕人同去。"

25王對押沙龍說："我兒，我們不必都去，恐怕使你耗費太多。"押沙龍再三請王，王仍是不肯去，只為他祝福。

26押沙龍說："王若不去，求王許我哥哥暗嫩同去。"

王說："何必要他去呢？" 27押沙龍再三求王，王就許暗嫩和王的眾子與他同去。

28押沙龍吩咐僕人說："你們注意，看暗嫩飲酒暢快的時候，我對你們說殺暗嫩，你們便殺他，不要懼怕。這不是我吩咐你們的嗎？你們只管壯膽奮勇。" 29押沙龍的僕人就照押沙龍所吩咐的，向暗嫩行了。王的眾子都起來，各人騎上騾子，逃跑了。

30他們還在路上，有風聲傳到大衛那裏，說："押沙龍將王的眾子都殺了，沒有留下一個。" 31王就起來，撕裂衣服，躺在地上。王的臣僕也都撕裂衣服，站在旁邊。

32大衛的長兄示米亞的兒子約拿達說："我主，不要以為王的眾子少年人都殺了，只有暗嫩一個人死了。自從暗嫩玷辱押沙龍妹子她瑪的那日，押沙龍就定意殺暗嫩了。33現在我主我王，不要把這事放在心上，以為王的眾子都死了，只有暗嫩一個人死了。"

34押沙龍逃跑了。

守望的少年人舉目觀看，見有許多人從山坡的路上來。

35約拿達對王說："看哪，王的眾子來了，果然與你僕人所說的相合。"

36話才說完，王的眾子都到了，放聲大哭。王和臣僕也都哭得甚慟。

37押沙龍逃到基述王亞米忽的兒子達買那裏去了。大衛天天為他兒子悲哀。

38押沙龍逃到基述，在那裏住了三年。39暗嫩死了以後，大衛王得了安慰，心裏切切想念押沙龍。

押沙龍回耶路撒冷

14 洗魯雅的兒子約押，知道王心裏想念押沙龍，²就打發人往提哥亞去，從那裏叫了一個聰明的婦人來，對她說：“請你假裝居喪的，穿上孝衣，不要用膏抹身，要裝作為死者許久悲哀的婦人，³進去見王，對王如此如此說。”於是約押將當說的話教導了婦人。

⁴提哥亞婦人到王面前，伏地叩拜，說：“王啊，求你拯救！”

⁵王問她說：“你有甚麼事呢？”

回答說：“婢女實在是寡婦，我丈夫死了。⁶我有兩個兒子，一日在田間爭鬥，沒有人解勸，這個就打死那個。⁷現在全家的人都起來攻擊婢女，說：‘你將那打死兄弟的交出來，我們好治死他，償他打死兄弟的命，滅絕那承受家業的。’這樣，他們要將我剩下的炭火滅盡，不與我丈夫留名留後在世上。”

⁸王對婦人說：“你回家去吧！我必為你下令。”

⁹提哥亞婦人又對王說：“我主我王，願這罪歸我和我父家，與王和王的位無干。”

¹⁰王說：“凡難為你的，你就帶他到我這裏來，他必不再攪擾你。”

¹¹婦人說：“願王記念耶和華你的神，不許報血仇的人施行滅絕，恐怕他們滅絕我的兒子。”王說：“我指着永生的耶和華起誓，你的兒子，連一根頭髮也不至落在地上。”

¹²婦人說：“求我主我王容婢女再說一句話。”王說：“你說吧！”

king*ᵃ* longed to go to Absalom, for he was consoled concerning Amnon's death.

Absalom Returns to Jerusalem

14 Joab son of Zeruiah knew that the king's heart longed for Absalom. ²So Joab sent someone to Tekoa and had a wise woman brought from there. He said to her, "Pretend you are in mourning. Dress in mourning clothes, and don't use any cosmetic lotions. Act like a woman who has spent many days grieving for the dead. ³Then go to the king and speak these words to him." And Joab put the words in her mouth.

⁴When the woman from Tekoa went*ᵇ* to the king, she fell with her face to the ground to pay him honor, and she said, "Help me, O king!"

⁵The king asked her, "What is troubling you?"

She said, "I am indeed a widow; my husband is dead. ⁶I your servant had two sons. They got into a fight with each other in the field, and no one was there to separate them. One struck the other and killed him. ⁷Now the whole clan has risen up against your servant; they say, 'Hand over the one who struck his brother down, so that we may put him to death for the life of his brother whom he killed; then we will get rid of the heir as well.' They would put out the only burning coal I have left, leaving my husband neither name nor descendant on the face of the earth."

⁸The king said to the woman, "Go home, and I will issue an order in your behalf."

⁹But the woman from Tekoa said to him, "My lord the king, let the blame rest on me and on my father's family, and let the king and his throne be without guilt."

¹⁰The king replied, "If anyone says anything to you, bring him to me, and he will not bother you again."

¹¹She said, "Then let the king invoke the LORD his God to prevent the avenger of blood from adding to the destruction, so that my son will not be destroyed."

"As surely as the LORD lives," he said, "not one hair of your son's head will fall to the ground."

¹²Then the woman said, "Let your servant speak a word to my lord the king."

"Speak," he replied.

a 39 Dead Sea Scrolls and some Septuagint manuscripts; Masoretic Text But |*the spirit of*|*David the king*
b 4 Many Hebrew manuscripts, Septuagint, Vulgate and Syriac; most Hebrew manuscripts spoke

¹³The woman said, "Why then have you devised a thing like this against the people of God? When the king says this, does he not convict himself, for the king has not brought back his banished son? ¹⁴Like water spilled on the ground, which cannot be recovered, so we must die. But God does not take away life; instead, he devises ways so that a banished person may not remain estranged from him.

¹⁵"And now I have come to say this to my lord the king because the people have made me afraid. Your servant thought, 'I will speak to the king; perhaps he will do what his servant asks. ¹⁶Perhaps the king will agree to deliver his servant from the hand of the man who is trying to cut off both me and my son from the inheritance God gave us.'

¹⁷"And now your servant says, 'May the word of my lord the king bring me rest, for my lord the king is like an angel of God in discerning good and evil. May the LORD your God be with you.'"

¹⁸Then the king said to the woman, "Do not keep from me the answer to what I am going to ask you."

"Let my lord the king speak," the woman said.

¹⁹The king asked, "Isn't the hand of Joab with you in all this?"

The woman answered, "As surely as you live, my lord the king, no one can turn to the right or to the left from anything my lord the king says. Yes, it was your servant Joab who instructed me to do this and who put all these words into the mouth of your servant. ²⁰Your servant Joab did this to change the present situation. My lord has wisdom like that of an angel of God—he knows everything that happens in the land."

²¹The king said to Joab, "Very well, I will do it. Go, bring back the young man Absalom."

²²Joab fell with his face to the ground to pay him honor, and he blessed the king. Joab said, "Today your servant knows that he has found favor in your eyes, my lord the king, because the king has granted his servant's request."

²³Then Joab went to Geshur and brought Absalom back to Jerusalem. ²⁴But the king said, "He must go to his own house; he must not see my face." So Absalom went to his own house and did not see the face of the king.

²⁵In all Israel there was not a man so highly praised for his handsome appearance as Absalom. From the top of his head to the sole of his foot there was no blemish in him. ²⁶Whenever he cut the hair of his head—he used to cut his hair from time to time when it became

¹³婦人說：「王為何也起意要害神的民呢？王不使那逃亡的人回來，王的這話，就是自證己錯了！¹⁴我們都是必死的，如同水潑在地上，不能收回。神並不奪取人的性命，乃設法使逃亡的人不至成為趕出回不來的。

¹⁵「我來將這話告訴我主我王，是因百姓使我懼怕。婢女想，不如將這話告訴王，或者王成就婢女所求的。¹⁶人要將我和我兒子從神的地業上一同除滅，王必應允救我脫離他的手。

¹⁷「婢女又想，我主我王的話必安慰我，因為我主我王能辨別是非，如同神的使者一樣。惟願耶和華你的神與你同在！」

¹⁸王對婦人說：「我要問你一句話，你一點不要瞞我。」

婦人說：「願我主我王說。」

¹⁹王說：「你這些話莫非是<u>約押</u>的主意嗎？」

婦人說：「我敢在我主我王面前起誓：王的話正對，不偏左右，是王的僕人<u>約押</u>吩咐我的，這些話是他教導我的。²⁰王的僕人<u>約押</u>如此行，為要挽回這事。我主的智慧卻如神使者的智慧，能知世上一切事。」

²¹王對<u>約押</u>說：「我應允你這事。你可以去，把那少年人<u>押沙龍</u>帶回來。」

²²<u>約押</u>就面伏於地叩拜，祝謝於王，又說：「王既應允僕人所求的，僕人今日知道在我主我王眼前蒙恩了。」

²³於是<u>約押</u>起身往<u>基述</u>去，將<u>押沙龍</u>帶回<u>耶路撒冷</u>。²⁴王說：「使他回自己家裏去，不要見我的面。」<u>押沙龍</u>就回自己家裏去，沒有見王的面。

²⁵<u>以色列</u>全地之中，無人像<u>押沙龍</u>那樣俊美，得人的稱讚，從腳底到頭頂毫無瑕疵。²⁶他的頭髮甚重，每到年底剪髮一次；所剪下來的，按王

的平稱一稱，重二百舍客勒。

²⁷押沙龍生了三個兒子，一個女兒。女兒名叫<u>她瑪</u>，是個容貌俊美的女子。

²⁸押沙龍住在<u>耶路撒冷</u>足有二年，沒有見王的面。²⁹押沙龍打發人去叫<u>約押</u>來，要託他去見王，<u>約押</u>卻不肯來。第二次打發人去叫他，他仍不肯來。³⁰所以押沙龍對僕人說："你們看，<u>約押</u>有一塊田，與我的田相近，其中有大麥，你們去放火燒了。"押沙龍的僕人就去放火燒了那田。

³¹於是<u>約押</u>起來，到了押沙龍家裏，問他說："你的僕人為何放火燒了我的田呢？"

³²押沙龍回答<u>約押</u>說："我打發人去請你來，好託你去見王，替我說：'我為何從<u>基述</u>回來呢？不如仍在那裏。'現在要許我見王的面，我若有罪，任憑王殺我就是了。"

³³於是<u>約押</u>去見王，將這話奏告王，王便叫來<u>押沙龍</u>。<u>押沙龍</u>來見王，在王面前俯伏於地，王就與<u>押沙龍</u>親嘴。

押沙龍的陰謀

15 此後，<u>押沙龍</u>為自己預備車馬，又派五十人在他前頭奔走。²<u>押沙龍</u>常常早晨起來，站在城門的道旁，凡有爭訟要去求王判斷的，<u>押沙龍</u>就叫他過來，問他說："你是哪一城的人？"回答說："僕人是<u>以色列</u>某支派的人。"³<u>押沙龍</u>對他說："你的事有情有理，無奈王沒有委人聽你伸訴。"⁴<u>押沙龍</u>又說："恨不得我作國中的士師，凡有爭訟求審判的，到我這裏來，我必秉公判斷。"

⁵若有人近前來要拜<u>押沙龍</u>，<u>押沙龍</u>就伸手拉住他，與他親嘴。⁶<u>以色列</u>人中，凡去見王求判斷的，<u>押沙龍</u>都是如此待他們。這樣，<u>押沙龍</u>暗中得了<u>以色列</u>人的心。

too heavy for him—he would weigh it, and its weight was two hundred shekels*ᵃ* by the royal standard.

²⁷Three sons and a daughter were born to Absalom. The daughter's name was Tamar, and she became a beautiful woman.

²⁸Absalom lived two years in Jerusalem without seeing the king's face. ²⁹Then Absalom sent for Joab in order to send him to the king, but Joab refused to come to him. So he sent a second time, but he refused to come. ³⁰Then he said to his servants, "Look, Joab's field is next to mine, and he has barley there. Go and set it on fire." So Absalom's servants set the field on fire.

³¹Then Joab did go to Absalom's house and he said to him, "Why have your servants set my field on fire?"

³²Absalom said to Joab, "Look, I sent word to you and said, 'Come here so I can send you to the king to ask, "Why have I come from Geshur? It would be better for me if I were still there!"' Now then, I want to see the king's face, and if I am guilty of anything, let him put me to death."

³³So Joab went to the king and told him this. Then the king summoned Absalom, and he came in and bowed down with his face to the ground before the king. And the king kissed Absalom.

Absalom's Conspiracy

15 In the course of time, Absalom provided himself with a chariot and horses and with fifty men to run ahead of him. ²He would get up early and stand by the side of the road leading to the city gate. Whenever anyone came with a complaint to be placed before the king for a decision, Absalom would call out to him, "What town are you from?" He would answer, "Your servant is from one of the tribes of Israel." ³Then Absalom would say to him, "Look, your claims are valid and proper, but there is no representative of the king to hear you." ⁴And Absalom would add, "If only I were appointed judge in the land! Then everyone who has a complaint or case could come to me and I would see that he gets justice."

⁵Also, whenever anyone approached him to bow down before him, Absalom would reach out his hand, take hold of him and kiss him. ⁶Absalom behaved in this way toward all the Israelites who came to the king asking for justice, and so he stole the hearts of the men of Israel.

a 26 That is, about 5 pounds (about 2.3 kilograms)

[7]At the end of four[a] years, Absalom said to the king, "Let me go to Hebron and fulfill a vow I made to the LORD. [8]While your servant was living at Geshur in Aram, I made this vow: 'If the LORD takes me back to Jerusalem, I will worship the LORD in Hebron.[b] '"

[9]The king said to him, "Go in peace." So he went to Hebron.

[10]Then Absalom sent secret messengers throughout the tribes of Israel to say, "As soon as you hear the sound of the trumpets, then say, 'Absalom is king in Hebron.' " [11]Two hundred men from Jerusalem had accompanied Absalom. They had been invited as guests and went quite innocently, knowing nothing about the matter. [12]While Absalom was offering sacrifices, he also sent for Ahithophel the Gilonite, David's counselor, to come from Giloh, his hometown. And so the conspiracy gained strength, and Absalom's following kept on increasing.

David Flees

[13]A messenger came and told David, "The hearts of the men of Israel are with Absalom."

[14]Then David said to all his officials who were with him in Jerusalem, "Come! We must flee, or none of us will escape from Absalom. We must leave immediately, or he will move quickly to overtake us and bring ruin upon us and put the city to the sword."

[15]The king's officials answered him, "Your servants are ready to do whatever our lord the king chooses."

[16]The king set out, with his entire household following him; but he left ten concubines to take care of the palace. [17]So the king set out, with all the people following him, and they halted at a place some distance away. [18]All his men marched past him, along with all the Kerethites and Pelethites; and all the six hundred Gittites who had accompanied him from Gath marched before the king.

[19]The king said to Ittai the Gittite, "Why should you come along with us? Go back and stay with King Absalom. You are a foreigner, an exile from your homeland. [20]You came only yesterday. And today shall I make you wander about with us, when I do not know where I am going? Go back, and take your countrymen. May kindness and faithfulness be with you."

[21]But Ittai replied to the king, "As surely as

[7]滿了四十年（註：有作"四年"的），押沙龍對王說："求你准我往希伯崙去，還我向耶和華所許的願。[8]因為僕人住在亞蘭的基述，曾許願說：'耶和華若使我再回耶路撒冷，我必侍奉他。'"

[9]王說："你平平安安地去吧！"押沙龍就起身，往希伯崙去了。

[10]押沙龍打發探子走遍以色列各支派，說："你們一聽見角聲就說：'押沙龍在希伯崙作王了！'"[11]押沙龍在耶路撒冷請了二百人與他同去，都是誠誠實實去的，並不知道其中的真情。[12]押沙龍獻祭的時候，打發人去將大衛的謀士、基羅人亞希多弗從他本城請了來。於是叛逆的勢派甚大，因為隨從押沙龍的人民，日漸增多。

大衛逃難

[13]有人報告大衛說："以色列人的心都歸向押沙龍了！"

[14]大衛就對耶路撒冷跟隨他的臣僕說："我們要起來逃走，不然都不能躲避押沙龍了。要速速地去，恐怕他忽然來到，加害於我們，用刀殺盡合城的人。"

[15]王的臣僕對王說："我主我王所定的，僕人都願遵行。"

[16]於是王帶着全家的人出去了，但留下十個妃嬪看守宮殿。[17]王出去，眾民都跟隨他，到伯墨哈，就住下了。[18]王的臣僕都在他面前過去。基利提人、比利提人，就是從迦特跟隨王來的六百人，也都在他面前過去。

[19]王對迦特人以太說："你是外邦逃來的人，為甚麼與我們同去呢？你可以回去，與新王同住，或者回你本地去吧！[20]你來的日子不多，我今日怎好叫你與我們一同飄流、沒有一定的住處呢？你不如帶你的弟兄回去吧！願耶和華用慈愛誠實待你。"

[21]以太對王說："我指着永生的

耶和華起誓，又敢在王面前起誓：無論生死，王在哪裏，僕人也必在那裏。」

²²大衛對以太說：「你前去過河吧！」於是迦特人以太帶着跟隨他的人和所有的婦人孩子，就都過去了。

²³本地的人都放聲大哭，眾民盡都過去。王也過了汲淪溪；眾民往曠野去了。

²⁴撒督和抬神約櫃的利未人也一同來了，將神的約櫃放下。亞比亞他上來，等着眾民從城裏出來過去。

²⁵王對撒督說：「你將神的約櫃抬回城去。我若在耶和華眼前蒙恩，他必使我回來，再見約櫃和他的居所。²⁶倘若他說：『我不喜悅你』，看哪！我在這裏，願他憑自己的意旨待我。」

²⁷王又對祭司撒督說：「你不是先見嗎？你可以安然回城。你兒子亞希瑪斯和亞比亞他的兒子約拿單，可以與你同去。²⁸我在曠野的渡口那裏，等你們報信給我。」²⁹於是撒督和亞比亞他將神的約櫃抬回耶路撒冷，他們就住在那裏。

³⁰大衛蒙頭赤腳上橄欖山，一面上一面哭。跟隨他的人也都蒙頭哭着上去。³¹有人告訴大衛說：「亞希多弗也在叛黨之中，隨從押沙龍。」大衛禱告說：「耶和華啊，求你使亞希多弗的計謀變為愚拙。」

³²大衛到了山頂敬拜神的地方，見亞基人戶篩衣服撕裂頭蒙灰塵來迎接他。³³大衛對他說：「你若與我同去必累贅我，³⁴你若回城去，對押沙龍說：『王啊，我願作你的僕人。我向來作你父親的僕人，現在我也照樣作你的僕人。』這樣，你就可以為我破壞亞希多弗的計謀。³⁵祭司撒督和亞比亞他，豈不都在那裏嗎？你在王宮裏聽見甚麼，就要告訴祭司撒督和亞比亞他。³⁶撒督的兒子亞希瑪斯，亞比亞他的兒子約拿單，也都在那裏。凡你們所聽見的，可以託這二人來報告我。」

the LORD lives, and as my lord the king lives, wherever my lord the king may be, whether it means life or death, there will your servant be."

²²David said to Ittai, "Go ahead, march on." So Ittai the Gittite marched on with all his men and the families that were with him.

²³The whole countryside wept aloud as all the people passed by. The king also crossed the Kidron Valley, and all the people moved on toward the desert.

²⁴Zadok was there, too, and all the Levites who were with him were carrying the ark of the covenant of God. They set down the ark of God, and Abiathar offered sacrifices[a] until all the people had finished leaving the city.

²⁵Then the king said to Zadok, "Take the ark of God back into the city. If I find favor in the LORD's eyes, he will bring me back and let me see it and his dwelling place again. ²⁶But if he says, 'I am not pleased with you,' then I am ready; let him do to me whatever seems good to him."

²⁷The king also said to Zadok the priest, "Aren't you a seer? Go back to the city in peace, with your son Ahimaaz and Jonathan son of Abiathar. You and Abiathar take your two sons with you. ²⁸I will wait at the fords in the desert until word comes from you to inform me." ²⁹So Zadok and Abiathar took the ark of God back to Jerusalem and stayed there.

³⁰But David continued up the Mount of Olives, weeping as he went; his head was covered and he was barefoot. All the people with him covered their heads too and were weeping as they went up. ³¹Now David had been told, "Ahithophel is among the conspirators with Absalom." So David prayed, "O LORD, turn Ahithophel's counsel into foolishness."

³²When David arrived at the summit, where people used to worship God, Hushai the Arkite was there to meet him, his robe torn and dust on his head. ³³David said to him, "If you go with me, you will be a burden to me. ³⁴But if you return to the city and say to Absalom, 'I will be your servant, O king; I was your father's servant in the past, but now I will be your servant,' then you can help me by frustrating Ahithophel's advice. ³⁵Won't the priests Zadok and Abiathar be there with you? Tell them anything you hear in the king's palace. ³⁶Their two sons, Ahimaaz son of Zadok and Jonathan son of Abiathar, are there with them. Send them to me with anything you hear."

a 24 Or Abiathar went up

³⁷So David's friend Hushai arrived at Jerusalem as Absalom was entering the city.

David and Ziba

16 When David had gone a short distance beyond the summit, there was Ziba, the steward of Mephibosheth, waiting to meet him. He had a string of donkeys saddled and loaded with two hundred loaves of bread, a hundred cakes of raisins, a hundred cakes of figs and a skin of wine.

²The king asked Ziba, "Why have you brought these?"

Ziba answered, "The donkeys are for the king's household to ride on, the bread and fruit are for the men to eat, and the wine is to refresh those who become exhausted in the desert."

³The king then asked, "Where is your master's grandson?"

Ziba said to him, "He is staying in Jerusalem, because he thinks, 'Today the house of Israel will give me back my grandfather's kingdom.'"

⁴Then the king said to Ziba, "All that belonged to Mephibosheth is now yours."

"I humbly bow," Ziba said. "May I find favor in your eyes, my lord the king."

Shimei Curses David

⁵As King David approached Bahurim, a man from the same clan as Saul's family came out from there. His name was Shimei son of Gera, and he cursed as he came out. ⁶He pelted David and all the king's officials with stones, though all the troops and the special guard were on David's right and left. ⁷As he cursed, Shimei said, "Get out, get out, you man of blood, you scoundrel! ⁸The LORD has repaid you for all the blood you shed in the household of Saul, in whose place you have reigned. The LORD has handed the kingdom over to your son Absalom. You have come to ruin because you are a man of blood!"

⁹Then Abishai son of Zeruiah said to the king, "Why should this dead dog curse my lord the king? Let me go over and cut off his head."

¹⁰But the king said, "What do you and I have in common, you sons of Zeruiah? If he is cursing because the LORD said to him, 'Curse David,' who can ask, 'Why do you do this?'"

¹¹David then said to Abishai and all his officials, "My son, who is of my own flesh, is trying to take my life. How much more, then, this Benjamite! Leave him alone; let him curse, for the LORD has told him to. ¹²It may be that the LORD will see my distress and repay me with good for the cursing I am receiving today."

---

³⁷於是大衛的朋友戶篩進了城；押沙龍也進了耶路撒冷。

大衛與洗巴

16 大衛剛過了山頂，見米非波設的僕人洗巴拉着備好了的兩匹驢，驢上馱着二百麵餅、一百葡萄餅、一百個夏天的果餅、一皮袋酒來迎接他。

²王問洗巴說："你帶這些來是甚麼意思呢？"

洗巴說："驢是給王的家眷騎的；麵餅和夏天的果餅是給少年人吃的；酒是給在曠野疲乏人喝的。"

³王問說："你主人的兒子在哪裏呢？"

洗巴回答王說："他仍在耶路撒冷，因他說：'以色列人今日必將我父的國歸還我。'"

⁴王對洗巴說："凡屬米非波設的都歸你了。"

洗巴說："我叩拜我主我王，願我在你眼前蒙恩。"

示每攻擊大衛

⁵大衛王到了巴戶琳，見有一個人出來，是掃羅族基拉的兒子，名叫示每。他一面走一面咒罵，⁶又拿石頭砍大衛王和王的臣僕；眾民和勇士都在王的左右。⁷示每咒罵說："你這流人血的壞人哪，去吧，去吧！⁸你流掃羅全家的血，接續他作王，耶和華把這罪歸在你身上，將這國交給你兒子押沙龍。現在你自取其禍，因為你是流人血的人。"

⁹洗魯雅的兒子亞比篩對王說："這死狗豈可咒罵我主我王呢？求你容我過去，割下他的頭來。"

¹⁰王說："洗魯雅的兒子，我與你們有何關涉呢？他咒罵，是因耶和華吩咐他說：'你要咒罵大衛。'如此，誰敢說你為甚麼這樣行呢？"

¹¹大衛又對亞比篩和眾臣僕說："我親生的兒子尚且尋索我的性命，何況這便雅憫人呢？由他咒罵吧！因為這是耶和華吩咐他的。¹²或者耶和華見我遭難，為我今日被這人咒罵，就施恩與我。"

¹³於是大衛和跟隨他的人往前行走。示每在大衛對面山坡，一面行走一面咒罵，又拿石頭砍他，拿土揚他。¹⁴王和跟隨他的眾人，疲倦乏力地到了一個地方，就在那裏歇息歇息。

戶篩與亞希多弗的主意

¹⁵押沙龍和以色列眾人來到耶路撒冷，亞希多弗也與他同來。¹⁶大衛的朋友亞基人戶篩去見押沙龍，對他說：「願王萬歲！願王萬歲！」

¹⁷押沙龍問戶篩說：「這是你恩待朋友嗎？為甚麼不與你的朋友同去呢？」

¹⁸戶篩對押沙龍說：「不然，耶和華和這民，並以色列眾人所揀選的，我必歸順他，與他同住。¹⁹再者，我當服侍誰呢？豈不是前王的兒子嗎？我怎樣服侍你父親，也必照樣服侍你。」

²⁰押沙龍對亞希多弗說：「你們出個主意，我們怎樣行才好？」

²¹亞希多弗對押沙龍說：「你父所留下看守宮殿的妃嬪，你可以與她們親近。以色列眾人聽見你父親憎惡你，凡歸順你人的手，就更堅強。」²²於是人為押沙龍在宮殿的平頂上支搭帳棚。押沙龍在以色列眾人眼前，與他父的妃嬪親近。

²³那時，亞希多弗所出的主意，好像人問神的話一樣，他昔日給大衛、今日給押沙龍所出的主意，都是這樣。

17 亞希多弗又對押沙龍說：「求你准我挑選一萬二千人，今夜我就起身追趕大衛。²趁他疲乏手軟，我忽然追上他，使他驚惶。跟隨他的民必都逃跑，我就單殺王一人，³使眾民都歸順你。你所尋找的人既然死了，眾民就如已經歸順你。這樣，也都平安無事了。」⁴押沙龍和以色列的長老都以這話為美。

⁵押沙龍說：「要召亞基人戶篩來，我們也要聽他怎樣說。」⁶戶篩到了押沙龍面前，押沙龍向他說：「亞希多弗是如此如此說的，我們照着他的話行可以不可以？若不可，你就說吧！」

---

¹³So David and his men continued along the road while Shimei was going along the hillside opposite him, cursing as he went and throwing stones at him and showering him with dirt. ¹⁴The king and all the people with him arrived at their destination exhausted. And there he refreshed himself.

The Advice of Hushai and Ahithophel

¹⁵Meanwhile, Absalom and all the men of Israel came to Jerusalem, and Ahithophel was with him. ¹⁶Then Hushai the Arkite, David's friend, went to Absalom and said to him, "Long live the king! Long live the king!"

¹⁷Absalom asked Hushai, "Is this the love you show your friend? Why didn't you go with your friend?"

¹⁸Hushai said to Absalom, "No, the one chosen by the LORD, by these people, and by all the men of Israel—his I will be, and I will remain with him. ¹⁹Furthermore, whom should I serve? Should I not serve the son? Just as I served your father, so I will serve you."

²⁰Absalom said to Ahithophel, "Give us your advice. What should we do?"

²¹Ahithophel answered, "Lie with your father's concubines whom he left to take care of the palace. Then all Israel will hear that you have made yourself a stench in your father's nostrils, and the hands of everyone with you will be strengthened." ²²So they pitched a tent for Absalom on the roof, and he lay with his father's concubines in the sight of all Israel.

²³Now in those days the advice Ahithophel gave was like that of one who inquires of God. That was how both David and Absalom regarded all of Ahithophel's advice.

17 Ahithophel said to Absalom, "I would*a* choose twelve thousand men and set out tonight in pursuit of David. ²I would*b* attack him while he is weary and weak. I would*b* strike him with terror, and then all the people with him will flee. I would*b* strike down only the king ³and bring all the people back to you. The death of the man you seek will mean the return of all; all the people will be unharmed." ⁴This plan seemed good to Absalom and to all the elders of Israel.

⁵But Absalom said, "Summon also Hushai the Arkite, so we can hear what he has to say." ⁶When Hushai came to him, Absalom said, "Ahithophel has given this advice. Should we do what he says? If not, give us your opinion."

---

a 1 Or Let me　　b 2 Or will

⁷Hushai replied to Absalom, "The advice Ahithophel has given is not good this time. ⁸You know your father and his men; they are fighters, and as fierce as a wild bear robbed of her cubs. Besides, your father is an experienced fighter; he will not spend the night with the troops. ⁹Even now, he is hidden in a cave or some other place. If he should attack your troops first,ᵃ whoever hears about it will say, 'There has been a slaughter among the troops who follow Absalom.' ¹⁰Then even the bravest soldier, whose heart is like the heart of a lion, will melt with fear, for all Israel knows that your father is a fighter and that those with him are brave.

¹¹"So I advise you: Let all Israel, from Dan to Beersheba—as numerous as the sand on the seashore—be gathered to you, with you yourself leading them into battle. ¹²Then we will attack him wherever he may be found, and we will fall on him as dew settles on the ground. Neither he nor any of his men will be left alive. ¹³If he withdraws into a city, then all Israel will bring ropes to that city, and we will drag it down to the valley until not even a piece of it can be found."

¹⁴Absalom and all the men of Israel said, "The advice of Hushai the Arkite is better than that of Ahithophel." For the LORD had determined to frustrate the good advice of Ahithophel in order to bring disaster on Absalom.

¹⁵Hushai told Zadok and Abiathar, the priests, "Ahithophel has advised Absalom and the elders of Israel to do such and such, but I have advised them to do so and so. ¹⁶Now send a message immediately and tell David, 'Do not spend the night at the fords in the desert; cross over without fail, or the king and all the people with him will be swallowed up.'"

¹⁷Jonathan and Ahimaaz were staying at En Rogel. A servant girl was to go and inform them, and they were to go and tell King David, for they could not risk being seen entering the city. ¹⁸But a young man saw them and told Absalom. So the two of them left quickly and went to the house of a man in Bahurim. He had a well in his courtyard, and they climbed down into it. ¹⁹His wife took a covering and spread it out over the opening of the well and scattered grain over it. No one knew anything about it.

²⁰When Absalom's men came to the woman at the house, they asked, "Where are Ahimaaz and Jonathan?"

---

⁷戶篩對押沙龍說：“亞希多弗這次所定的謀不善。”⁸戶篩又說：“你知道，你父親和跟隨他的人都是勇士，現在他們心裏惱怒，如同田野丟崽子的母熊一般；而且你父親是個戰士，必不和民一同住宿。⁹他現今或藏在坑中，或在別處，若有人首先被殺，凡聽見的必說：‘跟隨押沙龍的民被殺了’。¹⁰雖有人膽大如獅子，他的心也必消化。因為以色列人都知道你父親是英雄，跟隨他的人也都是勇士。

¹¹“依我之計，不如將以色列眾人，從但直到別是巴，如同海邊的沙那樣多，聚集到你這裏來，你也親自率領他們出戰。¹²這樣，我們在何處遇見他，就下到他那裏，如同露水下在地上一般，連他帶跟隨他的人，一個也不留下。¹³他若進了哪一座城，以色列眾人必帶繩子去，將那城拉到河裏，甚至連一塊小石頭都不剩下。”

¹⁴押沙龍和以色列眾人說：“亞基人戶篩的計謀，比亞希多弗的計謀更好！”這是因耶和華定意破壞亞希多弗的良謀，為要降禍與押沙龍。

¹⁵戶篩對祭司撒督和亞比亞他說：“亞希多弗為押沙龍和以色列的長老所定的計謀是如此如此；我所定的計謀是如此如此。¹⁶現在你們要急速打發人去，告訴大衛說：‘今夜不可住在曠野的渡口，務要過河。免得王和跟隨他的人都被吞滅。’”

¹⁷那時，約拿單和亞希瑪斯在隱羅結那裏等候，不敢進城，恐怕被人看見。有一個使女出來，將這話告訴他們，他們就去報信給大衛王。¹⁸然而有一個童子看見他們，就去告訴押沙龍。他們急忙跑到巴戶琳某人的家裏；那人院中有一口井，他們就下到井裏。¹⁹那家的婦人用蓋蓋上井口，又在上頭鋪上碎麥，事就沒有洩漏。

²⁰押沙龍的僕人來到那家，問婦人說：“亞希瑪斯和約拿單在哪裏？”

---

a 9 Or When some of the men fall at the first attack

婦人說：「他們過了河了。」僕人找他們，找不着，就回耶路撒冷去了。

21他們走後，二人從井裏上來，去告訴大衛王說：「亞希多弗如此如此定計害你，你們務要起來，快快過河。」22於是大衛和跟隨他的人都起來過約旦河。到了天亮，無一人不過約旦河的。

23亞希多弗見不依從他的計謀，就備上驢歸回本城。到了家，留下遺言，便弔死了，葬在他父親的墳墓裏。

24大衛到了瑪哈念，押沙龍和跟隨他的以色列人也都過了約旦河。25押沙龍立亞瑪撒作元帥代替約押。亞瑪撒是以實瑪利人（註：又作「以色列人」）以特拉的兒子。以特拉曾與拿轄的母親洗魯雅是姐妹。26押沙龍和以色列人都安營在基列地。

27大衛到了瑪哈念，亞捫族的拉巴人拿轄的兒子朔比，羅底巴人亞米利的兒子瑪吉，基列的羅基琳人巴西萊，28帶着被、褥、盆、碗、瓦器、小麥、大麥、麥麵、炒穀、豆子、紅豆、炒豆、29蜂蜜、奶油、綿羊、奶餅供給大衛和跟隨他的人吃。他們說：「民在曠野，必飢渴困乏了。」

押沙龍的死

18 大衛數點跟隨他的人，立千夫長、百夫長率領他們。2大衛打發軍兵出戰，分為三隊：一隊在約押手下，一隊在洗魯雅的兒子約押兄弟亞比篩手下，一隊在迦特人以太手下。大衛對軍兵說：「我必與你們一同出戰。」

3軍兵卻說：「你不可出戰。若是我們逃跑，敵人必不介意；我們陣亡一半，敵人也不介意。因為你一人強似我們萬人，你不如在城裏預備幫

The woman answered them, "They crossed over the brook."[a] The men searched but found no one, so they returned to Jerusalem.

21After the men had gone, the two climbed out of the well and went to inform King David. They said to him, "Set out and cross the river at once; Ahithophel has advised such and such against you." 22So David and all the people with him set out and crossed the Jordan. By daybreak, no one was left who had not crossed the Jordan.

23When Ahithophel saw that his advice had not been followed, he saddled his donkey and set out for his house in his hometown. He put his house in order and then hanged himself. So he died and was buried in his father's tomb.

24David went to Mahanaim, and Absalom crossed the Jordan with all the men of Israel. 25Absalom had appointed Amasa over the army in place of Joab. Amasa was the son of a man named Jether,[b] an Israelite[c] who had married Abigail,[d] the daughter of Nahash and sister of Zeruiah the mother of Joab. 26The Israelites and Absalom camped in the land of Gilead.

27When David came to Mahanaim, Shobi son of Nahash from Rabbah of the Ammonites, and Makir son of Ammiel from Lo Debar, and Barzillai the Gileadite from Rogelim 28brought bedding and bowls and articles of pottery. They also brought wheat and barley, flour and roasted grain, beans and lentils,[e] 29honey and curds, sheep, and cheese from cows' milk for David and his people to eat. For they said, "The people have become hungry and tired and thirsty in the desert."

Absalom's Death

18 David mustered the men who were with him and appointed over them commanders of thousands and commanders of hundreds. 2David sent the troops out—a third under the command of Joab, a third under Joab's brother Abishai son of Zeruiah, and a third under Ittai the Gittite. The king told the troops, "I myself will surely march out with you."

3But the men said, "You must not go out; if we are forced to flee, they won't care about us. Even if half of us die, they won't care; but you are worth ten thousand of us.[f] It would be better

---

a 20 Or "They passed by the sheep pen toward the water."
b 25 Hebrew Ithra, a variant of Jether   c 25 Hebrew and some Septuagint manuscripts; other Septuagint manuscripts (see also 1 Chron. 2:17) Ishmaelite or Jezreelite   d 25 Hebrew Abigal, a variant of Abigail   e 28 Most Septuagint manuscripts and Syriac; Hebrew lentils, and roasted grain   f 3 Two Hebrew manuscripts, some Septuagint manuscripts and Vulgate; most Hebrew manuscripts care; for now there are ten thousand like us

now for you to give us support from the city."

⁴The king answered, "I will do whatever seems best to you."

So the king stood beside the gate while all the men marched out in units of hundreds and of thousands. ⁵The king commanded Joab, Abishai and Ittai, "Be gentle with the young man Absalom for my sake." And all the troops heard the king giving orders concerning Absalom to each of the commanders.

⁶The army marched into the field to fight Israel, and the battle took place in the forest of Ephraim. ⁷There the army of Israel was defeated by David's men, and the casualties that day were great—twenty thousand men. ⁸The battle spread out over the whole countryside, and the forest claimed more lives that day than the sword.

⁹Now Absalom happened to meet David's men. He was riding his mule, and as the mule went under the thick branches of a large oak, Absalom's head got caught in the tree. He was left hanging in midair, while the mule he was riding kept on going.

¹⁰When one of the men saw this, he told Joab, "I just saw Absalom hanging in an oak tree."

¹¹Joab said to the man who had told him this, "What! You saw him? Why didn't you strike him to the ground right there? Then I would have had to give you ten shekels^a of silver and a warrior's belt."

¹²But the man replied, "Even if a thousand shekels^b were weighed out into my hands, I would not lift my hand against the king's son. In our hearing the king commanded you and Abishai and Ittai, 'Protect the young man Absalom for my sake.'^c ¹³And if I had put my life in jeopardy^d—and nothing is hidden from the king—you would have kept your distance from me."

¹⁴Joab said, "I'm not going to wait like this for you." So he took three javelins in his hand and plunged them into Absalom's heart while Absalom was still alive in the oak tree. ¹⁵And ten of Joab's armor-bearers surrounded Absalom, struck him and killed him.

¹⁶Then Joab sounded the trumpet, and the troops stopped pursuing Israel, for Joab halted them. ¹⁷They took Absalom, threw him into a big pit in the forest and piled up a large heap of

助我們。"

⁴王向他們說："你們以為怎樣好，我就怎樣行。"

於是王站在城門旁，軍兵或百或千地挨次出去了。⁵王囑咐約押、亞比篩、以太說："你們要為我的緣故寬待那少年人押沙龍。"王為押沙龍囑咐眾將的話，兵都聽見了。

⁶兵就出到田野迎着以色列人，在以法蓮樹林裏交戰。⁷以色列人敗在大衛的僕人面前；那日陣亡的甚多，共有二萬人。⁸因為在那裏四面打仗，死於樹林的，比死於刀劍的更多。

⁹押沙龍偶然遇見大衛的僕人。押沙龍騎着騾子，從大橡樹密枝底下經過，他的頭髮被樹枝繞住，就懸掛起來，所騎的騾子便離他去了。

¹⁰有個人看見，就告訴約押說："我看見押沙龍掛在橡樹上了。"

¹¹約押對報信的人說："你既看見他，為甚麼不將他打死落在地上呢？你若打死他，我就賞你十舍客勒銀子，一條帶子。"

¹²那人對約押說："我就是得你一千舍客勒銀子，我也不敢伸手害王的兒子，因為我們聽見王囑咐你和亞比篩並以太說：'你們要謹慎，不可害那少年人押沙龍。'¹³我若妄為害了他的性命，就是你自己也必與我為敵。（原來無論何事，都瞞不過王。）"

¹⁴約押說："我不能與你留連。"約押手拿三杆短槍，趁押沙龍在橡樹上還活着，就刺透他的心。¹⁵給約押拿兵器的十個少年人圍繞押沙龍，將他殺死。

¹⁶約押吹角，攔阻眾人，他們就回來，不再追趕以色列人。¹⁷他們將押沙龍丟在林中一個大坑裏，上頭堆

---

^a 11 That is, about 4 ounces (about 115 grams)　^b 12 That is, about 25 pounds (about 11 kilograms)　^c 12 A few Hebrew manuscripts, Septuagint, Vulgate and Syriac; most Hebrew manuscripts may be translated Absalom, whoever you may be.
^d 13 Or Otherwise, if I had acted treacherously toward him

起一大堆石頭。<u>以色列</u>眾人都逃跑，各回各家去了。

18<u>押沙龍</u>活着的時候，在<u>王谷</u>立了一根柱石，因他說：「我沒有兒子為我留名。」他就以自己的名稱那石柱叫<u>押沙龍</u>柱，直到今日。

大衛哀慟

19<u>撒督</u>的兒子<u>亞希瑪斯</u>說：「容我跑去，將耶和華向仇敵給王報仇的信息報與王知。」

20<u>約押</u>對他說：「你今日不可去報信，改日可以報信，因為今日王的兒子死了，所以你不可去報信。」

21<u>約押</u>對<u>古示</u>人說：「你去將所看見的告訴王。」<u>古示</u>人在<u>約押</u>面前下拜，就跑去了。

22<u>撒督</u>的兒子<u>亞希瑪斯</u>又對<u>約押</u>說：「無論怎樣，求你容我隨着<u>古示</u>人跑去。」

<u>約押</u>說：「我兒，你報這信息，既不得賞賜，何必要跑去呢？」

23他又說：「無論怎樣，我要跑去。」

<u>約押</u>說：「你跑去吧！」<u>亞希瑪斯</u>就從平原往前跑，跑過<u>古示</u>人去了。

24<u>大衛</u>正坐在城甕裏。守望的人上城門樓的頂上，舉目觀看，見有一個人獨自跑來。25守望的人就大聲告訴王。

王說：「他若獨自來，必是報口信的。」那人跑得漸漸近了。

26守望的人又見一人跑來，就對守城門的人說：「又有一人獨自跑來。」

王說：「這也必是報信的。」

27守望的人說：「我看前頭人的跑法好像<u>撒督</u>的兒子<u>亞希瑪斯</u>的跑法一樣。」

王說：「他是個好人，必是報好信息。」

28<u>亞希瑪斯</u>向王呼叫說：「平安了！」就在王面前臉伏於地叩拜說：「耶和華你的神是應當稱頌的，因他已將那舉手攻擊我主我王的人交給王了！」

29王問說：「少年人<u>押沙龍</u>平安

rocks over him. Meanwhile, all the Israelites fled to their homes.

18During his lifetime Absalom had taken a pillar and erected it in the King's Valley as a monument to himself, for he thought, "I have no son to carry on the memory of my name." He named the pillar after himself, and it is called Absalom's Monument to this day.

David Mourns

19Now Ahimaaz son of Zadok said, "Let me run and take the news to the king that the LORD has delivered him from the hand of his enemies."

20"You are not the one to take the news today," Joab told him. "You may take the news another time, but you must not do so today, because the king's son is dead."

21Then Joab said to a Cushite, "Go, tell the king what you have seen." The Cushite bowed down before Joab and ran off.

22Ahimaaz son of Zadok again said to Joab, "Come what may, please let me run behind the Cushite."

But Joab replied, "My son, why do you want to go? You don't have any news that will bring you a reward."

23He said, "Come what may, I want to run."

So Joab said, "Run!" Then Ahimaaz ran by way of the plain*a* and outran the Cushite.

24While David was sitting between the inner and outer gates, the watchman went up to the roof of the gateway by the wall. As he looked out, he saw a man running alone. 25The watchman called out to the king and reported it.

The king said, "If he is alone, he must have good news." And the man came closer and closer.

26Then the watchman saw another man running, and he called down to the gatekeeper, "Look, another man running alone!"

The king said, "He must be bringing good news, too."

27The watchman said, "It seems to me that the first one runs like Ahimaaz son of Zadok."

"He's a good man," the king said. "He comes with good news."

28Then Ahimaaz called out to the king, "All is well!" He bowed down before the king with his face to the ground and said, "Praise be to the LORD your God! He has delivered up the men who lifted their hands against my lord the king."

29The king asked, "Is the young man

a 23 That is, the plain of the Jordan

Absalom safe?"

Ahimaaz answered, "I saw great confusion just as Joab was about to send the king's servant and me, your servant, but I don't know what it was."

³⁰The king said, "Stand aside and wait here." So he stepped aside and stood there.

³¹Then the Cushite arrived and said, "My lord the king, hear the good news! The LORD has delivered you today from all who rose up against you."

³²The king asked the Cushite, "Is the young man Absalom safe?"

The Cushite replied, "May the enemies of my lord the king and all who rise up to harm you be like that young man."

³³The king was shaken. He went up to the room over the gateway and wept. As he went, he said: "O my son Absalom! My son, my son Absalom! If only I had died instead of you—O Absalom, my son, my son!"

19 Joab was told, "The king is weeping and mourning for Absalom." ²And for the whole army the victory that day was turned into mourning, because on that day the troops heard it said, "The king is grieving for his son." ³The men stole into the city that day as men steal in who are ashamed when they flee from battle. ⁴The king covered his face and cried aloud, "O my son Absalom! O Absalom, my son, my son!"

⁵Then Joab went into the house to the king and said, "Today you have humiliated all your men, who have just saved your life and the lives of your sons and daughters and the lives of your wives and concubines. ⁶You love those who hate you and hate those who love you. You have made it clear today that the commanders and their men mean nothing to you. I see that you would be pleased if Absalom were alive today and all of us were dead. ⁷Now go out and encourage your men. I swear by the LORD that if you don't go out, not a man will be left with you by nightfall. This will be worse for you than all the calamities that have come upon you from your youth till now."

⁸So the king got up and took his seat in the gateway. When the men were told, "The king is sitting in the gateway," they all came before him.

David Returns to Jerusalem

Meanwhile, the Israelites had fled to their homes. ⁹Throughout the tribes of Israel, the people were all arguing with each other, saying, "The king delivered us from the hand of our

不平安？"

亞希瑪斯回答說："約押打發王的僕人，那時僕人聽見眾民大聲喧嘩，卻不知道是甚麼事。"

³⁰王說："你退去，站在旁邊。"他就退去，站在旁邊。

³¹古示人也來到，說："有信息報給我主我王！耶和華今日向一切興起攻擊你的人給你報仇了。"

³²王問古示人說："少年人押沙龍平安不平安？"

古示人回答說："願我主我王的仇敵，和一切興起要殺害你的人，都與那少年人一樣。"

³³王就心裏傷慟，上城門樓去哀哭，一面走一面說："我兒押沙龍啊！我兒，我兒押沙龍啊！我恨不得替你死，押沙龍啊！我兒，我兒！"

19 有人告訴約押說："王為押沙龍哭泣悲哀。"²眾民聽說王為他兒子憂愁，他們得勝的歡樂卻變成悲哀。³那日眾民暗暗地進城，就如敗陣逃跑慚愧的民一般。⁴王蒙着臉，大聲哭號說："我兒押沙龍啊！押沙龍，我兒，我兒啊！"

⁵約押進去見王，說："你今日使你一切僕人臉面慚愧了。他們今日救了你的性命和你兒女妻妾的性命。⁶你卻愛那恨你的人，恨那愛你的人。你今日明明地不以將帥、僕人為念。我今日看明，若押沙龍活着，我們都死亡，你就喜悅了。⁷現在你當出去，安慰你僕人的心。我指着耶和華起誓：你若不出去，今夜必無一人與你同在一處；這禍患就比你從幼年到如今所遭的更甚！"

⁸於是王起來，坐在城門口。眾民聽說王坐在城門口，就都到王面前。

大衞返回耶路撒冷

以色列人已經逃跑，各回各家去了。⁹以色列眾支派的人紛紛議論說："王曾救我們脫離仇敵的手，又救我們脫離非利士人的手。現在他躲避押沙龍逃走了。¹⁰我們膏押沙龍治理我們，他已經陣亡。現在為甚麼不出一言請王回來呢？」

¹¹大衛王差人去見祭司撒督和亞比亞他，說：「你們當向猶大長老說：『以色列眾人已經有話請王回宮。你們為甚麼落在他們後頭呢？¹²你們是我的弟兄，是我的骨肉，為甚麼在人後頭請王回來呢？』¹³也要對亞瑪撒說：『你不是我的骨肉嗎？我若不立你替約押常作元帥，願神重重地降罰與我。』」

¹⁴如此就挽回猶大眾人的心，如同一人的心。他們便打發人去見王，說：「請王和王的一切臣僕回來。」¹⁵王就回來，到了約旦河。

猶大人來到吉甲，要去迎接王，請他過約旦河。¹⁶巴戶琳的便雅憫人基拉的兒子示每急忙與猶大人一同下去迎接大衛王。¹⁷跟從示每的有一千便雅憫人，還有掃羅家的僕人洗巴和他十五個兒子、二十個僕人，他們都趟過約旦河迎接王。¹⁸有擺渡船過去，渡王的家眷，任王使用。

王要過約旦河的時候，基拉的兒子示每就俯伏在王面前，¹⁹對王說：「我主我王出耶路撒冷的時候，僕人行悖逆的事。現在求我主不要因此加罪與僕人，不要記念，也不要放在心上。²⁰僕人明知自己有罪，所以約瑟全家之中，今日我首先下來迎接我主我王。」

²¹洗魯雅的兒子亞比篩說：「示每既咒罵耶和華的受膏者，不應當治死他嗎？」²²大衛說：「洗魯雅的兒子，我與你們有何關涉，使你們今日與我反對呢？今日在以色列中豈可治死人呢？我豈不知今日我作以色列的王嗎？」²³於是王對示每說：「你必不死。」王就向他起誓。

²⁴掃羅的孫子米非波設也下去迎接王。他自從王去的日子，直到王平平安安地回來，沒有修腳，沒有剃鬍

enemies; he is the one who rescued us from the hand of the Philistines. But now he has fled the country because of Absalom; ¹⁰and Absalom, whom we anointed to rule over us, has died in battle. So why do you say nothing about bringing the king back?"

¹¹King David sent this message to Zadok and Abiathar, the priests: "Ask the elders of Judah, 'Why should you be the last to bring the king back to his palace, since what is being said throughout Israel has reached the king at his quarters? ¹²You are my brothers, my own flesh and blood. So why should you be the last to bring back the king?' ¹³And say to Amasa, 'Are you not my own flesh and blood? May God deal with me, be it ever so severely, if from now on you are not the commander of my army in place of Joab.' "

¹⁴He won over the hearts of all the men of Judah as though they were one man. They sent word to the king, "Return, you and all your men." ¹⁵Then the king returned and went as far as the Jordan.

Now the men of Judah had come to Gilgal to go out and meet the king and bring him across the Jordan. ¹⁶Shimei son of Gera, the Benjamite from Bahurim, hurried down with the men of Judah to meet King David. ¹⁷With him were a thousand Benjamites, along with Ziba, the steward of Saul's household, and his fifteen sons and twenty servants. They rushed to the Jordan, where the king was. ¹⁸They crossed at the ford to take the king's household over and to do whatever he wished.

When Shimei son of Gera crossed the Jordan, he fell prostrate before the king ¹⁹and said to him, "May my lord not hold me guilty. Do not remember how your servant did wrong on the day my lord the king left Jerusalem. May the king put it out of his mind. ²⁰For I your servant know that I have sinned, but today I have come here as the first of the whole house of Joseph to come down and meet my lord the king."

²¹Then Abishai son of Zeruiah said, "Shouldn't Shimei be put to death for this? He cursed the LORD's anointed."

²²David replied, "What do you and I have in common, you sons of Zeruiah? This day you have become my adversaries! Should anyone be put to death in Israel today? Do I not know that today I am king over Israel?" ²³So the king said to Shimei, "You shall not die." And the king promised him on oath.

²⁴Mephibosheth, Saul's grandson, also went down to meet the king. He had not taken care of his feet or trimmed his mustache or washed his

clothes from the day the king left until the day he returned safely. ²⁵When he came from Jerusalem to meet the king, the king asked him, "Why didn't you go with me, Mephibosheth?"

²⁶He said, "My lord the king, since I your servant am lame, I said, 'I will have my donkey saddled and will ride on it, so I can go with the king.' But Ziba my servant betrayed me. ²⁷And he has slandered your servant to my lord the king. My lord the king is like an angel of God; so do whatever pleases you. ²⁸All my grandfather's descendants deserved nothing but death from my lord the king, but you gave your servant a place among those who sat at your table. So what right do I have to make any more appeals to the king?"

²⁹The king said to him, "Why say more? I order you and Ziba to divide the fields."

³⁰Mephibosheth said to the king, "Let him take everything, now that my lord the king has arrived home safely."

³¹Barzillai the Gileadite also came down from Rogelim to cross the Jordan with the king and to send him on his way from there. ³²Now Barzillai was a very old man, eighty years of age. He had provided for the king during his stay in Mahanaim, for he was a very wealthy man. ³³The king said to Barzillai, "Cross over with me and stay with me in Jerusalem, and I will provide for you."

³⁴But Barzillai answered the king, "How many more years will I live, that I should go up to Jerusalem with the king? ³⁵I am now eighty years old. Can I tell the difference between what is good and what is not? Can your servant taste what he eats and drinks? Can I still hear the voices of men and women singers? Why should your servant be an added burden to my lord the king? ³⁶Your servant will cross over the Jordan with the king for a short distance, but why should the king reward me in this way? ³⁷Let your servant return, that I may die in my own town near the tomb of my father and mother. But here is your servant Kimham. Let him cross over with my lord the king. Do for him whatever pleases you."

³⁸The king said, "Kimham shall cross over with me, and I will do for him whatever pleases you. And anything you desire from me I will do for you."

³⁹So all the people crossed the Jordan, and then the king crossed over. The king kissed Barzillai and gave him his blessing, and Barzillai returned to his home.

⁴⁰When the king crossed over to Gilgal, Kimham crossed with him. All the troops of

鬚，也沒有洗衣服。²⁵他來到耶路撒冷迎接王的時候，王問他說："米非波設，你為甚麼沒有與我同去呢？"

²⁶他回答說："我主我王，僕人是瘸腿的。那日我想要備驢騎上與王同去，無奈我的僕人欺哄了我，²⁷又在我主我王面前讒毀我。然而我主我王如同神的使者一般，你看怎樣好，就怎樣行吧！²⁸因為我祖全家的人，在我主我王面前，都算為死人；王卻使僕人在王的席上同人吃飯。我現在向王還能辨理訴冤嗎？"

²⁹王對他說："你何必再提你的事呢？我說，你與洗巴均分地土。"

³⁰米非波設對王說："我主我王既平平安安地回宮，就任憑洗巴都取了也可以。"

³¹基列人巴西萊從羅基琳下來，要送王過約旦河，就與王一同過了約旦河。³²巴西萊年紀老邁，已經八十歲了。王住在瑪哈念的時候，他就拿食物來供給王，他原是大富戶。³³王對巴西萊說："你與我同去，我要在耶路撒冷那裏養你的老。"

³⁴巴西萊對王說："我在世的年日還能有多少，使我與王同上耶路撒冷呢？³⁵僕人現在八十歲了，還能嘗出飲食的滋味，辨別美惡嗎？還能聽男女歌唱的聲音嗎？僕人何必累贅我主我王呢？³⁶僕人只要送王過約旦河，王何必賜我這樣的恩典呢？³⁷求你准我回去，好死在我本城，葬在我父母的墓旁。這裏有王的僕人金罕，讓他同我主我王過去，可以隨意待他。"

³⁸王說："金罕可以與我同去，我必照你的心願待他。你向我求甚麼，我都必為你成就。"

³⁹於是眾民過約旦河，王也過去。王與巴西萊親嘴，為他祝福。巴西萊就回本地去了。

⁴⁰王過去，到了吉甲，金罕也跟他過去。猶大眾民和以色列民的一

半，也都送王過去。

41以色列眾人來見王，對他說：
"我們弟兄猶大人為甚麼暗暗送王和
王的家眷，並跟隨王的人過約旦
河？"

42猶大眾人回答以色列人說：
"因為王與我們是親屬。你們為何因
這事發怒呢？我們吃了王的甚麼呢？
王賞賜了我們甚麼呢？"

43以色列人回答猶大人說："按
支派我們與王有十分的情分，在大衛
身上，我們也比你們更有情分。你們
為何藐視我們，請王回來，不先與我
們商量呢？"

但猶大人的話比以色列人的話
更硬。

示巴反叛大衛

20 在那裏恰巧有一個匪徒，名
叫示巴，是便雅憫人比基利
的兒子。他吹角說：

"我們與大衛無分，
　與耶西的兒子無涉。
　以色列人哪，你們各回各家去吧！"

2於是以色列人都離開大衛，跟
隨比基利的兒子示巴。但猶大人，從
約旦河直到耶路撒冷，都緊緊跟隨他
們的王。

3大衛王來到耶路撒冷，進了宮
殿，就把從前留下看守宮殿的十個妃
嬪禁閉在冷宮，養活她們，不與她們
親近。她們如同寡婦被禁，直到死的
日子。

4王對亞瑪撒說："你要在三日
之內將猶大人招聚了來，你也回到這
裏來。"5亞瑪撒就去招聚猶大人，
卻躭延過了王所限的日期。

6大衛對亞比篩說："現在恐怕
比基利的兒子示巴加害於我們，比押
沙龍更甚，你要帶領你主的僕人追趕
他，免得他得了堅固城，躲避我
們。"7約押的人和基利提人、比利
提人並所有的勇士，都跟著亞比篩，
從耶路撒冷出去，追趕比基利的兒子
示巴。

8他們到了基遍的大磐石那裏，

Judah and half the troops of Israel had taken the
king over.

41Soon all the men of Israel were coming to
the king and saying to him, "Why did our
brothers, the men of Judah, steal the king away
and bring him and his household across the
Jordan, together with all his men?"

42All the men of Judah answered the men of
Israel, "We did this because the king is closely
related to us. Why are you angry about it? Have
we eaten any of the king's provisions? Have we
taken anything for ourselves?"

43Then the men of Israel answered the men of
Judah, "We have ten shares in the king; and
besides, we have a greater claim on David than
you have. So why do you treat us with contempt? Were we not the first to speak of bringing back our king?"

But the men of Judah responded even more
harshly than the men of Israel.

Sheba Rebels Against David

20 Now a troublemaker named Sheba son
of Bicri, a Benjamite, happened to be
there. He sounded the trumpet and
shouted,

"We have no share in David,
　no part in Jesse's son!
Every man to his tent, O Israel!"

2So all the men of Israel deserted David to
follow Sheba son of Bicri. But the men of Judah
stayed by their king all the way from the Jordan
to Jerusalem.

3When David returned to his palace in
Jerusalem, he took the ten concubines he had
left to take care of the palace and put them in a
house under guard. He provided for them, but
did not lie with them. They were kept in con-
finement till the day of their death, living as
widows.

4Then the king said to Amasa, "Summon the
men of Judah to come to me within three days,
and be here yourself." 5But when Amasa went
to summon Judah, he took longer than the time
the king had set for him.

6David said to Abishai, "Now Sheba son of
Bicri will do us more harm than Absalom did.
Take your master's men and pursue him, or he
will find fortified cities and escape from us." 7So
Joab's men and the Kerethites and Pelethites
and all the mighty warriors went out under the
command of Abishai. They marched out from
Jerusalem to pursue Sheba son of Bicri.

8While they were at the great rock in Gibeon,

Amasa came to meet them. Joab was wearing his military tunic, and strapped over it at his waist was a belt with a dagger in its sheath. As he stepped forward, it dropped out of its sheath.

[9]Joab said to Amasa, "How are you, my brother?" Then Joab took Amasa by the beard with his right hand to kiss him. [10]Amasa was not on his guard against the dagger in Joab's hand, and Joab plunged it into his belly, and his intestines spilled out on the ground. Without being stabbed again, Amasa died. Then Joab and his brother Abishai pursued Sheba son of Bicri.

[11]One of Joab's men stood beside Amasa and said, "Whoever favors Joab, and whoever is for David, let him follow Joab!" [12]Amasa lay wallowing in his blood in the middle of the road, and the man saw that all the troops came to a halt there. When he realized that everyone who came up to Amasa stopped, he dragged him from the road into a field and threw a garment over him. [13]After Amasa had been removed from the road, all the men went on with Joab to pursue Sheba son of Bicri.

[14]Sheba passed through all the tribes of Israel to Abel Beth Maacah[a] and through the entire region of the Berites, who gathered together and followed him. [15]All the troops with Joab came and besieged Sheba in Abel Beth Maacah. They built a siege ramp up to the city, and it stood against the outer fortifications. While they were battering the wall to bring it down, [16]a wise woman called from the city, "Listen! Listen! Tell Joab to come here so I can speak to him." [17]He went toward her, and she asked, "Are you Joab?"

"I am," he answered.

She said, "Listen to what your servant has to say."

"I'm listening," he said.

[18]She continued, "Long ago they used to say, 'Get your answer at Abel,' and that settled it. [19]We are the peaceful and faithful in Israel. You are trying to destroy a city that is a mother in Israel. Why do you want to swallow up the LORD's inheritance?"

[20]"Far be it from me!" Joab replied, "Far be it from me to swallow up or destroy! [21]That is not the case. A man named Sheba son of Bicri, from the hill country of Ephraim, has lifted up his hand against the king, against David. Hand over this one man, and I'll withdraw from the city."

The woman said to Joab, "His head will be thrown to you from the wall."

亞瑪撒來迎接他們。那時約押穿着戰衣，腰束佩刀的帶子，刀在鞘內。約押前行，刀從鞘中掉出來。

[9]約押左手拾起刀來，對亞瑪撒說："我兄弟，你好啊！"就用右手抓住亞瑪撒的鬍子，要與他親嘴。[10]亞瑪撒沒有防備約押手裏所拿的刀，約押用刀刺入他的肚腹，他的腸子流在地上，沒有再刺他就死了。約押和他兄弟亞比篩往前追趕比基利的兒子示巴。

[11]有約押的一個少年人站在亞瑪撒屍身旁邊，對眾人說："誰喜悅約押，誰歸順大衛，就當跟隨約押去。"[12]亞瑪撒在道路上滾在自己的血裏。那人見眾民經過都站住，就把亞瑪撒的屍身從路上挪到田間，用衣服遮蓋。[13]屍身從路上挪移之後，眾民就都跟隨約押，去追趕比基利的兒子示巴。

[14]他走遍以色列各支派，直到伯瑪迦的亞比拉；並比利人的全地，那些地方的人也都聚集跟隨他。[15]約押和跟隨的人到了伯瑪迦的亞比拉，圍困示巴，就對着城築壘，跟隨約押的眾民用錘撞城，要使城塌陷。[16]有一個聰明婦人從城上呼叫說："聽啊，聽啊！請約押近前來，我好與他說話。"[17]約押就近前來。婦人問他說："你是約押不是？"

他說："我是。"
婦人說："求你聽婢女的話。"

約押說："我聽。"
[18]婦人說："古時有話說：'當先在亞比拉求問，然後事就定妥。'[19]我們這城的人，在以色列人中是和平、忠厚的。你為何要毀壞以色列中的大城，吞滅耶和華的產業呢？"

[20]約押回答說："我決不吞滅、毀壞。[21]乃因以法蓮山地的一個人、比基利的兒子示巴，舉手攻擊大衛王。你們若將他一人交出來，我便離城而去。"

婦人對約押說："那人的首級必從城牆上丟給你。"

22婦人就憑她的智慧去勸眾人。他們便將下比基利的兒子示巴的首級，丟給約押。約押吹角，眾人就離城而散，各歸各家去了。約押回耶路撒冷到王那裏。

23約押作以色列全軍的元帥；耶何耶大的兒子比拿雅統轄基利提人和比利提人；24亞多蘭掌管服苦的人；亞希律的兒子約沙法作史官；25示法作書記；撒督和亞比亞他作祭司長；26睚珥人以拉作大衛的宰相。

基遍人復仇

21大衛年間有饑荒，一連三年，大衛就求問耶和華。耶和華說："這饑荒是因掃羅和他流人血之家，殺死基遍人。"

2原來這基遍人不是以色列人，乃是亞摩利人中所剩的。以色列人曾向他們起誓，不殺滅他們，掃羅卻為以色列人和猶大人大發熱心，想要殺滅他們。大衛王召了他們來，3問他們說："我當為你們怎樣行呢？可用甚麼贖這罪，使你們為耶和華的產業祝福呢？"

4基遍人回答說："我們和掃羅與他家的事並不關乎金銀，也不要因我們的緣故殺一個以色列人。"

大衛說："你們怎樣說，我就為你們怎樣行。"

5他們對王說："那從前謀害我們，要滅我們，使我們不得再住以色列境內的人，6現在願將他的子孫七人交給我們，我們好在耶和華面前，將他們懸掛在耶和華揀選掃羅的基比亞。"

王說："我必交給你們。"

7王因為曾與掃羅的兒子約拿單指著耶和華起誓結盟，就愛惜掃羅的孫子、約拿單的兒子米非波設，不交出來，8卻把愛雅的女兒利斯巴給掃羅所生的兩個兒子亞摩尼、米非波設，和掃羅女兒米甲的姐姐給米何拉

22Then the woman went to all the people with her wise advice, and they cut off the head of Sheba son of Bicri and threw it to Joab. So he sounded the trumpet, and his men dispersed from the city, each returning to his home. And Joab went back to the king in Jerusalem.

23Joab was over Israel's entire army; Benaiah son of Jehoiada was over the Kerethites and Pelethites; 24Adoniram[a] was in charge of forced labor; Jehoshaphat son of Ahilud was recorder; 25Sheva was secretary; Zadok and Abiathar were priests; 26and Ira the Jairite was David's priest.

The Gibeonites Avenged

21During the reign of David, there was a famine for three successive years; so David sought the face of the LORD. The LORD said, "It is on account of Saul and his blood-stained house; it is because he put the Gibeonites to death."

2The king summoned the Gibeonites and spoke to them. (Now the Gibeonites were not a part of Israel but were survivors of the Amorites; the Israelites had sworn to [spare] them, but Saul in his zeal for Israel and Judah had tried to annihilate them.) 3David asked the Gibeonites, "What shall I do for you? How shall I make amends so that you will bless the LORD's inheritance?"

4The Gibeonites answered him, "We have no right to demand silver or gold from Saul or his family, nor do we have the right to put anyone in Israel to death."

"What do you want me to do for you?" David asked.

5They answered the king, "As for the man who destroyed us and plotted against us so that we have been decimated and have no place anywhere in Israel, 6let seven of his male descendants be given to us to be killed and exposed before the LORD at Gibeah of Saul—the LORD's chosen one."

So the king said, "I will give them to you."

7The king spared Mephibosheth son of Jonathan, the son of Saul, because of the oath before the LORD between David and Jonathan son of Saul. 8But the king took Armoni and Mephibosheth, the two sons of Aiah's daughter Rizpah, whom she had borne to Saul, together with the five sons of Saul's daughter Merab,[b]

---

a 24 Some Septuagint manuscripts (see also 1 Kings 4:6 and 5:14); Hebrew *Adoram*　b 8 Two Hebrew manuscripts, some Septuagint manuscripts and Syriac (see also 1 Samuel 18:19); most Hebrew and Septuagint manuscripts *Michal* whom she had borne to Adriel son of Barzillai the Meholathite. [9]He handed them over to the Gibeonites, who killed and exposed them on a hill before the LORD. All seven of them fell together; they were put to death during the first days of the harvest, just as the barley harvest was beginning.

[10]Rizpah daughter of Aiah took sackcloth and spread it out for herself on a rock. From the beginning of the harvest till the rain poured down from the heavens on the bodies, she did not let the birds of the air touch them by day or the wild animals by night. [11]When David was told what Aiah's daughter Rizpah, Saul's concubine, had done, [12]he went and took the bones of Saul and his son Jonathan from the citizens of Jabesh Gilead. (They had taken them secretly from the public square at Beth Shan, where the Philistines had hung them after they struck Saul down on Gilboa.) [13]David brought the bones of Saul and his son Jonathan from there, and the bones of those who had been killed and exposed were gathered up.

[14]They buried the bones of Saul and his son Jonathan in the tomb of Saul's father Kish, at Zela in Benjamin, and did everything the king commanded. After that, God answered prayer in behalf of the land.

Wars Against the Philistines

[15]Once again there was a battle between the Philistines and Israel. David went down with his men to fight against the Philistines, and he became exhausted. [16]And Ishbi-Benob, one of the descendants of Rapha, whose bronze spearhead weighed three hundred shekels[a] and who was armed with a new ⌊sword⌋, said he would kill David. [17]But Abishai son of Zeruiah came to David's rescue; he struck the Philistine down and killed him. Then David's men swore to him, saying, "Never again will you go out with us to battle, so that the lamp of Israel will not be extinguished."

[18]In the course of time, there was another battle with the Philistines, at Gob. At that time Sibbecai the Hushathite killed Saph, one of the descendants of Rapha.

[19]In another battle with the Philistines at Gob, Elhanan son of Jaare-Oregim[b] the Bethlehemite killed Goliath[c] the Gittite, who had a spear with a shaft like a weaver's rod.

[20]In still another battle, which took place at

人巴西萊兒子亞得列所生的五個兒子，[9]交在基遍人的手裏。基遍人就把他們在耶和華面前，懸掛在山上，這七人就一同死亡。被殺的時候正是收割的日子，就是動手割大麥的時候。

[10]愛雅的女兒利斯巴用麻布在磐石上搭棚，從動手收割的時候，直到天降雨在屍身上的時候，日間不容空中的雀鳥落在屍身上，夜間不讓田野的走獸前來糟踐。[11]有人將掃羅的妃嬪愛雅女兒利斯巴所行的這事告訴大衛。[12]大衛就去從基列雅比人那裏將掃羅和他兒子約拿單的骸骨搬了來，是因非利士人從前在基利波殺掃羅，將屍身懸掛在伯珊的街市上，基列雅比人把屍身偷了去。[13]大衛將掃羅和他兒子約拿單的骸骨從那裏搬了來，又收殮被懸掛七人的骸骨。

[14]將掃羅和他兒子約拿單的骸骨葬在便雅憫的洗拉，在掃羅父親基士的墳墓裏。眾人行了王所吩咐的。此後神垂聽國民所求的。

與非利士人爭戰

[15]非利士人與以色列人打仗，大衛帶領僕人下去，與非利士人接戰，大衛就疲乏了，[16]偉人的一個兒子以實比諾要殺大衛。他的銅槍重三百舍客勒，又佩着新刀。[17]但洗魯雅的兒子亞比篩幫助大衛，攻打非利士人，將他殺死。當日跟隨大衛的人向大衛起誓說："以後你不可再與我們一同出戰，恐怕熄滅以色列的燈。"

[18]後來，以色列人在歌伯與非利士人打仗，戶沙人西比該殺了偉人的一個兒子撒弗。

[19]又在歌伯與非利士人打仗，伯利恆人雅雷俄珥金的兒子伊勒哈難殺了迦特人歌利亞。這人的槍桿粗如織布的機軸。

[20]又在迦特打仗，那裏有一個身

a 16 That is, about 7 1/2 pounds (about 3.5 kilograms)
b 19 Or son of Jair the weaver   c 19 Hebrew and Septuagint;
1 Chron. 20:5 son of Jair killed Lahmi the brother of Goliath

量高大的人，手腳都是六指，共有二十四個指頭，他也是偉人的兒子。21這人向以色列人罵陣，大衛的哥哥示米亞的兒子約拿單就殺了他。

22這四個人是迦特偉人的兒子，都死在大衛和他僕人的手下。

大衛的頌歌

22 當耶和華救大衛脫離一切仇敵和掃羅之手的日子，他向耶和華念這詩，2說：

"耶和華是我的巖石，
　我的山寨，我的救主，
3我的神，我的磐石，我所投靠的。
　他是我的盾牌，是拯救我的角，
　是我的高臺，是我的避難所。
我的救主啊，
　你是救我脫離強暴的。
4我要求告當讚美的耶和華，
　這樣，我必從仇敵手中被救出來。

5"曾有死亡的波浪環繞我，
　匪類的急流使我驚懼，
6陰間的繩索纏繞我，
　死亡的網羅臨到我。
7我在急難中求告耶和華，
　向我的神呼求。
他從殿中聽了我的聲音，
　我的呼求入了他的耳中。

8"那時因他發怒，
　地就搖撼戰抖，
　天的根基也震動搖撼。
9從他鼻孔冒煙上騰，
　從他口中發火焚燒，
　連炭也着了。
10他又使天下垂，親自降臨，
　有黑雲在他腳下。
11他坐着基路伯飛行，
　在風的翅膀上顯現。
12他以黑暗和聚集的水，
　天空的厚雲為他四圍的行宮。
13因他面前的光輝
　炭都着了。
14耶和華從天上打雷，
　至高者發出聲音。

Gath, there was a huge man with six fingers on each hand and six toes on each foot—twenty-four in all. He also was descended from Rapha. 21When he taunted Israel, Jonathan son of Shimeah, David's brother, killed him.

22These four were descendants of Rapha in Gath, and they fell at the hands of David and his men.

David's Song of Praise

22 David sang to the LORD the words of this song when the LORD delivered him from the hand of all his enemies and from the hand of Saul. 2He said:

"The LORD is my rock, my fortress and my deliverer;
3　my God is my rock, in whom I take refuge, my shield and the horn[a] of my salvation.
He is my stronghold, my refuge and my savior—
　from violent men you save me.
4I call to the LORD, who is worthy of praise, and I am saved from my enemies.

5"The waves of death swirled about me;
　the torrents of destruction overwhelmed me.
6The cords of the grave[b] coiled around me;
　the snares of death confronted me.
7In my distress I called to the LORD;
　I called out to my God.
From his temple he heard my voice;
　my cry came to his ears.

8"The earth trembled and quaked,
　the foundations of the heavens[c] shook;
　they trembled because he was angry.
9Smoke rose from his nostrils;
　consuming fire came from his mouth,
　burning coals blazed out of it.
10He parted the heavens and came down;
　dark clouds were under his feet.
11He mounted the cherubim and flew;
　he soared[d] on the wings of the wind.
12He made darkness his canopy around him—
　the dark[e] rain clouds of the sky.
13Out of the brightness of his presence
　bolts of lightning blazed forth.
14The LORD thundered from heaven;
　the voice of the Most High resounded.

a 3 Horn here symbolizes strength.　　b 6 Hebrew Sheol
c 8 Hebrew; Vulgate and Syriac (see also Psalm 18:7)
mountains　　d 11 Many Hebrew manuscripts (see also Psalm 18:10); most Hebrew manuscripts appeared　　e 12 Septuagint and Vulgate (see also Psalm 18:11); Hebrew massed

¹⁵He shot arrows and scattered [the enemies],
　bolts of lightning and routed them.
¹⁶The valleys of the sea were exposed
　and the foundations of the earth laid bare
　at the rebuke of the L<small>ORD</small>,
　at the blast of breath from his nostrils.

¹⁷"He reached down from on high and took
　hold of me;
　he drew me out of deep waters.
¹⁸He rescued me from my powerful enemy,
　from my foes, who were too strong for me.
¹⁹They confronted me in the day of my disaster,
　but the L<small>ORD</small> was my support.
²⁰He brought me out into a spacious place;
　he rescued me because he delighted in me.

²¹"The L<small>ORD</small> has dealt with me according to my
　righteousness;
　according to the cleanness of my hands he
　has rewarded me.
²²For I have kept the ways of the L<small>ORD</small>;
　I have not done evil by turning from my
　God.
²³All his laws are before me;
　I have not turned away from his decrees.
²⁴I have been blameless before him
　and have kept myself from sin.
²⁵The L<small>ORD</small> has rewarded me according to my
　righteousness,
　according to my cleanness[a] in his sight.

²⁶"To the faithful you show yourself faithful,
　to the blameless you show yourself
　blameless,
²⁷to the pure you show yourself pure,
　but to the crooked you show yourself
　shrewd.
²⁸You save the humble,
　but your eyes are on the haughty to bring
　them low.
²⁹You are my lamp, O L<small>ORD</small>;
　the L<small>ORD</small> turns my darkness into light.
³⁰With your help I can advance against a troop[b];
　with my God I can scale a wall.

³¹"As for God, his way is perfect;
　the word of the L<small>ORD</small> is flawless.
　He is a shield
　for all who take refuge in him.
³²For who is God besides the L<small>ORD</small>?
　And who is the Rock except our God?

¹⁵他射出箭來，使仇敵四散；
　發出閃電，使他們擾亂。
¹⁶耶和華的斥責一發，
　鼻孔的氣一出，
　海底就出現，
　大地的根基也顯露。

¹⁷　"他從高天伸手抓住我，
　把我從大水中拉上來。

¹⁸他救我脫離我的勁敵和那些
　恨我的人，因為他們比我強盛。
¹⁹我遭遇災難的日子，他們來攻擊我，
　但耶和華是我的倚靠。
²⁰他又領我到寬闊之處，
　他救拔我，因他喜悅我。

²¹　"耶和華按着我的公義報答我，
　按着我手中的清潔賞賜我。

²²因為我遵守了耶和華的道，
　未曾作惡離開我的神。
²³他的一切典章常在我面前；
　他的律例，我也未曾離棄。
²⁴我在他面前作了完全人；
　我也保守自己遠離我的罪孽。
²⁵所以耶和華按我的公義，
　按我在他眼前的清潔賞賜我。

²⁶　"慈愛的人，你以慈愛待他；
　完全的人，你以完全待他；

²⁷清潔的人，你以清潔待他；
　乖僻的人，你以彎曲待他。

²⁸困苦的百姓，你必拯救。
　但你的眼目察看高傲的人，
　使他降卑。
²⁹耶和華啊，你是我的燈，
　耶和華必照明我的黑暗。
³⁰我藉着你衝入敵軍，
　藉着我的神跳過牆垣。

³¹　"至於神，他的道是完全的；
　耶和華的話，是煉淨的。
　凡投靠他的，
　他便作他們的盾牌。
³²除了耶和華，誰是神呢？
　除了我們的神，誰是磐石呢？

a 25 Hebrew; Septuagint and Vulgate (see also Psalm 18:24) *to
the cleanness of my hands*　b 30 Or *can run through a barricade*

33神是我堅固的保障，
　　他引導完全人行他的路。
34他使我的腳快如母鹿的蹄，
　　又使我在高處安穩。
35他教導我的手能以爭戰，
　　甚至我的膀臂能開銅弓。
36你把你的救恩給我作盾牌，
　　你的溫和使我為大。
37你使我腳下的地步寬闊；
　　我的腳未曾滑跌。

38 "我追趕我的仇敵，滅絕了他們，
　　未滅以先，我沒有歸回。
39我滅絕了他們，打傷了他們，
　　使他們不能起來；
　　他們都倒在我的腳下。
40因為你曾以力量束我的腰，
　　使我能爭戰；
　你也使那起來攻擊我的，
　　都服在我以下。
41你又使我的仇敵，
　　在我面前轉背逃跑，
　　叫我自己剪除那恨我的人。
42他們仰望，卻無人拯救，
　　就是呼求耶和華，他也不應允。
43我搗碎他們，如同地上的灰塵；
　　踐踏他們四散在地，
　　如同街上的泥土。

44 "你救我脫離我百姓的爭競，
　　保護我作列國的元首。
　　我素不認識的民必侍奉我。

45外邦人要投降我，
　　一聽見我的名聲，就必順從我。
46外邦人要衰殘，
　　戰戰兢兢地出他們的營寨。

47 "耶和華是活神。
　　願我的磐石被人稱頌；
　　願神那拯救我的磐石被人尊崇。
48這位神就是那為我伸冤，
　　使眾民服在我以下的。
49你救我脫離仇敵，又把我舉起，
　　高過那些起來攻擊我的；
　　你救我脫離強暴的人。
50耶和華啊，因此我要在外邦中
　　稱謝你，歌頌你的名。
51耶和華賜極大的救恩給他所立的王，
　　施慈愛給他的受膏者，
　　就是給大衛和他的後裔，
　　直到永遠。"

33It is God who arms me with strength[a]
　　and makes my way perfect.
34He makes my feet like the feet of a deer;
　　he enables me to stand on the heights.
35He trains my hands for battle;
　　my arms can bend a bow of bronze.
36You give me your shield of victory;
　　you stoop down to make me great.
37You broaden the path beneath me,
　　so that my ankles do not turn.

38"I pursued my enemies and crushed them;
　　I did not turn back till they were destroyed.
39I crushed them completely, and they could
　　not rise;
　　they fell beneath my feet.
40You armed me with strength for battle;
　　you made my adversaries bow at my feet.
41You made my enemies turn their backs in
　　flight,
　　and I destroyed my foes.
42They cried for help, but there was no one to
　　save them—
　　to the LORD, but he did not answer.
43I beat them as fine as the dust of the earth;
　　I pounded and trampled them like mud in
　　the streets.

44"You have delivered me from the attacks of
　　my people;
　　you have preserved me as the head of nations.
　　People I did not know are subject to me,
45 and foreigners come cringing to me;
　　as soon as they hear me, they obey me.
46They all lose heart;
　　they come trembling[b] from their strongholds.

47"The LORD lives! Praise be to my Rock!
　　Exalted be God, the Rock, my Savior!
48He is the God who avenges me,
　　who puts the nations under me,
49 who sets me free from my enemies.
　　You exalted me above my foes;
　　from violent men you rescued me.
50Therefore I will praise you, O LORD, among
　　the nations;
　　I will sing praises to your name.
51He gives his king great victories;
　　he shows unfailing kindness to his anointed,
　　to David and his descendants forever."

a 33 Dead Sea Scrolls, some Septuagint manuscripts, Vulgate
and Syriac (see also Psalm 18:32); Masoretic Text *who is my
strong refuge*　　b 46 Some Septuagint manuscripts and
Vulgate (see also Psalm 18:45); Masoretic Text *they arm
themselves.*

The Last Words of David

23 These are the last words of David:

"The oracle of David son of Jesse,
the oracle of the man exalted by the
Most High,
the man anointed by the God of Jacob,
Israel's singer of songs[a]

2"The Spirit of the LORD spoke through me;
his word was on my tongue.
3The God of Israel spoke,
the Rock of Israel said to me:
'When one rules over men in righteousness,
when he rules in the fear of God,
4he is like the light of morning at sunrise
on a cloudless morning,
like the brightness after rain
that brings the grass from the earth.'

5"Is not my house right with God?
Has he not made with me an everlasting
covenant,
arranged and secured in every part?
Will he not bring to fruition my salvation
and grant me my every desire?
6But evil men are all to be cast aside like thorns,
which are not gathered with the hand.
7Whoever touches thorns
uses a tool of iron or the shaft of a spear;
they are burned up where they lie."

David's Mighty Men

8These are the names of David's mighty men:
Josheb-Basshebeth,[b] a Tahkemonite,[c] was chief
of the Three; he raised his spear against eight
hundred men, whom he killed[d] in one encounter.

9Next to him was Eleazar son of Dodai the
Ahohite. As one of the three mighty men, he
was with David when they taunted the
Philistines gathered at Pas Dammim,[e] for battle.
Then the men of Israel retreated, 10but he stood
his ground and struck down the Philistines till
his hand grew tired and froze to the sword. The
LORD brought about a great victory that day.
The troops returned to Eleazar, but only to strip
the dead.

大衛末了的話

23 以下是大衛末了的話：

"耶西的兒子大衛得居高位，
是雅各神所膏的，
作以色列的美歌者說：

2 "耶和華的靈藉着我說，
他的話在我口中。
3 以色列的神、
以色列的磐石曉諭我說：
'那以公義治理人民的，
敬畏神執掌權柄，
4 他必像日出的晨光，
如無雲的清晨，
雨後的晴光，
使地發生嫩草。'

5 "我家在神面前並非如此，
神卻與我立永遠的約。
這約凡事堅穩，
關乎我的一切救恩
和我一切所想望的，
他豈不為我成就嗎？
6 但匪類都不像荊棘被丟棄；
人不敢用手拿它；
7 拿它的人必帶鐵器和槍桿，
終久它必被火焚燒。"

大衛的勇士

8 大衛勇士的名字，記在下面：
他革捫人約設巴設，又稱伊斯
尼人亞底挪，他是軍長的統領，一時
擊殺了八百人。
9 其次是亞合人朵多的兒子以利
亞撒。從前非利士人聚集要打仗，以
色列人迎着上去，有跟隨大衛的三個
勇士向非利士人罵陣，其中有以利亞
撒。10 他起來擊殺非利士人，直到手
臂疲乏，手粘住刀把。那日耶和華使
以色列人大獲全勝，眾民在以利亞撒
後頭專奪財物。

---

a 1 Or *Israel's beloved singer*   b 8 Hebrew; some Septuagint
manuscripts suggest *Ish-Bosheth*, that is, *Esh-Baal* (see also
1 Chron. 11:11 *Jashobeam*).   c 8 Probably a variant of
Hacmonite (see 1 Chron. 11:11)   d 8 Some Septuagint
manuscripts (see also 1 Chron. 11:11); Hebrew and other
Septuagint manuscripts *Three; it was Adino the Eznite who killed
eight hundred men*   e 9 See 1 Chron. 11:13; Hebrew *gathered
there.*

11其次是哈拉人亞基的兒子沙瑪。一日非利士人聚集成羣，在一塊長滿紅豆的田裏，眾民就在非利士人面前逃跑。12沙瑪卻站在那田間，擊殺非利士人，救護了那田。耶和華使以色列人大獲全勝。

13收割的時候，有三十個勇士中的三個人，下到亞杜蘭洞見大衛。非利士的軍兵在利乏音谷安營。14那時大衛在山寨，非利士人的防營在伯利恆。15大衛渴想，說：「甚願有人將伯利恆城門旁井裏的水打來給我喝。」16這三個勇士就闖過非利士人的營盤，從伯利恆城門旁的井裏打水，拿來奉給大衛。他卻不肯喝，將水奠在耶和華面前，17說：「耶和華啊，這三個人冒死去打水，這水好像他們的血一般，我斷不敢喝。」如此大衛不肯喝。

這是三個勇士所做的事。

18洗魯雅的兒子、約押的兄弟亞比篩是這三個勇士的首領。他舉槍殺了三百人，就在三個勇士裏得了名。19他在這三個勇士裏是最尊貴的，所以作他們的首領；只是不及前三個勇士。

20有甲薛勇士耶何耶大的兒子比拿雅行過大能的事：他殺了摩押人亞利伊勒的兩個兒子；又在下雪的時候下坑裏去，殺了一個獅子；21又殺了一個強壯的埃及人。埃及人手裏拿着槍，比拿雅只拿着棍子下去，從埃及人手裏奪過槍來，用那槍將他殺死。22這是耶何耶大的兒子比拿雅所行的事，就在三個勇士裏得了名。23他比那三十個勇士都尊貴，只是不及前三個勇士。大衛立他作護衛長。

24三十個勇士裏有：
約押的兄弟亞撒黑、
伯利恆人朵多的兒子伊勒哈難、

11Next to him was Shammah son of Agee the Hararite. When the Philistines banded together at a place where there was a field full of lentils, Israel's troops fled from them. 12But Shammah took his stand in the middle of the field. He defended it and struck the Philistines down, and the LORD brought about a great victory.

13During harvest time, three of the thirty chief men came down to David at the cave of Adullam, while a band of Philistines was encamped in the Valley of Rephaim. 14At that time David was in the stronghold, and the Philistine garrison was at Bethlehem. 15David longed for water and said, "Oh, that someone would get me a drink of water from the well near the gate of Bethlehem!" 16So the three mighty men broke through the Philistine lines, drew water from the well near the gate of Bethlehem and carried it back to David. But he refused to drink it; instead, he poured it out before the LORD. 17"Far be it from me, O LORD, to do this!" he said. "Is it not the blood of men who went at the risk of their lives?" And David would not drink it.

Such were the exploits of the three mighty men.

18Abishai the brother of Joab son of Zeruiah was chief of the Three.ᵃ He raised his spear against three hundred men, whom he killed, and so he became as famous as the Three. 19Was he not held in greater honor than the Three? He became their commander, even though he was not included among them.

20Benaiah son of Jehoiada was a valiant fighter from Kabzeel, who performed great exploits. He struck down two of Moab's best men. He also went down into a pit on a snowy day and killed a lion. 21And he struck down a huge Egyptian. Although the Egyptian had a spear in his hand, Benaiah went against him with a club. He snatched the spear from the Egyptian's hand and killed him with his own spear. 22Such were the exploits of Benaiah son of Jehoiada; he too was as famous as the three mighty men. 23He was held in greater honor than any of the Thirty, but he was not included among the Three. And David put him in charge of his bodyguard.

24Among the Thirty were:
Asahel the brother of Joab,
Elhanan son of Dodo from Bethlehem,

a 18 Most Hebrew manuscripts (see also 1 Chron. 11:20); two Hebrew manuscripts and Syriac Thirty

²⁵Shammah the Harodite,
Elika the Harodite,
²⁶Helez the Paltite,
Ira son of Ikkesh from Tekoa,
²⁷Abiezer from Anathoth,
Mebunnai*a* the Hushathite,
²⁸Zalmon the Ahohite,
Maharai the Netophathite,
²⁹Heled*b* son of Baanah the
Netophathite,
Ithai son of Ribai from Gibeah in
Benjamin,
³⁰Benaiah the Pirathonite,
Hiddai*c* from the ravines of Gaash,
³¹Abi-Albon the Arbathite,
Azmaveth the Barhumite,
³²Eliahba the Shaalbonite,
the sons of Jashen,
Jonathan ³³son of*d* Shammah the
Hararite,
Ahiam son of Sharar*e* the Hararite,
³⁴Eliphelet son of Ahasbai the Maacathite,
Eliam son of Ahithophel the Gilonite,
³⁵Hezro the Carmelite,
Paarai the Arbite,
³⁶Igal son of Nathan from Zobah,
the son of Hagri,*f*
³⁷Zelek the Ammonite,
Naharai the Beerothite, the armor-bearer
of Joab son of Zeruiah,
³⁸Ira the Ithrite,
Gareb the Ithrite
³⁹and Uriah the Hittite.
There were thirty-seven in all.

David Counts the Fighting Men

24 Again the anger of the LORD burned against Israel, and he incited David against them, saying, "Go and take a census of Israel and Judah."

²So the king said to Joab and the army commanders*g* with him, "Go throughout the tribes of Israel from Dan to Beersheba and enroll the fighting men, so that I may know how many there are."

---

a 27 Hebrew; some Septuagint manuscripts (see also 1 Chron. 11:29) Sibbecai　*b 29 Some Hebrew manuscripts and Vulgate (see also 1 Chron. 11:30); most Hebrew manuscripts* Heleb
c 30 Hebrew; some Septuagint manuscripts (see also 1 Chron. 11:32) Hurai　*d 33 Some Septuagint manuscripts (see also 1 Chron. 11:34); Hebrew does not have* son of.　*e 33 Hebrew; some Septuagint manuscripts (see also 1 Chron. 11:35)* Sacar
f 36 Some Septuagint manuscripts (see also 1 Chron. 11:38); Hebrew Haggadi　*g 2 Septuagint (see also verse 4 and 1 Chron. 21:2); Hebrew* Joab the army commander

---

²⁵哈律人沙瑪、
哈律人以利加、
²⁶帕勒提人希利斯、
提哥亞人益吉的兒子以拉、
²⁷亞拿突人亞比以謝、
戶沙人米本乃、
²⁸亞合人撒們、
尼陀法人瑪哈萊、
²⁹尼陀法人巴拿的兒子希立、
便雅憫族基比亞人
利拜的兒子以太、

³⁰比拉頓人比拿雅、
迦實溪人希太、
³¹伯亞拉巴人亞比亞本、
巴魯米人押斯瑪弗、
³²沙本人以利雅哈巴、
雅善兒子中的約拿單、
³³哈拉人沙瑪、
哈拉人沙拉的兒子亞希暗、

³⁴瑪迦人亞哈拜的兒子以利法列、
基羅人亞希多弗的兒子以連、
³⁵迦密人希斯萊、
亞巴人帕萊、
³⁶瑣巴人拿單的兒子以甲、
迦得人巴尼、
³⁷亞捫人洗勒、比érø人拿哈萊
（是給洗魯雅的兒子約押拿兵器
的）、
³⁸以帖人以拉、
以帖人迦立、
³⁹赫人烏利亞、
共有三十七人。

大衛數點軍兵

24 耶和華又向以色列人發怒，
就激動大衛，使他吩咐人去
數點以色列人和猶大人。

²大衛就吩咐跟隨他的元帥約押
說：「你去走遍以色列眾支派，從但
直到別是巴，數點百姓，我好知道他
們的數目。」

³約押對王說："無論百姓多少，願耶和華你的神再加增百倍，使我主我王親眼得見。我主我王何必喜悅行這事呢？"

⁴但王的命令勝過約押和眾軍長。約押和眾軍長就從王面前出去，數點以色列的百姓。

⁵他們過了約旦河，在迦得谷中城的右邊亞羅珥安營，與雅謝相對。⁶又到了基列和他停合示地。又到了但雅安，繞到西頓，⁷來到推羅的保障，並希未人和迦南人的各城。又到猶大南方的別是巴。

⁸他們走遍全地，過了九個月零二十天，就回到耶路撒冷。

⁹約押將百姓的總數奏告於王：以色列拿刀的勇士有八十萬；猶大有五十萬。

¹⁰大衛數點百姓以後，就心中自責，禱告耶和華說："我行這事大有罪了。耶和華啊，求你除掉僕人的罪孽，因我所行的甚是愚昧。"

¹¹大衛早晨起來，耶和華的話臨到先知迦得，就是大衛的先見，說：¹²"你去告訴大衛說，耶和華如此說：'我有三樣災，隨你選擇一樣，我好降與你。'"

¹³於是迦得來見大衛，對他說："你願意國中有七年的饑荒呢？是在你敵人面前逃跑，被追趕三個月呢？是在你國中有三日的瘟疫呢？現在你要揣摩思想，我好回覆那差我來的。"

¹⁴大衛對迦得說："我甚為難。我願落在耶和華的手裏，因為他有豐盛的憐憫，我不願落在人的手裏。"

¹⁵於是耶和華降瘟疫與以色列人，自早晨到所定的時候，從但直到別是巴，民間死了七萬人。¹⁶天使向耶路撒冷伸手要滅城的時候，耶和華

³But Joab replied to the king, "May the LORD your God multiply the troops a hundred times over, and may the eyes of my lord the king see it. But why does my lord the king want to do such a thing?"

⁴The king's word, however, overruled Joab and the army commanders; so they left the presence of the king to enroll the fighting men of Israel.

⁵After crossing the Jordan, they camped near Aroer, south of the town in the gorge, and then went through Gad and on to Jazer. ⁶They went to Gilead and the region of Tahtim Hodshi, and on to Dan Jaan and around toward Sidon. ⁷Then they went toward the fortress of Tyre and all the towns of the Hivites and Canaanites. Finally, they went on to Beersheba in the Negev of Judah.

⁸After they had gone through the entire land, they came back to Jerusalem at the end of nine months and twenty days.

⁹Joab reported the number of the fighting men to the king: In Israel there were eight hundred thousand able-bodied men who could handle a sword, and in Judah five hundred thousand.

¹⁰David was conscience-stricken after he had counted the fighting men, and he said to the LORD, "I have sinned greatly in what I have done. Now, O LORD, I beg you, take away the guilt of your servant. I have done a very foolish thing."

¹¹Before David got up the next morning, the word of the LORD had come to Gad the prophet, David's seer: ¹²"Go and tell David, 'This is what the LORD says: I am giving you three options. Choose one of them for me to carry out against you.'"

¹³So Gad went to David and said to him, "Shall there come upon you three*a* years of famine in your land? Or three months of fleeing from your enemies while they pursue you? Or three days of plague in your land? Now then, think it over and decide how I should answer the one who sent me."

¹⁴David said to Gad, "I am in deep distress. Let us fall into the hands of the LORD, for his mercy is great; but do not let me fall into the hands of men."

¹⁵So the LORD sent a plague on Israel from that morning until the end of the time designated, and seventy thousand of the people from Dan to Beersheba died. ¹⁶When the angel stretched out his hand to destroy Jerusalem, the

a 13 Septuagint (see also 1 Chron. 21:12); Hebrew seven

LORD was grieved because of the calamity and said to the angel who was afflicting the people, "Enough! Withdraw your hand." The angel of the LORD was then at the threshing floor of Araunah the Jebusite.

17When David saw the angel who was striking down the people, he said to the LORD, "I am the one who has sinned and done wrong. These are but sheep. What have they done? Let your hand fall upon me and my family."

David Builds an Altar

18On that day Gad went to David and said to him, "Go up and build an altar to the LORD on the threshing floor of Araunah the Jebusite." 19So David went up, as the LORD had commanded through Gad. 20When Araunah looked and saw the king and his men coming toward him, he went out and bowed down before the king with his face to the ground.

21Araunah said, "Why has my lord the king come to his servant?"

"To buy your threshing floor," David answered, "so I can build an altar to the LORD, that the plague on the people may be stopped."

22Araunah said to David, "Let my lord the king take whatever pleases him and offer it up. Here are oxen for the burnt offering, and here are threshing sledges and ox yokes for the wood. 23O king, Araunah gives all this to the king." Araunah also said to him, "May the LORD your God accept you."

24But the king replied to Araunah, "No, I insist on paying you for it. I will not sacrifice to the LORD my God burnt offerings that cost me nothing."

So David bought the threshing floor and the oxen and paid fifty shekels*a* of silver for them. 25David built an altar to the LORD there and sacrificed burnt offerings and fellowship offerings.*b* Then the LORD answered prayer in behalf of the land, and the plague on Israel was stopped.

後悔，就不降這災了，吩咐滅民的天使說：「夠了，住手吧！」那時耶和華的使者在耶布斯人亞勞拿的禾場那裏。

17大衛看見滅民的天使，就禱告耶和華說：「我犯了罪，行了惡；但這羣羊做了甚麼呢？願你的手攻擊我和我的父家。」

大衛築壇

18當日迦得來見大衛，對他說：「你上去，在耶布斯人亞勞拿的禾場上，為耶和華築一座壇。」19大衛就照着迦得奉耶和華名所說的話，上去了。20亞勞拿觀看，見王和他臣僕前來，就迎接出去，臉伏於地，向王下拜。

21說：「我主我王為何來到僕人這裏呢？」

大衛說：「我要買你這禾場，為耶和華築一座壇，使民間的瘟疫止住。」

22亞勞拿對大衛說：「我主我王，你喜悅用甚麼，就拿去獻祭。看哪，這裏有牛，可以作燔祭；有打糧的器具和套牛的軛，可以當柴燒。23王啊，這一切我亞勞拿都奉給你。」又對王說：「願耶和華你的神悅納你。」

24王對亞勞拿說：「不然，我必要按着價值向你買，我不肯用白得之物作燔祭，獻給耶和華我的神。」

大衛就用五十舍客勒銀子買了那禾場與牛。25大衛在那裏為耶和華築了一座壇，獻燔祭和平安祭。如此，耶和華垂聽國民所求的，瘟疫在以色列人中就止住了。

---

a 24 That is, about 1 1/4 pounds (about 0.6 kilogram)
b 25 Traditionally *peace offerings*

列王紀上

1 Kings

亞多尼雅自立為王

1 大衛王年紀老邁，雖用被遮蓋，仍不覺暖。²所以臣僕對他說：「不如為我主我王尋找一個處女，使她伺候王，奉養王，睡在王的懷中，好叫我主我王得暖。」

³於是，在以色列全境尋找美貌的童女，尋得書念的一個童女亞比煞，就帶到王那裏。⁴這童女極其美貌，她奉養王，伺候王，王卻沒有與她親近。

⁵那時，哈及的兒子亞多尼雅自尊，說：「我必作王。」就為自己預備車輛、馬兵，又派五十人在他前頭奔走。⁶他父親素來沒有使他憂悶，說：「你是做甚麼呢？」他甚俊美，生在押沙龍之後。

⁷亞多尼雅與洗魯雅的兒子約押，和祭司亞比亞他商議，二人就順從他，幫助他。⁸但祭司撒督、耶何耶大的兒子比拿雅、先知拿單、示每、利以，並大衛的勇士，都不順從亞多尼雅。

⁹一日，亞多尼雅在隱羅結旁、瑣希列磐石那裏，宰了牛羊、肥犢，請他的諸弟兄，就是王的眾子，並所有作王臣僕的猶大人；¹⁰惟獨先知拿單和比拿雅並勇士，與他的兄弟所羅門，他都沒有請。

¹¹拿單對所羅門的母親拔示巴說：「哈及的兒子亞多尼雅作王了，你沒有聽見嗎？我們的主大衛卻不知道。¹²現在我可以給你出個主意，好保全你和你兒子所羅門的性命。¹³你進去見大衛王，對他說：『我主我王啊，你不曾向婢女起誓說，你兒子所羅門必接續我作王，坐在我的位上嗎？現在亞多尼雅怎麼作了王呢？』¹⁴你還與王說話的時候，我也隨後進去，證實你的話。」

Adonijah Sets Himself Up as King

1 When King David was old and advanced in years, he could not keep warm even when they put covers over him. ²So his servants said to him, "Let us look for a young virgin to attend the king and take care of him. She can lie beside him so that our lord the king may keep warm."

³Then they searched throughout Israel for a beautiful girl and found Abishag, a Shunammite, and brought her to the king. ⁴The girl was very beautiful; she took care of the king and waited on him, but the king had no intimate relations with her.

⁵Now Adonijah, whose mother was Haggith, put himself forward and said, "I will be king." So he got chariots and horses*ᵃ* ready, with fifty men to run ahead of him. ⁶(His father had never interfered with him by asking, "Why do you behave as you do?" He was also very handsome and was born next after Absalom.)

⁷Adonijah conferred with Joab son of Zeruiah and with Abiathar the priest, and they gave him their support. ⁸But Zadok the priest, Benaiah son of Jehoiada, Nathan the prophet, Shimei and Rei*ᵇ* and David's special guard did not join Adonijah.

⁹Adonijah then sacrificed sheep, cattle and fattened calves at the Stone of Zoheleth near En Rogel. He invited all his brothers, the king's sons, and all the men of Judah who were royal officials, ¹⁰but he did not invite Nathan the prophet or Benaiah or the special guard or his brother Solomon.

¹¹Then Nathan asked Bathsheba, Solomon's mother, "Have you not heard that Adonijah, the son of Haggith, has become king without our lord David's knowing it? ¹²Now then, let me advise you how you can save your own life and the life of your son Solomon. ¹³Go in to King David and say to him, 'My lord the king, did you not swear to me your servant: "Surely Solomon your son shall be king after me, and he will sit on my throne"? Why then has Adonijah become king?' ¹⁴While you are still there talking to the king, I will come in and confirm what you have said."

a 5 Or charioteers　　b 8 Or and his friends

¹⁵So Bathsheba went to see the aged king in his room, where Abishag the Shunammite was attending him. ¹⁶Bathsheba bowed low and knelt before the king.

"What is it you want?" the king asked.

¹⁷She said to him, "My lord, you yourself swore to me your servant by the LORD your God: 'Solomon your son shall be king after me, and he will sit on my throne.' ¹⁸But now Adonijah has become king, and you, my lord the king, do not know about it. ¹⁹He has sacrificed great numbers of cattle, fattened calves, and sheep, and has invited all the king's sons, Abiathar the priest and Joab the commander of the army, but he has not invited Solomon your servant. ²⁰My lord the king, the eyes of all Israel are on you, to learn from you who will sit on the throne of my lord the king after him. ²¹Otherwise, as soon as my lord the king is laid to rest with his fathers, I and my son Solomon will be treated as criminals."

²²While she was still speaking with the king, Nathan the prophet arrived. ²³And they told the king, "Nathan the prophet is here." So he went before the king and bowed with his face to the ground.

²⁴Nathan said, "Have you, my lord the king, declared that Adonijah shall be king after you, and that he will sit on your throne? ²⁵Today he has gone down and sacrificed great numbers of cattle, fattened calves, and sheep. He has invited all the king's sons, the commanders of the army and Abiathar the priest. Right now they are eating and drinking with him and saying, 'Long live King Adonijah!' ²⁶But me your servant, and Zadok the priest, and Benaiah son of Jehoiada, and your servant Solomon he did not invite. ²⁷Is this something my lord the king has done without letting his servants know who should sit on the throne of my lord the king after him?"

David Makes Solomon King

²⁸Then King David said, "Call in Bathsheba." So she came into the king's presence and stood before him.

²⁹The king then took an oath: "As surely as the LORD lives, who has delivered me out of every trouble, ³⁰I will surely carry out today what I swore to you by the LORD, the God of Israel: Solomon your son shall be king after me, and he will sit on my throne in my place."

³¹Then Bathsheba bowed low with her face to the ground and, kneeling before the king, said, "May my lord King David live forever!"

³²King David said, "Call in Zadok the priest, Nathan the prophet and Benaiah son of

¹⁵拔示巴進入內室見王，王甚老邁，書念的童女亞比煞正伺候王。¹⁶拔示巴向王屈身下拜。

王說："你要甚麼？"

¹⁷她說："我主啊，你曾向婢女指着耶和華你的神起誓說：'你兒子所羅門必接續我作王，坐在我的位上。'¹⁸現在亞多尼雅作王了，我主我王卻不知道。¹⁹他宰了許多牛羊、肥犢，請了王的眾子和祭司亞比亞他，並元帥約押；惟獨王的僕人所羅門，他沒有請。²⁰我主我王啊，以色列眾人的眼目都仰望你，等你曉諭他們，在我主我王之後，誰坐你的位。²¹若不然，到我主我王與列祖同睡以後，我和我兒子所羅門必算為罪人了。"

²²拔示巴還與王說話的時候，先知拿單也進來了。²³有人奏告王說："先知拿單來了。"拿單進到王前，臉伏於地。

²⁴拿單說："我主我王果然應許亞多尼雅說：'你必接續我作王，坐在我的位上'嗎？²⁵他今日下去，宰了許多牛羊、肥犢，請了王的眾子和軍長，並祭司亞比亞他，他們正在亞多尼雅面前吃喝，說：'願亞多尼雅王萬歲！'²⁶惟獨我，就是你的僕人和祭司撒督、耶何耶大的兒子比拿雅，並王的僕人所羅門，他都沒有請。²⁷這事果然出乎我主我王嗎？王卻沒有告訴僕人們，在我主我王之後，誰坐你的位。"

大衛立所羅門為王

²⁸大衛王吩咐說："叫拔示巴來。"拔示巴就進來站在王面前。

²⁹王起誓說："我指着救我性命脫離一切苦難、永生的耶和華起誓。³⁰我既然指着耶和華以色列的神向你起誓說：'你兒子所羅門必接續我作王，坐在我的位上。'我今日就必照這話而行。"

³¹於是拔示巴臉伏於地，向王下拜，說："願我主大衛王萬歲！"

³²大衛王又吩咐說："將祭司撒督、先知拿單、耶何耶大的兒子比拿

雅召來。" 他們就都來到王面前。
33王對他們說：" 要帶領你們主的僕
人，使我兒子所羅門騎我的騾子，送
他下到基訓。34在那裏，祭司撒督和
先知拿單要膏他作以色列的王。你們
也要吹角，說：'願所羅門王萬
歲！' 35然後要跟隨他上來，使他坐
在我的位上，接續我作王。我已立他
作以色列和猶大的君。"

36耶何耶大的兒子比拿雅對王
說：" 阿們！願耶和華我主我王的神
也這樣命定。37耶和華怎樣與我主我
王同在，願他照樣與所羅門同在，使
他的國位比我主大衛王的國位更
大。"

38於是祭司撒督、先知拿單、耶
何耶大的兒子比拿雅和基利提人、比
利提人，都下去使所羅門騎大衛王的
騾子，將他送到基訓。39祭司撒督就
從帳幕中取了盛膏油的角來，用膏膏
所羅門。人就吹角，眾民都說：" 願
所羅門王萬歲！" 40眾民跟隨他上
來，且吹笛，大大歡呼，聲音震地。

41亞多尼雅和所請的眾客筵宴方
畢，聽見這聲音。約押聽見角聲，就
說：" 城中為何有這響聲呢？"

42他正說話的時候，祭司亞比亞
他的兒子約拿單來了。亞多尼雅對他
說：" 進來吧！你是個忠義的人，必
是報好信息。"

43約拿單對亞多尼雅說：" 我們
的主大衛王誠然立所羅門為王了。
44王差遣祭司撒督、先知拿單、耶何
耶大的兒子比拿雅和基利提人、比利
提人都去使所羅門騎王的騾子。45祭
司撒督和先知拿單在基訓已經膏他為
王。眾人都從那裏歡呼着上來，聲音
使城震動，這就是你們所聽見的聲
音。46並且所羅門登了國位。47王的
臣僕也來為我們的主大衛王祝福，
說：'願王的神使所羅門的名比王的
名更尊榮，使他的國位比王的國位更
大。' 王就在牀上屈身下拜。48王又
說：'耶和華以色列的神是應當稱頌
的！因他賜我一人今日坐在我的位
上，我也親眼看見了。'"

Jehoiada." When they came before the king, [33]he said to them: "Take your lord's servants with you and set Solomon my son on my own mule and take him down to Gihon. [34]There have Zadok the priest and Nathan the prophet anoint him king over Israel. Blow the trumpet and shout, 'Long live King Solomon!' [35]Then you are to go up with him, and he is to come and sit on my throne and reign in my place. I have appointed him ruler over Israel and Judah."

[36]Benaiah son of Jehoiada answered the king, "Amen! May the LORD, the God of my lord the king, so declare it. [37]As the LORD was with my lord the king, so may he be with Solomon to make his throne even greater than the throne of my lord King David!"

[38]So Zadok the priest, Nathan the prophet, Benaiah son of Jehoiada, the Kerethites and the Pelethites went down and put Solomon on King David's mule and escorted him to Gihon. [39]Zadok the priest took the horn of oil from the sacred tent and anointed Solomon. Then they sounded the trumpet and all the people shouted, "Long live King Solomon!" [40]And all the people went up after him, playing flutes and rejoicing greatly, so that the ground shook with the sound.

[41]Adonijah and all the guests who were with him heard it as they were finishing their feast. On hearing the sound of the trumpet, Joab asked, "What's the meaning of all the noise in the city?"

[42]Even as he was speaking, Jonathan son of Abiathar the priest arrived. Adonijah said, "Come in. A worthy man like you must be bringing good news."

[43]"Not at all!" Jonathan answered. "Our lord King David has made Solomon king. [44]The king has sent with him Zadok the priest, Nathan the prophet, Benaiah son of Jehoiada, the Kerethites and the Pelethites, and they have put him on the king's mule, [45]and Zadok the priest and Nathan the prophet have anointed him king at Gihon. From there they have gone up cheering, and the city resounds with it. That's the noise you hear. [46]Moreover, Solomon has taken his seat on the royal throne. [47]Also, the royal officials have come to congratulate our lord King David, saying, 'May your God make Solomon's name more famous than yours and his throne greater than yours!' And the king bowed in worship on his bed [48]and said, 'Praise be to the LORD, the God of Israel, who has allowed my eyes to see a successor on my throne today.'"

⁴⁹At this, all Adonijah's guests rose in alarm and dispersed. ⁵⁰But Adonijah, in fear of Solomon, went and took hold of the horns of the altar. ⁵¹Then Solomon was told, "Adonijah is afraid of King Solomon and is clinging to the horns of the altar. He says, 'Let King Solomon swear to me today that he will not put his servant to death with the sword.'"

⁵²Solomon replied, "If he shows himself to be a worthy man, not a hair of his head will fall to the ground; but if evil is found in him, he will die." ⁵³Then King Solomon sent men, and they brought him down from the altar. And Adonijah came and bowed down to King Solomon, and Solomon said, "Go to your home."

David's Charge to Solomon

2 When the time drew near for David to die, he gave a charge to Solomon his son.

²"I am about to go the way of all the earth," he said. "So be strong, show yourself a man, ³and observe what the LORD your God requires: Walk in his ways, and keep his decrees and commands, his laws and requirements, as written in the Law of Moses, so that you may prosper in all you do and wherever you go, ⁴and that the LORD may keep his promise to me: 'If your descendants watch how they live, and if they walk faithfully before me with all their heart and soul, you will never fail to have a man on the throne of Israel.'

⁵"Now you yourself know what Joab son of Zeruiah did to me—what he did to the two commanders of Israel's armies, Abner son of Ner and Amasa son of Jether. He killed them, shedding their blood in peacetime as if in battle, and with that blood stained the belt around his waist and the sandals on his feet. ⁶Deal with him according to your wisdom, but do not let his gray head go down to the grave[a] in peace.

⁷"But show kindness to the sons of Barzillai of Gilead and let them be among those who eat at your table. They stood by me when I fled from your brother Absalom.

⁸"And remember, you have with you Shimei son of Gera, the Benjamite from Bahurim, who called down bitter curses on me the day I went to Mahanaim. When he came down to meet me at the Jordan, I swore to him by the Lord: 'I will not put you to death by the sword.' ⁹But now, do not consider him innocent. You are a man of wisdom; you will know what to do to him.

---

^a 6 Hebrew *Sheol*; also in verse 9

---

⁴⁹亞多尼雅的眾客聽見這話就都驚懼，起來四散。⁵⁰亞多尼雅懼怕所羅門，就起來，去抓住祭壇的角。⁵¹有人告訴所羅門說：「亞多尼雅怕所羅門王，現在抓住祭壇的角，說：『願所羅門王今日向我起誓，必不用刀殺僕人。』」

⁵²所羅門說：「他若作忠義的人，連一根頭髮也不至落在地上；他若行惡，必要死亡。」⁵³於是，所羅門王差遣人，使亞多尼雅從壇上下來，他就來向所羅門王下拜。所羅門對他說：「你回家去吧！」

大衛對所羅門的臨終囑咐

2 大衛的死期臨近了，就囑咐他兒子所羅門說：

²「我現在要走世人必走的路，所以，你當剛強，作大丈夫，³遵守耶和華你神所吩咐的，照着摩西律法上所寫的行主的道，謹守他的律例、誡命、典章、法度。這樣，你無論做甚麼事，不拘往何處去，盡都亨通。⁴耶和華必成就向我所應許的話說：『你的子孫若謹慎自己的行為，盡心盡意、誠誠實實地行在我面前，就不斷人坐以色列的國位。』

⁵「你知道洗魯雅的兒子約押向我所行的，就是殺了以色列的兩個元帥——尼珥的兒子押尼珥和益帖的兒子亞瑪撒。他在太平之時流這二人的血，如在爭戰之時一樣，將這血染了腰間束的帶和腳上穿的鞋。⁶所以你要照你的智慧行，不容他白頭安然下陰間。

⁷「你當恩待基列人巴西萊的眾子，使他們常與你同席吃飯，因為我躲避你哥哥押沙龍的時候，他們拿食物來迎接我。⁸「在你這裏有巴戶琳的便雅憫人，基拉的兒子示每，我往瑪哈念去的那日，他用狠毒的言語咒罵我，後來卻下約旦河迎接我，我就指着耶和華向他起誓，說：『我必不用刀殺你。』⁹現在你不要以他為無罪，你是聰明人，必知道怎樣待他，使他白

頭見殺，流血下到陰間。"

10大衛與他列祖同睡，葬在大衛城。11大衛作以色列王四十年——在希伯崙作王七年，在耶路撒冷作王三十三年。12所羅門坐他父親大衛的位，他的國甚是堅固。

所羅門王位堅立

13哈及的兒子亞多尼雅去見所羅門的母親拔示巴，拔示巴問他說："你來是為平安嗎？"

回答說："是為平安。"14又說："我有話對你說。"

拔示巴說："你說吧。"

15亞多尼雅說："你知道國原是歸我的，以色列眾人也都仰望我作王。不料，國反歸了我兄弟，因他得國是出乎耶和華。16現在，我有一件事求你，望你不要推辭。"

拔示巴說："你說吧！"

17他說："求你請所羅門王將書念的女子亞比煞賜我為妻，因他必不推辭you。"

18拔示巴說："好，我必為你對王提說。"

19於是拔示巴去見所羅門王，要為亞多尼雅提說。王起來迎接，向她下拜，就坐在位上，吩咐人為王母設一座位，她便坐在王的右邊。

20拔示巴說："我有一件小事求你，望你不要推辭。"

王說："請母親說，我必不推辭。"

21拔示巴說："求你將書念的女子亞比煞賜給你哥哥亞多尼雅為妻。"

22所羅門王對他母親說："為何單替他求書念的女子亞比煞呢？也可以為他求國吧！他是我的哥哥，他有祭司亞比亞他和洗魯雅的兒子約押為輔佐。"

23所羅門王就指着耶和華起誓說："亞多尼雅這話是自己送命，不然，願神重重地降罰與我。24耶和華堅立我，使我坐在父親大衛的位上，照着所應許的話為我建立家室。現在我指着永生的耶和華起誓，亞多尼雅今日必被治死。"25於是，所羅門王差遣耶何耶大的兒子比拿雅將亞多尼雅殺死。

Bring his gray head down to the grave in blood."

10Then David rested with his fathers and was buried in the City of David. 11He had reigned forty years over Israel—seven years in Hebron and thirty-three in Jerusalem. 12So Solomon sat on the throne of his father David, and his rule was firmly established.

Solomon's Throne Established

13Now Adonijah, the son of Haggith, went to Bathsheba, Solomon's mother. Bathsheba asked him, "Do you come peacefully?"

He answered, "Yes, peacefully." 14Then he added, "I have something to say to you."

"You may say it," she replied.

15"As you know," he said, "the kingdom was mine. All Israel looked to me as their king. But things changed, and the kingdom has gone to my brother; for it has come to him from the LORD. 16Now I have one request to make of you. Do not refuse me."

"You may make it," she said.

17So he continued, "Please ask King Solomon—he will not refuse you—to give me Abishag the Shunammite as my wife."

18"Very well," Bathsheba replied, "I will speak to the king for you."

19When Bathsheba went to King Solomon to speak to him for Adonijah, the king stood up to meet her, bowed down to her and sat down on his throne. He had a throne brought for the king's mother, and she sat down at his right hand.

20"I have one small request to make of you," she said. "Do not refuse me."

The king replied, "Make it, my mother; I will not refuse you."

21So she said, "Let Abishag the Shunammite be given in marriage to your brother Adonijah."

22King Solomon answered his mother, "Why do you request Abishag the Shunammite for Adonijah? You might as well request the kingdom for him—after all, he is my older brother—yes, for him and for Abiathar the priest and Joab son of Zeruiah!"

23Then King Solomon swore by the LORD: "May God deal with me, be it ever so severely, if Adonijah does not pay with his life for this request! 24And now, as surely as the LORD lives—he who has established me securely on the throne of my father David and has founded a dynasty for me as he promised—Adonijah shall be put to death today!" 25So King Solomon gave orders to Benaiah son of Jehoiada, and he struck down Adonijah and he died.

²⁶To Abiathar the priest the king said, "Go back to your fields in Anathoth. You deserve to die, but I will not put you to death now, because you carried the ark of the Sovereign LORD before my father David and shared all my father's hardships." ²⁷So Solomon removed Abiathar from the priesthood of the LORD, fulfilling the word the LORD had spoken at Shiloh about the house of Eli.

²⁸When the news reached Joab, who had conspired with Adonijah though not with Absalom, he fled to the tent of the LORD and took hold of the horns of the altar. ²⁹King Solomon was told that Joab had fled to the tent of the LORD and was beside the altar. Then Solomon ordered Benaiah son of Jehoiada, "Go, strike him down!"

³⁰So Benaiah entered the tent of the LORD and said to Joab, "The king says, 'Come out!'"

But he answered, "No, I will die here."

Benaiah reported to the king, "This is how Joab answered me."

³¹Then the king commanded Benaiah, "Do as he says. Strike him down and bury him, and so clear me and my father's house of the guilt of the innocent blood that Joab shed. ³²The LORD will repay him for the blood he shed, because without the knowledge of my father David he attacked two men and killed them with the sword. Both of them—Abner son of Ner, commander of Israel's army, and Amasa son of Jether, commander of Judah's army—were better men and more upright than he. ³³May the guilt of their blood rest on the head of Joab and his descendants forever. But on David and his descendants, his house and his throne, may there be the LORD's peace forever."

³⁴So Benaiah son of Jehoiada went up and struck down Joab and killed him, and he was buried on his own land*ᵃ* in the desert. ³⁵The king put Benaiah son of Jehoiada over the army in Joab's position and replaced Abiathar with Zadok the priest.

³⁶Then the king sent for Shimei and said to him, "Build yourself a house in Jerusalem and live there, but do not go anywhere else. ³⁷The day you leave and cross the Kidron Valley, you can be sure you will die; your blood will be on your own head."

³⁸Shimei answered the king, "What you say is good. Your servant will do as my lord the king has said." And Shimei stayed in Jerusalem for a long time.

³⁹But three years later, two of Shimei's slaves ran off to Achish son of Maacah, king of Gath,

a 34 Or buried in his tomb

²⁶王對祭司亞比亞他說：「你回亞拿突歸自己的田地去吧！你本是該死的，但因你在我父親面前抬過主耶和華的約櫃，又與我父親同受一切苦難，所以我今日不將你殺死。」²⁷所羅門就革除亞比亞他，不許他作耶和華的祭司。這樣，便應驗耶和華在示羅論以利家所說的話。

²⁸約押雖然沒有歸從押沙龍，卻歸從了亞多尼雅。他聽見這風聲，就逃到耶和華的帳幕，抓住祭壇的角。²⁹有人告訴所羅門王說：「約押逃到耶和華的帳幕，現今在祭壇的旁邊。」所羅門就差遣耶何耶大的兒子比拿雅說：「你去將他殺死。」

³⁰比拿雅來到耶和華的帳幕，對約押說：「王吩咐說，你出來吧！」

他說：「我不出去，我要死在這裏。」比拿雅就去回覆王說，約押如此如此回答我。

³¹王說：「你可以照着他的話行，殺死他，將他葬埋，好叫約押流無辜人血的罪不歸我和我的父家了。³²耶和華必使約押流流人血的罪歸到他自己的頭上，因為他用刀殺了兩個比他又義又好的人，就是以色列元帥尼珥的兒子押尼珥和猶大元帥益帖的兒子亞瑪撒，我父親大衛卻不知道。³³故此，流這二人血的罪必歸到約押和他後裔的頭上，直到永遠；惟有大衛和他的後裔，並他的家與國，必從耶和華那裏得平安，直到永遠。」

³⁴於是耶何耶大的兒子比拿雅上去，將約押殺死，葬在曠野約押自己的墳墓裏（註：「墳墓」原文作「房屋」）。³⁵王就立耶何耶大的兒子比拿雅作元帥，代替約押，又使祭司撒督代替亞比亞他。

³⁶王差遣人將示每召來，對他說：「你要在耶路撒冷建造房屋居住，不可出來往別處去。³⁷你當確實地知道，你何日出來過汲淪溪，何日必死！你的罪（註：原文作「血」）必歸到自己的頭上。」

³⁸示每對王說：「這話甚好！我主我王怎樣說，僕人必怎樣行。」於是示每多日住在耶路撒冷。

³⁹過了三年，示每的兩個僕人逃到迦特王瑪迦的兒子亞吉那裏去。有

人告訴示每說：「你的僕人在迦特。」40示每起來，備上驢，往迦特到亞吉那裏去找他的僕人，就從迦特帶我僕人回來。

41有人告訴所羅門說：「示每出耶路撒冷往迦特去，回來了。」42王就差遣人將示每召了來，對他說：「我豈不是叫你指着耶和華起誓，並且警戒你說：『你當確實地知道，你哪日出來往別處去，哪日必死』嗎？你也對我說：『這話甚好，我必聽從。』43現在你為何不遵守你指着耶和華起的誓和我所吩咐你的命令呢？」

44王又對示每說：「你向我父親大衛所行的一切惡事，你自己心裏也知道，所以耶和華必使你的罪惡歸到自己的頭上。45惟有所羅門王必得福，並且大衛的國位必在耶和華面前堅定，直到永遠。」

46於是王吩咐耶何耶大的兒子比拿雅，他就去殺死示每。

這樣，便堅定了所羅門的國位。

所羅門求智慧

3所羅門與埃及王法老結親，娶了法老的女兒為妻，接她進入大衛城，直等到造完了自己的宮和耶和華的殿，並耶路撒冷周圍的城牆。2當那些日子，百姓仍在邱壇獻祭，因為還沒有為耶和華的名建殿。3所羅門愛耶和華，遵行他父親大衛的律例，只是還在邱壇獻祭燒香。

4所羅門王上基遍去獻祭，因為在那裏有極大的邱壇（註：「極大」或作「出名」），他在那壇上獻一千犧牲作燔祭。5在基遍，夜間夢中耶和華向所羅門顯現，對他說：「你願我賜你甚麼？你可以求。」

6所羅門說：「你僕人我父親大衛用誠實、公義、正直的心行在你面前，你就向他大施恩典；又為他存留大恩，賜他一個兒子坐在他的位上，正如今日一樣。

7「耶和華我的神啊，如今你使僕人接續我父親大衛作王，但我是幼

and Shimei was told, "Your slaves are in Gath." 40At this, he saddled his donkey and went to Achish at Gath in search of his slaves. So Shimei went away and brought the slaves back from Gath.

41When Solomon was told that Shimei had gone from Jerusalem to Gath and had returned, 42the king summoned Shimei and said to him, "Did I not make you swear by the LORD and warn you, 'On the day you leave to go anywhere else, you can be sure you will die'? At that time you said to me, 'What you say is good. I will obey.' 43Why then did you not keep your oath to the LORD and obey the command I gave you?"

44The king also said to Shimei, "You know in your heart all the wrong you did to my father David. Now the LORD will repay you for your wrongdoing. 45But King Solomon will be blessed, and David's throne will remain secure before the LORD forever."

46Then the king gave the order to Benaiah son of Jehoiada, and he went out and struck Shimei down and killed him.

The kingdom was now firmly established in Solomon's hands.

Solomon Asks for Wisdom

3Solomon made an alliance with Pharaoh king of Egypt and married his daughter. He brought her to the City of David until he finished building his palace and the temple of the LORD, and the wall around Jerusalem. 2The people, however, were still sacrificing at the high places, because a temple had not yet been built for the Name of the LORD. 3Solomon showed his love for the LORD by walking according to the statutes of his father David, except that he offered sacrifices and burned incense on the high places.

4The king went to Gibeon to offer sacrifices, for that was the most important high place, and Solomon offered a thousand burnt offerings on that altar. 5At Gibeon the LORD appeared to Solomon during the night in a dream, and God said, "Ask for whatever you want me to give you."

6Solomon answered, "You have shown great kindness to your servant, my father David, because he was faithful to you and righteous and upright in heart. You have continued this great kindness to him and have given him a son to sit on his throne this very day.

7"Now, O LORD my God, you have made your servant king in place of my father David. But I am only a little child and do not know how to carry out my duties. [8]Your servant is here among the people you have chosen, a great people, too numerous to count or number. [9]So give your servant a discerning heart to govern your people and to distinguish between right and wrong. For who is able to govern this great people of yours?"

[10]The Lord was pleased that Solomon had asked for this. [11]So God said to him, "Since you have asked for this and not for long life or wealth for yourself, nor have asked for the death of your enemies but for discernment in administering justice, [12]I will do what you have asked. I will give you a wise and discerning heart, so that there will never have been anyone like you, nor will there ever be. [13]Moreover, I will give you what you have not asked for—both riches and honor—so that in your lifetime you will have no equal among kings. [14]And if you walk in my ways and obey my statutes and commands as David your father did, I will give you a long life." [15]Then Solomon awoke—and he realized it had been a dream.

He returned to Jerusalem, stood before the ark of the Lord's covenant and sacrificed burnt offerings and fellowship offerings.[a] Then he gave a feast for all his court.

A Wise Ruling

[16]Now two prostitutes came to the king and stood before him. [17]One of them said, "My lord, this woman and I live in the same house. I had a baby while she was there with me. [18]The third day after my child was born, this woman also had a baby. We were alone; there was no one in the house but the two of us.

[19]"During the night this woman's son died because she lay on him. [20]So she got up in the middle of the night and took my son from my side while I your servant was asleep. She put him by her breast and put her dead son by my breast. [21]The next morning, I got up to nurse my son—and he was dead! But when I looked at him closely in the morning light, I saw that it wasn't the son I had borne."

[22]The other woman said, "No! The living one is my son; the dead one is yours."

But the first one insisted, "No! The dead one is yours; the living one is mine." And so they argued before the king.

[23]The king said, "This one says, 'My son is alive and your son is dead,' while that one says, 'No! Your son is dead and mine is alive.'"

童，不知道應當怎樣出入。[8]僕人住在你所揀選的民中，這民多得不可勝數。[9]所以求你賜我智慧，可以判斷你的民，能辨別是非。不然，誰能判斷這眾多的民呢？"

[10]所羅門因為求這事，就蒙主喜悅。[11]神對他說："你既然求這事，不為自己求壽、求富，也不求滅絕你仇敵的性命，單求智慧可以聽訟，[12]我就應允你所求的，賜你聰明智慧，甚至在你以前沒有像你的，在你以後也沒有像你的。[13]你所沒有求的，我也賜給你，就是富足、尊榮，使你在世的日子，列王中沒有一個能比你的。[14]你若效法你父親大衛，遵行我的道，謹守我的律例、誡命，我必使你長壽。"[15]所羅門醒了，不料是個夢。

他就回到耶路撒冷，站在耶和華的約櫃前，獻燔祭和平安祭，又為他眾臣僕設擺筵席。

智慧的斷案

[16]一日，有兩個妓女來，站在王面前。[17]一個說："我主啊，我和這婦人同住一房，她在房中的時候，我生了一個男孩。[18]我生孩子後第三日，這婦人也生了孩子。我們是同住的，除了我們二人之外，房中再沒有別人。

[19]"夜間，這婦人睡着的時候，壓死了她的孩子。[20]她半夜起來，趁我睡着，從我旁邊把我的孩子抱去，放在她懷裏，將她的死孩子放在我懷裏。[21]天要亮的時候，我起來要給我的孩子吃奶，不料，孩子死了。及至天亮，我細細地察看，不是我所生的孩子。"

[22]那婦人說："不然，活孩子是我的，死孩子是你的。"

這婦人說："不然，死孩子是你的，活孩子是我的。"她們在王面前如此爭論。

[23]王說："這婦人說：'活孩子是我的，死孩子是你的。'那婦人說：'不然，死孩子是你的，活孩子是我的。'"

---

a 15 Traditionally *peace offerings*

²⁴就吩咐说："拿刀來！"人就拿刀來。²⁵王说："將活孩子劈成兩半，一半給那婦人，一半給這婦人。"

²⁶活孩子的母親為自己的孩子心裏急痛，就说："求我主將活孩子給那婦人吧！萬不可殺他。"

那婦人说："這孩子也不歸我，也不歸你，把他劈了吧！"

²⁷王说："將活孩子給這婦人，萬不可殺他，這婦人實在是他的母親。"

²⁸以色列眾人聽見王這樣判斷，就都敬畏他，因為見他心裏有神的智慧，能以斷案。

所羅門的臣子和官吏

4 所羅門作以色列眾人的王。²他的臣子記在下面：

撒督的兒子亞撒利雅作祭司；
³示沙的兩個兒子以利何烈、亞希亞作書記；
亞希律的兒子約沙法作史官；
⁴耶何耶大的兒子比拿雅作元帥；
撒督和亞比亞他作祭司長；
⁵拿單的兒子亞撒利雅作眾長書；
王的朋友拿單的兒子撒布得作領袖；

⁶亞希煞作家宰；
亞比大的兒子亞多尼蘭掌管服苦的人。

⁷所羅門在以色列全地立了十二個官吏，使他們供給王和王家的食物，每年各人供給一月。⁸他們的名字記在下面：

在以法蓮山地有便戶珥；
⁹在瑪迦斯、沙賓、伯示麥、以倫伯哈南有便底甲；
¹⁰在亞魯泊有便希悉，他管理梭哥和希弗全地；
¹¹在多珥山岡（註：或作"全境"）有便亞比拿達，他娶了所羅門的女兒她法為妻；
¹²在他納和米吉多，並靠近撒拉他拿、耶斯列下邊的伯善全地，從伯善到亞伯米何拉

²⁴Then the king said, "Bring me a sword." So they brought a sword for the king. ²⁵He then gave an order: "Cut the living child in two and give half to one and half to the other."

²⁶The woman whose son was alive was filled with compassion for her son and said to the king, "Please, my lord, give her the living baby! Don't kill him!"

But the other said, "Neither I nor you shall have him. Cut him in two!"

²⁷Then the king gave his ruling: "Give the living baby to the first woman. Do not kill him; she is his mother."

²⁸When all Israel heard the verdict the king had given, they held the king in awe, because they saw that he had wisdom from God to administer justice.

Solomon's Officials and Governors

4 So King Solomon ruled over all Israel. ²And these were his chief officials:

Azariah son of Zadok—the priest;
³Elihoreph and Ahijah, sons of Shisha—secretaries;
Jehoshaphat son of Ahilud—recorder;
⁴Benaiah son of Jehoiada—commander in chief;
Zadok and Abiathar—priests;
⁵Azariah son of Nathan—in charge of the district officers;
Zabud son of Nathan—a priest and personal adviser to the king;
⁶Ahishar—in charge of the palace;
Adoniram son of Abda—in charge of forced labor.

⁷Solomon also had twelve district governors over all Israel, who supplied provisions for the king and the royal household. Each one had to provide supplies for one month in the year. ⁸These are their names:

Ben-Hur—in the hill country of Ephraim;
⁹Ben-Deker—in Makaz, Shaalbim, Beth Shemesh and Elon Bethhanan;
¹⁰Ben-Hesed—in Arubboth (Socoh and all the land of Hepher were his);
¹¹Ben-Abinadab—in Naphoth Dor[a] (he was married to Taphath daughter of Solomon);
¹²Baana son of Ahilud—in Taanach and Megiddo, and in all of Beth Shan next to Zarethan below Jezreel, from Beth Shan

a 11 Or in the heights of Dor

to Abel Meholah across to Jokmeam;

¹³Ben-Geber—in Ramoth Gilead (the settlements of Jair son of Manasseh in Gilead were his, as well as the district of Argob in Bashan and its sixty large walled cities with bronze gate bars);

¹⁴Ahinadab son of Iddo—in Mahanaim;

¹⁵Ahimaaz—in Naphtali (he had married Basemath daughter of Solomon);

¹⁶Baana son of Hushai—in Asher and in Aloth;

¹⁷Jehoshaphat son of Paruah—in Issachar;

¹⁸Shimei son of Ela—in Benjamin;

¹⁹Geber son of Uri—in Gilead (the country of Sihon king of the Amorites and the country of Og king of Bashan). He was the only governor over the district.

Solomon's Daily Provisions

²⁰The people of Judah and Israel were as numerous as the sand on the seashore; they ate, they drank and they were happy. ²¹And Solomon ruled over all the kingdoms from the River[a] to the land of the Philistines, as far as the border of Egypt. These countries brought tribute and were Solomon's subjects all his life.

²²Solomon's daily provisions were thirty cors[b] of fine flour and sixty cors[c] of meal, ²³ten head of stall-fed cattle, twenty of pasture-fed cattle and a hundred sheep and goats, as well as deer, gazelles, roebucks and choice fowl. ²⁴For he ruled over all the kingdoms west of the River, from Tiphsah to Gaza, and had peace on all sides. ²⁵During Solomon's lifetime Judah and Israel, from Dan to Beersheba, lived in safety, each man under his own vine and fig tree.

²⁶Solomon had four[d] thousand stalls for chariot horses, and twelve thousand horses.[e]

²⁷The district officers, each in his month, supplied provisions for King Solomon and all who came to the king's table. They saw to it that nothing was lacking. ²⁸They also brought to the proper place their quotas of barley and straw for the chariot horses and the other horses.

Solomon's Wisdom

²⁹God gave Solomon wisdom and very great insight, and a breadth of understanding as measureless as the sand on the seashore. ³⁰Solomon's wisdom was greater than the wisdom of

直到約念之外，有亞希律的兒子巴拿；

¹³在基列的拉末有便基別，他管理在基列的瑪拿西子孫睚珥的城邑，巴珊的亞珥歌伯地的大城六十座，都有城牆和銅閂；

¹⁴在瑪哈念有易多的兒子亞希拿達；

¹⁵在拿弗他利有亞希瑪斯，他也娶了所羅門的一個女兒巴實抹為妻；

¹⁶在亞設和亞祿有戶篩的兒子巴拿；

¹⁷在以薩迦有帕路亞的兒子約沙法；

¹⁸在便雅憫有以拉的兒子示每；

¹⁹在基列地，就是從前屬亞摩利王西宏和巴珊王噩之地，有烏利的兒子基別一人管理。

所羅門每日得豐富供應

²⁰猶大人和以色列人如同海邊的沙那樣多，都吃喝快樂。²¹所羅門統管諸國，從大河到非利士地，直到埃及的邊界。所羅門在世的日子，這些國都進貢服侍他。

²²所羅門每日所用的食物：細麵三十歌珥，粗麵六十歌珥，²³肥牛十隻，草場的牛二十隻，羊一百隻，還有鹿、羚羊、麃子並肥禽。²⁴所羅門管理大河西邊的諸王，以及從提弗薩直到迦薩的全地，四境盡都平安。²⁵所羅門在世的日子，從但到別是巴的猶大人和以色列人，都在自己的葡萄樹下和無花果樹下安然居住。

²⁶所羅門有套車的馬四萬，還有馬兵一萬二千。

²⁷那十二個官吏，各按各月供給所羅門王，並一切與他同席之人的食物，一無所缺。²⁸眾人各按各分，將養馬與快馬的大麥和乾草送到官吏那裏。

所羅門的智慧

²⁹神賜給所羅門極大的智慧聰明和廣大的心，如同海沙不可測量。³⁰所羅門的智慧超過東方人和埃及人

---

a 21 That is, the Euphrates; also in verse 24   b 22 That is, probably about 185 bushels (about 6.6 kiloliters)
c 22 That is, probably about 375 bushels (about 13.2 kiloliters)
d 26 Some Septuagint manuscripts (see also 2 Chron. 9:25); Hebrew forty   e 26 Or charioteers

的一切智慧。³¹他的智慧勝過萬人，勝過以斯拉人以探，並瑪曷的兒子希幔、甲各、達大的智慧，他的名聲傳揚在四圍的列國。³²他作箴言三千句，詩歌一千零五首。³³他講論草木，自黎巴嫩的香柏樹直到牆上長的牛膝草；又講論飛禽走獸、昆蟲水族。³⁴天下列王聽見所羅門的智慧，就都差人來聽他的智慧話。

建造聖殿的準備

5 推羅王希蘭，平素愛大衛。他聽見以色列人膏所羅門，接續他父親作王，就差遣臣僕來見他。²所羅門也差遣人去見希蘭，說：

³ “你知道我父親大衛因四圍的爭戰，不能為耶和華他神的名建殿，直等到耶和華使仇敵都服在他腳下。⁴現在耶和華我的神使我四圍平安，沒有仇敵，沒有災禍。⁵我定意要為耶和華我神的名建殿，是照耶和華應許我父親大衛的話說：‘我必使你兒子接續你坐你的位，他必為我的名建殿。’

⁶ “所以求你吩咐你的僕人，在黎巴嫩為我砍伐香柏木，我的僕人也必幫助他們。我必照你所定的，給你僕人的工價。因為你知道，在我們中間沒有人像西頓人善於砍伐樹木。”

⁷希蘭聽見所羅門的話，就甚喜悅，說：“今日應當稱頌耶和華，因他賜給大衛一個有智慧的兒子，治理這眾多的民。”

⁸希蘭打發人去見所羅門，說：

“你差遣人向我所提的那事，我都聽見了。論到香柏木和松木，我必照你的心願而行。⁹我的僕人必將這木料從黎巴嫩運到海裏，紮成筏子，浮海運到你所指定我的地方，在那裏拆開，你就可以收取。你也要成全我的心願，將食物給我的家。”

Preparations for Building the Temple

5 When Hiram king of Tyre heard that Solomon had been anointed king to succeed his father David, he sent his envoys to Solomon, because he had always been on friendly terms with David. ²Solomon sent back this message to Hiram:

³“You know that because of the wars waged against my father David from all sides, he could not build a temple for the Name of the LORD his God until the LORD put his enemies under his feet. ⁴But now the LORD my God has given me rest on every side, and there is no adversary or disaster. ⁵I intend, therefore, to build a temple for the Name of the LORD my God, as the LORD told my father David, when he said, ‘Your son whom I will put on the throne in your place will build the temple for my Name.’

⁶“So give orders that cedars of Lebanon be cut for me. My men will work with yours, and I will pay you for your men whatever wages you set. You know that we have no one so skilled in felling timber as the Sidonians.”

⁷When Hiram heard Solomon's message, he was greatly pleased and said, “Praise be to the LORD today, for he has given David a wise son to rule over this great nation.”

⁸So Hiram sent word to Solomon:

“I have received the message you sent me and will do all you want in providing the cedar and pine logs. ⁹My men will haul them down from Lebanon to the sea, and I will float them in rafts by sea to the place you specify. There I will separate them and you can take them away. And you are to grant my wish by providing food for my royal household.”

¹⁰In this way Hiram kept Solomon supplied with all the cedar and pine logs he wanted, ¹¹and Solomon gave Hiram twenty thousand cors*a* of wheat as food for his household, in addition to twenty thousand baths*b,c* of pressed olive oil. Solomon continued to do this for Hiram year after year. ¹²The LORD gave Solomon wisdom, just as he had promised him. There were peaceful relations between Hiram and Solomon, and the two of them made a treaty.

¹³King Solomon conscripted laborers from all Israel—thirty thousand men. ¹⁴He sent them off to Lebanon in shifts of ten thousand a month, so that they spent one month in Lebanon and two months at home. Adoniram was in charge of the forced labor. ¹⁵Solomon had seventy thousand carriers and eighty thousand stonecutters in the hills, ¹⁶as well as thirty-three hundred*d* foremen who supervised the project and directed the workmen. ¹⁷At the king's command they removed from the quarry large blocks of quality stone to provide a foundation of dressed stone for the temple. ¹⁸The craftsmen of Solomon and Hiram and the men of Gebal*e* cut and prepared the timber and stone for the building of the temple.

Solomon Builds the Temple

6 In the four hundred and eightieth*f* year after the Israelites had come out of Egypt, in the fourth year of Solomon's reign over Israel, in the month of Ziv, the second month, he began to build the temple of the LORD.

²The temple that King Solomon built for the LORD was sixty cubits long, twenty wide and thirty high.*g* ³The portico at the front of the main hall of the temple extended the width of the temple, that is twenty cubits,*h* and projected ten cubits*i* from the front of the temple. ⁴He made narrow clerestory windows in the temple. ⁵Against the walls of the main hall and inner sanctuary he built a structure around the building, in which there were side rooms. ⁶The lowest

¹⁰於是希蘭照着所羅門所要的，給他香柏木和松木。¹¹所羅門給希蘭麥子二萬歌珥，清油二十歌珥，作他家的食物。所羅門每年都是這樣給希蘭。¹²耶和華照着所應許的，賜智慧給所羅門。希蘭與所羅門和好，彼此立約。

¹³所羅門王從以色列人中挑取服苦的人共有三萬。¹⁴派他們輪流，每月一萬人上黎巴嫩去；一個月在黎巴嫩，兩個月在家裏，亞多尼蘭掌管他們。¹⁵所羅門用七萬扛抬的，八萬在山上鑿石頭的。¹⁶此外，所羅門用三千三百督工的監管工人。¹⁷王下令，人就鑿出又大又寶貴的石頭來，用以立殿的根基。¹⁸所羅門的匠人和希蘭的匠人，並迦巴勒人，都將石頭鑿好，預備木料和石頭建殿。

所羅門建造聖殿

6 以色列人出埃及地後四百八十年，所羅門作以色列王第四年西弗月，就是二月，開工建造耶和華的殿。

²所羅門王為耶和華所建的殿，長六十肘，寬二十肘，高三十肘。³殿前的廊子長二十肘，與殿的寬窄一樣，闊十肘。⁴又為殿做了嚴緊的窗櫺。⁵靠着殿牆，圍着外殿內殿，造了三層旁屋。⁶下層寬五肘，中層

---

a 11 That is, probably about 125,000 bushels (about 4,400 kiloliters)   *b 11 Septuagint (see also 2 Chron. 2:10); Hebrew twenty cors*   *c 11 That is, about 115,000 gallons (about 440 kiloliters)*   *d 16 Hebrew; some Septuagint manuscripts (see also 2 Chron. 2:2, 18) thirty-six hundred*   *e 18 That is, Byblos*   *f 1 Hebrew; Septuagint four hundred and fortieth*   *g 2 That is, about 90 feet (about 27 meters) long and 30 feet (about 9 meters) wide and 45 feet (about 13.5 meters) high*   *h 3 That is, about 30 feet (about 9 meters)*   *i 3 That is, about 15 feet (about 4.5 meters)*

寬六肘，上層寬七肘。殿外旁屋的梁木，擱在殿牆坎上，免得插入殿牆。

7建殿是用山中鑿成的石頭。建殿的時候，鎚子、斧子和別樣鐵器的響聲都沒有聽見。

8在殿右邊當中的旁屋有門，門內有旋螺的樓梯，可以上到第二層，從第二層可以上到第三層。9所羅門建殿，安置香柏木的棟梁，又用香柏木板遮蓋。10靠着殿所造的旁屋，每層高五肘，香柏木的棟梁，擱在殿牆坎上。

11耶和華的話臨到所羅門說：12 "論到你所建的這殿，你若遵行我的律例，謹守我的典章，遵從我的一切誡命，我必向你應驗我所應許你父親大衛的話。13我必住在以色列人中間，並不丟棄我民以色列。"

14所羅門建造殿宇，15殿裏面用香柏木板貼牆，從地到棚頂，都用木板遮蔽，又用松木板鋪地。16內殿，就是至聖所，長二十肘，從地到棚頂，用香柏木板遮蔽（註：或作 "隔斷"）。17內殿前的外殿，長四十肘。18殿裏一點石頭都不顯露，一概用香柏木遮蔽，上面刻着野瓜和初開的花。

19殿裏預備了內殿，好安放耶和華的約櫃。20內殿長二十肘，寬二十肘，高二十肘，牆面都貼上精金；又用香柏木做壇，包上精金。21所羅門用精金貼了殿內的牆，又用金鍊子掛在內殿前門扇，用金包裹。22全殿都貼上金子，直到貼完；內殿前的壇，也都用金包裹。

floor was five cubits*a* wide, the middle floor six cubits*b* and the third floor seven.*c* He made offset ledges around the outside of the temple so that nothing would be inserted into the temple walls.

7In building the temple, only blocks dressed at the quarry were used, and no hammer, chisel or any other iron tool was heard at the temple site while it was being built.

8The entrance to the lowest*d* floor was on the south side of the temple; a stairway led up to the middle level and from there to the third. 9So he built the temple and completed it, roofing it with beams and cedar planks. 10And he built the side rooms all along the temple. The height of each was five cubits, and they were attached to the temple by beams of cedar.

11The word of the LORD came to Solomon: 12"As for this temple you are building, if you follow my decrees, carry out my regulations and keep all my commands and obey them, I will fulfill through you the promise I gave to David your father. 13And I will live among the Israelites and will not abandon my people Israel."

14So Solomon built the temple and completed it. 15He lined its interior walls with cedar boards, paneling them from the floor of the temple to the ceiling, and covered the floor of the temple with planks of pine. 16He partitioned off twenty cubits*e* at the rear of the temple with cedar boards from floor to ceiling to form within the temple an inner sanctuary, the Most Holy Place. 17The main hall in front of this room was forty cubits*f* long. 18The inside of the temple was cedar, carved with gourds and open flowers. Everything was cedar; no stone was to be seen.

19He prepared the inner sanctuary within the temple to set the ark of the covenant of the LORD there. 20The inner sanctuary was twenty cubits long, twenty wide and twenty high.*g* He overlaid the inside with pure gold, and he also overlaid the altar of cedar. 21Solomon covered the inside of the temple with pure gold, and he extended gold chains across the front of the inner sanctuary, which was overlaid with gold. 22So he overlaid the whole interior with gold. He also overlaid with gold the altar that belonged to the inner sanctuary.

a 6 That is, about 7 1/2 feet (about 2.3 meters); also in verses 10 and 24   *b 6* That is, about 9 feet (about 2.7 meters)
c 6 That is, about 10 1/2 feet (about 3.1 meters)
d 8 Septuagint; Hebrew *middle*   *e 16* That is, about 30 feet (about 9 meters)   *f 17* That is, about 60 feet (about 18 meters)
g 20 That is, about 30 feet (about 9 meters) long, wide and high

23In the inner sanctuary he made a pair of cherubim of olive wood, each ten cubits[a] high. 24One wing of the first cherub was five cubits long, and the other wing five cubits—ten cubits from wing tip to wing tip. 25The second cherub also measured ten cubits, for the two cherubim were identical in size and shape. 26The height of each cherub was ten cubits. 27He placed the cherubim inside the innermost room of the temple, with their wings spread out. The wing of one cherub touched one wall, while the wing of the other touched the other wall, and their wings touched each other in the middle of the room. 28He overlaid the cherubim with gold.

29On the walls all around the temple, in both the inner and outer rooms, he carved cherubim, palm trees and open flowers. 30He also covered the floors of both the inner and outer rooms of the temple with gold.

31For the entrance of the inner sanctuary he made doors of olive wood with five-sided jambs. 32And on the two olive wood doors he carved cherubim, palm trees and open flowers, and overlaid the cherubim and palm trees with beaten gold. 33In the same way he made four-sided jambs of olive wood for the entrance to the main hall. 34He also made two pine doors, each having two leaves that turned in sockets. 35He carved cherubim, palm trees and open flowers on them and overlaid them with gold hammered evenly over the carvings.

36And he built the inner courtyard of three courses of dressed stone and one course of trimmed cedar beams.

37The foundation of the temple of the LORD was laid in the fourth year, in the month of Ziv. 38In the eleventh year in the month of Bul, the eighth month, the temple was finished in all its details according to its specifications. He had spent seven years building it.

Solomon Builds His Palace

7 It took Solomon thirteen years, however, to complete the construction of his palace. 2He built the Palace of the Forest of Lebanon a hundred cubits long, fifty wide and thirty high,[b] with four rows of cedar columns supporting trimmed cedar beams. 3It was roofed with cedar above the beams that rested on the columns—forty-five beams, fifteen to a row. 4Its windows were placed high in sets

[a] 23 That is, about 15 feet (about 4.5 meters) [b] 2 That is, about 150 feet (about 46 meters) long, 75 feet (about 23 meters) wide and 45 feet (about 13.5 meters) high

23他用橄欖木做兩個基路伯，各高十肘，安在內殿。24這一個基路伯有兩個翅膀，各長五肘，從這翅膀尖到那翅膀尖，共有十肘；25那一個基路伯的兩個翅膀也是十肘，兩個基路伯的尺寸、形像都是一樣。26這基路伯高十肘，那基路伯也是如此。27他將兩個基路伯安在內殿裏。基路伯的翅膀是張開的，這基路伯的一個翅膀挨着這邊的牆，那基路伯的一個翅膀挨着那邊的牆，裏邊的兩個翅膀，在殿中間彼此相接。28又用金子包裹二基路伯。

29內殿外殿周圍的牆上，都刻着基路伯、棕樹和初開的花。30內殿、外殿的地板都貼上金子。

31又用橄欖木製造內殿的門扇、門楣、門框，門口有牆的五分之一。32在橄欖木做的兩門扇上，刻着基路伯、棕樹和初開的花，都貼上金子。33又用橄欖木製造外殿的門框，門口有牆的四分之一。34用松木做門兩扇：這扇分兩扇，是摺疊的；那扇分兩扇，也是摺疊的。35上面刻着基路伯、棕樹和初開的花，都用金子貼了。

36他又用鑿成的石頭三層，香柏木一層，建築內院。

37所羅門在位第四年西弗月，立了耶和華殿的根基。38到十一年布勒月，就是八月，殿和一切屬殿的都按着樣式造成。他建殿的工夫共有七年。

所羅門建造自己的王宮

7 所羅門為自己建造宮室，十三年方才造成。2又建造黎巴嫩林宮，長一百肘，寬五十肘，高三十肘，有香柏木柱三（註：原文作“四”）行，柱上有香柏木柁梁。3其上以香柏木為蓋，每行柱子十五根，共有四十五根。4有窗戶三層，

窗與窗相對。⁵所有的門框都是厚木
見方的，有窗戶三層，窗與窗相對。

⁶並建造有柱子的廊子，長五十
肘，寬三十肘。在這廊前又有廊子，
廊外有柱子和臺階。

⁷又建造一廊，其中設立審判的
座位，這廊從地到頂，都用香柏木遮
蔽。⁸廊後院內有所羅門住的宮室，
工作與這工作相同。所羅門又為所娶
法老的女兒建造一宮，做法與這廊子
一樣。

⁹建造這一切所用的石頭都是寶
貴的，是按着尺寸鑿成的，是用鋸裏
外鋸齊的，從根基直到檐石，從外頭
直到大院，都是如此。¹⁰根基是寶貴
的大石頭，有長十肘的，有長八肘
的。¹¹上面有香柏木和按着尺寸鑿成
寶貴的石頭。¹²大院周圍有鑿成的石
頭三層，香柏木一層，都照耶和華殿
的內院和殿廊的樣式。

聖殿的設備

¹³所羅門王差遣人往推羅去，將
戶蘭召了來。¹⁴他是拿弗他利支派中
一個寡婦的兒子，他父親是推羅人，
作銅匠的。戶蘭滿有智慧、聰明、技
能，善於各樣銅作。他來到所羅門王
那裏，做王一切所要做的。

¹⁵他製造兩根銅柱，每根高十八
肘，圍十二肘。¹⁶又用銅鑄了兩個柱
頂安在柱上，各高五肘。¹⁷柱頂上有
裝修的網子和擰成的鏈索，每頂七
個。¹⁸網子周圍有兩行石榴遮蓋柱

of three, facing each other. ⁵All the doorways
had rectangular frames; they were in the front
part in sets of three, facing each other.ᵃ

⁶He made a colonnade fifty cubits long and
thirty wide.ᵇ In front of it was a portico, and in
front of that were pillars and an overhanging
roof.

⁷He built the throne hall, the Hall of Justice,
where he was to judge, and he covered it with
cedar from floor to ceiling.ᶜ ⁸And the palace in
which he was to live, set farther back, was similar in design. Solomon also made a palace like
this hall for Pharaoh's daughter, whom he had
married.

⁹All these structures, from the outside to the
great courtyard and from foundation to eaves,
were made of blocks of high-grade stone cut to
size and trimmed with a saw on their inner and
outer faces. ¹⁰The foundations were laid with
large stones of good quality, some measuring
ten cubitsᵈ and some eight.ᵉ ¹¹Above were high-
grade stones, cut to size, and cedar beams. ¹²The
great courtyard was surrounded by a wall of
three courses of dressed stone and one course of
trimmed cedar beams, as was the inner courtyard of the temple of the Lᴏʀᴅ with its portico.

The Temple's Furnishings

¹³King Solomon sent to Tyre and brought
Huram,ᶠ ¹⁴whose mother was a widow from the
tribe of Naphtali and whose father was a man of
Tyre and a craftsman in bronze. Huram was
highly skilled and experienced in all kinds of
bronze work. He came to King Solomon and did
all the work assigned to him.

¹⁵He cast two bronze pillars, each eighteen
cubits high and twelve cubits around,ᵍ by line.
¹⁶He also made two capitals of cast bronze to set
on the tops of the pillars; each capital was five
cubitsʰ high. ¹⁷A network of interwoven chains
festooned the capitals on top of the pillars,
seven for each capital. ¹⁸He made pomegranates
in two rowsⁱ encircling each network to decorate

a 5 The meaning of the Hebrew for this verse is uncertain.
b 6 That is, about 75 feet (about 23 meters) long and 45 feet
(about 13.5 meters) wide   *c 7* Vulgate and Syriac; Hebrew
floor   d 10 That is, about 15 feet (about 4.5 meters)
e 10 That is, about 12 feet (about 3.6 meters)   *f 13* Hebrew
Hiram, a variant of *Huram;* also in verses 40 and 45
g 15 That is, about 27 feet (about 8.1 meters) high and 18 feet
(about 5.4 meters) around   *h 16* That is, about 7 1/2 feet
(about 2.3 meters); also in verse 23   *i 18* Two Hebrew
manuscripts and Septuagint; most Hebrew manuscripts *made
the pillars, and there were two rows*

49the lampstands of pure gold (five on the right and five on the left, in front of the inner sanctuary);

the gold floral work and lamps and tongs;
50the pure gold basins, wick trimmers, sprinkling bowls, dishes and censers;

and the gold sockets for the doors of the innermost room, the Most Holy Place, and also for the doors of the main hall of the temple.

51When all the work King Solomon had done for the temple of the LORD was finished, he brought in the things his father David had dedicated—the silver and gold and the furnishings—and he placed them in the treasuries of the LORD's temple.

The Ark Brought to the Temple

8 Then King Solomon summoned into his presence at Jerusalem the elders of Israel, all the heads of the tribes and the chiefs of the Israelite families, to bring up the ark of the LORD's covenant from Zion, the City of David. 2All the men of Israel came together to King Solomon at the time of the festival in the month of Ethanim, the seventh month.

3When all the elders of Israel had arrived, the priests took up the ark, 4and they brought up the ark of the LORD and the Tent of Meeting and all the sacred furnishings in it. The priests and Levites carried them up, 5and King Solomon and the entire assembly of Israel that had gathered about him were before the ark, sacrificing so many sheep and cattle that they could not be recorded or counted.

6The priests then brought the ark of the LORD's covenant to its place in the inner sanctuary of the temple, the Most Holy Place, and put it beneath the wings of the cherubim. 7The cherubim spread their wings over the place of the ark and overshadowed the ark and its carrying poles. 8These poles were so long that their ends could be seen from the Holy Place in front of the inner sanctuary, but not from outside the Holy Place; and they are still there today. 9There was nothing in the ark except the two stone tablets that Moses had placed in it at Horeb, where the LORD made a covenant with the Israelites after they came out of Egypt.

10When the priests withdrew from the Holy Place, the cloud filled the temple of the LORD. 11And the priests could not perform their service because of the cloud, for the glory of the LORD filled his temple.

12Then Solomon said, "The LORD has said that

49內殿前的精金燈臺：右邊五個、左邊五個，並其上的金花、燈盞、蠟剪，

50與精金的杯、盤、鑷子、調羹、火鼎以及至聖所、內殿的門樞，和外殿的門樞。

51所羅門王做完了耶和華殿的一切工，就把他父大衛分別為聖的金銀和器皿，都帶來放在耶和華殿的府庫裏。

約櫃運入聖殿

8 那時，所羅門將以色列的長老和各支派的首領，並以色列的族長，招聚到耶路撒冷，要把耶和華的約櫃，從大衛城，就是錫安運上來。2以他念月，就是七月，在節前，以色列人都聚集到所羅門王那裏。

3以色列長老來到，祭司便抬起約櫃，4祭司和利未人將耶和華的約櫃運上來，又將會幕和會幕的一切聖器具都帶上來。5所羅門王和聚集到他那裏的以色列全會眾，一同在約櫃前獻牛羊為祭，多得不可勝數。

6祭司將耶和華的約櫃抬進內殿，就是至聖所，放在兩個基路伯的翅膀底下。7基路伯張着翅膀，在約櫃之上，遮掩約櫃和抬櫃的杠。8這杠甚長，杠頭在內殿前的聖所可以看見，在殿外卻不能看見，直到如今還在那裏。9約櫃裏惟有兩塊石版，就是以色列人出埃及地後，耶和華與他們立約的時候，摩西在何烈山所放的。除此以外，並無別物。

10祭司從聖所出來的時候，有雲充滿耶和華的殿，11甚至祭司不能站立供職，因為耶和華的榮光充滿了殿。

12那時所羅門說："耶和華曾

說，他必住在幽暗之處。¹³我已經建造殿宇作你的居所，為你永遠的住處。"

¹⁴王轉臉為<u>以色列</u>會眾祝福，<u>以色列</u>會眾就都站立。¹⁵<u>所羅門</u>說：

"耶和華<u>以色列</u>的神是應當稱頌的！因他親口向我父<u>大衛</u>所應許的，也親手成就了。¹⁶他說：'自從我領我民<u>以色列</u>出<u>埃及</u>以來，我未曾在<u>以色列</u>各支派中選擇一城，建造殿宇為我名的居所，但揀選<u>大衛</u>治理我民<u>以色列</u>。'"

¹⁷<u>所羅門</u>說："我父<u>大衛</u>曾立意要為耶和華<u>以色列</u>神的名建殿。¹⁸耶和華卻對我父<u>大衛</u>說：'你立意為我的名建殿，這意思甚好。¹⁹只是你不可建殿，惟你所生的兒子必為我名建殿。'

²⁰"現在耶和華成就了他所應許的話，使我接續我父<u>大衛</u>坐<u>以色列</u>的國位，又為耶和華<u>以色列</u>神的名建造了殿。²¹我也在其中為約櫃預備一處。約櫃內有耶和華的約，就是他領我們列祖出<u>埃及</u>地的時候，與他們所立的約。"

所羅門的獻殿禱告

²²<u>所羅門</u>當着<u>以色列</u>會眾，站在耶和華的壇前，向天舉手說：

²³"耶和華<u>以色列</u>的神啊！天上地下沒有神可比你的。你向那盡心行在你面前的僕人守約施慈愛；²⁴向你僕人我父<u>大衛</u>所應許的話現在應驗了，你親口應許，親手成就，正如今日一樣。

²⁵"耶和華<u>以色列</u>的神啊！你所應許你僕人我父<u>大衛</u>的話說：'你的子孫若謹慎自己的行為，在我面前行事像你所行的一樣，就不斷人坐<u>以色列</u>的國位。'現在求你應驗這話。²⁶<u>以色列</u>的神啊！求你成就向你僕人我父<u>大衛</u>所應許的話。

he would dwell in a dark cloud; ¹³I have indeed built a magnificent temple for you, a place for you to dwell forever."

¹⁴While the whole assembly of Israel was standing there, the king turned around and blessed them. ¹⁵Then he said:

"Praise be to the LORD, the God of Israel, who with his own hand has fulfilled what he promised with his own mouth to my father David. For he said, ¹⁶'Since the day I brought my people Israel out of Egypt, I have not chosen a city in any tribe of Israel to have a temple built for my Name to be there, but I have chosen David to rule my people Israel.'

¹⁷"My father David had it in his heart to build a temple for the Name of the LORD, the God of Israel. ¹⁸But the LORD said to my father David, 'Because it was in your heart to build a temple for my Name, you did well to have this in your heart. ¹⁹Nevertheless, you are not the one to build the temple, but your son, who is your own flesh and blood—he is the one who will build the temple for my Name.'

²⁰"The LORD has kept the promise he made: I have succeeded David my father and now I sit on the throne of Israel, just as the LORD promised, and I have built the temple for the Name of the LORD, the God of Israel. ²¹I have provided a place there for the ark, in which is the covenant of the LORD that he made with our fathers when he brought them out of Egypt."

Solomon's Prayer of Dedication

²²Then Solomon stood before the altar of the LORD in front of the whole assembly of Israel, spread out his hands toward heaven ²³and said:

"O LORD, God of Israel, there is no God like you in heaven above or on earth below—you who keep your covenant of love with your servants who continue wholeheartedly in your way. ²⁴You have kept your promise to your servant David my father; with your mouth you have promised and with your hand you have fulfilled it—as it is today.

²⁵"Now LORD, God of Israel, keep for your servant David my father the promises you made to him when you said, 'You shall never fail to have a man to sit before me on the throne of Israel, if only your sons are careful in all they do to walk before me as you have done.' ²⁶And now, O God of Israel, let your word that you promised your servant David my father come true.

27"But will God really dwell on earth? The heavens, even the highest heaven, cannot contain you. How much less this temple I have built! 28Yet give attention to your servant's prayer and his plea for mercy, O LORD my God. Hear the cry and the prayer that your servant is praying in your presence this day. 29May your eyes be open toward this temple night and day, this place of which you said, 'My Name shall be there,' so that you will hear the prayer your servant prays toward this place. 30Hear the supplication of your servant and of your people Israel when they pray toward this place. Hear from heaven, your dwelling place, and when you hear, forgive.

31"When a man wrongs his neighbor and is required to take an oath and he comes and swears the oath before your altar in this temple, 32then hear from heaven and act. Judge between your servants, condemning the guilty and bringing down on his own head what he has done. Declare the innocent not guilty, and so establish his innocence.

33"When your people Israel have been defeated by an enemy because they have sinned against you, and when they turn back to you and confess your name, praying and making supplication to you in this temple, 34then hear from heaven and forgive the sin of your people Israel and bring them back to the land you gave to their fathers.

35"When the heavens are shut up and there is no rain because your people have sinned against you, and when they pray toward this place and confess your name and turn from their sin because you have afflicted them, 36then hear from heaven and forgive the sin of your servants, your people Israel. Teach them the right way to live, and send rain on the land you gave your people for an inheritance.

37"When famine or plague comes to the land, or blight or mildew, locusts or grasshoppers, or when an enemy besieges them in any of their cities, whatever disaster or disease may come, 38and when a prayer or plea is made by any of your people Israel—each one aware of the afflictions of his own heart, and spreading out his hands toward this temple—39then hear from heaven, your dwelling place. Forgive and act; deal with each man according to all he does, since you know his heart (for you alone know the hearts of all men), 40so that they will fear you all the time they live in the land you gave our fathers.

27 "神果真住在地上嗎？看哪，天和天上的天，尚且不足你居住的，何況我所建的這殿呢？28惟求耶和華我的神垂顧僕人的禱告祈求，俯聽僕人今日在你面前的祈禱呼籲。29願你晝夜看顧這殿，就是你應許立為你名的居所；求你垂聽僕人向此處禱告的話。30你僕人和你民以色列向此處祈禱的時候，求你在天上你的居所垂聽，垂聽而赦免。

31 "人若得罪鄰舍，有人叫他起誓，他來到這殿在你的壇前起誓，32求你在天上垂聽，判斷你的僕人，定惡人有罪，照他所行的報應在他頭上；定義人有理，照他的義賞賜他。

33 "你的民以色列若得罪你，敗在仇敵面前，又歸向你，承認你的名，在這殿裏祈求禱告，34求你在天上垂聽，赦免你民以色列的罪，使他們歸回你賜給他們列祖之地。

35 "你的民因得罪你，你懲罰他們，使天閉塞不下雨，他們若向此處禱告，承認你的名，離開他們的罪，36求你在天上垂聽，赦免你僕人以色列民的罪，將當行的善道指教他們，且降雨在你的地，就是你賜給你民為業之地。

37 "國中若有饑荒、瘟疫、旱風、霉爛、蝗蟲、螞蚱，或有仇敵犯境圍困城邑，無論遭遇甚麼災禍疾病，38你的民以色列，或是眾人，或是一人，自覺有罪（註：原文作"災"），向這殿舉手，無論祈求甚麼，禱告甚麼，39求你在天上你的居所垂聽赦免。你是知道人心的，要照各人所行的待他們（惟有你知道世人的心），40使他們在你賜給我們列祖之地上，一生一世敬畏你。

41 "論到不屬你民以色列的外邦人，為你名從遠方而來，42（他們聽人論說你的大名和大能的膀臂，並伸出來的膀臂。）向這殿禱告，43求你在天上你的居所垂聽，照着外邦人所祈求的而行，使天下萬民都認識你的名，敬畏你像你的民以色列一樣，又使他們知道我建造的這殿，是稱為你名下的。

44 "你的民若奉你的差遣，無論往何處去與仇敵爭戰，向耶和華所選擇的城與我為你名所建造的殿禱告，45求你在天上垂聽他們的禱告祈求，使他們得勝。

46 "你的民若得罪你（世上沒有不犯罪的人），你向他們發怒，將他們交給仇敵，擄到仇敵之地，或遠或近，47他們若在擄到之地想起罪來，回心轉意，懇求你說：'我們有罪了，我們悖逆了，我們作惡了'；48他們若在擄到之地盡心盡性歸服你，又向自己的地，就是你賜給他們列祖之地和你所選擇的城，並我為你名所建造的殿禱告，49求你在天上你的居所垂聽他們的禱告祈求，為他們伸冤。50饒恕得罪你的民，赦免他們的一切過犯，使他們在擄他們的人面前蒙憐恤。51因為他們是你的子民，你的產業，是你從埃及領出來脫離鐵爐的。

52 "願你的眼目看顧僕人，聽你民以色列的祈求，無論何時向你祈求，願你垂聽。53主耶和華啊！你將他們從地上的萬民中分別出來作你的產業，是照你領我們列祖出埃及的時候，藉你僕人摩西所應許的話。"

54所羅門在耶和華的壇前屈膝跪着，向天舉手，在耶和華面前禱告祈求已畢，就起來，55站着大聲為以色列全會眾祝福，說：

41"As for the foreigner who does not belong to your people Israel but has come from a distant land because of your name—42for men will hear of your great name and your mighty hand and your outstretched arm—when he comes and prays toward this temple, 43then hear from heaven, your dwelling place, and do whatever the foreigner asks of you, so that all the peoples of the earth may know your name and fear you, as do your own people Israel, and may know that this house I have built bears your Name.

44"When your people go to war against their enemies, wherever you send them, and when they pray to the LORD toward the city you have chosen and the temple I have built for your Name, 45then hear from heaven their prayer and their plea, and uphold their cause.

46"When they sin against you—for there is no one who does not sin—and you become angry with them and give them over to the enemy, who takes them captive to his own land, far away or near; 47and if they have a change of heart in the land where they are held captive, and repent and plead with you in the land of their conquerors and say, 'We have sinned, we have done wrong, we have acted wickedly'; 48and if they turn back to you with all their heart and soul in the land of their enemies who took them captive, and pray to you toward the land you gave their fathers, toward the city you have chosen and the temple I have built for your Name; 49then from heaven, your dwelling place, hear their prayer and their plea, and uphold their cause. 50And forgive your people, who have sinned against you; forgive all the offenses they have committed against you, and cause their conquerors to show them mercy; 51for they are your people and your inheritance, whom you brought out of Egypt, out of that iron-smelting furnace.

52"May your eyes be open to your servant's plea and to the plea of your people Israel, and may you listen to them whenever they cry out to you. 53For you singled them out from all the nations of the world to be your own inheritance, just as you declared through your servant Moses when you, O Sovereign LORD, brought our fathers out of Egypt."

54When Solomon had finished all these prayers and supplications to the LORD, he rose from before the altar of the LORD, where he had been kneeling with his hands spread out toward heaven. 55He stood and blessed the whole assembly of Israel in a loud voice, saying:

56"Praise be to the LORD, who has given rest to his people Israel just as he promised. Not one word has failed of all the good promises he gave through his servant Moses. 57May the LORD our God be with us as he was with our fathers; may he never leave us nor forsake us. 58May he turn our hearts to him, to walk in all his ways and to keep the commands, decrees and regulations he gave our fathers. 59And may these words of mine, which I have prayed before the LORD, be near to the LORD our God day and night, that he may uphold the cause of his servant and the cause of his people Israel according to each day's need, 60so that all the peoples of the earth may know that the LORD is God and that there is no other. 61But your hearts must be fully committed to the LORD our God, to live by his decrees and obey his commands, as at this time."

The Dedication of the Temple

62Then the king and all Israel with him offered sacrifices before the LORD. 63Solomon offered a sacrifice of fellowship offerings*a* to the LORD: twenty-two thousand cattle and a hundred and twenty thousand sheep and goats. So the king and all the Israelites dedicated the temple of the LORD.

64On that same day the king consecrated the middle part of the courtyard in front of the temple of the LORD, and there he offered burnt offerings, grain offerings and the fat of the fellowship offerings, because the bronze altar before the LORD was too small to hold the burnt offerings, the grain offerings and the fat of the fellowship offerings.

65So Solomon observed the festival at that time, and all Israel with him—a vast assembly, people from Lebo*b* Hamath to the Wadi of Egypt. They celebrated it before the LORD our God for seven days and seven days more, fourteen days in all. 66On the following day he sent the people away. They blessed the king and then went home, joyful and glad in heart for all the good things the LORD had done for his servant David and his people Israel.

The LORD Appears to Solomon

9 When Solomon had finished building the temple of the LORD and the royal palace, and had achieved all he had desired to do, 2the LORD appeared to him a sec-

a 63 Traditionally peace offerings; *also in verse 64*
b 65 Or from the entrance to

---

56 "耶和華是應當稱頌的！因為他照着一切所應許的賜平安給他的民以色列人,凡藉他僕人摩西應許賜福的話,一句都沒有落空。57願耶和華我們的神與我們同在,像與我們列祖同在一樣,不撇下我們,不丟棄我們,58使我們的心歸向他,遵行他的道,謹守他吩咐我們列祖的誡命、律例、典章。59我在耶和華面前祈求的這些話,願耶和華我們的神晝夜垂念,每日為他僕人與他民以色列伸冤,60使地上的萬民都知道惟獨耶和華是神,並無別神。61所以你們當向耶和華我們的神存誠實的心,遵行他的律例,謹守他的誡命,至終如今日一樣。"

奉獻聖殿

62王和以色列眾民一同在耶和華面前獻祭。63所羅門向耶和華獻平安祭,用牛二萬二千,羊十二萬。這樣,王和以色列眾民,為耶和華的殿行奉獻之禮。

64當日王因耶和華殿前的銅壇太小,容不下燔祭、素祭和平安祭牲的脂油,便將耶和華殿前院子當中分別為聖,在那裏獻燔祭、素祭和平安祭牲的脂油。

65那時,所羅門和以色列眾人,就是從哈馬口直到埃及小河所有的以色列人,都聚集成為大會,在耶和華我們的神面前守節七日又七日,共十四日。66第八日,王遣散眾民,他們都為王祝福。因見耶和華向他僕人大衛和他民以色列所施的一切恩惠,就都心中喜樂,各歸各家去了。

主向所羅門顯現

9 所羅門建造耶和華殿和王宮,並一切所願意建造的都完畢了,2耶和華就二次向所羅門顯現，如先前在基遍向他顯現一樣，²對他說：

"你向我所禱告祈求的，我都應允了。我已將你所建的這殿分別為聖，使我的名永遠在其中，我的眼、我的心也必常在那裏。

⁴"你若效法你父大衛，存誠實正直的心行在我面前，遵行我一切所吩咐你的，謹守我的律例典章，⁵我就必堅固你的國位在以色列中，直到永遠，正如我應許你父大衛說：'你的子孫必不斷人坐以色列的國位。'

⁶"倘若你們和你們的子孫轉去不跟從我，不守我指示你們的誡命律例，去侍奉敬拜別神，⁷我就必將以色列人從我賜給他們的地上剪除，並且我為己名所分別為聖的殿，也必捨棄不顧，使以色列人在萬民中作笑談，被譏誚。⁸這殿雖然甚高，將來經過的人必驚訝、嗤笑，說：'耶和華為何向這地和這殿如此行呢？'⁹人必回答說：'是因此地的人離棄領他們列祖出埃及地之耶和華他們的神，去親近別神，侍奉敬拜他，所以耶和華使這一切災禍臨到他們。'"

所羅門的其他事蹟

¹⁰所羅門建造耶和華殿和王宮，這兩所二十年才完畢了。¹¹（推羅王希蘭曾照所羅門所要的，資助他香柏木、松木和金子）所羅門王就把加利利地的二十座城給了希蘭。¹²希蘭從推羅出來，察看所羅門給他的城邑，就不喜悅，¹³說："我兄啊，你給我的是甚麼城邑呢？"他就給這城邑之地起名叫迦步勒，直到今日。¹⁴希蘭給所羅門一百二十他連得金子。

¹⁵所羅門王挑取服苦的人，是為建造耶和華的殿、自己的宮、米羅、耶路撒冷的城牆、夏瑣、米吉多，並

ond time, as he had appeared to him at Gibeon. ³The LORD said to him:

"I have heard the prayer and plea you have made before me; I have consecrated this temple, which you have built, by putting my Name there forever. My eyes and my heart will always be there.

⁴"As for you, if you walk before me in integrity of heart and uprightness, as David your father did, and do all I command and observe my decrees and laws, ⁵I will establish your royal throne over Israel forever, as I promised David your father when I said, 'You shall never fail to have a man on the throne of Israel.'

⁶"But if you*ᵃ* or your sons turn away from me and do not observe the commands and decrees I have given you*ᵃ* and go off to serve other gods and worship them, ⁷then I will cut off Israel from the land I have given them and will reject this temple I have consecrated for my Name. Israel will then become a byword and an object of ridicule among all peoples. ⁸And though this temple is now imposing, all who pass by will be appalled and will scoff and say, 'Why has the LORD done such a thing to this land and to this temple?' ⁹People will answer, 'Because they have forsaken the LORD their God, who brought their fathers out of Egypt, and have embraced other gods, worshiping and serving them—that is why the LORD brought all this disaster on them.'"

Solomon's Other Activities

¹⁰At the end of twenty years, during which Solomon built these two buildings—the temple of the LORD and the royal palace— ¹¹King Solomon gave twenty towns in Galilee to Hiram king of Tyre, because Hiram had supplied him with all the cedar and pine and gold he wanted. ¹²But when Hiram went from Tyre to see the towns that Solomon had given him, he was not pleased with them. ¹³"What kind of towns are these you have given me, my brother?" he asked. And he called them the Land of Cabul,*ᵇ* a name they have to this day. ¹⁴Now Hiram had sent to the king 120 talents*ᶜ* of gold.

¹⁵Here is the account of the forced labor King Solomon conscripted to build the LORD's temple, his own palace, the supporting terraces,*ᵈ* the wall of Jerusalem, and Hazor, Megiddo and

---

a 6 The Hebrew is plural.　b 13 Cabul sounds like the Hebrew for good-for-nothing.　c 14 That is, about 4 1/2 tons (about 4 metric tons)　d 15 Or the Millo; also in verse 24

Gezer. 16(Pharaoh king of Egypt had attacked and captured Gezer. He had set it on fire. He killed its Canaanite inhabitants and then gave it as a wedding gift to his daughter, Solomon's wife. 17And Solomon rebuilt Gezer.) He built up Lower Beth Horon, 18Baalath, and Tadmor*a* in the desert, within his land, 19as well as all his store cities and the towns for his chariots and for his horses*b* —whatever he desired to build in Jerusalem, in Lebanon and throughout all the territory he ruled.

20All the people left from the Amorites, Hittites, Perizzites, Hivites and Jebusites (these peoples were not Israelites), 21that is, their descendants remaining in the land, whom the Israelites could not exterminate*c* —these Solomon conscripted for his slave labor force, as it is to this day. 22But Solomon did not make slaves of any of the Israelites; they were his fighting men, his government officials, his officers, his captains, and the commanders of his chariots and charioteers. 23They were also the chief officials in charge of Solomon's projects—550 officials supervising the men who did the work.

24After Pharaoh's daughter had come up from the City of David to the palace Solomon had built for her, he constructed the supporting terraces.

25Three times a year Solomon sacrificed burnt offerings and fellowship offerings*d* on the altar he had built for the LORD, burning incense before the LORD along with them, and so fulfilled the temple obligations.

26King Solomon also built ships at Ezion Geber, which is near Elath in Edom, on the shore of the Red Sea.*e* 27And Hiram sent his men—sailors who knew the sea—to serve in the fleet with Solomon's men. 28They sailed to Ophir and brought back 420 talents*f* of gold, which they delivered to King Solomon.

The Queen of Sheba Visits Solomon

10 When the queen of Sheba heard about the fame of Solomon and his relation to the name of the LORD, she came to test him with hard questions. 2Arriving at Jerusalem with a very great caravan—with camels carrying spices, large quantities of gold, and precious stones—she came to Solomon and talked with

---

基色。16先前埃及王法老上來攻取基色，用火焚燒，殺了城內居住的迦南人，將城賜給他女兒所羅門的妻作妝奩。17所羅門建造基色、下伯和崙、18巴拉，並國中曠野裏的達莫；19又建造所有的積貨城，並屯車和馬兵的城，與耶路撒冷、黎巴嫩，以及自己治理的全國中所願建造的。

20至於國中所剩下不屬以色列人的亞摩利人、赫人、比利洗人、希未人、耶布斯人，21就是以色列人不能滅盡的，所羅門挑取他們的後裔，作服苦的奴僕，直到今日。22惟有以色列人，所羅門不使他們作奴僕，乃是作他的戰士、臣僕、統領、軍長、車兵長、馬兵長。23所羅門有五百五十督工的，監管工人。

24法老的女兒，從大衛城搬到所羅門為她建造的宮裏，那時，所羅門才建造米羅。

25所羅門每年三次在他為耶和華所築的壇上獻燔祭和平安祭，又在耶和華面前的壇上燒香。這樣，他建造殿的工程完畢了。

26所羅門王在以東地紅海邊，靠近以祿的以旬迦別製造船隻。27希蘭差遣他的僕人，就是熟悉泛海的船家，與所羅門的僕人一同坐船航海。28他們到了俄斐，從那裏得了四百二十他連得金子，運到所羅門王那裏。

示巴女王來見所羅門

10 示巴女王聽見所羅門因耶和華之名所得的名聲，就來要用難解的話試問所羅門。2跟隨她到耶路撒冷的人甚多，又有駱駝馱著香料、寶石和許多金子。她來見了所羅門王，就把心裏所有的對所羅

---

a 18 The Hebrew may also be read *Tamar.*   *b 19* Or *charioteers*   *c 21* The Hebrew term refers to the irrevocable giving over of things or persons to the LORD, often by totally destroying them.   *d 25* Traditionally *peace offerings*   *e 26* Hebrew *Yam Suph;* that is, Sea of Reeds   *f 28* That is, about 16 tons (about 14.5 metric tons)

門都說出來。³所羅門王將她所問的都答上了，沒有一句不明白、不能答的。⁴示巴女王見所羅門大有智慧，和他所建造的宮室，⁵席上的珍饈美味，羣臣分列而坐，僕人兩旁侍立，以及他們的衣服裝飾，和酒政的衣服裝飾，又見他上耶和華殿的臺階（註：或作"他在耶和華殿裏所獻的燔祭"），就詫異得神不守舍。

⁶對王說："我在本國裏所聽見論到你的事和你的智慧實在是真的。⁷我先不信那些話，及至我來親眼見了，才知道人所告訴我的還不到一半。你的智慧和你的福分，越過我所聽見的風聲。⁸你的臣子、你的僕人常侍立在你面前聽你智慧的話，是有福的。⁹耶和華你的神是應當稱頌的！他喜悅你，使你坐以色列的國位。因為他永遠愛以色列，所以立你作王，使你秉公行義。"

¹⁰於是，示巴女王將一百二十他連得金子和寶石，與極多的香料，送給所羅門王。她送給王的香料，以後奉來的不再有這樣多。

¹¹希蘭的船隻從俄斐運了金子來，又從俄斐運了許多檀香木（註：或作"烏木"。下同）和寶石來。¹²王用檀香木為耶和華殿和王宮做欄杆，又為歌唱的人做琴瑟。以後再沒有這樣的檀香木進國來，也沒有人看見過，直到如今。

¹³示巴女王一切所要所求的，所羅門王都送給她，另外照自己的厚意餽送她。於是女王和她臣僕轉回本國去了。

所羅門的榮華

¹⁴所羅門每年所得的金子，共有六百六十六他連得。¹⁵另外還有商人和雜族的諸王，與國中的省長所進的金子（註："雜族"歷代志下9章14節作"阿拉伯"）。

¹⁶所羅門王用錘出來的金子打成擋牌二百面，每面用金子六百舍客

him about all that she had on her mind. ³Solomon answered all her questions; nothing was too hard for the king to explain to her. ⁴When the queen of Sheba saw all the wisdom of Solomon and the palace he had built, ⁵the food on his table, the seating of his officials, the attending servants in their robes, his cupbearers, and the burnt offerings he made at[a] the temple of the LORD, she was overwhelmed.

⁶She said to the king, "The report I heard in my own country about your achievements and your wisdom is true. ⁷But I did not believe these things until I came and saw with my own eyes. Indeed, not even half was told me; in wisdom and wealth you have far exceeded the report I heard. ⁸How happy your men must be! How happy your officials, who continually stand before you and hear your wisdom! ⁹Praise be to the LORD your God, who has delighted in you and placed you on the throne of Israel. Because of the LORD's eternal love for Israel, he has made you king, to maintain justice and righteousness."

¹⁰And she gave the king 120 talents[b] of gold, large quantities of spices, and precious stones. Never again were so many spices brought in as those the queen of Sheba gave to King Solomon.

¹¹(Hiram's ships brought gold from Ophir; and from there they brought great cargoes of almugwood[c] and precious stones. ¹²The king used the almugwood to make supports for the temple of the LORD and for the royal palace, and to make harps and lyres for the musicians. So much almugwood has never been imported or seen since that day.)

¹³King Solomon gave the queen of Sheba all she desired and asked for, besides what he had given her out of his royal bounty. Then she left and returned with her retinue to her own country.

Solomon's Splendor

¹⁴The weight of the gold that Solomon received yearly was 666 talents,[d] ¹⁵not including the revenues from merchants and traders and from all the Arabian kings and the governors of the land.

¹⁶King Solomon made two hundred large shields of hammered gold; six hundred bekas[e]

---

a 5 Or *the ascent by which he went up to*　　b 10 That is, about 4 1/2 tons (about 4 metric tons)　　c 11 Probably a variant of *algumwood*; also in verse 12　　d 14 That is, about 25 tons (about 23 metric tons)　　e 16 That is, about 7 1/2 pounds (about 3.5 kilograms) of gold went into each shield. [17]He also made three hundred small shields of hammered gold, with three minas[a] of gold in each shield. The king put them in the Palace of the Forest of Lebanon.

[18]Then the king made a great throne inlaid with ivory and overlaid with fine gold. [19]The throne had six steps, and its back had a rounded top. On both sides of the seat were armrests, with a lion standing beside each of them. [20]Twelve lions stood on the six steps, one at either end of each step. Nothing like it had ever been made for any other kingdom. [21]All King Solomon's goblets were gold, and all the household articles in the Palace of the Forest of Lebanon were pure gold. Nothing was made of silver, because silver was considered of little value in Solomon's days. [22]The king had a fleet of trading ships[b] at sea along with the ships of Hiram. Once every three years it returned, carrying gold, silver and ivory, and apes and baboons.

[23]King Solomon was greater in riches and wisdom than all the other kings of the earth. [24]The whole world sought audience with Solomon to hear the wisdom God had put in his heart. [25]Year after year, everyone who came brought a gift—articles of silver and gold, robes, weapons and spices, and horses and mules.

[26]Solomon accumulated chariots and horses; he had fourteen hundred chariots and twelve thousand horses,[c] which he kept in the chariot cities and also with him in Jerusalem. [27]The king made silver as common in Jerusalem as stones, and cedar as plentiful as sycamore-fig trees in the foothills. [28]Solomon's horses were imported from Egypt[d] and from Kue[e] —the royal merchants purchased them from Kue. [29]They imported a chariot from Egypt for six hundred shekels[f] of silver, and a horse for a hundred and fifty.[g] They also exported them to all the kings of the Hittites and of the Arameans.

Solomon's Wives

11 King Solomon, however, loved many foreign women besides Pharaoh's daughter—Moabites, Ammonites, Edomites, Sidonians and Hittites. [2]They were from nations about which the LORD had told the

---

a 17 That is, about 3 3/4 pounds (about 1.7 kilograms)
b 22 Hebrew of ships of Tarshish   c 26 Or charioteers
d 28 Or possibly Muzur, a region in Cilicia; also in verse 29
e 28 Probably Cilicia   f 29 That is, about 15 pounds (about 7 kilograms)   g 29 That is, about 3 3/4 pounds (about 1.7 kilograms)

勒；[17]又用錘出來的金子打成盾牌三百面，每面用金子三彌那，都放在黎巴嫩林宮裏。

[18]王用象牙製造一個寶座，用精金包裹。[19]寶座有六層臺階，座的後背是圓的，兩旁有扶手，靠近扶手有兩個獅子站立。[20]六層臺階上有十二個獅子站立，每層有兩個，左邊一個，右邊一個。在列國中沒有這樣做的。[21]所羅門王一切的飲器都是金子的。黎巴嫩林宮裏的一切器皿都是精金的。所羅門年間，銀子算不了甚麼。[22]因為王有他施船隻與希蘭的船隻一同航海，三年一次，裝載金銀、象牙、猿猴、孔雀回來。

[23]所羅門王的財寶與智慧勝過天下的列王。[24]普天下的王都求見所羅門，要聽神賜給他智慧的話。[25]他們各帶貢物，就是金器、銀器、衣服、軍械、香料、騾馬，每年有一定之例。

[26]所羅門聚集戰車馬兵，有戰車一千四百輛，馬兵一萬二千名，安置在屯車的城邑和耶路撒冷，就是王那裏。[27]王在耶路撒冷使銀子多如石頭，香柏木多如高原的桑樹。[28]所羅門的馬是從埃及帶來的，是王的商人一羣一羣按着定價買來的。[29]從埃及買來的車，每輛價銀六百舍客勒，馬每匹一百五十舍客勒。赫人諸王和亞蘭諸王所買的車馬，也是按這價值經他們手買來的。

所羅門的妃嬪

11 所羅門王在法老的女兒之外，又寵愛許多外邦女子，就是摩押女子、亞捫女子、以東女子、西頓女子、赫人女子。[2]論到這些國的人，耶和華曾曉諭以色列人說：

"你們不可與她們往來相通，因為她們必誘惑你們的心去隨從她們的神。" 所羅門卻戀愛這些女子。³所羅門有妃七百，都是公主；還有嬪三百。這些妃嬪誘惑他的心。⁴所羅門年老的時候，他的妃嬪誘惑他的心去隨從別神，不效法他父親大衛，誠誠實實地順服耶和華他的神。⁵因為所羅門隨從西頓人的女神亞斯她錄和亞捫人可憎的神米勒公。⁶所羅門行耶和華眼中看為惡的事，不效法他父親大衛專心順從耶和華。

⁷所羅門為摩押可憎的神基抹和亞捫人可憎的神摩洛，在耶路撒冷對面的山上建築邱壇。⁸他為那些向自己的神燒香獻祭的外邦女子，就是他娶來的妃嬪也是這樣行。

⁹耶和華向所羅門發怒，因為他的心偏離向他兩次顯現的耶和華以色列的神。¹⁰耶和華曾吩咐他不可隨從別神，他卻沒有遵守耶和華所吩咐的。¹¹所以耶和華對他說："你既行了這事，不遵守我所吩咐你守的約和律例，我必將你的國奪回，賜給你的臣子。¹²然而，因你父親大衛的緣故，我不在你活著的日子行這事，必從你兒子的手中將國奪回。¹³只是我不將全國奪回，要因我僕人大衛和我所選擇的耶路撒冷，還留一支派給你的兒子。"

所羅門的仇敵

¹⁴耶和華使以東人哈達興起，作所羅門的敵人，他是以東王的後裔。¹⁵先前大衛攻擊以東，元帥約押上去葬埋陣亡的人，將以東的男丁都殺了。¹⁶約押和以色列眾人在以東住了六個月，直到將以東的男丁盡都剪除。¹⁷那時哈達還是幼童；他和他父親的臣僕，幾個以東人逃往埃及。¹⁸他們從米甸起行，到了巴蘭；從巴蘭帶著幾個人來到埃及見埃及王法老。法老為他派定糧食，又給他房屋田地。

Israelites, "You must not intermarry with them, because they will surely turn your hearts after their gods." Nevertheless, Solomon held fast to them in love. ³He had seven hundred wives of royal birth and three hundred concubines, and his wives led him astray. ⁴As Solomon grew old, his wives turned his heart after other gods, and his heart was not fully devoted to the LORD his God, as the heart of David his father had been. ⁵He followed Ashtoreth the goddess of the Sidonians, and Molech*ᵃ* the detestable god of the Ammonites. ⁶So Solomon did evil in the eyes of the LORD; he did not follow the LORD completely, as David his father had done.

⁷On a hill east of Jerusalem, Solomon built a high place for Chemosh the detestable god of Moab, and for Molech the detestable god of the Ammonites. ⁸He did the same for all his foreign wives, who burned incense and offered sacrifices to their gods.

⁹The LORD became angry with Solomon because his heart had turned away from the LORD, the God of Israel, who had appeared to him twice. ¹⁰Although he had forbidden Solomon to follow other gods, Solomon did not keep the LORD's command. ¹¹So the LORD said to Solomon, "Since this is your attitude and you have not kept my covenant and my decrees, which I commanded you, I will most certainly tear the kingdom away from you and give it to one of your subordinates. ¹²Nevertheless, for the sake of David your father, I will not do it during your lifetime. I will tear it out of the hand of your son. ¹³Yet I will not tear the whole kingdom from him, but will give him one tribe for the sake of David my servant and for the sake of Jerusalem, which I have chosen."

Solomon's Adversaries

¹⁴Then the LORD raised up against Solomon an adversary, Hadad the Edomite, from the royal line of Edom. ¹⁵Earlier when David was fighting with Edom, Joab the commander of the army, who had gone up to bury the dead, had struck down all the men in Edom. ¹⁶Joab and all the Israelites stayed there for six months, until they had destroyed all the men in Edom. ¹⁷But Hadad, still only a boy, fled to Egypt with some Edomite officials who had served his father. ¹⁸They set out from Midian and went to Paran. Then taking men from Paran with them, they went to Egypt, to Pharaoh king of Egypt, who gave Hadad a house and land and provided him with food.

---

a 5 Hebrew *Milcom;* also in verse 33

¹⁹Pharaoh was so pleased with Hadad that he gave him a sister of his own wife, Queen Tahpenes, in marriage. ²⁰The sister of Tahpenes bore him a son named Genubath, whom Tahpenes brought up in the royal palace. There Genubath lived with Pharaoh's own children.

²¹While he was in Egypt, Hadad heard that David rested with his fathers and that Joab the commander of the army was also dead. Then Hadad said to Pharaoh, "Let me go, that I may return to my own country."

²²"What have you lacked here that you want to go back to your own country?" Pharaoh asked.

"Nothing," Hadad replied, "but do let me go!"

²³And God raised up against Solomon another adversary, Rezon son of Eliada, who had fled from his master, Hadadezer king of Zobah. ²⁴He gathered men around him and became the leader of a band of rebels when David destroyed the forces[a] of Zobah; the rebels went to Damascus, where they settled and took control. ²⁵Rezon was Israel's adversary as long as Solomon lived, adding to the trouble caused by Hadad. So Rezon ruled in Aram and was hostile toward Israel.

Jeroboam Rebels Against Solomon

²⁶Also, Jeroboam son of Nebat rebelled against the king. He was one of Solomon's officials, an Ephraimite from Zeredah, and his mother was a widow named Zeruah.

²⁷Here is the account of how he rebelled against the king: Solomon had built the supporting terraces[b] and had filled in the gap in the wall of the city of David his father. ²⁸Now Jeroboam was a man of standing, and when Solomon saw how well the young man did his work, he put him in charge of the whole labor force of the house of Joseph.

²⁹About that time Jeroboam was going out of Jerusalem, and Ahijah the prophet of Shiloh met him on the way, wearing a new cloak. The two of them were alone out in the country, ³⁰and Ahijah took hold of the new cloak he was wearing and tore it into twelve pieces. ³¹Then he said to Jeroboam, "Take ten pieces for yourself, for this is what the LORD, the God of Israel, says: 'See, I am going to tear the kingdom out of Solomon's hand and give you ten tribes. ³²But for the sake of my servant David and the city of Jerusalem, which I have chosen out of all the tribes of Israel, he will have one tribe. ³³I will do

¹⁹哈達在法老面前大蒙恩惠，以致法老將王后答比匿的妹子賜他為妻。²⁰答比匿的妹子給哈達生了一個兒子，名叫基努拔。答比匿使基努拔在法老的宮裏斷奶，基努拔就與法老的眾子一同住在法老的宮裏。

²¹哈達在埃及聽見大衛與他列祖同睡，元帥約押也死了，就對法老說：「求王容我回本國去。」

²²法老對他說：「你在我這裏有甚麼缺乏，你竟要回你本國去呢？」

他回答說：「我沒有缺乏甚麼，只是求王容我回去。」

²³神又使以利亞大的兒子利遜興起，作所羅門的敵人。他先前逃避主人瑣巴王哈大底謝。²⁴大衛擊殺瑣巴人的時候，利遜招聚了一羣人，自己作他們的頭目，往大馬士革居住，在那裏作王。²⁵所羅門活着的時候，哈達為患之外，利遜也作以色列的敵人。他恨惡以色列人，且作了亞蘭人的王。

耶羅波安背叛所羅門

²⁶所羅門的臣僕、尼八的兒子耶羅波安也舉手攻擊王。他是以法蓮支派的洗利達人，他母親是寡婦，名叫洗魯阿。

²⁷他舉手攻擊王的緣故，乃由先前所羅門建造米羅，修補他父親大衛城的破口。²⁸耶羅波安是大有才能的人。所羅門見這少年人殷勤，就派他監管約瑟家的一切工程。

²⁹一日，耶羅波安出了耶路撒冷，示羅人先知亞希雅在路上遇見他。亞希雅身上穿着一件新衣，他們二人在田野，以外並無別人。³⁰亞希雅將自己所穿的那件新衣撕成十二片，³¹對耶羅波安說：「你可以拿十片。耶和華以色列的神如此說：『我必將國從所羅門手裏奪回，將十個支派賜給你。（³²我因僕人大衛和我在以色列眾支派中所選擇的耶路撒冷城的緣故，仍給所羅門留一個支派。）』³³因

---

a 24 Hebrew destroyed them   b 27 Or the Millo

為他離棄我，敬拜西頓人的女神亞斯她錄、摩押的神基抹和亞捫人的神米勒公，沒有遵從我的道，行我眼中看為正的事，守我的律例典章，像他父親大衛一樣。

34 "'但我不從他手裏將全國奪回；使他終身為君，是因我所揀選的僕人大衛謹守我的誡命律例。35我必從他兒子的手裏將國奪回，以十個支派賜給你，36還留一個支派給他的兒子，使我僕人大衛在我所選擇立我名的耶路撒冷城裏，在我面前長有燈光。37我必揀選你，使你照心裏一切所願的，作王治理以色列。38你若聽從我一切所吩咐你的，遵行我的道，行我眼中看為正的事，謹守我的律例誡命，像我僕人大衛所行的，我就與你同在，為你立堅固的家，像我為大衛所立的一樣，將以色列人賜給你。39我必因所羅門所行的，使大衛後裔受患難，但不至於永遠。'"

40所羅門因此想要殺耶羅波安，耶羅波安卻起身逃往埃及，到了埃及王示撒那裏，就住在埃及，直到所羅門死了。

所羅門逝世

41所羅門其餘的事，凡他所行的和他的智慧，都寫在所羅門記上。42所羅門在耶路撒冷作以色列眾人的王共四十年。43所羅門與他列祖同睡，葬在他父親大衛的城裏。他兒子羅波安接續他作王。

以色列背叛羅波安

12 羅波安往示劍去，因為以色列人都到了示劍，要立他作王。2尼八的兒子耶羅波安先前躲避所羅門王，逃往埃及，住在那裏（他聽見這事）。3以色列人打發人去請他來，他就和以色列會眾都來見羅波安，對他說：4 "你父親使我們負重軛，做苦工，現在求你使我們做的苦工、負的重軛輕鬆些，我們就侍奉你。"

this because they have[a] forsaken me and worshiped Ashtoreth the goddess of the Sidonians, Chemosh the god of the Moabites, and Molech the god of the Ammonites, and have not walked in my ways, nor done what is right in my eyes, nor kept my statutes and laws as David, Solomon's father, did.

34 " 'But I will not take the whole kingdom out of Solomon's hand; I have made him ruler all the days of his life for the sake of David my servant, whom I chose and who observed my commands and statutes. 35I will take the kingdom from his son's hands and give you ten tribes. 36I will give one tribe to his son so that David my servant may always have a lamp before me in Jerusalem, the city where I chose to put my Name. 37However, as for you, I will take you, and you will rule over all that your heart desires; you will be king over Israel. 38If you do whatever I command you and walk in my ways and do what is right in my eyes by keeping my statutes and commands, as David my servant did, I will be with you. I will build you a dynasty as enduring as the one I built for David and will give Israel to you. 39I will humble David's descendants because of this, but not forever.' "

40Solomon tried to kill Jeroboam, but Jeroboam fled to Egypt, to Shishak the king, and stayed there until Solomon's death.

Solomon's Death

41As for the other events of Solomon's reign—all he did and the wisdom he displayed—are they not written in the book of the annals of Solomon? 42Solomon reigned in Jerusalem over all Israel forty years. 43Then he rested with his fathers and was buried in the city of David his father. And Rehoboam his son succeeded him as king.

Israel Rebels Against Rehoboam

12 Rehoboam went to Shechem, for all the Israelites had gone there to make him king. 2When Jeroboam son of Nebat heard this (he was still in Egypt, where he had fled from King Solomon), he returned from[b] Egypt. 3So they sent for Jeroboam, and he and the whole assembly of Israel went to Rehoboam and said to him: 4"Your father put a heavy yoke on us, but now lighten the harsh labor and the heavy yoke he put on us, and we will serve you."

a 33 Hebrew; Septuagint, Vulgate and Syriac *because he has*
b 2 Or *he remained in*

⁵Rehoboam answered, "Go away for three days and then come back to me." So the people went away.

⁶Then King Rehoboam consulted the elders who had served his father Solomon during his lifetime. "How would you advise me to answer these people?" he asked.

⁷They replied, "If today you will be a servant to these people and serve them and give them a favorable answer, they will always be your servants."

⁸But Rehoboam rejected the advice the elders gave him and consulted the young men who had grown up with him and were serving him. ⁹He asked them, "What is your advice? How should we answer these people who say to me, 'Lighten the yoke your father put on us'?"

¹⁰The young men who had grown up with him replied, "Tell these people who have said to you, 'Your father put a heavy yoke on us, but make our yoke lighter'—tell them, 'My little finger is thicker than my father's waist. ¹¹My father laid on you a heavy yoke; I will make it even heavier. My father scourged you with whips; I will scourge you with scorpions.'"

¹²Three days later Jeroboam and all the people returned to Rehoboam, as the king had said, "Come back to me in three days." ¹³The king answered the people harshly. Rejecting the advice given him by the elders, ¹⁴he followed the advice of the young men and said, "My father made your yoke heavy; I will make it even heavier. My father scourged you with whips; I will scourge you with scorpions." ¹⁵So the king did not listen to the people, for this turn of events was from the LORD, to fulfill the word the LORD had spoken to Jeroboam son of Nebat through Ahijah the Shilonite.

¹⁶When all Israel saw that the king refused to listen to them, they answered the king:

"What share do we have in David,
    what part in Jesse's son?
To your tents, O Israel!
Look after your own house, O David!"

So the Israelites went home. ¹⁷But as for the Israelites who were living in the towns of Judah, Rehoboam still ruled over them.

¹⁸King Rehoboam sent out Adoniram,ᵃ who was in charge of forced labor, but all Israel stoned him to death. King Rehoboam, however, managed to get into his chariot and escape to

ᵃ 18 Some Septuagint manuscripts and Syriac (see also 1 Kings 4:6 and 5:14); Hebrew *Adoram*

---

⁵羅波安對他們說："你們暫且去，第三日再來見我。"民就去了。

⁶羅波安之父所羅門在世的日子，有侍立在他面前的老年人，羅波安王和他們商議，說："你們給我出個甚麼主意，我好回覆這民。"

⁷老年人對他說："現在王若服侍這民如僕人，用好話回答他們，他們就永遠作王的僕人。"

⁸王卻不用老年人給他出的主意，就和那些與他一同長大在他面前侍立的少年人商議，⁹說："這民對我說：'你父親使我們負重軛，求你使我們輕鬆些。'你們給我出個甚麼主意，我好回覆他們。"

¹⁰那同他長大的少年人說："這民對我說：'你父親使我們負重軛，求你使我們輕鬆些。'王要對他們如此說：'我的小拇指頭比我父親的腰還粗。¹¹我父親使你們負重軛，我必使你們負更重的軛；我父親用鞭子責打你們，我要用蠍子鞭責打你們。'"

¹²耶羅波安和眾百姓遵着羅波安王所說"你們第三日再來見我"的那話，第三日他們果然來了。¹³王用嚴厲的話回答百姓，不用老年人給他所出的主意，¹⁴照着少年人所出的主意對民說："我父親使你們負重軛，我必使你們負更重的軛；我父親用鞭子責打你們，我要用蠍子鞭責打你們。"¹⁵王不肯依從百姓，這事乃出於耶和華，為要應驗他藉示羅人亞希雅對尼八的兒子耶羅波安所說的話。

¹⁶以色列眾民見王不依從他們，就對王說：

"我們與大衛有甚麼分兒呢？
與耶西的兒子並沒有關涉。
以色列人哪，各回各家去吧！
大衛家啊，自己顧自己吧！"

於是以色列人都回自己家裏去了。¹⁷惟獨住猶大城邑的以色列人，羅波安仍作他們的王。

¹⁸羅波安王差遣掌管服苦之人的亞多蘭往以色列人那裏去，以色列人就用石頭打死他。羅波安王急忙上

車，逃回耶路撒冷去了。¹⁹這樣，以色列人背叛大衛家，直到今日。

²⁰以色列眾人聽見耶羅波安回來了，就打發人去請他到會眾面前，立他作以色列眾人的王。除了猶大支派以外，沒有順從大衛家的。

²¹羅波安來到耶路撒冷，招聚猶大全家和便雅憫支派的人共十八萬，都是挑選的戰士，要與以色列家爭戰，好將國奪回，再歸所羅門的兒子羅波安。

²²但神的話臨到神人示瑪雅，說：²³"你去告訴所羅門的兒子猶大王羅波安和猶大、便雅憫全家，並其餘的民，說：²⁴'耶和華如此說：你們不可上去與你們的弟兄以色列人爭戰，各歸各家去吧！因為這事出於我。'"眾人就聽從耶和華的話，遵着耶和華的命回去了。

在伯特利和但立金牛犢

²⁵耶羅波安在以法蓮山地建築示劍，就住在其中。又從示劍出去，建築毘努伊勒。

²⁶耶羅波安心裏說："恐怕這國仍歸大衛家。²⁷這民若上耶路撒冷去，在耶和華的殿裏獻祭，他們的心必歸向他們的主猶大王羅波安，就把我殺了，仍歸猶大王羅波安。"

²⁸耶羅波安王就籌劃定妥，鑄造了兩個金牛犢，對眾民說："以色列人哪，你們上耶路撒冷去實在是難，這就是領你們出埃及地的神。"²⁹他就把牛犢一隻安在伯特利，一隻安在但。³⁰這事叫百姓陷在罪裏，因為他們往045去拜那牛犢。

³¹耶羅波安在邱壇那裏建殿，將那不屬利未人的凡民立為祭司。³²耶羅波安定八月十五日為節期，像在猶大的節期一樣，自己上壇獻祭。他在伯特利也這樣向他所鑄的牛犢獻祭，又將立為邱壇的祭司安置在伯特利。³³他在八月十五日，就是他私自所定的月日，為以色列人立作節期的日子，在伯特利上壇燒香。

Jerusalem. ¹⁹So Israel has been in rebellion against the house of David to this day.

²⁰When all the Israelites heard that Jeroboam had returned, they sent and called him to the assembly and made him king over all Israel. Only the tribe of Judah remained loyal to the house of David.

²¹When Rehoboam arrived in Jerusalem, he mustered the whole house of Judah and the tribe of Benjamin—a hundred and eighty thousand fighting men—to make war against the house of Israel and to regain the kingdom for Rehoboam son of Solomon.

²²But this word of God came to Shemaiah the man of God: ²³"Say to Rehoboam son of Solomon king of Judah, to the whole house of Judah and Benjamin, and to the rest of the people, ²⁴'This is what the LORD says: Do not go up to fight against your brothers, the Israelites. Go home, every one of you, for this is my doing.' " So they obeyed the word of the LORD and went home again, as the LORD had ordered.

Golden Calves at Bethel and Dan

²⁵Then Jeroboam fortified Shechem in the hill country of Ephraim and lived there. From there he went out and built up Peniel.ᵃ

²⁶Jeroboam thought to himself, "The kingdom will now likely revert to the house of David. ²⁷If these people go up to offer sacrifices at the temple of the LORD in Jerusalem, they will again give their allegiance to their lord, Rehoboam king of Judah. They will kill me and return to King Rehoboam."

²⁸After seeking advice, the king made two golden calves. He said to the people, "It is too much for you to go up to Jerusalem. Here are your gods, O Israel, who brought you up out of Egypt." ²⁹One he set up in Bethel, and the other in Dan. ³⁰And this thing became a sin; the people went even as far as Dan to worship the one there.

³¹Jeroboam built shrines on high places and appointed priests from all sorts of people, even though they were not Levites. ³²He instituted a festival on the fifteenth day of the eighth month, like the festival held in Judah, and offered sacrifices on the altar. This he did in Bethel, sacrificing to the calves he had made. And at Bethel he also installed priests at the high places he had made. ³³On the fifteenth day of the eighth month, a month of his own choosing, he offered sacrifices on the altar he had built at Bethel. So he instituted the festival for the Israelites and went up to the altar to make offerings.

a 25 Hebrew Penuel, a variant of Peniel

The Man of God From Judah

13 By the word of the LORD a man of God came from Judah to Bethel, as Jeroboam was standing by the altar to make an offering. ²He cried out against the altar by the word of the LORD: "O altar, altar! This is what the LORD says: 'A son named Josiah will be born to the house of David. On you he will sacrifice the priests of the high places who now make offerings here, and human bones will be burned on you.' " ³That same day the man of God gave a sign: "This is the sign the LORD has declared: The altar will be split apart and the ashes on it will be poured out."

⁴When King Jeroboam heard what the man of God cried out against the altar at Bethel, he stretched out his hand from the altar and said, "Seize him!" But the hand he stretched out toward the man shriveled up, so that he could not pull it back. ⁵Also, the altar was split apart and its ashes poured out according to the sign given by the man of God by the word of the LORD.

⁶Then the king said to the man of God, "Intercede with the LORD your God and pray for me that my hand may be restored." So the man of God interceded with the LORD, and the king's hand was restored and became as it was before.

⁷The king said to the man of God, "Come home with me and have something to eat, and I will give you a gift."

⁸But the man of God answered the king, "Even if you were to give me half your possessions, I would not go with you, nor would I eat bread or drink water here. ⁹For I was commanded by the word of the LORD: 'You must not eat bread or drink water or return by the way you came.' " ¹⁰So he took another road and did not return by the way he had come to Bethel.

¹¹Now there was a certain old prophet living in Bethel, whose sons came and told him all that the man of God had done there that day. They also told their father what he had said to the king. ¹²Their father asked them, "Which way did he go?" And his sons showed him which road the man of God from Judah had taken. ¹³So he said to his sons, "Saddle the donkey for me." And when they had saddled the donkey for him, he mounted it ¹⁴and rode after the man of God. He found him sitting under an oak tree and asked, "Are you the man of God who came from Judah?"

"I am," he replied.

¹⁵So the prophet said to him, "Come home with me and eat."

猶大來的神人

13 那時，有一個神人奉耶和華的命從猶大來到伯特利，耶羅波安正站在壇旁要燒香。²神人奉耶和華的命向壇呼叫，說："壇哪，壇哪！耶和華如此說：'大衛家裏必生一個兒子，名叫約西亞。他必將邱壇的祭司，就是在你上面燒香的，殺在你上面，人的骨頭也必燒在你上面。'"³當日，神人設個預兆，說："這壇必破裂，壇上的灰必傾撒。這是耶和華說的預兆。"

⁴耶羅波安王聽見神人向伯特利的壇所呼叫的話，就從壇上伸手，說："拿住他吧！"王向神人所伸的手就枯乾了，不能彎回；⁵壇也破裂了，壇上的灰傾撒了，正如神人奉耶和華的命所設的預兆。

⁶王對神人說："請你為我禱告，求耶和華你神的恩典，使我的手復原。"於是神人祈禱耶和華，王的手就復了原，仍如尋常一樣。

⁷王對神人說："請你同我回去吃飯，加添心力，我也必給你賞賜。"

⁸神人對王說："你就是把你的宮一半給我，我也不同你進去，也不在這地方吃飯喝水，⁹因為有耶和華的話囑咐我說：'不可在伯特利吃飯喝水，也不可從你去的原路回來。'"¹⁰於是神人從別的路回去，不從伯特利來的原路回去。

¹¹有一個老先知住在伯特利，他兒子們來將神人當日在伯特利所行的一切事和向王所說的話，都告訴了父親。¹²父親問他們說："神人從哪條路去了呢？"兒子們就告訴他。原來他們看見那從猶大來的神人所去的路。¹³老先知就吩咐他兒子們說："你們為我備好驢。"他們備好了驢，他就騎上，¹⁴去追趕神人，遇見他坐在橡樹底下，就問他說："你是從猶大來的神人不是？"

他說："是。"

¹⁵老先知對他說："請你同我回家吃飯。"

16神人說：「我不可同你回去進你的家，也不可在這裏同你吃飯喝水，17因為有耶和華的話囑咐我說：『你在那裏不可吃飯喝水，也不可從你去的原路回來。』」

18老先知對他說：「我也是先知，和你一樣。有天使奉耶和華的命對我說：『你去把他帶回你的家，叫他吃飯喝水。』」這都是老先知誆哄他。19於是神人同老先知回去，在他家裏吃飯喝水。

20二人坐席的時候，耶和華的話臨到那帶神人回來的先知。21他就對那從猶大來的神人說：「耶和華如此說：『你既違背耶和華的話，不遵守耶和華你神的命令，22反倒回來，在耶和華禁止你吃飯喝水的地方吃了喝了，因此你的屍身不得入你列祖的墳墓。』」

23吃喝完了，老先知為所帶回來的先知備驢。24他就去了。在路上有個獅子遇見他，將他咬死，屍身倒在路上，驢站在屍身旁邊，獅子也站在屍身旁邊。25有人從那裏經過，看見屍身倒在路上，獅子站在屍身旁邊，就來到老先知所住的城裏述說這事。

26那帶神人回來的先知聽見這事，就說：「這是那違背了耶和華命令的神人，所以耶和華把他交給獅子；獅子抓傷他，咬死他，是應驗耶和華對他說的話。」

27老先知就吩咐他兒子們說：「你們為我備驢。」他們就備了驢。28他去了，看見神人的屍身倒在路上，驢和獅子站在屍身旁邊，獅子卻沒有吃屍身，也沒有抓傷驢。29老先知就把神人的屍身馱在驢上，帶回自己的城裏，要哀哭他，葬埋他；30把他的屍身葬在自己的墳墓裏，哀哭他，說：「哀哉！我兄啊。」

31安葬之後，老先知對他兒子們說：「我死了，你們要葬我在神人的墳墓裏，使我的屍骨靠近他的屍骨。32因為他奉耶和華的命指着伯特利的

16The man of God said, "I cannot turn back and go with you, nor can I eat bread or drink water with you in this place. 17I have been told by the word of the LORD: 'You must not eat bread or drink water there or return by the way you came.'"

18The old prophet answered, "I too am a prophet, as you are. And an angel said to me by the word of the LORD: 'Bring him back with you to your house so that he may eat bread and drink water.'" (But he was lying to him.) 19So the man of God returned with him and ate and drank in his house.

20While they were sitting at the table, the word of the LORD came to the old prophet who had brought him back. 21He cried out to the man of God who had come from Judah, "This is what the LORD says: 'You have defied the word of the LORD and have not kept the command the LORD your God gave you. 22You came back and ate bread and drank water in the place where he told you not to eat or drink. Therefore your body will not be buried in the tomb of your fathers.'"

23When the man of God had finished eating and drinking, the prophet who had brought him back saddled his donkey for him. 24As he went on his way, a lion met him on the road and killed him, and his body was thrown down on the road, with both the donkey and the lion standing beside it. 25Some people who passed by saw the body thrown down there, with the lion standing beside the body, and they went and reported it in the city where the old prophet lived.

26When the prophet who had brought him back from his journey heard of it, he said, "It is the man of God who defied the word of the LORD. The LORD has given him over to the lion, which has mauled him and killed him, as the word of the LORD had warned him."

27The prophet said to his sons, "Saddle the donkey for me," and they did so. 28Then he went out and found the body thrown down on the road, with the donkey and the lion standing beside it. The lion had neither eaten the body nor mauled the donkey. 29So the prophet picked up the body of the man of God, laid it on the donkey, and brought it back to his own city to mourn for him and bury him. 30Then he laid the body in his own tomb, and they mourned over him and said, "Oh, my brother!"

31After burying him, he said to his sons, "When I die, bury me in the grave where the man of God is buried; lay my bones beside his bones. 32For the message he declared by the word of the LORD against the altar in Bethel and against all the shrines on the high places in the towns of Samaria will certainly come true."

33Even after this, Jeroboam did not change his evil ways, but once more appointed priests for the high places from all sorts of people. Anyone who wanted to become a priest he consecrated for the high places. 34This was the sin of the house of Jeroboam that led to its downfall and to its destruction from the face of the earth.

Ahijah's Prophecy Against Jeroboam

14 At that time Abijah son of Jeroboam became ill, 2and Jeroboam said to his wife, "Go, disguise yourself, so you won't be recognized as the wife of Jeroboam. Then go to Shiloh. Ahijah the prophet is there—the one who told me I would be king over this people. 3Take ten loaves of bread with you, some cakes and a jar of honey, and go to him. He will tell you what will happen to the boy." 4So Jeroboam's wife did what he said and went to Ahijah's house in Shiloh.

Now Ahijah could not see; his sight was gone because of his age. 5But the LORD had told Ahijah, "Jeroboam's wife is coming to ask you about her son, for he is ill, and you are to give her such and such an answer. When she arrives, she will pretend to be someone else."

6So when Ahijah heard the sound of her footsteps at the door, he said, "Come in, wife of Jeroboam. Why this pretense? I have been sent to you with bad news. 7Go, tell Jeroboam that this is what the LORD, the God of Israel, says: 'I raised you up from among the people and made you a leader over my people Israel. 8I tore the kingdom away from the house of David and gave it to you, but you have not been like my servant David, who kept my commands and followed me with all his heart, doing only what was right in my eyes. 9You have done more evil than all who lived before you. You have made for yourself other gods, idols made of metal; you have provoked me to anger and thrust me behind your back.

10" 'Because of this, I am going to bring disaster on the house of Jeroboam. I will cut off from Jeroboam every last male in Israel—slave or free. I will burn up the house of Jeroboam as one burns dung, until it is all gone. 11Dogs will eat those belonging to Jeroboam who die in the city, and the birds of the air will feed on those who die in the country. The LORD has spoken!'

12"As for you, go back home. When you set foot in your city, the boy will die. 13All Israel will mourn for him and bury him. He is the only

壇，和撒馬利亞各城有邱壇之殿所說的話，必定應驗。"

33這事以後，耶羅波安仍不離開他的惡道，將凡民立為邱壇的祭司；凡願意的，他都分別為聖，立為邱壇的祭司。34這事叫耶羅波安的家陷在罪裏，甚至他的家從地上除滅了。

亞希雅論耶羅波安的預言

14 那時，耶羅波安的兒子亞比雅病了。2耶羅波安對他的妻說："你可以起來改裝，使人不知道你是耶羅波安的妻，往示羅去，在那裏有先知亞希雅。他曾告訴我說：'你必作這民的王。'3現在你要帶十個餅與幾個薄餅和一瓶蜜去見他，他必告訴你兒子將要怎樣。"4耶羅波安的妻就這樣行，起身往示羅去，到了亞希雅的家。

亞希雅因年紀老邁，眼目發直，不能看見。5耶和華先曉諭亞希雅說："耶羅波安的妻要來問你，因她兒子病了，你當如此如此告訴她。她進來的時候，必裝作別的婦人。"

6她剛進門，亞希雅聽見她腳步的響聲，就說："耶羅波安的妻，進來吧！你為何裝別的婦人呢？我奉差遣將凶事告訴你。7你回去告訴耶羅波安說：'耶和華以色列的神如此說：我從民中將你高舉，立你作我民以色列的君，8將國從大衛家奪回賜給你，你卻不效法我僕人大衛，遵守我的誡命，一心順從我，行我眼中看為正的事。9你竟行惡，比那在你以先的更甚，為自己立了別神，鑄了偶像，惹我發怒，將我丟在背後。

10" '因此，我必使災禍臨到耶羅波安的家，將屬耶羅波安的男丁，無論困住的、自由的都從以色列中剪除，必除盡耶羅波安的家，如人除盡糞土一般。11凡屬耶羅波安的人，死在城中的，必被狗吃；死在田野的，必被空中的鳥吃。這是耶和華說的。'

12"所以你起身回家去吧！你的腳一進城，你兒子就必死了。13以色列眾人必為他哀哭，將他葬埋。凡屬耶羅波安的人，惟有他得入墳墓，因為在耶羅波安的家中，只有他向耶和華以色列的神顯出善行。

14 "耶和華必另立一王治理以色列。到了日期，他必剪除耶羅波安的家。那日期已經到了。15耶和華必擊打以色列人，使他們搖動，像水中的蘆葦一般；又將他們從耶和華賜給他們列祖的美地上拔出來，分散在大河那邊，因為他們做木偶，惹耶和華發怒。16因耶羅波安所犯的罪，又使以色列人陷在罪裏，耶和華必將以色列人交給仇敵。"

17耶羅波安的妻起身回去，到了得撒，剛到門檻，兒子就死了。18以色列眾人將他葬埋，為他哀哭，正如耶和華藉他僕人先知亞希雅所說的話。

19耶羅波安其餘的事，他怎樣爭戰，怎樣作王，都寫在以色列諸王記上。20耶羅波安作王二十二年，就與他列祖同睡。他兒子拿答接續他作王。

羅波安作猶大王

21所羅門的兒子羅波安作猶大王。所羅門的時候年四十一歲，在耶路撒冷，就是耶和華從以色列眾支派中所選擇立他名的城，作王十七年。羅波安的母親名叫拿瑪，是亞捫人。

22猶大人行耶和華眼中看為惡的事，犯罪觸動他的憤恨，比他們列祖更甚。23因為他們在各高岡上，各青翠樹下築壇，立柱像和木偶。24國中也有孌童。猶大人效法耶和華在以色列人面前所趕出的外邦人，行一切可憎惡的事。

25羅波安王第五年，埃及王示撒上來攻取耶路撒冷，26奪了耶和華殿和王宮裏的寶物，盡都帶走，又奪去所羅門製造的金盾牌，27羅波安王製

one belonging to Jeroboam who will be buried, because he is the only one in the house of Jeroboam in whom the LORD, the God of Israel, has found anything good.

14"The LORD will raise up for himself a king over Israel who will cut off the family of Jeroboam. This is the day! What? Yes, even now.[a] 15And the LORD will strike Israel, so that it will be like a reed swaying in the water. He will uproot Israel from this good land that he gave to their forefathers and scatter them beyond the River,[b] because they provoked the LORD to anger by making Asherah poles.[c] 16And he will give Israel up because of the sins Jeroboam has committed and has caused Israel to commit."

17Then Jeroboam's wife got up and left and went to Tirzah. As soon as she stepped over the threshold of the house, the boy died. 18They buried him, and all Israel mourned for him, as the LORD had said through his servant the prophet Ahijah.

19The other events of Jeroboam's reign, his wars and how he ruled, are written in the book of the annals of the kings of Israel. 20He reigned for twenty-two years and then rested with his fathers. And Nadab his son succeeded him as king.

Rehoboam King of Judah

21Rehoboam son of Solomon was king in Judah. He was forty-one years old when he became king, and he reigned seventeen years in Jerusalem, the city the LORD had chosen out of all the tribes of Israel in which to put his Name. His mother's name was Naamah; she was an Ammonite.

22Judah did evil in the eyes of the LORD. By the sins they committed they stirred up his jealous anger more than their fathers had done. 23They also set up for themselves high places, sacred stones and Asherah poles on every high hill and under every spreading tree. 24There were even male shrine prostitutes in the land; the people engaged in all the detestable practices of the nations the LORD had driven out before the Israelites.

25In the fifth year of King Rehoboam, Shishak king of Egypt attacked Jerusalem. 26He carried off the treasures of the temple of the LORD and the treasures of the royal palace. He took everything, including all the gold shields Solomon had made. 27So King Rehoboam made bronze

---

a 14 The meaning of the Hebrew for this sentence is uncertain. b 15 That is, the Euphrates   c 15 That is, symbols of the goddess Asherah; here and elsewhere in 1 Kings

shields to replace them and assigned these to the commanders of the guard on duty at the entrance to the royal palace. 28Whenever the king went to the LORD's temple, the guards bore the shields, and afterward they returned them to the guardroom.

29As for the other events of Rehoboam's reign, and all he did, are they not written in the book of the annals of the kings of Judah? 30There was continual warfare between Rehoboam and Jeroboam. 31And Rehoboam rested with his fathers and was buried with them in the City of David. His mother's name was Naamah; she was an Ammonite. And Abijah*a* his son succeeded him as king.

Abijah King of Judah

15 In the eighteenth year of the reign of Jeroboam son of Nebat, Abijah*b* became king of Judah, 2and he reigned in Jerusalem three years. His mother's name was Maacah daughter of Abishalom.*c*

3He committed all the sins his father had done before him; his heart was not fully devoted to the LORD his God, as the heart of David his forefather had been. 4Nevertheless, for David's sake the LORD his God gave him a lamp in Jerusalem by raising up a son to succeed him and by making Jerusalem strong. 5For David had done what was right in the eyes of the LORD and had not failed to keep any of the LORD's commands all the days of his life—except in the case of Uriah the Hittite.

6There was war between Rehoboam*d* and Jeroboam throughout ˻Abijah's˼ lifetime. 7As for the other events of Abijah's reign, and all he did, are they not written in the book of the annals of the kings of Judah? There was war between Abijah and Jeroboam. 8And Abijah rested with his fathers and was buried in the City of David. And Asa his son succeeded him as king.

Asa King of Judah

9In the twentieth year of Jeroboam king of Israel, Asa became king of Judah, 10and he reigned in Jerusalem forty-one years. His grandmother's name was Maacah daughter of Abishalom.

---

a 31 Some Hebrew manuscripts and Septuagint (see also 2 Chron. 12:16); most Hebrew manuscripts Abijam

b 1 Some Hebrew manuscripts and Septuagint (see also 2 Chron. 12:16); most Hebrew manuscripts Abijam; also in verses 7 and 8   c 2 A variant of Absalom; also in verse 10

d 6 Most Hebrew manuscripts; some Hebrew manuscripts and Syriac Abijam (that is, Abijah)

造銅盾牌代替那金盾牌，交給守王宮門的護衛長看守。28王每逢進耶和華的殿，護衛兵就拿這盾牌，隨後仍將盾牌送回，放在護衛房。

29羅波安其餘的事，凡他所行的，都寫在<u>猶大</u>列王記上。30<u>羅波安</u>與<u>耶羅波安</u>時常爭戰。31<u>羅波安</u>與他列祖同睡，葬在<u>大衛城</u>他列祖的墳地裏。他母親名叫<u>拿瑪</u>，是<u>亞捫</u>人。他兒子<u>亞比央</u>（註：又名"亞比雅"）接續他作王。

亞比央作猶大王

15 <u>尼八</u>的兒子<u>耶羅波安</u>王十八年，<u>亞比央</u>登基作<u>猶大王</u>。2在<u>耶路撒冷</u>作王三年。他母親名叫<u>瑪迦</u>，是<u>押沙龍</u>的女兒。

3<u>亞比央</u>行他父親在他以前所行的一切惡，他的心不像他祖<u>大衛</u>的心，誠誠實實地順服耶和華的神。4然而耶和華他的神，因<u>大衛</u>的緣故，仍使他在<u>耶路撒冷</u>有燈光，叫他兒子接續他作王，堅立<u>耶路撒冷</u>。5因為<u>大衛</u>除了<u>赫人烏利亞</u>那件事，都是行耶和華眼中看為正的事，一生沒有違背耶和華一切所吩咐的。

6<u>羅波安</u>在世的日子常與<u>耶羅波安</u>爭戰。7<u>亞比央</u>其餘的事，凡他所行的，都寫在<u>猶大</u>列王記上。<u>亞比央</u>常與<u>耶羅波安</u>爭戰。8<u>亞比央</u>與他列祖同睡，葬在<u>大衛</u>的城裏。他兒子<u>亞撒</u>接續他作王。

亞撒作猶大王

9<u>以色列王耶羅波安</u>二十年，<u>亞撒</u>登基作<u>猶大王</u>。10在<u>耶路撒冷</u>作王四十一年。他祖母名叫<u>瑪迦</u>，是<u>押沙龍</u>的女兒。

11亞撒效法他祖大衛行耶和華眼中看為正的事。12從國中除去孌童，又除掉他列祖所造的一切偶像。13並且貶了他祖母瑪迦太后的位，因她造了可憎的偶像亞舍拉。亞撒砍下她的偶像，燒在汲淪溪邊，14只是邱壇還沒有廢去。亞撒一生卻向耶和華存誠實的心。15亞撒將他父親所分別為聖與自己所分別為聖的金銀和器皿，都奉到耶和華的殿裏。

16亞撒和以色列王巴沙在世的日子常常爭戰。17以色列王巴沙上來要攻擊猶大，修築拉瑪，不許人從猶大王亞撒那裏出入。

18於是，亞撒將耶和華殿和王宮府庫裏所剩下的金銀，都交在他臣僕手中，打發他們往住大馬士革的亞蘭王希旬的孫子、他伯利們的兒子便哈達那裏去，19說：「你父曾與我父立約，我與你也要立約。現在我將金銀送你為禮物，求你廢掉你與以色列王巴沙所立的約，使他離開我。」

20便哈達聽從亞撒王的話，派軍長去攻擊以色列的城邑，他們就攻破以雲、但、亞伯伯瑪迦、基尼烈全境、拿弗他利全境。21巴沙聽見就停工，不修築拉瑪了，仍住在得撒。22於是亞撒王宣告猶大眾人，不准一個推辭，吩咐他們將巴沙修築拉瑪所用的石頭、木頭都運去，用以修築便雅憫的迦巴和米斯巴。

23亞撒其餘的事，凡他所行的，並他的勇力，與他所建築的城邑，都寫在猶大列王記上。亞撒年老的時候，腳上有病。24亞撒與他列祖同睡，葬在他祖大衛城他列祖的墳地裏。他兒子約沙法接續他作王。

拿答作以色列王

25猶大王亞撒第二年，耶羅波安的兒子拿答登基作以色列王共二年。26拿答行耶和華眼中看為惡的事，行他父親所行的，犯他父親使以色列人陷在罪裏的那罪。

11Asa did what was right in the eyes of the LORD, as his father David had done. 12He expelled the male shrine prostitutes from the land and got rid of all the idols his fathers had made. 13He even deposed his grandmother Maacah from her position as queen mother, because she had made a repulsive Asherah pole. Asa cut the pole down and burned it in the Kidron Valley. 14Although he did not remove the high places, Asa's heart was fully committed to the LORD all his life. 15He brought into the temple of the LORD the silver and gold and the articles that he and his father had dedicated.

16There was war between Asa and Baasha king of Israel throughout their reigns. 17Baasha king of Israel went up against Judah and fortified Ramah to prevent anyone from leaving or entering the territory of Asa king of Judah.

18Asa then took all the silver and gold that was left in the treasuries of the LORD's temple and of his own palace. He entrusted it to his officials and sent them to Ben-Hadad son of Tabrimmon, the son of Hezion, the king of Aram, who was ruling in Damascus. 19"Let there be a treaty between me and you," he said, "as there was between my father and your father. See, I am sending you a gift of silver and gold. Now break your treaty with Baasha king of Israel so he will withdraw from me."

20Ben-Hadad agreed with King Asa and sent the commanders of his forces against the towns of Israel. He conquered Ijon, Dan, Abel Beth Maacah and all Kinnereth in addition to Naphtali. 21When Baasha heard this, he stopped building Ramah and withdrew to Tirzah. 22Then King Asa issued an order to all Judah—no one was exempt—and they carried away from Ramah the stones and timber Baasha had been using there. With them King Asa built up Geba in Benjamin, and also Mizpah.

23As for all the other events of Asa's reign, all his achievements, all he did and the cities he built, are they not written in the book of the annals of the kings of Judah? In his old age, however, his feet became diseased. 24Then Asa rested with his fathers and was buried with them in the city of his father David. And Jehoshaphat his son succeeded him as king.

Nadab King of Israel

25Nadab son of Jeroboam became king of Israel in the second year of Asa king of Judah, and he reigned over Israel two years. 26He did evil in the eyes of the LORD, walking in the ways of his father and in his sin, which he had caused Israel to commit.

²⁷Baasha son of Ahijah of the house of Issachar plotted against him, and he struck him down at Gibbethon, a Philistine town, while Nadab and all Israel were besieging it. ²⁸Baasha killed Nadab in the third year of Asa king of Judah and succeeded him as king.

²⁹As soon as he began to reign, he killed Jeroboam's whole family. He did not leave Jeroboam anyone that breathed, but destroyed them all, according to the word of the LORD given through his servant Ahijah the Shilonite— ³⁰because of the sins Jeroboam had committed and had caused Israel to commit, and because he provoked the LORD, the God of Israel, to anger.

³¹As for the other events of Nadab's reign, and all he did, are they not written in the book of the annals of the kings of Israel? ³²There was war between Asa and Baasha king of Israel throughout their reigns.

Baasha King of Israel

³³In the third year of Asa king of Judah, Baasha son of Ahijah became king of all Israel in Tirzah, and he reigned twenty-four years. ³⁴He did evil in the eyes of the LORD, walking in the ways of Jeroboam and in his sin, which he had caused Israel to commit.

16 Then the word of the LORD came to Jehu son of Hanani against Baasha: ²"I lifted you up from the dust and made you leader of my people Israel, but you walked in the ways of Jeroboam and caused my people Israel to sin and to provoke me to anger by their sins. ³So I am about to consume Baasha and his house, and I will make your house like that of Jeroboam son of Nebat. ⁴Dogs will eat those belonging to Baasha who die in the city, and the birds of the air will feed on those who die in the country."

⁵As for the other events of Baasha's reign, what he did and his achievements, are they not written in the book of the annals of the kings of Israel? ⁶Baasha rested with his fathers and was buried in Tirzah. And Elah his son succeeded him as king.

⁷Moreover, the word of the LORD came through the prophet Jehu son of Hanani to Baasha and his house, because of all the evil he had done in the eyes of the LORD, provoking him to anger by the things he did, and becoming like the house of Jeroboam—and also because he destroyed it.

²⁷以薩迦人亞希雅的兒子巴沙背叛拿答，在非利士的基比頓殺了他。那時拿答和以色列眾人正圍困基比頓。²⁸在猶大王亞撒第三年巴沙殺了他，篡了他的位。

²⁹巴沙一作王，就殺了耶羅波安的全家。凡有氣息的，沒有留下一個，都滅盡了，正應驗耶和華藉他僕人示羅人亞希雅所說的話。³⁰這是因為耶羅波安所犯的罪使以色列人陷在罪裏，惹動耶和華以色列神的怒氣。

³¹拿答其餘的事，凡他所行的，都寫在以色列諸王記上。³²亞撒和以色列王巴沙在世的日子常常爭戰。

巴沙作以色列王

³³猶大王亞撒第三年，亞希雅的兒子巴沙在得撒登基作以色列眾人的王共二十四年。³⁴他行耶和華眼中看為惡的事，行耶羅波安所行的道，犯他使以色列人陷在罪裏的那罪。

16 耶和華的話臨到哈拿尼的兒子耶戶，責備巴沙說：²"我既從塵埃中提拔你，立你作我民以色列的君，你竟行耶羅波安所行的道，使我民以色列陷在罪裏，惹我發怒。³我必除盡你和你的家，使你的家像尼八的兒子耶羅波安的家一樣。⁴凡屬巴沙的人，死在城中的必被狗吃；死在田野的必被空中的鳥吃。"

⁵巴沙其餘的事，凡他所行的和他的勇力，都寫在以色列諸王記上。⁶巴沙與他列祖同睡，葬在得撒。他兒子以拉接續他作王。

⁷耶和華的話臨到哈拿尼的兒子先知耶戶，責備巴沙和他的家，因他行耶和華眼中看為惡的一切事，以他手所做的惹耶和華發怒，像耶羅波安的家一樣，又因他殺了耶羅波安的全家。

以拉作以色列王

⁸猶大王亞撒二十六年，巴沙的兒子以拉在得撒登基作以色列王共二年。

⁹有管理他一半戰車的臣子心利背叛他。當他在得撒家宰亞雜家裏喝醉的時候，¹⁰心利就進去殺了他，篡了他的位。這是猶大王亞撒二十七年的事。

¹¹心利一坐王位，就殺了巴沙的全家，連他的親屬、朋友也沒有留下一個男丁，¹²心利這樣滅絕巴沙的全家，正如耶和華藉先知耶戶責備巴沙的話。¹³這是因巴沙和他兒子以拉的一切罪，就是他們使以色列人陷在罪裏的那罪，以虛無的神惹耶和華以色列神的怒氣。

¹⁴以拉其餘的事，凡他所行的，都寫在以色列諸王記上。

心利作以色列王

¹⁵猶大王亞撒二十七年，心利在得撒作王七日。那時民正安營圍攻非利士的基比頓。¹⁶民在營中聽說心利背叛，又殺了王，故此以色列眾人當日在營中立元帥暗利作以色列王。¹⁷暗利率領以色列眾人從基比頓上去，圍困得撒。¹⁸心利見城破失，就進了王宮的衛所，放火焚燒宮殿，自焚而死。¹⁹這是因他犯罪，行耶和華眼中看為惡的事，行耶羅波安所行的，犯他使以色列人陷在罪裏的那罪。

²⁰心利其餘的事，和他背叛的情形，都寫在以色列諸王記上。

暗利作以色列王

²¹那時，以色列民分為兩半：一半隨從基納的兒子提比尼，要立他作王；一半隨從暗利。²²但隨從暗利的民，勝過隨從基納的兒子提比尼的民。提比尼死了，暗利就作了王。

Elah King of Israel

⁸In the twenty-sixth year of Asa king of Judah, Elah son of Baasha became king of Israel, and he reigned in Tirzah two years.

⁹Zimri, one of his officials, who had command of half his chariots, plotted against him. Elah was in Tirzah at the time, getting drunk in the home of Arza, the man in charge of the palace at Tirzah. ¹⁰Zimri came in, struck him down and killed him in the twenty-seventh year of Asa king of Judah. Then he succeeded him as king.

¹¹As soon as he began to reign and was seated on the throne, he killed off Baasha's whole family. He did not spare a single male, whether relative or friend. ¹²So Zimri destroyed the whole family of Baasha, in accordance with the word of the LORD spoken against Baasha through the prophet Jehu— ¹³because of all the sins Baasha and his son Elah had committed and had caused Israel to commit, so that they provoked the LORD, the God of Israel, to anger by their worthless idols.

¹⁴As for the other events of Elah's reign, and all he did, are they not written in the book of the annals of the kings of Israel?

Zimri King of Israel

¹⁵In the twenty-seventh year of Asa king of Judah, Zimri reigned in Tirzah seven days. The army was encamped near Gibbethon, a Philistine town. ¹⁶When the Israelites in the camp heard that Zimri had plotted against the king and murdered him, they proclaimed Omri, the commander of the army, king over Israel that very day there in the camp. ¹⁷Then Omri and all the Israelites with him withdrew from Gibbethon and laid siege to Tirzah. ¹⁸When Zimri saw that the city was taken, he went into the citadel of the royal palace and set the palace on fire around him. So he died, ¹⁹because of the sins he had committed, doing evil in the eyes of the LORD and walking in the ways of Jeroboam and in the sin he had committed and had caused Israel to commit.

²⁰As for the other events of Zimri's reign, and the rebellion he carried out, are they not written in the book of the annals of the kings of Israel?

Omri King of Israel

²¹Then the people of Israel were split into two factions; half supported Tibni son of Ginath for king, and the other half supported Omri. ²²But Omri's followers proved stronger than those of Tibni son of Ginath. So Tibni died and Omri became king.

²³In the thirty-first year of Asa king of Judah, Omri became king of Israel, and he reigned twelve years, six of them in Tirzah. ²⁴He bought the hill of Samaria from Shemer for two talents*a* of silver and built a city on the hill, calling it Samaria, after Shemer, the name of the former owner of the hill.

²⁵But Omri did evil in the eyes of the LORD and sinned more than all those before him. ²⁶He walked in all the ways of Jeroboam son of Nebat and in his sin, which he had caused Israel to commit, so that they provoked the LORD, the God of Israel, to anger by their worthless idols.

²⁷As for the other events of Omri's reign, what he did and the things he achieved, are they not written in the book of the annals of the kings of Israel? ²⁸Omri rested with his fathers and was buried in Samaria. And Ahab his son succeeded him as king.

Ahab Becomes King of Israel

²⁹In the thirty-eighth year of Asa king of Judah, Ahab son of Omri became king of Israel, and he reigned in Samaria over Israel twenty-two years. ³⁰Ahab son of Omri did more evil in the eyes of the LORD than any of those before him. ³¹He not only considered it trivial to commit the sins of Jeroboam son of Nebat, but he also married Jezebel daughter of Ethbaal king of the Sidonians, and began to serve Baal and worship him. ³²He set up an altar for Baal in the temple of Baal that he built in Samaria. ³³Ahab also made an Asherah pole and did more to provoke the LORD, the God of Israel, to anger than did all the kings of Israel before him.

³⁴In Ahab's time, Hiel of Bethel rebuilt Jericho. He laid its foundations at the cost of his firstborn son Abiram, and he set up its gates at the cost of his youngest son Segub, in accordance with the word of the LORD spoken by Joshua son of Nun.

Elijah Fed by Ravens

17 Now Elijah the Tishbite, from Tishbe*b* in Gilead, said to Ahab, "As the LORD, the God of Israel, lives, whom I serve, there will be neither dew nor rain in the next few years except at my word."

²Then the word of the LORD came to Elijah: ³"Leave here, turn eastward and hide in the Kerith Ravine, east of the Jordan. ⁴You will drink from the brook, and I have ordered the ravens to feed you there."

---

²³猶大王亞撒三十一年，暗利登基作以色列王共十二年，在得撒作王六年。²⁴暗利用二他連得銀子，向撒瑪買了撒馬利亞山，在山上造城，就按着山的原主撒瑪的名，給所造的城起名叫撒馬利亞。

²⁵暗利行耶和華眼中看為惡的事，比他以前的列王作惡更甚。²⁶因他行了尼八的兒子耶羅波安所行的，犯他使以色列人陷在罪裏的那罪，以虛無的神惹耶和華以色列神的怒氣。

²⁷暗利其餘的事和他所顯出的勇力，都寫在以色列諸王記上。²⁸暗利與他列祖同睡，葬在撒馬利亞。他兒子亞哈接續他作王。

亞哈作以色列王

²⁹猶大王亞撒三十八年，暗利的兒子亞哈登基作了以色列王。暗利的兒子亞哈在撒馬利亞作以色列王二十二年。³⁰暗利的兒子亞哈行耶和華眼中看為惡的事，比他以前的列王更甚，³¹犯了尼八的兒子耶羅波安所犯的罪。他還以為輕，又娶了西頓王謁巴力的女兒耶洗別為妻，去侍奉敬拜巴力。³²在撒馬利亞建造巴力的廟，在廟裏為巴力築壇。³³亞哈又做亞舍拉，他所行的惹耶和華以色列神的怒氣，比他以前的以色列諸王更甚。

³⁴亞哈在位的時候，有伯特利人希伊勒重修耶利哥城。立根基的時候，喪了長子亞比蘭；安門的時候，喪了幼子西割，正如耶和華藉嫩的兒子約書亞所說的話。

烏鴉供養以利亞

17 基列寄居的提斯比人以利亞對亞哈說：「我指着所侍奉永生耶和華以色列的神起誓，這幾年我若不禱告，必不降露，不下雨。」

²耶和華的話臨到以利亞說：³「你離開這裏往東去，藏在約旦河東邊的基立溪旁。⁴你要喝那溪裏的水，我已吩咐烏鴉在那裏供養你。」

---

a 24 That is, about 150 pounds (about 70 kilograms)   *b* 1 Or Tishbite, of the settlers

5於是，<u>以利亞</u>照着耶和華的話，去住在<u>約旦河東</u>的<u>基立溪旁</u>。6烏鴉早晚給他叼餅和肉來，他也喝那溪裏的水。

撒勒法的寡婦

7過了些日子，溪水就乾了，因為雨沒有下在地上。8耶和華的話臨到他說：9"你起身往<u>西頓</u>的<u>撒勒法</u>去（註："撒勒法"與路加福音4章26節同），住在那裏，我已吩咐那裏的一個寡婦供養你。" 10<u>以利亞</u>就起身往<u>撒勒法</u>去。到了城門，見有一個寡婦在那裏撿柴。<u>以利亞</u>呼叫她說："求你用器皿取點水來給我喝。" 11她去取水的時候，<u>以利亞</u>又呼叫她說："也求你拿點餅來給我！"

12她說："我指着永生耶和華你的神起誓，我沒有餅，罈內只有一把麵，瓶裏只有一點油。我現在找兩根柴，回裏要為我和我兒子做餅。我們吃了，死就死吧！"

13<u>以利亞</u>對她說："不要懼怕，可以照你所說的去做吧！只要先為我做一個小餅，拿來給我，然後為你和你的兒子做餅。14因為耶和華<u>以色列</u>的神如此說：'罈內的麵必不減少，瓶裏的油必不缺短，直到耶和華使雨降在地上的日子。'"

15婦人就照<u>以利亞</u>的話去行。她和她家中的人，並<u>以利亞</u>，吃了許多日子。16罈內的麵果不減少，瓶裏的油也不缺短，正如耶和華藉<u>以利亞</u>所說的話。

17這事以後，作那家主母的婦人，她兒子病了，病得甚重，以致身無氣息。18婦人對<u>以利亞</u>說："神人哪，我與你何干？你竟到我這裏來，使神想念我的罪，以致我的兒子死呢？"

19<u>以利亞</u>對她說："把你兒子交給我。" <u>以利亞</u>就從婦人懷中將孩子接過來，抱到他所住的樓中，放在自己的牀上。20就求告耶和華說："耶和華我的神啊！我寄居在這寡婦的家裏，你就降禍與她，使她的兒子死了嗎？" 21<u>以利亞</u>三次伏在孩子的身上求告耶和華說："耶和華我的神啊，求你使這孩子的靈魂仍入他的身體！"

5So he did what the LORD had told him. He went to the Kerith Ravine, east of the Jordan, and stayed there. 6The ravens brought him bread and meat in the morning and bread and meat in the evening, and he drank from the brook.

The Widow at Zarephath

7Some time later the brook dried up because there had been no rain in the land. 8Then the word of the LORD came to him: 9"Go at once to Zarephath of Sidon and stay there. I have commanded a widow in that place to supply you with food." 10So he went to Zarephath. When he came to the town gate, a widow was there gathering sticks. He called to her and asked, "Would you bring me a little water in a jar so I may have a drink?" 11As she was going to get it, he called, "And bring me, please, a piece of bread."

12"As surely as the LORD your God lives," she replied, "I don't have any bread—only a handful of flour in a jar and a little oil in a jug. I am gathering a few sticks to take home and make a meal for myself and my son, that we may eat it—and die."

13Elijah said to her, "Don't be afraid. Go home and do as you have said. But first make a small cake of bread for me from what you have and bring it to me, and then make something for yourself and your son. 14For this is what the LORD, the God of Israel, says: 'The jar of flour will not be used up and the jug of oil will not run dry until the day the LORD gives rain on the land.'"

15She went away and did as Elijah had told her. So there was food every day for Elijah and for the woman and her family. 16For the jar of flour was not used up and the jug of oil did not run dry, in keeping with the word of the LORD spoken by Elijah.

17Some time later the son of the woman who owned the house became ill. He grew worse and worse, and finally stopped breathing. 18She said to Elijah, "What do you have against me, man of God? Did you come to remind me of my sin and kill my son?"

19"Give me your son," Elijah replied. He took him from her arms, carried him to the upper room where he was staying, and laid him on his bed. 20Then he cried out to the LORD, "O LORD my God, have you brought tragedy also upon this widow I am staying with, by causing her son to die?" 21Then he stretched himself out on the boy three times and cried to the LORD, "O LORD my God, let this boy's life return to him!"

²²The LORD heard Elijah's cry, and the boy's life returned to him, and he lived. ²³Elijah picked up the child and carried him down from the room into the house. He gave him to his mother and said, "Look, your son is alive!"

²⁴Then the woman said to Elijah, "Now I know that you are a man of God and that the word of the LORD from your mouth is the truth."

Elijah and Obadiah

18 After a long time, in the third year, the word of the LORD came to Elijah: "Go and present yourself to Ahab, and I will send rain on the land." ²So Elijah went to present himself to Ahab.

Now the famine was severe in Samaria, ³and Ahab had summoned Obadiah, who was in charge of his palace. (Obadiah was a devout believer in the LORD. ⁴While Jezebel was killing off the LORD's prophets, Obadiah had taken a hundred prophets and hidden them in two caves, fifty in each, and had supplied them with food and water.) ⁵Ahab had said to Obadiah, "Go through the land to all the springs and valleys. Maybe we can find some grass to keep the horses and mules alive so we will not have to kill any of our animals." ⁶So they divided the land they were to cover, Ahab going in one direction and Obadiah in another.

⁷As Obadiah was walking along, Elijah met him. Obadiah recognized him, bowed down to the ground, and said, "Is it really you, my lord Elijah?"

⁸"Yes," he replied. "Go tell your master, 'Elijah is here.'"

⁹"What have I done wrong," asked Obadiah, "that you are handing your servant over to Ahab to be put to death? ¹⁰As surely as the LORD your God lives, there is not a nation or kingdom where my master has not sent someone to look for you. And whenever a nation or kingdom claimed you were not there, he made them swear they could not find you. ¹¹But now you tell me to go to my master and say, 'Elijah is here.' ¹²I don't know where the Spirit of the LORD may carry you when I leave you. If I go and tell Ahab and he doesn't find you, he will kill me. Yet I your servant have worshiped the LORD since my youth. ¹³Haven't you heard, my lord, what I did while Jezebel was killing the prophets of the LORD? I hid a hundred of the LORD's prophets in two caves, fifty in each, and supplied them with food and water. ¹⁴And now you tell me to go to my master and say, 'Elijah is here.' He will kill me!"

²²耶和華應允以利亞的話，孩子的靈魂仍入他的身體，他就活了。²³以利亞將孩子從樓上抱下來，進屋子交給他母親說："看哪，你的兒子活了！"

²⁴婦人對以利亞說："現在我知道你是神人，耶和華藉你口所說的話是真的。"

以利亞與俄巴底

18 過了許久，到第三年，耶和華的話臨到以利亞說："你去，使亞哈得見你，我要降雨在地上。"²以利亞就去，要使亞哈得見他。

那時，撒馬利亞有大饑荒。³亞哈將他的家宰俄巴底召了來。俄巴底甚是敬畏耶和華。⁴耶洗別殺耶和華眾先知的時候，俄巴底將一百個先知藏了，每五十人藏在一個洞裏，拿餅和水供養他們。⁵亞哈對俄巴底說："我們走遍這地，到一切水泉旁和一切溪邊，或者找得着青草，可以救活騾馬，免得絕了牲畜。"⁶於是二人分地遊行，亞哈獨走一路，俄巴底獨走一路。

⁷俄巴底在路上恰與以利亞相遇，俄巴底認出他來，就俯伏在地，說："你是我主以利亞不是？"

⁸回答說："是，你去告訴你主人說：'以利亞在這裏。'"

⁹俄巴底說："僕人有甚麼罪，你竟要將我交在亞哈手裏，使他殺我呢？¹⁰我指着永生耶和華你的神起誓，無論哪一邦、哪一國，我主都打發人去找你。若說你沒有在那裏，就必使那邦那國的人起誓說：實在是找不着你。¹¹現在你說：'要去告訴你主人說：以利亞在這裏。'¹²恐怕我一離開你，耶和華的靈就提你到我所不知道的地方去。這樣，我去告訴亞哈，他若找不着你，他必殺我；僕人卻是自幼敬畏耶和華的。¹³耶洗別殺耶和華眾先知的時候，我將耶和華的一百個先知藏了，每五十人藏在一個洞裏，拿餅和水供養他們，豈沒有人將這事告訴我主嗎？¹⁴現在你說：要去告訴我主人說：'以利亞在這裏。'他必殺我。"

¹⁵以利亞說：「我指着所侍奉永生的萬軍之耶和華起誓，我今日必使亞哈得見我。」

以利亞在迦密山上

¹⁶於是，俄巴底去迎着亞哈，告訴他，亞哈就去迎着以利亞。¹⁷亞哈見了以利亞，便說：「使以色列遭災的就是你嗎？」

¹⁸以利亞說：「使以色列遭災的不是我，乃是你和你父家，因為你們離棄耶和華的誡命，去隨從巴力。¹⁹現在你當差遣人，招聚以色列眾人和侍奉巴力的那四百五十個先知，並耶洗別所供養侍奉亞舍拉的那四百個先知，使他們都上迦密山去見我。」

²⁰亞哈就差遣人招聚以色列眾人和先知都上迦密山。²¹以利亞前來對眾民說：「你們心持兩意要到幾時呢？若耶和華是神，就當順從耶和華；若巴力是神，就當順從巴力。」

眾民一言不答。

²²以利亞對眾民說：「作耶和華先知的只剩下我一個人；巴力的先知卻有四百五十個人。²³當給我們兩隻牛犢。巴力的先知可以挑選一隻，切成塊子，放在柴上，不要點火；我也預備一隻牛犢，放在柴上，也不點火。²⁴你們求告你們神的名，我也求告耶和華的名。那降火顯應的神，就是神。」

眾民回答說：「這話甚好。」

²⁵以利亞對巴力的先知說：「你們既是人多，當先挑選一隻牛犢，預備好了，就求告你們神的名，卻不要點火。」²⁶他們將所得的牛犢預備好了。

從早晨到午間，求告巴力的名說：「巴力啊，求你應允我們！」卻沒有聲音，沒有應允的。他們在所築的壇四圍踴跳。

²⁷到了正午，以利亞嬉笑他們，說：「大聲求告吧！因為他是神，他或默想、或走到一邊、或行路、或睡覺，你們當叫醒他。」²⁸他們大聲求告，按着他們的規矩，用刀槍自割、自刺，直到身體流血。²⁹從午後直到獻晚祭的時候，他們狂呼亂叫，卻沒

¹⁵Elijah said, "As the LORD Almighty lives, whom I serve, I will surely present myself to Ahab today."

Elijah on Mount Carmel

¹⁶So Obadiah went to meet Ahab and told him, and Ahab went to meet Elijah. ¹⁷When he saw Elijah, he said to him, "Is that you, you troubler of Israel?"

¹⁸"I have not made trouble for Israel," Elijah replied. "But you and your father's family have. You have abandoned the LORD's commands and have followed the Baals. ¹⁹Now summon the people from all over Israel to meet me on Mount Carmel. And bring the four hundred and fifty prophets of Baal and the four hundred prophets of Asherah, who eat at Jezebel's table."

²⁰So Ahab sent word throughout all Israel and assembled the prophets on Mount Carmel. ²¹Elijah went before the people and said, "How long will you waver between two opinions? If the LORD is God, follow him; but if Baal is God, follow him."

But the people said nothing.

²²Then Elijah said to them, "I am the only one of the LORD's prophets left, but Baal has four hundred and fifty prophets. ²³Get two bulls for us. Let them choose one for themselves, and let them cut it into pieces and put it on the wood but not set fire to it. I will prepare the other bull and put it on the wood but not set fire to it. ²⁴Then you call on the name of your god, and I will call on the name of the LORD. The god who answers by fire—he is God."

Then all the people said, "What you say is good."

²⁵Elijah said to the prophets of Baal, "Choose one of the bulls and prepare it first, since there are so many of you. Call on the name of your god, but do not light the fire." ²⁶So they took the bull given them and prepared it.

Then they called on the name of Baal from morning till noon. "O Baal, answer us!" they shouted. But there was no response; no one answered. And they danced around the altar they had made.

²⁷At noon Elijah began to taunt them. "Shout louder!" he said. "Surely he is a god! Perhaps he is deep in thought, or busy, or traveling. Maybe he is sleeping and must be awakened." ²⁸So they shouted louder and slashed themselves with swords and spears, as was their custom, until their blood flowed. ²⁹Midday passed, and they continued their frantic prophesying until the time for the evening sacrifice. But there was no

response, no one answered, no one paid attention.

30Then Elijah said to all the people, "Come here to me." They came to him, and he repaired the altar of the LORD, which was in ruins. 31Elijah took twelve stones, one for each of the tribes descended from Jacob, to whom the word of the LORD had come, saying, "Your name shall be Israel." 32With the stones he built an altar in the name of the LORD, and he dug a trench around it large enough to hold two seahs*a* of seed. 33He arranged the wood, cut the bull into pieces and laid it on the wood. Then he said to them, "Fill four large jars with water and pour it on the offering and on the wood."

34"Do it again," he said, and they did it again.

"Do it a third time," he ordered, and they did it the third time. 35The water ran down around the altar and even filled the trench.

36At the time of sacrifice, the prophet Elijah stepped forward and prayed: "O LORD, God of Abraham, Isaac and Israel, let it be known today that you are God in Israel and that I am your servant and have done all these things at your command. 37Answer me, O LORD, answer me, so these people will know that you, O LORD, are God, and that you are turning their hearts back again."

38Then the fire of the LORD fell and burned up the sacrifice, the wood, the stones and the soil, and also licked up the water in the trench.

39When all the people saw this, they fell prostrate and cried, "The LORD—he is God! The LORD—he is God!"

40Then Elijah commanded them, "Seize the prophets of Baal. Don't let anyone get away!" They seized them, and Elijah had them brought down to the Kishon Valley and slaughtered there.

41And Elijah said to Ahab, "Go, eat and drink, for there is the sound of a heavy rain." 42So Ahab went off to eat and drink, but Elijah climbed to the top of Carmel, bent down to the ground and put his face between his knees.

43"Go and look toward the sea," he told his servant. And he went up and looked.

"There is nothing there," he said.

Seven times Elijah said, "Go back."

44The seventh time the servant reported, "A cloud as small as a man's hand is rising from the sea."

So Elijah said, "Go and tell Ahab, 'Hitch up your chariot and go down before the rain stops you.'"

---

a 32 That is, probably about 13 quarts (about 15 liters)

有聲音，沒有應允的，也沒有理會的。

30以利亞對眾民說："你們到我這裏來！"眾民就到他那裏。他便重修已經毀壞耶和華的壇。31以利亞照雅各子孫支派的數目，取了十二塊石頭（耶和華的話曾臨到雅各說："你的名要叫以色列"），32用這些石頭為耶和華的名築一座壇，在壇的四圍挖溝，可容穀種二細亞，33又在壇上擺好了柴，把牛犢切成塊子放在柴上，對眾人說："你們用四個桶盛滿水，倒在燔祭和柴上。"

34又說："倒第二次。"他們就倒第二次。

又說："倒第三次。"他們就倒第三次。35水流在壇的四圍，溝裏也滿了水。

36到了獻晚祭的時候，先知以利亞近前來，說："亞伯拉罕、以撒、以色列的神，耶和華啊！求你今日使人知道你是以色列的神，也知道我是你的僕人，又是奉你的命行這一切事。37耶和華啊，求你應允我，應允我！使這民知道你耶和華是神，又知道是你叫這民的心回轉。"

38於是，耶和華降下火來，燒盡燔祭、木柴、石頭、塵土，又燒乾溝裏的水。

39眾民看見了，就俯伏在地，說："耶和華是神！耶和華是神！"

40以利亞對他們說："拿住巴力的先知，不容一人逃脫！"眾人就拿住他們。以利亞帶他們到基順河邊，在那裏殺了他們。

41以利亞對亞哈說："你現在可以上去吃喝，因為有多雨的響聲了。"42亞哈就上去吃喝。以利亞上了迦密山頂，屈身在地，將臉伏在兩膝之中。

43對僕人說："你上去，向海觀看。"僕人就上去觀看，說："沒有甚麼。"他說："你再去觀看。"

如此七次。

44第七次僕人說："我看見有一小片雲從海裏上來，不過如人手那樣大。"

以利亞說："你上去告訴亞哈，當套車下去，免得被雨阻擋。"

⁴⁵霎時間，天因風雲黑暗，降下大雨。亞哈就坐車往耶斯列去了。⁴⁶耶和華的靈（註：原文作「手」）降在以利亞身上，他就束上腰，奔在亞哈前頭，直到耶斯列的城門。

以利亞逃往何烈山

19 亞哈將以利亞一切所行的和他用刀殺眾先知的事，都告訴耶洗別。²耶洗別就差遣人去見以利亞，告訴他說：「明日約在這時候，我若不使你的性命像那些人的性命一樣，願神明重重地降罰與我。」

³以利亞見這光景，就起來逃命，到了猶大的別是巴，將僕人留在那裏。⁴自己在曠野走了一日的路程，來到一棵羅騰樹下（註：羅騰，小樹名，松類。下同）；就坐在那裏求死，說：「耶和華啊，罷了！求你取我的性命，因為我不勝於我的列祖。」⁵他就躺在羅騰樹下睡着了。

有一個天使拍他，說：「起來吃吧！」⁶他觀看，見頭旁有一瓶水與炭火燒的餅，他就吃了喝了，仍然躺下。

⁷耶和華的使者第二次來拍他，說：「起來吃吧！因為你當走的路甚遠。」⁸他就起來吃了喝了，仗着這飲食的力，走了四十晝夜，到了神的山，就是何烈山。⁹他在那裏進了一個洞，就住在洞中。

主向以利亞顯現

耶和華的話臨到他說：「以利亞啊，你在這裏做甚麼？」

¹⁰他說：「我為耶和華萬軍之神大發熱心，因為以色列人背棄了你的約，毀壞了你的壇，用刀殺了你的先知，只剩下我一個人，他們還要尋索我的命。」

¹¹耶和華說：「你出來站在山上，在我面前。」那時，耶和華從那裏經過。

在他面前有烈風大作，崩山碎石，耶和華卻不在風中；風後地震，耶和華卻不在其中；¹²地震後有火，耶和華也不在火中；火後有微小的聲

Elijah Flees to Horeb

⁴⁵Meanwhile, the sky grew black with clouds, the wind rose, a heavy rain came on and Ahab rode off to Jezreel. ⁴⁶The power of the LORD came upon Elijah and, tucking his cloak into his belt, he ran ahead of Ahab all the way to Jezreel.

19 Now Ahab told Jezebel everything Elijah had done and how he had killed all the prophets with the sword. ²So Jezebel sent a messenger to Elijah to say, "May the gods deal with me, be it ever so severely, if by this time tomorrow I do not make your life like that of one of them."

³Elijah was afraid[a] and ran for his life. When he came to Beersheba in Judah, he left his servant there, ⁴while he himself went a day's journey into the desert. He came to a broom tree, sat down under it and prayed that he might die. "I have had enough, LORD," he said. "Take my life; I am no better than my ancestors." ⁵Then he lay down under the tree and fell asleep.

All at once an angel touched him and said, "Get up and eat." ⁶He looked around, and there by his head was a cake of bread baked over hot coals, and a jar of water. He ate and drank and then lay down again.

⁷The angel of the LORD came back a second time and touched him and said, "Get up and eat, for the journey is too much for you." ⁸So he got up and ate and drank. Strengthened by that food, he traveled forty days and forty nights until he reached Horeb, the mountain of God. ⁹There he went into a cave and spent the night.

The LORD Appears to Elijah

And the word of the LORD came to him: "What are you doing here, Elijah?"

¹⁰He replied, "I have been very zealous for the LORD God Almighty. The Israelites have rejected your covenant, broken down your altars, and put your prophets to death with the sword. I am the only one left, and now they are trying to kill me too."

¹¹The LORD said, "Go out and stand on the mountain in the presence of the LORD, for the LORD is about to pass by."

Then a great and powerful wind tore the mountains apart and shattered the rocks before the LORD, but the LORD was not in the wind. After the wind there was an earthquake, but the LORD was not in the earthquake. ¹²After the earthquake came a fire, but the LORD was not in the fire. And after the fire came a gentle whis-

a 3 Or Elijah saw

per. 13When Elijah heard it, he pulled his cloak over his face and went out and stood at the mouth of the cave.

Then a voice said to him, "What are you doing here, Elijah?"

14He replied, "I have been very zealous for the LORD God Almighty. The Israelites have rejected your covenant, broken down your altars, and put your prophets to death with the sword. I am the only one left, and now they are trying to kill me too."

15The LORD said to him, "Go back the way you came, and go to the Desert of Damascus. When you get there, anoint Hazael king over Aram. 16Also, anoint Jehu son of Nimshi king over Israel, and anoint Elisha son of Shaphat from Abel Meholah to succeed you as prophet. 17Jehu will put to death any who escape the sword of Hazael, and Elisha will put to death any who escape the sword of Jehu. 18Yet I reserve seven thousand in Israel—all whose knees have not bowed down to Baal and all whose mouths have not kissed him."

The Call of Elisha

19So Elijah went from there and found Elisha son of Shaphat. He was plowing with twelve yoke of oxen, and he himself was driving the twelfth pair. Elijah went up to him and threw his cloak around him. 20Elisha then left his oxen and ran after Elijah. "Let me kiss my father and mother good-by," he said, "and then I will come with you."

"Go back," Elijah replied. "What have I done to you?"

21So Elisha left him and went back. He took his yoke of oxen and slaughtered them. He burned the plowing equipment to cook the meat and gave it to the people, and they ate. Then he set out to follow Elijah and became his attendant.

Ben-Hadad Attacks Samaria

20 Now Ben-Hadad king of Aram mustered his entire army. Accompanied by thirty-two kings with their horses and chariots, he went up and besieged Samaria and attacked it. 2He sent messengers into the city to Ahab king of Israel, saying, "This is what Ben-Hadad says: 3'Your silver and gold are mine, and the best of your wives and children are mine.'"

4The king of Israel answered, "Just as you say, my lord the king. I and all I have are yours."

音。13以利亞聽見,就用外衣蒙上臉,出來站在洞口。

有聲音向他說:"以利亞啊,你在這裏做甚麼?"

14他說:"我為耶和華萬軍之神大發熱心,因為以色列人背棄了你的約,毀壞了你的壇,用刀殺了你的先知,只剩下我一個人,他們還要尋索我的命。"

15耶和華對他說:"你回去,從曠野往大馬士革去。到了那裏,就要膏哈薛作亞蘭王;16又膏寧示的孫子耶戶作以色列王;並膏亞伯米何拉人沙法的兒子以利沙作先知接續你。17將來躲避哈薛之刀的,必被耶戶所殺;躲避耶戶之刀的,必被以利沙所殺。18但我在以色列人中為自己留下七千人,是未曾向巴力屈膝的,未曾與巴力親嘴的。"

以利沙蒙召

19於是,以利亞離開那裏走了,遇見沙法的兒子以利沙耕地,在他前頭有十二對牛,自己趕着第十二對。以利亞到他那裏去,將自己的外衣搭在他身上。20以利沙就離開牛跑到以利亞那裏,說:"求你容我先與父母親嘴,然後我便跟隨你。"

以利亞對他說:"你回去吧!我向你做了甚麼呢?"

21以利沙就離開他回去,宰了一對牛,用套牛的器具煮肉給民吃,隨後就起身跟隨以利亞,服侍他。

便哈達攻擊撒馬利亞

20 亞蘭王便哈達聚集他的全軍,率領三十二個王,帶着車馬上來圍攻撒馬利亞。2又差遣使者進城見以色列王亞哈,對他說:"便哈達如此說:3'你的金銀都要歸我,你妻子兒女中最美的也要歸我。'"

4以色列王回答說:"我主我王啊,可以依着你的話,我與我所有的都歸你。"

⁵使者又來說："便哈達如此說:'我已差遣人去見你,要你將你的金銀、妻子兒女都給我。⁶但明日約在這時候,我還要差遣臣僕到你那裏,搜查你的家和你僕人的家,將你眼中一切所喜愛的都拿了去。'"

⁷以色列王召了國中的長老來,對他們說:"請你們看看,這人是怎樣地謀害我。他先差遣人到我這裏來,要我的妻子、兒女和金銀,我並沒有推辭他。"

⁸長老和百姓對王說:"不要聽從他,也不要應允他。"

⁹故此,以色列王對便哈達的使者說:"你們告訴我主我王說:'王頭一次差遣人向僕人所要的,僕人都依從;但這次所要的,我不能依從。'"使者就去回覆便哈達。

¹⁰便哈達又差遣人去見亞哈說:"撒馬利亞的塵土,若夠跟從我的人每人捧一捧的,願神明重重地降罰與我!"

¹¹以色列王說:"你告訴他說:'才頂盔貫甲的,休要像摘盔卸甲的誇口。'"

¹²便哈達和諸王正在帳幕裏喝酒,聽見這話,就對他臣僕說:"擺隊吧!"他們就擺隊攻城。

亞哈打敗便哈達

¹³有一個先知來見以色列王亞哈說:"耶和華如此說:'這一大羣人你看見了嗎?今日我必將他們交在你手裏,你就知道我是耶和華。'"

¹⁴亞哈說:"藉着誰呢?"他回答說:"耶和華說:'藉着跟從省長的少年人。'"

亞哈說:"要誰率領呢?"
他說:"要你親自率領。"

¹⁵於是,亞哈數點跟從省長的少年人,共有二百三十二名。後又數點以色列的眾兵,共有七千名。¹⁶午間,他們就出城。便哈達和幫助他的三十二個王,正在帳幕裏痛飲。¹⁷跟從省長的少年人先出城。

便哈達差遣人去探望,他們回報說:"有人從撒馬利亞出來了。"

¹⁸他說:"他們若為講和出來,要活捉他們;若為打仗出來,也要活

⁵The messengers came again and said, "This is what Ben-Hadad says: 'I sent to demand your silver and gold, your wives and your children. ⁶But about this time tomorrow I am going to send my officials to search your palace and the houses of your officials. They will seize everything you value and carry it away.' "

⁷The king of Israel summoned all the elders of the land and said to them, "See how this man is looking for trouble! When he sent for my wives and my children, my silver and my gold, I did not refuse him."

⁸The elders and the people all answered, "Don't listen to him or agree to his demands."

⁹So he replied to Ben-Hadad's messengers, "Tell my lord the king, 'Your servant will do all you demanded the first time, but this demand I cannot meet.' " They left and took the answer back to Ben-Hadad.

¹⁰Then Ben-Hadad sent another message to Ahab: "May the gods deal with me, be it ever so severely, if enough dust remains in Samaria to give each of my men a handful."

¹¹The king of Israel answered, "Tell him: 'One who puts on his armor should not boast like one who takes it off.' "

¹²Ben-Hadad heard this message while he and the kings were drinking in their tents,ᵃ and he ordered his men: "Prepare to attack." So they prepared to attack the city.

Ahab Defeats Ben-Hadad

¹³Meanwhile a prophet came to Ahab king of Israel and announced, "This is what the LORD says: 'Do you see this vast army? I will give it into your hand today, and then you will know that I am the LORD.' "

¹⁴"But who will do this?" asked Ahab.

The prophet replied, "This is what the LORD says: 'The young officers of the provincial commanders will do it.' "

"And who will start the battle?" he asked.

The prophet answered, "You will."

¹⁵So Ahab summoned the young officers of the provincial commanders, 232 men. Then he assembled the rest of the Israelites, 7,000 in all. ¹⁶They set out at noon while Ben-Hadad and the 32 kings allied with him were in their tents getting drunk. ¹⁷The young officers of the provincial commanders went out first.

Now Ben-Hadad had dispatched scouts, who reported, "Men are advancing from Samaria."

¹⁸He said, "If they have come out for peace, take them alive; if they have come out for war,

a 12 Or in Succoth; also in verse 16

take them alive."

¹⁹The young officers of the provincial commanders marched out of the city with the army behind them ²⁰and each one struck down his opponent. At that, the Arameans fled, with the Israelites in pursuit. But Ben-Hadad king of Aram escaped on horseback with some of his horsemen. ²¹The king of Israel advanced and overpowered the horses and chariots and inflicted heavy losses on the Arameans.

²²Afterward, the prophet came to the king of Israel and said, "Strengthen your position and see what must be done, because next spring the king of Aram will attack you again."

²³Meanwhile, the officials of the king of Aram advised him, "Their gods are gods of the hills. That is why they were too strong for us. But if we fight them on the plains, surely we will be stronger than they. ²⁴Do this: Remove all the kings from their commands and replace them with other officers. ²⁵You must also raise an army like the one you lost—horse for horse and chariot for chariot—so we can fight Israel on the plains. Then surely we will be stronger than they." He agreed with them and acted accordingly.

²⁶The next spring Ben-Hadad mustered the Arameans and went up to Aphek to fight against Israel. ²⁷When the Israelites were also mustered and given provisions, they marched out to meet them. The Israelites camped opposite them like two small flocks of goats, while the Arameans covered the countryside.

²⁸The man of God came up and told the king of Israel, "This is what the LORD says: 'Because the Arameans think the LORD is a god of the hills and not a god of the valleys, I will deliver this vast army into your hands, and you will know that I am the LORD.'"

²⁹For seven days they camped opposite each other, and on the seventh day the battle was joined. The Israelites inflicted a hundred thousand casualties on the Aramean foot soldiers in one day. ³⁰The rest of them escaped to the city of Aphek, where the wall collapsed on twenty-seven thousand of them. And Ben-Hadad fled to the city and hid in an inner room.

³¹His officials said to him, "Look, we have heard that the kings of the house of Israel are merciful. Let us go to the king of Israel with sackcloth around our waists and ropes around our heads. Perhaps he will spare your life."

³²Wearing sackcloth around their waists and ropes around their heads, they went to the king of Israel and said, "Your servant Ben-Hadad says: 'Please let me live.'"

捉他們。'"

¹⁹跟從省長的少年人出城，軍兵跟隨他們，²⁰各人遇見敵人就殺。亞蘭人逃跑，以色列人追趕他們。亞蘭王便哈達騎着馬和馬兵一同逃跑。²¹以色列王出城攻打車馬，大大擊殺亞蘭人。

²²那先知來見以色列王，對他說："你當自強，留心怎樣防備，因為到明年這時候，亞蘭王必上來攻擊你。"

²³亞蘭王的臣僕對亞蘭王說："以色列人的神是山神，所以他們勝過我們，但在平原與他們打仗，我們必定得勝。²⁴王當這樣行：把諸王革去，派軍長代替他們；²⁵又照着王喪失軍兵之數，再招募一軍，馬補馬，車補車，我們在平原與他們打仗，必定得勝。"王便聽臣僕的話去行。

²⁶次年，便哈達果然點齊亞蘭人上亞弗去，要與以色列人打仗。²⁷以色列人也點齊軍兵，預備食物，迎着亞蘭人出去，對着他們安營，好像兩小羣山羊羔。亞蘭人卻滿了地面。

²⁸有神人來見以色列王說："耶和華如此說：'亞蘭人既說我耶和華是山神，不是平原的神，所以我必將這一大羣人都交在你手中，你們就知道我是耶和華。'"

²⁹以色列人與亞蘭人相對安營七日，到第七日兩軍交戰。那一日以色列人殺了亞蘭人步兵十萬，³⁰其餘的逃入亞弗城，城牆塌倒，壓死剩下的二萬七千人。便哈達也逃入城，藏在嚴密的屋子裏。

³¹他的臣僕對他說："我們聽說以色列王都是仁慈的王，現在我們不如腰束麻布，頭套繩索，出去投降以色列王，或者他存留王的性命。"

³²於是他們腰束麻布，頭套繩索，去見以色列王，說："王的僕人便哈達說：'求王存留我的性命。'"

亞哈說："他還活着嗎？他是我的兄弟。"

³³這些人留心探出他的口氣來，便急忙就着他的話說：<u>"便哈達是王的兄弟。"</u>

王說："你們去請他來。"<u>便哈達</u>出來見王，王就請他上車。

³⁴<u>便哈達</u>對王說："我父從你父那裏所奪的城邑，我必歸還，你可以在<u>大馬士革</u>立街市，像我父在<u>撒馬利亞</u>所立的一樣。"

<u>亞哈</u>說："我照此立約，放你回去。"就與他立約，放他去了。

先知責亞哈

³⁵有先知的一個門徒，奉耶和華的命對他的同伴說："你打我吧！"那人不肯打他。

³⁶他就對那人說："你既不聽從耶和華的話，你一離開我，必有獅子咬死你。"那人一離開他，果然遇見獅子，把他咬死了。

³⁷先知的門徒又遇見一個人，對他說："你打我吧！"那人就打他，將他打傷。³⁸他就去了，用頭巾蒙眼，改換面目，在路旁等候王。³⁹王從那裏經過，他向王呼叫說："僕人在陣上的時候，有人帶了一個人來，對我說：'你看守這人，若把他失了，你的性命必代替他的性命，不然，你必交出一他連得銀子來。'⁴⁰僕人正在忙亂之間，那人就不見了。"

<u>以色列</u>王對他說："你自己定妥了，必照樣判斷你。"

⁴¹他急忙除掉蒙眼的頭巾，<u>以色列</u>王就認出他是一個先知。⁴²他對王說："耶和華如此說：'因你將我定要滅絕的人放去，你的命就必代替他的命，你的民也必代替他的民。'"⁴³於是，<u>以色列</u>王悶悶不樂地回到<u>撒馬利亞</u>，進了他的宮。

The king answered, "Is he still alive? He is my brother."

³³The men took this as a good sign and were quick to pick up his word. "Yes, your brother Ben-Hadad!" they said.

"Go and get him," the king said. When Ben-Hadad came out, Ahab had him come up into his chariot.

³⁴"I will return the cities my father took from your father," Ben-Hadad offered. "You may set up your own market areas in Damascus, as my father did in Samaria."

⌊Ahab said,⌋ "On the basis of a treaty I will set you free." So he made a treaty with him, and let him go.

A Prophet Condemns Ahab

³⁵By the word of the Lord one of the sons of the prophets said to his companion, "Strike me with your weapon," but the man refused.

³⁶So the prophet said, "Because you have not obeyed the Lord, as soon as you leave me a lion will kill you." And after the man went away, a lion found him and killed him.

³⁷The prophet found another man and said, "Strike me, please." So the man struck him and wounded him. ³⁸Then the prophet went and stood by the road waiting for the king. He disguised himself with his headband down over his eyes. ³⁹As the king passed by, the prophet called out to him, "Your servant went into the thick of the battle, and someone came to me with a captive and said, 'Guard this man. If he is missing, it will be your life for his life, or you must pay a talent^a of silver.' ⁴⁰While your servant was busy here and there, the man disappeared."

"That is your sentence," the king of Israel said. "You have pronounced it yourself."

⁴¹Then the prophet quickly removed the headband from his eyes, and the king of Israel recognized him as one of the prophets. ⁴²He said to the king, "This is what the Lord says: 'You have set free a man I had determined should die.^b Therefore it is your life for his life, your people for his people.'" ⁴³Sullen and angry, the king of Israel went to his palace in Samaria.

---

^a 39 That is, about 75 pounds (about 34 kilograms)
^b 42 The Hebrew term refers to the irrevocable giving over of things or persons to the Lord, often by totally destroying them.

Naboth's Vineyard

21 Some time later there was an incident involving a vineyard belonging to Naboth the Jezreelite. The vineyard was in Jezreel, close to the palace of Ahab king of Samaria. [2]Ahab said to Naboth, "Let me have your vineyard to use for a vegetable garden, since it is close to my palace. In exchange I will give you a better vineyard or, if you prefer, I will pay you whatever it is worth."

[3]But Naboth replied, "The LORD forbid that I should give you the inheritance of my fathers."

[4]So Ahab went home, sullen and angry because Naboth the Jezreelite had said, "I will not give you the inheritance of my fathers." He lay on his bed sulking and refused to eat.

[5]His wife Jezebel came in and asked him, "Why are you so sullen? Why won't you eat?"

[6]He answered her, "Because I said to Naboth the Jezreelite, 'Sell me your vineyard; or if you prefer, I will give you another vineyard in its place.' But he said, 'I will not give you my vineyard.'"

[7]Jezebel his wife said, "Is this how you act as king over Israel? Get up and eat! Cheer up. I'll get you the vineyard of Naboth the Jezreelite."

[8]So she wrote letters in Ahab's name, placed his seal on them, and sent them to the elders and nobles who lived in Naboth's city with him. [9]In those letters she wrote:

"Proclaim a day of fasting and seat Naboth in a prominent place among the people. [10]But seat two scoundrels opposite him and have them testify that he has cursed both God and the king. Then take him out and stone him to death."

[11]So the elders and nobles who lived in Naboth's city did as Jezebel directed in the letters she had written to them. [12]They proclaimed a fast and seated Naboth in a prominent place among the people. [13]Then two scoundrels came and sat opposite him and brought charges against Naboth before the people, saying, "Naboth has cursed both God and the king." So they took him outside the city and stoned him to death. [14]Then they sent word to Jezebel: "Naboth has been stoned and is dead."

[15]As soon as Jezebel heard that Naboth had been stoned to death, she said to Ahab, "Get up and take possession of the vineyard of Naboth the Jezreelite that he refused to sell you. He is no longer alive, but dead." [16]When Ahab heard that Naboth was dead, he got up and went down to take possession of Naboth's vineyard.

拿伯的葡萄園

21 這事以後，又有一事。耶斯列人拿伯在耶斯列有一個葡萄園，靠近撒馬利亞王亞哈的宮。[2]亞哈對拿伯說：“你將你的葡萄園給我作菜園，因為是靠近我的宮；我就把更好的葡萄園換給你，或是你要銀子，我就按着價值給你。”

[3]拿伯對亞哈說：“我敬畏耶和華，萬不敢將我先人留下的產業給你。”

[4]亞哈因耶斯列人拿伯說：“我不敢將我先人留下的產業給你”，就悶悶不樂地回宮，躺在牀上，轉臉向內，也不吃飯。

[5]王后耶洗別來問他說：“你為甚麼心裏這樣憂悶，不吃飯呢？”

[6]他回答說：“因我向耶斯列人拿伯說：‘你將你的葡萄園給我，我給你價銀，或是你願意，我就把別的葡萄園換給你’，他卻說：‘我不將我的葡萄園給你。’”

[7]王后耶洗別對亞哈說：“你現在是治理以色列國不是？只管起來，心裏暢暢快快地吃飯，我必將耶斯列人拿伯的葡萄園給你。”

[8]於是，託亞哈的名寫信，用王的印記，送給那些與拿伯同城居住的長老貴冑。[9]信上寫着說：

“你們當宣告禁食，叫拿伯坐在民間的高位上。[10]又叫兩個匪徒坐在拿伯對面，作見證告他說：‘你謗瀆神和王了’；隨後就把他拉出去用石頭打死。”

[11]那些與拿伯同城居住的長老貴冑，得了耶洗別的信，就照信而行，[12]宣告禁食，叫拿伯坐在民間的高位上。[13]有兩個匪徒來，坐在拿伯的對面，當着眾民作見證告他說：“拿伯謗瀆神和王了！”眾人就把他拉到城外，用石頭打死。[14]於是打發人去見耶洗別說：“拿伯被石頭打死了。”

[15]耶洗別聽見拿伯被石頭打死，就對亞哈說：“你起來得耶斯列人拿伯不肯為價銀給你的葡萄園吧！現在他已經死了。”[16]亞哈聽見拿伯死了，就起來，下去要得耶斯列人拿伯的葡萄園。

17耶和華的話臨到提斯比人以利亞說：18 "你起來，去見住撒馬利亞的以色列王亞哈。他下去要得拿伯的葡萄園，現今正在那裏。19你要對他說：'耶和華如此說：你殺了人，又得他的產業嗎？'又要對他說：'耶和華如此說：狗在何處舔拿伯的血，也必在何處舔你的血。'"

20亞哈對以利亞說："我仇敵啊，你找到我嗎？"

他回答說："我找到你了，因為你賣了自己，行耶和華眼中看為惡的事。21耶和華說：'我必使災禍臨到你，將你除盡，凡屬你的男丁，無論困住的、自由的，都從以色列中剪除。22我必使你的家像尼八的兒子耶羅波安的家，又像亞希雅的兒子巴沙的家，因為你惹我發怒，又使以色列人陷在罪裏。'

23 "論到耶洗別，耶和華也說：'狗在耶斯列的外郭必吃耶洗別的肉。'

24 "凡屬亞哈的人，死在城中的，必被狗吃；死在田野的，必被空中的鳥吃。"

(25從來沒有像亞哈的，因他自賣，行耶和華眼中看為惡的事，受了王后耶洗別的聳動，26就照耶和華在以色列人面前所趕出的亞摩利人，行了最可憎惡的事，信從偶像。)

27亞哈聽見這話，就撕裂衣服，禁食，身穿麻布，睡臥也穿着麻布，並且緩緩而行。

28耶和華的話臨到提斯比人以利亞說：29 "亞哈在我面前這樣自卑，你看見了嗎？因他在我面前自卑，他還在世的時候，我不降這禍；到他兒子的時候，我必降這禍與他的家。"

米該雅對亞哈的預言

22 亞蘭國和以色列國三年沒有爭戰。2到第三年，猶大王約沙法下去見以色列王。3以色列王對臣僕說："你們不知道基列的拉末是屬我們的嗎？我們豈可靜坐不動，不從亞蘭王手裏奪回來嗎？"

4亞哈問約沙法說："你肯同我去攻取基列的拉末嗎？"

17Then the word of the LORD came to Elijah the Tishbite: 18"Go down to meet Ahab king of Israel, who rules in Samaria. He is now in Naboth's vineyard, where he has gone to take possession of it. 19Say to him, 'This is what the LORD says: Have you not murdered a man and seized his property?' Then say to him, 'This is what the LORD says: In the place where dogs licked up Naboth's blood, dogs will lick up your blood—yes, yours!' "

20Ahab said to Elijah, "So you have found me, my enemy!"

"I have found you," he answered, "because you have sold yourself to do evil in the eyes of the LORD. 21I am going to bring disaster on you. I will consume your descendants and cut off from Ahab every last male in Israel—slave or free. 22I will make your house like that of Jeroboam son of Nebat and that of Baasha son of Ahijah, because you have provoked me to anger and have caused Israel to sin.'

23"And also concerning Jezebel the LORD says: 'Dogs will devour Jezebel by the wall of^a Jezreel.'

24"Dogs will eat those belonging to Ahab who die in the city, and the birds of the air will feed on those who die in the country."

25(There was never a man like Ahab, who sold himself to do evil in the eyes of the LORD, urged on by Jezebel his wife. 26He behaved in the vilest manner by going after idols, like the Amorites the LORD drove out before Israel.)

27When Ahab heard these words, he tore his clothes, put on sackcloth and fasted. He lay in sackcloth and went around meekly.

28Then the word of the LORD came to Elijah the Tishbite: 29"Have you noticed how Ahab has humbled himself before me? Because he has humbled himself, I will not bring this disaster in his day, but I will bring it on his house in the days of his son."

Micaiah Prophesies Against Ahab

22 For three years there was no war between Aram and Israel. 2But in the third year Jehoshaphat king of Judah went down to see the king of Israel. 3The king of Israel had said to his officials, "Don't you know that Ramoth Gilead belongs to us and yet we are doing nothing to retake it from the king of Aram?"

4So he asked Jehoshaphat, "Will you go with me to fight against Ramoth Gilead?"

a 23 Most Hebrew manuscripts; a few Hebrew manuscripts, Vulgate and Syriac (see also 2 Kings 9:26) the plot of ground at

Jehoshaphat replied to the king of Israel, "I am as you are, my people as your people, my horses as your horses." ⁵But Jehoshaphat also said to the king of Israel, "First seek the counsel of the LORD."

⁶So the king of Israel brought together the prophets—about four hundred men—and asked them, "Shall I go to war against Ramoth Gilead, or shall I refrain?"

"Go," they answered, "for the Lord will give it into the king's hand."

⁷But Jehoshaphat asked, "Is there not a prophet of the LORD here whom we can inquire of?"

⁸The king of Israel answered Jehoshaphat, "There is still one man through whom we can inquire of the LORD, but I hate him because he never prophesies anything good about me, but always bad. He is Micaiah son of Imlah."

"The king should not say that," Jehoshaphat replied.

⁹So the king of Israel called one of his officials and said, "Bring Micaiah son of Imlah at once."

¹⁰Dressed in their royal robes, the king of Israel and Jehoshaphat king of Judah were sitting on their thrones at the threshing floor by the entrance of the gate of Samaria, with all the prophets prophesying before them. ¹¹Now Zedekiah son of Kenaanah had made iron horns and he declared, "This is what the LORD says: 'With these you will gore the Arameans until they are destroyed.'"

¹²All the other prophets were prophesying the same thing. "Attack Ramoth Gilead and be victorious," they said, "for the LORD will give it into the king's hand."

¹³The messenger who had gone to summon Micaiah said to him, "Look, as one man the other prophets are predicting success for the king. Let your word agree with theirs, and speak favorably."

¹⁴But Micaiah said, "As surely as the LORD lives, I can tell him only what the LORD tells me."

¹⁵When he arrived, the king asked him, "Micaiah, shall we go to war against Ramoth Gilead, or shall I refrain?"

"Attack and be victorious," he answered, "for the LORD will give it into the king's hand."

¹⁶The king said to him, "How many times must I make you swear to tell me nothing but the truth in the name of the LORD?"

¹⁷Then Micaiah answered, "I saw all Israel scattered on the hills like sheep without a shepherd, and the LORD said, 'These people have no master. Let each one go home in peace.'"

約沙法對以色列王說："你我不分彼此，我的民與你的民一樣，我的馬與你的馬一樣。" ⁵約沙法對以色列王說："請你先求問耶和華。"

⁶於是以色列王招聚先知，約有四百人，問他們說："我上去攻取基列的拉末可以不可以？"

他們說："可以上去，因為主必將那城交在王的手裏。"

⁷約沙法說："這裏不是還有耶和華的先知，我們可以求問他嗎？"

⁸以色列王對約沙法說："還有一個人，是音拉的兒子米該雅，我們可以託他求問耶和華。只是我恨他，因為他指着我所說的預言，不說吉語，單說凶言。"

約沙法說："王不必這樣說。"

⁹以色列王就召了一個太監來，說："你快去，將音拉的兒子米該雅召來。"

¹⁰以色列王和猶大王約沙法在撒馬利亞城門前的空場上，各穿朝服，坐在位上。所有的先知都在他們面前說預言。¹¹基拿拿的兒子西底家造了兩個鐵角，說："耶和華如此說：'你要用這角牴觸亞蘭人，直到將他們滅盡。'"

¹²所有的先知也都這樣預言說："可以上基列的拉末去，必然得勝，因為耶和華必將那城交在王的手中。"

¹³那去召米該雅的使者對米該雅說："眾先知一口同音地都向王說吉言，你不如與他們說一樣的話，也說吉言。"

¹⁴米該雅說："我指着永生的耶和華起誓，耶和華對我說甚麼，我就說甚麼。"

¹⁵米該雅到王面前，王問他說："米該雅啊，我們上去攻取基列的拉末可以不可以？"

他回答說："可以上去，必然得勝，耶和華必將那城交在王的手中。"

¹⁶王對他說："我當囑咐你幾次，你才奉耶和華的名向我說實話呢？"

¹⁷米該雅說："我看見以色列眾民散在山上，如同沒有牧人的羊羣一般。耶和華說：'這民沒有主人，他們可以平平安安地各歸各家去。'"

¹⁸以色列王對約沙法說："我豈沒有告訴你，這人指着我所說的預言，不說吉語，單說凶言嗎？"

¹⁹米該雅說："你要聽耶和華的話。我看見耶和華坐在寶座上，天上的萬軍侍立在他左右。²⁰耶和華說：'誰去引誘亞哈上基列的拉末去陣亡呢？'

"這個就這樣說，那個就那樣說。²¹隨後有一個神靈出來，站在耶和華面前，說：'我去引誘他。'

²²"耶和華問他說：'你用何法呢？'他說：'我去要在他眾先知口中作謊言的靈。'

"耶和華說：'這樣，你必能引誘他，你去如此行吧！'

²³"現在耶和華使謊言的靈入了你這些先知的口，並且耶和華已經命定降禍與你。"

²⁴基拿拿的兒子西底家前來，打米該雅的臉，說："耶和華的靈從哪裏離開我與你說話呢？"

²⁵米該雅說："你進嚴密的屋子藏躲的那日，就必看見了。"

²⁶以色列王說："將米該雅帶回交給邑宰亞們和王的兒子約阿施，說：²⁷王如此說：'把這個人下在監裏，使他受苦，吃不飽、喝不足，等候我平平安安地回來。'"

²⁸米該雅說："你若能平平安安地回來，那就是耶和華沒有藉我說這話了。"又說："眾民哪，你們都要聽！"

亞哈在基列的拉末陣亡

²⁹以色列王和猶大王約沙法上基列的拉末去了。³⁰以色列王對約沙法說："我要改裝上陣，你可以仍穿王服。"以色列王就改裝上陣。

³¹先是亞蘭王吩咐他的三十二個車兵長說："他們的兵將，無論大小，你們都不可與他們爭戰，只要與以色列王爭戰。"³²車兵長看見約沙法，便說："這必是以色列王。"就轉過去與他爭戰，約沙法便呼喊。³³車兵長見不是以色列王，就轉去不追他了。

¹⁸The king of Israel said to Jehoshaphat, "Didn't I tell you that he never prophesies anything good about me, but only bad?"

¹⁹Micaiah continued, "Therefore hear the word of the LORD: I saw the LORD sitting on his throne with all the host of heaven standing around him on his right and on his left. ²⁰And the LORD said, 'Who will entice Ahab into attacking Ramoth Gilead and going to his death there?'

"One suggested this, and another that. ²¹Finally, a spirit came forward, stood before the LORD and said, 'I will entice him.'

²²"'By what means?' the LORD asked.

"'I will go out and be a lying spirit in the mouths of all his prophets,' he said.

"'You will succeed in enticing him,' said the LORD. 'Go and do it.'

²³"So now the LORD has put a lying spirit in the mouths of all these prophets of yours. The LORD has decreed disaster for you."

²⁴Then Zedekiah son of Kenaanah went up and slapped Micaiah in the face. "Which way did the spirit from^a the LORD go when he went from me to speak to you?" he asked.

²⁵Micaiah replied, "You will find out on the day you go to hide in an inner room."

²⁶The king of Israel then ordered, "Take Micaiah and send him back to Amon the ruler of the city and to Joash the king's son ²⁷and say, 'This is what the king says: Put this fellow in prison and give him nothing but bread and water until I return safely.'"

²⁸Micaiah declared, "If you ever return safely, the LORD has not spoken through me." Then he added, "Mark my words, all you people!"

Ahab Killed at Ramoth Gilead

²⁹So the king of Israel and Jehoshaphat king of Judah went up to Ramoth Gilead. ³⁰The king of Israel said to Jehoshaphat, "I will enter the battle in disguise, but you wear your royal robes." So the king of Israel disguised himself and went into battle.

³¹Now the king of Aram had ordered his thirty-two chariot commanders, "Do not fight with anyone, small or great, except the king of Israel." ³²When the chariot commanders saw Jehoshaphat, they thought, "Surely this is the king of Israel." So they turned to attack him, but when Jehoshaphat cried out, ³³the chariot commanders saw that he was not the king of Israel and stopped pursuing him.

[34]But someone drew his bow at random and hit the king of Israel between the sections of his armor. The king told his chariot driver, "Wheel around and get me out of the fighting. I've been wounded." [35]All day long the battle raged, and the king was propped up in his chariot facing the Arameans. The blood from his wound ran onto the floor of the chariot, and that evening he died. [36]As the sun was setting, a cry spread through the army: "Every man to his town; everyone to his land!"

[37]So the king died and was brought to Samaria, and they buried him there. [38]They washed the chariot at a pool in Samaria (where the prostitutes bathed),[a] and the dogs licked up his blood, as the word of the LORD had declared.

[39]As for the other events of Ahab's reign, including all he did, the palace he built and inlaid with ivory, and the cities he fortified, are they not written in the book of the annals of the kings of Israel? [40]Ahab rested with his fathers. And Ahaziah his son succeeded him as king.

Jehoshaphat King of Judah

[41]Jehoshaphat son of Asa became king of Judah in the fourth year of Ahab king of Israel. [42]Jehoshaphat was thirty-five years old when he became king, and he reigned in Jerusalem twenty-five years. His mother's name was Azubah daughter of Shilhi. [43]In everything he walked in the ways of his father Asa and did not stray from them; he did what was right in the eyes of the LORD. The high places, however, were not removed, and the people continued to offer sacrifices and burn incense there. [44]Jehoshaphat was also at peace with the king of Israel.

[45]As for the other events of Jehoshaphat's reign, the things he achieved and his military exploits, are they not written in the book of the annals of the kings of Judah? [46]He rid the land of the rest of the male shrine prostitutes who remained there even after the reign of his father Asa. [47]There was then no king in Edom; a deputy ruled.

[48]Now Jehoshaphat built a fleet of trading ships[b] to go to Ophir for gold, but they never set sail—they were wrecked at Ezion Geber. [49]At that time Ahaziah son of Ahab said to Jehoshaphat, "Let my men sail with your men," but Jehoshaphat refused.

[50]Then Jehoshaphat rested with his fathers and was buried with them in the city of David his father. And Jehoram his son succeeded him.

[34]有一人隨便開弓，恰巧射入以色列王的甲縫裏。王對趕車的說："我受了重傷，你轉過車來，拉我出陣吧！" [35]那日，陣勢越戰越猛，有人扶王站在車上，抵擋亞蘭人。到晚上，王就死了，血從傷處流在車中。 [36]約在日落的時候，有號令傳遍軍中說："各歸本城，各歸本地吧！"

[37]王既死了，眾人將他送到撒馬利亞，就葬在那裏。 [38]又有人把他的車，洗在撒馬利亞的池旁（妓女在那裏洗澡），狗來舔他的血，正如耶和華所說的話。

[39]亞哈其餘的事，凡他所行的和他所修造的象牙宮，並所建築的一切城邑，都寫在以色列諸王記上。 [40]亞哈與他列祖同睡。他兒子亞哈謝接續他作王。

約沙法作猶大王

[41]以色列王亞哈第四年，亞撒的兒子約沙法登基作了猶大王。 [42]約沙法登基的時候，年三十五歲，在耶路撒冷作王二十五年。他母親名叫阿蘇巴，乃示利希的女兒。 [43]約沙法行他父親亞撒所行的道，不偏離左右，行耶和華眼中看為正的事，只是邱壇還沒有廢去，百姓仍在那裏獻祭燒香。 [44]約沙法與以色列王和好。

[45]約沙法其餘的事和他所顯出的勇力，並他怎樣爭戰，都寫在猶大列王記上。 [46]約沙法將他父親亞撒在世所剩下的孌童都從國中除去了。 [47]那時，以東沒有王，有總督治理。

[48]約沙法製造他施船隻，要往俄斐去，將金子運來；只是沒有去，因為船在以旬迦別破壞了。 [49]亞哈的兒子亞哈謝對約沙法說："容我的僕人和你的僕人坐船同去吧！"約沙法卻不肯。

[50]約沙法與列祖同睡，葬在大衛城他列祖的墳地裏。他兒子約蘭接續他作王。

---

a 38 Or Samaria and cleaned the weapons   b 48 Hebrew of ships of Tarshish

亞哈謝作以色列王

⁵¹猶大王約沙法十七年，亞哈的兒子亞哈謝在撒馬利亞登基，作以色列王共二年。⁵²他行耶和華眼中看為惡的事，效法他的父母，又行尼八的兒子耶羅波安使以色列人陷在罪裏的事。⁵³他照他父親一切所行的，侍奉敬拜巴力，惹耶和華以色列神的怒氣。

Ahaziah King of Israel

⁵¹Ahaziah son of Ahab became king of Israel in Samaria in the seventeenth year of Jehoshaphat king of Judah, and he reigned over Israel two years. ⁵²He did evil in the eyes of the LORD, because he walked in the ways of his father and mother and in the ways of Jeroboam son of Nebat, who caused Israel to sin. ⁵³He served and worshiped Baal and provoked the LORD, the God of Israel, to anger, just as his father had done.

圖六：列王紀中的主要地方
MAP 6 : KEY PLACES IN 1 & 2 KINGS

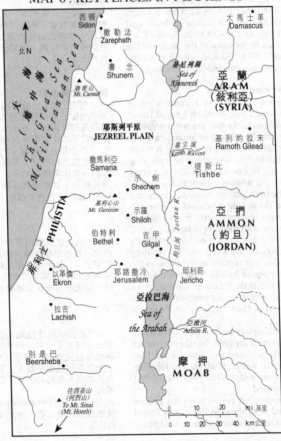

2 Kings

The LORD's Judgment on Ahaziah

1 After Ahab's death, Moab rebelled against Israel. ²Now Ahaziah had fallen through the lattice of his upper room in Samaria and injured himself. So he sent messengers, saying to them, "Go and consult Baal-Zebub, the god of Ekron, to see if I will recover from this injury."

³But the angel of the LORD said to Elijah the Tishbite, "Go up and meet the messengers of the king of Samaria and ask them, 'Is it because there is no God in Israel that you are going off to consult Baal-Zebub, the god of Ekron?' ⁴Therefore this is what the LORD says: 'You will not leave the bed you are lying on. You will certainly die!' " So Elijah went.

⁵When the messengers returned to the king, he asked them, "Why have you come back?"

⁶"A man came to meet us," they replied. "And he said to us, 'Go back to the king who sent you and tell him, "This is what the LORD says: Is it because there is no God in Israel that you are sending men to consult Baal-Zebub, the god of Ekron? Therefore you will not leave the bed you are lying on. You will certainly die!" ' "

⁷The king asked them, "What kind of man was it who came to meet you and told you this?"

⁸They replied, "He was a man with a garment of hair and with a leather belt around his waist."

The king said, "That was Elijah the Tishbite."

⁹Then he sent to Elijah a captain with his company of fifty men. The captain went up to Elijah, who was sitting on the top of a hill, and said to him, "Man of God, the king says, 'Come down!' "

¹⁰Elijah answered the captain, "If I am a man of God, may fire come down from heaven and consume you and your fifty men!" Then fire fell from heaven and consumed the captain and his men.

¹¹At this the king sent to Elijah another captain with his fifty men. The captain said to him, "Man of God, this is what the king says, 'Come down at once!' "

¹²"If I am a man of God," Elijah replied, "may fire come down from heaven and consume you and your fifty men!" Then the fire of God fell

列王紀下

主對亞哈謝的審判

1 亞哈死後，摩押背叛以色列。²亞哈謝在撒馬利亞，一日，從樓上的欄杆裏掉下來就病了，於是差遣使者說：「你們去問以革倫的神巴力西卜，我這病能好不能好？」

³但耶和華的使者對提斯比人以利亞說：「你起來，去迎着撒馬利亞王的使者，對他們說：『你們去問以革倫神巴力西卜，豈因以色列中沒有神嗎？』⁴所以耶和華如此說：『你必不下你所上的牀，必定要死！』」以利亞就去了。

⁵使者回來見王，王問他們說：「你們為甚麼回來呢？」

⁶使者回答說：「有一個人迎着我們來，對我們說：『你們回去見差你們來的王，對他說：耶和華如此說：你差人去問以革倫神巴力西卜，豈因以色列中沒有神嗎？所以，你必不下你所上的牀，必定要死！』」

⁷王問他們說：「迎着你們來告訴你們這話的，是怎樣的人？」

⁸回答說：「他身穿毛衣，腰束皮帶。」

王說：「這必是提斯比人以利亞。」

⁹於是王差遣五十夫長，帶領五十人去見以利亞，他就上到以利亞那裏；以利亞正坐在山頂上。五十夫長對他說：「神人哪，王吩咐你下來！」

¹⁰以利亞回答說：「我若是神人，願火從天上降下來，燒滅你和你那五十人！」於是有火從天上降下來，燒滅五十夫長和他那五十人。

¹¹王第二次差遣一個五十夫長，帶領五十人去見以利亞。五十夫長對以利亞說：「神人哪，王吩咐你快快下來！」

¹²以利亞回答說：「我若是神人，願火從天上降下來，燒滅你和你那五十人！」於是神的火從天上降下

來，燒滅五十夫長和他那五十人。

¹³王第三次差遣一個五十夫長，帶領五十人去。這五十夫長上去，雙膝跪在以利亞面前，哀求他說：“神人哪，願我的性命和你這五十個僕人的性命在你眼前看為寶貴。¹⁴已經有火從天上降下來，燒滅前兩次來的五十夫長和他們各自帶的五十人；現在願我的性命在你眼前看為寶貴！”

¹⁵耶和華的使者對以利亞說：“你同着他下去，不要怕他。”以利亞就起來，同着他下去見王。

¹⁶對王說：“耶和華如此說：你差人去問以革倫神巴力西卜，豈因以色列中沒有神可以求問嗎？所以你必不下所上的牀，必定要死！”¹⁷亞哈謝果然死了，正如耶和華藉以利亞所說的話。

因他沒有兒子，他兄弟約蘭接續他作王，正在猶大王約沙法的兒子約蘭第二年。¹⁸亞哈謝其餘所行的事都寫在以色列諸王記上。

以利亞被接升天

2 耶和華要用旋風接以利亞升天的時候，以利亞與以利沙從吉甲前往。²以利亞對以利沙說：“耶和華差我往伯特利去，你可以在這裏等候。”

以利沙說：“我指着永生的耶和華，又敢在你面前起誓，我必不離開你。”於是二人下到伯特利。

³住伯特利的先知門徒出來見以利沙，對他說：“耶和華今日要接你的師傅離開你，你知道不知道？”

他說：“我知道！你們不要做聲。”

⁴以利亞對以利沙說：“耶和華差我往耶利哥去，你可以在這裏等候。”

以利沙說：“我指着永生的耶和華，又敢在你面前起誓，我必不離開你。”於是二人到了耶利哥。

⁵住耶利哥的先知門徒就近以利沙，對他說：“耶和華今日要接你的師傅離開你，你知道不知道？”

from heaven and consumed him and his fifty men.

¹³So the king sent a third captain with his fifty men. This third captain went up and fell on his knees before Elijah. "Man of God," he begged, "please have respect for my life and the lives of these fifty men, your servants! ¹⁴See, fire has fallen from heaven and consumed the first two captains and all their men. But now have respect for my life!"

¹⁵The angel of the LORD said to Elijah, "Go down with him; do not be afraid of him." So Elijah got up and went down with him to the king.

¹⁶He told the king, "This is what the LORD says: Is it because there is no God in Israel for you to consult that you have sent messengers to consult Baal-Zebub, the god of Ekron? Because you have done this, you will never leave the bed you are lying on. You will certainly die!" ¹⁷So he died, according to the word of the LORD that Elijah had spoken.

Because Ahaziah had no son, Joram*a* succeeded him as king in the second year of Jehoram son of Jehoshaphat king of Judah. ¹⁸As for all the other events of Ahaziah's reign, and what he did, are they not written in the book of the annals of the kings of Israel?

Elijah Taken Up to Heaven

2 When the LORD was about to take Elijah up to heaven in a whirlwind, Elijah and Elisha were on their way from Gilgal. ²Elijah said to Elisha, "Stay here; the LORD has sent me to Bethel."

But Elisha said, "As surely as the LORD lives and as you live, I will not leave you." So they went down to Bethel.

³The company of the prophets at Bethel came out to Elisha and asked, "Do you know that the LORD is going to take your master from you today?"

"Yes, I know," Elisha replied, "but do not speak of it."

⁴Then Elijah said to him, "Stay here, Elisha; the LORD has sent me to Jericho."

And he replied, "As surely as the LORD lives and as you live, I will not leave you." So they went to Jericho.

⁵The company of the prophets at Jericho went up to Elisha and asked him, "Do you know that the LORD is going to take your master from you today?"

a 17 Hebrew Jehoram, a variant of Joram

"Yes, I know," he replied, "but do not speak of it."

⁶Then Elijah said to him, "Stay here; the LORD has sent me to the Jordan."

And he replied, "As surely as the LORD lives and as you live, I will not leave you." So the two of them walked on.

⁷Fifty men of the company of the prophets went and stood at a distance, facing the place where Elijah and Elisha had stopped at the Jordan. ⁸Elijah took his cloak, rolled it up and struck the water with it. The water divided to the right and to the left, and the two of them crossed over on dry ground.

⁹When they had crossed, Elijah said to Elisha, "Tell me, what can I do for you before I am taken from you?"

"Let me inherit a double portion of your spirit," Elisha replied.

¹⁰"You have asked a difficult thing," Elijah said, "yet if you see me when I am taken from you, it will be yours—otherwise not."

¹¹As they were walking along and talking together, suddenly a chariot of fire and horses of fire appeared and separated the two of them, and Elijah went up to heaven in a whirlwind. ¹²Elisha saw this and cried out, "My father! My father! The chariots and horsemen of Israel!" And Elisha saw him no more. Then he took hold of his own clothes and tore them apart.

¹³He picked up the cloak that had fallen from Elijah and went back and stood on the bank of the Jordan. ¹⁴Then he took the cloak that had fallen from him and struck the water with it. "Where now is the LORD, the God of Elijah?" he asked. When he struck the water, it divided to the right and to the left, and he crossed over.

¹⁵The company of the prophets from Jericho, who were watching, said, "The spirit of Elijah is resting on Elisha." And they went to meet him and bowed to the ground before him. ¹⁶"Look," they said, "we your servants have fifty able men. Let them go and look for your master. Perhaps the Spirit of the LORD has picked him up and set him down on some mountain or in some valley."

"No," Elisha replied, "do not send them."

¹⁷But they persisted until he was too ashamed to refuse. So he said, "Send them." And they sent fifty men, who searched for three days but did not find him. ¹⁸When they returned to Elisha, who was staying in Jericho, he said to them, "Didn't I tell you not to go?"

他說："我知道！你們不要做聲。"

⁶以利亞對以利沙說："耶和華差遣我往約旦河去，你可以在這裏等候。"

以利沙說："我指着永生的耶和華，又敢在你面前起誓，我必不離開你。"於是二人一同前往。

⁷有先知門徒去了五十人，遠遠地站在他們對面，二人在約旦河邊站住。⁸以利亞將自己的外衣捲起來，用以打水，水就左右分開，二人走乾地而過。

⁹過去之後，以利亞對以利沙說："我未曾被接去離開你，你要我為你做甚麼，只管求我。"

以利沙說："願感動你的靈加倍地感動我。"

¹⁰以利亞說："你所求的難得。雖然如此，我被接去離開你的時候，你若看見我，就必得着；不然，必得不着了。"

¹¹他們正走着說話，忽有火車火馬將二人隔開，以利亞就乘旋風升天去了。¹²以利沙看見，就呼叫說："我父啊！我父啊！以色列的戰車馬兵啊！"以後不再見他了。於是以利沙把自己的衣服撕為兩片。

¹³他拾起以利亞身上掉下來的外衣，回去站在約旦河邊。¹⁴他用以利亞身上掉下來的外衣打水，說："耶和華，以利亞的神在哪裏呢？"打水之後，水也左右分開，以利沙就過來了。

¹⁵住耶利哥的先知門徒從對面看見他，就說："感動以利亞的靈感動以利沙了。"他們就來迎接他，在他面前俯伏於地，¹⁶對他說："僕人這裏有五十個壯士，求你容他們去尋找你師傅，或者耶和華的靈將他提起來，投在某山某谷。"

以利沙說："你們不必打發人去。"

¹⁷他們再三催促他，他難以推辭，就說："你們打發人去吧！"他們便打發五十人去，尋找了三天，也沒有找着。¹⁸以利沙仍然在耶利哥，等候他們回到他那裏；他對他們說："我豈沒有告訴你們不必去嗎？"

治好惡水

¹⁹耶利哥城的人對以利沙說：「這城的地勢美好，我主看見了；只是水惡劣，土產不熟而落。」

²⁰以利沙說：「你們拿一個新瓶來裝鹽給我。」他們就拿來給他。

²¹他出到水源，將鹽倒在水中，說：「耶和華如此說：『我治好了這水，從此必不再使人死，也不再使地土不生產。』」²²於是那水治好了，直到今日，正如以利沙所說的。

以利沙被嘲笑

²³以利沙從那裏上伯特利去。正上去的時候，有些童子從城裏出來，戲笑他說：「禿頭的上去吧！禿頭的上去吧！」²⁴他回頭看見，就奉耶和華的名咒詛他們。於是有兩個母熊從林中出來，撕裂他們中間四十二個童子。²⁵以利沙從伯特利上迦密山，又從迦密山回到撒馬利亞。

摩押背叛

3 猶大王約沙法十八年，亞哈的兒子約蘭在撒馬利亞登基，作了以色列王十二年。²他行耶和華眼中看為惡的事，但不至像他父母所行的，因為除掉他父所造巴力的柱像。³然而，他貼近尼八的兒子耶羅波安使以色列人陷在罪裏的那罪，總不離開。

⁴摩押王米沙牧養許多羊，每年將十萬羊羔的毛和十萬公綿羊的毛給以色列王進貢。⁵亞哈死後，摩押背叛以色列王。⁶那時約蘭王出撒馬利亞，數點以色列眾人。⁷前行的時候，差人去見猶大王約沙法，說：「摩押王背叛我，你肯同我去攻打摩押嗎？」

他說：「我肯上去。你我不分彼此，我的民與你的民一樣，我的馬與你的馬一樣。」

⁸約蘭說：「我們從哪條路上去呢？」回答說：「從以東曠野的路上去。」

⁹於是，以色列王和猶大王，並

Healing of the Water

¹⁹The men of the city said to Elisha, "Look, our lord, this town is well situated, as you can see, but the water is bad and the land is unproductive."

²⁰"Bring me a new bowl," he said, "and put salt in it." So they brought it to him.

²¹Then he went out to the spring and threw the salt into it, saying, "This is what the LORD says: 'I have healed this water. Never again will it cause death or make the land unproductive.'" ²²And the water has remained wholesome to this day, according to the word Elisha had spoken.

Elisha Is Jeered

²³From there Elisha went up to Bethel. As he was walking along the road, some youths came out of the town and jeered at him. "Go on up, you baldhead!" they said. "Go on up, you baldhead!" ²⁴He turned around, looked at them and called down a curse on them in the name of the LORD. Then two bears came out of the woods and mauled forty-two of the youths. ²⁵And he went on to Mount Carmel and from there returned to Samaria.

Moab Revolts

3 Joram[a] son of Ahab became king of Israel in Samaria in the eighteenth year of Jehoshaphat king of Judah, and he reigned twelve years. ²He did evil in the eyes of the LORD, but not as his father and mother had done. He got rid of the sacred stone of Baal that his father had made. ³Nevertheless he clung to the sins of Jeroboam son of Nebat, which he had caused Israel to commit; he did not turn away from them.

⁴Now Mesha king of Moab raised sheep, and he had to supply the king of Israel with a hundred thousand lambs and with the wool of a hundred thousand rams. ⁵But after Ahab died, the king of Moab rebelled against the king of Israel. ⁶So at that time King Joram set out from Samaria and mobilized all Israel. ⁷He also sent this message to Jehoshaphat king of Judah: "The king of Moab has rebelled against me. Will you go with me to fight against Moab?"

"I will go with you," he replied. "I am as you are, my people as your people, my horses as your horses."

⁸"By what route shall we attack?" he asked.

"Through the Desert of Edom," he answered.

⁹So the king of Israel set out with the king of Judah and the king of Edom. After a round-

---

a 1 Hebrew *Jehoram,* a variant of *Joram;* also in verse 6 about march of seven days, the army had no more water for themselves or for the animals with them.

¹⁰"What!" exclaimed the king of Israel. "Has the LORD called us three kings together only to hand us over to Moab?"

¹¹But Jehoshaphat asked, "Is there no prophet of the LORD here, that we may inquire of the LORD through him?"

An officer of the king of Israel answered, "Elisha son of Shaphat is here. He used to pour water on the hands of Elijah.ᵃ "

¹²Jehoshaphat said, "The word of the LORD is with him." So the king of Israel and Jehoshaphat and the king of Edom went down to him.

¹³Elisha said to the king of Israel, "What do we have to do with each other? Go to the prophets of your father and the prophets of your mother."

"No," the king of Israel answered, "because it was the LORD who called us three kings together to hand us over to Moab."

¹⁴Elisha said, "As surely as the LORD Almighty lives, whom I serve, if I did not have respect for the presence of Jehoshaphat king of Judah, I would not look at you or even notice you. ¹⁵But now bring me a harpist."

While the harpist was playing, the hand of the LORD came upon Elisha ¹⁶and he said, "This is what the LORD says: Make this valley full of ditches. ¹⁷For this is what the LORD says: You will see neither wind nor rain, yet this valley will be filled with water, and you, your cattle and your other animals will drink. ¹⁸This is an easy thing in the eyes of the LORD; he will also hand Moab over to you. ¹⁹You will overthrow every fortified city and every major town. You will cut down every good tree, stop up all the springs, and ruin every good field with stones."

²⁰The next morning, about the time for offering the sacrifice, there it was—water flowing from the direction of Edom! And the land was filled with water.

²¹Now all the Moabites had heard that the kings had come to fight against them; so every man, young and old, who could bear arms was called up and stationed on the border. ²²When they got up early in the morning, the sun was shining on the water. To the Moabites across the way, the water looked red—like blood. ²³"That's blood!" they said. "Those kings must have fought and slaughtered each other. Now to the plunder, Moab!"

²⁴But when the Moabites came to the camp of Israel, the Israelites rose up and fought them

ᵃ 11 That is, he was Elijah's personal servant.

以東王，都一同去繞行七日的路程，軍隊和所帶的牲畜沒有水喝。

¹⁰以色列王說："哀哉！耶和華招聚我們這三王，乃要交在摩押人的手裏。"

¹¹約沙法說："這裏不是有耶和華的先知嗎？我們可以託他求問耶和華。"

以色列王的一個臣子回答說："這裏有沙法的兒子以利沙，就是從前服侍以利亞的（註：原文作"倒水在以利亞手上的"）。"

¹²約沙法說："他必有耶和華的話。"於是，以色列王和約沙法，並以東王，都下去見他。

¹³以利沙對以色列王說："我與你何干？去問你父親的先知和你母親的先知吧！"

以色列王對他說："不要這樣說，耶和華招聚我們這三王，乃要交在摩押人的手裏。"

¹⁴以利沙說："我指著所侍奉永生的萬軍耶和華起誓，我若不看猶大王約沙法的情面，必不理你，不顧你。¹⁵現在你們給我找一個彈琴的來。"

彈琴的時候，耶和華的靈（註：原文作"手"）就降在以利沙身上。¹⁶他便說："耶和華如此說：'你們要在這谷中滿處挖溝。'¹⁷因為耶和華如此說：'你們雖不見風，不見雨，這谷必滿了水，使你們和牲畜有水喝。'¹⁸在耶和華眼中這還算為小事，他也必將摩押人交在你們手中。¹⁹你們必攻破一切堅城美邑，砍伐各種佳樹，塞住一切水泉，用石頭糟踏一切美田。"

²⁰次日早晨，約在獻祭的時候，有水從以東而來，遍地就滿了水。

²¹摩押眾人聽見這三王上來要與他們爭戰，凡能頂盔貫甲的，無論老少，盡都聚集，站在邊界上。²²次日早晨，日光照在水上。摩押人起來，看見對面水紅如血，²³就說："這是血啊！必是三王互相擊殺，俱都滅亡。摩押人哪，我們現在去搶奪財物吧！"

²⁴摩押人到了以色列營，以色列人就起來攻打他們，以致他們在以色

列人面前逃跑。以色列人往前追殺摩押人，直殺入摩押的境內，25拆毀摩押的城邑。各人拋石填滿一切美田，塞住一切水泉，砍伐各種佳樹，只剩下吉珥哈列設的石牆，甩石的兵在四圍攻打那城。

26摩押王見陣勢甚大，難以對敵，就率領七百拿刀的兵，要衝過陣去到以東王那裏，卻是不能，27便將那應當接續他作王的長子，在城上獻為燔祭。以色列人遭遇耶和華的大怒（註：或作「招人痛恨」），於是三王離開摩押王，各回本國去了。

寡婦的油

4 有一個先知門徒的妻，哀求以利沙說：「你僕人我丈夫死了，他敬畏耶和華是你所知道的。現在有債主來，要取我兩個兒子作奴僕。」

2以利沙問她說：「我可以為你做甚麼呢？你告訴我，你家裏有甚麼？」

她說：「婢女家中除了一瓶油之外，沒有甚麼。」

3以利沙說：「你去，向你眾鄰舍借空器皿，不要少借。4回到家裏，關上門，你和你兒子在裏面，將油倒在所有的器皿裏，倒滿了的放在一邊。」

5於是，婦人離開以利沙去了，關上門，自己和兒子在裏面。兒子把器皿拿來，她就倒油，6器皿都滿了。她對兒子說：「再給我拿器皿來。」

兒子說：「再沒有器皿了。」油就止住了。

7婦人去告訴神人。神人說：「你去賣油還債，所剩的，你和你兒子可以靠着度日。」

書念婦人兒子復活

8一日，以利沙走到書念，在那裏有一個大戶的婦人強留他吃飯。此後，以利沙每過那裏經過，就進去吃飯。9婦人對丈夫說：「我看出那常從我們這裏經過的是聖潔的神人。10我們可以為他在牆上蓋一間小樓，在其中安放牀榻、桌子、椅子、燈臺，他來到我們這裏，就可以住在其間。」

11一日，以利沙來到那裏，就進了那樓躺臥。12以利沙吩咐僕人基哈

until they fled. And the Israelites invaded the land and slaughtered the Moabites. 25They destroyed the towns, and each man threw a stone on every good field until it was covered. They stopped up all the springs and cut down every good tree. Only Kir Hareseth was left with its stones in place, but men armed with slings surrounded it and attacked it as well.

26When the king of Moab saw that the battle had gone against him, he took with him seven hundred swordsmen to break through to the king of Edom, but they failed. 27Then he took his firstborn son, who was to succeed him as king, and offered him as a sacrifice on the city wall. The fury against Israel was great; they withdrew and returned to their own land.

The Widow's Oil

4 The wife of a man from the company of the prophets cried out to Elisha, "Your servant my husband is dead, and you know that he revered the LORD. But now his creditor is coming to take my two boys as his slaves."

2Elisha replied to her, "How can I help you? Tell me, what do you have in your house?"

"Your servant has nothing there at all," she said, "except a little oil."

3Elisha said, "Go around and ask all your neighbors for empty jars. Don't ask for just a few. 4Then go inside and shut the door behind you and your sons. Pour the oil into all the jars, and as each is filled, put it to one side."

5She left him and afterward shut the door behind her and her sons. They brought the jars to her and she kept pouring. 6When all the jars were full, she said to her son, "Bring me another one."

But he replied, "There is not a jar left." Then the oil stopped flowing.

7She went and told the man of God, and he said, "Go, sell the oil and pay your debts. You and your sons can live on what is left."

The Shunammite's Son Restored to Life

8One day Elisha went to Shunem. And a well-to-do woman was there, who urged him to stay for a meal. So whenever he came by, he stopped there to eat. 9She said to her husband, "I know that this man who often comes our way is a holy man of God. 10Let's make a small room on the roof and put in it a bed and a table, a chair and a lamp for him. Then he can stay there whenever he comes to us."

11One day when Elisha came, he went up to his room and lay down there. 12He said to his servant Gehazi, "Call the Shunammite." So he called her, and she stood before him. [13]Elisha said to him, "Tell her, 'You have gone to all this trouble for us. Now what can be done for you? Can we speak on your behalf to the king or the commander of the army?' "

She replied, "I have a home among my own people."

[14]"What can be done for her?" Elisha asked.

Gehazi said, "Well, she has no son and her husband is old."

[15]Then Elisha said, "Call her." So he called her, and she stood in the doorway. [16]"About this time next year," Elisha said, "you will hold a son in your arms."

"No, my lord," she objected. "Don't mislead your servant, O man of God!"

[17]But the woman became pregnant, and the next year about that same time she gave birth to a son, just as Elisha had told her.

[18]The child grew, and one day he went out to his father, who was with the reapers. [19]"My head! My head!" he said to his father.

His father told a servant, "Carry him to his mother." [20]After the servant had lifted him up and carried him to his mother, the boy sat on her lap until noon, and then he died. [21]She went up and laid him on the bed of the man of God, then shut the door and went out.

[22]She called her husband and said, "Please send me one of the servants and a donkey so I can go to the man of God quickly and return."

[23]"Why go to him today?" he asked. "It's not the New Moon or the Sabbath."

"It's all right," she said.

[24]She saddled the donkey and said to her servant, "Lead on; don't slow down for me unless I tell you." [25]So she set out and came to the man of God at Mount Carmel.

When he saw her in the distance, the man of God said to his servant Gehazi, "Look! There's the Shunammite! [26]Run to meet her and ask her, 'Are you all right? Is your husband all right? Is your child all right?' "

"Everything is all right," she said.

[27]When she reached the man of God at the mountain, she took hold of his feet. Gehazi came over to push her away, but the man of God said, "Leave her alone! She is in bitter distress, but the LORD has hidden it from me and has not told me why."

[28]"Did I ask you for a son, my lord?" she said. "Didn't I tell you, 'Don't raise my hopes'?"

[29]Elisha said to Gehazi, "Tuck your cloak into your belt, take my staff in your hand and run. If you meet anyone, do not greet him, and if any-

西說："你叫這書念婦人來。"他就把婦人叫了來。婦人站在以利沙面前。[13]以利沙吩咐僕人說："你對她說：'你既為我們費了許多心思，可以為你做甚麼呢？你向王或元帥有所求的沒有？'"

她回答說："我在我本鄉安居無事。"

[14]以利沙對僕人說："究竟當為她做甚麼呢？"基哈西說："她沒有兒子，她丈夫也老了。"

[15]以利沙說："再叫她來。"於是叫了她來，她就站在門口。[16]以利沙說："明年到這時候，你必抱一個兒子。"

她說："神人，我主啊！不要那樣欺哄婢女。"

[17]婦人果然懷孕，到了那時候，生了一個兒子，正如以利沙所說的。

[18]孩子漸漸長大，一日，到他父親和收割的人那裏。[19]他對父親說："我的頭啊，我的頭啊！"

他父親對僕人說："把他抱到他母親那裏。"[20]僕人抱去，交給他母親，孩子坐在母親的膝上，到晌午就死了。[21]他母親抱他上了樓，將他放在神人的牀上，關上門出來。

[22]呼叫她丈夫說："你叫一個僕人給我牽一匹驢來，我要快快地去見神人就回來。"

[23]丈夫說："今日不是月朔，也不是安息日，你為何要去見他呢？"

婦人說："平安無事。"

[24]於是備上驢，對僕人說："你快快趕着走，我若不吩咐你，就不要遲慢。"[25]婦人就往迦密山去見神人。

神人遠遠地看見她，對僕人基哈西說："看哪，書念的婦人來了。[26]你跑去迎接她，問她說：'你平安嗎？你丈夫平安嗎？孩子平安嗎？'"

她說："平安。"

[27]婦人上了山，到神人那裏，就抱住神人的腳。基哈西前來要推開她，神人說："由她吧！因為她心裏愁苦，耶和華向我隱瞞，沒有指示我。"

[28]婦人說："我何嘗向我主求過兒子呢？我豈沒有說過，不要欺哄我嗎？"

[29]以利沙吩咐基哈西說："你束上腰，手拿我的杖前去。若遇見人，不

要向他問安；人若向你問安，也不要回答；要把我的杖放在孩子臉上。"

30孩子的母親說："我指着永生的耶和華，又敢在你面前起誓，我必不離開你。"於是以利沙起身，隨着她去了。

31基哈西先去，把杖放在孩子臉上，卻沒有聲音，也沒有動靜。基哈西就迎着以利沙回來，告訴他說："孩子還沒有醒過來。"

32以利沙來到，進了屋子，看見孩子死了，放在自己的牀上。33他就關上門，只有自己和孩子在裏面。他便祈禱耶和華，34上牀伏在孩子身上，口對口、眼對眼、手對手，既伏在孩子身上，孩子的身體就漸漸溫和了。35然後他下來，在屋裏來往走了一趟，又上去伏在孩子身上，孩子打了七個噴嚏，就睜開眼睛了。

36以利沙叫基哈西說："你叫這書念婦人來。"於是叫了她來。以利沙說："將你兒子抱起來！"37婦人就進來，在以利沙腳前俯伏於地，抱起她兒子出去了。

鍋中有致死毒物

38以利沙又來到吉甲。那地正有饑荒，先知門徒坐在他面前，他吩咐僕人說："你將大鍋放在火上，給先知門徒熬湯。"

39有一個人去到田野掐菜，遇見一棵野瓜藤，就摘了一兜野瓜回來，切了擺在熬湯的鍋中。因為他們不知道是甚麼東西，40倒出來給人吃。吃的時候，都喊叫說："神人啊，鍋中有致死的毒物！"所以眾人不能吃了。

41以利沙說："拿點麵來。"就把麵撒在鍋中，說："倒出來，給眾人吃吧！"鍋中就沒有毒了。

餵飽一百人

42有一個人從巴力沙利沙來，帶着初熟大麥做的餅二十個，並新穗子裝在口袋裏，送給神人。神人說："把這些給眾人吃。"

43僕人說："這一點豈可擺給一百人吃呢？"

以利沙說："你只管給眾人吃吧！因為耶和華如此說：'眾人必吃了，還剩下。'"44僕人就擺在眾人

one greets you, do not answer. Lay my staff on the boy's face."

30But the child's mother said, "As surely as the LORD lives and as you live, I will not leave you." So he got up and followed her.

31Gehazi went on ahead and laid the staff on the boy's face, but there was no sound or response. So Gehazi went back to meet Elisha and told him, "The boy has not awakened."

32When Elisha reached the house, there was the boy lying dead on his couch. 33He went in, shut the door on the two of them and prayed to the LORD. 34Then he got on the bed and lay upon the boy, mouth to mouth, eyes to eyes, hands to hands. As he stretched himself out upon him, the boy's body grew warm. 35Elisha turned away and walked back and forth in the room and then got on the bed and stretched out upon him once more. The boy sneezed seven times and opened his eyes.

36Elisha summoned Gehazi and said, "Call the Shunammite." And he did. When she came, he said, "Take your son." 37She came in, fell at his feet and bowed to the ground. Then she took her son and went out.

Death in the Pot

38Elisha returned to Gilgal and there was a famine in that region. While the company of the prophets was meeting with him, he said to his servant, "Put on the large pot and cook some stew for these men."

39One of them went out into the fields to gather herbs and found a wild vine. He gathered some of its gourds and filled the fold of his cloak. When he returned, he cut them up into the pot of stew, though no one knew what they were. 40The stew was poured out for the men, but as they began to eat it, they cried out, "O man of God, there is death in the pot!" And they could not eat it.

41Elisha said, "Get some flour." He put it into the pot and said, "Serve it to the people to eat." And there was nothing harmful in the pot.

Feeding of a Hundred

42A man came from Baal Shalishah, bringing the man of God twenty loaves of barley bread baked from the first ripe grain, along with some heads of new grain. "Give it to the people to eat," Elisha said.

43"How can I set this before a hundred men?" his servant asked.

But Elisha answered, "Give it to the people to eat. For this is what the LORD says: 'They will eat and have some left over.'" 44Then he set it before them, and they ate and had some left over, according to the word of the LORD.

Naaman Healed of Leprosy

5 Now Naaman was commander of the army of the king of Aram. He was a great man in the sight of his master and highly regarded, because through him the LORD had given victory to Aram. He was a valiant soldier, but he had leprosy.[a]

2Now bands from Aram had gone out and had taken captive a young girl from Israel, and she served Naaman's wife. 3She said to her mistress, "If only my master would see the prophet who is in Samaria! He would cure him of his leprosy."

4Naaman went to his master and told him what the girl from Israel had said. 5"By all means, go," the king of Aram replied. "I will send a letter to the king of Israel." So Naaman left, taking with him ten talents[b] of silver, six thousand shekels[c] of gold and ten sets of clothing. 6The letter that he took to the king of Israel read: "With this letter I am sending my servant Naaman to you so that you may cure him of his leprosy."

7As soon as the king of Israel read the letter, he tore his robes and said, "Am I God? Can I kill and bring back to life? Why does this fellow send someone to me to be cured of his leprosy? See how he is trying to pick a quarrel with me!"

8When Elisha the man of God heard that the king of Israel had torn his robes, he sent him this message: "Why have you torn your robes? Have the man come to me and he will know that there is a prophet in Israel." 9So Naaman went with his horses and chariots and stopped at the door of Elisha's house. 10Elisha sent a messenger to say to him, "Go, wash yourself seven times in the Jordan, and your flesh will be restored and you will be cleansed."

11But Naaman went away angry and said, "I thought that he would surely come out to me and stand and call on the name of the LORD his God, wave his hand over the spot and cure me of my leprosy. 12Are not Abana and Pharpar, the rivers of Damascus, better than any of the waters of Israel? Couldn't I wash in them and be cleansed?" So he turned and went off in a rage.

13Naaman's servants went to him and said, "My father, if the prophet had told you to do some great thing, would you not have done it?

---

a 1 The Hebrew word was used for various diseases affecting the skin—not necessarily leprosy; also in verses 3, 6, 7, 11 and 27.   b 5 That is, about 750 pounds (about 340 kilograms)
c 5 That is, about 150 pounds (about 70 kilograms)

面前，他們吃了，果然還剩下，正如耶和華所說的。

乃縵大痲瘋得醫治

5 亞蘭王的元帥乃縵，在他主人面前為尊為大，因耶和華曾藉他使亞蘭人得勝；他又是大能的勇士，只是長了大痲瘋。

2先前亞蘭人成羣地出去，從以色列國擄了一個小女子，這女子就服侍乃縵的妻。3她對主母說：「巴不得我主人去見撒馬利亞的先知，必能治好他的大痲瘋。」

4乃縵進去，告訴他主人說，以色列國的女子如此如此說。5亞蘭王說：「你可以去，我也達信於以色列王。」於是，乃縵帶銀子十他連得、金子六千舍客勒、衣裳十套，就去了，6且帶信給以色列王，信上說：「我打發臣僕乃縵去見你，你接到這信，就要治好他的大痲瘋。」

7以色列王看了信，就撕裂衣服，說：「我豈是神，能使人死、使人活呢？這人竟打發人來，叫我治好他的大痲瘋。你們看一看，這人何以尋隙攻擊我呢？」

8神人以利沙聽見以色列王撕裂衣服，就打發人去見王，說：「你為甚麼撕了衣服呢？可使那人到我這裏來，他就知道以色列中有先知了。」9於是，乃縵帶着車馬到了以利沙的家，站在門前。10以利沙打發一個使者對乃縵說：「你去在約旦河中沐浴七回，你的肉就必復原，而得潔淨。」

11乃縵卻發怒走了，說：「我想他必定出來見我，站着求告耶和華他神的名，在患處以上搖手，治好這大痲瘋。12大馬士革的河亞罷拿和法珥法，豈不比以色列的一切水更好嗎？我在那裏沐浴不得潔淨嗎？」於是氣忿忿地轉身去了。

13他的僕人進前來對他說：「我父啊！先知若吩咐你做一件大事，你豈不做嗎？何況說你去沐浴而得潔淨呢？"¹⁴於是乃縵下去，照着神人的話，在約旦河裏沐浴七回，他的肉復原，好像小孩子的肉，他就潔淨了。

¹⁵乃縵帶着一切跟隨他的人，回到神人那裏，站在他面前說："如今我知道，除了以色列之外，普天下沒有神。現在求你收點僕人的禮物。"

¹⁶以利沙說："我指着所侍奉永生的耶和華起誓，我必不受。"乃縵再三地求他，他卻不受。

¹⁷乃縵說："你若不肯受，請將兩騾子馱的土賜給僕人。從今以後，僕人必不再將燔祭或平安祭獻與別神，只獻給耶和華。¹⁸惟有一件事，願耶和華饒恕你僕人：我主人進臨門廟叩拜的時候，我用手攙他在臨門廟，我也屈身。我在臨門廟屈身的這事，願耶和華饒恕我。"

¹⁹以利沙對他說："你可以平平安安地回去。"

乃縵就離開他去了，走了不遠，²⁰神人以利沙的僕人基哈西心裏說："我主人不願從這亞蘭人乃縵手裏受他帶來的禮物，我指着永生的耶和華起誓，我必跑去追上他，向他要些。"

²¹於是基哈西追趕乃縵。乃縵看見有人追趕，就急忙下車迎着他說："都平安嗎？"

²²說："都平安。我主人打發我來說：'剛才有兩個少年人，是先知門徒，從以法蓮山地來見我。請你賜他們一他連得銀子、兩套衣裳。'"

²³乃縵說："請受二他連得。"再三地請受，便將二他連得銀子裝在兩個口袋裏，又將兩套衣裳交給兩個僕人，他們就在基哈西前頭抬着走。²⁴到了山岡，基哈西從他們手中接過來，放在屋裏，打發他們回去。²⁵基哈西進去，站在他主人面前。

How much more, then, when he tells you, 'Wash and be cleansed'!" ¹⁴So he went down and dipped himself in the Jordan seven times, as the man of God had told him, and his flesh was restored and became clean like that of a young boy.

¹⁵Then Naaman and all his attendants went back to the man of God. He stood before him and said, "Now I know that there is no God in all the world except in Israel. Please accept now a gift from your servant."

¹⁶The prophet answered, "As surely as the LORD lives, whom I serve, I will not accept a thing." And even though Naaman urged him, he refused.

¹⁷"If you will not," said Naaman, "please let me, your servant, be given as much earth as a pair of mules can carry, for your servant will never again make burnt offerings and sacrifices to any other god but the LORD. ¹⁸But may the LORD forgive your servant for this one thing: When my master enters the temple of Rimmon to bow down and he is leaning on my arm and I bow there also—when I bow down in the temple of Rimmon, may the LORD forgive your servant for this."

¹⁹"Go in peace," Elisha said.

After Naaman had traveled some distance, ²⁰Gehazi, the servant of Elisha the man of God, said to himself, "My master was too easy on Naaman, this Aramean, by not accepting from him what he brought. As surely as the LORD lives, I will run after him and get something from him."

²¹So Gehazi hurried after Naaman. When Naaman saw him running toward him, he got down from the chariot to meet him. "Is everything all right?" he asked.

²²"Everything is all right," Gehazi answered. "My master sent me to say, 'Two young men from the company of the prophets have just come to me from the hill country of Ephraim. Please give them a talent*a* of silver and two sets of clothing.'"

²³"By all means, take two talents," said Naaman. He urged Gehazi to accept them, and then tied up the two talents of silver in two bags, with two sets of clothing. He gave them to two of his servants, and they carried them ahead of Gehazi. ²⁴When Gehazi came to the hill, he took the things from the servants and put them away in the house. He sent the men away and they left. ²⁵Then he went in and stood before his master Elisha.

a 22 That is, about 75 pounds (about 34 kilograms)

"Where have you been, Gehazi?" Elisha asked.

"Your servant didn't go anywhere," Gehazi answered.

26But Elisha said to him, "Was not my spirit with you when the man got down from his chariot to meet you? Is this the time to take money, or to accept clothes, olive groves, vineyards, flocks, herds, or menservants and maidservants? 27Naaman's leprosy will cling to you and to your descendants forever." Then Gehazi went from Elisha's presence and he was leprous, as white as snow.

An Axhead Floats

6 The company of the prophets said to Elisha, "Look, the place where we meet with you is too small for us. 2Let us go to the Jordan, where each of us can get a pole; and let us build a place there for us to live."

And he said, "Go."

3Then one of them said, "Won't you please come with your servants?"

"I will," Elisha replied. 4And he went with them.

They went to the Jordan and began to cut down trees. 5As one of them was cutting down a tree, the iron axhead fell into the water. "Oh, my lord," he cried out, "it was borrowed!"

6The man of God asked, "Where did it fall?" When he showed him the place, Elisha cut a stick and threw it there, and made the iron float.

7"Lift it out," he said. Then the man reached out his hand and took it.

Elisha Traps Blinded Arameans

8Now the king of Aram was at war with Israel. After conferring with his officers, he said, "I will set up my camp in such and such a place."

9The man of God sent word to the king of Israel: "Beware of passing that place, because the Arameans are going down there." 10So the king of Israel checked on the place indicated by the man of God. Time and again Elisha warned the king, so that he was on his guard in such places.

11This enraged the king of Aram. He summoned his officers and demanded of them, "Will you not tell me which of us is on the side of the king of Israel?"

12"None of us, my lord the king," said one of his officers, "but Elisha, the prophet who is in Israel, tells the king of Israel the very words you speak in your bedroom."

13"Go, find out where he is," the king

以利沙問他說："基哈西你從哪裏來？"

回答說："僕人沒有往哪裏去。"

26以利沙對他說："那人下車轉回迎你的時候，我的心豈沒有去呢？這豈是受銀子、衣裳、買橄欖園、葡萄園、牛羊、僕婢的時候呢？27因此，乃縵的大痲瘋必沾染你和你的後裔，直到永遠。"基哈西從以利沙面前退出去，就長了大痲瘋，像雪那樣白。

斧頭浮起

6 先知門徒對以利沙說："看哪，我們同你所住的地方過於窄小，2求你容我們往約旦河去，各人從那裏取一根木料建造房屋居住。"

他說："你們去吧！"

3有一人說："求你與僕人同去。"

回答說："我可以去。"4於是以利沙與他們同去。

到了約旦河，就砍伐樹木。5有一人砍樹的時候，斧頭掉在水裏，他就呼叫說："哀哉！我主啊，這斧子是借的。"

6神人問說："掉在哪裏了？"他將那地方指給以利沙看。以利沙砍了一根木頭，拋在水裏，斧頭就漂上來了。7以利沙說："拿起來吧！"那人就伸手拿起來了。

以利沙令亞蘭軍眼目昏迷

8亞蘭王與以色列人爭戰，和他的臣僕商議說："我要在某處某處安營。"

9神人打發人去見以色列王，說："你要謹慎，不要從某處經過，因為亞蘭人從那裏下來了。"10以色列王差人去窺探神人所告訴、所警戒他去的地方，就防備未受其害，不止一兩次。

11亞蘭王因這事心裏驚疑，召了臣僕來，對他們說："我們這裏有誰幫助以色列王，你們不指給我嗎？"

12有一個臣僕說："我主我王，無人幫助他，只有以色列中的先知以利沙，將王在臥房所說的話，告訴以色列王了。"

13王說："你們去探他在哪裏，

我好打發人去捉拿他。"有人告訴王
說："他在多坍。"¹⁴王就打發車馬和
大軍往那裏去。夜間到了，圍困那
城。

¹⁵神人的僕人清早起來出去，看
見車馬軍兵圍困了城。僕人對神人
說："哀哉！我主啊，我們怎樣行才
好呢？"

¹⁶神人說："不要懼怕！與我們
同在的，比與他們同在的更多。"

¹⁷以利沙禱告說："耶和華啊，
求你開這少年人的眼目，使他能看
見。"耶和華開他的眼目，他就看見
滿山有火車火馬圍繞以利沙。

¹⁸敵人下到以利沙那裏，以利沙
禱告耶和華說："求你使這些人的眼
目昏迷。"耶和華就照以利沙的話，
使他們的眼目昏迷。

¹⁹以利沙對他們說："這不是那
道，也不是那城，你們跟我去，我必
領你們到所尋找的人那裏。"於是，
領他們到了撒馬利亞。

²⁰他們進了撒馬利亞。以利沙禱
告說："耶和華啊，求你開這些人的
眼目，使他們能看見。"耶和華開他
們的眼目，他們就看見了。不料，是
在撒馬利亞的城中。

²¹以色列王見了他們。就問以利
沙說："我父啊，我可以擊殺他們
嗎？"

²²回答說："不可擊殺他們。就是
你用刀用弓擄來的，豈可擊殺他們嗎
（註：或作"也不可擊殺，何況這些人
呢？"）？當在他們面前設擺飲食，使
他們吃喝，回到他們的主人那裏。"
²³王就為他們預備了許多食物。他們吃
喝完了，打發他們回到他們主人那裏。
從此，亞蘭軍不再犯以色列境了。

圍城撒馬利亞的饑荒

²⁴此後，亞蘭王便哈達聚集他的
全軍，上來圍困撒馬利亞。²⁵於是撒
馬利亞被圍困，有饑荒，甚至一個驢
頭值銀八十舍客勒，二升鴿子糞值銀
五舍客勒。

²⁶一日，以色列王在城上經過，
有一個婦人向他呼叫說："我主、我
王啊，求你幫助！"

ordered, "so I can send men and capture him."
The report came back: "He is in Dothan." ¹⁴Then
he sent horses and chariots and a strong force
there. They went by night and surrounded the
city.

¹⁵When the servant of the man of God got up
and went out early the next morning, an army
with horses and chariots had surrounded the
city. "Oh, my lord, what shall we do?" the servant asked.

¹⁶"Don't be afraid," the prophet answered.
"Those who are with us are more than those
who are with them."

¹⁷And Elisha prayed, "O LORD, open his eyes
so he may see." Then the LORD opened the servant's eyes, and he looked and saw the hills full
of horses and chariots of fire all around Elisha.

¹⁸As the enemy came down toward him,
Elisha prayed to the LORD, "Strike these people
with blindness." So he struck them with blindness, as Elisha had asked.

¹⁹Elisha told them, "This is not the road and
this is not the city. Follow me, and I will lead
you to the man you are looking for." And he led
them to Samaria.

²⁰After they entered the city, Elisha said,
"LORD, open the eyes of these men so they can
see." Then the LORD opened their eyes and they
looked, and there they were, inside Samaria.

²¹When the king of Israel saw them, he asked
Elisha, "Shall I kill them, my father? Shall I kill
them?"

²²"Do not kill them," he answered. "Would
you kill men you have captured with your own
sword or bow? Set food and water before them
so that they may eat and drink and then go back
to their master." ²³So he prepared a great feast
for them, and after they had finished eating and
drinking, he sent them away, and they returned
to their master. So the bands from Aram
stopped raiding Israel's territory.

Famine in Besieged Samaria

²⁴Some time later, Ben-Hadad king of Aram
mobilized his entire army and marched up and
laid siege to Samaria. ²⁵There was a great famine
in the city; the siege lasted so long that a donkey's head sold for eighty shekels*ᵃ* of silver, and
a quarter of a cab*ᵇ* of seed pods*ᶜ* for five shekels.*ᵈ*

²⁶As the king of Israel was passing by on the
wall, a woman cried to him, "Help me, my lord
the king!"

a 25 That is, about 2 pounds (about 1 kilogram)　*b 25* That is,
probably about 1/2 pint (about 0.3 liter)　*c 25* Or *of dove's
dung*　*d 25* That is, about 2 ounces (about 55 grams)

27The king replied, "If the LORD does not help you, where can I get help for you? From the threshing floor? From the winepress?" 28Then he asked her, "What's the matter?"

She answered, "This woman said to me, 'Give up your son so we may eat him today, and tomorrow we'll eat my son.' 29So we cooked my son and ate him. The next day I said to her, 'Give up your son so we may eat him,' but she had hidden him."

30When the king heard the woman's words, he tore his robes. As he went along the wall, the people looked, and there, underneath, he had sackcloth on his body. 31He said, "May God deal with me, be it ever so severely, if the head of Elisha son of Shaphat remains on his shoulders today!"

32Now Elisha was sitting in his house, and the elders were sitting with him. The king sent a messenger ahead, but before he arrived, Elisha said to the elders, "Don't you see how this murderer is sending someone to cut off my head? Look, when the messenger comes, shut the door and hold it shut against him. Is not the sound of his master's footsteps behind him?"

33While he was still talking to them, the messenger came down to him. And ⌊the king⌋ said, "This disaster is from the LORD. Why should I wait for the LORD any longer?"

7 Elisha said, "Hear the word of the LORD. This is what the LORD says: About this time tomorrow, a seah*a* of flour will sell for a shekel*b* and two seahs*c* of barley for a shekel at the gate of Samaria."

2The officer on whose arm the king was leaning said to the man of God, "Look, even if the LORD should open the floodgates of the heavens, could this happen?"

"You will see it with your own eyes," answered Elisha, "but you will not eat any of it!"

The Siege Lifted

3Now there were four men with leprosy*d* at the entrance of the city gate. They said to each other, "Why stay here until we die? 4If we say, 'We'll go into the city'—the famine is there, and we will die. And if we stay here, we will die. So let's go over to the camp of the Arameans and

27王説：“耶和華不幫助你，我從何處幫助你？是從禾場、是從酒醡呢？” 28王問婦人説：“你有甚麼苦處？”

她回答説：“這婦人對我説：‘將你的兒子取來，我們今日可以吃，明日可以吃我的兒子。’ 29我們就煮了我的兒子吃了。次日我對她説：‘要將你的兒子取來，我們可以吃。’她卻將她的兒子藏起來了。”

30王聽見婦人的話，就撕裂衣服（王在城上經過），百姓看見王貼身穿着麻衣。31王説：“我今日若容沙法的兒子以利沙的頭仍在他項上，願神重重地降罰與我！”

32那時，以利沙正坐在家中，長老也與他同坐。王打發一個伺候他的人去，他還沒有到，以利沙對長老説：“你們看這兇手之子，打發人來斬我的頭。你們看看使者來到，就關上門，用門將他推出去。在他後頭不是有他主人腳步的響聲嗎？”

33正説話的時候，使者來到，王也到了，説：“這災禍是從耶和華那裏來的，我何必再仰望耶和華呢？”

7 以利沙説：“你們要聽耶和華的話。耶和華如此説：明日約到這時候，在撒馬利亞城門口，一細亞細麵要賣銀一舍客勒，二細亞大麥也要賣銀一舍客勒。”

2有一個攙扶王的軍長對神人説：“即便耶和華使天開了窗戶，也不能有這事。”

以利沙説：“你必親眼看見，卻不得吃。”

圍困解除

3在城門那裏有四個長大痲瘋的人，他們彼此説：“我們為何坐在這裏等死呢？4我們若説：‘進城去吧’，城裏有饑荒，必死在那裏；若在這裏坐着不動，也必是死。來吧！我們去投降亞蘭人的軍隊，他們若留

a 1 That is, probably about 7 quarts (about 7.3 liters); also in verses 16 and 18 　*b 1* That is, about 2/5 ounce (about 11 grams); also in verses 16 and 18 　*c 1* That is, probably about 13 quarts (about 15 liters); also in verses 16 and 18 　*d 3* The Hebrew word is used for various diseases affecting the skin—not necessarily leprosy; also in verse 8.

我們的活命，就活着；若殺我們，就死了吧！」

⁵黃昏的時候，他們起來往亞蘭人的營盤去；到了營邊，不見一人在那裏。⁶因為主使亞蘭人的軍隊聽見車馬的聲音，是大軍的聲音。他們就彼此說：「這必是以色列王賄買赫人的諸王和埃及人的諸王來攻擊我們。」⁷所以，在黃昏的時候，他們起來逃跑，撇下帳棚、馬、驢，營盤照舊，只顧逃命。

⁸那些長大痲瘋的到了營邊，進了帳棚，吃了喝了，且從其中拿出金銀和衣服來，去收藏了；回來，又進了一座帳棚，從其中拿出財物來，去收藏了。

⁹那時，他們彼此說：「我們所做的不好！今日是有好信息的日子，我們竟不做聲！若等到天亮，罪必臨到我們。來吧，我們與王家報信去！」

¹⁰他們就去叫守城門的，告訴他們說：「我們到了亞蘭人的營，不見一人在那裏，也無人聲，只有拴着的馬和驢，帳棚都照舊。」¹¹守城門的叫了眾守門的人來，他們就進去與王家報信。

¹²王夜間起來，對臣僕說：「我告訴你們亞蘭人向我們如何行：他們知道我們飢餓，所以離營，埋伏在田野，說：『以色列人出城的時候，我們就活捉他們，得以進城。』」

¹³有一個臣僕對王說：「我們不如用城裏剩下之馬中的五匹馬（馬和城裏剩下的以色列人都是一樣，快要滅絕），打發人去窺探。」

¹⁴於是取了兩輛車和馬，王差人去追尋亞蘭軍，說：「你們去窺探窺探。」¹⁵他們就追尋到約旦河，看見滿道上都是亞蘭人急跑時丟棄的衣服、器具。使者就回來報告王。¹⁶眾人就出去，擄掠亞蘭人的營盤。於是一細亞細麵賣銀一舍客勒，二細亞大麥也賣銀一舍客勒，正如耶和華所說的。

surrender. If they spare us, we live; if they kill us, then we die."

⁵At dusk they got up and went to the camp of the Arameans. When they reached the edge of the camp, not a man was there, ⁶for the Lord had caused the Arameans to hear the sound of chariots and horses and a great army, so that they said to one another, "Look, the king of Israel has hired the Hittite and Egyptian kings to attack us!" ⁷So they got up and fled in the dusk and abandoned their tents and their horses and donkeys. They left the camp as it was and ran for their lives.

⁸The men who had leprosy reached the edge of the camp and entered one of the tents. They ate and drank, and carried away silver, gold and clothes, and went off and hid them. They returned and entered another tent and took some things from it and hid them also.

⁹Then they said to each other, "We're not doing right. This is a day of good news and we are keeping it to ourselves. If we wait until daylight, punishment will overtake us. Let's go at once and report this to the royal palace."

¹⁰So they went and called out to the city gatekeepers and told them, "We went into the Aramean camp and not a man was there—not a sound of anyone—only tethered horses and donkeys, and the tents left just as they were." ¹¹The gatekeepers shouted the news, and it was reported within the palace.

¹²The king got up in the night and said to his officers, "I will tell you what the Arameans have done to us. They know we are starving; so they have left the camp to hide in the countryside, thinking, 'They will surely come out, and then we will take them alive and get into the city.'"

¹³One of his officers answered, "Have some men take five of the horses that are left in the city. Their plight will be like that of all the Israelites left here—yes, they will only be like all these Israelites who are doomed. So let us send them to find out what happened."

¹⁴So they selected two chariots with their horses, and the king sent them after the Aramean army. He commanded the drivers, "Go and find out what has happened." ¹⁵They followed them as far as the Jordan, and they found the whole road strewn with the clothing and equipment the Arameans had thrown away in their headlong flight. So the messengers returned and reported to the king. ¹⁶Then the people went out and plundered the camp of the Arameans. So a seah of flour sold for a shekel, and two seahs of barley sold for a shekel, as the LORD had said.

17Now the king had put the officer on whose arm he leaned in charge of the gate, and the people trampled him in the gateway, and he died, just as the man of God had foretold when the king came down to his house. 18It happened as the man of God had said to the king: "About this time tomorrow, a seah of flour will sell for a shekel and two seahs of barley for a shekel at the gate of Samaria."

19The officer had said to the man of God, "Look, even if the LORD should open the floodgates of the heavens, could this happen?" The man of God had replied, "You will see it with your own eyes, but you will not eat any of it!" 20And that is exactly what happened to him, for the people trampled him in the gateway, and he died.

The Shunammite's Land Restored

8 Now Elisha had said to the woman whose son he had restored to life, "Go away with your family and stay for a while wherever you can, because the LORD has decreed a famine in the land that will last seven years." 2The woman proceeded to do as the man of God said. She and her family went away and stayed in the land of the Philistines seven years.

3At the end of the seven years she came back from the land of the Philistines and went to the king to beg for her house and land. 4The king was talking to Gehazi, the servant of the man of God, and had said, "Tell me about all the great things Elisha has done." 5Just as Gehazi was telling the king how Elisha had restored the dead to life, the woman whose son Elisha had brought back to life came to beg the king for her house and land.

Gehazi said, "This is the woman, my lord the king, and this is her son whom Elisha restored to life." 6The king asked the woman about it, and she told him.

Then he assigned an official to her case and said to him, "Give back everything that belonged to her, including all the income from her land from the day she left the country until now."

Hazael Murders Ben-Hadad

7Elisha went to Damascus, and Ben-Hadad king of Aram was ill. When the king was told, "The man of God has come all the way up here," 8he said to Hazael, "Take a gift with you and go to meet the man of God. Consult the LORD through him; ask him, 'Will I recover from this illness?'"

9Hazael went to meet Elisha, taking with him as a gift forty camel-loads of all the finest wares

17王派攙扶他的那軍長，在城門口彈壓，眾人在那裏將他踐踏，他就死了，正如神人在王下來見他的時候所說的。18神人曾對王說：「明日約到這時候，在撒馬利亞城門口，二細亞大麥要賣銀一舍客勒，一細亞細麵也要賣銀一舍客勒。」

19那軍長對神人說：「即便耶和華使天開了窗戶，也不能有這事。」神人說：「你必親眼看見，卻不得吃。」20這話果然應驗在他身上，因為眾人在城門口將他踐踏，他就死了。

書念婦人得回田地

8 以利沙曾對所救活之子的那婦人說：「你和你的全家，要起身往你可住的地方去住，因為耶和華命饑荒降在這地七年。」2婦人就起身，照神人的話，帶着全家往非利士地去，住了七年。

3七年完了，那婦人從非利士地回來，就出去為自己的房屋田地哀告王。4那時王正與神人的僕人基哈西說：「請你將以利沙所行的一切大事告訴我。」5基哈西告訴王以利沙如何使死人復活，恰巧以利沙所救活她兒子的那婦人，為自己的房屋田地來哀告王。

基哈西說：「我主我王，這就是那婦人，這是她的兒子，就是以利沙所救活的。」6王問那婦人，她就把那事告訴王。

於是王為她派一個太監，說：「凡屬這婦人的都還給她，自從她離開本地直到今日，她田地的出產也都還給她。」

哈薛殺便哈達

7以利沙來到大馬士革，亞蘭王便哈達正患病。有人告訴王說：「神人來到這裏了。」8王就吩咐哈薛說：「你帶着禮物去見神人，託他求問耶和華，我這病能好不能好？」

9於是，哈薛用四十個駱駝，馱着大馬士革的各樣美物為禮物，去見以利沙。到了他那裏，站在他面前，說：「你兒子亞蘭王便哈達打發我來見你，他問說：『我這病能好不能好？』」

¹⁰以利沙對哈薛說：「你回去告訴他說，這病必能好；但耶和華指示我，他必要死。」¹¹神人定睛看着哈薛，甚致他慚愧。神人就哭了。

¹²哈薛說：「我主為甚麼哭？」

回答說：「因為我知道你必苦害以色列人，用火焚燒他們的保障，用刀殺死他們的壯丁，摔死他們的嬰孩，剖開他們的孕婦。」

¹³哈薛說：「你僕人算甚麼，不過是一條狗，焉能行這大事呢？」

以利沙回答說：「耶和華指示我，你必作亞蘭王。」

¹⁴哈薛離開以利沙，回去見他的主人。主人問他說：「以利沙對你說甚麼？」回答說：「他告訴我你必能好。」¹⁵次日，哈薛拿被窩浸在水中，蒙住王的臉，王就死了。於是哈薛篡了他的位。

約蘭作猶大王

¹⁶以色列王亞哈的兒子約蘭第五年，猶大王約沙法還在位的時候，約沙法的兒子約蘭登基，作了猶大王。¹⁷約蘭登基的時候年三十二歲，在耶路撒冷作王八年。¹⁸他行以色列諸王所行的，與亞哈家一樣；因為他娶了亞哈的女兒為妻，行耶和華眼中看為惡的事。¹⁹耶和華卻因他僕人大衛的緣故，仍不肯滅絕猶大，照他所應許大衛的話，永遠賜燈光與他的子孫。

²⁰約蘭年間，以東人背叛猶大，脫離他的權下，自己立王。²¹約蘭率領所有的戰車往撒益去，夜間起來，攻打圍困他的以東人和車兵長。猶大兵就逃跑，各回各家去了。²²這樣，以東人背叛猶大，脫離他的權下，直到今日。那時立拿人也背叛了。

²³約蘭其餘的事，凡他所行的，都寫在猶大列王記上。²⁴約蘭與他列

of Damascus. He went in and stood before him, and said, "Your son Ben-Hadad king of Aram has sent me to ask, 'Will I recover from this illness?' "

¹⁰Elisha answered, "Go and say to him, 'You will certainly recover'; but^a the LORD has revealed to me that he will in fact die." ¹¹He stared at him with a fixed gaze until Hazael felt ashamed. Then the man of God began to weep.

¹²"Why is my lord weeping?" asked Hazael.

"Because I know the harm you will do to the Israelites," he answered. "You will set fire to their fortified places, kill their young men with the sword, dash their little children to the ground, and rip open their pregnant women."

¹³Hazael said, "How could your servant, a mere dog, accomplish such a feat?"

"The LORD has shown me that you will become king of Aram," answered Elisha.

¹⁴Then Hazael left Elisha and returned to his master. When Ben-Hadad asked, "What did Elisha say to you?" Hazael replied, "He told me that you would certainly recover." ¹⁵But the next day he took a thick cloth, soaked it in water and spread it over the king's face, so that he died. Then Hazael succeeded him as king.

Jehoram King of Judah

¹⁶In the fifth year of Joram son of Ahab king of Israel, when Jehoshaphat was king of Judah, Jehoram son of Jehoshaphat began his reign as king of Judah. ¹⁷He was thirty-two years old when he became king, and he reigned in Jerusalem eight years. ¹⁸He walked in the ways of the kings of Israel, as the house of Ahab had done, for he married a daughter of Ahab. He did evil in the eyes of the LORD. ¹⁹Nevertheless, for the sake of his servant David, the LORD was not willing to destroy Judah. He had promised to maintain a lamp for David and his descendants forever.

²⁰In the time of Jehoram, Edom rebelled against Judah and set up its own king. ²¹So Jehoram^b went to Zair with all his chariots. The Edomites surrounded him and his chariot commanders, but he rose up and broke through by night; his army, however, fled back home. ²²To this day Edom has been in rebellion against Judah. Libnah revolted at the same time.

²³As for the other events of Jehoram's reign, and all he did, are they not written in the book of the annals of the kings of Judah? ²⁴Jehoram

^a 10 The Hebrew may also be read *Go and say, 'You will certainly not recover,' for.*　　^b 21 Hebrew *Joram,* a variant of *Jehoram*; also in verses 23 and 24

rested with his fathers and was buried with them in the City of David. And Ahaziah his son succeeded him as king.

Ahaziah King of Judah

25In the twelfth year of Joram son of Ahab king of Israel, Ahaziah son of Jehoram king of Judah began to reign. 26Ahaziah was twenty-two years old when he became king, and he reigned in Jerusalem one year. His mother's name was Athaliah, a granddaughter of Omri king of Israel. 27He walked in the ways of the house of Ahab and did evil in the eyes of the LORD, as the house of Ahab had done, for he was related by marriage to Ahab's family.

28Ahaziah went with Joram son of Ahab to war against Hazael king of Aram at Ramoth Gilead. The Arameans wounded Joram; 29so King Joram returned to Jezreel to recover from the wounds the Arameans had inflicted on him at Ramoth*a* in his battle with Hazael king of Aram.

Then Ahaziah son of Jehoram king of Judah went down to Jezreel to see Joram son of Ahab, because he had been wounded.

Jehu Anointed King of Israel

9 The prophet Elisha summoned a man from the company of the prophets and said to him, "Tuck your cloak into your belt, take this flask of oil with you and go to Ramoth Gilead. 2When you get there, look for Jehu son of Jehoshaphat, the son of Nimshi. Go to him, get him away from his companions and take him into an inner room. 3Then take the flask and pour the oil on his head and declare, 'This is what the LORD says: I anoint you king over Israel.' Then open the door and run; don't delay!"

4So the young man, the prophet, went to Ramoth Gilead. 5When he arrived, he found the army officers sitting together. "I have a message for you, commander," he said.

"For which of us?" asked Jehu.

"For you, commander," he replied.

6Jehu got up and went into the house. Then the prophet poured the oil on Jehu's head and declared, "This is what the LORD, the God of Israel, says: 'I anoint you king over the LORD's people Israel. 7You are to destroy the house of Ahab your master, and I will avenge the blood of my servants the prophets and the blood of all the LORD's servants shed by Jezebel. 8The whole house of Ahab will perish. I will cut off from

a 29 Hebrew Ramah, a variant of Ramoth

祖同睡，葬在大衛城他列祖的墳地裏。他兒子亞哈謝接續他作王。

亞哈謝作猶大王

25以色列王亞哈的兒子約蘭十二年，猶大王約蘭的兒子亞哈謝登基。26他登基的時候年二十二歲，在耶路撒冷作王一年。他母親名叫亞她利雅，是以色列王暗利的孫女。27亞哈謝效法亞哈家行耶和華眼中看為惡的事，與亞哈家一樣。因為他是亞哈家的女婿。

28他與亞哈的兒子約蘭同往基列的拉末去，與亞蘭王哈薛爭戰，亞蘭人打傷了約蘭，29約蘭王回到耶斯列，醫治在拉末與亞蘭王哈薛打仗的時候所受的傷。

猶大王約蘭的兒子亞哈謝因為亞哈的兒子約蘭病了，就下到耶斯列看望他。

耶戶受膏作以色列王

9 先知以利沙叫了一個先知門徒來，吩咐他說："你束上腰，手拿這瓶膏油，往基列的拉末去。2到了那裏，要尋找寧示的孫子、約沙法的兒子耶戶。使他從同僚中起來，帶他進嚴密的屋子，3將瓶裏的膏油倒在他頭上，說：'耶和華如此說：我膏你作以色列王。'說完了，就開門逃跑，不要遲延。"

4於是那少年先知往基列的拉末去了。5到了那裏，看見眾軍長都坐着，就說："將軍哪，我有話對你說。"

耶戶說："我們眾人裏，你要對哪一個說呢？"

回答說："將軍哪，我要對你說。"

6耶戶就起來，進了屋子，少年人將膏油倒在他頭上，對他說："耶和華以色列的神如此說：'我膏你作耶和華民以色列的王。7你要擊殺你主人亞哈的全家，我好在耶洗別身上伸我僕人眾先知和耶和華一切僕人流血的冤。8亞哈全家必都滅亡；凡屬亞哈的男丁，無論是困住的、自由的，我必從以色列中剪除，⁹使亞哈的家像尼八兒子耶羅波安的家，又像亞希雅兒子巴沙的家。¹⁰耶洗別必在耶斯列田裏被狗所吃，無人葬埋。'"說完了，少年人就開門逃跑了。

¹¹耶戶出來，回到他主人的臣僕那裏，有一人問他說："平安嗎？這狂妄的人來見你有甚麼事呢？"

回答說："你們認得那人，也知道他說甚麼。"

¹²他們說："這是假話，你據實地告訴我們。"回答說："他如此如此對我說。他說：'耶和華如此說：我膏你作以色列王。'"

¹³他們就急忙各將自己的衣服鋪在上層台階，使耶戶坐在其上。他們吹角，說："耶戶作王了！"

耶戶殺約蘭與亞哈謝

¹⁴這樣，寧示的孫子、約沙法的兒子耶戶，背叛約蘭。先是約蘭和以色列眾人因為亞蘭王哈薛的緣故，把守基列的拉末，¹⁵約蘭王回到耶斯列，醫治與亞蘭王哈薛打仗所受的傷。耶戶說："若合你們的意思，就不容人逃出城往耶斯列報信去。"¹⁶於是耶戶坐車往耶斯列去，因為約蘭病臥在那裏。猶大王亞哈謝已經下去看望他。

¹⁷有一個守望的人站在耶斯列的樓上，看見耶戶帶着一羣人來，就說："我看見一羣人。"

約蘭說："打發一個騎馬的去迎接他們，問他們：'平安不平安'？"

¹⁸騎馬的就去迎接耶戶，說："王問說：'平安不平安'？"

耶戶說："平安不平安與你何干？你轉在我後頭吧！"

守望的人又說："使者到了他們那裏，卻不回來。"

¹⁹王又打發一個騎馬的去。這人到了他們那裏，說："王問說：'平安不平安'？"

耶戶說："平安不平安與你何干？你轉在我後頭吧！"

²⁰守望的人又說："他到了他們那裏，也不回來。車趕得甚猛，像寧

Ahab every last male in Israel—slave or free. ⁹I will make the house of Ahab like the house of Jeroboam son of Nebat and like the house of Baasha son of Ahijah. ¹⁰As for Jezebel, dogs will devour her on the plot of ground at Jezreel, and no one will bury her.' " Then he opened the door and ran.

¹¹When Jehu went out to his fellow officers, one of them asked him, "Is everything all right? Why did this madman come to you?"

"You know the man and the sort of things he says," Jehu replied.

¹²"That's not true!" they said. "Tell us."

Jehu said, "Here is what he told me: 'This is what the LORD says: I anoint you king over Israel.' "

¹³They hurried and took their cloaks and spread them under him on the bare steps. Then they blew the trumpet and shouted, "Jehu is king!"

Jehu Kills Joram and Ahaziah

¹⁴So Jehu son of Jehoshaphat, the son of Nimshi, conspired against Joram. (Now Joram and all Israel had been defending Ramoth Gilead against Hazael king of Aram, ¹⁵but King Joram*ᵃ* had returned to Jezreel to recover from the wounds the Arameans had inflicted on him in the battle with Hazael king of Aram.) Jehu said, "If this is the way you feel, don't let anyone slip out of the city to go and tell the news in Jezreel." ¹⁶Then he got into his chariot and rode to Jezreel, because Joram was resting there and Ahaziah king of Judah had gone down to see him.

¹⁷When the lookout standing on the tower in Jezreel saw Jehu's troops approaching, he called out, "I see some troops coming."

"Get a horseman," Joram ordered. "Send him to meet them and ask, 'Do you come in peace?'"

¹⁸The horseman rode off to meet Jehu and said, "This is what the king says: 'Do you come in peace?' "

"What do you have to do with peace?" Jehu replied. "Fall in behind me."

The lookout reported, "The messenger has reached them, but he isn't coming back."

¹⁹So the king sent out a second horseman. When he came to them he said, "This is what the king says: 'Do you come in peace?' "

Jehu replied, "What do you have to do with peace? Fall in behind me."

²⁰The lookout reported, "He has reached them, but he isn't coming back either. The driv-

a 15 Hebrew Jehoram, a variant of Joram; also in verses 17 and 21-24

ing is like that of Jehu son of Nimshi—he drives like a madman."

21"Hitch up my chariot," Joram ordered. And when it was hitched up, Joram king of Israel and Ahaziah king of Judah rode out, each in his own chariot, to meet Jehu. They met him at the plot of ground that had belonged to Naboth the Jezreelite. 22When Joram saw Jehu he asked, "Have you come in peace, Jehu?"

"How can there be peace," Jehu replied, "as long as all the idolatry and witchcraft of your mother Jezebel abound?"

23Joram turned about and fled, calling out to Ahaziah, "Treachery, Ahaziah!"

24Then Jehu drew his bow and shot Joram between the shoulders. The arrow pierced his heart and he slumped down in his chariot. 25Jehu said to Bidkar, his chariot officer, "Pick him up and throw him on the field that belonged to Naboth the Jezreelite. Remember how you and I were riding together in chariots behind Ahab his father when the LORD made this prophecy about him: 26'Yesterday I saw the blood of Naboth and the blood of his sons, declares the LORD, and I will surely make you pay for it on this plot of ground, declares the LORD.'ᵃ Now then, pick him up and throw him on that plot, in accordance with the word of the LORD."

27When Ahaziah king of Judah saw what had happened, he fled up the road to Beth Haggan.ᵇ Jehu chased him, shouting, "Kill him too!" They wounded him in his chariot on the way up to Gur near Ibleam, but he escaped to Megiddo and died there. 28His servants took him by chariot to Jerusalem and buried him with his fathers in his tomb in the City of David. 29(In the eleventh year of Joram son of Ahab, Ahaziah had become king of Judah.)

Jezebel Killed

30Then Jehu went to Jezreel. When Jezebel heard about it, she painted her eyes, arranged her hair and looked out of a window. 31As Jehu entered the gate, she asked, "Have you come in peace, Zimri, you murderer of your master?"ᶜ

32He looked up at the window and called out, "Who is on my side? Who?" Two or three eunuchs looked down at him. 33"Throw her down!" Jehu said. So they threw her down, and some of her blood spattered the wall and the horses as they trampled her underfoot.

示的孫子耶戶的趕法。"

21約蘭吩咐說："套車！"人就給他套車。以色列王約蘭和猶大王亞哈謝，各坐自己的車出去迎接耶戶，在耶斯列人拿伯的田那裏遇見他。22約蘭見耶戶就說："耶戶啊，平安嗎？"

耶戶說："你母親耶洗別的淫行邪術這樣多，焉能平安呢？"

23約蘭就轉車逃跑，對亞哈謝說："亞哈謝啊，反了！"24耶戶開滿了弓，射中約蘭的脊背，箭從心窩穿出，約蘭就仆倒在車上。25耶戶對他的軍長畢甲說："你把他拋在耶斯列人拿伯的田間。你當追想，你我一同坐車跟隨他父亞哈的時候，耶和華對亞哈所說的預言，26說：'我昨日看見拿伯的血和他眾子的血，我必在這塊田上報應你。'這是耶和華說的。現在你要照着耶和華的話，把他拋在這田間。"

27猶大王亞哈謝見這光景，就從園亭之路逃跑。耶戶追趕他說："把這人也殺在車上。"到了靠近以伯蓮姑珥的坡上擊傷了他，他逃到米吉多，就死在那裏。28他的臣僕用車將他的屍首送到耶路撒冷，葬在大衛城他自己的墳墓裏，與他列祖同葬。29亞哈謝登基，作猶大王的時候，是在亞哈的兒子約蘭第十一年。

耶洗別被殺

30耶戶到了耶斯列。耶洗別聽見就擦粉、梳頭，從窗戶裏往外觀看。31耶戶進門的時候，耶洗別說："殺主人的心利啊，平安嗎？"

32耶戶抬頭向窗戶觀看，說："誰順從我？"有兩三個太監從窗戶往外看他。33耶戶說："把她扔下來！"他們就把她扔下來。她的血濺在牆上和馬上，於是把她踐踏了。

a 26 See 1 Kings 21:19.   b 27 Or fled by way of the garden house
c 31 Or "Did Zimri have peace, who murdered his master?"

³⁴耶戶進去，吃了喝了，吩咐說：「你們把這被咒詛的婦人葬埋了，因為她是王的女兒。」³⁵他們就去葬埋她，只尋得她的頭骨和腳，並手掌。³⁶他們回去告訴耶戶，耶戶說：「這正應驗耶和華藉他僕人提斯比人以利亞所說的話，說：在耶斯列田間，狗必吃耶洗別的肉；³⁷耶洗別的屍首必在耶斯列田間如同糞土，甚至人不能說：『這是耶洗別。』」

亞哈全家被殺

10 亞哈有七十個兒子在撒馬利亞。耶戶寫信送到撒馬利亞，通知耶斯列的首領，就是長老和教養亞哈眾子的人說：²「你們那裏既有你們主人的眾子和車馬、器械、堅固城，³接了這信，就可以在你們主人的眾子中，選擇一個賢能合宜的，使他坐他父親的位。你們也可以為你們主人的家爭戰。」

⁴他們卻甚懼怕，彼此說：「二王在他面前尚且站立不住，我們怎能站得住呢？」

⁵家宰、邑宰和長老，並教養眾子的人，打發人去見耶戶，說：「我們是你的僕人，凡你所吩咐我們的，都必遵行，我們不立誰作王，你看怎樣好就怎樣行。」

⁶耶戶又給他們寫信說：「你們若歸順我，聽從我的話，明日這時候，要將你們主人眾子的首級帶到耶斯列來見我。」

那時王的兒子七十人，都住在教養他們那城中的尊貴人家裏。⁷信一到，他們就把王的七十個兒子殺了，將首級裝在筐裏，送到耶斯列耶戶那裏。⁸有使者來告訴耶戶說：「他們將王眾子的首級送來了。」

耶戶說：「將首級在城門口堆作兩堆，擱到明日。」

⁹次日早晨，耶戶出來，站着對眾民說：「你們都是公義的。我背叛我主人，將他殺了。這些人卻是誰殺的呢？¹⁰由此可知，耶和華指着亞哈家所說的話，一句沒有落空，因為耶和華藉他僕人以利亞所說的話都成就

³⁴Jehu went in and ate and drank. "Take care of that cursed woman," he said, "and bury her, for she was a king's daughter." ³⁵But when they went out to bury her, they found nothing except her skull, her feet and her hands. ³⁶They went back and told Jehu, who said, "This is the word of the LORD that he spoke through his servant Elijah the Tishbite: On the plot of ground at Jezreel dogs will devour Jezebel's flesh.*ᵃ* ³⁷Jezebel's body will be like refuse on the ground in the plot at Jezreel, so that no one will be able to say, 'This is Jezebel.' "

Ahab's Family Killed

10 Now there were in Samaria seventy sons of the house of Ahab. So Jehu wrote letters and sent them to Samaria: to the officials of Jezreel,*ᵇ* to the elders and to the guardians of Ahab's children. He said, ²"As soon as this letter reaches you, since your master's sons are with you and you have chariots and horses, a fortified city and weapons, ³choose the best and most worthy of your master's sons and set him on his father's throne. Then fight for your master's house."

⁴But they were terrified and said, "If two kings could not resist him, how can we?"

⁵So the palace administrator, the city governor, the elders and the guardians sent this message to Jehu: "We are your servants and we will do anything you say. We will not appoint anyone as king; you do whatever you think best."

⁶Then Jehu wrote them a second letter, saying, "If you are on my side and will obey me, take the heads of your master's sons and come to me in Jezreel by this time tomorrow."

Now the royal princes, seventy of them, were with the leading men of the city, who were rearing them. ⁷When the letter arrived, these men took the princes and slaughtered all seventy of them. They put their heads in baskets and sent them to Jehu in Jezreel. ⁸When the messenger arrived, he told Jehu, "They have brought the heads of the princes."

Then Jehu ordered, "Put them in two piles at the entrance of the city gate until morning."

⁹The next morning Jehu went out. He stood before all the people and said, "You are innocent. It was I who conspired against my master and killed him, but who killed all these? ¹⁰Know then, that not a word the LORD has spoken against the house of Ahab will fail. The LORD has done what he promised through his servant

a 36 See 1 Kings 21:23.　　*b 1* Hebrew; some Septuagint manuscripts and Vulgate *of the city*

Elijah." 11So Jehu killed everyone in Jezreel who remained of the house of Ahab, as well as all his chief men, his close friends and his priests, leaving him no survivor.

12Jehu then set out and went toward Samaria. At Beth Eked of the Shepherds, 13he met some relatives of Ahaziah king of Judah and asked, "Who are you?"

They said, "We are relatives of Ahaziah, and we have come down to greet the families of the king and of the queen mother."

14"Take them alive!" he ordered. So they took them alive and slaughtered them by the well of Beth Eked—forty-two men. He left no survivor.

15After he left there, he came upon Jehonadab son of Recab, who was on his way to meet him. Jehu greeted him and said, "Are you in accord with me, as I am with you?"

"I am," Jehonadab answered.

"If so," said Jehu, "give me your hand." So he did, and Jehu helped him up into the chariot. 16Jehu said, "Come with me and see my zeal for the LORD." Then he had him ride along in his chariot.

17When Jehu came to Samaria, he killed all who were left there of Ahab's family; he destroyed them, according to the word of the LORD spoken to Elijah.

Ministers of Baal Killed

18Then Jehu brought all the people together and said to them, "Ahab served Baal a little; Jehu will serve him much. 19Now summon all the prophets of Baal, all his ministers and all his priests. See that no one is missing, because I am going to hold a great sacrifice for Baal. Anyone who fails to come will no longer live." But Jehu was acting deceptively in order to destroy the ministers of Baal.

20Jehu said, "Call an assembly in honor of Baal." So they proclaimed it. 21Then he sent word throughout Israel, and all the ministers of Baal came; not one stayed away. They crowded into the temple of Baal until it was full from one end to the other. 22And Jehu said to the keeper of the wardrobe, "Bring robes for all the ministers of Baal." So he brought out robes for them.

23Then Jehu and Jehonadab son of Recab went into the temple of Baal. Jehu said to the ministers of Baal, "Look around and see that no servants of the LORD are here with you—only ministers of Baal." 24So they went in to make sacrifices and burnt offerings. Now Jehu had posted eighty men outside with this warning: "If one of you lets any of the men I am placing in your hands escape, it will be your life for his life."

了。" 11凡亞哈家在耶斯列所剩下的人和他的大臣、密友、祭司，耶戶盡都殺了，沒有留下一個。

12耶戶起身往撒馬利亞去。在路上牧人剪羊毛之處，13遇見猶大王亞哈謝的弟兄，問他們說："你們是誰？"

回答說："我們是亞哈謝的弟兄，現在下去，要問王和太后的眾子安。"

14耶戶吩咐說："活捉他們！"跟從的人就活捉了他們，將他們殺在剪羊毛之處的坑邊，共四十二人，沒有留下一個。

15耶戶從那裏前行，恰遇利甲的兒子約拿達來迎接他，耶戶問他安，對他說："你誠心待我，像我誠心待你嗎？"

約拿達回答說："是。"

耶戶說："若是這樣，你向我伸手。"他就伸手，耶戶拉他上車。16耶戶說："你和我同去，看我為耶和華怎樣熱心。"於是請他坐在車上。

17到了撒馬利亞，就把撒馬利亞哈家剩下的人都殺了，直到滅盡，正如耶和華對以利亞所說的。

殺盡拜巴力者

18耶戶招聚眾民，對他們說："亞哈侍奉巴力還冷淡，耶戶卻更熱心。19現在我要給巴力獻大祭。應當叫巴力的眾先知和一切拜巴力的人，並巴力的眾祭司，都到我這裏來，不可缺少一個，凡不來的必不得活。"耶戶這樣行，是用詭計要殺盡拜巴力的人。

20耶戶說："要為巴力宣告嚴肅會。"於是宣告了。21耶戶差人走遍以色列地，凡拜巴力的人都來齊了，沒有一個不來的。他們進了巴力廟，巴力廟中從前邊直到後邊都滿了人。22耶戶吩咐掌管禮服的人說："拿出禮服來，給一切拜巴力的人穿。"他就拿出禮服來給了他們。

23耶戶和利甲的兒子約拿達進了巴力廟，對拜巴力的人說："你們察看察看，在你們這裏不可有那事奉耶和華的僕人，只可容留拜巴力的人。"24耶戶和約拿達進去獻平安祭和燔祭。耶戶先安排八十人在廟外，吩咐說："我將這些人交在你們手中，若有一人脫逃，誰放的，必叫他償命！"

²⁵耶戶獻完了燔祭，就出來吩咐護衛兵和軍長說："你們進去殺他們，不容一人出來。" 護衛兵和軍長就用刀殺他們，將屍首拋出去，便到巴力廟的城去了，²⁶將巴力廟中的柱像都拿出來燒了，²⁷毀壞了巴力柱像，拆毀了巴力廟作為廁所，直到今日。

²⁸這樣，耶戶在以色列中滅了巴力。²⁹只是耶戶不離開尼八的兒子耶羅波安使以色列人陷在罪裏的那罪，就是拜伯特利和但的金牛犢。

³⁰耶和華對耶戶說："因你辦好我眼中看為正的事，照我的心意待亞哈家，你的子孫必接續你坐以色列的國位，直到四代。" ³¹只是耶戶不盡心遵守耶和華以色列神的律法，不離開耶羅波安使以色列人陷在罪裏的那罪。

³²在那些日子，耶和華才割裂以色列國，使哈薛攻擊以色列的境界，³³乃是約旦河東、基列全地，從靠近亞嫩谷邊的亞羅珥起，就是基列和巴珊的迦得人、呂便人、瑪拿西人之地。

³⁴耶戶其餘的事，凡他所行的和他的勇力，都寫在以色列諸王記上。

³⁵耶戶與他列祖同睡，葬在撒馬利亞。他兒子約哈斯接續他作王。³⁶耶戶在撒馬利亞作以色列王二十八年。

亞她利雅與約阿施

11 亞哈謝的母親亞她利雅見她兒子死了，就起來剿滅王室。²但約蘭王的女兒、亞哈謝的妹子約示巴，將亞哈謝的兒子約阿施從那被殺的王子中偷出來，把他和他的乳母都藏在臥房裏，躲避亞她利雅，免得被殺。³約阿施和他的乳母藏在耶和華的殿裏六年，亞她利雅篡了國位。

²⁵As soon as Jehu had finished making the burnt offering, he ordered the guards and officers: "Go in and kill them; let no one escape." So they cut them down with the sword. The guards and officers threw the bodies out and then entered the inner shrine of the temple of Baal. ²⁶They brought the sacred stone out of the temple of Baal and burned it. ²⁷They demolished the sacred stone of Baal and tore down the temple of Baal, and people have used it for a latrine to this day.

²⁸So Jehu destroyed Baal worship in Israel. ²⁹However, he did not turn away from the sins of Jeroboam son of Nebat, which he had caused Israel to commit—the worship of the golden calves at Bethel and Dan.

³⁰The LORD said to Jehu, "Because you have done well in accomplishing what is right in my eyes and have done to the house of Ahab all I had in mind to do, your descendants will sit on the throne of Israel to the fourth generation." ³¹Yet Jehu was not careful to keep the law of the LORD, the God of Israel, with all his heart. He did not turn away from the sins of Jeroboam, which he had caused Israel to commit.

³²In those days the LORD began to reduce the size of Israel. Hazael overpowered the Israelites throughout their territory ³³east of the Jordan in all the land of Gilead (the region of Gad, Reuben and Manasseh), from Aroer by the Arnon Gorge through Gilead to Bashan.

³⁴As for the other events of Jehu's reign, all he did, and all his achievements, are they not written in the book of the annals of the kings of Israel?

³⁵Jehu rested with his fathers and was buried in Samaria. And Jehoahaz his son succeeded him as king. ³⁶The time that Jehu reigned over Israel in Samaria was twenty-eight years.

Athaliah and Joash

11 When Athaliah the mother of Ahaziah saw that her son was dead, she proceeded to destroy the whole royal family. ²But Jehosheba, the daughter of King Jehoram^a and sister of Ahaziah, took Joash son of Ahaziah and stole him away from among the royal princes, who were about to be murdered. She put him and his nurse in a bedroom to hide him from Athaliah; so he was not killed. ³He remained hidden with his nurse at the temple of the LORD for six years while Athaliah ruled the land.

a 2 Hebrew Joram, a variant of Jehoram

⁴In the seventh year Jehoiada sent for the commanders of units of a hundred, the Carites and the guards and had them brought to him at the temple of the LORD. He made a covenant with them and put them under oath at the temple of the LORD. Then he showed them the king's son. ⁵He commanded them, saying, "This is what you are to do: You who are in the three companies that are going on duty on the Sabbath—a third of you guarding the royal palace, ⁶a third at the Sur Gate, and a third at the gate behind the guard, who take turns guarding the temple— ⁷and you who are in the other two companies that normally go off Sabbath duty are all to guard the temple for the king. ⁸Station yourselves around the king, each man with his weapon in his hand. Anyone who approaches your ranks*ᵃ* must be put to death. Stay close to the king wherever he goes."

⁹The commanders of units of a hundred did just as Jehoiada the priest ordered. Each one took his men—those who were going on duty on the Sabbath and those who were going off duty—and came to Jehoiada the priest. ¹⁰Then he gave the commanders the spears and shields that had belonged to King David and that were in the temple of the LORD. ¹¹The guards, each with his weapon in his hand, stationed themselves around the king—near the altar and the temple, from the south side to the north side of the temple.

¹²Jehoiada brought out the king's son and put the crown on him; he presented him with a copy of the covenant and proclaimed him king. They anointed him, and the people clapped their hands and shouted, "Long live the king!"

¹³When Athaliah heard the noise made by the guards and the people, she went to the people at the temple of the LORD. ¹⁴She looked and there was the king, standing by the pillar, as the custom was. The officers and the trumpeters were beside the king, and all the people of the land were rejoicing and blowing trumpets. Then Athaliah tore her robes and called out, "Treason! Treason!"

¹⁵Jehoiada the priest ordered the commanders of units of a hundred, who were in charge of the troops: "Bring her out between the ranks*ᵇ* and put to the sword anyone who follows her." For the priest had said, "She must not be put to death in the temple of the LORD." ¹⁶So they seized her as she reached the place where the horses enter the palace grounds, and there she was put to death.

⁴第七年，耶何耶大打發人叫迦利人（註：或作"親兵"）和護衛兵的眾百夫長來，領他們進了耶和華的殿，與他們立約，使他們在耶和華殿裏起誓，又將王的兒子指給他們看，⁵吩咐他們說："你們當這樣行：凡安息日進班的三分之一要看守王宮；⁶三分之一要在蘇珥門；三分之一要在護衛兵院的後門。這樣把守王宮，攔阻閒人。⁷你們安息日所有出班的三分之二要在耶和華的殿裏護衛王，⁸各人手拿兵器，四圍護衛王。凡擅入你們班次的，必當治死。王出入的時候，你們當跟隨他。"

⁹眾百夫長就照着祭司耶何耶大一切所吩咐的去行，各帶所管安息日進班出班的人來見祭司耶何耶大。¹⁰祭司便將耶和華殿裏所藏大衛王的槍和盾牌交給百夫長。¹¹護衛兵手中各拿兵器，在壇和殿那裏，從殿右直到殿左，站在王子的四圍。

¹²祭司領王子出來，給他戴上冠冕，將律法書交給他，膏他作王。眾人就拍掌說："願王萬歲！"

¹³亞她利雅聽見護衛兵和民的聲音，就到民那裏，進耶和華的殿。¹⁴看見王照例站在柱旁，百夫長和吹號的人侍立在王左右，國中的眾民歡樂吹號。亞她利雅就撕裂衣服，喊叫說："反了！反了！"

¹⁵祭司耶何耶大吩咐管轄軍兵的百夫長說："將她趕出班外，凡跟隨她的，必用刀殺死！"因為祭司說，不可在耶和華殿裏殺她。¹⁶眾兵就閃開讓她去，她從馬路上王宮去，便在那裏被殺。

¹⁷耶何耶大使王和民與耶和華立約，作耶和華的民；又使王與民立約。¹⁸於是國民都到巴力廟，拆毀了廟，打碎壇和像，又在壇前將巴力的祭司瑪坦殺了。

祭司耶何耶大派官看守耶和華的殿，¹⁹又率領百夫長和迦利人（註：或作「親兵」）與護衛兵，以及國中的眾民，請王從耶和華殿下來，由護衛兵的門進入王宮。他就坐了王位。²⁰國民都歡樂，闔城那裏安靜。眾人已將亞她利雅在王宮那裏用刀殺了。

²¹約阿施登基的時候年方七歲。

約阿施修理聖殿

12 耶戶第七年，約阿施登基，在耶路撒冷作王四十年。他母親名叫西比亞，是別是巴人。²約阿施在祭司耶何耶大教訓他的時候，就行耶和華眼中看為正的事，³只是邱壇還沒有廢去，百姓仍在那裏獻祭燒香。

⁴約阿施對眾祭司說：「凡奉到耶和華殿分別為聖之物所值通用的銀子，或各人當納的身價，或樂意奉到耶和華殿的銀子，你們當從所認識的人收了來，修理殿的一切破壞之處。」

⁶無奈到了約阿施王二十三年，祭司仍未修理殿的破壞之處。⁷所以約阿施王召了大祭司耶何耶大和眾祭司來，對他們說：「你們怎麼不修理殿的破壞之處呢？從今以後，你們不要從所認識的人再收銀子，要將所收的交出來，修理殿的破壞之處。」⁸眾祭司答應不再收百姓的銀子，也不修理殿的破壞之處。

⁹祭司耶何耶大取了一個櫃子，在櫃蓋上鑽了一個窟窿，放於壇旁，在進耶和華殿的右邊。守門的祭司將

¹⁷Jehoiada then made a covenant between the LORD and the king and people that they would be the LORD's people. He also made a covenant between the king and the people. ¹⁸All the people of the land went to the temple of Baal and tore it down. They smashed the altars and idols to pieces and killed Mattan the priest of Baal in front of the altars.

Then Jehoiada the priest posted guards at the temple of the LORD. ¹⁹He took with him the commanders of hundreds, the Carites, the guards and all the people of the land, and together they brought the king down from the temple of the LORD and went into the palace, entering by way of the gate of the guards. The king then took his place on the royal throne, ²⁰and all the people of the land rejoiced. And the city was quiet, because Athaliah had been slain with the sword at the palace.

²¹Joash*ᵃ* was seven years old when he began to reign.

Joash Repairs the Temple

12 In the seventh year of Jehu, Joash*ᵇ* became king, and he reigned in Jerusalem forty years. His mother's name was Zibiah; she was from Beersheba. ²Joash did what was right in the eyes of the LORD all the years Jehoiada the priest instructed him. ³The high places, however, were not removed; the people continued to offer sacrifices and burn incense there.

⁴Joash said to the priests, "Collect all the money that is brought as sacred offerings to the temple of the LORD—the money collected in the census, the money received from personal vows and the money brought voluntarily to the temple. ⁵Let every priest receive the money from one of the treasurers, and let it be used to repair whatever damage is found in the temple."

⁶But by the twenty-third year of King Joash the priests still had not repaired the temple. ⁷Therefore King Joash summoned Jehoiada the priest and the other priests and asked them, "Why aren't you repairing the damage done to the temple? Take no more money from your treasurers, but hand it over for repairing the temple." ⁸The priests agreed that they would not collect any more money from the people and that they would not repair the temple themselves.

⁹Jehoiada the priest took a chest and bored a hole in its lid. He placed it beside the altar, on the right side as one enters the temple of the

---

a 21 Hebrew *Jehoash*, a variant of *Joash*　　*b 1* Hebrew *Jehoash*, a variant of *Joash*; also in verses 2, 4, 6, 7 and 18

LORD. The priests who guarded the entrance put into the chest all the money that was brought to the temple of the LORD. ¹⁰Whenever they saw that there was a large amount of money in the chest, the royal secretary and the high priest came, counted the money that had been brought into the temple of the LORD and put it into bags. ¹¹When the amount had been determined, they gave the money to the men appointed to supervise the work on the temple. With it they paid those who worked on the temple of the LORD—the carpenters and builders, ¹²the masons and stonecutters. They purchased timber and dressed stone for the repair of the temple of the LORD, and met all the other expenses of restoring the temple.

¹³The money brought into the temple was not spent for making silver basins, wick trimmers, sprinkling bowls, trumpets or any other articles of gold or silver for the temple of the LORD; ¹⁴it was paid to the workmen, who used it to repair the temple. ¹⁵They did not require an accounting from those to whom they gave the money to pay the workers, because they acted with complete honesty. ¹⁶The money from the guilt offerings and sin offerings was not brought into the temple of the LORD; it belonged to the priests.

¹⁷About this time Hazael king of Aram went up and attacked Gath and captured it. Then he turned to attack Jerusalem. ¹⁸But Joash king of Judah took all the sacred objects dedicated by his fathers—Jehoshaphat, Jehoram and Ahaziah, the kings of Judah—and the gifts he himself had dedicated and all the gold found in the treasuries of the temple of the LORD and of the royal palace, and he sent them to Hazael king of Aram, who then withdrew from Jerusalem.

¹⁹As for the other events of the reign of Joash, and all he did, are they not written in the book of the annals of the kings of Judah? ²⁰His officials conspired against him and assassinated him at Beth Millo, on the road down to Silla. ²¹The officials who murdered him were Jozabad son of Shimeath and Jehozabad son of Shomer. He died and was buried with his fathers in the City of David. And Amaziah his son succeeded him as king.

Jehoahaz King of Israel

13 In the twenty-third year of Joash son of Ahaziah king of Judah, Jehoahaz son of Jehu became king of Israel in Samaria, and he reigned seventeen years. ²He did evil in the eyes of the LORD by following the sins of Jeroboam son of Nebat, which he had caused Israel to commit, and he did not turn away from

奉到耶和華殿的一切銀子投在櫃裏。¹⁰他們見櫃裏的銀子多了，便叫王的書記和大祭司上來，將耶和華殿裏的銀子數算包起來。¹¹把所平的銀子交給督工的，就是耶和華殿裏辦事的人。他們把銀子轉交修理耶和華殿的木匠和工人，¹²並瓦匠、石匠，又買木料和鑿成的石頭，修理耶和華殿的破壞之處，以及修理殿的各樣使用。

¹³但那奉到耶和華殿的銀子，沒有用以做耶和華殿裏的銀杯、蠟剪、碗、號和別樣的金銀器皿，¹⁴乃將那銀子交給督工的人，修理耶和華的殿。¹⁵且將銀子交給辦事的人轉交做工的人，不與他們算賬，因為他們辦事誠實。¹⁶惟有贖愆祭、贖罪祭的銀子，沒有奉到耶和華的殿，都歸祭司。

¹⁷那時，亞蘭王哈薛上來攻打迦特，攻取了，就定意上來，攻打耶路撒冷。¹⁸猶大王約阿施將他列祖猶大王約沙法、約蘭、亞哈謝所分別為聖的物，和自己所分別為聖的物，並耶和華殿與王宮府庫裏所有的金子，都送給亞蘭王哈薛；哈薛就不上耶路撒冷來了。

¹⁹約阿施其餘的事，凡他所行的，都寫在猶大列王記上。²⁰約阿施的臣僕起來背叛，在下悉拉的米羅宮那裏將他殺了。²¹殺他的那臣僕就是示米押的兒子約撒甲和朔默的兒子約薩拔。眾人將他葬在大衛城他列祖的墳地裏，他兒子亞瑪謝接續他作王。

約哈斯作以色列王

13 猶大王亞哈謝的兒子約阿施二十三年，耶戶的兒子約哈斯在撒馬利亞登基，作以色列王十七年。²約哈斯行耶和華眼中看為惡的事，效法尼八的兒子耶羅波安使以色列人陷在罪裏的那罪，總不離開。³於是，耶和華的怒氣向以色列人發作，將他們屢次交在亞蘭王哈薛和他兒子便哈達的手裏。

⁴約哈斯懇求耶和華，耶和華就應允他，因為見以色列人所受亞蘭王的欺壓。⁵耶和華賜給以色列人一位拯救者，使他們脫離亞蘭人的手。於是以色列人仍舊安居在家裏。⁶然而，他們不離開耶羅波安家使以色列人陷在罪裏的那罪，仍然去行，並且在撒馬利亞留下亞舍拉。

⁷亞蘭王滅絕約哈斯的民，踐踏他們如禾場上的塵沙，只給約哈斯留下五十馬兵、十輛戰車、一萬步兵。

⁸約哈斯其餘的事，凡他所行的和他的勇力，都寫在以色列諸王記上。⁹約哈斯與他列祖同睡，葬在撒馬利亞。他兒子約阿施接續他作王。

約阿施作以色列王

¹⁰猶大王約阿施三十七年，約哈斯的兒子約阿施在撒馬利亞登基，作以色列王十六年。¹¹他行耶和華眼中看為惡的事，不離開尼八的兒子耶羅波安使以色列人陷在罪裏的一切罪，仍然去行。

¹²約阿施其餘的事，凡他所行的和他與猶大王亞瑪謝爭戰的勇力，都寫在以色列諸王記上。¹³約阿施與他列祖同睡，耶羅波安坐了他的位。約阿施與以色列諸王一同葬在撒馬利亞。

¹⁴以利沙得了必死的病，以色列王約阿施下來看他，伏在他臉上哭泣，說：“我父啊！我父啊！以色列的戰車馬兵啊！”

¹⁵以利沙對他說：“你取弓箭來。”王就取了弓箭來。¹⁶又對以色列王說：“你用手拿弓。”王就用手拿弓，以利沙按手在王的手上。

them. ³So the LORD's anger burned against Israel, and for a long time he kept them under the power of Hazael king of Aram and Ben-Hadad his son.

⁴Then Jehoahaz sought the LORD's favor, and the LORD listened to him, for he saw how severely the king of Aram was oppressing Israel. ⁵The LORD provided a deliverer for Israel, and they escaped from the power of Aram. So the Israelites lived in their own homes as they had before. ⁶But they did not turn away from the sins of the house of Jeroboam, which he had caused Israel to commit; they continued in them. Also, the Asherah pole*a* remained standing in Samaria.

⁷Nothing had been left of the army of Jehoahaz except fifty horsemen, ten chariots and ten thousand foot soldiers, for the king of Aram had destroyed the rest and made them like the dust at threshing time.

⁸As for the other events of the reign of Jehoahaz, all he did and his achievements, are they not written in the book of the annals of the kings of Israel? ⁹Jehoahaz rested with his fathers and was buried in Samaria. And Jehoash*b* his son succeeded him as king.

Jehoash King of Israel

¹⁰In the thirty-seventh year of Joash king of Judah, Jehoash son of Jehoahaz became king of Israel in Samaria, and he reigned sixteen years. ¹¹He did evil in the eyes of the LORD and did not turn away from any of the sins of Jeroboam son of Nebat, which he had caused Israel to commit; he continued in them.

¹²As for the other events of the reign of Jehoash, all he did and his achievements, including his war against Amaziah king of Judah, are they not written in the book of the annals of the kings of Israel? ¹³Jehoash rested with his fathers, and Jeroboam succeeded him on the throne. Jehoash was buried in Samaria with the kings of Israel.

¹⁴Now Elisha was suffering from the illness from which he died. Jehoash king of Israel went down to see him and wept over him. "My father! My father!" he cried. "The chariots and horsemen of Israel!"

¹⁵Elisha said, "Get a bow and some arrows," and he did so. ¹⁶"Take the bow in your hands," he said to the king of Israel. When he had taken it, Elisha put his hands on the king's hands.

a 6 That is, a symbol of the goddess Asherah; here and elsewhere in 2 Kings　*b 9* Hebrew *Joash*, a variant of *Jehoash*; also in verses 12-14 and 25

¹⁷"Open the east window," he said, and he opened it. "Shoot!" Elisha said, and he shot. "The LORD's arrow of victory, the arrow of victory over Aram!" Elisha declared. "You will completely destroy the Arameans at Aphek."

¹⁸Then he said, "Take the arrows," and the king took them. Elisha told him, "Strike the ground." He struck it three times and stopped. ¹⁹The man of God was angry with him and said, "You should have struck the ground five or six times; then you would have defeated Aram and completely destroyed it. But now you will defeat it only three times."

²⁰Elisha died and was buried.

Now Moabite raiders used to enter the country every spring. ²¹Once while some Israelites were burying a man, suddenly they saw a band of raiders; so they threw the man's body into Elisha's tomb. When the body touched Elisha's bones, the man came to life and stood up on his feet.

²²Hazael king of Aram oppressed Israel throughout the reign of Jehoahaz. ²³But the LORD was gracious to them and had compassion and showed concern for them because of his covenant with Abraham, Isaac and Jacob. To this day he has been unwilling to destroy them or banish them from his presence.

²⁴Hazael king of Aram died, and Ben-Hadad his son succeeded him as king. ²⁵Then Jehoash son of Jehoahaz recaptured from Ben-Hadad son of Hazael the towns he had taken in battle from his father Jehoahaz. Three times Jehoash defeated him, and so he recovered the Israelite towns.

Amaziah King of Judah

14 In the second year of Jehoash^a son of Jehoahaz king of Israel, Amaziah son of Joash king of Judah began to reign. ²He was twenty-five years old when he became king, and he reigned in Jerusalem twenty-nine years. His mother's name was Jehoaddin; she was from Jerusalem. ³He did what was right in the eyes of the LORD, but not as his father David had done. In everything he followed the example of his father Joash. ⁴The high places, however, were not removed; the people continued to offer sacrifices and burn incense there.

⁵After the kingdom was firmly in his grasp, he executed the officials who had murdered his father the king. ⁶Yet he did not put the sons of the assassins to death, in accordance with what

---

¹⁷說:"你開朝東的窗戶。"他就開了。以利沙說:"射箭吧!"他就射箭。以利沙說:"這是耶和華的得勝箭,就是戰勝亞蘭人的箭;因為你必在亞弗攻打亞蘭人,直到滅盡他們。"

¹⁸以利沙又說:"取幾枝箭來。"他就取了來。以利沙說:"打地吧!"他打了三次,便止住了。¹⁹神人向他發怒,說:"應當擊打五六次,就能攻打亞蘭人,直到滅盡。現在只能打敗亞蘭人三次。"

²⁰以利沙死了,人將他葬埋。

到了新年,有一羣摩押人犯境,²¹有人正葬死人,忽然看見一羣人,就把死人拋在以利沙的墳墓裏,一碰着以利沙的骸骨,死人就復活站起來了。

²²約哈斯年間,亞蘭王哈薛屢次欺壓以色列人。²³耶和華卻因與亞伯拉罕、以撒、雅各所立的約,仍施恩給以色列人,憐恤他們、眷顧他們,不肯滅盡他們,尚未趕逐他們離開自己面前。

²⁴亞蘭王哈薛死了,他兒子便哈達接續他作王。²⁵從前哈薛和約阿施的父親約哈斯爭戰,攻取了些城邑;現在約哈斯的兒子約阿施三次打敗哈薛的兒子便哈達,就收回了以色列的城邑。

亞瑪謝作猶大王

14 以色列王約哈斯的兒子約阿施第二年,猶大王約阿施的兒子亞瑪謝登基。²他登基的時候年二十五歲,在耶路撒冷作王二十九年。他母親名叫約耶但,是耶路撒冷人。³亞瑪謝行耶和華眼中看為正的事,但不如他祖大衛,乃效法他父約阿施一切所行的,⁴只是邱壇還沒有廢去,百姓仍在那裏獻祭燒香。

⁵國一堅定,就把殺他父王的臣僕殺了,⁶卻沒有治死殺王之人的兒

---

^a 1 Hebrew *Joash*, a variant of *Jehoash*; also in verses 13, 23 and 27

子，是照摩西律法書上耶和華所吩咐的說：「不可因子殺父，也不可因父殺子，各人要為本身的罪而死。」

7亞瑪謝在鹽谷殺了以東人一萬，又攻取了西拉，改名叫約帖，直到今日。

8那時，亞瑪謝差遣使者去見耶戶的孫子、約哈斯的兒子以色列王約阿施，說：「你來，我們二人相見於戰場。」

9以色列王約阿施差遣使者去見猶大王亞瑪謝說：「黎巴嫩的蒺藜差遣使者去見黎巴嫩的香柏樹，說：『將你的女兒給我兒子為妻。』後來黎巴嫩有一個野獸經過，把蒺藜踐踏了。10你打敗了以東人就心高氣傲，你以此為榮耀，在家裏安居就罷了，為何要惹禍，使自己和猶大國一同敗亡呢？」

11亞瑪謝卻不肯聽這話。於是以色列王約阿施上來，在猶大的伯示麥與猶大王亞瑪謝相見於戰場。12猶大人敗在以色列人面前，各自逃回家裏去了。13以色列王約阿施在伯示麥擒住亞哈謝的孫子、約阿施的兒子猶大王亞瑪謝，就來到耶路撒冷，拆毀耶路撒冷的城牆，從以法蓮門直到角門，共四百肘；14又將耶和華殿裏與王宮府庫裏所有的金銀和器皿都拿了去，並帶人去為質，就回撒馬利亞去了。

15約阿施其餘所行的事和他的勇力，並與猶大王亞瑪謝爭戰的事，都寫在以色列諸王記上。16約阿施與他列祖同睡，葬在撒馬利亞以色列諸王的墳地裏。他兒子耶羅波安接續他作王。

17以色列王約哈斯的兒子約阿施死後，猶大王約阿施的兒子亞瑪謝又活了十五年。18亞瑪謝其餘的事，都寫在猶大列王記上。

19耶路撒冷有人背叛亞瑪謝，他就逃到拉吉，叛黨卻打發人到拉吉將

is written in the Book of the Law of Moses where the LORD commanded: "Fathers shall not be put to death for their children, nor children put to death for their fathers; each is to die for his own sins."[a]

7He was the one who defeated ten thousand Edomites in the Valley of Salt and captured Sela in battle, calling it Joktheel, the name it has to this day.

8Then Amaziah sent messengers to Jehoash son of Jehoahaz, the son of Jehu, king of Israel, with the challenge: "Come, meet me face to face."

9But Jehoash king of Israel replied to Amaziah king of Judah: "A thistle in Lebanon sent a message to a cedar in Lebanon, 'Give your daughter to my son in marriage.' Then a wild beast in Lebanon came along and trampled the thistle underfoot. 10You have indeed defeated Edom and now you are arrogant. Glory in your victory, but stay at home! Why ask for trouble and cause your own downfall and that of Judah also?"

11Amaziah, however, would not listen, so Jehoash king of Israel attacked. He and Amaziah king of Judah faced each other at Beth Shemesh in Judah. 12Judah was routed by Israel, and every man fled to his home. 13Jehoash king of Israel captured Amaziah king of Judah, the son of Joash, the son of Ahaziah, at Beth Shemesh. Then Jehoash went to Jerusalem and broke down the wall of Jerusalem from the Ephraim Gate to the Corner Gate—a section about six hundred feet long.[b] 14He took all the gold and silver and all the articles found in the temple of the LORD and in the treasuries of the royal palace. He also took hostages and returned to Samaria.

15As for the other events of the reign of Jehoash, what he did and his achievements, including his war against Amaziah king of Judah, are they not written in the book of the annals of the kings of Israel? 16Jehoash rested with his fathers and was buried in Samaria with the kings of Israel. And Jeroboam his son succeeded him as king.

17Amaziah son of Joash king of Judah lived for fifteen years after the death of Jehoash son of Jehoahaz king of Israel. 18As for the other events of Amaziah's reign, are they not written in the book of the annals of the kings of Judah?

19They conspired against him in Jerusalem, and he fled to Lachish, but they sent men after

a 6 Deut. 24:16   b 13 Hebrew four hundred cubits (about 180 meters)

him to Lachish and killed him there. [20]He was brought back by horse and was buried in Jerusalem with his fathers, in the City of David.

[21]Then all the people of Judah took Azariah,[a] who was sixteen years old, and made him king in place of his father Amaziah. [22]He was the one who rebuilt Elath and restored it to Judah after Amaziah rested with his fathers.

Jeroboam II King of Israel

[23]In the fifteenth year of Amaziah son of Joash king of Judah, Jeroboam son of Jehoash king of Israel became king in Samaria, and he reigned forty-one years. [24]He did evil in the eyes of the LORD and did not turn away from any of the sins of Jeroboam son of Nebat, which he had caused Israel to commit. [25]He was the one who restored the boundaries of Israel from Lebo[b] Hamath to the Sea of the Arabah,[c] in accordance with the word of the LORD, the God of Israel, spoken through his servant Jonah son of Amittai, the prophet from Gath Hepher.

[26]The LORD had seen how bitterly everyone in Israel, whether slave or free, was suffering; there was no one to help them. [27]And since the LORD had not said he would blot out the name of Israel from under heaven, he saved them by the hand of Jeroboam son of Jehoash.

[28]As for the other events of Jeroboam's reign, all he did, and his military achievements, including how he recovered for Israel both Damascus and Hamath, which had belonged to Yaudi,[d] are they not written in the book of the annals of the kings of Israel? [29]Jeroboam rested with his fathers, the kings of Israel. And Zechariah his son succeeded him as king.

Azariah King of Judah

15 In the twenty-seventh year of Jeroboam king of Israel, Azariah son of Amaziah king of Judah began to reign. [2]He was sixteen years old when he became king, and he reigned in Jerusalem fifty-two years. His mother's name was Jecoliah; she was from Jerusalem. [3]He did what was right in the eyes of the LORD, just as his father Amaziah had done. [4]The high places, however, were not removed; the people continued to offer sacrifices and burn incense there.

[5]The LORD afflicted the king with leprosy[e] until the day he died, and he lived in a separate

他殺了。[20]人就用馬將他的屍首馱到耶路撒冷，葬在大衛城他列祖的墳地裏。

[21]猶大眾民ել立亞瑪謝的兒子亞撒利雅（註：又名"烏西雅"）接續他父作王，那時他年十六歲。[22]亞瑪謝與他列祖同睡之後，亞撒利雅收回以拉他仍歸猶大，又重新修理。

耶羅波安二世作以色列王

[23]猶大王約阿施的兒子亞瑪謝十五年，以色列王約阿施的兒子耶羅波安在撒馬利亞登基，作王四十一年。[24]他行耶和華眼中看為惡的事，不離開尼八的兒子耶羅波安使以色列人陷在罪裏的一切罪。[25]他收回以色列邊界之地，從哈馬口直到亞拉巴海，正如耶和華以色列的神藉他僕人迦特希弗人亞米太的兒子先知約拿所說的。

[26]因為耶和華看見以色列人甚是艱苦，無論困住的、自由的都沒有了，也無人幫助以色列人。[27]耶和華並沒有說要將以色列的名從天下塗抹，乃藉約阿施的兒子耶羅波安拯救他們。

[28]耶羅波安其餘的事，凡他所行的和他的勇力，他是怎樣爭戰，怎樣收回大馬土革和先前屬猶大的哈馬歸以色列，都寫在以色列諸王記上。[29]耶羅波安與他列祖以色列諸王同睡。他兒子撒迦利雅接續他作王。

亞撒利雅作猶大王

15 以色列王耶羅波安二十七年，猶大王亞瑪謝的兒子亞撒利雅登基，[2]他登基的時候年十六歲，在耶路撒冷作王五十二年。他母親名叫耶可利雅，是耶路撒冷人。[3]亞撒利雅行耶和華眼中看為正的事，效法他父親亞瑪謝一切所行的，[4]只是邱壇還沒有廢去，百姓仍在那裏獻祭燒香。

[5]耶和華降災與王，使他長大痲瘋，直到死日，他就住在別的宮裏。

---

a 21 Also called Uzziah   b 25 Or from the entrance to
c 25 That is, the Dead Sea   d 28 Or Judah   e 5 The Hebrew
word was used for various diseases affecting the skin—not
necessarily leprosy.

他的兒子約坦管理家事，治理國民。

⁶亞撒利雅其餘的事，凡他所行的，都寫在猶大列王記上。⁷亞撒利雅與他列祖同睡，葬在大衛城他列祖的墳地裏。他兒子約坦接續他作王。

撒迦利雅作以色列王

⁸猶大王亞撒利雅三十八年，耶羅波安的兒子撒迦利雅在撒馬利亞作以色列王六個月。⁹他行耶和華眼中看為惡的事，效法他列祖所行的，不離開尼八的兒子耶羅波安使以色列人陷在罪裏的那罪。

¹⁰雅比的兒子沙龍背叛他，在百姓面前擊殺他，篡了他的位。¹¹撒迦利雅其餘的事，都寫在以色列諸王記上。¹²這是從前耶和華應許雅戶說："你的子孫必坐以色列的國位直到四代。"這話果然應驗了。

沙龍作以色列王

¹³猶大王烏西雅（註：就是"亞撒利雅"）三十九年，雅比的兒子沙龍登基，在撒馬利亞作王一個月。¹⁴迦底的兒子米拿現從得撒上撒馬利亞，殺了雅比的兒子沙龍，篡了他的位。

¹⁵沙龍其餘的事和他背叛的情形，都寫在以色列諸王記上。

¹⁶那時，米拿現從得撒起，攻打提斐薩和其四境，擊殺城中一切的人，剖開其中所有的孕婦，都因他們沒有給他開城。

米拿現作以色列王

¹⁷猶大王亞撒利雅三十九年，迦底的兒子米拿現登基，在撒馬利亞作以色列王十年。¹⁸他行耶和華眼中看為惡的事，終身不離開尼八的兒子耶羅波安使以色列人陷在罪裏的那罪。

¹⁹亞述王普勒來攻擊以色列國，

house.^a Jotham the king's son had charge of the palace and governed the people of the land.

⁶As for the other events of Azariah's reign, and all he did, are they not written in the book of the annals of the kings of Judah? ⁷Azariah rested with his fathers and was buried near them in the City of David. And Jotham his son succeeded him as king.

Zechariah King of Israel

⁸In the thirty-eighth year of Azariah king of Judah, Zechariah son of Jeroboam became king of Israel in Samaria, and he reigned six months. ⁹He did evil in the eyes of the LORD, as his fathers had done. He did not turn away from the sins of Jeroboam son of Nebat, which he had caused Israel to commit.

¹⁰Shallum son of Jabesh conspired against Zechariah. He attacked him in front of the people,^b assassinated him and succeeded him as king. ¹¹The other events of Zechariah's reign are written in the book of the annals of the kings of Israel. ¹²So the word of the LORD spoken to Jehu was fulfilled: "Your descendants will sit on the throne of Israel to the fourth generation."^c

Shallum King of Israel

¹³Shallum son of Jabesh became king in the thirty-ninth year of Uzziah king of Judah, and he reigned in Samaria one month. ¹⁴Then Menahem son of Gadi went from Tirzah up to Samaria. He attacked Shallum son of Jabesh in Samaria, assassinated him and succeeded him as king.

¹⁵The other events of Shallum's reign, and the conspiracy he led, are written in the book of the annals of the kings of Israel.

¹⁶At that time Menahem, starting out from Tirzah, attacked Tiphsah and everyone in the city and its vicinity, because they refused to open their gates. He sacked Tiphsah and ripped open all the pregnant women.

Menahem King of Israel

¹⁷In the thirty-ninth year of Azariah king of Judah, Menahem son of Gadi became king of Israel, and he reigned in Samaria ten years. ¹⁸He did evil in the eyes of the LORD. During his entire reign he did not turn away from the sins of Jeroboam son of Nebat, which he had caused Israel to commit.

¹⁹Then Pul^d king of Assyria invaded the land,

---

a 5 Or in a house where he was relieved of responsibility
b 10 Hebrew; some Septuagint manuscripts in Ibleam
c 12 2 Kings 10:30   d 19 Also called Tiglath-Pileser

and Menahem gave him a thousand talents[a] of silver to gain his support and strengthen his own hold on the kingdom. 20Menahem exacted this money from Israel. Every wealthy man had to contribute fifty shekels[b] of silver to be given to the king of Assyria. So the king of Assyria withdrew and stayed in the land no longer.

21As for the other events of Menahem's reign, and all he did, are they not written in the book of the annals of the kings of Israel? 22Menahem rested with his fathers. And Pekahiah his son succeeded him as king.

Pekahiah King of Israel

23In the fiftieth year of Azariah king of Judah, Pekahiah son of Menahem became king of Israel in Samaria, and he reigned two years. 24Pekahiah did evil in the eyes of the LORD. He did not turn away from the sins of Jeroboam son of Nebat, which he had caused Israel to commit. 25One of his chief officers, Pekah son of Remaliah, conspired against him. Taking fifty men of Gilead with him, he assassinated Pekahiah, along with Argob and Arieh, in the citadel of the royal palace at Samaria. So Pekah killed Pekahiah and succeeded him as king.

26The other events of Pekahiah's reign, and all he did, are written in the book of the annals of the kings of Israel.

Pekah King of Israel

27In the fifty-second year of Azariah king of Judah, Pekah son of Remaliah became king of Israel in Samaria, and he reigned twenty years. 28He did evil in the eyes of the LORD. He did not turn away from the sins of Jeroboam son of Nebat, which he had caused Israel to commit.

29In the time of Pekah king of Israel, Tiglath-Pileser king of Assyria came and took Ijon, Abel Beth Maacah, Janoah, Kedesh and Hazor. He took Gilead and Galilee, including all the land of Naphtali, and deported the people to Assyria. 30Then Hoshea son of Elah conspired against Pekah son of Remaliah. He attacked and assassinated him, and then succeeded him as king in the twentieth year of Jotham son of Uzziah.

31As for the other events of Pekah's reign, and all he did, are they not written in the book of the annals of the kings of Israel?

Jotham King of Judah

32In the second year of Pekah son of Remaliah king of Israel, Jotham son of Uzziah

米拿現給他一千他連得銀子，請普勒幫助他堅定國位。20米拿現向以色列一切大富戶索要銀子，使他們各出五十舍客勒，就給了亞述王。於是亞述王回去，不在國中停留。

21米拿現其餘的事，凡他所行的，都寫在以色列諸王記上。22米拿現與他列祖同睡。他兒子比加轄接續他作王。

比加轄作以色列王

23猶大王亞撒利雅五十年，米拿現的兒子比加轄在撒馬利亞登基，作以色列王二年。24他行耶和華眼中看為惡的事，不離開尼八的兒子耶羅波安使以色列人陷在罪裏的那罪。25比加轄的將軍、利瑪利的兒子比加背叛他，在撒馬利亞王宮裏的衛所殺了他。亞珥歌伯和亞利耶並基列的五十人幫助比加，比加擊殺他，篡了他的位。

26比加轄其餘的事，凡他所行的，都寫在以色列諸王記上。

比加作以色列王

27猶大王亞撒利雅五十二年，利瑪利的兒子比加在撒馬利亞登基，作以色列王二十年。28他行耶和華眼中看為惡的事，不離開尼八的兒子耶羅波安使以色列人陷在罪裏的那罪。

29以色列王比加年間，亞述王提革拉毗列色來奪了以雲、亞伯伯瑪迦、亞挪、基低斯、夏瑣、基列、加利利和拿弗他利全地，將這些地方的居民都擄到亞述去了。30烏西雅的兒子約坦二十年，以拉的兒子何細亞背叛利瑪利的兒子比加，擊殺他，篡了他的位。

31比加其餘的事，凡他所行的，都寫在以色列諸王記上。

約坦作猶大王

32以色列王利瑪利的兒子比加第二年，猶大王烏西雅的兒子約坦登

a 19 That is, about 37 tons (about 34 metric tons)   b 20 That is, about 1 1/4 pounds (about 0.6 kilogram)

基。³³他登基的時候年二十五歲，在耶路撒冷作王十六年。他母親名叫耶路沙，是撒督的女兒。³⁴約坦行耶和華眼中看為正的事，效法他父親烏西雅一切所行的，³⁵只是邱壇還沒有廢去，百姓仍在那裏獻祭燒香。約坦建立耶和華殿的上門。

³⁶約坦其餘的事，凡他所行的，都寫在猶大列王記上。³⁷在那些日子，耶和華才使亞蘭王利汛和利瑪利的兒子比加去攻擊猶大。³⁸約坦與他列祖同睡，葬在他祖大衛城他列祖的墳地裏。他兒子亞哈斯接續他作王。

亞哈斯作猶大王

16 利瑪利的兒子比加十七年，猶大王約坦的兒子亞哈斯登基。²他登基的時候年二十歲，在耶路撒冷作王十六年。不像他祖大衛行耶和華他神眼中看為正的事，³卻效法以色列諸王所行的，又照着耶和華從以色列人面前趕出的外邦人所行可憎的事，使他的兒子經火，⁴並在邱壇上、山岡上、各青翠樹下獻祭燒香。

⁵亞蘭王利汛和以色列王利瑪利的兒子比加上來攻打耶路撒冷，圍困亞哈斯，卻不能勝他。⁶當時亞蘭王利汛收回以拉他歸與亞蘭，將猶大人從以拉他趕出去。亞蘭人（註：有作"以東人"的）就來到以拉他，住在那裏，直到今日。⁷亞哈斯差遣使者去見亞述王提革拉毗列色，說："我是你的僕人、你的兒子。現在亞蘭王和以色列王攻擊我，求你來救我脫離他們的手。"⁸亞哈斯將耶和華殿裏和王宮府庫裏所有的金銀都送給亞述王為禮物。⁹亞述王應允了他，就上去攻打大馬士革，將城攻取，殺了利汛，把居民擄到吉珥。

¹⁰亞哈斯王上大馬士革去迎接亞述王提革拉毗列色，在大馬士革看見

king of Judah began to reign. ³³He was twenty-five years old when he became king, and he reigned in Jerusalem sixteen years. His mother's name was Jerusha daughter of Zadok. ³⁴He did what was right in the eyes of the LORD, just as his father Uzziah had done. ³⁵The high places, however, were not removed; the people continued to offer sacrifices and burn incense there. Jotham rebuilt the Upper Gate of the temple of the LORD.

³⁶As for the other events of Jotham's reign, and what he did, are they not written in the book of the annals of the kings of Judah? ³⁷(In those days the LORD began to send Rezin king of Aram and Pekah son of Remaliah against Judah.) ³⁸Jotham rested with his fathers and was buried with them in the City of David, the city of his father. And Ahaz his son succeeded him as king.

Ahaz King of Judah

16 In the seventeenth year of Pekah son of Remaliah, Ahaz son of Jotham king of Judah began to reign. ²Ahaz was twenty years old when he became king, and he reigned in Jerusalem sixteen years. Unlike David his father, he did not do what was right in the eyes of the LORD his God. ³He walked in the ways of the kings of Israel and even sacrificed his son in[a] the fire, following the detestable ways of the nations the LORD had driven out before the Israelites. ⁴He offered sacrifices and burned incense at the high places, on the hilltops and under every spreading tree.

⁵Then Rezin king of Aram and Pekah son of Remaliah king of Israel marched up to fight against Jerusalem and besieged Ahaz, but they could not overpower him. ⁶At that time, Rezin king of Aram recovered Elath for Aram by driving out the men of Judah. Edomites then moved into Elath and have lived there to this day.

⁷Ahaz sent messengers to say to Tiglath-Pileser king of Assyria, "I am your servant and vassal. Come up and save me out of the hand of the king of Aram and of the king of Israel, who are attacking me." ⁸And Ahaz took the silver and gold found in the temple of the LORD and in the treasuries of the royal palace and sent it as a gift to the king of Assyria. ⁹The king of Assyria complied by attacking Damascus and capturing it. He deported its inhabitants to Kir and put Rezin to death.

¹⁰Then King Ahaz went to Damascus to meet Tiglath-Pileser king of Assyria. He saw an altar

a 3 Or even made his son pass through

in Damascus and sent to Uriah the priest a sketch of the altar, with detailed plans for its construction. [11]So Uriah the priest built an altar in accordance with all the plans that King Ahaz had sent from Damascus and finished it before King Ahaz returned. [12]When the king came back from Damascus and saw the altar, he approached it and presented offerings[a] on it. [13]He offered up his burnt offering and grain offering, poured out his drink offering, and sprinkled the blood of his fellowship offerings[b] on the altar. [14]The bronze altar that stood before the LORD he brought from the front of the temple—from between the new altar and the temple of the LORD—and put it on the north side of new altar.

[15]King Ahaz then gave these orders to Uriah the priest: "On the large new altar, offer the morning burnt offering and the evening grain offering, the king's burnt offering and his grain offering, and the burnt offering of all the people of the land, and their grain offering and their drink offering. Sprinkle on the altar all the blood of the burnt offerings and sacrifices. But I will use the bronze altar for seeking guidance." [16]And Uriah the priest did just as King Ahaz had ordered.

[17]King Ahaz took away the side panels and removed the basins from the movable stands. He removed the Sea from the bronze bulls that supported it and set it on a stone base. [18]He took away the Sabbath canopy[c] that had been built at the temple and removed the royal entryway outside the temple of the LORD, in deference to the king of Assyria.

[19]As for the other events of the reign of Ahaz, and what he did, are they not written in the book of the annals of the kings of Judah? [20]Ahaz rested with his fathers and was buried with them in the City of David. And Hezekiah his son succeeded him as king.

Hoshea Last King of Israel

17 In the twelfth year of Ahaz king of Judah, Hoshea son of Elah became king of Israel in Samaria, and he reigned nine years. [2]He did evil in the eyes of the LORD, but not like the kings of Israel who preceded him.

[3]Shalmaneser king of Assyria came up to attack Hoshea, who had been Shalmaneser's vassal and had paid him tribute. [4]But the king of Assyria discovered that Hoshea was a traitor,

一座壇，就照壇的規模樣式做法畫了圖樣，送到祭司烏利亞那裏。[11]祭司烏利亞照着亞哈斯王從大馬士革送來的圖樣，在亞哈斯王沒有從大馬士革回來之先，建築一座壇。[12]王從大馬士革回來看見壇，就近前來，在壇上獻祭，[13]燒燔祭、素祭，澆奠祭，將平安祭牲的血灑在壇上，[14]又將耶和華面前的銅壇，從耶和華殿和新壇的中間搬到新壇的北邊。

[15]亞哈斯王吩咐祭司烏利亞說：「早晨的燔祭、晚上的素祭、王的燔祭、素祭、國內眾民的燔祭、素祭、奠祭，都要燒在大壇上；燔祭牲和平安祭牲的血也要灑在這壇上；只是銅壇我要用以求問耶和華。」[16]祭司烏利亞就照着亞哈斯王所吩咐的行了。

[17]亞哈斯王打掉盆座四面鑲着的心子，把盆從座上挪下來，又將銅海從馱海的銅牛上搬下來，放在鋪石地。[18]又因亞述王的緣故，將耶和華殿為安息日所蓋的廊子和王從外入殿的廊子挪移，圍繞耶和華的殿。

[19]亞哈斯其餘所行的事，都寫在猶大列王記上。[20]亞哈斯與他列祖同睡，葬在大衛城他列祖的墳地裏。他兒子希西家接續他作王。

何細亞作以色列末後之王

17 猶大王亞哈斯十二年，以拉的兒子何細亞在撒馬利亞登基，作以色列王九年。[2]他行耶和華眼中看為惡的事，只是不像在他以前的以色列諸王。

[3]亞述王撒縵以色上來攻擊何細亞，何細亞就臣服他，給他進貢。[4]何細亞背叛，差人去見埃及王梭，

---

a 12 Or *and went up*　b 13 Traditionally *peace offerings*
c 18 Or *the dais of his throne* (see Septuagint)

不照往年所行的與亞述王進貢。亞述王知道了，就把他鎖禁，囚在監裏。 5 亞述王上來攻擊以色列遍地，上到撒馬利亞，圍困三年。 6 何細亞第九年，亞述王攻取了撒馬利亞，將以色列人擄到亞述，把他們安置在哈臘與歌散的哈博河邊，並瑪代人的城邑。

以色列人因犯罪被擄

7 這是因以色列人得罪那領他們出埃及地、脫離埃及王法老手的耶和華他們的神，去敬畏別神，8 隨從耶和華在他們面前所趕出外邦人的風俗和以色列諸王所立的條規。 9 以色列人暗中行不正的事，違背耶和華他們的神。在他們所有的城邑，從瞭望樓直到堅固城，建築邱壇； 10 在各高岡上、各青翠樹下立柱像和木偶； 11 在邱壇上燒香，效法耶和華在他們面前趕出的外邦人所行的；又行惡事惹動耶和華的怒氣； 12 且侍奉偶像，就是耶和華警戒他們不可行的。 13 但耶和華藉眾先知、先見勸戒以色列人和猶大人說：“當離開你們的惡行，謹守我的誡命律例，遵行我吩咐你們列祖，並藉我僕人眾先知所傳給你們的律法。”

14 他們卻不聽從，竟硬着頸項，效法他們列祖，不信服耶和華他們的神。 15 厭棄他的律例和他與他們列祖所立的約，並勸戒他們的話，隨從虛無的神，自己成為虛妄，效法周圍的外邦人，就是耶和華囑咐他們不可效法的。

16 離棄耶和華他們神的一切誡命，為自己鑄了兩個牛犢的像，立了亞舍拉，敬拜天上的萬象，侍奉巴力，17 又使他們的兒女經火，用占

for he had sent envoys to So[a] king of Egypt, and he no longer paid tribute to the king of Assyria, as he had done year by year. Therefore Shalmaneser seized him and put him in prison. 5The king of Assyria invaded the entire land, marched against Samaria and laid siege to it for three years. 6In the ninth year of Hoshea, the king of Assyria captured Samaria and deported the Israelites to Assyria. He settled them in Halah, in Gozan on the Habor River and in the towns of the Medes.

Israel Exiled Because of Sin

7All this took place because the Israelites had sinned against the LORD their God, who had brought them up out of Egypt from under the power of Pharaoh king of Egypt. They worshiped other gods 8and followed the practices of the nations the LORD had driven out before them, as well as the practices that the kings of Israel had introduced. 9The Israelites secretly did things against the LORD their God that were not right. From watchtower to fortified city they built themselves high places in all their towns. 10They set up sacred stones and Asherah poles on every high hill and under every spreading tree. 11At every high place they burned incense, as the nations whom the LORD had driven out before them had done. They did wicked things that provoked the LORD to anger. 12They worshiped idols, though the LORD had said, "You shall not do this."[b] 13The LORD warned Israel and Judah through all his prophets and seers: "Turn from your evil ways. Observe my commands and decrees, in accordance with the entire Law that I commanded your fathers to obey and that I delivered to you through my servants the prophets."

14But they would not listen and were as stiff-necked as their fathers, who did not trust in the LORD their God. 15They rejected his decrees and the covenant he had made with their fathers and the warnings he had given them. They followed worthless idols and themselves became worthless. They imitated the nations around them although the LORD had ordered them, "Do not do as they do," and they did the things the LORD had forbidden them to do.

16They forsook all the commands of the LORD their God and made for themselves two idols cast in the shape of calves, and an Asherah pole. They bowed down to all the starry hosts, and they worshiped Baal. 17They sacrificed their

a 4 Or *to Sais, to the; So* is possibly an abbreviation for *Osorkon.*
b 12 Exodus 20:4, 5

sons and daughters in*a* the fire. They practiced divination and sorcery and sold themselves to do evil in the eyes of the LORD, provoking him to anger.

18So the LORD was very angry with Israel and removed them from his presence. Only the tribe of Judah was left, 19and even Judah did not keep the commands of the LORD their God. They followed the practices Israel had introduced. 20Therefore the LORD rejected all the people of Israel; he afflicted them and gave them into the hands of plunderers, until he thrust them from his presence.

21When he tore Israel away from the house of David, they made Jeroboam son of Nebat their king. Jeroboam enticed Israel away from following the LORD and caused them to commit a great sin. 22The Israelites persisted in all the sins of Jeroboam and did not turn away from them 23until the LORD removed them from his presence, as he had warned through all his servants the prophets. So the people of Israel were taken from their homeland into exile in Assyria, and they are still there.

Samaria Resettled

24The king of Assyria brought people from Babylon, Cuthah, Avva, Hamath and Sepharvaim and settled them in the towns of Samaria to replace the Israelites. They took over Samaria and lived in its towns. 25When they first lived there, they did not worship the LORD; so he sent lions among them and they killed some of the people. 26It was reported to the king of Assyria: "The people you deported and resettled in the towns of Samaria do not know what the god of that country requires. He has sent lions among them, which are killing them off, because the people do not know what he requires."

27Then the king of Assyria gave this order: "Have one of the priests you took captive from Samaria go back to live there and teach the people what the god of the land requires." 28So one of the priests who had been exiled from Samaria came to live in Bethel and taught them how to worship the LORD.

29Nevertheless, each national group made its own gods in the several towns where they settled, and set them up in the shrines the people of Samaria had made at the high places. 30The men from Babylon made Succoth Benoth, the men from Cuthah made Nergal, and the men from Hamath made Ashima; 31the Avvites made Nibhaz and Tartak, and the Sepharvites burned

卜、行法術賣了自己，行耶和華眼中看為惡的事，惹動他的怒氣。

18所以耶和華向以色列人大大發怒，從自己面前趕出他們，只剩下猶大一個支派。19猶大人也不遵守耶和華他們神的誡命，隨從以色列人所立的條規。20耶和華就厭棄以色列全族，使他們受苦，把他們交在搶奪他們的人手中，以致趕出他們離開自己面前。

21將以色列國從大衞家奪回，他們就立尼八的兒子耶羅波安作王。耶羅波安引誘以色列人不隨從耶和華，陷在大罪裏。22以色列人犯耶羅波安所犯的一切罪，總不離開，23以致耶和華從自己面前趕出他們，正如藉他僕人眾先知所說的。這樣，以色列人從本地被擄到亞述，直到今日。

置異族於撒馬利亞

24亞述王從巴比倫、古他、亞瓦、哈馬，和西法瓦音遷移人來，安置在撒馬利亞的城邑，代替以色列人，他們就得了撒馬利亞，住在其中。25他們才住那裏的時候，不敬畏耶和華，所以耶和華叫獅子進入他們中間，咬死了些人。26有人告訴亞述王，說：「你所遷移安置在撒馬利亞各城的那些民，不知道那地之神的規矩，所以那神叫獅子進入他們中間，咬死他們。」

27亞述王就吩咐說：「叫所擄來的祭司回去一個，使他住在那裏，將那地之神的規矩指教那些民。」28於是有一個從撒馬利亞擄去的祭司回來，住在伯特利，指教他們怎樣敬畏耶和華。

29然而，各族之人在所住的城裏，各為自己製造神像，安置在撒馬利亞人所造有邱壇的殿中。30巴比倫人造疏割毗訥像；古他人造匿甲像；哈馬人造亞示瑪像；31亞瓦人造匿哈和他珥他像；西法瓦音人用火焚燒兒

---

a 17 Or They made their sons and daughters pass through

女，獻給西法瓦音的神亞得米勒和亞拿米勒。³²他們懼怕耶和華，也從他們中間立邱壇的祭司，為他們在有邱壇的殿中獻祭。³³他們又懼怕耶和華，又侍奉自己的神，從何邦遷移，就隨何邦的風俗。

³⁴他們直到如今仍照先前的風俗去行，不專心敬畏耶和華，不全守自己的規矩、典章，也不遵守耶和華吩咐雅各後裔的律法、誡命。雅各，就是從前耶和華起名叫以色列的。³⁵耶和華曾與他們立約，囑咐他們說："不可敬畏別神，不可跪拜侍奉他，也不可向他獻祭。³⁶但那用大能和伸出來的膀臂領你們出埃及地的耶和華，你們當敬畏、跪拜，向他獻祭。³⁷他給你們寫的律例、典章、律法、誡命，你們應當永遠謹守遵行，不可敬畏別神。³⁸我耶和華與你們所立的約你們不可忘記，也不可敬畏別神。³⁹但要敬畏耶和華你們的神，他必救你們脫離一切仇敵的手。"

⁴⁰他們卻不聽從，仍照先前的風俗去行。⁴¹如此這些民又懼怕耶和華，又侍奉他們的偶像。他們子子孫孫也都照樣行，效法他們的祖宗，直到今日。

希西家作猶大王

18 以色列王以拉的兒子何細亞第三年，猶大王亞哈斯的兒子希西家登基。²他登基的時候二十五歲，在耶路撒冷作王二十九年。他母親名叫亞比，是撒迦利雅的女兒。³希西家行耶和華眼中看為正的事，效法他祖大衛一切所行的。⁴他廢去邱壇，毀壞柱像，砍下木偶，打碎摩西所造的銅蛇，因為到那時以色列人仍向銅蛇燒香。希西家叫銅蛇為銅塊（註：或作"人稱銅蛇為銅像"）。

⁵希西家倚靠耶和華以色列的神，在他前後的猶大列王中沒有一個

their children in the fire as sacrifices to Adrammelech and Anammelech, the gods of Sepharvaim. ³²They worshiped the LORD, but they also appointed all sorts of their own people to officiate for them as priests in the shrines at the high places. ³³They worshiped the LORD, but they also served their own gods in accordance with the customs of the nations from which they had been brought.

³⁴To this day they persist in their former practices. They neither worship the LORD nor adhere to the decrees and ordinances, the laws and commands that the LORD gave the descendants of Jacob, whom he named Israel. ³⁵When the LORD made a covenant with the Israelites, he commanded them: "Do not worship any other gods or bow down to them, serve them or sacrifice to them. ³⁶But the LORD, who brought you up out of Egypt with mighty power and outstretched arm, is the one you must worship. To him you shall bow down and to him offer sacrifices. ³⁷You must always be careful to keep the decrees and ordinances, the laws and commands he wrote for you. Do not worship other gods. ³⁸Do not forget the covenant I have made with you, and do not worship other gods. ³⁹Rather, worship the LORD your God; it is he who will deliver you from the hand of all your enemies."

⁴⁰They would not listen, however, but persisted in their former practices. ⁴¹Even while these people were worshiping the LORD, they were serving their idols. To this day their children and grandchildren continue to do as their fathers did.

Hezekiah King of Judah

18 In the third year of Hoshea son of Elah king of Israel, Hezekiah son of Ahaz king of Judah began to reign. ²He was twenty-five years old when he became king, and he reigned in Jerusalem twenty-nine years. His mother's name was Abijah[a] daughter of Zechariah. ³He did what was right in the eyes of the LORD, just as his father David had done. ⁴He removed the high places, smashed the sacred stones and cut down the Asherah poles. He broke into pieces the bronze snake Moses had made, for up to that time the Israelites had been burning incense to it. (It was called[b] Nehushtan.[c])

⁵Hezekiah trusted in the LORD, the God of Israel. There was no one like him among all the

a 2 Hebrew *Abi*, a variant of *Abijah*　　b 4 Or *He called it*
c 4 *Nehushtan* sounds like the Hebrew for *bronze* and *snake* and *unclean thing*.

kings of Judah, either before him or after him.
⁶He held fast to the LORD and did not cease to
follow him; he kept the commands the LORD had
given Moses. ⁷And the LORD was with him; he
was successful in whatever he undertook. He
rebelled against the king of Assyria and did not
serve him. ⁸From watchtower to fortified city, he
defeated the Philistines, as far as Gaza and its
territory.

⁹In King Hezekiah's fourth year, which was
the seventh year of Hoshea son of Elah king of
Israel, Shalmaneser king of Assyria marched
against Samaria and laid siege to it. ¹⁰At the end
of three years the Assyrians took it. So Samaria
was captured in Hezekiah's sixth year, which
was the ninth year of Hoshea king of Israel.
¹¹The king of Assyria deported Israel to Assyria
and settled them in Halah, in Gozan on the
Habor River and in towns of the Medes. ¹²This
happened because they had not obeyed the
LORD their God, but had violated his covenant—
all that Moses the servant of the LORD commanded. They neither listened to the commands
nor carried them out.

¹³In the fourteenth year of King Hezekiah's
reign, Sennacherib king of Assyria attacked all
the fortified cities of Judah and captured them.
¹⁴So Hezekiah king of Judah sent this message
to the king of Assyria at Lachish: "I have done
wrong. Withdraw from me, and I will pay whatever you demand of me." The king of Assyria
exacted from Hezekiah king of Judah three hundred talents*a* of silver and thirty talents*b* of gold.
¹⁵So Hezekiah gave him all the silver that was
found in the temple of the LORD and in the treasuries of the royal palace.

¹⁶At this time Hezekiah king of Judah
stripped off the gold with which he had covered
the doors and doorposts of the temple of the
LORD, and gave it to the king of Assyria.

Sennacherib Threatens Jerusalem

¹⁷The king of Assyria sent his supreme commander, his chief officer and his field commander with a large army, from Lachish to King
Hezekiah at Jerusalem. They came up to Jerusalem and stopped at the aqueduct of the Upper
Pool, on the road to the Washerman's Field.
¹⁸They called for the king; and Eliakim son of
Hilkiah the palace administrator, Shebna the
secretary, and Joah son of Asaph the recorder
went out to them.

及他的。⁶因為他專靠耶和華，總不
離開，謹守耶和華所吩咐摩西的誡
命。⁷耶和華與他同在，他無論往何
處去，盡都亨通。他背叛，不肯侍奉
亞述王。⁸希西家攻擊非利士人，直
到迦薩，並迦薩的四境，從瞭望樓到
堅固城。

⁹希西家王第四年，就是以色列
王以拉的兒子何細亞第七年，亞述王
撒縵以色上來圍困撒馬利亞。¹⁰過了
三年就攻取了城。希西家第六年，以
色列王何細亞第九年，撒馬利亞被攻
取了。¹¹亞述王將以色列人擄到亞
述，把他們安置在哈臘與歌散的哈博
河邊，並瑪代人的城邑。¹²這都因他們
不聽從耶和華他們神的話，違背他的
約，就是耶和華僕人摩西吩咐他們所
當守的。

¹³希西家王十四年，亞述王西拿
基立上來攻擊猶大的一切堅固城，將
城攻取。¹⁴猶大王希西家差人往拉吉
去見亞述王，說：「我有罪了！求你
離開我，凡你罰我的，我必承當。」
於是亞述王罰猶大王希西家銀子三百
他連得、金子三十他連得。¹⁵希西家
就把耶和華殿裏和王宮府庫裏所有的
銀子都給了他。

¹⁶那時，猶大王希西家將耶和華
殿門上的金子和他自己包在柱上的金
子都刮下來，給了亞述王。

西拿基立恫嚇耶路撒冷

¹⁷亞述王從拉吉差遣他珥探、拉
伯撒利和拉伯沙基率領大軍往耶路撒
冷，到希西家王那裏去。他們上到耶
路撒冷，就站在上池的水溝旁，在漂
布地的大路上。¹⁸他們呼叫王的時
候，就有希勒家的兒子家宰以利亞
敬，並書記舍伯那和亞薩的兒子史官
約亞，出來見他們。

---

a 14 That is, about 11 tons (about 10 metric tons)   *b 14* That
is, about 1 ton (about 1 metric ton)

¹⁹拉伯沙基說："你們去告訴<u>希西家</u>說，<u>亞述</u>大王如此說：

"'你所倚靠的有甚麼可仗賴的呢？²⁰你說有打仗的計謀和能力，我看不過是虛話！你到底倚靠誰才背叛我呢？²¹看哪！你所倚靠的<u>埃及</u>，是那壓傷的葦杖。人若靠這杖，就必刺透他的手。<u>埃及</u>王法老向一切倚靠他的人也是這樣。²²你們若對我說：我們倚靠耶和華我們的神。<u>希西家</u>豈不是將神的邱壇和祭壇廢去，且對<u>猶大</u>和<u>耶路撒冷</u>的人說，你們當在<u>耶路撒冷</u>這壇前敬拜嗎？

²³"'現在你把當頭給我主<u>亞述王</u>，我給你二千匹馬，看你這一面騎馬的人夠不夠。²⁴若不然，怎能打敗我主臣僕中最小的軍長呢？你竟倚靠<u>埃及</u>的戰車馬兵嗎？²⁵現在我上來攻擊毀滅這地，豈沒有耶和華的意思嗎？耶和華吩咐我說，你上去攻擊毀滅這地吧！'"

²⁶<u>希勒家</u>的兒子<u>以利亞敬</u>和<u>舍伯那</u>並<u>約亞</u>，對拉伯沙基說："求你用<u>亞蘭</u>言語和僕人說話，因為我們懂得；不要用<u>猶大</u>言語和我們說話，達到城上百姓的耳中。"

²⁷拉伯沙基說："我主差遣我來，豈是單對你和你的主說這些話嗎？不也是對這些坐在城上，要與你們一同吃自己糞、喝自己尿的人說嗎？"

²⁸於是拉伯沙基站着，用<u>猶大</u>言語大聲喊着說："你們當聽<u>亞述</u>大王的話！²⁹王如此說：你們不要被<u>希西家</u>欺哄了，因他不能救你們脫離我的手。³⁰也不要聽<u>希西家</u>使你們倚靠耶和華，說'耶和華必要拯救我們，這城必不交在<u>亞述</u>王的手中。'

³¹"不要聽<u>希西家</u>的話。因<u>亞述</u>王如此說：你們要與我和好，出來投降我，各人就可以吃自己葡萄樹和無花果樹的果子，喝自己井裏的水。³²等我來領你們到一個地方，與你們

¹⁹The field commander said to them, "Tell Hezekiah:

"'This is what the great king, the king of Assyria, says: On what are you basing this confidence of yours? ²⁰You say you have strategy and military strength—but you speak only empty words. On whom are you depending, that you rebel against me? ²¹Look now, you are depending on Egypt, that splintered reed of a staff, which pierces a man's hand and wounds him if he leans on it! Such is Pharaoh king of Egypt to all who depend on him. ²²And if you say to me, "We are depending on the LORD our God"—isn't he the one whose high places and altars Hezekiah removed, saying to Judah and Jerusalem, "You must worship before this altar in Jerusalem"?

²³"'Come now, make a bargain with my master, the king of Assyria: I will give you two thousand horses—if you can put riders on them! ²⁴How can you repulse one officer of the least of my master's officials, even though you are depending on Egypt for chariots and horsemen^a? ²⁵Furthermore, have I come to attack and destroy this place without word from the LORD? The LORD himself told me to march against this country and destroy it.'"

²⁶Then Eliakim son of Hilkiah, and Shebna and Joah said to the field commander, "Please speak to your servants in Aramaic, since we understand it. Don't speak to us in Hebrew in the hearing of the people on the wall."

²⁷But the commander replied, "Was it only to your master and you that my master sent me to say these things, and not to the men sitting on the wall—who, like you, will have to eat their own filth and drink their own urine?"

²⁸Then the commander stood and called out in Hebrew: "Hear the word of the great king, the king of Assyria! ²⁹This is what the king says: Do not let Hezekiah deceive you. He cannot deliver you from my hand. ³⁰Do not let Hezekiah persuade you to trust in the LORD when he says, 'The LORD will surely deliver us; this city will not be given into the hand of the king of Assyria.'

³¹"Do not listen to Hezekiah. This is what the king of Assyria says: Make peace with me and come out to me. Then every one of you will eat from his own vine and fig tree and drink water from his own cistern, ³²until I come and take

a 24 Or charioteers

you to a land like your own, a land of grain and new wine, a land of bread and vineyards, a land of olive trees and honey. Choose life and not death!

"Do not listen to Hezekiah, for he is misleading you when he says, 'The LORD will deliver us.' ³³Has the god of any nation ever delivered his land from the hand of the king of Assyria? ³⁴Where are the gods of Hamath and Arpad? Where are the gods of Sepharvaim, Hena and Ivvah? Have they rescued Samaria from my hand? ³⁵Who of all the gods of these countries has been able to save his land from me? How then can the LORD deliver Jerusalem from my hand?"

³⁶But the people remained silent and said nothing in reply, because the king had commanded, "Do not answer him."

³⁷Then Eliakim son of Hilkiah the palace administrator, Shebna the secretary and Joah son of Asaph the recorder went to Hezekiah, with their clothes torn, and told him what the field commander had said.

Jerusalem's Deliverance Foretold

19 When King Hezekiah heard this, he tore his clothes and put on sackcloth and went into the temple of the LORD. ²He sent Eliakim the palace administrator, Shebna the secretary and the leading priests, all wearing sackcloth, to the prophet Isaiah son of Amoz. ³They told him, "This is what Hezekiah says: This day is a day of distress and rebuke and disgrace, as when children come to the point of birth and there is no strength to deliver them. ⁴It may be that the LORD your God will hear all the words of the field commander, whom his master, the king of Assyria, has sent to ridicule the living God, and that he will rebuke him for the words the LORD your God has heard. Therefore pray for the remnant that still survives."

⁵When King Hezekiah's officials came to Isaiah, ⁶Isaiah said to them, "Tell your master, 'This is what the LORD says: Do not be afraid of what you have heard—those words with which the underlings of the king of Assyria have blasphemed me. ⁷Listen! I am going to put such a spirit in him that when he hears a certain report, he will return to his own country, and there I will have him cut down with the sword.' "

⁸When the field commander heard that the king of Assyria had left Lachish, he withdrew and found the king fighting against Libnah.

⁹Now Sennacherib received a report that Tirhakah, the Cushite^a king ⌊of Egypt⌋, was

本地一樣，就是有五穀和新酒之地，有糧食和葡萄園之地，有橄欖樹和蜂蜜之地，好使你們存活，不至於死。

"希西家勸導你們，說'耶和華必拯救我們'；你們不要聽他的話。³³列國的神，有哪一個救他本國脫離亞述王的手呢？³⁴哈馬、亞珥拔的神在哪裏呢？西法瓦音、希拿、以瓦的神在哪裏呢？他們曾救撒馬利亞脫離我的手嗎？³⁵這些國的神有誰曾救自己的國脫離我的手呢？難道耶和華能救耶路撒冷脫離我的手嗎？"

³⁶百姓靜默不言，並不回答一句。因為王曾吩咐說："不要回答他。"

³⁷當下，希勒家的兒子家宰以利亞敬和書記舍伯那，並亞薩的兒子史官約亞都撕裂衣服，來到希西家那裏，將拉伯沙基的話告訴了他。

預言耶路撒冷得拯救

19 希西家王聽見，就撕裂衣服，披上麻布，進了耶和華的殿。²使家宰以利亞敬和書記舍伯那，並祭司中的長老都披上麻布，去見亞摩斯的兒子先知以賽亞。³對他說："希西家如此說："今日是急難、責罰、凌辱的日子，就如婦人將要生產嬰孩，卻沒有力量生產。⁴或者耶和華你的神聽見拉伯沙基的一切話，就是他主人亞述王打發他來辱罵永生神的話，耶和華你的神聽見這話，就發斥責。故此，求你為餘剩的民揚聲禱告。"

⁵希西家王的臣僕就去見以賽亞。⁶以賽亞對他們說："要這樣對你們的主人說：'耶和華如此說：你聽見亞述王的僕人褻瀆我的話，不要懼怕。⁷我必驚動（註：原文作"使靈進入"）他的心，他要聽見風聲，就歸回本地。我必使他在那裏倒在刀下。'"

⁸拉伯沙基回去，正遇見亞述王攻打立拿，原來他早聽見亞述王拔營離開拉吉。

⁹亞述王聽見人論古實王特哈加

說："他出來要與你爭戰。" 於是，亞述王又打發使者去見希西家，吩咐他們說：10 "你們對猶大王希西家如此說：不要聽你所倚靠的神來欺哄你，說 '耶路撒冷必不交在亞述王的手中。' 11你總聽說亞述諸王向列國所行的乃是盡行滅絕，難道你還能得救嗎？12我列祖所毀滅的，就是歌散、哈蘭、利色，和屬提拉撒的伊甸人，這些國的神何曾拯救這些國呢？13哈馬的王、亞珥拔的王、西法瓦音城的王、希拿和以瓦的王都在哪裏呢？"

希西家的禱告

14希西家從使者手裏接過書信來，看完了，就上耶和華的殿，將書信在耶和華面前展開。15希西家向耶和華禱告說："坐在二基路伯上耶和華以色列的神啊，你是天下萬國的神！你曾創造天地。16耶和華啊，求你側耳而聽！耶和華啊，求你睜眼而看！要聽西拿基立打發使者來辱罵永生神的話。

17 "耶和華啊！亞述諸王果然使列國和列國之地變為荒涼，18將列國的神像都扔在火裏，因為它本不是神，乃是人手所造的，是木頭石頭的，所以滅絕它。19耶和華我們的神啊，現在求你救我們脫離亞述王的手，使天下萬國都知道惟獨你耶和華是神！"

以賽亞預言西拿基立敗亡

20亞摩斯的兒子以賽亞就打發人去見希西家，說："耶和華以色列的神如此說：你既然求我攻擊亞述王西拿基立，我已聽見了。21耶和華論他這樣說：

　　"'錫安的處女藐視你、
　　　嗤笑你；
　　耶路撒冷的女子
　　　向你搖頭。
22你辱罵誰？褻瀆誰？
　　揚起聲來，
　　高舉眼目攻擊誰呢？
　　　乃是攻擊以色列的聖者！
23你藉你的使者辱罵主，

marching out to fight against him. So he again sent messengers to Hezekiah with this word: 10"Say to Hezekiah king of Judah: Do not let the god you depend on deceive you when he says, 'Jerusalem will not be handed over to the king of Assyria.' 11Surely you have heard what the kings of Assyria have done to all the countries, destroying them completely. And will you be delivered? 12Did the gods of the nations that were destroyed by my forefathers deliver them: the gods of Gozan, Haran, Rezeph and the people of Eden who were in Tel Assar? 13Where is the king of Hamath, the king of Arpad, the king of the city of Sepharvaim, or of Hena or Ivvah?"

Hezekiah's Prayer

14Hezekiah received the letter from the messengers and read it. Then he went up to the temple of the LORD and spread it out before the LORD. 15And Hezekiah prayed to the LORD: "O LORD, God of Israel, enthroned between the cherubim, you alone are God over all the kingdoms of the earth. You have made heaven and earth. 16Give ear, O LORD, and hear; open your eyes, O LORD, and see; listen to the words Sennacherib has sent to insult the living God.

17"It is true, O LORD, that the Assyrian kings have laid waste these nations and their lands. 18They have thrown their gods into the fire and destroyed them, for they were not gods but only wood and stone, fashioned by men's hands. 19Now, O LORD our God, deliver us from his hand, so that all kingdoms on earth may know that you alone, O LORD, are God."

Isaiah Prophesies Sennacherib's Fall

20Then Isaiah son of Amoz sent a message to Hezekiah: "This is what the LORD, the God of Israel, says: I have heard your prayer concerning Sennacherib king of Assyria. 21This is the word that the LORD has spoken against him:

　　" 'The Virgin Daughter of Zion
　　　despises you and mocks you.
　　The Daughter of Jerusalem
　　　tosses her head as you flee.
22Who is it you have insulted and blasphemed?
　　Against whom have you raised your voice
　　　and lifted your eyes in pride?
　　　Against the Holy One of Israel!
23By your messengers
　　you have heaped insults on the Lord.

a 9 That is, from the upper Nile region

And you have said,
"With my many chariots
I have ascended the heights of the mountains,
the utmost heights of Lebanon.
I have cut down its tallest cedars,
the choicest of its pines.
I have reached its remotest parts,
the finest of its forests.
24I have dug wells in foreign lands
and drunk the water there.
With the soles of my feet
I have dried up all the streams of Egypt."

25" 'Have you not heard?
Long ago I ordained it.
In days of old I planned it;
now I have brought it to pass,
that you have turned fortified cities
into piles of stone.
26Their people, drained of power,
are dismayed and put to shame.
They are like plants in the field,
like tender green shoots,
like grass sprouting on the roof,
scorched before it grows up.

27" 'But I know where you stay
and when you come and go
and how you rage against me.
28Because you rage against me
and your insolence has reached my ears,
I will put my hook in your nose
and my bit in your mouth,
and I will make you return
by the way you came.'

29"This will be the sign for you, O Hezekiah:

"This year you will eat what grows by itself,
and the second year what springs from that.
But in the third year sow and reap,
plant vineyards and eat their fruit.
30Once more a remnant of the house of Judah
will take root below and bear fruit above.
31For out of Jerusalem will come a remnant,
and out of Mount Zion a band of survivors.

The zeal of the LORD Almighty will accomplish
this.

32"Therefore this is what the LORD says concerning the king of Assyria:

"He will not enter this city
or shoot an arrow here.

並説:
我率領許多戰車上山頂,
到黎巴嫩極深之處;
我要砍伐其中高大的香柏樹
和佳美的松樹;
我必上極高之處,
進入肥田的樹林。

24我已經在外邦挖井喝水;

我必用腳掌踏乾
埃及的一切河。

25 "耶和華説:
'我早先所作的、
古時所立的,
就是現在藉你
使堅固城荒廢,變為亂堆,
這事你豈沒有聽見嗎?
26所以其中的居民力量甚小,
驚惶羞愧。
他們像野草、像青菜,
如房頂上的草,
又如未長成而枯乾的禾稼。

27 "'你坐下,你出去,你進來,
你向我發烈怒,
我都知道。
28因你向我發烈怒,
又因你狂傲的話達到我耳中,
我就要用鈎子鈎上你的鼻子,
把嚼環放在你口裏,
使你從你來的路轉回去。'

29 "以色列人哪,我賜你們一個證據:

"你們今年要吃自生的,
明年也要吃自長的;
至於後年,你們要耕種收割,
栽植葡萄園,吃其中的果子。
30猶大家所逃脱餘剩的,
仍要往下扎根,向上結果。
31必有餘剩的民,從耶路撒冷而出;
必有逃脱的人,從錫安山而來。

耶和華的熱心必成就這事。

32 "所以耶和華論亞述王如此説:

"他必不得來到這城,
也不在這裏射箭,

不得拿盾牌到城前，

　　也不築壘攻城。

33他從哪條路來，必從哪條路回去，

　　必不得來到這城。

　　　　　　　這是耶和華說的。

34因我為自己的緣故，

　　又為我僕人大衛的緣故，必保

　　護拯救這城。”

35當夜耶和華的使者出去，在亞述營中殺了十八萬五千人。清早有人起來一看，都是死屍了。36亞述王西拿基立就拔營回去，住在尼尼微。

37一日，在他的神尼斯洛廟裏叩拜，他兒子亞得米勒和沙利色用刀殺了他，就逃到亞拉臘地。他兒子以撒哈頓接續他作王。

希西家患重病愈

20那時，希西家病得要死。亞摩斯的兒子先知以賽亞去見他，對他說：“耶和華如此說：你當留遺命與你的家，因為你必死，不能活了。”

2希西家就轉臉朝牆，禱告耶和華說：3“耶和華啊，求你記念我在你面前怎樣存心完全的心，按誠實行事，又做你眼中所看為善的。”希西家就痛哭了。

4以賽亞出來，還沒有到中院（註：“院”或作“城”），耶和華的話就臨到他，說：5“你回去，告訴我民的君希西家說：‘耶和華你祖大衛的神如此說：我聽見了你的禱告，看見了你的眼淚，我必醫治你。到第三日，你必上到耶和華的殿。6我必加增你十五年的壽數；並且我要救你和這城脫離亞述王的手。我為自己和我僕人大衛的緣故，必保護這城。’”

7以賽亞說：“當取一塊無花果餅來。”人就取了來，貼在瘡上，王便痊愈了。

8希西家問以賽亞說：“耶和華必醫治我，到第三日，我能上耶和華的殿，有甚麼兆頭呢？”

9以賽亞說：“耶和華必成就他所說的，這是他給你的兆頭：你要日影向前進十度呢？是要往後退十度呢？”

He will not come before it with shield

　　or build a siege ramp against it.

33By the way that he came he will return;

　　he will not enter this city,

　　　　　　　declares the LORD.

34I will defend this city and save it,

　　for my sake and for the sake of David my

　　　servant."

35That night the angel of the LORD went out and put to death a hundred and eighty-five thousand men in the Assyrian camp. When the people got up the next morning—there were all the dead bodies! 36So Sennacherib king of Assyria broke camp and withdrew. He returned to Nineveh and stayed there.

37One day, while he was worshiping in the temple of his god Nisroch, his sons Adrammelech and Sharezer cut him down with the sword, and they escaped to the land of Ararat. And Esarhaddon his son succeeded him as king.

Hezekiah's Illness

20In those days Hezekiah became ill and was at the point of death. The prophet Isaiah son of Amoz went to him and said, "This is what the LORD says: Put your house in order, because you are going to die; you will not recover."

2Hezekiah turned his face to the wall and prayed to the LORD, 3"Remember, O LORD, how I have walked before you faithfully and with wholehearted devotion and have done what is good in your eyes." And Hezekiah wept bitterly.

4Before Isaiah had left the middle court, the word of the LORD came to him: 5"Go back and tell Hezekiah, the leader of my people, 'This is what the LORD, the God of your father David, says: I have heard your prayer and seen your tears; I will heal you. On the third day from now you will go up to the temple of the LORD. 6I will add fifteen years to your life. And I will deliver you and this city from the hand of the king of Assyria. I will defend this city for my sake and for the sake of my servant David.' "

7Then Isaiah said, "Prepare a poultice of figs." They did so and applied it to the boil, and he recovered.

8Hezekiah had asked Isaiah, "What will be the sign that the LORD will heal me and that I will go up to the temple of the LORD on the third day from now?"

9Isaiah answered, "This is the LORD's sign to you that the LORD will do what he has promised: Shall the shadow go forward ten steps, or shall it go back ten steps?"

¹⁰"It is a simple matter for the shadow to go forward ten steps," said Hezekiah. "Rather, have it go back ten steps."

¹¹Then the prophet Isaiah called upon the LORD, and the LORD made the shadow go back the ten steps it had gone down on the stairway of Ahaz.

Envoys From Babylon

¹²At that time Merodach-Baladan son of Baladan king of Babylon sent Hezekiah letters and a gift, because he had heard of Hezekiah's illness. ¹³Hezekiah received the messengers and showed them all that was in his storehouses—the silver, the gold, the spices and the fine oil—his armory and everything found among his treasures. There was nothing in his palace or in all his kingdom that Hezekiah did not show them.

¹⁴Then Isaiah the prophet went to King Hezekiah and asked, "What did those men say, and where did they come from?"

"From a distant land," Hezekiah replied. "They came from Babylon."

¹⁵The prophet asked, "What did they see in your palace?"

"They saw everything in my palace," Hezekiah said. "There is nothing among my treasures that I did not show them."

¹⁶Then Isaiah said to Hezekiah, "Hear the word of the LORD: ¹⁷The time will surely come when everything in your palace, and all that your fathers have stored up until this day, will be carried off to Babylon. Nothing will be left, says the LORD. ¹⁸And some of your descendants, your own flesh and blood, that will be born to you, will be taken away, and they will become eunuchs in the palace of the king of Babylon."

¹⁹"The word of the LORD you have spoken is good," Hezekiah replied. For he thought, "Will there not be peace and security in my lifetime?"

²⁰As for the other events of Hezekiah's reign, all his achievements and how he made the pool and the tunnel by which he brought water into the city, are they not written in the book of the annals of the kings of Judah? ²¹Hezekiah rested with his fathers. And Manasseh his son succeeded him as king.

Manasseh King of Judah

21 Manasseh was twelve years old when he became king, and he reigned in Jerusalem fifty-five years. His mother's name was Hephzibah. ²He did evil in the eyes of the LORD, following the detestable practices of the nations the LORD had driven out before the

¹⁰希西家回答説："日影向前進十度容易；我要日影往後退十度。"

¹¹先知以賽亞求告耶和華，耶和華就使亞哈斯的日晷向前進的日影，往後退了十度。

巴比倫使者到訪

¹²那時，巴比倫王巴拉但的兒子比羅達巴拉但聽見希西家病而痊愈，就送書信和禮物給他。¹³希西家聽從使者的話，就把他寶庫的金子、銀子、香料、貴重的膏油和他武庫的一切軍器，並他所有的財寶，都給他們看。他家中和他全國之內，希西家沒有一樣不給他們看的。

¹⁴於是先知以賽亞來見希西家王，問他説："這些人説甚麼？他們從哪裏來見你？"

希西家説："他們從遠方的巴比倫來。"

¹⁵以賽亞説："他們在你家裏看見了甚麼？"

希西家説："凡我家中所有的，他們都看見了；我財寶中沒有一樣不給他們看的。"

¹⁶以賽亞對希西家説："你要聽耶和華的話：¹⁷日子必到，凡你家裏所有的，並你列祖積蓄到如今的，都要被擄到巴比倫去，不留下一樣。這是耶和華説的。¹⁸並且從你本身所生的眾子，其中必有被擄去在巴比倫王宮裏當太監的。"

¹⁹希西家對以賽亞説："你所説耶和華的話甚好！若在我的年日中，有太平和穩固的景況，豈不是好嗎？"

²⁰希西家其餘的事和他的勇力，他怎樣挖池、挖溝、引水入城，都寫在猶大列王記上。²¹希西家與他列祖同睡。他兒子瑪拿西接續他作王。

瑪拿西作猶大王

21 瑪拿西登基的時候年十二歲，在耶路撒冷作王五十五年。他母親名叫協西巴。²瑪拿西行耶和華眼中看為惡的事，效法耶和華在以色列人面前趕出的外邦人所行可憎的事。³重新建築他父希西家所毀壞的邱壇，又為巴力築壇，做亞舍拉像，效法以色列王亞哈所行的，且敬拜侍奉天上的萬象；⁴在耶和華殿宇中築壇。耶和華曾指着這殿說："我必立我的名在耶路撒冷。"⁵他在耶和華殿的兩院中為天上的萬象築壇，⁶並使他的兒子經火，又觀兆，用法術，立交鬼的和行巫術的，多行耶和華眼中看為惡的事，惹動他的怒氣。

⁷又在殿內立雕刻的亞舍拉像。耶和華曾對大衛和他兒子所羅門說："我在以色列眾支派中所選擇的耶路撒冷和這殿，必立我的名，直到永遠。⁸以色列人若謹守遵行我一切所吩咐他們的和我僕人摩西所吩咐他們的一切律法，我就不再使他們挪移，離開我所賜給他們列祖之地。"⁹他們卻不聽從。瑪拿西引誘他們行惡，比耶和華在以色列人面前所滅的列國更甚。

¹⁰耶和華藉他僕人眾先知說：¹¹"因猶大王瑪拿西行這些可憎的惡事，比先前亞摩利人所行的更甚，使猶大人拜他的偶像，陷在罪裏。¹²所以耶和華以色列的神如此說：我必降禍與耶路撒冷和猶大，叫一切聽見的人無不耳鳴。¹³我必用量撒馬利亞的準繩和亞哈家的線鉈拉在耶路撒冷上，必擦淨耶路撒冷，如人擦盤，將盤倒扣。¹⁴我必棄掉所餘剩的子民（註：原文作"產業"），把他們交在仇敵手中，使他們成為一切仇敵擄掠之物。¹⁵是因他們自從列祖出埃及直到如今，常行我眼中看為惡的事，惹動我的怒氣。"

¹⁶瑪拿西行耶和華眼中看為惡的事，使猶大人陷在罪裏，又流許多無辜人的血，充滿了耶路撒冷，從這邊直到那邊。

¹⁷瑪拿西其餘的事，凡他所行的和他所犯的罪，都寫在猶大列王記

Israelites. ³He rebuilt the high places his father Hezekiah had destroyed; he also erected altars to Baal and made an Asherah pole, as Ahab king of Israel had done. He bowed down to all the starry hosts and worshiped them. ⁴He built altars in the temple of the LORD, of which the LORD had said, "In Jerusalem I will put my Name." ⁵In both courts of the temple of the LORD, he built altars to all the starry hosts. ⁶He sacrificed his own son in[a] the fire, practiced sorcery and divination, and consulted mediums and spiritists. He did much evil in the eyes of the LORD, provoking him to anger.

⁷He took the carved Asherah pole he had made and put it in the temple, of which the LORD had said to David and to his son Solomon, "In this temple and in Jerusalem, which I have chosen out of all the tribes of Israel, I will put my Name forever. ⁸I will not again make the feet of the Israelites wander from the land I gave their forefathers, if only they will be careful to do everything I commanded them and will keep the whole Law that my servant Moses gave them." ⁹But the people did not listen. Manasseh led them astray, so that they did more evil than the nations the LORD had destroyed before the Israelites.

¹⁰The LORD said through his servants the prophets: ¹¹"Manasseh king of Judah has committed these detestable sins. He has done more evil than the Amorites who preceded him and has led Judah into sin with his idols. ¹²Therefore this is what the LORD, the God of Israel, says: I am going to bring such disaster on Jerusalem and Judah that the ears of everyone who hears of it will tingle. ¹³I will stretch out over Jerusalem the measuring line used against Samaria and the plumb line used against the house of Ahab. I will wipe out Jerusalem as one wipes a dish, wiping it and turning it upside down. ¹⁴I will forsake the remnant of my inheritance and hand them over to their enemies. They will be looted and plundered by all their foes, ¹⁵because they have done evil in my eyes and have provoked me to anger from the day their forefathers came out of Egypt until this day."

¹⁶Moreover, Manasseh also shed so much innocent blood that he filled Jerusalem from end to end—besides the sin that he had caused Judah to commit, so that they did evil in the eyes of the LORD.

¹⁷As for the other events of Manasseh's reign, and all he did, including the sin he committed, are they not written in the book of the annals of

the kings of Judah? [18]Manasseh rested with his fathers and was buried in his palace garden, the garden of Uzza. And Amon his son succeeded him as king.

Amon King of Judah

[19]Amon was twenty-two years old when he became king, and he reigned in Jerusalem two years. His mother's name was Meshullemeth daughter of Haruz; she was from Jotbah. [20]He did evil in the eyes of the LORD, as his father Manasseh had done. [21]He walked in all the ways of his father; he worshiped the idols his father had worshiped, and bowed down to them. [22]He forsook the LORD, the God of his fathers, and did not walk in the way of the LORD.

[23]Amon's officials conspired against him and assassinated the king in his palace. [24]Then the people of the land killed all who had plotted against King Amon, and they made Josiah his son king in his place.

[25]As for the other events of Amon's reign, and what he did, are they not written in the book of the annals of the kings of Judah? [26]He was buried in his grave in the garden of Uzza. And Josiah his son succeeded him as king.

The Book of the Law Found

22 Josiah was eight years old when he became king, and he reigned in Jerusalem thirty-one years. His mother's name was Jedidah daughter of Adaiah; she was from Bozkath. [2]He did what was right in the eyes of the LORD and walked in all the ways of his father David, not turning aside to the right or to the left.

[3]In the eighteenth year of his reign, King Josiah sent the secretary, Shaphan son of Azaliah, the son of Meshullam, to the temple of the LORD. He said: [4]"Go up to Hilkiah the high priest and have him get ready the money that has been brought into the temple of the LORD, which the doorkeepers have collected from the people. [5]Have them entrust it to the men appointed to supervise the work on the temple. And have these men pay the workers who repair the temple of the LORD— [6]the carpenters, the builders and the masons. Also have them purchase timber and dressed stone to repair the temple. [7]But they need not account for the money entrusted to them, because they are acting faithfully."

[8]Hilkiah the high priest said to Shaphan the secretary, "I have found the Book of the Law in

上。[18]瑪拿西與他列祖同睡，葬在自己宮院烏撒的園內。他兒子亞們接續他作王。

亞們作猶大王

[19]亞們登基的時候年二十二歲，在耶路撒冷作王二年。他母親名叫米舒利密，是約提巴人哈魯斯的女兒。[20]亞們行耶和華眼中看為惡的事，與他父親瑪拿西所行的一樣。[21]行他父親一切所行的，敬奉他父親所敬奉的偶像，[22]離棄耶和華他列祖的神，不遵行耶和華的道。

[23]亞們王的臣僕背叛他，在宮裏殺了他。[24]但國民殺了那些背叛亞們王的人，立他兒子約西亞接續他作王。

[25]亞們其餘所行的事，都寫在猶大列王記上。[26]亞們葬在烏撒的園內自己的墳墓裏。他兒子約西亞接續他作王。

重獲律法書

22 約西亞登基的時候年八歲，在耶路撒冷作王三十一年。他母親名叫耶底大，是波斯加人亞大雅的女兒。[2]約西亞行耶和華眼中看為正的事，行他祖大衛一切所行的，不偏左右。

[3]約西亞王十八年，王差遣米書蘭的孫子、亞薩利的兒子、書記沙番上耶和華殿去，吩咐他說：[4]"你去見大祭司希勒家，使他將奉到耶和華殿的銀子，就是守門的從民中收聚的銀子，數算數算，[5]交給耶和華殿裏辦事的人，使他們轉交耶和華殿裏做工的人，好修理殿的破壞之處。[6]就是轉交木匠和工人，並瓦匠，又買木料和鑿成的石頭，修理殿宇。[7]將銀子交在辦事的人手裏，不與他們算賬，因為他們辦事誠實。"

[8]大祭司希勒家對書記沙番說："我在耶和華殿裏得了律法書。"希

勒家將書遞給沙番，沙番就看了。
9書記沙番到王那裏，回覆王說：
"你的僕人已將殿裏的銀子倒出數
算，交給耶和華殿裏辦事的人了。"
10書記沙番又對王說："祭司希勒家
遞給我一卷書。"沙番就在王面前讀
那書。

11王聽見律法書上的話，便撕裂
衣服，12吩咐祭司希勒家與沙番的兒
子亞希甘、米該亞的兒子亞革波、書
記沙番和王的臣僕亞撒雅說：13"你
們去，為我、為民、為猶大眾人，以
這書上的話求問耶和華。因為我們列
祖沒有聽從這書上的言語，沒有遵着
書上所吩咐我們的去行，耶和華就向
我們大發烈怒。"

14於是祭司希勒家和亞希甘、亞
革波、沙番、亞撒雅都去見女先知戶
勒大。戶勒大是掌管禮服沙龍的妻；
沙龍是哈珥哈斯的孫子、特瓦的兒
子。戶勒大住在耶路撒冷第二區。他
們請問於她。

15她對他們說："耶和華以色列
的神如此說：'你們可以回覆那差遣
你們來見我的人說，16耶和華如此
說：我必照着猶大王所讀那書上的一
切話，降禍與這地和其上的居民。
17因為他們離棄我，向別神燒香，用
他們手所做的惹我發怒，所以我的忿
怒必向這地發作，總不止息。'18然
而，差遣你們來求問耶和華的猶大
王，你們要這樣回覆他說："耶和華
以色列的神如此說：至於你所聽見的
話，19就是聽見我指着這地和其上的
居民所說，要使這地變為荒場、民受
咒詛的話，你便心裏傷服，在我面前
自卑，撕裂衣服，向我哭泣，因此我
應允了你。這是我耶和華說的。20我
必使你平平安安地歸到墳墓，到你列
祖那裏；我要降與這地的一切災禍，
你也不至親眼看見。'"

他們就回覆王去了。

the temple of the LORD." He gave it to Shaphan,
who read it. 9Then Shaphan the secretary went
to the king and reported to him: "Your officials
have paid out the money that was in the temple
of the LORD and have entrusted it to the workers
and supervisors at the temple." 10Then Shaphan
the secretary informed the king, "Hilkiah the
priest has given me a book." And Shaphan read
from it in the presence of the king.

11When the king heard the words of the Book
of the Law, he tore his robes. 12He gave these
orders to Hilkiah the priest, Ahikam son of
Shaphan, Acbor son of Micaiah, Shaphan the
secretary and Asaiah the king's attendant: 13"Go
and inquire of the LORD for me and for the people and for all Judah about what is written in
this book that has been found. Great is the
LORD's anger that burns against us because our
fathers have not obeyed the words of this book;
they have not acted in accordance with all that is
written there concerning us."

14Hilkiah the priest, Ahikam, Acbor, Shaphan
and Asaiah went to speak to the prophetess
Huldah, who was the wife of Shallum son of
Tikvah, the son of Harhas, keeper of the
wardrobe. She lived in Jerusalem, in the Second
District.

15She said to them, "This is what the LORD,
the God of Israel, says: Tell the man who sent
you to me, 16'This is what the LORD says: I am
going to bring disaster on this place and its people, according to everything written in the book
the king of Judah has read. 17Because they have
forsaken me and burned incense to other gods
and provoked me to anger by all the idols their
hands have made,a my anger will burn against
this place and will not be quenched.' 18Tell the
king of Judah, who sent you to inquire of the
LORD, 'This is what the LORD, the God of Israel,
says concerning the words you heard: 19Because
your heart was responsive and you humbled
yourself before the LORD when you heard what I
have spoken against this place and its people,
that they would become accursed and laid
waste, and because you tore your robes and
wept in my presence, I have heard you, declares
the LORD. 20Therefore I will gather you to your
fathers, and you will be buried in peace. Your
eyes will not see all the disaster I am going to
bring on this place.' "

So they took her answer back to the king.

a 17 Or by everything they have done

Josiah Renews the Covenant

23 Then the king called together all the elders of Judah and Jerusalem. [2]He went up to the temple of the LORD with the men of Judah, the people of Jerusalem, the priests and the prophets—all the people from the least to the greatest. He read in their hearing all the words of the Book of the Covenant, which had been found in the temple of the LORD. [3]The king stood by the pillar and renewed the covenant in the presence of the LORD—to follow the LORD and keep his commands, regulations and decrees with all his heart and all his soul, thus confirming the words of the covenant written in this book. Then all the people pledged themselves to the covenant.

[4]The king ordered Hilkiah the high priest, the priests next in rank and the doorkeepers to remove from the temple of the LORD all the articles made for Baal and Asherah and all the starry hosts. He burned them outside Jerusalem in the fields of the Kidron Valley and took the ashes to Bethel. [5]He did away with the pagan priests appointed by the kings of Judah to burn incense on the high places of the towns of Judah and on those around Jerusalem—those who burned incense to Baal, to the sun and moon, to the constellations and to all the starry hosts. [6]He took the Asherah pole from the temple of the LORD to the Kidron Valley outside Jerusalem and burned it there. He ground it to powder and scattered the dust over the graves of the common people. [7]He also tore down the quarters of the male shrine prostitutes, which were in the temple of the LORD and where women did weaving for Asherah.

[8]Josiah brought all the priests from the towns of Judah and desecrated the high places, from Geba to Beersheba, where the priests had burned incense. He broke down the shrines[a] at the gates—at the entrance to the Gate of Joshua, the city governor, which is on the left of the city gate. [9]Although the priests of the high places did not serve at the altar of the LORD in Jerusalem, they ate unleavened bread with their fellow priests.

[10]He desecrated Topheth, which was in the Valley of Ben Hinnom, so no one could use it to sacrifice his son or daughter in[b] the fire to Molech. [11]He removed from the entrance to the temple of the LORD the horses that the kings of Judah had dedicated to the sun. They were in

約西亞重立聖約

23 王差遣人招聚猶大和耶路撒冷的眾長老來。 [2]王和猶大眾人，與耶路撒冷的居民，並祭司、先知，和所有的百姓，無論大小，都一同上到耶和華的殿；王就把耶和華殿裏所得的約書念給他們聽。 [3]王站在柱旁，在耶和華面前立約，要盡心盡性地順從耶和華，遵守他的誡命、法度、律例，成就這書上所記的約言。眾民都服從這約。

[4]王吩咐大祭司希勒家和副祭司，並把門的，將那為巴力和亞舍拉，並天上萬象所造的器皿，都從耶和華殿裏搬出來，在耶路撒冷外汲淪溪旁的田間燒了，把灰拿到伯特利去。 [5]從前猶大列王所立拜偶像的祭司，在猶大城邑的邱壇和耶路撒冷的周圍燒香，現在王都廢去；又廢去向巴力和日、月、星、行星（註：「行星」或作「十二宮」），並天上萬象燒香的人； [6]又從耶和華殿裏，將亞舍拉搬到耶路撒冷外汲淪溪邊焚燒，打碎成灰，將灰撒在平民的墳上； [7]又拆毀耶和華殿裏孌童的屋子，就是婦女為亞舍拉織帳子的屋子。

[8]並且從猶大的城邑帶眾祭司來，污穢祭司燒香的邱壇，從迦巴直到別是巴；又拆毀城門旁的邱壇，這邱壇在邑宰約書亞門前，進城門的左邊。 [9]但是邱壇的祭司不登耶路撒冷耶和華的壇，只在他們弟兄中間吃無酵餅。

[10]又污穢欣嫩子谷的陀斐特，不許人在那裏使兒女經火獻給摩洛； [11]又將猶大列王在耶和華殿門旁，太

a 8 Or high places   b 10 Or to make his son or daughter pass through

監拿單米勒靠近遊廊的屋子，向日頭所獻的馬廢去，且用火焚燒日車。

12猶大列王在亞哈斯樓頂上所築的壇和瑪拿西在耶和華殿兩院中所築的壇，王都拆毀打碎了，就把灰倒在汲淪溪中。13從前以色列王所羅門在耶路撒冷前，邪僻山右邊，為西頓人可憎的神亞斯她錄、摩押人可憎的神基抹、亞捫人可憎的神米勒公所築的邱壇，王都污穢了，14又打碎柱像，砍下木偶，將人的骨頭充滿了那地方。

15他將伯特利的壇，就是叫以色列人陷在罪裏、尼八的兒子耶羅波安所築的那壇，都拆毀焚燒，打碎成灰，並焚燒了亞舍拉。16約西亞回頭，看見山上的墳墓，就打發人將墳墓裏的骸骨取出來，燒在壇上，污穢了壇，正如從前神人宣傳耶和華的話。

17約西亞問說：「我所看見的是甚麼碑？」

那城裏的人回答說：「先前有神人從猶大來，預先說王現在向伯特利壇所行的事，這就是他的墓碑。」

18約西亞說：「由他吧！不要挪移他的骸骨。」他們就不動他的骸骨，也不動從撒馬利亞來那先知的骸骨。

19從前以色列諸王在撒馬利亞的城邑建築邱壇的殿，惹動耶和華的怒氣，現在約西亞都廢去了，就如他在伯特利所行的一般；20又將邱壇的祭司都殺在壇上，並在壇上燒人的骨頭，就回耶路撒冷去了。

21王吩咐眾民說：「你們當照這約書上所寫的，向耶和華你們的神守逾越節。」22自從士師治理以色列人和以色列王、猶大王的時候，直到如今，實在沒有守過這樣的逾越節；

the court near the room of an official named Nathan-Melech. Josiah then burned the chariots dedicated to the sun.

12He pulled down the altars the kings of Judah had erected on the roof near the upper room of Ahaz, and the altars Manasseh had built in the two courts of the temple of the LORD. He removed them from there, smashed them to pieces and threw the rubble into the Kidron Valley. 13The king also desecrated the high places that were east of Jerusalem on the south of the Hill of Corruption—the ones Solomon king of Israel had built for Ashtoreth the vile goddess of the Sidonians, for Chemosh the vile god of Moab, and for Molech*a* the detestable god of the people of Ammon. 14Josiah smashed the sacred stones and cut down the Asherah poles and covered the sites with human bones.

15Even the altar at Bethel, the high place made by Jeroboam son of Nebat, who had caused Israel to sin—even that altar and high place he demolished. He burned the high place and ground it to powder, and burned the Asherah pole also. 16Then Josiah looked around, and when he saw the tombs that were there on the hillside, he had the bones removed from them and burned on the altar to defile it, in accordance with the word of the LORD proclaimed by the man of God who foretold these things.

17The king asked, "What is that tombstone I see?"

The men of the city said, "It marks the tomb of the man of God who came from Judah and pronounced against the altar of Bethel the very things you have done to it."

18"Leave it alone," he said. "Don't let anyone disturb his bones." So they spared his bones and those of the prophet who had come from Samaria.

19Just as he had done at Bethel, Josiah removed and defiled all the shrines at the high places that the kings of Israel had built in the towns of Samaria that had provoked the LORD to anger. 20Josiah slaughtered all the priests of those high places on the altars and burned human bones on them. Then he went back to Jerusalem.

21The king gave this order to all the people: "Celebrate the Passover to the LORD your God, as it is written in this Book of the Covenant." 22Not since the days of the judges who led Israel, nor throughout the days of the kings of Israel and the kings of Judah, had any such

a 13 Hebrew Milcom

Passover been observed. ²³But in the eighteenth year of King Josiah, this Passover was celebrated to the LORD in Jerusalem.

²⁴Furthermore, Josiah got rid of the mediums and spiritists, the household gods, the idols and all the other detestable things seen in Judah and Jerusalem. This he did to fulfill the requirements of the law written in the book that Hilkiah the priest had discovered in the temple of the LORD. ²⁵Neither before nor after Josiah was there a king like him who turned to the LORD as he did—with all his heart and with all his soul and with all his strength, in accordance with all the Law of Moses.

²⁶Nevertheless, the LORD did not turn away from the heat of his fierce anger, which burned against Judah because of all that Manasseh had done to provoke him to anger. ²⁷So the LORD said, "I will remove Judah also from my presence as I removed Israel, and I will reject Jerusalem, the city I chose, and this temple, about which I said, 'There shall my Name be.'ᵃ"

²⁸As for the other events of Josiah's reign, and all he did, are they not written in the book of the annals of the kings of Judah?

²⁹While Josiah was king, Pharaoh Neco king of Egypt went up to the Euphrates River to help the king of Assyria. King Josiah marched out to meet him in battle, but Neco faced him and killed him at Megiddo. ³⁰Josiah's servants brought his body in a chariot from Megiddo to Jerusalem and buried him in his own tomb. And the people of the land took Jehoahaz son of Josiah and anointed him and made him king in place of his father.

Jehoahaz King of Judah

³¹Jehoahaz was twenty-three years old when he became king, and he reigned in Jerusalem three months. His mother's name was Hamutal daughter of Jeremiah; she was from Libnah. ³²He did evil in the eyes of the LORD, just as his fathers had done. ³³Pharaoh Neco put him in chains at Riblah in the land of Hamathᵇ so that he might not reign in Jerusalem, and he imposed on Judah a levy of a hundred talentsᶜ of silver and a talentᵈ of gold. ³⁴Pharaoh Neco made Eliakim son of Josiah king in place of his father Josiah and changed Eliakim's name to Jehoiakim. But he took Jehoahaz and carried him off to Egypt, and there he died. ³⁵Jehoiakim

²³只有約西亞王十八年在耶路撒冷向耶和華守這逾越節。

²⁴凡猶大國和耶路撒冷所有交鬼的、行巫術的,與家中的神像和偶像,並一切可憎之物,約西亞盡都除掉,成就了祭司希勒家在耶和華殿裏所得律法書上所寫的話。²⁵在約西亞以前,沒有王像他盡心、盡性、盡力地歸向耶和華,遵行摩西的一切律法;在他以後,也沒有興起一個王像他。

²⁶然而,耶和華向猶大所發猛烈的怒氣仍不止息,是因瑪拿西諸事惹動他。²⁷耶和華說:「我必將猶大人從我面前趕出,如同趕出以色列人一般,我必棄掉我從前所選擇的這城耶路撒冷和我所立라我名的殿。」

²⁸約西亞其餘的事,凡他所行的,都寫在猶大列王記上。

²⁹約西亞年間,埃及王法老尼哥上到幼發拉底河攻擊亞述王,約西亞王去抵擋他。埃及王遇見約西亞在米吉多,就殺了他。³⁰他的臣僕用車將他的屍首從米吉多送到耶路撒冷,葬在他自己的墳墓裏。國民膏約西亞的兒子約哈斯,接續他父親作王。

約哈斯作猶大王

³¹約哈斯登基的時候年二十三歲,在耶路撒冷作王三個月。他母親名叫哈慕她,是立拿人耶利米的女兒。³²約哈斯行耶和華眼中看為惡的事,效法他列祖一切所行的。³³法老尼哥將約哈斯鎖禁在哈馬地的利比拉,不許他在耶路撒冷作王,又罰猶大國銀子一百他連得、金子一他連得。³⁴法老尼哥立約西亞的兒子以利亞敬接續他父親約西亞作王,給他改名叫約雅敬,卻將約哈斯帶到埃及,他就死在那裏。³⁵約雅敬將金銀給法

老，遵着法老的命向國民徵取金銀，按着各人的力量派定，索要金銀，好給法老尼哥。

約雅敬作猶大王

36約雅敬登基的時候年二十五歲，在耶路撒冷作王十一年。他母親名叫西布大，是魯瑪人毗大雅的女兒。37約雅敬行耶和華眼中看為惡的事，效法他列祖一切所行的。

24 約雅敬年間，巴比倫王尼布甲尼撒上到猶大，約雅敬便侍他三年，然後背叛他。2耶和華使迦勒底軍、亞蘭軍、摩押軍和亞捫人的軍來攻擊約雅敬，毀滅猶大，正如耶和華藉他僕人眾先知所說的。3這禍臨到猶大人，誠然是耶和華所命的，要將他們從自己面前趕出，是因瑪拿西所犯的一切罪，4又因他流無辜人的血，充滿了耶路撒冷。耶和華決不肯赦免。

5約雅敬其餘的事，凡他所行的，都寫在猶大列王記上。6約雅敬與他列祖同睡，他兒子約雅斤接續he作王。

7埃及王不再從他國中出來，因為巴比倫王將埃及王所管之地，從埃及小河直到幼發拉底河都奪去了。

約雅斤作猶大王

8約雅斤登基的時候，年十八歲，在耶路撒冷作王三個月。他母親名叫尼護施她，是耶路撒冷人以利拿單的女兒。9約雅斤行耶和華眼中看為惡的事，效法他父親一切所行的。

10那時，巴比倫王尼布甲尼撒的軍兵上到耶路撒冷，圍困城。11當他軍兵圍困城的時候，巴比倫王尼布甲尼撒親自來了。12猶大王約雅斤和他母親、臣僕、首領、太監一同出城，投降巴比倫王，巴比倫王便拿住他。

paid Pharaoh Neco the silver and gold he demanded. In order to do so, he taxed the land and exacted the silver and gold from the people of the land according to their assessments.

Jehoiakim King of Judah

36Jehoiakim was twenty-five years old when he became king, and he reigned in Jerusalem eleven years. His mother's name was Zebidah daughter of Pedaiah; she was from Rumah. 37And he did evil in the eyes of the LORD, just as his fathers had done.

24 During Jehoiakim's reign, Nebuchadnezzar king of Babylon invaded the land, and Jehoiakim became his vassal for three years. But then he changed his mind and rebelled against Nebuchadnezzar. 2The LORD sent Babylonian,*a* Aramean, Moabite and Ammonite raiders against him. He sent them to destroy Judah, in accordance with the word of the LORD proclaimed by his servants the prophets. 3Surely these things happened to Judah according to the LORD's command, in order to remove them from his presence because of the sins of Manasseh and all he had done, 4including the shedding of innocent blood. For he had filled Jerusalem with innocent blood, and the LORD was not willing to forgive.

5As for the other events of Jehoiakim's reign, and all he did, are they not written in the book of the annals of the kings of Judah? 6Jehoiakim rested with his fathers. And Jehoiachin his son succeeded him as king.

7The king of Egypt did not march out from his own country again, because the king of Babylon had taken all his territory, from the Wadi of Egypt to the Euphrates River.

Jehoiachin King of Judah

8Jehoiachin was eighteen years old when he became king, and he reigned in Jerusalem three months. His mother's name was Nehushta daughter of Elnathan; she was from Jerusalem. 9He did evil in the eyes of the LORD, just as his father had done.

10At that time the officers of Nebuchadnezzar king of Babylon advanced on Jerusalem and laid siege to it, 11and Nebuchadnezzar himself came up to the city while his officers were besieging it. 12Jehoiachin king of Judah, his mother, his attendants, his nobles and his officials all surrendered to him.

a 2 Or Chaldean

In the eighth year of the reign of the king of Babylon, he took Jehoiachin prisoner. [13]As the LORD had declared, Nebuchadnezzar removed all the treasures from the temple of the LORD and from the royal palace, and took away all the gold articles that Solomon king of Israel had made for the temple of the LORD. [14]He carried into exile all Jerusalem: all the officers and fighting men, and all the craftsmen and artisans—a total of ten thousand. Only the poorest people of the land were left.

[15]Nebuchadnezzar took Jehoiachin captive to Babylon. He also took from Jerusalem to Babylon the king's mother, his wives, his officials and the leading men of the land. [16]The king of Babylon also deported to Babylon the entire force of seven thousand fighting men, strong and fit for war, and a thousand craftsmen and artisans. [17]He made Mattaniah, Jehoiachin's uncle, king in his place and changed his name to Zedekiah.

Zedekiah King of Judah

[18]Zedekiah was twenty-one years old when he became king, and he reigned in Jerusalem eleven years. His mother's name was Hamutal daughter of Jeremiah; she was from Libnah. [19]He did evil in the eyes of the LORD, just as Jehoiakim had done. [20]It was because of the LORD's anger that all this happened to Jerusalem and Judah, and in the end he thrust them from his presence.

The Fall of Jerusalem

Now Zedekiah rebelled against the king of Babylon.

25 So in the ninth year of Zedekiah's reign, on the tenth day of the tenth month, Nebuchadnezzar king of Babylon marched against Jerusalem with his whole army. He encamped outside the city and built siege works all around it. [2]The city was kept under siege until the eleventh year of King Zedekiah. [3]By the ninth day of the [fourth[a] month the famine in the city had become so severe that there was no food for the people to eat. [4]Then the city wall was broken through, and the whole army fled at night through the gate between the two walls near the king's garden, though the Babylonians[b] were surrounding the city. They fled toward the Arabah,[c] [5]but the Babylonian[d] army pursued the king and over-

那時是巴比倫王第八年。[13]巴比倫王將耶和華殿和王宮裏的寶物都拿去了，將以色列王所羅門所造耶和華殿裏的金器都毀壞了，正如耶和華所說的。[14]又將耶路撒冷的眾民和眾首領，並所有大能的勇士共一萬人，連一切木匠、鐵匠都擄了去，除了國中極貧窮的人以外，沒有剩下的。

[15]並將約雅斤和王母、后妃、太監，與國中的大官，都從耶路撒冷擄到巴比倫去了，[16]又將一切勇士七千人和木匠、鐵匠一千人，都是能上陣的勇士，全擄到巴比倫去了。[17]巴比倫王立約雅斤的叔叔瑪探雅代替他作王，給瑪探雅改名叫西底家。

西底家作猶大王

[18]西底家登基的時候年二十一歲，在耶路撒冷作王十一年。他母親名叫哈慕他，是立拿人耶利米的女兒。[19]西底家行耶和華眼中看為惡的事，是照約雅敬一切所行的。[20]因此，耶和華的怒氣在耶路撒冷和猶大發作，以致將人民從自己面前趕出。

耶路撒冷失陷

西底家背叛巴比倫王。

25 他作王第九年十月初十日，巴比倫王尼布甲尼撒率領全軍來攻擊耶路撒冷，對城安營，四圍築壘攻城。[2]於是城被圍困，直到西底家王十一年。[3]四月初九日，城裏有大饑荒，甚至百姓都沒有糧食。[4]城被攻破，一切兵丁就在夜間從靠近王園兩城中間的門逃跑。迦勒底人正在四圍攻城，王就向亞拉巴逃走。[5]迦勒底的軍隊追趕王，在耶利哥的平原追上他，他的全軍都離開他四散了。6迦勒底人就拿住王，帶他到利比拉 巴比倫王那裏審判他。7在西底家眼前殺了他的眾子，並且剜了西底家的眼睛，用銅鏈鎖着他，帶到巴比倫去。

8巴比倫王尼布甲尼撒十九年五月初七日，巴比倫王的臣僕、護衛長尼布撒拉旦來到耶路撒冷，9用火焚燒耶和華的殿和王宮，又焚燒耶路撒冷的房屋，就是各大戶家的房屋。10跟從護衛長迦勒底的全軍，就拆毀耶路撒冷四圍的城牆。11那時護衛長尼布撒拉旦將城裏所剩下的百姓，並已經投降巴比倫王的人，以及大眾所剩下的人，都擄去了。12但護衛長留下些民中最窮的，使他們修理葡萄園，耕種田地。

13耶和華殿的銅柱，並耶和華殿的盆座和銅海、迦勒底人都打碎了，將那銅運到巴比倫去了；14又帶去鍋、鏟子、蠟剪、調羹、並所用的一切銅器，15火鼎、碗，無論金的銀的，護衛長也都帶去了。

16所羅門為耶和華殿所造的兩根銅柱、一個銅海，和幾個盆座，這一切的銅，多得無法可稱。17這一根柱子高十八肘，柱上有銅頂，高三肘，銅頂的周圍有網子和石榴，都是銅的。那一根柱子，照此一樣，也有網子。

18護衛長拿住大祭司西萊雅、副祭司西番亞和三個把門的，19又從城中拿住一個管理兵丁的官（註：或作"太監"），並在城裏所遇常見王面的五個人和檢點國民軍長的書記，以及城裏遇見的國民六十個人。20護衛長尼布撒拉旦將這些人帶到利比拉 巴比倫王那裏。21巴比倫王就把他們擊殺在哈馬地的利比拉。

took him in the plains of Jericho. All his soldiers were separated from him and scattered, 6and he was captured. He was taken to the king of Babylon at Riblah, where sentence was pronounced on him. 7They killed the sons of Zedekiah before his eyes. Then they put out his eyes, bound him with bronze shackles and took him to Babylon.

8On the seventh day of the fifth month, in the nineteenth year of Nebuchadnezzar king of Babylon, Nebuzaradan commander of the imperial guard, an official of the king of Babylon, came to Jerusalem. 9He set fire to the temple of the LORD, the royal palace and all the houses of Jerusalem. Every important building he burned down. 10The whole Babylonian army, under the commander of the imperial guard, broke down the walls around Jerusalem. 11Nebuzaradan the commander of the guard carried into exile the people who remained in the city, along with the rest of the populace and those who had gone over to the king of Babylon. 12But the commander left behind some of the poorest people of the land to work the vineyards and fields.

13The Babylonians broke up the bronze pillars, the movable stands and the bronze Sea that were at the temple of the LORD and they carried the bronze to Babylon. 14They also took away the pots, shovels, wick trimmers, dishes and all the bronze articles used in the temple service. 15The commander of the imperial guard took away the censers and sprinkling bowls—all that were made of pure gold or silver.

16The bronze from the two pillars, the Sea and the movable stands, which Solomon had made for the temple of the LORD, was more than could be weighed. 17Each pillar was twenty-seven feet[a] high. The bronze capital on top of one pillar was four and a half feet[b] high and was decorated with a network and pomegranates of bronze all around. The other pillar, with its network, was similar.

18The commander of the guard took as prisoners Seraiah the chief priest, Zephaniah the priest next in rank and the three doorkeepers. 19Of those still in the city, he took the officer in charge of the fighting men and five royal advisers. He also took the secretary who was chief officer in charge of conscripting the people of the land and sixty of his men who were found in the city. 20Nebuzaradan the commander took them all and brought them to the king of Babylon at Riblah. 21There at Riblah, in the land of Hamath, the king had them executed.

a 17 Hebrew eighteen cubits (about 8.1 meters)　　b 17 Hebrew three cubits (about 1.3 meters)

So Judah went into captivity, away from her land.

²²Nebuchadnezzar king of Babylon appointed Gedaliah son of Ahikam, the son of Shaphan, to be over the people he had left behind in Judah. ²³When all the army officers and their men heard that the king of Babylon had appointed Gedaliah as governor, they came to Gedaliah at Mizpah—Ishmael son of Nethaniah, Johanan son of Kareah, Seraiah son of Tanhumeth the Netophathite, Jaazaniah the son of the Maacathite, and their men. ²⁴Gedaliah took an oath to reassure them and their men. "Do not be afraid of the Babylonian officials," he said. "Settle down in the land and serve the king of Babylon, and it will go well with you."

²⁵In the seventh month, however, Ishmael son of Nethaniah, the son of Elishama, who was of royal blood, came with ten men and assassinated Gedaliah and also the men of Judah and the Babylonians who were with him at Mizpah. ²⁶At this, all the people from the least to the greatest, together with the army officers, fled to Egypt for fear of the Babylonians.

Jehoiachin Released

²⁷In the thirty-seventh year of the exile of Jehoiachin king of Judah, in the year Evil-Merodach[a] became king of Babylon, he released Jehoiachin from prison on the twenty-seventh day of the twelfth month. ²⁸He spoke kindly to him and gave him a seat of honor higher than those of the other kings who were with him in Babylon. ²⁹So Jehoiachin put aside his prison clothes and for the rest of his life ate regularly at the king's table. ³⁰Day by day the king gave Jehoiachin a regular allowance as long as he lived.

a 27 Also called Amel-Marduk

這樣，猶大人被擄去離開本地。

²²至於猶大國剩下的民，就是巴比倫王尼布甲尼撒所剩下的，巴比倫王立了沙番的孫子、亞希甘的兒子基大利作他們的省長。²³眾軍長和屬他們的人聽見巴比倫王立了基大利作省長，於是，軍長尼探雅的兒子以實瑪利、加利亞的兒子約哈難、尼陀法人單戶篾的兒子西萊雅、瑪迦人的兒子雅撒尼亞和屬他們的人，都到米斯巴見基大利。²⁴基大利向他們和屬他們的人起誓說：「你們不必懼怕迦勒底臣僕，只管住在這地服侍巴比倫王，就可以得福。」

²⁵七月間，宗室以利沙瑪的孫子、尼探雅的兒子以實瑪利，帶着十個人來，殺了基大利和同他在米斯巴的猶大人與迦勒底人。²⁶於是，眾民無論大小，連眾軍長，因為懼怕迦勒底人，都起身往埃及去了。

約雅斤獲釋

²⁷猶大王約雅斤被擄後三十七年，巴比倫王以未米羅達元年十二月二十七日，使猶大王約雅斤抬頭，提他出監，²⁸又對他說恩言，使他的位高過與他一同在巴比倫眾王的位，²⁹給他脫了囚服。他終身常在巴比倫王面前吃飯。³⁰王賜他所需用的食物，日日賜他一份，終身都是這樣。

歷代志上

從亞當到亞伯拉罕的歷史記錄

至挪亞的兒子

1 <u>亞當</u>生<u>塞特</u>；<u>塞特</u>生<u>以挪士</u>；²<u>以挪士</u>生<u>該南</u>；<u>該南</u>生<u>瑪勒列</u>；<u>瑪勒列</u>生<u>雅列</u>；³<u>雅列</u>生<u>以諾</u>；<u>以諾</u>生<u>瑪土撒拉</u>；<u>瑪土撒拉</u>生<u>拉麥</u>；⁴<u>拉麥</u>生<u>挪亞</u>；

<u>挪亞</u>生<u>閃</u>、<u>含</u>、<u>雅弗</u>。

雅弗的子孫

⁵<u>雅弗</u>的兒子是：

<u>歌篾</u>、<u>瑪各</u>、<u>瑪代</u>、<u>雅完</u>、<u>土巴</u>、<u>米設</u>、<u>提拉</u>。

⁶<u>歌篾</u>的兒子是：

<u>亞實基拿</u>、<u>低法</u>（註：“低法”在創世記10章3節作“利法”）、<u>陀迦瑪</u>。

⁷<u>雅完</u>的兒子是：

<u>以利沙</u>、<u>他施</u>、<u>基提</u>、<u>多單</u>（註：“多單”有作“羅單”的）。

含的子孫

⁸<u>含</u>的兒子是：

<u>古實</u>、<u>麥西</u>、<u>弗</u>、<u>迦南</u>。

⁹<u>古實</u>的兒子是：

<u>西巴</u>、<u>哈腓拉</u>、<u>撒弗他</u>、<u>拉瑪</u>、<u>撒弗提迦</u>。

<u>拉瑪</u>的兒子是：

<u>示巴</u>、<u>底但</u>。

¹⁰<u>古實</u>生<u>寧錄</u>，

他為世上英雄之首。

¹¹<u>麥西</u>生<u>路低人</u>、<u>亞拿米人</u>、<u>利哈比人</u>、<u>拿弗土希人</u>、¹²<u>帕斯魯細人</u>、<u>迦斯路希人</u>、<u>迦斐託人</u>；從<u>迦斐託</u>出來的有<u>非利士人</u>。

¹³<u>迦南</u>生長子<u>西頓</u>，又生<u>赫</u>，¹⁴和<u>耶布斯人</u>、<u>亞摩利人</u>、<u>革迦撒人</u>、

1 Chronicles

Historical Records From Adam to Abraham

To Noah's Sons

1 Adam, Seth, Enosh, ²Kenan, Mahalalel, Jared, ³Enoch, Methuselah, Lamech, Noah.

⁴The sons of Noah:[a]
Shem, Ham and Japheth.

The Japhethites

⁵The sons[b] of Japheth:
Gomer, Magog, Madai, Javan, Tubal, Meshech and Tiras.

⁶The sons of Gomer:
Ashkenaz, Riphath[c] and Togarmah.

⁷The sons of Javan:
Elishah, Tarshish, the Kittim and the Rodanim.

The Hamites

⁸The sons of Ham:
Cush, Mizraim,[d] Put and Canaan.

⁹The sons of Cush:
Seba, Havilah, Sabta, Raamah and Sabteca.

The sons of Raamah:
Sheba and Dedan.

¹⁰Cush was the father[e] of
Nimrod, who grew to be a mighty warrior on earth.

¹¹Mizraim was the father of
the Ludites, Anamites, Lehabites, Naphtuhites, ¹²Pathrusites, Casluhites (from whom the Philistines came) and Caphtorites.

¹³Canaan was the father of
Sidon his firstborn,[f] and of the Hittites, ¹⁴Jebusites, Amorites, Girgashites,

---

a 4 Septuagint; Hebrew does not have *The sons of Noah:*
b 5 Sons may mean *descendants* or *successors* or *nations*; also in verses 6-10, 17 and 20. *c 6* Many Hebrew manuscripts and Vulgate (see also Septuagint and Gen. 10:3); most Hebrew manuscripts *Diphath* *d 8* That is, Egypt; also in verse 11 *e 10* Father may mean *ancestor* or *predecessor* or *founder*; also in verses 11, 13, 18 and 20. *f 13* Or *of the Sidonians, the foremost*

15Hivites, Arkites, Sinites, 16Arvadites, Zemarites and Hamathites.

The Semites

17The sons of Shem:

Elam, Asshur, Arphaxad, Lud and Aram. The sons of Aram*a* :

Uz, Hul, Gether and Meshech.

18Arphaxad was the father of Shelah, and Shelah the father of Eber.

19Two sons were born to Eber:

One was named Peleg,*b* because in his time the earth was divided; his brother was named Joktan.

20Joktan was the father of

Almodad, Sheleph, Hazarmaveth, Jerah, 21Hadoram, Uzal, Diklah, 22Obal,*c* Abimael, Sheba, 23Ophir, Havilah and Jobab. All these were sons of Joktan.

24Shem, Arphaxad,*d* Shelah,
25Eber, Peleg, Reu,
26Serug, Nahor, Terah
27and Abram (that is, Abraham).

The Family of Abraham

28The sons of Abraham:

Isaac and Ishmael.

Descendants of Hagar

29These were their descendants:

Nebaioth the firstborn of Ishmael, Kedar, Adbeel, Mibsam, 30Mishma, Dumah, Massa, Hadad, Tema, 31Jetur, Naphish and Kedemah. These were the sons of Ishmael.

Descendants of Keturah

32The sons born to Keturah, Abraham's concubine:

Zimran, Jokshan, Medan, Midian, Ishbak and Shuah.

The sons of Jokshan:

Sheba and Dedan.

33The sons of Midian:

Ephah, Epher, Hanoch, Abida and Eldaah.

All these were descendants of Keturah.

15希未人、亞基人、西尼人、16亞瓦底人、洗瑪利人並哈馬人。

閃的子孫

17閃的兒子是：

以攔、亞述、亞法撒、路德、亞蘭、烏斯、戶勒、基帖、米設（註："米設"創世記10章23節作"瑪施"）。

18亞法撒生沙拉；

沙拉生希伯。

19希伯生了兩個兒子：

一個名叫法勒（註："法勒"就是"分"的意思），因為那時人就分地居住；法勒的兄弟名叫約坍。

20約坍生亞摩答、沙列、哈薩瑪非、耶拉、21哈多蘭、烏薩、德拉、22以巴錄、亞比瑪利、示巴、23阿斐、哈腓拉、約巴。這都是約坍的兒子。

24閃生亞法撒；亞法撒生沙拉；25沙拉生希伯；希伯生法勒；法勒生拉吳；26拉吳生西鹿；西鹿生拿鶴；拿鶴生他拉；27他拉生亞伯蘭，亞伯蘭就是亞伯拉罕。

亞伯拉罕的家族

28亞伯拉罕的兒子是：

以撒、以實瑪利。

夏甲的後裔

29以實瑪利的兒子記在下面：

以實瑪利的長子是尼拜約，其次是基達、押德別、米比衫、30米施瑪、度瑪、瑪撒、哈達、提瑪、31伊突、拿非施、基底瑪。這都是以實瑪利的兒子。

基土拉的後裔

32亞伯拉罕的妾基土拉所生的兒子就是：

心蘭、約珊、米但、米甸、伊施巴、書亞。

約珊的兒子是：

示巴、底但。

33米甸的兒子是：

以法、以弗、哈諾、亞比大、以勒大。

這都是基土拉的子孫。

---

a 17 One Hebrew manuscript and some Septuagint manuscripts (see also Gen. 10:23); most Hebrew manuscripts do not have this line. *b* 19 *Peleg* means *division.* *c* 22 Some Hebrew manuscripts and Syriac (see also Gen. 10:28); most Hebrew manuscripts *Ebal* *d* 24 Hebrew; some Septuagint manuscripts *Arphaxad, Cainan* (see also note at Gen. 11:10)

撒拉的後裔

³⁴亞伯拉罕生以撒。
　　以撒的兒子是：
　　以掃和以色列。

以掃的子孫

³⁵以掃的兒子是：
　　以利法、流珥、耶烏施、雅蘭、
　　可拉。
³⁶以利法的兒子是：
　　提幔、阿抹、洗玻、迦坦、基納
　　斯、亭納、亞瑪力。
³⁷流珥的兒子是：
　　拿哈、謝拉、沙瑪、米撒。

以東地的西珥人

³⁸西珥的兒子是：
　　羅坍、朔巴、祭便、亞拿、底
　　順、以察、底珊。
³⁹羅坍的兒子是：
　　何利、荷幔。羅坍的妹子是亭
　　納。
⁴⁰朔巴的兒子是：
　　亞勒文、瑪拿轄、以巴錄、示
　　非、阿南。
　　祭便的兒子是：
　　亞雅、亞拿。
⁴¹亞拿的兒子是：
　　底順。
　　底順的兒子是：
　　哈默蘭、伊是班、益蘭、基蘭。
⁴²以察的兒子是：
　　辟罕、撒番、亞干。
　　底珊的兒子是：
　　烏斯、亞蘭。

以東諸王

⁴³以色列人未有君王治理之先，在以
東地作王的記在下面：
　　有比珥的兒子比拉，他的京城名
　　叫亭哈巴。
⁴⁴比拉死了，波斯拉人謝拉的兒子約
巴接續他作王。

Descendants of Sarah

³⁴Abraham was the father of Isaac.
　　The sons of Isaac:
　　Esau and Israel.

Esau's Sons

³⁵The sons of Esau:
　　Eliphaz, Reuel, Jeush, Jalam and Korah.

³⁶The sons of Eliphaz:
　　Teman, Omar, Zepho,ᵃ Gatam and Kenaz;
　　by Timna: Amalek.ᵇ
³⁷The sons of Reuel:
　　Nahath, Zerah, Shammah and Mizzah.

The People of Seir in Edom

³⁸The sons of Seir:
　　Lotan, Shobal, Zibeon, Anah, Dishon,
　　Ezer and Dishan.
³⁹The sons of Lotan:
　　Hori and Homam. Timna was Lotan's
　　sister.
⁴⁰The sons of Shobal:
　　Alvan,ᶜ Manahath, Ebal, Shepho and
　　Onam.
　　The sons of Zibeon:
　　Aiah and Anah.
⁴¹The son of Anah:
　　Dishon.
　　The sons of Dishon:
　　Hemdan,ᵈ Eshban, Ithran and Keran.
⁴²The sons of Ezer:
　　Bilhan, Zaavan and Akan.ᵉ
　　The sons of Dishanᶠ:
　　Uz and Aran.

The Rulers of Edom

⁴³These were the kings who reigned in Edom
before any Israelite king reignedᵍ:
　　Bela son of Beor, whose city was named
　　Dinhabah.
⁴⁴When Bela died, Jobab son of Zerah from
Bozrah succeeded him as king.

---

a 36 Many Hebrew manuscripts, some Septuagint manuscripts
and Syriac (see also Gen. 36:11); most Hebrew manuscripts
Zephi   b 36 Some Septuagint manuscripts (see also Gen.
36:12); Hebrew *Gatam, Kenaz, Timna and Amalek   c 40* Many
Hebrew manuscripts and some Septuagint manuscripts (see
also Gen. 36:23); most Hebrew manuscripts *Alian*
d 41 Many Hebrew manuscripts and some Septuagint
manuscripts (see also Gen. 36:26); most Hebrew manuscripts
Hamran   e 42 Many Hebrew and Septuagint manuscripts
(see also Gen. 36:27); most Hebrew manuscripts *Zaavan, Jaakan*
f 42 Hebrew *Dishon,* a variant of *Dishan   g 43* Or *before an
Israelite king reigned over them*

⁴⁵When Jobab died, Husham from the land of the Temanites succeeded him as king.

⁴⁶When Husham died, Hadad son of Bedad, who defeated Midian in the country of Moab, succeeded him as king. His city was named Avith.

⁴⁷When Hadad died, Samlah from Masrekah succeeded him as king.

⁴⁸When Samlah died, Shaul from Rehoboth on the river[d] succeeded him as king.

⁴⁹When Shaul died, Baal-Hanan son of Acbor succeeded him as king.

⁵⁰When Baal-Hanan died, Hadad succeeded him as king. His city was named Pau,[b] and his wife's name was Mehetabel daughter of Matred, the daughter of Me-Zahab. ⁵¹Hadad also died.

The chiefs of Edom were:

Timna, Alvah, Jetheth, ⁵²Oholibamah, Elah, Pinon, ⁵³Kenaz, Teman, Mibzar, ⁵⁴Magdiel and Iram. These were the chiefs of Edom.

Israel's Sons

2 These were the sons of Israel:
Reuben, Simeon, Levi, Judah, Issachar, Zebulun, ²Dan, Joseph, Benjamin, Naphtali, Gad and Asher.

Judah

To Hezron's Sons

³The sons of Judah:

Er, Onan and Shelah. These three were born to him by a Canaanite woman, the daughter of Shua. Er, Judah's firstborn, was wicked in the LORD's sight; so the LORD put him to death. ⁴Tamar, Judah's daughter-in-law, bore him Perez and Zerah. Judah had five sons in all.

⁵The sons of Perez:

Hezron and Hamul.

⁶The sons of Zerah:

Zimri, Ethan, Heman, Calcol and Darda[c] —five in all.

⁴⁵約巴死了，提幔地的人戶珊接續他作王。

⁴⁶戶珊死了，比達的兒子哈達接續他作王。這哈達就是在摩押地殺敗米甸人的，他的京城名叫亞未得。

⁴⁷哈達死了，瑪士利加人桑拉接續他作王。

⁴⁸桑拉死了，大河邊的利河伯人掃羅接續他作王。

⁴⁹掃羅死了，亞革波的兒子巴勒哈南接續他作王。

⁵⁰巴勒哈南死了，哈達接續他作王，他的京城名叫巴伊。他的妻子名叫米希她別，是米薩合的孫女、瑪特列的女兒。⁵¹哈達死了。

以東人的族長有：

亨納族長、亞勒瓦族長、耶帖族長、⁵²亞何利巴瑪族長、以拉族長、比嫩族長、⁵³基納斯族長、提幔族長、米比薩族長、⁵⁴瑪基疊族長、以蘭族長。這都是以東人的族長。

以色列的眾子

2 以色列的兒子是：
呂便、西緬、利未、猶大、以薩迦、西布倫、²但、約瑟、便雅憫、拿弗他利、迦得、亞設。

猶大支派

至希斯崙的兒子

³猶大的兒子是：

珥、俄南、示拉，這三人是迦南人書亞女兒所生的。猶大的長子珥，在耶和華眼中看為惡，耶和華就使他死了。⁴他瑪給猶大生法勒斯和謝拉。猶大共有五個兒子。

⁵法勒斯的兒子是：

希斯崙、哈母勒。

⁶謝拉的兒子是：

心利、以探、希幔、甲各、大拉（註："大拉"即"達大"），共五人。

a 48 Possibly the Euphrates   b 50 Many Hebrew
manuscripts, some Septuagint manuscripts, Vulgate and
Syriac (see also Gen. 36:39); most Hebrew manuscripts *Pai*
c 6 Many Hebrew manuscripts, some Septuagint manuscripts
and Syriac (see also 1 Kings 4:31); most Hebrew manuscripts
Dara

7迦米的兒子是：

亞干，這亞干在當滅的物上犯了
罪，連累了以色列人。

8以探的兒子是：

亞撒利雅。

9希斯崙所生的兒子是：

耶拉篾、蘭、基路拜。

希斯崙之子蘭的後裔

10蘭生亞米拿達；亞米拿達生拿順，
拿順作猶大人的首領。11拿順生
撒門；撒門生波阿斯；12波阿斯
生俄備得；俄備得生耶西。

13耶西生長子以利押，次子亞比拿
達，三子示米亞（註：“示米亞”即
“沙瑪”，見撒母耳記上16章9節），14四
子拿坦業，五子拉代，15六子阿
鮮，七子大衛。16他們的姐妹是
洗魯雅和亞比該。洗魯雅的兒子
是亞比篩、約押、亞撒黑，共三
人。17亞比該生亞瑪撒。亞瑪撒
的父親是以實瑪利人益帖。

希斯崙之子迦勒

18希斯崙的兒子迦勒娶阿蘇巴和耶略
為妻。阿蘇巴的兒子是耶設、朔
罷、押墩。19阿蘇巴死了，迦勒
又娶以法她，生了戶珥。20戶珥
生烏利；烏利生比撒列。

21希斯崙正六十歲娶了基列父親瑪吉
的女兒，與她同房，瑪吉的女兒
生了西割。22西割生睚珥，睚珥
在基列地有二十三個城邑。23後
來基述人和亞蘭人奪了睚珥的城
邑，並基納和其鄉村，共六十
個。這都是基列父親瑪吉之子
的。

24希斯崙在迦勒以法他死後，他的妻
亞比雅給他生了亞施戶；亞施戶
是提哥亞的父親。

7The son of Carmi:

Achar,*a* who brought trouble on Israel by
violating the ban on taking devoted
things.*b*
8The son of Ethan:

Azariah.
9The sons born to Hezron were:

Jerahmeel, Ram and Caleb.*c*

From Ram Son of Hezron
10Ram was the father of

Amminadab, and Amminadab the father of
Nahshon, the leader of the people of Judah.
11Nahshon was the father of Salmon,*d*
Salmon the father of Boaz, 12Boaz the
father of Obed and Obed the father of Jesse.
13Jesse was the father of

Eliab his firstborn; the second son was
Abinadab, the third Shimea, 14the fourth
Nethanel, the fifth Raddai, 15the sixth
Ozem and the seventh David. 16Their sis-
ters were Zeruiah and Abigail. Zeruiah's
three sons were Abishai, Joab and
Asahel. 17Abigail was the mother of
Amasa, whose father was Jether the
Ishmaelite.

Caleb Son of Hezron
18Caleb son of Hezron had children by his wife
Azubah (and by Jerioth). These were her
sons: Jesher, Shobab and Ardon. 19When
Azubah died, Caleb married Ephrath,
who bore him Hur. 20Hur was the father
of Uri, and Uri the father of Bezalel.

21Later, Hezron lay with the daughter of Makir
the father of Gilead (he had married her
when he was sixty years old), and she
bore him Segub. 22Segub was the father
of Jair, who controlled twenty-three
towns in Gilead. 23(But Geshur and Aram
captured Havvoth Jair,*e* as well as Kenath
with its surrounding settlements—sixty
towns.) All these were descendants of
Makir the father of Gilead.

24After Hezron died in Caleb Ephrathah, Abijah
the wife of Hezron bore him Ashhur the
father*f* of Tekoa.

a 7 Achar means *trouble; Achar* is called *Achan* in Joshua.
b 7 The Hebrew term refers to the irrevocable giving over of
things or persons to the LORD, often by totally destroying
them.　*c 9* Hebrew *Kelubai,* a variant of *Caleb*
d 11 Septuagint (see also Ruth 4:21); Hebrew *Salma*　*e 23* Or
captured the settlements of Jair　*f 24 Father* may mean *civic
leader* or *military leader;* also in verses 42, 45, 49-52 and possibly
elsewhere.

Jerahmeel Son of Hezron

²⁵The sons of Jerahmeel the firstborn of Hezron:
　　Ram his firstborn, Bunah, Oren, Ozem
　　and*ᵃ* Ahijah. ²⁶Jerahmeel had another
　　wife, whose name was Atarah; she was
　　the mother of Onam.

²⁷The sons of Ram the firstborn of Jerahmeel:
　　Maaz, Jamin and Eker.

²⁸The sons of Onam:
　　Shammai and Jada.
　The sons of Shammai:
　　Nadab and Abishur.

²⁹Abishur's wife was named Abihail, who bore
　　him Ahban and Molid.

³⁰The sons of Nadab:
　　Seled and Appaim. Seled died without
　　children.

³¹The son of Appaim:
　　Ishi, who was the father of Sheshan.
　　Sheshan was the father of Ahlai.

³²The sons of Jada, Shammai's brother:
　　Jether and Jonathan. Jether died without
　　children.

³³The sons of Jonathan:
　　Peleth and Zaza.
　These were the descendants of Jerahmeel.

³⁴Sheshan had no sons—only daughters.
　　He had an Egyptian servant named Jarha.
　　³⁵Sheshan gave his daughter in marriage to
　　his servant Jarha, and she bore him Attai.

³⁶Attai was the father of Nathan,
　　Nathan the father of Zabad,
³⁷Zabad the father of Ephlal,
　　Ephlal the father of Obed,
³⁸Obed the father of Jehu,
　　Jehu the father of Azariah,
³⁹Azariah the father of Helez,
　　Helez the father of Eleasah,
⁴⁰Eleasah the father of Sismai,
　　Sismai the father of Shallum,
⁴¹Shallum the father of Jekamiah,
　　and Jekamiah the father of Elishama.

The Clans of Caleb

⁴²The sons of Caleb the brother of Jerahmeel:
　　Mesha his firstborn, who was the father
　　of Ziph, and his son Mareshah,*ᵇ* who was
　　the father of Hebron.

⁴³The sons of Hebron:
　　Korah, Tappuah, Rekem and Shema.
　　⁴⁴Shema was the father of Raham, and
　　Raham the father of Jorkeam. Rekem was

希斯崙之子耶拉篾

²⁵希斯崙的長子耶拉篾生長子蘭，又
　　生布拿、阿連、阿鮮、亞希雅。
　　²⁶耶拉篾又娶一妻名叫亞她拉，是
　　阿南的母親。

²⁷耶拉篾長子蘭的兒子是：
　　瑪斯、雅憫、以結。
²⁸阿南的兒子是：
　　沙買、雅大。
　沙買的兒子是：
　　拿答、亞比述。
²⁹亞比述的妻名叫亞比孩，亞比孩給
　　他生了亞辦和摩利。
³⁰拿答的兒子是：
　　西列、亞遍。西列死了沒有兒
　　子。
³¹亞遍的兒子是以示。
　　以示的兒子是示珊。
　　示珊的兒子是亞來。
³²沙買兄弟雅大的兒子是：
　　益帖、約拿單。益帖死了沒有兒
　　子。
³³約拿單的兒子是：
　　比勒、撒薩。
　這都是耶拉篾的子孫。
³⁴示珊沒有兒子，只有女兒。
　　示珊有一個僕人名叫耶哈，是埃
　　及人。³⁵示珊將女兒給了僕人耶
　　哈為妻，給他生了亞太。
³⁶亞太生拿單；
　　拿單生撒拔；
³⁷撒拔生以弗拉；
　　以弗拉生俄備得；
³⁸俄備得生耶戶；
　　耶戶生亞撒利雅；
³⁹亞撒利雅生希利斯；
　　希利斯生以利薩；
⁴⁰以利亞薩生西斯買；
　　西斯買生沙龍；
⁴¹沙龍生耶加米雅；
　　耶加米雅生以利沙瑪。

迦勒的家族

⁴²耶拉篾兄弟迦勒的長子米沙，是西
　　弗之祖瑪利沙的兒子，是希伯崙
　　之祖。

⁴³希伯崙的兒子是：
　　可拉、他普亞、利肯、示瑪。⁴⁴示瑪
　　生拉含，是約干之祖。利肯生

25 Or Oren and Ozem, by　　*b 42 The meaning of the Hebrew or this phrase is uncertain.*

沙買，45沙買的兒子是瑪雲；瑪雲
是伯夙之祖。

46迦勒的妾以法生哈蘭、摩撒、迦
謝。哈蘭生迦卸。

47雅代的兒子是：
利健、約坦、基珊、毘力、以法、
沙亞弗。

48迦勒的妾瑪迦生示別、特哈拿，
49又生麥瑪拿之祖沙亞弗、抹比
拿和基比亞之祖示法；迦勒的女
兒是押撒。

50迦勒的子孫就是以法她的長子戶珥
的兒子，記在下面：
基列耶琳之祖朔巴、51伯利恆之
祖薩瑪、伯迦得之祖哈勒。

52基列耶琳之祖朔巴的子孫是：
哈羅以和一半米努哈人（註："米
努哈人"即"瑪拿哈人"）。53基列耶
琳的諸族是以帖人、布特人、舒
瑪人、密來人，又從這些族中生
出瑣拉人和以實陶人來。

54薩瑪的子孫是：
伯利恆人、尼陀法人、亞他綠伯
約押人、一半瑪拿哈人、瑣利
人、55和住雅斯眾文士家的特
拉人、示米押人、蘇甲人。這都
是基尼人利甲家之祖哈末所生
的。

大衛的兒子

3 大衛在希伯崙所生的兒子記
在下面：
長子暗嫩是耶斯列人亞希暖
生的；
次子但以利是迦密人亞比該生
的；
2三子押沙龍是基述王達買的女兒
瑪迦生的；
四子亞多尼雅是哈及生的；
3五子示法提雅是亞比她生的；
六子以特念是大衛的妻以格拉生的。
4這六人都是大衛在希伯崙生的。
大衛在希伯崙作王七年零六個
月，在耶路撒冷作王三十三年。

5大衛在耶路撒冷所生的兒子是：

the father of Shammai. 45The son of
Shammai was Maon, and Maon was the
father of Beth Zur.

46Caleb's concubine Ephah was the mother of
Haran, Moza and Gazez. Haran was the
father of Gazez.

47The sons of Jahdai:
Regem, Jotham, Geshan, Pelet, Ephah
and Shaaph.

48Caleb's concubine Maacah was the mother of
Sheber and Tirhanah. 49She also gave
birth to Shaaph the father of Madmannah
and to Sheva the father of Macbenah and
Gibea. Caleb's daughter was Acsah.
50These were the descendants of Caleb.

The sons of Hur the firstborn of Ephrathah:
Shobal the father of Kiriath Jearim,
51Salma the father of Bethlehem, and
Hareph the father of Beth Gader.

52The descendants of Shobal the father of
Kiriath Jearim were:
Haroeh, half the Manahathites, 53and the
clans of Kiriath Jearim: the Ithrites,
Puthites, Shumathites and Mishraites.
From these descended the Zorathites and
Eshtaolites.

54The descendants of Salma:
Bethlehem, the Netophathites, Atroth
Beth Joab, half the Manahathites, the
Zorites, 55and the clans of scribes[a] who
lived at Jabez: the Tirathites, Shimeathites
and Sucathites. These are the Kenites
who came from Hammath, the father of
the house of Recab.[b]

The Sons of David

3 These were the sons of David born to
him in Hebron:
The firstborn was Amnon the son of
Ahinoam of Jezreel;
the second, Daniel the son of Abigail of
Carmel;
2the third, Absalom the son of Maacah
daughter of Talmai king of Geshur;
the fourth, Adonijah the son of Haggith;
3the fifth, Shephatiah the son of Abital;
and the sixth, Ithream, by his wife Eglah.
4These six were born to David in Hebron,
where he reigned seven years and six
months.
David reigned in Jerusalem thirty-three years,
5and these were the children born to him there:

a 55 Or of the Sopherites   *b 55 Or father of Beth Recab*

Shammua,[a] Shobab, Nathan and
Solomon. These four were by Bathsheba[b]
daughter of Ammiel. [6]There were also
Ibhar, Elishua,[c] Eliphelet, [7]Nogah,
Nepheg, Japhia, [8]Elishama, Eliada and
Eliphelet—nine in all. [9]All these were the
sons of David, besides his sons by his
concubines. And Tamar was their sister.

The Kings of Judah
[10]Solomon's son was Rehoboam,
Abijah his son,
Asa his son,
Jehoshaphat his son,
[11]Jehoram[d] his son,
Ahaziah his son,
Joash his son,
[12]Amaziah his son,
Azariah his son,
Jotham his son,
[13]Ahaz his son,
Hezekiah his son,
Manasseh his son,
[14]Amon his son,
Josiah his son.
[15]The sons of Josiah:
Johanan the firstborn,
Jehoiakim the second son,
Zedekiah the third,
Shallum the fourth.
[16]The successors of Jehoiakim:
Jehoiachin[e] his son,
and Zedekiah.

The Royal Line After the Exile
[17]The descendants of Jehoiachin the captive:
Shealtiel his son, [18]Malkiram, Pedaiah,
Shenazzar, Jekamiah, Hoshama and
Nedabiah.
[19]The sons of Pedaiah:
Zerubbabel and Shimei.
The sons of Zerubbabel:
Meshullam and Hananiah.
Shelomith was their sister.
[20]There were also five others:
Hashubah, Ohel, Berekiah, Hasadiah and
Jushab-Hesed.

示米亞、朔罷、拿單、所羅門，
這四人是亞米利的女兒拔書亞
（註：撒母耳記上11章，列王紀上1章作
"拔示巴"）生的；[6]還有益轄、以
利沙瑪、以利法列、[7]挪迦、尼
斐、雅非亞、[8]以利沙瑪、以利雅
大、以利法列，共九人。[9]這都是
大衛的兒子，還有他們的妹子她
瑪，妃嬪的兒子不在其內。

猶大諸王
[10]所羅門的兒子是羅波安；
羅波安的兒子是亞比雅；
亞比雅的兒子是亞撒；
亞撒的兒子是約沙法；
[11]約沙法的兒子是約蘭；
約蘭的兒子是約哈謝；
亞哈謝的兒子是約阿施；
[12]約阿施的兒子是亞瑪謝；
亞瑪謝的兒子是亞撒利雅；
亞撒利雅的兒子是約坦；
[13]約坦的兒子是亞哈斯；
亞哈斯的兒子是希西家；
希西家的兒子是瑪拿西；
[14]瑪拿西的兒子是亞們；
亞們的兒子是約西亞。
[15]約西亞的：
長子是約哈難，
次子是約雅敬，
三子是西底家，
四子是沙龍。
[16]約雅敬的兒子是：
耶哥尼雅
和西底家。

被擄以後王室的譜系
[17]耶哥尼雅被擄，他的兒子是：
撒拉鐵、[18]瑪基蘭、毘大雅、示
拿薩、耶加米、何沙瑪、尼大比
雅。
[19]毘大雅的兒子是：
所羅巴伯、示每。
所羅巴伯的兒子是：
米書蘭、哈拿尼雅，
他們的妹子名叫示羅密。
[20]米書蘭的兒子是：
哈舒巴、阿黑、比利家、哈撒
底、于沙希悉，共五人。

5 Hebrew *Shimea*, a variant of *Shammua*   b 5 One Hebrew
manuscript and Vulgate (see also Septuagint and 2 Samuel
5:3); most Hebrew manuscripts *Bathshua*   c 6 Two Hebrew
manuscripts (see also 2 Samuel 5:15 and 1 Chron. 14:5); most
Hebrew manuscripts *Elishama*   d 11 Hebrew *Joram*, a variant
of *Jehoram*   e 16 Hebrew *Jeconiah*, a variant of *Jehoiachin*; also
verse 17

²¹哈拿尼雅的兒子是：
　　毘拉提、耶篩亞，還有利法雅的
　　眾子、亞珥難的眾子、俄巴底亞
　　的眾子、示迦尼的眾子。
²²示迦尼的兒子是示瑪雅；
　　示瑪雅的兒子是：
　　哈突、以甲、巴利亞、尼利雅、
　　沙法，共六人。
²³尼利雅的兒子是：
　　以利約乃、希西家、亞斯利干，
　　共三人。
²⁴以利約乃的兒子是：
　　何大雅、以利亞實、毘萊雅、阿
　　谷、約哈難、第萊雅、阿拿尼，
　　共七人。

猶大支派的其他家族

4 猶大的兒子是：
　　法勒斯、希斯崙、迦米、戶
　　珥、朔巴。
²朔巴的兒子利亞雅生雅哈；雅哈生
　　亞戶買和拉哈，這是瑣拉人的諸
　　族。
³以坦之祖的兒子是：
　　耶斯列、伊施瑪、伊得巴，他們
　　的妹子名叫哈悉勒玻尼。⁴基多之
　　祖是毘努伊勒，戶沙之祖是以謝
　　珥。
　　這都是伯利恆之祖以法她的長子戶
　　珥所生的。

⁵提哥亞之祖亞施戶有兩個妻子：一
　　名希拉，一名拿拉。
⁶拿拉給亞施戶生亞戶撒、希弗、提
　　米尼、哈轄斯他利，這都是拿拉
　　的兒子。
⁷希拉的兒子是：
　　洗列、瑣轄、伊提南。⁸哥斯生
　　亞諾、瑣比巴，並哈崙兒子亞
　　哈黑的諸族。

⁹雅比斯比他眾弟兄更尊貴，他
母親給他起名叫雅比斯，意思說：
我生他甚是痛苦。¹⁰雅比斯求告以色
列的神說：「甚願你賜福與我，擴
張我的境界，常與我同在，保佑我
不遭患難，不受艱苦。」神就應允
他所求的。

²¹The descendants of Hananiah:
　　Pelatiah and Jeshaiah, and the sons of
　　Rephaiah, of Arnan, of Obadiah and of
　　Shecaniah.
²²The descendants of Shecaniah:
　　Shemaiah and his sons:
　　Hattush, Igal, Bariah, Neariah and
　　Shaphat—six in all.
²³The sons of Neariah:
　　Elioenai, Hizkiah and Azrikam—three in
　　all.
²⁴The sons of Elioenai:
　　Hodaviah, Eliashib, Pelaiah, Akkub,
　　Johanan, Delaiah and Anani—seven in
　　all.

Other Clans of Judah

4 The descendants of Judah:
　　Perez, Hezron, Carmi, Hur and Shobal.
²Reaiah son of Shobal was the father of
　　Jahath, and Jahath the father of Ahumai
　　and Lahad. These were the clans of the
　　Zorathites.
³These were the sons^a of Etam:
　　Jezreel, Ishma and Idbash. Their sister
　　was named Hazzelelponi. ⁴Penuel was
　　the father of Gedor, and Ezer the father of
　　Hushah.
　　These were the descendants of Hur, the first-
　　born of Ephrathah and father^b of
　　Bethlehem.
⁵Ashhur the father of Tekoa had two wives,
　　Helah and Naarah.
⁶Naarah bore him Ahuzzam, Hepher, Temeni
　　and Haahashtari. These were the descen-
　　dants of Naarah.
⁷The sons of Helah:
　　Zereth, Zohar, Ethnan, ⁸and Koz, who
　　was the father of Anub and Hazzobebah
　　and of the clans of Aharhel son of
　　Harum.

⁹Jabez was more honorable than his brothers.
His mother had named him Jabez,^c saying, "I
gave birth to him in pain." ¹⁰Jabez cried out to
the God of Israel, "Oh, that you would bless me
and enlarge my territory! Let your hand be with
me, and keep me from harm so that I will be free
from pain." And God granted his request.

---

*a 3 Some Septuagint manuscripts (see also Vulgate); Hebrew
father　b 4 Father may mean civic leader or military leader; also
in verses 12, 14, 17, 18 and possibly elsewhere.　c 9 Jabez
sounds like the Hebrew for pain.*

¹¹Kelub, Shuhah's brother, was the father of Mehir, who was the father of Eshton. ¹²Eshton was the father of Beth Rapha, Paseah and Tehinnah the father of Ir Nahash.^a These were the men of Recah.

¹³The sons of Kenaz:
Othniel and Seraiah.
The sons of Othniel:
Hathath and Meonothai.^b ¹⁴Meonothai was the father of Ophrah.
Seraiah was the father of Joab,
the father of Ge Harashim.^c It was called this because its people were craftsmen.

¹⁵The sons of Caleb son of Jephunneh:
Iru, Elah and Naam.
The son of Elah:
Kenaz.
¹⁶The sons of Jehallelel:
Ziph, Ziphah, Tiria and Asarel.
¹⁷The sons of Ezrah:
Jether, Mered, Epher and Jalon. One of Mered's wives gave birth to Miriam, Shammai and Ishbah the father of Eshtemoa. ¹⁸(His Judean wife gave birth to Jered the father of Gedor, Heber the father of Soco, and Jekuthiel the father of Zanoah.) These were the children of Pharaoh's daughter Bithiah, whom Mered had married.

¹⁹The sons of Hodiah's wife, the sister of Naham:
the father of Keilah the Garmite, and Eshtemoa the Maacathite.
²⁰The sons of Shimon:
Amnon, Rinnah, Ben-Hanan and Tilon.
The descendants of Ishi:
Zoheth and Ben-Zoheth.
²¹The sons of Shelah son of Judah:
Er the father of Lecah, Laadah the father of Mareshah and the clans of the linen workers at Beth Ashbea, ²²Jokim, the men of Cozeba, and Joash and Saraph, who ruled in Moab and Jashubi Lehem. (These records are from ancient times.) ²³They were the potters who lived at Netaim and Gederah; they stayed there and worked for the king.

¹¹書哈的弟兄基綠生米黑，米黑是伊施屯之祖。¹²伊施屯生伯拉巴、巴西亞，並珥拿轄之祖提欣拿。這都是利迦人。

¹³基納斯的兒子是：
俄陀聶、西萊雅。
俄陀聶的兒子是哈塔。¹⁴憫挪太生俄弗拉。

西萊雅生革夏納欣人之祖約押。他們都是匠人。

¹⁵耶孚尼的兒子是迦勒。迦勒的兒子是：
以路、以拉、拿安。
以拉的兒子是：
基納斯。
¹⁶耶哈利勒的兒子是：
西弗、西法、提利、亞撒列。
^{17、18}以斯拉的兒子是：
益帖、米列、以弗、雅倫。米列娶法老女兒比提雅為妻，生米利暗、沙買和以實提摩之祖益巴。米列又娶猶大女子為妻，生基多之祖雅列、梭哥之祖希伯和撒挪亞之祖耶古鐵。

¹⁹荷第雅的妻是拿含的妹子，她所生的兒子是：
迦米人基伊拉和瑪迦人以實提摩之祖。
²⁰示門的兒子是：
暗嫩、林拿、便哈南、提倫。
以示的兒子是：
梭黑與便梭黑。
²¹猶大的兒子是示拉。
示拉的兒子是利迦之祖珥、瑪利沙之祖拉大和屬亞實比族織細麻布的各家。²²還有約敬、哥西巴人、約阿施、薩拉，就是在摩押地掌權的，又有雅叔比利恆，這都是古時所記載的。²³這些人都是窰匠，是尼他應和基低拉的居民，與王同處，為王做工。

a 12 Or of the city of Nahash   b 13 Some Septuagint manuscripts and Vulgate; Hebrew does not have and Meonothai.   c 14 Ge Harashim means valley of craftsmen.

西緬支派

24西緬的兒子是：

尼母利、雅憫、雅立、謝拉、掃羅；25掃羅的兒子是沙龍；沙龍的兒子是米比衫；米比衫的兒子是米施瑪；26米施瑪的兒子是哈母利；哈母利的兒子是撒刻；撒刻的兒子是示每。

27示每有十六個兒子、六個女兒，他弟兄的兒女不多，他們各家不如猶大族的人丁增多。28西緬人住在別是巴、摩拉大、哈薩書亞、29辟拉、以森、陀臘、30彼土利、何珥瑪、洗革拉、31伯瑪嘉博、哈薩蘇撒、伯比利、沙拉音，這些城邑直到大衛王的時候都是屬西緬人的。32他們的五個城邑是以坦、亞因、臨門、陀健、亞珊。33還有屬城的鄉村，直到巴力。這是他們的住處，他們都有家譜。

34還有米所巴、雅米勒、亞瑪謝的兒子約沙、35約珥、約示比的兒子耶戶。約示比是西萊雅的兒子；西萊雅是亞薛的兒子。36還有以利約乃、雅哥巴、約朔海、亞帥雅、亞底業、耶西篾、比拿雅。37示非的兒子細撒，示非是亞龍的兒子；亞龍是耶大雅的兒子；耶大雅是申利的兒子；申利是示瑪雅的兒子。

38以上所記的人名，都是作族長的，他們宗族的人數增多。39他們往平原東邊基多口去，尋找牧放羊羣的草場，40尋得肥美的草場地，又寬闊、又平靜。從前住那裏的是含族的人。

41以上錄名的人，在猶大王希西家年間，來攻擊含族人的帳棚和那裏所有的米烏尼人，將他們滅盡，就住在他們的地方，直到今日。因為那裏有草場可以牧放羊羣。42這西緬人中，有五百人上西珥山，率領他們的是以示的兒子毘拉推、尼利雅、利法雅和烏薛，43殺了逃脫剩下的亞瑪力人，就住在那裏直到今日。

Simeon

24The descendants of Simeon:

Nemuel, Jamin, Jarib, Zerah and Shaul;
25Shallum was Shaul's son, Mibsam his son and Mishma his son.

26The descendants of Mishma:

Hammuel his son, Zaccur his son and Shimei his son.

27Shimei had sixteen sons and six daughters, but his brothers did not have many children; so their entire clan did not become as numerous as the people of Judah. 28They lived in Beersheba, Moladah, Hazar Shual, 29Bilhah, Ezem, Tolad, 30Bethuel, Hormah, Ziklag, 31Beth Marcaboth, Hazar Susim, Beth Biri and Shaaraim. These were their towns until the reign of David. 32Their surrounding villages were Etam, Ain, Rimmon, Token and Ashan—five towns— 33and all the villages around these towns as far as Baalath.[a] These were their settlements. And they kept a genealogical record.

34Meshobab, Jamlech, Joshah son of Amaziah, 35Joel, Jehu son of Joshibiah, the son of Seraiah, the son of Asiel, 36also Elioenai, Jaakobah, Jeshohaiah, Asaiah, Adiel, Jesimiel, Benaiah, 37and Ziza son of Shiphi, the son of Allon, the son of Jedaiah, the son of Shimri, the son of Shemaiah.

38The men listed above by name were leaders of their clans. Their families increased greatly, 39and they went to the outskirts of Gedor to the east of the valley in search of pasture for their flocks. 40They found rich, good pasture, and the land was spacious, peaceful and quiet. Some Hamites had lived there formerly.

41The men whose names were listed came in the days of Hezekiah king of Judah. They attacked the Hamites in their dwellings and also the Meunites who were there and completely destroyed[b] them, as is evident to this day. Then they settled in their place, because there was pasture for their flocks. 42And five hundred of these Simeonites, led by Pelatiah, Neariah, Rephaiah and Uzziel, the sons of Ishi, invaded the hill country of Seir. 43They killed the remaining Amalekites who had escaped, and they have lived there to this day.

---

a 33 Some Septuagint manuscripts (see also Joshua 19:8); Hebrew *Baal*　　*b 41* The Hebrew term refers to the irrevocable giving over of things or persons to the LORD, often by totally destroying them.

Reuben

5 The sons of Reuben the firstborn of Israel (he was the firstborn, but when he defiled his father's marriage bed, his rights as firstborn were given to the sons of Joseph son of Israel; so he could not be listed in the genealogical record in accordance with his birthright, ²and though Judah was the strongest of his brothers and a ruler came from him, the rights of the firstborn belonged to Joseph)— ³the sons of Reuben the firstborn of Israel:

Hanoch, Pallu, Hezron and Carmi.

⁴The descendants of Joel:

Shemaiah his son, Gog his son, Shimei his son, ⁵Micah his son, Reaiah his son, Baal his son,

⁶and Beerah his son, whom Tiglath-Pileser*a* king of Assyria took into exile. Beerah was a leader of the Reubenites.

⁷Their relatives by clans, listed according to their genealogical records:

Jeiel the chief, Zechariah, ⁸and Bela son of Azaz, the son of Shema, the son of Joel. They settled in the area from Aroer to Nebo and Baal Meon. ⁹To the east they occupied the land up to the edge of the desert that extends to the Euphrates River, because their livestock had increased in Gilead.

¹⁰During Saul's reign they waged war against the Hagrites, who were defeated at their hands; they occupied the dwellings of the Hagrites throughout the entire region east of Gilead.

Gad

¹¹The Gadites lived next to them in Bashan, as far as Salecah:

¹²Joel was the chief, Shapham the second, then Janai and Shaphat, in Bashan.

¹³Their relatives, by families, were:

Michael, Meshullam, Sheba, Jorai, Jacan, Zia and Eber—seven in all.

¹⁴These were the sons of Abihail son of Huri, the son of Jaroah, the son of Gilead, the son of Michael, the son of Jeshishai, the son of Jahdo, the son of Buz.

¹⁵Ahi son of Abdiel, the son of Guni, was head of their family.

呂便支派

5 以色列的長子原是呂便，因他污穢了父親的牀，他長子的名分就歸了約瑟；只是按家譜他不算長子。²猶大勝過一切弟兄，君王也是從他而出，長子的名分卻歸約瑟。³以色列長子呂便的兒子是：

哈諾、法路、希斯倫、迦米。

⁴約珥的兒子是示瑪雅；示瑪雅的兒子是歌革；歌革的兒子是示每；⁵示每的兒子是米迦；米迦的兒子是利亞雅；利亞雅的兒子是巴力；⁶巴力的兒子是備拉。這備拉作呂便支派的首領，被亞述王提革拉毘尼色擄去。⁷他的弟兄照着宗族、按着家譜作族長的是：

耶利、撒迦利雅、比拉。⁸比拉是亞撒的兒子；亞撒是示瑪的兒子；示瑪是約珥的兒子。約珥所住的地方是從亞羅珥直到尼波和巴力免，⁹又向東延到幼發拉底河這邊的曠野，因為他們在基列地牲畜增多。

¹⁰掃羅年間，他們與夏甲人爭戰，夏甲人倒在他們手下，他們就在基列東邊的全地，住在夏甲人的帳棚裏。

迦得支派

¹¹迦得的子孫在呂便對面，住在巴珊地，延到撒迦。¹²他們中間有作族長的約珥，有作副族長的沙番，還有雅乃和住在巴珊的沙法。¹³他們族弟兄是：

米迦勒、米書蘭、示巴、約賴、雅干、細亞、希伯，共七人。¹⁴這都是亞比孩的兒子。亞比孩是戶利的兒子；戶利是耶羅亞的兒子；耶羅亞是基列的兒子；基列是米迦勒的兒子；米迦勒是耶示篩的兒子；耶示篩是耶哈多的兒子；耶哈多是布斯的兒子。¹⁵還有古尼的孫子、押比疊的兒子亞希。這都是作族長的。

---

6 Hebrew Tilgath-Pilneser, a variant of Tiglath-Pileser; also in verse 26

¹⁶他們住在基列與巴珊和巴珊的鄉村，並沙崙的郊野，直到四圍的交界。

¹⁷這些人在猶大王約坦並在以色列王耶羅波安年間，都載入家譜。

¹⁸呂便人、迦得人和瑪拿西半支派的人，能拿盾牌和刀劍、拉弓射箭、出征善戰的勇士，共有四萬四千七百六十名。¹⁹他們與夏甲人、伊突人、拿非施人、挪答人爭戰。²⁰他們得了神的幫助，夏甲人和跟隨夏甲的人都交在他們手中。因為他們在陣上呼求神，倚賴神，神就應允他們。²¹他們擄掠了夏甲人的牲畜，有駱駝五萬、羊二十五萬、驢二千，又有人十萬。²²敵人被殺仆倒的甚多，因為這爭戰是出乎神。他們就住在敵人的地上，直到被擄的時候。

瑪拿西半支派

²³瑪拿西半支派的人住在那地，從巴珊延到巴力黑們、示尼珥與黑門山。

²⁴他們的族長是：以弗、以示、以列、亞斯列、耶利米、何達威雅、雅疊，都是大能的勇士，是有名的人，也是作族長的。²⁵他們得罪了他們列祖的神，隨從那地之民的神行邪淫；這民就是神在他們面前所除滅的。²⁶故此，以色列的神激動亞述王普勒和亞述王提革拉毘尼色的心，他們就把呂便人、迦得人、瑪拿西半支派的人擄到哈臘、哈博、哈拉與歌散河邊，直到今日還在那裏。

利未支派

6 利未的兒子是：
革順、哥轄、米拉利。
²歌轄的兒子是：
暗蘭、以斯哈、希伯倫、烏薛。
³暗蘭的兒子是：
亞倫、摩西，還有女兒米利暗。
亞倫的兒子是：
拿答、亞比戶、以利亞撒、以他瑪。
⁴以利亞撒生非尼哈；
非尼哈生亞比書；

¹⁶The Gadites lived in Gilead, in Bashan and its outlying villages, and on all the pasturelands of Sharon as far as they extended.

¹⁷All these were entered in the genealogical records during the reigns of Jotham king of Judah and Jeroboam king of Israel.

¹⁸The Reubenites, the Gadites and the half-tribe of Manasseh had 44,760 men ready for military service—able-bodied men who could handle shield and sword, who could use a bow, and who were trained for battle. ¹⁹They waged war against the Hagrites, Jetur, Naphish and Nodab. ²⁰They were helped in fighting them, and God handed the Hagrites and all their allies over to them, because they cried out to him during the battle. He answered their prayers, because they trusted in him. ²¹They seized the livestock of the Hagrites—fifty thousand camels, two hundred fifty thousand sheep and two thousand donkeys. They also took one hundred thousand people captive, ²²and many others fell slain, because the battle was God's. And they occupied the land until the exile.

The Half-Tribe of Manasseh

²³The people of the half-tribe of Manasseh were numerous; they settled in the land from Bashan to Baal Hermon, that is, to Senir (Mount Hermon).

²⁴These were the heads of their families: Epher, Ishi, Eliel, Azriel, Jeremiah, Hodaviah and Jahdiel. They were brave warriors, famous men, and heads of their families. ²⁵But they were unfaithful to the God of their fathers and prostituted themselves to the gods of the peoples of the land, whom God had destroyed before them. ²⁶So the God of Israel stirred up the spirit of Pul king of Assyria (that is, Tiglath-Pileser king of Assyria), who took the Reubenites, the Gadites and the half-tribe of Manasseh into exile. He took them to Halah, Habor, Hara and the river of Gozan, where they are to this day.

Levi

6 The sons of Levi:
Gershon, Kohath and Merari.
²The sons of Kohath:
Amram, Izhar, Hebron and Uzziel.
³The children of Amram:
Aaron, Moses and Miriam.
The sons of Aaron:
Nadab, Abihu, Eleazar and Ithamar.
⁴Eleazar was the father of Phinehas,
Phinehas the father of Abishua,

⁵Abishua the father of Bukki,
 Bukki the father of Uzzi,
⁶Uzzi the father of Zerahiah,
 Zerahiah the father of Meraioth,
⁷Meraioth the father of Amariah,
 Amariah the father of Ahitub,
⁸Ahitub the father of Zadok,
 Zadok the father of Ahimaaz,
⁹Ahimaaz the father of Azariah,
 Azariah the father of Johanan,
¹⁰Johanan the father of Azariah (it was he who served as priest in the temple Solomon built in Jerusalem),
¹¹Azariah the father of Amariah,
 Amariah the father of Ahitub,
¹²Ahitub the father of Zadok,
 Zadok the father of Shallum,
¹³Shallum the father of Hilkiah,
 Hilkiah the father of Azariah,
¹⁴Azariah the father of Seraiah,
 and Seraiah the father of Jehozadak.

¹⁵Jehozadak was deported when the LORD sent Judah and Jerusalem into exile by the hand of Nebuchadnezzar.

¹⁶The sons of Levi:
 Gershon,ᵃ Kohath and Merari.
¹⁷These are the names of the sons of Gershon:
 Libni and Shimei.
¹⁸The sons of Kohath:
 Amram, Izhar, Hebron and Uzziel.
¹⁹The sons of Merari:
 Mahli and Mushi.
These are the clans of the Levites listed according to their fathers:
²⁰Of Gershon:
 Libni his son, Jehath his son,
 Zimmah his son, ²¹Joah his son,
 Iddo his son, Zerah his son
 and Jeatherai his son.
²²The descendants of Kohath:
 Amminadab his son, Korah his son,
 Assir his son, ²³Elkanah his son,
 Ebiasaph his son, Assir his son,
²⁴Tahath his son, Uriel his son,
 Uzziah his son and Shaul his son.

²⁵The descendants of Elkanah:
 Amasai, Ahimoth,
²⁶Elkanah his son,ᵇ Zophai his son,
 Nahath his son, ²⁷Eliab his son,

⁵亞比書生布基；
 布基生烏西；
⁶烏西生西拉希雅；
 西拉希雅生米拉約；
⁷米拉約生亞瑪利雅；
 亞瑪利雅生亞希突；
⁸亞希突生撒督；
 撒督生亞希瑪斯；
⁹亞希瑪斯生亞撒利雅；
 亞撒利雅生約哈難；
¹⁰約哈難生亞撒利雅（這亞撒利雅在所羅門於耶路撒冷所建造的殿中，供祭司的職分）；
¹¹亞撒利雅生亞瑪利雅；
 亞瑪利雅生亞希突；
¹²亞希突生撒督；
 撒督生沙龍；
¹³沙龍生希勒家；
 希勒家生亞撒利雅；
¹⁴亞撒利雅生西萊雅；
 西萊雅生約薩答。

¹⁵當耶和華藉尼布甲尼撒的手擄掠猶大和耶路撒冷人的時候，這約薩答也被擄去。

¹⁶利未的兒子是：
 革順、哥轄、米拉利。
¹⁷革順的兒子名叫：
 立尼、示每。
¹⁸哥轄的兒子是：
 暗蘭、以斯哈、希伯倫、烏薛。
¹⁹米拉利的兒子是：
 抹利、母示。
這是按着利未人宗族分的各家：
²⁰革順的兒子是立尼；立尼的兒子是雅哈；雅哈的兒子是薪瑪；²¹薪瑪的兒子是約亞；約亞的兒子是易多；易多的兒子是謝拉；謝拉的兒子是耶特賴。
²²哥轄的兒子是亞米拿達；亞米拿達的兒子是可拉；可拉的兒子是亞惜；²³亞惜的兒子是以利加拿；以利加拿的兒子是以比雅撒；以比雅撒的兒子是亞惜；²⁴亞惜的兒子是他哈；他哈的兒子是烏列；烏列的兒子是烏西雅；烏西雅的兒子是少羅。
²⁵以利加拿的兒子是：
 亞瑪賽和亞希摩。
²⁶亞希摩的兒子是以利加拿；以利加拿的兒子是瑣菲；瑣菲的兒子是拿哈；²⁷拿哈的兒子是以利押；

以利押的兒子是<u>耶羅罕</u>；<u>耶羅罕</u>的兒子是<u>以利加拿</u>；<u>以利加拿</u>的兒子是<u>撒母耳</u>。

28<u>撒母耳</u>的長子是<u>約珥</u>，次子是<u>亞比亞</u>。

29<u>米拉利</u>的兒子是<u>抹利</u>；<u>抹利</u>的兒子是<u>立尼</u>；<u>立尼</u>的兒子是<u>示每</u>；<u>示每</u>的兒子是<u>烏撒</u>；

30<u>烏撒</u>的兒子是<u>示米亞</u>；<u>示米亞</u>的兒子是<u>哈基雅</u>；<u>哈基雅</u>的兒子是<u>亞帥雅</u>。

聖殿中的歌頌者

31約櫃安設之後，<u>大衛</u>派人在<u>耶和華</u>殿中管理歌唱的事。32他們就在會幕前當歌唱的差，及至<u>所羅門</u>在<u>耶路撒冷</u>建造了<u>耶和華</u>的殿，他們便按着班次供職。

33供職的人和他們的子孫記在下面：

哥轄的子孫中有歌唱的<u>希幔</u>。
<u>希幔</u>是<u>約珥</u>的兒子；
<u>約珥</u>是<u>撒母耳</u>的兒子；
34<u>撒母耳</u>是<u>以利加拿</u>的兒子；<u>以利加拿</u>是<u>耶羅罕</u>的兒子；<u>耶羅罕</u>是<u>以列</u>的兒子；<u>以列</u>是<u>陀亞</u>的兒子；
35<u>陀亞</u>是<u>蘇弗</u>的兒子；<u>蘇弗</u>是<u>以利加拿</u>的兒子；<u>以利加拿</u>是<u>瑪哈</u>的兒子；<u>瑪哈</u>是<u>亞瑪賽</u>的兒子；
36<u>亞瑪賽</u>是<u>以利加拿</u>的兒子；<u>以利加拿</u>是<u>約珥</u>的兒子；<u>約珥</u>是<u>亞撒利雅</u>的兒子；<u>亞撒利雅</u>是<u>西番雅</u>的兒子；
37<u>西番雅</u>是<u>他哈</u>的兒子；<u>他哈</u>是<u>亞惜</u>的兒子；<u>亞惜</u>是<u>以比雅撒</u>的兒子；<u>以比雅撒</u>是<u>可拉</u>的兒子；
38<u>可拉</u>是<u>以斯哈</u>的兒子；<u>以斯哈</u>是<u>哥轄</u>的兒子；<u>哥轄</u>是<u>利未</u>的兒子；<u>利未</u>是<u>以色列</u>的兒子。
39<u>希幔</u>的族兄<u>亞薩</u>是<u>比利家</u>的兒子，<u>亞薩</u>在<u>希幔</u>右邊供職。<u>比利家</u>是<u>示米亞</u>的兒子；
40<u>示米亞</u>是<u>米迦勒</u>的兒子；<u>米迦勒</u>是<u>巴西雅</u>的兒子；<u>巴西雅</u>是<u>瑪基雅</u>的兒子；41<u>瑪基雅</u>是<u>伊特尼</u>的兒子；<u>伊特尼</u>是<u>謝拉</u>的兒子；<u>謝拉</u>是<u>亞大雅</u>的兒子；
42<u>亞大雅</u>是<u>以探</u>的兒子；<u>以探</u>是<u>薪瑪</u>的兒子；<u>薪瑪</u>是<u>示每</u>的兒子；43<u>示每</u>是<u>雅哈</u>的兒子；<u>雅哈</u>是<u>革順</u>的兒子；<u>革順</u>是<u>利未</u>的兒子。

Jeroham his son, Elkanah his son
and Samuel his son.[a]
28The sons of Samuel:
Joel[b] the firstborn
and Abijah the second son.
29The descendants of Merari:
Mahli, Libni his son,
Shimei his son, Uzzah his son,
30Shimea his son, Haggiah his son
and Asaiah his son.

The Temple Musicians

31These are the men David put in charge of the music in the house of the LORD after the ark came to rest there. 32They ministered with music before the tabernacle, the Tent of Meeting, until Solomon built the temple of the LORD in Jerusalem. They performed their duties according to the regulations laid down for them.

33Here are the men who served, together with their sons:

From the Kohathites:
Heman, the musician,
the son of Joel, the son of Samuel,
34the son of Elkanah, the son of Jeroham,
the son of Eliel, the son of Toah,

35the son of Zuph, the son of Elkanah,
the son of Mahath, the son of Amasai,

36the son of Elkanah, the son of Joel,
the son of Azariah, the son of Zephaniah,

37the son of Tahath, the son of Assir,
the son of Ebiasaph, the son of Korah,

38the son of Izhar, the son of Kohath,
the son of Levi, the son of Israel;

39and Heman's associate Asaph, who served at his right hand:
Asaph son of Berekiah, the son of Shimea,
40the son of Michael, the son of Baaseiah,[c]
the son of Malkijah, 41the son of Ethni,
the son of Zerah, the son of Adaiah,

42the son of Ethan, the son of Zimmah,
the son of Shimei, 43the son of Jahath,
the son of Gershon, the son of Levi;

---

a 27 Some Septuagint manuscripts (see also 1 Samuel 1:19,20 and 1 Chron. 6:33,34); Hebrew does not have *and Samuel his son.* *b 28* Some Septuagint manuscripts and Syriac (see also 1 Samuel 8:2 and 1 Chron. 6:33); Hebrew does not have *Joel.* *c 40* Most Hebrew manuscripts; some Hebrew manuscripts, one Septuagint manuscript and Syriac *Maaseiah*

⁴⁴and from their associates, the Merarites, at his left hand:
Ethan son of Kishi, the son of Abdi, the son of Malluch, ⁴⁵the son of Hashabiah,
the son of Amaziah, the son of Hilkiah,

⁴⁶the son of Amzi, the son of Bani, the son of Shemer, ⁴⁷the son of Mahli, the son of Mushi, the son of Merari, the son of Levi.

⁴⁸Their fellow Levites were assigned to all the other duties of the tabernacle, the house of God. ⁴⁹But Aaron and his descendants were the ones who presented offerings on the altar of burnt offering and on the altar of incense in connection with all that was done in the Most Holy Place, making atonement for Israel, in accordance with all that Moses the servant of God had commanded.

⁵⁰These were the descendants of Aaron:
Eleazar his son, Phinehas his son, Abishua his son, ⁵¹Bukki his son, Uzzi his son, Zerahiah his son,

⁵²Meraioth his son, Amariah his son, Ahitub his son, ⁵³Zadok his son and Ahimaaz his son.

⁵⁴These were the locations of their settlements allotted as their territory (they were assigned to the descendants of Aaron who were from the Kohathite clan, because the first lot was for them):
⁵⁵They were given Hebron in Judah with its surrounding pasturelands. ⁵⁶But the fields and villages around the city were given to Caleb son of Jephunneh.
⁵⁷So the descendants of Aaron were given Hebron (a city of refuge), and Libnah,ᵃ Jattir, Eshtemoa, ⁵⁸Hilen, Debir, ⁵⁹Ashan, Juttahᵇ and Beth Shemesh, together with their pasturelands. ⁶⁰And from the tribe of Benjamin they were given Gibeon,ᶜ Geba, Alemeth and Anathoth, together with their pasturelands.
These towns, which were distributed among the Kohathite clans, were thirteen in all.
⁶¹The rest of Kohath's descendants were allotted ten towns from the clans of half the tribe of Manasseh.

---

⁴⁴他們的族弟兄米拉利的子孫，在他們左邊供職的有以探。以探是基示的兒子；基示是亞伯底的兒子；亞伯底是瑪鹿的兒子；⁴⁵瑪鹿是哈沙比雅的兒子；哈沙比雅是亞瑪謝的兒子；亞瑪謝是希勒家的兒子；

⁴⁶希勒家是暗西的兒子；暗西是巴尼的兒子；巴尼是沙麥的兒子；⁴⁷沙麥是末力的兒子；末力是母示的兒子；母示是米拉利的兒子；米拉利是利未的兒子。

⁴⁸他們的族弟兄利未人，也被派辦神殿中的一切事。⁴⁹亞倫和他的子孫在燔祭壇和香壇上獻祭燒香，又在至聖所辦理一切的事，為以色列人贖罪，是照神僕人摩西所吩咐的。

⁵⁰亞倫的兒子是以利亞撒；以利亞撒的兒子是非尼哈；非尼哈的兒子是亞比書；⁵¹亞比書的兒子是布基；布基的兒子是烏西；烏西的兒子是西拉希雅；

⁵²西拉希雅的兒子是米拉約；米拉約的兒子是亞瑪利雅；亞瑪利雅的兒子是亞希突；⁵³亞希突的兒子是撒督；撒督的兒子是亞希瑪斯。

⁵⁴他們的住處按着境內的營寨，記在下面：哥轄族亞倫的子孫先拈鬮得地：

⁵⁵在猶大地中得了希伯崙和四圍的郊野；⁵⁶只是屬城的田地和村莊都為耶孚尼的兒子迦勒所得。

⁵⁷亞倫的子孫得了逃城希伯崙，又得了立拿與其郊野，雅提珥、以實提莫與其郊野，⁵⁸希崙與其郊野，底璧與其郊野，⁵⁹亞珊與其郊野，伯示麥與其郊野。⁶⁰在便雅憫支派的地中，得了迦巴與其郊野，阿勒篾與其郊野，亞拿突與其郊野。他們諸家所得的城共十三座。

⁶¹哥轄族其餘的人又拈鬮，在瑪拿西半支派的地中得了十座城。

ᵃ 57 See Joshua 21:13; Hebrew given the cities of refuge: Hebron, Libnah.   ᵇ 59 Syriac (see also Septuagint and Joshua 21:16); Hebrew does not have Juttah.   ᶜ 60 See Joshua 21:17; Hebrew does not have Gibeon.

62革順族按着宗族在以薩迦支派
的地中、亞設支派的地中、拿弗他
利支派的地中、巴珊內瑪拿西支派
的地中得了十三座城。

63米拉利族按着宗族拈鬮，在呂
便支派的地中、迦得支派的地中、
西布倫支派的地中得了十二座城。

64以色列族人將這些城與其郊野給
了利未人。65這以上錄名的城，在猶
大、西緬、便雅憫三支派的地中，
以色列人拈鬮給了他們。

66哥轄族中，有幾家在以法蓮支
派的地中也得了城邑。

67在以法蓮山地，得了逃城示劍與
其郊野，又得了基色與其郊野，68約
緬與其郊野，伯和崙與其郊野，69亞
雅崙與其郊野，迦特臨門與其郊野。

70哥轄族其餘的人在瑪拿西半
支派的地中，得了亞乃與其郊
野，比連與其郊野。

71革順族在瑪拿西半支派的地中，
得了巴珊的哥蘭與其郊野，亞斯
他錄與其郊野。

72又在以薩迦支派的地中，
得了基低斯與其郊野，大比拉與
其郊野，73拉末與其郊野，亞年與
其郊野。

74在亞設支派的地中，
得了瑪沙與其郊野，押頓與其郊
野，75戶割與其郊野，利合與其
郊野。

76在拿弗他利支派的地中，
得了加利利的基低斯與其郊野，哈
們與其郊野，基列亭與其郊野。

77還有米拉利族的人在西布倫支派的
地中，
得了臨摩挪與其郊野，他泊與其
郊野。

78又在耶利哥的約旦河東，在呂便支
派的地中，得了曠野的比悉與其
郊野，雅哈撒與其郊野，79基底
莫與其郊野，米法押與其郊野。

80又在迦得支派的地中，得了基列
的拉末與其郊野，瑪哈念與其
郊野，81希實本與其郊野，雅謝
與其郊野。

62The descendants of Gershon, clan by clan,
were allotted thirteen towns from the tribes of
Issachar, Asher and Naphtali, and from the part
of the tribe of Manasseh that is in Bashan.

63The descendants of Merari, clan by clan,
were allotted twelve towns from the tribes of
Reuben, Gad and Zebulun.

64So the Israelites gave the Levites these
towns and their pasturelands. 65From the tribes
of Judah, Simeon and Benjamin they allotted the
previously named towns.

66Some of the Kohathite clans were given as
their territory towns from the tribe of Ephraim.

67In the hill country of Ephraim they were
given Shechem (a city of refuge), and Gezer,[a]
68Jokmeam, Beth Horon, 69Aijalon and Gath
Rimmon, together with their pasturelands.

70And from half the tribe of Manasseh the
Israelites gave Aner and Bileam, together with
their pasturelands, to the rest of the Kohathite
clans.

71The Gershonites received the following:
From the clan of the half-tribe of Manasseh
    they received Golan in Bashan and also
    Ashtaroth, together with their pasture-
    lands;
72from the tribe of Issachar
    they received Kedesh, Daberath, 73Ramoth
    and Anem, together with their pasture-
    lands;
74from the tribe of Asher
    they received Mashal, Abdon, 75Hukok and
    Rehob, together with their pasturelands;
76and from the tribe of Naphtali
    they received Kedesh in Galilee, Hammon
    and Kiriathaim, together with their pas-
    turelands.

77The Merarites (the rest of the Levites) received
the following:
From the tribe of Zebulun
    they received Jokneam, Kartah,[b] Rimmono
    and Tabor, together with their pasture-
    lands;
78from the tribe of Reuben across the Jordan east
of Jericho
    they received Bezer in the desert, Jahzah,
    79Kedemoth and Mephaath, together
    with their pasturelands;
80and from the tribe of Gad
    they received Ramoth in Gilead,
    Mahanaim, 81Heshbon and Jazer, togeth-
    er with their pasturelands.

a 67 See Joshua 21:21; Hebrew given the cities of refuge: Shechem,
Gezer.　b 77 See Septuagint and Joshua 21:34; Hebrew does
not have Jokneam, Kartah.

Issachar

7 The sons of Issachar:
Tola, Puah, Jashub and Shimron—four in all. [2]The sons of Tola:

Uzzi, Rephaiah, Jeriel, Jahmai, Ibsam and Samuel—heads of their families. During the reign of David, the descendants of Tola listed as fighting men in their genealogy numbered 22,600. [3]The son of Uzzi:

Izrahiah.

The sons of Izrahiah:

Michael, Obadiah, Joel and Isshiah. All five of them were chiefs. [4]According to their family genealogy, they had 36,000 men ready for battle, for they had many wives and children.

[5]The relatives who were fighting men belonging to all the clans of Issachar, as listed in their genealogy, were 87,000 in all.

Benjamin

[6]Three sons of Benjamin:
Bela, Beker and Jediael.

[7]The sons of Bela:

Ezbon, Uzzi, Uzziel, Jerimoth and Iri, heads of families—five in all. Their genealogical record listed 22,034 fighting men.

[8]The sons of Beker:

Zemirah, Joash, Eliezer, Elioenai, Omri, Jeremoth, Abijah, Anathoth and Alemeth. All these were the sons of Beker. [9]Their genealogical record listed the heads of families and 20,200 fighting men.

[10]The son of Jediael:

Bilhan.

The sons of Bilhan:

Jeush, Benjamin, Ehud, Kenaanah, Zethan, Tarshish and Ahishahar. [11]All these sons of Jediael were heads of families. There were 17,200 fighting men ready to go out to war.

[12]The Shuppites and Huppites were the descendants of Ir, and the Hushites the descendants of Aher.

Naphtali

[13]The sons of Naphtali:
Jahziel, Guni, Jezer and Shillem*ª* —the descendants of Bilhah.

ª 13 Some Hebrew and Septuagint manuscripts (see also Gen. 46:24 and Num. 26:49); most Hebrew manuscripts *Shallum*

以薩迦支派

7 以薩迦的兒子是：陀拉、普瓦、雅述（註：“雅述” 創世記第46章13節作 “約伯”）、伸崙，共四人。 [2]陀拉的兒子是：

烏西、利法雅、耶勒、雅買、易伯散、示母利。都是陀拉的族長，是大能的勇士。到大衛年間，他們的人數共有二萬二千六百名。 [3]烏西的兒子是：

伊斯拉希。

伊斯拉希的兒子是：

米迦勒、俄巴底亞、約珥、伊示雅，共五人，都是族長。 [4]他們所率領的按着宗族出戰的軍隊，共有三萬六千人，因為他們的妻和子眾多。

[5]他們的族弟兄在以薩迦各族中，都是大能的勇士。按着家譜計算，共有八萬七千人。

便雅憫支派

[6]便雅憫的兒子是：
比拉、比結、耶疊，共三人。

[7]比拉的兒子是：

以斯本、烏西、烏薛、耶利摩、以利，共五人。都是族長，是大能的勇士。按着家譜計算，他們的子孫共有二萬二千零三十四人。

[8]比結的兒子是：

細米拉、約阿施、以利以謝、以利約乃、暗利、耶利摩、亞比雅、亞拿突、亞拉篾。這都是比結的兒子。 [9]他們都是族長，是大能的勇士。按着家譜計算，他們的子孫共有二萬零二百人。

[10]耶疊的兒子是：

比勒罕。

比勒罕的兒子是：

耶烏施、便雅憫、以忽、基拿拿、細坦、他施、亞希沙哈。 [11]這都是耶疊的兒子，都是族長，是大能的勇士。他們的子孫能上陣打仗的，共有一萬七千二百人。

[12]還有以珥的兒子書品、戶品，並亞黑的兒子戶伸。

拿弗他利支派

[13]拿弗他利的兒子是：
雅薛、沽尼、耶色、沙龍。這都是辟拉的子孫。

瑪拿西支派

14瑪拿西的兒子：

亞斯列是他妾亞蘭人所生的，又生了基列之父瑪吉。15瑪吉娶的妻是戶品、書品的妹子，名叫瑪迦。

瑪拿西的次子名叫西羅非哈，西羅非哈但有幾個女兒。

16瑪吉的妻瑪迦生了一個兒子，起名叫毘利施。毘利施的兄弟名叫示利施；示利施的兒子是烏蘭和利金。

17烏蘭的兒子是：

比但。

這都是基列的子孫。基列是瑪吉的兒子；瑪吉是瑪拿西的兒子。18基列的妹子哈摩利吉生了伊施荷、亞比以謝、瑪拉。

19示米大的兒子是：

亞現、示劍、利克希、阿尼安。

以法蓮支派

20以法蓮的兒子是書提拉；書提拉的兒子是比列；比列的兒子是他哈；他哈的兒子是以拉大；以拉大的兒子是他哈；21他哈的兒子是撒拔；撒拔的兒子是書提拉。

以法蓮又生以謝、以列。這二人因為下去奪取迦特人的牲畜，被本地的迦特人殺了。22他們的父親以法蓮為他們悲哀了多日，他的弟兄都來安慰他。23以法蓮與妻同房，他妻就懷孕生了一子，以法蓮因為家裏遭禍，就給這兒子起名叫比利亞。24他的女兒名叫舍伊拉，就是建築上伯和崙、下伯和崙與烏羨舍伊拉的。

25比利阿的兒子是利法和利悉；利悉的兒子是他拉；他拉的兒子是他罕；26他罕的兒子是拉但；拉但的兒子是亞米忽；亞米忽的兒子是以利沙瑪；27以利沙瑪的兒子是嫩；嫩的兒子是約書亞。

28以法蓮人的地業和住處是伯特利與其村莊，東邊拿蘭，西邊基色與其村莊，示劍與其村莊，直到迦薩與其村莊。29還有靠近瑪拿西人的境界，伯善與其村莊，他納與其村莊，米吉多與其村莊，多珥與其村莊。以色列兒子約瑟的子孫住在這些地方。

Manasseh

14The descendants of Manasseh:

Asriel was his descendant through his Aramean concubine. She gave birth to Makir the father of Gilead. 15Makir took a wife from among the Huppites and Shuppites. His sister's name was Maacah. Another descendant was named Zelophehad, who had only daughters.

16Makir's wife Maacah gave birth to a son and named him Peresh. His brother was named Sheresh, and his sons were Ulam and Rakem.

17The son of Ulam:

Bedan.

These were the sons of Gilead son of Makir, the son of Manasseh. 18His sister Hammoleketh gave birth to Ishhod, Abiezer and Mahlah.

19The sons of Shemida were:

Ahian, Shechem, Likhi and Aniam.

Ephraim

20The descendants of Ephraim:

Shuthelah, Bered his son,
Tahath his son, Eleadah his son,
Tahath his son, 21Zabad his son
and Shuthelah his son.

Ezer and Elead were killed by the native-born men of Gath, when they went down to seize their livestock. 22Their father Ephraim mourned for them many days, and his relatives came to comfort him. 23Then he lay with his wife again, and she became pregnant and gave birth to a son. He named him Beriah,*a* because there had been misfortune in his family. 24His daughter was Sheerah, who built Lower and Upper Beth Horon as well as Uzzen Sheerah.

25Rephah was his son, Resheph his son,*b* Telah his son, Tahan his son,
26Ladan his son, Ammihud his son, Elishama his son, 27Nun his son and Joshua his son.

28Their lands and settlements included Bethel and its surrounding villages, Naaran to the east, Gezer and its villages to the west, and Shechem and its villages all the way to Ayyah and its villages. 29Along the borders of Manasseh were Beth Shan, Taanach, Megiddo and Dor, together with their villages. The descendants of Joseph son of Israel lived in these towns.

a 23 Beriah sounds like the Hebrew for misfortune.　　b 25 Some Septuagint manuscripts; Hebrew does not have his son.

Asher

³⁰The sons of Asher:

Imnah, Ishvah, Ishvi and Beriah. Their sister was Serah.

³¹The sons of Beriah:

Heber and Malkiel, who was the father of Birzaith.

³²Heber was the father of Japhlet, Shomer and Hotham and of their sister Shua.

³³The sons of Japhlet:

Pasach, Bimhal and Ashvath.

These were Japhlet's sons.

³⁴The sons of Shomer:

Ahi, Rohgah,^a Hubbah and Aram.

³⁵The sons of his brother Helem:

Zophah, Imna, Shelesh and Amal.

³⁶The sons of Zophah:

Suah, Harnepher, Shual, Beri, Imrah, ³⁷Bezer, Hod, Shamma, Shilshah, Ithran^b and Beera.

³⁸The sons of Jether:

Jephunneh, Pispah and Ara.

³⁹The sons of Ulla:

Arah, Hanniel and Rizia.

⁴⁰All these were descendants of Asher—heads of families, choice men, brave warriors and outstanding leaders. The number of men ready for battle, as listed in their genealogy, was 26,000.

The Genealogy of Saul the Benjamite

8 Benjamin was the father of Bela his first-born,

Ashbel the second son, Aharah the third, ²Nohah the fourth and Rapha the fifth.

³The sons of Bela were:

Addar, Gera, Abihud,^c ⁴Abishua, Naaman, Ahoah, ⁵Gera, Shephuphan and Huram.

⁶These were the descendants of Ehud, who were heads of families of those living in Geba and were deported to Manahath:

⁷Naaman, Ahijah, and Gera, who deported them and who was the father of Uzza and Ahihud.

⁸Sons were born to Shaharaim in Moab after he had divorced his wives Hushim and Baara. ⁹By his wife Hodesh he had Jobab, Zibia, Mesha, Malcam, ¹⁰Jeuz, Sakia and Mirmah. These were his sons, heads of families. ¹¹By Hushim he had Abitub and Elpaal.

亞設支派

³⁰亞設的兒子是：

音拿、亦施瓦、亦施韋、比利亞，還有他們的妹子西拉。

³¹比利亞的兒子是：

希別、瑪結；瑪結是比撒威的父親。

³²希別生雅弗勒、朔默、何坦和他們的妹子書雅。

³³雅弗勒的兒子是：

巴薩、賓哈、亞施法。

這都是雅弗勒的兒子。

³⁴朔默的兒子是：

亞希、羅迦、耶戶巴、亞蘭。

³⁵朔默兄弟希連的兒子是：

瑣法、音那、示利斯、亞抹。

³⁶瑣法的兒子是：

書亞、哈尼弗、書阿勒、比利、音拉、³⁷比悉、河得、珊瑪、施沙、益蘭、比拉。

³⁸益帖的兒子是：

耶孚尼、昆斯巴、亞拉。

³⁹烏拉的兒子是：

亞拉、漢尼業、利寫。

⁴⁰這都是亞設的子孫，都是族長，是精壯大能的勇士，也是首領中的頭目。按着家譜計算，他們的子孫能出戰的共有二萬六千人。

便雅憫人掃羅的族譜

8 便雅憫的長子比拉，

次子亞實別，

三子亞哈拉。

²四子挪哈，五子拉法。

³比拉的兒子是：

亞大、基拉、亞比忽、⁴亞比書、乃幔、亞何亞、⁵基拉、示孚汎、戶蘭。

⁶以忽的兒子作迦巴居民的族長，被擄到瑪拿轄；

⁷以忽的兒子乃幔、亞希亞、基拉也被擄去。基拉生烏撒、亞希忽。

⁸沙哈連休他二妻戶伸和巴拉之後，在摩押地生了兒子。⁹他與妻賀得同房，生了約巴、洗比雅、米沙、瑪拉干、¹⁰耶烏斯、沙迦、米瑪。他這些兒子都是族長。¹¹他的妻戶伸給他生的兒子有亞比突、以利巴力。

---

^a 34 Or *of his brother Shomer: Rohgah*   ^b 37 Possibly a variant of Jether   ^c 3 Or *Gera the father of Ehud*

12以利巴力的兒子是：

　希伯、米珊、沙麥。沙麥建立阿挪和羅德二城與其村莊。13又有比利亞和示瑪是亞雅崙居民的族長，是驅逐迦特人的。

14亞希約、沙煞、耶利末、15西巴第雅、亞拉得、亞得、16米迦勒、伊施巴、約哈都是比利亞的兒子。

17西巴第雅、米書蘭、希西基、希伯、18伊施米萊、伊斯利亞、約巴都是以利巴力的兒子。

19雅金、細基利、撒底、20以利乃、洗勒太、以列、21亞大雅、比拉雅、申拉都是示每的兒子。

22伊施班、希伯、以列、23亞伯頓、細基利、哈難、24哈拿尼雅、以攔、安陀提雅、25伊弗底雅、毘努伊勒都是沙煞的兒子。

26珊示萊、示哈利、亞他利雅、27雅利西、以利亞、細基利都是耶羅罕的兒子。

28這些人都是著名的族長，住在耶路撒冷。

29在基遍住的有基遍的父親耶利，他的妻名叫瑪迦。30他長子是亞伯頓，他又生蘇珥、基士、巴力、拿答、31基多、亞希約、撒迦、米基羅；32米基羅生示米暗。這些人和他們的弟兄，在耶路撒冷對面居住。

33尼珥生基士；基士生掃羅；掃羅生約拿單、麥基舒亞、亞比拿達、伊施巴力。

34約拿單的兒子是米力巴力（註：“米力巴力”撒母耳記下4章4節作“米非波設”）；米力巴力生米迦。

35米迦的兒子是：

　毘敦、米勒、他利亞、亞哈斯。

36亞哈斯生耶何阿達；耶何阿達生亞拉篾、亞斯瑪威、心利；心利生摩撒；37摩撒生比尼亞。比尼亞的兒子是拉法；拉法的兒子是以利亞薩；以利亞薩的兒子是亞悉。

38亞悉有六個兒子，他們的名字是：亞斯利干、波基路、以實瑪利、示亞利雅、俄巴底雅、哈難。這都是亞悉的兒子。

12The sons of Elpaal:

Eber, Misham, Shemed (who built Ono and Lod with its surrounding villages), 13and Beriah and Shema, who were heads of families of those living in Aijalon and who drove out the inhabitants of Gath.

14Ahio, Shashak, Jeremoth, 15Zebadiah, Arad, Eder, 16Michael, Ishpah and Joha were the sons of Beriah.

17Zebadiah, Meshullam, Hizki, Heber, 18Ishmerai, Izliah and Jobab were the sons of Elpaal.

19Jakim, Zicri, Zabdi, 20Elienai, Zillethai, Eliel, 21Adaiah, Beraiah and Shimrath were the sons of Shimei.

22Ishpan, Eber, Eliel, 23Abdon, Zicri, Hanan, 24Hananiah, Elam, Anthothijah, 25Iphdeiah and Penuel were the sons of Shashak.

26Shamsherai, Shehariah, Athaliah, 27Jaareshiah, Elijah and Zicri were the sons of Jeroham.

28All these were heads of families, chiefs as listed in their genealogy, and they lived in Jerusalem.

29Jeiel[a] the father[b] of Gibeon lived in Gibeon.

His wife's name was Maacah, 30and his firstborn son was Abdon, followed by Zur, Kish, Baal, Ner,[c] Nadab, 31Gedor, Ahio, Zeker 32and Mikloth, who was the father of Shimeah. They too lived near their relatives in Jerusalem.

33Ner was the father of Kish, Kish the father of Saul, and Saul the father of Jonathan, Malki-Shua, Abinadab and Esh-Baal.[d]

34The son of Jonathan:

Merib-Baal,[e] who was the father of Micah.

35The sons of Micah:

Pithon, Melech, Tarea and Ahaz.

36Ahaz was the father of Jehoaddah, Jehoaddah was the father of Alemeth, Azmaveth and Zimri, and Zimri was the father of Moza. 37Moza was the father of Binea; Raphah was his son, Eleasah his son and Azel his son.

38Azel had six sons, and these were their names: Azrikam, Bokeru, Ishmael, Sheariah, Obadiah and Hanan. All these were the sons of Azel.

a 29 Some Septuagint manuscripts (see also 1 Chron. 9:35); Hebrew does not have Jeiel.　b 29 Father may mean civic l eader or military leader.　c 30 Some Septuagint manuscripts (see also 1 Chron. 9:36); Hebrew does not have Ner.　d 33 Also known as Ish-Bosheth　e 34 Also known as Mephibosheth

39The sons of his brother Eshek:

Ulam his firstborn, Jeush the second son and Eliphelet the third. **40**The sons of Ulam were brave warriors who could handle the bow. They had many sons and grandsons—150 in all.

All these were the descendants of Benjamin.

9 All Israel was listed in the genealogies recorded in the book of the kings of Israel.

The People in Jerusalem

The people of Judah were taken captive to Babylon because of their unfaithfulness. **2**Now the first to resettle on their own property in their own towns were some Israelites, priests, Levites and temple servants.

3Those from Judah, from Benjamin, and from Ephraim and Manasseh who lived in Jerusalem were:

4Uthai son of Ammihud, the son of Omri, the son of Imri, the son of Bani, a descendant of Perez son of Judah.

5Of the Shilonites:

Asaiah the firstborn and his sons.

6Of the Zerahites:

Jeuel.

The people from Judah numbered 690.

7Of the Benjamites:

Sallu son of Meshullam, the son of Hodaviah, the son of Hassenuah;

8Ibneiah son of Jeroham; Elah son of Uzzi, the son of Micri; and Meshullam son of Shephatiah, the son of Reuel, the son of Ibnijah.

9The people from Benjamin, as listed in their genealogy, numbered 956. All these men were heads of their families.

10Of the priests:

Jedaiah; Jehoiarib; Jakin;

11Azariah son of Hilkiah, the son of Meshullam, the son of Zadok, the son of Meraioth, the son of Ahitub, the official in charge of the house of God;

12Adaiah son of Jeroham, the son of Pashhur, the son of Malkijah; and Maasai son of Adiel, the son of Jahzerah, the son of Meshullam, the son of Meshillemith, the son of Immer.

13The priests, who were heads of families, numbered 1,760. They were able men, responsible for ministering in the house of God.

39亞悉兄弟以設的長子是烏蘭，次子耶烏施，三子是以利法列。**40**烏蘭的兒子都是大能的勇士，是弓箭手。他們有許多的子孫，共一百五十名，都是便雅憫人。

9 以色列人都按家譜計算，寫在以色列諸王記上。

住在耶路撒冷的百姓

猶大人因犯罪就被擄到巴比倫。**2**先從巴比倫回來住在自己地業城邑中的有以色列人、祭司、利未人、尼提寧的首領。

3住在耶路撒冷的有猶大人、便雅憫人、以法蓮人、瑪拿西人。**4**猶大兒子法勒斯的子孫中有烏太。烏太是亞米忽的兒子；亞米忽是暗利的兒子；暗利是音利的兒子；音利是巴尼的兒子。

5示羅的子孫中有：

長子亞帥雅和他的眾子。

6謝拉的子孫中有：

耶烏利和他的弟兄，共六百九十人。

7便雅憫人中有：

哈西努的曾孫、何達威雅的孫子、米書蘭的兒子撒路；**8**又有耶羅罕的兒子伊比尼雅，米基立的孫子、烏西的兒子以拉；伊比尼雅的曾孫、流珥的孫子、示法提雅的兒子米書蘭，**9**和他們的族弟兄。按着家譜計算，共有九百五十六名。這些人都是他們的族長。

10祭司中有：

耶大雅、耶何雅立、雅斤，**11**還有管理神殿希勒家的兒子亞薩利雅。希勒家是米書蘭的兒子；米書蘭是撒督的兒子；撒督是米拉約的兒子；米拉約是亞希突的兒子。

12有瑪基雅的曾孫、巴施戶珥的孫子、耶羅罕的兒子亞大雅。又有亞第業的兒子瑪賽。亞第業是雅希細拉的兒子；雅希細拉是米書蘭的兒子；米書蘭是米實利密的兒子；米實利密是音麥的兒子。

13他們和眾弟兄都是族長，共有一千七百六十人，是善於做神殿使用之工的。

14利未人：

米拉利的子孫中有哈沙比雅的曾孫、押利甘的孫子、哈述的兒子示瑪雅；15有拔巴甲、黑勒施、迦拉並亞薩的曾孫、細基利的孫子、米迦的兒子瑪探雅；16又有耶杜頓的曾孫、迦拉的孫子、示瑪雅的兒子俄巴底；還有以利加拿的孫子、亞撒的兒子比利家。他們都住在尼陀法人的村莊。

17守門的是：

沙龍、亞谷、達們、亞希幔和他們的弟兄，沙龍為長。18從前這些人看守朝東的王門，如今是利未營中守門的。19可拉的曾孫、以比雅撒的孫子、可利的兒子沙龍，和他的族弟兄可拉人，都管理使用之工，並守會幕的門。他們的祖宗曾管理耶和華的營盤，又把守營門。20從前以利亞撒的兒子非尼哈管理他們，耶和華也與他同在。21米施利米雅的兒子撒迦利雅，是看守會幕之門的。

22被選守門的人共有二百一十二名，他們在自己的村莊，按着家譜計算，是大衛和先見撒母耳所派當這緊要職任的。23他們和他們的子孫，按着班次看守耶和華殿的門，就是會幕的門。24在東南西北四方都有守門的。25他們的族弟兄住在村莊，每七日來與他們換班。26這四個門領都是利未人，各有緊要的職任，看守神殿的倉庫。27他們住在神殿的四圍，是因委託他們守殿，要每日早晨開門。

28利未人中有管理使用器皿的，按着數目拿出拿入。29又有人管理器具和聖所的器皿，並細麵、酒、油、乳香、香料。30祭司中有人用香料做膏油。31利未人瑪他提雅是可拉

14Of the Levites:

Shemaiah son of Hasshub, the son of Azrikam, the son of Hashabiah, a Merarite; 15Bakbakkar, Heresh, Galal and Mattaniah son of Mica, the son of Zicri, the son of Asaph; 16Obadiah son of Shemaiah, the son of Galal, the son of Jeduthun; and Berekiah son of Asa, the son of Elkanah, who lived in the villages of the Netophathites.

17The gatekeepers:

Shallum, Akkub, Talmon, Ahiman and their brothers, Shallum their chief 18being stationed at the King's Gate on the east, up to the present time. These were the gatekeepers belonging to the camp of the Levites. 19Shallum son of Kore, the son of Ebiasaph, the son of Korah, and his fellow gatekeepers from his family (the Korahites) were responsible for guarding the thresholds of the Tent*a* just as their fathers had been responsible for guarding the entrance to the dwelling of the LORD. 20In earlier times Phinehas son of Eleazar was in charge of the gatekeepers, and the LORD was with him. 21Zechariah son of Meshelemiah was the gatekeeper at the entrance to the Tent of Meeting.

22Altogether, those chosen to be gatekeepers at the thresholds numbered 212. They were registered by genealogy in their villages. The gatekeepers had been assigned to their positions of trust by David and Samuel the seer. 23They and their descendants were in charge of guarding the gates of the house of the LORD—the house called the Tent. 24The gatekeepers were on the four sides: east, west, north and south. 25Their brothers in their villages had to come from time to time and share their duties for seven-day periods. 26But the four principal gatekeepers, who were Levites, were entrusted with the responsibility for the rooms and treasuries in the house of God. 27They would spend the night stationed around the house of God, because they had to guard it; and they had charge of the key for opening it each morning.

28Some of them were in charge of the articles used in the temple service; they counted them when they were brought in and when they were taken out. 29Others were assigned to take care of the furnishings and all the other articles of the sanctuary, as well as the flour and wine, and the oil, incense and spices. 30But some of the priests took care of mixing the spices. 31A Levite named

a 19 That is, the temple; also in verses 21 and 23

Mattithiah, the firstborn son of Shallum the Korahite, was entrusted with the responsibility for baking the offering bread. ³²Some of their Kohathite brothers were in charge of preparing for every Sabbath the bread set out on the table.

³³Those who were musicians, heads of Levite families, stayed in the rooms of the temple and were exempt from other duties because they were responsible for the work day and night.

³⁴All these were heads of Levite families, chiefs as listed in their genealogy, and they lived in Jerusalem.

The Genealogy of Saul

³⁵Jeiel the father*ª* of Gibeon lived in Gibeon.

His wife's name was Maacah, ³⁶and his firstborn son was Abdon, followed by Zur, Kish, Baal, Ner, Nadab, ³⁷Gedor, Ahio, Zechariah and Mikloth. ³⁸Mikloth was the father of Shimeam. They too lived near their relatives in Jerusalem.

³⁹Ner was the father of Kish, Kish the father of Saul, and Saul the father of Jonathan, Malki-Shua, Abinadab and Esh-Baal.*ᵇ*

⁴⁰The son of Jonathan:

Merib-Baal,*ᶜ* who was the father of Micah.

⁴¹The sons of Micah:

Pithon, Melech, Tahrea and Ahaz.*ᵈ*

⁴²Ahaz was the father of Jadah, Jadah*ᵉ* was the father of Alemeth, Azmaveth and Zimri, and Zimri was the father of Moza. ⁴³Moza was the father of Binea; Rephaiah was his son, Eleasah his son and Azel his son.

⁴⁴Azel had six sons, and these were their names: Azrikam, Bokeru, Ishmael, Sheariah, Obadiah and Hanan. These were the sons of Azel.

Saul Takes His Life

10 Now the Philistines fought against Israel; the Israelites fled before them, and many fell slain on Mount Gilboa. ²The Philistines pressed hard after Saul and his sons, and they killed his sons Jonathan, Abinadab and Malki-Shua. ³The fighting grew fierce around Saul, and when the archers overtook him, they wounded him.

---

a 35 Father may mean civic leader or military leader.   *b 39* Also known as Ish-Bosheth   *c 40* Also known as Mephibosheth   *d 41* Vulgate and Syriac (see also Septuagint and 1 Chron. 8:35); Hebrew does not have and Ahaz.   *e 42* Some Hebrew manuscripts and Septuagint (see also 1 Chron. 8:36); most Hebrew manuscripts Jarah, Jarah

---

族沙龍的長子，他緊要的職任是管理盤中烤的物。³²他們族弟兄哥轄子孫中，有管理陳設餅的，每安息日預備擺列。

³³歌唱的有利未人的族長，住在屬殿的房屋，晝夜供職，不做別樣的工。

³⁴以上都是利未人著名的族長，住在耶路撒冷。

掃羅的族譜

³⁵在基遍住的，有基遍的父親耶利。他的妻名叫瑪迦，³⁶他長子是亞伯頓，他又生蘇珥、基士、巴力、尼珥、拿答、³⁷基多、亞希約、撒迦利雅、米基羅。³⁸米基羅生示米暗。這些人和他們的弟兄在耶路撒冷對面居住。

³⁹尼珥生基士；基士生掃羅；掃羅生約拿單、麥基舒亞、亞比拿達、伊施巴力。

⁴⁰約拿單的兒子是：

米力巴力（註："米力巴力"即"米非波設"）；米力巴力生米迦。

⁴¹米迦的兒子是：

毘敦、米勒、他利亞、亞哈斯。

⁴²亞哈斯生雅拉；雅拉生亞拉篾、亞斯瑪威、心利；心利生摩撒；⁴³摩撒生比尼亞；比尼亞生利法雅。利法雅的兒子是以利亞薩；以利亞薩的兒子是亞悉。

⁴⁴亞悉有六個兒子，他們的名字是：亞斯利干、波基路、以實瑪利、示亞利雅、俄巴底雅、哈難，這都是亞悉的兒子。

掃羅自殺

10 非利士人與以色列人爭戰。以色列人在非利士人面前逃跑，在基利波山有被殺仆倒的。²非利士人緊追掃羅和他兒子們，就殺了掃羅的兒子約拿單、亞比拿達、麥基舒亞。³勢派甚大，掃羅被弓箭手追上，射傷甚重。

⁴就吩咐拿他兵器的人說：「你拔出刀來，將我刺死，免得那些未受割禮的人來凌辱我。」

但拿兵器的人甚懼怕，不肯刺他。⁵掃羅就自己伏在刀上死了。拿兵器的人見掃羅已死，也伏在刀上死了。⁶這樣，掃羅和他三個兒子，並他的全家都一同死亡。

⁷住平原的以色列眾人見以色列軍兵逃跑，掃羅和他兒子都死了，也就棄城逃跑，非利士人便來住在其中。

⁸次日，非利士人來剝那被殺之人的衣服，看見掃羅和他兒子仆倒在基利波山，⁹就剝了他的軍裝，割下他的首級，打發人到非利士地的四境（註：「到」或作「送到」）報信與他們的偶像和眾民；¹⁰又將掃羅的軍裝放在他們神的廟裏，將他的首級釘在大袞廟中。

¹¹基列雅比人聽見非利士人向掃羅所行的一切事，¹²他們中間所有的勇士就起身前去，將掃羅和他兒子的屍身送到雅比，將他們的屍骨葬在雅比的橡樹下，就禁食七日。

¹³這樣，掃羅死了。因為他干犯耶和華，沒有遵守耶和華的命，又因他求問交鬼的婦人，¹⁴沒有求問耶和華，所以耶和華使他被殺，把國歸於耶西的兒子大衛。

大衛作全以色列之王

11 以色列眾人聚集到希伯崙見大衛，說：「我們原是你的骨肉。²從前掃羅作王的時候，率領以色列人出入的是你，耶和華你的神也曾應許你說：『你必牧養我的民以色列，作以色列的君。』」³於是以色列的長老，都來到希伯崙見大衛王，大衛在希伯崙耶和華面前與他們立約。他們就膏大衛作以色列的王，是照耶和華藉撒母耳所說的話。

大衛攻佔耶路撒冷

⁴大衛和以色列眾人到了耶路撒冷，就是耶布斯，那時耶布斯人住在那裏。⁵耶布斯人對大衛說：「你決不能進這地方。」然而，大衛攻取錫安的保障，就是大衛的城。

⁴Saul said to his armor-bearer, "Draw your sword and run me through, or these uncircumcised fellows will come and abuse me."

But his armor-bearer was terrified and would not do it; so Saul took his own sword and fell on it. ⁵When the armor-bearer saw that Saul was dead, he too fell on his sword and died. ⁶So Saul and his three sons died, and all his house died together.

⁷When all the Israelites in the valley saw that the army had fled and that Saul and his sons had died, they abandoned their towns and fled. And the Philistines came and occupied them.

⁸The next day, when the Philistines came to strip the dead, they found Saul and his sons fallen on Mount Gilboa. ⁹They stripped him and took his head and his armor, and sent messengers throughout the land of the Philistines to proclaim the news among their idols and their people. ¹⁰They put his armor in the temple of their gods and hung up his head in the temple of Dagon.

¹¹When all the inhabitants of Jabesh Gilead heard of everything the Philistines had done to Saul, ¹²all their valiant men went and took the bodies of Saul and his sons and brought them to Jabesh. Then they buried their bones under the great tree in Jabesh, and they fasted seven days.

¹³Saul died because he was unfaithful to the LORD; he did not keep the word of the LORD and even consulted a medium for guidance, ¹⁴and did not inquire of the LORD. So the LORD put him to death and turned the kingdom over to David son of Jesse.

David Becomes King Over Israel

11 All Israel came together to David at Hebron and said, "We are your own flesh and blood. ²In the past, even while Saul was king, you were the one who led Israel on their military campaigns. And the LORD your God said to you, 'You will shepherd my people Israel, and you will become their ruler.' "

³When all the elders of Israel had come to King David at Hebron, he made a compact with them at Hebron before the LORD, and they anointed David king over Israel, as the LORD had promised through Samuel.

David Conquers Jerusalem

⁴David and all the Israelites marched to Jerusalem (that is, Jebus). The Jebusites who lived there ⁵said to David, "You will not get in here." Nevertheless, David captured the fortress of Zion, the City of David.

⁶David had said, "Whoever leads the attack on the Jebusites will become commander-in-chief." Joab son of Zeruiah went up first, and so he received the command.

⁷David then took up residence in the fortress, and so it was called the City of David. ⁸He built up the city around it, from the supporting terraces^a to the surrounding wall, while Joab restored the rest of the city. ⁹And David became more and more powerful, because the LORD Almighty was with him.

David's Mighty Men

¹⁰These were the chiefs of David's mighty men—they, together with all Israel, gave his kingship strong support to extend it over the whole land, as the LORD had promised— ¹¹this is the list of David's mighty men:

Jashobeam,^b a Hacmonite, was chief of the officers^c; he raised his spear against three hundred men, whom he killed in one encounter.

¹²Next to him was Eleazar son of Dodai the Ahohite, one of the three mighty men. ¹³He was with David at Pas Dammim when the Philistines gathered there for battle. At a place where there was a field full of barley, the troops fled from the Philistines. ¹⁴But they took their stand in the middle of the field. They defended it and struck the Philistines down, and the LORD brought about a great victory.

¹⁵Three of the thirty chiefs came down to David to the rock at the cave of Adullam, while a band of Philistines was encamped in the Valley of Rephaim. ¹⁶At that time David was in the stronghold, and the Philistine garrison was at Bethlehem. ¹⁷David longed for water and said, "Oh, that someone would get me a drink of water from the well near the gate of Bethlehem!" ¹⁸So the Three broke through the Philistine lines, drew water from the well near the gate of Bethlehem and carried it back to David. But he refused to drink it; instead, he poured it out before the LORD. ¹⁹"God forbid that I should do this!" he said. "Should I drink the blood of these men who went at the risk of their lives?" Because they risked their lives to bring it back, David would not drink it.

Such were the exploits of the three mighty men.

²⁰Abishai the brother of Joab was chief of the Three. He raised his spear against three hundred men, whom he killed, and so he became as famous as the Three. ²¹He was doubly honored

⁶大衛說："誰先攻打耶布斯人，必作首領元帥。"洗魯雅的兒子約押先上去，就作了元帥。

⁷大衛住在保障裏，所以那保障叫作大衛城。⁸大衛又從米羅起，四圍建築城牆，其餘的是約押修理。⁹大衛日見強盛，因為萬軍之耶和華與他同在。

大衛的勇士

¹⁰以下記錄跟隨大衛勇士的首領，就是奮勇幫助他得國、照着耶和華吩咐以色列人的話、與以色列人一同立他作王的。¹¹大衛勇士的數目記在下面：

哈革摩尼的兒子雅朔班，他是軍長的統領，一時舉槍殺了三百人。

¹²其次是亞合人朵多的兒子以利亞撒，他是三個勇士裏的一個。¹³他從前與大衛在巴斯達閔，非利士人聚集要打仗，那裏有一塊長滿大麥的田，眾民就在非利士人面前逃跑。¹⁴這勇士便站在那田間，擊殺非利士人，救護了那田。耶和華使以色列人大獲全勝。

¹⁵三十個勇士中的三個人下到磐石那裏，進了亞杜蘭洞見大衛，非利士的軍隊在利乏音谷安營。¹⁶那時大衛在山寨，非利士人的防營在伯利恆。¹⁷大衛渴想說："甚願有人將伯利恆城門旁井裏的水打來給我喝！"¹⁸這三個勇士就闖過非利士人的營盤，從伯利恆城門旁的井裏打水，拿來奉給大衛。他卻不肯喝，將水奠在耶和華面前，¹⁹說："我的神啊，這三個人冒死去打水，這水好像他們的血一般，我斷不敢喝！"如此，大衛不肯喝。

這是三個勇士所做的事。

²⁰約押的兄弟亞比篩，是這三個勇士的首領。他舉槍殺了三百人，就在三個勇士裏得了名。²¹他在這三個

a 8 Or *the Millo*   *b* 11 Possibly a variant of *Jashob-Baal*
c 11 Or *Thirty*; some Septuagint manuscripts *Three* (see also 2 Samuel 23:8)

勇士裏是最尊貴的，所以作他們的首領，只是不及前三個勇士。

22有甲薛勇士耶何耶大的兒子比拿雅，行過大能的事：他殺了摩押人亞利伊勒的兩個兒子，又在下雪的時候，下坑裏去殺了一個獅子，23又殺了一個埃及人。埃及人身高五肘，手裏拿着槍，槍桿粗如織布的機軸；比拿雅只拿着棍子下去，從埃及人手裏奪過槍來，用那槍將他刺死。24這是耶何耶大的兒子比拿雅所行的事，就在三個勇士裏得了名。25他比那三十個勇士都尊貴，只是不及前三個勇士。大衛立他作護衛長。

26軍中的勇士有：
　約押的兄弟亞撒黑、伯利恆人朵多的兒子伊勒哈難、
27哈律人沙瑪、
　比倫人希利斯、
28提哥亞人益吉的兒子以拉、
　亞拿突人亞比以謝、
29戶沙人西比該、
　亞合人以來、
30尼陀法人馬哈萊、
　尼陀法人巴拿的兒子希立、
31便雅憫族基比亞人利拜的兒子以太、
　比拉頓人比拿雅、
32迦實溪人戶萊、
　亞拉巴人亞比、
33巴路米人押斯瑪弗、
　沙本人以利雅哈巴、
34基孫人哈深的眾子、
　哈拉人沙基的兒子約拿單、
35哈拉人沙甲的兒子亞希暗、
　吾珥的兒子以利法勒、
36米基拉人希弗、
　比倫人亞希雅、
37迦密人希斯羅、
　伊斯拜的兒子拿萊、
38拿單的兄弟約珥、
　哈基利的兒子彌伯哈、
39亞捫人洗勒、
　比錄人拿哈萊，拿哈萊是給洗魯雅的兒子約押拿兵器的，
40以帖人以拉、
　以帖人迦立、
41赫人烏利亞、
　亞萊的兒子撒拔、

above the Three and became their commander, even though he was not included among them.

22Benaiah son of Jehoiada was a valiant fighter from Kabzeel, who performed great exploits. He struck down two of Moab's best men. He also went down into a pit on a snowy day and killed a lion. 23And he struck down an Egyptian who was seven and a half feet[a] tall. Although the Egyptian had a spear like a weaver's rod in his hand, Benaiah went against him with a club. He snatched the spear from the Egyptian's hand and killed him with his own spear. 24Such were the exploits of Benaiah son of Jehoiada; he too was as famous as the three mighty men. 25He was held in greater honor than any of the Thirty, but he was not included among the Three. And David put him in charge of his bodyguard.

26The mighty men were:
　Asahel the brother of Joab,
　Elhanan son of Dodo from Bethlehem,
27Shammoth the Harorite,
　Helez the Pelonite,
28Ira son of Ikkesh from Tekoa,
　Abiezer from Anathoth,
29Sibbecai the Hushathite,
　Ilai the Ahohite,
30Maharai the Netophathite,
　Heled son of Baanah the Netophathite,
31Ithai son of Ribai from Gibeah in Benjamin,
　Benaiah the Pirathonite,
32Hurai from the ravines of Gaash,
　Abiel the Arbathite,
33Azmaveth the Baharumite,
　Eliahba the Shaalbonite,
34the sons of Hashem the Gizonite,
　Jonathan son of Shagee the Hararite,
35Ahiam son of Sacar the Hararite,
　Eliphal son of Ur,
36Hepher the Mekerathite,
　Ahijah the Pelonite,
37Hezro the Carmelite,
　Naarai son of Ezbai,
38Joel the brother of Nathan,
　Mibhar son of Hagri,
39Zelek the Ammonite,
　Naharai the Berothite, the armor-bearer of Joab son of Zeruiah,
40Ira the Ithrite,
　Gareb the Ithrite,
41Uriah the Hittite,
　Zabad son of Ahlai,

a 23 Hebrew five cubits (about 2.3 meters)

⁴²Adina son of Shiza the Reubenite, who was chief of the Reubenites, and the thirty with him,

⁴³Hanan son of Maacah,
Joshaphat the Mithnite,

⁴⁴Uzzia the Ashterathite,
Shama and Jeiel the sons of Hotham the Aroerite,

⁴⁵Jediael son of Shimri,
his brother Joha the Tizite,

⁴⁶Eliel the Mahavite,
Jeribai and Joshaviah the sons of Elnaam,
Ithmah the Moabite,

⁴⁷Eliel, Obed and Jaasiel the Mezobaite.

Warriors Join David

12 These were the men who came to David at Ziklag, while he was banished from the presence of Saul son of Kish (they were among the warriors who helped him in battle; ²they were armed with bows and were able to shoot arrows or to sling stones right-handed or left-handed; they were kinsmen of Saul from the tribe of Benjamin):

³Ahiezer their chief and Joash the sons of Shemaah the Gibeathite; Jeziel and Pelet the sons of Azmaveth; Beracah, Jehu the Anathothite, ⁴and Ishmaiah the Gibeonite, a mighty man among the Thirty, who was a leader of the Thirty; Jeremiah, Jahaziel, Johanan, Jozabad the Gederathite, ⁵Eluzai, Jerimoth, Bealiah, Shemariah and Shephatiah the Haruphite; ⁶Elkanah, Isshiah, Azarel, Joezer and Jashobeam the Korahites; ⁷and Joelah and Zebadiah the sons of Jeroham from Gedor.

⁸Some Gadites defected to David at his stronghold in the desert. They were brave warriors, ready for battle and able to handle the shield and spear. Their faces were the faces of lions, and they were as swift as gazelles in the mountains. ⁹Ezer was the chief,

Obadiah the second in command, Eliab the third,

¹⁰Mishmannah the fourth, Jeremiah the fifth,

¹¹Attai the sixth, Eliel the seventh,

¹²Johanan the eighth, Elzabad the ninth,

¹³Jeremiah the tenth and Macbannai the eleventh.

¹⁴These Gadites were army commanders; the least was a match for a hundred, and the greatest for a thousand. ¹⁵It was they who crossed the Jordan in the first month when it was overflowing all its banks, and they put to flight everyone living in the valleys, to the east and to the west.

⁴²呂便人示撒的兒子亞第拿，他是呂便支派中的一個族長，率領三十人，

⁴³瑪迦的兒子哈難、彌特尼人約沙法、

⁴⁴亞施他拉人烏оба亞、亞羅珥人何坦的兒子沙瑪、耶利、

⁴⁵提洗人申利的兒子耶疊和他的兄弟約哈、

⁴⁶瑪哈未人以利業、伊利拿安的兒子耶利拜、約沙未雅、摩押人伊特瑪、

⁴⁷以利業、俄備得並米瑣八人雅西業。

投效大衛的勇士

12 大衛因怕基士的兒子掃羅，躲在洗革拉的時候，有勇士到他那裏幫助他打仗。²他們善於拉弓，能用左右兩手甩石射箭，都是便雅憫人掃羅的族弟兄：

³為首的是亞希以謝，其次是約阿施，都是基比亞人示瑪的兒子；還有亞斯瑪威的兒子耶薛和毘力；又有比拉迦，並亞拿突人耶戶、⁴基遍人以實買雅，他在三十人中是勇士，管理他們；且有耶利米、雅哈悉、約哈難和基得拉人約撒拔、⁵伊利烏賽、耶利摩、比亞利雅、示瑪利雅、哈律弗人示法提雅；⁶可拉人以利加拿、耶西亞、亞薩列、約以謝、雅朔班；⁷基多人耶羅罕的兒子猶拉和西巴第雅。

⁸迦得支派中有人到曠野的山寨投奔大衛，都是大能的勇士，能拿盾牌和槍的戰士。他們的面貌好像獅子，快跑如同山上的鹿。

⁹第一以薛，
第二俄巴底雅，
第三以利押，

¹⁰第四彌施瑪拿、第五耶利米，

¹¹第六亞太，第七以利業，

¹²第八約哈難，第九以利薩巴，

¹³第十耶利米，第十一末巴奈。

¹⁴這都是迦得人中的軍長，至小的能抵一百人，至大的能抵一千人。¹⁵正月，約旦河水漲過兩岸的時候，他們過河，使一切住平原的人東奔西逃。

16又有便雅憫和猶大人到山寨大衛那裏。17大衛出去迎接他們，對他們說：「你們若是和和平平地來幫助我，我心就與你們相契；你們若是將我這無罪的人賣在敵人手裏，願我們列祖的神察看責罰。」

18那時神的靈感動那三十個勇士的首領亞瑪撒，他就說：

「大衛啊，我們是歸於你的！
　耶西的兒子啊，我們是幫助你的！
願你平平安安，
　願幫助你的也都平安，
　　因為你的神幫助你。」

大衛就收留他們，立他們作軍長。

19大衛從前與非利士人同去，要與掃羅爭戰，有些瑪拿西人來投奔大衛，他們卻沒有幫助非利士人。因為非利士人的首領商議打發他們回去，說：「恐怕大衛拿我們的首級歸降他的主人掃羅。」20大衛往洗革拉去的時候，有瑪拿西人的千夫長押拿、約撒拔、耶疊、米迦勒、約撒拔、以利戶、洗勒太，都來投奔他。21這些人幫助大衛攻擊羣賊。他們都是大能的勇士，且作軍長。22那時，天天有人來幫助大衛，以致成了大軍，如神的軍一樣。

在希伯崙投效大衛之人

23預備打仗的兵來到希伯崙見大衛，要照着耶和華的話，將掃羅的國位歸與大衛。他們的數目如下：

24猶大支派，拿盾牌和槍預備打仗的，有六千八百人。
25西緬支派，能上陣大能的勇士，有七千一百人。
26利未支派有四千六百人。27耶何耶大是亞倫家的首領，跟從他的有三千七百人。28還有少年大能的勇士撒督，同着他的有族長二十二人。
29便雅憫支派、掃羅的族弟兄也有三千人，他們向來大半歸順掃羅家。
30以法蓮支派大能的勇士，在本族著名的有二萬零八百人。

16Other Benjamites and some men from Judah also came to David in his stronghold. 17David went out to meet them and said to them, "If you have come to me in peace, to help me, I am ready to have you unite with me. But if you have come to betray me to my enemies when my hands are free from violence, may the God of our fathers see it and judge you."

18Then the Spirit came upon Amasai, chief of the Thirty, and he said:

"We are yours, O David!
　We are with you, O son of Jesse!
Success, success to you,
　and success to those who help you,
　　for your God will help you."

So David received them and made them leaders of his raiding bands.

19Some of the men of Manasseh defected to David when he went with the Philistines to fight against Saul. (He and his men did not help the Philistines because, after consultation, their rulers sent him away. They said, "It will cost us our heads if he deserts to his master Saul.") 20When David went to Ziklag, these were the men of Manasseh who defected to him: Adnah, Jozabad, Jediael, Michael, Jozabad, Elihu and Zillethai, leaders of units of a thousand in Manasseh. 21They helped David against raiding bands, for all of them were brave warriors, and they were commanders in his army. 22Day after day men came to help David, until he had a great army, like the army of God.*a*

Others Join David at Hebron

23These are the numbers of the men armed for battle who came to David at Hebron to turn Saul's kingdom over to him, as the LORD had said:
24men of Judah, carrying shield and spear— 6,800 armed for battle;
25men of Simeon, warriors ready for battle— 7,100;
26men of Levi— 4,600, 27including Jehoiada, leader of the family of Aaron, with 3,700 men, 28and Zadok, a brave young warrior, with 22 officers from his family;
29men of Benjamin, Saul's kinsmen— 3,000, most of whom had remained loyal to Saul's house until then;
30men of Ephraim, brave warriors, famous in their own clans— 20,800;

a 22 Or a great and mighty army

³¹men of half the tribe of Manasseh, designated by name to come and make David king— 18,000;

³²men of Issachar, who understood the times and knew what Israel should do—200 chiefs, with all their relatives under their command;

³³men of Zebulun, experienced soldiers prepared for battle with every type of weapon, to help David with undivided loyalty—50,000;

³⁴men of Naphtali— 1,000 officers, together with 37,000 men carrying shields and spears;

³⁵men of Dan, ready for battle—28,600;

³⁶men of Asher, experienced soldiers prepared for battle—40,000;

³⁷and from east of the Jordan, men of Reuben, Gad and the half-tribe of Manasseh, armed with every type of weapon— 120,000.

³⁸All these were fighting men who volunteered to serve in the ranks. They came to Hebron fully determined to make David king over all Israel. All the rest of the Israelites were also of one mind to make David king. ³⁹The men spent three days there with David, eating and drinking, for their families had supplied provisions for them. ⁴⁰Also, their neighbors from as far away as Issachar, Zebulun and Naphtali came bringing food on donkeys, camels, mules and oxen. There were plentiful supplies of flour, fig cakes, raisin cakes, wine, oil, cattle and sheep, for there was joy in Israel.

Bringing Back the Ark

13 David conferred with each of his officers, the commanders of thousands and commanders of hundreds. ²He then said to the whole assembly of Israel, "If it seems good to you and if it is the will of the LORD our God, let us send word far and wide to the rest of our brothers throughout the territories of Israel, and also to the priests and Levites who are with them in their towns and pasturelands, to come and join us. ³Let us bring the ark of our God back to us, for we did not inquire of^a it^b during the reign of Saul." ⁴The whole assembly agreed to do this, because it seemed right to all the people.

⁵So David assembled all the Israelites, from the Shihor River in Egypt to Lebo^c Hamath, to bring the ark of God from Kiriath Jearim. ⁶David and all the Israelites with him went to Baalah of Judah (Kiriath Jearim) to bring up from there the

³¹瑪拿西半支派，冊上有名的共一萬八千人，都來立大衛作王。

³²以薩迦支派有二百族長，都通達時務，知道以色列人所當行的，他們族弟兄都聽從他們的命令。

³³西布倫支派能上陣，用各樣兵器打仗、行伍整齊、不生二心的，有五萬人。

³⁴拿弗他利支派有一千軍長，跟從他們拿盾牌和槍的有三萬七千人。

³⁵但支派，能擺陣的有二萬八千六百人。

³⁶亞設支派，能上陣打仗的有四萬人。

³⁷約旦河東的呂便支派、迦得支派、瑪拿西半支派，拿着各樣兵器打仗的有十二萬人。

³⁸以上都是能守行伍的戰士。他們都誠心來到希伯崙，要立大衛作以色列的王。以色列其餘的人也都一心要立大衛作王。³⁹他們在那裏三日，與大衛一同吃喝，因為他們的族弟兄給他們預備了。⁴⁰靠近他們的人，以及以薩迦、西布倫、拿弗他利人，將許多麵餅、無花果餅、乾葡萄、酒、油，用驢、駱駝、騾子、牛馱來，又帶了許多的牛和羊來，因為以色列人甚是歡樂。

運回約櫃

13 大衛與千夫長、百夫長，就是一切首領商議。²大衛對以色列全會眾說："你們若以為美，見這事是出於耶和華我們的神，我們就差遣人走遍以色列地，見我們未來的弟兄，又見住在有郊野之城的祭司利未人，使他們都到這裏來聚集。³我們要把神的約櫃運到我們這裏來，因為在掃羅年間，我們沒有在約櫃前求問神。"⁴全會眾都說："可以如此行，這事在眾民眼中都看為好。"

⁵於是，大衛將以色列人從埃及的西曷河直到哈馬口都招聚了來，要從基列耶琳將神的約櫃運來。⁶大衛率領以色列眾人上到巴拉，就是屬猶大的基列耶琳，要從那裏將約櫃運

---

a 3 Or we neglected   b 3 Or him   c 5 Or to the entrance to

來。這約櫃就是坐在二基路伯上耶和華神留名的約櫃。

⁷他們將神的約櫃從亞比拿達的家裏抬出來，放在新車上，烏撒和亞希約趕車。⁸大衛和以色列眾人在神前用琴、瑟、鑼、鼓、號作樂，極力跳舞歌唱。

⁹到了基頓的禾場（註：「基頓」撒母耳記下6章6節作「拿艮」），因為牛失前蹄（註：或作「驚跳」），烏撒就伸手扶住約櫃。¹⁰耶和華向他發怒，因他伸手扶住約櫃擊殺他，他就死在神面前。

¹¹大衛因耶和華擊殺（註：原文作「闖殺」）烏撒，心裏愁煩，就稱那地方為毘列斯烏撒，直到今日。

¹²那日大衛懼怕神，說：「神的約櫃怎可運到我這裏來？」¹³於是大衛不將約櫃運進大衛的城，卻運到迦特人俄別以東的家中。¹⁴神的約櫃在俄別以東家中三個月，耶和華賜福給俄別以東的家和他一切所有的。

大衛的宮室和家族

14 推羅王希蘭將香柏木運到大衛那裏，又差遣使者和石匠、木匠給大衛建造宮殿。²大衛就知道耶和華堅立他作以色列王，又為自己的民以色列，使他的國興旺。

³大衛在耶路撒冷又立后妃，又生兒女。⁴在耶路撒冷所生的眾子是沙母亞、朔罷、拿單、所羅門、⁵益轄、以利書亞、以法列、⁶挪迦、尼斐、雅非亞、⁷以利沙瑪、比利雅大、以利法列。

大衛打敗非利士人

⁸非利士人聽見大衛受膏作以色列眾人的王，非利士眾人就上來尋索大衛。大衛聽見，就出去迎敵。⁹非利士人來了，布散在利乏音谷。¹⁰大衛求問神，說：「我可以上去攻打非利士人嗎？你將他們交在我手裏嗎？」

耶和華說：「你可以上去，我必將他們交在你手裏。」

¹¹非利士人來到巴力毘拉心，大

ark of God the LORD, who is enthroned between the cherubim—the ark that is called by the Name.

⁷They moved the ark of God from Abinadab's house on a new cart, with Uzzah and Ahio guiding it. ⁸David and all the Israelites were celebrating with all their might before God, with songs and with harps, lyres, tambourines, cymbals and trumpets.

⁹When they came to the threshing floor of Kidon, Uzzah reached out his hand to steady the ark, because the oxen stumbled. ¹⁰The LORD's anger burned against Uzzah, and he struck him down because he had put his hand on the ark. So he died there before God.

¹¹Then David was angry because the LORD's wrath had broken out against Uzzah, and to this day that place is called Perez Uzzah.[a]

¹²David was afraid of God that day and asked, "How can I ever bring the ark of God to me?" ¹³He did not take the ark to be with him in the City of David. Instead, he took it aside to the house of Obed-Edom the Gittite. ¹⁴The ark of God remained with the family of Obed-Edom in his house for three months, and the LORD blessed his household and everything he had.

David's House and Family

14 Now Hiram king of Tyre sent messengers to David, along with cedar logs, stonemasons and carpenters to build a palace for him. ²And David knew that the LORD had established him as king over Israel and that his kingdom had been highly exalted for the sake of his people Israel.

³In Jerusalem David took more wives and became the father of more sons and daughters. ⁴These are the names of the children born to him there: Shammua, Shobab, Nathan, Solomon, ⁵Ibhar, Elishua, Elpelet, ⁶Nogah, Nepheg, Japhia, ⁷Elishama, Beeliada[b] and Eliphelet.

David Defeats the Philistines

⁸When the Philistines heard that David had been anointed king over all Israel, they went up in full force to search for him, but David heard about it and went out to meet them. ⁹Now the Philistines had come and raided the Valley of Rephaim; ¹⁰so David inquired of God: "Shall I go and attack the Philistines? Will you hand them over to me?"

The LORD answered him, "Go, I will hand them over to you."

¹¹So David and his men went up to Baal

---

a 11 Perez Uzzah means outbreak against Uzzah.   *b 7 A variant of Eliada*

Perazim, and there he defeated them. He said, "As waters break out, God has broken out against my enemies by my hand." So that place was called Baal Perazim.[a] 12The Philistines had abandoned their gods there, and David gave orders to burn them in the fire.

13Once more the Philistines raided the valley; 14so David inquired of God again, and God answered him, "Do not go straight up, but circle around them and attack them in front of the balsam trees. 15As soon as you hear the sound of marching in the tops of the balsam trees, move out to battle, because that will mean God has gone out in front of you to strike the Philistine army." 16So David did as God commanded him, and they struck down the Philistine army, all the way from Gibeon to Gezer.

17So David's fame spread throughout every land, and the LORD made all the nations fear him.

The Ark Brought to Jerusalem

15 After David had constructed buildings for himself in the City of David, he prepared a place for the ark of God and pitched a tent for it. 2Then David said, "No one but the Levites may carry the ark of God, because the LORD chose them to carry the ark of the LORD and to minister before him forever."

3David assembled all Israel in Jerusalem to bring up the ark of the LORD to the place he had prepared for it. 4He called together the descendants of Aaron and the Levites:

5From the descendants of Kohath,

Uriel the leader and 120 relatives;

6from the descendants of Merari,

Asaiah the leader and 220 relatives;

7from the descendants of Gershon,[b]

Joel the leader and 130 relatives;

8from the descendants of Elizaphan,

Shemaiah the leader and 200 relatives;

9from the descendants of Hebron,

Eliel the leader and 80 relatives;

10from the descendants of Uzziel,

Amminadab the leader and 112 relatives.

11Then David summoned Zadok and Abiathar the priests, and Uriel, Asaiah, Joel, Shemaiah, Eliel and Amminadab the Levites. 12He said to them, "You are the heads of the Levitical families; you and your fellow Levites are to consecrate yourselves and bring up the ark of the LORD, the God of Israel, to the place I have prepared for it. 13It was because you, the Levites, did not bring it up the first time that the LORD

衞在那裏殺敗他們。大衞說："神藉我的手沖破敵人，如同水沖去一般。"因此稱那地方為巴力毘拉心。12非利士人將神像撇在那裏，大衞吩咐人用火焚燒了。

13非利士人又布散在利乏音谷。14大衞又求問神。神說："不要一直地上去，要轉到他們後頭，從桑林對面攻打他們。15你聽見桑樹梢上有腳步的聲音，就要出戰，因為神已經在你前頭去攻打非利士人的軍隊。"16大衞就遵着神所吩咐的，攻打非利士人的軍隊，從基遍直到基色。

17於是大衞的名傳揚到列國，耶和華使列國都懼怕他。

約櫃運入耶路撒冷

15 大衞在大衞城為自己建造宮殿，又為神的約櫃預備地方，支搭帳幕。2那時大衞說："除了利未人之外，無人可抬神的約櫃，因為耶和華揀選他們抬神的約櫃，且永遠侍奉他。"

3大衞招聚以色列眾人到耶路撒冷，要將耶和華的約櫃抬到他所預備的地方。4大衞又聚集亞倫的子孫和利未人：

5哥轄子孫中有族長烏列和他的弟兄一百二十人；

6米拉利子孫中有族長亞帥雅和他的弟兄二百二十人；

7革順子孫中有族長約珥和他的弟兄一百三十人；

8以利撒反子孫中，有族長示瑪雅和他的弟兄二百人；

9希伯崙子孫中，有族長以列和他的弟兄八十人；

10烏薛子孫中有族長亞米拿達和他的弟兄一百一十二人。

11大衞將祭司撒督和亞比亞他，並利未人烏列、亞帥雅、約珥、示瑪雅、以列、亞米拿達召來，12對他們說："你們是利未人的族長，你們和你們的弟兄應當自潔，好將耶和華以色列神的約櫃抬到我所預備的地方。13因你們先前沒有抬這約櫃，按定例

a 11 Baal Perazim means the lord who breaks out.   b 7 Hebrew Gershom, a variant of Gershon

求問耶和華我們的神，所以他刑罰
（註：原文作「闖殺」）我們。」 14於是
祭司<u>利未人</u>自潔，好將耶和華以<u>以色
列</u>神的約櫃抬上來。 15<u>利未子</u>孫就用
杠、肩抬神的約櫃，是照耶和華藉
<u>摩西</u>所吩咐的。

16<u>大衛</u>吩咐<u>利未人</u>的族長，派他
們歌唱的弟兄用琴瑟和鈸作樂，歡
歡喜喜地大聲歌頌。

17於是<u>利未人</u>派<u>約珥</u>的兒子<u>希幔</u>
和他弟兄中<u>比利家</u>的兒子<u>亞薩</u>，並
他們族弟兄<u>米拉利</u>子孫裏<u>古沙雅</u>的
兒子<u>以探</u>；18其次還有他們的弟兄<u>撒
迦利雅</u>、<u>便雅薛</u>、<u>示米拉末</u>、<u>耶
歇</u>、<u>烏尼</u>、<u>以利押</u>、<u>比拿雅</u>、<u>瑪西
雅</u>、<u>瑪他提雅</u>、<u>以利斐利戶</u>、<u>彌克
尼雅</u>，並守門的<u>俄別以東</u>和<u>耶利</u>。

19這樣，派歌唱的<u>希幔</u>、<u>亞薩</u>、
<u>以探</u>敲銅鈸，大發響聲；20派<u>撒迦利
雅</u>、<u>雅薛</u>、<u>示米拉末</u>、<u>耶歇</u>、<u>烏
尼</u>、<u>以利押</u>、<u>瑪西雅</u>、<u>比拿雅</u>鼓
瑟，調用女音；21又派<u>瑪他提雅</u>、<u>以
利斐利戶</u>、<u>彌克尼雅</u>、<u>俄別以東</u>、
<u>耶利</u>、<u>亞撒西雅</u>領首彈琴，調用第
八。22<u>利未人</u>的族長<u>基拿尼雅</u>是歌唱
人的首領，又教訓人歌唱，因為他
精通此事。

23<u>比利家</u>、<u>以利加拿</u>，是約櫃前
守門的。24祭司<u>示巴尼</u>、<u>約沙法</u>、<u>拿
坦業</u>、<u>亞瑪賽</u>、<u>撒迦利雅</u>、<u>比拿
亞</u>、<u>以利以謝</u>，在神的約櫃前吹
號。<u>俄別以東</u>和<u>耶希亞</u>也是約櫃前
守門的。

25於是，<u>大衛</u>和<u>以色列</u>的長老並
千夫長，都去從<u>俄別以東</u>的家，歡
歡喜喜地將耶和華的約櫃抬上來。
26神賜恩與抬耶和華約櫃的<u>利未人</u>，
他們就獻上七隻公牛，七隻公羊。
27<u>大衛</u>和抬約櫃的<u>利未人</u>，並歌唱人
的首領<u>基拿尼雅</u>以及歌唱的人，都
穿着細麻布的外袍。<u>大衛</u>另外穿着
細麻布的以弗得。28這樣，<u>以色列</u>眾
人歡呼吹角、吹號、敲鈸、鼓瑟、
彈琴，大發響聲，將耶和華的約櫃
抬上來。

our God broke out in anger against us. We did
not inquire of him about how to do it in the prescribed way." [14]So the priests and Levites consecrated themselves in order to bring up the ark of
the LORD, the God of Israel. [15]And the Levites
carried the ark of God with the poles on their
shoulders, as Moses had commanded in accordance with the word of the LORD.

[16]David told the leaders of the Levites to
appoint their brothers as singers to sing joyful
songs, accompanied by musical instruments:
lyres, harps and cymbals.

[17]So the Levites appointed Heman son of Joel;
from his brothers, Asaph son of Berekiah; and
from their brothers the Merarites, Ethan son of
Kushaiah; [18]and with them their brothers next in
rank: Zechariah,[a] Jaaziel, Shemiramoth, Jehiel,
Unni, Eliab, Benaiah, Maaseiah, Mattithiah,
Eliphelehu, Mikneiah, Obed-Edom and Jeiel,[b]
the gatekeepers.

[19]The musicians Heman, Asaph and Ethan
were to sound the bronze cymbals; [20]Zechariah,
Aziel, Shemiramoth, Jehiel, Unni, Eliab, Maaseiah
and Benaiah were to play the lyres according to
alamoth,[c] [21]and Mattithiah, Eliphelehu, Mikneiah,
Obed-Edom, Jeiel and Azaziah were to play the
harps, directing according to *sheminith*.[c]
[22]Kenaniah the head Levite was in charge of the
singing; that was his responsibility because he
was skillful at it.

[23]Berekiah and Elkanah were to be doorkeepers for the ark. [24]Shebaniah, Joshaphat, Nethanel,
Amasai, Zechariah, Benaiah and Eliezer the
priests were to blow trumpets before the ark of
God. Obed-Edom and Jehiah were also to be
doorkeepers for the ark.

[25]So David and the elders of Israel and the
commanders of units of a thousand went to bring
up the ark of the covenant of the LORD from the
house of Obed-Edom, with rejoicing. [26]Because
God had helped the Levites who were carrying
the ark of the covenant of the LORD, seven bulls
and seven rams were sacrificed. [27]Now David
was clothed in a robe of fine linen, as were all the
Levites who were carrying the ark, and as were
the singers, and Kenaniah, who was in charge of
the singing of the choirs. David also wore a linen
ephod. [28]So all Israel brought up the ark of the
covenant of the LORD with shouts, with the
sounding of rams' horns and trumpets, and of
cymbals, and the playing of lyres and harps.

a 18 Three Hebrew manuscripts and most Septuagint
manuscripts (see also verse 20 and 1 Chron. 16:5); most
Hebrew manuscripts *Zechariah son and* or *Zechariah, Ben and*
b 18 Hebrew; Septuagint (see also verse 21) *Jeiel and Azaziah*
c 20 ,21 Probably a musical term

²⁹As the ark of the covenant of the LORD was entering the City of David, Michal daughter of Saul watched from a window. And when she saw King David dancing and celebrating, she despised him in her heart.

16 They brought the ark of God and set it inside the tent that David had pitched for it, and they presented burnt offerings and fellowship offerings^a before God. ²After David had finished sacrificing the burnt offerings and fellowship offerings, he blessed the people in the name of the LORD. ³Then he gave a loaf of bread, a cake of dates and a cake of raisins to each Israelite man and woman.

⁴He appointed some of the Levites to minister before the ark of the LORD, to make petition, to give thanks, and to praise the LORD, the God of Israel: ⁵Asaph was the chief, Zechariah second, then Jeiel, Shemiramoth, Jehiel, Mattithiah, Eliab, Benaiah, Obed-Edom and Jeiel. They were to play the lyres and harps, Asaph was to sound the cymbals, ⁶and Benaiah and Jahaziel the priests were to blow the trumpets regularly before the ark of the covenant of God.

David's Psalm of Thanks

⁷That day David first committed to Asaph and his associates this psalm of thanks to the LORD:

⁸Give thanks to the LORD, call on his name;
    make known among the nations what he has done.
⁹Sing to him, sing praise to him;
    tell of all his wonderful acts.
¹⁰Glory in his holy name;
    let the hearts of those who seek the LORD rejoice.
¹¹Look to the LORD and his strength;
    seek his face always.
¹²Remember the wonders he has done,
    his miracles, and the judgments he pronounced,
¹³O descendants of Israel his servant,
    O sons of Jacob, his chosen ones.

¹⁴He is the LORD our God;
    his judgments are in all the earth.
¹⁵He remembers^b his covenant forever,
    the word he commanded, for a thousand generations,
¹⁶the covenant he made with Abraham,
    the oath he swore to Isaac.

²⁹耶和華的約櫃進了大衛城的時候，掃羅的女兒米甲從窗戶裏觀看，見大衛王踴躍跳舞，心裏就輕視他。

16 眾人將神的約櫃請進去，安放在大衛所搭的帳幕裏，就在神面前獻燔祭和平安祭。²大衛獻完了燔祭和平安祭，就奉耶和華的名給民祝福，³並且分給以色列人，無論男女，每人一個餅、一塊肉、一個葡萄餅。

⁴大衛派幾個利未人在耶和華的約櫃前侍奉、頌揚、稱謝、讚美耶和華以色列的神。⁵為首的是亞薩，其次是撒迦利雅、雅薛、示米拉末、耶歇、瑪他提雅、以利押、比拿雅、俄別以東、耶利，鼓瑟彈琴；惟有亞薩敲鈸，大發響聲；⁶祭司比拿雅和雅哈悉常在神的約櫃前吹號。

大衛的頌歌

⁷那日，大衛初次藉亞薩和他的弟兄，以詩歌稱頌耶和華，說：

⁸你們要稱謝耶和華，
    求告他的名，
    在萬民中傳揚他的作為。
⁹要向他唱詩、歌頌，
    談論他一切奇妙的作為。
¹⁰要以他的聖名誇耀。
    尋求耶和華的人，
    心中應當歡喜。
¹¹要尋求耶和華與他的能力，
    時常尋求他的面。
¹²、¹³他僕人以色列的後裔、
    他所揀選雅各的子孫哪，
    你們要記念他奇妙的作為
    和他的奇事，
    並他口中的判語。

¹⁴他是耶和華我們的神，
    全地都有他的判斷。
¹⁵你們要記念他的約，直到永遠；
    他所吩咐的話，
    直到千代，
¹⁶就是與亞伯拉罕所立的約，
    向以撒所起的誓。

a 1 Traditionally peace offerings; also in verse 2   b 15 Some Septuagint manuscripts (see also Psalm 105:8); Hebrew Remember

17他又將這約向雅各定為律例；
　　向以色列定為永遠的約，
18說："我必將迦南地賜給你，
　　作你產業的分。"

19當時你們人丁有限，數目稀少，
　　並且在那地為寄居的。
20他們從這邦游行到那邦，
　　從這國行到那國。
21耶和華不容甚麼人欺負他們，
　　為他們的緣故責備君王，
22說："不可難為我受膏的人，
　　也不可惡待我的先知。"

23全地都要向耶和華歌唱！
　　天天傳揚他的救恩。
24在列邦中述說他的榮耀，
　　在萬民中述說他的奇事。
25因耶和華為大，當受極大的讚美；
　　他在萬神之上，當受敬畏！
26外邦的神都屬虛無，
　　惟獨耶和華創造諸天。
27有尊榮和威嚴在他面前，
　　有能力和喜樂在他聖所。
28民中的萬族啊，你們要將榮耀能力
　　歸給耶和華，都歸給耶和華！
29要將耶和華的名所當得的榮耀
　　歸給他，拿供物來奉到他面前；
　　當以聖潔的妝飾（註："的"或作"為"）
　　敬拜耶和華。
30全地要在他面前戰抖，
　　世界也堅定不得動搖。

31願天歡喜，願地快樂！
　　願人在列邦中說：
　　"耶和華作王了！"
32願海和其中所充滿的澎湃；
　　願田和其中所有的都歡樂。
33那時，林中的樹木
　　都要在耶和華面前歡呼，
　　因為他來要審判全地。

34應當稱謝耶和華，因他本為善，
　　他的慈愛永遠長存！
35要說："拯救我們的神啊，
　　求你救我們，聚集我們，
　　使我們脫離外邦，
　　我們好稱讚你的聖名，
　　以讚美你為誇勝。"
36耶和華以色列的神，
　　從亙古直到永遠，是應當稱頌的！

17He confirmed it to Jacob as a decree,
　　to Israel as an everlasting covenant:
18"To you I will give the land of Canaan
　　as the portion you will inherit."

19When they were but few in number,
　　few indeed, and strangers in it,
20they[a] wandered from nation to nation,
　　from one kingdom to another.
21He allowed no man to oppress them;
　　for their sake he rebuked kings:
22"Do not touch my anointed ones;
　　do my prophets no harm."

23Sing to the LORD, all the earth;
　　proclaim his salvation day after day.
24Declare his glory among the nations,
　　his marvelous deeds among all peoples.
25For great is the LORD and most worthy of praise;
　　he is to be feared above all gods.
26For all the gods of the nations are idols,
　　but the LORD made the heavens.
27Splendor and majesty are before him;
　　strength and joy in his dwelling place.
28Ascribe to the LORD, O families of nations,
　　ascribe to the LORD glory and strength,
29 ascribe to the LORD the glory due his name.
　　Bring an offering and come before him;
　　worship the LORD in the splendor of his[b]
　　　holiness.
30Tremble before him, all the earth!
　　The world is firmly established; it cannot be
　　　moved.
31Let the heavens rejoice, let the earth be glad;
　　let them say among the nations, "The LORD
　　　reigns!"
32Let the sea resound, and all that is in it;
　　let the fields be jubilant, and everything in them!
33Then the trees of the forest will sing,
　　they will sing for joy before the LORD,
　　for he comes to judge the earth.

34Give thanks to the LORD, for he is good;
　　his love endures forever.
35Cry out, "Save us, O God our Savior;
　　gather us and deliver us from the nations,
　　that we may give thanks to your holy name,
　　that we may glory in your praise."
36Praise be to the LORD, the God of Israel,
　　from everlasting to everlasting.

---

a 18-20 One Hebrew manuscript, Septuagint and Vulgate (see also Psalm 105:12); most Hebrew manuscripts inherit, / 19though you are but few in number, / few indeed, and strangers in it." / 20They　　b 29 Or LORD with the splendor of

Then all the people said "Amen" and "Praise the LORD."

37David left Asaph and his associates before the ark of the covenant of the LORD to minister there regularly, according to each day's requirements. 38He also left Obed-Edom and his sixty-eight associates to minister with them. Obed-Edom son of Jeduthun, and also Hosah, were gatekeepers.

39David left Zadok the priest and his fellow priests before the tabernacle of the LORD at the high place in Gibeon 40to present burnt offerings to the LORD on the altar of burnt offering regularly, morning and evening, in accordance with everything written in the Law of the LORD, which he had given Israel. 41With them were Heman and Jeduthun and the rest of those chosen and designated by name to give thanks to the LORD, "for his love endures forever." 42Heman and Jeduthun were responsible for the sounding of the trumpets and cymbals and for the playing of the other instruments for sacred song. The sons of Jeduthun were stationed at the gate.

43Then all the people left, each for his own home, and David returned home to bless his family.

God's Promise to David

17 After David was settled in his palace, he said to Nathan the prophet, "Here I am, living in a palace of cedar, while the ark of the covenant of the LORD is under a tent."

2Nathan replied to David, "Whatever you have in mind, do it, for God is with you."

3That night the word of God came to Nathan, saying:

4"Go and tell my servant David, 'This is what the LORD says: You are not the one to build me a house to dwell in. 5I have not dwelt in a house from the day I brought Israel up out of Egypt to this day. I have moved from one tent site to another, from one dwelling place to another. 6Wherever I have moved with all the Israelites, did I ever say to any of their leaders[a] whom I commanded to shepherd my people, "Why have you not built me a house of cedar?"'

7"Now then, tell my servant David, 'This is what the LORD Almighty says: I took you from the pasture and from following the flock, to be ruler over my people Israel. 8I have been with you wherever you have gone, and I have

a 6 Traditionally judges; also in verse 10

眾民都說：“阿們！”並且讚美耶和華。

37大衛派亞薩和他的弟兄在約櫃前常常侍奉耶和華，一日盡一日的職分。38又派俄別以東和他的弟兄六十八人，與耶杜頓的兒子俄別以東，並何薩作守門的。

39、40且派祭司撒督和他弟兄眾祭司，在基遍的邱壇耶和華的帳幕前燔祭壇上，每日早晚，照着耶和華律法書上所吩咐以色列人的，常給耶和華獻燔祭。41與他們一同被派的有希幔、耶杜頓和其餘被選名字錄在冊上的，稱謝耶和華，因他的慈愛永遠長存。42希幔、耶杜頓同着他們吹號、敲鈸，大發響聲，並用別的樂器隨着歌頌神。耶杜頓的子孫作守門的。

43於是眾民各歸各家，大衛也回去為家眷祝福。

神對大衛的應許

17 大衛住在自己宮中，對先知拿單說：“看哪，我住在香柏木的宮中，耶和華的約櫃反在幔子裏。”

2拿單對大衛說：“你可以照你的心意而行，因為神與你同在。”

3當夜，神的話臨到拿單，說：

4“你去告訴我僕人大衛說，耶和華如此說：‘你不可建造殿宇給我居住。5自從我領以色列人出埃及，直到今日，我未曾住過殿宇，乃從這會幕到那會幕，從這帳幕到那帳幕。6凡我同以色列人所走的地方，我何曾向以色列的一個士師，就是我吩咐牧養我民的說：你為何不給我建造香柏木的殿宇呢？’

7“現在你要告訴我僕人大衛說，萬軍之耶和華如此說：‘我從羊圈中將你召來，叫你不再跟從羊羣，立你作我民以色列的君。8你無論往哪裏去，我常與你同在，剪除你的一切仇敵。我必使你得大名，好像世上大大有名的人一樣。⁹我必為我民以色列選定一個地方，栽培他們，使他們住自己的地方，不再遷移。兇惡之子也不像從前擾害他們，¹⁰並不像我命士師治理我民以色列的時候一樣。

"'我必治服你的一切仇敵，並且我耶和華應許你，必為你建立家室。¹¹你壽數滿足歸你列祖的時候，我必使你的後裔接續你的位，我也必堅定他的國。¹²他必為我建造殿宇，我必堅定他的國位直到永遠。¹³我要作他的父，他要作我的子。並不使我的慈愛離開他，像離開在你以前的掃羅一樣。¹⁴我卻要將他永遠堅立在我家裏和我國裏；他的國位也必堅定，直到永遠。'"

¹⁵拿單就按這一切話，照這默示，告訴大衛。

大衛的禱告

¹⁶於是大衛王進去，坐在耶和華面前，說：

"耶和華神啊，我是誰？我的家算甚麼，你竟使我到這地步呢？¹⁷神啊，這在你眼中還看為小，又應許你僕人的家至於久遠。耶和華神啊，你看顧我好像看顧高貴的人。

¹⁸"你加給僕人的尊榮，我還有何言可說呢？因為你知道你的僕人。¹⁹耶和華啊，你行了這大事，並且顯明出來，是因你僕人的緣故，也是照你的心意。

²⁰"耶和華啊，照我們耳中聽見，沒有可比你的，除你以外再無神！²¹世上有何民能比你的民以色列呢？你神從埃及救贖他們作自己的子民，又在你贖出來的民面前行大而可畏的事，驅逐列邦人，顯出你的大名。²²你使以色列人作你的子民，直到永遠；你耶和華也作他們的神。

²³"耶和華啊，你所應許僕人和僕人家的話，求你堅定，直到

cut off all your enemies from before you. Now I will make your name like the names of the greatest men of the earth. ⁹And I will provide a place for my people Israel and will plant them so that they can have a home of their own and no longer be disturbed. Wicked people will not oppress them anymore, as they did at the beginning ¹⁰and have done ever since the time I appointed leaders over my people Israel. I will also subdue all your enemies.

"'I declare to you that the LORD will build a house for you: ¹¹When your days are over and you go to be with your fathers, I will raise up your offspring to succeed you, one of your own sons, and I will establish his kingdom. ¹²He is the one who will build a house for me, and I will establish his throne forever. ¹³I will be his father, and he will be my son. I will never take my love away from him, as I took it away from your predecessor. ¹⁴I will set him over my house and my kingdom forever; his throne will be established forever.'"

¹⁵Nathan reported to David all the words of this entire revelation.

David's Prayer

¹⁶Then King David went in and sat before the LORD, and he said:

"Who am I, O LORD God, and what is my family, that you have brought me this far? ¹⁷And as if this were not enough in your sight, O God, you have spoken about the future of the house of your servant. You have looked on me as though I were the most exalted of men, O LORD God.

¹⁸"What more can David say to you for honoring your servant? For you know your servant, ¹⁹O LORD. For the sake of your servant and according to your will, you have done this great thing and made known all these great promises.

²⁰"There is no one like you, O LORD, and there is no God but you, as we have heard with our own ears. ²¹And who is like your people Israel—the one nation on earth whose God went out to redeem a people for himself, and to make a name for yourself, and to perform great and awesome wonders by driving out nations from before your people, whom you redeemed from Egypt? ²²You made your people Israel your very own forever, and you, O LORD, have become their God.

²³"And now, LORD, let the promise you have made concerning your servant and his

house be established forever. Do as you promised, ²⁴so that it will be established and that your name will be great forever. Then men will say, 'The LORD Almighty, the God over Israel, is Israel's God!' And the house of your servant David will be established before you.

²⁵"You, my God, have revealed to your servant that you will build a house for him. So your servant has found courage to pray to you. ²⁶O LORD, you are God! You have promised these good things to your servant. ²⁷Now you have been pleased to bless the house of your servant, that it may continue forever in your sight; for you, O LORD, have blessed it, and it will be blessed forever."

David's Victories

18 In the course of time, David defeated the Philistines and subdued them, and he took Gath and its surrounding villages from the control of the Philistines.

²David also defeated the Moabites, and they became subject to him and brought tribute.

³Moreover, David fought Hadadezer king of Zobah, as far as Hamath, when he went to establish his control along the Euphrates River. ⁴David captured a thousand of his chariots, seven thousand charioteers and twenty thousand foot soldiers. He hamstrung all but a hundred of the chariot horses.

⁵When the Arameans of Damascus came to help Hadadezer king of Zobah, David struck down twenty-two thousand of them. ⁶He put garrisons in the Aramean kingdom of Damascus, and the Arameans became subject to him and brought tribute. The LORD gave David victory everywhere he went.

⁷David took the gold shields carried by the officers of Hadadezer and brought them to Jerusalem. ⁸From Tebah^a and Cun, towns that belonged to Hadadezer, David took a great quantity of bronze, which Solomon used to make the bronze Sea, the pillars and various bronze articles.

⁹When Tou king of Hamath heard that David had defeated the entire army of Hadadezer king of Zobah, ¹⁰he sent his son Hadoram to King David to greet him and congratulate him on his victory in battle over Hadadezer, who had been at war with Tou. Hadoram brought all kinds of articles of gold and silver and bronze.

¹¹King David dedicated these articles to the LORD, as he had done with the silver and gold he had taken from all these nations: Edom and

⁸ Hebrew *Tibhath*, a variant of *Tebah*

永遠，照你所說的而行。²⁴願你的名永遠堅立，被尊為大，說：『萬軍之耶和華是以色列的神，是治理以色列的神！』這樣，你僕人大衛的家必在你面前堅立。

²⁵"我的神啊，因你啓示僕人說：『我必為你建立家室。』所以僕人大膽在你面前祈禱。²⁶耶和華啊，惟有你是神，你也應許將這福氣賜給僕人。²⁷現在你喜悅賜福與僕人的家，可以永存在你面前。耶和華啊，你已經賜福，還要賜福到永遠。"

大衛的勝利

18 此後，大衛攻打非利士人，把他們治服，從他們手下奪取了迦特和屬迦特的村莊。

²又攻打摩押，摩押人就歸服大衛，給他進貢。

³瑣巴王哈大利謝（註：撒母耳記下8章3節作"哈大底謝"）往幼發拉底河去，要堅定自己的國權，大衛就攻打他，直到哈馬。⁴奪了他的戰車一千，馬兵七千，步兵二萬，將拉戰車的馬砍斷蹄筋，但留下一百輛車的馬。

⁵大馬士革的亞蘭人來幫助瑣巴王哈大利謝，大衛就殺了亞蘭人二萬二千。⁶於是大衛在大馬士革的亞蘭地設立防營，亞蘭人就歸服他，給他進貢。大衛無論往哪裏去，耶和華都使他得勝。

⁷他奪了哈大利謝臣僕所拿的金盾牌，帶到耶路撒冷。⁸大衛又從屬哈大利謝的提巴（註："提巴"或作"比他"）和均二城中，奪取了許多的銅。後來所羅門用此製造銅海、銅柱和一切的銅器。

⁹哈馬王陀烏聽見大衛殺敗瑣巴王哈大利謝的全軍，¹⁰就打發他兒子哈多蘭去見大衛王，問他的安，為他祝福，因為他殺敗了哈大利謝。原來陀烏與哈大利謝常常爭戰。哈多蘭帶了金銀銅的各樣器皿來。

¹¹大衛王將這些器皿並從各國奪來的金銀，就是從以東、摩押、亞

把、非利士、亞瑪力人所奪來的，都分別為聖獻給耶和華。

12洗魯雅的兒子亞比篩在鹽谷擊殺了以東的一萬八千人。13大衛在以東地設立防營，以東人就都歸服他。大衛無論往哪裏去，耶和華都使他得勝。

大衛的官員

14大衛作以色列眾人的王，又向眾民秉公行義。15洗魯雅的兒子約押作元帥；亞希律的兒子約沙法作史官；16亞希突的兒子撒督和亞比亞他的兒子亞希米勒作祭司長；沙威沙作書記；17耶何耶大的兒子比拿雅統轄基利提人和比利提人；大衛的眾子都在王的左右作領袖。

大衛與亞捫人爭戰

19 此後，亞捫人的王拿轄死了，他兒子接續他作王。2大衛說：「我要照哈嫩的父親拿轄厚待我的恩典厚待哈嫩。」於是大衛差遣使者為他喪父安慰他。

大衛的臣僕到了亞捫人的境內見哈嫩，要安慰他。3但亞捫人的首領對哈嫩說：「大衛差人來安慰你，你想他是尊敬你父親嗎？他的臣僕來見你不是為詳察窺探、傾覆這地嗎？」4哈嫩便將大衛臣僕的鬍鬚剃去一半，又割斷他們下半截的衣服，使他們露出下體，打發他們回去。

5有人將臣僕所遇的事告訴大衛，他就差人去迎接他們，因為他們甚覺羞恥；告訴他們說：「可以住在耶利哥，等到鬍鬚長起再回來。」

6亞捫人知道大衛憎惡他們，哈嫩和亞捫人就打發人拿一千他連得銀子，從美索不達米亞、亞蘭、瑪迦、瑣巴雇戰車和馬兵。7於是雇了三萬二千輛戰車和瑪迦王並他的軍兵。他們來安營在米底巴前，亞捫人也從他們的城裏出來，聚集交戰。

Moab, the Ammonites and the Philistines, and Amalek.

12Abishai son of Zeruiah struck down eighteen thousand Edomites in the Valley of Salt. 13He put garrisons in Edom, and all the Edomites became subject to David. The LORD gave David victory everywhere he went.

David's Officials

14David reigned over all Israel, doing what was just and right for all his people. 15Joab son of Zeruiah was over the army; Jehoshaphat son of Ahilud was recorder; 16Zadok son of Ahitub and Ahimelech*a* son of Abiathar were priests; Shavsha was secretary; 17Benaiah son of Jehoiada was over the Kerethites and Pelethites; and David's sons were chief officials at the king's side.

The Battle Against the Ammonites

19 In the course of time, Nahash king of the Ammonites died, and his son succeeded him as king. 2David thought, "I will show kindness to Hanun son of Nahash, because his father showed kindness to me." So David sent a delegation to express his sympathy to Hanun concerning his father.

When David's men came to Hanun in the land of the Ammonites to express sympathy to him, 3the Ammonite nobles said to Hanun, "Do you think David is honoring your father by sending men to you to express sympathy? Haven't his men come to you to explore and spy out the country and overthrow it?" 4So Hanun seized David's men, shaved them, cut off their garments in the middle at the buttocks, and sent them away.

5When someone came and told David about the men, he sent messengers to meet them, for they were greatly humiliated. The king said, "Stay at Jericho till your beards have grown, and then come back."

6When the Ammonites realized that they had become a stench in David's nostrils, Hanun and the Ammonites sent a thousand talents*b* of silver to hire chariots and charioteers from Aram Naharaim,*c* Aram Maacah and Zobah. 7They hired thirty-two thousand chariots and charioteers, as well as the king of Maacah with his troops, who came and camped near Medeba, while the Ammonites were mustered from their towns and moved out for battle.

a 16 Some Hebrew manuscripts, Vulgate and Syriac (see also 2 Samuel 8:17); most Hebrew manuscripts *Abimelech*
b 6 That is, about 37 tons (about 34 metric tons)　　c 6 That is, Northwest Mesopotamia

⁸On hearing this, David sent Joab out with the entire army of fighting men. ⁹The Ammonites came out and drew up in battle formation at the entrance to their city, while the kings who had come were by themselves in the open country.

¹⁰Joab saw that there were battle lines in front of him and behind him; so he selected some of the best troops in Israel and deployed them against the Arameans. ¹¹He put the rest of the men under the command of Abishai his brother, and they were deployed against the Ammonites. ¹²Joab said, "If the Arameans are too strong for me, then you are to rescue me; but if the Ammonites are too strong for you, then I will rescue you. ¹³Be strong and let us fight bravely for our people and the cities of our God. The LORD will do what is good in his sight."

¹⁴Then Joab and the troops with him advanced to fight the Arameans, and they fled before him. ¹⁵When the Ammonites saw that the Arameans were fleeing, they too fled before his brother Abishai and went inside the city. So Joab went back to Jerusalem.

¹⁶After the Arameans saw that they had been routed by Israel, they sent messengers and had Arameans brought from beyond the River,ᵃ with Shophach the commander of Hadadezer's army leading them.

¹⁷When David was told of this, he gathered all Israel and crossed the Jordan; he advanced against them and formed his battle lines opposite them. David formed his lines to meet the Arameans in battle, and they fought against him. ¹⁸But they fled before Israel, and David killed seven thousand of their charioteers and forty thousand of their foot soldiers. He also killed Shophach the commander of their army.

¹⁹When the vassals of Hadadezer saw that they had been defeated by Israel, they made peace with David and became subject to him.

So the Arameans were not willing to help the Ammonites anymore.

The Capture of Rabbah

20 In the spring, at the time when kings go off to war, Joab led out the armed forces. He laid waste the land of the Ammonites and went to Rabbah and besieged it, but David remained in Jerusalem. Joab attacked Rabbah and left it in ruins. ²David took the crown from the head of their kingᵇ —its weight was found to be a talentᶜ of gold, and it was set with precious stones—and it was placed on

⁸大衛聽見了，就差派約押統帶勇猛的全軍出去。⁹亞捫人出來在城門前擺陣；所來的諸王另在郊野擺陣。

¹⁰約押看見敵人在他的前後擺陣，就從以色列軍中挑選精兵，使他們對着亞蘭人擺陣。¹¹其餘的兵交與他兄弟亞比篩，對着亞捫人擺陣。¹²約押對亞比篩說："亞蘭人若強過我，你就來幫助我；亞捫人若強過你，我就去幫助你。¹³我們都當剛強，為本國的民和神的城邑作大丈夫。願耶和華憑他的意旨而行。"

¹⁴於是約押和跟隨他的人前進攻打亞蘭人。亞蘭人在約押面前逃跑。¹⁵亞捫人見亞蘭人逃跑，他們也在約押的兄弟亞比篩面前逃跑進城。約押就回耶路撒冷去了。

¹⁶亞蘭人見自己被以色列人打敗，就打發使者將大河那邊的亞蘭人調來，哈大利謝的將軍朔法率領他們。

¹⁷有人告訴大衛，他就聚集以色列眾人過約旦河，來到亞蘭人那裏，迎着他們擺陣。大衛既擺陣攻擊亞蘭人，亞蘭人就與他打仗。¹⁸亞蘭人在以色列人面前逃跑。大衛殺了亞蘭七千輛戰車的人、四萬步兵，又殺了亞蘭的將軍朔法。

¹⁹屬哈大利謝的諸王見自己被以色列人打敗，就與大衛和好，歸服他。

於是亞蘭人不敢再幫助亞捫人了。

攻取拉巴

20 過了一年，到列王出戰的時候，約押率領軍兵毀壞亞捫人的地，圍攻拉巴。大衛仍住在耶路撒冷。約押攻打拉巴，將城傾覆。²大衛奪了亞捫人之王所戴的金冠冕（註："王"或作"瑪勒堪"，"瑪勒堪"即"米勒公"，亞捫族之神名），其上的金子重一他連得，又嵌着寶石，人將這冠冕戴在大衛頭上。大衛從城裏奪

---

a 16 That is, the Euphrates   *b 2 Or of Milcom, that is, Molech*
c 2 That is, about 75 pounds (about 34 kilograms)

了許多財物，³將城裏的人拉出來，放在鋸下，或鐵耙下，或鐵斧下（註：或作「強他們用鋸，或用打糧食的鐵器，或用鐵斧做工」），大衛待亞捫各城的居民都是如此。其後大衛和眾軍都回耶路撒冷去了。

與非利士人爭戰

⁴後來，以色列人在基色與非利士人打仗。戶沙人西比該殺了偉人的一個兒子細派，非利士人就被制伏了。

⁵又與非利士人打仗，睚珥的兒子伊勒哈難殺了迦特人歌利亞的兄弟拉哈米，這人的槍桿粗如織布的機軸。

⁶又在迦特打仗，那裏有一個身量高大的人，手腳都是六指，共有二十四個指頭，他也是偉人的兒子。⁷這人向以色列人罵陣，大衛的哥哥示米亞的兒子約拿單就殺了他。

⁸這三個人是迦特偉人的兒子，都死在大衛和他僕人的手下。

大衛數點兵員之數

21 撒但起來攻擊以色列人，激動大衛數點他們。²大衛就吩咐約押和民中的首領說："你們去數點以色列人，從別是巴直到但，回來告訴我，我好知道他們的數目。"

³約押說："願耶和華使他的百姓比現在加增百倍。我主我王啊，他們不都是你的僕人嗎？我主為何吩咐行這事，為何使以色列人陷在罪裏呢？"

⁴但王的命令勝過約押。約押就出去，走遍以色列地，回到耶路撒冷，⁵將百姓的總數奏告大衛：以色列人拿刀的有一百一十萬；猶大人拿刀的有四十七萬。

⁶惟有利未人和便雅憫人沒有數在其中，因為約押厭惡王的這命令。⁷神不喜悅這數點百姓的事，便降災給以色列人。

⁸大衛禱告神說："我行這事大有罪了！現在求你除掉僕人的罪孽，因我所行的甚是愚昧。"

David's head. He took a great quantity of plunder from the city ³and brought out the people who were there, consigning them to labor with saws and with iron picks and axes. David did this to all the Ammonite towns. Then David and his entire army returned to Jerusalem.

War With the Philistines

⁴In the course of time, war broke out with the Philistines, at Gezer. At that time Sibbecai the Hushathite killed Sippai, one of the descendants of the Rephaites, and the Philistines were subjugated.

⁵In another battle with the Philistines, Elhanan son of Jair killed Lahmi the brother of Goliath the Gittite, who had a spear with a shaft like a weaver's rod.

⁶In still another battle, which took place at Gath, there was a huge man with six fingers on each hand and six toes on each foot—twenty-four in all. He also was descended from Rapha. ⁷When he taunted Israel, Jonathan son of Shimea, David's brother, killed him.

⁸These were descendants of Rapha in Gath, and they fell at the hands of David and his men.

David Numbers the Fighting Men

21 Satan rose up against Israel and incited David to take a census of Israel. ²So David said to Joab and the commanders of the troops, "Go and count the Israelites from Beersheba to Dan. Then report back to me so that I may know how many there are."

³But Joab replied, "May the LORD multiply his troops a hundred times over. My lord the king, are they not all my lord's subjects? Why does my lord want to do this? Why should he bring guilt on Israel?"

⁴The king's word, however, overruled Joab; so Joab left and went throughout Israel and then came back to Jerusalem. ⁵Joab reported the number of the fighting men to David: In all Israel there were one million one hundred thousand men who could handle a sword, including four hundred and seventy thousand in Judah.

⁶But Joab did not include Levi and Benjamin in the numbering, because the king's command was repulsive to him. ⁷This command was also evil in the sight of God; so he punished Israel.

⁸Then David said to God, "I have sinned greatly by doing this. Now, I beg you, take away the guilt of your servant. I have done a very foolish thing."

⁹The LORD said to Gad, David's seer, ¹⁰"Go and tell David, 'This is what the LORD says: I am giving you three options. Choose one of them for me to carry out against you.' "

¹¹So Gad went to David and said to him, "This is what the LORD says: 'Take your choice: ¹²three years of famine, three months of being swept away^a before your enemies, with their swords overtaking you, or three days of the sword of the LORD—days of plague in the land, with the angel of the LORD ravaging every part of Israel.' Now then, decide how I should answer the one who sent me."

¹³David said to Gad, "I am in deep distress. Let me fall into the hands of the LORD, for his mercy is very great; but do not let me fall into the hands of men."

¹⁴So the LORD sent a plague on Israel, and seventy thousand men of Israel fell dead. ¹⁵And God sent an angel to destroy Jerusalem. But as the angel was doing so, the LORD saw it and was grieved because of the calamity and said to the angel who was destroying the people, "Enough! Withdraw your hand." The angel of the LORD was then standing at the threshing floor of Araunah^b the Jebusite.

¹⁶David looked up and saw the angel of the LORD standing between heaven and earth, with a drawn sword in his hand extended over Jerusalem. Then David and the elders, clothed in sackcloth, fell facedown.

¹⁷David said to God, "Was it not I who ordered the fighting men to be counted? I am the one who has sinned and done wrong. These are but sheep. What have they done? O LORD my God, let your hand fall upon me and my family, but do not let this plague remain on your people."

¹⁸Then the angel of the LORD ordered Gad to tell David to go up and build an altar to the LORD on the threshing floor of Araunah the Jebusite. ¹⁹So David went up in obedience to the word that Gad had spoken in the name of the LORD.

²⁰While Araunah was threshing wheat, he turned and saw the angel; his four sons who were with him hid themselves. ²¹Then David approached, and when Araunah looked and saw him, he left the threshing floor and bowed down before David with his face to the ground.

²²David said to him, "Let me have the site of your threshing floor so I can build an altar to the LORD, that the plague on the people may be stopped. Sell it to me at the full price."

^a 12 Hebrew; Septuagint and Vulgate (see also 2 Samuel 24:13) of fleeing   ^b 15 Hebrew Ornan, a variant of Araunah; also in verses 18-28

⁹耶和華吩咐大衛的先見迦得說：¹⁰"你去告訴大衛說，耶和華如此說：'我有三樣災，隨你選擇一樣，我好降與你。'"

¹¹於是迦得來見大衛，對他說："耶和華如此說：'你可以隨意選擇：¹²或三年的饑荒；或敗在你敵人面前，被敵人的刀追殺三個月；或在你國中有耶和華的刀，就是三日的瘟疫，耶和華的使者在以色列的四境施行毀滅。'現在你要想一想，我好回覆那差我來的。"

¹³大衛對迦得說："我甚為難，我願落在耶和華的手裏，因為他有豐盛的憐憫；我不願落在人的手裏。"

¹⁴於是耶和華降瘟疫與以色列人，以色列人就死了七萬。¹⁵神差遣使者去滅耶路撒冷，剛要滅的時候，耶和華看見後悔，就不降這災了，吩咐滅城的天使說："夠了，住手吧！"那時，耶和華的使者站在耶布斯人阿珥楠的禾場那裏。

¹⁶大衛舉目，看見耶和華的使者站在天地間，手裏有拔出來的刀，伸在耶路撒冷以上。大衛和長老都身穿麻衣，面伏於地。

¹⁷大衛禱告神說："吩咐數點百姓的不是我嗎？我犯了罪、行了惡，但這羣羊做了甚麼呢？願耶和華我神的手攻擊我和我的父家，不要攻擊你的民，降瘟疫與他們。"

¹⁸耶和華的使者吩咐迦得去告訴大衛，叫他上去，在耶布斯人阿珥楠的禾場上，為耶和華築一座壇。¹⁹大衛就照着迦得奉耶和華名所說的話上去了。

²⁰那時，阿珥楠正打麥子，回頭看見天使，就和他四個兒子都藏起來了。²¹大衛到了阿珥楠那裏，阿珥楠看見大衛，就從禾場上出去，臉伏於地，向他下拜。

²²大衛對阿珥楠說："你將這禾場與相連之地賣給我，我必給你足價，我好在其上為耶和華築一座壇，使民間的瘟疫止住。"

²³阿珥楠對大衛說：“你可以用這禾場，願我主我王照你所喜悅的去行。我也將牛給你作燔祭，把打糧的器具當柴燒，拿麥子作素祭。這些都送給你。”

²⁴大衛王對阿珥楠說：“不然，我必要用足價向你買，我不用你的物獻給耶和華，也不用白得之物獻為燔祭。”

²⁵於是，大衛為那塊地平了六百舍客勒金子給阿珥楠。²⁶大衛在那裏為耶和華築了一座壇，獻燔祭和平安祭，求告耶和華，耶和華就應允他，使火從天降在燔祭壇上。

²⁷耶和華吩咐使者，他就收刀入鞘。²⁸那時，大衛見耶和華在耶布斯人阿珥楠的禾場上應允了他，就在那裏獻祭。²⁹摩西在曠野所造之耶和華的帳幕和燔祭壇，都在基遍的高處。³⁰只是大衛不敢前去求問神，因為懼怕耶和華使者的刀。

³¹大衛說：“這就是耶和華神的殿，為以色列人獻燔祭的壇。”

預備建造聖殿

22 大衛吩咐聚集住以色列地的外邦人，從其中派石匠鑿石頭，要建造神的殿。²大衛備許多鐵，作門上的釘子和鈎子；又預備許多銅，多得無法可稱；³又預備無數的香柏木，因為西頓人和推羅人給大衛運了許多香柏木來。

⁴大衛說：“我兒子所羅門還年幼嬌嫩，要為耶和華建造的殿宇，必須高大輝煌，使名譽榮耀傳遍萬國！所以我要為殿預備材料。”於是，大衛在未死之先，預備的材料甚多。

⁵大衛召了他兒子所羅門來，囑咐他給耶和華以色列的神建造殿宇。⁶對所羅門說：“我兒啊，我心裏本想為耶和華我神的名建造殿宇，⁷只是耶和華的話臨到我說：

²³Araunah said to David, "Take it! Let my lord the king do whatever pleases him. Look, I will give the oxen for the burnt offerings, the threshing sledges for the wood, and the wheat for the grain offering. I will give all this."

²⁴But King David replied to Araunah, "No, I insist on paying the full price. I will not take for the LORD what is yours, or sacrifice a burnt offering that costs me nothing."

²⁵So David paid Araunah six hundred shekels[a] of gold for the site. ²⁶David built an altar to the LORD there and sacrificed burnt offerings and fellowship offerings.[b] He called on the LORD, and the LORD answered him with fire from heaven on the altar of burnt offering.

²⁷Then the LORD spoke to the angel, and he put his sword back into its sheath. ²⁸At that time, when David saw that the LORD had answered him on the threshing floor of Araunah the Jebusite, he offered sacrifices there. ²⁹The tabernacle of the LORD, which Moses had made in the desert, and the altar of burnt offering were at that time on the high place at Gibeon. ³⁰But David could not go before it to inquire of God, because he was afraid of the sword of the angel of the LORD.

22 Then David said, "The house of the LORD God is to be here, and also the altar of burnt offering for Israel."

Preparations for the Temple

²So David gave orders to assemble the aliens living in Israel, and from among them he appointed stonecutters to prepare dressed stone for building the house of God. ³He provided a large amount of iron to make nails for the doors of the gateways and for the fittings, and more bronze than could be weighed. ⁴He also provided more cedar logs than could be counted, for the Sidonians and Tyrians had brought large numbers of them to David.

⁵David said, "My son Solomon is young and inexperienced, and the house to be built for the LORD should be of great magnificence and fame and splendor in the sight of all the nations. Therefore I will make preparations for it." So David made extensive preparations before his death.

⁶Then he called for his son Solomon and charged him to build a house for the LORD, the God of Israel. ⁷David said to Solomon: "My son, I had it in my heart to build a house for the Name of the LORD my God. ⁸But this word of the

---

a 25 That is, about 15 pounds (about 7 kilograms)
b 26 Traditionally peace offerings

LORD came to me: 'You have shed much blood and have fought many wars. You are not to build a house for my Name, because you have shed much blood on the earth in my sight. ⁹But you will have a son who will be a man of peace and rest, and I will give him rest from all his enemies on every side. His name will be Solomon,ᵃ and I will grant Israel peace and quiet during his reign. ¹⁰He is the one who will build a house for my Name. He will be my son, and I will be his father. And I will establish the throne of his kingdom over Israel forever.'

¹¹"Now, my son, the LORD be with you, and may you have success and build the house of the LORD your God, as he said you would. ¹²May the LORD give you discretion and understanding when he puts you in command over Israel, so that you may keep the law of the LORD your God. ¹³Then you will have success if you are careful to observe the decrees and laws that the LORD gave Moses for Israel. Be strong and courageous. Do not be afraid or discouraged.

¹⁴"I have taken great pains to provide for the temple of the LORD a hundred thousand talentsᵇ of gold, a million talentsᶜ of silver, quantities of bronze and iron too great to be weighed, and wood and stone. And you may add to them. ¹⁵You have many workmen: stonecutters, masons and carpenters, as well as men skilled in every kind of work ¹⁶in gold and silver, bronze and iron—craftsmen beyond number. Now begin the work, and the LORD be with you."

¹⁷Then David ordered all the leaders of Israel to help his son Solomon. ¹⁸He said to them, "Is not the LORD your God with you? And has he not granted you rest on every side? For he has handed the inhabitants of the land over to me, and the land is subject to the LORD and to his people. ¹⁹Now devote your heart and soul to seeking the LORD your God. Begin to build the sanctuary of the LORD God, so that you may bring the ark of the covenant of the LORD and the sacred articles belonging to God into the temple that will be built for the Name of the LORD."

The Levites

23 When David was old and full of years, he made his son Solomon king over Israel.

²He also gathered together all the leaders of Israel, as well as the priests and Levites. ³The Levites thirty years old or more were counted,

'你流了多人的血,打了多次大仗,你不可為我的名建造殿宇,因為你在我眼前使多人的血流在地上。⁸你要生一個兒子,他必作太平的人。我必使他安靜,不被四圍的仇敵擾亂。他的名要叫所羅門(註:即「太平」之意)。他在位的日子,我必使以色列人平安康泰。⁹他必為我的名建造殿宇。他要作我的子,我要作他的父。他作以色列王,我必堅定他的國位,直到永遠。'

¹⁰ "我兒啊,現今願耶和華與你同在,使你亨通,照他指着你說的話,建造耶和華你神的殿。¹¹但願耶和華賜與你聰明智慧,好治理以色列國,遵行耶和華你神的律法。¹²你若謹守遵行耶和華藉摩西吩咐以色列的律例典章,就得亨通。你當剛強壯膽,不要懼怕,也不要驚惶。

¹³ "我在困難之中為耶和華的殿預備了金子十萬他連得,銀子一百萬他連得,銅和鐵多得無法可稱。我也預備了木頭、石頭,你還可以增添。¹⁴你有許多匠人,就是石匠、木匠,和一切能做各樣工的巧匠,¹⁵並有無數的金、銀、銅、鐵。你當起來辦事,願耶和華與你同在。"

¹⁶大衛又吩咐以色列的眾首領幫助他兒子所羅門,說:¹⁷ "耶和華你們的神不是與你們同在嗎?不是叫你們四圍都平安嗎?因他已將這地的居民交在我手中,這地就在耶和華與他百姓面前制伏了。¹⁸現在你們應當立定心意,尋求耶和華你們的神;也當起來建造耶和華神的聖所,好將耶和華的約櫃和供奉神的聖器皿,都搬進為耶和華名建造的殿裏。"

利未人

23 大衛年紀老邁,日子滿足,就立他兒子所羅門作以色列的王。

²大衛招聚以色列的眾首領和祭司利未人。³利未人從三十歲以外的

---

⁹ *Solomon* sounds like and may be derived from the Hebrew for *peace.* *b 14* That is, about 3,750 tons (about 3,450 metric tons) *c 14* That is, about 37,500 tons (about 34,500 metric tons)

都被數點，他們男丁的數目共有三萬八千。⁴其中有二萬四千人管理耶和華殿的事；有六千人作官長和士師；⁵有四千人作守門的；又有四千人用<u>大衛</u>所做的樂器頌讚耶和華。

⁶<u>大衛</u>將<u>利未</u>人<u>革順</u>、<u>哥轄</u>、<u>米拉利</u>的子孫分了班次。

<u>革順</u>的子孫
⁷<u>革順</u>的子孫有：
　<u>拉但</u>和<u>示每</u>。
⁸<u>拉但</u>的：
　長子是<u>耶歇</u>，還有<u>細坦</u>和<u>約珥</u>，
　共三人。
⁹<u>示每</u>的兒子是：
　<u>示羅密</u>、<u>哈薛</u>、<u>哈蘭</u>三人。
　這是<u>拉但</u>族的族長。

¹⁰<u>示每</u>的兒子是：
　<u>雅哈</u>、<u>細拿</u>、<u>耶烏施</u>、<u>比利亞</u>，
　共四人。

¹¹<u>雅哈</u>是長子，<u>細撒</u>是次子。但<u>耶烏施</u>和<u>比利亞</u>的子孫不多，所以算為一族。

<u>哥轄</u>的子孫
¹²<u>哥轄</u>的兒子是：
　<u>暗蘭</u>、<u>以斯哈</u>、<u>希伯倫</u>、<u>烏薛</u>，
　共四人。
¹³<u>暗蘭</u>的兒子是：
　<u>亞倫</u>、<u>摩西</u>。
　<u>亞倫</u>和他的子孫分出來，好分別至聖的物，在耶和華面前燒香，侍奉他，奉他的名祝福，直到永遠。¹⁴至於神人<u>摩西</u>，他的子孫，名字記在<u>利未</u>支派的冊上。

¹⁵<u>摩西</u>的兒子是：
　<u>革舜</u>和<u>以利以謝</u>。
¹⁶<u>革舜</u>的：
　長子是<u>細布業</u>。
¹⁷<u>以利以謝</u>的兒子是：
　<u>利哈比雅</u>。
　<u>以利以謝</u>沒有別的兒子，但<u>利哈比雅</u>的子孫甚多。

and the total number of men was thirty-eight thousand. ⁴David said, "Of these, twenty-four thousand are to supervise the work of the temple of the LORD and six thousand are to be officials and judges. ⁵Four thousand are to be gatekeepers and four thousand are to praise the LORD with the musical instruments I have provided for that purpose."

⁶David divided the Levites into groups corresponding to the sons of Levi: Gershon, Kohath and Merari.

Gershonites
⁷Belonging to the Gershonites:
　Ladan and Shimei.
⁸The sons of Ladan:
　Jehiel the first, Zetham and Joel—three in all.
⁹The sons of Shimei:
　Shelomoth, Haziel and Haran—three in all.
　These were the heads of the families of Ladan.
¹⁰And the sons of Shimei:
　Jahath, Ziza,ᵃ Jeush and Beriah.
　These were the sons of Shimei—four in all.
¹¹Jahath was the first and Ziza the second, but Jeush and Beriah did not have many sons; so they were counted as one family with one assignment.

Kohathites
¹²The sons of Kohath:
　Amram, Izhar, Hebron and Uzziel—four in all.
¹³The sons of Amram:
　Aaron and Moses.
　Aaron was set apart, he and his descendants forever, to consecrate the most holy things, to offer sacrifices before the LORD, to minister before him and to pronounce blessings in his name forever. ¹⁴The sons of Moses the man of God were counted as part of the tribe of Levi.
¹⁵The sons of Moses:
　Gershom and Eliezer.
¹⁶The descendants of Gershom:
　Shubael was the first.
¹⁷The descendants of Eliezer:
　Rehabiah was the first.
　Eliezer had no other sons, but the sons of Rehabiah were very numerous.

---

a 10 One Hebrew manuscript, Septuagint and Vulgate (see also verse 11); most Hebrew manuscripts *Zina*

¹⁸The sons of Izhar:

　　Shelomith was the first.

¹⁹The sons of Hebron:

　　Jeriah the first, Amariah the second, Jahaziel the third and Jekameam the fourth.

²⁰The sons of Uzziel:

　　Micah the first and Isshiah the second.

Merarites

²¹The sons of Merari:

　　Mahli and Mushi.

　The sons of Mahli:

　　Eleazar and Kish.

²²Eleazar died without having sons: he had only daughters. Their cousins, the sons of Kish, married them.

²³The sons of Mushi:

　　Mahli, Eder and Jerimoth—three in all.

²⁴These were the descendants of Levi by their families—the heads of families as they were registered under their names and counted individually, that is, the workers twenty years old or more who served in the temple of the LORD. ²⁵For David had said, "Since the LORD, the God of Israel, has granted rest to his people and has come to dwell in Jerusalem forever, ²⁶the Levites no longer need to carry the tabernacle or any of the articles used in its service." ²⁷According to the last instructions of David, the Levites were counted from those twenty years old or more.

²⁸The duty of the Levites was to help Aaron's descendants in the service of the temple of the LORD: to be in charge of the courtyards, the side rooms, the purification of all sacred things and the performance of other duties at the house of God. ²⁹They were in charge of the bread set out on the table, the flour for the grain offerings, the unleavened wafers, the baking and the mixing, and all measurements of quantity and size. ³⁰They were also to stand every morning to thank and praise the LORD. They were to do the same in the evening ³¹and whenever burnt offerings were presented to the LORD on Sabbaths and at New Moon festivals and at appointed feasts. They were to serve before the LORD regularly in the proper number and in the way prescribed for them.

³²And so the Levites carried out their responsibilities for the Tent of Meeting, for the Holy Place and, under their brothers the descendants of Aaron, for the service of the temple of the LORD.

¹⁸以斯哈的：

　　長子是示羅密。

¹⁹希伯倫的：

　　長子是耶利雅，次子是亞瑪利亞，三子是雅哈悉，四子是耶加面。

²⁰烏薛的：

　　長子是米迦，次子是耶西雅。

米拉利的子孫

²¹米拉利的兒子是：

　　抹利、母示。

　抹利的兒子是：

　　以利亞撒、基士。

²²以利亞撒死了，沒有兒子，只有女兒，他們本族基士的兒子娶了她們為妻。

²³母示的兒子是：

　　末力、以得、耶利摩，共三人。

²⁴以上利未子孫作族長的，照着男丁的數目，從二十歲以外，都辦耶和華殿的事務。²⁵大衛說："耶和華以色列的神，已經使他的百姓平安，他永遠住在耶路撒冷。²⁶利未人不必再抬帳幕和其中所用的一切器皿了。"²⁷照着大衛臨終所吩咐的，利未人從二十歲以外的都被數點。

²⁸他們的職任是服侍亞倫的子孫，在耶和華的殿和院子並屋中辦事，潔淨一切聖物，就是辦神殿的事務，²⁹並管理陳設餅、素祭的細麵或無酵薄餅，或用盤烤，或用油調和的物，又管理各樣的升斗尺度。³⁰每日早晚，站立稱謝讚美耶和華，³¹又在安息日、月朔並節期，按數照例，將燔祭常常獻給耶和華。

³²又看守會幕和聖所，並守耶和華吩咐他們弟兄亞倫子孫的，辦耶和華殿的事。

祭司的班次

24 亞倫子孫的班次記在下面：

亞倫的兒子是<u>拿答</u>、<u>亞比戶</u>、<u>以利亞撒</u>、<u>以他瑪</u>。²<u>拿答</u>、<u>亞比戶</u>死在他們父親之先，沒有留下兒子，故此，<u>以利亞撒</u>、<u>以他瑪</u>供祭司的職分。³<u>以利亞撒</u>的子孫<u>撒督</u>和<u>以他瑪</u>的子孫<u>亞希米勒</u>，同着<u>大衛</u>將他們的族弟兄分成班次。⁴<u>以利亞撒</u>子孫中為首的比<u>以他瑪</u>子孫中為首的更多。分班如下：<u>以利亞撒</u>的子孫中有十六個族長；<u>以他瑪</u>的子孫中，有八個族長。⁵都掣籤分立，彼此一樣。在聖所和神面前作首領的有<u>以利亞撒</u>的子孫，也有<u>以他瑪</u>的子孫。

⁶作書記的<u>利未人</u>拿坦業的兒子<u>示瑪雅</u>在王和首領，與祭司<u>撒督</u>、<u>亞比亞他</u>的兒子<u>亞希米勒</u>，並祭司<u>利未人</u>的族長面前，記錄他們的名字。在<u>以利亞撒</u>的子孫中取一族；在<u>以他瑪</u>的子孫中取一族。

⁷掣籤的時候，第一掣出來的是<u>耶何雅立</u>，第二是<u>耶大雅</u>，
⁸第三是<u>哈琳</u>，
第四是<u>梭琳</u>，
⁹第五是<u>瑪基雅</u>，
第六是<u>米雅民</u>，
¹⁰第七是<u>哈歌斯</u>，
第八是<u>亞比雅</u>，
¹¹第九是<u>耶書亞</u>，
第十是<u>示迦尼</u>，
¹²第十一是<u>以利亞實</u>，
第十二是<u>雅金</u>，
¹³第十三是<u>胡巴</u>，
第十四是<u>耶是比押</u>，
¹⁴第十五是<u>璧迦</u>，
第十六是<u>音麥</u>，
¹⁵第十七是<u>希悉</u>，
第十八是<u>哈闢悉</u>，
¹⁶第十九是<u>毘他希雅</u>，
第二十是<u>以西結</u>，
¹⁷第二十一是<u>雅斤</u>，
第二十二是<u>迦末</u>，
¹⁸第二十三是<u>第來雅</u>，
第二十四是<u>瑪西亞</u>。

¹⁹這就是他們的班次，要照耶和華<u>以色列</u>的神藉他們祖宗<u>亞倫</u>所吩咐的條例，進入耶和華的殿辦理事務。

The Divisions of Priests

24 These were the divisions of the sons of Aaron:

The sons of Aaron were Nadab, Abihu, Eleazar and Ithamar. ²But Nadab and Abihu died before their father did, and they had no sons; so Eleazar and Ithamar served as the priests. ³With the help of Zadok a descendant of Eleazar and Ahimelech a descendant of Ithamar, David separated them into divisions for their appointed order of ministering. ⁴A larger number of leaders were found among Eleazar's descendants than among Ithamar's, and they were divided accordingly: sixteen heads of families from Eleazar's descendants and eight heads of families from Ithamar's descendants. ⁵They divided them impartially by drawing lots, for there were officials of the sanctuary and officials of God among the descendants of both Eleazar and Ithamar.

⁶The scribe Shemaiah son of Nethanel, a Levite, recorded their names in the presence of the king and of the officials: Zadok the priest, Ahimelech son of Abiathar and the heads of families of the priests and of the Levites—one family being taken from Eleazar and then one from Ithamar.

⁷The first lot fell to Jehoiarib,
    the second to Jedaiah,
⁸the third to Harim,
    the fourth to Seorim,
⁹the fifth to Malkijah,
    the sixth to Mijamin,
¹⁰the seventh to Hakkoz,
    the eighth to Abijah,
¹¹the ninth to Jeshua,
    the tenth to Shecaniah,
¹²the eleventh to Eliashib,
    the twelfth to Jakim,
¹³the thirteenth to Huppah,
    the fourteenth to Jeshebeab,
¹⁴the fifteenth to Bilgah,
    the sixteenth to Immer,
¹⁵the seventeenth to Hezir,
    the eighteenth to Happizzez,
¹⁶the nineteenth to Pethahiah,
    the twentieth to Jehezkel,
¹⁷the twenty-first to Jakin,
    the twenty-second to Gamul,
¹⁸the twenty-third to Delaiah
    and the twenty-fourth to Maaziah.

¹⁹This was their appointed order of ministering when they entered the temple of the LORD, according to the regulations prescribed for them by their forefather Aaron, as the LORD, the God of Israel, had commanded him.

The Rest of the Levites

20As for the rest of the descendants of Levi:
from the sons of Amram: Shubael;
    from the sons of Shubael: Jehdeiah.
      21As for Rehabiah, from his sons:
      Isshiah was the first.
22From the Izharites: Shelomoth;
    from the sons of Shelomoth: Jahath.
23The sons of Hebron: Jeriah the first,*a* Amariah
    the second, Jahaziel the third and
    Jekameam the fourth.
24The son of Uzziel: Micah;
    from the sons of Micah: Shamir.
      25The brother of Micah: Isshiah;
      from the sons of Isshiah: Zechariah.
26The sons of Merari: Mahli and Mushi.
    The son of Jaaziah: Beno.
27The sons of Merari:
    from Jaaziah: Beno, Shoham, Zaccur and
    Ibri.
28From Mahli: Eleazar, who had no sons.

29From Kish: the son of Kish: Jerahmeel.
30And the sons of Mushi: Mahli, Eder and
    Jerimoth.

These were the Levites, according to their families. 31They also cast lots, just as their brothers the descendants of Aaron did, in the presence of King David and of Zadok, Ahimelech, and the heads of families of the priests and of the Levites. The families of the oldest brother were treated the same as those of the youngest.

The Singers

25 David, together with the commanders of the army, set apart some of the sons of Asaph, Heman and Jeduthun for the ministry of prophesying, accompanied by harps, lyres and cymbals. Here is the list of the men who performed this service:

2From the sons of Asaph:
    Zaccur, Joseph, Nethaniah and Asarelah. The sons of Asaph were under the supervision of Asaph, who prophesied under the king's supervision.
3As for Jeduthun, from his sons:
    Gedaliah, Zeri, Jeshaiah, Shimei,*b* Hashabiah and Mattithiah, six in all, under the super-

a 23 Two Hebrew manuscripts and some Septuagint manuscripts (see also 1 Chron. 23:19); most Hebrew manuscripts The sons of Jeriah: *b 3 One Hebrew manuscript and some Septuagint manuscripts (see also verse 17); most Hebrew manuscripts do not have* Shimei.

其餘的利未人

20利未其餘的子孫如下：
暗蘭的子孫裏有：書巴業；
書巴業的子孫裏有：耶希底亞。
    21利哈比雅的子孫裏有：
    長子伊示雅。
22以斯哈的子孫裏有：示羅摩；
示羅摩的子孫裏有：雅哈。
23希伯倫的子孫裏有：長子耶利雅，
    次子亞瑪利亞，三子雅哈悉，四
    子耶加面。
24烏薛的子孫裏有：米迦；
米迦的子孫裏有：沙密。
    25米迦的兄弟是：伊示雅；
    伊示雅的子孫裏有：撒迦利雅。
26米拉利的兒子是：抹利、母示、雅
西雅；雅西雅的兒子有比挪。
27米拉利的子孫裏有：
    雅西雅的兒子比挪、朔含、撒
    刻、伊比利。
28抹利的兒子是：以利亞撒；以利亞
撒沒有兒子。
29基士的子孫裏有：耶拉篾。
30母示的兒子是：末力、以得、耶利
摩。

按着宗族這都是利未的子孫。
31他們在大衛王和撒督，並亞希米
勒與祭司利未人的族長面前掣籤，
正如他們弟兄亞倫的子孫一般。各
族的長者與兄弟沒有分別。

歌頌者

25 大衛和眾首領分派亞薩、希
幔並耶杜頓的子孫彈琴、鼓
瑟、敲鈸、唱歌（註："唱歌"原
文作"說預言"。本章同。）他們供職的人
數記在下面：

2亞薩的兒子：
    撒刻、約瑟、尼探雅、亞薩利拉都
歸亞薩指教，遵王的旨意唱歌。

3耶杜頓的兒子：
    基大利、西利、耶篩亞、哈沙比
雅、瑪他提雅、示每，共六人，都

歸他們父親耶杜頓指教，彈琴、唱歌、稱謝頌讚耶和華。

4希幔的兒子：

布基雅、瑪探雅、烏薛、細布業、耶利摩、哈拿尼雅、哈拿尼、以利亞他、基大利提、羅幔提以謝、約施比加沙、瑪羅提、何提、瑪哈秀。5這都是希幔的兒子，吹角頌讚。希幔奉神之命作王的先見。神賜給希幔十四個兒子、三個女兒。

6都歸他們父親指教，在耶和華的殿唱歌、敲鈸、彈琴、鼓瑟，辦神殿的事務。亞薩、耶杜頓、希幔都是王所命定的。7他們和他們的弟兄學習頌讚耶和華，善於歌唱的，共有二百八十八人。8這些人無論大小，為師的、為徒的，都一同掣籤分了班次。

9掣籤的時候，

第一掣出來的是
亞薩的兒子約瑟。
第二是基大利，
他和他弟兄並兒子共十二人。
10第三是撒刻，
他和他兒子並弟兄共十二人。
11第四是伊洗利，
他和他兒子並弟兄共十二人。
12第五是尼探雅，
他和他兒子並弟兄共十二人。
13第六是布基雅，
他和他兒子並弟兄共十二人。
14第七是耶薩利拉，
他和他兒子並弟兄共十二人。
15第八是耶篩亞，
他和他兒子並弟兄共十二人。
16第九是瑪探雅，
他和他兒子並弟兄共十二人。
17第十是示每，
他和他兒子並弟兄共十二人。
18第十一是亞薩烈，
他和他兒子並弟兄共十二人。
19第十二是哈沙比雅，
他和他兒子並弟兄共十二人。
20第十三是書巴業，
他和他兒子並弟兄共十二人。

vision of their father Jeduthun, who prophesied, using the harp in thanking and praising the LORD.

4As for Heman, from his sons:

Bukkiah, Mattaniah, Uzziel, Shubael and Jerimoth; Hananiah, Hanani, Eliathah, Giddalti and Romamti-Ezer; Joshbekashah, Mallothi, Hothir and Mahazioth. 5All these were sons of Heman the king's seer. They were given him through the promises of God to exalt him.*a* God gave Heman fourteen sons and three daughters.

6All these men were under the supervision of their fathers for the music of the temple of the LORD, with cymbals, lyres and harps, for the ministry at the house of God. Asaph, Jeduthun and Heman were under the supervision of the king. 7Along with their relatives—all of them trained and skilled in music for the LORD—they numbered 288. 8Young and old alike, teacher as well as student, cast lots for their duties.

9The first lot, which was for
  Asaph, fell to Joseph,
  his sons and relatives,*b*   12*c*
  the second to Gedaliah,
  he and his relatives and sons,   12
10the third to Zaccur,
  his sons and relatives,   12
11the fourth to Izri,*d*
  his sons and relatives,   12
12the fifth to Nethaniah,
  his sons and relatives,   12
13the sixth to Bukkiah,
  his sons and relatives,   12
14the seventh to Jesarelah,*e*
  his sons and relatives,   12
15the eighth to Jeshaiah,
  his sons and relatives,   12
16the ninth to Mattaniah,
  his sons and relatives,   12
17the tenth to Shimei,
  his sons and relatives,   12
18the eleventh to Azarel,*f*
  his sons and relatives,   12
19the twelfth to Hashabiah,
  his sons and relatives,   12
20the thirteenth to Shubael,
  his sons and relatives,   12

a 5 Hebrew *exalt the horn*   *b 9* See Septuagint; Hebrew does not have *his sons and relatives.*   *c 9* See the total in verse 7; Hebrew does not have *twelve.*   *d 11* A variant of *Zeri*   *e 14* A variant of *Asarelah*   *f 18* A variant of *Uzziel*

²¹the fourteenth to Mattithiah,
his sons and relatives, 12
²²the fifteenth to Jerimoth,
his sons and relatives, 12
²³the sixteenth to Hananiah,
his sons and relatives, 12
²⁴the seventeenth to Joshbekashah,
his sons and relatives, 12
²⁵the eighteenth to Hanani,
his sons and relatives, 12
²⁶the nineteenth to Mallothi,
his sons and relatives, 12
²⁷the twentieth to Eliathah,
his sons and relatives, 12
²⁸the twenty-first to Hothir,
his sons and relatives, 12
²⁹the twenty-second to Giddalti,
his sons and relatives, 12
³⁰the twenty-third to Mahazioth,
his sons and relatives, 12
³¹the twenty-fourth to Romamti-Ezer,
his sons and relatives, 12

The Gatekeepers

26 The divisions of the gatekeepers:

From the Korahites: Meshelemiah son of Kore, one of the sons of Asaph.
²Meshelemiah had sons:
Zechariah the firstborn,
Jediael the second,
Zebadiah the third,
Jathniel the fourth,
³Elam the fifth,
Jehohanan the sixth
and Eliehoenai the seventh.
⁴Obed-Edom also had sons:
Shemaiah the firstborn,
Jehozabad the second,
Joah the third,
Sacar the fourth,
Nethanel the fifth,
⁵Ammiel the sixth,
Issachar the seventh
and Peullethai the eighth.
(For God had blessed Obed-Edom.)

⁶His son Shemaiah also had sons, who were leaders in their father's family because they were very capable men. ⁷The sons of Shemaiah: Othni, Rephael, Obed and Elzabad; his relatives Elihu and Semakiah were also able men. ⁸All these were descendants of Obed-Edom; they and their sons and their relatives were capable men with the strength to do the work— descendants of Obed-Edom, 62 in all.

²¹第十四是瑪他提雅，
他和他兒子並弟兄共十二人。
²²第十五是耶利摩，
他和他兒子並弟兄共十二人。
²³第十六是哈拿尼雅，
他和他兒子並弟兄共十二人。
²⁴第十七是約施比加沙，
他和他兒子並弟兄共十二人。
²⁵第十八是哈拿尼，
他和他兒子並弟兄共十二人。
²⁶第十九是瑪羅提，
他和他兒子並弟兄共十二人。
²⁷第二十是以利亞他，
他和他兒子並弟兄共十二人。
²⁸第二十一是何提，
他和他兒子並弟兄共十二人。
²⁹第二十二是基大利提，
他和他兒子並弟兄共十二人。
³⁰第二十三是瑪哈秀，
他和他兒子並弟兄共十二人。
³¹第二十四是羅幔提以謝，
他和他兒子並弟兄共十二人。

守門者

26 守門的班次記在下面：

可拉族亞薩的子孫中有：可利的兒子米施利米雅。
²米施利米雅的：
長子是撒迦利亞，
次子是耶疊，
三子是西巴第雅，
四子是耶提聶，
³五子是以攔，
六子是約哈難，
七子是以利約乃。
⁴俄別以東的：
長子是示瑪雅，
次子是約薩拔，
三子是約亞，
四子是沙甲，
五子是拿坦業，
⁵六子是亞米利，
七子是以薩迦，
八子是毘烏利太，
因為神賜福與俄別以東。

⁶他的兒子示瑪雅有幾個兒子，都是大能的壯士，掌管父親的家。⁷示瑪雅的兒子是俄得尼、利法益、俄備得、以利薩巴。以利薩巴的弟兄是壯士，還有以利戶和西瑪迦。⁸這都是俄別以東的子孫，他們和他們的兒子並弟兄，都是善於辦事的壯士。俄別以東的子孫共六十二人。

⁹米施利米雅的兒子和弟兄都是壯士，共十八人。

¹⁰米拉利子孫何薩有幾個兒子：
長子是申利，他原不是長子，是他父親立他作長子，¹¹次子是希勒家，三子是底巴利雅，四子是撒迦利亞。何薩的兒子並弟兄共十三人。

¹²這些人都是守門的班長，與他們的弟兄一同在耶和華殿裏按班供職。¹³他們無論大小，都按着宗族掣籤，分守各門。

¹⁴掣籤守東門的是示利米雅。他的兒子撒迦利亞是精明的謀士，掣籤守北門。¹⁵俄別以東守南門。他的兒子守庫房。¹⁶書聘與何薩守西門，在靠近沙利基門，通往往上去的街道上，班與班相對。

¹⁷每日東門有六個利未人，北門有四個，南門有四個，庫房有兩個，又有兩個輪班替換。¹⁸在西面街道上有四個，在遊廊上有兩個。

¹⁹以上是可拉子孫和米拉利子孫守門的班次。

掌管府庫及其他的官員
²⁰利未子孫中有亞希雅掌管神殿的府庫和聖物的府庫。

²¹革順族拉但子孫裏，作族長的是革順族拉但的子孫耶希伊利。²²耶希伊利的兒子西坦和他兄弟約珥掌管耶和華殿裏的府庫。

²³暗蘭族、以斯哈族、希伯倫族、烏泄族，也有職分。

²⁴摩西的孫子、革舜的兒子細布業掌管府庫。²⁵還有他的弟兄以利以謝。以利以謝的兒子是利哈比雅；利哈比雅的兒子是耶篩亞；耶篩亞的兒子是約蘭；約蘭的兒子是細基利；細基利的兒子是示羅密。²⁶這示羅密和他的弟兄掌管府庫的聖物，就是大衛王和眾

⁹Meshelemiah had sons and relatives, who were able men—18 in all.

¹⁰Hosah the Merarite had sons:
Shimri the first (although he was not the firstborn, his father had appointed him the first), ¹¹Hilkiah the second, Tabaliah the third and Zechariah the fourth. The sons and relatives of Hosah were 13 in all.

¹²These divisions of the gatekeepers, through their chief men, had duties for ministering in the temple of the LORD, just as their relatives had. ¹³Lots were cast for each gate, according to their families, young and old alike.

¹⁴The lot for the East Gate fell to Shelemiah.ᵃ Then lots were cast for his son Zechariah, a wise counselor, and the lot for the North Gate fell to him. ¹⁵The lot for the South Gate fell to Obed-Edom, and the lot for the storehouse fell to his sons. ¹⁶The lots for the West Gate and the Shalleketh Gate on the upper road fell to Shuppim and Hosah.

Guard was alongside of guard: ¹⁷There were six Levites a day on the east, four a day on the north, four a day on the south and two at a time at the storehouse. ¹⁸As for the court to the west, there were four at the road and two at the court itself.

¹⁹These were the divisions of the gatekeepers who were descendants of Korah and Merari.

The Treasurers and Other Officials
²⁰Their fellow Levites wereᵇ in charge of the treasuries of the house of God and the treasuries for the dedicated things.

²¹The descendants of Ladan, who were Gershonites through Ladan and who were heads of families belonging to Ladan the Gershonite, were Jehieli, ²²the sons of Jehieli, Zetham and his brother Joel. They were in charge of the treasuries of the temple of the LORD.

²³From the Amramites, the Izharites, the Hebronites and the Uzzielites:

²⁴Shubael, a descendant of Gershom son of Moses, was the officer in charge of the treasuries. ²⁵His relatives through Eliezer: Rehabiah his son, Jeshaiah his son, Joram his son, Zicri his son and Shelomith his son. ²⁶Shelomith and his relatives were in charge of all the treasuries for the things dedicated by King David, by the heads of families who were the commanders of

a 14 A variant of Meshelemiah   b 20 Septuagint; Hebrew As for the Levites, Ahijah was

thousands and commanders of hundreds, and by the other army commanders. 27Some of the plunder taken in battle they dedicated for the repair of the temple of the LORD. 28And everything dedicated by Samuel the seer and by Saul son of Kish, Abner son of Ner and Joab son of Zeruiah, and all the other dedicated things were in the care of Shelomith and his relatives.

29From the Izharites: Kenaniah and his sons were assigned duties away from the temple, as officials and judges over Israel.

30From the Hebronites: Hashabiah and his relatives—seventeen hundred able men—were responsible in Israel west of the Jordan for all the work of the LORD and for the king's service. 31As for the Hebronites, Jeriah was their chief according to the genealogical records of their families. In the fortieth year of David's reign a search was made in the records, and capable men among the Hebronites were found at Jazer in Gilead. 32Jeriah had twenty-seven hundred relatives, who were able men and heads of families, and King David put them in charge of the Reubenites, the Gadites and the half-tribe of Manasseh for every matter pertaining to God and for the affairs of the king.

Army Divisions

27 This is the list of the Israelites—heads of families, commanders of thousands and commanders of hundreds, and their officers, who served the king in all that concerned the army divisions that were on duty month by month throughout the year. Each division consisted of 24,000 men.

2In charge of the first division, for the first month, was Jashobeam son of Zabdiel. There were 24,000 men in his division. 3He was a descendant of Perez and chief of all the army officers for the first month.

4In charge of the division for the second month was Dodai the Ahohite; Mikloth was the leader of his division. There were 24,000 men in his division.

5The third army commander, for the third month, was Benaiah son of Jehoiada the priest. He was chief and there were 24,000 men in his division. 6This was the Benaiah who was a mighty man among the Thirty and was over the Thirty. His son Ammizabad was in charge of his division.

族長、千夫長、百夫長並軍長所分別為聖的物。27他們將爭戰時所奪的財物分別為聖,以備修造耶和華的殿。28先見撒母耳、基士的兒子掃羅、尼珥的兒子押尼珥、洗魯雅的兒子約押所分別為聖的物,都歸示羅密和他的弟兄掌管。

29以斯哈族有基拿尼雅和他眾子作官長和士師,管理以色列的外事。

30希伯倫族有哈沙比雅和他弟兄一千七百人,都是壯士,在約旦河西,以色列地辦理耶和華與王的事。31希伯倫族中有耶利雅作族長。大衛作王第四十年,在基列的雅謝,從這族中尋得大能的勇士。32耶利雅的弟兄有二千七百人,都是壯士,且作族長。大衛王派他們在呂便支派、迦得支派、瑪拿西半支派中辦理神和王的事。

軍隊的班次

27 以色列人的族長、千夫長、百夫長和官長,都分定班次,每班是二萬四千人,週年按月輪流,替換出入服侍王。

2正月第一班的班長是撒巴第業的兒子雅朔班,他班內有二萬四千人。3他是法勒斯的子孫,統管正月班的一切軍長。

4二月的班長是亞哈希人朵代,還有副官密基羅,他班內有二萬四千人。

5三月第三班的班長(註:原文作"軍長"。下同)是祭司耶何耶大的兒子比拿雅,他班內有二萬四千人。6這比拿雅是那三十人中的勇士,管理那三十人;他班內又有他兒子暗米薩拔。

7四月第四班的班長是約押的兄弟亞撒黑，接續他的是他兒子西巴第雅，他班內有二萬四千人。

8五月第五班的班長是伊斯拉人珊合，他班內有二萬四千人。

9六月第六班的班長是提哥亞人益吉的兒子以拉，他班內有二萬四千人。

10七月第七班的班長是以法蓮族比倫人希利斯，他班內有二萬四千人。

11八月第八班的班長是謝拉族戶沙人西比該，他班內有二萬四千人。

12九月第九班的班長是便雅憫族亞拿突人亞比以謝，他班內有二萬四千人。

13十月第十班的班長是謝拉族尼陀法人瑪哈萊，他班內有二萬四千人。

14十一月第十一班的班長是以法蓮族比拉頓人比拿雅，他班內有二萬四千人。

15十二月第十二班的班長是俄陀聶族尼陀法人黑玳，他班內有二萬四千人。

各支派的首領

16管理以色列眾支派的記在下面：

管呂便人的是細基利的兒子以利以謝；管西緬人的是瑪迦的兒子示法提雅；

17管利未人的是基母利的兒子哈沙比雅；管亞倫子孫的是撒督；

18管猶大人的是大衛的一個哥哥以利戶；管以薩迦人的是米迦勒的兒子暗利；

19管西布倫人的是俄巴第雅的兒子伊施瑪雅；管拿弗他利人的是亞斯列的兒子耶利摩；

20管以法蓮人的是阿撒細雅的兒子何細亞；管瑪拿西半支派的是毘大雅的兒子約珥；

21管基列地瑪拿西那半支派的是撒迦利亞的兒子易多；管便雅憫人的是押尼珥的兒子雅西業；

22管但人的是耶羅罕的兒子亞薩列。以上是以色列眾支派的首領。

23以色列人二十歲以內的，大衛沒有記其數目，因耶和華曾應許說：必加增以色列人如天上的星那

7The fourth, for the fourth month, was Asahel the brother of Joab; his son Zebadiah was his successor. There were 24,000 men in his division.

8The fifth, for the fifth month, was the commander Shamhuth the Izrahite. There were 24,000 men in his division.

9The sixth, for the sixth month, was Ira the son of Ikkesh the Tekoite. There were 24,000 men in his division.

10The seventh, for the seventh month, was Helez the Pelonite, an Ephraimite. There were 24,000 men in his division.

11The eighth, for the eighth month, was Sibbecai the Hushathite, a Zerahite. There were 24,000 men in his division.

12The ninth, for the ninth month, was Abiezer the Anathothite, a Benjamite. There were 24,000 men in his division.

13The tenth, for the tenth month, was Maharai the Netophathite, a Zerahite. There were 24,000 men in his division.

14The eleventh, for the eleventh month, was Benaiah the Pirathonite, an Ephraimite. There were 24,000 men in his division.

15The twelfth, for the twelfth month, was Heldai the Netophathite, from the family of Othniel. There were 24,000 men in his division.

Officers of the Tribes

16The officers over the tribes of Israel:

over the Reubenites: Eliezer son of Zicri;
over the Simeonites: Shephatiah son of Maacah;

17over Levi: Hashabiah son of Kemuel;
over Aaron: Zadok;

18over Judah: Elihu, a brother of David;
over Issachar: Omri son of Michael;

19over Zebulun: Ishmaiah son of Obadiah;
over Naphtali: Jerimoth son of Azriel;

20over the Ephraimites: Hoshea son of Azaziah;
over half the tribe of Manasseh: Joel son of Pedaiah;

21over the half-tribe of Manasseh in Gilead: Iddo son of Zechariah;
over Benjamin: Jaasiel son of Abner;

22over Dan: Azarel son of Jeroham.

These were the officers over the tribes of Israel.

23David did not take the number of the men twenty years old or less, because the LORD had promised to make Israel as numerous as the stars in the sky. [24]Joab son of Zeruiah began to count the men but did not finish. Wrath came on Israel on account of this numbering, and the number was not entered in the book[a] of the annals of King David.

The King's Overseers

[25]Azmaveth son of Adiel was in charge of the royal storehouses.

Jonathan son of Uzziah was in charge of the storehouses in the outlying districts, in the towns, the villages and the watchtowers.

[26]Ezri son of Kelub was in charge of the field workers who farmed the land.

[27]Shimei the Ramathite was in charge of the vineyards.

Zabdi the Shiphmite was in charge of the produce of the vineyards for the wine vats.

[28]Baal-Hanan the Gederite was in charge of the olive and sycamore-fig trees in the western foothills.

Joash was in charge of the supplies of olive oil.

[29]Shitrai the Sharonite was in charge of the herds grazing in Sharon.

Shaphat son of Adlai was in charge of the herds in the valleys.

[30]Obil the Ishmaelite was in charge of the camels.

Jehdeiah the Meronothite was in charge of the donkeys.

[31]Jaziz the Hagrite was in charge of the flocks.

All these were the officials in charge of King David's property.

[32]Jonathan, David's uncle, was a counselor, a man of insight and a scribe. Jehiel son of Hacmoni took care of the king's sons.

[33]Ahithophel was the king's counselor.

Hushai the Arkite was the king's friend. [34]Ahithophel was succeeded by Jehoiada son of Benaiah and by Abiathar.

Joab was the commander of the royal army.

David's Plans for the Temple

28 David summoned all the officials of Israel to assemble at Jerusalem: the officers over the tribes, the commanders of the divisions in the service of the king, the commanders of thousands and commanders of hundreds, and the officials in charge of all the property and livestock belonging to the king and his sons, together with the palace officials, the mighty men and all the brave warriors.

---

a 24 Septuagint; Hebrew number

樣多。[24]洗魯雅的兒子約押動手數點；當時耶和華的烈怒臨到以色列人，因此沒有點完，數目也沒有寫在大衛王記上。

王的產業管理人

[25]掌管王府庫的是亞疊的兒子押斯馬威；

掌管田野城邑村莊保障之倉庫的是烏西雅的兒子約拿單；

[26]掌管耕田種地的是基綠的兒子以斯利；

[27]掌管葡萄園的是拉瑪人示每；

掌管葡萄園酒窖的是實弗米人撒巴底；

[28]掌管高原橄欖樹和桑樹的是基第利人巴勒哈南；

掌管油庫的是約阿施；

[29]掌管沙崙牧放牛羣的是沙崙人施提賚；

掌管山谷牧養牛羣的是亞第賚的兒子沙法；

[30]掌管駝羣的是以實瑪利人阿比勒；

掌管驢羣的是米崙人耶希底亞；

掌管羊羣的是夏甲人雅悉。

[31]這都是給大衛王掌管產業的。

[32]大衛的叔叔約拿單作謀士，這人有智慧，又作書記。哈摩尼的兒子耶歇作王眾子的師傅。

[33]亞希多弗也作王的謀士。

亞基人戶篩作王的陪伴。[34]亞希多弗之後，有比拿雅的兒子耶何耶大和亞比亞他，接續他作謀士。

約押作王的元帥。

大衛建造聖殿的計劃

28 大衛招聚以色列各支派的首領和輪班服侍王的軍長與千夫長、百夫長，掌管王和王子產業、牲畜的，並太監，以及大能的勇士，都到耶路撒冷來。

²大衛王就站起來，說："我的弟兄、我的百姓啊，你們當聽我言！我心裏本想建造殿宇，安放耶和華的約櫃，作為我神的腳凳，我已經預備建造的材料。³只是神對我說：'你不可為我的名建造殿宇，因你是戰士，流了人的血。'

⁴"然而耶和華以色列的神，在我父的全家揀選我作以色列的王，直到永遠。因他揀選猶大為首領；在猶大支派中揀選我父家；在我父的眾子裏喜悅我，立我作以色列眾人的王。⁵耶和華賜我許多兒子，在我兒子中揀選所羅門坐耶和華的國位，治理以色列人。⁶耶和華對我說：'你兒子所羅門必建造我的殿和院宇，因為我揀選他作我的子；我也必作他的父。⁷他若恆久遵行我的誡命典章，如今日一樣，我就必堅定他的國位，直到永遠。'

⁸"現今在耶和華的會中，以色列眾人眼前所說的，我們的神也聽見了。你們應當尋求耶和華你們神的一切誡命，謹守遵行，如此你們可以承受這美地，遺留給你們的子孫永遠為業。

⁹"我兒所羅門哪，你當認識耶和華你父的神，誠心樂意地侍奉他。因為他鑒察眾人的心，知道一切的思意念。你若尋求他，他必使你尋見；你若離棄他，他必永遠丟棄你！¹⁰你當謹慎，因耶和華揀選你建造殿宇作為聖所。你當剛強去行。"

¹¹大衛將殿的遊廊、旁屋、府庫、樓房、內殿和施恩所的樣式，指示他兒子所羅門。¹²又將被靈感動所得的樣式，就是耶和華神殿的院子、周圍的房屋、殿的府庫和聖物府庫的一切樣式都指示他。¹³又指示他祭司和利未人的班次，與耶和華殿裏各樣的工作，並耶和華殿裏一切器皿的樣式，¹⁴以及各樣應用金器的分兩，和各樣應用銀器的分兩，

²King David rose to his feet and said: "Listen to me, my brothers and my people. I had it in my heart to build a house as a place of rest for the ark of the covenant of the LORD, for the footstool of our God, and I made plans to build it. ³But God said to me, 'You are not to build a house for my Name, because you are a warrior and have shed blood.'

⁴"Yet the LORD, the God of Israel, chose me from my whole family to be king over Israel forever. He chose Judah as leader, and from the house of Judah he chose my family, and from my father's sons he was pleased to make me king over all Israel. ⁵Of all my sons—and the LORD has given me many—he has chosen my son Solomon to sit on the throne of the kingdom of the LORD over Israel. ⁶He said to me: 'Solomon your son is the one who will build my house and my courts, for I have chosen him to be my son, and I will be his father. ⁷I will establish his kingdom forever if he is unswerving in carrying out my commands and laws, as is being done at this time.'

⁸"So now I charge you in the sight of all Israel and of the assembly of the LORD, and in the hearing of our God: Be careful to follow all the commands of the LORD your God, that you may possess this good land and pass it on as an inheritance to your descendants forever.

⁹"And you, my son Solomon, acknowledge the God of your father, and serve him with wholehearted devotion and with a willing mind, for the LORD searches every heart and understands every motive behind the thoughts. If you seek him, he will be found by you; but if you forsake him, he will reject you forever. ¹⁰Consider now, for the LORD has chosen you to build a temple as a sanctuary. Be strong and do the work."

¹¹Then David gave his son Solomon the plans for the portico of the temple, its buildings, its storerooms, its upper parts, its inner rooms and the place of atonement. ¹²He gave him the plans of all that the Spirit had put in his mind for the courts of the temple of the LORD and all the surrounding rooms, for the treasuries of the temple of God and for the treasuries for the dedicated things. ¹³He gave him instructions for the divisions of the priests and Levites, and for all the work of serving in the temple of the LORD, as well as for all the articles to be used in its service. ¹⁴He designated the weight of gold for all the gold articles to be used in various kinds of service, and the weight of silver for all the silver articles to be used in various kinds of service:

[15]the weight of gold for the gold lampstands and their lamps, with the weight for each lampstand and its lamps; and the weight of silver for each silver lampstand and its lamps, according to the use of each lampstand; [16]the weight of gold for each table for consecrated bread; the weight of silver for the silver tables; [17]the weight of pure gold for the forks, sprinkling bowls and pitchers; the weight of gold for each gold dish; the weight of silver for each silver dish; [18]and the weight of the refined gold for the altar of incense. He also gave him the plan for the chariot, that is, the cherubim of gold that spread their wings and shelter the ark of the covenant of the LORD.

[19]"All this," David said, "I have in writing from the hand of the LORD upon me, and he gave me understanding in all the details of the plan."

[20]David also said to Solomon his son, "Be strong and courageous, and do the work. Do not be afraid or discouraged, for the LORD God, my God, is with you. He will not fail you or forsake you until all the work for the service of the temple of the LORD is finished. [21]The divisions of the priests and Levites are ready for all the work on the temple of God, and every willing man skilled in any craft will help you in all the work. The officials and all the people will obey your every command."

Gifts for Building the Temple

29 Then King David said to the whole assembly: "My son Solomon, the one whom God has chosen, is young and inexperienced. The task is great, because this palatial structure is not for man but for the LORD God. [2]With all my resources I have provided for the temple of my God—gold for the gold work, silver for the silver, bronze for the bronze, iron for the iron and wood for the wood, as well as onyx for the settings, turquoise,[a] stones of various colors, and all kinds of fine stone and marble—all of these in large quantities. [3]Besides, in my devotion to the temple of my God I now give my personal treasures of gold and silver for the temple of my God, over and above everything I have provided for this holy temple: [4]three thousand talents[b] of gold (gold of Ophir) and seven thousand talents[c] of refined silver, for the overlaying of the walls of the buildings,

[15]金燈臺和金燈的分兩，銀燈臺和銀燈的分兩，輕重各都合宜，[16]陳設餅金桌子的分兩，銀桌子的分兩，[17]精金的肉叉子、盤子和爵的分兩，各金碗與各銀碗的分兩，[18]精金香壇的分兩，並用金子做基路伯（註：原文作「用金子做車式的基路伯」）。基路伯張開翅膀，遮掩耶和華的約櫃。

[19]大衛說：「這一切工作的樣式，都是耶和華用手劃出來使我明白的。」

[20]大衛又對他兒子所羅門說：「你當剛強壯膽去行！不要懼怕，也不要驚惶。因為耶和華神就是我的神，與你同在；他必不撇下你，也不丟棄你，直到耶和華殿的工作都完畢了。[21]有祭司和利未人的各班，為要辦理神殿各樣的事；又有靈巧的人在各樣的工作上樂意幫助你；並有眾首領和眾民一心聽從你的命令。」

為建造聖殿奉獻

29 大衛王對會眾說：「我兒子所羅門是神特選的，還年幼嬌嫩。這工程甚大，因這殿不是為人，乃是為耶和華神建造的。[2]我為我神的殿已經盡力，預備金子做金器，銀子做銀器，銅做銅器，鐵做鐵器，木做木器，還有紅瑪瑙可鑲嵌的寶石，彩石和一切的寶石，並許多漢白玉。[3]且因我心中愛慕我神的殿，就在預備建造聖殿的材料之外，又將我自己積蓄的金銀獻上，建造我神的殿，[4]就是俄斐金三千他連得，精煉的銀子七千他連得，以貼殿牆。

---

a 2 The meaning of the Hebrew for this word is uncertain.
b 4 That is, about 110 tons (about 100 metric tons)
c 4 That is, about 260 tons (about 240 metric tons)

⁵金子做金器，銀子做銀器，並藉匠人的手製造一切。今日有誰樂意將自己獻給耶和華呢？"

⁶於是，眾族長和以色列各支派的首領、千夫長、百夫長，並監管王工的官長，都樂意獻上。⁷他們為神殿的使用獻上金子五千他連得零一萬達利克，銀子一萬他連得，銅一萬八千他連得，鐵十萬他連得。⁸凡有寶石的都交給革順人耶歇，送入耶和華殿的府庫。⁹因這些人誠心樂意獻給耶和華，百姓就歡喜，大衛王也大大歡喜。

大衛的禱告

¹⁰所以，大衛在會眾面前稱頌耶和華說：

"耶和華我們的父，

以色列的神，

是應當稱頌，直到永永遠遠的！

¹¹"耶和華啊，尊大、能力、

榮耀、強勝、威嚴

都是你的；

凡天上地下的都是你的；

國度也是你的，

並且你為至高，為萬有之首。

¹²"豐富尊榮都從你而來，

你也治理萬物。

在你手裏有大能大力，

使人尊大強盛都出於你。

¹³"我們的神啊，現在我們稱謝你，

讚美你榮耀之名！

¹⁴"我算甚麼，我的民算甚麼，竟能如此樂意奉獻？因為萬物都從你而來，我們把從你而得的獻給你！¹⁵我們在你面前是客旅、是寄居的，與我們列祖一樣。我們在世的日子如影兒，不能長存（註：或作"沒有長存的指望"）。¹⁶耶和華我們的神啊，我們預備這許多材料，要為你的聖名建造殿宇，都是從你而來，都是屬你的。¹⁷我的神啊，我知道你

⁵for the gold work and the silver work, and for all the work to be done by the craftsmen. Now, who is willing to consecrate himself today to the LORD?"

⁶Then the leaders of families, the officers of the tribes of Israel, the commanders of thousands and commanders of hundreds, and the officials in charge of the king's work gave willingly. ⁷They gave toward the work on the temple of God five thousand talents*a* and ten thousand darics*b* of gold, ten thousand talents*c* of silver, eighteen thousand talents*d* of bronze and a hundred thousand talents*e* of iron. ⁸Any who had precious stones gave them to the treasury of the temple of the LORD in the custody of Jehiel the Gershonite. ⁹The people rejoiced at the willing response of their leaders, for they had given freely and wholeheartedly to the LORD. David the king also rejoiced greatly.

David's Prayer

¹⁰David praised the LORD in the presence of the whole assembly, saying,

"Praise be to you, O LORD,

God of our father Israel,

from everlasting to everlasting.

¹¹Yours, O LORD, is the greatness and the power

and the glory and the majesty and the splendor,

for everything in heaven and earth is yours.

Yours, O LORD, is the kingdom;

you are exalted as head over all.

¹²Wealth and honor come from you;

you are the ruler of all things.

In your hands are strength and power

to exalt and give strength to all.

¹³Now, our God, we give you thanks,

and praise your glorious name.

¹⁴"But who am I, and who are my people, that we should be able to give as generously as this? Everything comes from you, and we have given you only what comes from your hand. ¹⁵We are aliens and strangers in your sight, as were all our forefathers. Our days on earth are like a shadow, without hope. ¹⁶O LORD our God, as for all this abundance that we have provided for building you a temple for your Holy Name, it comes from your hand, and all of it belongs to you. ¹⁷I know, my God, that you test the heart

a 7 That is, about 190 tons (about 170 metric tons)　　*b 7* That is, about 185 pounds (about 84 kilograms)　　*c 7* That is, about 375 tons (about 345 metric tons)　　*d 7* That is, about 675 tons (about 610 metric tons)　　*e 7* That is, about 3,750 tons (about 3,450 metric tons)

and are pleased with integrity. All these things have I given willingly and with honest intent. And now I have seen with joy how willingly your people who are here have given to you. [18]O LORD, God of our fathers Abraham, Isaac and Israel, keep this desire in the hearts of your people forever, and keep their hearts loyal to you. [19]And give my son Solomon the whole-hearted devotion to keep your commands, requirements and decrees and to do everything to build the palatial structure for which I have provided."

[20]Then David said to the whole assembly, "Praise the LORD your God." So they all praised the LORD, the God of their fathers; they bowed low and fell prostrate before the LORD and the king.

Solomon Acknowledged as King

[21]The next day they made sacrifices to the LORD and presented burnt offerings to him: a thousand bulls, a thousand rams and a thousand male lambs, together with their drink offerings, and other sacrifices in abundance for all Israel. [22]They ate and drank with great joy in the presence of the LORD that day.

Then they acknowledged Solomon son of David as king a second time, anointing him before the LORD to be ruler and Zadok to be priest. [23]So Solomon sat on the throne of the LORD as king in place of his father David. He prospered and all Israel obeyed him. [24]All the officers and mighty men, as well as all of King David's sons, pledged their submission to King Solomon.

[25]The LORD highly exalted Solomon in the sight of all Israel and bestowed on him royal splendor such as no king over Israel ever had before.

The Death of David

[26]David son of Jesse was king over all Israel. [27]He ruled over Israel forty years—seven in Hebron and thirty-three in Jerusalem. [28]He died at a good old age, having enjoyed long life, wealth and honor. His son Solomon succeeded him as king.

[29]As for the events of King David's reign, from beginning to end, they are written in the records of Samuel the seer, the records of Nathan the prophet and the records of Gad the seer, [30]together with the details of his reign and power, and the circumstances that surrounded him and Israel and the kingdoms of all the other lands.

察驗人心，喜悅正直。我以正直的心樂意獻上這一切物。現在我喜歡見你的民在這裏都樂意奉獻與你。[18]耶和華我們列祖亞伯拉罕、以撒、以色列的神啊，求你使你的民，常存這樣的心思意念，堅定他們的心歸向你。[19]又求你賜我兒子所羅門誠實的心，遵守你的命令、法度、律例，成就這一切的事，用我所預備的建造殿宇。"

[20]大衛對全會眾說："你們應當稱頌耶和華你們的神。"於是會眾稱頌耶和華他們列祖的神，低頭拜耶和華與王。

所羅門被立為王

[21]次日，他們向耶和華獻平安祭和燔祭，就是獻公牛一千隻，公綿羊一千隻，羊羔一千隻，並同獻的奠祭，又為以色列眾人獻許多的祭。那日，他們在耶和華面前吃喝，大大歡樂。

[22]他們奉耶和華的命，再膏大衛的兒子所羅門作王，又膏撒督作祭司。[23]於是所羅門坐在耶和華所賜的位上，接續他父親大衛作王，萬事亨通。以色列眾人也都聽從他。[24]眾首領和勇士，並大衛王的眾子，都順服所羅門王。

[25]耶和華使所羅門在以色列眾人眼前甚為尊大，極其威嚴，勝過在他以前的以色列王。

大衛壽終

[26]耶西的兒子大衛作以色列眾人的王。[27]作王共四十年：在希伯崙作王七年，在耶路撒冷作王三十三年。[28]他年紀老邁，日子滿足，享受豐富、尊榮，就死了。他兒子所羅門接續他作王。

[29]大衛始終的事，都寫在先見撒母耳的書上和先知拿單並先見迦得的書上。[30]他的國事和他的勇力，以及他和以色列並列國所經過的事，都寫在這書上。

歷代志下

2 Chronicles

所羅門求智慧

1 大衛的兒子所羅門國位堅固。耶和華他的神與他同在，使他甚為尊大。

2 所羅門吩咐以色列眾人，就是千夫長、百夫長、審判官、首領與族長都來。3 所羅門和會眾都往基遍的邱壇去，因那裏有神的會幕，就是耶和華僕人摩西在曠野所製造的。4 只是神的約櫃，大衛已經從基列耶琳搬到他所預備的地方，因他曾在耶路撒冷為約櫃支搭了帳幕。5 並且戶珥的孫子、烏利的兒子比撒列所造的銅壇，也在基遍耶和華的會幕前。所羅門和會眾都就近壇前。6 所羅門上到耶和華面前會幕的銅壇那裏，獻一千犧牲為燔祭。

7 當夜，神向所羅門顯現，對他說："你願我賜你甚麼，你可以求。"

8 所羅門對神說："你曾向我父大衛大施慈愛，使我接續他作王。9 耶和華神啊！現在求你成就向我父大衛所應許的話。因你立我作這民的王，他們如同地上塵沙那樣多，10 求你賜我智慧聰明，我好在這民前出入，不然，誰能判斷這眾多的民呢？"

11 神對所羅門說："我已立你作我民的王。你既有這心意，並不求資財豐富尊榮，也不求滅絕那恨你之人的性命，又不求大壽數，只求智慧聰明好判斷我的民；12 我必賜你智慧聰明，也必賜你資財豐富尊榮。在你以前的列王都沒有這樣，在你以後也必沒有這樣的。"

13 於是，所羅門從基遍邱壇會幕前回到耶路撒冷，治理以色列人。

Solomon Asks for Wisdom

1 Solomon son of David established himself firmly over his kingdom, for the LORD his God was with him and made him exceedingly great.

2 Then Solomon spoke to all Israel—to the commanders of thousands and commanders of hundreds, to the judges and to all the leaders in Israel, the heads of families— 3 and Solomon and the whole assembly went to the high place at Gibeon, for God's Tent of Meeting was there, which Moses the LORD's servant had made in the desert. 4 Now David had brought up the ark of God from Kiriath Jearim to the place he had prepared for it, because he had pitched a tent for it in Jerusalem. 5 But the bronze altar that Bezalel son of Uri, the son of Hur, had made was in Gibeon in front of the tabernacle of the LORD; so Solomon and the assembly inquired of him there. 6 Solomon went up to the bronze altar before the LORD in the Tent of Meeting and offered a thousand burnt offerings on it.

7 That night God appeared to Solomon and said to him, "Ask for whatever you want me to give you."

8 Solomon answered God, "You have shown great kindness to David my father and have made me king in his place. 9 Now, LORD God, let your promise to my father David be confirmed, for you have made me king over a people who are as numerous as the dust of the earth. 10 Give me wisdom and knowledge, that I may lead this people, for who is able to govern this great people of yours?"

11 God said to Solomon, "Since this is your heart's desire and you have not asked for wealth, riches or honor, nor for the death of your enemies, and since you have not asked for a long life but for wisdom and knowledge to govern my people over whom I have made you king, 12 therefore wisdom and knowledge will be given you. And I will also give you wealth, riches and honor, such as no king who was before you ever had and none after you will have."

13 Then Solomon went to Jerusalem from the high place at Gibeon, from before the Tent of Meeting. And he reigned over Israel.

14Solomon accumulated chariots and horses; he had fourteen hundred chariots and twelve thousand horses,[a] which he kept in the chariot cities and also with him in Jerusalem. 15The king made silver and gold as common in Jerusalem as stones, and cedar as plentiful as sycamore-fig trees in the foothills. 16Solomon's horses were imported from Egypt[b] and from Kue[c] —the royal merchants purchased them from Kue. 17They imported a chariot from Egypt for six hundred shekels[d] of silver, and a horse for a hundred and fifty.[e] They also exported them to all the kings of the Hittites and of the Arameans.

Preparations for Building the Temple

2 Solomon gave orders to build a temple for the Name of the LORD and a royal palace for himself. 2He conscripted seventy thousand men as carriers and eighty thousand as stonecutters in the hills and thirty-six hundred as foremen over them.

3Solomon sent this message to Hiram[f] king of Tyre:

"Send me cedar logs as you did for my father David when you sent him cedar to build a palace to live in. 4Now I am about to build a temple for the Name of the LORD my God and to dedicate it to him for burning fragrant incense before him, for setting out the consecrated bread regularly, and for making burnt offerings every morning and evening and on Sabbaths and New Moons and at the appointed feasts of the LORD our God. This is a lasting ordinance for Israel.

5"The temple I am going to build will be great, because our God is greater than all other gods. 6But who is able to build a temple for him, since the heavens, even the highest heavens, cannot contain him? Who then am I to build a temple for him, except as a place to burn sacrifices before him?

7"Send me, therefore, a man skilled to work in gold and silver, bronze and iron, and in purple, crimson and blue yarn, and experienced in the art of engraving, to work in Judah and Jerusalem with my skilled craftsmen, whom my father David provided.

8"Send me also cedar, pine and algum[g] logs

14所羅門聚集戰車馬兵，有戰車一千四百輛，馬兵一萬二千名，安置在屯車的城邑和耶路撒冷，就是王那裏。15王在耶路撒冷使金銀多如石頭，香柏木多如高原的桑樹。16所羅門的馬是從埃及帶來的，是王的商人一羣一羣按着定價買來的。17他們從埃及買來的車，每輛價銀六百舍客勒，馬每匹一百五十舍客勒。赫人諸王和亞蘭諸王所買的車馬，也是按這價值經他們手買來的。

建造聖殿的準備

2 所羅門定意要為耶和華的名建造殿宇，又為自己的國建造宮室。2所羅門就挑選七萬扛抬的，八萬在山上鑿石頭的，三千六百督工的。

3所羅門差人去見推羅王希蘭說：

"你曾運香柏木與我父大衞建宮居住，求你也這樣待我。4我要為耶和華我神的名建造殿宇，分別為聖獻給他，在他面前焚燒美香，常擺陳設餅，每早晚、安息日、月朔，並耶和華我們神所定的節期獻燔祭，這是以色列人永遠的定例。

5"我所要建造的殿宇甚大，因為我們的神至大，超乎諸神。6天和天上的天，尚且不足他居住的，誰能為他建造殿宇呢？我是誰，能為他建造殿宇嗎？不過在他面前燒香而已。

7"現在求你差一個巧匠來，就是善用金、銀、銅、鐵，和紫色、朱紅色、藍色線，並精於雕刻之工的巧匠，與我父大衞在猶大和耶路撒冷所預備的巧匠一同做工。

8"又求你從黎巴嫩運些香柏

---

a 14 Or charioteers   b 16 Or possibly Muzur, a region in Cilicia; also in verse 17   c 16 Probably Cilicia   d 17 That is, about 15 pounds (about 7 kilograms)   e 17 That is, about 3 3/4 pounds (about 1.7 kilograms)   f 3 Hebrew Huram, a variant of Hiram; also in verses 11 and 12   g 8 Probably a variant of almug; possibly juniper

木、松木、檀香木到我這裏來，因我知道你的僕人善於砍伐黎巴嫩的樹木，我的僕人也必與你的僕人同工。⁹這樣，可以給我預備許多的木料，因我要建造的殿宇高大出奇。¹⁰你的僕人砍伐樹木，我必給他們打好了的小麥二萬歌珥，大麥二萬歌珥，酒二萬罷特，油二萬罷特。"

¹¹推羅王希蘭寫信回答所羅門說：

"耶和華因為愛他的子民，所以立你作他們的王。"

¹²又說：

"創造天地的耶和華以色列的神，是應當稱頌的！他賜給大衛王一個有智慧的兒子，使他有謀略聰明，可以為耶和華建造殿宇，又為自己的國建造宮室。¹³現在我打發一個精巧有聰明的人去，他是我父親希蘭所用的，¹⁴是但支派一個婦人的兒子。他父親是推羅人，他善用金、銀、銅、鐵、石、木，和紫色、藍色、朱紅色線，與細麻製造各物，又精於雕刻，又能想出各樣的巧工。請你派定這人與你的巧匠和你父我主大衛的巧匠，一同做工。¹⁵我主所說的小麥、大麥、酒、油，願我主運來給眾僕人。¹⁶我們必照你所需用的，從黎巴嫩砍伐樹木，紮成筏子，浮海運到約帕；你可以從那裏運到耶路撒冷。"

¹⁷所羅門仿照他父親大衛數點住在以色列地所有寄居的外邦人，共有十五萬三千六百名。¹⁸使七萬人扛抬材料，八萬人在山上鑿石頭，三千六百人督理工作。

所羅門建造聖殿

3 所羅門就在耶路撒冷、耶和華向他父大衛顯現的摩利亞山上，就是耶布斯人阿珥楠

from Lebanon, for I know that your men are skilled in cutting timber there. My men will work with yours ⁹to provide me with plenty of lumber, because the temple I build must be large and magnificent. ¹⁰I will give your servants, the woodsmen who cut the timber, twenty thousand cors^a of ground wheat, twenty thousand cors of barley, twenty thousand baths^b of wine and twenty thousand baths of olive oil."

¹¹Hiram king of Tyre replied by letter to Solomon:

"Because the LORD loves his people, he has made you their king."

¹²And Hiram added:

"Praise be to the LORD, the God of Israel, who made heaven and earth! He has given King David a wise son, endowed with intelligence and discernment, who will build a temple for the LORD and a palace for himself.

¹³"I am sending you Huram-Abi, a man of great skill, ¹⁴whose mother was from Dan and whose father was from Tyre. He is trained to work in gold and silver, bronze and iron, stone and wood, and with purple and blue and crimson yarn and fine linen. He is experienced in all kinds of engraving and can execute any design given to him. He will work with your craftsmen and with those of my lord, David your father.

¹⁵"Now let my lord send his servants the wheat and barley and the olive oil and wine he promised, ¹⁶and we will cut all the logs from Lebanon that you need and will float them in rafts by sea down to Joppa. You can then take them up to Jerusalem."

¹⁷Solomon took a census of all the aliens who were in Israel, after the census his father David had taken; and they were found to be 153,600. ¹⁸He assigned 70,000 of them to be carriers and 80,000 to be stonecutters in the hills, with 3,600 foremen over them to keep the people working.

Solomon Builds the Temple

3 Then Solomon began to build the temple of the LORD in Jerusalem on Mount Moriah, where the LORD had appeared

a 10 That is, probably about 125,000 bushels (about 4,400 kiloliters)　　*b 10* That is, probably about 115,000 gallons (about 440 kiloliters)

to his father David. It was on the threshing floor of Araunah*a* the Jebusite, the place provided by David. ²He began building on the second day of the second month in the fourth year of his reign.

³The foundation Solomon laid for building the temple of God was sixty cubits long and twenty cubits wide*b* (using the cubit of the old standard). ⁴The portico at the front of the temple was twenty cubits*c* long across the width of the building and twenty cubits*d* high.

He overlaid the inside with pure gold. ⁵He paneled the main hall with pine and covered it with fine gold and decorated it with palm tree and chain designs. ⁶He adorned the temple with precious stones. And the gold he used was gold of Parvaim. ⁷He overlaid the ceiling beams, doorframes, walls and doors of the temple with gold, and he carved cherubim on the walls.

⁸He built the Most Holy Place, its length corresponding to the width of the temple—twenty cubits long and twenty cubits wide. He overlaid the inside with six hundred talents*e* of fine gold. ⁹The gold nails weighed fifty shekels.*f* He also overlaid the upper parts with gold.

¹⁰In the Most Holy Place he made a pair of sculptured cherubim and overlaid them with gold. ¹¹The total wingspan of the cherubim was twenty cubits. One wing of the first cherub was five cubits*g* long and touched the temple wall, while its other wing, also five cubits long, touched the wing of the other cherub. ¹²Similarly one wing of the second cherub was five cubits long and touched the other temple wall, and its other wing, also five cubits long, touched the wing of the first cherub. ¹³The wings of these cherubim extended twenty cubits. They stood on their feet, facing the main hall.*h*

¹⁴He made the curtain of blue, purple and crimson yarn and fine linen, with cherubim worked into it.

¹⁵In the front of the temple he made two pillars, which ⌊together⌋ were thirty-five cubits*i* long, each with a capital on top measuring five cubits. ¹⁶He made interwoven chains*j* and put

---

的禾場上、大衛所指定的地方預備好了，開工建造耶和華的殿。²所羅門作王第四年二月初二日開工建造。

³所羅門建築神殿的根基，乃是這樣：長六十肘，寬二十肘，都按着古時的尺寸。⁴殿前的廊子長二十肘，與殿的寬窄一樣，高一百二十肘，裏面貼上精金。

⁵大殿的牆，都用松木板遮蔽，又貼了精金，上面雕刻棕樹和鏈子；⁶又用寶石裝飾殿牆，使殿華美。所用的金子都是巴瓦音的金子。⁷又用金子貼殿和殿的棟梁、門檻、牆壁、門扇，牆上雕刻基路伯。

⁸又建造至聖所，長二十肘，與殿的寬窄一樣；寬也是二十肘，貼上精金，共用金子六百他連得。⁹金釘重五十舍客勒。樓房都貼上金子。

¹⁰在至聖所按造像的法子造兩個基路伯，用金子包裹。¹¹兩個基路伯的翅膀共長二十肘。這基路伯的一個翅膀長五肘，挨着殿這邊的牆；那一個翅膀也長五肘，與那基路伯的翅膀相接。¹²那基路伯的一個翅膀長五肘，挨着殿那邊的牆；那一個翅膀也長五肘，與這基路伯的翅膀相接。¹³兩個基路伯張開翅膀，共長二十肘，面向外殿而立。

¹⁴又用藍色、紫色、朱紅色線和細麻織幔子，在其上繡出基路伯來。

¹⁵在殿前造了兩根柱子，高三十五肘，每柱頂高五肘。¹⁶又照聖所內

---

a 1 Hebrew *Ornan*, a variant of *Araunah*   *b 3* That is, about 90 feet (about 27 meters) long and 30 feet (about 9 meters) wide   *c 4* That is, about 30 feet (about 9 meters); also in verses 8, 11 and 13   *d 4* Some Septuagint and Syriac manuscripts; Hebrew *and a hundred and twenty*   *e 8* That is, about 23 tons (about 21 metric tons)   *f 9* That is, about 1 1/4 pounds (about 0.6 kilogram)   *g 11* That is, about 7 1/2 feet (about 2.3 meters); also in verse 15   *h 13* Or *facing inward*   *i 15* That is, about 52 feet (about 16 meters)   *j 16* Or possibly *made chains in the inner sanctuary;* the meaning of the Hebrew for this phrase is uncertain.

鏈子的樣式做鏈子，安在柱頂上；又做一百石榴，安在鏈子上。¹⁷將兩根柱子立在殿前，一根在右邊，一根在左邊；右邊的起名叫<u>雅斤</u>，左邊的起名叫<u>波阿斯</u>。

聖殿的設備

4 他又製造一座銅壇，長二十肘，寬二十肘，高十肘。²又鑄一個銅海，樣式是圓的，高五肘，徑十肘，圍三十肘。³海周圍有野瓜的樣式，每肘十瓜，共有兩行，是鑄海的時候鑄上的（註：“野瓜”原文作“牛”）。

⁴有十二隻銅牛馱海，三隻向北，三隻向西，三隻向南，三隻向東。海在牛上，牛尾向內；⁵海厚一掌，邊如杯邊，又如百合花，可容三千罷特。

⁶又製造十個盆：五個放在右邊，五個放在左邊。獻燔祭所用之物都洗在其內，但海是為祭司沐浴的。

⁷他又照所定的樣式造十個金燈臺，放在殿裏：五個在右邊，五個在左邊。

⁸又造十張桌子，放在殿裏：五張在右邊，五張在左邊。又造一百個金碗。

⁹又建立祭司院和大院，並院門，用銅包裹門扇。¹⁰將海安在殿門的右邊，就是南邊。

¹¹<u>戶蘭</u>又造了盆、鏟、碗。

這樣，他為<u>所羅門</u>王做完了神殿的工。

them on top of the pillars. He also made a hundred pomegranates and attached them to the chains. ¹⁷He erected the pillars in the front of the temple, one to the south and one to the north. The one to the south he named Jakin^a and the one to the north Boaz.^b

The Temple's Furnishings

4 He made a bronze altar twenty cubits long, twenty cubits wide and ten cubits high.^c ²He made the Sea of cast metal, circular in shape, measuring ten cubits from rim to rim and five cubits^d high. It took a line of thirty cubits^e to measure around it. ³Below the rim, figures of bulls encircled it—ten to a cubit.^f The bulls were cast in two rows in one piece with the Sea.

⁴The Sea stood on twelve bulls, three facing north, three facing west, three facing south and three facing east. The Sea rested on top of them, and their hindquarters were toward the center. ⁵It was a handbreadth^g in thickness, and its rim was like the rim of a cup, like a lily blossom. It held three thousand baths.^h

⁶He then made ten basins for washing and placed five on the south side and five on the north. In them the things to be used for the burnt offerings were rinsed, but the Sea was to be used by the priests for washing.

⁷He made ten gold lampstands according to the specifications for them and placed them in the temple, five on the south side and five on the north.

⁸He made ten tables and placed them in the temple, five on the south side and five on the north. He also made a hundred gold sprinkling bowls.

⁹He made the courtyard of the priests, and the large court and the doors for the court, and overlaid the doors with bronze. ¹⁰He placed the Sea on the south side, at the southeast corner.

¹¹He also made the pots and shovels and sprinkling bowls.

So Huram finished the work he had undertaken for King Solomon in the temple of God:

---

^a 17 *Jakin* probably means *he establishes.*　　*b* 17 *Boaz* probably means *in him is strength.*　　*c* 1 That is, about 30 feet (about 9 meters) long and wide, and about 15 feet (about 4.5 meters) high　　*d* 2 That is, about 7 1/2 feet (about 2.3 meters) *e*2 That is, about 45 feet (about 13.5 meters)　　*f* 3 That is, about 1 1/2 feet (about 0.5 meter)　　*g* 5 That is, about 3 inches (about 8 centimeters)　　*h*5 That is, about 17,500 gallons (about 66 kiloliters)

[12]the two pillars;

the two bowl-shaped capitals on top of the pillars;

the two sets of network decorating the two bowl-shaped capitals on top of the pillars;

[13]the four hundred pomegranates for the two sets of network (two rows of pomegranates for each network, decorating the bowl-shaped capitals on top of the pillars);

[14]the stands with their basins;

[15]the Sea and the twelve bulls under it;

[16]the pots, shovels, meat forks and all related articles.

All the objects that Huram-Abi made for King Solomon for the temple of the LORD were of polished bronze. [17]The king had them cast in clay molds in the plain of the Jordan between Succoth and Zarethan.[a] [18]All these things that Solomon made amounted to so much that the weight of the bronze was not determined.

[19]Solomon also made all the furnishings that were in God's temple:

the golden altar;

the tables on which was the bread of the Presence;

[20]the lampstands of pure gold with their lamps, to burn in front of the inner sanctuary as prescribed;

[21]the gold floral work and lamps and tongs (they were solid gold);

[22]the pure gold wick trimmers, sprinkling bowls, dishes and censers; and the gold doors of the temple: the inner doors to the Most Holy Place and the doors of the main hall.

5 When all the work Solomon had done for the temple of the LORD was finished, he brought in the things his father David had dedicated—the silver and gold and all the furnishings—and he placed them in the treasuries of God's temple.

The Ark Brought to the Temple

[2]Then Solomon summoned to Jerusalem the elders of Israel, all the heads of the tribes and the chiefs of the Israelite families, to bring up the ark of the LORD's covenant from Zion, the City of David. [3]And all the men of Israel came together to the king at the time of the festival in the seventh month.

[12]所造的就是兩根柱子和柱上兩個如球的頂，並兩個蓋柱頂的網子，

[13]和四百石榴，安在兩個網子上。
每網兩行，蓋着兩個柱上如球的頂。

[14]盆座和其上的盆，

[15]海和海下的十二隻牛，

[16]盆、鏟子、肉鍤子，與耶和華殿裏的一切器皿，

都是巧匠戶蘭用光亮的銅為所羅門王造成的。[17]是在約旦平原、疏割和撒利但中間，藉膠泥鑄成的。[18]所羅門製造的這一切甚多，銅的輕重無法可查。

[19]所羅門又造神殿裏的金壇和陳設餅的桌子，

[20]並精金的燈臺和燈盞，
可以照例點在內殿前。

[21]燈臺上的花和燈盞，並蠟剪都是金的，且是純金的。

[22]又用精金製造鑷子、盤子、調羹、火鼎。至於殿門和至聖所的門扇，並殿的門扇，都是金子妝飾的。

5 所羅門做完了耶和華殿的一切工，就把他父大衛分別為聖的金銀和器皿都帶來，放在神殿的府庫裏。

約櫃運入聖殿

[2]那時所羅門將以色列的長老、各支派的首領，並以色列的族長招聚到耶路撒冷，要把耶和華的約櫃從大衛城就是錫安運上來。[3]於是，以色列眾人在七月節前都聚集到王那裏。

---

*a 17 Hebrew Zeredatha, a variant of Zarethan

4以色列眾長老來到，利未人便抬起約櫃，5祭司利未人將約櫃運上來，又將會幕和會幕的一切聖器具都帶上來。6所羅門王和聚集到他那裏的以色列全會眾，都在約櫃前獻牛羊為祭，多得不可勝數。

7祭司將耶和華的約櫃抬進內殿，就是至聖所，放在兩個基路伯的翅膀底下。8基路伯張着翅膀在約櫃之上，遮掩約櫃和抬櫃的杠。9這杠甚長，杠頭在內殿前可以看見，在殿外卻不能看見，直到如今還在那裏。10約櫃裏惟有兩塊石版，就是以色列人出埃及後，耶和華與他們立約的時候，摩西在何烈山所放的。除此以外，並無別物。

11當時，在那裏所有的祭司都已自潔，並不分班供職。12他們出聖所的時候，歌唱的利未人亞薩、希幔、耶杜頓和他們的眾子、眾弟兄都穿細麻布衣服，站在壇的東邊敲鈸、鼓瑟、彈琴。同着他們有一百二十個祭司吹號。13吹號的、歌唱的都一齊發聲，聲合為一，讚美感謝耶和華。吹號、敲鈸，用各種樂器，揚聲讚美耶和華說：

"耶和華本為善，
　他的慈愛永遠長存！"

那時，耶和華的殿有雲充滿，14甚至祭司不能站立供職，因為耶和華的榮光充滿了神的殿。

6 那時，所羅門說："耶和華曾說他必住在幽暗之處，2但我已經建造殿宇作你的居所，為你永遠的住處。"
3王轉臉為以色列會眾祝福，以色列會眾就都站立。4所羅門說：

"耶和華以色列的神是應當稱頌的！因他親口向我父大衛所應許的，也親手成就了。5他說：

4When all the elders of Israel had arrived, the Levites took up the ark, 5and they brought up the ark and the Tent of Meeting and all the sacred furnishings in it. The priests, who were Levites, carried them up; 6and King Solomon and the entire assembly of Israel that had gathered about him were before the ark, sacrificing so many sheep and cattle that they could not be recorded or counted.

7The priests then brought the ark of the LORD's covenant to its place in the inner sanctuary of the temple, the Most Holy Place, and put it beneath the wings of the cherubim. 8The cherubim spread their wings over the place of the ark and covered the ark and its carrying poles. 9These poles were so long that their ends, extending from the ark, could be seen from in front of the inner sanctuary, but not from outside the Holy Place; and they are still there today. 10There was nothing in the ark except the two tablets that Moses had placed in it at Horeb, where the LORD made a covenant with the Israelites after they came out of Egypt.

11The priests then withdrew from the Holy Place. All the priests who were there had consecrated themselves, regardless of their divisions. 12All the Levites who were musicians—Asaph, Heman, Jeduthun and their sons and relatives—stood on the east side of the altar, dressed in fine linen and playing cymbals, harps and lyres. They were accompanied by 120 priests sounding trumpets. 13The trumpeters and singers joined in unison, as with one voice, to give praise and thanks to the LORD. Accompanied by trumpets, cymbals and other instruments, they raised their voices in praise to the LORD and sang:

"He is good;
　his love endures forever."

Then the temple of the LORD was filled with a cloud, 14and the priests could not perform their service because of the cloud, for the glory of the LORD filled the temple of God.

6 Then Solomon said, "The LORD has said that he would dwell in a dark cloud; 2I have built a magnificent temple for you, a place for you to dwell forever."

3While the whole assembly of Israel was standing there, the king turned around and blessed them. 4Then he said:

"Praise be to the LORD, the God of Israel, who with his hands has fulfilled what he promised with his mouth to my father David. For he said, 5'Since the day I brought my people out of Egypt, I have not chosen a city in any tribe of Israel to have a temple built for my Name to be there, nor have I chosen anyone to be the leader over my people Israel. ⁶But now I have chosen Jerusalem for my Name to be there, and I have chosen David to rule my people Israel.'

⁷"My father David had it in his heart to build a temple for the Name of the LORD, the God of Israel. ⁸But the LORD said to my father David, 'Because it was in your heart to build a temple for my Name, you did well to have this in your heart. ⁹Nevertheless, you are not the one to build the temple, but your son, who is your own flesh and blood—he is the one who will build the temple for my Name.'

¹⁰"The LORD has kept the promise he made. I have succeeded David my father and now I sit on the throne of Israel, just as the LORD promised, and I have built the temple for the Name of the LORD, the God of Israel. ¹¹There I have placed the ark, in which is the covenant of the LORD that he made with the people of Israel."

Solomon's Prayer of Dedication

¹²Then Solomon stood before the altar of the LORD in front of the whole assembly of Israel and spread out his hands. ¹³Now he had made a bronze platform, five cubits^a long, five cubits wide and three cubits^b high, and had placed it in the center of the outer court. He stood on the platform and then knelt down before the whole assembly of Israel and spread out his hands toward heaven. ¹⁴He said:

"O LORD, God of Israel, there is no God like you in heaven or on earth—you who keep your covenant of love with your servants who continue wholeheartedly in your way. ¹⁵You have kept your promise to your servant David my father; with your mouth you have promised and with your hand you have fulfilled it—as it is today.

¹⁶"Now LORD, God of Israel, keep for your servant David my father the promises you made to him when you said, 'You shall never fail to have a man to sit before me on the throne of Israel, if only your sons are careful in all they do to walk before me according to my law, as you have done.' ¹⁷And now, O LORD, God of Israel, let your word that you promised your servant David come true.

'自從我領我民出埃及地以來,我未曾在以色列眾支派中選擇一城建造殿宇為我名的居所,也未曾揀選一人作我民以色列的君。⁶但選擇耶路撒冷為我名的居所,又揀選大衛治理我民以色列。'"

⁷所羅門說:"我父大衛曾立意要為耶和華以色列神的名建殿。⁸耶和華卻對我父大衛說:'你立意要為我的名建殿,這意思甚好。⁹只是你不可建殿,惟你所生的兒子必為我名建殿。'

¹⁰"現在耶和華成就了他所應許的話,使我接續我父大衛坐以色列的國位,是照耶和華所說的,又為耶和華以色列神的名建造了殿。¹¹我將約櫃安置在其中,櫃內有耶和華的約,就是他與以色列人所立的約。"

所羅門獻殿的禱告

¹²所羅門當着以色列會眾,站在耶和華的壇前,舉起手來。¹³所羅門曾造一個銅臺,長五肘、寬五肘、高三肘,放在院中,就站在臺上,當着以色列的會眾跪下,向天舉手,¹⁴說:

"耶和華以色列的神啊,天上地下沒有神可比你的!你向那盡心行在你面前的僕人守約施慈愛;¹⁵向你僕人我父大衛所應許的話,現在應驗了。你親口應許,親手成就,正如今日一樣。

¹⁶"耶和華以色列的神啊,你所應許你僕人我父大衛的話說:'你的子孫若謹慎自己的行為,遵守我的律法,像你在我面前所行的一樣,就不斷人坐以色列的國位。'現在求你應驗這話。¹⁷耶和華以色列的神啊,求你成就向你僕人大衛所應許的話。

---

^a 13 That is, about 7 1/2 feet (about 2.3 meters)
^b 13 That is, about 4 1/2 feet (about 1.3 meters)

18 "神果真與世人同住在地上嗎？看哪，天和天上的天尚且不足你居住的，何況我所建的這殿呢！ 19惟求耶和華我的神，垂顧僕人的禱告祈求，俯聽僕人在你面前的祈禱呼籲。 20願你晝夜看顧這殿，就是你應許立為你名的居所，求你垂聽僕人向此處禱告的話。 21你僕人和你民以色列向此處祈禱的時候，求你從天上你的居所垂聽，垂聽而赦免。

22 "人若得罪鄰舍，有人叫他起誓，他來到這殿，在你的壇前起誓， 23求你從天上垂聽，判斷你的僕人，定惡人有罪，照他所行的報應在他頭上；定義人有理，照他的義賞賜他。

24 "你的民以色列若得罪你，敗在仇敵面前，又回心轉意承認你的名，在這殿裏向你祈求禱告， 25求你從天上垂聽，赦免你民以色列的罪，使他們歸回你賜給他們和他們列祖之地。

26 "你的民因得罪你，你懲罰他們，使天閉塞不下雨，他們若向此處禱告，承認你的名，離開他們的罪， 27求你在天上垂聽，赦免你僕人和你民以色列的罪，將當行的善道指教他們，且降雨在你的地，就是你賜給你民為業之地。

28 "國中若有饑荒、瘟疫、旱風、霉爛、蝗蟲、螞蚱，或有仇敵犯境，圍困城邑，無論遭遇甚麼災禍疾病， 29你的民以色列，或是眾人，或是一人，自覺災禍甚苦，向這殿舉手，無論祈求甚麼、禱告甚麼， 30求你從天上你的居所垂聽赦免。你是知道人心的，要照各人所行的待他們（惟

18"But will God really dwell on earth with men? The heavens, even the highest heavens, cannot contain you. How much less this temple I have built! 19Yet give attention to your servant's prayer and his plea for mercy, O LORD my God. Hear the cry and the prayer that your servant is praying in your presence. 20May your eyes be open toward this temple day and night, this place of which you said you would put your Name there. May you hear the prayer your servant prays toward this place. 21Hear the supplications of your servant and of your people Israel when they pray toward this place. Hear from heaven, your dwelling place; and when you hear, forgive.

22"When a man wrongs his neighbor and is required to take an oath and he comes and swears the oath before your altar in this temple, 23then hear from heaven and act. Judge between your servants, repaying the guilty by bringing down on his own head what he has done. Declare the innocent not guilty and so establish his innocence.

24"When your people Israel have been defeated by an enemy because they have sinned against you and when they turn back and confess your name, praying and making supplication before you in this temple, 25then hear from heaven and forgive the sin of your people Israel and bring them back to the land you gave to them and their fathers.

26"When the heavens are shut up and there is no rain because your people have sinned against you, and when they pray toward this place and confess your name and turn from their sin because you have afflicted them, 27then hear from heaven and forgive the sin of your servants, your people Israel. Teach them the right way to live, and send rain on the land you gave your people for an inheritance.

28"When famine or plague comes to the land, or blight or mildew, locusts or grasshoppers, or when enemies besiege them in any of their cities, whatever disaster or disease may come, 29and when a prayer or plea is made by any of your people Israel—each one aware of his afflictions and pains, and spreading out his hands toward this temple— 30then hear from heaven, your dwelling place. Forgive, and deal with each man according to all he does, since you know his heart (for you alone know the hearts of men), ³¹so that they will fear you and walk in your ways all the time they live in the land you gave our fathers.

³²"As for the foreigner who does not belong to your people Israel but has come from a distant land because of your great name and your mighty hand and your outstretched arm—when he comes and prays toward this temple, ³³then hear from heaven, your dwelling place, and do whatever the foreigner asks of you, so that all the peoples of the earth may know your name and fear you, as do your own people Israel, and may know that this house I have built bears your Name.

³⁴"When your people go to war against their enemies, wherever you send them, and when they pray to you toward this city you have chosen and the temple I have built for your Name, ³⁵then hear from heaven their prayer and their plea, and uphold their cause.

³⁶"When they sin against you—for there is no one who does not sin—and you become angry with them and give them over to the enemy, who takes them captive to a land far away or near; ³⁷and if they have a change of heart in the land where they are held captive, and repent and plead with you in the land of their captivity and say, 'We have sinned, we have done wrong and acted wickedly'; ³⁸and if they turn back to you with all their heart and soul in the land of their captivity where they were taken, and pray toward the land you gave their fathers, toward the city you have chosen and toward the temple I have built for your Name; ³⁹then from heaven, your dwelling place, hear their prayer and their pleas, and uphold their cause. And forgive your people, who have sinned against you.

⁴⁰"Now, my God, may your eyes be open and your ears attentive to the prayers offered in this place.

⁴¹"Now arise, O LORD God, and come to your resting place,
　　you and the ark of your might.
May your priests, O LORD God, be clothed with salvation,
　　may your saints rejoice in your goodness.
⁴²O LORD God, do not reject your anointed one.
　　Remember the great love promised to David your servant."

有你知道世人的心），³¹使他們在你賜給我們列祖之地上一生一世敬畏你，遵行你的道。

³²"論到不屬你民以色列的外邦人，為你的大名和大能的手，並伸出來的膀臂，從遠方而來，向這殿禱告，³³求你從天上你的居所垂聽，照着外邦人所祈求的而行，使天下萬民都認識你的名，敬畏你，像你的民以色列一樣。又使他們知道我建造的這殿，是稱為你名下的。

³⁴"你的民若奉你的差遣，無論往何處去與仇敵爭戰，向你所選擇的城與我為你名所建造的殿禱告，³⁵求你從天上垂聽他們的禱告祈求，使他們得勝。

³⁶"你的民若得罪你（世上沒有不犯罪的人），你向他們發怒，將他們交給仇敵擄到或遠或近之地；³⁷他們若在擄到之地想起罪來，回心轉意，懇求你說：'我們有罪了！我們悖逆了！我們作惡了！'³⁸他們若在擄到之地盡心盡性歸服你，又向自己的地，就是你賜給他們列祖之地和你所選擇的城，並我為你名所建造的殿禱告，³⁹求你從天上你的居所垂聽你民的禱告祈求，為他們伸冤，赦免他們的過犯。

⁴⁰"我的神啊，現在求你睜眼看、側耳聽在此處所獻的禱告。

⁴¹"耶和華神啊，求你起來，
　　和你有能力的約櫃
　　　　同入安息之所。
耶和華神啊，
　　願你的祭司披上救恩；
　　願你的聖民蒙福歡樂。
⁴²耶和華神啊，
　　求你不要厭棄你的受膏者，
　　要記念向你僕人大衛
　　　　所施的慈愛。"

奉獻聖殿

7 所羅門祈禱已畢，就有火從天上降下來，燒盡燔祭和別的祭。耶和華的榮光充滿了殿。²因耶和華的榮光充滿了耶和華殿，所以祭司不能進殿。³那火降下，耶和華的榮光在殿上的時候，以色列眾人看見，就在鋪石地俯伏叩拜，稱謝耶和華說：

"耶和華本為善，
　他的慈愛永遠長存！"

⁴王和眾民在耶和華面前獻祭。⁵所羅門王用牛二萬二千，羊十二萬獻祭。這樣，王和眾民為神的殿行奉獻之禮。⁶祭司侍立，各供其職；利未人也拿著耶和華的樂器，就是大衛王造出來，藉利未人頌讚耶和華的（他的慈愛永遠長存）。祭司在眾人面前吹號，以色列人都站立。

⁷所羅門因他所造的銅壇容不下燔祭、素祭和脂油，便將耶和華殿前院子當中分別為聖，在那裏獻燔祭和平安祭牲的脂油。

⁸那時，所羅門和以色列眾人，就是從哈馬口直到埃及小河所有的以色列人都聚集成為大會，守節七日。⁹第八日設立嚴肅會，行奉獻壇的禮七日，守節七日。¹⁰七月二十三日，王遣散眾民。他們因見耶和華向大衛和所羅門與他民以色列所施的恩惠，就都心中喜樂，各歸各家去了。

主向所羅門顯現

¹¹所羅門造成了耶和華殿和王宮，在耶和華殿和王宮凡他心中所要做的，都順順利利地做成了。¹²夜間耶和華向所羅門顯現，對他說：

The Dedication of the Temple

7 When Solomon finished praying, fire came down from heaven and consumed the burnt offering and the sacrifices, and the glory of the LORD filled the temple. ²The priests could not enter the temple of the LORD because the glory of the LORD filled it. ³When all the Israelites saw the fire coming down and the glory of the LORD above the temple, they knelt on the pavement with their faces to the ground, and they worshiped and gave thanks to the LORD, saying,

"He is good;
　his love endures forever."

⁴Then the king and all the people offered sacrifices before the LORD. ⁵And King Solomon offered a sacrifice of twenty-two thousand head of cattle and a hundred and twenty thousand sheep and goats. So the king and all the people dedicated the temple of God. ⁶The priests took their positions, as did the Levites with the LORD's musical instruments, which King David had made for praising the LORD and which were used when he gave thanks, saying, "His love endures forever." Opposite the Levites, the priests blew their trumpets, and all the Israelites were standing.

⁷Solomon consecrated the middle part of the courtyard in front of the temple of the LORD, and there he offered burnt offerings and the fat of the fellowship offerings,ᵃ because the bronze altar he had made could not hold the burnt offerings, the grain offerings and the fat portions.

⁸So Solomon observed the festival at that time for seven days, and all Israel with him—a vast assembly, people from Leboᵇ Hamath to the Wadi of Egypt. ⁹On the eighth day they held an assembly, for they had celebrated the dedication of the altar for seven days and the festival for seven days more. ¹⁰On the twenty-third day of the seventh month he sent the people to their homes, joyful and glad in heart for the good things the LORD had done for David and Solomon and for his people Israel.

The LORD Appears to Solomon

¹¹When Solomon had finished the temple of the LORD and the royal palace, and had succeeded in carrying out all he had in mind to do in the temple of the LORD and in his own palace, ¹²the LORD appeared to him at night and said:

a 7 Traditionally peace offerings　　*b 8 Or from the entrance to*

"I have heard your prayer and have chosen this place for myself as a temple for sacrifices. 13"When I shut up the heavens so that there is no rain, or command locusts to devour the land or send a plague among my people, 14if my people, who are called by my name, will humble themselves and pray and seek my face and turn from their wicked ways, then will I hear from heaven and will forgive their sin and will heal their land. 15Now my eyes will be open and my ears attentive to the prayers offered in this place. 16I have chosen and consecrated this temple so that my Name may be there forever. My eyes and my heart will always be there.

17"As for you, if you walk before me as David your father did, and do all I command, and observe my decrees and laws, 18I will establish your royal throne, as I covenanted with David your father when I said, 'You shall never fail to have a man to rule over Israel.'

19"But if you*a* turn away and forsake the decrees and commands I have given you*b* and go off to serve other gods and worship them, 20then I will uproot Israel from my land, which I have given them, and will reject this temple I have consecrated for my Name. I will make it a byword and an object of ridicule among all peoples. 21And though this temple is now so imposing, all who pass by will be appalled and say, 'Why has the LORD done such a thing to this land and to this temple?' 22People will answer, 'Because they have forsaken the LORD, the God of their fathers, who brought them out of Egypt, and have embraced other gods, worshiping and serving them—that is why he brought all this disaster on them.'"

Solomon's Other Activities

8 At the end of twenty years, during which Solomon built the temple of the LORD and his own palace, 2Solomon rebuilt the villages that Hiram*c* had given him, and settled Israelites in them. 3Solomon then went to Hamath Zobah and captured it. 4He also built up Tadmor in the desert and all the store cities he had built in Hamath. 5He rebuilt Upper Beth Horon and Lower Beth Horon as fortified cities, with walls and with gates and bars, 6as well as Baalath and all his store cities, and all

"我已聽了你的禱告，也選擇這地方作為祭祀我的殿宇。13"我若使天閉塞不下雨，或使蝗蟲吃這地的出產，或使瘟疫流行在我民中，14這稱為我名下的子民，若是自卑、禱告，尋求我的面，轉離他們的惡行，我必從天上垂聽，赦免他們的罪，醫治他們的地。15我必睜眼看、側耳聽在此處所獻的禱告。16現在我已選擇這殿，分別為聖，使我的名永在其中。我的眼、我的心也必常在那裏。

17 "你若在我面前效法你父大衞所行的，遵行我一切所吩咐你的，謹守我的律例、典章，18我就必堅固你的國位，正如我與你父大衞所立的約，說：'你的子孫必不斷人作以色列的王。'

19 "倘若你們轉去丟棄我指示你們的律例誡命，去侍奉敬拜別神，20我就必將以色列人從我賜給他們的地上拔出根來，並且我為己名所分別為聖的殿也必捨棄不顧，使他在萬民中作笑談、被譏誚。21這殿雖然甚高，將來經過的人必驚訝說：'耶和華為何向這地和這殿如此行呢？' 22人必回答說：'是因此地的人離棄耶和華他們列祖的神，就是領他們出埃及地的神，去親近別神，敬拜侍奉他，所以耶和華使這一切災禍臨到他們。'"

所羅門的其他事蹟

8 所羅門建造耶和華殿和王宮，二十年才完畢了。2以後，所羅門重新修築希蘭送給他的那些城邑，使以色列人住在那裏。3所羅門往哈馬瑣巴去，攻取了那地方。4所羅門建造曠野裏的達莫，又建造哈馬所有的積貨城，5又建造上伯和崙、下伯和崙作為保障，都有牆、有門、有閂；6又建造巴拉和所有的積貨城，並屯車輛馬兵的

---

a 19 The Hebrew is plural.　　b 19 The Hebrew is plural.
c 2 Hebrew Huram, a variant of Hiram; also in verse 18

城，與耶路撒冷、黎巴嫩以及自己治理的全國中所願意建造的。

7至於國中所剩下不屬以色列人的赫人、亞摩利人、比利洗人、希未人、耶布斯人，8就是以色列人未曾滅絕的，所羅門挑取他們的後裔作服苦的奴僕，直到今日。9惟有以色列人，所羅門不使他們當奴僕做工，乃是作他的戰士、軍長的統領、車兵長、馬兵長。10所羅門王有二百五十督工的，監管工人。

11所羅門將法老的女兒帶出大衛城，上到為她建造的宮裏。因所羅門說：「耶和華約櫃所到之處都為聖地，所以我的妻不可住在以色列王大衛的宮裏。」

12所羅門在耶和華的壇上，就是在廊子前他所築的壇上，與耶和華獻燔祭。13又遵着摩西的吩咐，在安息日、月朔，並一年三節，就是除酵節、七七節、住棚節，獻每日所當獻的祭。14所羅門照着他父大衛所定的例，派定祭司的班次，使他們各供己事；又使利未人各盡其職，讚美耶和華，在祭司面前做每日所當做的；又派守門的按着班次看守各門，因為神人大衛是這樣吩咐的。15王所吩咐眾祭司和利未人的，無論是管府庫，或辦別的事，他們都不違背。

16所羅門建造耶和華的殿，從立根基直到成功的日子，工料俱備。這樣，耶和華的殿全然完畢。

17那時，所羅門往以東地靠海的以旬迦別和以祿去。18希蘭差遣他的臣僕，將船隻和熟悉泛海的僕人，送到所羅門那裏。他們同着所羅門的僕人到了俄斐，得了四百五十他連得金子，運到所羅門王那裏。

the cities for his chariots and for his horses[a] — whatever he desired to build in Jerusalem, in Lebanon and throughout all the territory he ruled.

7All the people left from the Hittites, Amorites, Perizzites, Hivites and Jebusites (these peoples were not Israelites), 8that is, their descendants remaining in the land, whom the Israelites had not destroyed—these Solomon conscripted for his slave labor force, as it is to this day. 9But Solomon did not make slaves of the Israelites for his work; they were his fighting men, commanders of his captains, and commanders of his chariots and charioteers. 10They were also King Solomon's chief officials—two hundred and fifty officials supervising the men.

11Solomon brought Pharaoh's daughter up from the City of David to the palace he had built for her, for he said, "My wife must not live in the palace of David king of Israel, because the places the ark of the LORD has entered are holy."

12On the altar of the LORD that he had built in front of the portico, Solomon sacrificed burnt offerings to the LORD, 13according to the daily requirement for offerings commanded by Moses for Sabbaths, New Moons and the three annual feasts—the Feast of Unleavened Bread, the Feast of Weeks and the Feast of Tabernacles. 14In keeping with the ordinance of his father David, he appointed the divisions of the priests for their duties, and the Levites to lead the praise and to assist the priests according to each day's requirement. He also appointed the gatekeepers by divisions for the various gates, because this was what David the man of God had ordered. 15They did not deviate from the king's commands to the priests or to the Levites in any matter, including that of the treasuries.

16All Solomon's work was carried out, from the day the foundation of the temple of the LORD was laid until its completion. So the temple of the LORD was finished.

17Then Solomon went to Ezion Geber and Elath on the coast of Edom. 18And Hiram sent him ships commanded by his own officers, men who knew the sea. These, with Solomon's men, sailed to Ophir and brought back four hundred and fifty talents[b] of gold, which they delivered to King Solomon.

---

a 6 Or charioteers　　b 18 That is, about 17 tons (about 16 metric tons)

The Queen of Sheba Visits Solomon

9 When the queen of Sheba heard of Solomon's fame, she came to Jerusalem to test him with hard questions. Arriving with a very great caravan — with camels carrying spices, large quantities of gold, and precious stones—she came to Solomon and talked with him about all she had on her mind. [2]Solomon answered all her questions; nothing was too hard for him to explain to her. [3]When the queen of Sheba saw the wisdom of Solomon, as well as the palace he had built, [4]the food on his table, the seating of his officials, the attending servants in their robes, the cupbearers in their robes and the burnt offerings he made at[a] the temple of the LORD, she was overwhelmed.

[5]She said to the king, "The report I heard in my own country about your achievements and your wisdom is true. [6]But I did not believe what they said until I came and saw with my own eyes. Indeed, not even half the greatness of your wisdom was told me; you have far exceeded the report I heard. [7]How happy your men must be! How happy your officials, who continually stand before you and hear your wisdom! [8]Praise be to the LORD your God, who has delighted in you and placed you on his throne as king to rule for the LORD your God. Because of the love of your God for Israel and his desire to uphold them forever, he has made you king over them, to maintain justice and righteousness."

[9]Then she gave the king 120 talents[b] of gold, large quantities of spices, and precious stones. There had never been such spices as those the queen of Sheba gave to King Solomon.

[10](The men of Hiram and the men of Solomon brought gold from Ophir; they also brought algumwood[c] and precious stones. [11]The king used the algumwood to make steps for the temple of the LORD and for the royal palace, and to make harps and lyres for the musicians. Nothing like them had ever been seen in Judah.)

[12]King Solomon gave the queen of Sheba all she desired and asked for; he gave her more than she had brought to him. Then she left and returned with her retinue to her own country.

Solomon's Splendor

[13]The weight of the gold that Solomon received yearly was 666 talents,[d] [14]not including the revenues brought in by merchants and

示巴女王來見所羅門

9 示巴女王聽見所羅門的名聲，就來到耶路撒冷，要用難解的話試問所羅門。跟隨她的人甚多，又有駱駝馱着香料、寶石和許多金子。她來見了所羅門，就把心裏所有的對所羅門都說出來。[2]所羅門將她所問的都答上了，沒有一句不明白、不能答的。[3]示巴女王見所羅門的智慧和他所建造的宮室、[4]席上的珍饈美味、羣臣分列而坐、僕人兩旁侍立、以及他們的衣服裝飾、酒政和酒政的衣服裝飾、又見他上耶和華殿的臺階，就詫異得神不守舍。

[5]對王說："我在本國裏所聽見論到你的事和你的智慧，實在是真的！[6]我先不信那些話，及至我來親眼見了，才知道你的大智慧，人所告訴我的，還不到一半！你的實跡，越過我所聽見的名聲。[7]你的羣臣、你的僕人常侍立在你面前聽你智慧的話，是有福的。[8]耶和華你的神是應當稱頌的！他喜悅你，使你坐他的國位，為耶和華你的神作王。因為你的神愛以色列人，要永遠堅立他們，所以立你作他們的王，使你秉公行義。"

[9]於是，示巴女王將一百二十他連得金子和寶石，與極多的香料送給所羅門王。她送給王的香料，以後再沒有這樣的。

[10]希蘭的僕人和所羅門的僕人從俄斐運了金子來，也運了檀香木（註：或作"烏木"。下同）和寶石來。[11]王用檀香木為耶和華殿和王宮做臺，又為歌唱的人做琴瑟；猶大地從來沒有見過這樣的。

[12]所羅門王按示巴女王所帶來的還她禮物，另外照她一切所要所求的，都送給她。於是女王和她臣僕轉回本國去了。

所羅門的榮華

[13]所羅門每年所得的金子共有六百六十六他連得。[14]另外還有商人所

---

a 4 Or *the ascent by which he went up to*　　b 9 That is, about 4 1/2 tons (about 4 metric tons)　　c 10 Probably a variant of *almugwood*　　d 13 That is, about 25 tons (about 23 metric tons)

進的金子，並且阿拉伯諸王、與屬國的省長，都帶金銀給所羅門。

¹⁵所羅門王用錘出來的金子打成擋牌二百面，每面用金子六百舍客勒；¹⁶又用錘出來的金子打成盾牌三百面，每面用金子三百舍客勒，都放在黎巴嫩林宮裏。

¹⁷王用象牙製造一個大寶座，用精金包裹。¹⁸寶座有六層臺階，又有金腳凳與寶座相連。寶座兩旁有扶手，靠近扶手有兩個獅子站立。¹⁹六層臺階上有十二個獅子站立，每層有兩個：左邊一個，右邊一個；在列國中沒有這樣做的。²⁰所羅門王一切的飲器都是金的；黎巴嫩林宮裏的一切器皿都是精金的。所羅門年間，銀子算不了甚麼。²¹因為王的船隻與希蘭的僕人一同往他施去，他施船隻三年一次裝載金、銀、象牙、猿猴、孔雀回來。

²²所羅門王的財寶與智慧勝過天下的列王。²³普天下的王都求見所羅門，要聽神賜給他智慧的話。²⁴他們各帶貢物，就是金器、銀器、衣服、軍械、香料、騾馬，每年有一定之例。

²⁵所羅門有套車的馬四千棚，有馬兵一萬二千，安置在屯車的城邑和耶路撒冷，就是王那裏。²⁶所羅門統管諸王，從大河到非利士地直到埃及的邊界。²⁷王在耶路撒冷使銀子多如石頭，香柏木多如高原的桑樹。²⁸有人從埃及和各國為所羅門趕馬羣來。

所羅門壽終

²⁹所羅門其餘的事，自始至終，不都寫在先知拿單的書上和示羅人亞希雅的預言書上，並先見易多論尼八兒子耶羅波安的默示書上嗎？

traders. Also all the kings of Arabia and the governors of the land brought gold and silver to Solomon.

¹⁵King Solomon made two hundred large shields of hammered gold; six hundred bekas^a of hammered gold went into each shield. ¹⁶He also made three hundred small shields of hammered gold, with three hundred bekas^b of gold in each shield. The king put them in the Palace of the Forest of Lebanon.

¹⁷Then the king made a great throne inlaid with ivory and overlaid with pure gold. ¹⁸The throne had six steps, and a footstool of gold was attached to it. On both sides of the seat were armrests, with a lion standing beside each of them. ¹⁹Twelve lions stood on the six steps, one at either end of each step. Nothing like it had ever been made for any other kingdom. ²⁰All King Solomon's goblets were gold, and all the household articles in the Palace of the Forest of Lebanon were pure gold. Nothing was made of silver, because silver was considered of little value in Solomon's day. ²¹The king had a fleet of trading ships^c manned by Hiram's^d men. Once every three years it returned, carrying gold, silver and ivory, and apes and baboons.

²²King Solomon was greater in riches and wisdom than all the other kings of the earth. ²³All the kings of the earth sought audience with Solomon to hear the wisdom God had put in his heart. ²⁴Year after year, everyone who came brought a gift—articles of silver and gold, and robes, weapons and spices, and horses and mules.

²⁵Solomon had four thousand stalls for horses and chariots, and twelve thousand horses,^e which he kept in the chariot cities and also with him in Jerusalem. ²⁶He ruled over all the kings from the River^f to the land of the Philistines, as far as the border of Egypt. ²⁷The king made silver as common in Jerusalem as stones, and cedar as plentiful as sycamore-fig trees in the foothills. ²⁸Solomon's horses were imported from Egypt^g and from all other countries.

Solomon's Death

²⁹As for the other events of Solomon's reign, from beginning to end, are they not written in the records of Nathan the prophet, in the prophecy of Ahijah the Shilonite and in the visions of Iddo the seer concerning Jeroboam

---

a 15 That is, about 7 1/2 pounds (about 3.5 kilograms)
b 16 That is, about 3 3/4 pounds (about 1.7 kilograms)
c 21 Hebrew *of ships that could go to Tarshish*　　*d 21* Hebrew *Huram,* a variant of *Hiram*　　*e 25* Or *charioteers*　　*f 26* That is, the Euphrates　　*g 28* Or possibly *Muzur,* a region in Cilicia

son of Nebat? [30]Solomon reigned in Jerusalem over all Israel forty years. [31]Then he rested with his fathers and was buried in the city of David his father. And Rehoboam his son succeeded him as king.

Israel Rebels Against Rehoboam

10 Rehoboam went to Shechem, for all the Israelites had gone there to make him king. [2]When Jeroboam son of Nebat heard this (he was in Egypt, where he had fled from King Solomon), he returned from Egypt. [3]So they sent for Jeroboam, and he and all Israel went to Rehoboam and said to him: [4]"Your father put a heavy yoke on us, but now lighten the harsh labor and the heavy yoke he put on us, and we will serve you."

[5]Rehoboam answered, "Come back to me in three days." So the people went away.

[6]Then King Rehoboam consulted the elders who had served his father Solomon during his lifetime. "How would you advise me to answer these people?" he asked.

[7]They replied, "If you will be kind to these people and please them and give them a favorable answer, they will always be your servants."

[8]But Rehoboam rejected the advice the elders gave him and consulted the young men who had grown up with him and were serving him. [9]He asked them, "What is your advice? How should we answer these people who say to me, 'Lighten the yoke your father put on us'?"

[10]The young men who had grown up with him replied, "Tell the people who have said to you, 'Your father put a heavy yoke on us, but make our yoke lighter'—tell them, 'My little finger is thicker than my father's waist. [11]My father laid on you a heavy yoke; I will make it even heavier. My father scourged you with whips; I will scourge you with scorpions.' "

[12]Three days later Jeroboam and all the people returned to Rehoboam, as the king had said, "Come back to me in three days." [13]The king answered them harshly. Rejecting the advice of the elders, [14]he followed the advice of the young men and said, "My father made your yoke heavy; I will make it even heavier. My father scourged you with whips; I will scourge you with scorpions." [15]So the king did not listen to the people, for this turn of events was from God, to fulfill the word the LORD had spoken to Jeroboam son of Nebat through Ahijah the Shilonite.

[16]When all Israel saw that the king refused to listen to them, they answered the king:

[30]所羅門在耶路撒冷作以色列眾人的王共四十年。[31]所羅門與他列祖同睡，葬在他父大衛城裏。他兒子羅波安接續他作王。

以色列背叛羅波安

10 羅波安往示劍去，因為以色列人都到了示劍，要立他作王。[2]尼八的兒子耶羅波安先前躲避所羅門王，逃往埃及，住在那裏。他聽見這事，就從埃及回來。[3]以色列人打發人去請他。他就和以色列眾人來見羅波安，對他說：[4]"你父親使我們負重軛、做苦工。現在求你使我們做的苦工、負的重軛輕鬆些，我們就侍奉你。"

[5]羅波安對他們說："第三日再來見我吧！"民就去了。

[6]羅波安之父所羅門在世的日子，有侍立在他面前的老年人，羅波安王和他們商議，說："你們給我出個甚麼主意，我好回覆這民。"

[7]老年人對他說："王若恩待這民，使他們喜悅，用好話回覆他們，他們就永遠作王的僕人。"

[8]王卻不用老年人給他出的主意，就和那些與他一同長大、在他面前侍立的少年人商議，[9]說："這民對我說：'你父親使我們負重軛，求你使我們輕鬆些。'你們給我出個甚麼主意，我好回覆他們。"

[10]那同他長大的少年人說："這民對王說：'你父親使我們負重軛，求你使我們輕鬆些。'王要對他們如此說：'我的小拇指比我父親的腰還粗。[11]我父親使你們負重軛，我必使你們負更重的軛；我父親用鞭子責打你們，我要用蠍子鞭責打你們！'"

[12]耶羅波安和眾百姓遵着羅波安王所說"你們第三日再來見我"的那話，第三日他們果然來了。[13]羅波安王用嚴厲的話回覆他們，不用老年人所出的主意，[14]照着少年人所出的主意對他們說："我父親使你們負重軛，我必使你們負更重的軛；我父親用鞭子責打你們，我要用蠍子鞭責打你們！"[15]王不肯依從百姓，這事乃出於神，為要應驗耶和華藉示羅人亞希雅對尼八兒子耶羅波安所說的話。

[16]以色列眾民見王不依從他們，就對王說：

"我們與大衛有甚麼分兒呢？
　　與耶西的兒子並沒有關涉！
以色列人哪，各回各家去吧！
　　大衛家啊，自己顧自己吧！"

於是，以色列眾人都回自己家裏去了，¹⁷惟獨住在猶大城邑的以色列人，羅波安仍作他們的王。

¹⁸羅波安王差遣掌管服苦之人的哈多蘭往以色列人那裏去，以色列人就用石頭打死他。羅波安王急忙上車，逃回耶路撒冷去了。¹⁹這樣，以色列人背叛大衛家，直到今日。

11 羅波安來到耶路撒冷，招聚猶大家和便雅憫家，共十八萬人，都是挑選的戰士，要與以色列人爭戰，好將國奪回再歸自己。

²但耶和華的話臨到神人示瑪雅說：³ "你去告訴所羅門的兒子猶大王羅波安和住猶大、便雅憫的以色列眾人說：⁴ '耶和華如此說：你們不可上去與你們的弟兄爭戰，各歸各家去吧！因為這事出於我。'"眾人就聽從耶和華的話歸回，不去與耶羅波安爭戰。

羅波安鞏固猶大設防

⁵羅波安住在耶路撒冷，在猶大地修築城邑，⁶為保障修築伯利恆、以坦、提哥亞、⁷伯夙、梭哥、亞杜蘭、⁸迦特、瑪利沙、西弗、⁹亞多萊音、拉吉、亞西加、¹⁰瑣拉、亞雅崙、希伯崙；這都是猶大和便雅憫的堅固城。¹¹羅波安又堅固各處的保障，在其中安置軍長，又預備下糧食、油、酒。¹²他在各城裏預備盾牌和槍，且使城極其堅固。猶大和便雅憫都歸了他。

¹³以色列全地的祭司和利未人，都從四方來歸羅波安。¹⁴利未人撇下他們的郊野和產業，來到猶大與耶路撒冷，是因耶羅波安和他的兒子拒絕他們，不許他們供祭司職分侍奉耶和華。¹⁵耶羅波安為邱壇、為鬼魔（註：原文作 "公山羊"）、為自己所鑄造的牛犢設立祭司。¹⁶以色列各支派中，凡立定心意尋求耶和華以色列神的，都隨從利未人，來到耶路撒冷祭祀耶和華他們列祖的神。¹⁷這樣，就堅固猶大國，使所羅門的兒

"What share do we have in David,
　　what part in Jesse's son?
To your tents, O Israel!
　　Look after your own house, O David!"

So all the Israelites went home. ¹⁷But as for the Israelites who were living in the towns of Judah, Rehoboam still ruled over them.

¹⁸King Rehoboam sent out Adoniram,ᵃ who was in charge of forced labor, but the Israelites stoned him to death. King Rehoboam, however, managed to get into his chariot and escape to Jerusalem. ¹⁹So Israel has been in rebellion against the house of David to this day.

11 When Rehoboam arrived in Jerusalem, he mustered the house of Judah and Benjamin—a hundred and eighty thousand fighting men—to make war against Israel and to regain the kingdom for Rehoboam.

²But this word of the LORD came to Shemaiah the man of God: ³"Say to Rehoboam son of Solomon king of Judah and to all the Israelites in Judah and Benjamin, ⁴'This is what the LORD says: Do not go up to fight against your brothers. Go home, every one of you, for this is my doing.'" So they obeyed the words of the LORD and turned back from marching against Jeroboam.

Rehoboam Fortifies Judah

⁵Rehoboam lived in Jerusalem and built up towns for defense in Judah: ⁶Bethlehem, Etam, Tekoa, ⁷Beth Zur, Soco, Adullam, ⁸Gath, Mareshah, Ziph, ⁹Adoraim, Lachish, Azekah, ¹⁰Zorah, Aijalon and Hebron. These were fortified cities in Judah and Benjamin. ¹¹He strengthened their defenses and put commanders in them, with supplies of food, olive oil and wine. ¹²He put shields and spears in all the cities, and made them very strong. So Judah and Benjamin were his.

¹³The priests and Levites from all their districts throughout Israel sided with him. ¹⁴The Levites even abandoned their pasturelands and property, and came to Judah and Jerusalem because Jeroboam and his sons had rejected them as priests of the LORD. ¹⁵And he appointed his own priests for the high places and for the goat and calf idols he had made. ¹⁶Those from every tribe of Israel who set their hearts on seeking the LORD, the God of Israel, followed the Levites to Jerusalem to offer sacrifices to the LORD, the God of their fathers. ¹⁷They strengthened the kingdom of Judah and supported

a 18 Hebrew *Hadoram*, a variant of *Adoniram*

Rehoboam son of Solomon three years, walking in the ways of David and Solomon during this time.

Rehoboam's Family

[18]Rehoboam married Mahalath, who was the daughter of David's son Jerimoth and of Abihail, the daughter of Jesse's son Eliab. [19]She bore him sons: Jeush, Shemariah and Zaham. [20]Then he married Maacah daughter of Absalom, who bore him Abijah, Attai, Ziza and Shelomith. [21]Rehoboam loved Maacah daughter of Absalom more than any of his other wives and concubines. In all, he had eighteen wives and sixty concubines, twenty-eight sons and sixty daughters.

[22]Rehoboam appointed Abijah son of Maacah to be the chief prince among his brothers, in order to make him king. [23]He acted wisely, dispersing some of his sons throughout the districts of Judah and Benjamin, and to all the fortified cities. He gave them abundant provisions and took many wives for them.

Shishak Attacks Jerusalem

12 After Rehoboam's position as king was established and he had become strong, he and all Israel[a] with him abandoned the law of the LORD. [2]Because they had been unfaithful to the LORD, Shishak king of Egypt attacked Jerusalem in the fifth year of King Rehoboam. [3]With twelve hundred chariots and sixty thousand horsemen and the innumerable troops of Libyans, Sukkites and Cushites[b] that came with him from Egypt, [4]he captured the fortified cities of Judah and came as far as Jerusalem.

[5]Then the prophet Shemaiah came to Rehoboam and to the leaders of Judah who had assembled in Jerusalem for fear of Shishak, and he said to them, "This is what the LORD says, 'You have abandoned me; therefore, I now abandon you to Shishak.'"

[6]The leaders of Israel and the king humbled themselves and said, "The LORD is just."

[7]When the LORD saw that they humbled themselves, this word of the LORD came to Shemaiah: "Since they have humbled themselves, I will not destroy them but will soon give them deliverance. My wrath will not be poured out on Jerusalem through Shishak. [8]They will, however, become subject to him, so that they may learn the difference between serving me and serving the kings of other lands."

子羅波安強盛三年，因為他們三年遵行大衛和所羅門的道。

羅波安之家室

[18]羅波安娶大衛兒子耶利摩的女兒瑪哈拉為妻，又娶耶西兒子以利押的女兒亞比孩為妻，[19]從她生了幾個兒子，就是耶烏施、示瑪利雅、撒罕。[20]後來又娶押沙龍的女兒瑪迦（註：13章2節作"烏列的女兒米該雅"），從她生了亞比雅、亞太、細撒、示羅密。[21]羅波安娶十八個妻，立六十個妾，生二十八個兒子，六十個女兒。他卻愛押沙龍的女兒瑪迦，比愛別的妻妾更甚。

[22]羅波安立瑪迦的兒子亞比雅作太子，在他弟兄中為首，因為想要立他接續作王。[23]羅波安辦事精明，使他眾子分散在猶大和便雅憫全地各堅固城裏，又賜他們許多糧食，為他們多尋妻子。

示撒攻打耶路撒冷

12 羅波安的國堅立，他強盛的時候，就離棄耶和華的律法，以色列人也都隨從他。[2]羅波安王第五年，埃及王示撒上來攻打耶路撒冷，因為王和民得罪了耶和華。[3]示撒帶戰車一千二百輛，馬兵六萬，並且跟從他出埃及的路比人、蘇基人和古實人，多得不可勝數。[4]他攻取了猶大的堅固城，就來到耶路撒冷。

[5]那時，猶大的首領因為示撒就聚集在耶路撒冷。有先知示瑪雅去見羅波安和眾首領，對他們説："耶和華如此説：'你們離棄了我，所以我使你們落在示撒手裏'"

[6]於是，王和以色列的眾首領都自卑説："耶和華是公義的！"

[7]耶和華見他們自卑，耶和華的話就臨到示瑪雅説："他們既自卑，我必不滅絕他們；必使他們略得拯救，我不藉着示撒的手，將我的怒氣倒在耶路撒冷。[8]然而他們必作示撒的僕人，好叫他們知道，服侍我與服侍外邦人有何分別。"

---

a 1 That is, Judah, as frequently in 2 Chronicles   b 3 That is, people from the upper Nile region

9於是，埃及王示撒上來攻取耶路撒冷，奪了耶和華殿和王宮裏的寶物，盡都帶走；又奪去所羅門製造的金盾牌。10羅波安王製造銅盾牌代替那金盾牌，交給守王宮門的護衛長看守。11王每逢進耶和華的殿，護衛兵就拿這盾牌，隨後仍將盾牌送回，放在護衛房。

12王自卑的時候，耶和華的怒氣就轉消了，不將他滅盡，並且在猶大中間也有善益的事。

13羅波安王自強，在耶路撒冷作王，他登基的時候年四十一歲，在耶路撒冷，就是耶和華從以色列眾支派中所選擇立他名的城，作王十七年。羅波安的母親名叫拿瑪，是亞捫人。14羅波安行惡，因他不立定心意尋求耶和華。

15羅波安所行的事，自始至終不都寫在先知示瑪雅和先見易多的史記上嗎？羅波安與耶羅波安時常爭戰。16羅波安與他列祖同睡，葬在大衛城裏。他兒子亞比雅接續他作王。

亞比雅作猶大王

13 耶羅波安王十八年，亞比雅登基作猶大王，2在耶路撒冷作王三年。他母親名叫米該亞（註：「米該亞」又作「瑪迦」），是基比亞人烏列的女兒。

亞比雅常與耶羅波安爭戰。3有一次，亞比雅率領挑選的兵四十萬擺陣，都是勇敢的戰士；耶羅波安也挑選大能的勇士八十萬，對亞比雅擺陣。

4亞比雅站在以法蓮山地中的洗瑪臉山上，說：「耶羅波安和以色列眾人哪，要聽我說！5耶和華以色列的神曾立鹽約（註：「鹽」即「不廢壞」的意思），將以色列國永遠賜給大衛和他的子孫，你們不知道嗎？6無奈大衛兒子所羅門的臣僕、尼八兒子耶羅波安起來背叛他的主人。7有

9When Shishak king of Egypt attacked Jerusalem, he carried off the treasures of the temple of the LORD and the treasures of the royal palace. He took everything, including the gold shields Solomon had made. 10So King Rehoboam made bronze shields to replace them and assigned these to the commanders of the guard on duty at the entrance to the royal palace. 11Whenever the king went to the LORD's temple, the guards went with him, bearing the shields, and afterward they returned them to the guardroom.

12Because Rehoboam humbled himself, the LORD's anger turned from him, and he was not totally destroyed. Indeed, there was some good in Judah.

13King Rehoboam established himself firmly in Jerusalem and continued as king. He was forty-one years old when he became king, and he reigned seventeen years in Jerusalem, the city the LORD had chosen out of all the tribes of Israel in which to put his Name. His mother's name was Naamah; she was an Ammonite. 14He did evil because he had not set his heart on seeking the LORD.

15As for the events of Rehoboam's reign, from beginning to end, are they not written in the records of Shemaiah the prophet and of Iddo the seer that deal with genealogies? There was continual warfare between Rehoboam and Jeroboam. 16Rehoboam rested with his fathers and was buried in the City of David. And Abijah his son succeeded him as king.

Abijah King of Judah

13 In the eighteenth year of the reign of Jeroboam, Abijah became king of Judah, 2and he reigned in Jerusalem three years. His mother's name was Maacah,[a] a daughter[b] of Uriel of Gibeah.

There was war between Abijah and Jeroboam. 3Abijah went into battle with a force of four hundred thousand able fighting men, and Jeroboam drew up a battle line against him with eight hundred thousand able troops.

4Abijah stood on Mount Zemaraim, in the hill country of Ephraim, and said, "Jeroboam and all Israel, listen to me! 5Don't you know that the LORD, the God of Israel, has given the kingship of Israel to David and his descendants forever by a covenant of salt? 6Yet Jeroboam son of Nebat, an official of Solomon son of David, rebelled against his master. 7Some worthless scoundrels

a 2 Most Septuagint manuscripts and Syriac (see also 2 Chron. 11:20 and 1 Kings 15:2); Hebrew Micaiah
b 2 Or granddaughter

gathered around him and opposed Rehoboam son of Solomon when he was young and indecisive and not strong enough to resist them.

⁸"And now you plan to resist the kingdom of the LORD, which is in the hands of David's descendants. You are indeed a vast army and have with you the golden calves that Jeroboam made to be your gods. ⁹But didn't you drive out the priests of the LORD, the sons of Aaron, and the Levites, and make priests of your own as the peoples of other lands do? Whoever comes to consecrate himself with a young bull and seven rams may become a priest of what are not gods.

¹⁰"As for us, the LORD is our God, and we have not forsaken him. The priests who serve the LORD are sons of Aaron, and the Levites assist them. ¹¹Every morning and evening they present burnt offerings and fragrant incense to the LORD. They set out the bread on the ceremonially clean table and light the lamps on the gold lampstand every evening. We are observing the requirements of the LORD our God. But you have forsaken him. ¹²God is with us; he is our leader. His priests with their trumpets will sound the battle cry against you. Men of Israel, do not fight against the LORD, the God of your fathers, for you will not succeed."

¹³Now Jeroboam had sent troops around to the rear, so that while he was in front of Judah the ambush was behind them. ¹⁴Judah turned and saw that they were being attacked at both front and rear. Then they cried out to the LORD. The priests blew their trumpets ¹⁵and the men of Judah raised the battle cry. At the sound of their battle cry, God routed Jeroboam and all Israel before Abijah and Judah. ¹⁶The Israelites fled before Judah, and God delivered them into their hands. ¹⁷Abijah and his men inflicted heavy losses on them, so that there were five hundred thousand casualties among Israel's able men. ¹⁸The men of Israel were subdued on that occasion, and the men of Judah were victorious because they relied on the LORD, the God of their fathers.

¹⁹Abijah pursued Jeroboam and took from him the towns of Bethel, Jeshanah and Ephron, with their surrounding villages. ²⁰Jeroboam did not regain power during the time of Abijah. And the LORD struck him down and he died.

²¹But Abijah grew in strength. He married fourteen wives and had twenty-two sons and sixteen daughters.

²²The other events of Abijah's reign, what he did and what he said, are written in the annotations of the prophet Iddo.

些無賴的匪徒聚集跟從他，逞強攻擊所羅門的兒子羅波安；那時羅波安還幼弱，不能抵擋他們。

⁸"現在你們有意抗拒大衞子孫手下所治耶和華的國，你們的人也甚多，你們那裏又有耶羅波安為你們所造當作神的金牛犢。⁹你們不是驅逐耶和華的祭司亞倫的後裔和利未人嗎？不是照着外邦人的惡俗為自己立祭司嗎？無論何人牽一隻公牛犢、七隻公綿羊，將自己分別出來，就可作虛無之神的祭司。

¹⁰"至於我們，耶和華是我們的神！我們並沒有離棄他。我們有侍奉耶和華的祭司，都是亞倫的後裔，並有利未人各盡其職。¹¹每日早晚向耶和華獻燔祭，燒美香，又在精金的桌子上擺陳設餅；又有金燈臺和燈盞，每晚點起，因為我們遵守耶和華我們神的命，惟有你們離棄了他。¹²率領我們的是神，我們這裏也有神的祭司拿號向你們吹出大聲。以色列人哪！不要與耶和華你們列祖的神爭戰，因你們必不能亨通。"

¹³耶羅波安卻在猶大人的後頭設伏兵。這樣，以色列人在猶大人的前頭，伏兵在猶大人的後頭。¹⁴猶大人回頭觀看，見前後都有敵兵，就呼求耶和華，祭司也吹號。¹⁵於是猶大人吶喊；猶大人吶喊的時候，神就使耶羅波安和以色列眾人敗在亞比雅與猶大人面前。¹⁶以色列人在猶大人面前逃跑，神將他們交在猶大人手裏。¹⁷亞比雅和他的軍兵大大殺戮以色列人。以色列人仆倒死亡的精兵有五十萬。¹⁸那時，以色列人被制伏了，猶大人得勝，是因倚靠耶和華他們列祖的神。

¹⁹亞比雅追趕耶羅波安，攻取了他的幾座城，就是伯特利和屬伯特利的鎮市，耶沙拿和屬耶沙拿的鎮市，以法拉音（註：或作"以弗倫"）和屬以法拉音的鎮市。²⁰亞比雅在世的時候，耶羅波安不能再強盛，耶和華攻擊他，他就死了。

²¹亞比雅卻漸漸強盛，娶妻妾十四個，生了二十二個兒子，十六個女兒。

²²亞比雅其餘的事和他的言行，都寫在先知易多的傳上。

14

亞比雅與他列祖同睡，葬在大衛城裏。他兒子亞撒接續他作王。亞撒年間，國中太平十年。

亞撒作猶大王

2 亞撒行耶和華他神眼中看為善為正的事，3 除掉外邦神的壇和邱壇，打碎柱像，砍下木偶，4 吩咐猶大人尋求耶和華他們列祖的神，遵行他的律法、誡命；5 又在猶大各城邑除掉邱壇和日像，那時國享太平；6 又在猶大建造了幾座堅固城，國中太平數年，沒有戰爭。因為耶和華賜他平安。

7 他對猶大人說：“我們要建造這些城邑，四圍築牆、蓋樓、安門、做閂；地還屬我們，是因尋求耶和華我們的神。我們既尋求他，他就賜我們四境平安。”於是建造城邑，諸事亨通。

8 亞撒的軍兵，出自猶大拿盾牌拿槍的三十萬人；出自便雅憫拿盾牌拉弓的二十八萬人。這都是大能的勇士。

9 有古實王謝拉率領軍兵一百萬，戰車三百輛，出來攻擊猶大人，到了瑪利沙。10 於是亞撒出去與他迎敵，就在瑪利沙的洗法谷彼此擺陣。

11 亞撒呼求耶和華他的神，說：“耶和華啊，惟有你能幫助軟弱的，勝過強盛的。耶和華我們的神啊，求你幫助我們！因為我們仰賴你，奉你的名來攻擊這大軍。耶和華啊，你是我們的神，不要容人勝過你。”

12 於是，耶和華使古實人敗在亞撒和猶大人面前；古實人就逃跑了。13 亞撒和跟隨他的軍兵追趕他們，直到基拉耳。古實人被殺的甚多，不能再強盛，因為敗在耶和華與他軍兵面前。猶大人就奪了許多財物，14 又打破基拉耳四圍的城邑。耶和華使其中的人都甚恐懼。猶大人又將所有的城擄掠一空，因其中

14

And Abijah rested with his fathers and was buried in the City of David. Asa his son succeeded him as king, and in his days the country was at peace for ten years.

Asa King of Judah

2 Asa did what was good and right in the eyes of the LORD his God. 3 He removed the foreign altars and the high places, smashed the sacred stones and cut down the Asherah poles.[a] 4 He commanded Judah to seek the LORD, the God of their fathers, and to obey his laws and commands. 5 He removed the high places and incense altars in every town in Judah, and the kingdom was at peace under him. 6 He built up the fortified cities of Judah, since the land was at peace. No one was at war with him during those years, for the LORD gave him rest.

7 "Let us build up these towns," he said to Judah, "and put walls around them, with towers, gates and bars. The land is still ours, because we have sought the LORD our God; we sought him and he has given us rest on every side." So they built and prospered.

8 Asa had an army of three hundred thousand men from Judah, equipped with large shields and with spears, and two hundred and eighty thousand from Benjamin, armed with small shields and with bows. All these were brave fighting men.

9 Zerah the Cushite marched out against them with a vast army[b] and three hundred chariots, and came as far as Mareshah. 10 Asa went out to meet him, and they took up battle positions in the Valley of Zephathah near Mareshah.

11 Then Asa called to the LORD his God and said, "LORD, there is no one like you to help the powerless against the mighty. Help us, O LORD our God, for we rely on you, and in your name we have come against this vast army. O LORD, you are our God; do not let man prevail against you."

12 The LORD struck down the Cushites before Asa and Judah. The Cushites fled, 13 and Asa and his army pursued them as far as Gerar. Such a great number of Cushites fell that they could not recover; they were crushed before the LORD and his forces. The men of Judah carried off a large amount of plunder. 14 They destroyed all the villages around Gerar, for the terror of the LORD had fallen upon them. They plundered all these villages, since there was much booty

---

a 3 That is, symbols of the goddess Asherah; here and elsewhere in 2 Chronicles　b 9 Hebrew with an army of a thousand thousands or with an army of thousands upon thousands

there. ¹⁵They also attacked the camps of the herdsmen and carried off droves of sheep and goats and camels. Then they returned to Jerusalem.

Asa's Reform

15 The Spirit of God came upon Azariah son of Oded. ²He went out to meet Asa and said to him, "Listen to me, Asa and all Judah and Benjamin. The LORD is with you when you are with him. If you seek him, he will be found by you, but if you forsake him, he will forsake you. ³For a long time Israel was without the true God, without a priest to teach and without the law. ⁴But in their distress they turned to the LORD, the God of Israel, and sought him, and he was found by them. ⁵In those days it was not safe to travel about, for all the inhabitants of the lands were in great turmoil. ⁶One nation was being crushed by another and one city by another, because God was troubling them with every kind of distress. ⁷But as for you, be strong and do not give up, for your work will be rewarded."

⁸When Asa heard these words and the prophecy of Azariah son of*a* Oded the prophet, he took courage. He removed the detestable idols from the whole land of Judah and Benjamin and from the towns he had captured in the hills of Ephraim. He repaired the altar of the LORD that was in front of the portico of the LORD's temple.

⁹Then he assembled all Judah and Benjamin and the people from Ephraim, Manasseh and Simeon who had settled among them, for large numbers had come over to him from Israel when they saw that the LORD his God was with him.

¹⁰They assembled at Jerusalem in the third month of the fifteenth year of Asa's reign. ¹¹At that time they sacrificed to the LORD seven hundred head of cattle and seven thousand sheep and goats from the plunder they had brought back. ¹²They entered into a covenant to seek the LORD, the God of their fathers, with all their heart and soul. ¹³All who would not seek the LORD, the God of Israel, were to be put to death, whether small or great, man or woman. ¹⁴They took an oath to the LORD with loud acclamation, with shouting and with trumpets and horns. ¹⁵All Judah rejoiced about the oath because they had sworn it wholeheartedly. They sought God eagerly, and he was found by them. So the LORD gave them rest on every side.

---

a 8 Vulgate and Syriac (see also Septuagint and verse 1); Hebrew does not have *Azariah son of.*

的財物甚多；¹⁵又毀壞了羣畜的圈，奪取許多的羊和駱駝，就回耶路撒冷去了。

亞撒的革新

15 神的靈感動俄德的兒子亞撒利雅。²他出來迎接亞撒，對他說："亞撒和猶大、便雅憫眾人哪，要聽我說！你們若順從耶和華，耶和華必與你們同在；你們若尋求他，就必尋見；你們若離棄他，他必離棄你們。³以色列人不信真神，沒有訓誨的祭司，也沒有律法，已經好久了。⁴但他們在急難的時候，歸向耶和華以色列的神，尋求他，他就被他們尋見。⁵那時出入的人，不得平安；列國的居民，都遭大亂。⁶這國攻擊那國，這城攻擊那城，互相破壞，因為神用各樣災難擾亂他們。⁷現在你們要剛強，不要手軟，因你們所行的，必得賞賜。"

⁸亞撒聽見這話和俄德兒子先知亞撒利雅的預言，就壯起膽來，在猶大、便雅憫全地，並以法蓮山地所奪的各城，將可憎之物盡都除掉；又在耶和華殿的廊前，重新修築耶和華的壇。

⁹又招聚猶大、便雅憫的眾人，並他們中間寄居的以法蓮人、瑪拿西人、西緬人。有許多以色列人歸降亞撒，因見耶和華他的神與他同在。

¹⁰亞撒十五年三月，他們都聚集在耶路撒冷。¹¹當日他們從所取的擄物中，將牛七百隻、羊七千隻獻給耶和華。¹²他們就立約，要盡心盡性地尋求耶和華他們列祖的神；¹³凡不尋求耶和華以色列神的，無論大小、男女，必被治死。¹⁴他們就大聲歡呼，吹號、吹角，向耶和華起誓。¹⁵猶大眾人為所起的誓歡喜。因他們是盡心起誓，盡意尋求耶和華，耶和華就被他們尋見，且賜他們四境平安。

16亞撒王貶了他祖母瑪迦太后的位，因她造了可憎的偶像亞舍拉。亞撒砍下她的偶像，搗得粉碎，燒在汲淪溪邊。17只是邱壇還沒有從以色列中廢去，然而亞撒的心一生誠實。18亞撒將他父所分別為聖、與自己所分別為聖的金銀和器皿都奉到神的殿裏。

19從這時直到亞撒三十五年，都沒有爭戰的事。

亞撒的晚年

16 亞撒三十六年，以色列王巴沙上來攻擊猶大，修築拉瑪，不許人從猶大王亞撒那裏出入。

2於是亞撒從耶和華殿和王宮的府庫裏拿出金銀來，送與住大馬士革的亞蘭王便哈達，說：3"你父曾與我父立約，我與你也要立約。現在我將金銀送給你，求你廢掉你與以色列王巴沙所立的約，使他離開我。"

4便哈達聽從亞撒王的話，派軍長去攻擊以色列的城邑，他們就攻破以雲、但、亞伯瑪音和拿弗他利一切的積貨城。5巴沙聽見就停工，不修築拉瑪了。6於是，亞撒王率領猶大眾人，將巴沙修築拉瑪所用的石頭、木頭都運去，用以修築迦巴和米斯巴。

7那時，先見哈拿尼來見猶大王亞撒，對他說："因你仰賴亞蘭王，沒有仰賴耶和華你的神，所以亞蘭王的軍兵脫離了你的手。8古實人、路比人的軍隊不是甚大嗎？戰車馬兵不是極多嗎？只因你仰賴耶和華，他便將他們交在你手裏。9耶和華的眼目遍察全地，要顯大能幫助向他心存誠實的人。你這事行得愚昧，此後，你必有爭戰的事。"

10亞撒因此惱恨先見，將他囚在監裏。那時，亞撒也虐待一些人民。

16King Asa also deposed his grandmother Maacah from her position as queen mother, because she had made a repulsive Asherah pole. Asa cut the pole down, broke it up and burned it in the Kidron Valley. 17Although he did not remove the high places from Israel, Asa's heart was fully committed ⌊to the LORD⌋ all his life. 18He brought into the temple of God the silver and gold and the articles that he and his father had dedicated.

19There was no more war until the thirty-fifth year of Asa's reign.

Asa's Last Years

16 In the thirty-sixth year of Asa's reign Baasha king of Israel went up against Judah and fortified Ramah to prevent anyone from leaving or entering the territory of Asa king of Judah.

2Asa then took the silver and gold out of the treasuries of the LORD's temple and of his own palace and sent it to Ben-Hadad king of Aram, who was ruling in Damascus. 3"Let there be a treaty between me and you," he said, "as there was between my father and your father. See, I am sending you silver and gold. Now break your treaty with Baasha king of Israel so he will withdraw from me."

4Ben-Hadad agreed with King Asa and sent the commanders of his forces against the towns of Israel. They conquered Ijon, Dan, Abel Maim[a] and all the store cities of Naphtali. 5When Baasha heard this, he stopped building Ramah and abandoned his work. 6Then King Asa brought all the men of Judah, and they carried away from Ramah the stones and timber Baasha had been using. With them he built up Geba and Mizpah.

7At that time Hanani the seer came to Asa king of Judah and said to him: "Because you relied on the king of Aram and not on the LORD your God, the army of the king of Aram has escaped from your hand. 8Were not the Cushites[b] and Libyans a mighty army with great numbers of chariots and horsemen[c]? Yet when you relied on the LORD, he delivered them into your hand. 9For the eyes of the LORD range throughout the earth to strengthen those whose hearts are fully committed to him. You have done a foolish thing, and from now on you will be at war."

10Asa was angry with the seer because of this; he was so enraged that he put him in prison. At the same time Asa brutally oppressed some of the people.

---

a 4 Also known as *Abel Beth Maacah*　　b 8 That is, people from the upper Nile region　　c 8 Or *charioteers*

11The events of Asa's reign, from beginning to end, are written in the book of the kings of Judah and Israel. 12In the thirty-ninth year of his reign Asa was afflicted with a disease in his feet. Though his disease was severe, even in his illness he did not seek help from the LORD, but only from the physicians. 13Then in the forty-first year of his reign Asa died and rested with his fathers. 14They buried him in the tomb that he had cut out for himself in the City of David. They laid him on a bier covered with spices and various blended perfumes, and they made a huge fire in his honor.

Jehoshaphat King of Judah

17 Jehoshaphat his son succeeded him as king and strengthened himself against Israel. 2He stationed troops in all the fortified cities of Judah and put garrisons in Judah and in the towns of Ephraim that his father Asa had captured.

3The LORD was with Jehoshaphat because in his early years he walked in the ways his father David had followed. He did not consult the Baals 4but sought the God of his father and followed his commands rather than the practices of Israel. 5The LORD established the kingdom under his control; and all Judah brought gifts to Jehoshaphat, so that he had great wealth and honor. 6His heart was devoted to the ways of the LORD; furthermore, he removed the high places and the Asherah poles from Judah.

7In the third year of his reign he sent his officials Ben-Hail, Obadiah, Zechariah, Nethanel and Micaiah to teach in the towns of Judah. 8With them were certain Levites—Shemaiah, Nethaniah, Zebadiah, Asahel, Shemiramoth, Jehonathan, Adonijah, Tobijah and Tob-Adonijah—and the priests Elishama and Jehoram. 9They taught throughout Judah, taking with them the Book of the Law of the LORD; they went around to all the towns of Judah and taught the people.

10The fear of the LORD fell on all the kingdoms of the lands surrounding Judah, so that they did not make war with Jehoshaphat. 11Some Philistines brought Jehoshaphat gifts and silver as tribute, and the Arabs brought him flocks: seven thousand seven hundred rams and seven thousand seven hundred goats.

12Jehoshaphat became more and more powerful; he built forts and store cities in Judah 13and had large supplies in the towns of Judah. He also kept experienced fighting men in Jerusalem. 14Their enrollment by families was as follows:

11亞撒所行的事，自始至終都寫在猶大和以色列諸王記上。12亞撒作王三十九年，他腳上有病，而且甚重。病的時候沒有求耶和華，只求醫生。13他作王四十一年而死，與他列祖同睡，14葬在大衛城自己所鑿的墳墓裏，放在牀上，其牀堆滿各樣馨香的香料，就是按做香的作法調和的香料；又為他燒了許多的物件。

約沙法作猶大王

17 亞撒的兒子約沙法接續他作王，奮勇自強，防備以色列人。2安置軍兵在猶大一切堅固城裏，又安置防兵在猶大地和他父亞撒所得以法蓮的城邑中。

3耶和華與約沙法同在，因為他行他祖大衛初行的道，不尋求巴力，4只尋求他父親的神，遵行他的誡命，不效法以色列人的行為。5所以耶和華堅定他的國，猶大眾人給他進貢；約沙法大有尊榮貲財。6他高興遵行耶和華的道，並且從猶大除掉一切邱壇和木偶。

7他作王第三年，就差遣臣子便亥伊勒、俄巴底、撒迦利雅、拿坦業、米該亞往猶大各城去教訓百姓。8同着他們有利未人示瑪雅、尼探雅、西巴第雅、亞撒黑、示米拉末、約拿單、亞多尼雅、多比雅、駝巴多尼雅，又有祭司以利沙瑪、約蘭同着他們。9他們帶着耶和華的律法書，走遍猶大各城教訓百姓。

10耶和華使猶大四圍的列國都甚恐懼，不敢與約沙法爭戰。11有些非利士人與約沙法送禮物、納貢銀。阿拉伯人也送他公綿羊七千七百隻，公山羊七千七百隻。

12約沙法日漸強大，在猶大建造營寨和積貨城。13他在猶大城邑中有許多工程。又在耶路撒冷有戰士，就是大能的勇士。14他們的數目，按着宗族記在下面：

猶大族的千夫長押拿為首，
　率領大能的勇士三十萬；

15其次是千夫長約哈難，率領大
　能的勇士二十八萬；
16其次是細基利的兒子亞瑪斯
　雅，他為耶和華犧牲自己，
　率領大能的勇士二十萬；
17便雅憫族：
　是大能的勇士以利雅大，率領
　拿弓箭和盾牌的二十萬；
18其次是約薩拔，率領預備打仗
　的十八萬。

19這都是伺候王的，還有王在猶大全
地堅固城所安置的不在其內。

米該雅預言警告亞哈

18 約沙法大有尊榮資財，就與
亞哈結親。2過了幾年，他下
到撒馬利亞去見亞哈。亞哈
為他和跟從他的人宰了許多牛羊，
勸他與自己同去攻取基列的拉末。
3以色列王亞哈問猶大王約沙法說：
"你肯同我去攻取基列的拉末
嗎？"

他回答說："你我不分彼此，
我的民與你的民一樣，必與你同去
爭戰。"4約沙法對以色列王說：
"請你先求問耶和華。"

5於是，以色列王招聚先知四百
人，問他們說："我們上去攻取基
列的拉末可以不可以？"

他們說："可以上去。因為神
必將那城交在王的手裏。"

6約沙法說："這裏不是還有耶
和華的先知，我們可以求問他
嗎？"

7以色列王對約沙法說："還有
一個人，是音拉的兒子米該雅，我
們可以託他求問耶和華。只是我恨
他，因為他指著我所說的預言，不
說吉語，常說凶言。"

約沙法說："王不必這樣說。"

8以色列王就召了一個太監來，
說："你快去將音拉的兒子米該雅
召來。"

9以色列王和猶大王約沙法在撒
馬利亞城門前的空場上，各穿朝服
坐在位上。所有的先知都在他們面
前說預言。10基拿拿的兒子西底家造

From Judah, commanders of units of 1,000:
　Adnah the commander, with 300,000
　fighting men;
15next, Jehohanan the commander, with
　280,000;
16next, Amasiah son of Zicri, who volun-
　teered himself for the service of the
　LORD, with 200,000.
17From Benjamin:
　Eliada, a valiant soldier, with 200,000 men
　armed with bows and shields;
18next, Jehozabad, with 180,000 men armed
　for battle.

19These were the men who served the king,
besides those he stationed in the fortified cities
throughout Judah.

Micaiah Prophesies Against Ahab

18 Now Jehoshaphat had great wealth and
honor, and he allied himself with Ahab
by marriage. 2Some years later he went
down to visit Ahab in Samaria. Ahab slaughtered many sheep and cattle for him and the people with him and urged him to attack Ramoth
Gilead. 3Ahab king of Israel asked Jehoshaphat
king of Judah, "Will you go with me against
Ramoth Gilead?"

Jehoshaphat replied, "I am as you are, and my
people as your people; we will join you in the
war." 4But Jehoshaphat also said to the king of
Israel, "First seek the counsel of the LORD."

5So the king of Israel brought together the
prophets—four hundred men—and asked them,
"Shall we go to war against Ramoth Gilead, or
shall I refrain?"

"Go," they answered, "for God will give it
into the king's hand."

6But Jehoshaphat asked, "Is there not a
prophet of the LORD here whom we can inquire
of?"

7The king of Israel answered Jehoshaphat,
"There is still one man through whom we can
inquire of the LORD, but I hate him because he
never prophesies anything good about me, but
always bad. He is Micaiah son of Imlah."

"The king should not say that," Jehoshaphat
replied.

8So the king of Israel called one of his officials
and said, "Bring Micaiah son of Imlah at once."

9Dressed in their royal robes, the king of
Israel and Jehoshaphat king of Judah were sitting on their thrones at the threshing floor by
the entrance to the gate of Samaria, with all the
prophets prophesying before them. 10Now
Zedekiah son of Kenaanah had made iron horns,

and he declared, "This is what the LORD says: 'With these you will gore the Arameans until they are destroyed.' "

¹¹All the other prophets were prophesying the same thing. "Attack Ramoth Gilead and be victorious," they said, "for the LORD will give it into the king's hand."

¹²The messenger who had gone to summon Micaiah said to him, "Look, as one man the other prophets are predicting success for the king. Let your word agree with theirs, and speak favorably."

¹³But Micaiah said, "As surely as the LORD lives, I can tell him only what my God says."

¹⁴When he arrived, the king asked him, "Micaiah, shall we go to war against Ramoth Gilead, or shall I refrain?"

"Attack and be victorious," he answered, "for they will be given into your hand."

¹⁵The king said to him, "How many times must I make you swear to tell me nothing but the truth in the name of the LORD?"

¹⁶Then Micaiah answered, "I saw all Israel scattered on the hills like sheep without a shepherd, and the LORD said, 'These people have no master. Let each one go home in peace.' "

¹⁷The king of Israel said to Jehoshaphat, "Didn't I tell you that he never prophesies anything good about me, but only bad?"

¹⁸Micaiah continued, "Therefore hear the word of the LORD: I saw the LORD sitting on his throne with all the host of heaven standing on his right and on his left. ¹⁹And the LORD said, 'Who will entice Ahab king of Israel into attacking Ramoth Gilead and going to his death there?'

"One suggested this, and another that. ²⁰Finally, a spirit came forward, stood before the LORD and said, 'I will entice him.'

" 'By what means?' the LORD asked.

²¹" 'I will go and be a lying spirit in the mouths of all his prophets,' he said.

" 'You will succeed in enticing him,' said the LORD. 'Go and do it.'

²²"So now the LORD has put a lying spirit in the mouths of these prophets of yours. The LORD has decreed disaster for you."

²³Then Zedekiah son of Kenaanah went up and slapped Micaiah in the face. "Which way did the spirit from*ᵃ* the LORD go when he went from me to speak to you?" he asked.

²⁴Micaiah replied, "You will find out on the day you go to hide in an inner room."

a 23 Or Spirit of

了兩個鐵角，說："耶和華如此說：'你要用這角牴觸亞蘭人，直到將他們滅盡。'"

¹¹所有的先知也都這樣預言，說："可以上基列的拉末去，必然得勝，因為耶和華必將那城交在王的手中。"

¹²那去召米該雅的使者對米該雅說："眾先知一口同音地都向王說吉言，你不如與他們說一樣的話，也說吉言。"

¹³米該雅說："我指着永生的耶和華起誓，我的神說甚麼，我就說甚麼！"

¹⁴米該雅到王面前，王問他說："米該雅啊，我們上去攻取基列的拉末可以不可以？"

他說："可以上去，必然得勝，敵人必交在你們手裏。"

¹⁵王對他說："我當囑咐你幾次，你才奉耶和華的名向我說實話呢？"

¹⁶米該雅說："我看見以色列眾民散在山上，如同沒有牧人的羊羣一般。耶和華說：'這民沒有主人，他們可以平平安安地各歸各家去。'"

¹⁷以色列王對約沙法說："我豈沒有告訴你，這人指着我所說的預言，不說吉語，單說凶言嗎？"

¹⁸米該雅說："你們要聽耶和華的話。我看見耶和華坐在寶座上，天上的萬軍侍立在他左右。¹⁹耶和華說：'誰去引誘以色列王亞哈上基列的拉末去陣亡呢？'

"這個就這樣說，那個就那樣說。²⁰隨後有一個神靈出來，站在耶和華面前說：'我去引誘他！'

"耶和華問他說：'你用何法呢？'

²¹"他說：'我去，要在他眾先知口中作謊言的靈。'

"耶和華說：'這樣，你必能引誘他，你去如此行吧！'

²²"現在耶和華使謊言的靈，入了你這些先知的口，並且耶和華已經命定降禍與你。"

²³基拿拿的兒子西底家前來打米該雅的臉，說："耶和華的靈從哪裏離開我與你說話呢？"

²⁴米該雅說："你進嚴密的屋子藏躲的那日，就必看見了。"

25以色列王說："將米該雅帶回，交給邑宰亞們和王的兒子約阿施，說：26'王如此說：把這個人下在監裏，使他受苦，吃不飽、喝不足，等候我平平安安地回來。'"

27米該雅說："你若能平安回來，那就是耶和華沒有藉我說這話了。"又說："眾民哪，你們都要聽！"

亞哈在基列的拉末陣亡

28以色列王和猶大王約沙法上基列的拉末去了。29以色列王對約沙法說："我要改裝上陣，你可以仍穿王服。"於是以色列王改裝，他們就上陣去了。

30先是亞蘭王吩咐車兵長說："他們的兵將，無論大小，你們都不可與他們爭戰，只要與以色列王爭戰。"31車兵長看見約沙法便說："這必是以色列王。"就轉過去與他爭戰。約沙法一呼喊，耶和華就幫助他，神又感動他們離開他。32車兵長見不是以色列王，就轉去不追他了。

33有一人隨便開弓，恰巧射入以色列王的甲縫裏。王對趕車的說："我受了重傷，你轉過來吧，拉我出陣吧！"34那日，陣勢越戰越猛，以色列王勉強站在車上抵擋亞蘭人，直到晚上。約在日落的時候，王就死了。

19 猶大王約沙法平平安安地回耶路撒冷，到宮裏去了。2先見哈拿尼的兒子耶戶出來迎接約沙法王，對他說："你豈當幫助惡人，愛那恨惡耶和華的人呢？因此，耶和華的忿怒臨到你。3然而，你還有善行，因你從國中除掉木偶，立定心意尋求神。"

約沙法設立審判官

4約沙法住在耶路撒冷。以後又出巡民間，從別是巴直到以法蓮山地，引導民歸向耶和華他們列祖的神。5又在猶大國中遍地的堅固城裏，設立審判官，6對他們說："你們辦事應當謹慎，因為你們判斷不

25The king of Israel then ordered, "Take Micaiah and send him back to Amon the ruler of the city and to Joash the king's son, 26and say, 'This is what the king says: Put this fellow in prison and give him nothing but bread and water until I return safely.' "

27Micaiah declared, "If you ever return safely, the LORD has not spoken through me." Then he added, "Mark my words, all you people!"

Ahab Killed at Ramoth Gilead

28So the king of Israel and Jehoshaphat king of Judah went up to Ramoth Gilead. 29The king of Israel said to Jehoshaphat, "I will enter the battle in disguise, but you wear your royal robes." So the king of Israel disguised himself and went into battle.

30Now the king of Aram had ordered his chariot commanders, "Do not fight with anyone, small or great, except the king of Israel." 31When the chariot commanders saw Jehoshaphat, they thought, "This is the king of Israel." So they turned to attack him, but Jehoshaphat cried out, and the LORD helped him. God drew them away from him, 32for when the chariot commanders saw that he was not the king of Israel, they stopped pursuing him.

33But someone drew his bow at random and hit the king of Israel between the sections of his armor. The king told the chariot driver, "Wheel around and get me out of the fighting. I've been wounded." 34All day long the battle raged, and the king of Israel propped himself up in his chariot facing the Arameans until evening. Then at sunset he died.

19 When Jehoshaphat king of Judah returned safely to his palace in Jerusalem, 2Jehu the seer, the son of Hanani, went out to meet him and said to the king, "Should you help the wicked and love*a* those who hate the LORD? Because of this, the wrath of the LORD is upon you. 3There is, however, some good in you, for you have rid the land of the Asherah poles and have set your heart on seeking God."

Jehoshaphat Appoints Judges

4Jehoshaphat lived in Jerusalem, and he went out again among the people from Beersheba to the hill country of Ephraim and turned them back to the LORD, the God of their fathers. 5He appointed judges in the land, in each of the fortified cities of Judah. 6He told them, "Consider carefully what you do, because you are not judg-

a 2 Or and make alliances with

ing for man but for the LORD, who is with you whenever you give a verdict. [7]Now let the fear of the LORD be upon you. Judge carefully, for with the LORD our God there is no injustice or partiality or bribery."

[8]In Jerusalem also, Jehoshaphat appointed some of the Levites, priests and heads of Israelite families to administer the law of the LORD and to settle disputes. And they lived in Jerusalem. [9]He gave them these orders: "You must serve faithfully and wholeheartedly in the fear of the LORD. [10]In every case that comes before you from your fellow countrymen who live in the cities— whether bloodshed or other concerns of the law, commands, decrees or ordinances—you are to warn them not to sin against the LORD; otherwise his wrath will come on you and your brothers. Do this, and you will not sin.

[11]"Amariah the chief priest will be over you in any matter concerning the LORD, and Zebadiah son of Ishmael, the leader of the tribe of Judah, will be over you in any matter concerning the king, and the Levites will serve as officials before you. Act with courage, and may the LORD be with those who do well."

Jehoshaphat Defeats Moab and Ammon

20 After this, the Moabites and Ammonites with some of the Meunites[a] came to make war on Jehoshaphat.

[2]Some men came and told Jehoshaphat, "A vast army is coming against you from Edom,[b] from the other side of the Sea.[c] It is already in Hazazon Tamar" (that is, En Gedi). [3]Alarmed, Jehoshaphat resolved to inquire of the LORD, and he proclaimed a fast for all Judah. [4]The people of Judah came together to seek help from the LORD; indeed, they came from every town in Judah to seek him.

[5]Then Jehoshaphat stood up in the assembly of Judah and Jerusalem at the temple of the LORD in the front of the new courtyard [6]and said:

"O LORD, God of our fathers, are you not the God who is in heaven? You rule over all the kingdoms of the nations. Power and might are in your hand, and no one can withstand you. [7]O our God, did you not drive out the inhabitants of this land before your people Israel and give it forever to the descendants of Abraham your friend? [8]They have lived in it and have built in it a sanctuary for your Name, saying,

是為人，乃是為耶和華。判斷的時候，他必與你們同在。[7]現在你們應當敬畏耶和華，謹慎辦事，因為耶和華我們的神沒有不義，不偏待人，也不受賄賂。"

[8]約沙法從利未人和祭司，並以色列族長中派定人，在耶路撒冷為耶和華判斷，聽民間的爭訟，就回耶路撒冷去了。[9]約沙法囑咐他們說："你們當敬畏耶和華，忠心誠實辦事。[10]住在各城裏你們的弟兄，若有爭訟的事來到你們這裏，或為流血，或犯律法、誡命、律例、典章，你們要警戒他們，免得他們得罪耶和華，以致他的忿怒臨到你們和你們的弟兄。這樣行，你們就沒有罪了。

[11]"凡屬耶和華的事，有大祭司亞瑪利雅管理你們；凡屬王的事，有猶大支派的族長以實瑪利的兒子西巴第雅管理你們。在你們面前有利未人作官長，你們應當壯膽辦事，願耶和華與善人同在。"

約沙法打敗摩押和亞捫

20 此後，摩押人和亞捫人，又有米烏尼人，一同來攻擊約沙法。

[2]有人來報告約沙法說："從海外亞蘭那邊（註："亞蘭"又作"以東"），有大軍來攻擊你，如今他們在哈洗遜他瑪，就是隱基底。"[3]約沙法便懼怕，定意尋求耶和華，在猶大全地宣告禁食。[4]於是猶大人聚會，求耶和華幫助，猶大各城都有人出來尋求耶和華。

[5]約沙法就在猶大和耶路撒冷的會中，站在耶和華殿的新院前，[6]說：

"耶和華我們列祖的神啊，你不是天上的神嗎？你不是萬邦萬國的主宰嗎？在你手中有大能大力，無人能抵擋你。[7]我們的神啊，你不是曾在你民以色列人面前驅逐這地的居民，將這地賜給你朋友亞伯拉罕的後裔永遠為業嗎？[8]他們住在這地，又為你的名建造聖所，

---

[a] 1 Some Septuagint manuscripts; Hebrew *Ammonites*
[b] 2 One Hebrew manuscript; most Hebrew manuscripts, Septuagint and Vulgate *Aram*   [c] 2 That is, the Dead Sea

說：⁹'倘有禍患臨到我們，或刀兵災殃，或瘟疫饑荒，我們在急難的時候，站在這殿前向你呼求，你必垂聽而拯救，因為你的名在這殿裏。'

¹⁰"從前以色列人出埃及地的時候，你不容以色列人侵犯亞捫人、摩押人和西珥山人。以色列人就離開他們，不滅絕他們。¹¹看哪，他們怎樣報復我們，要來驅逐我們出離你的地，就是你賜給我們為業之地。¹²我們的神啊，你不懲罰他們嗎？因為我們無力抵擋這來攻擊我們的大軍，我們也不知道怎樣行，我們的眼目單仰望你。"

¹³猶大眾人和他們的嬰孩、妻子、兒女，都站在耶和華面前。

¹⁴那時，耶和華的靈在會中臨到利未人亞薩的後裔、瑪探雅的玄孫、耶利的曾孫、比拿雅的孫子、撒迦利雅的兒子雅哈悉。

¹⁵他說："猶大眾人、耶路撒冷的居民和約沙法王，你們請聽！耶和華對你們如此說：'不要因這大軍恐懼驚惶，因為勝敗不在乎你們，乃在乎神。¹⁶明日你們要下去迎敵，他們是從洗斯坡上來，你們必在耶魯伊勒曠野前的谷口遇見他們。¹⁷猶大和耶路撒冷人哪，這次你們不要爭戰，要擺陣站着，看耶和華為你們施行拯救。不要恐懼，也不要驚惶，明日當出去迎敵，因為耶和華與你們同在。'"

¹⁸約沙法就面伏於地，猶大眾人和耶路撒冷的居民也俯伏在耶和華面前，叩拜耶和華。¹⁹哥轄族和可拉族的利未人都起來，用極大的聲音讚美耶和華以色列的神。

²⁰次日清早，眾人起來往提哥亞的曠野去。出去的時候，約沙法站着說："猶大人和耶路撒冷的居民哪，要聽我說！信耶和華你們的神，就必立穩；信他的先知，就必亨通。"²¹約沙法既與民商議了，就設立歌唱的人頌讚耶和華，使他們

⁹'If calamity comes upon us, whether the sword of judgment, or plague or famine, we will stand in your presence before this temple that bears your Name and will cry out to you in our distress, and you will hear us and save us.'

¹⁰"But now here are men from Ammon, Moab and Mount Seir, whose territory you would not allow Israel to invade when they came from Egypt; so they turned away from them and did not destroy them. ¹¹See how they are repaying us by coming to drive us out of the possession you gave us as an inheritance. ¹²O our God, will you not judge them? For we have no power to face this vast army that is attacking us. We do not know what to do, but our eyes are upon you."

¹³All the men of Judah, with their wives and children and little ones, stood there before the LORD.

¹⁴Then the Spirit of the LORD came upon Jahaziel son of Zechariah, the son of Benaiah, the son of Jeiel, the son of Mattaniah, a Levite and descendant of Asaph, as he stood in the assembly.

¹⁵He said: "Listen, King Jehoshaphat and all who live in Judah and Jerusalem! This is what the LORD says to you: 'Do not be afraid or discouraged because of this vast army. For the battle is not yours, but God's. ¹⁶Tomorrow march down against them. They will be climbing up by the Pass of Ziz, and you will find them at the end of the gorge in the Desert of Jeruel. ¹⁷You will not have to fight this battle. Take up your positions; stand firm and see the deliverance the LORD will give you, O Judah and Jerusalem. Do not be afraid; do not be discouraged. Go out to face them tomorrow, and the LORD will be with you.'"

¹⁸Jehoshaphat bowed with his face to the ground, and all the people of Judah and Jerusalem fell down in worship before the LORD. ¹⁹Then some Levites from the Kohathites and Korahites stood up and praised the LORD, the God of Israel, with very loud voice.

²⁰Early in the morning they left for the Desert of Tekoa. As they set out, Jehoshaphat stood and said, "Listen to me, Judah and people of Jerusalem! Have faith in the LORD your God and you will be upheld; have faith in his prophets and you will be successful." ²¹After consulting the people, Jehoshaphat appointed men to sing to

the LORD and to praise him for the splendor of
his^a holiness as they went out at the head of the
army, saying:

"Give thanks to the LORD,
for his love endures forever."

²²As they began to sing and praise, the LORD
set ambushes against the men of Ammon and
Moab and Mount Seir who were invading Judah,
and they were defeated. ²³The men of Ammon
and Moab rose up against the men from Mount
Seir to destroy and annihilate them. After they
finished slaughtering the men from Seir, they
helped to destroy one another.

²⁴When the men of Judah came to the place
that overlooks the desert and looked toward the
vast army, they saw only dead bodies lying on
the ground; no one had escaped. ²⁵So Jehoshaphat and his men went to carry off their plunder, and they found among them a great amount
of equipment and clothing^b and also articles of
value—more than they could take away. There
was so much plunder that it took three days to
collect it. ²⁶On the fourth day they assembled in
the Valley of Beracah, where they praised the
LORD. This is why it is called the Valley of
Beracah^c to this day.

²⁷Then, led by Jehoshaphat, all the men of
Judah and Jerusalem returned joyfully to Jerusalem, for the LORD had given them cause to
rejoice over their enemies. ²⁸They entered Jerusalem and went to the temple of the LORD with
harps and lutes and trumpets.

²⁹The fear of God came upon all the king-
doms of the countries when they heard how the
LORD had fought against the enemies of Israel.
³⁰And the kingdom of Jehoshaphat was at peace,
for his God had given him rest on every side.

The End of Jehoshaphat's Reign

³¹So Jehoshaphat reigned over Judah. He was
thirty-five years old when he became king of
Judah, and he reigned in Jerusalem twenty-five
years. His mother's name was Azubah daughter
of Shilhi. ³²He walked in the ways of his father
Asa and did not stray from them; he did what
was right in the eyes of the LORD. ³³The high
places, however, were not removed, and the
people still had not set their hearts on the God
of their fathers.

穿上聖潔的禮服，走在軍前讚美耶和
華說：

"當稱謝耶和華，
因他的慈愛永遠長存！"

²²眾人方唱歌讚美的時候，耶和
華就派伏兵擊殺那來攻擊<u>猶大</u>人的<u>亞
門</u>人、<u>摩押</u>人和<u>西珥山</u>人，他們就被
打敗了。²³因為<u>亞門</u>人和<u>摩押</u>人起來
擊殺住<u>西珥山</u>的人，將他們滅盡；滅
盡住<u>西珥山</u>的人之後，他們又彼此自
相擊殺。

²⁴<u>猶大</u>人來到曠野的望樓，向那
大軍觀看，見屍橫遍地，沒有一個逃
脫的。²⁵<u>約沙法</u>和他的百姓就來收取
敵人的財物。在屍首中見了許多財
物、珍寶，他們剝脫下來的多得不可
攜帶，因為甚多，直收取了三日。
²⁶第四日，眾人聚集在<u>比拉迦</u>（註：就
是"稱頌"的意思）谷，在那裏稱頌耶和
華。因此那地方名叫<u>比拉迦</u>谷，直到
今日。

²⁷<u>猶大</u>人和<u>耶路撒冷</u>人都歡歡喜
喜地回<u>耶路撒冷</u>，<u>約沙法</u>率領他們。
因為耶和華使他們戰勝仇敵，就歡喜
快樂。²⁸他們彈琴、鼓瑟、吹號，來
到<u>耶路撒冷</u>，進了耶和華的殿。

²⁹列邦諸國聽見耶和華戰敗<u>以色
列</u>的仇敵，就甚懼怕。³⁰這樣，<u>約沙
法</u>的國得享太平，因為神賜他四境平
安。

約沙法王朝的終結

³¹<u>約沙法</u>作<u>猶大</u>王，登基的時候
年三十五歲，在<u>耶路撒冷</u>作王二十五
年。他母親名叫<u>阿蘇巴</u>，乃<u>示利希</u>的
女兒。³²<u>約沙法</u>效法他父<u>亞撒</u>所行
的，不偏左右，行耶和華眼中看為正
的事。³³只是邱壇還沒有廢去，百姓
也沒有立定心意歸向他們列祖的神。

---

a 21 Or him with the splendor of　　*b 25* Some Hebrew
manuscripts and Vulgate; most Hebrew manuscripts *corpses*
c 26 Beracah means *praise.*

³⁴約沙法其餘的事，自始至終都寫在哈拿尼的兒子耶戶的書上，也載入以色列諸王記上。

³⁵此後，猶大王約沙法與以色列王亞哈謝交好。亞哈謝行惡太甚。³⁶二王合夥造船要往他施去，遂在以旬迦別造船。³⁷那時，瑪利沙人、多大瓦的兒子以利以謝向約沙法預言說："因你與亞哈謝交好，耶和華必破壞你所造的。"後來那船果然破壞，不能往他施去了。

21 約沙法與他列祖同睡，葬在大衛城他列祖的墳地裏。他兒子約蘭接續他作王。²約蘭有幾個兄弟，就是約沙法的兒子亞撒利雅、耶歇、撒迦利雅、亞撒利雅、米迦勒、示法提雅，這都是以色列王約沙法的兒子。³他們的父親將許多金銀、財寶和猶大地的堅固城，賜給他們；但將國賜給約蘭，因為他是長子。

約蘭作猶大王

⁴約蘭興起坐他父的位，奮勇自強，就用刀殺了他的眾兄弟和以色列的幾個首領。⁵約蘭登基的時候年三十二歲，在耶路撒冷作王八年。⁶他行以色列諸王的道，與亞哈家一樣。因他娶了亞哈的女兒為妻，行耶和華眼中看為惡的事。⁷耶和華卻因自己與大衛所立的約，不肯滅大衛的家，照他所應許的，永遠賜燈光與大衛和他的子孫。

⁸約蘭年間，以東人背叛猶大，脫離他的權下，自己立王。⁹約蘭就率領軍長和所有的戰車，夜間起來，攻擊圍困他的以東人和車兵長。¹⁰這樣，以東人背叛猶大，脫離他的權下，直到今日。

那時，立拿人也背叛了，因為約蘭離棄耶和華他列祖的神。¹¹他又

³⁴The other events of Jehoshaphat's reign, from beginning to end, are written in the annals of Jehu son of Hanani, which are recorded in the book of the kings of Israel.

³⁵Later, Jehoshaphat king of Judah made an alliance with Ahaziah king of Israel, who was guilty of wickedness. ³⁶He agreed with him to construct a fleet of trading ships.*ᵃ* After these were built at Ezion Geber, ³⁷Eliezer son of Dodavahu of Mareshah prophesied against Jehoshaphat, saying, "Because you have made an alliance with Ahaziah, the LORD will destroy what you have made." The ships were wrecked and were not able to set sail to trade.*ᵇ*

21 Then Jehoshaphat rested with his fathers and was buried with them in the City of David. And Jehoram his son succeeded him as king. ²Jehoram's brothers, the sons of Jehoshaphat, were Azariah, Jehiel, Zechariah, Azariahu, Michael and Shephatiah. All these were sons of Jehoshaphat king of Israel.*ᶜ* ³Their father had given them many gifts of silver and gold and articles of value, as well as fortified cities in Judah, but he had given the kingdom to Jehoram because he was his firstborn son.

Jehoram King of Judah

⁴When Jehoram established himself firmly over his father's kingdom, he put all his brothers to the sword along with some of the princes of Israel. ⁵Jehoram was thirty-two years old when he became king, and he reigned in Jerusalem eight years. ⁶He walked in the ways of the kings of Israel, as the house of Ahab had done, for he married a daughter of Ahab. He did evil in the eyes of the LORD. ⁷Nevertheless, because of the covenant the LORD had made with David, the LORD was not willing to destroy the house of David. He had promised to maintain a lamp for him and his descendants forever.

⁸In the time of Jehoram, Edom rebelled against Judah and set up its own king. ⁹So Jehoram went there with his officers and all his chariots. The Edomites surrounded him and his chariot commanders, but he rose up and broke through by night. ¹⁰To this day Edom has been in rebellion against Judah.

Libnah revolted at the same time, because Jehoram had forsaken the LORD, the God of his fathers. ¹¹He had also built high places on the

---

a 36 Hebrew of ships that could go to Tarshish *b 37 Hebrew sail for Tarshish* *c 2 That is, Judah, as frequently in 2 Chronicles*

hills of Judah and had caused the people of Jerusalem to prostitute themselves and had led Judah astray.

¹²Jehoram received a letter from Elijah the prophet, which said:

"This is what the LORD, the God of your father David, says: 'You have not walked in the ways of your father Jehoshaphat or of Asa king of Judah. ¹³But you have walked in the ways of the kings of Israel, and you have led Judah and the people of Jerusalem to prostitute themselves, just as the house of Ahab did. You have also murdered your own brothers, members of your father's house, men who were better than you. ¹⁴So now the LORD is about to strike your people, your sons, your wives and everything that is yours, with a heavy blow. ¹⁵You yourself will be very ill with a lingering disease of the bowels, until the disease causes your bowels to come out.'"

¹⁶The LORD aroused against Jehoram the hostility of the Philistines and of the Arabs who lived near the Cushites. ¹⁷They attacked Judah, invaded it and carried off all the goods found in the king's palace, together with his sons and wives. Not a son was left to him except Ahaziah,[a] the youngest.

¹⁸After all this, the LORD afflicted Jehoram with an incurable disease of the bowels. ¹⁹In the course of time, at the end of the second year, his bowels came out because of the disease, and he died in great pain. His people made no fire in his honor, as they had for his fathers.

²⁰Jehoram was thirty-two years old when he became king, and he reigned in Jerusalem eight years. He passed away, to no one's regret, and was buried in the City of David, but not in the tombs of the kings.

Ahaziah King of Judah

22 The people of Jerusalem made Ahaziah, Jehoram's youngest son, king in his place, since the raiders, who came with the Arabs into the camp, had killed all the older sons. So Ahaziah son of Jehoram king of Judah began to reign.

²Ahaziah was twenty-two[b] years old when he became king, and he reigned in Jerusalem one year. His mother's name was Athaliah, a granddaughter of Omri.

在猶大諸山建築邱壇，使耶路撒冷的居民行邪淫，誘惑猶大人。

¹²先知以利亞達信與約蘭說：

"耶和華你祖大衛的神如此說：'因為你不行你父約沙法和猶大王亞撒的道，¹³乃行以色列諸王的道，使猶大人和耶路撒冷的居民行邪淫，像亞哈家一樣，又殺了你父家比你好的諸兄弟。¹⁴故此，耶和華降大災與你的百姓和你的妻子、兒女，並你一切所有的。¹⁵你的腸子必患病，日加沉重，以致你的腸子墜落下來。'"

¹⁶以後，耶和華激動非利士人和靠近古實的阿拉伯人來攻擊約蘭。¹⁷他們上來攻擊猶大，侵入境內，擄掠了王宮裏所有的財貨和他的妻子、兒女。除了他小兒子約哈斯（註：又名"亞哈謝"）之外，沒有留下一個兒子。

¹⁸這些事以後，耶和華使約蘭的腸子患不能醫治的病。¹⁹他患此病纏綿日久，過了二年，腸子墜落下來，病重而死。他的民沒有為他燒甚麼物件，像從前為他列祖所燒的一樣。

²⁰約蘭登基的時候年三十二歲，在耶路撒冷作王八年。他去世無人思慕，眾人葬他在大衛城，只是不在列王的墳墓裏。

亞哈謝作猶大王

22 耶路撒冷的居民立約蘭的小兒子亞哈謝接續他作王，因為跟隨阿拉伯人來攻營的軍兵，曾殺了亞哈謝的眾長子。這樣，猶大王約蘭的兒子亞哈謝作了王。

²亞哈謝登基的時候年四十二歲（註：列王紀下8章26節作"二十二歲"），在耶路撒冷作王一年。他母親名叫亞她利雅，是暗利的孫女。

a 17 Hebrew Jehoahaz, a variant of Ahaziah   b 2 Some Septuagint manuscripts and Syriac (see also 2 Kings 8:26); Hebrew forty-two

³亞哈謝也行亞哈家的道，因為他母親給他主謀，使他行惡。⁴他行耶和華眼中看為惡的事，像亞哈家一樣。因他父親死後有亞哈家的人給他主謀，以致敗壞。⁵他聽從亞哈家的計謀，同以色列王亞哈的兒子約蘭往基列的拉末去，與亞蘭王哈薛爭戰。亞蘭人打傷了約蘭。⁶約蘭回到耶斯列，醫治在拉末與亞蘭王哈薛打仗所受的傷。

猶大王約蘭的兒子亞撒利雅（註：即"亞哈謝"），因為亞哈的兒子約蘭病了，就下到耶斯列看望他。

⁷亞哈謝去見約蘭，就被害了，這是出乎神。因為他到了，就同約蘭出去攻擊寧示的孫子耶戶；這耶戶是耶和華所膏，使他剪除亞哈家的。⁸耶戶討亞哈家罪的時候，遇見猶大的眾首領和亞哈謝的眾侄子服侍亞哈謝，就把他們都殺了。⁹亞哈謝藏在撒馬利亞，耶戶尋找他，眾人將他拿住，送到耶戶那裏，就殺了他，將他葬埋。因他們說："他是那盡心尋求耶和華之約沙法的兒子。"這樣，亞哈謝的家無力保守國權。

亞她利雅與約阿施

¹⁰亞哈謝的母親亞她利雅見她兒子死了，就起來剿滅猶大王室。¹¹但王的女兒約示巴，將亞哈謝的兒子約阿施從那被殺的王子中偷出來，把他和他的乳母都藏在臥房裏。約示巴是約蘭王的女兒，亞哈謝的妹子，祭司耶何耶大的妻。她收藏約阿施，躲避亞她利雅，免得被殺。¹²約阿施和她們一同藏在神殿裏六年。亞她利雅篡了國位。

³He too walked in the ways of the house of Ahab, for his mother encouraged him in doing wrong. ⁴He did evil in the eyes of the LORD, as the house of Ahab had done, for after his father's death they became his advisers, to his undoing. ⁵He also followed their counsel when he went with Joram*a* son of Ahab king of Israel to war against Hazael king of Aram at Ramoth Gilead. The Arameans wounded Joram; ⁶so he returned to Jezreel to recover from the wounds they had inflicted on him at Ramoth*b* in his battle with Hazael king of Aram.

Then Ahaziah*c* son of Jehoram king of Judah went down to Jezreel to see Joram son of Ahab because he had been wounded.

⁷Through Ahaziah's visit to Joram, God brought about Ahaziah's downfall. When Ahaziah arrived, he went out with Joram to meet Jehu son of Nimshi, whom the LORD had anointed to destroy the house of Ahab. ⁸While Jehu was executing judgment on the house of Ahab, he found the princes of Judah and the sons of Ahaziah's relatives, who had been attending Ahaziah, and he killed them. ⁹He then went in search of Ahaziah, and his men captured him while he was hiding in Samaria. He was brought to Jehu and put to death. They buried him, for they said, "He was a son of Jehoshaphat, who sought the LORD with all his heart." So there was no one in the house of Ahaziah powerful enough to retain the kingdom.

Athaliah and Joash

¹⁰When Athaliah the mother of Ahaziah saw that her son was dead, she proceeded to destroy the whole royal family of the house of Judah. ¹¹But Jehosheba,*d* the daughter of King Jehoram, took Joash son of Ahaziah and stole him away from among the royal princes who were about to be murdered and put him and his nurse in a bedroom. Because Jehosheba,*d* the daughter of King Jehoram and wife of the priest Jehoiada, was Ahaziah's sister, she hid the child from Athaliah so she could not kill him. ¹²He remained hidden with them at the temple of God for six years while Athaliah ruled the land.

23 In the seventh year Jehoiada showed his strength. He made a covenant with the commanders of units of a hundred: Azariah son of Jeroham, Ishmael son of Jehohanan, Azariah son of Obed, Maaseiah son of Adaiah, and Elishaphat son of Zicri. ²They went throughout Judah and gathered the Levites and the heads of Israelite families from all the towns. When they came to Jerusalem, ³the whole assembly made a covenant with the king at the temple of God.

Jehoiada said to them, "The king's son shall reign, as the LORD promised concerning the descendants of David. ⁴Now this is what you are to do: A third of you priests and Levites who are going on duty on the Sabbath are to keep watch at the doors, ⁵a third of you at the royal palace and a third at the Foundation Gate, and all the other men are to be in the courtyards of the temple of the LORD. ⁶No one is to enter the temple of the LORD except the priests and Levites on duty; they may enter because they are consecrated, but all the other men are to guard what the LORD has assigned to them.ᵃ ⁷The Levites are to station themselves around the king, each man with his weapons in his hand. Anyone who enters the temple must be put to death. Stay close to the king wherever he goes."

⁸The Levites and all the men of Judah did just as Jehoiada the priest ordered. Each one took his men—those who were going on duty on the Sabbath and those who were going off duty—for Jehoiada the priest had not released any of the divisions. ⁹Then he gave the commanders of units of a hundred the spears and the large and small shields that had belonged to King David and that were in the temple of God. ¹⁰He stationed all the men, each with his weapon in his hand, around the king—near the altar and the temple, from the south side to the north side of the temple.

¹¹Jehoiada and his sons brought out the king's son and put the crown on him; they presented him with a copy of the covenant and proclaimed him king. They anointed him and shouted, "Long live the king!"

¹²When Athaliah heard the noise of the people running and cheering the king, she went to them at the temple of the LORD. ¹³She looked, and there was the king, standing by his pillar at the entrance. The officers and the trumpeters were beside the king, and all the people of the land were rejoicing and blowing trumpets, and

23 第七年，耶何耶大奮勇自強，將百夫長耶羅罕的兒子亞撒利雅，約哈難的兒子以實瑪利，俄備得的兒子亞撒利雅，亞大雅的兒子瑪西雅，細基利的兒子以利沙法召來，與他們立約。²他們走遍猶大，從猶大各城裏招聚利未人和以色列的眾族長到耶路撒冷來。³會眾在神殿裏與王立約。

耶何耶大對他們說："看哪，王的兒子必當作王，正如耶和華指着大衛子孫所應許的話。"⁴又說："你們當這樣行：祭司和利未人，凡安息日進班的，三分之一要把守各門，⁵三分之一要在王宮，三分之一要在基址門；眾百姓要在耶和華殿的院內。⁶除了祭司和供職的利未人之外，不准別人進耶和華的殿；惟獨他們可以進去，因為他們聖潔。眾百姓要遵守耶和華所吩咐的。⁷利未人要手中各拿兵器，四圍護衛王。凡擅入殿宇的，必當治死。王出入的時候，你們當跟隨他。"

⁸利未人和猶大眾人都照着祭司耶何耶大一切所吩咐的去行，各帶所管安息日進班出班的人來，因為祭司耶何耶大不許他們下班。⁹祭司耶何耶大便將神殿裏所藏大衛王的槍、盾牌、擋牌交給百夫長；¹⁰又分派眾民手中各拿兵器，在壇和殿那裏，從殿右直到殿左，站在王子的四圍。

¹¹於是領王子出來，給他戴上冠冕，將律法書交給他，立他作王。耶何耶大和眾子膏他，眾人說："願王萬歲！"

¹²亞她利雅聽見民奔走、讚美王的聲音，就到民那裏，進耶和華的殿。¹³看見王站在殿門的柱旁，百夫長和吹號的人侍立在王左右，國民都

歡樂吹號，又有歌唱的，用各樣的樂器，領人歌唱讚美，<u>亞她利雅</u>就撕裂衣服，喊叫說：「反了！反了！」¹⁴祭司<u>耶何耶大</u>帶管轄軍兵的百夫長出來，吩咐他們說：「將她趕到班外，凡跟隨她的必用刀殺死！」因為祭司說：「不可在耶和華殿裏殺她。」¹⁵眾兵就閃開，讓她去；她走到王宮的<u>馬門</u>，便在那裏把她殺了。

¹⁶<u>耶何耶大</u>與眾民和王立約，都要作耶和華的民。¹⁷於是眾民都到<u>巴力廟</u>，拆毀了廟，打碎壇和像，又在壇前將<u>巴力</u>的祭司<u>瑪坦</u>殺了。

¹⁸<u>耶何耶大</u>派官看守耶和華的殿，是在祭司<u>利未人</u>手下。這祭司<u>利未人</u>是<u>大衛</u>分派在耶和華殿中，照<u>摩西</u>律法上所寫的，給耶和華獻燔祭，又按<u>大衛</u>所定的例，歡樂歌唱；¹⁹且設立守門的把守耶和華殿的各門，無論為何事，不潔淨的人都不准進去。

²⁰又率領百夫長和貴冑，與民間的官長，並國中的眾民，請王從耶和華殿下來，由上門進入王宮，立王坐在國位上。²¹國民都歡樂，合城都安靜。眾人已將<u>亞她利雅</u>用刀殺了。

約阿施修理聖殿

24 <u>約阿施</u>登基的時候年七歲，在<u>耶路撒冷</u>作王四十年。他母親名叫<u>西比亞</u>，是<u>別是巴</u>人。²祭司<u>耶何耶大</u>在世的時候，<u>約阿施</u>行耶和華眼中看為正的事。³<u>耶何耶大</u>為他娶了兩個妻，並且生兒養女。

⁴此後，<u>約阿施</u>有意重修耶和華的殿，⁵便召聚眾祭司和<u>利未人</u>，吩咐他們說：「你們要往<u>猶大</u>各城去，使<u>以色列</u>眾人捐納銀子，每年可以修理你們神的殿，你們要急速辦理這事。」只是<u>利未人</u>不急速辦理。

singers with musical instruments were leading the praises. Then Athaliah tore her robes and shouted, "Treason! Treason!"

¹⁴Jehoiada the priest sent out the commanders of units of a hundred, who were in charge of the troops, and said to them: "Bring her out between the ranks*a* and put to the sword anyone who follows her." For the priest had said, "Do not put her to death at the temple of the LORD." ¹⁵So they seized her as she reached the entrance of the Horse Gate on the palace grounds, and there they put her to death.

¹⁶Jehoiada then made a covenant that he and the people and the king*b* would be the LORD's people. ¹⁷All the people went to the temple of Baal and tore it down. They smashed the altars and idols and killed Mattan the priest of Baal in front of the altars.

¹⁸Then Jehoiada placed the oversight of the temple of the LORD in the hands of the priests, who were Levites, to whom David had made assignments in the temple, to present the burnt offerings of the LORD as written in the Law of Moses, with rejoicing and singing, as David had ordered. ¹⁹He also stationed doorkeepers at the gates of the LORD's temple so that no one who was in any way unclean might enter.

²⁰He took with him the commanders of hundreds, the nobles, the rulers of the people and all the people of the land and brought the king down from the temple of the LORD. They went into the palace through the Upper Gate and seated the king on the royal throne, ²¹and all the people of the land rejoiced. And the city was quiet, because Athaliah had been slain with the sword.

Joash Repairs the Temple

24 Joash was seven years old when he became king, and he reigned in Jerusalem forty years. His mother's name was Zibiah; she was from Beersheba. ²Joash did what was right in the eyes of the LORD all the years of Jehoiada the priest. ³Jehoiada chose two wives for him, and he had sons and daughters.

⁴Some time later Joash decided to restore the temple of the LORD. ⁵He called together the priests and Levites and said to them, "Go to the towns of Judah and collect the money due annually from all Israel, to repair the temple of your God. Do it now." But the Levites did not act at once.

a 14 Or out from the precincts   b 16 Or covenant between the LORD and the people and the king that they (see 2 Kings 11:17)

⁶Therefore the king summoned Jehoiada the chief priest and said to him, "Why haven't you required the Levites to bring in from Judah and Jerusalem the tax imposed by Moses the servant of the LORD and by the assembly of Israel for the Tent of the Testimony?"

⁷Now the sons of that wicked woman Athaliah had broken into the temple of God and had used even its sacred objects for the Baals.

⁸At the king's command, a chest was made and placed outside, at the gate of the temple of the LORD. ⁹A proclamation was then issued in Judah and Jerusalem that they should bring to the LORD the tax that Moses the servant of God had required of Israel in the desert. ¹⁰All the officials and all the people brought their contributions gladly, dropping them into the chest until it was full. ¹¹Whenever the chest was brought in by the Levites to the king's officials and they saw that there was a large amount of money, the royal secretary and the officer of the chief priest would come and empty the chest and carry it back to its place. They did this regularly and collected a great amount of money. ¹²The king and Jehoiada gave it to the men who carried out the work required for the temple of the LORD. They hired masons and carpenters to restore the LORD's temple, and also workers in iron and bronze to repair the temple.

¹³The men in charge of the work were diligent, and the repairs progressed under them. They rebuilt the temple of God according to its original design and reinforced it. ¹⁴When they had finished, they brought the rest of the money to the king and Jehoiada, and with it were made articles for the LORD's temple: articles for the service and for the burnt offerings, and also dishes and other objects of gold and silver. As long as Jehoiada lived, burnt offerings were presented continually in the temple of the LORD.

¹⁵Now Jehoiada was old and full of years, and he died at the age of a hundred and thirty. ¹⁶He was buried with the kings in the City of David, because of the good he had done in Israel for God and his temple.

The Wickedness of Joash

¹⁷After the death of Jehoiada, the officials of Judah came and paid homage to the king, and he listened to them. ¹⁸They abandoned the temple of the LORD, the God of their fathers, and worshiped Asherah poles and idols. Because of their guilt, God's anger came upon Judah and Jerusalem. ¹⁹Although the LORD sent prophets to the people to bring them back to him, and though they testified against them, they would not listen.

⁶王召了大祭司<u>耶和華大</u>來，對他說："從前耶和華的僕人<u>摩西</u>為法櫃的帳幕，與<u>以色列</u>會眾所定的捐項，你為何不叫<u>利未</u>人照這例從<u>猶大</u>和<u>耶路撒冷</u>帶來，作殿的費用呢？"

⁷因為那惡婦<u>亞她利雅</u>的眾子曾拆毀神的殿，又用耶和華殿中分別為聖的物供奉<u>巴力</u>。

⁸於是王下令，眾人做了一櫃，放在耶和華殿的門外。⁹又通告<u>猶大</u>和<u>耶路撒冷</u>的百姓，要將神僕人<u>摩西</u>在曠野所吩咐<u>以色列</u>人的捐項，給耶和華送來。¹⁰眾首領和百姓都歡歡喜喜地將銀子送來，投入櫃中，直到捐完。¹¹<u>利未</u>人見銀子多了，就把櫃抬到王所派的司事面前。王的書記和大祭司的屬員來將櫃倒空，仍放在原處。日日都是這樣，積蓄的銀子甚多。¹²王與<u>耶和華大</u>將銀子交給耶和華殿裏辦事的人，他們就雇了石匠、木匠重修耶和華的殿，又雇了鐵匠、銅匠修理耶和華的殿。

¹³工人操作，漸漸修成，將神殿修造得與從前一樣，而且甚是堅固。¹⁴工程完了，他們就把其餘的銀子拿到王與<u>耶和華大</u>面前，用以製造耶和華殿供奉所用的器皿和調羹，並金銀的器皿。<u>耶和華大</u>在世的時候，眾人常在耶和華殿裏獻燔祭。

¹⁵<u>耶和華大</u>年紀老邁，日子滿足而死，死的時候年一百三十歲。¹⁶葬在<u>大衛城</u>列王的墳墓裏，因為他在<u>以色列</u>人中行善，又侍奉神，修理神的殿。

約阿施的惡行

¹⁷<u>耶和華大</u>死後，<u>猶大</u>的眾首領來朝拜王，王就聽從他們。¹⁸他們離棄耶和華他們列祖神的殿，去侍奉<u>亞舍拉</u>和偶像。因他們這罪，就有忿怒臨到<u>猶大</u>和<u>耶路撒冷</u>。¹⁹但神仍遣先知到他們那裏，引導他們歸向耶和華。這先知警戒他們，他們卻不肯聽。

²⁰那時，神的靈感動祭司耶何耶大的兒子撒迦利亞，他就站在上面對民說：「神如此說：『你們為何干犯耶和華的誡命，以致不得亨通呢？因為你們離棄耶和華，所以他也離棄你們。』」

²¹眾民同心謀害撒迦利亞，就照王的吩咐，在耶和華殿的院內，用石頭打死他。²²這樣，約阿施王不想念撒迦利亞的父親耶何耶大向自己所施的恩，殺了他的兒子。撒迦利亞臨死的時候說：「願耶和華鑒察伸冤！」

²³滿了一年，亞蘭的軍兵上來攻擊約阿施，來到猶大和耶路撒冷，殺了民中的眾首領，將所掠的財貨送到大馬士革王那裏。²⁴亞蘭的軍兵雖來了一小隊，耶和華卻將大隊的軍兵交在他們手裏，是因猶大人離棄耶和華他們列祖的神，所以藉亞蘭人懲罰約阿施。²⁵亞蘭人離開約阿施的時候，他患重病。臣僕背叛他，要報祭司耶何耶大兒子流血之仇，殺他在牀上，葬他在大衛城，只是不葬在列王的墳墓裏。

²⁶背叛他的是亞捫婦人示米押的兒子撒拔和摩押婦人示米利的兒子約薩拔。²⁷至於他的眾子和他所受的警戒，並他重修神殿的事，都寫在列王的傳上。他兒子亞瑪謝接續他作王。

亞瑪謝作猶大王

25 亞瑪謝登基的時候年二十五歲，在耶路撒冷作王二十九年。他母親名叫約耶但，是耶路撒冷人。²亞瑪謝行耶和華眼中看為正的事，只是心不專誠。³國一堅定，就把殺他父王的臣僕殺了，⁴卻沒有治死他們的兒子，是照摩西律法書上耶和華所吩咐的，說：「不可因子殺父，也不可因父殺子，各人要為本身的罪而死。」

²⁰Then the Spirit of God came upon Zechariah son of Jehoiada the priest. He stood before the people and said, "This is what God says: 'Why do you disobey the LORD's commands? You will not prosper. Because you have forsaken the LORD, he has forsaken you.'"

²¹But they plotted against him, and by order of the king they stoned him to death in the courtyard of the LORD's temple. ²²King Joash did not remember the kindness Zechariah's father Jehoiada had shown him but killed his son, who said as he lay dying, "May the LORD see this and call you to account."

²³At the turn of the year,[a] the army of Aram marched against Joash; it invaded Judah and Jerusalem and killed all the leaders of the people. They sent all the plunder to their king in Damascus. ²⁴Although the Aramean army had come with only a few men, the LORD delivered into their hands a much larger army. Because Judah had forsaken the LORD, the God of their fathers, judgment was executed on Joash. ²⁵When the Arameans withdrew, they left Joash severely wounded. His officials conspired against him for murdering the son of Jehoiada the priest, and they killed him in his bed. So he died and was buried in the City of David, but not in the tombs of the kings.

²⁶Those who conspired against him were Zabad,[b] son of Shimeath an Ammonite woman, and Jehozabad, son of Shimrith[c] a Moabite woman. ²⁷The account of his sons, the many prophecies about him, and the record of the restoration of the temple of God are written in the annotations on the book of the kings. And Amaziah his son succeeded him as king.

Amaziah King of Judah

25 Amaziah was twenty-five years old when he became king, and he reigned in Jerusalem twenty-nine years. His mother's name was Jehoaddin[d]; she was from Jerusalem. ²He did what was right in the eyes of the LORD, but not wholeheartedly. ³After the kingdom was firmly in his control, he executed the officials who had murdered his father the king. ⁴Yet he did not put their sons to death, but acted in accordance with what is written in the Law, in the Book of Moses, where the LORD commanded: "Fathers shall not be put to death for their children, nor children put to death for their fathers; each is to die for his own sins."[e]

---

a 23 Probably in the spring　　*b 26* A variant of *Jozabad*
c 26 A variant of *Shomer*　　*d 1* Hebrew *Jehoaddan*, a variant of *Jehoaddin*　　*e 4* Deut. 24:16

⁵Amaziah called the people of Judah together and assigned them according to their families to commanders of thousands and commanders of hundreds for all Judah and Benjamin. He then mustered those twenty years old or more and found that there were three hundred thousand men ready for military service, able to handle the spear and shield. ⁶He also hired a hundred thousand fighting men from Israel for a hundred talents^a of silver.

⁷But a man of God came to him and said, "O king, these troops from Israel must not march with you, for the LORD is not with Israel—not with any of the people of Ephraim. ⁸Even if you go and fight courageously in battle, God will overthrow you before the enemy, for God has the power to help or to overthrow."

⁹Amaziah asked the man of God, "But what about the hundred talents I paid for these Israelite troops?"

The man of God replied, "The LORD can give you much more than that."

¹⁰So Amaziah dismissed the troops who had come to him from Ephraim and sent them home. They were furious with Judah and left for home in a great rage.

¹¹Amaziah then marshaled his strength and led his army to the Valley of Salt, where he killed ten thousand men of Seir. ¹²The army of Judah also captured ten thousand men alive, took them to the top of a cliff and threw them down so that all were dashed to pieces.

¹³Meanwhile the troops that Amaziah had sent back and had not allowed to take part in the war raided Judean towns from Samaria to Beth Horon. They killed three thousand people and carried off great quantities of plunder.

¹⁴When Amaziah returned from slaughtering the Edomites, he brought back the gods of the people of Seir. He set them up as his own gods, bowed down to them and burned sacrifices to them. ¹⁵The anger of the LORD burned against Amaziah, and he sent a prophet to him, who said, "Why do you consult this people's gods, which could not save their own people from your hand?"

¹⁶While he was still speaking, the king said to him, "Have we appointed you an adviser to the king? Stop! Why be struck down?"

So the prophet stopped but said, "I know that God has determined to destroy you, because you have done this and have not listened to my counsel."

⁵亞瑪謝招聚猶大人，按着猶大和便雅憫的宗族，設立千夫長、百夫長。又數點人數，從二十歲以外，能拿槍、拿盾牌出去打仗的精兵，共有三十萬。⁶又用銀子一百他連得，從以色列招募了十萬大能的勇士。

⁷有一個神人來見亞瑪謝，對他說："王啊，不要使以色列的軍兵與你同去，因為耶和華不與以色列人以法蓮的後裔同在。⁸你若一定要去，就奮勇爭戰吧！但神必使你敗在敵人面前，因為神能助人得勝；也能使人傾敗！"

⁹亞瑪謝問神人說："我給了以色列軍的那一百他連得銀子怎麼樣呢？"

神人回答說："耶和華能把更多的賜給你。"

¹⁰於是，亞瑪謝將那從以法蓮來的軍兵分別出來，叫他們回家去，故此，他們甚惱怒猶大人，氣忿忿地回家去了。

¹¹亞瑪謝壯起膽來，率領他的民到鹽谷，殺了西珥人一萬。¹²猶大人又生擒了一萬帶到山崖上，從那裏把他們扔下去，以致他們都摔碎了。

¹³但亞瑪謝所打發回去、不許一同出征的那些軍兵，攻打猶大各城，從撒馬利亞直到伯和崙，殺了三千人，搶了許多財物。

¹⁴亞瑪謝殺了以東人回來，就把西珥的神像帶回，立為自己的神，在他面前叩拜燒香。¹⁵因此，耶和華的怒氣向亞瑪謝發作，就差一個先知去見他，說："這些神不能救他的民脫離你的手，你為何尋求他呢？"

¹⁶先知與王說話的時候，王對他說："誰立你作王的謀士呢？你住口吧！為何找打呢？"

先知就止住了，又說："你行這事不聽從我的勸戒，我知道神定意要滅你。"

^a 6 That is, about 3 3/4 tons (about 3.4 metric tons); also in verse 9

¹⁷猶大王亞瑪謝與羣臣商議，就差遣使者去見耶戶的孫子、約哈斯的兒子、以色列王約阿施說：“你來，我們二人相見於戰場。”

¹⁸以色列王約阿施差遣使者去見猶大王亞瑪謝說：“黎巴嫩的蒺藜差遣使者去見黎巴嫩的香柏樹，說：‘將你的女兒給我兒子為妻。’後來黎巴嫩有一個野獸經過，把蒺藜踐踏了。¹⁹你說：‘看哪，我打敗了以東人。’你就心高氣傲，以致矜誇。你在家裏安居就罷了，為何要惹禍使自己和猶大國一同敗亡呢？”

²⁰亞瑪謝卻不肯聽從，這是出乎神，好將他們交在敵人手裏，因為他們尋求以東的神。²¹於是，以色列王約阿施上來，在猶大的伯示麥與猶大王亞瑪謝相見於戰場。²²猶大人敗在以色列人面前，各自逃回家裏去了。²³以色列王約阿施，在伯示麥擒住約哈斯（註：就是“亞哈謝”）的孫子、約阿施的兒子、猶大王亞瑪謝，將他帶到耶路撒冷。又拆毀耶路撒冷的城牆，從以法蓮門直到角門，共四百肘；²⁴又將俄別以東所看守神殿裏的一切金銀和器皿，與王宮裏的財寶都拿了去，並帶人去為質，就回撒利亞去了。

²⁵以色列王約哈斯的兒子約阿施死後，猶大王約阿施的兒子亞瑪謝又活了十五年。²⁶亞瑪謝其餘的事，自始至終不都寫在猶大和以色列諸王記上嗎？²⁷自從亞瑪謝離棄耶和華之後，在耶路撒冷有人背叛他，他就逃到拉吉。叛黨卻打發人到拉吉將他殺了。²⁸人就用馬將他的屍首馱回，葬在猶大京城、他列祖的墳地裏。

烏西雅作猶大王

26 猶大眾民立亞瑪謝的兒子烏西雅（註：又名“亞撒利雅”）接續他父作王，那時他年十六歲。²亞瑪謝與他列祖同睡之後，烏西雅收回以祿仍歸猶大，又重新修理。

¹⁷After Amaziah king of Judah consulted his advisers, he sent this challenge to Jehoash^a son of Jehoahaz, the son of Jehu, king of Israel: "Come, meet me face to face."

¹⁸But Jehoash king of Israel replied to Amaziah king of Judah: "A thistle in Lebanon sent a message to a cedar in Lebanon, 'Give your daughter to my son in marriage.' Then a wild beast in Lebanon came along and trampled the thistle underfoot. ¹⁹You say to yourself that you have defeated Edom, and now you are arrogant and proud. But stay at home! Why ask for trouble and cause your own downfall and that of Judah also?"

²⁰Amaziah, however, would not listen, for God so worked that he might hand them over to Jehoash, because they sought the gods of Edom. ²¹So Jehoash king of Israel attacked. He and Amaziah king of Judah faced each other at Beth Shemesh in Judah. ²²Judah was routed by Israel, and every man fled to his home. ²³Jehoash king of Israel captured Amaziah king of Judah, the son of Joash, the son of Ahaziah,^b at Beth Shemesh. Then Jehoash brought him to Jerusalem and broke down the wall of Jerusalem from the Ephraim Gate to the Corner Gate—a section about six hundred feet^c long. ²⁴He took all the gold and silver and all the articles found in the temple of God that had been in the care of Obed-Edom, together with the palace treasures and the hostages, and returned to Samaria.

²⁵Amaziah son of Joash king of Judah lived for fifteen years after the death of Jehoash son of Jehoahaz king of Israel. ²⁶As for the other events of Amaziah's reign, from beginning to end, are they not written in the book of the kings of Judah and Israel? ²⁷From the time that Amaziah turned away from following the LORD, they conspired against him in Jerusalem and he fled to Lachish, but they sent men after him to Lachish and killed him there. ²⁸He was brought back by horse and was buried with his fathers in the City of Judah.

Uzziah King of Judah

26 Then all the people of Judah took Uzziah,^d who was sixteen years old, and made him king in place of his father Amaziah. ²He was the one who rebuilt Elath and restored it to Judah after Amaziah rested with his fathers.

*a 17 Hebrew Joash, a variant of Jehoash; also in verses 18, 21, 23 and 25　　b 23 Hebrew Jehoahaz, a variant of Ahaziah
c 23 Hebrew four hundred cubits (about 180 meters)　　d 1 Also called Azariah*

³Uzziah was sixteen years old when he became king, and he reigned in Jerusalem fifty-two years. His mother's name was Jecoliah; she was from Jerusalem. ⁴He did what was right in the eyes of the LORD, just as his father Amaziah had done. ⁵He sought God during the days of Zechariah, who instructed him in the fear^a of God. As long as he sought the LORD, God gave him success.

⁶He went to war against the Philistines and broke down the walls of Gath, Jabneh and Ashdod. He then rebuilt towns near Ashdod and elsewhere among the Philistines. ⁷God helped him against the Philistines and against the Arabs who lived in Gur Baal and against the Meunites. ⁸The Ammonites brought tribute to Uzziah, and his fame spread as far as the border of Egypt, because he had become very powerful.

⁹Uzziah built towers in Jerusalem at the Corner Gate, at the Valley Gate and at the angle of the wall, and he fortified them. ¹⁰He also built towers in the desert and dug many cisterns, because he had much livestock in the foothills and in the plain. He had people working his fields and vineyards in the hills and in the fertile lands, for he loved the soil.

¹¹Uzziah had a well-trained army, ready to go out by divisions according to their numbers as mustered by Jeiel the secretary and Maaseiah the officer under the direction of Hananiah, one of the royal officials. ¹²The total number of family leaders over the fighting men was 2,600. ¹³Under their command was an army of 307,500 men trained for war, a powerful force to support the king against his enemies. ¹⁴Uzziah provided shields, spears, helmets, coats of armor, bows and slingstones for the entire army. ¹⁵In Jerusalem he made machines designed by skillful men for use on the towers and on the corner defenses to shoot arrows and hurl large stones. His fame spread far and wide, for he was greatly helped until he became powerful.

¹⁶But after Uzziah became powerful, his pride led to his downfall. He was unfaithful to the LORD his God, and entered the temple of the LORD to burn incense on the altar of incense. ¹⁷Azariah the priest with eighty other courageous priests of the LORD followed him in. ¹⁸They confronted him and said, "It is not right for you, Uzziah, to burn incense to the LORD. That is for the priests, the descendants of Aaron, who have been consecrated to burn incense. Leave the

³烏西雅登基的時候年十六歲，在耶路撒冷作王五十二年。他母親名叫耶可利雅，是耶路撒冷人。⁴烏西雅行耶和華眼中看為正的事，效法他父亞瑪謝一切所行的。⁵通曉神默示撒迦利亞在世的時候，烏西雅定意尋求神；他尋求，耶和華神就使他亨通。

⁶他出去攻擊非利士人，拆毀了迦特城、雅比尼城和亞實突城；在非利士人中、在亞實突境內，又建築了些城。⁷神幫助他攻擊非利士人和住在姑珥巴力的阿拉伯人，並米烏尼人。⁸亞捫人給烏西雅進貢，他的名聲傳到埃及，因他甚是強盛。

⁹烏西雅在耶路撒冷的角門和谷門，並城牆轉彎之處建築城樓，且甚堅固；¹⁰又在曠野與高原和平原建築望樓，挖了許多井，因他的牲畜甚多；又在山地和佳美之地，有農夫和修理葡萄園的人，因為他喜悅農事。

¹¹烏西雅又有軍兵，照書記耶利和官長瑪西雅所數點的，在王的一個將軍哈拿尼雅手下，分隊出戰。¹²族長、大能勇士的總數，共有二千六百人。¹³他們手下的軍兵，共有三十萬七千五百人，都有大能，善於爭戰，幫助王攻擊仇敵。¹⁴烏西雅為全軍預備盾牌、槍、盔、甲、弓和甩石的機弦；¹⁵又在耶路撒冷使巧匠做機器，安在城樓和角樓上，用以射箭發石。烏西雅的名聲傳到遠方，因為他得了非常的幫助，甚是強盛。

¹⁶他既強盛，就心高氣傲，以致行事邪僻，干犯耶和華他的神，進耶和華的殿，要在香壇上燒香。¹⁷祭司亞撒利雅率領耶和華勇敢的祭司八十人，跟隨他進去。¹⁸他們就阻擋烏西雅王，對他說：“烏西雅啊，給耶和華燒香不是你的事，乃是亞倫子孫承接聖職祭司的事。你出聖殿吧！因為

---

a 5 Many Hebrew manuscripts, Septuagint and Syriac; other Hebrew manuscripts *vision*

你犯了罪，你行這事，耶和華神必不使你得榮耀。"

19烏西雅就發怒，手拿香爐要燒香。他向祭司發怒的時候，在耶和華殿中香壇旁眾祭司面前，額上忽然發出大痲瘋。20大祭司亞撒利雅和眾祭司觀看，見他額上發出大痲瘋，就催他出殿；他自己也急速出去，因為耶和華降災與他。

21烏西雅王長大痲瘋直到死日，因此住在別的宮裏，與耶和華的殿隔絕。他兒子約坦管理家事，治理國民。

22烏西雅其餘的事，自始至終都是亞摩斯的兒子、先知以賽亞所記的。23烏西雅與他列祖同睡，葬在王陵的田間他列祖的墳地裏，因為人說，他是長大痲瘋的。他兒子約坦接續他作王。

約坦作猶大王

27 約坦登基的時候年二十五歲，在耶路撒冷作王十六年。他母親名叫耶路沙，是撒督的女兒。2約坦行耶和華眼中看為正的事，效法他父烏西雅一切所行的，只是不入耶和華的殿。百姓還行邪僻的事。3約坦建立耶和華殿的上門。在俄斐勒城上多有建造，4又在猶大山地建造城邑，在樹林中建築營寨和高樓。

5約坦與亞捫人的王打仗，勝了他們，當年他們進貢銀一百他連得，小麥一萬歌珥，大麥一萬歌珥。第二年、第三年也是這樣。

6約坦在耶和華他神面前行正道，以致日漸強盛。

7約坦其餘的事和一切爭戰，並他的行為，都寫在以色列和猶大列

sanctuary, for you have been unfaithful; and you will not be honored by the LORD God."

19Uzziah, who had a censer in his hand ready to burn incense, became angry. While he was raging at the priests in their presence before the incense altar in the LORD's temple, leprosy*a* broke out on his forehead. 20When Azariah the chief priest and all the other priests looked at him, they saw that he had leprosy on his forehead, so they hurried him out. Indeed, he himself was eager to leave, because the LORD had afflicted him.

21King Uzziah had leprosy until the day he died. He lived in a separate house*b* —leprous, and excluded from the temple of the LORD. Jotham his son had charge of the palace and governed the people of the land.

22The other events of Uzziah's reign, from beginning to end, are recorded by the prophet Isaiah son of Amoz. 23Uzziah rested with his fathers and was buried near them in a field for burial that belonged to the kings, for people said, "He had leprosy." And Jotham his son succeeded him as king.

Jotham King of Judah

27 Jotham was twenty-five years old when he became king, and he reigned in Jerusalem sixteen years. His mother's name was Jerusha daughter of Zadok. 2He did what was right in the eyes of the LORD, just as his father Uzziah had done, but unlike him he did not enter the temple of the LORD. The people, however, continued their corrupt practices. 3Jotham rebuilt the Upper Gate of the temple of the LORD and did extensive work on the wall at the hill of Ophel. 4He built towns in the Judean hills and forts and towers in the wooded areas.

5Jotham made war on the king of the Ammonites and conquered them. That year the Ammonites paid him a hundred talents*c* of silver, ten thousand cors*d* of wheat and ten thousand cors of barley. The Ammonites brought him the same amount also in the second and third years.

6Jotham grew powerful because he walked steadfastly before the LORD his God.

7The other events in Jotham's reign, including all his wars and the other things he did, are written in the book of the kings of Israel and Judah.

---

a 19 The Hebrew word was used for various diseases affecting the skin—not necessarily leprosy; also in verses 20, 21 and 23.
b 21 Or *in a house where he was relieved of responsibilities*
c 5 That is, about 3 3/4 tons (about 3.4 metric tons)　　*d 5* That is, probably about 62,000 bushels (about 2,200 kiloliters)

8He was twenty-five years old when he became king, and he reigned in Jerusalem sixteen years. 9Jotham rested with his fathers and was buried in the City of David. And Ahaz his son succeeded him as king.

Ahaz King of Judah

28 Ahaz was twenty years old when he became king, and he reigned in Jerusalem sixteen years. Unlike David his father, he did not do what was right in the eyes of the LORD. 2He walked in the ways of the kings of Israel and also made cast idols for worshiping the Baals. 3He burned sacrifices in the Valley of Ben Hinnom and sacrificed his sons in the fire, following the detestable ways of the nations the LORD had driven out before the Israelites. 4He offered sacrifices and burned incense at the high places, on the hilltops and under every spreading tree.

5Therefore the LORD his God handed him over to the king of Aram. The Arameans defeated him and took many of his people as prisoners and brought them to Damascus.

He was also given into the hands of the king of Israel, who inflicted heavy casualties on him. 6In one day Pekah son of Remaliah killed a hundred and twenty thousand soldiers in Judah—because Judah had forsaken the LORD, the God of their fathers. 7Zicri, an Ephraimite warrior, killed Maaseiah the king's son, Azrikam the officer in charge of the palace, and Elkanah, second to the king. 8The Israelites took captive from their kinsmen two hundred thousand wives, sons and daughters. They also took a great deal of plunder, which they carried back to Samaria.

9But a prophet of the LORD named Oded was there, and he went out to meet the army when it returned to Samaria. He said to them, "Because the LORD, the God of your fathers, was angry with Judah, he gave them into your hand. But you have slaughtered them in a rage that reaches to heaven. 10And now you intend to make the men and women of Judah and Jerusalem your slaves. But aren't you also guilty of sins against the LORD your God? 11Now listen to me! Send back your fellow countrymen you have taken as prisoners, for the LORD's fierce anger rests on you."

12Then some of the leaders in Ephraim—Azariah son of Jehohanan, Berekiah son of Meshillemoth, Jehizkiah son of Shallum, and Amasa son of Hadlai—confronted those who were arriving from the war. 13"You must not bring those prisoners here," they said, "or we will be guilty before the LORD. Do you intend to

王記上。8他登基的時候年二十五歲，在耶路撒冷作王十六年。9約坦與他列祖同睡，葬在大衛城裏。他兒子亞哈斯接續他作王。

亞哈斯作猶大王

28 亞哈斯登基的時候年二十歲，在耶路撒冷作王十六年。不像他祖大衛行耶和華眼中看為正的事，2卻行以色列諸王的道，又鑄造巴力的像；3並且在欣嫩子谷燒香，用火焚燒他的兒女，行耶和華在以色列人面前所驅逐的外邦人那可憎的事；4並在邱壇上、山岡上、各青翠樹下獻祭燒香。

5所以耶和華他的神將他交在亞蘭王手裏。亞蘭王打敗他，擄了他許多的民，帶到大馬士革去。

神又將他交在以色列王手裏。以色列王向他大行殺戮。6利瑪利的兒子比加一日殺了猶大人十二萬，都是勇士。因為他們離棄了耶和華他們列祖的神。7有一個以法蓮中的勇士，名叫細基利，殺了王的兒子瑪西雅和管理王宮的押斯利甘，並宰相以利加拿。8以色列人擄了他們的弟兄，連婦人帶兒女共有二十萬，又掠了許多的財物，帶到撒馬利亞去了。

9但那裏有耶和華的一個先知，名叫俄德，出來迎接往撒馬利亞去的軍兵，對他們說："因為耶和華你們列祖的神惱怒猶大人，所以將他們交在你們手裏，你們竟怒氣沖天，大行殺戮！10如今你們又有意強逼猶大人和耶路撒冷人作你們的奴婢。你們豈不也有得罪耶和華你們神的事嗎？11現在你們當聽我說！要將擄來的弟兄釋放回去，因為耶和華向你們已經大發烈怒。"

12於是以法蓮人的幾個族長，就是約哈難的兒子亞撒利雅、米實利末的兒子比利家、沙龍的兒子耶希西家、哈得萊的兒子亞瑪撒，起來攔擋出兵回來的人，13對他們說："你們不可帶進這被擄的人來！你們想要使我們得罪耶和華，加增我們的罪惡過犯？因為我們的罪過甚大，已經有烈怒臨到以色列人了！"

14於是帶兵器的人，將擄來的人口和掠來的財物都留在眾首領和會眾的面前。15以上提名的那些人就站起，使被擄的人前來，其中有赤身的，就從所掠的財物中拿出衣服和鞋來，給他們穿；又給他們吃喝，用膏抹他們。其中有軟弱的，就使他們騎驢，送到棕樹城耶利哥他們弟兄那裏。隨後就回撒馬利亞去了。

16那時，亞哈斯王差遣人去見亞述諸王，求他們幫助。17因為以東人又來攻擊猶大，擄掠子民。18非利士人也來侵佔高原和猶大南方的城邑，取了伯示麥、亞雅崙、基低羅、梭哥和屬梭哥的鄉村，亭納和屬亭納的鄉村，瑾鎮和屬瑾鎮的鄉村，就住在那裏。19因為以色列王亞哈斯在猶大放肆，大大干犯耶和華，所以耶和華使猶大卑微。20亞述王提革拉毘尼色上來，卻沒有幫助他，反倒欺凌他。21亞哈斯從耶和華殿裏和王宮中，並首領家內所取的財寶給了亞述王，這也無濟於事。

22這亞哈斯王在急難的時候，越發得罪耶和華。23他祭祀攻擊他的大馬士革之神，說："因為亞蘭王的神幫助他們，我也獻祭與他，他好幫助我。"但那些神使他和以色列眾敗亡了。

24亞哈斯將神殿裏的器皿都聚了來，毀壞了，且封鎖耶和華殿的門，在耶路撒冷各處的拐角建築祭壇；25又在猶大各城建立邱壇，與別神燒香，惹動耶和華他列祖神的怒氣。

26亞哈斯其餘的事和他的行為，自始至終都寫在猶大和以色列諸王記上。27亞哈斯與他列祖同睡，葬在耶路撒冷城裏，沒有送入以色列諸王的墳墓中。他兒子希西家接續他作王。

add to our sin and guilt? For our guilt is already great, and his fierce anger rests on Israel."

14So the soldiers gave up the prisoners and plunder in the presence of the officials and all the assembly. 15The men designated by name took the prisoners, and from the plunder they clothed all who were naked. They provided them with clothes and sandals, food and drink, and healing balm. All those who were weak they put on donkeys. So they took them back to their fellow countrymen at Jericho, the City of Palms, and returned to Samaria.

16At that time King Ahaz sent to the king[a] of Assyria for help. 17The Edomites had again come and attacked Judah and carried away prisoners, 18while the Philistines had raided towns in the foothills and in the Negev of Judah. They captured and occupied Beth Shemesh, Aijalon and Gederoth, as well as Soco, Timnah and Gimzo, with their surrounding villages. 19The LORD had humbled Judah because of Ahaz king of Israel,[b] for he had promoted wickedness in Judah and had been most unfaithful to the LORD. 20Tiglath-Pileser[c] king of Assyria came to him, but he gave him trouble instead of help. 21Ahaz took some of the things from the temple of the LORD and from the royal palace and from the princes and presented them to the king of Assyria, but that did not help him.

22In his time of trouble King Ahaz became even more unfaithful to the LORD. 23He offered sacrifices to the gods of Damascus, who had defeated him; for he thought, "Since the gods of the kings of Aram have helped them, I will sacrifice to them so they will help me." But they were his downfall and the downfall of all Israel.

24Ahaz gathered together the furnishings from the temple of God and took them away.[d] He shut the doors of the LORD's temple and set up altars at every street corner in Jerusalem. 25In every town in Judah he built high places to burn sacrifices to other gods and provoked the LORD, the God of his fathers, to anger.

26The other events of his reign and all his ways, from beginning to end, are written in the book of the kings of Judah and Israel. 27Ahaz rested with his fathers and was buried in the city of Jerusalem, but he was not placed in the tombs of the kings of Israel. And Hezekiah his son succeeded him as king.

a 16 One Hebrew manuscript, Septuagint and Vulgate (see also 2 Kings 16:7); most Hebrew manuscripts kings
b 19 That is, Judah, as frequently in 2 Chronicles
c 20 Hebrew Tilgath-Pilneser, a variant of Tiglath-Pileser
d 24 Or and cut them up

Hezekiah Purifies the Temple

29 Hezekiah was twenty-five years old when he became king, and he reigned in Jerusalem twenty-nine years. His mother's name was Abijah daughter of Zechariah. ²He did what was right in the eyes of the LORD, just as his father David had done.

³In the first month of the first year of his reign, he opened the doors of the temple of the LORD and repaired them. ⁴He brought in the priests and the Levites, assembled them in the square on the east side ⁵and said: "Listen to me, Levites! Consecrate yourselves now and consecrate the temple of the LORD, the God of your fathers. Remove all defilement from the sanctuary. ⁶Our fathers were unfaithful; they did evil in the eyes of the LORD our God and forsook him. They turned their faces away from the LORD's dwelling place and turned their backs on him. ⁷They also shut the doors of the portico and put out the lamps. They did not burn incense or present any burnt offerings at the sanctuary to the God of Israel. ⁸Therefore, the anger of the LORD has fallen on Judah and Jerusalem; he has made them an object of dread and horror and scorn, as you can see with your own eyes. ⁹This is why our fathers have fallen by the sword and why our sons and daughters and our wives are in captivity. ¹⁰Now I intend to make a covenant with the LORD, the God of Israel, so that his fierce anger will turn away from us. ¹¹My sons, do not be negligent now, for the LORD has chosen you to stand before him and serve him, to minister before him and to burn incense."

¹²Then these Levites set to work:

from the Kohathites,

Mahath son of Amasai and Joel son of Azariah;

from the Merarites,

Kish son of Abdi and Azariah son of Jehallelel;

from the Gershonites,

Joah son of Zimmah and Eden son of Joah;

¹³from the descendants of Elizaphan,

Shimri and Jeiel;

from the descendants of Asaph,

Zechariah and Mattaniah;

¹⁴from the descendants of Heman,

Jehiel and Shimei;

from the descendants of Jeduthun,

Shemaiah and Uzziel.

¹⁵When they had assembled their brothers and consecrated themselves, they went in to purify the temple of the LORD, as the king had ordered, following the word of the LORD. ¹⁶The

希西家潔淨聖殿

29 希西家登基的時候年二十五歲，在耶路撒冷作王二十九年。他母親名叫亞比雅，是撒迦利雅的女兒。²希西家行耶和華眼中看為正的事，效法他祖大衛一切所行的。

³元年正月，開了耶和華殿的門，重新修理。⁴他召眾祭司和利未人來，聚集在東邊的寬闊處，⁵對他們說：「利未人哪，當聽我說！現在你們要潔淨自己，又潔淨耶和華你們列祖神的殿，從聖所中除去污穢之物。⁶我們列祖犯了罪，行耶和華我們神眼中看為惡的事，離棄他，轉臉背向他的居所，⁷封鎖廊門，吹滅燈火，不在聖所中向以色列神燒香或獻燔祭。⁸因此，耶和華的忿怒臨到猶大和耶路撒冷，將其中的人拋來拋去，令人驚駭、嗤笑，正如你們親眼所見的。⁹所以我們的祖宗倒在刀下，我們的妻子兒女也被擄掠。¹⁰現在我心中有意，與耶和華以色列的神立約，好使他的烈怒轉離我們。¹¹我的眾子啊，現在不要懈怠，因為耶和華揀選你們站在他面前侍奉他，與他燒香。」

¹²於是，利未人哥轄的子孫亞瑪賽的兒子瑪哈，

亞撒利雅的兒子約珥；

米拉利的子孫亞伯底的兒子基士；

耶哈利勒的兒子亞撒利雅；

革順的子孫薪瑪的兒子約亞；

約亞的兒子伊甸；

¹³以利撒反的子孫申利和耶利，

亞薩的子孫撒迦利雅和瑪探雅；

¹⁴希幔的子孫耶歇和示每；

耶杜頓的子孫示瑪雅和烏薛。

¹⁵起來聚集他們的弟兄，潔淨自己，照着王的吩咐、耶和華的命令，進去潔淨耶和華的殿。¹⁶祭司進入

耶和華的殿要潔淨殿，將殿中所有污穢之物搬到耶和華殿的院內，利未人接去，搬到外頭汲淪溪邊。17從正月初一日潔淨起，初八日到了耶和華的殿廊，用八日的工夫潔淨耶和華的殿，到正月十六日才潔淨完了。

18於是，他們晉見希西家王說："我們已將耶和華的全殿和燔祭壇，並壇的一切器皿、陳設餅的桌子與桌子的一切器皿都潔淨了。19並且亞哈斯王在位犯罪的時候所廢棄的器皿，我們預備齊全，且潔淨了，現今都在耶和華的壇前。"

20希西家王清早起來，聚集城裏的首領都上耶和華的殿。21牽了七隻公牛，七隻公羊，七隻羊羔，七隻公山羊，要為國、為殿、為猶大人作贖罪祭。王吩咐亞倫的子孫眾祭司，獻在耶和華的壇上，22就宰了公牛，祭司接血灑在壇上；宰了公羊，把血灑在壇上；又宰了羊羔，也把血灑在壇上。23把那作贖罪祭的公山羊牽到王和會眾面前，他們就按手在其上。24祭司宰了羊，將血獻在壇上作贖罪祭，為以色列眾人贖罪，因為王吩咐將燔祭和贖罪祭為以色列眾人獻上。

25王又派利未人在耶和華殿中敲鈸、鼓瑟、彈琴，乃照大衛和他先見迦得，並先知拿單所吩咐的，就是耶和華藉先知所吩咐的。26利未人拿大衛的樂器，祭司拿號，一同站立。

27希西家吩咐在壇上獻燔祭。燔祭一獻，就唱讚美耶和華的歌，用號，並用以色列王大衛的樂器相和。28會眾都敬拜，歌唱的歌唱，吹號的吹號，如此直到燔祭獻完了。

priests went into the sanctuary of the LORD to purify it. They brought out to the courtyard of the LORD's temple everything unclean that they found in the temple of the LORD. The Levites took it and carried it out to the Kidron Valley. 17They began the consecration on the first day of the first month, and by the eighth day of the month they reached the portico of the LORD. For eight more days they consecrated the temple of the LORD itself, finishing on the sixteenth day of the first month.

18Then they went in to King Hezekiah and reported: "We have purified the entire temple of the LORD, the altar of burnt offering with all its utensils, and the table for setting out the consecrated bread, with all its articles. 19We have prepared and consecrated all the articles that King Ahaz removed in his unfaithfulness while he was king. They are now in front of the LORD's altar."

20Early the next morning King Hezekiah gathered the city officials together and went up to the temple of the LORD. 21They brought seven bulls, seven rams, seven male lambs and seven male goats as a sin offering for the kingdom, for the sanctuary and for Judah. The king commanded the priests, the descendants of Aaron, to offer these on the altar of the LORD. 22So they slaughtered the bulls, and the priests took the blood and sprinkled it on the altar; next they slaughtered the rams and sprinkled their blood on the altar; then they slaughtered the lambs and sprinkled their blood on the altar. 23The goats for the sin offering were brought before the king and the assembly, and they laid their hands on them. 24The priests then slaughtered the goats and presented their blood on the altar for a sin offering to atone for all Israel, because the king had ordered the burnt offering and the sin offering for all Israel.

25He stationed the Levites in the temple of the LORD with cymbals, harps and lyres in the way prescribed by David and Gad the king's seer and Nathan the prophet; this was commanded by the LORD through his prophets. 26So the Levites stood ready with David's instruments, and the priests with their trumpets.

27Hezekiah gave the order to sacrifice the burnt offering on the altar. As the offering began, singing to the LORD began also, accompanied by trumpets and the instruments of David king of Israel. 28The whole assembly bowed in worship, while the singers sang and the trumpeters played. All this continued until the sacrifice of the burnt offering was completed.

²⁹When the offerings were finished, the king and everyone present with him knelt down and worshiped. ³⁰King Hezekiah and his officials ordered the Levites to praise the LORD with the words of David and of Asaph the seer. So they sang praises with gladness and bowed their heads and worshiped.

³¹Then Hezekiah said, "You have now dedicated yourselves to the LORD. Come and bring sacrifices and thank offerings to the temple of the LORD." So the assembly brought sacrifices and thank offerings, and all whose hearts were willing brought burnt offerings.

³²The number of burnt offerings the assembly brought was seventy bulls, a hundred rams and two hundred male lambs—all of them for burnt offerings to the LORD. ³³The animals consecrated as sacrifices amounted to six hundred bulls and three thousand sheep and goats. ³⁴The priests, however, were too few to skin all the burnt offerings; so their kinsmen the Levites helped them until the task was finished and until other priests had been consecrated, for the Levites had been more conscientious in consecrating themselves than the priests had been. ³⁵There were burnt offerings in abundance, together with the fat of the fellowship offerings[a] and the drink offerings that accompanied the burnt offerings.

So the service of the temple of the LORD was reestablished. ³⁶Hezekiah and all the people rejoiced at what God had brought about for his people, because it was done so quickly.

Hezekiah Celebrates the Passover

30 Hezekiah sent word to all Israel and Judah and also wrote letters to Ephraim and Manasseh, inviting them to come to the temple of the LORD in Jerusalem and celebrate the Passover to the LORD, the God of Israel. ²The king and his officials and the whole assembly in Jerusalem decided to celebrate the Passover in the second month. ³They had not been able to celebrate it at the regular time because not enough priests had consecrated themselves and the people had not assembled in Jerusalem. ⁴The plan seemed right both to the king and to the whole assembly. ⁵They decided to send a proclamation throughout Israel, from Beersheba to Dan, calling the people to come to Jerusalem and celebrate the Passover to the LORD, the God of Israel. It had not been celebrated in large numbers according to what was written.

²⁹獻完了祭，王和一切跟隨的人都俯伏敬拜。³⁰希西家王與眾首領又吩咐利未人用大衛和先見亞薩的詩詞頌讚耶和華。他們就歡歡喜喜地頌讚耶和華，低頭敬拜。

³¹希西家說：“你們既然歸耶和華為聖，就要前來把祭物和感謝祭奉到耶和華殿裏。”會眾就把祭物和感謝祭奉來，凡甘心樂意的也將燔祭奉來。

³²會眾所奉的燔祭如下：公牛七十隻，公羊一百隻，羊羔二百隻，這都是作燔祭獻給耶和華的。³³又有分別為聖之物：公牛六百隻，綿羊三千隻。³⁴但祭司太少，不能剝盡燔祭牲的皮，所以他們的弟兄利未人幫助他們，直等燔祭的事完了，又等別的祭司自潔了。因為利未人誠心自潔，勝過祭司。³⁵燔祭和平安祭牲的脂油，並燔祭同獻的奠祭甚多。

這樣，耶和華殿中的事務俱都齊備了（註：或作“就整頓了”）。³⁶這事辦得甚速，希西家和眾民都喜樂，是因神為眾民所預備的。

希西家守逾越節

30 希西家差遣人去見以色列和猶大眾人，又寫信給以法蓮和瑪拿西人，叫他們到耶路撒冷耶和華的殿，向耶和華以色列的神守逾越節。²因為王和眾首領，並耶路撒冷全會眾已經商議，要在二月內守逾越節。³正月（註：原文作“那時”）間他們不能守，因為自潔的祭司尚不敷用，百姓也沒有聚集在耶路撒冷。⁴王與全會眾都以這事為善。⁵於是定了命令傳遍以色列，從別是巴直到但，使他們都來，在耶路撒冷向耶和華以色列的神守逾越節。因為照所寫的例，守這節的不多了（註：或作“因為民許久沒有照所寫的例守節了”）。

---

a 35 Traditionally *peace offerings*

⁶驛卒就把王和眾首領的信，遵着王命，傳遍以色列和猶大。信內說：

"以色列人哪，你們當轉向耶和華亞伯拉罕、以撒、以色列的神，好叫他轉向你們這脫離亞述王手的餘民。⁷你們不要效法你們列祖和你們的弟兄。他們干犯耶和華他們列祖的神，以致耶和華丟棄他們，使他們敗亡（註：或作"令人驚駭"），正如你們所見的。⁸現在不要像你們列祖硬着頸項，只要歸順耶和華，進入他的聖所，就是永遠成聖的居所；又要侍奉耶和華你們的神，好使他的烈怒轉離你們。⁹你們若轉向耶和華，你們的弟兄和兒女，必在擄掠他們的人面前蒙憐恤，得以歸回這地，因為耶和華你們的神有恩典、施憐憫。你們若轉向他，他必不轉臉不顧你們。"

¹⁰驛卒就由這城跑到那城，傳遍了以法蓮、瑪拿西、直到西布倫。那裏的人卻戲笑他們，譏誚他們。¹¹然而亞設、瑪拿西、西布倫中也有人自卑，來到耶路撒冷。¹²神也感動猶大人，使他們一心遵行王與眾首領憑耶和華之言所發的命令。

¹³二月，有許多人在耶路撒冷聚集，成為大會，要守除酵節。¹⁴他們起來，把耶路撒冷的祭壇和燒香的壇盡都除去，拋在汲淪溪中。

¹⁵二月十四日，宰了逾越節的羊羔。祭司與利未人覺得慚愧，就潔淨自己，把燔祭奉到耶和華殿中。¹⁶遵着神人摩西的律法，照例站在自己的地方，祭司從利未人手裏接過血來，灑在壇上。¹⁷會中有許多人尚未自潔，所以利未人為一切不潔之人宰逾越節的羊羔，使他們在耶和華面前成為聖潔。¹⁸、¹⁹以法蓮、瑪拿西、以薩迦、西布倫，有許多人尚未自潔，他們卻也吃逾越節的羊羔，不合所記錄的定例。希西家為他們禱告說："凡專心尋求神，就是耶和華他列祖之神的，雖不照着聖所潔淨之禮自潔，求至善的耶和華

"People of Israel, return to the LORD, the God of Abraham, Isaac and Israel, that he may return to you who are left, who have escaped from the hand of the kings of Assyria. 7Do not be like your fathers and brothers, who were unfaithful to the LORD, the God of their fathers, so that he made them an object of horror, as you see. 8Do not be stiff-necked, as your fathers were; submit to the LORD. Come to the sanctuary, which he has consecrated forever. Serve the LORD your God, so that his fierce anger will turn away from you. 9If you return to the LORD, then your brothers and your children will be shown compassion by their captors and will come back to this land, for the LORD your God is gracious and compassionate. He will not turn his face from you if you return to him."

10The couriers went from town to town in Ephraim and Manasseh, as far as Zebulun, but the people scorned and ridiculed them. 11Nevertheless, some men of Asher, Manasseh and Zebulun humbled themselves and went to Jerusalem. 12Also in Judah the hand of God was on the people to give them unity of mind to carry out what the king and his officials had ordered, following the word of the LORD.

13A very large crowd of people assembled in Jerusalem to celebrate the Feast of Unleavened Bread in the second month. 14They removed the altars in Jerusalem and cleared away the incense altars and threw them into the Kidron Valley.

15They slaughtered the Passover lamb on the fourteenth day of the second month. The priests and the Levites were ashamed and consecrated themselves and brought burnt offerings to the temple of the LORD. 16Then they took up their regular positions as prescribed in the Law of Moses the man of God. The priests sprinkled the blood handed to them by the Levites. 17Since many in the crowd had not consecrated themselves, the Levites had to kill the Passover lambs for all those who were not ceremonially clean and could not consecrate their lambs to the LORD. 18Although most of the many people who came from Ephraim, Manasseh, Issachar and Zebulun had not purified themselves, yet they ate the Passover, contrary to what was written. But Hezekiah prayed for them, saying, "May the LORD, who is good, pardon everyone 19who sets his heart on seeking God—the LORD, the God of his fathers—even if he is not clean according to the rules of the sanctuary." [20]And the LORD heard Hezekiah and healed the people.

[21]The Israelites who were present in Jerusalem celebrated the Feast of Unleavened Bread for seven days with great rejoicing, while the Levites and priests sang to the LORD every day, accompanied by the LORD's instruments of praise.[a]

[22]Hezekiah spoke encouragingly to all the Levites, who showed good understanding of the service of the LORD. For the seven days they ate their assigned portion and offered fellowship offerings[b] and praised the LORD, the God of their fathers.

[23]The whole assembly then agreed to celebrate the festival seven more days; so for another seven days they celebrated joyfully. [24]Hezekiah king of Judah provided a thousand bulls and seven thousand sheep and goats for the assembly, and the officials provided them with a thousand bulls and ten thousand sheep and goats. A great number of priests consecrated themselves. [25]The entire assembly of Judah rejoiced, along with the priests and Levites and all who had assembled from Israel, including the aliens who had come from Israel and those who lived in Judah. [26]There was great joy in Jerusalem, for since the days of Solomon son of David king of Israel there had been nothing like this in Jerusalem. [27]The priests and the Levites stood to bless the people, and God heard them, for their prayer reached heaven, his holy dwelling place.

31 When all this had ended, the Israelites who were there went out to the towns of Judah, smashed the sacred stones and cut down the Asherah poles. They destroyed the high places and the altars throughout Judah and Benjamin and in Ephraim and Manasseh. After they had destroyed all of them, the Israelites returned to their own towns and to their own property.

Contributions for Worship

[2]Hezekiah assigned the priests and Levites to divisions—each of them according to their duties as priests or Levites—to offer burnt offerings and fellowship offerings,[b] to minister, to give thanks and to sing praises at the gates of the LORD's dwelling. [3]The king contributed from his own possessions for the morning and evening

也饒恕他。"[20]耶和華垂聽希西家的禱告，就饒恕（註：原文作"醫治"）百姓。

[21]在耶路撒冷的以色列人，大大喜樂，守除酵節七日。利未人和祭司用響亮的樂器，日日頌讚耶和華。

[22]希西家慰勞一切善於侍奉耶和華的利未人。於是眾人吃節筵七日，又獻平安祭，且向耶和華他們列祖的神認罪。

[23]全會眾商議，要再守節七日，於是歡歡喜喜地又守節七日。[24]猶大王希西家賜給會眾公牛一千隻，羊七千隻為祭物；眾首領也賜給會眾公牛一千隻，羊一萬隻；並有許多的祭司潔淨自己。[25]猶大全會眾、祭司利未人，並那從以色列地來的會眾和寄居的人，以及猶大寄居的人，盡都喜樂。[26]這樣，在耶路撒冷大有喜樂，自從以色列王大衛兒子所羅門的時候，在耶路撒冷沒有這樣的喜樂。[27]那時，祭司利未人起來，為民祝福。他們的聲音，蒙神垂聽；他們的禱告，達到天上的聖所。

31 這事既都完畢，在那裏的以色列眾人就到猶大的城邑，打碎柱像、砍斷木偶，又在猶大、便雅憫、以法蓮、瑪拿西遍地，將邱壇和祭壇拆毀淨盡。於是以色列眾人各回各城，各歸各地。

為敬拜作奉獻

[2]希西家派定祭司利未人的班次，各按各職獻燔祭和平安祭，又在耶和華殿（註：原文作"營"）門內侍奉、稱謝、頌讚耶和華。[3]王又從自己的產業中定出分來為燔祭，就是早晚的燔祭，和安息日、月朔、並節期

---

a 21 Or priests praised the LORD every day with resounding instruments belonging to the LORD   *b 22,2 Traditionally peace offerings*

的燔祭，都是按耶和華律法上所載的。⁴又吩咐住耶路撒冷的百姓，將祭司利未人所應得的分給他們，使他們專心遵守耶和華的律法。⁵諭旨一出，以色列人就把初熟的五穀、新酒、油、蜜和田地的出產多多送來，又把各物的十分之一送來的極多。⁶住猶大各城的以色列人和猶大人，也將牛羊的十分之一，並分別為聖歸耶和華他們神之物，就是十分取一之物，盡都送來積成堆壘。⁷從三月積起，到七月才完。⁸希西家和眾首領來，看見堆壘，就稱頌耶和華，又為耶和華的民以色列人祝福。

⁹希西家向祭司利未人查問這堆壘。¹⁰撒督家的大祭司亞撒利雅回答說："自從民將供物送到耶和華殿以來，我們不但吃飽，且剩下的甚多。因為耶和華賜福與他的民，所剩下的才這樣豐盛。"

¹¹希西家吩咐在耶和華殿裏預備倉房，他們就預備了。¹²他們誠心將供物和十分取一之物，並分別為聖之物，都搬入倉內。利未人歌楠雅掌管這事，他兄弟示每為副管。¹³耶歇、亞撒細雅、拿哈、亞撒黑、耶利末、約撒拔、以列、伊斯瑪基雅、瑪哈、比拿雅都是督理，在歌楠雅和他兄弟示每的手下，是希西家王和管理神殿的亞撒利雅所派的。

¹⁴守東門的利未人音拿的兒子可利，掌管樂意獻與神的禮物，發放獻與耶和華的供物和至聖的物。¹⁵在他手下有伊甸、珉雅珉、耶書亞、示瑪雅、亞瑪利雅、示迦尼雅，在祭司的各城裏供緊要的職任，無論弟兄大小，都按着班次分給他們。

¹⁶按家譜，三歲以外的男丁，凡每日進耶和華殿按班次供職的，也分給他。¹⁷又按宗族家譜分給祭司，按班次職任分給二十歲以外的利未

burnt offerings and for the burnt offerings on the Sabbaths, New Moons and appointed feasts as written in the Law of the LORD. ⁴He ordered the people living in Jerusalem to give the portion due the priests and Levites so they could devote themselves to the Law of the LORD. ⁵As soon as the order went out, the Israelites generously gave the firstfruits of their grain, new wine, oil and honey and all that the fields produced. They brought a great amount, a tithe of everything. ⁶The men of Israel and Judah who lived in the towns of Judah also brought a tithe of their herds and flocks and a tithe of the holy things dedicated to the LORD their God, and they piled them in heaps. ⁷They began doing this in the third month and finished in the seventh month. ⁸When Hezekiah and his officials came and saw the heaps, they praised the LORD and blessed his people Israel.

⁹Hezekiah asked the priests and Levites about the heaps; ¹⁰and Azariah the chief priest, from the family of Zadok, answered, "Since the people began to bring their contributions to the temple of the LORD, we have had enough to eat and plenty to spare, because the LORD has blessed his people, and this great amount is left over."

¹¹Hezekiah gave orders to prepare storerooms in the temple of the LORD, and this was done. ¹²Then they faithfully brought in the contributions, tithes and dedicated gifts. Conaniah, a Levite, was in charge of these things, and his brother Shimei was next in rank. ¹³Jehiel, Azaziah, Nahath, Asahel, Jerimoth, Jozabad, Eliel, Ismakiah, Mahath and Benaiah were supervisors under Conaniah and Shimei his brother, by appointment of King Hezekiah and Azariah the official in charge of the temple of God.

¹⁴Kore son of Imnah the Levite, keeper of the East Gate, was in charge of the freewill offerings given to God, distributing the contributions made to the LORD and also the consecrated gifts. ¹⁵Eden, Miniamin, Jeshua, Shemaiah, Amariah and Shecaniah assisted him faithfully in the towns of the priests, distributing to their fellow priests according to their divisions, old and young alike.

¹⁶In addition, they distributed to the males three years old or more whose names were in the genealogical records—all who would enter the temple of the LORD to perform the daily duties of their various tasks, according to their responsibilities and their divisions. ¹⁷And they distributed to the priests enrolled by their families in the genealogical records and likewise to the Levites twenty years old or more, according to their responsibilities and their divisions.

18They included all the little ones, the wives, and the sons and daughters of the whole community listed in these genealogical records. For they were faithful in consecrating themselves.

19As for the priests, the descendants of Aaron, who lived on the farm lands around their towns or in any other towns, men were designated by name to distribute portions to every male among them and to all who were recorded in the genealogies of the Levites.

20This is what Hezekiah did throughout Judah, doing what was good and right and faithful before the LORD his God. 21In everything that he undertook in the service of God's temple and in obedience to the law and the commands, he sought his God and worked wholeheartedly. And so he prospered.

Sennacherib Threatens Jerusalem

32 After all that Hezekiah had so faithfully done, Sennacherib king of Assyria came and invaded Judah. He laid siege to the fortified cities, thinking to conquer them for himself. 2When Hezekiah saw that Sennacherib had come and that he intended to make war on Jerusalem, 3he consulted with his officials and military staff about blocking off the water from the springs outside the city, and they helped him. 4A large force of men assembled, and they blocked all the springs and the stream that flowed through the land. "Why should the kings*a* of Assyria come and find plenty of water?" they said. 5Then he worked hard repairing all the broken sections of the wall and building towers on it. He built another wall outside that one and reinforced the supporting terraces*b* of the City of David. He also made large numbers of weapons and shields.

6He appointed military officers over the people and assembled them before him in the square at the city gate and encouraged them with these words: 7"Be strong and courageous. Do not be afraid or discouraged because of the king of Assyria and the vast army with him, for there is a greater power with us than with him. 8With him is only the arm of flesh, but with us is the LORD our God to help us and to fight our battles." And the people gained confidence from what Hezekiah the king of Judah said.

9Later, when Sennacherib king of Assyria and all his forces were laying siege to Lachish, he sent his officers to Jerusalem with this message for Hezekiah king of Judah and for all the people of Judah who were there:

人。18又按家譜計算，分給他們會中的妻子、兒女，因他們身供要職，自潔成聖。

19按名派定的人，要把應得的，分給亞倫子孫，住在各城郊野祭司所有的男丁和一切載入家譜的利未人。

20希西家在猶大遍地這樣辦理，行耶和華他神眼中看為善為正為忠的事。21凡他所行的，無論是辦神殿的事，是遵律法守誠命，是尋求他的神，都是盡心去行，無不亨通。

西拿基立恫嚇耶路撒冷

32 這虔誠的事以後，亞述王西拿基立來侵入猶大，圍困一切堅固城，想要攻破佔據。2希西家見西拿基立來定意要攻打耶路撒冷，3就與首領和勇士商議塞住城外的泉源，他們就都幫助他。4於是有許多人聚集，塞了一切泉源，並通流國中的小河，說："亞述王來，為何讓他得著許多水呢？"5希西家力圖自強，就修築所有拆毀的城牆，高與城樓相齊，在城外又築一城，堅固大衛城的米羅，製造了許多軍器、盾牌。

6設立軍長管理百姓，將他們招聚在城門的寬闊處，用話勉勵他們說：7"你們當剛強壯膽，不要因亞述王和跟隨他的大軍恐懼、驚慌，因為與我們同在的，比與他們同在的更大！8與他們同在的是肉臂，與我們同在的是耶和華我們的神！他必幫助我們，為我們爭戰。"百姓就靠猶大王希西家的話，安然無懼了。

9此後，亞述王西拿基立和他的全軍攻打拉吉，就差遣臣僕到耶路撒冷見猶大王希西家和一切在耶路撒冷的猶大人，說：

---

a 4 Hebrew; Septuagint and Syriac king   b 5 Or the Millo

10 "亞述王西拿基立如此說：你們倚靠甚麼還在耶路撒冷受困呢？ 11希西家對你們說：'耶和華我們的神必救我們脫離亞述王的手。'這不是誘惑你們，使你們受飢渴而死嗎？ 12這希西家豈不是廢去耶和華的邱壇和祭壇，吩咐猶大與耶路撒冷的人說：'你們當在一個壇前敬拜，在其上燒香'嗎？

13 "我與我列祖向列邦所行的，你們豈不知道嗎？列邦的神何嘗能救自己的國脫離我手呢？ 14我列祖所滅的國，那些神中誰能救自己的民脫離我手呢？難道你們的神能救你們脫離我手嗎？ 15所以你們不要叫希西家這樣欺哄誘惑你們，也不要信他！因為沒有一國一邦的神能救自己的民脫離我手和我列祖的手，何況你們的神，更不能救你們脫離我的手。"

16西拿基立的臣僕還有別的話毀謗耶和華神和他僕人希西家。 17西拿基立也寫信毀謗耶和華神以色列的神說："列邦的神既不能救他的民脫離我手，希西家的神也不能救他的民脫離我手了。" 18亞述王的臣僕用猶大言語向耶路撒冷城上的民大聲呼叫，要驚嚇他們、擾亂他們，以便取城。 19他們論耶路撒冷的神，如同論世上人手所造的神一樣。

20希西家王和亞摩斯的兒子先知以賽亞因此禱告，向天呼求。 21耶和華就差遣一個使者進入亞述王營中，把所有大能的勇士和官長、將帥盡都滅了。亞述王滿面含羞地回到本國，進了他神的廟中，有他親生的兒子在那裏用刀殺了他。

22這樣，耶和華救希西家和耶路撒冷的居民，脫離亞述王西拿基立的手，也脫離一切仇敵的手，又賜他們四境平安。 23有許多人到耶路撒冷，將供物獻與耶和華，又將寶物送給猶大王希西家。此後，希西家在列邦人的眼中看為尊大。

10"This is what Sennacherib king of Assyria says: On what are you basing your confidence, that you remain in Jerusalem under siege? 11When Hezekiah says, 'The LORD our God will save us from the hand of the king of Assyria,' he is misleading you, to let you die of hunger and thirst. 12Did not Hezekiah himself remove this god's high places and altars, saying to Judah and Jerusalem, 'You must worship before one altar and burn sacrifices on it'?

13"Do you not know what I and my fathers have done to all the peoples of the other lands? Were the gods of those nations ever able to deliver their land from my hand? 14Who of all the gods of these nations that my fathers destroyed has been able to save his people from me? How then can your god deliver you from my hand? 15Now do not let Hezekiah deceive you and mislead you like this. Do not believe him, for no god of any nation or kingdom has been able to deliver his people from my hand or the hand of my fathers. How much less will your god deliver you from my hand!"

16Sennacherib's officers spoke further against the LORD God and against his servant Hezekiah. 17The king also wrote letters insulting the LORD, the God of Israel, and saying this against him: "Just as the gods of the peoples of the other lands did not rescue their people from my hand, so the god of Hezekiah will not rescue his people from my hand." 18Then they called out in Hebrew to the people of Jerusalem who were on the wall, to terrify them and make them afraid in order to capture the city. 19They spoke about the God of Jerusalem as they did about the gods of the other peoples of the world—the work of men's hands.

20King Hezekiah and the prophet Isaiah son of Amoz cried out in prayer to heaven about this. 21And the LORD sent an angel, who annihilated all the fighting men and the leaders and officers in the camp of the Assyrian king. So he withdrew to his own land in disgrace. And when he went into the temple of his god, some of his sons cut him down with the sword.

22So the LORD saved Hezekiah and the people of Jerusalem from the hand of Sennacherib king of Assyria and from the hand of all others. He took care of them*a* on every side. 23Many brought offerings to Jerusalem for the LORD and valuable gifts for Hezekiah king of Judah. From then on he was highly regarded by all the nations.

---

a 22 Hebrew; Septuagint and Vulgate He gave them rest

Hezekiah's Pride, Success and Death

²⁴In those days Hezekiah became ill and was at the point of death. He prayed to the LORD, who answered him and gave him a miraculous sign. ²⁵But Hezekiah's heart was proud and he did not respond to the kindness shown him; therefore the LORD's wrath was on him and on Judah and Jerusalem. ²⁶Then Hezekiah repented of the pride of his heart, as did the people of Jerusalem; therefore the LORD's wrath did not come upon them during the days of Hezekiah.

²⁷Hezekiah had very great riches and honor, and he made treasuries for his silver and gold and for his precious stones, spices, shields and all kinds of valuables. ²⁸He also made buildings to store the harvest of grain, new wine and oil; and he made stalls for various kinds of cattle, and pens for the flocks. ²⁹He built villages and acquired great numbers of flocks and herds, for God had given him very great riches.

³⁰It was Hezekiah who blocked the upper outlet of the Gihon spring and channeled the water down to the west side of the City of David. He succeeded in everything he undertook. ³¹But when envoys were sent by the rulers of Babylon to ask him about the miraculous sign that had occurred in the land, God left him to test him and to know everything that was in his heart.

³²The other events of Hezekiah's reign and his acts of devotion are written in the vision of the prophet Isaiah son of Amoz in the book of the kings of Judah and Israel. ³³Hezekiah rested with his fathers and was buried on the hill where the tombs of David's descendants are. All Judah and the people of Jerusalem honored him when he died. And Manasseh his son succeeded him as king.

Manasseh King of Judah

33 Manasseh was twelve years old when he became king, and he reigned in Jerusalem fifty-five years. ²He did evil in the eyes of the LORD, following the detestable practices of the nations the LORD had driven out before the Israelites. ³He rebuilt the high places his father Hezekiah had demolished; he also erected altars to the Baals and made Asherah poles. He bowed down to all the starry hosts and worshiped them. ⁴He built altars in the temple of the LORD, of which the LORD had said, "My Name will remain in Jerusalem forever." ⁵In both courts of the temple of the LORD, he built altars to all the starry hosts. ⁶He sacrificed his sons in^a the fire in the Valley of Ben Hinnom, practiced

a 6 Or He made his sons pass through

希西家的驕傲、成就和死

²⁴那時希西家病得要死，就禱告耶和華，耶和華應允他，賜他一個兆頭。²⁵希西家卻沒有照他所蒙的恩，報答耶和華，因他心裏驕傲，所以忿怒要臨到他和猶大並耶路撒冷。²⁶但希西家和耶路撒冷的居民，覺得心裏驕傲，就一同自卑，以致耶和華的忿怒在希西家的日子沒有臨到他們。

²⁷希西家大有尊榮資財。建造府庫，收藏金銀、寶石、香料、盾牌和各樣的寶器；²⁸又建造倉房，收藏五穀、新酒和油，又為各類牲畜蓋棚立圈；²⁹並且建立城邑，還有許多的羊羣牛羣，因為神賜他極多的財產。

³⁰這希西家也塞住基訓的上源，引水直下，流在大衞城的西邊。希西家所行的事，盡都亨通。³¹惟有一件事，就是巴比倫王差遣使者來見希西家，訪問國中所現的奇事；這件事神離開他，要試驗他，好知道他心內如何。

³²希西家其餘的事和他的善行，都寫在亞摩斯的兒子先知以賽亞的默示書上和猶大、以色列的諸王記上。³³希西家與他列祖同睡，葬在大衞子孫的高陵上。他死的時候，猶大人和耶路撒冷的居民都尊敬他。他兒子瑪拿西接續他作王。

瑪拿西作猶大王

33 瑪拿西登基的時候年十二歲，在耶路撒冷作王五十五年。²他行耶和華眼中看為惡的事，效法耶和華在以色列人面前趕出的外邦人那可憎的事。³重新建築他父希西家所拆毀的邱壇，又為巴力築壇、做木偶，且敬拜侍奉天上的萬象。⁴在耶和華的殿宇中築壇。耶和華曾指着這殿說：“我的名必永遠在耶路撒冷。”⁵他在耶和華殿的兩院中為天上的萬象築壇；⁶並在欣嫩子谷使他的兒女經火；又觀兆、用法

術、行邪術、立交鬼的和行巫術
的，多行耶和華眼中看為惡的事，
惹動他的怒氣。
7又在神殿內立雕刻的偶像。神
曾對大衛和他兒子所羅門說：“我
在以色列各支派中所選擇的耶路撒
冷和這殿，必立我的名直到永遠。
8以色列人若謹守遵行我藉摩西所吩
咐他們的一切法度、律例、典章，
我就不再使他們挪移離開我所賜給
他們列祖之地。”9瑪拿西引誘猶大
和耶路撒冷的居民，以致他們行惡
比耶和華在以色列人面前所滅的列
國更甚。

10耶和華警戒瑪拿西和他的百
姓，他們卻是不聽。11所以耶和華使
亞述王的將帥來攻擊他們，用鐃鉤
鉤住瑪拿西，用銅鍊鎖住他，帶到
巴比倫去。12他在急難的時候就懇求
耶和華他的神，且在他列祖的神面
前極其自卑。13他祈禱耶和華，耶和
華就允准他的祈求，垂聽他的禱
告，使他歸回耶路撒冷，仍坐國
位。瑪拿西這才知道惟獨耶和華是
神。

14此後，瑪拿西在大衛城外，從
谷內基訓西邊直到魚門口，建築城
牆，環繞俄斐勒，這牆築得甚高；
又在猶大各堅固城內，設立勇敢的
軍長。

15並除掉外邦人的神像與耶和華
殿中的偶像；又將他在耶和華殿的
山上和耶路撒冷所築的各壇都拆
毀，拋在城外。16重修耶和華的祭
壇，在壇上獻平安祭、感謝祭，吩
咐猶大人侍奉耶和華以色列的神。
17百姓卻仍在邱壇上獻祭，只獻給耶
和華他們的神。

18瑪拿西其餘的事和禱告他神的
話，並先見奉耶和華以色列神的名
警戒他的言語，都寫在以色列諸王
記上。19他的禱告，與神怎樣應允
他，他未自卑以前的罪愆過犯，並
在何處建築邱壇，設立亞舍拉和雕

sorcery, divination and witchcraft, and consulted mediums and spiritists. He did much evil in
the eyes of the LORD, provoking him to anger.

7He took the carved image he had made and
put it in God's temple, of which God had said to
David and to his son Solomon, "In this temple
and in Jerusalem, which I have chosen out of all
the tribes of Israel, I will put my Name forever. 8I
will not again make the feet of the Israelites leave
the land I assigned to your forefathers, if only
they will be careful to do everything I commanded them concerning all the laws, decrees and
ordinances given through Moses." 9But Manasseh led Judah and the people of Jerusalem
astray, so that they did more evil than the nations
the LORD had destroyed before the Israelites.

10The LORD spoke to Manasseh and his people, but they paid no attention. 11So the LORD
brought against them the army commanders of
the king of Assyria, who took Manasseh prisoner, put a hook in his nose, bound him with
bronze shackles and took him to Babylon. 12In
his distress he sought the favor of the LORD his
God and humbled himself greatly before the God
of his fathers. 13And when he prayed to him, the
LORD was moved by his entreaty and listened to
his plea; so he brought him back to Jerusalem
and to his kingdom. Then Manasseh knew that
the LORD is God.

14Afterward he rebuilt the outer wall of the
City of David, west of the Gihon spring in the
valley, as far as the entrance of the Fish Gate and
encircling the hill of Ophel; he also made it much
higher. He stationed military commanders in all
the fortified cities in Judah.

15He got rid of the foreign gods and removed
the image from the temple of the LORD, as well
as all the altars he had built on the temple hill
and in Jerusalem; and he threw them out of the
city. 16Then he restored the altar of the LORD and
sacrificed fellowship offerings*a* and thank offerings on it, and told Judah to serve the LORD, the
God of Israel. 17The people, however, continued
to sacrifice at the high places, but only to the
LORD their God.

18The other events of Manasseh's reign,
including his prayer to his God and the words
the seers spoke to him in the name of the LORD,
the God of Israel, are written in the annals of the
kings of Israel.*b* 19His prayer and how God was
moved by his entreaty, as well as all his sins and
unfaithfulness, and the sites where he built high

a 16 Traditionally *peace offerings*　　*b 18* That is, Judah, as frequently in 2 Chronicles

places and set up Asherah poles and idols before he humbled himself—all are written in the records of the seers.[a] [20]Manasseh rested with his fathers and was buried in his palace. And Amon his son succeeded him as king.

Amon King of Judah

[21]Amon was twenty-two years old when he became king, and he reigned in Jerusalem two years. [22]He did evil in the eyes of the LORD, as his father Manasseh had done. Amon worshiped and offered sacrifices to all the idols Manasseh had made. [23]But unlike his father Manasseh, he did not humble himself before the LORD; Amon increased his guilt.

[24]Amon's officials conspired against him and assassinated him in his palace. [25]Then the people of the land killed all who had plotted against King Amon, and they made Josiah his son king in his place.

Josiah's Reforms

34 Josiah was eight years old when he became king, and he reigned in Jerusalem thirty-one years. [2]He did what was right in the eyes of the LORD and walked in the ways of his father David, not turning aside to the right or to the left.

[3]In the eighth year of his reign, while he was still young, he began to seek the God of his father David. In his twelfth year he began to purge Judah and Jerusalem of high places, Asherah poles, carved idols and cast images. [4]Under his direction the altars of the Baals were torn down; he cut to pieces the incense altars that were above them, and smashed the Asherah poles, the idols and the images. These he broke to pieces and scattered over the graves of those who had sacrificed to them. [5]He burned the bones of the priests on their altars, and so he purged Judah and Jerusalem. [6]In the towns of Manasseh, Ephraim and Simeon, as far as Naphtali, and in the ruins around them, [7]he tore down the altars and the Asherah poles and crushed the idols to powder and cut to pieces all the incense altars throughout Israel. Then he went back to Jerusalem.

[8]In the eighteenth year of Josiah's reign, to purify the land and the temple, he sent Shaphan son of Azaliah and Maaseiah the ruler of the city, with Joah son of Joahaz, the recorder, to repair the temple of the LORD his God.

刻的偶像，都寫在何賽的書上。[20]瑪拿西與他列祖同睡，葬在自己的宮院裏。他兒子亞們接續他作王。

亞們作猶大王

[21]亞們登基的時候年二十二歲，在耶路撒冷作王二年。[22]他行耶和華眼中看為惡的事，效法他父瑪拿西所行的，祭祀侍奉他父瑪拿西所雕刻的偶像，[23]不在耶和華面前像他父瑪拿西自卑。這亞們所犯的罪，越犯越大。

[24]他的臣僕背叛，在宮裏殺了他。[25]但國民殺了那些背叛亞們王的人，立他兒子約西亞接續他作王。

約西亞的改革

34 約西亞登基的時候年八歲，在耶路撒冷作王三十一年。[2]他行耶和華眼中看為正的事，效法他祖大衛所行的，不偏左右。

[3]他作王第八年，尚且年幼，就尋求他祖大衛的神。到了十二年，才潔淨猶大和耶路撒冷，除掉邱壇、木偶、雕刻的像和鑄造的像。[4]眾人在他面前拆毀巴力的壇，砍斷壇上高高的日像；又把木偶和雕刻的像，並鑄造的像打碎成灰，撒在祭偶像人的墳上；[5]將他們祭司的骸骨燒在壇上；潔淨了猶大和耶路撒冷。[6]又在瑪拿西、以法蓮、西緬、拿弗他利各城和四圍破壞之處，都這樣行。[7]又拆毀祭壇，把木偶和雕刻的像打碎成灰，砍斷以色列遍地所有的日像，就回耶路撒冷去了。

[8]約西亞王十八年，淨地淨殿之後，就差遣亞薩利雅的兒子沙番、邑宰瑪西雅、約哈斯的兒子史官約亞去修理耶和華他神的殿。

---

a 19 One Hebrew manuscript and Septuagint; most Hebrew manuscripts *of Hozai*

9他們就去見大祭司希勒家，將奉到神殿的銀子交給他。這銀子是看守殿門的利未人從瑪拿西、以法蓮和一切以色列剩下的人，以及猶大、便雅憫眾人，並耶路撒冷的居民收來的。10又將這銀子交給耶和華殿裏督工的，轉交修理耶和華殿的工匠，11就是交給木匠、石匠，買鑿成的石頭和架木與棟梁，修猶大王所毀壞的殿。

12這些人辦事誠實。督工的是利未人米拉利的子孫雅哈、俄巴底。督催的是哥轄的子孫撒迦利亞、米書蘭，還有善於作樂的利未人。13他們又監管扛抬的人，督催一切做工的。利未人中，也有作書記、作司事、作守門的。

重獲律法書

14他們將奉到耶和華殿的銀子運出來的時候，祭司希勒家偶然得了摩西所傳耶和華的律法書。15希勒家對書記沙番說：「我在耶和華殿裏得了律法書。」遂將書遞給沙番。

16沙番把書拿到王那裏，回覆王說：凡交給僕人們辦的都辦理了。17耶和華殿裏的銀子倒出來，交給督工的和匠人的手裏了。」18書記沙番又對王說：「祭司希勒家遞給我一卷書。」沙番就在王面前讀那書。

19王聽見律法上的話，就撕裂衣服，20吩咐希勒家與沙番的兒子亞希甘、米迦的兒子亞比頓、書記沙番和王的臣僕亞撒雅說：21「你們去為我、為以色列和猶大剩下的人，以這書上的話去問耶和華，因我們列祖沒有遵守耶和華的言語，沒有照這書上所記的去行，耶和華的烈怒就倒在我們身上。」

9They went to Hilkiah the high priest and gave him the money that had been brought into the temple of God, which the Levites who were the doorkeepers had collected from the people of Manasseh, Ephraim and the entire remnant of Israel and from all the people of Judah and Benjamin and the inhabitants of Jerusalem. 10Then they entrusted it to the men appointed to supervise the work on the LORD's temple. These men paid the workers who repaired and restored the temple. 11They also gave money to the carpenters and builders to purchase dressed stone, and timber for joists and beams for the buildings that the kings of Judah had allowed to fall into ruin.

12The men did the work faithfully. Over them to direct them were Jahath and Obadiah, Levites descended from Merari, and Zechariah and Meshullam, descended from Kohath. The Levites—all who were skilled in playing musical instruments— 13had charge of the laborers and supervised all the workers from job to job. Some of the Levites were secretaries, scribes and doorkeepers.

The Book of the Law Found

14While they were bringing out the money that had been taken into the temple of the LORD, Hilkiah the priest found the Book of the Law of the LORD that had been given through Moses. 15Hilkiah said to Shaphan the secretary, "I have found the Book of the Law in the temple of the LORD." He gave it to Shaphan.

16Then Shaphan took the book to the king and reported to him: "Your officials are doing everything that has been committed to them. 17They have paid out the money that was in the temple of the LORD and have entrusted it to the supervisors and workers." 18Then Shaphan the secretary informed the king, "Hilkiah the priest has given me a book." And Shaphan read from it in the presence of the king.

19When the king heard the words of the Law, he tore his robes. 20He gave these orders to Hilkiah, Ahikam son of Shaphan, Abdon son of Micah,a Shaphan the secretary and Asaiah the king's attendant: 21"Go and inquire of the LORD for me and for the remnant in Israel and Judah about what is written in this book that has been found. Great is the LORD's anger that is poured out on us because our fathers have not kept the word of the LORD; they have not acted in accordance with all that is written in this book."

a 20 Also called Acbor son of Micaiah

²²Hilkiah and those the king had sent with him^a went to speak to the prophetess Huldah, who was the wife of Shallum son of Tokhath,^b the son of Hasrah,^c keeper of the wardrobe. She lived in Jerusalem, in the Second District.

²³She said to them, "This is what the LORD, the God of Israel, says: Tell the man who sent you to me, ²⁴'This is what the LORD says: I am going to bring disaster on this place and its people—all the curses written in the book that has been read in the presence of the king of Judah. ²⁵Because they have forsaken me and burned incense to other gods and provoked me to anger by all that their hands have made,^d my anger will be poured out on this place and will not be quenched.' ²⁶Tell the king of Judah, who sent you to inquire of the LORD, 'This is what the LORD, the God of Israel, says concerning the words you heard: ²⁷Because your heart was responsive and you humbled yourself before God when you heard what he spoke against this place and its people, and because you humbled yourself before me and tore your robes and wept in my presence, I have heard you, declares the LORD. ²⁸Now I will gather you to your fathers, and you will be buried in peace. Your eyes will not see all the disaster I am going to bring on this place and on those who live here.' "

So they took her answer back to the king.

²⁹Then the king called together all the elders of Judah and Jerusalem. ³⁰He went up to the temple of the LORD with the men of Judah, the people of Jerusalem, the priests and the Levites—all the people from the least to the greatest. He read in their hearing all the words of the Book of the Covenant, which had been found in the temple of the LORD. ³¹The king stood by his pillar and renewed the covenant in the presence of the LORD—to follow the LORD and keep his commands, regulations and decrees with all his heart and all his soul, and to obey the words of the covenant written in this book.

³²Then he had everyone in Jerusalem and Benjamin pledge themselves to it; the people of Jerusalem did this in accordance with the covenant of God, the God of their fathers.

³³Josiah removed all the detestable idols from all the territory belonging to the Israelites, and he had all who were present in Israel serve the LORD their God. As long as he lived, they did not fail to follow the LORD, the God of their fathers.

a 22 One Hebrew manuscript, Vulgate and Syriac; most Hebrew manuscripts do not have had sent with him. b 22 Also called Tikvah   c 22 Also called Harhas   d 25 Or by everything they have done

²²於是，希勒家和王所派的眾人都去見女先知戶勒大。戶勒大是掌管禮服沙龍的妻，沙龍是哈斯拉的孫子、特瓦的兒子。戶勒大住在耶路撒冷第二區。他們請問於她。

²³她對他們說："耶和華以色列的神如此說：'你們可以回覆那差遣你們來見我的人說，²⁴耶和華如此說：我必照着在猶大王面前所讀那書上的一切咒詛，降禍與這地和其上的居民。²⁵因為他們離棄我，向別神燒香，用他們手所做的惹我發怒，所以我的忿怒如火倒在這地上，總不息滅。' ²⁶然而差遣你們來求問耶和華的猶大王，你們要這樣回覆他說：'耶和華以色列的神如此說：至於你所聽見的話，²⁷就是聽見我指着這地和其上居民所說的話，你便心裏敬服，在我面前自卑，撕裂衣服，向我哭泣，因此我應允了你。這是我耶和華說的。²⁸我必使你平平安安地歸到墳墓，到你列祖那裏。我要降與這地和其上居民的一切災禍，你也不至親眼看見。' "

他們就回覆王去了。

²⁹王差遣人招聚猶大和耶路撒冷的眾長老來。³⁰王和猶大眾人，與耶路撒冷的居民，並祭司利未人，以及所有的百姓，無論大小，都一同上到耶和華的殿。王就把殿裏所得的約書念給他們聽。³¹王站在他的地位上，在耶和華面前立約，要盡心盡性地順從耶和華，遵守他的誡命、法度、律例，成就這書上所記的約言。

³²又使住耶路撒冷和便雅憫的人都服從這約。於是耶路撒冷的居民，都遵行他們列祖之神的約。

³³約西亞從以色列各處，將一切可憎之物，盡都除掉，使以色列境內的人，都侍奉耶和華他們的神。約西亞在世的日子，就跟從耶和華他們列祖的神，總不離開。

約西亞守逾越節

約西亞在耶路撒冷向耶和華守逾越節。正月十四日，就宰了逾越節的羊羔。²王分派祭司各盡其職，又勉勵他們辦耶和華殿中的事。³對那歸耶和華為聖、教訓以色列人的利未人說："你們將要約櫃安放在以色列王大衛兒子所羅門建造的殿裏，不必再用肩扛抬。現在要侍奉耶和華你們的神，服侍他的民以色列。⁴你們應當按着宗族，照着班次，遵以色列王大衛和他兒子所羅門所寫的，自己預備。

⁵"要按着你們的弟兄這民宗族的班次，站在聖所，每班中要利未宗族的幾個人。⁶要宰逾越節的羊羔，潔淨自己，為你們的弟兄預備了，好遵行耶和華藉摩西所吩咐的話。"

⁷約西亞從羣畜中賜給在那裏所有的人民，綿羊羔和山羊羔三萬隻，牛三千隻，作逾越節的祭物。這都是出自王的產業中。

⁸約西亞的眾首領也樂意將犧牲給百姓和祭司利未人；又有管理神殿的希勒家、撒迦利亞、耶歇，將羊羔二千六百隻，牛三百隻，給祭司作逾越節的祭物。⁹利未人的族長歌楠雅和他兩個兄弟示瑪雅、拿坦業，與哈沙比雅、耶利、約撒拔，將羊羔五千隻，牛五百隻，給利未人作逾越節的祭物。

¹⁰這樣，供獻的事齊備了。祭司站在自己的地方，利未人按着班次站立，都是照王所吩咐的。¹¹利未人宰了逾越節的羊羔，祭司從他們手裏接過血來灑在壇上；利未人剝皮，¹²將燔祭搬來，按着宗族的班次分給眾民，好照摩西書上所寫的，獻給耶和華；獻牛也是這樣。¹³他們按着常例，用火烤逾越節的羊羔，別的聖物用鍋、用釜、用罐煮了，速速地送給眾民。¹⁴然後為自己和祭司預備祭物，因為祭司亞倫的子孫獻燔祭和脂油，直到晚上。所以利未人為自己和祭司亞倫的子孫預備祭物。

Josiah Celebrates the Passover

35 Josiah celebrated the Passover to the LORD in Jerusalem, and the Passover lamb was slaughtered on the fourteenth day of the first month. ²He appointed the priests to their duties and encouraged them in the service of the LORD's temple. ³He said to the Levites, who instructed all Israel and who had been consecrated to the LORD: "Put the sacred ark in the temple that Solomon son of David king of Israel built. It is not to be carried about on your shoulders. Now serve the LORD your God and his people Israel. ⁴Prepare yourselves by families in your divisions, according to the directions written by David king of Israel and by his son Solomon.

⁵"Stand in the holy place with a group of Levites for each subdivision of the families of your fellow countrymen, the lay people. ⁶Slaughter the Passover lambs, consecrate yourselves and prepare ⌊the lambs⌋ for your fellow countrymen, doing what the LORD commanded through Moses."

⁷Josiah provided for all the lay people who were there a total of thirty thousand sheep and goats for the Passover offerings, and also three thousand cattle—all from the king's own possessions.

⁸His officials also contributed voluntarily to the people and the priests and Levites. Hilkiah, Zechariah and Jehiel, the administrators of God's temple, gave the priests twenty-six hundred Passover offerings and three hundred cattle. ⁹Also Conaniah along with Shemaiah and Nethanel, his brothers, and Hashabiah, Jeiel and Jozabad, the leaders of the Levites, provided five thousand Passover offerings and five hundred head of cattle for the Levites.

¹⁰The service was arranged and the priests stood in their places with the Levites in their divisions as the king had ordered. ¹¹The Passover lambs were slaughtered, and the priests sprinkled the blood handed to them, while the Levites skinned the animals. ¹²They set aside the burnt offerings to give them to the subdivisions of the families of the people to offer to the LORD, as is written in the Book of Moses. They did the same with the cattle. ¹³They roasted the Passover animals over the fire as prescribed, and boiled the holy offerings in pots, caldrons and pans and served them quickly to all the people. ¹⁴After this, they made preparations for themselves and for the priests, because the priests, the descendants of Aaron, were sacrificing the burnt offerings and the fat portions until nightfall. So the Levites made preparations for themselves and for the Aaronic priests.

¹⁵The musicians, the descendants of Asaph, were in the places prescribed by David, Asaph, Heman and Jeduthun the king's seer. The gatekeepers at each gate did not need to leave their posts, because their fellow Levites made the preparations for them.

¹⁶So at that time the entire service of the LORD was carried out for the celebration of the Passover and the offering of burnt offerings on the altar of the LORD, as King Josiah had ordered. ¹⁷The Israelites who were present celebrated the Passover at that time and observed the Feast of Unleavened Bread for seven days. ¹⁸The Passover had not been observed like this in Israel since the days of the prophet Samuel; and none of the kings of Israel had ever celebrated such a Passover as did Josiah, with the priests, the Levites and all Judah and Israel who were there with the people of Jerusalem. ¹⁹This Passover was celebrated in the eighteenth year of Josiah's reign.

The Death of Josiah

²⁰After all this, when Josiah had set the temple in order, Neco king of Egypt went up to fight at Carchemish on the Euphrates, and Josiah marched out to meet him in battle. ²¹But Neco sent messengers to him, saying, "What quarrel is there between you and me, O king of Judah? It is not you I am attacking at this time, but the house with which I am at war. God has told me to hurry; so stop opposing God, who is with me, or he will destroy you."

²²Josiah, however, would not turn away from him, but disguised himself to engage him in battle. He would not listen to what Neco had said at God's command but went to fight him on the plain of Megiddo.

²³Archers shot King Josiah, and he told his officers, "Take me away; I am badly wounded." ²⁴So they took him out of his chariot, put him in the other chariot he had and brought him to Jerusalem, where he died. He was buried in the tombs of his fathers, and all Judah and Jerusalem mourned for him.

²⁵Jeremiah composed laments for Josiah, and to this day all the men and women singers commemorate Josiah in the laments. These became a tradition in Israel and are written in the Laments.

²⁶The other events of Josiah's reign and his acts of devotion, according to what is written in the Law of the Lord— ²⁷all the events, from beginning to end, are written in the book of the kings of Israel and Judah. ¹And the people of the land took Jehoahaz son of Josiah and made him king in Jerusalem in place of his father.

¹⁵歌唱的亞薩之子孫，照着大衛、亞薩、希幔和王的先見耶杜頓所吩咐的，站在自己的地位上。守門的看守各門，不用離開他們的職事，因為他們的弟兄利未人給他們預備祭物。

¹⁶當日，供奉耶和華的事齊備了，就照約西亞王的吩咐守逾越節，獻燔祭在耶和華的壇上。¹⁷當時，在耶路撒冷的以色列人守逾越節，又守除酵節七日。¹⁸自從先知撒母耳以來，在以色列中沒有守過這樣的逾越節；以色列諸王也沒有守過像約西亞、祭司、利未人、在那裏的猶大人和以色列人，以及耶路撒冷居民所守的逾越節。¹⁹這逾越節是約西亞作王十八年守的。

約西亞的死

²⁰這事以後，約西亞修完了殿，有埃及王尼哥上來，要攻擊靠近幼發拉底河的迦基米施，約西亞出去抵擋他。²¹他差遣使者來見約西亞說："猶大王啊，我與你何干？我今世不是要攻擊你，乃是要攻擊與我爭戰之家，並且神吩咐我速行，你不要干預神的事，免得他毀滅你，因為神是與我同在。"

²²約西亞卻不肯轉去離開他，改裝要與他打仗，不聽從神藉尼哥之口所說的話，便來到米吉多平原爭戰。

²³弓箭手射中約西亞王。王對他的臣僕說："我受了重傷，你拉我出陣吧！"²⁴他的臣僕扶他下了戰車，上了次車，送他到耶路撒冷，他就死了，葬在他列祖的墳墓裏。猶大人和耶路撒冷人都為他悲哀。

²⁵耶利米為約西亞作哀歌。所有歌唱的男女也唱哀歌，追悼約西亞，直到今日；而且在以色列中成了定例。這歌載在哀歌書上。

²⁶約西亞其餘的事和他遵着耶和華律法上所記而行的善事，²⁷並他自始至終所行的，都寫在以色列和猶大列王記上。

36 國民立約西亞的兒子約哈斯，在耶路撒冷接續他父作王。

約哈斯作猶大王

²約哈斯登基的時候年二十三歲，在耶路撒冷作王三個月，³埃及王在耶路撒冷廢了他；又罰猶大國銀子一百他連得，金子一他連得。⁴埃及王尼哥立約哈斯的哥哥以利雅敬作猶大和耶路撒冷的王，改名叫約雅敬，又將約哈斯帶到埃及去了。

約雅敬作猶大王

⁵約雅敬登基的時候年二十五歲，在耶路撒冷作王十一年，行耶和華他神眼中看為惡的事。⁶巴比倫王尼布甲尼撒上來攻擊他，用銅鏈鎖着他，要將他帶到巴比倫去。⁷尼布甲尼撒又將耶和華殿裏的器皿帶到巴比倫，放在他神的廟裏（註：或作"自己的宮裏"）。

⁸約雅敬其餘的事和他所行可憎的事，並他一切的行為，都寫在以色列和猶大列王記上。他兒子約雅斤接續他作王。

約雅斤作猶大王

⁹約雅斤登基的時候年八歲（註：列王記下24章8節作"十八歲"），在耶路撒冷作王三個月零十天，行耶和華眼中看為惡的事。¹⁰過了一年，尼布甲尼撒差遣人將約雅斤和耶和華殿裏各樣寶貴的器皿帶到巴比倫，就立約雅斤的叔叔（註：原文作"兄"）西底家作猶大和耶路撒冷的王。

西底家作猶大王

¹¹西底家登基的時候年二十一歲，在耶路撒冷作王十一年，¹²行耶和華他神眼中看為惡的事。先知耶利米以耶和華的話勸他，他仍不在耶利米面前自卑。¹³尼布甲尼撒曾使他指着神起誓，他卻背叛，強項硬心，不歸服耶和華以色列的神。¹⁴眾祭司長和百姓也大大犯罪，效法外

Jehoahaz King of Judah

²Jehoahaz[a] was twenty-three years old when he became king, and he reigned in Jerusalem three months. ³The king of Egypt dethroned him in Jerusalem and imposed on Judah a levy of a hundred talents[b] of silver and a talent[c] of gold. ⁴The king of Egypt made Eliakim, a brother of Jehoahaz, king over Judah and Jerusalem and changed Eliakim's name to Jehoiakim. But Neco took Eliakim's brother Jehoahaz and carried him off to Egypt.

Jehoiakim King of Judah

⁵Jehoiakim was twenty-five years old when he became king, and he reigned in Jerusalem eleven years. He did evil in the eyes of the LORD his God. ⁶Nebuchadnezzar king of Babylon attacked him and bound him with bronze shackles to take him to Babylon. ⁷Nebuchadnezzar also took to Babylon articles from the temple of the LORD and put them in his temple[d] there.

⁸The other events of Jehoiakim's reign, the detestable things he did and all that was found against him, are written in the book of the kings of Israel and Judah. And Jehoiachin his son succeeded him as king.

Jehoiachin King of Judah

⁹Jehoiachin was eighteen[e] years old when he became king, and he reigned in Jerusalem three months and ten days. He did evil in the eyes of the LORD. ¹⁰In the spring, King Nebuchadnezzar sent for him and brought him to Babylon, together with articles of value from the temple of the LORD, and he made Jehoiachin's uncle[f] Zedekiah, king over Judah and Jerusalem.

Zedekiah King of Judah

¹¹Zedekiah was twenty-one years old when he became king, and he reigned in Jerusalem eleven years. ¹²He did evil in the eyes of the LORD his God and did not humble himself before Jeremiah the prophet, who spoke the word of the LORD. ¹³He also rebelled against King Nebuchadnezzar, who had made him take an oath in God's name. He became stiff-necked and hardened his heart and would not turn to the LORD, the God of Israel. ¹⁴Furthermore, all the leaders of the

---

a 2 Hebrew *Joahaz*, a variant of *Jehoahaz*; also in verse 4
b 3 That is, about 3 3/4 tons (about 3.4 metric tons)　　*c* 3 That is, about 75 pounds (about 34 kilograms)　　*d* 7 Or *palace*
e 9 One Hebrew manuscript, some Septuagint manuscripts and Syriac (see also 2 Kings 24:8); most Hebrew manuscripts *eight*　　*f* 10 Hebrew *brother*, that is, relative (see 2 Kings 24:17)

priests and the people became more and more unfaithful, following all the detestable practices of the nations and defiling the temple of the LORD, which he had consecrated in Jerusalem.

The Fall of Jerusalem

[15]The LORD, the God of their fathers, sent word to them through his messengers again and again, because he had pity on his people and on his dwelling place. [16]But they mocked God's messengers, despised his words and scoffed at his prophets until the wrath of the LORD was aroused against his people and there was no remedy. [17]He brought up against them the king of the Babylonians,[a] who killed their young men with the sword in the sanctuary, and spared neither young man nor young woman, old man or aged. God handed all of them over to Nebuchadnezzar. [18]He carried to Babylon all the articles from the temple of God, both large and small, and the treasures of the LORD's temple and the treasures of the king and his officials. [19]They set fire to God's temple and broke down the wall of Jerusalem; they burned all the palaces and destroyed everything of value there.

[20]He carried into exile to Babylon the remnant, who escaped from the sword, and they became servants to him and his sons until the kingdom of Persia came to power. [21]The land enjoyed its sabbath rests; all the time of its desolation it rested, until the seventy years were completed in fulfillment of the word of the LORD spoken by Jeremiah.

[22]In the first year of Cyrus king of Persia, in order to fulfill the word of the LORD spoken by Jeremiah, the LORD moved the heart of Cyrus king of Persia to make a proclamation throughout his realm and to put it in writing:

[23]"This is what Cyrus king of Persia says:

" 'The LORD, the God of heaven, has given me all the kingdoms of the earth and he has appointed me to build a temple for him at Jerusalem in Judah. Anyone of his people among you—may the LORD his God be with him, and let him go up.' "

邦人一切可憎的事，污穢耶和華在<u>耶路撒冷</u>分別為聖的殿。

耶路撒冷失陷

[15]耶和華他們列祖的神，因為愛惜自己的民和他的居所，從早起來差遣使者去警戒他們。[16]他們卻嬉笑神的使者，藐視他的言語，譏誚他的先知，以致耶和華的忿怒向他的百姓發作，無法可救。[17]所以，耶和華使<u>迦勒底</u>人的王來攻擊他們。在他們聖殿裏用刀殺了他們的壯丁，不憐恤他們的少男處女、老人白叟。耶和華將他們都交在<u>迦勒底</u>王手裏。[18]<u>迦勒底</u>王將神殿裏的大小器皿，與耶和華殿裏的財寶，並王和眾首領的財寶，都帶到<u>巴比倫</u>去了。[19]<u>迦勒底</u>人焚燒神的殿，拆毀<u>耶路撒冷</u>的城牆，用火燒了城裏的宮殿，毀壞了城裏寶貴的器皿。

[20]凡脫離刀劍的，<u>迦勒底</u>王都擄到<u>巴比倫</u>去，作他和他子孫的僕婢，直到<u>波斯</u>國興起來。[21]這就應驗耶和華藉<u>耶利米</u>口所說的話：地享受安息。因為地土荒涼便守安息，直滿了七十年。

[22]<u>波斯</u>王<u>塞魯士</u>元年，耶和華為要應驗藉<u>耶利米</u>口所說的話，就激動<u>波斯</u>王<u>塞魯士</u>的心，使他下詔通告全國，說：

[23] "<u>波斯</u>王<u>塞魯士</u>如此說：
" '耶和華天上的神，已將天下萬國賜給我，又囑咐我在<u>猶大</u>的<u>耶路撒冷</u>為他建造殿宇。你們中間凡作他子民的，可以上去，願耶和華他的神與他同在。' "

a 17 Or Chaldeans

以斯拉記

Ezra

塞魯士助被擄的人歸回

1 波斯王塞魯士元年，耶和華為要應驗藉耶利米口所說的話，就激動波斯王塞魯士的心，使他下詔通告全國說：

² "波斯王塞魯士如此說：
" '耶和華天上的神，已將天下萬國賜給我，又囑咐我在猶大的耶路撒冷為他建造殿宇。³ 在你們中間凡作他子民的，可以上猶大的耶路撒冷，在耶路撒冷重建耶和華以色列神的殿（只有他是神），願神與這人同在。⁴ 凡剩下的人，無論寄居何處，那地的人要用金銀、財物、牲畜幫助他；另外也要為耶路撒冷神的殿，甘心獻上禮物。' "

⁵ 於是，猶大和便雅憫的族長、祭司、利未人，就是一切被神激動他心的人，都起來，要上耶路撒冷去建造耶和華的殿。⁶ 他們四圍的人就拿銀器、金子、財物、牲畜、珍寶幫助他們（註：原文作"堅固他們的手"），另外還有甘心獻的禮物。⁷ 塞魯士王也將耶和華殿的器皿拿出來，這器皿是尼布甲尼撒從耶路撒冷掠來，放在自己神之廟中的。⁸ 波斯王塞魯士派庫官米提利達將這器皿拿出來，按數交給猶大的首領設巴薩。

⁹ 器皿的數目記在下面：

金盤三十個，
銀盤一千個，
刀二十九把，
¹⁰ 金碗三十個，
銀碗之次的四百一十個，
別樣的器皿一千件。

Cyrus Helps the Exiles to Return

1 In the first year of Cyrus king of Persia, in order to fulfill the word of the LORD spoken by Jeremiah, the LORD moved the heart of Cyrus king of Persia to make a proclamation throughout his realm and to put it in writing:

²"This is what Cyrus king of Persia says:
" 'The LORD, the God of heaven, has given me all the kingdoms of the earth and he has appointed me to build a temple for him at Jerusalem in Judah. ³Anyone of his people among you—may his God be with him, and let him go up to Jerusalem in Judah and build the temple of the LORD, the God of Israel, the God who is in Jerusalem. ⁴And the people of any place where survivors may now be living are to provide him with silver and gold, with goods and livestock, and with freewill offerings for the temple of God in Jerusalem.' "

⁵Then the family heads of Judah and Benjamin, and the priests and Levites—everyone whose heart God had moved—prepared to go up and build the house of the LORD in Jerusalem. ⁶All their neighbors assisted them with articles of silver and gold, with goods and livestock, and with valuable gifts, in addition to all the freewill offerings. ⁷Moreover, King Cyrus brought out the articles belonging to the temple of the LORD, which Nebuchadnezzar had carried away from Jerusalem and had placed in the temple of his god.[a] ⁸Cyrus king of Persia had them brought by Mithredath the treasurer, who counted them out to Sheshbazzar the prince of Judah.

⁹This was the inventory:

gold dishes	30
silver dishes	1,000
silver pans[b]	29
¹⁰gold bowls	30
matching silver bowls	410
other articles	1,000

---

a 7 Or gods　　b 9 The meaning of the Hebrew for this word is uncertain.

¹¹In all, there were 5,400 articles of gold and of silver. Sheshbazzar brought all these along when the exiles came up from Babylon to Jerusalem.

The List of the Exiles Who Returned

2 Now these are the people of the province who came up from the captivity of the exiles, whom Nebuchadnezzar king of Babylon had taken captive to Babylon (they returned to Jerusalem and Judah, each to his own town, ²in company with Zerubbabel, Jeshua, Nehemiah, Seraiah, Reelaiah, Mordecai, Bilshan, Mispar, Bigvai, Rehum and Baanah):

The list of the men of the people of Israel:

³the descendants of Parosh	2,172
⁴of Shephatiah	372
⁵of Arah	775
⁶of Pahath-Moab (through the line of Jeshua and Joab)	2,812
⁷of Elam	1,254
⁸of Zattu	945
⁹of Zaccai	760
¹⁰of Bani	642
¹¹of Bebai	623
¹²of Azgad	1,222
¹³of Adonikam	666
¹⁴of Bigvai	2,056
¹⁵of Adin	454
¹⁶of Ater (through Hezekiah)	98
¹⁷of Bezai	323
¹⁸of Jorah	112
¹⁹of Hashum	223
²⁰of Gibbar	95
²¹the men of Bethlehem	123
²²of Netophah	56
²³of Anathoth	128
²⁴of Azmaveth	42
²⁵of Kiriath Jearim,^a Kephirah and Beeroth	743
²⁶of Ramah and Geba	621
²⁷of Micmash	122
²⁸of Bethel and Ai	223
²⁹of Nebo	52
³⁰of Magbish	156
³¹of the other Elam	1,254
³²of Harim	320
³³of Lod, Hadid and Ono	725
³⁴of Jericho	345
³⁵of Senaah	3,630

^a 25 See Septuagint (see also Neh. 7:29); Hebrew *Kiriath Arim*.

¹¹金銀器皿共有五千四百件。被擄的人從巴比倫上耶路撒冷的時候,設巴薩將這一切都帶上來。

被擄歸回者之名單

2 巴比倫王尼布甲尼撒從前擄到巴比倫之猶大省的人,現在他們的子孫從被擄到之地回耶路撒冷和猶大,各歸本城。²他們是同着所羅巴伯、耶書亞、尼希米、西萊雅、利來雅、末底改、必珊、米斯拔、比革瓦伊、利宏、巴拿回來的。

³以色列人民的數目記在下面:

巴錄的子孫二千一百七十二名;
  ⁴示法提雅的子孫三百七十二名;
  ⁵亞拉的子孫七百七十五名;
  ⁶巴哈摩押的後裔,就是耶書亞和約押的子孫二千八百一十二名;
  ⁷以攔的子孫一千二百五十四名;
  ⁸薩土的子孫九百四十五名;
  ⁹薩改的子孫七百六十名;
  ¹⁰巴尼的子孫六百四十二名;
  ¹¹比拜的子孫六百二十三名;
  ¹²押甲的子孫一千二百二十二名;
  ¹³亞多尼甘的子孫六百六十六名;
  ¹⁴比革瓦伊的子孫二千零五十六名;
  ¹⁵亞丁的子孫四百五十四名;
  ¹⁶亞特的後裔,就是希西家的子孫九十八名;
  ¹⁷比賽的子孫三百二十三名;
  ¹⁸約拉的子孫一百一十二名;
  ¹⁹哈順的子孫二百二十三名;
  ²⁰吉罷珥人九十五名;
  ²¹伯利恆人一百二十三名;
  ²²尼陀法人五十六名;
  ²³亞拿突人一百二十八名;
  ²⁴亞斯瑪弗人四十二名;
  ²⁵基列耶琳人、基非拉人、比錄人共七百四十三名;
  ²⁶拉瑪人、迦巴人共六百二十一名;
  ²⁷默瑪人一百二十二名;
  ²⁸伯特利人、艾人共二百二十三名;
  ²⁹尼波人五十二名;
  ³⁰末必人一百五十六名;
  ³¹別的以攔子孫一千二百五十四名;
  ³²哈琳的子孫三百二十名;
  ³³羅德人、哈第人、阿挪人共七百二十五名;
  ³⁴耶利哥人三百四十五名;
  ³⁵西拿人三千六百三十名。

³⁶祭司：

耶書亞家耶大雅的子孫九百七十三名；
　³⁷音麥的子孫一千零五十二名；
　³⁸巴施戶珥的子孫一千二百四十七名；
　³⁹哈琳的子孫一千零一十七名。

⁴⁰利未人：

何達威雅的後裔，就是耶書亞和甲篾的子孫七十四名。

⁴¹歌唱的：

亞薩的子孫一百二十八名。

⁴²守門的：

沙龍的子孫、亞特的子孫、達們的子孫、亞谷的子孫、哈底大的子孫、朔拜的子孫共一百三十九名。

⁴³尼提寧 (註：就是"殿役") ：

西哈的子孫、哈蘇巴的子孫、答巴俄的子孫、
　⁴⁴基綠的子孫、西亞的子孫、巴頓的子孫、
　⁴⁵利巴拿的子孫、哈迦巴的子孫、亞谷的子孫、
　⁴⁶哈甲的子孫、薩買的子孫、哈難的子孫、
　⁴⁷吉德的子孫、迦哈的子孫、利亞雅的子孫、
　⁴⁸利汛的子孫、尼哥大的子孫、迦散的子孫、
　⁴⁹烏撒的子孫、巴西亞的子孫、比賽的子孫、
　⁵⁰押拿的子孫、米烏寧的子孫、尼普心的子孫、
　⁵¹巴卜的子孫、哈古巴的子孫、哈忽的子孫、
　⁵²巴洗律的子孫、米希大的子孫、哈沙的子孫、
　⁵³巴柯的子孫、西西拉的子孫、答瑪的子孫、
　⁵⁴尼細亞的子孫、哈提法的子孫。

⁵⁵所羅門僕人的後裔，就是瑣太的子孫、瑣斐列的子孫、比路大的子孫、
　⁵⁶雅拉的子孫、達昆的子孫、吉德的子孫、

³⁶The priests:

the descendants of Jedaiah (through
　the family of Jeshua)　　　　973
　³⁷of Immer　　　　1,052
　³⁸of Pashhur　　　　1,247
　³⁹of Harim　　　　1,017

⁴⁰The Levites:

the descendants of Jeshua and
　Kadmiel (through the line of Hodaviah)　74

⁴¹The singers:

the descendants of Asaph　　　　128

⁴²The gatekeepers of the temple:

the descendants of
　Shallum, Ater, Talmon,
　Akkub, Hatita and Shobai　　　　139

⁴³The temple servants:

the descendants of
　Ziha, Hasupha, Tabbaoth,
　⁴⁴Keros, Siaha, Padon,

　⁴⁵Lebanah, Hagabah, Akkub,

　⁴⁶Hagab, Shalmai, Hanan,

　⁴⁷Giddel, Gahar, Reaiah,

　⁴⁸Rezin, Nekoda, Gazzam,

　⁴⁹Uzza, Paseah, Besai,

　⁵⁰Asnah, Meunim, Nephussim,

　⁵¹Bakbuk, Hakupha, Harhur,

　⁵²Bazluth, Mehida, Harsha,

　⁵³Barkos, Sisera, Temah,

　⁵⁴Neziah and Hatipha

⁵⁵The descendants of the servants of Solomon:

the descendants of
　Sotai, Hassophereth, Peruda,
　⁵⁶Jaala, Darkon, Giddel,

⁵⁷Shephatiah, Hattil,
   Pokereth-Hazzebaim and Ami

⁵⁸The temple servants and the descendants
   of the servants of Solomon   392

⁵⁹The following came up from the towns of
Tel Melah, Tel Harsha, Kerub, Addon and
Immer, but they could not show that their
families were descended from Israel:

⁶⁰The descendants of
   Delaiah, Tobiah and Nekoda   652

⁶¹And from among the priests:

The descendants of
   Hobaiah, Hakkoz and Barzillai (a man who
   had married a daughter of Barzillai the
   Gileadite and was called by that name).

⁶²These searched for their family records,
but they could not find them and so were
excluded from the priesthood as unclean.
⁶³The governor ordered them not to eat any of
the most sacred food until there was a priest
ministering with the Urim and Thummim.

⁶⁴The whole company numbered 42,360,
⁶⁵besides their 7,337 menservants and maid-
servants; and they also had 200 men and
women singers. ⁶⁶They had 736 horses, 245
mules, ⁶⁷435 camels and 6,720 donkeys.

⁶⁸When they arrived at the house of the LORD
in Jerusalem, some of the heads of the families
gave freewill offerings toward the rebuilding of
the house of God on its site. ⁶⁹According to their
ability they gave to the treasury for this work
61,000 drachmas^a of gold, 5,000 minas^b of silver
and 100 priestly garments.
⁷⁰The priests, the Levites, the singers, the
gatekeepers and the temple servants settled in
their own towns, along with some of the other
people, and the rest of the Israelites settled in
their towns.

Rebuilding the Altar

3 When the seventh month came and the
Israelites had settled in their towns, the
people assembled as one man in Jeru-
salem. ²Then Jeshua son of Jozadak and his fellow priests and Zerubbabel son of Shealtiel and
his associates began to build the altar of the God

⁵⁷示法提雅的子孫、哈替的子孫、玻
黑列哈斯巴音的子孫、亞米的子
孫。

⁵⁸尼提寧和所羅門僕人的後裔共三百
九十二名。

⁵⁹從特米拉、特哈薩、基綠、
押但、音麥上來的，不能指明他們
的宗族譜系是以色列人不是。

⁶⁰他們是：第來雅的子孫、多比雅的
子孫、尼哥大的子孫，共六百五十
二名。

⁶¹祭司中：

哈巴雅的子孫、哈哥斯的子孫、巴
西萊的子孫，因為他們的先祖娶了
基列人巴西萊的女兒為妻，所以起
名叫巴西萊。

⁶²這三家的人，在族譜之中尋
查自己的譜系，卻尋不著，因此算
為不潔，不准供祭司的職任。⁶³省
長對他們說：“不可吃至聖的物，
直到有用烏陵和土明決疑的祭司興
起來。”

⁶⁴會眾共有四萬二千三百六十
名。⁶⁵此外，還有他們的僕婢七千
三百三十七名，又有歌唱的男女二
百名。⁶⁶他們有馬七百三十六匹，
騾子二百四十五匹，⁶⁷駱駝四百三
十五隻，驢六千七百二十匹。

⁶⁸有些族長到了耶路撒冷耶和華
殿的地方，便為神的殿甘心獻上禮
物，要重新建造。⁶⁹他們量力捐入工
程庫的金子六萬一千達利克、銀子五
千彌拿，並祭司的禮服一百件。

⁷⁰於是祭司、利未人，民中的一
些人、歌唱的、守門的、尼提寧，並
以色列眾人，各住在自己的城裏。

重建祭壇

3 到了七月，以色列人住在各
城，那時他們如同一人，聚
集在耶路撒冷。²約薩達的兒
子耶書亞和他的弟兄眾祭司，並撒拉
鐵的兒子所羅巴伯與他的弟兄，都起
來建築以色列神的壇，要照神人摩西

---

^a 69 That is, about 1,100 pounds (about 500 kilograms)
^b 69 That is, about 3 tons (about 2.9 metric tons)

律法書上所寫的，在壇上獻燔祭。³他們在原有的根基上築壇，因懼怕鄰國的民，又在其上向耶和華早晚獻燔祭；⁴又照律法書上所寫的守住棚節，按數照例，獻每日所當獻的燔祭。⁵其後獻常獻的燔祭，並在月朔與耶和華的一切聖節獻祭，又向耶和華獻各人的甘心祭。⁶從七月初一日起，他們就向耶和華獻燔祭，但耶和華殿的根基尚未立定。

重建聖殿

⁷他們又將銀子給石匠、木匠，把糧食、酒、油給西頓人、推羅人，使他們將香柏樹從黎巴嫩運到海裏，浮海運到約帕，是照波斯王塞魯士所允准的。

⁸百姓到了耶路撒冷神殿的地方。第二年二月，撒拉鐵的兒子所羅巴伯，約薩達的兒子耶書亞和其餘的弟兄，就是祭司、利未人、並一切被擄歸回耶路撒冷的人，都興工建造；又派利未人，從二十歲以外的，督理建造耶和華殿的工作。⁹於是猶大（註：在2章40節作"何達威雅"）的後裔，就是耶書亞和他的子孫與弟兄、甲篾和他的子孫、利未人希拿達的子孫與弟兄，都一同起來，督理那在神殿做工的人。

¹⁰匠人立耶和華殿根基的時候，祭司皆穿禮服吹號，亞薩的子孫利未人敲鈸，照以色列王大衛所定的例，都站着讚美耶和華。¹¹他們彼此唱和、讚美稱謝耶和華說：

"他本為善，
　他向以色列人永發慈愛。"

他們讚美耶和華的時候，眾民大聲呼喊，因耶和華殿的根基已經立定。¹²然而有許多祭司、利未人、族長，就是見過舊殿的老年人，現在親眼看見立這殿的根基，便大聲哭號，也有

of Israel to sacrifice burnt offerings on it, in accordance with what is written in the Law of Moses the man of God. ³Despite their fear of the peoples around them, they built the altar on its foundation and sacrificed burnt offerings on it to the LORD, both the morning and evening sacrifices. ⁴Then in accordance with what is written, they celebrated the Feast of Tabernacles with the required number of burnt offerings prescribed for each day. ⁵After that, they presented the regular burnt offerings, the New Moon sacrifices and the sacrifices for all the appointed sacred feasts of the LORD, as well as those brought as freewill offerings to the LORD. ⁶On the first day of the seventh month they began to offer burnt offerings to the LORD, though the foundation of the LORD's temple had not yet been laid.

Rebuilding the Temple

⁷Then they gave money to the masons and carpenters, and gave food and drink and oil to the people of Sidon and Tyre, so that they would bring cedar logs by sea from Lebanon to Joppa, as authorized by Cyrus king of Persia.

⁸In the second month of the second year after their arrival at the house of God in Jerusalem, Zerubbabel son of Shealtiel, Jeshua son of Jozadak and the rest of their brothers (the priests and the Levites and all who had returned from the captivity to Jerusalem) began the work, appointing Levites twenty years of age and older to supervise the building of the house of the LORD. ⁹Jeshua and his sons and brothers and Kadmiel and his sons (descendants of Hodaviah[a]) and the sons of Henadad and their sons and brothers—all Levites—joined together in supervising those working on the house of God.

¹⁰When the builders laid the foundation of the temple of the LORD, the priests in their vestments and with trumpets, and the Levites (the sons of Asaph) with cymbals, took their places to praise the LORD, as prescribed by David king of Israel. ¹¹With praise and thanksgiving they sang to the LORD:

"He is good;
　his love to Israel endures forever."

And all the people gave a great shout of praise to the LORD, because the foundation of the house of the LORD was laid. ¹²But many of the older priests and Levites and family heads, who had seen the former temple, wept aloud when they saw the foundation of this temple being laid,

---

a 9 Hebrew *Yehudah,* probably a variant of *Hodaviah*

while many others shouted for joy. [13]No one could distinguish the sound of the shouts of joy from the sound of weeping, because the people made so much noise. And the sound was heard far away.

Opposition to the Rebuilding

4 When the enemies of Judah and Benjamin heard that the exiles were building a temple for the LORD, the God of Israel, [2]they came to Zerubbabel and to the heads of the families and said, "Let us help you build because, like you, we seek your God and have been sacrificing to him since the time of Esarhaddon king of Assyria, who brought us here."

[3]But Zerubbabel, Jeshua and the rest of the heads of the families of Israel answered, "You have no part with us in building a temple to our God. We alone will build it for the LORD, the God of Israel, as King Cyrus, the king of Persia, commanded us."

[4]Then the peoples around them set out to discourage the people of Judah and make them afraid to go on building.[a] [5]They hired counselors to work against them and frustrate their plans during the entire reign of Cyrus king of Persia and down to the reign of Darius king of Persia.

Later Opposition Under Xerxes and Artaxerxes

[6]At the beginning of the reign of Xerxes,[b] they lodged an accusation against the people of Judah and Jerusalem.

[7]And in the days of Artaxerxes king of Persia, Bishlam, Mithredath, Tabeel and the rest of his associates wrote a letter to Artaxerxes. The letter was written in Aramaic script and in the Aramaic language.[c,d]

[8]Rehum the commanding officer and Shimshai the secretary wrote a letter against Jerusalem to Artaxerxes the king as follows:

[9]Rehum the commanding officer and Shimshai the secretary, together with the rest of their associates—the judges and officials over the men from Tripolis, Persia,[e] Erech and Babylon, the Elamites of Susa, [10]and the other people whom the great and honorable Ashurbanipal[f] deported and settled in the city of Samaria and elsewhere in Trans-Euphrates.

---

a 4 Or *and troubled them as they built*   *b 6* Hebrew *Ahasuerus,* a variant of Xerxes' Persian name   *c 7* Or *written in Aramaic and translated*   *d 7* The text of Ezra 4:8-6:18 is in Aramaic.
e 9 Or *officials, magistrates and governors over the men from*
f 10 Aramaic *Osnappar,* a variant of *Ashurbanipal*

許多人大聲歡呼，[13]甚至百姓不能分辨歡呼的聲音和哭號的聲音，因為眾人大聲呼喊，聲音聽到遠處。

反對重建工程

4 猶大和便雅憫的敵人，聽說被擄歸回的人為耶和華以色列的神建造殿宇，[2]就去見所羅巴伯和以色列的族長，對他們說："請容我們與你們一同建造，因為我們尋求你們的神，與你們一樣。自從亞述王以撒哈頓帶我們上這地以來，我們常祭祀神。"

[3]但所羅巴伯、耶書亞和其餘以色列的族長對他們說："我們建造神的殿與你們無干，我們自己為耶和華以色列的神協力建造，是照波斯王塞魯士所吩咐的。"

[4]那地的民，就在猶大人建造的時候，使他們的手發軟，擾亂他們。[5]從波斯王塞魯士年間，直到波斯王大利烏登基的時候，賄買謀士，要敗壞他們的謀算。

亞哈隨魯及亞達薛西年間反對重建

[6]在亞哈隨魯才登基的時候，上本控告猶大和耶路撒冷的居民。

[7]亞達薛西年間，比施蘭、米特利達、他別和他們的同黨，上本奏告波斯王亞達薛西，本章是用亞蘭文字、亞蘭方言。

[8]省長利宏、書記伸帥要控告耶路撒冷人，也上本奏告亞達薛西王：

[9]省長利宏、書記伸帥和同黨的底拿人、亞法薩提迦人、他毘拉人、亞法撒人、亞基衛人、巴比倫人、書珊迦人、底亥人、以攔人，[10]和尊大的亞斯那巴所遷移、安置在撒馬利亞城，並大河西一帶地方的人等，

11 上奏亞達薛西王說:

河西的臣民云云;

12 王該知道,從王那裏上到我們這裏的猶大人,已經到耶路撒冷重建這反叛惡劣的城,築立根基,建造城牆。

13 如今王該知道,他們若建造這城,城牆完畢,就不再與王進貢、交課、納稅,終久王必受虧損。14 我們既食御鹽,不忍見王吃虧,因此奏告於王。15 請王考察先王的實錄,必在其上查知這城是反叛的城,與列王和各省有害。自古以來,其中常有悖逆的事,因此這城曾被拆毀。16 我們謹奏王知,這城若再建造,城牆完畢,河西之地王就無分了。

17 那時王諭:

覆省長利宏、書記伸帥和他們的同黨,就是住撒馬利亞、並河西一帶地方的人,說:

願你們平安云云。

18 你們所上的本,已經明讀在我面前。19 我已命人考查,得知此城古來果然背叛列王,其中常有反叛悖逆的事。20 從前耶路撒冷也有大君王統管河西全地,人就給他們進貢、交課、納稅。21 現在你們要出告示,命這些人停工,使這城不得建造,等我降旨。22 你們當謹慎,不可遲延。為何容害加重,使王受虧損呢?

23 亞達薛西王的上諭讀在利宏和書記伸帥,並他們的同黨面前,他們

11(This is a copy of the letter they sent him.)

To King Artaxerxes,

From your servants, the men of Trans-Euphrates:

12The king should know that the Jews who came up to us from you have gone to Jerusalem and are rebuilding that rebellious and wicked city. They are restoring the walls and repairing the foundations.

13Furthermore, the king should know that if this city is built and its walls are restored, no more taxes, tribute or duty will be paid, and the royal revenues will suffer. 14Now since we are under obligation to the palace and it is not proper for us to see the king dishonored, we are sending this message to inform the king, 15so that a search may be made in the archives of your predecessors. In these records you will find that this city is a rebellious city, troublesome to kings and provinces, a place of rebellion from ancient times. That is why this city was destroyed. 16We inform the king that if this city is built and its walls are restored, you will be left with nothing in Trans-Euphrates.

17The king sent this reply:

To Rehum the commanding officer, Shimshai the secretary and the rest of their associates living in Samaria and elsewhere in Trans-Euphrates:

Greetings.

18The letter you sent us has been read and translated in my presence. 19I issued an order and a search was made, and it was found that this city has a long history of revolt against kings and has been a place of rebellion and sedition. 20Jerusalem has had powerful kings ruling over the whole of Trans-Euphrates, and taxes, tribute and duty were paid to them. 21Now issue an order to these men to stop work, so that this city will not be rebuilt until I so order. 22Be careful not to neglect this matter. Why let this threat grow, to the detriment of the royal interests?

23As soon as the copy of the letter of King Artaxerxes was read to Rehum and Shimshai the secretary and their associates, they went immediately to the Jews in Jerusalem and compelled them by force to stop.

24Thus the work on the house of God in Jerusalem came to a standstill until the second year of the reign of Darius king of Persia.

Tattenai's Letter to Darius

5 Now Haggai the prophet and Zechariah the prophet, a descendant of Iddo, prophesied to the Jews in Judah and Jerusalem in the name of the God of Israel, who was over them. 2Then Zerubbabel son of Shealtiel and Jeshua son of Jozadak set to work to rebuild the house of God in Jerusalem. And the prophets of God were with them, helping them.

3At that time Tattenai, governor of Trans-Euphrates, and Shethar-Bozenai and their associates went to them and asked, "Who authorized you to rebuild this temple and restore this structure?" 4They also asked, "What are the names of the men constructing this building?"*a* 5But the eye of their God was watching over the elders of the Jews, and they were not stopped until a report could go to Darius and his written reply be received.

6This is a copy of the letter that Tattenai, governor of Trans-Euphrates, and Shethar-Bozenai and their associates, the officials of Trans-Euphrates, sent to King Darius. 7The report they sent him read as follows:

To King Darius:

Cordial greetings.

8The king should know that we went to the district of Judah, to the temple of the great God. The people are building it with large stones and placing the timbers in the walls. The work is being carried on with diligence and is making rapid progress under their direction.

9We questioned the elders and asked them, "Who authorized you to rebuild this temple and restore this structure?" 10We also asked them their names, so that we could write down the names of their leaders for your information.

11This is the answer they gave us:

"We are the servants of the God of heaven and earth, and we are rebuilding the temple

就急忙往耶路撒冷去見猶大人，用勢力強迫他們停工。

24於是，在耶路撒冷神殿的工程就停止了，直停到波斯王大利烏第二年。

達乃奏告大利烏王

5 那時先知哈該和易多的孫子撒迦利亞，奉以色列神的名，向猶大和耶路撒冷的猶大人說勸勉的話。2於是，撒拉鐵的兒子所羅巴伯和約薩達的兒子耶書亞，都起來動手建造耶路撒冷神的殿，有神的先知在那裏幫助他們。

3當時，河西的總督達乃和示他波斯乃，並他們的同黨，來問說："誰降旨讓你們建造這殿，修成這牆呢？" 4我們便告訴他們，建造這殿的人叫甚麼名字。5神的眼目看顧猶大的長老，以致總督等沒有叫他們停工，直到這事奏告大利烏，得着他的回諭。

6河西的總督達乃和示他波斯乃，並他們的同黨，就是住河西的亞法薩迦人，上本奏告大利烏王。7本上寫着說：

願大利烏王

諸事平安！

8王該知道，我們往猶大省去，到了至大神的殿，這殿是用大石建造的，梁木插入牆內，工作甚速，他們手下亨通。

9我們就問那些長老說："誰降旨讓你們建造這殿、修成這牆呢？" 10又問他們的名字，要記錄他們首領的名字，奏告於王。

11他們回答說：

"我們是天地之神的僕人，重建

---

a 4 See Septuagint; Aramaic 4 We told them the names of the men constructing this building.

前多年所建造的殿，就是<u>以色列</u>的一位大君王建造修成的。¹²只因我們列祖惹天上的神發怒，神把他們交在迦勒底人巴比倫王<u>尼布甲尼撒</u>的手中，他就拆毀這殿，又將百姓擄到<u>巴比倫</u>。

¹³ "然而<u>巴比倫</u>王<u>塞魯士</u>元年，他降旨允准建造建造神的這殿。¹⁴神殿中的金銀、器皿，就是<u>尼布甲尼撒從耶路撒冷</u>的殿中掠去帶到<u>巴比倫</u>廟裏的。

"<u>塞魯士</u>從<u>巴比倫</u>廟裏取出來，交給派為省長的，名叫<u>設巴薩</u>，¹⁵對他說：'可以將這些器皿帶去，放在<u>耶路撒冷</u>的殿中，在原處建造神的殿。'¹⁶於是，這<u>設巴薩</u>來建立<u>耶路撒冷</u>神殿的根基。這殿從那時直到如今，尚未造成。"

¹⁷現在王若以為美，請察<u>巴比倫</u>王的府庫，看<u>塞魯士</u>王降旨，允准在<u>耶路撒冷</u>建造神的殿沒有？王的心意如何，請降旨曉諭我們。

大利烏王的命令

6 於是<u>大利烏</u>王降旨，要尋察典籍庫內，就是在<u>巴比倫</u>藏寶物之處，²在<u>瑪代省亞馬他</u>城的宮內尋得一卷，其中記着說：

³<u>塞魯士</u>王元年，他降旨論到<u>耶路撒冷</u>神的殿：

要建造這殿為獻祭之處，堅立殿的根基。殿高六十肘、寬六十肘，⁴用三層大石頭、一層新木頭，經費要出於王庫。⁵並且神殿的金銀器皿，就是<u>尼布甲尼撒從耶路撒冷</u>的殿中掠到<u>巴比倫</u>的，要歸還帶到<u>耶路撒冷</u>的殿中，各按原處放在神的殿裏。

that was built many years ago, one that a great king of Israel built and finished. ¹²But because our fathers angered the God of heaven, he handed them over to Nebuchadnezzar the Chaldean, king of Babylon, who destroyed this temple and deported the people to Babylon.

¹³"However, in the first year of Cyrus king of Babylon, King Cyrus issued a decree to rebuild this house of God. ¹⁴He even removed from the temple*^a* of Babylon the gold and silver articles of the house of God, which Nebuchadnezzar had taken from the temple in Jerusalem and brought to the temple*^a* in Babylon.

"Then King Cyrus gave them to a man named Sheshbazzar, whom he had appointed governor, ¹⁵and he told him, 'Take these articles and go and deposit them in the temple in Jerusalem. And rebuild the house of God on its site.' ¹⁶So this Sheshbazzar came and laid the foundations of the house of God in Jerusalem. From that day to the present it has been under construction but is not yet finished."

¹⁷Now if it pleases the king, let a search be made in the royal archives of Babylon to see if King Cyrus did in fact issue a decree to rebuild this house of God in Jerusalem. Then let the king send us his decision in this matter.

The Decree of Darius

6 King Darius then issued an order, and they searched in the archives stored in the treasury at Babylon. ²A scroll was found in the citadel of Ecbatana in the province of Media, and this was written on it:

Memorandum:

³In the first year of King Cyrus, the king issued a decree concerning the temple of God in Jerusalem:

Let the temple be rebuilt as a place to present sacrifices, and let its foundations be laid. It is to be ninety feet*^b* high and ninety feet wide, ⁴with three courses of large stones and one of timbers. The costs are to be paid by the royal treasury. ⁵Also, the gold and silver articles of the house of God, which Nebuchadnezzar took from the temple in Jerusalem and brought to Babylon, are to be returned to their places in the temple in Jerusalem; they are to be deposited in the house of God.

---

a 14 Or palace   b 3 Aramaic sixty cubits (about 27 meters)

6Now then, Tattenai, governor of Trans-Euphrates, and Shethar-Bozenai and you, their fellow officials of that province, stay away from there. 7Do not interfere with the work on this temple of God. Let the governor of the Jews and the Jewish elders rebuild this house of God on its site.

8Moreover, I hereby decree what you are to do for these elders of the Jews in the construction of this house of God:

The expenses of these men are to be fully paid out of the royal treasury, from the revenues of Trans-Euphrates, so that the work will not stop. 9Whatever is needed—young bulls, rams, male lambs for burnt offerings to the God of heaven, and wheat, salt, wine and oil, as requested by the priests in Jerusalem—must be given them daily without fail, 10so that they may offer sacrifices pleasing to the God of heaven and pray for the well-being of the king and his sons.

11Furthermore, I decree that if anyone changes this edict, a beam is to be pulled from his house and he is to be lifted up and impaled on it. And for this crime his house is to be made a pile of rubble. 12May God, who has caused his Name to dwell there, overthrow any king or people who lifts a hand to change this decree or to destroy this temple in Jerusalem.

I Darius have decreed it. Let it be carried out with diligence.

Completion and Dedication of the Temple

13Then, because of the decree King Darius had sent, Tattenai, governor of Trans-Euphrates, and Shethar-Bozenai and their associates carried it out with diligence. 14So the elders of the Jews continued to build and prosper under the preaching of Haggai the prophet and Zechariah, a descendant of Iddo. They finished building the temple according to the command of the God of Israel and the decrees of Cyrus, Darius and Artaxerxes, kings of Persia. 15The temple was completed on the third day of the month Adar, in the sixth year of the reign of King Darius.

16Then the people of Israel—the priests, the Levites and the rest of the exiles—celebrated the dedication of the house of God with joy. 17For the dedication of this house of God they offered a hundred bulls, two hundred rams, four hundred male lambs and, as a sin offering for all Israel, twelve male goats, one for each of the

6現在河西的總督達乃和示他波斯乃，並你們的同黨，就是住河西的亞法薩迦人，你們當遠離他們，7不要攔阻神殿的工作，任憑猶大人的省長和猶大人的長老在原處建造神的這殿。

8我又降旨，吩咐你們向猶大人的長老為建造神的殿當怎樣行：

就是從河西的款項中，急速撥取貢銀作他們的經費，免得躭誤工作。9他們與天上的神獻燔祭所需用的公牛犢、公綿羊、綿羊羔，並所用的麥子、鹽、酒、油，都要照耶路撒冷祭司的話，每日供給他們，不得有誤！10好叫他們獻馨香的祭給天上的神，又為王和王眾子的壽命祈禱。

11我再降旨，無論誰更改這命令，必從他房屋中拆出一根梁來，把他舉起，懸在其上，又使他的房屋成為糞堆。12若有王和民伸手更改這命令，拆毀這殿，願那使耶路撒冷的殿作為他名居所的神，將他們滅絕。

我大利烏降這旨意，當速速遵行。

聖殿竣工及獻殿

13於是，河西總督達乃和示他波斯乃，並他們的同黨，因大利烏王所發的命令，就急速遵行。14猶大長老因先知哈該和易多的孫子撒迦利亞所說勸勉的話，就建造這殿，凡事亨通。他們遵著以色列神的命令和波斯王塞魯士、大利烏、亞達薛西的旨意，建造完畢。15大利烏王第六年，亞達月初三日，這殿修成了。

16以色列的祭司和利未人，並其餘被擄歸回的人，都歡歡喜喜地行奉獻神殿的禮。17行奉獻神殿的禮就獻公牛一百隻、公綿羊二百隻、綿羊羔四百隻，又照以色列支派的數目，獻公山羊十二隻，為以色列眾人作贖罪祭。18且派祭司和利未人,按着班次在耶路撒冷侍奉神,是照摩西律法書上所寫的。

逾越節

19正月十四日,被擄歸回的人守逾越節。20原來祭司和利未人一同自潔,無一人不潔淨。利未人為被擄歸回的眾人和他們的弟兄眾祭司,並為自己宰逾越節的羊羔。21從擄到之地歸回的以色列人,和一切除掉所染外邦人污穢、歸附他們、要尋求耶和華以色列神的人,都吃這羊羔,22歡歡喜喜地守除酵節七日,因為耶和華使他們歡喜,又使亞述王的心轉向他們,堅固他們的手,作以色列神殿的工程。

以斯拉來到耶路撒冷

7 這事以後,波斯王亞達薛西年間,有個以斯拉,他是西萊雅的兒子;西萊雅是亞撒利雅的兒子;亞撒利雅是希勒家的兒子;2希勒家是沙龍的兒子;沙龍是撒督的兒子;撒督是亞希突的兒子;3亞希突是亞瑪利雅的兒子;亞瑪利雅是亞撒利雅的兒子;亞撒利雅是米拉約的兒子;4米拉約是西拉希雅的兒子;西拉希雅是烏西的兒子;烏西是布基的兒子;5布基是亞比書的兒子;亞比書是非尼哈的兒子;非尼哈是以利亞撒的兒子;以利亞撒是大祭司亞倫的兒子。6這以斯拉從巴比倫上來,他是敏捷的文士,通達耶和華以色列神所賜摩西的律法書。王允准他一切所求的,是因耶和華神的手幫助他。7亞達薛西王第七年,以色列人、祭司、利未人、歌唱的、守門的、尼提寧,有上耶路撒冷的。

8王第七年五月,以斯拉到了耶路撒冷。9正月初一日,他從巴比倫起程,因他神施恩的手幫助他,五月初一日就到了耶路撒冷。10以斯拉定志考究遵行耶和華的律法,又將律例典章教訓以色列人。

tribes of Israel. 18And they installed the priests in their divisions and the Levites in their groups for the service of God at Jerusalem, according to what is written in the Book of Moses.

The Passover

19On the fourteenth day of the first month, the exiles celebrated the Passover. 20The priests and Levites had purified themselves and were all ceremonially clean. The Levites slaughtered the Passover lamb for all the exiles, for their brothers the priests and for themselves. 21So the Israelites who had returned from the exile ate it, together with all who had separated themselves from the unclean practices of their Gentile neighbors in order to seek the LORD, the God of Israel. 22For seven days they celebrated with joy the Feast of Unleavened Bread, because the LORD had filled them with joy by changing the attitude of the king of Assyria, so that he assisted them in the work on the house of God, the God of Israel.

Ezra Comes to Jerusalem

7 After these things, during the reign of Artaxerxes king of Persia, Ezra son of Seraiah, the son of Azariah, the son of Hilkiah, 2the son of Shallum, the son of Zadok, the son of Ahitub, 3the son of Amariah, the son of Azariah, the son of Meraioth, 4the son of Zerahiah, the son of Uzzi, the son of Bukki, 5the son of Abishua, the son of Phinehas, the son of Eleazar, the son of Aaron the chief priest— 6this Ezra came up from Babylon. He was a teacher well versed in the Law of Moses, which the LORD, the God of Israel, had given. The king had granted him everything he asked, for the hand of the LORD his God was on him. 7Some of the Israelites, including priests, Levites, singers, gatekeepers and temple servants, also came up to Jerusalem in the seventh year of King Artaxerxes.

8Ezra arrived in Jerusalem in the fifth month of the seventh year of the king. 9He had begun his journey from Babylon on the first day of the first month, and he arrived in Jerusalem on the first day of the fifth month, for the gracious hand of his God was on him. 10For Ezra had devoted himself to the study and observance of the Law of the LORD, and to teaching its decrees and laws in Israel.

King Artaxerxes' Letter to Ezra

[11]This is a copy of the letter King Artaxerxes had given to Ezra the priest and teacher, a man learned in matters concerning the commands and decrees of the LORD for Israel:

[12a]Artaxerxes, king of kings,

To Ezra the priest, a teacher of the Law of the God of heaven:

Greetings.

[13]Now I decree that any of the Israelites in my kingdom, including priests and Levites, who wish to go to Jerusalem with you, may go. [14]You are sent by the king and his seven advisers to inquire about Judah and Jerusalem with regard to the Law of your God, which is in your hand. [15]Moreover, you are to take with you the silver and gold that the king and his advisers have freely given to the God of Israel, whose dwelling is in Jerusalem, [16]together with all the silver and gold you may obtain from the province of Babylon, as well as the freewill offerings of the people and priests for the temple of their God in Jerusalem. [17]With this money be sure to buy bulls, rams and male lambs, together with their grain offerings and drink offerings, and sacrifice them on the altar of the temple of your God in Jerusalem.

[18]You and your brother Jews may then do whatever seems best with the rest of the silver and gold, in accordance with the will of your God. [19]Deliver to the God of Jerusalem all the articles entrusted to you for worship in the temple of your God. [20]And anything else needed for the temple of your God that you may have occasion to supply, you may provide from the royal treasury.

[21]Now I, King Artaxerxes, order all the treasurers of Trans-Euphrates to provide with diligence whatever Ezra the priest, a teacher of the Law of the God of heaven, may ask of you— [22]up to a hundred talents[b] of silver, a hundred cors[c] of wheat, a hundred baths[c] of wine, a hundred baths[d] of olive oil, and salt without limit. [23]Whatever the God of heaven has prescribed, let it be done with diligence for the temple of the God of heaven. Why

---

a 12 The text of Ezra 7:12-26 is in Aramaic.
b 22 That is, about 3 3/4 tons (about 3.4 metric tons)
c 22 That is, probably about 600 bushels (about 22 kiloliters)
d 22 That is, probably about 600 gallons (about 2.2 kiloliters)

亞達薛西王給以斯拉的諭旨

[11]祭司以斯拉是通達耶和華誡命和賜以色列之律例的文士。亞達薛西王賜給他諭旨，上面寫着說：

[12]諸王之王亞達薛西，

達於祭司以斯拉、通達天上神律法大德的文士云云：

[13]住在我國中的以色列人、祭司、利未人，凡甘心上耶路撒冷去的，我降旨准他們與你同去。[14]王與七個謀士既然差你去，照你手中神的律法書，察問猶大和耶路撒冷的景況；[15]又帶金銀，就是王和謀士columns為士心所獻給住耶路撒冷、以色列神的；[16]並帶你在巴比倫全省所得的金銀和百姓、祭司樂意獻給耶路撒冷他們神殿的禮物。[17]所以你當用這金銀，急速買公牛、公綿羊、綿羊羔，和同獻的素祭奠祭之物，獻在耶路撒冷你們神殿的壇上。

[18]剩下的金銀，你和你的弟兄看着怎樣好，就怎樣用，總要遵着你們神的旨意。[19]所交給你神殿中使用的器皿，你要交在耶路撒冷神面前。[20]你神殿裏，若再有需用的經費，你可以從王的府庫裏支取。

[21]我亞達薛西王，又降旨與河西的一切庫官，說：通達天上神律法的文士祭司以斯拉，無論向你們要甚麼，你們要速速地備辦，[22]就是銀子直到一百他連得、麥子一百柯珥、酒一百罷特、油一百罷特、鹽不計其數，也要給他。[23]凡天上之神所吩咐的，當為天上神的殿詳

細辦理，為何使忿怒臨到王和王眾子的國呢？24我又曉諭你們，至於祭司、利未人、歌唱的、守門的和尼提寧，並在神殿當差的人，不可叫他們進貢、交課、納稅。

25以斯拉啊，要照着你神賜你的智慧，將所有明白你神律法的人立為士師、審判官，治理河西的百姓，使他們教訓一切不明白神律法的人。26凡不遵行你神律法和王命令的人，就當速速定他的罪，或治死、或充軍、或抄家、或囚禁。

27以斯拉說：「耶和華我們列祖的神是應當稱頌的，因他使王起這心意修飾耶路撒冷耶和華的殿；28又在王和謀士，並大能的軍長面前施恩於我。因耶和華我神的手幫助我，我就得以堅強，從以色列中招聚首領，與我一同上來。」

隨以斯拉歸回的族長名單

8 當亞達薛西王年間，同我從巴比倫上來的人，他們的族長和他們的家譜記在下面：

2屬非尼哈的子孫有革順；屬以他瑪的子孫有但以理；屬大衛的子孫有哈突；3屬巴錄的後裔，就是示迦尼的子孫有撒迦利亞，同着他，按家譜計算，男丁一百五十人；

4屬巴哈摩押的子孫有西拉希雅的兒子以利約乃，同着他有男丁二百；

5屬示迦尼的子孫有雅哈悉的兒子，同着他有男丁三百；

6屬亞丁的子孫有約拿單的兒子以別，同着他有男丁五十；

7屬以攔的子孫有亞他利雅的兒子耶篩亞，同着他有男丁七十；

8屬示法提雅的子孫有米迦勒的兒子西巴第雅，同着他有男丁八十；

9屬約押的子孫有耶歇的兒子俄巴底亞，同着他有男丁二百一十八；

should there be wrath against the realm of the king and of his sons? 24You are also to know that you have no authority to impose taxes, tribute or duty on any of the priests, Levites, singers, gatekeepers, temple servants or other workers at this house of God.

25And you, Ezra, in accordance with the wisdom of your God, which you possess, appoint magistrates and judges to administer justice to all the people of Trans-Euphrates—all who know the laws of your God. And you are to teach any who do not know them. 26Whoever does not obey the law of your God and the law of the king must surely be punished by death, banishment, confiscation of property, or imprisonment.

27Praise be to the LORD, the God of our fathers, who has put it into the king's heart to bring honor to the house of the LORD in Jerusalem in this way 28and who has extended his good favor to me before the king and his advisers and all the king's powerful officials. Because the hand of the LORD my God was on me, I took courage and gathered leading men from Israel to go up with me.

List of the Family Heads Returning With Ezra

8 These are the family heads and those registered with them who came up with me from Babylon during the reign of King Artaxerxes:

2of the descendants of Phinehas, Gershom;
of the descendants of Ithamar, Daniel;
of the descendants of David, Hattush 3of the descendants of Shecaniah;

of the descendants of Parosh, Zechariah, and with him were registered 150 men;
4of the descendants of Pahath-Moab, Eliehoenai son of Zerahiah, and with him 200 men;
5of the descendants of Zattu,a Shecaniah son of Jahaziel, and with him 300 men;
6of the descendants of Adin, Ebed son of Jonathan, and with him 50 men;
7of the descendants of Elam, Jeshaiah son of Athaliah, and with him 70 men;
8of the descendants of Shephatiah, Zebadiah son of Michael, and with him 80 men;
9of the descendants of Joab, Obadiah son of Jehiel, and with him 218 men;

a 5 Some Septuagint manuscripts (also 1 Esdras 8:32); Hebrew does not have Zattu.

¹⁰of the descendants of Bani,^a Shelomith son of Josiphiah, and with him 160 men;

¹¹of the descendants of Bebai, Zechariah son of Bebai, and with him 28 men;

¹²of the descendants of Azgad, Johanan son of Hakkatan, and with him 110 men;

¹³of the descendants of Adonikam, the last ones, whose names were Eliphelet, Jeuel and Shemaiah, and with them 60 men;

¹⁴of the descendants of Bigvai, Uthai and Zaccur, and with them 70 men.

The Return to Jerusalem

¹⁵I assembled them at the canal that flows toward Ahava, and we camped there three days. When I checked among the people and the priests, I found no Levites there. ¹⁶So I summoned Eliezer, Ariel, Shemaiah, Elnathan, Jarib, Elnathan, Nathan, Zechariah and Meshullam, who were leaders, and Joiarib and Elnathan, who were men of learning, ¹⁷and I sent them to Iddo, the leader in Casiphia. I told them what to say to Iddo and his kinsmen, the temple servants in Casiphia, so that they might bring attendants to us for the house of our God. ¹⁸Because the gracious hand of our God was on us, they brought us Sherebiah, a capable man, from the descendants of Mahli son of Levi, the son of Israel, and Sherebiah's sons and brothers, 18 men; ¹⁹and Hashabiah, together with Jeshaiah from the descendants of Merari, and his brothers and nephews, 20 men. ²⁰They also brought 220 of the temple servants—a body that David and the officials had established to assist the Levites. All were registered by name.

²¹There, by the Ahava Canal, I proclaimed a fast, so that we might humble ourselves before our God and ask him for a safe journey for us and our children, with all our possessions. ²²I was ashamed to ask the king for soldiers and horsemen to protect us from enemies on the road, because we had told the king, "The gracious hand of our God is on everyone who looks to him, but his great anger is against all who forsake him." ²³So we fasted and petitioned our God about this, and he answered our prayer.

²⁴Then I set apart twelve of the leading priests, together with Sherebiah, Hashabiah and ten of their brothers, ²⁵and I weighed out to them the offering of silver and gold and the articles that the king, his advisers, his officials and all Israel present there had donated for the

¹⁰屬示羅密的子孫有約細斐的兒子，同着他有男丁一百六十；

¹¹屬比拜的子孫有比拜的兒子撒迦利亞，同着他有男丁二十八；

¹²屬押甲的子孫，有哈加坦的兒子約哈難，同着他有男丁一百一十；

¹³屬亞多尼干的子孫，就是末尾的，他們的名字是以利法列、耶利、示瑪雅，同着他們有男丁六十；

¹⁴屬比革瓦伊的子孫，有烏太和撒布，同着他們有男丁七十。

回耶路撒冷

¹⁵我招聚這些人在流入亞哈瓦的河邊，我們在那裏住了三日。我查看百姓和祭司，見沒有利未人在那裏，¹⁶就召首領以利以謝、亞列、示瑪雅、以利拿單、雅立、以利拿單、拿單、撒迦利亞、米書蘭，又召教習約雅立和以利拿單。¹⁷我打發他們往迦西斐雅地方去，見那裏的首領易多，又告訴他們當向易多和他的弟兄尼提寧說甚麼話，叫他們為我們神的殿帶使用的人來。¹⁸蒙我們神施恩的手幫助我們，他們在以色列的曾孫、利未的孫子、抹利的後裔中帶一個通達人來；還有示利比和他的眾子與弟兄共一十八人；¹⁹又有哈沙比雅，同着他有米拉利的子孫耶篩亞，並他的眾子和弟兄共二十人。²⁰從前大衛和眾首領派尼提寧寧服侍利未人，現在從這尼提寧中也帶了二百二十人來，都是按名指定的。

²¹那時，我在亞哈瓦河邊宣告禁食，為要在我們神面前克苦己心，求他使我們和婦人孩子，並一切所有的，都得平坦的道路。²²我求王撥步兵馬兵幫助我們抵擋路上的仇敵，本以為羞恥，因我曾對王說：“我們神施恩的手，必幫助一切尋求他的；但他的能力和忿怒，必攻擊一切離棄他的。”²³所以我們禁食祈求我們的神，他就應允了我們。

²⁴我分派祭司長十二人，就是示利比、哈沙比雅和他們的弟兄十人，²⁵將王和謀士、軍長，並在那裏的以色列眾人，為我們神殿所獻的金銀和

a 10 Some Septuagint manuscripts (also 1 Esdras 8:36); Hebrew does not have *Bani*.

器皿,都秤了交給他們。²⁶我秤了交在他們手中的銀子有六百五十他連得,銀器重一百他連得;金子一百他連得,²⁷金碗二十個,重一千達利克;上等光銅的器皿兩個,寶貴如金。

²⁸我對他們說:"你們歸耶和華為聖,器皿也為聖;金銀是甘心獻給耶和華你們列祖之神的。²⁹你們當警醒看守,直到你們在耶路撒冷耶和華殿的庫內,在祭司長和利未族長,並以色列的各族長面前過了秤。"³⁰於是祭司、利未人按着分量接受金銀和器皿,要帶到耶路撒冷我們神的殿裏。

³¹正月十二日,我們從亞哈瓦河邊起行,要往耶路撒冷去。我們神的手保佑我們,救我們脫離仇敵和路上埋伏之人的手。³²我們到了耶路撒冷,在那裏住了三日。

³³第四日,在我們神的殿裏把金銀和器皿都秤了,交在祭司烏利亞的兒子米利末的手中,同着他有非尼哈的兒子以利亞撒,還有利未人耶書亞的兒子約撒拔和賓內的兒子挪亞底。³⁴當時都點了數目,按着分量寫在冊上。

³⁵從擄到之地歸回的人向以色列的神獻燔祭,就是為以色列眾人獻公牛十二隻、公綿羊九十六隻、綿羊羔七十七隻,又獻公山羊十二隻作贖罪祭,這都是向耶和華焚獻的。³⁶他們將王的諭旨交給王所派的總督與河西的省長,他們就幫助百姓,又供給神殿裏所需用的。

以斯拉為與異族通婚之事祈禱

9 這事做完了,眾首領來見我,說:"以色列民和祭司並利未人,沒有離絕迦南人、赫人、比利洗人、耶布斯人、亞捫人、摩押人、埃及人、亞摩利人,仍效法這些國的民,行可憎的事。²因他們為自己和兒子娶了這些外邦女子為妻,以致

house of our God. ²⁶I weighed out to them 650 talents[a] of silver, silver articles weighing 100 talents,[b] 100 talents[b] of gold, ²⁷20 bowls of gold valued at 1,000 darics,[c] and two fine articles of polished bronze, as precious as gold.

²⁸I said to them, "You as well as these articles are consecrated to the LORD. The silver and gold are a freewill offering to the LORD, the God of your fathers. ²⁹Guard them carefully until you weigh them out in the chambers of the house of the LORD in Jerusalem before the leading priests and the Levites and the family heads of Israel." ³⁰Then the priests and Levites received the silver and gold and sacred articles that had been weighed out to be taken to the house of our God in Jerusalem.

³¹On the twelfth day of the first month we set out from the Ahava Canal to go to Jerusalem. The hand of our God was on us, and he protected us from enemies and bandits along the way. ³²So we arrived in Jerusalem, where we rested three days.

³³On the fourth day, in the house of our God, we weighed out the silver and gold and the sacred articles into the hands of Meremoth son of Uriah, the priest. Eleazar son of Phinehas was with him, and so were the Levites Jozabad son of Jeshua and Noadiah son of Binnui. ³⁴Everything was accounted for by number and weight, and the entire weight was recorded at that time.

³⁵Then the exiles who had returned from captivity sacrificed burnt offerings to the God of Israel: twelve bulls for all Israel, ninety-six rams, seventy-seven male lambs and, as a sin offering, twelve male goats. All this was a burnt offering to the LORD. ³⁶They also delivered the king's orders to the royal satraps and to the governors of Trans-Euphrates, who then gave assistance to the people and to the house of God.

Ezra's Prayer About Intermarriage

9 After these things had been done, the leaders came to me and said, "The people of Israel, including the priests and the Levites, have not kept themselves separate from the neighboring peoples with their detestable practices, like those of the Canaanites, Hittites, Perizzites, Jebusites, Ammonites, Moabites, Egyptians and Amorites. ²They have taken some of their daughters as wives for themselves and their sons, and have mingled

a 26 That is, about 25 tons (about 22 metric tons)　　b 26 That is, about 3 3/4 tons (about 3.4 metric tons)　　c 27 That is, about 19 pounds (about 8.5 kilograms)

the holy race with the peoples around them. And the leaders and officials have led the way in this unfaithfulness."

³When I heard this, I tore my tunic and cloak, pulled hair from my head and beard and sat down appalled. ⁴Then everyone who trembled at the words of the God of Israel gathered around me because of this unfaithfulness of the exiles. And I sat there appalled until the evening sacrifice.

⁵Then, at the evening sacrifice, I rose from my self-abasement, with my tunic and cloak torn, and fell on my knees with my hands spread out to the LORD my God ⁶and prayed:

"O my God, I am too ashamed and disgraced to lift up my face to you, my God, because our sins are higher than our heads and our guilt has reached to the heavens. ⁷From the days of our forefathers until now, our guilt has been great. Because of our sins, we and our kings and our priests have been subjected to the sword and captivity, to pillage and humiliation at the hand of foreign kings, as it is today.

⁸"But now, for a brief moment, the LORD our God has been gracious in leaving us a remnant and giving us a firm place in his sanctuary, and so our God gives light to our eyes and a little relief in our bondage. ⁹Though we are slaves, our God has not deserted us in our bondage. He has shown us his kindness in the sight of the kings of Persia: He has granted us new life to rebuild the house of our God and repair its ruins, and he has given us a wall of protection in Judah and Jerusalem.

¹⁰"But now, O our God, what can we say after this? For we have disregarded the commands ¹¹you gave through your servants the prophets when you said: 'The land you are entering to possess is a land polluted by the corruption of its peoples. By their detestable practices they have filled it with their impurity from one end to the other. ¹²Therefore, do not give your daughters in marriage to their sons or take their daughters for your sons. Do not seek a treaty of friendship with them at any time, that you may be strong and eat the good things of the land and leave it to your children as an everlasting inheritance.'

¹³"What has happened to us is a result of our evil deeds and our great guilt, and yet, our God, you have punished us less than our sins have deserved and have given us a remnant like this. ¹⁴Shall we again break your commands and intermarry with the peoples

聖潔的種類和這些國的民混雜，而且首領和官長在這事上為罪魁。"

³我一聽見這事，就撕裂衣服和外袍，拔了頭髮和鬍鬚，驚懼憂悶而坐。⁴凡為以色列神言語戰兢的，都因這被擄歸回之人所犯的罪，聚集到我這裏來，我就驚懼憂悶而坐，直到獻晚祭的時候。

⁵獻晚祭的時候，我起來，心中愁苦，穿着撕裂的衣袍，雙膝跪下向耶和華我的神舉手，⁶說：

"我的神啊，我抱愧蒙羞，不敢向我神仰面，因為我們的罪孽滅頂，我們的罪惡滔天。⁷從我們列祖直到今日，我們的罪惡甚重。因我們的罪孽，我們和君王、祭司都交在外邦列王的手中，殺害、擄掠、搶奪、臉上蒙羞，正如今日的光景。

⁸"現在耶和華我們的神暫且施恩與我們，給我們留些逃脫的人，使我們安穩如釘子，釘在他的聖所，我們的神好光照我們的眼目，使我們在受轄制之中稍微復興。⁹我們是奴僕，然而在受轄制之中，我們的神仍沒有丟棄我們，在波斯王眼前向我們施恩，叫我們復興，能重建我們神的殿，修其毀壞之處，使我們在猶大和耶路撒冷有牆垣。

¹⁰"我們的神啊，既是如此，我們還有甚麼話可說呢？因為我們已經離棄你的命令，¹¹就是你藉你僕人眾先知所吩咐的，說：'你們要去得為業之地是污穢之地，因列國之民的污穢和可憎的事，叫全地從這邊直到那邊滿了污穢。¹²所以不可將你們的女兒嫁他們的兒子；也不可為你們的兒子娶他們的女兒。永不可求他們的平安和他們的利益，這樣你們就可以強盛，吃這地的美物，並遺留這地給你們的子孫永遠為業。'

¹³"神啊，我們因自己的惡行和大罪，遭遇了這一切的事，並且你刑罰我們輕於我們罪所當得的，又給我們留下這些人。¹⁴我們豈可再違背你的命令，與這行可憎之事的民

結親呢？若這樣行，你豈不向我們發怒，將我們滅絕，以致沒有一個剩下逃脫的人嗎？15耶和華以色列的神啊！因你是公義的，我們這剩下的人才得逃脫，正如今日的光景。看哪，我們在你面前有罪惡，因此無人在你面前站立得住。」

百姓認罪

10 以斯拉禱告、認罪、哭泣，俯伏在神殿前的時候，有以色列中的男女孩童聚集到以斯拉那裏，成了大會，眾民無不痛哭。2屬以攔的子孫、耶歇的兒子示迦尼對以斯拉說：「我們在此地娶了外邦女子為妻，干犯了我們的神，然而以色列人還有指望。3現在當與我們的神立約，休這一切的妻，離絕她們所生的，照着我主和那信神命令戰兢之人所議定的，按律法而行。4你起來，這是你當辦的事，我們必幫助你，你當奮勉而行。」

5以斯拉便起來，使祭司長和利未人，並以色列眾人起誓說：必照這話去行；他們就起了誓。6以斯拉從神殿前起來，進入以利亞實的兒子約哈難的屋裏，到了那裏不吃飯，也不喝水，因為被擄歸回之人所犯的罪，心裏悲傷。

7他們通告猶大和耶路撒冷被擄歸回的人，叫他們在耶路撒冷聚集。8凡不遵首領和長老所議定三日之內不來的，就必抄他的家，使他離開被擄歸回之人的會。

9於是，猶大和便雅憫眾人，三日之內都聚集在耶路撒冷。那日正是九月二十日，眾人都坐在神殿前的寬闊處；因這事，又因下大雨，就都戰兢。10祭司以斯拉站起來，對他們說：「你們有罪了，因你們娶了外邦的女子為妻，增添以色列人的罪惡。11現在當向耶和華你們列祖的神認罪，遵行他的旨意，離絕這些國的民和外邦的女子。」

12會眾都大聲回答說：「我們必照着你的話行，13只是百姓眾多，又

who commit such detestable practices? Would you not be angry enough with us to destroy us, leaving us no remnant or survivor? 15O LORD, God of Israel, you are righteous! We are left this day as a remnant. Here we are before you in our guilt, though because of it not one of us can stand in your presence."

The People's Confession of Sin

10 While Ezra was praying and confessing, weeping and throwing himself down before the house of God, a large crowd of Israelites—men, women and children—gathered around him. They too wept bitterly. 2Then Shecaniah son of Jehiel, one of the descendants of Elam, said to Ezra, "We have been unfaithful to our God by marrying foreign women from the peoples around us. But in spite of this, there is still hope for Israel. 3Now let us make a covenant before our God to send away all these women and their children, in accordance with the counsel of my lord and of those who fear the commands of our God. Let it be done according to the Law. 4Rise up; this matter is in your hands. We will support you, so take courage and do it."

5So Ezra rose up and put the leading priests and Levites and all Israel under oath to do what had been suggested. And they took the oath. 6Then Ezra withdrew from before the house of God and went to the room of Jehohanan son of Eliashib. While he was there, he ate no food and drank no water, because he continued to mourn over the unfaithfulness of the exiles.

7A proclamation was then issued throughout Judah and Jerusalem for all the exiles to assemble in Jerusalem. 8Anyone who failed to appear within three days would forfeit all his property, in accordance with the decision of the officials and elders, and would himself be expelled from the assembly of the exiles.

9Within the three days, all the men of Judah and Benjamin had gathered in Jerusalem. And on the twentieth day of the ninth month, all the people were sitting in the square before the house of God, greatly distressed by the occasion and because of the rain. 10Then Ezra the priest stood up and said to them, "You have been unfaithful; you have married foreign women, adding to Israel's guilt. 11Now make confession to the LORD, the God of your fathers, and do his will. Separate yourselves from the peoples around you and from your foreign wives."

12The whole assembly responded with a loud voice: "You are right! We must do as you say. 13But there are many people here and it is the rainy season; so we cannot stand outside. Besides, this matter cannot be taken care of in a day or two, because we have sinned greatly in this thing. [14]Let our officials act for the whole assembly. Then let everyone in our towns who has married a foreign woman come at a set time, along with the elders and judges of each town, until the fierce anger of our God in this matter is turned away from us." [15]Only Jonathan son of Asahel and Jahzeiah son of Tikvah, supported by Meshullam and Shabbethai the Levite, opposed this.

[16]So the exiles did as was proposed. Ezra the priest selected men who were family heads, one from each family division, and all of them designated by name. On the first day of the tenth month they sat down to investigate the cases, [17]and by the first day of the first month they finished dealing with all the men who had married foreign women.

Those Guilty of Intermarriage

[18]Among the descendants of the priests, the following had married foreign women:

From the descendants of Jeshua son of Jozadak, and his brothers: Maaseiah, Eliezer, Jarib and Gedaliah. [19](They all gave their hands in pledge to put away their wives, and for their guilt they each presented a ram from the flock as a guilt offering.)

[20]From the descendants of Immer:
Hanani and Zebadiah.
[21]From the descendants of Harim:
Maaseiah, Elijah, Shemaiah, Jehiel and Uzziah.
[22]From the descendants of Pashhur:
Elioenai, Maaseiah, Ishmael, Nethanel, Jozabad and Elasah.

[23]Among the Levites:

Jozabad, Shimei, Kelaiah (that is, Kelita), Pethahiah, Judah and Eliezer.
[24]From the singers:
Eliashib.
From the gatekeepers:
Shallum, Telem and Uri.

[25]And among the other Israelites:

From the descendants of Parosh:
Ramiah, Izziah, Malkijah, Mijamin, Eleazar, Malkijah and Benaiah.

逢大雨的時令，我們不能站在外頭，這也不是一兩天辦完的事。因我們在這事上犯了大罪，[14]不如為全會眾派首領辦理。凡我們城邑中娶外邦女子為妻的，當按所定的日期，同着本城的長老和士師而來，直到辦完這事，神的烈怒就轉離我們了。" [15]惟有亞撒黑的兒子約拿單、特瓦的兒子雅哈謝，阻擋（註：或作"總辦"）這事，並有米書蘭和利未人沙比太幫助他們。

[16]被擄歸回的人如此而行。祭司以斯拉和些族長按着宗族，都指名見派，在十月初一日，一同在座查辦這事。[17]到正月初一日，才查清娶外邦女子的人數。

犯異族通婚罪之人

[18]在祭司中查出娶外邦女子為妻的：

就是耶書亞的子孫約薩達的兒子，和他弟兄瑪西雅、以利以謝、雅立、基大利，[19]他們便應許必休他們的妻。他們因有罪，就獻羣中的一隻公綿羊贖罪。

[20]音麥的子孫中有：
哈拿尼、西巴第雅。
[21]哈琳的子孫中有：
瑪西雅、以利雅、示瑪雅、耶歇、烏西雅。
[22]巴施戶珥的子孫中有：
以利約乃、瑪西雅、以實瑪利、拿坦業、約撒拔、以利亞撒。

[23]利未人中有：
約撒拔、示每、基拉雅，基拉雅就是基利他，還有毘他希雅、猶大、以利以謝。
[24]歌唱的人中有：
以利亞實。
守門的人中有：
沙龍、提聯、烏利。

[25]以色列人巴錄的子孫中有：

拉米、耶西雅、瑪基雅、米雅民、以利亞撒、瑪基雅、比拿雅。

26以攔的子孫中有：
　瑪他尼、撒迦利亞、耶歇、押
　底、耶利末、以利雅。
27薩土的子孫中有：
　以利約乃、以利亞實、瑪他尼、
　耶利末、撒拔、亞西撒。
28比拜的子孫中有：
　約哈難、哈拿尼雅、薩拜、亞勒。
29巴尼的子孫中有：
　米書蘭、瑪鹿、亞大雅、雅述、
　示押、耶利末。
30巴哈摩押的子孫中有：
　阿底拿、基拉、比拿雅、瑪西
　雅、瑪他尼、比撒列、賓內、瑪
　拿西。
31哈琳的子孫中有：
　以利以謝、伊示雅、瑪基雅、示
　瑪雅、西緬、32便雅憫、瑪鹿、
　示瑪利雅。
33哈順的子孫中有：
　瑪特乃、瑪達他、撒拔、以利法
　列、耶利買、瑪拿西、示每。
34巴尼的子孫中有：
　瑪玳、暗蘭、烏益、35比拿雅、比底
　雅、基祿、36瓦尼雅、米利末、以利
　亞實、37瑪他尼、瑪特乃、雅掃、
38巴尼、賓內、示每、39示利米雅、
　拿單、亞大雅、40瑪拿底拜、沙
　賽、沙賴、41亞薩利、示利米
　雅、示瑪利雅、42沙龍、亞瑪利
　雅、約瑟。
43尼波的子孫中有：
　耶利、瑪他提雅、撒拔、西比
　拿、雅玳、約珥、比拿雅。

44這些人都娶了外邦女子為妻，
其中也有生了兒女的。

26From the descendants of Elam:
　Mattaniah, Zechariah, Jehiel, Abdi,
　Jeremoth and Elijah.
27From the descendants of Zattu:
　Elioenai, Eliashib, Mattaniah, Jeremoth,
　Zabad and Aziza.
28From the descendants of Bebai:
　Jehohanan, Hananiah, Zabbai and Athlai.
29From the descendants of Bani:
　Meshullam, Malluch, Adaiah, Jashub,
　Sheal and Jeremoth.
30From the descendants of Pahath-Moab:
　Adna, Kelal, Benaiah, Maaseiah,
　Mattaniah, Bezalel, Binnui and
　Manasseh.
31From the descendants of Harim:
　Eliezer, Ishijah, Malkijah, Shemaiah,
　Shimeon, 32Benjamin, Malluch and
　Shemariah.
33From the descendants of Hashum:
　Mattenai, Mattattah, Zabad, Eliphelet,
　Jeremai, Manasseh and Shimei.
34From the descendants of Bani:
　Maadai, Amram, Uel, 35Benaiah, Bedeiah,
　Keluhi, 36Vaniah, Meremoth, Eliashib,
　37Mattaniah, Mattenai and Jaasu.
38From the descendants of Binnui:a
　Shimei, 39Shelemiah, Nathan, Adaiah,
　40Macnadebai, Shashai, Sharai, 41Azarel,
　Shelemiah, Shemariah, 42Shallum,
　Amariah and Joseph.
43From the descendants of Nebo:
　Jeiel, Mattithiah, Zabad, Zebina, Jaddai,
　Joel and Benaiah.

44All these had married foreign women, and
some of them had children by these wives.b

a 37,38 See Septuagint (also 1 Esdras 9:34); Hebrew Jaasu
38 and Bani and Binnui,　b 44 Or and they sent them away with
their children

Nehemiah

尼希米記

Nehemiah's Prayer

1 The words of Nehemiah son of Hacaliah:

In the month of Kislev in the twentieth year, while I was in the citadel of Susa, ²Hanani, one of my brothers, came from Judah with some other men, and I questioned them about the Jewish remnant that survived the exile, and also about Jerusalem.

³They said to me, "Those who survived the exile and are back in the province are in great trouble and disgrace. The wall of Jerusalem is broken down, and its gates have been burned with fire."

⁴When I heard these things, I sat down and wept. For some days I mourned and fasted and prayed before the God of heaven. ⁵Then I said:

"O Lᴏʀᴅ, God of heaven, the great and awesome God, who keeps his covenant of love with those who love him and obey his commands, ⁶let your ear be attentive and your eyes open to hear the prayer your servant is praying before you day and night for your servants, the people of Israel. I confess the sins we Israelites, including myself and my father's house, have committed against you. ⁷We have acted very wickedly toward you. We have not obeyed the commands, decrees and laws you gave your servant Moses.

⁸"Remember the instruction you gave your servant Moses, saying, 'If you are unfaithful, I will scatter you among the nations, ⁹but if you return to me and obey my commands, then even if your exiled people are at the farthest horizon, I will gather them from there and bring them to the place I have chosen as a dwelling for my Name.'

¹⁰"They are your servants and your people, whom you redeemed by your great strength and your mighty hand. ¹¹O Lord, let your ear be attentive to the prayer of this your servant and to the prayer of your servants who delight in revering your name. Give your servant success today by granting him favor in the presence of this man."

I was cupbearer to the king.

尼希米的禱告

1 哈迦利亞的兒子尼希米的言語如下：

亞達薛西王二十年基斯流月，我在書珊城的宮中。²那時，有我一個弟兄哈拿尼，同着幾個人從猶大來。我問他們那些被擄歸回剩下逃脫的猶大人和耶路撒冷的光景。

³他們對我說：「那些被擄歸回剩下的人，在猶大省遭大難，受凌辱；並且耶路撒冷的城牆拆毀，城門被火焚燒。」

⁴我聽見這話，就坐下哭泣，悲哀幾日，在天上的神面前禁食祈禱說：

⁵「耶和華天上的神，大而可畏的神啊，你向愛你、守你誡命的人守約施慈愛。⁶願你睜眼看，側耳聽，你僕人晝夜在你面前為你眾僕人以色列民的祈禱，承認我們以色列人向你所犯的罪。我與我父家都有罪了。⁷我們向你所行的甚是邪惡，沒有遵守你藉着僕人摩西所吩咐的誡命、律例、典章。

⁸「求你記念所吩咐你僕人摩西的話說：『你們若犯罪，我就把你們分散在萬民中；⁹但你們若歸向我，謹守遵行我的誡命，你們被趕散的人，雖在天涯，我也必從那裏將他們招聚回來，帶到我所選擇立為我名的居所。』

¹⁰「這都是你的僕人、你的百姓，就是你用大力和大能的手所救贖的。¹¹主啊，求你側耳聽你僕人的祈禱，和喜愛敬畏你名眾僕人的祈禱，使你僕人現今亨通，在王面前蒙恩。」

我是作王酒政的。

亞達薛西差尼希米去耶路撒冷

2 亞達薛西王二十年尼散月，在王面前擺酒，我拿起酒來奉給王。我素來在王面前沒有愁容。²王對我說："你既沒有病，為甚麼面帶愁容呢？這不是別的，必是你心中愁煩。"

於是我甚懼怕。³我對王說："願王萬歲！我列祖墳墓所在的那城荒涼，城門被火焚燒，我豈能面無愁容嗎？"

⁴王問我說："你要求甚麼？"於是我默禱天上的神。⁵我對王說："僕人若在王眼前蒙恩，王若喜歡，求王差遣我往猶大，到我列祖墳墓所在的那城去，我好重新建造。"

⁶那時，王后坐在王的旁邊。王問我說："你去要多少日子？幾時回來？"我就定了日期。於是王喜歡差遣我去。

⁷我又對王說："王若喜歡，求王賜我詔書，通知大河西的省長准我經過，直到猶大；⁸又賜詔書，通知管理王園林的亞薩，使他給我木料，做殿營樓之門的橫梁和城牆，與我自己房屋使用的。"王就允准我，因我神施恩的手幫助我。⁹王派了軍長和馬兵護送我。我到了河西的省長那裏，將王的詔書交給他們。

¹⁰和倫人參巴拉，並為奴的亞捫人多比雅，聽見有人來為以色列人求好處，就甚惱怒。

尼希米巡視耶路撒冷城牆

¹¹我到了耶路撒冷，在那裏住了三日。¹²我夜間起來，有幾個人也一同起來；但神使我心裏要為耶路撒冷做甚麼事，我並沒有告訴人。除了我騎的牲口以外，也沒有別的牲口在我那裏。

¹³當夜我出了谷門，往野狗井去（註："野狗"或作"龍"），到了糞廠門，察看耶路撒冷的城牆，見城牆拆毀，城門被火焚燒。¹⁴我又往前，到了泉門和王池，但所騎的牲口沒

Artaxerxes Sends Nehemiah to Jerusalem

2 In the month of Nisan in the twentieth year of King Artaxerxes, when wine was brought for him, I took the wine and gave it to the king. I had not been sad in his presence before; ²so the king asked me, "Why does your face look so sad when you are not ill? This can be nothing but sadness of heart."

I was very much afraid, ³but I said to the king, "May the king live forever! Why should my face not look sad when the city where my fathers are buried lies in ruins, and its gates have been destroyed by fire?"

⁴The king said to me, "What is it you want?"

Then I prayed to the God of heaven, ⁵and I answered the king, "If it pleases the king and if your servant has found favor in his sight, let him send me to the city in Judah where my fathers are buried so that I can rebuild it."

⁶Then the king, with the queen sitting beside him, asked me, "How long will your journey take, and when will you get back?" It pleased the king to send me; so I set a time.

⁷I also said to him, "If it pleases the king, may I have letters to the governors of Trans-Euphrates, so that they will provide me safe-conduct until I arrive in Judah? ⁸And may I have a letter to Asaph, keeper of the king's forest, so he will give me timber to make beams for the gates of the citadel by the temple and for the city wall and for the residence I will occupy?" And because the gracious hand of my God was upon me, the king granted my requests. ⁹So I went to the governors of Trans-Euphrates and gave them the king's letters. The king had also sent army officers and cavalry with me.

¹⁰When Sanballat the Horonite and Tobiah the Ammonite official heard about this, they were very much disturbed that someone had come to promote the welfare of the Israelites.

Nehemiah Inspects Jerusalem's Walls

¹¹I went to Jerusalem, and after staying there three days ¹²I set out during the night with a few men. I had not told anyone what my God had put in my heart to do for Jerusalem. There were no mounts with me except the one I was riding on.

¹³By night I went out through the Valley Gate toward the Jackal[a] Well and the Dung Gate, examining the walls of Jerusalem, which had been broken down, and its gates, which had been destroyed by fire. ¹⁴Then I moved on toward the Fountain Gate and the King's Pool,

a 13 Or Serpent or Fig

but there was not enough room for my mount to get through; [15]so I went up the valley by night, examining the wall. Finally, I turned back and reentered through the Valley Gate. [16]The officials did not know where I had gone or what I was doing, because as yet I had said nothing to the Jews or the priests or nobles or officials or any others who would be doing the work.

[17]Then I said to them, "You see the trouble we are in: Jerusalem lies in ruins, and its gates have been burned with fire. Come, let us rebuild the wall of Jerusalem, and we will no longer be in disgrace." [18]I also told them about the gracious hand of my God upon me and what the king had said to me.

They replied, "Let us start rebuilding." So they began this good work.

[19]But when Sanballat the Horonite, Tobiah the Ammonite official and Geshem the Arab heard about it, they mocked and ridiculed us. "What is this you are doing?" they asked. "Are you rebelling against the king?"

[20]I answered them by saying, "The God of heaven will give us success. We his servants will start rebuilding, but as for you, you have no share in Jerusalem or any claim or historic right to it."

Builders of the Wall

3 Eliashib the high priest and his fellow priests went to work and rebuilt the Sheep Gate. They dedicated it and set its doors in place, building as far as the Tower of the Hundred, which they dedicated, and as far as the Tower of Hananel. [2]The men of Jericho built the adjoining section, and Zaccur son of Imri built next to them.

[3]The Fish Gate was rebuilt by the sons of Hassenaah. They laid its beams and put its doors and bolts and bars in place. [4]Meremoth son of Uriah, the son of Hakkoz, repaired the next section. Next to him Meshullam son of Berekiah, the son of Meshezabel, made repairs, and next to him Zadok son of Baana also made repairs. [5]The next section was repaired by the men of Tekoa, but their nobles would not put their shoulders to the work under their supervisors. [a]

[6]The Jeshanah[b] Gate was repaired by Joiada son of Paseah and Meshullam son of Besodeiah. They laid its beams and put its doors and bolts and bars in place. [7]Next to them, repairs were made by men from Gibeon and Mizpah— Melatiah of Gibeon and Jadon of Meronoth—

有地方過去。[15]於是夜間沿溪而上，察看城牆。又轉身進入谷門，就回來了。[16]我往哪裏去，我做甚麼事，官長都不知道。我還沒有告訴猶大平民、祭司、貴冑、官長和其餘做工的人。

[17]以後，我對他們說：「我們所遭的難，耶路撒冷怎樣荒涼，城門被火焚燒，你們都看見了。來吧！我們重建耶路撒冷的城牆，免得再受凌辱。」[18]我告訴他們我神施恩的手怎樣幫助我，並王對我所說的話。

他們就說：「我們起來建造吧！」於是他們奮勇做這善工。

[19]但和倫人參巴拉，並為奴的亞捫人多比雅和阿拉伯人基善聽見就嗤笑我們，藐視我們，說：「你們做甚麼呢？要背叛王嗎？」

[20]我回答他們說：「天上的神必使我們亨通。我們作他僕人的，要起來建造；你們卻在耶路撒冷無分、無權、無記念。」

重建城牆者

3 那時，大祭司以利亞實和他的弟兄眾祭司起來建立羊門，分別為聖，安立門扇，又築城牆到哈米亞樓，直到哈楠業樓，分別為聖。[2]其次是耶利哥人建造。其次是音利的兒子撒刻建造。

[3]哈西拿的子孫建立魚門，架橫梁、安門扇和閂、鎖。[4]其次是哈哥斯的孫子、烏利亞的兒子米利末修造。其次是米示薩別的孫子、比利迦的兒子米書蘭修造。其次是巴拿的兒子撒督修造。[5]其次是提哥亞人修造。但是他們的貴冑不用肩擔他們主的工作。（註：「肩」原文作「頸項」）。

[6]巴西亞的兒子耶何耶大與比所玳的兒子米書蘭修造古門，架橫梁、安門扇和閂、鎖。[7]其次是基遍人米拉提，米倫人雅頓與基遍人，並屬

河西總督所管的米斯巴人修造。⁸其次是銀匠哈海雅的兒子烏薛修造。其次是做香的哈拿尼雅修造。這些人修堅耶路撒冷，直到寬牆。⁹其次是管理耶路撒冷一半、戶珥的兒子利法雅修造。¹⁰其次是哈路抹的兒子耶大雅，對着自己的房屋修造。其次是哈沙尼的兒子哈突修造。¹¹哈琳的兒子瑪基雅和巴哈摩押的兒子哈述修造一段，並修造爐樓。¹²其次是管理耶路撒冷那一半、哈羅黑的兒子沙龍和他的女兒們修造。

¹³哈嫩和撒挪亞的居民修造谷門，立門、安門扇和閂、鎖，又建築城牆一千肘，直到糞廠門。

¹⁴管理伯哈基琳，利甲的兒子瑪基雅修造糞廠門，立門、安門扇和閂、鎖。

¹⁵管理米斯巴，各荷西的兒子沙崙修造泉門，立門、蓋門頂、安門扇和閂、鎖，又修造靠近王園西羅亞池的牆垣，直到那從大衛城下來的臺階。¹⁶其次是管理伯夙一半，押卜的兒子尼希米修造，直到大衛墳地的對面，又到挖成的池子，並勇士的房屋。

¹⁷其次是利未人巴尼的兒子利宏修造。其次是管理基伊拉一半，哈沙比雅為他所管的本境修造。¹⁸其次是利未人弟兄中管理基伊拉那一半，希拿達的兒子巴瓦伊修造。¹⁹其次是管理米斯巴，耶書亞的兒子以謝修造一段，對着武庫的上坡、城牆轉彎之處。²⁰其次是薩拜的兒子巴錄竭力修造一段，從城牆轉彎，直

places under the authority of the governor of Trans-Euphrates. ⁸Uzziel son of Harhaiah, one of the goldsmiths, repaired the next section; and Hananiah, one of the perfume-makers, made repairs next to that. They restored*a* Jerusalem as far as the Broad Wall. ⁹Rephaiah son of Hur, ruler of a half-district of Jerusalem, repaired the next section. ¹⁰Adjoining this, Jedaiah son of Harumaph made repairs opposite his house, and Hattush son of Hashabneiah made repairs next to him. ¹¹Malkijah son of Harim and Hasshub son of Pahath-Moab repaired another section and the Tower of the Ovens. ¹²Shallum son of Hallohesh, ruler of a half-district of Jeru-salem, repaired the next section with the help of his daughters.

¹³The Valley Gate was repaired by Hanun and the residents of Zanoah. They rebuilt it and put its doors and bolts and bars in place. They also repaired five hundred yards*b* of the wall as far as the Dung Gate.

¹⁴The Dung Gate was repaired by Malkijah son of Recab, ruler of the district of Beth Hakkerem. He rebuilt it and put its doors and bolts and bars in place.

¹⁵The Fountain Gate was repaired by Shallun son of Col-Hozeh, ruler of the district of Mizpah. He rebuilt it, roofing it over and putting its doors and bolts and bars in place. He also repaired the wall of the Pool of Siloam,*c* by the King's Garden, as far as the steps going down from the City of David. ¹⁶Beyond him, Nehemiah son of Azbuk, ruler of a half-district of Beth Zur, made repairs up to a point opposite the tombs*d* of David, as far as the artificial pool and the House of the Heroes.

¹⁷Next to him, the repairs were made by the Levites under Rehum son of Bani. Beside him, Hashabiah, ruler of half the district of Keilah, carried out repairs for his district. ¹⁸Next to him, the repairs were made by their countrymen under Binnui*e* son of Henadad, ruler of the other half-district of Keilah. ¹⁹Next to him, Ezer son of Jeshua, ruler of Mizpah, repaired another section, from a point facing the ascent to the armory as far as the angle. ²⁰Next to him, Baruch son of Zabbai zealously repaired another section, from the angle to the entrance of the

---

a 8 Or *They left out part of*　　*b 13* Hebrew *a thousand cubits* (about 450 meters)　　*c 15* Hebrew *Shelah,* a variant of *Shiloah,* that is, Siloam　　*d 16* Hebrew; Septuagint, some Vulgate manuscripts and Syriac *tomb*　　*e 18* Two Hebrew manuscripts and Syriac (see also Septuagint and verse 24); most Hebrew manuscripts *Bavvai*

house of Eliashib the high priest. [21]Next to him, Meremoth son of Uriah, the son of Hakkoz, repaired another section, from the entrance of Eliashib's house to the end of it.

[22]The repairs next to him were made by the priests from the surrounding region. [23]Beyond them, Benjamin and Hasshub made repairs in front of their house; and next to them, Azariah son of Maaseiah, the son of Ananiah, made repairs beside his house. [24]Next to him, Binnui son of Henadad repaired another section, from Azariah's house to the angle and the corner, [25]and Palal son of Uzai worked opposite the angle and the tower projecting from the upper palace near the court of the guard. Next to him, Pedaiah son of Parosh [26]and the temple servants living on the hill of Ophel made repairs up to a point opposite the Water Gate toward the east and the projecting tower. [27]Next to them, the men of Tekoa repaired another section, from the great projecting tower to the wall of Ophel.

[28]Above the Horse Gate, the priests made repairs, each in front of his own house. [29]Next to them, Zadok son of Immer made repairs opposite his house. Next to him, Shemaiah son of Shecaniah, the guard at the East Gate, made repairs. [30]Next to him, Hananiah son of Shelemiah, and Hanun, the sixth son of Zalaph, repaired another section. Next to them, Meshullam son of Berekiah made repairs opposite his living quarters. [31]Next to him, Malkijah, one of the goldsmiths, made repairs as far as the house of the temple servants and the merchants, opposite the Inspection Gate, and as far as the room above the corner; [32]and between the room above the corner and the Sheep Gate the goldsmiths and merchants made repairs.

Opposition to the Rebuilding

4 When Sanballat heard that we were rebuilding the wall, he became angry and was greatly incensed. He ridiculed the Jews, [2]and in the presence of his associates and the army of Samaria, he said, "What are those feeble Jews doing? Will they restore their wall? Will they offer sacrifices? Will they finish in a day? Can they bring the stones back to life from those heaps of rubble—burned as they are?"

[3]Tobiah the Ammonite, who was at his side, said, "What they are building—if even a fox climbed up on it, he would break down their wall of stones!"

[4]Hear us, O our God, for we are despised. Turn their insults back on their own heads. Give

到大祭司以利亞實的府門。[21]其次是哈哥斯的孫子、烏利亞的兒子米利末修造一段，從以利亞實的府門，直到以利亞實府的盡頭。

[22]其次是住平原的祭司修造。[23]其次是便雅憫與哈述對着自己的房屋修造。其次是亞難尼的孫子、瑪西雅的兒子亞撒利雅在靠近自己的房屋修造。[24]其次是希拿達的兒子賓內修造一段，從亞撒利雅的房屋直到城牆轉彎，又到城角。[25]烏賽的兒子巴拉修造對着城牆的轉彎和王上宮凸出來的城樓，靠近護衛院的那一段。其次是巴錄的兒子毘大雅修造。（[26]尼提單住在俄斐勒，直到朝東水門的對面和凸出來的城樓。）[27]其次是提哥亞人又修一段，對着那凸出來的大樓，直到俄斐勒的牆。

[28]從馬門往上，眾祭司各對自己的房屋修造。[29]其次是音麥的兒子撒督對着自己的房屋修造。其次是守東門示迦尼的兒子示瑪雅修造。[30]其次是示利米雅的兒子哈拿尼雅和薩拉的第六子哈嫩又修一段。其次是比利迦的兒子米書蘭對着自己的房屋修造。[31]其次是銀匠瑪基雅修造到尼提寧和商人的房屋，對着哈米弗甲門，直到城的角樓。[32]銀匠與商人在城的角樓和羊門中間修造。

仇敵阻撓重建工程

4 參巴拉聽見我們修造城牆，就發怒，大大惱恨，before嗤笑猶大人。[2]對他弟兄和撒馬利亞的軍兵說：“這些軟弱的猶大人做甚麼呢？要保護自己嗎？要獻祭嗎？要一日成功嗎？要從土堆裏拿出火燒的石頭再立牆嗎？”

[3]亞捫人多比雅站在旁邊，說：“他們所修造的石牆，就是狐狸上去也必跐倒！”

[4]我們的神啊，求你垂聽！因為我們被藐視。求你使他們的毀謗歸於

他們的頭上，使他們在擄到之地作為掠物。⁵不要遮掩他們的罪孽，不要使他們的罪惡從你面前塗抹，因為他們在修造的人眼前惹動你的怒氣。

⁶這樣，我們修造城牆，城牆就都連絡，高至一半，因為百姓專心做工。

⁷參巴拉、多比雅、阿拉伯人、亞捫人、亞實突人聽見修造耶路撒冷城牆，着手進行堵塞破裂的地方，就甚發怒。⁸大家同謀要來攻擊耶路撒冷，使城內擾亂，⁹然而我們禱告我們的神，又因他們的緣故，就派人看守，晝夜防備。

¹⁰猶大人說："灰土尚多，扛抬的人力氣已經衰敗，所以我們不能建造城牆。"

¹¹我們的敵人且說："趁他們不知不見，我們進入他們中間殺他們，使工作止住。"

¹²那靠近敵人居住的猶大人，十次從各處來見我們說："你們必要回到我們那裏。"

¹³所以我使百姓各按宗族拿刀、拿槍、拿弓，站在城牆後邊低窪的空處。¹⁴我察看了，就起來對貴冑、官長和其餘的人說："不要怕他們，當記念主是大而可畏的。你們要為弟兄、兒女、妻子、家產爭戰！"

¹⁵仇敵聽見我們知道他們的心意，見神也破壞他們的計謀，就不來了。我們都回到城牆那裏，各做各的工。

¹⁶從那日起，我的僕人一半做工，一半拿槍、拿盾牌、拿弓、穿鎧甲（註："穿"或作"拿"）。官長都站在猶大眾人的後邊。¹⁷修造城牆的，扛抬材料的，都一手做工，一手拿兵器。¹⁸修造的人都腰間佩刀修造，吹角的人在我旁邊。

¹⁹我對貴冑、官長和其餘的人說："這工程浩大，我們在城牆上相離甚遠，²⁰你們聽見角聲在哪裏，就聚集到我們那裏去。我們的神必為我們爭戰。"

them over as plunder in a land of captivity. ⁵Do not cover up their guilt or blot out their sins from your sight, for they have thrown insults in the face of[a] the builders.

⁶So we rebuilt the wall till all of it reached half its height, for the people worked with all their heart.

⁷But when Sanballat, Tobiah, the Arabs, the Ammonites and the men of Ashdod heard that the repairs to Jerusalem's walls had gone ahead and that the gaps were being closed, they were very angry. ⁸They all plotted together to come and fight against Jerusalem and stir up trouble against it. ⁹But we prayed to our God and posted a guard day and night to meet this threat.

¹⁰Meanwhile, the people in Judah said, "The strength of the laborers is giving out, and there is so much rubble that we cannot rebuild the wall."

¹¹Also our enemies said, "Before they know it or see us, we will be right there among them and will kill them and put an end to the work."

¹²Then the Jews who lived near them came and told us ten times over, "Wherever you turn, they will attack us."

¹³Therefore I stationed some of the people behind the lowest points of the wall at the exposed places, posting them by families, with their swords, spears and bows. ¹⁴After I looked things over, I stood up and said to the nobles, the officials and the rest of the people, "Don't be afraid of them. Remember the Lord, who is great and awesome, and fight for your brothers, your sons and your daughters, your wives and your homes."

¹⁵When our enemies heard that we were aware of their plot and that God had frustrated it, we all returned to the wall, each to his own work.

¹⁶From that day on, half of my men did the work, while the other half were equipped with spears, shields, bows and armor. The officers posted themselves behind all the people of Judah ¹⁷who were building the wall. Those who carried materials did their work with one hand and held a weapon in the other, ¹⁸and each of the builders wore his sword at his side as he worked. But the man who sounded the trumpet stayed with me.

¹⁹Then I said to the nobles, the officials and the rest of the people, "The work is extensive and spread out, and we are widely separated from each other along the wall. ²⁰Wherever you hear the sound of the trumpet, join us there. Our God will fight for us!"

a 5 Or have provoked you to anger before

²¹So we continued the work with half the men holding spears, from the first light of dawn till the stars came out. ²²At that time I also said to the people, "Have every man and his helper stay inside Jerusalem at night, so they can serve us as guards by night and workmen by day." ²³Neither I nor my brothers nor my men nor the guards with me took off our clothes; each had his weapon, even when he went for water.ᵃ

Nehemiah Helps the Poor

5 Now the men and their wives raised a great outcry against their Jewish brothers. ²Some were saying, "We and our sons and daughters are numerous; in order for us to eat and stay alive, we must get grain."

³Others were saying, "We are mortgaging our fields, our vineyards and our homes to get grain during the famine."

⁴Still others were saying, "We have had to borrow money to pay the king's tax on our fields and vineyards. ⁵Although we are of the same flesh and blood as our countrymen and though our sons are as good as theirs, yet we have to subject our sons and daughters to slavery. Some of our daughters have already been enslaved, but we are powerless, because our fields and our vineyards belong to others."

⁶When I heard their outcry and these charges, I was very angry. ⁷I pondered them in my mind and then accused the nobles and officials. I told them, "You are exacting usury from your own countrymen!" So I called together a large meeting to deal with them ⁸and said: "As far as possible, we have bought back our Jewish brothers who were sold to the Gentiles. Now you are selling your brothers, only for them to be sold back to us!" They kept quiet, because they could find nothing to say.

⁹So I continued, "What you are doing is not right. Shouldn't you walk in the fear of our God to avoid the reproach of our Gentile enemies? ¹⁰I and my brothers and my men are also lending the people money and grain. But let the exacting of usury stop! ¹¹Give back to them immediately their fields, vineyards, olive groves and houses, and also the usury you are charging them—the hundredth part of the money, grain, new wine and oil."

¹²"We will give it back," they said. "And we will not demand anything more from them. We will do as you say."

Then I summoned the priests and made the nobles and officials take an oath to do what they had promised. ¹³I also shook out the folds of my

²¹於是我們做工，一半拿兵器，從天亮直到星宿出現的時候。²²那時，我又對百姓說："各人和他的僕人當在耶路撒冷住宿，好在夜間保守我們，白晝做工。"²³這樣，我和弟兄、僕人、並跟從我的兵丁，都不脫衣服，出去打水也帶兵器。

尼希米救助貧民

5 百姓和他們的妻大大呼號，埋怨他們的弟兄猶大人。²有的說："我們和兒女人口眾多，要去得糧食度命。"

³有的說："我們典了田地、葡萄園、房屋，要得糧食充飢。"

⁴有的說："我們已經指着田地、葡萄園，借了錢給王納稅。⁵我們的身體與我們弟兄的身體一樣；我們的兒女與他們的兒女一般。現在我們將要使兒女作人的僕婢，我們的女兒已有為婢的。我們並無力拯救，因為我們的田地、葡萄園已經歸了別人。"

⁶我聽見他們呼號，說這些話，便甚發怒。⁷我心裏籌劃，就斥責貴冑和官長說："你們各人向弟兄取利！"於是我招聚大會攻擊他們。⁸我對他們說："我們盡力贖回我們弟兄，就是賣與外邦的猶大人；你們還要賣弟兄，使我們贖回來嗎？"他們就靜默不語，無話可答。

⁹我又說："你們所行的不善！你們行事不當敬畏我們的神嗎？不然，難免我們的仇敵外邦人毀謗我們。¹⁰我和我的弟兄與僕人也將銀錢、糧食借給百姓，我們大家都當免去利息。¹¹如今我勸你們將他們的田地、葡萄園、橄欖園、房屋，並向他們所取的銀錢、糧食、新酒和油，百分之一的利息都歸還他們。"

¹²眾人說："我們必歸還，不再向他們索要，必照你的話行。"

我就召了祭司來，叫眾人起誓，必照着所應許的而行。¹³我也抖

ᵃ 23 The meaning of the Hebrew for this clause is uncertain.

着胸前的衣襟說：「凡不成就這應許的，願神照樣抖他離開家產和他勞碌得來的，直到抖空了。」

會眾都說：「阿們！」又讚美耶和華。百姓就照着所應許的去行。

14自從我奉派作猶大地的省長，就是從亞達薛西王二十年直到三十二年，共十二年之久，我與我弟兄都沒有吃省長的俸祿。15在我以前的省長，加重百姓的擔子，每日索要糧食和酒，並銀子四十舍客勒，就是他們的僕人也轄制百姓；但我因敬畏神，不這樣行。16並且我恆心修造城牆，並沒有置買田地，我的僕人也都聚集在那裏做工。

17除了從四圍外邦中來的猶大人以外，有猶大平民和官長一百五十人在我席上吃飯。18每日預備一隻公牛、六隻肥羊，又預備些飛禽，每十日一次，多預備各樣的酒。雖然如此，我並不要省長的俸祿，因為百姓服役甚重。

19我的神啊，求你記念我為這百姓所行的一切事，施恩與我。

進一步阻撓重建工程

6 參巴拉、多比雅、阿拉伯人基善和我們其餘的仇敵，聽見我已經修完了城牆，其中沒有破裂之處（那時我還沒有安門扇）。2參巴拉和基善就打發人來見我，說：「請你來，我們在阿挪平原的一個村莊相會。」

他們卻想害我。3於是我差遣人去見他們說：「我現在辦理大工，不能下去！焉能停工，下去見你們呢？」4他們這樣四次打發人來見我，我都如此回答他們。

5參巴拉第五次打發僕人來見我，手裏拿着未封的信，6信上寫着說：

robe and said, "In this way may God shake out of his house and possessions every man who does not keep this promise. So may such a man be shaken out and emptied!"

At this the whole assembly said, "Amen," and praised the LORD. And the people did as they had promised.

[14]Moreover, from the twentieth year of King Artaxerxes, when I was appointed to be their governor in the land of Judah, until his thirty-second year—twelve years—neither I nor my brothers ate the food allotted to the governor. [15]But the earlier governors—those preceding me—placed a heavy burden on the people and took forty shekels[a] of silver from them in addition to food and wine. Their assistants also lorded it over the people. But out of reverence for God I did not act like that. [16]Instead, I devoted myself to the work on this wall. All my men were assembled there for the work; we[b] did not acquire any land.

[17]Furthermore, a hundred and fifty Jews and officials ate at my table, as well as those who came to us from the surrounding nations. [18]Each day one ox, six choice sheep and some poultry were prepared for me, and every ten days an abundant supply of wine of all kinds. In spite of all this, I never demanded the food allotted to the governor, because the demands were heavy on these people.

[19]Remember me with favor, O my God, for all I have done for these people.

Further Opposition to the Rebuilding

6 When word came to Sanballat, Tobiah, Geshem the Arab and the rest of our enemies that I had rebuilt the wall and not a gap was left in it—though up to that time I had not set the doors in the gates— [2]Sanballat and Geshem sent me this message: "Come, let us meet together in one of the villages[c] on the plain of Ono."

But they were scheming to harm me; [3]so I sent messengers to them with this reply: "I am carrying on a great project and cannot go down. Why should the work stop while I leave it and go down to you?" [4]Four times they sent me the same message, and each time I gave them the same answer.

[5]Then, the fifth time, Sanballat sent his aide to me with the same message, and in his hand was an unsealed letter [6]in which was written:

a 15 That is, about 1 pound (about 0.5 kilogram)　　*b 16* Most Hebrew manuscripts; some Hebrew manuscripts, Septuagint, Vulgate and Syriac I　　*c 2* Or *in Kephirim*

"It is reported among the nations—and Geshem*a* says it is true—that you and the Jews are plotting to revolt, and therefore you are building the wall. Moreover, according to these reports you are about to become their king 7and have even appointed prophets to make this proclamation about you in Jeru-salem: 'There is a king in Judah!' Now this report will get back to the king; so come, let us confer together."

8I sent him this reply: "Nothing like what you are saying is happening; you are just making it up out of your head."

9They were all trying to frighten us, thinking, "Their hands will get too weak for the work, and it will not be completed."

⌊But I prayed,⌋ "Now strengthen my hands."

10One day I went to the house of Shemaiah son of Delaiah, the son of Mehetabel, who was shut in at his home. He said, "Let us meet in the house of God, inside the temple, and let us close the temple doors, because men are coming to kill you—by night they are coming to kill you."

11But I said, "Should a man like me run away? Or should one like me go into the temple to save his life? I will not go!" 12I realized that God had not sent him, but that he had prophesied against me because Tobiah and Sanballat had hired him. 13He had been hired to intimidate me so that I would commit a sin by doing this, and then they would give me a bad name to discredit me.

14Remember Tobiah and Sanballat, O my God, because of what they have done; remember also the prophetess Noadiah and the rest of the prophets who have been trying to intimidate me.

The Completion of the Wall

15So the wall was completed on the twenty-fifth of Elul, in fifty-two days. 16When all our enemies heard about this, all the surrounding nations were afraid and lost their self-confidence, because they realized that this work had been done with the help of our God.

17Also, in those days the nobles of Judah were sending many letters to Tobiah, and replies from Tobiah kept coming to them. 18For many in Judah were under oath to him, since he was son-in-law to Shecaniah son of Arah, and his son Jehohanan had married the daughter of Meshullam son of Berekiah. 19Moreover, they kept reporting to me his good deeds and then telling him what I said. And Tobiah sent letters to intimidate me.

"外邦人中有風聲，<u>迦施慕</u>（註：就是"基善"，見2章19節）也說，你和<u>猶大</u>人謀反，修造城牆，你要作他們的王。7你又派先知在<u>耶路撒冷</u>指著你宣講說：'在<u>猶大</u>有王。'現在這話必傳與王知，所以請你來，與我們彼此商議。"

8我就差遣人去見他說："你所說的這事，一概沒有，是你心裏捏造的。"

9他們都要使我們懼怕，意思說，"他們的手必軟弱，以致工作不能成就"。

"神啊，求你堅固我的手"。

10我到了<u>米希大別</u>的孫子、<u>第來雅</u>的兒子<u>示瑪雅</u>家裏。那時，他閉門不出。他說："我們不如在神的殿裏會面，將殿門關鎖，因為他們要來殺你，就是夜裏來殺你。"

11我說："像我這樣的人，豈要逃跑呢？像我這樣的人，豈能進入殿裏保全生命呢？我不進去！"12我看明神沒有差遣他，是他自己說這話攻擊我，是<u>多比雅</u>和<u>參巴拉</u>賄買了他。13賄買他的緣故，是要叫我懼怕，依從他犯罪，他們好傳揚惡言毀謗我。

14我的神啊！<u>多比雅</u>、<u>參巴拉</u>、女先知<u>挪亞底</u>和其餘的先知，要叫我懼怕，求你記念他們所行的這些事。

城牆重建完成

15以祿月二十五日，城牆修完了，共修了五十二天。16我們一切仇敵，四圍的外邦人，聽見了便懼怕，愁眉不展，因為見這工作完成，是出乎我們的神。

17在那些日子，<u>猶大</u>的貴冑屢次寄信與<u>多比雅</u>，<u>多比雅</u>也來信與他們。18在<u>猶大</u>有許多人與<u>多比雅</u>結盟，因他是<u>亞拉</u>的兒子、<u>示迦尼</u>的女婿，並且他的兒子<u>約哈難</u>娶了<u>比利迦</u>兒子<u>米書蘭</u>的女兒為妻。19他們常在我面前說<u>多比雅</u>的善行，也將我的話傳與他。<u>多比雅</u>又常寄信來，要叫我懼怕。

a 6 Hebrew *Gashmu*, a variant of *Geshem*

7 城牆修完，我安了門扇，守門的、歌唱的和利未人都已派定。²我就派我的弟兄哈拿尼和營樓的宰官哈拿尼雅管理耶路撒冷。因為哈拿尼雅是忠信的，又敬畏神過於眾人。³我吩咐他們說："等到太陽上升，才可開耶路撒冷的城門；人尚看守的時候，就要關門上閂。也當派耶路撒冷的居民各按班次，看守自己房屋對面之處。"

被擄歸回者名單

⁴城是廣大，其中的民卻稀少，房屋還沒有建造。⁵我的神感動我心，招聚貴冑、官長和百姓，要照家譜計算。我找着第一次上來之人的家譜，其上寫着：

⁶巴比倫王尼布甲尼撒從前擄去猶大省的人，現在他們的子孫從被擄到之地回耶路撒冷和猶大，各歸本城。⁷他們是同着所羅巴伯、耶書亞、尼希米、亞撒利雅、拉米、拿哈瑪尼、末底改、必珊、米斯毘列、比革瓦伊、尼宏、巴拿回來的。

⁸以色列人民的數目記在下面：

巴錄的子孫二千一百七十二名；
⁹示法提雅的子孫三百七十二名；
¹⁰亞拉的子孫六百五十二名；
¹¹巴哈摩押的後裔，就是耶書亞和約押的子孫二千八百一十八名；
¹²以攔的子孫一千二百五十四名；
¹³薩土的子孫八百四十五名；
¹⁴薩改的子孫七百六十名；
¹⁵賓內的子孫六百四十八名；
¹⁶比拜的子孫六百二十八名；
¹⁷押甲的子孫二千三百二十二名；
¹⁸亞多尼干的子孫六百六十七名；
¹⁹比革瓦伊的子孫二千零六十七名；
²⁰亞丁的子孫六百五十五名；
²¹亞特的後裔，就是希西家的子孫．九十八名；
²²哈順的子孫三百二十八名；
²³比賽的子孫三百二十四名；
²⁴哈拉的子孫一百一十二名；
²⁵基遍人九十五名；

7 After the wall had been rebuilt and I had set the doors in place, the gatekeepers and the singers and the Levites were appointed. ²I put in charge of Jerusalem my brother Hanani, along with*ᵈ* Hananiah the commander of the citadel, because he was a man of integrity and feared God more than most men do. ³I said to them, "The gates of Jerusalem are not to be opened until the sun is hot. While the gatekeepers are still on duty, have them shut the doors and bar them. Also appoint residents of Jerusalem as guards, some at their posts and some near their own houses."

The List of the Exiles Who Returned

⁴Now the city was large and spacious, but there were few people in it, and the houses had not yet been rebuilt. ⁵So my God put it into my heart to assemble the nobles, the officials and the common people for registration by families. I found the genealogical record of those who had been the first to return. This is what I found written there:

⁶These are the people of the province who came up from the captivity of the exiles whom Nebuchadnezzar king of Babylon had taken captive (they returned to Jerusalem and Judah, each to his own town, ⁷in company with Zerubbabel, Jeshua, Nehemiah, Azariah, Raamiah, Nahamani, Mordecai, Bilshan, Mispereth, Bigvai, Nehum and Baanah):

The list of the men of Israel:

⁸the descendants of Parosh	2,172
⁹of Shephatiah	372
¹⁰of Arah	652
¹¹of Pahath-Moab (through the line of Jeshua and Joab)	2,818
¹²of Elam	1,254
¹³of Zattu	845
¹⁴of Zaccai	760
¹⁵of Binnui	648
¹⁶of Bebai	628
¹⁷of Azgad	2,322
¹⁸of Adonikam	667
¹⁹of Bigvai	2,067
²⁰of Adin	655
²¹of Ater (through Hezekiah)	98
²²of Hashum	328
²³of Bezai	324
²⁴of Hariph	112
²⁵of Gibeon	95

a 2 Or Hanani, that is,

26the men of Bethlehem and Netophah	188
27of Anathoth	128
28of Beth Azmaveth	42
29of Kiriath Jearim, Kephirah and Beeroth	743
30of Ramah and Geba	621
31of Micmash	122
32of Bethel and Ai	123
33of the other Nebo	52
34of the other Elam	1,254
35of Harim	320
36of Jericho	345
37of Lod, Hadid and Ono	721
38of Senaah	3,930

39The priests:

the descendants of Jedaiah (through the family of Jeshua)	973
40of Immer	1,052
41of Pashhur	1,247
42of Harim	1,017

43The Levites:

the descendants of Jeshua (through Kadmiel through the line of Hodaviah) 74

44The singers:

the descendants of Asaph 148

45The gatekeepers:

the descendants of Shallum, Ater, Talmon, Akkub, Hatita and Shobai 138

46The temple servants:

the descendants of Ziha, Hasupha, Tabbaoth, 47Keros, Sia, Padon,

48Lebana, Hagaba, Shalmai,

49Hanan, Giddel, Gahar,

50Reaiah, Rezin, Nekoda,

51Gazzam, Uzza, Paseah,

26伯利恆人和尼陀法人共一百八十八名；

27亞拿突人一百二十八名；

28伯亞斯瑪弗人四十二名；

29基列耶琳人、基非拉人、比錄人共七百四十三名；

30拉瑪人和迦巴人共六百二十一名；

31默瑪人一百二十二名；

32伯特利人和艾人共一百二十三名；

33別的尼波人五十二名；

34別的以攔子孫一千二百五十四名；

35哈琳的子孫三百二十名；

36耶利哥人三百四十五名；

37羅德人、哈第人、阿挪人共七百二十一名；

38西拿人三千九百三十名。

39祭司；

耶書亞家、耶大雅的子孫九百七十三名；

40音麥的子孫一千零五十二名；

41巴施戶珥的子孫一千二百四十七名；

42哈琳的子孫一千零一十七名。

43利未人：

何達威的後裔，就是耶書亞和甲篾的子孫七十四名。

44歌唱的：

亞薩的子孫一百四十八名。

45守門的：

沙龍的子孫、亞特的子孫、達們的子孫、亞谷的子孫、哈底大的子孫、朔拜的子孫共一百三十八名。

46尼提寧（註：就是“殿役”）：

西哈的子孫、哈蘇巴的子孫、答巴俄的子孫、

47基綠的子孫、西亞的子孫、巴頓的子孫、

48利巴拿的子孫、哈迦巴的子孫、薩買的子孫、

49哈難的子孫、吉德的子孫、迦哈的子孫、

50利亞雅的子孫、利汛的子孫、尼哥大的子孫、

51迦散的子孫、烏撒的子孫、巴西亞的子孫、

⁵²比賽的子孫、米烏寧的子孫、尼
普心的子孫、

⁵³巴卜的子孫、哈古巴的子孫、哈
忽的子孫、

⁵⁴巴洗律的子孫、米希大的子孫、
哈沙的子孫、

⁵⁵巴柯的子孫、西西拉的子孫、答
瑪的子孫、

⁵⁶尼細亞的子孫、哈提法的子孫。

⁵⁷所羅門僕人的後裔：

就是瑣太的子孫、瑣斐列的子孫、
比路大的子孫、

⁵⁸雅拉的子孫、達昆的子孫、
吉德的子孫、

⁵⁹示法提雅的子孫、哈替的子孫、
玻黑列哈斯巴音的子孫、亞們
的子孫。

⁶⁰尼提寧和所羅門僕人的後裔
共三百九十二名。

⁶¹從特米拉、特哈薩、基綠、
亞頓、音麥上來的，不能指明他
們的宗族譜系是以色列人不是。

⁶²他們是第萊雅的子孫、多比雅的
子孫、尼哥大的子孫，共六百
四十二名。

⁶³祭司中：

哈巴雅的子孫、哈哥斯的子孫、
巴西萊的子孫，因為他們的先
祖娶了基列人巴西萊的女兒為
妻，所以起名叫巴西萊。
⁶⁴這三家的人，在族譜之中尋
查自己的譜系，卻尋不着，因此
算為不潔，不准供祭司的職任。
⁶⁵省長對他們說：“不可吃至聖的
物，直到有用烏陵和土明決疑的
祭司興起來。”

⁶⁶會眾共有四萬二千三百六十
名。⁶⁷此外，還有他們的僕婢七千三
百三十七名，又有歌唱的男女二百
四十五名。⁶⁸他們有馬七百三十六
匹，騾子二百四十五匹，⁶⁹駱駝四
百三十五隻，驢六千七百二十四。

⁷⁰有些族長為工程捐助。省長

⁵²Besai, Meunim, Nephussim,

⁵³Bakbuk, Hakupha, Harhur,

⁵⁴Bazluth, Mehida, Harsha,

⁵⁵Barkos, Sisera, Temah,

⁵⁶Neziah and Hatipha

⁵⁷The descendants of the servants of Solomon:

the descendants of
Sotai, Sophereth, Perida,
⁵⁸Jaala, Darkon, Giddel,

⁵⁹Shephatiah, Hattil,
Pokereth-Hazzebaim and Amon

⁶⁰The temple servants and the descendants
of the servants of Solomon　392

⁶¹The following came up from the towns of
Tel Melah, Tel Harsha, Kerub, Addon and
Immer, but they could not show that their
families were descended from Israel:

⁶²the descendants of
Delaiah, Tobiah and Nekoda　642

⁶³And from among the priests:

the descendants of
Hobaiah, Hakkoz and Barzillai (a man
who had married a daughter of Barzillai
the Gileadite and was called by that name).
⁶⁴These searched for their family records,
but they could not find them and so were
excluded from the priesthood as unclean.
⁶⁵The governor, therefore, ordered them not
to eat any of the most sacred food until there
should be a priest ministering with the Urim
and Thummim.

⁶⁶The whole company numbered 42,360,
⁶⁷besides their 7,337 menservants and maid-
servants; and they also had 245 men and
women singers. ⁶⁸There were 736 horses, 245
mules,^a ⁶⁹435 camels and 6,720 donkeys.

⁷⁰Some of the heads of the families con-

^a 68 Some Hebrew manuscripts (see also Ezra 2:66); most
Hebrew manuscripts do not have this verse.

tributed to the work. The governor gave to the treasury 1,000 drachmas[b] of gold, 50 bowls and 530 garments for priests. [71]Some of the heads of the families gave to the treasury for the work 20,000 drachmas[c] of gold and 2,200 minas[d] of silver. [72]The total given by the rest of the people was 20,000 drachmas of gold, 2,000 minas[e] of silver and 67 garments for priests.

[73]The priests, the Levites, the gatekeepers, the singers and the temple servants, along with certain of the people and the rest of the Israelites, settled in their own towns.

Ezra Reads the Law

8 When the seventh month came and the Israelites had settled in their towns, [1]all the people assembled as one man in the square before the Water Gate. They told Ezra the scribe to bring out the Book of the Law of Moses, which the LORD had commanded for Israel.

[2]So on the first day of the seventh month Ezra the priest brought the Law before the assembly, which was made up of men and women and all who were able to understand. [3]He read it aloud from daybreak till noon as he faced the square before the Water Gate in the presence of the men, women and others who could understand. And all the people listened attentively to the Book of the Law.

[4]Ezra the scribe stood on a high wooden platform built for the occasion. Beside him on his right stood Mattithiah, Shema, Anaiah, Uriah, Hilkiah and Maaseiah; and on his left were Pedaiah, Mishael, Malkijah, Hashum, Hashbaddanah, Zechariah and Meshullam.

[5]Ezra opened the book. All the people could see him because he was standing above them; and as he opened it, the people all stood up. [6]Ezra praised the LORD, the great God; and all the people lifted their hands and responded, "Amen! Amen!" Then they bowed down and worshiped the LORD with their faces to the ground.

[7]The Levites—Jeshua, Bani, Sherebiah, Jamin, Akkub, Shabbethai, Hodiah, Maaseiah, Kelita, Azariah, Jozabad, Hanan and Pelaiah—instructed the people in the Law while the people were standing there. [8]They read from the Book of the Law of God, making it clear[e] and giving the meaning so that the people could understand what was being read.

a 70 That is, about 19 pounds (about 8.5 kilograms)
b 71 That is, about 375 pounds (about 170 kilograms); also in verse 72　c 71 That is, about 1 1/3 tons (about 1.2 metric tons)
d 72 That is, about 1 1/4 tons (about 1.1 metric tons)
e 8 Or God, translating it

捐入庫中的金子一千達利克，碗五十個，祭司的禮服五百三十件。 [71]又有族長捐入工程庫的金子二萬達利克，銀子二千二百彌拿。 [72]其餘百姓所捐的金子二萬達利克，銀子二千彌拿，祭司的禮服六十七件。

[73]於是，祭司、<u>利未人</u>、守門的、歌唱的、民中的一些人、尼提寧，並<u>以色列</u>眾人，各住在自己的城裏。

以斯拉宣讀律法

<u>以色列</u>人住在自己的城裏。 **8** 到了七月，[1]那時，他們如同一人聚集在<u>水門</u>前的寬闊處，請文士<u>以斯拉</u>將耶和華藉摩西傳給<u>以色列</u>人的律法書帶來。

[2]七月初一日，祭司<u>以斯拉</u>將律法書帶到聽了能明白的男女會眾面前。 [3]在<u>水門</u>前的寬闊處，從清早到晌午，在眾男女一切聽了能明白的人面前，讀這律法書。眾民側耳而聽。

[4]文士<u>以斯拉</u>站在為這事特備的木臺上。<u>瑪他提雅</u>、<u>示瑪</u>、<u>亞奈雅</u>、<u>烏利亞</u>、<u>希勒家</u>和<u>瑪西雅</u>站在他的右邊；<u>毘大雅</u>、<u>米沙利</u>、<u>瑪基雅</u>、<u>哈順</u>、<u>哈拔大拿</u>、<u>撒迦利亞</u>和<u>米書蘭</u>站在他的左邊。

[5]<u>以斯拉</u>站在眾民以上，在眾民眼前展開這書。他一展開，眾民就都站起來。 [6]<u>以斯拉</u>稱頌耶和華至大的神，眾民都舉手應聲說："阿們！阿們！"就低頭，面伏於地，敬拜耶和華。

[7]<u>耶書亞</u>、<u>巴尼</u>、<u>示利比</u>、<u>雅憫</u>、<u>亞谷</u>、<u>沙比太</u>、<u>荷第雅</u>、<u>瑪西雅</u>、<u>基利他</u>、<u>亞撒利雅</u>、<u>約撒拔</u>、<u>哈難</u>、<u>毘萊雅</u>和<u>利未</u>人使百姓明白律法；百姓都站在自己的地方。 [8]他們清清楚楚地念神的律法書，講明意思，使百姓明白所念的。

⁹省長尼希米和作祭司的文士以斯拉，並教訓百姓的利未人，對眾民說：「今日是耶和華你們神的聖日，不要悲哀哭泣。」這是因為眾民聽見律法書上的話都哭了。

¹⁰又對他們說：「你們去吃肥美的，喝甘甜的，有不能預備的，就分給他；因為今日是我們主的聖日。你們不要憂愁，因靠耶和華而得的喜樂是你們的力量。」

¹¹於是利未人使眾民靜默，說：「今日是聖日；不要做聲，也不要憂愁。」

¹²眾民都去吃喝，也分給人，大大快樂，因為他們明白所教訓他們的話。

¹³次日，眾民的族長、祭司和利未人都聚集到文士以斯拉那裏，要留心聽律法上的話。¹⁴他們見律法上寫着，耶和華藉摩西吩咐以色列人，要在七月節住棚，¹⁵並要在各城和耶路撒冷宣傳報告說：「你們當上山，將橄欖樹、野橄欖樹、番石榴樹、棕樹和各樣茂密樹的枝子取來，照着所寫的搭棚。」

¹⁶於是百姓出去，取了樹枝來，各人在自己的房頂上，或院內，或神殿的院內，或水門的寬闊處，或以法蓮門的寬闊處搭棚。¹⁷從擄到之地歸回的全會眾就搭棚，住在棚裏。從嫩的兒子約書亞的時候直到這日，以色列人沒有這樣行。於是眾人大大喜樂。

¹⁸從頭一天直到末一天，以斯拉每日念神的律法書。眾人守節七日，第八日照例有嚴肅會。

以色列人認罪

9 這月二十四日，以色列人聚集禁食，身穿麻衣，頭蒙灰塵。²以色列人（註：「人」原文作「種類」）就與一切外邦人離絕，站着承認自己的罪惡和列祖的罪孽。³那日的四分之一，站在自己的地

⁹Then Nehemiah the governor, Ezra the priest and scribe, and the Levites who were instructing the people said to them all, "This day is sacred to the LORD your God. Do not mourn or weep." For all the people had been weeping as they listened to the words of the Law.

¹⁰Nehemiah said, "Go and enjoy choice food and sweet drinks, and send some to those who have nothing prepared. This day is sacred to our Lord. Do not grieve, for the joy of the LORD is your strength."

¹¹The Levites calmed all the people, saying, "Be still, for this is a sacred day. Do not grieve."

¹²Then all the people went away to eat and drink, to send portions of food and to celebrate with great joy, because they now understood the words that had been made known to them.

¹³On the second day of the month, the heads of all the families, along with the priests and the Levites, gathered around Ezra the scribe to give attention to the words of the Law. ¹⁴They found written in the Law, which the LORD had commanded through Moses, that the Israelites were to live in booths during the feast of the seventh month ¹⁵and that they should proclaim this word and spread it throughout their towns and in Jerusalem: "Go out into the hill country and bring back branches from olive and wild olive trees, and from myrtles, palms and shade trees, to make booths"—as it is written.ᵃ

¹⁶So the people went out and brought back branches and built themselves booths on their own roofs, in their courtyards, in the courts of the house of God and in the square by the Water Gate and the one by the Gate of Ephraim. ¹⁷The whole company that had returned from exile built booths and lived in them. From the days of Joshua son of Nun until that day, the Israelites had not celebrated it like this. And their joy was very great.

¹⁸Day after day, from the first day to the last, Ezra read from the Book of the Law of God. They celebrated the feast for seven days, and on the eighth day, in accordance with the regulation, there was an assembly.

The Israelites Confess Their Sins

9 On the twenty-fourth day of the same month, the Israelites gathered together, fasting and wearing sackcloth and having dust on their heads. ²Those of Israelite descent had separated themselves from all foreigners. They stood in their places and confessed their sins and the wickedness of their fathers. ³They stood where they were and read from the

a 15 See Lev. 23:37-40.

Book of the Law of the LORD their God for a quarter of the day, and spent another quarter in confession and in worshiping the LORD their God. 4Standing on the stairs were the Levites—Jeshua, Bani, Kadmiel, Shebaniah, Bunni, Sherebiah, Bani and Kenani—who called with loud voices to the LORD their God. 5And the Levites—Jeshua, Kadmiel, Bani, Hashabneiah, Sherebiah, Hodiah, Shebaniah and Pethahiah—said: "Stand up and praise the LORD your God, who is from everlasting to everlasting.ª"

"Blessed be your glorious name, and may it be exalted above all blessing and praise. 6You alone are the LORD. You made the heavens, even the highest heavens, and all their starry host, the earth and all that is on it, the seas and all that is in them. You give life to everything, and the multitudes of heaven worship you.

7"You are the LORD God, who chose Abram and brought him out of Ur of the Chaldeans and named him Abraham. 8You found his heart faithful to you, and you made a covenant with him to give to his descendants the land of the Canaanites, Hittites, Amorites, Perizzites, Jebusites and Girgashites. You have kept your promise because you are righteous.

9"You saw the suffering of our forefathers in Egypt; you heard their cry at the Red Sea.b 10You sent miraculous signs and wonders against Pharaoh, against all his officials and all the people of his land, for you knew how arrogantly the Egyptians treated them. You made a name for yourself, which remains to this day. 11You divided the sea before them, so that they passed through it on dry ground, but you hurled their pursuers into the depths, like a stone into mighty waters. 12By day you led them with a pillar of cloud, and by night with a pillar of fire to give them light on the way they were to take.

13"You came down on Mount Sinai; you spoke to them from heaven. You gave them regulations and laws that are just and right, and decrees and commands that are good. 14You made known to them your holy Sabbath and gave them commands, decrees and laws through your servant Moses. 15In their hunger you gave them bread from heaven and in their thirst you brought them water from the rock; you told them to go in and take possession of the land you had sworn with uplifted hand to give them.

方,念耶和華他們神的律法書;又四分之一認罪,敬拜耶和華他們的神。4耶書亞、巴尼、甲篾、示巴尼、布尼、示利比、巴尼、基拿尼站在利未人的臺上,大聲哀求耶和華他們的神。5利未人耶書亞、甲篾、巴尼、哈沙尼、示利比、荷第雅、示巴尼、毘他希雅說:"你們要站起來稱頌耶和華你們的神,永世無盡。"

"耶和華啊,你榮耀之名是應當稱頌的,超乎一切稱頌和讚美!6你,惟獨你,是耶和華!你造了天和天上的天,並天上的萬象,地和地上的萬物,海和海中所有的,這一切都是你所保存的;天軍也都敬拜你。

7"你是耶和華神,曾揀選亞伯蘭,領他出迦勒底的吾珥,給他改名叫亞伯拉罕。8你見他在你面前心裏誠實,就與他立約,應許把迦南人、赫人、亞摩利人、比利洗人、耶布斯人、革迦撒人之地,賜給他的後裔,且應驗了你的話,因為你是公義的。

9"你曾看見我們列祖在埃及所受的困苦,垂聽他們在紅海邊的哀求,10就施行神蹟奇事在法老和他一切臣僕、並他國中的眾民身上,你也得了名聲,正如今日一樣,因為你知道他們向我們列祖行事狂傲。11你又在我們列祖面前把海分開,使他們在海中行走乾地,將追趕他們的人拋在深海,如石頭拋在大水中。12並且白晝用雲柱引導他們,黑夜用火柱照亮他們當行的路。

13"你也降臨在西奈山,從天上與他們說話,賜給他們正直的典章、真實的律法、美好的條例與誡命。14又使他們知道你的安息聖日,並藉你僕人摩西傳給他們誡命、條例、律法。15從天上賜下糧食充他們的飢,從磐石使水流出解他們的渴,又吩咐他們進去得你起誓應許賜給他們的地。

a 5 Or *God for ever and ever*   b 9 Hebrew *Yam Suph*; that is, Sea of Reeds

16 「但我們的列祖行事狂傲，硬着頸項不聽從你的誡命；17不肯順從，也不記念你在他們中間所行的奇事，竟硬着頸項，居心背逆，自立首領，要回他們為奴之地。但你是樂意饒恕人，有恩典，有憐憫，不輕易發怒，有豐盛慈愛的神，並不丟棄他們。18他們雖然鑄了一隻牛犢，彼此說‘這是領你出埃及的神’，因而大大惹動你的怒氣。

19 「你還是大施憐憫，在曠野不丟棄他們。白晝，雲柱不離開他們，仍引導他們行路；黑夜，火柱也不離開他們，仍照亮他們當行的路。20你也賜下你良善的靈教訓他們，未嘗不賜嗎哪使他們餬口，並賜水解他們的渴。21在曠野四十年，你養育他們，他們就一無所缺：衣服沒有穿破，腳也沒有腫。

22 「並且，你將列國之地照分賜給他們，他們就得了西宏之地、岳實本王之地和巴珊王噩之地。23你也使他們的子孫多如天上的星，帶他們到你所應許他們列祖進入得為業之地。24這樣，他們進去得了那地，你在他們面前制伏那地的居民，就是迦南人；將迦南人和其君王、並那地的居民，都交在他們手裏，讓他們任意而待。25他們得了堅固的城邑、肥美的地土、充滿各樣美物的房屋、鑿成的水井、葡萄園、橄欖園，並許多果木樹。他們就吃而得飽，身體肥胖，因你的大恩，心中快樂。

26 「然而，他們不順從，竟背叛你。將你的律法丟在背後，殺害那勸他們歸向你的眾先知，大大惹動你的怒氣。27所以你將他們交在敵人的手中，磨難他們。他們遭難的時候哀求你，你就從天上

16"But they, our forefathers, became arrogant and stiff-necked, and did not obey your commands. 17They refused to listen and failed to remember the miracles you performed among them. They became stiff-necked and in their rebellion appointed a leader in order to return to their slavery. But you are a forgiving God, gracious and compassionate, slow to anger and abounding in love. Therefore you did not desert them, 18even when they cast for themselves an image of a calf and said, 'This is your god, who brought you up out of Egypt,' or when they committed awful blasphemies.

19"Because of your great compassion you did not abandon them in the desert. By day the pillar of cloud did not cease to guide them on their path, nor the pillar of fire by night to shine on the way they were to take. 20You gave your good Spirit to instruct them. You did not withhold your manna from their mouths, and you gave them water for their thirst. 21For forty years you sustained them in the desert; they lacked nothing, their clothes did not wear out nor did their feet become swollen.

22"You gave them kingdoms and nations, allotting to them even the remotest frontiers. They took over the country of Sihon[a] king of Heshbon and the country of Og king of Bashan. 23You made their sons as numerous as the stars in the sky, and you brought them into the land that you told their fathers to enter and possess. 24Their sons went in and took possession of the land. You subdued before them the Canaanites, who lived in the land; you handed the Canaanites over to them, along with their kings and the peoples of the land, to deal with them as they pleased. 25They captured fortified cities and fertile land; they took possession of houses filled with all kinds of good things, wells already dug, vineyards, olive groves and fruit trees in abundance. They ate to the full and were well-nourished; they reveled in your great goodness.

26"But they were disobedient and rebelled against you; they put your law behind their backs. They killed your prophets, who had admonished them in order to turn them back to you; they committed awful blasphemies. 27So you handed them over to their enemies, who oppressed them. But when they were oppressed they cried out to you. From heaven

a 22 One Hebrew manuscript and Septuagint; most Hebrew manuscripts Sihon, that is, the country of the

you heard them, and in your great compassion you gave them deliverers, who rescued them from the hand of their enemies.

28"But as soon as they were at rest, they again did what was evil in your sight. Then you abandoned them to the hand of their enemies so that they ruled over them. And when they cried out to you again, you heard from heaven, and in your compassion you delivered them time after time.

29"You warned them to return to your law, but they became arrogant and disobeyed your commands. They sinned against your ordinances, by which a man will live if he obeys them. Stubbornly they turned their backs on you, became stiff-necked and refused to listen. 30For many years you were patient with them. By your Spirit you admonished them through your prophets. Yet they paid no attention, so you handed them over to the neighboring peoples. 31But in your great mercy you did not put an end to them or abandon them, for you are a gracious and merciful God.

32"Now therefore, O our God, the great, mighty and awesome God, who keeps his covenant of love, do not let all this hardship seem trifling in your eyes—the hardship that has come upon us, upon our kings and leaders, upon our priests and prophets, upon our fathers and all your people, from the days of the kings of Assyria until today. 33In all that has happened to us, you have been just; you have acted faithfully, while we did wrong. 34Our kings, our leaders, our priests and our fathers did not follow your law; they did not pay attention to your commands or the warnings you gave them. 35Even while they were in their kingdom, enjoying your great goodness to them in the spacious and fertile land you gave them, they did not serve you or turn from their evil ways.

36"But see, we are slaves today, slaves in the land you gave our forefathers so they could eat its fruit and the other good things it produces. 37Because of our sins, its abundant harvest goes to the kings you have placed over us. They rule over our bodies and our cattle as they please. We are in great distress.

The Agreement of the People

38"In view of all this, we are making a binding agreement, putting it in writing, and our leaders, our Levites and our priests are affixing their seals to it."

垂聽，照你的大憐憫賜給他們拯救者，救他們脫離敵人的手。

28 "但他們得平安之後，又在你面前行惡，所以你丟棄他們在仇敵的手中，使仇敵轄制他們。然而他們轉回哀求你，你仍從天上垂聽，屢次照你的憐憫拯救他們。

29 "又警戒他們，要使他們歸服你的律法。他們卻行事狂傲，不聽從你的誡命，干犯你的典章（人若遵行就必因此活著），扭轉肩頭，硬著頸項，不肯聽從。30但你多年寬容他們，又用你的靈藉眾先知勸戒他們，他們仍不聽從，所以你將他們交在列國之民的手中。31然而你大發憐憫，不全然滅絕他們，也不丟棄他們；因為你是有恩典、有憐憫的神。"

32 "我們的神啊，你是至大、至能、至可畏、至守約施慈愛的神。我們的君王、首領、祭司、先知、列祖和你的眾民，從亞述列王的時候直到今日所遭遇的苦難，現在求你不要以為小。33在一切臨到我們的事上，你卻是公義的；因你所行的是誠實，我們所作的是邪惡。34我們的君王、首領、祭司、列祖都不遵守你的律法，不聽從你的誡命和你警戒他們的話。35他們在本國裏沾你大恩的時候，在你所賜給他們這廣大肥美之地上，不侍奉你，也不轉離他們的惡行。

36 "我們現今作了奴僕；至於你所賜給我們列祖享受其上的土產，並美物之地，看哪，我們在這地上作了奴僕！37這地許多出產歸了列王，就是你因我們的罪所派轄制我們的。他們任意轄制我們的身體和牲畜，我們遭了大難。

百姓簽名立約

38 "因這一切的事，我們立確實的約，寫在冊上。我們的首領、利未人和祭司都簽了名。"

10

簽名的是：

哈迦利亞的兒子、省長尼希米和西底家。

2祭司：西萊雅、亞撒利雅、耶利米、
3巴施戶珥、亞瑪利雅、瑪基雅、
4哈突、示巴尼、瑪鹿、
5哈琳、米利末、俄巴底亞、
6但以理、近頓、巴錄、
7米書蘭、亞比雅、米雅民、
8瑪西亞、璧該、示瑪雅。

9又有利未人：

就是亞散尼的兒子耶書亞、希拿達的子孫賓內、甲篾，
10還有他們的弟兄示巴尼、荷第雅、基利他、毘萊雅、哈難、
11米迦、利合、哈沙比雅、
12撒刻、示利比、示巴尼、
13荷第雅、巴尼、比尼努。

14又有民的首領：

就是巴錄、巴哈摩押、以攔、薩土、巴尼、
15布尼、押甲、比拜、
16亞多尼雅、比革瓦伊、亞丁、
17亞特、希西家、押朔、
18荷第雅、哈順、比賽、
19哈拉、亞拿突、尼拜、
20抹比押、米書蘭、希悉、
21米示薩別、撒督、押杜亞、
22毘拉提、哈難、亞奈雅、
23何細亞、哈拿尼雅、哈述、
24哈羅黑、毘利哈、朔百、
25利宏、哈沙拿、瑪西雅、
26亞希雅、哈難、亞難、
27瑪鹿、哈琳、巴拿。

28 "其餘的民、祭司、利未人、守門的、歌唱的、尼提寧和一切離絕鄰邦居民、歸服神律法的，並他們的妻子、兒女，凡有知識能明白的，29都隨從他們貴冑的弟兄，發咒起誓，必遵行神藉他僕人摩西所傳的律法，謹守遵行耶和華我們主的一切誡命、典章、律例。

30 "並不將我們的女兒嫁給這地的居民，也不為我們的兒子娶他們的女兒。

10

Those who sealed it were:

Nehemiah the governor, the son of Hacaliah.

Zedekiah, 2Seraiah, Azariah, Jeremiah,
3Pashhur, Amariah, Malkijah,
4Hattush, Shebaniah, Malluch,
5Harim, Meremoth, Obadiah,
6Daniel, Ginnethon, Baruch,
7Meshullam, Abijah, Mijamin,
8Maaziah, Bilgai and Shemaiah.
These were the priests.

9The Levites:

Jeshua son of Azaniah, Binnui of the sons of Henadad, Kadmiel,
10and their associates: Shebaniah,
Hodiah, Kelita, Pelaiah, Hanan,
11Mica, Rehob, Hashabiah,
12Zaccur, Sherebiah, Shebaniah,
13Hodiah, Bani and Beninu.

14The leaders of the people:

Parosh, Pahath-Moab, Elam, Zattu, Bani,
15Bunni, Azgad, Bebai,
16Adonijah, Bigvai, Adin,
17Ater, Hezekiah, Azzur,
18Hodiah, Hashum, Bezai,
19Hariph, Anathoth, Nebai,
20Magpiash, Meshullam, Hezir,
21Meshezabel, Zadok, Jaddua,
22Pelatiah, Hanan, Anaiah,
23Hoshea, Hananiah, Hasshub,
24Hallohesh, Pilha, Shobek,
25Rehum, Hashabnah, Maaseiah,
26Ahiah, Hanan, Anan,
27Malluch, Harim and Baanah.

28"The rest of the people—priests, Levites, gatekeepers, singers, temple servants and all who separated themselves from the neighboring peoples for the sake of the Law of God, together with their wives and all their sons and daughters who are able to understand—29all these now join their brothers the nobles, and bind themselves with a curse and an oath to follow the Law of God given through Moses the servant of God and to obey carefully all the commands, regulations and decrees of the LORD our Lord.
30"We promise not to give our daughters in marriage to the peoples around us or take their daughters for our sons.

31"When the neighboring peoples bring merchandise or grain to sell on the Sabbath, we will not buy from them on the Sabbath or on any holy day. Every seventh year we will forgo working the land and will cancel all debts.

32"We assume the responsibility for carrying out the commands to give a third of a shekel*ᵃ* each year for the service of the house of our God: 33for the bread set out on the table; for the regular grain offerings and burnt offerings; for the offerings on the Sabbaths, New Moon festivals and appointed feasts; for the holy offerings; for sin offerings to make atonement for Israel; and for all the duties of the house of our God.

34"We—the priests, the Levites and the people—have cast lots to determine when each of our families is to bring to the house of our God at set times each year a contribution of wood to burn on the altar of the LORD our God, as it is written in the Law.

35"We also assume responsibility for bringing to the house of the LORD each year the first-fruits of our crops and of every fruit tree.

36"As it is also written in the Law, we will bring the firstborn of our sons and of our cattle, of our herds and of our flocks to the house of our God, to the priests ministering there.

37"Moreover, we will bring to the storerooms of the house of our God, to the priests, the first of our ground meal, of our ⌊grain⌋ offerings, of the fruit of all our trees and of our new wine and oil. And we will bring a tithe of our crops to the Levites, for it is the Levites who collect the tithes in all the towns where we work. 38A priest descended from Aaron is to accompany the Levites when they receive the tithes, and the Levites are to bring a tenth of the tithes up to the house of our God, to the storerooms of the treasury. 39The people of Israel, including the Levites, are to bring their contributions of grain, new wine and oil to the storerooms where the articles for the sanctuary are kept and where the ministering priests, the gatekeepers and the singers stay.

"We will not neglect the house of our God."

The New Residents of Jerusalem

11 Now the leaders of the people settled in Jerusalem, and the rest of the people cast lots to bring one out of every ten to live in Jerusalem, the holy city, while the remaining nine were to stay in their own towns. 2The peo-

31 "這地的居民若在安息日,或甚麼聖日,帶了貨物或糧食來賣給我們,我們必不買。每逢第七年必不耕種,凡欠我們債的必不追討。

32 "我們又為自己定例:每年各人捐銀一舍客勒三分之一,為我們神殿的使用,33就是為陳設餅、常獻的素祭和燔祭,安息日、月朔、節期所獻的與聖物,並以色列人的贖罪祭,以及我們神殿裏一切的費用。

34 "我們的祭司、利未人和百姓都掣籤,看每年是哪一族,按定期將獻祭的柴奉到我們神的殿裏,照着律法上所寫的,燒在耶和華我們神的壇上。

35 "又定每年將我們地上初熟的土產和各樣樹上初熟的果子,都奉到耶和華的殿裏。

36 "又照律法上所寫的,將我們頭胎的兒子和首生的牛羊,都奉到我們神的殿,交給我們神殿裏供職的祭司。

37 "並要初熟之麥子所磨的麵和舉祭、各樣樹上初熟的果子、新酒與油奉給祭司,收在我們神殿的庫房裏,把我們地上所產的十分之一奉給利未人,因利未人在我們一切城邑的土產中,當取十分之一。38利未人取十分之一的時候,亞倫的子孫中,當有一個祭司與利未人同在。利未人也當從十分之一中,取十分之一,奉到我們神殿的屋子裏,收在庫房中。39以色列人和利未人要將五穀、新酒和油為舉祭,奉到收存聖所器皿的屋子裏,就是供職的祭司、守門的、歌唱的所住的屋子。

"這樣,我們就不離棄我們神的殿。"

耶路撒冷的新居民

11 百姓的首領住在耶路撒冷,其餘的百姓掣籤,每十人中使一人來住在聖城耶路撒冷,那九人住在別的城邑。2凡甘心

---

a 32 That is, about 1/8 ounce (about 4 grams)

樂意住在耶路撒冷的，百姓都為他們祝福。

3以色列人、祭司、利未人、尼提寧和所羅門僕人的後裔，都住在猶大城邑，各在自己的地業中。本省的首領住在耶路撒冷的記在下面。4其中有些猶大人和便雅憫人：

猶大人中有：

法勒斯的子孫、烏西雅的兒子亞他雅。烏西雅是撒迦利雅的兒子；撒迦利雅是亞瑪利雅的兒子；亞瑪利雅是示法提雅的兒子；示法提雅是瑪勒列的兒子。5又有巴錄的兒子瑪西雅。巴錄是谷何西的兒子；谷何西是哈賽雅的兒子；哈賽雅是亞大雅的兒子；亞大雅是約雅立的兒子；約雅立是撒迦利雅的兒子；撒迦利雅是示羅尼的兒子。6住在耶路撒冷、法勒斯的子孫共四百六十八名，都是勇士。

7便雅憫人中有：

米書蘭的兒子撒路。米書蘭是約葉的兒子；約葉是毘大雅的兒子；毘大雅是哥賴雅的兒子；哥賴雅是瑪西雅的兒子；瑪西雅是以鐵的兒子；以鐵是耶篩亞的兒子。8其次有迦拜、撒來的子孫共九百二十八名。9細基利的兒子約珥是他們的長官，哈西努亞的兒子猶大是耶路撒冷的副官。

10祭司中有：

雅斤，又有約雅立的兒子耶大雅，11還有管理神殿的西萊雅。西萊雅是希勒家的兒子；希勒家是米書蘭的兒子；米書蘭是撒督的兒子；撒督是米拉約的兒子；米拉約是亞希突的兒子。12還有他們的弟兄在殿裏供職的，共八百二十二名。又有耶羅罕的兒子亞大雅。耶羅罕是毘拉利的兒子；毘拉利是暗洗的兒子；暗洗是撒瑪利亞的兒子；撒瑪利亞是巴施戶珥的兒子；巴施戶珥是瑪基雅的兒子。13還有他的弟兄作族長的，二百四十二名。又有亞薩列的兒子亞瑪帥。亞薩列是亞哈賽的兒子；亞哈賽是米實利末的兒子；米實利末是音麥的兒子。14還有他們弟兄大能的勇士共一百二十八名。哈基多琳的兒子撒巴第業是他們的長官。

ple commended all the men who volunteered to live in Jerusalem.

3These are the provincial leaders who settled in Jerusalem (now some Israelites, priests, Levites, temple servants and descendants of Solomon's servants lived in the towns of Judah, each on his own property in the various towns, 4while other people from both Judah and Benjamin lived in Jerusalem):

From the descendants of Judah:

Athaiah son of Uzziah, the son of Zechariah, the son of Amariah, the son of Shephatiah, the son of Mahalalel, a descendant of Perez; 5and Maaseiah son of Baruch, the son of Col-Hozeh, the son of Hazaiah, the son of Adaiah, the son of Joiarib, the son of Zechariah, a descendant of Shelah. 6The descendants of Perez who lived in Jerusalem totaled 468 able men.

7From the descendants of Benjamin:

Sallu son of Meshullam, the son of Joed, the son of Pedaiah, the son of Kolaiah, the son of Maaseiah, the son of Ithiel, the son of Jeshaiah, 8and his followers, Gabbai and Sallai—928 men. 9Joel son of Zicri was their chief officer, and Judah son of Hassenuah was over the Second District of the city.

10From the priests:

Jedaiah; the son of Joiarib; Jakin; 11Seraiah son of Hilkiah, the son of Meshullam, the son of Zadok, the son of Meraioth, the son of Ahitub, supervisor in the house of God, 12and their associates, who carried on work for the temple—822 men; Adaiah son of Jeroham, the son of Pelaliah, the son of Amzi, the son of Zechariah, the son of Pashhur, the son of Malkijah, 13and his associates, who were heads of families—242 men; Amashsai son of Azarel, the son of Ahzai, the son of Meshillemoth, the son of Immer, 14and his*a* associates, who were able men—128. Their chief officer was Zabdiel son of Haggedolim.

a 14 Most Septuagint manuscripts; Hebrew *their*

¹⁵From the Levites:

Shemaiah son of Hasshub, the son of Azrikam, the son of Hashabiah, the son of Bunni; ¹⁶Shabbethai and Jozabad, two of the heads of the Levites, who had charge of the outside work of the house of God; ¹⁷Mattaniah son of Mica, the son of Zabdi, the son of Asaph, the director who led in thanksgiving and prayer; Bakbukiah, second among his associates; and Abda son of Shammua, the son of Galal, the son of Jeduthun. ¹⁸The Levites in the holy city totaled 284.

¹⁹The gatekeepers:

Akkub, Talmon and their associates, who kept watch at the gates—172 men.

²⁰The rest of the Israelites, with the priests and Levites, were in all the towns of Judah, each on his ancestral property.

²¹The temple servants lived on the hill of Ophel, and Ziha and Gishpa were in charge of them.

²²The chief officer of the Levites in Jerusalem was Uzzi son of Bani, the son of Hashabiah, the son of Mattaniah, the son of Mica. Uzzi was one of Asaph's descendants, who were the singers responsible for the service of the house of God. ²³The singers were under the king's orders, which regulated their daily activity.

²⁴Pethahiah son of Meshezabel, one of the descendants of Zerah son of Judah, was the king's agent in all affairs relating to the people.

²⁵As for the villages with their fields, some of the people of Judah lived in Kiriath Arba and its surrounding settlements, in Dibon and its settlements, in Jekabzeel and its villages, ²⁶in Jeshua, in Moladah, in Beth Pelet, ²⁷in Hazar Shual, in Beersheba and its settlements, ²⁸in Ziklag, in Meconah and its settlements, ²⁹in En Rimmon, in Zorah, in Jarmuth, ³⁰Zanoah, Adullam and their villages, in Lachish and its fields, and in Azekah and its settlements. So they were living all the way from Beersheba to the Valley of Hinnom.

³¹The descendants of the Benjamites from Geba lived in Micmash, Aija, Bethel and its settlements, ³²in Anathoth, Nob and Ananiah, ³³in Hazor, Ramah and Gittaim, ³⁴in Hadid, Zeboim and Neballat, ³⁵in Lod and Ono, and in the Valley of the Craftsmen.

³⁶Some of the divisions of the Levites of Judah settled in Benjamin.

¹⁵利未人中有：

哈述的兒子示瑪雅。哈述是押利甘的兒子；押利甘是哈沙比雅的兒子；哈沙比雅是布尼的兒子。¹⁶又有利未人的族長沙比太和約撒拔，管理神殿的外事。¹⁷祈禱的時候，為稱謝領首的是米迦的兒子瑪他尼。米迦是撒底的兒子；撒底是亞薩的兒子；又有瑪他尼弟兄中的八布迦為副。還有沙母亞的兒子押大。沙母亞是加拉的兒子；加拉是耶杜頓的兒子。¹⁸在聖城的利未人共二百八十四名。

¹⁹守門的是：

亞谷和達們，並守門的弟兄，共一百七十二名。

²⁰其餘的以色列人、祭司、利未人，都住在猶大的一切城邑，各在自己的地業中。

²¹尼提寧卻住在俄斐勒，西哈和基斯帕管理他們。

²²在耶路撒冷，利未人的長官，管理神殿事務的是歌唱者亞薩的子孫、巴尼的兒子烏西。巴尼是哈沙比雅的兒子；哈沙比雅是瑪他尼的兒子；瑪他尼是米迦的兒子。²³王為唱歌的出命令，每日供給他們必有一定之糧。

²⁴猶大兒子謝拉的子孫、米示薩別的兒子毗他希雅，輔助王辦理猶大民的事。

²⁵至於村莊和屬村莊的田地，有猶大人住在基列亞巴和屬基列亞巴的鄉村；底本和屬底本的鄉村；葉甲薛和屬葉甲薛的村莊；²⁶耶書亞、摩拉大、伯帕列、²⁷哈薩書亞、別是巴和屬別是巴的鄉村；²⁸洗革拉、米哥拿和屬米哥拿的鄉村；²⁹音臨門、瑣拉、耶末、³⁰撒挪亞、亞杜蘭和屬這兩處的村莊；拉吉和屬拉吉的田地；亞西加和屬亞西加的鄉村。他們所住的地方，是從別是巴直到欣嫩谷。

³¹便雅憫人從迦巴起，住在密抹、亞雅、伯特利和屬伯特利的鄉村，³²亞拿突、挪伯、亞難雅、³³夏瑣、拉瑪、基他音、³⁴哈疊、洗編、尼八拉、³⁵羅德、阿挪、匠人之谷。

³⁶利未人中有幾班曾住在猶大地歸於便雅憫的。

祭司與利未人

12 同着撒拉鐵的兒子所羅巴伯和耶書亞回來的祭司與利未人記在下面。祭司是：

西萊雅、耶利米、以斯拉、²亞瑪利雅、瑪鹿、哈突、³示迦尼、利宏、米利末、⁴易多、近頓、亞比雅、⁵米雅民、瑪底雅、璧迦、⁶示瑪雅、約雅立、耶大雅、⁷撒路、亞木、希勒家、耶大雅。這些人在耶書亞的時候作祭司和他們弟兄的首領。

⁸利未人是：耶書亞、賓內、甲篾、示利比、猶大、瑪他尼。這瑪他尼和他的弟兄管理稱謝的事。⁹他們的弟兄八布迦和烏尼，照自己的班次，與他們相對。

¹⁰耶書亞生約雅金；約雅金生以利亞實；以利亞實生耶何耶大；¹¹耶何耶大生約拿單；約拿單生押杜亞。

¹²在約雅金的時候，祭司作族長的：

西萊雅族（註：或作"班"。本段同）有米拉雅；

耶利米族有哈拿尼雅；

¹³以斯拉族有米書蘭；

亞瑪利雅族有約哈難；

¹⁴米利古族有約拿單；

示巴尼族有約瑟；

¹⁵哈琳族有押拿；

米拉約族有希勒愷；

¹⁶易多族有撒迦利亞；

近頓族有米書蘭；

¹⁷亞比雅族有細基利；

米拿民族某；摩亞底族有毘勒太；

¹⁸璧迦族有沙母亞；

示瑪雅族有約拿單；

¹⁹約雅立族有瑪特乃；

耶大雅族有烏西；

²⁰撒來族有加萊；

亞木族有希伯；

²¹希勒家族有哈沙比雅；

耶大雅族有拿坦業。

²²至於利未人，當以利亞實、耶何耶大、約哈難、押杜亞的時候，他們的族長記在冊上；波斯王大利烏在位的時候，作族長的祭司也記在冊上。²³利未人作族長的，記在歷

Priests and Levites

12 These were the priests and Levites who returned with Zerubbabel son of Shealtiel and with Jeshua:

Seraiah, Jeremiah, Ezra,
²Amariah, Malluch, Hattush,
³Shecaniah, Rehum, Meremoth,
⁴Iddo, Ginnethon,[a] Abijah,
⁵Mijamin,[b] Moadiah, Bilgah,
⁶Shemaiah, Joiarib, Jedaiah,
⁷Sallu, Amok, Hilkiah and Jedaiah.

These were the leaders of the priests and their associates in the days of Jeshua.

⁸The Levites were Jeshua, Binnui, Kadmiel, Sherebiah, Judah, and also Mattaniah, who, together with his associates, was in charge of the songs of thanksgiving. ⁹Bakbukiah and Unni, their associates, stood opposite them in the services.

¹⁰Jeshua was the father of Joiakim, Joiakim the father of Eliashib, Eliashib the father of Joiada, ¹¹Joiada the father of Jonathan, and Jonathan the father of Jaddua.

¹²In the days of Joiakim, these were the heads of the priestly families:

of Seraiah's family, Meraiah;
of Jeremiah's, Hananiah;
¹³of Ezra's, Meshullam;
of Amariah's, Jehohanan;
¹⁴of Malluch's, Jonathan;
of Shecaniah's,[c] Joseph;
¹⁵of Harim's, Adna;
of Meremoth's,[d] Helkai;
¹⁶of Iddo's, Zechariah;
of Ginnethon's, Meshullam;
¹⁷of Abijah's, Zicri;
of Miniamin's and of Moadiah's, Piltai;
¹⁸of Bilgah's, Shammua;
of Shemaiah's, Jehonathan;
¹⁹of Joiarib's, Mattenai;
of Jedaiah's, Uzzi;
²⁰of Sallu's, Kallai;
of Amok's, Eber;
²¹of Hilkiah's, Hashabiah;
of Jedaiah's, Nethanel.

²²The family heads of the Levites in the days of Eliashib, Joiada, Johanan and Jaddua, as well as those of the priests, were recorded in the reign of Darius the Persian. ²³The family heads among the descendants of Levi up to the time of

---

a 4 Many Hebrew manuscripts and Vulgate (see also Neh. 12:16); most Hebrew manuscripts *Ginnethoi*　b 5 A variant of *Miniamin*　c 14 Very many Hebrew manuscripts, some Septuagint manuscripts and Syriac (see also Neh. 12:3); most Hebrew manuscripts *Shebaniah's*　d 15 Some Septuagint manuscripts (see also Neh. 12:3); Hebrew *Meraioth's*

Johanan son of Eliashib were recorded in the book of the annals. ²⁴And the leaders of the Levites were Hashabiah, Sherebiah, Jeshua son of Kadmiel, and their associates, who stood opposite them to give praise and thanksgiving, one section responding to the other, as prescribed by David the man of God.

²⁵Mattaniah, Bakbukiah, Obadiah, Meshullam, Talmon and Akkub were gatekeepers who guarded the storerooms at the gates. ²⁶They served in the days of Joiakim son of Jeshua, the son of Jozadak, and in the days of Nehemiah the governor and of Ezra the priest and scribe.

Dedication of the Wall of Jerusalem

²⁷At the dedication of the wall of Jerusalem, the Levites were sought out from where they lived and were brought to Jerusalem to celebrate joyfully the dedication with songs of thanksgiving and with the music of cymbals, harps and lyres. ²⁸The singers also were brought together from the region around Jerusalem—from the villages of the Netophathites, ²⁹from Beth Gilgal, and from the area of Geba and Azmaveth, for the singers had built villages for themselves around Jerusalem. ³⁰When the priests and Levites had purified themselves ceremonially, they purified the people, the gates and the wall.

³¹I had the leaders of Judah go up on top[a] of the wall. I also assigned two large choirs to give thanks. One was to proceed on top[b] of the wall to the right, toward the Dung Gate. ³²Hoshaiah and half the leaders of Judah followed them, ³³along with Azariah, Ezra, Meshullam, ³⁴Judah, Benjamin, Shemaiah, Jeremiah, ³⁵as well as some priests with trumpets, and also Zechariah son of Jonathan, the son of Shemaiah, the son of Mattaniah, the son of Micaiah, the son of Zaccur, the son of Asaph, ³⁶and his associates—Shemaiah, Azarel, Milalai, Gilalai, Maai, Nethanel, Judah and Hanani—with musical instruments [prescribed by] David the man of God. Ezra the scribe led the procession. ³⁷At the Fountain Gate they continued directly up the steps of the City of David on the ascent to the wall and passed above the house of David to the Water Gate on the east.

³⁸The second choir proceeded in the opposite direction. I followed them on top[c] of the wall, together with half the people—past the Tower of the Ovens to the Broad Wall, ³⁹over the Gate of Ephraim, the Jeshanah[d] Gate, the Fish Gate,

史上，直到以利亞實的兒子約哈難的時候。²⁴利未人的族長是哈沙比雅、示利比、甲篾的兒子耶書亞，與他們弟兄的班次相對，照着神人大衛的命令，一班一班地讚美稱謝。

²⁵瑪他尼、八布迦、俄巴底亞、米書蘭、達們、亞谷是守門的，就是在庫房那裏守門。²⁶這都是在約撒達的孫子、耶書亞的兒子約雅金和省長尼希米，並祭司文士以斯拉的時候，有職任的。

耶路撒冷城牆的奉獻禮

²⁷耶路撒冷城牆告成的時候，眾民就把各處的利未人招到耶路撒冷，要稱謝、歌唱、敲鈸、鼓瑟、彈琴，歡歡喜喜地行告成之禮。²⁸、²⁹歌唱的人從耶路撒冷的周圍和尼陀法的村莊，與伯吉甲，又從迦巴和押瑪弗的田地聚集，因為歌唱的人在耶路撒冷四圍，為自己立了村莊。³⁰祭司和利未人就潔淨自己，也潔淨百姓和城門，並城牆。

³¹我帶猶大的首領上城，使稱謝的人分為兩大隊，排列而行：第一隊在城上往右邊向糞廠門行走，³²在他們後頭的有何沙雅與猶大首領的一半，³³又有亞撒利雅、以斯拉、米書蘭、³⁴猶大、便雅憫、示瑪雅、耶利米。³⁵還有些吹號之祭司的子孫，約拿單的兒子撒迦利亞。約拿單是示瑪雅的兒子；示瑪雅是瑪他尼的兒子；瑪他尼是米該亞的兒子；米該亞是撒刻的兒子；撒刻是亞薩的兒子。³⁶又有撒迦利亞的弟兄示瑪雅、亞撒利、米拉萊、基拉萊、瑪艾、拿坦業、猶大、哈拿尼，都拿着神人大衛的樂器，文士以斯拉引領他們。³⁷他們經過泉門往前，從大衛城的臺階，隨地勢而上，在大衛宮殿以上，直行到朝東的水門。

³⁸第二隊稱謝的人要與那一隊相迎而行。我和民的一半跟隨他們，在城牆上過了爐樓，直到寬牆。³⁹又過了以法蓮門、古門、魚

---

a 31 Or go alongside   b 31 Or proceed alongside   c 38 Or them alongside   d 39 Or Old

門、哈楠業樓、哈米亞樓，直到羊門，就在護衛門站住。

40於是這兩隊稱謝的人，連我和官長的一半，站在神的殿裏。41還有祭司以利亞金、瑪西雅、米拿民、米該雅、以利約乃、撒迦利亞、哈楠尼亞吹號。42又有瑪西雅、示瑪雅、以利亞撒、烏西、約哈難、瑪基雅、以攔和以謝奏樂。歌唱的就大聲歌唱，伊斯拉希雅管理他們。43那日眾人獻大祭而歡樂，因為神使他們大大歡樂，連婦女帶孩童也都歡樂，甚至耶路撒冷中的歡聲聽到遠處。

44當日派人管理庫房，將舉祭、初熟之物和所取的十分之一，就是按各城田地，照律法所定歸給祭司和利未人的分，都收在裏頭。猶大人因祭司和利未人供職，就歡樂了。45祭司利未人遵守神所吩咐的，並守潔淨的禮。歌唱的、守門的，照着大衛和他兒子所羅門的命令，也如此行。46古時，在大衛和亞薩的日子，有歌唱的伶長，並有讚美稱謝神的詩歌。47當所羅巴伯和尼希米的時候，以色列眾人將歌唱的、守門的每日所當得的分供給他們。又給利未人當得的分；利未人又給亞倫的子孫當得的分。

尼希米末後的改革

13 當日，人念摩西的律法書給百姓聽，遇見書上寫着說："亞捫人和摩押人永不可入神的會，2因為他們沒有拿食物和水來迎接以色列人，且雇了巴蘭咒詛他們；但我們的神使那咒詛變為祝福。"3以色列民聽見這律法，就與一切閑雜人絕交。

4先是蒙派管理我們神殿中庫房的祭司以利亞實與多比雅結親，5便為他預備一間大屋子，就是從前收存素祭、乳香、器皿，和照命令供給利未人、歌唱的、守門的五穀、新酒和油的十分之一，並歸祭司舉祭的屋子。

the Tower of Hananel and the Tower of the Hundred, as far as the Sheep Gate. At the Gate of the Guard they stopped.

40The two choirs that gave thanks then took their places in the house of God; so did I, together with half the officials, 41as well as the priests—Eliakim, Maaseiah, Miniamin, Micaiah, Elioenai, Zechariah and Hananiah with their trumpets—42and also Maaseiah, Shemaiah, Eleazar, Uzzi, Jehohanan, Malkijah, Elam and Ezer. The choirs sang under the direction of Jezrahiah. 43And on that day they offered great sacrifices, rejoicing because God had given them great joy. The women and children also rejoiced. The sound of rejoicing in Jerusalem could be heard far away.

44At that time men were appointed to be in charge of the storerooms for the contributions, firstfruits and tithes. From the fields around the towns they were to bring into the storerooms the portions required by the Law for the priests and the Levites, for Judah was pleased with the ministering priests and Levites. 45They performed the service of their God and the service of purification, as did also the singers and gatekeepers, according to the commands of David and his son Solomon. 46For long ago, in the days of David and Asaph, there had been directors for the singers and for the songs of praise and thanksgiving to God. 47So in the days of Zerubbabel and of Nehemiah, all Israel contributed the daily portions for the singers and gatekeepers. They also set aside the portion for the other Levites, and the Levites set aside the portion for the descendants of Aaron.

Nehemiah's Final Reforms

13 On that day the Book of Moses was read aloud in the hearing of the people and there it was found written that no Ammonite or Moabite should ever be admitted into the assembly of God, 2because they had not met the Israelites with food and water but had hired Balaam to call a curse down on them. (Our God, however, turned the curse into a blessing.) 3When the people heard this law, they excluded from Israel all who were of foreign descent.

4Before this, Eliashib the priest had been put in charge of the storerooms of the house of our God. He was closely associated with Tobiah, 5and he had provided him with a large room formerly used to store the grain offerings and incense and temple articles, and also the tithes of grain, new wine and oil prescribed for the Levites, singers and gatekeepers, as well as the contributions for the priests.

⁶But while all this was going on, I was not in Jerusalem, for in the thirty-second year of Artaxerxes king of Babylon I had returned to the king. Some time later I asked his permission ⁷and came back to Jerusalem. Here I learned about the evil thing Eliashib had done in providing Tobiah a room in the courts of the house of God. ⁸I was greatly displeased and threw all Tobiah's household goods out of the room. ⁹I gave orders to purify the rooms, and then I put back into them the equipment of the house of God, with the grain offerings and the incense.

¹⁰I also learned that the portions assigned to the Levites had not been given to them, and that all the Levites and singers responsible for the service had gone back to their own fields. ¹¹So I rebuked the officials and asked them, "Why is the house of God neglected?" Then I called them together and stationed them at their posts.

¹²All Judah brought the tithes of grain, new wine and oil into the storerooms. ¹³I put Shelemiah the priest, Zadok the scribe, and a Levite named Pedaiah in charge of the storerooms and made Hanan son of Zaccur, the son of Mattaniah, their assistant, because these men were considered trustworthy. They were made responsible for distributing the supplies to their brothers.

¹⁴Remember me for this, O my God, and do not blot out what I have so faithfully done for the house of my God and its services.

¹⁵In those days I saw men in Judah treading winepresses on the Sabbath and bringing in grain and loading it on donkeys, together with wine, grapes, figs and all other kinds of loads. And they were bringing all this into Jerusalem on the Sabbath. Therefore I warned them against selling food on that day. ¹⁶Men from Tyre who lived in Jerusalem were bringing in fish and all kinds of merchandise and selling them in Jerusalem on the Sabbath to the people of Judah. ¹⁷I rebuked the nobles of Judah and said to them, "What is this wicked thing you are doing—desecrating the Sabbath day? ¹⁸Didn't your forefathers do the same things, so that our God brought all this calamity upon us and upon this city? Now you are stirring up more wrath against Israel by desecrating the Sabbath."

¹⁹When evening shadows fell on the gates of Jerusalem before the Sabbath, I ordered the doors to be shut and not opened until the Sabbath was over. I stationed some of my own men at the gates so that no load could be brought in on the Sabbath day. ²⁰Once or twice the mer-

⁶那時，我不在耶路撒冷。因為巴比倫王亞達薛西三十二年，我回到王那裏。過了多日，我向王告假。⁷我來到耶路撒冷，就知道以利亞實為多比雅在神殿的院內預備屋子的那件惡事。⁸我甚惱怒，就把多比雅的一切家具從屋裏都拋出去，⁹吩咐人潔淨這屋子，遂將神殿的器皿和素祭乳香又搬進去。

¹⁰我見利未人所當得的分，無人供給他們，甚至供職的利未人與歌唱的俱各奔回自己的田地去了。¹¹我就斥責官長說：“為何離棄神的殿呢？”我便招聚利未人，使他們照舊供職。

¹²猶大眾人就把五穀、新酒和油的十分之一，送入庫房。¹³我派祭司示利米雅、文士撒督和利未人毘大雅作庫官管理庫房；副官是哈難。哈難是撒刻的兒子；撒刻是瑪他尼的兒子。這些人都是忠信的，他們的職分是將所供給的分給他們的弟兄。

¹⁴我的神啊，求你因這事記念我，不要塗抹我為神的殿與其中的禮節所行的善。

¹⁵那些日子，我在猶大見有人在安息日醉酒（註：原文作“踹酒醡”），搬運禾捆，馱在驢上，又把酒、葡萄、無花果，和各樣的擔子，在安息日擔入耶路撒冷，我就在他們賣食物的那日，警戒他們。¹⁶又有推羅人住在耶路撒冷，他們把魚和各樣貨物運進來，在安息日賣給猶大人。¹⁷我就斥責猶大的貴冑說：“你們怎麼行這惡事，犯了安息日呢？¹⁸從前你們列祖豈不是這樣行，以致我們神使一切災禍臨到我們和這城嗎？現在你們還犯安息日，使忿怒越發臨到以色列？！”

¹⁹在安息日的前一日，耶路撒冷城門有黑影的時候，我就吩咐人將門關鎖，不過安息日不准開放。我又派我幾個僕人管理城門，免得有人在安息日擔甚麼擔子進城。²⁰於是商人和

販賣各樣貨物的，一兩次住宿在耶路撒冷城外。²¹我就警戒他們說：「你們為何在城外住宿呢？若再這樣，我必下手拿辦你們。」從此以後，他們在安息日不再來了。²²我吩咐利未人潔淨自己，來守城門，使安息日為聖。

我的神啊，求你因這事記念我，照你的大慈愛憐恤我。

²³那些日子，我也見猶大人娶了亞實突、亞捫、摩押的女子為妻。²⁴他們的兒女說話，一半是亞實突的話，不會說猶大的話，所說的是照着各族的方言。²⁵我就斥責他們，咒詛他們，打了他們幾個人，拔下他們的頭髮，叫他們指着神起誓，必不將自己的女兒嫁給外邦人的兒子，也不為自己和兒子娶他們的女兒。²⁶我又說：「以色列王所羅門不是在這樣的事上犯罪嗎？在多國中並沒有一王像他，且蒙他神所愛，神立他作以色列全國的王，然而連他也被外邦女子引誘犯罪。²⁷如此，我豈聽你們行這大惡，娶外邦女子干犯我們的神呢？」

²⁸大祭司以利亞實的孫子、耶何耶大的一個兒子，是和倫人參巴拉的女婿，我就從我這裏把他趕出去。

²⁹我的神啊，求你記念他們的罪，因為他們玷污了祭司的職任，違背你與祭司利未人所立的約。

³⁰這樣，我潔淨他們，使他們離絕一切外邦人，派定祭司和利未人的班次，使他們各盡其職。³¹我又派百姓按定期獻柴和初熟的土產。

我的神啊，求你記念我，施恩與我。

chants and sellers of all kinds of goods spent the night outside Jerusalem. ²¹But I warned them and said, "Why do you spend the night by the wall? If you do this again, I will lay hands on you." From that time on they no longer came on the Sabbath. ²²Then I commanded the Levites to purify themselves and go and guard the gates in order to keep the Sabbath day holy.

Remember me for this also, O my God, and show mercy to me according to your great love.

²³Moreover, in those days I saw men of Judah who had married women from Ashdod, Ammon and Moab. ²⁴Half of their children spoke the language of Ashdod or the language of one of the other peoples, and did not know how to speak the language of Judah. ²⁵I rebuked them and called curses down on them. I beat some of the men and pulled out their hair. I made them take an oath in God's name and said: "You are not to give your daughters in marriage to their sons, nor are you to take their daughters in marriage for your sons or for yourselves. ²⁶Was it not because of marriages like these that Solomon king of Israel sinned? Among the many nations there was no king like him. He was loved by his God, and God made him king over all Israel, but even he was led into sin by foreign women. ²⁷Must we hear now that you too are doing all this terrible wickedness and are being unfaithful to our God by marrying foreign women?"

²⁸One of the sons of Joiada son of Eliashib the high priest was son-in-law to Sanballat the Horonite. And I drove him away from me.

²⁹Remember them, O my God, because they defiled the priestly office and the covenant of the priesthood and of the Levites.

³⁰So I purified the priests and the Levites of everything foreign, and assigned them duties, each to his own task. ³¹I also made provision for contributions of wood at designated times, and for the firstfruits.

Remember me with favor, O my God.

Esther

以斯帖記

Queen Vashti Deposed

1 This is what happened during the time of Xerxes,[a] the Xerxes who ruled over 127 provinces stretching from India to Cush[b] : [2]At that time King Xerxes reigned from his royal throne in the citadel of Susa, [3]and in the third year of his reign he gave a banquet for all his nobles and officials. The military leaders of Persia and Media, the princes, and the nobles of the provinces were present.

[4]For a full 180 days he displayed the vast wealth of his kingdom and the splendor and glory of his majesty. [5]When these days were over, the king gave a banquet, lasting seven days, in the enclosed garden of the king's palace, for all the people from the least to the greatest, who were in the citadel of Susa. [6]The garden had hangings of white and blue linen, fastened with cords of white linen and purple material to silver rings on marble pillars. There were couches of gold and silver on a mosaic pavement of porphyry, marble, mother-of-pearl and other costly stones. [7]Wine was served in goblets of gold, each one different from the other, and the royal wine was abundant, in keeping with the king's liberality. [8]By the king's command each guest was allowed to drink in his own way, for the king instructed all the wine stewards to serve each man what he wished.

[9]Queen Vashti also gave a banquet for the women in the royal palace of King Xerxes.

[10]On the seventh day, when King Xerxes was in high spirits from wine, he commanded the seven eunuchs who served him—Mehuman, Biztha, Harbona, Bigtha, Abagtha, Zethar and Carcas— [11]to bring before him Queen Vashti, wearing her royal crown, in order to display her beauty to the people and nobles, for she was lovely to look at. [12]But when the attendants delivered the king's command, Queen Vashti refused to come. Then the king became furious and burned with anger.

[13]Since it was customary for the king to consult experts in matters of law and justice, he spoke with the wise men who understood the

王后瓦實提被廢

1 亞哈隨魯作王，從印度直到古實，統管一百二十七省。 [2]亞哈隨魯王在書珊城的宮登基。 [3]在位第三年，為他一切首領、臣僕設擺筵席，有波斯和瑪代的權貴，就是各省的貴冑與首領，在他面前。

[4]他把他榮耀之國的豐富和他美好威嚴的尊貴，給他們看了許多日，就是一百八十日。 [5]這日子滿了，又為所有住書珊城的大小人民，在御園的院子裏設擺筵席七日。 [6]有白色、綠色、藍色的帳子，用細麻繩、紫色繩從銀環內繫在白玉石柱上，有金銀的牀榻擺在紅、白、黃、黑玉石的鋪石地上。 [7]用金器皿賜酒，器皿各有不同。御酒甚多，足顯王的厚意。 [8]喝酒有例，不准勉強人，因王吩咐宮裏的一切臣宰，讓人各隨己意。

[9]王后瓦實提在亞哈隨魯王的宮內，也為婦女設擺筵席。

[10]第七日，亞哈隨魯王飲酒，心中快樂，就吩咐在他面前侍立的七個太監米戶幔、比斯他、哈波拿、比革他、亞拔他、西達、甲迦， [11]請王后瓦實提頭戴王后的冠冕到王面前，使各等臣民看她的美貌，因為她容貌甚美。 [12]王后瓦實提卻不肯遵太監所傳的王命而來，所以王甚發怒，心如火燒。

[13]、[14]那時，在王左右常見王面、國中坐高位的，有波斯和瑪代的七個大臣，就是甲示拿、示達、押瑪他、

---

a 1 Hebrew *Ahasuerus*, a variant of Xerxes' Persian name; here and throughout Esther　　b 1 That is, the upper Nile region

他施斯、米力、瑪西拿、米母王，都是達時務的明哲人。按王的常規，辦事必先詢問知例明法的人。王問他們說：

15 "王后瓦實提不遵太監所傳的王命，照例應當怎樣辦理呢？"

16米母王在王和眾首領面前回答說："王后瓦實提這事不但得罪王，並且有害於王各省的臣民。17因為王后這事必傳到眾婦人的耳中，說亞哈隨魯王吩咐王后瓦實提到王面前，她卻不來。她們就藐視自己的丈夫。18今日波斯和瑪代的眾夫人聽見王后這事，必向王的大臣照樣行，從此必大開藐視和忿怒之端。

19 "王若以為美，就降旨寫在波斯和瑪代人的例中，永不更改，不准瓦實提再到王面前，將她王后的位分賜給比她選好的人。20所降的旨意傳遍通國（國度本來廣大），所有的婦人，無論丈夫貴賤都必尊敬他。"

21王和眾首領都以米母王的話為美，王就照這話去行。22發詔書，用各省的文字、各族的方言通知各省，使為丈夫的在家中作主，各說本地的方言。

以斯帖被立為后

2 這事以後，亞哈隨魯王的忿怒止息，就想念瓦實提和她所行的，並怎樣降旨辦她。2於是王的侍臣對王說："不如為王尋找美貌的處女。3王可以派官在國中的各省，招聚美貌的處女到書珊城（註：或作"宮"）的女院，交給掌管女子的太監希該，給她們當用的香品。4王所喜愛的女子可以立為王后，代替瓦實提。"王以這事為美，就如此行。

times [14]and were closest to the king—Carshena, Shethar, Admatha, Tarshish, Meres, Marsena and Memucan, the seven nobles of Persia and Media who had special access to the king and were highest in the kingdom.

[15]"According to law, what must be done to Queen Vashti?" he asked. "She has not obeyed the command of King Xerxes that the eunuchs have taken to her."

[16]Then Memucan replied in the presence of the king and the nobles, "Queen Vashti has done wrong, not only against the king but also against all the nobles and the peoples of all the provinces of King Xerxes. [17]For the queen's conduct will become known to all the women, and so they will despise their husbands and say, 'King Xerxes commanded Queen Vashti to be brought before him, but she would not come.' [18]This very day the Persian and Median women of the nobility who have heard about the queen's conduct will respond to all the king's nobles in the same way. There will be no end of disrespect and discord.

[19]"Therefore, if it pleases the king, let him issue a royal decree and let it be written in the laws of Persia and Media, which cannot be repealed, that Vashti is never again to enter the presence of King Xerxes. Also let the king give her royal position to someone else who is better than she. [20]Then when the king's edict is proclaimed throughout all his vast realm, all the women will respect their husbands, from the least to the greatest."

[21]The king and his nobles were pleased with this advice, so the king did as Memucan proposed. [22]He sent dispatches to all parts of the kingdom, to each province in its own script and to each people in its own language, proclaiming in each people's tongue that every man should be ruler over his own household.

Esther Made Queen

2 Later when the anger of King Xerxes had subsided, he remembered Vashti and what she had done and what he had decreed about her. [2]Then the king's personal attendants proposed, "Let a search be made for beautiful young virgins for the king. [3]Let the king appoint commissioners in every province of his realm to bring all these beautiful girls into the harem at the citadel of Susa. Let them be placed under the care of Hegai, the king's eunuch, who is in charge of the women; and let beauty treatments be given to them. [4]Then let the girl who pleases the king be queen instead of Vashti." This advice appealed to the king, and he followed it.

⁵Now there was in the citadel of Susa a Jew of the tribe of Benjamin, named Mordecai son of Jair, the son of Shimei, the son of Kish, ⁶who had been carried into exile from Jerusalem by Nebuchadnezzar king of Babylon, among those taken captive with Jehoiachin*a* king of Judah. ⁷Mordecai had a cousin named Hadassah, whom he had brought up because she had neither father nor mother. This girl, who was also known as Esther, was lovely in form and features, and Mordecai had taken her as his own daughter when her father and mother died.

⁸When the king's order and edict had been proclaimed, many girls were brought to the citadel of Susa and put under the care of Hegai. Esther also was taken to the king's palace and entrusted to Hegai, who had charge of the harem. ⁹The girl pleased him and won his favor. Immediately he provided her with her beauty treatments and special food. He assigned to her seven maids selected from the king's palace and moved her and her maids into the best place in the harem.

¹⁰Esther had not revealed her nationality and family background, because Mordecai had forbidden her to do so. ¹¹Every day he walked back and forth near the courtyard of the harem to find out how Esther was and what was happening to her.

¹²Before a girl's turn came to go in to King Xerxes, she had to complete twelve months of beauty treatments prescribed for the women, six months with oil of myrrh and six with perfumes and cosmetics. ¹³And this is how she would go to the king: Anything she wanted was given her to take with her from the harem to the king's palace. ¹⁴In the evening she would go there and in the morning return to another part of the harem to the care of Shaashgaz, the king's eunuch who was in charge of the concubines. She would not return to the king unless he was pleased with her and summoned her by name.

¹⁵When the turn came for Esther (the girl Mordecai had adopted, the daughter of his uncle Abihail) to go to the king, she asked for nothing other than what Hegai, the king's eunuch who was in charge of the harem, suggested. And Esther won the favor of everyone who saw her. ¹⁶She was taken to King Xerxes in the royal residence in the tenth month, the month of Tebeth, in the seventh year of his reign.

¹⁷Now the king was attracted to Esther more than to any of the other women, and she won

⁵書珊城有一個猶大人，名叫末底改，是便雅憫人基士的曾孫、示每的孫子、睚珥的兒子。⁶從前巴比倫王尼布甲尼撒將猶大王耶哥尼雅（註：又名「約雅斤」）和百姓從耶路撒冷擄去，末底改也在其內。⁷末底改撫養他叔叔的女兒哈大沙（後名以斯帖），因為她沒有父母。這女子又容貌俊美，她父母死了，末底改就收她為自己的女兒。

⁸王的諭旨傳出，就招聚許多女子到書珊城，交給掌管女子的希該；以斯帖也送入王宮，交付希該。⁹希該喜悅以斯帖，就恩待她，急忙給她需用的香品和她所當得的分，又派所當得的七個宮女服侍她，使她和她的宮女搬入女院上好的房屋。

¹⁰以斯帖未曾將籍貫宗族告訴人，因為末底改囑咐她不可叫人知道。¹¹末底改天天在女院前邊行走，要知道以斯帖平安不平安，並後事如何。

¹²眾女子照例先潔淨身體十二個月：六個月用沒藥油，六個月用香料和潔身之物。滿了日期，然後挨次進去見亞哈隨魯王。¹³女子進去見王是這樣：從女院到王宮的時候，凡她所要的都必給她。¹⁴晚上進去，次日回到女子第二院，交給掌管妃嬪的太監沙甲；除非王喜愛她，再提名召她，就不再進去見王。

¹⁵末底改叔叔亞比孩的女兒，就是末底改收為自己女兒的以斯帖，按次序當進去見王的時候，除了掌管女子的太監希該所派定給她的，她別無所求。凡看見以斯帖的都喜悅她。¹⁶亞哈隨魯王第七年十月，就是提別月，以斯帖被引入宮見王。

¹⁷王愛以斯帖過於愛眾女，她在王眼前蒙寵愛比眾處女更甚。王就

a 6 Hebrew *Jeconiah,* a variant of *Jehoiachin*

把王后的冠冕戴在她頭上，立她為王后，代替瓦實提。18王因以斯帖的緣故給翠首領和臣僕設擺大筵席，又豁免各省的租稅，並照王的厚意大頒賞賜。

末底改告發害王陰謀

19第二次招聚處女的時候，末底改坐在朝門。20以斯帖照着末底改所囑咐的，還沒有將籍貫宗族告訴人，因為以斯帖遵末底改的命，如撫養她的時候一樣。

21當那時候，末底改坐在朝門，王的太監中有兩個守門的辟探和提列，惱恨亞哈隨魯王，想要下手害他。22末底改知道了，就告訴王后以斯帖。以斯帖奉末底改的名，報告於王。23究察這事，果然是實，就把二人掛在木頭上，將這事在王面前寫於歷史上。

哈曼圖謀除滅猶大人

3 這事以後，亞哈隨魯王抬舉亞甲族哈米大他的兒子哈曼，使他高升，叫他的爵位超過與他同事的一切臣宰。2在朝門的一切臣僕，都跪拜哈曼，因為王如此吩咐；惟獨末底改不跪不拜。

3在朝門的臣僕問末底改說："你為何違背王的命令呢？"4他們天天勸他，他還是不聽。他們就告訴哈曼，要看末底改的事站得住站不住，因他已經告訴他們自己是猶大人。

5哈曼見末底改不跪不拜，他就怒氣填胸。6他們已將末底改的本族告訴哈曼。他以為下手害末底改一人是小事，就要滅絕亞哈隨魯王通國所有的猶大人，就是末底改的本族。

his favor and approval more than any of the other virgins. So he set a royal crown on her head and made her queen instead of Vashti. 18And the king gave a great banquet, Esther's banquet, for all his nobles and officials. He proclaimed a holiday throughout the provinces and distributed gifts with royal liberality.

Mordecai Uncovers a Conspiracy

19When the virgins were assembled a second time, Mordecai was sitting at the king's gate. 20But Esther had kept secret her family background and nationality just as Mordecai had told her to do, for she continued to follow Mordecai's instructions as she had done when he was bringing her up.

21During the time Mordecai was sitting at the king's gate, Bigthana[a] and Teresh, two of the king's officers who guarded the doorway, became angry and conspired to assassinate King Xerxes. 22But Mordecai found out about the plot and told Queen Esther, who in turn reported it to the king, giving credit to Mordecai. 23And when the report was investigated and found to be true, the two officials were hanged on a gallows.[b] All this was recorded in the book of the annals in the presence of the king.

Haman's Plot to Destroy the Jews

3 After these events, King Xerxes honored Haman son of Hammedatha, the Agagite, elevating him and giving him a seat of honor higher than that of all the other nobles. 2All the royal officials at the king's gate knelt down and paid honor to Haman, for the king had commanded this concerning him. But Mordecai would not kneel down or pay him honor.

3Then the royal officials at the king's gate asked Mordecai, "Why do you disobey the king's command?" 4Day after day they spoke to him but he refused to comply. Therefore they told Haman about it to see whether Mordecai's behavior would be tolerated, for he had told them he was a Jew.

5When Haman saw that Mordecai would not kneel down or pay him honor, he was enraged. 6Yet having learned who Mordecai's people were, he scorned the idea of killing only Mordecai. Instead Haman looked for a way to destroy all Mordecai's people, the Jews, throughout the whole kingdom of Xerxes.

---

a 21 Hebrew *Bigthan,* a variant of *Bigthana*　　*b 23* Or *were hung* (or *impaled*) *on poles*; similarly elsewhere in Esther

⁷In the twelfth year of King Xerxes, in the first month, the month of Nisan, they cast the *pur* (that is, the lot) in the presence of Haman to select a day and month. And the lot fell on^a the twelfth month, the month of Adar.

⁸Then Haman said to King Xerxes, "There is a certain people dispersed and scattered among the peoples in all the provinces of your kingdom whose customs are different from those of all other people and who do not obey the king's laws; it is not in the king's best interest to tolerate them. ⁹If it pleases the king, let a decree be issued to destroy them, and I will put ten thousand talents^b of silver into the royal treasury for the men who carry out this business."

¹⁰So the king took his signet ring from his finger and gave it to Haman son of Hammedatha, the Agagite, the enemy of the Jews. ¹¹"Keep the money," the king said to Haman, "and do with the people as you please."

¹²Then on the thirteenth day of the first month the royal secretaries were summoned. They wrote out in the script of each province and in the language of each people all Haman's orders to the king's satraps, the governors of the various provinces and the nobles of the various peoples. These were written in the name of King Xerxes himself and sealed with his own ring. ¹³Dispatches were sent by couriers to all the king's provinces with the order to destroy, kill and annihilate all the Jews—young and old, women and little children—on a single day, the thirteenth day of the twelfth month, the month of Adar, and to plunder their goods. ¹⁴A copy of the text of the edict was to be issued as law in every province and made known to the people of every nationality so they would be ready for that day.

¹⁵Spurred on by the king's command, the couriers went out, and the edict was issued in the citadel of Susa. The king and Haman sat down to drink, but the city of Susa was bewildered.

Mordecai Persuades Esther to Help

4 When Mordecai learned of all that had been done, he tore his clothes, put on sackcloth and ashes, and went out into the city, wailing loudly and bitterly. ²But he went only as far as the king's gate, because no one clothed in sackcloth was allowed to enter it. ³In every province to which the edict and order of the king came, there was great mourning

---

⁷亞哈隨魯王十二年正月，就是尼散月，人在哈曼面前，按日日月月擲普珥，就是擲籤，要定何月何日為吉，擇定了十二月，就是亞達月。

⁸哈曼對亞哈隨魯王說：「有一種民，散居在王國各省的民中，他們的律例與萬民的律例不同，也不守王的律例，所以容留他們與王無益。 ⁹王若以為美，請下旨意滅絕他們，我就捐一萬他連得銀子，交給掌管國帑的人，納入王的府庫。」

¹⁰於是王從自己手上摘下戒指，給猶大人的仇敵，亞甲族哈米大他的兒子哈曼。 ¹¹王對哈曼說：「這銀子仍賜給你，這民也交給你，你可以隨意待他們。」

¹²正月十三日，就召了王的書記來，照着哈曼一切所吩咐的，用各省的文字、各族的方言，奉亞哈隨魯王的名寫旨意，傳與總督和各省的省長，並各族的首領。又用王的戒指蓋印，¹³交給驛卒傳到王的各省，吩咐將猶大人，無論老少婦女孩子，在一日之間，十二月，就是亞達月，十三日，全然剪除，殺戮滅絕，並奪他們的財為掠物。 ¹⁴抄錄這旨意，頒行各省，宣告各族，使他們預備等候那日。

¹⁵驛卒奉王命急忙起行，旨意也傳遍書珊城。王同哈曼坐下飲酒，書珊城的民，卻都慌亂。

末底改說服以斯帖救本族

4 末底改知道所做的這一切事，就撕裂衣服，穿麻衣，蒙灰塵，在城中行走，痛哭哀號。 ²到了朝門前停住腳步，因為穿麻衣的不可進朝門。 ³王的諭旨所到的各省各處，猶大人大大悲哀，禁

---

^a 7 Septuagint; Hebrew does not have *And the lot fell on*.

^b 9 That is, about 375 tons (about 345 metric tons)

食哭泣哀號，穿麻衣躺在灰中的甚多。

4王后以斯帖的宮女和太監來把這事告訴以斯帖，她甚是憂愁，就送衣服給末底改穿，要他脫下麻衣，他卻不受。5以斯帖就把王所派伺候她的一個太監，名叫哈他革召來，吩咐他去見末底改，要知道這是甚麼事，是甚麼緣故。

6於是，哈他革出到朝門前的寬闊處見末底改。7末底改將自己所遇的事，並哈曼為滅絕猶大人，應許捐入王庫的銀數，都告訴了他。8又將所抄寫傳遍書珊城要滅絕猶大人的旨意交給哈他革，要給以斯帖看，又要給她說明，並囑咐她進去見王，為本族的人在王面前懇切祈求。

9哈他革回來，將末底改的話告訴以斯帖。10以斯帖就吩咐哈他革去見末底改說：11「王的一切臣僕和各省的人民，都知道有一個定例：若不蒙召，擅入內院見王的，無論男女必被治死；除非王向他伸出金杖，不得存活。現在我沒有蒙召進去見王已經三十日了。」

12人就把以斯帖這話告訴末底改。13末底改託人回覆以斯帖說：「你莫想在王宮裏強過一切猶大人，得免這禍。14此時你若閉口不言，猶大人必從別處得解脫，蒙拯救；你和你父家必至滅亡。焉知你得了王后的位分，不是為現今的機會嗎？」

15以斯帖就吩咐人回報末底改說：16「你當去招聚書珊城所有的猶大人，為我禁食三晝三夜，不吃不喝；我和我的宮女也要這樣禁食。然後我違例進去見王，我若死就死吧！」

17於是末底改照以斯帖一切所吩咐的去行。

among the Jews, with fasting, weeping and wailing. Many lay in sackcloth and ashes.

4When Esther's maids and eunuchs came and told her about Mordecai, she was in great distress. She sent clothes for him to put on instead of his sackcloth, but he would not accept them. 5Then Esther summoned Hathach, one of the king's eunuchs assigned to attend her, and ordered him to find out what was troubling Mordecai and why.

6So Hathach went out to Mordecai in the open square of the city in front of the king's gate. 7Mordecai told him everything that had happened to him, including the exact amount of money Haman had promised to pay into the royal treasury for the destruction of the Jews. 8He also gave him a copy of the text of the edict for their annihilation, which had been published in Susa, to show to Esther and explain it to her, and he told him to urge her to go into the king's presence to beg for mercy and plead with him for her people.

9Hathach went back and reported to Esther what Mordecai had said. 10Then she instructed him to say to Mordecai, 11"All the king's officials and the people of the royal provinces know that for any man or woman who approaches the king in the inner court without being summoned the king has but one law: that he be put to death. The only exception to this is for the king to extend the gold scepter to him and spare his life. But thirty days have passed since I was called to go to the king."

12When Esther's words were reported to Mordecai, 13he sent back this answer: "Do not think that because you are in the king's house you alone of all the Jews will escape. 14For if you remain silent at this time, relief and deliverance for the Jews will arise from another place, but you and your father's family will perish. And who knows but that you have come to royal position for such a time as this?"

15Then Esther sent this reply to Mordecai: 16"Go, gather together all the Jews who are in Susa, and fast for me. Do not eat or drink for three days, night or day. I and my maids will fast as you do. When this is done, I will go to the king, even though it is against the law. And if I perish, I perish."

17So Mordecai went away and carried out all of Esther's instructions.

Esther's Request to the King

5 On the third day Esther put on her royal robes and stood in the inner court of the palace, in front of the king's hall. The king was sitting on his royal throne in the hall, facing the entrance. [2]When he saw Queen Esther standing in the court, he was pleased with her and held out to her the gold scepter that was in his hand. So Esther approached and touched the tip of the scepter.

[3]Then the king asked, "What is it, Queen Esther? What is your request? Even up to half the kingdom, it will be given you."

[4]"If it pleases the king," replied Esther, "let the king, together with Haman, come today to a banquet I have prepared for him."

[5]"Bring Haman at once," the king said, "so that we may do what Esther asks."

So the king and Haman went to the banquet Esther had prepared. [6]As they were drinking wine, the king again asked Esther, "Now what is your petition? It will be given you. And what is your request? Even up to half the kingdom, it will be granted."

[7]Esther replied, "My petition and my request is this: [8]If the king regards me with favor and if it pleases the king to grant my petition and fulfill my request, let the king and Haman come tomorrow to the banquet I will prepare for them. Then I will answer the king's question."

Haman's Rage Against Mordecai

[9]Haman went out that day happy and in high spirits. But when he saw Mordecai at the king's gate and observed that he neither rose nor showed fear in his presence, he was filled with rage against Mordecai. [10]Nevertheless, Haman restrained himself and went home.

Calling together his friends and Zeresh, his wife, [11]Haman boasted to them about his vast wealth, his many sons, and all the ways the king had honored him and how he had elevated him above the other nobles and officials. [12]"And that's not all," Haman added. "I'm the only person Queen Esther invited to accompany the king to the banquet she gave. And she has invited me along with the king tomorrow. [13]But all this gives me no satisfaction as long as I see that Jew Mordecai sitting at the king's gate."

[14]His wife Zeresh and all his friends said to him, "Have a gallows built, seventy-five feet[a] high, and ask the king in the morning to have Mordecai hanged on it. Then go with the king to

---

以斯帖有求於王

5 第三日，以斯帖穿上朝服，進王宮的內院，對殿站立。王在殿裏坐在寶座上，對着殿門。²王見王后以斯帖站在院內，就施恩於她，向她伸出手中的金杖，以斯帖便向前摸杖頭。

³王對她說："王后以斯帖啊，你要甚麼？你求甚麼？就是國的一半也必賜給你。"

⁴以斯帖說："王若以為美，就請王帶着哈曼今日赴我所預備的筵席。"

⁵王說："叫哈曼速速照以斯帖的話去行。"

於是，王帶着哈曼赴以斯帖所預備的筵席。⁶在酒席筵前，王又問以斯帖說："你要甚麼？我必賜給你；你求甚麼？就是國的一半也必為你成就。"

⁷以斯帖回答說："我有所要，我有所求。⁸我若在王眼前蒙恩，王若願意賜我所要的，准我所求的，就請王帶着哈曼再赴我所要預備的筵席。明日我必照王所問的說明。"

哈曼惱怒末底改

⁹那日哈曼心中快樂，歡歡喜喜地出來，但見末底改在朝門不站起來，連身也不動，就滿心惱怒末底改。¹⁰哈曼暫且忍耐回家，叫人請他朋友和他妻子細利斯來。

¹¹哈曼將他富厚的榮耀、眾多的兒女，和王抬舉他使他超乎首領臣僕之上，都述說給他們聽。¹²哈曼又說："王后以斯帖預備筵席，除了我之外，不許別人隨王赴席。明日王后又請我隨王赴席；¹³只是我見猶大人末底改坐在朝門，雖有這一切榮耀，也與我無益。"

¹⁴他的妻細利斯和他一切的朋友對他說："不如立一個五丈高的木架，明早求王將末底改掛在其上，然

後你可以歡歡喜喜地隨王赴席。"
哈曼以這話為美，就叫人做了木架。

末底改得尊榮

6 那夜王睡不着覺，就吩咐人取歷史來，念給他聽。²正遇見書上寫着說：王的太監中有兩個守門的辟探和提列，想要下手害亞哈隨魯王，末底改將這事告訴王后。

³王說："末底改行了這事，賜他甚麼尊榮爵位沒有？"

伺候王的臣僕回答說："沒有賜他甚麼。"

⁴王說："誰在院子裏？"（那時哈曼正進王宮的外院，要求王將末底改掛在他所預備的木架上。）

⁵臣僕說："哈曼站在院內。"

王說："叫他進來。"

⁶哈曼就進去。王問他說："王所悅尊榮的人，當如何待他呢？"

哈曼心裏說："王所喜悅尊榮的，不是我是誰呢？"⁷哈曼就回答說："王所喜悅尊榮的人，⁸當將王常穿的朝服和戴冠的御馬，⁹都交給王極尊貴的一個大臣，命他將衣服給王所喜悅尊榮的人穿上，使他騎上馬，走遍城裏的街市，在他面前宣告說：'王所喜悅尊榮的人，就如此待他。'"

¹⁰王對哈曼說："你速速將這衣服和馬，照你所說的，向坐在朝門的猶大人末底改去行。凡你所說的，一樣不可缺。"

¹¹於是哈曼將朝服給末底改穿上，使他騎上馬走遍城裏的街市，在他面前宣告說："王所喜悅尊榮的人，就如此待他。"

¹²末底改仍回到朝門；哈曼卻憂憂悶悶地蒙着頭，急忙回家去了，¹³將所遇的一切事，詳細說給他的妻細利斯和他的眾朋友聽。

他的智慧人和他的妻細利斯對他說："你在末底改面前始而敗落，他如果是猶大人，你必不能

the dinner and be happy." This suggestion delighted Haman, and he had the gallows built.

Mordecai Honored

6 That night the king could not sleep; so he ordered the book of the chronicles, the record of his reign, to be brought in and read to him. ²It was found recorded there that Mordecai had exposed Bigthana and Teresh, two of the king's officers who guarded the doorway, who had conspired to assassinate King Xerxes.

³"What honor and recognition has Mordecai received for this?" the king asked.

"Nothing has been done for him," his attendants answered.

⁴The king said, "Who is in the court?" Now Haman had just entered the outer court of the palace to speak to the king about hanging Mordecai on the gallows he had erected for him.

⁵His attendants answered, "Haman is standing in the court."

"Bring him in," the king ordered.

⁶When Haman entered, the king asked him, "What should be done for the man the king delights to honor?"

Now Haman thought to himself, "Who is there that the king would rather honor than me?" ⁷So he answered the king, "For the man the king delights to honor, ⁸have them bring a royal robe the king has worn and a horse the king has ridden, one with a royal crest placed on its head. ⁹Then let the robe and horse be entrusted to one of the king's most noble princes. Let them robe the man the king delights to honor, and lead him on the horse through the city streets, proclaiming before him, 'This is what is done for the man the king delights to honor!' "

¹⁰"Go at once," the king commanded Haman. "Get the robe and the horse and do just as you have suggested for Mordecai the Jew, who sits at the king's gate. Do not neglect anything you have recommended."

¹¹So Haman got the robe and the horse. He robed Mordecai, and led him on horseback through the city streets, proclaiming before him, "This is what is done for the man the king delights to honor!"

¹²Afterward Mordecai returned to the king's gate. But Haman rushed home, with his head covered in grief, ¹³and told Zeresh his wife and all his friends everything that had happened to him.

His advisers and his wife Zeresh said to him, "Since Mordecai, before whom your downfall has started, is of Jewish origin, you cannot stand

against him—you will surely come to ruin!"
[14]While they were still talking with him, the
king's eunuchs arrived and hurried Haman
away to the banquet Esther had prepared.

Haman Hanged

7 So the king and Haman went to dine
with Queen Esther, [2]and as they were
drinking wine on that second day, the
king again asked, "Queen Esther, what is your
petition? It will be given you. What is your
request? Even up to half the kingdom, it will be
granted."

[3]Then Queen Esther answered, "If I have
found favor with you, O king, and if it pleases
your majesty, grant me my life—this is my petition. And spare my people—this is my request.
[4]For I and my people have been sold for destruction and slaughter and annihilation. If we
had merely been sold as male and female slaves,
I would have kept quiet, because no such distress would justify disturbing the king.[a]"

[5]King Xerxes asked Queen Esther, "Who is
he? Where is the man who has dared to do such
a thing?"

[6]Esther said, "The adversary and enemy is
this vile Haman."

Then Haman was terrified before the king and
queen. [7]The king got up in a rage, left his wine
and went out into the palace garden. But Haman,
realizing that the king had already decided his
fate, stayed behind to beg Queen Esther for his
life.

[8]Just as the king returned from the palace
garden to the banquet hall, Haman was falling
on the couch where Esther was reclining.

The king exclaimed, "Will he even molest the
queen while she is with me in the house?"

As soon as the word left the king's mouth,
they covered Haman's face. [9]Then Harbona, one
of the eunuchs attending the king, said, "A gallows seventy-five feet[b] high stands by Haman's
house. He had it made for Mordecai, who spoke
up to help the king."

The king said, "Hang him on it!" [10]So they
hanged Haman on the gallows he had prepared
for Mordecai. Then the king's fury subsided.

The King's Edict in Behalf of the Jews

8 That same day King Xerxes gave Queen
Esther the estate of Haman, the enemy
of the Jews. And Mordecai came into

勝他,終必在他面前敗落。" [14]他們
還與哈曼說話的時候,王的太監來催
哈曼快去赴以斯帖所預備的筵席。

哈曼被掛

7 王帶着哈曼來赴王后以斯帖
的筵席。[2]這第二次在酒席筵
前,王又問以斯帖說:"王
后以斯帖啊,你要甚麼?我必賜給
你;你求甚麼?就是國的一半,也必
為你成就。"

[3]王后以斯帖回答說:"我若在
王眼前蒙恩,王若以為美,我所願
的,是願王將我的性命賜給我;我所
求的,是求王將我的本族賜給我。
[4]因我和我的本族被賣了,要剪除殺
戮滅絕我們。我們若被賣為奴為婢,
我也閉口不言,但王的損失,敵人萬
不能補足。"

[5]亞哈隨魯王問王后以斯帖說:
"擅敢起意如此行的是誰?這人在哪
裏呢?"

[6]以斯帖說:"仇人敵人就是這
惡人哈曼!"

哈曼在王和王后面前就甚驚
惶。[7]王便大怒,起來離開酒席往御
園去了。哈曼見王定意要加罪與他,
就起來,求王后以斯帖救命。

[8]王從御園回到酒席之處,見哈
曼伏在以斯帖所靠的榻上。

王說:"他竟敢在宮內,在我面
前,凌辱王后嗎?"

這話一出王口,人就蒙了哈曼的
臉。[9]伺候王的一個太監名叫哈波
拿,說:"哈曼為那救王有功的末底
改做了五丈高的木架,現今立在哈曼
家裏!"

王說:"把哈曼掛在其上!" [10]於
是人將哈曼掛在他為末底改所預備的
木架上。王的忿怒這才止息。

王為猶大人寫諭旨

8 當日,亞哈隨魯王把猶大人
仇敵哈曼的家產賜給王后以
斯帖。末底改也來到王面

---

*a 4 Or quiet, but the compensation our adversary offers cannot be
compared with the loss the king would suffer   b 9 Hebrew fifty
cubits (about 23 meters)*

前，因為以斯帖已經告訴王末底改
是她的親屬。²王摘下自己的戒指，
就是從哈曼追回的，給了末底改。
以斯帖派末底改管理哈曼的家產。

³以斯帖又俯伏在王腳前，流淚
哀告，求他除掉亞甲族哈曼害猶大
人的惡謀。⁴王向以斯帖伸出金杖，
以斯帖就起來，站在王前，

⁵說：“亞甲族哈米大他的兒子
哈曼設謀傳旨，要殺滅在王各省的
猶大人。現今王若願意，我若在王
眼前蒙恩，王若以為美，若喜悅
我，請王另下旨意，廢除哈曼所傳
的那旨意。⁶我何忍見我本族的人受
害？何忍見我同宗的人被滅呢？”

⁷亞哈隨魯王對王后以斯帖和猶
大人末底改說：“因哈曼要下手害
猶大人，我已將他的家產賜給以斯
帖，人也將he曼掛在木架上。⁸現在
你們可以隨意奉王的名寫諭旨給猶
大人，用王的戒指蓋印，因為奉王
名所寫、用王戒指蓋印的諭旨，人
都不能廢除。”

⁹三月，就是西彎月，二十三
日，將王的書記召來，按著末底改
所吩咐的，用各省的文字、各族的
方言，並猶大人的文字方言寫諭
旨，傳給那從印度直到古實一百二
十七省的猶大人和總督省長首領。
¹⁰末底改奉亞哈隨魯王的名寫諭旨，
用王的戒指蓋印，交給騎御馬、圈
快馬的驛卒，傳到各處。

¹¹、¹²諭旨中，王准各省各城的
猶大人在一日之間，十二月，就是
亞達月，十三日，聚集保護性命，
剪除殺戮滅絕那要攻擊猶大人的一
切仇敵和他們的妻子兒女，奪取他
們的財為掠物。¹³抄錄這諭旨，頒行
各省，宣告各族，使猶大人預備等

the presence of the king, for Esther had told
how he was related to her. ²The king took off his
signet ring, which he had reclaimed from
Haman, and presented it to Mordecai. And
Esther appointed him over Haman's estate.

³Esther again pleaded with the king, falling at
his feet and weeping. She begged him to put an
end to the evil plan of Haman the Agagite,
which he had devised against the Jews. ⁴Then
the king extended the gold scepter to Esther and
she arose and stood before him.

⁵"If it pleases the king," she said, "and if he
regards me with favor and thinks it the right
thing to do, and if he is pleased with me, let an
order be written overruling the dispatches that
Haman son of Hammedatha, the Agagite,
devised and wrote to destroy the Jews in all the
king's provinces. ⁶For how can I bear to see disaster fall on my people? How can I bear to see
the destruction of my family?"

⁷King Xerxes replied to Queen Esther and to
Mordecai the Jew, "Because Haman attacked the
Jews, I have given his estate to Esther, and they
have hanged him on the gallows. ⁸Now write
another decree in the king's name in behalf of
the Jews as seems best to you, and seal it with
the king's signet ring—for no document written
in the king's name and sealed with his ring can
be revoked."

⁹At once the royal secretaries were summoned—on the twenty-third day of the third
month, the month of Sivan. They wrote out all
Mordecai's orders to the Jews, and to the satraps,
governors and nobles of the 127 provinces
stretching from India to Cush.ᵃ These orders
were written in the script of each province and
the language of each people and also to the Jews
in their own script and language. ¹⁰Mordecai
wrote in the name of King Xerxes, sealed the
dispatches with the king's signet ring, and sent
them by mounted couriers, who rode fast horses
especially bred for the king.

¹¹The king's edict granted the Jews in every
city the right to assemble and protect themselves; to destroy, kill and annihilate any armed
force of any nationality or province that might
attack them and their women and children; and
to plunder the property of their enemies. ¹²The
day appointed for the Jews to do this in all the
provinces of King Xerxes was the thirteenth day
of the twelfth month, the month of Adar. ¹³A
copy of the text of the edict was to be issued as
law in every province and made known to the

a 9 That is, the upper Nile region

people of every nationality so that the Jews would be ready on that day to avenge themselves on their enemies.

¹⁴The couriers, riding the royal horses, raced out, spurred on by the king's command. And the edict was also issued in the citadel of Susa.

¹⁵Mordecai left the king's presence wearing royal garments of blue and white, a large crown of gold and a purple robe of fine linen. And the city of Susa held a joyous celebration. ¹⁶For the Jews it was a time of happiness and joy, gladness and honor. ¹⁷In every province and in every city, wherever the edict of the king went, there was joy and gladness among the Jews, with feasting and celebrating. And many people of other nationalities became Jews because fear of the Jews had seized them.

Triumph of the Jews

9 On the thirteenth day of the twelfth month, the month of Adar, the edict commanded by the king was to be carried out. On this day the enemies of the Jews had hoped to overpower them, but now the tables were turned and the Jews got the upper hand over those who hated them. ²The Jews assembled in their cities in all the provinces of King Xerxes to attack those seeking their destruction. No one could stand against them, because the people of all the other nationalities were afraid of them. ³And all the nobles of the provinces, the satraps, the governors and the king's administrators helped the Jews, because fear of Mordecai had seized them. ⁴Mordecai was prominent in the palace; his reputation spread throughout the provinces, and he became more and more powerful.

⁵The Jews struck down all their enemies with the sword, killing and destroying them, and they did what they pleased to those who hated them. ⁶In the citadel of Susa, the Jews killed and destroyed five hundred men. ⁷They also killed Parshandatha, Dalphon, Aspatha, ⁸Poratha, Adalia, Aridatha, ⁹Parmashta, Arisai, Aridai and Vaizatha, ¹⁰the ten sons of Haman son of Hammedatha, the enemy of the Jews. But they did not lay their hands on the plunder.

¹¹The number of those slain in the citadel of Susa was reported to the king that same day. ¹²The king said to Queen Esther, "The Jews have killed and destroyed five hundred men and the ten sons of Haman in the citadel of Susa. What have they done in the rest of the king's provinces? Now what is your petition? It will be given you. What is your request? It will also be granted."

候那日，在仇敵身上報仇。

¹⁴於是，騎快馬的驛卒被王命催促，急忙起行。諭旨也傳遍書珊城。

¹⁵末底改穿着藍色、白色的朝服，頭戴大金冠冕，又穿紫色細麻布的外袍，從王面前出來。書珊城的人民都歡呼快樂。¹⁶猶大人有光榮，歡喜快樂而得尊貴。¹⁷王的諭旨所到的各省各城，猶大人都歡喜快樂，設擺筵宴，以那日為吉日。那國的人民，有許多因懼怕猶大人，就入了猶大籍。

猶大人得勝

9 十二月，乃亞達月，十三日，王的諭旨將要舉行，就是猶大人的仇敵盼望轄制他們的日子，猶大人反倒轄制恨他們的人。²猶大人在亞哈隨魯王各省的城裏聚集，下手擊殺那要害他們的人。無人能敵擋他們，因為各族都懼怕他們。³各省的首領、總督、省長和辦理王事的人，因懼怕末底改，就都幫助猶大人。⁴末底改在朝中為大，名聲傳遍各省，日漸昌盛。

⁵猶大人用刀擊殺一切仇敵，任意殺滅恨他們的人。⁶在書珊城，猶大人殺滅了五百人。⁷又殺巴珊大他、達分、亞斯帕他、⁸破拉他、亞大利雅、亞利大他、⁹帕瑪斯他、亞利賽、亞利代、瓦耶撒他；¹⁰這十人都是哈米大他的孫子、猶大人仇敵哈曼的兒子。猶大人卻沒有下手奪取財物。

¹¹當日，將書珊城被殺的人數呈在王前。¹²王對王后以斯帖說："猶大人在書珊城殺滅了五百人，又殺了哈曼的十個兒子，在王的各省不知如何呢？現在你要甚麼？我必賜給你；你還求甚麼？也必為你成就。"

13以斯帖说：“王若以為美，求你准書珊的猶大人，明日也照今日的旨意行，並將哈曼十個兒子的屍首掛在木架上。”

14王便允准如此行。旨意傳在書珊，人就把哈曼十個兒子的屍首掛起來了。15亞達月十四日，書珊的猶大人又聚集在書珊，殺了三百人，卻沒有下手奪取財物。

16在王各省其餘的猶大人，也都聚集保護性命，殺了恨他們的人七萬五千，卻沒有下手奪取財物。這樣，就脫離仇敵，得享平安。17亞達月十三日，行了這事；十四日安息，以這日為設筵歡樂的日子。

慶祝普珥日

18但書珊的猶大人，這十三、十四日聚集殺戮仇敵；十五日安息，以這日為設筵歡樂的日子。

19所以住無城牆鄉村的猶大人，如今都以亞達月十四日為設筵歡樂的吉日，彼此餽送禮物。

20末底改記錄這事，寫信與亞哈隨魯王各省遠近所有的猶大人，21囑咐他們每年守亞達月十四十五兩日，22以這月的兩日為猶大人脫離仇敵得平安、轉憂為喜、轉悲為樂的吉日。在這兩日設筵歡樂，彼此餽送禮物，賙濟窮人。

23於是，猶大人按着末底改所寫與他們的信，應承照初次所守的守為永例。24是因猶大人的仇敵亞甲族哈米大他的兒子哈曼，設謀殺害猶大人，掣普珥，就是掣籤，為要殺盡滅絕他們。25這事報告於王，王便降旨使哈曼謀害猶大人的惡事，歸到他自己的頭上，並吩咐把他和他的眾子都掛在木架上。26照着普珥的名字，猶大人就稱這兩日為普珥日。他們因這信上的話，又因所

13"If it pleases the king," Esther answered, "give the Jews in Susa permission to carry out this day's edict tomorrow also, and let Haman's ten sons be hanged on gallows."

14So the king commanded that this be done. An edict was issued in Susa, and they hanged the ten sons of Haman. 15The Jews in Susa came together on the fourteenth day of the month of Adar, and they put to death in Susa three hundred men, but they did not lay their hands on the plunder.

16Meanwhile, the remainder of the Jews who were in the king's provinces also assembled to protect themselves and get relief from their enemies. They killed seventy-five thousand of them but did not lay their hands on the plunder. 17This happened on the thirteenth day of the month of Adar, and on the fourteenth they rested and made it a day of feasting and joy.

Purim Celebrated

18The Jews in Susa, however, had assembled on the thirteenth and fourteenth, and then on the fifteenth they rested and made it a day of feasting and joy.

19That is why rural Jews—those living in villages—observe the fourteenth of the month of Adar as a day of joy and feasting, a day for giving presents to each other.

20Mordecai recorded these events, and he sent letters to all the Jews throughout the provinces of King Xerxes, near and far, 21to have them celebrate annually the fourteenth and fifteenth days of the month of Adar 22as the time when the Jews got relief from their enemies, and as the month when their sorrow was turned into joy and their mourning into a day of celebration. He wrote them to observe the days as days of feasting and joy and giving presents of food to one another and gifts to the poor.

23So the Jews agreed to continue the celebration they had begun, doing what Mordecai had written to them. 24For Haman son of Hammedatha, the Agagite, the enemy of all the Jews, had plotted against the Jews to destroy them and had cast the pur (that is, the lot) for their ruin and destruction. 25But when the plot came to the king's attention,[a] he issued written orders that the evil scheme Haman had devised against the Jews should come back onto his own head, and that he and his sons should be hanged on the gallows. 26(Therefore these days were called Purim, from the word pur.) Because of everything written in this letter and because of what

a 25 Or when Esther came before the king

they had seen and what had happened to them, ²⁷the Jews took it upon themselves to establish the custom that they and their descendants and all who join them should without fail observe these two days every year, in the way prescribed and at the time appointed. ²⁸These days should be remembered and observed in every generation by every family, and in every province and in every city. And these days of Purim should never cease to be celebrated by the Jews, nor should the memory of them die out among their descendants.

²⁹So Queen Esther, daughter of Abihail, along with Mordecai the Jew, wrote with full authority to confirm this second letter concerning Purim. ³⁰And Mordecai sent letters to all the Jews in the 127 provinces of the kingdom of Xerxes—words of goodwill and assurance— ³¹to establish these days of Purim at their designated times, as Mordecai the Jew and Queen Esther had decreed for them, and as they had established for themselves and their descendants in regard to their times of fasting and lamentation. ³²Esther's decree confirmed these regulations about Purim, and it was written down in the records.

The Greatness of Mordecai

10 King Xerxes imposed tribute throughout the empire, to its distant shores. ²And all his acts of power and might, together with a full account of the greatness of Mordecai to which the king had raised him, are they not written in the book of the annals of the kings of Media and Persia? ³Mordecai the Jew was second in rank to King Xerxes, preeminent among the Jews, and held in high esteem by his many fellow Jews, because he worked for the good of his people and spoke up for the welfare of all the Jews.

看見、所遇見的事，²⁷就應承自己與後裔，並歸附他們的人，每年按時必守這兩日，永遠不廢。²⁸各省各城、家家戶戶、世世代代記念遵守這兩日，使這普珥日在猶大人中不可廢掉，在他們後裔中也不可忘記。

²⁹亞比孩的女兒王后以斯帖和猶大人末底改，以全權寫第二封信，堅囑猶大人守這普珥日。³⁰用和平誠實話寫信給亞哈隨魯王國中一百二十七省所有的猶大人，³¹勸他們按時守這普珥日，禁食呼求，是照猶大人末底改和王后以斯帖所囑咐的，也照猶大人為自己與後裔所應承的。³²以斯帖命定守普珥日，這事也記錄在書上。

末底改蒙高舉為大

10 亞哈隨魯王使旱地和海島的人民都進貢。²他以權柄能力所行的，並他抬舉末底改使他高升的事，豈不都寫在瑪代和波斯王的歷史上嗎？³猶大人末底改作亞哈隨魯王的宰相，在猶大人中為大，得他眾弟兄的喜悅，為本族的人求好處，向他們説和平的話。

約伯記　Job

序幕

1 烏斯地有一個人，名叫約伯；那人完全正直，敬畏神，遠離惡事。²他生了七個兒子，三個女兒。³他的家產有七千羊，三千駱駝，五百對牛，五百母驢，並有許多僕婢。這人在東方人中就為至大。

⁴他的兒子按着日子，各在自己家裏設擺筵宴，就打發人去請了他們的三個姐妹來，與他們一同吃喝。⁵筵宴的日子過了，約伯打發人去叫他們自潔。他清早起來，按着他們眾人的數目獻燔祭。因為他說："恐怕我兒子犯了罪，心中棄掉神。"約伯常常這樣行。

約伯初受試煉

⁶有一天，神的眾子來侍立在耶和華面前，撒但也來在其中。⁷耶和華問撒但說："你從哪裏來？"

撒但回答說："我從地上走來走去，往返而來。"

⁸耶和華問撒但說："你曾用心察看我的僕人約伯沒有？地上再沒有人像他完全正直，敬畏神，遠離惡事。"

⁹撒但回答耶和華說："約伯敬畏神豈是無故呢？¹⁰你豈不是四面圈上籬笆圍護他和他的家，並他一切所有的嗎？他手所做的都蒙你賜福；他的家產也在地上增多。¹¹你且伸手毀他一切所有的，他必當面棄掉你。"

¹²耶和華對撒但說："凡他所有的都在你手中，只是不可伸手加害於他。"

於是撒但從耶和華面前退去。

¹³有一天，約伯的兒女正在他們

Prologue

1 In the land of Uz there lived a man whose name was Job. This man was blameless and upright; he feared God and shunned evil. ²He had seven sons and three daughters, ³and he owned seven thousand sheep, three thousand camels, five hundred yoke of oxen and five hundred donkeys, and had a large number of servants. He was the greatest man among all the people of the East.

⁴His sons used to take turns holding feasts in their homes, and they would invite their three sisters to eat and drink with them. ⁵When a period of feasting had run its course, Job would send and have them purified. Early in the morning he would sacrifice a burnt offering for each of them, thinking, "Perhaps my children have sinned and cursed God in their hearts." This was Job's regular custom.

Job's First Test

⁶One day the angels*a* came to present themselves before the LORD, and Satan*b* also came with them. ⁷The LORD said to Satan, "Where have you come from?"

Satan answered the LORD, "From roaming through the earth and going back and forth in it."

⁸Then the LORD said to Satan, "Have you considered my servant Job? There is no one on earth like him; he is blameless and upright, a man who fears God and shuns evil."

⁹"Does Job fear God for nothing?" Satan replied. ¹⁰"Have you not put a hedge around him and his household and everything he has? You have blessed the work of his hands, so that his flocks and herds are spread throughout the land. ¹¹But stretch out your hand and strike everything he has, and he will surely curse you to your face."

¹²The LORD said to Satan, "Very well, then, everything he has is in your hands, but on the man himself do not lay a finger."

Then Satan went out from the presence of the LORD.

¹³One day when Job's sons and daughters

a 6 Hebrew the sons of God   b 6 Satan means accuser.

were feasting and drinking wine at the oldest brother's house, [14]a messenger came to Job and said, "The oxen were plowing and the donkeys were grazing nearby, [15]and the Sabeans attacked and carried them off. They put the servants to the sword, and I am the only one who has escaped to tell you!"

[16]While he was still speaking, another messenger came and said, "The fire of God fell from the sky and burned up the sheep and the servants, and I am the only one who has escaped to tell you!"

[17]While he was still speaking, another messenger came and said, "The Chaldeans formed three raiding parties and swept down on your camels and carried them off. They put the servants to the sword, and I am the only one who has escaped to tell you!"

[18]While he was still speaking, yet another messenger came and said, "Your sons and daughters were feasting and drinking wine at the oldest brother's house, [19]when suddenly a mighty wind swept in from the desert and struck the four corners of the house. It collapsed on them and they are dead, and I am the only one who has escaped to tell you!"

[20]At this, Job got up and tore his robe and shaved his head. Then he fell to the ground in worship [21]and said:

"Naked I came from my mother's womb,
  and naked I will depart.[a]
The LORD gave and the LORD has taken away;
  may the name of the LORD be praised."

[22]In all this, Job did not sin by charging God with wrongdoing.

Job's Second Test

2 On another day the angels[b] came to present themselves before the LORD, and Satan also came with them to present himself before him. [2]And the LORD said to Satan, "Where have you come from?"

Satan answered the LORD, "From roaming through the earth and going back and forth in it."

[3]Then the LORD said to Satan, "Have you considered my servant Job? There is no one on earth like him; he is blameless and upright, a man who fears God and shuns evil. And he still maintains his integrity, though you incited me against him to ruin him without any reason."

[4]"Skin for skin!" Satan replied. "A man will

長兄的家裏吃飯喝酒，[14]有報信的來見約伯說："牛正耕地，驢在旁邊吃草，[15]示巴人忽然闖來，把牲畜擄去，並用刀殺了僕人；惟有我一人逃脫，來報信給你。"

[16]他還說話的時候，又有人來說："神從天上降下火來，將羣羊和僕人都燒滅了；惟有我一人逃脫，來報信給你。"

[17]他還說話的時候，又有人來說："迦勒底人分作三隊，忽然闖來，把駱駝擄去，並用刀殺了僕人；惟有我一人逃脫，來報信給你。"

[18]他還說話的時候，又有人來說："你的兒女正在他們長兄的家裏吃飯喝酒，[19]不料有狂風從曠野颳來，擊打房屋的四角，房屋倒塌在少年人身上，他們就都死了；惟有我一人逃脫，來報信給你。"

[20]約伯便起來，撕裂外袍，剃了頭，伏在地上下拜，[21]說：

"我赤身出於母胎，
  也必赤身歸回。
賞賜的是耶和華，收取的也是耶和華；
  耶和華的名是應當稱頌的。"

[22]在這一切的事上，約伯並不犯罪，也不以神為愚妄（註：或作"也不妄評神"）。

約伯再受試煉

2 又有一天，神的眾子來侍立在耶和華面前，撒但也來在其中。[2]耶和華問撒但說："你從哪裏來？"

撒但回答說："我從地上走來走去，往返而來。"

[3]耶和華問撒但說："你曾用心察看我的僕人約伯沒有？地上再沒有人像他完全正直，敬畏神，遠離惡事。你雖激動我攻擊他，無故地毀滅他，他仍然持守他的純正。"

[4]撒但回答耶和華說："人以

皮代皮，情願捨去一切所有的保全性命。⁵你且伸手傷他的骨頭和他的肉，他必當面棄掉你。

⁶耶和華對撒但說：「他在你手中，只要存留他的性命。」

⁷於是撒但從耶和華面前退去，擊打<u>約伯</u>，使他從腳掌到頭頂長毒瘡。⁸<u>約伯</u>就坐在爐灰中，拿瓦片刮身體。

⁹他的妻子對他說：「你仍然持守你的純正嗎？你棄掉神，死了吧！」

¹⁰<u>約伯</u>卻對她說：「你說話像愚頑的婦人一樣。嗳！難道我們從神手裏得福，不也受禍嗎？」

在這一切的事上，<u>約伯</u>並不以口犯罪。

約伯的三友

¹¹<u>約伯</u>的三個朋友，<u>提幔</u>人<u>以利法</u>、<u>書亞</u>人<u>比勒達</u>、<u>拿瑪</u>人<u>瑣法</u>，聽說有這一切的災禍臨到他身上，各人就從本處約會同來，為他悲傷，安慰他。¹²他們遠遠地舉目觀看，認不出他來，就放聲大哭。各人撕裂外袍，把塵土向天揚起來，落在自己的頭上。¹³他們就同他七天七夜坐在地上，一個人也不向他說句話，因為他極其痛苦。

約伯發言

3 此後，<u>約伯</u>開口咒詛自己的生日，²說：

³「願我生的那日
　和說懷了男胎的那夜都滅沒。
⁴願那日變為黑暗，
　願神不從上面尋找它，
　願亮光不照於其上。
⁵願黑暗和死蔭
　　索取那日，
　願密雲停在其上，
　願日蝕恐嚇它。
⁶願那夜被幽暗奪取，
　不在年中的日子同樂，
　也不入月中的數目。

⁷願那夜沒有生育，
　其間也沒有歡樂的聲音。
⁸願那咒詛日子且能惹動鱷魚的，
　咒詛那夜。

give all he has for his own life. ⁵But stretch out your hand and strike his flesh and bones, and he will surely curse you to your face."

⁶The LORD said to Satan, "Very well, then, he is in your hands; but you must spare his life."

⁷So Satan went out from the presence of the LORD and afflicted Job with painful sores from the soles of his feet to the top of his head. ⁸Then Job took a piece of broken pottery and scraped himself with it as he sat among the ashes.

⁹His wife said to him, "Are you still holding on to your integrity? Curse God and die!"

¹⁰He replied, "You are talking like a foolish*a* woman. Shall we accept good from God, and not trouble?"

In all this, Job did not sin in what he said.

Job's Three Friends

¹¹When Job's three friends, Eliphaz the Temanite, Bildad the Shuhite and Zophar the Naamathite, heard about all the troubles that had come upon him, they set out from their homes and met together by agreement to go and sympathize with him and comfort him. ¹²When they saw him from a distance, they could hardly recognize him; they began to weep aloud, and they tore their robes and sprinkled dust on their heads. ¹³Then they sat on the ground with him for seven days and seven nights. No one said a word to him, because they saw how great his suffering was.

Job Speaks

3 After this, Job opened his mouth and cursed the day of his birth. ²He said:

³"May the day of my birth perish,
　and the night it was said, 'A boy is born!'
⁴That day—may it turn to darkness;
　may God above not care about it;
　may no light shine upon it.
⁵May darkness and deep shadow*b* claim it once
　　more;
　may a cloud settle over it;
　may blackness overwhelm its light.
⁶That night—may thick darkness seize it;
　may it not be included among the days of the
　　year
　nor be entered in any of the months.
⁷May that night be barren;
　may no shout of joy be heard in it.
⁸May those who curse days*c* curse that day,
　those who are ready to rouse Leviathan.

---

a 10 The Hebrew word rendered *foolish* denotes moral deficiency.　*b 5* Or *and the shadow of death*　*c 8* Or *the sea*

⁹May its morning stars become dark;
  may it wait for daylight in vain
  and not see the first rays of dawn,
¹⁰for it did not shut the doors of the womb on me
  to hide trouble from my eyes.

¹¹"Why did I not perish at birth,
  and die as I came from the womb?
¹²Why were there knees to receive me
  and breasts that I might be nursed?
¹³For now I would be lying down in peace;
  I would be asleep and at rest
¹⁴with kings and counselors of the earth,
  who built for themselves places now lying in
    ruins,
¹⁵with rulers who had gold,
  who filled their houses with silver.
¹⁶Or why was I not hidden in the ground like a
    stillborn child,
  like an infant who never saw the light of day?
¹⁷There the wicked cease from turmoil,
  and there the weary are at rest.
¹⁸Captives also enjoy their ease;
  they no longer hear the slave driver's shout.
¹⁹The small and the great are there,
  and the slave is freed from his master.

²⁰"Why is light given to those in misery,
  and life to the bitter of soul,
²¹to those who long for death that does not
    come,
  who search for it more than for hidden
    treasure,
²²who are filled with gladness
  and rejoice when they reach the grave?
²³Why is life given to a man
  whose way is hidden,
  whom God has hedged in?
²⁴For sighing comes to me instead of food;
  my groans pour out like water.
²⁵What I feared has come upon me;
  what I dreaded has happened to me.
²⁶I have no peace, no quietness;
  I have no rest, but only turmoil."

Eliphaz

4 Then Eliphaz the Temanite replied:

  ²"If someone ventures a word with
you, will you be impatient?
  But who can keep from speaking?
³Think how you have instructed many,
  how you have strengthened feeble hands.
⁴Your words have supported those who
    stumbled;
  you have strengthened faltering knees.

⁹願那夜黎明的星宿變為黑暗，
  盼亮卻不亮，也不見早晨的光線
  （註："光線"原文作"眼皮"）。
¹⁰因沒有把懷我胎的門關閉，
  也沒有將患難對我的眼隱藏。

¹¹ "我為何不出母胎而死？
  為何不出母腹絕氣？
¹²為何有膝接收我？
  為何有奶哺養我？
¹³不然，
  我就早已躺臥安睡，
¹⁴和地上
  為自己重造荒邱的
    君王、謀士，
¹⁵或與有金子、將銀子裝滿了房屋的
  王子一同安息。
¹⁶或像隱而未現、不到期而落的胎，
  歸於無有，
  如同未見光的嬰孩。
¹⁷在那裏惡人止息攪擾，
  困乏人得享安息，
¹⁸被囚的人同得安逸，
  不聽見督工的聲音。
¹⁹大小都在那裏，
  奴僕脫離主人的轄制。

²⁰ "受患難的人為何有光賜給他呢？
  心中愁苦的人為何有生命賜給他呢？
²¹他們切望死，
  卻不得死；
  求死，
  勝於求隱藏的珍寶。
²²他們尋見墳墓就快樂，
  極其歡喜。
²³人的道路既然遮隱，
  神又把他四面圍困，
  為何有光賜給他呢？
²⁴我未曾吃飯，就發出歎息；
  我唉哼的聲音湧出如水。
²⁵因我所恐懼的臨到我身；
  我所懼怕的迎我而來。
²⁶我不得安逸，不得平靜，
  也不得安息，卻有患難來到。"

以利法回答

4 提幔人以利法回答說：

  ² "人若想與你說話，
  你就厭煩嗎？
  但誰能忍住不說呢？
³你素來教導許多的人，
  又堅固軟弱的手。
⁴你的言語
  曾扶助那將要跌倒的人，
  你又使軟弱的膝穩固。

⁵但現在禍患臨到你，
　　　你就昏迷；
　　挨近你，你便驚惶。
⁶你的倚靠，不是在你敬畏神嗎？
　　你的盼望，不是在你行事純正嗎？

⁷ “請你追想：
　　無辜的人有誰滅亡？
　　正直的人在何處剪除？
⁸按我所見，耕罪孽、種毒害的人
　　都照樣收割。
⁹神一出氣，他們就滅亡；
　　神一發怒，他們就消沒。
¹⁰獅子的吼叫和猛獅的聲音盡都止息，
　　少壯獅子的牙齒也都敲掉，
¹¹老獅子因絕食而死，
　　母獅之子也都離散。

¹² “我暗暗地得了默示，
　　我耳朵也聽其細微的聲音。
¹³在思念夜中異象之間，
　　世人沉睡的時候，
¹⁴恐懼、戰兢臨到我身，
　　使我百骨打戰。
¹⁵有靈從我面前經過，
　　我身上的毫毛直立。
¹⁶那靈停住，
　　我卻不能辨其形狀。
　　有影像在我眼前，
　　我在靜默中聽見有聲音說：
¹⁷ ‘必死的人豈能比神公義嗎？
　　人豈能比造他的主潔淨嗎？
¹⁸主不信靠他的臣僕，
　　並且指他的使者為愚昧；
¹⁹何況那住在土房、
　　根基在塵土裏、
　　　被蠹蟲所毀壞的人呢？
²⁰早晚之間
　　就被毀滅，
　　永歸無有，無人理會。
²¹他帳棚的繩索豈不從中抽出來呢？
　　他死，且是無智慧而死。’

5 “你且呼求，
　　有誰答應你？
　　諸聖者之中，
　　你轉向哪一位呢？
²忿怒害死愚妄人；
　　嫉妒殺死癡迷人。
³我曾見愚妄人扎下根，
　　但我忽然咒詛他的住處。
⁴他的兒女遠離穩妥的地步，
　　在城門口被壓，並無人搭救。

⁵But now trouble comes to you, and you are
　　discouraged;
　it strikes you, and you are dismayed.
⁶Should not your piety be your confidence
　and your blameless ways your hope?

⁷“Consider now: Who, being innocent, has ever
　　perished?
　Where were the upright ever destroyed?
⁸As I have observed, those who plow evil
　and those who sow trouble reap it.
⁹At the breath of God they are destroyed;
　at the blast of his anger they perish.
¹⁰The lions may roar and growl,
　yet the teeth of the great lions are broken.
¹¹The lion perishes for lack of prey,
　and the cubs of the lioness are scattered.

¹²“A word was secretly brought to me,
　my ears caught a whisper of it.
¹³Amid disquieting dreams in the night,
　when deep sleep falls on men,
¹⁴fear and trembling seized me
　and made all my bones shake.
¹⁵A spirit glided past my face,
　and the hair on my body stood on end.
¹⁶It stopped,
　but I could not tell what it was.
　A form stood before my eyes,
　and I heard a hushed voice:
¹⁷‘Can a mortal be more righteous than God?
　Can a man be more pure than his Maker?
¹⁸If God places no trust in his servants,
　if he charges his angels with error,
¹⁹how much more those who live in houses of
　　clay,
　whose foundations are in the dust,
　who are crushed more readily than a moth!
²⁰Between dawn and dusk they are broken to
　　pieces;
　unnoticed, they perish forever.
²¹Are not the cords of their tent pulled up,
　so that they die without wisdom?’[a]

5 “Call if you will, but who will answer
　　you?
　　To which of the holy ones will you
　　turn?
²Resentment kills a fool,
　and envy slays the simple.
³I myself have seen a fool taking root,
　but suddenly his house was cursed.
⁴His children are far from safety,
　crushed in court without a defender.

a 21 Some interpreters end the quotation after verse 17.

⁵The hungry consume his harvest,
   taking it even from among thorns,
   and the thirsty pant after his wealth.
⁶For hardship does not spring from the soil,
   nor does trouble sprout from the ground.
⁷Yet man is born to trouble
   as surely as sparks fly upward.

⁸"But if it were I, I would appeal to God;
   I would lay my cause before him.
⁹He performs wonders that cannot be fathomed,
   miracles that cannot be counted.
¹⁰He bestows rain on the earth;
   he sends water upon the countryside.
¹¹The lowly he sets on high,
   and those who mourn are lifted to safety.
¹²He thwarts the plans of the crafty,
   so that their hands achieve no success.
¹³He catches the wise in their craftiness,
   and the schemes of the wily are swept away.
¹⁴Darkness comes upon them in the daytime;
   at noon they grope as in the night.
¹⁵He saves the needy from the sword in their
     mouth;
   he saves them from the clutches of the
     powerful.
¹⁶So the poor have hope,
   and injustice shuts its mouth.

¹⁷"Blessed is the man whom God corrects;
   so do not despise the discipline of the
     Almighty.[a]
¹⁸For he wounds, but he also binds up;
   he injures, but his hands also heal.
¹⁹From six calamities he will rescue you;
   in seven no harm will befall you.
²⁰In famine he will ransom you from death,
   and in battle from the stroke of the sword.
²¹You will be protected from the lash of the
     tongue,
   and need not fear when destruction comes.
²²You will laugh at destruction and famine,
   and need not fear the beasts of the earth.
²³For you will have a covenant with the stones
     of the field,
   and the wild animals will be at peace with
     you.
²⁴You will know that your tent is secure;
   you will take stock of your property and find
     nothing missing.
²⁵You will know that your children will be
     many,
   and your descendants like the grass of the
     earth.

⁵他的莊稼有飢餓的人吃盡了，
   就是在荊棘裏的也搶去了；
   他的財寶，有網羅張口吞滅了。
⁶禍患原不是從土中出來；
   患難也不是從地裏發生。
⁷人生在世必遇患難，
   如同火星飛騰。

⁸"至於我，我必仰望神，
   把我的事情託付他。
⁹他行大事不可測度，
   行奇事不可勝數。
¹⁰降雨在地上，
   賜水於田裏。
¹¹將卑微的安置在高處，
   將哀痛的舉到穩妥之地。
¹²破壞狡猾人的計謀，
   使他們所謀的不得成就。
¹³他叫有智慧的中了自己的詭計，
   使狡詐人的計謀速速滅亡。
¹⁴他們白晝遇見黑暗，
   午間摸索如在夜間。
¹⁵神拯救窮乏人，
   脫離他們口中的刀
     和強暴人的手。
¹⁶這樣，貧寒的人有指望，
   罪孽之輩必塞口無言。

¹⁷"神所懲治的人是有福的，
   所以你不可輕看
     全能者的管教。
¹⁸因為他打破，又纏裹；
   他擊傷，用手醫治。
¹⁹你六次遭難，他必救你；
   就是七次，災禍也無法害你。
²⁰在饑荒中，他必救你脫離死亡；
   在爭戰中，他必救你脫離刀劍的權力。
²¹你必被隱藏，
   不受口舌之害；
   災殃臨到，你也不懼怕。
²²你遇見災害饑饉，就必嬉笑；
   地上的野獸，你也不懼怕。
²³因為你必與
   田間的石頭立約；
   田裏的野獸
   也必與你和好。
²⁴你必知道你帳棚平安，
   要查看你的羊圈，
   一無所失。
²⁵也必知道你的後裔
     將來發達，
   你的子孫
   像地上的青草。

---

a 17 Hebrew *Shaddai*; here and throughout Job

²⁶你必壽高年邁才歸墳墓，
　　好像禾捆到時收藏。

²⁷ "這理我們已經考察，本是如此。
　　你須要聽，要知道是與自己有益。"

約伯回答

6

約伯回答說：

² "惟願我的煩惱稱一稱，
　　我一切的災害放在天平裏，
³現今都比海沙更重，
　　所以我的言語急躁。
⁴因全能者的箭射入我身，
　　其毒，我的靈喝盡了；
　　神的驚嚇擺陣攻擊我。
⁵野驢有草豈能叫喚？
　　牛有料豈能吼叫？
⁶物淡而無鹽豈可吃呢？
　　蛋青有甚麼滋味呢？
⁷看為可厭的食物，
　　我心不肯挨近。

⁸ "惟願我得着所求的，
　　願神賜我所切望的——
⁹就是願神把我壓碎，
　　伸手將我剪除。
¹⁰我因沒有違棄那聖者的言語，
　　就可以此為安慰，
　　在不止息的痛苦中
　　　　還可踊躍。

¹¹ "我有甚麼氣力使我等候？
　　我有甚麼結局使我忍耐？

¹²我的氣力豈是石頭的氣力？
　　我的肉身豈是銅的呢？
¹³在我豈不是毫無幫助嗎？
　　智慧豈不是從我心中趕出淨盡嗎？

¹⁴ "那將要灰心、離棄全能者、
　　不敬畏神的人，
　　他的朋友
　　　　當以慈愛待他。
¹⁵我的弟兄詭詐，
　　好像溪水，
　　又像溪水流乾的河道。
¹⁶這河，因結冰發黑，
　　有雪藏在其中；
¹⁷天氣漸暖，就隨時消化；
　　日頭炎熱，便從原處乾涸。
¹⁸結伴的客旅離棄大道，
　　順河偏行，到荒野之地死亡。

²⁶You will come to the grave in full vigor,
　　like sheaves gathered in season.

²⁷"We have examined this, and it is true.
　　So hear it and apply it to yourself."

Job

6

Then Job replied:

²"If only my anguish could be weighed
　　and all my misery be placed on the scales!
³It would surely outweigh the sand of the seas—
　　no wonder my words have been impetuous.
⁴The arrows of the Almighty are in me,
　　my spirit drinks in their poison;
　　God's terrors are marshaled against me.
⁵Does a wild donkey bray when it has grass,
　　or an ox bellow when it has fodder?
⁶Is tasteless food eaten without salt,
　　or is there flavor in the white of an egg^a?
⁷I refuse to touch it;
　　such food makes me ill.

⁸"Oh, that I might have my request,
　　that God would grant what I hope for,
⁹that God would be willing to crush me,
　　to let loose his hand and cut me off!
¹⁰Then I would still have this consolation—
　　my joy in unrelenting pain—
　　that I had not denied the words of the Holy
　　　　One.

¹¹"What strength do I have, that I should still
　　hope?
　　What prospects, that I should be patient?
¹²Do I have the strength of stone?
　　Is my flesh bronze?
¹³Do I have any power to help myself,
　　now that success has been driven from me?

¹⁴"A despairing man should have the devotion
　　of his friends,
　　even though he forsakes the fear of the
　　　　Almighty.
¹⁵But my brothers are as undependable as
　　intermittent streams,
　　as the streams that overflow
¹⁶when darkened by thawing ice
　　and swollen with melting snow,
¹⁷but that cease to flow in the dry season,
　　and in the heat vanish from their channels.
¹⁸Caravans turn aside from their routes;
　　they go up into the wasteland and perish.

a 6 The meaning of the Hebrew for this phrase is uncertain.

¹⁹The caravans of Tema look for water,
the traveling merchants of Sheba look in
hope.
²⁰They are distressed, because they had been
confident;
they arrive there, only to be disappointed.
²¹Now you too have proved to be of no help;
you see something dreadful and are afraid.
²²Have I ever said, 'Give something on my
behalf,
pay a ransom for me from your wealth,
²³deliver me from the hand of the enemy,
ransom me from the clutches of the
ruthless'?

²⁴"Teach me, and I will be quiet;
show me where I have been wrong.
²⁵How painful are honest words!
But what do your arguments prove?
²⁶Do you mean to correct what I say,
and treat the words of a despairing man as
wind?
²⁷You would even cast lots for the fatherless
and barter away your friend.

²⁸"But now be so kind as to look at me.
Would I lie to your face?
²⁹Relent, do not be unjust;
reconsider, for my integrity is at stake.[a]
³⁰Is there any wickedness on my lips?
Can my mouth not discern malice?

7 "Does not man have hard service on
earth?
Are not his days like those of a hired
man?
²Like a slave longing for the evening shadows,
or a hired man waiting eagerly for his wages,
³so I have been allotted months of futility,
and nights of misery have been assigned to
me.
⁴When I lie down I think, 'How long before I
get up?'
The night drags on, and I toss till dawn.
⁵My body is clothed with worms and scabs,
my skin is broken and festering.

⁶"My days are swifter than a weaver's shuttle,
and they come to an end without hope.
⁷Remember, O God, that my life is but a breath;
my eyes will never see happiness again.
⁸The eye that now sees me will see me no
longer;
you will look for me, but I will be no more.

¹⁹提瑪結伴的客旅瞻望,
示巴同夥的人等候。

²⁰他們因失了盼望
就抱愧,
來到那裏便蒙羞。
²¹現在你們正是這樣,
看見驚嚇的事便懼怕。
²²我豈說,
'請你們供給我,
從你們的財物中送禮物給我'?
²³豈說,
'拯救我脫離敵人的手'嗎?
'救贖我脫離強暴人的手'嗎?

²⁴"請你們教導我,我便不做聲;
使我明白在何事上有錯。
²⁵正直的言語力量何其大!
但你們責備,是責備甚麼呢?
²⁶絕望人的講論既然如風,
你們還想要
駁正言語嗎?
²⁷你們想為孤兒拈鬮,
以朋友當貨物。

²⁸"現在請你們看看我,
我決不當面說謊。
²⁹請你們轉意,不要不公;
請再轉意,我的事有理。
³⁰我的舌上,豈有不義嗎?
我的口裏豈不辨好惡嗎?

7 "人在世上
豈無爭戰嗎?
他的日子
不像雇工人的日子嗎?
²像奴僕切慕黑影,
像雇工人盼望工價;
³我也照樣經過困苦的日月,
夜間的疲乏
為我而定。
⁴我躺臥的時候便說,
我何時起來,黑夜就過去呢?
我盡是反來覆去,直到天亮。
⁵我的肉體以蟲子和塵土為衣,
我的皮膚才收了口又重新破裂。

⁶"我的日子比梭更快,
都消耗在無指望之中。
⁷求你想念,我的生命不過是一口氣,
我的眼睛必不再見福樂。
⁸觀看我的人,
他的眼必不再見我;
你的眼目要看我,我卻不在了。

<hr />

a 29 Or *my righteousness still stands*

⁹雲彩消散而過；
　　照樣，人下陰間
　　　也不再上來。
¹⁰他不再回自己的家，
　　故土也不再認識他。

¹¹ “我不禁止我口；
　　我靈愁苦，要發出言語；
　　我心苦惱，要吐露哀情。
¹²我對神說：我豈是洋海，
　　豈是大魚，你竟防守我呢？
¹³若說，我的牀必安慰我，
　　我的榻必解釋我的苦情；
¹⁴你就用夢驚駭我，
　　用異象恐嚇我。
¹⁵甚至我寧肯噎死，寧肯死亡，
　　勝似留我這一身的骨頭。
¹⁶我厭棄性命，不願永活。
　　你任憑我吧，因我的日子都是虛空。

¹⁷ “人算甚麼，你竟看他為大，
　　將他放在心上？
¹⁸每早鑒察他，
　　時刻試驗他。
¹⁹你到何時才轉眼不看我，
　　才任憑我咽下唾沫呢？
²⁰鑒察人的主啊，
　　我若有罪，於你何妨？
　　為何以我當你的箭靶子，
　　使我厭棄自己的性命？
²¹為何不赦免我的過犯，
　　除掉我的罪孽？
　　我現今要躺臥在塵土中，
　　你要殷勤地尋找我，
　　我卻不在了。”

比勒達發言

8 書亞人比勒達回答說：

²“這些話你要說到幾時？
　　口中的言語如狂風要到幾時呢？
³神豈能偏離公平？
　　全能者豈能偏離公義？
⁴或者你的兒女得罪了他，
　　他使他們受報應。
⁵你若殷勤地尋求神，
　　向全能者懇求；
⁶你若清潔正直，
　　他必定為你起來，
　　使你公義的居所興旺。

⁹As a cloud vanishes and is gone,
　　so he who goes down to the grave[a] does not
　　　return.
¹⁰He will never come to his house again;
　　his place will know him no more.

¹¹“Therefore I will not keep silent;
　　I will speak out in the anguish of my spirit,
　　I will complain in the bitterness of my soul.
¹²Am I the sea, or the monster of the deep,
　　that you put me under guard?
¹³When I think my bed will comfort me
　　and my couch will ease my complaint,
¹⁴even then you frighten me with dreams
　　and terrify me with visions,
¹⁵so that I prefer strangling and death,
　　rather than this body of mine.
¹⁶I despise my life; I would not live forever.
　　Let me alone; my days have no meaning.

¹⁷“What is man that you make so much of him,
　　that you give him so much attention,
¹⁸that you examine him every morning
　　and test him every moment?
¹⁹Will you never look away from me,
　　or let me alone even for an instant?
²⁰If I have sinned, what have I done to you,
　　O watcher of men?
　　Why have you made me your target?
　　Have I become a burden to you?[b]
²¹Why do you not pardon my offenses
　　and forgive my sins?
　　For I will soon lie down in the dust;
　　you will search for me, but I will be no more.”

Bildad

8 Then Bildad the Shuhite replied:

²“How long will you say such things?
　　Your words are a blustering wind.
³Does God pervert justice?
　　Does the Almighty pervert what is right?
⁴When your children sinned against him,
　　he gave them over to the penalty of their sin.
⁵But if you will look to God
　　and plead with the Almighty,
⁶if you are pure and upright,
　　even now he will rouse himself on your
　　　behalf
　　and restore you to your rightful place.

a 9 Hebrew *Sheol*　　*b 20* A few manuscripts of the Masoretic
Text, an ancient Hebrew scribal tradition and Septuagint;
most manuscripts of the Masoretic Text *I have become a burden
to myself.*

7Your beginnings will seem humble,
   so prosperous will your future be.

8"Ask the former generations
   and find out what their fathers learned,
9for we were born only yesterday and know
    nothing,
   and our days on earth are but a shadow.
10Will they not instruct you and tell you?
   Will they not bring forth words from their
    understanding?
11Can papyrus grow tall where there is no
    marsh?
   Can reeds thrive without water?
12While still growing and uncut,
   they wither more quickly than grass.
13Such is the destiny of all who forget God;
   so perishes the hope of the godless.
14What he trusts in is fragile[a];
   what he relies on is a spider's web.
15He leans on his web, but it gives way;
   he clings to it, but it does not hold.
16He is like a well-watered plant in the
    sunshine,
   spreading its shoots over the garden;
17it entwines its roots around a pile of rocks
   and looks for a place among the stones.
18But when it is torn from its spot,
   that place disowns it and says, 'I never saw
    you.'
19Surely its life withers away,
   and[b] from the soil other plants grow.

20"Surely God does not reject a blameless man
   or strengthen the hands of evildoers.
21He will yet fill your mouth with laughter
   and your lips with shouts of joy.
22Your enemies will be clothed in shame,
   and the tents of the wicked will be no more."

Job

9

Then Job replied:

2"Indeed, I know that this is true.
  But how can a mortal be righteous before
    God?
3Though one wished to dispute with him,
   he could not answer him one time out of a
    thousand.
4His wisdom is profound, his power is vast.
  Who has resisted him and come out
    unscathed?

7你起初雖然微小，
　　終久必甚發達。

8 "請你考問前代，
　　追念他們的列祖所查究的。
9 （我們不過從昨日才有，
　　一無所知，
　　我們在世的日子好像影兒。）
10他們豈不指教你、
　　告訴你從心裏
　　　發出言語來呢？
11蒲草沒有泥豈能發長？
　　蘆荻沒有水豈能生發？

12尚青的時候，還沒有割下，
　　比百樣的草先枯槁。
13凡忘記神的人，景況也是這樣；
　　不虔敬人的指望要滅沒。
14他所仰賴的必折斷；
　　他所倚靠的是蜘蛛網。
15他要倚靠房屋，房屋卻站立不住；
　　他要抓住房屋，房屋卻不能存留。
16他在日光之下發青，
　　蔓子爬滿了園子。

17他的根盤繞石堆，
　　扎入石地。
18他若從本地被拔出，
　　那地就不認識他，說：
　　　'我沒有見過你'。
19看哪，這就是他道中之樂，
　　以後必另有人從地而生。

20 " 神必不丟棄完全人，
　　也不扶助邪惡人。
21他還要以喜笑充滿你的口，
　　以歡呼充滿你的嘴。
22恨惡你的要披戴慚愧；
　　惡人的帳棚，必歸於無有。"

約伯解釋

9

約伯回答說：

2 "我真知道是這樣。
　但人在神面前
　　怎能成為義呢？
3若願意與他爭辯，
　　千中之一
　　　也不能回答。
4他心裏有智慧，且大有能力。
　　誰向神剛硬
　　　而得亨通呢？

a 14 The meaning of the Hebrew for this word is uncertain.
b 19 Or *Surely all the joy it has* / *is that*

⁵他發怒，把山翻倒挪移，
　　山並不知覺。
⁶他使地震動，離其本位，
　　地的柱子就搖撼。
⁷他吩咐日頭不出來，就不出來；
　　又封閉眾星。
⁸他獨自鋪張蒼天，
　　步行在海浪之上。
⁹他造北斗、參星、昴星，
　　並南方的密宮。
¹⁰他行大事，不可測度，
　　行奇事，不可勝數。
¹¹他從我旁邊經過，我卻不看見；
　　他在我面前行走，我倒不知覺。
¹²他奪取，誰能阻擋？
　　誰敢問他：「你做甚麼？」
¹³神必不收回他的怒氣；
　　扶助拉哈伯的，屈身在他以下。

¹⁴「既是這樣，我怎敢回答他，
　　怎敢選擇言語與他辯論呢？
¹⁵我雖有義，
　　也不回答他，
　　只要向那審判我的懇求。
¹⁶我若呼籲，他應允我；
　　我仍不信他真聽我的聲音。
¹⁷他用暴風折斷我，
　　無故地加增我的損傷。
¹⁸我就是喘一口氣，他都不容，
　　倒使我滿心苦惱。
¹⁹若論力量，他真有能力；
　　若論審判，
　　他說誰能將我傳來呢？
²⁰我雖有義，
　　自己的口要定我為有罪；
　　我雖完全，
　　我口必顯我為彎曲。

²¹「我本完全，
　　不顧自己，
　　我厭惡我的性命。
²²善惡無分，都是一樣，
　　所以我說：
　　『完全人和惡人，他都滅絕。』
²³若忽然遭殺害之禍，
　　他必戲笑無辜的人遇難。
²⁴世界交在惡人手中，
　　蒙蔽世界審判官的臉，
　　若不是他是誰呢？

²⁵「我的日子比跑信的更快，
　　急速過去，不見福樂。

⁵He moves mountains without their knowing it
　　and overturns them in his anger.
⁶He shakes the earth from its place
　　and makes its pillars tremble.
⁷He speaks to the sun and it does not shine;
　　he seals off the light of the stars.
⁸He alone stretches out the heavens
　　and treads on the waves of the sea.
⁹He is the Maker of the Bear and Orion,
　　the Pleiades and the constellations of the
　　　south.
¹⁰He performs wonders that cannot be fathomed,
　　miracles that cannot be counted.
¹¹When he passes me, I cannot see him;
　　when he goes by, I cannot perceive him.
¹²If he snatches away, who can stop him?
　　Who can say to him, 'What are you doing?'
¹³God does not restrain his anger;
　　even the cohorts of Rahab cowered at his feet.

¹⁴"How then can I dispute with him?
　　How can I find words to argue with him?
¹⁵Though I were innocent, I could not answer
　　　him;
　　I could only plead with my Judge for mercy.
¹⁶Even if I summoned him and he responded,
　　I do not believe he would give me a hearing.
¹⁷He would crush me with a storm
　　and multiply my wounds for no reason.
¹⁸He would not let me regain my breath
　　but would overwhelm me with misery.
¹⁹If it is a matter of strength, he is mighty!
　　And if it is a matter of justice, who will
　　　summon him^a?
²⁰Even if I were innocent, my mouth would
　　　condemn me;
　　if I were blameless, it would pronounce me
　　　guilty.

²¹"Although I am blameless,
　　I have no concern for myself;
　　I despise my own life.
²²It is all the same; that is why I say,
　　'He destroys both the blameless and the
　　　wicked.'
²³When a scourge brings sudden death,
　　he mocks the despair of the innocent.
²⁴When a land falls into the hands of the wicked,
　　he blindfolds its judges.
　　If it is not he, then who is it?

²⁵"My days are swifter than a runner;
　　they fly away without a glimpse of joy.

a 19 See Septuagint; Hebrew me.

26They skim past like boats of papyrus,
　　like eagles swooping down on their prey.
27If I say, 'I will forget my complaint,
　　I will change my expression, and smile,'
28I still dread all my sufferings,
　　for I know you will not hold me innocent.
29Since I am already found guilty,
　　why should I struggle in vain?
30Even if I washed myself with soap[a]
　　and my hands with washing soda,
31you would plunge me into a slime pit
　　so that even my clothes would detest me.

32"He is not a man like me that I might answer
　　him,
　　that we might confront each other in court.
33If only there were someone to arbitrate
　　between us,
　　to lay his hand upon us both,
34someone to remove God's rod from me,
　　so that his terror would frighten me no more.
35Then I would speak up without fear of him,
　　but as it now stands with me, I cannot.

10 "I loathe my very life;
　　therefore I will give free rein to my
　　complaint
　　and speak out in the bitterness of my soul.
2I will say to God: Do not condemn me,
　　but tell me what charges you have against
　　me.
3Does it please you to oppress me,
　　to spurn the work of your hands,
　　while you smile on the schemes of the
　　wicked?
4Do you have eyes of flesh?
　　Do you see as a mortal sees?
5Are your days like those of a mortal
　　or your years like those of a man,
6that you must search out my faults
　　and probe after my sin—
7though you know that I am not guilty
　　and that no one can rescue me from your
　　hand?

8"Your hands shaped me and made me.
　　Will you now turn and destroy me?
9Remember that you molded me like clay.
　　Will you now turn me to dust again?
10Did you not pour me out like milk
　　and curdle me like cheese,
11clothe me with skin and flesh
　　and knit me together with bones and
　　sinews?

26我的日子過去如快船，
　　如急落抓食的鷹。
27我若說：'我要忘記我的哀情，
　　除去我的愁容，心中暢快。'
28我因愁苦而懼怕，
　　知道你必不以我為無辜。
29我必被你定為有罪，
　　我何必徒然勞苦呢？
30我若用雪水洗身，
　　用鹼潔淨我的手，
31你還要扔我在坑裏；
　　我的衣服都憎惡我。

32"他本不像我是人，
　　使我可以回答他，
　　又使我們可以同聽審判。
33我們中間
　　沒有聽訟的人，
　　可以向我們兩造按手。
34願他把杖離開我，
　　不使驚惶威嚇我；
35我就說話，也不懼怕他，
　　現在我卻不是那樣。

10 "我厭煩我的性命，
　　必由着自己述說我的哀情，
　　因心裏苦惱，
　　我要說話。
2對神說：不要定我有罪，
　　要指示我，
　　你為何與我爭辯。
3你手所造的，
　　你又欺壓，又藐視，
　　卻光照惡人的計謀，
　　這事你以為美嗎？
4你的眼豈是肉眼？
　　你查看豈像人查看嗎？
5你的日子豈像人的日子？
　　你的年歲豈像人的年歲？
6就追問我的罪孽，
　　尋察我的罪過嗎？
7其實，你知道我沒有罪惡，
　　並沒有能救我脫離你手的。

8"你的手創造我，造就我的四肢百體，
　　你還要毀滅我？
9求你記念，製造我如摶泥一般，
　　你還要使我歸於塵土嗎？
10你不是倒出我來好像奶，
　　使我凝結如同奶餅嗎？
11你以皮和肉為衣給我穿上，
　　用骨與筋把我全體聯絡。

a 30 Or *snow*

¹²你將生命和慈愛賜給我，
　　你也眷顧保全我的心靈。

¹³"然而你待我的這些事，
　　早已藏在你心裏，
　　我知道你久有此意。
¹⁴我若犯罪，你就察看我，
　　並不赦免我的罪孽。
¹⁵我若行惡，便有了禍；
　　我若為義，也不敢抬頭，
　　正是滿心羞愧，
　　眼見我的苦情。
¹⁶我若昂首自得，
　　你就追捕我如獅子，
　　又在我身上顯出奇能。
¹⁷你重立見證攻擊我，
　　向我加增惱怒，
　　如軍兵更換着攻擊我。

¹⁸"你為何使我出母胎呢？
　　不如我當時氣絕，無人得見我。
¹⁹這樣，
　　就如沒有我一般，
　　一出母胎就被送入墳墓。
²⁰、²¹我的日子不是甚少嗎？
　　求你停手寬容我，
　　叫我在往而不返之先，
　　就是往黑暗和死蔭之地以先，
　　可以稍得暢快。
²²那地甚是幽暗，
　　是死蔭混沌之地，
　　那裏的光好像幽暗。"

瑣法回答

11
拿瑪人瑣法回答說：

²"這許多的言語豈不該回答嗎？
　　多嘴多舌的人豈可稱為義嗎？
³你誇大的話，豈能使人不做聲嗎？
　　你戲笑的時候，
　　豈沒有人叫你害羞嗎？
⁴你說：'我的道理純全，
　　我在你眼前潔淨。'
⁵惟願神說話，
　　願他開口攻擊你，
⁶並將智慧的奧秘指示你，
　　他有諸般的智識。
　　所以當知道：神追討你，
　　比你罪孽該得的還少。

¹²You gave me life and showed me kindness,
　　and in your providence watched over my
　　　spirit.

¹³"But this is what you concealed in your heart,
　　and I know that this was in your mind:
¹⁴If I sinned, you would be watching me
　　and would not let my offense go unpunished.
¹⁵If I am guilty—woe to me!
　　Even if I am innocent, I cannot lift my head,
　　for I am full of shame
　　and drowned in*^a* my affliction.
¹⁶If I hold my head high, you stalk me like a lion
　　and again display your awesome power
　　　against me.
¹⁷You bring new witnesses against me
　　and increase your anger toward me;
　　your forces come against me wave upon
　　　wave.

¹⁸"Why then did you bring me out of the womb?
　　I wish I had died before any eye saw me.
¹⁹If only I had never come into being,
　　or had been carried straight from the womb
　　　to the grave!
²⁰Are not my few days almost over?
　　Turn away from me so I can have a moment's
　　　joy
²¹before I go to the place of no return,
　　to the land of gloom and deep shadow,*^b*
²²to the land of deepest night,
　　of deep shadow and disorder,
　　where even the light is like darkness."

Zophar

11
Then Zophar the Naamathite replied:

²"Are all these words to go unanswered?
　　Is this talker to be vindicated?
³Will your idle talk reduce men to silence?
　　Will no one rebuke you when you mock?

⁴You say to God, 'My beliefs are flawless
　　and I am pure in your sight.'
⁵Oh, how I wish that God would speak,
　　that he would open his lips against you
⁶and disclose to you the secrets of wisdom,
　　for true wisdom has two sides.
　　Know this: God has even forgotten some of
　　　your sin.

*a 15 Or and aware of　　b 21 Or and the shadow of death; also in
verse 22*

⁷"Can you fathom the mysteries of God?
  Can you probe the limits of the Almighty?
⁸They are higher than the heavens—what can
    you do?
  They are deeper than the depths of the
    grave^a—what can you know?
⁹Their measure is longer than the earth
  and wider than the sea.

¹⁰"If he comes along and confines you in prison
  and convenes a court, who can oppose him?
¹¹Surely he recognizes deceitful men;
  and when he sees evil, does he not take note?
¹²But a witless man can no more become wise
  than a wild donkey's colt can be born a man.^b

¹³"Yet if you devote your heart to him
  and stretch out your hands to him,
¹⁴if you put away the sin that is in your hand
  and allow no evil to dwell in your tent,
¹⁵then you will lift up your face without shame;
  you will stand firm and without fear.
¹⁶You will surely forget your trouble,
  recalling it only as waters gone by.
¹⁷Life will be brighter than noonday,
  and darkness will become like morning.
¹⁸You will be secure, because there is hope;
  you will look about you and take your rest in
    safety.
¹⁹You will lie down, with no one to make you
    afraid,
  and many will court your favor.
²⁰But the eyes of the wicked will fail,
  and escape will elude them;
  their hope will become a dying gasp."

Job

12

Then Job replied:

²"Doubtless you are the people,
  and wisdom will die with you!
³But I have a mind as well as you;
  I am not inferior to you.
  Who does not know all these things?

⁴"I have become a laughingstock to my friends,
  though I called upon God and he answered—
  a mere laughingstock, though righteous and
    blameless!
⁵Men at ease have contempt for misfortune
  as the fate of those whose feet are slipping.

⁷"你考察，就能測透神嗎？
  你豈能盡情測透全能者嗎？
⁸他的智慧高於天，
  你還能做甚麼？
  深於陰間，
  你還能知道甚麼？
⁹其量，
  比地長，比海寬。

¹⁰"他若經過，將人拘禁，
  招人受審，誰能阻擋他呢？
¹¹他本知道虛妄的人；
  人的罪孽，他雖不留意，
  還是無所不見。
¹²空虛的人卻毫無知識，
  人生在世好像野驢的駒子。

¹³"你若將心安正，
  又向主舉手；
¹⁴你手裏若有罪孽，就當遠遠地除掉，
  也不容非義住在你帳棚之中。
¹⁵那時，你必仰起臉來，毫無斑點；
  你也必堅固，無所懼怕。
¹⁶你必忘記你的苦楚，
  就是想起也如流過去的水一樣。
¹⁷你在世的日子要比正午更明，
  雖有黑暗，仍像早晨。
¹⁸你因有指望，就必穩固，
  也必四圍巡查，
  坦然安息。
¹⁹你躺臥
  無人驚嚇，
  且有許多人向你求恩。
²⁰但惡人的眼目必要失明，
  他們無路可逃，
  他們的指望就是氣絕。"

約伯發言

12

約伯回答說：

²"你們真是子民哪！
  你們死亡，智慧也就滅沒了。
³但我也有聰明，與你們一樣，
  並非不及你們。
  你們所說的，誰不知道呢？

⁴"我這求告神，蒙他應允的人，
  竟成了朋友所譏笑的；
  公義完全人，
  竟受了人的譏笑！
⁵安逸的人心裏藐視災禍，
  這災禍常常等待滑腳的人。

⁶強盜的帳棚興旺，
　　惹神的人穩固，
　　神多將財物送到他們手中。

⁷ "你且問走獸，走獸必指教你；
　　又問空中的飛鳥，飛鳥必告訴你；
⁸或與地說話，地必指教你，
　　海中的魚也必向你說明。
⁹看這一切，
　　誰不知道是耶和華的手做成的呢？
¹⁰凡活物的生命和人類的氣息
　　都在他手中。
¹¹耳朵豈不試驗言語，
　　正如上膛嘗食物嗎？
¹²年老的有智慧，
　　壽高的有知識？

¹³ "在神有智慧和能力，
　　他有謀略和知識；
¹⁴他拆毀的，就不能再建造；
　　他捆住人，便不得開釋。
¹⁵他把水留住，水便枯乾；
　　他再發出水來，水就翻地。
¹⁶在他有能力和智慧，
　　被誘惑的與誘惑人的都是屬他。
¹⁷他把謀士剝衣擄去，
　　又使審判官變成愚人。
¹⁸他放鬆君王的綁，
　　又用帶子捆他們的腰。
¹⁹他把祭司剝衣擄去，
　　又使有能的人傾敗。
²⁰他廢去忠信人的講論，
　　又奪去老人的聰明。
²¹他使君王蒙羞被辱，
　　放鬆有力之人的腰帶。
²²他將深奧的事從黑暗中彰顯，
　　使死蔭顯為光明。
²³他使邦國興旺而又毀滅，
　　他使邦國開廣而又擄去；
²⁴他將地上民中首領的聰明奪去，
　　使他們在荒廢無路之地漂流。

²⁵他們無光，在黑暗中摸索，
　　又使他們東倒西歪，
　　像醉酒的人一樣。

13 "這一切我眼都見過，
　　我耳都聽過，而且明白。
²你們所知道的，我也知道，
　　並非不及你們。
³我真要對全能者說話，
　　我願與神理論。

⁶The tents of marauders are undisturbed,
　　and those who provoke God are secure—
　　those who carry their god in their hands.ᵃ

⁷"But ask the animals, and they will teach you,
　　or the birds of the air, and they will tell you;
⁸or speak to the earth, and it will teach you,
　　or let the fish of the sea inform you.
⁹Which of all these does not know
　　that the hand of the LORD has done this?
¹⁰In his hand is the life of every creature
　　and the breath of all mankind.
¹¹Does not the ear test words
　　as the tongue tastes food?
¹²Is not wisdom found among the aged?
　　Does not long life bring understanding?

¹³"To God belong wisdom and power;
　　counsel and understanding are his.
¹⁴What he tears down cannot be rebuilt;
　　the man he imprisons cannot be released.
¹⁵If he holds back the waters, there is drought;
　　if he lets them loose, they devastate the land.
¹⁶To him belong strength and victory;
　　both deceived and deceiver are his.
¹⁷He leads counselors away stripped
　　and makes fools of judges.
¹⁸He takes off the shackles put on by kings
　　and ties a loinclothᵇ around their waist.
¹⁹He leads priests away stripped
　　and overthrows men long established.
²⁰He silences the lips of trusted advisers
　　and takes away the discernment of elders.
²¹He pours contempt on nobles
　　and disarms the mighty.
²²He reveals the deep things of darkness
　　and brings deep shadows to the light.
²³He makes nations great, and destroys them;
　　he enlarges nations, and disperses them.
²⁴He deprives the leaders of the earth of their
　　reason;
　　he sends them wandering through a
　　trackless waste.
²⁵They grope in darkness with no light;
　　he makes them stagger like drunkards.

13 "My eyes have seen all this,
　　my ears have heard and understood it.
²What you know, I also know;
　　I am not inferior to you.
³But I desire to speak to the Almighty
　　and to argue my case with God.

a 6 Or secure / in what God's hand brings them　　b 18 Or shackles
of kings / and ties a belt

⁴You, however, smear me with lies;
　you are worthless physicians, all of you!
⁵If only you would be altogether silent!
　For you, that would be wisdom.
⁶Hear now my argument;
　listen to the plea of my lips.
⁷Will you speak wickedly on God's behalf?
　Will you speak deceitfully for him?
⁸Will you show him partiality?
　Will you argue the case for God?
⁹Would it turn out well if he examined you?
　Could you deceive him as you might deceive
　　men?
¹⁰He would surely rebuke you
　if you secretly showed partiality.
¹¹Would not his splendor terrify you?
　Would not the dread of him fall on you?
¹²Your maxims are proverbs of ashes;
　your defenses are defenses of clay.

¹³"Keep silent and let me speak;
　then let come to me what may.
¹⁴Why do I put myself in jeopardy
　and take my life in my hands?
¹⁵Though he slay me, yet will I hope in him;
　I will surely^a defend my ways to his face.
¹⁶Indeed, this will turn out for my deliverance,
　for no godless man would dare come before
　　him!
¹⁷Listen carefully to my words;
　let your ears take in what I say.
¹⁸Now that I have prepared my case,
　I know I will be vindicated.
¹⁹Can anyone bring charges against me?
　If so, I will be silent and die.

²⁰"Only grant me these two things, O God,
　and then I will not hide from you:
²¹Withdraw your hand far from me,
　and stop frightening me with your terrors.
²²Then summon me and I will answer,
　or let me speak, and you reply.
²³How many wrongs and sins have I
　　committed?
　Show me my offense and my sin.
²⁴Why do you hide your face
　and consider me your enemy?
²⁵Will you torment a windblown leaf?
　Will you chase after dry chaff?
²⁶For you write down bitter things against me
　and make me inherit the sins of my youth.
²⁷You fasten my feet in shackles;
　you keep close watch on all my paths
　by putting marks on the soles of my feet.

a 15 Or He will surely slay me; I have no hope — / yet I will

⁴你們是編造謊言的，
　都是無用的醫生。
⁵惟願你們全然不做聲，
　這就算為你們的智慧。
⁶請你們聽我的辯論，
　留心聽我口中的分訴。
⁷你們要為神說不義的話嗎？
　為他說詭詐的言語嗎？
⁸你們要為神徇情嗎？
　要為他爭論嗎？
⁹他查出你們來，這豈是好嗎？
　人欺哄人，
　你們也要照樣欺哄他嗎？
¹⁰你們若暗中徇情，
　他必要責備你們。
¹¹他的尊榮，豈不叫你們懼怕嗎？
　他的驚嚇，豈不臨到你們嗎？
¹²你們以為可記念的箴言，
　是爐灰的箴言；
　你們以為可靠的堅壘，是淤泥的堅壘！
¹³"你們不要做聲，任憑我吧！
　讓我說話，無論如何我都承當。
¹⁴我何必把我的肉掛在牙上，
　將我的命放在手中？
¹⁵他必殺我，我雖無指望，
　然而我在他面前
　還要辯明我所行的。
¹⁶這要成為我的拯救，
　因為不虔誠的人不得到他面前。
¹⁷你們要細聽我的言語，
　使我所辯論的入你們的耳中。
¹⁸我已陳明我的案。
　知道自己有義。
¹⁹有誰與我爭論，
　我就情願緘默不言，氣絕而亡。

²⁰"惟有兩件不要向我施行，
　我就不躲開你的面：
²¹就是把你的手縮回，遠離我身，
　又不使你的驚惶威嚇我。
²²這樣，你呼叫，我就回答；
　或是讓我說話，你回答我。
²³我的罪孽和罪過有多少呢？
　求你叫我知道
　　我的過犯與罪愆。
²⁴你為何掩面、
　拿我當仇敵呢？
²⁵你要驚動被風吹的葉子嗎？
　要追趕枯乾的碎稭嗎？
²⁶你按罪狀刑罰我，
　又使我擔當幼年的罪孽。
²⁷也把我的腳上了木狗，
　並窺察我一切的道路，
　為我的腳掌劃定界限。

28 "我已經像滅絕的爛物，
　　像蟲蛀的衣裳。

14 "人為婦人所生，
　　日子短少，多有患難。
2 出來如花，
　　又被割下；
　　飛去如影，不能存留。
3 這樣的人你豈睜眼看他嗎？
　　又叫我來受審嗎？

4 誰能使潔淨之物出於污穢之中呢？
　　無論誰也不能！
5 人的日子既然限定，
　　他的月數在你那裏，
　　你也派定他的界限，使他不能越過；
6 便求你轉眼不看他，使他得歇息，
　　直等他像雇工人完畢他的日子。

7 "樹若被砍下，
　　還可指望發芽，
　　嫩枝生長不息。
8 其根雖然衰老在地裏，
　　幹也死在土中；
9 及至得了水氣，還要發芽，
　　又長枝條，像新栽的樹一樣。
10 但人死亡而消滅，
　　他氣絕，竟在何處呢？
11 海中的水絕盡，
　　江河消散乾涸。
12 人也是如此，躺下不再起來，
　　等到天沒有了，
　　仍不得復醒，
　　也不得從睡中喚醒。

13 惟願你把我藏在陰間，
　　存於隱密處，等你的忿怒過去；
　　願你為我
　　定了日期記念我。
14 人若死了豈能再活呢？
　　我只要在我一切爭戰的日子，
　　等我被釋放的時候來到（註："被
　　釋放"或作"改變"）。
15 你呼叫，我便回答；
　　你手所做的，你必羨慕。
16 但如今你數點我的腳步，
　　豈不窺察我的罪過嗎？
17 我的過犯被你封在囊中，
　　也縫嚴了我的罪孽。

18 "山崩變為無有，
　　磐石挪開原處。

28"So man wastes away like something rotten,
　　like a garment eaten by moths.

14 "Man born of woman
　　is of few days and full of trouble.
2 He springs up like a flower and
　　withers away;
　　like a fleeting shadow, he does not endure.
3 Do you fix your eye on such a one?
　　Will you bring him[a] before you for
　　judgment?
4 Who can bring what is pure from the impure?
　　No one!
5 Man's days are determined;
　　you have decreed the number of his months
　　and have set limits he cannot exceed.
6 So look away from him and let him alone,
　　till he has put in his time like a hired man.

7"At least there is hope for a tree:
　　If it is cut down, it will sprout again,
　　and its new shoots will not fail.
8 Its roots may grow old in the ground
　　and its stump die in the soil,
9 yet at the scent of water it will bud
　　and put forth shoots like a plant.
10 But man dies and is laid low;
　　he breathes his last and is no more.
11 As water disappears from the sea
　　or a riverbed becomes parched and dry,
12 so man lies down and does not rise;
　　till the heavens are no more, men will not
　　awake
　　or be roused from their sleep.

13"If only you would hide me in the grave[b]
　　and conceal me till your anger has passed!
　　If only you would set me a time
　　and then remember me!
14 If a man dies, will he live again?
　　All the days of my hard service
　　I will wait for my renewal[c] to come.
15 You will call and I will answer you;
　　you will long for the creature your hands
　　have made.
16 Surely then you will count my steps
　　but not keep track of my sin.
17 My offenses will be sealed up in a bag;
　　you will cover over my sin.

18"But as a mountain erodes and crumbles
　　and as a rock is moved from its place,

a 3 Septuagint, Vulgate and Syriac; Hebrew *me*　　*b 13* Hebrew
Sheol　　*c 14* Or *release*

¹⁹as water wears away stones
   and torrents wash away the soil,
   so you destroy man's hope.
²⁰You overpower him once for all, and he is
   gone;
   you change his countenance and send him
    away.
²¹If his sons are honored, he does not know it;
   if they are brought low, he does not see it.
²²He feels but the pain of his own body
   and mourns only for himself."

Eliphaz

15 Then Eliphaz the Temanite replied:

²"Would a wise man answer with
   empty notions
   or fill his belly with the hot east wind?
³Would he argue with useless words,
   with speeches that have no value?
⁴But you even undermine piety
   and hinder devotion to God.
⁵Your sin prompts your mouth;
   you adopt the tongue of the crafty.
⁶Your own mouth condemns you, not mine;
   your own lips testify against you.

⁷"Are you the first man ever born?
   Were you brought forth before the hills?
⁸Do you listen in on God's council?
   Do you limit wisdom to yourself?
⁹What do you know that we do not know?
   What insights do you have that we do not
    have?
¹⁰The gray-haired and the aged are on our side,
   men even older than your father.
¹¹Are God's consolations not enough for you,
   words spoken gently to you?
¹²Why has your heart carried you away,
   and why do your eyes flash,
¹³so that you vent your rage against God
   and pour out such words from your mouth?

¹⁴"What is man, that he could be pure,
   or one born of woman, that he could be
    righteous?
¹⁵If God places no trust in his holy ones,
   if even the heavens are not pure in his eyes,
¹⁶how much less man, who is vile and corrupt,
   who drinks up evil like water!

¹⁷"Listen to me and I will explain to you;
   let me tell you what I have seen,
¹⁸what wise men have declared,
   hiding nothing received from their fathers

¹⁹水流消磨石頭,
   所流溢的,洗去地上的塵土;
   你也照樣滅絕人的指望。
²⁰你攻擊人常常得勝,
   使他去世;
   你改變他的容貌,
   叫他往而不回。
²¹他兒子得尊榮,他也不知道;
   降為卑,他也不覺得,
²²但知身上疼痛,
   心中悲哀。"

以利法再發言

15 提幔人以利法回答說:

²"智慧人豈可用
   虛空的知識回答,
   用東風充滿肚腹呢?
³他豈可用無益的話
   和無濟於事的言語理論呢?
⁴你是廢棄敬畏的意,
   在神面前阻止敬虔的心。
⁵你的罪孽指教你的口,
   你選用詭詐人的舌頭。
⁶你自己的口定你有罪,並非是我;
   你自己的嘴見證你的不是。

⁷"你豈是頭一個被生的人嗎?
   你受造在諸山之先嗎?
⁸你曾聽見神的密旨嗎?
   你還將智慧獨自得盡嗎?
⁹你知道甚麼是我們不知道的呢?
   你明白甚麼是我們不明白的呢?
¹⁰我們這裏有白髮的和年紀老邁的,
   比你父親還老。
¹¹神用溫和的話安慰你,
   你以為太小嗎?
¹²你的心為何將你逼去?
   你的眼為何冒出火星?
¹³使你的靈反對神,
   也任你的口發這言語?

¹⁴"人是甚麼,竟算為潔淨呢?
   婦人所生的是甚麼,
   竟算為義呢?
¹⁵神不信靠他的眾聖者,
   在他眼前天也不潔淨!
¹⁶何況那污穢可憎、
   喝罪孽如水的世人呢?

¹⁷"我指示你,你要聽!
   我要述說所看見的,
¹⁸就是智慧人從列祖所受、
   傳說而不隱瞞的。

19（這地惟獨賜給他們，
　並沒有外人從他們中間經過。）
20惡人一生之日勤勞痛苦，
　強暴人一生的年數
　也是如此。
21驚嚇的聲音常在他耳中；
　在平安時搶奪的必臨到他那裏。
22他不信自己能從黑暗中轉回；
　他被刀劍等候。
23他漂流在外求食，說：
　'哪裏有食物呢？'
　他知道黑暗的日子
　在他手邊預備好了。
24急難困苦叫他害怕，而且勝了他，
　好像君王預備上陣一樣。
25他伸手攻擊神，
　以驕傲攻擊全能者，
26挺着頸項，
　用盾牌的厚凸面向全能者直闖。

27"是因他的臉蒙上脂油，
　腰積成肥肉，
28他曾住在荒涼城邑，
　無人居住
　將成亂堆的房屋。
29他不得富足，
　財物不得常存，
　產業在地上也不加增。
30他不得出離黑暗，
　火焰必將他的枝子燒乾，
　因神口中的氣，
　他要滅亡（註："滅亡"原文作"走去"）。
31他不用倚靠虛假
　欺哄自己，
　因虛假必成為他的報應。
32他的日期未到之先，這事必成就；
　他的枝子不得青綠。
33他必像葡萄樹的葡萄，
　未熟而落；
　又像橄欖樹的花，一開而謝。
34原來不敬虔之輩必無生育；
　受賄賂之人的帳棚必被火燒。
35他們所懷的是毒害，
　所生的是罪孽，
　心裏所預備的是詭詐。"

約伯回答

16

約伯回答說：

2"這樣的話我聽了許多。
　你們安慰人，反叫人愁煩。
3虛空的言語有窮盡嗎？
　有甚麼話惹動你回答呢？

19(to whom alone the land was given
　when no alien passed among them):
20All his days the wicked man suffers torment,
　the ruthless through all the years stored up
　for him.
21Terrifying sounds fill his ears;
　when all seems well, marauders attack him.
22He despairs of escaping the darkness;
　he is marked for the sword.
23He wanders about—food for vultures[a];
　he knows the day of darkness is at hand.
24Distress and anguish fill him with terror;
　they overwhelm him, like a king poised to
　attack,
25because he shakes his fist at God
　and vaunts himself against the Almighty,
26defiantly charging against him
　with a thick, strong shield.

27"Though his face is covered with fat
　and his waist bulges with flesh,
28he will inhabit ruined towns
　and houses where no one lives,
　houses crumbling to rubble.
29He will no longer be rich and his wealth will
　not endure,
　nor will his possessions spread over the land.
30He will not escape the darkness;
　a flame will wither his shoots,
　and the breath of God's mouth will carry
　him away.
31Let him not deceive himself by trusting what
　is worthless,
　for he will get nothing in return.
32Before his time he will be paid in full,
　and his branches will not flourish.
33He will be like a vine stripped of its unripe
　grapes,
　like an olive tree shedding its blossoms.
34For the company of the godless will be barren,
　and fire will consume the tents of those who
　love bribes.
35They conceive trouble and give birth to evil;
　their womb fashions deceit."

Job

16

Then Job replied:

2"I have heard many things like these;
　miserable comforters are you all!
3Will your long-winded speeches never end?
　What ails you that you keep on arguing?

a 23 Or about, looking for food

⁴I also could speak like you,
　　if you were in my place;
　I could make fine speeches against you
　　and shake my head at you.
⁵But my mouth would encourage you;
　　comfort from my lips would bring you relief.

⁶"Yet if I speak, my pain is not relieved;
　　and if I refrain, it does not go away.
⁷Surely, O God, you have worn me out;
　　you have devastated my entire household.
⁸You have bound me—and it has become a
　　witness;
　my gauntness rises up and testifies against me.
⁹God assails me and tears me in his anger
　　and gnashes his teeth at me;
　my opponent fastens on me his piercing eyes.
¹⁰Men open their mouths to jeer at me;
　　they strike my cheek in scorn
　　and unite together against me.
¹¹God has turned me over to evil men
　　and thrown me into the clutches of the
　　wicked.
¹²All was well with me, but he shattered me;
　　he seized me by the neck and crushed me.
　He has made me his target;
¹³　his archers surround me.
　Without pity, he pierces my kidneys
　　and spills my gall on the ground.
¹⁴Again and again he bursts upon me;
　　he rushes at me like a warrior.

¹⁵"I have sewed sackcloth over my skin
　　and buried my brow in the dust.
¹⁶My face is red with weeping,
　　deep shadows ring my eyes;
¹⁷yet my hands have been free of violence
　　and my prayer is pure.

¹⁸"O earth, do not cover my blood;
　　may my cry never be laid to rest!
¹⁹Even now my witness is in heaven;
　　my advocate is on high.
²⁰My intercessor is my friend[a]
　　as my eyes pour out tears to God;
²¹on behalf of a man he pleads with God
　　as a man pleads for his friend.

²²"Only a few years will pass
　　before I go on the journey of no return.

17

　¹My spirit is broken,
　my days are cut short,
　the grave awaits me.

⁴我也能說你們那樣的話。
　你們若處在我的境遇，
　我也會聯絡言語攻擊你們，
　又能向你們搖頭。
⁵但我必用口堅固你們，
　用嘴消解你們的憂愁。

⁶「我雖說話，憂愁仍不得消解；
　我雖停住不說，憂愁就離開我嗎？
⁷但現在神使我困倦，
　使親友遠離我，
⁸又抓住我，作見證攻擊我。
　我身體的枯瘦，
　也當面見證我的不是。
⁹主發怒撕裂我，逼迫我，
　向我切齒；
　我的敵人怒目看我。
¹⁰他們向我開口，
　打我的臉羞辱我，
　聚會攻擊我。
¹¹神把我交給不敬虔的人，
　把我扔到
　惡人的手中。
¹²我素來安逸，他折斷我，
　揪住我的頸項把我摔碎，
　又立我為他的箭靶子。
¹³他的弓箭手四面圍繞我，
　他破裂我的肺腑，並不留情，
　把我的膽傾倒在地上。
¹⁴將我破裂又破裂，
　如同勇士向我直闖。

¹⁵「我縫麻布在我皮膚上，
　把我的角放在塵土中。
¹⁶我的臉因哭泣發紫，
　在我的眼皮上有死蔭。
¹⁷我的手中卻無強暴，
　我的祈禱也是清潔。

¹⁸「地啊，不要遮蓋我的血，
　不要阻擋我的哀求！
¹⁹現今，在天有我的見證，
　在上有我的中保。
²⁰我的朋友譏誚我，
　我卻向神眼淚汪汪。
²¹願人得與神辯白，
　如同人與朋友辯白一樣。

²²「因為再過幾年，
　我必走那往而不返之路。

17

　¹我的心靈消耗，
　我的日子滅盡，
　墳墓為我預備好了。

---

a 20 Or My friends treat me with scorn

² 真有戲笑我的在我這裏，
　我眼常見他們惹動我。

³ "願主拿憑據給我，自己為我作保。
　在你以外誰肯與我擊掌呢？

⁴ "因你使他們心不明理，
　所以你必不高舉他們。
⁵ 控告他的朋友，以朋友為可搶奪的，
　連他兒女的眼睛也要失明。

⁶ "神使我作了民中的笑談；
　他們也吐唾沫在我臉上。
⁷ 我的眼睛因憂愁昏花，
　我的百體好像影兒。
⁸ 正直人因此必驚奇，
　無辜的人要興起攻擊不敬虔之輩。
⁹ 然而義人
　要持守所行的道；
　手潔的人
　要力上加力。

¹⁰ "至於你們眾人，可以再來辯論吧！
　你們中間，我找不着一個智慧人。
¹¹ 我的日子已經過了，
　我的謀算、我心所想望的
　　已經斷絕。
¹² 他們以黑夜為白晝，說：
　'亮光近乎黑暗。'

¹³ 我若盼望陰間為我的房屋，
　若下榻在黑暗中，
¹⁴ 若對朽壞說：'你是我的父'，
　對蟲說：'你是我的母親姐妹'，
¹⁵ 這樣，我的指望在哪裏呢？
　我所指望的誰能看見呢？
¹⁶ 等到安息在塵土中，
　這指望必下到
　　陰間的門閂那裏了。"

比勒達發言

18

書亞人比勒達回答說：

² "你尋索言語要到幾時呢？
　你可以揣摩思想，然後我們就說話。
³ 我們為何算為畜生，
　在你眼中看作污穢呢？
⁴ 你這惱怒將自己撕裂的，
　難道大地為你見棄，
　磐石挪開原處嗎？

⁵ "惡人的亮光必要熄滅，
　他的火焰必不照耀。

²Surely mockers surround me;
　my eyes must dwell on their hostility.

³"Give me, O God, the pledge you demand.
　Who else will put up security for me?

⁴You have closed their minds to understanding;
　therefore you will not let them triumph.
⁵If a man denounces his friends for reward,
　the eyes of his children will fail.

⁶"God has made me a byword to everyone,
　a man in whose face people spit.
⁷My eyes have grown dim with grief;
　my whole frame is but a shadow.
⁸Upright men are appalled at this;
　the innocent are aroused against the ungodly.
⁹Nevertheless, the righteous will hold to their
　　ways,
　and those with clean hands will grow
　　stronger.

¹⁰"But come on, all of you, try again!
　I will not find a wise man among you.
¹¹My days have passed, my plans are
　　shattered,
　and so are the desires of my heart.
¹²These men turn night into day;
　in the face of darkness they say, 'Light is
　　near.'

¹³If the only home I hope for is the grave,ᵃ
　if I spread out my bed in darkness,
¹⁴if I say to corruption, 'You are my father,'
　and to the worm, 'My mother' or 'My sister,'
¹⁵where then is my hope?
　Who can see any hope for me?
¹⁶Will it go down to the gates of deathᵇ?
　Will we descend together into the dust?"

Bildad

18

Then Bildad the Shuhite replied:

²"When will you end these speeches?
　Be sensible, and then we can talk.
³Why are we regarded as cattle
　and considered stupid in your sight?
⁴You who tear yourself to pieces in your anger,
　is the earth to be abandoned for your sake?
　Or must the rocks be moved from their
　　place?

⁵"The lamp of the wicked is snuffed out;
　the flame of his fire stops burning.

a 13 Hebrew Sheol　　b 16 Hebrew Sheol

⁶The light in his tent becomes dark;
　the lamp beside him goes out.
⁷The vigor of his step is weakened;
　his own schemes throw him down.
⁸His feet thrust him into a net
　and he wanders into its mesh.
⁹A trap seizes him by the heel;
　a snare holds him fast.
¹⁰A noose is hidden for him on the ground;
　a trap lies in his path.
¹¹Terrors startle him on every side
　and dog his every step.
¹²Calamity is hungry for him;
　disaster is ready for him when he falls.
¹³It eats away parts of his skin;
　death's firstborn devours his limbs.
¹⁴He is torn from the security of his tent
　and marched off to the king of terrors.
¹⁵Fire resides*a* in his tent;
　burning sulfur is scattered over his dwelling.
¹⁶His roots dry up below
　and his branches wither above.
¹⁷The memory of him perishes from the earth;
　he has no name in the land.
¹⁸He is driven from light into darkness
　and is banished from the world.
¹⁹He has no offspring or descendants among his
　people,
　no survivor where once he lived.
²⁰Men of the west are appalled at his fate;
　men of the east are seized with horror.
²¹Surely such is the dwelling of an evil man;
　such is the place of one who knows not
　God."

Job

19

Then Job replied:

²"How long will you torment me
　and crush me with words?
³Ten times now you have reproached me;
　shamelessly you attack me.
⁴If it is true that I have gone astray,
　my error remains my concern alone.
⁵If indeed you would exalt yourselves above me
　and use my humiliation against me,
⁶then know that God has wronged me
　and drawn his net around me.

⁷"Though I cry, 'I've been wronged!' I get no
　response;
　though I call for help, there is no justice.
⁸He has blocked my way so I cannot pass;
　he has shrouded my paths in darkness.

a 15 Or Nothing he had remains

⁶他帳棚中的亮光要變為黑暗，
　他以上的燈也必熄滅。
⁷他堅強的腳步必見狹窄，
　自己的計謀必將他絆倒。
⁸因為他被自己的腳陷入網中，
　走在纏人的網羅上。
⁹圈套必抓住他的腳跟，
　機關必擒獲他。
¹⁰活扣為他藏在土內，
　翻絆為他藏在路上。
¹¹四面的驚嚇要使他害怕，
　並且追趕他的腳跟。
¹²他的力量必因飢餓衰敗；
　禍患要在他旁邊等候。
¹³他本身的肢體要被吞吃，
　死亡的長子要吞吃他的肢體。
¹⁴他要從所倚靠的帳棚被拔出來，
　帶到驚嚇的王那裏。
¹⁵不屬他的，必住在他的帳棚裏，
　硫磺必撒在他所住之處。
¹⁶下邊，他的根本要枯乾；
　上邊，他的枝子要剪除。
¹⁷他的記念在地上必然滅亡；
　他的名字在街上也不存留。
¹⁸他必從光明中被攆到黑暗裏，
　必被趕出世界。
¹⁹在本民中必無子無孫；
　在寄居之地
　也無一人存留。
²⁰以後來的，要驚奇他的日子，
　好像以前去的，受了驚駭。
²¹不義之人的住處總是這樣；
　此乃不認識神之人的地步。"

約伯回答

19

約伯回答說：

²"你們攪擾我的心，
　用言語壓碎我，要到幾時呢？
³你們這十次羞辱我，
　你們苦待我也不以為恥。
⁴果真我有錯，
　這錯乃是在我。
⁵你們果然要向我誇大，
　以我的羞辱為證指責我；
⁶就該知道是神傾覆我，
　用網羅圍繞我。

⁷"我因委曲呼叫，
　卻不蒙應允；
　我呼求，卻不得公斷。
⁸神用籬笆攔住我的道路，
　使我不得經過，
　又使我的路徑黑暗。

⁹他剝去我的榮光，
　摘去我頭上的冠冕。
¹⁰他在四圍攻擊我，
　我便歸於死亡，
　將我的指望如樹拔出來。
¹¹他的忿怒向我發作，
　以我為敵人。
¹²他的軍旅一齊上來，
　修築戰路攻擊我，
　在我帳棚的四圍安營。

¹³"他把我的弟兄隔在遠處，
　使我所認識的
　全然與我生疏。
¹⁴我的親戚與我斷絕，
　我的密友都忘記我。
¹⁵在我家寄居的和我的使女
　都以我為外人；
　我在他們眼中看為外邦人。
¹⁶我呼喚僕人，
　雖用口求他，
　他還是不回答。
¹⁷我口的氣味，我妻子厭惡，
　我的懇求，我同胞也憎嫌。
¹⁸連小孩子也藐視我；
　我若起來，他們都嘲笑我。
¹⁹我的密友都憎惡我；
　我平日所愛的人向我翻臉。
²⁰我的皮肉緊貼骨頭，
　我只剩牙皮逃脫了。

²¹"我朋友啊，可憐我！可憐我！
　因為神的手攻擊我。
²²你們為甚麼彷彿神逼迫我，
　吃我的肉還以為不足呢？

²³"惟願我的言語現在寫上，
　都記錄在書上；
²⁴用鐵筆鐫刻，
　用鉛灌在磐石上，
　直存到永遠。
²⁵我知道我的救贖主活着，
　末了必站立在地上。
²⁶我這皮肉滅絕之後，
　我必在肉體之外得見神。
²⁷我自己要見他，
　親眼要看他，並不像外人。
　我的心腸在我裏面消滅了。

⁹He has stripped me of my honor
　and removed the crown from my head.
¹⁰He tears me down on every side till I am
　gone;
　he uproots my hope like a tree.
¹¹His anger burns against me;
　he counts me among his enemies.
¹²His troops advance in force;
　they build a siege ramp against me
　and encamp around my tent.

¹³"He has alienated my brothers from me;
　my acquaintances are completely estranged
　from me.
¹⁴My kinsmen have gone away;
　my friends have forgotten me.
¹⁵My guests and my maidservants count me a
　stranger;
　they look upon me as an alien.
¹⁶I summon my servant, but he does not
　answer,
　though I beg him with my own mouth.
¹⁷My breath is offensive to my wife;
　I am loathsome to my own brothers.
¹⁸Even the little boys scorn me;
　when I appear, they ridicule me.
¹⁹All my intimate friends detest me;
　those I love have turned against me.
²⁰I am nothing but skin and bones;
　I have escaped with only the skin of my
　teeth.[a]

²¹"Have pity on me, my friends, have pity,
　for the hand of God has struck me.
²²Why do you pursue me as God does?
　Will you never get enough of my flesh?

²³"Oh, that my words were recorded,
　that they were written on a scroll,
²⁴that they were inscribed with an iron tool on[b]
　lead,
　or engraved in rock forever!
²⁵I know that my Redeemer[c] lives,
　and that in the end he will stand upon the
　earth.[d]
²⁶And after my skin has been destroyed,
　yet[e] in[f] my flesh I will see God;
²⁷I myself will see him
　with my own eyes—I, and not another.
　How my heart yearns within me!

a 20 Or only my gums   b 24 Or and   c 25 Or defender
d 25 Or upon my grave   e 26 Or And after I awake, / though this
(body) has been destroyed, / then   f 26 Or / apart from

²⁸"If you say, 'How we will hound him,
 since the root of the trouble lies in him,^a'
²⁹you should fear the sword yourselves;
 for wrath will bring punishment by the sword,
 and then you will know that there is
 judgment.^b "

Zophar

²⁸"你們若説'我們逼迫他要何等的
　　重呢？惹事的根乃在乎他'，
²⁹你們就當懼怕刀劍，
　　因為忿怒惹動刀劍的刑罰，
　　使你們知道有報應（註：原文作"審
　　判"）。"

瑣法回答

20 Then Zophar the Naamathite replied:

²"My troubled thoughts prompt me to
 answer
 because I am greatly disturbed.
³I hear a rebuke that dishonors me,
 and my understanding inspires me to reply.

20 拿瑪人瑣法回答説：

²"我心中急躁，
　　所以我的思念
　　叫我回答。
³我已聽見那羞辱我、責備我的話，
　　我的悟性叫我回答！

⁴"Surely you know how it has been from of old,
 ever since man^c was placed on the earth,
⁵that the mirth of the wicked is brief,
 the joy of the godless lasts but a moment.
⁶Though his pride reaches to the heavens
 and his head touches the clouds,
⁷he will perish forever, like his own dung;
 those who have seen him will say, 'Where is
 he?'
⁸Like a dream he flies away, no more to be found,
 banished like a vision of the night.
⁹The eye that saw him will not see him again;
 his place will look on him no more.
¹⁰His children must make amends to the poor;
 his own hands must give back his wealth.
¹¹The youthful vigor that fills his bones
 will lie with him in the dust.

⁴"你豈不知亙古以來，
　　自從人生在地，
⁵惡人誇勝是暫時的，
　　不敬虔人的喜樂不過轉眼之間嗎？
⁶他的尊榮雖達到天上，
　　頭雖頂到雲中，
⁷他終必滅亡，像自己的糞一樣；
　　素來見他的人要説：
　　'他在哪裏呢？'
⁸他必飛去如夢，不再尋見；
　　速被趕去，如夜間的異象。
⁹親眼見過他的必不再見他；
　　他的本處也再見不着他。
¹⁰他的兒女要求窮人的恩，
　　他的手要賠還不義之財。
¹¹他的骨頭雖然有青年之力，
　　卻要和他一同躺臥在塵土中。

¹²"Though evil is sweet in his mouth
 and he hides it under his tongue,
¹³though he cannot bear to let it go
 and keeps it in his mouth,
¹⁴yet his food will turn sour in his stomach;
 it will become the venom of serpents within
 him.
¹⁵He will spit out the riches he swallowed;
 God will make his stomach vomit them up.
¹⁶He will suck the poison of serpents;
 the fangs of an adder will kill him.
¹⁷He will not enjoy the streams,
 the rivers flowing with honey and cream.
¹⁸What he toiled for he must give back uneaten;
 he will not enjoy the profit from his trading.
¹⁹For he has oppressed the poor and left them
 destitute;
 he has seized houses he did not build.

¹²"他口內雖以惡為甘甜，
　　藏在舌頭底下，
¹³愛戀不捨，
　　含在口中；
¹⁴他的食物在肚裏卻要化為酸，
　　在他裏面
　　成為虺蛇的惡毒。
¹⁵他吞了財寶，還要吐出；
　　神要從他腹中掏出來。
¹⁶他必吸飲虺蛇的毒氣，
　　蝮蛇的舌頭也必殺他。
¹⁷流奶與蜜之河，
　　他不得再見。
¹⁸他勞碌得來的要賠還，
　　不得享用（註：原文作"吞下"），
　　不能照所得的財貨歡樂。
¹⁹他欺壓窮人，且又離棄，
　　強取非自己所蓋的房屋（註：或作
　　"強取房屋不得再建造"）。

a 28 Many Hebrew manuscripts, Septuagint and Vulgate;
most Hebrew manuscripts me
b 29 Or / that you may come to know the Almighty　c 4 Or Adam

²⁰「他因貪而無厭，
　　所喜悦的
　　連一樣也不能保守。
²¹其餘的沒有一樣他不吞滅，
　　所以他的福樂不能長久。
²²他在滿足有餘的時候，
　　必到狹窄的地步；
　　凡受苦楚的人，
　　都必加手在他身上。
²³他正要充滿肚腹的時候，
　　神必將猛烈的忿怒降在他身上；
　　正在他吃飯的時候，
　　要將這忿怒像雨降在他身上。
²⁴他要躲避鐵器，
　　銅弓的箭要將他射透。
²⁵他把箭一抽，就從他身上出來；
　　發光的箭頭從他膽中出來，
　　有驚惶臨在他身上。
²⁶他的財寶歸於黑暗，
　　人所不吹的火，要把他燒滅；
　　要把他帳棚中所剩下的燒燬。
²⁷天要顯明他的罪孽，
　　地要興起攻擊他。
²⁸他的家產必然過去，
　　神發怒的日子，他的貨物都要消滅。
²⁹這是惡人從神所得的分，
　　是神為他所定的產業。」

約伯答辯

21

²⁰"Surely he will have no respite from his
　　craving;
　　he cannot save himself by his treasure.
²¹Nothing is left for him to devour;
　　his prosperity will not endure.
²²In the midst of his plenty, distress will
　　overtake him;
　　the full force of misery will come upon
　　him.
²³When he has filled his belly,
　　God will vent his burning anger against
　　him
　　and rain down his blows upon him.
²⁴Though he flees from an iron weapon,
　　a bronze-tipped arrow pierces him.
²⁵He pulls it out of his back,
　　the gleaming point out of his liver.
　　Terrors will come over him;
²⁶　total darkness lies in wait for his treasures.
　　A fire unfanned will consume him
　　and devour what is left in his tent.
²⁷The heavens will expose his guilt;
　　the earth will rise up against him.
²⁸A flood will carry off his house,
　　rushing waters[a] on the day of God's wrath.
²⁹Such is the fate God allots the wicked,
　　the heritage appointed for them by God."

Job

21

約伯回答説：

²"你們要細聽我的言語，
　　就算是你們安慰我的。
³請寬容我，我又要説話；
　　説了以後，任憑你們嗤笑吧！

⁴「我豈是向人訴冤，
　　為何不焦急呢？
⁵你們要看着我而驚奇，
　　用手搗口。
⁶我每逢思想，心就驚惶，
　　渾身戰兢。
⁷惡人為何存活，
　　享大壽數，勢力強盛呢？
⁸他們眼見
　　兒孫和他們
　　一同堅立。
⁹他們的家宅平安無懼；
　　神的杖也不加在他們身上。
¹⁰他們的公牛孳生而不斷絕；
　　母牛下犢而不掉胎。

Then Job replied:

²"Listen carefully to my words;
　　let this be the consolation you give me.
³Bear with me while I speak,
　　and after I have spoken, mock on.

⁴"Is my complaint directed to man?
　　Why should I not be impatient?
⁵Look at me and be astonished;
　　clap your hand over your mouth.
⁶When I think about this, I am terrified;
　　trembling seizes my body.
⁷Why do the wicked live on,
　　growing old and increasing in power?
⁸They see their children established around
　　them,
　　their offspring before their eyes.
⁹Their homes are safe and free from fear;
　　the rod of God is not upon them.
¹⁰Their bulls never fail to breed;
　　their cows calve and do not miscarry.

*a 28 Or The possessions in his house will be carried off, / washed
away*

11They send forth their children as a flock;
 their little ones dance about.
12They sing to the music of tambourine and
 harp;
 they make merry to the sound of the flute.
13They spend their years in prosperity
 and go down to the grave^a in peace.^{b}
14Yet they say to God, 'Leave us alone!
 We have no desire to know your ways.
15Who is the Almighty, that we should serve
 him?
 What would we gain by praying to him?'
16But their prosperity is not in their own hands,
 so I stand aloof from the counsel of the
 wicked.

17"Yet how often is the lamp of the wicked
 snuffed out?
 How often does calamity come upon them,
 the fate God allots in his anger?
18How often are they like straw before the
 wind,
 like chaff swept away by a gale?
19It is said, 'God stores up a man's
 punishment for his sons.'
 Let him repay the man himself, so that he
 will know it!
20Let his own eyes see his destruction;
 let him drink of the wrath of the Almighty.^{c}
21For what does he care about the family he
 leaves behind
 when his allotted months come to an end?

22"Can anyone teach knowledge to God,
 since he judges even the highest?
23One man dies in full vigor,
 completely secure and at ease,
24his body^d well nourished,
 his bones rich with marrow.
25Another man dies in bitterness of soul,
 never having enjoyed anything good.
26Side by side they lie in the dust,
 and worms cover them both.

27"I know full well what you are thinking,
 the schemes by which you would wrong me.
28You say, 'Where now is the great man's
 house,
 the tents where wicked men lived?'
29Have you never questioned those who travel?
 Have you paid no regard to their accounts—

11他們打發小孩子出去,多如羊羣,
 他們的兒女踊躍跳舞。
12他們隨着琴鼓歌唱,
 又因簫聲歡喜。
13他們度日諸事亨通,
 轉眼下入陰間。
14他們對神說:「離開我們吧!
 我們不願曉得你的道。
15全能者是誰,
 我們何必侍奉他呢?
 求告他有甚麼益處呢?」
16看哪,他們亨通不在乎自己,
 惡人所謀定的
  離我好遠。

17「惡人的燈何嘗熄滅?
 患難何嘗臨到他們呢?
 神何嘗發怒,
 向他們分散災禍呢?
18他們何嘗像風前的碎稭,
 如暴風颳去的糠粃呢?
19你們說:『神為惡人的兒女
 積蓄罪孽。』
 我說:『不如本人受報,
 好使他親自知道。』
20願他親眼看見自己敗亡,
 親自飲全能者的忿怒。
21他的歲月既盡,
 他還顧他本家嗎?

22「神既審判那在高位的,
 誰能將知識教訓他呢?
23有人至死身體強壯,
 盡得平靖安逸,
24他的奶桶充滿,
 他的骨髓滋潤。
25有人至死心中痛苦,
 終身未嘗福樂的滋味。
26他們一樣躺臥在塵土中,
 都被蟲子遮蓋。

27「我知道你們的意思,
 並誣害我的計謀。
28你們說:
 『霸者的房屋在哪裏?
 惡人住過的帳棚在哪裏?』
29你們豈沒有詢問過路的人嗎?
 不知道他們所引的證據嗎?

a 13 Hebrew *Sheol* *b* 13 Or *in an instant* *c* 17-20 Verses 17
and 18 may be taken as exclamations and 19 and 20 as
declarations. *d* 24 The meaning of the Hebrew for this word
is uncertain.

³⁰就是惡人
　　在禍患的日子得存留，
　　在發怒的日子得逃脫。
³¹他所行的，有誰當面給他說明？
　　他所做的，有誰報應他呢？
³²然而他要被抬到塋地，
　　並有人看守墳墓。
³³他要以谷中的土塊為甘甜，
　　在他以先去的無數，
　　在他以後去的更多。

³⁴「你們對答的話中既都錯謬，
　　怎麼徒然安慰我呢？」

以利法回答

22 提幔人以利法回答說：

²「人豈能使神有益呢？
　　智慧人但能有益於己。
³你為人公義，
　　豈叫全能者喜悅呢？
　　你行為完全，
　　豈能使他得利呢？

⁴「豈是因你敬畏他，
　　就責備你、審判你嗎？
⁵你的罪惡豈不是大嗎？
　　你的罪孽也沒有窮盡。
⁶因你無故強取弟兄的物
　　為當頭，
　　剝去貧寒人的衣服。

⁷困乏的人，你沒有給他水喝；
　　飢餓的人，你沒有給他食物。
⁸有能力的人
　　就得地土，
　　尊貴的人也住在其中。
⁹你打發寡婦空手回去，
　　折斷孤兒的膀臂。
¹⁰因此，有網羅環繞你，
　　有恐懼忽然使你驚惶，
¹¹或有黑暗蒙蔽你，
　　並有洪水淹沒你。

¹²「神豈不是在高天嗎？
　　你看星宿何其高呢？
¹³你說：『神知道甚麼？
　　他豈能看透幽暗施行審判呢？
¹⁴密雲將他遮蓋，使他不能看見；
　　他周遊穹蒼。』

³⁰that the evil man is spared from the day of
　　calamity,
　　that he is delivered from^a the day of wrath?
³¹Who denounces his conduct to his face?
　　Who repays him for what he has done?
³²He is carried to the grave,
　　and watch is kept over his tomb.
³³The soil in the valley is sweet to him;
　　all men follow after him,
　　and a countless throng goes^b before him.

³⁴"So how can you console me with your
　　nonsense?
　　Nothing is left of your answers but
　　falsehood!"

Eliphaz

22 Then Eliphaz the Temanite replied:

²"Can a man be of benefit to God?
　　Can even a wise man benefit him?
³What pleasure would it give the Almighty if
　　you were righteous?
　　What would he gain if your ways were
　　blameless?

⁴"Is it for your piety that he rebukes you
　　and brings charges against you?
⁵Is not your wickedness great?
　　Are not your sins endless?
⁶You demanded security from your brothers for
　　no reason;
　　you stripped men of their clothing, leaving
　　them naked.
⁷You gave no water to the weary
　　and you withheld food from the hungry,
⁸though you were a powerful man, owning
　　land—
　　an honored man, living on it.
⁹And you sent widows away empty-handed
　　and broke the strength of the fatherless.
¹⁰That is why snares are all around you,
　　why sudden peril terrifies you,
¹¹why it is so dark you cannot see,
　　and why a flood of water covers you.

¹²"Is not God in the heights of heaven?
　　And see how lofty are the highest stars!
¹³Yet you say, 'What does God know?
　　Does he judge through such darkness?
¹⁴Thick clouds veil him, so he does not see us
　　as he goes about in the vaulted heavens.'

*a 30 Or man is reserved for the day of calamity, / that he is brought
forth to*　　*b 33 Or / as a countless throng went*

15Will you keep to the old path
　　that evil men have trod?
16They were carried off before their time,
　　their foundations washed away by a flood.
17They said to God, 'Leave us alone!
　　What can the Almighty do to us?'
18Yet it was he who filled their houses with
　　　good things,
　　so I stand aloof from the counsel of the
　　　wicked.

19"The righteous see their ruin and rejoice;
　　the innocent mock them, saying,
20'Surely our foes are destroyed,
　　and fire devours their wealth.'

21"Submit to God and be at peace with him;
　　in this way prosperity will come to you.
22Accept instruction from his mouth
　　and lay up his words in your heart.
23If you return to the Almighty, you will be
　　　restored:
　　If you remove wickedness far from your tent
24and assign your nuggets to the dust,
　　your gold of Ophir to the rocks in the
　　　ravines,
25then the Almighty will be your gold,
　　the choicest silver for you.
26Surely then you will find delight in the
　　　Almighty
　　and will lift up your face to God.
27You will pray to him, and he will hear you,
　　and you will fulfill your vows.
28What you decide on will be done,
　　and light will shine on your ways.
29When men are brought low and you say, 'Lift
　　　them up!'
　　then he will save the downcast.
30He will deliver even one who is not innocent,
　　who will be delivered through the cleanness
　　　of your hands."

Job

23　Then Job replied:

2"Even today my complaint is bitter;
　　his hand*a* is heavy in spite of*b* my groaning.
3If only I knew where to find him;
　　if only I could go to his dwelling!
4I would state my case before him
　　and fill my mouth with arguments.
5I would find out what he would answer me,
　　and consider what he would say.

15你要依從上古的道嗎？
　　這道是惡人所行的。
16他們未到死期，忽然除滅，
　　根基毀壞，好像被江河沖去。
17他們向神說：'離開我們吧！'
　　又說：'全能者能把我們
　　　怎麼樣呢？'
18哪知神以美物充滿他們的房屋；
　　但惡人所謀定的
　　　離我好遠。

19"義人看見他們的結局就歡喜，
　　無辜的人嗤笑他們，
20說：'那起來攻擊我們的，
　　果然被剪除，
　　其餘的都被火燒滅。'

21"你要認識神，就得平安；
　　福氣也必臨到你。
22你當領受他口中的教訓，
　　將他的言語存在心裏。
23你若歸向全能者，
　　從你帳棚中遠除不義，
　　就必得建立。
24要將你的珍寶丟在塵土裏，
　　將俄斐的黃金
　　　丟在溪河石頭之間，
25全能者就必為你的珍寶，
　　作你的寶銀。
26你就要
　　以全能者為喜樂，
　　向神仰起臉來。
27你要禱告他，他就聽你；
　　你也要還你的願。
28你定意要做何事，必然給你成就；
　　亮光也必照耀你的路。
29人使你降卑，
　　你仍可說：'必得高升。'
　　謙卑的人，神必然拯救。
30人非無辜，神且要搭救他，
　　他因你手中清潔，
　　必蒙拯救。"

約伯發言

23　約伯回答說：

2"如今我的哀告還算為悖逆；
　　我的責罰比我的唉哼還重。
3惟願我能知道在哪裏可以尋見神，
　　能到他的臺前，
4我就在他面前將我的案件陳明，
　　滿口辯白。
5我必知道他回答我的言語，
　　明白他向我所說的話。

a 2 Septuagint and Syriac; Hebrew / the hand on me　　b 2 Or
heavy on me in

6他豈用大能與我爭辯嗎？
　　必不這樣！他必理會我。
7在他那裏，
　　正直人可以與他辯論；
　　這樣，我必永遠脫離
　　　那審判我的。

8 "只是我往前行，他不在那裏；
　　往後退，也不能見他。
9他在左邊行事，
　　我卻不能看見；
　　在右邊隱藏，
　　我也不能見他。
10然而他知道我所行的路，
　　他試煉我之後，
　　我必如精金。
11我腳追隨他的步履，
　　我謹守他的道，並不偏離。
12他嘴唇的命令
　　我未曾背棄，
　　我看重他口中的言語，
　　過於我需用的飲食。

13 "只是他心志已定，
　　誰能使他轉意呢？
　　他心裏所願的，就行出來。
14他向我所定的，就必做成；
　　這類的事他還有許多。
15所以我在他面前驚惶，
　　我思念這事，便懼怕他。
16神使我喪膽，
　　全能者使我驚惶。
17我的恐懼，不是因為黑暗，
　　也不是因為幽暗蒙蔽我的臉。

24 "全能者
　　既定期罰惡，
　　為何不使認識他的人
　　看見那日子呢？
2有人挪移地界，
　　搶奪羣畜而牧養。
3他們拉去孤兒的驢，
　　強取寡婦的牛為當頭。
4他們使窮人離開正道，
　　世上的貧民盡都隱藏。
5這些貧窮人如同野驢出到曠野，
　　殷勤尋找食物。
　　他們靠着野地
　　給兒女餬口；
6收割別人田間的禾稼，
　　摘取惡人餘剩的葡萄。
7終夜赤身無衣，
　　天氣寒冷
　　毫無遮蓋。
8在山上被大雨淋濕，
　　因沒有避身之處就挨近磐石。

6Would he oppose me with great power?
　　No, he would not press charges against me.
7There an upright man could present his case
　　before him,
　　and I would be delivered forever from my
　　　judge.

8"But if I go to the east, he is not there;
　　if I go to the west, I do not find him.
9When he is at work in the north, I do not see
　　him;
　　when he turns to the south, I catch no
　　　glimpse of him.
10But he knows the way that I take;
　　when he has tested me, I will come forth as
　　　gold.
11My feet have closely followed his steps;
　　I have kept to his way without turning aside.
12I have not departed from the commands of his
　　lips;
　　I have treasured the words of his mouth
　　　more than my daily bread.

13"But he stands alone, and who can oppose
　　him?
　　He does whatever he pleases.
14He carries out his decree against me,
　　and many such plans he still has in store.
15That is why I am terrified before him;
　　when I think of all this, I fear him.
16God has made my heart faint;
　　the Almighty has terrified me.
17Yet I am not silenced by the darkness,
　　by the thick darkness that covers my face.

24 "Why does the Almighty not set times
　　for judgment?
　　Why must those who know him look in
　　vain for such days?
2Men move boundary stones;
　　they pasture flocks they have stolen.
3They drive away the orphan's donkey
　　and take the widow's ox in pledge.
4They thrust the needy from the path
　　and force all the poor of the land into hiding.
5Like wild donkeys in the desert,
　　the poor go about their labor of foraging food;
　　the wasteland provides food for their
　　　children.
6They gather fodder in the fields
　　and glean in the vineyards of the wicked.
7Lacking clothes, they spend the night naked;
　　they have nothing to cover themselves in the
　　　cold.
8They are drenched by mountain rains
　　and hug the rocks for lack of shelter.

14And these are but the outer fringe of his works;
how faint the whisper we hear of him!
Who then can understand the thunder of his power?"

27

And Job continued his discourse:

2"As surely as God lives, who has denied me justice,
the Almighty, who has made me taste bitterness of soul,
3as long as I have life within me,
the breath of God in my nostrils,
4my lips will not speak wickedness,
and my tongue will utter no deceit.
5I will never admit you are in the right;
till I die, I will not deny my integrity.
6I will maintain my righteousness and never let go of it;
my conscience will not reproach me as long as I live.

7"May my enemies be like the wicked,
my adversaries like the unjust!
8For what hope has the godless when he is cut off,
when God takes away his life?
9Does God listen to his cry
when distress comes upon him?
10Will he find delight in the Almighty?
Will he call upon God at all times?

11"I will teach you about the power of God;
the ways of the Almighty I will not conceal.
12You have all seen this yourselves.
Why then this meaningless talk?

13"Here is the fate God allots to the wicked,
the heritage a ruthless man receives from the Almighty:
14However many his children, their fate is the sword;
his offspring will never have enough to eat.
15The plague will bury those who survive him,
and their widows will not weep for them.
16Though he heaps up silver like dust
and clothes like piles of clay,
17what he lays up the righteous will wear,
and the innocent will divide his silver.
18The house he builds is like a moth's cocoon,
like a hut made by a watchman.
19He lies down wealthy, but will do so no more;
when he opens his eyes, all is gone.

14看哪，
這不過是神工作的些微，
我們所聽於他的是何等細微的聲音！
他大能的雷聲
誰能明透呢？"

27

約伯接着說：

2"神奪去我的理，
全能者使我心中愁苦。
我指着永生的神起誓：
3（我的生命尚在我裏面，
神所賜呼吸之氣仍在我的鼻孔內。）
4我的嘴決不說非義之言；
我的舌也不說詭詐之語。
5我斷不以你們為是；
我至死必不以自己為不正。
6我持定我的義，
必不放鬆；
在世的日子，
我心必不責備我。

7"願我的仇敵如惡人一樣，
願那起來攻擊我的，
如不義之人一般。
8不敬虔的人雖然得利，
神奪取其命的時候，
還有甚麼指望呢？
9患難臨到他，
神豈能聽他的呼求？
10他豈以全能者為樂，
隨時求告神呢？

11"神的作為，我要指教你們；
全能者所行的，我也不隱瞞。
12你們自己也都見過，
為何全然變為虛妄呢？

13"神為惡人所定的分，
強暴人從全能者所得的報（註："報"
原文作"產業"）乃是這樣：
14倘或他的兒女增多，
還是被刀所殺；
他的子孫必不得飽食。
15他所遺留的人必死而埋葬，
他的寡婦也不哀哭。
16他雖積蓄銀子如塵沙，
預備衣服如泥土，
17他只管預備，義人卻要穿上；
他的銀子，無辜的人要分取。
18他建造房屋如蟲做窩，
又如守望者所搭的棚。
19他雖富足躺臥，卻不得收殮，
轉眼之間就不在了。

²⁰驚恐如波濤將他追上；
　暴風在夜間將他颳去。
²¹東風把他飄去，
　又颳他離開本處。
²²神要向他射箭，並不留情；
　他恨不得逃脫神的手。
²³人要向他拍掌，
　並要發叱聲，使他離開本處。

28 “銀子有礦，
　　　煉金有方。
²鐵從地裏挖出，
　銅從石中熔化。
³人為黑暗定界限，
　查究幽暗陰翳的石頭，
　直到極處。
⁴在無人居住之處刨開礦穴，
　過路的人也想不到他們；
　又與人遠離，懸在空中搖來搖去。
⁵至於地，能出糧食，
　地內好像被火翻起來。
⁶地中的石頭有藍寶石，
　並有金沙。
⁷礦中的路鷙鳥不得知道，
　鷹眼也未見過。
⁸狂傲的野獸未曾行過；
　猛烈的獅子也未曾經過。
⁹人伸手鑿開堅石，
　傾倒山根。
¹⁰在磐石中鑿出水道，
　親眼看見各樣寶物。
¹¹他封閉水不得滴流，
　使隱藏的物顯露出來。

¹² “然而，智慧有何處可尋？
　聰明之處在哪裏呢？
¹³智慧的價值無人能知，
　在活人之地也無處可尋。
¹⁴深淵說：‘不在我內！’
　滄海說：‘不在我中！’
¹⁵智慧非用黃金可得，
　也不能平白銀為它的價值。
¹⁶俄斐金和貴重的紅瑪瑙，
　並藍寶石，不足與較量。
¹⁷黃金和玻璃不足與比較，
　精金的器皿不足與兌換。
¹⁸珊瑚、水晶都不足論，
　智慧的價值勝過珍珠 (註：或作
　“紅寶石”)。
¹⁹古實的紅璧璽不足與比較，
　精金也不足與較量。
²⁰ “智慧從何處來呢？
　聰明之處在哪裏呢？

²⁰Terrors overtake him like a flood;
　a tempest snatches him away in the night.
²¹The east wind carries him off, and he is gone;
　it sweeps him out of his place.
²²It hurls itself against him without mercy
　as he flees headlong from its power.
²³It claps its hands in derision
　and hisses him out of his place.

28 “There is a mine for silver
　　　and a place where gold is refined.
²Iron is taken from the earth,
　and copper is smelted from ore.
³Man puts an end to the darkness;
　he searches the farthest recesses
　for ore in the blackest darkness.
⁴Far from where people dwell he cuts a shaft,
　in places forgotten by the foot of man;
　far from men he dangles and sways.
⁵The earth, from which food comes,
　is transformed below as by fire;
⁶sapphires[a] come from its rocks,
　and its dust contains nuggets of gold.
⁷No bird of prey knows that hidden path,
　no falcon’s eye has seen it.
⁸Proud beasts do not set foot on it,
　and no lion prowls there.
⁹Man’s hand assaults the flinty rock
　and lays bare the roots of the mountains.
¹⁰He tunnels through the rock;
　his eyes see all its treasures.
¹¹He searches[b] the sources of the rivers
　and brings hidden things to light.

¹²“But where can wisdom be found?
　Where does understanding dwell?
¹³Man does not comprehend its worth;
　it cannot be found in the land of the living.
¹⁴The deep says, ‘It is not in me’;
　the sea says, ‘It is not with me.’
¹⁵It cannot be bought with the finest gold,
　nor can its price be weighed in silver.
¹⁶It cannot be bought with the gold of Ophir,
　with precious onyx or sapphires.
¹⁷Neither gold nor crystal can compare with it,
　nor can it be had for jewels of gold.
¹⁸Coral and jasper are not worthy of mention;
　the price of wisdom is beyond rubies.
¹⁹The topaz of Cush cannot compare with it;
　it cannot be bought with pure gold.

²⁰“Where then does wisdom come from?
　Where does understanding dwell?

*a 6 Or lapis lazuli; also in verse 16　b 11 Septuagint, Aquila
and Vulgate; Hebrew He dams up*

²¹It is hidden from the eyes of every living thing,
    concealed even from the birds of the air.
²²Destruction^a and Death say,
    'Only a rumor of it has reached our ears.'
²³God understands the way to it
    and he alone knows where it dwells,
²⁴for he views the ends of the earth
    and sees everything under the heavens.
²⁵When he established the force of the wind
    and measured out the waters,
²⁶when he made a decree for the rain
    and a path for the thunderstorm,
²⁷then he looked at wisdom and appraised it;
    he confirmed it and tested it.
²⁸And he said to man,
    'The fear of the Lord—that is wisdom,
    and to shun evil is understanding.' "

29

Job continued his discourse:

²"How I long for the months gone by,
    for the days when God watched over me,
³when his lamp shone upon my head
    and by his light I walked through darkness!
⁴Oh, for the days when I was in my prime,
    when God's intimate friendship blessed my
      house,
⁵when the Almighty was still with me
    and my children were around me,
⁶when my path was drenched with cream
    and the rock poured out for me streams of
      olive oil.

⁷"When I went to the gate of the city
    and took my seat in the public square,
⁸the young men saw me and stepped aside
    and the old men rose to their feet;
⁹the chief men refrained from speaking
    and covered their mouths with their hands;
¹⁰the voices of the nobles were hushed,
    and their tongues stuck to the roof of their
      mouths.
¹¹Whoever heard me spoke well of me,
    and those who saw me commended me,
¹²because I rescued the poor who cried for help,
    and the fatherless who had none to assist
      him.
¹³The man who was dying blessed me;
    I made the widow's heart sing.
¹⁴I put on righteousness as my clothing;
    justice was my robe and my turban.
¹⁵I was eyes to the blind
    and feet to the lame.

²¹是向一切有生命的眼目隱藏，
    向空中的飛鳥掩蔽。
²²滅沒和死亡說：
    '我們風聞其名。'
²³神明白智慧的道路，
    曉得智慧的所在。
²⁴因他鑒察直到地極，
    遍觀普天之下。
²⁵要為風定輕重，
    又度量諸水。
²⁶他為雨露定命令，
    為雷電定道路。
²⁷那時他看見智慧，而且述說；
    他堅定，並且查究。
²⁸他對人說：
    '敬畏主就是智慧；
    遠離惡便是聰明！'"

29

約伯又接着說：

²"惟願我的景況如從前的月份，
    如神保守我的日子。
³那時他的燈照在我頭上，
    我藉他的光行過黑暗。
⁴我願如壯年的時候，
    那時我在帳棚中，
    神待我有密友之情；
⁵全能者仍與我同在，
    我的兒女都環繞我。
⁶奶多可洗我的腳，
    磐石為我出油成河。

⁷"我出到城門，
    在街上設立座位；
⁸少年人見我而迴避，
    老年人也起身站立；
⁹王子都停止說話，
    用手摀口；
¹⁰首領靜默無聲，
    舌頭貼住上膛。
¹¹耳朵聽我的，就稱我有福；
    眼睛看我的，便稱讚我；
¹²因我拯救
    哀求的困苦人
    和無人幫助的孤兒。
¹³將要滅亡的為我祝福；
    我也使寡婦心中歡樂。
¹⁴我以公義為衣服，
    以公平為外袍和冠冕。
¹⁵我為瞎子的眼，
    瘸子的腳。

^a 22 Hebrew *Abaddon*

¹⁶我為窮乏人的父，
　　素不認識的人，我查明他的案件。
¹⁷我打破不義之人的牙牀，
　　從他牙齒中奪了所搶的。

¹⁸"我便說，'我必死在家中（註：原
　　文作"窩中"），
　　必增添我的日子，多如塵沙。
¹⁹我的根長到水邊，
　　露水終夜霑在我的枝上。
²⁰我的榮耀在身上增新，
　　我的弓在手中日強'。

²¹"人聽見我而仰望，
　　靜默等候我的指教。
²²我說話之後，他們就不再說；
　　我的言語像雨露滴在他們身上。
²³他們仰望我如仰望雨，
　　又張開口如切慕春雨。
²⁴他們不敢自信，
　　我就向他們含笑；
　　他們不使我臉上的光改變。
²⁵我為他們選擇道路，又坐首位。
　　我如君王在軍隊中居住，
　　又如弔喪的安慰傷心的人。

30

"但如今，
比我年少的人戲笑我；
其人之父我曾藐視，
不肯安在看守我羊羣的狗中。
²他們壯年的氣力
　　既已衰敗，
　　其手之力與我何益呢？
³他們因窮乏飢餓，身體枯瘦，
　　在荒廢淒涼的幽暗中
　　齦乾燥之地，
⁴在草叢之中採鹹草，
　　羅騰的根為他們的食物（註："羅
　　騰"，小樹名，松類）。
⁵他們從人中被趕出，
　　人追喊他們如賊一般。
⁶以致他們住在荒谷之間，
　　在地洞和巖穴中，
⁷在草叢中叫喚，
　　在荊棘下聚集。
⁸這都是愚頑下賤人的兒女，
　　他們被鞭打，趕出境外。

⁹"現在這些人以我為歌曲，
　　以我為笑談。
¹⁰他們厭惡我，躲在旁邊站着，
　　不住地吐唾沫在我臉上。

¹⁶I was a father to the needy;
　　I took up the case of the stranger.
¹⁷I broke the fangs of the wicked
　　and snatched the victims from their teeth.

¹⁸"I thought, 'I will die in my own house,
　　my days as numerous as the grains of sand.
¹⁹My roots will reach to the water,
　　and the dew will lie all night on my branches.
²⁰My glory will remain fresh in me,
　　the bow ever new in my hand.'

²¹"Men listened to me expectantly,
　　waiting in silence for my counsel.
²²After I had spoken, they spoke no more;
　　my words fell gently on their ears.
²³They waited for me as for showers
　　and drank in my words as the spring rain.
²⁴When I smiled at them, they scarcely believed it;
　　the light of my face was precious to them.^a
²⁵I chose the way for them and sat as their chief;
　　I dwelt as a king among his troops;
　　I was like one who comforts mourners.

30

"But now they mock me,
men younger than I,
whose fathers I would have disdained
to put with my sheep dogs.
²Of what use was the strength of their hands to me,
　　since their vigor had gone from them?
³Haggard from want and hunger,
　　they roamed^b the parched land
　　in desolate wastelands at night.
⁴In the brush they gathered salt herbs,
　　and their food^c was the root of the broom tree.
⁵They were banished from their fellow men,
　　shouted at as if they were thieves.
⁶They were forced to live in the dry stream beds,
　　among the rocks and in holes in the ground.
⁷They brayed among the bushes
　　and huddled in the undergrowth.
⁸A base and nameless brood,
　　they were driven out of the land.

⁹"And now their sons mock me in song;
　　I have become a byword among them.
¹⁰They detest me and keep their distance;
　　they do not hesitate to spit in my face.

^a 24 The meaning of the Hebrew for this clause is uncertain.
^b 3 Or *gnawed*　　^c 4 Or *fuel*

¹¹Now that God has unstrung my bow and
    afflicted me,
  they throw off restraint in my presence.
¹²On my right the tribe^a attacks;
  they lay snares for my feet,
  they build their siege ramps against me.
¹³They break up my road;
  they succeed in destroying me—
  without anyone's helping them.^b
¹⁴They advance as through a gaping breach;
  amid the ruins they come rolling in.
¹⁵Terrors overwhelm me;
  my dignity is driven away as by the wind,
  my safety vanishes like a cloud.

¹⁶"And now my life ebbs away;
  days of suffering grip me.
¹⁷Night pierces my bones;
  my gnawing pains never rest.
¹⁸In his great power God becomes like
    clothing to me^c;
  he binds me like the neck of my garment.
¹⁹He throws me into the mud,
  and I am reduced to dust and ashes.

²⁰"I cry out to you, O God, but you do not
    answer;
  I stand up, but you merely look at me.
²¹You turn on me ruthlessly;
  with the might of your hand you attack me.
²²You snatch me up and drive me before the
    wind;
  you toss me about in the storm.
²³I know you will bring me down to death,
  to the place appointed for all the living.

²⁴"Surely no one lays a hand on a broken man
  when he cries for help in his distress.
²⁵Have I not wept for those in trouble?
  Has not my soul grieved for the poor?
²⁶Yet when I hoped for good, evil came;
  when I looked for light, then came darkness.
²⁷The churning inside me never stops;
  days of suffering confront me.
²⁸I go about blackened, but not by the sun;
  I stand up in the assembly and cry for help.
²⁹I have become a brother of jackals,
  a companion of owls.
³⁰My skin grows black and peels;
  my body burns with fever.
³¹My harp is tuned to mourning,
  and my flute to the sound of wailing.

---

a 12 The meaning of the Hebrew for this word is uncertain.
b 13 Or me. / 'No one can help him,' they say.   *c 18 Hebrew;*
Septuagint God grasps my clothing

¹¹鬆開他們的繩索
  苦待我，
  在我面前脫去韁頭。
¹²這等下流人在我右邊起來，
  推開我的腳，
  築成戰路來攻擊我。
¹³這些無人幫助的，
  毀壞我的道，
  加增我的災。
¹⁴他們來如同闖進大破口，
  在毀壞之間，滾在我身上。
¹⁵驚恐臨到我，
  驅逐我的尊榮如風；
  我的福祿如雲過去。

¹⁶"現在我心極其悲傷，
  困苦的日子將我抓住。
¹⁷夜間我裏面的骨頭刺我，
  疼痛不止，好像齦我。
¹⁸因神的大力，
  我的外衣污穢不堪，
  又如裏衣的領子將我纏住。
¹⁹神把我扔在淤泥中，
  我就像塵土和爐灰一般。

²⁰"主啊，我呼求你，
  你不應允我；
  我站起來，你就定睛看我。
²¹你向我變心，待我殘忍，
  又用大能追逼我。
²²把我提在風中，
  使我駕風而行，
  又使我消滅在烈風中。
²³我知道要使我臨到死地，
  到那為眾生所定的陰宅。

²⁴"然而人仆倒，豈不伸手？
  遇災難，豈不求救呢？
²⁵人遭難，我豈不為他哭泣呢？
  人窮乏，我豈不為他憂愁呢？
²⁶我仰望得好處，災禍就到了；
  我等待光明，黑暗便來了。
²⁷我心裏煩擾不安，
  困苦的日子臨到我身。
²⁸我沒有日光就哀哭行去（註：或作"我
    面發黑並非因日曬"），
  我在會中站着求救。
²⁹我與野狗為弟兄，與鴕鳥為同伴。
³⁰我的皮膚黑而脫落；
  我的骨頭因熱燒焦。
³¹所以我的琴音變為悲音；
  我的簫聲變為哭聲。

31

“我與眼睛立約，
怎能戀戀瞻望處女呢？
2從至上的神所得之分，
從至高全能者所得之業是甚麼呢？
3豈不是禍患臨到不義的，
災害臨到作孽的呢？
4神豈不是察看我的道路，
數點我的腳步呢？

5“我若與虛謊同行，
腳若追隨詭詐；
6我若被公道的天平稱度，
使神可以知道我的純正；
7我的腳步若偏離正路，
我的心若隨着我的眼目，
若有玷污粘在我手上，
8就願我所種的別人吃；
我田所產的被拔出來。

9“我若受迷惑，向婦人起淫念，
在鄰舍的門外蹲伏，
10就願我的妻子給別人推磨，
別人也與她同室。
11因為這是大罪，
是審判官當罰的罪孽。
12這本是火焚燒，直到燬滅，
必拔除我所有的家產。

13“我的僕婢
與我爭辯的時候，
我若藐視不聽他們的情節，
14神興起，我怎樣行呢？
他察問，我怎樣回答呢？
15造我在腹中的，
不也是造他嗎？
將他與我摶在腹中的，
豈不是一位嗎？

16“我若不容貧寒人得其所願，
或叫寡婦眼中失望；
17或獨自吃我一點食物，
孤兒沒有與我同吃；
18（從幼年時孤兒與我同長，
好像父子一樣；
我從出母腹就扶助 (註：“扶助”原
文作“引領”) 寡婦。）
19我若見人因無衣死亡，
或見窮乏人身無遮蓋；
20我若不使他
因我羊的毛得暖
為我祝福；
21我若在城門口見有幫助我的，
舉手攻擊孤兒，

31

“I made a covenant with my eyes
not to look lustfully at a girl.
2For what is man's lot from God above,
his heritage from the Almighty on high?
3Is it not ruin for the wicked,
disaster for those who do wrong?
4Does he not see my ways
and count my every step?

5“If I have walked in falsehood
or my foot has hurried after deceit—
6let God weigh me in honest scales
and he will know that I am blameless—
7if my steps have turned from the path,
if my heart has been led by my eyes,
or if my hands have been defiled,
8then may others eat what I have sown,
and may my crops be uprooted.

9“If my heart has been enticed by a woman,
or if I have lurked at my neighbor's door,
10then may my wife grind another man's grain,
and may other men sleep with her.
11For that would have been shameful,
a sin to be judged.
12It is a fire that burns to Destruction*a*;
it would have uprooted my harvest.

13“If I have denied justice to my menservants
and maidservants
when they had a grievance against me,
14what will I do when God confronts me?
What will I answer when called to account?
15Did not he who made me in the womb make
them?
Did not the same one form us both within
our mothers?

16“If I have denied the desires of the poor
or let the eyes of the widow grow weary,
17if I have kept my bread to myself,
not sharing it with the fatherless—
18but from my youth I reared him as would a
father,
and from my birth I guided the widow—
19if I have seen anyone perishing for lack of
clothing,
or a needy man without a garment,
20and his heart did not bless me
for warming him with the fleece from my
sheep,
21if I have raised my hand against the fatherless,
knowing that I had influence in court,

a 12 Hebrew Abaddon

²²then let my arm fall from the shoulder,
   let it be broken off at the joint.
²³For I dreaded destruction from God,
   and for fear of his splendor I could not do
      such things.

²⁴"If I have put my trust in gold
   or said to pure gold, 'You are my security,'
²⁵if I have rejoiced over my great wealth,
   the fortune my hands had gained,
²⁶if I have regarded the sun in its radiance
   or the moon moving in splendor,
²⁷so that my heart was secretly enticed
   and my hand offered them a kiss of homage,
²⁸then these also would be sins to be judged,
   for I would have been unfaithful to God on
      high.

²⁹"If I have rejoiced at my enemy's misfortune
   or gloated over the trouble that came to
      him—
³⁰I have not allowed my mouth to sin
   by invoking a curse against his life—
³¹if the men of my household have never said,
   'Who has not had his fill of Job's meat?'—
³²but no stranger had to spend the night in the
      street,
   for my door was always open to the
      traveler—
³³if I have concealed my sin as men do,^a
   by hiding my guilt in my heart
³⁴because I so feared the crowd
   and so dreaded the contempt of the clans
   that I kept silent and would not go outside

³⁵("Oh, that I had someone to hear me!
   I sign now my defense—let the Almighty
      answer me;
   let my accuser put his indictment in writing.
³⁶Surely I would wear it on my shoulder,
   I would put it on like a crown.
³⁷I would give him an account of my every step;
   like a prince I would approach him.)—

³⁸"if my land cries out against me
   and all its furrows are wet with tears,
³⁹if I have devoured its yield without payment
   or broken the spirit of its tenants,
⁴⁰then let briers come up instead of wheat
   and weeds instead of barley."

The words of Job are ended.

²²情願我的肩頭從缺盆骨脫落，
   我的膀臂從羊矢骨折斷。
²³因神降的災禍使我恐懼；
   因他的威嚴，
   我不能妄為。

²⁴ "我若以黃金為指望，
   對精金說‘你是我的倚靠’；
²⁵我若因財物豐裕，
   因我手多得資財而歡喜；
²⁶我若見太陽發光，
   明月行在空中，
²⁷心就暗暗被引誘，
   口便親手；
²⁸這也是審判官當罰的罪孽，
   又是我背棄在上的神。

²⁹ "我若見恨我的遭報就歡喜，
   見他遭災便高興；

³⁰ （我沒有容口犯罪，
   咒詛他的生命。）
³¹若我帳棚的人未嘗說，
   ‘誰不以主人的食物吃飽呢？’
³² （從來我沒有容客旅
      在街上住宿，
   卻開門迎接行路的人。）
³³我若像亞當（註：“亞當”或作“別人”）
   遮掩我的過犯，將罪孽藏在懷中，
³⁴因懼怕大眾，
   又因宗族藐視我，使我驚恐，
   以致閉口無言，杜門不出。

³⁵ "惟願有一位肯聽我！
    （看哪，在這裏
      有我所劃的押，
   願全能者回答我。）
³⁶願那敵我者所寫的狀詞在我這裏，
   我必帶在肩上，又綁在頭上為冠冕。
³⁷我必向他述說我腳步的數目，
   必如君王進到他面前。

³⁸ "我若奪取田地，這地向我喊冤，
   犁溝一同哭泣；
³⁹我若吃地的出產不給價值，
   或叫原主喪命；
⁴⁰願這地長蒺藜代替麥子，
   長惡草代替大麥。"

約伯的話說完了。

a 33 Or as Adam did

以利戶

32 於是這三個人，因約伯自以
為義，就不再回答他。²那時
有布西人蘭族巴拉迦的兒子
以利戶向約伯發怒，因約伯自以為
義，不以神為義，³他又向約伯的三
個朋友發怒，因為他們想不出回答
的話來，仍以約伯為有罪。⁴以利
戶要與約伯說話，就等候他們，因
為他們比自己年老。⁵以利戶見這三
個人口中無話回答，就怒氣發作。

⁶布西人巴拉迦的兒子以利戶回
答說：
"我年輕，
　你們老邁，
因此我退讓，
　不敢向你們陳說我的意見。
⁷我說：'年老的當先說話；
　壽高的當以智慧教訓人。'
⁸但在人裏面有靈，
　全能者的氣
　　使人有聰明。
⁹尊貴的不都有智慧；
　壽高的不都能明白公平。

¹⁰"因此我說，你們要聽我言，
　我也要陳說我的意見。
¹¹你們查究所要說的話，
　那時我等候你們的話，
　側耳聽你們的辯論，
¹²留心聽你們，
　誰知你們中間無一人折服約伯，
　駁倒他的話。
¹³你們切不可說：'我們尋得智慧；
　神能勝他，人卻不能。'
¹⁴約伯沒有
　　向我爭辯，
我也不用你們的話
　　回答他。

¹⁵"他們驚奇，不再回答，
　一言不發。
¹⁶我豈因他們不說話，
　站住不再回答，仍舊等候呢？
¹⁷我也要回答我的一分話，
　陳說我的意見。
¹⁸因為我的言語滿懷，
　我裏面的靈激動我。
¹⁹我的胸懷如盛酒之囊
　沒有出氣之縫，

Elihu

32 So these three men stopped answering
Job, because he was righteous in his
own eyes. ²But Elihu son of Barakel the
Buzite, of the family of Ram, became very angry
with Job for justifying himself rather than God.
³He was also angry with the three friends,
because they had found no way to refute Job,
and yet had condemned him.ᵃ ⁴Now Elihu had
waited before speaking to Job because they were
older than he. ⁵But when he saw that the three
men had nothing more to say, his anger was
aroused.

⁶So Elihu son of Barakel the Buzite said:

"I am young in years,
　and you are old;
that is why I was fearful,
　not daring to tell you what I know.
⁷I thought, 'Age should speak;
　advanced years should teach wisdom.'
⁸But it is the spiritᵇ in a man,
　the breath of the Almighty, that gives him
　　understanding.
⁹It is not only the oldᶜ who are wise,
　not only the aged who understand what is
　　right.

¹⁰"Therefore I say: Listen to me;
　I too will tell you what I know.
¹¹I waited while you spoke,
　I listened to your reasoning;
　while you were searching for words,
¹² I gave you my full attention.
But not one of you has proved Job wrong;
　none of you has answered his arguments.
¹³Do not say, 'We have found wisdom;
　let God refute him, not man.'
¹⁴But Job has not marshaled his words against
　me,
　and I will not answer him with your
　　arguments.

¹⁵"They are dismayed and have no more to say;
　words have failed them.
¹⁶Must I wait, now that they are silent,
　now that they stand there with no reply?
¹⁷I too will have my say;
　I too will tell what I know.
¹⁸For I am full of words,
　and the spirit within me compels me;
¹⁹inside I am like bottled-up wine,

---

a 3 Masoretic Text; an ancient Hebrew scribal tradition *Job, and
so had condemned God*　　*b 8* Or *Spirit*; also in verse 18　　*c 9* Or
many; or *great*

like new wineskins ready to burst.
²⁰I must speak and find relief;
　I must open my lips and reply.
²¹I will show partiality to no one,
　nor will I flatter any man;
²²for if I were skilled in flattery,
　my Maker would soon take me away.

33

"But now, Job, listen to my words;
　pay attention to everything I say.
²I am about to open my mouth;
　my words are on the tip of my tongue.
³My words come from an upright heart;
　my lips sincerely speak what I know.
⁴The Spirit of God has made me;
　the breath of the Almighty gives me life.
⁵Answer me then, if you can;
　prepare yourself and confront me.
⁶I am just like you before God;
　I too have been taken from clay.
⁷No fear of me should alarm you,
　nor should my hand be heavy upon you.

⁸"But you have said in my hearing—
　I heard the very words—
⁹'I am pure and without sin;
　I am clean and free from guilt.
¹⁰Yet God has found fault with me;
　he considers me his enemy.
¹¹He fastens my feet in shackles;
　he keeps close watch on all my paths.'

¹²"But I tell you, in this you are not right,
　for God is greater than man.
¹³Why do you complain to him
　that he answers none of man's words^a?
¹⁴For God does speak—now one way, now another—
　though man may not perceive it.
¹⁵In a dream, in a vision of the night,
　when deep sleep falls on men
　as they slumber in their beds,
¹⁶he may speak in their ears
　and terrify them with warnings,
¹⁷to turn man from wrongdoing
　and keep him from pride,
¹⁸to preserve his soul from the pit,^b
　his life from perishing by the sword.^c
¹⁹Or a man may be chastened on a bed of pain
　with constant distress in his bones,
²⁰so that his very being finds food repulsive
　and his soul loathes the choicest meal.

又如新皮袋快要破裂。
²⁰我要說話，使我舒暢，
　我要開口回答。
²¹我必不看人的情面，
　也不奉承人。
²²我不曉得奉承，若奉承，
　造我的主必快快除滅我。

33

"約伯啊，請聽我的話，
　留心聽我一切的言語！
²我現在開口，
　用舌發言，
³我的言語要發明心中所存的正直；
　我所知道的，我嘴唇要誠實地說出。
⁴神的靈造我，
　全能者的氣使我得生。
⁵你若回答我，
　就站起來在我面前陳明。
⁶我在神面前與你一樣，
　也是用土造成。
⁷我不用威嚴驚嚇你，
　也不用勢力重壓你。

⁸"你所說的，我聽見了，
　也聽見你的言語，說：
⁹'我是清潔無過的，我是無辜的，
　在我裏面也沒有罪孽。
¹⁰神找機會攻擊我，
　以我為仇敵，
¹¹把我的腳上了木狗，
　窺察我一切的道路。'

¹²"我要回答你說：你這話無理，
　因神比世人更大！
¹³你為何與他爭論呢？
　因他的事都不對人解說？
¹⁴神說一次、兩次，
　世人卻不理會。
¹⁵人躺在牀上
　沉睡的時候，
　神就用夢和夜間的異象，
¹⁶開通他們的耳朵，
　將當受的教訓印在他們心上，
¹⁷好叫人不從自己的謀算，不行驕傲
　的事（註：原文作"將驕傲向人隱藏"）；
¹⁸攔阻人不陷於坑裏，
　不死在刀下。
¹⁹人在牀上被懲治，
　骨頭中不住地疼痛，
²⁰以致他的口厭棄食物，
　心厭惡美味。

<sub>a 13 Or that he does not answer for any of his actions　　b 18 Or
preserve him from the grave　　c 18 Or from crossing the River</sub>

21他的肉消瘦，不得再見，
　　先前不見的骨頭都凸出來。
22他的靈魂臨近深坑，
　　他的生命臨於滅命的。

23 "一千天使中，
　　若有一個作傳話的與神同在，
　　指示人所當行的事，
24神就給他開恩，說：
　　'救贖他免得下坑，
　　我已經得了贖價。'
25他的肉要比孩童的肉更嫩，
　　他就返老還童。
26他禱告神，神就喜悅他，
　　使他歡呼朝見神的面；
　　神又看他為義。
27他在人前歌唱說：
　　'我犯了罪，顛倒是非，
　　這事與我無益。
28神救贖我的靈魂
　　免入深坑，
　　我的生命也必見光。'

29 "神兩次、三次
　　向人行這一切的事，
30為要從深坑救回人的靈魂，
　　使他被光照耀，與活人一樣。

31 "約伯啊，你當側耳聽我的話，
　　不要做聲，等我講說。
32你若有話說，就可以回答我，
　　你只管說，因我願以你為是。
33若不然，你就聽我說，
　　你不要做聲，
　　我便將智慧教訓你。"

34 以利戶又說：

2 "你們智慧人要聽我的話；
　　有知識的人要留心聽我說！
3因為耳朵試驗話語，
　　好像上膛嘗食物。
4我們當選擇何為是，
　　彼此知道何為善。

5 "約伯曾說：
　　'我是公義，神奪去我的理。
6我雖有理，
　　還算為說謊言的；
　　我雖無過，
　　受的傷還不能醫治。'

21His flesh wastes away to nothing,
　　and his bones, once hidden, now stick out.
22His soul draws near to the pit,[a]
　　and his life to the messengers of death.[b]

23"Yet if there is an angel on his side
　　as a mediator, one out of a thousand,
　　to tell a man what is right for him,
24to be gracious to him and say,
　　'Spare him from going down to the pit[c];
　　I have found a ransom for him'—
25then his flesh is renewed like a child's;
　　it is restored as in the days of his youth.
26He prays to God and finds favor with him,
　　he sees God's face and shouts for joy;
　　he is restored by God to his righteous state.
27Then he comes to men and says,
　　"I sinned, and perverted what was right,
　　but I did not get what I deserved.
28He redeemed my soul from going down to
　　the pit,[d]
　　and I will live to enjoy the light.'

29"God does all these things to a man—
　　twice, even three times—
30to turn back his soul from the pit,[e]
　　that the light of life may shine on him.

31"Pay attention, Job, and listen to me;
　　be silent, and I will speak.
32If you have anything to say, answer me;
　　speak up, for I want you to be cleared.
33But if not, then listen to me;
　　be silent, and I will teach you wisdom."

34 Then Elihu said:

2"Hear my words, you wise men;
　　listen to me, you men of learning.
3For the ear tests words
　　as the tongue tastes food.
4Let us discern for ourselves what is right;
　　let us learn together what is good.

5"Job says, 'I am innocent,
　　but God denies me justice.
6Although I am right,
　　I am considered a liar;
　　although I am guiltless,
　　his arrow inflicts an incurable wound.'

---

a 22 Or *He draws near to the grave*　　b 22 Or *to the dead*
c 24 Or *grave*　　d 28 Or *redeemed me from going down to the
grave*　　e 30 Or *turn him back from the grave*

7What man is like Job,
who drinks scorn like water?
8He keeps company with evildoers;
he associates with wicked men.
9For he says, 'It profits a man nothing
when he tries to please God.'

10"So listen to me, you men of understanding.
Far be it from God to do evil,
from the Almighty to do wrong.
11He repays a man for what he has done;
he brings upon him what his conduct
deserves.
12It is unthinkable that God would do wrong,
that the Almighty would pervert justice.
13Who appointed him over the earth?
Who put him in charge of the whole world?
14If it were his intention
and he withdrew his spirit[a] and breath,
15all mankind would perish together
and man would return to the dust.

16"If you have understanding, hear this;
listen to what I say.
17Can he who hates justice govern?
Will you condemn the just and mighty One?
18Is he not the One who says to kings, 'You are
worthless,'
and to nobles, 'You are wicked,'
19who shows no partiality to princes
and does not favor the rich over the poor,
for they are all the work of his hands?
20They die in an instant, in the middle of the
night;
the people are shaken and they pass away;
the mighty are removed without human
hand.

21"His eyes are on the ways of men;
he sees their every step.
22There is no dark place, no deep shadow,
where evildoers can hide.
23God has no need to examine men further,
that they should come before him for
judgment.
24Without inquiry he shatters the mighty
and sets up others in their place.
25Because he takes note of their deeds,
he overthrows them in the night and they
are crushed.
26He punishes them for their wickedness
where everyone can see them,
27because they turned from following him
and had no regard for any of his ways.

7誰像約伯，
喝譏誚如同喝水呢？
8他與作孽的結伴，
和惡人同行。
9他說：'人以神為樂，
總是無益。'

10"所以你們明理的人，要聽我的話。
神斷不至行惡，
全能者斷不至作孽！
11他必按人所做的報應人，
使各人照所行的得報。
12神必不作惡，
全能者也不偏離公平！
13誰派他治理地、
安定全世界呢？
14他若專心為己，
將靈和氣收歸自己，
15凡有血氣的就必一同死亡，
世人必仍歸塵土。

16"你若明理，就當聽我的話，
留心聽我言語的聲音；
17難道恨惡公平的，可以掌權嗎？
那有公義的、有大能的，
豈可定他有罪嗎？
18他對君王說'你是鄙陋的'；
對貴臣說'你是邪惡的'。
19他待王子不徇情面，
也不看重富足的過於貧窮的，
因為都是他手所造。
20在轉眼之間，半夜之中，
他們就死亡。
百姓被震動而去世；
有權力的被奪去
非借人手。

21"神注目觀看人的道路，
看明人的腳步。
22沒有黑暗、陰翳能
給作孽的藏身。
23神審判人，
不必使人到他面前
再三鑒察。
24他用難測之法打破有能力的人，
設立別人代替他們。
25他原知道他們的行為，
使他們在夜間
傾倒滅亡。
26他在眾人眼前擊打他們，
如同擊打惡人一樣。
27因為他們偏行不跟從他，
也不留心他的道；

²⁸甚至使貧窮人的哀聲
　　達到他那裏，
　他也聽見困苦人的哀聲。
²⁹他使人安靜，
　　誰能擾亂（註：或作"定罪"）呢？
　他掩面，誰能見他呢？
　　無論待一國或一人都是如此——
³⁰使不虔敬的人不得作王，
　　免得有人牢籠百姓。

³¹"有誰對神説：
　　'我受了責罰，不再犯罪。
³²我所看不明的，求你指教我；
　　我若作了孽，必不再作'
³³他施行報應，豈要隨你的心願，
　　叫你推辭不受嗎？
　選定的是你，不是我。
　你所知道的只管説吧！

³⁴"明理的人和聽我話的智慧人
　　必對我説：
³⁵'約伯説話沒有知識，
　　言語中毫無智慧。'
³⁶願約伯被試驗到底，
　　因他回答像惡人一樣。
³⁷他在罪上又加悖逆；
　　在我們中間拍手，
　用許多言語輕慢神。"

35 以利户又説：

² "你以為有理，
　　或以為你的公義勝於神的公義，
³才説：'這與我有甚麼益處？
　　我不犯罪，比犯罪有甚麼好處呢？'

⁴ "我要回答你
　　和在你這裏的朋友。
⁵你要向天觀看，
　　瞻望那高於你的穹蒼。
⁶你若犯罪，能使神受何害呢？
　　你的過犯加增，
　　能使神受何損呢？
⁷你若是公義，還能加增他甚麼呢？
　　他從你手裏還接受甚麼呢？
⁸你的過惡或能害你這類的人；
　　你的公義或能叫世人得益處。

⁹ "人因多受欺壓就哀求，
　　因受能者的轄制（註："轄制"原文
　　作"膀臂"）便求救；
¹⁰卻無人説：'造我的神在哪裏？
　　他使人夜間歌唱，

²⁸They caused the cry of the poor to come
　　before him,
　so that he heard the cry of the needy.
²⁹But if he remains silent, who can condemn
　　him?
　If he hides his face, who can see him?
　Yet he is over man and nation alike,
³⁰ to keep a godless man from ruling,
　　from laying snares for the people.

³¹"Suppose a man says to God,
　　'I am guilty but will offend no more.
³²Teach me what I cannot see;
　　if I have done wrong, I will not do so again.'
³³Should God then reward you on your terms,
　　when you refuse to repent?
　You must decide, not I;
　so tell me what you know.

³⁴"Men of understanding declare,
　　wise men who hear me say to me,
³⁵'Job speaks without knowledge;
　　his words lack insight.'
³⁶Oh, that Job might be tested to the utmost
　　for answering like a wicked man!
³⁷To his sin he adds rebellion;
　　scornfully he claps his hands among us
　and multiplies his words against God."

35 Then Elihu said:

²"Do you think this is just?
　　You say, 'I will be cleared by God.'ᵃ
³Yet you ask him, 'What profit is it to me,ᵇ
　　and what do I gain by not sinning?'

⁴"I would like to reply to you
　　and to your friends with you.
⁵Look up at the heavens and see;
　　gaze at the clouds so high above you.
⁶If you sin, how does that affect him?
　　If your sins are many, what does that do to
　　him?
⁷If you are righteous, what do you give to him,
　　or what does he receive from your hand?
⁸Your wickedness affects only a man like yourself,
　　and your righteousness only the sons of men.

⁹"Men cry out under a load of oppression;
　　they plead for relief from the arm of the
　　powerful.
¹⁰But no one says, 'Where is God my Maker,
　　who gives songs in the night,

a 2 Or My righteousness is more than God's　　b 3 Or you

¹¹who teaches more to us than to^a the beasts of
the earth
and makes us wiser than^b the birds of the air?'
¹²He does not answer when men cry out
because of the arrogance of the wicked.
¹³Indeed, God does not listen to their empty plea;
the Almighty pays no attention to it.
¹⁴How much less, then, will he listen
when you say that you do not see him,
that your case is before him
and you must wait for him,
¹⁵and further, that his anger never punishes
and he does not take the least notice of
wickedness.^c
¹⁶So Job opens his mouth with empty talk;
without knowledge he multiplies words."

36
Elihu continued:

²"Bear with me a little longer and I will
show you
that there is more to be said in God's behalf.
³I get my knowledge from afar;
I will ascribe justice to my Maker.
⁴Be assured that my words are not false;
one perfect in knowledge is with you.

⁵"God is mighty, but does not despise men;
he is mighty, and firm in his purpose.
⁶He does not keep the wicked alive
but gives the afflicted their rights.
⁷He does not take his eyes off the righteous;
he enthrones them with kings
and exalts them forever.
⁸But if men are bound in chains,
held fast by cords of affliction,
⁹he tells them what they have done—
that they have sinned arrogantly.
¹⁰He makes them listen to correction
and commands them to repent of their evil.
¹¹If they obey and serve him,
they will spend the rest of their days in
prosperity
and their years in contentment.
¹²But if they do not listen,
they will perish by the sword^d
and die without knowledge.

¹³"The godless in heart harbor resentment;
even when he fetters them, they do not cry
for help.

¹¹教訓我們勝於地上的走獸，
使我們有聰明
勝於空中的飛鳥。'
¹²他們在那裏，
因惡人的驕傲呼求，卻無人答應。
¹³虛妄的呼求，神必不垂聽；
全能者也必不眷顧。
¹⁴何況你說，
你不得見他。
你的案件在他面前，
你等候他吧！
¹⁵但如今因他未曾發怒降罰，
也不甚理會狂傲。

¹⁶所以約伯開口說虛妄的話，
多發無知識的言語。"

36
以利戶又接着說：

²"你再容我片時，
我就指示你，
因我還有話為神說。
³我要將所知道的從遠處引來，
將公義歸給造我的主。
⁴我的言語真不虛謊，
有知識全備的與你同在。

⁵"神有大能，並不藐視人，
他的智慧甚廣。
⁶他不保護惡人的性命，
卻為困苦人伸冤。
⁷他時常看顧義人，
使他們和君王同坐寶座，
永遠要被高舉。
⁸他們若被鎖鏈捆住，
被苦難的繩索纏住，
⁹他就把他們的作為和過犯指示他們，
叫他們知道有驕傲的行動。
¹⁰他也開通他們的耳朵得受教訓，
吩咐他們離開罪孽轉回。
¹¹他們若聽從侍奉他，
就必度日亨通，
歷年福樂。

¹²若不聽從，
就要被刀殺滅，
無知無識而死。

¹³"那心中不敬虔的人積蓄怒氣；
神捆綁他們，
他們竟不求救，

a 11 Or *teaches us by*   b 11 Or *us wise by*   c 15 Symmachus,
Theodotion and Vulgate; the meaning of the Hebrew for this
word is uncertain.   d 12 Or *will cross the River*

14必在青年時死亡，
　　與污穢人一樣喪命。
15神藉著困苦救拔困苦人，
　　趁他們受欺壓，
　　開通他們的耳朵。

16　"神也必引你出離患難，
　　進入寬闊不狹窄之地；
　　擺在你席上的，
　　必滿有肥甘。
17但你滿口
　　　　有惡人批評的言語，
　　判斷和刑罰抓住你。
18不可容忿怒觸動你，使你不服責罰，
　　也不可因贖價大就偏行。
19你的呼求（註："呼求"或作"資財"），
　　或是你一切的勢力，
　　果有靈驗，叫你不受患難嗎？
20不要切慕黑夜，
　　就是眾民在本處被除滅的時候。
21你要謹慎，不可重看罪孽，
　　因你選擇罪孽過於選擇苦難。

22　"神行事有高大的能力，
　　教訓人的有誰像他呢？
23誰派定他的道路？
　　誰能說，'你所行的不義'？
24你不可忘記稱讚他所行的為大，
　　就是人所歌頌的。
25他所行的，萬人都看見；
　　世人也從遠處觀看。
26神為大，我們不能全知；
　　他的年數不能測度。

27　"他吸取水點，
　　這水點從雲霧中就變成雨；
28雲彩將雨落下，
　　沛然降與世人。
29誰能明白雲彩如何鋪張，
　　和神行宮的雷聲呢？

30他將亮光普照在自己的四圍，
　　他又遮覆海底。
31他用這些審判眾民，
　　且賜豐富的糧食。
32他以電光遮手，
　　命閃電擊中敵人（註：或作"中了靶子"）。
33所發的雷聲顯明他的作為，
　　又向牲畜指明要起暴風。

14They die in their youth,
　　among male prostitutes of the shrines.
15But those who suffer he delivers in their
　　suffering;
　　he speaks to them in their affliction.

16"He is wooing you from the jaws of distress
　　to a spacious place free from restriction,
　　to the comfort of your table laden with
　　　choice food.
17But now you are laden with the judgment due
　　the wicked;
　　judgment and justice have taken hold of you.
18Be careful that no one entices you by riches;
　　do not let a large bribe turn you aside.
19Would your wealth
　　or even all your mighty efforts
　　sustain you so you would not be in distress?
20Do not long for the night,
　　to drag people away from their homes.a
21Beware of turning to evil,
　　which you seem to prefer to affliction.

22"God is exalted in his power.
　　Who is a teacher like him?
23Who has prescribed his ways for him,
　　or said to him, 'You have done wrong'?
24Remember to extol his work,
　　which men have praised in song.
25All mankind has seen it;
　　men gaze on it from afar.
26How great is God—beyond our understanding!
　　The number of his years is past finding out.

27"He draws up the drops of water,
　　which distill as rain to the streamsb;
28the clouds pour down their moisture
　　and abundant showers fall on mankind.
29Who can understand how he spreads out the
　　clouds,
　　how he thunders from his pavilion?
30See how he scatters his lightning about him,
　　bathing the depths of the sea.
31This is the way he governsc the nations
　　and provides food in abundance.
32He fills his hands with lightning
　　and commands it to strike its mark.
33His thunder announces the coming storm;
　　even the cattle make known its approach.d

a 20 The meaning of the Hebrew for verses 18-20 is uncertain.
b 27 Or distill from the mist as rain　　c 31 Or nourishes
d 33 Or announces his coming— / the One zealous against evil

37

"At this my heart pounds
and leaps from its place.
[2]Listen! Listen to the roar of his voice,
to the rumbling that comes from his mouth.
[3]He unleashes his lightning beneath the whole
heaven
and sends it to the ends of the earth.
[4]After that comes the sound of his roar;
he thunders with his majestic voice.
When his voice resounds,
he holds nothing back.
[5]God's voice thunders in marvelous ways;
he does great things beyond our understanding.
[6]He says to the snow, 'Fall on the earth,'
and to the rain shower, 'Be a mighty
downpour.'
[7]So that all men he has made may know his work,[a]
he stops every man from his labor.[a]
[8]The animals take cover;
they remain in their dens.
[9]The tempest comes out from its chamber,
the cold from the driving winds.
[10]The breath of God produces ice,
and the broad waters become frozen.
[11]He loads the clouds with moisture;
he scatters his lightning through them.
[12]At his direction they swirl around
over the face of the whole earth
to do whatever he commands them.
[13]He brings the clouds to punish men,
or to water his earth[b] and show his love.

[14]"Listen to this, Job;
stop and consider God's wonders.
[15]Do you know how God controls the clouds
and makes his lightning flash?
[16]Do you know how the clouds hang poised,
those wonders of him who is perfect in
knowledge?
[17]You who swelter in your clothes
when the land lies hushed under the south
wind,
[18]can you join him in spreading out the skies,
hard as a mirror of cast bronze?

[19]"Tell us what we should say to him;
we cannot draw up our case because of our
darkness.
[20]Should he be told that I want to speak?
Would any man ask to be swallowed up?
[21]Now no one can look at the sun,
bright as it is in the skies
after the wind has swept them clean.

*a 7 Or / he fills all men with fear by his power　　b 13 Or to favor
them*

37

"因此我心戰兢，
從原處移動。
[2]聽啊，神轟轟的聲音，
是他口中所發的響聲。
[3]他發響聲
震遍天下，
發電光閃到地極。
[4]隨後人聽見
有雷聲轟轟，
大發威嚴，
雷電接連不斷。
[5]神發出奇妙的雷聲，
他行大事，我們不能測透。
[6]他對雪說「要降在地上」，
對大雨和暴雨
也是這樣說。
[7]他封住各人的手，
叫所造的萬人都曉得他的作為。
[8]百獸進入穴中，
臥在洞內。
[9]暴風出於南宮，
寒冷出於北方。
[10]神噓氣成冰，
寬闊之水也都凝結。
[11]他使密雲盛滿水氣，
布散電光之雲；
[12]這雲，是藉他的指引游行旋轉，
得以在全地面上
行他一切所吩咐的。
[13]或為責罰，或為潤地，
或為施行慈愛。

[14]"約伯啊，你要留心聽，
要站立思想神奇妙的作為。
[15]神如何吩咐這些，
如何使雲中的電光照耀，你知道嗎？
[16]雲彩如何浮於空中，
那知識全備者奇妙的作為，
你知道嗎？
[17]南風使地寂靜，
你的衣服就如火熱，
你知道嗎？
[18]你豈能與神同鋪穹蒼嗎？
這穹蒼堅硬，如同鑄成的鏡子。

[19]"我們愚昧不能陳說，
請你指教我們
該對他說甚麼話。
[20]人豈可說，我願與他說話？
豈有人自願滅亡嗎？
[21]現在有雲遮蔽，
人不得見穹蒼的光亮；
但風吹過，天又發晴。

22金光出於北方，
　　在神那裏有可怕的威嚴。
23論到全能者，我們不能測度；
　　他大有能力，
　　有公平和大義，
　　必不苦待人。
24所以人敬畏他，
　　凡自以為心中有智慧的人，
　　他都不顧念。"

主發言

38 那時，耶和華從旋風中回答
約伯說：

2"誰用無知的言語
　　使我的旨意暗昧不明？
3你要如勇士束腰；
　　我問你，
　　你可以指示我。

4"我立大地根基的時候，
　　你在哪裏呢？
　　你若有聰明，只管說吧！
5你若曉得就說，
　　是誰定地的尺度？
　　是誰把準繩拉在其上？
6地的根基安置在何處？
　　地的角石是誰安放的？
7那時，晨星一同歌唱，
　　神的眾子也都歡呼。

8"海水衝出，如出胎胞。
　　那時誰將它關閉呢？
9是我用雲彩當海的衣服，
　　用幽暗當包裹它的布，
10為它定界限，
　　又安門和閂，
11說：'你只可到這裏，
　　不可越過，
　　你狂傲的浪要到此止住。'

12"你自生以來，曾命定晨光
　　使清晨的日光知道本位，
13叫這光普照地的四極，
　　將惡人從其中驅逐出來嗎？
14因這光，地面改變如泥上印印，
　　萬物出現如衣服一樣。
15亮光不照惡人，
　　強橫的膀臂也必折斷。

16"你曾進到海源，
　　或在深淵的隱密處行走嗎？

The LORD Speaks

38 Then the LORD answered Job out of the
storm. He said:

2"Who is this that darkens my counsel
　　with words without knowledge?
3Brace yourself like a man;
　　I will question you,
　　and you shall answer me.

4"Where were you when I laid the earth's
　　foundation?
　　Tell me, if you understand.
5Who marked off its dimensions? Surely you
　　know!
　　Who stretched a measuring line across it?
6On what were its footings set,
　　or who laid its cornerstone—
7while the morning stars sang together
　　and all the angels[b] shouted for joy?

8"Who shut up the sea behind doors
　　when it burst forth from the womb,
9when I made the clouds its garment
　　and wrapped it in thick darkness,
10when I fixed limits for it
　　and set its doors and bars in place,
11when I said, 'This far you may come and no
　　farther;
　　here is where your proud waves halt'?

12"Have you ever given orders to the morning,
　　or shown the dawn its place,
13that it might take the earth by the edges
　　and shake the wicked out of it?
14The earth takes shape like clay under a seal;
　　its features stand out like those of a garment.
15The wicked are denied their light,
　　and their upraised arm is broken.

16"Have you journeyed to the springs of the sea
　　or walked in the recesses of the deep?

a 24 Or for he does not have regard for any who think they are wise.
b 7 Hebrew the sons of God

¹⁷Have the gates of death been shown to you?
  Have you seen the gates of the shadow of
  death^a?
¹⁸Have you comprehended the vast expanses of
  the earth?
  Tell me, if you know all this.

¹⁹"What is the way to the abode of light?
  And where does darkness reside?
²⁰Can you take them to their places?
  Do you know the paths to their dwellings?
²¹Surely you know, for you were already born!
  You have lived so many years!

²²"Have you entered the storehouses of the snow
  or seen the storehouses of the hail,
²³which I reserve for times of trouble,
  for days of war and battle?
²⁴What is the way to the place where the
  lightning is dispersed,
  or the place where the east winds are
  scattered over the earth?
²⁵Who cuts a channel for the torrents of rain,
  and a path for the thunderstorm,
²⁶to water a land where no man lives,
  a desert with no one in it,
²⁷to satisfy a desolate wasteland
  and make it sprout with grass?
²⁸Does the rain have a father?
  Who fathers the drops of dew?
²⁹From whose womb comes the ice?
  Who gives birth to the frost from the heavens
³⁰when the waters become hard as stone,
  when the surface of the deep is frozen?

³¹"Can you bind the beautiful^b Pleiades?
  Can you loose the cords of Orion?
³²Can you bring forth the constellations in their
  seasons^c
  or lead out the Bear^d with its cubs?
³³Do you know the laws of the heavens?
  Can you set up [God's^e] dominion over the
  earth?

³⁴"Can you raise your voice to the clouds
  and cover yourself with a flood of water?
³⁵Do you send the lightning bolts on their way?
  Do they report to you, 'Here we are'?
³⁶Who endowed the heart^f with wisdom
  or gave understanding to the mind^f?

¹⁷死亡的門曾向你顯露嗎？
  死蔭的門你曾見過嗎？
¹⁸地的廣大你能明透嗎？
  你若全知道，
  只管說吧！

¹⁹"光明的居所從何而至？
  黑暗的本位在於何處？
²⁰你能帶到本境，
  能看明其室之路嗎？
²¹你總知道，因為你早已生在世上，
  你日子的數目也多。

²²"你曾進入雪庫，
  或見過雹倉嗎？
²³這雪雹乃是我為降災，
  並打仗和爭戰的日子所預備的。
²⁴光亮
  從何路分開？
  東風
  從何路分散遍地？
²⁵誰為雨水分道？
  誰為雷電開路？
²⁶使雨降在無人之地，
  無人居住的曠野？
²⁷使荒廢淒涼之地得以豐足，
  青草得以發生？
²⁸雨有父嗎？
  露水珠是誰生的呢？
²⁹冰出於誰的胎？
  天上的霜是誰生的呢？
³⁰諸水堅硬（註：或作"隱藏"）如石頭，
  深淵之面凝結成冰。

³¹"你能繫住昴星的結嗎？
  能解開參星的帶嗎？
³²你能按時領出十二宮嗎？
  能引導北斗和隨它的眾星嗎（註：
  "星"原文作"子"）？
³³你知道天的定例嗎？
  能使地歸在天的權下嗎？

³⁴"你能向雲彩揚起聲來，
  使傾盆的雨遮蓋你嗎？
³⁵你能發出閃電，叫它行去，
  使它對你說，'我們在這裏'？
³⁶誰將智慧放在懷中？
  誰將聰明賜於心內？

*a 17 Or gates of deep shadows   b 31 Or the twinkling; or the
chains of the   c 32 Or the morning star in its season   d 32 Or
out Leo   e 33 Or his; or their   f 36 The meaning of the
Hebrew for this word is uncertain.*

37、38 誰能用智慧數算雲彩呢？
　　塵土聚集成團，
　　土塊緊緊結連，
　　那時，誰能傾倒天上的瓶呢？

39、40 「母獅子在洞中蹲伏，
　　少壯獅子在隱密處埋伏，
　　你能為牠們抓取食物，
　　使牠們飽足嗎？
41 烏鴉之雛，因無食物飛來飛去，
　　哀告神；
　　那時，誰為牠預備食物呢？

39 「山巖間的野山羊
　　幾時生產，你知道嗎？
　　母鹿下犢之期，
　　你能察定嗎？
2 牠們懷胎的月數，你能數算嗎？
　　牠們幾時生產，你能曉得嗎？
3 牠們屈身將子生下，
　　就除掉疼痛。
4 這子漸漸肥壯，在荒野長大，
　　去而不回。

5 「誰放野驢出去自由？
　　誰解開快驢的繩索？
6 我使曠野作牠的住處，
　　使鹹地當牠的居所。
7 牠嗤笑城內的喧嚷，
　　不聽趕牲口的喝聲。
8 遍山是牠的草場，
　　牠尋找各樣青綠之物。

9 「野牛豈肯服侍你？
　　豈肯住在你的槽旁？
10 你豈能用套繩將野牛籠在犁溝之間？
　　牠豈肯隨你耙山谷之地？
11 豈可因牠的力大就倚靠牠？
　　豈可把你的工交給牠做嗎？
12 豈可信靠牠把你的糧食運到家，
　　又收聚你禾場上的穀嗎？

13 「鴕鳥的翅膀歡然搧展，
　　豈是顯慈愛的翎毛和羽毛嗎？

14 因牠把蛋留在地上，
　　在塵土中使得溫暖，
15 卻想不到被腳踹碎，
　　或被野獸踐踏。

16 「牠忍心待雛，
　　似乎不是自己的；
　　雖然徒受勞苦，也不為雛懼怕。
17 因為神使牠沒有智慧，
　　也未將悟性賜給牠。

37 Who has the wisdom to count the clouds?
　　Who can tip over the water jars of the heavens
38 when the dust becomes hard
　　and the clods of earth stick together?

39 "Do you hunt the prey for the lioness
　　and satisfy the hunger of the lions
40 when they crouch in their dens
　　or lie in wait in a thicket?
41 Who provides food for the raven
　　when its young cry out to God
　　and wander about for lack of food?

39 "Do you know when the mountain
　　goats give birth?
　　Do you watch when the doe bears her
　　fawn?
2 Do you count the months till they bear?
　　Do you know the time they give birth?
3 They crouch down and bring forth their young;
　　their labor pains are ended.
4 Their young thrive and grow strong in the wilds;
　　they leave and do not return.

5 "Who let the wild donkey go free?
　　Who untied his ropes?
6 I gave him the wasteland as his home,
　　the salt flats as his habitat.
7 He laughs at the commotion in the town;
　　he does not hear a driver's shout.
8 He ranges the hills for his pasture
　　and searches for any green thing.

9 "Will the wild ox consent to serve you?
　　Will he stay by your manger at night?
10 Can you hold him to the furrow with a harness?
　　Will he till the valleys behind you?
11 Will you rely on him for his great strength?
　　Will you leave your heavy work to him?
12 Can you trust him to bring in your grain
　　and gather it to your threshing floor?

13 "The wings of the ostrich flap joyfully,
　　but they cannot compare with the pinions
　　and feathers of the stork.
14 She lays her eggs on the ground
　　and lets them warm in the sand,
15 unmindful that a foot may crush them,
　　that some wild animal may trample them.

16 She treats her young harshly, as if they were
　　not hers;
　　she cares not that her labor was in vain,
17 for God did not endow her with wisdom
　　or give her a share of good sense.

¹⁸Yet when she spreads her feathers to run,
　she laughs at horse and rider.

¹⁹"Do you give the horse his strength
　or clothe his neck with a flowing mane?
²⁰Do you make him leap like a locust,
　striking terror with his proud snorting?
²¹He paws fiercely, rejoicing in his strength,
　and charges into the fray.
²²He laughs at fear, afraid of nothing;
　he does not shy away from the sword.
²³The quiver rattles against his side,
　along with the flashing spear and lance.
²⁴In frenzied excitement he eats up the ground;
　he cannot stand still when the trumpet sounds.
²⁵At the blast of the trumpet he snorts, 'Aha!'
　He catches the scent of battle from afar,
　the shout of commanders and the battle cry.

²⁶"Does the hawk take flight by your wisdom
　and spread his wings toward the south?
²⁷Does the eagle soar at your command
　and build his nest on high?
²⁸He dwells on a cliff and stays there at night;
　a rocky crag is his stronghold.
²⁹From there he seeks out his food;
　his eyes detect it from afar.
³⁰His young ones feast on blood,
　and where the slain are, there is he."

40

The LORD said to Job:

²"Will the one who contends with the
　Almighty correct him?
Let him who accuses God answer him!"

³Then Job answered the LORD:

⁴"I am unworthy—how can I reply to you?
　I put my hand over my mouth.
⁵I spoke once, but I have no answer—
　twice, but I will say no more."

⁶Then the LORD spoke to Job out of the storm:

⁷"Brace yourself like a man;
　I will question you,
　and you shall answer me.

⁸"Would you discredit my justice?
　Would you condemn me to justify yourself?
⁹Do you have an arm like God's,
　and can your voice thunder like his?
¹⁰Then adorn yourself with glory and splendor,
　and clothe yourself in honor and majesty.

¹⁸牠幾時挺身展開翅膀，
　就嗤笑馬和騎馬的人。

¹⁹"馬的大力是你所賜的嗎？
　牠頸項上挓挲的鬃
　　是你給牠披上的嗎？
²⁰是你叫牠跳躍像蝗蟲嗎？
　牠噴氣之威使人驚惶。
²¹牠在谷中刨地自喜其力；
　牠出去迎接佩帶兵器的人。
²²牠嗤笑可怕的事，並不驚惶，
　也不因刀劍退回。
²³箭袋和發亮的槍，並短槍，
　在牠身上錚錚有聲。
²⁴牠發猛烈的怒氣將地吞下，
　一聽角聲就不耐站立。
²⁵角每發聲，牠說，'呵哈！'
　牠從遠處聞着戰氣，
　又聽見軍長大發雷聲和兵丁吶喊。

²⁶"鷹雀飛翔，展開翅膀一直向南，
　豈是藉你的智慧嗎？
²⁷大鷹上騰，在高處搭窩，
　豈是聽你的吩咐嗎？
²⁸牠住在山巖，
　以山峯和堅固之所為家，
²⁹從那裏窺看食物，
　眼睛遠遠觀望。
³⁰牠的雛也咂血，
　被殺的人在哪裏，牠也在那裏。"

40

耶和華又對約伯說：

²"強辯的豈可
　與全能者爭論嗎？
　與神辯駁的，可以回答這些吧！"

³於是約伯回答耶和華說：

⁴"我是卑賤的！我用甚麼回答你呢？
　只好用手摀口。
⁵我說了一次，再不回答；
　說了兩次，就不再說。"

⁶於是耶和華從旋風中回答約伯說：

⁷"你要如勇士束腰；
　我問你，
　你可以指示我。

⁸"你豈可廢棄我所擬定的？
　豈可定我有罪，好顯自己為義嗎？
⁹你有神那樣的膀臂嗎？
　你能像他發雷聲嗎？
¹⁰你要以榮耀莊嚴為妝飾，
　以尊榮威嚴為衣服；

¹¹要發出你滿溢的怒氣，
　　見一切驕傲的人，使他降卑；
¹²見一切驕傲的人，將他制伏，
　　把惡人踐踏在本處。
¹³將他們一同隱藏在塵土中；
　　把他們的臉蒙蔽在隱密處。
¹⁴我就認你右手
　　能以救自己。

¹⁵"你且觀看河馬。
　　我造你也造牠，
　　牠吃草與牛一樣。
¹⁶牠的氣力在腰間，
　　能力在肚腹的筋上。
¹⁷牠搖動尾巴如香柏樹，
　　牠大腿的筋互相聯絡。
¹⁸牠的骨頭好像銅管，
　　牠的肢體彷彿鐵棍。
¹⁹牠在神所造的物中為首，
　　創造牠的
　　給牠刀劍。
²⁰諸山給牠出食物，
　　也是百獸遊玩之處。
²¹牠伏在蓮葉之下，
　　臥在蘆葦隱密處和水窪子裏。
²²蓮葉的陰涼遮蔽牠，
　　溪旁的柳樹環繞牠。
²³河水氾濫，牠不發戰，
　　就是約旦河的水漲到牠口邊，
　　也是安然。
²⁴在牠防備的時候，誰能捉拿牠？
　　誰能牢籠牠、穿牠的鼻子呢？

41 "你能用魚鉤
　　釣上鱷魚嗎？
　　能用繩子壓下牠的舌頭嗎？
²你能用繩索穿牠的鼻子嗎？
　　能用鉤穿牠的腮骨嗎？
³牠豈向你連連懇求，
　　説柔和的話嗎？
⁴豈肯與你立約，
　　使你拿牠永遠作奴僕嗎？
⁵你豈可拿牠當雀鳥玩耍嗎？
　　豈可為你的幼女將牠拴住嗎？
⁶搭夥的漁夫，豈可拿牠當貨物嗎？
　　能把牠分給商人嗎？
⁷你能用倒鉤槍扎滿牠的皮，
　　能用魚叉叉滿牠的頭嗎？
⁸你按手在牠身上，
　　想與牠爭戰
　　就不再這樣行吧！

¹¹Unleash the fury of your wrath,
　　look at every proud man and bring him low,
¹²look at every proud man and humble him,
　　crush the wicked where they stand.
¹³Bury them all in the dust together;
　　shroud their faces in the grave.
¹⁴Then I myself will admit to you
　　that your own right hand can save you.

¹⁵"Look at the behemoth,^a
　　which I made along with you
　　and which feeds on grass like an ox.
¹⁶What strength he has in his loins,
　　what power in the muscles of his belly!
¹⁷His tail^b sways like a cedar;
　　the sinews of his thighs are close-knit.
¹⁸His bones are tubes of bronze,
　　his limbs like rods of iron.
¹⁹He ranks first among the works of God,
　　yet his Maker can approach him with his
　　sword.
²⁰The hills bring him their produce,
　　and all the wild animals play nearby.
²¹Under the lotus plants he lies,
　　hidden among the reeds in the marsh.
²²The lotuses conceal him in their shadow;
　　the poplars by the stream surround him.
²³When the river rages, he is not alarmed;
　　he is secure, though the Jordan should surge
　　against his mouth.
²⁴Can anyone capture him by the eyes,^c
　　or trap him and pierce his nose?

41 "Can you pull in the leviathan^d with a
　　fishhook
　　or tie down his tongue with a rope?
²Can you put a cord through his nose
　　or pierce his jaw with a hook?
³Will he keep begging you for mercy?
　　Will he speak to you with gentle words?
⁴Will he make an agreement with you
　　for you to take him as your slave for life?
⁵Can you make a pet of him like a bird
　　or put him on a leash for your girls?
⁶Will traders barter for him?
　　Will they divide him up among the merchants?
⁷Can you fill his hide with harpoons
　　or his head with fishing spears?
⁸If you lay a hand on him,
　　you will remember the struggle and never
　　do it again!

^a 15 Possibly the hippopotamus or the elephant
^b 17 Possibly trunk　　^c 24 Or by a water hole　　^d 1 Possibly the
crocodile

9Any hope of subduing him is false;
  the mere sight of him is overpowering.
10No one is fierce enough to rouse him.
  Who then is able to stand against me?
11Who has a claim against me that I must pay?
  Everything under heaven belongs to me.

12"I will not fail to speak of his limbs,
  his strength and his graceful form.
13Who can strip off his outer coat?
  Who would approach him with a bridle?
14Who dares open the doors of his mouth,
  ringed about with his fearsome teeth?
15His back has*a* rows of shields
  tightly sealed together;
16each is so close to the next
  that no air can pass between.
17They are joined fast to one another;
  they cling together and cannot be parted.
18His snorting throws out flashes of light;
  his eyes are like the rays of dawn.
19Firebrands stream from his mouth;
  sparks of fire shoot out.
20Smoke pours from his nostrils
  as from a boiling pot over a fire of reeds.
21His breath sets coals ablaze,
  and flames dart from his mouth.
22Strength resides in his neck;
  dismay goes before him.
23The folds of his flesh are tightly joined;
  they are firm and immovable.
24His chest is hard as rock,
  hard as a lower millstone.
25When he rises up, the mighty are terrified;
  they retreat before his thrashing.
26The sword that reaches him has no effect,
  nor does the spear or the dart or the javelin.
27Iron he treats like straw
  and bronze like rotten wood.
28Arrows do not make him flee;
  slingstones are like chaff to him.
29A club seems to him but a piece of straw;
  he laughs at the rattling of the lance.
30His undersides are jagged potsherds,
  leaving a trail in the mud like a threshing
    sledge.
31He makes the depths churn like a boiling caldron
  and stirs up the sea like a pot of ointment.
32Behind him he leaves a glistening wake;
  one would think the deep had white hair.
33Nothing on earth is his equal—
  a creature without fear.
34He looks down on all that are haughty;
  he is king over all that are proud."

a 15 Or His pride is his

9人指望捉拿牠是徒然的；
  一見牠，豈不喪膽嗎？
10沒有那麼兇猛的人敢惹牠。
  這樣，誰能在我面前站立得住呢？
11誰先給我甚麼，使我償還呢？
  天下萬物都是我的。

12"論到鱷魚的肢體和其大力，
  並美好的骨骼，我不能緘默不言。
13誰能剝牠的外衣？
  誰能進牠上下牙骨之間呢？
14誰能開牠的腮頰？
  牠牙齒四圍是可畏的。
15牠以堅固的鱗甲為可誇，
  緊緊合閉，封得嚴密。
16這鱗甲一一相連，
  甚至氣不得透入其間，
17都是互相聯絡、膠結，不能分離。
18牠打噴嚏，就發出光來；
  牠眼睛好像早晨的光線 (註："光線"
  原文作"眼皮")。
19從牠口中發出燒着的火把，
  與飛迸的火星；
20從牠鼻孔冒出烟來，
  如燒開的鍋和點着的蘆葦。
21牠的氣點着煤炭，
  有火焰從牠口中發出。
22牠頸項中存着勁力，
  在牠面前的都恐嚇蹦跳。
23牠的肉塊互相聯絡，
  緊貼其身，不能搖動。
24牠的心結實如石頭，
  如下磨石那樣結實。
25牠一起來，勇士都驚恐，
  心裏慌亂，便都昏迷。
26人若用刀，用槍，用標槍，
  用尖槍扎牠，都是無用。
27牠以鐵為乾草，
  以銅為爛木。
28箭不能恐嚇牠使牠逃避；
  彈石在牠看為碎稭，
29棍棒算為禾稭；
  牠嗤笑短槍颼的響聲。
30牠肚腹下如尖瓦片，
  牠如釘耙
    經過淤泥。
31牠使深淵開滾如鍋，
  使洋海如鍋中的膏油。
32牠行的路隨後發光，
  令人想深淵如同白髮。
33在地上沒有像牠造的
  那樣無所懼怕。
34凡高大的，牠無不藐視；
  牠在驕傲的水族上作王。"

約伯回答

42

約伯回答耶和華說：
2 "我知道你萬事都能做，
你的旨意不能攔阻。
3 誰用無知的言語
使你的旨意隱藏呢？
我所說的是我不明白的；
這些事太奇妙是我不知道的。

4 "求你聽我，我要說話；
我問你，
求你指示我。
5 我從前風聞有你，
現在親眼看見你。
6 因此我厭惡自己（註："自己或作"我的
言語"），在塵土和爐灰中懊悔。"

結語

7 耶和華對約伯說話以後，就對
提幔人以利法說："我的怒氣向你
和你兩個朋友發作，因為你們議論
我，不如我的僕人約伯說的是。8 現
在你們要取七隻公牛，七隻公羊，
到我僕人約伯那裏去，為自己獻上
燔祭，我的僕人約伯就為你們祈
禱。我因悅納他，就不按你們的愚
妄辦你們。你們議論我，不如我的
僕人約伯說的是。"9 於是提幔人以
利法、書亞人比勒達、拿瑪人瑣
法，照着耶和華所吩咐的去行。耶
和華就悅納約伯。

10 約伯為他的朋友祈禱，耶和華
就使約伯從苦境轉回（註："苦境"原文
作"擄掠"），並且耶和華賜給他的比
他從前所有的加倍。11 約伯的弟兄姐
妹和以先所認識的人都來見他，在他
家裏一同吃飯；又論到耶和華所降與
他的一切災禍，都為他悲傷安慰他，
每人也送他一塊銀子和一個金環。
12 這樣，耶和華後來賜福給約伯
比先前更多。他有一萬四千羊，六
千駱駝，一千對牛，一千母驢。13 他
也有七個兒子，三個女兒。14 他給長
女起名叫耶米瑪，次女叫基洗亞，
三女叫基連哈樸。15 在那全地的婦女
中，找不着像約伯的女兒那樣美
貌。她們的父親使她們在弟兄中得
產業。

16 此後，約伯又活了一百四十
年，得見他的兒孫，直到四代。17 這
樣，約伯年紀老邁，日子滿足而死。

Job

42

Then Job replied to the LORD:
2 "I know that you can do all things;
no plan of yours can be thwarted.
3 You asked, 'Who is this that obscures my
counsel without knowledge?'
Surely I spoke of things I did not understand,
things too wonderful for me to know.

4 "You said, 'Listen now, and I will speak;
I will question you,
and you shall answer me.'
5 My ears had heard of you
but now my eyes have seen you.
6 Therefore I despise myself
and repent in dust and ashes."

Epilogue

7 After the LORD had said these things to Job,
he said to Eliphaz the Temanite, "I am angry
with you and your two friends, because you
have not spoken of me what is right, as my servant Job has. 8 So now take seven bulls and seven
rams and go to my servant Job and sacrifice a
burnt offering for yourselves. My servant Job
will pray for you, and I will accept his prayer
and not deal with you according to your folly.
You have not spoken of me what is right, as my
servant Job has." 9 So Eliphaz the Temanite,
Bildad the Shuhite and Zophar the Naamathite
did what the LORD told them; and the LORD
accepted Job's prayer.

10 After Job had prayed for his friends, the
LORD made him prosperous again and gave him
twice as much as he had before. 11 All his brothers
and sisters and everyone who had known him
before came and ate with him in his house. They
comforted and consoled him over all the trouble
the LORD had brought upon him, and each one
gave him a piece of silver[a] and a gold ring.
12 The LORD blessed the latter part of Job's life
more than the first. He had fourteen thousand
sheep, six thousand camels, a thousand yoke of
oxen and a thousand donkeys. 13 And he also
had seven sons and three daughters. 14 The first
daughter he named Jemimah, the second Keziah
and the third Keren-Happuch. 15 Nowhere in all
the land were there found women as beautiful
as Job's daughters, and their father granted
them an inheritance along with their brothers.

16 After this, Job lived a hundred and forty years;
he saw his children and their children to the fourth
generation. 17 And so he died, old and full of years.

*a 11 Hebrew him a kesitah; a kesitah was a unit of money of
unknown weight and value.*

Psalms

BOOK I

Psalms 1-41

Psalm 1

¹Blessed is the man
   who does not walk in the counsel of the
      wicked
   or stand in the way of sinners
   or sit in the seat of mockers.
²But his delight is in the law of the LORD,
   and on his law he meditates day and night.
³He is like a tree planted by streams of water,
   which yields its fruit in season
   and whose leaf does not wither.
   Whatever he does prospers.

⁴Not so the wicked!
   They are like chaff
   that the wind blows away.
⁵Therefore the wicked will not stand in the
      judgment,
   nor sinners in the assembly of the righteous.

⁶For the LORD watches over the way of the
      righteous,
   but the way of the wicked will perish.

Psalm 2

¹Why do the nations conspire[a]
   and the peoples plot in vain?
²The kings of the earth take their stand
   and the rulers gather together
   against the LORD
   and against his Anointed One.[b]
³"Let us break their chains," they say,
   "and throw off their fetters."

⁴The One enthroned in heaven laughs;
   the LORD scoffs at them.
⁵Then he rebukes them in his anger
   and terrifies them in his wrath, saying,

詩篇

卷一

詩篇 1-41

第一篇

¹不從惡人的計謀，
   不站罪人的道路，
   不坐褻慢人的座位。

²惟喜愛耶和華的律法，
   晝夜思想，這人便為有福！
³他要像一棵樹栽在溪水旁，
   按時候結果子，
   葉子也不枯乾。
   凡他所做的盡都順利。

⁴惡人並不是這樣，
   乃像糠粃
   被風吹散。
⁵因此當審判的時候，
   惡人必站立不住；
   罪人在義人的會中也是如此。

⁶因為耶和華知道義人的道路，
   惡人的道路卻必滅亡。

第二篇

¹外邦為甚麼爭鬧？
   萬民為甚麼謀算虛妄的事？
²世上的君王一齊起來，
   臣宰一同商議，
   要敵擋耶和華
   並他的受膏者，
³說："我們要掙開他們的捆綁，
   脫去他們的繩索。"

⁴那坐在天上的必發笑；
   主必嗤笑他們。
⁵那時，他要在怒中責備他們，
   在烈怒中驚嚇他們，

---

a 1 Hebrew; Septuagint *rage*   *b* 2 Or *anointed one*

⁶說：“我已經立我的君
　　在錫安我的聖山上了。”

⁷受膏者說，我要傳聖旨：

　耶和華曾對我說：
　　“你是我的兒子，我今日生你。
⁸你求我，
　　我就將列國賜你為基業，
　　將地極賜你為田產。
⁹你必用鐵杖打破他們，
　　你必將他們
　　　如同窰匠的瓦器摔碎。”
¹⁰現在，你們君王應當省悟，
　　你們世上的審判官該受管教！
¹¹當存畏懼侍奉耶和華，
　　又當存戰兢而快樂。
¹²當以嘴親子，恐怕他發怒，
　　你們便在道中滅亡，
　　因為他的怒氣快要發作。
　　凡投靠他的，都是有福的。

第三篇

大衛逃避他兒子押沙龍的時候作的詩。

¹耶和華啊，我的敵人何其加增！
　　有許多人起來攻擊我；
²有許多人議論我說：
　　“他得不着神的幫助。”　　　細拉

³但你耶和華是我四圍的盾牌，
　　是我的榮耀，
　　又是叫我抬起頭來的。
⁴我用我的聲音求告耶和華，
　　他就從他的聖山上應允我。　細拉

⁵我躺下睡覺，我醒着，
　　耶和華都保佑我。
⁶雖有成萬的百姓來周圍攻擊我，
　　我也不怕。

⁷耶和華啊，求你起來！
　　我的神啊，求你救我！
　　因為你打了我一切仇敵的腮骨，
　　敲碎了惡人的牙齒。

⁸救恩屬乎耶和華，
　　願你賜福給你的百姓。　　細拉

⁶"I have installed my King^{*a*}
　　on Zion, my holy hill."

⁷I will proclaim the decree of the LORD:

　He said to me, "You are my Son^{*b*};
　　today I have become your Father.^{*c*}
⁸Ask of me,
　　and I will make the nations your inheritance,
　　the ends of the earth your possession.
⁹You will rule them with an iron scepter^{*d*};
　　you will dash them to pieces like pottery."

¹⁰Therefore, you kings, be wise;
　　be warned, you rulers of the earth.
¹¹Serve the LORD with fear
　　and rejoice with trembling.
¹²Kiss the Son, lest he be angry
　　and you be destroyed in your way,
　　for his wrath can flare up in a moment.
　　Blessed are all who take refuge in him.

Psalm 3

A psalm of David. When he fled from his son Absalom.

¹O LORD, how many are my foes!
　　How many rise up against me!
²Many are saying of me,
　　"God will not deliver him."　　*Selah^e*

³But you are a shield around me, O LORD;
　　you bestow glory on me and lift^{*f*} up my
　　head.
⁴To the LORD I cry aloud,
　　and he answers me from his holy hill.　*Selah*

⁵I lie down and sleep;
　　I wake again, because the LORD sustains me.
⁶I will not fear the tens of thousands
　　drawn up against me on every side.

⁷Arise, O LORD!
　　Deliver me, O my God!
　　Strike all my enemies on the jaw;
　　break the teeth of the wicked.

⁸From the LORD comes deliverance.
　　May your blessing be on your people.　*Selah*

a 6 Or *king*　*b* 7 Or *son;* also in verse 12　*c* 7 Or *have begotten you*　*d* 9 Or *will break them with a rod of iron*　*e* 2 A word of uncertain meaning, occurring frequently in the Psalms; possibly a musical term　*f* 3 Or *LORD, / my Glorious One, who lifts*

Psalm 4

For the director of music. With stringed instruments.
A psalm of David.

¹Answer me when I call to you,
  O my righteous God.
Give me relief from my distress;
  be merciful to me and hear my prayer.

²How long, O men, will you turn my glory into
  shame*a*?
How long will you love delusions and seek
  false gods*b*?   *Selah*
³Know that the LORD has set apart the godly for
  himself;
the LORD will hear when I call to him.

⁴In your anger do not sin;
  when you are on your beds,
search your hearts and be silent.   *Selah*
⁵Offer right sacrifices
  and trust in the LORD.

⁶Many are asking, "Who can show us any
  good?"
Let the light of your face shine upon us,
  O LORD.
⁷You have filled my heart with greater joy
  than when their grain and new wine
  abound.
⁸I will lie down and sleep in peace,
  for you alone, O LORD,
  make me dwell in safety.

Psalm 5

For the director of music. For flutes. A psalm of David.

¹Give ear to my words, O LORD,
  consider my sighing.
²Listen to my cry for help,
  my King and my God,
  for to you I pray.
³In the morning, O LORD, you hear my voice;
  in the morning I lay my requests before you
  and wait in expectation.

⁴You are not a God who takes pleasure in evil;
  with you the wicked cannot dwell.
⁵The arrogant cannot stand in your presence;
  you hate all who do wrong.

第四篇

大衛的詩，交與伶長。用絲弦的樂器。

¹顯我為義的神啊，
  我呼籲的時候，求你應允我！
我在困苦中，你曾使我寬廣；
  現在求你憐恤我，聽我的禱告。

²你們這上流人哪，你們將我的尊榮
  變為羞辱要到幾時呢？
你們喜愛虛妄、
  尋找虛假要到幾時呢？   細拉
³你們要知道，耶和華已經分別
  虔誠人歸他自己。
我求告耶和華，他必聽我。

⁴你們應當畏懼，不可犯罪；
  在牀上的時候，
要心裏思想，並要肅靜。   細拉
⁵當獻上公義的祭，
  又當倚靠耶和華。

⁶有許多人說：
  "誰能指示我們甚麼好處？"
耶和華啊，求你仰起臉來，
  光照我們！
⁷你使我心裏快樂，
  勝過那豐收五穀新酒的人。

⁸我必安然躺下睡覺，
  因為獨有你耶和華
  使我安然居住。

第五篇

大衛的詩，交與伶長。用吹的樂器。

¹耶和華啊，求你留心聽我的言語，
  顧念我的心思。
²我的王我的神啊，
  求你垂聽我呼求的聲音，
  因為我向你祈禱！
³耶和華啊，早晨你必聽我的聲音；
  早晨我必向你陳明我的心意，
  並要警醒。

⁴因為你不是喜悅惡事的神，
  惡人不能與你同居。
⁵狂傲人不能站在你眼前；
  凡作孽的，都是你所恨惡的。

---

a 2 Or you dishonor my Glorious One   b 2 Or seek lies

⁶說謊言的，你必滅絕；
　　好流人血弄詭詐的，
　　都為耶和華所憎惡。

⁷至於我，我必憑你豐盛的慈愛
　　進入你的居所；
　我必存敬畏你的心
　　向你的聖殿下拜。
⁸耶和華啊，求你因我的仇敵，
　　憑你的公義引領我，
　　使你的道路在我面前正直。

⁹因為他們的口中沒有誠實；
　　他們的心裏滿有邪惡。
　他們的喉嚨是敞開的墳墓；
　　他們用舌頭諂媚人。
¹⁰神啊，求你定他們的罪。
　　願他們因自己的計謀跌倒；
　願你在他們許多的過犯中把他們
　　逐出，因為他們背叛了你。

¹¹凡投靠你的，願他們喜樂，
　　時常歡呼。
　因為你護庇他們，
　　又願那愛你名的人
　　都靠你歡欣。
¹²因為你必賜福與義人，
　　耶和華啊，你必用恩惠如同盾牌
　　四面護衛他。

第六篇

大衛的詩，交與伶長。用絲弦的樂器，調用第八。

¹耶和華啊，求你不要在怒中責備我，
　　也不要在烈怒中懲罰我。
²耶和華啊，求你可憐我，因為我
　　軟弱！耶和華啊，求你醫治我，
　　因為我的骨頭發戰！
³我心也大大地驚惶。耶和華啊，
　　你要到幾時才救我呢？
⁴耶和華啊，求你轉回搭救我；
　　因你的慈愛拯救我。
⁵因為在死地無人記念你，
　　在陰間有誰稱謝你？

⁶我因唉哼而困乏，
　　我每夜流淚，把牀榻漂起，
　　把褥子濕透。
⁷我因憂愁眼睛乾癟，
　　又因我一切的敵人眼睛昏花。

⁶You destroy those who tell lies;
　　bloodthirsty and deceitful men
　　the LORD abhors.

⁷But I, by your great mercy,
　　will come into your house;
　in reverence will I bow down
　　toward your holy temple.
⁸Lead me, O LORD, in your righteousness
　　because of my enemies—
　　make straight your way before me.

⁹Not a word from their mouth can be trusted;
　　their heart is filled with destruction.
　Their throat is an open grave;
　　with their tongue they speak deceit.
¹⁰Declare them guilty, O God!
　　Let their intrigues be their downfall.
　Banish them for their many sins,
　　for they have rebelled against you.

¹¹But let all who take refuge in you be glad;
　　let them ever sing for joy.
　Spread your protection over them,
　　that those who love your name may rejoice
　　in you.
¹²For surely, O LORD, you bless the righteous;
　　you surround them with your favor as with
　　a shield.

Psalm 6

For the director of music. With stringed instruments.
According to *sheminith*.^a A psalm of David.

¹O LORD, do not rebuke me in your anger
　　or discipline me in your wrath.
²Be merciful to me, LORD, for I am faint;
　　O LORD, heal me, for my bones are in agony.
³My soul is in anguish.
　　How long, O LORD, how long?

⁴Turn, O LORD, and deliver me;
　　save me because of your unfailing love.
⁵No one remembers you when he is dead.
　　Who praises you from the grave^b?

⁶I am worn out from groaning;
　　all night long I flood my bed with weeping
　　and drench my couch with tears.
⁷My eyes grow weak with sorrow;
　　they fail because of all my foes.

a Title: Probably a musical term　　*b* 5 Hebrew *Sheol*

⁸Away from me, all you who do evil,
for the LORD has heard my weeping.
⁹The LORD has heard my cry for mercy;
the LORD accepts my prayer.
¹⁰All my enemies will be ashamed and
dismayed;
they will turn back in sudden disgrace.

Psalm 7

*A shiggaion^a of David, which he sang to the LORD
concerning Cush, a Benjamite.*

¹O LORD my God, I take refuge in you;
save and deliver me from all who pursue
me,
²or they will tear me like a lion
and rip me to pieces with no one to rescue
me.

³O LORD my God, if I have done this
and there is guilt on my hands—
⁴if I have done evil to him who is at peace with
me
or without cause have robbed my foe—
⁵then let my enemy pursue and overtake me;
let him trample my life to the ground
and make me sleep in the dust.　　　*Selah*

⁶Arise, O LORD, in your anger;
rise up against the rage of my enemies.
Awake, my God; decree justice.
⁷Let the assembled peoples gather around you.
Rule over them from on high;
⁸　let the LORD judge the peoples.
Judge me, O LORD, according to my
righteousness,
according to my integrity, O Most High.
⁹O righteous God,
who searches minds and hearts,
bring to an end the violence of the wicked
and make the righteous secure.

¹⁰My shield^b is God Most High,
who saves the upright in heart.
¹¹God is a righteous judge,
a God who expresses his wrath every day.
¹²If he does not relent,
he^c will sharpen his sword;
he will bend and string his bow.
¹³He has prepared his deadly weapons;
he makes ready his flaming arrows.

⁸你們一切作孽的人，離開我吧！
因為耶和華聽了我哀哭的聲音。
⁹耶和華聽了我的懇求，
耶和華必收納我的禱告！
¹⁰我的一切仇敵都必羞愧，
大大驚惶；
他們必要退後，忽然羞愧。

第七篇

大衛指着便雅憫人古實的話，
向耶和華唱的流離歌。

¹耶和華我的神啊，我投靠你，
求你救我脫離一切追趕我的人，
將我救拔出來！
²恐怕他們像獅子撕裂我，
甚至撕碎，無人搭救。

³耶和華我的神啊，我若行了這事，
若有罪孽在我手裏，
⁴我若以惡報那與我交好的人，
（連那無故與我為敵的，
我也救了他。）
⁵就任憑仇敵追趕我，直到追上，
將我的性命踏在地下，
使我的榮耀歸於灰塵。　　　細拉

⁶耶和華啊，求你在怒中起來，
挺身而立，抵擋我敵人的暴怒！
求你為我興起，
你已經命定施行審判！
⁷願眾民的會環繞你；
願你從其上歸於高位！
⁸耶和華向眾民施行審判。
耶和華啊，求你按我的公義
和我心中的純正判斷我。
⁹願惡人的惡斷絕；
願你堅立義人！
因為公義的神
察驗人的心腸肺腑。

¹⁰神是我的盾牌，
他拯救心裏正直的人。
¹¹神是公義的審判者，
又是天天向惡人發怒的神。
¹²若有人不回頭，
他的刀必磨快，
弓必上弦，預備妥當了；
¹³他也預備了殺人的器械，
他所射的是火箭。

a Title: Probably a literary or musical term　　*b* 10 Or *sovereign*
c 12 Or *If a man does not repent, / God*

¹⁴試看惡人因奸惡而劬勞，
　　所懷的是毒害，
　　所生的是虛假。
¹⁵他掘了坑，又挖深了，
　　竟掉在自己所挖的阱裏。
¹⁶他的毒害必臨到他自己的頭上；
　　他的強暴必落到他自己的腦袋上。

¹⁷我要照着耶和華的公義稱謝他，
　　歌頌耶和華至高者的名。

第八篇

大衛的詩，交與伶長。用迦特樂器。

¹耶和華我們的主啊，
　　你的名在全地何其美！

　你將你的榮耀
　　彰顯於天。
²你因敵人的緣故，
　　從嬰孩和吃奶的口中建立了能力，
　使仇敵和報仇的
　　閉口無言。

³我觀看
　　你指頭所造的天，
　並你所陳設的
　　月亮星宿，
⁴便說，人算甚麼，你竟顧念他？
　　世人算甚麼，你竟眷顧他？
⁵你叫他比天使（註：或作"神"）
　　微小一點，
　並賜他榮耀尊貴為冠冕。

^{6、7、8}你派他管理你手所造的，
　　使萬物，
　就是一切的牛羊、
　　田野的獸、
　空中的鳥、
　　海裏的魚，
　凡經行海道的，
　　都服在他的腳下。

⁹耶和華我們的主啊，
　　你的名在全地何其美！

¹⁴He who is pregnant with evil
　　and conceives trouble gives birth to
　　　disillusionment.
¹⁵He who digs a hole and scoops it out
　　falls into the pit he has made.
¹⁶The trouble he causes recoils on himself;
　　his violence comes down on his own head.

¹⁷I will give thanks to the LORD because of his
　　righteousness
　and will sing praise to the name of the LORD
　　Most High.

Psalm 8

For the director of music. According to *gittith.*[a]
A psalm of David.

¹O LORD, our Lord,
　　how majestic is your name in all the earth!

　You have set your glory
　　above the heavens.
²From the lips of children and infants
　　you have ordained praise[b]
　because of your enemies,
　　to silence the foe and the avenger.

³When I consider your heavens,
　　the work of your fingers,
　the moon and the stars,
　　which you have set in place,
⁴what is man that you are mindful of him,
　　the son of man that you care for him?
⁵You made him a little lower than the heavenly
　　beings[c]
　and crowned him with glory and honor.

⁶You made him ruler over the works of your
　　hands;
　you put everything under his feet:
⁷all flocks and herds,
　　and the beasts of the field,
⁸the birds of the air,
　　and the fish of the sea,
　all that swim the paths of the seas.

⁹O LORD, our Lord,
　　how majestic is your name in all the earth!

---

a Title: Probably a musical term　　*b 2 Or strength*　　*c 5 Or than God*

Psalm 9[a]

For the director of music. To [the tune of] "The Death of
the Son." A psalm of David.

[1]I will praise you, O LORD, with all my heart;
　　I will tell of all your wonders.
[2]I will be glad and rejoice in you;
　　I will sing praise to your name, O Most
　　　High.

[3]My enemies turn back;
　　they stumble and perish before you.
[4]For you have upheld my right and my cause;
　　you have sat on your throne, judging
　　　righteously.
[5]You have rebuked the nations and destroyed
　　　the wicked;
　　you have blotted out their name for ever and
　　　ever.
[6]Endless ruin has overtaken the enemy,
　　you have uprooted their cities;
　　even the memory of them has perished.

[7]The LORD reigns forever;
　　he has established his throne for judgment.
[8]He will judge the world in righteousness;
　　he will govern the peoples with justice.
[9]The LORD is a refuge for the oppressed,
　　a stronghold in times of trouble.
[10]Those who know your name will trust in you,
　　for you, LORD, have never forsaken those
　　　who seek you.

[11]Sing praises to the LORD, enthroned in Zion;
　　proclaim among the nations what he has
　　　done.
[12]For he who avenges blood remembers;
　　he does not ignore the cry of the afflicted.

[13]O LORD, see how my enemies persecute me!
　　Have mercy and lift me up from the gates of
　　　death,
[14]that I may declare your praises
　　in the gates of the Daughter of Zion
　　and there rejoice in your salvation.
[15]The nations have fallen into the pit they have
　　　dug;
　　their feet are caught in the net they have
　　　hidden.

---

[a] Psalms 9 and 10 may have been originally a single acrostic
poem, the stanzas of which begin with the successive letters of
the Hebrew alphabet. In the Septuagint they constitute one
psalm.

第九篇

大衛的詩,交與伶長。調用"慕拉便"。

[1]我要一心稱謝耶和華;
　　我要傳揚你一切奇妙的作為!
[2]我要因你歡喜快樂;
　　至高者啊,我要歌頌你的名!

[3]我的仇敵轉身退去的時候,
　　他們一見你的面就跌倒滅亡。
[4]因為你已經為我伸冤,為我辨屈;
　　你坐在寶座上,
　　按公義審判。
[5]你曾斥責外邦,
　　你曾滅絕惡人;
　　你曾塗抹他們的名,
　　直到永永遠遠。
[6]仇敵到了盡頭,他們被毀壞,
　　直到永遠;他們拆毀他們的城邑,
　　連他們的名號都歸於無有。

[7]惟耶和華坐着為王,直到永遠!
　　他已經為審判設擺他的寶座。
[8]他要按公義審判世界,
　　按正直判斷萬民。
[9]耶和華又要給受欺壓的人作高臺,
　　在患難的時候作高臺。
[10]耶和華啊,
　　認識你名的人要倚靠你,
　　因你沒有離棄尋求你的人。

[11]應當歌頌居錫安的耶和華,
　　將他所行的
　　傳揚在眾民中。
[12]因為那追討流人血之罪的,
　　他記念受屈的人,
　　不忘記困苦人的哀求。

[13]耶和華啊,你是從死birth
　　把我提拔起來的;求你憐恤我,
　　看那恨我的人所加給我的苦難,
[14]好叫我述說你一切的美德。
　　我必在錫安城(註:"城"原文作"女
　　子")的門因你的救恩歡樂。
[15]外邦人陷在
　　自己所掘的坑中;
　　他們的腳在自己暗設的網羅裏
　　纏住了。

¹⁶耶和華已將自己顯明了，
　　他已施行審判；惡人被自己手
　　　　所做的纏住了（註：或作"他叫惡
　　　　人被自己手所做的累住了"）。　細拉
¹⁷惡人，就是忘記神的外邦人，
　　都必歸到陰間。
¹⁸窮乏人必不永久被忘；
　　困苦人的指望必不永遠落空。
¹⁹耶和華啊，求你起來，不容人得勝，
　　願外邦人在你面前受審判！
²⁰耶和華啊，求你使外邦人恐懼，
　　願他們知道自己不過是人！　細拉

第十篇

¹耶和華啊，你為甚麼站在遠處？
　　在患難的時候，為甚麼隱藏？

²惡人在驕橫中把困苦人追得火急，
　　願他們陷在自己所設的計謀裏。
³因為惡人以心願自誇，貪財的背棄
　　耶和華，並且輕慢他（註：或作"他
　　祝福貪財的，卻輕慢耶和華"）。
⁴惡人面帶驕傲，說：
　　"耶和華必不追究。"
　　他一切所想的，都以為沒有神。
⁵凡他所做的，時常穩固；
　　你的審判超過他的眼界。
　　至於他一切的敵人，
　　他都向他們噴氣。
⁶他心裏說："我必不動搖，
　　世世代代不遭災難。"
⁷他滿口是咒罵、詭詐、欺壓，
　　舌底是毒害、奸惡。
⁸他在村莊埋伏等候，
　　他在隱密處殺害無辜的人。
　　他的眼睛窺探無倚無靠的人。
⁹他埋伏在暗地，如獅子蹲在洞中。
　　他埋伏，要擄去困苦人；
　　他拉網，就把困苦人擄去。

¹⁰他屈身蹲伏，無倚無靠的人就倒在他
　　爪牙之下（註："爪牙"或作"強暴人"）。
¹¹他心裏說："神竟忘記了，
　　他掩面永不觀看。"

¹²耶和華啊，求你起來！神啊，
　　求你舉手，不要忘記困苦人！

¹⁶The LORD is known by his justice;
　　the wicked are ensnared by the work of their
　　　hands. *Higgaion.^a Selah*
¹⁷The wicked return to the grave,^b
　　all the nations that forget God.
¹⁸But the needy will not always be forgotten,
　　nor the hope of the afflicted ever perish.

¹⁹Arise, O LORD, let not man triumph;
　　let the nations be judged in your presence.
²⁰Strike them with terror, O LORD;
　　let the nations know they are but men. *Selah*

Psalm 10^c

¹Why, O LORD, do you stand far off?
　　Why do you hide yourself in times of
　　　trouble?

²In his arrogance the wicked man hunts down
　　the weak,
　　who are caught in the schemes he devises.
³He boasts of the cravings of his heart;
　　he blesses the greedy and reviles the LORD.
⁴In his pride the wicked does not seek him;
　　in all his thoughts there is no room for God.
⁵His ways are always prosperous;
　　he is haughty and your laws are far from
　　　him;
　　he sneers at all his enemies.
⁶He says to himself, "Nothing will shake me;
　　I'll always be happy and never have
　　　trouble."
⁷His mouth is full of curses and lies and threats;
　　trouble and evil are under his tongue.
⁸He lies in wait near the villages;
　　from ambush he murders the innocent,
　　watching in secret for his victims.
⁹He lies in wait like a lion in cover;
　　he lies in wait to catch the helpless;
　　he catches the helpless and drags them off in
　　　his net.
¹⁰His victims are crushed, they collapse;
　　they fall under his strength.
¹¹He says to himself, "God has forgotten;
　　he covers his face and never sees."

¹²Arise, LORD! Lift up your hand, O God.
　　Do not forget the helpless.

---

a 16 Or *Meditation; possibly a musical notation　　b 17* Hebrew
Sheol　　c Psalms 9 and 10 may have been originally a single
acrostic poem, the stanzas of which begin with the successive
letters of the Hebrew alphabet. In the Septuagint they
constitute one psalm.

¹³Why does the wicked man revile God?
Why does he say to himself,
"He won't call me to account"?
¹⁴But you, O God, do see trouble and grief;
you consider it to take it in hand.
The victim commits himself to you;
you are the helper of the fatherless.
¹⁵Break the arm of the wicked and evil man;
call him to account for his wickedness
that would not be found out.

¹⁶The LORD is King for ever and ever;
the nations will perish from his land.
¹⁷You hear, O LORD, the desire of the afflicted;
you encourage them, and you listen to their
cry,
¹⁸defending the fatherless and the oppressed,
in order that man, who is of the earth, may
terrify no more.

Psalm 11

For the director of music. Of David.

¹In the LORD I take refuge.
How then can you say to me:
"Flee like a bird to your mountain.
²For look, the wicked bend their bows;
they set their arrows against the strings
to shoot from the shadows
at the upright in heart.
³When the foundations are being destroyed,
what can the righteous do*ᵃ*?"

⁴The LORD is in his holy temple;
the LORD is on his heavenly throne.
He observes the sons of men;
his eyes examine them.
⁵The LORD examines the righteous,
but the wicked*ᵇ* and those who love violence
his soul hates.
⁶On the wicked he will rain
fiery coals and burning sulfur;
a scorching wind will be their lot.

⁷For the LORD is righteous,
he loves justice;
upright men will see his face.

¹³惡人為何輕慢神，
心裏說：
"你必不追究"？
¹⁴其實你已經觀看，因為奸惡毒害，
你都看見了，為要以手施行報應。
無倚無靠的人把自己交託你，
你向來是幫助孤兒的。
¹⁵願你打斷惡人的膀臂；
至於壞人，願你追究他的惡，
直到淨盡。

¹⁶耶和華永永遠遠為王，
外邦人從他的地已經滅絕了。
¹⁷耶和華啊，謙卑人的心願，
你早已知道（註：原文作"聽見"）；
你必預備他們的心，
也必側耳聽他們的祈求，
¹⁸為要給孤兒和受欺壓的人伸冤，
使強橫的人不再威嚇他們。

第十一篇

大衛的詩，交與伶長。

¹我是投靠耶和華，
你們怎麼對我說：
"你當像鳥飛往你的山去。
²看哪，惡人彎弓，
把箭搭在弦上，
要在暗中
射那心裏正直的人。
³根基若毀壞，
義人還能做甚麼呢？"

⁴耶和華在他的聖殿裏，
耶和華的寶座在天上；
他的慧眼
察看世人。
⁵耶和華試驗義人；
惟有惡人和喜愛強暴的人，
他心裏恨惡。
⁶他要向惡人密布網羅，
有烈火、硫磺、熱風
作他們杯中的分。

⁷因為耶和華是公義的，
他喜愛公義，
正直人必得見他的面。

---

*a 3 Or what is the Righteous One doing   b 5 Or The LORD, the
Righteous One, examines the wicked, |*

第十二篇

大衛的詩，交與伶長。調用第八。

1耶和華啊，求你幫助！
　　因虔誠人斷絕了，
　　世人中間的忠信人沒有了。
2人人向鄰舍說謊，他們說話，
　　是嘴唇油滑，心口不一。
3凡油滑的嘴唇和誇大的舌頭，
　　耶和華必要剪除。
4他們曾說：「我們必能以舌頭得勝，
　　我們的嘴唇是我們自己的，
　　誰能作我們的主呢？」
5耶和華說：「因為困苦人的冤屈
　　和貧窮人的歎息，
　我現在要起來，
　　把他安置在
　　　他所切慕的穩妥之地。」
6耶和華的言語是純淨的言語，
　　如同銀子
　　在泥爐中煉過七次。

7耶和華啊，你必保護他們，
　　你必保佑他們永遠脫離這世代的人。
8下流人在世人中升高，
　　就有惡人到處遊行。

第十三篇

大衛的詩，交與伶長。

1耶和華啊，你忘記我要到幾時呢？
　　要到永遠嗎？
　　你掩面不顧我要到幾時呢？
2我心裏籌算，終日愁苦要到幾時呢？
　　我的仇敵升高壓制我要到幾時呢？

3耶和華我的神啊，求你看顧我，
　　應允我，使我眼目光明，
　　免得我沉睡至死；
4免得我的仇敵說：「我勝了他」；
　　免得我的敵人
　　在我搖動的時候喜樂。

5但我倚靠你的慈愛，
　　我的心因你的救恩快樂。
6我要向耶和華歌唱，
　　因他用厚恩待我。

Psalm 12

For the director of music. According to *sheminith.*[a]
A psalm of David.

1Help, LORD, for the godly are no more;
　　the faithful have vanished from among men.
2Everyone lies to his neighbor;
　　their flattering lips speak with deception.

3May the LORD cut off all flattering lips
　　and every boastful tongue
4that says, "We will triumph with our tongues;
　　we own our lips[b]—who is our master?"

5"Because of the oppression of the weak
　　and the groaning of the needy,
　I will now arise," says the LORD.
　　"I will protect them from those who malign
　　them."
6And the words of the LORD are flawless,
　　like silver refined in a furnace of clay,
　　purified seven times.

7O LORD, you will keep us safe
　　and protect us from such people forever.
8The wicked freely strut about
　　when what is vile is honored among men.

Psalm 13

For the director of music. A psalm of David.

1How long, O LORD? Will you forget me forever?
　　How long will you hide your face from me?
2How long must I wrestle with my thoughts
　　and every day have sorrow in my heart?
　　How long will my enemy triumph over me?

3Look on me and answer, O LORD my God.
　　Give light to my eyes, or I will sleep in
　　death;
4my enemy will say, "I have overcome him,"
　　and my foes will rejoice when I fall.

5But I trust in your unfailing love;
　　my heart rejoices in your salvation.
6I will sing to the LORD,
　　for he has been good to me.

*a Title: Probably a musical term   b 4 Or / our lips are our
plowshares*

Psalm 14

For the director of music. Of David.

[1]The fool[a] says in his heart,
　"There is no God."
They are corrupt, their deeds are vile;
　there is no one who does good.

[2]The LORD looks down from heaven
　on the sons of men
to see if there are any who understand,
　any who seek God.
[3]All have turned aside,
　they have together become corrupt;
there is no one who does good,
　not even one.

[4]Will evildoers never learn—
　those who devour my people as men eat
　　bread
and who do not call on the LORD?
[5]There they are, overwhelmed with dread,
　for God is present in the company of the
　　righteous.
[6]You evildoers frustrate the plans of the poor,
　but the LORD is their refuge.

[7]Oh, that salvation for Israel would come out of
　　Zion!
When the LORD restores the fortunes of his
　　people,
let Jacob rejoice and Israel be glad!

Psalm 15

A psalm of David.

[1]LORD, who may dwell in your sanctuary?
　Who may live on your holy hill?

[2]He whose walk is blameless
　and who does what is righteous,
who speaks the truth from his heart
[3]　and has no slander on his tongue,
who does his neighbor no wrong
　and casts no slur on his fellowman,
[4]who despises a vile man
　but honors those who fear the LORD,
who keeps his oath
　even when it hurts,

a 1 The Hebrew words rendered *fool* in Psalms denote one
who is morally deficient.

第十四篇

大衛的詩，交與伶長。

[1]愚頑人心裏說：
　"沒有神。"
他們都是邪惡，行了可憎惡的事；
　沒有一個人行善。

[2]耶和華從天上
　垂看世人，
要看有明白的沒有，
　有尋求神的沒有。
[3]他們都偏離正路，
　一同變為污穢；
並沒有行善的，
　連一個也沒有！

[4]作孽的都沒有知識嗎？
　他們吞吃我的百姓
　　如同吃飯一樣，
並不求告耶和華。
[5]他們在那裏大大地害怕，
　因為神在義人的族類中。

[6]你們叫困苦人的謀算變為羞辱，
　然而耶和華是他的避難所。

[7]但願以色列的救恩從錫安而出，
　耶和華救回他被擄的子民。
那時，雅各要快樂，
　以色列要歡喜。

第十五篇

大衛的詩。

[1]耶和華啊，誰能寄居你的帳幕？
　誰能住在你的聖山？

[2]就是行為正直，
　作事公義，
　心裏說實話的人。
[3]他不以舌頭讒謗人，
　不惡待朋友，
　也不隨夥毀謗鄰里。
[4]他眼中藐視匪類，
　卻尊重那敬畏耶和華的人。
他發了誓，雖然自己吃虧，
　也不更改。

⁵他不放債取利，
　　不受賄賂以害無辜。

行這些事的人
　　必永不動搖。

第十六篇

大衛的金詩。

¹神啊，求你保佑我，
　　因為我投靠你。

²我的心哪，你曾對耶和華說：
　　"你是我的主，
　　我的好處不在你以外。"
³論到世上的聖民，
　　他們又美又善，是我最喜悅的。
⁴以別神代替耶和華的（註：或作"送禮
　　物給別神的"），
　　他們的愁苦必加增。
　　他們所澆奠的血我不獻上；
　　我嘴唇也不提別神的名號。
⁵耶和華是我的產業，
　　是我杯中的分；
　　我所得的，你為我持守。
⁶用繩量給我的地界，
　　坐落在佳美之處；
　　我的產業實在美好。

⁷我必稱頌那指教我的耶和華；
　　我的心腸在夜間也警戒我。
⁸我將耶和華常擺在我面前，
　　因他在我右邊，
　　我便不至搖動。

⁹因此，我的心歡喜，我的靈（註：原
　　文作"榮耀"）快樂，
　　我的肉身也要安然居住。
¹⁰因為你必不將我的靈魂
　　撇在陰間，
　　也不叫你的聖者見朽壞。
¹¹你必將生命的道路指示我；
　　在你面前有滿足的喜樂，
　　在你右手中有永遠的福樂。

⁵who lends his money without usury
　　and does not accept a bribe against the
　　　innocent.

He who does these things
　　will never be shaken.

Psalm 16

A *miktam*[a] of David.

¹Keep me safe, O God,
　　for in you I take refuge.

²I said to the LORD, "You are my Lord;
　　apart from you I have no good thing."
³As for the saints who are in the land,
　　they are the glorious ones in whom is all my
　　　delight.[b]
⁴The sorrows of those will increase
　　who run after other gods.
　　I will not pour out their libations of blood
　　or take up their names on my lips.

⁵LORD, you have assigned me my portion and
　　my cup;
　　you have made my lot secure.
⁶The boundary lines have fallen for me in
　　pleasant places;
　　surely I have a delightful inheritance.

⁷I will praise the LORD, who counsels me;
　　even at night my heart instructs me.
⁸I have set the LORD always before me.
　　Because he is at my right hand,
　　I will not be shaken.

⁹Therefore my heart is glad and my tongue
　　rejoices;
　　my body also will rest secure,
¹⁰because you will not abandon me to the
　　grave,[c]
　　nor will you let your Holy One[d] see decay.
¹¹You have made[e] known to me the path of life;
　　you will fill me with joy in your presence,
　　with eternal pleasures at your right hand.

*a Title: Probably a literary or musical term　b 3 Or As for the
pagan priests who are in the land / and the nobles in whom all
delight, I said:　c 10 Hebrew Sheol　d 10 Or your faithful one
e 11 Or You will make*

Psalm 17

A prayer of David.

¹Hear, O LORD, my righteous plea;
    listen to my cry.
    Give ear to my prayer—
    it does not rise from deceitful lips.
²May my vindication come from you;
    may your eyes see what is right.

³Though you probe my heart and examine me
        at night,
    though you test me, you will find nothing;
    I have resolved that my mouth will not sin.
⁴As for the deeds of men—
    by the word of your lips
    I have kept myself
    from the ways of the violent.
⁵My steps have held to your paths;
    my feet have not slipped.

⁶I call on you, O God, for you will answer me;
    give ear to me and hear my prayer.
⁷Show the wonder of your great love,
    you who save by your right hand
    those who take refuge in you from their foes.
⁸Keep me as the apple of your eye;
    hide me in the shadow of your wings
⁹from the wicked who assail me,
    from my mortal enemies who surround me.

¹⁰They close up their callous hearts,
    and their mouths speak with arrogance.
¹¹They have tracked me down, they now
        surround me,
    with eyes alert, to throw me to the ground.
¹²They are like a lion hungry for prey,
    like a great lion crouching in cover.

¹³Rise up, O LORD, confront them, bring them
        down;
    rescue me from the wicked by your sword.
¹⁴O LORD, by your hand save me from such
        men,
    from men of this world whose reward is in
        this life.

    You still the hunger of those you cherish;
        their sons have plenty,
    and they store up wealth for their children.
¹⁵And I—in righteousness I will see your face;
    when I awake, I will be satisfied with seeing
        your likeness.

第十七篇

大衛的祈禱。

¹耶和華啊,求你聽聞公義,
    側耳聽我的呼籲!
    求你留心聽我
    這不出於詭詐嘴唇的祈禱。
²願我的判語從你面前發出;
    願你的眼睛觀看公正。

³你已經試驗我的心,
    你在夜間鑒察我,
    你熬煉我,卻找不着甚麼,
    我立志叫我口中沒有過失。
⁴論到人的行為,
    我藉着你嘴唇的言語
        自己謹守,
    不行強暴人的道路。
⁵我的腳踏定了你的路徑;
    我的兩腳未曾滑跌。

⁶神啊,我曾求告你,因為你必應允我;
    求你向我側耳,聽我的言語!
⁷求你顯出你奇妙的慈愛來,
    你是那用右手拯救投靠你的,
    脫離起來攻擊他們的人。
⁸求你保護我,如同保護眼中的瞳人;
    將我隱藏在你翅膀的蔭下,
⁹使我脫離那欺壓我的惡人,
    就是圍困我要害我命的仇敵。

¹⁰他們的心被脂油包裹;
    他們用口說驕傲的話。
¹¹他們圍困了我們的腳步,
    他們瞪着眼,
    要把我們推倒在地。
¹²他像獅子急要抓食,
    又像少壯獅子蹲伏在暗處。

¹³耶和華啊,求你起來,
    前去迎敵,將他打倒,
    用你的刀救護我命脫離惡人。
¹⁴耶和華啊,
    求你用手救我脫離世人,
    脫離那只在今生有福分的世人!

    你把你的財寶充滿他們的肚腹;
        他們因有兒女就心滿意足,
    將其餘的財物留給他們的嬰孩。
¹⁵至於我,我必在義中見你的面;
    我醒了的時候,得見你的形像(註:
        "見"或作"着"),就心滿意足了。

第十八篇

耶和華的僕人大衛的詩，交與伶長。當耶和華
　救他脫離一切仇敵和掃羅之手的日子，
　　他向耶和華念這詩的話，說：

¹耶和華我的力量啊，我愛你！

²耶和華是我的巖石，我的山寨，
　　我的救主，我的神，
　　我的磐石，我所投靠的。
　他是我的盾牌，是拯救我的角，
　　是我的高臺。
³我要求告當讚美的耶和華，
　　這樣我必從仇敵手中被救出來。

⁴曾有死亡的繩索纏繞我，
　　匪類的急流使我驚懼；
⁵陰間的繩索纏繞我，
　　死亡的網羅臨到我。
⁶我在急難中求告耶和華，
　　向我的神呼求。
　他從殿中聽了我的聲音，
　　我在他面前的呼求入了他的耳中。

⁷那時，因他發怒，
　　地就搖撼戰抖；
　　山的根基也震動搖撼。
⁸從他鼻孔冒煙上騰；
　　從他口中發火焚燒，
　　連炭也著了。
⁹他又使天下垂，親自降臨，
　　有黑雲在他腳下。
¹⁰他坐着基路伯飛行；
　　他藉着風的翅膀快飛。
¹¹他以黑暗為藏身之處，
　　以水的黑暗、天空的厚雲
　　為他四圍的行宮。
¹²因他面前的光輝，
　　他的厚雲行過，
　　便有冰雹火炭。
¹³耶和華也在天上打雷，
　　至高者發出聲音，便有冰雹火炭。
¹⁴他射出箭來，
　　使仇敵四散；
　　多多發出閃電，使他們擾亂。
¹⁵耶和華啊，你的斥責一發，
　　你鼻孔的氣一出，
　　海底就出現，
　　大地的根基也顯露。

Psalm 18

For the director of music. Of David the servant of the LORD.
He sang to the Lord the words of this song when the Lord
delivered him from the hand of all his enemies and from
the hand of Saul. He said:

¹I love you, O LORD, my strength.

²The LORD is my rock, my fortress and my
　　deliverer;
　my God is my rock, in whom I take refuge.
　He is my shield and the horn*ᵃ* of my
　　salvation, my stronghold.
³I call to the LORD, who is worthy of praise,
　　and I am saved from my enemies.

⁴The cords of death entangled me;
　　the torrents of destruction overwhelmed me.
⁵The cords of the grave*ᵇ* coiled around me;
　　the snares of death confronted me.
⁶In my distress I called to the LORD;
　　I cried to my God for help.
　From his temple he heard my voice;
　　my cry came before him, into his ears.

⁷The earth trembled and quaked,
　　and the foundations of the mountains shook;
　　they trembled because he was angry.
⁸Smoke rose from his nostrils;
　　consuming fire came from his mouth,
　　burning coals blazed out of it.
⁹He parted the heavens and came down;
　　dark clouds were under his feet.
¹⁰He mounted the cherubim and flew;
　　he soared on the wings of the wind.
¹¹He made darkness his covering, his canopy
　　around him—
　　the dark rain clouds of the sky.
¹²Out of the brightness of his presence clouds
　　advanced,
　　with hailstones and bolts of lightning.
¹³The LORD thundered from heaven;
　　the voice of the Most High resounded.*ᶜ*
¹⁴He shot his arrows and scattered the
　　enemies,
　　great bolts of lightning and routed them.
¹⁵The valleys of the sea were exposed
　　and the foundations of the earth laid bare
　　at your rebuke, O LORD,
　　at the blast of breath from your nostrils.

a 2 Horn here symbolizes strength.　　b 5 Hebrew Sheol
c 13 Some Hebrew manuscripts and Septuagint (see also 2
Samuel 22:14); most Hebrew manuscripts resounded, / amid
hailstones and bolts of lightning

¹⁶He reached down from on high and took hold
 of me;
 he drew me out of deep waters.
¹⁷He rescued me from my powerful enemy,
 from my foes, who were too strong for me.
¹⁸They confronted me in the day of my disaster,
 but the LORD was my support.
¹⁹He brought me out into a spacious place;
 he rescued me because he delighted in me.

²⁰The LORD has dealt with me according to my
 righteousness;
 according to the cleanness of my hands he
 has rewarded me.
²¹For I have kept the ways of the LORD;
 I have not done evil by turning from my
 God.
²²All his laws are before me;
 I have not turned away from his decrees.
²³I have been blameless before him
 and have kept myself from sin.
²⁴The LORD has rewarded me according to my
 righteousness,
 according to the cleanness of my hands in his
 sight.

²⁵To the faithful you show yourself faithful,
 to the blameless you show yourself
 blameless,
²⁶to the pure you show yourself pure,
 but to the crooked you show yourself
 shrewd.
²⁷You save the humble
 but bring low those whose eyes are haughty.
²⁸You, O LORD, keep my lamp burning;
 my God turns my darkness into light.
²⁹With your help I can advance against a troop[a]
 with my God I can scale a wall.

³⁰As for God, his way is perfect;
 the word of the LORD is flawless.
 He is a shield
 for all who take refuge in him.
³¹For who is God besides the LORD?
 And who is the Rock except our God?
³²It is God who arms me with strength
 and makes my way perfect.
³³He makes my feet like the feet of a deer;
 he enables me to stand on the heights.
³⁴He trains my hands for battle;
 my arms can bend a bow of bronze.
³⁵You give me your shield of victory,
 and your right hand sustains me;
 you stoop down to make me great.

¹⁶他從高天伸手
 抓住我,
 把我從大水中拉上來。
¹⁷他救我脫離我的勁敵和那些
 恨我的人,因為他們比我強盛。
¹⁸我遭遇災難的日子,他們來攻擊我,
 但耶和華是我的倚靠。
¹⁹他又領我到寬闊之處,
 他救拔我,因我喜悅我。

²⁰耶和華按着我的公義
 報答我,
 按着我手中的清潔
 賞賜我。
²¹因為我遵守了耶和華的道,
 未曾作惡
 離開我的神。
²²他的一切典章常在我面前,
 他的律例我也未曾丟棄。
²³我在他面前作了完全人,
 我也保守自己遠離我的罪孽。
²⁴所以耶和華
 按我的公義,
 按我在他眼前手中的清潔
 償還我。

²⁵慈愛的人,你以慈愛待他;
 完全的人,你以完全待他;
²⁶清潔的人,你以清潔待他;
 乖僻的人,你以彎曲待他。
²⁷困苦的百姓,你必拯救;
 高傲的眼目,你必使他降卑。
²⁸你必點着我的燈;
 耶和華我的神必照明我的黑暗。
²⁹我藉着你衝入敵軍,
 藉着我的神跳過牆垣。

³⁰至於神,他的道是完全的;
 耶和華的話是煉淨的。
 凡投靠他的,
 他便作他們的盾牌。
³¹除了耶和華,誰是神呢?
 除了我們的神,誰是磐石呢?
³²惟有那以力量束我的腰,
 使我行為完全的,他是神。
³³他使我的腳快如母鹿的蹄,
 又使我在高處安穩。
³⁴他教導我的手能以爭戰,
 甚至我的膀臂能開銅弓。
³⁵你把你的救恩給我作盾牌,
 你的右手扶持我,
 你的溫和使我為大。

a 29 Or can run through a barricade

³⁶你使我腳下的地步寬闊；
　　我的腳未曾滑跌。

³⁷我要追趕我的仇敵，並要追上他們；
　　不將他們滅絕，我總不歸回。
³⁸我要打傷他們，使他們不能起來，
　　他們必倒在我的腳下。
³⁹因為你曾以力量束我的腰，
　　使我能爭戰；
　　你也使那起來攻擊我的，
　　都服在我以下。
⁴⁰你又使我的仇敵在我面前轉背逃跑，
　　叫我能以剪除那恨我的人。
⁴¹他們呼求，卻無人拯救；
　　就是呼求耶和華，他也不應允。
⁴²我搗碎他們，如同風前的灰塵，
　　倒出他們，如同街上的泥土。

⁴³你救我
　　脫離百姓的爭競，
　　立我作列國的元首，
　　我素不認識的民必侍奉我。
⁴⁴他們一聽見我的名聲，就必順從我；
　　外邦人要投降我。
⁴⁵外邦人要衰殘，
　　戰戰兢兢地出他們的營寨。

⁴⁶耶和華是活神；願我的磐石被人
　　稱頌！願救我的神被人尊崇！
⁴⁷這位神，就是那為我伸冤、
　　使眾民服在我以下的。
⁴⁸你救我脫離仇敵，又把我舉起，
　　高過那些起來攻擊我的；
　　你救我脫離強暴的人。
⁴⁹耶和華啊，
　　因此我要在外邦中稱謝你，
　　歌頌你的名。
⁵⁰耶和華賜極大的救恩給他所立的王，
　　施慈愛給他的受膏者，
　　就是給大衛和他的後裔，直到永遠。

第十九篇

大衛的詩，交與伶長。

¹諸天述說神的榮耀；
　　穹蒼傳揚他的手段。
²這日到那日發出言語；
　　這夜到那夜傳出知識。
³無言無語，
　　也無聲音可聽。
⁴它的量帶通遍天下，
　　它的言語傳到地極。

³⁶You broaden the path beneath me,
　　so that my ankles do not turn.

³⁷I pursued my enemies and overtook them;
　　I did not turn back till they were destroyed.
³⁸I crushed them so that they could not rise;
　　they fell beneath my feet.
³⁹You armed me with strength for battle;
　　you made my adversaries bow at my feet.
⁴⁰You made my enemies turn their backs in
　　flight,
　　and I destroyed my foes.
⁴¹They cried for help, but there was no one to
　　save them—
　　to the LORD, but he did not answer.
⁴²I beat them as fine as dust borne on the wind;
　　I poured them out like mud in the streets.

⁴³You have delivered me from the attacks of the
　　people;
　　you have made me the head of nations;
　　people I did not know are subject to me.
⁴⁴As soon as they hear me, they obey me;
　　foreigners cringe before me.
⁴⁵They all lose heart;
　　they come trembling from their strongholds.

⁴⁶The LORD lives! Praise be to my Rock!
　　Exalted be God my Savior!
⁴⁷He is the God who avenges me,
　　who subdues nations under me,
⁴⁸　who saves me from my enemies.
　　You exalted me above my foes;
　　from violent men you rescued me.
⁴⁹Therefore I will praise you among the nations,
　　O LORD;
　　I will sing praises to your name.
⁵⁰He gives his king great victories;
　　he shows unfailing kindness to his anointed,
　　to David and his descendants forever.

Psalm 19

For the director of music. A psalm of David.

¹The heavens declare the glory of God;
　　the skies proclaim the work of his hands.
²Day after day they pour forth speech;
　　night after night they display knowledge.
³There is no speech or language
　　where their voice is not heard.^a
⁴Their voice^b goes out into all the earth,
　　their words to the ends of the world.

*a 3 Or They have no speech, there are no words; | no sound is heard
from them　b 4 Septuagint, Jerome and Syriac; Hebrew line*

In the heavens he has pitched a tent for the
    sun,
5 which is like a bridegroom coming forth
    from his pavilion,
    like a champion rejoicing to run his course.
6It rises at one end of the heavens
    and makes its circuit to the other;
    nothing is hidden from its heat.

7The law of the LORD is perfect,
    reviving the soul.
    The statutes of the LORD are trustworthy,
    making wise the simple.
8The precepts of the LORD are right,
    giving joy to the heart.
    The commands of the LORD are radiant,
    giving light to the eyes.
9The fear of the LORD is pure,
    enduring forever.
    The ordinances of the LORD are sure
    and altogether righteous.
10They are more precious than gold,
    than much pure gold;
    they are sweeter than honey,
    than honey from the comb.
11By them is your servant warned;
    in keeping them there is great reward.

12Who can discern his errors?
    Forgive my hidden faults.
13Keep your servant also from willful sins;
    may they not rule over me.
    Then will I be blameless,
    innocent of great transgression.

14May the words of my mouth and the
    meditation of my heart
    be pleasing in your sight,
    O LORD, my Rock and my Redeemer.

Psalm 20

For the director of music. A psalm of David.

1May the LORD answer you when you are in
    distress;
    may the name of the God of Jacob protect
    you.
2May he send you help from the sanctuary
    and grant you support from Zion.
3May he remember all your sacrifices
    and accept your burnt offerings.   Selah
4May he give you the desire of your heart
    and make all your plans succeed.

神在其間
    為太陽安設帳幕，
5太陽如同新郎出洞房，
    又如勇士歡然奔路。

6它從天這邊出來，
    繞到天那邊，
    沒有一物被隱藏不得它的熱氣。

7耶和華的律法全備，
    能甦醒人心；
    耶和華的法度確定，
    能使愚人有智慧；
8耶和華的訓詞正直，
    能快活人的心；
    耶和華的命令清潔，
    能明亮人的眼目；
9耶和華的道理潔淨，
    存到永遠；
    耶和華的典章真實，
    全然公義。
10都比金子可羨慕，
    且比極多的精金可羨慕；
    比蜜甘甜，
    且比蜂房下滴的蜜甘甜。
11況且你的僕人因此受警戒，
    守著這些便有大賞。

12誰能知道自己的錯失呢？
    願你赦免我隱而未現的過錯。
13求你攔阻僕人不犯任意妄為的罪，
    不容這罪轄制我，
    我便完全，
    免犯大罪。

14耶和華我的磐石，
    我的救贖主啊！
    願我口中的言語，心裏的意念，
    在你面前蒙悅納。

第二十篇

大衛的詩，交與伶長。

1願耶和華在你遭難的日子
    應允你；
    願名為雅各神的
    高舉你。
2願他從聖所救助你，
    從錫安堅固你。
3記念你的一切供獻，
    悅納你的燔祭。   細拉
4將你心所願的賜給你，
    成就你的一切籌算。

⁵我們要因你的救恩誇勝，
　　要奉我們神的名
　　豎立旌旗。
　願耶和華成就你一切所求的。

⁶現在我知道耶和華救護他的受膏者，
　　必從他的聖天上應允他，
　　用右手的能力救護他。
⁷有人靠車，有人靠馬，
　　但我們要提到耶和華
　　我們神的名。
⁸他們都屈身仆倒；
　　我們卻起來，立得正直。

⁹求耶和華施行拯救，
　　我們呼求的時候，願王應允我們！

第二十一篇

大衛的詩，交與伶長。

¹耶和華啊，王必因你的能力歡喜；
　　因你的救恩，他的快樂何其大！
²他心裏所願的，你已經賜給他；
　　他嘴唇所求的，你未嘗不應允。
　　　　　　　　　　　　　細拉
³你以美福迎接他，
　　把精金的冠冕戴在他頭上。
⁴他向你求壽，你便賜給他，
　　就是日子長久，直到永遠。
⁵他因你的救恩
　　大有榮耀，
　　你又將尊榮威嚴
　　加在他身上。
⁶你使他有洪福，直到永遠，
　　又使他在你面前
　　歡喜快樂。
⁷王倚靠耶和華，
　　因至高者的慈愛
　　必不搖動。

⁸你的手要搜出你的一切仇敵，
　　你的右手要搜出那些恨你的人。
⁹你發怒的時候，
　　要使他們如在炎熱的火爐中。
　耶和華要在他的震怒中吞滅他們，
　　那火要把他們燒盡了。
¹⁰你必從世上滅絕他們的子孫（註：
　　"子孫"原文作"果子"），
　　從人間滅絕他們的後裔。
¹¹因為他們有意加害於你，
　　他們想出計謀，
　　卻不能做成。
¹²你必使他們轉背逃跑，

⁵We will shout for joy when you are victorious
　　and will lift up our banners in the name of
　　our God.
　May the L<small>ORD</small> grant all your requests.

⁶Now I know that the L<small>ORD</small> saves his anointed;
　　he answers him from his holy heaven
　　with the saving power of his right hand.
⁷Some trust in chariots and some in horses,
　　but we trust in the name of the L<small>ORD</small> our
　　God.
⁸They are brought to their knees and fall,
　　but we rise up and stand firm.

⁹O L<small>ORD</small>, save the king!
　Answer^a us when we call!

Psalm 21

For the director of music. A psalm of David.

¹O L<small>ORD</small>, the king rejoices in your strength.
　　How great is his joy in the victories you give!
²You have granted him the desire of his heart
　　and have not withheld the request of his lips.
　　　　　　　　　　　　　Selah

³You welcomed him with rich blessings
　　and placed a crown of pure gold on his head.
⁴He asked you for life, and you gave it to him—
　　length of days, for ever and ever.
⁵Through the victories you gave, his glory is
　　great;
　　you have bestowed on him splendor and
　　majesty.
⁶Surely you have granted him eternal blessings
　　and made him glad with the joy of your
　　presence.
⁷For the king trusts in the L<small>ORD</small>;
　　through the unfailing love of the Most High
　　he will not be shaken.

⁸Your hand will lay hold on all your enemies;
　　your right hand will seize your foes.
⁹At the time of your appearing
　　you will make them like a fiery furnace.
　In his wrath the L<small>ORD</small> will swallow them up,
　　and his fire will consume them.
¹⁰You will destroy their descendants from the
　　earth,
　　their posterity from mankind.
¹¹Though they plot evil against you
　　and devise wicked schemes, they cannot
　　succeed;
¹²for you will make them turn their backs

a 9 Or save! / O King, answer

when you aim at them with drawn bow.

¹³Be exalted, O LORD, in your strength;
    we will sing and praise your might.

Psalm 22

For the director of music. To the tune of "The Doe of the
Morning." A psalm of David.

¹My God, my God, why have you forsaken me?
    Why are you so far from saving me,
        so far from the words of my groaning?
²O my God, I cry out by day, but you do not
    answer,
        by night, and am not silent.

³Yet you are enthroned as the Holy One;
    you are the praise of Israel.^a
⁴In you our fathers put their trust;
    they trusted and you delivered them.
⁵They cried to you and were saved;
    in you they trusted and were not disappointed.

⁶But I am a worm and not a man,
    scorned by men and despised by the people.
⁷All who see me mock me;
    they hurl insults, shaking their heads:
⁸"He trusts in the LORD;
    let the LORD rescue him.
    Let him deliver him,
        since he delights in him."

⁹Yet you brought me out of the womb;
    you made me trust in you
        even at my mother's breast.
¹⁰From birth I was cast upon you;
    from my mother's womb you have been my
        God.
¹¹Do not be far from me,
    for trouble is near
        and there is no one to help.

¹²Many bulls surround me;
    strong bulls of Bashan encircle me.
¹³Roaring lions tearing their prey
    open their mouths wide against me.
¹⁴I am poured out like water,
    and all my bones are out of joint.
    My heart has turned to wax;
        it has melted away within me.
¹⁵My strength is dried up like a potsherd,
    and my tongue sticks to the roof of my
        mouth;

向他們的臉搭箭在弦。
¹³耶和華啊，
    願你因自己的能力顯為至高！
    這樣，我們就唱詩歌頌你的大能！

第二十二篇

大衛的詩，交與伶長。調用"朝鹿"。

¹我的神，我的神！為甚麼離棄我？
    為甚麼遠離不救我，
    不聽我唉哼的言語？
²我的神啊，
    我白日呼求，你不應允；
    夜間呼求，並不住聲。

³但你是聖潔的，是用以色列的讚美
    為寶座的（註："寶座"或作"居所"）。
⁴我們的祖宗倚靠你，
    他們倚靠你，你便解救他們。
⁵他們哀求你，便蒙解救；
    他們倚靠你，就不羞愧。

⁶但我是蟲，不是人，
    被眾人羞辱，被百姓藐視。
⁷凡看見我的都嗤笑我；
    他們撇嘴搖頭，說：
⁸"他把自己交託耶和華，
    耶和華可以救他吧！
    耶和華既喜悅他，
    可以搭救他吧！"

⁹但你是叫我出母腹的，
    我在母懷裏，
    你就使我有倚靠的心。
¹⁰我自出母胎就被交在你手裏，
    從我母親生我，
    你就是我的神。
¹¹求你不要遠離我，
    因為急難臨近了，
    沒有人幫助我。

¹²有許多公牛圍繞我，
    巴珊大力的公牛四面困住我；
¹³牠們向我張口，
    好像抓撕吼叫的獅子。
¹⁴我如水被倒出來，
    我的骨頭都脫了節，
    我心在我裏面
    如蠟熔化。
¹⁵我的精力枯乾，如同瓦片；
    我的舌頭貼在我牙牀上。

a 3 Or Yet you are holy, / enthroned on the praises of Israel

你將我安置在死地的塵土中。
16犬類圍着我，
　　惡黨環繞我；
　　他們扎了我的手、我的腳。
17我的骨頭，我都能數過；
　　他們瞪着眼看我。
18他們分我的外衣，
　　為我的裏衣拈鬮。

19耶和華啊，求你不要遠離我！
　　我的救主啊，求你快來幫助我！
20求你救我的靈魂脫離刀劍，
　　救我的生命脫離犬類（註：「生命」
　　　原文作「獨一者」），
21救我脫離獅子的口；你已經應允我，
　　使我脫離野牛的角。
22我要將你的名傳與我的弟兄，
　　在會中我要讚美你！
23你們敬畏耶和華的人要讚美他！
　　雅各的後裔都要榮耀他！
　　以色列的後裔都要懼怕他！
24因為他沒有藐視憎惡受苦的人，
　　也沒有向他掩面；
　　那受苦之人呼籲的時候，
　　他就垂聽。

25我在大會中讚美你的話
　　是從你而來的；
　　我要在敬畏耶和華的人面前
　　還我的願。
26謙卑的人必吃得飽足，
　　尋求耶和華的人必讚美他。
　　願你們的心永遠活着！
27地的四極都要想念耶和華，
　　並且歸順他；
　　列國的萬族
　　都要在你面前敬拜。
28因為國權是耶和華的；
　　他是管理萬國的。

29地上一切豐肥的人
　　必吃喝而敬拜；
　　凡下到塵土中
　　不能存活自己性命的人，
　　都要在他面前下拜。
30他必有後裔侍奉他；
　　主所行的事
　　必傳與後代！
31他們必來把他的公義
　　傳給將要生的民，
　　言明這事是他所行的。

you lay me[a] in the dust of death.
16Dogs have surrounded me;
　　a band of evil men has encircled me,
　　they have pierced[b] my hands and my feet.
17I can count all my bones;
　　people stare and gloat over me.
18They divide my garments among them
　　and cast lots for my clothing.

19But you, O Lord, be not far off;
　　O my Strength, come quickly to help me.
20Deliver my life from the sword,
　　my precious life from the power of the dogs.
21Rescue me from the mouth of the lions;
　　save[c] me from the horns of the wild oxen.

22I will declare your name to my brothers;
　　in the congregation I will praise you.
23You who fear the Lord, praise him!
　　All you descendants of Jacob, honor him!
　　Revere him, all you descendants of Israel!
24For he has not despised or disdained
　　the suffering of the afflicted one;
　　he has not hidden his face from him
　　but has listened to his cry for help.

25From you comes the theme of my praise in the
　　great assembly;
　　before those who fear you[d] will I fulfill my
　　vows.
26The poor will eat and be satisfied;
　　they who seek the Lord will praise him—
　　may your hearts live forever!
27All the ends of the earth
　　will remember and turn to the Lord,
　　and all the families of the nations
　　will bow down before him,
28for dominion belongs to the Lord
　　and he rules over the nations.

29All the rich of the earth will feast and
　　worship;
　　all who go down to the dust will kneel
　　before him—
　　those who cannot keep themselves alive.
30Posterity will serve him;
　　future generations will be told about the
　　Lord.
31They will proclaim his righteousness
　　to a people yet unborn—
　　for he has done it.

a 15 Or / I am laid　　b 16 Some Hebrew manuscripts,
Septuagint and Syriac; most Hebrew manuscripts / like the
lion,　　c 21 Or / you have heard　　d 25 Hebrew him

Psalm 23

A psalm of David.

[1]The LORD is my shepherd, I shall not be in
　want.
[2]　He makes me lie down in green pastures,
　he leads me beside quiet waters,
[3]　he restores my soul.
He guides me in paths of righteousness
　for his name's sake.
[4]Even though I walk
　through the valley of the shadow of death,[a]
I will fear no evil,
　for you are with me;
your rod and your staff,
　they comfort me.

[5]You prepare a table before me
　in the presence of my enemies.
You anoint my head with oil;
　my cup overflows.
[6]Surely goodness and love will follow me
　all the days of my life,
and I will dwell in the house of the LORD
　forever.

Psalm 24

Of David. A psalm.

[1]The earth is the LORD's, and everything in it,
　the world, and all who live in it;
[2]for he founded it upon the seas
　and established it upon the waters.

[3]Who may ascend the hill of the LORD?
　Who may stand in his holy place?
[4]He who has clean hands and a pure heart,
　who does not lift up his soul to an idol
　or swear by what is false.[b]
[5]He will receive blessing from the LORD
　and vindication from God his Savior.
[6]Such is the generation of those who seek him,
　who seek your face, O God of Jacob.[c]　*Selah*

[7]Lift up your heads, O you gates;
　be lifted up, you ancient doors,
　that the King of glory may come in.
[8]Who is this King of glory?
　The LORD strong and mighty,
　the LORD mighty in battle.

第二十三篇

大衛的詩。

[1]耶和華是我的牧者，
　我必不至缺乏。
[2]他使我躺臥在青草地上，
　領我在可安歇的水邊。
[3]他使我的靈魂甦醒，
　為自己的名
　引導我走義路。
[4]我雖然行過
　死蔭的幽谷，
　也不怕遭害，
因為你與我同在；
　你的杖，你的竿，
　都安慰我。

[5]在我敵人面前，
　你為我擺設筵席。
你用油膏了我的頭，
　使我的福杯滿溢。
[6]我一生一世
　必有恩惠慈愛隨著我，
我且要住在耶和華的殿中，
　直到永遠！

第二十四篇

大衛的詩。

[1]地和其中所充滿的，
　世界和住在其間的，都屬耶和華。
[2]他把地建立在海上，
　安定在大水之上。

[3]誰能登耶和華的山？
　誰能站在他的聖所？
[4]就是手潔心清，
　不向虛妄，
　起誓不懷詭詐的人。
[5]他必蒙耶和華賜福，
　又蒙救他的神使他成義。
[6]這是尋求耶和華的族類，
　是尋求你面的雅各。　　　　細拉

[7]眾城門哪，你們要抬起頭來！
　永久的門戶，你們要被舉起！
　那榮耀的王將要進來。
[8]榮耀的王是誰呢？
　就是有力有能的耶和華，
　在戰場上有能的耶和華。

---

a 4 Or *through the darkest valley*　b 4 Or *swear falsely*
c 6 Two Hebrew manuscripts and Syriac (see also Septuagint);
most Hebrew manuscripts *face, Jacob*

9眾城門哪，你們要抬起頭來！
　永久的門戶，你們要把頭抬起！
　那榮耀的王將要進來！
10榮耀的王是誰呢？
　萬軍之耶和華，
　他是榮耀的王！　　　　細拉

第二十五篇

大衛的詩。

1耶和華啊，我的心仰望你。
2我的神啊，我素來倚靠你。
　求你不要叫我羞愧，
　不要叫我的仇敵向我誇勝。
3凡等候你的
　必不羞愧；
　惟有那無故行奸詐的
　必要羞愧。

4耶和華啊，求你將你的道指示我，
　將你的路教訓我！
5求你以你的真理引導我，教訓我，
　因為你是救我的神，
　我終日等候你。
6耶和華啊，
　求你記念你的憐憫和慈愛，
　因為這是亙古以來所常有的。
7求你不要記念我幼年的罪愆
　和我的過犯。
　耶和華啊，求你因你的恩惠，
　按你的慈愛記念我。

8耶和華是良善正直的，
　所以他必指示罪人走正路。
9他必按公平引領謙卑人，
　將他的道教訓他們。
10凡遵守他的約
　和他法度的人，
　耶和華都以慈愛誠實待他。
11耶和華啊，求你因你的名赦免
　我的罪，因為我的罪重大。
12誰敬畏耶和華，
　耶和華必指示他
　當選擇的道路。
13他必安然居住，
　他的後裔必承受地土。
14耶和華與敬畏他的人親密，
　他必將自己的約指示他們。
15我的眼目時常仰望耶和華，
　因為他必將我的腳
　從網裏拉出來。

9Lift up your heads, O you gates;
　lift them up, you ancient doors,
　that the King of glory may come in.
10Who is he, this King of glory?
　The LORD Almighty—
　he is the King of glory.　　　*Selah*

Psalm 25[a]

Of David.

1To you, O LORD, I lift up my soul;
2　in you I trust, O my God.
　Do not let me be put to shame,
　nor let my enemies triumph over me.
3No one whose hope is in you
　will ever be put to shame,
　but they will be put to shame
　who are treacherous without excuse.

4Show me your ways, O LORD,
　teach me your paths;
5guide me in your truth and teach me,
　for you are God my Savior,
　and my hope is in you all day long.
6Remember, O LORD, your great mercy and
　love,
　for they are from of old.
7Remember not the sins of my youth
　and my rebellious ways;
　according to your love remember me,
　for you are good, O LORD.

8Good and upright is the LORD;
　therefore he instructs sinners in his ways.
9He guides the humble in what is right
　and teaches them his way.
10All the ways of the LORD are loving and faithful
　for those who keep the demands of his
　covenant.
11For the sake of your name, O LORD,
　forgive my iniquity, though it is great.
12Who, then, is the man that fears the LORD?
　He will instruct him in the way chosen for
　him.
13He will spend his days in prosperity,
　and his descendants will inherit the land.
14The LORD confides in those who fear him;
　he makes his covenant known to them.
15My eyes are ever on the LORD,
　for only he will release my feet from the
　snare.

a This psalm is an acrostic poem, the verses of which begin
with the successive letters of the Hebrew alphabet.

16Turn to me and be gracious to me,
　for I am lonely and afflicted.
17The troubles of my heart have multiplied;
　free me from my anguish.
18Look upon my affliction and my distress
　and take away all my sins.
19See how my enemies have increased
　and how fiercely they hate me!
20Guard my life and rescue me;
　let me not be put to shame,
　for I take refuge in you.
21May integrity and uprightness protect me,
　because my hope is in you.

22Redeem Israel, O God,
　from all their troubles!

Psalm 26

Of David.

1Vindicate me, O LORD,
　for I have led a blameless life;
　I have trusted in the LORD
　without wavering.
2Test me, O LORD, and try me,
　examine my heart and my mind;
3for your love is ever before me,
　and I walk continually in your truth.
4I do not sit with deceitful men,
　nor do I consort with hypocrites;
5I abhor the assembly of evildoers
　and refuse to sit with the wicked.
6I wash my hands in innocence,
　and go about your altar, O LORD,
7proclaiming aloud your praise
　and telling of all your wonderful deeds.
8I love the house where you live, O LORD,
　the place where your glory dwells.

9Do not take away my soul along with sinners,
　my life with bloodthirsty men,
10in whose hands are wicked schemes,
　whose right hands are full of bribes.
11But I lead a blameless life;
　redeem me and be merciful to me.

12My feet stand on level ground;
　in the great assembly I will praise the LORD.

Psalm 27

Of David.

1The LORD is my light and my salvation—
　whom shall I fear?

16求你轉向我，憐恤我，
　因為我是孤獨困苦。
17我心裏的愁苦甚多，
　求你救我脫離我的禍患。
18求你看顧我的困苦、我的艱難，
　赦免我一切的罪。
19求你察看我的仇敵，
　因為他們人多，並且痛痛地恨我。
20求你保護我的性命，搭救我，
　使我不至羞愧，
　因為我投靠你。
21願純全正直保守我，
　因為我等候你。

22神啊，求你救贖以色列
　脫離他一切的愁苦。

第二十六篇

大衛的詩。

1耶和華啊，求你為我伸冤，
　因我向來行事純全，
　我又倚靠耶和華
　並不搖動。
2耶和華啊，求你察看我，試驗我，
　熬煉我的肺腑心腸；
3因為你的慈愛常在我眼前，
　我也按你的真理而行。
4我沒有和虛謊人同坐，
　也不與瞞哄人的同羣；
5我恨惡惡人的會，
　必不與惡人同坐。
6耶和華啊，我要洗手表明無辜，
　才環繞你的祭壇；
7我好發稱謝的聲音，
　也要述說你一切奇妙的作為。
8耶和華啊，我喜愛你所住的殿
　和你顯榮耀的居所。

9不要把我的靈魂和罪人一同除掉；
　不要把我的性命和流人血的
　一同除掉。
10他們的手中有奸惡，
　右手滿有賄賂。
11至於我，卻要行事純全。
　求你救贖我，憐恤我！
12我的腳站在平坦地方，
　在眾會中我要稱頌耶和華！

第二十七篇

大衛的詩。

1耶和華是我的亮光，是我的拯救，
　我還怕誰呢？

耶和華是我性命的保障（註：“保障”或
　　作“力量”），我還懼誰呢？
2那作惡的，
　　就是我的仇敵，
　　前來吃我肉的時候，
　　就絆跌仆倒。
3雖有軍兵安營攻擊我，
　　我的心也不害怕；
　　雖然興起刀兵攻擊我，
　　我必仍舊安穩。

4有一件事，我曾求耶和華，
　　我仍要尋求：
　　就是一生一世
　　住在耶和華的殿中，
　　瞻仰他的榮美，
　　在他的殿裏求問。
5因為我遭遇患難，
　　他必暗暗地保守我；
　　在他亭子裏，把我藏在他帳幕的
　　隱密處，將我高舉在磐石上。
6現在我得以昂首，
　　高過四面的仇敵；
　　我要在他的帳幕裏
　　歡然獻祭，
　　我要唱詩歌頌耶和華！

7耶和華啊，我用聲音呼籲的時候，
　　求你垂聽，
　　並求你憐恤我，應允我。
8你説：“你們當尋求我的面。”
　　那時我心向你説：“耶和華啊，
　　你的面我正要尋求。”
9不要向我掩面，
　　不要發怒趕逐僕人，
　　你向來是幫助我的。
　　救我的神啊，不要丟棄我，
　　也不要離棄我。
10我父母離棄我，耶和華必收留我。
11耶和華啊，求你將你的道指教我，
　　因我仇敵的緣故
　　引導我走平坦的路。
12求你不要把我交給敵人，遂其所願；
　　因為妄作見證的和口吐兇言的，
　　起來攻擊我。
13我若不信在活人之地
　　得見耶和華的恩惠，
　　就早已喪膽了。
14要等候耶和華！
　　當壯膽，堅固你的心。
　　我再説：要等候耶和華！

The LORD is the stronghold of my life—
　　of whom shall I be afraid?
2When evil men advance against me
　　to devour my flesh,[a]
when my enemies and my foes attack me,
　　they will stumble and fall.
3Though an army besiege me,
　　my heart will not fear;
though war break out against me,
　　even then will I be confident.

4One thing I ask of the LORD,
　　this is what I seek:
that I may dwell in the house of the LORD
　　all the days of my life,
to gaze upon the beauty of the LORD
　　and to seek him in his temple.
5For in the day of trouble
　　he will keep me safe in his dwelling;
he will hide me in the shelter of his tabernacle
　　and set me high upon a rock.
6Then my head will be exalted
　　above the enemies who surround me;
at his tabernacle will I sacrifice with shouts of
　　　　joy;
I will sing and make music to the LORD.

7Hear my voice when I call, O LORD;
　　be merciful to me and answer me.
8My heart says of you, "Seek his[b] face!"
　　Your face, LORD, I will seek.
9Do not hide your face from me,
　　do not turn your servant away in anger;
　　you have been my helper.
Do not reject me or forsake me,
　　O God my Savior.
10Though my father and mother forsake me,
　　the LORD will receive me.
11Teach me your way, O LORD;
　　lead me in a straight path
　　because of my oppressors.
12Do not turn me over to the desire of my foes,
　　for false witnesses rise up against me,
　　breathing out violence.

13I am still confident of this:
　　I will see the goodness of the LORD
　　in the land of the living.
14Wait for the LORD;
　　be strong and take heart
　　and wait for the LORD.

a 2 Or to slander me　　b 8 Or To you, O my heart, he has said,
"Seek my

Psalm 28

Of David.

¹To you I call, O LORD my Rock;
  do not turn a deaf ear to me.
  For if you remain silent,
    I will be like those who have gone down to
    the pit.
²Hear my cry for mercy
  as I call to you for help,
  as I lift up my hands
    toward your Most Holy Place.

³Do not drag me away with the wicked,
  with those who do evil,
  who speak cordially with their neighbors
    but harbor malice in their hearts.
⁴Repay them for their deeds
  and for their evil work;
  repay them for what their hands have done
    and bring back upon them what they
    deserve.
⁵Since they show no regard for the works of the
    LORD
  and what his hands have done,
  he will tear them down
    and never build them up again.

⁶Praise be to the LORD,
  for he has heard my cry for mercy.
⁷The LORD is my strength and my shield;
  my heart trusts in him, and I am helped.
  My heart leaps for joy
    and I will give thanks to him in song.

⁸The LORD is the strength of his people,
  a fortress of salvation for his anointed one.
⁹Save your people and bless your inheritance;
  be their shepherd and carry them forever.

Psalm 29

A psalm of David.

¹Ascribe to the LORD, O mighty ones,
  ascribe to the LORD glory and strength.
²Ascribe to the LORD the glory due his name;
  worship the Lord in the splendor of his*ᵃ*
    holiness.

³The voice of the LORD is over the waters;
  the God of glory thunders,
  the LORD thunders over the mighty waters.

a 2 Or LORD *with the splendor of*

第二十八篇

大衛的詩。

¹耶和華啊，我要求告你；
  我的磐石啊，不要向我緘默；
  倘若你向我閉口，
    我就如將死的人一樣。

²我呼求你，
  向你至聖所舉手的時候，
  求你垂聽我懇求的聲音！

³不要把我和惡人並作孽的
    一同除掉；
  他們與鄰舍說和平話，
    心裏卻是奸惡。
⁴願你按着他們所做的，
  並他們所行的惡事待他們。
  願你照着他們手所做的待他們，
    將他們所應得的報應
    加給他們。
⁵他們既然不留心
  耶和華所行的
  和他手所做的，
  他就必毀壞他們，
    不建立他們。

⁶耶和華是應當稱頌的，
  因為他聽了我懇求的聲音。
⁷耶和華是我的力量，是我的盾牌；
  我心裏倚靠他，就得幫助；
  所以我心中歡樂，
    我必用詩歌頌讚他！

⁸耶和華是他百姓的力量，
  又是他受膏者得救的保障。
⁹求你拯救你的百姓，賜福給你的產業，
  牧養他們，扶持他們，直到永遠！

第二十九篇

大衛的詩。

¹神的眾子啊，你們要將榮耀能力
  歸給耶和華，歸給耶和華。
²要將耶和華的名所當得的榮耀
  歸給他，以聖潔的妝飾（註：“的”
    或作“為”）敬拜耶和華。

³耶和華的聲音發在水上，
  榮耀的神打雷，
  耶和華打雷在大水之上。

⁴耶和華的聲音大有能力；
　　耶和華的聲音滿有威嚴。
⁵耶和華的聲音震破香柏樹；
　　耶和華震碎
　　　黎巴嫩的香柏樹。
⁶他也使之跳躍如牛犢，
　　使黎巴嫩和西連跳躍如野牛犢。
⁷耶和華的聲音
　　使火焰分岔。
⁸耶和華的聲音震動曠野；
　　耶和華震動加低斯的曠野。
⁹耶和華的聲音驚動母鹿落胎，
　　樹木也脫落淨光。
　　凡在他殿中的，都稱說他的榮耀。

¹⁰洪水泛濫之時，耶和華坐着為王；
　　耶和華坐着為王，直到永遠。
¹¹耶和華必賜力量給他的百姓，
　　耶和華必賜平安的福給他的百姓。

第三十篇

大衛在獻殿的時候，作這詩歌。

¹耶和華啊，我要尊崇你，
　　因為你曾提拔我，
　　不叫仇敵向我誇耀。
²耶和華我的神啊，我曾呼求你，
　　你醫治了我。
³耶和華啊，
　　你曾把我的靈魂從陰間救上來，
　　使我存活，不至於下坑。
⁴耶和華的聖民哪，你們要歌頌他，
　　稱讚他可記念的聖名。
⁵因為他的怒氣不過是轉眼之間；
　　他的恩典乃是一生之久。
　　一宿雖然有哭泣，
　　早晨便必歡呼。

⁶至於我，我凡事平順，便說：
　　「我永不動搖。」
⁷耶和華啊，你曾施恩，
　　叫我的江山穩固；
　　你掩了面
　　我就驚惶。

⁸耶和華啊，我曾求告你。
　　我向耶和華懇求，說：
⁹「我被害流血，下到坑中，
　　有甚麼益處呢？
　　塵土豈能稱讚你，
　　傳說你的誠實嗎？

⁴The voice of the LORD is powerful;
　　the voice of the LORD is majestic.
⁵The voice of the LORD breaks the cedars;
　　the LORD breaks in pieces the cedars of
　　　Lebanon.
⁶He makes Lebanon skip like a calf,
　　Sirionᵃ like a young wild ox.
⁷The voice of the LORD strikes
　　with flashes of lightning.
⁸The voice of the LORD shakes the desert;
　　the LORD shakes the Desert of Kadesh.
⁹The voice of the LORD twists the oaksᵇ
　　and strips the forests bare.
　　And in his temple all cry, "Glory!"

¹⁰The LORD sitsᶜ enthroned over the flood;
　　the LORD is enthroned as King forever.
¹¹The LORD gives strength to his people;
　　the LORD blesses his people with peace.

Psalm 30

A psalm. A song. For the dedication of the temple.ᵈ Of David.

¹I will exalt you, O LORD,
　　for you lifted me out of the depths
　　and did not let my enemies gloat over me.
²O LORD my God, I called to you for help
　　and you healed me.
³O LORD, you brought me up from the graveᵉ;
　　you spared me from going down into the pit.

⁴Sing to the LORD, you saints of his;
　　praise his holy name.
⁵For his anger lasts only a moment,
　　but his favor lasts a lifetime;
　　weeping may remain for a night,
　　but rejoicing comes in the morning.

⁶When I felt secure, I said,
　　"I will never be shaken."
⁷O LORD, when you favored me,
　　you made my mountainᶠ stand firm;
　　but when you hid your face,
　　I was dismayed.

⁸To you, O LORD, I called;
　　to the Lord I cried for mercy:
⁹"What gain is there in my destruction,ᵍ
　　in my going down into the pit?
　　Will the dust praise you?
　　Will it proclaim your faithfulness?

ᵃ 6 That is, Mount Hermon　　ᵇ 9 Or LORD makes the deer give
birth　　ᶜ 10 Or sat　　ᵈ Title: Or palace　　ᵉ 3 Hebrew Sheol
ᶠ 7 Or hill country　　ᵍ 9 Or there if I am silenced

¹⁰Hear, O L<small>ORD</small>, and be merciful to me;
  O L<small>ORD</small>, be my help."

¹¹You turned my wailing into dancing;
  you removed my sackcloth and clothed me
    with joy,
¹²that my heart may sing to you and not be
    silent.
  O Lord my God, I will give you thanks
    forever.

Psalm 31

For the director of music. A psalm of David.

¹In you, O L<small>ORD</small>, I have taken refuge;
  let me never be put to shame;
  deliver me in your righteousness.
²Turn your ear to me,
  come quickly to my rescue;
  be my rock of refuge,
  a strong fortress to save me.
³Since you are my rock and my fortress,
  for the sake of your name lead and guide me.
⁴Free me from the trap that is set for me,
  for you are my refuge.
⁵Into your hands I commit my spirit;
  redeem me, O L<small>ORD</small>, the God of truth.

⁶I hate those who cling to worthless idols;
  I trust in the L<small>ORD</small>.
⁷I will be glad and rejoice in your love,
  for you saw my affliction
  and knew the anguish of my soul.
⁸You have not handed me over to the enemy
  but have set my feet in a spacious place.

⁹Be merciful to me, O L<small>ORD</small>, for I am in distress;
  my eyes grow weak with sorrow,
  my soul and my body with grief.
¹⁰My life is consumed by anguish
  and my years by groaning;
  my strength fails because of my affliction,^a
  and my bones grow weak.
¹¹Because of all my enemies,
  I am the utter contempt of my neighbors;
  I am a dread to my friends—
  those who see me on the street flee from me.
¹²I am forgotten by them as though I were dead;
  I have become like broken pottery.
¹³For I hear the slander of many;
  there is terror on every side;
  they conspire against me
  and plot to take my life.

a 10 Or guilt

---

¹⁰耶和華啊，求你應允我，憐恤我！
  耶和華啊，求你幫助我！」

¹¹你已將我的哀哭變為跳舞，
  將我的麻衣脫去，
  給我披上喜樂。
¹²好叫我的靈（註：原文作"榮耀"）
  歌頌你，並不住聲。
  耶和華我的神啊，
  我要稱謝你，直到永遠！

第三十一篇

大衛的詩，交與伶長。

¹耶和華啊，我投靠你，
  求你使我永不羞愧，
  憑你的公義搭救我。
²求你側耳而聽，
  快快救我！
  作我堅固的磐石，
  拯救我的保障。
³因為你是我的巖石，我的山寨，
  所以求你為你名的緣故
  引導我，指點我。
⁴求你救我脫離人為我暗設的網羅，
  因為你是我的保障。
⁵我將我的靈魂交在你手裏。
  耶和華誠實的神啊，你救贖了我。
⁶我恨惡那信奉虛無之神的人，
  我卻倚靠耶和華。
⁷我要為你的慈愛高興歡喜，
  因為你見過我的困苦，
  知道我心中的艱難。
⁸你未曾把我交在仇敵手裏；
  你使我的腳站在寬闊之處。
⁹耶和華啊，求你憐恤我，
  因為我在急難之中。
  我的眼睛因憂愁而乾癟，
  連我的身心也不安舒。
¹⁰我的生命為愁苦所消耗，
  我的年歲為歎息所曠廢；
  我的力量因我的罪孽衰敗，
  我的骨頭也枯乾。
¹¹我因一切敵人成了羞辱，
  在我的鄰舍跟前更甚；
  那認識我的都懼怕我，
  在外頭看見我的都躲避我。
¹²我被人忘記，如同死人，無人記念。
  我好像破碎的器皿。
¹³我聽見了許多人的讒謗，
  四圍都是驚嚇。
  他們一同商議攻擊我的時候，
  就圖謀要害我的性命。

14耶和華啊，我仍舊倚靠你；
　我說："你是我的神！"
15我終身的事在你手中，
　求你救我脫離仇敵的手
　和那些逼迫我的人。
16求你使你的臉光照僕人，
　憑你的慈愛拯救我。
17耶和華啊，求你叫我不至羞愧，
　因為我曾呼籲你；
　求你使惡人羞愧，
　使他們在陰間緘默無聲。
18那撒謊的人逞驕傲輕慢，
　出狂妄的話攻擊義人，
　願他的嘴啞而無言。

19敬畏你、投靠你的人，
　你為他們所積存的，
　在世人面前
　所施行的恩惠
　是何等大呢！
20你必把他們藏在你面前的隱密處，
　免得遇見人的計謀；
　你必暗暗地保守他們在亭子裏，
　免受口舌的爭鬧。

21耶和華是應當稱頌的！
　因為他在堅固城裏
　向我施展奇妙的慈愛。
22至於我，我曾急促地說：
　"我從你眼前被隔絕。"
　然而，我呼求你的時候，
　你仍聽我懇求的聲音。

23耶和華的聖民哪，你們都要愛他！
　耶和華保護誠實人，
　足足報應行事驕傲的人。
24凡仰望耶和華的人，
　你們都要壯膽，堅固你們的心。

第三十二篇

大衛的訓誨詩

1得赦免其過、
　遮蓋其罪的，
　這人是有福的！
2凡心裏沒有詭詐、
　耶和華不算為有罪的，
　這人是有福的！

3我閉口不認罪的時候，
　因終日唉哼
　而骨頭枯乾。

14But I trust in you, O LORD;
　I say, "You are my God."
15My times are in your hands;
　deliver me from my enemies
　and from those who pursue me.
16Let your face shine on your servant;
　save me in your unfailing love.
17Let me not be put to shame, O LORD,
　for I have cried out to you;
　but let the wicked be put to shame
　and lie silent in the grave.*a*
18Let their lying lips be silenced,
　for with pride and contempt
　they speak arrogantly against the righteous.

19How great is your goodness,
　which you have stored up for those who fear
　　you,
　which you bestow in the sight of men
　on those who take refuge in you.
20In the shelter of your presence you hide them
　from the intrigues of men;
　in your dwelling you keep them safe
　from accusing tongues.

21Praise be to the LORD,
　for he showed his wonderful love to me
　when I was in a besieged city.
22In my alarm I said,
　"I am cut off from your sight!"
　Yet you heard my cry for mercy
　when I called to you for help.

23Love the LORD, all his saints!
　The LORD preserves the faithful,
　but the proud he pays back in full.
24Be strong and take heart,
　all you who hope in the LORD.

Psalm 32

Of David. A *maskil.b*

1Blessed is he
　whose transgressions are forgiven,
　whose sins are covered.
2Blessed is the man
　whose sin the LORD does not count against
　　him
　and in whose spirit is no deceit.

3When I kept silent,
　my bones wasted away
　through my groaning all day long.

a 17 Hebrew Sheol　b Title: Probably a literary or musical term

⁴For day and night
   your hand was heavy upon me;
my strength was sapped
   as in the heat of summer.   *Selah*
⁵Then I acknowledged my sin to you
   and did not cover up my iniquity.
I said, "I will confess
   my transgressions to the LORD"—
and you forgave
   the guilt of my sin.   *Selah*

⁶Therefore let everyone who is godly pray to you
   while you may be found;
surely when the mighty waters rise,
   they will not reach him.
⁷You are my hiding place;
   you will protect me from trouble
and surround me with songs of deliverance.   *Selah*

⁸I will instruct you and teach you in the way
   you should go;
I will counsel you and watch over you.
⁹Do not be like the horse or the mule,
   which have no understanding
but must be controlled by bit and bridle
   or they will not come to you.
¹⁰Many are the woes of the wicked,
   but the LORD's unfailing love
surrounds the man who trusts in him.

¹¹Rejoice in the LORD and be glad, you righteous;
   sing, all you who are upright in heart!

Psalm 33

¹Sing joyfully to the LORD, you righteous;
   it is fitting for the upright to praise him.
²Praise the LORD with the harp;
   make music to him on the ten-stringed lyre.
³Sing to him a new song;
   play skillfully, and shout for joy.

⁴For the word of the LORD is right and true;
   he is faithful in all he does.
⁵The LORD loves righteousness and justice;
   the earth is full of his unfailing love.

⁶By the word of the LORD were the heavens
   made,
their starry host by the breath of his mouth.
⁷He gathers the waters of the sea into jars*ᵃ*;
   he puts the deep into storehouses.
⁸Let all the earth fear the LORD;

a 7 Or sea as into a heap

---

⁴黑夜白日，
   你的手在我身上沉重；
我的精液耗盡，
   如同夏天的乾旱。   細拉
⁵我向你陳明我的罪，
   不隱瞞我的惡。
我說：「我要向耶和華
   承認我的過犯。」
你就赦免
   我的罪惡。   細拉

⁶為此，凡虔誠人都當
   趁你可尋找的時候禱告你；
大水泛溢的時候，
   必不能到他那裏。
⁷你是我藏身之處，
   你必保佑我脫離苦難，
以得救的樂歌四面環繞我。
    細拉

⁸我要教導你，
   指示你當行的路；
我要定睛在你身上勸戒你。
⁹你不可像那無知的騾馬，
   必用嚼環轡頭勒住牠，
不然，
   就不能馴服。
¹⁰惡人必多受苦楚；
   惟獨倚靠耶和華的，
必有慈愛四面環繞他。

¹¹你們義人應當靠耶和華歡喜快樂；
   你們心裏正直的人都當歡呼。

第三十三篇

¹義人哪，你們應當靠耶和華歡樂；
   正直人的讚美是合宜的。
²你們應當彈琴稱謝耶和華，
   用十弦瑟歌頌他。
³應當向他唱新歌，
   彈得巧妙，聲音洪亮。

⁴因為耶和華的言語正直，
   凡他所做的，盡都誠實。
⁵他喜愛仁義公平，
   遍地滿了耶和華的慈愛。

⁶諸天藉耶和華的命而造；
   萬象藉他口中的氣而成。

⁷他聚集海水如壘，
   收藏深洋在庫房。
⁸願全地都敬畏耶和華；

願世上的居民都懼怕他。
9因為他說有，就有；
　　命立，就立。
10耶和華使列國的籌算歸於無有，
　　使眾民的思念無有功效。
11耶和華的籌算永遠立定，
　　他心中的思念萬代常存。

12以耶和華為神的，那國是有福的！
　　他所揀選為自己產業的，
　　那民是有福的！
13耶和華從天上觀看，
　　他看見一切的世人；
14從他的居所往外察看
　　地上一切的居民，
15他是那造成他們眾人心的，
　　留意他們一切作為的。
16君王不能因兵多得勝；
　　勇士不能因力大得救。
17靠馬得救是枉然的；
　　馬也不能因力大救人。
18耶和華的眼目
　　看顧敬畏他的人
　　和仰望他慈愛的人，
19要救他們的命脫離死亡，
　　並使他們在饑荒中存活。

20我們的心向來等候耶和華，
　　他是我們的幫助，我們的盾牌。
21我們的心必靠他歡喜，
　　因為我們向來倚靠他的聖名。
22耶和華啊，
　　求你照着我們所仰望你的，
　　向我們施行慈愛。

第三十四篇

大衛在亞比米勒面前裝瘋，被他趕出去，
就作這詩。

1我要時時稱頌耶和華，
　　讚美他的話必常在我口中。
2我的心必因耶和華誇耀；
　　謙卑人聽見，就要喜樂。
3你們和我當稱耶和華為大，
　　一同高舉他的名。

4我曾尋求耶和華，他就應允我，
　　救我脫離了一切的恐懼。
5凡仰望他的，便有光榮；
　　他們的臉，必不蒙羞。
6我這困苦人呼求，耶和華便垂聽，
　　救我脫離一切患難。

let all the people of the world revere him.
9For he spoke, and it came to be;
　　he commanded, and it stood firm.
10The LORD foils the plans of the nations;
　　he thwarts the purposes of the peoples.
11But the plans of the LORD stand firm forever,
　　the purposes of his heart through all
　　　generations.

12Blessed is the nation whose God is the LORD,
　　the people he chose for his inheritance.
13From heaven the LORD looks down
　　and sees all mankind;
14from his dwelling place he watches
　　all who live on earth—
15he who forms the hearts of all,
　　who considers everything they do.
16No king is saved by the size of his army;
　　no warrior escapes by his great strength.
17A horse is a vain hope for deliverance;
　　despite all its great strength it cannot save.
18But the eyes of the LORD are on those who fear
　　him,
　　on those whose hope is in his unfailing love,
19to deliver them from death
　　and keep them alive in famine.

20We wait in hope for the LORD;
　　he is our help and our shield.
21In him our hearts rejoice,
　　for we trust in his holy name.
22May your unfailing love rest upon us,
　　O LORD,
　　even as we put our hope in you.

Psalm 34[a]

Of David. When he pretended to be insane before Abimelech,
who drove him away, and he left.

1I will extol the LORD at all times;
　　his praise will always be on my lips.
2My soul will boast in the LORD;
　　let the afflicted hear and rejoice.
3Glorify the LORD with me;
　　let us exalt his name together.

4I sought the LORD, and he answered me;
　　he delivered me from all my fears.
5Those who look to him are radiant;
　　their faces are never covered with shame.
6This poor man called, and the LORD heard him;
　　he saved him out of all his troubles.

a This psalm is an acrostic poem, the verses of which begin
with the successive letters of the Hebrew alphabet.

⁷The angel of the LORD encamps around those
　who fear him,
　and he delivers them.

⁸Taste and see that the LORD is good;
　blessed is the man who takes refuge in him.
⁹Fear the LORD, you his saints,
　for those who fear him lack nothing.
¹⁰The lions may grow weak and hungry,
　but those who seek the LORD lack no good
　　thing.

¹¹Come, my children, listen to me;
　I will teach you the fear of the LORD.
¹²Whoever of you loves life
　and desires to see many good days,
¹³keep your tongue from evil
　and your lips from speaking lies.
¹⁴Turn from evil and do good;
　seek peace and pursue it.

¹⁵The eyes of the LORD are on the righteous
　and his ears are attentive to their cry;
¹⁶the face of the LORD is against those who do
　　evil,
　to cut off the memory of them from the
　　earth.

¹⁷The righteous cry out, and the LORD hears
　them;
　he delivers them from all their troubles.
¹⁸The LORD is close to the brokenhearted
　and saves those who are crushed in spirit.

¹⁹A righteous man may have many troubles,
　but the LORD delivers him from them all;
²⁰he protects all his bones,
　not one of them will be broken.

²¹Evil will slay the wicked;
　the foes of the righteous will be condemned.
²²The LORD redeems his servants;
　no one will be condemned who takes refuge
　　in him.

Psalm 35

Of David.

¹Contend, O LORD, with those who contend
　with me;
　fight against those who fight against me.
²Take up shield and buckler;
　arise and come to my aid.

⁷耶和華的使者，
　在敬畏他的人四圍
　安營搭救他們。

⁸你們要嘗嘗主恩的滋味，
　便知道他是美善；
　投靠他的人有福了！
⁹耶和華的聖民哪，你們當敬畏他，
　因敬畏他的一無所缺。
¹⁰少壯獅子還缺食忍餓；
　但尋求耶和華的，
　甚麼好處都不缺。
¹¹眾弟子啊，你們當來聽我的話！
　我要將敬畏耶和華的道教訓你們。
¹²有何人喜好存活，
　愛慕長壽，得享美福，
¹³就要禁止舌頭不出惡言，
　嘴唇不説詭詐的話。
¹⁴要離惡行善，
　尋求和睦，一心追趕。

¹⁵耶和華的眼目看顧義人；
　他的耳朵聽他們的呼求。
¹⁶耶和華向行惡的人變臉，
　要從世上
　　除滅他們的名號。

¹⁷義人呼求，
　耶和華聽見了，
　便救他們脱離一切患難。
¹⁸耶和華靠近傷心的人，
　拯救靈性痛悔的人。

¹⁹義人多有苦難，
　但耶和華救他脱離這一切，
²⁰又保全他一身的骨頭，
　連一根也不折斷。

²¹惡必害死惡人；
　恨惡義人的，必被定罪！
²²耶和華救贖他僕人的靈魂，
　凡投靠他的，必不至定罪！

第三十五篇

大衛的詩。

¹耶和華啊，
　與我相爭的，求你與他們相爭；
　與我相戰的，求你與他們相戰。
²拿着大小的盾牌，
　起來幫助我！

³抽出槍來，
　　擋住那追趕我的。
　求你對我的靈魂說：
　　「我是拯救你的。」

⁴願那尋索我命的，
　　蒙羞受辱；
　願那謀害我的，
　　退後羞愧。
⁵願他們像風前的糠，
　　有耶和華的使者
　　趕逐他們。
⁶願他們的道路又暗又滑，
　　有耶和華的使者追趕他們。
⁷因他們無故地為我暗設網羅，
　　無故地挖坑，要害我的性命。
⁸願災禍忽然臨到他身上；
　　願他暗設的網纏住自己；
　　願他落在其中遭災禍！
⁹我的心必靠耶和華快樂，
　　靠他的救恩高興。
¹⁰我的骨頭都要說：
　　「耶和華啊，誰能像你，
　救護困苦人
　　脫離那比他強壯的，
　救護困苦窮乏人
　　脫離那搶奪他的？」

¹¹兇惡的見證人起來，
　　盤問我所不知道的事。

¹²他們向我以惡報善，
　　使我的靈魂孤苦。
¹³至於我，當他們有病的時候，
　　我便穿麻衣，禁食，刻苦己心，
　我所求的
　　都歸到自己的懷中。
¹⁴我這樣行，
　　好像他是我的朋友、我的弟兄；
　我屈身悲哀，
　　如同人為母親哀痛。
¹⁵我在患難中，他們卻歡喜，大家聚集；
　　我所不認識的那些下流人
　　　聚集攻擊我，
　　他們不住地把我撕裂。
¹⁶他們如同席上好嬉笑的狂妄人
　　向我咬牙。
¹⁷主啊，你看着不理要到幾時呢？
　　求你救我的靈魂脫離他們的殘害；
　　救我的生命脫離少壯獅子（註：
　　　"生命"原文作"獨一者"）！
¹⁸我在大會中要稱謝你，
　　在眾民中要讚美你。

³Brandish spear and javelin^a
　　against those who pursue me.
　Say to my soul,
　　"I am your salvation."

⁴May those who seek my life
　　be disgraced and put to shame;
　may those who plot my ruin
　　be turned back in dismay.
⁵May they be like chaff before the wind,
　　with the angel of the LORD driving them
　　　away;
⁶may their path be dark and slippery,
　　with the angel of the LORD pursuing them.
⁷Since they hid their net for me without cause
　　and without cause dug a pit for me,
⁸may ruin overtake them by surprise—
　　may the net they hid entangle them,
　　may they fall into the pit, to their ruin.
⁹Then my soul will rejoice in the LORD
　　and delight in his salvation.
¹⁰My whole being will exclaim,
　　"Who is like you, O LORD?
　You rescue the poor from those too strong for
　　them,
　　the poor and needy from those who rob
　　them."

¹¹Ruthless witnesses come forward;
　　they question me on things I know nothing
　　　about.
¹²They repay me evil for good
　　and leave my soul forlorn.
¹³Yet when they were ill, I put on sackcloth
　　and humbled myself with fasting.
　When my prayers returned to me
　　　unanswered,
¹⁴　I went about mourning
　　as though for my friend or brother.
　I bowed my head in grief
　　as though weeping for my mother.
¹⁵But when I stumbled, they gathered in glee;
　　attackers gathered against me when I was
　　　unaware.
　They slandered me without ceasing.
¹⁶Like the ungodly they maliciously mocked^b;
　　they gnashed their teeth at me.
¹⁷O LORD, how long will you look on?
　　Rescue my life from their ravages,
　　my precious life from these lions.
¹⁸I will give you thanks in the great assembly;
　　among throngs of people I will praise you.

*a 3 Or and block the way　　b 16 Septuagint; Hebrew may mean
ungodly circle of mockers.*

19Let not those gloat over me
 who are my enemies without cause;
let not those who hate me without reason
 maliciously wink the eye.
20They do not speak peaceably,
 but devise false accusations
against those who live quietly in the land.
21They gape at me and say, "Aha! Aha!
 With our own eyes we have seen it."

22O LORD, you have seen this; be not silent.
 Do not be far from me, O LORD.
23Awake, and rise to my defense!
 Contend for me, my God and Lord.
24Vindicate me in your righteousness, O LORD
  my God;
 do not let them gloat over me.
25Do not let them think, "Aha, just what we
  wanted!"
 or say, "We have swallowed him up."

26May all who gloat over my distress
 be put to shame and confusion;
may all who exalt themselves over me
 be clothed with shame and disgrace.
27May those who delight in my vindication
 shout for joy and gladness;
may they always say, "The LORD be exalted,
 who delights in the well-being of his servant."
28My tongue will speak of your righteousness
 and of your praises all day long.

Psalm 36

For the director of music. Of David the servant of the LORD.

1An oracle is within my heart
 concerning the sinfulness of the wicked:a
There is no fear of God
 before his eyes.
2For in his own eyes he flatters himself
 too much to detect or hate his sin.
3The words of his mouth are wicked and deceitful;
 he has ceased to be wise and to do good.
4Even on his bed he plots evil;
 he commits himself to a sinful course
 and does not reject what is wrong.

5Your love, O LORD, reaches to the heavens,
 your faithfulness to the skies.
6Your righteousness is like the mighty
  mountains,
 your justice like the great deep.
O LORD, you preserve both man and beast.

a 1 Or heart: / Sin proceeds from the wicked.

19求你不容那無理與我為仇的
  向我誇耀;
 不容那無故恨我的
  向我擠眼。
20因為他們不說和平話,
  倒想出詭詐的言語
 害地上的安靜人。
21他們大大張口攻擊我,說:"阿哈!
 阿哈!我們的眼已經看見了。"
22耶和華啊,你已經看見了,
  求你不要閉口!
 主啊,求你不要遠離我!
23我的神、我的主啊,求你奮興醒起,
  判清我的事,伸明我的冤!
24耶和華我的神啊,
  求你按你的公義判斷我,
 不容他們向我誇耀。
25不容他們心裏說:
  "阿哈,遂我們的心願了!"
 不容他們說:
  "我們已經把他吞了!"
26願那喜歡我遭難的
  一同抱愧蒙羞;
 願那向我妄自尊大的
  披慚愧,蒙羞辱;
27願那喜悅我冤屈得伸的(註:"冤屈得
 伸"原文作"公義")歡呼快樂,
 願他們常說:"當尊耶和華為大!
 耶和華喜悅他的僕人平安。"
28我的舌頭要終日論說你的公義,
  時常讚美你。

第三十六篇

耶和華的僕人大衛的詩,交與伶長。

1惡人的罪過在他心裏說:
  "我眼中不怕神!"

2他自誇自媚,以為他的罪孽
  終不顯露,不被恨惡。
3他口中的言語盡是罪孽詭詐,
  他與智慧善行已經斷絕。
4他在牀上圖謀罪孽,
  定意行不善的道,
 不憎惡惡事。

5耶和華啊,你的慈愛上及諸天,
  你的信實達到穹蒼。
6你的公義好像高山,
  你的判斷如同深淵。
 耶和華啊,
  人民、牲畜,你都救護。

7神啊，
　你的慈愛何其寶貴！
　世人投靠在你翅膀的蔭下。
8他們必因你殿裏的肥甘得以飽足；
　你也必叫他們喝你樂河的水。

9因為在你那裏有生命的源頭，
　在你的光中，我們必得見光。

10願你常施慈愛給認識你的人，
　常以公義待心裏正直的人。
11不容驕傲人的腳踐踏我；
　不容兇惡人的手趕逐我。

12在那裏，作孽的人已經仆倒。
　他們被推倒，不能再起來。

第三十七篇

大衛的詩。

1不要為作惡的心懷不平，
　也不要向那行不義的生出嫉妒。
2因為他們如草快被割下，
　又如青菜快要枯乾。

3你當倚靠耶和華而行善，
　住在地上，以他的信實為糧；
4又要以耶和華為樂，
　他就將你心裏所求的賜給你。

5當將你的事交託耶和華，
　並倚靠他，他就必成全。
6他要使你的公義
　如光發出，
　使你的公平
　明如正午。

7你當默然倚靠耶和華，
　耐性等候他；
　不要因那道路通達的
　和那惡謀成就的心懷不平。

8當止住怒氣，離棄忿怒；
　不要心懷不平，以致作惡。
9因為作惡的必被剪除，
　惟有等候耶和華的
　必承受地土。

7 　How priceless is your unfailing love!
　Both high and low among men
　　find[a] refuge in the shadow of your wings.
8They feast on the abundance of your house;
　you give them drink from your river of
　　delights.
9For with you is the fountain of life;
　in your light we see light.

10Continue your love to those who know you,
　your righteousness to the upright in heart.
11May the foot of the proud not come against
　　me,
　nor the hand of the wicked drive me away.
12See how the evildoers lie fallen—
　thrown down, not able to rise!

Psalm 37[b]

Of David.

1Do not fret because of evil men
　or be envious of those who do wrong;
2for like the grass they will soon wither,
　like green plants they will soon die away.

3Trust in the LORD and do good;
　dwell in the land and enjoy safe pasture.
4Delight yourself in the LORD
　and he will give you the desires of your
　　heart.

5Commit your way to the LORD;
　trust in him and he will do this:
6He will make your righteousness shine like the
　　dawn,
　the justice of your cause like the noonday
　　sun.

7Be still before the LORD and wait patiently for
　　him;
　do not fret when men succeed in their ways,
　when they carry out their wicked schemes.

8Refrain from anger and turn from wrath;
　do not fret—it leads only to evil.
9For evil men will be cut off,
　but those who hope in the LORD will inherit
　　the land.

a 7 Or love, O God! / Men find; or love! / Both heavenly beings and
men / find   b This psalm is an acrostic poem, the stanzas of
which begin with the successive letters of the Hebrew
alphabet.

¹⁰A little while, and the wicked will be no more;
  though you look for them, they will not be
    found.
¹¹But the meek will inherit the land
  and enjoy great peace.

¹²The wicked plot against the righteous
  and gnash their teeth at them;
¹³but the Lord laughs at the wicked,
  for he knows their day is coming.

¹⁴The wicked draw the sword
  and bend the bow
to bring down the poor and needy,
  to slay those whose ways are upright.
¹⁵But their swords will pierce their own hearts,
  and their bows will be broken.

¹⁶Better the little that the righteous have
  than the wealth of many wicked;
¹⁷for the power of the wicked will be broken,
  but the Lᴏʀᴅ upholds the righteous.

¹⁸The days of the blameless are known to the
  Lᴏʀᴅ,
  and their inheritance will endure forever.
¹⁹In times of disaster they will not wither;
  in days of famine they will enjoy plenty.

²⁰But the wicked will perish:
  The Lᴏʀᴅ's enemies will be like the beauty of
    the fields,
  they will vanish—vanish like smoke.

²¹The wicked borrow and do not repay,
  but the righteous give generously;
²²those the Lᴏʀᴅ blesses will inherit the land,
  but those he curses will be cut off.

²³If the Lᴏʀᴅ delights in a man's way,
  he makes his steps firm;
²⁴though he stumble, he will not fall,
  for the Lᴏʀᴅ upholds him with his hand.

²⁵I was young and now I am old,
  yet I have never seen the righteous forsaken
  or their children begging bread.
²⁶They are always generous and lend freely;
  their children will be blessed.

²⁷Turn from evil and do good;
  then you will dwell in the land forever.
²⁸For the Lᴏʀᴅ loves the just
  and will not forsake his faithful ones.

¹⁰還有片時，惡人要歸於無有。
  你就是細察他的住處，
  也要歸於無有。
¹¹但謙卑人必承受地土，
  以豐盛的平安為樂。

¹²惡人設謀害義人，
  又向他咬牙。
¹³主要笑他，
  因見他受罰的日子將要來到。

¹⁴惡人已經弓上弦，
  刀出鞘，
  要打倒困苦窮乏的人，
  要殺害行動正直的人。
¹⁵他們的刀必刺入自己的心；
  他們的弓必被折斷。

¹⁶一個義人所有的雖少，
  強過許多惡人的富餘。
¹⁷因為惡人的膀臂必被折斷；
  但耶和華是扶持義人。

¹⁸耶和華知道
    完全人的日子，
  他們的產業要存到永遠。
¹⁹他們在急難的時候不至羞愧；
  在饑荒的日子必得飽足。

²⁰惡人卻要滅亡，
  耶和華的仇敵要像羊羔的脂油（註：
    或作「像草地的華美」），
  他們要消滅，要如煙消滅。

²¹惡人借貸而不償還；
  義人卻恩待人，並且施捨。
²²蒙耶和華賜福的，必承受地土；
  被他咒詛的，必被剪除。

²³義人的腳步被耶和華立定，
  他的道路，耶和華也喜愛。
²⁴他雖失腳，也不至全身仆倒，
  因為耶和華用手攙扶他（註：或作
    "攙扶他的手"）。

²⁵我從前年幼，現在年老，
  卻未見過義人被棄，
  也未見過他的後裔討飯。
²⁶他終日恩待人，借給人，
  他的後裔也蒙福。

²⁷你當離惡行善，
  就可永遠安居。
²⁸因為耶和華喜愛公平，
  不撇棄他的聖民。

他們永蒙保佑，
　　但惡人的後裔
　　必被剪除。
29義人必承受地土，
　　永居其上。

30義人的口談論智慧，
　　他的舌頭講說公平。
31神的律法在他心裏，
　　他的腳總不滑跌。

32惡人窺探義人，
　　想要殺他。
33耶和華必不撇他
　　在惡人手中，
　　當審判的時候，
　　也不定他的罪。

34你當等候耶和華，
　　遵守他的道，
　　他就抬舉你，使你承受地土。
　　惡人被剪除的時候，你必看見。

35我見過惡人大有勢力，
　　好像一棵青翠樹在本土生發。
36有人從那裏經過，
　　不料，他沒有了，
　　我也尋找他，卻尋不着。

37你要細察那完全人，觀看那正直人，
　　因為和平人有好結局。
38至於犯法的人，必一同滅絕，
　　惡人終必剪除。

39但義人得救，
　　是由於耶和華，
　　他在患難時作他們的營寨。
40耶和華幫助他們，解救他們；
　　他解救他們脫離惡人，
　　把他們救出來，
　　因為他們投靠他。

第三十八篇

大衛的紀念詩。

1耶和華啊，求你不要在怒中責備我，
　　不要在烈怒中懲罰我。
2因為你的箭射入我身，
　　你的手壓住我。
3因你的惱怒，
　　我的肉無一完全；
　　因我的罪過，
　　我的骨頭也不安寧。

They will be protected forever,
　　but the offspring of the wicked will be cut
　　　　off;
29the righteous will inherit the land
　　and dwell in it forever.

30The mouth of the righteous man utters wisdom,
　　and his tongue speaks what is just.
31The law of his God is in his heart;
　　his feet do not slip.

32The wicked lie in wait for the righteous,
　　seeking their very lives;
33but the LORD will not leave them in their
　　power
　　or let them be condemned when brought to
　　trial.

34Wait for the LORD
　　and keep his way.
He will exalt you to inherit the land;
　　when the wicked are cut off, you will see it.

35I have seen a wicked and ruthless man
　　flourishing like a green tree in its native soil,
36but he soon passed away and was no more;
　　though I looked for him, he could not be
　　found.

37Consider the blameless, observe the upright;
　　there is a future[a] for the man of peace.
38But all sinners will be destroyed;
　　the future[b] of the wicked will be cut off.

39The salvation of the righteous comes from the
　　LORD;
　　he is their stronghold in time of trouble.
40The LORD helps them and delivers them;
　　he delivers them from the wicked and saves
　　them,
　　because they take refuge in him.

Psalm 38

A psalm of David. A petition.

1O LORD, do not rebuke me in your anger
　　or discipline me in your wrath.
2For your arrows have pierced me,
　　and your hand has come down upon me.
3Because of your wrath there is no health in my
　　body;
　　my bones have no soundness because of my
　　sin.

a 37 Or there will be posterity　　b 38 Or posterity

⁴My guilt has overwhelmed me
　like a burden too heavy to bear.

⁵My wounds fester and are loathsome
　because of my sinful folly.
⁶I am bowed down and brought very low;
　all day long I go about mourning.
⁷My back is filled with searing pain;
　there is no health in my body.
⁸I am feeble and utterly crushed;
　I groan in anguish of heart.

⁹All my longings lie open before you, O Lord;
　my sighing is not hidden from you.
¹⁰My heart pounds, my strength fails me;
　even the light has gone from my eyes.
¹¹My friends and companions avoid me
　because of my wounds;
　my neighbors stay far away.
¹²Those who seek my life set their traps,
　those who would harm me talk of my ruin;
　all day long they plot deception.

¹³I am like a deaf man, who cannot hear,
　like a mute, who cannot open his mouth;
¹⁴I have become like a man who does not hear,
　whose mouth can offer no reply.
¹⁵I wait for you, O LORD;
　you will answer, O Lord my God.
¹⁶For I said, "Do not let them gloat
　or exalt themselves over me when my foot
　slips."

¹⁷For I am about to fall,
　and my pain is ever with me.
¹⁸I confess my iniquity;
　I am troubled by my sin.
¹⁹Many are those who are my vigorous enemies;
　those who hate me without reason are
　numerous.
²⁰Those who repay my good with evil
　slander me when I pursue what is good.

²¹O LORD, do not forsake me;
　be not far from me, O my God.
²²Come quickly to help me,
　O Lord my Savior.

Psalm 39

For the director of music. For Jeduthun. A psalm of David.

¹I said, "I will watch my ways
　and keep my tongue from sin;
　I will put a muzzle on my mouth
　as long as the wicked are in my presence."

⁴我的罪孽高過我的頭，
　如同重擔叫我擔當不起。

⁵因我的愚昧，
　我的傷發臭流膿。
⁶我疼痛，大大拳曲，
　終日哀痛。
⁷我滿腰是火，
　我的肉無一完全。
⁸我被壓傷，身體疲倦，
　因心裏不安，我就唉哼。

⁹主啊，我的心願都在你面前；
　我的歎息不向你隱瞞。
¹⁰我心跳動，我力衰微，
　連我眼中的光也沒有了。
¹¹我的良朋密友，
　因我的災病都躲在旁邊站着；
　我的親戚本家也遠遠地站立。
¹²那尋索我命的設下網羅；
　那想要害我的，口出惡言，
　終日思想詭計。

¹³但我如聾子不聽，
　像啞巴不開口。
¹⁴我如不聽見的人，
　口中沒有回話。
¹⁵耶和華啊，我仰望你！
　主我的神啊，你必應允我！
¹⁶我曾說："恐怕他們向我誇耀。
　我失腳的時候，
　他們向我誇大。"

¹⁷我幾乎跌倒，
　我的痛苦常在我面前。
¹⁸我要承認我的罪孽，
　我要因我的罪憂愁。
¹⁹但我的仇敵又活潑、又強壯，
　無理恨我的
　增多了。
²⁰以惡報善的與我作對，
　因我是追求良善。

²¹耶和華啊，求你不要撇棄我！
　我的神啊，求你不要遠離我！
²²拯救我的主啊，
　求你快快幫助我！

第三十九篇

大衛的詩，交與伶長耶杜頓。

¹我曾說："我要謹慎我的言行，
　免得我舌頭犯罪。
　惡人在我面前的時候，
　我要用嚼環勒住我的口。"

²我默然無聲，
　　連好話也不出口，
　　我的愁苦就發動了。
³我的心在我裏面發熱。
　　我默想的時候，火就燒起，
　　我便用舌頭說話：

⁴ "耶和華啊，求你叫我曉得
　　我身之終，我的壽數幾何，
　　叫我知道我的生命不長。
⁵你使我的年日窄如手掌；
　　我一生的年數，
　　在你面前如同無有。
　　各人最穩妥的時候，
　　真是全然虛幻！　　　　　　細拉
⁶世人行動實係幻影；
　　他們忙亂，真是枉然；
　　積蓄財寶，不知將來有誰收取。

⁷ "主啊，如今我等甚麼呢？
　　我的指望在乎你！
⁸求你救我脫離一切的過犯，
　　不要使我受愚頑人的羞辱。
⁹因我所遭遇的是出於你，
　　我就默然不語。
¹⁰求你把你的責罰從我身上免去，
　　因你手的責打，我便消滅。
¹¹你因人的罪惡懲罰他的時候，
　　叫他的笑容消滅（註："的笑容"或
　　　作"所喜愛的"），如衣被蟲所咬。
　　世人真是虛幻！　　　　　　細拉
¹² "耶和華啊，求你聽我的禱告，
　　留心聽我的呼求！
　　我流淚，求你不要靜默無聲，
　　因為我在你面前是客旅，
　　是寄居的，像我列祖一般。
¹³求你寬容我，使我在去而不返之先
　　可以力量復原。"

第四十篇

大衛的詩，交與伶長。

¹我曾耐性等候耶和華，
　　他垂聽我的呼求。
²他從禍坑裏、從淤泥中
　　把我拉上來，
　　使我的腳立在磐石上，
　　使我腳步穩當。
³他使我口唱新歌，
　　就是讚美我們神的話。
　　許多人必看見而懼怕，
　　並要倚靠耶和華。

⁴那倚靠耶和華，
　　不理會狂傲

²But when I was silent and still,
　　not even saying anything good,
　　my anguish increased.
³My heart grew hot within me,
　　and as I meditated, the fire burned;
　　then I spoke with my tongue:

⁴"Show me, O LORD, my life's end
　　and the number of my days;
　　let me know how fleeting is my life.
⁵You have made my days a mere handbreadth;
　　the span of my years is as nothing before
　　　you.
　　Each man's life is but a breath.　　　*Selah*
⁶Man is a mere phantom as he goes to and fro:
　　He bustles about, but only in vain;
　　he heaps up wealth, not knowing who will
　　　get it.

⁷"But now, Lord, what do I look for?
　　My hope is in you.
⁸Save me from all my transgressions;
　　do not make me the scorn of fools.
⁹I was silent; I would not open my mouth,
　　for you are the one who has done this.
¹⁰Remove your scourge from me;
　　I am overcome by the blow of your hand.
¹¹You rebuke and discipline men for their sin;
　　you consume their wealth like a moth—
　　each man is but a breath.　　　*Selah*

¹²"Hear my prayer, O LORD,
　　listen to my cry for help;
　　be not deaf to my weeping.
　　For I dwell with you as an alien,
　　a stranger, as all my fathers were.
¹³Look away from me, that I may rejoice again
　　before I depart and am no more."

Psalm 40

For the director of music. Of David. A psalm.

¹I waited patiently for the LORD;
　　he turned to me and heard my cry.
²He lifted me out of the slimy pit,
　　out of the mud and mire;
　　he set my feet on a rock
　　and gave me a firm place to stand.
³He put a new song in my mouth,
　　a hymn of praise to our God.
　　Many will see and fear
　　and put their trust in the LORD.

⁴Blessed is the man
　　who makes the LORD his trust,

who does not look to the proud,
　to those who turn aside to false gods.[a]
5 Many, O LORD my God,
　are the wonders you have done.
The things you planned for us
　no one can recount to you;
were I to speak and tell of them,
　they would be too many to declare.

6 Sacrifice and offering you did not desire,
　but my ears you have pierced[b,c];
burnt offerings and sin offerings
　you did not require.
7 Then I said, "Here I am, I have come—
　it is written about me in the scroll.[d]
8 I desire to do your will, O my God;
　your law is within my heart."

9 I proclaim righteousness in the great assembly;
　I do not seal my lips,
　as you know, O LORD.
10 I do not hide your righteousness in my heart;
　I speak of your faithfulness and salvation.
I do not conceal your love and your truth
　from the great assembly.

11 Do not withhold your mercy from me,
　O LORD;
　may your love and your truth always protect
　me.
12 For troubles without number surround me;
　my sins have overtaken me, and I cannot see.
They are more than the hairs of my head,
　and my heart fails within me.

13 Be pleased, O LORD, to save me;
　O LORD, come quickly to help me.
14 May all who seek to take my life
　be put to shame and confusion;
may all who desire my ruin
　be turned back in disgrace.
15 May those who say to me, "Aha! Aha!"
　be appalled at their own shame.
16 But may all who seek you
　rejoice and be glad in you;
may those who love your salvation always
　say,
　"The LORD be exalted!"

17 Yet I am poor and needy;
　may the Lord think of me.

和偏向虛假之輩的，
　這人便為有福！
5 耶和華我的神啊，
　你所行的奇事，
並你向我們所懷的意念甚多，
　不能向你陳明；
若要陳明，
　其事不可勝數。

6 祭物和禮物，你不喜悅，
　你已經開通我的耳朵；
燔祭和贖罪祭
　非你所要。
7 那時我說："看哪，我來了！
　我的事在經卷上已經記載了。
8 我的神啊，我樂意照你的旨意行；
　你的律法在我心裏。"

9 我在大會中宣傳公義的佳音，
　我必不止住我的嘴唇，
　耶和華啊，這是你所知道的。
10 我未曾把你的公義藏在心裏，
　我已陳明你的信實和你的救恩。
我在大會中未曾隱瞞
　你的慈愛和誠實。

11 耶和華啊，
　求你不要向我止住你的慈悲；
　願你的慈愛和誠實常常保佑我。

12 因有無數的禍患圍困我，
　我的罪孽追上了我，使我不能昂首。
這罪孽比我的頭髮還多，
　我就心寒膽戰。

13 耶和華啊，求你開恩搭救我！
　耶和華啊，求你速速幫助我！
14 願那些尋找我、要滅我命的，
　一同抱愧蒙羞；
願那些喜悅我受害的，
　退後受辱！
15 願那些對我說："阿哈、阿哈"的，
　因羞愧而敗亡！
16 願一切尋求你的，
　因你高興歡喜；
願那些喜愛你救恩的，
　常說：
　"當尊耶和華為大！"

17 但我是困苦窮乏的，
　主仍顧念我。

---

a 4 Or to falsehood　b 6 Hebrew; Septuagint but a body you
have prepared for me (see also Symmachus and Theodotion)
c 6 Or opened　d 7 Or come / with the scroll written for me

你是幫助我的，搭救我的。
神啊，求你不要躭延！

第四十一篇

大衛的詩，交與伶長。

¹眷顧貧窮的有福了！
　　他遭難的日子，耶和華必搭救他！
²耶和華必保全他，
　　使他存活；
　　他必在地上享福。
　求你不要把他交給仇敵，
　　遂其所願。
³他病重在榻，耶和華必扶持他；
　　他在病中，你必給他鋪牀。

⁴我曾說："耶和華啊，求你憐恤我，
　　醫治我，因為我得罪了你。"
⁵我的仇敵用惡言議論我說：
　　"他幾時死，他的名才滅亡呢？"
⁶他來看我，
　　就說假話，
　　他心存奸惡，
　　走到外邊才說出來。

⁷一切恨我的，都交頭接耳地議論我；
　　他們設計要害我。
⁸他們說："有怪病貼在他身上；
　　他已躺臥，
　　必不能再起來。"
⁹連我知己的朋友，
　　我所倚靠吃過我飯的，
　　也用腳踢我。

¹⁰耶和華啊，求你憐恤我，
　　使我起來，好報復他們。
¹¹因我的仇敵不得向我誇勝，
　　我從此便知道你喜愛我。
¹²你因我純正就扶持我，
　　使我永遠站在你的面前。

¹³耶和華以色列的神是應當稱頌的，
　　從亙古直到永遠。
　　　　阿們！阿們！

Psalm 41

For the director of music. A psalm of David.

¹Blessed is he who has regard for the weak;
　　the LORD delivers him in times of trouble.
²The LORD will protect him and preserve his
　　　life;
　　he will bless him in the land
　　and not surrender him to the desire of his
　　　foes.
³The LORD will sustain him on his sickbed
　　and restore him from his bed of illness.

⁴I said, "O LORD, have mercy on me;
　　heal me, for I have sinned against you."
⁵My enemies say of me in malice,
　　"When will he die and his name perish?"
⁶Whenever one comes to see me,
　　he speaks falsely, while his heart gathers
　　　slander;
　　then he goes out and spreads it abroad.

⁷All my enemies whisper together against me;
　　they imagine the worst for me, saying,
⁸"A vile disease has beset him;
　　he will never get up from the place where he
　　　lies."
⁹Even my close friend, whom I trusted,
　　he who shared my bread,
　　has lifted up his heel against me.

¹⁰But you, O LORD, have mercy on me;
　　raise me up, that I may repay them.
¹¹I know that you are pleased with me,
　　for my enemy does not triumph over me.
¹²In my integrity you uphold me
　　and set me in your presence forever.

¹³Praise be to the LORD, the God of Israel,
　　from everlasting to everlasting.
　　　　Amen and Amen.

BOOK II

Psalms 42-72

Psalm 42[a]

For the director of music. A *maskil*[b] of the Sons of Korah.

[1]As the deer pants for streams of water,
  so my soul pants for you, O God.
[2]My soul thirsts for God, for the living God.
  When can I go and meet with God?
[3]My tears have been my food
  day and night,
  while men say to me all day long,
  "Where is your God?"
[4]These things I remember
  as I pour out my soul:
  how I used to go with the multitude,
  leading the procession to the house of God,
  with shouts of joy and thanksgiving
  among the festive throng.

[5]Why are you downcast, O my soul?
  Why so disturbed within me?
  Put your hope in God,
  for I will yet praise him,
  my Savior and [6]my God.

My[c] soul is downcast within me;
  therefore I will remember you
  from the land of the Jordan,
  the heights of Hermon—from Mount Mizar.
[7]Deep calls to deep
  in the roar of your waterfalls;
  all your waves and breakers
  have swept over me.

[8]By day the LORD directs his love,
  at night his song is with me—
  a prayer to the God of my life.

[9]I say to God my Rock,
  "Why have you forgotten me?
  Why must I go about mourning,
  oppressed by the enemy?"
[10]My bones suffer mortal agony
  as my foes taunt me,
  saying to me all day long,
  "Where is your God?"

---

a In many Hebrew manuscripts Psalms 42 and 43 constitute
one psalm.   *b* Title: Probably a literary or musical term
c 5,6 A few Hebrew manuscripts, Septuagint and Syriac; most
Hebrew manuscripts *praise him for his saving help.* / [6]*O my God, my*

卷二

詩篇 42-72

第四十二篇

可拉後裔的訓誨詩,交與伶長。

[1]神啊,我的心切慕你,
  如鹿切慕溪水。
[2]我的心渴想神,就是永生神;
  我幾時得朝見神呢?
[3]我晝夜以眼淚當飲食,
  人不住地對我說:
  "你的神在哪裏呢?"

[4]我從前與眾人同往,
  用歡呼稱讚的聲音
    領他們到神的殿裏,
  大家守節。
  我追想這些事,
  我的心極其悲傷。

[5]我的心哪,你為何憂悶?
  為何在我裏面煩躁?
  應當仰望神,
  因他笑臉幫助我,
  我還要稱讚他。

[6]我的神啊,
  我的心在我裏面憂悶,
  所以我從約旦地、
  從黑門嶺、從米薩山記念你。
[7]你的瀑布發聲,
  深淵就與深淵響應,
  你的波浪洪濤
  漫過我身。

[8]白晝,耶和華必向我施慈愛;
  黑夜,我要歌頌
  禱告賜我生命的神。

[9]我要對神我的磐石說:
  "你為何忘記我呢?
  我為何因仇敵的欺壓
  時常哀痛呢?"
[10]我的敵人辱罵我,
  好像打碎我的骨頭,
  不住地對我說:
  "你的神在哪裏呢?"

11我的心哪，你為何憂悶？
　　為何在我裏面煩躁？
　　應當仰望神，因我還要稱讚他。
　　他是我臉上的光榮（註：原文作"幫
　　　助"），是我的神。

第四十三篇

1神啊，
　　求你伸我的冤，
　　向不虔誠的國為我辨屈；
　　求你救我脫離詭詐不義的人。
2因為你是賜我力量的神，
　　為何丟棄我呢？
　　我為何因仇敵的欺壓
　　時常哀痛呢？
3求你發出你的亮光和真實，
　　好引導我，
　　帶我到你的聖山，
　　到你的居所！
4我就走到神的祭壇，
　　到我最喜樂的神那裏。
　　神啊，我的神！
　　我要彈琴稱讚你！

5我的心哪，你為何憂悶？
　　為何在我裏面煩躁？
　　應當仰望神，因我還要稱讚他。
　　他是我臉上的光榮（註：原文作"幫
　　　助"），是我的神。

第四十四篇

可拉後裔的訓誨詩，交與伶長。

1神啊，你在古時，
　　我們列祖的日子所行的事，
　　我們親耳聽見了；
　　我們的列祖也給我們述說過。
2你曾用手趕出外邦人，
　　卻栽培了我們列祖；
　　你苦待列邦，
　　卻叫我們列祖發達。
3因為他們
　　不是靠自己的刀劍得地土，
　　也不是靠自己的膀臂得勝，
　　乃是靠你的右手、你的膀臂
　　和你臉上的亮光，因為你喜悅他們。

4神啊，你是我的王，
　　求你出令使雅各得勝！

11Why are you downcast, O my soul?
　　Why so disturbed within me?
　Put your hope in God,
　　for I will yet praise him,
　　my Savior and my God.

Psalm 43[a]

1Vindicate me, O God,
　　and plead my cause against an ungodly
　　　nation;
　　rescue me from deceitful and wicked men.
2You are God my stronghold.
　　Why have you rejected me?
　　Why must I go about mourning,
　　oppressed by the enemy?
3Send forth your light and your truth,
　　let them guide me;
　　let them bring me to your holy mountain,
　　to the place where you dwell.
4Then will I go to the altar of God,
　　to God, my joy and my delight.
　　I will praise you with the harp,
　　O God, my God.

5Why are you downcast, O my soul?
　　Why so disturbed within me?
　Put your hope in God,
　　for I will yet praise him,
　　my Savior and my God.

Psalm 44

For the director of music. Of the Sons of Korah. A maskil.[b]

1We have heard with our ears, O God;
　　our fathers have told us
　　what you did in their days,
　　in days long ago.
2With your hand you drove out the nations
　　and planted our fathers;
　　you crushed the peoples
　　and made our fathers flourish.
3It was not by their sword that they won the
　　　land,
　　nor did their arm bring them victory;
　　it was your right hand, your arm,
　　and the light of your face, for you loved them.

4You are my King and my God,
　　who decrees[c] victories for Jacob.

a In many Hebrew manuscripts Psalms 42 and 43 constitute
one psalm.　b Title: Probably a literary or musical term
c 4 Septuagint, Aquila and Syriac; Hebrew King, O God; /
command

⁵Through you we push back our enemies;
    through your name we trample our foes.
⁶I do not trust in my bow,
    my sword does not bring me victory;
⁷but you give us victory over our enemies,
    you put our adversaries to shame.
⁸In God we make our boast all day long,
    and we will praise your name forever.   *Selah*

⁹But now you have rejected and humbled us;
    you no longer go out with our armies.
¹⁰You made us retreat before the enemy,
    and our adversaries have plundered us.
¹¹You gave us up to be devoured like sheep
    and have scattered us among the nations.
¹²You sold your people for a pittance,
    gaining nothing from their sale.

¹³You have made us a reproach to our neighbors,
    the scorn and derision of those around us.
¹⁴You have made us a byword among the
        nations;
    the peoples shake their heads at us.
¹⁵My disgrace is before me all day long,
    and my face is covered with shame
¹⁶at the taunts of those who reproach and revile
        me,
    because of the enemy, who is bent on
        revenge.

¹⁷All this happened to us,
    though we had not forgotten you
    or been false to your covenant.
¹⁸Our hearts had not turned back;
    our feet had not strayed from your path.
¹⁹But you crushed us and made us a haunt for
        jackals
    and covered us over with deep darkness.

²⁰If we had forgotten the name of our God
    or spread out our hands to a foreign god,
²¹would not God have discovered it,
    since he knows the secrets of the heart?
²²Yet for your sake we face death all day long;
    we are considered as sheep to be
        slaughtered.

²³Awake, O Lord! Why do you sleep?
    Rouse yourself! Do not reject us forever.
²⁴Why do you hide your face
    and forget our misery and oppression?

²⁵We are brought down to the dust;
    our bodies cling to the ground.
²⁶Rise up and help us;
    redeem us because of your unfailing love.

⁵我們靠你要推倒我們的敵人,
    靠你的名
    要踐踏那起來攻擊我們的人。
⁶因為我必不靠我的弓,
    我的刀也不能使我得勝。
⁷惟你救了我們脫離敵人,
    使恨我們的人羞愧。
⁸我們終日因神誇耀,
    還要永遠稱謝你的名。   細拉

⁹但如今你丟棄了我們,使我們受辱,
    不和我們的軍兵同去。
¹⁰你使我們向敵人轉身退後,
    那恨我們的人任意搶奪。
¹¹你使我們當作快要被吃的羊,
    把我們分散在列邦中。
¹²你賣了你的子民,也不賺利,
    所得的價值,並不加添你的資財。

¹³你使我們受鄰國的羞辱,
    被四圍的人嗤笑譏刺。
¹⁴你使我們在列邦中
    作了笑談,
    使眾民向我們搖頭。
¹⁵我的凌辱終日在我面前,
    我臉上的羞愧將我遮蔽,
¹⁶都因那辱罵毀謗人的聲音,
    又因仇敵
    和報仇人的緣故。

¹⁷這都臨到我們身上,
    我們卻沒有忘記你,
    也沒有違背你的約。
¹⁸我們的心沒有退後,
    我們的腳也沒有偏離你的路。
¹⁹你在野狗之處
    壓傷我們,
    用死蔭遮蔽我們。

²⁰倘若我們忘了神的名,
    或向別神舉手,
²¹神豈不鑒察這事嗎?
    因為他曉得人心裏的隱秘。
²²我們為你的緣故終日被殺,
    人看我們
    如將宰的羊。

²³主啊,求你睡醒,為何儘睡呢?
    求你興起,不要永遠丟棄我們。
²⁴你為何掩面,
    不顧我們所遭的苦難
    和所受的欺壓?

²⁵我們的性命伏於塵土,
    我們的肚腹緊貼地面。
²⁶求你起來幫助我們,
    憑你的慈愛救贖我們!

第四十五篇

可拉後裔的訓誨詩，又是愛慕歌，交與伶長。
調用"百合花"。

1 我心裏湧出美辭。
　我論到我為王做的事，
　我的舌頭是快手筆。

2 你比世人更美，
　在你嘴裏滿有恩惠，
　所以神賜福給你，直到永遠。

3 大能者啊，
　願你腰間佩刀，
　大有榮耀和威嚴！

4 為真理、謙卑、公義
　赫然坐車前往，
　無不得勝。
　你的右手必顯明可畏的事。

5 你的箭鋒快，
　射中王敵之心，
　萬民仆倒在你以下。

6 神啊，
　你的寶座是永永遠遠的，
　你的國權是正直的。

7 你喜愛公義，恨惡罪惡，
　所以神，就是你的神，
　用喜樂油膏你，
　勝過膏你的同伴。

8 你的衣服
　都有沒藥、沉香、肉桂的香氣，
　象牙宮中有絲弦樂器的聲音，
　使你歡喜。

9 有君王的女兒
　在你尊貴婦女之中；
　王后佩戴俄斐金飾
　站在你右邊。

10 女子啊，你要聽，要想，要側耳而聽！
　不要記念你的民和你的父家，

11 王就羨慕你的美貌，
　因為他是你的主，你當敬拜他。

12 推羅的民（註："民"原文作"女子"）
　必來送禮，
　民中的富足人也必向你求恩。

13 王女在宮裏
　極其榮華，
　她的衣服是用金線繡的。

14 她要穿錦繡的衣服，
　被引到王前；
　隨從她的陪伴童女
　也要被帶到你面前。

Psalm 45

For the director of music. To [the tune of] "Lilies." Of the Sons of Korah. A *maskil*.[a] A wedding song.

1 My heart is stirred by a noble theme
　as I recite my verses for the king;
　my tongue is the pen of a skillful writer.

2 You are the most excellent of men
　and your lips have been anointed with grace,
　since God has blessed you forever.

3 Gird your sword upon your side, O mighty one;
　clothe yourself with splendor and majesty.

4 In your majesty ride forth victoriously
　in behalf of truth, humility and righteousness;
　let your right hand display awesome deeds.

5 Let your sharp arrows pierce the hearts of the king's enemies;
　let the nations fall beneath your feet.

6 Your throne, O God, will last for ever and ever;
　a scepter of justice will be the scepter of your kingdom.

7 You love righteousness and hate wickedness;
　therefore God, your God, has set you above your companions
　by anointing you with the oil of joy.

8 All your robes are fragrant with myrrh and aloes and cassia;
　from palaces adorned with ivory
　the music of the strings makes you glad.

9 Daughters of kings are among your honored women;
　at your right hand is the royal bride in gold of Ophir.

10 Listen, O daughter, consider and give ear:
　Forget your people and your father's house.

11 The king is enthralled by your beauty;
　honor him, for he is your lord.

12 The Daughter of Tyre will come with a gift,[b]
　men of wealth will seek your favor.

13 All glorious is the princess within [her chamber];
　her gown is interwoven with gold.

14 In embroidered garments she is led to the king;
　her virgin companions follow her
　and are brought to you.

a Title: Probably a literary or musical term　*b* 12 Or *A Tyrian robe is among the gifts*

¹⁵They are led in with joy and gladness;
   they enter the palace of the king.

¹⁶Your sons will take the place of your fathers;
   you will make them princes throughout the
   land.
¹⁷I will perpetuate your memory through all
   generations;
   therefore the nations will praise you for ever
   and ever.

Psalm 46

For the director of music. Of the Sons of Korah.
According to *alamoth.*^a A song.

¹God is our refuge and strength,
   an ever-present help in trouble.
²Therefore we will not fear, though the earth
   give way
   and the mountains fall into the heart of the sea,
³though its waters roar and foam
   and the mountains quake with their surging.
                   Selah

⁴There is a river whose streams make glad the
   city of God,
   the holy place where the Most High dwells.
⁵God is within her, she will not fall;
   God will help her at break of day.
⁶Nations are in uproar, kingdoms fall;
   he lifts his voice, the earth melts.

⁷The LORD Almighty is with us;
   the God of Jacob is our fortress.   *Selah*

⁸Come and see the works of the LORD,
   the desolations he has brought on the earth.
⁹He makes wars cease to the ends of the earth;
   he breaks the bow and shatters the spear,
   he burns the shields^b with fire.
¹⁰"Be still, and know that I am God;
   I will be exalted among the nations,
   I will be exalted in the earth."

¹¹The LORD Almighty is with us;
   the God of Jacob is our fortress.   *Selah*

Psalm 47

For the director of music. Of the Sons of Korah. A psalm.

¹Clap your hands, all you nations;
   shout to God with cries of joy.

---

a Title: Probably a musical term   *b* 9 Or *chariots*

---

¹⁵她們要歡喜快樂被引導，
   她們要進入王宮。

¹⁶你的子孫要接續你的列祖，
   你要立他們
     在全地作王。
¹⁷我必叫你的名
   被萬代記念，
   所以萬民要永永遠遠
   稱謝你。

第四十六篇

可拉後裔的詩歌，交與伶長。調用女音。

¹神是我們的避難所，是我們的力量，
   是我們在患難中隨時的幫助！
²所以
   地雖改變，
   山雖搖動到海心，
³其中的水雖匉訇翻騰，
   山雖因海漲而戰抖，
   我們也不害怕。   細拉

⁴有一道河，
   這河的分汊，使神的城歡喜；
   這城就是至高者居住的聖所。
⁵神在其中，城必不動搖；
   到天一亮，神必幫助這城。
⁶外邦喧嚷，列國動搖。
   神發聲，地便熔化。

⁷萬軍之耶和華與我們同在；
   雅各的神是我們的避難所！   細拉

⁸你們來看耶和華的作為，
   看他使地怎樣荒涼。
⁹他止息刀兵，直到地極；
   他折弓、斷槍，
   把戰車焚燒在火中。
¹⁰ "你們要休息，要知道我是神！
   我必在外邦中被尊崇，
   在遍地上也被尊崇。"

¹¹萬軍之耶和華與我們同在；
   雅各的神是我們的避難所。

第四十七篇

可拉後裔的詩，交與伶長。

¹萬民哪，你們都要拍掌，
   要用誇勝的聲音向神呼喊！

2因為耶和華至高者是可畏的，
　　他是治理全地的大君王。
3他叫萬民服在我們以下，
　　又叫列邦服在我們腳下。
4他為我們選擇產業，
　　就是他所愛之雅各的榮耀。　　細拉

5神上升，有喊聲相送；
　　耶和華上升，有角聲相送。
6你們要向神歌頌，歌頌！
　　向我們王歌頌，歌頌！

7因為神是全地的王，
　　你們要用悟性歌頌！
8神作王治理萬國，
　　神坐在他的聖寶座上。
9列邦的君王聚集，
　　要作亞伯拉罕之神的民，
　　因為世界的盾牌是屬神的，
　　他為至高。

第四十八篇

可拉後裔的詩歌。

1耶和華本為大！在我們神的城中，
　　在他的聖山上，該受大讚美！
2錫安山，
　　大君王的城，
　　在北面居高華美，
　　為全地所喜悅。

3神在其宮中
　　自顯為避難所。

4看哪，眾王會合，
　　一同經過。
5他們見了這城，
　　就驚奇喪膽，急忙逃跑。
6他們在那裏被戰兢疼痛抓住，
　　好像產難的婦人一樣。
7神啊，
　　你用東風打破他施的船隻。

8我們在萬軍之耶和華的城中，
　　就是我們神的城中所看見的，
　　正如我們所聽見的。
　　神必堅立這城，
　　直到永遠！　　　　　　　細拉

2How awesome is the LORD Most High,
　　the great King over all the earth!
3He subdued nations under us,
　　peoples under our feet.
4He chose our inheritance for us,
　　the pride of Jacob, whom he loved.　　*Selah*

5God has ascended amid shouts of joy,
　　the LORD amid the sounding of trumpets.
6Sing praises to God, sing praises;
　　sing praises to our King, sing praises.

7For God is the King of all the earth;
　　sing to him a psalm*a* of praise.
8God reigns over the nations;
　　God is seated on his holy throne.
9The nobles of the nations assemble
　　as the people of the God of Abraham,
　　for the kings*b* of the earth belong to God;
　　he is greatly exalted.

Psalm 48

A song. A psalm of the Sons of Korah.

1Great is the LORD, and most worthy of praise,
　　in the city of our God, his holy mountain.
2It is beautiful in its loftiness,
　　the joy of the whole earth.
　　Like the utmost heights of Zaphon*c* is Mount
　　　Zion,
　　the*d* city of the Great King.
3God is in her citadels;
　　he has shown himself to be her fortress.

4When the kings joined forces,
　　when they advanced together,
5they saw [her] and were astounded;
　　they fled in terror.
6Trembling seized them there,
　　pain like that of a woman in labor.
7You destroyed them like ships of Tarshish
　　shattered by an east wind.

8As we have heard,
　　so have we seen
　　in the city of the LORD Almighty,
　　in the city of our God:
　　God makes her secure forever.　　*Selah*

---

a 7 Or *a maskil* (probably a literary or musical term)　　*b* 9 Or
shields　　*c* 2 *Zaphon* can refer to a sacred mountain or the
direction north.　　*d* 2 Or *earth, / Mount Zion, on the northern
side / of the*

9Within your temple, O God,
  we meditate on your unfailing love.
10Like your name, O God,
  your praise reaches to the ends of the earth;
  your right hand is filled with righteousness.
11Mount Zion rejoices,
  the villages of Judah are glad
  because of your judgments.

12Walk about Zion, go around her,
  count her towers,
13consider well her ramparts,
  view her citadels,
  that you may tell of them to the next
    generation.
14For this God is our God for ever and ever;
  he will be our guide even to the end.

Psalm 49

For the director of music. Of the Sons of Korah. A psalm.

1Hear this, all you peoples;
  listen, all who live in this world,
2both low and high,
  rich and poor alike:
3My mouth will speak words of wisdom;
  the utterance from my heart will give
    understanding.
4I will turn my ear to a proverb;
  with the harp I will expound my riddle:

5Why should I fear when evil days come,
  when wicked deceivers surround me—
6those who trust in their wealth
  and boast of their great riches?
7No man can redeem the life of another
  or give to God a ransom for him—
8the ransom for a life is costly,
  no payment is ever enough—
9that he should live on forever
  and not see decay.

10For all can see that wise men die;
  the foolish and the senseless alike perish
  and leave their wealth to others.
11Their tombs will remain their houses[a] forever,
  their dwellings for endless generations,
  though they had[b] named lands after
    themselves.

9神啊，我們在你的殿中，
  想念你的慈愛。
10神啊，你受的讚美，
  正與你的名相稱，直到地極！
  你的右手滿了公義。
11因你的判斷，
  <u>錫安山應當歡喜</u>，
  <u>猶大</u>的城邑應當快樂（註：「城邑」
  原文作「女子」）。

12你們當周遊<u>錫安</u>，四圍旋繞，
  數點城樓，
13細看他的外郭，
  察看他的宮殿，
  為要傳說到後代。

14因為這神永永遠遠為我們的神，
  他必作我們引路的，直到死時。

第四十九篇

可拉後裔的詩，交與伶長。

1萬民哪，你們都當聽這話！
  世上一切的居民，
2無論上流下流，
  富足貧窮，都當留心聽！
3我口要說智慧的言語；
  我心要想通達的道理。

4我要側耳聽比喻，
  用琴解謎語。

5在患難的日子，奸惡隨我腳跟，
  四面環繞我，我何必懼怕？
6那些倚仗財貨
  自誇錢財多的人，
7一個也無法贖自己的弟兄，
  也不能替他將贖價給神，
8、9叫他長遠活着，
  不見朽壞，
  因為贖他生命的價值極貴，
  只可永遠罷休。

10他必見智慧人死，
  又見愚頑人和畜類人一同滅亡，
  將他們的財貨留給別人。
11他們心裏思想，他們的家室必永存，
  住宅必留到萬代；
  他們以自己的名
  稱自己的地。

---

a 11 Septuagint and Syriac; Hebrew In their thoughts their
houses will remain   b 11 Or / for they have

¹²但人居尊貴中不能長久，
　　如同死亡的畜類一樣。

¹³他們行的這道，
　　本為自己的愚昧，
　但他們以後的人
　　還佩服他們的話語。　　　　細拉
¹⁴他們如同羊羣派定下陰間，
　　死亡必作他們的牧者。
　到了早晨，
　　正直人必管轄他們。
　他們的美容必被陰間所滅，
　　以致無處可存。
¹⁵只是神必救贖我的靈魂
　　脫離陰間的權柄，
　　因他必收納我。　　　　細拉
¹⁶見人發財、家室增榮的時候，
　　你不要懼怕。
¹⁷因為他死的時候，
　　甚麼也不能帶去，
　他的榮耀不能隨他下去。
¹⁸他活着的時候，
　　雖然自誇為有福
　　（你若利己，人必誇獎你），
¹⁹他仍必歸到他歷代的祖宗那裏，
　　永不見光！

²⁰人在尊貴中而不醒悟，
　　就如死亡的畜類一樣。

第五十篇

亞薩的詩。

¹大能者神耶和華，
　　已經發言招呼天下，
　從日出之地
　　到日落之處。
²從全美的錫安中，
　　神已經發光了。
³我們的神要來，決不閉口，
　　有烈火在他面前吞滅，
　有暴風在他四圍大颳。
⁴他招呼上天下地，
　　為要審判他的民，
⁵說："招聚我的聖民到我這裏來，
　　就是那些用祭物與我立約的人。"
⁶諸天必表明他的公義，
　　因為神是施行審判的。　　　細拉

⁷　"我的民哪，你們當聽我的話；
　　以色列啊，我要勸戒你。
　我是神，是你的神！

¹²But man, despite his riches, does not endure;
　　he is^a like the beasts that perish.

¹³This is the fate of those who trust in
　　themselves,
　and of their followers, who approve their
　　sayings.　　　　　　　　　　　Selah
¹⁴Like sheep they are destined for the grave,^b
　　and death will feed on them.
　The upright will rule over them in the
　　morning;
　their forms will decay in the grave,^b
　　far from their princely mansions.
¹⁵But God will redeem my life^c from the grave;
　　he will surely take me to himself.　Selah

¹⁶Do not be overawed when a man grows rich,
　　when the splendor of his house increases;
¹⁷for he will take nothing with him when he
　　dies,
　his splendor will not descend with him.
¹⁸Though while he lived he counted himself
　　blessed—
　and men praise you when you prosper—
¹⁹he will join the generation of his fathers,
　　who will never see the light [of life].

²⁰A man who has riches without understanding
　　is like the beasts that perish.

Psalm 50

A psalm of Asaph.

¹The Mighty One, God, the LORD,
　　speaks and summons the earth
　from the rising of the sun to the place where
　　it sets.
²From Zion, perfect in beauty,
　　God shines forth.
³Our God comes and will not be silent;
　　a fire devours before him,
　and around him a tempest rages.
⁴He summons the heavens above,
　　and the earth, that he may judge his people:
⁵"Gather to me my consecrated ones,
　　who made a covenant with me by sacrifice."
⁶And the heavens proclaim his righteousness,
　　for God himself is judge.　　　　Selah

⁷"Hear, O my people, and I will speak,
　　O Israel, and I will testify against you:
　I am God, your God.

---

a 12 Hebrew; Septuagint and Syriac read verse 12 the same as
verse 20.　　*b 14* Hebrew *Sheol;* also in verse 15.　　*c 15* Or *soul*

8I do not rebuke you for your sacrifices
    or your burnt offerings, which are ever
      before me.
9I have no need of a bull from your stall
    or of goats from your pens,
10for every animal of the forest is mine,
    and the cattle on a thousand hills.
11I know every bird in the mountains,
    and the creatures of the field are mine.
12If I were hungry I would not tell you,
    for the world is mine, and all that is in it.
13Do I eat the flesh of bulls
    or drink the blood of goats?
14Sacrifice thank offerings to God,
    fulfill your vows to the Most High,
15and call upon me in the day of trouble;
    I will deliver you, and you will honor me."

16But to the wicked, God says:

"What right have you to recite my laws
    or take my covenant on your lips?
17You hate my instruction
    and cast my words behind you.
18When you see a thief, you join with him;
    you throw in your lot with adulterers.
19You use your mouth for evil
    and harness your tongue to deceit.
20You speak continually against your brother
    and slander your own mother's son.
21These things you have done and I kept silent;
    you thought I was altogether*a* like you.
    But I will rebuke you
    and accuse you to your face.

22"Consider this, you who forget God,
    or I will tear you to pieces, with none to rescue:
23He who sacrifices thank offerings honors me,
    and he prepares the way
    so that I may show him*b* the salvation of
      God."

Psalm 51

For the director of music. A psalm of David.
When the prophet Nathan came to him after David had
committedadultery with Bathsheba.

1Have mercy on me, O God,
    according to your unfailing love;
    according to your great compassion
    blot out my transgressions.

8我並不因你的祭物責備你，
    你的燔祭
      常在我面前。
9我不從你家中取公牛，
    也不從你圈內取山羊。
10因為樹林中的百獸是我的，
    千山上的牲畜也是我的。
11山中的飛鳥，我都知道；
    野地的走獸也都屬我。
12我若是飢餓，我不用告訴你，
    因為世界和其中所充滿的都是我的。
13我豈吃公牛的肉呢？
    我豈喝山羊的血呢？
14你們要以感謝為祭獻與神，
    又要向至高者還你的願。
15並要在患難之日求告我，
    我必搭救你，你也要榮耀我。"

16但神對惡人說：

"你怎敢傳說我的律例，
    口中提到我的約呢？
17其實你恨惡管教，
    將我的言語丟在背後。
18你見了盜賊，就樂意與他同夥，
    又與行姦淫的人一同有分。
19你口任說惡言；
    你舌編造詭詐。
20你坐着毀謗你的兄弟，
    讒毀你親母的兒子。
21你行了這些事，我還閉口不言，
    你想我恰和你一樣；
    其實我要責備你，
    將這些事擺在你眼前。

22 "你們忘記神的，要思想這事，
    免得我把你們撕碎，無人搭救。
23凡以感謝獻上為祭的便是榮耀我，
    那按正路而行的，
    我必使他得着我的救恩。"

第五十一篇

大衛與拔示巴同室以後，先知拿單來見他。他作
這詩，交與伶長。

1神啊，
    求你按你的慈愛憐恤我，
    按你豐盛的慈悲
    塗抹我的過犯！

---

*a 21 Or thought the 'I AM' was   b 23 Or and to him who
considers his way / I will show*

²求你將我的罪孽洗除淨盡，
　　並潔除我的罪！
³因為我知道我的過犯，
　　我的罪常在我面前。
⁴我向你犯罪，惟獨得罪了你，
　　在你眼前行了這惡，
　以致你責備我的時候顯為公義；
　　判斷我的時候顯為清正。
⁵我是在罪孽裏生的，
　　在我母親懷胎的時候
　　　就有了罪。
⁶你所喜愛的是內裏誠實；
　　你在我隱密處必使我得智慧。

⁷求你用牛膝草潔淨我，我就乾淨；
　　求你洗滌我，我就比雪更白。
⁸求你使我得聽歡喜快樂的聲音，
　　使你所壓傷的骨頭可以踴躍。
⁹求你掩面不看我的罪，
　　塗抹我一切的罪孽。

¹⁰神啊，求你為我造清潔的心，
　　使我裏面重新有正直的靈（註："正
　直"或作"堅定"）。
¹¹不要丟棄我，使我離開你的面；
　　不要從我收回你的聖靈。
¹²求你使我仍得救恩之樂，
　　賜我樂意的靈扶持我；
¹³我就把你的道指教有過犯的人，
　　罪人必歸順你。
¹⁴神啊，你是拯救我的神，
　　求你救我脫離流人血的罪，
　我的舌頭
　　就高聲歌唱你的公義。
¹⁵主啊，求你使我嘴唇張開，
　　我的口便傳揚讚美你的話。
¹⁶你本不喜愛祭物，
　　若喜愛，我就獻上；
　燔祭你也不喜悅。
¹⁷神所要的祭，就是憂傷的靈。
　　神啊，憂傷痛悔的心，
　　你必不輕看。

¹⁸求你隨你的美意善待錫安，
　　建造耶路撒冷的城牆。
¹⁹那時，你必喜愛公義的祭和燔祭，
　　並全牲的燔祭；
　那時，人必將公牛獻在你壇上。

²Wash away all my iniquity
  and cleanse me from my sin.
³For I know my transgressions,
  and my sin is always before me.
⁴Against you, you only, have I sinned
  and done what is evil in your sight,
 so that you are proved right when you speak
  and justified when you judge.
⁵Surely I was sinful at birth,
  sinful from the time my mother conceived
  me.
⁶Surely you desire truth in the inner parts*a*;
  you teach*b* me wisdom in the inmost place.

⁷Cleanse me with hyssop, and I will be clean;
  wash me, and I will be whiter than snow.
⁸Let me hear joy and gladness;
  let the bones you have crushed rejoice.
⁹Hide your face from my sins
  and blot out all my iniquity.

¹⁰Create in me a pure heart, O God,
  and renew a steadfast spirit within me.
¹¹Do not cast me from your presence
  or take your Holy Spirit from me.
¹²Restore to me the joy of your salvation
  and grant me a willing spirit, to sustain me.

¹³Then I will teach transgressors your ways,
  and sinners will turn back to you.
¹⁴Save me from bloodguilt, O God,
  the God who saves me,
  and my tongue will sing of your
   righteousness.
¹⁵O LORD, open my lips,
  and my mouth will declare your praise.
¹⁶You do not delight in sacrifice, or I would
   bring it;
  you do not take pleasure in burnt offerings.
¹⁷The sacrifices of God are*c* a broken spirit;
  a broken and contrite heart,
  O God, you will not despise.

¹⁸In your good pleasure make Zion prosper;
  build up the walls of Jerusalem.
¹⁹Then there will be righteous sacrifices,
  whole burnt offerings to delight you;
  then bulls will be offered on your altar.

---

a 6 The meaning of the Hebrew for this phrase is uncertain.
b 6 Or *you desired . . . ; / you taught*   *c 17* Or *My sacrifice,*
O God, is

Psalm 52

For the director of music. A *maskil*[a] of David. When Doeg the Edomite had gone to Saul and told him: "David has gone to the house of Ahimelech."

1 Why do you boast of evil, you mighty man?
 Why do you boast all day long,
 you who are a disgrace in the eyes of God?
2 Your tongue plots destruction;
 it is like a sharpened razor,
 you who practice deceit.
3 You love evil rather than good,
 falsehood rather than speaking the truth.
 Selah
4 You love every harmful word,
 O you deceitful tongue!

5 Surely God will bring you down to everlasting ruin:
 He will snatch you up and tear you from your tent;
 he will uproot you from the land of the living.
 Selah
6 The righteous will see and fear;
 they will laugh at him, saying,
7 "Here now is the man
 who did not make God his stronghold
 but trusted in his great wealth
 and grew strong by destroying others!"

8 But I am like an olive tree
 flourishing in the house of God;
 I trust in God's unfailing love
 for ever and ever.
9 I will praise you forever for what you have done;
 in your name I will hope, for your name is good.
 I will praise you in the presence of your saints.

Psalm 53

For the director of music. According to *mahalath*.[b] A *maskil*[a] of David.

1 The fool says in his heart,
 "There is no God."
 They are corrupt, and their ways are vile;
 there is no one who does good.

第五十二篇

以東人多益來告訴掃羅說:"大衛到了亞希米勒家。"那時,大衛作這訓誨詩,交與伶長。

1 勇士啊,
 你為何以作惡自誇?
 神的慈愛是常存的。
2 你的舌頭邪惡詭詐,
 好像剃頭刀,
 快利傷人。
3 你愛惡勝似愛善,
 又愛說謊,不愛說公義。
 細拉
4 詭詐的舌頭啊,
 你愛說一切毀滅的話。

5 神也要毀滅你,
 直到永遠;
 他要把你拿去,
 從你的帳棚中抽出,
 從活人之地將你拔出。
 細拉
6 義人要看見而懼怕,
 並要笑他。
7 說:"看哪,
 這就是那不以神為他力量的人,
 只倚仗他豐富的財物,
 在邪惡上堅立自己。"

8 至於我,
 就像神殿中的青橄欖樹,
 我永永遠遠
 倚靠神的慈愛!
9 我要稱謝你,直到永遠,
 因為你行了這事;
 我也要在你聖民面前
 仰望你的名,
 這名本為美好。

第五十三篇

大衛的訓誨詩,交與伶長。調用"麻哈拉"。

1 愚頑人心裏說:
 "沒有神!"
 他們都是邪惡,行了可憎惡的罪孽,
 沒有一個人行善。

---

a Title: Probably a literary or musical term   *b* Title: Probably a musical term

²神從天上垂看世人，
　　要看有明白的沒有，
　　有尋求他的沒有？

³他們各人都退後，
　　一同變為污穢；
　　並沒有行善的，
　　連一個也沒有！

⁴作孽的沒有知識嗎？
　　他們吞吃我的百姓
　　　如同吃飯一樣，
　　並不求告神。
⁵他們在無可懼怕之處，
　　就大大害怕，
　　因為神把那安營攻擊你之人的骨頭
　　散開了。
　　你使他們蒙羞，
　　因為神棄絕了他們。

⁶但願以色列的救恩
　　從錫安而出，
　　神救回他被擄的子民。
　　那時，雅各要快樂，
　　以色列要歡喜。

第五十四篇

西弗人來對掃羅說："大衛豈不是在我們那裏藏
身嗎？"那時，大衛作這訓誨詩，交與伶長。
用絲弦的樂器。

¹神啊，求你以你的名救我，
　　憑你的大能為我伸冤。
²神啊，求你聽我的禱告，
　　留心聽我口中的言語。

³因為外人起來攻擊我，
　　強暴人尋索我的命。
　　他們眼中沒有神。   細拉

⁴神是幫助我的，
　　是扶持我命的。

⁵他要報應我仇敵所行的惡，
　　求你憑你的誠實滅絕他們。

⁶我要把甘心祭獻給你；
　　耶和華啊，我要稱讚你的名，
　　這名本為美好。
⁷他從一切的急難中把我救出來，
　　我的眼睛也看見了我仇敵遭報。

²God looks down from heaven
　　on the sons of men
　to see if there are any who understand,
　　any who seek God.
³Everyone has turned away,
　　they have together become corrupt;
　there is no one who does good,
　　not even one.

⁴Will the evildoers never learn—
　　those who devour my people as men eat
　　bread
　and who do not call on God?
⁵There they were, overwhelmed with dread,
　where there was nothing to dread.
　God scattered the bones of those who
　　attacked you;
　you put them to shame, for God despised
　　them.

⁶Oh, that salvation for Israel would come out of
　　Zion!
　When God restores the fortunes of his
　　people,
　let Jacob rejoice and Israel be glad!

Psalm 54

For the director of music. With stringed instruments. A maskil[a]
of David. When the Ziphites had gone to Saul and said, "Is
not David hiding among us?"

¹Save me, O God, by your name;
　　vindicate me by your might.
²Hear my prayer, O God;
　　listen to the words of my mouth.

³Strangers are attacking me;
　　ruthless men seek my life—
　men without regard for God.   Selah

⁴Surely God is my help;
　　the Lord is the one who sustains me.

⁵Let evil recoil on those who slander me;
　　in your faithfulness destroy them.

⁶I will sacrifice a freewill offering to you;
　　I will praise your name, O LORD,
　　for it is good.
⁷For he has delivered me from all my troubles,
　　and my eyes have looked in triumph on my
　　foes.

a Title: Probably a literary or musical term

Psalm 55

For the director of music. With stringed instruments.
A *maskil*[a] of David.

¹Listen to my prayer, O God,
  do not ignore my plea;
2 hear me and answer me.
  My thoughts trouble me and I am distraught
3 at the voice of the enemy,
    at the stares of the wicked;
  for they bring down suffering upon me
    and revile me in their anger.

⁴My heart is in anguish within me;
  the terrors of death assail me.
⁵Fear and trembling have beset me;
  horror has overwhelmed me.
⁶I said, "Oh, that I had the wings of a dove!
  I would fly away and be at rest—
⁷I would flee far away
  and stay in the desert;   *Selah*
⁸I would hurry to my place of shelter,
  far from the tempest and storm."

⁹Confuse the wicked, O Lord, confound their
    speech,
  for I see violence and strife in the city.
¹⁰Day and night they prowl about on its walls;
  malice and abuse are within it.
¹¹Destructive forces are at work in the city;
  threats and lies never leave its streets.

¹²If an enemy were insulting me,
  I could endure it;
  if a foe were raising himself against me,
  I could hide from him.
¹³But it is you, a man like myself,
  my companion, my close friend,
¹⁴with whom I once enjoyed sweet fellowship
  as we walked with the throng at the house of
    God.

¹⁵Let death take my enemies by surprise;
  let them go down alive to the grave,[b]
  for evil finds lodging among them.

¹⁶But I call to God,
  and the LORD saves me.
¹⁷Evening, morning and noon
  I cry out in distress,
  and he hears my voice.
¹⁸He ransoms me unharmed

第五十五篇

大衛的訓誨詩，交與伶長。用絲弦的樂器。

¹神啊，求你留心聽我的禱告，
  不要隱藏不聽我的懇求！
²求你側耳聽我，應允我。
  我哀歎不安，發聲唉哼。
³都因仇敵的聲音，
  惡人的欺壓，
  因為他們將罪孽加在我身上，
  發怒氣逼迫我。

⁴我心在我裏面甚是疼痛，
  死的驚惶臨到我身。
⁵恐懼戰兢歸到我身，
  驚恐漫過了我。
⁶我說："但願我有翅膀像鴿子，
  我就飛去得享安息。
⁷我必遠遊，
  宿在曠野。   細拉
⁸我必速速逃到避所，
  脫離狂風暴雨。"

⁹主啊，求你吞滅他們，
  變亂他們的舌頭，
  因為我在城中見了強暴爭競的事。
¹⁰他們在城牆上晝夜繞行，
  在城內也有罪孽和奸惡。
¹¹邪惡在其中，
  欺壓和詭詐不離街市。

¹²原來不是仇敵辱罵我，
  若是仇敵，還可忍耐；
  也不是恨我的人向我狂大，
  若是恨我的人，就必躲避他。
¹³不料是你！你原與我平等，
  是我的同伴，是我知己的朋友。
¹⁴我們素常彼此談論，以為甘甜，
  我們與羣眾在神的殿中同行。

¹⁵願死亡忽然臨到他們，
  願他們活活地下入陰間；
  因為他們的住處，
  他們的心中，都是邪惡。
¹⁶至於我，我要求告神，
  耶和華必拯救我。
¹⁷我要晚上、早晨、晌午
  哀聲悲歎，
  他也必聽我的聲音。
¹⁸他救贖我命脫離攻擊我的人，

---

a Title: Probably a literary or musical term   *b* 15 Hebrew
Sheol

使我得享平安，
　　因為與我相爭的人甚多。
¹⁹那沒有更變、
　　不敬畏神的人，
　　從太古常存的神，
　　必聽見而苦待他。

²⁰他背了約，
　　伸手攻擊與他和好的人。
²¹他的口如奶油光滑，
　　他的心卻懷着爭戰；
　　他的話比油柔和，
　　其實是拔出來的刀。

²²你要把你的重擔卸給耶和華，
　　他必撫養你，
　　他永不叫義人動搖。
²³神啊，
　　你必使惡人下入滅亡的坑；
　　流人血、行詭詐的人
　　必活不到半世。

但我要倚靠你。

第五十六篇

非利士人在迦特拿住大衛。那時，他作這金
詩，交與伶長。調用“遠方無聲鴿”。

¹神啊，求你憐憫我！
　　因為人要把我吞了，
　　終日攻擊欺壓我。
²我的仇敵終日要把我吞了，
　　因逞驕傲攻擊我的人甚多。

³我懼怕的時候
　　要倚靠你。
⁴我倚靠神，我要讚美他的話；
　　我倚靠神，必不懼怕。
　　血氣之輩能把我怎麼樣呢？

⁵他們終日顛倒我的話，
　　他們一切的心思都是要害我。
⁶他們聚集、埋伏，
　　窺探我的腳蹤，
　　等候要害我的命。

⁷他們豈能因罪孽逃脫嗎？
　　神啊，求你在怒中使眾民墮落。
⁸我幾次流離，你都記數。
　　求你把我眼淚裝在你的皮袋裏，
　　這不都記在你冊子上嗎？

from the battle waged against me,
　　even though many oppose me.
¹⁹God, who is enthroned forever,
　　will hear them and afflict them—　　　*Selah*
men who never change their ways
　　and have no fear of God.

²⁰My companion attacks his friends;
　　he violates his covenant.
²¹His speech is smooth as butter,
　　yet war is in his heart;
his words are more soothing than oil,
　　yet they are drawn swords.

²²Cast your cares on the LORD
　　and he will sustain you;
he will never let the righteous fall.
²³But you, O God, will bring down the wicked
　　into the pit of corruption;
bloodthirsty and deceitful men
　　will not live out half their days.

But as for me, I trust in you.

Psalm 56

For the director of music. To [the tune of]"A Dove on Distant
Oaks." Of David. A *miktam*.ᵃ When the Philistines had seized
him in Gath.

¹Be merciful to me, O God, for men hotly
　　pursue me;
　　all day long they press their attack.
²My slanderers pursue me all day long;
　　many are attacking me in their pride.

³When I am afraid,
　　I will trust in you.
⁴In God, whose word I praise,
　　in God I trust; I will not be afraid.
　　What can mortal man do to me?

⁵All day long they twist my words;
　　they are always plotting to harm me.
⁶They conspire, they lurk,
　　they watch my steps,
　　eager to take my life.

⁷On no account let them escape;
　　in your anger, O God, bring down the nations.
⁸Record my lament;
　　list my tears on your scrollᵇ —
　　are they not in your record?

---

a Title: Probably a literary or musical term　　*b* 8 Or / *put my
tears in your wineskin*

⁹Then my enemies will turn back
  when I call for help.
  By this I will know that God is for me.
¹⁰In God, whose word I praise,
  in the LORD, whose word I praise—
¹¹in God I trust; I will not be afraid.
  What can man do to me?

¹²I am under vows to you, O God;
  I will present my thank offerings to you.
¹³For you have delivered me^a from death
  and my feet from stumbling,
  that I may walk before God
  in the light of life.^b

Psalm 57

For the director of music. [To the tune of] "Do Not Destroy."
Of David. A *miktam*.^c When he had fled from Saul into
the cave.

¹Have mercy on me, O God, have mercy on me,
  for in you my soul takes refuge.
  I will take refuge in the shadow of your wings
  until the disaster has passed.

²I cry out to God Most High,
  to God, who fulfills [his purpose] for me.
³He sends from heaven and saves me,
  rebuking those who hotly pursue me;   *Selah*
  God sends his love and his faithfulness.

⁴I am in the midst of lions;
  I lie among ravenous beasts—
  men whose teeth are spears and arrows,
  whose tongues are sharp swords.

⁵Be exalted, O God, above the heavens;
  let your glory be over all the earth.

⁶They spread a net for my feet—
  I was bowed down in distress.
  They dug a pit in my path—
  but they have fallen into it themselves.   *Selah*

⁷My heart is steadfast, O God,
  my heart is steadfast;
  I will sing and make music.
⁸Awake, my soul!
  Awake, harp and lyre!
  I will awaken the dawn.

---

⁹我呼求的日子，
  我的仇敵都要轉身退後。
  神幫助我，這是我所知道的。
¹⁰我倚靠神，我要讚美他的話；
  我倚靠耶和華，我要讚美他的話！
¹¹我倚靠神，必不懼怕。
  人能把我怎麼樣呢？

¹²神啊，我向你所許的願在我身上，
  我要將感謝祭獻給你。
¹³因為你救我的命脫離死亡，
  你豈不是救護我的腳不跌倒，
  使我在生命光中
  行在神面前嗎？

第五十七篇

大衛逃避掃羅，藏在洞裏。那時，他作這金詩，
  交與伶長。調用「休要毀壞」。

¹神啊，求你憐憫我，憐憫我！
  因為我的心投靠你。
  我要投靠在你翅膀的蔭下，
  等到災害過去。

²我要求告至高的神，
  就是為我成全諸事的神。
³那要吞我的人辱罵我的時候，
  神從天上必施恩救我，
  也必向我發出慈愛和誠實。

⁴我的性命在獅子中間；
  我躺臥在性如烈火的世人當中。
  他們的牙齒是槍、箭；
  他們的舌頭是快刀。

⁵神啊，願你崇高過於諸天！
  願你的榮耀高過全地！

⁶他們為我的腳設下網羅，
  壓制我的心。
  他們在我面前挖了坑，
  自己反掉在其中。   細拉

⁷神啊，我心堅定，
  我心堅定！
  我要唱詩，我要歌頌！
⁸我的靈啊（註：原文作"榮耀"），
  你當醒起！
  琴瑟啊，你們當醒起！
  我自己要極早醒起。

---

^a 13 Or *my soul*   ^b 13 Or *the land of the living*   ^c Title:
Probably a literary or musical term

9主啊，我要在萬民中稱謝你，
　　在列邦中歌頌你！
10因為你的慈愛高及諸天；
　　你的誠實達到穹蒼。

11神啊，願你崇高過於諸天！
　　願你的榮耀高過全地！

第五十八篇

大衛的金詩，交與伶長。調用“休要毀壞”。

1世人哪，
　　你們默然不語，真合公義嗎？
　　施行審判，豈按正直嗎？
2不然，你們是心中作惡，
　　你們在地上
　　秤出你們手所行的強暴。
3惡人一出母胎，就與神疏遠，
　　一離母腹，便走錯路，說謊話。
4他們的毒氣好像蛇的毒氣，
　　他們好像塞耳的聾虺，
5不聽行法術的聲音，
　　雖用極靈的咒語，也是不聽。

6神啊，求你敲碎他們口中的牙；
　　耶和華啊，
　　求你敲掉少壯獅子的大牙！
7願他們消滅如急流的水一般；
　　他們瞅準射箭的時候，
　　願箭頭彷彿砍斷。
8願他們像蝸牛消化過去，
　　又像婦人墜落未見天日的胎。

9你們用荊棘燒火，
　　鍋還未熱，
　他要用旋風
　　把青的和燒着的一齊颳去。
10義人見仇敵遭報就歡喜，
　　要在惡人的血中洗腳。

11因此，人必說：
　　“義人誠然有善報，
　　在地上果有施行判斷的神。”

9I will praise you, O LORD, among the nations;
　　I will sing of you among the peoples.
10For great is your love, reaching to the heavens;
　　your faithfulness reaches to the skies.

11Be exalted, O God, above the heavens;
　　let your glory be over all the earth.

Psalm 58

For the director of music. ⌊To the tune of⌋ "Do Not Destroy."
Of David. A *miktam.*[a]

1Do you rulers indeed speak justly?
　　Do you judge uprightly among men?
2No, in your heart you devise injustice,
　　and your hands mete out violence on the
　　earth.
3Even from birth the wicked go astray;
　　from the womb they are wayward and speak
　　lies.
4Their venom is like the venom of a snake,
　　like that of a cobra that has stopped its ears,
5that will not heed the tune of the charmer,
　　however skillful the enchanter may be.

6Break the teeth in their mouths, O God;
　　tear out, O LORD, the fangs of the lions!
7Let them vanish like water that flows away;
　　when they draw the bow, let their arrows be
　　blunted.
8Like a slug melting away as it moves along,
　　like a stillborn child, may they not see the
　　sun.

9Before your pots can feel ⌊the heat of⌋ the
　　thorns—
　　whether they be green or dry—the wicked
　　will be swept away.[b]
10The righteous will be glad when they are
　　avenged,
　　when they bathe their feet in the blood of the
　　wicked.
11Then men will say,
　　"Surely the righteous still are rewarded;
　　surely there is a God who judges the earth."

a Title: Probably a literary or musical term　　*b* 9 The meaning
of the Hebrew for this verse is uncertain.

Psalm 59

For the director of music. ⌊To the tune of⌋ "Do Not Destroy."
Of David. A *miktam.*[a] When Saul had sent men to watch
David's house in order to kill him.

¹Deliver me from my enemies, O God;
   protect me from those who rise up against
   me.
²Deliver me from evildoers
   and save me from bloodthirsty men.

³See how they lie in wait for me!
   Fierce men conspire against me
   for no offense or sin of mine, O LORD.
⁴I have done no wrong, yet they are ready to
   attack me.
   Arise to help me; look on my plight!
⁵O LORD God Almighty, the God of Israel,
   rouse yourself to punish all the nations;
   show no mercy to wicked traitors.   *Selah*

⁶They return at evening,
   snarling like dogs,
   and prowl about the city.
⁷See what they spew from their mouths—
   they spew out swords from their lips,
   and they say, "Who can hear us?"
⁸But you, O LORD, laugh at them;
   you scoff at all those nations.

⁹O my Strength, I watch for you;
   you, O God, are my fortress, ¹⁰my loving
   God.

   God will go before me
   and will let me gloat over those who slander
   me.
¹¹But do not kill them, O LORD our shield,[b]
   or my people will forget.
   In your might make them wander about,
   and bring them down.
¹²For the sins of their mouths,
   for the words of their lips,
   let them be caught in their pride.
   For the curses and lies they utter,
¹³ consume them in wrath,
   consume them till they are no more.
   Then it will be known to the ends of the earth
   that God rules over Jacob.   *Selah*

¹⁴They return at evening,
   snarling like dogs,
   and prowl about the city.

第五十九篇

掃羅打發人窺探大衛的房屋，要殺他。那時，大
衛作這金詩，交與伶長。調用「休要毀壞」。

¹我的神啊，求你救我脫離仇敵！
   把我安置在高處，
   得脫那些起來攻擊我的人；
²求你救我脫離作孽的人
   和喜愛流人血的人。
³因為他們埋伏，要害我的命。
   有能力的人聚集來攻擊我。
   耶和華啊，這不是為我的過犯，
   也不是為我的罪愆。
⁴我雖然無過，
   他們預備整齊，跑來攻擊我。
   求你興起鑒察，幫助我。
⁵萬軍之神耶和華以色列的神啊，
   求你興起，懲治萬邦！
   不要憐憫行詭詐的惡人！   細拉

⁶他們晚上轉回，
   叫號如狗，
   圍城繞行。
⁷他們口中噴吐惡言，
   嘴裏有刀。
   他們說：「有誰聽見？」
⁸但你耶和華必笑話他們，
   你要嗤笑萬邦。

⁹我的力量啊，我必仰望你，
   因為神是我的高臺。

¹⁰我的神要以慈愛迎接我。
   神要叫我看見
   我仇敵遭報。
¹¹不要殺他們，恐怕我的民忘記。
   主啊，你是我們的盾牌，
   求你用你的能力使他們四散，
   且降為卑。
¹²因他們口中的罪
   和嘴裏的言語，
   並咒罵虛謊的話，
   願他們在驕傲之中被纏住了。
¹³求你發怒，使他們消滅，
   以至歸於無有，
   叫他們知道神在雅各中間掌權，
   直到地極。   細拉

¹⁴到了晚上，任憑他們轉回，
   任憑他們叫號如狗，
   圍城繞行。

---

a Title: Probably a literary or musical term   *b* 11 Or *sovereign*

15他們必走來走去，尋找食物，
　　若不得飽，就終夜在外。
16但我要歌頌你的力量，
　　早晨要高唱你的慈愛；
　　因為你作過我的高臺，
　　在我急難的日子作過我的避難所。
17我的力量啊，我要歌頌你，
　　因為神是我的高臺，
　　是賜恩與我的神。

第六十篇

大衛與兩河間的亞蘭並瑣巴的亞蘭爭戰的時
候，約押轉回，在鹽谷攻擊以東，殺了一萬二
千人。那時，大衛作這金詩，叫人學習，交與
伶長。調用「為證的百合花」。

1神啊，你丟棄了我們，
　　使我們破敗。
　　你向我們發怒，求你使我們復興。
2你使地震動，而且崩裂。
　　求你將裂口醫好，因為地搖動。
3你叫你的民遇見艱難；
　　你叫我們喝那使人東倒西歪的酒。

4你把旌旗
　　賜給敬畏你的人，
　　可以為真理揚起來。　　　　細拉

5求你應允我們，用右手拯救我們，
　　好叫你所親愛的人得救。
6神已經指着他的聖潔說（註：「說」或
　　作「應許我」）：
　　「我要歡樂，我要分開示劍，
　　丈量疏割谷。
7基列是我的，瑪拿西也是我的，
　　以法蓮是護衛我頭的，
　　猶大是我的杖。
8摩押是我的沐浴盆，
　　我要向以東拋鞋。
　　非利士啊，你還能因我歡呼嗎？」
9誰能領我進堅固城？
　　誰能引我到以東地？
10神啊，你不是丟棄了我們嗎？
　　神啊，你不和我們的軍兵同去嗎？
11求你幫助我們攻擊敵人，
　　因為人的幫助是枉然的。
12我們倚靠神，才得施展大能，
　　因為踐踏我們敵人的就是他。

15They wander about for food
　　and howl if not satisfied.
16But I will sing of your strength,
　　in the morning I will sing of your love;
　　for you are my fortress,
　　my refuge in times of trouble.

17O my Strength, I sing praise to you;
　　you, O God, are my fortress, my loving God.

Psalm 60

For the director of music. To the tune of "The Lily of
the Covenant." A *miktam*[a] of David. For teaching.
When he fought Aram Naharaim[b] and Aram Zobah,[c]
and when Joab returned and struck down twelve thousand
Edomites in the Valley of Salt.

1You have rejected us, O God, and burst forth
　　upon us;
　　you have been angry—now restore us!
2You have shaken the land and torn it open;
　　mend its fractures, for it is quaking.
3You have shown your people desperate times;
　　you have given us wine that makes us stagger.

4But for those who fear you, you have raised a
　　banner
　　to be unfurled against the bow.　　*Selah*

5Save us and help us with your right hand,
　　that those you love may be delivered.
6God has spoken from his sanctuary:
　　"In triumph I will parcel out Shechem
　　and measure off the Valley of Succoth.
7Gilead is mine, and Manasseh is mine;
　　Ephraim is my helmet,
　　Judah my scepter.
8Moab is my washbasin,
　　upon Edom I toss my sandal;
　　over Philistia I shout in triumph."

9Who will bring me to the fortified city?
　　Who will lead me to Edom?
10Is it not you, O God, you who have rejected us
　　and no longer go out with our armies?
11Give us aid against the enemy,
　　for the help of man is worthless.
12With God we will gain the victory,
　　and he will trample down our enemies.

---

a Title: Probably a literary or musical term　　*b* Title: That is,
Arameans of Northwest Mesopotamia　　*c* Title: That is,
Arameans of central Syria

Psalm 61

For the director of music. With stringed instruments.
Of David.

¹Hear my cry, O God;
  listen to my prayer.

²From the ends of the earth I call to you,
  I call as my heart grows faint;
  lead me to the rock that is higher than I.
³For you have been my refuge,
  a strong tower against the foe.

⁴I long to dwell in your tent forever
  and take refuge in the shelter of your wings.
                             Selah
⁵For you have heard my vows, O God;
  you have given me the heritage of those who
    fear your name.

⁶Increase the days of the king's life,
  his years for many generations.
⁷May he be enthroned in God's presence forever;
  appoint your love and faithfulness to protect
  him.

⁸Then will I ever sing praise to your name
  and fulfill my vows day after day.

Psalm 62

For the director of music. For Jeduthun. A psalm of David.

¹My soul finds rest in God alone;
  my salvation comes from him.
²He alone is my rock and my salvation;
  he is my fortress, I will never be shaken.

³How long will you assault a man?
  Would all of you throw him down—
  this leaning wall, this tottering fence?
⁴They fully intend to topple him
  from his lofty place;
  they take delight in lies.
  With their mouths they bless,
  but in their hearts they curse.   *Selah*

⁵Find rest, O my soul, in God alone;
  my hope comes from him.
⁶He alone is my rock and my salvation;
  he is my fortress, I will not be shaken.
⁷My salvation and my honor depend on God*a*;
  he is my mighty rock, my refuge.

a 7 Or / God Most High is my salvation and my honor

第六十一篇

大衛的詩,交與伶長。用絲弦的樂器。

¹神啊,求你聽我的呼求,
  側耳聽我的禱告。

²我心裏發昏的時候,
  我要從地極求告你,
  求你領我到那比我更高的磐石。
³因為你作過我的避難所,
  作過我的堅固臺,脫離仇敵。

⁴我要永遠住在你的帳幕裏,
  我要投靠在你翅膀下的隱密處。
                          細拉
⁵神啊,你原是聽了我所許的願,
  你將產業賜給敬畏你名的人。

⁶你要加添王的壽數,
  他的年歲必存到世世。
⁷他必永遠坐在神面前;
  願你預備慈愛和誠實保佑他。

⁸這樣,我要歌頌你的名,
  直到永遠,好天天還我所許的願。

第六十二篇

大衛的詩,照耶杜頓的作法,交與伶長。

¹我的心默默無聲,專等候神;
  我的救恩是從他而來。
²惟獨他是我的磐石,我的拯救;
  他是我的高臺,我必不很動搖。

³你們大家攻擊一人,把他毀壞,
  如同毀壞歪斜的牆、將倒的壁,
  要到幾時呢?
⁴他們彼此商議,
  專要從他的尊位上把他推下;
  他們喜愛謊話,
    口雖祝福,
    心卻咒詛。   細拉

⁵我的心哪,你當默默無聲,專等候神,
  因為我的盼望是從他而來。
⁶惟獨他是我的磐石,我的拯救;
  他是我的高臺,我必不動搖。
⁷我的拯救,我的榮耀,都在乎神;
  我力量的磐石,我的避難所,
  都在乎神。

8你們眾民當時時倚靠他，
　　在他面前傾心吐意。
　　神是我們的避難所。　　　　　細拉

9下流人真是虛空，
　　上流人也是虛假；
　　放在天平裏就必浮起，
　　他們一共比空氣還輕。
10不要仗勢欺人，
　　也不要因搶奪而驕傲；
　　若財寶加增，
　　　　不要放在心上。

11神說了一次、兩次，
　　我都聽見，
　　就是能力都屬乎神。
12主啊，慈愛也是屬乎你，
　　因為你照着各人所行的報應他。

8Trust in him at all times, O people;
　　pour out your hearts to him,
　　for God is our refuge.　　　　*Selah*

9Lowborn men are but a breath,
　　the highborn are but a lie;
　　if weighed on a balance, they are nothing;
　　together they are only a breath.
10Do not trust in extortion
　　or take pride in stolen goods;
　　though your riches increase,
　　do not set your heart on them.

11One thing God has spoken,
　　two things have I heard:
　　that you, O God, are strong,
12 and that you, O LORD, are loving.
　　Surely you will reward each person
　　according to what he has done.

第六十三篇

大衛在猶大曠野的時候，作了這詩。

1神啊，你是我的神！
　　我要切切地尋求你；
　　在乾旱疲乏
　　　無水之地，
　　我渴想你，
　　　我的心切慕你。

2我在聖所中曾如此瞻仰你，
　　為要見你的能力和你的榮耀。
3因你的慈愛比生命更好，
　　我的嘴唇要頌讚你。
4我還活的時候要這樣稱頌你，
　　我要奉你的名舉手。
5、6我在牀上記念你，
　　在夜更的時候思想你。

我的心就像飽足了骨髓肥油，
　　我也要以歡樂的嘴唇讚美你。

7因為你曾幫助我，
　　我就在你翅膀的蔭下歡呼。
8我心緊緊地跟隨你；
　　你的右手扶持我。

9但那些尋索要滅我命的人，
　　必往地底下去。
10他們必被刀劍所殺
　　被野狗所吃。

Psalm 63

A psalm of David. When he was in the Desert of Judah.

1O God, you are my God,
　　earnestly I seek you;
　　my soul thirsts for you,
　　my body longs for you,
　　in a dry and weary land
　　where there is no water.

2I have seen you in the sanctuary
　　and beheld your power and your glory.
3Because your love is better than life,
　　my lips will glorify you.
4I will praise you as long as I live,
　　and in your name I will lift up my hands.
5My soul will be satisfied as with the richest of
　　foods;
　　with singing lips my mouth will praise you.

6On my bed I remember you;
　　I think of you through the watches of the
　　night.
7Because you are my help,
　　I sing in the shadow of your wings.
8My soul clings to you;
　　your right hand upholds me.

9They who seek my life will be destroyed;
　　they will go down to the depths of the earth.
10They will be given over to the sword
　　and become food for jackals.

11But the king will rejoice in God;
    all who swear by God's name will praise him,
    while the mouths of liars will be silenced.

Psalm 64

For the director of music. A psalm of David.

1Hear me, O God, as I voice my complaint;
    protect my life from the threat of the enemy.
2Hide me from the conspiracy of the wicked,
    from that noisy crowd of evildoers.

3They sharpen their tongues like swords
    and aim their words like deadly arrows.
4They shoot from ambush at the innocent man;
    they shoot at him suddenly, without fear.

5They encourage each other in evil plans,
    they talk about hiding their snares;
    they say, "Who will see them*a*?"
6They plot injustice and say,
    "We have devised a perfect plan!"
    Surely the mind and heart of man are
      cunning.

7But God will shoot them with arrows;
    suddenly they will be struck down.
8He will turn their own tongues against them
    and bring them to ruin;
    all who see them will shake their heads in
      scorn.

9All mankind will fear;
    they will proclaim the works of God
    and ponder what he has done.
10Let the righteous rejoice in the LORD
    and take refuge in him;
    let all the upright in heart praise him!

Psalm 65

For the director of music. A psalm of David. A song.

1Praise awaits*b* you, O God, in Zion;
    to you our vows will be fulfilled.
2O you who hear prayer,
    to you all men will come.
3When we were overwhelmed by sins,
    you forgave*c* our transgressions.
4Blessed are those you choose
    and bring near to live in your courts!

a 5 Or *us*   *b 1* Or *befits*; the meaning of the Hebrew for this
word is uncertain.   *c 3* Or *made atonement for*

11但是王必因神歡喜,
    凡指着他發誓的,必要誇口,
    因為說謊之人的口必被塞住。

第六十四篇

大衛的詩,交與伶長。

1神啊,我哀歎的時候,
    求你聽我的聲音,
    求你保護我的性命不受仇敵的驚恐。
2求你把我隱藏,使我脫離作惡之人
    的暗謀和作孽之人的擾亂。
3他們磨舌如刀,發出苦毒的言語,
    好像比準了的箭,
4要在暗地射完全人。
    他們忽然射他,並不懼怕。

5他們彼此勉勵設下惡計;
    他們商量暗設網羅說:
    "誰能看見?"
6他們圖謀奸惡說:
    "我們是極力圖謀的。"
    他們各人的意念心思是深的。

7但神要射他們,
    他們忽然被箭射傷。
8他們必然絆跌,
    被自己的舌頭所害;
    凡看見他們的必都搖頭。

9眾人都要害怕,
    要傳揚神的工作,
    並且明白他的作為。
10義人必因耶和華歡喜,
    並要投靠他;
    凡心裏正直的人都要誇口。

第六十五篇

大衛的詩歌,交與伶長。

1神啊,錫安的人都等候讚美你,
    所許的願也要向你償還。
2聽禱告的主啊,
    凡有血氣的都要來就你。
3罪孽勝了我,
    至於我們的過犯,你都要赦免。
4你所揀選、
    使他親近你、住在你院中的,
    這人便為有福!

我們必因你居所、
　　你聖殿的美福
　　知足了。

5 拯救我們的神啊，
　　你必以威嚴
　　秉公義應允我們；
　你本是一切地極
　　和海上遠處的人所倚靠的。
6 他既以大能束腰，
　　就用力量安定諸山，
7 使諸海的響聲
　　和其中波浪的響聲，
　　並萬民的喧嘩，都平靜了。
8 住在地極的人，
　　因你的神蹟懼怕；
　　你使日出日落之地都歡呼。

9 你眷顧地，降下透雨，
　　使地大得肥美。
　神的河滿了水，
　　你這樣澆灌了地，
　　好為人預備五穀。
10 你澆透地的犂溝，
　　潤平犂脊，
　降甘霖使地軟和；
　　其中發長的，蒙你賜福。
11 你以恩典為年歲的冠冕，
　　你的路徑都滴下脂油。
12 滴在曠野的草場上。
　　小山以歡樂束腰，
13 草場以羊羣為衣，
　　谷中也長滿了五穀。
　　這一切都歡呼歌唱！

第六十六篇

一篇詩歌，交與伶長。

1 全地都當向神歡呼！
2 歌頌他名的榮耀，
　　用讚美的言語將他的榮耀發明。
3 當對神說：“你的作為何等可畏！
　　因你的大能，
　　仇敵要477降你。
4 全地要敬拜你，
　　歌頌你，
　　要歌頌你的名。”　　　　細拉

5 你們來看神所行的，
　　他向世人所作之事是可畏的。
6 他將海變成乾地，
　　眾民步行過河，
　　我們在那裏因他歡喜。

We are filled with the good things of your
　　house,
　of your holy temple.

5 You answer us with awesome deeds of
　　righteousness,
　　O God our Savior,
　the hope of all the ends of the earth
　　and of the farthest seas,
6 who formed the mountains by your power,
　　having armed yourself with strength,
7 who stilled the roaring of the seas,
　　the roaring of their waves,
　　and the turmoil of the nations.
8 Those living far away fear your wonders;
　　where morning dawns and evening fades
　　you call forth songs of joy.

9 You care for the land and water it;
　　you enrich it abundantly.
　The streams of God are filled with water
　　to provide the people with grain,
　　for so you have ordained it.[a]
10 You drench its furrows
　　and level its ridges;
　　you soften it with showers
　　and bless its crops.
11 You crown the year with your bounty,
　　and your carts overflow with abundance.
12 The grasslands of the desert overflow;
　　the hills are clothed with gladness.
13 The meadows are covered with flocks
　　and the valleys are mantled with grain;
　　they shout for joy and sing.

Psalm 66

For the director of music. A song. A psalm.

1 Shout with joy to God, all the earth!
2 　Sing the glory of his name;
　　make his praise glorious!
3 Say to God, “How awesome are your deeds!
　　So great is your power
　　that your enemies cringe before you.
4 All the earth bows down to you;
　　they sing praise to you,
　　they sing praise to your name.”　　　Selah

5 Come and see what God has done,
　　how awesome his works in man's behalf!
6 He turned the sea into dry land,
　　they passed through the waters on foot—
　　come, let us rejoice in him.

a 9 Or for that is how you prepare the land

⁷He rules forever by his power,
  his eyes watch the nations—
  let not the rebellious rise up against him.
                                    Selah

⁸Praise our God, O peoples,
  let the sound of his praise be heard;
⁹he has preserved our lives
  and kept our feet from slipping.
¹⁰For you, O God, tested us;
  you refined us like silver.
¹¹You brought us into prison
  and laid burdens on our backs.
¹²You let men ride over our heads;
  we went through fire and water,
  but you brought us to a place of abundance.

¹³I will come to your temple with burnt
    offerings
  and fulfill my vows to you—
¹⁴vows my lips promised and my mouth spoke
  when I was in trouble.
¹⁵I will sacrifice fat animals to you
  and an offering of rams;
  I will offer bulls and goats.   *Selah*

¹⁶Come and listen, all you who fear God;
  let me tell you what he has done for me.
¹⁷I cried out to him with my mouth;
  his praise was on my tongue.
¹⁸If I had cherished sin in my heart,
  the Lord would not have listened;
¹⁹but God has surely listened
  and heard my voice in prayer.
²⁰Praise be to God,
  who has not rejected my prayer
  or withheld his love from me!

Psalm 67

For the director of music. With stringed instruments.
A psalm. A song.

¹May God be gracious to us and bless us
  and make his face shine upon us,   *Selah*
²that your ways may be known on earth,
  your salvation among all nations.

³May the peoples praise you, O God;
  may all the peoples praise you.
⁴May the nations be glad and sing for joy,
  for you rule the peoples justly
  and guide the nations of the earth.   *Selah*
⁵May the peoples praise you, O God;
  may all the peoples praise you.

⁷他用權能治理萬民,直到永遠。
  他的眼睛鑒察列邦,
  悖逆的人不可自高。
                                    細拉

⁸萬民哪,你們當稱頌我們的神!
  使人得聽讚美他的聲音。
⁹他使我們的生命存活,
  也不叫我們的腳搖動。
¹⁰神啊,你曾試驗我們,
  熬煉我們,如熬煉銀子一樣。
¹¹你使我們進入網羅,
  把重擔放在我們的身上。
¹²你使人坐車軋我們的頭。
  我們經過水火,
  你卻使我們到豐富之地。

¹³我要用燔祭
  進你的殿,
  向你還我的願——
¹⁴就是在急難時,
  我嘴唇所發的、口中所許的。
¹⁵我要把肥牛作燔祭,
  將公羊的香祭獻給你,
  又把公牛和山羊獻上。   細拉

¹⁶凡敬畏神的人,你們都來聽!
  我要述說他為我所行的事。
¹⁷我曾用口求告他,
  我的舌頭也稱他為高。
¹⁸我若心裏注重罪孽,
  主必不聽。
¹⁹但神實在聽見了,
  他側耳聽了我禱告的聲音。
²⁰神是應當稱頌的!
  他並沒有推卻我的禱告,
  也沒有叫他的慈愛離開我。

第六十七篇

一篇詩歌,交與伶長。用絲弦的樂器。

¹願神憐憫我們,賜福與我們,
  用臉光照我們,   細拉
²好叫世界得知你的道路,
  萬國得知你的救恩。

³神啊,願列邦稱讚你,
  願萬民都稱讚你!
⁴願萬國都快樂歡呼,
  因為你必按公正審判萬民,
  引導世上的萬國。   細拉
⁵神啊,願列邦稱讚你,
  願萬民都稱讚你!

6地已經出了土產；
　　神，就是我們的神要賜福與我們。
7神要賜福與我們，
　　地的四極都要敬畏他。

第六十八篇

大衛的詩歌，交與伶長。

1願神興起，使他的仇敵四散，
　　叫那恨他的人，從他面前逃跑。
2他們被驅逐，
　　如煙被風吹散；
　惡人見神之面而消滅，
　　如蠟被火熔化。
3惟有義人必然歡喜，
　　在神面前高興快樂。

4你們當向神唱詩，歌頌他的名！
　　為那坐車行過曠野的修平大路。
　他的名是耶和華，
　　要在他面前歡樂。
5神在他的聖所作孤兒的父，
　　作寡婦的伸冤者。
6神叫孤獨的有家，
　　使被囚的出來享福；
　惟有悖逆的住在乾燥之地。

7神啊，
　　你曾在你百姓前頭出來，
　　在曠野行走。　　　　　　細拉

8那時，地見神的面而震動，
　　天也落雨，
　西奈山見以色列神的面
　　也震動。
9神啊，你降下大雨，
　　你產業以色列疲乏的時候，
　　你使他堅固。
10你的會眾住在其中。
　　神啊，你的恩惠是為困苦人
　　預備的。
11主發命令，
　　傳好信息的婦女
　　成了大群。
12統兵的君王逃跑了，逃跑了；
　　在家等候的婦女分受所奪的。
13你們安臥在羊圈的時候，
　　好像鴿子的翅膀鍍白銀，
　　翎毛鍍黃金一般。

6Then the land will yield its harvest,
　　and God, our God, will bless us.
7God will bless us,
　　and all the ends of the earth will fear him.

Psalm 68

For the director of music. Of David. A psalm. A song.

1May God arise, may his enemies be scattered;
　　may his foes flee before him.
2As smoke is blown away by the wind,
　　may you blow them away;
　as wax melts before the fire,
　　may the wicked perish before God.
3But may the righteous be glad
　　and rejoice before God;
　　may they be happy and joyful.

4Sing to God, sing praise to his name,
　　extol him who rides on the clouds[a] —
　his name is the LORD—
　　and rejoice before him.
5A father to the fatherless, a defender of widows,
　　is God in his holy dwelling.
6God sets the lonely in families,[b]
　　he leads forth the prisoners with singing;
　　but the rebellious live in a sun-scorched
　　land.

7When you went out before your people,
　　O God,
　when you marched through the wasteland,
　　　　　　　　　　　　　　Selah
8the earth shook,
　　the heavens poured down rain,
　before God, the One of Sinai,
　　before God, the God of Israel.
9You gave abundant showers, O God;
　　you refreshed your weary inheritance.
10Your people settled in it,
　　and from your bounty, O God, you provided
　　for the poor.

11The LORD announced the word,
　　and great was the company of those who
　　proclaimed it:
12"Kings and armies flee in haste;
　　in the camps men divide the plunder.
13Even while you sleep among the campfires,[c]
　　the wings of ⌊my⌋ dove are sheathed with
　　silver,
　　its feathers with shining gold."

a 4 Or / prepare the way for him who rides through the deserts
b 6 Or the desolate in a homeland　c 13 Or saddlebags

¹⁴When the Almighty^a scattered the kings in the land,
    it was like snow fallen on Zalmon.

¹⁵The mountains of Bashan are majestic mountains;
    rugged are the mountains of Bashan.
¹⁶Why gaze in envy, O rugged mountains,
    at the mountain where God chooses to reign,
    where the LORD himself will dwell forever?
¹⁷The chariots of God are tens of thousands
    and thousands of thousands;
    the Lord ⌊has come⌋ from Sinai into his sanctuary.
¹⁸When you ascended on high,
    you led captives in your train;
    you received gifts from men,
    even from^b the rebellious—
    that you,^c O LORD God, might dwell there.

¹⁹Praise be to the Lord, to God our Savior,
    who daily bears our burdens.   *Selah*
²⁰Our God is a God who saves;
    from the Sovereign LORD comes escape from death.

²¹Surely God will crush the heads of his enemies,
    the hairy crowns of those who go on in their sins.
²²The Lord says, "I will bring them from Bashan;
    I will bring them from the depths of the sea,
²³that you may plunge your feet in the blood of your foes,
    while the tongues of your dogs have their share."

²⁴Your procession has come into view, O God,
    the procession of my God and King into the sanctuary.
²⁵In front are the singers, after them the musicians;
    with them are the maidens playing tambourines.
²⁶Praise God in the great congregation;
    praise the LORD in the assembly of Israel.
²⁷There is the little tribe of Benjamin, leading them,
    there the great throng of Judah's princes,
    and there the princes of Zebulun and of Naphtali.

¹⁴全能者在境內
    趕散列王的時候，
    勢如飄雪在撒們。

¹⁵巴珊山是神的山，
    巴珊山是多峯多嶺的山。
¹⁶你們多峯多嶺的山哪，
    為何斜看神所願居住的山？
    耶和華必住這山，直到永遠。
¹⁷神的車輦累萬盈千，
    主在其中，
    好像在西奈聖山一樣。

¹⁸你已經升上高天
    擄掠仇敵；
    你在人間，
    就是在悖逆的人間受了供獻，
    叫耶和華神可以與他們同住。
¹⁹天天背負我們重擔的主，
    就是拯救我們的神，
    是應當稱頌的。   細拉
²⁰神是為我們施行諸般救恩的神；
    人能脫離死亡
    是在乎主耶和華。

²¹但神要打破
    他仇敵的頭，
    就是那常犯罪之人的髮頂。

²²主說：
    "我要使眾民從巴珊而歸，
    使他們從深海而回，
²³使你打碎仇敵，
    你的腳踹在血中，
    使你狗的舌頭
    從其中得分。"

²⁴神啊，你是我的神，我的王；
    人已經看見你行走，
    進入聖所。
²⁵歌唱的行在前，
    作樂的隨在後，
    都在擊鼓的童女中間。
²⁶從以色列源頭而來的，
    當在各會中稱頌主神。
²⁷在那裏有統管他們的小便雅憫，
    有猶大的首領和他們的羣眾，
    有西布倫的首領，
    有拿弗他利的首領。

---

a 14 Hebrew *Shaddai*   *b* 18 Or *gifts for men, / even*
c 18 Or *they*

²⁸以色列的能力是神所賜的。
　　神啊，求你堅固
　　　你為我們所成全的事。
²⁹因你耶路撒冷的殿，
　　列王必帶貢物獻給你。
³⁰求你叱喝蘆葦中的野獸和羣公牛，
　　並列邦中的牛犢，
　　把銀塊踹在腳下；
　　神已經趕散
　　好爭戰的列邦。
³¹埃及的公侯要出來朝見神；
　　古實人要急忙舉手禱告。

³²世上的列國啊，你們要向神歌唱；
　　願你們歌頌主，
³³歌頌那自古駕行在諸天以上的主。
　　他發出聲音，是極大的聲音。
³⁴你們要將能力歸給神，
　　他的威榮在以色列之上，
　　他的能力是在穹蒼。
³⁵神啊，你從聖所顯為可畏。
　　以色列的神是那將力量權能
　　　賜給他百姓的。

　　神是應當稱頌的！

第六十九篇

大衛的詩，交與伶長。調用“百合花”。

¹神啊，求你救我，
　　因為眾水要淹沒我！
²我陷在深淤泥中，
　　沒有立腳之地；
　　我到了深水中，
　　大水漫過我身。
³我因呼求困乏，
　　喉嚨發乾；
　　我因等候神，
　　眼睛失明。
⁴無故恨我的，
　　比我頭髮還多；
　　無理與我為仇、要把我剪除的，
　　甚為強盛。
　　我沒有搶奪的，
　　要叫我償還。

⁵神啊，我的愚昧，你原知道；
　　我的罪愆不能隱瞞。

⁶萬軍的主耶和華啊，
　　求你叫那等候你的，

²⁸Summon your power, O God*a*;
　　show us your strength, O God, as you have
　　　done before.
²⁹Because of your temple at Jerusalem
　　kings will bring you gifts.
³⁰Rebuke the beast among the reeds,
　　the herd of bulls among the calves of the
　　　nations.
　　Humbled, may it bring bars of silver.
　　Scatter the nations who delight in war.
³¹Envoys will come from Egypt;
　　Cush*b* will submit herself to God.

³²Sing to God, O kingdoms of the earth,
　　sing praise to the Lord,　　　　　　*Selah*
³³to him who rides the ancient skies above,
　　who thunders with mighty voice.
³⁴Proclaim the power of God,
　　whose majesty is over Israel,
　　whose power is in the skies.
³⁵You are awesome, O God, in your sanctuary;
　　the God of Israel gives power and strength to
　　　his people.

　　Praise be to God!

Psalm 69

For the director of music. To [the tune of] "Lilies." Of David.

¹Save me, O God,
　　for the waters have come up to my neck.
²I sink in the miry depths,
　　where there is no foothold.
　　I have come into the deep waters;
　　the floods engulf me.
³I am worn out calling for help;
　　my throat is parched.
　　My eyes fail,
　　looking for my God.
⁴Those who hate me without reason
　　outnumber the hairs of my head;
　　many are my enemies without cause,
　　those who seek to destroy me.
　　I am forced to restore
　　what I did not steal.

⁵You know my folly, O God;
　　my guilt is not hidden from you.

⁶May those who hope in you
　　not be disgraced because of me,

a 28 Many Hebrew manuscripts, Septuagint and Syriac; most
Hebrew manuscripts *Your God has summoned power for you*
b 31 That is, the upper Nile region

O Lord, the LORD Almighty;
  may those who seek you
    not be put to shame because of me,
    O God of Israel.
⁷For I endure scorn for your sake,
  and shame covers my face.
⁸I am a stranger to my brothers,
  an alien to my own mother's sons;
⁹for zeal for your house consumes me,
  and the insults of those who insult you fall
    on me.
¹⁰When I weep and fast,
  I must endure scorn;
¹¹when I put on sackcloth,
  people make sport of me.
¹²Those who sit at the gate mock me,
  and I am the song of the drunkards.

¹³But I pray to you, O LORD,
  in the time of your favor;
  in your great love, O God,
  answer me with your sure salvation.
¹⁴Rescue me from the mire,
  do not let me sink;
  deliver me from those who hate me,
  from the deep waters.
¹⁵Do not let the floodwaters engulf me
  or the depths swallow me up
  or the pit close its mouth over me.
¹⁶Answer me, O LORD, out of the goodness of
    your love;
  in your great mercy turn to me.
¹⁷Do not hide your face from your servant;
  answer me quickly, for I am in trouble.
¹⁸Come near and rescue me;
  redeem me because of my foes.

¹⁹You know how I am scorned, disgraced and
    shamed;
  all my enemies are before you.
²⁰Scorn has broken my heart
  and has left me helpless;
  I looked for sympathy, but there was none,
  for comforters, but I found none.
²¹They put gall in my food
  and gave me vinegar for my thirst.

²²May the table set before them become a snare;
  may it become retribution andᵃ a trap.
²³May their eyes be darkened so they cannot
    see,
  and their backs be bent forever.
²⁴Pour out your wrath on them;
  let your fierce anger overtake them.

不要因我蒙羞；
以色列的神啊，
  求你叫那尋求你的，
  不要因我受辱。
⁷因我為你的緣故受了辱罵，
  滿面羞愧。
⁸我的弟兄看我為外路人，
  我的同胞看我為外邦人。
⁹因我為你的殿心裏焦急，如同火燒，
  並且辱罵你人的辱罵
    都落在我身上。
¹⁰我哭泣，以禁食刻苦我心，
  這倒算為我的羞辱。
¹¹我拿麻布當衣裳，
  就成了他們的笑談。
¹²坐在城門口的談論我，
  酒徒也以我為歌曲。

¹³但我在悅納的時候，
  向你耶和華祈禱。
神啊，求你按你豐盛的慈愛，
  憑你拯救的誠實應允我。
¹⁴求你搭救我出離淤泥，
  不叫我陷在其中；
  求你使我脫離那些恨我的人，
  使我出離深水。
¹⁵求你不容大水漫過我，
  不容深淵吞滅我，
  不容坑坎在我以上合口。
¹⁶耶和華啊，求你應允我，
  因為你的慈愛本為美好；
  求你按你豐盛的慈悲，回轉眷顧我。
¹⁷不要掩面不顧你的僕人，
  我是在急難之中，
  求你速速地應允我！
¹⁸求你親近我，救贖我，
  求你因我的仇敵把我贖回！

¹⁹你知道我受的
  辱罵、欺凌、羞辱；
  我的敵人都在你面前。
²⁰辱罵傷破了我的心，
  我又滿了憂愁。
  我指望有人體恤，卻沒有一個；
  我指望有人安慰，卻找不著一個。
²¹他們拿苦膽給我當食物；
  我渴了，他們拿醋給我喝。

²²願他們的筵席在他們面前變為網羅，
  在他們平安的時候變為機檻。
²³願他們的眼睛昏矇，
  不得看見；
  願你使他們的腰常常戰抖。
²⁴求你將你的惱恨倒在他們身上；
  叫你的烈怒追上他們。

a 22 Or snare / and their fellowship become

25願他們的住處變為荒場；
　　願他們的帳棚無人居住。
26因為你所擊打的，他們就逼迫；
　　你所擊傷的，他們戲說他的愁苦。
27願你在他們的罪上加罪，
　　不容他們在你面前稱義。
28願他們從生命冊上被塗抹，
　　不得記錄在義人之中。

29但我是困苦憂傷的；
　　神啊，願你的救恩將我安置在高處。

30我要以詩歌讚美神的名，
　　以感謝稱他為大！
31這便叫耶和華喜悅，勝似獻牛，
　　或是獻有角有蹄的公牛。
32謙卑的人看見了就喜樂，
　　尋求神的人，願你們的心甦醒。
33因為耶和華聽了窮乏人，
　　不藐視被囚的人。

34願天和地，
　　洋海和其中一切的動物都讚美他。
35因為神要拯救錫安，
　　建造猶大的城邑。
　　他的民要在那裏居住，得以為業。
36他僕人的後裔要承受為業。
　　愛他名的人也要住在其中。

第七十篇

大衛的記念詩，交與伶長。

1神啊，求你快快搭救我！
　　耶和華啊，求你速速幫助我！
2願那些尋索我命的，
　　抱愧蒙羞；
　　願那些喜悅我遭害的，
　　退後受辱！
3願那些對我說「阿哈！阿哈！」的，
　　因羞愧退後。
4願一切尋求你的，
　　因你高興歡喜；
　　願那些喜愛你救恩的常說：
　　「當尊神為大！」

5但我是困苦窮乏的。
　　神啊，求你速速到我這裏來！
　　你是幫助我的，搭救我的。
　　耶和華啊，求你不要耽延！

25May their place be deserted;
　　let there be no one to dwell in their tents.
26For they persecute those you wound
　　and talk about the pain of those you hurt.
27Charge them with crime upon crime;
　　do not let them share in your salvation.
28May they be blotted out of the book of life
　　and not be listed with the righteous.

29I am in pain and distress;
　　may your salvation, O God, protect me.

30I will praise God's name in song
　　and glorify him with thanksgiving.
31This will please the LORD more than an ox,
　　more than a bull with its horns and hoofs.
32The poor will see and be glad—
　　you who seek God, may your hearts live!
33The LORD hears the needy
　　and does not despise his captive people.

34Let heaven and earth praise him,
　　the seas and all that move in them,
35for God will save Zion
　　and rebuild the cities of Judah.
　　Then people will settle there and possess it;
36　the children of his servants will inherit it,
　　and those who love his name will dwell
　　　there.

Psalm 70

For the director of music. Of David. A petition.

1Hasten, O God, to save me;
　　O LORD, come quickly to help me.
2May those who seek my life
　　be put to shame and confusion;
　　may all who desire my ruin
　　be turned back in disgrace.
3May those who say to me, "Aha! Aha!"
　　turn back because of their shame.
4But may all who seek you
　　rejoice and be glad in you;
　　may those who love your salvation always
　　　say,
　　"Let God be exalted!"

5Yet I am poor and needy;
　　come quickly to me, O God.
　　You are my help and my deliverer;
　　O LORD, do not delay.

Psalm 71

¹In you, O LORD, I have taken refuge;
  let me never be put to shame.
²Rescue me and deliver me in your
    righteousness;
  turn your ear to me and save me.
³Be my rock of refuge,
  to which I can always go;
  give the command to save me,
  for you are my rock and my fortress.
⁴Deliver me, O my God, from the hand of the
    wicked,
  from the grasp of evil and cruel men.

⁵For you have been my hope, O Sovereign
    LORD,
  my confidence since my youth.
⁶From birth I have relied on you;
  you brought me forth from my mother's
    womb.
  I will ever praise you.
⁷I have become like a portent to many,
  but you are my strong refuge.
⁸My mouth is filled with your praise,
  declaring your splendor all day long.

⁹Do not cast me away when I am old;
  do not forsake me when my strength is gone.
¹⁰For my enemies speak against me;
  those who wait to kill me conspire together.
¹¹They say, "God has forsaken him;
  pursue him and seize him,
  for no one will rescue him."
¹²Be not far from me, O God;
  come quickly, O my God, to help me.
¹³May my accusers perish in shame;
  may those who want to harm me
  be covered with scorn and disgrace.

¹⁴But as for me, I will always have hope;
  I will praise you more and more.
¹⁵My mouth will tell of your righteousness,
  of your salvation all day long,
  though I know not its measure.
¹⁶I will come and proclaim your mighty acts,
  O Sovereign LORD;
  I will proclaim your righteousness, yours
    alone.
¹⁷Since my youth, O God, you have taught me,
  and to this day I declare your marvelous
    deeds.
¹⁸Even when I am old and gray,
  do not forsake me, O God,
  till I declare your power to the next generation,
  your might to all who are to come.

第七十一篇

¹耶和華啊，我投靠你，
  求你叫我永不羞愧。
²求你憑你的公義搭救我，
  救拔我；
  側耳聽我，拯救我！
³求你作我常住的磐石。
  你已經命定要救我，
  因為你是我的巖石，
  我的山寨。
⁴我的神啊，
  求你救我脫離惡人的手，
  脫離不義和殘暴之人的手。

⁵主耶和華啊，
  你是我所盼望的，
  從我年幼，你是我所倚靠的。
⁶我從出母胎被你扶持，
  使我出母腹的是你。
  我必常常讚美你！
⁷許多人以我為怪，
  但你是我堅固的避難所。
⁸你的讚美，你的榮耀，
  終日必滿了我的口。

⁹我年老的時候，求你不要丟棄我；
  我力氣衰弱的時候，求你不要離棄我。
¹⁰我的仇敵議論我，
  那些窺探要害我命的彼此商議，
¹¹說："神已經離棄他，
  我們追趕他，捉拿他吧！
  因為沒有人搭救。"
¹²神啊，求你不要遠離我！
  我的神啊，求你速速幫助我！
¹³願那與我性命為敵的，羞愧被滅；
  願那謀害我的，受辱蒙羞。

¹⁴我卻要常常盼望，
  並要越發讚美你。
¹⁵我的口終日要述說你的公義
  和你的救恩，
  因我不計其數。
¹⁶我要來說
  主耶和華大能的事，
  我單要提說
  你的公義。
¹⁷神啊，自我年幼時，你就教訓我；
  直到如今，
  我傳揚你奇妙的作為。
¹⁸神啊，我到年老髮白的時候，
  求你不要離棄我！
  等我將你的能力指示下代，
  將你的大能指示後世的人。

¹⁹神啊，
　　你的公義甚高！
　行過大事的神啊，
　　誰能像你？
²⁰你是叫我們
　　多經歷重大急難的，
　必使我們復活，
　　從地的深處救上來。

²¹求你使我越發昌大，
　　又轉來安慰我。

²²我的神啊，我要鼓瑟稱讚你，
　　稱讚你的誠實！
　以色列的聖者啊，
　　我要彈琴歌頌你！
²³我歌頌你的時候，
　　我的嘴唇和你所贖我的靈魂
　　都必歡呼。
²⁴並且我的舌頭
　　必終日講論你的公義，
　因為那些謀害我的人
　　已經蒙羞受辱了。

第七十二篇

所羅門的詩。

¹神啊，求你將判斷的權柄賜給王，
　　將公義賜給王的兒子。
²他要按公義審判你的民，
　　按公平審判你的困苦人。
³大山小山
　　都要因公義
　　　使民得享平安。
⁴他必為民中的困苦人伸冤，
　　拯救窮乏之輩，
　　壓碎那欺壓人的。

⁵太陽還存，月亮還在，
　　人要敬畏你，直到萬代。
⁶他必降臨，像雨降在已割的草地上，
　　如甘霖滋潤田地。
⁷在他的日子，義人要發旺，
　　大有平安，
　　好像月亮長存。

⁸他要執掌權柄，從這海直到那海，
　　從大河直到地極。
⁹住在曠野的，必在他面前下拜；
　　他的仇敵必要舔土。

¹⁹Your righteousness reaches to the skies,
　O God,
　　you who have done great things.
　Who, O God, is like you?
²⁰Though you have made me see troubles,
　　many and bitter,
　　you will restore my life again;
　from the depths of the earth
　　you will again bring me up.
²¹You will increase my honor
　　and comfort me once again.

²²I will praise you with the harp
　　for your faithfulness, O my God;
　I will sing praise to you with the lyre,
　　O Holy One of Israel.
²³My lips will shout for joy
　　when I sing praise to you—
　　I, whom you have redeemed.
²⁴My tongue will tell of your righteous acts
　　all day long,
　for those who wanted to harm me
　　have been put to shame and confusion.

Psalm 72

Of Solomon.

¹Endow the king with your justice, O God,
　　the royal son with your righteousness.
²He will^a judge your people in righteousness,
　　your afflicted ones with justice.
³The mountains will bring prosperity to the
　　people,
　　the hills the fruit of righteousness.
⁴He will defend the afflicted among the people
　　and save the children of the needy;
　　he will crush the oppressor.

⁵He will endure^b as long as the sun,
　　as long as the moon, through all generations.
⁶He will be like rain falling on a mown field,
　　like showers watering the earth.
⁷In his days the righteous will flourish;
　　prosperity will abound till the moon is no
　　more.

⁸He will rule from sea to sea
　　and from the River^c to the ends of the earth.^d
⁹The desert tribes will bow before him
　　and his enemies will lick the dust.

---

*a 2 Or May he; similarly in verses 3-11 and 17　　b 5 Septuagint;
Hebrew You will be feared　　c 8 That is, the Euphrates
d 8 Or the end of the land*

¹⁰The kings of Tarshish and of distant shores
　　will bring tribute to him;
　　the kings of Sheba and Seba
　　will present him gifts.
¹¹All kings will bow down to him
　　and all nations will serve him.

¹²For he will deliver the needy who cry out,
　　the afflicted who have no one to help.
¹³He will take pity on the weak and the needy
　　and save the needy from death.
¹⁴He will rescue them from oppression and
　　violence,
　　for precious is their blood in his sight.

¹⁵Long may he live!
　　May gold from Sheba be given him.
　　May people ever pray for him
　　and bless him all day long.
¹⁶Let grain abound throughout the land;
　　on the tops of the hills may it sway.
　　Let its fruit flourish like Lebanon;
　　let it thrive like the grass of the field.
¹⁷May his name endure forever;
　　may it continue as long as the sun.

　　All nations will be blessed through him,
　　and they will call him blessed.

¹⁸Praise be to the LORD God, the God of Israel,
　　who alone does marvelous deeds.
¹⁹Praise be to his glorious name forever;
　　may the whole earth be filled with his glory.
　　　　Amen and Amen.

²⁰This concludes the prayers of David son of
　　Jesse.

BOOK III

Psalms 73-89

Psalm 73

A psalm of Asaph.

¹Surely God is good to Israel,
　　to those who are pure in heart.

²But as for me, my feet had almost slipped;
　　I had nearly lost my foothold.
³For I envied the arrogant
　　when I saw the prosperity of the wicked.

¹⁰他施和海島的王
　　要進貢；
　　示巴和西巴的王
　　要獻禮物。
¹¹諸王都要叩拜他；
　　萬國都要侍奉他。

¹²因為窮乏人呼求的時候，他要搭救；
　　沒有人幫助的困苦人，他也要搭救。
¹³他要憐恤貧寒和窮乏的人，
　　拯救窮苦人的性命。
¹⁴他要救贖他們
　　脫離欺壓和強暴；
　　他們的血在他眼中看為寶貴。

¹⁵他們要存活！
　　示巴的金子要奉給他。
　　人要常常為他禱告，
　　終日稱頌他。
¹⁶在地的山頂上，五穀必然茂盛（註：
　　　“五穀必然茂盛”或作“有一把五穀”），
　　所結的穀實要響動。
　　如黎巴嫩的樹林，
　　城裏的人要發旺如地上的草。
¹⁷他的名要存到永遠，
　　要留傳如日之久。
　　人要因他蒙福，
　　萬國要稱他有福。

¹⁸獨行奇事的耶和華以色列的神，
　　是應當稱頌的。
¹⁹他榮耀的名也當稱頌，直到永遠。
　　願他的榮耀充滿全地。
　　　　阿們！阿們！

²⁰耶西的兒子大衛的祈禱完畢。

卷三

詩篇 73-89

第七十三篇

亞薩的詩。

¹神實在恩待以色列
　　那些清心的人。

²至於我，我的腳幾乎失閃，
　　我的腳險些滑跌。
³我見惡人和狂傲人享平安，
　　就心懷不平。

⁴他們死的時候沒有疼痛，
　　他們的力氣卻也壯實。
⁵他們不像別人受苦，
　　也不像別人遭災。

⁶所以，驕傲如鍊子戴在他們的項上；
　　強暴像衣裳遮住他們的身體。
⁷他們的眼睛因體胖而凸出；
　　他們所得的過於心裏所想的。
⁸他們譏笑人，憑惡意說欺壓人的話；
　　他們說話自高。
⁹他們的口褻瀆上天；
　　他們的舌毀謗全地。

¹⁰所以神的民歸到這裏，
　　喝盡了滿杯的苦水。
¹¹他們說："神怎能曉得？
　　至高者豈有知識呢？"

¹²看哪，這就是惡人，
　　他們既是常享安逸，財寶便加增。

¹³我實在徒然潔淨了我的心；
　　徒然洗手表明無辜。

¹⁴因為我終日遭災難，
　　每早晨受懲治。

¹⁵我若說，"我要這樣講"，
　　這就是以奸詐待你的眾子。
¹⁶我思索怎能明白這事，
　　眼看實係為難。
¹⁷等我進了神的聖所，
　　思想他們的結局。

¹⁸你實在把他們安在滑地，
　　使他們掉在沉淪之中。
¹⁹他們轉眼之間成了何等的荒涼！
　　他們被驚恐滅盡了。
²⁰人睡醒了，怎樣看夢，
　　主啊，你醒了，
　　也必照樣輕看他們的影像。

²¹因而我心裏發酸，
　　肺腑被刺。
²²我這樣愚昧無知，
　　在你面前如畜類一般。

²³然而我常與你同在，
　　你攙着我的右手。

⁴They have no struggles;
　　their bodies are healthy and strong.ᵃ
⁵They are free from the burdens common to
　　man;
　　they are not plagued by human ills.
⁶Therefore pride is their necklace;
　　they clothe themselves with violence.
⁷From their callous hearts comes iniquityᵇ;
　　the evil conceits of their minds know no limits.
⁸They scoff, and speak with malice;
　　in their arrogance they threaten oppression.
⁹Their mouths lay claim to heaven,
　　and their tongues take possession of the
　　earth.
¹⁰Therefore their people turn to them
　　and drink up waters in abundance.ᶜ
¹¹They say, "How can God know?
　　Does the Most High have knowledge?"

¹²This is what the wicked are like—
　　always carefree, they increase in wealth.

¹³Surely in vain have I kept my heart pure;
　　in vain have I washed my hands in
　　innocence.
¹⁴All day long I have been plagued;
　　I have been punished every morning.

¹⁵If I had said, "I will speak thus,"
　　I would have betrayed your children.
¹⁶When I tried to understand all this,
　　it was oppressive to me
¹⁷till I entered the sanctuary of God;
　　then I understood their final destiny.

¹⁸Surely you place them on slippery ground;
　　you cast them down to ruin.
¹⁹How suddenly are they destroyed,
　　completely swept away by terrors!
²⁰As a dream when one awakes,
　　so when you arise, O Lord,
　　you will despise them as fantasies.

²¹When my heart was grieved
　　and my spirit embittered,
²²I was senseless and ignorant;
　　I was a brute beast before you.

²³Yet I am always with you;
　　you hold me by my right hand.

a 4 With a different word division of the Hebrew; Masoretic
Text *struggles at their death; / their bodies are healthy*   *b 7* Syriac
(see also Septuagint); Hebrew *Their eyes bulge with fat*
c 10 The meaning of the Hebrew for this verse is uncertain.

²⁴You guide me with your counsel,
and afterward you will take me into glory.
²⁵Whom have I in heaven but you?
And earth has nothing I desire besides you.
²⁶My flesh and my heart may fail,
but God is the strength of my heart
and my portion forever.

²⁷Those who are far from you will perish;
you destroy all who are unfaithful to you.
²⁸But as for me, it is good to be near God.
I have made the Sovereign LORD my refuge;
I will tell of all your deeds.

Psalm 74

A maskil[a] of Asaph.

¹Why have you rejected us forever, O God?
Why does your anger smolder against the
sheep of your pasture?
²Remember the people you purchased of old,
the tribe of your inheritance, whom you
redeemed—
Mount Zion, where you dwelt.
³Turn your steps toward these everlasting
ruins,
all this destruction the enemy has brought
on the sanctuary.

⁴Your foes roared in the place where you met
with us;
they set up their standards as signs.
⁵They behaved like men wielding axes
to cut through a thicket of trees.
⁶They smashed all the carved paneling
with their axes and hatchets.
⁷They burned your sanctuary to the ground;
they defiled the dwelling place of your
Name.
⁸They said in their hearts, "We will crush them
completely!"
They burned every place where God was
worshiped in the land.
⁹We are given no miraculous signs;
no prophets are left,
and none of us knows how long this will be.

¹⁰How long will the enemy mock you, O God?
Will the foe revile your name forever?
¹¹Why do you hold back your hand, your right
hand?
Take it from the folds of your garment and
destroy them!

²⁴你要以你的訓言引導我，
以後引接我到榮耀裏。
²⁵除你以外，在天上我有誰呢？
除你以外，
在地上我也沒有所愛慕的！
²⁶我的肉體和我的心腸衰殘，
但神是我心裏的力量，
又是我的福分，直到永遠。

²⁷遠離你的，必要死亡；
凡離棄你行邪淫的，你都滅絕了。
²⁸但我親近神是與我有益，
我以主耶和華為我的避難所，
好叫我述說你一切的作為。

第七十四篇

亞薩的訓誨詩。

¹神啊，你為何永遠丟棄我們呢？
你為何向你草場的羊發怒
如煙冒出呢？
²求你記念你古時所得來的會眾，
就是你所贖作你產業支派的，
並記念你向來所居住的錫安山。

³求你舉步
去看那日久荒涼之地，
仇敵在聖所中
所行的一切惡事。

⁴你的敵人
在你會中吼叫；
他們豎了自己的旗為記號。
⁵他們好像人揚起斧子
砍伐林中的樹。
⁶聖所中一切雕刻的，
他們現在用斧子、錘子打壞了。
⁷他們用火焚燒你的聖所，
褻瀆你名的居所，
拆毀到地。
⁸他們心裏說：
"我們要盡行毀滅。"
他們就在遍地
把神的會所都燒燬了。
⁹我們不見我們的標幟，不再有先知，
我們內中也沒有人知道
這災禍要到幾時呢！

¹⁰神啊，敵人辱罵要到幾時呢？
仇敵褻瀆你的名要到永遠嗎？
¹¹你為甚麼
縮回你的右手？
求你從懷中伸出來，
毀滅他們。

---

a Title: Probably a literary or musical term

12神自古以來為我的王——
　　在地上施行拯救。
13你曾用能力將海分開，
　　將水中大魚的頭打破。

14你曾砸碎鱷魚的頭，
　　把牠給曠野的禽獸為食物（註：
　　"禽獸"原文作"民"）。

15你曾分裂磐石，
　　水便成了溪河，
　　你使長流的江河乾了。
16白晝屬你，黑夜也屬你；
　　亮光和日頭是你所預備的。
17地的一切疆界是你所立的；
　　夏天和冬天是你所定的。

18耶和華啊，仇敵辱罵，
　　愚頑民褻瀆了你的名，
　　求你記念這事。
19不要將你斑鳩的性命
　　交給野獸；
　　不要永遠忘記
　　你困苦人的性命。
20求你顧念所立的約，
　　因為地上黑暗之處，
　　都滿了強暴的居所。
21不要叫受欺壓的人蒙羞回去；
　　要叫困苦窮乏的人讚美你的名。

22神啊，求你起來，為自己伸訴，
　　要記念愚頑人怎樣終日辱罵你。
23不要忘記你敵人的聲音；
　　那起來敵你之人的喧嘩
　　時常上升。

第七十五篇

亞薩的詩歌，交與伶長。
調用"休要毀壞"。

1神啊，我們稱謝你，我們稱謝你！
　　因為你的名相近，
　　人都述說你奇妙的作為。

2 "我到了所定的日期，
　　必按正直施行審判。
3地和其上的居民都消化了。
　　我曾立了地的柱子。　　　細拉
4我對狂傲人說：'不要行事狂傲。'
　　對兇惡人說：'不要舉角！

5不要把你們的角高舉；
　　不要挺着頸項說話。'"

12But you, O God, are my king from of old;
　　you bring salvation upon the earth.
13It was you who split open the sea by your
　　power;
　　you broke the heads of the monster in the
　　waters.
14It was you who crushed the heads of
　　Leviathan
　　and gave him as food to the creatures of the
　　desert.
15It was you who opened up springs and
　　streams;
　　you dried up the ever flowing rivers.
16The day is yours, and yours also the night;
　　you established the sun and moon.
17It was you who set all the boundaries of the
　　earth;
　　you made both summer and winter.

18Remember how the enemy has mocked you,
　　O LORD,
　　how foolish people have reviled your name.
19Do not hand over the life of your dove to wild
　　beasts;
　　do not forget the lives of your afflicted
　　people forever.
20Have regard for your covenant,
　　because haunts of violence fill the dark
　　places of the land.
21Do not let the oppressed retreat in disgrace;
　　may the poor and needy praise your name.

22Rise up, O God, and defend your cause;
　　remember how fools mock you all day long.
23Do not ignore the clamor of your adversaries,
　　the uproar of your enemies, which rises
　　continually.

Psalm 75

For the director of music. To the tune of "Do Not Destroy."
A psalm of Asaph. A song.

1We give thanks to you, O God,
　　we give thanks, for your Name is near;
　　men tell of your wonderful deeds.

2You say, "I choose the appointed time;
　　it is I who judge uprightly.
3When the earth and all its people quake,
　　it is I who hold its pillars firm.　　*Selah*
4To the arrogant I say, 'Boast no more,'
　　and to the wicked, 'Do not lift up your
　　horns.
5Do not lift your horns against heaven;
　　do not speak with outstretched neck.' "

⁶No one from the east or the west
　　or from the desert can exalt a man.
⁷But it is God who judges:
　　He brings one down, he exalts another.
⁸In the hand of the LORD is a cup
　　full of foaming wine mixed with spices;
　　he pours it out, and all the wicked of the earth
　　drink it down to its very dregs.

⁹As for me, I will declare this forever;
　　I will sing praise to the God of Jacob.
¹⁰I will cut off the horns of all the wicked,
　　but the horns of the righteous will be lifted
　　up.

Psalm 76

For the director of music. With stringed instruments.
A psalm of Asaph. A song.

¹In Judah God is known;
　　his name is great in Israel.
²His tent is in Salem,
　　his dwelling place in Zion.
³There he broke the flashing arrows,
　　the shields and the swords, the weapons of
　　war.　　　　　　　　　　　　*Selah*

⁴You are resplendent with light,
　　more majestic than mountains rich with
　　game.
⁵Valiant men lie plundered,
　　they sleep their last sleep;
　　not one of the warriors
　　can lift his hands.
⁶At your rebuke, O God of Jacob,
　　both horse and chariot lie still.
⁷You alone are to be feared.
　　Who can stand before you when you are
　　angry?
⁸From heaven you pronounced judgment,
　　and the land feared and was quiet—
⁹when you, O God, rose up to judge,
　　to save all the afflicted of the land.　*Selah*
¹⁰Surely your wrath against men brings you
　　praise,
　　and the survivors of your wrath are
　　restrained.^a

¹¹Make vows to the LORD your God and fulfill
　　them;
　　let all the neighboring lands
　　bring gifts to the One to be feared.

---

a 10 Or Surely the wrath of men brings you praise, / and with the remainder of wrath you arm yourself

⁶因為高舉非從東，非從西，
　　也非從南而來。
⁷惟有神斷定：
　　他使這人降卑，使那人升高。
⁸耶和華手裏有杯，其中的酒起沫，
　　杯內滿了攙雜的酒。
　　他倒出來，地上的惡人
　　必都喝這酒的渣滓，而且喝盡。

⁹但我要宣揚，直到永遠，
　　我要歌頌雅各的神！
¹⁰惡人一切的角，我要砍斷；
　　惟有義人的角必被高舉。

第七十六篇

亞薩的詩歌，交與伶長。用絲弦的樂器。

¹在猶大，神為人所認識；
　　在以色列，他的名為大。
²在撒冷，有他的帳幕，
　　在錫安，有他的居所。
³他在那裏折斷弓上的火箭，
　　並盾牌、刀劍和爭戰的兵器。
　　　　　　　　　　　　　　細拉

⁴你從有野食之山而來，
　　有光華和榮美。

⁵心中勇敢的人都被搶奪，
　　他們睡了長覺，
　　沒有一個英雄能措手。

⁶雅各的神啊，你的斥責一發，
　　坐車的、騎馬的都沉睡了。
⁷惟獨你是可畏的。
　　你怒氣一發，
　　誰能在你面前站得住呢？
^{8、9}你從天上使人聽判斷。
　　神起來施行審判，
　　要救地上一切謙卑的人。
　　那時地就懼怕而靜默。　　細拉
¹⁰人的忿怒
　　要成全你的榮美，
　　人的餘怒，
　　你要禁止。

¹¹你們許願，
　　當向耶和華你們的神還願。
　　在他四面的人，
　　都當拿貢物獻給那可畏的主。

¹²他要挫折王子的驕氣，
　他向地上的君王顯威可畏。

第七十七篇

亞薩的詩，照耶杜頓的作法，交與伶長。

¹我要向神發聲呼求；
　我向神發聲，他必留心聽我。
²我在患難之日尋求主，
　我在夜間不住地舉手禱告，
　我的心不肯受安慰。

³我想念神，就煩躁不安；
　我沉吟悲傷，心便發昏。　　　細拉
⁴你叫我不能閉眼。
　我煩亂不安，甚至不能說話。
⁵我追想古時之日，
　上古之年。
⁶我想起夜間的歌曲，
　捫心自問，我心裏也仔細省察：

⁷　"難道主要永遠丟棄我，
　不再施恩嗎？
⁸難道他的慈愛永遠窮盡，
　他的應許世世廢棄嗎？
⁹難道神忘記開恩，
　因發怒就止住他的慈悲嗎？"
　　　　　　　　　　　　　細拉

¹⁰我便說："這是我的懦弱，
　但我要追念至高者
　顯出右手之年代。"
¹¹我要提說耶和華所行的，
　我要記念你古時的奇事；
¹²我也要思想你的經營，
　默念你的作為。

¹³神啊，你的作為是潔淨的，
　有何神大如神呢？
¹⁴你是行奇事的神。
　你曾在列邦中彰顯你的能力。
¹⁵你曾用你的膀臂
　贖了你的民，
　就是雅各和約瑟的子孫。　　　細拉

¹⁶ 神啊，諸水見你，
　一見就都驚惶；
　深淵也都戰抖。
¹⁷雲中倒出水來，
　天空發出響聲，
　你的箭也飛行四方。
¹⁸你的雷聲在旋風中，
　電光照亮世界，
　大地戰抖震動。

¹²He breaks the spirit of rulers;
　he is feared by the kings of the earth.

Psalm 77

For the director of music. For Jeduthun. Of Asaph. A psalm.

¹I cried out to God for help;
　I cried out to God to hear me.
²When I was in distress, I sought the LORD;
　at night I stretched out untiring hands
　and my soul refused to be comforted.

³I remembered you, O God, and I groaned;　　*Selah*
　I mused, and my spirit grew faint.
⁴You kept my eyes from closing;
　I was too troubled to speak.
⁵I thought about the former days,
　the years of long ago;
⁶I remembered my songs in the night.
　My heart mused and my spirit inquired:

⁷"Will the LORD reject forever?
　Will he never show his favor again?
⁸Has his unfailing love vanished forever?
　Has his promise failed for all time?
⁹Has God forgotten to be merciful?
　Has he in anger withheld his compassion?"　　*Selah*

¹⁰Then I thought, "To this I will appeal:
　the years of the right hand of the Most
　High."
¹¹I will remember the deeds of the LORD;
　yes, I will remember your miracles of long ago.
¹²I will meditate on all your works
　and consider all your mighty deeds.

¹³Your ways, O God, are holy.
　What god is so great as our God?
¹⁴You are the God who performs miracles;
　you display your power among the peoples.
¹⁵With your mighty arm you redeemed your
　people,
　the descendants of Jacob and Joseph.　　*Selah*

¹⁶The waters saw you, O God,
　the waters saw you and writhed;
　the very depths were convulsed.
¹⁷The clouds poured down water,
　the skies resounded with thunder;
　your arrows flashed back and forth.
¹⁸Your thunder was heard in the whirlwind,
　your lightning lit up the world;
　the earth trembled and quaked.

¹⁹Your path led through the sea,
   your way through the mighty waters,
   though your footprints were not seen.

²⁰You led your people like a flock
   by the hand of Moses and Aaron.

Psalm 78

A maskil[a] of Asaph.

¹O my people, hear my teaching;
   listen to the words of my mouth.
²I will open my mouth in parables,
   I will utter hidden things, things from of
      old—
³what we have heard and known,
   what our fathers have told us.
⁴We will not hide them from their children;
   we will tell the next generation
   the praiseworthy deeds of the LORD,
      his power, and the wonders he has done.
⁵He decreed statutes for Jacob
   and established the law in Israel,
   which he commanded our forefathers
      to teach their children,
⁶so the next generation would know them,
   even the children yet to be born,
   and they in turn would tell their children.
⁷Then they would put their trust in God
   and would not forget his deeds
      but would keep his commands.
⁸They would not be like their forefathers—
   a stubborn and rebellious generation,
   whose hearts were not loyal to God,
      whose spirits were not faithful to him.

⁹The men of Ephraim, though armed with
      bows,
   turned back on the day of battle;
¹⁰they did not keep God's covenant
   and refused to live by his law.
¹¹They forgot what he had done,
   the wonders he had shown them.
¹²He did miracles in the sight of their fathers
   in the land of Egypt, in the region of Zoan.
¹³He divided the sea and led them through;
   he made the water stand firm like a wall.
¹⁴He guided them with the cloud by day
   and with light from the fire all night.
¹⁵He split the rocks in the desert
   and gave them water as abundant as the
      seas;

¹⁹你的道在海中，
   你的路在大水中，
   你的腳蹤無人知道。

²⁰你曾藉<u>摩西</u>和<u>亞倫</u>的手
   引導你的百姓，好像羊羣一般。

第七十八篇

亞薩的訓誨詩

¹我的民哪，你們要留心聽我的訓誨，
   側耳聽我口中的話。
²我要開口說比喻，
   我要說出
      古時的謎語。
³是我們所聽見、所知道的，
   也是我們的祖宗告訴我們的。
⁴我們不將這些事向他們的子孫隱瞞，
   要述耶和華的美德和他的能力，
   並他奇妙的作為，
      述說給後代聽。
⁵因為，他在<u>雅各</u>中立法度，
   在<u>以色列</u>中設律法，
   是他吩咐我們祖宗
      要傳給子孫的，
⁶使將要生的後代子孫可以曉得，
   他們也要起來
      告訴他們的子孫，
⁷好叫他們仰望神，
   不忘記神的作為，
      惟要守他的命令。
⁸不要像他們的祖宗，
   是頑梗悖逆、
      居心不正之輩，
   向着神心不誠實。

⁹<u>以法蓮</u>的子孫
   帶着兵器，拿着弓，
   臨陣之日，轉身退後。
¹⁰他們不遵守神的約，
   不肯照他的律法行，
¹¹又忘記他所行的
   和他顯給他們奇妙的作為。
¹²他在<u>埃及</u>地、在<u>瑣安</u>田、
   在他們祖宗的眼前施行奇事。
¹³他將海分裂，使他們過去，
   又叫水立起如壘。
¹⁴他白日用雲彩，
   終夜用火光引導他們。
¹⁵他在曠野分裂磐石，
   多多地給他們水喝，
   如從深淵而出。

---

a Title: Probably a literary or musical term

¹⁶他使水從磐石湧出，
　　叫水如江河下流。

¹⁷他們卻仍舊得罪他，
　　在乾燥之地悖逆至高者。
¹⁸他們心中試探神，
　　隨自己所欲的求食物，
¹⁹並且妄論神說：
　　"神在曠野豈能擺設筵席嗎？
²⁰他曾擊打磐石，使水湧出，
　　成了江河。
　　他還能賜糧食嗎？
　　還能為他的百姓預備肉嗎？"
²¹所以耶和華聽見
　　就發怒。
　　有烈火向雅各燒起，
　　有怒氣向以色列上騰。
²²因為他們不信服神，
　　不倚賴他的救恩。
²³他卻吩咐天空，
　　又敞開天上的門，
²⁴降嗎哪像雨給他們吃，
　　將天上的糧食賜給他們。
²⁵各人（註：或作"人"）吃大能者的食物。
　　他賜下糧食，使他們飽足。
²⁶他領東風起在天空，
　　又用能力引了南風來。
²⁷他降肉像雨在他們當中，多如塵土，
　　又降飛鳥，多如海沙。
²⁸落在他們的營中，
　　在他們住處的四面。
²⁹他們吃了，而且飽足，
　　這樣，就隨了他們所欲的。
³⁰他們貪而無厭，
　　食物還在
　　　他們口中的時候，
³¹神的怒氣就向他們上騰，
　　殺了他們內中的肥壯人，
　　打倒以色列的少年人。

³²雖是這樣，他們仍舊犯罪，
　　不信他奇妙的作為。
³³因此，他叫他們的日子全歸虛空，
　　叫他們的年歲盡屬驚恐。
³⁴他殺他們的時候，
　　他們才求問他，
　　回心轉意，切切地尋求神。
³⁵他們也追念神是他們的磐石，
　　至高的神是他們的救贖主。
³⁶他們卻用口諂媚他，
　　用舌向他說謊。

³⁷因他們的心向他不正，
　　在他的約上也不忠心。
³⁸但他有憐憫，
　　赦免他們的罪孽，

¹⁶he brought streams out of a rocky crag
　　and made water flow down like rivers.

¹⁷But they continued to sin against him,
　　rebelling in the desert against the Most High.
¹⁸They willfully put God to the test
　　by demanding the food they craved.
¹⁹They spoke against God, saying,
　　"Can God spread a table in the desert?
²⁰When he struck the rock, water gushed out,
　　and streams flowed abundantly.
　　But can he also give us food?
　　Can he supply meat for his people?"
²¹When the LORD heard them, he was very
　　　angry;
　　his fire broke out against Jacob,
　　and his wrath rose against Israel,
²²for they did not believe in God
　　or trust in his deliverance.
²³Yet he gave a command to the skies above
　　and opened the doors of the heavens;
²⁴he rained down manna for the people to eat,
　　he gave them the grain of heaven.
²⁵Men ate the bread of angels;
　　he sent them all the food they could eat.
²⁶He let loose the east wind from the heavens
　　and led forth the south wind by his power.
²⁷He rained meat down on them like dust,
　　flying birds like sand on the seashore.
²⁸He made them come down inside their camp,
　　all around their tents.
²⁹They ate till they had more than enough,
　　for he had given them what they craved.
³⁰But before they turned from the food they
　　　craved,
　　even while it was still in their mouths,
³¹God's anger rose against them;
　　he put to death the sturdiest among them,
　　cutting down the young men of Israel.

³²In spite of all this, they kept on sinning;
　　in spite of his wonders, they did not believe.
³³So he ended their days in futility
　　and their years in terror.
³⁴Whenever God slew them, they would seek
　　　him;
　　they eagerly turned to him again.
³⁵They remembered that God was their Rock,
　　that God Most High was their Redeemer.
³⁶But then they would flatter him with their
　　　mouths,
　　lying to him with their tongues;
³⁷their hearts were not loyal to him,
　　they were not faithful to his covenant.
³⁸Yet he was merciful;
　　he forgave their iniquities

and did not destroy them.
Time after time he restrained his anger
and did not stir up his full wrath.
³⁹He remembered that they were but flesh,
a passing breeze that does not return.

⁴⁰How often they rebelled against him in the
desert
and grieved him in the wasteland!
⁴¹Again and again they put God to the test;
they vexed the Holy One of Israel.
⁴²They did not remember his power—
the day he redeemed them from the
oppressor,
⁴³the day he displayed his miraculous signs in
Egypt,
his wonders in the region of Zoan.
⁴⁴He turned their rivers to blood;
they could not drink from their streams.
⁴⁵He sent swarms of flies that devoured them,
and frogs that devastated them.
⁴⁶He gave their crops to the grasshopper,
their produce to the locust.
⁴⁷He destroyed their vines with hail
and their sycamore-figs with sleet.
⁴⁸He gave over their cattle to the hail,
their livestock to bolts of lightning.
⁴⁹He unleashed against them his hot anger,
his wrath, indignation and hostility—
a band of destroying angels.
⁵⁰He prepared a path for his anger;
he did not spare them from death
but gave them over to the plague.
⁵¹He struck down all the firstborn of Egypt,
the firstfruits of manhood in the tents of
Ham.
⁵²But he brought his people out like a flock;
he led them like sheep through the desert.
⁵³He guided them safely, so they were unafraid;
but the sea engulfed their enemies.
⁵⁴Thus he brought them to the border of his
holy land,
to the hill country his right hand had taken.
⁵⁵He drove out nations before them
and allotted their lands to them as an
inheritance;
he settled the tribes of Israel in their homes.

⁵⁶But they put God to the test
and rebelled against the Most High;
they did not keep his statutes.
⁵⁷Like their fathers they were disloyal and
faithless,
as unreliable as a faulty bow.
⁵⁸They angered him with their high places;
they aroused his jealousy with their idols.

不滅絕他們；
而且屢次消他的怒氣，
不發盡他的忿怒。
³⁹他想到他們不過是血氣，
是一陣去而不返的風。

⁴⁰他們在曠野悖逆他，
在荒地叫他擔憂，
何其多呢！
⁴¹他們再三試探神，
惹動以色列的聖者。
⁴²他們不追念他的能力（註：原文
作"手"），
和贖他們脫離敵人的日子。
⁴³他怎樣在埃及地
顯神蹟，
在瑣安田顯奇事，
⁴⁴把他們的江河並河汊的水都變為血，
使他們不能喝。
⁴⁵他叫蒼蠅成羣落在他們當中，
嘬盡他們，又叫青蛙滅了他們。
⁴⁶把他們的土產交給螞蚱，
把他們辛苦得來的交給蝗蟲。
⁴⁷他降冰雹打壞他們的葡萄樹，
下嚴霜打壞他們的桑樹。
⁴⁸又把他們的牲畜交給冰雹，
把他們的羣畜交給閃電。
⁴⁹他使猛烈的怒氣和忿怒、惱恨、苦難
成了一羣降災的使者，
臨到他們。
⁵⁰他為自己的怒氣修平了路，
將他們交給瘟疫，
使他們死亡。
⁵¹在埃及擊殺一切長子，
在含的帳棚中，
擊殺他們強壯時頭生的。
⁵²他卻領出自己的民如羊，
在曠野引他們如羊羣。
⁵³他領他們穩穩妥妥的，
使他們不至害怕；
海卻淹沒他們的仇敵。
⁵⁴他帶他們到自己聖地的邊界，
到他右手所得的這山地。
⁵⁵他在他們面前趕出外邦人，
用繩子將外邦的地量給他們為業，
叫以色列支派的人
住在他們的帳棚裏。
⁵⁶他們仍舊試探、
悖逆至高的神，
不守他的法度，
⁵⁷反倒退後，行詭詐，
像他們的祖宗一樣。
他們改變，如同翻背的弓。
⁵⁸因他們的邱壇惹了他的怒氣；
因他們雕刻的偶像觸動他的憤恨。

59神聽見就發怒，
　　極其憎惡<u>以色列</u>人，
60甚至他離棄<u>示羅</u>的帳幕，
　　就是他在人間所搭的帳棚。
61又將他的約櫃（註：原文作“能力”）
　　交與人擄去；
　　將他的榮耀交在敵人手中。
62並將他的百姓交與刀劍，
　　向他的產業發怒。
63少年人被火燒滅，處女也無喜歌。
64祭司倒在刀下，
　　寡婦卻不哀哭。

65那時，主像世人睡醒，
　　像勇士飲酒呼喊。
66他就打退了他的敵人，
　　叫他們永蒙羞辱。
67並且他棄掉<u>約瑟</u>的帳棚，
　　不揀選<u>以法蓮</u>支派，
68卻揀選<u>猶大</u>支派，
　　他所喜愛的<u>錫安山</u>。
69蓋造他的聖所，好像高峯，
　　又像他建立永存之地。
70又揀選他的僕人<u>大衛</u>，
　　從羊圈中將他召來；
71叫他不再跟從那些帶奶的母羊，
　　為要牧養自己的百姓<u>雅各</u>
　　和自己的產業<u>以色列</u>。
72於是，
　　他按心中的純正牧養他們；
　　用手中的巧妙引導他們。

第七十九篇

亞薩的詩。

1神啊，
　　外邦人進入你的產業，
　　污穢你的聖殿，
　　使耶路撒冷變成荒堆。
2把你僕人的屍首，
　　交與天空的飛鳥為食；
　　把你聖民的肉，
　　交與地上的野獸。

3在耶路撒冷周圍
　　流他們的血如水，
　　無人葬埋。
4我們成為鄰國的羞辱，
　　成為我們四圍人的嗤笑譏刺。

5耶和華啊，這到幾時呢？
　　你要動怒到永遠嗎？
　　你的憤恨要如火焚燒嗎？
6願你將你的忿怒
　　倒在那不認識你的外邦，

59When God heard them, he was very angry;
　　he rejected Israel completely.
60He abandoned the tabernacle of Shiloh,
　　the tent he had set up among men.
61He sent the ark of his might into captivity,
　　his splendor into the hands of the enemy.
62He gave his people over to the sword;
　　he was very angry with his inheritance.
63Fire consumed their young men,
　　and their maidens had no wedding songs;
64their priests were put to the sword,
　　and their widows could not weep.

65Then the Lord awoke as from sleep,
　　as a man wakes from the stupor of wine.
66He beat back his enemies;
　　he put them to everlasting shame.
67Then he rejected the tents of Joseph,
　　he did not choose the tribe of Ephraim;
68but he chose the tribe of Judah,
　　Mount Zion, which he loved.
69He built his sanctuary like the heights,
　　like the earth that he established forever.
70He chose David his servant
　　and took him from the sheep pens;
71from tending the sheep he brought him
　　to be the shepherd of his people Jacob,
　　of Israel his inheritance.
72And David shepherded them with integrity of heart;
　　with skillful hands he led them.

Psalm 79

A psalm of Asaph.

1O God, the nations have invaded your inheritance;
　　they have defiled your holy temple,
　　they have reduced Jerusalem to rubble.
2They have given the dead bodies of your servants
　　as food to the birds of the air,
　　the flesh of your saints to the beasts of the earth.
3They have poured out blood like water
　　all around Jerusalem,
　　and there is no one to bury the dead.
4We are objects of reproach to our neighbors,
　　of scorn and derision to those around us.

5How long, O LORD? Will you be angry forever?
　　How long will your jealousy burn like fire?
6Pour out your wrath on the nations
　　that do not acknowledge you,

on the kingdoms
  that do not call on your name;
7for they have devoured Jacob
  and destroyed his homeland.
8Do not hold against us the sins of the fathers;
  may your mercy come quickly to meet us,
  for we are in desperate need.

9Help us, O God our Savior,
  for the glory of your name;
  deliver us and forgive our sins
  for your name's sake.
10Why should the nations say,
  "Where is their God?"
  Before our eyes, make known among the
    nations
  that you avenge the outpoured blood of your
    servants.
11May the groans of the prisoners come before
    you;
  by the strength of your arm
  preserve those condemned to die.

12Pay back into the laps of our neighbors seven
    times
  the reproach they have hurled at you,
    O Lord.
13Then we your people, the sheep of your
    pasture,
  will praise you forever;
  from generation to generation
  we will recount your praise.

Psalm 80

For the director of music. To [the tune of] "The Lilies of the
Covenant." Of Asaph. A psalm.

1Hear us, O Shepherd of Israel,
  you who lead Joseph like a flock;
  you who sit enthroned between the cherubim,
    shine forth
2   before Ephraim, Benjamin and Manasseh.
  Awaken your might;
  come and save us.

3Restore us, O God;
  make your face shine upon us,
  that we may be saved.

4O LORD God Almighty,
  how long will your anger smolder
  against the prayers of your people?
5You have fed them with the bread of tears;
  you have made them drink tears by the
    bowlful.

和那不求告你名的國度。

7因為他們吞了雅各,
  把他的住處變為荒場。
8求你不要記念我們先祖的罪孽,
  向我們追討;
  願你的慈悲快迎著我們,
  因為我們落到極卑微的地步。
9拯救我們的神啊,
  求你因你名的榮耀幫助我們;
  為你名的緣故搭救我們,
  赦免我們的罪。
10為何容外邦人說:
  "他們的神在哪裏呢?"
  願你使外邦人知道
  你在我們眼前,
  伸你僕人流血的冤。

11願被囚之人的歎息
  達到你面前;
  願你按你的大能力,
  存留那些將要死的人。

12主啊,願你將我們鄰邦
  所羞辱你的羞辱,
  加七倍
  歸到他們身上!
13這樣,你的民,
  你草場的羊要稱謝你,
  直到永遠;
  要述說讚美你的話,
  直到萬代!

第八十篇

亞薩的詩,交與伶長。調用"為證的百合花"。

1領約瑟如領羊羣之以色列的牧者啊,
  求你留心聽!
  坐在二基路伯上的啊,
  求你發出光來!
2在以法蓮、便雅憫、瑪拿西前面,
  施展你的大能,
  來救我們。

3神啊,求你使我們回轉(註:"回轉"
    或作"復興"),使你的臉發光,
  我們便要得救。

4耶和華萬軍之神啊,
  你向你百姓的禱告發怒,
  要到幾時呢?
5你以眼淚當食物給他們吃,
  又多量出眼淚給他們喝。

6你使鄰邦因我們紛爭，
　　我們的仇敵彼此戲笑。

7萬軍之神啊，求你使我們回轉，
　　使你的臉發光，
　　我們便要得救！

8你從埃及挪出一棵葡萄樹，
　　趕出外邦人，把這樹栽上。
9你在這樹根前預備了地方，
　　它就深深扎根，爬滿了地。
10它的影子遮滿了山，
　　枝子好像佳美的香柏樹。
11它發出枝子，長到大海，
　　發出蔓子，延到大河。

12你為何拆毀這樹的籬笆，
　　任憑一切過路的人摘取？
13林中出來的野豬把它糟蹋；
　　野地的走獸拿它當食物。
14萬軍之神啊，求你回轉，
　　從天上垂看，
　　眷顧這葡萄樹，
15保護你右手所栽的，
　　和你為自己所堅固的枝子。

16這樹已經被火焚燒，被刀砍伐；
　　他們因你臉上的怒容就滅亡了。
17願你的手
　　扶持你右邊的人，
　　就是你為自己所堅固的人子。
18這樣，我們便不退後離開你；
　　求你救活我們，
　　我們就要求告你的名。

19耶和華萬軍之神啊，
　　求你使我們回轉，
　　使你的臉發光，我們便要得救！

第八十一篇

亞薩的詩，交與伶長。用迦特樂器。

1你們當向神我們的力量大聲歡呼，
　　向雅各的神發聲歡樂！
2唱起詩歌，打手鼓，
　　彈美琴與瑟。

3當在月朔並月望，
　　我們過節的日期吹角，

4因這是為以色列定的律例，
　　是雅各神的典章。

6You have made us a source of contention to
　　our neighbors,
　　and our enemies mock us.

7Restore us, O God Almighty;
　　make your face shine upon us,
　　that we may be saved.

8You brought a vine out of Egypt;
　　you drove out the nations and planted it.
9You cleared the ground for it,
　　and it took root and filled the land.
10The mountains were covered with its shade,
　　the mighty cedars with its branches.
11It sent out its boughs to the Sea,*a*
　　its shoots as far as the River.*b*

12Why have you broken down its walls
　　so that all who pass by pick its grapes?
13Boars from the forest ravage it
　　and the creatures of the field feed on it.
14Return to us, O God Almighty!
　　Look down from heaven and see!
　Watch over this vine,
15　the root your right hand has planted,
　　the son*c* you have raised up for yourself.

16Your vine is cut down, it is burned with fire;
　　at your rebuke your people perish.
17Let your hand rest on the man at your right
　　hand,
　　the son of man you have raised up for yourself.
18Then we will not turn away from you;
　　revive us, and we will call on your name.

19Restore us, O LORD God Almighty;
　　make your face shine upon us,
　　that we may be saved.

Psalm 81

For the director of music. According to *gittith.d* Of Asaph.

1Sing for joy to God our strength;
　　shout aloud to the God of Jacob!
2Begin the music, strike the tambourine,
　　play the melodious harp and lyre.

3Sound the ram's horn at the New Moon,
　　and when the moon is full, on the day of our
　　Feast;
4this is a decree for Israel,
　　an ordinance of the God of Jacob.

a 11 Probably the Mediterranean　　*b 11* That is, the Euphrates
c 15 Or *branch*　　*d* Title: Probably a musical term

⁵He established it as a statute for Joseph
　　when he went out against Egypt,
　where we heard a language we did not
　　understand.ᵃ

⁶He says, "I removed the burden from their
　　shoulders;
　their hands were set free from the basket.
⁷In your distress you called and I rescued you,
　　I answered you out of a thundercloud;
　I tested you at the waters of Meribah.   *Selah*

⁸"Hear, O my people, and I will warn you—
　　if you would but listen to me, O Israel!
⁹You shall have no foreign god among you;
　　you shall not bow down to an alien god.
¹⁰I am the Lord your God,
　　who brought you up out of Egypt.
　Open wide your mouth and I will fill it.

¹¹"But my people would not listen to me;
　　Israel would not submit to me.
¹²So I gave them over to their stubborn hearts
　　to follow their own devices.

¹³"If my people would but listen to me,
　　if Israel would follow my ways,
¹⁴how quickly would I subdue their enemies
　　and turn my hand against their foes!
¹⁵Those who hate the Lord would cringe before
　　him,
　and their punishment would last forever.
¹⁶But you would be fed with the finest of wheat;
　　with honey from the rock I would satisfy
　　you."

Psalm 82

A psalm of Asaph.

¹God presides in the great assembly;
　　he gives judgment among the "gods":

²"How long will youᵇ defend the unjust
　　and show partiality to the wicked?   *Selah*
³Defend the cause of the weak and fatherless;
　　maintain the rights of the poor and oppressed.
⁴Rescue the weak and needy;
　　deliver them from the hand of the wicked.

⁵"They know nothing, they understand nothing.
　　They walk about in darkness;
　all the foundations of the earth are shaken.

⁵他去攻擊埃及地的時候，
　　在約瑟中間立此為證。
　我在那裏
　　聽見我所不明白的言語。

⁶神說：
　"我使你的肩得脫重擔，
　　你的手放下筐子。
⁷你在急難中呼求，我就搭救你，
　　我在雷的隱密處應允你，
　在米利巴水那裏試驗你。   細拉

⁸"我的民哪，你當聽，我要勸戒你；
　　以色列啊，甚願你肯聽從我。
⁹在你當中不可有別的神，
　　外邦的神你也不可下拜。
¹⁰我是耶和華你的神，
　　曾把你從埃及地領上來。
　你要大大張口，我就給你充滿。

¹¹"無奈我的民不聽我的聲音；
　　以色列全不理我。
¹²我便任憑他們心裏剛硬，
　　隨自己的計謀而行。

¹³"甚願我的民肯聽從我，
　　以色列肯行我的道，
¹⁴我便速速治服他們的仇敵，
　　反手攻擊他們的敵人。
¹⁵恨耶和華的人
　　必來投降，
　但他的百姓必永久長存。
¹⁶他也必拿上好的麥子給他們吃，
　　又拿從磐石出的蜂蜜
　　叫他們飽足。"

第八十二篇

亞薩的詩。

¹神站在有權力者的會中，
　　在諸神中行審判，

²說："你們審判不秉公義，
　　徇惡人的情面，要到幾時呢？細拉
³你們當為貧寒的人和孤兒伸冤，
　　當為困苦和窮乏的人施行公義。
⁴當保護貧寒和窮乏的人，
　　救他們脫離惡人的手。

⁵"你們仍不知道，也不明白，
　　在黑暗中走來走去；
　地的根基都搖動了。

ᵃ 5 Or / *and we heard a voice we had not known*   ᵇ 2 The
Hebrew is plural.

⁶ "我曾說：' 你們是神，
　　都是至高者的兒子。'
⁷ 然而你們要死，與世人一樣；
　　要仆倒，像王子中的一位。"

⁸ 神啊，求你起來審判世界，
　　因為你要得萬邦為業。

第八十三篇

亞薩的詩歌。

¹ 神啊，求你不要靜默；
　　神啊，求你不要閉口，也不要不做聲。
² 因為你的仇敵喧嚷，
　　恨你的抬起頭來。
³ 他們同謀奸詐，要害你的百姓；
　　彼此商議，要害你所隱藏的人。
⁴ 他們說："來吧，我們將他們剪滅，
　　使他們不再成國；
　　使以色列的名
　　不再被人記念。"

⁵ 他們同心商議，
　　彼此結盟，要抵擋你，
⁶ 就是住帳棚的以東人和以實瑪利人，
　　摩押和夏甲人，
⁷ 迦巴勒、亞捫和亞瑪力、
　　非利士並推羅的居民。
⁸ 亞述也與他們連合，
　　他們作羅得子孫的幫手。

細拉

⁹ 求你待他們如待米甸，
　　如在基順河
　　待西西拉和耶賓一樣。
¹⁰ 他們在隱多珥滅亡，
　　成了地上的糞土。
¹¹ 求你叫他們的首領像俄立和西伊伯，
　　叫他們的王子都像西巴和撒慕拿。
¹² 他們說："我們要得神的住處，
　　作為自己的產業。"

¹³ 我的神啊，求你叫他們像旋風的
　　塵土，像風前的碎稭。
¹⁴ 火怎樣焚燒樹林，
　　火焰怎樣燒着山嶺，
¹⁵ 求你也照樣用狂風追趕他們，
　　用暴雨恐嚇他們。
¹⁶ 願你使他們滿面羞恥，
　　好叫他們尋求你耶和華的名。

¹⁷ 願他們永遠羞愧驚惶，
　　願他們慚愧滅亡。

⁶"I said, 'You are "gods";
　　you are all sons of the Most High.'
⁷But you will die like mere men;
　　you will fall like every other ruler."

⁸Rise up, O God, judge the earth,
　　for all the nations are your inheritance.

Psalm 83

A song. A psalm of Asaph.

¹O God, do not keep silent;
　　be not quiet, O God, be not still.
²See how your enemies are astir,
　　how your foes rear their heads.
³With cunning they conspire against your people;
　　they plot against those you cherish.
⁴"Come," they say, "let us destroy them as a
　　nation,
　　that the name of Israel be remembered no
　　more."

⁵With one mind they plot together;
　　they form an alliance against you—
⁶the tents of Edom and the Ishmaelites,
　　of Moab and the Hagrites,
⁷Gebal,^a Ammon and Amalek,
　　Philistia, with the people of Tyre.
⁸Even Assyria has joined them
　　to lend strength to the descendants of Lot.

Selah

⁹Do to them as you did to Midian,
　　as you did to Sisera and Jabin at the river
　　Kishon,
¹⁰who perished at Endor
　　and became like refuse on the ground.
¹¹Make their nobles like Oreb and Zeeb,
　　all their princes like Zebah and Zalmunna,
¹²who said, "Let us take possession
　　of the pasturelands of God."

¹³Make them like tumbleweed, O my God,
　　like chaff before the wind.
¹⁴As fire consumes the forest
　　or a flame sets the mountains ablaze,
¹⁵so pursue them with your tempest
　　and terrify them with your storm.
¹⁶Cover their faces with shame
　　so that men will seek your name, O LORD.

¹⁷May they ever be ashamed and dismayed;
　　may they perish in disgrace.

a 7 That is, Byblos

¹⁸Let them know that you, whose name is the
LORD—
　　that you alone are the Most High over all the
　　earth.

Psalm 84

For the director of music. According to *gittith.*[a] Of the Sons of
Korah. A psalm.

¹How lovely is your dwelling place,
　　O LORD Almighty!
²My soul yearns, even faints,
　　for the courts of the LORD;
my heart and my flesh cry out
　　for the living God.

³Even the sparrow has found a home,
　　and the swallow a nest for herself,
　　where she may have her young—
a place near your altar,
　　O LORD Almighty, my King and my God.
⁴Blessed are those who dwell in your house;
　　they are ever praising you.　　　　　*Selah*

⁵Blessed are those whose strength is in you,
　　who have set their hearts on pilgrimage.
⁶As they pass through the Valley of Baca,
　　they make it a place of springs;
　　the autumn rains also cover it with pools.[b]
⁷They go from strength to strength,
　　till each appears before God in Zion.

⁸Hear my prayer, O LORD God Almighty;
　　listen to me, O God of Jacob.　　　*Selah*
⁹Look upon our shield,[c] O God;
　　look with favor on your anointed one.

¹⁰Better is one day in your courts
　　than a thousand elsewhere;
I would rather be a doorkeeper in the house
　　of my God
than dwell in the tents of the wicked.
¹¹For the LORD God is a sun and shield;
　　the LORD bestows favor and honor;
no good thing does he withhold
　　from those whose walk is blameless.

¹²O LORD Almighty,
　　blessed is the man who trusts in you.

¹⁸使他們知道：
　　惟獨你名為耶和華的，
　　是全地以上的至高者。

第八十四篇

可拉後裔的詩，交與伶長。用迦特樂器。

¹萬軍之耶和華啊，
　　你的居所何等可愛！
²我羨慕渴想
　　耶和華的院宇，
　　我的心腸、我的肉體
　　向永生神呼籲（註：或作"歡呼"）。

³萬軍之耶和華，
　　我的王、我的神啊，
　　在你祭壇那裏，
　　麻雀為自己找着房屋，
　　燕子為自己找着菢雛之窩。
⁴如此住在你殿中的，便為有福，
　　他們仍要讚美你！　　　　　細拉

⁵靠你有力量、心中想往錫安大道的，
　　這人便為有福！
⁶他們經過流淚谷，
　　叫這谷變為泉源之地，
　　並有秋雨之福蓋滿了全谷。
⁷他們行走，力上加力，
　　各人到錫安朝見神。

⁸耶和華萬軍之神啊，求你聽我的禱告！
　　雅各的神啊，求你留心聽！　　細拉
⁹神啊，你是我們的盾牌，
　　求你垂顧觀看你受膏者的面。

¹⁰在你的院宇住一日，
　　勝似在別處住千日；
　　寧可在我神殿中看門，
　　不願住在惡人的帳棚裏。
¹¹因為耶和華神是日頭、是盾牌，
　　要賜下恩惠和榮耀。
　　他未嘗留下一樣好處
　　不給那些行動正直的人。

¹²萬軍之耶和華啊，
　　倚靠你的人便為有福！

---

a Title: Probably a musical term　　*b* 6 Or *blessings*
c 9 Or *sovereign*

第八十五篇

可拉後裔的詩，交與伶長。

¹耶和華啊，你已經向你的地施恩，
　　救回被擄的雅各。
²你赦免了你百姓的罪孽，
　　遮蓋了他們一切的過犯。　　細拉
³你收轉了所發的忿怒
　　和你猛烈的怒氣。

⁴拯救我們的神啊，求你使我們回轉，
　　叫你的惱恨向我們止息。
⁵你要向我們發怒到永遠嗎？
　　你要將你的怒氣
　　　延留到萬代嗎？
⁶你不再將我們救活，
　　使你的百姓靠你歡喜嗎？
⁷耶和華啊，
　　求你使我們得見你的慈愛，
　　又將你的救恩賜給我們。
⁸我要聽神耶和華所說的話，
　　因為他必應許將平安
　　賜給他的百姓、他的聖民；
　　他們卻不可再轉去妄行。
⁹他的救恩誠然與敬畏他的人相近，
　　叫榮耀住在我們的地上。
¹⁰慈愛和誠實彼此相遇；
　　公義和平安彼此相親。
¹¹誠實從地而生；
　　公義從天而現。
¹²耶和華必將好處賜給我們，
　　我們的地也要多出土產。
¹³公義要行在他面前，
　　叫他的腳蹤成為可走的路。

第八十六篇

大衛的祈禱

¹耶和華啊，求你側耳應允我，
　　因我是困苦窮乏的。
²求你保存我的性命，因我是虔誠人。
　　我的神啊，
　　求你拯救這倚靠你的僕人。
³主啊，求你憐憫我，
　　因我終日求告你。
⁴主啊，求你使僕人心裏歡喜，
　　因為我的心仰望你。

⁵主啊，你本為良善，樂意饒恕人，
　　有豐盛的慈愛，賜給凡求告你的人。
⁶耶和華啊，求你留心聽我的禱告，
　　垂聽我懇求的聲音！

Psalm 85

For the director of music. Of the Sons of Korah. A psalm.

¹You showed favor to your land, O LORD;
　　you restored the fortunes of Jacob.
²You forgave the iniquity of your people
　　and covered all their sins.　　*Selah*
³You set aside all your wrath
　　and turned from your fierce anger.

⁴Restore us again, O God our Savior,
　　and put away your displeasure toward us.
⁵Will you be angry with us forever?
　　Will you prolong your anger through all
　　　generations?
⁶Will you not revive us again,
　　that your people may rejoice in you?
⁷Show us your unfailing love, O LORD,
　　and grant us your salvation.

⁸I will listen to what God the LORD will say;
　　he promises peace to his people, his saints—
　　but let them not return to folly.
⁹Surely his salvation is near those who fear him,
　　that his glory may dwell in our land.

¹⁰Love and faithfulness meet together;
　　righteousness and peace kiss each other.
¹¹Faithfulness springs forth from the earth,
　　and righteousness looks down from heaven.
¹²The LORD will indeed give what is good,
　　and our land will yield its harvest.
¹³Righteousness goes before him
　　and prepares the way for his steps.

Psalm 86

A prayer of David.

¹Hear, O LORD, and answer me,
　　for I am poor and needy.
²Guard my life, for I am devoted to you.
　　You are my God; save your servant
　　who trusts in you.
³Have mercy on me, O Lord,
　　for I call to you all day long.
⁴Bring joy to your servant,
　　for to you, O Lord,
　　I lift up my soul.

⁵You are forgiving and good, O Lord,
　　abounding in love to all who call to you.
⁶Hear my prayer, O LORD;
　　listen to my cry for mercy.

⁷In the day of my trouble I will call to you,
  for you will answer me.

⁸Among the gods there is none like you,
  O Lord;
  no deeds can compare with yours.
⁹All the nations you have made
  will come and worship before you, O Lord;
  they will bring glory to your name.
¹⁰For you are great and do marvelous deeds;
  you alone are God.

¹¹Teach me your way, O LORD,
  and I will walk in your truth;
  give me an undivided heart,
  that I may fear your name.
¹²I will praise you, O Lord my God, with all my
  heart;
  I will glorify your name forever.
¹³For great is your love toward me;
  you have delivered me from the depths of
  the grave.ᵃ

¹⁴The arrogant are attacking me, O God;
  a band of ruthless men seeks my life—
  men without regard for you.
¹⁵But you, O Lord, are a compassionate and
  gracious God,
  slow to anger, abounding in love and
  faithfulness.
¹⁶Turn to me and have mercy on me;
  grant your strength to your servant
  and save the son of your maidservant.ᵇ
¹⁷Give me a sign of your goodness,
  that my enemies may see it and be put to
  shame,
  for you, O LORD, have helped me and
  comforted me.

Psalm 87

Of the Sons of Korah. A psalm. A song.

¹He has set his foundation on the holy
  mountain;
2 the LORD loves the gates of Zion
  more than all the dwellings of Jacob.
³Glorious things are said of you,
  O city of God: *Selah*
⁴"I will record Rahabᶜ and Babylon
  among those who acknowledge me—

⁷我在患難之日要求告你，
  因為你必應允我。

⁸主啊，
  諸神之中沒有可比你的，
  你的作為也無可比。
⁹主啊，
  你所造的萬民都要來敬拜你，
  他們也要榮耀你的名。
¹⁰因你為大，且行奇妙的事，
  惟獨你是神。

¹¹耶和華啊，求你將你的道指教我，
  我要照你的真理行；
  求你使我專心
    敬畏你的名。
¹²主我的神啊，
  我要一心稱讚你，
  我要榮耀你的名，直到永遠！
¹³因為你向我發的慈愛是大的，
  你救了我的靈魂，
  免入極深的陰間。

¹⁴神啊，驕傲的人起來攻擊我，
  又有一黨強橫的人尋索我的命，
  他們沒有將你放在眼中。
¹⁵主啊，你是有憐憫、
  有恩典的神，
  不輕易發怒，
  並有豐盛的慈愛和誠實。
¹⁶求你向我轉臉，憐恤我，
  將你的力量賜給僕人，
  救你婢女的兒子。
¹⁷求你向我顯出恩待我的憑據，
  叫恨我的人看見便羞愧，
  因為你耶和華幫助我，
  安慰我。

第八十七篇

可拉後裔的詩歌

¹耶和華所立的根基
  在聖山上。
²他愛錫安的門，
  勝於愛雅各一切的住處。
³神的城啊，
  有榮耀的事乃指着你說的。   細拉
⁴我要提起拉哈伯和巴比倫人，
  是在認識我之中的；

---

a 13 Hebrew *Sheol*   *b* 16 Or *save your faithful son*   *c* 4 A poetic
name for Egypt

看哪，非利士和推羅並古實人，
　個個生在那裏。

5論到錫安，必說：
　"這一個那一個都生在其中。
　而且至高者必親自堅立這城。"
6當耶和華記錄萬民的時候，
　他要點出
　這一個生在那裏。　　　　　細拉
7歌唱的、跳舞的都要說：
　"我的泉源都在你裏面。"

第八十八篇

可拉後裔的詩歌，就是以斯拉人希幔的
訓誨詩，交與伶長。調用"麻哈拉利暗俄"。

1耶和華拯救我的神啊，
　我晝夜在你面前呼籲。
2願我的禱告達到你面前，
　求你側耳聽我的呼求！

3因為我心裏滿了患難，
　我的性命臨近陰間。
4我算和下坑的人同列，
　如同無力的人一樣（註："無力"或
　作"沒有幫助"）。
5我被丟在死人中，
　好像被殺的人躺在墳墓裏。
　他們是你不再記念的，
　與你隔絕了。

6你把我放在極深的坑裏，
　在黑暗地方，在深處。
7你的忿怒重壓我身，
　你用一切的波浪困住我。
　　　　　　　　　　細拉
8你把我所認識的隔在遠處，
　使我為他們所憎惡。
　我被拘困，不得出來。
9我的眼睛因困苦而乾癟。

耶和華啊，我天天求告你，
　向你舉手。
10你豈要行奇事給死人看嗎？
　難道陰魂還能起來稱讚你嗎？
　　　　　　　　　　細拉
11豈能在墳墓裏述說你的慈愛嗎？
　豈能在滅亡中述說你的信實嗎？

Philistia too, and Tyre, along with Cush[a] —
　and will say, 'This[b] one was born in Zion.' "

5Indeed, of Zion it will be said,
　"This one and that one were born in her,
　and the Most High himself will establish her."
6The LORD will write in the register of the
　peoples:
　"This one was born in Zion."　　　Selah
7As they make music they will sing,
　"All my fountains are in you."

Psalm 88

A song. A psalm of the Sons of Korah. For the director of
music. According to *mahalath leannoth*.[c] A *maskil*[d] of Heman
the Ezrahite.

1O LORD, the God who saves me,
　day and night I cry out before you.
2May my prayer come before you;
　turn your ear to my cry.

3For my soul is full of trouble
　and my life draws near the grave.[e]
4I am counted among those who go down to the
　pit;
　I am like a man without strength.
5I am set apart with the dead,
　like the slain who lie in the grave,
　whom you remember no more,
　who are cut off from your care.

6You have put me in the lowest pit,
　in the darkest depths.
7Your wrath lies heavily upon me;
　you have overwhelmed me with all your
　waves.　　　　　　　　Selah
8You have taken from me my closest friends
　and have made me repulsive to them.
　I am confined and cannot escape;
9　my eyes are dim with grief.

I call to you, O LORD, every day;
　I spread out my hands to you.
10Do you show your wonders to the dead?
　Do those who are dead rise up and praise
　you?　　　　　　　　　Selah
11Is your love declared in the grave,
　your faithfulness in Destruction[f]?

---

a 4 That is, the upper Nile region　　*b* 4 Or *"O Rahab and
Babylon, / Philistia, Tyre and Cush, / I will record concerning those
who acknowledge me: / 'This*　　*c* Title: Possibly a tune, "The
Suffering of Affliction"　　*d* Title: Probably a literary or
musical term　　*e* 3 Hebrew *Sheol*　　*f* 11 Hebrew *Abaddon*

¹²Are your wonders known in the place of
    darkness,
  or your righteous deeds in the land of
    oblivion?

¹³But I cry to you for help, O LORD;
  in the morning my prayer comes before you.
¹⁴Why, O LORD, do you reject me
  and hide your face from me?

¹⁵From my youth I have been afflicted and close
    to death;
  I have suffered your terrors and am in
    despair.
¹⁶Your wrath has swept over me;
  your terrors have destroyed me.
¹⁷All day long they surround me like a flood;
  they have completely engulfed me.
¹⁸You have taken my companions and loved
    ones from me;
  the darkness is my closest friend.

Psalm 89

A *maskil*[a] of Ethan the Ezrahite.

¹I will sing of the LORD's great love forever;
  with my mouth I will make your faithfulness
    known through all generations.
²I will declare that your love stands firm forever,
  that you established your faithfulness in
    heaven itself.

³You said, "I have made a covenant with my
    chosen one,
  I have sworn to David my servant,
⁴'I will establish your line forever
  and make your throne firm through all
    generations.' "   *Selah*

⁵The heavens praise your wonders, O LORD,
  your faithfulness too, in the assembly of the
    holy ones.
⁶For who in the skies above can compare with
    the LORD?
  Who is like the LORD among the heavenly
    beings?
⁷In the council of the holy ones God is greatly
    feared;
  he is more awesome than all who surround
    him.
⁸O LORD God Almighty, who is like you?
  You are mighty, O LORD, and your
    faithfulness surrounds you.

a Title: Probably a literary or musical term

¹²你的奇事
  豈能在幽暗裏被知道嗎？
你的公義
  豈能在忘記之地被知道嗎？

¹³耶和華啊，我呼求你！
  我早晨的禱告要達到你面前。
¹⁴耶和華啊，你為何丟棄我？
  為何掩面不顧我？

¹⁵我自幼受苦，
  幾乎死亡；
  我受你的驚恐，
  甚至慌張。
¹⁶你的烈怒漫過我身；
  你的驚嚇把我剪除。
¹⁷這些終日如水環繞我，
  一齊都來圍困我。
¹⁸你把我的良朋密友隔在遠處，
  使我所認識的人進入黑暗裏。

第八十九篇

以斯拉人以探的訓誨詩。

¹我要歌唱耶和華的慈愛直到永遠，
  我要用口將你的信實傳與萬代！

²因我曾說，
  你的慈悲必建立到永遠，
  你的信實必堅立在天上。

³ "我與我所揀選的人立了約，
  向我的僕人大衛起了誓：

⁴ '我要建立你的後裔，直到永遠；
  要建立你的寶座，直到萬代。'"
      細拉

⁵耶和華啊，諸天要稱讚你的奇事，
  在聖者的會中，
  要稱讚你的信實。
⁶在天空
  誰能比耶和華呢？
神的眾子中，
  誰能像耶和華呢？
⁷他在聖者的會中，
  是大有威嚴的神，
比一切在他四圍的
  更可畏懼。
⁸耶和華萬軍之神啊，
  哪一個大能者像你耶和華？
  你的信實是在你的四圍。

⁹你管轄海的狂傲，
　　波浪翻騰，你就使它平靜了。
¹⁰你打碎了<u>拉哈伯</u>，似乎是已殺的人；
　　你用有能的膀臂
　　打散了你的仇敵。
¹¹天屬你，地也屬你；
　　世界和其中所充滿的，
　　都為你所建立。
¹²南北為你所創造，
　　<u>他泊</u>和<u>黑門</u>都因你的名歡呼。
¹³你有大能的膀臂，
　　你的手有力，你的右手也高舉。

¹⁴公義和公平是你寶座的根基；
　　慈愛和誠實行在你前面。

¹⁵知道向你歡呼的，
　　那民是有福的！
　　耶和華啊，
　　他們在你臉上的光裏行走。
¹⁶他們因你的名終日歡樂，
　　因你的公義得以高舉。
¹⁷你是他們力量的榮耀，
　　因為你喜悅我們，
　　我們的角必被高舉。
¹⁸我們的盾牌屬耶和華；
　　我們的王屬<u>以色列</u>的聖者。
¹⁹當時，你在異象中
　　曉諭你的聖民，說：
　　"我已把救助之力
　　加在那有能者的身上，
　　我高舉那從民中所揀選的。
²⁰我尋得我的僕人<u>大衛</u>，
　　用我的聖膏膏他。
²¹我的手必使他堅立，
　　我的膀臂也必堅固他。
²²仇敵必不勒索他，
　　兇惡之子也不苦害他。
²³我要在他面前打碎他的敵人，
　　擊殺那恨他的人。
²⁴只是我的信實和我的慈愛
　　要與他同在，
　　因我的名，他的角必被高舉。
²⁵我要使他的左手伸到海上，
　　右手伸到河上。
²⁶他要稱呼我說：'你是我的父，
　　是我的神，是拯救我的磐石。'
²⁷我也要立他為長子，
　　為世上最高的君王。
²⁸我要為他存留我的慈愛，直到永遠，
　　我與他立的約必要堅定。
²⁹我也要使他的後裔存到永遠，
　　使他的寶座如天之久。

⁹You rule over the surging sea;
　　when its waves mount up, you still them.
¹⁰You crushed Rahab like one of the slain;
　　with your strong arm you scattered your
　　enemies.
¹¹The heavens are yours, and yours also the
　　earth;
　　you founded the world and all that is in it.
¹²You created the north and the south;
　　Tabor and Hermon sing for joy at your name.
¹³Your arm is endued with power;
　　your hand is strong, your right hand exalted.

¹⁴Righteousness and justice are the foundation
　　of your throne;
　　love and faithfulness go before you.
¹⁵Blessed are those who have learned to acclaim
　　you,
　　who walk in the light of your presence,
　　O Lᴏʀᴅ.
¹⁶They rejoice in your name all day long;
　　they exult in your righteousness.
¹⁷For you are their glory and strength,
　　and by your favor you exalt our horn.ᵃ
¹⁸Indeed, our shieldᵇ belongs to the Lᴏʀᴅ,
　　our king to the Holy One of Israel.
¹⁹Once you spoke in a vision,
　　to your faithful people you said:
　　"I have bestowed strength on a warrior;
　　I have exalted a young man from among the
　　people.
²⁰I have found David my servant;
　　with my sacred oil I have anointed him.
²¹My hand will sustain him;
　　surely my arm will strengthen him.
²²No enemy will subject him to tribute;
　　no wicked man will oppress him.
²³I will crush his foes before him
　　and strike down his adversaries.
²⁴My faithful love will be with him,
　　and through my name his hornᶜ will be
　　exalted.
²⁵I will set his hand over the sea,
　　his right hand over the rivers.
²⁶He will call out to me, 'You are my Father,
　　my God, the Rock my Savior.'
²⁷I will also appoint him my firstborn,
　　the most exalted of the kings of the earth.
²⁸I will maintain my love to him forever,
　　and my covenant with him will never fail.
²⁹I will establish his line forever,
　　his throne as long as the heavens endure.

a 17 Horn here symbolizes strong one.　　b 18 Or sovereign
c 24 Horn here symbolizes strength.

³⁰"If his sons forsake my law
　　and do not follow my statutes,
³¹if they violate my decrees
　　and fail to keep my commands,
³²I will punish their sin with the rod,
　　their iniquity with flogging;
³³but I will not take my love from him,
　　nor will I ever betray my faithfulness.
³⁴I will not violate my covenant
　　or alter what my lips have uttered.
³⁵Once for all, I have sworn by my holiness—
　　and I will not lie to David—
³⁶that his line will continue forever
　　and his throne endure before me like the sun;
³⁷it will be established forever like the moon,
　　the faithful witness in the sky."　　　*Selah*

³⁸But you have rejected, you have spurned,
　　you have been very angry with your
　　　anointed one.
³⁹You have renounced the covenant with your
　　servant
　　and have defiled his crown in the dust.
⁴⁰You have broken through all his walls
　　and reduced his strongholds to ruins.
⁴¹All who pass by have plundered him;
　　he has become the scorn of his neighbors.
⁴²You have exalted the right hand of his foes;
　　you have made all his enemies rejoice.
⁴³You have turned back the edge of his sword
　　and have not supported him in battle.
⁴⁴You have put an end to his splendor
　　and cast his throne to the ground.
⁴⁵You have cut short the days of his youth;
　　you have covered him with a mantle of
　　shame.　　　*Selah*

⁴⁶How long, O LORD? Will you hide yourself
　　forever?
　　How long will your wrath burn like fire?
⁴⁷Remember how fleeting is my life.
　　For what futility you have created all men!
⁴⁸What man can live and not see death,
　　or save himself from the power of the grave^a?
　　　Selah
⁴⁹O Lord, where is your former great love,
　　which in your faithfulness you swore to
　　David?
⁵⁰Remember, Lord, how your servant has^b been
　　mocked,
　　how I bear in my heart the taunts of all the
　　nations,

³⁰"倘若他的子孫離棄我的律法，
　　不照我的典章行，
³¹背棄我的律例，
　　不遵守我的誡命，
³²我就要用杖責罰他們的過犯，
　　用鞭責罰他們的罪孽。
³³只是我必不將我的慈愛全然收回，
　　也必不叫我的信實廢棄。
³⁴我必不背棄我的約，
　　也不改變我口中所出的。
³⁵我一次指着自己的聖潔起誓，
　　我決不向大衞說謊。
³⁶他的後裔要存到永遠，
　　他的寶座在我面前如日之恆一般；
³⁷又如月亮永遠堅立，
　　如天上確實的見證。"　　　細拉

³⁸但你惱怒你的受膏者，
　　就丟掉棄絕他。
³⁹你厭惡了與僕人所立的約，
　　將他的冠冕踐踏於地。
⁴⁰你拆毀了他一切的籬笆，
　　使他的保障變為荒場。
⁴¹凡過路的人都搶奪他，
　　他成為鄰邦的羞辱。
⁴²你高舉了他敵人的右手，
　　你叫他一切的仇敵歡喜。
⁴³你叫他的刀劍捲刃，
　　叫他在爭戰之中站立不住。
⁴⁴你使他的光輝止息，
　　將他的寶座推倒於地。
⁴⁵你減少他青年的日子，
　　又使他蒙羞。
　　　細拉

⁴⁶耶和華啊，這要到幾時呢？
　　你要將自己隱藏到永遠嗎？
　　你的忿怒如火焚燒，要到幾時呢？
⁴⁷求你想念我的時候是何等的短少。
　　你創造世人，
　　要使他們歸何等的虛空呢！　　細拉
⁴⁸誰能常活免死，
　　救他的靈魂脫離陰間的權柄呢？　細拉
⁴⁹主啊，
　　你從前憑你的信實向大衞立誓，
　　要施行的慈愛在哪裏呢？
⁵⁰主啊，
　　求你記念僕人們所受的羞辱，
　　記念我怎樣將一切強盛民的羞辱
　　存在我懷裏。

a 48 Hebrew *Sheol*　　*b 50* Or *your servants have*

51耶和華啊，
　　你的仇敵用這羞辱，
　羞辱了你的僕人，
　　羞辱了你受膏者的腳蹤。

52耶和華是應當稱頌的，直到永遠。
　　阿們！阿們！

卷四

詩篇 90-106

第九十篇

神人摩西的祈禱

1主啊，你世世代代
　　作我們的居所。
2諸山未曾生出，
　　地與世界你未曾造成，
　從亙古到永遠，
　　你是神！

3你使人歸於塵土，說：
　　"你們世人要歸回。"
4在你看來，
　　千年如已過的昨日，
　　又如夜間的一更。
5你叫他們如水沖去，他們如睡一覺。
　　早晨，他們如生長的草，
6早晨發芽生長，
　　晚上割下枯乾。

7我們因你的怒氣而消滅，
　　因你的忿怒而驚惶。
8你將我們的罪孽擺在你面前，
　　將我們的隱惡擺在你面光之中。
9我們經過的日子都在你震怒之下；
　　我們度盡的年歲好像一聲歎息。
10我們一生的年日是七十歲，
　　若是強壯可到八十歲；
　但其中所矜誇的不過是勞苦愁煩，
　　轉眼成空，我們便如飛而去。

11誰曉得你怒氣的權勢？
　　誰按着你該受的敬畏
　　　曉得你的忿怒呢？
12求你指教我們怎樣數算自己的日子，
　　好叫我們得着智慧的心。

13耶和華啊，我們要等到幾時呢？
　　求你轉回，為你的僕人後悔。

51the taunts with which your enemies have
　　mocked, O LORD,
　with which they have mocked every step of
　　your anointed one.

52Praise be to the LORD forever!
　　Amen and Amen.

BOOK IV

Psalms 90-106

Psalm 90

A prayer of Moses the man of God.

1Lord, you have been our dwelling place
　　throughout all generations.
2Before the mountains were born
　　or you brought forth the earth and the
　　　world,
　from everlasting to everlasting you are God.

3You turn men back to dust,
　　saying, "Return to dust, O sons of men."
4For a thousand years in your sight
　　are like a day that has just gone by,
　　or like a watch in the night.
5You sweep men away in the sleep of death;
　　they are like the new grass of the morning—
6though in the morning it springs up new,
　　by evening it is dry and withered.

7We are consumed by your anger
　　and terrified by your indignation.
8You have set our iniquities before you,
　　our secret sins in the light of your presence.
9All our days pass away under your wrath;
　　we finish our years with a moan.
10The length of our days is seventy years—
　　or eighty, if we have the strength;
　yet their span*a* is but trouble and sorrow,
　　for they quickly pass, and we fly away.

11Who knows the power of your anger?
　　For your wrath is as great as the fear that is
　　　due you.
12Teach us to number our days aright,
　　that we may gain a heart of wisdom.

13Relent, O LORD! How long will it be?
　　Have compassion on your servants.

a 10 Or yet the best of them

¹⁴Satisfy us in the morning with your unfailing love,
    that we may sing for joy and be glad all our days.
¹⁵Make us glad for as many days as you have afflicted us,
    for as many years as we have seen trouble.
¹⁶May your deeds be shown to your servants,
    your splendor to their children.

¹⁷May the favor^a of the Lord our God rest upon us;
    establish the work of our hands for us—
    yes, establish the work of our hands.

Psalm 91

¹He who dwells in the shelter of the Most High
    will rest in the shadow of the Almighty.^b
²I will say^c of the LORD, "He is my refuge and my fortress,
    my God, in whom I trust."

³Surely he will save you from the fowler's snare
    and from the deadly pestilence.
⁴He will cover you with his feathers,
    and under his wings you will find refuge;
    his faithfulness will be your shield and rampart.
⁵You will not fear the terror of night,
    nor the arrow that flies by day,
⁶nor the pestilence that stalks in the darkness,
    nor the plague that destroys at midday.
⁷A thousand may fall at your side,
    ten thousand at your right hand,
    but it will not come near you.
⁸You will only observe with your eyes
    and see the punishment of the wicked.

⁹If you make the Most High your dwelling—
    even the LORD, who is my refuge—
¹⁰then no harm will befall you,
    no disaster will come near your tent.
¹¹For he will command his angels concerning you
    to guard you in all your ways;
¹²they will lift you up in their hands,
    so that you will not strike your foot against a stone.
¹³You will tread upon the lion and the cobra;
    you will trample the great lion and the serpent.

¹⁴"Because he loves me," says the LORD, "I will rescue him;

¹⁴求你使我們
      早早飽得你的慈愛，
      好叫我們一生一世
      歡呼喜樂。
¹⁵求你照着你使我們受苦的日子
      和我們遭難的年歲，
      叫我們喜樂。
¹⁶願你的作為向你僕人顯現；
      願你的榮耀向他們子孫顯明。

¹⁷願主我們神的榮美歸於我們身上。
      願你堅立我們手所做的工；
    我們手所做的工，
      願你堅立。

第九十一篇

¹住在至高者隱密處的，
      必住在全能者的蔭下。
²我要論到耶和華說：
      "他是我的避難所，是我的山寨，
      是我的神，是我所倚靠的。"

³他必救你脫離捕鳥人的網羅
      和毒害的瘟疫。
⁴他必用自己的翎毛遮蔽你，
      你要投靠在他的翅膀底下。
    他的誠實
      是大小的盾牌。
⁵你必不怕黑夜的驚駭，
      或是白日飛的箭；
⁶也不怕黑夜行的瘟疫，
      或是午間滅人的毒病。
⁷雖有千人仆倒在你旁邊，
      萬人仆倒在你右邊，
      這災卻不得臨近你。
⁸你惟親眼觀看，
      見惡人遭報。

⁹耶和華是我的避難所；
      你已將至高者當你的居所，
¹⁰禍患必不臨到你，
      災害也不挨近你的帳棚。
¹¹因他要為你吩咐他的使者，
      在你行的一切道路上保護你。
¹²他們要用手托着你，
      免得你的腳
      碰在石頭上。
¹³你要踹在獅子和虺蛇的身上，
      踐踏少壯獅子和大蛇。

¹⁴神說："因為他專心愛我，
      我就要搭救他；

a 17 Or beauty   b 1 Hebrew Shaddai   c 2 Or He says

因為他知道我的名，
　　我要把他安置在高處。
15他若求告我，我就應允他；
　　他在急難中，我要與他同在；
　　我要搭救他，使他尊貴。
16我要使他足享長壽，
　　將我的救恩顯明給他。"

第九十二篇

安息日的詩歌。

1稱謝耶和華，
　　歌頌你至高者的名！
2、3用十弦的樂器和瑟，
　　用琴彈幽雅的聲音，
　　早晨傳揚你的慈愛，
　　每夜傳揚你的信實，這本為美事！

4因你耶和華藉着你的作為叫我高興；
　　我要因你手的工作歡呼。
5耶和華啊，你的工作何其大，
　　你的心思極其深！
6畜類人不曉得，
　　愚頑人也不明白。
7惡人茂盛如草，
　　一切作孽之人發旺的時候，
　　正是他們要滅亡，直到永遠。

8惟你耶和華是至高，直到永遠！

9耶和華啊，
　　你的仇敵都要滅亡，
　　一切作孽的也要離散。
10你卻高舉了我的角，
　　如野牛的角；
　　我是被新油膏了的。
11我眼睛看見
　　仇敵遭報；
　　我耳朵聽見
　　那些起來攻擊我的惡人受罰。

12義人要發旺如棕樹，
　　生長如黎巴嫩的香柏樹。
13他們栽於耶和華的殿中，
　　發旺在我們神的院裏。
14他們年老的時候仍要結果子，
　　要滿了汁漿而常發青。
15好顯明耶和華是正直的。
　　他是我的磐石，在他毫無不義。

I will protect him, for he acknowledges my
　　name.
15He will call upon me, and I will answer him;
　　I will be with him in trouble,
　　I will deliver him and honor him.
16With long life will I satisfy him
　　and show him my salvation."

Psalm 92

A psalm. A song. For the Sabbath day.

1It is good to praise the LORD
　　and make music to your name, O Most High,
2to proclaim your love in the morning
　　and your faithfulness at night,
3to the music of the ten-stringed lyre
　　and the melody of the harp.

4For you make me glad by your deeds, O LORD;
　　I sing for joy at the works of your hands.
5How great are your works, O LORD,
　　how profound your thoughts!
6The senseless man does not know,
　　fools do not understand,
7that though the wicked spring up like grass
　　and all evildoers flourish,
　　they will be forever destroyed.

8But you, O LORD, are exalted forever.

9For surely your enemies, O LORD,
　　surely your enemies will perish;
　　all evildoers will be scattered.
10You have exalted my horn[a] like that of a wild
　　ox;
　　fine oils have been poured upon me.
11My eyes have seen the defeat of my
　　adversaries;
　　my ears have heard the rout of my wicked
　　foes.

12The righteous will flourish like a palm tree,
　　they will grow like a cedar of Lebanon;
13planted in the house of the LORD,
　　they will flourish in the courts of our God.
14They will still bear fruit in old age,
　　they will stay fresh and green,
15proclaiming, "The LORD is upright;
　　he is my Rock, and there is no wickedness in
　　him."

a 10 *Horn* here symbolizes strength.

Psalm 93

¹The LORD reigns, he is robed in majesty;
  the LORD is robed in majesty
  and is armed with strength.
 The world is firmly established;
  it cannot be moved.
²Your throne was established long ago;
  you are from all eternity.

³The seas have lifted up, O LORD,
  the seas have lifted up their voice;
  the seas have lifted up their pounding
    waves.
⁴Mightier than the thunder of the great waters,
  mightier than the breakers of the sea—
  the LORD on high is mighty.

⁵Your statutes stand firm;
  holiness adorns your house
  for endless days, O LORD.

Psalm 94

¹O LORD, the God who avenges,
  O God who avenges, shine forth.
²Rise up, O Judge of the earth;
  pay back to the proud what they deserve.
³How long will the wicked, O LORD,
  how long will the wicked be jubilant?

⁴They pour out arrogant words;
  all the evildoers are full of boasting.
⁵They crush your people, O LORD;
  they oppress your inheritance.
⁶They slay the widow and the alien;
  they murder the fatherless.
⁷They say, "The LORD does not see;
  the God of Jacob pays no heed."

⁸Take heed, you senseless ones among the
    people;
  you fools, when will you become wise?
⁹Does he who implanted the ear not hear?
  Does he who formed the eye not see?
¹⁰Does he who disciplines nations not punish?
  Does he who teaches man lack knowledge?
¹¹The LORD knows the thoughts of man;
  he knows that they are futile.

¹²Blessed is the man you discipline, O LORD,
  the man you teach from your law;
¹³you grant him relief from days of trouble,
  till a pit is dug for the wicked.
¹⁴For the LORD will not reject his people;
  he will never forsake his inheritance.

第九十三篇

¹耶和華作王，他以威嚴為衣穿上。
  耶和華以能力為衣，
    以能力束腰，
  世界就堅定，
    不得動搖。
²你的寶座從太初立定，
  你從亙古就有。

³耶和華啊，
    大水揚起，
  大水發聲，
    波浪澎湃。
⁴耶和華在高處大有能力，
  勝過諸水的響聲，
    洋海的大浪。

⁵耶和華啊，你的法度最的確；
  你的殿永稱為聖，
    是合宜的。

第九十四篇

¹耶和華啊，你是伸冤的神。
  伸冤的神啊，求你發出光來。
²審判世界的主啊，求你挺身而立，
  使驕傲人受應得的報應。
³耶和華啊，惡人誇勝要到幾時呢？
  要到幾時呢？

⁴他們絮絮叨叨說傲慢的話，
  一切作孽的人都自己誇張。
⁵耶和華啊，他們強壓你的百姓，
  苦害你的產業。
⁶他們殺死寡婦和寄居的，
  又殺害孤兒。
⁷他們說：「耶和華必不看見，
  雅各的神必不思念。」

⁸你們民間的畜類人當思想；
  你們愚頑人
    到幾時才有智慧呢？
⁹造耳朵的，難道自己不聽見嗎？
  造眼睛的，難道自己不看見嗎？
¹⁰管教列邦的，就是叫人得知識的，
  難道自己不懲治人嗎？
¹¹耶和華知道
  人的意念是虛妄的。

¹²耶和華啊，你所管教、
  用律法所教訓的人是有福的！
¹³你使他在遭難的日子得享平安；
  惟有惡人陷在所挖的坑中。
¹⁴因為耶和華必不丟棄他的百姓，
  也不離棄他的產業。

¹⁵審判要轉向公義，
　　心裏正直的，
　　必都隨從。

¹⁶誰肯為我起來攻擊作惡的？
　　誰肯為我站起抵擋作孽的？

¹⁷若不是耶和華幫助我，
　　我就住在寂靜之中了。

¹⁸我正說"我失了腳"，
　　耶和華啊，那時你的慈愛扶助我。
¹⁹我心裏多憂多疑，
　　你安慰我，就使我歡樂。
²⁰那藉着律例架弄殘害、
　　在位上行奸惡的，
　　豈能與你相交嗎？
²¹他們大家聚集攻擊義人，
　　將無辜的人定為死罪。
²²但耶和華向來作了我的高臺，
　　我的神作了我投靠的磐石。
²³他叫他們的罪孽歸到他們身上。
　　他們正在行惡之中，他要剪除他們；
　　耶和華我們的神要把他們剪除。

第九十五篇

¹來啊，我們要向耶和華歌唱；
　　向拯救我們的磐石歡呼！

²我們要來感謝他，
　　用詩歌向他歡呼！

³因耶和華為大神，
　　為大王，超乎萬神之上。
⁴地的深處在他手中，
　　山的高峯也屬他。
⁵海洋屬他，是他造的；
　　旱地也是他手造成的。

⁶來啊，我們要屈身敬拜，
　　在造我們的耶和華面前跪下。
⁷因為他是我們的神，
　　我們是他草場的羊，
　　是他手下的民。

　　惟願你們今天聽他的話。
⁸你們不可硬着心，
　　像當日在米利巴，
　　就是在曠野的瑪撒。
⁹那時，你們的祖宗試我探我，
　　並且觀看我的作為。
¹⁰四十年之久，
　　我厭煩那世代，說：

¹⁵Judgment will again be founded on
　　righteousness,
　　and all the upright in heart will follow it.

¹⁶Who will rise up for me against the wicked?
　　Who will take a stand for me against
　　evildoers?
¹⁷Unless the LORD had given me help,
　　I would soon have dwelt in the silence of
　　death.
¹⁸When I said, "My foot is slipping,"
　　your love, O LORD, supported me.
¹⁹When anxiety was great within me,
　　your consolation brought joy to my soul.

²⁰Can a corrupt throne be allied with you—
　　one that brings on misery by its decrees?
²¹They band together against the righteous
　　and condemn the innocent to death.
²²But the LORD has become my fortress,
　　and my God the rock in whom I take refuge.
²³He will repay them for their sins
　　and destroy them for their wickedness;
　　the LORD our God will destroy them.

Psalm 95

¹Come, let us sing for joy to the LORD;
　　let us shout aloud to the Rock of our
　　salvation.
²Let us come before him with thanksgiving
　　and extol him with music and song.

³For the LORD is the great God,
　　the great King above all gods.
⁴In his hand are the depths of the earth,
　　and the mountain peaks belong to him.
⁵The sea is his, for he made it,
　　and his hands formed the dry land.

⁶Come, let us bow down in worship,
　　let us kneel before the LORD our Maker;
⁷for he is our God
　　and we are the people of his pasture,
　　the flock under his care.

　　Today, if you hear his voice,
⁸　do not harden your hearts as you did at
　　Meribah,^a
　　as you did that day at Massah^b in the desert,
⁹where your fathers tested and tried me,
　　though they had seen what I did.
¹⁰For forty years I was angry with that
　　generation;

a 8 Meribah means quarreling. b 8 Massah means testing.

I said, "They are a people whose hearts go astray,
and they have not known my ways."
¹¹So I declared on oath in my anger,
"They shall never enter my rest."

Psalm 96

¹Sing to the LORD a new song;
sing to the LORD, all the earth.
²Sing to the LORD, praise his name;
proclaim his salvation day after day.
³Declare his glory among the nations,
his marvelous deeds among all peoples.

⁴For great is the LORD and most worthy of praise;
he is to be feared above all gods.
⁵For all the gods of the nations are idols,
but the LORD made the heavens.
⁶Splendor and majesty are before him;
strength and glory are in his sanctuary.

⁷Ascribe to the LORD, O families of nations,
ascribe to the LORD glory and strength.
⁸Ascribe to the LORD the glory due his name;
bring an offering and come into his courts.
⁹Worship the LORD in the splendor of his[a]
holiness;
tremble before him, all the earth.

¹⁰Say among the nations, "The LORD reigns."
The world is firmly established, it cannot be moved;
he will judge the peoples with equity.
¹¹Let the heavens rejoice, let the earth be glad;
let the sea resound, and all that is in it;
¹² let the fields be jubilant, and everything in them.
Then all the trees of the forest will sing for joy;
¹³ they will sing before the LORD, for he comes,
he comes to judge the earth.
He will judge the world in righteousness
and the peoples in his truth.

Psalm 97

¹The LORD reigns, let the earth be glad;
let the distant shores rejoice.

²Clouds and thick darkness surround him;
righteousness and justice are the foundation
of his throne.
³Fire goes before him
and consumes his foes on every side.

---

a 9 Or LORD *with the splendor of*

"這是心裏迷糊的百姓,
竟不曉得我的作為！"
¹¹所以我在怒中起誓說:
"他們斷不可進入我的安息！"

第九十六篇

¹你們要向耶和華唱新歌,
全地都要向耶和華歌唱！
²要向耶和華歌唱,稱頌他的名,
天天傳揚他的救恩。
³在列邦中述說他的榮耀,
在萬民中述說他的奇事。

⁴因耶和華為大,當受極大的讚美;
他在萬神之上,當受敬畏！
⁵外邦的神都屬虛無,
惟獨耶和華創造諸天。
⁶有尊榮和威嚴在他面前,
有能力與華美在他聖所。

⁷民中的萬族啊,你們要將榮耀能力
歸給耶和華,都歸給耶和華！
⁸要將耶和華的名所當得的榮耀
歸給他,拿供物來進入他的院宇。
⁹當以聖潔的妝飾 (註: "的"或作"為")
敬拜耶和華。
全地要在他面前戰抖。

¹⁰人在列邦中要說:
"耶和華作王,
世界就堅定,不得動搖;
他要按公正審判眾民。"
¹¹願天歡喜,願地快樂！
願海和其中所充滿的澎湃！
¹²願田和其中所有的都歡樂！
那時,林中的樹木
都要在耶和華面前歡呼。
¹³因為他來了,他來要審判全地。
他要按公義審判世界,
按他的信實審判萬民。

第九十七篇

¹耶和華作王,願地快樂,
願眾海島歡喜！

²密雲和幽暗在他的四圍;
公義和公平
是他寶座的根基。
³有烈火在他前頭行,
燒滅他四圍的敵人。

⁴他的閃電光照世界，
　　大地看見便震動。
⁵諸山見耶和華的面，
　　就是全地之主的面，便消化如蠟。
⁶諸天表明他的公義，
　　萬民看見他的榮耀。

⁷願一切侍奉雕刻的偶像、
　　靠虛無之神自誇的，都蒙羞愧。
　　萬神哪，你們都當拜他。

⁸耶和華啊，錫安聽見你的判斷
　　就歡喜，猶大的城邑（註：原文作
　　"女子"）也都快樂。
⁹因為你耶和華至高，
　　超乎全地；
　　你被尊崇，遠超萬神之上。

¹⁰你們愛耶和華的都當恨惡罪惡；
　　他保護聖民的性命，
　　搭救他們
　　　　脫離惡人的手。
¹¹散佈亮光是為義人；
　　預備喜樂是為正直人。
¹²你們義人當靠耶和華歡喜，
　　稱謝他可記念的聖名。

第九十八篇

一篇詩。

¹你們要向耶和華唱新歌！
　　因為他行過奇妙的事，
　　他的右手和聖臂
　　施行救恩。
²耶和華發明了他的救恩，
　　在列邦人眼前顯出公義。
³記念他向以色列家所發的慈愛，
　　所憑的信實，
　　地的四極都看見
　　我們神的救恩。

⁴全地都要向耶和華歡樂，
　　要發起大聲，歡呼歌頌！
⁵要用琴歌頌耶和華，
　　用琴和詩歌的聲音歌頌他！
⁶用號和角聲，
　　在大君王耶和華面前歡呼！

⁷願海和其中所充滿的澎湃，
　　世界和住在其間的也要發聲。
⁸願大水拍手，
　　願諸山在耶和華面前一同歡呼。
⁹因為他來
　　要審判遍地，

⁴His lightning lights up the world;
　　the earth sees and trembles.
⁵The mountains melt like wax before the LORD,
　　before the Lord of all the earth.
⁶The heavens proclaim his righteousness,
　　and all the peoples see his glory.

⁷All who worship images are put to shame,
　　those who boast in idols—
　　worship him, all you gods!

⁸Zion hears and rejoices
　　and the villages of Judah are glad
　　because of your judgments, O LORD.
⁹For you, O LORD, are the Most High over all
　　the earth;
　　you are exalted far above all gods.

¹⁰Let those who love the LORD hate evil,
　　for he guards the lives of his faithful ones
　　and delivers them from the hand of the
　　　　wicked.
¹¹Light is shed upon the righteous
　　and joy on the upright in heart.
¹²Rejoice in the LORD, you who are righteous,
　　and praise his holy name.

Psalm 98

A psalm.

¹Sing to the LORD a new song,
　　for he has done marvelous things;
　　his right hand and his holy arm
　　have worked salvation for him.
²The LORD has made his salvation known
　　and revealed his righteousness to the nations.
³He has remembered his love
　　and his faithfulness to the house of Israel;
　　all the ends of the earth have seen
　　the salvation of our God.

⁴Shout for joy to the LORD, all the earth,
　　burst into jubilant song with music;
⁵make music to the LORD with the harp,
　　with the harp and the sound of singing,
⁶with trumpets and the blast of the ram's horn—
　　shout for joy before the LORD, the King.

⁷Let the sea resound, and everything in it,
　　the world, and all who live in it.
⁸Let the rivers clap their hands,
　　let the mountains sing together for joy;
⁹let them sing before the LORD,
　　for he comes to judge the earth.

He will judge the world in righteousness
    and the peoples with equity.

Psalm 99

¹The LORD reigns,
    let the nations tremble;
he sits enthroned between the cherubim,
    let the earth shake.
²Great is the LORD in Zion;
    he is exalted over all the nations.
³Let them praise your great and awesome name—
    he is holy.

⁴The King is mighty, he loves justice—
    you have established equity;
in Jacob you have done
    what is just and right.
⁵Exalt the LORD our God
    and worship at his footstool;
    he is holy.

⁶Moses and Aaron were among his priests,
    Samuel was among those who called on his
        name;
they called on the LORD
    and he answered them.
⁷He spoke to them from the pillar of cloud;
    they kept his statutes and the decrees he
        gave them.

⁸O LORD our God,
    you answered them;
you were to Israel^a a forgiving God,
    though you punished their misdeeds.^b
⁹Exalt the LORD our God
    and worship at his holy mountain,
for the LORD our God is holy.

Psalm 100

A psalm. For giving thanks.

¹Shout for joy to the LORD, all the earth.
² Worship the LORD with gladness;
    come before him with joyful songs.
³Know that the LORD is God.
    It is he who made us, and we are his^c;
    we are his people, the sheep of his pasture.

⁴Enter his gates with thanksgiving
    and his courts with praise;
    give thanks to him and praise his name.

他要按公義審判世界，
    按公正審判萬民。

第九十九篇

¹耶和華作王，
    萬民當戰抖！
他坐在二基路伯上，
    地當動搖！
²耶和華在錫安為大，
    他超乎萬民之上。
³他們當稱讚他大而可畏的名，
    他本為聖！

⁴王有能力，
    喜愛公平，
    堅立公正，
    在雅各中施行公平和公義。
⁵你們當尊崇耶和華我們的神，
    在他腳凳前下拜；
    他本為聖！

⁶在他的祭司中有摩西和亞倫，
    在求告他名的人中有撒母耳。
他們求告耶和華，
    他就應允他們。
⁷他在雲柱中對他們說話；
    他們遵守他的法度
        和他所賜給他們的律例。

⁸耶和華我們的神啊，
    你應允他們。
你是赦免他們的神，
    卻按他們所行的報應他們。
⁹你們要尊崇耶和華我們的神，
    在他的聖山下拜，
因為耶和華我們的神本為聖。

第一百篇

稱謝詩。

¹普天下當向耶和華歡呼！
²你們當樂意侍奉耶和華，
    當來向他歌唱！
³你們當曉得耶和華是神。
    我們是他造的，也是屬他的；
    我們是他的民，也是他草場的羊。

⁴當稱謝進入他的門，
    當讚美進入他的院；
    當感謝他，稱頌他的名。

---

*a 8 Hebrew them b 8 Or / an avenger of the wrongs done to
them c 3 Or and not we ourselves*

⁵因為耶和華本為善，
　　他的慈愛存到永遠，
　　他的信實直到萬代！

第一百零一篇

大衛的詩

¹我要歌唱慈愛和公平；
　　耶和華啊，我要向你歌頌！
²我要用智慧行完全的道。
　　你幾時到我這裏來呢？

我要存完全的心
　　行在我家中。
³邪僻的事，
　　我都不擺在我眼前。

悖逆人所做的事，我甚恨惡，
　　不容沾在我身上。
⁴彎曲的心思，我必遠離；
　　一切的惡人（註：或作"惡事"），
　　我不認識。
⁵在暗中讒謗他鄰居的，
　　我必將他滅絕；
　　眼目高傲、心裏驕縱的，
　　我必不容他。

⁶我眼要看國中的誠實人，
　　叫他們與我同住；
　　行為完全的，
　　他要伺候我。

⁷行詭詐的，
　　必不得住在我家裏；
　　說謊話的，
　　必不得立在我眼前。

⁸我每日早晨
　　要滅絕國中所有的惡人，
　　好把一切作孽的
　　從耶和華的城裏剪除。

第一百零二篇

困苦人發昏的時候，在耶和華面前
吐露苦情的禱告。

¹耶和華啊，求你聽我的禱告，
　　容我的呼求達到你面前。
²我在急難的日子，
　　求你向我側耳，不要向我掩面；
　　我呼求的日子，
　　求你快快應允我。

⁵For the LORD is good and his love endures
　　forever;
　　his faithfulness continues through all
　　generations.

Psalm 101

Of David. A psalm.

¹I will sing of your love and justice;
　　to you, O LORD, I will sing praise.
²I will be careful to lead a blameless life—
　　when will you come to me?

I will walk in my house
　　with blameless heart.
³I will set before my eyes
　　no vile thing.

The deeds of faithless men I hate;
　　they will not cling to me.
⁴Men of perverse heart shall be far from me;
　　I will have nothing to do with evil.

⁵Whoever slanders his neighbor in secret,
　　him will I put to silence;
　　whoever has haughty eyes and a proud heart,
　　him will I not endure.

⁶My eyes will be on the faithful in the land,
　　that they may dwell with me;
　　he whose walk is blameless
　　will minister to me.

⁷No one who practices deceit
　　will dwell in my house;
　　no one who speaks falsely
　　will stand in my presence.

⁸Every morning I will put to silence
　　all the wicked in the land;
　　I will cut off every evildoer
　　from the city of the LORD.

Psalm 102

A prayer of an afflicted man. When he is faint and pours out
his lament before the LORD.

¹Hear my prayer, O LORD;
　　let my cry for help come to you.
²Do not hide your face from me
　　when I am in distress.
　　Turn your ear to me;
　　when I call, answer me quickly.

³For my days vanish like smoke;
　　my bones burn like glowing embers.
⁴My heart is blighted and withered like grass;
　　I forget to eat my food.
⁵Because of my loud groaning
　　I am reduced to skin and bones.
⁶I am like a desert owl,
　　like an owl among the ruins.
⁷I lie awake; I have become
　　like a bird alone on a roof.
⁸All day long my enemies taunt me;
　　those who rail against me use my name as a
　　　　curse.
⁹For I eat ashes as my food
　　and mingle my drink with tears
¹⁰because of your great wrath,
　　for you have taken me up and thrown me
　　　　aside.
¹¹My days are like the evening shadow;
　　I wither away like grass.

¹²But you, O LORD, sit enthroned forever;
　　your renown endures through all generations.
¹³You will arise and have compassion on Zion,
　　for it is time to show favor to her;
　　the appointed time has come.
¹⁴For her stones are dear to your servants;
　　her very dust moves them to pity.
¹⁵The nations will fear the name of the LORD,
　　all the kings of the earth will revere your
　　　　glory.
¹⁶For the LORD will rebuild Zion
　　and appear in his glory.
¹⁷He will respond to the prayer of the destitute;
　　he will not despise their plea.

¹⁸Let this be written for a future generation,
　　that a people not yet created may praise the
　　　　LORD:
¹⁹"The LORD looked down from his sanctuary
　　　　on high,
　　from heaven he viewed the earth,
²⁰to hear the groans of the prisoners
　　and release those condemned to death."
²¹So the name of the LORD will be declared in
　　　　Zion
　　and his praise in Jerusalem
²²when the peoples and the kingdoms
　　assemble to worship the LORD.

²³In the course of my life[a] he broke my strength;
　　he cut short my days.
²⁴So I said:

---

³因為我的年日如煙雲消滅；
　　我的骨頭如火把燒着。
⁴我的心被傷，如草枯乾，
　　甚至我忘記吃飯。
⁵因我唉哼的聲音，
　　我的肉緊貼骨頭。
⁶我如同曠野的鵜鶘，
　　我好像荒場的鴞鳥。
⁷我警醒不睡，
　　我像房頂上孤單的麻雀。
⁸我的仇敵終日辱罵我，
　　向我猖狂的人
　　　　指着我賭咒。
⁹我吃過爐灰，如同吃飯；
　　我所喝的與眼淚攙雜。
¹⁰這都因你的惱恨和忿怒；
　　你把我拾起來，
　　　　又把我擲下去。
¹¹我的年日如日影偏斜；
　　我也如草枯乾。

¹²惟你耶和華必存到永遠，
　　你可記念的名也存到萬代。
¹³你必起來憐恤錫安，
　　因現在是可憐他的時候，
　　日期已經到了。
¹⁴你的僕人原來喜悅他的石頭，
　　可憐他的塵土。
¹⁵列國要敬畏耶和華的名；
　　世上諸王
　　　　都敬畏你的榮耀。
¹⁶因為耶和華建造了錫安，
　　在他榮耀裏顯現。
¹⁷他垂聽窮人的禱告，
　　並不藐視他們的祈求。

¹⁸這必為後代的人記下，
　　將來受造的民
　　　　要讚美耶和華，
¹⁹因為他從至高的聖所垂看。
　　耶和華從天
　　　　向地觀察，
²⁰要垂聽被囚之人的歎息，
　　要釋放將要死的人，
²¹使人在錫安傳揚耶和華的名，
　　在耶路撒冷
　　　　傳揚讚美他的話，
²²就是在萬民和列國聚會
　　侍奉耶和華的時候。

²³他使我的力量中道衰弱，
　　使我的年日短少。
²⁴我說：

---

a 23 Or *By his power*

"我的神啊，
　　不要使我中年去世；
　　你的年數世世無窮。
25你起初立了地的根基，
　　天也是你手所造的。

26天地都要滅沒，你卻要長存；
　　天地都要如外衣漸漸舊了。
　你要將天地如裏衣更換，
　　天地就都改變了。
27惟有你永不改變，
　　你的年數沒有窮盡！
28你僕人的子孫要長存，
　　他們的後裔要堅立在你面前。"

第一百零三篇

大衛的詩。

1我的心哪，你要稱頌耶和華，
　　凡在我裏面的，也要稱頌他的聖名！
2我的心哪，你要稱頌耶和華，
　　不可忘記他的一切恩惠！
3他赦免你的一切罪孽，
　　醫治你的一切疾病。
4他救贖你的命脫離死亡，
　　以仁愛和慈悲為你的冠冕。
5他用美物使你所願的得以知足，
　　以致你如鷹返老還童。

6耶和華施行公義，
　　為一切受屈的人伸冤。

7他使摩西知道他的法則，
　　叫以色列人曉得他的作為。
8耶和華有憐憫，有恩典，
　　不輕易發怒，且有豐盛的慈愛。
9他不長久責備，
　　也不永遠懷怒。
10他沒有按我們的罪過待我們，
　　也沒有照我們的罪孽報應我們。
11天離地何等的高，他的慈愛
　　向敬畏他的人也是何等的大！
12東離西有多遠，
　　他叫我們的過犯
　　離我們也有多遠！
13父親怎樣憐恤他的兒女，
　　耶和華也怎樣憐恤
　　敬畏他的人！
14因為他知道我們的本體，
　　思念我們不過是塵土。
15至於世人，他的年日如草一樣，
　　他發旺如野地的花；

Psalm 103

Of David.

1Praise the LORD, O my soul;
　　all my inmost being, praise his holy name.
2Praise the LORD, O my soul,
　　and forget not all his benefits—
3who forgives all your sins
　　and heals all your diseases,
4who redeems your life from the pit
　　and crowns you with love and compassion,
5who satisfies your desires with good things
　　so that your youth is renewed like the eagle's.

6The LORD works righteousness
　　and justice for all the oppressed.

7He made known his ways to Moses,
　　his deeds to the people of Israel:
8The LORD is compassionate and gracious,
　　slow to anger, abounding in love.
9He will not always accuse,
　　nor will he harbor his anger forever;
10he does not treat us as our sins deserve
　　or repay us according to our iniquities.
11For as high as the heavens are above the earth,
　　so great is his love for those who fear him;
12as far as the east is from the west,
　　so far has he removed our transgressions
　　from us.
13As a father has compassion on his children,
　　so the LORD has compassion on those who
　　fear him;
14for he knows how we are formed,
　　he remembers that we are dust.
15As for man, his days are like grass,
　　he flourishes like a flower of the field;

16the wind blows over it and it is gone,
　　and its place remembers it no more.
17But from everlasting to everlasting
　　the LORD's love is with those who fear him,
　　and his righteousness with their children's
　　　children—
18with those who keep his covenant
　　and remember to obey his precepts.

19The LORD has established his throne in heaven,
　　and his kingdom rules over all.

20Praise the LORD, you his angels,
　　you mighty ones who do his bidding,
　　who obey his word.
21Praise the LORD, all his heavenly hosts,
　　you his servants who do his will.
22Praise the LORD, all his works
　　everywhere in his dominion.

Praise the LORD, O my soul.

Psalm 104

1Praise the LORD, O my soul.

O LORD my God, you are very great;
　　you are clothed with splendor and majesty.
2He wraps himself in light as with a garment;
　　he stretches out the heavens like a tent
3and lays the beams of his upper chambers on
　　　their waters.
He makes the clouds his chariot
　　and rides on the wings of the wind.
4He makes winds his messengers,[a]
　　flames of fire his servants.

5He set the earth on its foundations;
　　it can never be moved.
6You covered it with the deep as with a garment;
　　the waters stood above the mountains.
7But at your rebuke the waters fled,
　　at the sound of your thunder they took to
　　　flight;
8they flowed over the mountains,
　　they went down into the valleys,
　　to the place you assigned for them.
9You set a boundary they cannot cross;
　　never again will they cover the earth.

10He makes springs pour water into the ravines;
　　it flows between the mountains.
11They give water to all the beasts of the field;
　　the wild donkeys quench their thirst.

16經風一吹，便歸無有，
　　他的原處，也不再認識他。
17但耶和華的慈愛歸於敬畏他的人，
　　從亙古到永遠；
他的公義
　　也歸於子子孫孫，
18就是那些遵守他的約，
　　記念他的訓詞而遵行的人。

19耶和華在天上立定寶座，
　　他的權柄（註：原文作"國"）統管萬有。

20聽從他命令、成全他旨意、
　　有大能的天使，
　　都要稱頌耶和華！
21你們作他的諸軍，作他的僕役，
　　行他所喜悅的，都要稱頌耶和華！
22你們一切被他造的，
　　在他所治理的各處，
　　都要稱頌耶和華。
我的心哪，你要稱頌耶和華！

第一百零四篇

1我的心哪，你要稱頌耶和華！

耶和華我的神啊，你為至大！
　　你以尊榮威嚴為衣服。
2披上亮光，如披外袍；
　　鋪張穹蒼，如鋪幔子。
3在水中
　　立樓閣的棟梁，
用雲彩為車輦，
　　藉着風的翅膀而行。
4以風為使者，
　　以火焰為僕役。

5將地立在根基上，
　　使地永不動搖。
6你用深水遮蓋地面，猶如衣裳；
　　諸水高過山嶺。
7你的斥責一發，水便奔逃；
　　你的雷聲一發，水便奔流。

8諸山升上，諸谷沉下（註：或作"隨山上
翻，隨谷下流"），
　　歸你為它所安定之地。
9你定了界限，使水不能過去，
　　不再轉回遮蓋地面。

10耶和華使泉源湧在山谷，
　　流在山間。
11使野地的走獸有水喝，
　　野驢得解其渴。

a 4 Or angels

¹²天上的飛鳥在水旁住宿，
　　在樹枝上啼叫。
¹³他從樓閣中澆灌山嶺，
　　因他作為的功效，
　　地就豐足。
¹⁴他使草生長，給六畜吃，
　　使菜蔬發長，供給人用，
　　使人從地裏能得食物，
¹⁵又得酒能悅人心，
　　得油能潤人面，
　　得糧能養人心。
¹⁶佳美的樹木，就是黎巴嫩的香柏樹，
　　是耶和華所栽種的，都滿了汁漿。
¹⁷雀鳥在其上搭窩，
　　至於鶴，松樹是牠的房屋。
¹⁸高山為野山羊的住所；
　　巖石為沙番的藏處。

¹⁹你安置月亮為定節令，
　　日頭自知沉落。
²⁰你造黑暗為夜，
　　林中的百獸就都爬出來。
²¹少壯獅子吼叫，要抓食，
　　向神尋求食物。
²²日頭一出，獸便躲避，
　　臥在洞裏。
²³人出去做工，
　　勞碌直到晚上。

²⁴耶和華啊，你所造的何其多！
　　都是你用智慧造成的，
　　遍地滿了你的豐富。
²⁵那裏有海，又大又廣，
　　其中有無數的動物，
　　大小活物都有。
²⁶那裏有船行走，
　　有你所造的鱷魚游泳在其中。

²⁷這都仰望你
　　按時給牠食物。
²⁸你給牠們，
　　牠們便拾起來；
　　你張手，
　　牠們飽得美食。
²⁹你掩面，
　　牠們便驚惶；
　　你收回牠們的氣，
　　牠們就死亡，歸於塵土。
³⁰你發出你的靈，
　　牠們便受造。
　　你使地面更換為新。

¹²The birds of the air nest by the waters;
　　they sing among the branches.
¹³He waters the mountains from his upper
　　chambers;
　　the earth is satisfied by the fruit of his work.
¹⁴He makes grass grow for the cattle,
　　and plants for man to cultivate—
　　bringing forth food from the earth:
¹⁵wine that gladdens the heart of man,
　　oil to make his face shine,
　　and bread that sustains his heart.
¹⁶The trees of the Lord are well watered,
　　the cedars of Lebanon that he planted.
¹⁷There the birds make their nests;
　　the stork has its home in the pine trees.
¹⁸The high mountains belong to the wild goats;
　　the crags are a refuge for the coneys.ᵃ

¹⁹The moon marks off the seasons,
　　and the sun knows when to go down.
²⁰You bring darkness, it becomes night,
　　and all the beasts of the forest prowl.
²¹The lions roar for their prey
　　and seek their food from God.
²²The sun rises, and they steal away;
　　they return and lie down in their dens.
²³Then man goes out to his work,
　　to his labor until evening.

²⁴How many are your works, O Lord!
　　In wisdom you made them all;
　　the earth is full of your creatures.
²⁵There is the sea, vast and spacious,
　　teeming with creatures beyond number—
　　living things both large and small.
²⁶There the ships go to and fro,
　　and the leviathan, which you formed to
　　frolic there.

²⁷These all look to you
　　to give them their food at the proper time.
²⁸When you give it to them,
　　they gather it up;
　　when you open your hand,
　　they are satisfied with good things.
²⁹When you hide your face,
　　they are terrified;
　　when you take away their breath,
　　they die and return to the dust.
³⁰When you send your Spirit,
　　they are created,
　　and you renew the face of the earth.

a 18 That is, the hyrax or rock badger

³¹May the glory of the LORD endure forever;
    may the LORD rejoice in his works—
³²he who looks at the earth, and it trembles,
    who touches the mountains, and they smoke.

³³I will sing to the LORD all my life;
    I will sing praise to my God as long as I live.
³⁴May my meditation be pleasing to him,
    as I rejoice in the LORD.
³⁵But may sinners vanish from the earth
    and the wicked be no more.

Praise the LORD, O my soul.

Praise the LORD.*ᵃ*

Psalm 105

¹Give thanks to the LORD, call on his name;
    make known among the nations what he has
    done.
²Sing to him, sing praise to him;
    tell of all his wonderful acts.
³Glory in his holy name;
    let the hearts of those who seek the LORD
    rejoice.
⁴Look to the LORD and his strength;
    seek his face always.

⁵Remember the wonders he has done,
    his miracles, and the judgments he
    pronounced,
⁶O descendants of Abraham his servant,
    O sons of Jacob, his chosen ones.
⁷He is the LORD our God;
    his judgments are in all the earth.

⁸He remembers his covenant forever,
    the word he commanded, for a thousand
    generations,
⁹the covenant he made with Abraham,
    the oath he swore to Isaac.
¹⁰He confirmed it to Jacob as a decree,
    to Israel as an everlasting covenant:
¹¹"To you I will give the land of Canaan
    as the portion you will inherit."

¹²When they were but few in number,
    few indeed, and strangers in it,
¹³they wandered from nation to nation,
    from one kingdom to another.
¹⁴He allowed no one to oppress them;
    for their sake he rebuked kings:

---

³¹願耶和華的榮耀存到永遠；
    願耶和華喜悅自己所造的。
³²他看地，地便震動；
    他摸山，山就冒煙。

³³我要一生向耶和華唱詩，
    我還活的時候，要向我神歌頌！
³⁴願他以我的默念為甘甜，
    我要因耶和華歡喜！
³⁵願罪人從世上消滅，
    願惡人歸於無有。

我的心哪，要稱頌耶和華！
你們要讚美耶和華（註：原文作"哈利
路亞"。下同）！

第一百零五篇

¹你們要稱謝耶和華，
    求告他的名，
    在萬民中傳揚他的作為。
²要向他唱詩歌頌，
    談論他一切奇妙的作為。
³要以他的聖名誇耀，
    尋求耶和華的人，
    心中應當歡喜。
⁴要尋求耶和華與他的能力，
    時常尋求他的面。

⁵、⁶他僕人亞伯拉罕的後裔，
    他所揀選雅各的子孫哪，
    你們要記念他奇妙的作為
    和他的奇事，
    並他口中的判語。
⁷他是耶和華我們的神，
    全地都有他的判斷。

⁸他記念他的約，直到永遠，
    他所吩咐的話，
    直到千代，
⁹就是與亞伯拉罕所立的約，
    向以撒所起的誓。
¹⁰他又將這約向雅各定為律例，
    向以色列定為永遠的約，
¹¹說："我必將迦南地賜給你，
    作你產業的分。"

¹²當時他們人丁有限，數目稀少，
    並且在那地為寄居的。
¹³他們從這邦遊到那邦，
    從這國行到那國。
¹⁴他不容甚麼人欺負他們，
    為他們的緣故責備君王，

---

*a 35 Hebrew Hallelu Yah; in the Septuagint this line stands at
the beginning of Psalm 105.*

¹⁵說：「不可難為我受膏的人，
　　也不可惡待我的先知。」

¹⁶他命饑荒降在那地上，
　　將所倚靠的糧食全行斷絕，
¹⁷在他們以先打發一個人去——
　　約瑟被賣為奴僕。
¹⁸人用腳鐐傷他的腳，
　　他被鐵鏈捆拘。
¹⁹耶和華的話試煉他，
　　直等到他所說的應驗了。
²⁰王打發人把他解開，
　　就是治理眾民的，把他釋放，
²¹立他作王家的主，
　　掌管他一切所有的，
²²使他隨意捆綁他的臣宰，
　　將智慧教導他的長老。

²³以色列也到了埃及，
　　雅各在含地寄居。
²⁴耶和華使他的百姓生養眾多，
　　使他們比敵人強盛，
²⁵使敵人的心轉去恨他的百姓，
　　並用詭計待他的僕人。
²⁶他打發他的僕人摩西
　　和他所揀選的亞倫，
²⁷在敵人中間
　　顯他的神蹟，
　　在含地顯他的奇事。
²⁸他命黑暗，就有黑暗，
　　沒有違背他說的。
²⁹他叫埃及的水變為血，
　　叫他們的魚死了。
³⁰在他們的地上
　　以及王宮的內室，
　　青蛙多多滋生。
³¹他說一聲，蒼蠅就成羣而來，
　　並有虱子進入他們四境。
³²他給他們降下冰雹為雨，
　　在他們的地上降下火焰。
³³他也擊打他們的葡萄樹和無花果樹，
　　毀壞他們境內的樹木。
³⁴他說一聲，就有蝗蟲、螞蚱上來，
　　不計其數；
³⁵吃盡了他們地上各樣的
　　菜蔬和田地的出產。
³⁶他又擊殺
　　他們國內一切的長子，
　　就是他們強壯時頭生的。

³⁷他領自己的百姓
　　帶銀子、金子出來，
　　他支派中沒有一個軟弱的。
³⁸他們出來的時候，埃及人便歡喜，
　　原來埃及人懼怕他們。

¹⁵"Do not touch my anointed ones;
　　do my prophets no harm."

¹⁶He called down famine on the land
　　and destroyed all their supplies of food;
¹⁷and he sent a man before them—
　　Joseph, sold as a slave.
¹⁸They bruised his feet with shackles,
　　his neck was put in irons,
¹⁹till what he foretold came to pass,
　　till the word of the LORD proved him true.
²⁰The king sent and released him,
　　the ruler of peoples set him free.
²¹He made him master of his household,
　　ruler over all he possessed,
²²to instruct his princes as he pleased
　　and teach his elders wisdom.

²³Then Israel entered Egypt;
　　Jacob lived as an alien in the land of Ham.
²⁴The LORD made his people very fruitful;
　　he made them too numerous for their foes,
²⁵whose hearts he turned to hate his people,
　　to conspire against his servants.
²⁶He sent Moses his servant,
　　and Aaron, whom he had chosen.
²⁷They performed his miraculous signs among them,
　　his wonders in the land of Ham.
²⁸He sent darkness and made the land dark—
　　for had they not rebelled against his words?
²⁹He turned their waters into blood,
　　causing their fish to die.
³⁰Their land teemed with frogs,
　　which went up into the bedrooms of their rulers.
³¹He spoke, and there came swarms of flies,
　　and gnats throughout their country.
³²He turned their rain into hail,
　　with lightning throughout their land;
³³he struck down their vines and fig trees
　　and shattered the trees of their country.
³⁴He spoke, and the locusts came,
　　grasshoppers without number;
³⁵they ate up every green thing in their land,
　　ate up the produce of their soil.
³⁶Then he struck down all the firstborn in their land,
　　the firstfruits of all their manhood.

³⁷He brought out Israel, laden with silver and gold,
　　and from among their tribes no one faltered.
³⁸Egypt was glad when they left,
　　because dread of Israel had fallen on them.

³⁹He spread out a cloud as a covering,
and a fire to give light at night.
⁴⁰They asked, and he brought them quail
and satisfied them with the bread of heaven.
⁴¹He opened the rock, and water gushed out;
like a river it flowed in the desert.

⁴²For he remembered his holy promise
given to his servant Abraham.
⁴³He brought out his people with rejoicing,
his chosen ones with shouts of joy;
⁴⁴he gave them the lands of the nations,
and they fell heir to what others had toiled
for—
⁴⁵that they might keep his precepts
and observe his laws.

Praise the LORD.^a

Psalm 106

¹Praise the LORD.^b

Give thanks to the LORD, for he is good;
his love endures forever.
²Who can proclaim the mighty acts of the LORD
or fully declare his praise?
³Blessed are they who maintain justice,
who constantly do what is right.
⁴Remember me, O LORD, when you show favor
to your people,
come to my aid when you save them,
⁵that I may enjoy the prosperity of your chosen
ones,
that I may share in the joy of your nation
and join your inheritance in giving praise.

⁶We have sinned, even as our fathers did;
we have done wrong and acted wickedly.
⁷When our fathers were in Egypt,
they gave no thought to your miracles;
they did not remember your many kindnesses,
and they rebelled by the sea, the Red Sea.^c
⁸Yet he saved them for his name's sake,
to make his mighty power known.
⁹He rebuked the Red Sea, and it dried up;
he led them through the depths as through a
desert.
¹⁰He saved them from the hand of the foe;
from the hand of the enemy he redeemed
them.

³⁹他鋪張雲彩當遮蓋，
夜間使火光照。
⁴⁰他們一求，他就使鵪鶉飛來，
並用天上的糧食叫他們飽足。
⁴¹他打開磐石，水就湧出；
在乾旱之處，水流成河。

⁴²這都因他記念他的聖言
和他的僕人亞伯拉罕。
⁴³他帶領百姓歡樂而出，
帶領選民歡呼前往。
⁴⁴他將列國的地賜給他們——
他們便承受
眾民勞碌得來的，
⁴⁵好使他們遵他的律例，
守他的律法。

你們要讚美耶和華！

第一百零六篇

¹你們要讚美耶和華！

要稱謝耶和華，因他本為善，
他的慈愛永遠長存！
²誰能傳說耶和華的大能？
誰能表明他一切的美德？
³凡遵守公平、常行公義的，
這人便為有福！
⁴耶和華啊，你用恩惠待你的百姓，
求你也用這恩惠記念我，
開你的救恩眷顧我，
⁵使我見你選民的福，
樂你國民的樂，
與你的產業一同誇耀。

⁶我們與我們的祖宗一同犯罪，
我們作了孽，行了惡。
⁷我們的祖宗在埃及
不明白你的奇事，
不記念你豐盛的慈愛，
反倒在紅海行了悖逆。
⁸然而他因自己的名拯救他們，
為要彰顯他的大能，
⁹並且斥責紅海，海便乾了，
他帶領他們經過深處，
如同經過曠野。
¹⁰他拯救他們脫離恨他們人的手，
從仇敵手中救贖他們。

a 45 Hebrew Hallelu Yah   b 1 Hebrew Hallelu Yah; also in
verse 48   c 7 Hebrew Yam Suph; that is, Sea of Reeds; also in
verses 9 and 22

11水淹沒他們的敵人，
　　沒有一個存留。
12那時他們才信了他的話，
　　歌唱讚美他。

13等不多時，他們就忘了他的作為，
　　不仰望他的指教，
14反倒在曠野大起慾心，
　　在荒地試探神。
15他將他們所求的賜給他們，
　　卻使他們的心靈軟弱。

16他們又在營中嫉妒摩西
　　和耶和華的聖者亞倫。

17地裂開吞下大坍，
　　掩蓋亞比蘭一黨的人。
18有火在他們的黨中發起，
　　有火焰燒燬了惡人。

19他們在何烈山造了牛犢，
　　叩拜鑄成的像。
20如此將他們榮耀的主
　　換為吃草之牛的像。
21忘了神，他們的救主，
　　他曾在埃及行大事，
22在含地行奇事，
　　在紅海行可畏的事。
23所以他說要滅絕他們，
　　若非有他所揀選的摩西站在當中
　　　（註：原文作 "破口"），
　　使他的忿怒轉消，
　　恐怕他就滅絕他們。
24他們又藐視那美地，
　　不信他的話。
25在自己帳棚內發怨言，
　　不聽耶和華的聲音。
26所以他對他們起誓，
　　必叫他們倒在曠野，
27叫他們的後裔倒在列國之中，
　　分散在各地。

28他們又與巴力毗珥連合，
　　且吃了祭死神（註：或作 "人"）的物。
29他們這樣行，
　　惹耶和華發怒，
　　便有瘟疫流行在他們中間。
30那時非尼哈站起，刑罰惡人，
　　瘟疫這才止息。
31那就算為他的義，
　　世世代代直到永遠。

32他們在米利巴水
　　又叫耶和華發怒，
　　甚至摩西也受了虧損，

11The waters covered their adversaries;
　　not one of them survived.
12Then they believed his promises
　　and sang his praise.

13But they soon forgot what he had done
　　and did not wait for his counsel.
14In the desert they gave in to their craving;
　　in the wasteland they put God to the test.
15So he gave them what they asked for,
　　but sent a wasting disease upon them.

16In the camp they grew envious of Moses
　　and of Aaron, who was consecrated to the
　　　LORD.
17The earth opened up and swallowed Dathan;
　　it buried the company of Abiram.
18Fire blazed among their followers;
　　a flame consumed the wicked.

19At Horeb they made a calf
　　and worshiped an idol cast from metal.
20They exchanged their Glory
　　for an image of a bull, which eats grass.
21They forgot the God who saved them,
　　who had done great things in Egypt,
22miracles in the land of Ham
　　and awesome deeds by the Red Sea.
23So he said he would destroy them—
　　had not Moses, his chosen one,
　　stood in the breach before him
　　to keep his wrath from destroying them.

24Then they despised the pleasant land;
　　they did not believe his promise.
25They grumbled in their tents
　　and did not obey the LORD.
26So he swore to them with uplifted hand
　　that he would make them fall in the desert,
27make their descendants fall among the nations
　　and scatter them throughout the lands.

28They yoked themselves to the Baal of Peor
　　and ate sacrifices offered to lifeless gods;
29they provoked the LORD to anger by their
　　　wicked deeds,
　　and a plague broke out among them.
30But Phinehas stood up and intervened,
　　and the plague was checked.
31This was credited to him as righteousness
　　for endless generations to come.

32By the waters of Meribah they angered the
　　　LORD,
　　and trouble came to Moses because of them;

²⁰He sent forth his word and healed them;
   he rescued them from the grave.
²¹Let them give thanks to the LORD for his
   unfailing love
   and his wonderful deeds for men.
²²Let them sacrifice thank offerings
   and tell of his works with songs of joy.

²³Others went out on the sea in ships;
   they were merchants on the mighty waters.
²⁴They saw the works of the LORD,
   his wonderful deeds in the deep.
²⁵For he spoke and stirred up a tempest
   that lifted high the waves.
²⁶They mounted up to the heavens and went
   down to the depths;
   in their peril their courage melted away.
²⁷They reeled and staggered like drunken men;
   they were at their wits' end.
²⁸Then they cried out to the LORD in their trouble,
   and he brought them out of their distress.
²⁹He stilled the storm to a whisper;
   the waves of the sea were hushed.
³⁰They were glad when it grew calm,
   and he guided them to their desired haven.
³¹Let them give thanks to the LORD for his
   unfailing love
   and his wonderful deeds for men.
³²Let them exalt him in the assembly of the people
   and praise him in the council of the elders.

³³He turned rivers into a desert,
   flowing springs into thirsty ground,
³⁴and fruitful land into a salt waste,
   because of the wickedness of those who
   lived there.
³⁵He turned the desert into pools of water
   and the parched ground into flowing springs;
³⁶there he brought the hungry to live,
   and they founded a city where they could
   settle.
³⁷They sowed fields and planted vineyards
   that yielded a fruitful harvest;
³⁸he blessed them, and their numbers greatly
   increased,
   and he did not let their herds diminish.

³⁹Then their numbers decreased, and they were
   humbled
   by oppression, calamity and sorrow;
⁴⁰he who pours contempt on nobles
   made them wander in a trackless waste.
⁴¹But he lifted the needy out of their affliction
   and increased their families like flocks.

²⁰他發命醫治他們，
   救他們脫離死亡。
²¹但願人因耶和華的慈愛
   和他向人所行的奇事
   都稱讚他。
²²願他們以感謝為祭獻給他，
   歡呼述說他的作為。

²³在海上坐船，
   在大水中經理事務的，
²⁴他們看見耶和華的作為，
   並他在深水中的奇事。
²⁵因他一吩咐，狂風就起來，
   海中的波浪也揚起。
²⁶他們上到天空，下到海底，
   他們的心因患難便消化。
²⁷他們搖搖幌幌，東倒西歪，
   好像醉酒的人；
   他們的智慧無法可施。
²⁸於是，他們在苦難中哀求耶和華，
   他從他們的禍患中領出他們來。
²⁹他使狂風止息，
   波浪就平靜。
³⁰風息浪靜，他們便歡喜，
   他就引他們到所願去的海口。
³¹但願人因耶和華的慈愛
   和他向人所行的奇事
   都稱讚他。
³²願他們在民的會中尊崇他，
   在長老的位上讚美他。

³³他使江河變為曠野，
   叫水泉變為乾渴之地，
³⁴使肥地變為鹼地，
   這都因其間居民的罪惡。
³⁵他使曠野變為水潭，
   叫旱地變為水泉。
³⁶他使飢餓的人
   住在那裏，
   好建造可住的城邑，
³⁷又種田地，栽葡萄園，
   得享所出的土產。
³⁸他又賜福給他們，
   叫他們生養眾多，
   也不叫他們的牲畜減少。

³⁹他們又因暴虐、
   患難、愁苦，
   就減少且卑下。
⁴⁰他使君王蒙羞被辱，
   使他們在荒廢無路之地漂流。
⁴¹他卻將窮乏人安置在高處，脫離苦難，
   使他的家屬多如羊羣。

⁴²正直人看見就歡喜，
　罪孽之輩必塞口無言。

⁴³凡有智慧的，必在這些事上留心，
　也必思想耶和華的慈愛。

第一百零八篇

大衛的詩歌。

¹神啊，我心堅定！
　我口（註：原文作"榮耀"）要唱詩歌頌！
²琴瑟啊，你們當醒起！
　我自己要極早醒起。
³耶和華啊，我要在萬民中稱謝你，
　在列邦中歌頌你！
⁴因為你的慈愛大過諸天；
　你的誠實達到穹蒼。
⁵神啊，願你崇高過於諸天！
　願你的榮耀高過全地！

⁶求你應允我們，用右手拯救我們，
　好叫你所親愛的人得救。
⁷神已經指著他的聖潔說（註："說"或
　作"應許我"）："我要歡樂，
　我要分開示劍，丈量疏割谷。
⁸基列是我的，瑪拿西是我的，
　以法蓮是護衛我頭的，
　猶大是我的杖；
⁹摩押是我的沐浴盆，
　我要向以東拋鞋，
　我必因勝非利士呼喊。"

¹⁰誰能領我進堅固城？
　誰能引我到以東地？
¹¹神啊，你不是丟棄了我們嗎？
　神啊，你不和我們的軍兵同去嗎？
¹²求你幫助我們攻擊敵人，
　因為人的幫助是枉然的。
¹³我們倚靠神，才得施展大能，
　因為踐踏我們敵人的就是他。

第一百零九篇

大衛的詩，交與伶長。

¹我所讚美的神啊，
　求你不要閉口不言。
²因為惡人的嘴和詭詐人的口，
　已經張開攻擊我，
　他們用撒謊的舌頭
　對我說話。
³他們圍繞我，說怨恨的話，
　又無故地攻打我。

⁴²The upright see and rejoice,
　but all the wicked shut their mouths.

⁴³Whoever is wise, let him heed these things
　and consider the great love of the LORD.

Psalm 108

A song. A psalm of David.

¹My heart is steadfast, O God;
　I will sing and make music with all my soul.
²Awake, harp and lyre!
　I will awaken the dawn.
³I will praise you, O LORD, among the nations;
　I will sing of you among the peoples.
⁴For great is your love, higher than the heavens;
　your faithfulness reaches to the skies.
⁵Be exalted, O God, above the heavens,
　and let your glory be over all the earth.

⁶Save us and help us with your right hand,
　that those you love may be delivered.
⁷God has spoken from his sanctuary:
　"In triumph I will parcel out Shechem
　and measure off the Valley of Succoth.
⁸Gilead is mine, Manasseh is mine;
　Ephraim is my helmet,
　Judah my scepter.
⁹Moab is my washbasin,
　upon Edom I toss my sandal;
　over Philistia I shout in triumph."

¹⁰Who will bring me to the fortified city?
　Who will lead me to Edom?
¹¹Is it not you, O God, you who have rejected us
　and no longer go out with our armies?
¹²Give us aid against the enemy,
　for the help of man is worthless.
¹³With God we will gain the victory,
　and he will trample down our enemies.

Psalm 109

For the director of music. Of David. A psalm.

¹O God, whom I praise,
　do not remain silent,
²for wicked and deceitful men
　have opened their mouths against me;
　they have spoken against me with lying
　tongues.
³With words of hatred they surround me;
　they attack me without cause.

⁴In return for my friendship they accuse me,
    but I am a man of prayer.
⁵They repay me evil for good,
    and hatred for my friendship.

⁶Appoint^a an evil man^b to oppose him;
    let an accuser^c stand at his right hand.
⁷When he is tried, let him be found guilty,
    and may his prayers condemn him.
⁸May his days be few;
    may another take his place of leadership.
⁹May his children be fatherless
    and his wife a widow.
¹⁰May his children be wandering beggars;
    may they be driven^d from their ruined homes.
¹¹May a creditor seize all he has;
    may strangers plunder the fruits of his labor.
¹²May no one extend kindness to him
    or take pity on his fatherless children.
¹³May his descendants be cut off,
    their names blotted out from the next
        generation.
¹⁴May the iniquity of his fathers be remembered
        before the LORD;
    may the sin of his mother never be blotted
        out.
¹⁵May their sins always remain before the LORD,
    that he may cut off the memory of them from
        the earth.

¹⁶For he never thought of doing a kindness,
    but hounded to death the poor
    and the needy and the brokenhearted.
¹⁷He loved to pronounce a curse—
    may it^e come on him;
    he found no pleasure in blessing—
    may it be^f far from him.
¹⁸He wore cursing as his garment;
    it entered into his body like water,
    into his bones like oil.
¹⁹May it be like a cloak wrapped about him,
    like a belt tied forever around him.
²⁰May this be the LORD's payment to my
        accusers,
    to those who speak evil of me.

²¹But you, O Sovereign LORD,
    deal well with me for your name's sake;
    out of the goodness of your love, deliver me.
²²For I am poor and needy,
    and my heart is wounded within me.

⁴他們與我為敵以報我愛，
    但我專心祈禱。
⁵他們向我以惡報善，
    以恨報愛。

⁶願你派一個惡人轄制他，
    派一個對頭站在他右邊。
⁷他受審判的時候，願他出來擔當罪名，
    願他的祈禱反成為罪。
⁸願他的年日短少，
    願別人得他的職分。
⁹願他的兒女為孤兒，
    他的妻子為寡婦。
¹⁰願他的兒女漂流討飯，
    從他們荒涼之處出來求食。
¹¹願強暴的債主牢籠他一切所有的，
    願外人搶他勞碌得來的。
¹²願無人向他延綿施恩，
    願無人可憐他的孤兒。
¹³願他的後人斷絕，
    名字被塗抹，
    不傳於下代。
¹⁴願他祖宗的罪孽
    被耶和華記念，
    願他母親的罪過
    不被塗抹。
¹⁵願這些罪常在耶和華面前，
    使他的名號
        斷絕於世！

¹⁶因為他不想施恩，
    卻逼迫困苦窮乏的和傷心的人，
    要把他們治死。
¹⁷他愛咒罵，
    咒罵就臨到他；
    他不喜愛福樂，
    福樂就與他遠離。
¹⁸他拿咒罵當衣服穿上，
    這咒罵就如水進他裏面，
    像油入他的骨頭。
¹⁹願這咒罵當他遮身的衣服，
    當他常束的腰帶。
²⁰這就是我對頭
    和用惡言議論我的人，
    從耶和華那裏所受的報應。

²¹主耶和華啊，求你為你的名恩待我，
    因你的慈愛美好，
    求你搭救我！
²²因為我困苦窮乏，
    內心受傷。

a 6 Or {They say:} "Appoint (with quotation marks at the end of
verse 19)   *b 6 Or the Evil One   c 6 Or let Satan*
d 10 Septuagint; Hebrew sought   e 17 Or curse, / and it has
f 17 Or blessing, / and it is

²³我如日影漸漸偏斜而去；
　　我如蝗蟲被抖出來。
²⁴我因禁食，膝骨軟弱；
　　我身上的肉也漸漸瘦了。
²⁵我受他們的羞辱，
　　他們看見我便搖頭。

²⁶耶和華我的神啊，求你幫助我，
　　照你的慈愛拯救我。
²⁷使他們知道這是你的手，
　　是你耶和華所行的事。
²⁸任憑他們咒罵，惟願你賜福；
　　他們幾時起來就必蒙羞，
　　你的僕人卻要歡喜。
²⁹願我的對頭披戴羞辱，
　　願他們以自己的羞愧為外袍遮身。

³⁰我要用口極力稱讚耶和華，
　　我要在眾人中間讚美他！
³¹因為他必站在
　　窮乏人的右邊，
　　要救他脫離審判他靈魂的人。

第一百一十篇

大衛的詩。

¹耶和華對我主說：
　　"你坐在我的右邊，
　　等我使你仇敵
　　作你的腳凳。"

²耶和華必使你從錫安
　　伸出能力的杖來，
　　你要在你仇敵中掌權。
³當你掌權的日子（註：或作"行軍的日子"），
　　你的民要以聖潔的妝飾為衣（註：
　　　或作"以聖潔為妝飾"），
　　甘心犧牲自己；
　　你的民多如清晨的甘露（註：或作"你
　　　少年時光耀如清晨的甘露"）。
⁴耶和華起了誓，
　　決不後悔，說：
　　"你是照着麥基洗德的等次
　　永遠為祭司。"

⁵在你右邊的主，
　　當他發怒的日子，必打傷列王。
⁶他要在列邦中刑罰惡人，
　　屍首就遍滿各處，
　　他要在許多國中打破仇敵的頭。
⁷他要喝路旁的河水，
　　因此必抬起頭來。

²³I fade away like an evening shadow;
　I am shaken off like a locust.
²⁴My knees give way from fasting;
　my body is thin and gaunt.
²⁵I am an object of scorn to my accusers;
　when they see me, they shake their heads.

²⁶Help me, O LORD my God;
　save me in accordance with your love.
²⁷Let them know that it is your hand,
　that you, O LORD, have done it.
²⁸They may curse, but you will bless;
　when they attack they will be put to shame,
　but your servant will rejoice.
²⁹My accusers will be clothed with disgrace
　and wrapped in shame as in a cloak.

³⁰With my mouth I will greatly extol the LORD;
　in the great throng I will praise him.
³¹For he stands at the right hand of the needy
　one,
　to save his life from those who condemn him.

Psalm 110

Of David. A psalm.

¹The LORD says to my Lord:
　"Sit at my right hand
　until I make your enemies
　a footstool for your feet."

²The LORD will extend your mighty scepter
　from Zion;
　you will rule in the midst of your enemies.
³Your troops will be willing
　on your day of battle.
　Arrayed in holy majesty,
　from the womb of the dawn
　you will receive the dew of your youth.ᵃ

⁴The LORD has sworn
　and will not change his mind:
　"You are a priest forever,
　in the order of Melchizedek."

⁵The Lord is at your right hand;
　he will crush kings on the day of his wrath.
⁶He will judge the nations, heaping up the dead
　and crushing the rulers of the whole earth.
⁷He will drink from a brook beside the wayᵇ;
　therefore he will lift up his head.

*a 3 Or / your young men will come to you like the dew   b 7 Or /
The One who grants succession will set him in authority*

Psalm 111[a]

¹Praise the LORD.[b]

I will extol the LORD with all my heart
  in the council of the upright and in the
    assembly.

²Great are the works of the LORD;
  they are pondered by all who delight in
    them.
³Glorious and majestic are his deeds,
  and his righteousness endures forever.
⁴He has caused his wonders to be remembered;
  the LORD is gracious and compassionate.
⁵He provides food for those who fear him;
  he remembers his covenant forever.
⁶He has shown his people the power of his
    works,
  giving them the lands of other nations.
⁷The works of his hands are faithful and just;
  all his precepts are trustworthy.
⁸They are steadfast for ever and ever,
  done in faithfulness and uprightness.
⁹He provided redemption for his people;
  he ordained his covenant forever—
  holy and awesome is his name.

¹⁰The fear of the LORD is the beginning of wisdom;
  all who follow his precepts have good
    understanding.
  To him belongs eternal praise.

Psalm 112[a]

¹Praise the LORD.[b]

Blessed is the man who fears the LORD,
  who finds great delight in his commands.

²His children will be mighty in the land;
  the generation of the upright will be blessed.
³Wealth and riches are in his house,
  and his righteousness endures forever.
⁴Even in darkness light dawns for the upright,
  for the gracious and compassionate and
    righteous man.[c]
⁵Good will come to him who is generous and
    lends freely,
  who conducts his affairs with justice.

*a This psalm is an acrostic poem, the lines of which begin with
the successive letters of the Hebrew alphabet.   b 1 Hebrew
Hallelu Yah   c 4 Or / for (the LORD) is gracious and
compassionate and righteous*

第一百一十一篇

¹你們要讚美耶和華！

我要在正直人的大會中，
  並公會中，
    一心稱謝耶和華。

²耶和華的作為本為大，
  凡喜愛的都必考察。

³他所行的是尊榮和威嚴；
  他的公義存到永遠。
⁴他行了奇事，使人記念；
  耶和華有恩惠，有憐憫。
⁵他賜糧食給敬畏他的人；
  他必永遠記念他的約。
⁶他向百姓顯出大能的作為，
  把外邦的地
    賜給他們為業。
⁷他手所行的，是誠實公平，
  他的訓詞都是確實的。
⁸是永永遠遠堅定的，
  是按誠實正直設立的。
⁹他向百姓施行救贖，
  命定他的約，直到永遠；
  他的名聖而可畏。

¹⁰敬畏耶和華是智慧的開端；
  凡遵行他命令的是聰明人。
  耶和華是永遠當讚美的！

第一百一十二篇

¹你們要讚美耶和華！

敬畏耶和華，甚喜愛他命令的，
  這人便為有福！

²他的後裔在世必強盛，
  正直人的代代必要蒙福。
³他家中有貨物，有錢財；
  他的公義存到永遠！
⁴正直人在黑暗中，有光向他發現。
  他有恩惠，有憐憫，
  有公義。
⁵施恩與人、借貸與人的，
  這人事情順利；
  他被審判的時候，
    要訴明自己的冤。

⁶他永不動搖，
　　義人被記念，直到永遠。
⁷他必不怕兇惡的信息；
　　他心堅定，倚靠耶和華。
⁸他心確定，總不懼怕，
　　直到他看見敵人遭報。
⁹他施捨錢財，賙濟貧窮；
　　他的仁義存到永遠。
　　他的角必被高舉，大有榮耀。

¹⁰惡人看見便惱恨，
　　必咬牙而消化；
　　惡人的心願要歸滅絕。

第一百一十三篇

¹你們要讚美耶和華！

　耶和華的僕人哪，
　　你們要讚美，讚美耶和華的名！
²耶和華的名是應當稱頌的，
　　從今時直到永遠！
³從日出之地
　　到日落之處，
　　耶和華的名是應當讚美的！

⁴耶和華超乎萬民之上，
　　他的榮耀高過諸天！
⁵誰像耶和華我們的神呢？
　　他坐在至高之處，
⁶自己謙卑，
　　觀看天上地下的事。

⁷他從灰塵裏抬舉貧寒人，
　　從糞堆中提拔窮乏人，
⁸使他們與王子同坐，
　　就是與本國的王子同坐；
⁹他使不能生育的婦人安居家中，
　　為多子的樂母。

　你們要讚美耶和華！

第一百一十四篇

¹以色列出了埃及，
　雅各家
　　離開說異言之民。
²那時猶大為主的聖所，
　　以色列為他所治理的國度。

³滄海看見就奔逃，
　　約旦河也倒流。

⁶Surely he will never be shaken;
　　a righteous man will be remembered forever.
⁷He will have no fear of bad news;
　　his heart is steadfast, trusting in the LORD.
⁸His heart is secure, he will have no fear;
　　in the end he will look in triumph on his foes.
⁹He has scattered abroad his gifts to the poor,
　　his righteousness endures forever;
　　his horn*a* will be lifted high in honor.

¹⁰The wicked man will see and be vexed,
　　he will gnash his teeth and waste away;
　　the longings of the wicked will come to nothing.

Psalm 113

¹Praise the LORD.*b*

　Praise, O servants of the LORD,
　　praise the name of the LORD.
²Let the name of the LORD be praised,
　　both now and forevermore.
³From the rising of the sun to the place where it
　　sets,
　　the name of the LORD is to be praised.

⁴The LORD is exalted over all the nations,
　　his glory above the heavens.
⁵Who is like the LORD our God,
　　the One who sits enthroned on high,
⁶who stoops down to look
　　on the heavens and the earth?

⁷He raises the poor from the dust
　　and lifts the needy from the ash heap;
⁸he seats them with princes,
　　with the princes of their people.
⁹He settles the barren woman in her home
　　as a happy mother of children.

　Praise the LORD.

Psalm 114

¹When Israel came out of Egypt,
　　the house of Jacob from a people of foreign
　　tongue,
²Judah became God's sanctuary,
　　Israel his dominion.

³The sea looked and fled,
　　the Jordan turned back;

---

a 9 Horn here symbolizes dignity.　*b 1* Hebrew *Hallelu Yah*;
also in verse 9

⁴the mountains skipped like rams,
    the hills like lambs.

⁵Why was it, O sea, that you fled,
    O Jordan, that you turned back,
⁶you mountains, that you skipped like rams,
    you hills, like lambs?

⁷Tremble, O earth, at the presence of the Lord,
    at the presence of the God of Jacob,
⁸who turned the rock into a pool,
    the hard rock into springs of water.

Psalm 115

¹Not to us, O LORD, not to us
    but to your name be the glory,
    because of your love and faithfulness.

²Why do the nations say,
    "Where is their God?"
³Our God is in heaven;
    he does whatever pleases him.
⁴But their idols are silver and gold,
    made by the hands of men.
⁵They have mouths, but cannot speak,
    eyes, but they cannot see;
⁶they have ears, but cannot hear,
    noses, but they cannot smell;
⁷they have hands, but cannot feel,
    feet, but they cannot walk;
    nor can they utter a sound with their throats.
⁸Those who make them will be like them,
    and so will all who trust in them.

⁹O house of Israel, trust in the LORD—
    he is their help and shield.
¹⁰O house of Aaron, trust in the LORD—
    he is their help and shield.
¹¹You who fear him, trust in the LORD—
    he is their help and shield.

¹²The LORD remembers us and will bless us:
    He will bless the house of Israel,
    he will bless the house of Aaron,
¹³he will bless those who fear the LORD—
    small and great alike.

¹⁴May the LORD make you increase,
    both you and your children.
¹⁵May you be blessed by the LORD,
    the Maker of heaven and earth.

¹⁶The highest heavens belong to the LORD,
    but the earth he has given to man.

⁴大山踊躍如公羊，
    小山跳舞如羊羔。

⁵滄海啊，你為何奔逃？
    約旦哪，你為何倒流？
⁶大山哪，你為何踊躍如公羊？
    小山哪，你為何跳舞如羊羔？

⁷大地啊，你見主的面，
    就是雅各神的面，便要震動。
⁸他叫磐石變為水池，
    叫堅石變為泉源。

第一百一十五篇

¹耶和華啊，榮耀不要歸與我們，
    不要歸與我們，要因你的慈愛
    和誠實歸在你的名下！

²為何容外邦人說：
    "他們的神在哪裏呢？"
³然而我們的神在天上，
    都隨自己的意旨行事。
⁴他們的偶像是金的銀的，
    是人手所造的。
⁵有口卻不能言，
    有眼卻不能看；
⁶有耳卻不能聽，
    有鼻卻不能聞；
⁷有手卻不能摸，
    有腳卻不能走；
    有喉嚨也不能出聲。
⁸造他的要和他一樣，
    凡靠他的也要如此。

⁹以色列啊，你要倚靠耶和華！
    他是你的幫助和你的盾牌。
¹⁰亞倫家啊，你們要倚靠耶和華！
    他是你們的幫助和你們的盾牌。
¹¹你們敬畏耶和華的，要倚靠耶和華！
    他是你們的幫助和你們的盾牌。

¹²耶和華向來眷念我們，
    他還要賜福給我們：
    要賜福給以色列的家，
    賜福給亞倫的家。
¹³凡敬畏耶和華的，
    無論大小，主必賜福給他。

¹⁴願耶和華叫你們
    和你們的子孫日見加增。
¹⁵你們蒙了
    造天地之耶和華的福。

¹⁶天，是耶和華的天；
    地，他卻給了世人。

¹⁷死人不能讚美耶和華，
　　下到寂靜中的也都不能。
¹⁸但我們要稱頌耶和華，
　　從今時直到永遠！

你們要讚美耶和華！

第一百一十六篇

¹我愛耶和華，
　　因為他聽了我的聲音和我的懇求。
²他既向我側耳，
　　我一生要求告他。

³死亡的繩索纏繞我，
　　陰間的痛苦抓住我，
　　我遭遇患難愁苦。
⁴那時，我便求告耶和華的名，說：
　　"耶和華啊，求你救我的靈魂！"

⁵耶和華有恩惠，有公義，
　　我們的神以憐憫為懷。
⁶耶和華保護愚人，
　　我落到卑微的地步，他救了我。

⁷我的心哪，你要仍歸安樂，
　　因為耶和華用厚恩待你。

⁸主啊，
　　你救我的命免了死亡，
　救我的眼免了流淚，
　救我的腳免了跌倒。
⁹我要在耶和華面前
　　行活人之路。
¹⁰我因信，所以如此說話：
　　"我受了極大的困苦。"
¹¹我曾急促地說：
　　"人都是說謊的！"

¹²我拿甚麼報答耶和華
　　向我所賜的一切厚恩？
¹³我要舉起救恩的杯，
　　稱揚耶和華的名！
¹⁴我要在他眾民面前
　　向耶和華還我的願。

¹⁵在耶和華眼中，
　　看聖民之死極為寶貴。
¹⁶耶和華啊，我真是你的僕人；
　　我是你的僕人，
　　是你婢女的兒子。
　　你已經解開我的綁索。

---

¹⁷It is not the dead who praise the L<small>ORD</small>,
　　those who go down to silence;
¹⁸it is we who extol the L<small>ORD</small>,
　　both now and forevermore.

Praise the L<small>ORD</small>.^{*a*}

Psalm 116

¹I love the L<small>ORD</small>, for he heard my voice;
　　he heard my cry for mercy.
²Because he turned his ear to me,
　　I will call on him as long as I live.

³The cords of death entangled me,
　　the anguish of the grave^{*b*} came upon me;
　　I was overcome by trouble and sorrow.
⁴Then I called on the name of the L<small>ORD</small>:
　　"O L<small>ORD</small>, save me!"

⁵The L<small>ORD</small> is gracious and righteous;
　　our God is full of compassion.
⁶The L<small>ORD</small> protects the simplehearted;
　　when I was in great need, he saved me.

⁷Be at rest once more, O my soul,
　　for the L<small>ORD</small> has been good to you.

⁸For you, O L<small>ORD</small>, have delivered my soul from
　　death,
　　my eyes from tears,
　　my feet from stumbling,
⁹that I may walk before the L<small>ORD</small>
　　in the land of the living.
¹⁰I believed; therefore^{*c*} I said,
　　"I am greatly afflicted."
¹¹And in my dismay I said,
　　"All men are liars."

¹²How can I repay the L<small>ORD</small>
　　for all his goodness to me?
¹³I will lift up the cup of salvation
　　and call on the name of the L<small>ORD</small>.
¹⁴I will fulfill my vows to the L<small>ORD</small>
　　in the presence of all his people.

¹⁵Precious in the sight of the L<small>ORD</small>
　　is the death of his saints.
¹⁶O L<small>ORD</small>, truly I am your servant;
　　I am your servant, the son of your
　　　maidservant^{*d*};
　　you have freed me from my chains.

---

a 18 Hebrew *Hallelu Yah*　　*b* 3 Hebrew *Sheol*　　*c* 10 Or *believed
even when*　　*d* 16 Or *servant, your faithful son*

¹⁷I will sacrifice a thank offering to you
and call on the name of the LORD.
¹⁸I will fulfill my vows to the LORD
in the presence of all his people,
¹⁹in the courts of the house of the LORD—
in your midst, O Jerusalem.

Praise the LORD.^a

Psalm 117

¹Praise the LORD, all you nations;
extol him, all you peoples.
²For great is his love toward us,
and the faithfulness of the LORD endures
forever.

Praise the LORD.^a

Psalm 118

¹Give thanks to the LORD, for he is good;
his love endures forever.

²Let Israel say:
"His love endures forever."
³Let the house of Aaron say:
"His love endures forever."
⁴Let those who fear the LORD say:
"His love endures forever."

⁵In my anguish I cried to the LORD,
and he answered by setting me free.
⁶The LORD is with me; I will not be afraid.
What can man do to me?
⁷The LORD is with me; he is my helper.
I will look in triumph on my enemies.

⁸It is better to take refuge in the LORD
than to trust in man.
⁹It is better to take refuge in the LORD
than to trust in princes.

¹⁰All the nations surrounded me,
but in the name of the LORD I cut them off.
¹¹They surrounded me on every side,
but in the name of the LORD I cut them off.
¹²They swarmed around me like bees,
but they died out as quickly as burning
thorns;
in the name of the LORD I cut them off.

¹³I was pushed back and about to fall,
but the LORD helped me.

---

¹⁷我要以感謝為祭獻給你，
又要求告耶和華的名。
¹⁸、¹⁹我要在他眾民面前，
在耶和華殿的院內，
在耶路撒冷當中，
向耶和華還我的願。

你們要讚美耶和華！

第一百一十七篇

¹萬國啊，你們都當讚美耶和華！
萬民哪，你們都當頌讚他！
²因為他向我們大施慈愛，
耶和華的誠實存到永遠。

你們要讚美耶和華！

第一百一十八篇

¹你們要稱謝耶和華，因他本為善，
他的慈愛永遠長存！

²願以色列說：
"他的慈愛永遠長存！"
³願亞倫的家說：
"他的慈愛永遠長存！"
⁴願敬畏耶和華的說：
"他的慈愛永遠長存！"

⁵我在急難中求告耶和華，
他就應允我，把我安置在寬闊之地。
⁶有耶和華幫助我，我必不懼怕，
人能把我怎麼樣呢？
⁷在那幫助我的人中，有耶和華幫助我，
所以我要看見那恨我的人遭報。

⁸投靠耶和華，
強似倚賴人；
⁹投靠耶和華，
強似倚賴王子。

¹⁰萬民圍繞我，
我靠耶和華的名，必剿滅他們。
¹¹他們環繞我，圍困我，
我靠耶和華的名，必剿滅他們。
¹²他們如同蜂子圍繞我，
好像燒荊棘的火，必被熄滅；
我靠耶和華的名，必剿滅他們。

¹³你推我，要叫我跌倒，
但耶和華幫助了我。

---

a 19,2 Hebrew Hallelu Yah

14耶和華是我的力量，是我的詩歌，
　　他也成了我的拯救。

15在義人的帳棚裏，
　　有歡呼拯救的聲音：
　　"耶和華的右手
　　　施展大能！
16耶和華的右手高舉，
　　耶和華的右手施展大能！"

17我必不至於死，仍要存活，
　　並要傳揚耶和華的作為。
18耶和華雖嚴嚴地懲治我，
　　卻未曾將我交於死亡。

19給我敞開義門，
　　我要進去稱謝耶和華！
20這是耶和華的門，
　　義人要進去。
21我要稱謝你，因為你已經應允我，
　　又成了我的拯救。

22匠人所棄的石頭，
　　已成了房角的頭塊石頭。
23這是耶和華所做的，
　　在我們眼中看為希奇。
24這是耶和華所定的日子，
　　我們在其中要高興歡喜。

25耶和華啊，求你拯救！
　　耶和華啊，求你使我們亨通！
26奉耶和華名來的是應當稱頌的！
　　我們從耶和華的殿中
　　　為你們祝福。
27耶和華是神！
　　他光照了我們。
　　理當用繩索把祭牲拴住，
　　牽到壇角那裏。

28你是我的神，我要稱謝你！
　　你是我的神，我要尊崇你！

29你們要稱謝耶和華，因他本為善，
　　他的慈愛永遠長存！

第一百一十九篇

1行為完全、遵行耶和華律法的，
　　這人便為有福！

14The LORD is my strength and my song;
　　he has become my salvation.

15Shouts of joy and victory
　　resound in the tents of the righteous:
　　"The LORD's right hand has done mighty
　　　things!
16　The LORD's right hand is lifted high;
　　the LORD's right hand has done mighty things!"

17I will not die but live,
　　and will proclaim what the LORD has done.
18The LORD has chastened me severely,
　　but he has not given me over to death.

19Open for me the gates of righteousness;
　　I will enter and give thanks to the LORD.
20This is the gate of the LORD
　　through which the righteous may enter.
21I will give you thanks, for you answered me;
　　you have become my salvation.

22The stone the builders rejected
　　has become the capstone;
23the LORD has done this,
　　and it is marvelous in our eyes.
24This is the day the LORD has made;
　　let us rejoice and be glad in it.

25O LORD, save us;
　　O LORD, grant us success.
26Blessed is he who comes in the name of the
　　LORD.
　　From the house of the LORD we bless you.ᵃ
27The LORD is God,
　　and he has made his light shine upon us.
　　With boughs in hand, join in the festal procession
　　upᵇ to the horns of the altar.

28You are my God, and I will give you thanks;
　　you are my God, and I will exalt you.

29Give thanks to the LORD, for he is good;
　　his love endures forever.

Psalm 119ᶜ

Aleph

1Blessed are they whose ways are blameless,
　　who walk according to the law of the LORD.

a 26 The Hebrew is plural.　b 27 Or *Bind the festal sacrifice
with ropes / and take it*　c This psalm is an acrostic poem; the
verses of each stanza begin with the same letter of the Hebrew
alphabet.

2Blessed are they who keep his statutes
　and seek him with all their heart.
3They do nothing wrong;
　they walk in his ways.
4You have laid down precepts
　that are to be fully obeyed.
5Oh, that my ways were steadfast
　in obeying your decrees!
6Then I would not be put to shame
　when I consider all your commands.
7I will praise you with an upright heart
　as I learn your righteous laws.
8I will obey your decrees;
　do not utterly forsake me.

Beth

9How can a young man keep his way pure?
　By living according to your word.
10I seek you with all my heart;
　do not let me stray from your commands.
11I have hidden your word in my heart
　that I might not sin against you.
12Praise be to you, O LORD;
　teach me your decrees.
13With my lips I recount
　all the laws that come from your mouth.
14I rejoice in following your statutes
　as one rejoices in great riches.
15I meditate on your precepts
　and consider your ways.
16I delight in your decrees;
　I will not neglect your word.

Gimel

17Do good to your servant, and I will live;
　I will obey your word.
18Open my eyes that I may see
　wonderful things in your law.
19I am a stranger on earth;
　do not hide your commands from me.
20My soul is consumed with longing
　for your laws at all times.
21You rebuke the arrogant, who are cursed
　and who stray from your commands.
22Remove from me scorn and contempt,
　for I keep your statutes.
23Though rulers sit together and slander me,
　your servant will meditate on your decrees.
24Your statutes are my delight;
　they are my counselors.

2遵守他的法度，一心尋求他的，
　這人便為有福！
3這人不做非義的事，
　但遵行他的道。
4耶和華啊，你曾將你的訓詞
　吩咐我們，為要我們殷勤遵守。
5但願我行事堅定，
　得以遵守你的律例。
6我看重你的一切命令，
　就不至於羞愧。
7我學了你公義的判語，
　就要以正直的心稱謝你。
8我必守你的律例，
　求你總不要丟棄我。

9少年人用甚麼潔淨他的行為呢？
　是要遵行你的話。
10我一心尋求了你，
　求你不要叫我偏離你的命令。
11我將你的話藏在心裏，
　免得我得罪你。
12耶和華啊，你是應當稱頌的！
　求你將你的律例教訓我。
13我用嘴唇傳揚你
　口中的一切典章。
14我喜悅你的法度，
　如同喜悅一切的財物。
15我要默想你的訓詞，
　看重你的道路。
16我要在你的律例中自樂，
　我不忘記你的話。

17求你用厚恩待你的僕人，使我存活，
　我就遵守你的話。
18求你開我的眼睛，
　使我看出你律法中的奇妙。
19我是在地上作寄居的，
　求你不要向我隱瞞你的命令。
20我時常切慕你的典章，
　甚至心碎。
21受咒詛，偏離你命令的驕傲人，
　你已經責備他們。
22求你除掉我所受的羞辱和藐視，
　因我遵守你的法度。
23雖有首領坐着妄論我，
　你僕人卻思想你的律例。
24你的法度是我所喜樂的，
　是我的謀士。

25我的性命幾乎歸於塵土，
　　求你照你的話將我救活。
26我述說我所行的，你應允了我，
　　求你將你的律例教訓我。
27求你使我明白你的訓詞，
　　我就思想你的奇事。

28我的心因愁苦而消化，
　　求你照你的話使我堅立！
29求你使我離開奸詐的道，
　　開恩將你的律法賜給我。
30我揀選了忠信的道，
　　將你的典章擺在我面前。
31我持守你的法度，
　　耶和華啊，求你不要叫我羞愧！
32你開廣我心的時候，
　　我就往你命令的道上直奔。

33耶和華啊，求你將你的律例指教我，
　　我必遵守到底。
34求你賜我悟性，我便遵守你的律法，
　　且要一心遵守。
35求你叫我遵行你的命令，
　　因為這是我所喜樂的。
36求你使我的心趨向你的法度，
　　不趨向非義之財。
37求你叫我轉眼不看虛假，
　　又叫我在你的道中生活。
38你向敬畏你的人所應許的話，
　　求你向僕人堅定。
39求你使我所怕的羞辱遠離我，
　　因你的典章本為美。
40我羨慕你的訓詞，
　　求你使我在你的公義上生活。

41耶和華啊，願你照你的話，
　　使你的慈愛，就是你的救恩，
　　臨到我身上；
42我就有話回答那羞辱我的，
　　因我倚靠你的話。
43求你叫真理的話總不離開我口，
　　因我仰望你的典章。
44我要常守你的律法，
　　直到永永遠遠。
45我要自由而行（註：或作"我要行在寬闊
　　之地"），
　　因我素來考究你的訓詞。

Daleth

25I am laid low in the dust;
　　preserve my life according to your word.
26I recounted my ways and you answered me;
　　teach me your decrees.
27Let me understand the teaching of your
　　precepts;
　　then I will meditate on your wonders.

28My soul is weary with sorrow;
　　strengthen me according to your word.
29Keep me from deceitful ways;
　　be gracious to me through your law.
30I have chosen the way of truth;
　　I have set my heart on your laws.
31I hold fast to your statutes, O LORD;
　　do not let me be put to shame.
32I run in the path of your commands,
　　for you have set my heart free.

He

33Teach me, O LORD, to follow your decrees;
　　then I will keep them to the end.
34Give me understanding, and I will keep your law
　　and obey it with all my heart.
35Direct me in the path of your commands,
　　for there I find delight.
36Turn my heart toward your statutes
　　and not toward selfish gain.
37Turn my eyes away from worthless things;
　　preserve my life according to your word.[a]
38Fulfill your promise to your servant,
　　so that you may be feared.
39Take away the disgrace I dread,
　　for your laws are good.
40How I long for your precepts!
　　Preserve my life in your righteousness.

Waw

41May your unfailing love come to me, O LORD,
　　your salvation according to your promise;
42then I will answer the one who taunts me,
　　for I trust in your word.
43Do not snatch the word of truth from my
　　mouth,
　　for I have put my hope in your laws.
44I will always obey your law,
　　for ever and ever.
45I will walk about in freedom,
　　for I have sought out your precepts.

a 37 Two manuscripts of the Masoretic Text and Dead Sea
Scrolls; most manuscripts of the Masoretic Text *life in your way*

⁴⁶I will speak of your statutes before kings
and will not be put to shame,
⁴⁷for I delight in your commands
because I love them.
⁴⁸I lift up my hands to^a your commands, which
I love,
and I meditate on your decrees.

Zayin

⁴⁹Remember your word to your servant,
for you have given me hope.
⁵⁰My comfort in my suffering is this:
Your promise preserves my life.
⁵¹The arrogant mock me without restraint,
but I do not turn from your law.
⁵²I remember your ancient laws, O LORD,
and I find comfort in them.
⁵³Indignation grips me because of the wicked,
who have forsaken your law.
⁵⁴Your decrees are the theme of my song
wherever I lodge.
⁵⁵In the night I remember your name, O LORD,
and I will keep your law.
⁵⁶This has been my practice:
I obey your precepts.

Heth

⁵⁷You are my portion, O LORD;
I have promised to obey your words.
⁵⁸I have sought your face with all my heart;
be gracious to me according to your promise.
⁵⁹I have considered my ways
and have turned my steps to your statutes.
⁶⁰I will hasten and not delay
to obey your commands.
⁶¹Though the wicked bind me with ropes,
I will not forget your law.
⁶²At midnight I rise to give you thanks
for your righteous laws.
⁶³I am a friend to all who fear you,
to all who follow your precepts.
⁶⁴The earth is filled with your love, O LORD;
teach me your decrees.

Teth

⁶⁵Do good to your servant
according to your word, O LORD.
⁶⁶Teach me knowledge and good judgment,
for I believe in your commands.
⁶⁷Before I was afflicted I went astray,
but now I obey your word.

^a 48 Or for

⁴⁶我也要在君王面前論說你的法度，
並不至於羞愧。
⁴⁷我要在你的命令中自樂，
這命令素來是我所愛的。
⁴⁸我又要遵行（註：原文作"舉手"）
你的命令，
這命令素來是我所愛的。
我也要思想你的律例。

⁴⁹求你記念向你僕人所應許的話，
叫我有盼望。
⁵⁰這話將我救活了。
我在患難中，因此得安慰。
⁵¹驕傲的人甚侮慢我，
我卻未曾偏離你的律法。
⁵²耶和華啊，我記念你
從古以來的典章，就得了安慰。
⁵³我見惡人離棄你的律法，
就怒氣發作，猶如火燒。
⁵⁴我在世寄居，
素來以你的律例為詩歌。
⁵⁵耶和華啊，我夜間記念你的名，
遵守你的律法。
⁵⁶我所以如此，
是因我守你的訓詞。

⁵⁷耶和華是我的福分。
我曾說，我要遵守你的言語。
⁵⁸我一心求過你的恩，
願你照你的話憐憫我。
⁵⁹我思想我所行的道，
就轉步歸向你的法度。
⁶⁰我急忙遵守你的命令，
並不遲延。
⁶¹惡人的繩索纏繞我，
我卻沒有忘記你的律法。
⁶²我因你公義的典章，
半夜必起來稱謝你。
⁶³凡敬畏你、守你訓詞的人，
我都與他作伴。
⁶⁴耶和華啊，你的慈愛遍滿大地，
求你將你的律例教訓我！

⁶⁵耶和華啊，
你向來是照你的話善待僕人。
⁶⁶求你將精明和知識賜給我，
因我信了你的命令。
⁶⁷我未受苦以先走迷了路，
現在卻遵守你的話。

68你本為善，所行的也善，
　　求你將你的律例教訓我。
69驕傲人
　　編造謊言攻擊我，
　　我卻要一心守你的訓詞。
70他們心蒙脂油，
　　我卻喜愛你的律法。
71我受苦是與我有益，
　　為要使我學習你的律例。
72你口中的訓言（註：或作"律法"）
　　與我有益，
　　勝於千萬的金銀。

73你的手製造我，建立我。
　　求你賜我悟性，
　　可以學習你的命令。
74敬畏你的人見我，
　　就要歡喜，
　　因我仰望你的話。
75耶和華啊，
　　我知道你的判語是公義的；
　　你使我受苦是以誠實待我。
76求你照着應許僕人的話，
　　以慈愛安慰我。
77願你的慈悲臨到我，使我存活，
　　因你的律法是我所喜愛的。
78願驕傲人蒙羞，
　　因為他們無理地傾覆我，
　　但我要思想你的訓詞。
79願敬畏你的人歸向我，
　　他們就知道你的法度。
80願我的心
　　在你的律例上完全，
　　使我不至蒙羞。

81我心渴想你的救恩，
　　仰望你的應許。
82我因盼望你的應許，眼睛失明，
　　說："你何時安慰我？"
83我好像煙薰的皮袋，
　　卻不忘記你的律例。
84你僕人的年日有多少呢？
　　你幾時向逼迫我的人施行審判呢？
85不從你律法的驕傲人
　　為我掘了坑。
86你的命令盡都誠實；
　　他們無理地逼迫我，
　　求你幫助我。
87他們幾乎把我從世上滅絕，
　　但我沒有離棄你的訓詞。
88求你照你的慈愛將我救活，
　　我就遵守你口中的法度。

68You are good, and what you do is good;
　　teach me your decrees.
69Though the arrogant have smeared me with
　　lies,
　　I keep your precepts with all my heart.
70Their hearts are callous and unfeeling,
　　but I delight in your law.
71It was good for me to be afflicted
　　so that I might learn your decrees.
72The law from your mouth is more precious to
　　me
　　than thousands of pieces of silver and gold.

Yodh

73Your hands made me and formed me;
　　give me understanding to learn your
　　commands.
74May those who fear you rejoice when they see
　　me,
　　for I have put my hope in your word.
75I know, O LORD, that your laws are righteous,
　　and in faithfulness you have afflicted me.
76May your unfailing love be my comfort,
　　according to your promise to your servant.
77Let your compassion come to me that I may
　　live,
　　for your law is my delight.
78May the arrogant be put to shame for
　　wronging me without cause;
　　but I will meditate on your precepts.
79May those who fear you turn to me,
　　those who understand your statutes.
80May my heart be blameless toward your
　　decrees,
　　that I may not be put to shame.

Kaph

81My soul faints with longing for your salvation,
　　but I have put my hope in your word.
82My eyes fail, looking for your promise;
　　I say, "When will you comfort me?"
83Though I am like a wineskin in the smoke,
　　I do not forget your decrees.
84How long must your servant wait?
　　When will you punish my persecutors?
85The arrogant dig pitfalls for me,
　　contrary to your law.
86All your commands are trustworthy;
　　help me, for men persecute me without
　　cause.
87They almost wiped me from the earth,
　　but I have not forsaken your precepts.
88Preserve my life according to your love,
　　and I will obey the statutes of your mouth.

Lamedh

89Your word, O LORD, is eternal;
  it stands firm in the heavens.
90Your faithfulness continues through all
    generations;
  you established the earth, and it endures.
91Your laws endure to this day,
  for all things serve you.
92If your law had not been my delight,
  I would have perished in my affliction.
93I will never forget your precepts,
  for by them you have preserved my life.
94Save me, for I am yours;
  I have sought out your precepts.
95The wicked are waiting to destroy me,
  but I will ponder your statutes.
96To all perfection I see a limit;
  but your commands are boundless.

Mem

97Oh, how I love your law!
  I meditate on it all day long.
98Your commands make me wiser than my
    enemies,
  for they are ever with me.
99I have more insight than all my teachers,
  for I meditate on your statutes.
100I have more understanding than the elders,
  for I obey your precepts.
101I have kept my feet from every evil path
  so that I might obey your word.
102I have not departed from your laws,
  for you yourself have taught me.
103How sweet are your words to my taste,
  sweeter than honey to my mouth!
104I gain understanding from your precepts;
  therefore I hate every wrong path.

Nun

105Your word is a lamp to my feet
  and a light for my path.
106I have taken an oath and confirmed it,
  that I will follow your righteous laws.
107I have suffered much;
  preserve my life, O LORD, according to
    your word.
108Accept, O LORD, the willing praise of my
    mouth,
  and teach me your laws.
109Though I constantly take my life in my hands,
  I will not forget your law.
110The wicked have set a snare for me,
  but I have not strayed from your precepts.

89耶和華啊，你的話安定在天，
  直到永遠。
90你的誠實存到萬代；
  你堅定了地，
  地就長存。
91天地照你的安排存到今日；
  萬物都是你的僕役。
92我若不是喜愛你的律法，
  早就在苦難中滅絕了。
93我永不忘記你的訓詞，
  因你用這訓詞將我救活了。
94我是屬你的，求你救我，
  因我尋求了你的訓詞。
95惡人等待我，要滅絕我，
  我卻要揣摩你的法度。
96我看萬事盡都有限，
  惟有你的命令極其寬廣。

97我何等愛慕你的律法，
  終日不住地思想。
98你的命令
  常存在我心裏，
  使我比仇敵有智慧。
99我比我的師傅更通達，
  因我思想你的法度；
100我比年老的更明白，
  因我守了你的訓詞。
101我禁止我腳走一切的邪路，
  為要遵守你的話。
102我沒有偏離你的典章，
  因為你教訓了我。
103你的言語在我上膛何等甘美，
  在我口中比蜜更甜！
104我藉着你的訓詞得以明白，
  所以我恨一切的假道。

105你的話是我腳前的燈，
  是我路上的光。
106你公義的典章，我曾起誓遵守，
  我必按誓而行。
107我甚是受苦；
  耶和華啊，
  求你照你的話將我救活！
108耶和華啊，
  求你悅納我口中的讚美為供物，
  又將你的典章教訓我！
109我的性命常在危險之中，
  我卻不忘記你的律法。
110惡人為我設下網羅，
  我卻沒有偏離你的訓詞。

111我以你的法度為永遠的產業，
　　因這是我心中所喜愛的。
112我的心專向你的律例，
　　永遠遵行，一直到底。

113心懷二意的人為我所恨；
　　但你的律法為我所愛。
114你是我藏身之處，又是我的盾牌；
　　我甚仰望你的話語。
115作惡的人哪，你們離開我吧！
　　我好遵守我神的命令。
116求你照你的話扶持我，
　　使我存活，
　　也不叫我因失望而害羞。
117求你扶持我，我便得救，
　　時常看重你的律例。
118凡偏離你律例的人，你都輕棄他們，
　　因為他們的詭詐必歸虛空。
119凡地上的惡人，你除掉他，
　　好像除掉渣滓，
　　因此我愛你的法度。
120我因懼怕你，肉就發抖，
　　我也怕你的判語。

121我行過公平和公義，
　　求你不要撇下我給欺壓我的人。
122求你為僕人作保，使我得好處，
　　不容驕傲人欺壓我。
123我因盼望你的救恩和你公義的話，
　　眼睛失明。
124求你照你的慈愛待僕人，
　　將你的律例教訓我。
125我是你的僕人，求你賜我悟性，
　　使我得知你的法度。
126這是耶和華降罰的時候，
　　因人廢了你的律法。
127所以我愛你的命令勝於金子，
　　更勝於精金。
128你一切的訓詞，
　　在萬事上我都以為正直，
　　我卻恨惡一切假道。

129你的法度奇妙，
　　所以我一心謹守。
130你的言語一解開，就發出亮光，
　　使愚人通達。
131我張口而氣喘，
　　因我切慕你的命令。

111Your statutes are my heritage forever;
　they are the joy of my heart.
112My heart is set on keeping your decrees
　to the very end.

Samekh

113I hate double-minded men,
　but I love your law.
114You are my refuge and my shield;
　I have put my hope in your word.
115Away from me, you evildoers,
　that I may keep the commands of my God!
116Sustain me according to your promise, and I
　　will live;
　do not let my hopes be dashed.
117Uphold me, and I will be delivered;
　I will always have regard for your decrees.
118You reject all who stray from your decrees,
　for their deceitfulness is in vain.
119All the wicked of the earth you discard like
　　dross;
　therefore I love your statutes.
120My flesh trembles in fear of you;
　I stand in awe of your laws.

Ayin

121I have done what is righteous and just;
　do not leave me to my oppressors.
122Ensure your servant's well-being;
　let not the arrogant oppress me.
123My eyes fail, looking for your salvation,
　looking for your righteous promise.
124Deal with your servant according to your
　　love
　and teach me your decrees.
125I am your servant; give me discernment
　that I may understand your statutes.
126It is time for you to act, O LORD;
　your law is being broken.
127Because I love your commands
　more than gold, more than pure gold,
128and because I consider all your precepts
　　right,
　I hate every wrong path.

Pe

129Your statutes are wonderful;
　therefore I obey them.
130The unfolding of your words gives light;
　it gives understanding to the simple.
131I open my mouth and pant,
　longing for your commands.

¹³²Turn to me and have mercy on me,
as you always do to those who love your name.
¹³³Direct my footsteps according to your word;
let no sin rule over me.
¹³⁴Redeem me from the oppression of men,
that I may obey your precepts.
¹³⁵Make your face shine upon your servant
and teach me your decrees.
¹³⁶Streams of tears flow from my eyes,
for your law is not obeyed.

Tsadhe

¹³⁷Righteous are you, O Lord,
and your laws are right.
¹³⁸The statutes you have laid down are
righteous;
they are fully trustworthy.
¹³⁹My zeal wears me out,
for my enemies ignore your words.
¹⁴⁰Your promises have been thoroughly tested,
and your servant loves them.
¹⁴¹Though I am lowly and despised,
I do not forget your precepts.
¹⁴²Your righteousness is everlasting
and your law is true.
¹⁴³Trouble and distress have come upon me,
but your commands are my delight.
¹⁴⁴Your statutes are forever right;
give me understanding that I may live.

Qoph

¹⁴⁵I call with all my heart; answer me, O Lord,
and I will obey your decrees.
¹⁴⁶I call out to you; save me
and I will keep your statutes.
¹⁴⁷I rise before dawn and cry for help;
I have put my hope in your word.
¹⁴⁸My eyes stay open through the watches of
the night,
that I may meditate on your promises.
¹⁴⁹Hear my voice in accordance with your love;
preserve my life, O Lord, according to your
laws.
¹⁵⁰Those who devise wicked schemes are near,
but they are far from your law.
¹⁵¹Yet you are near, O Lord,
and all your commands are true.
¹⁵²Long ago I learned from your statutes
that you established them to last forever.

Resh

¹⁵³Look upon my suffering and deliver me,
for I have not forgotten your law.

¹³²求你轉向我，憐憫我，
好像你素常待那些愛你名的人。
¹³³求你用你的話使我腳步穩當，
不許甚麼罪孽轄制我。
¹³⁴求你救我脫離人的欺壓，
我要遵守你的訓詞。
¹³⁵求你用臉光照僕人，
又將你的律例教訓我。
¹³⁶我的眼淚下流成河，
因為他們不守你的律法。

¹³⁷耶和華啊，你是公義的，
你的判語也是正直的！
¹³⁸你所命定的法度
是憑公義和至誠。
¹³⁹我心焦急，如同火燒，
因我敵人忘記你的言語。
¹⁴⁰你的話極其精煉，
所以你的僕人喜愛。
¹⁴¹我微小，被人藐視，
卻不忘記你的訓詞。
¹⁴²你的公義永遠長存，
你的律法盡都真實。
¹⁴³我遭遇患難愁苦，
你的命令卻是我所喜愛的。
¹⁴⁴你的法度永遠是公義的，
求你賜我悟性，我就活了。

¹⁴⁵耶和華啊，我一心呼籲你，
求你應允我，我必謹守你的律例！
¹⁴⁶我向你呼籲，求你救我！
我要遵守你的法度。
¹⁴⁷我趁天未亮呼求，
我仰望了你的言語；
¹⁴⁸我趁夜更未換
將眼睜開，
為要思想你的話語。
¹⁴⁹求你照你的慈愛聽我的聲音；
耶和華啊，
求你照你的典章將我救活。
¹⁵⁰追求奸惡的人臨近了，
他們遠離你的律法。
¹⁵¹耶和華啊，你與我相近，
你一切的命令盡都真實！
¹⁵²我因學你的法度，
久已知道是你永遠立定的。

¹⁵³求你看顧我的苦難，搭救我，
因我不忘記你的律法。

154求你為我辨屈，救贖我，
　　照你的話將我救活。
155救恩遠離惡人，
　　因為他們不尋求你的律例。
156耶和華啊，你的慈悲本為大，
　　求你照你的典章將我救活！
157逼迫我的，抵擋我的很多，
　　我卻沒有偏離你的法度。
158我看見奸惡的人就甚憎惡，
　　因為他們不遵守你的話。
159你看我怎樣愛你的訓詞，
　　耶和華啊，
　　求你照你的慈愛將我救活！
160你話的總綱是真實，
　　你一切公義的典章是永遠長存！

161首領無故地逼迫我，
　　但我的心畏懼你的言語。
162我喜愛你的話，
　　好像人得了許多擄物。
163謊話是我所恨惡所憎嫌的；
　　惟你的律法是我所愛的。
164我因你公義的典章，
　　一天七次讚美你。
165愛你律法的人有大平安，
　　甚麼都不能使他們絆腳。
166耶和華啊，我仰望了你的救恩，
　　遵行了你的命令。
167我心裏守了你的法度；
　　這法度我甚喜愛。
168我遵守了你的訓詞和法度，
　　因我一切所行的都在你面前。

169耶和華啊，
　　願我的呼籲達到你面前，
　　照你的話賜我悟性。
170願我的懇求達到你面前，
　　照你的話搭救我。
171願我的嘴發出讚美的話，
　　因為你將律例教訓我。
172願我的舌頭歌唱你的話，
　　因你一切的命令盡都公義。
173願你用手幫助我，
　　因我揀選了你的訓詞。
174耶和華啊，我切慕你的救恩，
　　你的律法也是我所喜愛的。
175願我的性命存活，得以讚美你！
　　願你的典章幫助我！
176我如亡羊走迷了路，
　　求你尋找僕人，
　　因我不忘記你的命令。

154Defend my cause and redeem me;
　　preserve my life according to your promise.
155Salvation is far from the wicked,
　　for they do not seek out your decrees.
156Your compassion is great, O LORD;
　　preserve my life according to your laws.
157Many are the foes who persecute me,
　　but I have not turned from your statutes.
158I look on the faithless with loathing,
　　for they do not obey your word.
159See how I love your precepts;
　　preserve my life, O LORD, according to your
　　love.
160All your words are true;
　　all your righteous laws are eternal.

Sin and Shin

161Rulers persecute me without cause,
　　but my heart trembles at your word.
162I rejoice in your promise
　　like one who finds great spoil.
163I hate and abhor falsehood
　　but I love your law.
164Seven times a day I praise you
　　for your righteous laws.
165Great peace have they who love your law,
　　and nothing can make them stumble.
166I wait for your salvation, O LORD,
　　and I follow your commands.
167I obey your statutes,
　　for I love them greatly.
168I obey your precepts and your statutes,
　　for all my ways are known to you.

Taw

169May my cry come before you, O LORD;
　　give me understanding according to your
　　word.
170May my supplication come before you;
　　deliver me according to your promise.
171May my lips overflow with praise,
　　for you teach me your decrees.
172May my tongue sing of your word,
　　for all your commands are righteous.
173May your hand be ready to help me,
　　for I have chosen your precepts.
174I long for your salvation, O LORD,
　　and your law is my delight.
175Let me live that I may praise you,
　　and may your laws sustain me.
176I have strayed like a lost sheep.
　　Seek your servant,
　　for I have not forgotten your commands.

Psalm 120

A song of ascents.

¹I call on the LORD in my distress,
   and he answers me.
²Save me, O LORD, from lying lips
   and from deceitful tongues.

³What will he do to you,
   and what more besides, O deceitful tongue?
⁴He will punish you with a warrior's sharp
    arrows,
   with burning coals of the broom tree.

⁵Woe to me that I dwell in Meshech,
   that I live among the tents of Kedar!
⁶Too long have I lived
   among those who hate peace.
⁷I am a man of peace;
   but when I speak, they are for war.

Psalm 121

A song of ascents.

¹I lift up my eyes to the hills—
   where does my help come from?
²My help comes from the LORD,
   the Maker of heaven and earth.

³He will not let your foot slip—
   he who watches over you will not slumber;
⁴indeed, he who watches over Israel
   will neither slumber nor sleep.

⁵The LORD watches over you—
   the LORD is your shade at your right hand;
⁶the sun will not harm you by day,
   nor the moon by night.

⁷The LORD will keep you from all harm—
   he will watch over your life;
⁸the LORD will watch over your coming and
    going
   both now and forevermore.

Psalm 122

A song of ascents. Of David.

¹I rejoiced with those who said to me,
   "Let us go to the house of the LORD."
²Our feet are standing
   in your gates, O Jerusalem.

第一百二十篇

上行（註：或作"登階"。下同）之詩。

¹我在急難中求告耶和華，
   他就應允我。
²耶和華啊，求你救我
   脫離說謊的嘴唇和詭詐的舌頭。

³詭詐的舌頭啊，要給你甚麼呢？
   要拿甚麼加給你呢？
⁴就是勇士的利箭和羅騰（註："羅騰"
     小樹名，松類）木的炭火。

⁵我寄居在米設，
   住在基達帳棚之中有禍了！
⁶我與那恨惡和睦的人
   許久同住。
⁷我願和睦，
   但我發言，他們就要爭戰。

第一百二十一篇

上行之詩。

¹我要向山舉目，
   我的幫助從何而來？
²我的幫助
   從造天地的耶和華而來。

³他必不叫你的腳搖動，
   保護你的必不打盹！
⁴保護以色列的，
   也不打盹，也不睡覺。

⁵保護你的是耶和華，
   耶和華在你右邊蔭庇你。
⁶白日，太陽必不傷你；
   夜間，月亮必不害你。

⁷耶和華要保護你，免受一切的災害。
   他要保護你的性命。
⁸你出你入，
   耶和華要保護你，
   從今時直到永遠。

第一百二十二篇

大衛上行之詩。

¹人對我說"我們往耶和華的殿去"，
   我就歡喜。
²耶路撒冷啊，
   我們的腳站在你的門內。

³耶路撒冷被建造，
　　如同連絡整齊的一座城。
⁴眾支派，就是耶和華的支派，
　　上那裏去，按以色列的常例（註：
　　或作「作以色列的證據」）
　　稱讚耶和華的名。
⁵因為在那裏設立審判的寶座，
　　就是大衛家的寶座。

⁶你們要為耶路撒冷求平安。
　　耶路撒冷啊，愛你的人必然興旺。
⁷願你城中平安，
　　願你宮內興旺！
⁸因我弟兄和同伴的緣故，
　　我要說：「願平安在你中間！」
⁹因耶和華我們神殿的緣故，
　　我要為你求福。

第一百二十三篇

上行之詩。

¹坐在天上的主啊，
　　我向你舉目。
²看哪，僕人的眼睛
　　怎樣望主人的手，
　使女的眼睛
　　怎樣望主母的手，
　我們的眼睛
　　也照樣望耶和華我們的神，
　　直到他憐憫我們。
³耶和華啊，
　　求你憐憫我們，憐憫我們！
　　因為我們被藐視，已到極處。
⁴我們被那些安逸人的譏誚
　　和驕傲人的藐視，已到極處。

第一百二十四篇

大衛上行之詩。

¹以色列人要說，
　　若不是耶和華幫助我們，
²若不是耶和華幫助我們，
　　當人起來攻擊我們，
³向我們發怒的時候，
　　就把我們活活地吞了。
⁴那時，波濤必漫過我們，
　　河水必淹沒我們，
⁵狂傲的水
　　必淹沒我們。
⁶耶和華是應當稱頌的，
　　他沒有把我們當野食
　　交給他們吞吃（註：原文作「牙齒」）。
⁷我們好像雀鳥，
　　從捕鳥人的網羅裏逃脫；

³Jerusalem is built like a city
　　that is closely compacted together.
⁴That is where the tribes go up,
　　the tribes of the LORD,
　to praise the name of the LORD
　　according to the statute given to Israel.
⁵There the thrones for judgment stand,
　　the thrones of the house of David.

⁶Pray for the peace of Jerusalem:
　　"May those who love you be secure.
⁷May there be peace within your walls
　　and security within your citadels."
⁸For the sake of my brothers and friends,
　　I will say, "Peace be within you."
⁹For the sake of the house of the LORD our God,
　　I will seek your prosperity.

Psalm 123

A song of ascents.

¹I lift up my eyes to you,
　　to you whose throne is in heaven.
²As the eyes of slaves look to the hand of their
　　master,
　as the eyes of a maid look to the hand of her
　　mistress,
　so our eyes look to the LORD our God,
　　till he shows us his mercy.

³Have mercy on us, O LORD, have mercy on us,
　　for we have endured much contempt.
⁴We have endured much ridicule from the
　　proud,
　much contempt from the arrogant.

Psalm 124

A song of ascents. Of David.

¹If the LORD had not been on our side—
　　let Israel say—
²if the LORD had not been on our side
　　when men attacked us,
³when their anger flared against us,
　　they would have swallowed us alive;
⁴the flood would have engulfed us,
　　the torrent would have swept over us,
⁵the raging waters
　　would have swept us away.

⁶Praise be to the LORD,
　　who has not let us be torn by their teeth.
⁷We have escaped like a bird
　　out of the fowler's snare;

the snare has been broken,
and we have escaped.
[8]Our help is in the name of the LORD,
the Maker of heaven and earth.

Psalm 125

A song of ascents.

[1]Those who trust in the LORD are like Mount
Zion,
which cannot be shaken but endures forever.
[2]As the mountains surround Jerusalem,
so the LORD surrounds his people
both now and forevermore.

[3]The scepter of the wicked will not remain
over the land allotted to the righteous,
for then the righteous might use
their hands to do evil.

[4]Do good, O LORD, to those who are good,
to those who are upright in heart.
[5]But those who turn to crooked ways
the LORD will banish with the evildoers.

Peace be upon Israel.

Psalm 126

A song of ascents.

[1]When the LORD brought back the captives to[a]
Zion,
we were like men who dreamed.[b]
[2]Our mouths were filled with laughter,
our tongues with songs of joy.
Then it was said among the nations,
"The LORD has done great things for them."
[3]The LORD has done great things for us,
and we are filled with joy.

[4]Restore our fortunes,[c] O LORD,
like streams in the Negev.
[5]Those who sow in tears
will reap with songs of joy.
[6]He who goes out weeping,
carrying seed to sow,
will return with songs of joy,
carrying sheaves with him.

網羅破裂，
我們逃脫了。
[8]我們得幫助，
是在乎倚靠造天地之耶和華的名。

第一百二十五篇

上行之詩。

[1]倚靠耶和華的人
好像錫安山，
永不動搖。
[2]眾山怎樣圍繞耶路撒冷，
耶和華也照樣圍繞他的百姓，
從今時直到永遠。

[3]惡人的杖
不常落在義人的分上，
免得義人
伸手作惡。

[4]耶和華啊，求你善待那些為善
和心裏正直的人。
[5]至於那偏行彎曲道路的人，
耶和華必使他和作惡的人
一同出去受刑。
願平安歸於以色列！

第一百二十六篇

上行之詩。

[1]當耶和華將那些被擄的
帶回錫安的時候，
我們好像做夢的人。
[2]我們滿口喜笑、
滿舌歡呼的時候，
外邦中就有人說：
"耶和華為他們行了大事！"
[3]耶和華果然為我們行了大事，
我們就歡喜。

[4]耶和華啊，求你使我們被擄的人歸回，
好像南地的河水復流！
[5]流淚撒種的，
必歡呼收割！
[6]那帶種
流淚出去的，
必要歡歡樂樂地
帶禾捆回來！

---

a 1 Or LORD *restored the fortunes of*   *b* 1 Or *men restored to*
health   *c* 4 Or *Bring back our captives*

第一百二十七篇

所羅門上行之詩。

¹若不是耶和華建造房屋，
　　建造的人就枉然勞力；
　若不是耶和華看守城池，
　　看守的人就枉然警醒。
²你們清晨早起，夜晚安歇，
　吃勞碌得來的飯，本是枉然；
　惟有耶和華所親愛的，
　　必叫他安然睡覺。

³兒女是耶和華所賜的產業，
　所懷的胎是他所給的賞賜。
⁴少年時所生的兒女，
　好像勇士手中的箭。
⁵箭袋充滿的人，
　便為有福。
　他們在城門口
　和仇敵說話的時候，
　必不至於羞愧。

第一百二十八篇

上行之詩。

¹凡敬畏耶和華、遵行他道的人，
　便為有福。
²你要吃勞碌得來的，
　你要享福，事情順利。
³你妻子在你的內室，
　好像多結果子的葡萄樹；
　你兒女圍繞你的桌子，
　好像橄欖栽子。
⁴看哪，敬畏耶和華的人，
　必要這樣蒙福！

⁵願耶和華從錫安賜福給你；
　願你一生一世
　　看見耶路撒冷的好處。
⁶願你看見你兒女的兒女。

願平安歸於以色列！

第一百二十九篇

上行之詩。

¹以色列當說：
　"從我幼年以來，
　敵人屢次苦害我。

Psalm 127

A song of ascents. Of Solomon.

¹Unless the LORD builds the house,
　its builders labor in vain.
　Unless the LORD watches over the city,
　the watchmen stand guard in vain.
²In vain you rise early
　and stay up late,
　toiling for food to eat—
　for he grants sleep to*ᵃ* those he loves.

³Sons are a heritage from the LORD,
　children a reward from him.
⁴Like arrows in the hands of a warrior
　are sons born in one's youth.
⁵Blessed is the man
　whose quiver is full of them.
　They will not be put to shame
　when they contend with their enemies in the
　gate.

Psalm 128

A song of ascents.

¹Blessed are all who fear the LORD,
　who walk in his ways.
²You will eat the fruit of your labor;
　blessings and prosperity will be yours.
³Your wife will be like a fruitful vine
　within your house;
　your sons will be like olive shoots
　around your table.
⁴Thus is the man blessed
　who fears the LORD.

⁵May the LORD bless you from Zion
　all the days of your life;
　may you see the prosperity of Jerusalem,
⁶　and may you live to see your children's
　children.

Peace be upon Israel.

Psalm 129

A song of ascents.

¹They have greatly oppressed me from my
　youth—
　let Israel say—

a 2 Or eat— / for while they sleep he provides for

²they have greatly oppressed me from my
    youth,
  but they have not gained the victory over me.
³Plowmen have plowed my back
  and made their furrows long.
⁴But the LORD is righteous;
  he has cut me free from the cords of the
    wicked.

⁵May all who hate Zion
  be turned back in shame.
⁶May they be like grass on the roof,
  which withers before it can grow;
⁷with it the reaper cannot fill his hands,
  nor the one who gathers fill his arms.
⁸May those who pass by not say,
  "The blessing of the LORD be upon you;
  we bless you in the name of the LORD."

Psalm 130

A song of ascents.

¹Out of the depths I cry to you, O LORD;
² O Lord, hear my voice.
  Let your ears be attentive
    to my cry for mercy.

³If you, O LORD, kept a record of sins,
  O Lord, who could stand?
⁴But with you there is forgiveness;
  therefore you are feared.

⁵I wait for the LORD, my soul waits,
  and in his word I put my hope.
⁶My soul waits for the Lord
  more than watchmen wait for the morning,
  more than watchmen wait for the morning.

⁷O Israel, put your hope in the LORD,
  for with the LORD is unfailing love
  and with him is full redemption.
⁸He himself will redeem Israel
  from all their sins.

Psalm 131

A song of ascents. Of David.

¹My heart is not proud, O LORD,
  my eyes are not haughty;
  I do not concern myself with great matters
  or things too wonderful for me.
²But I have stilled and quieted my soul;
  like a weaned child with its mother,
  like a weaned child is my soul within me.

²從我幼年以來，
    敵人屢次苦害我，
    卻沒有勝了我。
³如同扶犁的在我背上扶犁而耕，
    耕的犁溝甚長。”
⁴耶和華是公義的，
    他砍斷了惡人的繩索。

⁵願恨惡錫安的
    都蒙羞退後。
⁶願他們像房頂上的草，
    未長成而枯乾。
⁷收割的不夠一把，
    捆禾的也不滿懷；
⁸過路的也不說：
    “願耶和華所賜的福歸與你們；
    我們奉耶和華的名給你們祝福。”

第一百三十篇

上行之詩。

¹耶和華啊，我從深處向你求告。
²主啊，求你聽我的聲音，
    願你側耳聽我
      懇求的聲音！

³主耶和華啊，你若究察罪孽，
    誰能站得住呢？
⁴但在你有赦免之恩，
    要叫人敬畏你。

⁵我等候耶和華，我的心等候，
    我也仰望他的話。
⁶我的心等候主，
    勝於守夜的等候天亮，
    勝於守夜的等候天亮。

⁷以色列啊，你當仰望耶和華！
    因他有慈愛，
    有豐盛的救恩。
⁸他必救贖以色列
    脫離一切的罪孽。

第一百三十一篇

大衛上行之詩。

¹耶和華啊，我的心不狂傲，
    我的眼不高大，
    重大和測不透的事，
    我也不敢行。
²我的心平穩安靜，
    好像斷過奶的孩子在他母親的懷中；
    我的心在我裏面真像斷過奶的孩子。

³以色列啊，你當仰望耶和華，
　　從今時直到永遠！

第一百三十二篇

上行之詩。

¹耶和華啊，
　　求你記念大衛所受的一切苦難。

²他怎樣向耶和華起誓，
　　向雅各的大能者許願，
³說："我必不進我的帳幕，
　　也不上我的床榻；
⁴我不容我的眼睛睡覺，
　　也不容我的眼目打盹；
⁵直等我為耶和華尋得所在，
　　為雅各的大能者尋得居所。"

⁶我們聽說約櫃在以法他，
　　我們在基列耶琳就尋見了。
⁷我們要進他的居所，
　　在他腳凳前下拜。
⁸耶和華啊，求你興起，
　　和你有能力的約櫃同入安息之所。
⁹願你的祭司披上公義，
　　願你的聖民歡呼。

¹⁰求你因你僕人大衛的緣故，
　　不要厭棄你的受膏者。

¹¹耶和華向大衛憑誠實起了誓，
　　必不反覆，說：
　"我要使你所生的，
　　坐在你的寶座上。
¹²你的眾子若守我的約
　　和我所教訓他們的法度，
　他們的子孫
　　必永遠坐在你的寶座上。"

¹³因為耶和華揀選了錫安，
　　願意當作自己的居所，
¹⁴說："這是我永遠安息之所，
　　我要住在這裏，
　　因為是我所願意的。
¹⁵我要使其中的糧食豐滿，
　　使其中的窮人飽足。
¹⁶我要使祭司披上救恩，
　　聖民大聲歡呼。

¹⁷ "我要叫大衛的角在那裏發生；

³O Israel, put your hope in the LORD
　　both now and forevermore.

Psalm 132

A song of ascents.

¹O LORD, remember David
　　and all the hardships he endured.

²He swore an oath to the LORD
　　and made a vow to the Mighty One of Jacob:
³"I will not enter my house
　　or go to my bed—
⁴I will allow no sleep to my eyes,
　　no slumber to my eyelids,
⁵till I find a place for the LORD,
　　a dwelling for the Mighty One of Jacob."

⁶We heard it in Ephrathah,
　　we came upon it in the fields of Jaar^{a,b}
⁷"Let us go to his dwelling place;
　　let us worship at his footstool—
⁸arise, O LORD, and come to your resting place,
　　you and the ark of your might.
⁹May your priests be clothed with
　　righteousness;
　　may your saints sing for joy."

¹⁰For the sake of David your servant,
　　do not reject your anointed one.

¹¹The LORD swore an oath to David,
　　a sure oath that he will not revoke:
　"One of your own descendants
　　I will place on your throne—
¹²if your sons keep my covenant
　　and the statutes I teach them,
　then their sons will sit
　　on your throne for ever and ever."

¹³For the LORD has chosen Zion,
　　he has desired it for his dwelling:
¹⁴"This is my resting place for ever and ever;
　　here I will sit enthroned, for I have desired
　　it—
¹⁵I will bless her with abundant provisions;
　　her poor will I satisfy with food.
¹⁶I will clothe her priests with salvation,
　　and her saints will ever sing for joy.

¹⁷"Here I will make a horn^{c} grow for David

a 6 That is, Kiriath Jearim　b 6 Or heard of it in Ephrathah, / we
found it in the fields of Jaar. (And no quotes around verses 7-9)
c 17 Horn here symbolizes strong one, that is, king.

and set up a lamp for my anointed one.
18I will clothe his enemies with shame,
　　but the crown on his head will be
　　resplendent."

Psalm 133

A song of ascents. Of David.

1How good and pleasant it is
　　when brothers live together in unity!
2It is like precious oil poured on the head,
　　running down on the beard,
　　running down on Aaron's beard,
　　down upon the collar of his robes.
3It is as if the dew of Hermon
　　were falling on Mount Zion.
　　For there the LORD bestows his blessing,
　　even life forevermore.

Psalm 134

A song of ascents.

1Praise the LORD, all you servants of the LORD
　　who minister by night in the house of the
　　LORD.
2Lift up your hands in the sanctuary
　　and praise the LORD.

3May the LORD, the Maker of heaven and earth,
　　bless you from Zion.

Psalm 135

1Praise the LORD.ª

Praise the name of the LORD;
　　praise him, you servants of the LORD,
2you who minister in the house of the LORD,
　　in the courts of the house of our God.

3Praise the LORD, for the LORD is good;
　　sing praise to his name, for that is pleasant.
4For the LORD has chosen Jacob to be his own,
　　Israel to be his treasured possession.

5I know that the LORD is great,
　　that our Lord is greater than all gods.
6The LORD does whatever pleases him,
　　in the heavens and on the earth,
　　in the seas and all their depths.
7He makes clouds rise from the ends of the
　　earth;

a 1 Hebrew *Hallelu Yah*; also in verses 3 and 21

我為我的受膏者預備明燈。
18我要使他的仇敵披上羞恥，
　　但他的冠冕要在頭上發光。"

第一百三十三篇

大衛上行之詩。

1看哪，弟兄和睦同居，
　　是何等的善，何等的美！
2這好比那貴重的油
　　澆在亞倫的頭上，
　　流到鬍鬚，
　　又流到他的衣襟。
3又好比黑門的甘露
　　降在錫安山。
　　因為在那裏有耶和華所命定的福，
　　就是永遠的生命。

第一百三十四篇

上行之詩。

1耶和華的僕人，
　　夜間站在耶和華殿中的，
　　你們當稱頌耶和華！
2你們當向聖所舉手，
　　稱頌耶和華！

3願造天地的耶和華，
　　從錫安賜福給你們。

第一百三十五篇

1．2你們要讚美耶和華！

你們要讚美耶和華的名！
　　耶和華的僕人站在耶和華殿中，
　　站在我們神殿院中的，
　　你們要讚美他！

3你們要讚美耶和華，耶和華本為善；
　　要歌頌他的名，因為這是美好的。
4耶和華揀選雅各歸自己，
　　揀選以色列特作自己的子民。

5原來我知道耶和華為大，
　　也知道我們的主超乎萬神之上。
6耶和華在天上、在地下，
　　在海中，在一切的深處，
　　都隨自己的意旨而行。
7他使雲霧
　　從地極上騰，

造電隨雨而閃，
　　從府庫中帶出風來。

8他將埃及頭生的，
　　連人帶牲畜都擊殺了。
9埃及啊，
　　他施行神蹟奇事在你當中，
　　在法老和他一切臣僕身上。
10他擊殺許多的民，
　　又殺戮大能的王，
11就是亞摩利王西宏
　　和巴珊王噩，
　　並迦南一切的國王，
12將他們的地
　　賞賜他的百姓以色列為業。

13耶和華啊，你的名存到永遠！
　　耶和華啊，
　　你可記念的名存到萬代！
14耶和華要為他的百姓伸冤，
　　為他的僕人後悔。

15外邦的偶像是金的、銀的，
　　是人手所造的。
16有口卻不能言，
　　有眼卻不能看；
17有耳卻不能聽，
　　口中也沒有氣息。
18造他的要和他一樣，
　　凡靠他的也要如此！

19以色列家啊，你們要稱頌耶和華！
　　亞倫家啊，你們要稱頌耶和華！
20利未家啊，你們要稱頌耶和華！
　　你們敬畏耶和華的，
　　要稱頌耶和華！
21住在耶路撒冷的耶和華，
　　該從錫安受稱頌。
　　你們要讚美耶和華！

第一百三十六篇

1你們要稱謝耶和華，因他本為善，
　　　　　他的慈愛永遠長存！
2你們要稱謝萬神之神，
　　　　　因他的慈愛永遠長存！
3你們要稱謝萬主之主，
　　　　　因他的慈愛永遠長存！

4稱謝那獨行大奇事的，
　　　　　因他的慈愛永遠長存！
5稱謝那用智慧造天的，
　　　　　因他的慈愛永遠長存！
6稱謝那鋪地在水以上的，
　　　　　因他的慈愛永遠長存！

he sends lightning with the rain
and brings out the wind from his storehouses.

8He struck down the firstborn of Egypt,
the firstborn of men and animals.
9He sent his signs and wonders into your midst,
O Egypt,
against Pharaoh and all his servants.
10He struck down many nations
and killed mighty kings—
11Sihon king of the Amorites,
Og king of Bashan
and all the kings of Canaan—
12and he gave their land as an inheritance,
an inheritance to his people Israel.

13Your name, O LORD, endures forever,
your renown, O LORD, through all
generations.
14For the LORD will vindicate his people
and have compassion on his servants.

15The idols of the nations are silver and gold,
made by the hands of men.
16They have mouths, but cannot speak,
eyes, but they cannot see;
17they have ears, but cannot hear,
nor is there breath in their mouths.
18Those who make them will be like them,
and so will all who trust in them.

19O house of Israel, praise the LORD;
O house of Aaron, praise the LORD;
20O house of Levi, praise the LORD;
you who fear him, praise the LORD.
21Praise be to the LORD from Zion,
to him who dwells in Jerusalem.

Praise the LORD.

Psalm 136

1Give thanks to the LORD, for he is good.
　　　　　His love endures forever.
2Give thanks to the God of gods.
　　　　　His love endures forever.
3Give thanks to the Lord of lords:
　　　　　His love endures forever.

4to him who alone does great wonders,
　　　　　His love endures forever.
5who by his understanding made the heavens,
　　　　　His love endures forever.
6who spread out the earth upon the waters,
　　　　　His love endures forever.

⁷who made the great lights—
His love endures forever.
⁸the sun to govern the day,
His love endures forever.
⁹the moon and stars to govern the night;
His love endures forever.

¹⁰to him who struck down the firstborn of Egypt
His love endures forever.
¹¹and brought Israel out from among them
His love endures forever.
¹²with a mighty hand and outstretched arm;
His love endures forever.

¹³to him who divided the Red Sea^a asunder
His love endures forever.
¹⁴and brought Israel through the midst of it,
His love endures forever.
¹⁵but swept Pharaoh and his army into the Red Sea;

¹⁶to him who led his people through the desert,
His love endures forever.
¹⁷who struck down great kings,
His love endures forever.
¹⁸and killed mighty kings—
His love endures forever.
¹⁹Sihon king of the Amorites
His love endures forever.
²⁰and Og king of Bashan—
His love endures forever.
²¹and gave their land as an inheritance,
His love endures forever.
²²an inheritance to his servant Israel;
His love endures forever.

²³to the One who remembered us in our low estate
His love endures forever.
²⁴and freed us from our enemies,
His love endures forever.
²⁵and who gives food to every creature.
His love endures forever.

²⁶Give thanks to the God of heaven.
His love endures forever.

Psalm 137

¹By the rivers of Babylon we sat and wept
when we remembered Zion.
²There on the poplars
we hung our harps,

a 13 Hebrew Yam Suph; that is, Sea of Reeds; also in verse 15

⁷稱謝那造成大光的，
因他的慈愛永遠長存！
⁸他造日頭管白晝，
因他的慈愛永遠長存！
⁹他造月亮星宿管黑夜，
因他的慈愛永遠長存！

¹⁰稱謝那擊殺埃及人之長子的，
因他的慈愛永遠長存！
¹¹他領以色列人從他們中間出來，
因他的慈愛永遠長存！
¹²他施展大能的手和伸出來的膀臂，
因他的慈愛永遠長存！

¹³稱謝那分裂紅海的，
¹⁴他領以色列從其中經過，
因他的慈愛永遠長存！
¹⁵卻把法老和他的軍兵
推翻在紅海裏，
因他的慈愛永遠長存！

¹⁶稱謝那引導自己的民行走曠野的，
因他的慈愛永遠長存！
¹⁷稱謝那擊殺大君王的，
因他的慈愛永遠長存！
¹⁸他殺戮有名的君王，
因他的慈愛永遠長存！
¹⁹就是殺戮亞摩利王西宏，
因他的慈愛永遠長存！
²⁰又殺巴珊王噩，
因他的慈愛永遠長存！
²¹他將他們的地賜他的百姓為業，
因他的慈愛永遠長存！
²²就是賜他的僕人以色列為業，
因他的慈愛永遠長存！

²³他顧念我們
在卑微的地步，
因他的慈愛永遠長存！
²⁴他救拔我們脫離敵人，
因他的慈愛永遠長存！
²⁵他賜糧食給凡有血氣的，
因他的慈愛永遠長存！

²⁶你們要稱謝天上的神，
因他的慈愛永遠長存！

第一百三十七篇

¹我們曾在巴比倫的河邊坐下，
一追想錫安就哭了。
²我們把琴
掛在那裏的柳樹上，

3因為在那裏，擄掠我們的要我們唱歌；
　　搶奪我們的要我們作樂，説：
　　"給我們唱一首錫安歌吧！"

4我們怎能在外邦
　　唱耶和華的歌呢？
5耶路撒冷啊，我若忘記你，
　　情願我的右手忘記技巧。
6我若不記念你，
　　若不看耶路撒冷
　　過於我所最喜樂的，
　　情願我的舌頭貼於上膛。

7耶路撒冷遭難的日子，
　　以東人説："拆毀，拆毀，
　　　直拆到根基！"
　　耶和華啊，求你記念這仇。
8將要被滅的巴比倫城啊（註："城"原
　　文作"女子"），
　　報復你像你待我們的，
　　那人便為有福！
9拿你的嬰孩摔在磐石上的，
　　那人便為有福！

第一百三十八篇

大衛的詩。

1我要一心稱謝你，
　　在諸神面前頌讚你！
2我要向你的聖殿下拜，
　　為你的慈愛和誠實稱讚你的名；
　　因你使你的話顯為大，
　　過於你所應許的（註：或作"超乎你
　　的名聲"）。
3我呼求的日子，你就應允我，
　　鼓勵我，使我心裏有能力。

4耶和華啊，
　　地上的君王都要稱謝你，
　　因他們聽見了你口中的言語。
5他們要歌頌耶和華的作為，
　　因耶和華大有榮耀。

6耶和華雖高，
　　仍看顧低微的人；
　　他卻從遠處看出驕傲的人。
7我雖行在患難中，
　　你必將我救活；
　　我的仇敵發怒，
　　你必伸手抵擋他們，
　　你的右手也必救我。
8耶和華必成全關乎我的事。
　　耶和華啊，你的慈愛永遠長存！
　　求你不要離棄你手所造的。

3for there our captors asked us for songs,
　　our tormentors demanded songs of joy;
　　they said, "Sing us one of the songs of Zion!"

4How can we sing the songs of the LORD
　　while in a foreign land?
5If I forget you, O Jerusalem,
　　may my right hand forget its skill.
6May my tongue cling to the roof of my mouth
　　if I do not remember you,
　if I do not consider Jerusalem
　　my highest joy.

7Remember, O LORD, what the Edomites did
　　on the day Jerusalem fell.
　"Tear it down," they cried,
　　"tear it down to its foundations!"

8O Daughter of Babylon, doomed to destruction,
　　happy is he who repays you
　　for what you have done to us—
9he who seizes your infants
　　and dashes them against the rocks.

Psalm 138

Of David.

1I will praise you, O LORD, with all my heart;
　　before the "gods" I will sing your praise.
2I will bow down toward your holy temple
　　and will praise your name
　　for your love and your faithfulness,
　for you have exalted above all things
　　your name and your word.
3When I called, you answered me;
　　you made me bold and stouthearted.

4May all the kings of the earth praise you,
　　O LORD,
　　when they hear the words of your mouth.
5May they sing of the ways of the LORD,
　　for the glory of the LORD is great.

6Though the LORD is on high, he looks upon the
　　lowly,
　　but the proud he knows from afar.
7Though I walk in the midst of trouble,
　　you preserve my life;
　you stretch out your hand against the anger of
　　my foes,
　　with your right hand you save me.
8The LORD will fulfill his purpose for me;
　　your love, O LORD, endures forever—
　　do not abandon the works of your hands.

Psalm 139

For the director of music. Of David. A psalm.

¹O LORD, you have searched me
  and you know me.
²You know when I sit and when I rise;
  you perceive my thoughts from afar.
³You discern my going out and my lying down;
  you are familiar with all my ways.
⁴Before a word is on my tongue
  you know it completely, O LORD.

⁵You hem me in—behind and before;
  you have laid your hand upon me.
⁶Such knowledge is too wonderful for me,
  too lofty for me to attain.

⁷Where can I go from your Spirit?
  Where can I flee from your presence?
⁸If I go up to the heavens, you are there;
  if I make my bed in the depths,^a you are
    there.
⁹If I rise on the wings of the dawn,
  if I settle on the far side of the sea,
¹⁰even there your hand will guide me,
  your right hand will hold me fast.

¹¹If I say, "Surely the darkness will hide me
  and the light become night around me,"
¹²even the darkness will not be dark to you;
  the night will shine like the day,
  for darkness is as light to you.

¹³For you created my inmost being;
  you knit me together in my mother's womb.
¹⁴I praise you because I am fearfully and
    wonderfully made;
  your works are wonderful,
  I know that full well.
¹⁵My frame was not hidden from you
  when I was made in the secret place.
  When I was woven together in the depths of
    the earth,
¹⁶ your eyes saw my unformed body.
  All the days ordained for me
  were written in your book
  before one of them came to be.

¹⁷How precious to^b me are your thoughts,
    O God!
  How vast is the sum of them!
¹⁸Were I to count them,
  they would outnumber the grains of sand.

a 8 Hebrew Sheol   b 17 Or concerning

第一百三十九篇

大衛的詩,交與伶長。

¹耶和華啊,你已經鑒察我、
  認識我。
²我坐下,我起來,你都曉得,
  你從遠處知道我的意念;
³我行路,我躺臥,你都細察,
  你也深知我一切所行的。
⁴耶和華啊,我舌頭上的話,
  你沒有一句不知道的。

⁵你在我前後環繞我,
  按手在我身上。
⁶這樣的知識奇妙,是我不能測的;
  至高,是我不能及的。

⁷我往哪裏去躲避你的靈?
  我往哪裏逃躲避你的面?
⁸我若升到天上,你在那裏;
  我若在陰間下榻,你也在那裏。

⁹我若展開清晨的翅膀,
  飛到海極居住;
¹⁰就是在那裏,你的手必引導我,
  你的右手也必扶持我。

¹¹我若說:"黑暗必定遮蔽我,
  我周圍的亮光必成為黑夜,"
¹²黑暗也不能遮蔽我使你不見,
  黑夜卻如白晝發亮。
  黑暗和光明,在你看都是一樣。

¹³我的肺腑是你所造的。
  我在母腹中,你已覆庇我。
¹⁴我要稱謝你,
  因我受造奇妙可畏。
  你的作為奇妙,
  這是我心深知道的。
¹⁵我在暗中受造,
  在地的深處被聯絡。
  那時,我的形體並不向你隱藏。
¹⁶我未成形的體質,
  你的眼早已看見了。
  你所定的日子,我尚未度一日(註:
      或作"我被造的肢體尚未有其一"),
  你都寫在你的冊上了。

¹⁷神啊,
  你的意念向我何等寶貴,
  其數何等眾多!
¹⁸我若數點,
  比海沙更多。

我睡醒的時候，
　仍和你同在。

¹⁹神啊，你必要殺戮惡人，
　所以你們好流人血的，離開我去吧！
²⁰因為他們說惡言頂撞你，
　你的仇敵也妄稱你的名。
²¹耶和華啊，
　恨惡你的，我豈不恨惡他們嗎？
　攻擊你的，我豈不憎嫌他們嗎？
²²我切切地恨惡他們，以他們為仇敵。

²³神啊，求你鑒察我，知道我的心思，
　試煉我，知道我的意念。
²⁴看在我裏面有甚麼惡行沒有，
　引導我走永生的道路。

第一百四十篇

大衛的詩，交與伶長。

¹耶和華啊，求你拯救我脫離兇惡的人，
　保護我脫離強暴的人。
²他們心中圖謀奸惡，
　常常聚集要爭戰。
³他們使舌頭尖利如蛇，
　嘴裏有虺蛇的毒氣。　　　　細拉

⁴耶和華啊，
　求你拯救我脫離惡人的手，
　保護我脫離強暴的人。
　他們圖謀推我跌倒。
⁵驕傲人為我暗設網羅和繩索，
　他們在路旁鋪下網，
　設下圈套。　　　　細拉

⁶我曾對耶和華說，你是我的神。
　耶和華啊，求你留心聽我懇求的聲音！
⁷主耶和華——我救恩的力量啊，
　在爭戰的日子，你遮蔽了我的頭。
⁸耶和華啊，求你不要遂惡人的心願，
　不要成就他們的計謀，
　恐怕他們自高。　　　　細拉

⁹至於那些昂首圍困我的人，
　願他們嘴唇的奸惡，
　陷害（註：原文作"遮蔽"）自己。
¹⁰願火炭落在他們身上，
　願他們被丟在火中，
　拋在深坑裏，不能再起來。
¹¹說惡言的人在地上必堅立不住。
　禍患必獵取強暴的人，將他打倒。

¹²我知道耶和華必為困苦人伸冤，
　必為窮乏人辨屈。

When I awake,
I am still with you.

¹⁹If only you would slay the wicked, O God!
　Away from me, you bloodthirsty men!
²⁰They speak of you with evil intent;
　your adversaries misuse your name.
²¹Do I not hate those who hate you, O LORD,
　and abhor those who rise up against you?
²²I have nothing but hatred for them;
　I count them my enemies.

²³Search me, O God, and know my heart;
　test me and know my anxious thoughts.
²⁴See if there is any offensive way in me,
　and lead me in the way everlasting.

Psalm 140

For the director of music. A psalm of David.

¹Rescue me, O LORD, from evil men;
　protect me from men of violence,
²who devise evil plans in their hearts
　and stir up war every day.
³They make their tongues as sharp as a serpent's;
　the poison of vipers is on their lips. *Selah*

⁴Keep me, O LORD, from the hands of the
　wicked;
　protect me from men of violence
　who plan to trip my feet.
⁵Proud men have hidden a snare for me;
　they have spread out the cords of their net
　and have set traps for me along my path.
　　　　　　　　　　　　　　　Selah

⁶O LORD, I say to you, "You are my God."
　Hear, O LORD, my cry for mercy.
⁷O Sovereign LORD, my strong deliverer,
　who shields my head in the day of battle—
⁸do not grant the wicked their desires, O LORD;
　do not let their plans succeed,
　or they will become proud. *Selah*

⁹Let the heads of those who surround me
　be covered with the trouble their lips have
　caused.
¹⁰Let burning coals fall upon them;
　may they be thrown into the fire,
　into miry pits, never to rise.
¹¹Let slanderers not be established in the land;
　may disaster hunt down men of violence.

¹²I know that the LORD secures justice for the poor
　and upholds the cause of the needy.

¹³Surely the righteous will praise your name
   and the upright will live before you.

Psalm 141

A psalm of David.

¹O LORD, I call to you; come quickly to me.
   Hear my voice when I call to you.
²May my prayer be set before you like incense;
   may the lifting up of my hands be like the
      evening sacrifice.

³Set a guard over my mouth, O LORD;
   keep watch over the door of my lips.
⁴Let not my heart be drawn to what is evil,
   to take part in wicked deeds
   with men who are evildoers;
   let me not eat of their delicacies.

⁵Let a righteous man^a strike me—it is a
      kindness;
   let him rebuke me—it is oil on my head.
   My head will not refuse it.

   Yet my prayer is ever against the deeds of
      evildoers;
⁶   their rulers will be thrown down from the
      cliffs,
   and the wicked will learn that my words
      were well spoken.
⁷⌊They will say,⌋ "As one plows and breaks up
      the earth,
   so our bones have been scattered at the
      mouth of the grave.^b"

⁸But my eyes are fixed on you, O Sovereign
      LORD;
   in you I take refuge—do not give me over to
      death.
⁹Keep me from the snares they have laid for me,
   from the traps set by evildoers.
¹⁰Let the wicked fall into their own nets,
   while I pass by in safety.

Psalm 142

A maskil^c of David. When he was in the cave. A prayer.

¹I cry aloud to the LORD;
   I lift up my voice to the LORD for mercy.
²I pour out my complaint before him;
   before him I tell my trouble.

---

¹³義人必要稱讚你的名，
   正直人必住在你面前。

第一百四十一篇

大衛的詩。

¹耶和華啊，我曾求告你，
   求你快快臨到我這裏！
   我求告你的時候，
      願你留心聽我的聲音！
²願我的禱告如香陳列在你面前；
   願我舉手祈求，如獻晚祭。
³耶和華啊，求你禁止我的口，
   把守我的嘴。
⁴求你不叫我的心
   偏向邪惡，
   以致我和作孽的人同行惡事；
   也不叫我吃他們的美食。

⁵任憑義人擊打我，這算為仁慈；
   任憑他責備我，
   這算為頭上的膏油。
   我的頭不要躲閃。

   正在他們行惡的時候，
      我仍要祈禱。
⁶他們的審判官
   被扔在巖下，
   眾人要聽我的話，
      因為這話甘甜。
⁷我們的骨頭
   散在墓旁，
   好像人耕田、
      刨地的土塊。

⁸主耶和華啊，
   我的眼目仰望你，
   我投靠你——求你不要將我
      撇得孤苦。
⁹求你保護我脫離惡人為我設的網羅
   和作孽之人的圈套。
¹⁰願惡人落在自己的網裏，
   我卻得以逃脫。

第一百四十二篇

大衛在洞裏作的訓誨詩，乃是祈禱。

¹我發聲哀告耶和華，
   發聲懇求耶和華。
²我在他面前吐露我的苦情，
   陳說我的患難。

---

a 5 Or Let the Righteous One   b 7 Hebrew Sheol
c Title: Probably a literary or musical term

³我的靈在我裏面發昏的時候，
　　你知道我的道路。
　在我行的路上，
　　敵人為我暗設網羅。
⁴求你向我右邊觀看，
　　因為沒有人認識我。
　我無處避難，
　　也沒有人眷顧我。

⁵耶和華啊，我曾向你哀求，
　　我說："你是我的避難所，
　　在活人之地，你是我的福分。"
⁶求你側耳聽我的呼求，
　　因我落到極卑之地；
　求你救我脫離逼迫我的人，
　　因為他們比我強盛。
⁷求你領我出離被囚之地，
　　我好稱讚你的名。

　義人必環繞我，
　　因為你是用厚恩待我。

第一百四十三篇

大衛的詩。

¹耶和華啊，求你聽我的禱告，
　　留心聽我的懇求，
　憑你的信實和公義
　　應允我。
²求你不要審問僕人，因為在你面前，
　　凡活着的人沒有一個是義的。

³原來仇敵逼迫我，
　　將我打倒在地，
　使我住在幽暗之處，
　　像死了許久的人一樣。
⁴所以我的靈在我裏面發昏，
　　我的心在我裏面悽慘。

⁵我追想古時之日，
　　思想你的一切作為，
　　默念你手的工作。
⁶我向你舉手，我的心渴想你，
　　如乾旱之地盼雨一樣。

細拉

⁷耶和華啊，求你速速應允我！
　　我心神耗盡。
　不要向我掩面，
　　免得我像那些下坑的人一樣。

⁸求你使我清晨
　　得聽你慈愛之言，
　　因我倚靠你；

³When my spirit grows faint within me,
　　it is you who know my way.
　In the path where I walk
　　men have hidden a snare for me.
⁴Look to my right and see;
　　no one is concerned for me.
　I have no refuge;
　　no one cares for my life.

⁵I cry to you, O LORD;
　　I say, "You are my refuge,
　　my portion in the land of the living."
⁶Listen to my cry,
　　for I am in desperate need;
　rescue me from those who pursue me,
　　for they are too strong for me.
⁷Set me free from my prison,
　　that I may praise your name.

Then the righteous will gather about me
　because of your goodness to me.

Psalm 143

A psalm of David.

¹O LORD, hear my prayer,
　　listen to my cry for mercy;
　in your faithfulness and righteousness
　　come to my relief.
²Do not bring your servant into judgment,
　　for no one living is righteous before you.

³The enemy pursues me,
　　he crushes me to the ground;
　he makes me dwell in darkness
　　like those long dead.
⁴So my spirit grows faint within me;
　　my heart within me is dismayed.

⁵I remember the days of long ago;
　　I meditate on all your works
　　and consider what your hands have done.
⁶I spread out my hands to you;
　　my soul thirsts for you like a parched land.

Selah

⁷Answer me quickly, O LORD;
　　my spirit fails.
　Do not hide your face from me
　　or I will be like those who go down to the
　　　pit.
⁸Let the morning bring me word of your
　　　unfailing love,
　for I have put my trust in you.

Show me the way I should go,
　for to you I lift up my soul.
⁹Rescue me from my enemies, O LORD,
　for I hide myself in you.
¹⁰Teach me to do your will,
　for you are my God;
may your good Spirit
　lead me on level ground.

¹¹For your name's sake, O LORD, preserve my
　life;
　in your righteousness, bring me out of trouble.
¹²In your unfailing love, silence my enemies;
　destroy all my foes,
　for I am your servant.

Psalm 144

Of David.

¹Praise be to the LORD my Rock,
　who trains my hands for war,
　my fingers for battle.
²He is my loving God and my fortress,
　my stronghold and my deliverer,
　my shield, in whom I take refuge,
　who subdues peoples*ᵃ* under me.

³O LORD, what is man that you care for him,
　the son of man that you think of him?
⁴Man is like a breath;
　his days are like a fleeting shadow.

⁵Part your heavens, O LORD, and come down;
　touch the mountains, so that they smoke.
⁶Send forth lightning and scatter [the enemies];
　shoot your arrows and rout them.
⁷Reach down your hand from on high;
　deliver me and rescue me
　from the mighty waters,
　from the hands of foreigners
⁸whose mouths are full of lies,
　whose right hands are deceitful.

⁹I will sing a new song to you, O God;
　on the ten-stringed lyre I will make music to
　you,
¹⁰to the One who gives victory to kings,
　who delivers his servant David from the
　deadly sword.

---

*a 2 Many manuscripts of the Masoretic Text, Dead Sea Scrolls,
Aquila, Jerome and Syriac; most manuscripts of the Masoretic
Text subdues my people*

求你使我知道當行的路,
　因我的心仰望你。
⁹耶和華啊,求你救我脫離我的仇敵,
　我往你那裏藏身。
¹⁰求你指教我遵行你的旨意,
　因你是我的神。
你的靈本為善,
　求你引我到平坦之地。

¹¹耶和華啊,求你為你的名將我救活;
　憑你的公義,
　將我從患難中領出來。
¹²憑你的慈愛剪除我的仇敵,
　滅絕一切苦待我的人,
　因我是你的僕人。

第一百四十四篇

大衛的詩。

¹耶和華我的磐石是應當稱頌的;
　他教導我的手爭戰,
　教導我的指頭打仗。
²他是我慈愛的主,我的山寨,
　我的高臺,我的救主,
　我的盾牌,是我所投靠的,
　他使我的百姓服在我以下。

³耶和華啊,人算甚麼,你竟認識他?
　世人算甚麼,你竟顧念他?
⁴人好像一口氣,
　他的年日如同影兒快快過去。

⁵耶和華啊,求你使天下垂,
　親自降臨,摸山,山就冒煙。
⁶求你發出閃電,使他們四散;
　射出你的箭,使他們擾亂。
⁷求你從上伸手
　救拔我,
　救我出離大水,
　救我脫離外邦人的手。
⁸他們的口說謊話,
　他們的右手起假誓。

⁹神啊,
　我要向你唱新歌,
　用十弦瑟向你歌頌。
¹⁰你是那拯救君王的,
　你是那救僕人大衛
　脫離害命之刀的。

¹¹求你救拔我，
　　救我脫離外邦人的手。
他們的口說謊話，
　　他們的右手起假誓。

¹²我們的兒子
　　從幼年好像樹栽子長大；
我們的女兒如同殿角石，
　　是按建宮的樣式鑿成的。
¹³我們的倉盈滿，
　　能出各樣的糧食；
我們的羊
　　在田間孳生千萬。
¹⁴我們的牛馱着滿馱，
　　沒有人闖進來搶奪，
　　也沒有人出去爭戰。
我們的街市上也沒有哭號的聲音。

¹⁵遇見這光景的百姓便為有福。
　　有耶和華為他們的神，
　　這百姓便為有福！

第一百四十五篇

大衛的讚美詩。

¹我的神、我的王啊，我要尊崇你，
　　我要永永遠遠稱頌你的名！
²我要天天稱頌你，
　　也要永永遠遠讚美你的名！

³耶和華本為大，該受大讚美，
　　其大無法測度。
⁴這代要對那代
　　　頌讚你的作為，
　　也要傳揚你的大能。
⁵我要默念
　　你威嚴的尊榮，
　　和你奇妙的作為。

⁶人要傳說你可畏之事的能力，
　　我也要傳揚你的大德。

⁷他們記念你的大恩，就要傳出來，
　　並要歌唱你的公義。

⁸耶和華有恩惠，有憐憫，
　　不輕易發怒，大有慈愛。

¹¹Deliver me and rescue me
　　from the hands of foreigners
whose mouths are full of lies,
　　whose right hands are deceitful.

¹²Then our sons in their youth
　　will be like well-nurtured plants,
and our daughters will be like pillars
　　carved to adorn a palace.
¹³Our barns will be filled
　　with every kind of provision.
Our sheep will increase by thousands,
　　by tens of thousands in our fields;
¹⁴ our oxen will draw heavy loads.ᵃ
There will be no breaching of walls,
　　no going into captivity,
　　no cry of distress in our streets.

¹⁵Blessed are the people of whom this is true;
　　blessed are the people whose God is the
　　LORD.

Psalm 145ᵇ

A psalm of praise. Of David.

¹I will exalt you, my God the King;
　　I will praise your name for ever and ever.
²Every day I will praise you
　　and extol your name for ever and ever.

³Great is the LORD and most worthy of praise;
　　his greatness no one can fathom.
⁴One generation will commend your works to
　　　another;
　　they will tell of your mighty acts.
⁵They will speak of the glorious splendor of
　　　your majesty,
　　and I will meditate on your wonderful
　　　works.ᶜ
⁶They will tell of the power of your awesome
　　　works,
　　and I will proclaim your great deeds.
⁷They will celebrate your abundant goodness
　　and joyfully sing of your righteousness.

⁸The LORD is gracious and compassionate,
　　slow to anger and rich in love.

*a 14 Or our chieftains will be firmly established　　b This psalm is
an acrostic poem, the verses of which (including verse 13b)
begin with the successive letters of the Hebrew alphabet.
c 5 Dead Sea Scrolls and Syriac (see also Septuagint);
Masoretic Text On the glorious splendor of your majesty / and on
your wonderful works I will meditate*

9The LORD is good to all;
    he has compassion on all he has made.
10All you have made will praise you, O LORD;
    your saints will extol you.
11They will tell of the glory of your kingdom
    and speak of your might,
12so that all men may know of your mighty acts
    and the glorious splendor of your kingdom.
13Your kingdom is an everlasting kingdom,
    and your dominion endures through all
    generations.

    The LORD is faithful to all his promises
    and loving toward all he has made.[a]
14The LORD upholds all those who fall
    and lifts up all who are bowed down.
15The eyes of all look to you,
    and you give them their food at the proper
    time.
16You open your hand
    and satisfy the desires of every living thing.

17The LORD is righteous in all his ways
    and loving toward all he has made.
18The LORD is near to all who call on him,
    to all who call on him in truth.
19He fulfills the desires of those who fear him;
    he hears their cry and saves them.
20The LORD watches over all who love him,
    but all the wicked he will destroy.

21My mouth will speak in praise of the LORD.
    Let every creature praise his holy name
    for ever and ever.

Psalm 146

1Praise the LORD.[b]

    Praise the LORD, O my soul.
2   I will praise the LORD all my life;
    I will sing praise to my God as long as I live.

3Do not put your trust in princes,
    in mortal men, who cannot save.
4When their spirit departs, they return to the
    ground;
    on that very day their plans come to nothing.

5Blessed is he whose help is the God of Jacob,
    whose hope is in the LORD his God,

9耶和華善待萬民，
    他的慈悲覆庇他一切所造的。
10耶和華啊，你一切所造的都要稱謝你；
    你的聖民也要稱頌你，
11傳說你國的榮耀，
    談論你的大能，
12好叫世人知道你大能的作為，
    並你國度威嚴的榮耀。
13你的國是永遠的國，
    你執掌的權柄
    存到萬代。

14凡跌倒的，耶和華將他們扶持；
    凡被壓下的，將他們扶起。
15萬民都舉目仰望你，
    你隨時
      給他們食物。
16你張手，
    使有生氣的都隨願飽足。

17耶和華在他一切所行的，無不公義；
    在他一切所做的都有慈愛。
18凡求告耶和華的，就是誠心求告他的，
    耶和華便與他們相近。
19敬畏他的，他必成就他們的心願，
    也必聽他們的呼求，拯救他們。
20耶和華保護一切愛他的人，
    卻要滅絕一切的惡人。

21我的口要說出讚美耶和華的話，
    惟願凡有血氣的，
    都永永遠遠稱頌他的聖名！

第一百四十六篇

1你們要讚美耶和華！

    我的心哪，你要讚美耶和華！
2我一生要讚美耶和華。
    我還活的時候，要歌頌我的神。

3你們不要倚靠君王，
    不要倚靠世人，他一點不能幫助。
4他的氣一斷，
    就歸回塵土；
    他所打算的，當日就消滅了。

5以雅各的神為幫助、
    仰望耶和華他神的，
    這人便為有福！

---

a 13 One manuscript of the Masoretic Text, Dead Sea Scrolls
and Syriac (see also Septuagint); most manuscripts of the
Masoretic Text do not have the last two lines of verse 13.
b 1 Hebrew *Hallelu Yah*; also in verse 10

⁶耶和華造天、地、
　　海和其中的萬物，
　　他守誠實，直到永遠。
⁷他為受屈的伸冤，
　　賜食物與飢餓的，
　　耶和華釋放被囚的。
⁸耶和華開了瞎子的眼睛，
　　耶和華扶起被壓下的人，
　　耶和華喜愛義人。
⁹耶和華保護寄居的，
　　扶持孤兒和寡婦，
　　卻使惡人的道路彎曲。

¹⁰耶和華要作王，直到永遠。
　　錫安哪，你的神要作王，
　　直到萬代！
　　你們要讚美耶和華！

第一百四十七篇

¹你們要讚美耶和華！

因歌頌我們的神為善為美，
　　讚美的話是合宜的。

²耶和華建造耶路撒冷，
　　聚集以色列中被趕散的人。
³他醫好傷心的人，
　　裹好他們的傷處。

⁴他數點星宿的數目，
　　一一稱他的名。
⁵我們的主為大，最有能力。
　　他的智慧無法測度！
⁶耶和華扶持謙卑人，
　　將惡人傾覆於地。

⁷你們要以感謝向耶和華歌唱，
　　用琴向我們的神歌頌。
⁸他用雲遮天，
　　為地降雨，
　　使草生長在山上。
⁹他賜食給走獸
　　和啼叫的小烏鴉。

¹⁰他不喜悅馬的力大，
　　不喜愛人的腿快。
¹¹耶和華喜愛敬畏他
　　和盼望他慈愛的人。

¹²耶路撒冷啊，你要頌讚耶和華！
　　錫安哪，你要讚美你的神！
¹³因為他堅固了你的門閂，
　　賜福給你中間的兒女。

⁶the Maker of heaven and earth,
　　the sea, and everything in them—
　　the LORD, who remains faithful forever.
⁷He upholds the cause of the oppressed
　　and gives food to the hungry.
　　The LORD sets prisoners free,
8　　the LORD gives sight to the blind,
　　the LORD lifts up those who are bowed down,
　　the LORD loves the righteous.
⁹The LORD watches over the alien
　　and sustains the fatherless and the widow,
　　but he frustrates the ways of the wicked.

¹⁰The LORD reigns forever,
　　your God, O Zion, for all generations.

Praise the LORD.

Psalm 147

¹Praise the LORD.ᵃ

How good it is to sing praises to our God,
　　how pleasant and fitting to praise him!

²The LORD builds up Jerusalem;
　　he gathers the exiles of Israel.
³He heals the brokenhearted
　　and binds up their wounds.

⁴He determines the number of the stars
　　and calls them each by name.
⁵Great is our Lord and mighty in power;
　　his understanding has no limit.
⁶The LORD sustains the humble
　　but casts the wicked to the ground.

⁷Sing to the LORD with thanksgiving;
　　make music to our God on the harp.
⁸He covers the sky with clouds;
　　he supplies the earth with rain
　　and makes grass grow on the hills.
⁹He provides food for the cattle
　　and for the young ravens when they call.

¹⁰His pleasure is not in the strength of the horse,
　　nor his delight in the legs of a man;
¹¹the LORD delights in those who fear him,
　　who put their hope in his unfailing love.

¹²Extol the LORD, O Jerusalem;
　　praise your God, O Zion,
¹³for he strengthens the bars of your gates
　　and blesses your people within you.

a 1 Hebrew *Hallelu Yah;* also in verse 20

¹⁴He grants peace to your borders
 and satisfies you with the finest of wheat.

¹⁵He sends his command to the earth;
 his word runs swiftly.
¹⁶He spreads the snow like wool
 and scatters the frost like ashes.
¹⁷He hurls down his hail like pebbles.
 Who can withstand his icy blast?
¹⁸He sends his word and melts them;
 he stirs up his breezes, and the waters flow.

¹⁹He has revealed his word to Jacob,
 his laws and decrees to Israel.
²⁰He has done this for no other nation;
 they do not know his laws.

Praise the LORD.

Psalm 148

¹Praise the LORD.*

Praise the LORD from the heavens,
 praise him in the heights above.
²Praise him, all his angels,
 praise him, all his heavenly hosts.
³Praise him, sun and moon,
 praise him, all you shining stars.
⁴Praise him, you highest heavens
 and you waters above the skies.
⁵Let them praise the name of the LORD,
 for he commanded and they were created.
⁶He set them in place for ever and ever;
 he gave a decree that will never pass away.

⁷Praise the LORD from the earth,
 you great sea creatures and all ocean depths,
⁸lightning and hail, snow and clouds,
 stormy winds that do his bidding,
⁹you mountains and all hills,
 fruit trees and all cedars,
¹⁰wild animals and all cattle,
 small creatures and flying birds,
¹¹kings of the earth and all nations,
 you princes and all rulers on earth,
¹²young men and maidens,
 old men and children.

¹³Let them praise the name of the LORD,
 for his name alone is exalted;
 his splendor is above the earth and the
  heavens.

¹⁴他使你境內平安,
 用上好的麥子使你滿足。

¹⁵他發命在地,
 他的話頒行最快。
¹⁶他降雪如羊毛,
 撒霜如爐灰。
¹⁷他擲下冰雹如碎渣,
 他發出寒冷,誰能當得起呢?
¹⁸他一出令,這些都就消化;
 他使風颳起,水便流動。

¹⁹他將他的道指示雅各,
 將他的律例、典章指示以色列。
²⁰別國他都沒有這樣待過,
 至於他的典章,他們向來沒有知道。

你們要讚美耶和華!

第一百四十八篇

¹你們要讚美耶和華!

從天上讚美耶和華,
 在高處讚美他。
²他的眾使者都要讚美他,
 他的諸軍都要讚美他。
³日頭、月亮,你們要讚美他!
 放光的星宿,你們要讚美他!
⁴天上的天和天上的水,
 你們都要讚美他!
⁵願這些都讚美耶和華的名,
 因他一吩咐便都造成。
⁶他將這些立定,直到永永遠遠。
 他定了命,不能廢去 (註:"廢去"
  或作"越過")。
⁷所有在地上的,
 大魚和一切深洋,
⁸火與冰雹,雪和霧氣,
 成就他命的狂風,
⁹大山和小山,
 結果的樹木和一切香柏樹,
¹⁰野獸和一切牲畜、
 昆蟲和飛鳥,
¹¹世上的君王和萬民,
 首領和世上一切審判官,
¹²少年人和處女,老年人和孩童,
 都當讚美耶和華!

¹³願這些都讚美耶和華的名;
 因為獨有他的名被尊崇,
 他的榮耀在天地之上。

_a 1 Hebrew *Hallelu Yah*; also in verse 14

14他將他百姓的角高舉，
　　因為他（註：「因此他」或作「他使」）
　　一切聖民以色列人，
　　就是與他相近的百姓，都讚美他。
你們要讚美耶和華！

第一百四十九篇

1你們要讚美耶和華！

向耶和華唱新歌，
　　在聖民的會中讚美他！

2願以色列因造他的主歡喜；
　　願錫安的民因他們的王快樂。
3願他們跳舞讚美他的名，
　　擊鼓、彈琴歌頌他！

4因為耶和華喜愛他的百姓，
　　他要用救恩當作謙卑人的妝飾。
5願聖民因所得的榮耀高興，
　　願他們在牀上歡呼！

6願他們口中稱讚神為高，
　　手裏有兩刃的刀，
7為要報復列邦，
　　刑罰萬民。
8要用鏈子捆他們的君王，
　　用鐵鐐鎖他們的大臣，
9要在他們身上施行所記錄的審判。
　　他的聖民都有這榮耀。

你們要讚美耶和華！

第一百五十篇

1你們要讚美耶和華！

在神的聖所讚美他，
　　在他顯能力的穹蒼讚美他！
2要因他大能的作為讚美他，
　　按着他極美的大德讚美他。
3要用角聲讚美他，
　　鼓瑟、彈琴讚美他！
4擊鼓、跳舞讚美他，
　　用絲弦的樂器和簫的聲音讚美他。
5用大響的鈸讚美他，
　　用高聲的鈸讚美他。

6凡有氣息的，都要讚美耶和華！

你們要讚美耶和華！

14He has raised up for his people a horn,*a*
　　the praise of all his saints,
　　of Israel, the people close to his heart.

　　Praise the LORD.

Psalm 149

1Praise the LORD.*b*

Sing to the LORD a new song,
　　his praise in the assembly of the saints.

2Let Israel rejoice in their Maker;
　　let the people of Zion be glad in their King.
3Let them praise his name with dancing
　　and make music to him with tambourine and
　　　　harp.
4For the LORD takes delight in his people;
　　he crowns the humble with salvation.
5Let the saints rejoice in this honor
　　and sing for joy on their beds.

6May the praise of God be in their mouths
　　and a double-edged sword in their hands,
7to inflict vengeance on the nations
　　and punishment on the peoples,
8to bind their kings with fetters,
　　their nobles with shackles of iron,
9to carry out the sentence written against them.
　　This is the glory of all his saints.

　　Praise the LORD.

Psalm 150

1Praise the LORD.*c*

Praise God in his sanctuary;
　　praise him in his mighty heavens.
2Praise him for his acts of power;
　　praise him for his surpassing greatness.
3Praise him with the sounding of the trumpet,
　　praise him with the harp and lyre,
4praise him with tambourine and dancing,
　　praise him with the strings and flute,
5praise him with the clash of cymbals,
　　praise him with resounding cymbals.

6Let everything that has breath praise the LORD.

　　Praise the LORD.

---

a 14 *Horn* here symbolizes strong one, that is, king.
b 1 Hebrew *Hallelu Yah; also in verse 9*　　*c* 1 Hebrew *Hallelu Yah; also in verse 6*

Proverbs

箴言

Prologue: Purpose and Theme

前言：目的與主題

1 The proverbs of Solomon son of David, king of Israel:

1 <u>以色列王大衞兒子所羅門</u>的箴言：

²for attaining wisdom and discipline;
  for understanding words of insight;
³for acquiring a disciplined and prudent life,
  doing what is right and just and fair;
⁴for giving prudence to the simple,
  knowledge and discretion to the young—
⁵let the wise listen and add to their learning,
  and let the discerning get guidance—
⁶for understanding proverbs and parables,
  the sayings and riddles of the wise.

²要使人曉得智慧和訓誨，
  分辨通達的言語，
³使人處事領受智慧、仁義、
  公平、正直的訓誨，
⁴使愚人靈明，
  使少年人有知識和謀略，
⁵使智慧人聽見，增長學問，
  使聰明人得着智謀，
⁶使人明白箴言和譬喻，
  懂得智慧人的言詞和謎語。

⁷The fear of the LORD is the beginning of
  knowledge,
  but fools*ᵃ* despise wisdom and discipline.

⁷敬畏耶和華是知識的開端；
  愚妄人藐視智慧和訓誨。

Exhortations to Embrace Wisdom

勸要有智慧

Warning Against Enticement

警告不要受引誘

⁸Listen, my son, to your father's instruction
  and do not forsake your mother's teaching.
⁹They will be a garland to grace your head
  and a chain to adorn your neck.

⁸我兒，要聽你父親的訓誨，
  不可離棄你母親的法則（註：或作
  "指教"），
⁹因為這要作你頭上的華冠，
  你項上的金鏈。

¹⁰My son, if sinners entice you,
  do not give in to them.
¹¹If they say, "Come along with us;
  let's lie in wait for someone's blood,
  let's waylay some harmless soul;
¹²let's swallow them alive, like the grave,*ᵇ*
  and whole, like those who go down to the pit;
¹³we will get all sorts of valuable things
  and fill our houses with plunder;
¹⁴throw in your lot with us,
  and we will share a common purse"—
¹⁵my son, do not go along with them,
  do not set foot on their paths;
¹⁶for their feet rush into sin,
  they are swift to shed blood.
¹⁷How useless to spread a net

¹⁰我兒，惡人若引誘你，
  你不可隨從。
¹¹他們若說："你與我們同去，
  我們要埋伏流人之血，
  要蹲伏害無罪之人。
¹²我們好像陰間，把他們活活吞下；
  他們如同下坑的人，被我們囫圇吞了。
¹³我們必得各樣寶物，
  將所擄來的裝滿房屋。
¹⁴你與我們大家同分，
  我們共用一個囊袋。"
¹⁵我兒，不要與他們同行一道，
  禁止你腳走他們的路！
¹⁶因為他們的腳奔跑行惡，
  他們急速流人的血，
¹⁷好像飛鳥，

*a 7 The Hebrew words rendered fool in Proverbs, and often
elsewhere in the Old Testament, denote one who is morally
deficient. b 12 Hebrew Sheol*

網羅設在眼前仍不躲避。

18這些人埋伏，是為自流己血；
　　蹲伏，是為自害己命。

19凡貪戀財利的，
　　　　所行之路都是如此；
　　這貪戀之心乃奪去得財者之命。

警告不要拒絕智慧

20智慧在街市上呼喊，
　　在寬闊處發聲，
21在熱鬧街頭喊叫，
　　在城門口、在城中發出言語，

22說：“你們愚昧人喜愛愚昧，
　　褻慢人喜歡褻慢，
　　愚頑人恨惡知識，
　　要到幾時呢？
23你們當因我的責備回轉，
　　我要將我的靈澆灌你們，
　　將我的話指示你們。
24我呼喚，你們不肯聽從；
　　我伸手，無人理會。

25反輕棄我一切的勸戒，
　　不肯受我的責備。
26你們遭災難，我就發笑；
　　驚恐臨到你們，我必嗤笑。
27驚恐臨到你們，好像狂風；
　　災難來到，如同暴風，
　　急難痛苦臨到你們身上。

28“那時，你們必呼求我，我卻不答應；
　　懇切地尋找我，卻尋不見。
29因為你們恨惡知識，
　　不喜愛敬畏耶和華，
30不聽我的勸戒，
　　藐視我一切的責備，
31所以必吃自結的果子，
　　充滿自設的計謀。
32愚昧人背道，必殺己身；
　　愚頑人安逸，必害己命。

33惟有聽從我的，必安然居住，
　　得享安靜，不怕災禍。”

智慧使人有好德行

2 我兒，你若領受我的言語，
　　存記我的命令，
　　2側耳聽智慧，

in full view of all the birds!

18These men lie in wait for their own blood;
they waylay only themselves!

19Such is the end of all who go after ill-gotten
gain;
it takes away the lives of those who get it.

Warning Against Rejecting Wisdom

20Wisdom calls aloud in the street,
she raises her voice in the public squares;
21at the head of the noisy streets*a* she cries out,
in the gateways of the city she makes her
speech:

22“How long will you simple ones*b* love your
simple ways?
How long will mockers delight in mockery
and fools hate knowledge?
23If you had responded to my rebuke,
I would have poured out my heart to you
and made my thoughts known to you.
24But since you rejected me when I called
and no one gave heed when I stretched out
my hand,
25since you ignored all my advice
and would not accept my rebuke,
26I in turn will laugh at your disaster;
I will mock when calamity overtakes you—
27when calamity overtakes you like a storm,
when disaster sweeps over you like a
whirlwind,
when distress and trouble overwhelm you.

28“Then they will call to me but I will not answer;
they will look for me but will not find me.
29Since they hated knowledge
and did not choose to fear the LORD,
30since they would not accept my advice
and spurned my rebuke,
31they will eat the fruit of their ways
and be filled with the fruit of their schemes.
32For the waywardness of the simple will kill
them,
and the complacency of fools will destroy
them;
33but whoever listens to me will live in safety
and be at ease, without fear of harm.”

Moral Benefits of Wisdom

2 My son, if you accept my words
and store up my commands within you,
2turning your ear to wisdom

*a 21 Hebrew; Septuagint / on the tops of the walls　　b 22 The
Hebrew word rendered simple in Proverbs generally denotes
one without moral direction and inclined to evil.*

and applying your heart to understanding,
³and if you call out for insight
  and cry aloud for understanding,
⁴and if you look for it as for silver
  and search for it as for hidden treasure,
⁵then you will understand the fear of the LORD
  and find the knowledge of God.
⁶For the LORD gives wisdom,
  and from his mouth come knowledge and
    understanding.
⁷He holds victory in store for the upright,
  he is a shield to those whose walk is
    blameless,
⁸for he guards the course of the just
  and protects the way of his faithful ones.

⁹Then you will understand what is right and
    just
  and fair—every good path.
¹⁰For wisdom will enter your heart,
  and knowledge will be pleasant to your soul.
¹¹Discretion will protect you,
  and understanding will guard you.

¹²Wisdom will save you from the ways of
    wicked men,
  from men whose words are perverse,
¹³who leave the straight paths
  to walk in dark ways,
¹⁴who delight in doing wrong
  and rejoice in the perverseness of evil,
¹⁵whose paths are crooked
  and who are devious in their ways.

¹⁶It will save you also from the adulteress,
  from the wayward wife with her seductive
    words,
¹⁷who has left the partner of her youth
  and ignored the covenant she made before
    God.^a
¹⁸For her house leads down to death
  and her paths to the spirits of the dead.
¹⁹None who go to her return
  or attain the paths of life.

²⁰Thus you will walk in the ways of good men
  and keep to the paths of the righteous.
²¹For the upright will live in the land,
  and the blameless will remain in it;
²²but the wicked will be cut off from the land,
  and the unfaithful will be torn from it.

專心求聰明，
³呼求明哲，
  揚聲求聰明，
⁴尋找它，如尋找銀子，
  搜求它，如搜求隱藏的珍寶，
⁵你就明白敬畏耶和華，
  得以認識神。
⁶因為耶和華賜人智慧，
  知識和聰明都由他口而出。

⁷他給正直人存留真智慧，
  給行為純正的人作盾牌，

⁸為要保守公平人的路，
  護庇虔敬人的道。

⁹你也必明白仁義、公平、
  正直，一切的善道。

¹⁰智慧必入你心，
  你的靈要以知識為美。
¹¹謀略必護衛你，
  聰明必保守你，

¹²要救你脫離惡道（註："惡道"或作"惡
    人的道"），
  脫離說乖謬話的人。
¹³那等人捨棄正直的路，
  行走黑暗的道，
¹⁴歡喜作惡，
  喜愛惡人的乖僻，
¹⁵在他們的道中彎曲，
  在他們的路上偏僻。

¹⁶智慧要救你脫離淫婦，
  就是那油嘴滑舌的外女。

¹⁷她離棄幼年的配偶，
  忘了神的盟約。

¹⁸她的家陷入死地，
  她的路偏向陰間。
¹⁹凡到她那裏去的，不得轉回，
  也得不着生命的路。

²⁰智慧必使你行善人的道，
  守義人的路。
²¹正直人必在世上居住，
  完全人必在地上存留；
²²惟有惡人必然剪除，
  奸詐的必然拔出。

---

a 17 Or covenant of her God

再述智慧的好處

3 我兒，不要忘記我的法則
（註：或作「指教」），
你心要謹守我的誡命，

2因為他必將長久的日子、
生命的年數與平安加給你。

3不可使慈愛、誠實離開你，
要繫在你頸項上，
刻在你心版上。

4這樣，你必在神和世人眼前蒙恩寵，
有聰明。

5你要專心仰賴耶和華，
不可倚靠自己的聰明，

6在你一切所行的事上都要認定他，
他必指引你的路。

7不要自以為有智慧，
要敬畏耶和華，遠離惡事。

8這便醫治你的肚臍，
滋潤你的百骨。

9你要以財物和一切初熟的土產
尊榮耶和華。

10這樣，你的倉房必充滿有餘，
你的酒醡有新酒盈溢。

11我兒，你不可輕看耶和華的管教（註：
或作「懲治」），
也不可厭煩他的責備，

12因為耶和華所愛的，他必責備，
正如父親責備所喜愛的兒子。

13得智慧、得聰明的，
這人便為有福。

14因為得智慧勝過得銀子，
其利益強如精金。

15比珍珠（註：或作「紅寶石」）寶貴，
你一切所喜愛的，都不足與比較。

16她右手有長壽，
左手有富貴。

17她的道是安樂，
她的路全是平安。

18她與持守她的作生命樹，
持定她的，俱各有福。

19耶和華以智慧立地，
以聰明定天；

20以知識使深淵裂開，
使天空滴下甘露。

Further Benefits of Wisdom

3 My son, do not forget my teaching,
but keep my commands in your heart,
2for they will prolong your life many
years
and bring you prosperity.

3Let love and faithfulness never leave you;
bind them around your neck,
write them on the tablet of your heart.
4Then you will win favor and a good name
in the sight of God and man.

5Trust in the LORD with all your heart
and lean not on your own understanding;
6in all your ways acknowledge him,
and he will make your paths straight.^{a}

7Do not be wise in your own eyes;
fear the LORD and shun evil.
8This will bring health to your body
and nourishment to your bones.

9Honor the LORD with your wealth,
with the firstfruits of all your crops;
10then your barns will be filled to overflowing,
and your vats will brim over with new wine.

11My son, do not despise the LORD's discipline
and do not resent his rebuke,
12because the LORD disciplines those he loves,
as a father^b the son he delights in.

13Blessed is the man who finds wisdom,
the man who gains understanding,
14for she is more profitable than silver
and yields better returns than gold.
15She is more precious than rubies;
nothing you desire can compare with her.
16Long life is in her right hand;
in her left hand are riches and honor.
17Her ways are pleasant ways,
and all her paths are peace.
18She is a tree of life to those who embrace her;
those who lay hold of her will be blessed.

19By wisdom the LORD laid the earth's
foundations,
by understanding he set the heavens in
place;
20by his knowledge the deeps were divided,
and the clouds let drop the dew.

---

a 6 Or will direct your paths   *b 12 Hebrew; Septuagint / and he punishes*

²¹My son, preserve sound judgment and discernment,
　do not let them out of your sight;
²²they will be life for you,
　an ornament to grace your neck.
²³Then you will go on your way in safety,
　and your foot will not stumble;
²⁴when you lie down, you will not be afraid;
　when you lie down, your sleep will be sweet.
²⁵Have no fear of sudden disaster
　or of the ruin that overtakes the wicked,
²⁶for the LORD will be your confidence
　and will keep your foot from being snared.

²⁷Do not withhold good from those who deserve it,
　when it is in your power to act.
²⁸Do not say to your neighbor,
　"Come back later; I'll give it tomorrow"—
　when you now have it with you.

²⁹Do not plot harm against your neighbor,
　who lives trustfully near you.
³⁰Do not accuse a man for no reason—
　when he has done you no harm.

³¹Do not envy a violent man
　or choose any of his ways,
³²for the LORD detests a perverse man
　but takes the upright into his confidence.

³³The LORD's curse is on the house of the wicked,
　but he blesses the home of the righteous.
³⁴He mocks proud mockers
　but gives grace to the humble.
³⁵The wise inherit honor,
　but fools he holds up to shame.

Wisdom Is Supreme

4 Listen, my sons, to a father's instruction;
　pay attention and gain understanding.
²I give you sound learning,
　so do not forsake my teaching.
³When I was a boy in my father's house,
　still tender, and an only child of my mother,
⁴he taught me and said,
　"Lay hold of my words with all your heart;
　keep my commands and you will live.
⁵Get wisdom, get understanding;
　do not forget my words or swerve from them.
⁶Do not forsake wisdom, and she will protect you;
　love her, and she will watch over you.
⁷Wisdom is supreme; therefore get wisdom.

²¹我兒，要謹守真智慧和謀略，
　不可使她離開你的眼目。

²²這樣，她必作你的生命，
　頸項的美飾。
²³你就坦然行路，
　不至碰腳。
²⁴你躺下，必不懼怕；
　你躺臥，睡得香甜。
²⁵忽然來的驚恐，不要害怕，
　惡人遭毀滅，也不要恐懼，
²⁶因為耶和華是你所倚靠的，
　他必保守你的腳不陷入網羅。

²⁷你手若有行善的力量，不可推辭，
　就當向那應得的人施行。

²⁸你那富若有現成的，不可對鄰舍說：
　"去吧！明天再來，我必給你。"

²⁹你的鄰舍既在你附近安居，
　你不可設計害他。
³⁰人未曾加害與你，
　不可無故與他相爭。

³¹不可嫉妒強暴的人，
　也不可選擇他所行的路。
³²因為乖僻人為耶和華所憎惡；
　正直人為他所親密。

³³耶和華咒詛惡人的家庭，
　賜福與義人的居所。
³⁴他譏誚那好譏誚的人，
　賜恩給謙卑的人；
³⁵智慧人必承受尊榮；
　愚昧人高陞也成為羞辱。

智慧崇高無比

4 眾子啊，要聽父親的教訓，
　留心得知聰明。
²因我所給你們的是好教訓，
　不可離棄我的法則（註：或作"指教"）。
³我在父親面前為孝子，
　在母親眼中為獨一的嬌兒。
⁴父親教訓我說：
　"你心要存記我的言語，
　遵守我的命令，便得存活。
⁵要得智慧，要得聰明，
　不可忘記，
　也不可偏離我口中的言語。
⁶不可離棄智慧，智慧就護衛你；
　要愛她，她就保守你。

⁷智慧為首，所以要得智慧，

在你一切所得之內必得聰明（註：
　或作「用你一切所得的去換聰明」）。
8高舉智慧，她就使你高陞；
　懷抱智慧，她就使你尊榮。
9她必將華冠加在你頭上，
　把榮冕交給你。」

10我兒，你要聽受我的言語，
　就必延年益壽。
11我已指教你走智慧的道，
　引導你行正直的路。
12你行走，腳步必不致狹窄；
　你奔跑，也不致跌倒。

13要持定訓誨，不可放鬆；
　必當謹守，因為她是你的生命。
14不可行惡人的路，
　不要走壞人的道。
15要躲避，不可經過；
　要轉身而去。
16這等人若不行惡，不得睡覺；
　不使人跌倒，睡臥不安。

17因為他們以奸惡吃餅，
　以強暴喝酒。

18但義人的路好像黎明的光，
　越照越明，直到日午。

19惡人的道好像幽暗，
　自己不知因甚麼跌倒。

20我兒，要留心聽我的言詞，
　側耳聽我的話語。
21都不可離你的眼目，
　要存記在你心中。
22因為得着它的，就得了生命，
　又得了醫全體的良藥。
23你要保守你心，勝過保守一切（註：
　　或作「你要切切保守你心」），
　因為一生的果效，是由心發出。
24你要除掉邪僻的口，
　棄絕乖謬的嘴。
25你的眼目要向前正看，你的眼睛
　　（註：原文作「皮」）當向前直觀。
26要修平你腳下的路，
　堅定你一切的道。
27不可偏向左右，
　要使你的腳離開邪惡。

Though it cost all you have,*a* get understanding.
8Esteem her, and she will exalt you;
　embrace her, and she will honor you.
9She will set a garland of grace on your head
　and present you with a crown of splendor."

10Listen, my son, accept what I say,
　and the years of your life will be many.
11I guide you in the way of wisdom
　and lead you along straight paths.
12When you walk, your steps will not be hampered;
　when you run, you will not stumble.
13Hold on to instruction, do not let it go;
　guard it well, for it is your life.
14Do not set foot on the path of the wicked
　or walk in the way of evil men.
15Avoid it, do not travel on it;
　turn from it and go on your way.
16For they cannot sleep till they do evil;
　they are robbed of slumber till they make someone fall.
17They eat the bread of wickedness
　and drink the wine of violence.

18The path of the righteous is like the first gleam of dawn,
　shining ever brighter till the full light of day.
19But the way of the wicked is like deep darkness;
　they do not know what makes them stumble.

20My son, pay attention to what I say;
　listen closely to my words.
21Do not let them out of your sight,
　keep them within your heart;
22for they are life to those who find them
　and health to a man's whole body.
23Above all else, guard your heart,
　for it is the wellspring of life.
24Put away perversity from your mouth;
　keep corrupt talk far from your lips.
25Let your eyes look straight ahead,
　fix your gaze directly before you.
26Make level*b* paths for your feet
　and take only ways that are firm.
27Do not swerve to the right or the left;
　keep your foot from evil.

a 7 Or Whatever else you get   b 26 Or Consider the

Warning Against Adultery

5 My son, pay attention to my wisdom,
    listen well to my words of insight,
²that you may maintain discretion
    and your lips may preserve knowledge.
³For the lips of an adulteress drip honey,
    and her speech is smoother than oil;
⁴but in the end she is bitter as gall,
    sharp as a double-edged sword.
⁵Her feet go down to death;
    her steps lead straight to the grave.^a
⁶She gives no thought to the way of life;
    her paths are crooked, but she knows it not.

⁷Now then, my sons, listen to me;
    do not turn aside from what I say.
⁸Keep to a path far from her,
    do not go near the door of her house,
⁹lest you give your best strength to others
    and your years to one who is cruel,
¹⁰lest strangers feast on your wealth
    and your toil enrich another man's house.
¹¹At the end of your life you will groan,
    when your flesh and body are spent.
¹²You will say, "How I hated discipline!
    How my heart spurned correction!
¹³I would not obey my teachers
    or listen to my instructors.
¹⁴I have come to the brink of utter ruin
    in the midst of the whole assembly."

¹⁵Drink water from your own cistern,
    running water from your own well.
¹⁶Should your springs overflow in the streets,
    your streams of water in the public squares?
¹⁷Let them be yours alone,
    never to be shared with strangers.
¹⁸May your fountain be blessed,
    and may you rejoice in the wife of your
    youth.
¹⁹A loving doe, a graceful deer—
    may her breasts satisfy you always,
    may you ever be captivated by her love.
²⁰Why be captivated, my son, by an adulteress?
    Why embrace the bosom of another man's
    wife?

²¹For a man's ways are in full view of the LORD,
    and he examines all his paths.
²²The evil deeds of a wicked man ensnare him;
    the cords of his sin hold him fast.
²³He will die for lack of discipline,
    led astray by his own great folly.

a 5 Hebrew Sheol

警告不要犯淫亂

5 我兒，要留心我智慧的話語，
    側耳聽我聰明的言詞，
²為要使你謹守謀略，
    嘴唇保存知識。
³因為淫婦的嘴滴下蜂蜜，
    她的口比油更滑，
⁴至終卻苦似茵蔯，
    快如兩刃的刀。
⁵她的腳下入死地，
    她腳步踏住陰間，
⁶以致她找不着生命平坦的道。
    她的路變遷不定，自己還不知道。

⁷眾子啊，現在要聽從我，
    不可離棄我口中的話，
⁸你所行的道要離她遠，
    不可就近她的房門。
⁹恐怕將你的尊榮給別人，
    將你的歲月給殘忍的人；
¹⁰恐怕外人滿得你的力量，
    你勞碌得來的，歸入外人的家。
¹¹終久，你皮肉和身體消毀，
    你就悲歎，
¹²說：「我怎麼恨惡訓誨，
    心中藐視責備，
¹³也不聽從我師傅的話，
    又不側耳聽那教訓我的人。
¹⁴我在聖會裏，
    幾乎落在諸般惡中。」

¹⁵你要喝自己池中的水，
    飲自己井裏的活水。
¹⁶你的泉源豈可漲溢在外？
    你的河水豈可流在街上？
¹⁷惟獨歸你一人，
    不可與外人同用。
¹⁸要使你的泉源蒙福，
    要喜悅你幼年所娶的妻。
¹⁹她如可愛的麀鹿，可喜的母鹿。
    願她的胸懷使你時時知足，
    她的愛情使你常常戀慕。
²⁰我兒，你為何戀慕淫婦？
    為何抱外女的胸懷？

²¹因為人所行的道都在耶和華眼前，
    他也修平人一切的路。
²²惡人必被自己的罪孽捉住，
    他必被自己的罪惡如繩索纏繞。
²³他因不受訓誨，就必死亡；
    又因愚昧過甚，必走差了路。

警告愚昧的人

6 我兒，
　　你若為朋友作保，
　　替外人擊掌，
²你就被口中的話語纏住，
　　被嘴裏的言語捉住。

³我兒，你既落在朋友手中，
　　就當這樣行，才可救自己：
　　你要自卑，
　　去懇求你的朋友。

⁴不要容你的眼睛睡覺，
　　不要容你的眼皮打盹。
⁵要救自己，
　　如鹿脫離獵戶的手，
　　如鳥脫離捕鳥人的手。

⁶懶惰人哪，你去察看螞蟻的動作，
　　就可得智慧！
⁷螞蟻沒有元帥，
　　沒有官長，沒有君王，
⁸尚且在夏天預備食物，
　　在收割時聚斂糧食。

⁹懶惰人哪，你要睡到幾時呢？
　　你何時睡醒呢？
¹⁰再睡片時，打盹片時，
　　抱着手躺臥片時，
¹¹你的貧窮就必如強盜速來，
　　你的缺乏彷彿拿兵器的人來到。

¹²無賴的惡徒，
　　行動就用乖僻的口，
¹³用眼傳神，
　　用腳示意，
　　用指點劃，
¹⁴心中乖僻，
　　常設惡謀，布散紛爭。
¹⁵所以災難必忽然臨到他身；
　　他必頃刻敗壞，無法可治。

¹⁶耶和華所恨惡的有六樣，
　　連他心所憎惡的共有七樣：
¹⁷就是高傲的眼，
　　撒謊的舌，
　　流無辜人血的手，
¹⁸圖謀惡計的心，
　　飛跑行惡的腳，
¹⁹吐謊言的假見證，
　　並弟兄中布散紛爭的人。

Warnings Against Folly

6 My son, if you have put up security for
　　your neighbor,
　　if you have struck hands in pledge for
　　another,
²if you have been trapped by what you said,
　　ensnared by the words of your mouth,
³then do this, my son, to free yourself,
　　since you have fallen into your neighbor's
　　hands:
　　Go and humble yourself;
　　press your plea with your neighbor!
⁴Allow no sleep to your eyes,
　　no slumber to your eyelids.
⁵Free yourself, like a gazelle from the hand of
　　the hunter,
　　like a bird from the snare of the fowler.

⁶Go to the ant, you sluggard;
　　consider its ways and be wise!
⁷It has no commander,
　　no overseer or ruler,
⁸yet it stores its provisions in summer
　　and gathers its food at harvest.

⁹How long will you lie there, you sluggard?
　　When will you get up from your sleep?
¹⁰A little sleep, a little slumber,
　　a little folding of the hands to rest—
¹¹and poverty will come on you like a bandit
　　and scarcity like an armed man.ᵃ

¹²A scoundrel and villain,
　　who goes about with a corrupt mouth,
¹³ who winks with his eye,
　　signals with his feet
　　and motions with his fingers,
¹⁴ who plots evil with deceit in his heart—
　　he always stirs up dissension.
¹⁵Therefore disaster will overtake him in an
　　instant;
　　he will suddenly be destroyed—without
　　remedy.

¹⁶There are six things the LORD hates,
　　seven that are detestable to him:
¹⁷ haughty eyes,
　　a lying tongue,
　　hands that shed innocent blood,
¹⁸ a heart that devises wicked schemes,
　　feet that are quick to rush into evil,
¹⁹ a false witness who pours out lies
　　and a man who stirs up dissension among
　　brothers.

a 11 Or like a vagrant / and scarcity like a beggar

Warning Against Adultery

²⁰My son, keep your father's commands
　　and do not forsake your mother's teaching.
²¹Bind them upon your heart forever;
　　fasten them around your neck.
²²When you walk, they will guide you;
　　when you sleep, they will watch over you;
　　when you awake, they will speak to you.
²³For these commands are a lamp,
　　this teaching is a light,
　　and the corrections of discipline
　　are the way to life,
²⁴keeping you from the immoral woman,
　　from the smooth tongue of the wayward
　　　wife.

²⁵Do not lust in your heart after her beauty
　　or let her captivate you with her eyes,
²⁶for the prostitute reduces you to a loaf of
　　　bread,
　　and the adulteress preys upon your very life.

²⁷Can a man scoop fire into his lap
　　without his clothes being burned?
²⁸Can a man walk on hot coals
　　without his feet being scorched?
²⁹So is he who sleeps with another man's wife;
　　no one who touches her will go unpunished.

³⁰Men do not despise a thief if he steals
　　to satisfy his hunger when he is starving.
³¹Yet if he is caught, he must pay sevenfold,
　　though it costs him all the wealth of his
　　　house.
³²But a man who commits adultery lacks
　　　judgment;
　　whoever does so destroys himself.
³³Blows and disgrace are his lot,
　　and his shame will never be wiped away;
³⁴for jealousy arouses a husband's fury,
　　and he will show no mercy when he takes
　　　revenge.
³⁵He will not accept any compensation;
　　he will refuse the bribe, however great it is.

Warning Against the Adulteress

7 My son, keep my words
　　and store up my commands within you.
²Keep my commands and you will live;
　　guard my teachings as the apple of your eye.
³Bind them on your fingers;
　　write them on the tablet of your heart.
⁴Say to wisdom, "You are my sister,"
　　and call understanding your kinsman;
⁵they will keep you from the adulteress,
　　from the wayward wife with her seductive
　　　words.

警告不要犯淫亂

²⁰我兒，要謹守你父親的誡命，
　　不可離棄你母親的法則（註：或作
　　　"指教"），
²¹要常繫在你心上，
　　掛在你項上。
²²你行走，它必引導你；
　　你躺臥，它必保守你；
　　你睡醒，它必與你談論。
²³因為誡命是燈，
　　法則（註：或作"指教"）是光，
　　訓誨的責備是生命的道，
²⁴能保你遠離惡婦，
　　遠離外女諂媚的舌頭。

²⁵你心中不要戀慕她的美色，
　　也不要被她眼皮勾引。
²⁶因為妓女能使人只剩一塊餅，
　　淫婦獵取人寶貴的生命。

²⁷人若懷裏搋火，
　　衣服豈能不燒呢？
²⁸人若在火炭上走，
　　腳豈能不燙呢？
²⁹親近鄰舍之妻的，也是如此。
　　凡挨近她的，不免受罰。

³⁰賊因飢餓偷竊充飢，
　　人不藐視他，
³¹若被找著，他必賠還七倍，
　　必將家中所有的盡都償還。

³²與婦人行淫的，便是無知；
　　行這事的，必喪掉生命。

³³他必受傷損，必被凌辱，
　　他的羞恥不得塗抹。
³⁴因為人的嫉恨成了烈怒，
　　報仇的時候決不留情。

³⁵甚麼贖價，他都不顧；
　　你雖送許多禮物，他也不肯干休。

警告遠離淫婦

7 我兒，你要遵守我的言語，
　　將我的命令存記在心。
²遵守我的命令就得存活；
　　保守我的法則（註：或作"指教"），
　　好像保守眼中的瞳人。
³繫在你指頭上，刻在你心版上。
⁴對智慧說："你是我的姊妹"，
　　稱呼聰明為你的親人，
⁵她就保你遠離淫婦，
　　遠離說諂媚話的外女。

⁶我曾在我房屋的窗戶內，
　　從我窗櫺之間往外觀看，
⁷見愚蒙人內，
　　少年人中，
　　分明有一個無知的少年人，
⁸從街上經過，走近淫婦的巷口，
　　直往她家的路去。
⁹在黃昏，或晚上，
　　或半夜，或黑暗之中。

¹⁰看哪，有一個婦人來迎接他，
　　是妓女的打扮，有詭詐的心思。

¹¹這婦人喧嚷，不守約束，
　　在家裏停不住腳，
¹²有時在街市上，有時在寬闊處，
　　或在各巷口蹲伏。
¹³拉住那少年人，與他親嘴，
　　臉無羞恥對他說：

¹⁴ “平安祭在我這裏，
　　今日才還了我所許的願。
¹⁵因此，我出來迎接你，
　　懇切求見你的面，恰巧遇見了你。
¹⁶我已經用繡花毯子和埃及線織的
　　花紋布鋪了我的床。
¹⁷我又用沒藥、沉香、桂皮
　　薰了我的榻。
¹⁸你來，我們可以飽享愛情，直到
　　早晨，我們可以彼此親愛歡樂。
¹⁹因為我丈夫不在家，
　　出門行遠路，
²⁰他手拿銀囊，
　　必到月望才回家。”

²¹淫婦用許多巧言誘他隨從，
　　用諂媚的嘴唇勾引他同行。
²²少年人立刻跟隨她，
　　好像牛往宰殺之地，
　　又像愚昧人帶鎖鏈去受刑罰，
²³直等箭穿透他的肝，
　　如同雀鳥急入網羅，
　　卻不知是自喪己命。

²⁴眾子啊，現在要聽從我，
　　留心聽我口中的話！
²⁵你的心不可偏向淫婦的道，
　　不要入她的迷途。
²⁶因為被她傷害仆倒的不少，
　　被她殺戮的而且甚多。
²⁷她的家是在陰間之路，
　　下到死亡之宮。

⁶At the window of my house
　　I looked out through the lattice.
⁷I saw among the simple,
　　I noticed among the young men,
　　a youth who lacked judgment.
⁸He was going down the street near her corner,
　　walking along in the direction of her house
⁹at twilight, as the day was fading,
　　as the dark of night set in.

¹⁰Then out came a woman to meet him,
　　dressed like a prostitute and with crafty
　　　intent.
¹¹(She is loud and defiant,
　　her feet never stay at home;
¹²now in the street, now in the squares,
　　at every corner she lurks.)
¹³She took hold of him and kissed him
　　and with a brazen face she said:

¹⁴"I have fellowship offerings^a at home;
　　today I fulfilled my vows.
¹⁵So I came out to meet you;
　　I looked for you and have found you!
¹⁶I have covered my bed
　　with colored linens from Egypt.
¹⁷I have perfumed my bed
　　with myrrh, aloes and cinnamon.
¹⁸Come, let's drink deep of love till morning;
　　let's enjoy ourselves with love!
¹⁹My husband is not at home;
　　he has gone on a long journey.
²⁰He took his purse filled with money
　　and will not be home till full moon."

²¹With persuasive words she led him astray;
　　she seduced him with her smooth talk.
²²All at once he followed her
　　like an ox going to the slaughter,
　　like a deer^b stepping into a noose^c
²³ till an arrow pierces his liver,
　　like a bird darting into a snare,
　　little knowing it will cost him his life.

²⁴Now then, my sons, listen to me;
　　pay attention to what I say.
²⁵Do not let your heart turn to her ways
　　or stray into her paths.
²⁶Many are the victims she has brought down;
　　her slain are a mighty throng.
²⁷Her house is a highway to the grave,^d
　　leading down to the chambers of death.

---

a 14 Traditionally *peace offerings*   *b 22* Syriac (see also Septuagint); Hebrew *fool*   *c 22* The meaning of the Hebrew for this line is uncertain.   *d 27* Hebrew *Sheol*

Wisdom's Call

8 Does not wisdom call out?
Does not understanding raise her voice?
[2]On the heights along the way,
where the paths meet, she takes her stand;
[3]beside the gates leading into the city,
at the entrances, she cries aloud:
[4]"To you, O men, I call out;
I raise my voice to all mankind.
[5]You who are simple, gain prudence;
you who are foolish, gain understanding.
[6]Listen, for I have worthy things to say;
I open my lips to speak what is right.
[7]My mouth speaks what is true,
for my lips detest wickedness.
[8]All the words of my mouth are just;
none of them is crooked or perverse.
[9]To the discerning all of them are right;
they are faultless to those who have
knowledge.
[10]Choose my instruction instead of silver,
knowledge rather than choice gold,
[11]for wisdom is more precious than rubies,
and nothing you desire can compare with
her.

[12]"I, wisdom, dwell together with prudence;
I possess knowledge and discretion.
[13]To fear the LORD is to hate evil;
I hate pride and arrogance,
evil behavior and perverse speech.
[14]Counsel and sound judgment are mine;
I have understanding and power.
[15]By me kings reign
and rulers make laws that are just;
[16]by me princes govern,
and all nobles who rule on earth.[a]
[17]I love those who love me,
and those who seek me find me.
[18]With me are riches and honor,
enduring wealth and prosperity.
[19]My fruit is better than fine gold;
what I yield surpasses choice silver.
[20]I walk in the way of righteousness,
along the paths of justice,
[21]bestowing wealth on those who love me
and making their treasuries full.

[22]"The LORD brought me forth as the first of his
works,[b,c]
before his deeds of old;

智慧的呼喚

8 智慧豈不呼叫？
聰明豈不發聲？
[2]她在道旁高處的頂上，
在十字路口站立。
[3]在城門旁，在城門口，
在城門洞，大聲說：
[4]"眾人哪，我呼叫你們，
我向世人發聲，
[5]說：愚蒙人哪，你們要會悟靈明；
愚昧人哪，你們當心裏明白！
[6]你們當聽，因我要說極美的話，
我張嘴要論正直的事。
[7]我的口要發出真理；
我的嘴憎惡邪惡。
[8]我口中的言語都是公義，
並無彎曲乖僻。
[9]有聰明的以為明顯；
得知識的以為正直。

[10]你們當受我的教訓，不受白銀，
寧得知識，勝過黃金。
[11]因為智慧比珍珠（註：或作"紅寶石"）
更美，
一切可喜愛的，都不足與比較。

[12]"我智慧以靈明為居所，
又尋得知識和謀略。
[13]敬畏耶和華，在乎恨惡邪惡。
那驕傲、狂妄並惡道，
以及乖謬的口，都為我所恨惡。
[14]我有謀略和真知識，
我乃聰明，我有能力。
[15]帝王藉我坐國位；
君王藉我定公平。
[16]王子和首領，世上一切的審判官，
都是藉我掌權。
[17]愛我的，我也愛他；
懇切尋求我的，必尋得見。
[18]豐富尊榮在我；
恆久的財並公義也在我。
[19]我的果實勝過黃金，強如精金；
我的出產超乎高銀。
[20]我在公義的道上走，
在公平的路中行，
[21]使愛我的承受貨財，
並充滿他們的府庫。

[22]"在耶和華造化的起頭，
在太初創造萬物之先，
就有了我。

---

*a 16 Many Hebrew manuscripts and Septuagint; most Hebrew
manuscripts and nobles—all righteous rulers   b 22 Or way; or
dominion   c 22 Or The LORD possessed me at the beginning of his
work; or The LORD brought me forth at the beginning of his work*

23從互古，從太初，
　未有世界以前，我已被立。
24沒有深淵，
　沒有大水的泉源，我已生出。

25大山未曾奠定，
　小山未有之先，我已生出。
26耶和華還沒有創造大地和田野，
　並世上的土質，我已生出。
27他立高天，
　我在那裏；
　他在淵面的周圍劃出圓圈，
28上使穹蒼堅硬，
　下使淵源穩固，
29為滄海定出界限，
　使水不越過他的命令，
　立定大地的根基。

30那時，我在他那裏為工師，
　日日為他所喜愛，
　常常在他面前踴躍，
31踴躍在他為人預備可住之地，
　也喜悅住在世人之間。

32"眾子啊，現在要聽從我，
　因為謹守我道的，便為有福。
33要聽教訓，就得智慧，
　不可棄絕。
34聽從我，日日在我門口仰望，
　在我門旁邊等候的，
　那人便為有福。
35因為尋得我的，就尋得生命，
　也必蒙耶和華的恩惠。
36得罪我的，卻害了自己的性命；
　恨惡我的，都喜愛死亡。"

智慧和愚昧的邀請

9 智慧建造房屋，
　鑿成七根柱子，
2宰殺牲畜，
　調和旨酒，
　設擺筵席。
3打發使女出去，
　自己在城中至高處呼叫，
4說："誰是愚蒙人，可以轉到這裏
　來！"又對那無知的人說：
5"你們來，吃我的餅，
　喝我調和的酒。
6你們愚蒙人，要捨棄愚蒙，就得存活，
　並要走光明的道。

7"指斥褻慢人的必受辱罵；

23I was appointed[a] from eternity,
　from the beginning, before the world began.
24When there were no oceans, I was given birth,
　when there were no springs abounding with
　　water;
25before the mountains were settled in place,
　before the hills, I was given birth,
26before he made the earth or its fields
　or any of the dust of the world.
27I was there when he set the heavens in place,
　when he marked out the horizon on the face
　　of the deep,
28when he established the clouds above
　and fixed securely the fountains of the deep,
29when he gave the sea its boundary
　so the waters would not overstep his
　　command,
and when he marked out the foundations of
　　the earth.
30 Then I was the craftsman at his side.
　I was filled with delight day after day,
　rejoicing always in his presence,
31rejoicing in his whole world
　and delighting in mankind.

32"Now then, my sons, listen to me;
　blessed are those who keep my ways.
33Listen to my instruction and be wise;
　do not ignore it.
34Blessed is the man who listens to me,
　watching daily at my doors,
　waiting at my doorway.
35For whoever finds me finds life
　and receives favor from the LORD.
36But whoever fails to find me harms himself;
　all who hate me love death."

Invitations of Wisdom and of Folly

9 Wisdom has built her house;
　she has hewn out its seven pillars.
2She has prepared her meat and mixed
　her wine;
　she has also set her table.
3She has sent out her maids, and she calls
　from the highest point of the city.
4"Let all who are simple come in here!"
　she says to those who lack judgment.
5"Come, eat my food
　and drink the wine I have mixed.
6Leave your simple ways and you will live;
　walk in the way of understanding.

7"Whoever corrects a mocker invites insult;

a 23 Or fashioned

whoever rebukes a wicked man incurs
  abuse.
[8]Do not rebuke a mocker or he will hate you;
  rebuke a wise man and he will love you.
[9]Instruct a wise man and he will be wiser still;
  teach a righteous man and he will add to his
  learning.

[10]"The fear of the LORD is the beginning of
  wisdom,
  and knowledge of the Holy One is
  understanding.
[11]For through me your days will be many,
  and years will be added to your life.
[12]If you are wise, your wisdom will reward
  you;
  if you are a mocker, you alone will suffer."

[13]The woman Folly is loud;
  she is undisciplined and without knowledge.
[14]She sits at the door of her house,
  on a seat at the highest point of the city,
[15]calling out to those who pass by,
  who go straight on their way.
[16]"Let all who are simple come in here!"
  she says to those who lack judgment.
[17]"Stolen water is sweet;
  food eaten in secret is delicious!"
[18]But little do they know that the dead are
  there,
  that her guests are in the depths of the
  grave.[a]

Proverbs of Solomon

10 The proverbs of Solomon:

A wise son brings joy to his father,
but a foolish son grief to his mother.

[2]Ill-gotten treasures are of no value,
  but righteousness delivers from death.

[3]The LORD does not let the righteous go hungry
  but he thwarts the craving of the wicked.

[4]Lazy hands make a man poor,
  but diligent hands bring wealth.

[5]He who gathers crops in summer is a wise son,
  but he who sleeps during harvest is a
  disgraceful son.

[6]Blessings crown the head of the righteous,

a 18 Hebrew Sheol

責備惡人的必被玷污。

[8]不要責備褻慢人，恐怕他恨你；
  要責備智慧人，他必愛你。
[9]教導智慧人，他就越發有智慧；
  指示義人，他就增長學問。

[10]"敬畏耶和華是智慧的開端，
  認識至聖者便是聰明！

[11]你藉着我，日子必增多，
  年歲也必加添。
[12]你若有智慧，是與自己有益；
  你若褻慢，就必獨自擔當。"

[13]愚昧的婦人喧嚷，
  她是愚蒙，一無所知。
[14]她坐在自己的家門口，
  坐在城中高處的座位上，
[15]呼叫過路的，
  就是直行其道的人，
[16]說："誰是愚蒙人，
  可以轉到這裏來！"
  又對那無知的人說：
[17]"偷來的水是甜的，
  暗吃的餅是好的。"
[18]人卻不知有陰魂在她那裏，
  她的客在陰間的深處。

所羅門的箴言

10 所羅門的箴言：

智慧之子使父親歡樂；
愚昧之子叫母親擔憂。

[2]不義之財毫無益處，
  惟有公義能救人脫離死亡。

[3]耶和華不使義人受飢餓；
  惡人所欲的，他必推開。

[4]手懶的，要受貧窮；
  手勤的，卻要富足。

[5]夏天聚斂的，是智慧之子；
  收割時沉睡的，是貽羞之子。

[6]福祉臨到義人的頭；

強暴蒙蔽惡人的口。

but violence overwhelms the mouth of the wicked.[a]

7義人的記念被稱讚；
　惡人的名字必朽爛。

7The memory of the righteous will be a blessing,
　but the name of the wicked will rot.

8心中智慧的，必受命令；
　口裏愚妄的，必致傾倒。

8The wise in heart accept commands,
　but a chattering fool comes to ruin.

9行正直路的，步步安穩；
　走彎曲道的，必致敗露。

9The man of integrity walks securely,
　but he who takes crooked paths will be found out.

10以眼傳神的，使人憂患；
　口裏愚妄的，必致傾倒。

10He who winks maliciously causes grief,
　and a chattering fool comes to ruin.

11義人的口是生命的泉源；
　強暴蒙蔽惡人的口。

11The mouth of the righteous is a fountain of life,
　but violence overwhelms the mouth of the wicked.

12恨，能挑啓爭端；
　愛，能遮掩一切過錯。

12Hatred stirs up dissension,
　but love covers over all wrongs.

13明哲人嘴裏有智慧；
　無知人背上受刑杖。

13Wisdom is found on the lips of the discerning,
　but a rod is for the back of him who lacks judgment.

14智慧人積存知識；
　愚妄人的口速致敗壞。

14Wise men store up knowledge,
　but the mouth of a fool invites ruin.

15富戶的財物是他的堅城；
　窮人的貧乏是他的敗壞。

15The wealth of the rich is their fortified city,
　but poverty is the ruin of the poor.

16義人的勤勞致生；
　惡人的進項致死（註："死"原文作 "罪"）。

16The wages of the righteous bring them life,
　but the income of the wicked brings them punishment.

17謹守訓誨的，乃在生命的道上；
　違棄責備的，便失迷了路。

17He who heeds discipline shows the way to life,
　but whoever ignores correction leads others astray.

18隱藏怨恨的，有說謊的嘴；
　口出讒謗的，是愚妄的人。

18He who conceals his hatred has lying lips,
　and whoever spreads slander is a fool.

19多言多語難免有過；
　禁止嘴唇是有智慧。

19When words are many, sin is not absent,
　but he who holds his tongue is wise.

20義人的舌乃似高銀；
　惡人的心所值無幾。

20The tongue of the righteous is choice silver,
　but the heart of the wicked is of little value.

21義人的口教養多人；
　愚昧人因無知而死亡。

21The lips of the righteous nourish many,
　but fools die for lack of judgment.

a 6 Or *but the mouth of the wicked conceals violence*; also in verse 11

22The blessing of the LORD brings wealth,
and he adds no trouble to it.

23A fool finds pleasure in evil conduct,
but a man of understanding delights in
wisdom.

24What the wicked dreads will overtake him;
what the righteous desire will be granted.

25When the storm has swept by, the wicked are
gone,
but the righteous stand firm forever.

26As vinegar to the teeth and smoke to the eyes,
so is a sluggard to those who send him.

27The fear of the LORD adds length to life,
but the years of the wicked are cut short.

28The prospect of the righteous is joy,
but the hopes of the wicked come to nothing.

29The way of the LORD is a refuge for the
righteous,
but it is the ruin of those who do evil.

30The righteous will never be uprooted,
but the wicked will not remain in the land.

31The mouth of the righteous brings forth
wisdom,
but a perverse tongue will be cut out.

32The lips of the righteous know what is fitting,
but the mouth of the wicked only what is
perverse.

11 The LORD abhors dishonest scales,
but accurate weights are his delight.

2When pride comes, then comes disgrace,
but with humility comes wisdom.

3The integrity of the upright guides them,
but the unfaithful are destroyed by their
duplicity.

4Wealth is worthless in the day of wrath,
but righteousness delivers from death.

5The righteousness of the blameless makes a
straight way for them,
but the wicked are brought down by their
own wickedness.

22耶和華所賜的福，使人富足，
並不加上憂慮。

23愚妄人以行惡為戲耍；
明哲人卻以智慧為樂。

24惡人所怕的必臨到他；
義人所願的必蒙應允。

25暴風一過，
惡人歸於無有；
義人的根基卻是永久。

26懶惰人叫差他的人如醋倒牙，
如煙薰目。

27敬畏耶和華使人日子加多，
但惡人的年歲必被減少。

28義人的盼望必得喜樂；
惡人的指望必致滅沒。

29耶和華的道是正直人的保障，
卻成了作孽人的敗壞。

30義人永不挪移；
惡人不得住在地上。

31義人的口滋生智慧；
乖謬的舌必被割斷。

32義人的嘴能令人喜悅；
惡人的口說乖謬的話。

11 詭詐的天平
為耶和華所憎惡；
公平的法碼為他所喜悅。

2驕傲來，羞恥也來；
謙遜人卻有智慧。

3正直人的純正必引導自己；
奸詐人的乖僻必毀滅自己。

4發怒的日子，資財無益；
惟有公義能救人脫離死亡。

5完全人的義必指引他的路，
但惡人必因自己的惡跌倒。

⁶正直人的義，必拯救自己；
　　奸詐人必陷在自己的罪孽中。

⁷惡人一死，他的指望必滅絕；
　　罪人的盼望，也必滅沒。

⁸義人得脫離患難，
　　有惡人來代替他。

⁹不虔敬的人用口敗壞鄰舍；
　　義人卻因知識得救。

¹⁰義人享福，合城喜樂；
　　惡人滅亡，人都歡呼。

¹¹城因正直人祝福便高舉，
　　卻因邪惡人的口就傾覆。

¹²藐視鄰舍的，毫無智慧；
　　明哲人卻靜默不言。

¹³往來傳舌的，洩漏密事；
　　心中誠實的，遮隱事情。

¹⁴無智謀，民就敗落，
　　謀士多，人便安居。

¹⁵為外人作保的，必受虧損；
　　恨惡擊掌的，卻得安穩。

¹⁶恩德的婦女得尊榮；
　　強暴的男子得資財。

¹⁷仁慈的人善待自己；
　　殘忍的人擾害己身。

¹⁸惡人經營，得虛浮的工價；
　　撒義種的，得實在的果效。

¹⁹恆心為義的，必得生命；
　　追求邪惡的，必致死亡。

²⁰心中乖僻的，為耶和華所憎惡；
　　行事完全的，為他所喜悅。

⁶The righteousness of the upright delivers them,
　　but the unfaithful are trapped by evil desires.

⁷When a wicked man dies, his hope perishes;
　　all he expected from his power comes to
　　nothing.

⁸The righteous man is rescued from trouble,
　　and it comes on the wicked instead.

⁹With his mouth the godless destroys his
　　neighbor,
　　but through knowledge the righteous
　　escape.

¹⁰When the righteous prosper, the city rejoices;
　　when the wicked perish, there are shouts of
　　joy.

¹¹Through the blessing of the upright a city is
　　exalted,
　　but by the mouth of the wicked it is
　　destroyed.

¹²A man who lacks judgment derides his
　　neighbor,
　　but a man of understanding holds his tongue.

¹³A gossip betrays a confidence,
　　but a trustworthy man keeps a secret.

¹⁴For lack of guidance a nation falls,
　　but many advisers make victory sure.

¹⁵He who puts up security for another will
　　surely suffer,
　　but whoever refuses to strike hands in
　　pledge is safe.

¹⁶A kindhearted woman gains respect,
　　but ruthless men gain only wealth.

¹⁷A kind man benefits himself,
　　but a cruel man brings trouble on himself.

¹⁸The wicked man earns deceptive wages,
　　but he who sows righteousness reaps a sure
　　reward.

¹⁹The truly righteous man attains life,
　　but he who pursues evil goes to his death.

²⁰The LORD detests men of perverse heart
　　but he delights in those whose ways are
　　blameless.

²¹Be sure of this: The wicked will not go
　　unpunished,
　　but those who are righteous will go free.

²²Like a gold ring in a pig's snout
　　is a beautiful woman who shows no
　　discretion.

²³The desire of the righteous ends only in good,
　　but the hope of the wicked only in wrath.

²⁴One man gives freely, yet gains even more;
　　another withholds unduly, but comes to
　　poverty.

²⁵A generous man will prosper;
　　he who refreshes others will himself be
　　refreshed.

²⁶People curse the man who hoards grain,
　　but blessing crowns him who is willing to
　　sell.

²⁷He who seeks good finds goodwill,
　　but evil comes to him who searches for it.

²⁸Whoever trusts in his riches will fall,
　　but the righteous will thrive like a green leaf.

²⁹He who brings trouble on his family will
　　inherit only wind,
　　and the fool will be servant to the wise.

³⁰The fruit of the righteous is a tree of life,
　　and he who wins souls is wise.

³¹If the righteous receive their due on earth,
　　how much more the ungodly and the sinner!

12
Whoever loves discipline loves
knowledge,
but he who hates correction is stupid.

²A good man obtains favor from the LORD,
　　but the LORD condemns a crafty man.

³A man cannot be established through
　　wickedness,
　　but the righteous cannot be uprooted.

⁴A wife of noble character is her husband's
　　crown,
　　but a disgraceful wife is like decay in his
　　bones.

²¹惡人雖然連手，必不免受罰；
　　義人的後裔，必得拯救。

²²婦女美貌而無見識，
　　如同金環帶在豬鼻上。

²³義人的心願，盡得好處；
　　惡人的指望，致干忿怒。

²⁴有施散的，卻更增添；
　　有吝惜過度的，反致窮乏。

²⁵好施捨的，必得豐裕；
　　滋潤人的，必得滋潤。

²⁶屯糧不賣的，民必咒詛他；
　　情願出賣的，人必為他祝福。

²⁷懇切求善的，就求得恩惠；
　　惟獨求惡的，惡必臨到他身。

²⁸倚仗自己財物的，必跌倒；
　　義人必發旺如青葉。

²⁹擾害己家的，必承受清風；
　　愚昧人必作慧心人的僕人。

³⁰義人所結的果子就是生命樹，
　　有智慧的必能得人。

³¹看哪，義人在世尚且受報，
　　何況惡人和罪人呢？

12
喜愛管教的，就是喜愛知識；
恨惡責備的，卻是畜類。

²善人必蒙耶和華的恩惠；
　　設詭計的人，耶和華必定他的罪。

³人靠惡行不能堅立；
　　義人的根，必不動搖。

⁴才德的婦人是丈夫的冠冕；
　　貽羞的婦人
　　　　如同朽爛在她丈夫的骨中。

⁵義人的思念是公平；
　　惡人的計謀是詭詐。

⁶惡人的言論是埋伏流人的血；
　　正直人的口必拯救人。

⁷惡人傾覆，歸於無有；
　　義人的家，必站得住。

⁸人必按自己的智慧被稱讚；
　　心中乖謬的，必被藐視。

⁹被人輕賤，卻有僕人，
　　強如自尊，缺少食物。

¹⁰義人顧惜他牲畜的命；
　　惡人的憐憫也是殘忍。

¹¹耕種自己田地的，必得飽食；
　　追隨虛浮的，卻是無知。

¹²惡人想得壞人的網羅；
　　義人的根得以結實。

¹³惡人嘴中的過錯，是自己的網羅；
　　但義人必脫離患難。

¹⁴人因口所結的果子，必飽得美福；
　　人手所做的，必為自己的報應。

¹⁵愚妄人所行的，在自己眼中看為正直；
　　惟智慧人肯聽人的勸教。

¹⁶愚妄人的惱怒立時顯露；
　　通達人能忍辱藏羞。

¹⁷說出真話的，顯明公義；
　　作假見證的，顯出詭詐。

¹⁸說話浮躁的，如刀刺人；
　　智慧人的舌頭，卻為醫人的良藥。

¹⁹口吐真言，永遠堅立；
　　舌說謊話，只存片時。

²⁰圖謀惡事的，心存詭詐；
　　勸人和睦的，便得喜樂。

⁵The plans of the righteous are just,
　　but the advice of the wicked is deceitful.

⁶The words of the wicked lie in wait for blood,
　　but the speech of the upright rescues them.

⁷Wicked men are overthrown and are no more,
　　but the house of the righteous stands firm.

⁸A man is praised according to his wisdom,
　　but men with warped minds are despised.

⁹Better to be a nobody and yet have a servant
　　than pretend to be somebody and have no
　　food.

¹⁰A righteous man cares for the needs of his
　　animal,
　　but the kindest acts of the wicked are cruel.

¹¹He who works his land will have abundant
　　food,
　　but he who chases fantasies lacks judgment.

¹²The wicked desire the plunder of evil men,
　　but the root of the righteous flourishes.

¹³An evil man is trapped by his sinful talk,
　　but a righteous man escapes trouble.

¹⁴From the fruit of his lips a man is filled with
　　good things
　　as surely as the work of his hands rewards
　　him.

¹⁵The way of a fool seems right to him,
　　but a wise man listens to advice.

¹⁶A fool shows his annoyance at once,
　　but a prudent man overlooks an insult.

¹⁷A truthful witness gives honest testimony,
　　but a false witness tells lies.

¹⁸Reckless words pierce like a sword,
　　but the tongue of the wise brings healing.

¹⁹Truthful lips endure forever,
　　but a lying tongue lasts only a moment.

²⁰There is deceit in the hearts of those who plot
　　evil,
　　but joy for those who promote peace.

²¹No harm befalls the righteous,
  but the wicked have their fill of trouble.

²²The LORD detests lying lips,
  but he delights in men who are truthful.

²³A prudent man keeps his knowledge to
    himself,
  but the heart of fools blurts out folly.

²⁴Diligent hands will rule,
  but laziness ends in slave labor.

²⁵An anxious heart weighs a man down,
  but a kind word cheers him up.

²⁶A righteous man is cautious in friendship,ᵃ
  but the way of the wicked leads them astray.

²⁷The lazy man does not roastᵇ his game,
  but the diligent man prizes his possessions.

²⁸In the way of righteousness there is life;
  along that path is immortality.

13 A wise son heeds his father's
    instruction,
  but a mocker does not listen to rebuke.

²From the fruit of his lips a man enjoys good
    things,
  but the unfaithful have a craving for
    violence.

³He who guards his lips guards his life,
  but he who speaks rashly will come to ruin.

⁴The sluggard craves and gets nothing,
  but the desires of the diligent are fully
    satisfied.

⁵The righteous hate what is false,
  but the wicked bring shame and disgrace.

⁶Righteousness guards the man of integrity,
  but wickedness overthrows the sinner.

⁷One man pretends to be rich, yet has nothing;
  another pretends to be poor, yet has great
    wealth.

⁸A man's riches may ransom his life,
  but a poor man hears no threat.

---

²¹義人不遭災害，
  惡人滿受禍患。

²²說謊言的嘴，為耶和華所憎惡；
  行事誠實的，為他所喜悅。

²³通達人隱藏知識；
  愚昧人的心，彰顯愚昧。

²⁴殷勤人的手必掌權；
  懶惰的人必服苦。

²⁵人心憂慮，屈而不伸；
  一句良言，使心歡樂。

²⁶義人引導他的鄰舍；
  惡人的道叫人失迷。

²⁷懶惰的人，不烤打獵所得的；
  殷勤的人，卻得寶貴的財物。

²⁸在公義的道上有生命；
  其路之中並無死亡。

13 智慧子聽父親的教訓；
  褻慢人不聽責備。

²人因口所結的果子，必享美福；
  奸詐人必遭強暴。

³謹守口的，得保生命；
  大張嘴的，必致敗亡。

⁴懶惰人羨慕，卻無所得；
  殷勤人必得豐裕。

⁵義人恨惡謊言；
  惡人有臭名，且致慚愧。

⁶行為正直的，有公義保守；
  犯罪的，被邪惡傾覆。

⁷假作富足的，卻一無所有；
  裝作窮乏的，卻廣有財物。

⁸人的資財，是他生命的贖價，
  窮乏人卻聽不見威嚇的話。

ᵃ 26 Or *man is a guide to his neighbor*   ᵇ 27 The meaning of the
Hebrew for this word is uncertain.

9義人的光明亮（註：“明亮”原文作“歡喜”）；惡人的燈要熄滅。

10驕傲只啟爭競；
　聽勸言的，卻有智慧。

11不勞而得之財，必然消耗；
　勤勞積蓄的，必見加增。

12所盼望的遲延未得，令人心憂；
　所願意的臨到，卻是生命樹。

13藐視訓言的，自取滅亡；
　敬畏誡命的，必得善報。

14智慧人的法則（註：或作“指教”）
　是生命的泉源，
　可以使人離開死亡的網羅。

15美好的聰明，使人蒙恩；
　奸詐人的道路，崎嶇難行。

16凡通達人都憑知識行事；
　愚昧人張揚自己的愚昧。

17奸惡的使者，必陷在禍患裏；
　忠信的使臣，乃醫人的良藥。

18棄絕管教的，必致貧受辱；
　領受責備的，必得尊榮。

19所欲的成就，心覺甘甜；
　遠離惡事，為愚昧人所憎惡。

20與智慧人同行的，必得智慧；
　和愚昧人做伴的，必受虧損。

21禍患追趕罪人；
　義人必得善報。

22善人給子孫遺留產業；
　罪人為義人積存資財。

23窮人耕種，多得糧食；
　但因不義，有消滅的。

9The light of the righteous shines brightly,
but the lamp of the wicked is snuffed out.

10Pride only breeds quarrels,
but wisdom is found in those who take advice.

11Dishonest money dwindles away,
but he who gathers money little by little makes it grow.

12Hope deferred makes the heart sick,
but a longing fulfilled is a tree of life.

13He who scorns instruction will pay for it,
but he who respects a command is rewarded.

14The teaching of the wise is a fountain of life,
turning a man from the snares of death.

15Good understanding wins favor,
but the way of the unfaithful is hard.*a*

16Every prudent man acts out of knowledge,
but a fool exposes his folly.

17A wicked messenger falls into trouble,
but a trustworthy envoy brings healing.

18He who ignores discipline comes to poverty and shame,
but whoever heeds correction is honored.

19A longing fulfilled is sweet to the soul,
but fools detest turning from evil.

20He who walks with the wise grows wise,
but a companion of fools suffers harm.

21Misfortune pursues the sinner,
but prosperity is the reward of the righteous.

22A good man leaves an inheritance for his children's children,
but a sinner's wealth is stored up for the righteous.

23A poor man's field may produce abundant food,
but injustice sweeps it away.

a 15 Or unfaithful does not endure

24He who spares the rod hates his son,
 but he who loves him is careful to discipline
  him.

25The righteous eat to their hearts' content,
 but the stomach of the wicked goes hungry.

14 The wise woman builds her house,
 but with her own hands the foolish one
 tears hers down.

2He whose walk is upright fears the LORD,
 but he whose ways are devious despises
  him.

3A fool's talk brings a rod to his back,
 but the lips of the wise protect them.

4Where there are no oxen, the manger is empty,
 but from the strength of an ox comes an
  abundant harvest.

5A truthful witness does not deceive,
 but a false witness pours out lies.

6The mocker seeks wisdom and finds none,
 but knowledge comes easily to the
  discerning.

7Stay away from a foolish man,
 for you will not find knowledge on his lips.

8The wisdom of the prudent is to give thought
 to their ways,
 but the folly of fools is deception.

9Fools mock at making amends for sin,
 but goodwill is found among the upright.

10Each heart knows its own bitterness,
 and no one else can share its joy.

11The house of the wicked will be destroyed,
 but the tent of the upright will flourish.

12There is a way that seems right to a man,
 but in the end it leads to death.

13Even in laughter the heart may ache,
 and joy may end in grief.

14The faithless will be fully repaid for their
 ways,
 and the good man rewarded for his.

24不忍用杖打兒子的，是恨惡他；
 疼愛兒子的，隨時管教。

25義人吃得飽足；
 惡人肚腹缺糧。

14 智慧婦人，建立家室；
 愚妄婦人，親手拆毀。

2行動正直的，敬畏耶和華；
 行事乖僻的，卻藐視他。

3愚妄人口中驕傲，如杖責打己身；
 智慧人的嘴，必保守自己。

4家裏無牛，槽頭乾淨；
 土產加多，乃憑牛力。

5誠實見證人，不說謊話；
 假見證人，吐出謊言。

6褻慢人尋智慧，卻尋不着；
 聰明人易得知識。

7到愚昧人面前，
 不見他嘴中有知識。

8通達人的智慧，在乎明白自己道；
 愚昧人的愚妄，乃是詭詐（註：或
  作"自欺"）。

9愚妄人犯罪，以為戲耍（註：或作"贖
  愆祭愚弄愚妄人"）；
 正直人互相喜悅。

10心中的苦楚，自己知道；
 心裏的喜樂，外人無干。

11奸惡人的房屋必傾倒；
 正直人的帳棚必興盛。

12有一條路人以為正，
 至終成為死亡之路。

13人在喜笑中，心也憂愁；
 快樂至極，就生愁苦。

14心中背道的，必滿得自己的結果；
 善人必從自己的行為得以知足。

15愚蒙人是話都信；
　通達人步步謹慎。

15A simple man believes anything,
　but a prudent man gives thought to his
　　steps.

16智慧人懼怕，就遠離惡事；
　愚妄人卻狂傲自恃。

16A wise man fears the Lord and shuns evil,
　but a fool is hotheaded and reckless.

17輕易發怒的，行事愚妄；
　設立詭計的，被人恨惡。

17A quick-tempered man does foolish things,
　and a crafty man is hated.

18愚蒙人得愚昧為產業；
　通達人得知識為冠冕。

18The simple inherit folly,
　but the prudent are crowned with
　　knowledge.

19壞人俯伏在善人面前；
　惡人俯伏在義人門口。

19Evil men will bow down in the presence of
　　the good,
　and the wicked at the gates of the righteous.

20貧窮人連鄰舍也恨他；
　富足人朋友最多。

20The poor are shunned even by their
　　neighbors,
　but the rich have many friends.

21藐視鄰舍的，這人有罪；
　憐憫貧窮的，這人有福。

21He who despises his neighbor sins,
　but blessed is he who is kind to the needy.

22謀惡的，豈非走入迷途嗎？
　謀善的，必得慈愛和誠實。

22Do not those who plot evil go astray?
　But those who plan what is good find*a* love
　　and faithfulness.

23諸般勤勞都有益處；
　嘴上多言乃致窮乏。

23All hard work brings a profit,
　but mere talk leads only to poverty.

24智慧人的財，為自己的冠冕；
　愚妄人的愚昧，終是愚昧。

24The wealth of the wise is their crown,
　but the folly of fools yields folly.

25作真見證的，救人性命；
　吐出謊言的，施行詭詐。

25A truthful witness saves lives,
　but a false witness is deceitful.

26敬畏耶和華的，大有倚靠，
　他的兒女，也有避難所。

26He who fears the Lord has a secure fortress,
　and for his children it will be a refuge.

27敬畏耶和華，就是生命的泉源，
　可以使人離開死亡的網羅。

27The fear of the Lord is a fountain of life,
　turning a man from the snares of death.

28帝王榮耀在乎民多；
　君王衰敗在乎民少。

28A large population is a king's glory,
　but without subjects a prince is ruined.

29不輕易發怒的，大有聰明；
　性情暴躁的，大顯愚妄。

29A patient man has great understanding,
　but a quick-tempered man displays folly.

30心中安靜，是肉體的生命；
　嫉妒是骨中的朽爛。

30A heart at peace gives life to the body,
　but envy rots the bones.

a 22 Or show

³¹He who oppresses the poor shows contempt
　　for their Maker,
　but whoever is kind to the needy honors
　　God.

³²When calamity comes, the wicked are brought
　　down,
　but even in death the righteous have a
　　refuge.

³³Wisdom reposes in the heart of the discerning
　and even among fools she lets herself be
　　known.ᵃ

³⁴Righteousness exalts a nation,
　but sin is a disgrace to any people.

³⁵A king delights in a wise servant,
　but a shameful servant incurs his wrath.

15 A gentle answer turns away wrath,
　　but a harsh word stirs up anger.

²The tongue of the wise commends knowledge,
　but the mouth of the fool gushes folly.

³The eyes of the LORD are everywhere,
　keeping watch on the wicked and the good.

⁴The tongue that brings healing is a tree of life,
　but a deceitful tongue crushes the spirit.

⁵A fool spurns his father's discipline,
　but whoever heeds correction shows
　　prudence.

⁶The house of the righteous contains great
　　treasure,
　but the income of the wicked brings them
　　trouble.

⁷The lips of the wise spread knowledge;
　not so the hearts of fools.

⁸The LORD detests the sacrifice of the wicked,
　but the prayer of the upright pleases him.

⁹The LORD detests the way of the wicked
　but he loves those who pursue righteousness.

¹⁰Stern discipline awaits him who leaves the
　　path;
　he who hates correction will die.

³¹欺壓貧寒的，是辱沒造他的主；
　憐憫窮乏的，乃是尊敬主。

³²惡人在所行的惡上必被推倒；
　義人臨死，有所投靠。

³³智慧存在聰明人心中；
　愚昧人心裏所存的，顯而易見。

³⁴公義使邦國高舉；
　罪惡是人民的羞辱。

³⁵智慧的臣子蒙王恩惠；
　貽羞的僕人遭其震怒。

15 回答柔和，使怒消退；
　　言語暴戾，觸動怒氣。

²智慧人的舌，善發知識；
　愚昧人的口，吐出愚昧。

³耶和華的眼目，無處不在，
　惡人善人，他都鑒察。

⁴溫良的舌是生命樹；
　乖謬的嘴使人心碎。

⁵愚妄人藐視父親的管教；
　領受責備的，得着見識。

⁶義人家中，多有財寶；
　惡人得利，反受擾害。

⁷智慧人的嘴，播揚知識；
　愚昧人的心，並不如此。

⁸惡人獻祭，為耶和華所憎惡；
　正直人祈禱，為他所喜悅。

⁹惡人的道路，為耶和華所憎惡；
　追求公義的，為他所喜愛。

¹⁰捨棄正路的，必受嚴刑；
　恨惡責備的，必致死亡。

---

*a 33 Hebrew; Septuagint and Syriac / but in the heart of fools she
is not known*

11 陰間和滅亡，尚在耶和華眼前，
　　何況世人的心呢？

11 Death and Destruction[a] lie open before the
　　LORD—
　　how much more the hearts of men!

12 褻慢人不愛受責備，
　　他也不就近智慧人。

12 A mocker resents correction;
　　he will not consult the wise.

13 心中喜樂，面帶笑容；
　　心裏憂愁，靈被損傷。

13 A happy heart makes the face cheerful,
　　but heartache crushes the spirit.

14 聰明人心求知識；
　　愚昧人口吃愚昧。

14 The discerning heart seeks knowledge,
　　but the mouth of a fool feeds on folly.

15 困苦人的日子都是愁苦；
　　心中歡暢的，常享豐筵。

15 All the days of the oppressed are wretched,
　　but the cheerful heart has a continual feast.

16 少有財寶，敬畏耶和華，
　　強如多有財寶，煩亂不安。

16 Better a little with the fear of the LORD
　　than great wealth with turmoil.

17 吃素菜，彼此相愛，
　　強如吃肥牛，彼此相恨。

17 Better a meal of vegetables where there is love
　　than a fattened calf with hatred.

18 暴怒的人挑啓爭端；
　　忍怒的人止息紛爭。

18 A hot-tempered man stirs up dissension,
　　but a patient man calms a quarrel.

19 懶惰人的道，像荊棘的籬笆；
　　正直人的路，是平坦的大道。

19 The way of the sluggard is blocked with
　　thorns,
　　but the path of the upright is a highway.

20 智慧子使父親喜樂；
　　愚昧人藐視母親。

20 A wise son brings joy to his father,
　　but a foolish man despises his mother.

21 無知的人以愚妄為樂；
　　聰明的人按正直而行。

21 Folly delights a man who lacks judgment,
　　but a man of understanding keeps a straight
　　course.

22 不先商議，所謀無效；
　　謀士眾多，所謀乃成。

22 Plans fail for lack of counsel,
　　but with many advisers they succeed.

23 口善應對，自覺喜樂，
　　話合其時，何等美好。

23 A man finds joy in giving an apt reply—
　　and how good is a timely word!

24 智慧人從生命的道上升，
　　使他遠離在下的陰間。

24 The path of life leads upward for the wise
　　to keep him from going down to the grave.[b]

25 耶和華必拆毀驕傲人的家，
　　卻要立定寡婦的地界。

25 The LORD tears down the proud man's house
　　but he keeps the widow's boundaries intact.

26 惡謀為耶和華所憎惡；
　　良言乃為純淨。

26 The LORD detests the thoughts of the wicked,
　　but those of the pure are pleasing to him.

27 貪戀財利的，擾害己家；
　　恨惡賄賂的，必得存活。

27 A greedy man brings trouble to his family,
　　but he who hates bribes will live.

a 11 Hebrew *Sheol and Abaddon*　　b 24 Hebrew *Sheol*

28The heart of the righteous weighs its answers,
   but the mouth of the wicked gushes evil.

29The LORD is far from the wicked
   but he hears the prayer of the righteous.

30A cheerful look brings joy to the heart,
   and good news gives health to the bones.

31He who listens to a life-giving rebuke
   will be at home among the wise.

32He who ignores discipline despises himself,
   but whoever heeds correction gains
   understanding.

33The fear of the LORD teaches a man wisdom,*a*
   and humility comes before honor.

16 To man belong the plans of the heart,
   but from the Lord comes the reply of
   the tongue.

2All a man's ways seem innocent to him,
   but motives are weighed by the LORD.

3Commit to the LORD whatever you do,
   and your plans will succeed.

4The LORD works out everything for his own
   ends—
   even the wicked for a day of disaster.

5The LORD detests all the proud of heart.
   Be sure of this: They will not go unpunished.

6Through love and faithfulness sin is atoned
   for;
   through the fear of the LORD a man avoids
   evil.

7When a man's ways are pleasing to the LORD,
   he makes even his enemies live at peace with
   him.

8Better a little with righteousness
   than much gain with injustice.

9In his heart a man plans his course,
   but the LORD determines his steps.

10The lips of a king speak as an oracle,
   and his mouth should not betray justice.

28義人的心，思量如何回答；
   惡人的口，吐出惡言。

29耶和華遠離惡人，
   卻聽義人的禱告。

30眼有光，使心喜樂；
   好信息，使骨滋潤。

31聽從生命責備的，
   必常在智慧人中。

32棄絕管教的，輕看自己的生命；
   聽從責備的，卻得智慧。

33敬畏耶和華，是智慧的訓誨；
   尊榮以前，必有謙卑。

16 心中的謀算在乎人，
   舌頭的應對由於耶和華。

2人一切所行的，在自己眼中看為清潔，
   惟有耶和華衡量人心。

3你所做的，要交託耶和華，
   你所謀的，就必成立。

4耶和華所造的，各適其用，
   就是惡人，也為禍患的日子所造。

5凡心裏驕傲的，為耶和華所憎惡，
   雖然連手，他必不免受罰。

6因憐憫誠實，罪孽得贖；
   敬畏耶和華的，遠離惡事。

7人所行的，若蒙耶和華喜悅，
   耶和華也使他的仇敵與他和好。

8多有財利，行事不義，
   不如少有財利，行事公義。

9人心籌算自己的道路，
   惟耶和華指引他的腳步。

10王的嘴中有神語，
   審判之時，他的口必不差錯。

a 33 Or Wisdom teaches the fear of the LORD

11公道的天平和秤都屬耶和華；
　囊中一切法碼都為他所定。

11Honest scales and balances are from the LORD;
　all the weights in the bag are of his making.

12作惡，為王所憎惡，
　因國位是靠公義堅立。

12Kings detest wrongdoing,
　for a throne is established through
　　righteousness.

13公義的嘴，為王所喜悅；
　說正直話的，為王所喜愛。

13Kings take pleasure in honest lips;
　they value a man who speaks the truth.

14王的震怒如殺人的使者，
　但智慧人能止息王怒。

14A king's wrath is a messenger of death,
　but a wise man will appease it.

15王的臉光使人有生命；
　王的恩典好像春雲時雨。

15When a king's face brightens, it means life;
　his favor is like a rain cloud in spring.

16得智慧勝似得金子；
　選聰明強如選銀子。

16How much better to get wisdom than gold,
　to choose understanding rather than silver!

17正直人的道，是遠離惡事；
　謹守己路的，是保全性命。

17The highway of the upright avoids evil;
　he who guards his way guards his life.

18驕傲在敗壞以先；
　狂心在跌倒之前。

18Pride goes before destruction,
　a haughty spirit before a fall.

19心裏謙卑與窮乏人來往，
　強如將擄物與驕傲人同分。

19Better to be lowly in spirit and among the
　　oppressed
　than to share plunder with the proud.

20謹守訓言的，必得好處；
　倚靠耶和華的，便為有福！

20Whoever gives heed to instruction prospers,
　and blessed is he who trusts in the LORD.

21心中有智慧，必稱為通達人；
　嘴中的甜言，加增人的學問。

21The wise in heart are called discerning,
　and pleasant words promote instruction.[a]

22人有智慧就有生命的泉源；
　愚昧人必被愚昧懲治。

22Understanding is a fountain of life to those
　　who have it,
　but folly brings punishment to fools.

23智慧人的心教訓他的口，
　又使他的嘴增長學問。

23A wise man's heart guides his mouth,
　and his lips promote instruction.[b]

24良言如同蜂房，
　使心覺甘甜，使骨得醫治。

24Pleasant words are a honeycomb,
　sweet to the soul and healing to the bones.

25有一條路，人以為正，
　至終成為死亡之路。

25There is a way that seems right to a man,
　but in the end it leads to death.

26勞力人的胃口，使他勞力，
　因為他的口腹催逼他。

26The laborer's appetite works for him;
　his hunger drives him on.

27匪徒圖謀奸惡，
　嘴上彷彿有燒焦的火。

27A scoundrel plots evil,
　and his speech is like a scorching fire.

*a 21 Or words make a man persuasive   b 23 Or mouth / and
makes his lips persuasive*

²⁸A perverse man stirs up dissension,
and a gossip separates close friends.

²⁹A violent man entices his neighbor
and leads him down a path that is not good.

³⁰He who winks with his eye is plotting
perversity;
he who purses his lips is bent on evil.

³¹Gray hair is a crown of splendor;
it is attained by a righteous life.

³²Better a patient man than a warrior,
a man who controls his temper than one who
takes a city.

³³The lot is cast into the lap,
but its every decision is from the LORD.

17 Better a dry crust with peace and quiet
than a house full of feasting,^a with strife.

²A wise servant will rule over a disgraceful son,
and will share the inheritance as one of the
brothers.

³The crucible for silver and the furnace for gold,
but the LORD tests the heart.

⁴A wicked man listens to evil lips;
a liar pays attention to a malicious tongue.

⁵He who mocks the poor shows contempt for
their Maker;
whoever gloats over disaster will not go
unpunished.

⁶Children's children are a crown to the aged,
and parents are the pride of their children.

⁷Arrogant^b lips are unsuited to a fool—
how much worse lying lips to a ruler!

⁸A bribe is a charm to the one who gives it;
wherever he turns, he succeeds.

⁹He who covers over an offense promotes love,
but whoever repeats the matter separates
close friends.

¹⁰A rebuke impresses a man of discernment
more than a hundred lashes a fool.

---

²⁸乖僻人播散紛爭；
傳舌的離間密友。

²⁹強暴人誘惑鄰舍，
領他走不善之道。

³⁰眼目緊合的，圖謀乖僻；
嘴唇緊閉的，成就邪惡。

³¹白髮是榮耀的冠冕，
在公義的道上，必能得着。

³²不輕易發怒的，勝過勇士；
治服己心的，強如取城。

³³籤放在懷裏，
定事由耶和華。

17 設筵滿屋，大家相爭，
不如有塊乾餅，大家相安。

²僕人辦事聰明，必管轄貽羞之子，
又在眾子中同分產業。

³鼎為煉銀，爐為煉金；
惟有耶和華熬煉人心。

⁴行惡的，留心聽奸詐之言；
說謊的，側耳聽邪惡之語。

⁵戲笑窮人的，是辱沒造他的主；
幸災樂禍的，必不免受罰。

⁶子孫為老人的冠冕；
父親是兒女的榮耀。

⁷愚頑人說美言本不相宜，
何況君王說謊話呢？

⁸賄賂在餽送的人眼中看為寶玉，
隨處運動都得順利。

⁹遮掩人過的，尋求人愛；
屢次挑錯的，離間密友。

¹⁰一句責備話深入聰明人的心，
強如責打愚昧人一百下。

---

a 1 Hebrew sacrifices   b 7 Or Eloquent

11惡人只尋背叛，
　　所以必有嚴厲的使者奉差攻擊他。

11An evil man is bent only on rebellion;
　　a merciless official will be sent against him.

12寧可遇見丟崽子的母熊，
　　不可遇見正行愚妄的愚昧人。

12Better to meet a bear robbed of her cubs
　　than a fool in his folly.

13以惡報善的，
　　禍患必不離他的家。

13If a man pays back evil for good,
　　evil will never leave his house.

14紛爭的起頭如水放開，
　　所以在爭鬧之先，必當止息爭競。

14Starting a quarrel is like breaching a dam;
　　so drop the matter before a dispute breaks
　　out.

15定惡人為義的，定義人為惡的，
　　這都為耶和華所憎惡。

15Acquitting the guilty and condemning the
　　innocent—
　　the LORD detests them both.

16愚昧人既無聰明，
　　為何手拿價銀買智慧呢？

16Of what use is money in the hand of a fool,
　　since he has no desire to get wisdom?

17朋友乃時常親愛；
　　弟兄為患難而生。

17A friend loves at all times,
　　and a brother is born for adversity.

18在鄰舍面前擊掌作保，
　　乃是無知的人。

18A man lacking in judgment strikes hands in
　　pledge
　　and puts up security for his neighbor.

19喜愛爭競的，是喜愛過犯；
　　高立家門的，乃自取敗壞。

19He who loves a quarrel loves sin;
　　he who builds a high gate invites destruction.

20心存邪僻的，尋不着好處；
　　舌弄是非的，陷在禍患中。

20A man of perverse heart does not prosper;
　　he whose tongue is deceitful falls into
　　trouble.

21生愚昧子的，必自愁苦；
　　愚頑人的父毫無喜樂。

21To have a fool for a son brings grief;
　　there is no joy for the father of a fool.

22喜樂的心，乃是良藥；
　　憂傷的靈，使骨枯乾。

22A cheerful heart is good medicine,
　　but a crushed spirit dries up the bones.

23惡人暗中受賄賂，
　　為要顛倒判斷。

23A wicked man accepts a bribe in secret
　　to pervert the course of justice.

24明哲人眼前有智慧；
　　愚昧人眼望地極。

24A discerning man keeps wisdom in view,
　　but a fool's eyes wander to the ends of the
　　earth.

25愚昧子使父親愁煩，
　　使母親憂苦。

25A foolish son brings grief to his father
　　and bitterness to the one who bore him.

26刑罰義人為不善；
　　責打君子為不義。

26It is not good to punish an innocent man,
　　or to flog officials for their integrity.

27寡少言語的有知識；
　　性情溫良的有聰明。

27A man of knowledge uses words with restraint,
　　and a man of understanding is even-
　　tempered.

28Even a fool is thought wise if he keeps silent,
and discerning if he holds his tongue.

18
An unfriendly man pursues selfish
ends;
he defies all sound judgment.

2A fool finds no pleasure in understanding
but delights in airing his own opinions.

3When wickedness comes, so does contempt,
and with shame comes disgrace.

4The words of a man's mouth are deep waters,
but the fountain of wisdom is a bubbling
brook.

5It is not good to be partial to the wicked
or to deprive the innocent of justice.

6A fool's lips bring him strife,
and his mouth invites a beating.

7A fool's mouth is his undoing,
and his lips are a snare to his soul.

8The words of a gossip are like choice morsels;
they go down to a man's inmost parts.

9One who is slack in his work
is brother to one who destroys.

10The name of the LORD is a strong tower;
the righteous run to it and are safe.

11The wealth of the rich is their fortified city;
they imagine it an unscalable wall.

12Before his downfall a man's heart is proud,
but humility comes before honor.

13He who answers before listening—
that is his folly and his shame.

14A man's spirit sustains him in sickness,
but a crushed spirit who can bear?

15The heart of the discerning acquires
knowledge;
the ears of the wise seek it out.

16A gift opens the way for the giver
and ushers him into the presence of the
great.

28愚昧人若靜默不言，也可算為智慧，
閉口不說，也可算為聰明。

18
與眾寡合的，
獨自尋求心願，
並惱恨一切真智慧。

2愚昧人不喜愛明哲，
只喜愛顯露心意。

3惡人來，藐視隨來；
羞恥到，辱罵同到。

4人口中的言語，如同深水；
智慧的泉源，好像湧流的河水。

5瞻徇惡人的情面，
偏斷義人的案件，都為不善。

6愚昧人張嘴啟爭端，
開口招鞭打。

7愚昧人的口自取敗壞，
他的嘴是他生命的網羅。

8傳舌人的言語，
如同美食深入人的心腹。

9做工懈怠的，
與浪費人為弟兄。

10耶和華的名是堅固臺，
義人奔入，便得安穩。

11富足人的財物是他的堅城，
在他心想，猶如高牆。

12敗壞之先，人心驕傲；
尊榮以前，必有謙卑。

13未曾聽完先回答的，
便是他的愚昧和羞辱。

14人有疾病，心能忍耐；
心靈憂傷，誰能承當呢？

15聰明人的心得知識，
智慧人的耳求知識。

16人的禮物為他開路，
引他到高位的人面前。

¹⁷先訴情由的，似乎有理，
　　但鄰舍來到，就察出實情。

¹⁸掣籤能止息爭競，
　　也能解散強勝的人。

¹⁹弟兄結怨，勸他和好，
　　比取堅固城還難，
　　這樣的爭競，
　　如同堅寨的門閂。

²⁰人口中所結的果子，必充滿肚腹；
　　他嘴所出的，必使他飽足。

²¹生死在舌頭的權下，
　　喜愛它的，必吃它所結的果子。

²²得着賢妻的，是得着好處，
　　也是蒙了耶和華的恩惠。

²³貧窮人說哀求的話，
　　富足人用威嚇的話回答。

²⁴濫交朋友的，自取敗壞；
　　但有一朋友，比弟兄更親密。

19 行為純正的貧窮人，
　　勝過乖謬愚妄的富足人。

²心無知識的，乃為不善；
　　腳步急快的，難免犯罪。

³人的愚昧傾敗他的道，
　　他的心也抱怨耶和華。

⁴財物使朋友增多，
　　但窮人朋友遠離。

⁵作假見證的，必不免受罰；
　　吐出謊言的，終不能逃脫。

⁶好施散的，有多人求他的恩情；
　　愛送禮的，人都為他的朋友。

⁷貧窮人，弟兄都恨他，
　　何況他的朋友，更遠離他！
　　他用言語追隨，
　　他們卻走了。

¹⁷The first to present his case seems right,
　　till another comes forward and questions
　　him.

¹⁸Casting the lot settles disputes
　　and keeps strong opponents apart.

¹⁹An offended brother is more unyielding than
　　a fortified city,
　　and disputes are like the barred gates of a
　　citadel.

²⁰From the fruit of his mouth a man's stomach
　　is filled;
　　with the harvest from his lips he is satisfied.

²¹The tongue has the power of life and death,
　　and those who love it will eat its fruit.

²²He who finds a wife finds what is good
　　and receives favor from the LORD.

²³A poor man pleads for mercy,
　　but a rich man answers harshly.

²⁴A man of many companions may come to
　　ruin,
　　but there is a friend who sticks closer than a
　　brother.

19 Better a poor man whose walk is
　　blameless
　　than a fool whose lips are perverse.

²It is not good to have zeal without knowledge,
　　nor to be hasty and miss the way.

³A man's own folly ruins his life,
　　yet his heart rages against the LORD.

⁴Wealth brings many friends,
　　but a poor man's friend deserts him.

⁵A false witness will not go unpunished,
　　and he who pours out lies will not go free.

⁶Many curry favor with a ruler,
　　and everyone is the friend of a man who
　　gives gifts.

⁷A poor man is shunned by all his relatives—
　　how much more do his friends avoid him!
　　Though he pursues them with pleading,
　　they are nowhere to be found.^a

a 7 The meaning of the Hebrew for this sentence is uncertain.

⁸He who gets wisdom loves his own soul;
he who cherishes understanding prospers.

⁹A false witness will not go unpunished,
and he who pours out lies will perish.

¹⁰It is not fitting for a fool to live in luxury—
how much worse for a slave to rule over
princes!

¹¹A man's wisdom gives him patience;
it is to his glory to overlook an offense.

¹²A king's rage is like the roar of a lion,
but his favor is like dew on the grass.

¹³A foolish son is his father's ruin,
and a quarrelsome wife is like a constant
dripping.

¹⁴Houses and wealth are inherited from
parents,
but a prudent wife is from the LORD.

¹⁵Laziness brings on deep sleep,
and the shiftless man goes hungry.

¹⁶He who obeys instructions guards his life,
but he who is contemptuous of his ways will
die.

¹⁷He who is kind to the poor lends to the LORD,
and he will reward him for what he has
done.

¹⁸Discipline your son, for in that there is hope;
do not be a willing party to his death.

¹⁹A hot-tempered man must pay the penalty;
if you rescue him, you will have to do it
again.

²⁰Listen to advice and accept instruction,
and in the end you will be wise.

²¹Many are the plans in a man's heart,
but it is the LORD's purpose that prevails.

²²What a man desires is unfailing love^a;
better to be poor than a liar.

²³The fear of the LORD leads to life:
Then one rests content, untouched by
trouble.

a 22 Or A man's greed is his shame

---

⁸得着智慧的，愛惜生命；
保守聰明的，必得好處。

⁹作假見證的，不免受罰；
吐出謊言的，也必滅亡。

¹⁰愚昧人宴樂度日，是不合宜的，
何況僕人管轄王子呢？

¹¹人有見識，就不輕易發怒，
寬恕人的過失，便是自己的榮耀。

¹²王的忿怒，好像獅子吼叫；
他的恩典，卻如草上的甘露。

¹³愚昧的兒子，是父親的禍患；
妻子的爭吵，如雨連連滴漏。

¹⁴房屋錢財是祖宗所遺留的；
惟有賢慧的妻是耶和華所賜的。

¹⁵懶惰使人沉睡，
懈怠的人必受飢餓。

¹⁶謹守誡命的，保全生命；
輕忽己路的，必致死亡。

¹⁷憐憫貧窮的，就是借給耶和華，
他的善行，耶和華必償還。

¹⁸趁有指望，管教你的兒子，
你的心不可任他死亡。

¹⁹暴怒的人必受刑罰；
你若救他，必須再救。

²⁰你要聽勸教、受訓誨，
使你終久有智慧。

²¹人心多有計謀，
惟有耶和華的籌算，才能立定。

²²施行仁慈的，令人愛慕；
窮人強如說謊言的。

²³敬畏耶和華的，得着生命，
他必恆久知足，不遭禍患。

²⁴懶惰人放手在盤子裏，
　　就是向口撒回，他也不肯。

²⁵鞭打褻慢人，愚蒙人必長見識；
　　責備明哲人，他就明白知識。

²⁶虐待父親、攆出母親的，
　　是貽羞致辱之子。

²⁷我兒，不可聽了教訓，
　　而又偏離知識的言語。

²⁸匪徒作見證戲笑公平；
　　惡人的口吞下罪孽。

²⁹刑罰是為褻慢人預備的；
　　鞭打是為愚昧人的背預備的。

20 酒能使人褻慢，
　　濃酒使人喧嚷，
　　凡因酒錯誤的，就無智慧。

²王的威嚇，如同獅子吼叫；
　　惹動他怒的，是自害己命。

³遠離紛爭，是人的尊榮；
　　愚妄人都愛爭鬧。

⁴懶惰人因冬寒不肯耕種，
　　到收割的時候，
　　　他必討飯而無所得。

⁵人心懷藏謀略，好像深水，
　　惟明哲人才能汲引出來。

⁶人多述說自己的仁慈，
　　但忠信人誰能遇着呢？

⁷行為純正的義人，
　　他的子孫是有福的！

⁸王坐在審判的位上，
　　以眼目驅散諸惡。

⁹誰能說，我潔淨了我的心，
　　我脫淨了我的罪？

¹⁰兩樣的法碼、兩樣的升斗，
　　都為耶和華所憎惡。

¹¹孩童的動作，是清潔、是正直，
　　都顯明他的本性。

²⁴The sluggard buries his hand in the dish;
　　he will not even bring it back to his mouth!

²⁵Flog a mocker, and the simple will learn
　　prudence;
　　rebuke a discerning man, and he will gain
　　knowledge.

²⁶He who robs his father and drives out his
　　mother
　　is a son who brings shame and disgrace.

²⁷Stop listening to instruction, my son,
　　and you will stray from the words of
　　knowledge.

²⁸A corrupt witness mocks at justice,
　　and the mouth of the wicked gulps down
　　evil.

²⁹Penalties are prepared for mockers,
　　and beatings for the backs of fools.

20 Wine is a mocker and beer a brawler;
　　whoever is led astray by them is not
　　wise.

²A king's wrath is like the roar of a lion;
　　he who angers him forfeits his life.

³It is to a man's honor to avoid strife,
　　but every fool is quick to quarrel.

⁴A sluggard does not plow in season;
　　so at harvest time he looks but finds nothing.

⁵The purposes of a man's heart are deep waters,
　　but a man of understanding draws them out.

⁶Many a man claims to have unfailing love,
　　but a faithful man who can find?

⁷The righteous man leads a blameless life;
　　blessed are his children after him.

⁸When a king sits on his throne to judge,
　　he winnows out all evil with his eyes.

⁹Who can say, "I have kept my heart pure;
　　I am clean and without sin"?

¹⁰Differing weights and differing measures—
　　the LORD detests them both.

¹¹Even a child is known by his actions,
　　by whether his conduct is pure and right.

¹²Ears that hear and eyes that see—
 the LORD has made them both.

¹³Do not love sleep or you will grow poor;
 stay awake and you will have food to spare.

¹⁴"It's no good, it's no good!" says the buyer;
 then off he goes and boasts about his
 purchase.

¹⁵Gold there is, and rubies in abundance,
 but lips that speak knowledge are a rare jewel.

¹⁶Take the garment of one who puts up security
 for a stranger;
 hold it in pledge if he does it for a wayward
 woman.

¹⁷Food gained by fraud tastes sweet to a man,
 but he ends up with a mouth full of gravel.

¹⁸Make plans by seeking advice;
 if you wage war, obtain guidance.

¹⁹A gossip betrays a confidence;
 so avoid a man who talks too much.

²⁰If a man curses his father or mother,
 his lamp will be snuffed out in pitch
 darkness.

²¹An inheritance quickly gained at the beginning
 will not be blessed at the end.

²²Do not say, "I'll pay you back for this wrong!"
 Wait for the LORD, and he will deliver you.

²³The LORD detests differing weights,
 and dishonest scales do not please him.

²⁴A man's steps are directed by the LORD.
 How then can anyone understand his own
 way?

²⁵It is a trap for a man to dedicate something
 rashly
 and only later to consider his vows.

²⁶A wise king winnows out the wicked;
 he drives the threshing wheel over them.

²⁷The lamp of the LORD searches the spirit of a
 man^a;
 it searches out his inmost being.

---

¹²能聽的耳，能看的眼，
 都是耶和華所造的。

¹³不要貪睡，免致貧窮；
 眼要睜開，你就吃飽。

¹⁴買物的說：“不好，不好！”
 及至買去，他便自誇。

¹⁵有金子和許多珍珠（註：或作“紅寶石”），
 惟有知識的嘴，乃為貴重的珍寶。

¹⁶誰為生人作保，就拿誰的衣服；
 誰為外人作保，誰就要承當。

¹⁷以虛謊而得的食物，人覺甘甜，
 但後來他的口必充滿塵沙。

¹⁸計謀都憑籌算立定；
 打仗要憑智謀。

¹⁹往來傳舌的，洩漏密事；
 大張嘴的，不可與他結交。

²⁰咒罵父母的，
 他的燈必滅，變為漆黑的黑暗。

²¹起初速得的產業，
 終久卻不為福。

²²你不要說：“我要以惡報惡”；
 要等候耶和華，他必拯救你。

²³兩樣的法碼，為耶和華所憎惡；
 詭詐的天平，也為不善。

²⁴人的腳步為耶和華所定，
 人豈能明白自己的路呢？

²⁵人冒失說，這是聖物，
 許願之後才查問，就是自陷網羅。

²⁶智慧的王簸散惡人，
 用碌碡滾軋他們。

²⁷人的靈是耶和華的燈，
 鑒察人的心腹。

---

a 27 Or The spirit of man is the LORD's lamp

28王因仁慈和誠實，
　　得以保全他的國位，
　　也因仁慈立穩。

29強壯乃少年人的榮耀；
　　白髮為老年人的尊榮。

30鞭傷除淨人的罪惡；
　　責打能入人的心腹。

21
王的心在耶和華手中，
好像隴溝的水隨意流轉。

2人所行的，在自己眼中都看為正，
　　惟有耶和華衡量人心。

3行仁義公平，
　　比獻祭更蒙耶和華悅納。

4惡人發達(註："發達"原文作"燈")，
　　眼高心傲，這乃是罪。

5殷勤籌劃的，足致豐裕；
　　行事急躁的，都必缺乏。

6用詭詐之舌求財的，就是自己取死；
　　所得之財，乃是吹來吹去的浮雲。

7惡人的強暴，必將自己掃除，
　　因他們不肯按公平行事。

8負罪之人的路，甚是彎曲；
　　至於清潔的人，
　　他所行的乃是正直。

9寧可住在房頂的角上，
　　不在寬闊的房屋，
　　與爭吵的婦人同住。

10惡人的心，樂人受禍，
　　他眼並不憐恤鄰舍。

11褻慢的人受刑罰，
　　愚蒙的人就得智慧；
　　智慧人受訓誨，
　　便得知識。

12義人思想惡人的家，
　　知道惡人傾倒，必致滅亡。

28Love and faithfulness keep a king safe;
　　through love his throne is made secure.

29The glory of young men is their strength,
　　gray hair the splendor of the old.

30Blows and wounds cleanse away evil,
　　and beatings purge the inmost being.

21
The king's heart is in the hand of the LORD;
　　he directs it like a watercourse
　　wherever he pleases.

2All a man's ways seem right to him,
　　but the LORD weighs the heart.

3To do what is right and just
　　is more acceptable to the LORD than sacrifice.

4Haughty eyes and a proud heart,
　　the lamp of the wicked, are sin!

5The plans of the diligent lead to profit
　　as surely as haste leads to poverty.

6A fortune made by a lying tongue
　　is a fleeting vapor and a deadly snare.a

7The violence of the wicked will drag them away,
　　for they refuse to do what is right.

8The way of the guilty is devious,
　　but the conduct of the innocent is upright.

9Better to live on a corner of the roof
　　than share a house with a quarrelsome wife.

10The wicked man craves evil;
　　his neighbor gets no mercy from him.

11When a mocker is punished, the simple gain wisdom;
　　when a wise man is instructed, he gets knowledge.

12The Righteous Oneb takes note of the house of the wicked
　　and brings the wicked to ruin.

a 6 Some Hebrew manuscripts, Septuagint and Vulgate; most Hebrew manuscripts vapor for those who seek death　　b 12 Or The righteous man

13If a man shuts his ears to the cry of the poor,
　　he too will cry out and not be answered.

14A gift given in secret soothes anger,
　　and a bribe concealed in the cloak pacifies
　　　great wrath.

15When justice is done, it brings joy to the
　　　righteous
　　but terror to evildoers.

16A man who strays from the path of
　　　understanding
　　comes to rest in the company of the dead.

17He who loves pleasure will become poor;
　　whoever loves wine and oil will never be
　　　rich.

18The wicked become a ransom for the
　　　righteous,
　　and the unfaithful for the upright.

19Better to live in a desert
　　than with a quarrelsome and ill-tempered
　　　wife.

20In the house of the wise are stores of choice
　　　food and oil,
　　but a foolish man devours all he has.

21He who pursues righteousness and love
　　finds life, prosperity*a* and honor.

22A wise man attacks the city of the mighty
　　and pulls down the stronghold in which
　　　they trust.

23He who guards his mouth and his tongue
　　keeps himself from calamity.

24The proud and arrogant man—"Mocker" is
　　　his name;
　　he behaves with overweening pride.

25The sluggard's craving will be the death of
　　　him,
　　because his hands refuse to work.
26All day long he craves for more,
　　but the righteous give without sparing.

27The sacrifice of the wicked is detestable—
　　how much more so when brought with evil
　　　intent!

a 21 Or righteousness

13塞耳不聽窮人哀求的，
　　他將來呼籲也不蒙應允。

14暗中送的禮物，挽回怒氣；
　　懷中揣的賄賂，止息暴怒。

15秉公行義，使義人喜樂，
　　使作孽的人敗壞。

16迷離通達道路的，
　　必住在陰魂的會中。

17愛宴樂的，必致窮乏；
　　好酒，愛膏油的，必不富足。

18惡人作了義人的贖價；
　　奸詐人代替正直人。

19寧可住在曠野，
　　不與爭吵使氣的婦人同住。

20智慧人家中積蓄寶物膏油；
　　愚昧人隨得來隨吞下。

21追求公義仁慈的，
　　就尋得生命、公義和尊榮。

22智慧人爬上勇士的城牆，
　　傾覆他所倚靠的堅壘。

23謹守口與舌的，
　　就保守自己免受災難。

24心驕氣傲的人，名叫褻慢，
　　他行事狂妄，都出於驕傲。

25懶惰人的心願，將他殺害，
　　因為他手不肯做工。
26有終日貪得無饜的；
　　義人施捨而不吝惜。

27惡人的祭物是可憎的，
　　何況他存惡意來獻呢？

28作假見證的必滅亡；
　　惟有聽真情而言的，其言長存。

28A false witness will perish,
　　and whoever listens to him will be destroyed
　　forever.[a]

29惡人臉無羞恥；
　　正直人行事堅定。

29A wicked man puts up a bold front,
　　but an upright man gives thought to his
　　ways.

30沒有人能以智慧、聰明、謀略
　　敵擋耶和華。

30There is no wisdom, no insight, no plan
　　that can succeed against the LORD.

31馬是為打仗之日預備的，
　　得勝乃在乎耶和華。

31The horse is made ready for the day of battle,
　　but victory rests with the LORD.

22

美名勝過大財；
　　恩寵強如金銀。

A good name is more desirable than
　　great riches;
　　to be esteemed is better than silver or
　　gold.

2富戶窮人在世相遇，
　　都為耶和華所造。

2Rich and poor have this in common:
　　The LORD is the Maker of them all.

3通達人見禍藏躲；
　　愚蒙人前往受害。

3A prudent man sees danger and takes refuge,
　　but the simple keep going and suffer for it.

4敬畏耶和華心存謙卑，
　　就得富有、尊榮、生命為賞賜。

4Humility and the fear of the LORD
　　bring wealth and honor and life.

5乖僻人的路上，
　　有荊棘和網羅，
　　保守自己生命的，
　　必要遠離。

5In the paths of the wicked lie thorns and
　　snares,
　　but he who guards his soul stays far from
　　them.

6教養孩童，使他走當行的道，
　　就是到老他也不偏離。

6Train[b] a child in the way he should go,
　　and when he is old he will not turn from it.

7富戶管轄窮人，
　　欠債的是債主的僕人。

7The rich rule over the poor,
　　and the borrower is servant to the lender.

8撒罪孽的，必收災禍；
　　他逞怒的杖，也必廢掉。

8He who sows wickedness reaps trouble,
　　and the rod of his fury will be destroyed.

9眼目慈善的，就必蒙福，
　　因他將食物分給窮人。

9A generous man will himself be blessed,
　　for he shares his food with the poor.

10趕出褻慢人，爭端就消除，
　　紛爭和羞辱也必止息。

10Drive out the mocker, and out goes strife;
　　quarrels and insults are ended.

11喜愛清心的人，
　　因他嘴上的恩言，
　　王必與他為友。

11He who loves a pure heart and whose speech
　　is gracious
　　will have the king for his friend.

*a 28 Or / but the words of an obedient man will live on   b 6 Or
Start*

¹²The eyes of the LORD keep watch over
knowledge,
but he frustrates the words of the unfaithful.

¹³The sluggard says, "There is a lion outside!"
or, "I will be murdered in the streets!"

¹⁴The mouth of an adulteress is a deep pit;
he who is under the LORD's wrath will fall
into it.

¹⁵Folly is bound up in the heart of a child,
but the rod of discipline will drive it far from
him.

¹⁶He who oppresses the poor to increase his
wealth
and he who gives gifts to the rich—both
come to poverty.

Sayings of the Wise

¹⁷Pay attention and listen to the sayings of the
wise;
apply your heart to what I teach,
¹⁸for it is pleasing when you keep them in your
heart
and have all of them ready on your lips.
¹⁹So that your trust may be in the LORD,
I teach you today, even you.
²⁰Have I not written thirty^a sayings for you,
sayings of counsel and knowledge,
²¹teaching you true and reliable words,
so that you can give sound answers
to him who sent you?

²²Do not exploit the poor because they are poor
and do not crush the needy in court,
²³for the LORD will take up their case
and will plunder those who plunder them.

²⁴Do not make friends with a hot-tempered
man,
do not associate with one easily angered,
²⁵or you may learn his ways
and get yourself ensnared.

²⁶Do not be a man who strikes hands in pledge
or puts up security for debts;
²⁷if you lack the means to pay,
your very bed will be snatched from under
you.

¹²耶和華的眼目眷顧聰明人，
卻傾敗奸詐人的言語。

¹³懶惰人說："外頭有獅子，
我在街上就必被殺。"

¹⁴淫婦的口為深坑，
耶和華所憎惡的，必陷在其中。

¹⁵愚蒙迷住孩童的心，
用管教的杖可以遠遠趕除。

¹⁶欺壓貧窮為要利己的，
並送禮與富戶的，都必缺乏。

智慧人的言語

¹⁷你須側耳聽受智慧人的言語，
留心領會我的知識；

¹⁸你若心中記存，
嘴上咬定，這便為美！

¹⁹我今日以此特別指教你，
為要使你倚靠耶和華。
²⁰謀略和知識的美事，
我豈沒有寫給你嗎？
²¹要使你知道真言的實理，
你好將真言回覆
那打發你來的人。

²²貧窮人，
你不可因他貧窮就搶奪他的物，
也不可在城門口欺壓困苦人。
²³因耶和華必為他辨屈，
搶奪他的，
耶和華必奪取那人的命。
²⁴好生氣的人，不可與他結交；
暴怒的人，不可與他來往，
²⁵恐怕你效法他的行為，
自己就陷在網羅裏。

²⁶不要與人擊掌，
不要為欠債的作保。
²⁷你若沒有甚麼償還，
何必使人奪去你睡臥的牀呢？

---

a 20 Or not formerly written; or not written excellent

28你先祖所立的地界，
　你不可挪移。

29你看見辦事殷勤的人嗎？
　他必站在君王面前，
　必不站在下賤人面前。

23 你若與官長坐席，
　　要留意在你面前的是誰。
2你若是貪食的，
　就當拿刀放在喉嚨上。
3不可貪戀他的美食，
　因為是哄人的食物。

4不要勞碌求富，
　休仗自己的聰明。
5你豈要定睛在虛無的錢財上嗎？
　因錢財必長翅膀，
　如鷹向天飛去。

6不要吃惡眼人的飯，
　也不要貪他的美味。
7因為他心怎樣思量，
　他為人就是怎樣。
　他雖對你說：「請吃，請喝」，
　他的心卻與你相背。
8你所吃的那點食物必吐出來；
　你所說的甘美言語也必落空。

9你不要說話給愚昧人聽，
　因他必藐視你智慧的言語。

10不可挪移古時的地界，
　也不可侵入孤兒的田地。
11因他們的救贖主大有能力；
　他必向你為他們辨屈。

12你要留心領受訓誨，
　側耳聽從知識的言語。

13不可不管教孩童，
　你用杖打他，他必不至於死。
14你要用杖打他，
　就可以救他的靈魂免下陰間。

15我兒，你心若存智慧，
　我的心也甚歡喜；
16你的嘴若說正直話，
　我的心腸也必快樂。

17你心中不要嫉妒罪人，
　只要終日敬畏耶和華。

28Do not move an ancient boundary stone
　set up by your forefathers.

29Do you see a man skilled in his work?
　He will serve before kings;
　he will not serve before obscure men.

23 When you sit to dine with a ruler,
　　note well what[a] is before you,
2and put a knife to your throat
　if you are given to gluttony.
3Do not crave his delicacies,
　for that food is deceptive.

4Do not wear yourself out to get rich;
　have the wisdom to show restraint.
5Cast but a glance at riches, and they are gone,
　for they will surely sprout wings
　and fly off to the sky like an eagle.

6Do not eat the food of a stingy man,
　do not crave his delicacies;
7for he is the kind of man
　who is always thinking about the cost.[b]
　"Eat and drink," he says to you,
　but his heart is not with you.
8You will vomit up the little you have eaten
　and will have wasted your compliments.

9Do not speak to a fool,
　for he will scorn the wisdom of your words.

10Do not move an ancient boundary stone
　or encroach on the fields of the fatherless,
11for their Defender is strong;
　he will take up their case against you.

12Apply your heart to instruction
　and your ears to words of knowledge.

13Do not withhold discipline from a child;
　if you punish him with the rod, he will not
　die.
14Punish him with the rod
　and save his soul from death.[c]

15My son, if your heart is wise,
　then my heart will be glad;
16my inmost being will rejoice
　when your lips speak what is right.

17Do not let your heart envy sinners,
　but always be zealous for the fear of the LORD.

---

a 1 Or who　　b 7 Or for as he thinks within himself, / so he is; or
for as he puts on a feast, / so he is　　c 14 Hebrew Sheol

¹⁸There is surely a future hope for you,
 and your hope will not be cut off.
¹⁹Listen, my son, and be wise,
 and keep your heart on the right path.
²⁰Do not join those who drink too much wine
 or gorge themselves on meat,
²¹for drunkards and gluttons become poor,
 and drowsiness clothes them in rags.

²²Listen to your father, who gave you life,
 and do not despise your mother when she is
  old.
²³Buy the truth and do not sell it;
 get wisdom, discipline and understanding.
²⁴The father of a righteous man has great joy;
 he who has a wise son delights in him.
²⁵May your father and mother be glad;
 may she who gave you birth rejoice!

²⁶My son, give me your heart
 and let your eyes keep to my ways,
²⁷for a prostitute is a deep pit
 and a wayward wife is a narrow well.
²⁸Like a bandit she lies in wait,
 and multiplies the unfaithful among men.

²⁹Who has woe? Who has sorrow?
 Who has strife? Who has complaints?
 Who has needless bruises? Who has
  bloodshot eyes?
³⁰Those who linger over wine,
 who go to sample bowls of mixed wine.
³¹Do not gaze at wine when it is red,
 when it sparkles in the cup,
 when it goes down smoothly!
³²In the end it bites like a snake
 and poisons like a viper.
³³Your eyes will see strange sights
 and your mind imagine confusing things.
³⁴You will be like one sleeping on the high seas,
 lying on top of the rigging.
³⁵"They hit me," you will say, "but I'm not
  hurt!
 They beat me, but I don't feel it!
 When will I wake up
  so I can find another drink?"

24 Do not envy wicked men,
 do not desire their company;
  ²for their hearts plot violence,
 and their lips talk about making trouble.

³By wisdom a house is built,
 and through understanding it is established;
⁴through knowledge its rooms are filled
 with rare and beautiful treasures.

¹⁸因為至終必有善報，
 你的指望也不至斷絕。
¹⁹我兒，你當聽，當存智慧，
 好在正道上引導你的心。
²⁰好飲酒的，好吃肉的，
 不要與他們來往。
²¹因為好酒貪食的，必致貧窮；
 好睡覺的，必穿破爛衣服。

²²你要聽從生你的父親；
 你母親老了，也不可藐視她。
²³你當買真理，就是智慧、
 訓誨和聰明也都不可賣。
²⁴義人的父親，必大得快樂；
 人生智慧的兒子，必因他歡喜。
²⁵你要使父母歡喜，
 使生你的快樂。

²⁶我兒，要將你的心歸我，
 你的眼目也要喜悅我的道路。
²⁷妓女是深坑，
 外女是窄阱。
²⁸她埋伏好像強盜，
 她使人中多有奸詐的。

²⁹誰有禍患？誰有憂愁？
 誰有爭鬥？
 誰有哀歎（註：或作"怨言"）？
 誰無故受傷？誰眼目紅赤？
³⁰就是那流連飲酒，
 常去尋找調和酒的人。
³¹、³²酒發紅，在杯中閃爍，
 你不可觀看，
雖然下咽舒暢，
 終久是咬你如蛇，
 刺你如毒蛇。
³³你眼必看見異怪的事（註："異怪的事"
   或作"淫婦"），
 你心必發出乖謬的話。
³⁴你必像躺在海中，
 或像臥在桅杆上。
³⁵你必說："人打我，我卻未受傷；
 人鞭打我，我竟不覺得。
 我幾時清醒，
  我仍去尋酒。"

24 你不要嫉妒惡人，
 也不要起意與他們相處，
  ²因為他們的心圖謀強暴，
 他們的口談論奸惡。

³房屋因智慧建造，
 又因聰明立穩，
⁴其中因知識
 充滿各樣美好寶貴的財物。

⁵智慧人大有能力，
  有知識的人力上加力。
⁶你去打仗，要憑智謀；
  謀士眾多，人便得勝。

⁷智慧極高，非愚昧人所能及，
  所以在城門內不敢開口。

⁸設計作惡的，
  必稱為奸人。
⁹愚妄人的思念乃是罪惡，
  褻慢者為人所憎惡。

¹⁰你在患難之日若膽怯，
  你的力量就微小。

¹¹人被拉到死地，你要解救；
  人將被殺，你須攔阻。
¹²你若說：「這事我未曾知道」，
  那衡量人心的豈不明白嗎？
  保守你命的，豈不知道嗎？
  他豈不按各人所行的
  報應各人嗎？

¹³我兒，你要吃蜜，因為是好的，
  吃蜂房下滴的蜜，便覺甘甜。
¹⁴你心得了智慧，也必覺得如此。
  你若尋著，至終必有善報；
  你的指望，也不至斷絕。

¹⁵你這惡人，
  不要埋伏攻擊義人的家，
  不要毀壞他安居之所。
¹⁶因為義人雖七次跌倒，
  仍必興起；
  惡人卻被禍患傾倒。

¹⁷你仇敵跌倒，你不要歡喜；
  他傾倒，你心不要快樂，

¹⁸恐怕耶和華看見就不喜悅，
  將怒氣從仇敵身上轉過來。

¹⁹不要為作惡的心懷不平，
  也不要嫉妒惡人，
²⁰因為惡人終不得善報，
  惡人的燈，也必熄滅。

²¹我兒，你要敬畏耶和華與君王，
  不要與反覆無常的人結交，
²²因為他們的災難
  必忽然而起。
  耶和華與君王所施行的毀滅，
  誰能知道呢？

⁵A wise man has great power,
  and a man of knowledge increases strength;
⁶for waging war you need guidance,
  and for victory many advisers.

⁷Wisdom is too high for a fool;
  in the assembly at the gate he has nothing to
    say.

⁸He who plots evil
  will be known as a schemer.
⁹The schemes of folly are sin,
  and men detest a mocker.

¹⁰If you falter in times of trouble,
  how small is your strength!

¹¹Rescue those being led away to death;
  hold back those staggering toward slaughter.
¹²If you say, "But we knew nothing about this,"
  does not he who weighs the heart perceive it?
  Does not he who guards your life know it?
  Will he not repay each person according to
    what he has done?

¹³Eat honey, my son, for it is good;
  honey from the comb is sweet to your taste.
¹⁴Know also that wisdom is sweet to your soul;
  if you find it, there is a future hope for you,
  and your hope will not be cut off.

¹⁵Do not lie in wait like an outlaw against a
    righteous man's house,
  do not raid his dwelling place;
¹⁶for though a righteous man falls seven times,
  he rises again,
  but the wicked are brought down by calamity.

¹⁷Do not gloat when your enemy falls;
  when he stumbles, do not let your heart
    rejoice,
¹⁸or the LORD will see and disapprove
  and turn his wrath away from him.

¹⁹Do not fret because of evil men
  or be envious of the wicked,
²⁰for the evil man has no future hope,
  and the lamp of the wicked will be snuffed
    out.

²¹Fear the LORD and the king, my son,
  and do not join with the rebellious,
²²for those two will send sudden destruction
    upon them,
  and who knows what calamities they can
    bring?

Further Sayings of the Wise

²³These also are sayings of the wise:

To show partiality in judging is not good:
²⁴Whoever says to the guilty, "You are
    innocent"—
  peoples will curse him and nations denounce
    him.
²⁵But it will go well with those who convict the
    guilty,
  and rich blessing will come upon them.

²⁶An honest answer
  is like a kiss on the lips.

²⁷Finish your outdoor work
  and get your fields ready;
  after that, build your house.

²⁸Do not testify against your neighbor without
    cause,
  or use your lips to deceive.
²⁹Do not say, "I'll do to him as he has done to me;
  I'll pay that man back for what he did."

³⁰I went past the field of the sluggard,
  past the vineyard of the man who lacks
    judgment;
³¹thorns had come up everywhere,
  the ground was covered with weeds,
  and the stone wall was in ruins.
³²I applied my heart to what I observed
  and learned a lesson from what I saw:
³³A little sleep, a little slumber,
  a little folding of the hands to rest—
³⁴and poverty will come on you like a bandit
  and scarcity like an armed man.^a

More Proverbs of Solomon

25 These are more proverbs of Solomon,
copied by the men of Hezekiah king of
Judah:

²It is the glory of God to conceal a matter;
  to search out a matter is the glory of kings.

³As the heavens are high and the earth is deep,
  so the hearts of kings are unsearchable.

⁴Remove the dross from the silver,
  and out comes material for^b the silversmith;

*a 34 Or like a vagrant / and scarcity like a beggar   b 4 Or comes a
vessel from*

續智慧人的言語

²³以下也是智慧人的箴言：

審判時看人情面是不好的。
²⁴對惡人說"你是義人"的，
  這人萬民必咒詛，列邦必憎惡。

²⁵責備惡人的，必得喜悅，
  美好的福也必臨到他。

²⁶應對正直的，
  猶如與人親嘴。

²⁷你要在外頭預備工料，
  在田間辦理整齊，
  然後建造房屋。

²⁸不可無故作見證陷害鄰舍，
  也不可用嘴欺騙人。
²⁹不可說："人怎樣待我，
  我也怎樣待他，
  我必照他所行的報復他。"
³⁰我經過懶惰人的田地、
  無知人的葡萄園，

³¹荊棘長滿了地皮，
  刺草遮蓋了田面，
  石牆也坍塌了。
³²我看見就留心思想，
  我看着就領了訓誨。
³³再睡片時，打盹片時，
  抱着手躺臥片時，
³⁴你的貧窮，就必如強盜速來，
  你的缺乏，彷彿拿兵器的人來到。

所羅門更多的箴言

25 以下也是所羅門的箴言，是猶
大王希西家的人所謄錄的。

²將事隱秘，乃神的榮耀；
  將事察清，乃君王的榮耀。

³天之高，地之厚，
  君王之心也測不透。

⁴除去銀子的渣滓，就有銀子出來，
  銀匠能以做器皿；

⁵除去王面前的惡人，
　　國位就靠公義堅立。

⁶不要在王面前妄自尊大，
　　不要在大人的位上站立。
⁷寧可有人說：“請你上來”，
　　強如在你觀見的王子面
　　前叫你退下。

⁸不要冒失出去與人爭競，
　　免得至終被他羞辱，
　　你就不知道怎樣行了。

⁹你與鄰舍爭訟，要與他一人辯論，
　　不可洩漏人的密事，
¹⁰恐怕聽見的人罵你，
　　你的臭名就難以脫離。

¹¹一句話說得合宜，
　　就如金蘋果在銀網子裏。

¹²智慧人的勸戒，
　　在順從的人耳中，
　　好像金耳環和精金的妝飾。

¹³忠信的使者，
　　叫差他的人心裏舒暢，
　　就如在收割時，
　　有冰雪的涼氣。

¹⁴空誇贈送禮物的，
　　好像無雨的風雲。

¹⁵恆常忍耐可以勸動君王，
　　柔和的舌頭能折斷骨頭。

¹⁶你得了蜜嗎？只可吃夠而已，
　　恐怕你過飽就嘔吐出來。
¹⁷你的腳要少進鄰舍的家，
　　恐怕他厭煩你，恨惡你。

¹⁸作假見證陷害鄰舍的，
　　就是大槌，是利刀，是快箭。

¹⁹患難時倚靠不忠誠的人，
　　好像破壞的牙，錯骨縫的腳。

⁵remove the wicked from the king's presence,
　and his throne will be established through
　　righteousness.

⁶Do not exalt yourself in the king's presence,
　and do not claim a place among great men;
⁷it is better for him to say to you, "Come up
　　here,"
　than for him to humiliate you before a
　　nobleman.

What you have seen with your eyes
⁸　do not bring^a hastily to court,
　for what will you do in the end
　　if your neighbor puts you to shame?

⁹If you argue your case with a neighbor,
　do not betray another man's confidence,
¹⁰or he who hears it may shame you
　and you will never lose your bad reputation.

¹¹A word aptly spoken
　is like apples of gold in settings of silver.

¹²Like an earring of gold or an ornament of fine
　　gold
　is a wise man's rebuke to a listening ear.

¹³Like the coolness of snow at harvest time
　is a trustworthy messenger to those who
　　send him;
　he refreshes the spirit of his masters.

¹⁴Like clouds and wind without rain
　is a man who boasts of gifts he does not give.

¹⁵Through patience a ruler can be persuaded,
　and a gentle tongue can break a bone.

¹⁶If you find honey, eat just enough—
　too much of it, and you will vomit.
¹⁷Seldom set foot in your neighbor's house—
　too much of you, and he will hate you.

¹⁸Like a club or a sword or a sharp arrow
　is the man who gives false testimony against
　　his neighbor.

¹⁹Like a bad tooth or a lame foot
　is reliance on the unfaithful in times of
　　trouble.

a 7,8 Or nobleman / on whom you had set your eyes. / ⁸ Do not go

²⁰Like one who takes away a garment on a cold
 day,
  or like vinegar poured on soda,
 is one who sings songs to a heavy heart.

²¹If your enemy is hungry, give him food to eat;
  if he is thirsty, give him water to drink.
²²In doing this, you will heap burning coals on
 his head,
  and the LORD will reward you.

²³As a north wind brings rain,
  so a sly tongue brings angry looks.

²⁴Better to live on a corner of the roof
  than share a house with a quarrelsome wife.

²⁵Like cold water to a weary soul
  is good news from a distant land.

²⁶Like a muddied spring or a polluted well
  is a righteous man who gives way to the
  wicked.

²⁷It is not good to eat too much honey,
  nor is it honorable to seek one's own honor.

²⁸Like a city whose walls are broken down
  is a man who lacks self-control.

26 Like snow in summer or rain in harvest,
     honor is not fitting for a fool.

²Like a fluttering sparrow or a darting swallow,
  an undeserved curse does not come to rest.

³A whip for the horse, a halter for the donkey,
  and a rod for the backs of fools!

⁴Do not answer a fool according to his folly,
  or you will be like him yourself.

⁵Answer a fool according to his folly,
  or he will be wise in his own eyes.

⁶Like cutting off one's feet or drinking violence
  is the sending of a message by the hand of a
  fool.

⁷Like a lame man's legs that hang limp
  is a proverb in the mouth of a fool.

⁸Like tying a stone in a sling
  is the giving of honor to a fool.

²⁰對傷心的人唱歌，
  就如冷天脫衣服，
  又如鹼上倒醋。

²¹你的仇敵若餓了，就給他飯吃；
  若渴了，就給他水喝。
²²因為你這樣行，
  就是把炭火堆在他的頭上，
  耶和華也必賞賜你。

²³北風生雨，
  讒謗人的舌頭也生怒容。

²⁴寧可住在房頂的角上，
  不在寬闊的房屋
  與爭吵的婦人同住。

²⁵有好消息從遠方來，
  就如拿涼水給口渴的人喝。

²⁶義人在惡人面前退縮，
  好像趟渾之泉，弄濁之井。

²⁷吃蜜過多是不好的；
  考究自己的榮耀也是可厭的。

²⁸人不制伏自己的心，
  好像毀壞的城邑，沒有牆垣。

26 夏天落雪，收割時下雨，
     都不相宜；
     愚昧人得尊榮也是如此。
²麻雀往來，燕子翻飛，
  這樣，無故的咒詛也必不臨到。

³鞭子是為打馬，轡頭是為勒驢；
  刑杖是為打愚昧人的背。

⁴不要照愚昧人的愚妄話回答他，
  恐怕你與他一樣。

⁵要照愚昧人的愚妄話回答他，
  免得他自以為有智慧。

⁶藉愚昧人手寄信的，
  是砍斷自己的腳，自受損害（註：
  "自受"原文作"喝"）。

⁷瘸子的腳空存無用；
  箴言在愚昧人的口中也是如此。

⁸將尊榮給愚昧人的，
  好像人把石子包在機弦裏。

9箴言在愚昧人的口中，
　　好像荊棘刺入醉漢的手。

10雇愚昧人的，與雇過路人的，
　　就像射傷眾人的弓箭手。

11愚昧人行愚妄事，行了又行，
　　就如狗轉過來吃牠所吐的。

12你見自以為有智慧的人嗎？
　　愚昧人比他更有指望。

13懶惰人說："道上有猛獅，
　　街上有壯獅。"

14門在樞紐轉動，
　　懶惰人在牀上也是如此。

15懶惰人放手在盤子裏，
　　就是向口撒回也以為勞乏。

16懶惰人看自己，
　　比七個善於應對的人更有智慧。

17過路被事激動，
　　管理不干己的爭競，
　　好像人揪住狗耳。

18、19人欺凌鄰舍，卻說：
　　"我豈不是戲耍嗎？"
　　他就像瘋狂的人，
　　拋擲火把、利箭與殺人的兵器（註：
　　"殺人的兵器"原文作"死亡"）。

20火缺了柴，就必熄滅；
　　無人傳舌，爭競便止息。

21好爭競的人煽惑爭端，
　　就如餘火加炭，火上加柴一樣。

22傳舌人的言語，如同美食，
　　深入人的心腹。

23火熱的嘴，奸惡的心，
　　好像銀渣包的瓦器。

24怨恨人的，用嘴粉飾，
　　心裏卻藏着詭詐。
25他用甜言蜜語，你不可信他，
　　因為他心中有七樣可憎惡的。

26他雖用詭詐遮掩自己的怨恨，
　　他的邪惡必在會中顯露。

9Like a thornbush in a drunkard's hand
　　is a proverb in the mouth of a fool.

10Like an archer who wounds at random
　　is he who hires a fool or any passer-by.

11As a dog returns to its vomit,
　　so a fool repeats his folly.

12Do you see a man wise in his own eyes?
　　There is more hope for a fool than for him.

13The sluggard says, "There is a lion in the road,
　　a fierce lion roaming the streets!"

14As a door turns on its hinges,
　　so a sluggard turns on his bed.

15The sluggard buries his hand in the dish;
　　he is too lazy to bring it back to his mouth.

16The sluggard is wiser in his own eyes
　　than seven men who answer discreetly.

17Like one who seizes a dog by the ears
　　is a passer-by who meddles in a quarrel not
　　his own.

18Like a madman shooting
　　firebrands or deadly arrows
19is a man who deceives his neighbor
　　and says, "I was only joking!"

20Without wood a fire goes out;
　　without gossip a quarrel dies down.

21As charcoal to embers and as wood to fire,
　　so is a quarrelsome man for kindling strife.

22The words of a gossip are like choice morsels;
　　they go down to a man's inmost parts.

23Like a coating of glaze*a* over earthenware
　　are fervent lips with an evil heart.

24A malicious man disguises himself with his lips,
　　but in his heart he harbors deceit.
25Though his speech is charming, do not believe
　　him,
　　for seven abominations fill his heart.
26His malice may be concealed by deception,
　　but his wickedness will be exposed in the
　　assembly.

*a 23 With a different word division of the Hebrew; Masoretic
Text of silver dross*

²⁷If a man digs a pit, he will fall into it;
    if a man rolls a stone, it will roll back on him.

²⁸A lying tongue hates those it hurts,
    and a flattering mouth works ruin.

27

Do not boast about tomorrow,
    for you do not know what a day may
    bring forth.

²Let another praise you, and not your own
    mouth;
    someone else, and not your own lips.

³Stone is heavy and sand a burden,
    but provocation by a fool is heavier than both.

⁴Anger is cruel and fury overwhelming,
    but who can stand before jealousy?

⁵Better is open rebuke
    than hidden love.

⁶Wounds from a friend can be trusted,
    but an enemy multiplies kisses.

⁷He who is full loathes honey,
    but to the hungry even what is bitter tastes
    sweet.

⁸Like a bird that strays from its nest
    is a man who strays from his home.

⁹Perfume and incense bring joy to the heart,
    and the pleasantness of one's friend springs
    from his earnest counsel.

¹⁰Do not forsake your friend and the friend of
    your father,
    and do not go to your brother's house when
    disaster strikes you—
    better a neighbor nearby than a brother far
    away.

¹¹Be wise, my son, and bring joy to my heart;
    then I can answer anyone who treats me
    with contempt.

¹²The prudent see danger and take refuge,
    but the simple keep going and suffer for it.

¹³Take the garment of one who puts up security
    for a stranger;
    hold it in pledge if he does it for a wayward
    woman.

²⁷挖陷坑的，自己必掉在其中；
    滾石頭的，石頭必反滾在他身上。

²⁸虛謊的舌，恨他所壓傷的人；
    諂媚的口，敗壞人的事。

27

不要為明日自誇，
    因為一日要生何事，
    你尚且不能知道。

²要別人誇獎你，不可用口自誇；
    等外人稱讚你，不可用嘴自稱。

³石頭重，沙土沉，
    愚妄人的惱怒，比這兩樣更重。

⁴忿怒為殘忍，怒氣為狂瀾，
    惟有嫉妒，誰能敵得住呢？

⁵當面的責備，
    強如背地的愛情。

⁶朋友加的傷痕，出於忠誠；
    仇敵連連親嘴，卻是多餘。

⁷人吃飽了，厭惡蜂房的蜜；
    人飢餓了，一切苦物都覺甘甜。

⁸人離本處飄流，
    好像雀鳥離窩遊飛。

⁹膏油與香料，使人心喜悅，
    朋友誠實的勸教也是如此甘美。

¹⁰你的朋友和父親的朋友，
    你都不可離棄。
    你遭難的日子，
    不要上弟兄的家去；
    相近的鄰舍，
    強如遠方的弟兄。

¹¹我兒，你要作智慧人，
    好叫我的心歡喜，
    使我可以回答那譏誚我的人。

¹²通達人見禍藏躲；
    愚蒙人前往受害。

¹³誰為生人作保，就拿誰的衣服；
    誰為外女作保，誰就承當。

14清晨起來，大聲給朋友祝福的，
　　就算是咒詛他。

15大雨之日，連連滴漏，
　　和爭吵的婦人一樣；
16想攔阻她的，便是攔阻風，
　　也是右手抓油。

17鐵磨鐵，磨出刃來；
　　朋友相感（註：原文作"磨朋友的臉"），
　　也是如此。

18看守無花果樹的，
　　必吃樹上的果子；
　　敬奉主人的，必得尊榮。

19水中照臉，彼此相符；
　　人與人，心也相對。

20陰間和滅亡永不滿足，
　　人的眼目也是如此。

21鼎為煉銀，爐為煉金，
　　人的稱讚也試煉人。

22你雖用杵將愚妄人
　　與打碎的麥子一同搗在臼中，
　　他的愚妄還是離不了他。

23你要詳細知道你羊群的景況，
　　留心料理你的牛群；
24因為資財不能永有，
　　冠冕豈能存到萬代？
25乾草割去，嫩草發現，
　　山上的菜蔬也被收斂。

26羊羔之毛是為你作衣服；
　　山羊是為作田地的價值；
27並有母山羊奶夠你吃，
　　也夠你的家眷吃，
　　且夠養你的婢女。

28 惡人雖無人追趕也逃跑；
　　義人卻膽壯像獅子。

2邦國因有罪過，
　　君王就多更換；
　　因有聰明知識的人，
　　國必長存。

3窮人欺壓貧民，
　　好像暴雨沖沒糧食。

14If a man loudly blesses his neighbor early in
　　the morning,
　　it will be taken as a curse.

15A quarrelsome wife is like
　　a constant dripping on a rainy day;
16restraining her is like restraining the wind
　　or grasping oil with the hand.

17As iron sharpens iron,
　　so one man sharpens another.

18He who tends a fig tree will eat its fruit,
　　and he who looks after his master will be
　　honored.

19As water reflects a face,
　　so a man's heart reflects the man.

20Death and Destruction*a* are never satisfied,
　　and neither are the eyes of man.

21The crucible for silver and the furnace for gold,
　　but man is tested by the praise he receives.

22Though you grind a fool in a mortar,
　　grinding him like grain with a pestle,
　　you will not remove his folly from him.

23Be sure you know the condition of your flocks,
　　give careful attention to your herds;
24for riches do not endure forever,
　　and a crown is not secure for all generations.
25When the hay is removed and new growth
　　appears
　　and the grass from the hills is gathered in,
26the lambs will provide you with clothing,
　　and the goats with the price of a field.
27You will have plenty of goats' milk
　　to feed you and your family
　　and to nourish your servant girls.

28 The wicked man flees though no one
　　pursues,
　　but the righteous are as bold as a lion.

2When a country is rebellious, it has many
　　rulers,
　　but a man of understanding and knowledge
　　maintains order.

3A ruler*b* who oppresses the poor
　　is like a driving rain that leaves no crops.

a 20 Hebrew Sheol and Abaddon　　b 3 Or A poor man

⁴Those who forsake the law praise the wicked,
  but those who keep the law resist them.

⁵Evil men do not understand justice,
  but those who seek the LORD understand it
  fully.

⁶Better a poor man whose walk is blameless
  than a rich man whose ways are perverse.

⁷He who keeps the law is a discerning son,
  but a companion of gluttons disgraces his
  father.

⁸He who increases his wealth by exorbitant
  interest
  amasses it for another, who will be kind to
  the poor.

⁹If anyone turns a deaf ear to the law,
  even his prayers are detestable.

¹⁰He who leads the upright along an evil path
  will fall into his own trap,
  but the blameless will receive a good
  inheritance.

¹¹A rich man may be wise in his own eyes,
  but a poor man who has discernment sees
  through him.

¹²When the righteous triumph, there is great
  elation;
  but when the wicked rise to power, men go
  into hiding.

¹³He who conceals his sins does not prosper,
  but whoever confesses and renounces them
  finds mercy.

¹⁴Blessed is the man who always fears the LORD,
  but he who hardens his heart falls into
  trouble.

¹⁵Like a roaring lion or a charging bear
  is a wicked man ruling over a helpless
  people.

¹⁶A tyrannical ruler lacks judgment,
  but he who hates ill-gotten gain will enjoy a
  long life.

¹⁷A man tormented by the guilt of murder
  will be a fugitive till death;
  let no one support him.

---

⁴違棄律法的，誇獎惡人；
  遵守律法的，卻與惡人相爭。

⁵壞人不明白公義；
  惟有尋求耶和華的，無不明白。

⁶行為純正的窮乏人，
  勝過行事乖僻的富足人。

⁷謹守律法的是智慧之子；
  與貪食人作伴的，卻羞辱其父。

⁸人以厚利加增財物，
  是給那憐憫窮人者積蓄的。

⁹轉耳不聽律法的，
  他的祈禱也為可憎。

¹⁰誘惑正直人行惡道的，
  必掉在自己的坑裏，
  惟有完全人，
  必承受福分。

¹¹富足人自以為有智慧，
  但聰明的貧窮人能將他查透。

¹²義人得志，有大榮耀；
  惡人興起，人就躲藏。

¹³遮掩自己罪過的，必不亨通；
  承認離棄罪過的，必蒙憐恤。

¹⁴常存敬畏的，便為有福；
  心存剛硬的，必陷在禍患裏。

¹⁵暴虐的君王轄制貧民，
  好像吼叫的獅子、覓食的熊。

¹⁶無知的君多行暴虐；
  以貪財為可恨的，必年長日久。

¹⁷背負流人血之罪的，
  必往坑裏奔跑，
  誰也不可攔阻他。

¹⁸行動正直的，必蒙拯救；
　　行事彎曲的，立時跌倒。

¹⁹耕種自己田地的，必得飽食；
　　追隨虛浮的，足受窮乏。

²⁰誠實人必多得福，
　　想要急速發財的，不免受罰。

²¹看人的情面，乃為不好；
　　人因一塊餅枉法，也為不好。

²²人有惡眼想要急速發財，
　　卻不知窮乏必臨到他身。

²³責備人的，後來蒙人喜悅，
　　多於那用舌頭諂媚人的。

²⁴偷竊父母的說：
　　“這不是罪”，
　　此人就是與強盜同類。

²⁵心中貪婪的，挑起爭端；
　　倚靠耶和華的，必得豐裕。

²⁶心中自是的，便是愚昧人；
　　憑智慧行事的，必蒙拯救。

²⁷賙濟貧窮的，不致缺乏；
　　佯為不見的，必多受咒詛。

²⁸惡人興起，人就躲藏；
　　惡人敗亡，義人增多。

29 人屢次受責罰，
　　仍然硬着頸項，
　　他必頃刻敗壞，
　　無法可治。

²義人增多，民就喜樂；
　　惡人掌權，民就歎息。

³愛慕智慧的，使父親喜樂；
　　與妓女結交的，卻浪費錢財。

¹⁸He whose walk is blameless is kept safe,
　　but he whose ways are perverse will
　　　suddenly fall.

¹⁹He who works his land will have abundant
　　food,
　　but the one who chases fantasies will have
　　　his fill of poverty.

²⁰A faithful man will be richly blessed,
　　but one eager to get rich will not go
　　　unpunished.

²¹To show partiality is not good—
　　yet a man will do wrong for a piece of bread.

²²A stingy man is eager to get rich
　　and is unaware that poverty awaits him.

²³He who rebukes a man will in the end gain
　　　more favor
　　than he who has a flattering tongue.

²⁴He who robs his father or mother
　　and says, "It's not wrong"—
　　he is partner to him who destroys.

²⁵A greedy man stirs up dissension,
　　but he who trusts in the LORD will prosper.

²⁶He who trusts in himself is a fool,
　　but he who walks in wisdom is kept safe.

²⁷He who gives to the poor will lack nothing,
　　but he who closes his eyes to them receives
　　　many curses.

²⁸When the wicked rise to power, people go
　　into hiding;
　　but when the wicked perish, the righteous
　　　thrive.

29 A man who remains stiff-necked after
　　many rebukes
　　will suddenly be destroyed—without
　　remedy.

²When the righteous thrive, the people rejoice;
　　when the wicked rule, the people groan.

³A man who loves wisdom brings joy to his
　　father,
　　but a companion of prostitutes squanders his
　　　wealth.

⁴By justice a king gives a country stability,
    but one who is greedy for bribes tears it
      down.

⁵Whoever flatters his neighbor
    is spreading a net for his feet.

⁶An evil man is snared by his own sin,
    but a righteous one can sing and be glad.

⁷The righteous care about justice for the poor,
    but the wicked have no such concern.

⁸Mockers stir up a city,
    but wise men turn away anger.

⁹If a wise man goes to court with a fool,
    the fool rages and scoffs, and there is no
      peace.

¹⁰Bloodthirsty men hate a man of integrity
    and seek to kill the upright.

¹¹A fool gives full vent to his anger,
    but a wise man keeps himself under control.

¹²If a ruler listens to lies,
    all his officials become wicked.

¹³The poor man and the oppressor have this in
    common:
    The LORD gives sight to the eyes of both.

¹⁴If a king judges the poor with fairness,
    his throne will always be secure.

¹⁵The rod of correction imparts wisdom,
    but a child left to himself disgraces his mother.

¹⁶When the wicked thrive, so does sin,
    but the righteous will see their downfall.

¹⁷Discipline your son, and he will give you
    peace;
    he will bring delight to your soul.

¹⁸Where there is no revelation, the people cast
    off restraint;
    but blessed is he who keeps the law.

¹⁹A servant cannot be corrected by mere words;
    though he understands, he will not respond.

²⁰Do you see a man who speaks in haste?
    There is more hope for a fool than for him.

⁴王藉公平，使國堅定；
    索要賄賂，使國傾敗。

⁵諂媚鄰舍的，
    就是設網羅絆他的腳。

⁶惡人犯罪，自陷網羅，
    惟獨義人，歡呼喜樂。

⁷義人知道查明窮人的案，
    惡人沒有聰明，就不得而知。

⁸褻慢人煽惑通城；
    智慧人止息眾怒。

⁹智慧人與愚妄人相爭，
    或怒或笑，總不能使他止息。

¹⁰好流人血的，恨惡完全人，
    索取正直人的性命。

¹¹愚妄人怒氣全發；
    智慧人忍氣含怒。

¹²君王若聽謊言，
    他一切臣僕都是奸惡。

¹³貧窮人、強暴人在世相遇，
    他們的眼目，都蒙耶和華光照。

¹⁴君王憑誠實判斷窮人，
    他的國位必永遠堅立。

¹⁵杖打和責備能加增智慧；
    放縱的兒子使母親羞愧。

¹⁶惡人加多，過犯也加多，
    義人必看見他們跌倒。

¹⁷管教你的兒子，他就使你得安息，
    也必使你心裏喜樂。

¹⁸沒有異象（註：或作"默示"），
      民就放肆；
    惟遵守律法的，便為有福！

¹⁹只用言語，僕人不肯受管教，
    他雖然明白，也不留意。

²⁰你見言語急躁的人嗎？
    愚昧人比他更有指望。

21 人將僕人從小嬌養，
 　　這僕人終久必成了他的兒子。

22 好氣的人，挑啓爭端；
 　　暴怒的人，多多犯罪。

23 人的高傲，必使他卑下；
 　　心裏謙遜的，必得尊榮。

24 人與盜賊分贓，
 　　是恨惡自己的性命；
 　他聽見叫人發誓的聲音，
 　　卻不言語。

25 懼怕人的，陷入網羅；
 　　惟有倚靠耶和華的，必得安穩。

26 求王恩的人多，
 　　定人事乃在耶和華。

27 為非作歹的，被義人憎嫌；
 　　行事正直的，被惡人憎惡。

亞古珥的言語

30 雅基的兒子亞古珥的言語，
　　就是真言。

這人對以鐵和烏甲說：

2 "我比眾人更蠢笨，
 　　也沒有人的聰明。
3 我沒有學好智慧，
 　　也不認識至聖者。
4 誰升天又降下來？
 　　誰聚風在掌握中？

誰包水在衣服裏？
 　　誰立定地的四極？
 　他名叫甚麼？他兒子名叫甚麼？
 　　你知道嗎？

5 "神的言語句句都是煉淨的！
 　　投靠他的，他便作他們的盾牌。
6 他的言語，你不可加添，
 　　恐怕他責備你，
 　　你就顯為說謊言的。

7 "我求你兩件事，
 　　在我未死之先，不要不賜給我：
8 求你使虛假和謊言遠離我；
 　　使我也不貧窮，也不富足，
 　　賜給我需用的飲食。

21 If a man pampers his servant from youth,
 　　he will bring grief*a* in the end.

22 An angry man stirs up dissension,
 　　and a hot-tempered one commits many sins.

23 A man's pride brings him low,
 　　but a man of lowly spirit gains honor.

24 The accomplice of a thief is his own enemy;
 　　he is put under oath and dare not testify.

25 Fear of man will prove to be a snare,
 　　but whoever trusts in the LORD is kept safe.

26 Many seek an audience with a ruler,
 　　but it is from the LORD that man gets justice.

27 The righteous detest the dishonest;
 　　the wicked detest the upright.

Sayings of Agur

30 The sayings of Agur son of Jakeh—an
oracle*b*:

This man declared to Ithiel,
 　　to Ithiel and to Ucal:*c*

2 "I am the most ignorant of men;
 　　I do not have a man's understanding.
3 I have not learned wisdom,
 　　nor have I knowledge of the Holy One.
4 Who has gone up to heaven and come down?
 　　Who has gathered up the wind in the hollow
 　　　of his hands?

Who has wrapped up the waters in his cloak?
 　　Who has established all the ends of the earth?
 　What is his name, and the name of his son?
 　　Tell me if you know!

5 "Every word of God is flawless;
 　　he is a shield to those who take refuge in him.
6 Do not add to his words,
 　　or he will rebuke you and prove you a liar.

7 "Two things I ask of you, O LORD;
 　　do not refuse me before I die:
8 Keep falsehood and lies far from me;
 　　give me neither poverty nor riches,
 　　but give me only my daily bread.

a 21 The meaning of the Hebrew for this word is uncertain.
b 1 Or *Jakeh of Massa*　*c 1* Masoretic Text; with a different
word division of the Hebrew *declared,* "*I am weary, O God; / I
am weary, O God, and faint.*

9Otherwise, I may have too much and disown
you
　and say, 'Who is the LORD?'
Or I may become poor and steal,
　and so dishonor the name of my God.

10"Do not slander a servant to his master,
　or he will curse you, and you will pay for it.

11"There are those who curse their fathers
　and do not bless their mothers;
12those who are pure in their own eyes
　and yet are not cleansed of their filth;
13those whose eyes are ever so haughty,
　whose glances are so disdainful;
14those whose teeth are swords
　and whose jaws are set with knives
to devour the poor from the earth,
　the needy from among mankind.

15"The leech has two daughters.
　'Give! Give!' they cry.

"There are three things that are never
　satisfied,
four that never say, 'Enough!':
16the grave,*a* the barren womb,
　land, which is never satisfied with water,
　and fire, which never says, 'Enough!'

17"The eye that mocks a father,
　that scorns obedience to a mother,
will be pecked out by the ravens of the valley,
　will be eaten by the vultures.

18"There are three things that are too amazing
　for me,
four that I do not understand:
19the way of an eagle in the sky,
　the way of a snake on a rock,
the way of a ship on the high seas,
　and the way of a man with a maiden.

20"This is the way of an adulteress:
　She eats and wipes her mouth
and says, 'I've done nothing wrong.'

21"Under three things the earth trembles,
　under four it cannot bear up:
22a servant who becomes king,
　a fool who is full of food,
23an unloved woman who is married,
　and a maidservant who displaces her
　mistress.

a 16 Hebrew Sheol

9恐怕我飽足不認你，説：

　　'耶和華是誰呢？'
又恐怕我貧窮就偷竊，
　以致褻瀆我神的名。

10 "你不要向主人讒謗僕人，
　恐怕他咒詛你，你便算為有罪。

11 "有一宗人（註："宗"原文作"代"。下
　同），咒詛父親，不給母親祝福。
12有一宗人，自以為清潔，
　卻沒有洗去自己的污穢。
13有一宗人，眼目何其高傲，
　眼皮也是高舉。
14有一宗人，牙如劍、齒如刀，
　要吞滅地上的困苦人，
　　和世間的窮乏人。

15 "螞蟥有兩個女兒，
　常説：'給呀，給呀！'

"有三樣不知足的，
　連不説夠的共有四樣：

16就是陰間和石胎，
　浸水不足的地，
　並火。

17 "戲笑父親，
　藐視而不聽從母親的，
他的眼睛必為谷中的烏鴉啄出來，
　為鷹雛所吃。

18 "我所測不透的奇妙有三樣，
　連我所不知道的共有四樣：

19就是鷹在空中飛的道，
　蛇在磐石上爬的道，
船在海中行的道，
　男與女交合的道。

20 "淫婦的道，也是這樣：
　她吃了把嘴一擦，就説：
　'我沒有行惡。'

21 "使地震動的有三樣，
　連地擔不起的共有四樣：
22就是僕人作王，
　愚頑人吃飽，
23醜惡的女子出嫁，
　婢女接續主母。

24 "地上有四樣小物，
　　卻甚聰明：
25螞蟻是無力之類，
　　卻在夏天預備糧食；
26沙番是軟弱之類，
　　卻在磐石中造房；
27蝗蟲沒有君王，
　　卻分隊而出；
28守宮用爪抓牆，
　　卻住在王宮。

29 "步行威武的有三樣，
　　連行走威武的共有四樣：

30就是獅子乃百獸中最為猛烈，
　　無所躲避的；
31獵狗、公山羊，
　　和無人能敵的君王。

32 "你若行事愚頑，
　　自高自傲，
　　或是懷了惡念，
　　就當用手搗口。
33搖牛奶必成奶油，
　　扭鼻子必出血，
　　照樣，激動怒氣必起爭端。"

利慕伊勒王的言語

31 利慕伊勒王的言語，是他母
　　 親教訓他的真言：

2 "我的兒啊，我腹中生的兒啊，
　　我許願得的兒啊，
　　我當怎樣教訓你呢？
3不要將你的精力給婦女，
　　也不要有敗壞君王的行為。
4 "利慕伊勒啊，
　　君王喝酒，君王喝酒不相宜；
　　王子說，濃酒在那裏也不相宜。
5恐怕喝了就忘記律例，
　　顛倒一切困苦人的是非。
6可以把濃酒給將亡的人喝，
　　把清酒給苦心的人喝，
7讓他喝了，就忘記他的貧窮，
　　不再記念他的苦楚。

8 "你當為啞巴（註：或作"不能自辯的"）
　　開口，
　　為一切孤獨的伸冤。
9你當開口按公義判斷，
　　為困苦和窮乏的辨屈。"

24"Four things on earth are small,
　　yet they are extremely wise:
25Ants are creatures of little strength,
　　yet they store up their food in the summer;
26coneys*a* are creatures of little power,
　　yet they make their home in the crags;
27locusts have no king,
　　yet they advance together in ranks;
28a lizard can be caught with the hand,
　　yet it is found in kings' palaces.

29"There are three things that are stately in their
　　stride,
　　four that move with stately bearing:
30a lion, mighty among beasts,
　　who retreats before nothing;
31a strutting rooster, a he-goat,
　　and a king with his army around him.*b*

32"If you have played the fool and exalted
　　yourself,
　　or if you have planned evil,
　　clap your hand over your mouth!
33For as churning the milk produces butter,
　　and as twisting the nose produces blood,
　　so stirring up anger produces strife."

Sayings of King Lemuel

31 The sayings of King Lemuel—an oracle*c*
　　 his mother taught him:

2"O my son, O son of my womb,
　　O son of my vows,*d*
3do not spend your strength on women,
　　your vigor on those who ruin kings.

4"It is not for kings, O Lemuel—
　　not for kings to drink wine,
　　not for rulers to crave beer,
5lest they drink and forget what the law decrees,
　　and deprive all the oppressed of their rights.
6Give beer to those who are perishing,
　　wine to those who are in anguish;
7let them drink and forget their poverty
　　and remember their misery no more.

8"Speak up for those who cannot speak for
　　themselves,
　　for the rights of all who are destitute.
9Speak up and judge fairly;
　　defend the rights of the poor and needy."

a 26 That is, the hyrax or rock badger　　*b 31 Or king secure
against revolt*　　*c 1 Or of Lemuel king of Massa, which
d 2 Or | the answer to my prayers*

Epilogue: The Wife of Noble Character

^{10a} A wife of noble character who can find?
　She is worth far more than rubies.
¹¹Her husband has full confidence in her
　and lacks nothing of value.
¹²She brings him good, not harm,
　all the days of her life.
¹³She selects wool and flax
　and works with eager hands.
¹⁴She is like the merchant ships,
　bringing her food from afar.
¹⁵She gets up while it is still dark;
　she provides food for her family
　and portions for her servant girls.
¹⁶She considers a field and buys it;
　out of her earnings she plants a vineyard.
¹⁷She sets about her work vigorously;
　her arms are strong for her tasks.
¹⁸She sees that her trading is profitable,
　and her lamp does not go out at night.
¹⁹In her hand she holds the distaff
　and grasps the spindle with her fingers.
²⁰She opens her arms to the poor
　and extends her hands to the needy.
²¹When it snows, she has no fear for her
　household;
　for all of them are clothed in scarlet.
²²She makes coverings for her bed;
　she is clothed in fine linen and purple.
²³Her husband is respected at the city gate,
　where he takes his seat among the elders of
　the land.
²⁴She makes linen garments and sells them,
　and supplies the merchants with sashes.
²⁵She is clothed with strength and dignity;
　she can laugh at the days to come.
²⁶She speaks with wisdom,
　and faithful instruction is on her tongue.
²⁷She watches over the affairs of her household
　and does not eat the bread of idleness.
²⁸Her children arise and call her blessed;
　her husband also, and he praises her:
²⁹"Many women do noble things,
　but you surpass them all."
³⁰Charm is deceptive, and beauty is fleeting;
　but a woman who fears the LORD is to be
　praised.
³¹Give her the reward she has earned,
　and let her works bring her praise at the city
　gate.

後語：才德的婦人

¹⁰才德的婦人誰能得着呢？
　她的價值遠勝過珍珠。
¹¹她丈夫心裏倚靠她，
　必不缺少利益。
¹²她一生
　使丈夫有益無損。
¹³她尋找羊羢和麻，
　甘心用手做工。
¹⁴她好像商船
　從遠方運糧來。
¹⁵未到黎明她就起來，
　把食物分給家中的人，
　將當做的工分派婢女。
¹⁶她想得田地就買來，
　用手所得之利，栽種葡萄園。
¹⁷她以能力束腰，
　使膀臂有力。
¹⁸她覺得所經營的有利，
　她的燈終夜不滅。
¹⁹她手拿撚線竿，
　手把紡線車。
²⁰她張手賙濟困苦人，
　伸手幫補窮乏人。
²¹她不因下雪為家裏的人擔心，
　因為全家都穿着朱紅衣服。
²²她為自己製作繡花毯子，
　她的衣服是細麻和紫色布做的。
²³她丈夫在城門口
　與本地的長老同坐，
　為眾人所認識。
²⁴她做細麻布衣裳出賣，
　又將腰帶賣與商家。
²⁵能力和威儀是她的衣服。
　她想到日後的景況就喜笑。
²⁶她開口就發智慧，
　她舌上有仁慈的法則。
²⁷她觀察家務，
　並不吃閒飯。
²⁸她的兒女起來稱她有福，
　她的丈夫也稱讚她。
²⁹說："才德的女子很多，
　惟獨你超過一切！"
³⁰艷麗是虛假的，美容是虛浮的，
　惟敬畏耶和華的婦女必得稱讚！
³¹願她享受操作所得的；
　願她的工作，在城門口榮耀她。

---

a 10 Verses 10-31 are an acrostic, each verse beginning with a
successive letter of the Hebrew alphabet.

傳道書

Ecclesiastes

凡事都是虛空

1 在耶路撒冷作王，<u>大衛</u>的兒子，傳道者的言語。

² 傳道者說：
　　"虛空的虛空，
　虛空的虛空，
　凡事都是虛空。"

³ 人一切的勞碌，就是他在日光之下
　　的勞碌，有甚麼益處呢？
⁴ 一代過去，一代又來，
　　地卻永遠長存。
⁵ 日頭出來，日頭落下，
　　急歸所出之地。
⁶ 風往南颳，
　又向北轉，
　不住地旋轉，
　而且返回轉行原道。
⁷ 江河都往海裏流，
　　海卻不滿；
　江河從何處流，
　　仍歸還何處。
⁸ 萬事令人厭煩（註：或作"萬物滿有困
　　乏"），人不能說盡。
　眼看，看不飽；
　耳聽，聽不足。
⁹ 已有的事，後必再有；
　　已行的事，後必再行。
　日光之下，並無新事。
¹⁰ 豈有一件事人能指着說：
　　"這是新的"？
　哪知，
　　在我們以前的世代早已有了。
¹¹ 已過的世代，
　　無人記念；
　將來的世代，
　　後來的人也不記念。

智慧是虛空

¹² 我傳道者在<u>耶路撒冷</u>作過以<u>色
列</u>的王。¹³ 我專心用智慧尋求查究天
下所做的一切事，乃知神叫世人所
經練的是極重的勞苦。¹⁴ 我見日光之

Everything Is Meaningless

1 The words of the Teacher,[a] son of David, king in Jerusalem:

² "Meaningless! Meaningless!"
　says the Teacher.
　"Utterly meaningless!
　Everything is meaningless."

³ What does man gain from all his labor
　at which he toils under the sun?
⁴ Generations come and generations go,
　but the earth remains forever.
⁵ The sun rises and the sun sets,
　and hurries back to where it rises.
⁶ The wind blows to the south
　and turns to the north;
　round and round it goes,
　ever returning on its course.
⁷ All streams flow into the sea,
　yet the sea is never full.
　To the place the streams come from,
　there they return again.
⁸ All things are wearisome,
　more than one can say.
　The eye never has enough of seeing,
　nor the ear its fill of hearing.
⁹ What has been will be again,
　what has been done will be done again;
　there is nothing new under the sun.
¹⁰ Is there anything of which one can say,
　"Look! This is something new"?
　It was here already, long ago;
　it was here before our time.
¹¹ There is no remembrance of men of old,
　and even those who are yet to come
　will not be remembered
　by those who follow.

Wisdom Is Meaningless

¹² I, the Teacher, was king over Israel in Jerusalem. ¹³ I devoted myself to study and to explore by wisdom all that is done under heaven. What a heavy burden God has laid on men! ¹⁴ I have seen all the things that are done under

a 1 Or leader of the assembly; also in verses 2 and 12

the sun; all of them are meaningless, a chasing after the wind.

15What is twisted cannot be straightened;
    what is lacking cannot be counted.

16I thought to myself, "Look, I have grown and increased in wisdom more than anyone who has ruled over Jerusalem before me; I have experienced much of wisdom and knowledge." 17Then I applied myself to the understanding of wisdom, and also of madness and folly, but I learned that this, too, is a chasing after the wind.

18For with much wisdom comes much sorrow;
    the more knowledge, the more grief.

Pleasures Are Meaningless

2 I thought in my heart, "Come now, I will test you with pleasure to find out what is good." But that also proved to be meaningless. 2"Laughter," I said, "is foolish. And what does pleasure accomplish?" 3I tried cheering myself with wine, and embracing folly—my mind still guiding me with wisdom. I wanted to see what was worthwhile for men to do under heaven during the few days of their lives.

4I undertook great projects: I built houses for myself and planted vineyards. 5I made gardens and parks and planted all kinds of fruit trees in them. 6I made reservoirs to water groves of flourishing trees. 7I bought male and female slaves and had other slaves who were born in my house. I also owned more herds and flocks than anyone in Jerusalem before me. 8I amassed silver and gold for myself, and the treasure of kings and provinces. I acquired men and women singers, and a harem^a as well—the delights of the heart of man. 9I became greater by far than anyone in Jerusalem before me. In all this my wisdom stayed with me.

10I denied myself nothing my eyes desired;
    I refused my heart no pleasure.
My heart took delight in all my work,
    and this was the reward for all my labor.
11Yet when I surveyed all that my hands had done
    and what I had toiled to achieve,
everything was meaningless, a chasing after
    the wind;
    nothing was gained under the sun.

下所做的一切事，都是虛空，都是捕風。

15彎曲的不能變直；
    缺少的不能足數。

16我心裏議論說："我得了大智慧，勝過我以前在耶路撒冷的眾人，而且我心中多經歷智慧和知識的事。"17我又專心察明智慧、狂妄和愚昧，乃知這也是捕風。

18因為多有智慧，就多有愁煩；
    加增知識的，就加增憂傷。

享樂是虛空

2 我心裏說："來吧！我以喜樂試試你，你好享福。"誰知，這也是虛空。2我指嬉笑說："這是狂妄"；論喜樂說："有何功效呢？" 3我心裏察究，如何用酒使我肉體舒暢，我心卻仍以智慧引導我；又如何持住愚昧，等我看明世人，在天下一生當行何事為美。

4我為自己動大工程，建造房屋，栽種葡萄園；5修造園囿，在其中栽種各樣果木樹；6挖造水池，用以澆灌嫩小的樹木。7我買了僕婢，也有生在家中的僕婢；又有許多牛羣羊羣，勝過以前在耶路撒冷眾人所有的。8我又為自己積蓄金銀和君王的財寶，並各省的財寶；又得唱歌的男女和世人所喜愛的物，並許多的妃嬪。9這樣，我就日見昌盛，勝過以前在耶路撒冷的眾人。我的智慧仍然存留。

10凡我眼所求的，
    我沒有留下不給他的；
我心所樂的，我沒有禁止不享受的；
    因我的心為我一切所勞碌的快樂，
    這就是我從勞碌中所得的分。
11後來，我察看我手所經營的一切事
    和我勞碌所成的功，
誰知都是虛空，都是捕風，
    在日光之下毫無益處。

---

a 8 The meaning of the Hebrew for this phrase is uncertain.

智愚皆是虛空

¹²我轉念觀看智慧、
　　狂妄和愚昧。
　在王以後而來的人
　　還能做甚麼呢？
　　也不過行早先所行的就是了。
¹³我便看出智慧勝過愚昧，
　　如同光明勝過黑暗。
¹⁴智慧人的眼目光明（註："光明"原文作
　　"在他頭上"）；
　　愚昧人在黑暗裏行。
　我卻看明有一件事，
　　這兩等人都必遇見。

¹⁵我就心裏說：
　"愚昧人所遇見的，我也必遇見，
　　我為何更有智慧呢？"
　我心裏說：
　　"這也是虛空。"
¹⁶智慧人和愚昧人一樣，
　　永遠無人記念，
　　因為日後都被忘記；
　可歎智慧人死亡，與愚昧人無異。

勞碌是虛空

¹⁷我所以恨惡生命，因為在日光之下所行的事，我都以為煩惱，都是虛空，都是捕風。¹⁸我恨惡一切的勞碌，就是我在日光之下的勞碌，因為我得來的必留給我以後的人。¹⁹那人是智慧，是愚昧，誰能知道？他竟要管理我勞碌所得的，就是我在日光之下用智慧所得的。這也是虛空。²⁰故此，我轉想我在日光之下所勞碌的一切工作，心便絕望。²¹因為有人用智慧、知識、靈巧所勞碌得來的，卻要留給未曾勞碌的人為分。這也是虛空，也是大患！²²人在日光之下勞碌累心，在他一切的勞碌上得著甚麼呢？²³因為他日日憂慮，他的勞苦成為愁煩，連夜間心也不安。這也是虛空。

²⁴人莫強如吃喝，且在勞碌中享福，我看這也是出於神的手。²⁵論到吃用、享福，誰能勝過我呢？²⁶神喜悅誰，就給誰智慧、知識和喜樂，惟有罪人，神使他勞苦，叫他將所收聚的、所堆積的歸給神所喜悅的人。這也是虛空，也是捕風。

Wisdom and Folly Are Meaningless

¹²Then I turned my thoughts to consider
　wisdom,
　and also madness and folly.
What more can the king's successor do
　than what has already been done?
¹³I saw that wisdom is better than folly,
　just as light is better than darkness.
¹⁴The wise man has eyes in his head,
　while the fool walks in the darkness;
　but I came to realize
　that the same fate overtakes them both.

¹⁵Then I thought in my heart,

"The fate of the fool will overtake me also.
　What then do I gain by being wise?"
I said in my heart,
　"This too is meaningless."
¹⁶For the wise man, like the fool, will not be
　long remembered;
　in days to come both will be forgotten.
　Like the fool, the wise man too must die!

Toil Is Meaningless

¹⁷So I hated life, because the work that is done under the sun was grievous to me. All of it is meaningless, a chasing after the wind. ¹⁸I hated all the things I had toiled for under the sun, because I must leave them to the one who comes after me. ¹⁹And who knows whether he will be a wise man or a fool? Yet he will have control over all the work into which I have poured my effort and skill under the sun. This too is meaningless. ²⁰So my heart began to despair over all my toilsome labor under the sun. ²¹For a man may do his work with wisdom, knowledge and skill, and then he must leave all he owns to someone who has not worked for it. This too is meaningless and a great misfortune. ²²What does a man get for all the toil and anxious striving with which he labors under the sun? ²³All his days his work is pain and grief; even at night his mind does not rest. This too is meaningless.

²⁴A man can do nothing better than to eat and drink and find satisfaction in his work. This too, I see, is from the hand of God, ²⁵for without him, who can eat or find enjoyment? ²⁶To the man who pleases him, God gives wisdom, knowledge and happiness, but to the sinner he gives the task of gathering and storing up wealth to hand it over to the one who pleases God. This too is meaningless, a chasing after the wind.

A Time for Everything

3 There is a time for everything,
and a season for every activity under
heaven:

2 a time to be born and a time to die,
a time to plant and a time to uproot,
3 a time to kill and a time to heal,
a time to tear down and a time to build,
4 a time to weep and a time to laugh,
a time to mourn and a time to dance,
5 a time to scatter stones and a time to gather
them,
a time to embrace and a time to refrain,
6 a time to search and a time to give up,
a time to keep and a time to throw away,
7 a time to tear and a time to mend,
a time to be silent and a time to speak,
8 a time to love and a time to hate,
a time for war and a time for peace.

9What does the worker gain from his toil? 10I
have seen the burden God has laid on men. 11He
has made everything beautiful in its time. He
has also set eternity in the hearts of men; yet
they cannot fathom what God has done from
beginning to end. 12I know that there is nothing
better for men than to be happy and do good
while they live. 13That everyone may eat and
drink, and find satisfaction in all his toil—this is
the gift of God. 14I know that everything God
does will endure forever; nothing can be added
to it and nothing taken from it. God does it so
that men will revere him.

15Whatever is has already been,
and what will be has been before;
and God will call the past to account.*a*

16And I saw something else under the sun:

In the place of
judgment—wickedness was there,
in the place of
justice—wickedness was there.

17I thought in my heart,

"God will bring to judgment
both the righteous and the wicked,
for there will be a time for every activity,
a time for every deed."

18I also thought, "As for men, God tests them

a 15 Or God calls back the past

萬事都有定時

3 凡事都有定期，
天下萬務都有定時。

2生有時，死有時；
栽種有時，拔出所栽種的也有時；
3殺戮有時，醫治有時；
拆毀有時，建造有時；
4哭有時，笑有時；
哀慟有時，跳舞有時；
5拋擲石頭有時，
堆聚石頭有時；
懷抱有時，不懷抱有時；
6尋找有時，失落有時；
保守有時，捨棄有時；
7撕裂有時，縫補有時；
靜默有時，言語有時；
8喜愛有時，恨惡有時；
爭戰有時，和好有時。

9這樣看來，做事的人在他的勞
碌上有甚麼益處呢？10我見神叫世人
勞苦，使他們在其中受經練。11神造
萬物，各按其時成為美好，又將永生
安置在世人心裏（註：“永生”原文作
“永遠”）。然而神從始至終的作為，
人不能參透。12我知道世人，莫強如
終身喜樂行善，13並且人人吃喝，在
他一切勞碌中享福，這也是神的恩
賜。14我知道神一切所做的都必永
存，無所增添，無所減少。神這樣
行，是要人在他面前存敬畏的心。

15現今的事早先就有了，
將來的事早已也有了，
並且神使已過的事重新再來（註：
或作“並且神再尋回已過的事”）。

16我又見日光之下：

在審判之處
有奸惡，
在公義之處
也有奸惡。

17我心裏說：

“神必審判
義人和惡人，
因為在那裏，各樣事務，
一切工作，都有定時。”

18我心裏說：“這乃為世人的緣

故，是神要試驗他們，使他們覺得
自己不過像獸一樣。¹⁹因為世人遭遇
的，獸也遭遇，所遭遇的都是一
樣：這個怎樣死，那個也怎樣死，
氣息都是一樣。人不能強於獸，都
是虛空。²⁰都歸一處，都是出於塵
土，也都歸於塵土。²¹誰知道人的靈
是往上升，獸的魂是下入地呢？"

²²故此，我見人莫強如在他經營
的事上喜樂，因為這是他的分；他
身後的事，誰能使他回來得見呢？

欺壓、勞碌、無朋友

4 我又轉念，見日光之下所行
的一切欺壓：

看哪，受欺壓的流淚，
　　且無人安慰；
欺壓他們的有勢力，
　　也無人安慰他們。
²因此，
　　我讚歎那早已死的死人，
　　勝過那還活着的活人。

³並且
　　我以為那未曾生的，
就是未見過日光之下惡事的，
比這兩等人更強。

⁴我又見人為一切的勞碌和各樣
靈巧的工作，就被鄰舍嫉妒。這也
是虛空，也是捕風。

⁵愚昧人抱着手，
吃自己的肉。
⁶滿了一把，得享安靜，
強如滿了兩把，
勞碌捕風。

⁷我又轉念，見日光之下有一件
虛空的事：

⁸有人孤單無二，
　　無子無兄，
竟勞碌不息，
　　眼目也不以錢財為足。
他說："我勞勞碌碌，
　　刻苦自己，不享福樂，
　　到底是為誰呢？"
這也是虛空，
　　是極重的勞苦。

so that they may see that they are like the animals. ¹⁹Man's fate is like that of the animals; the same fate awaits them both: As one dies, so dies the other. All have the same breath*a*; man has no advantage over the animal. Everything is meaningless. ²⁰All go to the same place; all come from dust, and to dust all return. ²¹Who knows if the spirit of man rises upward and if the spirit of the animal*b* goes down into the earth?"

²²So I saw that there is nothing better for a man than to enjoy his work, because that is his lot. For who can bring him to see what will happen after him?

Oppression, Toil, Friendlessness

4 Again I looked and saw all the oppression that was taking place under the sun:

I saw the tears of the oppressed—
　　and they have no comforter;
power was on the side of their oppressors—
　　and they have no comforter.
²And I declared that the dead,
　　who had already died,
are happier than the living,
　　who are still alive.
³But better than both
　　is he who has not yet been,
who has not seen the evil
　　that is done under the sun.

⁴And I saw that all labor and all achievement spring from man's envy of his neighbor. This too is meaningless, a chasing after the wind.

⁵The fool folds his hands
　　and ruins himself.
⁶Better one handful with tranquillity
　　than two handfuls with toil
　　and chasing after the wind.

⁷Again I saw something meaningless under the sun:

⁸There was a man all alone;
　　he had neither son nor brother.
There was no end to his toil,
　　yet his eyes were not content with his wealth.
"For whom am I toiling," he asked,
　　"and why am I depriving myself of
　　　enjoyment?"
This too is meaningless—
　　a miserable business!

---

*a 19 Or spirit   b 21 Or Who knows the spirit of man, which rises
upward, or the spirit of the animal, which*

9Two are better than one,
  because they have a good return for their
    work:
10If one falls down,
  his friend can help him up.
  But pity the man who falls
  and has no one to help him up!
11Also, if two lie down together, they will keep
    warm.
  But how can one keep warm alone?
12Though one may be overpowered,
  two can defend themselves.
  A cord of three strands is not quickly broken.

Advancement Is Meaningless

13Better a poor but wise youth than an old
but foolish king who no longer knows how to
take warning. 14The youth may have come from
prison to the kingship, or he may have been
born in poverty within his kingdom. 15I saw that
all who lived and walked under the sun followed the youth, the king's successor. 16There
was no end to all the people who were before
them. But those who came later were not
pleased with the successor. This too is meaningless, a chasing after the wind.

Stand in Awe of God

5 Guard your steps when you go to the
house of God. Go near to listen rather
than to offer the sacrifice of fools, who
do not know that they do wrong.

2Do not be quick with your mouth,
  do not be hasty in your heart
  to utter anything before God.
  God is in heaven
  and you are on earth,
  so let your words be few.
3As a dream comes when there are many cares,
  so the speech of a fool when there are many
    words.

4When you make a vow to God, do not delay
in fulfilling it. He has no pleasure in fools; fulfill
your vow. 5It is better not to vow than to make a
vow and not fulfill it. 6Do not let your mouth
lead you into sin. And do not protest to the
⌊temple⌋ messenger, "My vow was a mistake."
Why should God be angry at what you say and
destroy the work of your hands? 7Much dream-
ing and many words are meaningless. Therefore
stand in awe of God.

Riches Are Meaningless

8If you see the poor oppressed in a district,

9兩個人總比一個人好，
  因為二人勞碌同得美好的果效。

10若是跌倒，
  這人可以扶起他的同伴；
  若是孤身跌倒，
  沒有別人扶起他來，
  這人就有禍了！
11再者，二人同睡，就都暖和；
  一人獨睡，怎能暖和呢？
12有人攻勝孤身一人，
  若有二人便能敵擋他；
  三股合成的繩子不容易折斷。

高升是虛空

13貧窮而有智慧的少年人，勝過
年老不肯納諫的愚昧王。14這人是從
監牢中出來作王；在他國中，生來原
是貧窮的。15我見日光之下一切行動
的活人，都隨從那第二位，就是起來
代替老王的少年人。16他所治理的眾
人，就是他的百姓，多得無數。在他
後來的人，尚且不喜悅他。這真是虛
空，也是捕風。

要敬畏神

5 你到神的殿要謹慎腳步，因為
近前聽，勝過愚昧人獻祭
（註：或作"勝過獻愚昧人的祭"），
他們本不知道所做的是惡。

2你在神面前
  不可冒失開口，
  也不可心急發言，
  因為神在天上，
  你在地下，
  所以你的言語要寡少。
3事務多，就令人做夢；
  言語多，就顯出愚昧。

4你向神許願，償還不可遲延，
因他不喜悅愚昧人，所以你許的願應
當償還。5你許願不還，不如不許。
6不可任你的口使肉體犯罪，也不可
在祭司（註：原文作"使者"）面前說是
錯許了。為何使神因你的聲音發怒，
敗壞你手所做的呢？7多夢和多言，
其中多有虛幻。你只要敬畏神。

財富是虛空

8你若在一省之中見窮人受欺

壓，並奪去公義、公平的事，不要因此詫異。因有一位高過居高位的鑒察，在他們以上還有更高的。⁹況且地的益處歸眾人，就是君王也受田地的供應。

¹⁰貪愛銀子的，
　　不因得銀子知足；
　貪愛豐富的，
　　也不因得利益知足。
　這也是虛空。

¹¹貨物增添，
　　吃的人也增添，
　物主得甚麼益處呢？
　　不過眼看而已。

¹²勞碌的人不拘吃多吃少，
　　睡得香甜；
　富足人的豐滿，
　　卻不容他睡覺。

¹³我見日光之下，有一宗大禍患：

　　就是財主積存資財，反害自己。
¹⁴因遭遇禍患，這些資財就消滅；
　　那人若生了兒子，
　　手裏也一無所有。
¹⁵他怎樣從母胎赤身而來，
　　也必照樣赤身而去；
　他所勞碌得來的，
　　手中分毫不能帶去。

¹⁶他來的情形怎樣，
　　他去的情形也怎樣。

　這也是一宗大禍患。
　　他為風勞碌有甚麼益處呢？
¹⁷並且他終身在黑暗中吃喝，
　　多有煩惱，又有病患嘔氣。

¹⁸我所見為善為美的，就是人在神賜他一生的日子吃喝，享受日光之下勞碌得來的好處，因為這是他的分。¹⁹神賜人資財豐富，使他能以吃用，能取自己的分，在他勞碌中喜樂，這乃是神的恩賜。²⁰他不多思念自己一生的年日，因為神應他的心使他喜樂。

6 我見日光之下有一宗禍患重壓在人身上：²就是人蒙神賜他資財、豐富、尊榮，以致他心裏所願的一樣都不缺，只是神使他不能吃用，反有外人來吃用。

and justice and rights denied, do not be surprised at such things; for one official is eyed by a higher one, and over them both are others higher still. ⁹The increase from the land is taken by all; the king himself profits from the fields.

¹⁰Whoever loves money never has money
　　enough;
　whoever loves wealth is never satisfied with
　　his income.
　This too is meaningless.

¹¹As goods increase,
　　so do those who consume them.
　And what benefit are they to the owner
　　except to feast his eyes on them?

¹²The sleep of a laborer is sweet,
　　whether he eats little or much,
　but the abundance of a rich man
　　permits him no sleep.

¹³I have seen a grievous evil under the sun:

　　wealth hoarded to the harm of its owner,
¹⁴ or wealth lost through some misfortune,
　　so that when he has a son
　　there is nothing left for him.
¹⁵Naked a man comes from his mother's womb,
　　and as he comes, so he departs.
　He takes nothing from his labor
　　that he can carry in his hand.

¹⁶This too is a grievous evil:

　As a man comes, so he departs,
　　and what does he gain,
　　since he toils for the wind?
¹⁷All his days he eats in darkness,
　　with great frustration, affliction and anger.

¹⁸Then I realized that it is good and proper for a man to eat and drink, and to find satisfaction in his toilsome labor under the sun during the few days of life God has given him—for this is his lot. ¹⁹Moreover, when God gives any man wealth and possessions, and enables him to enjoy them, to accept his lot and be happy in his work—this is a gift of God. ²⁰He seldom reflects on the days of his life, because God keeps him occupied with gladness of heart.

6 I have seen another evil under the sun, and it weighs heavily on men: ²God gives a man wealth, possessions and honor, so that he lacks nothing his heart desires, but God does not enable him to enjoy them, and a stranger enjoys them instead. This is meaningless, a grievous evil.

³A man may have a hundred children and live many years; yet no matter how long he lives, if he cannot enjoy his prosperity and does not receive proper burial, I say that a stillborn child is better off than he. ⁴It comes without meaning, it departs in darkness, and in darkness its name is shrouded. ⁵Though it never saw the sun or knew anything, it has more rest than does that man— ⁶even if he lives a thousand years twice over but fails to enjoy his prosperity. Do not all go to the same place?

⁷All man's efforts are for his mouth,
　　yet his appetite is never satisfied.
⁸What advantage has a wise man
　　over a fool?
　What does a poor man gain
　　by knowing how to conduct himself before
　　　others?
⁹Better what the eye sees
　　than the roving of the appetite.
　This too is meaningless,
　　a chasing after the wind.

¹⁰Whatever exists has already been named,
　　and what man is has been known;
　no man can contend
　　with one who is stronger than he.
¹¹The more the words,
　　the less the meaning,
　and how does that profit anyone?

¹²For who knows what is good for a man in life, during the few and meaningless days he passes through like a shadow? Who can tell him what will happen under the sun after he is gone?

Wisdom

7 A good name is better than fine perfume,
　　and the day of death better than the day
　　of birth.
²It is better to go to a house of mourning
　　than to go to a house of feasting,
　for death is the destiny of every man;
　　the living should take this to heart.
³Sorrow is better than laughter,
　　because a sad face is good for the heart.
⁴The heart of the wise is in the house of
　　mourning,
　but the heart of fools is in the house of
　　pleasure.
⁵It is better to heed a wise man's rebuke
　　than to listen to the song of fools.

這是虛空，也是禍患。

³人若生一百個兒子，活許多歲數，以致他的年日甚多，心裏卻不得滿享福樂，又不得埋葬；據我說，那不到期而落的胎比他倒好。⁴因為虛虛而來，暗暗而去，名字被黑暗遮蔽，⁵並且沒有見過天日，也毫無知覺，這胎比那人倒享安息。⁶那人雖然活千年，再活千年，卻不享福，眾人豈不都歸一個地方去嗎？

⁷人的勞碌都為口腹，
　　心裏卻不知足。
⁸這樣看來，
　　智慧人比愚昧人有甚麼長處呢？
　窮人在眾人面前知道如何行，
　　有甚麼長處呢？
⁹眼睛所看的，
　　比心裏妄想的倒好。
　這也是虛空，
　　也是捕風。

¹⁰先前所有的，早已起了名，
　　並知道何為人，
　他也不能
　　與那比自己力大的相爭。
¹¹加增虛浮的事既多，
　　這與人有甚麼益處呢？

¹²人一生虛度的日子，就如影兒經過，誰知道甚麼與他有益呢？誰能告訴他身後在日光之下有甚麼事呢？

智慧

7 名譽強如美好的膏油；
　　人死的日子，
　　勝過人生的日子。
²往遭喪的家去，
　　強如往宴樂的家去，
　因為死是眾人的結局，
　　活人也必將這事放在心上。
³憂愁強如喜笑，
　　因為面帶愁容，終必使心喜樂。
⁴智慧人的心，
　　在遭喪之家；
　愚昧人的心，
　　在快樂之家。
⁵聽智慧人的責備，
　　強如聽愚昧人的歌唱。

⁶愚昧人的笑聲，
　　好像鍋下燒荊棘的爆聲。
　　這也是虛空。

⁷勒索使智慧人變為愚妄，
　　賄賂能敗壞人的慧心。

⁸事情的終局，強如事情的起頭；
　　存心忍耐的，勝過居心驕傲的。
⁹你不要心裏急躁惱怒，
　　因為惱怒存在愚昧人的懷中。

¹⁰不要說："先前的日子強過如今的
　　日子，是甚麼緣故呢？"
　　你這樣問，不是出於智慧。

¹¹智慧和產業並好，而且見天日的人，
　　得智慧更為有益。
¹²因為智慧護庇人，
　　好像銀錢護庇人一樣。
　　惟獨智慧能保全智慧人的生命。
　　這就是知識的益處。

¹³你要察看神的作為：

　　因神使為曲的，
　　誰能變為直呢？
¹⁴遇亨通的日子，你當喜樂；
　　遭患難的日子，你當思想。
　　因為神使這兩樣並列，
　　為的是叫人查不出
　　身後有甚麼事。

¹⁵有義人行義，反致滅亡；
　　有惡人行惡，倒享長壽。

　　這都是我在虛度之日中所見過的。

¹⁶不要行義過分，
　　也不要過於自逞智慧，
　　何必自取敗亡呢？
¹⁷不要行惡過分，
　　也不要為人愚昧，
　　何必不到期而死呢？
¹⁸你持守這個為美，
　　那個也不要鬆手；
　　因為敬畏神的人，
　　必從這兩樣出來。

¹⁹智慧使有智慧的人
　　比城中十個官長更有能力。

⁶Like the crackling of thorns under the pot,
　　so is the laughter of fools.
　　This too is meaningless.

⁷Extortion turns a wise man into a fool,
　　and a bribe corrupts the heart.

⁸The end of a matter is better than its beginning,
　　and patience is better than pride.
⁹Do not be quickly provoked in your spirit,
　　for anger resides in the lap of fools.

¹⁰Do not say, "Why were the old days better
　　than these?"
　　For it is not wise to ask such questions.

¹¹Wisdom, like an inheritance, is a good thing
　　and benefits those who see the sun.
¹²Wisdom is a shelter
　　as money is a shelter,
　　but the advantage of knowledge is this:
　　that wisdom preserves the life of its possessor.

¹³Consider what God has done:

　　Who can straighten
　　what he has made crooked?
¹⁴When times are good, be happy;
　　but when times are bad, consider:
　　God has made the one
　　as well as the other.
　　Therefore, a man cannot discover
　　anything about his future.

¹⁵In this meaningless life of mine I have seen
　　both of these:

　　a righteous man perishing in his righteousness,
　　and a wicked man living long in his
　　　wickedness.

¹⁶Do not be overrighteous,
　　neither be overwise—
　　why destroy yourself?
¹⁷Do not be overwicked,
　　and do not be a fool—
　　why die before your time?
¹⁸It is good to grasp the one
　　and not let go of the other.
　　The man who fears God will avoid all
　　　⌊extremes⌋.^a

¹⁹Wisdom makes one wise man more powerful
　　than ten rulers in a city.

²⁰There is not a righteous man on earth
  who does what is right and never sins.

²¹Do not pay attention to every word people say,
  or you may hear your servant cursing you—
²²for you know in your heart
  that many times you yourself have cursed
    others.

  ²³All this I tested by wisdom and I said,

  "I am determined to be wise"—
    but this was beyond me.
²⁴Whatever wisdom may be,
  it is far off and most profound—
  who can discover it?
²⁵So I turned my mind to understand,
  to investigate and to search out wisdom and
    the scheme of things
  and to understand the stupidity of wickedness
  and the madness of folly.

²⁶I find more bitter than death
  the woman who is a snare,
  whose heart is a trap
  and whose hands are chains.
  The man who pleases God will escape her,
  but the sinner she will ensnare.

  ²⁷"Look," says the Teacher,^a "this is what I
have discovered:

  "Adding one thing to another to discover the
    scheme of things—
²⁸ while I was still searching
  but not finding—
  I found one [upright] man among a thousand,
  but not one [upright] woman among them all.
²⁹This only have I found:
  God made mankind upright,
  but men have gone in search of many
    schemes."

8 Who is like the wise man?
  Who knows the explanation of things?
  Wisdom brightens a man's face
  and changes its hard appearance.

Obey the King

  ²Obey the king's command, I say, because
you took an oath before God. ³Do not be in a
hurry to leave the king's presence. Do not stand
up for a bad cause, for he will do whatever he
pleases. ⁴Since a king's word is supreme, who

^a 27 Or leader of the assembly

---

²⁰時常行善而不犯罪的義人，
  世上實在沒有。

²¹人所説的一切話，你不要放在心上，
  恐怕聽見你的僕人咒詛你。
²²因為你心裏知道，
  自己也曾屢次咒詛別人。

  ²³我曾用智慧試驗這一切事，我説：

  "要得智慧"，
    智慧卻離我遠。
²⁴萬事之理，
  離我甚遠，而且最深，
  誰能測透呢？
²⁵我轉念，一心要知道，
  要考察，要尋求
    智慧和萬事的理由，
  又要知道邪惡為愚昧，
  愚昧為狂妄。

²⁶我得知有等婦人，
  比死還苦，
  她的心是網羅，
  手是鎖鍊。
  凡蒙神喜悦的人，必能躲避她；
  有罪的人，卻被她纏住了。

^{27、28}傳道者説：
  "看哪，一千男子中，
    我找到一個正直人；
  但眾女子中，
    沒有找到一個。
  我將這事一一比較，
    要尋求其理，
  我心仍要尋找，
    卻未曾找到。
²⁹我所找到的只有一件：
    就是神造人原是正直，
    但他們尋出許多巧計。"

8 誰如智慧人呢？
  誰知道事情的解釋呢？
  人的智慧使他的臉發光，
  並使他臉上的暴氣改變。

服從君王

  ²我勸你遵守王的命令，既指神
起誓，理當如此。³不要急躁離開王的
面前，不要固執行惡，因為他凡事都
隨自己的心意而行。⁴王的話本有權

力，誰敢問他說：「你做甚麼呢？」

5凡遵守命令的，
　　必不經歷禍患；
　智慧人的心，能辨明時候和定理
　　（註：原文作"審判"。下節同）。
6各樣事務成就，
　　都有時候和定理，
　　因為人的苦難重壓在他身上。

7他不知道將來的事，
　　因為將來如何，誰能告訴他呢？
8無人有權力掌管生命，將生命留住；
　　也無人有權力掌管死期。
　　這場爭戰，無人能免，
　　邪惡也不能救那好行邪惡的人。

9這一切我都見過，也專心查考日光之下所做的一切事。有時這人管轄那人，令人受害。10我見惡人埋葬，歸入墳墓；又見行正直事的離開聖地，在城中被人忘記。這也是虛空。

11因為斷定罪名，不立刻施刑，所以世人滿心作惡。12罪人雖然作惡百次，倒享長久的年日。然而我準知道，敬畏神的，就是在他面前敬畏的人，終久必得福樂。13惡人卻不得福樂，也不得長久的年日；這年日好像影兒，因他不敬畏神。

14世上有一件虛空的事，就是義人所遭遇的，反照惡人所行的；又有惡人所遭遇的，反照義人所行的。我說，這也是虛空。15我就稱讚快樂，原來人在日光之下，莫強如吃喝快樂，因為他在日光之下，神賜他一生的年日，要從勞碌中時常享受所得的。

16我專心求智慧，要看世上所做的事。（有晝夜不睡覺，不合眼的。）17我就看見神一切的作為，知道人查不出日光之下所做的事；任憑他費多少力尋查，都查不出來，就是智慧人雖想知道，也是查不出來。

can say to him, "What are you doing?"

5Whoever obeys his command will come to no harm,
　and the wise heart will know the proper time and procedure.
6For there is a proper time and procedure for every matter,
　though a man's misery weighs heavily upon him.

7Since no man knows the future,
　who can tell him what is to come?
8No man has power over the wind to contain it[a];
　so no one has power over the day of his death.
As no one is discharged in time of war,
　so wickedness will not release those who practice it.

9All this I saw, as I applied my mind to everything done under the sun. There is a time when a man lords it over others to his own[b] hurt. 10Then too, I saw the wicked buried—those who used to come and go from the holy place and receive praise[c] in the city where they did this. This too is meaningless.

11When the sentence for a crime is not quickly carried out, the hearts of the people are filled with schemes to do wrong. 12Although a wicked man commits a hundred crimes and still lives a long time, I know that it will go better with God-fearing men, who are reverent before God. 13Yet because the wicked do not fear God, it will not go well with them, and their days will not lengthen like a shadow.

14There is something else meaningless that occurs on earth: righteous men who get what the wicked deserve, and wicked men who get what the righteous deserve. This too, I say, is meaningless. 15So I commend the enjoyment of life, because nothing is better for a man under the sun than to eat and drink and be glad. Then joy will accompany him in his work all the days of the life God has given him under the sun.

16When I applied my mind to know wisdom and to observe man's labor on earth—his eyes not seeing sleep day or night— 17then I saw all that God has done. No one can comprehend what goes on under the sun. Despite all his efforts to search it out, man cannot discover its meaning. Even if a wise man claims he knows, he cannot really comprehend it.

a 8 Or over his spirit to retain it   b 9 Or to their   c 10 Some Hebrew manuscripts and Septuagint (Aquila); most Hebrew manuscripts and are forgotten

A Common Destiny for All

9 So I reflected on all this and concluded that the righteous and the wise and what they do are in God's hands, but no man knows whether love or hate awaits him. [2]All share a common destiny—the righteous and the wicked, the good and the bad,[a] the clean and the unclean, those who offer sacrifices and those who do not.

As it is with the good man,
  so with the sinner;
as it is with those who take oaths,
  so with those who are afraid to take them.

[3]This is the evil in everything that happens under the sun: The same destiny overtakes all. The hearts of men, moreover, are full of evil and there is madness in their hearts while they live, and afterward they join the dead. [4]Anyone who is among the living has hope[b]—even a live dog is better off than a dead lion!

[5]For the living know that they will die,
  but the dead know nothing;
they have no further reward,
  and even the memory of them is forgotten.
[6]Their love, their hate
  and their jealousy have long since vanished;
never again will they have a part
  in anything that happens under the sun.

[7]Go, eat your food with gladness, and drink your wine with a joyful heart, for it is now that God favors what you do. [8]Always be clothed in white, and always anoint your head with oil. [9]Enjoy life with your wife, whom you love, all the days of this meaningless life that God has given you under the sun— all your meaningless days. For this is your lot in life and in your toilsome labor under the sun. [10]Whatever your hand finds to do, do it with all your might, for in the grave,[c] where you are going, there is neither working nor planning nor knowledge nor wisdom.

[11]I have seen something else under the sun:

The race is not to the swift
  or the battle to the strong,
nor does food come to the wise
  or wealth to the brilliant

臨到眾人的事都是一樣

9 我將這一切事放在心上，詳細考究，就知道義人和智慧人，並他們的作為都在神手中；或是愛，或是恨，都在他們的前面，人不能知道。[2]凡臨到眾人的事都是一樣：義人和惡人都遭遇一樣的事；好人，潔淨人和不潔淨人，獻祭的與不獻祭的，也是一樣。

好人如何，
  罪人也如何；
起誓的如何，
  怕起誓的也如何。

[3]在日光之下所行的一切事上，有一件禍患，就是眾人所遭遇的都是一樣，並且世人的心充滿了惡。活着的時候心裏狂妄，後來就歸死人那裏去了。[4]與一切活人相連的，那人還有指望，因為活着的狗比死了的獅子更強。

[5]活着的人知道必死，
  死了的人毫無所知，
也不再得賞賜，
  他們的名無人記念。
[6]他們的愛，他們的恨，
  他們的嫉妒，早都消滅了。
在日光之下所行的一切事上，
  他們永不再有分了。

[7]你只管去歡歡喜喜吃你的飯，心中快樂喝你的酒，因為神已經悅納你的作為。[8]你的衣服當時常潔白，你頭上也不要缺少膏油。[9]在你一生虛空的年日，就是神賜你在日光之下虛空的年日，當同你所愛的妻快活度日，因為那是你生前在日光之下勞碌的事上所得的分。[10]凡你手所當做的事，要盡力去做，因為在你所必去的陰間，沒有工作，沒有謀算，沒有知識，也沒有智慧。

[11]我又轉念，見日光之下：

快跑的未必能贏，
  力戰的未必得勝；
智慧的未必得糧食，
  明哲的未必得資財，

---

a 2 Septuagint (Aquila), Vulgate and Syriac; Hebrew does not have and the bad.   b 4 Or What then is to be chosen? With all who live, there is hope   c 10 Hebrew Sheol

靈巧的未必得喜悅；
　　所臨到眾人的，是在乎當時的機會。

12原來人也不知道自己的定期：

魚被惡網圍住，
　　鳥被網羅捉住，
禍患忽然臨到的時候，
　　世人陷在其中，也是如此。

智慧勝過愚昧

13我見日光之下有一樣智慧，據我看乃是廣大。14就是有一小城，其中的人數稀少，有大君王來攻擊，修築營壘，將城圍困。15城中有一個貧窮的智慧人，他用智慧救了那城，卻沒有人記念那窮人。16我就說："智慧勝過勇力。"然而那貧窮人的智慧被人藐視，他的話也無人聽從。

17寧可在安靜之中
　　聽智慧人的言語，
不聽掌管愚昧人的喊聲。
18智慧勝過打仗的兵器，
　　但一個罪人能敗壞許多善事。

10

死蒼蠅使做香的膏油發出臭氣。這樣，一點愚昧，也能敗壞智慧和尊榮。
2智慧人的心居右，
　　愚昧人的心居左。
3並且愚昧人行路顯出無知，
　　對眾人說，
　　他是愚昧人。
4掌權者的心若向你發怒，
　　不要離開你的本位，
　　因為柔和能免大過。

5我見日光之下有一件禍患，
　　似乎出於掌權的錯誤：
6就是愚昧人立在高位，
　　富足人坐在低位。
7我見過僕人騎馬，
　　王子像僕人在地上步行。

8挖陷坑的，自己必掉在其中；
　　拆牆垣的，必為蛇所咬。
9鑿開（註：或作"挪移"）石頭的，
　　必受損傷；
劈開木頭的，
　　必遭危險。

or favor to the learned;
　　but time and chance happen to them all.

12Moreover, no man knows when his hour will come:

As fish are caught in a cruel net,
　　or birds are taken in a snare,
so men are trapped by evil times
　　that fall unexpectedly upon them.

Wisdom Better Than Folly

13I also saw under the sun this example of wisdom that greatly impressed me: 14There was once a small city with only a few people in it. And a powerful king came against it, surrounded it and built huge siegeworks against it. 15Now there lived in that city a man poor but wise, and he saved the city by his wisdom. But nobody remembered that poor man. 16So I said, "Wisdom is better than strength." But the poor man's wisdom is despised, and his words are no longer heeded.

17The quiet words of the wise are more to be heeded
　　than the shouts of a ruler of fools.
18Wisdom is better than weapons of war,
　　but one sinner destroys much good.

10

As dead flies give perfume a bad smell,
　　so a little folly outweighs wisdom and honor.
2The heart of the wise inclines to the right,
　　but the heart of the fool to the left.
3Even as he walks along the road,
　　the fool lacks sense
　　and shows everyone how stupid he is.
4If a ruler's anger rises against you,
　　do not leave your post;
　　calmness can lay great errors to rest.

5There is an evil I have seen under the sun,
　　the sort of error that arises from a ruler:
6Fools are put in many high positions,
　　while the rich occupy the low ones.
7I have seen slaves on horseback,
　　while princes go on foot like slaves.

8Whoever digs a pit may fall into it;
　　whoever breaks through a wall may be bitten by a snake.
9Whoever quarries stones may be injured by them;
　　whoever splits logs may be endangered by them.

¹⁰If the ax is dull
　　and its edge unsharpened,
　　more strength is needed
　　but skill will bring success.

¹¹If a snake bites before it is charmed,
　　there is no profit for the charmer.

¹²Words from a wise man's mouth are gracious,
　　but a fool is consumed by his own lips.
¹³At the beginning his words are folly;
　　at the end they are wicked madness—
¹⁴　and the fool multiplies words.

No one knows what is coming—
　　who can tell him what will happen after him?

¹⁵A fool's work wearies him;
　　he does not know the way to town.

¹⁶Woe to you, O land whose king was a
　　servant^a
　　and whose princes feast in the morning.
¹⁷Blessed are you, O land whose king is of
　　noble birth
　　and whose princes eat at a proper time—
　　for strength and not for drunkenness.

¹⁸If a man is lazy, the rafters sag;
　　if his hands are idle, the house leaks.

¹⁹A feast is made for laughter,
　　and wine makes life merry,
　　but money is the answer for everything.

²⁰Do not revile the king even in your thoughts,
　　or curse the rich in your bedroom,
　　because a bird of the air may carry your
　　words,
　　and a bird on the wing may report what you say.

Bread Upon the Waters

11 Cast your bread upon the waters,
for after many days you will find it
again.
²Give portions to seven, yes to eight,
　　for you do not know what disaster may
　　come upon the land.

³If clouds are full of water,
　　they pour rain upon the earth.
Whether a tree falls to the south or to the north,
　　in the place where it falls, there will it lie.

---

¹⁰鐵器鈍了，
　　若不將刃磨快，
　　就必多費氣力；
　　但得智慧指教，便有益處。

¹¹未行法術以先，蛇若咬人，
　　後行法術也是無益。

¹²智慧人的口說出恩言；
　　愚昧人的嘴吞滅自己。
¹³他口中的言語起頭是愚昧；
　　他話的末尾是奸惡的狂妄。
¹⁴愚昧人多有言語。

人卻不知將來有甚麼事，
　　他身後的事，誰能告訴他呢？

¹⁵凡愚昧人，他的勞碌使自己困乏，
　　因為連進城的路，他也不知道。

¹⁶邦國啊，你的王若是孩童，
　　你的羣臣早晨宴樂，
　　你就有禍了！
¹⁷邦國啊，你的王若是貴冑之子，
　　你的羣臣按時吃喝，
　　為要補力，不為酒醉，
　　你就有福了！

¹⁸因人懶惰，房頂塌下；
　　因人手懶，房屋滴漏。

¹⁹設擺筵席，是為喜笑。
　　酒能使人快活，
　　錢能叫萬事應心。

²⁰你不可咒詛君王，
　　也不可心懷此念，
　　在你臥房也不可咒詛富戶，
　　因為空中的鳥必傳揚這聲音，
　　有翅膀的也必述說這事。

糧食撒在水面

11 當將你的糧食撒在水面，
因為日久必能得着。
²你要分給七人，或分給八人，
　　因為你不知道
　　將來有甚麼災禍臨到地上。

³雲若滿了雨，
　　就必傾倒在地上。
樹若向南倒，或向北倒，
　　樹倒在何處，就存在何處。

---

a 16 Or king is a child

⁴看風的必不撒種；
　　望雲的必不收割。

⁵風從何道來，
　　骨頭在懷孕婦人的胎中如何長成，
　　你尚且不得知道，
　　這樣，行萬事之神的作為，
　　你更不得知道。

⁶早晨要撒你的種，
　　晚上也不要歇你的手，
　　因為你不知道哪一樣發旺：
　　或是早撒的、或是晚撒的，
　　或是兩樣都好。

當趁年輕記念造你的主
⁷光本是佳美的，
　　眼見日光也是可悅的。
⁸人活多年，
　　就當快樂多年；
　然而也當想到黑暗的日子，
　　因為這日子必多，
　　所要來的都是虛空。

⁹少年人哪，你在幼年時當快樂。
　　在幼年的日子，
　　使你的心歡暢，
　行你心所願行的，
　　看你眼所愛看的；
　卻要知道，為這一切的事，
　　神必審問你。
¹⁰所以你當從心中除掉愁煩，
　　從肉體克去邪惡，
　　因為一生的開端和幼年之時，
　　都是虛空的。

12 你趁著年幼、
　　　衰敗的日子尚未來到，
　　　就是你所說，
　我毫無喜樂的那些年日
　　未曾臨近之先，當記念造你的主！
²不要等到日頭、光明、
　　月亮、星宿變為黑暗，
　　雨後雲彩反回；
³看守房屋的發顫，
　　有力的屈身，
　推磨的稀少就止息，
　　從窗戶往外看的都昏暗；

⁴街門關閉，
　　推磨的響聲微小；
　雀鳥一叫，人就起來，
　　歌唱的女子也都衰微。
⁵人怕高處，
　　路上有驚慌；

⁴Whoever watches the wind will not plant;
　　whoever looks at the clouds will not reap.

⁵As you do not know the path of the wind,
　　or how the body is formed^a in a mother's
　　　womb,
　so you cannot understand the work of God,
　　the Maker of all things.

⁶Sow your seed in the morning,
　　and at evening let not your hands be idle,
　for you do not know which will succeed,
　　whether this or that,
　　or whether both will do equally well.

Remember Your Creator While Young
⁷Light is sweet,
　　and it pleases the eyes to see the sun.
⁸However many years a man may live,
　　let him enjoy them all.
　But let him remember the days of darkness,
　　for they will be many.
　Everything to come is meaningless.

⁹Be happy, young man, while you are young,
　　and let your heart give you joy in the days of
　　　your youth.
　Follow the ways of your heart
　　and whatever your eyes see,
　but know that for all these things
　　God will bring you to judgment.
¹⁰So then, banish anxiety from your heart
　　and cast off the troubles of your body,
　　for youth and vigor are meaningless.

12 Remember your Creator
　　　in the days of your youth,
　　　before the days of trouble come
　　and the years approach when you will say,
　　"I find no pleasure in them"—
²before the sun and the light
　　and the moon and the stars grow dark,
　　and the clouds return after the rain;
³when the keepers of the house tremble,
　　and the strong men stoop,
　when the grinders cease because they are few,
　　and those looking through the windows
　　　grow dim;
⁴when the doors to the street are closed
　　and the sound of grinding fades;
　when men rise up at the sound of birds,
　　but all their songs grow faint;
⁵when men are afraid of heights
　　and of dangers in the streets;

a 5 Or know how life (or *the spirit*) / *enters the body being formed*

when the almond tree blossoms
and the grasshopper drags himself along
and desire no longer is stirred.
Then man goes to his eternal home
and mourners go about the streets.

杏樹開花，
蚱蜢成為重擔；
人所願的也都廢掉。
因為人歸他永遠的家，
弔喪的在街上往來。

⁶Remember him—before the silver cord is
severed,
or the golden bowl is broken;
before the pitcher is shattered at the spring,
or the wheel broken at the well,
⁷and the dust returns to the ground it came
from,
and the spirit returns to God who gave it.

⁶銀鏈折斷，
金罐破裂，
瓶子在泉旁損壞，
水輪在井口破爛；
⁷塵土仍歸於地，
靈仍歸於賜靈的神。

⁸"Meaningless! Meaningless!" says the Teacher.ᵃ
"Everything is meaningless!"

⁸傳道者說："虛空的虛空，
凡事都是虛空！"

The Conclusion of the Matter

⁹Not only was the Teacher wise, but also he imparted knowledge to the people. He pondered and searched out and set in order many proverbs. ¹⁰The Teacher searched to find just the right words, and what he wrote was upright and true.

¹¹The words of the wise are like goads, their collected sayings like firmly embedded nails— given by one Shepherd. ¹²Be warned, my son, of anything in addition to them.

Of making many books there is no end, and much study wearies the body.

¹³Now all has been heard;
here is the conclusion of the matter:
Fear God and keep his commandments,
for this is the whole ⌊duty⌋ of man.
¹⁴For God will bring every deed into judgment,
including every hidden thing,
whether it is good or evil.

結論

⁹再者，傳道者因有智慧，仍將知識教訓眾人；又默想，又考查，又陳說許多箴言。¹⁰傳道者專心尋求可喜悅的言語，是憑正直寫的誠實話。

¹¹智慧人的言語好像刺棍；會中之師的言語又像釘穩的釘子，都是一個牧者所賜的。¹²我兒，還有一層，你當受勸戒：

著書多，沒有窮盡；讀書多，身體疲倦。

¹³這些事都已聽見了，
總意就是敬畏神，
謹守他的誡命，
這是人所當盡的本分。
（註：或作"這是眾人的本分"）
¹⁴因為人所做的事，
連一切隱藏的事，
無論是善是惡，
神都必審問。

ᵃ 8 Or the leader of the assembly; also in verses 9 and 10

雅歌

Song of Songs

1

所羅門的歌，是歌中的雅歌。

1

Solomon's Song of Songs.

新婦

² 願他用口與我親嘴，
　　因你的愛情比酒更美。
³ 你的膏油馨香，
　　你的名如同倒出來的香膏，
　　所以眾童女都愛你。
⁴ 願你吸引我，我們就快跑跟隨你。
　　王帶我進了內室。

Beloved[a]

² Let him kiss me with the kisses of his mouth—
　　for your love is more delightful than wine.
³ Pleasing is the fragrance of your perfumes;
　　your name is like perfume poured out.
　　No wonder the maidens love you!
⁴ Take me away with you—let us hurry!
　　Let the king bring me into his chambers.

朋友

　我們必因你歡喜快樂；
　　我們要稱讚你的愛情，
　　勝似稱讚美酒。

Friends

　We rejoice and delight in you[b];
　　we will praise your love more than wine.

新婦

　她們愛你是理所當然的！

Beloved

　How right they are to adore you!

⁵ 耶路撒冷的眾女子啊，
　　我雖然黑，卻是秀美，
　　如同基達的帳棚，
　　好像所羅門的幔子；
⁶ 不要因日頭把我曬黑了，
　　就輕看我。
　我同母的弟兄向我發怒，
　　他們使我看守葡萄園；
　　我自己的葡萄園卻沒有看守。
⁷ 我心所愛的啊，求你告訴我，
　　你在何處牧羊？
　　晌午在何處使羊歇臥？
　我何必在你同伴的羊羣旁邊，
　　好像蒙着臉的人呢？

⁵ Dark am I, yet lovely,
　　O daughters of Jerusalem,
　　dark like the tents of Kedar,
　　like the tent curtains of Solomon.[c]
⁶ Do not stare at me because I am dark,
　　because I am darkened by the sun.
　My mother's sons were angry with me
　　and made me take care of the vineyards;
　　my own vineyard I have neglected.
⁷ Tell me, you whom I love, where you graze
　　　your flock
　　and where you rest your sheep at midday.
　Why should I be like a veiled woman
　　beside the flocks of your friends?

朋友

⁸ 你這女子中極美麗的，
　　你若不知道，
　　只管跟隨羊羣的腳蹤去，
　把你的山羊羔
　　牧放在牧人帳棚的旁邊。

Friends

⁸ If you do not know, most beautiful of women,
　　follow the tracks of the sheep
　　and graze your young goats
　　by the tents of the shepherds.

a Primarily on the basis of the gender of the Hebrew pronouns
used, male and female speakers are indicated in the margins
by the captions *Lover* and *Beloved* respectively. The words of
others are marked *Friends*. In some instances the divisions and
their captions are debatable.　　*b* 4 The Hebrew is masculine
singular.　　*c* 5 Or *Salma*

Lover

⁹I liken you, my darling, to a mare
  harnessed to one of the chariots of Pharaoh.
¹⁰Your cheeks are beautiful with earrings,
  your neck with strings of jewels.
¹¹We will make you earrings of gold,
  studded with silver.

Beloved

¹²While the king was at his table,
  my perfume spread its fragrance.
¹³My lover is to me a sachet of myrrh
  resting between my breasts.
¹⁴My lover is to me a cluster of henna blossoms
  from the vineyards of En Gedi.

Lover

¹⁵How beautiful you are, my darling!
  Oh, how beautiful!
  Your eyes are doves.

Beloved

¹⁶How handsome you are, my lover!
  Oh, how charming!
  And our bed is verdant.

Lover

¹⁷The beams of our house are cedars;
  our rafters are firs.

Beloved[a]

2 I am a rose[b] of Sharon,
  a lily of the valleys.

Lover

²Like a lily among thorns
  is my darling among the maidens.

Beloved

³Like an apple tree among the trees of the forest
  is my lover among the young men.
I delight to sit in his shade,
  and his fruit is sweet to my taste.
⁴He has taken me to the banquet hall,
  and his banner over me is love.
⁵Strengthen me with raisins,
  refresh me with apples,
  for I am faint with love.
⁶His left arm is under my head,
  and his right arm embraces me.
⁷Daughters of Jerusalem, I charge you
  by the gazelles and by the does of the field:
Do not arouse or awaken love
  until it so desires.

a 1 Or Lover   b 1 Possibly a member of the crocus family

新郎

⁹我的佳偶，
  我將你比法老車上套的駿馬。
¹⁰你的兩腮因髮辮而秀美；
  你的頸項因珠串而華麗。
¹¹我們要為你編上金辮，
  鑲上銀釘。

新婦

¹²王正坐席的時候，
  我的哪噠香膏發出香味。
¹³我以我的良人為一袋沒藥，
  常在我懷中。
¹⁴我以我的良人為一棵鳳仙花，
  在隱基底葡萄園中。

新郎

¹⁵我的佳偶，你甚美麗！
  你甚美麗！
  你的眼好像鴿子眼。

新婦

¹⁶我的良人哪，
  你甚美麗可愛！
  我們以青草為牀榻。

新郎

¹⁷以香柏樹為房屋的棟梁，
  以松樹為椽子。

新婦

2 我是沙崙的玫瑰花（註：或作"水仙花"），
  是谷中的百合花。

新郎

²我的佳偶在女子中，
  好像百合花在荊棘內。

新婦

³我的良人在男子中，
  如同蘋果樹在樹林中，
我歡歡喜喜坐在他的蔭下，
  嘗他果子的滋味，覺得甘甜。
⁴他帶我入筵宴所，
  以愛為旗在我以上。
⁵求你們給我葡萄乾增補我力，
  給我蘋果暢快我心，
  因我思愛成病。
⁶他的左手在我頭下；
  他的右手將我抱住。
⁷耶路撒冷的眾女子啊，我指着羚羊
  或田野的母鹿囑咐你們：
不要驚動，不要叫醒我所親愛的，
  等他自己情願（註："不要叫醒云云"
  或作"不要激動愛情，等他自發"）。

⁸聽啊，
　　是我良人的聲音；
　　看哪，
　　他蹦山越嶺而來！
⁹我的良人好像羚羊，或像小鹿。
　　他站在我們牆壁後，
　　從窗戶往裏觀看，
　　從窗櫺往裏窺探。
¹⁰我良人對我說：
　　“我的佳偶，我的美人！
　　起來，與我同去！
¹¹因為冬天已往，
　　雨水止住過去了。
¹²地上百花開放、
　　百鳥鳴叫的時候（註：或作“修理葡萄樹的時候”）已經來到，
　　斑鳩的聲音在我們境內也聽見了。
¹³無花果樹的果子漸漸成熟；
　　葡萄樹開花放香。
　　我的佳偶，我的美人！
　　起來，與我同去！”

新郎

¹⁴我的鴿子啊，你在磐石穴中，
　　在陡巖的隱密處。
　　求你容我得見你的面貌，
　　得聽你的聲音；
　　因為你的聲音柔和，
　　你的面貌秀美。
¹⁵要給我們擒拿狐狸，
　　就是毀壞葡萄園的小狐狸，
　　因為我們的葡萄正在開花。

新婦

¹⁶良人屬我，我也屬他；
　　他在百合花中牧放羣羊。
¹⁷我的良人哪，求你等到天起涼風、
　　日影飛去的時候，
　　你要轉回，
　　好像羚羊
　　或像小鹿
　　在比特山上。

3 我夜間躺臥在牀上，
　　尋找我心所愛的；
　　我尋找他，卻尋不見。
²我說：我要起來，遊行城中，
　　在街市上，在寬闊處，
　　尋找我心所愛的。
　　我尋找他，卻尋不見。
³城中巡邏看守的人遇見我，
　　我問他們：
　　“你們看見我心所愛的沒有？”

⁸Listen! My lover!
　　Look! Here he comes,
　　leaping across the mountains,
　　bounding over the hills.
⁹My lover is like a gazelle or a young stag.
　　Look! There he stands behind our wall,
　　gazing through the windows,
　　peering through the lattice.
¹⁰My lover spoke and said to me,
　　"Arise, my darling,
　　my beautiful one, and come with me.
¹¹See! The winter is past;
　　the rains are over and gone.
¹²Flowers appear on the earth;
　　the season of singing has come,
　　the cooing of doves
　　is heard in our land.
¹³The fig tree forms its early fruit;
　　the blossoming vines spread their fragrance.
　　Arise, come, my darling;
　　my beautiful one, come with me."

Lover

¹⁴My dove in the clefts of the rock,
　　in the hiding places on the mountainside,
　　show me your face,
　　let me hear your voice;
　　for your voice is sweet,
　　and your face is lovely.
¹⁵Catch for us the foxes,
　　the little foxes
　　that ruin the vineyards,
　　our vineyards that are in bloom.

Beloved

¹⁶My lover is mine and I am his;
　　he browses among the lilies.
¹⁷Until the day breaks
　　and the shadows flee,
　　turn, my lover,
　　and be like a gazelle
　　or like a young stag
　　on the rugged hills.^a

3 All night long on my bed
　　I looked for the one my heart loves;
　　I looked for him but did not find him.
²I will get up now and go about the city,
　　through its streets and squares;
　　I will search for the one my heart loves.
　　So I looked for him but did not find him.
³The watchmen found me
　　as they made their rounds in the city.
　　"Have you seen the one my heart loves?"

a 17 Or the hills of Bether

⁴Scarcely had I passed them
　　when I found the one my heart loves.
I held him and would not let him go
　　till I had brought him to my mother's house,
　　to the room of the one who conceived me.
⁵Daughters of Jerusalem, I charge you
　　by the gazelles and by the does of the field:
Do not arouse or awaken love
　　until it so desires.

⁶Who is this coming up from the desert
　　like a column of smoke,
perfumed with myrrh and incense
　　made from all the spices of the merchant?
⁷Look! It is Solomon's carriage,
　　escorted by sixty warriors,
　　the noblest of Israel,
⁸all of them wearing the sword,
　　all experienced in battle,
each with his sword at his side,
　　prepared for the terrors of the night.
⁹King Solomon made for himself the carriage;
　　he made it of wood from Lebanon.
¹⁰Its posts he made of silver,
　　its base of gold.
Its seat was upholstered with purple,
　　its interior lovingly inlaid
　　by^a the daughters of Jerusalem.
¹¹Come out, you daughters of Zion,
　　and look at King Solomon wearing the crown,
　　the crown with which his mother crowned
　　him
on the day of his wedding,
　　the day his heart rejoiced.

Lover

4

　　How beautiful you are, my darling!
　　Oh, how beautiful!
　　Your eyes behind your veil are doves.
Your hair is like a flock of goats
　　descending from Mount Gilead.
²Your teeth are like a flock of sheep just shorn,
　　coming up from the washing.
Each has its twin;
　　not one of them is alone.
³Your lips are like a scarlet ribbon;
　　your mouth is lovely.
Your temples behind your veil
　　are like the halves of a pomegranate.
⁴Your neck is like the tower of David,
　　built with elegance^b;
on it hang a thousand shields,
　　all of them shields of warriors.

⁴我剛離開他們，
　　就遇見我心所愛的。
我拉住他，不容他走，
　　領他入我母家，
　　到懷我者的內室。
⁵耶路撒冷的眾女子啊，
　　我指着羚羊或田野的母鹿
　　囑咐你們：
不要驚動、不要叫醒我所親愛的，
　　等他自己情願（註：“不要叫醒云云
　　或作“不要激動愛情，等他自發”）。
⁶那從曠野上來、形狀如煙柱的，
　　以沒藥和乳香
　　並商人各樣香粉薰的是誰呢？
⁷看哪，是所羅門的轎！
　　四圍有六十個勇士，
　　都是以色列中的勇士；
⁸手都持刀，
　　善於爭戰，
腰間佩刀，
　　防備夜間有驚慌。
⁹所羅門王用黎巴嫩木
　　為自己製造一乘華轎。
¹⁰轎柱是用銀做的，
　　轎底是用金做的，
坐墊是紫色的，
　　其中所鋪的
　　乃耶路撒冷眾女子的愛情。
¹¹錫安的眾女子啊，
　　你們出去觀看所羅門王，
　　頭戴冠冕，
就是在他婚筵的日子、
　　心中喜樂的時候，
　　他母親給他戴上的。

新郎

4

　　我的佳偶，你甚美麗！
　　你甚美麗！
　　你的眼在帕子內好像鴿子眼。
你的頭髮如同山羊羣
　　臥在基列山旁。
²你的牙齒如新剪毛的一羣母羊，
　　洗淨上來，個個都有雙生，
　　沒有一隻喪掉子的。

³你的唇好像一條朱紅線，
　　你的嘴也秀美。
你的兩太陽在帕子內
　　如同一塊石榴。
⁴你的頸項
　　好像大衛建造收藏軍器的高臺，
其上懸掛一千盾牌，
　　都是勇士的籐牌。

---

a 10 Or *its inlaid interior a gift of love / from*　　*b 4* The meaning
of the Hebrew for this word is uncertain.

5你的兩乳
　　好像百合花中吃草的一對小鹿，
　　就是母鹿雙生的。
6我要往沒藥山和乳香岡去，
　　直等到天起涼風，
　　日影飛去的時候回來。

7我的佳偶，你全然美麗，
　　毫無瑕疵！

8我的新婦，
　　求你與我一同離開黎巴嫩，
　　與我一同離開黎巴嫩。
　從亞瑪拿頂，
　　從示尼珥與黑門頂，
　從有獅子的洞，
　　從有豹子的山往下觀看。
9我妹子，我新婦，你奪了我的心！
　　你用眼一看，
　　用你項上的一條金鏈，
　　奪了我的心。
10我妹子，我新婦，
　　你的愛情何其美！
　你的愛情
　　比酒更美，
　你膏油的香氣
　　勝過一切香品。
11我新婦，你的嘴唇滴蜜，
　　好像蜂房滴蜜；
　你的舌下有蜜有奶，
　　你衣服的香氣如黎巴嫩的香氣。

12我妹子，我新婦，乃是關鎖的園，
　　禁閉的井，封閉的泉源。
13你園內所種的結了石榴，
　　有佳美的果子，
　　並鳳仙花與哪噠樹。
14有哪噠和番紅花，
　　菖蒲和桂樹，
　並各樣乳香木、
　　沒藥、沉香，
　　與一切上等的果品。
15你是園中的泉，
　　活水的井，
　　從黎巴嫩流下來的溪水。

新婦
16北風啊，興起！
　　南風啊，吹來！
　吹在我的園內，
　　使其中的香氣發出來。
　願我的良人進入自己園裏，
　　吃他佳美的果子。

5Your two breasts are like two fawns,
　　like twin fawns of a gazelle
　　that browse among the lilies.
6Until the day breaks
　　and the shadows flee,
　I will go to the mountain of myrrh
　　and to the hill of incense.
7All beautiful you are, my darling;
　　there is no flaw in you.

8Come with me from Lebanon, my bride,
　　come with me from Lebanon.
　Descend from the crest of Amana,
　　from the top of Senir, the summit of
　　　Hermon,
　from the lions' dens
　　and the mountain haunts of the leopards.
9You have stolen my heart, my sister, my bride;
　　you have stolen my heart
　with one glance of your eyes,
　　with one jewel of your necklace.
10How delightful is your love, my sister, my
　　bride!
　How much more pleasing is your love than
　　wine,
　and the fragrance of your perfume than any
　　spice!
11Your lips drop sweetness as the honeycomb,
　　my bride;
　milk and honey are under your tongue.
　The fragrance of your garments is like that of
　　Lebanon.
12You are a garden locked up, my sister, my bride;
　　you are a spring enclosed, a sealed fountain.
13Your plants are an orchard of pomegranates
　　with choice fruits,
　　with henna and nard,
14 nard and saffron,
　　calamus and cinnamon,
　　with every kind of incense tree,
　　with myrrh and aloes
　　and all the finest spices.
15You are^a a garden fountain,
　　a well of flowing water
　　streaming down from Lebanon.

Beloved
16Awake, north wind,
　　and come, south wind!
　Blow on my garden,
　　that its fragrance may spread abroad.
　Let my lover come into his garden
　　and taste its choice fruits.

a 15 Or *I am* (spoken by the *Beloved*)

Lover

5

I have come into my garden, my sister,
my bride;
I have gathered my myrrh with my
spice.
I have eaten my honeycomb and my honey;
I have drunk my wine and my milk.

Friends

Eat, O friends, and drink;
drink your fill, O lovers.

Beloved

²I slept but my heart was awake.
Listen! My lover is knocking:
"Open to me, my sister, my darling,
my dove, my flawless one.
My head is drenched with dew,
my hair with the dampness of the night."
³I have taken off my robe—
must I put it on again?
I have washed my feet—
must I soil them again?
⁴My lover thrust his hand through the latch-
opening;
my heart began to pound for him.
⁵I arose to open for my lover,
and my hands dripped with myrrh,
my fingers with flowing myrrh,
on the handles of the lock.
⁶I opened for my lover,
but my lover had left; he was gone.
My heart sank at his departure.ᵃ
I looked for him but did not find him.
I called him but he did not answer.
⁷The watchmen found me
as they made their rounds in the city.
They beat me, they bruised me;
they took away my cloak,
those watchmen of the walls!
⁸O daughters of Jerusalem, I charge you—
if you find my lover,
what will you tell him?
Tell him I am faint with love.

Friends

⁹How is your beloved better than others,
most beautiful of women?
How is your beloved better than others,
that you charge us so?

Beloved

¹⁰My lover is radiant and ruddy,
outstanding among ten thousand.

a 6 Or heart had gone out to him when he spoke

新郎

5

我妹子，我新婦，
我進了我的園中，
採了我的沒藥和香料。

吃了我的蜜房和蜂蜜，
喝了我的酒和奶。

朋友

我的朋友們，請吃！
我所親愛的，請喝！且多多的喝！

新婦

²我身睡臥，我心卻醒。
這是我良人的聲音，他敲門說：
"我的妹子，我的佳偶，
我的鴿子，我的完全人，
求你給我開門，因我的頭滿了露水，
我的頭髮被夜露滴濕。"
³我回答說：
"我脫了衣裳，怎能再穿上呢？
我洗了腳，怎能再玷污呢？"
⁴我的良人從門孔伸進手來，
我便因他動了心。

⁵我起來，要給我良人開門；
我的兩手滴下沒藥，
我的指頭有沒藥汁滴在門閂上。

⁶我給我的良人開了門；
我的良人卻已轉身走了。
他說話的時候，我神不守舍；
我尋找他，竟尋不見；
我呼叫他，他卻不回答。
⁷城中巡邏看守的人遇見我，
打了我，
傷了我；
看守城牆的人
奪去我的披肩。
⁸耶路撒冷的眾女子啊，
我囑咐你們：
若遇見我的良人，
要告訴他，我因思愛成病。

朋友

⁹你這女子中極美麗的，
你的良人比別人的良人有何強處？
你的良人比別人的良人有何強處？
你就這樣囑咐我們？

新婦

¹⁰我的良人白而且紅，
超乎萬人之上。

11他的頭像至精的金子；
　　他的頭髮厚密纍垂，
　　黑如烏鴉。
12他的眼
　　如溪水旁的鴿子眼，
　用奶洗淨，
　　安得合式。
13他的兩腮如香花畦，
　　如香草臺。
　他的嘴唇像百合花，
　　且滴下沒藥汁。
14他的兩手好像金管，
　　鑲嵌水蒼玉。
　他的身體如同雕刻的象牙，
　　周圍鑲嵌藍寶石。
15他的腿好像白玉石柱，
　　安在精金座上。
　他的形狀如黎巴嫩，
　　且佳美如香柏樹。
16他的口極其甘甜，
　　他全然可愛。
　耶路撒冷的眾女子啊，
　　這是我的良人，這是我的朋友。

朋友

6 你這女子中極美麗的，
　　你的良人往何處去了？
　　你的良人轉向何處去了？
　　我們好與你同去尋找他。

新婦

2我的良人下入自己園中，
　　到香花畦，
　在園內牧放羣羊，
　　採百合花。
3我屬我的良人，我的良人也屬我；
　　他在百合花中牧放羣羊。

新郎

4我的佳偶啊，你美麗如得撒，
　　秀美如耶路撒冷，
　　威武如展開旌旗的軍隊。
5求你掉轉眼目不看我，
　　因你的眼目使我驚亂。
　你的頭髮如同山羊羣，
　　臥在基列山旁。
6你的牙齒如一羣母羊，
　　洗淨上來，
　個個都有雙生，
　　沒有一隻喪掉子的。
7你的兩太陽在帕子內
　　如同一塊石榴。
8有六十王后，
　　八十妃嬪，

11His head is purest gold;
　　his hair is wavy
　　and black as a raven.
12His eyes are like doves
　　by the water streams,
　washed in milk,
　　mounted like jewels.
13His cheeks are like beds of spice
　　yielding perfume.
　His lips are like lilies
　　dripping with myrrh.
14His arms are rods of gold
　　set with chrysolite.
　His body is like polished ivory
　　decorated with sapphires.[a]
15His legs are pillars of marble
　　set on bases of pure gold.
　His appearance is like Lebanon,
　　choice as its cedars.
16His mouth is sweetness itself;
　　he is altogether lovely.
　This is my lover, this my friend,
　　O daughters of Jerusalem.

Friends

6 Where has your lover gone,
　　most beautiful of women?
　　Which way did your lover turn,
　　that we may look for him with you?

Beloved

2My lover has gone down to his garden,
　　to the beds of spices,
　　to browse in the gardens
　　and to gather lilies.
3I am my lover's and my lover is mine;
　　he browses among the lilies.

Lover

4You are beautiful, my darling, as Tirzah,
　　lovely as Jerusalem,
　　majestic as troops with banners.
5Turn your eyes from me;
　　they overwhelm me.
　Your hair is like a flock of goats
　　descending from Gilead.
6Your teeth are like a flock of sheep
　　coming up from the washing.
　Each has its twin,
　　not one of them is alone.
7Your temples behind your veil
　　are like the halves of a pomegranate.
8Sixty queens there may be,
　　and eighty concubines,

a 14 Or lapis lazuli

and virgins beyond number;
⁹but my dove, my perfect one, is unique,
  the only daughter of her mother,
  the favorite of the one who bore her.
The maidens saw her and called her blessed;
  the queens and concubines praised her.

Friends
¹⁰Who is this that appears like the dawn,
  fair as the moon, bright as the sun,
  majestic as the stars in procession?

Lover
¹¹I went down to the grove of nut trees
  to look at the new growth in the valley,
  to see if the vines had budded
  or the pomegranates were in bloom.
¹²Before I realized it,
  my desire set me among the royal chariots of
    my people.ᵃ

Friends
¹³Come back, come back, O Shulammite;
  come back, come back, that we may gaze on
    you!

Lover
Why would you gaze on the Shulammite
  as on the dance of Mahanaim?

7 How beautiful your sandaled feet,
  O prince's daughter!
  Your graceful legs are like jewels,
  the work of a craftsman's hands.
²Your navel is a rounded goblet
  that never lacks blended wine.
Your waist is a mound of wheat
  encircled by lilies.
³Your breasts are like two fawns,
  twins of a gazelle.
⁴Your neck is like an ivory tower.
Your eyes are the pools of Heshbon
  by the gate of Bath Rabbim.
Your nose is like the tower of Lebanon
  looking toward Damascus.
⁵Your head crowns you like Mount Carmel.
Your hair is like royal tapestry;
  the king is held captive by its tresses.
⁶How beautiful you are and how pleasing,
  O love, with your delights!
⁷Your stature is like that of the palm,
  and your breasts like clusters of fruit.

a 12 Or among the chariots of Amminadab; or among the chariots of the people of the prince

並有無數的童女。
⁹我的鴿子，我的完全人，
  只有這一個，是她母親獨生的，
  是生養她者所寶愛的。
眾女子見了就稱她有福；
  王后妃嬪見了也讚美她。

朋友
¹⁰那向外觀看如晨光發現，
  美麗如月亮，皎潔如日頭，
  威武如展開旌旗軍隊的是誰呢？

新郎
¹¹我下入核桃園，
  要看谷中青綠的植物，
  要看葡萄發芽沒有，
  石榴開花沒有。
¹²不知不覺，
  我的心將我安置在
  我尊長的車中。

朋友
¹³回來，回來，書拉密女！
  你回來，你回來，
  使我們得觀看你！

新郎
你們為何要觀看書拉密女，
  像觀看瑪哈念跳舞的呢？

7 王女啊，
  你的腳在鞋中何其美好！
  你的大腿圓潤好像美玉，
  是巧匠的手做成的。
²你的肚臍如圓杯，
  不缺調和的酒。
你的腰如一堆麥子，
  周圍有百合花。
³你的兩乳好像一對小鹿，
  就是母鹿雙生的。
⁴你的頸項如象牙臺；
  你的眼目像希實本
  巴特拉併門旁的水池；
  你的鼻子彷彿朝大馬士革的
  黎巴嫩塔；
⁵你的頭在你身上好像迦密山，
  你頭上的髮是紫黑色。
  王的心因這下垂的髮綹繫住了。
⁶我所愛的，你何其美好！何其可悅！
  使人歡暢喜樂！
⁷你的身量好像棕樹；
  你的兩乳如同其上的果子，
  纍纍下垂。

8我説：「我要上這棕樹，
　　抓住枝子。」
　願你的兩乳好像葡萄纍纍下垂；
　　你鼻子的氣味香如蘋果；
9你的口如上好的酒。

新婦

　女子説：為我的良人下咽舒暢，
　　流入睡覺人的嘴中。
10我屬我的良人，
　　他也戀慕我！
11我的良人，來吧！你我可以往田間去，
　　你我可以在村莊住宿。
12我們早晨起來往葡萄園去，
　　看看葡萄發芽開花沒有，
　　石榴放蕊沒有；
　　我在那裏要將我的愛情給你。
13風茄放香，
　　在我們的門內
　　有各樣新陳佳美的果子；
　　我的良人，這都是我為你存留的。

8 巴不得你像我的兄弟，
　　像吃我母親奶的兄弟！
　我在外頭遇見你，
　　就與你親嘴，
　　誰也不輕看我。
2我必引導你，
　　領你進我母親的家，
　我可以領受教訓，
　　也就使你喝石榴汁釀的香酒。

3他的左手必在我頭下；
　　他的右手必將我抱住。
4耶路撒冷的眾女子啊，我囑咐你們：
　　不要驚動，不要叫醒我所親愛的，
　　等他自己情願（註：「不要叫醒云云」
　　或作「不要激動愛情，等他自發」）。

朋友

5那靠着良人
　　從曠野上來的是誰呢？

新婦

　我在蘋果樹下叫醒你，
　　你母親在那裏為你劬勞，
　　生養你的在那裏為你劬勞。
6求你將我放在心上如印記，
　　帶在你臂上如戳記；
　　因為愛情如死之堅強，
　　嫉恨如陰間之殘忍。

8I said, "I will climb the palm tree;
　　I will take hold of its fruit."
May your breasts be like the clusters of the vine,
　　the fragrance of your breath like apples,
9　and your mouth like the best wine.

Beloved

May the wine go straight to my lover,
　　flowing gently over lips and teeth.[a]
10I belong to my lover,
　　and his desire is for me.
11Come, my lover, let us go to the countryside,
　　let us spend the night in the villages.[b]
12Let us go early to the vineyards
　　to see if the vines have budded,
　　if their blossoms have opened,
　　and if the pomegranates are in bloom—
　　there I will give you my love.
13The mandrakes send out their fragrance,
　　and at our door is every delicacy,
　　both new and old,
　　that I have stored up for you, my lover.

8 If only you were to me like a brother,
　　who was nursed at my mother's breasts!
　Then, if I found you outside,
　　I would kiss you,
　　and no one would despise me.
2I would lead you
　　and bring you to my mother's house—
　　she who has taught me.
　I would give you spiced wine to drink,
　　the nectar of my pomegranates.
3His left arm is under my head
　　and his right arm embraces me.
4Daughters of Jerusalem, I charge you:
　　Do not arouse or awaken love
　　until it so desires.

Friends

5Who is this coming up from the desert
　　leaning on her lover?

Beloved

Under the apple tree I roused you;
　　there your mother conceived you,
　　there she who was in labor gave you birth.
6Place me like a seal over your heart,
　　like a seal on your arm;
　　for love is as strong as death,
　　its jealousy[c] unyielding as the grave.[d]

---

a 9 Septuagint, Aquila, Vulgate and Syriac; Hebrew *lips of sleepers*　*b 11* Or *henna bushes*　*c 6* Or *ardor*　*d 6* Hebrew *Sheol*

It burns like blazing fire,
   like a mighty flame.[a]
[7]Many waters cannot quench love;
   rivers cannot wash it away.
  If one were to give
   all the wealth of his house for love,
   it[b] would be utterly scorned.

Friends
[8]We have a young sister,
   and her breasts are not yet grown.
  What shall we do for our sister
   for the day she is spoken for?
[9]If she is a wall,
   we will build towers of silver on her.
  If she is a door,
   we will enclose her with panels of cedar.

Beloved
[10]I am a wall,
   and my breasts are like towers.
  Thus I have become in his eyes
   like one bringing contentment.
[11]Solomon had a vineyard in Baal Hamon;
   he let out his vineyard to tenants.
  Each was to bring for its fruit
   a thousand shekels[c] of silver.
[12]But my own vineyard is mine to give;
   the thousand shekels are for you,
     O Solomon,
  and two hundred[d] are for those who tend its
   fruit.

Lover
[13]You who dwell in the gardens
   with friends in attendance,
   let me hear your voice!

Beloved
[14]Come away, my lover,
   and be like a gazelle
  or like a young stag
   on the spice-laden mountains.

所發的電光，是火焰的電光，
　　是耶和華的烈焰。
[7]愛情，眾水不能息滅，
　　大水也不能淹沒，
　若有人拿家中所有的財寶
　　要換愛情，
　　就全被藐視。

朋友
[8]我們有一小妹，
　　她的兩乳尚未長成，
　人來提親的日子，
　　我們當為她怎樣辦理？
[9]她若是牆，
　　我們要在其上建造銀塔；
　她若是門，
　　我們要用香柏木板圍護她。

新婦
[10]我是牆，
　　我兩乳像其上的樓。
　那時我在他眼中
　　像得平安的人。
[11]所羅門在巴力哈們有一葡萄園，
　　他將這葡萄園交給看守的人，
　為其中的果子，
　　必交一千舍客勒銀子。
[12]我自己的葡萄園在我面前；
　　所羅門哪，
　一千舍客勒歸你，
　　二百舍客勒歸看守果子的人。

新郎
[13]你這住在園中的，
　　同伴都要聽你的聲音，
　　求你使我也得聽見。

新婦
[14]我的良人哪，
　　求你快來！
　如羚羊或小鹿
　　在香草山上。

a 6 Or / *like the very flame of the Lord*   *b 7* Or *he*   *c 11* That is,
about 25 pounds (about 11.5 kilograms); also in verse 12
d 12 That is, about 5 pounds (about 2.3 kilograms)

以賽亞書

Isaiah

1 當烏西雅、約坦、亞哈斯、希西家作猶大王的時候，亞摩斯的兒子以賽亞得默示，論到猶大和耶路撒冷。

悖逆的國民

2 天哪，要聽！地啊，側耳而聽！
　　因為耶和華說：
　"我養育兒女，將他們養大，
　　他們竟悖逆我。
3 牛認識主人，
　　驢認識主人的槽；
　以色列卻不認識，
　　我的民卻不留意。"

4 嗐！犯罪的國民，
　　擔着罪孽的百姓；
　行惡的種類，
　　敗壞的兒女！
　他們離棄耶和華，
　　藐視以色列的聖者，
　　與他生疏，往後退步。

5 你們為甚麼屢次悖逆？
　　還要受責打嗎？
　你們已經滿頭疼痛，
　　全心發昏。
6 從腳掌到頭頂，
　　沒有一處完全的，
　盡是傷口、青腫
　　與新打的傷痕，
　都沒有收口，
　　沒有纏裹，
　　也沒有用膏滋潤。

7 你們的地土已經荒涼，
　　你們的城邑被火焚燬，
　你們的田地
　　在你們眼前為外邦人所侵吞。
　既被外邦人傾覆，就成為荒涼。
8 僅存錫安城（註："城"原文作"女子"），
　　好像葡萄園的草棚，
　瓜田的茅屋，
　　被圍困的城邑。
9 若不是萬軍之耶和華
　　給我們稍留餘種，
　我們早已像所多瑪、
　　蛾摩拉的樣子了。

1 The vision concerning Judah and Jerusalem that Isaiah son of Amoz saw during the reigns of Uzziah, Jotham, Ahaz and Hezekiah, kings of Judah.

A Rebellious Nation

2 Hear, O heavens! Listen, O earth!
　　For the LORD has spoken:
　"I reared children and brought them up,
　　but they have rebelled against me.
3 The ox knows his master,
　　the donkey his owner's manger,
　but Israel does not know,
　　my people do not understand."

4 Ah, sinful nation,
　　a people loaded with guilt,
　a brood of evildoers,
　　children given to corruption!
　They have forsaken the LORD;
　　they have spurned the Holy One of Israel
　　and turned their backs on him.

5 Why should you be beaten anymore?
　　Why do you persist in rebellion?
　Your whole head is injured,
　　your whole heart afflicted.
6 From the sole of your foot to the top of your
　　　head
　there is no soundness—
　only wounds and welts
　　and open sores,
　not cleansed or bandaged
　　or soothed with oil.

7 Your country is desolate,
　　your cities burned with fire;
　your fields are being stripped by foreigners
　　right before you,
　　laid waste as when overthrown by strangers.
8 The Daughter of Zion is left
　　like a shelter in a vineyard,
　like a hut in a field of melons,
　　like a city under siege.
9 Unless the LORD Almighty
　　had left us some survivors,
　we would have become like Sodom,
　　we would have been like Gomorrah.

¹⁰Hear the word of the LORD,
  you rulers of Sodom;
listen to the law of our God,
  you people of Gomorrah!
¹¹"The multitude of your sacrifices—
  what are they to me?" says the LORD.
"I have more than enough of burnt offerings,
  of rams and the fat of fattened animals;
I have no pleasure
  in the blood of bulls and lambs and goats.
¹²When you come to appear before me,
  who has asked this of you,
  this trampling of my courts?
¹³Stop bringing meaningless offerings!
  Your incense is detestable to me.
New Moons, Sabbaths and convocations—
  I cannot bear your evil assemblies.
¹⁴Your New Moon festivals and your appointed
    feasts
  my soul hates.
They have become a burden to me;
  I am weary of bearing them.
¹⁵When you spread out your hands in prayer,
  I will hide my eyes from you;
even if you offer many prayers,
  I will not listen.
Your hands are full of blood;
¹⁶ wash and make yourselves clean.
Take your evil deeds
  out of my sight!
Stop doing wrong,
¹⁷ learn to do right!
Seek justice,
  encourage the oppressed.^a
Defend the cause of the fatherless,
  plead the case of the widow.

¹⁸"Come now, let us reason together,"
  says the LORD.
"Though your sins are like scarlet,
  they shall be as white as snow;
though they are red as crimson,
  they shall be like wool.
¹⁹If you are willing and obedient,
  you will eat the best from the land;
²⁰but if you resist and rebel,
  you will be devoured by the sword."
    For the mouth of the LORD has spoken.

²¹See how the faithful city
  has become a harlot!
She once was full of justice;
  righteousness used to dwell in her—
  but now murderers!

a 17 Or / rebuke the oppressor

¹⁰你們這所多瑪的官長啊,
  要聽耶和華的話!
你們這蛾摩拉的百姓啊,
  要側耳聽我們神的訓誨!
¹¹耶和華說:「你們所獻的許多祭物
  與我何益呢?
公綿羊的燔祭和肥畜的脂油,
  我已經夠了;
公牛的血,羊羔的血,
  公山羊的血,我都不喜悅。
¹²你們來朝見我,
  誰向你們討這些,
  使你們踐踏我的院宇呢?
¹³你們不要再獻虛浮的供物!
  香品是我所憎惡的;
月朔和安息日,並宣召的大會,
  也是我所憎惡的;
作罪孽,又守嚴肅會,我也不能容忍。
¹⁴你們的月朔和節期,
  我心裏恨惡,我都以為麻煩;
我擔當,
  便不耐煩。
¹⁵你們舉手禱告,
  我必遮眼不看;
就是你們多多地祈禱,
  我也不聽。
你們的手都滿了殺人的血。
¹⁶你們要洗濯、自潔,
  從我眼前
    除掉你們的惡行;
要止住作惡,
¹⁷學習行善,
  尋求公平,
解救受欺壓的,
  給孤兒伸冤,
  為寡婦辨屈。」

¹⁸耶和華說:
  「你們來,我們彼此辯論。
你們的罪雖像硃紅,
  必變成雪白;
雖紅如丹顏,
  必白如羊毛。
¹⁹你們若甘心聽從,
  必吃地上的美物;
²⁰若不聽從,反倒悖逆,
  必被刀劍吞滅。
      這是耶和華親口說的。

²¹可歎,
  忠信的城變為妓女!
從前充滿了公平,
  公義居在其中,
  現今卻有兇手居住。

22你的銀子變為渣滓；
　　你的酒用水攙對。
23你的官長居心悖逆，
　　與盜賊作伴，
　各都喜愛賄賂，
　追求贓私。
　他們不為孤兒伸冤，
　寡婦的案件
　　　也不得呈到他們面前。
24因此，主萬軍之耶和華
　　以色列的大能者說：
　"哎！我要向我的對頭雪恨，
　　向我的敵人報仇。
25我必反手加在你身上，
　煉盡你的渣滓，
　除淨你的雜質。
26我也必復還你的審判官，
　　像起初一樣；
　復還你的謀士，像起先一般。
　然後，你必稱為公義之城，
　　忠信之邑。"

27錫安必因公平得蒙救贖，
　其中歸正的人必因公義得蒙救贖。
28但悖逆的和犯罪的必一同敗亡；
　離棄耶和華的必致消滅。

29那等人必因
　你們所喜愛的橡樹抱愧，
　你們必因
　　所選擇的園子蒙羞。

30因為你們必如葉子枯乾的橡樹，
　好像無水澆灌的園子。
31有權勢的必如麻瓤，
　他的工作好像火星，
　都要一同焚燬，
　無人撲滅。

主的山

2 亞摩斯的兒子以賽亞得默示，論到猶大和耶路撒冷。

2末後的日子，

耶和華殿的山
　　必堅立，
　　超乎諸山，
　高舉過於萬嶺，
　萬民都要流歸這山。

3必有許多國的民前往，說：

"來吧！
　我們登耶和華的山，
　奔雅各神的殿；

22Your silver has become dross,
　　your choice wine is diluted with water.
23Your rulers are rebels,
　　companions of thieves;
　they all love bribes
　　and chase after gifts.
　They do not defend the cause of the
　　　fatherless;
　　the widow's case does not come before them.
24Therefore the Lord, the LORD Almighty,
　　the Mighty One of Israel, declares:
　"Ah, I will get relief from my foes
　　and avenge myself on my enemies.
25I will turn my hand against you;
　I will thoroughly purge away your dross
　　and remove all your impurities.
26I will restore your judges as in days of old,
　　your counselors as at the beginning.
　Afterward you will be called
　　the City of Righteousness,
　　the Faithful City."

27Zion will be redeemed with justice,
　　her penitent ones with righteousness.
28But rebels and sinners will both be broken,
　　and those who forsake the LORD will perish.

29"You will be ashamed because of the sacred
　　oaks
　in which you have delighted;
　you will be disgraced because of the gardens
　　that you have chosen.
30You will be like an oak with fading leaves,
　　like a garden without water.
31The mighty man will become tinder
　　and his work a spark;
　both will burn together,
　　with no one to quench the fire."

The Mountain of the LORD

2 This is what Isaiah son of Amoz saw
　concerning Judah and Jerusalem:

2In the last days

the mountain of the LORD's temple will be
　　established
　as chief among the mountains;
　it will be raised above the hills,
　　and all nations will stream to it.

3Many peoples will come and say,

"Come, let us go up to the mountain of the
　　LORD,
　to the house of the God of Jacob.

9The look on their faces testifies against them;
  they parade their sin like Sodom;
  they do not hide it.
Woe to them!
  They have brought disaster upon themselves.

10Tell the righteous it will be well with them,
  for they will enjoy the fruit of their deeds.
11Woe to the wicked! Disaster is upon them!
  They will be paid back for what their hands
    have done.

12Youths oppress my people,
  women rule over them.
O my people, your guides lead you astray;
  they turn you from the path.

13The LORD takes his place in court;
  he rises to judge the people.
14The LORD enters into judgment
  against the elders and leaders of his people:
  "It is you who have ruined my vineyard;
  the plunder from the poor is in your houses.
15What do you mean by crushing my people
  and grinding the faces of the poor?"
        declares the Lord, the LORD Almighty.

16The LORD says,
  "The women of Zion are haughty,
  walking along with outstretched necks,
  flirting with their eyes,
  tripping along with mincing steps,
  with ornaments jingling on their ankles.
17Therefore the Lord will bring sores on the
    heads of the women of Zion;
  the LORD will make their scalps bald."

18In that day the Lord will snatch away their
finery: the bangles and headbands and crescent
necklaces, 19the earrings and bracelets and veils,
20the headdresses and ankle chains and sashes,
the perfume bottles and charms, 21the signet
rings and nose rings, 22the fine robes and the
capes and cloaks, the purses 23and mirrors, and
the linen garments and tiaras and shawls.

24Instead of fragrance there will be a stench;
  instead of a sash, a rope;
instead of well-dressed hair, baldness;
  instead of fine clothing, sackcloth;
  instead of beauty, branding.
25Your men will fall by the sword,
  your warriors in battle.
26The gates of Zion will lament and mourn;
  destitute, she will sit on the ground.

9他們的面色證明自己的不正;
  他們述說自己的罪惡,
  並不隱瞞,好像所多瑪一樣。
他們有禍了,
  因為作惡自害。

10你們要論義人説:他必享福樂,
  因為要吃自己行為所結的果子。
11惡人有禍了,他必遭災難!
  因為要照自己手所行的受報應。

12至於我的百姓,孩童欺壓他們,
  婦女轄管他們。
我的百姓啊,引導你的使你走錯,
  並毀壞你所行的道路。

13耶和華起來辯論,
  站着審判眾民。
14耶和華必審問
  他民中的長老和首領,説:
  "吃盡葡萄園果子的就是你們;
  向貧窮人所奪的都在你們家中。"
15主萬軍之耶和華説:
  "你們為何壓制我的百姓,
  搓磨貧窮人的臉呢?"

16耶和華又説:
  "因為錫安的女子狂傲,
  行走挺項,
  賣弄眼目,
  俏步徐行,
  腳下玎璫。
17所以主必使錫安的女子
  頭長禿瘡;
  耶和華又使她們赤露下體。"

18到那日,主必除掉她們華美的
腳釧、髮網、月牙圈、19耳環、手
鐲、蒙臉的帕子、20華冠、足鏈、華
帶、香盒、符囊、21戒指、鼻環、22吉
服、外套、雲肩、荷包、23手鏡、細
麻衣、裹頭巾、蒙身的帕子。

24必有臭爛代替馨香,
  繩子代替腰帶,
  光禿代替美髮,
  麻衣緊腰代替華服,
  烙傷代替美容。
25你的男丁必倒在刀下;
  你的勇士必死在陣上。
26錫安(註:原文作"她")的城門
  必悲傷、哀號;
  她必荒涼坐在地上。

4

在那日，七個女人
必拉住一個男人，
說：「我們吃自己的食物，
穿自己的衣服，
但求你許我們歸你名下，
求你除掉我們的羞恥。」

主的苗

2到那日，耶和華發生的苗必華
美尊榮，地的出產必為以色列逃脫
的人顯為榮華茂盛。3、4主以公義的
靈和焚燒的靈，將錫安女子的污穢
洗去，又將耶路撒冷中殺人的血除
淨。那時，剩在錫安、留在耶路撒
冷的，就是一切住耶路撒冷、在生
命冊上記名的，必稱為聖。5耶和華
也必在錫安全山，並各會眾以上，
使白日有煙雲，黑夜有火焰的光，
因為在全榮耀之上必有遮蔽。6必有
亭子，白日可以得蔭避暑，也可以
作為藏身之處，躲避狂風暴雨。

葡萄園之歌

5

我要為我所親愛的唱歌，
是我所愛者的歌，
論他葡萄園的事。
我所親愛的有葡萄園在肥美的山岡上。
2他刨挖園子，撿去石頭，
栽種上等的葡萄樹，
在園中蓋了一座樓，
又鑿出壓酒池，
指望結好葡萄，
反倒結了野葡萄。

3耶路撒冷的居民和猶大人哪，
請你們現今在我與我的葡萄園中，
斷定是非。
4我為我葡萄園
所做之外，
還有甚麼可做的呢？
我指望結好葡萄，
怎麼倒結了野葡萄呢？
5現在我告訴你們，
我要向我葡萄園怎樣行：
我必撤去籬笆，
使它被吞滅；
拆毀牆垣，
使它被踐踏。
6我必使它荒廢，
不再修理，不再鋤刨，
荊棘蒺藜倒要生長。

4

In that day seven women
will take hold of one man
and say, "We will eat our own food
and provide our own clothes;
only let us be called by your name.
Take away our disgrace!"

The Branch of the LORD

2In that day the Branch of the LORD will be
beautiful and glorious, and the fruit of the land
will be the pride and glory of the survivors in
Israel. 3Those who are left in Zion, who remain
in Jerusalem, will be called holy, all who are
recorded among the living in Jerusalem. 4The
Lord will wash away the filth of the women of
Zion; he will cleanse the bloodstains from Jerusalem by a spirit*a* of judgment and a spirit*a* of
fire. 5Then the LORD will create over all of Mount
Zion and over those who assemble there a cloud
of smoke by day and a glow of flaming fire by
night; over all the glory will be a canopy. 6It will
be a shelter and shade from the heat of the day,
and a refuge and hiding place from the storm
and rain.

The Song of the Vineyard

5

I will sing for the one I love
a song about his vineyard:
My loved one had a vineyard
on a fertile hillside.
2He dug it up and cleared it of stones
and planted it with the choicest vines.
He built a watchtower in it
and cut out a winepress as well.
Then he looked for a crop of good grapes,
but it yielded only bad fruit.

3"Now you dwellers in Jerusalem and men of
Judah,
judge between me and my vineyard.
4What more could have been done for my
vineyard
than I have done for it?
When I looked for good grapes,
why did it yield only bad?
5Now I will tell you
what I am going to do to my vineyard:
I will take away its hedge,
and it will be destroyed;
I will break down its wall,
and it will be trampled.
6I will make it a wasteland,
neither pruned nor cultivated,
and briers and thorns will grow there.

a 4 Or the Spirit

I will command the clouds
    not to rain on it."

我也必命雲
不降雨在其上。

⁷The vineyard of the LORD Almighty
    is the house of Israel,
and the men of Judah
    are the garden of his delight.
And he looked for justice, but saw bloodshed;
    for righteousness, but heard cries of distress.

⁷萬軍之耶和華的葡萄園，
　就是以色列家；
他所喜愛的樹，就是猶大人。
他指望的是公平，誰知倒有暴虐
　（註：或作"倒流人血"）；
指望的是公義，誰知倒有冤聲。

Woes and Judgments

⁸Woe to you who add house to house
    and join field to field
till no space is left
    and you live alone in the land.

災禍與審判

⁸禍哉！那些以房接房、
以地連地，
以致不留餘地的，
只顧自己獨居境內。

⁹The LORD Almighty has declared in my hearing:

⁹我耳聞萬軍之耶和華說：

"Surely the great houses will become desolate,
    the fine mansions left without occupants.
¹⁰A ten-acre^a vineyard will produce only a bath^b
    of wine,
a homer^c of seed only an ephah^d of grain."

"必有許多又大又美的房屋
　成為荒涼，無人居住。
¹⁰三十畝葡萄園只出一罷特酒；
一賀梅珥穀種
　只結一伊法糧食。"

¹¹Woe to those who rise early in the morning
    to run after their drinks,
who stay up late at night
    till they are inflamed with wine.
¹²They have harps and lyres at their banquets,
    tambourines and flutes and wine,
but they have no regard for the deeds of the
    LORD,
no respect for the work of his hands.
¹³Therefore my people will go into exile
    for lack of understanding;
their men of rank will die of hunger
    and their masses will be parched with thirst.
¹⁴Therefore the grave^e enlarges its appetite
    and opens its mouth without limit;
into it will descend their nobles and masses
    with all their brawlers and revelers.
¹⁵So man will be brought low
    and mankind humbled,
the eyes of the arrogant humbled.
¹⁶But the LORD Almighty will be exalted by his
    justice,
and the holy God will show himself holy by
    his righteousness.

¹¹禍哉！
那些清早起來追求濃酒，
留連到夜深，
甚至因酒發燒的人。
¹²他們在筵席上彈琴、鼓瑟、
擊鼓、吹笛、飲酒，
卻不顧念
　耶和華的作為，
也不留心他手所做的。
¹³所以我的百姓
因無知就被擄去。
他們的尊貴人甚是飢餓，
羣眾極其乾渴。
¹⁴故此，陰間擴張其欲，
開了無限量的口；
他們的榮耀、羣眾、繁華，
並快樂的人，都落在其中。
¹⁵卑賤人被壓服，
尊貴人降為卑，
眼目高傲的人也降為卑。
¹⁶惟有萬軍之耶和華
因公平而崇高；
聖者神
因公義顯為聖。

---

^a 10 Hebrew *ten-yoke*, that is, the land plowed by 10 yoke of
oxen in one day
^b 10 That is, probably about 6 gallons (about 22 liters)
^c 10 That is, probably about 6 bushels (about 220 liters)
^d 10 That is, probably about 3/5 bushel (about 22 liters)
^e 14 Hebrew *Sheol*

¹⁷那時，羊羔必來吃草，
　　如同在自己的草場；
　　豐肥人的荒場被遊行的人吃盡。
¹⁸禍哉！
　　那些以虛假之細繩牽罪孽的人！
　　他們又像以套繩拉罪惡，
¹⁹說："任他急速行，
　　趕快成就他的作為，
　　使我們看看；
　　任以色列聖者所謀劃的
　　臨近成就，
　　使我們知道。"

²⁰禍哉！那些稱惡為善、
　　稱善為惡，
　　以暗為光、
　　以光為暗，
　　以苦為甜、
　　以甜為苦的人！

²¹禍哉！那些自以為有智慧，
　　自看為通達的人！

²²禍哉！那些勇於飲酒，
　　以能力調濃酒的人！
²³他們因受賄賂，就稱惡人為義，
　　將義人的義奪去。
²⁴火苗怎樣吞滅碎稭，
　　乾草怎樣落在火焰之中，
　　照樣，他們的根必像朽物，
　　他們的花必像灰塵飛騰；
　　因為他們厭棄
　　萬軍之耶和華的訓誨，
　　藐視以色列聖者的言語。

²⁵所以，耶和華的怒氣
　　向他的百姓發作。
　　他的手伸出攻擊他們，
　　山嶺就震動；
　　他們的屍首在街市上
　　好像糞土。

雖然如此，他的怒氣還未轉消，
　　他的手仍伸不縮。

²⁶他必豎立大旗，招遠方的國民，
　　發嘶聲叫他們從地極而來！
　　看哪，
　　他們必急速奔來。
²⁷其中沒有疲倦的、絆跌的；
　　沒有打盹的、睡覺的；
　　腰帶並不放鬆，
　　鞋帶也不折斷。

¹⁷Then sheep will graze as in their own pasture;
　　lambs will feed^a among the ruins of the rich.

¹⁸Woe to those who draw sin along with cords
　　　of deceit,
　　and wickedness as with cart ropes,
¹⁹to those who say, "Let God hurry,
　　let him hasten his work
　　so we may see it.
　Let it approach,
　　let the plan of the Holy One of Israel come,
　　so we may know it."

²⁰Woe to those who call evil good
　　　and good evil,
　　who put darkness for light
　　and light for darkness,
　　who put bitter for sweet
　　and sweet for bitter.

²¹Woe to those who are wise in their own eyes
　　and clever in their own sight.

²²Woe to those who are heroes at drinking wine
　　and champions at mixing drinks,
²³who acquit the guilty for a bribe,
　　but deny justice to the innocent.
²⁴Therefore, as tongues of fire lick up straw
　　and as dry grass sinks down in the flames,
　　so their roots will decay
　　and their flowers blow away like dust;
　for they have rejected the law of the LORD
　　　Almighty
　　and spurned the word of the Holy One of
　　　Israel.
²⁵Therefore the LORD's anger burns against his
　　　people;
　　his hand is raised and he strikes them down.
　The mountains shake,
　　and the dead bodies are like refuse in the
　　　streets.

Yet for all this, his anger is not turned away,
　　his hand is still upraised.

²⁶He lifts up a banner for the distant nations,
　　he whistles for those at the ends of the earth.
　Here they come,
　　swiftly and speedily!
²⁷Not one of them grows tired or stumbles,
　　not one slumbers or sleeps;
　　not a belt is loosened at the waist,
　　not a sandal thong is broken.

²⁸Their arrows are sharp,
    all their bows are strung;
  their horses' hoofs seem like flint,
    their chariot wheels like a whirlwind.
²⁹Their roar is like that of the lion,
    they roar like young lions;
  they growl as they seize their prey
    and carry it off with no one to rescue.
³⁰In that day they will roar over it
    like the roaring of the sea.
  And if one looks at the land,
    he will see darkness and distress;
    even the light will be darkened by the clouds.

Isaiah's Commission

6 In the year that King Uzziah died, I saw the Lord seated on a throne, high and exalted, and the train of his robe filled the temple. ²Above him were seraphs, each with six wings: With two wings they covered their faces, with two they covered their feet, and with two they were flying. ³And they were calling to one another:

  "Holy, holy, holy is the Lord Almighty;
    the whole earth is full of his glory."

⁴At the sound of their voices the doorposts and thresholds shook and the temple was filled with smoke.

⁵"Woe to me!" I cried. "I am ruined! For I am a man of unclean lips, and I live among a people of unclean lips, and my eyes have seen the King, the Lord Almighty."

⁶Then one of the seraphs flew to me with a live coal in his hand, which he had taken with tongs from the altar. ⁷With it he touched my mouth and said, "See, this has touched your lips; your guilt is taken away and your sin atoned for."

⁸Then I heard the voice of the Lord saying, "Whom shall I send? And who will go for us?"
And I said, "Here am I. Send me!"

⁹He said, "Go and tell this people:

  " 'Be ever hearing, but never understanding;
  be ever seeing, but never perceiving.'
¹⁰Make the heart of this people calloused;
  make their ears dull
  and close their eyes.^a

---

a 9,10 Hebrew; Septuagint 'You will be ever hearing, but never understanding; / you will be ever seeing, but never perceiving.' /
¹⁰ This people's heart has become calloused; / they hardly hear with their ears, / and they have closed their eyes

---

²⁸他們的箭快利，
    弓也上了弦；
  馬蹄算如堅石，
    車輪好像旋風。
²⁹他們要吼叫，像母獅子，
    咆哮，像少壯獅子；
  他們要咆哮抓食，
    坦然叼去，無人救回。
³⁰那日，他們要向以色列人吼叫，
    像海浪匉訇。
  人若望地，
    只見黑暗艱難，
    光明在雲中變為昏暗。

以賽亞奉差遣

6 當烏西雅王崩的那年，我見主坐在高高的寶座上。他的衣裳垂下，遮滿聖殿。²其上有撒拉弗侍立，各有六個翅膀：用兩個翅膀遮臉，兩個翅膀遮腳，兩個翅膀飛翔。³彼此呼喊說：

  "聖哉！聖哉！聖哉！
    萬軍之耶和華，
    他的榮光充滿全地！"

⁴因呼喊者的聲音，門檻的根基震動，殿充滿了煙雲。

⁵那時我說："禍哉！我滅亡了！因為我是嘴唇不潔的人，又住在嘴唇不潔的民中；又因我眼見大君王萬軍之耶和華。"

⁶有一撒拉弗飛到我跟前，手裏拿着紅炭，是用火剪從壇上取下來的，⁷將炭沾我的口，說："看哪，這炭沾了你的嘴，你的罪孽便除掉，你的罪惡就赦免了。"

⁸我又聽見主的聲音說："我可以差遣誰呢？誰肯為我們去呢？"
  我說："我在這裏，請差遣我！"
⁹他說："你去告訴這百姓說：

  " '你們聽是要聽見，卻不明白；
  看是要看見，卻不曉得。'
¹⁰要使這百姓心蒙脂油，
  耳朵發沉，
  眼睛昏迷；

恐怕眼睛看見，
　　耳朵聽見，
　　心裏明白，
　　回轉過來，便得醫治。"

11 我就說："主啊！這到幾時為止呢？"
　　他說：

"直到城邑荒涼，
　　無人居住，
　　房屋空閒無人，
　　地土極其荒涼，
12 並且耶和華將人遷到遠方，
　　在這境內撇下的地土很多。
13 境內剩下的人若還有十分之一，
　　也必被吞滅。
　　像栗樹、橡樹，
　　雖被砍伐，樹不子卻仍存留，
　　這聖潔的種類
　　在國中也是如此。"

以馬內利的兆頭

7 烏西雅的孫子、約坦的兒子猶大王亞哈斯在位的時候，亞蘭王利汛和利瑪利的兒子以色列王比加上來攻打耶路撒冷，卻不能攻取。

2 有人告訴大衛家說："亞蘭與以法蓮已經同盟。"王的心和百姓的心都跳動，好像林中的樹被風吹動一樣。

3 耶和華對以賽亞說："你和你的兒子施亞雅述出去，到上池的水溝頭，在漂布地的大路上去迎接亞哈斯。4 對他說：'你要謹慎安靜，不要因亞蘭王利汛和利瑪利的兒子——這兩個冒煙的火把頭所發的烈怒害怕，也不要心裏膽怯。5 因為亞蘭和以法蓮，並利瑪利的兒子設惡謀害你，6 說：我們可以上去攻擊猶大，擾亂他，攻破他，在其中立他比勒的兒子為王。7 所以主耶和華如此說：

"'這所謀的必立不住，
　　也不得成就。
8 原來亞蘭的首城是大馬士革，
　　大馬士革的首領是利汛。
　　六十五年之內，
　　以法蓮必然破壞，
　　不再成為國民。

Otherwise they might see with their eyes,
　　hear with their ears,
　　understand with their hearts,
　　and turn and be healed."

11 Then I said, "For how long, O Lord?"
And he answered:

"Until the cities lie ruined
　　and without inhabitant,
until the houses are left deserted
　　and the fields ruined and ravaged,
12 until the LORD has sent everyone far away
　　and the land is utterly forsaken.
13 And though a tenth remains in the land,
　　it will again be laid waste.
But as the terebinth and oak
　　leave stumps when they are cut down,
　　so the holy seed will be the stump in the
　　　land."

The Sign of Immanuel

7 When Ahaz son of Jotham, the son of Uzziah, was king of Judah, King Rezin of Aram and Pekah son of Remaliah king of Israel marched up to fight against Jerusalem, but they could not overpower it.

2 Now the house of David was told, "Aram has allied itself with[a] Ephraim"; so the hearts of Ahaz and his people were shaken, as the trees of the forest are shaken by the wind.

3 Then the LORD said to Isaiah, "Go out, you and your son Shear-Jashub,[b] to meet Ahaz at the end of the aqueduct of the Upper Pool, on the road to the Washerman's Field. 4 Say to him, 'Be careful, keep calm and don't be afraid. Do not lose heart because of these two smoldering stubs of firewood—because of the fierce anger of Rezin and Aram and of the son of Remaliah. 5 Aram, Ephraim and Remaliah's son have plotted your ruin, saying, 6 "Let us invade Judah; let us tear it apart and divide it among ourselves, and make the son of Tabeel king over it." 7 Yet this is what the Sovereign LORD says:

" 'It will not take place,
　　it will not happen,
8 for the head of Aram is Damascus,
　　and the head of Damascus is only Rezin.
　　Within sixty-five years
　　Ephraim will be too shattered to be a people.

---

a 2 Or *has set up camp in*　　*b 3 Shear-Jashub* means *a remnant will return.*

⁹The head of Ephraim is Samaria,
　and the head of Samaria is only Remaliah's
　son.
　If you do not stand firm in your faith,
　you will not stand at all.' "

¹⁰Again the LORD spoke to Ahaz, ¹¹"Ask the
LORD your God for a sign, whether in the deepest depths or in the highest heights."

¹²But Ahaz said, "I will not ask; I will not put
the LORD to the test."

¹³Then Isaiah said, "Hear now, you house of
David! Is it not enough to try the patience of
men? Will you try the patience of my God also?
¹⁴Therefore the Lord himself will give youᵃ a
sign: The virgin will be with child and will give
birth to a son, andᵇ will call him Immanuel.ᶜ
¹⁵He will eat curds and honey when he knows
enough to reject the wrong and choose the right.
¹⁶But before the boy knows enough to reject the
wrong and choose the right, the land of the two
kings you dread will be laid waste. ¹⁷The LORD
will bring on you and on your people and on
the house of your father a time unlike any since
Ephraim broke away from Judah—he will bring
the king of Assyria."

¹⁸In that day the LORD will whistle for flies
from the distant streams of Egypt and for bees
from the land of Assyria. ¹⁹They will all come
and settle in the steep ravines and in the crevices
in the rocks, on all the thornbushes and at all the
water holes. ²⁰In that day the Lord will use a
razor hired from beyond the Riverᵈ —the king
of Assyria—to shave your head and the hair of
your legs, and to take off your beards also. ²¹In
that day, a man will keep alive a young cow and
two goats. ²²And because of the abundance of
the milk they give, he will have curds to eat. All
who remain in the land will eat curds and honey.
²³In that day, in every place where there were a
thousand vines worth a thousand silver shekels,ᵉ
there will be only briers and thorns. ²⁴Men will
go there with bow and arrow, for the land will
be covered with briers and thorns. ²⁵As for all
the hills once cultivated by the hoe, you will no
longer go there for fear of the briers and thorns;
they will become places where cattle are turned
loose and where sheep run.

⁹以法蓮的首城是撒馬利亞，
　撒馬利亞的首領
　是利瑪利的兒子。
你們若是不信，
　定然不得立穩。’ ”

¹⁰耶和華又曉諭亞哈斯說：¹¹ “你
向耶和華你的神求一個兆頭，或求顯
在深處，或求顯在高處。”
¹²亞哈斯說： “我不求！我不試
探耶和華。”

¹³以賽亞說： “大衛家啊，你們
當聽！你們使人厭煩豈算小事，還要
使我的神厭煩嗎？¹⁴因此，主自己要
給你們一個兆頭，必有童女懷孕生
子，給他起名叫以馬內利（註：就是
“神與我們同在”的意思）。¹⁵到他曉得棄
惡擇善的時候，他必吃奶油與蜂蜜。
¹⁶因為在這孩子還不曉得棄惡擇善之
先，你所憎惡的那二王之地必致見
棄。¹⁷耶和華必使亞述王攻擊你的日
子臨到你和你的百姓，並你的父家。
自從以法蓮離開猶大以來，未曾有這
樣的日子。”

¹⁸那時，耶和華要發嘶聲，使埃
及江河源頭的蒼蠅和亞述地的蜂子飛
來；¹⁹都必飛來，落在荒涼的谷內、
磐石的穴裏和一切荊棘籬笆中，並一
切的草場上。²⁰那時，主必用大河外
賃的剃頭刀，就是亞述王，剃去頭髮
和腳上的毛，並要剃淨鬍鬚。²¹那
時，一個人要養活一隻母牛犢，兩隻
母綿羊。²²因為出的奶多，他就得吃
奶油；在境內所剩的人都要吃奶油與
蜂蜜。²³從前，凡種一千棵葡萄樹，
值銀一千舍客勒的地方，到那時，必
長荊棘和蒺藜。²⁴人上那裏去，必帶
弓箭，因為遍地滿了荊棘和蒺藜。
²⁵所有用鋤刨挖的山地，你因怕荊棘
和蒺藜，不敢上那裏去；只可成了放
牛之處，為羊踐踏之地。

---

a 14 The Hebrew is plural.　*b 14* Masoretic Text; Dead Sea
Scrolls *and he* or *and they*　*c 14 Immanuel* means *God with us.*
d 20 That is, the Euphrates　*e 23* That is, about 25 pounds
(about 11.5 kilograms)

亞述是主的工具

8 耶和華對我說：「你取一個大牌，拿人所用的筆（註：或作「人常用的字」），寫上瑪黑珥沙勒哈施罷斯（註：就是「擄掠速臨，搶奪快到」的意思）。²我要用誠實的見證人，祭司烏利亞和耶比利家的兒子撒迦利亞記這事。」

³我以賽亞與妻子（註：原文作「女先知」）同室。她懷孕生子，耶和華就對我說：「給他起名叫瑪黑珥沙勒哈施罷斯。⁴因為在這小孩子不曉得叫父叫母之先，大馬士革的財寶和撒馬利亞的擄物，必在亞述王面前搬了去。」

⁵耶和華又曉諭我說：

6 「這百姓既厭棄西羅亞緩流的水，
　喜悅利汛和利瑪利的兒子；
7因此，主必使大河翻騰的水
　猛然沖來，
　就是亞述王和他所有的威勢，
　必漫過一切的水道，
　漲過兩岸；
8必沖入猶太，
　漲溢氾濫，
　直到頸項。
　以馬內利啊，
　他展開翅膀，
　遍滿你的地！」

9列國的人民哪，任憑你們喧嚷，
　終必破壞；
　遠方的眾人哪，當側耳而聽！
　任憑你們束起腰來，終必破壞，
　你們束起腰來，終必破壞。
10任憑你們同謀，終歸無有；
　任憑你們言定，終不成立。
　因為神與我們同在。

敬畏神

11耶和華以大能的手，指教我不可行這百姓所行的道，對我這樣說：

12 「這百姓說同謀背叛，
　你們不要說同謀背叛。
　他們所怕的，你們不要怕，
　也不要畏懼。

Assyria, the LORD's Instrument

8 The LORD said to me, "Take a large scroll and write on it with an ordinary pen: Maher-Shalal-Hash-Baz.[a] ²And I will call in Uriah the priest and Zechariah son of Jeberekiah as reliable witnesses for me."

³Then I went to the prophetess, and she conceived and gave birth to a son. And the LORD said to me, "Name him Maher-Shalal-Hash-Baz. ⁴Before the boy knows how to say 'My father' or 'My mother,' the wealth of Damascus and the plunder of Samaria will be carried off by the king of Assyria."

⁵The LORD spoke to me again:

6"Because this people has rejected
　the gently flowing waters of Shiloah
　and rejoices over Rezin
　and the son of Remaliah,
7therefore the Lord is about to bring against them
　the mighty floodwaters of the River[b] —
　the king of Assyria with all his pomp.
It will overflow all its channels,
　run over all its banks
8and sweep on into Judah, swirling over it,
　passing through it and reaching up to the neck.
Its outspread wings will cover the breadth of
　your land,
　O Immanuel[c]!"

9Raise the war cry,[d] you nations, and be
　shattered!
　Listen, all you distant lands.
　Prepare for battle, and be shattered!
　Prepare for battle, and be shattered!
10Devise your strategy, but it will be thwarted;
　propose your plan, but it will not stand,
　for God is with us.[e]

Fear God

11The LORD spoke to me with his strong hand upon me, warning me not to follow the way of this people. He said:

12"Do not call conspiracy
　everything that these people call conspiracy[f];
　do not fear what they fear,
　and do not dread it.

---

a 1 Maher-Shalal-Hash-Baz means quick to the plunder, swift to the spoil; also in verse 3.　　b 7 That is, the Euphrates
c 8 Immanuel means God with us.　　d 9 Or Do your worst
e 10 Hebrew Immanuel　　f 12 Or Do not call for a treaty / every time these people call for a treaty

¹³The LORD Almighty is the one you are to
　　regard as holy,
　he is the one you are to fear,
　he is the one you are to dread,
¹⁴and he will be a sanctuary;
　but for both houses of Israel he will be
　a stone that causes men to stumble
　and a rock that makes them fall.
　And for the people of Jerusalem he will be
　a trap and a snare.
¹⁵Many of them will stumble;
　they will fall and be broken,
　they will be snared and captured."

¹⁶Bind up the testimony
　and seal up the law among my disciples.
¹⁷I will wait for the LORD,
　who is hiding his face from the house of Jacob.
　I will put my trust in him.

¹⁸Here am I, and the children the LORD has
given me. We are signs and symbols in Israel
from the LORD Almighty, who dwells on Mount
Zion.

¹⁹When men tell you to consult mediums and
spiritists, who whisper and mutter, should not a
people inquire of their God? Why consult the
dead on behalf of the living? ²⁰To the law and to
the testimony! If they do not speak according
to this word, they have no light of dawn.
²¹Distressed and hungry, they will roam through
the land; when they are famished, they will
become enraged and, looking upward, will curse
their king and their God. ²²Then they will look
toward the earth and see only distress and darkness and fearful gloom, and they will be thrust
into utter darkness.

To Us a Child Is Born

9 Nevertheless, there will be no more
gloom for those who were in distress. In
the past he humbled the land of
Zebulun and the land of Naphtali, but in the
future he will honor Galilee of the Gentiles, by
the way of the sea, along the Jordan—

²The people walking in darkness
　have seen a great light;
　on those living in the land of the shadow of
　　death*ᵃ*
　a light has dawned.
³You have enlarged the nation
　and increased their joy;

¹³但要尊萬軍之耶和華為聖，
　　以他為你們所當怕的、
　　所當畏懼的。

¹⁴他必作為聖所，
　卻向以色列兩家
　　作絆腳的石頭、
　　跌人的磐石；
　向耶路撒冷的居民
　　作為圈套和網羅。
¹⁵許多人必在其上絆腳跌倒，
　　而且跌碎，
　　並陷入網羅被纏住。"

¹⁶你要捲起律法書，
　　在我門徒中間封住訓誨。
¹⁷我要等候
　　那掩面不顧雅各家的耶和華，
　我也要仰望他。

¹⁸看哪，我與耶和華所給我的兒
女，就是從住在錫安山萬軍之耶和華
來的，在以色列中作為預兆和奇蹟。

¹⁹有人對你們說："當求問那些
交鬼的和行巫術的，就是聲音綿蠻、
言語微細的。"你們便回答說："百
姓不當求問自己的神嗎？豈可為活人
求問死人呢？" ²⁰人當以訓誨和法度
為標準，他們所說的若不與此相符，
必不得見晨光。²¹他們必經過這地，
受艱難、受飢餓；飢餓的時候，心中
焦躁，咒罵自己的君王和自己的神。
²²仰觀上天，俯察下地，不料，盡是
艱難、黑暗和幽暗的痛苦。他們必被
趕入烏黑的黑暗中去。

有一嬰孩為我們而生

9 但那受過痛苦的，必不再見
幽暗。從前神使西布倫地和
拿弗他利地被藐視，末後卻
使這沿海的路，約旦河外，外邦人的
加利利地得着榮耀——

²在黑暗中行走的百姓，
　　看見了大光；
　住在死蔭之地的人，
　　有光照耀他們。

³你使這國民繁多，
　　加增他們的喜樂；

---

a 2 Or land of darkness

他們在你面前歡喜，
　好像收割的歡喜，
像人分擄物
　那樣的快樂。
⁴因為他們所負的重軛
　和肩頭上的杖，
並欺壓他們人的棍，
　你都已經折斷，
好像在米甸的日子一樣。
⁵戰士在亂殺之間所穿戴的盔甲，
　並那滾在血中的衣服，
都必作為可燒的，
　當作火柴。
⁶因有一嬰孩為我們而生，
　有一子賜給我們，
　政權必擔在他的肩頭上。
他名稱為
　奇妙策士、全能的神、
　永在的父、和平的君。
⁷他的政權與平安
　必加增無窮。
他必在大衛的寶座上
　治理他的國，
以公平公義
　使國堅定穩固，
　從今直到永遠。
萬軍之耶和華的熱心
　必成就這事。

主向以色列發怒

⁸主使一言入於雅各家，
　落於以色列家。
⁹這眾百姓，
　就是以法蓮和撒馬利亞的居民，
都要知道，
　他們憑驕傲自大的心說：
¹⁰ "磚牆塌了，
　我們卻要鑿石頭建築；
桑樹砍了，
　我們卻要換香柏樹。"
¹¹因此，耶和華要高舉利汛的敵人
　來攻擊以色列，
　並要激動以色列的仇敵。
¹²東有亞蘭人，
　西有非利士人；
　他們張口要吞吃以色列。

雖然如此，耶和華的怒氣還未轉消，
　他的手仍伸不縮。

¹³這百姓還沒有歸向擊打他們的主，
　也沒有尋求萬軍之耶和華。

they rejoice before you
　as people rejoice at the harvest,
as men rejoice
　when dividing the plunder.
⁴For as in the day of Midian's defeat,
　you have shattered
the yoke that burdens them,
　the bar across their shoulders,
　the rod of their oppressor.
⁵Every warrior's boot used in battle
　and every garment rolled in blood
will be destined for burning,
　will be fuel for the fire.
⁶For to us a child is born,
　to us a son is given,
　and the government will be on his shoulders.
And he will be called
　Wonderful Counselor,ᵃ Mighty God,
　Everlasting Father, Prince of Peace.
⁷Of the increase of his government and peace
　there will be no end.
He will reign on David's throne
　and over his kingdom,
establishing and upholding it
　with justice and righteousness
　from that time on and forever.
The zeal of the LORD Almighty
　will accomplish this.

The LORD's Anger Against Israel

⁸The Lord has sent a message against Jacob;
　it will fall on Israel.
⁹All the people will know it—
　Ephraim and the inhabitants of Samaria—
who say with pride
　and arrogance of heart,
¹⁰"The bricks have fallen down,
　but we will rebuild with dressed stone;
the fig trees have been felled,
　but we will replace them with cedars."
¹¹But the LORD has strengthened Rezin's foes
　against them
　and has spurred their enemies on.
¹²Arameans from the east and Philistines from
　the west
　have devoured Israel with open mouth.

Yet for all this, his anger is not turned away,
　his hand is still upraised.

¹³But the people have not returned to him who
　struck them,
　nor have they sought the LORD Almighty.

---

a 6 Or Wonderful, Counselor

¹⁴So the L<small>ORD</small> will cut off from Israel both head
　　and tail,
　　both palm branch and reed in a single day;
¹⁵the elders and prominent men are the head,
　　the prophets who teach lies are the tail.
¹⁶Those who guide this people mislead them,
　　and those who are guided are led astray.
¹⁷Therefore the Lord will take no pleasure in
　　the young men,
　　nor will he pity the fatherless and widows,
　for everyone is ungodly and wicked,
　　every mouth speaks vileness.

　Yet for all this, his anger is not turned away,
　　his hand is still upraised.

¹⁸Surely wickedness burns like a fire;
　　it consumes briers and thorns,
　it sets the forest thickets ablaze,
　　so that it rolls upward in a column of smoke.
¹⁹By the wrath of the L<small>ORD</small> Almighty
　　the land will be scorched
　and the people will be fuel for the fire;
　　no one will spare his brother.
²⁰On the right they will devour,
　　but still be hungry;
　on the left they will eat,
　　but not be satisfied.
　Each will feed on the flesh of his own
　　offspring^a:
²¹Manasseh will feed on Ephraim, and
　　Ephraim on Manasseh;
　together they will turn against Judah.

　Yet for all this, his anger is not turned away,
　　his hand is still upraised.

10 Woe to those who make unjust laws,
　　to those who issue oppressive decrees,
　　²to deprive the poor of their rights
　and withhold justice from the oppressed of
　　my people,
　making widows their prey
　　and robbing the fatherless.
³What will you do on the day of reckoning,
　　when disaster comes from afar?
　To whom will you run for help?
　Where will you leave your riches?
⁴Nothing will remain but to cringe among the
　　captives
　or fall among the slain.

　Yet for all this, his anger is not turned away,
　　his hand is still upraised.

^a *20 Or arm*

¹⁴因此，耶和華一日之間
　　必從以色列中剪除頭與尾、
　　棕枝與蘆葦。
¹⁵長老和尊貴人就是頭，
　　以謊言教人的先知就是尾。
¹⁶因為引導這百姓的，
　　使他們走錯了路，
　　被引導的都必敗亡。
¹⁷所以，主必不喜悅他們的少年人，
　　也不憐恤他們的孤兒寡婦。
　因為各人是褻瀆的、是行惡的，
　　並且各人的口都說愚妄的話。

　雖然如此，耶和華的怒氣還未轉消，
　　他的手仍伸不縮。

¹⁸邪惡像火焚燒，
　　燒滅荊棘和蒺藜，
　在稠密的樹林中着起來，
　　就成為煙柱，旋轉上騰。
¹⁹因萬軍之耶和華的烈怒，
　　地都燒遍，
　百姓成為火柴，
　　無人憐愛弟兄。
²⁰有人右邊搶奪，
　　仍受飢餓；
　左邊吞吃，
　　仍不飽足。
　各人吃自己膀臂上的肉。
²¹瑪拿西吞吃（註：或作"攻擊"。下同）
　　以法蓮，
　以法蓮吞吃瑪拿西，
　　又一同攻擊猶大。

　雖然如此，耶和華的怒氣還未轉消，
　　他的手仍伸不縮。

10 禍哉！那些設立不義之律例的
　　和記錄奸詐之判語的，
　　²為要屈枉窮乏人，
　奪去我民中
　　困苦人的理，
　以寡婦當作擄物，
　　以孤兒當作掠物。
³到降罰的日子，有災禍從遠方臨到。
　　那時，你們怎樣行呢？
　你們向誰逃奔求救呢？
　你們的榮耀（註：或作"財寶"）
　　存留何處呢？
⁴他們只得屈身在被擄的人以下，
　　仆倒在被殺的人以下。

　雖然如此，耶和華的怒氣還未轉消，
　　他的手仍伸不縮。

神對亞述的審判

5 "亞述是我怒氣的棍，
　　手中拿我惱恨的杖。
6 我要打發他攻擊褻瀆的國民，
　　吩咐他攻擊我所惱怒的百姓，
　　搶財為擄物，奪貨為掠物，
　　將他們踐踏，
　　像街上的泥土一樣！
7 然而，他不是這樣的意思，
　　他心也不這樣打算。
　　他心裏倒想毀滅，
　　剪除不少的國。
8 他說："我的臣僕豈不都是王嗎？
9 迦勒挪豈不像迦基米施嗎？
　　哈瑪豈不像亞珥拔嗎？
　　撒馬利亞豈不像大馬士革嗎？
10 我手已經搆到有偶像的國，
　　這些國雕刻的偶像，
　　過於耶路撒冷和撒馬利亞的偶像。
11 我怎樣待撒馬利亞和其中的偶像，
　　豈不照樣待耶路撒冷
　　和其中的偶像嗎？'"

12 主在錫安山和耶路撒冷成就他
一切工作的時候，主說："我必罰
亞述王自大的心和他高傲眼目的榮
耀。13 因為他說：

" '我所成就的事，
　　是靠我手的能力和我的智慧，
　　我本有聰明。
我挪移列國的地界，
　　搶奪他們所積蓄的財寶，
　　並且我像勇士，
　　使坐寶座的降為卑。
14 我的手搆到列國的財寶，
　　好像人搆到鳥窩；
　　我也得了全地，
　　好像人拾起所棄的雀蛋。
　　沒有動翅膀的，
　　沒有張嘴的，也沒有鳴叫的。'"

15 斧豈可向用斧砍木的自誇呢？
　　鋸豈可向用鋸的自大呢？
　　好比棍掄起那舉棍的，
　　好比杖舉起那非木的人。
16 因此，主萬軍之耶和華，
　　必使亞述王的肥壯人
　　變為瘦弱，
　　在他的榮華之下必有火着起，
　　如同焚燒一樣。
17 以色列的光必如火，
　　他的聖者必如火焰。

God's Judgment on Assyria

5"Woe to the Assyrian, the rod of my anger,
　　in whose hand is the club of my wrath!
6I send him against a godless nation,
　　I dispatch him against a people who anger me,
　　to seize loot and snatch plunder,
　　and to trample them down like mud in the
　　　streets.
7But this is not what he intends,
　　this is not what he has in mind;
　　his purpose is to destroy,
　　to put an end to many nations.
8'Are not my commanders all kings?' he says.
9　'Has not Calno fared like Carchemish?
　　Is not Hamath like Arpad,
　　and Samaria like Damascus?
10As my hand seized the kingdoms of the idols,
　　kingdoms whose images excelled those of
　　　Jerusalem and Samaria—
11shall I not deal with Jerusalem and her images
　　as I dealt with Samaria and her idols?' "

12When the Lord has finished all his work
against Mount Zion and Jerusalem, he will say,
"I will punish the king of Assyria for the willful
pride of his heart and the haughty look in his
eyes. 13For he says:

" 'By the strength of my hand I have done this,
　　and by my wisdom, because I have
　　　understanding.
I removed the boundaries of nations,
　　I plundered their treasures;
　　like a mighty one I subdued*a* their kings.
14As one reaches into a nest,
　　so my hand reached for the wealth of the
　　　nations;
　　as men gather abandoned eggs,
　　so I gathered all the countries;
　　not one flapped a wing,
　　or opened its mouth to chirp.' "

15Does the ax raise itself above him who swings it,
　　or the saw boast against him who uses it?
　　As if a rod were to wield him who lifts it up,
　　or a club brandish him who is not wood!
16Therefore, the Lord, the LORD Almighty,
　　will send a wasting disease upon his sturdy
　　　warriors;
　　under his pomp a fire will be kindled
　　like a blazing flame.
17The Light of Israel will become a fire,
　　their Holy One a flame;

a 13 Or / I subdued the mighty,

in a single day it will burn and consume
 his thorns and his briers.
¹⁸The splendor of his forests and fertile fields
 it will completely destroy,
 as when a sick man wastes away.
¹⁹And the remaining trees of his forests will be
  so few
 that a child could write them down.

The Remnant of Israel

²⁰In that day the remnant of Israel,
 the survivors of the house of Jacob,
will no longer rely on him
 who struck them down
but will truly rely on the LORD,
 the Holy One of Israel.
²¹A remnant will return,ᵃ a remnant of Jacob
 will return to the Mighty God.
²²Though your people, O Israel, be like the sand
  by the sea,
 only a remnant will return.
Destruction has been decreed,
 overwhelming and righteous.
²³The Lord, the LORD Almighty, will carry out
 the destruction decreed upon the whole land.

²⁴Therefore, this is what the Lord, the LORD
Almighty, says:

"O my people who live in Zion,
 do not be afraid of the Assyrians,
who beat you with a rod
 and lift up a club against you, as Egypt did.
²⁵Very soon my anger against you will end
 and my wrath will be directed to their
  destruction."

²⁶The LORD Almighty will lash them with a
  whip,
 as when he struck down Midian at the rock
  of Oreb;
and he will raise his staff over the waters,
 as he did in Egypt.
²⁷In that day their burden will be lifted from
  your shoulders,
 their yoke from your neck;
the yoke will be broken
 because you have grown so fat.ᵇ

²⁸They enter Aiath;
 they pass through Migron;
 they store supplies at Micmash.

在一日之間，
 將亞述王的荊棘和蒺藜焚燒淨盡。
¹⁸又將他樹林和肥田的榮耀
 全然燒盡，
 好像拿軍旗的昏過去一樣。
¹⁹他林中剩下的樹
 必稀少，
 就是孩子也能寫其數。

以色列的餘民

²⁰到那日，以色列所剩下的
 和雅各家所逃脫的，
不再倚靠
 那擊打他們的，
卻要誠實倚靠耶和華
 以色列的聖者。
²¹所剩下的，就是雅各家所剩下的，
 必歸回全能的神。
²²以色列啊，
 你的百姓雖多如海沙，
 惟有剩下的歸回。
原來滅絕的事已定，
 必有公義施行，如水漲溢。
²³因為主萬軍之耶和華在全地之中，
 必成就所定規的結局。

²⁴所以主萬軍之耶和華如此說：

"住錫安我的百姓啊，
 亞述王雖然用棍擊打你，
又照埃及的樣子舉杖攻擊你，
 你卻不要怕他。
²⁵因為還有一點點時候，
 向你們發的忿恨就要完畢，
我的怒氣要向他發作，使他滅亡。"

²⁶萬軍之耶和華
 要興起鞭來攻擊他，
 好像在俄立磐石那裏
 殺戮米甸人一樣。
耶和華的杖要向海伸出，
 把杖舉起，像在埃及一樣。
²⁷到那日，亞述王的重擔
 必離開你的肩頭，
他的軛必離開你的頸項，
 那軛也必因肥壯的緣故撐斷（註：
  或作"因膏油的緣故毀壞"）。

²⁸亞述王來到亞葉，
 經過米磯崙，
 在密抹安放輜重。

---

a 21 Hebrew *shear-jashub;* also in verse 22 *b* 27 Hebrew;
Septuagint *broken / from your shoulders*

²⁹他們過了隘口，
　在迦巴住宿。
　拉瑪人戰兢，
　掃羅的基比亞人逃跑。
³⁰迦琳的居民哪（註：“居民”原文作“女
　子”），要高聲呼喊！
　萊煞人哪，須聽！
　哀哉，困苦的亞拿突啊！
³¹瑪得米那人躲避，
　基柄的居民逃遁。
³²當那日，亞述王要在挪伯歇兵，
　向錫安女子的山，
　就是耶路撒冷的山，掄手攻他。

³³看哪，主萬軍之耶和華
　以驚嚇削去樹枝，
　長高的必被砍下，
　高大的必被伐倒。
³⁴稠密的樹林，他要用鐵器砍下；
　黎巴嫩的樹木必被大能者伐倒。

耶西的枝子

11 從耶西的本（註：原文作“不”）
必發一條，
從他根生的枝子必結果實。
²耶和華的靈必住在他身上，
　就是使他有智慧和聰明的靈、
　謀略和能力的靈、
　知識和敬畏耶和華的靈。

³他必以敬畏耶和華為樂。

　行審判不憑眼見，
　斷是非也不憑耳聞；
⁴卻要以公義審判貧窮人，
　以正直
　　判斷世上的謙卑人。
　以口中的杖
　　擊打世界；
　以嘴裏的氣
　　殺戮惡人。
⁵公義必當他的腰帶，
　信實必當他脅下的帶子。

⁶豺狼必與綿羊羔同居，
　豹子與山羊羔同臥；
　少壯獅子與牛犢並肥畜同羣；
　小孩子要牽引牠們。
⁷牛必與熊同食，
　牛犢必與小熊同臥；
　獅子必吃草與牛一樣。
⁸吃奶的孩子必玩耍在虺蛇的洞口，
　斷奶的嬰兒
　　必按手在毒蛇的穴上。

²⁹They go over the pass, and say,
　"We will camp overnight at Geba."
　Ramah trembles;
　Gibeah of Saul flees.
³⁰Cry out, O Daughter of Gallim!
　Listen, O Laishah!
　Poor Anathoth!
³¹Madmenah is in flight;
　the people of Gebim take cover.
³²This day they will halt at Nob;
　they will shake their fist
　at the mount of the Daughter of Zion,
　at the hill of Jerusalem.

³³See, the Lord, the LORD Almighty,
　will lop off the boughs with great power.
　The lofty trees will be felled,
　the tall ones will be brought low.
³⁴He will cut down the forest thickets with an ax;
　Lebanon will fall before the Mighty One.

The Branch From Jesse

11 A shoot will come up from the stump of
Jesse;
from his roots a Branch will bear fruit.
²The Spirit of the LORD will rest on him—
　the Spirit of wisdom and of understanding,
　the Spirit of counsel and of power,
　the Spirit of knowledge and of the fear of the
　　LORD—
³and he will delight in the fear of the LORD.

He will not judge by what he sees with his eyes,
　or decide by what he hears with his ears;
⁴but with righteousness he will judge the needy,
　with justice he will give decisions for the
　　poor of the earth.
He will strike the earth with the rod of his
　　mouth;
　with the breath of his lips he will slay the
　　wicked.
⁵Righteousness will be his belt
　and faithfulness the sash around his waist.

⁶The wolf will live with the lamb,
　the leopard will lie down with the goat,
　the calf and the lion and the yearling*a* together;
　and a little child will lead them.
⁷The cow will feed with the bear,
　their young will lie down together,
　and the lion will eat straw like the ox.
⁸The infant will play near the hole of the cobra,
　and the young child put his hand into the
　　viper's nest.

a 6 Hebrew; Septuagint lion will feed

⁹They will neither harm nor destroy
　　on all my holy mountain,
　for the earth will be full of the knowledge of
　　the LORD
　　as the waters cover the sea.

¹⁰In that day the Root of Jesse will stand as a
banner for the peoples; the nations will rally to
him, and his place of rest will be glorious. ¹¹In
that day the Lord will reach out his hand a second time to reclaim the remnant that is left of
his people from Assyria, from Lower Egypt, from
Upper Egypt,ᵃ from Cush,ᵇ from Elam, from
Babylonia,ᶜ from Hamath and from the islands
of the sea.

¹²He will raise a banner for the nations
　　and gather the exiles of Israel;
　he will assemble the scattered people of Judah
　　from the four quarters of the earth.
¹³Ephraim's jealousy will vanish,
　　and Judah's enemiesᵈ will be cut off;
　Ephraim will not be jealous of Judah,
　　nor Judah hostile toward Ephraim.
¹⁴They will swoop down on the slopes of
　　Philistia to the west;
　together they will plunder the people to the
　　east.
　They will lay hands on Edom and Moab,
　　and the Ammonites will be subject to them.
¹⁵The LORD will dry up
　　the gulf of the Egyptian sea;
　with a scorching wind he will sweep his hand
　　over the Euphrates River.ᵉ
　He will break it up into seven streams
　　so that men can cross over in sandals.
¹⁶There will be a highway for the remnant of his
　　people
　that is left from Assyria,
　as there was for Israel
　　when they came up from Egypt.

Songs of Praise

12 In that day you will say:

　"I will praise you, O LORD.
　Although you were angry with me,
　your anger has turned away
　　and you have comforted me.
²Surely God is my salvation;
　I will trust and not be afraid.

⁹在我聖山的遍處，
　　這一切都不傷人、不害物，
　因為認識耶和華的知識
　　要充滿遍地，
　　好像水充滿洋海一般。

¹⁰到那日，耶西的根立作萬民的
大旗，外邦人必尋求他，他安息之所
大有榮耀。¹¹當那日，主必二次伸手
救回自己百姓中所餘剩的，就是在亞
述、埃及、巴忒羅、古實、以攔、示
拿、哈馬，並眾海島所剩下的。

¹²他必向列國豎立大旗，
　　招回以色列被趕散的人，
　又從地的四方
　　聚集分散的猶大人。
¹³以法蓮的嫉妒就必消散，
　　擾害猶大的必被剪除。
　以法蓮必不嫉妒猶大，
　　猶大也不擾害以法蓮。
¹⁴他們要向西飛，
　　撲在非利士人的肩頭上（註："肩頭
　　　上"或作"西界"），
　　一同擄掠東方人，
　伸手按住以東和摩押，
　　亞捫人也必順服他們。
¹⁵耶和華必使
　　埃及海汊枯乾，
　掄手用暴熱的風
　　使大河分為七條，
　令人過去
　　不至濕腳。
¹⁶為主餘剩的百姓，
　　就是從亞述剩下回來的，
　必有一條大道，
　　如當日以色列
　　從埃及地上來一樣。

頌歌

12 到那日，你必說：

　"耶和華啊，我要稱謝你！
　因為你雖然向我發怒，
　你的怒氣卻已轉消，
　　你又安慰了我。
²看哪！神是我的拯救，
　　我要倚靠他，並不懼怕；

ᵃ 11 Hebrew *from Pathros*　　ᵇ 11 That is, the upper Nile region
ᶜ 11 Hebrew *Shinar*　　ᵈ 13 Or *hostility*　　ᵉ 15 Hebrew *the River*

因為主耶和華是我的力量，
　　是我的詩歌，
他也成了我的拯救。"
³所以，你們必從救恩的泉源
　　歡然取水。

⁴在那日，你們要說：

"當稱謝耶和華，求告他的名，
　　將他所行的
　　　　傳揚在萬民中，
　　提說他的名已被尊崇。
⁵你們要向耶和華唱歌，
　　因他所行的甚是美好！
　　但願這事普傳天下。
⁶錫安的居民哪，當揚聲歡呼，
　　因為在你們中間的以色列聖者
　　　　乃為至大。"

論巴比倫的預言

13 亞摩斯的兒子以賽亞得默
示，論巴比倫。

²應當在淨光的山豎立大旗，
　　向羣眾揚聲招手，
使他們進入
　　貴冑的門。
³我吩咐我所挑出來的人，
　　我招呼我的勇士，
就是那矜誇高傲之輩，
　　為要成就我怒中所定的。

⁴山間有多人的聲音，
　　好像是大國人民。
有許多國的民
　　聚集鬨嚷的聲音，
這是萬軍之耶和華點齊軍隊，
　　預備打仗。
⁵他們從遠方來，
　　從天邊來，
就是耶和華並他惱恨的兵器，
　　要毀滅這全地。

⁶你們要哀號，
　　因為耶和華的日子臨近了！
這日來到，好像毀滅從全能者來到。
⁷所以人手都必軟弱，
　　人心都必消化。
⁸他們必驚惶悲痛，
　　愁苦必將他們抓住。
他們疼痛，好像產難的婦人一樣，
　　彼此驚奇相看，
　　臉如火焰。

The LORD, the LORD, is my strength and my
　　song;
　he has become my salvation."
³With joy you will draw water
　from the wells of salvation.

⁴In that day you will say:

"Give thanks to the LORD, call on his name;
　make known among the nations what he has
　　done,
　and proclaim that his name is exalted.
⁵Sing to the LORD, for he has done glorious
　　things;
　let this be known to all the world.
⁶Shout aloud and sing for joy, people of Zion,
　for great is the Holy One of Israel among
　　you."

A Prophecy Against Babylon

13 An oracle concerning Babylon that Isaiah
son of Amoz saw:

²Raise a banner on a bare hilltop,
　　shout to them;
　beckon to them
　　to enter the gates of the nobles.
³I have commanded my holy ones;
　I have summoned my warriors to carry out
　　my wrath—
　those who rejoice in my triumph.

⁴Listen, a noise on the mountains,
　like that of a great multitude!
Listen, an uproar among the kingdoms,
　like nations massing together!
The LORD Almighty is mustering
　an army for war.
⁵They come from faraway lands,
　from the ends of the heavens—
the LORD and the weapons of his wrath—
　to destroy the whole country.

⁶Wail, for the day of the LORD is near;
　it will come like destruction from the
　　Almighty.ᵃ
⁷Because of this, all hands will go limp,
　every man's heart will melt.
⁸Terror will seize them,
　pain and anguish will grip them;
　they will writhe like a woman in labor.
They will look aghast at each other,
　their faces aflame.

a 6 Hebrew Shaddai

9See, the day of the LORD is coming
　　—a cruel day, with wrath and fierce anger—
　to make the land desolate
　　and destroy the sinners within it.
10The stars of heaven and their constellations
　　will not show their light.
　The rising sun will be darkened
　　and the moon will not give its light.
11I will punish the world for its evil,
　　the wicked for their sins.
　I will put an end to the arrogance of the haughty
　　and will humble the pride of the ruthless.
12I will make man scarcer than pure gold,
　　more rare than the gold of Ophir.
13Therefore I will make the heavens tremble;
　　and the earth will shake from its place
　at the wrath of the LORD Almighty,
　　in the day of his burning anger.

14Like a hunted gazelle,
　　like sheep without a shepherd,
　each will return to his own people,
　　each will flee to his native land.
15Whoever is captured will be thrust through;
　　all who are caught will fall by the sword.
16Their infants will be dashed to pieces before
　　　their eyes;
　their houses will be looted and their wives
　　ravished.

17See, I will stir up against them the Medes,
　　who do not care for silver
　and have no delight in gold.
18Their bows will strike down the young men;
　　they will have no mercy on infants
　　nor will they look with compassion on
　　　children.
19Babylon, the jewel of kingdoms,
　　the glory of the Babylonians'ᵃ pride,
　will be overthrown by God
　　like Sodom and Gomorrah.
20She will never be inhabited
　　or lived in through all generations;
　no Arab will pitch his tent there,
　　no shepherd will rest his flocks there.
21But desert creatures will lie there,
　　jackals will fill her houses;
　there the owls will dwell,
　　and there the wild goats will leap about.
22Hyenas will howl in her strongholds,
　　jackals in her luxurious palaces.
　Her time is at hand,
　　and her days will not be prolonged.

9耶和華的日子臨到，
　必有殘忍、忿恨、烈怒，
使這地荒涼，
　從其中除滅罪人。
10天上的眾星羣宿
　都不發光，
日頭一出，就變黑暗；
　月亮也不放光。
11我必因邪惡刑罰世界，
　因罪孽刑罰惡人，
使驕傲人的狂妄止息，
　制伏強暴人的狂傲。
12我必使人比精金還少，
　使人比俄斐純金更少！
13我萬軍之耶和華
　在忿恨中發烈怒的日子，
必使天震動，
　使地搖撼，離其本位。

14人必像被追趕的鹿，
　像無人收聚的羊，
各歸回本族，
　各逃到本土。
15凡被仇敵追上的，必被刺死；
　凡被捉住的，必被刀殺。
16他們的嬰孩，
　必在他們眼前摔碎；
他們的房屋，必被搶奪；
　他們的妻子，必被玷污。

17我必激動瑪代人來攻擊他們，
　瑪代人不注重銀子，
也不喜愛金子。
18他們必用弓擊碎少年人，
　不憐憫婦人所生的，
　眼也不顧惜孩子。
19巴比倫素來為列國的榮耀，
　為迦勒底人所矜誇的華美，
必像神所傾覆的所多瑪、
　蛾摩拉一樣。
20其內必永無人煙，
　世世代代無人居住，
阿拉伯人也不在那裏支搭帳棚，
　牧羊的人也不使羊羣臥在那裏。
21只有曠野的走獸臥在那裏，
　咆哮的獸滿了房屋；
鴕鳥住在那裏，
　野山羊在那裏跳舞。
22豺狼必在她宮中呼號，
　野狗必在她華美殿內吼叫。
巴比倫受罰的時候臨近，
　她的日子必不長久。

a 19 Or Chaldeans'

14

耶和華要憐恤雅各，
必再揀選以色列，
將他們安置在本地，
寄居的必與他們聯合，
緊貼雅各家。
2外邦人
必將他們帶回本土；
以色列家
必在耶和華的地上
得外邦人為僕婢，
也要擄掠先前擄掠他們的，
轄制先前欺壓他們的。

3當耶和華使你脫離愁苦、煩惱，並人勉強你做的苦工，得享安息的日子，4你必題這詩歌論巴比倫王說：

欺壓人的何竟息滅？
強暴的何竟止息？
5耶和華折斷了惡人的杖，
轄制人的圭，
6就是在忿怒中
連連攻擊眾民的，
在怒氣中轄制列國，
行逼迫無人阻止的。
7現在全地得安息、享平靜，
人皆發聲歡呼。
8松樹和黎巴嫩的香柏樹
都因你歡樂，說：
"自從你仆倒，
再無人上來砍伐我們。"

9你下到陰間，
陰間就因你震動，
來迎接你。
又因你驚動
在世曾為首領的陰魂，
並使那曾為列國君王的，
都離位站起。
10他們都要發言
對你說：
"你也變為軟弱像我們一樣嗎？
你也成了我們的樣子嗎？"
11你的威勢
和你琴瑟的聲音
都下到陰間。
你下鋪的是蟲，
上蓋的是蛆。

12明亮之星，早晨之子啊！
你何竟從天墜落？

14

The LORD will have compassion on Jacob;
once again he will choose Israel
and will settle them in their own land.
Aliens will join them
and unite with the house of Jacob.
2Nations will take them
and bring them to their own place.
And the house of Israel will possess the nations
as menservants and maidservants in the
LORD's land.
They will make captives of their captors
and rule over their oppressors.

3On the day the LORD gives you relief from suffering and turmoil and cruel bondage, 4you will take up this taunt against the king of Babylon:

How the oppressor has come to an end!
How his fury[a] has ended!
5The LORD has broken the rod of the wicked,
the scepter of the rulers,
6which in anger struck down peoples
with unceasing blows,
and in fury subdued nations
with relentless aggression.
7All the lands are at rest and at peace;
they break into singing.
8Even the pine trees and the cedars of Lebanon
exult over you and say,
"Now that you have been laid low,
no woodsman comes to cut us down."

9The grave[b] below is all astir
to meet you at your coming;
it rouses the spirits of the departed to greet
you—
all those who were leaders in the world;
it makes them rise from their thrones—
all those who were kings over the nations.
10They will all respond,
they will say to you,
"You also have become weak, as we are;
you have become like us."
11All your pomp has been brought down to the
grave,
along with the noise of your harps;
maggots are spread out beneath you
and worms cover you.

12How you have fallen from heaven,
O morning star, son of the dawn!

a 4 Dead Sea Scrolls, Septuagint and Syriac; the meaning of
the word in the Masoretic Text is uncertain.　b 9 Hebrew
Sheol; also in verses 11 and 15

You have been cast down to the earth,
　you who once laid low the nations!
¹³You said in your heart,
　"I will ascend to heaven;
　I will raise my throne
　　above the stars of God;
　I will sit enthroned on the mount of assembly,
　　on the utmost heights of the sacred
　　　mountain.ᵃ
¹⁴I will ascend above the tops of the clouds;
　I will make myself like the Most High."
¹⁵But you are brought down to the grave,
　to the depths of the pit.

¹⁶Those who see you stare at you,
　they ponder your fate:
　"Is this the man who shook the earth
　and made kingdoms tremble,
¹⁷the man who made the world a desert,
　who overthrew its cities
　and would not let his captives go home?"

¹⁸All the kings of the nations lie in state,
　each in his own tomb.
¹⁹But you are cast out of your tomb
　like a rejected branch;
you are covered with the slain,
　with those pierced by the sword,
　those who descend to the stones of the pit.
Like a corpse trampled underfoot,
²⁰　you will not join them in burial,
for you have destroyed your land
　and killed your people.

The offspring of the wicked
　will never be mentioned again.
²¹Prepare a place to slaughter his sons
　for the sins of their forefathers;
they are not to rise to inherit the land
　and cover the earth with their cities.

²²"I will rise up against them,"
　declares the LORD Almighty.
"I will cut off from Babylon her name and
　　survivors,
　her offspring and descendants,"
　　　　　declares the LORD.
²³"I will turn her into a place for owls
　and into swampland;
I will sweep her with the broom of destruction,"
declares the LORD Almighty.

你這攻敗列國的，
　何竟被砍倒在地上？
¹³你心裏曾說：
　"我要升到天上！
我要高舉我的寶座
　在神眾星以上；
我要坐在
　聚會的山上，
　在北方的極處；
¹⁴我要升到高雲之上，
　我要與至上者同等。"
¹⁵然而你必墜落陰間，
　到坑中極深之處。

¹⁶凡看見你的，都要定睛看你，
　留意看你，說：
"使大地戰抖，
　使列國震動，
¹⁷使世界如同荒野，使城邑傾覆，
　不釋放被擄的人歸家，
　是這個人嗎？"

¹⁸列國的君王
　俱各在自己陰宅的榮耀中安睡。
¹⁹惟獨你被拋棄，不得入你的墳墓，
　好像可憎的枝子；
以被殺的人為衣，
　就是被刀刺透，
　墜落坑中石頭那裏的；
你又像被踐踏的屍首一樣。
²⁰你不得與君王同葬，
　因為你敗壞你的國，
　殺戮你的民。

惡人後裔的名，
　必永不提說。
²¹先人既有罪孽，
　就要預備殺戮他的子孫，
免得他們興起來，得了遍地，
　在世上修滿城邑。

²²萬軍之耶和華說：
　"我必興起攻擊他們，
將巴比倫的名號
　和所餘剩的人，
　連子帶孫一並剪除。"
　　　　　這是耶和華說的。
²³ "我必使巴比倫為箭豬所得，
　又變為水池。
我要用滅亡的掃箒掃淨她。"
　這是萬軍之耶和華說的。

a 13 Or the north; Hebrew Zaphon

論亞述的預言

²⁴萬軍之耶和華起誓說：

"我怎樣思想，必照樣成就；
　　我怎樣定意，必照樣成立，
²⁵就是在我地上打折亞述人，
　　在我山上將他踐踏。
他加的軛必離開以色列人；
　　他加的重擔
　　必離開他們的肩頭。"

²⁶這是向全地所定的旨意，
　　這是向萬國所伸出的手。
²⁷萬軍之耶和華既然定意，
　　誰能廢棄呢？
他的手已經伸出，
　　誰能轉回呢？

論非利士的預言

²⁸亞哈斯王崩的那年，就有以下
的默示：

²⁹非利士全地啊，
　　不要因擊打你的杖折斷就喜樂。
因為從蛇的根
　　必生出毒蛇，
牠所生的，是火焰的飛龍。
³⁰貧寒人的長子必有所食；
　　窮乏人必安然躺臥。
我必以飢荒治死你的根；
　　你所餘剩的人必被殺戮。

³¹門哪，應當哀號！城哪，應當呼喊！
　　非利士全地啊，你都消化了！
因為有煙從北方出來，
　　他行伍中並無亂隊的。
³²可怎樣回答外邦的使者呢（註："外
邦"或指"非利士"）？
　　必說："耶和華建立了錫安，
　　他百姓中的困苦人
　　必投奔在其中。"

論摩押的預言

15

論摩押的默示：

一夜之間，摩押的亞珥
　　變為荒廢，歸於無有。
一夜之間，摩押的基珥變為荒廢，
　　歸於無有。
²他們上巴益，又往底本，
　　到高處去哭泣。
摩押人因尼波和米底巴哀號，
　　各人頭上光禿，
　　鬍鬚剃淨。

A Prophecy Against Assyria

²⁴The Lᴏʀᴅ Almighty has sworn,

"Surely, as I have planned, so it will be,
　　and as I have purposed, so it will stand.
²⁵I will crush the Assyrian in my land;
　　on my mountains I will trample him down.
His yoke will be taken from my people,
　　and his burden removed from their
　　　shoulders."

²⁶This is the plan determined for the whole
　　world;
　　this is the hand stretched out over all nations.
²⁷For the Lᴏʀᴅ Almighty has purposed, and
　　who can thwart him?
His hand is stretched out, and who can turn
　　it back?

A Prophecy Against the Philistines

²⁸This oracle came in the year King Ahaz
died:

²⁹Do not rejoice, all you Philistines,
　　that the rod that struck you is broken;
from the root of that snake will spring up a
　　viper,
　　its fruit will be a darting, venomous serpent.
³⁰The poorest of the poor will find pasture,
　　and the needy will lie down in safety.
But your root I will destroy by famine;
　　it will slay your survivors.

³¹Wail, O gate! Howl, O city!
　　Melt away, all you Philistines!
A cloud of smoke comes from the north,
　　and there is not a straggler in its ranks.
³²What answer shall be given
　　to the envoys of that nation?
"The Lᴏʀᴅ has established Zion,
　　and in her his afflicted people will find
　　　refuge."

A Prophecy Against Moab

15

An oracle concerning Moab:

Ar in Moab is ruined,
　　destroyed in a night!
Kir in Moab is ruined,
　　destroyed in a night!
²Dibon goes up to its temple,
　　to its high places to weep;
Moab wails over Nebo and Medeba.
Every head is shaved
　　and every beard cut off.

³In the streets they wear sackcloth;
   on the roofs and in the public squares
  they all wail,
   prostrate with weeping.
⁴Heshbon and Elealeh cry out,
   their voices are heard all the way to Jahaz.
  Therefore the armed men of Moab cry out,
   and their hearts are faint.
⁵My heart cries out over Moab;
   her fugitives flee as far as Zoar,
  as far as Eglath Shelishiyah.
  They go up the way to Luhith,
   weeping as they go;
  on the road to Horonaim
   they lament their destruction.
⁶The waters of Nimrim are dried up
   and the grass is withered;
  the vegetation is gone
   and nothing green is left.
⁷So the wealth they have acquired and stored up
   they carry away over the Ravine of the
     Poplars.
⁸Their outcry echoes along the border of Moab;
   their wailing reaches as far as Eglaim,
  their lamentation as far as Beer Elim.
⁹Dimon's*ᵃ* waters are full of blood,
   but I will bring still more upon Dimon*ᵃ* —
  a lion upon the fugitives of Moab
   and upon those who remain in the land.

16 Send lambs as tribute
   to the ruler of the land,
   from Sela, across the desert,
   to the mount of the Daughter of Zion.
²Like fluttering birds
   pushed from the nest,
  so are the women of Moab
   at the fords of the Arnon.

³"Give us counsel,
   render a decision.
  Make your shadow like night—
   at high noon.
  Hide the fugitives,
   do not betray the refugees.
⁴Let the Moabite fugitives stay with you;
   be their shelter from the destroyer."

The oppressor will come to an end,
   and destruction will cease;
  the aggressor will vanish from the land.

³他們在街市上都腰束麻布，
   在房頂上和寬闊處
     俱各哀號，
     眼淚汪汪。
⁴希實本和以利亞利悲哀的聲音
   達到雅雜，
  所以摩押帶兵器的高聲喊嚷，
   人心戰兢。
⁵我心為摩押悲哀；
   她的貴冑（註：或作"逃民"）
     逃到瑣珥，
   到伊基拉、施利施亞。
  他們上魯希坡隨走隨哭；
   在何羅念的路上，
   因毀滅舉起哀聲。
⁶因為寧林的水成為乾涸，
   青草枯乾、
   嫩草滅沒，
   青綠之物一無所有。
⁷因此，摩押人所得的財物
   和所積蓄的
   都要運過柳樹河。
⁸哀聲遍聞摩押的四境；
   哀號的聲音達到以基蓮；
   哀號的聲音達到比珥以琳。
⁹底們的水充滿了血；
   我還要加增底們的災難，
   叫獅子來追上摩押逃脫的民
   和那地上所餘剩的人。

16 你們當將羊羔奉給那地掌權的，
   從西拉往曠野，
   送到錫安城的山（註："城"原文
     作"女子"）。
²摩押的居民（註："居民"原文作"女子"）
   在亞嫩渡口，
  必像遊飛的鳥，
   如拆窩的雛。

³ "求你獻謀略、
   行公平，
  使你的影子
   在午間如黑夜，
  隱藏被趕散的人，
   不可顯露逃民。
⁴求你容我這被趕散的人和你同居。
   至於摩押，求你作她的隱密處，
   脫離滅命者的面。"

勒索人的歸於無有，
   毀滅的事止息了，
   欺壓人的從國中除滅了。

a 9 Masoretic Text; Dead Sea Scrolls, some Septuagint manuscripts and Vulgate Dibon

5必有寶座因慈愛堅立，
　　必有一位誠誠實實坐在其上，
　　在大衞帳幕中施行審判，
尋求公平，
　　速行公義。

6我們聽說摩押人驕傲，
　　是極其驕傲；
聽說她狂妄、驕傲、忿怒，
　　她誇大的話是虛空的。
7因此，摩押人必為摩押哀號，
　　人人都要哀號。
你們摩押人要為吉珥哈列設的
　　葡萄餅哀歎，極其憂傷。
8因為希實本的田地
　　和西比瑪的葡萄樹都衰殘了。
列國的君主
　　折斷其上美好的枝子；
這枝子長到雅謝
　　延到曠野，
嫩枝向外探出，
　　直探過鹽海。
9因此，我要為西比瑪的葡萄樹哀哭，
　　與雅謝人哀哭一樣。
希實本、以利亞利啊，
　　我要以眼淚澆灌你，
因為有交戰吶喊的聲音
　　臨到你夏天的果子，
並你收割的莊稼。
10從肥美的田中奪去了歡喜快樂；
　　在葡萄園裏必無歌唱，
　　也無歡呼的聲音。
踹酒的在酒醡中不得踹出酒來，
　　我使她歡呼的聲音止息。
11因此，我心腹為摩押哀鳴如琴；
　　我心腸為吉珥哈列設也是如此。
12摩押人朝見的時候，
　　在高處疲乏，
又到他聖所祈禱，也不蒙應允。

　　13這是耶和華從前論摩押的話。
14但現在耶和華說：「三年之內，照
雇工的年數，摩押的榮耀與她的羣
眾必被藐視，餘剩的人甚少無
幾。」

論大馬士革的預言

17 論大馬士革的默示：

看哪，大馬士革已被廢棄，
不再為城，必變作亂堆！
2亞羅珥的城邑已被撤棄，
　　必成為牧羊之處；

5In love a throne will be established;
　　in faithfulness a man will sit on it—
　　one from the house[a] of David—
one who in judging seeks justice
　　and speeds the cause of righteousness.

6We have heard of Moab's pride—
　　her overweening pride and conceit,
　　her pride and her insolence—
　　but her boasts are empty.
7Therefore the Moabites wail,
　　they wail together for Moab.
Lament and grieve
　　for the men[b] of Kir Hareseth.
8The fields of Heshbon wither,
　　the vines of Sibmah also.
The rulers of the nations
　　have trampled down the choicest vines,
which once reached Jazer
　　and spread toward the desert.
Their shoots spread out
　　and went as far as the sea.
9So I weep, as Jazer weeps,
　　for the vines of Sibmah.
O Heshbon, O Elealeh,
　　I drench you with tears!
The shouts of joy over your ripened fruit
　　and over your harvests have been stilled.
10Joy and gladness are taken away from the
　　orchards;
no one sings or shouts in the vineyards;
no one treads out wine at the presses,
　　for I have put an end to the shouting.
11My heart laments for Moab like a harp,
　　my inmost being for Kir Hareseth.
12When Moab appears at her high place,
　　she only wears herself out;
when she goes to her shrine to pray,
　　it is to no avail.

13This is the word the LORD has already spoken concerning Moab. 14But now the LORD says:
"Within three years, as a servant bound by contract would count them, Moab's splendor and
all her many people will be despised, and her
survivors will be very few and feeble."

An Oracle Against Damascus

17 An oracle concerning Damascus:

"See, Damascus will no longer be a city
　　but will become a heap of ruins.
2The cities of Aroer will be deserted
　　and left to flocks, which will lie down,

---

a 5 Hebrew tent　b 7 Or "raisin cakes," a wordplay

with no one to make them afraid.

³The fortified city will disappear from Ephraim,
and royal power from Damascus;
the remnant of Aram will be
like the glory of the Israelites,"
declares the LORD Almighty.

⁴"In that day the glory of Jacob will fade;
the fat of his body will waste away.

⁵It will be as when a reaper gathers the standing
grain
and harvests the grain with his arm—
as when a man gleans heads of grain
in the Valley of Rephaim.

⁶Yet some gleanings will remain,
as when an olive tree is beaten,
leaving two or three olives on the topmost
branches,
four or five on the fruitful boughs,"
declares the LORD, the God of Israel.

⁷In that day men will look to their Maker
and turn their eyes to the Holy One of Israel.

⁸They will not look to the altars,
the work of their hands,
and they will have no regard for the Asherah
poles*
and the incense altars their fingers have
made.

⁹In that day their strong cities, which they left
because of the Israelites, will be like places abandoned to thickets and undergrowth. And all will
be desolation.

¹⁰You have forgotten God your Savior;
you have not remembered the Rock, your
fortress.
Therefore, though you set out the finest plants
and plant imported vines,

¹¹though on the day you set them out, you
make them grow,
and on the morning when you plant them,
you bring them to bud,
yet the harvest will be as nothing
in the day of disease and incurable pain.

¹²Oh, the raging of many nations—
they rage like the raging sea!
Oh, the uproar of the peoples—
they roar like the roaring of great waters!

¹³Although the peoples roar like the roar of
surging waters,
when he rebukes them they flee far away,

羊在那裏躺臥，無人驚嚇。

³以法蓮不再有保障；
大馬士革不再有國權；
亞蘭所餘下的，
必像以色列人的榮耀消滅一樣。
這是萬軍之耶和華說的。

⁴"到那日，雅各的榮耀必至枵薄，
他肥胖的身體必漸瘦弱；

⁵就必像收割的人
收斂禾稼，
用手割取穗子，
又像人在利乏音谷
拾取遺落的穗子。

⁶其間所剩下的不多，
好像人打橄欖樹，
在儘上的枝梢上只剩兩三個果子，
在多果樹的旁枝上
只剩四五個果子。"
這是耶和華以色列的神說的。

⁷當那日，人必仰望造他們的主，
眼目重看以色列的聖者。

⁸他們必不仰望祭壇，
就是自己手所築的，
也不重看
自己指頭所做的，
無論是木偶、
是日像。

⁹在那日，他們的堅固城必像樹
林中和山頂上所撇棄的地方，就是從
前在以色列人面前被人撇棄的。這
樣，地就荒涼了。

¹⁰因你忘記救你的神，
不記念你能力的磐石，
所以，
你栽上佳美的樹秧子，
插上異樣的栽子，

¹¹栽種的日子，
你周圍圈上籬笆，
又到早晨
使你所種的開花，
但在愁苦極其傷痛的日子，
所收割的都飛去了。

¹²唉！多民鬨嚷，
好像海浪匉訇；
列邦奔騰，
好像猛水滔滔，

¹³列邦奔騰，
好像多水滔滔；
但神斥責他們，他們就遠遠逃避，

---

a 8 That is, symbols of the goddess Asherah

又被追趕，如同山上的風前糠，
　　又如暴風前的旋風土。
14到晚上有驚嚇，
　　未到早晨他們就沒有了。
這是擄掠我們之人所得的分，
　　是搶奪我們之人的報應！

論古實的預言

18 唉！古實河外
　　翅膀刷刷響聲之地，
2差遣使者在水面上，
　　坐蒲草船過海。

先知說："你們快行的使者，
　　要到高大光滑的民那裏去。
自從開國以來，那民極其可畏，
　　是分地界踐踏人的，
　　他們的地有江河分開。"

3世上一切的居民
　　和地上所住的人哪，
山上豎立大旗的時候，
　　你們要看！
吹角的時候，
　　你們要聽！
4耶和華對我這樣說：
　　"我要安靜，
　　在我的居所觀看，
如同日光中的清熱，
　　又如露水的雲霧在收割的熱天。"
5收割之先，
　　花開已謝，
　　花也成了將熟的葡萄；
他必用鐮刀
　　削去嫩枝，
　　又砍掉蔓延的枝條。
6都要撇給山間的鷙鳥
　　和地上的野獸。
夏天鷙鳥要宿在其上；
　　冬天野獸都臥在其中。

7到那時，

這高大光滑的民，
　　就是從開國以來極其可畏、
分地界踐踏人的，
　　他們的地有江河分開。

他們必將禮物奉給萬軍之耶和華，
就是奉到錫安山，耶和華安置他名
的地方。

driven before the wind like chaff on the hills,
　　like tumbleweed before a gale.
14In the evening, sudden terror!
　　Before the morning, they are gone!
This is the portion of those who loot us,
　　the lot of those who plunder us.

A Prophecy Against Cush

18 Woe to the land of whirring wings[a]
　　along the rivers of Cush,[b]
2which sends envoys by sea
　　in papyrus boats over the water.

Go, swift messengers,
　　to a people tall and smooth-skinned,
　　to a people feared far and wide,
an aggressive nation of strange speech,
　　whose land is divided by rivers.

3All you people of the world,
　　you who live on the earth,
when a banner is raised on the mountains,
　　you will see it,
and when a trumpet sounds,
　　you will hear it.
4This is what the LORD says to me:
　　"I will remain quiet and will look on from
　　　　my dwelling place,
like shimmering heat in the sunshine,
　　like a cloud of dew in the heat of harvest."
5For, before the harvest, when the blossom is
　　gone
and the flower becomes a ripening grape,
　　he will cut off the shoots with pruning knives,
　　and cut down and take away the spreading
　　　　branches.
6They will all be left to the mountain birds of prey
　　and to the wild animals;
the birds will feed on them all summer,
　　the wild animals all winter.

7At that time gifts will be brought to the LORD
Almighty

from a people tall and smooth-skinned,
　　from a people feared far and wide,
an aggressive nation of strange speech,
　　whose land is divided by rivers—

the gifts will be brought to Mount Zion, the
place of the Name of the LORD Almighty.

a 1 Or of locusts   b 1 That is, the upper Nile region

A Prophecy About Egypt

19 An oracle concerning Egypt:

See, the LORD rides on a swift cloud
and is coming to Egypt.
The idols of Egypt tremble before him,
and the hearts of the Egyptians melt within
them.
2 "I will stir up Egyptian against Egyptian—
brother will fight against brother,
neighbor against neighbor,
city against city,
kingdom against kingdom.
3 The Egyptians will lose heart,
and I will bring their plans to nothing;
they will consult the idols and the spirits of
the dead,
the mediums and the spiritists.
4 I will hand the Egyptians over
to the power of a cruel master,
and a fierce king will rule over them,"
declares the Lord, the LORD Almighty.

5 The waters of the river will dry up,
and the riverbed will be parched and dry.
6 The canals will stink;
the streams of Egypt will dwindle and dry
up.
The reeds and rushes will wither,
7 also the plants along the Nile,
at the mouth of the river.
Every sown field along the Nile
will become parched, will blow away and be
no more.
8 The fishermen will groan and lament,
all who cast hooks into the Nile;
those who throw nets on the water
will pine away.
9 Those who work with combed flax will despair,
the weavers of fine linen will lose hope.
10 The workers in cloth will be dejected,
and all the wage earners will be sick at heart.

11 The officials of Zoan are nothing but fools;
the wise counselors of Pharaoh give
senseless advice.
How can you say to Pharaoh,
"I am one of the wise men,
a disciple of the ancient kings"?

12 Where are your wise men now?
Let them show you and make known
what the LORD Almighty
has planned against Egypt.

論埃及的預言

19 論埃及的默示：

看哪！耶和華乘駕快雲，
臨到埃及。
埃及的偶像在他面前戰兢；
埃及人的心在裏面消化。
2 "我必激動埃及人攻擊埃及人，
弟兄攻擊弟兄，
鄰舍攻擊鄰舍，
這城攻擊那城，
這國攻擊那國。
3 埃及人的心神必在裏面耗盡，
我必敗壞他們的謀略。
他們必求問
偶像和念咒的、
交鬼的、行巫術的。
4 我必將埃及人
交在殘忍主的手中，
強暴王必轄制他們。"
這是主萬軍之耶和華說的。

5 海中的水必絕盡，
河也消沒乾涸，
6 江河要變臭，
埃及的河水
都必減少枯乾，
葦子和蘆荻都必衰殘。
7 靠尼羅河旁的草田，
並沿尼羅河所種的田
都必枯乾。
莊稼被風吹去，
歸於無有。
8 打魚的必哀哭，
在尼羅河一切釣魚的必悲傷，
在水上撒網的
必都衰弱。
9 用梳好的麻造物的和織白布的
都必羞愧。
10 國柱必被打碎，
所有傭工的，心必愁煩。

11 瑣安的首領極其愚昧；
法老大有智慧的謀士所籌劃的
成為愚謀。
你們怎敢對法老說：
"我是智慧人的子孫，
我是古王的後裔"？

12 你的智慧人在哪裏呢？
萬軍之耶和華
向埃及所定的旨意，
他們可以知道，可以告訴你吧！

¹³瑣安的首領都變為愚昧，
　　挪弗的首領都受了迷惑；
　　當埃及支派房角石的，
　　　　使埃及人走錯了路。
¹⁴耶和華使乖謬的靈攙入埃及中間，
　　首領使埃及一切所做的都有差錯，
　　好像醉酒之人嘔吐的時候，
　　東倒西歪一樣。
¹⁵埃及中無論是頭與尾，棕枝與蘆葦，
　　所做之工都不成就。

¹⁶到那日，埃及人必像婦人一樣，他們必因萬軍之耶和華在埃及以上所掄的手戰兢懼怕。¹⁷猶大地必使埃及驚恐。向誰提起猶大地，誰就懼怕。這是因萬軍之耶和華向埃及所定的旨意。

¹⁸當那日，埃及地必有五城的人說迦南的方言，又指着萬軍之耶和華起誓。有一城，必稱為滅亡城。

¹⁹當那日，在埃及地中必有為耶和華築的一座壇；在埃及的邊界上必有為耶和華立的一根柱。²⁰這都要在埃及地為萬軍之耶和華作記號和證據。埃及人因為受人的欺壓哀求耶和華，他就差遣一位救主作護衛者，拯救他們。²¹耶和華必被埃及人所認識，在那日，埃及人必認識耶和華，也要獻祭物和供物敬拜他，並向耶和華許願還願。²²耶和華必擊打埃及，又擊打又醫治，埃及人就歸向耶和華。他必應允他們的禱告，醫治他們。

²³當那日，必有從埃及通亞述去的大道，亞述人要進入埃及，埃及人也進入亞述，埃及人要與亞述人一同敬拜耶和華。²⁴當那日以色列必與埃及、亞述三國一律，使地上的人得福，²⁵因為萬軍之耶和華賜福給他們，說："埃及我的百姓，亞述我手的工作，以色列我的產業，都有福了！"

論埃及與古實的預言

20 亞述王撒珥根打發他珥探到亞實突的那年，他珥探就攻打亞實突，將城攻取。²那

¹³The officials of Zoan have become fools,
　　the leaders of Memphis^a are deceived;
　　the cornerstones of her peoples
　　have led Egypt astray.
¹⁴The LORD has poured into them
　　a spirit of dizziness;
　　they make Egypt stagger in all that she does,
　　as a drunkard staggers around in his vomit.
¹⁵There is nothing Egypt can do—
　　head or tail, palm branch or reed.

¹⁶In that day the Egyptians will be like women. They will shudder with fear at the uplifted hand that the LORD Almighty raises against them. ¹⁷And the land of Judah will bring terror to the Egyptians; everyone to whom Judah is mentioned will be terrified, because of what the LORD Almighty is planning against them.

¹⁸In that day five cities in Egypt will speak the language of Canaan and swear allegiance to the LORD Almighty. One of them will be called the City of Destruction.^b

¹⁹In that day there will be an altar to the LORD in the heart of Egypt, and a monument to the LORD at its border. ²⁰It will be a sign and witness to the LORD Almighty in the land of Egypt. When they cry out to the LORD because of their oppressors, he will send them a savior and defender, and he will rescue them. ²¹So the LORD will make himself known to the Egyptians, and in that day they will acknowledge the LORD. They will worship with sacrifices and grain offerings; they will make vows to the LORD and keep them. ²²The LORD will strike Egypt with a plague; he will strike them and heal them. They will turn to the LORD, and he will respond to their pleas and heal them.

²³In that day there will be a highway from Egypt to Assyria. The Assyrians will go to Egypt and the Egyptians to Assyria. The Egyptians and Assyrians will worship together. ²⁴In that day Israel will be the third, along with Egypt and Assyria, a blessing on the earth. ²⁵The LORD Almighty will bless them, saying, "Blessed be Egypt my people, Assyria my handiwork, and Israel my inheritance."

A Prophecy Against Egypt and Cush

20 In the year that the supreme commander, sent by Sargon king of Assyria, came to Ashdod and attacked and captured it— ²at that time the LORD spoke through

---

a 13 Hebrew *Noph*　　*b 18* Most manuscripts of the Masoretic Text; some manuscripts of the Masoretic Text, Dead Sea Scrolls and Vulgate *City of the Sun* (that is, Heliopolis)

Isaiah son of Amoz. He said to him, "Take off the sackcloth from your body and the sandals from your feet." And he did so, going around stripped and barefoot.

³Then the LORD said, "Just as my servant Isaiah has gone stripped and barefoot for three years, as a sign and portent against Egypt and Cush,ᵃ ⁴so the king of Assyria will lead away stripped and barefoot the Egyptian captives and Cushite exiles, young and old, with buttocks bared—to Egypt's shame. ⁵Those who trusted in Cush and boasted in Egypt will be afraid and put to shame. ⁶In that day the people who live on this coast will say, 'See what has happened to those we relied on, those we fled to for help and deliverance from the king of Assyria! How then can we escape?' "

A Prophecy Against Babylon

21 An oracle concerning the Desert by the Sea:

Like whirlwinds sweeping through the
    southland,
an invader comes from the desert,
    from a land of terror.

²A dire vision has been shown to me:
    The traitor betrays, the looter takes loot.
Elam, attack! Media, lay siege!
    I will bring to an end all the groaning she
    caused.

³At this my body is racked with pain,
    pangs seize me, like those of a woman in
    labor;
I am staggered by what I hear,
    I am bewildered by what I see.
⁴My heart falters,
    fear makes me tremble;
the twilight I longed for
    has become a horror to me.

⁵They set the tables,
    they spread the rugs,
    they eat, they drink!
Get up, you officers,
    oil the shields!

⁶This is what the Lord says to me:

"Go, post a lookout
    and have him report what he sees.

時，耶和華曉諭亞摩斯的兒子以賽亞說："你去解掉你腰間的麻布，脫下你腳上的鞋。"以賽亞就這樣做，露身赤腳行走。

³耶和華說："我僕人以賽亞怎樣露身赤腳行走三年，作為關乎埃及和古實的預兆奇蹟，⁴照樣，亞述王也必擄去埃及人，掠去古實人，無論老少，都露身赤腳，現出下體，使埃及蒙羞。⁵以色列人必因所仰望的古實，所誇耀的埃及，驚惶羞愧。⁶那時，這沿海一帶的居民必說：'看哪，我們素所仰望的，就是我們為脫離亞述王逃往求救的，不過是如此！我們怎能逃脫呢？'"

論巴比倫的預言

21 論海旁曠野的默示：

有仇敵從曠野，
    從可怕之地而來，
好像南方的旋風，
    猛然掃過。

²令人悽慘的異象已默示於我：
    詭詐的行詭詐，毀滅的行毀滅。
以攔哪，你要上去！
    瑪代啊，你要圍困！
主說："我使一切歎息止住。"

³所以我滿腰疼痛，
    痛苦將我抓住，
好像產難的婦人一樣。
我疼痛甚至不能聽，
    我驚惶甚至不能看。
⁴我心慌張，
    驚恐威嚇我。
我所羨慕的黃昏
    變為我的戰兢。

⁵他們擺設筵席，
    派人守望，
    又吃又喝。
首領啊！你們起來，
    用油抹盾牌。

⁶主對我如此說：

"你去設立守望的，
    使他將所看見的述說。

ᵃ 3 That is, the upper Nile region; also in verse 5

7他看見軍隊，
　　就是騎馬的一對一對地來，
又看見驢隊、
　　駱駝隊，
　　就要側耳細聽。"

8他像獅子吼叫，說：

"主啊，
　　我日日常站在望樓上，
整夜立在我守望所。
9看哪，有一隊軍兵騎着馬
　　一對一對地來。
他就說：
　　'巴比倫傾倒了！傾倒了！
他一切雕刻的神像
　　都打碎於地！'"

10我被打的禾稼，我場上的穀啊，
　　我從萬軍之耶和華
　　以色列的神那裏所聽見的，
　　都告訴你們了。

論以東的預言
11論度瑪的默示：

有人聲從西珥呼問我說：
　　"守望的啊，夜裏如何？
　　守望的啊，夜裏如何？"
12守望的說：
　　"早晨將到，黑夜也來。
你們若要問就可以問，
　　可以回頭再來。"

論阿拉伯的預言
13論阿拉伯的默示：

底但結伴的客旅啊，
　　你們必在阿拉伯的樹林中住宿。
14提瑪地的居民拿水來，
　　送給口渴的，
拿餅來迎接逃避的。
15因為他們逃避刀劍
　　和出了鞘的刀，
並上了弦的弓
　　與刀兵的重災。

16主對我這樣說："一年之內，
照雇工的年數，基達的一切榮耀必
歸於無有；17弓箭手所餘剩的，就是

7When he sees chariots
　　with teams of horses,
riders on donkeys
　　or riders on camels,
let him be alert,
　　fully alert."

8And the lookout[a] shouted,

"Day after day, my lord, I stand on the
　　watchtower;
every night I stay at my post.
9Look, here comes a man in a chariot
　　with a team of horses.
And he gives back the answer:
　　'Babylon has fallen, has fallen!
All the images of its gods
　　lie shattered on the ground!' "

10O my people, crushed on the threshing floor,
　　I tell you what I have heard
from the LORD Almighty,
　　from the God of Israel.

A Prophecy Against Edom
11An oracle concerning Dumah[b]:

Someone calls to me from Seir,
　　"Watchman, what is left of the night?
　　Watchman, what is left of the night?"
12The watchman replies,
　　"Morning is coming, but also the night.
If you would ask, then ask;
　　and come back yet again."

A Prophecy Against Arabia
13An oracle concerning Arabia:

You caravans of Dedanites,
　　who camp in the thickets of Arabia,
14 bring water for the thirsty;
you who live in Tema,
　　bring food for the fugitives.
15They flee from the sword,
　　from the drawn sword,
from the bent bow
　　and from the heat of battle.

16This is what the Lord says to me: "Within
one year, as a servant bound by contract would
count it, all the pomp of Kedar will come to an
end. 17The survivors of the bowmen, the war-

---

a 8 Dead Sea Scrolls and Syriac; Masoretic Text A lion
b 11 Dumah means silence or stillness, a wordplay on Edom.

riors of Kedar, will be few." The LORD, the God of Israel, has spoken.

A Prophecy About Jerusalem

22 An oracle concerning the Valley of Vision:

What troubles you now,
    that you have all gone up on the roofs,
2O town full of commotion,
    O city of tumult and revelry?
    Your slain were not killed by the sword,
    nor did they die in battle.
3All your leaders have fled together;
    they have been captured without using the bow.
    All you who were caught were taken prisoner together,
    having fled while the enemy was still far away.
4Therefore I said, "Turn away from me;
    let me weep bitterly.
Do not try to console me
    over the destruction of my people."

5The Lord, the LORD Almighty, has a day
    of tumult and trampling and terror
    in the Valley of Vision,
a day of battering down walls
    and of crying out to the mountains.
6Elam takes up the quiver,
    with her charioteers and horses;
    Kir uncovers the shield.
7Your choicest valleys are full of chariots,
    and horsemen are posted at the city gates;
8   the defenses of Judah are stripped away.

And you looked in that day
    to the weapons in the Palace of the Forest;
9you saw that the City of David
    had many breaches in its defenses;
you stored up water
    in the Lower Pool.
10You counted the buildings in Jerusalem
    and tore down houses to strengthen the wall.
11You built a reservoir between the two walls
    for the water of the Old Pool,
but you did not look to the One who made it,
    or have regard for the One who planned it long ago.

12The Lord, the LORD Almighty,
    called you on that day
to weep and to wail,
    to tear out your hair and put on sackcloth.

基達人的勇士，必然稀少。"因為這是耶和華以色列的神說的。

論耶路撒冷的預言

22 論異象谷的默示：

有甚麼事使你這滿城的人
    都上房頂呢？
2你這滿處吶喊、大有喧嘩的城，
    歡樂的邑啊，
    你中間被殺的，並不是被刀殺，
    也不是因打仗死亡。
3你所有的官長
    一同逃跑，
    都為弓箭手所捆綁。
你中間一切被找到的，
    都一同被捆綁，
    他們本是逃往遠方的。

4所以我說："你們轉眼不看我，
    我要痛哭，
不要因我眾民（註：原文作"民女"）的
    毀滅，就竭力安慰我。"

5因為主萬軍之耶和華
    使異象谷有潰亂、
    踐踏、煩擾的日子。
城被攻破，
    哀聲達到山間。
6以攔帶着箭袋，
    還有坐戰車的和馬兵；
    吉珥揭開盾牌。
7你嘉美的谷遍滿戰車，
    也有馬兵在城門前排列。
8他去掉猶大的遮蓋。

那日，
    你就仰望林庫內的軍器。
9你們看見
    大衛城的破口很多，
    便聚積下池的水；
10又數點耶路撒冷的房屋，
    將房屋拆毀，修補城牆；
11又在兩道城牆中間挖一個聚水池，
    可盛舊池的水；
卻不仰望做這事的主，
    也不顧念從古定這事的。

12當那日，主萬軍之耶和華
    叫人哭泣哀號，
頭上光禿，
    身披麻布。

¹³誰知，人倒歡喜快樂，
　　宰牛殺羊，
　　吃肉喝酒，
　　說：“我們吃喝吧！
　　因為明天要死了。”

¹⁴萬軍之耶和華親自默示我說：“這罪孽直到你們死，斷不得赦免！”這是主萬軍之耶和華說的。

¹⁵主萬軍之耶和華這樣說：

“你去見掌銀庫的，
　　就是家宰舍伯那，對他說：
¹⁶你在這裏
　　做甚麼呢？
　有甚麼人竟在這裏鑿墳墓，
　就是在高處為自己鑿墳墓，
　在磐石中為自己鑿出安身之所？

¹⁷“看哪，耶和華必像大有力的人，
　　將你緊緊纏裹，
　　竭力拋去。
¹⁸他必將你滾成一團，
　　拋在寬闊之地，好像拋球一樣。
　你這主人家的羞辱，
　　必在那裏坐你榮耀的車，
　　也必在那裏死亡。
¹⁹我必趕逐你離開官職，
　　你必從你的原位撤下。

²⁰“到那日，我必召我僕人希勒家的兒子以利亞敬來，²¹將你的外袍給他穿上，將你的腰帶給他繫緊，將你的政權交在他手中，他必作耶路撒冷居民和猶大家的父。²²我必將大衛家的鑰匙放在他肩頭上，他開，無人能關；他關，無人能開。²³我必將他安穩，像釘子釘在堅固處。他必作為他父家榮耀的寶座。²⁴他父家所有的榮耀，連兒女帶子孫，都掛在他身上，好像一切小器皿，從杯子到酒瓶掛上一樣。”

²⁵萬軍之耶和華說：“當那日，釘在堅固處的釘子必壓斜，被砍斷落地；掛在其上的重擔必被剪斷。”因為這是耶和華說的。

---

¹³But see, there is joy and revelry,
　　slaughtering of cattle and killing of sheep,
　　eating of meat and drinking of wine!
　“Let us eat and drink,” you say,
　　“for tomorrow we die!”

¹⁴The Lord Almighty has revealed this in my hearing: “Till your dying day this sin will not be atoned for,” says the Lord, the Lord Almighty.

¹⁵This is what the Lord, the Lord Almighty, says:

　“Go, say to this steward,
　　to Shebna, who is in charge of the palace:
¹⁶What are you doing here and who gave you permission
　to cut out a grave for yourself here,
　hewing your grave on the height
　　and chiseling your resting place in the rock?

¹⁷“Beware, the Lord is about to take firm hold of you
　　and hurl you away, O you mighty man.
¹⁸He will roll you up tightly like a ball
　　and throw you into a large country.
　There you will die
　　and there your splendid chariots will remain—
　　you disgrace to your master’s house!
¹⁹I will depose you from your office,
　　and you will be ousted from your position.

²⁰“In that day I will summon my servant, Eliakim son of Hilkiah. ²¹I will clothe him with your robe and fasten your sash around him and hand your authority over to him. He will be a father to those who live in Jerusalem and to the house of Judah. ²²I will place on his shoulder the key to the house of David; what he opens no one can shut, and what he shuts no one can open. ²³I will drive him like a peg into a firm place; he will be a seat[a] of honor for the house of his father. ²⁴All the glory of his family will hang on him: its offspring and offshoots—all its lesser vessels, from the bowls to all the jars.

²⁵“In that day,” declares the Lord Almighty, “the peg driven into the firm place will give way; it will be sheared off and will fall, and the load hanging on it will be cut down.” The Lord has spoken.

---

^a 23 Or *throne*

A Prophecy About Tyre

23 An oracle concerning Tyre:

Wail, O ships of Tarshish!
  For Tyre is destroyed
    and left without house or harbor.
  From the land of Cyprus[a]
    word has come to them.

[2]Be silent, you people of the island
  and you merchants of Sidon,
    whom the seafarers have enriched.
[3]On the great waters
  came the grain of the Shihor;
  the harvest of the Nile[b] was the revenue of
    Tyre,
  and she became the marketplace of the
    nations.

[4]Be ashamed, O Sidon, and you, O fortress of
    the sea,
  for the sea has spoken:
"I have neither been in labor nor given birth;
  I have neither reared sons nor brought up
    daughters."
[5]When word comes to Egypt,
  they will be in anguish at the report from
    Tyre.

[6]Cross over to Tarshish;
  wail, you people of the island.
[7]Is this your city of revelry,
  the old, old city,
  whose feet have taken her
    to settle in far-off lands?
[8]Who planned this against Tyre,
  the bestower of crowns,
  whose merchants are princes,
  whose traders are renowned in the earth?
[9]The LORD Almighty planned it,
  to bring low the pride of all glory
  and to humble all who are renowned on the
    earth.

[10]Till[c] your land as along the Nile,
  O Daughter of Tarshish,
  for you no longer have a harbor.
[11]The LORD has stretched out his hand over the
    sea
  and made its kingdoms tremble.

---

*a 1 Hebrew Kittim   b 2,3 Masoretic Text; one Dead Sea Scroll
Sidon, / who cross over the sea; / your envoys ³Ware on the great
waters. / The grain of the Shihor, / the harvest of the Nile,
c 10 Dead Sea Scrolls and some Septuagint manuscripts;
Masoretic Text Go through*

論推羅的預言

23 論推羅的默示：

他施的船隻都要哀號，
  因為推羅變為荒場，
甚至沒有房屋，
  沒有可進之路。
這消息是從基提地得來的。

[2]沿海的居民，就是素來
    靠航海西頓的商家得豐盛的，
  你們當靜默無言。
[3]在大水之上，
  西曷的糧食、
  尼羅河的莊稼
  是推羅的進項，
  他作列國的大碼頭。

[4]西頓哪，你當慚愧！
  因為大海說，
  就是海中的保障說：
"我沒有劬勞，也沒有生產，
  沒有養育男子，
  也沒有撫養童女。"
[5]這風聲傳到埃及，
  埃及人為推羅的風聲
    極其疼痛。

[6]推羅人哪，你們當過到他施去。
  沿海的居民哪，你們都當哀號！
[7]這是你們歡樂的城，
  從上古而有的嗎？
其中的居民
  往遠方寄居。
[8]推羅本是賜冠冕的，
  她的商家是王子，
  她的買賣人是世上的尊貴人。
  遭遇如此，是誰定的呢？
[9]是萬軍之耶和華所定的！
  為要污辱一切高傲的榮耀，
  使地上一切的尊貴人被藐視。

[10]他施的民哪（註："民"原文作"女"），
  可以流行你的地，好像尼羅河，
  不再有腰帶拘緊你。
[11]耶和華已經
  向海伸手，
  震動列國。

至於迦南，
　　他已經吩咐拆毀其中的保障。
12他又說：「受欺壓西頓的居民哪
　　（註：「居民」原文作「處女」），
　　你必不得再歡樂。
起來！過到基提去，
　　就是在那裏也不得安歇。」
13看哪，
　　迦勒底人之地向來沒有這民，
這國是亞述人
　　為住曠野的人所立的。
現在他們建築戍樓，
　　拆毀推羅的宮殿，
　　使她成為荒涼。

14他施的船隻都要哀號，
　　因為你們的保障變為荒場。

15到那時，推羅必被忘記七十
年，照着一王的年日。七十年後，
推羅的景況必像妓女所唱的歌：

16「你這被忘記的妓女啊，
　　拿琴周流城內，
巧彈多唱，
　　使人再想念你。」

17七十年後，耶和華必眷顧推
羅，她就仍得利息（註：原文作「雇
價」，下同），與地上的萬國交易（註：
原文作「行淫」）。18她的貨財和利息要
歸耶和華為聖，必不積攢存留，因
為她的貨財必為住在耶和華面前的
人所得，使他們吃飽，穿耐久的衣
服。

主使大地荒涼

24 看哪，
　　耶和華使地空虛，
　　　　變為荒涼；
又翻轉大地，
　　將居民分散。
2那時
　　百姓怎樣，祭司也怎樣；
　　僕人怎樣，主人也怎樣；
　　婢女怎樣，主母也怎樣；
　　買物的怎樣，賣物的也怎樣；
　　放債的怎樣，借債的也怎樣；
　　取利的怎樣，出利的也怎樣。
3地必全然空虛，
　　盡都荒涼。
　　　　因為這話是耶和華說的。

He has given an order concerning Phoenicia[a]
　　that her fortresses be destroyed.
12He said, "No more of your reveling,
　　O Virgin Daughter of Sidon, now crushed!

"Up, cross over to Cyprus[b];
　　even there you will find no rest."
13Look at the land of the Babylonians,[c]
　　this people that is now of no account!
The Assyrians have made it
　　a place for desert creatures;
they raised up their siege towers,
　　they stripped its fortresses bare
　　and turned it into a ruin.

14Wail, you ships of Tarshish;
　　your fortress is destroyed!

15At that time Tyre will be forgotten for seventy years, the span of a king's life. But at the end of these seventy years, it will happen to Tyre as in the song of the prostitute:

16"Take up a harp, walk through the city,
　　O prostitute forgotten;
play the harp well, sing many a song,
　　so that you will be remembered."

17At the end of seventy years, the LORD will deal with Tyre. She will return to her hire as a prostitute and will ply her trade with all the kingdoms on the face of the earth. 18Yet her profit and her earnings will be set apart for the LORD; they will not be stored up or hoarded. Her profits will go to those who live before the LORD, for abundant food and fine clothes.

The LORD's Devastation of the Earth

24 See, the LORD is going to lay waste the earth
　　and devastate it;
he will ruin its face
　　and scatter its inhabitants—
2it will be the same
　　for priest as for people,
　　for master as for servant,
　　for mistress as for maid,
　　for seller as for buyer,
　　for borrower as for lender,
　　for debtor as for creditor.
3The earth will be completely laid waste
　　and totally plundered.
　　　　The LORD has spoken this word.

a 11 Hebrew Canaan　　b 12 Hebrew Kittim　　c 13 Or Chaldeans

⁴The earth dries up and withers,
　　the world languishes and withers,
　　the exalted of the earth languish.
⁵The earth is defiled by its people;
　　they have disobeyed the laws,
　　violated the statutes
　　and broken the everlasting covenant.
⁶Therefore a curse consumes the earth;
　　its people must bear their guilt.
　　Therefore earth's inhabitants are burned up,
　　and very few are left.
⁷The new wine dries up and the vine withers;
　　all the merrymakers groan.
⁸The gaiety of the tambourines is stilled,
　　the noise of the revelers has stopped,
　　the joyful harp is silent.
⁹No longer do they drink wine with a song;
　　the beer is bitter to its drinkers.
¹⁰The ruined city lies desolate;
　　the entrance to every house is barred.
¹¹In the streets they cry out for wine;
　　all joy turns to gloom,
　　all gaiety is banished from the earth.
¹²The city is left in ruins,
　　its gate is battered to pieces.
¹³So will it be on the earth
　　and among the nations,
　　as when an olive tree is beaten,
　　or as when gleanings are left after the grape
　　　　harvest.

¹⁴They raise their voices, they shout for joy;
　　from the west they acclaim the LORD's
　　　　majesty.
¹⁵Therefore in the east give glory to the LORD;
　　exalt the name of the LORD, the God of Israel,
　　in the islands of the sea.
¹⁶From the ends of the earth we hear singing:
　　"Glory to the Righteous One."

But I said, "I waste away, I waste away!
　　Woe to me!
The treacherous betray!
　　With treachery the treacherous betray!"
¹⁷Terror and pit and snare await you,
　　O people of the earth.
¹⁸Whoever flees at the sound of terror
　　will fall into a pit;
whoever climbs out of the pit
　　will be caught in a snare.

The floodgates of the heavens are opened,
　　the foundations of the earth shake.
¹⁹The earth is broken up,
　　the earth is split asunder,
　　the earth is thoroughly shaken.

⁴地上悲哀衰殘，
　　世界敗落衰殘，
　　地上居高位的人也敗落了。
⁵地被其上的居民污穢，
　　因為他們犯了律法，
　　廢了律例，
　　背了永約。
⁶所以地被咒詛吞滅，
　　住在其上的顯為有罪。
　　地上的居民被火焚燒，
　　剩下的人稀少。
⁷新酒悲哀，葡萄樹衰殘；
　　心中歡樂的俱都歎息。
⁸擊鼓之樂止息，
　　宴樂人的聲音完畢，
　　彈琴之樂也止息了。
⁹人必不得飲酒唱歌；
　　喝濃酒的，必以為苦。
¹⁰荒涼的城拆毀了，各家關門閉戶，
　　使人都不得進去。
¹¹在街上因酒有悲歎的聲音，
　　一切喜樂變為昏暗，
　　地上的歡樂歸於無有。
¹²城中只有荒涼，
　　城門拆毀淨盡。
¹³在地上的
　　萬民中，
　　必像打過的橄欖樹，
　　又像已摘的葡萄
　　所剩無幾。

¹⁴這些人要高聲歡呼，
　　他們為耶和華的威嚴，
　　從海那裏揚起聲來。
¹⁵因此，你們要在東方榮耀耶和華，
　　在眾海島榮耀耶和華
　　以色列神的名。
¹⁶我們聽見從地極有人歌唱，說：
　　"榮耀歸於義人。"

我卻說："我消滅了，我消滅了，
　　我有禍了！
詭詐的行詭詐，
　　詭詐的大行詭詐！"
¹⁷地上的居民哪，
　　恐懼、陷坑、網羅都臨近你。
¹⁸躲避恐懼聲音的
　　必墜入陷坑；
從陷坑上來的
　　必被網羅纏住。

因為天上的窗戶都開了，
　　地的根基也震動了。
¹⁹地全然破壞，
　　盡都崩裂，
　　大大地震動了。

20地要東倒西歪，好像醉酒的人；
　又搖來搖去，好像吊牀。
罪過在其上沉重，
　必然塌陷，不能復起。

21到那日，耶和華在高處
　必懲罰高處的眾軍，
　在地上必懲罰地上的列王。
22他們必被聚集，
　像囚犯被聚在牢獄中，
　並要囚在監牢裏，
　多日之後便被討罪（註：或作“眷顧”）。
23那時，月亮要蒙羞，日頭要慚愧。
　因為萬軍之耶和華必在錫安山、
　在耶路撒冷作王，
　在敬畏他的長老面前必有榮耀。

讚美主

25 耶和華啊，你是我的神，
　我要尊崇你，
　我要稱讚你的名！
因為你以忠信誠實行過奇妙的事，
　成就你古時所定的。
2你使城變為亂堆，
　使堅固城變為荒場，
　使外邦人宮殿的城不再為城，
　永遠不再建造。
3所以，剛強的民必榮耀你，
　強暴之國的城必敬畏你。
4因為當強暴人催逼人的時候，
　如同暴風直吹牆壁，
　你就作貧窮人的保障，
　作困乏人急難中的保障，
　作躲暴風之處，
　作避炎熱的陰涼。
5你要壓制外邦人的喧嘩，
　好像乾燥地的熱氣下落；
　禁止強暴人的凱歌，
　好像熱氣被雲影消化。

6在這山上，
　萬軍之耶和華必為萬民
　用肥甘設擺筵席，
　用陳酒和滿髓的肥甘，
　並澄清的陳酒，設擺筵席。
7他又必在這山上
　除滅遮蓋萬民之物
　和遮蔽萬國蒙臉的帕子。
8他已經吞滅死亡直到永遠。
　主耶和華必擦去
　各人臉上的眼淚，
　又除掉普天下
　他百姓的羞辱，
　　　因為這是耶和華說的。

20The earth reels like a drunkard,
　it sways like a hut in the wind;
so heavy upon it is the guilt of its rebellion
　that it falls—never to rise again.

21In that day the LORD will punish
　the powers in the heavens above
　and the kings on the earth below.
22They will be herded together
　like prisoners bound in a dungeon;
they will be shut up in prison
　and be punished*a* after many days.
23The moon will be abashed, the sun ashamed;
　for the LORD Almighty will reign
on Mount Zion and in Jerusalem,
　and before its elders, gloriously.

Praise to the LORD

25 O LORD, you are my God;
　I will exalt you and praise your name,
　for in perfect faithfulness
you have done marvelous things,
　things planned long ago.
2You have made the city a heap of rubble,
　the fortified town a ruin,
　the foreigners' stronghold a city no more;
　it will never be rebuilt.
3Therefore strong peoples will honor you;
　cities of ruthless nations will revere you.
4You have been a refuge for the poor,
　a refuge for the needy in his distress,
a shelter from the storm
　and a shade from the heat.
For the breath of the ruthless
　is like a storm driving against a wall
5　and like the heat of the desert.
You silence the uproar of foreigners;
　as heat is reduced by the shadow of a cloud,
so the song of the ruthless is stilled.

6On this mountain the LORD Almighty will
　　prepare
　a feast of rich food for all peoples,
　a banquet of aged wine—
　the best of meats and the finest of wines.
7On this mountain he will destroy
　the shroud that enfolds all peoples,
　the sheet that covers all nations;
8　he will swallow up death forever.
　The Sovereign LORD will wipe away the tears
　from all faces;
he will remove the disgrace of his people
　from all the earth.
　　　　　The LORD has spoken.

a 22 Or released

9In that day they will say,

"Surely this is our God;
　　we trusted in him, and he saved us.
This is the LORD, we trusted in him;
　　let us rejoice and be glad in his salvation."

10The hand of the LORD will rest on this
　　mountain;
but Moab will be trampled under him
　　as straw is trampled down in the manure.
11They will spread out their hands in it,
　　as a swimmer spreads out his hands to
　　　swim.
God will bring down their pride
　　despite the cleverness[a] of their hands.
12He will bring down your high fortified walls
　　and lay them low;
he will bring them down to the ground,
　　to the very dust.

A Song of Praise

26 In that day this song will be sung in the
land of Judah:

We have a strong city;
　　God makes salvation
　　its walls and ramparts.
2Open the gates
　　that the righteous nation may enter,
　　the nation that keeps faith.
3You will keep in perfect peace
　　him whose mind is steadfast,
　　because he trusts in you.
4Trust in the LORD forever,
　　for the LORD, the LORD, is the Rock eternal.
5He humbles those who dwell on high,
　　he lays the lofty city low;
he levels it to the ground
　　and casts it down to the dust.
6Feet trample it down—
　　the feet of the oppressed,
　　the footsteps of the poor.

7The path of the righteous is level;
　　O upright One, you make the way of the
　　　righteous smooth.
8Yes, LORD, walking in the way of your laws,[b]
　　we wait for you;
your name and renown
　　are the desire of our hearts.
9My soul yearns for you in the night;
　　in the morning my spirit longs for you.

9到那日，人必說：

"看哪，這是我們的神，
　　我們素來等候他，他必拯救我們。
這是耶和華，我們素來等候他，
　　我們必因他的救恩歡喜快樂。"

10耶和華的手
　　必按在這山上；
摩押人在所居之地必被踐踏，
　　好像乾草被踐踏在糞池的水中。
11他必在其中伸開手，
　　好像洑水的
　　　伸開手洑水一樣，
但耶和華必使他的驕傲
　　和他手所行的詭計一併敗落。
12耶和華使你城上的堅固高臺
　　傾倒，
拆平，
　　直到塵埃。

一首讚美的詩歌

26 當那日，在猶大地人必唱這
歌說：

我們有堅固的城；
　　耶和華要將救恩定為城牆、
　　為外郭。
2敞開城門，
　　使守信的義民
　　得以進入。
3堅心倚賴你的，
　　你必保守他十分平安，
　　因為他倚靠你。
4你們當倚靠耶和華直到永遠，
　　因為耶和華是永久的磐石。
5他使住高處的與高城一併敗落，
　　將城拆毀，
拆平，
　　直到塵埃。
6要被腳踐踏，
　　就是被困苦人的腳
　　和窮乏人的腳踐踏。

7義人的道是正直的，
　　你為正直的主，
　　必修平義人的路。
8耶和華啊，
　　我們在你行審判的路上等候你；
我們心裏所羨慕的是你的名，
　　就是你那可記念的名。
9夜間，我心中羨慕你，
　　我裏面的靈切切尋求你。

a 11 The meaning of the Hebrew for this word is uncertain.
b 8 Or judgments

因為你在世上行審判的時候，
地上的居民就學習公義。
10以恩惠待惡人，
他仍不學習公義；
在正直的地上，
他必行事不義，
也不注意耶和華的威嚴。
11耶和華啊！你的手高舉，
他們仍然不看；
卻要看你為百姓發的熱心，
因而抱愧，
並且有火
燒滅你的敵人。

12耶和華啊！你必派定我們得平安，
因為我們所做的事，
都是你給我們成就的。
13耶和華我們的神啊！
在你以外曾有別的主管轄我們，
但我們專要倚靠你，提你的名。
14他們死了，必不能再活；
他們去世，必不能再起；
因為你刑罰他們，毀滅他們，
他們的名號就全然消滅。
15耶和華啊，你增添國民，
你增添國民；
你得了榮耀，
又擴張地的四境。

16耶和華啊，他們在急難中尋求你，
你的懲罰臨到他們身上，
他們就傾心吐膽禱告你。
17婦人懷孕，臨產疼痛，
在痛苦之中喊叫；
耶和華啊，我們在你面前也是如此。
18我們也曾懷孕疼痛，
所產的竟像風一樣。
我們在地上未曾行甚麼拯救的事；
世上的居民也未曾敗落。

19死人（註：原文作「你的死人」）要復活，
屍首（原文作「我的屍首」）要興起。
睡在塵埃的啊，
要醒起歌唱！
因你的甘露好像菜蔬上的甘露，
地也要交出死人來。

20我的百姓啊，你們要來進入內室，
關上門，
隱藏片時，
等到忿怒過去。
21因為耶和華從他的居所出來，
要刑罰地上居民的罪孽。

When your judgments come upon the earth,
　　the people of the world learn righteousness.
10Though grace is shown to the wicked,
　　they do not learn righteousness;
even in a land of uprightness they go on
　　　doing evil
　　and regard not the majesty of the LORD.
11O LORD, your hand is lifted high,
　　but they do not see it.
Let them see your zeal for your people and be
　　　put to shame;
　　let the fire reserved for your enemies
　　　consume them.

12LORD, you establish peace for us;
　　all that we have accomplished you have
　　　done for us.
13O LORD, our God, other lords besides you
　　　have ruled over us,
　　but your name alone do we honor.
14They are now dead, they live no more;
　　those departed spirits do not rise.
You punished them and brought them to ruin;
　　you wiped out all memory of them.
15You have enlarged the nation, O LORD;
　　you have enlarged the nation.
You have gained glory for yourself;
　　you have extended all the borders of the land.

16LORD, they came to you in their distress;
　　when you disciplined them,
　　they could barely whisper a prayer.[a]
17As a woman with child and about to give birth
　　writhes and cries out in her pain,
　　so were we in your presence, O LORD.
18We were with child, we writhed in pain,
　　but we gave birth to wind.
We have not brought salvation to the earth;
　　we have not given birth to people of the world.

19But your dead will live;
　　their bodies will rise.
You who dwell in the dust,
　　wake up and shout for joy.
Your dew is like the dew of the morning;
　　the earth will give birth to her dead.

20Go, my people, enter your rooms
　　and shut the doors behind you;
hide yourselves for a little while
　　until his wrath has passed by.
21See, the LORD is coming out of his dwelling
　　to punish the people of the earth for their sins.

a 16 The meaning of the Hebrew for this clause is uncertain.

The earth will disclose the blood shed upon her;
she will conceal her slain no longer.

Deliverance of Israel

27 In that day,

the LORD will punish with his sword,
his fierce, great and powerful sword,
Leviathan the gliding serpent,
Leviathan the coiling serpent;
he will slay the monster of the sea.

2In that day—

"Sing about a fruitful vineyard:
3 I, the LORD, watch over it;
I water it continually.
I guard it day and night
so that no one may harm it.
4 I am not angry.
If only there were briers and thorns
confronting me!
I would march against them in battle;
I would set them all on fire.
5Or else let them come to me for refuge;
let them make peace with me,
yes, let them make peace with me."

6In days to come Jacob will take root,
Israel will bud and blossom
and fill all the world with fruit.

7Has ⌊the LORD⌋ struck her
as he struck down those who struck her?
Has she been killed
as those were killed who killed her?
8By warfare[a] and exile you contend with her—
with his fierce blast he drives her out,
as on a day the east wind blows.
9By this, then, will Jacob's guilt be atoned for,
and this will be the full fruitage of the
removal of his sin:
When he makes all the altar stones
to be like chalk stones crushed to pieces,
no Asherah poles[b] or incense altars
will be left standing.
10The fortified city stands desolate,
an abandoned settlement, forsaken like the
desert;
there the calves graze,
there they lie down;
they strip its branches bare.

地也必露出其中的血，
不再掩蓋被殺的人。

以色列必蒙拯救

27 到那日，

耶和華必用
他剛硬有力的大刀
刑罰鱷魚，就是那快行的蛇；
刑罰鱷魚，就是那曲行的蛇，
並殺海中的大魚。

2當那日，有出酒的葡萄園，
你們要指這園唱歌說：

3 "我耶和華是看守葡萄園的，
我必時刻澆灌，
晝夜看守，
免得有人損害。
4我心中不存忿怒；
惟願荊棘蒺藜
與我交戰，
我就勇往直前，
把他一同焚燒。
5不然，讓他持住我的能力，
使他與我和好，
願他與我和好。"

6將來雅各要扎根，
以色列要發芽開花，
他們的果實必充滿世界。

7主擊打他們，
豈像擊打那些擊打他們的人嗎？
他們被殺戮，
豈像被他們所殺戮的嗎？
8你打發他們去，是相機宜與他們相爭；
颳東風的日子，
就用暴風將他們逐去。
9所以，雅各的罪孽得赦免，
他的罪過得除掉的果效，
全在乎此，
就是他叫祭壇的石頭
變為打碎的灰石，
以致木偶和日像
不再立起。
10因為堅固城變為淒涼，
成了撇下離棄的居所，
像曠野一樣；
牛犢必在那裏吃草，
在那裏躺臥，
並吃盡其中的樹枝。

---

a 8 See Septuagint; the meaning of the Hebrew for this word is
uncertain.　　b 9 That is, symbols of the goddess Asherah

11 枝條枯乾，必被折斷，
　　婦女要來點火燒着。
　　因為這百姓蒙昧無知，
　　所以，創造他們的必不憐恤他們；
　　造成他們的也不施恩與他們。

12 以色列人哪，到那日，耶和華
必從大河直到埃及小河，將你們一一
地收集，如同人打樹拾果一樣。13 當
那日，必大發角聲，在亞述地將要
滅亡的，並在埃及地被趕散的，都
要來，他們就在耶路撒冷聖山上敬
拜耶和華。

以法蓮有禍了

28 禍哉！以法蓮的酒徒，
　　　住在肥美谷的山上，
　　　他們心裏高傲，
　　　以所誇的為冠冕，
　　　猶如將殘之花。
2 看哪，主有一大能大力者，
　　像一陣冰雹，
　　像毀滅的暴風，
　　像漲溢的大水，
　　他必用手將冠冕摔落於地。
3 以法蓮高傲的酒徒，
　　他的冠冕必被踏在腳下。
4 那榮美將殘之花，
　　就是在肥美谷山上的，
　　必像夏令以前初熟的無花果；
　　看見這果的就注意，
　　一到手中
　　就吞吃了。

5 到那日，
　　萬軍之耶和華
　　必作他餘剩之民的
　　榮冠華冕，
6 也作了在位上
　　行審判者公平之靈，
　　並城門口
　　打退仇敵者的力量。

7 就是這地的人，也因酒搖搖晃晃，
　　因濃酒東倒西歪。
　　祭司和先知因濃酒搖搖晃晃，
　　被酒所困，
　　因濃酒東倒西歪。
　　他們錯解默示，
　　謬行審判。
8 因為各席上滿了嘔吐的污穢，
　　無一處乾淨。

11 When its twigs are dry, they are broken off
　　and women come and make fires with them.
　　For this is a people without understanding;
　　so their Maker has no compassion on them,
　　and their Creator shows them no favor.

12 In that day the LORD will thresh from the
flowing Euphrates[a] to the Wadi of Egypt, and
you, O Israelites, will be gathered up one by
one. 13 And in that day a great trumpet will
sound. Those who were perishing in Assyria and
those who were exiled in Egypt will come and
worship the LORD on the holy mountain in Jerusalem.

Woe to Ephraim

28 Woe to that wreath, the pride of
　　Ephraim's drunkards,
　　　to the fading flower, his glorious beauty,
　　set on the head of a fertile valley—
　　to that city, the pride of those laid low by wine!
2 See, the Lord has one who is powerful and
　　　strong.
　　Like a hailstorm and a destructive wind,
　　like a driving rain and a flooding downpour,
　　he will throw it forcefully to the ground.
3 That wreath, the pride of Ephraim's drunkards,
　　will be trampled underfoot.
4 That fading flower, his glorious beauty,
　　set on the head of a fertile valley,
　　will be like a fig ripe before harvest—
　　as soon as someone sees it and takes it in his
　　　hand,
　　he swallows it.

5 In that day the LORD Almighty
　　will be a glorious crown,
　　a beautiful wreath
　　for the remnant of his people.
6 He will be a spirit of justice
　　to him who sits in judgment,
　　a source of strength
　　to those who turn back the battle at the gate.

7 And these also stagger from wine
　　and reel from beer:
　　Priests and prophets stagger from beer
　　and are befuddled with wine;
　　they reel from beer,
　　they stagger when seeing visions,
　　they stumble when rendering decisions.
8 All the tables are covered with vomit
　　and there is not a spot without filth.

⁹"Who is it he is trying to teach?
   To whom is he explaining his message?
   To children weaned from their milk,
     to those just taken from the breast?
¹⁰For it is:
   Do and do, do and do,
   rule on rule, rule on rule ᵃ;
   a little here, a little there."

¹¹Very well then, with foreign lips and strange
    tongues
   God will speak to this people,
¹²to whom he said,
   "This is the resting place, let the weary rest";
   and, "This is the place of repose"—
   but they would not listen.
¹³So then, the word of the Lᴏʀᴅ to them will
    become:
   Do and do, do and do,
   rule on rule, rule on rule;
   a little here, a little there—
   so that they will go and fall backward,
   be injured and snared and captured.

¹⁴Therefore hear the word of the Lᴏʀᴅ, you
    scoffers
   who rule this people in Jerusalem.
¹⁵You boast, "We have entered into a covenant
    with death,
   with the grave ᵇ we have made an agreement.
   When an overwhelming scourge sweeps by,
    it cannot touch us,
   for we have made a lie our refuge
   and falsehood ᶜ our hiding place."

¹⁶So this is what the Sovereign Lᴏʀᴅ says:

"See, I lay a stone in Zion,
   a tested stone,
   a precious cornerstone for a sure foundation;
   the one who trusts will never be dismayed.
¹⁷I will make justice the measuring line
   and righteousness the plumb line;
   hail will sweep away your refuge, the lie,
   and water will overflow your hiding place.
¹⁸Your covenant with death will be annulled;
   your agreement with the grave will not
    stand.
   When the overwhelming scourge sweeps by,
   you will be beaten down by it.

⁹譏誚先知的說：
   "他要將知識指教誰呢？
   要使誰明白傳言呢？
   是那剛斷奶離懷的嗎？
¹⁰他竟
   命上加命、令上加令，
   律上加律、例上加例，
   這裏一點、那裏一點。"

¹¹先知說："不然，主要藉
   異邦人的嘴唇和外邦人的舌頭
   對這百姓說話。"
¹²他曾對他們說：
   "你們要使疲乏人得安息，
   這樣才得安息，才得舒暢。"
   他們卻不肯聽。
¹³所以
   耶和華向他們說的話是：
   命上加命、令上加令，
   律上加律、例上加例，
   這裏一點、那裏一點，
   以致他們前行仰面跌倒，
   而且跌碎，並陷入網羅被纏住。

¹⁴所以，你們這些褻慢的人，
   就是轄管住在耶路撒冷這百姓的，
   要聽耶和華的話。
¹⁵你們曾說：
   "我們與死亡立約，
   與陰間結盟。
   敵軍（註：原文作"鞭子"）如水漲漫
    經過的時候，必不臨到我們。
   因我們以謊言為避所，
   在虛假以下藏身。"

¹⁶所以主耶和華如此說：

"看哪，我在錫安放一塊石頭，
   作為根基，是試驗過的石頭，
   是穩固根基，寶貴的房角石，
   信靠的人必不着急。
¹⁷我必以公平為準繩，
   以公義為線鉈。
   冰雹必沖去謊言的避所；
   大水必漫過藏身之處。
¹⁸你們與死亡所立的約必然廢掉；
   與陰間所結的盟必立不住。
   敵軍（註：原文作"鞭子"）如水漲漫
    經過的時候，
   你們必被他踐踏；

---

a 10 Hebrew *sav lasav sav lasav / kav lakav kav lakav* (possibly
meaningless sounds; perhaps a mimicking of the prophet's
words); also in verse 13   *b 15* Hebrew *Sheol*; also in verse 18
c 15 Or *false gods*

19每逢經過必將你們擄去。
　因為每早晨他必經過，
　白晝黑夜都必如此。”

明白傳言的
　必受驚恐。
20原來牀榻短，使人不能舒身；
　被窩窄，使人不能遮體。
21耶和華必興起，
　像在毘拉心山；
他必發怒，
　像在基遍谷，
好做成他的工，就是非常的工；
　成就他的事，就是奇異的事。
22現在你們不可褻慢，
　恐怕捆你們的綁索更結實了。
因為我從主萬軍之耶和華那裏聽見，
　已經決定在全地上
　施行滅絕的事。

23你們當側耳聽我的聲音，
　留心聽我的言語。
24那耕地為要撒種的，
　豈是常常耕地呢？
　豈是常常開墾耙地呢？

25他拉平了地面，
　豈不就撒種小茴香，
　播種大茴香，
按行列種小麥，
　在定處種大麥，
　在田邊種粗麥呢？
26因為他的神教導他務農相宜，
　並且指教他。

27原來打小茴香，不用尖利的器具，
　軋大茴香，也不用碌碡（註：原文
　　作“車輪”。下同）；
　但用杖打小茴香，用棍打大茴香。
28做餅的糧食是用磨磨碎，
　因它不必常打；
雖用碌碡
　和馬打散，
　卻不磨它。
29這也是出於萬軍之耶和華，
　他的謀略奇妙，
　他的智慧廣大。

大衛城有禍了

29 唉！亞利伊勒，亞利伊勒，
　大衛安營的城！
任憑你年上加年，
　節期照常周流。

19As often as it comes it will carry you away;
　morning after morning, by day and by night,
　it will sweep through.”

The understanding of this message
　will bring sheer terror.
20The bed is too short to stretch out on,
　the blanket too narrow to wrap around you.
21The LORD will rise up as he did at Mount
　　Perazim,
　he will rouse himself as in the Valley of
　　Gibeon—
to do his work, his strange work,
　and perform his task, his alien task.
22Now stop your mocking,
　or your chains will become heavier;
　the Lord, the LORD Almighty, has told me
　of the destruction decreed against the whole
　　land.

23Listen and hear my voice;
　pay attention and hear what I say.
24When a farmer plows for planting, does he
　　plow continually?
　Does he keep on breaking up and harrowing
　　the soil?
25When he has leveled the surface,
　does he not sow caraway and scatter
　　cummin?
Does he not plant wheat in its place,[a]
　barley in its plot,[a]
　and spelt in its field?
26His God instructs him
　and teaches him the right way.

27Caraway is not threshed with a sledge,
　nor is a cartwheel rolled over cummin;
caraway is beaten out with a rod,
　and cummin with a stick.
28Grain must be ground to make bread;
　so one does not go on threshing it forever.
Though he drives the wheels of his threshing
　　cart over it,
　his horses do not grind it.
29All this also comes from the LORD Almighty,
　wonderful in counsel and magnificent in
　　wisdom.

Woe to David's City

29 Woe to you, Ariel, Ariel,
　the city where David settled!
Add year to year
　and let your cycle of festivals go on.

a 25 The meaning of the Hebrew for this word is uncertain.

²Yet I will besiege Ariel;
　　she will mourn and lament,
　　she will be to me like an altar hearth.ᵃ
³I will encamp against you all around;
　　I will encircle you with towers
　　and set up my siege works against you.
⁴Brought low, you will speak from the ground;
　　your speech will mumble out of the dust.
　　Your voice will come ghostlike from the earth;
　　out of the dust your speech will whisper.

⁵But your many enemies will become like fine
　　　dust,
　　the ruthless hordes like blown chaff.
　　Suddenly, in an instant,
⁶　the LORD Almighty will come
　　with thunder and earthquake and great noise,
　　with windstorm and tempest and flames of a
　　　devouring fire.
⁷Then the hordes of all the nations that fight
　　　against Ariel,
　　that attack her and her fortress and besiege
　　　her,
　　will be as it is with a dream,
　　with a vision in the night—
⁸as when a hungry man dreams that he is eating,
　　but he awakens, and his hunger remains;
　　as when a thirsty man dreams that he is
　　　drinking,
　　but he awakens faint, with his thirst
　　　unquenched.
　　So will it be with the hordes of all the nations
　　　that fight against Mount Zion.

⁹Be stunned and amazed,
　　blind yourselves and be sightless;
　　be drunk, but not from wine,
　　stagger, but not from beer.
¹⁰The LORD has brought over you a deep sleep:
　　He has sealed your eyes (the prophets);
　　he has covered your heads (the seers).

¹¹For you this whole vision is nothing but
words sealed in a scroll. And if you give the
scroll to someone who can read, and say to him,
"Read this, please," he will answer, "I can't; it is
sealed." ¹²Or if you give the scroll to someone
who cannot read, and say, "Read this, please,"
he will answer, "I don't know how to read."

²我終必使亞利伊勒困難，
　　她必悲傷哀號，
　　我卻仍以她為亞利伊勒。
³我必四圍安營攻擊你，
　　屯兵圍困你，
　　築壘攻擊你。
⁴你必敗落，從地中說話。
　　你的言語必微細出於塵埃。
　　你的聲音必像那交鬼者的聲音出於地；
　　你的言語低低微微出於塵埃。

⁵你仇敵的羣眾，卻要像細塵；
　　強暴人的羣眾，
　　也要像飛糠。
　　這事必頃刻之間忽然臨到。
⁶萬軍之耶和華必用
　　雷轟、地震、大聲、
　　　旋風、暴風，並吞滅的火焰，
　　向他討罪。
⁷那時，攻擊亞利伊勒列國的羣眾，
　　就是一切攻擊亞利伊勒
　　　和她的保障，
　　並使她困難的，
　　必如夢景，
　　如夜間的異象。
⁸又必像飢餓的人夢中吃飯，
　　醒了仍覺腹空，
　　或像口渴的人
　　夢中喝水，
　　醒了仍覺發昏，
　　心裏想喝。
　　攻擊錫安山列國的羣眾
　　也必如此。

⁹你們等候驚奇吧！
　　你們宴樂昏迷吧！
　　他們醉了，卻非因酒；
　　他們東倒西歪，卻非因濃酒。
¹⁰因為耶和華將沉睡的靈澆灌你們，
　　封閉你們的眼，蒙蓋你們的頭。
　　你們的眼就是先知，
　　你們的頭就是先見。
¹¹所有的默示，你們看如封住的
書卷，人將這書卷交給識字的，說：
"請念吧！"他說："我不能念，因
為是封住了。" ¹²又將這書卷交給不
識字的人，說："請念吧！"他說：
"我不識字。"

_a 2 The Hebrew for altar hearth sounds like the Hebrew for
Ariel._

13主説：

　"因為這百姓親近我，
　　用嘴唇尊敬我，
　　心卻遠離我。
　他們敬畏我，
　　不過是領受人的吩咐。
14所以，我在這百姓中
　　要行奇妙的事，
　　就是奇妙又奇妙的事。
　他們智慧人的智慧必然消滅；
　　聰明人的聰明必然隱藏。"
15禍哉！那些向耶和華深藏謀略的，
　　又在暗中行事，説：
　"誰看見我們呢？
　　誰知道我們呢？"
16你們把事顛倒了，
　　豈可看窰匠如泥嗎？
　被製作的物豈可論製作物的説：
　　"他沒有製作我？"
　或是被創造的物論造物的説：
　　"他沒有聰明？"

17黎巴嫩變為肥田，
　　肥田看如樹林，
　　不是只有一點點時候嗎？
18那時，
　　聾子必聽見這書上的話；
　瞎子的眼
　　必從迷矇黑暗中得以看見。
19謙卑人必因耶和華增添歡喜；
　人間貧窮的必因以色列的聖者快樂。
20因為強暴人已歸無有，
　　褻慢人已經滅絕；
　一切找機會作孽的
　　都被剪除。
21他們在爭訟的事上，
　　定無罪的為有罪，
　為城門口責備人的設下網羅，
　　用虛無的事
　　　屈枉義人。

22所以，救贖亞伯拉罕的耶和華
論雅各家如此説：

　"雅各必不再羞愧，
　　面容也不至變色。
23但他看見他的眾子，
　　就是我手的工作在他那裏，
　他們必尊我的名為聖，
　　必尊雅各的聖者為聖，
　　必敬畏以色列的神。

13The Lord says:

"These people come near to me with their mouth
　and honor me with their lips,
　but their hearts are far from me.
Their worship of me
　is made up only of rules taught by men.[a]
14Therefore once more I will astound these
　people
　with wonder upon wonder;
　the wisdom of the wise will perish,
　the intelligence of the intelligent will vanish."
15Woe to those who go to great depths
　to hide their plans from the LORD,
who do their work in darkness and think,
　"Who sees us? Who will know?"
16You turn things upside down,
　as if the potter were thought to be like the clay!
Shall what is formed say to him who formed it,
　"He did not make me"?
Can the pot say of the potter,
　"He knows nothing"?

17In a very short time, will not Lebanon be
　turned into a fertile field
and the fertile field seem like a forest?
18In that day the deaf will hear the words of the
　scroll,
　and out of gloom and darkness
　the eyes of the blind will see.
19Once more the humble will rejoice in the LORD;
　the needy will rejoice in the Holy One of Israel.
20The ruthless will vanish,
　the mockers will disappear,
　and all who have an eye for evil will be cut
　　down—
21those who with a word make a man out to be
　　guilty,
　who ensnare the defender in court
　and with false testimony deprive the
　　innocent of justice.

22Therefore this is what the LORD, who redeemed Abraham, says to the house of Jacob:

"No longer will Jacob be ashamed;
　no longer will their faces grow pale.
23When they see among them their children,
　the work of my hands,
　they will keep my name holy;
　they will acknowledge the holiness of the
　　Holy One of Jacob,
　and will stand in awe of the God of Israel.

*a 13 Hebrew; Septuagint They worship me in vain; / their
teachings are but rules taught by men*

²⁴Those who are wayward in spirit will gain understanding;
those who complain will accept instruction."

Woe to the Obstinate Nation

30 "Woe to the obstinate children,"
declares the LORD,
"to those who carry out plans that are not mine,
forming an alliance, but not by my Spirit,
heaping sin upon sin;

²who go down to Egypt
without consulting me;
who look for help to Pharaoh's protection,
to Egypt's shade for refuge.

³But Pharaoh's protection will be to your shame,
Egypt's shade will bring you disgrace.

⁴Though they have officials in Zoan
and their envoys have arrived in Hanes,

⁵everyone will be put to shame
because of a people useless to them,
who bring neither help nor advantage,
but only shame and disgrace."

⁶An oracle concerning the animals of the Negev:

Through a land of hardship and distress,
of lions and lionesses,
of adders and darting snakes,
the envoys carry their riches on donkeys' backs,
their treasures on the humps of camels,
to that unprofitable nation,

⁷ to Egypt, whose help is utterly useless.
Therefore I call her
Rahab the Do-Nothing.

⁸Go now, write it on a tablet for them,
inscribe it on a scroll,
that for the days to come
it may be an everlasting witness.

⁹These are rebellious people, deceitful children,
children unwilling to listen to the LORD's instruction.

¹⁰They say to the seers,
"See no more visions!"
and to the prophets,
"Give us no more visions of what is right!
Tell us pleasant things,
prophesy illusions.

¹¹Leave this way,
get off this path,
and stop confronting us
with the Holy One of Israel!"

---

²⁴心中迷糊的
必得明白；
發怨言的必受訓誨。"

悖逆的國民有禍了

30 耶和華說：
"禍哉！這悖逆的兒女。
他們同謀，
卻不由於我，
結盟，卻不由於我的靈，
以致罪上加罪。

²起身下埃及去，
並沒有求問我。
要靠法老的力量加添自己的力量，
並投在埃及的蔭下。

³所以法老的力量必作你們的羞辱；
投在埃及的蔭下，
要為你們的慚愧。

⁴他們的首領已在瑣安；
他們的使臣到了哈內斯。

⁵他們必因
那不利於他們的民蒙羞。
那民並非幫助，也非利益，
只作羞恥淩辱。"

⁶論南方牲畜的默示：

他們把財物馱在驢駒的脊背上，
將寶物馱在駱駝的肉鞍上，
經過艱難困苦之地，
就是公獅、母獅、
蝮蛇、火焰的飛龍之地，
往那不利於他們的民那裏去。

⁷埃及的幫助是徒然無益的，
所以我稱她為
"坐而不動的拉哈伯"。

⁸現今你去，在他們面前將這話
刻在版上、寫在書上，
以便傳留後世，
直到永永遠遠。

⁹因為他們是悖逆的百姓、
說謊的兒女，
不肯聽從耶和華訓誨的兒女。

¹⁰他們對先見說：
"不要望見不吉利的事！"
對先知說：
"不要向我們講正直的話，
要向我們說柔和的話，
言虛幻的事。

¹¹你們要離棄正道，
偏離直路，
不要在我們面前
再提說以色列的聖者！"

12所以，以色列的聖者如此說：

"因為你們藐視這訓誨的話，
　　倚賴欺壓和乖僻，
　　以此為可靠的。
13故此，這罪孽在你們身上，
　　好像將要破裂凸出來的高牆，
　　頃刻之間忽然坍塌。
14要被打碎，
　　好像把窰匠的瓦器打碎，
　　毫不顧惜，
　　甚至碎塊中找不到一片可用以
　　　從爐內取火，
　　　從池中舀水。"

15主耶和華以色列的聖者曾如此說：

"你們得救在乎歸回安息；
　　你們得力在乎平靜安穩。
　　你們竟自不肯。
16你們卻說：'不然，我們要騎馬
　　　奔走。'所以你們必然奔走。
　　又說：'我們要騎飛快的牲口。'
　　所以追趕你們的也必飛快。
17一人叱喝，
　　必令千人逃跑；
　　五人叱喝，
　　你們都必逃跑。
　　以致剩下的，
　　好像山頂的旗杆，
　　岡上的大旗。"

18耶和華必然等候，要施恩給你們；
　　必然興起，好憐憫你們。
　　因為耶和華是公平的神，
　　凡等候他的都是有福的！

19百姓必在錫安在耶路撒冷居
住，不再哭泣。主必因你哀求的
聲音施恩給你；他聽見的時候，就
必應允你。20主雖然以艱難給你當
餅，以困苦給你當水，你的教師卻
不再隱藏，你眼必看見你的教師。
21你或向左、或向右，你必聽見後邊
有聲音說："這是正路，要行在其
間。"22你把雕刻偶像所包的銀子和鑄
造偶像所鍍的金子，你要玷污、要
拋棄，好像污穢之物，對偶像說：
"去吧！"

23你將種子撒在地裏，主必降雨
在其上，並使地所出的糧肥美豐

12Therefore, this is what the Holy One of Israel says:

"Because you have rejected this message,
　relied on oppression
　and depended on deceit,
13this sin will become for you
　like a high wall, cracked and bulging,
　that collapses suddenly, in an instant.
14It will break in pieces like pottery,
　shattered so mercilessly
　that among its pieces not a fragment will be
　　found
　for taking coals from a hearth
　or scooping water out of a cistern."

15This is what the Sovereign LORD, the Holy One of Israel, says:

"In repentance and rest is your salvation,
　in quietness and trust is your strength,
　but you would have none of it.
16You said, 'No, we will flee on horses.'
　Therefore you will flee!
　You said, 'We will ride off on swift horses.'
　Therefore your pursuers will be swift!
17A thousand will flee
　at the threat of one;
　at the threat of five
　you will all flee away,
　till you are left
　like a flagstaff on a mountaintop,
　like a banner on a hill."

18Yet the LORD longs to be gracious to you;
　he rises to show you compassion.
For the LORD is a God of justice.
　Blessed are all who wait for him!

19O people of Zion, who live in Jerusalem, you will weep no more. How gracious he will be when you cry for help! As soon as he hears, he will answer you. 20Although the Lord gives you the bread of adversity and the water of affliction, your teachers will be hidden no more; with your own eyes you will see them. 21Whether you turn to the right or to the left, your ears will hear a voice behind you, saying, "This is the way; walk in it." 22Then you will defile your idols overlaid with silver and your images covered with gold; you will throw them away like a menstrual cloth and say to them, "Away with you!"

23He will also send you rain for the seed you sow in the ground, and the food that comes from the land will be rich and plentiful. In that day your cattle will graze in broad meadows. ²⁴The oxen and donkeys that work the soil will eat fodder and mash, spread out with fork and shovel. ²⁵In the day of great slaughter, when the towers fall, streams of water will flow on every high mountain and every lofty hill. ²⁶The moon will shine like the sun, and the sunlight will be seven times brighter, like the light of seven full days, when the LORD binds up the bruises of his people and heals the wounds he inflicted.

²⁷See, the Name of the LORD comes from afar,
    with burning anger and dense clouds of
        smoke;
    his lips are full of wrath,
        and his tongue is a consuming fire.
²⁸His breath is like a rushing torrent,
    rising up to the neck.
He shakes the nations in the sieve of
        destruction;
    he places in the jaws of the peoples
        a bit that leads them astray.
²⁹And you will sing
    as on the night you celebrate a holy festival;
    your hearts will rejoice
        as when people go up with flutes
to the mountain of the LORD,
    to the Rock of Israel.
³⁰The LORD will cause men to hear his majestic
        voice
    and will make them see his arm coming down
    with raging anger and consuming fire,
    with cloudburst, thunderstorm and hail.
³¹The voice of the LORD will shatter Assyria;
    with his scepter he will strike them down.
³²Every stroke the LORD lays on them
    with his punishing rod
will be to the music of tambourines and harps,
    as he fights them in battle with the blows of
        his arm.
³³Topheth has long been prepared;
    it has been made ready for the king.
Its fire pit has been made deep and wide,
    with an abundance of fire and wood;
the breath of the LORD,
    like a stream of burning sulfur,
    sets it ablaze.

Woe to Those Who Rely on Egypt

31 Woe to those who go down to Egypt for
        help,
        who rely on horses,
who trust in the multitude of their chariots
    and in the great strength of their horsemen,
but do not look to the Holy One of Israel,
    or seek help from the LORD.

盛。到那時,你的牲畜必在寬闊的草場吃草。²⁴耕地的牛和驢駒必吃加鹽的料,這料是用木杴和杈子揚淨的。²⁵在大行殺戮的日子,高臺倒塌的時候,各高山岡陵必有川流河湧。²⁶當耶和華纏裹他百姓的損處、醫治他民鞭傷的日子,月光必像日光,日光必加七倍,像七日的光一樣。

²⁷看哪,耶和華的名從遠方來,
    怒氣燒起,
    密煙上騰;
他的嘴唇滿有忿恨,
    他的舌頭像吞滅的火。
²⁸他的氣如漲溢的河水,
    直漲到頸項,
    要用毀滅的篩籮
    篩淨列國;
    並且在眾民的口中
    必有使人錯行的嚼環。
²⁹你們必唱歌,
    像守聖節的夜間一樣,
    並且心中喜樂,
    像人吹笛,
    上耶和華的山,
    到以色列的磐石那裏。
³⁰耶和華必使人聽他威嚴的聲音,
    又顯他降罰的膀臂
        和他怒中的忿恨,
    並吞滅的火焰
        與霹雷、暴風、冰雹。
³¹亞述人必因耶和華的聲音驚惶,
    耶和華必用杖擊打他。
³²耶和華必將命定的杖加在他身上,
    每打一下,
    人必擊鼓彈琴。
打仗的時候,
    耶和華必掄起手來與他交戰。
³³原來陀斐特又深又寬,
    早已為王預備好了,
其中堆的是火
    與許多木柴。
耶和華的氣
    如一股硫磺火,
    使它着起來。

倚靠埃及的人有禍了

31 禍哉!
    那些下埃及求幫助的,
        是因仗賴馬匹,
倚靠甚多的車輛,
    並倚靠強壯的馬兵,
卻不仰望以色列的聖者,
    也不求問耶和華。

²其實耶和華有智慧，他必降災禍，
　　並不反悔自己的話，
　　卻要興起攻擊那作惡之家，
　　又攻擊那行孽幫助人的。
³埃及人不過是人，並不是神；
　　他們的馬不過是血肉，並不是靈。
　耶和華一伸手，
　　那幫助人的必絆跌；
　　那受幫助的也必跌倒，
　　都一同滅亡。

⁴耶和華對我如此說：

　"獅子和少壯獅子
　　護食咆哮，
　就是喊許多牧人來
　　攻擊牠，
　牠總不因他們的聲音驚惶，
　　也不因他們的喧嘩縮伏。
　如此，萬軍之耶和華
　　也必降臨在錫安山岡上爭戰。
⁵雀鳥怎樣搧翅覆雛，
　萬軍之耶和華
　　也要照樣保護耶路撒冷，
　他必保護拯救，要越門保守它。"

　⁶以色列人哪，你們要深深地悖逆
耶和華，現今要歸向他。⁷到那日，
各人必將他金偶像、銀偶像，就是
親手所造、陷自己在罪中的，都拋
棄了。
⁸"亞述人必倒在刀下，並非人的刀；
　　有刀要將他吞滅，並非人的刀。
　他必逃避這刀，
　　他的少年人
　　必成為服苦的。
⁹他的磐石
　　必因驚嚇挪去，
　他的首領
　　必因大旗驚惶。"
　這是那有火在錫安、
　　有爐在耶路撒冷的耶和華說的。

公義的國度

32 看哪，必有一王憑公義行政，
　　必有首領藉公平掌權。
²必有一人
　　像避風所
　　和避暴雨的隱密處，
　又像河流在乾旱之地，
　　像大磐石的影子
　　在疲乏之地。

³那能看的人，
　　眼不再昏迷；
　能聽的人，耳必得聽聞。

²Yet he too is wise and can bring disaster;
　he does not take back his words.
He will rise up against the house of the wicked,
　against those who help evildoers.
³But the Egyptians are men and not God;
　their horses are flesh and not spirit.
When the LORD stretches out his hand,
　he who helps will stumble,
　he who is helped will fall;
　both will perish together.

⁴This is what the LORD says to me:

"As a lion growls,
　a great lion over his prey—
and though a whole band of shepherds
　is called together against him,
he is not frightened by their shouts
　or disturbed by their clamor—
so the LORD Almighty will come down
　to do battle on Mount Zion and on its heights.
⁵Like birds hovering overhead,
　the LORD Almighty will shield Jerusalem;
he will shield it and deliver it,
　he will 'pass over' it and will rescue it."

⁶Return to him you have so greatly revolted
against, O Israelites. ⁷For in that day every one
of you will reject the idols of silver and gold
your sinful hands have made.

⁸"Assyria will fall by a sword that is not of man;
　a sword, not of mortals, will devour them.
They will flee before the sword
　and their young men will be put to forced
　　labor.
⁹Their stronghold will fall because of terror;
　at sight of the battle standard their
　　commanders will panic,"
declares the LORD,
　whose fire is in Zion,
　whose furnace is in Jerusalem.

The Kingdom of Righteousness

32 See, a king will reign in righteousness
　　and rulers will rule with justice.
²Each man will be like a shelter from
　　the wind
and a refuge from the storm,
　like streams of water in the desert
　and the shadow of a great rock in a thirsty
　　land.

³Then the eyes of those who see will no longer
　be closed,
and the ears of those who hear will listen.

⁴The mind of the rash will know and understand,
and the stammering tongue will be fluent
and clear.
⁵No longer will the fool be called noble
nor the scoundrel be highly respected.
⁶For the fool speaks folly,
his mind is busy with evil:
He practices ungodliness
and spreads error concerning the LORD;
the hungry he leaves empty
and from the thirsty he withholds water.
⁷The scoundrel's methods are wicked,
he makes up evil schemes
to destroy the poor with lies,
even when the plea of the needy is just.
⁸But the noble man makes noble plans,
and by noble deeds he stands.

The Women of Jerusalem

⁹You women who are so complacent,
rise up and listen to me;
you daughters who feel secure,
hear what I have to say!
¹⁰In little more than a year
you who feel secure will tremble;
the grape harvest will fail,
and the harvest of fruit will not come.
¹¹Tremble, you complacent women;
shudder, you daughters who feel secure!
Strip off your clothes,
put sackcloth around your waists.
¹²Beat your breasts for the pleasant fields,
for the fruitful vines
¹³and for the land of my people,
a land overgrown with thorns and briers—
yes, mourn for all houses of merriment
and for this city of revelry.
¹⁴The fortress will be abandoned,
the noisy city deserted;
citadel and watchtower will become a
wasteland forever,
the delight of donkeys, a pasture for flocks,
¹⁵till the Spirit is poured upon us from on high,
and the desert becomes a fertile field,
and the fertile field seems like a forest.
¹⁶Justice will dwell in the desert
and righteousness live in the fertile field.
¹⁷The fruit of righteousness will be peace;
the effect of righteousness will be quietness
and confidence forever.
¹⁸My people will live in peaceful dwelling places,
in secure homes,
in undisturbed places of rest.
¹⁹Though hail flattens the forest
and the city is leveled completely,

⁴冒失人的心，必明白知識；
結巴人的舌，
必說話通快。
⁵愚頑人不再稱為高明；
吝嗇人不再稱為大方。
⁶因為愚頑人必說愚頑話，
心裏想作罪孽，
慣行褻瀆的事，
說錯謬的話攻擊耶和華，
使飢餓的人無食可吃，
使口渴的人無水可喝。
⁷吝嗇人所用的法子是惡的，
他圖謀惡計，用謊言毀滅謙卑人；
窮乏人講公理的時候，
他也是這樣行。
⁸高明人卻謀高明事，
在高明事上也必永存。

耶路撒冷的婦女

⁹安逸的婦女啊，
起來聽我的聲音！
無慮的女子啊，
側耳聽我的言語！
¹⁰無慮的女子啊，
再過一年多，必受騷擾；
因為無葡萄可摘，
無果子（註：或作「禾稼」）可收。
¹¹安逸的婦女啊，要戰兢；
無慮的女子啊，要受騷擾，
脫去衣服，赤着身體，
腰束麻布。
¹²她們必為美好的田地
和多結果的葡萄樹搥胸哀哭。
¹³荊棘蒺藜
必長在我百姓的地上，
又長在歡樂的城中
和一切快樂的房屋上。
¹⁴因為宮殿必被撇下，
多民的城必被離棄；
山岡望樓永為洞穴，
作野驢所喜樂的，
為羊群的草場。
¹⁵等到聖靈從上澆灌我們，
曠野就變為肥田，
肥田看如樹林。
¹⁶那時，公平要居在曠野，
公義要居在肥田。
¹⁷公義的果效必是平安；
公義的效驗必是平穩，
直到永遠。
¹⁸我的百姓必住在平安的居所，
安穩的住處，
平靜的安歇所。
¹⁹但要降冰雹打倒樹林，
城必全然拆平。

²⁰你們在各水邊撒種、
　牧放牛驢的
　　有福了。

受苦與救助

33 禍哉！你這毀滅人的，
　自己倒不被毀滅；
　行事詭詐的，
　人倒不以詭詐待你。
你毀滅罷休了，
　自己必被毀滅；
你行完了詭詐，
　人必以詭詐待你。

²耶和華啊，求你施恩於我們，
　我們等候你。
求你每早晨作我們的膀臂，
　遭難的時候為我們的拯救。
³喧嚷的響聲一發，眾民奔逃；
　你一興起，列國四散。
⁴你們所擄的必被斂盡，好像螞蚱吃
　（註：原文作「斂」）盡禾稼；
　人要蹦在其上，好像蝗蟲一樣。

⁵耶和華被尊崇，因他居在高處，
　他以公平公義充滿錫安。
⁶你一生一世必得安穩，
　有豐盛的救恩
　　並智慧和知識，
　你以敬畏耶和華為至寶。

⁷看哪！他們的豪傑在外頭哀號；
　求和的使臣痛痛哭泣。
⁸大路荒涼，
　行人止息；
敵人背約，
　藐視城邑，
　不顧人民。
⁹地上悲哀衰殘，
　黎巴嫩羞愧枯乾；
　沙崙像曠野，
　巴珊和迦密的樹林凋殘。

¹⁰耶和華說：“現在我要起來，
　我要興起，
　我要勃然而興！
¹¹你們要懷的是糠秕，
　要生的是碎稭，
　你們的氣就是吞滅自己的火。
¹²列邦必像已燒的石灰，
　像已割的荊棘在火中焚燒。”

Distress and Help

33 Woe to you, O destroyer,
　you who have not been destroyed!
　Woe to you, O traitor,
　you who have not been betrayed!
When you stop destroying,
　you will be destroyed;
when you stop betraying,
　you will be betrayed.

²O Lord, be gracious to us;
　we long for you.
Be our strength every morning,
　our salvation in time of distress.
³At the thunder of your voice, the peoples flee;
　when you rise up, the nations scatter.
⁴Your plunder, O nations, is harvested as by
　young locusts;
　like a swarm of locusts men pounce on it.

⁵The Lord is exalted, for he dwells on high;
　he will fill Zion with justice and righteousness.
⁶He will be the sure foundation for your times,
　a rich store of salvation and wisdom and
　knowledge;
　the fear of the Lord is the key to this treasure.^a

⁷Look, their brave men cry aloud in the streets;
　the envoys of peace weep bitterly.
⁸The highways are deserted,
　no travelers are on the roads.
The treaty is broken,
　its witnesses^b are despised,
　no one is respected.
⁹The land mourns^c and wastes away;
　Lebanon is ashamed and withers;
Sharon is like the Arabah,
　and Bashan and Carmel drop their leaves.

¹⁰"Now will I arise," says the Lord.
　"Now will I be exalted;
　now will I be lifted up.
¹¹You conceive chaff,
　you give birth to straw;
　your breath is a fire that consumes you.
¹²The peoples will be burned as if to lime;
　like cut thornbushes they will be set ablaze."

a 6 Or is a treasure from him　　*b 8 Dead Sea Scrolls; Masoretic
Text / the cities*　　*c 9 Or dries up*

¹³You who are far away, hear what I have done;
   you who are near, acknowledge my power!
¹⁴The sinners in Zion are terrified;
   trembling grips the godless:
   "Who of us can dwell with the consuming fire?
   Who of us can dwell with everlasting
     burning?"
¹⁵He who walks righteously
   and speaks what is right,
who rejects gain from extortion
   and keeps his hand from accepting bribes,
who stops his ears against plots of murder
   and shuts his eyes against contemplating
    evil—
¹⁶this is the man who will dwell on the heights,
   whose refuge will be the mountain fortress.
His bread will be supplied,
   and water will not fail him.

¹⁷Your eyes will see the king in his beauty
   and view a land that stretches afar.
¹⁸In your thoughts you will ponder the former
   terror:
   "Where is that chief officer?
   Where is the one who took the revenue?
   Where is the officer in charge of the towers?"
¹⁹You will see those arrogant people no more,
   those people of an obscure speech,
   with their strange, incomprehensible tongue.

²⁰Look upon Zion, the city of our festivals;
   your eyes will see Jerusalem,
   a peaceful abode, a tent that will not be moved;
its stakes will never be pulled up,
   nor any of its ropes broken.
²¹There the LORD will be our Mighty One.
   It will be like a place of broad rivers and
    streams.
No galley with oars will ride them,
   no mighty ship will sail them.
²²For the LORD is our judge,
   the LORD is our lawgiver,
   the LORD is our king;
   it is he who will save us.

²³Your rigging hangs loose:
   The mast is not held secure,
   the sail is not spread.
Then an abundance of spoils will be divided
   and even the lame will carry off plunder.
²⁴No one living in Zion will say, "I am ill";
   and the sins of those who dwell there will be
    forgiven.

¹³你們遠方的人當聽我所行的；
   你們近處的人當承認我的大能。
¹⁴錫安中的罪人都懼怕；
   不敬虔的人被戰兢抓住：
   "我們中間誰能與吞滅的火同住？
   我們中間
    誰能與永火同住呢？"
¹⁵行事公義，
   說話正直，
憎惡欺壓的財利，
   擺手不受賄賂，
塞耳不聽流血的話，
   閉眼不看邪惡事的——

¹⁶他必居高處，
   他的保障是磐石的堅壘；
他的糧必不缺乏（註：原文作"賜給"），
   他的水必不斷絕。

¹⁷你的眼必見王的榮美，
   必見遼闊之地。
¹⁸你的心
   必思想那驚嚇的事，
自問說："記數目的在哪裏呢？
   平貢銀的在哪裏呢？
   數戍樓的在哪裏呢？"
¹⁹你必不見那強暴的民，
   就是說話深奧，你不能明白，
   言語呢喃，你不能懂得的。

²⁰你要看錫安——我們守聖節的城；
   你的眼必見耶路撒冷
   為安靜的居所，為不挪移的帳幕，
橛子永不拔出，
   繩索一根也不折斷。
²¹在那裏，
   耶和華必顯威嚴與我們同在，
   當作江河寬闊之地；
其中必沒有盪槳搖櫓的船來往，
   也沒有威武的船經過。
²²因為耶和華是審判我們的，
   耶和華是給我們設律法的，
耶和華是我們的王，
   他必拯救我們。

²³你的繩索鬆開，
   不能栽穩桅杆，
   也不能揚起篷來。
那時許多擄來的物被分了，
   瘸腿的把掠物奪去了。
²⁴城內居民必不說"我病了"，
   其中居住的百姓，
   罪孽都赦免了。

對列國的審判

34 列國啊，要近前來聽！
眾民哪，要側耳而聽！
地和其上所充滿的，
世界和其中一切所出的，都應當聽！
2 因為耶和華向萬國發忿恨，
向他們的全軍發烈怒，
將他們滅盡，
交出他們受殺戮。
3 被殺的必然拋棄，
屍首臭氣上騰，
諸山被他們的血融化。

4 天上的萬象都要消沒；
天被捲起，好像書卷。
其上的萬象要殘敗，
像葡萄樹的葉子殘敗，
又像無花果樹的葉子殘敗一樣。

5 因為我的刀在天上已經喝足。
這刀必臨到以東
和我所咒詛的民，要施行審判。
6 耶和華的刀滿了血，
用脂油和羊羔、
公山羊的血，
並公綿羊腰子的脂油滋潤的。
因為耶和華在波斯拉有獻祭的事，
在以東地大行殺戮。
7 野牛、牛犢和公牛
要一同下來。
他們的地喝醉了血；
他們的塵土因脂油肥潤。

8 因耶和華有報仇之日，
為錫安的爭辯有報應之年。
9 以東的河水要變為石油，
塵埃要變為硫磺，
地土成為燒着的石油，
10 晝夜總不熄滅，
煙氣永遠上騰，
必世世代代
成為荒廢，
永永遠遠無人經過。
11 鵜鶘、箭豬卻要得為業；
貓頭鷹、烏鴉要住在其間，
耶和華必將空虛的準繩、
混沌的線鉈
拉在其上。
12 以東人要召貴冑來治國，
那裏卻無一個，
首領也都歸於無有。

Judgment Against the Nations

34 Come near, you nations, and listen;
pay attention, you peoples!
Let the earth hear, and all that is in it,
the world, and all that comes out of it!
2 The LORD is angry with all nations;
his wrath is upon all their armies.
He will totally destroy[a] them,
he will give them over to slaughter.
3 Their slain will be thrown out,
their dead bodies will send up a stench;
the mountains will be soaked with their
blood.
4 All the stars of the heavens will be dissolved
and the sky rolled up like a scroll;
all the starry host will fall
like withered leaves from the vine,
like shriveled figs from the fig tree.

5 My sword has drunk its fill in the heavens;
see, it descends in judgment on Edom,
the people I have totally destroyed.
6 The sword of the LORD is bathed in blood,
it is covered with fat—
the blood of lambs and goats,
fat from the kidneys of rams.
For the LORD has a sacrifice in Bozrah
and a great slaughter in Edom.
7 And the wild oxen will fall with them,
the bull calves and the great bulls.
Their land will be drenched with blood,
and the dust will be soaked with fat.

8 For the LORD has a day of vengeance,
a year of retribution, to uphold Zion's cause.
9 Edom's streams will be turned into pitch,
her dust into burning sulfur;
her land will become blazing pitch!
10 It will not be quenched night and day;
its smoke will rise forever.
From generation to generation it will lie
desolate;
no one will ever pass through it again.
11 The desert owl[b] and screech owl[b] will possess it;
the great owl[b] and the raven will nest there.
God will stretch out over Edom
the measuring line of chaos
and the plumb line of desolation.
12 Her nobles will have nothing there to be
called a kingdom,
all her princes will vanish away.

---

a 2 The Hebrew term refers to the irrevocable giving over of
things or persons to the LORD, often by totally destroying
them; also in verse 5.　　*b 11* The precise identification of these
birds is uncertain.

¹³Thorns will overrun her citadels,
　　nettles and brambles her strongholds.
　She will become a haunt for jackals,
　　a home for owls.
¹⁴Desert creatures will meet with hyenas,
　　and wild goats will bleat to each other;
　there the night creatures will also repose
　　and find for themselves places of rest.
¹⁵The owl will nest there and lay eggs,
　　she will hatch them, and care for her young
　　　under the shadow of her wings;
　there also the falcons will gather,
　　each with its mate.

¹⁶Look in the scroll of the LORD and read:

None of these will be missing,
　not one will lack her mate.
For it is his mouth that has given the order,
　and his Spirit will gather them together.
¹⁷He allots their portions;
　his hand distributes them by measure.
They will possess it forever
　and dwell there from generation to generation.

Joy of the Redeemed

35 The desert and the parched land will be glad;
　　the wilderness will rejoice and blossom.
Like the crocus, ²it will burst into bloom;
　it will rejoice greatly and shout for joy.
The glory of Lebanon will be given to it,
　the splendor of Carmel and Sharon;
　they will see the glory of the LORD,
　the splendor of our God.

³Strengthen the feeble hands,
　steady the knees that give way;
⁴say to those with fearful hearts,
　"Be strong, do not fear;
　your God will come,
　he will come with vengeance;
　with divine retribution
　he will come to save you."

⁵Then will the eyes of the blind be opened
　and the ears of the deaf unstopped.
⁶Then will the lame leap like a deer,
　and the mute tongue shout for joy.
Water will gush forth in the wilderness
　and streams in the desert.
⁷The burning sand will become a pool,
　the thirsty ground bubbling springs.
In the haunts where jackals once lay,
　grass and reeds and papyrus will grow.

---

¹³以東的宮殿要長荊棘，
　　保障要長蒺藜和刺草；
　要作野狗的住處、
　　鴕鳥的居所。
¹⁴曠野的走獸要和豺狼相遇，
　　野山羊要與伴偶對叫；
　夜間的怪物必在那裏棲身，
　　自找安歇之處。
¹⁵箭蛇要在那裏做窩，
　　下蛋，菢蛋，生子，
　　聚子在其影下；
　鷂鷹各與伴偶
　　聚集在那裏。

¹⁶你們要查考宣讀耶和華的書：

這都無一缺少，
　無一沒有伴偶；
因為我的口已經吩咐，
　他的靈將牠們聚集。
¹⁷他也為牠們拈鬮，
　又親手用準繩給牠們分地，
　牠們必永得為業，
　世世代代住在其間。

蒙救贖的喜樂

35 曠野和乾旱之地
　　必然歡喜，
　　沙漠也必快樂，
又像玫瑰開花，²必開花繁盛，
　樂上加樂，而且歡呼。
黎巴嫩的榮耀
　並迦密與沙崙的華美，必賜給它。
人必看見耶和華的榮耀，
　我們神的華美。

³你們要使軟弱的手堅壯，
　無力的膝穩固。
⁴對膽怯的人說：
　"你們要剛強，不要懼怕。
看哪！
　你們的神必來報仇，
　必來施行極大的報應；
　他必來拯救你們。"

⁵那時瞎子的眼必睜開，
　聾子的耳必開通。
⁶那時瘸子必跳躍像鹿，
　啞吧的舌頭必能歌唱。
在曠野必有水發出，
　在沙漠必有河湧流。
⁷發光的沙（註：或作"蜃樓"）要變為
　水池，乾渴之地要變為泉源；
　在野狗躺臥之處
　必有青草、蘆葦和蒲草。

8在那裏必有一條大道，
　稱為聖路。
污穢人不得經過，
　必專為贖民行走；
　行路的人雖愚昧，也不至失迷。
9在那裏必沒有獅子，
　猛獸也不登這路，
　在那裏都遇不見，
只有贖民在那裏行走。
10並且耶和華救贖的民必歸回，
　歌唱來到錫安。
永樂必歸到他們的頭上，
　他們必得着歡喜快樂，
　憂愁歎息盡都逃避。

西拿基立恫嚇耶路撒冷

36 希西家王十四年，亞述王西拿基立上來攻擊猶大的一切堅固城，將城攻取。2亞述王從拉吉差遣拉伯沙基率領大軍往耶路撒冷，到希西家王那裏去。他就站在上池的水溝旁，在漂布地的大路上。3於是希勒家的兒子家宰以利亞敬，並書記舍伯那和亞薩的兒子史官約亞，出來見拉伯沙基。

4拉伯沙基對他們說：

"你們去告訴希西家，說亞述大王如此說：'你所倚靠的有甚麼可仗賴的呢？5你說有打仗的計謀和能力，我看不過是虛話！你到底倚靠誰才背叛我呢？6看哪！你所倚靠的埃及，是那壓傷的葦杖。人若靠這杖，就必刺透他的手。埃及王法老向一切倚靠他的人也是這樣。7你若對我說：我們倚靠耶和華我們的神。希西家豈不是將神的邱壇和祭壇廢去，且對猶大和耶路撒冷的人說，你們當在這壇前敬拜嗎？

8 "'現在你把當頭給我主亞述王，我給你二千匹馬，看你這一面騎馬的人夠不夠。9若不然，怎能打敗我主臣僕中最小的軍長呢？你竟倚靠埃及的戰車馬兵嗎？10現在我上來攻擊毀滅這地，

Sennacherib Threatens Jerusalem

36 In the fourteenth year of King Hezekiah's reign, Sennacherib king of Assyria attacked all the fortified cities of Judah and captured them. 2Then the king of Assyria sent his field commander with a large army from Lachish to King Hezekiah at Jerusalem. When the commander stopped at the aqueduct of the Upper Pool, on the road to the Washerman's Field, 3Eliakim son of Hilkiah the palace administrator, Shebna the secretary, and Joah son of Asaph the recorder went out to him.

4The field commander said to them, "Tell Hezekiah,

" 'This is what the great king, the king of Assyria, says: On what are you basing this confidence of yours? 5You say you have strategy and military strength—but you speak only empty words. On whom are you depending, that you rebel against me? 6Look now, you are depending on Egypt, that splintered reed of a staff, which pierces a man's hand and wounds him if he leans on it! Such is Pharaoh king of Egypt to all who depend on him. 7And if you say to me, "We are depending on the LORD our God"—isn't he the one whose high places and altars Hezekiah removed, saying to Judah and Jerusalem, "You must worship before this altar"?

8" 'Come now, make a bargain with my master, the king of Assyria: I will give you two thousand horses—if you can put riders on them! 9How then can you repulse one officer of the least of my master's officials, even though you are depending on Egypt for chariots and horsemen? 10Furthermore, have I come to attack and destroy this land without

a 8 Or / the simple will not stray from it

the LORD? The LORD himself told me to march against this country and destroy it.' "

[11]Then Eliakim, Shebna and Joah said to the field commander, "Please speak to your servants in Aramaic, since we understand it. Don't speak to us in Hebrew in the hearing of the people on the wall."

[12]But the commander replied, "Was it only to your master and you that my master sent me to say these things, and not to the men sitting on the wall—who, like you, will have to eat their own filth and drink their own urine?"

[13]Then the commander stood and called out in Hebrew, "Hear the words of the great king, the king of Assyria! [14]This is what the king says: Do not let Hezekiah deceive you. He cannot deliver you! [15]Do not let Hezekiah persuade you to trust in the LORD when he says, 'The LORD will surely deliver us; this city will not be given into the hand of the king of Assyria.'

[16]"Do not listen to Hezekiah. This is what the king of Assyria says: Make peace with me and come out to me. Then every one of you will eat from his own vine and fig tree and drink water from his own cistern, [17]until I come and take you to a land like your own—a land of grain and new wine, a land of bread and vineyards.

[18]"Do not let Hezekiah mislead you when he says, 'The LORD will deliver us.' Has the god of any nation ever delivered his land from the hand of the king of Assyria? [19]Where are the gods of Hamath and Arpad? Where are the gods of Sepharvaim? Have they rescued Samaria from my hand? [20]Who of all the gods of these countries has been able to save his land from me? How then can the LORD deliver Jerusalem from my hand?"

[21]But the people remained silent and said nothing in reply, because the king had commanded, "Do not answer him."

[22]Then Eliakim son of Hilkiah the palace administrator, Shebna the secretary, and Joah son of Asaph the recorder went to Hezekiah, with their clothes torn, and told him what the field commander had said.

Jerusalem's Deliverance Foretold

37 When King Hezekiah heard this, he tore his clothes and put on sackcloth and went into the temple of the LORD. [2]He sent Eliakim the palace administrator, Shebna the secretary, and the leading priests, all wearing sackcloth, to the prophet Isaiah son of Amoz. [3]They told him, "This is what Hezekiah says: This day is a day of distress and rebuke and

豈沒有耶和華的意思嗎？耶和華吩咐我說，你上去攻擊毀滅這地吧！'"

[11]以利亞敬、舍伯那、約亞對拉伯沙基說："求你用亞蘭言語和僕人說話，因為我們懂得；不要用猶大言語和我們說話，達到城上百姓的耳中。"

[12]拉伯沙基說："我主差遣我來，豈是單對你和你的主說這些話嗎？不也是對這些坐在城上、要與你們一同吃自己糞、喝自己尿的人說嗎？"

[13]於是拉伯沙基站着，用猶大言語大聲喊着說："你們當聽亞述大王的話！[14]王如此說：'你們不要被希西家欺哄了，因他不能拯救你們。[15]也不要聽希西家使你們倚靠耶和華，說耶和華必要拯救我們，這城必不交在亞述王的手中。'

[16]"不要聽希西家的話。因亞述王如此說：你們要與我和好，出來投降我，各人就可以吃自己葡萄樹和無花果樹的果子，喝自己井裏的水。[17]等我來領你們到一個地方，與你們本地一樣，就是有五穀和新酒之地，有糧食和葡萄園之地。

[18]"你們要謹防，恐怕希西家勸導你們說：'耶和華必拯救我們。'列國的神有哪一個救他本國脫離亞述王的手呢？[19]哈馬和亞珥拔的神在哪裏呢？西法瓦音的神在哪裏呢？他們曾救撒馬利亞脫離我的手嗎？[20]這些國的神有誰曾救自己的國脫離我的手呢？難道耶和華能救耶路撒冷脫離我的手嗎？"

[21]百姓靜默不言，並不回答一句，因為王曾吩咐說："不要回答他。"

[22]當下希勒家的兒子家宰以利亞敬和書記舍伯那，並亞薩的兒子史官約亞，都撕裂衣服，來到希西家那裏，將拉伯沙基的話告訴了他。

預言耶路撒冷得解救

37 希西家王聽見，就撕裂衣服，披上麻布，進了耶和華的殿。[2]使家宰以利亞敬和書記舍伯那，並祭司中的長老，都披上麻布，去見亞摩斯的兒子先知以賽亞。[3]對他說："希西家如此說：今日是急難、責罰、凌辱的日子，就如婦人將要生產嬰孩，卻沒有力量生產。4或者耶和華你的神聽見拉伯沙基的話，就是他主人亞述王打發他來辱罵永生神的話，耶和華你的神聽見這話就發斥責。故此，求你為餘剩的民揚聲禱告。"

5希西家王的臣僕就去見以賽亞。6以賽亞對他們說："要這樣對你們的主人說，耶和華如此說：'你聽見亞述王的僕人褻瀆我的話，不要懼怕。7我必驚動（註：原文作"使靈進入"）他的心，他要聽見風聲就歸回本地，我必使他在那裏倒在刀下。'"

8拉伯沙基回去，正遇見亞述王攻打立拿，原來他早聽見亞述王拔營離開拉吉。

9亞述王聽見人論古實王特哈加說："他出來要與你爭戰。"亞述王一聽見，就打發使者去見希西家，吩咐他們說：10"你們對猶大王希西家如此說：不要聽你所倚靠的神哄你說：'耶路撒冷必不交在亞述王的手中。'11你總聽說亞述諸王向列國所行的乃是盡行滅絕，難道你還能得救嗎？12我列祖所毀滅的，就是歌散、哈蘭、利色和屬提拉撒的伊甸人，這些國的神何曾拯救這些國呢？13哈馬的王、亞珥拔的王、西法瓦音城的王、希拿和以瓦的王都在哪裏呢？"

希西家的祈禱

14希西家從使者手裏接過書信來，看完了，就上耶和華的殿，將書信在耶和華面前展開。15希西家向耶和華禱告說：16"坐在二基路伯上萬軍之耶和華以色列的神啊，你，惟有你，是天下萬國的神！你曾創造天地。17耶和華啊，求你側耳而聽！耶和華啊，求你睜眼而看！要聽西拿基立的一切話，他是打發使者來辱罵永生神的。

18"耶和華啊！亞述諸王果然使列國和列國之地變為荒涼，19將列國的神像都扔在火裏，因為他本不是神，乃是人手所造的，是木頭、石頭的，所以滅絕他。20耶和華我們的神啊，現在求你救我們脫離亞述王

disgrace, as when children come to the point of birth and there is no strength to deliver them. 4It may be that the LORD your God will hear the words of the field commander, whom his master, the king of Assyria, has sent to ridicule the living God, and that he will rebuke him for the words the LORD your God has heard. Therefore pray for the remnant that still survives."

5When King Hezekiah's officials came to Isaiah, 6Isaiah said to them, "Tell your master, 'This is what the LORD says: Do not be afraid of what you have heard—those words with which the underlings of the king of Assyria have blasphemed me. 7Listen! I am going to put a spirit in him so that when he hears a certain report, he will return to his own country, and there I will have him cut down with the sword.'"

8When the field commander heard that the king of Assyria had left Lachish, he withdrew and found the king fighting against Libnah.

9Now Sennacherib received a report that Tirhakah, the Cushite[a] king of Egypt, was marching out to fight against him. When he heard it, he sent messengers to Hezekiah with this word: 10"Say to Hezekiah king of Judah: Do not let the god you depend on deceive you when he says, 'Jerusalem will not be handed over to the king of Assyria.' 11Surely you have heard what the kings of Assyria have done to all the countries, destroying them completely. And will you be delivered? 12Did the gods of the nations that were destroyed by my forefathers deliver them—the gods of Gozan, Haran, Rezeph and the people of Eden who were in Tel Assar? 13Where is the king of Hamath, the king of Arpad, the king of the city of Sepharvaim, or of Hena or Ivvah?"

Hezekiah's Prayer

14Hezekiah received the letter from the messengers and read it. Then he went up to the temple of the LORD and spread it out before the LORD. 15And Hezekiah prayed to the LORD: 16"O LORD Almighty, God of Israel, enthroned between the cherubim, you alone are God over all the kingdoms of the earth. You have made heaven and earth. 17Give ear, O LORD, and hear; open your eyes, O LORD, and see; listen to all the words Sennacherib has sent to insult the living God.

18"It is true, O LORD, that the Assyrian kings have laid waste all these peoples and their lands. 19They have thrown their gods into the fire and destroyed them, for they were not gods but only wood and stone, fashioned by human hands. 20Now, O LORD our God, deliver us from his hand, so that all kingdoms on earth may know that you alone, O LORD, are God.[a]

Sennacherib's Fall

[21]Then Isaiah son of Amoz sent a message to Hezekiah: "This is what the LORD, the God of Israel, says: Because you have prayed to me concerning Sennacherib king of Assyria, [22]this is the word the LORD has spoken against him:

"The Virgin Daughter of Zion
　　despises and mocks you.
The Daughter of Jerusalem
　　tosses her head as you flee.
[23]Who is it you have insulted and blasphemed?
　　Against whom have you raised your voice
and lifted your eyes in pride?
　　Against the Holy One of Israel!
[24]By your messengers
　　you have heaped insults on the Lord.
And you have said,
　'With my many chariots
I have ascended the heights of the mountains,
　　the utmost heights of Lebanon.
I have cut down its tallest cedars,
　　the choicest of its pines.
I have reached its remotest heights,
　　the finest of its forests.
[25]I have dug wells in foreign lands[b]
　　and drunk the water there.
With the soles of my feet
　　I have dried up all the streams of Egypt.'

[26]"Have you not heard?
　　Long ago I ordained it.
In days of old I planned it;
　　now I have brought it to pass,
that you have turned fortified cities
　　into piles of stone.
[27]Their people, drained of power,
　　are dismayed and put to shame.
They are like plants in the field,
　　like tender green shoots,
like grass sprouting on the roof,
　　scorched[c] before it grows up.

[28]"But I know where you stay
　　and when you come and go
　　and how you rage against me.

a 20 Dead Sea Scrolls (see also 2 Kings 19:19); Masoretic Text
alone are the LORD　　b 25 Dead Sea Scrolls (see also 2 Kings
19:24); Masoretic Text does not have *in foreign lands*.
c 27 Some manuscripts of the Masoretic Text, Dead Sea Scrolls
and some Septuagint manuscripts (see also 2 Kings 19:26);
most manuscripts of the Masoretic Text *roof | and terraced fields*

的手，使天下萬國都知道惟有你是耶和華！"

西拿基立的敗亡

[21]亞摩斯的兒子以賽亞就打發人去見希西家，說："耶和華以色列的神如此說，你既然求我攻擊亞述王西拿基立，[22]所以耶和華論他這樣說：

"錫安的處女
　藐視你、嗤笑你；
耶路撒冷的女子
　向你搖頭。
[23]你辱罵誰？褻瀆誰？
　揚起聲來，
高舉眼目攻擊誰呢？
　乃是攻擊以色列的聖者！
[24]你藉你的臣僕
　辱罵主說：

'我率領許多戰車
　上山頂，
　到黎巴嫩極深之處；
我要砍伐其中高大的香柏樹
　和佳美的松樹；
我必上極高之處，
　進入肥田的樹林。
[25]我已經挖井喝水；
　我必用腳掌
　踏乾埃及的一切河。'

[26]"耶和華說：
　你豈沒有聽見
　　我早先所做的、
　　古時所立的嗎？
現在藉你使堅固城荒廢，
　變為亂堆。
[27]所以其中的居民力量甚小，
　驚惶羞愧。
他們像野草、
　像青菜，
如房頂上的草，
　又如田間未長成的禾稼。

[28]"你坐下，
　你出去，你進來，
　你向我發烈怒，我都知道。

29因為你向我發烈怒，
　　又因你狂傲的話
　　　達到我耳中，
　　我就要用鉤子鉤上你的鼻子，
　　　把嚼環放在你口裏，
　　　使你從原路轉回去。

　30 "以色列人哪，我賜你們一個
證據：
"你們今年要吃自生的，
　　明年也要吃自長的；
　　至於後年，你們要耕種收割，
　　栽植葡萄園，吃其中的果子。
31猶大家所逃脫餘剩的，
　　仍要往下扎根，向上結果。
32必有餘剩的民從耶路撒冷而出；
　　必有逃脫的人從錫安山而來。
　　萬軍之耶和華的熱心
　　必成就這事。

　33 "所以耶和華論亞述王如此
說：

"他必不得來到這城，
　　也不在這裏射箭，
　　不得拿盾牌到城前，
　　也不築壘攻城。
34他從哪條路來，必從那條路回去，
　　必不得來到這城。"
　　　　　　　這是耶和華說的。
35 "因我為自己的緣故，
　　又為我僕人大衛的緣故，
　　必保護拯救這城。"

36耶和華的使者出去，在亞述營
中殺了十八萬五千人。清早有人起
來一看，都是死屍了。37亞述王西拿
基立就拔營回去，住在尼尼微。

38一日，在他的神尼斯洛廟裏叩
拜，他兒子亞得米勒和沙利色用刀
殺了他，就逃到亞拉臘地。他兒子
以撒哈頓接續他作王。

希西家患病

38 那時希西家病得要死。亞摩
斯的兒子先知以賽亞去見
他，對他說："耶和華如此
說：你當留遺命與你的家，因為你
必死，不能活了。"

29Because you rage against me
　　and because your insolence has reached my
　　　ears,
I will put my hook in your nose
　　and my bit in your mouth,
and I will make you return
　　by the way you came.

　30This will be the sign for you, O Hezekiah:

"This year you will eat what grows by itself,
　　and the second year what springs from that.
But in the third year sow and reap,
　　plant vineyards and eat their fruit.
31Once more a remnant of the house of Judah
　　will take root below and bear fruit above.
32For out of Jerusalem will come a remnant,
　　and out of Mount Zion a band of survivors.
The zeal of the LORD Almighty
　　will accomplish this.

33"Therefore this is what the LORD says concerning the king of Assyria:

"He will not enter this city
　　or shoot an arrow here.
He will not come before it with shield
　　or build a siege ramp against it.
34By the way that he came he will return;
　　he will not enter this city,"
　　　　　　　declares the LORD.
35"I will defend this city and save it,
　　for my sake and for the sake of David my
　　　servant!"

36Then the angel of the LORD went out and
put to death a hundred and eighty-five thousand
men in the Assyrian camp. When the people got
up the next morning—there were all the dead
bodies! 37So Sennacherib king of Assyria broke
camp and withdrew. He returned to Nineveh
and stayed there.

38One day, while he was worshiping in the
temple of his god Nisroch, his sons Adrammelech
and Sharezer cut him down with the sword, and
they escaped to the land of Ararat. And Esarhaddon his son succeeded him as king.

Hezekiah's Illness

38 In those days Hezekiah became ill and
was at the point of death. The prophet
Isaiah son of Amoz went to him and
said, "This is what the LORD says: Put your house
in order, because you are going to die; you will
not recover."

2Hezekiah turned his face to the wall and prayed to the LORD, 3"Remember, O LORD, how I have walked before you faithfully and with wholehearted devotion and have done what is good in your eyes." And Hezekiah wept bitterly.

4Then the word of the LORD came to Isaiah: 5"Go and tell Hezekiah, 'This is what the LORD, the God of your father David, says: I have heard your prayer and seen your tears; I will add fifteen years to your life. 6And I will deliver you and this city from the hand of the king of Assyria. I will defend this city.

7" 'This is the LORD's sign to you that the LORD will do what he has promised: 8I will make the shadow cast by the sun go back the ten steps it has gone down on the stairway of Ahaz.' " So the sunlight went back the ten steps it had gone down.

9A writing of Hezekiah king of Judah after his illness and recovery:

10I said, "In the prime of my life
　　must I go through the gates of death*a*
　　and be robbed of the rest of my years?"
11I said, "I will not again see the LORD,
　　the LORD, in the land of the living;
　　no longer will I look on mankind,
　　or be with those who now dwell in this world.*b*
12Like a shepherd's tent my house
　　has been pulled down and taken from me.
　　Like a weaver I have rolled up my life,
　　and he has cut me off from the loom;
　　day and night you made an end of me.
13I waited patiently till dawn,
　　but like a lion he broke all my bones;
　　day and night you made an end of me.
14I cried like a swift or thrush,
　　I moaned like a mourning dove.
　　My eyes grew weak as I looked to the heavens.
　　I am troubled; O Lord, come to my aid!"

15But what can I say?
　　He has spoken to me, and he himself has
　　　　done this.
　　I will walk humbly all my years
　　because of this anguish of my soul.
16Lord, by such things men live;
　　and my spirit finds life in them too.
　　You restored me to health
　　and let me live.
17Surely it was for my benefit
　　that I suffered such anguish.

2希西家就轉臉朝牆，禱告耶和華說：3"耶和華啊，求你記念我在你面前怎樣存完全的心，按誠實行事，又做你眼中所看為善的。"希西家就痛哭了。

4耶和華的話臨到以賽亞說：5"你去告訴希西家說，耶和華你祖大衛的神如此說：我聽見了你的禱告，看見了你的眼淚。我必加增你十五年的壽數；6並且我要救你和這城脫離亞述王的手，也要保護這城。

7"我耶和華必成就我所說的，我先給你一個兆頭，8就是叫亞哈斯的日晷，向前進的日影往後退十度。"於是前進的日影，果然在日晷上往後退了十度。

9猶大王希西家患病已經痊愈，就作詩說：

10我說："正在我中年（註：或作"晌午"）
　　之日，必進入陰間的門；
　　我餘剩的年歲不得享受。"
11我說："我必不得見耶和華，
　　就是在活人之地不見耶和華；
　　我與世上的居民
　　不再見面。
12我的住處被遷去離開我，
　　好像牧人的帳棚一樣。
　　我將性命捲起，像織布的捲布一樣；
　　耶和華必將我從機頭剪斷，
　　從早到晚，他要使我完結。
13我使自己安靜，直到天亮；
　　他像獅子折斷我一切的骨頭，
　　從早到晚，他要使我完結。
14我像燕子呢喃，像白鶴鳴叫，
　　又像鴿子哀鳴；
　　我因仰觀，眼睛困倦。
　　耶和華啊，我受欺壓，
　　求你為我作保。"
15我可說甚麼呢？
　　他應許我的，
　　也給我成就了。
　　我因心裏的苦楚，
　　在一生的年日必悄悄而行。
16主啊，人得存活，乃在乎此；
　　我靈存活，也全在此。
　　所以求你使我痊愈，
　　仍然存活。
17看哪，我受大苦，
　　本為使我得平安；

a 10 Hebrew *Sheol*　　*b 11* A few Hebrew manuscripts; most Hebrew manuscripts *in the place of cessation*

你因愛我的靈魂（註：或作"生命"），
便救我脫離敗壞的坑，
因為你將我一切的罪
扔在你的背後。
18 原來陰間不能稱謝你，
死亡不能頌揚你，
下坑的人
不能盼望你的誠實。
19 只有活人，活人必稱謝你，
像我今日稱謝你一樣。
為父的，
必使兒女知道你的誠實。

20 耶和華肯救我，
所以我們要一生一世，
在耶和華殿中，
用絲弦的樂器唱我的詩歌。

21 以賽亞說："當取一塊無花果
餅來，貼在瘡上，王必痊愈。"
22 希西家問說："我能上耶和華
的殿，有甚麼兆頭呢？"

巴比倫使者來訪

39 那時，巴比倫王巴拉但的兒
子米羅達巴拉但聽見希西家
病而痊愈，就送書信和禮物
給他。2 希西家喜歡見使者，就把自
己寶庫的金子、銀子、香料、貴重
的膏油和他武庫的一切軍器，並所
有的寶貝都給他們看。他家中和全
國之內，希西家沒有一樣不給他們
看的。

3 於是先知以賽亞來見希西家
王，問他說："這些人說甚麼？他
們從哪裏來見你？"

希西家說："他們從遠方的巴
比倫來見我。"

4 以賽亞說："他們在你家裏看
見了甚麼？"

希西家說："凡我家中所有
的，他們都看見了；我財寶中沒有
一樣不給他們看的。"

5 以賽亞對希西家說："你要聽
萬軍之耶和華的話：6 日子必到，凡
你家裏所有的，並你列祖積蓄到如
今的，都要被擄到巴比倫去，不留
下一樣。這是耶和華說的。7 並且從
你本身所生的眾子，其中必有被擄
去，在巴比倫王宮裏當太監的。"

In your love you kept me
　from the pit of destruction;
　you have put all my sins
　　behind my back.
18 For the grave*a* cannot praise you,
　death cannot sing your praise;
　those who go down to the pit
　cannot hope for your faithfulness.
19 The living, the living—they praise you,
　as I am doing today;
　fathers tell their children
　about your faithfulness.

20 The LORD will save me,
　and we will sing with stringed instruments
all the days of our lives
　in the temple of the LORD.

21 Isaiah had said, "Prepare a poultice of figs
and apply it to the boil, and he will recover."

22 Hezekiah had asked, "What will be the sign
that I will go up to the temple of the LORD?"

Envoys From Babylon

39 At that time Merodach-Baladan son of
Baladan king of Babylon sent Hezekiah
letters and a gift, because he had heard
of his illness and recovery. 2 Hezekiah received
the envoys gladly and showed them what was
in his storehouses—the silver, the gold, the
spices, the fine oil, his entire armory and everything found among his treasures. There was
nothing in his palace or in all his kingdom that
Hezekiah did not show them.

3 Then Isaiah the prophet went to King Hezekiah and asked, "What did those men say, and
where did they come from?"

"From a distant land," Hezekiah replied.
"They came to me from Babylon."

4 The prophet asked, "What did they see in
your palace?"

"They saw everything in my palace," Hezekiah said. "There is nothing among my treasures
that I did not show them."

5 Then Isaiah said to Hezekiah, "Hear the word
of the LORD Almighty: 6 The time will surely come
when everything in your palace, and all that
your fathers have stored up until this day, will
be carried off to Babylon. Nothing will be left,
says the LORD. 7 And some of your descendants,
your own flesh and blood who will be born to
you, will be taken away, and they will become
eunuchs in the palace of the king of Babylon."

a 18 Hebrew Sheol

⁸"The word of the LORD you have spoken is good," Hezekiah replied. For he thought, "There will be peace and security in my lifetime."

Comfort for God's People

40 Comfort, comfort my people,
    says your God.
²Speak tenderly to Jerusalem,
  and proclaim to her
that her hard service has been completed,
    that her sin has been paid for,
that she has received from the LORD's hand
    double for all her sins.

³A voice of one calling:
  "In the desert prepare
  the way for the LORD^a;
  make straight in the wilderness
  a highway for our God.^b
⁴Every valley shall be raised up,
  every mountain and hill made low;
the rough ground shall become level,
  the rugged places a plain.
⁵And the glory of the LORD will be revealed,
  and all mankind together will see it.
      For the mouth of the LORD has spoken."

⁶A voice says, "Cry out."
  And I said, "What shall I cry?"

  "All men are like grass,
  and all their glory is like the flowers of the field.
⁷The grass withers and the flowers fall,
  because the breath of the LORD blows on them.
  Surely the people are grass.
⁸The grass withers and the flowers fall,
  but the word of our God stands forever."

⁹You who bring good tidings to Zion,
  go up on a high mountain.
You who bring good tidings to Jerusalem,^c
  lift up your voice with a shout,
lift it up, do not be afraid;
  say to the towns of Judah,
  "Here is your God!"
¹⁰See, the Sovereign LORD comes with power,
  and his arm rules for him.
See, his reward is with him,
  and his recompense accompanies him.

---

a 3 Or A voice of one calling in the desert: | "Prepare the way for the LORD b 3 Hebrew; Septuagint make straight the paths of our God c 9 Or O Zion, bringer of good tidings, | go up on a high mountain. | O Jerusalem, bringer of good tidings

⁸希西家對以賽亞説："你所説耶和華的話甚好！因為在我的年日中，必有太平和穩固的景況。"

對神子民的安慰

40 你們的神説：你們要安慰，
  安慰我的百姓。
²要對耶路撒冷説安慰的話，
  又向他宣告説，
他爭戰的日子已滿了；
  他的罪孽赦免了，
他為自己的一切罪，
  從耶和華手中加倍受罰。

³有人聲喊着説：
  "在曠野預備耶和華的路（註：或作
    "在曠野，有人聲喊着説："當預備耶和
    華的路"），
  在沙漠地修平我們神的道。
⁴一切山窪都要填滿，
  大小山岡都要削平。
高高低低的要改為平坦，
  崎崎嶇嶇的必成為平原。
⁵耶和華的榮耀必然顯現，
  凡有血氣的必一同看見。
    因為這是耶和華親口説的。"

⁶有人聲説："你喊叫吧！"
  有一個説："我喊叫甚麼呢？"

  説："凡有血氣的盡都如草，
  他的美容
    都像野地的花。
⁷草必枯乾，花必凋殘，
  因為耶和華的氣吹在其上；
  百姓誠然是草。
⁸草必枯乾，花必凋殘，
  惟有我們神的話必永遠立定！"

⁹報好信息給錫安的啊，
  你要登高山；
報好信息給耶路撒冷的啊，
  你要極力揚聲，
揚聲不要懼怕，
  對猶大的城邑説：
  "看哪，你們的神！"
¹⁰主耶和華必象大能者臨到，
  他的膀臂必為他掌權。
他的賞賜在他那裏，
  他的報應在他面前。

11他必像牧人
　　牧養自己的羊羣，
　用膀臂聚集羊羔抱在懷中，
　　慢慢引導那乳養小羊的。

12誰曾用手心
　　量諸水，
　用手虎口
　　量蒼天？
　用升斗盛大地的塵土，
　　用秤稱山嶺，用天平平岡陵呢？
13誰曾測度耶和華的心（註：或作“誰曾
　　指示耶和華的靈”），
　　或作他的謀士指教他呢？
14他與誰商議，誰教導他，
　　誰將公平的路指示他，
　又將知識教訓他，
　　將通達的道指教他呢？

15看哪，萬民都像水桶的一滴，
　　又算如天平上的微塵；
　他舉起眾海島，
　　好像極微之物。
16黎巴嫩的樹林不夠當柴燒，
　　其中的走獸也不夠作燔祭。
17萬民在他面前好像虛無，
　　被他看為不及虛無，
　　乃為虛空。

18你們究竟將誰比神，
　　用甚麼形像與神比較呢？
19偶像是匠人鑄造，
　　銀匠用金包裹，
　　為它鑄造銀鍊。
20窮乏獻不起這樣供物的，
　　就揀選不能朽壞的樹木，
　為自己尋找巧匠，
　　立起不能搖動的偶像。

21你們豈不曾知道嗎？
　　你們豈不曾聽見嗎？
　從起初沒有人告訴你們嗎？
　　自從立地的根基，
　　你們豈沒有明白嗎？
22神坐在地球大圈之上，
　　地上的居民好像蝗蟲。
　他鋪張穹蒼如幔子，
　　展開諸天如可住的帳棚。
23他使君王歸於虛無，
　　使地上的審判官成為虛空。
24他們是剛才栽上（註：“剛才”或作“不
　　曾”。下同），剛才種上，
　　根也剛才扎在地裏；

11He tends his flock like a shepherd:
　He gathers the lambs in his arms
　　and carries them close to his heart;
　he gently leads those that have young.

12Who has measured the waters in the hollow
　　of his hand,
　or with the breadth of his hand marked off
　　the heavens?
　Who has held the dust of the earth in a basket,
　　or weighed the mountains on the scales
　　and the hills in a balance?
13Who has understood the mind*a* of the LORD,
　　or instructed him as his counselor?
14Whom did the LORD consult to enlighten him,
　　and who taught him the right way?
　Who was it that taught him knowledge
　　or showed him the path of understanding?

15Surely the nations are like a drop in a bucket;
　　they are regarded as dust on the scales;
　he weighs the islands as though they were
　　fine dust.
16Lebanon is not sufficient for altar fires,
　　nor its animals enough for burnt offerings.
17Before him all the nations are as nothing;
　　they are regarded by him as worthless
　　and less than nothing.

18To whom, then, will you compare God?
　　What image will you compare him to?
19As for an idol, a craftsman casts it,
　　and a goldsmith overlays it with gold
　　and fashions silver chains for it.
20A man too poor to present such an offering
　　selects wood that will not rot.
　He looks for a skilled craftsman
　　to set up an idol that will not topple.

21Do you not know?
　　Have you not heard?
　Has it not been told you from the beginning?
　　Have you not understood since the earth
　　was founded?
22He sits enthroned above the circle of the earth,
　　and its people are like grasshoppers.
　He stretches out the heavens like a canopy,
　　and spreads them out like a tent to live in.
23He brings princes to naught
　　and reduces the rulers of this world to nothing.
24No sooner are they planted,
　　no sooner are they sown,
　　no sooner do they take root in the ground,

a 13 Or Spirit; or spirit

than he blows on them and they wither,
  and a whirlwind sweeps them away like chaff.

25"To whom will you compare me?
  Or who is my equal?" says the Holy One.
26Lift your eyes and look to the heavens:
  Who created all these?
He who brings out the starry host one by one,
  and calls them each by name.
Because of his great power and mighty
    strength,
  not one of them is missing.

27Why do you say, O Jacob,
  and complain, O Israel,
"My way is hidden from the LORD;
  my cause is disregarded by my God"?
28Do you not know?
  Have you not heard?
The LORD is the everlasting God,
  the Creator of the ends of the earth.
He will not grow tired or weary,
  and his understanding no one can fathom.
29He gives strength to the weary
  and increases the power of the weak.
30Even youths grow tired and weary,
  and young men stumble and fall;
31but those who hope in the LORD
  will renew their strength.
They will soar on wings like eagles;
  they will run and not grow weary,
  they will walk and not be faint.

The Helper of Israel

41 "Be silent before me, you islands!
  Let the nations renew their strength!
  Let them come forward and speak;
  let us meet together at the place of judgment.

2"Who has stirred up one from the east,
  calling him in righteousness to his service*a*?
He hands nations over to him
  and subdues kings before him.
He turns them to dust with his sword,
  to windblown chaff with his bow.
3He pursues them and moves on unscathed,
  by a path his feet have not traveled before.
4Who has done this and carried it through,
  calling forth the generations from the
    beginning?
I, the LORD—with the first of them
  and with the last—I am he."

a 2 Or / whom victory meets at every step

他一吹在其上，便都枯乾，
  旋風將他們吹去，像碎稭一樣。

25那聖者說：「你們將誰比我，
  叫他與我相等呢？
26你們向上舉目，
  看誰創造這萬象，
按數目領出，
  他一一稱其名，
因他的權能，
  又因他的大能大力，
連一個都不缺。」

27雅各啊，你為何說：
  「我的道路向耶和華隱藏？」
以色列啊，你為何言：
  「我的冤屈神並不查問？」
28你豈不曾知道嗎？
  你豈不曾聽見嗎？
永在的神耶和華，
  創造地極的主，
並不疲乏，也不困倦，
  他的智慧無法測度。
29疲乏的，他賜能力；
  軟弱的，他加力量。
30就是少年人也要疲乏困倦，
  強壯的也必全然跌倒；
31但那等候耶和華的，
  必從新得力。
他們必如鷹展翅上騰；
  他們奔跑卻不困倦，
  行走卻不疲乏。

以色列的幫助者

41 眾海島啊，當在我面前靜默！
  眾民當從新得力，
  都要近前來才可以說話，
  我們可以彼此辯論。

2 「誰從東方興起一人，
  憑公義召他來到腳前呢？
耶和華將列國交給他，
  使他管轄君王，
把他們如灰塵交與他的刀，
  如風吹的碎稭交與他的弓。
3他追趕他們，
  走他所未走的道，坦然前行。
4誰行做成就這事，
  從起初宣召歷代呢？
就是我耶和華；
  我是首先的，
  也與末後的同在。

5海島看見就都害怕；
　　地極也都戰兢，
　　就近前來。
6他們各人幫助鄰舍，
　　各人對弟兄說："壯膽吧！"
7木匠勉勵銀匠，
　　用鎚打光的
　　　勉勵打砧的，
　　論銲工說："銲得好！"
　　又用釘子釘穩，免得偶像動搖。

8"惟你以色列我的僕人，
　　雅各我所揀選的，
　　我朋友亞伯拉罕的後裔，
9你是我從地極所領（註：原文作"抓"）
　　來的，從地角所召來的，
　　且對你說：'你是我的僕人'，
　　我揀選你，並不棄絕你。
10你不要害怕，因為我與你同在；
　　不要驚惶，因為我是你的神。
　　我必堅固你，我必幫助你，
　　我必用我公義的右手扶持你。

11"凡向你發怒的
　　必都抱愧蒙羞，
　　與你相爭的必如無有，
　　並要滅亡。
12與你爭競的，
　　你要找他們也找不着；
　　與你爭戰的必如無有，
　　成為虛無。
13因為我耶和華你的神
　　必攙扶你的右手，
　　對你說：不要害怕！
　　我必幫助你。
14你這蟲雅各和你們以色列人，
　　不要害怕！
　　耶和華說：我必幫助你。"
　　你的救贖主就是以色列的聖者。
15"看哪，我已使你成為
　　有快齒打糧的新器具；
　　你要把山嶺打得粉碎，
　　使岡陵如同糠粃。
16你要把它簸揚，
　　風要吹去，
　　旋風要把它颳散。
　　你倒要以耶和華為喜樂，
　　以以色列的聖者為誇耀。

17"困苦窮乏人尋求水
　　卻沒有，
　　他們因口渴，舌頭乾燥。
　　我耶和華必應允他們，
　　我以色列的神必不離棄他們。

5The islands have seen it and fear;
　　the ends of the earth tremble.
　　They approach and come forward;
6　each helps the other
　　and says to his brother, "Be strong!"
7The craftsman encourages the goldsmith,
　　and he who smooths with the hammer
　　spurs on him who strikes the anvil.
　　He says of the welding, "It is good."
　　He nails down the idol so it will not topple.

8"But you, O Israel, my servant,
　　Jacob, whom I have chosen,
　　you descendants of Abraham my friend,
9I took you from the ends of the earth,
　　from its farthest corners I called you.
　　I said, 'You are my servant';
　　I have chosen you and have not rejected you.
10So do not fear, for I am with you;
　　do not be dismayed, for I am your God.
　　I will strengthen you and help you;
　　I will uphold you with my righteous right
　　　hand.

11"All who rage against you
　　will surely be ashamed and disgraced;
　　those who oppose you
　　will be as nothing and perish.
12Though you search for your enemies,
　　you will not find them.
　　Those who wage war against you
　　will be as nothing at all.
13For I am the LORD, your God,
　　who takes hold of your right hand
　　and says to you, Do not fear;
　　I will help you.
14Do not be afraid, O worm Jacob,
　　O little Israel,
　　for I myself will help you," declares the LORD,
　　your Redeemer, the Holy One of Israel.
15"See, I will make you into a threshing sledge,
　　new and sharp, with many teeth.
　　You will thresh the mountains and crush them,
　　and reduce the hills to chaff.
16You will winnow them, the wind will pick
　　them up,
　　and a gale will blow them away.
　　But you will rejoice in the LORD
　　and glory in the Holy One of Israel.

17"The poor and needy search for water,
　　but there is none;
　　their tongues are parched with thirst.
　　But I the LORD will answer them;
　　I, the God of Israel, will not forsake them.

¹⁸I will make rivers flow on barren heights,
　　and springs within the valleys.
　I will turn the desert into pools of water,
　　and the parched ground into springs.
¹⁹I will put in the desert
　　the cedar and the acacia, the myrtle and the
　　　olive.
　I will set pines in the wasteland,
　　the fir and the cypress together,
²⁰so that people may see and know,
　　may consider and understand,
　that the hand of the LORD has done this,
　　that the Holy One of Israel has created it.

²¹"Present your case," says the LORD.
　　"Set forth your arguments," says Jacob's
　　　King.
²²"Bring in your idols to tell us
　　what is going to happen.
　Tell us what the former things were,
　　so that we may consider them
　　and know their final outcome.
　Or declare to us the things to come,
²³　tell us what the future holds,
　　so we may know that you are gods.
　Do something, whether good or bad,
　　so that we will be dismayed and filled with
　　　fear.
²⁴But you are less than nothing
　　and your works are utterly worthless;
　he who chooses you is detestable.

²⁵"I have stirred up one from the north, and he
　　comes—
　one from the rising sun who calls on my name.
　He treads on rulers as if they were mortar,
　　as if he were a potter treading the clay.
²⁶Who told of this from the beginning, so we
　　could know,
　　or beforehand, so we could say, 'He was
　　　right'?
　No one told of this,
　　no one foretold it,
　　no one heard any words from you.
²⁷I was the first to tell Zion, 'Look, here they are!'
　　I gave to Jerusalem a messenger of good
　　　tidings.
²⁸I look but there is no one—
　　no one among them to give counsel,
　　no one to give answer when I ask them.
²⁹See, they are all false!
　　Their deeds amount to nothing;
　　their images are but wind and confusion.

¹⁸我要在淨光的高處開江河，
　　在谷中開泉源；
　我要使沙漠變為水池，
　　使乾地變為湧泉。
¹⁹我要在曠野種上
　　香柏樹、皂莢樹、番石榴樹
　　　和野橄欖樹；
　我在沙漠要把松樹、杉樹，
　　並黃楊樹一同栽植；
²⁰好叫人看見、知道、
　　思想、明白，
　這是耶和華的手所做的，
　　是以色列的聖者所造的。"

²¹耶和華對假神說：
　　"你們要呈上你們的案件。"
　雅各的君說：
　　"你們要聲明你們確實的理由。"
²²　"可以聲明、
　　指示我們將來必遇的事，
　說明先前的是甚麼事，
　　好叫我們思索、得知事的結局，
　　或者把將來的事指示我們。
²³要說明後來的事，
　　好叫我們知道你們是神。
　你們或降福，或降禍，
　　使我們驚奇，
　　一同觀看。
²⁴看哪，你們屬乎虛無，
　　你們的作為也屬乎虛空。
　那選擇你們的是可憎惡的。

²⁵　"我從北方興起一人，
　　他是求告我名的，
　　從日出之地而來。
　他必臨到掌權的，好像臨到灰泥，
　　彷彿窰匠蹋泥一樣。
²⁶誰從起初指明這事，
　　使我們知道呢？
　誰從先前說明，
　　使我們說他不錯呢？
　誰也沒有指明，
　　誰也沒有說明；
　　誰也沒有聽見你們的話。
²⁷我首先對錫安說：看哪，
　　我要將一位報好信息的
　　賜給耶路撒冷。
²⁸我看的時候並沒有人；
　　我問的時候，他們中間也沒有
　　　謀士可以回答一句。
²⁹看哪，他們和他們的工作
　　都是虛空，且是虛無。
　他們所鑄的偶像都是風，
　　都是虛的。"

主的僕人

42 "看哪，我的僕人，我所扶持、
所揀選、心裏所喜悅的。
我已將我的靈賜給他，
他必將公理傳給外邦。
²他不喧嚷，不揚聲，
也不使街上聽見他的聲音。
³壓傷的蘆葦，他不折斷；
將殘的燈火，他不吹滅。
他憑真實將公理傳開。
⁴他不灰心，也不喪膽，
直到他在地上設立公理，
海島都等候他的訓誨。"

⁵創造諸天，
鋪張穹蒼，
將地和地所出的
一併鋪開，
賜氣息給地上的眾人，
又賜靈性給行在其上之人的
神耶和華，他如此說：
⁶"我耶和華憑公義召你，
必攙扶你的手，
保守你，使你作眾民的中保（註：
"中保"原文作"約"），
作外邦人的光，
⁷開瞎子的眼，
領被囚的出牢獄，
領坐黑暗的出監牢。

⁸"我是耶和華，這是我的名。
我必不將我的榮耀歸給假神，
也不將我的稱讚歸給雕刻的偶像。
⁹看哪！先前的事已經成就，
現在我將新事說明，
這事未發以先，
我就說給你們聽。"

讚美主的歌

¹⁰航海的和海中所有的，
海島和其上的居民，
都當向耶和華唱新歌，
從地極讚美他！
¹¹曠野和其中的城邑，
並基達人居住的村莊都當揚聲；
西拉的居民當歡呼，
在山頂上吶喊！
¹²他們當將榮耀歸給耶和華，
在海島中傳揚他的頌讚。
¹³耶和華必像勇士出去，
必像戰士激動熱心，
要喊叫，大聲吶喊，
要用大力攻擊仇敵。

The Servant of the LORD

42 "Here is my servant, whom I uphold,
my chosen one in whom I delight;
I will put my Spirit on him
and he will bring justice to the nations.
²He will not shout or cry out,
or raise his voice in the streets.
³A bruised reed he will not break,
and a smoldering wick he will not snuff out.
In faithfulness he will bring forth justice;
⁴ he will not falter or be discouraged
till he establishes justice on earth.
In his law the islands will put their hope."

⁵This is what God the LORD says—
he who created the heavens and stretched
them out,
who spread out the earth and all that comes
out of it,
who gives breath to its people,
and life to those who walk on it:
⁶"I, the LORD, have called you in righteousness;
I will take hold of your hand.
I will keep you and will make you
to be a covenant for the people
and a light for the Gentiles,
⁷to open eyes that are blind,
to free captives from prison
and to release from the dungeon those who
sit in darkness.

⁸"I am the LORD; that is my name!
I will not give my glory to another
or my praise to idols.
⁹See, the former things have taken place,
and new things I declare;
before they spring into being
I announce them to you."

Song of Praise to the LORD

¹⁰Sing to the LORD a new song,
his praise from the ends of the earth,
you who go down to the sea, and all that is in it,
you islands, and all who live in them.
¹¹Let the desert and its towns raise their voices;
let the settlements where Kedar lives rejoice.
Let the people of Sela sing for joy;
let them shout from the mountaintops.
¹²Let them give glory to the LORD
and proclaim his praise in the islands.
¹³The LORD will march out like a mighty man,
like a warrior he will stir up his zeal;
with a shout he will raise the battle cry
and will triumph over his enemies.

14"For a long time I have kept silent,
  I have been quiet and held myself back.
But now, like a woman in childbirth,
  I cry out, I gasp and pant.
15I will lay waste the mountains and hills
  and dry up all their vegetation;
I will turn rivers into islands
  and dry up the pools.
16I will lead the blind by ways they have not
    known,
  along unfamiliar paths I will guide them;
I will turn the darkness into light before them
  and make the rough places smooth.
These are the things I will do;
  I will not forsake them.
17But those who trust in idols,
  who say to images, 'You are our gods,'
  will be turned back in utter shame.

Israel Blind and Deaf

18"Hear, you deaf;
  look, you blind, and see!
19Who is blind but my servant,
  and deaf like the messenger I send?
Who is blind like the one committed to me,
  blind like the servant of the LORD?
20You have seen many things, but have paid no
    attention;
  your ears are open, but you hear nothing."
21It pleased the LORD
  for the sake of his righteousness
  to make his law great and glorious.
22But this is a people plundered and looted,
  all of them trapped in pits
  or hidden away in prisons.
They have become plunder,
  with no one to rescue them;
they have been made loot,
  with no one to say, "Send them back."

23Which of you will listen to this
  or pay close attention in time to come?
24Who handed Jacob over to become loot,
  and Israel to the plunderers?
Was it not the LORD,
  against whom we have sinned?
For they would not follow his ways;
  they did not obey his law.
25So he poured out on them his burning anger,
  the violence of war.
It enveloped them in flames, yet they did not
    understand;
  it consumed them, but they did not take it to
    heart.

---

14 "我許久閉口不言，
　　靜默不語；
　　現在我要喊叫像產難的婦人，
　　我要急氣而喘哮。
15我要使大山小岡變為荒場，
　　使其上的花草都枯乾；
　　我要使江河變為洲島，
　　使水池都乾涸。
16我要引瞎子
　　行不認識的道，
　　領他們走不知道的路；
　　在他們面前使黑暗變為光明，
　　使彎曲變為平直。
　　這些事我都要行，
　　並不離棄他們。
17倚靠雕刻的偶像，
　　對鑄造的偶像說：'你是我們的神'，
　　這等人要退後，全然蒙羞。"

以色列眼瞎耳聾

18 "你們這耳聾的，聽吧！
　　你們這眼瞎的，看吧！
　　使你們能看見。
19誰比我的僕人眼瞎呢？
　　誰比我差遣的使者耳聾呢？
　　誰瞎眼像那與我和好的？
　　誰瞎眼像耶和華的僕人呢？
20你看見許多事卻不領會；
　　耳朵開通卻不聽見。"
21耶和華因自己公義的緣故，
　　喜歡使律法 (註：或作"訓誨")
　　為大、為尊。
22但這百姓是被搶被奪的，
　　都牢籠在坑中，
　　隱藏在獄裏。
他們作掠物，
　　無人拯救；
作擄物，
　　無人說交還。

23你們中間誰肯側耳聽此，
　　誰肯留心而聽，以防將來呢？
24誰將雅各交出當作擄物，
　　將以色列交給搶奪的呢？
　　豈不是耶和華嗎？
　　就是我們所得罪的那位。
他們不肯遵行他的道，
　　也不聽從他的訓誨。
25所以，他將猛烈的怒氣
　　和爭戰的勇力，
　　傾倒在以色列的身上；
　　在他四圍如火著起，他還不知道，
　　燒着他，他也不介意。

以色列的唯一救主

43 雅各啊，創造你的耶和華；以色列啊，造成你的那位，現在如此說：

"你不要害怕！因為我救贖了你。
我曾提你的名召你，
你是屬我的。

2 你從水中經過，
我必與你同在；
你趟過江河，
水必不漫過你；
你從火中行過，
必不被燒，
火焰也不着在你身上。

3 因為我是耶和華你的神，
是以色列的聖者、你的救主。
我已經使埃及作你的贖價，
使古實和西巴代替你。

4 因我看你為寶為尊，
又因我愛你，
所以我使人代替你，
使列邦人替換你的生命。

5 不要害怕，因我與你同在！
我必領你的後裔從東方來，
又從西方招聚你。

6 我要對北方說：'交出來！'
對南方說：'不要拘留！'
將我的眾子從遠方帶來，
將我的眾女從地極領回，

7 就是凡稱為我名下的人，
是我為自己的榮耀創造的，
是我所做成、所造作的。"

8 你要將有眼而瞎、
有耳而聾的民都帶出來。

9 任憑萬國聚集，
任憑眾民會合，
其中誰能將此聲明，
並將先前的事說給我們聽呢？
他們可以帶出見證來，自顯為是，
或者他們聽見便說：
"這是真的。"

10 耶和華說："你們是我的見證，
我所揀選的僕人。
既是這樣，便可以知道，且信服我，
又明白我就是耶和華。
在我以前沒有真神（註："真"原文作
"造作的"），在我以後也必沒有。

11 惟有我是耶和華，
除我以外沒有救主。

12 我曾指示，我曾拯救，我曾說明，
並且在你們中間沒有別神。"
所以耶和華說：
"你們是我的見證，我也是神。

Israel's Only Savior

43 But now, this is what the LORD says—
he who created you, O Jacob,
he who formed you, O Israel:
"Fear not, for I have redeemed you;
I have summoned you by name; you are
mine.

2 When you pass through the waters,
I will be with you;
and when you pass through the rivers,
they will not sweep over you.
When you walk through the fire,
you will not be burned;
the flames will not set you ablaze.

3 For I am the LORD, your God,
the Holy One of Israel, your Savior;
I give Egypt for your ransom,
Cush[a] and Seba in your stead.

4 Since you are precious and honored in my sight,
and because I love you,
I will give men in exchange for you,
and people in exchange for your life.

5 Do not be afraid, for I am with you;
I will bring your children from the east
and gather you from the west.

6 I will say to the north, 'Give them up!'
and to the south, 'Do not hold them back.'
Bring my sons from afar
and my daughters from the ends of the earth—

7 everyone who is called by my name,
whom I created for my glory,
whom I formed and made."

8 Lead out those who have eyes but are blind,
who have ears but are deaf.

9 All the nations gather together
and the peoples assemble.
Which of them foretold this
and proclaimed to us the former things?
Let them bring in their witnesses to prove
they were right,
so that others may hear and say, "It is true."

10 "You are my witnesses," declares the LORD,
"and my servant whom I have chosen,
so that you may know and believe me
and understand that I am he.
Before me no god was formed,
nor will there be one after me.

11 I, even I, am the LORD,
and apart from me there is no savior.

12 I have revealed and saved and proclaimed—
I, and not some foreign god among you.
You are my witnesses," declares the LORD,
"that I am God.

a 3 That is, the upper Nile region

13　Yes, and from ancient days I am he.
　　No one can deliver out of my hand.
　　When I act, who can reverse it?"

God's Mercy and Israel's Unfaithfulness

14This is what the LORD says—
　　your Redeemer, the Holy One of Israel:
　　"For your sake I will send to Babylon
　　and bring down as fugitives all the
　　　　Babylonians,ᵃ
　　in the ships in which they took pride.
15I am the LORD, your Holy One,
　　Israel's Creator, your King."

16This is what the LORD says—
　　he who made a way through the sea,
　　a path through the mighty waters,
17who drew out the chariots and horses,
　　the army and reinforcements together,
　　and they lay there, never to rise again,
　　extinguished, snuffed out like a wick:
18"Forget the former things;
　　do not dwell on the past.
19See, I am doing a new thing!
　　　Now it springs up; do you not perceive it?
　　I am making a way in the desert
　　and streams in the wasteland.
20The wild animals honor me,
　　the jackals and the owls,
　　because I provide water in the desert
　　and streams in the wasteland,
　　to give drink to my people, my chosen,
21　the people I formed for myself
　　that they may proclaim my praise.

22"Yet you have not called upon me, O Jacob,
　　you have not wearied yourselves for me,
　　　　O Israel.
23You have not brought me sheep for burnt
　　　　offerings,
　　nor honored me with your sacrifices.
　　I have not burdened you with grain offerings
　　nor wearied you with demands for incense.
24You have not bought any fragrant calamus for
　　　　me,
　　or lavished on me the fat of your sacrifices.
　　But you have burdened me with your sins
　　and wearied me with your offenses.

25"I, even I, am he who blots out
　　your transgressions, for my own sake,
　　and remembers your sins no more.

13自從有日子以來，我就是神。
　　誰也不能救人脫離我手，
　　我要行事誰能阻止呢？"

神的慈愛與以色列的不忠

14耶和華你們的救贖主——
　　以色列的聖者如此說：
　　"因你們的緣故，
　　我已經打發人到巴比倫去，
　　並且我要使迦勒底人如逃民，
　　都坐自己喜樂的船下來。
15我是耶和華——你們的聖者，
　　是創造以色列的，是你們的君王。"

16耶和華
　　在滄海中開道，
　　在大水中開路，
17使車輛、馬匹、軍兵、勇士都出來，
　　一同躺下，不再起來，
　　他們滅沒，好像熄滅的燈火。
18耶和華如此說：
　　"你們不要記念從前的事，
　　也不要思想古時的事。
19看哪，我要做一件新事，
　　如今要發現，你們豈不知道嗎？
　　我必在曠野開道路，
　　在沙漠開江河。
20野地的走獸必尊重我，
　　野狗和駝鳥也必如此。
　　因我使曠野有水，
　　使沙漠有河，
　　好賜給我的百姓、我的選民喝。
21這百姓是我為自己所造的，
　　好述說我的美德。

22　"雅各啊，你並沒有求告我；
　　以色列啊，
　　你倒厭煩我。
23你沒有將你的羊帶來
　　給我作燔祭，
　　也沒有用祭物尊敬我；
　　我沒有因供物使你服勞，
　　也沒有因乳香使你厭煩。
24你沒有用銀子
　　為我買菖蒲，
　　也沒有用祭物的脂油使我飽足；
　　倒使我因你的罪惡服勞，
　　使我因你的罪孽厭煩。

25　"惟有我為自己的緣故
　　塗抹你的過犯，
　　我也不記念你的罪惡。

---

a 14 Or Chaldeans

26你要提醒我，
　　　你我可以一同辯論；
　　　你可以將你的理陳明，自顯為義。
27你的始祖犯罪，
　　　你的師傅違背我。
28所以我要辱沒
　　　　聖所的首領，
　　　使雅各成為咒詛，
　　　使以色列成為辱罵。

以色列蒙揀選

44 "我的僕人雅各，
　　我所揀選的以色列啊，
　　現在你當聽！
2造作你，
　　　又從你出胎造就你，
　　　並要幫助你的耶和華如此說：
　我的僕人雅各，
　　　我所揀選的耶書崙哪，不要害怕！
3因為我要將水澆灌口渴的人，
　　　將河澆灌乾旱之地；
　　我要將我的靈澆灌你的後裔，
　　　將我的福澆灌你的子孫。
4他們要發生在草中，
　　　像溪水旁的柳樹。
5這個要說：我是屬耶和華的；
　　　那個要以雅各的名自稱；
　　又一個要親手寫：歸耶和華的（註：
　　　　或作"在手上寫歸耶和華"），
　　　並自稱為以色列。

主，非偶像

6 "耶和華以色列的君──
　　　以色列的救贖主，
　　萬軍之耶和華如此說：
　　　我是首先的，我是末後的，
　　　除我以外再沒有真神！
7自從我設立古時的民，
　　　誰能像我宣告，
　　並且指明，
　　　　又為自己陳說呢？
　　讓他將未來的事
　　　和必成的事說明。
8你們不要恐懼，也不要害怕，
　　　我豈不是從上古就說明
　　　　指示你們嗎？
　　並且你們是我的見證。
　除我以外，豈有真神嗎？
　　　誠然沒有磐石，我不知道一個！"

9製造雕刻偶像的盡都虛空；
　　　他們所喜悅的都無益處。

26Review the past for me,
　　let us argue the matter together;
　　state the case for your innocence.
27Your first father sinned;
　　your spokesmen rebelled against me.
28So I will disgrace the dignitaries of your
　　　temple,
　　and I will consign Jacob to destruction[a]
　　and Israel to scorn.

Israel the Chosen

44 "But now listen, O Jacob, my servant,
　　Israel, whom I have chosen.
　　2This is what the LORD says—
　he who made you, who formed you in the
　　　womb,
　　and who will help you:
　Do not be afraid, O Jacob, my servant,
　　Jeshurun, whom I have chosen.
3For I will pour water on the thirsty land,
　　and streams on the dry ground;
　I will pour out my Spirit on your offspring,
　　and my blessing on your descendants.
4They will spring up like grass in a meadow,
　　like poplar trees by flowing streams.
5One will say, 'I belong to the LORD';
　　another will call himself by the name of Jacob;
　still another will write on his hand, 'The
　　　LORD's,'
　　and will take the name Israel.

The LORD, Not Idols

6"This is what the LORD says—
　　Israel's King and Redeemer, the LORD
　　　Almighty:
　I am the first and I am the last;
　　apart from me there is no God.
7Who then is like me? Let him proclaim it.
　　Let him declare and lay out before me
　what has happened since I established my
　　　ancient people,
　　and what is yet to come—
　　yes, let him foretell what will come.
8Do not tremble, do not be afraid.
　　Did I not proclaim this and foretell it long
　　　ago?
　You are my witnesses. Is there any God
　　　besides me?
　　No, there is no other Rock; I know not one."

9All who make idols are nothing,
　　and the things they treasure are worthless.

---

a 28 The Hebrew term refers to the irrevocable giving over of
things or persons to the LORD, often by totally destroying
them.

Those who would speak up for them are blind;
  they are ignorant, to their own shame.

10Who shapes a god and casts an idol,
  which can profit him nothing?

11He and his kind will be put to shame;
  craftsmen are nothing but men.
Let them all come together and take their stand;
  they will be brought down to terror and
    infamy.

12The blacksmith takes a tool
  and works with it in the coals;
he shapes an idol with hammers,
  he forges it with the might of his arm.
He gets hungry and loses his strength;
  he drinks no water and grows faint.

13The carpenter measures with a line
  and makes an outline with a marker;
he roughs it out with chisels
  and marks it with compasses.
He shapes it in the form of man,
  of man in all his glory,
  that it may dwell in a shrine.

14He cut down cedars,
  or perhaps took a cypress or oak.
He let it grow among the trees of the forest,
  or planted a pine, and the rain made it grow.

15It is man's fuel for burning;
  some of it he takes and warms himself,
  he kindles a fire and bakes bread.
But he also fashions a god and worships it;
  he makes an idol and bows down to it.

16Half of the wood he burns in the fire;
  over it he prepares his meal,
  he roasts his meat and eats his fill.
He also warms himself and says,
  "Ah! I am warm; I see the fire."

17From the rest he makes a god, his idol;
  he bows down to it and worships.
He prays to it and says,
  "Save me; you are my god."

18They know nothing, they understand nothing;
  their eyes are plastered over so they cannot
    see,
  and their minds closed so they cannot
    understand.

19No one stops to think,
  no one has the knowledge or understanding
    to say,
"Half of it I used for fuel;
  I even baked bread over its coals,
  I roasted meat and I ate.
Shall I make a detestable thing from what is
    left?
Shall I bow down to a block of wood?"

他們的見證無所看見,
  無所知曉,他們便覺羞愧。

10誰製造神像,
  鑄造無益的偶像?

11看哪,他的同伴都必羞愧!
  工匠也不過是人,
任他們聚會,任他們站立,
  都必懼怕,
  一同羞愧。

12鐵匠把鐵
  在火炭中燒熱,
用鎚打鐵器,
  用他有力的膀臂錘成;
他飢餓而無力,
  不喝水而發倦。

13木匠拉線,
  用筆劃出樣子,
用鉋子鉋成形狀,
  用圓尺劃了模樣,
仿照人的體態,
  做成人形,
  好住在房屋中。

14他砍伐香柏樹,
  又取柞(註:或作「青桐」)樹和橡樹,
  在樹林中選定了一棵。
他栽種松樹,得雨長養。

15這樹,人可用以燒火。
  他自己取些烤火,
  又燒着烤餅,
  而且做神像跪拜,
  做雕刻的偶像向他叩拜。

16他把一分燒在火中,
  把一分烤肉吃飽。
自己烤火說:
  「阿哈!我暖和了!
  我見火了!」

17他用剩下的做了一神,
  就是雕刻的偶像。
他向這偶像俯伏叩拜,禱告它說:
  「求你拯救我,因你是我的神。」

18他們不知道,也不思想,
  因為耶和華閉住他們的眼,
    不能看見;
  塞住他們的心,
    不能明白。

19誰心裏也不醒悟,
  也沒有知識,沒有聰明,
  能說:
  「我曾拿一分在火中燒了,
  在炭火上烤過餅,
  我也烤過肉吃,
這剩下的
  我豈要做可憎的物嗎?
  我豈可向木不子叩拜呢?」

20他以灰為食，心中昏迷，
　　使他偏邪，
他不能自救，也不能說：
　　"我右手中豈不是有虛謊嗎？"

21 "雅各、以色列啊，
　　你是我的僕人，要記念這些事。
以色列啊，你是我的僕人，
　　我造就你，必不忘記你。
22我塗抹了你的過犯，像厚雲消散；
　　我塗抹了你的罪惡，如薄雲滅沒。
你當歸向我，
　　因我救贖了你。"

23諸天哪，應當歌唱！
　　因為耶和華做成這事。
地的深處啊，應當歡呼！
眾山應當發聲歌唱，
　　樹林和其中所有的樹都當如此。
因為耶和華救贖了雅各，
　　並要因以色列榮耀自己。

耶路撒冷必有人居住

24 "從你出胎，
　　造就你的救贖主耶和華如此說：

我耶和華是創造萬物的，
　　是獨自鋪張諸天、
　　鋪開大地的。
　　誰與我同在呢？

25使說假話的兆頭失效，
　　使占卜的癲狂，
使智慧人退後，
　　使他的知識變為愚拙。
26使我僕人的話語立定，
　　我使者的謀算成就。

論到耶路撒冷說：'必有人居住。'
論到猶大的城邑說：'必被建造，
　　其中的荒場我也必興起。'
27對深淵說：'你乾了吧！
　　我也要使你的江河乾涸。'
28論塞魯士說：'他是我的牧人，
　　必成就我所喜悅的，
必下令建造耶路撒冷，
　　發命立穩聖殿的根基。'

45 "我耶和華
　　所膏的塞魯士，
　　我攙扶他的右手，
使列國降伏在他面前。
我也要放鬆列王的腰帶，
　　使城門在他面前敞開，
　　不得關閉。我對他如此說：

20He feeds on ashes, a deluded heart misleads
　　　him;
　　he cannot save himself, or say,
　　"Is not this thing in my right hand a lie?"

21"Remember these things, O Jacob,
　　for you are my servant, O Israel.
　　I have made you, you are my servant;
　　O Israel, I will not forget you.
22I have swept away your offenses like a cloud,
　　your sins like the morning mist.
　　Return to me,
　　for I have redeemed you."

23Sing for joy, O heavens, for the LORD has done
　　　this;
　　shout aloud, O earth beneath.
　　Burst into song, you mountains,
　　you forests and all your trees,
　　for the LORD has redeemed Jacob,
　　he displays his glory in Israel.

Jerusalem to Be Inhabited

24"This is what the LORD says—
　　your Redeemer, who formed you in the womb:

I am the LORD,
　　who has made all things,
　　who alone stretched out the heavens,
　　who spread out the earth by myself,

25who foils the signs of false prophets
　　and makes fools of diviners,
　　who overthrows the learning of the wise
　　and turns it into nonsense,
26who carries out the words of his servants
　　and fulfills the predictions of his messengers,

who says of Jerusalem, 'It shall be inhabited,'
　　of the towns of Judah, 'They shall be built,'
　　and of their ruins, 'I will restore them,'
27who says to the watery deep, 'Be dry,
　　and I will dry up your streams,'
28who says of Cyrus, 'He is my shepherd
　　and will accomplish all that I please;
　　he will say of Jerusalem, "Let it be rebuilt,"
　　and of the temple, "Let its foundations be
　　　laid."'

45 "This is what the LORD says to his
　　anointed,
　　to Cyrus, whose right hand I take hold of
to subdue nations before him
　　and to strip kings of their armor,
to open doors before him
　　so that gates will not be shut:

²I will go before you
　　and will level the mountains[a];
　I will break down gates of bronze
　　and cut through bars of iron.
³I will give you the treasures of darkness,
　　riches stored in secret places,
　so that you may know that I am the LORD,
　　the God of Israel, who summons you by
　　name.
⁴For the sake of Jacob my servant,
　　of Israel my chosen,
　I summon you by name
　　and bestow on you a title of honor,
　　though you do not acknowledge me.
⁵I am the LORD, and there is no other;
　　apart from me there is no God.
　I will strengthen you,
　　though you have not acknowledged me,
⁶so that from the rising of the sun
　　to the place of its setting
　men may know there is none besides me.
　I am the LORD, and there is no other.
⁷I form the light and create darkness,
　　I bring prosperity and create disaster;
　I, the LORD, do all these things.

⁸"You heavens above, rain down righteousness;
　　let the clouds shower it down.
　Let the earth open wide,
　　let salvation spring up,
　let righteousness grow with it;
　　I, the LORD, have created it.

⁹"Woe to him who quarrels with his Maker,
　　to him who is but a potsherd among the
　　potsherds on the ground.
　Does the clay say to the potter,
　　'What are you making?'
　Does your work say,
　　'He has no hands'?
¹⁰Woe to him who says to his father,
　　'What have you begotten?'
　or to his mother,
　　'What have you brought to birth?'

¹¹"This is what the LORD says—
　　the Holy One of Israel, and its Maker:
　Concerning things to come,
　　do you question me about my children,
　　or give me orders about the work of my
　　hands?
¹²It is I who made the earth
　　and created mankind upon it.

²我必在你前面行，
　　修平崎嶇之地。
　我必打破銅門，
　　砍斷鐵閂。
³我要將暗中的寶物
　　和隱密的財寶賜給你，
　使你知道提名召你的，
　　就是我耶和華，
　　以色列的神。
⁴因我僕人雅各，
　　我所揀選以色列的緣故，
　我就提名召你；
　　你雖不認識我，
　　我也加給你名號。
⁵我是耶和華，在我以外並沒有別神。
　　除了我以外再沒有神。
　你雖不認識我，
　　我必給你束腰。
⁶從日出之地
　　到日落之處，
　使人都知道除了我以外，沒有別神。
　　我是耶和華，在我以外並沒有別神。
⁷我造光，又造暗；
　　我施平安，又降災禍，
　造作這一切的是我耶和華。

⁸"諸天哪，自上而滴，
　　穹蒼降下公義；
　地面開裂，
　　產出救恩，
　使公義一同發生。
　　這都是我耶和華所造的。

⁹禍哉！那與造他的主爭論的，
　　他不過是地上瓦片中的
　　一塊瓦片。
　泥土豈可對摶弄他的說：
　　'你做甚麼呢？'
　所做的物豈可說：
　　'你沒有手呢？'
¹⁰禍哉！那對父親說：
　　'你生的是甚麼呢？'
　或對母親（註：原文作"婦人"）說：
　　'你產的是甚麼呢？'

¹¹"耶和華、以色列的聖者，
　　就是造就以色列的如此說：
　將來的事你們可以問我，
　　至於我的眾子，
　　並我手的工作，你們可以求我命定
　　（註："求我命定"原文作"吩咐我"）。
¹²我造地，
　　又造人在地上；

_a 2 Dead Sea Scrolls and Septuagint; the meaning of the word
in the Masoretic Text is uncertain._

我親手鋪張諸天，
　　天上萬象也是我所命定的。
13我憑公義興起塞魯士（註：“塞魯士”
　　　　　　　原文作“他”）
　　又要修直他一切道路。
他必建造我的城，
　　釋放我被擄的民，
不是為工價，也不是為賞賜。
　　這是萬軍之耶和華說的。”

14耶和華如此說：

“埃及勞碌得來的
　　和古實的貨物
　　必歸你，
身量高大的西巴人必投降你，
　　也要屬你。
他們必帶着鎖鏈
　　過來隨從你，
又向你下拜，
　　祈求你說：
‘神真在你們中間，此外再沒有別神！
再沒有別的神！’”

15救主以色列的神啊，
　　你實在是自隱的神。
16凡製造偶像的
　　都必抱愧蒙羞，
都要一同歸於慚愧。
17惟有以色列必蒙耶和華的拯救，
　　得永遠的救恩。
你們必不蒙羞，也不抱愧，
　　直到永世無盡。

18創造諸天的耶和華，
　　製造成全大地的神，
他創造堅定大地，
　　並非使地荒涼，
　　是要給人居住。

他如此說：
　　“我是耶和華，
　　再沒有別神！
19我沒有在
　　隱密黑暗之地說話；
我沒有對雅各的後裔說：
　　‘你們尋求我是徒然的。’
我耶和華所講的是公義，
　　所說的是正直。

20　“你們從列國逃脫的人，
　　要一同聚集前來。

My own hands stretched out the heavens;
　I marshaled their starry hosts.
13I will raise up Cyrus[a] in my righteousness:
　I will make all his ways straight.
He will rebuild my city
　and set my exiles free,
but not for a price or reward,
　says the LORD Almighty."

14This is what the LORD says:

"The products of Egypt and the merchandise
　　of Cush,[b]
and those tall Sabeans—
　they will come over to you
　and will be yours;
they will trudge behind you,
　coming over to you in chains.
They will bow down before you
　and plead with you, saying,
'Surely God is with you, and there is no other;
　there is no other god.' "

15Truly you are a God who hides himself,
　O God and Savior of Israel.
16All the makers of idols will be put to shame
　　and disgraced;
　they will go off into disgrace together.
17But Israel will be saved by the LORD
　with an everlasting salvation;
you will never be put to shame or disgraced,
　to ages everlasting.

18For this is what the LORD says—
　he who created the heavens,
　　he is God;
he who fashioned and made the earth,
　he founded it;
he did not create it to be empty,
　but formed it to be inhabited—
he says:
　"I am the LORD,
　　and there is no other.
19I have not spoken in secret,
　from somewhere in a land of darkness;
I have not said to Jacob's descendants,
　'Seek me in vain.'
I, the LORD, speak the truth;
　I declare what is right.

20"Gather together and come;
　assemble, you fugitives from the nations.

Ignorant are those who carry about idols of
　　wood,
who pray to gods that cannot save.
[21]Declare what is to be, present it—
　　let them take counsel together.
Who foretold this long ago,
　　who declared it from the distant past?
Was it not I, the LORD?
　　And there is no God apart from me,
a righteous God and a Savior;
　　there is none but me.

[22]"Turn to me and be saved,
　　all you ends of the earth;
for I am God, and there is no other.
[23]By myself I have sworn,
　　my mouth has uttered in all integrity
a word that will not be revoked:
　　Before me every knee will bow;
by me every tongue will swear.
[24]They will say of me, 'In the LORD alone
　　are righteousness and strength.' "
All who have raged against him
　　will come to him and be put to shame.
[25]But in the LORD all the descendants of Israel
　　will be found righteous and will exult.

Gods of Babylon

46 Bel bows down, Nebo stoops low;
their idols are borne by beasts of burden.[a]
The images that are carried about are
　　burdensome,
a burden for the weary.
[2]They stoop and bow down together;
　　unable to rescue the burden,
they themselves go off into captivity.

[3]"Listen to me, O house of Jacob,
　　all you who remain of the house of Israel,
you whom I have upheld since you were
　　conceived,
and have carried since your birth.
[4]Even to your old age and gray hairs
　　I am he, I am he who will sustain you.
I have made you and I will carry you;
　　I will sustain you and I will rescue you.

[5]"To whom will you compare me or count me
　　equal?
To whom will you liken me that we may be
　　compared?
[6]Some pour out gold from their bags
　　and weigh out silver on the scales;

那些抬着雕刻木偶，
　　禱告不能救人之神的，
毫無知識。
[21]你們要述說陳明你們的理，
　　讓他們彼此商議。
誰從古時指明？
　　誰從上古述說？
不是我耶和華嗎？
　　除了我以外，再沒有神！
我是公義的神，又是救主，
　　除了我以外，再沒有別神！

[22]"地極的人都當仰望我，
　　就必得救。
因為我是神，再沒有別神！
[23]我指着自己起誓，
　　我口所出的話是憑公義，
並不反回。
　　萬膝必向我跪拜，
萬口必憑我起誓。
[24]人論我說：'公義、能力，
　　惟獨在乎耶和華。'"
人都必歸向他，
　　凡向他發怒的，必至蒙羞。
[25]以色列的後裔都必因耶和華
　　得稱為義，並要誇耀。

巴比倫的偶像

46 彼勒屈身，尼波彎腰；
巴比倫的偶像
駄在獸和牲畜上。
他們所抬的如今成了重駄，
　　使牲畜疲乏。
[2]都一同彎腰屈身，
　　不能保全重駄，
自己倒被擄去。

[3]雅各家、以色列家一切餘剩的
　　要聽我言：
"你們自從生下，
　　就蒙我保抱；
自從出胎，便蒙我懷搋。
[4]直到你們年老，我仍這樣；
　　直到你們髮白，我仍懷搋。
我已造作，也必保抱；
　　我必懷抱，也必拯救。

[5]"你們將誰與我相比，
　　與我同等，
可以與我比較，
　　使我們相同呢？
[6]那從囊中抓金子、
　　用天平平銀子的人，

---

a 1 Or *are but beasts and cattle*

雇銀匠製造神像，
　　他們又俯伏又叩拜。
7他們將神像抬起，扛在肩上，
　　安置在定處，它就站立，
　　不離本位。
　　人呼求它，它不能答應，
　　也不能救人脫離患難。

8 "你們當想念這事，自己作大丈夫。
　　悖逆的人哪，要心裏思想。
9你們要追念上古的事，
　　因為我是神，並無別神；
　　我是神，再沒有能比我的！
10我從起初指明末後的事，
　　從古時言明未成的事，
　　說：我的籌算必立定，
　　凡我所喜悅的，我必成就。
11我召鷙鳥從東方來，
　　召那成就我籌算的人
　　　　從遠方來。
　　我已說出，也必成就；
　　我已謀定，也必作成。
12你們這些心中頑梗、
　　遠離公義的，當聽我言。
13我使我的公義臨近，
　　必不遠離。
　　我的救恩必不遲延。
　　我要為以色列、我的榮耀，
　　在錫安施行救恩。

巴比倫的傾覆

47 "巴比倫的處女啊，
　　下來坐在塵埃；
　　迦勒底的閨女啊，
　　沒有寶座，要坐在地上。
　　因為你不再稱為
　　柔弱嬌嫩的。
2要用磨磨麵，
　　揭去帕子，
　　脫去長衣，
　　露腿趟河。
3你的下體必被露出，
　　你的醜陋必被看見。
　　我要報仇，
　　誰也不寬容。"

4我們救贖主的名
　　是萬軍之耶和華，
　　以色列的聖者。

5 "迦勒底的閨女啊，
　　你要默然靜坐，進入暗中，
　　因為你不再稱為
　　列國的主母。

they hire a goldsmith to make it into a god,
　and they bow down and worship it.
7They lift it to their shoulders and carry it;
　they set it up in its place, and there it stands.
　From that spot it cannot move.
　Though one cries out to it, it does not answer;
　it cannot save him from his troubles.

8"Remember this, fix it in mind,
　take it to heart, you rebels.
9Remember the former things, those of long ago;
　I am God, and there is no other;
　I am God, and there is none like me.
10I make known the end from the beginning,
　from ancient times, what is still to come.
　I say: My purpose will stand,
　and I will do all that I please.
11From the east I summon a bird of prey;
　from a far-off land, a man to fulfill my
　　purpose.
　What I have said, that will I bring about;
　what I have planned, that will I do.
12Listen to me, you stubborn-hearted,
　you who are far from righteousness.
13I am bringing my righteousness near,
　it is not far away;
　and my salvation will not be delayed.
　I will grant salvation to Zion,
　my splendor to Israel.

The Fall of Babylon

47 "Go down, sit in the dust,
　Virgin Daughter of Babylon;
　sit on the ground without a throne,
　Daughter of the Babylonians.[a]
　No more will you be called
　tender or delicate.
2Take millstones and grind flour;
　take off your veil.
　Lift up your skirts, bare your legs,
　and wade through the streams.
3Your nakedness will be exposed
　and your shame uncovered.
　I will take vengeance;
　I will spare no one."

4Our Redeemer—the LORD Almighty is his
　name—
　is the Holy One of Israel.

5"Sit in silence, go into darkness,
　Daughter of the Babylonians;
　no more will you be called
　queen of kingdoms.

a 1 Or Chaldeans; also in verse 5

⁶I was angry with my people
    and desecrated my inheritance;
I gave them into your hand,
    and you showed them no mercy.
Even on the aged
    you laid a very heavy yoke.
⁷You said, 'I will continue forever—
    the eternal queen!'
But you did not consider these things
    or reflect on what might happen.

⁸"Now then, listen, you wanton creature,
    lounging in your security
and saying to yourself,
    'I am, and there is none besides me.
I will never be a widow
    or suffer the loss of children.'
⁹Both of these will overtake you
    in a moment, on a single day:
loss of children and widowhood.
They will come upon you in full measure,
    in spite of your many sorceries
    and all your potent spells.
¹⁰You have trusted in your wickedness
    and have said, 'No one sees me.'
Your wisdom and knowledge mislead you
    when you say to yourself,
    'I am, and there is none besides me.'
¹¹Disaster will come upon you,
    and you will not know how to conjure it away.
A calamity will fall upon you
    that you cannot ward off with a ransom;
a catastrophe you cannot foresee
    will suddenly come upon you.

¹²"Keep on, then, with your magic spells
    and with your many sorceries,
    which you have labored at since childhood.
Perhaps you will succeed,
    perhaps you will cause terror.
¹³All the counsel you have received has only
        worn you out!
Let your astrologers come forward,
those stargazers who make predictions month
        by month,
let them save you from what is coming upon
        you.
¹⁴Surely they are like stubble;
    the fire will burn them up.
They cannot even save themselves
    from the power of the flame.
Here are no coals to warm anyone;
    here is no fire to sit by.
¹⁵That is all they can do for you—
    these you have labored with
    and trafficked with since childhood.

⁶我向我的百姓發怒,
    使我的產業被褻瀆,
    將他們交在你手中,
    你毫不憐憫他們,
把極重的軛
    加在老年人身上。
⁷你自己說:
    '我必永為主母',
所以你不將這事放在心上,
    也不思想這事的結局。

⁸"你這專好宴樂、安然居住的,
    現在當聽這話。
你心中說:
    '惟有我,除我以外再沒有別的,
我必不至寡居,
    也不遭喪子之事。'
⁹哪知,喪子、寡居這兩件事,
    在一日轉眼之間必臨到你,
正在你多行邪術、
    廣施符咒的時候,
這兩件事
    必全然臨到你身上。
¹⁰你素來倚仗自己的惡行說:
    '無人看見我。'
你的智慧、聰明使你偏邪,
    並且你心裏說:
    '惟有我,除我以外再沒有別的。'
¹¹因此,禍患要臨到你身,
    你不知何時發現(註:"何時發現"或
        作"如何驅逐"),
災害落在你身上,你也不能除掉,
    所不知道的毀滅
    也必忽然臨到你身。

¹²"站起來吧!
    用你從幼年勞神施行的符咒
    和你許多的邪術,
或者可得益處,
    或者可得強勝。
¹³你籌劃太多,
    以致疲倦。
讓那些觀天象的、看星宿的、
    在月朔說預言的,
    都站起來,
救你脫離
    所要臨到你的事。
¹⁴他們要像碎稭
    被火焚燒,
不能救自己
    脫離火焰之力,
這火並非可烤的炭火,
    也不是可以坐在其前的火。
¹⁵你所勞神的事
    都要這樣與你無益。
從幼年與你貿易的,

也都各奔各鄉，
　　無人救你。

頑梗的以色列

48 ¹「雅各家稱為以色列名下、
從猶大水源出來的，
當聽我言！
你們指着耶和華的名起誓，
　　提說以色列的神，
　　卻不憑誠實，不憑公義。
² （他們自稱為聖城的人，
　　所倚靠的是名為萬軍之耶和華——
　　以色列的神。）
³ 主說：早先的事，我從古時說明，
　　已經出了我的口，
　　也是我所指示的。
　　我忽然行作，事便成就。
⁴ 因為我素來知道你是頑梗的，
　　你的頸項是鐵的，
　　你的額是銅的。
⁵ 所以我從古時將這事給你說明，
　　在未成以先
　　　指示你，
　　免得你說：
　　　'這些事是我的偶像所行的，
　　是我雕刻的偶像
　　和我鑄造的偶像所命定的。'
⁶ 你已經聽見，現在要看見這一切，
　　你不說明嗎？

　　"從今以後，我將新事，
　　就是你所不知道的隱密事指示你。
⁷ 這事是現今造的，並非從古就有；
　　在今日以先，你也未曾聽見，
　　免得你說：
　　　'這事我早已知道了。'
⁸ 你未曾聽見，未曾知道，
　　你的耳朵從來未曾開通。
　　我原知道你行事極其詭詐，
　　你自從出胎以來，便稱為悖逆的。
⁹ 我為我的名暫且忍怒，
　　為我的頌讚
　　　向你容忍，
　　不將你剪除。
¹⁰ 我熬煉你，卻不像熬煉銀子；
　　你在苦難的爐中，我揀選你。
¹¹ 我為自己的緣故必行這事，
　　我焉能使我的名被褻瀆？
　　我必不將我的榮耀歸給假神。

以色列得釋

¹² 「雅各、我所選召的以色列啊，
　　當聽我言：
　　我是耶和華，
　　我是首先的，也是末後的。

Each of them goes on in his error;
　　there is not one that can save you.

Stubborn Israel

48 "Listen to this, O house of Jacob,
　　you who are called by the name of Israel
　　and come from the line of Judah,
you who take oaths in the name of the LORD
　　and invoke the God of Israel—
　　but not in truth or righteousness—
²you who call yourselves citizens of the holy city
　　and rely on the God of Israel—
　　the LORD Almighty is his name:
³I foretold the former things long ago,
　　my mouth announced them and I made
　　　them known;
　　then suddenly I acted, and they came to pass.
⁴For I knew how stubborn you were;
　　the sinews of your neck were iron,
　　your forehead was bronze.
⁵Therefore I told you these things long ago;
　　before they happened I announced them to
　　　you
so that you could not say,
　　'My idols did them;
　　my wooden image and metal god ordained
　　　them.'
⁶You have heard these things; look at them all.
　　Will you not admit them?

　　"From now on I will tell you of new things,
　　of hidden things unknown to you.
⁷They are created now, and not long ago;
　　you have not heard of them before today.
So you cannot say,
　　'Yes, I knew of them.'
⁸You have neither heard nor understood;
　　from of old your ear has not been open.
Well do I know how treacherous you are;
　　you were called a rebel from birth.
⁹For my own name's sake I delay my wrath;
　　for the sake of my praise I hold it back from
　　　you,
　　so as not to cut you off.
¹⁰See, I have refined you, though not as silver;
　　I have tested you in the furnace of affliction.
¹¹For my own sake, for my own sake, I do this.
　　How can I let myself be defamed?
　　I will not yield my glory to another.

Israel Freed

¹²"Listen to me, O Jacob,
　　Israel, whom I have called:
I am he;
　　I am the first and I am the last.

¹³My own hand laid the foundations of the earth,
　and my right hand spread out the heavens;
when I summon them,
　they all stand up together.

¹⁴"Come together, all of you, and listen:
　Which of the idols has foretold these things?
The LORD's chosen ally
　will carry out his purpose against Babylon;
　his arm will be against the Babylonians.^a
¹⁵I, even I, have spoken;
　yes, I have called him.
I will bring him,
　and he will succeed in his mission.

¹⁶Come near me and listen to this:

"From the first announcement I have not
　spoken in secret;
　at the time it happens, I am there."

And now the Sovereign LORD has sent me,
　with his Spirit.

¹⁷This is what the LORD says—
　your Redeemer, the Holy One of Israel:
"I am the LORD your God,
　who teaches you what is best for you,
　who directs you in the way you should go.
¹⁸If only you had paid attention to my commands,
　your peace would have been like a river,
　your righteousness like the waves of the sea.
¹⁹Your descendants would have been like the
　　sand,
　your children like its numberless grains;
　their name would never be cut off
　nor destroyed from before me."

²⁰Leave Babylon,
　flee from the Babylonians!
Announce this with shouts of joy
　and proclaim it.
Send it out to the ends of the earth;
　say, "The LORD has redeemed his servant
　　Jacob."
²¹They did not thirst when he led them through
　　the deserts;
　he made water flow for them from the rock;
　he split the rock
　and water gushed out.

²²"There is no peace," says the LORD, "for the
　wicked."

¹³我手立了地的根基；
　我右手鋪張諸天。
我一招呼
　便都立住。

¹⁴"你們都當聚集而聽：
　他們（註：或作"偶像"）內中
　誰說過這些事？
耶和華所愛的人，
　必向巴比倫行他所喜悅的事，
　他的膀臂也要加在迦勒底人身上。
¹⁵惟有我曾說過，
　我又選召他，領他來，
　他的道路就必亨通。

¹⁶"你們要就近我來聽這話：

"我從起頭
　並未曾在隱密處說話，
　自從有這事，我就在那裏。"

現在主耶和華差遣我和他的靈來
（註：或作"耶和華和他的靈差遣我來"）。

¹⁷耶和華你的救贖主——
　以色列的聖者如此說：
"我是耶和華你的神，
　教訓你使你得益處，
　引導你所當行的路。
¹⁸甚願你素來聽從我的命令，
　你的平安就如河水，
　你的公義就如海浪。
¹⁹你的後裔
　也必多如海沙，
　你腹中所生的也必多如沙粒。
他的名在我面前必不剪除，
　也不滅絕。"

²⁰你們要從巴比倫出來，
　從迦勒底人中逃脫，
以歡呼的聲音
　傳揚說：
"耶和華救贖了他的僕人雅各！"
　你們要將這事
　宣揚到地極。
²¹耶和華引導他們經過沙漠，
　他們並不乾渴；
他為他們使水從磐石而流，
　分裂磐石，
　水就湧出。

²²耶和華說：
"惡人必不得平安！"

^a 14 Or Chaldeans; also in verse 20

主的僕人

49 眾海島啊，當聽我言！
　　遠方的眾民哪，留心而聽！
　　自我出胎，耶和華就選召我；
自出母腹，
　　他就提我的名。
2他使我的口如快刀，
　　將我藏在他手蔭之下；
又使我成為磨亮的箭，
　　將我藏在他箭袋之中。
3對我說："你是我的僕人以色列，
　　我必因你得榮耀。"
4我卻說："我勞碌是徒然，
　　我盡力是虛無虛空；
然而，
　　我當得的理必在耶和華那裏，
　　我的賞賜必在我神那裏。"

5耶和華從我出胎，
　　造就我
　　　作他的僕人，
要使雅各歸向他，
　　使以色列到他那裏聚集。
　　（原來耶和華看我為尊貴，
　　我的神也成為我的力量。）
6現在他說：
　　"你作我的僕人，
　　使雅各眾支派復興，
　　使以色列中得保全的歸回
　　　尚為小事；
　　我還要使你作外邦人的光，
　　　叫你施行我的救恩，直到地極。"

7救贖主——
　　以色列的聖者耶和華，
　　對那被人所藐視、
　　本國所憎惡、
　　官長所虐待的如此說：
　　"君王要看見就站起，
　　　首領也要下拜，
都因信實的耶和華，
　　就是揀選你以色列的聖者。"

以色列的復興

8耶和華如此說：

　　"在悅納的時候，我應允了你；
　　在拯救的日子，我濟助了你。
　　我要保護你，使你作眾民的中保
　　　（註："中保"原文作"約"），
　　復興遍地，
　　　使人承受荒涼之地為業。
9對那被捆綁的人說：'出來吧！'
　　對那在黑暗的人說：'顯露吧！'

　　他們在路上必得飲食，

The Servant of the LORD

49 Listen to me, you islands;
　　hear this, you distant nations:
　Before I was born the LORD called me;
　from my birth he has made mention of my
　　name.
2He made my mouth like a sharpened sword,
　in the shadow of his hand he hid me;
　he made me into a polished arrow
　　and concealed me in his quiver.
3He said to me, "You are my servant,
　Israel, in whom I will display my splendor."
4But I said, "I have labored to no purpose;
　I have spent my strength in vain and for
　　nothing.
　Yet what is due me is in the LORD's hand,
　and my reward is with my God."

5And now the LORD says—
　he who formed me in the womb to be his
　　servant
　to bring Jacob back to him
　and gather Israel to himself,
　for I am honored in the eyes of the LORD
　and my God has been my strength—
6he says:
　"It is too small a thing for you to be my servant
　to restore the tribes of Jacob
　and bring back those of Israel I have kept.
　I will also make you a light for the Gentiles,
　that you may bring my salvation to the ends
　　of the earth."

7This is what the LORD says—
　the Redeemer and Holy One of Israel—
　to him who was despised and abhorred by
　　the nation,
　to the servant of rulers:
　"Kings will see you and rise up,
　princes will see and bow down,
　because of the LORD, who is faithful,
　the Holy One of Israel, who has chosen you."

Restoration of Israel

8This is what the LORD says:

　"In the time of my favor I will answer you,
　and in the day of salvation I will help you;
　I will keep you and will make you
　to be a covenant for the people,
　to restore the land
　and to reassign its desolate inheritances,
9to say to the captives, 'Come out,'
　and to those in darkness, 'Be free!'

　"They will feed beside the roads

and find pasture on every barren hill.
¹⁰They will neither hunger nor thirst,
    nor will the desert heat or the sun beat upon them.
He who has compassion on them will guide them
    and lead them beside springs of water.
¹¹I will turn all my mountains into roads,
    and my highways will be raised up.
¹²See, they will come from afar—
    some from the north, some from the west,
    some from the region of Aswan.ᵃ"

¹³Shout for joy, O heavens;
    rejoice, O earth;
    burst into song, O mountains!
For the LORD comforts his people
    and will have compassion on his afflicted ones.

¹⁴But Zion said, "The LORD has forsaken me,
    the Lord has forgotten me."

¹⁵"Can a mother forget the baby at her breast
    and have no compassion on the child she has borne?
Though she may forget,
    I will not forget you!
¹⁶See, I have engraved you on the palms of my hands;
    your walls are ever before me.
¹⁷Your sons hasten back,
    and those who laid you waste depart from you.
¹⁸Lift up your eyes and look around;
    all your sons gather and come to you.
As surely as I live," declares the LORD,
    "you will wear them all as ornaments;
    you will put them on, like a bride.

¹⁹"Though you were ruined and made desolate
    and your land laid waste,
now you will be too small for your people,
    and those who devoured you will be far away.
²⁰The children born during your bereavement
    will yet say in your hearing,
'This place is too small for us;
    give us more space to live in.'
²¹Then you will say in your heart,
    'Who bore me these?
I was bereaved and barren;
    I was exiled and rejected.
Who brought these up?
I was left all alone,
    but these—where have they come from?' "

在一切淨光的高處必有食物。
¹⁰不飢不渴，
    炎熱和烈日
    必不傷害他們，
因為憐恤他們的，
    必引導他們，
    領他們到水泉旁邊。
¹¹我必使我的眾山成為大道；
    我的大路也被修高。
¹²看哪，這些從遠方來；
    這些從北方、從西方來；
    這些從秦國來（註："秦"原文作"希尼"）。"

¹³諸天哪，應當歡呼！
    大地啊，應當快樂！
    眾山哪，應當發聲歌唱！
因為耶和華已經安慰他的百姓，
    也要憐恤他困苦之民。

¹⁴錫安說："耶和華離棄了我，
    主忘記了我。"

¹⁵"婦人焉能忘記她吃奶的嬰孩，
    不憐恤
      她所生的兒子？
即或有忘記的，
    我卻不忘記你。
¹⁶看哪，
    我將你銘刻在我掌上；
    你的牆垣常在我眼前。
¹⁷你的兒女必急速歸回，
    毀壞你的、使你荒廢的，
    必都離你出去。
¹⁸你舉目向四方觀看，
    他們都聚集來到你這裏。"
耶和華說："我指着我的永生起誓，
    你必要以他們為妝飾佩戴，
    以他們為華帶束腰像新婦一樣。

¹⁹"至於你荒廢淒涼之處，
    並你被毀壞之地，
現今眾民居住必顯為太窄；
    吞滅你的必離你遙遠。
²⁰你必聽見
    喪子之後所生的兒女說：
'這地方我居住太窄，
    求你給我地方居住。'
²¹那時你心裏必說：
    '我既喪子獨居，
是被擄的，漂流在外，
    誰給我生這些，
    誰將這些養大呢？
撇下我一人獨居的時候，
    這些在哪裏呢？'

---

a 12 Dead Sea Scrolls; Masoretic Text *Sinim*

22主耶和華如此說：

"我必向列國舉手，
　向萬民豎立大旗，
他們必將你的眾子懷中抱來，
　將你的眾女肩上扛來。
23列王必作你的養父，
　王后必作你的乳母；
他們必將臉伏地，
　向你下拜，
　並舔你腳上的塵土。
你便知道我是耶和華！
　等候我的
　必不至羞愧。"

24勇士搶去的豈能奪回，
　該擄掠的豈能解救嗎？

25但耶和華如此說：

"就是勇士所擄掠的，也可以奪回；
　強暴人所搶的，也可以解救。
與你相爭的，
　我必與他相爭，
　我要拯救你的兒女。
26並且我必使那欺壓你的
　吃自己的肉，
也要以自己的血喝醉，
　好像喝甜酒一樣。
凡有血氣的，
　必都知道我耶和華是你的救主，
　是你的救贖主，是雅各的大能者。"

以色列的犯罪與僕人的順服

50 耶和華如此說：

"我休你們的母親，
　休書在哪裏呢？
我將你們賣給
　我哪一個債主呢？
你們被賣，
　是因你們的罪孽；
你們的母親被休，
　是因你們的過犯。
2我來的時候，為何無人等候呢？
　我呼喚的時候，
　為何無人答應呢？
我的膀臂豈是縮短、不能救贖嗎？
　我豈無拯救之力嗎？
看哪，我一斥責，海就乾了！
　我使江河變為曠野，
其中的魚因無水腥臭，
　乾渴而死。

22This is what the Sovereign LORD says:

"See, I will beckon to the Gentiles,
　I will lift up my banner to the peoples;
they will bring your sons in their arms
　and carry your daughters on their shoulders.
23Kings will be your foster fathers,
　and their queens your nursing mothers.
They will bow down before you with their
　　faces to the ground;
they will lick the dust at your feet.
Then you will know that I am the LORD;
　those who hope in me will not be
　　disappointed."

24Can plunder be taken from warriors,
　or captives rescued from the fierce[a]?

25But this is what the LORD says:

"Yes, captives will be taken from warriors,
　and plunder retrieved from the fierce;
I will contend with those who contend with
　　you,
　and your children I will save.
26I will make your oppressors eat their own
　　flesh;
they will be drunk on their own blood, as
　　with wine.
Then all mankind will know
　that I, the LORD, am your Savior,
　your Redeemer, the Mighty One of Jacob."

Israel's Sin and the Servant's Obedience

50 This is what the LORD says:

"Where is your mother's certificate of
　　divorce
with which I sent her away?
Or to which of my creditors
　did I sell you?
Because of your sins you were sold;
　because of your transgressions your mother
　　was sent away.
2When I came, why was there no one?
　When I called, why was there no one to
　　answer?
Was my arm too short to ransom you?
　Do I lack the strength to rescue you?
By a mere rebuke I dry up the sea,
　I turn rivers into a desert;
their fish rot for lack of water
　and die of thirst.

---

a 24 Dead Sea Scrolls, Vulgate and Syriac (see also Septuagint
and verse 25); Masoretic Text *righteous*

³I clothe the sky with darkness
  and make sackcloth its covering."
⁴The Sovereign LORD has given me an
    instructed tongue,
  to know the word that sustains the weary.
  He wakens me morning by morning,
    wakens my ear to listen like one being taught.
⁵The Sovereign LORD has opened my ears,
    and I have not been rebellious;
  I have not drawn back.
⁶I offered my back to those who beat me,
    my cheeks to those who pulled out my beard;
  I did not hide my face
    from mocking and spitting.
⁷Because the Sovereign LORD helps me,
    I will not be disgraced.
  Therefore have I set my face like flint,
    and I know I will not be put to shame.
⁸He who vindicates me is near.
    Who then will bring charges against me?
  Let us face each other!
  Who is my accuser?
    Let him confront me!
⁹It is the Sovereign LORD who helps me.
    Who is he that will condemn me?
  They will all wear out like a garment;
    the moths will eat them up.

¹⁰Who among you fears the LORD
    and obeys the word of his servant?
  Let him who walks in the dark,
    who has no light,
  trust in the name of the LORD
    and rely on his God.
¹¹But now, all you who light fires
    and provide yourselves with flaming torches,
  go, walk in the light of your fires
    and of the torches you have set ablaze.
  This is what you shall receive from my hand:
    You will lie down in torment.

Everlasting Salvation for Zion

51 "Listen to me, you who pursue
      righteousness
    and who seek the LORD:
  Look to the rock from which you were cut
    and to the quarry from which you were hewn;
²look to Abraham, your father,
    and to Sarah, who gave you birth.
  When I called him he was but one,
    and I blessed him and made him many.
³The LORD will surely comfort Zion
    and will look with compassion on all her ruins;
  he will make her deserts like Eden,
    her wastelands like the garden of the LORD.

³我使諸天以黑暗為衣服，
  以麻布為遮蓋。"
⁴主耶和華賜我受教者的舌頭，
    使我知道怎樣用言語
  扶助疲乏的人。
  主每早晨提醒，提醒我的耳朵，
    使我能聽，像受教者一樣。
⁵主耶和華開通我的耳朵，
    我並沒有違背，
  也沒有退後。
⁶人打我的背，我任他打；
    人拔我腮頰的鬍鬚，我由他拔；
  人辱我，吐我，
    我並不掩面。
⁷主耶和華必幫助我，
    所以我不抱愧。
  我硬着臉面好像堅石，
    我也知道我必不至蒙羞。
⁸稱我為義的與我相近；
    誰與我爭論？
  可以與我一同站立！
  誰與我作對？
    可以就近我來！
⁹主耶和華要幫助我，
    誰能定我有罪呢？
  他們都像衣服漸漸舊了，
    為蛀蟲所咬。

¹⁰你們中間誰是敬畏耶和華、
    聽從他僕人之話的？
  這人行在暗中，
    沒有亮光。
  當倚靠耶和華的名，
    仗賴自己的神。
¹¹凡你們點火，
    用火把圍繞自己的，
  可以行在你們的火焰裏，
    並你們所點的火把中。
  這是我手所定的。
    你們必躺在悲慘之中。

對錫安的永遠拯救

51 "你們這追求公義、
      尋求耶和華的，
    當聽我言！
  你們要追想被鑿而出的磐石，
    被挖而出的巖穴。
²要追想你們的祖宗亞伯拉罕
    和生養你們的撒拉。
  因為亞伯拉罕獨自一人的時候，
    我選召他，賜福與他，使他人數增多。
³耶和華已經安慰錫安
    和錫安一切的荒場，
  使曠野像伊甸，
    使沙漠像耶和華的園囿；

在其中必有歡喜、快樂、
　感謝和歌唱的聲音。

4 "我的百姓啊，要向我留心；
　我的國民哪，要向我側耳。
　因為訓誨必從我而出；
　我必堅定我的公理為萬民之光。
5 我的公義臨近，
　我的救恩發出，
　我的膀臂要審判萬民；
　海島都要等候我，
　倚賴我的膀臂。
6 你們要向天舉目，觀看下地，
　因為天必像煙雲消散，
　地必如衣服漸漸舊了，
　其上的居民也要如此死亡（註：
　　"如此死亡" 或作 "像蠓蟲死亡"）；
　惟有我的救恩永遠長存，
　我的公義也不廢掉。

7 "知道公義、將我訓誨
　存在心中的民，要聽我言！
　不要怕人的辱罵，
　也不要因人的毀謗驚惶。
8 因為蛀蟲必咬他們，好像咬衣服；
　蟲子必咬他們，如同咬羊羢。
　惟有我的公義永遠長存，
　我的救恩直到萬代。"

9 耶和華的膀臂啊，興起！興起！
　以能力為衣穿上，
　像古時的年日、
　上古的世代興起一樣。
　從前砍碎拉哈伯、
　刺透大魚的，不是你嗎？
10 使海與深淵的水乾涸、
　使海的深處
　變為贖民經過之路的，
　不是你嗎？
11 耶和華救贖的民必歸回，
　歌唱來到錫安；
　永樂必歸到他們的頭上。
　他們必得着歡喜快樂，
　憂愁歎息盡都逃避。

12 "惟有我，是安慰你們的。
　你是誰，竟怕那必死的人，
　怕那要變如草的世人，
13 卻忘記鋪張諸天、
　立定地基、
　創造你的耶和華？
　又因欺壓者圖謀毀滅
　要發的暴怒，
　整天害怕！
　其實那欺壓者的暴怒在哪裏呢？
14 被擄去的快得釋放，

Joy and gladness will be found in her,
　thanksgiving and the sound of singing.

4"Listen to me, my people;
　hear me, my nation:
　The law will go out from me;
　my justice will become a light to the nations.
5My righteousness draws near speedily,
　my salvation is on the way,
　and my arm will bring justice to the nations.
　The islands will look to me
　and wait in hope for my arm.
6Lift up your eyes to the heavens,
　look at the earth beneath;
　the heavens will vanish like smoke,
　the earth will wear out like a garment
　and its inhabitants die like flies.
　But my salvation will last forever,
　my righteousness will never fail.

7"Hear me, you who know what is right,
　you people who have my law in your hearts:
　Do not fear the reproach of men
　or be terrified by their insults.
8For the moth will eat them up like a garment;
　the worm will devour them like wool.
　But my righteousness will last forever,
　my salvation through all generations."

9Awake, awake! Clothe yourself with strength,
　O arm of the LORD;
　awake, as in days gone by,
　as in generations of old.
　Was it not you who cut Rahab to pieces,
　who pierced that monster through?
10Was it not you who dried up the sea,
　the waters of the great deep,
　who made a road in the depths of the sea
　so that the redeemed might cross over?
11The ransomed of the LORD will return.
　They will enter Zion with singing;
　everlasting joy will crown their heads.
　Gladness and joy will overtake them,
　and sorrow and sighing will flee away.

12"I, even I, am he who comforts you.
　Who are you that you fear mortal men,
　the sons of men, who are but grass,
13that you forget the LORD your Maker,
　who stretched out the heavens
　and laid the foundations of the earth,
　that you live in constant terror every day
　because of the wrath of the oppressor,
　who is bent on destruction?
　For where is the wrath of the oppressor?
14 The cowering prisoners will soon be set free;

they will not die in their dungeon,
   nor will they lack bread.
¹⁵For I am the LORD your God,
   who churns up the sea so that its waves roar—
   the LORD Almighty is his name.
¹⁶I have put my words in your mouth
   and covered you with the shadow of my
      hand—
I who set the heavens in place,
   who laid the foundations of the earth,
   and who say to Zion, 'You are my people.' "

The Cup of the LORD's Wrath

¹⁷Awake, awake!
   Rise up, O Jerusalem,
you who have drunk from the hand of the LORD
   the cup of his wrath,
you who have drained to its dregs
   the goblet that makes men stagger.
¹⁸Of all the sons she bore
   there was none to guide her;
of all the sons she reared
   there was none to take her by the hand.
¹⁹These double calamities have come upon you—
   who can comfort you?—
ruin and destruction, famine and sword—
   who can^a console you?
²⁰Your sons have fainted;
   they lie at the head of every street,
   like antelope caught in a net.
They are filled with the wrath of the LORD
   and the rebuke of your God.

²¹Therefore hear this, you afflicted one,
   made drunk, but not with wine.
²²This is what your Sovereign LORD says,
   your God, who defends his people:
"See, I have taken out of your hand
   the cup that made you stagger;
from that cup, the goblet of my wrath,
   you will never drink again.
²³I will put it into the hands of your tormentors,
   who said to you,
   'Fall prostrate that we may walk over you.'
And you made your back like the ground,
   like a street to be walked over."

52

Awake, awake, O Zion,
   clothe yourself with strength.
Put on your garments of splendor,
O Jerusalem, the holy city.
The uncircumcised and defiled
   will not enter you again.

a 19 Dead Sea Scrolls, Septuagint, Vulgate and Syriac;
Masoretic Text / *how can I*

必不死而下坑，
　　他的食物也不至缺乏。
¹⁵我是耶和華你的神，
　　攪動大海，使海中的波浪匉訇，
　　萬軍之耶和華是我的名。
¹⁶我將我的話傳給你，
　　用我的手影
　　遮蔽你，
　　為要栽定諸天，
　　立定地基，
　　又對錫安說：你是我的百姓。"

耶和華忿怒的杯

¹⁷耶路撒冷啊，興起！興起！
　　站起來！
你從耶和華手中
　　喝了他忿怒之杯，
喝了那使人東倒西歪的爵，
　　以致喝盡。
¹⁸她所生育的諸子中，
　　沒有一個引導她的；
她所養大的諸子中，
　　沒有一個攙扶她的。
¹⁹荒涼、毀滅、饑荒、刀兵，
　　這幾樣臨到你，
誰為你舉哀？
　　我如何能安慰你呢？
²⁰你的眾子發昏，
　　在各市口上躺臥，
　　好像黃羊在網羅之中，
都滿了耶和華的忿怒、
　　你神的斥責。

²¹因此，你這困苦卻非因酒而醉的，
　　要聽我言。
²²你的主耶和華，
　　就是為他百姓辨屈的神如此說：
"看哪，我已將那使人東倒西歪的杯，
　　就是我忿怒的爵，
從你手中接過來，
　　你必不至再喝。
²³我必將這杯遞在苦待你的人手中。
他們曾對你說：
　　'你屈身，由我們踐踏過去吧！'
你便以背為地，
　　好像街市，任人經過。"

52

錫安啊，興起！興起！
披上你的能力！
聖城耶路撒冷啊，
穿上你華美的衣服！
因為從今以後，
未受割禮、不潔淨的，
必不再進入你中間。

²耶路撒冷啊，要抖下塵土，
　　起來坐在位上！
　錫安被擄的居民哪（註："居民"原文
　　作"女子"），要解開你頸項的鎖鏈！

³耶和華如此說：

"你們是無價被賣的，
　也必無銀被贖。"

⁴主耶和華如此說：

"起先我的百姓下到埃及，在那裏寄居，
　又有亞述人無故欺壓他們。"

⁵耶和華說：
"我的百姓
　既是無價被擄去，
　如今我在這裏
　做甚麼呢？"

　耶和華說：
　"轄制他們的人呼叫，
　我的名整天受褻瀆。
⁶所以，我的百姓必知道我的名，
　到那日他們必知道
　　說這話的就是我。
　看哪，是我！"

⁷那報佳音、
　傳平安、
　報好信、
　傳救恩的，
　對錫安說：
　"你的神作王了！"
　這人的腳登山何等佳美！

⁸聽啊，你守望之人的聲音，
　他們揚起聲來，一同歌唱。
　因為耶和華歸回錫安的時候，
　他們必親眼看見。

⁹耶路撒冷的荒場啊，
　要發起歡聲，一同歌唱！
　因為耶和華安慰了他的百姓，
　救贖了耶路撒冷。

¹⁰耶和華在萬國眼前露出聖臂，
　地極的人都看見我們神的救恩了。

¹¹你們離開吧！離開吧！
　從巴比倫出來，
　不要沾不潔淨的物，
　要從其中出來。
　你們扛抬耶和華器皿的人哪，
　務要自潔。

¹²你們出來必不至急忙，
　也不至奔逃，

²Shake off your dust;
　rise up, sit enthroned, O Jerusalem.
Free yourself from the chains on your neck,
　O captive Daughter of Zion.

³For this is what the LORD says:

"You were sold for nothing,
　and without money you will be redeemed."

⁴For this is what the Sovereign LORD says:

"At first my people went down to Egypt to live;
　lately, Assyria has oppressed them.

⁵"And now what do I have here?" declares
the LORD.

"For my people have been taken away for
　nothing,
　and those who rule them mock,ᵃ
　　　　　　　　　　　　declares the LORD.
"And all day long
　my name is constantly blasphemed.
⁶Therefore my people will know my name;
　therefore in that day they will know
that it is I who foretold it.
　Yes, it is I."

⁷How beautiful on the mountains
　are the feet of those who bring good news,
who proclaim peace,
　who bring good tidings,
who proclaim salvation,
who say to Zion,
　"Your God reigns!"

⁸Listen! Your watchmen lift up their voices;
　together they shout for joy.
When the LORD returns to Zion,
　they will see it with their own eyes.

⁹Burst into songs of joy together,
　you ruins of Jerusalem,
for the LORD has comforted his people,
　he has redeemed Jerusalem.

¹⁰The LORD will lay bare his holy arm
　in the sight of all the nations,
and all the ends of the earth will see
　the salvation of our God.

¹¹Depart, depart, go out from there!
　Touch no unclean thing!
Come out from it and be pure,
　you who carry the vessels of the LORD.

¹²But you will not leave in haste
　or go in flight;

a 5 Dead Sea Scrolls and Vulgate; Masoretic Text wail

for the LORD will go before you,
　　the God of Israel will be your rear guard.

The Suffering and Glory of the Servant

[13]See, my servant will act wisely[a];
　　he will be raised and lifted up and highly
　　　exalted.
[14]Just as there were many who were appalled at
　　him[b]—
　　his appearance was so disfigured beyond
　　　that of any man
　　and his form marred beyond human
　　　likeness—
[15]so will he sprinkle many nations,[c]
　　and kings will shut their mouths because of
　　　him.
　　For what they were not told, they will see,
　　and what they have not heard, they will
　　　understand.

53 Who has believed our message
　　　and to whom has the arm of the LORD
　　　been revealed?
[2]He grew up before him like a tender shoot,
　　and like a root out of dry ground.
　　He had no beauty or majesty to attract us to
　　　him,
　　nothing in his appearance that we should
　　　desire him.
[3]He was despised and rejected by men,
　　a man of sorrows, and familiar with suffering.
　　Like one from whom men hide their faces
　　he was despised, and we esteemed him not.

[4]Surely he took up our infirmities
　　and carried our sorrows,
　　yet we considered him stricken by God,
　　smitten by him, and afflicted.
[5]But he was pierced for our transgressions,
　　he was crushed for our iniquities;
　　the punishment that brought us peace was
　　　upon him,
　　and by his wounds we are healed.
[6]We all, like sheep, have gone astray,
　　each of us has turned to his own way;
　　and the LORD has laid on him
　　the iniquity of us all.
[7]He was oppressed and afflicted,
　　yet he did not open his mouth;
　　he was led like a lamb to the slaughter,
　　and as a sheep before her shearers is silent,
　　so he did not open his mouth.

因為耶和華必在你們前頭行；
　　以色列的神必作你們的後盾。

僕人的受苦與榮耀

[13]我的僕人行事必有智慧（註：或作“行
　　事通達”），
　　必被高舉上升，且成為至高。
[14]許多人
　　因他（註：原文作“你”）驚奇，
　　（他的面貌
　　　比別人憔悴，
　　他的形容
　　　比世人枯槁。）
[15]這樣，他必洗淨（註：或作“鼓動”）
　　許多國民，
　　君王要向他閉口。
　　因所未曾傳與他們的，他們必看見；
　　未曾聽見的，他們要明白。

53 我們所傳的（註：或作“所傳與我
　　　們的”）有誰信呢？
　　　耶和華的膀臂向誰顯露呢？
[2]他在耶和華面前生長如嫩芽，
　　像根出於乾地。
　　他無佳形美容，
　　我們看見他的時候，
　　也無美貌
　　使我們羨慕他。
[3]他被藐視，被人厭棄，
　　多受痛苦，常經憂患。
　　他被藐視，好像被人掩面不看的一樣；
　　我們也不尊重他。

[4]他誠然擔當我們的憂患，
　　背負我們的痛苦；
　　我們卻以為他受責罰，
　　被神擊打苦待了。
[5]哪知他為我們的過犯受害，
　　為我們的罪孽壓傷。
　　因他受的刑罰，
　　　我們得平安；
　　因他受的鞭傷，我們得醫治。
[6]我們都如羊走迷，
　　各人偏行己路。
　　耶和華使我們眾人的罪孽
　　都歸在他身上。
[7]他被欺壓，
　　在受苦的時候卻不開口（註：或作
　　　“他受欺壓，卻自卑不開口”）。
　　他像羊羔被牽到宰殺之地，
　　又像羊在剪毛的人手下無聲，
　　他也是這樣不開口。

a 13 Or will prosper　　b 14 Hebrew you　　c 15 Hebrew;
Septuagint so will many nations marvel at him

8因受欺壓和審判，
　他被奪去，
　至於他同世的人，
　誰想他受鞭打、
　　從活人之地被剪除，
　是因我百姓的罪過呢？
9他雖然未行強暴，
　口中也沒有詭詐，
　人還使他與惡人同埋；
　誰知死的時候與財主同葬。

10耶和華卻定意（註：或作「喜悅」）
　將他壓傷，使他受痛苦；
　耶和華以他為贖罪祭（註：或作「他獻
　　本身為贖罪祭」）。
　他必看見後裔，並且延長年日，
　耶和華所喜悅的事
　　必在他手中亨通。
11他必看見自己勞苦的功效，
　便心滿意足。
　有許多人因認識我的義僕
　得稱為義，
　並且他要擔當他們的罪孽。
12所以，
　我要使他與位大的同分，
　與強盛的均分擄物。
　因為他將命傾倒，以至於死。
　他也被列在罪犯之中。
　他卻擔當多人的罪，
　又為罪犯代求。

錫安未來的榮耀

54 　"你這不懷孕、
　　不生養的要歌唱！
　你這未曾經過產難的
　　要發聲歌唱，
　揚聲歡呼！
　因為沒有丈夫的
　　比有丈夫的兒女更多。"
　　　　　　　這是耶和華說的。
2 "要擴張你帳幕之地，
　張大你居所的幔子，
　　不要限止；
　要放長你的繩子，
　堅固你的橛子。
3因為你要
　向左向右開展，

8By oppression[a] and judgment he was taken
　away.
　And who can speak of his descendants?
For he was cut off from the land of the living;
　for the transgression of my people he was
　stricken.[b]
9He was assigned a grave with the wicked,
　and with the rich in his death,
though he had done no violence,
　nor was any deceit in his mouth.

10Yet it was the LORD's will to crush him and
　cause him to suffer,
　and though the LORD makes[c] his life a guilt
　offering,
he will see his offspring and prolong his days,
　and the will of the LORD will prosper in his
　hand.
11After the suffering of his soul,
　he will see the light [of life][d] and be satisfied[e];
by his knowledge[f] my righteous servant will
　justify many,
　and he will bear their iniquities.
12Therefore I will give him a portion among the
　great,[g]
and he will divide the spoils with the strong,[h]
because he poured out his life unto death,
　and was numbered with the transgressors.
For he bore the sin of many,
　and made intercession for the transgressors.

The Future Glory of Zion

54 　"Sing, O barren woman,
　　you who never bore a child;
　burst into song, shout for joy,
　you who were never in labor;
because more are the children of the desolate
　woman
　than of her who has a husband,"
　　　　　　　　　　　　says the LORD.
2"Enlarge the place of your tent,
　stretch your tent curtains wide,
　do not hold back;
　lengthen your cords,
　strengthen your stakes.
3For you will spread out to the right and to the
　left;

*a 8 Or From arrest　b 8 Or away. / Yet who of his generation
considered / that he was cut off from the land of the living / for the
transgression of my people, / to whom the blow was due?
c 10 Hebrew though you make　d 11 Dead Sea Scrolls (see also
Septuagint); Masoretic Text does not have the light [of life].
e 11 Or (with Masoretic Text)　11He will see the result of the
suffering of his soul / and be satisfied　f 11 Or by knowledge of
him　g 12 Or many　h 12 Or numerous*

your descendants will dispossess nations
and settle in their desolate cities.

4"Do not be afraid; you will not suffer shame.
Do not fear disgrace; you will not be
humiliated.
You will forget the shame of your youth
and remember no more the reproach of your
widowhood.
5For your Maker is your husband—
the LORD Almighty is his name—
the Holy One of Israel is your Redeemer;
he is called the God of all the earth.
6The LORD will call you back
as if you were a wife deserted and distressed
in spirit—
a wife who married young,
only to be rejected," says your God.
7"For a brief moment I abandoned you,
but with deep compassion I will bring you
back.
8In a surge of anger
I hid my face from you for a moment,
but with everlasting kindness
I will have compassion on you,"
says the LORD your Redeemer.

9"To me this is like the days of Noah,
when I swore that the waters of Noah would
never again cover the earth.
So now I have sworn not to be angry with you,
never to rebuke you again.
10Though the mountains be shaken
and the hills be removed,
yet my unfailing love for you will not be shaken
nor my covenant of peace be removed,"
says the LORD, who has compassion on you.

11"O afflicted city, lashed by storms and not
comforted,
I will build you with stones of turquoise,*a*
your foundations with sapphires.*b*
12I will make your battlements of rubies,
your gates of sparkling jewels,
and all your walls of precious stones.
13All your sons will be taught by the LORD,
and great will be your children's peace.
14In righteousness you will be established:
Tyranny will be far from you;
you will have nothing to fear.
Terror will be far removed;
it will not come near you.

你的後裔必得多國為業，
又使荒涼的城邑有人居住。"

4 "不要懼怕，
因你必不至蒙羞；
也不要抱愧，
因你必不至受辱。
你必忘記幼年的羞愧，
不再記念你寡居的羞辱。
5因為造你的是你的丈夫，
萬軍之耶和華是他的名；
救贖你的是以色列的聖者，
他必稱為全地之神。
6耶和華召你，
如召被離棄
心中憂傷的妻，
就是幼年所娶被棄的妻。"
這是你神所說的。
7 "我離棄你不過片時，
卻要施大恩
將你收回。
8我的怒氣漲溢，
頃刻之間向你掩面，
卻要以永遠的慈愛
憐恤你。"
這是耶和華你的救贖主說的。

9 "這事在我好像挪亞的洪水。
我怎樣起誓不再使挪亞的洪水
漫過遍地，
我也照樣起誓不再向你發怒，
也不斥責你。
10大山可以挪開，
小山可以遷移；
但我的慈愛必不離開你，
我平安的約也不遷移。"
這是憐恤你的耶和華說的。

11 "你這受困苦
被風飄蕩不得安慰的人哪，
我必以彩色安置你的石頭，
以藍寶石立定你的根基；
12又以紅寶石造你的女牆，
以紅玉造你的城門，
以寶石造你四圍的邊界（註：或作
"外郭"）。
13你的兒女都要受耶和華的教訓，
你的兒女必大享平安。
14你必因公義得堅立，
必遠離欺壓，不至害怕；
你必遠離驚嚇，
驚嚇必不臨近你。

---

a 11 The meaning of the Hebrew for this word is uncertain.
b 11 Or lapis lazuli

15即或有人聚集，卻不由於我；
　　凡聚集攻擊你的，必因你仆倒
　　　　（註："因你仆倒"或作"投降你"）。

16 "吹噓炭火、
　　打造合用器械的鐵匠
　　是我所造；
　　殘害人、行毀滅的
　　也是我所造。
17凡為攻擊你造成的器械，必不利用；
　　凡在審判時興起用舌攻擊你的，
　　　你必定他為有罪。
　　這是耶和華僕人的產業，
　　是他們從我所得的義。"
　　　　　　　　　這是耶和華說的。

邀請乾渴者

55 "你們一切乾渴的
　　都當就近水來，
　　沒有銀錢的也可以來。
　你們都來，買了吃，
　　不用銀錢，不用價值，
　　也來買酒和奶。
2你們為何花錢（註：原文作"平銀"）
　　買那不足為食物的？
　　用勞碌得來的買那不使人飽足的呢？
　　你們要留意聽我的話，
　　就能吃那美物，得享肥甘，心中喜樂。
3你們當就近我來，
　　側耳而聽，就必得活。
　我必與你們立永約，
　　就是應許大衛那可靠的恩典。
4我已立他作萬民的見證，
　　為萬民的君王和司令。
5你素不認識的國民，你也必召來；
　　素不認識你的國民，
　　也必向你奔跑，
　都因耶和華你的神，
　　以色列的聖者，
　　因為他已經榮耀你。"

6當趁耶和華可尋找的時候尋找他，
　　相近的時候求告他。
7惡人當離棄自己的道路，
　　不義的人當除掉自己的意念。
　歸向耶和華，耶和華就必憐恤他；
　　當歸向我們的神，
　　因為神必廣行赦免。
8耶和華說：
　　"我的意念非同你們的意念，
　　我的道路非同你們的道路。
9 "天怎樣高過天，
　　照樣我的道路高過你們的道路，
　　我的意念高過你們的意念。

16"See, it is I who created the blacksmith
　who fans the coals into flame
　and forges a weapon fit for its work.
　And it is I who have created the destroyer to
　　work havoc;
17　no weapon forged against you will prevail,
　and you will refute every tongue that
　　accuses you.
This is the heritage of the servants of the LORD,
　and this is their vindication from me,"
　　　　　　　declares the LORD.

Invitation to the Thirsty

55 "Come, all you who are thirsty,
　come to the waters;
　and you who have no money,
　come, buy and eat!
　Come, buy wine and milk
　without money and without cost.
2Why spend money on what is not bread,
　and your labor on what does not satisfy?
Listen, listen to me, and eat what is good,
　and your soul will delight in the richest of
　　fare.
3Give ear and come to me;
　hear me, that your soul may live.
I will make an everlasting covenant with you,
　my faithful love promised to David.
4See, I have made him a witness to the peoples,
　a leader and commander of the peoples.
5Surely you will summon nations you know not,
　and nations that do not know you will
　　hasten to you,
　because of the LORD your God,
　the Holy One of Israel,
　for he has endowed you with splendor."

6Seek the LORD while he may be found;
　call on him while he is near.
7Let the wicked forsake his way
　and the evil man his thoughts.
Let him turn to the LORD, and he will have
　mercy on him,
　and to our God, for he will freely pardon.
8"For my thoughts are not your thoughts,
　neither are your ways my ways,"
　　　　　　　declares the LORD.
9"As the heavens are higher than the earth,
　so are my ways higher than your ways
　and my thoughts than your thoughts.

¹⁰As the rain and the snow
come down from heaven,
and do not return to it
without watering the earth
and making it bud and flourish,
so that it yields seed for the sower and bread
for the eater,
¹¹so is my word that goes out from my mouth:
It will not return to me empty,
but will accomplish what I desire
and achieve the purpose for which I sent it.
¹²You will go out in joy
and be led forth in peace;
the mountains and hills
will burst into song before you,
and all the trees of the field
will clap their hands.
¹³Instead of the thornbush will grow the pine tree,
and instead of briers the myrtle will grow.
This will be for the LORD's renown,
for an everlasting sign,
which will not be destroyed."

Salvation for Others

56 This is what the LORD says:

"Maintain justice
and do what is right,
for my salvation is close at hand
and my righteousness will soon be revealed.
²Blessed is the man who does this,
the man who holds it fast,
who keeps the Sabbath without desecrating it,
and keeps his hand from doing any evil."

³Let no foreigner who has bound himself to the
LORD say,
"The Lord will surely exclude me from his
people."
And let not any eunuch complain,
"I am only a dry tree."

⁴For this is what the LORD says:

"To the eunuchs who keep my Sabbaths,
who choose what pleases me
and hold fast to my covenant—
⁵to them I will give within my temple and its
walls
a memorial and a name
better than sons and daughters;
I will give them an everlasting name
that will not be cut off.
⁶And foreigners who bind themselves to the LORD
to serve him,

¹⁰雨雪
從天而降，
並不返回，
卻滋潤地土，
使地上發芽結實，
使撒種的有種，
使要吃的有糧。
¹¹我口所出的話也必如此，
決不徒然返回，
卻要成就我所喜悅的，
在我發它去成就的事上（註："發它
去成就"或作"所命定"）必然亨通。
¹²你們必歡歡喜喜而出來，
平平安安蒙引導；
大山小山
必在你們面前發聲歌唱，
田野的樹木也都拍掌。
¹³松樹長出，代替荊棘；
番石榴長出，代替蒺藜。
這要為耶和華留名，
作為永遠的證據，
不能剪除。"

其他民族將蒙拯救

56 耶和華如此說：

"你們當守公平，
行公義，
因我的救恩臨近，
我的公義將要顯現。
²謹守安息日而不干犯，
禁止己手而不作惡；
如此行、如此持守的人
便為有福。"

³與耶和華聯合的外邦人
不要說：
"耶和華必定將我從他民中
分別出來。"
太監也不要說：
"我是枯樹。"

⁴因為耶和華如此說：

"那些謹守我的安息日，
揀選我所喜悅的事，
持守我約的太監，
⁵我必使他們在我殿中，
在我牆內有記念、
有名號，
比有兒女的更美。
我必賜他們永遠的名，
不能剪除。
⁶還有那些與耶和華聯合的外邦人，
要侍奉他，

要愛耶和華的名，
　　要作他的僕人，
就是凡守安息日不干犯，
　　又持守他（註：原文作「我」）約的人。
7我必領他們到我的聖山，
　　使他們在禱告我的殿中喜樂。
他們的燔祭和平安祭，
　　在我壇上必蒙悅納。
因我的殿
　　必稱為萬民禱告的殿！"
8主耶和華——
　　就是招聚以色列被趕散的，說：
"在這被招聚的人以外，
　　我還要招聚別人歸併他們。"

神對惡人的指責

9田野的諸獸都來吞吃吧！
　　林中的諸獸也要如此。
10他看守的人是瞎眼的，
　　都沒有知識，
都是啞巴狗，
　　不能叫喚；
但知做夢、躺臥、
　　貪睡。
11這些狗貪食，
　　不知飽足。
這些牧人不能明白，
　　各人偏行己路，
　　各從各方求自己的利益。
12他們說："來吧！我去拿酒，
　　我們飽飲濃酒，
明日必和今日一樣，
　　就是宴樂無量極大之日。"

57 義人死亡，
　　　無人放在心上；
　　　虔誠人被收去，
　　無人思念。
這義人被收去
　　是免了將來的禍患。
2他們得享（註：原文作「進入」）平安，
　　素行正直的，各人在墳裏（註：原
　　文作「牀上」）安歇。

3 "你們這些巫婆的兒子，
　　姦夫和妓女的種子，
　　都要前來！
4你們向誰戲笑、
　　向誰張口吐舌呢？
你們豈不是悖逆的兒女、
　　虛謊的種類呢？
5你們在橡樹中間，
　　在各青翠樹下慾火攻心；
在山谷間，
　　在石穴下殺了兒女。

to love the name of the LORD,
　　and to worship him,
all who keep the Sabbath without desecrating it
　　and who hold fast to my covenant—
7these I will bring to my holy mountain
　　and give them joy in my house of prayer.
Their burnt offerings and sacrifices
　　will be accepted on my altar;
for my house will be called
　　a house of prayer for all nations."
8The Sovereign LORD declares—
　　he who gathers the exiles of Israel:
"I will gather still others to them
　　besides those already gathered."

God's Accusation Against the Wicked

9Come, all you beasts of the field,
　　come and devour, all you beasts of the forest!
10Israel's watchmen are blind,
　　they all lack knowledge;
they are all mute dogs,
　　they cannot bark;
they lie around and dream,
　　they love to sleep.
11They are dogs with mighty appetites;
　　they never have enough.
They are shepherds who lack understanding;
　　they all turn to their own way,
　　each seeks his own gain.
12"Come," each one cries, "let me get wine!
　　Let us drink our fill of beer!
And tomorrow will be like today,
　　or even far better."

57 The righteous perish,
　　　and no one ponders it in his heart;
　　　devout men are taken away,
　　and no one understands
that the righteous are taken away
　　to be spared from evil.
2Those who walk uprightly
　　enter into peace;
they find rest as they lie in death.

3"But you—come here, you sons of a sorceress,
　　you offspring of adulterers and prostitutes!
4Whom are you mocking?
　　At whom do you sneer
　　and stick out your tongue?
Are you not a brood of rebels,
　　the offspring of liars?
5You burn with lust among the oaks
　　and under every spreading tree;
you sacrifice your children in the ravines
　　and under the overhanging crags.

⁶The idols among the smooth stones of the
  ravines are your portion;
  they, they are your lot.
  Yes, to them you have poured out drink
    offerings
  and offered grain offerings.
  In the light of these things, should I relent?
⁷You have made your bed on a high and lofty
  hill;
  there you went up to offer your sacrifices.
⁸Behind your doors and your doorposts
  you have put your pagan symbols.
  Forsaking me, you uncovered your bed,
  you climbed into it and opened it wide;
  you made a pact with those whose beds you
    love,
  and you looked on their nakedness.
⁹You went to Molech*a* with olive oil
  and increased your perfumes.
  You sent your ambassadors*b* far away;
  you descended to the grave*c* itself!
¹⁰You were wearied by all your ways,
  but you would not say, 'It is hopeless.'
  You found renewal of your strength,
  and so you did not faint.

¹¹"Whom have you so dreaded and feared
  that you have been false to me,
  and have neither remembered me
  nor pondered this in your hearts?
  Is it not because I have long been silent
  that you do not fear me?
¹²I will expose your righteousness and your
    works,
  and they will not benefit you.
¹³When you cry out for help,
  let your collection of idols save you!
  The wind will carry all of them off,
  a mere breath will blow them away.
  But the man who makes me his refuge
  will inherit the land
  and possess my holy mountain."

Comfort for the Contrite

¹⁴And it will be said:

  "Build up, build up, prepare the road!
  Remove the obstacles out of the way of my
    people."
¹⁵For this is what the high and lofty One says—
  he who lives forever, whose name is holy:
  "I live in a high and holy place,
  but also with him who is contrite and lowly
    in spirit,

⁶在谷中光滑石頭裏
  有你的分,
  這些就是你所得的分。
  你也向他澆了奠祭、
  獻了供物,
  因這事
  我豈能容忍嗎?
⁷你在高而又高的山上
  安設牀榻,
  也上那裏去獻祭。
⁸你在門後、
  在門框後立起你的記念,
  向外人赤露,
  又上去擴張牀榻,
  與他們立約。
  你在那裏看見他們的牀
  就甚喜愛。
⁹你把油帶到王那裏,
  又多加香料,
  打發使者往遠方去,
  自卑自賤直到陰間。
¹⁰你因路遠疲倦,
  卻不說這是枉然;
  你以為有復興之力,
  所以不覺疲憊。

¹¹"你怕誰?因誰恐懼?
  竟說謊,
  不記念我,
  又不將這事放在心上!
  我不是許久閉口不言,
  你仍不怕我嗎?
¹²我要指明你的公義;
  至於你所行的,
  都必與你無益。
¹³你哀求的時候,
  讓你所聚集的拯救你吧!
  風要把他們颳散,
  一口氣要把他們都吹去;
  但那投靠我的
  必得地土,
  必承受我的聖山為業。"

痛悔者得安慰

¹⁴耶和華要說:

  "你們修築修築,預備道路,
  將絆腳石
  從我百姓的路中除掉!"
¹⁵因為那至高至上、
  永遠長存 (註:原文作"住在永遠")
  名為聖者的如此說:
  "我住在至高至聖的所在,
  也與心靈痛悔、謙卑的人同居;

---

a 9 Or *to the king*   *b 9* Or *idols*   *c 9* Hebrew *Sheol*

要使謙卑人的靈甦醒，
也使痛悔人的心甦醒。
16我必不永遠相爭，
也不長久發怒，
恐怕我所造的人與靈性
都必發昏。
17因他貪婪的罪孽，
我就發怒擊打他。
我向他掩面發怒，
他卻仍然隨心背道。
18我看見他所行的道，也要醫治他，
又要引導他，
使他和那一同傷心的人再得安慰。
19我造就嘴唇的果子，
願平安康泰歸與遠處的人，
也歸與近處的人；並且我要醫治他。”
這是耶和華說的。
20惟獨惡人，好像翻騰的海不得平靜；
其中的水常湧出污穢和淤泥來。
21我的神說：
“惡人必不得平安！”

真正的禁食

58 “你要大聲喊叫，不可止息；
揚起聲來，好像吹角。
向我百姓說明他們的過犯，
向雅各家說明他們的罪惡。
2他們天天尋求我，
樂意明白我的道，
好像行義的國民，
不離棄他們神的典章，
向我求問公義的判語，
喜悅親近神。
3他們說：‘我們禁食，
你為何不看見呢？
我們刻苦己心，
你為何不理會呢？’

“看哪，你們禁食的日子
仍求利益，
勒逼人為你們做苦工。
4你們禁食，卻互相爭競，
以兇惡的拳頭打人。
你們今日禁食，
不得使你們的聲音聽聞於上。
5這樣禁食，豈是我所揀選、
使人刻苦己心的日子嗎？
豈是叫人垂頭像葦子，
用麻布和爐灰鋪在他以下嗎？
你這可稱為禁食、
為耶和華所悅納的日子嗎？

6 “我所揀選的禁食，
不是要鬆開兇惡的繩，
解下軛上的索，

to revive the spirit of the lowly
and to revive the heart of the contrite.
16I will not accuse forever,
nor will I always be angry,
for then the spirit of man would grow faint
before me—
the breath of man that I have created.
17I was enraged by his sinful greed;
I punished him, and hid my face in anger,
yet he kept on in his willful ways.
18I have seen his ways, but I will heal him;
I will guide him and restore comfort to him,
19 creating praise on the lips of the mourners in
Israel.
Peace, peace, to those far and near,"
says the LORD. "And I will heal them."
20But the wicked are like the tossing sea,
which cannot rest,
whose waves cast up mire and mud.
21"There is no peace," says my God, "for the
wicked."

True Fasting

58 "Shout it aloud, do not hold back.
Raise your voice like a trumpet.
Declare to my people their rebellion
and to the house of Jacob their sins.
2For day after day they seek me out;
they seem eager to know my ways,
as if they were a nation that does what is right
and has not forsaken the commands of its God.
They ask me for just decisions
and seem eager for God to come near them.
3'Why have we fasted,' they say,
'and you have not seen it?
Why have we humbled ourselves,
and you have not noticed?'

"Yet on the day of your fasting, you do as you
please
and exploit all your workers.
4Your fasting ends in quarreling and strife,
and in striking each other with wicked fists.
You cannot fast as you do today
and expect your voice to be heard on high.
5Is this the kind of fast I have chosen,
only a day for a man to humble himself?
Is it only for bowing one's head like a reed
and for lying on sackcloth and ashes?
Is that what you call a fast,
a day acceptable to the LORD?

6"Is not this the kind of fasting I have chosen:
to loose the chains of injustice
and untie the cords of the yoke,

to set the oppressed free
and break every yoke?
[7]Is it not to share your food with the hungry
and to provide the poor wanderer with
shelter—
when you see the naked, to clothe him,
and not to turn away from your own flesh
and blood?
[8]Then your light will break forth like the dawn,
and your healing will quickly appear;
then your righteousness[a] will go before you,
and the glory of the LORD will be your rear
guard.
[9]Then you will call, and the LORD will answer;
you will cry for help, and he will say: Here
am I.

"If you do away with the yoke of oppression,
with the pointing finger and malicious talk,
[10]and if you spend yourselves in behalf of the
hungry
and satisfy the needs of the oppressed,
then your light will rise in the darkness,
and your night will become like the noonday.
[11]The LORD will guide you always;
he will satisfy your needs in a sun-scorched
land
and will strengthen your frame.
You will be like a well-watered garden,
like a spring whose waters never fail.
[12]Your people will rebuild the ancient ruins
and will raise up the age-old foundations;
you will be called Repairer of Broken Walls,
Restorer of Streets with Dwellings.

[13]"If you keep your feet from breaking the
Sabbath
and from doing as you please on my holy day,
if you call the Sabbath a delight
and the LORD's holy day honorable,
and if you honor it by not going your own way
and not doing as you please or speaking idle
words,
[14]then you will find your joy in the LORD,
and I will cause you to ride on the heights of
the land
and to feast on the inheritance of your father
Jacob."
The mouth of the LORD has spoken.

Sin, Confession and Redemption

59 Surely the arm of the LORD is not too
short to save,
nor his ear too dull to hear.

使被欺壓的得自由，
折斷一切的軛嗎？
[7]不是要把你的餅分給飢餓的人，
將飄流的窮人
接到你家中，
見赤身的給他衣服遮體，
顧恤自己的骨肉
而不掩藏嗎？
[8]這樣，你的光就必發現如早晨的光，
你所得的醫治要速速發明。
你的公義必在你前面行；
耶和華的榮光
必作你的後盾。
[9]那時你求告，耶和華必應允；
你呼求，他必說：
我在這裏。

"你若從你中間除掉重軛
和指摘人的指頭，並發惡言的事，
[10]你心若向飢餓的人
發憐憫，
使困苦的人得滿足，
你的光就必在黑暗中發現，
你的幽暗必變如正午。
[11]耶和華也必時常引導你，
在乾旱之地，
使你心滿意足，
骨頭強壯。
你必像澆灌的園子，
又像水流不絕的泉源。
[12]那些出於你的人，
必修造久已荒廢之處。
你要建立拆毀累代的根基，
你必稱為補破口的，
和重修路徑與人居住的。
[13] "你若在安息日掉轉（註：或作"謹
慎"）你的腳步，
在我聖日不以操作為喜樂，
稱安息日為可喜樂的，
稱耶和華的聖日為可尊重的，
而且尊敬這日，不辦自己的私事，
不隨自己的私意，
不說自己的私話，
[14]你就以耶和華為樂。
耶和華要使你
乘駕地的高處，
又以你祖雅各的產業
養育你。"
這是耶和華親口說的。

罪，悔改與救贖

59 耶和華的膀臂並非縮短，
不能拯救，
耳朵並非發沉，不能聽見。

2但你們的罪孽
　　使你們與神隔絕。
　你們的罪惡
　　使他掩面不聽你們。
3因為你們的手被血沾染，
　　你們的指頭被罪孽沾污；
　你們的嘴唇說謊言，
　　你們的舌頭出惡語。
4無一人按公義告狀，
　　無一人憑誠實辨白。
　都倚靠虛妄，說謊言；
　　所懷的是毒害，所生的是罪孽。
5他們菢毒蛇蛋，
　　結蜘蛛網。
　人吃這蛋必死，
　　這蛋被踏，必出蝮蛇。
6所結的網不能成為衣服；
　　所做的
　　　也不能遮蓋自己。
　他們的行為都是罪孽；
　　手所做的都是強暴。
7他們的腳奔跑行惡，
　　他們急速流無辜人的血。
　意念都是罪孽，
　　所經過的路都荒涼毀滅。
8平安的路，他們不知道；
　　所行的事沒有公平。
　他們為自己修彎曲的路；
　　凡行此路的，都不知道平安。

9因此，公平離我們遠，
　　公義追不上我們。
　我們指望光亮，卻是黑暗；
　　指望光明，卻行幽暗。
10我們摸索牆壁，好像瞎子；
　　我們摸索，如同無目之人。
　我們晌午絆腳，如在黃昏一樣；
　　我們在肥壯人中，像死人一般。
11我們咆哮如熊，
　　哀鳴如鴿；
　指望公平，卻是沒有；
　　指望救恩，卻遠離我們。

12我們的過犯在你面前增多，
　　罪惡作見證告我們；
　過犯與我們同在。
　　至於我們的罪孽，我們都知道：
13就是悖逆不認識耶和華，
　　轉去不跟從我們的神，
　說欺壓和叛逆的話，
　　心懷謊言，隨即說出。
14並且公平轉而退後，
　　公義站在遠處；
　誠實在街上仆倒，
　　正直也不得進入。

2But your iniquities have separated
　　you from your God;
　your sins have hidden his face from you,
　　so that he will not hear.
3For your hands are stained with blood,
　　your fingers with guilt.
　Your lips have spoken lies,
　　and your tongue mutters wicked things.
4No one calls for justice;
　　no one pleads his case with integrity.
　They rely on empty arguments and speak lies;
　　they conceive trouble and give birth to evil.
5They hatch the eggs of vipers
　　and spin a spider's web.
　Whoever eats their eggs will die,
　　and when one is broken, an adder is hatched.
6Their cobwebs are useless for clothing;
　　they cannot cover themselves with what they
　　　make.
　Their deeds are evil deeds,
　　and acts of violence are in their hands.
7Their feet rush into sin;
　　they are swift to shed innocent blood.
　Their thoughts are evil thoughts;
　　ruin and destruction mark their ways.
8The way of peace they do not know;
　　there is no justice in their paths.
　They have turned them into crooked roads;
　　no one who walks in them will know peace.

9So justice is far from us,
　　and righteousness does not reach us.
　We look for light, but all is darkness;
　　for brightness, but we walk in deep shadows.
10Like the blind we grope along the wall,
　　feeling our way like men without eyes.
　At midday we stumble as if it were twilight;
　　among the strong, we are like the dead.
11We all growl like bears;
　　we moan mournfully like doves.
　We look for justice, but find none;
　　for deliverance, but it is far away.

12For our offenses are many in your sight,
　　and our sins testify against us.
　Our offenses are ever with us,
　　and we acknowledge our iniquities:
13rebellion and treachery against the LORD,
　　turning our backs on our God,
　fomenting oppression and revolt,
　　uttering lies our hearts have conceived.
14So justice is driven back,
　　and righteousness stands at a distance;
　truth has stumbled in the streets,
　　honesty cannot enter.

¹⁵Truth is nowhere to be found,
  and whoever shuns evil becomes a prey.
The LORD looked and was displeased
  that there was no justice.
¹⁶He saw that there was no one,
  he was appalled that there was no one to
    intervene;
so his own arm worked salvation for him,
  and his own righteousness sustained him.
¹⁷He put on righteousness as his breastplate,
  and the helmet of salvation on his head;
he put on the garments of vengeance
  and wrapped himself in zeal as in a cloak.
¹⁸According to what they have done,
  so will he repay
wrath to his enemies
  and retribution to his foes;
he will repay the islands their due.
¹⁹From the west, men will fear the name of the
    LORD,
  and from the rising of the sun, they will
    revere his glory.
For he will come like a pent-up flood
  that the breath of the LORD drives along.^a

²⁰"The Redeemer will come to Zion,
  to those in Jacob who repent of their sins,"
                              declares the LORD.

²¹"As for me, this is my covenant with them,"
says the LORD. "My Spirit, who is on you, and
my words that I have put in your mouth will
not depart from your mouth, or from the mouths
of your children, or from the mouths of their
descendants from this time on and forever,"
says the LORD.

The Glory of Zion

60 "Arise, shine, for your light has come,
  and the glory of the LORD rises upon
    you.
²See, darkness covers the earth
  and thick darkness is over the peoples,
but the LORD rises upon you
  and his glory appears over you.
³Nations will come to your light,
  and kings to the brightness of your dawn.

⁴"Lift up your eyes and look about you:
  All assemble and come to you;
your sons come from afar,
  and your daughters are carried on the arm.

^a 19 Or When the enemy comes in like a flood, / the Spirit of the
LORD will put him to flight

¹⁵誠實少見，
  離惡的人反成掠物。
那時，耶和華看見沒有公平，
  甚不喜悅。
¹⁶他見無人拯救，
  無人代求，
  甚為詫異，
就用自己的膀臂施行拯救，
  以公義扶持自己。
¹⁷他以公義為鎧甲（註：或作"護心鏡"），
  以拯救為頭盔，
  以報仇為衣服，
  以熱心為外袍。
¹⁸他必按
  人的行為施報，
  惱怒他的敵人，
  報復他的仇敵，
  向眾海島施行報應。
¹⁹如此，人從日落之處
  必敬畏耶和華的名；
從日出之地，
  也必敬畏他的榮耀。
因為仇敵好像急流的河水沖來，
  是耶和華之氣所驅逐的。

²⁰ "必有一位救贖主來到錫安，
  雅各族中轉離過犯的人那裏。"
                    這是耶和華說的。

²¹耶和華說："至於我與他們所
立的約乃是這樣：我加給你的靈，傳
給你的話，必不離你的口，也不離你
後裔與你後裔之後裔的口，從今直到
永遠！"這是耶和華說的。

錫安的榮耀

60 "興起，發光！
  因為你的光已經來到！
  耶和華的榮耀發現照耀你。
²看哪，黑暗遮蓋大地，
  幽暗遮蓋萬民，
耶和華卻要顯現照耀你，
  他的榮耀要發現在你身上。
³萬國要來就你的光，
  君王要來就你發現的光輝。

⁴ "你舉目向四方觀看，
  眾人都聚集來到你這裏。
你的眾子從遠方而來，
  你的眾女也被懷抱而來。

⁵那時你看見就有光榮；
　　你心又跳動又寬暢。
　因為大海豐盛的貨物必轉來歸你，
　　列國的財寶也必來歸你。
⁶成羣的駱駝並米甸和以法的獨峯駝
　　必遮滿你。
　示巴的眾人都必來到；
　要奉上黃金乳香，
　　又要傳說耶和華的讚美。
⁷基達的羊羣都必聚集到你這裏，
　　尼拜約的公羊要供你使用；
　在我壇上必蒙悅納，
　　我必榮耀我榮耀的殿。

⁸「那些飛來如雲，
　　又如鴿子向窗戶飛回的是誰呢？
⁹眾海島必等候我，
　　首先是他施的船隻，
　將你的眾子連他們的金銀
　　從遠方一同帶來，
　都為耶和華你神的名，
　　又為以色列的聖者，
　　因為他已經榮耀了你。

¹⁰「外邦人必建築你的城牆，
　　他們的王必服侍你。
　我曾發怒擊打你，
　　現今卻施恩憐恤你。
¹¹你的城門必時常開放，
　　晝夜不關，
　使人把列國的財物
　　帶來歸你，
　　並將他們的君王牽引而來。
¹²哪一邦哪一國不侍奉你，
　　就必滅亡，
　也必全然荒廢。

¹³「黎巴嫩的榮耀，就是松樹、
　　杉樹、黃楊樹，都必一同歸你。
　為要修飾我聖所之地，
　　我也要使我腳踏之處得榮耀。
¹⁴素來苦待你的，
　　他的子孫都必屈身來就你；
　藐視你的，
　　都要在你腳下跪拜。
　他們要稱你為‘耶和華的城’，
　　為‘以色列聖者的錫安’。

¹⁵「你雖然被撇棄、被厭惡，
　　甚至無人經過，
　我卻使你變為永遠的榮華，
　　成為累代的喜樂。
¹⁶你也必吃萬國的奶，
　　又吃君王的奶。

⁵Then you will look and be radiant,
　your heart will throb and swell with joy;
the wealth on the seas will be brought to you,
　to you the riches of the nations will come.
⁶Herds of camels will cover your land,
　young camels of Midian and Ephah.
And all from Sheba will come,
　bearing gold and incense
and proclaiming the praise of the LORD.
⁷All Kedar's flocks will be gathered to you,
　the rams of Nebaioth will serve you;
they will be accepted as offerings on my altar,
　and I will adorn my glorious temple.

⁸"Who are these that fly along like clouds,
　like doves to their nests?
⁹Surely the islands look to me;
　in the lead are the ships of Tarshish,[a]
bringing your sons from afar,
　with their silver and gold,
to the honor of the LORD your God,
　the Holy One of Israel,
　for he has endowed you with splendor.

¹⁰"Foreigners will rebuild your walls,
　and their kings will serve you.
Though in anger I struck you,
　in favor I will show you compassion.
¹¹Your gates will always stand open,
　they will never be shut, day or night,
so that men may bring you the wealth of the
　　nations—
　their kings led in triumphal procession.
¹²For the nation or kingdom that will not serve
　　you will perish;
　it will be utterly ruined.

¹³"The glory of Lebanon will come to you,
　the pine, the fir and the cypress together,
to adorn the place of my sanctuary;
　and I will glorify the place of my feet.
¹⁴The sons of your oppressors will come
　　bowing before you;
　all who despise you will bow down at your
　　feet
and will call you the City of the LORD,
　Zion of the Holy One of Israel.

¹⁵"Although you have been forsaken and hated,
　with no one traveling through,
I will make you the everlasting pride
　and the joy of all generations.
¹⁶You will drink the milk of nations
　and be nursed at royal breasts.

a 9 Or the trading ships

Then you will know that I, the LORD, am your
  Savior,
  your Redeemer, the Mighty One of Jacob.
[17]Instead of bronze I will bring you gold,
  and silver in place of iron.
Instead of wood I will bring you bronze,
  and iron in place of stones.
I will make peace your governor
  and righteousness your ruler.
[18]No longer will violence be heard in your land,
  nor ruin or destruction within your borders,
but you will call your walls Salvation
  and your gates Praise.
[19]The sun will no more be your light by day,
  nor will the brightness of the moon shine on
    you,
for the LORD will be your everlasting light,
  and your God will be your glory.
[20]Your sun will never set again,
  and your moon will wane no more;
the LORD will be your everlasting light,
  and your days of sorrow will end.
[21]Then will all your people be righteous
  and they will possess the land forever.
They are the shoot I have planted,
  the work of my hands,
for the display of my splendor.
[22]The least of you will become a thousand,
  the smallest a mighty nation.
I am the LORD;
  in its time I will do this swiftly."

The Year of the LORD's Favor

61 The Spirit of the Sovereign LORD is on me,
  because the LORD has anointed me
  to preach good news to the poor.
He has sent me to bind up the brokenhearted,
  to proclaim freedom for the captives
  and release from darkness for the prisoners,[a]
[2]to proclaim the year of the LORD's favor
  and the day of vengeance of our God,
to comfort all who mourn,
[3] and provide for those who grieve in Zion—
to bestow on them a crown of beauty
  instead of ashes,
the oil of gladness
  instead of mourning,
and a garment of praise
  instead of a spirit of despair.
They will be called oaks of righteousness,
  a planting of the LORD
for the display of his splendor.

你便知道我耶和華是你的救主，
  是你的救贖主，
  雅各的大能者。
[17]我要拿金子代替銅，
  拿銀子代替鐵，
  拿銅代替木頭，
  拿鐵代替石頭；
並要以和平為你的官長，
  以公義為你的監督。
[18]你地上不再聽見強暴的事，
  境內不再聽見荒涼毀滅的事。
你必稱你的牆為‘拯救’，
  稱你的門為‘讚美’。
[19]日頭不再作你白晝的光，
  月亮也不再
    發光照耀你；
耶和華卻要作你永遠的光，
  你神要為你的榮耀！
[20]你的日頭不再下落，
  你的月亮也不退縮；
因為耶和華必作你永遠的光，
  你悲哀的日子也完畢了。
[21]你的居民都成為義人，
  永遠得地為業，
是我種的栽子，
  我手的工作，
  使我得榮耀。
[22]至小的族要加增千倍，
  微弱的國必成為強盛；
我耶和華
  要按定期速成這事。”

主悅納之年

61 主耶和華的靈在我身上，
  因為耶和華用膏膏我，
  叫我傳好信息給謙卑的人
    （註：或作“傳福音給貧窮的人”），
差遣我醫好傷心的人，
  報告被擄的得釋放，
  被囚的出監牢；
[2]報告耶和華的恩年，
  和我們神報仇的日子，
安慰一切悲哀的人；
[3]賜華冠與錫安悲哀的人，
  代替灰塵，
喜樂油
  代替悲哀，
讚美衣
  代替憂傷之靈。
使他們稱為公義樹，
  是耶和華所栽的，
  叫他得榮耀。

---

a 1 Hebrew; Septuagint *the blind*

⁴他們必修造已久的荒場，
　　建立先前淒涼之處，
　　重修歷代荒涼之城。
⁵那時，外人必起來牧放你們的羊羣，
　　外邦人必作你們耕種田地的、
　　修理葡萄園的。
⁶你們倒要稱為耶和華的祭司，
　　人必稱你們為我們神的僕役。
　　你們必吃用列國的財物，
　　因得他們的榮耀自誇。

⁷你們必得加倍的好處，
　　代替所受的羞辱；
　　分中所得的喜樂，
　　必代替所受的凌辱。
　　在境內必得加倍的產業，
　　永遠之樂必歸與你們（註：原文作
　　"他們"）。

⁸"因為我耶和華喜愛公平，
　　恨惡搶奪和罪孽。
　　我要憑誠實施行報應，
　　並要與我的百姓立永約。
⁹他們的後裔
　　必在列國中被人認識，
　　他們的子孫在眾民中也是如此。
　　凡看見他們的，
　　必認他們是耶和華賜福的後裔。"

¹⁰我因耶和華大大歡喜，
　　我的心靠神快樂。
　　因他以拯救為衣給我穿上，
　　以公義為袍給我披上。
　　好像新郎戴上華冠，
　　又像新婦佩戴妝飾。
¹¹田地怎樣使百穀發芽，
　　園子怎樣使所種的發生，
　　主耶和華必照樣
　　　使公義和讚美，
　　　在萬民中發出。

錫安的新名

62 我因錫安必不靜默，
　　為耶路撒冷必不息聲，
　　直到他的公義
　　　如光輝發出，
　　　他的救恩如明燈發亮。
²列國必見你的公義，
　　列王必見你的榮耀。
　　你必得新名的稱呼，
　　是耶和華親口所起的。
³你在耶和華的手中
　　要作為華冠，
　　在你神的掌上必作為冕旒。
⁴你必不再稱為"撇棄的"，
　　你的地也不再稱為"荒涼的"；

⁴They will rebuild the ancient ruins
　　and restore the places long devastated;
　they will renew the ruined cities
　　that have been devastated for generations.
⁵Aliens will shepherd your flocks;
　　foreigners will work your fields and vineyards.
⁶And you will be called priests of the LORD,
　　you will be named ministers of our God.
　You will feed on the wealth of nations,
　　and in their riches you will boast.

⁷Instead of their shame
　　my people will receive a double portion,
　and instead of disgrace
　　they will rejoice in their inheritance;
　and so they will inherit a double portion in
　　their land,
　　and everlasting joy will be theirs.

⁸"For I, the LORD, love justice;
　　I hate robbery and iniquity.
　In my faithfulness I will reward them
　　and make an everlasting covenant with them.
⁹Their descendants will be known among the
　　nations
　　and their offspring among the peoples.
　All who see them will acknowledge
　　that they are a people the LORD has blessed."

¹⁰I delight greatly in the LORD;
　　my soul rejoices in my God.
　For he has clothed me with garments of salvation
　　and arrayed me in a robe of righteousness,
　as a bridegroom adorns his head like a priest,
　　and as a bride adorns herself with her jewels.
¹¹For as the soil makes the sprout come up
　　and a garden causes seeds to grow,
　so the Sovereign LORD will make
　　righteousness and praise
　　spring up before all nations.

Zion's New Name

62 For Zion's sake I will not keep silent,
　　for Jerusalem's sake I will not remain
　　quiet,
　till her righteousness shines out like the dawn,
　　her salvation like a blazing torch.
²The nations will see your righteousness,
　　and all kings your glory;
　you will be called by a new name
　　that the mouth of the LORD will bestow.
³You will be a crown of splendor in the LORD's
　　hand,
　　a royal diadem in the hand of your God.
⁴No longer will they call you Deserted,
　　or name your land Desolate.

But you will be called Hephzibah,[a]
and your land Beulah;[b]
for the LORD will take delight in you,
and your land will be married.
[5]As a young man marries a maiden,
so will your sons[c] marry you;
as a bridegroom rejoices over his bride,
so will your God rejoice over you.

[6]I have posted watchmen on your walls,
O Jerusalem;
they will never be silent day or night.
You who call on the LORD,
give yourselves no rest,
[7]and give him no rest till he establishes Jerusalem
and makes her the praise of the earth.

[8]The LORD has sworn by his right hand
and by his mighty arm:
"Never again will I give your grain
as food for your enemies,
and never again will foreigners drink the new
wine
for which you have toiled;
[9]but those who harvest it will eat it
and praise the LORD,
and those who gather the grapes will drink it
in the courts of my sanctuary."

[10]Pass through, pass through the gates!
Prepare the way for the people.
Build up, build up the highway!
Remove the stones.
Raise a banner for the nations.

[11]The LORD has made proclamation
to the ends of the earth:
"Say to the Daughter of Zion,
'See, your Savior comes!
See, his reward is with him,
and his recompense accompanies him.' "
[12]They will be called the Holy People,
the Redeemed of the LORD;
and you will be called Sought After,
the City No Longer Deserted.

God's Day of Vengeance and Redemption

63
Who is this coming from Edom,
from Bozrah, with his garments stained
crimson?
Who is this, robed in splendor,
striding forward in the greatness of his
strength?

a 4 *Hephzibah* means *my delight is in her.* b 4 *Beulah* means
married. c 5 Or *Builder*

你卻要稱為"我所喜悅的",
你的地也必稱為"有夫之婦"。
因為耶和華喜悅你,
你的地也必歸他。
[5]少年人怎樣娶處女,你的眾民(註:
"民"原文作"子")也要照樣娶你;
新郎怎樣喜悅新婦,
你的神也要照樣喜悅你。

[6]耶路撒冷啊,
我在你城上設立守望的,
他們晝夜必不靜默。
呼籲耶和華的,你們不要歇息,
[7]也不要使他歇息,
直等他建立耶路撒冷,
使耶路撒冷在地上成為可讚美的。

[8]耶和華指着自己的右手
和大能的膀臂起誓說:
"我必不再將你的五穀
給你仇敵作食物;
外邦人
也不再喝
你勞碌得來的新酒。
[9]惟有那收割的要吃,
並讚美耶和華,
那聚斂的
要在我聖所的院內喝。"

[10]你們當從門經過經過,
預備百姓的路;
修築修築大道,
撿去石頭,
為萬民豎立大旗。

[11]看哪,耶和華曾宣告到地極,
對錫安的居民(註:"民"原文作"女子")
說:
"你的拯救者來到,
他的賞賜在他那裏;
他的報應在他面前。"
[12]人必稱他們為"聖民",
為"耶和華的贖民",
你也必稱為"被眷顧、
不撇棄的城"。

神忿怒與拯救的日子

63
這從以東的波斯拉來,
穿紅衣服、
裝扮華美、
能力廣大、
大步行走的
是誰呢?

"就是我，是憑公義說話，
　　以大能施行拯救。"

²你的裝扮為何有紅色？
　　你的衣服為何像踹酒醡的呢？

³　"我獨自踹酒醡，
　　　眾民中無一人與我同在。
　　我發怒將他們踹下，
　　　發烈怒將他們踐踏；
　　他們的血濺在我衣服上，
　　　並且污染了我一切的衣裳。
⁴因為報仇之日在我心中，
　　救贖我民之年已經來到。
⁵我仰望，見無人幫助；
　　我詫異，沒有人扶持。
　　所以我自己的膀臂為我施行拯救，
　　我的烈怒將我扶持。
⁶我發怒，踹下眾民；
　　發烈怒，使他們沉醉，
　　又將他們的血倒在地上。"

頌讚與禱告

⁷我要照耶和華一切
　　　所賜給我們的，
　　提起他的慈愛和美德，
　　並他向以色列家所施的大恩，
　　這恩是照他的憐恤
　　　和豐盛的慈愛
　　　賜給他們的。
⁸他說："他們誠然是我的百姓，
　　不行虛假的子民。"
　　這樣，他就作了他們的救主。
⁹他們在一切苦難中，他也同受苦難，
　　並且他面前的使者拯救他們。
　　他以慈愛和憐憫救贖他們，
　　在古時的日子常保抱他們、
　　懷搋他們。
¹⁰他們竟悖逆，
　　使主的聖靈擔憂；
　　他就轉作他們的仇敵，
　　親自攻擊他們。

¹¹那時，他們（註：原文作"他"）想起
　　　古時的日子，
　　摩西和他百姓說：
　　將百姓和牧養他全羣的人
　　　從海裏領上來的在哪裏呢？
　　將他的聖靈降在他們中間的
　　　在哪裏呢？
¹²使他榮耀的膀臂
　　在摩西的右手邊行動，
　　在他們前面ľ使水分開，
　　要建立自己永遠的名，

"It is I, speaking in righteousness,
　　mighty to save."

²Why are your garments red,
　　like those of one treading the winepress?

³"I have trodden the winepress alone;
　　from the nations no one was with me.
　I trampled them in my anger
　　and trod them down in my wrath;
　their blood spattered my garments,
　　and I stained all my clothing.
⁴For the day of vengeance was in my heart,
　　and the year of my redemption has come.
⁵I looked, but there was no one to help,
　　I was appalled that no one gave support;
　so my own arm worked salvation for me,
　　and my own wrath sustained me.
⁶I trampled the nations in my anger;
　　in my wrath I made them drunk
　　and poured their blood on the ground."

Praise and Prayer

⁷I will tell of the kindnesses of the LORD,
　　the deeds for which he is to be praised,
　　according to all the LORD has done for us—
　yes, the many good things he has done
　　for the house of Israel,
　　according to his compassion and many
　　　kindnesses.
⁸He said, "Surely they are my people,
　　sons who will not be false to me";
　　and so he became their Savior.
⁹In all their distress he too was distressed,
　　and the angel of his presence saved them.
　In his love and mercy he redeemed them;
　　he lifted them up and carried them
　　all the days of old.
¹⁰Yet they rebelled
　　and grieved his Holy Spirit.
　So he turned and became their enemy
　　and he himself fought against them.

¹¹Then his people recalled*ᵃ* the days of old,
　　the days of Moses and his people—
　where is he who brought them through the
　　　sea,
　with the shepherd of his flock?
　Where is he who set
　　his Holy Spirit among them,
¹²who sent his glorious arm of power
　　to be at Moses' right hand,
　who divided the waters before them,
　　to gain for himself everlasting renown,

a 11 Or But may he recall

¹³who led them through the depths?
　Like a horse in open country,
　　they did not stumble;
¹⁴like cattle that go down to the plain,
　they were given rest by the Spirit of the LORD.
　This is how you guided your people
　　to make for yourself a glorious name.

¹⁵Look down from heaven and see
　from your lofty throne, holy and glorious.
　Where are your zeal and your might?
　　Your tenderness and compassion are
　　　withheld from us.
¹⁶But you are our Father,
　though Abraham does not know us
　or Israel acknowledge us;
　you, O LORD, are our Father,
　our Redeemer from of old is your name.
¹⁷Why, O LORD, do you make us wander from
　　your ways
　and harden our hearts so we do not revere
　　you?
　Return for the sake of your servants,
　　the tribes that are your inheritance.
¹⁸For a little while your people possessed your
　　holy place,
　but now our enemies have trampled down
　　your sanctuary.
¹⁹We are yours from of old;
　but you have not ruled over them,
　they have not been called by your name.ᵃ

64 Oh, that you would rend the heavens
　　and come down,
　　that the mountains would tremble
　　before you!
²As when fire sets twigs ablaze
　and causes water to boil,
　come down to make your name known to
　　your enemies
　and cause the nations to quake before you!
³For when you did awesome things that we did
　　not expect,
　you came down, and the mountains
　　trembled before you.
⁴Since ancient times no one has heard,
　no ear has perceived,
　no eye has seen any God besides you,
　who acts on behalf of those who wait for him.
⁵You come to the help of those who gladly do
　　right,
　who remember your ways.

a 19 Or We are like those you have never ruled, / like those never
called by your name

¹³帶領他們經過深處，
　如馬行走曠野，
　　使他們不至絆跌的在哪裏呢？
¹⁴耶和華的靈使他們得安息，
　彷彿牲畜下到山谷。
　照樣，你也引導你的百姓，
　　要建立自己榮耀的名。

¹⁵求你從天上垂顧，
　從你聖潔榮耀的居所觀看。
　你的熱心和你大能的作為在哪裏呢？
　你愛慕的心腸和憐憫
　　向我們止住了。
¹⁶亞伯拉罕雖然不認識我們，
　以色列也不承認我們，
　你卻是我們的父。
　耶和華啊，你是我們的父；
　從萬古以來，
　你名稱為“我們的救贖主”。
¹⁷耶和華啊，
　你為何使我們走差離開你的道，
　使我們心裏剛硬不敬畏你呢？
　求你為你僕人─
　　為你產業支派的緣故轉回來。
¹⁸你的聖民
　不過暫時得這產業，
　我們的敵人
　　已經踐踏你的聖所。
¹⁹我們好像
　你未曾治理的人，
　又像未曾得稱你名下的人。

64 願你
　　裂天而降，
　　願山
　在你面前震動。
²好像火燒乾柴，
　又像火將水燒開。
　使你敵人
　　知道你的名，
　使列國在你面前發顫。
³你曾行
　　我們不能逆料可畏的事。
　那時你降臨，
　山嶺在你面前震動。
⁴從古以來人未曾聽見、
　未曾耳聞、
　未曾眼見在你以外有甚麼神
　為等候他的人行事。
⁵你迎接
　那歡喜行義、
　記念你道的人；

你曾發怒，
　　我們仍犯罪。
　　這景況已久，我們還能得救嗎？
6我們都像不潔淨的人，
　　所有的義都像污穢的衣服；
我們都像葉子漸漸枯乾，
　　我們的罪孽好像風把我們吹去。
7並且無人求告你的名，
　　無人奮力抓住你，
原來你掩面不顧我們，
　　使我們因罪孽消化。

8耶和華啊，現在你仍是我們的父！
　　我們是泥，你是窰匠，
　　我們都是你手的工作。
9耶和華啊，求你不要大發震怒，
　　也不要永遠記念罪孽。
求你垂顧我們，
　　我們都是你的百姓。
10你的聖邑變為曠野，
　　錫安變為曠野，耶路撒冷成為荒場。
11我們聖潔華美的殿，
　　就是我們列祖讚美你的所在，
　　被火焚燒；
我們所羨慕的美地盡都荒廢。
12耶和華啊，有這些事，
　　你還忍得住嗎？
你仍靜默，
　　使我們深受苦難嗎？

審判與拯救

65 「素來沒有訪問我的，
　　現在求問我；
　　沒有尋找我的，
我叫他們遇見；
沒有稱為我名下的，我對他們說：
　　『我在這裏！我在這裏！』
2我整天伸手
　　招呼那悖逆的百姓，
他們隨自己的意念
　　行不善之道。
3這百姓時常
　　當面惹我發怒：
在園中獻祭，
　　在壇（註：原文作“磚”）上燒香；
4在墳墓間坐着，
　　在隱密處住宿；
吃豬肉，
　　他們器皿中有可憎之物做的湯；
5且對人說：『你站開吧！不要挨近我，
　　因為我比你聖潔。』
主說：『這些人是我鼻中的煙，
　　是整天燒着的火。』
6、7看哪，這都寫在我面前，
　　我必不靜默，
　　必施行報應，

But when we continued to sin against them,
　　you were angry.
　　How then can we be saved?
6All of us have become like one who is unclean,
　　and all our righteous acts are like filthy rags;
we all shrivel up like a leaf,
　　and like the wind our sins sweep us away.
7No one calls on your name
　　or strives to lay hold of you;
for you have hidden your face from us
　　and made us waste away because of our sins.

8Yet, O LORD, you are our Father.
　　We are the clay, you are the potter;
　　we are all the work of your hand.
9Do not be angry beyond measure, O LORD;
　　do not remember our sins forever.
Oh, look upon us, we pray,
　　for we are all your people.
10Your sacred cities have become a desert;
　　even Zion is a desert, Jerusalem a desolation.
11Our holy and glorious temple, where our
　　fathers praised you,
　　has been burned with fire,
and all that we treasured lies in ruins.
12After all this, O LORD, will you hold yourself
　　back?
　　Will you keep silent and punish us beyond
　　measure?

Judgment and Salvation

65 "I revealed myself to those who did not
　　ask for me;
　　I was found by those who did not seek
　　me.
To a nation that did not call on my name,
　　I said, 'Here am I, here am I.'
2All day long I have held out my hands
　　to an obstinate people,
who walk in ways not good,
　　pursuing their own imaginations—
3a people who continually provoke me
　　to my very face,
offering sacrifices in gardens
　　and burning incense on altars of brick;
4who sit among the graves
　　and spend their nights keeping secret vigil;
who eat the flesh of pigs,
　　and whose pots hold broth of unclean meat;
5who say, 'Keep away; don't come near me,
　　for I am too sacred for you!'
Such people are smoke in my nostrils,
　　a fire that keeps burning all day.
6"See, it stands written before me:
　　I will not keep silent but will pay back in full;
　　I will pay it back into their laps—

7both your sins and the sins of your fathers,"
　　says the LORD.
　　"Because they burned sacrifices on the
　　　　mountains
　　and defied me on the hills,
　I will measure into their laps
　　the full payment for their former deeds."

　8This is what the LORD says:

　"As when juice is still found in a cluster of
　　　　grapes
　　and men say, 'Don't destroy it,
　　there is yet some good in it,'
　so will I do in behalf of my servants;
　　I will not destroy them all.
9I will bring forth descendants from Jacob,
　　and from Judah those who will possess my
　　　　mountains;
　my chosen people will inherit them,
　　and there will my servants live.
10Sharon will become a pasture for flocks,
　　and the Valley of Achor a resting place for
　　　　herds,
　　for my people who seek me.

11"But as for you who forsake the LORD
　　and forget my holy mountain,
　who spread a table for Fortune
　　and fill bowls of mixed wine for Destiny,
12I will destine you for the sword,
　　and you will all bend down for the slaughter;
　for I called but you did not answer,
　I spoke but you did not listen.
　You did evil in my sight
　　and chose what displeases me."

　13Therefore this is what the Sovereign LORD
says:

　"My servants will eat,
　　but you will go hungry;
　my servants will drink,
　　but you will go thirsty;
　my servants will rejoice,
　　but you will be put to shame.
14My servants will sing
　　out of the joy of their hearts,
　but you will cry out
　　from anguish of heart
　　and wail in brokenness of spirit.
15You will leave your name
　　to my chosen ones as a curse;
　the Sovereign LORD will put you to death,
　　but to his servants he will give another name.

必將你們的罪孽
　和你們列祖的罪孽，
就是在山上燒香，
　在岡上褻瀆我的罪孽，
　一同報應在他們後人懷中。
我先要把他們所行的量給他們。"
　　　　　　這是耶和華說的。

8耶和華如此說：

"葡萄中尋得新酒，
　人就說：
　'不要毀壞，
　　因為福在其中。'
我因我僕人的緣故也必照樣而行，
　不將他們全然毀滅。
9我必從雅各中領出後裔，
　從猶大中領出
　　承受我眾山的。
我的選民必承受，
　我的僕人要在那裏居住。
10沙崙平原必成為羊羣的圈；
　亞割谷必成為
　　牛羣躺臥之處，
　都為尋求我的民所得。

11"但你們這些離棄耶和華，
　忘記我的聖山，
給時運擺筵席（註：原文作"桌子"），
　給天命盛滿調和酒的，
12我要命定你們歸在刀下，
　都必屈身被殺。
因為我呼喚，你們沒有答應；
　我說話，你們沒有聽從，
反倒行我眼中看為惡的，
　揀選我所不喜悅的。"

13所以主耶和華如此說：

"我的僕人必得吃，
　你們卻飢餓；
我的僕人必得喝，
　你們卻乾渴；
我的僕人必歡喜，
　你們卻蒙羞。
14我的僕人
　因心中高興歡呼，
你們卻
　因心中憂愁哀哭，
　又因心裏憂傷哀號。
15你們必留下自己的名，
　為我選民指着賭咒。
主耶和華必殺你們，
　另起別名稱呼他的僕人。

16這樣，在地上為自己求福的，
　　必憑真實的神求福；
在地上起誓的，
　　必指真實的神起誓；
因為從前的患難已經忘記，
　　也從我眼前隱藏了。

新天新地

17 "看哪，
　　我造新天新地；
從前的事不再被記念，
　　也不再追想。
18你們當因我所造的
　　永遠歡喜快樂！
因我造耶路撒冷為人所喜，
　　造其中的居民為人所樂。
19我必因耶路撒冷歡喜，
　　因我的百姓快樂。
其中必不再聽見哭泣的聲音
　　和哀號的聲音。

20 "其中必沒有
　　數日夭亡的嬰孩，
　　也沒有壽數不滿的老者；
因為百歲死的
　　仍算孩童，
有百歲死的罪人
　　算被咒詛。
21他們要建造房屋，自己居住；
　　栽種葡萄園，吃其中的果子。
22他們建造的，
　　別人不得住；
他們栽種的，
　　別人不得吃。
因為我民的日子必像樹木的日子，
　　我選民親手勞碌得來的
　　必長久享用。
23他們必不徒然勞碌，
　　所生產的，也不遭災害。
因為都是蒙耶和華賜福的後裔，
　　他們的子孫也是如此。
24他們尚未求告，我就應允；
　　正說話的時候，我就垂聽。
25豺狼必與羊羔同食，
　　獅子必吃草與牛一樣，
　　塵土必作蛇的食物。
在我聖山的遍處，
　　這一切都不傷人、不害物。"
　　　　　　　　　這是耶和華說的。

審判與盼望

66 耶和華如此說：

"天是我的座位，

16Whoever invokes a blessing in the land
　　will do so by the God of truth;
he who takes an oath in the land
　　will swear by the God of truth.
For the past troubles will be forgotten
　　and hidden from my eyes.

New Heavens and a New Earth

17"Behold, I will create
　　new heavens and a new earth.
The former things will not be remembered,
　　nor will they come to mind.
18But be glad and rejoice forever
　　in what I will create,
for I will create Jerusalem to be a delight
　　and its people a joy.
19I will rejoice over Jerusalem
　　and take delight in my people;
the sound of weeping and of crying
　　will be heard in it no more.

20"Never again will there be in it
　　an infant who lives but a few days,
　　or an old man who does not live out his years;
he who dies at a hundred
　　will be thought a mere youth;
he who fails to reach[a] a hundred
　　will be considered accursed.
21They will build houses and dwell in them;
　　they will plant vineyards and eat their fruit.
22No longer will they build houses and others
　　live in them,
　　or plant and others eat.
For as the days of a tree,
　　so will be the days of my people;
my chosen ones will long enjoy
　　the works of their hands.
23They will not toil in vain
　　or bear children doomed to misfortune;
for they will be a people blessed by the LORD,
　　they and their descendants with them.
24Before they call I will answer;
　　while they are still speaking I will hear.
25The wolf and the lamb will feed together,
　　and the lion will eat straw like the ox,
　　but dust will be the serpent's food.
They will neither harm nor destroy
　　on all my holy mountain,"
　　　　　　　　　says the LORD.

Judgment and Hope

66 This is what the LORD says:

"Heaven is my throne,

a 20 Or / the sinner who reaches

and the earth is my footstool.
Where is the house you will build for me?
Where will my resting place be?
²Has not my hand made all these things,
and so they came into being?"
declares the LORD.

"This is the one I esteem:
he who is humble and contrite in spirit,
and trembles at my word.
³But whoever sacrifices a bull
is like one who kills a man,
and whoever offers a lamb,
like one who breaks a dog's neck;
whoever makes a grain offering
is like one who presents pig's blood,
and whoever burns memorial incense,
like one who worships an idol.
They have chosen their own ways,
and their souls delight in their abominations;
⁴so I also will choose harsh treatment for them
and will bring upon them what they dread.
For when I called, no one answered,
when I spoke, no one listened.
They did evil in my sight
and chose what displeases me."

⁵Hear the word of the LORD,
you who tremble at his word:
"Your brothers who hate you,
and exclude you because of my name, have
said,
'Let the LORD be glorified,
that we may see your joy!'
Yet they will be put to shame.
⁶Hear that uproar from the city,
hear that noise from the temple!
It is the sound of the LORD
repaying his enemies all they deserve.

⁷"Before she goes into labor,
she gives birth;
before the pains come upon her,
she delivers a son.
⁸Who has ever heard of such a thing?
Who has ever seen such things?
Can a country be born in a day
or a nation be brought forth in a moment?
Yet no sooner is Zion in labor
than she gives birth to her children.
⁹Do I bring to the moment of birth
and not give delivery?" says the LORD.
"Do I close up the womb
when I bring to delivery?" says your God.
¹⁰"Rejoice with Jerusalem and be glad for her,
all you who love her;

地是我的腳凳。
你們要為我造何等的殿宇？
哪裏是我安息的地方呢？"
²耶和華說：
"這一切都是我手所造的，
所以就都有了。

"但我所看顧的，就是虛心痛悔、
因我話而戰兢的人（註："虛心"原
文作"貧窮"）。
³假冒為善的宰牛，
好像殺人，
獻羊羔，
好像打折狗項，
獻供物，
好像獻豬血，
燒乳香，
好像稱頌偶像。
這等人揀選自己的道路，
心裏喜悅行可憎惡的事。
⁴我也必揀選迷惑他們的事，
使他們所懼怕的臨到他們。
因為我呼喚，無人答應；
我說話，他們不聽從；
反倒行我眼中看為惡的，
揀選我所不喜悅的。"

⁵你們因耶和華言語戰兢的人，
當聽他的話：
"你們的弟兄，就是恨惡你們、
因我名趕出你們的，
曾說：
'願耶和華得榮耀，
使我們得見你們的喜樂'，
但蒙羞的究竟是他們。
⁶有喧嘩的聲音出自城中，
有聲音出於殿中，
是耶和華向仇敵
施行報應的聲音。

⁷"錫安未曾劬勞
就生產；
未覺疼痛
就生出男孩。
⁸國豈能一日而生？
民豈能一時而產？
因為錫安一劬勞，
便生下兒女。
這樣的事誰曾聽見、
誰曾看見呢？"
⁹耶和華說："我既使她臨產，
豈不使她生產呢？"
你的神說："我既使她生產，
豈能使她閉胎不生呢？"
¹⁰"你們愛慕耶路撒冷的，
都要與她一同歡喜快樂；

你們為她悲哀的，
都要與她一同樂上加樂；
11使你們在她安慰的懷中
吃奶得飽，
使他們得她豐盛的榮耀，
猶如擠奶，滿心喜樂。”

12耶和華如此說：

“我要使平安延及她，好像江河；
使列國的榮耀延及她，
如同漲溢的河。
你們要從中享受（註：原文作“哺”），
你們必蒙抱在肋旁，搖弄在膝上。
13母親怎樣安慰兒子，
我就照樣安慰你們。
你們也必因（註：或作“在”）
耶路撒冷得安慰。”

14你們看見，就心中快樂，
你們的骨頭必得滋潤，像嫩草一樣。
而且耶和華的手向他僕人所行的，
必被人知道；
他也要向仇敵發惱恨。
15看哪，耶和華必在火中降臨。
他的車輦像旋風，
以烈怒施行報應，
以火焰施行責罰。
16因為耶和華在一切有血氣的人身上，
必以火與刀施行審判，
被耶和華所殺的必多。

17“那些分別為聖、潔淨自己
的，進入園內。跟在其中一個人的
後頭吃豬肉和倉鼠，並可憎之物，
他們必一同滅絕。”這是耶和華說
的。

18“我知道他們的行為和他們的
意念。時候將到，我必將萬民萬族
（註：“族”原文作“舌”）聚來，看見我
的榮耀。”

19“我要顯神蹟（註：或作“記
號”）在他們中間，逃脫的我要差到
列國去，就是到他施、普勒、拉弓
的路德和土巴、雅完，並素來沒有
聽見我名聲、沒有看見我榮耀遼遠
的海島，他們必將我的榮耀傳揚在
列國中。20他們必將你們的弟兄從列
國中送回，使他們或騎馬，或坐
車，坐轎，騎騾子，騎獨峯駝，到
我的聖山耶路撒冷，作為供物獻給
耶和華，好像以色列人用潔淨的器
皿盛供物奉到耶和華的殿中。”這

rejoice greatly with her,
all you who mourn over her.
11For you will nurse and be satisfied
at her comforting breasts;
you will drink deeply
and delight in her overflowing abundance."

12For this is what the LORD says:

"I will extend peace to her like a river,
and the wealth of nations like a flooding
stream;
you will nurse and be carried on her arm
and dandled on her knees.
13As a mother comforts her child,
so will I comfort you;
and you will be comforted over Jerusalem."

14When you see this, your heart will rejoice
and you will flourish like grass;
the hand of the LORD will be made known to
his servants,
but his fury will be shown to his foes.
15See, the LORD is coming with fire,
and his chariots are like a whirlwind;
he will bring down his anger with fury,
and his rebuke with flames of fire.
16For with fire and with his sword
the LORD will execute judgment upon all men,
and many will be those slain by the LORD.

17"Those who consecrate and purify themselves to go into the gardens, following the one
in the midst of[a] those who eat the flesh of pigs
and rats and other abominable things—they will
meet their end together," declares the LORD.

18"And I, because of their actions and their
imaginations, am about to come[b] and gather all
nations and tongues, and they will come and see
my glory.

19"I will set a sign among them, and I will
send some of those who survive to the nations—
to Tarshish, to the Libyans[c] and Lydians (famous
as archers), to Tubal and Greece, and to the distant islands that have not heard of my fame or
seen my glory. They will proclaim my glory
among the nations. 20And they will bring all your
brothers, from all the nations, to my holy mountain in Jerusalem as an offering to the LORD—on
horses, in chariots and wagons, and on mules
and camels," says the LORD. "They will bring
them, as the Israelites bring their grain offerings,

---

a 17 Or gardens behind one of your temples, and
b 18 The meaning of the Hebrew for this clause is uncertain.
c 19 Some Septuagint manuscripts Put (Libyans); Hebrew Pul

to the temple of the LORD in ceremonially clean vessels. [21]And I will select some of them also to be priests and Levites," says the LORD.

[22]"As the new heavens and the new earth that I make will endure before me," declares the LORD, "so will your name and descendants endure. [23]From one New Moon to another and from one Sabbath to another, all mankind will come and bow down before me," says the LORD. [24]"And they will go out and look upon the dead bodies of those who rebelled against me; their worm will not die, nor will their fire be quenched, and they will be loathsome to all mankind."

是耶和華說的。[21]耶和華說："我也必從他們中間取人為祭司，為<u>利未</u>人。"

[22]耶和華說："我所要造的新天新地，怎樣在我面前長存，你們的後裔和你們的名字也必照樣長存！[23]每逢月朔、安息日，凡有血氣的必來在我面前下拜。這是耶和華說的。[24]他們必出去觀看那些違背我人的屍首，因為他們的蟲是不死的，他們的火是不滅的。凡有血氣的都必憎惡他們。"

表八：舊約中所提的主要偶像
TABLE 8 : MAJOR IDOLS MENTIONED IN OLD TESTAMENT

名字 Name	經文 Reference	民族 People	代表 Represent	禮儀 Ritual
亞斯她錄 (亞舍拉) Ashtoreth (Asherah)	王上 1Ki 18:19 王上 1Ki 11:5	西頓、迦南、腓尼基 Sidon, Canaan, Phoenicia	愛神(女)、生育、多產 Goddess of love, childbirth, fertility	淫亂(廟妓) Prostitution
巴力 Baal	王上 1Ki 16:31	迦南 Canaan	風雨、豐收、力量 Rain, harvest, fertility, strength	淫亂(廟妓) Prostitution
比勒 (米羅達) Bel (Marduk)	賽 Isa 46:1 耶 Jer 50:2	巴比倫 Babylon	戰神、守護神、日神、天氣、命運、創造 War, guarding god, sun, weather, destiny, creation	淫亂(廟妓)、獻孩為祭 Prostitution, child sacrifice
基抹 Chemosh	民 Nu 21:29	摩押 Moab 亞捫 Ammon	國族的神 National god	獻孩為祭 Child sacrifice
大袞 Dagon	士 Jdg 16:23	非利士 Philistia	豐收、五穀、農藝 Harvest, grain, success in farming	獻孩為祭 Child sacrifice
摩洛 Molech 米勒公 Milcom	王上 1Ki 11:7 王上 1Ki 11:5	亞捫 Ammon	國族的神 National god	獻孩為祭 Child sacrifice
尼波 Nebo (米羅達之子) (Son of Marduk)	賽 Isa 46:1	巴比倫 Babylon	學識、天文、科學 Learning, astronomy, science	
臨門 Rimmon	王下 2Ki 5:18	亞蘭 Aram (敍利亞 Syria)		

耶利米書

1 便雅憫地亞拿突城的祭司中，希勒家的兒子耶利米的話記在下面。²猶大王亞們的兒子約西亞在位十三年，耶和華的話臨到耶利米。³從猶大王約西亞的兒子約雅敬在位的時候，直到猶大王約西亞的兒子西底家在位的末年，就是十一年五月間耶路撒冷人被擄的時候，耶和華的話也常臨到耶利米。

耶利米蒙召

⁴耶利米說，耶和華的話臨到我說：

⁵ "我未將你造在腹中，
　我已曉得你；
你未出母胎，我已分別你為聖；
　我已派你作列國的先知。"

⁶我就說："主耶和華啊，我不知怎樣說，因為我是年幼的。"

⁷耶和華對我說："你不要說'我是年幼的'，因為我差遣你到誰那裏去，你都要去；我吩咐你說甚麼話，你都要說。⁸你不要懼怕他們，因為我與你同在，要拯救你。"這是耶和華說的。

⁹於是耶和華伸手按我的口，對我說："我已將當說的話傳給你。¹⁰看哪，我今日立你在列邦列國之上，為要施行拔出、拆毀、毀壞、傾覆，又要建立、栽植。"

¹¹耶和華的話又臨到我說："耶利米，你看見甚麼？"

我說："我看見一根杏樹枝。"

¹²耶和華對我說："你看得不錯，因為我留意保守我的話，使得成就。"

¹³耶和華的話第二次臨到我說："你看見甚麼？"

我說："我看見一個燒開的鍋，從北而傾。"

¹⁴耶和華對我說："必有災禍從北方發出，臨到這地的一切居民。"¹⁵耶和華說："看哪，我要召

Jeremiah

1 The words of Jeremiah son of Hilkiah, one of the priests at Anathoth in the territory of Benjamin. ²The word of the LORD came to him in the thirteenth year of the reign of Josiah son of Amon king of Judah, ³and through the reign of Jehoiakim son of Josiah king of Judah, down to the fifth month of the eleventh year of Zedekiah son of Josiah king of Judah, when the people of Jerusalem went into exile.

The Call of Jeremiah

⁴The word of the LORD came to me, saying,

⁵"Before I formed you in the womb I knew[a]
　you,
　before you were born I set you apart;
　I appointed you as a prophet to the nations."

⁶"Ah, Sovereign LORD," I said, "I do not know how to speak; I am only a child."

⁷But the LORD said to me, "Do not say, 'I am only a child.' You must go to everyone I send you to and say whatever I command you. ⁸Do not be afraid of them, for I am with you and will rescue you," declares the LORD.

⁹Then the LORD reached out his hand and touched my mouth and said to me, "Now, I have put my words in your mouth. ¹⁰See, today I appoint you over nations and kingdoms to uproot and tear down, to destroy and overthrow, to build and to plant."

¹¹The word of the LORD came to me: "What do you see, Jeremiah?"

"I see the branch of an almond tree," I replied.

¹²The LORD said to me, "You have seen correctly, for I am watching[b] to see that my word is fulfilled."

¹³The word of the LORD came to me again: "What do you see?"

"I see a boiling pot, tilting away from the north," I answered.

¹⁴The LORD said to me, "From the north disaster will be poured out on all who live in the land. ¹⁵I am about to summon all the peoples of

---

a 5 Or *chose*　　*b 12* The Hebrew for *watching* sounds like the Hebrew for *almond tree.*

the northern kingdoms," declares the LORD.

> "Their kings will come and set up their
> thrones
> in the entrance of the gates of Jerusalem;
> they will come against all her surrounding
> walls
> and against all the towns of Judah.

¹⁶I will pronounce my judgments on my people
because of their wickedness in forsaking me,
in burning incense to other gods
and in worshiping what their hands have
made.

¹⁷"Get yourself ready! Stand up and say to
them whatever I command you. Do not be terrified by them, or I will terrify you before them.
¹⁸Today I have made you a fortified city, an iron
pillar and a bronze wall to stand against the
whole land—against the kings of Judah, its officials, its priests and the people of the land.
¹⁹They will fight against you but will not overcome you, for I am with you and will rescue
you," declares the LORD.

Israel Forsakes God

2 The word of the LORD came to me: ²"Go
and proclaim in the hearing of Jerusalem:

> " 'I remember the devotion of your youth,
> how as a bride you loved me
> and followed me through the desert,
> through a land not sown.
> ³Israel was holy to the LORD,
> the firstfruits of his harvest;
> all who devoured her were held guilty,
> and disaster overtook them,' "
>
> declares the LORD.

⁴Hear the word of the LORD, O house of Jacob,
all you clans of the house of Israel.

⁵This is what the LORD says:

> "What fault did your fathers find in me,
> that they strayed so far from me?
> They followed worthless idols
> and became worthless themselves.
> ⁶They did not ask, 'Where is the LORD,
> who brought us up out of Egypt
> and led us through the barren wilderness,
> through a land of deserts and rifts,
> a land of drought and darkness,ᵃ

a 6 Or and the shadow of death

北方列國的眾族。

> "他們要來，
> 各安座位
> 在耶路撒冷的城門口，
> 周圍攻擊城牆，
> 又要攻擊猶大的一切城邑。

¹⁶至於這民的一切惡，
> 就是離棄我，
> 向別神燒香，
> 跪拜自己手所造的，
> 我要發出我的判語攻擊他們。

¹⁷ "所以你當束腰，起來將我所
吩咐你的一切話告訴他們。不要因他
們驚惶，免得我使你在他們面前驚
惶。¹⁸看哪，我今日使你成為堅城、
鐵柱、銅牆，與全地和猶大的君王、
首領、祭司，並地上的眾民反對。
¹⁹他們要攻擊你，卻不能勝你，因為
我與你同在，要拯救你。"這是耶和
華說的。

以色列離棄神

2 耶和華的話臨到我說：² "你
去向耶路撒冷人的耳中喊叫
說，耶和華如此說：

> " '你幼年的恩愛，婚姻的愛情，
> 你怎樣在曠野，
> 在未曾耕種之地跟隨我，
> 我都記得。
> ³那時以色列歸耶和華為聖，
> 作為土產初熟的果子；
> 凡吞吃她的必算為有罪，
> 災禍必臨到他們。' "
>
> 這是耶和華說的。

⁴雅各家、以色列家的各族啊，
你們當聽耶和華的話。

⁵耶和華如此說：

> "你們的列祖見我有甚麼不義，
> 竟遠離我，
> 隨從虛無的神，
> 自己成為虛妄的呢？
> ⁶他們也不說：
> 那領我們從埃及地上來，
> 引導我們經過曠野、
> 沙漠有深坑之地，
> 和乾旱死蔭、

無人經過、無人居住之地的
　　耶和華在哪裏呢？’

7我領你們進入肥美之地，
　　使你們得吃其中的果子和美物。
但你們進入的時候，
　　就玷污我的地，
　　使我的產業成為可憎的。
8祭司都不說：
　　‘耶和華在哪裏呢？’
傳講律法的都不認識我，
官長違背我，
先知藉巴力說預言，
　　隨從無益的神。”

9耶和華說：
　　“我因此必與你們爭辯，
　　也必與你們的子孫爭辯。

10你們且過到基提海島去察看，
　　打發人往基達去留心查考，
　　看曾有這樣的事沒有？
11豈有一國換了他的神嗎？
　　其實這不是神！
但我的百姓將他們的榮耀
　　換了那無益的神。
12諸天哪，要因此驚奇，
　　極其恐慌，甚為淒涼！”
　　　　　　　　這是耶和華說的。

13 “因為我的百姓做了兩件惡事，
　　就是離棄我這活水的泉源，
　　為自己鑿出池子，
　　是破裂不能存水的池子。
14以色列是僕人嗎？
　　是家中生的奴僕嗎？
　　為何成為掠物呢？
15少壯獅子向他咆哮，
　　大聲吼叫，
使他的地荒涼，
　　城邑也都焚燒，無人居住。
16挪弗人和答比匿人
　　也打破你的頭頂。
17這事臨到你身上，不是你自招的嗎？
　　不是因耶和華你神引你行路
　　的時候，你離棄他嗎？
18現今你為何在埃及路上
　　要喝西曷的水呢？
你為何在亞述路上
　　要喝大河的水呢？
19你自己的惡必懲治你；
　　你背道的事必責備你。

a land where no one travels and no one
　　lives?'

7I brought you into a fertile land
　　to eat its fruit and rich produce.
But you came and defiled my land
　　and made my inheritance detestable.
8The priests did not ask,
　　'Where is the LORD?'
Those who deal with the law did not know
　　me;
　　the leaders rebelled against me.
The prophets prophesied by Baal,
　　following worthless idols.

9"Therefore I bring charges against you again,"
　　　　　　　declares the LORD.
　　"And I will bring charges against your
　　children's children.
10Cross over to the coasts of Kittim[a] and look,
　　send to Kedar[b] and observe closely;
　　see if there has ever been anything like this:
11Has a nation ever changed its gods?
　　(Yet they are not gods at all.)
But my people have exchanged their[c] Glory
　　for worthless idols.
12Be appalled at this, O heavens,
　　and shudder with great horror,"
　　　　　　　declares the LORD.
13"My people have committed two sins:
　　They have forsaken me,
　　the spring of living water,
and have dug their own cisterns,
　　broken cisterns that cannot hold water.
14Is Israel a servant, a slave by birth?
　　Why then has he become plunder?
15Lions have roared;
　　they have growled at him.
They have laid waste his land;
　　his towns are burned and deserted.
16Also, the men of Memphis[d] and Tahpanhes
　　have shaved the crown of your head.[e]
17Have you not brought this on yourselves
　　by forsaking the LORD your God
　　when he led you in the way?
18Now why go to Egypt
　　to drink water from the Shihor[f]?
And why go to Assyria
　　to drink water from the River[g]?
19Your wickedness will punish you;
　　your backsliding will rebuke you.

---

a 10 That is, Cyprus and western coastlands　*b 10* The home
of Bedouin tribes in the Syro-Arabian desert　*c 11* Masoretic
Text; an ancient Hebrew scribal tradition *my*　*d 16* Hebrew
Noph　*e 16* Or *have cracked your skull*　*f 18* That is, a branch
of the Nile　*g 18* That is, the Euphrates

Consider then and realize
　how evil and bitter it is for you
when you forsake the LORD your God
　and have no awe of me,"
　　　　declares the Lord, the LORD Almighty.

20"Long ago you broke off your yoke
　and tore off your bonds;
　you said, 'I will not serve you!'
Indeed, on every high hill
　and under every spreading tree
　you lay down as a prostitute.

21I had planted you like a choice vine
　of sound and reliable stock.
How then did you turn against me
　into a corrupt, wild vine?

22Although you wash yourself with soda
　and use an abundance of soap,
　the stain of your guilt is still before me,"
　　　　declares the Sovereign LORD.

23"How can you say, 'I am not defiled;
　I have not run after the Baals'?
See how you behaved in the valley;
　consider what you have done.
You are a swift she-camel
　running here and there,

24a wild donkey accustomed to the desert,
　sniffing the wind in her craving—
　in her heat who can restrain her?
Any males that pursue her need not tire
　themselves;
　at mating time they will find her.

25Do not run until your feet are bare
　and your throat is dry.
But you said, 'It's no use!
　I love foreign gods,
　and I must go after them.'

26"As a thief is disgraced when he is caught,
　so the house of Israel is disgraced—
they, their kings and their officials,
　their priests and their prophets.

27They say to wood, 'You are my father,'
　and to stone, 'You gave me birth.'
They have turned their backs to me
　and not their faces;
yet when they are in trouble, they say,
　'Come and save us!'

28Where then are the gods you made for
　yourselves?
Let them come if they can save you
　when you are in trouble!
For you have as many gods
　as you have towns, O Judah.

由此可知可見，
　你離棄耶和華你的神，
不存敬畏我的心，
　乃為惡事，為苦事。"
　　　　這是主萬軍之耶和華說的。

20 "我在古時折斷你的軛，
　　解開你的繩索，
　你說：'我必不侍奉耶和華。'
因為你在各高岡上、
　各青翠樹下屈身行淫。
（註：或作"我在古時折斷你的軛，解開你的
繩索，你就說：'我必不侍奉別神？'誰知你
在各高岡上、各青翠樹下仍屈身行淫。"）

21然而我栽你是上等的葡萄樹，
　　全然是真種子，你怎麼向我變為
　　　外邦葡萄樹的壞枝子呢？

22你雖用鹼、多用肥皂洗濯，
　你罪孽的痕跡仍然在我面前顯出。"
　　　　這是主耶和華說的。

23 "你怎能說：'我沒有玷污，
　　沒有隨從眾巴力'？
你看你谷中的路，
　就知道你所行的如何。
你是快行的獨峰駝，
　狂奔亂走；

24你是野驢慣在曠野，
　慾心發動時吸風，
　起性的時候誰能使牠轉去呢？
凡尋找牠的
　必不至疲乏，
　在牠的月份必能尋見。

25我說：'你不要使腳上無鞋，
　　喉嚨乾渴。'
你倒說：'這是枉然。
　我喜愛別神，
　我必隨從他們。'

26 "賊被捉拿，怎樣羞愧，
　以色列家和他們的
　　　君王、首領、祭司、先知
　　　也都照樣羞愧。

27他們向木頭說：'你是我的父'；
　向石頭說：'你是生我的'。
他們以背向我，
　不以面向我，
及至遭遇患難的時候卻說：
　'起來拯救我們！'

28你為自己做的神
　在哪裏呢？
你遭遇患難的時候，
　叫他們起來拯救你吧！
猶大啊，你神的數目
　與你城的數目相等。"

29耶和華說：
"你們為何與我爭辯呢？
你們都違背了我。
30我責打你們的兒女是徒然的，
他們不受懲治。
你們自己的刀吞滅你們的先知，
好像殘害的獅子。

31 "這世代的人哪，你們要看明
耶和華的話：

"我豈向以色列作曠野呢？
或作幽暗之地呢？
我的百姓為何說：'我們脫離約束，
再不歸向你了'？
32處女豈能忘記她的妝飾呢？
新婦豈能忘記她的美衣呢？
我的百姓卻忘記了
我無數的日子。
33你怎麼修飾你的道路要求愛情呢？
就是惡劣的婦人
你也叫她們行你的路。
34並且你的衣襟上
有無辜窮人的血。
你殺他們並不是遇見他們挖窟窿，
乃是因這一切的事。
35你還說：'我無辜，
耶和華的怒氣必定向我消了。'
看哪，我必審問你！
因你自說：'我沒有犯罪。'
36你為何東跑西奔，
要更換你的路呢？
你必因埃及蒙羞，
像從前因亞述蒙羞一樣。
37你也必兩手抱頭
從埃及出來。
因為耶和華已經棄絕你所倚靠的，
你必不因他們得順利。

3 "有話說，人若休妻，
妻離他而去，
作了別人的妻，
前夫豈能再收回她來？
若收回她來，
那地豈不是大大玷污了嗎？
但你和許多親愛的行邪淫，
還可以歸向我了？"
這是耶和華說的。
2 "你向淨光的高處舉目觀看，
你在何處
沒有淫行呢？
你坐在道旁等候，
好像阿拉伯人在曠野埋伏一樣，

29"Why do you bring charges against me?
You have all rebelled against me,"
declares the LORD.
30"In vain I punished your people;
they did not respond to correction.
Your sword has devoured your prophets
like a ravening lion.

31"You of this generation, consider the word
of the LORD:

"Have I been a desert to Israel
or a land of great darkness?
Why do my people say, 'We are free to roam;
we will come to you no more'?
32Does a maiden forget her jewelry,
a bride her wedding ornaments?
Yet my people have forgotten me,
days without number.
33How skilled you are at pursuing love!
Even the worst of women can learn from
your ways.
34On your clothes men find
the lifeblood of the innocent poor,
though you did not catch them breaking in.
Yet in spite of all this
35 you say, 'I am innocent;
he is not angry with me.'
But I will pass judgment on you
because you say, 'I have not sinned.'
36Why do you go about so much,
changing your ways?
You will be disappointed by Egypt
as you were by Assyria.
37You will also leave that place
with your hands on your head,
for the LORD has rejected those you trust;
you will not be helped by them.

3 "If a man divorces his wife
and she leaves him and marries another
man,
should he return to her again?
Would not the land be completely defiled?
But you have lived as a prostitute with many
lovers—
would you now return to me?"
declares the LORD.
2"Look up to the barren heights and see.
Is there any place where you have not been
ravished?
By the roadside you sat waiting for lovers,
sat like a nomad[a] in the desert.

a 2 Or an Arab

You have defiled the land
with your prostitution and wickedness.
³Therefore the showers have been withheld,
and no spring rains have fallen.
Yet you have the brazen look of a prostitute;
you refuse to blush with shame.
⁴Have you not just called to me:
'My Father, my friend from my youth,
⁵will you always be angry?
Will your wrath continue forever?'
This is how you talk,
but you do all the evil you can."

Unfaithful Israel

⁶During the reign of King Josiah, the LORD said to me, "Have you seen what faithless Israel has done? She has gone up on every high hill and under every spreading tree and has committed adultery there. ⁷I thought that after she had done all this she would return to me but she did not, and her unfaithful sister Judah saw it. ⁸I gave faithless Israel her certificate of divorce and sent her away because of all her adulteries. Yet I saw that her unfaithful sister Judah had no fear; she also went out and committed adultery. ⁹Because Israel's immorality mattered so little to her, she defiled the land and committed adultery with stone and wood. ¹⁰In spite of all this, her unfaithful sister Judah did not return to me with all her heart, but only in pretense," declares the LORD.

¹¹The LORD said to me, "Faithless Israel is more righteous than unfaithful Judah. ¹²Go, proclaim this message toward the north:

" 'Return, faithless Israel,' declares the LORD,
'I will frown on you no longer,
for I am merciful,' declares the LORD,
'I will not be angry forever.
¹³Only acknowledge your guilt—
you have rebelled against the LORD your God,
you have scattered your favors to foreign gods
under every spreading tree,
and have not obeyed me,' "

declares the LORD.

¹⁴"Return, faithless people," declares the LORD, "for I am your husband. I will choose you—one from a town and two from a clan—and bring you to Zion. ¹⁵Then I will give you shepherds after my own heart, who will lead you with knowledge and understanding. ¹⁶In those days, when your numbers have increased greatly in the land," declares the LORD, "men will no longer say, 'The ark of the covenant of the LORD.' It will never enter their minds or be

並且你的淫行邪惡
玷污了全地。
³因此甘霖停止，
春（註：原文作"晚"）雨不降，
你還是有娼妓之臉，
不顧羞恥。
⁴從今以後，你豈不向我呼叫說：
'我父啊，你是我幼年的恩主。
⁵耶和華豈永遠懷怒，
存留到底嗎？'
看哪，你又發惡言、又行壞事，
隨自己的私意而行（註：或作"你雖這樣說，還是行惡，放縱惡心"）。"

不忠貞的以色列

⁶約西亞王在位的時候，耶和華又對我說："背道的以色列所行的，你看見沒有？她上各高山，在各青翠樹下行淫。⁷她行這些事以後，我說：'她必歸向我。'她卻不歸向我。她奸詐的妹妹猶大也看見了。⁸背道的以色列行淫，我為這緣故給她休書休她。我看見她奸詐的妹妹猶大還不懼怕，也去行淫。⁹因以色列輕忽了她的淫亂，和石頭木頭行淫，地就被玷污了。¹⁰雖有這一切的事，她奸詐的妹妹猶大還不一心歸向我，不過是假意歸我。"這是耶和華說的。

¹¹耶和華對我說："背道的以色列比奸詐的猶大還顯為義。¹²你去向北方宣告說，耶和華說：

" '背道的以色列啊，回來吧！
我必不怒目看你們，
因為我是慈愛的，
我必不永遠存怒。'
這是耶和華說的。
¹³'只要承認你的罪孽，
就是你違背耶和華你的神，
在各青翠樹下，向別神東奔西跑，
沒有聽從我的話。'"
這是耶和華說的。

¹⁴耶和華說："背道的兒女啊，回來吧！因為我作你們的丈夫，並且我必將你們從一城取一人，從一族取兩人，帶到錫安。¹⁵我也必將合我心的牧者賜給你們，他們必以知識和智慧教養你們。"¹⁶耶和華說："你們在國中生養眾多。當那些日子，人必不再提說耶和華的約櫃，不追想、不

記念，不覺缺少，也不再製造。¹⁷那時，人必稱耶路撒冷為耶和華的寶座，萬國必到耶路撒冷，在耶和華立名的地方聚集。他們必不再隨從自己頑梗的惡心行事。¹⁸當那些日子，猶大家要和以色列家同行，從北方之地一同來到我賜給你們列祖為業之地。

¹⁹ "我說：

" '我怎樣將你安置在兒女之中，
　　賜給你美地，
　　就是萬國中肥美的產業。'
　我又說：你們必稱我為父，
　　也不再轉去不跟從我。
²⁰以色列家，你們向我行詭詐，
　　真像妻子行詭詐
　　離開她丈夫一樣。"
　　　　　　　　　這是耶和華說的。

²¹在淨光的高處聽見人聲，
　　就是以色列人
　　哭泣懇求之聲，
　乃因他們走彎曲之道，
　　忘記耶和華他們的神。

²² "你們這背道的兒女啊，回來吧！
　我要醫治你們背道的病。"

"看哪，我們來到你這裏，
　　因你是耶和華我們的神。
²³仰望從小山或從大山的喧嚷中
　　得幫助，真是枉然的。
　以色列得救，
　　誠然在乎耶和華我們的神。
²⁴從我們幼年以來，那可恥的偶像
　　將我們列祖所勞碌得來的
　　　羊羣、牛羣，
　　和他們的兒女都吞吃了。
²⁵我們在羞恥中躺臥吧！
　願慚愧蓋著我們遮蓋。
　因為從立國（註：原文作 "幼年"）以來，
　我們和我們的列祖
　　常常得罪耶和華我們的神，
　　沒有聽從耶和華我們神的話。"

4 耶和華說："以色列啊，
　　你若回來歸向我，

　若從我眼前
　　除掉我可憎的偶像，
　　你就不被遷移。
²你必憑誠實、公平、公義，
　　指着永生的耶和華起誓；

remembered; it will not be missed, nor will another one be made. ¹⁷At that time they will call Jerusalem The Throne of the LORD, and all nations will gather in Jerusalem to honor the name of the LORD. No longer will they follow the stubbornness of their evil hearts. ¹⁸In those days the house of Judah will join the house of Israel, and together they will come from a northern land to the land I gave your forefathers as an inheritance.

¹⁹"I myself said,

" 'How gladly would I treat you like sons
　and give you a desirable land,
　the most beautiful inheritance of any nation.'
I thought you would call me 'Father'
　and not turn away from following me.
²⁰But like a woman unfaithful to her husband,
　so you have been unfaithful to me, O house
　of Israel,"
　　　　　　　　　declares the LORD.

²¹A cry is heard on the barren heights,
　the weeping and pleading of the people of
　　Israel,
because they have perverted their ways
　and have forgotten the LORD their God.

²²"Return, faithless people;
　I will cure you of backsliding."

"Yes, we will come to you,
　for you are the LORD our God.
²³Surely the idolatrous commotion on the hills
　and mountains is a deception;
surely in the LORD our God
　is the salvation of Israel.
²⁴From our youth shameful gods have consumed
　the fruits of our fathers' labor—
　their flocks and herds,
　their sons and daughters.
²⁵Let us lie down in our shame,
　and let our disgrace cover us.
We have sinned against the LORD our God,
　both we and our fathers;
from our youth till this day
　we have not obeyed the LORD our God."

4 "If you will return, O Israel,
　return to me,"
　　　　　　　　　declares the LORD.
"If you put your detestable idols out of my
　　sight
　and no longer go astray,
²and if in a truthful, just and righteous way
　you swear, 'As surely as the LORD lives,'

then the nations will be blessed by him
　　and in him they will glory."

³This is what the LORD says to the men of
Judah and to Jerusalem:

"Break up your unplowed ground
　　and do not sow among thorns.
⁴Circumcise yourselves to the LORD,
　　circumcise your hearts,
　　you men of Judah and people of Jerusalem,
or my wrath will break out and burn like fire
　　because of the evil you have done—
burn with no one to quench it.

Disaster From the North

⁵"Announce in Judah and proclaim in
　　　　Jerusalem and say:
'Sound the trumpet throughout the land!'
Cry aloud and say:
'Gather together!
Let us flee to the fortified cities!'
⁶Raise the signal to go to Zion!
　　Flee for safety without delay!
For I am bringing disaster from the north,
　　even terrible destruction."

⁷A lion has come out of his lair;
　　a destroyer of nations has set out.
He has left his place
　　to lay waste your land.
Your towns will lie in ruins
　　without inhabitant.
⁸So put on sackcloth,
　　lament and wail,
for the fierce anger of the LORD
　　has not turned away from us.

⁹"In that day," declares the LORD,
　　"the king and the officials will lose heart,
the priests will be horrified,
　　and the prophets will be appalled."

¹⁰Then I said, "Ah, Sovereign LORD, how
completely you have deceived this people and
Jerusalem by saying, 'You will have peace,'
when the sword is at our throats."

¹¹At that time this people and Jerusalem will
be told, "A scorching wind from the barren
heights in the desert blows toward my people,
but not to winnow or cleanse; ¹²a wind too
strong for that comes from me.ᵃ Now I pronounce my judgments against them."

列國必因耶和華稱自己為有福,
　　也必因他誇耀。'"

³耶和華對猶大和耶路撒冷人如
此説:

"要開墾你們的荒地,
　　不要撒種在荊棘中!
猶大人和耶路撒冷的居民哪,
　　你們當自行割禮歸耶和華,
　　將心裏的污穢除掉;
恐怕我的忿怒因你們的惡行發作,
　　如火着起,
　　甚至無人能以熄滅!

災禍從北方而來

⁵ "你們當傳揚在猶大,
　　宣告在耶路撒冷説:
　　'你們當在國中吹角!'
高聲呼叫説:
　　'你們當聚集,
　　我們好進入堅固城!'
⁶應當向錫安豎立大旗,
　　要逃避,不要遲延!
因我必使災禍與大毀滅
　　從北方來到。"

⁷有獅子從密林中上來,
　　是毀壞列國的。
牠已經動身,出離本處,
　　要使你的地荒涼,
使你的城邑變為荒場,
　　無人居住。
⁸因此,你們當腰束麻布,
　　大聲哀號,
因為耶和華的烈怒
　　沒有向我們轉消。

⁹耶和華説: "到那時
　　君王和首領的心都要消滅,
祭司都要驚奇,
　　先知都要詫異。"

¹⁰我説: "哀哉!主耶和華啊,
你真是大大地欺哄這百姓和耶路撒
冷,説: '你們必得平安。'其實刀
劍害及性命了。"

¹¹那時,必有話對這百姓和耶路
撒冷説: "有一陣熱風從曠野淨光的
高處向我的眾民 (註:原文作「民女」)
颳來,不是為簸揚,也不是為揚淨。
¹²必有一陣更大的風從這些地方為我
颳來;現在我又必發出判語攻擊他
們。"

ᵃ 12 Or *comes at my command*

¹³看哪，仇敵必如雲上來，
　　他的戰車如旋風，
　　他的馬匹比鷹更快。
　　我們有禍了！我們敗落了！
¹⁴耶路撒冷啊，你當洗去心中的惡，
　　使你可以得救。
　　惡念存在你心裏要到幾時呢？
¹⁵有聲音從但傳揚，
　　從以法蓮山報禍患。
¹⁶"你們當傳給列國，
　　報告攻擊耶路撒冷的事說：
　　'有探望的人從遠方來到，
　　　向猶大的城邑大聲吶喊。
¹⁷他們周圍攻擊耶路撒冷，
　　好像看守田園的，
　　因為她背叛了我。'"
　　　　　　　　　這是耶和華說的。
¹⁸"你的行動，你的作為，
　　招惹這事，
　　這是你罪惡的結果，
　　實在是苦，
　　是害及你心了！"

¹⁹我的肺腑啊，我的肺腑啊，
　　我心疼痛！
　　我心在我裏面
　　　煩躁不安，
　　我不能靜默不言，
　　因為我已經聽見
　　角聲和打仗的喊聲。
²⁰毀壞的信息連絡不絕，
　　因為全地荒廢。
　　我的帳棚忽然毀壞；
　　我的幔子頃刻破裂。
²¹我看見大旗，聽見角聲，
　　要到幾時呢？

²²耶和華說：
　　"我的百姓愚頑，
　　　不認識我，
　　他們是愚昧無知的兒女，
　　有智慧行惡，
　　沒有知識行善。"

²³先知說：我觀看地，
　　不料，地是空虛混沌；
　　我觀看天，
　　天也無光。
²⁴我觀看大山，
　　不料，盡都震動，
　　小山也都搖來搖去。
²⁵我觀看，不料，無人，
　　空中的飛鳥也都躲避。
²⁶我觀看，不料，肥田變為荒地，
　　一切城邑在耶和華面前，
　　因他的烈怒都被拆毀。

¹³Look! He advances like the clouds,
　　his chariots come like a whirlwind,
　his horses are swifter than eagles.
　　Woe to us! We are ruined!
¹⁴O Jerusalem, wash the evil from your heart
　　and be saved.
　How long will you harbor wicked thoughts?
¹⁵A voice is announcing from Dan,
　　proclaiming disaster from the hills of Ephraim.
¹⁶"Tell this to the nations,
　　proclaim it to Jerusalem:
　'A besieging army is coming from a distant
　　land,
　raising a war cry against the cities of Judah.
¹⁷They surround her like men guarding a field,
　　because she has rebelled against me,' "
　　　　　　　　　　　　　declares the LORD.
¹⁸"Your own conduct and actions
　　have brought this upon you.
　This is your punishment.
　　How bitter it is!
　　How it pierces to the heart!"

¹⁹Oh, my anguish, my anguish!
　　I writhe in pain.
　Oh, the agony of my heart!
　　My heart pounds within me,
　　I cannot keep silent.
　For I have heard the sound of the trumpet;
　　I have heard the battle cry.
²⁰Disaster follows disaster;
　　the whole land lies in ruins.
　In an instant my tents are destroyed,
　　my shelter in a moment.
²¹How long must I see the battle standard
　　and hear the sound of the trumpet?

²²"My people are fools;
　　they do not know me.
　They are senseless children;
　　they have no understanding.
　They are skilled in doing evil;
　　they know not how to do good."

²³I looked at the earth,
　　and it was formless and empty;
　and at the heavens,
　　and their light was gone.
²⁴I looked at the mountains,
　　and they were quaking;
　all the hills were swaying.
²⁵I looked, and there were no people;
　　every bird in the sky had flown away.
²⁶I looked, and the fruitful land was a desert;
　　all its towns lay in ruins
　before the LORD, before his fierce anger.

²⁷This is what the LORD says:

"The whole land will be ruined,
   though I will not destroy it completely.
²⁸Therefore the earth will mourn
   and the heavens above grow dark,
because I have spoken and will not relent,
   I have decided and will not turn back."

²⁹At the sound of horsemen and archers
   every town takes to flight.
Some go into the thickets;
   some climb up among the rocks.
All the towns are deserted;
   no one lives in them.

³⁰What are you doing, O devastated one?
   Why dress yourself in scarlet
   and put on jewels of gold?
Why shade your eyes with paint?
   You adorn yourself in vain.
Your lovers despise you;
   they seek your life.

³¹I hear a cry as of a woman in labor,
   a groan as of one bearing her first child—
the cry of the Daughter of Zion gasping for
      breath,
   stretching out her hands and saying,
"Alas! I am fainting;
   my life is given over to murderers."

Not One Is Upright

5 "Go up and down the streets of
   Jerusalem,
   look around and consider,
   search through her squares.
If you can find but one person
   who deals honestly and seeks the truth,
   I will forgive this city.
²Although they say, 'As surely as the LORD
      lives,'
   still they are swearing falsely."

³O LORD, do not your eyes look for truth?
   You struck them, but they felt no pain;
   you crushed them, but they refused
      correction.
They made their faces harder than stone
   and refused to repent.
⁴I thought, "These are only the poor;
   they are foolish,
for they do not know the way of the LORD,
   the requirements of their God.
⁵So I will go to the leaders
   and speak to them;

²⁷耶和華如此說：

"全地必然荒涼，
   我卻不毀滅淨盡。
²⁸因此，地要悲哀，
   在上的天也必黑暗。
因為我言已出，我意已定，
   必不後悔，也不轉意不做。"

²⁹各城的人因馬兵和弓箭手的響聲
   就都逃跑，
進入密林，
   爬上磐石；
各城被撇下，
   無人住在其中。

³⁰你淒涼的時候要怎樣行呢？
   你雖穿上朱紅衣服，
   佩戴黃金裝飾，
用顏料修飾眼目，
   這樣標緻是枉然的！
戀愛你的藐視你，
   並且尋索你的性命。

³¹我聽見有聲音，
   彷彿婦人產難的聲音，
好像生頭胎疼痛的聲音，
   是錫安女子的聲音（註："女子"就
      是指"民"的意思）。她喘著氣，
   挓挲手，說："我有禍了！
在殺人的跟前，我的心發昏了。"

沒有一個正直的人

5 "你們當在耶路撒冷的街上
   跑來跑去，
   在寬闊處尋找，
看看有一人行公義、
   求誠實沒有？
若有，
   我就赦免這城。
²其中的人，
   雖然指著永生的耶和華起誓，
   所起的誓實在是假的。"

³耶和華啊，
   你的眼目，不是看顧誠實嗎？
你擊打他們，他們卻不傷慟；
   你毀滅他們，他們仍不受懲治。
他們使臉剛硬過於磐石，
   不肯回頭。
⁴我說："這些人實在是貧窮的，
   是愚昧的，
因為不曉得耶和華的作為
   和他們神的法則。
⁵我要去見尊大的人，
   對他們說話，

因為他們曉得耶和華的作為
　　和他們神的法則。"
哪知,
　　這些人齊心將軛折斷,
　　掙開繩索。
6因此,林中的獅子必害死他們,
　　晚上 (註:或作"野地") 的豺狼
　　必滅絕他們,
　　豹子要在城外窺伺他們,
　　凡出城的必被撕碎;
　　因為他們的罪過極多,
　　背道的事也加增了。

7 "我怎能赦免你呢?
　　你的兒女離棄我,
　　又指着那不是神的起誓。
　　我使他們飽足,
　　他們就行姦淫,
　　成羣地聚集在娼妓家裏。
8他們像餵飽的馬到處亂跑,
　　各向他鄰舍的妻發嘶聲。"
9耶和華說:
　　"我豈不因這些事討罪呢?
　　豈不報復這樣的國民呢?

10 "你們要上她葡萄園的牆毀行毀壞,
　　但不可毀壞淨盡,
　　只可除掉她的枝子,
　　因為不屬耶和華。
11原來以色列家和猶大家
　　大行詭詐攻擊我。"
　　　　　　　　這是耶和華說的。

12他們不認耶和華,說:
　　"這並不是他,
　　災禍必不臨到我們,
　　刀劍和飢荒,我們也看不見。
13先知的話必成為風,
　　道也不在他們裏面。
　　這災必臨到他們身上。"

14所以耶和華萬軍之神如此說:

"因為百姓說這話,
　　我必使我的話在你口中為火,
　　使他們為柴,
　　這火便將他們燒滅。"
15耶和華說:"以色列家啊,
　　我必使一國的民
　　從遠方來攻擊你,
　　是強盛的國,是從古而有的國。
　　他們的言語你不曉得,
　　他們的話你不明白。

surely they know the way of the LORD,
　the requirements of their God."
But with one accord they too had broken off
　the yoke
and torn off the bonds.
6Therefore a lion from the forest will attack
　them,
a wolf from the desert will ravage them,
a leopard will lie in wait near their towns
　to tear to pieces any who venture out,
for their rebellion is great
　and their backslidings many.

7"Why should I forgive you?
　Your children have forsaken me
　and sworn by gods that are not gods.
I supplied all their needs,
　yet they committed adultery
　and thronged to the houses of prostitutes.
8They are well-fed, lusty stallions,
　each neighing for another man's wife.
9Should I not punish them for this?"
　declares the LORD.
　"Should I not avenge myself
　on such a nation as this?

10"Go through her vineyards and ravage them,
　but do not destroy them completely.
Strip off her branches,
　for these people do not belong to the LORD.
11The house of Israel and the house of Judah
　have been utterly unfaithful to me,"
　　　　　　　　declares the LORD.

12They have lied about the LORD;
　they said, "He will do nothing!
No harm will come to us;
　we will never see sword or famine.
13The prophets are but wind
　and the word is not in them;
　so let what they say be done to them."

14Therefore this is what the LORD God Almighty says:

"Because the people have spoken these
　words,
I will make my words in your mouth a fire
　and these people the wood it consumes.
15O house of Israel," declares the LORD,
　"I am bringing a distant nation against
　　you—
an ancient and enduring nation,
a people whose language you do not know,
　whose speech you do not understand.

¹⁶Their quivers are like an open grave;
   all of them are mighty warriors.
¹⁷They will devour your harvests and food,
   devour your sons and daughters;
   they will devour your flocks and herds,
   devour your vines and fig trees.
With the sword they will destroy
   the fortified cities in which you trust.

¹⁸"Yet even in those days," declares the LORD,
"I will not destroy you completely. ¹⁹And when
the people ask, 'Why has the LORD our God
done all this to us?' you will tell them, 'As you
have forsaken me and served foreign gods in
your own land, so now you will serve foreigners
in a land not your own.'

²⁰"Announce this to the house of Jacob
   and proclaim it in Judah:
²¹Hear this, you foolish and senseless people,
   who have eyes but do not see,
   who have ears but do not hear:
²²Should you not fear me?" declares the LORD.
   "Should you not tremble in my presence?
I made the sand a boundary for the sea,
   an everlasting barrier it cannot cross.
The waves may roll, but they cannot prevail;
   they may roar, but they cannot cross it.
²³But these people have stubborn and rebellious
      hearts;
   they have turned aside and gone away.
²⁴They do not say to themselves,
   'Let us fear the LORD our God,
who gives autumn and spring rains in season,
who assures us of the regular weeks of
      harvest.'
²⁵Your wrongdoings have kept these away;
   your sins have deprived you of good.

²⁶"Among my people are wicked men
   who lie in wait like men who snare birds
   and like those who set traps to catch men.
²⁷Like cages full of birds,
   their houses are full of deceit;
   they have become rich and powerful
²⁸ and have grown fat and sleek.
Their evil deeds have no limit;
   they do not plead the case of the fatherless to
      win it,
   they do not defend the rights of the poor.
²⁹Should I not punish them for this?"
   declares the LORD.
   "Should I not avenge myself
      on such a nation as this?

¹⁶他們的箭袋是敞開的墳墓，
   他們都是勇士。
¹⁷他們必吃盡你的莊稼和你的糧食，
   是你兒女該吃的；
必吃盡你的牛羊，
   吃盡你的葡萄和無花果；
又必用刀
   毀壞你所倚靠的堅固城。"

¹⁸耶和華說："就是到那時，我
也不將你們毀滅淨盡。¹⁹百姓若說：
'耶和華我們的神為甚麼向我們行這
一切事呢？' 你就對他們說：'你們
怎樣離棄耶和華（註：原文作"我"），
在你們的地上侍奉外邦神，也必照樣
在不屬你們的地上侍奉外邦人。'

²⁰ "當傳揚在雅各家，
   報告在猶大，說：
²¹愚昧無知的百姓啊，
   你們有眼不看，
   有耳不聽，現在當聽這話。"
²²耶和華說："你們怎麼不懼怕我呢？
   我以永遠的定例，
   用沙為海的界限，水不得越過。
因此，你們在我面前還不戰兢嗎？
   波浪雖然翻騰，卻不能逾越；
   雖然匉訇，卻不能過去。
²³但這百姓
   有背叛忤逆的心，
   他們叛我而去。
²⁴心內也不說：
   '我們應當敬畏耶和華我們的神，
他按時賜雨，就是秋雨春雨，
   又為我們定收割的節令，
   永存不廢。'
²⁵你們的罪孽，使這些事轉離你們；
   你們的罪惡使你們不能得福。

²⁶ "因為在我民中有惡人，
   他們埋伏窺探，好像捕鳥的人，
   他們設立圈套陷害人。
²⁷籠內怎樣滿了雀鳥，
   他們的房中也照樣充滿詭詐。
   所以他們得成為大，而且富足。
²⁸他們肥胖光潤，
   作惡過甚，
不為人伸冤，
   就是不為孤兒伸冤，
不使他亨通，也不為窮人辨屈。"
²⁹耶和華說：
   "我豈不因這些事討罪呢？
   豈不報復這樣的國民呢？

30 "國中有可驚駭、
　　可憎惡的事:

31就是先知說假預言,
　　祭司藉他們把持權柄,
　　我的百姓也喜愛這些事。
　　到了結局你們怎樣行呢?"

耶路撒冷被圍攻

6 "便雅憫人哪,
　　你們要逃出耶路撒冷,
　　在提哥亞吹角,
　　在伯哈基琳立號旗。
　　因為有災禍與大毀滅
　　從北方張望。

2秀美嬌嫩的錫安女子（註:"女子"
　　就是指"民"的意思）,我必剪除。

3牧人必引他們的羊羣
　　到她那裏,
　　在她周圍支搭帳棚,
　　各在自己所佔之地使羊吃草。"

4 "你們要準備攻擊她,
　　起來吧!我們可以趁午時上去。
　　哀哉!日已漸斜,
　　晚影拖長了。

5起來吧!
　　我們夜間上去毀壞她的宮殿。"

6因為萬軍之耶和華如此說:

"你們要砍伐樹木,
　　築壘攻打耶路撒冷。
　　這就是那該罰的城,
　　其中盡是欺壓。

7井怎樣湧出水來,
　　這城也照樣湧出惡來。
　　在其間常聽見有強暴毀滅的事,
　　病患損傷也常在我面前。

8耶路撒冷啊,你當受教,
　　免得我心與你生疏,
　　免得我使你荒涼,
　　成為無人居住之地。"

9萬軍之耶和華曾如此說:

"敵人必擄盡以色列剩下的民,
　　如同摘淨葡萄一樣。
　　你要像摘葡萄的人摘了又摘,
　　回手放在筐子裏。"

10現在我可以向誰說話作見證,
　　使他們聽呢?
　　他們的耳朵未受割禮,
　　不能聽見。

30"A horrible and shocking thing
　has happened in the land:
31The prophets prophesy lies,
　the priests rule by their own authority,
and my people love it this way.
　But what will you do in the end?

Jerusalem Under Siege

6 "Flee for safety, people of Benjamin!
　Flee from Jerusalem!
　Sound the trumpet in Tekoa!
Raise the signal over Beth Hakkerem!
For disaster looms out of the north,
　even terrible destruction.
2I will destroy the Daughter of Zion,
　so beautiful and delicate.
3Shepherds with their flocks will come against
　her;
　they will pitch their tents around her,
　each tending his own portion."

4"Prepare for battle against her!
　Arise, let us attack at noon!
But, alas, the daylight is fading,
　and the shadows of evening grow long.
5So arise, let us attack at night
　and destroy her fortresses!"

6This is what the LORD Almighty says:

"Cut down the trees
　and build siege ramps against Jerusalem.
This city must be punished;
　it is filled with oppression.
7As a well pours out its water,
　so she pours out her wickedness.
Violence and destruction resound in her;
　her sickness and wounds are ever before me.
8Take warning, O Jerusalem,
　or I will turn away from you
and make your land desolate
　so no one can live in it."

9This is what the LORD Almighty says:

"Let them glean the remnant of Israel
　as thoroughly as a vine;
pass your hand over the branches again,
　like one gathering grapes."

10To whom can I speak and give warning?
　Who will listen to me?
Their ears are closed[a]
　so they cannot hear.

a 10 Hebrew uncircumcised

The word of the LORD is offensive to them;
　they find no pleasure in it.
11But I am full of the wrath of the LORD,
　and I cannot hold it in.

"Pour it out on the children in the street
　and on the young men gathered together;
both husband and wife will be caught in it,
　and the old, those weighed down with years.
12Their houses will be turned over to others,
　together with their fields and their wives,
when I stretch out my hand
　against those who live in the land,"
　　　　　　　　　　　declares the LORD.
13"From the least to the greatest,
　all are greedy for gain;
prophets and priests alike,
　all practice deceit.
14They dress the wound of my people
　as though it were not serious.
'Peace, peace,' they say,
　when there is no peace.
15Are they ashamed of their loathsome
　conduct?
　No, they have no shame at all;
　they do not even know how to blush.
So they will fall among the fallen;
　they will be brought down when I punish
　them,"
　　　　　　　　　　　says the LORD.

16This is what the LORD says:

"Stand at the crossroads and look;
　ask for the ancient paths,
ask where the good way is, and walk in it,
　and you will find rest for your souls.
But you said, 'We will not walk in it.'
17I appointed watchmen over you and said,
　'Listen to the sound of the trumpet!'
But you said, 'We will not listen.'
18Therefore hear, O nations;
　observe, O witnesses,
　what will happen to them.
19Hear, O earth:
　I am bringing disaster on this people,
　the fruit of their schemes,
because they have not listened to my words
　and have rejected my law.
20What do I care about incense from Sheba
　or sweet calamus from a distant land?
Your burnt offerings are not acceptable;
　your sacrifices do not please me."

看哪，耶和華的話，
　他們以為羞辱，不以為喜悦。
11因此我被耶和華的忿怒充滿，
　難以含忍。

"我要傾在街中的孩童
　和聚會的少年人身上，
連夫帶妻，並年老的與日子滿足的
　都必被擒拿。
12他們的房屋、田地和妻子
　都必轉歸別人。
我要伸手
　攻擊這地的居民！"
　　　　　　　　　這是耶和華説的。
13"因為他們從最小的到至大的
　都一味地貪婪；
從先知到祭司
　都行事虛謊。
14他們輕輕忽忽地
　醫治我百姓的損傷，
説：'平安了！平安了！'
　其實沒有平安！
15他們行可憎的事，
　知道慚愧嗎？
不然，他們毫不慚愧，
　也不知羞恥。
因此，他們必在仆倒的人中仆倒，
　我向他們討罪的時候，
　他們必致跌倒。"
　　　　　　　　　這是耶和華説的。

16耶和華如此説：

"你們當站在路上察看，
　訪問古道，
哪是善道，便行在其間；
　這樣，你們心裏必得安息。
他們卻説：'我們不行在其間。'
17我設立守望的人照管你們，説：
　'要聽角聲。'
他們卻説：'我們不聽。'
18列國啊，因此你們當聽；
　會眾啊，
　要知道他們必遭遇的事！
19地啊，當聽：
　我必使災禍臨到這百姓，
　就是他們意念所結的果子，
　因為他們不聽從我的言語。
至於我的訓誨（註：或作"律法"），
　他們也厭棄了。
20從示巴出的乳香，
　從遠方出的菖蒲（註：或作"甘蔗"），
　奉來給我有何益呢？
你們的燔祭不蒙悦納，
　你們的平安祭我也不喜悦。"

²¹所以耶和華如此說：

"我要將絆腳石放在這百姓前面，
　　父親和兒子
　　要一同跌在其上；
　　鄰舍與朋友也都滅亡。"

²²耶和華如此說：

"看哪，
　　有一種民從北方而來，
　　並有一大國被激動，
　　從地極來到。
²³他們拿弓和槍，
　　性情殘忍，不施憐憫。
　　他們的聲音，像海浪匐訇。
　　錫安城啊（註："城"原文作"女子"），
　　他們騎馬，都擺隊伍，
　　如上戰場的人要攻擊你。"

²⁴我們聽見他們的風聲，
　　手就發軟，
痛苦將我們抓住，
　　疼痛彷彿產難的婦人。
²⁵你們不要往田野去，
　　也不要行在路上，
因四圍有
　　仇敵的刀劍和驚嚇。
²⁶我民哪（註："民"原文作"民女"），
　　應當腰束麻布，滾在灰中；
你要悲傷，
　　如喪獨生子痛痛哭號，
因為滅命的
　　要忽然臨到我們。

²⁷"我使你在我民中為高臺、為保障
　　（註："高臺"或作"試驗人的"），
　　使你知道
　　試驗他們的行動。
²⁸他們都是極悖逆的，
　　往來讒謗人。
　　他們是銅是鐵，
　　都行壞事。
²⁹風箱吹火，
　　鉛被燒毀，
他們煉而又煉，終是徒然；
　　因為惡劣的還未除掉。
³⁰人必稱他們為被棄的銀渣，
　　因為耶和華已經棄掉他們。"

假宗教虛謊無益

7 耶和華的話臨到耶利米說：²"你當站在耶和華殿的門口，在那裏宣傳這話說：

²¹Therefore this is what the LORD says:

"I will put obstacles before this people.
　　Fathers and sons alike will stumble over
　　　them;
　　neighbors and friends will perish."

²²This is what the LORD says:

"Look, an army is coming
　　from the land of the north;
a great nation is being stirred up
　　from the ends of the earth.
²³They are armed with bow and spear;
　　they are cruel and show no mercy.
They sound like the roaring sea
　　as they ride on their horses;
they come like men in battle formation
　　to attack you, O Daughter of Zion."

²⁴We have heard reports about them,
　　and our hands hang limp.
Anguish has gripped us,
　　pain like that of a woman in labor.
²⁵Do not go out to the fields
　　or walk on the roads,
for the enemy has a sword,
　　and there is terror on every side.
²⁶O my people, put on sackcloth
　　and roll in ashes;
mourn with bitter wailing
　　as for an only son,
for suddenly the destroyer
　　will come upon us.

²⁷"I have made you a tester of metals
　　and my people the ore,
that you may observe
　　and test their ways.
²⁸They are all hardened rebels,
　　going about to slander.
They are bronze and iron;
　　they all act corruptly.
²⁹The bellows blow fiercely
　　to burn away the lead with fire,
but the refining goes on in vain;
　　the wicked are not purged out.
³⁰They are called rejected silver,
　　because the LORD has rejected them."

False Religion Worthless

7 This is the word that came to Jeremiah from the LORD: ²"Stand at the gate of the LORD's house and there proclaim this message:

" 'Hear the word of the LORD, all you people of Judah who come through these gates to worship the LORD. ³This is what the LORD Almighty, the God of Israel, says: Reform your ways and your actions, and I will let you live in this place. ⁴Do not trust in deceptive words and say, "This is the temple of the LORD, the temple of the LORD, the temple of the LORD!" ⁵If you really change your ways and your actions and deal with each other justly, ⁶if you do not oppress the alien, the fatherless or the widow and do not shed innocent blood in this place, and if you do not follow other gods to your own harm, ⁷then I will let you live in this place, in the land I gave your forefathers for ever and ever. ⁸But look, you are trusting in deceptive words that are worthless.

⁹" 'Will you steal and murder, commit adultery and perjury,ᵃ burn incense to Baal and follow other gods you have not known, ¹⁰and then come and stand before me in this house, which bears my Name, and say, "We are safe"—safe to do all these detestable things? ¹¹Has this house, which bears my Name, become a den of robbers to you? But I have been watching! declares the LORD.

¹²" 'Go now to the place in Shiloh where I first made a dwelling for my Name, and see what I did to it because of the wickedness of my people Israel. ¹³While you were doing all these things, declares the LORD, I spoke to you again and again, but you did not listen; I called you, but you did not answer. ¹⁴Therefore, what I did to Shiloh I will now do to the house that bears my Name, the temple you trust in, the place I gave to you and your fathers. ¹⁵I will thrust you from my presence, just as I did all your brothers, the people of Ephraim.'

¹⁶"So do not pray for this people nor offer any plea or petition for them; do not plead with me, for I will not listen to you. ¹⁷Do you not see what they are doing in the towns of Judah and in the streets of Jerusalem? ¹⁸The children gather wood, the fathers light the fire, and the women knead the dough and make cakes of bread for the Queen of Heaven. They pour out drink offerings to other gods to provoke me to anger. ¹⁹But am I the one they are provoking? declares the LORD. Are they not rather harming themselves, to their own shame?

²⁰" 'Therefore this is what the Sovereign LORD says: My anger and my wrath will be poured out on this place, on man and beast, on the trees of the field and on the fruit of the ground, and it will burn and not be quenched.

---

a 9 Or and swear by false gods

" '你們進這些門敬拜耶和華的一切<u>猶大</u>人,當聽耶和華的話。³萬軍之耶和華<u>以色列</u>的神如此說:你們改正行動作為,我就使你們在這地方仍然居住。⁴你們不要倚靠虛謊的話,說:這些是耶和華的殿,是耶和華的殿,是耶和華的殿。⁵你們若實在改正行動作為,在人和鄰舍中間誠然施行公平,⁶不欺壓寄居的和孤兒寡婦,在這地方不流無辜人的血,也不隨從別神陷害自己,⁷我就使你們在這地方仍然居住,就是我古時所賜給你們列祖的地,直到永遠。⁸看哪,你們倚靠虛謊無益的話。

⁹" '你們偷盜、殺害、姦淫、起假誓、向<u>巴力</u>燒香,並隨從素不認識的別神;¹⁰且來到這稱為我名下的殿,在我面前敬拜。又說:我們可以自由了!你們這樣的舉動是要行那些可憎的事嗎?¹¹這稱為我名下的殿,在你們眼中豈可看為賊窩嗎?我都看見了。這是耶和華說的。

¹²" '你們且往<u>示羅</u>去,就是我先前立為我名的居所,察看我因這百姓<u>以色列</u>的罪惡,向那地所行的如何。¹³耶和華說:現在因你們行了這一切的事,我也從早起來警戒你們,你們卻不聽從;呼喚你們,你們卻不答應。¹⁴所以我要向這稱為我名下、你們所倚靠的殿,與我所賜給你們和你們列祖的地施行,照我從前向<u>示羅</u>所行的一樣。¹⁵我必將你們從我眼前趕出,正如趕出你們的眾弟兄,就是<u>以法蓮</u>的一切後裔。'

¹⁶"所以你不要為這百姓祈禱。不要為他們呼求禱告,也不要向我為他們祈求,因我不聽允你。¹⁷他們在<u>猶大</u>城邑中和<u>耶路撒冷</u>街上所行的,你沒有看見嗎?¹⁸孩子撿柴,父親燒火,婦女摶麵做餅,獻給天后,又向別神澆奠祭,惹我發怒。¹⁹耶和華說:'他們豈是惹我發怒呢?不是自己惹禍,以致臉上慚愧嗎?

²⁰" '所以主耶和華如此說:看哪,我必將我的怒氣和忿怒傾在這地方的人和牲畜身上,並田野的樹木和地裏的出產上,必如火着起,不能熄滅。

²¹ "『萬軍之耶和華以色列的神如此說：你們將燔祭加在平安祭上，吃肉吧！²²因為我將你們列祖從埃及地領出來的那日，燔祭平安祭的事我並沒有提說，也沒有吩咐他們。²³我只吩咐他們這一件說：你們當聽從我的話，我就作你們的神，你們也作我的子民；你們行我所吩咐的一切道，就可以得福！²⁴他們卻不聽從，不側耳而聽，竟隨從自己的計謀和頑梗的惡心，向後不向前。²⁵自從你們列祖出埃及地的那日，直到今日，我差遣我的僕人眾先知到你們那裏去，每日從早起來差遣他們。²⁶你們卻不聽從，不側耳而聽，竟硬着頸項行惡，比你們列祖更甚。』

²⁷ "你要將這一切的話告訴他們，他們卻不聽從；呼喚他們，他們卻不答應。²⁸你要對他們說：『這就是不聽從耶和華他們神的話，不受教訓的國民，從他們的口中，誠實滅絕了。』²⁹耶路撒冷啊，要剪髮拋棄，在淨光的高處舉哀。因為耶和華丟掉離棄了惹他忿怒的世代。

殺戮谷

³⁰ "耶和華說：『猶大人行我眼中看為惡的事，將可憎之物設立在稱為我名下的殿中，污穢這殿。³¹他們在欣嫩子谷建築陀斐特的邱壇，好在火中焚燒自己的兒女。這並不是我所吩咐的，也不是我心所起的意。』³²耶和華說：『因此日子將到，這地方不再稱為陀斐特和欣嫩子谷，反倒稱為殺戮谷，因為要在陀斐特葬埋屍首，甚至無處可葬。³³並且這百姓的屍首，必給空中的飛鳥和地上的野獸作食物，並無人嚇趕。³⁴那時，我必使猶大城邑中和耶路撒冷街上，歡喜和快樂的聲音，新郎和新婦的聲音都止息了，因為地必成為荒場。』

8 "耶和華說：『到那時，人必將猶大王的骸骨和他首領的骸骨、祭司的骸骨、先知的骸骨，並耶路撒冷居民的骸骨，都從墳墓中取出來，²拋散在日頭、月亮和天上眾星之下，就是他們從

²¹ " 'This is what the LORD Almighty, the God of Israel, says: Go ahead, add your burnt offerings to your other sacrifices and eat the meat yourselves! ²²For when I brought your forefathers out of Egypt and spoke to them, I did not just give them commands about burnt offerings and sacrifices, ²³but I gave them this command: Obey me, and I will be your God and you will be my people. Walk in all the ways I command you, that it may go well with you. ²⁴But they did not listen or pay attention; instead, they followed the stubborn inclinations of their evil hearts. They went backward and not forward. ²⁵From the time your forefathers left Egypt until now, day after day, again and again I sent you my servants the prophets. ²⁶But they did not listen to me or pay attention. They were stiff-necked and did more evil than their forefathers.'

²⁷"When you tell them all this, they will not listen to you; when you call to them, they will not answer. ²⁸Therefore say to them, 'This is the nation that has not obeyed the LORD its God or responded to correction. Truth has perished; it has vanished from their lips. ²⁹Cut off your hair and throw it away; take up a lament on the barren heights, for the LORD has rejected and abandoned this generation that is under his wrath.

The Valley of Slaughter

³⁰" 'The people of Judah have done evil in my eyes, declares the LORD. They have set up their detestable idols in the house that bears my Name and have defiled it. ³¹They have built the high places of Topheth in the Valley of Ben Hinnom to burn their sons and daughters in the fire—something I did not command, nor did it enter my mind. ³²So beware, the days are coming, declares the LORD, when people will no longer call it Topheth or the Valley of Ben Hinnom, but the Valley of Slaughter, for they will bury the dead in Topheth until there is no more room. ³³Then the carcasses of this people will become food for the birds of the air and the beasts of the earth, and there will be no one to frighten them away. ³⁴I will bring an end to the sounds of joy and gladness and to the voices of bride and bridegroom in the towns of Judah and the streets of Jerusalem, for the land will become desolate.

8 " 'At that time, declares the LORD, the bones of the kings and officials of Judah, the bones of the priests and prophets, and the bones of the people of Jerusalem will be removed from their graves. ²They will be exposed to the sun and the moon and all the stars of the heavens, which they have loved and served and which they have followed and consulted and worshiped. They will not be gathered up or buried, but will be like refuse lying on the ground. ³Wherever I banish them, all the survivors of this evil nation will prefer death to life, declares the LORD Almighty.'

Sin and Punishment

⁴"Say to them, 'This is what the LORD says:

" 'When men fall down, do they not get up?
    When a man turns away, does he not return?
⁵Why then have these people turned away?
    Why does Jerusalem always turn away?
They cling to deceit;
    they refuse to return.
⁶I have listened attentively,
    but they do not say what is right.
No one repents of his wickedness,
    saying, "What have I done?"
Each pursues his own course
    like a horse charging into battle.
⁷Even the stork in the sky
    knows her appointed seasons,
and the dove, the swift and the thrush
    observe the time of their migration.
But my people do not know
    the requirements of the LORD.

⁸" 'How can you say, "We are wise,
    for we have the law of the LORD,"
when actually the lying pen of the scribes
    has handled it falsely?
⁹The wise will be put to shame;
    they will be dismayed and trapped.
Since they have rejected the word of the LORD,
    what kind of wisdom do they have?
¹⁰Therefore I will give their wives to other men
    and their fields to new owners.
From the least to the greatest,
    all are greedy for gain;
prophets and priests alike,
    all practice deceit.
¹¹They dress the wound of my people
    as though it were not serious.
"Peace, peace," they say,
    when there is no peace.
¹²Are they ashamed of their loathsome conduct?
    No, they have no shame at all;
    they do not even know how to blush.
So they will fall among the fallen;
    they will be brought down when they are punished,

                                      says the LORD.

前所喜愛、所侍奉、所隨從、所求問、所敬拜的。這些骸骨不再收殮，不再葬埋，必在地面上成為糞土。³並且這惡族所剩下的民，在我所趕他們到的各處，寧可揀死不揀生。這是萬軍之耶和華說的。'

罪與懲罰

⁴"你要對他們說，耶和華如此說：

" '人跌倒，不再起來嗎？
    人轉去，不再轉來嗎？
⁵這耶路撒冷的民
    為何恆久背道呢？
他們守定詭詐，
    不肯回頭。
⁶我留心聽，
    聽見他們說不正直的話，
無人悔改惡行，說：
    我做的是甚麼呢？
他們各人轉奔己路，
    如馬直闖戰場。
⁷空中的鸛鳥
    知道來去的定期，
斑鳩、燕子與白鶴，
    也守候當來的時令；
我的百姓，
    卻不知道耶和華的法則。

⁸" '你們怎麼說：我們有智慧，
    耶和華的律法在我們這裏？
看哪，
    文士的假筆舞弄虛假。
⁹智慧人慚愧，
    驚惶，被擒拿；
他們棄掉耶和華的話，
    心裏還有甚麼智慧呢？
¹⁰所以我必將他們的妻子給別人，
    將他們的田地給別人為業。
因為他們從最小的到至大的
    都一味地貪婪；
從先知到祭司
    都行事虛謊。
¹¹他們輕輕忽忽地
    醫治我百姓的損傷，
說：平安了！平安了！
    其實沒有平安。
¹²他們行可憎的事
    知道慚愧嗎？
不然，他們毫不慚愧，
    也不知羞恥。
因此他們必在仆倒的人中仆倒；
    我向他們討罪的時候，
    他們必致跌倒。

                          這是耶和華說的。'

¹³"耶和華說：
'我必使他們全然滅絕。
　葡萄樹上必沒有葡萄，
無花果樹上必沒有果子，
　葉子也必枯乾。
我所賜給他們的，
　必離開他們過去。'"

¹⁴"我們為何靜坐不動呢？
　我們當聚集，進入堅固城，
在那裏靜默不言；
因為耶和華我們的神
　使我們靜默不言，
又將苦膽水給我們喝，
　都因我們得罪了耶和華。
¹⁵我們指望平安，
　卻得不着好處；
指望痊愈的時候，
　不料，受了驚惶。
¹⁶聽見從但那裏
　敵人的馬噴鼻氣，
他的壯馬發嘶聲，
　全地就都震動；
因為他們來吞滅這地
　和其上所有的，
吞滅這城與其中的居民。"

¹⁷"看哪，我必使毒蛇到你們中間，
　是不服法術的，
必咬你們。"

　　　　　　　這是耶和華說的。

¹⁸我有憂愁，願能自慰，
　我心在我裏面發昏！
¹⁹聽啊，是我百姓的哀聲
　從極遠之地而來，說：
"耶和華不在錫安嗎？
　錫安的王不在其中嗎？"

耶和華說："他們為甚麼以雕刻
　偶像和外邦虛無的神，
惹我發怒呢？"

²⁰"麥秋已過，
　夏令已完，
我們還未得救！"

²¹先知說：因我百姓的損傷，
　我也受了損傷。
我哀痛，驚惶將我抓住。
²²在基列豈沒有乳香呢？
　在那裏豈沒有醫生呢？
我百姓為何不得痊愈呢？

¹³" 'I will take away their harvest,
　　　　　　　　declares the LORD.
There will be no grapes on the vine.
There will be no figs on the tree,
　and their leaves will wither.
What I have given them
　will be taken from them.[a] '"

¹⁴"Why are we sitting here?
　Gather together!
Let us flee to the fortified cities
　and perish there!
For the LORD our God has doomed us to perish
　and given us poisoned water to drink,
　because we have sinned against him.
¹⁵We hoped for peace
　but no good has come,
for a time of healing
　but there was only terror.
¹⁶The snorting of the enemy's horses
　is heard from Dan;
at the neighing of their stallions
　the whole land trembles.
They have come to devour
　the land and everything in it,
the city and all who live there."

¹⁷"See, I will send venomous snakes among you,
　vipers that cannot be charmed,
　and they will bite you,"
　　　　　　　declares the LORD.

¹⁸O my Comforter[b] in sorrow,
　my heart is faint within me.
¹⁹Listen to the cry of my people
　from a land far away:
"Is the LORD not in Zion?
　Is her King no longer there?"

　"Why have they provoked me to anger with
　　their images,
　with their worthless foreign idols?"

²⁰"The harvest is past,
　the summer has ended,
and we are not saved."

²¹Since my people are crushed, I am crushed;
　I mourn, and horror grips me.
²²Is there no balm in Gilead?
　Is there no physician there?
Why then is there no healing
　for the wound of my people?

---

a 13 The meaning of the Hebrew for this sentence is uncertain.
b 18 The meaning of the Hebrew for this word is uncertain.

9

¹Oh, that my head were a spring of water
and my eyes a fountain of tears!
I would weep day and night
for the slain of my people.
²Oh, that I had in the desert
a lodging place for travelers,
so that I might leave my people
and go away from them;
for they are all adulterers,
a crowd of unfaithful people.

³"They make ready their tongue
like a bow, to shoot lies;
it is not by truth
that they triumph[a] in the land.
They go from one sin to another;
they do not acknowledge me,"
declares the LORD.
⁴"Beware of your friends;
do not trust your brothers.
For every brother is a deceiver,[b]
and every friend a slanderer.
⁵Friend deceives friend,
and no one speaks the truth.
They have taught their tongues to lie;
they weary themselves with sinning.
⁶You[c] live in the midst of deception;
in their deceit they refuse to acknowledge
me,"
declares the LORD.

⁷Therefore this is what the LORD Almighty says:

"See, I will refine and test them,
for what else can I do
because of the sin of my people?
⁸Their tongue is a deadly arrow;
it speaks with deceit.
With his mouth each speaks cordially to his
neighbor,
but in his heart he sets a trap for him.
⁹Should I not punish them for this?"
declares the LORD.
"Should I not avenge myself
on such a nation as this?"

¹⁰I will weep and wail for the mountains
and take up a lament concerning the desert
pastures.
They are desolate and untraveled,
and the lowing of cattle is not heard.

9

¹但願我的頭為水，
我的眼為淚的泉源，
我好為我百姓（註：原文作"民
女"。⁷節同）中被殺的人
晝夜哭泣。
²惟願我在曠野
有行路人住宿之處，
使我可以離開我的民出去。
因他們都是行姦淫的，
是行詭詐的一黨。

³"他們彎起舌頭弓一樣，
為要說謊話。
他們在國中增長勢力，
不是為行誠實，
乃是惡上加惡，
並不認識我。"
這是耶和華說的。
⁴"你們各人當謹防鄰舍，
不可信靠弟兄；
因為弟兄盡行欺騙，
鄰舍都往來讒謗人。
⁵他們各人欺哄鄰舍，
不說真話；
他們教舌頭學習說謊，
勞勞碌碌地作孽。
⁶你的住處在詭詐的人中，
他們因行詭詐，
不肯認識我。"
這是耶和華說的。

⁷所以萬軍之耶和華如此說：

"看哪，我要將他們熔化熬煉，
不然，我因我百姓的罪
該怎樣行呢？
⁸他們的舌頭是毒箭，
說話詭詐；
人與鄰舍口說和平話，
心卻謀害他。"

⁹耶和華說：
"我豈不因這些事
討他們的罪呢？
豈不報復這樣的國民呢？"

¹⁰我要為山嶺哭泣悲哀，
為曠野的草場揚聲哀號；
因為都已乾焦，
甚至無人經過。
人也聽不見牲畜鳴叫，

---

*a 3 Or lies; / they are not valiant for truth   b 4 Or a deceiving
Jacob   c 6 That is, Jeremiah (the Hebrew is singular)*

空中的飛鳥和地上的野獸
　都已逃去。

11 "我必使耶路撒冷變為亂堆，
　　為野狗的住處；
　也必使猶大的城邑變為荒場
　　無人居住。"

12 誰是智慧人，可以明白這事？耶和華的口向誰說過，使他可以傳說？遍地為何滅亡，乾焦好像曠野，甚至無人經過呢？

13 耶和華說："因為這百姓離棄我，在他們面前所設立的律法沒有遵行，也沒有聽從我的話。14 只隨從自己頑梗的心行事，照他們列祖所教訓的隨從眾巴力。" 15 所以萬軍之耶和華以色列的神如此說："看哪，我必將茵蔯給這百姓吃，又將苦膽水給他們喝。16 我要把他們散在列邦中，就是他們和他們列祖素不認識的列邦。我也要使刀劍追殺他們，直到將他們滅盡。"

17 萬軍之耶和華如此說：

"你們應當思想，
　將善唱哀歌的婦女召來，
　又打發人召善哭的婦女來。
18 叫她們速速
　為我們舉哀，
　使我們眼淚汪汪，
　使我們的眼皮湧出水來。
19 因為聽見哀聲出於錫安，說：
　'我們怎樣敗落了！
　我們大大地慚愧！
　我們撇下地土，
　人也拆毀了我們的房屋。'"

20 婦女們哪，你們當聽耶和華的話，
　領受他口中的言語；
　又當教導你們的兒女舉哀，
　各人教導鄰舍唱哀歌。
21 因為死亡上來，進了我們的窗戶，
　入了我們的宮殿，
　要從外邊剪除孩童，
　從街上剪除少年人。

22 你當說："耶和華如此說：

"'人的屍首
　必倒在田野像糞土，
　又像收割的人遺落的一把禾稼，
　無人收取。'"

The birds of the air have fled
　and the animals are gone.

11 "I will make Jerusalem a heap of ruins,
　a haunt of jackals;
and I will lay waste the towns of Judah
　so no one can live there."

12 What man is wise enough to understand this? Who has been instructed by the LORD and can explain it? Why has the land been ruined and laid waste like a desert that no one can cross?

13 The LORD said, "It is because they have forsaken my law, which I set before them; they have not obeyed me or followed my law. 14 Instead, they have followed the stubbornness of their hearts; they have followed the Baals, as their fathers taught them." 15 Therefore, this is what the LORD Almighty, the God of Israel, says: "See, I will make this people eat bitter food and drink poisoned water. 16 I will scatter them among nations that neither they nor their fathers have known, and I will pursue them with the sword until I have destroyed them."

17 This is what the LORD Almighty says:

"Consider now! Call for the wailing women
　to come;
send for the most skillful of them.
18 Let them come quickly
　and wail over us
till our eyes overflow with tears
　and water streams from our eyelids.
19 The sound of wailing is heard from Zion:
　'How ruined we are!
　How great is our shame!
We must leave our land
　because our houses are in ruins.'"

20 Now, O women, hear the word of the LORD;
　open your ears to the words of his mouth.
Teach your daughters how to wail;
　teach one another a lament.
21 Death has climbed in through our windows
　and has entered our fortresses;
it has cut off the children from the streets
　and the young men from the public squares.

22 Say, "This is what the LORD declares:

" 'The dead bodies of men will lie
　like refuse on the open field,
like cut grain behind the reaper,
　with no one to gather them.' "

23This is what the LORD says:

"Let not the wise man boast of his wisdom
　or the strong man boast of his strength
　or the rich man boast of his riches,
24but let him who boasts boast about this:
　that he understands and knows me,
　that I am the LORD, who exercises kindness,
　justice and righteousness on earth,
　for in these I delight,"
　　　　　　　　　　　declares the LORD.

25"The days are coming," declares the LORD, "when I will punish all who are circumcised only in the flesh— 26Egypt, Judah, Edom, Ammon, Moab and all who live in the desert in distant places.*a* For all these nations are really uncircumcised, and even the whole house of Israel is uncircumcised in heart."

God and Idols

10 Hear what the LORD says to you, O house of Israel. 2This is what the LORD says:

"Do not learn the ways of the nations
　or be terrified by signs in the sky,
　though the nations are terrified by them.
3For the customs of the peoples are worthless;
　they cut a tree out of the forest,
　and a craftsman shapes it with his chisel.
4They adorn it with silver and gold;
　they fasten it with hammer and nails
　so it will not totter.
5Like a scarecrow in a melon patch,
　their idols cannot speak;
　they must be carried
　because they cannot walk.
Do not fear them;
　they can do no harm
　nor can they do any good."

6No one is like you, O LORD;
　you are great,
　and your name is mighty in power.
7Who should not revere you,
　O King of the nations?
　This is your due.
Among all the wise men of the nations
　and in all their kingdoms,
　there is no one like you.
8They are all senseless and foolish;
　they are taught by worthless wooden idols.

a 26 Or desert and who clip the hair by their foreheads

23耶和華如此說:

"智慧人不要因他的智慧誇口,
　勇士不要因他的勇力誇口,
　財主不要因他的財物誇口。
24誇口的卻因他有聰明,
　認識我是耶和華,
　又知道我喜悅在世上施行慈愛、
　公平和公義,
　以此誇口。"
　　　　　　　　　這是耶和華說的。

25耶和華說:"看哪,日子將到,我要刑罰一切受過割禮,心卻未受割禮的,26就是埃及、猶大、以東、亞捫人、摩押人和一切住在曠野剃周圍頭髮的。因為列國人都沒有受割禮,以色列人心中也沒有受割禮。"

神與偶像

10 以色列家啊,要聽耶和華對你們所說的話。2耶和華如此說:

"你們不要效法列國的行為,
　也不要為天象驚惶,
　因列國為此事驚惶。
3眾民的風俗是虛空的,
　他們在樹林中用斧子砍伐一棵樹,
　匠人用手工造成偶像。
4他們用金銀妝飾它,
　用釘子和錘子釘穩,
　使它不動搖。
5它好像棕樹,是鏇成的,
　不能說話,
　不能行走,
　必須有人抬着。
你們不要怕它,
　它不能降禍,
　也無力降福。"

6耶和華啊,沒有能比你的;
　你本為大,
　有大能大力的名!
7萬國的王啊,
　誰不敬畏你?
　敬畏你本是合宜的;
　因為在列國的智慧人中,
　雖有政權的尊榮,
　也不能比你。
8他們盡都是畜類,是愚昧的。
　偶像的訓誨算甚麼呢?
　偶像不過是木頭!

9有銀子打成片，是從他施帶來的，
　　並有從烏法來的金子，
　　都是匠人和銀匠的手工；
　　又有藍色紫色料的衣服，
　　都是巧匠的工作。
10惟耶和華是真神，
　　是活神，是永遠的王！
　　他一發怒，大地震動；
　　他一惱恨，列國都擔當不起。

　　11 「你們要對他們如此說：‘不
是那創造天地的神，必從地上從天
下被除滅！’”

12耶和華用能力創造大地，
　　用智慧建立世界，
　　用聰明鋪張穹蒼。

13他一發聲，
　　空中便有多水激動，
　　他使雲霧
　　從地極上騰；
　　他造電隨雨而閃，
　　從他府庫中帶出風來。

14各人都成了畜類，毫無知識；
　　各銀匠都因他雕刻的偶像羞愧。
　　他所鑄的偶像本是虛假的，
　　其中並無氣息；
15都是虛無的，是迷惑人的工作。
　　到追討的時候，必被除滅。
16雅各的分不像這些，
　　因他是造作萬有的主。
　　以色列也是他產業的支派——
　　萬軍之耶和華是他的名。

將臨的災禍

17受圍困的人哪，當收拾你的財物，
　　從國中帶出去。
18因為耶和華如此說：
　　“這時候，我必將此地的居民，
　　好像用機弦甩出去，
　　又必加害在他們身上，
　　使他們覺悟。”

19民說：禍哉！我受損傷，
　　我的傷痕極其重大。
　　我卻說：
　　“這真是我的痛苦，必須忍受。”
20我的帳棚毀壞，
　　我的繩索折斷。
　　我的兒女離我出去，沒有了；
　　無人再支搭我的帳棚，
　　掛起我的幔子。

9Hammered silver is brought from Tarshish
　　and gold from Uphaz.
What the craftsman and goldsmith have made
　　is then dressed in blue and purple—
　　all made by skilled workers.
10But the LORD is the true God;
　　he is the living God, the eternal King.
When he is angry, the earth trembles;
　　the nations cannot endure his wrath.

11"Tell them this: 'These gods, who did not
make the heavens and the earth, will perish
from the earth and from under the heavens.' "[a]

12But God made the earth by his power;
　　he founded the world by his wisdom
　　and stretched out the heavens by his
　　　understanding.
13When he thunders, the waters in the heavens
　　　roar;
　　he makes clouds rise from the ends of the
　　　earth.
He sends lightning with the rain
　　and brings out the wind from his storehouses.

14Everyone is senseless and without knowledge;
　　every goldsmith is shamed by his idols.
His images are a fraud;
　　they have no breath in them.
15They are worthless, the objects of mockery;
　　when their judgment comes, they will perish.
16He who is the Portion of Jacob is not like these,
　　for he is the Maker of all things,
including Israel, the tribe of his inheritance—
　　the LORD Almighty is his name.

Coming Destruction

17Gather up your belongings to leave the land,
　　you who live under siege.
18For this is what the LORD says:
　　"At this time I will hurl out
　　those who live in this land;
　　I will bring distress on them
　　so that they may be captured."

19Woe to me because of my injury!
　　My wound is incurable!
Yet I said to myself,
　　"This is my sickness, and I must endure it."
20My tent is destroyed;
　　all its ropes are snapped.
My sons are gone from me and are no more;
　　no one is left now to pitch my tent
　　or to set up my shelter.

a 11 The text of this verse is in Aramaic.

21The shepherds are senseless
　and do not inquire of the LORD;
so they do not prosper
　and all their flock is scattered.
22Listen! The report is coming—
　a great commotion from the land of the
　　　north!
It will make the towns of Judah desolate,
　a haunt of jackals.

Jeremiah's Prayer

23I know, O LORD, that a man's life is not his
　own;
　it is not for man to direct his steps.
24Correct me, LORD, but only with justice—
　not in your anger,
　lest you reduce me to nothing.
25Pour out your wrath on the nations
　that do not acknowledge you,
　on the peoples who do not call on your
　　name.
For they have devoured Jacob;
　they have devoured him completely
　and destroyed his homeland.

The Covenant Is Broken

11 This is the word that came to Jeremiah from the LORD: 2"Listen to the terms of this covenant and tell them to the people of Judah and to those who live in Jerusalem. 3Tell them that this is what the LORD, the God of Israel, says: 'Cursed is the man who does not obey the terms of this covenant— 4the terms I commanded your forefathers when I brought them out of Egypt, out of the iron-smelting furnace.' I said, 'Obey me and do everything I command you, and you will be my people, and I will be your God. 5Then I will fulfill the oath I swore to your forefathers, to give them a land flowing with milk and honey'—the land you possess today."

I answered, "Amen, LORD."

6The LORD said to me, "Proclaim all these words in the towns of Judah and in the streets of Jerusalem: 'Listen to the terms of this covenant and follow them. 7From the time I brought your forefathers up from Egypt until today, I warned them again and again, saying, "Obey me." 8But they did not listen or pay attention; instead, they followed the stubbornness of their evil hearts. So I brought on them all the curses of the covenant I had commanded them to follow but that they did not keep.' "

9Then the LORD said to me, "There is a conspiracy among the people of Judah and those

21因為牧人都成為畜類，
　沒有求問耶和華，
所以不得順利，
　他們的羊羣也都分散。
22有風聲！
　看哪，敵人來了！
有大擾亂從北方出來，
要使猶大城邑，變為荒涼，
　成為野狗的住處。

耶利米的祈禱

23耶和華啊，
　我曉得人的道路不由自己；
　行路的人也不能定自己的腳步。
24耶和華啊，求你從寬懲治我，
　不要在你的怒中懲治我，
　恐怕使我歸於無有。
25願你將忿怒傾在
　不認識你的列國中，
和不求告你名的各族上。
因為他們吞了雅各，
　不但吞了，
而且滅絕，
　把他的住處變為荒場。

違背聖約

11 耶和華的話臨到耶利米說：2"當聽這約的話，告訴猶大人和耶路撒冷的居民。3對他們說：'耶和華以色列的神如此說：不聽從這約之話的人，必受咒詛。4這約，是我將你們列祖從埃及地領出來，脫離鐵爐的那日所吩咐他們的，說：你們要聽從我的話，照我一切所吩咐的去行。這樣，你們就作我的子民，我也作你們的神。5我好堅定向你們列祖所起的誓，給他們流奶與蜜之地，正如今日一樣。' "

我就回答說："耶和華啊，阿們！"

6耶和華對我說："你要在猶大城邑中和耶路撒冷街市上，宣告這一切話說：'你們當聽從遵行這約的話。7因為我將你們列祖從埃及地領出來的那日，直到今日，都是從早起來，切切告誡他們，說：你們當聽從我的話。8他們卻不聽從，不側耳而聽，竟隨從自己頑梗的惡心去行。所以我使這約中一切咒詛的話臨到他們身上。這約是我吩咐他們行的，他們卻不去行。'"

9耶和華對我說："在猶大人和耶路撒冷居民中有同謀背叛的事。

10他們轉去效法他們的先祖，不肯聽我的話，犯罪作孽，又隨從別神，侍奉它。以色列家和猶大家背了我與他們列祖所立的約。11所以耶和華如此說：'我必使災禍臨到他們，是他們不能逃脫的。他們必向我哀求，我卻不聽。12那時猶大城邑的人和耶路撒冷的居民，要去哀求他們燒香所供奉的神，只是遭難的時候，這些神毫不拯救他們。13猶大啊，你神的數目與你城的數目相等；你為那可恥的巴力所築燒香的壇，也與耶路撒冷街道的數目相等。'

14 "所以你不要為這百姓祈禱，不要為他們呼求禱告。因為他們遭難向我哀求的時候，我必不應允。

15 "我所親愛的，
　　既行許多淫亂，
　　聖肉也離了你，
　　你在我殿中做甚麼呢？
　　你作惡就喜樂。"

16從前耶和華給你起名叫青橄欖樹，
　　又華美又結好果子；
　　如今他用鬨嚷之聲，
　　點火在其上，
　　枝子也被折斷。

17原來栽培你的萬軍之耶和華已經說，要降禍攻擊你，是因以色列家和猶大家行惡，向巴力燒香，惹我發怒，是自作自受。

害耶利米的陰謀

18耶和華指示我，我就知道。你將他們所行的給我指明。19我卻像羊順的羊羔被牽到宰殺之地；我並不知道他們設計謀害我，說：

"我們把樹連果子都滅了吧！
　　將他從活人之地剪除，
　　使他的名不再被記念。"

who live in Jerusalem. 10They have returned to the sins of their forefathers, who refused to listen to my words. They have followed other gods to serve them. Both the house of Israel and the house of Judah have broken the covenant I made with their forefathers. 11Therefore this is what the LORD says: 'I will bring on them a disaster they cannot escape. Although they cry out to me, I will not listen to them. 12The towns of Judah and the people of Jerusalem will go and cry out to the gods to whom they burn incense, but they will not help them at all when disaster strikes. 13You have as many gods as you have towns, O Judah; and the altars you have set up to burn incense to that shameful god Baal are as many as the streets of Jerusalem.'

14"Do not pray for this people nor offer any plea or petition for them, because I will not listen when they call to me in the time of their distress.

15"What is my beloved doing in my temple
　　as she works out her evil schemes with
　　　　many?
　　Can consecrated meat avert your
　　　　punishment?
　　When you engage in your wickedness,
　　　　then you rejoice.a "

16The LORD called you a thriving olive tree
　　with fruit beautiful in form.
　　But with the roar of a mighty storm
　　he will set it on fire,
　　and its branches will be broken.

17The LORD Almighty, who planted you, has decreed disaster for you, because the house of Israel and the house of Judah have done evil and provoked me to anger by burning incense to Baal.

Plot Against Jeremiah

18Because the LORD revealed their plot to me, I knew it, for at that time he showed me what they were doing. 19I had been like a gentle lamb led to the slaughter; I did not realize that they had plotted against me, saying,

"Let us destroy the tree and its fruit;
　　let us cut him off from the land of the living,
　　that his name be remembered no more."

a 15 Or Could consecrated meat avert your punishment? / Then you would rejoice

20But, O LORD Almighty, you who judge righteously
and test the heart and mind,
let me see your vengeance upon them,
for to you I have committed my cause.

21"Therefore this is what the LORD says about the men of Anathoth who are seeking your life and saying, 'Do not prophesy in the name of the LORD or you will die by our hands'— 22therefore this is what the LORD Almighty says: 'I will punish them. Their young men will die by the sword, their sons and daughters by famine. 23Not even a remnant will be left to them, because I will bring disaster on the men of Anathoth in the year of their punishment.'"

Jeremiah's Complaint

12 You are always righteous, O LORD,
when I bring a case before you.
Yet I would speak with you about your justice:
Why does the way of the wicked prosper?
Why do all the faithless live at ease?
2You have planted them, and they have taken root;
they grow and bear fruit.
You are always on their lips
but far from their hearts.
3Yet you know me, O LORD;
you see me and test my thoughts about you.
Drag them off like sheep to be butchered!
Set them apart for the day of slaughter!
4How long will the land lie parched*a*
and the grass in every field be withered?
Because those who live in it are wicked,
the animals and birds have perished.
Moreover, the people are saying,
"He will not see what happens to us."

God's Answer

5"If you have raced with men on foot
and they have worn you out,
how can you compete with horses?
If you stumble in safe country,*b*
how will you manage in the thickets by*c* the Jordan?
6Your brothers, your own family—
even they have betrayed you;
they have raised a loud cry against you.
Do not trust them,
though they speak well of you.

20按公義判斷，
察驗人肺腑心腸的
萬軍之耶和華啊！
我卻要見你在他們身上報仇，
因我將我的案件向你稟明了。

21「所以耶和華論到尋索你命的亞拿突人如此說：『他們說：你不要奉耶和華的名說預言，免得你死在我們手中。』22所以萬軍之耶和華如此說：『看哪，我必刑罰他們。他們的少年人必被刀劍殺死；他們的兒女必因饑荒滅亡。23並且沒有餘剩的人留給他們。因為在追討之年，我必使災禍臨到亞拿突人。』」

耶利米的埋怨

12 耶和華啊，
我與你爭辯的時候，
你顯為義。
但有一件，我還要與你理論：
惡人的道路為何亨通呢？
大行詭詐的為何得安逸呢？
2你栽培了他們，
他們也扎了根，
長大，而且結果。
他們的口是與你相近，
心卻與你遠離。
3耶和華啊，你曉得我，看見我，
察驗我向你是怎樣的心。
求你將他們拉出來，好像將宰的羊，
叫他們等候殺戮的日子。
4這地悲哀，
通國的青草枯乾，要到幾時呢？
因其上居民的惡行，
牲畜和飛鳥都滅絕了。
他們曾說：
「他看不見我們的結局。」

神的答覆

5耶和華說：
「你若與步行的人同跑，尚且覺累，
怎能與馬賽跑呢？
你在平安之地，雖然安穩，
在約旦河邊的叢林
要怎樣行呢？
6因為連你弟兄和你父家
都用奸詐待你。
他們也在你後邊大聲喊叫。
雖向你說好話，
你也不要信他們。

---

a 4 Or *land mourn*   *b* 5 Or *If you put your trust in a land of safety*
c 5 Or *the flooding of*

7 "我離了我的殿宇，
　　撇棄我的產業，
　　將我心裏所親愛的
　　交在她仇敵的手中。
8 我的產業向我
　　如林中的獅子，
　　她發聲攻擊我，
　　因此我恨惡她。
9 我的產業向我
　　豈如斑點的鷙鳥呢？
　　鷙鳥豈在她四圍攻擊她呢？
　　你們要去聚集田野的百獸，
　　帶來吞吃吧！
10 許多牧人毀壞我的葡萄園，
　　踐踏我的分，
　　使我美好的分
　　變為荒涼的曠野。
11 他們使地荒涼，
　　地既荒涼，便向我悲哀；
　　全地荒涼，
　　因無人介意。
12 滅命的都來到曠野中
　　一切淨光的高處；
　　耶和華的刀，
　　從地這邊直到地那邊，盡行殺滅。
　　凡有血氣的，都不得平安。
13 他們種的是麥子，收的是荊棘，
　　勞勞苦苦，卻毫無益處。
　　因耶和華的烈怒，
　　你們必為自己的土產羞愧。"

14 耶和華如此說："一切惡鄰，就是佔據我使百姓以色列所承受產業的，我要將他們拔出本地，又要將猶大家從他們中間拔出來。15 我拔出他們以後，我必轉過來憐憫他們，把他們再帶回來，各歸本業，各歸故土。16 他們若殷勤學習我百姓的道，指着我的名起誓說：'我指着永生的耶和華起誓'，正如他們從前教我百姓指着巴力起誓，他們就必建立在我百姓中間。17 他們若是不聽，我必拔出那國，拔出而且毀滅。"這是耶和華說的。

麻布腰帶

13 耶和華對我如此說："你去買一根麻布帶子束腰，不可放在水中。" 2 我就照着耶和華的話，買了一根帶子束腰。

3 耶和華的話第二次臨到我說：4 "要拿着你所買的腰帶，就是你腰上的帶子，起來往幼發拉底河去，

---

7 "I will forsake my house,
　　abandon my inheritance;
　I will give the one I love
　　into the hands of her enemies.
8 My inheritance has become to me
　　like a lion in the forest.
　She roars at me;
　　therefore I hate her.
9 Has not my inheritance become to me
　　like a speckled bird of prey
　　that other birds of prey surround and attack?
　Go and gather all the wild beasts;
　　bring them to devour.
10 Many shepherds will ruin my vineyard
　　and trample down my field;
　they will turn my pleasant field
　　into a desolate wasteland.
11 It will be made a wasteland,
　　parched and desolate before me;
　the whole land will be laid waste
　　because there is no one who cares.
12 Over all the barren heights in the desert
　　destroyers will swarm,
　for the sword of the LORD will devour
　　from one end of the land to the other;
　　no one will be safe.
13 They will sow wheat but reap thorns;
　　they will wear themselves out but gain nothing.
　So bear the shame of your harvest
　　because of the LORD's fierce anger."

14 This is what the LORD says: "As for all my wicked neighbors who seize the inheritance I gave my people Israel, I will uproot them from their lands and I will uproot the house of Judah from among them. 15 But after I uproot them, I will again have compassion and will bring each of them back to his own inheritance and his own country. 16 And if they learn well the ways of my people and swear by my name, saying, 'As surely as the LORD lives'—even as they once taught my people to swear by Baal—then they will be established among my people. 17 But if any nation does not listen, I will completely uproot and destroy it," declares the LORD.

A Linen Belt

13 This is what the LORD said to me: "Go and buy a linen belt and put it around your waist, but do not let it touch water." 2 So I bought a belt, as the LORD directed, and put it around my waist.

3 Then the word of the LORD came to me a second time: 4 "Take the belt you bought and are wearing around your waist, and go now to

Perath[a] and hide it there in a crevice in the rocks." [5]So I went and hid it at Perath, as the LORD told me.

[6]Many days later the LORD said to me, "Go now to Perath and get the belt I told you to hide there." [7]So I went to Perath and dug up the belt and took it from the place where I had hidden it, but now it was ruined and completely useless.

[8]Then the word of the LORD came to me: [9]"This is what the LORD says: 'In the same way I will ruin the pride of Judah and the great pride of Jerusalem. [10]These wicked people, who refuse to listen to my words, who follow the stubbornness of their hearts and go after other gods to serve and worship them, will be like this belt—completely useless! [11]For as a belt is bound around a man's waist, so I bound the whole house of Israel and the whole house of Judah to me,' declares the LORD, 'to be my people for my renown and praise and honor. But they have not listened.'

Wineskins

[12]"Say to them: 'This is what the LORD, the God of Israel, says: Every wineskin should be filled with wine.' And if they say to you, 'Don't we know that every wineskin should be filled with wine?' [13]then tell them, 'This is what the LORD says: I am going to fill with drunkenness all who live in this land, including the kings who sit on David's throne, the priests, the prophets and all those living in Jerusalem. [14]I will smash them one against the other, fathers and sons alike, declares the LORD. I will allow no pity or mercy or compassion to keep me from destroying them.' "

Threat of Captivity

[15]Hear and pay attention,
　　do not be arrogant,
　　for the LORD has spoken.
[16]Give glory to the LORD your God
　　before he brings the darkness,
before your feet stumble
　　on the darkening hills.
You hope for light,
　　but he will turn it to thick darkness
　　and change it to deep gloom.
[17]But if you do not listen,
　　I will weep in secret
　　because of your pride;
my eyes will weep bitterly,
　　overflowing with tears,
because the LORD's flock will be taken captive.

a 4 Or possibly the Euphrates; also in verses 5-7

將腰帶藏在那裏的磐石穴中。" [5]我就去，照着耶和華所吩咐我的，將腰帶藏在<u>幼發拉底河</u>邊。

[6]過了多日，耶和華對我說："你起來往<u>幼發拉底河</u>去，將我吩咐你藏在那裏的腰帶取出來。" [7]我就往<u>幼發拉底河</u>去，將腰帶從我所藏的地方刨出來。見腰帶已經變壞，毫無用了。

[8]耶和華的話臨到我說：[9]"耶和華如此說：'我必照樣敗壞<u>猶大</u>的驕傲和<u>耶路撒冷</u>的大驕傲。[10]這惡民不肯聽我的話，按自己頑梗的心而行，隨從別神，侍奉敬拜，他們也必像這腰帶變為無用。' [11]耶和華說：'腰帶怎樣緊貼人腰，照樣，我也使<u>以色列</u>全家和<u>猶大</u>全家緊貼我，好叫他們屬我為子民，使我得名聲，得頌讚，得榮耀。他們卻不肯聽。'

酒罈

[12]"所以你要對他們說：'耶和華<u>以色列</u>的神如此說：各罈都要盛滿了酒。' 他們必對你說：'我們豈不確知各罈都要盛滿了酒呢？' [13]你就要對他們說：'耶和華如此說：我必使這地的一切居民，就是<u>坐大衛寶座</u>的君王和祭司，與先知，<u>並耶路撒冷</u>的一切居民，都酩酊大醉。[14]耶和華說：我要使他們彼此相碰，就是父與子彼此相碰；我必不可憐、不顧惜、不憐憫，以致滅絕他們。'"

被擄的威脅

[15]你們當聽，當側耳而聽，
　　不要驕傲！
　　因為耶和華已經說了。
[16]耶和華你們的神
　　未使黑暗來到，
你們的腳未在昏暗山上絆跌之先，
　　當將榮耀歸給他，
免得你們盼望光明，
　　他使光明變為死蔭，
　　成為幽暗。
[17]你們若不聽這話，
　　我必因你們的驕傲，
　　在暗地哭泣；
我眼必痛哭流淚，
　　因為耶和華的羣眾被擄去了。

18你要對君王和太后說：
　　"你們當自卑，坐在下邊。
　因為你們的頭巾，就是你們的華冠，
　　已經脫落了。"
19南方的城盡都關閉，
　　無人開放。
　猶大全被擄掠，
　　且擄掠淨盡。

20你們要舉目觀看從北方來的人。
　　先前賜給你的羣眾，
　就是你佳美的羣眾，
　　如今在哪裏呢？
21耶和華立你自己所交的朋友為首，
　　轄制你，
　那時你還有甚麼話說呢？
　痛苦豈不將你抓住
　　像產難的婦人嗎？
22你若心裏說：
　　"這一切事為何臨到我呢？"
　你的衣襟揭起，
　　你的腳跟受傷，
　是因你的罪孽甚多。
23古實人豈能改變皮膚呢？
　　豹豈能改變斑點呢？
　若能，
　　你們這習慣行惡的便能行善了。

24所以我必用曠野的風吹散他們，
　　像吹過的碎稭一樣。
25耶和華說：
　　"這是你所當得的，
　是我量給你的分；
　　因為你忘記我，
　倚靠虛假（註：或譯"偶像"）。
26所以我要揭起你的衣襟，
　　蒙在你臉上，顯出你的醜陋。
27你那些可憎惡之事，
　　就是在田野的山上行姦淫，
　發嘶聲，作淫亂的事，
　　我都看見了。
　耶路撒冷啊，你有禍了！
　　你不肯潔淨，還要到幾時呢？"

乾旱，饑荒，刀劍

14 耶和華論到乾旱之災的話臨到耶利米：

2　"猶大悲哀，
　　城門衰敗，
　眾人披上黑衣坐在地上，
　　耶路撒冷的哀聲上達。

18Say to the king and to the queen mother,
　"Come down from your thrones,
　for your glorious crowns
　　will fall from your heads."
19The cities in the Negev will be shut up,
　and there will be no one to open them.
　All Judah will be carried into exile,
　carried completely away.

20Lift up your eyes and see
　those who are coming from the north.
　Where is the flock that was entrusted to you,
　　the sheep of which you boasted?
21What will you say when ⌊the LORD⌋ sets over
　　you
　those you cultivated as your special allies?
　Will not pain grip you
　like that of a woman in labor?
22And if you ask yourself,
　"Why has this happened to me?"—
　it is because of your many sins
　　that your skirts have been torn off
　and your body mistreated.
23Can the Ethiopian*a* change his skin
　or the leopard its spots?
　Neither can you do good
　who are accustomed to doing evil.

24"I will scatter you like chaff
　driven by the desert wind.
25This is your lot,
　the portion I have decreed for you,"
　　　　　　　　　　　　declares the LORD,
　"because you have forgotten me
　and trusted in false gods.
26I will pull up your skirts over your face
　that your shame may be seen—
27your adulteries and lustful neighings,
　your shameless prostitution!
　I have seen your detestable acts
　on the hills and in the fields.
　Woe to you, O Jerusalem!
　How long will you be unclean?"

Drought, Famine, Sword

14 This is the word of the LORD to Jeremiah concerning the drought:

2"Judah mourns,
　her cities languish;
　they wail for the land,
　and a cry goes up from Jerusalem.

a 23 Hebrew *Cushite* (probably a person from the upper Nile region)

3The nobles send their servants for water;
　　they go to the cisterns
　　but find no water.
They return with their jars unfilled;
　　dismayed and despairing,
　　they cover their heads.
4The ground is cracked
　　because there is no rain in the land;
　　the farmers are dismayed
　　and cover their heads.
5Even the doe in the field
　　deserts her newborn fawn
　　because there is no grass.
6Wild donkeys stand on the barren heights
　　and pant like jackals;
　　their eyesight fails
　　for lack of pasture."

7Although our sins testify against us,
　　O Lord, do something for the sake of your
　　　name.
For our backsliding is great;
　　we have sinned against you.
8O Hope of Israel,
　　its Savior in times of distress,
　　why are you like a stranger in the land,
　　like a traveler who stays only a night?
9Why are you like a man taken by surprise,
　　like a warrior powerless to save?
You are among us, O LORD,
　　and we bear your name;
　　do not forsake us!

10This is what the LORD says about this people:

　　"They greatly love to wander;
　　　they do not restrain their feet.
　　So the LORD does not accept them;
　　　he will now remember their wickedness
　　　and punish them for their sins."

11Then the LORD said to me, "Do not pray for
the well-being of this people. 12Although they
fast, I will not listen to their cry; though they
offer burnt offerings and grain offerings, I will
not accept them. Instead, I will destroy them
with the sword, famine and plague."

13But I said, "Ah, Sovereign LORD, the
prophets keep telling them, 'You will not see the
sword or suffer famine. Indeed, I will give you
lasting peace in this place.' "

14Then the LORD said to me, "The prophets
are prophesying lies in my name. I have not sent
them or appointed them or spoken to them.
They are prophesying to you false visions, div-

3他們的貴冑打發家僮打水，
　　他們來到水池，
　　見沒有水，
　　就拿着空器皿，
　　蒙羞慚愧，
　　抱頭而回。
4耕地的
　　也蒙羞抱頭，
　　因為無雨降在地上，
　　地都乾裂。
5田野的母鹿生下小鹿，
　　就撇棄，
　　因為無草。
6野驢站在淨光的高處，
　　喘氣好像野狗，
　　因為無草，
　　眼目失明。"

7耶和華啊，
　　我們的罪孽雖然作見證告我們，
　　還求你為你名的緣故行事。
　　我們本是多次背道，
　　得罪了你。
8以色列所盼望
　　在患難時作他救主的啊，
　　你為何在這地像寄居的，
　　又像行路的只住一宵呢？
9你為何像受驚的人，
　　像不能救人的勇士呢？
耶和華啊，你仍在我們中間，
　　我們也稱為你名下的人，
　　求你不要離開我們。

10耶和華對這百姓如此說：

　　"這百姓喜愛妄行（註：原文作"飄流"），
　　不禁止腳步，
　　所以耶和華不悅納他們，
　　現今要記念他們的罪孽，
　　追討他們的罪惡。"

11耶和華又對我說："不要為這
百姓祈禱求好處。12他們禁食的時
候，我不聽他們的呼求；他們獻燔祭
和素祭，我也不悅納。我卻要用刀
劍、饑荒、瘟疫滅絕他們。"

13我就說："唉！主耶和華啊，
那些先知常對他們說：'你們必不看
見刀劍，也不遭遇饑荒，耶和華要在
這地方賜你們長久的平安。' "

14耶和華對我說："那些先知託
我的名假預言，我並沒有打發他
們，沒有吩咐他們，也沒有對他們說
話。他們向你們預言的，乃是虛假的

異象和占卜，並虛無的事，以及本
心的詭詐。15所以耶和華如此說：論
到託我名說預言的那些先知，我並
沒有打發他們。他們還說這地不能
有刀劍饑荒，其實那些先知必被刀
劍饑荒滅絕。16聽他們說預言的百
姓，必因饑荒刀劍拋在耶路撒冷的
街道上，無人葬埋。他們連妻子帶
兒女，都是如此。我必將他們的惡
倒在他們身上（註：或作「我必使他們罪
惡的報應臨到他們身上」）。

17 "你要將這話對他們說：

" '願我眼淚汪汪，
　　晝夜不息，
因為我百姓（註：原文作「民的處女」）
　　受了裂口破壞的大傷。
18我若出往田間，
　　就見有被刀殺的；
我若進入城內，
　　就見有因饑荒患病的。
連先知帶祭司在國中往來，
　　也是毫無知識（註：或作「不知怎樣
　　才好」）。' "

19你全然棄掉猶大嗎？
　　你心厭惡錫安嗎？
為何擊打我們，
　　以致無法醫治呢？
我們指望平安，
　　卻得不着好處；
指望痊愈，
　　不料，受了驚惶。
20耶和華啊，我們承認自己的罪惡，
　　和我們列祖的罪孽，
　　因我們得罪了你。
21求你為你名的緣故，不厭惡我們，
　　不辱沒你榮耀的寶座；
求你追念，
　　不要背了與我們所立的約。
22外邦人虛無的神中，
　　有能降雨的嗎？天能自降甘霖嗎？
耶和華我們的神啊，
　　能如此的不是你嗎？
所以我們仍要等候你，
　　因為這一切都是你所造的。

15 耶和華對我說："雖有摩西
和撒母耳站在我面前代求，
我的心也不顧惜這百姓。你
將他們從我眼前趕出，叫他們去

inations, idolatries*a* and the delusions of their
own minds. 15Therefore, this is what the LORD
says about the prophets who are prophesying in
my name: I did not send them, yet they are saying, 'No sword or famine will touch this land.'
Those same prophets will perish by sword and
famine. 16And the people they are prophesying
to will be thrown out into the streets of Jerusalem because of the famine and sword. There
will be no one to bury them or their wives, their
sons or their daughters. I will pour out on them
the calamity they deserve.

17"Speak this word to them:

" 'Let my eyes overflow with tears
　　night and day without ceasing;
for my virgin daughter—my people—
　　has suffered a grievous wound,
　　a crushing blow.
18If I go into the country,
　　I see those slain by the sword;
if I go into the city,
　　I see the ravages of famine.
Both prophet and priest
　　have gone to a land they know not.' "

19Have you rejected Judah completely?
　　Do you despise Zion?
Why have you afflicted us
　　so that we cannot be healed?
We hoped for peace
　　but no good has come,
for a time of healing
　　but there is only terror.
20O LORD, we acknowledge our wickedness
　　and the guilt of our fathers;
　　we have indeed sinned against you.
21For the sake of your name do not despise us;
　　do not dishonor your glorious throne.
Remember your covenant with us
　　and do not break it.
22Do any of the worthless idols of the nations
　　bring rain?
Do the skies themselves send down showers?
No, it is you, O LORD our God.
Therefore our hope is in you,
　　for you are the one who does all this.

15 Then the LORD said to me: "Even if
Moses and Samuel were to stand before
me, my heart would not go out to this
people. Send them away from my presence! Let

a 14 Or visions, worthless divinations

them go! ²And if they ask you, 'Where shall we go?' tell them, 'This is what the LORD says:

" 'Those destined for death, to death;
    those for the sword, to the sword;
    those for starvation, to starvation;
    those for captivity, to captivity.'

³"I will send four kinds of destroyers against them," declares the LORD, "the sword to kill and the dogs to drag away and the birds of the air and the beasts of the earth to devour and destroy. ⁴I will make them abhorrent to all the kingdoms of the earth because of what Manasseh son of Hezekiah king of Judah did in Jerusalem.

⁵"Who will have pity on you, O Jerusalem?
    Who will mourn for you?
    Who will stop to ask how you are?
⁶You have rejected me," declares the LORD.
    "You keep on backsliding.
So I will lay hands on you and destroy you;
    I can no longer show compassion.
⁷I will winnow them with a winnowing fork
    at the city gates of the land.
I will bring bereavement and destruction on
        my people,
    for they have not changed their ways.
⁸I will make their widows more numerous
    than the sand of the sea.
At midday I will bring a destroyer
    against the mothers of their young men;
suddenly I will bring down on them
    anguish and terror.
⁹The mother of seven will grow faint
    and breathe her last.
Her sun will set while it is still day;
    she will be disgraced and humiliated.
I will put the survivors to the sword
    before their enemies,"
                        declares the LORD.

¹⁰Alas, my mother, that you gave me birth,
    a man with whom the whole land strives
        and contends!
I have neither lent nor borrowed,
    yet everyone curses me.

¹¹The LORD said,

"Surely I will deliver you for a good purpose;
    surely I will make your enemies plead with
        you
    in times of disaster and times of distress.

吧！²他們問你說：'我們往哪裏去呢？'你便告訴他們：'耶和華如此說：

" '定為死亡的，必至死亡；
    定為刀殺的，必交刀殺；
    定為飢荒的，必遭飢荒；
    定為擄掠的，必被擄掠。'"

³耶和華說："我命定四樣害他們，就是：刀劍殺戮，狗類撕裂，空中的飛鳥和地上的野獸吞吃毀滅。⁴又必使他們在天下萬國中拋來拋去，都因猶大王希西家的兒子瑪拿西在耶路撒冷所行的事。

⁵"耶路撒冷啊，誰可憐你呢？
    誰為你悲傷呢？
    誰轉身問你的安呢？"
⁶耶和華說："你棄絕了我，
    轉身退後，
因此我伸手攻擊你、毀壞你。
    我後悔，甚不耐煩。
⁷我在境內各城門口（註：或作"我在這地邊界的關口"）用簸箕簸了我的百姓，
    使他們喪掉兒女。
我毀滅他們，
    他們仍不轉離所行的道。
⁸他們的寡婦在我面前
    比海沙更多。
我使滅命的午間來，
    攻擊少年人的母親，
使痛苦驚嚇
    忽然臨到她身上。
⁹生過七子的婦人
    力衰氣絕，
尚在白晝，日頭忽落，
    她抱愧蒙羞。
其餘的人，我必在他們敵人跟前，
    交與刀劍。"
                        這是耶和華說的。

¹⁰我的母親哪，我有禍了！
    因你生我作為遍地相爭相競的人。
我素來沒有借貸與人，
    人也沒有借貸與我，
    人人卻都咒罵我。

¹¹耶和華說：

"我必要堅固你，
    使你得好處；
災禍苦難臨到的時候，
    我必要使仇敵央求你。

12 "人豈能將銅與鐵,
　　就是北方的鐵折斷呢?

13 我必因你在四境之內
　　所犯的一切罪,
把你的貨物財寶當掠物,
　　白白地交給仇敵。

14 我也必使仇敵帶這掠物
　　到你所不認識的地去,
因我怒中起的火
　　要將你們焚燒。"

15 耶和華啊,你是知道的,
　　求你記念我,眷顧我,
向逼迫我的人為我報仇;
不要向他們忍怒取我的命,
　　要知道我為你的緣故受了凌辱。

16 耶和華萬軍之神啊,
　　我得着你的言語,就當食物吃了,
你的言語是我心中的歡喜快樂,
　　因我是稱為你名下的人。

17 我沒有坐在宴樂人的會中,
　　也沒有歡樂;
我因你的感動 (註:"感動"原文作"手")
　　獨自靜坐,因你使我滿心憤恨。

18 我的痛苦為何長久不止呢?
　　我的傷痕為何無法醫治,
不能痊愈呢?
難道你待我有詭詐,
　　像流乾的河道嗎?

19 耶和華如此說:
"你若歸回,我就將你再帶來,
　　使你站在我面前;
你若將寶貴的和下賤的分別出來,
　　你就可以當作我的口。
他們必歸向你,
　　你卻不可歸向他們。

20 我必使你向這百姓
　　成為堅固的銅牆;
他們必攻擊你,
　　卻不能勝你,
因我與你同在,
　　要拯救你、搭救你。"
　　　　　　　　　　　這是耶和華說的。

21 "我必搭救你脫離惡人的手,
救贖你脫離強暴人的手。"

災難的日子

16 耶和華的話又臨到我說: 2 "你在這地方不可娶妻,生兒養女。" 3 因為論到在這地方所生的兒女,又論到在這國中生

12 "Can a man break iron—
iron from the north—or bronze?

13 Your wealth and your treasures
I will give as plunder, without charge,
because of all your sins
throughout your country.

14 I will enslave you to your enemies
in[a] a land you do not know,
for my anger will kindle a fire
that will burn against you."

15 You understand, O LORD;
remember me and care for me.
Avenge me on my persecutors.
You are long-suffering—do not take me away;
think of how I suffer reproach for your sake.

16 When your words came, I ate them;
they were my joy and my heart's delight,
for I bear your name,
O LORD God Almighty.

17 I never sat in the company of revelers,
never made merry with them;
I sat alone because your hand was on me
and you had filled me with indignation.

18 Why is my pain unending
and my wound grievous and incurable?
Will you be to me like a deceptive brook,
like a spring that fails?

19 Therefore this is what the LORD says:

"If you repent, I will restore you
that you may serve me;
if you utter worthy, not worthless, words,
you will be my spokesman.
Let this people turn to you,
but you must not turn to them.

20 I will make you a wall to this people,
a fortified wall of bronze;
they will fight against you
but will not overcome you,
for I am with you
to rescue and save you,"

declares the LORD.

21 "I will save you from the hands of the wicked
and redeem you from the grasp of the cruel."

Day of Disaster

16 Then the word of the LORD came to me: 2 "You must not marry and have sons or daughters in this place." 3 For this is what the LORD says about the sons and daugh-

---

a 14 Some Hebrew manuscripts, Septuagint and Syriac (see also Jer. 17:4); most Hebrew manuscripts I will cause your enemies to bring you / into

ters born in this land and about the women who are their mothers and the men who are their fathers: 4"They will die of deadly diseases. They will not be mourned or buried but will be like refuse lying on the ground. They will perish by sword and famine, and their dead bodies will become food for the birds of the air and the beasts of the earth."

5For this is what the LORD says: "Do not enter a house where there is a funeral meal; do not go to mourn or show sympathy, because I have withdrawn my blessing, my love and my pity from this people," declares the LORD. 6"Both high and low will die in this land. They will not be buried or mourned, and no one will cut himself or shave his head for them. 7No one will offer food to comfort those who mourn for the dead—not even for a father or a mother—nor will anyone give them a drink to console them.

8"And do not enter a house where there is feasting and sit down to eat and drink. 9For this is what the LORD Almighty, the God of Israel, says: Before your eyes and in your days I will bring an end to the sounds of joy and gladness and to the voices of bride and bridegroom in this place.

10"When you tell these people all this and they ask you, 'Why has the LORD decreed such a great disaster against us? What wrong have we done? What sin have we committed against the LORD our God?' 11then say to them, 'It is because your fathers forsook me,' declares the LORD, 'and followed other gods and served and worshiped them. They forsook me and did not keep my law. 12But you have behaved more wickedly than your fathers. See how each of you is following the stubbornness of his evil heart instead of obeying me. 13So I will throw you out of this land into a land neither you nor your fathers have known, and there you will serve other gods day and night, for I will show you no favor.'

14"However, the days are coming," declares the LORD, "when men will no longer say, 'As surely as the LORD lives, who brought the Israelites up out of Egypt,' 15but they will say, 'As surely as the LORD lives, who brought the Israelites up out of the land of the north and out of all the countries where he had banished them.' For I will restore them to the land I gave their forefathers.

16"But now I will send for many fishermen," declares the LORD, "and they will catch them. After that I will send for many hunters, and they will hunt them down on every mountain and hill and from the crevices of the rocks. 17My eyes

養他們的父母，耶和華如此說：4"他們必死得甚苦，無人哀哭，必不得葬埋；必在地上像糞土，必被刀劍和饑荒滅絕；他們的屍首必給空中的飛鳥和地上的野獸作食物。"

5耶和華如此說："不要進入喪家，不要去哀哭，也不要為他們悲傷，因我已將我的平安、慈愛、憐憫從這百姓奪去了。"這是耶和華說的。"6連大帶小，都必在這地死亡，不得葬埋。人必不為他們哀哭，不用刀割身，也不使頭光禿。7他們有喪事，人必不為他們擘餅，因死人安慰他們。他們喪父喪母，人也不給他們一杯酒安慰他們。

8"你不可進入宴樂的家，與他們同坐吃喝。9因為萬軍之耶和華以色列的神如此說：你們還活着的日子在你們眼前，我必使歡喜和快樂的聲音、新郎和新婦的聲音從這地方止息了。

10"你將這一切的話指示這百姓，他們問你說：'耶和華為甚麼說，要降這大災禍攻擊我們呢？我們有甚麼罪孽呢？我們向耶和華我們的神犯了甚麼罪呢？'11你就對他們說：'耶和華說：因為你們列祖離棄我，隨從別神，侍奉敬拜，不遵守我的律法。12而且你們行惡比你們列祖更甚；因為各人隨從自己頑梗的惡心行事，甚至不聽從我。13所以我必將你們從這地趕出，直趕到你們和你們列祖素不認識的地，你們在那裏必晝夜侍奉別神，因為我必不向你們施恩。'"

14耶和華說："日子將到，人必不再指着那領以色列人從埃及地上來之永生的耶和華起誓，15卻要指着那領以色列人從北方之地，並趕他們到的各國上來之永生的耶和華起誓，並且我要領他們再入我從前賜給他們列祖之地。"

16耶和華說："我要召許多打魚的，把以色列人打上來，然後我要召許多打獵的，從各山上、各岡上、各石穴中獵取他們。17因我的眼目察看他們的一切行為，他們不能在我面前遮掩；他們的罪孽，也不能在我眼前隱藏。¹⁸我先要加倍報應他們的罪孽和罪惡，因為他們用可憎之屍玷污我的地土，又用可厭之物充滿我的產業。"

¹⁹耶和華啊，
　你是我的力量，是我的保障，
　在苦難之日是我的避難所。
列國人必從地極來到你這裏，說：
　"我們列祖所承受的，
　不過是虛假，
　是虛空無益之物。
²⁰人豈可為自己製造神呢？
　其實這不是神！"

²¹耶和華說："我要使他們知道，
　就是這一次使他們知道
　我的手和我的能力；
　他們就知道
　我的名是耶和華了。"

17 "猶大的罪，
　是用鐵筆、
　用金鋼鑽記錄的，
　銘刻在他們的心版上
　和壇角上。
²他們的兒女，
　記念他們高岡上、
　青翠樹旁的壇和木偶。

³我田野的山哪，
　我必因你
　在四境之內所犯的罪，
把你的貨物，財寶，
　並邱壇當掠物交給仇敵。
⁴並且你因自己的罪，
　必失去我所賜給你的產業。
我也必使你在你所不認識的地上，
　服侍你的仇敵。
因為你使我怒中起火，
　直燒到永遠。"

⁵耶和華如此說：

"倚靠人血肉的膀臂，
　心中離棄耶和華的，
　那人有禍了！
⁶因他必像沙漠的杜松，
　不見福樂來到，

are on all their ways; they are not hidden from me, nor is their sin concealed from my eyes. ¹⁸I will repay them double for their wickedness and their sin, because they have defiled my land with the lifeless forms of their vile images and have filled my inheritance with their detestable idols."

¹⁹O LORD, my strength and my fortress,
　my refuge in time of distress,
to you the nations will come
　from the ends of the earth and say,
"Our fathers possessed nothing but false
　gods,
　worthless idols that did them no good.
²⁰Do men make their own gods?
　Yes, but they are not gods!"

²¹"Therefore I will teach them—
　this time I will teach them
　my power and might.
Then they will know
　that my name is the LORD.

17 "Judah's sin is engraved with an iron
　tool,
　inscribed with a flint point,
on the tablets of their hearts
　and on the horns of their altars.
²Even their children remember
　their altars and Asherah poles[a]
beside the spreading trees
　and on the high hills.
³My mountain in the land
　and your[b] wealth and all your treasures
I will give away as plunder,
　together with your high places,
　because of sin throughout your country.
⁴Through your own fault you will lose
　the inheritance I gave you.
I will enslave you to your enemies
　in a land you do not know,
for you have kindled my anger,
　and it will burn forever."

⁵This is what the LORD says:

"Cursed is the one who trusts in man,
　who depends on flesh for his strength
　and whose heart turns away from the LORD.
⁶He will be like a bush in the wastelands;
　he will not see prosperity when it comes.

a 2 That is, symbols of the goddess Asherah　b 2,3 Or hills /
³and the mountains of the land. / Your

He will dwell in the parched places of the
    desert,
  in a salt land where no one lives.

卻要住曠野乾旱之處，
  無人居住的鹹地。

7"But blessed is the man who trusts in the LORD,
  whose confidence is in him.
8He will be like a tree planted by the water
  that sends out its roots by the stream.
  It does not fear when heat comes;
  its leaves are always green.
  It has no worries in a year of drought
  and never fails to bear fruit."

7 "倚靠耶和華，以耶和華為可靠的，
  那人有福了！
8他必像樹栽於水旁，
  在河邊扎根，
  炎熱來到，並不懼怕，
  葉子仍必青翠，
  在乾旱之年毫無掛慮，
  而且結果不止。"

9The heart is deceitful above all things
  and beyond cure.
  Who can understand it?

9人心比萬物都詭詐，
  壞到極處，
  誰能識透呢？

10"I the LORD search the heart
  and examine the mind,
  to reward a man according to his conduct,
  according to what his deeds deserve."

10 "我耶和華是鑒察人心，
  試驗人肺腑的，
  要照各人所行的
  和他做事的結果報應他。"

11Like a partridge that hatches eggs it did not lay
  is the man who gains riches by unjust means.
  When his life is half gone, they will desert him,
  and in the end he will prove to be a fool.

11那不按正道得財的，
  好像鷓鴣孵不是自己下的蛋；
  到了中年，那財都必離開他，
  他終久成為愚頑人。

12A glorious throne, exalted from the beginning,
  is the place of our sanctuary.
13O LORD, the hope of Israel,
  all who forsake you will be put to shame.
  Those who turn away from you will be
    written in the dust
  because they have forsaken the LORD,
  the spring of living water.

12我們的聖所是榮耀的寶座，
  從太初安置在高處。
13耶和華以色列的盼望啊，
  凡離棄你的必至蒙羞。
  耶和華說：離開我的，
  他們的名字必寫在土裏，
  因為他們離棄我
  這活水的泉源。

14Heal me, O LORD, and I will be healed;
  save me and I will be saved,
  for you are the one I praise.
15They keep saying to me,
  "Where is the word of the LORD?
  Let it now be fulfilled!"
16I have not run away from being your
    shepherd;
  you know I have not desired the day of
    despair.
  What passes my lips is open before you.
17Do not be a terror to me;
  you are my refuge in the day of disaster.
18Let my persecutors be put to shame,
  but keep me from shame;
  let them be terrified,
  but keep me from terror.
  Bring on them the day of disaster;
  destroy them with double destruction.

14耶和華啊，求你醫治我，我便痊愈；
  拯救我，我便得救；
  因你是我所讚美的。
15他們對我說：
  "耶和華的話在哪裏呢？
  叫這話應驗吧！"
16至於我，那跟從你作牧人的職分，
  我並沒有急忙離棄，
  也沒有想那災殃的日子，
  這是你知道的。
  我口中所出的言語都在你面前。
17不要使我因你驚恐；
  當災禍的日子，你是我的避難所。
18願那些逼迫我的蒙羞，
  卻不要使我蒙羞；
  使他們驚惶，
  卻不要使我驚惶；
  使災禍的日子臨到他們，
  以加倍的毀壞毀壞他們。

以安息日為聖日

19耶和華對我如此說：「你去站在平民的門口，就是猶大君王出入的門，又站在耶路撒冷的各門口，20對他們說：『你們這猶大君王和猶大眾人，並耶路撒冷的一切居民，凡從這些門進入的，都當聽耶和華的話。21耶和華如此說：你們要謹慎，不要在安息日擔甚麼擔子過耶路撒冷的各門；22也不要在安息日從家中擔出擔子去。無論何工都不可做，只要以安息日為聖日，正如我所吩咐你們列祖的。』23他們卻不聽從，不側耳而聽，竟硬着頸項不聽，不受教訓。24耶和華說：你們若留意聽從我，在安息日不擔甚麼擔子進入這城的各門，只以安息日為聖日，在那日無論何工都不做，25那時就有坐大衛寶座的君王和首領，他們與猶大人，並耶路撒冷的居民，或坐車，或騎馬進入這城的各門。而且這城必存到永遠。26也必有人從猶大城邑和耶路撒冷四圍的各處，從便雅憫地、高原、山地、並南地而來，都帶燔祭、平安祭、素祭和乳香，並感謝祭，到耶和華的殿去。27你們若不聽從我，不以安息日為聖日，仍在安息日擔擔子進入耶路撒冷的各門，我必在各門中點火，這火也必燒毀耶路撒冷的宮殿，不能熄滅。』」

在窰匠的家裏

18 耶和華的話臨到耶利米說：2「你起來，下到窰匠的家裏去，我在那裏要使你聽我的話。」3我就下到窰匠的家裏去，正遇他轉輪做器皿。4窰匠用泥做的器皿，在他手中做壞了，他又用這泥另做別的器皿。窰匠看怎樣好，就怎樣做。

5耶和華的話就臨到我說：6「耶和華說：以色列家啊，我待你們，豈不能照這窰匠弄泥麼？以色列家啊，泥在窰匠的手中怎樣，你們在我的手中也怎樣。7我何時論到一邦或一國說：要拔出、拆毀、毀壞；8我所說的那一邦，若是轉意離開他們的惡，我就必後悔，不將我想要施行的災禍降與他們；9我何時論到

Keeping the Sabbath Holy

19This is what the LORD said to me: "Go and stand at the gate of the people, through which the kings of Judah go in and out; stand also at all the other gates of Jerusalem. 20Say to them, 'Hear the word of the LORD, O kings of Judah and all people of Judah and everyone living in Jerusalem who come through these gates. 21This is what the LORD says: Be careful not to carry a load on the Sabbath day or bring it through the gates of Jerusalem. 22Do not bring a load out of your houses or do any work on the Sabbath, but keep the Sabbath day holy, as I commanded your forefathers. 23Yet they did not listen or pay attention; they were stiff-necked and would not listen or respond to discipline. 24But if you are careful to obey me, declares the LORD, and bring no load through the gates of this city on the Sabbath, but keep the Sabbath day holy by not doing any work on it, 25then kings who sit on David's throne will come through the gates of this city with their officials. They and their officials will come riding in chariots and on horses, accompanied by the men of Judah and those living in Jerusalem, and this city will be inhabited forever. 26People will come from the towns of Judah and the villages around Jerusalem, from the territory of Benjamin and the western foothills, from the hill country and the Negev, bringing burnt offerings and sacrifices, grain offerings, incense and thank offerings to the house of the LORD. 27But if you do not obey me to keep the Sabbath day holy by not carrying any load as you come through the gates of Jerusalem on the Sabbath day, then I will kindle an unquenchable fire in the gates of Jerusalem that will consume her fortresses.' "

At the Potter's House

18 This is the word that came to Jeremiah from the LORD: 2"Go down to the potter's house, and there I will give you my message." 3So I went down to the potter's house, and I saw him working at the wheel. 4But the pot he was shaping from the clay was marred in his hands; so the potter formed it into another pot, shaping it as seemed best to him.

5Then the word of the LORD came to me: 6"O house of Israel, can I not do with you as this potter does?" declares the LORD. "Like clay in the hand of the potter, so are you in my hand, O house of Israel. 7If at any time I announce that a nation or kingdom is to be uprooted, torn down and destroyed, 8and if that nation I warned repents of its evil, then I will relent and not inflict on it the disaster I had planned. 9And if at another time I announce that a nation or king-dom is to be built up and planted, [10]and if it does evil in my sight and does not obey me, then I will reconsider the good I had intended to do for it.

[11]"Now therefore say to the people of Judah and those living in Jerusalem, 'This is what the LORD says: Look! I am preparing a disaster for you and devising a plan against you. So turn from your evil ways, each one of you, and re-form your ways and your actions.' [12]But they will reply, 'It's no use. We will continue with our own plans; each of us will follow the stub-bornness of his evil heart.' "

[13]Therefore this is what the LORD says:

"Inquire among the nations:
　Who has ever heard anything like this?
A most horrible thing has been done
　by Virgin Israel.
[14]Does the snow of Lebanon
　ever vanish from its rocky slopes?
Do its cool waters from distant sources
　ever cease to flow?[a]
[15]Yet my people have forgotten me;
　they burn incense to worthless idols,
which made them stumble in their ways
　and in the ancient paths.
They made them walk in bypaths
　and on roads not built up.
[16]Their land will be laid waste,
　an object of lasting scorn;
all who pass by will be appalled
　and will shake their heads.
[17]Like a wind from the east,
　I will scatter them before their enemies;
I will show them my back and not my face
　in the day of their disaster."

[18]They said, "Come, let's make plans against Jeremiah; for the teaching of the law by the priest will not be lost, nor will counsel from the wise, nor the word from the prophets. So come, let's attack him with our tongues and pay no attention to anything he says."

[19]Listen to me, O LORD;
　hear what my accusers are saying!
[20]Should good be repaid with evil?
　Yet they have dug a pit for me.
Remember that I stood before you
　and spoke in their behalf
to turn your wrath away from them.

a 14 The meaning of the Hebrew for this sentence is uncertain.

一邦或一國說：要建立、栽植；[10]他們若行我眼中看為惡的事，不聽從我的話，我就必後悔，不將我所說的福氣賜給他們。

[11]"現在你要對猶大人和耶路撒冷的居民說：'耶和華如此說：我造出災禍攻擊你們，定意刑罰你們。你們各人當回頭離開所行的惡道，改正你們的行動作為。'[12]他們卻說：'這是枉然！我們要照自己的計謀去行，各人隨自己頑梗的惡心做事。'"

[13]所以耶和華如此說：

"你們且往各國訪問，
　有誰聽見這樣的事，
以色列民（註：原文作"處女"）
　行了一件極可憎惡的事。
[14]黎巴嫩的雪
　從田野的磐石上豈能斷絕呢？
　從遠處流下的涼水豈能乾涸呢？

[15]我的百姓竟忘記我，
　向假神燒香，
使他們在所行的路上，
　在古道上絆跌，
使他們行
　沒有修築的斜路，
[16]以致他們的地令人驚駭，
　常常嗤笑，
凡經過這地的，
　必驚駭搖頭。
[17]我必在仇敵面前分散他們，
　好像用東風吹散一樣。
遭難的日子，我必以背向他們，
　不以面向他們。"

[18]他們就說："來吧！我們可以設計謀害耶利米。因為我們有祭司講律法，智慧人設謀略，先知說預言，都不能斷絕。來吧！我們可以用舌頭擊打他，不要理會他的一切話。"

[19]耶和華啊，求你理會我，
　且聽那些與我爭競之人的話。
[20]豈可以惡報善呢？
　他們竟挖坑要害我的性命。
求你記念我怎樣站在你面前
　為他們代求，
　要使你的忿怒向他們轉消。

21故此，願你將他們的兒女
　　交與饑荒和刀劍；
　　願他們的妻無子，且作寡婦；
　　又願他們的男人被死亡所滅，
　　他們的少年人在陣上被刀擊殺。
22你使敵軍忽然臨到他們的時候，
　　願人聽見哀聲
　　　從他們的屋內發出，
　　因他們挖坑要捉拿我，
　　暗設網羅要絆我的腳。
23耶和華啊，他們要殺我的那一切
　　計謀，你都知道。
　　不要赦免他們的罪孽，
　　也不要從你面前塗抹他們的罪惡，
　　要叫他們在你面前跌倒，
　　願你發怒的時候罰辦他們。

19 耶和華如此說："你去買窰匠的瓦瓶，又帶百姓中的長老和祭司中的長老，2出去到欣嫩子谷，哈珥西（註："哈珥西"就是"瓦片"的意思）的門口那裏，宣告我所吩咐你的話，3說："猶大君王和耶路撒冷的居民哪，當聽耶和華的話！萬軍之耶和華以色列的神如此說：我必使災禍臨到這地方，凡聽見的人都必耳鳴；4因為他們和他們列祖，並猶大君王離棄我，將這地方看為平常，在這裏向素不認識的別神燒香，又使這地方滿了無辜人的血。5又建築巴力的邱壇，好在火中焚燒自己的兒子，作為燔祭獻給巴力。這不是我所吩咐的，不是我所提說的，也不是我心所起的意。6耶和華說：因此，日子將到，這地方不再稱為陀斐特和欣嫩子谷，反倒稱為殺戮谷。

7 "'我必在這地方使猶大和耶路撒冷的計謀落空，也必使他們在仇敵面前倒於刀下，並尋索其命的人手下。他們的屍首，我必給空中的飛鳥和地上的野獸作食物。8我必使這城令人驚駭嗤笑；凡經過的人，必因這城所遭的災驚駭嗤笑。9我必使他們在圍困窘迫之中，就是仇敵和尋索其命的人窘迫他們的時候，各人吃自己兒女的肉和朋友的肉。'

21So give their children over to famine;
　hand them over to the power of the sword.
Let their wives be made childless and widows;
　let their men be put to death,
　their young men slain by the sword in battle.
22Let a cry be heard from their houses
　when you suddenly bring invaders against
　　them,
　for they have dug a pit to capture me
　and have hidden snares for my feet.
23But you know, O LORD,
　all their plots to kill me.
Do not forgive their crimes
　or blot out their sins from your sight.
Let them be overthrown before you;
　deal with them in the time of your anger.

19 This is what the LORD says: "Go and buy a clay jar from a potter. Take along some of the elders of the people and of the priests 2and go out to the Valley of Ben Hinnom, near the entrance of the Potsherd Gate. There proclaim the words I tell you, 3and say, 'Hear the word of the LORD, O kings of Judah and people of Jerusalem. This is what the LORD Almighty, the God of Israel, says: Listen! I am going to bring a disaster on this place that will make the ears of everyone who hears of it tingle. 4For they have forsaken me and made this a place of foreign gods; they have burned sacrifices in it to gods that neither they nor their fathers nor the kings of Judah ever knew, and they have filled this place with the blood of the innocent. 5They have built the high places of Baal to burn their sons in the fire as offerings to Baal—something I did not command or mention, nor did it enter my mind. 6So beware, the days are coming, declares the LORD, when people will no longer call this place Topheth or the Valley of Ben Hinnom, but the Valley of Slaughter.

7" 'In this place I will ruin[a] the plans of Judah and Jerusalem. I will make them fall by the sword before their enemies, at the hands of those who seek their lives, and I will give their carcasses as food to the birds of the air and the beasts of the earth. 8I will devastate this city and make it an object of scorn; all who pass by will be appalled and will scoff because of all its wounds. 9I will make them eat the flesh of their sons and daughters, and they will eat one another's flesh during the stress of the siege imposed on them by the enemies who seek their lives.'

a 7 The Hebrew for ruin sounds like the Hebrew for jar (see verses 1 and 10).

10"Then break the jar while those who go with you are watching, 11and say to them, 'This is what the LORD Almighty says: I will smash this nation and this city just as this potter's jar is smashed and cannot be repaired. They will bury the dead in Topheth until there is no more room. 12This is what I will do to this place and to those who live here, declares the LORD. I will make this city like Topheth. 13The houses in Jerusalem and those of the kings of Judah will be defiled like this place, Topheth—all the houses where they burned incense on the roofs to all the starry hosts and poured out drink offerings to other gods.' "

14Jeremiah then returned from Topheth, where the LORD had sent him to prophesy, and stood in the court of the LORD's temple and said to all the people, 15"This is what the LORD Almighty, the God of Israel, says: 'Listen! I am going to bring on this city and the villages around it every disaster I pronounced against them, because they were stiff-necked and would not listen to my words.' "

Jeremiah and Pashhur

20 When the priest Pashhur son of Immer, the chief officer in the temple of the LORD, heard Jeremiah prophesying these things, 2he had Jeremiah the prophet beaten and put in the stocks at the Upper Gate of Benjamin at the LORD's temple. 3The next day, when Pashhur released him from the stocks, Jeremiah said to him, "The LORD's name for you is not Pashhur, but Magor-Missabib.ᵃ 4For this is what the LORD says: 'I will make you a terror to yourself and to all your friends; with your own eyes you will see them fall by the sword of their enemies. I will hand all Judah over to the king of Babylon, who will carry them away to Babylon or put them to the sword. 5I will hand over to their enemies all the wealth of this city—all its products, all its valuables and all the treasures of the kings of Judah. They will take it away as plunder and carry it off to Babylon. 6And you, Pashhur, and all who live in your house will go into exile to Babylon. There you will die and be buried, you and all your friends to whom you have prophesied lies.' "

Jeremiah's Complaint

7O LORD, you deceivedᵇ me, and I was deceivedᵇ;
  you overpowered me and prevailed.
I am ridiculed all day long;
  everyone mocks me.

10 "你要在同去的人眼前打碎那瓶，11對他們說：'萬軍之耶和華如此說：我要照樣打碎這民和這城，正如人打碎窰匠的瓦器，以致不能再復圓。並且人要在陀斐特葬埋屍首，甚至無處可葬。12耶和華說：我必向這地方和其中的居民如此行，使這城與陀斐特一樣。13耶路撒冷的房屋和猶大君王的宮殿，是已經被玷污的，就是他們在其上向天上的萬象燒香，向別神澆奠祭的宮殿房屋，都必與陀斐特一樣。'"

14耶利米從陀斐特，就是耶和華差他去說預言的地方回來，站在耶和華殿的院中，對眾人說：15"萬軍之耶和華以色列的神如此說：'我必使我所說的一切災禍臨到這城和屬城的一切城邑，因為他們硬着頸項，不聽我的話。'"

耶利米與巴施戶珥

20 祭司音麥的兒子巴施戶珥作耶和華殿的總管，聽見耶利米預言這些事，2他就打先知耶利米，用耶和華殿裏便雅憫高門內的枷，將他枷在那裏。3次日，巴施戶珥將耶利米開枷釋放。於是耶利米對他說："耶和華不是叫你的名為巴施戶珥，乃是叫你瑪歌珥米撒畢（註：就是"四面驚嚇"的意思），4因耶和華如此說：'我必使你自覺驚嚇，你也必使眾朋友驚嚇；他們必倒在仇敵的刀下，你也必親眼看見。我必將猶大人全交在巴比倫王的手中；他要將他們擄到巴比倫去，也要用刀將他們殺戮。5並且我要將這城中的一切貨財和勞碌得來的，並一切珍寶，以及猶大君王所有的寶物，都交在他們仇敵的手中，仇敵要當作掠物，帶到巴比倫去。6你這巴施戶珥和一切住在你家中的人都必被擄去，你和你的眾朋友，就是你向他們說假預言的都必到巴比倫去，要死在那裏，葬在那裏。'"

耶利米的埋怨

7耶和華啊，你曾勸導我，
  我也聽了你的勸導。
你比我有力量，且勝了我；
  我終日成為笑話，人人都戲弄我。

ᵃ 3 *Magor-Missabib* means *terror on every side.*　ᵇ 7 Or *persuaded*

⁸我每逢講論的時候，就發出哀聲，
　我喊叫說：有強暴和毀滅！
因為耶和華的話
　終日成了我的凌辱、譏刺。
⁹我若說﹕“我不再提耶和華，
　也不再奉他的名講論”，
我便心裏覺得似乎有燒着的火
　閉塞在我骨中，
我就含忍不住，
　不能自禁。
¹⁰我聽見了許多人的譏謗，
　四圍都是驚嚇，
就是我知己的朋友也都窺探我，
　願我跌倒，說：
“告他吧！我們也要告他！
　或者他被引誘，
我們就能勝他，
　在他身上報仇。”
¹¹然而耶和華與我同在，
　好像甚可怕的勇士。
因此，逼迫我的必都絆跌，
　不能得勝；
他們必大大蒙羞，
　就是受永不忘記的羞辱，
　因為他們行事沒有智慧。
¹²試驗義人，察看人肺腑心腸的
　萬軍之耶和華啊，
求你容我見你在他們身上報仇，
　因我將我的案件向你稟明了。
¹³你們要向耶和華唱歌，
　讚美耶和華！
因他救了窮人的性命
　脫離惡人的手。
¹⁴願我生的那日受咒詛！
　願我母親產我的那日不蒙福！
¹⁵給我父親報信說
　“你得了兒子”，
使我父親甚歡喜的，
　願那人受咒詛！
¹⁶願那人像耶和華所傾覆
　而不後悔的城邑；
願他早晨聽見哀聲，
　晌午聽見吶喊。
¹⁷因他在我未出胎的時候不殺我，
　使我母親成了我的墳墓，
　胎就時常重大。
¹⁸我為何出胎
　見勞碌愁苦，
　使我的年日因羞愧消滅呢？

⁸Whenever I speak, I cry out
　proclaiming violence and destruction.
So the word of the LORD has brought me
　insult and reproach all day long.
⁹But if I say, "I will not mention him
　or speak any more in his name,"
his word is in my heart like a fire,
　a fire shut up in my bones.
I am weary of holding it in;
　indeed, I cannot.
¹⁰I hear many whispering,
　"Terror on every side!
　Report him! Let's report him!"
All my friends
　are waiting for me to slip, saying,
　"Perhaps he will be deceived;
then we will prevail over him
　and take our revenge on him."
¹¹But the LORD is with me like a mighty warrior;
　so my persecutors will stumble and not
　　prevail.
They will fail and be thoroughly disgraced;
　their dishonor will never be forgotten.
¹²O LORD Almighty, you who examine the
　righteous
and probe the heart and mind,
let me see your vengeance upon them,
　for to you I have committed my cause.
¹³Sing to the LORD!
　Give praise to the LORD!
He rescues the life of the needy
　from the hands of the wicked.
¹⁴Cursed be the day I was born!
　May the day my mother bore me not be
　　blessed!
¹⁵Cursed be the man who brought my father
　the news,
　who made him very glad, saying,
　"A child is born to you—a son!"
¹⁶May that man be like the towns
　the LORD overthrew without pity.
May he hear wailing in the morning,
　a battle cry at noon.
¹⁷For he did not kill me in the womb,
　with my mother as my grave,
　her womb enlarged forever.
¹⁸Why did I ever come out of the womb
　to see trouble and sorrow
　and to end my days in shame?

God Rejects Zedekiah's Request

21 The word came to Jeremiah from the LORD when King Zedekiah sent to him Pashhur son of Malkijah and the priest Zephaniah son of Maaseiah. They said: ²"Inquire now of the LORD for us because Nebuchadnezzar[a] king of Babylon is attacking us. Perhaps the LORD will perform wonders for us as in times past so that he will withdraw from us."

³But Jeremiah answered them, "Tell Zedekiah, ⁴This is what the LORD, the God of Israel, says: I am about to turn against you the weapons of war that are in your hands, which you are using to fight the king of Babylon and the Babylonians[b] who are outside the wall besieging you. And I will gather them inside this city. ⁵I myself will fight against you with an outstretched hand and a mighty arm in anger and fury and great wrath. ⁶I will strike down those who live in this city—both men and animals—and they will die of a terrible plague. ⁷After that, declares the LORD, I will hand over Zedekiah king of Judah, his officials and the people in this city who survive the plague, sword and famine, to Nebuchadnezzar king of Babylon and to their enemies who seek their lives. He will put them to the sword; he will show them no mercy or pity or compassion.'

⁸"Furthermore, tell the people, 'This is what the LORD says: See, I am setting before you the way of life and the way of death. ⁹Whoever stays in this city will die by the sword, famine or plague. But whoever goes out and surrenders to the Babylonians who are besieging you will live; he will escape with his life. ¹⁰I have determined to do this city harm and not good, declares the LORD. It will be given into the hands of the king of Babylon, and he will destroy it with fire.'

¹¹"Moreover, say to the royal house of Judah, 'Hear the word of the LORD; ¹²O house of David, this is what the LORD says:

" 'Administer justice every morning;
　rescue from the hand of his oppressor
　the one who has been robbed,
or my wrath will break out and burn like fire
　because of the evil you have done—
burn with no one to quench it.
¹³I am against you, ⌐Jerusalem,⌐
　you who live above this valley
　on the rocky plateau,

　　　　　　　　declares the LORD—

---

a 2 Hebrew *Nebuchadrezzar*, of which *Nebuchadnezzar* is a variant; here and often in Jeremiah and Ezekiel　b 4 Or *Chaldeans*; also in verse 9

神拒絕西底家的請求

21 耶和華的話臨到耶利米。那時，西底家王打發瑪基雅的兒子巴施戶珥和瑪西雅的兒子祭司西番雅去見耶利米，說：²"請你為我們求問耶和華，因為巴比倫王尼布甲尼撒來攻擊我們，或者耶和華照他一切奇妙的作為待我們，使巴比倫王離開我們上去。"

³耶利米對他們說："你們當對西底家這樣說：⁴'耶和華以色列的神如此說：我要使你們手中的兵器，就是你們在城外與巴比倫王和圍困你們的迦勒底人打仗的兵器翻轉過來，又要使這些都聚集在這城中。⁵並且我要在怒氣、忿怒和大惱恨中，用伸出來的手，並大能的膀臂，親自攻擊你們。⁶又要擊打這城的居民，連人帶牲畜都必遭遇大瘟疫死亡。⁷以後我要將猶大王西底家和他的臣僕百姓，就是在城內，從瘟疫、刀劍、饑荒中剩下的人，都交在巴比倫王尼布甲尼撒的手中和他們仇敵，並尋索其命的人手中。巴比倫王必用刀擊殺他們，不顧惜、不可憐、不憐憫。這是耶和華說的。'

⁸"你要對這百姓說：'耶和華如此說：看哪，我將生命的路和死亡的路擺在你們面前。⁹住在這城裏的必遭刀劍、饑荒、瘟疫而死；但出去歸降圍困你們迦勒底人的必得存活，要以自己的命為掠物。¹⁰耶和華說：我向這城變臉，降禍不降福，這城必交在巴比倫王的手中，他必用火焚燒。'

¹¹"至於猶大王的家，你們當聽耶和華的話。¹²大衛家啊，耶和華如此說：

" '你們每早晨要施行公平，
　拯救被搶奪的
　脫離欺壓人的手，
恐怕我的忿怒因你們的惡行發作，
　如火着起，
　甚至無人能以熄滅。
¹³耶和華說：
　住山谷
　和平原磐石上的居民，

你們說：誰能下來攻擊我們，
　　誰能進入我們的住處呢？
　　看哪，我與你們為敵。
¹⁴耶和華又說：
　　我必按你們做事的結果刑罰你們，
　　我也必使火在耶路撒冷的林中著起，
　　將他四圍所有的盡行燒滅。'"

審判臨到惡王

22 耶和華如此說："你下到猶大王的宮中，在那裏說這話。²說：'坐大衛寶座的猶大王啊，你和你的臣僕，並進入城門的百姓，都當聽耶和華的話！³耶和華如此說：你們要施行公平和公義，拯救被搶奪的脫離欺壓人的手；不可虧負寄居的和孤兒寡婦，不可以強暴待他們，在這地方也不可流無辜人的血。⁴你們若認真行這事，就必有坐大衛寶座的君王和他的臣僕、百姓，或坐車、或騎馬，從這城的各門進入。⁵你們若不聽這些話，耶和華說：我指著自己起誓，這城必變為荒場。'"

⁶耶和華論到猶大王的家如此說：

"我看你如基列，
　　如黎巴嫩頂，
然而，我必使你變為曠野，
　　為無人居住的城邑。
⁷我要預備行毀滅的人，
　　各拿器械攻擊你，
他們要砍下你佳美的香柏樹，
　　扔在火中。

⁸"許多國的民要經過這城，各人對鄰舍說：'耶和華為何向這大城如此行呢？'⁹他們必回答說：'是因離棄了耶和華他們神的約，侍奉敬拜別神。'"

¹⁰不要為死人哭號，
　　不要為他悲傷，
卻要為離家出外的人大大哭號，
　　因為他不得再回來，
　　也不得再見他的本國。

¹¹因為耶和華論到從這地方出去的猶大王約西亞的兒子沙龍（註：列王紀下23章30節名約哈斯），就是接續他父親約西亞作王的，這樣說："他必不得

you who say, "Who can come against us?
　　Who can enter our refuge?"
¹⁴I will punish you as your deeds deserve,
　　　　　　declares the LORD.
I will kindle a fire in your forests
　　that will consume everything around you.' "

Judgment Against Evil Kings

22 This is what the LORD says: "Go down to the palace of the king of Judah and proclaim this message there: ²'Hear the word of the LORD, O king of Judah, you who sit on David's throne—you, your officials and your people who come through these gates. ³This is what the LORD says: Do what is just and right. Rescue from the hand of his oppressor the one who has been robbed. Do no wrong or violence to the alien, the fatherless or the widow, and do not shed innocent blood in this place. ⁴For if you are careful to carry out these commands, then kings who sit on David's throne will come through the gates of this palace, riding in chariots and on horses, accompanied by their officials and their people. ⁵But if you do not obey these commands, declares the LORD, I swear by myself that this palace will become a ruin.' "

⁶For this is what the LORD says about the palace of the king of Judah:

"Though you are like Gilead to me,
　　like the summit of Lebanon,
I will surely make you like a desert,
　　like towns not inhabited.
⁷I will send destroyers against you,
　　each man with his weapons,
and they will cut up your fine cedar beams
　　and throw them into the fire.

⁸"People from many nations will pass by this city and will ask one another, 'Why has the LORD done such a thing to this great city?' ⁹And the answer will be: 'Because they have forsaken the covenant of the LORD their God and have worshiped and served other gods.' "

¹⁰Do not weep for the dead [king] or mourn his loss;
　　rather, weep bitterly for him who is exiled,
because he will never return
　　nor see his native land again.

¹¹For this is what the LORD says about Shallum[a] son of Josiah, who succeeded his father as king of Judah but has gone from this place: "He will

a 11 Also called Jehoahaz

never return. ¹²He will die in the place where they have led him captive; he will not see this land again."

¹³"Woe to him who builds his palace by unrighteousness,
　　his upper rooms by injustice,
making his countrymen work for nothing,
　　not paying them for their labor.
¹⁴He says, 'I will build myself a great palace
　　with spacious upper rooms.'
So he makes large windows in it,
　　panels it with cedar
　　and decorates it in red.

¹⁵"Does it make you a king
　　to have more and more cedar?
Did not your father have food and drink?
　　He did what was right and just,
　　so all went well with him.
¹⁶He defended the cause of the poor and needy,
　　and so all went well.
Is that not what it means to know me?"
　　declares the LORD.
¹⁷"But your eyes and your heart
　　are set only on dishonest gain,
on shedding innocent blood
　　and on oppression and extortion."

¹⁸Therefore this is what the LORD says about Jehoiakim son of Josiah king of Judah:

"They will not mourn for him:
　　'Alas, my brother! Alas, my sister!'
They will not mourn for him:
　　'Alas, my master! Alas, his splendor!'
¹⁹He will have the burial of a donkey—
　　dragged away and thrown
　　outside the gates of Jerusalem."

²⁰"Go up to Lebanon and cry out,
　　let your voice be heard in Bashan,
cry out from Abarim,
　　for all your allies are crushed.
²¹I warned you when you felt secure,
　　but you said, 'I will not listen!'
This has been your way from your youth;
　　you have not obeyed me.
²²The wind will drive all your shepherds away,
　　and your allies will go into exile.
Then you will be ashamed and disgraced
　　because of all your wickedness.
²³You who live in 'Lebanon,^a'
　　who are nestled in cedar buildings,

a 23 That is, the palace in Jerusalem (see 1 Kings 7:2)

再回到這裏來，¹²卻要死在被擄去的地方，必不得再見這地。"

¹³ "那行不義蓋房、
　　行不公造樓、
　　白白使用人的手工
　　不給工價的、
　　有禍了！
¹⁴他說：'我要為自己蓋廣大的房、
　　寬敞的樓，
　　為自己開窗戶。'
這樓房的護牆板是香柏木的，
　　樓房是丹色油漆的。

¹⁵ "難道你作王
　　是在乎造香柏木樓房爭勝嗎？
你的父親豈不是也吃、也喝、
　　也施行公平和公義嗎？
　　那時他得了福樂？
¹⁶他為困苦和窮乏人伸冤，
　　那時就得了福樂！
認識我不在乎此嗎？"
　　這是耶和華說的。
¹⁷ "惟有你的眼和你的心
　　專顧貪婪，
流無辜人的血，
　　行欺壓和強暴。"

¹⁸所以，耶和華論到猶大王約西亞的兒子約雅敬如此說：
"人必不為他舉哀說：
　　'哀哉，我的哥哥！'
　　或說：'哀哉，我的姐姐！'
也不為他舉哀說：
　　'哀哉，我的主！'
　　或說：'哀哉，我主的榮華！'
¹⁹他被埋葬，好像埋驢一樣，
　　要拉出去
　　扔在耶路撒冷的城門之外。"

²⁰ "你要上黎巴嫩哀號，
　　在巴珊揚聲，
從亞巴琳哀號，
　　因為你所親愛的都毀滅了。
²¹你興盛的時候，我對你說話，
　　你卻說：'我不聽。'
你自幼年以來總是這樣，
　　不聽從我的話。
²²你的牧人要被風吞吃，
　　你所親愛的必被擄去；
那時，你必因你一切的惡
　　抱愧蒙羞。
²³你這住黎巴嫩在香柏樹上搭窩的，
　　有痛苦臨到你，

好像疼痛臨到產難的婦人，
　　那時你何等可憐！」

24耶和華說：「<u>猶大王約雅敬的
兒子哥尼雅</u>（註：又名耶哥尼雅。下同）雖
是我右手上帶印的戒指，我憑我的
永生起誓，也必將你從其上摘下
來。25並且我必將你交給尋索你命的
人和你所懼怕的人手中，就是<u>巴比
倫王尼布甲尼撒和迦勒底人</u>的手
中。26我也必將你和生你的母親趕到
別國，並不是你們生的地方，你們
必死在那裏。27但心中甚想歸回之
地，必不得歸回。」
28哥尼雅這人是被輕看、
　　破壞的器皿嗎？
　是無人喜愛的器皿嗎？
他和他的後裔
　　為何被趕到不認識之地呢？
29地啊，地啊，地啊，
　　當聽耶和華的話！
30耶和華如此說：
「要寫明這人算為無子，
　是平生不得享通的，
　因為他後裔中再無一人得享通，
　能坐在<u>大衛</u>的寶座上
　　治理<u>猶大</u>。」

公義的苗裔

23 耶和華說：「那些殘害、趕
散我草場之羊的牧人，有禍
了！」2耶和華<u>以色列</u>的神斥
責那些牧養他百姓的牧人，如此
說：「你們趕散我的羊羣，並沒有
看顧他們。我必討你們這行惡的
罪。」這是耶和華說的。3「我要將
我羊羣中所餘剩的，從我趕他們到
的各國內招聚出來，領他們歸回本
圈，他們也必生養眾多。4我必設立
照管他們的牧人，牧養他們。他們
不再懼怕，不再驚惶，也不缺少一
個。」這是耶和華說的。

5耶和華說：「日子將到，
　我要給<u>大衛</u>興起
　　一個公義的苗裔；
　他必掌王權，行事有智慧，
　　在地上施行公平和公義。

---

how you will groan when pangs come upon
  you,
  pain like that of a woman in labor!

24"As surely as I live," declares the LORD,
"even if you, Jehoiachin[a] son of Jehoiakim king
of Judah, were a signet ring on my right hand, I
would still pull you off. 25I will hand you over
to those who seek your life, those you fear—to
Nebuchadnezzar king of Babylon and to the
Babylonians.[b] 26I will hurl you and the mother
who gave you birth into another country, where
neither of you was born, and there you both will
die. 27You will never come back to the land you
long to return to."

28Is this man Jehoiachin a despised, broken pot,
  an object no one wants?
Why will he and his children be hurled out,
  cast into a land they do not know?
29O land, land, land,
  hear the word of the LORD!
30This is what the LORD says:
"Record this man as if childless,
  a man who will not prosper in his lifetime,
for none of his offspring will prosper,
  none will sit on the throne of David
  or rule anymore in Judah."

The Righteous Branch

23 "Woe to the shepherds who are destroying and scattering the sheep of my pasture!" declares the LORD. 2Therefore this
is what the LORD, the God of Israel, says to the
shepherds who tend my people: "Because you
have scattered my flock and driven them away
and have not bestowed care on them, I will
bestow punishment on you for the evil you have
done," declares the LORD. 3"I myself will gather
the remnant of my flock out of all the countries
where I have driven them and will bring them
back to their pasture, where they will be fruitful
and increase in number. 4I will place shepherds
over them who will tend them, and they will no
longer be afraid or terrified, nor will any be
missing," declares the LORD.

5"The days are coming," declares the LORD,
  "when I will raise up to David[c] a righteous
    Branch,
  a King who will reign wisely
  and do what is just and right in the land.

---

a 24 Hebrew *Coniah*, a variant of *Jehoiachin*; also in verse 28
b 25 Or *Chaldeans*　　c 5 Or *up from David's line*

⁶In his days Judah will be saved
    and Israel will live in safety.
This is the name by which he will be called:
    The LORD Our Righteousness.

⁷"So then, the days are coming," declares the
LORD, "when people will no longer say, 'As
surely as the LORD lives, who brought the
Israelites up out of Egypt,' ⁸but they will say,
'As surely as the LORD lives, who brought the
descendants of Israel up out of the land of the
north and out of all the countries where he had
banished them.' Then they will live in their own
land."

Lying Prophets
    ⁹Concerning the prophets:

My heart is broken within me;
    all my bones tremble.
I am like a drunken man,
    like a man overcome by wine,
because of the LORD
    and his holy words.
¹⁰The land is full of adulterers;
    because of the curse^a the land lies parched^b
    and the pastures in the desert are withered.
The ⌊prophets⌋ follow an evil course
    and use their power unjustly.

¹¹"Both prophet and priest are godless;
    even in my temple I find their wickedness,"
                         declares the LORD.
¹²"Therefore their path will become slippery;
    they will be banished to darkness
    and there they will fall.
I will bring disaster on them
    in the year they are punished,"
                         declares the LORD.

¹³"Among the prophets of Samaria
    I saw this repulsive thing:
They prophesied by Baal
    and led my people Israel astray.
¹⁴And among the prophets of Jerusalem
    I have seen something horrible:
They commit adultery and live a lie.
They strengthen the hands of evildoers,
    so that no one turns from his wickedness.
They are all like Sodom to me;
    the people of Jerusalem are like Gomorrah."

⁶在他的日子，猶大必得救，
    以色列也要安然居住。
他的名必稱為：
    耶和華我們的義。"

⁷耶和華說："日子將到，人必不再
指着那領以色列人從埃及地上來永生
的耶和華起誓，⁸卻要指着那領以色
列家的後裔從北方，和趕他們到的各
國中上來永生的耶和華起誓。他們必
住在本地。"

說謊言的先知
⁹論到那些先知，

我心在我裏面憂傷，
    我骨頭都發顫。
因耶和華和他的聖言，
    我像醉酒的人，
    像被酒所勝的人。

¹⁰地滿了行淫的人，
    因妄自賭咒，地就悲哀，
    曠野的草場都枯乾了。
他們所行的道乃是惡的，
    他們的勇力使得不正。
¹¹"連先知帶祭司，都是褻瀆的，
    就是在我殿中，
    我也看見他們的惡。"
                  這是耶和華說的。
¹²"因此，他們的道路
    必像黑暗中的滑地，他們必被追趕，
    在這路中仆倒；
因為當追討之年，
    我必使災禍臨到他們。"
                  這是耶和華說的。

¹³"我在撒馬利亞的先知中
    曾見愚妄，
他們藉巴力說預言，
    使我的百姓以色列走錯了路。
¹⁴我在耶路撒冷的先知中
    曾見可憎惡的事：
他們行姦淫，做事虛妄；
    又堅固惡人的手，
    甚至無人回頭離開他的惡。
他們在我面前都像所多瑪，
    耶路撒冷的居民都像蛾摩拉。"

---

a 10 Or because of these things   *b 10 Or land mourns*

¹⁵所以萬軍之耶和華論到先知如此說：

"我必將茵蔯給他們吃，
　　又將苦膽水給他們喝，
　因為褻瀆的事
　　出於耶路撒冷的先知，
　　流行遍地。"

¹⁶萬軍之耶和華如此說：

"這些先知向你們說預言，
　　你們不要聽他們的話。
　他們以虛空教訓你們，
　所說的異象，是出於自己的心，
　　不是出於耶和華的口。
¹⁷他們常對藐視我的人說：
　'耶和華說：你們必享平安。'
　又對一切按自己頑梗之心
　　而行的人說：
　'必沒有災禍臨到你們。'
¹⁸有誰站在耶和華的會中，
　　得以聽見並會悟他的話呢？
　有誰留心聽他的話呢？

¹⁹看哪，耶和華的忿怒好像暴風，
　　已經發出；
　是暴烈的旋風，
　　必轉到惡人的頭上。
²⁰耶和華的怒氣必不轉消，
　　直到他心中所擬定的
　　成就了。
　末後的日子
　　你們要全然明白。
²¹我沒有打發那些先知，
　　他們竟自奔跑；
　我沒有對他們說話，
　　他們竟自預言。
²²他們若是站在我的會中，
　　就必使我的百姓
　　　聽我的話，
　又使他們回頭離開惡道
　　和他們所行的惡。"

²³耶和華說：
"我豈為近處的神呢？
　不也為遠處的神嗎？"
²⁴耶和華說：
"人豈能在隱密處藏身，
　使我看不見他呢？"
耶和華說：
"我豈不充滿天地嗎？

²⁵ "我已聽見那些先知所說的，
就是託我名說的假預言，他們說：

¹⁵Therefore, this is what the LORD Almighty says concerning the prophets:

"I will make them eat bitter food
　and drink poisoned water,
because from the prophets of Jerusalem
　ungodliness has spread throughout the
　　land."

¹⁶This is what the LORD Almighty says:

"Do not listen to what the prophets are
　　prophesying to you;
　they fill you with false hopes.
They speak visions from their own minds,
　not from the mouth of the LORD.
¹⁷They keep saying to those who despise me,
　'The LORD says: You will have peace.'
And to all who follow the stubbornness of
　　their hearts
　they say, 'No harm will come to you.'
¹⁸But which of them has stood in the council of
　　the LORD
　to see or to hear his word?
　Who has listened and heard his word?
¹⁹See, the storm of the LORD
　will burst out in wrath,
　a whirlwind swirling down
　on the heads of the wicked.
²⁰The anger of the LORD will not turn back
　until he fully accomplishes
　　the purposes of his heart.
In days to come
　you will understand it clearly.
²¹I did not send these prophets,
　yet they have run with their message;
　I did not speak to them,
　yet they have prophesied.
²²But if they had stood in my council,
　they would have proclaimed my words to
　　my people
and would have turned them from their evil
　　ways
　and from their evil deeds.

²³"Am I only a God nearby,"
　　　　　　　　　　declares the LORD,
　"and not a God far away?
²⁴Can anyone hide in secret places
　so that I cannot see him?"
　　　　　　　　　　declares the LORD.
　"Do not I fill heaven and earth?"
　　　　　　　　　　declares the LORD.

²⁵"I have heard what the prophets say who prophesy lies in my name. They say, 'I had a

dream! I had a dream!' 26How long will this continue in the hearts of these lying prophets, who prophesy the delusions of their own minds? 27They think the dreams they tell one another will make my people forget my name, just as their fathers forgot my name through Baal worship. 28Let the prophet who has a dream tell his dream, but let the one who has my word speak it faithfully. For what has straw to do with grain?" declares the LORD. 29"Is not my word like fire," declares the LORD, "and like a hammer that breaks a rock in pieces?

30"Therefore," declares the LORD, "I am against the prophets who steal from one another words supposedly from me. 31Yes," declares the LORD, "I am against the prophets who wag their own tongues and yet declare, 'The LORD declares.' 32Indeed, I am against those who prophesy false dreams," declares the LORD. "They tell them and lead my people astray with their reckless lies, yet I did not send or appoint them. They do not benefit these people in the least," declares the LORD.

False Oracles and False Prophets

33"When these people, or a prophet or a priest, ask you, 'What is the oracle[a] of the LORD?' say to them, 'What oracle?[b] I will forsake you, declares the LORD.' 34If a prophet or a priest or anyone else claims, 'This is the oracle of the LORD,' I will punish that man and his household. 35This is what each of you keeps on saying to his friend or relative: 'What is the LORD's answer?' or 'What has the LORD spoken?' 36But you must not mention 'the oracle of the LORD' again, because every man's own word becomes his oracle and so you distort the words of the living God, the LORD Almighty, our God. 37This is what you keep saying to a prophet: 'What is the LORD's answer to you?' or 'What has the LORD spoken?' 38Although you claim, 'This is the oracle of the LORD,' this is what the LORD says: You used the words, 'This is the oracle of the LORD,' even though I told you that you must not claim, 'This is the oracle of the LORD.' 39Therefore, I will surely forget you and cast you out of my presence along with the city I gave to you and your fathers. 40I will bring upon you everlasting disgrace—everlasting shame that will not be forgotten."

'我做了夢,我做了夢!' 26說假預言的先知,就是預言本心詭詐的先知,他們這樣存心要到幾時呢? 27他們各人將所做的夢對鄰舍述說,想要使我的百姓忘記我的名,正如他們列祖因巴力忘記我的名一樣。 28得夢的先知,可以述說那夢;得我話的人,可以誠實講說我的話。糠粃怎能與麥子比較呢?" 這是耶和華說的。 29耶和華說:"我的話豈不像火,又像能打碎磐石的大錘嗎?"

30耶和華說:"那些先知各從鄰舍偷竊我的言語,因此我必與他們反對。" 31耶和華說:"那些先知用舌頭說是耶和華說的,我必與他們反對。" 32耶和華說:"那些以幻夢為預言,又述說這夢,以謊言和矜誇使我百姓走錯了路的,我必與他們反對。我沒有打發他們,也沒有吩咐他們。他們與這百姓毫無益處。" 這是耶和華說的。

假默示和假先知

33"無論是百姓,是先知,是祭司,問你說:'耶和華有甚麼默示呢?'你就對他們說:'甚麼默示啊?耶和華說:我要撇棄你們。' 34無論是先知,是祭司,是百姓,說'耶和華的默示',我必刑罰那人和他的家。 35你們各人要對鄰舍,各人要對弟兄如此說:'耶和華回答甚麼?耶和華說了甚麼呢?' 36'耶和華的默示'你們不可再提,各人所說的話必作自己的重擔(註:"重擔"和"默示"原文同)。因為你們謬用永生神萬軍之耶和華我們神的言語。 37你們要對先知如此說:'耶和華回答你甚麼?耶和華說了甚麼呢?' 38你們若說'耶和華的默示',耶和華就如此說:因你們說'耶和華的默示'這句話,我也打發人到你們那裏去,告訴你們不可說'耶和華的默示'。 39所以我必全然忘記你們,將你們和我所賜給你們並你們列祖的城撇棄了。 40又必使永遠的凌辱和長久的羞恥臨到你們,是不能忘記的。"

---

a 33 Or burden (see Septuagint and Vulgate)   b 33 Hebrew; Septuagint and Vulgate 'You are the burden. (The Hebrew for oracle and burden is the same.)

兩筐無花果

24 巴比倫王尼布甲尼撒，將猶大王約雅敬的兒子耶哥尼雅和猶大的首領並工匠、鐵匠，從耶路撒冷擄去，帶到巴比倫。這事以後，耶和華指給我看，有兩筐無花果放在耶和華的殿前。 2一筐是極好的無花果，好像是初熟的；一筐是極壞的無花果，壞得不可吃。

3於是耶和華問我說：「耶利米你看見甚麼？」

我說：「我看見無花果：好的極好，壞的極壞，壞得不可吃。」

4耶和華的話臨到我說：5「耶和華以色列的神如此說：『被擄去的猶大人，就是我打發離開這地到迦勒底人之地去的，我必看顧他們如這好無花果，使他們得好處。6我要眷顧他們，使他們得好處，領他們歸回這地。我也要建立他們，必不拆毀；栽植他們，並不拔出。7我要賜他們認識我的心，知道我是耶和華。他們要作我的子民，我要作他們的神，因為他們要一心歸向我。』

8「耶和華如此說：『我必將猶大王西底家和他的首領，以及剩在這地耶路撒冷的餘民，並住在埃及地的猶大人都交出來，好像那極壞、壞得不可吃的無花果。9我必使他們交出來，在天下萬國中拋來拋去，遭遇災禍。在我趕逐他們到的各處，成為凌辱、笑談、譏刺、咒詛。10我必使刀劍、饑荒、瘟疫臨到他們，直到他們從我所賜給他們和他們列祖之地滅絕。』」

被擄七十年

25 猶大王約西亞的兒子約雅敬第四年，就是巴比倫王尼布甲尼撒的元年，耶和華論猶大眾民的話臨到耶利米。2先知耶利米就將這話對猶大眾人和耶路撒冷的一切居民說：3「從猶大王亞們的兒子約西亞十三年直到今日，這二十三年之內，常有耶和華的話臨到我，我也對你們傳說，就是從早起來傳說，只是你們沒有聽從。

Two Baskets of Figs

24 After Jehoiachin[a] son of Jehoiakim king of Judah and the officials, the craftsmen and the artisans of Judah were carried into exile from Jerusalem to Babylon by Nebuchadnezzar king of Babylon, the LORD showed me two baskets of figs placed in front of the temple of the LORD. 2One basket had very good figs, like those that ripen early; the other basket had very poor figs, so bad they could not be eaten.

3Then the LORD asked me, "What do you see, Jeremiah?"

"Figs," I answered. "The good ones are very good, but the poor ones are so bad they cannot be eaten."

4Then the word of the LORD came to me: 5"This is what the LORD, the God of Israel, says: 'Like these good figs, I regard as good the exiles from Judah, whom I sent away from this place to the land of the Babylonians.[b] 6My eyes will watch over them for their good, and I will bring them back to this land. I will build them up and not tear them down; I will plant them and not uproot them. 7I will give them a heart to know me, that I am the LORD. They will be my people, and I will be their God, for they will return to me with all their heart.

8" 'But like the poor figs, which are so bad they cannot be eaten,' says the LORD, 'so will I deal with Zedekiah king of Judah, his officials and the survivors from Jerusalem, whether they remain in this land or live in Egypt. 9I will make them abhorrent and an offense to all the kingdoms of the earth, a reproach and a byword, an object of ridicule and cursing, wherever I banish them. 10I will send the sword, famine and plague against them until they are destroyed from the land I gave to them and their fathers.' "

Seventy Years of Captivity

25 The word came to Jeremiah concerning all the people of Judah in the fourth year of Jehoiakim son of Josiah king of Judah, which was the first year of Nebuchadnezzar king of Babylon. 2So Jeremiah the prophet said to all the people of Judah and to all those living in Jerusalem: 3For twenty-three years—from the thirteenth year of Josiah son of Amon king of Judah until this very day—the word of the LORD has come to me and I have spoken to you again and again, but you have not listened.

---

a 1 Hebrew *Jeconiah*, a variant of *Jehoiachin*　　*b 5* Or *Chaldeans*

⁴And though the LORD has sent all his servants the prophets to you again and again, you have not listened or paid any attention. ⁵They said, "Turn now, each of you, from your evil ways and your evil practices, and you can stay in the land the LORD gave to you and your fathers for ever and ever. ⁶Do not follow other gods to serve and worship them; do not provoke me to anger with what your hands have made. Then I will not harm you."

⁷"But you did not listen to me," declares the LORD, "and you have provoked me with what your hands have made, and you have brought harm to yourselves."

⁸Therefore the LORD Almighty says this: "Because you have not listened to my words, ⁹I will summon all the peoples of the north and my servant Nebuchadnezzar king of Babylon," declares the LORD, "and I will bring them against this land and its inhabitants and against all the surrounding nations. I will completely destroy^a them and make them an object of horror and scorn, and an everlasting ruin. ¹⁰I will banish from them the sounds of joy and gladness, the voices of bride and bridegroom, the sound of millstones and the light of the lamp. ¹¹This whole country will become a desolate wasteland, and these nations will serve the king of Babylon seventy years.

¹²"But when the seventy years are fulfilled, I will punish the king of Babylon and his nation, the land of the Babylonians,^b for their guilt," declares the LORD, "and will make it desolate forever. ¹³I will bring upon that land all the things I have spoken against it, all that are written in this book and prophesied by Jeremiah against all the nations. ¹⁴They themselves will be enslaved by many nations and great kings; I will repay them according to their deeds and the work of their hands."

The Cup of God's Wrath

¹⁵This is what the LORD, the God of Israel, said to me: "Take from my hand this cup filled with the wine of my wrath and make all the nations to whom I send you drink it. ¹⁶When they drink it, they will stagger and go mad because of the sword I will send among them."

¹⁷So I took the cup from the LORD's hand and made all the nations to whom he sent me drink it: ¹⁸Jerusalem and the towns of Judah, its kings and officials, to make them a ruin and an object

⁴耶和華也從早起來，差遣他的僕人眾先知到你們這裏來（只是你們沒有聽從，也沒有側耳而聽），⁵說：「你們各人當回頭，離開惡道和所作的惡，便可居住耶和華古時所賜給你們和你們列祖之地，直到永遠。⁶不可隨從別神侍奉敬拜，以你們手所做的惹我發怒，這樣，我就不加害與你們。」

⁷「然而你們沒有聽從我，竟以手所做的惹我發怒，陷害自己。」這是耶和華說的。

⁸所以萬軍之耶和華如此說：「因為你們沒有聽從我的話，⁹我必召北方的眾族和我僕人巴比倫王尼布甲尼撒來攻擊這地，和這地的居民，並四圍一切的國民。我要將他們盡行滅絕，以致他們令人驚駭、嗤笑，並且永久荒涼。這是耶和華說的。¹⁰我又要使歡喜和快樂的聲音，新郎和新婦的聲音，推磨的聲音和燈的亮光，從他們中間止息。¹¹這全地必然荒涼，令人驚駭，這些國民要服侍巴比倫王七十年。

¹²「七十年滿了以後，我必刑罰巴比倫王和那國民，並迦勒底人之地，因他們的罪孽使那地永遠荒涼。」這是耶和華說的。¹³「我也必使我向那地所說的話，就是記在這書上的話，是耶利米向這些國民說的預言，都臨到那地。¹⁴因為有多國和大君王必使迦勒底人作奴僕，我也必照他們的行為，按他們手所做的報應他們。」

神忿怒的杯

¹⁵耶和華以色列的神對我如此說：「你從我手中接這杯忿怒的酒，使我所差遣你去的各國的民喝。¹⁶他們喝了就要東倒西歪，並要發狂，因我使刀劍臨到他們中間。」

¹⁷我就從耶和華的手中接了這杯，給耶和華所差遣我去的各國的民喝。¹⁸就是耶路撒冷和猶大的城邑，並耶路撒冷的君王與首領，使這城邑

---

^a 9 The Hebrew term refers to the irrevocable giving over of things or persons to the LORD, often by totally destroying them.   ^b 12 Or Chaldeans

荒涼，令人驚駭、嗤笑、咒詛，正如今日一樣。19 又有埃及王法老和他的臣僕、首領，以及他的眾民，20 並雜族的人民和烏斯地的諸王，與非利士地的諸王、亞實基倫、迦薩、以革倫，以及亞實突剩下的人；21 以東、摩押、亞捫人，22 推羅的諸王、西頓的諸王，海島的諸王，23 底但、提瑪、布斯和一切剃周圍頭髮的；24 阿拉伯的諸王，住曠野雜族人民的諸王，25 心利的諸王、以攔的諸王、瑪代的諸王，26 北方遠近的諸王，以及天下、地上的萬國喝了，以後示沙克（註：就是「巴比倫」）王也要喝。

27 "你要對他們說：'萬軍之耶和華以色列的神如此說：你們要喝，且要喝醉，要嘔吐，且要跌倒，不得再起來，都因我使刀劍臨到你們中間。'28 他們若不肯從你手接這杯喝，你就要對他們說：'萬軍之耶和華如此說：你們一定要喝！29 我既從稱為我名下的城起首施行災禍，你們能盡免刑罰嗎？你們必不能免，因為我要命刀劍臨到地上一切的居民。這是萬軍之耶和華說的。'

30 "所以你要向他們預言這一切的話，攻擊他們，說：

" '耶和華必從高天吼叫，
　　從聖所發聲，
　　向自己的羊羣大聲吼叫，
他要向地上一切的居民吶喊，
　　像踹葡萄的一樣。
31 必有響聲達到地極，
　　因為耶和華與列國相爭，
凡有血氣的他必審問，
　　至於惡人，
　　他必交給刀劍。'

這是耶和華說的。

32 萬軍之耶和華如此說：
"看哪，
　　必有災禍從這國發到那國，
　　並有大暴風從地極颳起。"

33 到那日，從地這邊直到地那邊，都有耶和華所殺戮的。必無人哀哭，不得收殮，不得葬埋，必在地上成為糞土。

of horror and scorn and cursing, as they are today; [19]Pharaoh king of Egypt, his attendants, his officials and all his people, [20]and all the foreign people there; all the kings of Uz; all the kings of the Philistines (those of Ashkelon, Gaza, Ekron, and the people left at Ashdod); [21]Edom, Moab and Ammon; [22]all the kings of Tyre and Sidon; the kings of the coastlands across the sea; [23]Dedan, Tema, Buz and all who are in distant places[a]; [24]all the kings of Arabia and all the kings of the foreign people who live in the desert; [25]all the kings of Zimri, Elam and Media; [26]and all the kings of the north, near and far, one after the other—all the kingdoms on the face of the earth. And after all of them, the king of Sheshach[b] will drink it too.

[27]"Then tell them, 'This is what the LORD Almighty, the God of Israel, says: Drink, get drunk and vomit, and fall to rise no more because of the sword I will send among you.' [28]But if they refuse to take the cup from your hand and drink, tell them, 'This is what the LORD Almighty says: You must drink it! [29]See, I am beginning to bring disaster on the city that bears my Name, and will you indeed go unpunished? You will not go unpunished, for I am calling down a sword upon all who live on the earth, declares the LORD Almighty.'

[30]"Now prophesy all these words against them and say to them:

" 'The LORD will roar from on high;
he will thunder from his holy dwelling
and roar mightily against his land.
He will shout like those who tread the grapes,
shout against all who live on the earth.
[31]The tumult will resound to the ends of the earth,
for the Lord will bring charges against the nations;
he will bring judgment on all mankind
and put the wicked to the sword,' "

declares the LORD.

[32]This is what the LORD Almighty says:
"Look! Disaster is spreading
from nation to nation;
a mighty storm is rising
from the ends of the earth."

[33]At that time those slain by the LORD will be everywhere—from one end of the earth to the other. They will not be mourned or gathered up or buried, but will be like refuse lying on the ground.

a 23 Or who clip the hair by their foreheads　b 26 Sheshach is a cryptogram for Babylon.

34Weep and wail, you shepherds;
　　roll in the dust, you leaders of the flock.
　For your time to be slaughtered has come;
　　you will fall and be shattered like fine
　　　pottery.
35The shepherds will have nowhere to flee,
　　the leaders of the flock no place to escape.
36Hear the cry of the shepherds,
　　the wailing of the leaders of the flock,
　for the LORD is destroying their pasture.
37The peaceful meadows will be laid waste
　　because of the fierce anger of the LORD.
38Like a lion he will leave his lair,
　　and their land will become desolate
　because of the sword[a] of the oppressor
　and because of the LORD's fierce anger.

Jeremiah Threatened With Death

26 Early in the reign of Jehoiakim son of Josiah king of Judah, this word came from the LORD: 2"This is what the LORD says: Stand in the courtyard of the LORD's house and speak to all the people of the towns of Judah who come to worship in the house of the LORD. Tell them everything I command you; do not omit a word. 3Perhaps they will listen and each will turn from his evil way. Then I will relent and not bring on them the disaster I was planning because of the evil they have done. 4Say to them, 'This is what the LORD says: If you do not listen to me and follow my law, which I have set before you, 5and if you do not listen to the words of my servants the prophets, whom I have sent to you again and again (though you have not listened), 6then I will make this house like Shiloh and this city an object of cursing among all the nations of the earth.' "

7The priests, the prophets and all the people heard Jeremiah speak these words in the house of the LORD. 8But as soon as Jeremiah finished telling all the people everything the LORD had commanded him to say, the priests, the prophets and all the people seized him and said, "You must die! 9Why do you prophesy in the LORD's name that this house will be like Shiloh and this city will be desolate and deserted?" And all the people crowded around Jeremiah in the house of the LORD.

10When the officials of Judah heard about these things, they went up from the royal palace to the house of the LORD and took their places at the entrance of the New Gate of the LORD's house. 11Then the priests and the prophets said

34牧人哪，你們當哀號、呼喊；
　　羣眾的頭目啊，你們要滾在灰中，
　因為你們被殺戮分散的日子
　　足呈來到。
　你們要跌碎，好像美器打碎一樣。
35牧人無路逃跑；
　　羣眾的頭目也無法逃脫。
36聽啊，有牧人呼喊，
　　有羣眾頭目哀號的聲音，
　因為耶和華使他們的草場變為荒場。
37耶和華發出猛烈的怒氣，
　　平安的羊圈就都寂靜無聲。
38他離了隱密處像獅子一樣，
　　他們的地，因刀劍兇猛的欺壓，
　又因他猛烈的怒氣，
　　都成為可驚駭的。

以死恐嚇耶利米

26 猶大王約西亞的兒子約雅敬登基的時候，有這話從耶和華臨到耶利米說：2"耶和華如此說：你站在耶和華殿的院內，對猶大眾城邑的人，就是到耶和華殿來禮拜的，說我所吩咐你的一切話，一字不可刪減。3或者他們肯聽從，各人回頭離開惡道，使我後悔不將我因他們所行的惡，想要施行的災禍降與他們。4你要對他們說：'耶和華如此說：你們若不聽從我，不遵行我設立在你們面前的律法，5不聽我從早起來差遣到你們那裏去我僕人眾先知的話（你們還是沒有聽從），6我就必使這殿如示羅，使這城為地上萬國所咒詛的。' "

7耶利米在耶和華殿中說的這些話，祭司、先知與眾民都聽見了。8耶利米說完了耶和華所吩咐他對眾人說的一切話，祭司、先知與眾民都來抓住他，說："你必要死！9你為何託耶和華的名預言，說這殿必如示羅，這城必變為荒場無人居住呢？"於是眾民都在耶和華的殿中，聚集到耶利米那裏。

10猶大的首領聽見這事，就從王宮上到耶和華的殿，坐在耶和華殿的新門口。11祭司、先知對首領和眾民

---

a 38 Some Hebrew manuscripts and Septuagint (see also Jer. 46:16 and 50:16); most Hebrew manuscripts anger

説："這人是該死的！因為他説預言攻擊這城，正如你們親耳所聽見的。"

12耶利米就對眾首領和眾民説："耶和華差遣我預言，攻擊這殿和這城，説你們所聽見的這一切話。13現在要改正你們的行動作為，聽從耶和華你們神的話，他就必後悔，不將所説的災禍降與你們。14至於我，我在你們手中，你們眼看何為善，何為正，就那樣待我吧！15但你們要確實地知道，若把我治死，就使無辜人的血歸到你們和這城，並其中的居民了，因為耶和華實在差遣我到你們這裏來，將這一切話傳與你們耳中。"

16首領和眾民就對祭司、先知説："這人是不該死的，因為他是奉耶和華我們神的名向我們説話。"

17國中的長老就有幾個人起來，對聚會的眾民説：18"當猶大王希西家的日子，有摩利沙人彌迦對猶大眾人預言説："萬軍之耶和華如此説：

" '錫安必被耕種像一塊田，
　耶路撒冷必變為亂堆，
　這殿的山
　必像叢林的高處。'

19 "猶大王希西家和猶大眾人豈是把他治死呢？希西家豈不是敬畏耶和華，懇求他的恩嗎？耶和華就後悔，不把自己所説的災禍降與我們。若治死這人，我們就作了大惡，自害己命！"

20又有一個人奉耶和華的名説預言，是基列耶琳人示瑪雅的兒子烏利亞。他照耶和華的一切話説預言，攻擊這城和這地。21約雅敬王和他眾勇士、眾首領聽見了烏利亞的話，王就想要把他治死。烏利亞聽見就懼怕，逃往埃及去了。22約雅敬王便打發亞革波的兒子以利拿單，帶領幾個人往埃及去。23他們就從埃及將烏利亞帶出來，送到約雅敬王那裏，王用刀殺了他，把他的屍首拋在平民的墳地中。

to the officials and all the people, "This man should be sentenced to death because he has prophesied against this city. You have heard it with your own ears!"

12Then Jeremiah said to all the officials and all the people: "The LORD sent me to prophesy against this house and this city all the things you have heard. 13Now reform your ways and your actions and obey the LORD your God. Then the LORD will relent and not bring the disaster he has pronounced against you. 14As for me, I am in your hands; do with me whatever you think is good and right. 15Be assured, however, that if you put me to death, you will bring the guilt of innocent blood on yourselves and on this city and on those who live in it, for in truth the LORD has sent me to you to speak all these words in your hearing."

16Then the officials and all the people said to the priests and the prophets, "This man should not be sentenced to death! He has spoken to us in the name of the LORD our God."

17Some of the elders of the land stepped forward and said to the entire assembly of people, 18"Micah of Moresheth prophesied in the days of Hezekiah king of Judah. He told all the people of Judah, 'This is what the LORD Almighty says:

" 'Zion will be plowed like a field,
　Jerusalem will become a heap of rubble,
　the temple hill a mound overgrown with
　　thickets.'a

19"Did Hezekiah king of Judah or anyone else in Judah put him to death? Did not Hezekiah fear the LORD and seek his favor? And did not the LORD relent, so that he did not bring the disaster he pronounced against them? We are about to bring a terrible disaster on ourselves!"

20(Now Uriah son of Shemaiah from Kiriath Jearim was another man who prophesied in the name of the LORD; he prophesied the same things against this city and this land as Jeremiah did. 21When King Jehoiakim and all his officers and officials heard his words, the king sought to put him to death. But Uriah heard of it and fled in fear to Egypt. 22King Jehoiakim, however, sent Elnathan son of Acbor to Egypt, along with some other men. 23They brought Uriah out of Egypt and took him to King Jehoiakim, who had him struck down with a sword and his body thrown into the burial place of the common people.)

a 18 Micah 3:12

24Furthermore, Ahikam son of Shaphan supported Jeremiah, and so he was not handed over to the people to be put to death.

Judah to Serve Nebuchadnezzar

27 Early in the reign of Zedekiah[a] son of Josiah king of Judah, this word came to Jeremiah from the LORD: 2This is what the LORD said to me: "Make a yoke out of straps and crossbars and put it on your neck. 3Then send word to the kings of Edom, Moab, Ammon, Tyre and Sidon through the envoys who have come to Jerusalem to Zedekiah king of Judah. 4Give them a message for their masters and say, 'This is what the LORD Almighty, the God of Israel, says: "Tell this to your masters: 5With my great power and outstretched arm I made the earth and its people and the animals that are on it, and I give it to anyone I please. 6Now I will hand all your countries over to my servant Nebuchadnezzar king of Babylon; I will make even the wild animals subject to him. 7All nations will serve him and his son and his grandson until the time for his land comes; then many nations and great kings will subjugate him.

8" ' "If, however, any nation or kingdom will not serve Nebuchadnezzar king of Babylon or bow its neck under his yoke, I will punish that nation with the sword, famine and plague, declares the LORD, until I destroy it by his hand. 9So do not listen to your prophets, your diviners, your interpreters of dreams, your mediums or your sorcerers who tell you, 'You will not serve the king of Babylon.' 10They prophesy lies to you that will only serve to remove you far from your lands; I will banish you and you will perish. 11But if any nation will bow its neck under the yoke of the king of Babylon and serve him, I will let that nation remain in its own land to till it and to live there, declares the LORD." ' "

12I gave the same message to Zedekiah king of Judah. I said, "Bow your neck under the yoke of the king of Babylon; serve him and his people, and you will live. 13Why will you and your people die by the sword, famine and plague with which the LORD has threatened any nation that will not serve the king of Babylon? 14Do not listen to the words of the prophets who say to you, 'You will not serve the king of Babylon,' for they are prophesying lies to you. 15'I have not sent them,' declares the LORD. 'They are proph-

---

a 1 A few Hebrew manuscripts and Syriac (see also Jer. 27:3, 12 and 28:1); most Hebrew manuscripts Jehoiakim (Most Septuagint manuscripts do not have this verse.)

24然而，沙番的兒子亞希甘保護耶利米，不交在百姓的手中治死他。

猶大要服侍尼布甲尼撒

27 猶大王約西亞的兒子約雅敬（註："約雅敬"是"西底家"的別名。看第3節）登基的時候，有這話從耶和華臨到耶利米說：2耶和華對我如此說："你做繩索與軛，加在自己的頸項上，3藉那些來到耶路撒冷見猶大王西底家的使臣之手，把繩索與軛送到以東王、摩押王、亞捫王、推羅王、西頓王那裏，4囑咐使臣傳與他們的主人說，萬軍之耶和華以色列的神如此說：5 '我用大能和伸出來的膀臂，創造大地和地上的人民、牲畜，我看給誰相宜，就把地給誰。6現在我將這些地都交給我僕人巴比倫王尼布甲尼撒的手，我也將田野的走獸給他使用。7列國都必服侍他和他的兒孫，直到他本國遭報的日期來到。那時，多國和大君王，要使他作他們的奴僕。

8 " '無論哪一邦哪一國，不肯服侍這巴比倫王尼布甲尼撒，也不把頸項放在巴比倫王的軛下，我必用刀劍、饑荒、瘟疫刑罰那邦，直到我藉巴比倫王的手將他們毀滅。這是耶和華說的。9至於你們，不可聽從你們的先知和占卜的、圓夢的、觀兆的，以及行邪術的。他們告訴你們說：你們不至服侍巴比倫王。10他們向你們說假預言，要叫你們遷移，遠離本地，以致我將你們趕出去，使你們滅亡。11但哪一邦肯把頸項放在巴比倫王的軛下服侍他，我必使那邦仍在本地存留，得以耕種居住。這是耶和華說的。' "

12我就照這一切的話，對猶大王西底家說："要把你們的頸項放在巴比倫王的軛下，服侍他和他的百姓，便得存活。13你和你的百姓為何要因刀劍、饑荒、瘟疫死亡，正如耶和華論到不服侍巴比倫王的那國說的話呢？14不可聽那些先知對你們所說的話。他們說："你們不至服侍巴比倫王'，其實他們向你們說假預言。15耶和華說："我並沒有打發他們，他們卻託我的名說假預言，好使我將你們和向你們說預言的那些先知，趕出去一同滅亡。’”

16我又對祭司和這眾民說：“耶和華如此說：你們不可聽那先知對你們所說的預言。他們說：‘耶和華殿中的器皿快要從巴比倫帶回來。’其實他們向你們說假預言。17不可聽從他們，只管服侍巴比倫王，便得存活，這城何至變為荒場呢？18他們若是先知，有耶和華的話臨到他們，讓他們祈求萬軍之耶和華，使那在耶和華殿中和猶大王宮內，並耶路撒冷剩下的器皿，不被帶到巴比倫去。19因為萬軍之耶和華論到柱子、銅海、盆座，並剩在這城裏的器皿，20就是巴比倫王尼布甲尼撒擄掠猶大王約雅敬的兒子耶哥尼雅，和猶大、耶路撒冷一切貴胄的時候所沒有掠去的器皿。21論到那在耶和華殿中和猶大王宮內，並耶路撒冷剩下的器皿，萬軍之耶和華以色列的神如此說：22‘必被帶到巴比倫存在那裏，直到我眷顧以色列人的日子。那時，我必將這器皿帶回來交還此地。’這是耶和華說的。”

假先知哈拿尼雅

28 當年，就是猶大王西底家登基第四年五月，基遍人押朔的兒子先知哈拿尼雅，在耶和華的殿中當着祭司和眾民對我說：2“萬軍之耶和華以色列的神如此說：‘我已經折斷巴比倫王的軛，3二年之內，我要將巴比倫王尼布甲尼撒從這地掠到巴比倫的器皿，就是耶和華殿中的一切器皿都帶回此地。4我又要將猶大王約雅敬的兒子耶哥尼雅和被擄到巴比倫去的一切猶大人帶回此地，因為我要折斷巴比倫王的軛。’這是耶和華說的。”

5先知耶利米當着祭司和站在耶和華殿裏的眾民對先知哈拿尼雅說：6“阿們！願耶和華如此行！願

esying lies in my name. Therefore, I will banish you and you will perish, both you and the prophets who prophesy to you.' "

16Then I said to the priests and all these people, "This is what the LORD says: Do not listen to the prophets who say, 'Very soon now the articles from the LORD's house will be brought back from Babylon.' They are prophesying lies to you. 17Do not listen to them. Serve the king of Babylon, and you will live. Why should this city become a ruin? 18If they are prophets and have the word of the LORD, let them plead with the LORD Almighty that the furnishings remaining in the house of the LORD and in the palace of the king of Judah and in Jerusalem not be taken to Babylon. 19For this is what the LORD Almighty says about the pillars, the Sea, the movable stands and the other furnishings that are left in this city, 20which Nebuchadnezzar king of Babylon did not take away when he carried Jehoiachin[a] son of Jehoiakim king of Judah into exile from Jerusalem to Babylon, along with all the nobles of Judah and Jerusalem— 21yes, this is what the LORD Almighty, the God of Israel, says about the things that are left in the house of the LORD and in the palace of the king of Judah and in Jerusalem: 22'They will be taken to Babylon and there they will remain until the day I come for them,' declares the LORD. 'Then I will bring them back and restore them to this place.' "

The False Prophet Hananiah

28 In the fifth month of that same year, the fourth year, early in the reign of Zedekiah king of Judah, the prophet Hananiah son of Azzur, who was from Gibeon, said to me in the house of the LORD in the presence of the priests and all the people: 2"This is what the LORD Almighty, the God of Israel, says: 'I will break the yoke of the king of Babylon. 3Within two years I will bring back to this place all the articles of the LORD's house that Nebuchadnezzar king of Babylon removed from here and took to Babylon. 4I will also bring back to this place Jehoiachin[b] son of Jehoiakim king of Judah and all the other exiles from Judah who went to Babylon,' declares the LORD, 'for I will break the yoke of the king of Babylon.' "

5Then the prophet Jeremiah replied to the prophet Hananiah before the priests and all the people who were standing in the house of the LORD. 6He said, "Amen! May the LORD do so!

---

a 20 Hebrew Jeconiah, a variant of Jehoiachin　*b 4 Hebrew Jeconiah, a variant of Jehoiachin*

May the LORD fulfill the words you have prophesied by bringing the articles of the LORD's house and all the exiles back to this place from Babylon. ⁷Nevertheless, listen to what I have to say in your hearing and in the hearing of all the people: ⁸From early times the prophets who preceded you and me have prophesied war, disaster and plague against many countries and great kingdoms. ⁹But the prophet who prophesies peace will be recognized as one truly sent by the LORD only if his prediction comes true."

¹⁰Then the prophet Hananiah took the yoke off the neck of the prophet Jeremiah and broke it, ¹¹and he said before all the people, "This is what the LORD says: 'In the same way will I break the yoke of Nebuchadnezzar king of Babylon off the neck of all the nations within two years.' " At this, the prophet Jeremiah went on his way.

¹²Shortly after the prophet Hananiah had broken the yoke off the neck of the prophet Jeremiah, the word of the LORD came to Jeremiah: ¹³"Go and tell Hananiah, 'This is what the LORD says: You have broken a wooden yoke, but in its place you will get a yoke of iron. ¹⁴This is what the LORD Almighty, the God of Israel, says: I will put an iron yoke on the necks of all these nations to make them serve Nebuchadnezzar king of Babylon, and they will serve him. I will even give him control over the wild animals.' "

¹⁵Then the prophet Jeremiah said to Hananiah the prophet, "Listen, Hananiah! The LORD has not sent you, yet you have persuaded this nation to trust in lies. ¹⁶Therefore, this is what the LORD says: 'I am about to remove you from the face of the earth. This very year you are going to die, because you have preached rebellion against the LORD.' "

¹⁷In the seventh month of that same year, Hananiah the prophet died.

A Letter to the Exiles

29 This is the text of the letter that the prophet Jeremiah sent from Jerusalem to the surviving elders among the exiles and to the priests, the prophets and all the other people Nebuchadnezzar had carried into exile from Jerusalem to Babylon. ²(This was after King Jehoiachin*ᵃ* and the queen mother, the court officials and the leaders of Judah and Jerusalem, the craftsmen and the artisans had gone into exile from Jerusalem.) ³He entrusted the letter to Elasah son of Shaphan and to

---

耶和華成就你所預言的話，將耶和華殿中的器皿和一切被擄去的人，從巴比倫帶回此地。⁷然而，我向你和眾民耳中所要說的話，你應當聽：⁸從古以來，在你我以前的先知，向多國和大邦說預言，論到爭戰、災禍、瘟疫的事。⁹先知預言的平安，到話語成就的時候，人便知道他真是耶和華所差來的。"

¹⁰於是，先知哈拿尼雅將先知耶利米頸項上的軛取下來，折斷了。¹¹哈拿尼雅又當著眾民說："耶和華如此說：二年之內，我必照樣從列國人的頸項上，折斷巴比倫王尼布甲尼撒的軛。"於是先知耶利米就走了。

¹²先知哈拿尼雅把先知耶利米頸項上的軛折斷以後，耶和華的話臨到耶利米說：¹³"你去告訴哈拿尼雅說：'耶和華如此說：你折斷木軛，卻換了鐵軛！¹⁴因為萬軍之耶和華以色列的神如此說：我已將鐵軛加在這些國的頸項上，使他們服侍巴比倫王尼布甲尼撒，他們總要服侍他，我也把田野的走獸給了他。'"

¹⁵於是，先知耶利米對先知哈拿尼雅說："哈拿尼雅啊，你應當聽！耶和華並沒有差遣你，你竟使這百姓倚靠謊言。¹⁶所以耶和華如此說：'看哪，我要叫你去世，你今年必死！因為你向耶和華說了叛逆的話。'"

¹⁷這樣，先知哈拿尼雅當年七月間就死了。

致被擄者的信

29 先知耶利米從耶路撒冷寄信與被擄的祭司、先知和眾民，並生存的長老，就是尼布甲尼撒從耶路撒冷擄到巴比倫去的。²（這在耶哥尼雅王和太后、太監，並猶大、耶路撒冷的首領，以及工匠、鐵匠都離了耶路撒冷以後。）³他藉沙番的兒子以利亞薩和希勒家的兒子基瑪利的手寄去。他們二人是

---

a 2 Hebrew Jeconiah, a variant of Jehoiachin

猶大王<u>西底家</u>打發往<u>巴比倫</u>去見<u>尼布甲尼撒</u>王的。

⁴信上說：萬軍之耶和華<u>以色列</u>的神對一切被擄去的，就是我使他們從<u>耶路撒冷</u>被擄到巴比倫的人，如此說：⁵"你們要蓋造房屋，住在其中；栽種田園，吃其中所產的；⁶娶妻生兒女，為你們的兒子娶妻，使你們的女兒嫁人，生兒養女，在那裏生養眾多，不至減少。⁷我所使你們被擄到的那城，你們要為那城求平安，為那城禱告耶和華。因為那城得平安，你們也隨着得平安。⁸萬軍之耶和華<u>以色列</u>的神如此說："不要被你們中間的先知和占卜的誘惑，也不要聽信自己所做的夢，⁹因為他們託我的名對你們說假預言，我並沒有差遣他們。"這是耶和華說的。

¹⁰耶和華如此說："為巴比倫所定的七十年滿了以後，我要眷顧你們，向你們成就我的恩言，使你們仍回此地。"¹¹耶和華說："我知道我向你們所懷的意念，是賜平安的意念，不是降災禍的意念，要叫你們末後有指望。¹²你們要呼求我，禱告我，我就應允你們。¹³你們尋求我，若專心尋求我，就必尋見。"¹⁴耶和華說："我必被你們尋見，我也必使你們被擄的人歸回，將你們從各國中和我所趕你們到的各處招聚了來，又將你們帶回我使你們被擄掠離開的地方。"這是耶和華說的。

¹⁵你們說："耶和華在<u>巴比倫</u>為我們興起先知。"¹⁶所以耶和華論到坐<u>大衛</u>寶座的王和住在這城裏的一切百姓，就是未曾與你們一同被擄的弟兄，¹⁷萬軍之耶和華如此說："看哪，我必使刀劍、饑荒、瘟疫臨到他們，使他們像極壞的無花果，壞得不可吃。¹⁸我必用刀劍、饑荒、瘟疫追趕他們，使他們在天下萬國拋來拋去，在我所趕他們到的各國中，令人咒詛、驚駭、嗤笑、羞辱。"¹⁹耶和華說："這

Gemariah son of Hilkiah, whom Zedekiah king of Judah sent to King Nebuchadnezzar in Babylon. It said:

⁴This is what the L ORD Almighty, the God of Israel, says to all those I carried into exile from Jerusalem to Babylon: ⁵"Build houses and settle down; plant gardens and eat what they produce. ⁶Marry and have sons and daughters; find wives for your sons and give your daughters in marriage, so that they too may have sons and daughters. Increase in number there; do not decrease. ⁷Also, seek the peace and prosperity of the city to which I have carried you into exile. Pray to the L ORD for it, because if it prospers, you too will prosper." ⁸Yes, this is what the L ORD Almighty, the God of Israel, says: "Do not let the prophets and diviners among you deceive you. Do not listen to the dreams you encourage them to have. ⁹They are prophesying lies to you in my name. I have not sent them," declares the L ORD.

¹⁰This is what the L ORD says: "When seventy years are completed for Babylon, I will come to you and fulfill my gracious promise to bring you back to this place. ¹¹For I know the plans I have for you," declares the L ORD, "plans to prosper you and not to harm you, plans to give you hope and a future. ¹²Then you will call upon me and come and pray to me, and I will listen to you. ¹³You will seek me and find me when you seek me with all your heart. ¹⁴I will be found by you," declares the L ORD, "and will bring you back from captivity.^a I will gather you from all the nations and places where I have banished you," declares the L ORD, "and will bring you back to the place from which I carried you into exile."

¹⁵You may say, "The L ORD has raised up prophets for us in Babylon," ¹⁶but this is what the L ORD says about the king who sits on David's throne and all the people who remain in this city, your countrymen who did not go with you into exile— ¹⁷yes, this is what the L ORD Almighty says: "I will send the sword, famine and plague against them and I will make them like poor figs that are so bad they cannot be eaten. ¹⁸I will pursue them with the sword, famine and plague and will make them abhorrent to all the kingdoms of the earth and an object of cursing and horror, of scorn and reproach, among all the nations where I drive them. ¹⁹For they have not lis-

a 14 Or will restore your fortunes

tened to my words," declares the LORD, "words that I sent to them again and again by my servants the prophets. And you exiles have not listened either," declares the LORD.

20Therefore, hear the word of the LORD, all you exiles whom I have sent away from Jerusalem to Babylon. 21This is what the LORD Almighty, the God of Israel, says about Ahab son of Kolaiah and Zedekiah son of Maaseiah, who are prophesying lies to you in my name: "I will hand them over to Nebuchadnezzar king of Babylon, and he will put them to death before your very eyes. 22Because of them, all the exiles from Judah who are in Babylon will use this curse: 'The LORD treat you like Zedekiah and Ahab, whom the king of Babylon burned in the fire.' 23For they have done outrageous things in Israel; they have committed adultery with their neighbors' wives and in my name have spoken lies, which I did not tell them to do. I know it and am a witness to it," declares the LORD.

Message to Shemaiah

24Tell Shemaiah the Nehelamite, 25"This is what the LORD Almighty, the God of Israel, says: You sent letters in your own name to all the people in Jerusalem, to Zephaniah son of Maaseiah the priest, and to all the other priests. You said to Zephaniah, 26'The LORD has appointed you priest in place of Jehoiada to be in charge of the house of the LORD; you should put any madman who acts like a prophet into the stocks and neck-irons. 27So why have you not reprimanded Jeremiah from Anathoth, who poses as a prophet among you? 28He has sent this message to us in Babylon: It will be a long time. Therefore build houses and settle down; plant gardens and eat what they produce.' "

29Zephaniah the priest, however, read the letter to Jeremiah the prophet. 30Then the word of the LORD came to Jeremiah: 31"Send this message to all the exiles: 'This is what the LORD says about Shemaiah the Nehelamite: Because Shemaiah has prophesied to you, even though I did not send him, and has led you to believe a lie, 32this is what the LORD says: I will surely punish Shemaiah the Nehelamite and his descendants. He will have no one left among this people, nor will he see the good things I will do for my people, declares the LORD, because he has preached rebellion against me.' "

是因為他們沒有聽從我的話，就是我從早起來差遣我僕人眾先知去說的，無奈他們不聽。"這是耶和華說的。

20所以你們一切被擄去的，就是我從耶路撒冷打發到巴比倫去的，當聽耶和華的話。21萬軍之耶和華以色列的神，論到哥賴雅的兒子亞哈，並瑪西雅的兒子西底家如此說："他們是託我名向你們說假預言的，我必將他們交在巴比倫王尼布甲尼撒的手中，他要在你們眼前殺害他們。22住巴比倫一切被擄的猶大人必藉這二人賭咒說：'願耶和華使你像巴比倫王在火中燒的西底家和亞哈一樣。'23這二人是在以色列中行了醜事，與鄰舍的妻行淫，又假託我名說我未曾吩咐他們的話。知道的是我，作見證的也是我。"這是耶和華說的。

給示瑪雅的信息

24論到尼希蘭人示瑪雅，你當說：25"萬軍之耶和華以色列的神如此說：你曾用自己的名寄信給耶路撒冷的眾民和祭司瑪西雅的兒子西番雅，並眾祭司說：26'耶和華已經立你西番雅為祭司，代替祭司耶何耶大，使耶和華殿中有官長，好將一切狂妄自稱為先知的人用枷拘住，用鎖鎖住。27現在亞拿突人耶利米向你們自稱為先知，你們為何沒有責備他呢？28因為他寄信給我們在巴比倫的人說：被擄的事必長久，你們要蓋造房屋，住在其中；栽種田園，吃其中所產的。'"

29祭司西番雅就把這信念給先知耶利米聽。30於是耶和華的話臨到耶利米說：31"你當寄信給一切被擄的人說：'耶和華論到尼希蘭人示瑪雅說：因為示瑪雅向你們說預言，我並沒有差遣他，他使你們倚靠謊言。32所以耶和華如此說：我必刑罰尼希蘭人示瑪雅和他的後裔，他必無一人存留住在這民中，也不得見我所要賜與我百姓的福樂，因為他向耶和華說了叛逆的話。這是耶和華說的。'"

以色列的復興

30 耶和華的話臨到耶利米說：2 "耶和華以色列的神如此說：'你將我對你說過的一切話都寫在書上。' 3 耶和華說：'日子將到，我要使我的百姓以色列和猶大被擄的人歸回；我也要使他們回到我所賜給他們列祖之地，他們就得這地為業。' 這是耶和華說的。"

4 以下是耶和華論到以色列和猶大所說的話：5 "耶和華如此說：

" '我們聽見聲音，
　是戰抖懼怕而不平安的聲音。
6 你們且訪問看看，
　男人有產難嗎？
我怎麼看見
　人人用手掐腰，
　像產難的婦人，
　臉面都變青了呢？
7 哀哉！那日為大，
　無日可比，
這是雅各遭難的時候，
　但他必被救出來。'

8 "萬軍之耶和華說：'到那日，
　我必從你頸項上折斷仇敵的軛，
扭開他的繩索，
　外邦人不得再使你作他們的奴僕。
9 你們卻要侍奉耶和華你們的神，
　和我為你們
　　所要興起的王大衛。'

10 "故此耶和華說：
'我的僕人雅各啊，不要懼怕；
　以色列啊，不要驚惶；
因我要從遠方拯救你，
　從被擄到之地
　　拯救你的後裔。
雅各必回來得享平靖安逸，
　無人使他驚怕。
11 因我與你同在，要拯救你，
　也要將所趕散你到的那些國
　　滅絕淨盡，
　卻不將你滅絕淨盡，
倒要從寬懲治你，
　萬不能不罰你（註："不罰你"或作
　"以你為無罪"）。'
　　　　　這是耶和華說的。

12 "耶和華如此說：

" '你的損傷無法醫治，
　你的傷痕極其重大。

Restoration of Israel

30 This is the word that came to Jeremiah from the LORD: 2 This is what the LORD, the God of Israel, says: 'Write in a book all the words I have spoken to you. 3 The days are coming,' declares the LORD, 'when I will bring my people Israel and Judah back from captivity[a] and restore them to the land I gave their forefathers to possess,' says the LORD."

4 These are the words the LORD spoke concerning Israel and Judah: 5 "This is what the LORD says:

" 'Cries of fear are heard—
　terror, not peace.
6 Ask and see:
　Can a man bear children?
Then why do I see every strong man
　with his hands on his stomach like a woman
　　in labor,
　every face turned deathly pale?
7 How awful that day will be!
　None will be like it.
It will be a time of trouble for Jacob,
　but he will be saved out of it.

8 " 'In that day,' declares the LORD Almighty,
　'I will break the yoke off their necks
and will tear off their bonds;
　no longer will foreigners enslave them.
9 Instead, they will serve the LORD their God
　and David their king,
　whom I will raise up for them.

10 " 'So do not fear, O Jacob my servant;
　do not be dismayed, O Israel,'
　　　　　　　　　declares the LORD.
'I will surely save you out of a distant place,
　your descendants from the land of their
　　exile.
Jacob will again have peace and security,
　and no one will make him afraid.
11 I am with you and will save you,'
　declares the LORD.
'Though I completely destroy all the nations
　among which I scatter you,
I will not completely destroy you.
I will discipline you but only with justice;
　I will not let you go entirely unpunished.'

12 "This is what the LORD says:

" 'Your wound is incurable,
　your injury beyond healing.

a 3 Or will restore the fortunes of my people Israel and Judah

¹³There is no one to plead your cause,
no remedy for your sore,
no healing for you.
¹⁴All your allies have forgotten you;
they care nothing for you.
I have struck you as an enemy would
and punished you as would the cruel,
because your guilt is so great
and your sins so many.
¹⁵Why do you cry out over your wound,
your pain that has no cure?
Because of your great guilt and many sins
I have done these things to you.

¹⁶" 'But all who devour you will be devoured;
all your enemies will go into exile.
Those who plunder you will be plundered;
all who make spoil of you I will despoil.
¹⁷But I will restore you to health
and heal your wounds,'

                       declares the LORD,
'because you are called an outcast,
Zion for whom no one cares.'

¹⁸"This is what the LORD says:

" 'I will restore the fortunes of Jacob's tents
and have compassion on his dwellings;
the city will be rebuilt on her ruins,
and the palace will stand in its proper place.
¹⁹From them will come songs of thanksgiving
and the sound of rejoicing.
I will add to their numbers,
and they will not be decreased;
I will bring them honor,
and they will not be disdained.
²⁰Their children will be as in days of old,
and their community will be established
before me;
I will punish all who oppress them.
²¹Their leader will be one of their own;
their ruler will arise from among them.
I will bring him near and he will come close to
me,
for who is he who will devote himself
to be close to me?'

                       declares the LORD.
²²" 'So you will be my people,
and I will be your God.' "

²³See, the storm of the LORD
will burst out in wrath,
a driving wind swirling down
on the heads of the wicked.
²⁴The fierce anger of the LORD will not turn back
until he fully accomplishes

¹³無人為你分訴，
使你的傷痕得以纏裹；
你沒有醫治的良藥。
¹⁴你所親愛的都忘記你，
不來探問（註：或作"理會"）你。
我因你的罪孽甚大，
罪惡眾多，
曾用仇敵加的傷害傷害你，
用殘忍者的懲治懲治你。
¹⁵你為何因損傷哀號呢？
你的痛苦無法醫治，
我因你的罪孽甚大，罪惡眾多，
曾將這些加在你身上。

¹⁶" '故此，凡吞吃你的，必被吞吃；
你的敵人個個都被擄去。
擄掠你的，必成為擄物；
搶奪你的，必成為掠物。'
¹⁷耶和華說：'我必使你痊愈，
醫好你的傷痕，
都因人稱你為被趕散的，說：
這是錫安，
無人來探問（註：或作"理會"）的。'

¹⁸"耶和華如此說：

" '我必使雅各被擄去的帳棚歸回，
也必顧惜他的住處。
城必建造在原舊的山岡，
宮殿也照舊有人居住。
¹⁹必有感謝和歡樂的聲音
從其中發出。
我要使他們增多，
不致減少；
使他們尊榮，
不致卑微。
²⁰他們的兒女要如往日；
他們的會眾
堅立在我面前。
凡欺壓他們的，我必刑罰他。
²¹他們的君王必是屬乎他們的，
掌權的必從他們中間而出。
我要使他就近我，
他也要親近我，
不然，
誰有膽量親近我呢？'
這是耶和華說的。
²²" '你們要作我的子民，
我要作你們的神。' "

²³看哪，耶和華的忿怒
好像暴風已經發出；
是掃滅的暴風，
必轉到惡人的頭上。
²⁴耶和華的烈怒必不轉消，
直到他心中所擬定的成就了。

末後的日子
你們要明白！

31 耶和華說：“那時我必作以
色列各家的神，他們必作我
的子民。”

²耶和華如此說：

“脫離刀劍的就是以色列人，
　我使他享安息的時候，
　他曾在曠野蒙恩。”

　　³古時（註：或作“從遠方”）耶和華
向以色列（註：原文作“我”）顯現，說：
“我以永遠的愛愛你，
　因此我以慈愛吸引你。
⁴以色列的民哪（註：“民”原文作“處女”），
　我要再建立你，你就被建立；
　你必再以擊鼓為美，
　與歡樂的人一同跳舞而出。
⁵又必在撒馬利亞的山上
　栽種葡萄園，
　栽種的人
　要享用所結的果子。
⁶日子必到，
　以法蓮山上守望的人必呼叫說：
‘起來吧！我們可以上錫安，
　到耶和華我們的神那裏去。’”

⁷耶和華如此說：

“你們當為雅各歡樂歌唱，
　因萬國中為首的歡呼。
　當傳揚頌讚說：‘耶和華啊，
　求你拯救你的百姓
　以色列所剩下的人。’
⁸我必將他們從北方領來，
　從地極招聚，
　同着他們來的
　有瞎子、瘸子、
　　孕婦、產婦，
　他們必成為大幫回到這裏來。
⁹他們要哭泣而來，
　我要照他們懇求的引導他們，
　使他們在河水旁走正直的路，
　在其上不致絆跌，
　因為我是以色列的父，
　以法蓮是我的長子。

¹⁰“列國啊，要聽耶和華的話，
　傳揚在遠處的海島說：
‘趕散以色列的，必招聚他，
　又看守他，好像牧人看守羊羣。’

31 "At that time," declares the LORD, "I
will be the God of all the clans of Israel,
and they will be my people."
²This is what the LORD says:

"The people who survive the sword
　will find favor in the desert;
　I will come to give rest to Israel."

³The LORD appeared to us in the past,ᵃ saying:

"I have loved you with an everlasting love;
　I have drawn you with loving-kindness.
⁴I will build you up again
　and you will be rebuilt, O Virgin Israel.
Again you will take up your tambourines
　and go out to dance with the joyful.
⁵Again you will plant vineyards
　on the hills of Samaria;
the farmers will plant them
　and enjoy their fruit.
⁶There will be a day when watchmen cry out
　on the hills of Ephraim,
'Come, let us go up to Zion,
　to the LORD our God.' "

⁷This is what the LORD says:

"Sing with joy for Jacob;
　shout for the foremost of the nations.
Make your praises heard, and say,
　'O LORD, save your people,
　the remnant of Israel.'
⁸See, I will bring them from the land of the
　north
　and gather them from the ends of the earth.
Among them will be the blind and the lame,
　expectant mothers and women in labor;
　a great throng will return.
⁹They will come with weeping;
　they will pray as I bring them back.
I will lead them beside streams of water
　on a level path where they will not stumble,
because I am Israel's father,
　and Ephraim is my firstborn son.

¹⁰"Hear the word of the LORD, O nations;
　proclaim it in distant coastlands:
'He who scattered Israel will gather them
　and will watch over his flock like a shepherd.'

ᵃ 3 Or LORD has appeared to us from afar

¹¹For the LORD will ransom Jacob
 and redeem them from the hand of those
  stronger than they.
¹²They will come and shout for joy on the
  heights of Zion;
 they will rejoice in the bounty of the LORD—
 the grain, the new wine and the oil,
 the young of the flocks and herds.
 They will be like a well-watered garden,
 and they will sorrow no more.
¹³Then maidens will dance and be glad,
 young men and old as well.
 I will turn their mourning into gladness;
 I will give them comfort and joy instead of
  sorrow.
¹⁴I will satisfy the priests with abundance,
 and my people will be filled with my bounty,"
                                    declares the LORD.

¹⁵This is what the LORD says:

"A voice is heard in Ramah,
 mourning and great weeping,
Rachel weeping for her children
 and refusing to be comforted,
 because her children are no more."

¹⁶This is what the LORD says:

"Restrain your voice from weeping
 and your eyes from tears,
for your work will be rewarded,"
                                    declares the LORD.
 "They will return from the land of the enemy.
¹⁷So there is hope for your future,"
                                    declares the LORD.
 "Your children will return to their own land.

¹⁸"I have surely heard Ephraim's moaning:
 'You disciplined me like an unruly calf,
 and I have been disciplined.
Restore me, and I will return,
 because you are the LORD my God.
¹⁹After I strayed,
 I repented;
after I came to understand,
 I beat my breast.
I was ashamed and humiliated
 because I bore the disgrace of my youth.'
²⁰Is not Ephraim my dear son,
 the child in whom I delight?
Though I often speak against him,
 I still remember him.
Therefore my heart yearns for him;
 I have great compassion for him,"
                                    declares the LORD.

¹¹因耶和華救贖了雅各，
　救贖他脫離
　　比他更強之人的手。
¹²他們要來到
　錫安的高處歌唱，
　又流歸耶和華施恩之地，
　就是有五穀、新酒和油，
　　並羊羔、牛犢之地。
　他們的心必像澆灌的園子，
　　他們也不再有一點愁煩。
¹³那時處女必歡樂跳舞，
　年少的年老的，也必一同歡樂，
　因為我要使他們的悲哀變為歡喜，
　並要安慰他們，
　　使他們的愁煩轉為快樂。
¹⁴我必以肥油使祭司的心滿足；
　我的百姓也要因我的恩惠知足。"
　　　　　　　　這是耶和華說的。

¹⁵耶和華如此說：

"在拉瑪聽見
　號咷痛哭的聲音，
　是拉結哭她兒女，
　不肯受安慰，
　　因為他們都不在了。"

¹⁶耶和華如此說：

"你禁止聲音不要哀哭，
　禁止眼目不要流淚，
　因你所做之工，必有賞賜，
　　他們必從敵國歸回。"
　　　　　　　　這是耶和華說的。
¹⁷耶和華說：
"你末後必有指望，
　你的兒女必回到自己的境界。

¹⁸"我聽見以法蓮為自己悲歎說：
　'你責罰我，我便受責罰，
　像不慣負軛的牛犢一樣。
　求你使我回轉，我便回轉，
　　因為你是耶和華我的神。
¹⁹我回轉以後，
　就真正懊悔；
　受教以後，
　　就拍腿歎息；
　我因擔當幼年的凌辱，
　　就抱愧蒙羞。"
²⁰耶和華說：
"以法蓮是我的愛子嗎？
　是可喜悅的孩子嗎？
　我每逢責備他，
　　仍深顧念他，
　所以我的心腸戀慕他，
　　我必要憐憫他。"

21 "以色列民哪（註："民"原文作"處女"），
　　你當為自己設立指路碑，
　　豎起引路柱。
　你要留心向大路，
　　就是你所去的原路；
　你當回轉，回轉到你這些城邑。
22 背道的民哪（註："民"原文作"女子"），
　　你反來覆去要到幾時呢？
　耶和華在地上造了一件新事，
　　就是女子護衛男子。"

23 萬軍之耶和華以色列的神如此
說："我使被擄之人歸回的時候，
他們在猶大和其中的城邑必再這
樣說：'公義的居所啊，聖山哪，
願耶和華賜福給你！' 24 猶大和屬猶
大城邑的人，農夫和放羊的人，要
一同住在其中。25 疲乏的人，我使他
飽飫；愁煩的人，我使他知足。"

26 先知說："我醒了，覺着睡得
香甜！"
27 耶和華說："日子將到，我要
把人的種和牲畜的種，播種在以色
列家和猶大家。28 我先前怎樣留意將
他們拔出、拆毀、毀壞、傾覆、苦
害，也必照樣留意將他們建立、栽
植。"這是耶和華說的。29 "當那些
日子，人不再說：

'父親吃了酸葡萄，
　兒子的牙酸倒了。'

30 但各人必因自己的罪死亡；
　凡吃酸葡萄的，
　　自己的牙必酸倒。"

31 耶和華說：
　　"日子將到，
　我要與以色列家
　　和猶大家另立新約。
32 不像我拉着
　　　他們祖宗的手，
　領他們出埃及地的時候，
　　與他們所立的約。
　我雖作他們的丈夫，
　　他們卻背了我的約。"
　　　　　　　這是耶和華說的。
33 耶和華說："那些日子以後，
　我與以色列家
　　所立的約乃是這樣：

21 "Set up road signs;
　　put up guideposts.
　Take note of the highway,
　　the road that you take.
　Return, O Virgin Israel,
　　return to your towns.
22 How long will you wander,
　　O unfaithful daughter?
　The LORD will create a new thing on earth—
　　a woman will surround[a] a man."

23 This is what the LORD Almighty, the God of
Israel, says: "When I bring them back from captivity,[b] the people in the land of Judah and in its
towns will once again use these words: 'The
LORD bless you, O righteous dwelling, O sacred
mountain.' 24 People will live together in Judah
and all its towns—farmers and those who move
about with their flocks. 25 I will refresh the weary
and satisfy the faint."

26 At this I awoke and looked around. My
sleep had been pleasant to me.

27 "The days are coming," declares the LORD,
"when I will plant the house of Israel and the
house of Judah with the offspring of men and of
animals. 28 Just as I watched over them to uproot
and tear down, and to overthrow, destroy and
bring disaster, so I will watch over them to build
and to plant," declares the LORD. 29 "In those
days people will no longer say,

'The fathers have eaten sour grapes,
　and the children's teeth are set on edge.'

30 Instead, everyone will die for his own sin;
whoever eats sour grapes—his own teeth will be
set on edge.

31 "The time is coming," declares the LORD,
　　"when I will make a new covenant
　with the house of Israel
　　and with the house of Judah.
32 It will not be like the covenant
　　I made with their forefathers
　when I took them by the hand
　　to lead them out of Egypt,
　because they broke my covenant,
　　though I was a husband to[c] them,[d]"
　　　　　　　declares the LORD.
33 "This is the covenant I will make with the
　　house of Israel
　after that time," declares the LORD.

---

*a 22 Or will go about [seeking]; or will protect　b 23 Or I restore
their fortunes　c 32 Hebrew; Septuagint and Syriac / and I
turned away from　d 32 Or was their master*

"I will put my law in their minds
  and write it on their hearts.
I will be their God,
  and they will be my people.
34No longer will a man teach his neighbor,
  or a man his brother, saying, 'Know the
    Lord,'
because they will all know me,
  from the least of them to the greatest,"
          declares the LORD.
"For I will forgive their wickedness
  and will remember their sins no more."

35This is what the LORD says,

he who appoints the sun
  to shine by day,
who decrees the moon and stars
  to shine by night,
who stirs up the sea
  so that its waves roar—
  the LORD Almighty is his name:
36"Only if these decrees vanish from my sight,"
  declares the LORD,
"will the descendants of Israel ever cease
  to be a nation before me."

37This is what the LORD says:

"Only if the heavens above can be measured
  and the foundations of the earth below be
    searched out
will I reject all the descendants of Israel
  because of all they have done,"
          declares the LORD.

38"The days are coming," declares the LORD,
"when this city will be rebuilt for me from the
Tower of Hananel to the Corner Gate. 39The
measuring line will stretch from there straight to
the hill of Gareb and then turn to Goah. 40The
whole valley where dead bodies and ashes are
thrown, and all the terraces out to the Kidron
Valley on the east as far as the corner of the
Horse Gate, will be holy to the LORD. The city
will never again be uprooted or demolished."

Jeremiah Buys a Field

32 This is the word that came to Jeremiah
from the LORD in the tenth year of
Zedekiah king of Judah, which was the
eighteenth year of Nebuchadnezzar. 2The army
of the king of Babylon was then besieging Jerusalem, and Jeremiah the prophet was confined
in the courtyard of the guard in the royal palace
of Judah.

我要將我的律法放在他們裏面，
  寫在他們心上。
我要作他們的神，
  他們要作我的子民。
34他們各人不再教導自己的鄰舍
  和自己的弟兄說：
'你該認識耶和華。'
  因為他們從最小的到至大的，
  都必認識我。
我要赦免他們的罪孽，
  不再記念他們的罪惡。"
          這是耶和華說的。

35那使太陽白日發光，
  使星月有定例，
黑夜發亮，
  又攪動大海，
使海中波浪匉訇的——
  萬軍之耶和華是他的名。

他如此說：
36 "這些定例若能在我面前廢掉，
  以色列的後裔也就在我面前斷絕，
  永遠不再成國。"
          這是耶和華說的。

37耶和華如此說：

"若能量度上天，
  尋察下地的根基，
我就因以色列後裔
  一切所行的
棄絕他們。"
          這是耶和華說的。

38耶和華說："日子將到，這城
必為耶和華建造，從哈楠業樓直到角
門。39準繩要往外量出，直到迦立
山，又轉到歌亞。40拋屍的全谷和倒
灰之處，並一切田地，直到汲淪溪，
又直到東方馬門的拐角，都要歸耶和
華為聖，不再拔出，不再傾覆，直到
永遠。"

耶利米買田

32 猶大王西底家第十年，就是
尼布甲尼撒十八年，耶和華
的話臨到耶利米。2那時巴比
倫王的軍隊圍困耶路撒冷，先知耶利
米囚在護衛兵的院內，在猶大王的宮
中。

³因為猶大王西底家已將他囚禁，說：「你為甚麼預言說：『耶和華如此說：我必將這城交在巴比倫王的手中，他必攻取這城。⁴猶大王西底家必不能逃脫迦勒底人的手，定要交在巴比倫王的手中，要口對口彼此說話，眼對眼彼此相看。⁵巴比倫王必將西底家帶到巴比倫，西底家必住在那裏，直到我眷顧他的時候。你們雖與迦勒底人爭戰，卻不順利。這是耶和華說的。』」

⁶耶利米說：「耶和華的話臨到我說：⁷你叔叔沙龍的兒子哈拿篾必來見你，說：『我在亞拿突的那地，求你買來，因你買這地是合乎贖回之理。』

⁸「我叔叔的兒子哈拿篾果然照耶和華的話，來到護衛兵的院內，對我說：『我在便雅憫境內亞拿突的那塊地，求你買來，因你買來是合乎承受之理，是你當贖的，你為自己買來吧！』

「我耶利米就知道這是耶和華的話。⁹我便向我叔叔的兒子哈拿篾買了亞拿突的那塊地，平了十七舍客勒銀子給他。¹⁰我在契上畫押，將契封緘，又請見證人來，並用天平將銀子平給他。¹¹我便將照例按規敵立的買契，就是封緘的那一張和敵著的那一張，¹²當著我叔叔的兒子哈拿篾和畫押作見證的人，並坐在護衛兵院內的一切猶大人眼前，交給瑪西雅的孫子、尼利亞的兒子巴錄。

¹³「當著他們眾人眼前，我囑咐巴錄說：¹⁴『萬軍之耶和華以色列的神如此說：要將這封緘的和敵著的兩張契放在瓦器裏，可以存留多日。¹⁵因為萬軍之耶和華以色列的神如此說：將來在這地必有人再買房屋、田地和葡萄園。』

¹⁶「我將買契交給尼利亞的兒子巴錄以後，便禱告耶和華說：

¹⁷「主耶和華啊，你曾用大能和伸出來的膀臂創造天地，在你沒有難成的事。¹⁸你施慈愛與千萬人，又將父親的罪孽報應在他後世子孫的懷中，是至大全能的

³Now Zedekiah king of Judah had imprisoned him there, saying, "Why do you prophesy as you do? You say, 'This is what the LORD says: I am about to hand this city over to the king of Babylon, and he will capture it. ⁴Zedekiah king of Judah will not escape out of the hands of the Babylonians[a] but will certainly be handed over to the king of Babylon, and will speak with him face to face and see him with his own eyes. ⁵He will take Zedekiah to Babylon, where he will remain until I deal with him, declares the LORD. If you fight against the Babylonians, you will not succeed.' "

⁶Jeremiah said, "The word of the LORD came to me: ⁷Hanamel son of Shallum your uncle is going to come to you and say, 'Buy my field at Anathoth, because as nearest relative it is your right and duty to buy it.'

⁸"Then, just as the LORD had said, my cousin Hanamel came to me in the courtyard of the guard and said, 'Buy my field at Anathoth in the territory of Benjamin. Since it is your right to redeem it and possess it, buy it for yourself.'

"I knew that this was the word of the LORD; ⁹so I bought the field at Anathoth from my cousin Hanamel and weighed out for him seventeen shekels[b] of silver. ¹⁰I signed and sealed the deed, had it witnessed, and weighed out the silver on the scales. ¹¹I took the deed of purchase—the sealed copy containing the terms and conditions, as well as the unsealed copy—¹²and I gave this deed to Baruch son of Neriah, the son of Mahseiah, in the presence of my cousin Hanamel and of the witnesses who had signed the deed and of all the Jews sitting in the courtyard of the guard.

¹³"In their presence I gave Baruch these instructions: ¹⁴This is what the LORD Almighty, the God of Israel, says: Take these documents, both the sealed and unsealed copies of the deed of purchase, and put them in a clay jar so they will last a long time. ¹⁵For this is what the LORD Almighty, the God of Israel, says: Houses, fields and vineyards will again be bought in this land.'

¹⁶"After I had given the deed of purchase to Baruch son of Neriah, I prayed to the LORD:

¹⁷"Ah, Sovereign LORD, you have made the heavens and the earth by your great power and outstretched arm. Nothing is too hard for you. ¹⁸You show love to thousands but bring the punishment for the fathers' sins into the laps of their children after them. O great and

powerful God, whose name is the LORD Almighty, [19]great are your purposes and mighty are your deeds. Your eyes are open to all the ways of men; you reward everyone according to his conduct and as his deeds deserve. [20]You performed miraculous signs and wonders in Egypt and have continued them to this day, both in Israel and among all mankind, and have gained the renown that is still yours. [21]You brought your people Israel out of Egypt with signs and wonders, by a mighty hand and an outstretched arm and with great terror. [22]You gave them this land you had sworn to give their forefathers, a land flowing with milk and honey. [23]They came in and took possession of it, but they did not obey you or follow your law; they did not do what you commanded them to do. So you brought all this disaster upon them.

[24]"See how the siege ramps are built up to take the city. Because of the sword, famine and plague, the city will be handed over to the Babylonians who are attacking it. What you said has happened, as you now see. [25]And though the city will be handed over to the Babylonians, you, O Sovereign LORD, say to me, 'Buy the field with silver and have the transaction witnessed.' "

[26]Then the word of the LORD came to Jeremiah: [27]"I am the LORD, the God of all mankind. Is anything too hard for me? [28]Therefore, this is what the LORD says: I am about to hand this city over to the Babylonians and to Nebuchadnezzar king of Babylon, who will capture it. [29]The Babylonians who are attacking this city will come in and set it on fire; they will burn it down, along with the houses where the people provoked me to anger by burning incense on the roofs to Baal and by pouring out drink offerings to other gods.

[30]"The people of Israel and Judah have done nothing but evil in my sight from their youth; indeed, the people of Israel have done nothing but provoke me with what their hands have made, declares the LORD. [31]From the day it was built until now, this city has so aroused my anger and wrath that I must remove it from my sight. [32]The people of Israel and Judah have provoked me by all the evil they have done—they, their kings and officials, their priests and prophets, the men of Judah and the people of Jerusalem. [33]They turned their backs to me and not their faces; though I taught them again and again, they would not listen or respond to discipline. [34]They set up their abominable idols in

神，萬軍之耶和華是你的名。[19]謀事有大略，行事有大能，注目觀看世人一切的舉動，為要照各人所行的和他做事的結果報應他。[20]在埃及地顯神蹟奇事，直到今日在以色列和別人中間也是如此，使自己得了名聲，正如今日一樣。[21]用神蹟奇事和大能的手，並伸出來的膀臂與大可畏的事，領你的百姓以色列出了埃及。[22]將這地賜給他們，就是你向他們列祖起誓應許賜給他們流奶與蜜之地。[23]他們進入這地得了為業，卻不聽從你的話，也不遵行你的律法。你一切所吩咐他們行的，他們一無所行，因此你使這一切的災禍臨到他們。

[24]"看哪！敵人已經來到，築壘要攻取這城；城也因刀劍、饑荒、瘟疫交在攻城的迦勒底人手中。你所說的話都成就了，你也看見了。[25]主耶和華啊，你對我說：'要用銀子為自己買那塊地，又請見證人。'其實這城已交在迦勒底人的手中了。' "

[26]耶和華的話臨到耶利米說：[27]"我是耶和華，是凡有血氣者的神，豈有我難成的事嗎？[28]耶和華如此說：我必將這城交付迦勒底人的手和巴比倫王尼布甲尼撒的手，他必攻取這城。[29]攻城的迦勒底人必來放火焚燒這城和其中的房屋。在這房屋上，人曾向巴力燒香，向別神澆奠，惹我發怒。

[30]"以色列人和猶大人，自從幼年以來，專行我眼中看為惡的事；以色列人盡以手所做的惹我發怒。這是耶和華說的。[31]這城自從建造的那日，直到今日，常惹我的怒氣和忿怒，使我將這城從我面前除掉。[32]是因以色列人和猶大人一切的邪惡，就是他們和他們的君王、首領、祭司、先知，並猶大的眾人，以及耶路撒冷的居民所行的，惹我發怒。[33]他們以背向我，不以面向我。我雖從早起來教訓他們，他們卻不聽從，不受教訓，[34]竟把可憎之物設立在稱為我名

下的殿中，污穢了這殿。³⁵他們在欣嫩子谷建築巴力的邱壇，好使自己的兒女經火歸摩洛，他們行這可憎的事，使猶大陷在罪裏。這並不是我所吩咐的，也不是我心所起的意。

³⁶「現在論到這城，就是你們所說，已經由刀劍、饑荒、瘟疫交在巴比倫王手中的，耶和華以色列的神如此說：³⁷我在怒氣、忿怒和大惱恨中，將以色列人趕到各國。日後，我必從那裏將他們招聚出來，領他們回到此地，使他們安然居住。³⁸他們要作我的子民，我要作他們的神。³⁹我要使他們彼此同心同道，好叫他們永遠敬畏我，使他們和他們後世的子孫得福樂。⁴⁰又要與他們立永遠的約，必隨着他們施恩，並不離開他們，且使他們有敬畏我的心，不離開我。⁴¹我必歡喜施恩與他們，要盡心盡意、誠誠實實將他們栽於此地。

⁴²「因為耶和華如此說：我怎樣使這一切大禍臨到這百姓，我也要照樣使我所應許他們的一切福樂都臨到他們。⁴³你們說：『這地是荒涼、無人民、無牲畜，是交付迦勒底人手之地。』日後，在這境內必有人置買田地。⁴⁴在便雅憫地、耶路撒冷四圍的各處、猶大的城邑、山地的城邑、高原的城邑並南地的城邑，人必用銀子買田地，在契上畫押，將契封緘，請出見證人，因為我必使被擄的人歸回。這是耶和華說的。」

復興的應許

33 耶利米還囚在護衛兵的院內，耶和華的話第二次臨到他說：² 「成就的是耶和華，造作為要建立的也是耶和華，耶和華是他的名。他如此說：³ 『你求告我，我就應允你，並將你所不知道，又大又難的事指示你。』⁴論到這城中的房屋和猶大王的宮室，就是拆毀為擋敵人高壘和刀劍的，耶和華以色列的神如此說：⁵ 『人要與迦勒底人爭戰，正是拿死屍充滿這房屋，就是我在怒氣和忿怒中所殺

the house that bears my Name and defiled it. ³⁵They built high places for Baal in the Valley of Ben Hinnom to sacrifice their sons and daughters[a] to Molech, though I never commanded, nor did it enter my mind, that they should do such a detestable thing and so make Judah sin.

³⁶"You are saying about this city, 'By the sword, famine and plague it will be handed over to the king of Babylon'; but this is what the LORD, the God of Israel, says: ³⁷I will surely gather them from all the lands where I banish them in my furious anger and great wrath; I will bring them back to this place and let them live in safety. ³⁸They will be my people, and I will be their God. ³⁹I will give them singleness of heart and action, so that they will always fear me for their own good and the good of their children after them. ⁴⁰I will make an everlasting covenant with them: I will never stop doing good to them, and I will inspire them to fear me, so that they will never turn away from me. ⁴¹I will rejoice in doing them good and will assuredly plant them in this land with all my heart and soul.

⁴²"This is what the LORD says: As I have brought all this great calamity on this people, so I will give them all the prosperity I have promised them. ⁴³Once more fields will be bought in this land of which you say, 'It is a desolate waste, without men or animals, for it has been handed over to the Babylonians.' ⁴⁴Fields will be bought for silver, and deeds will be signed, sealed and witnessed in the territory of Benjamin, in the villages around Jerusalem, in the towns of Judah and in the towns of the hill country, of the western foothills and of the Negev, because I will restore their fortunes,[b] declares the LORD."

Promise of Restoration

33 While Jeremiah was still confined in the courtyard of the guard, the word of the LORD came to him a second time: ²"This is what the LORD says, he who made the earth, the LORD who formed it and established it—the LORD is his name: ³'Call to me and I will answer you and tell you great and unsearchable things you do not know.' ⁴For this is what the LORD, the God of Israel, says about the houses in this city and the royal palaces of Judah that have been torn down to be used against the siege ramps and the sword ⁵in the fight with the Babylonians[c]: 'They will be filled with the dead bodies of the men I will slay in my anger and

---

a 35 Or to make their sons and daughters pass through the fire
b 44 Or will bring them back from captivity　*c 5 Or Chaldeans*

wrath. I will hide my face from this city because of all its wickedness.

6 " 'Nevertheless, I will bring health and healing to it; I will heal my people and will let them enjoy abundant peace and security. 7I will bring Judah and Israel back from captivity[a] and will rebuild them as they were before. 8I will cleanse them from all the sin they have committed against me and will forgive all their sins of rebellion against me. 9Then this city will bring me renown, joy, praise and honor before all nations on earth that hear of all the good things I do for it; and they will be in awe and will tremble at the abundant prosperity and peace I provide for it.'

10"This is what the LORD says: 'You say about this place, "It is a desolate waste, without men or animals." Yet in the towns of Judah and the streets of Jerusalem that are deserted, inhabited by neither men nor animals, there will be heard once more 11the sounds of joy and gladness, the voices of bride and bridegroom, and the voices of those who bring thank offerings to the house of the LORD, saying,

"Give thanks to the LORD Almighty,
　for the LORD is good;
　his love endures forever."

For I will restore the fortunes of the land as they were before,' says the LORD.

12"This is what the LORD Almighty says: 'In this place, desolate and without men or animals—in all its towns there will again be pastures for shepherds to rest their flocks. 13In the towns of the hill country, of the western foothills and of the Negev, in the territory of Benjamin, in the villages around Jerusalem and in the towns of Judah, flocks will again pass under the hand of the one who counts them,' says the LORD.

14" 'The days are coming,' declares the LORD, "when I will fulfill the gracious promise I made to the house of Israel and to the house of Judah.

15" 'In those days and at that time
I will make a righteous Branch sprout from
　David's line;
he will do what is just and right in the land.
16In those days Judah will be saved
and Jerusalem will live in safety.
This is the name by which it[b] will be called:
　The LORD Our Righteousness.'

a 7 Or will restore the fortunes of Judah and Israel　　b 16 Or he

的人，因他們的一切惡，我就掩面不顧這城。

6 " '看哪，我要使這城得以痊愈安舒，使城中的人得醫治，又將豐盛的平安和誠實顯明與他們。7我也要使猶大被擄的和以色列被擄的歸回，並建立他們和起初一樣。8我要除淨他們的一切罪，就是向我所犯的罪；又要赦免他們的一切罪，就是干犯我、違背我的罪。9這城要在地上萬國人面前使我得頌讚、得榮耀，名為可喜可樂之城。萬國人因聽見我向這城所賜的福樂、所施的恩惠平安，就懼怕戰兢。'

10 "耶和華如此說：'你們論這地方說：是荒廢無人民、無牲畜之地。但在這荒涼無人民無牲畜的猶大城邑和耶路撒冷的街上，11必再聽見有歡喜和快樂的聲音，新郎和新婦的聲音，並聽見有人說：

要稱謝萬軍之耶和華，
　因耶和華本為善，
　他的慈愛永遠長存！

又有奉感謝祭到耶和華殿中之人的聲音，因為我必使這地被擄的人歸回，和起初一樣。' 這是耶和華說的。

12 "萬軍之耶和華如此說：'在這荒廢無人民無牲畜之地，並其中所有的城邑，必再有牧人的住處。他們要使羊群躺臥在那裏。13在山地的城邑、高原的城邑、南地的城邑、便雅憫地、耶路撒冷四圍的各處和猶大的城邑，必再有羊群從數點的人手下經過。' 這是耶和華說的。

14 "耶和華說：'日子將到，我應許以色列家和猶大家的恩言必然成就。

15 " '當那日子，那時候，
　我必使大衛
　　公義的苗裔長起來；
　他必在地上施行公平和公義。
16在那日子猶大必得救，
　耶路撒冷必安然居住，
　他的名必稱為
　　耶和華我們的義。'

¹⁷因為耶和華如此說：「大衛必永不斷人坐在以色列家的寶座上；¹⁸祭司利未人在我面前也不斷人獻燔祭、燒素祭，時常辦理獻祭的事。」」

¹⁹耶和華的話臨到耶利米說：²⁰「耶和華如此說：『你們若能廢棄我所立白日黑夜的約，使白日黑夜不按時輪轉，²¹就能廢棄我與我僕人大衛所立的約，使他沒有兒子在他的寶座上為王。並能廢棄我與侍奉我的祭司利未人所立的約。²²天上的萬象不能數算，海邊的塵沙也不能斗量；我必照樣使我僕人大衛的後裔和侍奉我的利未人多起來。』」

²³耶和華的話臨到耶利米說：²⁴「你沒有揣摩這百姓的話嗎？他們說：『耶和華所揀選的二族，他已經棄絕了。』他們這樣藐視我的百姓，以為不再成國。²⁵耶和華如此說：『若是我立白日黑夜的約不能存住，若是我未曾安排天地的定例，²⁶我就棄絕雅各的後裔和我僕人大衛的後裔，不使大衛的後裔治理亞伯拉罕、以撒、雅各的後裔。因為我必使他們被擄的人歸回，也必憐憫他們。』」

對西底家的警告

34 巴比倫王尼布甲尼撒率領他的全軍和地上屬他的各國各邦，攻打耶路撒冷和屬耶路撒冷所有的城邑。那時，耶和華的話臨到耶利米說：²「耶和華以色列的神說：你去告訴猶大王西底家：『耶和華如此說：我要將這城交付巴比倫王的手，他必用火焚燒。³你必不能逃脫他的手，定被拿住，交在他的手中。你的眼要見巴比倫王的眼，他要口對口和你說話，你必到巴比倫去。

⁴「『猶大王西底家啊，你還要聽耶和華的話。耶和華論到你如此說：你必不被刀劍殺死，⁵你必平安而死，人必為你焚燒物件，好像為你列祖，就是在你以前的先王焚燒

¹⁷For this is what the LORD says: 'David will never fail to have a man to sit on the throne of the house of Israel, ¹⁸nor will the priests, who are Levites, ever fail to have a man to stand before me continually to offer burnt offerings, to burn grain offerings and to present sacrifices.'"

¹⁹The word of the LORD came to Jeremiah: ²⁰"This is what the LORD says: 'If you can break my covenant with the day and my covenant with the night, so that day and night no longer come at their appointed time, ²¹then my covenant with David my servant—and my covenant with the Levites who are priests ministering before me—can be broken and David will no longer have a descendant to reign on his throne. ²²I will make the descendants of David my servant and the Levites who minister before me as countless as the stars of the sky and as measureless as the sand on the seashore.'"

²³The word of the LORD came to Jeremiah: ²⁴"Have you not noticed that these people are saying, 'The LORD has rejected the two kingdoms*ᵃ* he chose'? So they despise my people and no longer regard them as a nation. ²⁵This is what the LORD says: 'If I have not established my covenant with day and night and the fixed laws of heaven and earth, ²⁶then I will reject the descendants of Jacob and David my servant and will not choose one of his sons to rule over the descendants of Abraham, Isaac and Jacob. For I will restore their fortunes*ᵇ* and have compassion on them.'"

Warning to Zedekiah

34 While Nebuchadnezzar king of Babylon and all his army and all the kingdoms and peoples in the empire he ruled were fighting against Jerusalem and all its surrounding towns, this word came to Jeremiah from the LORD: ²"This is what the LORD, the God of Israel, says: Go to Zedekiah king of Judah and tell him, 'This is what the LORD says: I am about to hand this city over to the king of Babylon, and he will burn it down. ³You will not escape from his grasp but will surely be captured and handed over to him. You will see the king of Babylon with your own eyes, and he will speak with you face to face. And you will go to Babylon.

⁴"'Yet hear the promise of the LORD, O Zedekiah king of Judah. This is what the LORD says concerning you: You will not die by the sword; ⁵you will die peacefully. As people made a funeral fire in honor of your fathers, the former kings who preceded you, so they will make

a 24 Or families   b 26 Or will bring them back from captivity

a fire in your honor and lament, "Alas, O master!" I myself make this promise, declares the LORD.' "

⁶Then Jeremiah the prophet told all this to Zedekiah king of Judah, in Jerusalem, ⁷while the army of the king of Babylon was fighting against Jerusalem and the other cities of Judah that were still holding out—Lachish and Azekah. These were the only fortified cities left in Judah.

Freedom for Slaves

⁸The word came to Jeremiah from the LORD after King Zedekiah had made a covenant with all the people in Jerusalem to proclaim freedom for the slaves. ⁹Everyone was to free his Hebrew slaves, both male and female; no one was to hold a fellow Jew in bondage. ¹⁰So all the officials and people who entered into this covenant agreed that they would free their male and female slaves and no longer hold them in bondage. They agreed, and set them free. ¹¹But afterward they changed their minds and took back the slaves they had freed and enslaved them again.

¹²Then the word of the LORD came to Jeremiah: ¹³"This is what the LORD, the God of Israel, says: I made a covenant with your forefathers when I brought them out of Egypt, out of the land of slavery. I said, ¹⁴'Every seventh year each of you must free any fellow Hebrew who has sold himself to you. After he has served you six years, you must let him go free.'ᵃ Your fathers, however, did not listen to me or pay attention to me. ¹⁵Recently you repented and did what is right in my sight: Each of you proclaimed freedom to his countrymen. You even made a covenant before me in the house that bears my Name. ¹⁶But now you have turned around and profaned my name; each of you has taken back the male and female slaves you had set free to go where they wished. You have forced them to become your slaves again.

¹⁷"Therefore, this is what the LORD says: You have not obeyed me; you have not proclaimed freedom for your fellow countrymen. So I now proclaim 'freedom' for you, declares the LORD— 'freedom' to fall by the sword, plague and famine. I will make you abhorrent to all the kingdoms of the earth. ¹⁸The men who have violated my covenant and have not fulfilled the terms of the covenant they made before me, I will treat like the calf they cut in two and then walked between its pieces. ¹⁹The leaders of

a 14 Deut. 15:12

一般。　人必為你舉哀說：哀哉！我主啊。耶和華說，這話是我說的。'"

⁶於是，先知耶利米在耶路撒冷將這一切話告訴猶大王西底家。⁷那時，巴比倫王的軍隊正攻打耶路撒冷，又攻打猶大所剩下的城邑，就是拉吉和亞西加。原來猶大的堅固城只剩下這兩座。

奴僕得自由

⁸、⁹西底家王與耶路撒冷的眾民立約，要向他們宣告自由，叫各人任他希伯來的僕人和婢女自由出去，誰也不可使他的一個猶大弟兄作奴僕。（此後，有耶和華的話臨到耶利米。）¹⁰所有立約的首領和眾民，就任他的僕人婢女自由出去，誰也不再叫他們作奴僕。大家都順從，將他們釋放了。¹¹後來卻又反悔，叫所任去自由的僕人婢女回來，勉強他們仍為僕婢。

¹²因此，耶和華的話臨到耶利米說：¹³"耶和華以色列的神如此說：我將你們的列祖從埃及地為奴之家領出來的時候，與他們立約說：¹⁴'你的一個希伯來弟兄若賣給你，服侍你六年，到第七年你們各人就要任他自由出去。'只是你們列祖不聽從我，也不側耳而聽。¹⁵如今你們回轉，行我眼中看為正的事，各人向鄰舍宣告自由，並且在稱為我名下的殿中，在我面前立約。¹⁶你們卻又反悔，褻瀆我的名，各人叫所任去隨意自由的僕人婢女回來，勉強他們仍為僕婢。

¹⁷"所以耶和華如此說：你們沒有聽從我，各人向弟兄鄰舍宣告自由。看哪！我向你們宣告一樣自由，就是使你們自由於刀劍、饑荒、瘟疫之下，並且使你們在天下萬國中拋來拋去。這是耶和華說的。¹⁸、¹⁹猶大的首領、耶路撒冷的首領、太監、祭司和國中的眾民曾將牛犢劈開，分成兩半，從其中經過，在我面前立約。

後來又違背我的約，不遵行這約上的話。20我必將他們交在仇敵和尋索其命的人手中，他們的屍首必給空中的飛鳥和地上的野獸作食物。

21"並且我必將猶大王西底家和他的首領交在他們仇敵和尋索其命的人，與那暫離你們而去巴比倫王軍隊的手中。22耶和華說：我必吩咐他們回到這城，攻打這城，將城攻取，用火焚燒。我也要使猶大的城邑變為荒場無人居住。"

利甲族

35 當猶大王約西亞之子約雅敬的時候，耶和華的話臨到耶利米說：2"你去見利甲族的人，和他們說話，領他們進入耶和華殿的一間屋子，給他們酒喝。"

3我就將哈巴洗尼雅的孫子、雅利米雅的兒子雅撒尼亞和他弟兄，並他眾子，以及利甲全族的人，4領到耶和華的殿，進入神人伊基大利的兒子哈難眾子的屋子。那屋子在首領的屋子旁邊，在沙龍之子把門的瑪西雅屋子以上。5於是我在利甲族人面前設擺盛滿酒的碗和杯，對他們說："請你們喝酒。"

6他們卻說："我們不喝酒。因為我們先祖利甲的兒子約拿達曾吩咐我們說：'你們與你們的子孫永不可喝酒，7也不可蓋房、撒種、栽種葡萄園，但一生的年日要住帳棚，使你們的日子在寄居之地得以延長。'8凡我們先祖利甲的兒子約拿達所吩咐我們的話，我們都聽從了。我們和我們的妻子兒女，一生的年日都不喝酒，9也不蓋房居住，也沒有葡萄園、田地和種子，10但住帳棚，聽從我們先祖約拿達的話，照他所吩咐我們的去行。11巴比倫王尼布甲尼撒上此地來，我們因怕迦勒底的軍隊和亞蘭的軍隊，就說，'來吧！我們到耶路撒冷去。'這樣，我們才住在耶路撒冷。"

Judah and Jerusalem, the court officials, the priests and all the people of the land who walked between the pieces of the calf, 20I will hand over to their enemies who seek their lives. Their dead bodies will become food for the birds of the air and the beasts of the earth.

21"I will hand Zedekiah king of Judah and his officials over to their enemies who seek their lives, to the army of the king of Babylon, which has withdrawn from you. 22I am going to give the order, declares the LORD, and I will bring them back to this city. They will fight against it, take it and burn it down. And I will lay waste the towns of Judah so no one can live there."

The Recabites

35 This is the word that came to Jeremiah from the LORD during the reign of Jehoiakim son of Josiah king of Judah: 2"Go to the Recabite family and invite them to come to one of the side rooms of the house of the LORD and give them wine to drink."

3So I went to get Jaazaniah son of Jeremiah, the son of Habazziniah, and his brothers and all his sons—the whole family of the Recabites. 4I brought them into the house of the LORD, into the room of the sons of Hanan son of Igdaliah the man of God. It was next to the room of the officials, which was over that of Maaseiah son of Shallum the doorkeeper. 5Then I set bowls full of wine and some cups before the men of the Recabite family and said to them, "Drink some wine."

6But they replied, "We do not drink wine, because our forefather Jonadab son of Recab gave us this command: 'Neither you nor your descendants must ever drink wine. 7Also you must never build houses, sow seed or plant vineyards; you must never have any of these things, but must always live in tents. Then you will live a long time in the land where you are nomads.' 8We have obeyed everything our forefather Jonadab son of Recab commanded us. Neither we nor our wives nor our sons and daughters have ever drunk wine 9or built houses to live in or had vineyards, fields or crops. 10We have lived in tents and have fully obeyed everything our forefather Jonadab commanded us. 11But when Nebuchadnezzar king of Babylon invaded this land, we said, 'Come, we must go to Jerusalem to escape the Babylonian[a] and Aramean armies.' So we have remained in Jerusalem."

a 11 Or *Chaldean*

¹²Then the word of the LORD came to Jeremiah, saying: ¹³"This is what the LORD Almighty, the God of Israel, says: Go and tell the men of Judah and the people of Jerusalem, 'Will you not learn a lesson and obey my words?' declares the LORD. ¹⁴Jonadab son of Recab ordered his sons not to drink wine and this command has been kept. To this day they do not drink wine, because they obey their forefather's command. But I have spoken to you again and again, yet you have not obeyed me. ¹⁵Again and again I sent all my servants the prophets to you. They said, "Each of you must turn from your wicked ways and reform your actions; do not follow other gods to serve them. Then you will live in the land I have given to you and your fathers." But you have not paid attention or listened to me. ¹⁶The descendants of Jonadab son of Recab have carried out the command their forefather gave them, but these people have not obeyed me.'

¹⁷"Therefore, this is what the LORD God Almighty, the God of Israel, says: 'Listen! I am going to bring on Judah and on everyone living in Jerusalem every disaster I pronounced against them. I spoke to them, but they did not listen; I called to them, but they did not answer.'"

¹⁸Then Jeremiah said to the family of the Recabites, "This is what the LORD Almighty, the God of Israel, says: 'You have obeyed the command of your forefather Jonadab and have followed all his instructions and have done everything he ordered.' ¹⁹Therefore, this is what the LORD Almighty, the God of Israel, says: 'Jonadab son of Recab will never fail to have a man to serve me.'"

Jehoiakim Burns Jeremiah's Scroll

36 In the fourth year of Jehoiakim son of Josiah king of Judah, this word came to Jeremiah from the LORD: ²"Take a scroll and write on it all the words I have spoken to you concerning Israel, Judah and all the other nations from the time I began speaking to you in the reign of Josiah till now. ³Perhaps when the people of Judah hear about every disaster I plan to inflict on them, each of them will turn from his wicked way; then I will forgive their wickedness and their sin."

⁴So Jeremiah called Baruch son of Neriah, and while Jeremiah dictated all the words the LORD had spoken to him, Baruch wrote them on the scroll. ⁵Then Jeremiah told Baruch, "I am restricted; I cannot go to the LORD's temple. ⁶So you go to the house of the LORD on a day of fasting and read to the people from the scroll the

¹²耶和華的話臨到耶利米說：¹³"萬軍之耶和華以色列的神如此說：你去對猶大人和耶路撒冷的居民說：'耶和華說：你們不受教訓，不聽從我的話嗎？¹⁴利甲的兒子約拿達所吩咐他子孫不可喝酒的話，他們已經遵守，直到今日也不喝酒，因為他們聽從先祖的吩咐。我從早起來警戒你們，你們卻不聽從我。¹⁵我從早起來差遣我的僕人眾先知去，說：你們各人當回頭，離開惡道，改正行為，不隨從侍奉別神，就必住在我所賜給你們和你們列祖的地上。只是你們沒有聽從我，也沒有側耳而聽。¹⁶利甲的兒子約拿達的子孫，能遵守先人所吩咐他們的命，這百姓卻沒有聽從我！'

¹⁷"因此，耶和華萬軍之神以色列的神如此說：'我要使我所說的一切災禍臨到猶大和耶路撒冷的一切居民。因為我對他們說話，他們沒有聽從；我呼喚他們，他們沒有答應。'"

¹⁸耶利米對利甲族的人說："萬軍之耶和華以色列的神如此說：'因你們聽從你們先祖約拿達的吩咐，謹守他的一切誡命，照他所吩咐你們的去行。'¹⁹所以萬軍之耶和華以色列的神如此說：'利甲的兒子約拿達必永不缺人侍立在我面前。'"

約雅敬燒燬耶利米的書卷

36 猶大王約西亞的兒子約雅敬第四年，耶和華的話臨到耶利米說：²"你取一書卷，將我對你說攻擊以色列和猶大，並各國的一切話，從我對你說話的那日，是從約西亞的日子起，直到今日，都寫在其上。³或者猶大家聽見我想要降與他們的一切災禍，各人就回頭，離開惡道，我好赦免他們的罪孽和罪惡。"

⁴所以，耶利米召了尼利亞的兒子巴錄來，巴錄就從耶利米口中，將耶和華對耶利米所說的一切話寫在書卷上。⁵耶利米吩咐巴錄說："我被拘管，不能進耶和華的殿。⁶所以你要去，趁禁食的日子，在耶和華殿中

將耶和華的話，就是你從我口中所寫在書卷上的話，念給百姓和一切從猶大城邑出來的人聽。⁷或者他們在耶和華面前懇求，各人回頭，離開惡道，因為耶和華向這百姓所說要發的怒氣和忿怒是大的。」

⁸尼利亞的兒子巴錄就照先知耶利米一切所吩咐的去行，在耶和華的殿中從書上念耶和華的話。⁹猶大王約西亞的兒子約雅敬第五年九月，耶路撒冷的眾民和那從猶大城邑來到耶路撒冷的眾民，在耶和華面前宣告禁食的日子。¹⁰巴錄就在耶和華殿的上院，耶和華殿的新門口，沙番的兒子文士基瑪利雅的屋內，念書上耶利米的話給眾民聽。

¹¹沙番的孫子、基瑪利雅的兒子米該亞聽見書上耶和華的一切話，¹²他就下到王宮，進入文士的屋子。眾首領，就是文士以利沙瑪、示瑪雅的兒子第萊雅、亞革波的兒子以利拿單、沙番的兒子基瑪利雅、哈拿尼雅的兒子西底家和其餘的首領都坐在那裏。¹³於是米該亞對他們述說他所聽見的一切話，就是巴錄向百姓念那書的時候所聽見的。¹⁴眾首領就打發古示的曾孫示利米雅的孫子尼探雅的兒子猶底到巴錄那裏，對他說：「你將所念給百姓聽的書卷拿在手中，到我們這裏來。」尼利亞的兒子巴錄就手拿書卷，來到他們那裏。¹⁵他們對他說：「請你坐下，念給我們聽。」

巴錄就念給他們聽。¹⁶他們聽見這一切話就害怕，面面相觀，對巴錄說：「我們必須將這一切話告訴王。」¹⁷他們問巴錄說：「請你告訴我們，你怎樣從他口中寫這一切話呢？」

¹⁸巴錄回答說：「他用口向我說這一切話，我就用筆墨寫在書上。」

¹⁹眾首領對巴錄說：「你和耶利米要去藏起來，不可叫人知道你們在哪裏。」

²⁰眾首領進院見王，卻先把書卷存在文士以利沙瑪的屋內，以後將這一切話說給王聽。²¹王就打發猶底去拿這書卷來，他便從文士以利沙瑪的屋內取來，念給王和王左右侍立的眾首領聽。²²那時正是九月，王

words of the LORD that you wrote as I dictated. Read them to all the people of Judah who come in from their towns. ⁷Perhaps they will bring their petition before the LORD, and each will turn from his wicked ways, for the anger and wrath pronounced against this people by the LORD are great."

⁸Baruch son of Neriah did everything Jeremiah the prophet told him to do; at the LORD's temple he read the words of the LORD from the scroll. ⁹In the ninth month of the fifth year of Jehoiakim son of Josiah king of Judah, a time of fasting before the LORD was proclaimed for all the people in Jerusalem and those who had come from the towns of Judah. ¹⁰From the room of Gemariah son of Shaphan the secretary, which was in the upper courtyard at the entrance of the New Gate of the temple, Baruch read to all the people at the LORD's temple the words of Jeremiah from the scroll.

¹¹When Micaiah son of Gemariah, the son of Shaphan, heard all the words of the LORD from the scroll, ¹²he went down to the secretary's room in the royal palace, where all the officials were sitting: Elishama the secretary, Delaiah son of Shemaiah, Elnathan son of Acbor, Gemariah son of Shaphan, Zedekiah son of Hananiah, and all the other officials. ¹³After Micaiah told them everything he had heard Baruch read to the people from the scroll, ¹⁴all the officials sent Jehudi son of Nethaniah, the son of Shelemiah, the son of Cushi, to say to Baruch, "Bring the scroll from which you have read to the people and come." So Baruch son of Neriah went to them with the scroll in his hand. ¹⁵They said to him, "Sit down, please, and read it to us."

So Baruch read it to them. ¹⁶When they heard all these words, they looked at each other in fear and said to Baruch, "We must report all these words to the king." ¹⁷Then they asked Baruch, "Tell us, how did you come to write all this? Did Jeremiah dictate it?"

¹⁸"Yes," Baruch replied, "he dictated all these words to me, and I wrote them in ink on the scroll."

¹⁹Then the officials said to Baruch, "You and Jeremiah, go and hide. Don't let anyone know where you are."

²⁰After they put the scroll in the room of Elishama the secretary, they went to the king in the courtyard and reported everything to him. ²¹The king sent Jehudi to get the scroll, and Jehudi brought it from the room of Elishama the secretary and read it to the king and all the officials standing beside him. ²²It was the ninth month and the king was sitting in the winter

apartment, with a fire burning in the firepot in front of him. 23Whenever Jehudi had read three or four columns of the scroll, the king cut them off with a scribe's knife and threw them into the firepot, until the entire scroll was burned in the fire. 24The king and all his attendants who heard all these words showed no fear, nor did they tear their clothes. 25Even though Elnathan, Delaiah and Gemariah urged the king not to burn the scroll, he would not listen to them. 26Instead, the king commanded Jerahmeel, a son of the king, Seraiah son of Azriel and Shelemiah son of Abdeel to arrest Baruch the scribe and Jeremiah the prophet. But the LORD had hidden them.

27After the king burned the scroll containing the words that Baruch had written at Jeremiah's dictation, the word of the LORD came to Jeremiah: 28"Take another scroll and write on it all the words that were on the first scroll, which Jehoiakim king of Judah burned up. 29Also tell Jehoiakim king of Judah, 'This is what the LORD says: You burned that scroll and said, "Why did you write on it that the king of Babylon would certainly come and destroy this land and cut off both men and animals from it?" 30Therefore, this is what the LORD says about Jehoiakim king of Judah: He will have no one to sit on the throne of David; his body will be thrown out and exposed to the heat by day and the frost by night. 31I will punish him and his children and his attendants for their wickedness; I will bring on them and those living in Jerusalem and the people of Judah every disaster I pronounced against them, because they have not listened.' "

32So Jeremiah took another scroll and gave it to the scribe Baruch son of Neriah, and as Jeremiah dictated, Baruch wrote on it all the words of the scroll that Jehoiakim king of Judah had burned in the fire. And many similar words were added to them.

Jeremiah in Prison

37 Zedekiah son of Josiah was made king of Judah by Nebuchadnezzar king of Babylon; he reigned in place of Jehoiachin*a* son of Jehoiakim. 2Neither he nor his attendants nor the people of the land paid any attention to the words the LORD had spoken through Jeremiah the prophet.

3King Zedekiah, however, sent Jehucal son of Shelemiah with the priest Zephaniah son of Maaseiah to Jeremiah the prophet with this message: "Please pray to the LORD our God for us."

a 1 Hebrew Coniah, a variant of Jehoiachin

坐在過冬的房屋裏，王的前面火盆中有燒着的火。23猶底念了三、四篇（註：或作"行"），王就用文士的刀將書卷割破，扔在火盆中，直到全卷在火中燒盡了。24王和聽見這一切話的臣僕都不懼怕，也不撕裂衣服。25以利拿單和第萊雅，並基瑪利雅懇求王不要燒這書卷，他卻不聽。26王就吩咐哈米勒的兒子（註：或作"王的兒子"）耶拉篾和亞斯列的兒子西萊雅，並亞伯疊的兒子示利米雅，去捉拿文士巴錄和先知耶利米。耶和華卻將他們隱藏。

27王燒了書卷。其上有巴錄從耶利米口中所寫的話。以後，耶和華的話臨到耶利米說：28"你再取一卷，將猶大王約雅敬所燒第一卷上的一切話寫在其上。29論到猶大王約雅敬要說：'耶和華如此說：你燒了書卷，說：你為甚麼在其上寫着說，巴比倫王必要來毀滅這地，使這地上絕了人民牲畜呢？30所以耶和華論到猶大王約雅敬說：他後裔中必沒有人坐在大衛的寶座上；他的屍首必被拋棄，白日受炎熱，黑夜受寒霜。31我必因他和他後裔，並他臣僕的罪孽刑罰他們。我要使我所說的一切災禍臨到他們和耶路撒冷的居民，並猶大人；只是他們不聽。'"

32於是耶利米又取一書卷，交給尼利亞的兒子文士巴錄，他就從耶利米的口中寫了猶大王約雅敬所燒前卷上的一切話，另外又添了許多相彷的話。

耶利米在監牢裏

37 約西亞的兒子西底家代替約雅敬的兒子哥尼雅為王，是巴比倫王尼布甲尼撒立在猶大地作王的。2但西底家和他的臣僕，並國中的百姓，都不聽從耶和華藉先知耶利米所說的話。

3西底家王打發示利米雅的兒子猶甲和祭司瑪西雅的兒子西番雅，去見先知耶利米，說："求你為我們禱告耶和華我們的神。"

⁴那時耶利米在民中出入，因為他們還沒有把他囚在監裏。法老的軍隊已經從埃及出來，那圍困耶路撒冷的迦勒底人聽見他們的風聲，就拔營離開耶路撒冷去了。

⁶耶和華的話臨到先知耶利米說：⁷「耶和華以色列的神如此說：猶大王打發你們來求問我，你們要如此對他說：『那出來幫助你們法老的軍隊，必回埃及本國去。⁸迦勒底人必再來攻打這城，並要攻取，用火焚燒。』

⁹「耶和華如此說：你們不要自欺說：『迦勒底人必定離開我們』，因為他們必不離開。¹⁰你們即便殺敗了與你們爭戰的迦勒底全軍，但剩下受傷的人，也必各人從帳棚裏起來，用火焚燒這城。」

¹¹迦勒底的軍隊因怕法老的軍隊，拔營離開耶路撒冷的時候，¹²耶利米就離在民中出入離耶路撒冷，要往便雅憫地去，在那裏得自己的地業。¹³他到了便雅憫門那裏，有守門官名叫伊利雅，是哈拿尼亞的孫子、示利米雅的兒子，他就拿住先知耶利米，說：「你是投降迦勒底人哪！」

¹⁴耶利米說：「你這是謊話，我並不是投降迦勒底人。」伊利雅不聽他的話，就拿住他，解到首領那裏。¹⁵首領惱怒耶利米，就打了他，將他囚在文士約拿單的房屋中，因為他們以這房屋當作監牢。

¹⁶耶利米來到獄中，進入牢房，在那裏囚了多日。¹⁷西底家王打發人提出他來，在自己的宮內私下問他說：「從耶和華有甚麼話臨到沒有？」耶利米說：「有！」又說：「你必交在巴比倫王手中。」

¹⁸耶利米又對西底家王說：「我在甚麼事上得罪你，或你的臣僕，或這百姓，你竟將我囚在監裏呢？¹⁹對你們預言巴比倫王必不來攻擊你們和這地的先知，現今在哪裏呢？²⁰主我的王啊，求你現在垂聽，准我在你面前的懇求：不要使我回到文士約拿單的房屋中，免得我死在那裏。」

⁴Now Jeremiah was free to come and go among the people, for he had not yet been put in prison. ⁵Pharaoh's army had marched out of Egypt, and when the Babylonians[a] who were besieging Jerusalem heard the report about them, they withdrew from Jerusalem.

⁶Then the word of the LORD came to Jeremiah the prophet: ⁷"This is what the LORD, the God of Israel, says: Tell the king of Judah, who sent you to inquire of me, 'Pharaoh's army, which has marched out to support you, will go back to its own land, to Egypt. ⁸Then the Babylonians will return and attack this city; they will capture it and burn it down.'

⁹"This is what the LORD says: Do not deceive yourselves, thinking, 'The Babylonians will surely leave us.' They will not! ¹⁰Even if you were to defeat the entire Babylonian[b] army that is attacking you and only wounded men were left in their tents, they would come out and burn this city down."

¹¹After the Babylonian army had withdrawn from Jerusalem because of Pharaoh's army, ¹²Jeremiah started to leave the city to go to the territory of Benjamin to get his share of the property among the people there. ¹³But when he reached the Benjamin Gate, the captain of the guard, whose name was Irijah son of Shelemiah, the son of Hananiah, arrested him and said, "You are deserting to the Babylonians!"

¹⁴"That's not true!" Jeremiah said. "I am not deserting to the Babylonians." But Irijah would not listen to him; instead, he arrested Jeremiah and brought him to the officials. ¹⁵They were angry with Jeremiah and had him beaten and imprisoned in the house of Jonathan the secretary, which they had made into a prison.

¹⁶Jeremiah was put into a vaulted cell in a dungeon, where he remained a long time. ¹⁷Then King Zedekiah sent for him and had him brought to the palace, where he asked him privately, "Is there any word from the LORD?"

"Yes," Jeremiah replied, "you will be handed over to the king of Babylon."

¹⁸Then Jeremiah said to King Zedekiah, "What crime have I committed against you or your officials or this people, that you have put me in prison? ¹⁹Where are your prophets who prophesied to you, 'The king of Babylon will not attack you or this land'? ²⁰But now, my lord the king, please listen. Let me bring my petition before you: Do not send me back to the house of Jonathan the secretary, or I will die there."

---

a 5 Or *Chaldeans;* also in verses 8, 9, 13 and 14   *b 10* Or *Chaldean;* also in verse 11

21King Zedekiah then gave orders for Jeremiah to be placed in the courtyard of the guard and given bread from the street of the bakers each day until all the bread in the city was gone. So Jeremiah remained in the courtyard of the guard.

Jeremiah Thrown Into a Cistern

38 Shephatiah son of Mattan, Gedaliah son of Pashhur, Jehucal[a] son of Shelemiah, and Pashhur son of Malkijah heard what Jeremiah was telling all the people when he said, 2"This is what the LORD says: 'Whoever stays in this city will die by the sword, famine or plague, but whoever goes over to the Babylonians[b] will live. He will escape with his life; he will live.' 3And this is what the LORD says: 'This city will certainly be handed over to the army of the king of Babylon, who will capture it.' "

4Then the officials said to the king, "This man should be put to death. He is discouraging the soldiers who are left in this city, as well as all the people, by the things he is saying to them. This man is not seeking the good of these people but their ruin."

5"He is in your hands," King Zedekiah answered. "The king can do nothing to oppose you."

6So they took Jeremiah and put him into the cistern of Malkijah, the king's son, which was in the courtyard of the guard. They lowered Jeremiah by ropes into the cistern; it had no water in it, only mud, and Jeremiah sank down into the mud.

7But Ebed-Melech, a Cushite,[c] an official[d] in the royal palace, heard that they had put Jeremiah into the cistern. While the king was sitting in the Benjamin Gate, 8Ebed-Melech went out of the palace and said to him, 9"My lord the king, these men have acted wickedly in all they have done to Jeremiah the prophet. They have thrown him into a cistern, where he will starve to death when there is no longer any bread in the city."

10Then the king commanded Ebed-Melech the Cushite, "Take thirty men from here with you and lift Jeremiah the prophet out of the cistern before he dies."

11So Ebed-Melech took the men with him and went to a room under the treasury in the palace. He took some old rags and worn-out clothes from there and let them down with ropes to Jeremiah in the cistern. 12Ebed-Melech the

21於是西底家王下令，他們就把耶利米交在護衛兵的院中，每天從餅舖街取一個餅給他，直到城中的餅用盡了。這樣，耶利米仍在護衛兵的院中。

耶利米被投進淤泥牢獄中

38 瑪坦的兒子示法提雅、巴施戶珥的兒子基大利、示利米雅的兒子猶甲、瑪基雅的兒子巴示戶珥聽見耶利米對眾人所說的話，說：2"耶和華如此說：'住在這城裏的必遭刀劍、饑荒、瘟疫而死；但出去歸降迦勒底人的，必得存活，就是以自己命為掠物的，必得存活。'3耶和華如此說：'這城必要交在巴比倫王軍隊的手中，他必攻取這城。'"

4於是首領對王說："求你將這人治死，因他向城裏剩下的兵丁和眾民說這樣的話，使他們的手發軟。這人不是求這百姓得平安，乃是叫他們受災禍。"

5西底家王說："他在你們手中，無論何事，王也不能與你們反對。"

6他們就拿住耶利米，下在哈米勒的兒子（註：或作"王的兒子"）瑪基雅的牢獄裏。那牢獄在護衛兵的院中。他們用繩子將耶利米繫下去。牢獄裏沒有水，只有淤泥，耶利米就陷在淤泥中。

7在王宮的太監古實人以伯米勒，聽見他們將耶利米下了牢獄（那時王坐在便雅憫門口），8以伯米勒就從王宮裏出來，對王說：9"主我的王啊，這些人向先知耶利米一味地行惡，將他下在牢獄中，他在那裏必因飢餓而死，因為城中再沒有糧食。"

10王就吩咐古實人以伯米勒說："你從這裏帶領三十人，趁着先知耶利米未死以前，將他從牢獄中提上來。"

11於是以伯米勒帶領這些人同去，進入王宮，到庫房以下，從那裏取了些碎布和破爛的衣服，用繩子縋下牢獄去到耶利米那裏。12古實人以

---

a 1 Hebrew *Jucal*, a variant of *Jehucal*　b 2 Or *Chaldeans*; also in verses 18, 19 and 23　c 7 Probably from the upper Nile region　d 7 Or *a eunuch*

伯米勒對耶利米說：“你用這些碎布和破爛的衣服放在繩子上，墊你的胳肢窩。”耶利米就照樣行了。¹³這樣，他們用繩子將耶利米從牢獄裏拉上來。耶利米仍在護衛兵的院中。

西底家再次詢問耶利米

¹⁴西底家王打發人帶領先知耶利米，進耶和華殿中第三門裏見王。王就對耶利米說：“我要問你一件事，你絲毫不可向我隱瞞。”

¹⁵耶利米對西底家說：“我若告訴你，你豈不定要殺我嗎？我若勸戒你，你必不聽從我。”

¹⁶西底家王就私下向耶利米說：“我指着那造我們生命之永生的耶和華起誓，我必不殺你，也不將你交在尋索你命的人手中。”

¹⁷耶利米對西底家說：“耶和華萬軍之神、以色列的神如此說：‘你若出去歸降巴比倫王的首領，你的命就必存活，這城也不至被火焚燒，你和你的全家都必存活’；¹⁸你若不出去歸降巴比倫王的首領，這城必交在迦勒底人手中，他們必用火焚燒，你也不得脫離他們的手。’”

¹⁹西底家王對耶利米說：“我怕那些投降迦勒底人的猶大人，恐怕迦勒底人將我交在他們手中，他們戲弄我。”

²⁰耶利米說：“迦勒底人必不將你交出。求你聽從我對你所說耶和華的話，這樣，你必得好處，你的命也必存活，²¹你若不肯出去，耶和華指示我的話乃是這樣：²²猶大王宮裏所剩的婦女必都帶到巴比倫王的首領那裏。這些婦女必說：

“‘你知己的朋友催逼你，
　勝過你；
見你的腳陷入淤泥中，
　就轉身退後了。’

²³“人必將你的后妃和你的兒女帶到迦勒底人那裏。你也不得脫離他們的手，必被巴比倫王的手捉住，你也必使這城被火焚燒。”

Cushite said to Jeremiah, "Put these old rags and worn-out clothes under your arms to pad the ropes." Jeremiah did so, ¹³and they pulled him up with the ropes and lifted him out of the cistern. And Jeremiah remained in the courtyard of the guard.

Zedekiah Questions Jeremiah Again

¹⁴Then King Zedekiah sent for Jeremiah the prophet and had him brought to the third entrance to the temple of the LORD. "I am going to ask you something," the king said to Jeremiah. "Do not hide anything from me."

¹⁵Jeremiah said to Zedekiah, "If I give you an answer, will you not kill me? Even if I did give you counsel, you would not listen to me."

¹⁶But King Zedekiah swore this oath secretly to Jeremiah: "As surely as the LORD lives, who has given us breath, I will neither kill you nor hand you over to those who are seeking your life."

¹⁷Then Jeremiah said to Zedekiah, "This is what the LORD God Almighty, the God of Israel, says: 'If you surrender to the officers of the king of Babylon, your life will be spared and this city will not be burned down; you and your family will live. ¹⁸But if you will not surrender to the officers of the king of Babylon, this city will be handed over to the Babylonians and they will burn it down; you yourself will not escape from their hands.'"

¹⁹King Zedekiah said to Jeremiah, "I am afraid of the Jews who have gone over to the Babylonians, for the Babylonians may hand me over to them and they will mistreat me."

²⁰"They will not hand you over," Jeremiah replied. "Obey the LORD by doing what I tell you. Then it will go well with you, and your life will be spared. ²¹But if you refuse to surrender, this is what the LORD has revealed to me: ²²All the women left in the palace of the king of Judah will be brought out to the officials of the king of Babylon. Those women will say to you:

" 'They misled you and overcame you—
　those trusted friends of yours.
Your feet are sunk in the mud;
　your friends have deserted you.'

²³"All your wives and children will be brought out to the Babylonians. You yourself will not escape from their hands but will be captured by the king of Babylon; and this city will*a* be burned down."

a 23 Or and you will cause this city to

²⁴Then Zedekiah said to Jeremiah, "Do not let anyone know about this conversation, or you may die. ²⁵If the officials hear that I talked with you, and they come to you and say, 'Tell us what you said to the king and what the king said to you; do not hide it from us or we will kill you,' ²⁶then tell them, 'I was pleading with the king not to send me back to Jonathan's house to die there.' "

²⁷All the officials did come to Jeremiah and question him, and he told them everything the king had ordered him to say. So they said no more to him, for no one had heard his conversation with the king.

²⁸And Jeremiah remained in the courtyard of the guard until the day Jerusalem was captured.

The Fall of Jerusalem

39 This is how Jerusalem was taken: ¹In the ninth year of Zedekiah king of Judah, in the tenth month, Nebuchadnezzar king of Babylon marched against Jerusalem with his whole army and laid siege to it. ²And on the ninth day of the fourth month of Zedekiah's eleventh year, the city wall was broken through. ³Then all the officials of the king of Babylon came and took seats in the Middle Gate: Nergal-Sharezer of Samgar, Nebo-Sarsekim[a] a chief officer, Nergal-Sharezer a high official and all the other officials of the king of Babylon. ⁴When Zedekiah king of Judah and all the soldiers saw them, they fled; they left the city at night by way of the king's garden, through the gate between the two walls, and headed toward the Arabah.[b]

⁵But the Babylonian[c] army pursued them and overtook Zedekiah in the plains of Jericho. They captured him and took him to Nebuchadnezzar king of Babylon at Riblah in the land of Hamath, where he pronounced sentence on him. ⁶There at Riblah the king of Babylon slaughtered the sons of Zedekiah before his eyes and also killed all the nobles of Judah. ⁷Then he put out Zedekiah's eyes and bound him with bronze shackles to take him to Babylon.

⁸The Babylonians[d] set fire to the royal palace and the houses of the people and broke down the walls of Jerusalem. ⁹Nebuzaradan commander of the imperial guard carried into exile to Babylon the people who remained in the city, along with those who had gone over to him, and the rest of the people. ¹⁰But Nebuzaradan the commander of the guard left behind in the land

---

²⁴西底家對耶利米說:"不要使人知道這些話,你就不至於死,²⁵首領若聽見了我與你說話,就來見你,問你說:'你對王說甚麼話不要向我們隱瞞,我們就不殺你;王向你說甚麼話,也要告訴我們。'²⁶你就對他們說:'我在王面前懇求不要叫我回到約拿單的房屋死在那裏。'"

²⁷隨後眾首領來見耶利米,問他,他就照王所吩咐的一切話回答他們。他們不再與他說話,因為事情沒有洩漏。

²⁸於是耶利米仍在護衛兵的院中,直到耶路撒冷被攻取的日子。

耶路撒冷淪陷

39 ¹猶大王西底家第九年十月,巴比倫王尼布甲尼撒率領全軍來圍困耶路撒冷。²西底家十一年四月初九日,城被攻破。³耶路撒冷被攻取的時候,巴比倫王的首領尼甲沙利薛、三甲尼波、撒西金、拉撒力、尼甲沙利薛、拉墨,並巴比倫王其餘的一切首領,都來坐在中門。⁴猶大王西底家和一切兵丁看見他們,就在夜間從靠近王園兩城中間的門出城逃跑,往亞拉巴逃去。

⁵迦勒底的軍隊追趕他們,在耶利哥的平原追上西底家,將他拿住,帶到哈馬地的利比拉、巴比倫王尼布甲尼撒那裏。尼布甲尼撒就審判他。⁶巴比倫王在利比拉、西底家眼前殺了他的眾子,又殺了猶大的一切貴冑。⁷並且剜西底家的眼睛,用銅鏈鎖着他,要帶到巴比倫去。

⁸迦勒底人用火焚燒王宮和百姓的房屋,又拆毀耶路撒冷的城牆。⁹那時,護衛長尼布撒拉旦將城裏所剩下的百姓和投降他的逃民,以及其餘的民都擄到巴比倫去了。¹⁰護衛長尼布撒拉旦卻將民中毫無所有的窮人

---

a 3 Or Nergal-Sharezer, Samgar-Nebo, Sarsekim   b 4 Or the Jordan Valley   c 5 Or Chaldean   d 8 Or Chaldeans

留在<u>猶大</u>地，當時給他們葡萄園和田地。

11<u>巴比倫</u>王<u>尼布甲尼撒</u>提到<u>耶利米</u>，囑咐護衛長<u>尼布撒拉旦</u>說：12 "你領他去，好好地看待他，切不可害他。他對你怎麼說，你就向他怎麼行。" 13護衛長<u>尼布撒拉旦</u>和<u>尼布沙斯班</u>、<u>拉撒力</u>、<u>尼甲沙利薛</u>、<u>拉墨</u>並<u>巴比倫</u>王的一切官長，14打發人去將<u>耶利米</u>從護衛兵院中提出來，交與<u>沙番</u>的孫子、<u>亞希甘</u>的兒子<u>基大利</u>帶回家去。於是<u>耶利米</u>住在民中。

15<u>耶利米</u>還囚在護衛兵院中的時候，耶和華的話臨到他說：16 "你去告訴<u>古實人以伯米勒</u>說，萬軍之耶和華<u>以色列</u>的神如此說：'我說降禍不降福的話必臨到這城，到那時必在你面前成就了。17耶和華說：到那日我必拯救你，你必不至交在你所怕的人手中。18我定要搭救你，你不至倒在刀下，卻要以自己的命為掠物，因你倚靠我。這是耶和華說的。'"

耶利米獲釋

40 <u>耶利米</u>鎖在<u>耶路撒冷</u>和<u>猶大</u>被擄到<u>巴比倫</u>的人中，護衛長<u>尼布撒拉旦</u>將他從拉瑪釋放以後，耶和華的話臨到<u>耶利米</u>。2護衛長將<u>耶利米</u>叫來，對他說："耶和華你的神曾說要降這禍與此地。3耶和華使這禍臨到，照他所說的行了，因為你們得罪耶和華，沒有聽從他的話，所以這事臨到你們。4現在我解開你手上的鏈子，你若看與我同往<u>巴比倫</u>去好，就可以去，我必厚待你；你若看與我同往<u>巴比倫</u>去不好，就不必去。看哪，全地在你面前，你以為哪裏美好，哪裏合宜，只管上那裏去吧！" 5<u>耶利米</u>還沒有回去，護衛長說："你可以回到<u>沙番</u>的孫子、<u>亞希甘</u>的兒子<u>基大利</u>那裏去，現在<u>巴比倫</u>王立他作<u>猶大</u>城邑的省長。你可以在他那裏住在民中，不然，你看哪裏合宜就可以上那裏去。"

of Judah some of the poor people, who owned nothing; and at that time he gave them vineyards and fields.

11Now Nebuchadnezzar king of Babylon had given these orders about Jeremiah through Nebuzaradan commander of the imperial guard: 12"Take him and look after him; don't harm him but do for him whatever he asks." 13So Nebuzaradan the commander of the guard, Nebushazban a chief officer, Nergal-Sharezer a high official and all the other officers of the king of Babylon 14sent and had Jeremiah taken out of the courtyard of the guard. They turned him over to Gedaliah son of Ahikam, the son of Shaphan, to take him back to his home. So he remained among his own people.

15While Jeremiah had been confined in the courtyard of the guard, the word of the LORD came to him: 16"Go and tell Ebed-Melech the Cushite, 'This is what the LORD Almighty, the God of Israel, says: I am about to fulfill my words against this city through disaster, not prosperity. At that time they will be fulfilled before your eyes. 17But I will rescue you on that day, declares the LORD; you will not be handed over to those you fear. 18I will save you; you will not fall by the sword but will escape with your life, because you trust in me, declares the LORD.' "

Jeremiah Freed

40 The word came to Jeremiah from the LORD after Nebuzaradan commander of the imperial guard had released him at Ramah. He had found Jeremiah bound in chains among all the captives from Jerusalem and Judah who were being carried into exile to Babylon. 2When the commander of the guard found Jeremiah, he said to him, "The LORD your God decreed this disaster for this place. 3And now the LORD has brought it about; he has done just as he said he would. All this happened because you people sinned against the LORD and did not obey him. 4But today I am freeing you from the chains on your wrists. Come with me to Babylon, if you like, and I will look after you; but if you do not want to, then don't come. Look, the whole country lies before you; go wherever you please." 5However, before Jeremiah turned to go,a Nebuzaradan added, "Go back to Gedaliah son of Ahikam, the son of Shaphan, whom the king of Babylon has appointed over the towns of Judah, and live with him among the people, or go anywhere else you please."

a 5 Or Jeremiah answered

Then the commander gave him provisions and a present and let him go. [6]So Jeremiah went to Gedaliah son of Ahikam at Mizpah and stayed with him among the people who were left behind in the land.

Gedaliah Assassinated

[7]When all the army officers and their men who were still in the open country heard that the king of Babylon had appointed Gedaliah son of Ahikam as governor over the land and had put him in charge of the men, women and children who were the poorest in the land and who had not been carried into exile to Babylon, [8]they came to Gedaliah at Mizpah—Ishmael son of Nethaniah, Johanan and Jonathan the sons of Kareah, Seraiah son of Tanhumeth, the sons of Ephai the Netophathite, and Jaazaniah[a] the son of the Maacathite, and their men. [9]Gedaliah son of Ahikam, the son of Shaphan, took an oath to reassure them and their men. "Do not be afraid to serve the Babylonians,[b]" he said. "Settle down in the land and serve the king of Babylon, and it will go well with you. [10]I myself will stay at Mizpah to represent you before the Babylonians who come to us, but you are to harvest the wine, summer fruit and oil, and put them in your storage jars, and live in the towns you have taken over."

[11]When all the Jews in Moab, Ammon, Edom and all the other countries heard that the king of Babylon had left a remnant in Judah and had appointed Gedaliah son of Ahikam, the son of Shaphan, as governor over them, [12]they all came back to the land of Judah, to Gedaliah at Mizpah, from all the countries where they had been scattered. And they harvested an abundance of wine and summer fruit.

[13]Johanan son of Kareah and all the army officers still in the open country came to Gedaliah at Mizpah [14]and said to him, "Don't you know that Baalis king of the Ammonites has sent Ishmael son of Nethaniah to take your life?" But Gedaliah son of Ahikam did not believe them.

[15]Then Johanan son of Kareah said privately to Gedaliah in Mizpah, "Let me go and kill Ishmael son of Nethaniah, and no one will know it. Why should he take your life and cause all the Jews who are gathered around you to be scattered and the remnant of Judah to perish?"

[16]But Gedaliah son of Ahikam said to Johanan son of Kareah, "Don't do such a thing! What you are saying about Ishmael is not true."

於是護衛長送他糧食和禮物，釋放他去了。[6]耶利米就到米斯巴見亞希甘的兒子基大利，在他那裏住在境內剩下的民中。

基大利被謀殺

[7]在田野的一切軍長和屬他們的人，聽見巴比倫王立了亞希甘的兒子基大利作境內的省長，並將沒有擄到巴比倫的男人、婦女、孩童和境內極窮的人全交給他，[8]於是軍長尼探雅的兒子以實瑪利，加利亞的兩個兒子約哈難和約拿單，單戶篾的兒子西萊雅，並尼陀法人以斐的眾子，瑪迦人的兒子耶撒尼亞和屬他們的人，都到米斯巴見基大利。[9]沙番的孫子、亞希甘的兒子基大利向他們和屬他們的人起誓說：“不要怕服侍迦勒底人，只管住在這地服侍巴比倫王，就可以得福。[10]至於我，我要住在米斯巴，伺候那到我們這裏來的迦勒底人；只是你們當積蓄酒、油和夏天的果子，收在器皿裏，住在你們所佔的城邑中。”

[11]在摩押地和亞捫人中，在以東地和各國的一切猶大人，聽見巴比倫王留下些猶大人，並立沙番的孫子、亞希甘的兒子基大利管理他們。[12]這一切猶大人，就從所趕到的各處回來，到猶大地的米斯巴基大利那裏，又積蓄了許多的酒，並夏天的果子。

[13]加利亞的兒子約哈難和在田野的一切軍長，來到米斯巴見基大利，[14]對他說：“亞捫人的王巴利斯打發尼探雅的兒子以實瑪利來要你的命，你知道嗎？”亞希甘的兒子基大利卻不信他們的話。

[15]加利亞的兒子約哈難在米斯巴私下對基大利說：“求你容我去殺尼探雅的兒子以實瑪利，必無人知道。何必讓他要你的命，使聚集到你這裏來的猶大人都分散，以致猶大剩下的人都滅亡呢？”

[16]亞希甘的兒子基大利對加利亞的兒子約哈難說：“你不可行這事，你所論以實瑪利的話是假的。”

---

a 8 Hebrew *Jezaniah,* a variant of *Jaazaniah*   *b 9* Or *Chaldeans;* also in verse 10

41 七月間，王的大臣宗室以利沙瑪的孫子、尼探雅的兒子以實瑪利帶着十個人，來到米斯巴見亞希甘的兒子基大利。他們在米斯巴一同吃飯。²尼探雅的兒子以實瑪利和同他來的那十個人起來，用刀殺了沙番的孫子、亞希甘的兒子基大利，就是巴比倫王所立為全地省長的。³以實瑪利又殺了在米斯巴、基大利那裏的一切猶大人和所遇見的迦勒底兵丁。

⁴他殺了基大利，無人知道。⁵第二天，有八十人從示劍和示羅，並撒馬利亞來，鬍鬚剃去，衣服撕裂，身體劃破，手拿素祭和乳香，要奉到耶和華的殿。⁶尼探雅的兒子以實瑪利出米斯巴迎接他們，隨走隨哭。遇見了他們，就對他們說："你們可以來見亞希甘的兒子基大利"。⁷他們到了城中，尼探雅的兒子以實瑪利和同着他的人就將他們殺了，拋在坑內。⁸只是他們中間有十個人對以實瑪利說："不要殺我們，因為我們有許多大麥、小麥、油、蜜藏在田間。"於是他住了手，沒有將他們殺在弟兄中間。⁹以實瑪利將所殺之人的屍首都拋在坑裏基大利的旁邊。這坑是從前亞撒王因怕以色列王巴沙所挖的。尼探雅的兒子以實瑪利將那些被殺的人填滿了坑。

¹⁰以實瑪利將米斯巴剩下的人，就是眾公主和仍住在米斯巴所有的百姓，原是護衛長尼布撒拉旦交給亞希甘的兒子基大利的，都擄去了。尼探雅的兒子以實瑪利擄了他們，要往亞捫人那裏去。

¹¹加利亞的兒子約哈難和同着他的眾軍長，聽見尼探雅的兒子以實瑪利所行的一切惡，¹²就帶領眾人前往，要和尼探雅的兒子以實瑪利爭戰，在基遍的大水旁（註：或作"大水池旁"）遇見他。¹³以實瑪利那裏的眾人看見加利亞的兒子約哈難和同着他的眾軍長就都歡喜。¹⁴這樣，以實瑪利從米斯巴所擄去的眾人，都轉身

41 In the seventh month Ishmael son of Nethaniah, the son of Elishama, who was of royal blood and had been one of the king's officers, came with ten men to Gedaliah son of Ahikam at Mizpah. While they were eating together there, ²Ishmael son of Nethaniah and the ten men who were with him got up and struck down Gedaliah son of Ahikam, the son of Shaphan, with the sword, killing the one whom the king of Babylon had appointed as governor over the land. ³Ishmael also killed all the Jews who were with Gedaliah at Mizpah, as well as the Babylonianᵃ soldiers who were there.

⁴The day after Gedaliah's assassination, before anyone knew about it, ⁵eighty men who had shaved off their beards, torn their clothes and cut themselves came from Shechem, Shiloh and Samaria, bringing grain offerings and incense with them to the house of the LORD. ⁶Ishmael son of Nethaniah went out from Mizpah to meet them, weeping as he went. When he met them, he said, "Come to Gedaliah son of Ahikam." ⁷When they went into the city, Ishmael son of Nethaniah and the men who were with him slaughtered them and threw them into a cistern. ⁸But ten of them said to Ishmael, "Don't kill us! We have wheat and barley, oil and honey, hidden in a field." So he let them alone and did not kill them with the others. ⁹Now the cistern where he threw all the bodies of the men he had killed along with Gedaliah was the one King Asa had made as part of his defense against Baasha king of Israel. Ishmael son of Nethaniah filled it with the dead.

¹⁰Ishmael made captives of all the rest of the people who were in Mizpah—the king's daughters along with all the others who were left there, over whom Nebuzaradan commander of the imperial guard had appointed Gedaliah son of Ahikam. Ishmael son of Nethaniah took them captive and set out to cross over to the Ammonites.

¹¹When Johanan son of Kareah and all the army officers who were with him heard about all the crimes Ishmael son of Nethaniah had committed, ¹²they took all their men and went to fight Ishmael son of Nethaniah. They caught up with him near the great pool in Gibeon. ¹³When all the people Ishmael had with him saw Johanan son of Kareah and the army officers who were with him, they were glad. ¹⁴All the people Ishmael had taken captive at Mizpah turned and went over to Johanan son of Kareah.

a 3 Or Chaldean

15But Ishmael son of Nethaniah and eight of his men escaped from Johanan and fled to the Ammonites.

Flight to Egypt

16Then Johanan son of Kareah and all the army officers who were with him led away all the survivors from Mizpah whom he had recovered from Ishmael son of Nethaniah after he had assassinated Gedaliah son of Ahikam: the soldiers, women, children and court officials he had brought from Gibeon. 17And they went on, stopping at Geruth Kimham near Bethlehem on their way to Egypt 18to escape the Babylonians.*a* They were afraid of them because Ishmael son of Nethaniah had killed Gedaliah son of Ahikam, whom the king of Babylon had appointed as governor over the land.

42 Then all the army officers, including Johanan son of Kareah and Jezaniah*b* son of Hoshaiah, and all the people from the least to the greatest approached 2Jeremiah the prophet and said to him, "Please hear our petition and pray to the LORD your God for this entire remnant. For as you now see, though we were once many, now only a few are left. 3Pray that the LORD your God will tell us where we should go and what we should do."

4"I have heard you," replied Jeremiah the prophet. "I will certainly pray to the LORD your God as you have requested; I will tell you everything the LORD says and will keep nothing back from you."

5Then they said to Jeremiah, "May the LORD be a true and faithful witness against us if we do not act in accordance with everything the LORD your God sends you to tell us. 6Whether it is favorable or unfavorable, we will obey the LORD our God, to whom we are sending you, so that it will go well with us, for we will obey the LORD our God."

7Ten days later the word of the LORD came to Jeremiah. 8So he called together Johanan son of Kareah and all the army officers who were with him and all the people from the least to the greatest. 9He said to them, "This is what the LORD, the God of Israel, to whom you sent me to present your petition, says: 10'If you stay in this land, I will build you up and not tear you down; I will plant you and not uproot you, for I am grieved over the disaster I have inflicted on you. 11Do not be afraid of the king of Babylon, whom you now fear. Do not be afraid of him, declares

a 18 Or Chaldeans   b 1 Hebrew; Septuagint (see also 43:2) Azariah

歸加利亞的兒子約哈難去了。15尼探雅的兒子以實瑪利和八個人脫離約哈難的手,逃往亞捫人那裏去了。

逃往埃及

16尼探雅的兒子以實瑪利殺了亞希甘的兒子基大利,從米斯巴將剩下的一切百姓、兵丁、婦女、孩童、太監擄到基遍之後,加利亞的兒子約哈難和同著他的眾軍長,將他們都奪回來,17帶到靠近伯利恆的金罕寓(註:或作"基羅特金罕")住下,要進入埃及去。18因為尼探雅的兒子以實瑪利殺了巴比倫王所立為省長的亞希甘的兒子基大利,約哈難懼怕迦勒底人。

42 眾軍長和加利亞的兒子約哈難,並何沙雅的兒子耶撒雅亞(註:"耶撒尼亞"又名"亞撒利雅"。見43章2節)以及眾百姓,從最小的到至大的都進前來,2對先知耶利米說:"求你准我們在你面前祈求,為我們這剩下的人禱告耶和華你的神。我們本來眾多,現在剩下的極少,這是你親眼所見的。3願耶和華你的神指示我們所當走的路,所當做的事。"

4先知耶利米對他們說:"我已經聽見你們了,我必照著你們的話禱告耶和華你們的神。耶和華無論回答甚麼,我必都告訴你們,毫不隱瞞。"

5於是他們對耶利米說:"我們若不照耶和華你的神差遣你來說的一切話行,願耶和華在我們中間作真實誠信的見證。6我們現在請你到耶和華我們的神面前,他說的無論是好是歹,我們都必聽從!我們聽從耶和華我們神的話,就可以得福。"

7過了十天,耶和華的話臨到耶利米。8他就將加利亞的兒子約哈難和同著他的眾軍長,並眾百姓,從最小的到至大的都叫了來,9對他們說:"耶和華以色列的神,就是你們請我在他面前為你們祈求的主,如此說:10'你們若仍住在這地,我就建立你們,必不拆毀;栽植你們,並不拔出,因我為降與你們的災禍後悔了。11不要怕你們所怕的巴比倫王。耶和華說:不要怕他,因為我與你們

同在，要拯救你們脫離他的手。¹²我也要使他發憐憫，好憐憫你們，叫你們歸回本地。’

¹³“倘若你們說：‘我們不住在這地’，以致不聽從耶和華你們神的話，¹⁴說：‘我們不住這地，卻要進入埃及地，在那裏看不見爭戰，聽不見角聲，也不至無食飢餓。我們必住在那裏。’¹⁵你們所剩下的猶大人哪，現在要聽耶和華的話！萬軍之耶和華以色列的神如此說：‘你們若定意要進入埃及，在那裏寄居，¹⁶你們所懼怕的刀劍，在埃及地必追上你們！你們所懼怕的饑荒在埃及要緊緊地跟隨你們！你們必死在那裏。¹⁷凡定意要進入埃及在那裏寄居的，必遭刀劍、饑荒、瘟疫而死，無一人存留，逃脫我所降與他們的災禍。’¹⁸萬軍之耶和華以色列的神如此說：‘我怎樣將我的怒氣和忿怒傾在耶路撒冷的居民身上，你們進入埃及的時候，我也必照樣將我的忿怒傾在你們身上，以致你們令人辱罵、驚駭、咒詛、羞辱，你們不得再見這地方。’

¹⁹“所剩下的猶大人哪，耶和華論到你們說：‘不要進入埃及去！’你們要確實地知道我今日警教你們了。²⁰你們行詭詐自害，因為你們請我到耶和華你們的神那裏，說：‘求你為我們禱告耶和華我們神，照耶和華我們的神一切所說的告訴我們，我們就必遵行。’²¹我今日將這話告訴你們：耶和華你們的神為你們的事，差遣我到你們那裏說的，你們卻一樣沒有聽從。²²現在你們要確實地知道，你們在所要去寄居之地必遭刀劍、饑荒、瘟疫而死。”

43 耶利米向眾百姓說完了耶和華他們神的一切話，就是耶和華他們神差遣他去所說的一切話。²何沙雅的兒子亞撒利雅和加利亞的兒子約哈難，並一切狂傲的人，就對耶利米說：“你說謊言！耶和華我們的神並沒有差遣你來說：‘你們不可進入埃及在那裏寄居。’³這是尼利亞的兒子巴錄挑唆你害我們，要將我們交在迦勒底人的手中，使我們有被殺的，有被擄到巴比倫去的。”

⁴於是加利亞的兒子約哈難和一切軍長，並眾百姓，不聽從耶和華的話住在猶大地。⁵、⁶加利亞的兒子

the LORD, for I am with you and will save you and deliver you from his hands. ¹²I will show you compassion so that he will have compassion on you and restore you to your land.'

¹³"However, if you say, 'We will not stay in this land,' and so disobey the LORD your God, ¹⁴and if you say, 'No, we will go and live in Egypt, where we will not see war or hear the trumpet or be hungry for bread,' ¹⁵then hear the word of the LORD, O remnant of Judah. This is what the LORD Almighty, the God of Israel, says: 'If you are determined to go to Egypt and you do go to settle there, ¹⁶then the sword you fear will overtake you there, and the famine you dread will follow you into Egypt, and there you will die. ¹⁷Indeed, all who are determined to go to Egypt to settle there will die by the sword, famine and plague; not one of them will survive or escape the disaster I will bring on them.' ¹⁸This is what the LORD Almighty, the God of Israel, says: 'As my anger and wrath have been poured out on those who lived in Jerusalem, so will my wrath be poured out on you when you go to Egypt. You will be an object of cursing and horror, of condemnation and reproach; you will never see this place again.'

¹⁹"O remnant of Judah, the LORD has told you, 'Do not go to Egypt.' Be sure of this: I warn you today ²⁰that you made a fatal mistake[a] when you sent me to the LORD your God and said, 'Pray to the LORD our God for us; tell us everything he says and we will do it.' ²¹I have told you today, but you still have not obeyed the LORD your God in all he sent me to tell you. ²²So now, be sure of this: You will die by the sword, famine and plague in the place where you want to go to settle."

43 When Jeremiah finished telling the people all the words of the LORD their God—everything the LORD had sent him to tell them— ²Azariah son of Hoshaiah and Johanan son of Kareah and all the arrogant men said to Jeremiah, "You are lying! The LORD our God has not sent you to say, 'You must not go to Egypt to settle there.' ³But Baruch son of Neriah is inciting you against us to hand us over to the Babylonians,[b] so they may kill us or carry us into exile to Babylon."

⁴So Johanan son of Kareah and all the army officers and all the people disobeyed the LORD's command to stay in the land of Judah. ⁵Instead,

a 20 Or you erred in your hearts   b 3 Or Chaldeans

Johanan son of Kareah and all the army officers led away all the remnant of Judah who had come back to live in the land of Judah from all the nations where they had been scattered. ⁶They also led away all the men, women and children and the king's daughters whom Nebuzaradan commander of the imperial guard had left with Gedaliah son of Ahikam, the son of Shaphan, and Jeremiah the prophet and Baruch son of Neriah. ⁷So they entered Egypt in disobedience to the LORD and went as far as Tahpanhes.

⁸In Tahpanhes the word of the LORD came to Jeremiah: ⁹"While the Jews are watching, take some large stones with you and bury them in clay in the brick pavement at the entrance to Pharaoh's palace in Tahpanhes. ¹⁰Then say to them, 'This is what the LORD Almighty, the God of Israel, says: I will send for my servant Nebuchadnezzar king of Babylon, and I will set his throne over these stones I have buried here; he will spread his royal canopy above them. ¹¹He will come and attack Egypt, bringing death to those destined for death, captivity to those destined for captivity, and the sword to those destined for the sword. ¹²Heᵃ will set fire to the temples of the gods of Egypt; he will burn their temples and take their gods captive. As a shepherd wraps his garment around him, so will he wrap Egypt around himself and depart from there unscathed. ¹³There in the temple of the sunᵇ in Egypt he will demolish the sacred pillars and will burn down the temples of the gods of Egypt.' "

Disaster Because of Idolatry

44 This word came to Jeremiah concerning all the Jews living in Lower Egypt—in Migdol, Tahpanhes and Memphisᶜ—and in Upper Egyptᵈ: ²"This is what the LORD Almighty, the God of Israel, says: You saw the great disaster I brought on Jerusalem and on all the towns of Judah. Today they lie deserted and in ruins ³because of the evil they have done. They provoked me to anger by burning incense and by worshiping other gods that neither they nor you nor your fathers ever knew. ⁴Again and again I sent my servants the prophets, who said, 'Do not do this detestable thing that I hate!' ⁵But they did not listen or pay attention; they did not turn from their wickedness or stop burning incense to other gods. ⁶Therefore, my fierce anger was poured out; it raged against the towns of Judah and the streets of Jerusalem and made them the desolate ruins they are today.

約哈難和一切軍長卻將所剩下的<u>猶大</u>人，就是從被趕到各國回來，在<u>猶大</u>地寄居的男人、婦女、孩童和眾公主，並護衛長<u>尼布撒拉旦</u>所留在<u>沙番</u>的孫子、<u>亞希甘</u>的兒子<u>基大利</u>那裏的眾人，與先知<u>耶利米</u>，以及<u>尼利亞</u>的兒子<u>巴錄</u>，⁷都帶入<u>埃及</u>地，到了<u>答比匿</u>。這是因他們不聽從耶和華的話。

⁸在<u>答比匿</u>，耶和華的話臨到<u>耶利米</u>說，⁹"你在<u>猶大</u>人眼前要用手拿幾塊大石頭，藏在砌磚的灰泥中，就是在<u>答比匿</u>法老的宮門那裏，¹⁰對他們說：'萬軍之耶和華<u>以色列</u>的神如此說：我必召我的僕人<u>巴比倫</u>王<u>尼布甲尼撒</u>來，在所藏的石頭上，我要安置他的寶座。他必將光華的寶帳支搭在其上。¹¹他要來攻擊<u>埃及</u>地。定為死亡的，必至死亡；定為擄掠的，必被擄掠；定為刀殺的，必交刀殺。¹²我要在<u>埃及</u>的廟中使火着起，<u>巴比倫</u>王要將廟宇焚燒，神像擄去，他要得（註："得"原文作"披上"）<u>埃及</u>地，好像牧人披上外衣，從那裏安然而去。¹³他必打碎<u>埃及</u>地<u>伯示麥</u>的柱像，用火焚燒<u>埃及</u>神的廟宇。'"

拜偶像的災禍

44 有臨到<u>耶利米</u>的話，論及一切住在<u>埃及</u>地的<u>猶大</u>人，就是住在<u>密奪</u>、<u>答比匿</u>、<u>挪弗</u>、<u>巴忒羅</u>境內的<u>猶大</u>人，說：²"萬軍之耶和華<u>以色列</u>的神如此說：我所降與<u>耶路撒冷</u>和<u>猶大</u>各城的一切災禍，你們都看見了。那些城邑今日荒涼，無人居住。³這是因居民所行的惡，去燒香侍奉別神，就是他們和你們，並你們列祖所不認識的神，惹我發怒。⁴我從早起來差遣我的僕人眾先知去說：'你們切不要行我所厭惡這可憎之事。'⁵他們卻不聽從，不側耳而聽，不轉離惡事，仍向別神燒香。⁶因此，我的怒氣和忿怒都倒出來，在<u>猶大</u>城邑中和<u>耶路撒冷</u>的街市上，如火着起，以致都荒廢淒涼，正如今日一樣。

ᵃ 12 Or I   ᵇ 13 Or in Heliopolis   ᶜ 1 Hebrew Noph
ᵈ 1 Hebrew in Pathros

7 "現在耶和華萬軍之神、以色列的神如此說：你們為何作這大惡自害己命，使你們的男人、婦女、嬰孩和吃奶的都從猶大中剪除，不留一人呢？ 8 就是因你們手所做的，在所去寄居的埃及地，向別神燒香惹我發怒，使你們被剪除，在天下萬國中令人咒詛羞辱。 9 你們列祖的惡行，猶大列王和他們后妃的惡行，你們自己和你們妻子的惡行，就是在猶大地、耶路撒冷街上所行的，你們都忘了嗎？ 10 如今還沒有懊悔，沒有懼怕，沒有遵行我在你們和你們列祖面前所設立的法度律例。

11 "所以萬軍之耶和華以色列的神如此說：我必向你們變臉降災，以致剪除猶大眾人。 12 那定意進入埃及地，在那裏寄居的，就是所剩下的猶大人，我必使他們盡都滅絕。必在埃及地仆倒，必因刀劍、饑荒滅絕，從最小的到至大的都必遭刀劍饑荒而死，以致令人辱罵、驚駭、咒詛、羞辱。 13 我怎樣用刀劍、饑荒、瘟疫刑罰耶路撒冷，也必照樣刑罰那些住在埃及地的猶大人。 14 甚至那進入埃及地寄居的，就是所剩下的猶大人，都不得逃脫，也不得存留歸回猶大地，他們心中甚想歸回居住之地；除了逃脫的以外，一個都不能歸回。

15 那些住在埃及地巴忒羅知道自己妻子向別神燒香的，與旁邊站立的眾婦女，聚集成羣，回答耶利米說： 16 "論到你奉耶和華的名向我們所說的話，我們必不聽從。 17 我們定要成就我們口中所出的一切話，向天后燒香、澆奠祭，按着我們與我們列祖、君王、首領在猶大的城邑中和耶路撒冷的街市上素常所行的一樣。因為那時我們吃飽飯、享福樂，並不見災禍。 18 自從我們停止向天后燒香、澆奠祭，我們倒缺乏一切，又因刀劍饑荒滅絕。"

7"Now this is what the LORD God Almighty, the God of Israel, says: Why bring such great disaster on yourselves by cutting off from Judah the men and women, the children and infants, and so leave yourselves without a remnant? 8Why provoke me to anger with what your hands have made, burning incense to other gods in Egypt, where you have come to live? You will destroy yourselves and make yourselves an object of cursing and reproach among all the nations on earth. 9Have you forgotten the wickedness committed by your fathers and by the kings and queens of Judah and the wickedness committed by you and your wives in the land of Judah and the streets of Jerusalem? 10To this day they have not humbled themselves or shown reverence, nor have they followed my law and the decrees I set before you and your fathers.

11"Therefore, this is what the LORD Almighty, the God of Israel, says: I am determined to bring disaster on you and to destroy all Judah. 12I will take away the remnant of Judah who were determined to go to Egypt to settle there. They will all perish in Egypt; they will fall by the sword or die from famine. From the least to the greatest, they will die by sword or famine. They will become an object of cursing and horror, of condemnation and reproach. 13I will punish those who live in Egypt with the sword, famine and plague, as I punished Jerusalem. 14None of the remnant of Judah who have gone to live in Egypt will escape or survive to return to the land of Judah, to which they long to return and live; none will return except a few fugitives."

15Then all the men who knew that their wives were burning incense to other gods, along with all the women who were present—a large assembly—and all the people living in Lower and Upper Egypt,a said to Jeremiah, 16"We will not listen to the message you have spoken to us in the name of the LORD! 17We will certainly do everything we said we would: We will burn incense to the Queen of Heaven and will pour out drink offerings to her just as we and our fathers, our kings and our officials did in the towns of Judah and in the streets of Jerusalem. At that time we had plenty of food and were well off and suffered no harm. 18But ever since we stopped burning incense to the Queen of Heaven and pouring out drink offerings to her, we have had nothing and have been perishing by sword and famine."

a 15 Hebrew in Egypt and Pathros

[19]The women added, "When we burned incense to the Queen of Heaven and poured out drink offerings to her, did not our husbands know that we were making cakes like her image and pouring out drink offerings to her?"

[20]Then Jeremiah said to all the people, both men and women, who were answering him, [21]"Did not the LORD remember and think about the incense burned in the towns of Judah and the streets of Jerusalem by you and your fathers, your kings and your officials and the people of the land? [22]When the LORD could no longer endure your wicked actions and the detestable things you did, your land became an object of cursing and a desolate waste without inhabitants, as it is today. [23]Because you have burned incense and have sinned against the LORD and have not obeyed him or followed his law or his decrees or his stipulations, this disaster has come upon you, as you now see."

[24]Then Jeremiah said to all the people, including the women, "Hear the word of the LORD, all you people of Judah in Egypt. [25]This is what the LORD Almighty, the God of Israel, says: You and your wives have shown by your actions what you promised when you said, 'We will certainly carry out the vows we made to burn incense and pour out drink offerings to the Queen of Heaven.'

"Go ahead then, do what you promised! Keep your vows! [26]But hear the word of the LORD, all Jews living in Egypt: 'I swear by my great name,' says the LORD, 'that no one from Judah living anywhere in Egypt will ever again invoke my name or swear, "As surely as the Sovereign LORD lives." [27]For I am watching over them for harm, not for good; the Jews in Egypt will perish by sword and famine until they are all destroyed. [28]Those who escape the sword and return to the land of Judah from Egypt will be very few. Then the whole remnant of Judah who came to live in Egypt will know whose word will stand—mine or theirs.

[29]" 'This will be the sign to you that I will punish you in this place,' declares the LORD, 'so that you will know that my threats of harm against you will surely stand.' [30]This is what the LORD says: 'I am going to hand Pharaoh Hophra king of Egypt over to his enemies who seek his life, just as I handed Zedekiah king of Judah over to Nebuchadnezzar king of Babylon, the enemy who was seeking his life.' "

[19]婦女說：“我們向天后燒香、澆奠祭，做天后像的餅供奉她，向她澆奠祭，是外乎我們的丈夫嗎？”

[20]耶利米對一切那樣回答他的男人婦女說：[21]“你們與你們列祖、君王、首領、並國內的百姓，在猶大城邑中和耶路撒冷街市上所燒的香，耶和華豈不記念，心中豈不思想嗎？[22]耶和華因你們所作的惡，所行可憎的事，不能再容忍。所以你們的地荒涼，令人驚駭、咒詛，無人居住，正如今日一樣。[23]你們燒香，得罪耶和華，沒有聽從他的話，沒有遵行他的律法、條例、法度，所以你們遭遇這災禍，正如今日一樣。”

[24]耶利米又對眾民和眾婦女說：“你們在埃及地的一切猶大人，當聽耶和華的話。[25]萬軍之耶和華以色列的神如此說：你們和你們的妻都口中說、手裏做，說：‘我們定要償還所許的願，向天后燒香、澆奠祭。’

“現在你們只管堅定所許的願而償還吧！[26]所以你們住在埃及地的一切猶大人，當聽耶和華的話。耶和華說：‘我指着我的大名起誓，在埃及全地，我的名不再被猶大一個人的口稱呼說：我指着主永生的耶和華起誓。[27]我向他們留意降禍不降福，在埃及地的一切猶大人必因刀劍、饑荒所滅，直到滅盡。[28]脫離刀劍、從埃及地歸回猶大地的人數很少；那進入埃及地要在那裏寄居的，就是所剩下的猶大人，必知道是誰的話立得住，是我的話呢？是他們的話呢？’

[29]“耶和華說：‘我在這地方刑罰你們，必有預兆，使你們知道我降禍與你們的話，必要立得住。’[30]耶和華如此說：‘我必將埃及王法老合弗拉交在他仇敵和尋索其命的人手中，像我將猶大王西底家交在他仇敵和尋索其命的巴比倫王尼布甲尼撒手中一樣。’”

給巴錄的信息

45 猶大王約西亞的兒子約雅敬第四年，尼利亞的兒子巴錄將先知耶利米口中所說的話寫在書上。耶利米說：²「巴錄啊，耶和華以色列的神說：³「巴錄（註：原文作"你"）曾說：哀哉！耶和華將憂愁加在我的痛苦上，我因唉哼而困乏，不得安歇。」

⁴「你要這樣告訴他，耶和華如此說：『我所建立的，我必拆毀；我所栽植的，我必拔出。在全地我都如此行。⁵你為自己圖謀大事嗎？不要圖謀！我必使災禍臨到凡有血氣的。但你無論往哪裏去，我必使你以自己的命為掠物。』這是耶和華說的。」

論埃及的信息

46 耶和華論列國的話臨到先知耶利米。

²論到關乎埃及王法老尼哥的軍隊：

這軍隊安營在幼發拉底河邊的迦基米施，是巴比倫王尼布甲尼撒在猶大王約西亞的兒子約雅敬第四年所打敗的。

³ 「你們要預備大小盾牌，
　　往前上陣，
⁴你們套上車，
　　騎上馬，
頂盔站立，
磨槍貫甲。

⁵我為何看見他們
　　驚惶轉身退後呢？

他們的勇士打敗了，
　　急忙逃跑，
並不回頭，
　　驚嚇四圍都有！」
　　　　　　　這是耶和華說的。
⁶ 「不要容快跑的逃避；
　　不要容勇士逃脫（註：或作"快跑的不能逃避，勇士不能逃脫"）。

他們在北方幼發拉底河邊
　　絆跌仆倒。

⁷ 「像尼羅河漲發，
　　像江河之水翻騰的是誰呢？

A Message to Baruch

45 This is what Jeremiah the prophet told Baruch son of Neriah in the fourth year of Jehoiakim son of Josiah king of Judah, after Baruch had written on a scroll the words Jeremiah was then dictating: ²This is what the LORD, the God of Israel, says to you, Baruch: ³You said, 'Woe to me! The LORD has added sorrow to my pain; I am worn out with groaning and find no rest.'

⁴The LORD said, "Say this to him: 'This is what the LORD says: I will overthrow what I have built and uproot what I have planted, throughout the land. ⁵Should you then seek great things for yourself? Seek them not. For I will bring disaster on all people, declares the LORD, but wherever you go I will let you escape with your life.' "

A Message About Egypt

46 This is the word of the LORD that came to Jeremiah the prophet concerning the nations:

²Concerning Egypt:

This is the message against the army of Pharaoh Neco king of Egypt, which was defeated at Carchemish on the Euphrates River by Nebuchadnezzar king of Babylon in the fourth year of Jehoiakim son of Josiah king of Judah:

³"Prepare your shields, both large and small,
　　and march out for battle!
⁴Harness the horses,
　　mount the steeds!
Take your positions
　　with helmets on!
Polish your spears,
　　put on your armor!
⁵What do I see?
　　They are terrified,
they are retreating,
　　their warriors are defeated.
They flee in haste
　　without looking back,
and there is terror on every side,"
　　　　　　　declares the LORD.
⁶"The swift cannot flee
　　nor the strong escape.
In the north by the River Euphrates
　　they stumble and fall.

⁷"Who is this that rises like the Nile,
　　like rivers of surging waters?

[8]Egypt rises like the Nile,
　　like rivers of surging waters.
She says, 'I will rise and cover the earth;
　　I will destroy cities and their people.'
[9]Charge, O horses!
　　Drive furiously, O charioteers!
March on, O warriors—
　　men of Cush[a] and Put who carry shields,
　　men of Lydia who draw the bow.
[10]But that day belongs to the Lord, the LORD
　　Almighty—
　　a day of vengeance, for vengeance on his foes.
The sword will devour till it is satisfied,
　　till it has quenched its thirst with blood.
For the Lord, the LORD Almighty, will offer
　　sacrifice
　　in the land of the north by the River Euphrates.

[11]"Go up to Gilead and get balm,
　　O Virgin Daughter of Egypt.
But you multiply remedies in vain;
　　there is no healing for you.
[12]The nations will hear of your shame;
　　your cries will fill the earth.
One warrior will stumble over another;
　　both will fall down together."

[13]This is the message the LORD spoke to
Jeremiah the prophet about the coming of
Nebuchadnezzar king of Babylon to attack
Egypt:

[14]"Announce this in Egypt, and proclaim it in
　　Migdol;
　　proclaim it also in Memphis[b] and Tahpanhes:
'Take your positions and get ready,
　　for the sword devours those around you.'
[15]Why will your warriors be laid low?
　　They cannot stand, for the LORD will push
　　them down.
[16]They will stumble repeatedly;
　　they will fall over each other.
They will say, 'Get up, let us go back
　　to our own people and our native lands,
　　away from the sword of the oppressor.'
[17]There they will exclaim,
　　'Pharaoh king of Egypt is only a loud noise;
　　he has missed his opportunity.'

[18]"As surely as I live," declares the King,
　　whose name is the LORD Almighty,

[8]埃及像尼羅河漲發，
　　像江河的水翻騰。
她說：'我要漲發遮蓋遍地，
　　我要毀滅城邑和其中的居民。'
[9]馬匹上去吧！
　　車輛急行吧！
勇士，就是手拿盾牌的古實人
　　和弗人（註：又作 "利比亞人"），
　　並拉弓的路德族，都出去吧！
[10]那日是主萬軍之耶和華
　　報仇的日子，
　　要向敵人報仇！
刀劍必吞吃得飽，
　　飲血飲足；
因為主萬軍之耶和華
　　在北方幼發拉底河邊
　　有獻祭的事。

[11]"埃及的民哪（註："民" 原文作 "處女"），
　　可以上基列取乳香去；
你雖多服良藥，
　　總是徒然，不得治好。
[12]列國聽見你的羞辱，
　　遍地滿了你的哀聲，
勇士與勇士彼此相碰，
　　一齊跌倒。"

[13]耶和華對先知耶利米所說的
話，論到巴比倫王尼布甲尼撒要來攻
擊埃及地：

[14]"你們要傳揚在埃及，宣告在密奪，
　　報告在挪弗、答比匿說：
'要站起出隊，自作準備，
　　因為刀劍在你四圍
　　施行吞滅的事。'
[15]你的壯士為何被沖去呢？
　　他們站立不住，
　　因為耶和華驅逐他們，
[16]使多人絆跌，
　　他們也彼此撞倒，說：
'起來吧！
　　我們再往本民本地去，
　　好躲避欺壓的刀劍。'
[17]他們在那裏喊叫說：
'埃及王法老不過是個聲音（註：
　　"不過是個聲音" 或作 "已經敗亡"），
　　他已錯過所定的時候了。'"
[18]君王，名為萬軍之耶和華的說：
　　"我指着我的永生起誓，

a 9 That is, the upper Nile region　　b 14 Hebrew Noph; also in
verse 19

尼布甲尼撒（註：原文作“他”）來的
　　勢派必像他泊在眾山之中，
　　像迦密在海邊一樣。
19 住在埃及的民哪（註：“民”原文作“女
　子”），要預備擄去時所用的物件，
　因為挪弗必成為荒場，
　　且被燒燬，無人居住。

20 “埃及是肥美的母牛犢，
　　但出於北方的毀滅（註：“毀滅”或
　　　作“牛虻”）來到了！來到了！
21 其中的雇勇
　　好像圈裏的肥牛犢，
　他們轉身退後，一齊逃跑，
　　站立不住，
　因為他們遭難的日子、
　追討的時候已經臨到。
22 其中的聲音好像蛇行一樣，
　　敵人要成隊而來，
　如砍伐樹木的手
　　拿斧子攻擊她。”
23 耶和華說：“埃及的樹林，
　　雖然不能尋察（註：或作“穿不過”），
　敵人卻要砍伐，
　　因他們多於蝗蟲，
　　不可勝數。
24 埃及的民（註：“民”原文作“女子”）
　　必然蒙羞，
　　必交在北方人的手中。”
25 萬軍之耶和華以色列的神說：
　“我必刑罰挪的亞捫（註：埃及尊大之
　神）和法老，並埃及與埃及的神，以
　及君王，也必刑罰法老和倚靠他的
　人。26 我要將他們交付尋索其命之人
　的手和巴比倫王尼布甲尼撒與他臣
　僕的手。以後埃及必再有人居住，
　與從前一樣。”這是耶和華說的。

27 “我的僕人雅各啊，不要懼怕！
　　以色列啊，不要驚惶！
　因我要從遠方拯救你，
　　從被擄到之地拯救你的後裔。
　雅各必回來，得享平靖安逸，
　　無人使他害怕。
28 我的僕人雅各啊，不要懼怕！
　　因我與你同在。
　我要將我所趕你到的那些國
　　滅絕淨盡，
　卻不將你滅絕淨盡，
　倒要從寬懲治你，
　萬不能不罰你（註：“不罰你”或作
　“以你為無罪”）。”
　　　　　　　　　　這是耶和華說的。

"one will come who is like Tabor among the
　mountains,
　like Carmel by the sea.
19 Pack your belongings for exile,
　you who live in Egypt,
　for Memphis will be laid waste
　and lie in ruins without inhabitant.

20 "Egypt is a beautiful heifer,
　but a gadfly is coming
　against her from the north.
21 The mercenaries in her ranks
　are like fattened calves.
　They too will turn and flee together,
　they will not stand their ground,
　for the day of disaster is coming upon them,
　the time for them to be punished.
22 Egypt will hiss like a fleeing serpent
　as the enemy advances in force;
　they will come against her with axes,
　like men who cut down trees.
23 They will chop down her forest,"
　　　　　　　　　declares the LORD,
　"dense though it be.
　They are more numerous than locusts,
　they cannot be counted.
24 The Daughter of Egypt will be put to shame,
　handed over to the people of the north."

25 The LORD Almighty, the God of Israel, says:
"I am about to bring punishment on Amon god
of Thebes,[a] on Pharaoh, on Egypt and her gods
and her kings, and on those who rely on Pharaoh. 26 I will hand them over to those who seek
their lives, to Nebuchadnezzar king of Babylon
and his officers. Later, however, Egypt will be
inhabited as in times past," declares the LORD.

27 "Do not fear, O Jacob my servant;
　do not be dismayed, O Israel.
　I will surely save you out of a distant place,
　your descendants from the land of their exile.
　Jacob will again have peace and security,
　and no one will make him afraid.
28 Do not fear, O Jacob my servant,
　for I am with you," declares the LORD.
　"Though I completely destroy all the nations
　among which I scatter you,
　I will not completely destroy you.
　I will discipline you but only with justice;
　I will not let you go entirely unpunished."

a 25 Hebrew No

A Message About the Philistines

47 This is the word of the LORD that came to Jeremiah the prophet concerning the Philistines before Pharaoh attacked Gaza:

²This is what the LORD says:

"See how the waters are rising in the north;
     they will become an overflowing torrent.
They will overflow the land and everything in it,
     the towns and those who live in them.
The people will cry out;
     all who dwell in the land will wail
³at the sound of the hoofs of galloping steeds,
     at the noise of enemy chariots
     and the rumble of their wheels.
Fathers will not turn to help their children;
     their hands will hang limp.
⁴For the day has come
     to destroy all the Philistines
and to cut off all survivors
     who could help Tyre and Sidon.
The LORD is about to destroy the Philistines,
     the remnant from the coasts of Caphtor.ᵃ
⁵Gaza will shave her head in mourning;
     Ashkelon will be silenced.
O remnant on the plain,
     how long will you cut yourselves?

⁶" 'Ah, sword of the LORD,' ⌐you cry,⌐
     'how long till you rest?
Return to your scabbard;
     cease and be still.'
⁷But how can it rest
     when the LORD has commanded it,
when he has ordered it
     to attack Ashkelon and the coast?"

A Message About Moab

48 Concerning Moab:

This is what the LORD Almighty, the God of Israel, says:

"Woe to Nebo, for it will be ruined.
     Kiriathaim will be disgraced and captured;
the strongholdᵇ will be disgraced and
          shattered.
²Moab will be praised no more;
     in Heshbonᶜ men will plot her downfall:
'Come, let us put an end to that nation.'

論非利士人的信息

47 法老攻擊迦薩之先，有耶和華論非利士人的話臨到先知耶利米：

²耶和華如此說：

"有水從北方發起，
     成為漲溢的河，
要漲過遍地和其中所有的，
     並城其中所住的。
人必呼喊，
     境內的居民都必哀號。
³聽見敵人壯馬蹄跳的響聲
     和戰車隆隆、
     車輪轟轟，
為父的手就發軟，
     不回頭看顧兒女。
⁴因為日子將到，
     要毀滅一切非利士人，
剪除幫助推羅、西頓
     所剩下的人。
原來耶和華必毀滅非利士人，
     就是迦斐託海島餘剩的人。
⁵迦薩成了光禿；
     平原中所剩的亞實基倫
     歸於無有。
你用刀割身，要到幾時呢？

⁶ " '耶和華的刀劍哪，
     你到幾時才止息呢？
你要入鞘
     安靖不動。'
⁷耶和華既吩咐你攻擊
     亞實基倫和海邊之地，
他已經派定你，
     焉能止息呢？"

論摩押的信息

48 論摩押：

萬軍之耶和華以色列的神如此說：

"尼波有禍了！因變為荒場。
     基列亭蒙羞被攻取；
     米斯迦蒙羞被毀壞。

²摩押不再被稱讚，
     有人在希實本設計謀害她，說：
'來吧！我們將她剪除，
     不再成國。'

ᵃ 4 That is, Crete   ᵇ 1 Or / Misgab   ᶜ 2 The Hebrew for Heshbon sounds like the Hebrew for plot.

瑪得緬哪，你也必默默無聲，
　　刀劍必追趕你。
³從何羅念
　　有喊荒涼大毀滅的哀聲。
⁴摩押毀滅了！
　　她的孩童（註：或作"僮僕"）
　　發哀聲，使人聽見。
⁵人上魯希坡隨走隨哭，
　　因為在何羅念的下坡，
　　聽見毀滅的哀聲。
⁶你們要奔逃，自救性命，
　　獨自居住，好像曠野的杜松。
⁷你因倚靠自己所做的和自己的財寶，
　　必被攻取。
　　基抹和屬他的祭司、
　　首領也要一同被擄去。
⁸行毀滅的必來到各城，
　　並無一城得免。
　　山谷必至敗落，
　　平原必被毀壞，
　　正如耶和華所說的。
⁹要將翅膀給摩押，
　　使她可以飛去。
　　她的城邑必至荒涼，
　　無人居住。

¹⁰"懶惰為耶和華行事的，
　　必受咒詛！
　　禁止刀劍不經血的，
　　必受咒詛！

¹¹"摩押自幼年以來常享安逸，
　　如酒在渣滓上澄清，
　　沒有從這器皿倒在那器皿裏，
　　也未曾被擄去。
　　因此，她的原味尚存，
　　香氣未變。"
¹²耶和華說：
　　"日子將到，
　　我必打發倒酒的往她那裏去，
　　將她倒出來，
　　倒空她的器皿，
　　打碎她的罈子。
¹³摩押必因基抹羞愧，
　　像以色列家從前倚靠伯特利的神
　　羞愧一樣。

¹⁴"你們怎麼說'我們是勇士，
　　是有勇力打仗的'呢？
¹⁵摩押變為荒場，
　　敵人上去進了她的城邑。

You too, O Madmen,[a] will be silenced;
　　the sword will pursue you.
³Listen to the cries from Horonaim,
　　cries of great havoc and destruction.
⁴Moab will be broken;
　　her little ones will cry out.[b]
⁵They go up the way to Luhith,
　　weeping bitterly as they go;
on the road down to Horonaim
　　anguished cries over the destruction are heard.
⁶Flee! Run for your lives;
　　become like a bush[c] in the desert.
⁷Since you trust in your deeds and riches,
　　you too will be taken captive,
and Chemosh will go into exile,
　　together with his priests and officials.
⁸The destroyer will come against every town,
　　and not a town will escape.
The valley will be ruined
　　and the plateau destroyed,
　　because the LORD has spoken.
⁹Put salt on Moab,
　　for she will be laid waste[d];
her towns will become desolate,
　　with no one to live in them.

¹⁰"A curse on him who is lax in doing the
　　　LORD's work!
A curse on him who keeps his sword from
　　　bloodshed!

¹¹"Moab has been at rest from youth,
　　like wine left on its dregs,
not poured from one jar to another—
　　she has not gone into exile.
So she tastes as she did,
　　and her aroma is unchanged.
¹²But days are coming,"
　　declares the LORD,
　　"when I will send men who pour from jars,
　　and they will pour her out;
they will empty her jars
　　and smash her jugs.
¹³Then Moab will be ashamed of Chemosh,
　　as the house of Israel was ashamed
　　when they trusted in Bethel.

¹⁴"How can you say, 'We are warriors,
　　men valiant in battle'?
¹⁵Moab will be destroyed and her towns
　　　invaded;

*a 2 The name of the Moabite town Madmen sounds like the
Hebrew for be silenced.　b 4 Hebrew; Septuagint / proclaim it
to Zoar　c 6 Or like Aroer　d 9 Or Give wings to Moab, / for she
will fly away*

her finest young men will go down in the
　　slaughter,"
declares the King, whose name is the LORD
　　Almighty.
16"The fall of Moab is at hand;
　　her calamity will come quickly.
17Mourn for her, all who live around her,
　　all who know her fame;
say, 'How broken is the mighty scepter,
　　how broken the glorious staff!'

18"Come down from your glory
　　and sit on the parched ground,
　　O inhabitants of the Daughter of Dibon,
for he who destroys Moab
　　will come up against you
　　and ruin your fortified cities.
19Stand by the road and watch,
　　you who live in Aroer.
Ask the man fleeing and the woman escaping,
　　ask them, 'What has happened?'
20Moab is disgraced, for she is shattered.
　　Wail and cry out!
Announce by the Arnon
　　that Moab is destroyed.
21Judgment has come to the plateau—
　　to Holon, Jahzah and Mephaath,
22　to Dibon, Nebo and Beth Diblathaim,
23　to Kiriathaim, Beth Gamul and Beth Meon,
24　to Kerioth and Bozrah—
　　to all the towns of Moab, far and near.
25Moab's horn*a* is cut off;
　　her arm is broken,"
　　　　　　　　　　　　declares the LORD.

26"Make her drunk,
　　for she has defied the LORD.
Let Moab wallow in her vomit;
　　let her be an object of ridicule.
27Was not Israel the object of your ridicule?
　　Was she caught among thieves,
that you shake your head in scorn
　　whenever you speak of her?
28Abandon your towns and dwell among the rocks,
　　you who live in Moab.
Be like a dove that makes its nest
　　at the mouth of a cave.

29"We have heard of Moab's pride—
　　her overweening pride and conceit,
her pride and arrogance
　　and the haughtiness of her heart.
30I know her insolence but it is futile,"
　　　　　　　　　　　　declares the LORD,

她所特選的少年人下去
　　遭了殺戮。"
這是君王、
　　名為萬軍之耶和華說的。
16 "摩押的災殃臨近；
　　她的苦難速速來到。
17凡在她四圍的和認識她名的，
　　你們都要為她悲傷，說：
'那結實的杖和那美好的棍，
　　何竟折斷了呢？'

18 "住在<u>底本</u>的民哪（註："民"原文作
　　"女子"），要從你榮耀的位上下來，
　　坐受乾渴，
因毀滅<u>摩押</u>的
　　上來攻擊你，
　　毀壞了你的保障。
19住<u>亞羅珥</u>的啊，
　　要站在道旁觀望，
問逃避的男人和逃脫的女人說：
　　'是甚麼事呢？'
20<u>摩押</u>因毀壞蒙羞，
　　你們要哀號呼喊！
要在<u>亞嫩</u>旁邊報告說：
　　<u>摩押</u>變為荒場！
21刑罰臨到平原之地的
　　<u>何倫</u>、<u>雅雜</u>、<u>米法押</u>、
22<u>底本</u>、<u>尼波</u>、<u>伯低比拉太音</u>、
23<u>基列亭</u>、<u>伯迦末</u>、<u>伯米恩</u>、
24<u>加略</u>、<u>波斯拉</u>
　　和<u>摩押</u>地遠近所有的城邑。
25<u>摩押</u>的角砍斷了，
　　<u>摩押</u>的膀臂折斷了。"
　　　　　　　　　這是耶和華說的。

26 "你們要使<u>摩押</u>沉醉，
　　因她向耶和華誇大。
她要在自己所吐之中打滾，
　　又要被人嗤笑。
27<u>摩押</u>啊，你不曾嗤笑<u>以色列</u>嗎？
　　她豈是在賊中查出來的呢？
　　你每逢提到她便搖頭。
28<u>摩押</u>的居民哪，
　　要離開城邑，
　　住在山崖裏，
　　像鴿子在深淵口上搭窩。

29 "我們聽說<u>摩押</u>人驕傲，
　　是極其驕傲；
聽說她自高自傲，
　　並且狂妄，居心自大。"
30耶和華說：
　　"我知道她的忿怒是虛空的；

---

a 25 Horn here symbolizes strength.

她誇大的話一無所成。
31因此，我要為摩押哀號，
　　為摩押全地呼喊。
　　人必為吉珥哈列設人歎息。
32西比瑪的葡萄樹啊，我為你哀哭，
　　甚於雅謝人哀哭。
　你的枝子蔓延過海，
　　直長到雅謝海。
　那行毀滅的，已經臨到
　　你夏天的果子和你所摘的葡萄。
33肥田和摩押地的歡喜快樂
　　都被奪去，
　我使酒醡的酒絕流，
　　無人踹酒歡呼；
　那歡呼卻變為仇敵的吶喊（註：原文
　　作"那歡呼卻不是歡呼"）。

34　"希實本人發的哀聲
　　達到以利亞利，直達到雅雜，
　從瑣珥達到何羅念，
　　直到伊基拉施利施亞，
　　因為寧林的水必然乾涸。"
35耶和華說：
　"我必在摩押地
　　使那在邱壇獻祭的，
　和那向他的神燒香的
　　都斷絕了。
36　"我心腹為摩押哀鳴如簫，
　　我心腸為吉珥哈列設人
　　也是如此，
　　因摩押人所得的財物都滅沒了。
37各人頭上光禿，
　　鬍鬚剪短，
　手有劃傷，
　　腰束麻布。
38在摩押的各房頂上
　　和街市上，
　　處處有人哀哭。
　因我打碎摩押，
　　好像打碎無人喜悅的器皿。"
　　　　　　　　這是耶和華說的。
39　"摩押何等毀壞！何等哀號！
　　何等羞愧轉背！
　這樣，
　　摩押必令四圍的人嗤笑驚駭。"

40耶和華如此說：

　"仇敵必如大鷹飛起，
　　展開翅膀，攻擊摩押。
41加略被攻取，
　　保障也被佔據。

"and her boasts accomplish nothing.
31Therefore I wail over Moab,
　for all Moab I cry out,
　I moan for the men of Kir Hareseth.
32I weep for you, as Jazer weeps,
　O vines of Sibmah.
　Your branches spread as far as the sea;
　　they reached as far as the sea of Jazer.
　The destroyer has fallen
　　on your ripened fruit and grapes.
33Joy and gladness are gone
　from the orchards and fields of Moab.
　I have stopped the flow of wine from the
　　presses;
　no one treads them with shouts of joy.
　Although there are shouts,
　　they are not shouts of joy.

34"The sound of their cry rises
　from Heshbon to Elealeh and Jahaz,
　from Zoar as far as Horonaim and Eglath
　　Shelishiyah,
　for even the waters of Nimrim are dried up.
35In Moab I will put an end
　to those who make offerings on the high
　　places
　and burn incense to their gods,"
　　　　　　　　declares the LORD.
36"So my heart laments for Moab like a flute;
　it laments like a flute for the men of Kir
　　Hareseth.
　The wealth they acquired is gone.
37Every head is shaved
　and every beard cut off;
　every hand is slashed
　and every waist is covered with sackcloth.
38On all the roofs in Moab
　and in the public squares
　there is nothing but mourning,
　for I have broken Moab
　like a jar that no one wants,"
　　　　　　　　declares the LORD.
39"How shattered she is! How they wail!
　How Moab turns her back in shame!
　Moab has become an object of ridicule,
　an object of horror to all those around her."

40This is what the LORD says:

　"Look! An eagle is swooping down,
　spreading its wings over Moab.
41Kerioth[a] will be captured
　and the strongholds taken.

In that day the hearts of Moab's warriors
　will be like the heart of a woman in labor.
[42]Moab will be destroyed as a nation
　because she defied the LORD.
[43]Terror and pit and snare await you,
　O people of Moab,"
　　　　　　　　　　　　　declares the LORD.
[44]"Whoever flees from the terror
　will fall into a pit,
whoever climbs out of the pit
　will be caught in a snare;
for I will bring upon Moab
　the year of her punishment,"
　　　　　　　　　　　　　declares the LORD.

[45]"In the shadow of Heshbon
　the fugitives stand helpless,
for a fire has gone out from Heshbon,
　a blaze from the midst of Sihon;
it burns the foreheads of Moab,
　the skulls of the noisy boasters.
[46]Woe to you, O Moab!
　The people of Chemosh are destroyed;
your sons are taken into exile
　and your daughters into captivity.

[47]"Yet I will restore the fortunes of Moab
　in days to come,"
　　　　　　　　　　　　　declares the LORD.

Here ends the judgment on Moab.

A Message About Ammon

49 Concerning the Ammonites:

　　This is what the LORD says:

"Has Israel no sons?
　Has she no heirs?
Why then has Molech[a] taken possession of
　Gad?
Why do his people live in its towns?
[2]But the days are coming,"
　declares the LORD,
"when I will sound the battle cry
　against Rabbah of the Ammonites;
it will become a mound of ruins,
　and its surrounding villages will be set on
　fire.
Then Israel will drive out
　those who drove her out,"
　　　　　　　　　　　　　says the LORD.
[3]"Wail, O Heshbon, for Ai is destroyed!
　Cry out, O inhabitants of Rabbah!

a 1 Or their king; Hebrew malcam; also in verse 3

到那日，摩押的勇士心中疼痛
　如臨產的婦人。
[42]摩押必被毀滅，不再成國，
　因她向耶和華誇大。"
[43]耶和華說：
　"摩押的居民哪，
　恐懼、陷坑、網羅都臨近你。
[44]"躲避恐懼的
　必墜入陷坑；
從陷坑上來的
　必被網羅纏住。
因我必使追討之年
　臨到摩押。"
　　　　　　　　　　這是耶和華說的。

[45]"躲避的人
　無力站在希實本的影下，
因為有火從希實本發出，
　有火焰出於西宏的城，
燒盡摩押的角
　和鬨嚷人的頭頂。
[46]摩押啊，你有禍了！
　屬基抹的民滅亡了！
因你的眾子都被擄去，
　你的眾女也被擄去。"

[47]耶和華說：
　"到末後，
　我還要使被擄的摩押人歸回。"

摩押受審判的話到此為止。

論亞捫的信息

49 論亞捫人：

　　耶和華如此說：

"以色列沒有兒子嗎？
　沒有後嗣嗎？
瑪勒堪為何得迦得之地為業呢？
　屬他的民為何住其中的城邑呢？"

[2]耶和華說：
"日子將到，
　我必使人聽見打仗的喊聲，
　是攻擊亞捫人拉巴的喊聲。
拉巴要成為亂堆，
　屬他的鄉村（註：原文作"女子"）
　要被火焚燒。
先前得以色列地為業的，此時
　以色列倒要得他們的地為業。"
　　　　　　　　這是耶和華說的。
[3]"希實本哪，你要哀號！
　因為愛地變為荒場。
拉巴的居民哪（註："居民"原文作
　"女子"），

要呼喊，以麻布束腰；
　要哭號，在籬笆中跑來跑去，
因瑪勒堪和屬他的祭司、
　首領要一同被擄去。

4背道的民哪（註："民"原文作"女子"），
　你們為何因有山谷，
　就是水流的山谷誇張呢？
為何倚靠財寶說：
　'誰能來到我們這裏呢？'"

5主萬軍之耶和華說：
"我要使恐嚇從四圍的人中
　臨到你們，
你們必被趕出，
　各人一直前往，
　沒有人收聚逃民。

6 "後來我還要使
　被擄的亞捫人歸回。"
　　這是耶和華說的。

論以東的信息

7論以東：

萬軍之耶和華如此說：

"提幔中再沒有智慧嗎？
　明哲人不再有謀略嗎？
　他們的智慧盡歸無有嗎？
8底但的居民哪，
　要轉身逃跑，住在深密處；
因為我向以掃追討的時候，
　必使災殃臨到他。
9摘葡萄的若來到他那裏，
　豈不剩下些葡萄呢？
盜賊若夜間而來，
　豈不毀壞
　　直到夠了呢？
10我卻使以掃赤露，
　顯出他的隱密處，
　他不能自藏。
他的後裔、弟兄、鄰舍盡都滅絕，
　他也歸於無有。
11你撇下孤兒，我必保全他們的命，
　你的寡婦可以倚靠我。"

12耶和華如此說："原不該喝那杯的一定要喝。你能盡免刑罰嗎？你必不能免，一定要喝！"13耶和華說："我指着自己起誓，波斯拉必令人驚駭、羞辱、咒詛，並且荒涼。他的一切城邑必變為永遠的荒場。"

Put on sackcloth and mourn;
　rush here and there inside the walls,
for Molech will go into exile,
　together with his priests and officials.
4Why do you boast of your valleys,
　boast of your valleys so fruitful?
O unfaithful daughter,
　you trust in your riches and say,
　'Who will attack me?'
5I will bring terror on you
　from all those around you,"
　　　　　　declares the Lord,
　　　　　　　the LORD Almighty.
"Every one of you will be driven away,
　and no one will gather the fugitives.

6"Yet afterward, I will restore the fortunes of
　the Ammonites,"
　　　　　　declares the LORD.

A Message About Edom

7Concerning Edom:

This is what the LORD Almighty says:

"Is there no longer wisdom in Teman?
　Has counsel perished from the prudent?
　Has their wisdom decayed?
8Turn and flee, hide in deep caves,
　you who live in Dedan,
for I will bring disaster on Esau
　at the time I punish him.
9If grape pickers came to you,
　would they not leave a few grapes?
If thieves came during the night,
　would they not steal only as much as they
　　wanted?
10But I will strip Esau bare;
　I will uncover his hiding places,
　so that he cannot conceal himself.
His children, relatives and neighbors will perish,
　and he will be no more.
11Leave your orphans; I will protect their lives.
　Your widows too can trust in me."

12This is what the LORD says: "If those who do not deserve to drink the cup must drink it, why should you go unpunished? You will not go unpunished, but must drink it. 13I swear by myself," declares the LORD, "that Bozrah will become a ruin and an object of horror, of reproach and of cursing; and all its towns will be in ruins forever."

¹⁴I have heard a message from the LORD:
   An envoy was sent to the nations to say,
   "Assemble yourselves to attack it!
   Rise up for battle!"

¹⁵"Now I will make you small among the nations,
   despised among men.
¹⁶The terror you inspire
   and the pride of your heart have deceived you,
   you who live in the clefts of the rocks,
   who occupy the heights of the hill.
   Though you build your nest as high as the
      eagle's,
   from there I will bring you down,"
                              declares the LORD.
¹⁷"Edom will become an object of horror;
   all who pass by will be appalled and will scoff
   because of all its wounds.
¹⁸As Sodom and Gomorrah were overthrown,
   along with their neighboring towns,"
                              says the LORD,
   "so no one will live there;
   no man will dwell in it.

¹⁹"Like a lion coming up from Jordan's thickets
   to a rich pastureland,
   I will chase Edom from its land in an instant.
   Who is the chosen one I will appoint for this?
   Who is like me and who can challenge me?
   And what shepherd can stand against me?"
²⁰Therefore, hear what the LORD has planned
      against Edom,
   what he has purposed against those who live
      in Teman:
   The young of the flock will be dragged away;
   he will completely destroy their pasture
      because of them.
²¹At the sound of their fall the earth will
      tremble;
   their cry will resound to the Red Sea.^a
²²Look! An eagle will soar and swoop down,
   spreading its wings over Bozrah.
   In that day the hearts of Edom's warriors
   will be like the heart of a woman in labor.

A Message About Damascus

²³Concerning Damascus:

"Hamath and Arpad are dismayed,
   for they have heard bad news.
They are disheartened,
   troubled like^b the restless sea.

¹⁴我從耶和華那裏聽見信息，
   並有使者被差往列國去，說：
   "你們聚集來攻擊以東，
   要起來爭戰！"

¹⁵ "我使他在列國中為最小，
   在世人中被藐視。
¹⁶住在山穴中
      據守山頂的啊，
   論到你的威嚇，
      你因心中的狂傲自欺，
   你雖如大鷹
      高高搭窩，
   我卻從那裏拉下你來。"
                        這是耶和華說的。
¹⁷ "以東必令人驚駭；
   凡經過的人就受驚駭，
   又因他一切的災禍嗤笑。"
¹⁸耶和華說：
   "必無人住在那裏，
   也無人在其中寄居。
   要像所多瑪、蛾摩拉和鄰近的城邑
   傾覆的時候一樣。

¹⁹ "仇敵必像獅子從約旦河邊的叢林
      上來，攻擊堅固的居所。
   轉眼之間，
   我要使以東人逃跑離開這地。
   誰蒙揀選，我就派誰治理這地。
   誰能比我呢？誰能épée我定規日期呢？
   有何牧人能在我面前站立得住呢？"
²⁰你們要聽耶和華攻擊以東
      所說的謀略，
   和他攻擊提幔居民
      所定的旨意。
   仇敵定要將他們羣眾微弱的拉去，
   定要使他們的居所荒涼。
²¹因他們仆倒的聲音，地就震動。
   人在紅海那裏
      必聽見呼喊的聲音。
²²仇敵必如大鷹飛起，
   展開翅膀攻擊波斯拉。
   到那日，以東的勇士心中疼痛，
   如臨產的婦人。

論大馬士革的信息

²³論大馬士革：

"哈馬和亞珥拔蒙羞，
   因他們聽見兇惡的信息
      就消化了。
   海上有憂愁，不得平靜。

---

^a 21 Hebrew *Yam Suph*; that is, Sea of Reeds   ^b 23 Hebrew *on*
or *by*

24大馬士革發軟，
　　轉身逃跑。
戰兢將她捉住，
　　痛苦憂愁將她抓住，
　　如產難的婦人一樣。
25我所喜樂
　　可稱讚的城，
　　為何被撇棄了呢？
26她的少年人，必仆倒在街上。
　　當那日，一切兵丁必默默無聲。」
　　　　　　這是萬軍之耶和華說的。
27「我必在大馬士革城中使火着起，
　　燒滅便哈達的宮殿。」

論基達和夏瑣的信息

28論巴比倫王尼布甲尼撒所攻打
的基達和夏瑣的諸國：

耶和華如此說：

「迦勒底人哪，起來上基達去，
　　毀滅東方人。
29他們的帳棚和羊羣都要奪去，
　　將幔子和一切器皿，
　　並駱駝為自己掠去。
　人向他們喊着說：
　　『四圍都有驚嚇。』」

30耶和華說：
「夏瑣的居民哪，
　　要逃奔遠方，住在深密處。
　因為巴比倫王尼布甲尼撒
　　設計謀害你們，
　　起意攻擊你們。」

31耶和華說：
「迦勒底人哪，起來，
　　上安逸無慮的居民那裏去。
　他們是無門無門，
　　獨自居住的。
32他們的駱駝必成為掠物；
　　他們眾多的牲畜必成為擄物。
　我必將剃周圍頭髮的人
　　分散四方（註：「方」原文作「風」），
　使災殃
　　從四圍臨到他們。」
　　　　　　這是耶和華說的。

33「夏瑣必成為野狗的住處，
　　永遠淒涼。
　必無人住在那裏，
　　也無人在其中寄居。」

24Damascus has become feeble,
　　she has turned to flee
　　and panic has gripped her;
anguish and pain have seized her,
　　pain like that of a woman in labor.
25Why has the city of renown not been
　　abandoned,
　　the town in which I delight?
26Surely, her young men will fall in the streets;
　　all her soldiers will be silenced in that day,"
　　　　　　declares the LORD Almighty.
27"I will set fire to the walls of Damascus;
　　it will consume the fortresses of Ben-Hadad."

A Message About Kedar and Hazor

28Concerning Kedar and the kingdoms of
Hazor, which Nebuchadnezzar king of Babylon
attacked:

This is what the LORD says:

"Arise, and attack Kedar
　　and destroy the people of the East.
29Their tents and their flocks will be taken;
　　their shelters will be carried off
　　with all their goods and camels.
Men will shout to them,
　　'Terror on every side!'

30"Flee quickly away!
　　Stay in deep caves, you who live in Hazor,"
　　　　　　declares the LORD.

"Nebuchadnezzar king of Babylon has plotted
　　against you;
　　he has devised a plan against you.

31"Arise and attack a nation at ease,
　　which lives in confidence,"
　　　　　　declares the LORD,
　"a nation that has neither gates nor bars;
　　its people live alone.
32Their camels will become plunder,
　　and their large herds will be booty.
I will scatter to the winds those who are in
　　distant places[a]
　　and will bring disaster on them from every
　　side,"
　　　　　　declares the LORD.

33"Hazor will become a haunt of jackals,
　　a desolate place forever.
No one will live there;
　　no man will dwell in it."

a 32 Or who clip the hair by their foreheads

A Message About Elam

34This is the word of the LORD that came to Jeremiah the prophet concerning Elam, early in the reign of Zedekiah king of Judah:

35This is what the LORD Almighty says:

"See, I will break the bow of Elam,
　the mainstay of their might.
36I will bring against Elam the four winds
　from the four quarters of the heavens;
I will scatter them to the four winds,
　and there will not be a nation
　where Elam's exiles do not go.
37I will shatter Elam before their foes,
　before those who seek their lives;
I will bring disaster upon them,
　even my fierce anger,"
　　　　　　　　　　　declares the LORD.
"I will pursue them with the sword
　until I have made an end of them.
38I will set my throne in Elam
　and destroy her king and officials,"
　　　　　　　　　　　declares the LORD.

39"Yet I will restore the fortunes of Elam
　in days to come,"
　　　　　　　　　　　declares the LORD.

A Message About Babylon

50 This is the word the LORD spoke through Jeremiah the prophet concerning Babylon and the land of the Babylonians[a]:

2"Announce and proclaim among the nations,
　lift up a banner and proclaim it;
　keep nothing back, but say,
'Babylon will be captured;
　Bel will be put to shame,
　Marduk filled with terror.
Her images will be put to shame
　and her idols filled with terror.'
3A nation from the north will attack her
　and lay waste her land.
No one will live in it;
　both men and animals will flee away.

4"In those days, at that time,"
　　　　　　　　　　　declares the LORD,
"the people of Israel and the people of Judah together
　will go in tears to seek the LORD their God.

a 1 Or Chaldeans; also in verses 8, 25, 35 and 45

論以攔的信息

34猶大王西底家登基的時候，耶和華論以攔的話臨到先知耶利米説：

35萬軍之耶和華如此説：

"我必折斷以攔人的弓，
　就是他們為首的權力。
36我要使四風從天的四方颳來，
　臨到以攔人，將他們分散四方
　　（註："方"原文作"風"）。
這被趕散的人，
　沒有一國不到的。"
37耶和華説：
"我必使以攔人在仇敵
　和尋索其命的人面前驚惶；
我也必使災禍，
　就是我的烈怒臨到他們；
又必使刀劍追殺他們，
　直到將他們滅盡。
38我要在以攔設立我的寶座，
　從那裏除滅君王和首領。"
　　　　　　　　這是耶和華説的。

39"到末後，
　我還要使被擄的以攔人歸回。"
　　　　　　　　這是耶和華説的。

論巴比倫的信息

50 耶和華藉先知耶利米論巴比倫和迦勒底人之地所説的話：

2"你們要在萬國中傳揚報告，
　豎立大旗；
　要報告，不可隱瞞，説：
'巴比倫被攻取，
　彼勒蒙羞，
　米羅達驚惶。
巴比倫的神像都蒙羞，
　她的偶像都驚惶。'
3因有一國從北方上來攻擊她，
　使她的地荒涼，
無人居住，
　連人帶牲畜都逃走了。"

4耶和華説：
"當那日子，那時候，
　以色列人要和猶大人同來，
隨走隨哭，
　尋求耶和華他們的神。

⁵他們必訪問錫安，
　　又面向這裏說：
　　來吧！
　　你們要與耶和華聯合為
　　永遠不忘的約。

⁶ “我的百姓作了迷失的羊，
　　牧人使他們走差路，
　　使他們轉到山上。
　　他們從大山走到小山，
　　竟忘了安歇之處。
⁷凡遇見他們的，就把他們吞滅。
　　敵人說：‘我們沒有罪，
　　因他們得罪那
　　作公義居所的耶和華，
　　就是他們列祖所仰望的耶和華。’

⁸ “我民哪，你們要從巴比倫中逃走，
　　從迦勒底人之地出去，
　　要像羊羣前面走的公山羊。
⁹因我必激動聯合的大國
　　從北方上來
　　　攻擊巴比倫，
　　他們要擺陣攻擊她，
　　她必從那裏被攻取。
　　他們的箭好像善射之勇士的箭，
　　　一枝也不徒然返回。
¹⁰迦勒底必成為掠物；
　　凡擄掠她的都必心滿意足。”
　　　　　　這是耶和華說的。

¹¹ “搶奪我產業的啊，
　　你們因歡喜快樂，
　　且像踹穀撒歡的母牛犢，
　　又像發嘶聲的壯馬。
¹²你們的母巴比倫就極其抱愧，
　　生你們的必然蒙羞。
　　她要列在諸國之末，
　　成為曠野、旱地、沙漠。
¹³因耶和華的忿怒，
　　必無人居住，
　　要全然荒涼。
　　凡經過巴比倫的，
　　要受驚駭，
　　又因她所遭的災殃嗤笑。

¹⁴ “所有拉弓的，
　　你們要在巴比倫的四圍擺陣，
　　射箭攻擊她，不要愛惜箭枝，
　　因她得罪了耶和華。
¹⁵你們要在她四圍吶喊！
　　她已經投降，外郭坍塌了，
　　城牆拆毀了。

⁵They will ask the way to Zion
　　and turn their faces toward it.
They will come and bind themselves to the
　　LORD
　　in an everlasting covenant
　　that will not be forgotten.

⁶“My people have been lost sheep;
　　their shepherds have led them astray
　　and caused them to roam on the mountains.
They wandered over mountain and hill
　　and forgot their own resting place.
⁷Whoever found them devoured them;
　　their enemies said, ‘We are not guilty,
　　for they sinned against the LORD, their true
　　　pasture,
　　the LORD, the hope of their fathers.’

⁸“Flee out of Babylon;
　　leave the land of the Babylonians,
　　and be like the goats that lead the flock.
⁹For I will stir up and bring against Babylon
　　an alliance of great nations from the land of
　　　the north.
They will take up their positions against her,
　　and from the north she will be captured.
Their arrows will be like skilled warriors
　　who do not return empty-handed.
¹⁰So Babylonia^a will be plundered;
　　all who plunder her will have their fill,”
　　　　　　　　　　　declares the LORD.

¹¹“Because you rejoice and are glad,
　　you who pillage my inheritance,
　　because you frolic like a heifer threshing grain
　　and neigh like stallions,
¹²your mother will be greatly ashamed;
　　she who gave you birth will be disgraced.
She will be the least of the nations—
　　a wilderness, a dry land, a desert.
¹³Because of the LORD's anger she will not be
　　inhabited
　　but will be completely desolate.
All who pass Babylon will be horrified and
　　scoff
　　because of all her wounds.

¹⁴“Take up your positions around Babylon,
　　all you who draw the bow.
Shoot at her! Spare no arrows,
　　for she has sinned against the LORD.
¹⁵Shout against her on every side!
　　She surrenders, her towers fall,
　　her walls are torn down.

_a 10 Or *Chaldea*

Since this is the vengeance of the LORD,
  take vengeance on her;
  do to her as she has done to others.
¹⁶Cut off from Babylon the sower,
  and the reaper with his sickle at harvest.
Because of the sword of the oppressor
  let everyone return to his own people,
  let everyone flee to his own land.

¹⁷"Israel is a scattered flock
  that lions have chased away.
The first to devour him
  was the king of Assyria;
the last to crush his bones
  was Nebuchadnezzar king of Babylon."

¹⁸Therefore this is what the LORD Almighty,
the God of Israel, says:

"I will punish the king of Babylon and his land
  as I punished the king of Assyria.
¹⁹But I will bring Israel back to his own pasture
  and he will graze on Carmel and Bashan;
his appetite will be satisfied
  on the hills of Ephraim and Gilead.
²⁰In those days, at that time,"
  declares the LORD,
"search will be made for Israel's guilt,
  but there will be none,
and for the sins of Judah,
  but none will be found,
for I will forgive the remnant I spare.

²¹"Attack the land of Merathaim
  and those who live in Pekod.
Pursue, kill and completely destroy^a them,"
                    declares the LORD.
"Do everything I have commanded you.
²²The noise of battle is in the land,
  the noise of great destruction!
²³How broken and shattered
  is the hammer of the whole earth!
How desolate is Babylon
  among the nations!
²⁴I set a trap for you, O Babylon,
  and you were caught before you knew it;
you were found and captured
  because you opposed the LORD.
²⁵The LORD has opened his arsenal
  and brought out the weapons of his wrath,
for the Sovereign LORD Almighty has work to do
  in the land of the Babylonians.

因為這是耶和華報仇的事,
  你們要向巴比倫報仇;
  她怎樣待人,也要怎樣待她。
¹⁶你們要將巴比倫撒種的
  和收割時拿鐮刀的都剪除了。
他們各人因怕欺壓的刀劍,
  必歸回本族,
  逃到本土。

¹⁷"以色列是打散的羊,
  是被獅子趕出的。
首先是亞述王
  將他吞滅;
末後是巴比倫王尼布甲尼撒
  將他的骨頭折斷。"

¹⁸所以萬軍之耶和華以色列的神
如此說:

"我必罰巴比倫王和他的地,
  像我從前罰亞述王一樣。
¹⁹我必再容領以色列回他的草場,
  他必在迦密和巴珊吃草,
又在以法蓮山上和基列境內
  得以飽足。"
²⁰耶和華說:
"當那日子,那時候,
  雖尋以色列的罪孽,
  一無所有;
雖尋猶大的罪惡,
  也無所見,
  因為我所留下的人,我必赦免。"

²¹耶和華說:
"上去攻擊米拉大翁之地,
  又攻擊比割的居民。
要追殺滅盡,
  照我一切所吩咐你的去行。
²²境內有打仗
  和大毀滅的響聲。
²³全地的大錘
  何竟砍斷破壞?
巴比倫在列國中
  何竟荒涼?
²⁴巴比倫哪,我為你設下網羅,
  你不知不覺被纏住。
你被尋着,也被捉住,
  因為你與耶和華爭競。
²⁵耶和華已經開了武庫,
  拿出他惱恨的兵器,
因為主萬軍之耶和華
  在迦勒底人之地有當做的事。

---

^a 21 The Hebrew term refers to the irrevocable giving over of
things or persons to the LORD, often by totally destroying
them, also in verse 26.

26你們要從極遠的邊界來攻擊她，
　　開她的倉廩，
　　將她堆如高堆，
　毀滅淨盡，
　　絲毫不留。
27要殺她的一切牛犢，
　　使他們下去遭遇殺戮。
　他們有禍了！
　　因為追討他們的日子已經來到。
28有從巴比倫之地
　　逃避出來的人，
　在錫安揚聲報告
　　耶和華我們的神報仇，
　　就是為他的殿報仇。

29　"招集一切弓箭手
　　來攻擊巴比倫。
　要在巴比倫四圍安營，
　　不要容一人逃脫，
　照着她所做的報應她；
　　她怎樣待人，也要怎樣待她，
　　因為她向耶和華以色列的聖者
　發了狂傲。
30所以她的少年人必仆倒在街上；
　　當那日，一切兵丁必默默無聲。"
　　　　　　　　　　　這是耶和華說的。
31主萬軍之耶和華說：
　　"你這狂傲的啊，我與你反對！
　因為我追討你的日子
　　已經來到。
32狂傲的必絆跌仆倒，
　　無人扶起。
　我也必使火在她的城邑中着起來，
　　將她四圍所有的盡行燒滅。"

33萬軍之耶和華如此說：

　"以色列人和猶大人
　　一同受欺壓；
　凡擄掠他們的，
　　都緊緊抓住他們，不肯釋放。
34他們的救贖主大有能力，
　　萬軍之耶和華是他的名。
　他必伸清他們的冤，
　　好使全地得平安，
　並攪擾巴比倫的居民。"

35耶和華說：
　"有刀劍臨到迦勒底人
　　和巴比倫的居民，
　　並他的首領與智慧人。
36有刀劍臨到矜誇的人，
　　他們就成為愚昧；
　有刀劍臨到他的勇士，
　　他們就驚惶。

26Come against her from afar.
　Break open her granaries;
　　pile her up like heaps of grain.
Completely destroy her
　and leave her no remnant.
27Kill all her young bulls;
　let them go down to the slaughter!
Woe to them! For their day has come,
　the time for them to be punished.
28Listen to the fugitives and refugees from
　　Babylon
　declaring in Zion
how the LORD our God has taken vengeance,
　vengeance for his temple.

29"Summon archers against Babylon,
　all those who draw the bow.
Encamp all around her;
　let no one escape.
Repay her for her deeds;
　do to her as she has done.
For she has defied the LORD,
　the Holy One of Israel.
30Therefore, her young men will fall in the streets;
　all her soldiers will be silenced in that day,"
　　　　　　　　　　declares the LORD.
31"See, I am against you, O arrogant one,"
　declares the Lord, the LORD Almighty,
　"for your day has come,
　the time for you to be punished.
32The arrogant one will stumble and fall
　and no one will help her up;
I will kindle a fire in her towns
　that will consume all who are around her."

33This is what the LORD Almighty says:

"The people of Israel are oppressed,
　and the people of Judah as well.
All their captors hold them fast,
　refusing to let them go.
34Yet their Redeemer is strong;
　the LORD Almighty is his name.
He will vigorously defend their cause
　so that he may bring rest to their land,
　but unrest to those who live in Babylon.

35"A sword against the Babylonians!"
　declares the LORD—
　"against those who live in Babylon
　and against her officials and wise men!
36A sword against her false prophets!
　They will become fools.
A sword against her warriors!
　They will be filled with terror.

¹²Lift up a banner against the walls of Babylon!
  Reinforce the guard,
station the watchmen,
  prepare an ambush!
The LORD will carry out his purpose,
  his decree against the people of Babylon.
¹³You who live by many waters
  and are rich in treasures,
your end has come,
  the time for you to be cut off.
¹⁴The LORD Almighty has sworn by himself:
  I will surely fill you with men, as with a
    swarm of locusts,
  and they will shout in triumph over you.

¹⁵"He made the earth by his power;
  he founded the world by his wisdom
  and stretched out the heavens by his
    understanding.
¹⁶When he thunders, the waters in the heavens
    roar;
  he makes clouds rise from the ends of the
    earth.
He sends lightning with the rain
  and brings out the wind from his storehouses.

¹⁷"Every man is senseless and without
    knowledge;
  every goldsmith is shamed by his idols.
His images are a fraud;
  they have no breath in them.
¹⁸They are worthless, the objects of mockery;
  when their judgment comes, they will perish.
¹⁹He who is the Portion of Jacob is not like these,
  for he is the Maker of all things,
including the tribe of his inheritance—
  the LORD Almighty is his name.

²⁰"You are my war club,
  my weapon for battle—
with you I shatter nations,
  with you I destroy kingdoms,
²¹with you I shatter horse and rider,
  with you I shatter chariot and driver,
²²with you I shatter man and woman,
  with you I shatter old man and youth,
  with you I shatter young man and maiden,
²³with you I shatter shepherd and flock,
  with you I shatter farmer and oxen,
  with you I shatter governors and officials.

²⁴"Before your eyes I will repay Babylon and all who live in Babylonia^a for all the wrong they have done in Zion," declares the LORD.

a 24 Or Chaldea; also in verse 35

---

¹²你們要豎立大旗，
  攻擊巴比倫的城牆，
要堅固瞭望臺，
  派定守望的設下埋伏，
因為耶和華指着巴比倫居民
  所說的話，所定的意，
  他已經作成。
¹³住在眾水之上多有財寶的啊，
  你的結局到了！
  你貪婪之量滿了！
¹⁴萬軍之耶和華指着自己起誓說：
  "我必使敵人充滿你，
像螞蚱一樣，
  他們必吶喊攻擊你。

¹⁵"耶和華用能力創造大地，
  用智慧建立世界，
  用聰明鋪張穹蒼。
¹⁶他一發聲，
  空中便有多水激動，
他使雲霧
  從地極上騰。
他造電隨雨而閃，
  從他府庫中帶出風來。

¹⁷"各人都成了畜類，
  毫無知識。
各銀匠都因他的偶像羞愧；
  他所鑄的偶像本是虛假的，
  其中並無氣息。
¹⁸都是虛無的，是迷惑人的工作，
  到追討的時候，必被除滅。
¹⁹雅各的分不像這些，
  因他是造作萬有的主，
以色列也是他產業的支派。
  萬軍之耶和華是他的名。

²⁰"你是我爭戰的斧子
  和打仗的兵器，
我要用你打碎列國，
  用你毀滅列邦；
²¹用你打碎馬和騎馬的，
  用你打碎戰車和坐在其上的；
²²用你打碎男人和女人，
  用你打碎老年人和少年人，
  用你打碎壯丁和處女；
²³用你打碎牧人和他的羣畜，
  用你打碎農夫和他一對牛，
  用你打碎省長和副省長。"

²⁴耶和華說："我必在你們眼前報復巴比倫人和迦勒底居民在錫安所行的諸惡。"

25耶和華說：“你這行毀滅的山哪，
　　就是毀滅天下的山，
　　我與你反對！
我必向你伸手，
　　將你從山巖滾下去，
　　使你成為燒燬的山。
26人必不從你那裏
　　　取石頭為房角石，
　　也不取石頭為根基石；
　　你必永遠荒涼。”
　　　　　　　這是耶和華說的。

27 “要在境內豎立大旗，
　　在各國中吹角，
　使列國預備攻擊巴比倫，
　　將亞拉臘、米尼、亞實基拿
　　　各國招來攻擊她，
　又派軍長來攻擊她，
　　使馬匹上來如螞蚱，
28使列國和瑪代君王，
　　與省長和副省長，
　　並他們所管全地之人，
　　都預備攻擊她。
29地必震動而瘠苦；
　　因耶和華向巴比倫
　　　所定的旨意成立了，
　　使巴比倫之地荒涼，
　　無人居住。
30巴比倫的勇士止息爭戰，
　　藏在堅壘之中。
　他們的勇力衰盡，
　　好像婦女一樣。
　巴比倫的住處有火着起，
　　門閂都折斷了。
31跑報的要彼此相遇，
　　送信的要互相迎接，
　報告巴比倫王說：
　　城的四方被攻取了，
32渡口被佔據了，
　　葦塘被火燒了，
　　兵丁也驚慌了。”

　　　33萬軍之耶和華以色列的神如此
說：

“巴比倫城（註：“城”原文作“女子”）
　　像踹穀的禾場；
　再過片時，
　　收割她的時候就到了。”

34以色列人說：
“巴比倫王尼布甲尼撒吞滅我，
　　壓碎我，
　　使我成為空虛的器皿。

25"I am against you, O destroying mountain,
　　you who destroy the whole earth,"
　　　　　　　declares the LORD.
 "I will stretch out my hand against you,
　　roll you off the cliffs,
　　and make you a burned-out mountain.
26No rock will be taken from you for a
　　　cornerstone,
　　nor any stone for a foundation,
　　for you will be desolate forever,"
　　　　　　　declares the LORD.

27"Lift up a banner in the land!
　　Blow the trumpet among the nations!
　Prepare the nations for battle against her;
　　summon against her these kingdoms:
　　Ararat, Minni and Ashkenaz.
　Appoint a commander against her;
　　send up horses like a swarm of locusts.
28Prepare the nations for battle against her—
　　the kings of the Medes,
　　their governors and all their officials,
　　and all the countries they rule.
29The land trembles and writhes,
　　for the LORD's purposes against Babylon
　　　stand—
　　to lay waste the land of Babylon
　　so that no one will live there.
30Babylon's warriors have stopped fighting;
　　they remain in their strongholds.
　Their strength is exhausted;
　　they have become like women.
　Her dwellings are set on fire;
　　the bars of her gates are broken.
31One courier follows another
　　and messenger follows messenger
　to announce to the king of Babylon
　　that his entire city is captured,
32the river crossings seized,
　　the marshes set on fire,
　　and the soldiers terrified."

33This is what the LORD Almighty, the God of
Israel, says:

　"The Daughter of Babylon is like a threshing
　　floor
　　at the time it is trampled;
　　the time to harvest her will soon come."

34"Nebuchadnezzar king of Babylon has
　　devoured us,
　　he has thrown us into confusion,
　　he has made us an empty jar.

Like a serpent he has swallowed us
　and filled his stomach with our delicacies,
　and then has spewed us out.
³⁵May the violence done to our flesh^a be upon
　　Babylon,"
　say the inhabitants of Zion.
"May our blood be on those who live in
　　Babylonia,"
　says Jerusalem.

³⁶Therefore, this is what the LORD says:

"See, I will defend your cause
　and avenge you;
I will dry up her sea
　and make her springs dry.
³⁷Babylon will be a heap of ruins,
　a haunt of jackals,
an object of horror and scorn,
　a place where no one lives.
³⁸Her people all roar like young lions,
　they growl like lion cubs.
³⁹But while they are aroused,
　I will set out a feast for them
　and make them drunk,
so that they shout with laughter—
　then sleep forever and not awake,"
　　　　　　　　　　　　　declares the LORD.
⁴⁰"I will bring them down
　like lambs to the slaughter,
　like rams and goats.

⁴¹"How Sheshach^b will be captured,
　the boast of the whole earth seized!
What a horror Babylon will be
　among the nations!
⁴²The sea will rise over Babylon;
　its roaring waves will cover her.
⁴³Her towns will be desolate,
　a dry and desert land,
a land where no one lives,
　through which no man travels.
⁴⁴I will punish Bel in Babylon
　and make him spew out what he has
　　swallowed.
The nations will no longer stream to him.
　And the wall of Babylon will fall.

⁴⁵"Come out of her, my people!
　Run for your lives!
　Run from the fierce anger of the LORD.
⁴⁶Do not lose heart or be afraid
　when rumors are heard in the land;

他像大魚將我吞下，
　用我的美物充滿他的肚腹，
　又將我趕出去。"
³⁵錫安的居民要說：
　"巴比倫以強暴待我，
　損害我的身體，願這罪歸給她。"
耶路撒冷人要說：
　"願流我們血的罪，
　歸到迦勒底的居民。"

³⁶所以耶和華如此說：

"我必為你伸冤，
　為你報仇；
我必使巴比倫的海枯竭，
　使她的泉源乾涸。
³⁷巴比倫必成為亂堆，
　為野狗的住處，
令人驚駭、嗤笑，
　並且無人居住。
³⁸他們要像少壯獅子咆哮，
　像小獅子吼叫；
³⁹他們火熱的時候，
　我必為他們設擺酒席，
　使他們沉醉，
好叫他們快樂，
　睡了長覺，永不醒起。"
　　　　　　　　這是耶和華說的。
⁴⁰"我必使他們像羊羔，
　像公綿羊和公山羊，
　下到宰殺之地。

⁴¹"示沙克（註：就是"巴比倫"）
　何竟被攻取？
天下所稱讚的何竟被佔據？
　巴比倫在列國中何竟變為荒場？
⁴²海水漲起，漫過巴比倫，
　她被許多海浪遮蓋。
⁴³她的城邑，變為荒場、
　旱地、沙漠，
無人居住，
　無人經過之地。
⁴⁴我必刑罰巴比倫的彼勒，
　使他吐出所吞的，
萬民必不再流歸他那裏。
　巴比倫的城牆也必坍塌了。

⁴⁵"我的民哪，你們要從其中出去，
　各人拯救自己，
　躲避耶和華的烈怒。
⁴⁶你們不要心驚膽怯，
　也不要因境內
　所聽見的風聲懼怕；

a 35 Or done to us and to our children　　b 41 Sheshach is a
cryptogram for Babylon.

因為這年有風聲傳來，
　　那年也有風聲傳來，
　　境內有強暴的事，官長攻擊官長。
47日子將到，
　　我必刑罰巴比倫雕刻的偶像。
她全地必然抱愧；
　　她被殺的人必在其中仆倒。
48那時，天地和其中所有的，
　　必因巴比倫歡呼；
因為行毀滅的
　　要從北方來到她那裏。”
　　　　　　　　　　　這是耶和華說的。

49 “巴比倫怎樣使以色列
　　　　被殺的人仆倒，
　　照樣，她全地被殺的人
　　　　也必在巴比倫仆倒。
50你們躲避刀劍的要快走，
　　　　不要站住。
　　要在遠方記念耶和華，
　　　　心中追想耶路撒冷。
51 “我們聽見辱罵就蒙羞，
　　　　滿面慚愧，
　　因為外邦人進入
　　　　耶和華殿的聖所。

52耶和華說：
　　 “日子將到，
　　我必刑罰巴比倫雕刻的偶像，
　　通國受傷的人必唉哼。
53巴比倫雖升到天上，
　　雖使她堅固的高處更堅固，
　　還有行毀滅的
　　　　從我這裏到她那裏。”
　　　　　　　　　　　這是耶和華說的。
54 “有哀號的聲音從巴比倫出來；
　　有大毀滅的響聲
　　　　從迦勒底人之地發出。
55因耶和華使巴比倫變為荒場，
　　使其中的大聲滅絕。
　　仇敵彷彿眾水波浪匉訇，
　　響聲已經發出。
56這是行毀滅的臨到巴比倫，
　　巴比倫的勇士被捉拿，
　　他們的弓折斷了，
　　因為耶和華是施行報應的神，
　　　　必定施行報應。”
57君王，名為萬軍之耶和華的說：
　　 “我必使巴比倫的首領、智慧人、
　　　　省長、副省長和勇士都沉醉，
　　使他們睡了長覺，
　　　　永不醒起。”

one rumor comes this year, another the next,
　　rumors of violence in the land
　　and of ruler against ruler.
47For the time will surely come
　　when I will punish the idols of Babylon;
　　her whole land will be disgraced
　　and her slain will all lie fallen within her.
48Then heaven and earth and all that is in them
　　will shout for joy over Babylon,
for out of the north
　　destroyers will attack her,"
　　　　　　　　　　　declares the LORD.

49"Babylon must fall because of Israel's slain,
　　just as the slain in all the earth
　　have fallen because of Babylon.
50You who have escaped the sword,
　　leave and do not linger!
Remember the LORD in a distant land,
　　and think on Jerusalem."

51"We are disgraced,
　　for we have been insulted
　　and shame covers our faces,
because foreigners have entered
　　the holy places of the LORD's house."

52"But days are coming," declares the LORD,
　　"when I will punish her idols,
and throughout her land
　　the wounded will groan.
53Even if Babylon reaches the sky
　　and fortifies her lofty stronghold,
I will send destroyers against her,"
　　　　　　　　　　　declares the LORD.

54"The sound of a cry comes from Babylon,
　　the sound of great destruction
　　from the land of the Babylonians.a
55The LORD will destroy Babylon;
　　he will silence her noisy din.
Waves [of enemies] will rage like great waters;
　　the roar of their voices will resound.
56A destroyer will come against Babylon;
　　her warriors will be captured,
　　and their bows will be broken.
For the LORD is a God of retribution;
　　he will repay in full.
57I will make her officials and wise men drunk,
　　her governors, officers and warriors as well;
they will sleep forever and not awake,"
　　　　declares the King, whose name is the LORD
　　　　Almighty.

a 54 Or Chaldeans

58This is what the LORD Almighty says:

"Babylon's thick wall will be leveled
  and her high gates set on fire;
the peoples exhaust themselves for nothing,
  the nations' labor is only fuel for the flames."

59This is the message Jeremiah gave to the staff officer Seraiah son of Neriah, the son of Mahseiah, when he went to Babylon with Zedekiah king of Judah in the fourth year of his reign. 60Jeremiah had written on a scroll about all the disasters that would come upon Babylon—all that had been recorded concerning Babylon. 61He said to Seraiah, "When you get to Babylon, see that you read all these words aloud. 62Then say, 'O LORD, you have said you will destroy this place, so that neither man nor animal will live in it; it will be desolate forever.' 63When you finish reading this scroll, tie a stone to it and throw it into the Euphrates. 64Then say, 'So will Babylon sink to rise no more because of the disaster I will bring upon her. And her people will fall.'"

The words of Jeremiah end here.

The Fall of Jerusalem

52 Zedekiah was twenty-one years old when he became king, and he reigned in Jerusalem eleven years. His mother's name was Hamutal daughter of Jeremiah; she was from Libnah. 2He did evil in the eyes of the LORD, just as Jehoiakim had done. 3It was because of the LORD's anger that all this happened to Jerusalem and Judah, and in the end he thrust them from his presence.

Now Zedekiah rebelled against the king of Babylon.

4So in the ninth year of Zedekiah's reign, on the tenth day of the tenth month, Nebuchadnezzar king of Babylon marched against Jerusalem with his whole army. They camped outside the city and built siege works all around it. 5The city was kept under siege until the eleventh year of King Zedekiah.

6By the ninth day of the fourth month the famine in the city had become so severe that there was no food for the people to eat. 7Then the city wall was broken through, and the whole army fled. They left the city at night through the gate between the two walls near the king's garden, though the Babylonians*a* were surrounding the city. They fled toward the Arabah,*b* 8but the

a 7 Or Chaldeans; also in verse 17   *b 7 Or the Jordan Valley*

58萬軍之耶和華如此說：

"巴比倫寬闊的城牆必然傾倒，
  她高大的城門必被火焚燒。
眾民所勞碌的必致虛空；
  列國所勞碌的被火焚燒，
  他們都必困乏。"

59猶大王西底家在位第四年，上巴比倫去的時候，瑪西雅的孫子、尼利亞的兒子西萊雅與王同去（西萊雅是王宮的大臣），先知耶利米有話吩咐他。60耶利米將一切要臨到巴比倫的災禍，就是論到巴比倫的一切話寫在書上。61耶利米對西萊雅說："你到了巴比倫務要念這書上的話。62又說："耶和華啊，你曾論到這地方說：'要剪除，甚至連人帶牲畜沒有在這裏居住的，必永遠荒涼。'63你念完了這書，就把一塊石頭拴在書上，扔在幼發拉底河中，64說：'巴比倫因耶和華所要降與她的災禍，必如此沉下去，不再興起，人民也必困乏。'"

耶利米的話到此為止。

耶路撒冷淪陷

52 西底家登基的時候，年二十一歲，在耶路撒冷作王十一年。他母親名叫哈慕她，是立拿人耶利米的女兒。2西底家行耶和華眼中看為惡的事，是照約雅敬一切所行的。3因此，耶和華的怒氣在耶路撒冷和猶大發作，以致將人民從自己的面前趕出。

4西底家背叛巴比倫王。

他作王第九年十月初十日，巴比倫王尼布甲尼撒率領全軍來攻擊耶路撒冷，對城安營，四圍築壘攻城。5於是城被圍困，直到西底家王十一年。

6四月初九日，城裏有大饑荒，甚至百姓都沒有糧食。7城被攻破，一切兵丁就在夜間從靠近王園兩城中間的門出城逃跑，迦勒底人正在四圍攻城，他們就往亞拉巴逃去。8迦勒底的軍隊追趕西底家王，在耶利哥的平原追上他。他的全軍都離開他四散了。

9迦勒底人就拿住王，帶他到哈馬地的利比拉巴比倫王那裏，巴比倫王便審判他。10巴比倫王在西底家眼前殺了他的眾子，又在利比拉殺了猶大的一切首領，11並且剜了西底家的眼睛，用銅鏈鎖着他，帶到巴比倫去，將他囚在監裏，直到他死的日子。

12巴比倫王尼布甲尼撒十九年五月初十日，在巴比倫王面前侍立的護衛長尼布撒拉旦進入耶路撒冷，13用火焚燒耶和華的殿和王宮，又焚燒耶路撒冷的房屋，就是各大戶家的房屋。14跟從護衛長迦勒底的全軍，就拆毀耶路撒冷四圍的城牆。15那時護衛長尼布撒拉旦將民中最窮的和城裏所剩下的百姓，並已經投降巴比倫王的人，以及大眾所剩下的人都擄去了。16但護衛長尼布撒拉旦留下些民中最窮的，使他們修理葡萄園，耕種田地。

17耶和華殿的銅柱並殿內的盆座和銅海，迦勒底人都打碎了，將那銅運到巴比倫去了。18又帶去鍋、鏟子、蠟剪、盤子、調羹，並所用的一切銅器，19杯、火鼎、碗、盆、燈臺、調羹、爵，無論金的銀的，護衛長也都帶去了。

20所羅門為耶和華殿所造的兩根銅柱，一個銅海，並座下的十二隻銅牛，這一切的銅多得無法可稱。21這一根柱子高十八肘，厚四指，是空的，圍十二肘。22柱上有銅頂，高五肘，銅頂的周圍有網子和石榴，

Babylonian[a] army pursued King Zedekiah and overtook him in the plains of Jericho. All his soldiers were separated from him and scattered, 9and he was captured.

He was taken to the king of Babylon at Riblah in the land of Hamath, where he pronounced sentence on him. 10There at Riblah the king of Babylon slaughtered the sons of Zedekiah before his eyes; he also killed all the officials of Judah. 11Then he put out Zedekiah's eyes, bound him with bronze shackles and took him to Babylon, where he put him in prison till the day of his death.

12On the tenth day of the fifth month, in the nineteenth year of Nebuchadnezzar king of Babylon, Nebuzaradan commander of the imperial guard, who served the king of Babylon, came to Jerusalem. 13He set fire to the temple of the LORD, the royal palace and all the houses of Jerusalem. Every important building he burned down. 14The whole Babylonian army under the commander of the imperial guard broke down all the walls around Jerusalem. 15Nebuzaradan the commander of the guard carried into exile some of the poorest people and those who remained in the city, along with the rest of the craftsmen[b] and those who had gone over to the king of Babylon. 16But Nebuzaradan left behind the rest of the poorest people of the land to work the vineyards and fields.

17The Babylonians broke up the bronze pillars, the movable stands and the bronze Sea that were at the temple of the LORD and they carried all the bronze to Babylon. 18They also took away the pots, shovels, wick trimmers, sprinkling bowls, dishes and all the bronze articles used in the temple service. 19The commander of the imperial guard took away the basins, censers, sprinkling bowls, pots, lampstands, dishes and bowls used for drink offerings—all that were made of pure gold or silver.

20The bronze from the two pillars, the Sea and the twelve bronze bulls under it, and the movable stands, which King Solomon had made for the temple of the LORD, was more than could be weighed. 21Each of the pillars was eighteen cubits high and twelve cubits in circumference[c]; each was four fingers thick, and hollow. 22The bronze capital on top of the one pillar was five cubits[d] high and was decorated with a network and pomegranates of bronze all around. The

a 8 Or Chaldean; also in verse 14   b 15 Or populace
c 21 That is, about 27 feet (about 8.1 meters) high and 18 feet
(about 5.4 meters) in circumference   d 22 That is, about
7 1/2 feet (about 2.3 meters)

that were hers in days of old.
When her people fell into enemy hands,
    there was no one to help her.
Her enemies looked at her
    and laughed at her destruction.

[8]Jerusalem has sinned greatly
    and so has become unclean.
All who honored her despise her,
    for they have seen her nakedness;
she herself groans
    and turns away.

[9]Her filthiness clung to her skirts;
    she did not consider her future.
Her fall was astounding;
    there was none to comfort her.
"Look, O LORD, on my affliction,
    for the enemy has triumphed."

[10]The enemy laid hands
    on all her treasures;
she saw pagan nations
    enter her sanctuary—
those you had forbidden
    to enter your assembly.

[11]All her people groan
    as they search for bread;
they barter their treasures for food
    to keep themselves alive.
"Look, O LORD, and consider,
    for I am despised."

[12]"Is it nothing to you, all you who pass by?
    Look around and see.
Is any suffering like my suffering
    that was inflicted on me,
that the LORD brought on me
    in the day of his fierce anger?

[13]"From on high he sent fire,
    sent it down into my bones.
He spread a net for my feet
    and turned me back.
He made me desolate,
    faint all the day long.

[14]"My sins have been bound into a yoke[a];
    by his hands they were woven together.
They have come upon my neck
    and the Lord has sapped my strength.
He has handed me over

一切的樂境。
她百姓落在敵人手中,
    無人救濟,
敵人看見,
    就因她的荒涼嗤笑。

[8]耶路撒冷大大犯罪,
    所以成為不潔之物,
素來尊敬她的,
    見她赤露就都藐視她;
她自己也歎息退後。

[9]她的污穢是在衣襟上,
    她不思想自己的結局,
所以非常的敗落,
    無人安慰她。
她說:"耶和華啊,
    求你看我的苦難,因為仇敵誇大。"

[10]敵人伸手
    奪取她的美物。
她眼見外邦人
    進入她的聖所;
論這外邦人,
    你曾吩咐不可入你的會中。

[11]她的民都歎息,
    尋求食物;
他們用美物換糧食,
    要救性命。
他們說:"耶和華啊,求你觀看,
    因為我甚是卑賤。"

[12]"你們一切過路的人哪,
    這事你們不介意嗎?
你們要觀看,
    有像這臨到我的痛苦沒有?
就是耶和華在他發烈怒的日子
    使我所受的苦。

[13]"他從高天使火進入我的骨頭,
    剋制了我;
他鋪下網羅,絆我的腳,
    使我轉回,
他使我
    終日淒涼發昏。

[14]"我罪過的軛
    是他手所綁的,
猶如軛繩縛在我頸項上,
    他使我的力量衰敗。
主將我交在

---

a 14 Most Hebrew manuscripts; Septuagint He kept watch over my sins

我所不能敵擋的人手中。

15 "主輕棄我中間的一切勇士，
　　招聚多人（註：原文作"大會"）
攻擊我，
　　要壓碎我的少年人。
主將猶大居民踹下，
　　像在酒醡中一樣。

16 "我因這些事哭泣，
　　我眼淚汪汪，
因為那當安慰我、
　　救我性命的，離我甚遠。
我的兒女孤苦，
　　因為仇敵得了勝。"

17 錫安舉手，
　　無人安慰。
耶和華論雅各已經出令，
　　使四圍的人作他仇敵，
耶路撒冷在他們中間
　　像不潔之物。

18 "耶和華是公義的！
　　他這樣待我，
是因我違背他的命令。
眾民哪，請聽我的話，
　　看我的痛苦，
我的處女和少年人都被擄去。

19 "我招呼我所親愛的，
　　他們卻愚弄我。
我的祭司和長老，
　　正尋求食物救性命的時候，
就在城中絕氣。

20 "耶和華啊，求你觀看，
　　因為我在急難中！
我心腸擾亂，我心在我裏面翻轉，
　　因我大大悖逆。
在外刀劍使人喪子；
　　在家猶如死亡。

21 "聽見我歎息的有人；
　　安慰我的卻無人！
我的仇敵都聽見我所遭的患難；
　　因你做這事，他們都喜樂。
你必使你報告的日子來到，
　　他們就像我一樣。

22 "願他們的惡行
　　都呈在你面前；
你怎樣因我的一切罪過待我，

to those I cannot withstand.

15 "The Lord has rejected
　　all the warriors in my midst;
he has summoned an army against me
　　toᵃ crush my young men.
In his winepress the Lord has trampled
　　the Virgin Daughter of Judah.

16 "This is why I weep
　　and my eyes overflow with tears.
No one is near to comfort me,
　　no one to restore my spirit.
My children are destitute
　　because the enemy has prevailed."

17 Zion stretches out her hands,
　　but there is no one to comfort her.
The LORD has decreed for Jacob
　　that his neighbors become his foes;
Jerusalem has become
　　an unclean thing among them.

18 "The LORD is righteous,
　　yet I rebelled against his command.
Listen, all you peoples;
　　look upon my suffering.
My young men and maidens
　　have gone into exile.

19 "I called to my allies
　　but they betrayed me.
My priests and my elders
　　perished in the city
while they searched for food
　　to keep themselves alive.

20 "See, O LORD, how distressed I am!
　　I am in torment within,
and in my heart I am disturbed,
　　for I have been most rebellious.
Outside, the sword bereaves;
　　inside, there is only death.

21 "People have heard my groaning,
　　but there is no one to comfort me.
All my enemies have heard of my distress;
　　they rejoice at what you have done.
May you bring the day you have announced
　　so they may become like me.

22 "Let all their wickedness come before you;
　　deal with them
as you have dealt with me

a 15 Or has set a time for me / when he will

because of all my sins.
My groans are many
　and my heart is faint."

2 ᵃHow the Lord has covered the
　　Daughter of Zion
　　with the cloud of his anger ᵇ!
He has hurled down the splendor of Israel
　from heaven to earth;
he has not remembered his footstool
　in the day of his anger.

²Without pity the Lord has swallowed up
　all the dwellings of Jacob;
in his wrath he has torn down
　the strongholds of the Daughter of Judah.
He has brought her kingdom and its princes
　down to the ground in dishonor.

³In fierce anger he has cut off
　every horn ᶜ of Israel.
He has withdrawn his right hand
　at the approach of the enemy.
He has burned in Jacob like a flaming fire
　that consumes everything around it.

⁴Like an enemy he has strung his bow;
　his right hand is ready.
Like a foe he has slain
　all who were pleasing to the eye;
he has poured out his wrath like fire
　on the tent of the Daughter of Zion.

⁵The Lord is like an enemy;
　he has swallowed up Israel.
He has swallowed up all her palaces
　and destroyed her strongholds.
He has multiplied mourning and lamentation
　for the Daughter of Judah.

⁶He has laid waste his dwelling like a garden;
　he has destroyed his place of meeting.
The Lord has made Zion forget
　her appointed feasts and her Sabbaths;
in his fierce anger he has spurned
　both king and priest.

⁷The Lord has rejected his altar
　and abandoned his sanctuary.
He has handed over to the enemy

求你照樣待他們，
　因我歎息甚多，
　心中發昏。」

2 主何竟發怒，
　　使黑雲遮蔽錫安城？
　　他將以色列的華美
從天扔在地上；
在他發怒的日子
　並不記念自己的腳凳。

²主吞滅雅各一切的住處，
　並不顧惜。
他發怒傾覆猶大民的保障，
　使這保障坍倒在地。
他辱沒這國
　和其中的首領。

³他發烈怒，
　把以色列的角全然砍斷，
　在仇敵面前收回右手。
他像火焰四圍吞滅，
　將雅各燒燬。

⁴他張弓，好像仇敵；
　他站着舉起右手，
如同敵人將悅人眼目的，
　盡行殺戮。
在錫安百姓的帳棚上，
　倒出他的忿怒像火一樣。

⁵主如仇敵吞滅以色列
　和錫安的一切宮殿，
拆毀百姓的保障；
　在猶大民中，
　加增悲傷哭號。

⁶他強取自己的帳幕，
　好像是園中的窩棚，
　毀壞他的聚會之處。
耶和華使聖節和安息日
　在錫安都被忘記，
又在怒氣的憤恨中藐視君王和祭司。

⁷耶和華丟棄自己的祭壇，
　憎惡自己的聖所。
將宮殿的牆垣

---

a This chapter is an acrostic poem, the verses of which begin
with the successive letters of the Hebrew alphabet.   b 1 Or
*How the Lord in his anger / has treated the Daughter of Zion with
contempt*   c 3 Or / *all the strength; or every king; horn here*
symbolizes strength.

交付仇敵，
他們在耶和華的殿中喧嚷，
　　像在聖會之日一樣。

8耶和華定意
　　拆毀錫安的城牆，
他拉了準繩，
　　不將手收回，
　　定要毀滅。
他使外郭和城牆都悲哀，
　　一同衰敗。

9錫安的門，
　　都陷入地內，
主將她的門閂毀壞折斷。
她的君王和首領落在
　　沒有律法的列國中；
她的先知
　　不得見耶和華的異象。

10錫安城的長老坐在地上
　　默默無聲，
他們揚起塵土落在頭上，
　　腰束麻布；
耶路撒冷的處女，
　　垂頭至地。

11我眼中流淚，
　　以致失明；
我的心腸擾亂，肝膽塗地；
　　都因我眾民遭毀滅，
又因孩童和吃奶的
　　在城內街上發昏。

12那時，
　　他們在城內街上發昏，
好像受傷的，
　　在母親的懷裏將要喪命，
對母親說：
　　"穀、酒在哪裏呢？"

13耶路撒冷的民哪，
　　我可用甚麼向你證明呢？
　　我可用甚麼與你相比呢？
錫安的民哪，
　　我可拿甚麼和你比較，
　　好安慰你呢？
因為你的裂口大如海，
　　誰能醫治你呢？

14你的先知為你見虛假
　　和愚昧的異象，
並沒有顯露你的罪孽，
　　使你被擄的歸回，
卻為你見虛假的默示

the walls of her palaces;
they have raised a shout in the house of the
　　LORD
　　as on the day of an appointed feast.

8The LORD determined to tear down
　　the wall around the Daughter of Zion.
He stretched out a measuring line
　　and did not withhold his hand from
　　destroying.
He made ramparts and walls lament;
　　together they wasted away.

9Her gates have sunk into the ground;
　　their bars he has broken and destroyed.
Her king and her princes are exiled among
　　the nations,
　　the law is no more,
and her prophets no longer find
　　visions from the LORD.

10The elders of the Daughter of Zion
　　sit on the ground in silence;
they have sprinkled dust on their heads
　　and put on sackcloth.
The young women of Jerusalem
　　have bowed their heads to the ground.

11My eyes fail from weeping,
　　I am in torment within,
my heart is poured out on the ground
　　because my people are destroyed,
because children and infants faint
　　in the streets of the city.

12They say to their mothers,
　　"Where is bread and wine?"
as they faint like wounded men
　　in the streets of the city,
as their lives ebb away
　　in their mothers' arms.

13What can I say for you?
　　With what can I compare you,
　　O Daughter of Jerusalem?
To what can I liken you,
　　that I may comfort you,
　　O Virgin Daughter of Zion?
Your wound is as deep as the sea.
　　Who can heal you?

14The visions of your prophets
　　were false and worthless;
they did not expose your sin
　　to ward off your captivity.
The oracles they gave you

were false and misleading.

¹⁵All who pass your way
  clap their hands at you;
they scoff and shake their heads
  at the Daughter of Jerusalem:
"Is this the city that was called
  the perfection of beauty,
  the joy of the whole earth?"

¹⁶All your enemies open their mouths
  wide against you;
they scoff and gnash their teeth
  and say, "We have swallowed her up.
This is the day we have waited for;
  we have lived to see it."

¹⁷The LORD has done what he planned;
  he has fulfilled his word,
  which he decreed long ago.
He has overthrown you without pity,
  he has let the enemy gloat over you,
  he has exalted the horn^a of your foes.

¹⁸The hearts of the people
  cry out to the Lord.
O wall of the Daughter of Zion,
  let your tears flow like a river
  day and night;
give yourself no relief,
  your eyes no rest.

¹⁹Arise, cry out in the night,
  as the watches of the night begin;
pour out your heart like water
  in the presence of the Lord.
Lift up your hands to him
  for the lives of your children,
who faint from hunger
  at the head of every street.

²⁰"Look, O LORD, and consider:
  Whom have you ever treated like this?
Should women eat their offspring,
  the children they have cared for?
Should priest and prophet be killed
  in the sanctuary of the Lord?

²¹"Young and old lie together
  in the dust of the streets;
my young men and maidens
  have fallen by the sword.
You have slain them in the day of your anger;
  you have slaughtered them without pity.

---

a 17 Horn here symbolizes strength.

和使你被趕出本境的緣故。

¹⁵凡過路的
  都向你拍掌。
他們向耶路撒冷城嗤笑、
  搖頭，說：
  "難道人所稱為全美的，
  稱為全地所喜悅的，
  就是這城嗎？"

¹⁶你的仇敵都向你大大張口。
  他們嗤笑，
  又切齒說：
  "我們吞滅她，
  這真是我們所盼望的日子臨到了！
  我們親眼看見了！"

¹⁷耶和華成就了他所定的，
  應驗了他古時所命定的。
他傾覆了，並不顧惜，
  使你的仇敵向你誇耀，
  使你敵人的角也被高舉。

¹⁸錫安民的心
  哀求主。
錫安的城牆啊，
  願你流淚如河，
  晝夜不息；
願你眼中的瞳人
  淚流不止。

¹⁹夜間，
  每逢交更的時候要起來呼喊，
在主面前
  傾心如水。
你的孩童在各市口上
  受餓發昏，
你要為他們的性命
  向主舉手禱告。

²⁰"耶和華啊，求你觀看！
  見你向誰這樣行？
婦人豈可吃自己所生育、
  手裏所搖弄的嬰孩嗎？
祭司和先知豈可在主的聖所中
  被殺戮嗎？

²¹"少年人和老年人
  都在街上躺臥；
我的處女和壯丁
  都倒在刀下。
你發怒的日子殺死他們。
  你殺了，並不顧惜。

22 "你招聚四圍驚嚇我的，
　　像在大會的日子
　　招聚人一樣。
　耶和華發怒的日子，
　　無人逃脫，無人存留；
　我所搖弄所養育的嬰孩，
　　仇敵都殺淨了。"

3
　　我是因耶和華忿怒的杖，
　　遭遇困苦的人。
　2他引導我，
　使我行在黑暗中，
　　不行在光明裏。
3他真是終日再三反手攻擊我！

4他使我的皮肉枯乾，他折斷（註：或
　作"壓傷"）我的骨頭。
5他築壘攻擊我，用苦楚（註：原文作
　"苦膽"）和艱難圍困我。
6他使我住在幽暗之處
　像死了許久的人一樣。

7他用籬笆圍住我，使我不能出去，
　他使我的銅鏈沉重。
8我哀號求救，
　他使我的禱告不得上達。
9他用鑿過的石頭擋住我的道；
　他使我的路彎曲。

10他向我如熊埋伏，
　如獅子在隱密處。
11他使我轉離正路，
　將我撕碎，使我淒涼。
12他張弓
　將我當作箭靶子。

13他把箭袋中的箭
　射入我的肺腑。
14我成了眾民的笑話；
　他們終日以我為歌曲。
15他用苦楚充滿我，
　使我飽用茵蔯。

16他又用沙石磣斷我的牙，
　用灰塵將我蒙蔽。
17你使我遠離平安，
　我忘記好處。
18我就說："我的力量衰敗，
　我在耶和華那裏毫無指望！"

19耶和華啊，求你記念我如茵蔯

22"As you summon to a feast day,
　so you summoned against me terrors on
　　every side.
In the day of the LORD's anger
　no one escaped or survived;
　those I cared for and reared,
　　my enemy has destroyed."

3
　　a I am the man who has seen affliction
　　by the rod of his wrath.
　　2He has driven me away and made me
　　walk
in darkness rather than light;
3indeed, he has turned his hand against me
　again and again, all day long.

4He has made my skin and my flesh grow old
　and has broken my bones.
5He has besieged me and surrounded me
　with bitterness and hardship.
6He has made me dwell in darkness
　like those long dead.

7He has walled me in so I cannot escape;
　he has weighed me down with chains.
8Even when I call out or cry for help,
　he shuts out my prayer.
9He has barred my way with blocks of stone;
　he has made my paths crooked.

10Like a bear lying in wait,
　like a lion in hiding,
11he dragged me from the path and mangled me
　and left me without help.
12He drew his bow
　and made me the target for his arrows.

13He pierced my heart
　with arrows from his quiver.
14I became the laughingstock of all my people;
　they mock me in song all day long.
15He has filled me with bitter herbs
　and sated me with gall.

16He has broken my teeth with gravel;
　he has trampled me in the dust.
17I have been deprived of peace;
　I have forgotten what prosperity is.
18So I say, "My splendor is gone
　and all that I had hoped from the LORD."

19I remember my affliction and my wandering,

a This chapter is an acrostic poem; the verses of each stanza
begin with the successive letters of the Hebrew alphabet, and
the verses within each stanza begin with the same letter.

the bitterness and the gall.
20 I well remember them,
and my soul is downcast within me.
21 Yet this I call to mind
and therefore I have hope:

22 Because of the LORD's great love we are not
consumed,
for his compassions never fail.
23 They are new every morning;
great is your faithfulness.
24 I say to myself, "The LORD is my portion;
therefore I will wait for him."

25 The LORD is good to those whose hope is in him,
to the one who seeks him;
26 it is good to wait quietly
for the salvation of the LORD.
27 It is good for a man to bear the yoke
while he is young.

28 Let him sit alone in silence,
for the LORD has laid it on him.
29 Let him bury his face in the dust—
there may yet be hope.
30 Let him offer his cheek to one who would
strike him,
and let him be filled with disgrace.

31 For men are not cast off
by the Lord forever.
32 Though he brings grief, he will show
compassion,
so great is his unfailing love.
33 For he does not willingly bring affliction
or grief to the children of men.

34 To crush underfoot
all prisoners in the land,
35 to deny a man his rights
before the Most High,
36 to deprive a man of justice—
would not the Lord see such things?

37 Who can speak and have it happen
if the Lord has not decreed it?
38 Is it not from the mouth of the Most High
that both calamities and good things come?
39 Why should any living man complain
when punished for his sins?

40 Let us examine our ways and test them,
and let us return to the LORD.
41 Let us lift up our hearts and our hands
to God in heaven, and say:
42 "We have sinned and rebelled

和苦膽的困苦窘迫。
20 我心想念這些，
就在裏面憂悶。
21 我想起這事，
心裏就有指望。

22 我們不至消滅，
是出於耶和華諸般的慈愛，
是因他的憐憫不至斷絕。
23 每早晨這都是新的；
你的誠實極其廣大！
24 我心裏說："耶和華是我的分，
因此，我要仰望他。"

25 凡等候耶和華、心裏尋求他的，
耶和華必施恩給他。
26 人仰望耶和華，靜默等候他的救恩，
這原是好的。
27 人在幼年負軛，
這原是好的。

28 他當獨坐無言，
因為這是耶和華加在他身上的。
29 他當口貼塵埃，
或者有指望。
30 他當由人打他的腮頰，
要滿受凌辱。

31 因為主必不永遠丟棄人。

32 主雖使人憂愁，
還要照他諸般的慈愛發憐憫。

33 因他並不甘心使人受苦，
使人憂愁。

34 人將世上被囚的踹（註：原文作"壓"）
在腳下，
35 或在至高者面前屈枉人，

36 或在人的訟事上顛倒是非，
這都是主看不上的。

37 除非主命定，
誰能說成就成呢？
38 禍福不都出於
至高者的口嗎？
39 活人因自己的罪受罰，
為何發怨言呢？

40 我們當深深考察自己的行為，
再歸向耶和華。
41 我們當誠心向天上的神
舉手禱告：
42 "我們犯罪背逆，

你並不赦免。

and you have not forgiven.

43 "你自被怒氣遮蔽，
　　追趕我們；
　　你施行殺戮，並不顧惜。
44 你以黑雲遮蔽自己，
　　以致禱告不得透入。
45 你使我們在萬民中
　　成為污穢和渣滓。

43 "You have covered yourself with anger and
　　pursued us;
　　you have slain without pity.
44 You have covered yourself with a cloud
　　so that no prayer can get through.
45 You have made us scum and refuse
　　among the nations.

46 "我們的仇敵
　　都向我們大大張口。
47 恐懼和陷坑，
　　殘害和毀滅，都臨近我們。"
48 因我眾民遭的毀滅，
　　我就眼淚下流如河。

46 "All our enemies have opened their mouths
　　wide against us.
47 We have suffered terror and pitfalls,
　　ruin and destruction."
48 Streams of tears flow from my eyes
　　because my people are destroyed.

49 我的眼多多流淚，
　　總不止息，
50 直等耶和華垂顧，
　　從天觀看。
51 因我本城的眾民，
　　我的眼，使我的心傷痛。

49 My eyes will flow unceasingly,
　　without relief,
50 until the LORD looks down
　　from heaven and sees.
51 What I see brings grief to my soul
　　because of all the women of my city.

52 無故與我為仇的追趕我，
　　像追雀鳥一樣。
53 他們使我的命在牢獄中斷絕，
　　並將一塊石頭拋在我身上。
54 眾水流過我頭，
　　我說："我命斷絕了！"

52 Those who were my enemies without cause
　　hunted me like a bird.
53 They tried to end my life in a pit
　　and threw stones at me;
54 the waters closed over my head,
　　and I thought I was about to be cut off.

55 耶和華啊，
　　我從深牢中求告你的名。
56 你曾聽見我的聲音；
　　我求你解救，你不要掩耳不聽。
57 我求告你的日子，你臨近我，
　　說："不要懼怕！"

55 I called on your name, O LORD,
　　from the depths of the pit.
56 You heard my plea: "Do not close your ears
　　to my cry for relief."
57 You came near when I called you,
　　and you said, "Do not fear."

58 主啊，你伸明了我的冤，
　　你救贖了我的命。
59 耶和華啊，你見了我受的委屈，
　　求你為我伸冤。
60 他們仇恨我、
　　謀害我，你都看見了。

58 O Lord, you took up my case;
　　you redeemed my life.
59 You have seen, O LORD, the wrong done to me.
　　Uphold my cause!
60 You have seen the depth of their vengeance,
　　all their plots against me.

61 耶和華啊，你聽見他們辱罵我的話，
　　知道他們向我所設的計，
62 並那些起來攻擊我的人口中所說的
　　話，以及終日向我所設的計謀。
63 求你觀看，他們坐下、起來，
　　都以我為歌曲。

61 O LORD, you have heard their insults,
　　all their plots against me—
62 what my enemies whisper and mutter
　　against me all day long.
63 Look at them! Sitting or standing,
　　they mock me in their songs.

64 耶和華啊，你要按着他們手所做的，
　　向他們施行報應。
65 你要使他們心裏剛硬，
　　使你的咒詛臨到他們。

64 Pay them back what they deserve, O LORD,
　　for what their hands have done.
65 Put a veil over their hearts,
　　and may your curse be on them!

⁶⁶Pursue them in anger and destroy them
  from under the heavens of the LORD.

4 | ^aHow the gold has lost its luster,
    the fine gold become dull!
    The sacred gems are scattered
  at the head of every street.

²How the precious sons of Zion,
  once worth their weight in gold,
  are now considered as pots of clay,
  the work of a potter's hands!

³Even jackals offer their breasts
  to nurse their young,
  but my people have become heartless
  like ostriches in the desert.

⁴Because of thirst the infant's tongue
  sticks to the roof of its mouth;
  the children beg for bread,
  but no one gives it to them.

⁵Those who once ate delicacies
  are destitute in the streets.
  Those nurtured in purple
  now lie on ash heaps.

⁶The punishment of my people
  is greater than that of Sodom,
  which was overthrown in a moment
  without a hand turned to help her.

⁷Their princes were brighter than snow
  and whiter than milk,
  their bodies more ruddy than rubies,
  their appearance like sapphires.^b

⁸But now they are blacker than soot;
  they are not recognized in the streets.
  Their skin has shriveled on their bones;
  it has become as dry as a stick.

⁹Those killed by the sword are better off
  than those who die of famine;
  racked with hunger, they waste away
  for lack of food from the field.

¹⁰With their own hands compassionate women
  have cooked their own children,
  who became their food
  when my people were destroyed.

a This chapter is an acrostic poem, the verses of which begin
with the successive letters of the Hebrew alphabet.   b 7 Or
lapis lazuli

⁶⁶你要發怒追趕他們，
  從耶和華的天下除滅他們。

4 | 黃金何其失光！
    純金何其變色！
    聖所的石頭倒在各市口上。

²錫安寶貴的眾子
  好比精金，
  現在何竟算為窰匠
  手所做的瓦瓶？

³野狗尚且把奶乳
  哺其子，
  我民的婦人倒成為殘忍，
  好像曠野的鴕鳥一般。

⁴吃奶孩子的舌頭
  因乾渴貼住上膛；
  孩童求餅，
  無人擘給他們。

⁵素來吃美好食物的，
  現今在街上變為孤寒；
  素來臥朱紅褥子的，
  現今躺臥糞堆。

⁶都因我眾民的罪孽
  比所多瑪的罪還大；
  所多瑪雖然無人加手於她，
  還是轉眼之間被傾覆。

⁷錫安的貴冑素來比雪純淨，
  比奶更白；
  他們的身體比紅寶玉（註：或作"珊
      瑚"）更紅，
  像光潤的藍寶石一樣。

⁸現在他們的面貌比煤炭更黑，
  以致在街上無人認識；
  他們的皮膚緊貼骨頭，
  枯乾如同槁木。

⁹餓死的不如被刀殺的，
  因為這是缺了田間的土產，
  就身體衰弱，
  漸漸消滅。

¹⁰慈心的婦人，
  當我眾民被毀滅的時候，
  親手煮自己的兒女
  作為食物。

11耶和華發怒成就他所定的，
　　倒出他的烈怒，
　　在錫安使火着起，
　　燒燬錫安的根基。

12地上的君王
　　和世上的居民，
　　都不信敵人和仇敵
　　能進耶路撒冷的城門。

13這都因她先知的罪惡
　　和祭司的罪孽，
　　他們在城中
　　流了義人的血。

14他們在街上
　　如瞎子亂走，
　　又被血玷污，
　　以致人不能摸他們的衣服。

15人向他們喊着說："不潔淨的，
　　躲開，躲開！不要挨近我！"
　　他們逃走飄流的時候，
　　列國中有人說：
　　"他們不可仍在這裏寄居。"

16耶和華發怒，將他們分散，
　　不再眷顧他們。
　　人不重看祭司，
　　也不厚待長老。

17我們仰望人來幫助，
　　以致眼目失明，還是枉然。
　　我們所盼望的，
　　竟盼望一個不能救人的國！

18仇敵追趕我們的腳步像打獵的，
　　以致我們不敢在自己的街上行走。
　　我們的結局臨近，我們的日子滿足，
　　我們的結局來到了。

19追趕我們的
　　比空中的鷹更快；
　　他們在山上追逼我們，
　　在曠野埋伏，等候我們。

20耶和華的受膏者好比我們鼻中的氣，
　　在他們的坑中被捉住；
　　我們曾論到他說："我們必在他蔭
　　下，在列國中存活。"

21住烏斯地的以東民哪，
　　只管歡喜快樂，
　　苦杯也必傳到你那裏；
　　你必喝醉，以致露體。

11The LORD has given full vent to his wrath;
　　he has poured out his fierce anger.
　　He kindled a fire in Zion
　　that consumed her foundations.

12The kings of the earth did not believe,
　　nor did any of the world's people,
　　that enemies and foes could enter
　　the gates of Jerusalem.

13But it happened because of the sins of her
　　　prophets
　　and the iniquities of her priests,
　　who shed within her
　　the blood of the righteous.

14Now they grope through the streets
　　like men who are blind.
　　They are so defiled with blood
　　that no one dares to touch their garments.

15"Go away! You are unclean!" men cry to them.
　　"Away! Away! Don't touch us!"
　　When they flee and wander about,
　　people among the nations say,
　　"They can stay here no longer."

16The LORD himself has scattered them;
　　he no longer watches over them.
　　The priests are shown no honor,
　　the elders no favor.

17Moreover, our eyes failed,
　　looking in vain for help;
　　from our towers we watched
　　for a nation that could not save us.

18Men stalked us at every step,
　　so we could not walk in our streets.
　　Our end was near, our days were numbered,
　　for our end had come.

19Our pursuers were swifter
　　than eagles in the sky;
　　they chased us over the mountains
　　and lay in wait for us in the desert.

20The LORD's anointed, our very life breath,
　　was caught in their traps.
　　We thought that under his shadow
　　we would live among the nations.

21Rejoice and be glad, O Daughter of Edom,
　　you who live in the land of Uz.
　　But to you also the cup will be passed;
　　you will be drunk and stripped naked.

²²O Daughter of Zion, your punishment will
    end;
  he will not prolong your exile.
But, O Daughter of Edom, he will punish
    your sin
  and expose your wickedness.

5 Remember, O LORD, what has happened
    to us;
    look, and see our disgrace.
²Our inheritance has been turned over to aliens,
  our homes to foreigners.
³We have become orphans and fatherless,
  our mothers like widows.
⁴We must buy the water we drink;
  our wood can be had only at a price.
⁵Those who pursue us are at our heels;
  we are weary and find no rest.
⁶We submitted to Egypt and Assyria
  to get enough bread.
⁷Our fathers sinned and are no more,
  and we bear their punishment.
⁸Slaves rule over us,
  and there is none to free us from their hands.
⁹We get our bread at the risk of our lives
  because of the sword in the desert.
¹⁰Our skin is hot as an oven,
  feverish from hunger.
¹¹Women have been ravished in Zion,
  and virgins in the towns of Judah.
¹²Princes have been hung up by their hands;
  elders are shown no respect.
¹³Young men toil at the millstones;
  boys stagger under loads of wood.
¹⁴The elders are gone from the city gate;
  the young men have stopped their music.
¹⁵Joy is gone from our hearts;
  our dancing has turned to mourning.
¹⁶The crown has fallen from our head.
  Woe to us, for we have sinned!
¹⁷Because of this our hearts are faint,
  because of these things our eyes grow dim
¹⁸for Mount Zion, which lies desolate,
  with jackals prowling over it.

¹⁹You, O LORD, reign forever;
  your throne endures from generation to
    generation.
²⁰Why do you always forget us?
  Why do you forsake us so long?
²¹Restore us to yourself, O LORD, that we may
    return;
  renew our days as of old
²²unless you have utterly rejected us
  and are angry with us beyond measure.

²²錫安的民哪，
  你罪孽的刑罰受足了，
  耶和華必不使你再被擄去。
以東的民哪，
  他必追討你的罪孽，
  顯露你的罪惡。

5 耶和華啊，
  求你記念我們所遭遇的事，
  觀看我們所受的凌辱。
²我們的產業歸與外邦人；
  我們的房屋歸與外路人。
³我們是無父的孤兒；
  我們的母親好像寡婦。
⁴我們出錢才得水喝；
  我們的柴是人賣給我們的。
⁵追趕我們的，到了我們的頸項上；
  我們疲乏不得歇息。
⁶我們投降埃及人和亞述人，
  為要得糧吃飽。
⁷我們列祖犯罪，而今不在了，
  我們擔當他們的罪孽。
⁸奴僕轄制我們，
  無人救我們脫離他們的手。
⁹因為曠野的刀劍，
  我們冒着險才得糧食。
¹⁰因飢餓燥熱，
  我們的皮膚就黑如爐。
¹¹敵人在錫安玷污婦人，
  在猶大的城邑玷污處女。
¹²他們吊起首領的手，
  也不尊敬老人的面。
¹³少年人扛磨石，
  孩童背木柴，都絆跌了。
¹⁴老年人在城門口斷絕；
  少年人不再作樂。
¹⁵我們心中的快樂止息，
  跳舞變為悲哀。
¹⁶冠冕從我們的頭上落下；
  我們犯罪了，我們有禍了！
¹⁷這些事我們心裏發昏，
  我們的眼睛昏花。
¹⁸錫安山荒涼，
  野狗（註：或作"狐狸"）行在其上。

¹⁹耶和華啊，
  你存到永遠，
  你的寶座存到萬代。
²⁰你為何永遠忘記我們？
  為何許久離棄我們？
²¹耶和華啊，求你使我們向你回轉，
  我們便得回轉；
  求你復新我們的日子，像古時一樣。
²²你竟全然棄絕我們，
  向我們大發烈怒。

以西結書　Ezekiel

四活物與主的榮耀

1 當三十年四月初五日，<u>以西結</u>（註：原文作"我"）在迦巴魯河邊被擄的人中，天就開了，得見神的異象。

² 正是 <u>約雅斤</u>王被擄去第五年四月初五日，³ 在<u>迦勒底</u>人之地、<u>迦巴魯</u>河邊，耶和華的話特特臨到<u>布西</u>的兒子祭司<u>以西結</u>，耶和華的靈（註：原文作"手"）降在他身上。

⁴ 我觀看，見狂風從北方颳來，隨着有一朵包括閃爍火的大雲，周圍有光輝，從其中的火內發出好像光耀的精金；⁵ 又從其中顯出四個活物的形像來。他們的形狀是這樣：有人的形像，⁶ 各有四個臉面，四個翅膀；⁷ 他們的腿是直的，腳掌好像牛犢之蹄，都燦爛如光明的銅；⁸ 在四面的翅膀以下有人的手。這四個活物的臉和翅膀乃是這樣：⁹ 翅膀彼此相接，行走並不轉身，俱各直往前行。

¹⁰ 至於臉的形像：前面各有人的臉，右面各有獅子的臉，左面各有牛的臉，後面各有鷹的臉。¹¹ 各展開上邊的兩個翅膀相接，各以下邊的兩個翅膀遮體。¹² 他們俱各直往前行，靈往哪裏去，他們就往哪裏去，行走並不轉身。¹³ 至於四活物的形像，就如燒着火炭的形狀，又如火把的形狀。火在四活物中間上下來，這火有光輝，從火中發出閃電。¹⁴ 這活物往來奔走，好像電光一閃。

¹⁵ 我正觀看活物的時候，見活物的臉旁，各有一輪在地上。¹⁶ 輪的形狀和顏色（註：原文作"做法"）好像水

The Living Creatures and the Glory of the LORD

1 In the[a] thirtieth year, in the fourth month on the fifth day, while I was among the exiles by the Kebar River, the heavens were opened and I saw visions of God.

²On the fifth of the month—it was the fifth year of the exile of King Jehoiachin— ³the word of the LORD came to Ezekiel the priest, the son of Buzi,[b] by the Kebar River in the land of the Babylonians.[c] There the hand of the LORD was upon him.

⁴I looked, and I saw a windstorm coming out of the north—an immense cloud with flashing lightning and surrounded by brilliant light. The center of the fire looked like glowing metal, ⁵and in the fire was what looked like four living creatures. In appearance their form was that of a man, ⁶but each of them had four faces and four wings. ⁷Their legs were straight; their feet were like those of a calf and gleamed like burnished bronze. ⁸Under their wings on their four sides they had the hands of a man. All four of them had faces and wings, ⁹and their wings touched one another. Each one went straight ahead; they did not turn as they moved.

¹⁰Their faces looked like this: Each of the four had the face of a man, and on the right side each had the face of a lion, and on the left the face of an ox; each also had the face of an eagle. ¹¹Such were their faces. Their wings were spread out upward; each had two wings, one touching the wing of another creature on either side, and two wings covering its body. ¹²Each one went straight ahead. Wherever the spirit would go, they would go, without turning as they went. ¹³The appearance of the living creatures was like burning coals of fire or like torches. Fire moved back and forth among the creatures; it was bright, and lightning flashed out of it. ¹⁴The creatures sped back and forth like flashes of lightning.

¹⁵As I looked at the living creatures, I saw a wheel on the ground beside each creature with its four faces. ¹⁶This was the appearance and structure of the wheels: They sparkled like

a 1 Or [my]　b 3 Or Ezekiel son of Buzi the priest　c 3 Or Chaldeans

chrysolite, and all four looked alike. Each appeared to be made like a wheel intersecting a wheel. [17]As they moved, they would go in any one of the four directions the creatures faced; the wheels did not turn about[a] as the creatures went. [18]Their rims were high and awesome, and all four rims were full of eyes all around.

[19]When the living creatures moved, the wheels beside them moved; and when the living creatures rose from the ground, the wheels also rose. [20]Wherever the spirit would go, they would go, and the wheels would rise along with them, because the spirit of the living creatures was in the wheels. [21]When the creatures moved, they also moved; when the creatures stood still, they also stood still; and when the creatures rose from the ground, the wheels rose along with them, because the spirit of the living creatures was in the wheels.

[22]Spread out above the heads of the living creatures was what looked like an expanse, sparkling like ice, and awesome. [23]Under the expanse their wings were stretched out one toward the other, and each had two wings covering its body. [24]When the creatures moved, I heard the sound of their wings, like the roar of rushing waters, like the voice of the Almighty,[b] like the tumult of an army. When they stood still, they lowered their wings.

[25]Then there came a voice from above the expanse over their heads as they stood with lowered wings. [26]Above the expanse over their heads was what looked like a throne of sapphire,[c] and high above on the throne was a figure like that of a man. [27]I saw that from what appeared to be his waist up he looked like glowing metal, as if full of fire, and that from there down he looked like fire; and brilliant light surrounded him. [28]Like the appearance of a rainbow in the clouds on a rainy day, so was the radiance around him.

This was the appearance of the likeness of the glory of the Lord. When I saw it, I fell facedown, and I heard the voice of one speaking.

Ezekiel's Call

2 He said to me, "Son of man, stand up on your feet and I will speak to you." [2]As he spoke, the Spirit came into me and raised me to my feet, and I heard him speaking to me.

[3]He said: "Son of man, I am sending you to the Israelites, to a rebellious nation that has rebelled against me; they and their fathers have

蒼玉。四輪都是一個樣式，形狀和做法好像輪中套輪。[17]輪行走的時候，向四方都能直行，並不掉轉。[18]至於輪輞，高而可畏；四個輪輞周圍滿有眼睛。

[19]活物行走，輪也在旁邊行走；活物從地上升，輪也都上升。[20]靈往哪裏去，活物就往哪裏去；活物上升，輪也在活物旁邊上升，因為活物的靈在輪中。[21]那些行走，這些也行走；那些站住，這些也站住。那些從地上升，輪也在旁邊上升，因為活物的靈在輪中。

[22]活物的頭以上有穹蒼的形像，看着像可畏的水晶，鋪張在活物的頭以上。[23]穹蒼以下，活物的翅膀直張，彼此相對，每活物有兩個翅膀遮體。[24]活物行走的時候，我聽見翅膀的響聲，像大水的聲音，像全能者的聲音，也像軍隊鬨嚷的聲音。活物站住的時候，便將翅膀垂下。

[25]在他們頭以上的穹蒼之上有聲音。他們站住的時候，便將翅膀垂下。[26]在他們頭以上的穹蒼之上有寶座的形像，彷彿藍寶石；在寶座形像以上有彷彿人的形狀。[27]我見從他腰以上有彷彿光耀的精金，周圍都有火的形狀；又見從他腰以下有彷彿火的形狀，周圍也有光輝。[28]下雨的日子，雲中虹的形狀怎樣，周圍光輝的形狀也是怎樣。

這就是耶和華榮耀的形像。我一看見就俯伏在地，又聽見一位說話的聲音。

以西結的蒙召

2 他對我說：「人子啊，你站起來，我要和你說話。」[2]他對我說話的時候，靈就進入我裏面，使我站起來，我便聽見那位對我說話的聲音。

[3]他對我說：「人子啊，我差你往悖逆的國民以色列人那裏去。他們是悖逆我的，他們和他們的列祖違背

---

a 17 Or aside   b 24 Hebrew Shaddai   c 26 Or lapis lazuli

我，直到今日。⁴這眾子面無羞恥、心裏剛硬。我差你往他們那裏去，你要對他們說：'主耶和華如此說。' ⁵他們或聽，或不聽（他們是悖逆之家），必知道在他們中間有了先知。⁶人子啊，雖有荊棘和蒺藜在你那裏，你又住在蠍子中間，總不要怕他們，也不要怕他們的話；他們雖是悖逆之家，還不要怕他們的話，也不要因他們的臉色驚惶。⁷他們或聽，或不聽，你只管將我的話告訴他們。他們是極其悖逆的。⁸人子啊，要聽我對你所說的話，不要悖逆像那悖逆之家，你要開口吃我所賜給你的。"

⁹我觀看，見有一隻手向我伸出來，手中有一書卷。¹⁰他將書卷在我面前展開，內外都寫着字，其上所寫的有哀號、歎息、悲痛的話。

3 他對我說："人子啊，要吃你所得的，要吃這書卷，好去對以色列家講說。" ²於是我開口，他就使我吃這書卷。

³又對我說："人子啊，要吃我所賜給你的這書卷，充滿你的肚腹。"我就吃了，口中覺其甜如蜜。

⁴他對我說："人子啊，你往以色列家那裏去，將我的話對他們講說。⁵你奉差遣不是往那說話深奧、言語難懂的民那裏去，乃是往以色列家去。⁶不是往那說話深奧、言語難懂的多國去，他們的話語是你不懂得的；我若差你往他們那裏去，他們必聽從你。⁷以色列家卻不肯聽從你，因為他們不肯聽從我；原來以色列全家是額堅心硬的人。⁸看哪，我使你的臉硬過他們的臉，使你的額硬過他們的額。⁹我使你的額像金鋼鑽，比火石更硬。他們雖是悖逆之家，你不要怕他們，也不要因他們的臉色驚惶。"

¹⁰他又對我說："人子啊，我對你所說的一切話，要心裏領會，耳中聽聞。¹¹你往你本國被擄的子民那裏去，他們或聽，或不聽，你要對他們講說，告訴他們：'這是主耶和華說的。'

¹²那時，靈將我舉起，我就聽見在我身後有震動轟轟的聲音，說："從耶和華的所在顯出來的榮耀是該稱頌的！" ¹³我又聽見那活物翅膀

been in revolt against me to this very day. ⁴The people to whom I am sending you are obstinate and stubborn. Say to them, 'This is what the Sovereign LORD says.' ⁵And whether they listen or fail to listen—for they are a rebellious house—they will know that a prophet has been among them. ⁶And you, son of man, do not be afraid of them or their words. Do not be afraid, though briers and thorns are all around you and you live among scorpions. Do not be afraid of what they say or terrified by them, though they are a rebellious house. ⁷You must speak my words to them, whether they listen or fail to listen, for they are rebellious. ⁸But you, son of man, listen to what I say to you. Do not rebel like that rebellious house; open your mouth and eat what I give you."

⁹Then I looked, and I saw a hand stretched out to me. In it was a scroll, ¹⁰which he unrolled before me. On both sides of it were written words of lament and mourning and woe.

3 And he said to me, "Son of man, eat what is before you, eat this scroll; then go and speak to the house of Israel." ²So I opened my mouth, and he gave me the scroll to eat.

³Then he said to me, "Son of man, eat this scroll I am giving you and fill your stomach with it." So I ate it, and it tasted as sweet as honey in my mouth.

⁴He then said to me: "Son of man, go now to the house of Israel and speak my words to them. ⁵You are not being sent to a people of obscure speech and difficult language, but to the house of Israel— ⁶not to many peoples of obscure speech and difficult language, whose words you cannot understand. Surely if I had sent you to them, they would have listened to you. ⁷But the house of Israel is not willing to listen to you because they are not willing to listen to me, for the whole house of Israel is hardened and obstinate. ⁸But I will make you as unyielding and hardened as they are. ⁹I will make your forehead like the hardest stone, harder than flint. Do not be afraid of them or terrified by them, though they are a rebellious house."

¹⁰And he said to me, "Son of man, listen carefully and take to heart all the words I speak to you. ¹¹Go now to your countrymen in exile and speak to them. Say to them, 'This is what the Sovereign LORD says,' whether they listen or fail to listen."

¹²Then the Spirit lifted me up, and I heard behind me a loud rumbling sound—May the glory of the LORD be praised in his dwelling place!— ¹³the sound of the wings of the living

creatures brushing against each other and the sound of the wheels beside them, a loud rumbling sound. [14]The Spirit then lifted me up and took me away, and I went in bitterness and in the anger of my spirit, with the strong hand of the LORD upon me. [15]I came to the exiles who lived at Tel Abib near the Kebar River. And there, where they were living, I sat among them for seven days—overwhelmed.

Warning to Israel

[16]At the end of seven days the word of the LORD came to me: [17]"Son of man, I have made you a watchman for the house of Israel; so hear the word I speak and give them warning from me. [18]When I say to a wicked man, 'You will surely die,' and you do not warn him or speak out to dissuade him from his evil ways in order to save his life, that wicked man will die for[a] his sin, and I will hold you accountable for his blood. [19]But if you do warn the wicked man and he does not turn from his wickedness or from his evil ways, he will die for his sin; but you will have saved yourself.

[20]"Again, when a righteous man turns from his righteousness and does evil, and I put a stumbling block before him, he will die. Since you did not warn him, he will die for his sin. The righteous things he did will not be remembered, and I will hold you accountable for his blood. [21]But if you do warn the righteous man not to sin and he does not sin, he will surely live because he took warning, and you will have saved yourself."

[22]The hand of the LORD was upon me there, and he said to me, "Get up and go out to the plain, and there I will speak to you." [23]So I got up and went out to the plain. And the glory of the LORD was standing there, like the glory I had seen by the Kebar River, and I fell facedown.

[24]Then the Spirit came into me and raised me to my feet. He spoke to me and said: "Go, shut yourself inside your house. [25]And you, son of man, they will tie with ropes; you will be bound so that you cannot go out among the people. [26]I will make your tongue stick to the roof of your mouth so that you will be silent and unable to rebuke them, though they are a rebellious house. [27]But when I speak to you, I will open your mouth and you shall say to them, 'This is what the Sovereign LORD says.' Whoever will listen let him listen, and whoever will refuse let him refuse; for they are a rebellious house.

相碰，與活物旁邊輪子旋轉震動轟轟的響聲。[14]於是靈將我舉起帶我而去。我心中甚苦，靈性忿激，並且耶和華的靈（註：原文作「手」）在我身上大有能力。[15]我就來到提勒亞畢，住在迦巴魯河邊被擄的人那裏，到他們所住的地方，在他們中間憂憂悶悶地坐了七日。

警戒以色列人

[16]過了七日，耶和華的話臨到我說：[17]「人子啊，我立你作以色列家守望的人，所以你要聽我口中的話，替我警戒他們。[18]我何時指著惡人說：『他必要死』，你若不警戒他，也不勸戒他，使他離開惡行，拯救他的性命，這惡人必死在罪孽之中；我卻要向你討他喪命的罪（註：原文作「血」）。[19]倘若你警戒惡人，他仍不轉離罪惡，也不離開惡行，他必死在罪孽之中；你卻救自己脫離了罪。

[20]「再者，義人何時離義而犯罪，我將絆腳石放在他面前，他就必死。因你沒有警戒他，他必死在罪中，他素來所行的義不被記念，我卻要向你討他喪命的罪（註：原文作「血」）。[21]倘若你警戒義人，使他不犯罪，他就不犯罪，他因受警戒就必存活，你也救自己脫離了罪。」

[22]耶和華的靈（註：原文作「手」）在那裏降在我身上。他對我說：「你起來往平原去，我要在那裏和你說話。」[23]於是我起來往平原去。不料，耶和華的榮耀，正如我在迦巴魯河邊所見的一樣，停在那裏，我就俯伏於地。

[24]靈就進入我裏面，使我站起來。耶和華對我說：「你進房屋去，將門關上。[25]人子啊，人必用繩索捆綁你，你就不能出去在他們中間來往。[26]我必使你的舌頭貼住上膛，以致你啞口，不能作責備他們的人，他們原是悖逆之家。[27]但我對你說話的時候，必使你開口，你就要對他們說：『主耶和華如此說。』聽的可以聽，不聽的任他不聽，因為他們是悖逆之家。

---

a 18 Or in; also in verses 19 and 20

耶路撒冷被圍困的預兆

4 "人子啊，你要拿一塊磚擺在你面前，將一座耶路撒冷城畫在其上。²又圍困這城，造臺築壘，安營攻擊，在四圍安設撞錘攻城，³又要拿個鐵鏊放在你和城的中間，作為鐵牆。你要對面攻擊這城，使城被困，這樣，好作以色列家的預兆。

⁴ "你要向左側臥，承當以色列家的罪孽；要按你向左側臥的日數，擔當他們的罪孽，⁵因為我已將他們作孽的年數，定為你向左側臥的日數，就是三百九十日，你要這樣擔當以色列家的罪孽。

⁶ "再者，你滿了這些日子，還要向右側臥，擔當猶大家的罪孽。我給你定規側臥四十日，一日頂一年。⁷你要露出膀臂，面向被困的耶路撒冷，說預言攻擊這城。⁸我用繩索捆綁你，使你不能輾轉，直等你滿了困城的日子。

⁹ "你要取小麥、大麥、豆子、紅豆、小米、粗麥，裝在一個器皿中，用以為自己做餅。要按你側臥的三百九十日吃這餅。¹⁰你所吃的要按分兩吃：每日二十舍客勒，按時而吃。¹¹你喝水也要按制子：每日喝一欣六分之一，按時而喝。¹²你吃這餅像吃大麥餅一樣，要用人糞在眾人眼前燒烤。"¹³耶和華說："以色列人在我所趕他們到的各國中，也必這樣吃不潔淨的食物。"

¹⁴我說："哎！主耶和華啊，我素來未曾被玷污，從幼年到如今沒有吃過自死的，或被野獸撕裂的，那可憎的肉也未曾入我的口。"

¹⁵於是他對我說："看哪，我給你牛糞代替人糞，你要將你的餅烤在其上。"

¹⁶他又對我說："人子啊，我必在耶路撒冷折斷他們的杖，就是斷絕他們的糧。他們吃餅要按分兩，憂慮而吃；喝水也要按制子，驚惶而喝。¹⁷使他們缺糧、缺水，彼此驚惶，因自己的罪孽消滅。

Siege of Jerusalem Symbolized

4 "Now, son of man, take a clay tablet, put it in front of you and draw the city of Jerusalem on it. ²Then lay siege to it: Erect siege works against it, build a ramp up to it, set up camps against it and put battering rams around it. ³Then take an iron pan, place it as an iron wall between you and the city and turn your face toward it. It will be under siege, and you shall besiege it. This will be a sign to the house of Israel.

⁴"Then lie on your left side and put the sin of the house of Israel upon yourself.ᵃ You are to bear their sin for the number of days you lie on your side. ⁵I have assigned you the same number of days as the years of their sin. So for 390 days you will bear the sin of the house of Israel.

⁶"After you have finished this, lie down again, this time on your right side, and bear the sin of the house of Judah. I have assigned you 40 days, a day for each year. ⁷Turn your face toward the siege of Jerusalem and with bared arm prophesy against her. ⁸I will tie you up with ropes so that you cannot turn from one side to the other until you have finished the days of your siege.

⁹"Take wheat and barley, beans and lentils, millet and spelt; put them in a storage jar and use them to make bread for yourself. You are to eat it during the 390 days you lie on your side. ¹⁰Weigh out twenty shekelsᵇ of food to eat each day and eat it at set times. ¹¹Also measure out a sixth of a hincᶜ of water and drink it at set times. ¹²Eat the food as you would a barley cake; bake it in the sight of the people, using human excrement for fuel." ¹³The Lᴏʀᴅ said, "In this way the people of Israel will eat defiled food among the nations where I will drive them."

¹⁴Then I said, "Not so, Sovereign Lᴏʀᴅ! I have never defiled myself. From my youth until now I have never eaten anything found dead or torn by wild animals. No unclean meat has ever entered my mouth."

¹⁵"Very well," he said, "I will let you bake your bread over cow manure instead of human excrement."

¹⁶He then said to me: "Son of man, I will cut off the supply of food in Jerusalem. The people will eat rationed food in anxiety and drink rationed water in despair, ¹⁷for food and water will be scarce. They will be appalled at the sight of each other and will waste away because ofᵈ their sin.

a 4 Or your side　　b 10 That is, about 8 ounces (about 0.2 kilogram)　　c 11 That is, about 2/3 quart (about 0.6 liter)　　d 17 Or away in

5 "Now, son of man, take a sharp sword and use it as a barber's razor to shave your head and your beard. Then take a set of scales and divide up the hair. [2]When the days of your siege come to an end, burn a third of the hair with fire inside the city. Take a third and strike it with the sword all around the city. And scatter a third to the wind. For I will pursue them with drawn sword. [3]But take a few strands of hair and tuck them away in the folds of your garment. [4]Again, take a few of these and throw them into the fire and burn them up. A fire will spread from there to the whole house of Israel.

[5]"This is what the Sovereign LORD says: This is Jerusalem, which I have set in the center of the nations, with countries all around her. [6]Yet in her wickedness she has rebelled against my laws and decrees more than the nations and countries around her. She has rejected my laws and has not followed my decrees.

[7]"Therefore this is what the Sovereign LORD says: You have been more unruly than the nations around you and have not followed my decrees or kept my laws. You have not even[a] conformed to the standards of the nations around you.

[8]"Therefore this is what the Sovereign LORD says: I myself am against you, Jerusalem, and I will inflict punishment on you in the sight of the nations. [9]Because of all your detestable idols, I will do to you what I have never done before and will never do again. [10]Therefore in your midst fathers will eat their children, and children will eat their fathers. I will inflict punishment on you and will scatter all your survivors to the winds. [11]Therefore as surely as I live, declares the Sovereign LORD, because you have defiled my sanctuary with all your vile images and detestable practices, I myself will withdraw my favor; I will not look on you with pity or spare you. [12]A third of your people will die of the plague or perish by famine inside you; a third will fall by the sword outside your walls; and a third I will scatter to the winds and pursue with drawn sword.

[13]"Then my anger will cease and my wrath against them will subside, and I will be avenged. And when I have spent my wrath upon them, they will know that I the LORD have spoken in my zeal.

[14]"I will make you a ruin and a reproach among the nations around you, in the sight of

---

5 "人子啊，你要拿一把快刀，當作剃頭刀，用這刀剃你的頭髮和你的鬍鬚，用天平將鬚髮平分。[2]圍困城的日子滿了，你要將三分之一在城中用火焚燒，將三分之一在城的四圍用刀砍碎，將三分之一任風吹散，我也要拔刀追趕。[3]你要從其中取幾根包在衣襟裏，[4]再從這幾根中取些扔在火中焚燒，從裏面必有火出來燒入<u>以色列</u>全家。

[5]"主耶和華如此說：這就是<u>耶路撒冷</u>。我曾將她安置在列邦之中，列國都在她的四圍。[6]她行惡，違背我的典章，過於列國；干犯我的律例，過於四圍的列邦。因為她棄掉我的典章。至於我的律例，她並沒有遵行。

[7]"所以主耶和華如此說：因為你們紛爭過於四圍的列國，也不遵行我的律例，不謹守我的典章，並以遵從四圍列國的惡規尚不滿意。

[8]"所以主耶和華如此說：看哪，我與你反對，必在列國的眼前，在你中間，施行審判。[9]並且因你一切可憎的事，我要在你中間行我所未曾行的，以後我也不再照着行。[10]在你中間父親要吃兒子，兒子要吃父親。我必向你施行審判，我必將你所剩下的分散四方（註："方"原文作"風"）。[11]主耶和華說：我指着我的永生起誓，因你用一切可憎的物、可厭的事玷污了我的聖所，故此，我定要使你人數減少，我眼必不顧惜你，也不可憐你。[12]你的民三分之一必遭瘟疫而死，在你中間必因饑荒消滅；三分之一必在你四圍倒在刀下；我必將三分之一分散四方（註："方"原文作"風"），並要拔刀追趕他們。

[13]"我要這樣成就怒中所定的，我向他們發的忿怒止息了，自己就得着安慰；我在他們身上成就怒中所定的，那時，他們就知道我耶和華所說的是出於熱心。[14]"並且我必使你在四圍的列國中，在經過的眾人眼前，成了荒涼和

---

a 7 Most Hebrew manuscripts; some Hebrew manuscripts and Syriac *You have*

羞辱。¹⁵這樣，我必以怒氣和忿怒，並烈怒的責備，向你施行審判。那時，你就在四圍的列國中成為羞辱、譏刺、警戒、驚駭。這是我耶和華說的。¹⁶那時，我要將滅人，使人饑荒的惡箭，就是射去滅人的，射在你們身上，並要加增你們的饑荒，斷絕你們所倚靠的糧食；¹⁷又要使饑荒和惡獸到你那裏，叫你喪子，瘟疫和流血的事也必盛行在你那裏，我也要使刀劍臨到你。這是我耶和華說的。"

向以色列的眾山說預言

6 耶和華的話臨到我說：²"人子啊，你要面向以色列的眾山說預言。³說：'以色列的眾山哪，要聽主耶和華的話！主耶和華對大山、小岡、水溝、山谷如此說：我必使刀劍臨到你們，也必毀滅你們的邱壇。⁴你們的祭壇必然荒涼，你們的日像必被打碎，我要使你們被殺的人倒在你們的偶像面前，⁵我也要將以色列人的屍首放在他們的偶像面前，將你們的骸骨拋散在你們祭壇的四圍。⁶在你們一切的住處，城邑要變為荒場，邱壇必然淒涼，使你們的祭壇荒廢，將你們的偶像打碎。你們的日像被砍倒，你們的工作被毀滅。⁷被殺的人必倒在你們中間，你們就知道我是耶和華。

⁸"'你們分散在各國的時候，我必在列邦中使你們有剩下脫離刀劍的人。⁹那脫離刀劍的人必在所擄到的各國中記念我，為他們心中何等傷破，是因他們起淫心，遠離我，眼對偶像行邪淫。他們因行一切可憎的惡事，必厭惡自己。¹⁰他們必知道我是耶和華，我說要使這災禍臨到他們身上，並非空話。

¹¹"'主耶和華如此說：你當拍手頓足說：哀哉！以色列家行這一切可憎的惡事，他們必倒在刀劍、饑荒、瘟疫之下。¹²在遠處的，必遭瘟疫而死；在近處的，必倒在刀劍之下；那存留被圍困的，必因饑荒而死。我必這樣在他們身上成就我

all who pass by. ¹⁵You will be a reproach and a taunt, a warning and an object of horror to the nations around you when I inflict punishment on you in anger and in wrath and with stinging rebuke. I the LORD have spoken. ¹⁶When I shoot at you with my deadly and destructive arrows of famine, I will shoot to destroy you. I will bring more and more famine upon you and cut off your supply of food. ¹⁷I will send famine and wild beasts against you, and they will leave you childless. Plague and bloodshed will sweep through you, and I will bring the sword against you. I the LORD have spoken."

A Prophecy Against the Mountains of Israel

6 The word of the LORD came to me: ²"Son of man, set your face against the mountains of Israel; prophesy against them ³and say: 'O mountains of Israel, hear the word of the Sovereign LORD. This is what the Sovereign LORD says to the mountains and hills, to the ravines and valleys: I am about to bring a sword against you, and I will destroy your high places. ⁴Your altars will be demolished and your incense altars will be smashed; and I will slay your people in front of your idols. ⁵I will lay the dead bodies of the Israelites in front of their idols, and I will scatter your bones around your altars. ⁶Wherever you live, the towns will be laid waste and the high places demolished, so that your altars will be laid waste and devastated, your idols smashed and ruined, your incense altars broken down, and what you have made wiped out. ⁷Your people will fall slain among you, and you will know that I am the LORD.

⁸"'But I will spare some, for some of you will escape the sword when you are scattered among the lands and nations. ⁹Then in the nations where they have been carried captive, those who escape will remember me—how I have been grieved by their adulterous hearts, which have turned away from me, and by their eyes, which have lusted after their idols. They will loathe themselves for the evil they have done and for all their detestable practices. ¹⁰And they will know that I am the LORD; I did not threaten in vain to bring this calamity on them.

¹¹"'This is what the Sovereign LORD says: Strike your hands together and stamp your feet and cry out "Alas!" because of all the wicked and detestable practices of the house of Israel, for they will fall by the sword, famine and plague. ¹²He that is far away will die of the plague, and he that is near will fall by the sword, and he that survives and is spared will die of famine. So will I spend my wrath upon

them. 13And they will know that I am the LORD, when their people lie slain among their idols around their altars, on every high hill and on all the mountaintops, under every spreading tree and every leafy oak—places where they offered fragrant incense to all their idols. 14And I will stretch out my hand against them and make the land a desolate waste from the desert to Diblah[a] —wherever they live. Then they will know that I am the LORD.' "

The End Has Come

7 The word of the LORD came to me: 2"Son of man, this is what the Sovereign LORD says to the land of Israel: The end! The end has come upon the four corners of the land. 3The end is now upon you and I will unleash my anger against you. I will judge you according to your conduct and repay you for all your detestable practices. 4I will not look on you with pity or spare you; I will surely repay you for your conduct and the detestable practices among you. Then you will know that I am the LORD.

5"This is what the Sovereign LORD says: Disaster! An unheard-of[b] disaster is coming. 6The end has come! The end has come! It has roused itself against you. It has come! 7Doom has come upon you—you who dwell in the land. The time has come, the day is near; there is panic, not joy, upon the mountains. 8I am about to pour out my wrath on you and spend my anger against you; I will judge you according to your conduct and repay you for all your detestable practices. 9I will not look on you with pity or spare you; I will repay you in accordance with your conduct and the detestable practices among you. Then you will know that it is I the LORD who strikes the blow.

10"The day is here! It has come! Doom has burst forth, the rod has budded, arrogance has blossomed! 11Violence has grown into[c] a rod to punish wickedness; none of the people will be left, none of that crowd—no wealth, nothing of value. 12The time has come, the day has arrived. Let not the buyer rejoice nor the seller grieve, for wrath is upon the whole crowd. 13The seller will not recover the land he has sold as long as both of them live, for the vision concerning the whole crowd will not be reversed. Because of their sins, not one of them will preserve his life.

---

a 14 Most Hebrew manuscripts; a few Hebrew manuscripts Riblah   b 5 Most Hebrew manuscripts; some Hebrew manuscripts and Syriac Disaster after   c 11 Or The violent one has become

---

怒中所定的。13他們被殺的人，倒在他們祭壇四圍的偶像中，就是各高岡、各山頂、各青翠樹下、各茂密的橡樹下，乃是他們獻馨香的祭牲給一切偶像的地方。那時，他們就知道我是耶和華。14我必伸手攻擊他們，使他們的地從曠野到第伯拉他一切住處極其荒涼。他們就知道我是耶和華。' "

結局已經臨到

7 耶和華的話又臨到我說：2"人子啊，主耶和華對以色列地如此說：結局到了！結局到了地的四境。3現在你的結局已經臨到，我必使我的怒氣歸與你，也必按你的行為審判你，照你一切可憎的事刑罰你。4我眼必不顧惜你，也不可憐你，卻要按你所行的報應你，照你中間可憎的事刑罰你。你就知道我是耶和華。

5 "主耶和華如此說：有一災，獨有一災，看哪，臨近了！6結局來了，結局來了！向你興起。看哪，來到了！7境內的居民哪，所定的災臨到你，時候到了，日子近了，乃是鬧嚷，並非在山上歡呼的日子。8我快要將我的忿怒傾在你身上，向你成就我怒中所定的，按你的行為審判你，照你一切可憎的事刑罰你。9我眼必不顧惜你，也不可憐你，必按你所行的報應你，照你中間可憎的事刑罰你。你就知道擊打你的是我耶和華。

10 "看哪，看哪！日子快到了，所定的災已經發出！杖已經開花，驕傲已經發芽。11強暴興起，成了罰惡的杖。以色列人，或是他們的羣眾，或是他們的財寶，無一存留，他們中間也沒有得尊榮的。12時候到了，日子近了，買主不可歡喜，賣主不可愁煩，因為烈怒已經臨到他們眾人身上。13賣主雖然存活，卻不能歸回再得所賣的，因為這異象關乎他們眾人。誰都不得歸回，也沒有人在他的罪孽中堅立自己。¹⁴他們已經吹角，預備齊全，卻無一人出戰，因為我的烈怒臨到他們眾人身上。

¹⁵ "在外有刀劍，在內有瘟疫、饑荒；在田野的必遭刀劍而死，在城中的必有飢荒、瘟疫吞滅他。¹⁶其中所逃脫的，就必逃脫，各人因自己的罪孽在山上發出悲聲，好像谷中的鴿子哀鳴。¹⁷手都發軟，膝弱如水。¹⁸要用麻布束腰，被戰兢所蓋，各人臉上羞愧，頭上光禿。¹⁹他們要將銀子拋在街上，金子看如污穢之物。當耶和華發怒的日子，他們的金銀不能救他們，不能使心裏知足，也不能使肚腹飽滿，因為這金銀作了他們罪孽的絆腳石。²⁰論到耶和華妝飾華美的殿，他建立得威嚴，他們卻在其中製造可憎可厭的偶像，所以這殿我使他們看如污穢之物。²¹我必將這殿交付外邦人為掠物，交付地上的惡人為擄物，他們也必褻瀆這殿。²²我必轉臉不顧以色列人，他們褻瀆我隱密之所，強盜也必進去褻瀆。

²³ "要製造鎖鏈，因為這地遍滿流血的罪，城邑充滿強暴的事。²⁴所以我必使列國中最惡的人來佔據他們的房屋；我必使強暴人的驕傲止息，他們的聖所都要被褻瀆。²⁵毀滅臨近了！他們要求平安，卻無平安可得。²⁶災害加上災害，風聲接連風聲。他們必向先知求異象，但祭司講的律法，長老設的謀略，都必斷絕。²⁷君要悲哀，王要披淒涼為衣，國民的手都發顫。我必照他們的行為待他們，按他們應得的審判他們。他們就知道我是耶和華。"

聖殿中拜偶像

8 第六年六月初五日，我坐在家中，猶大的眾長老坐在我面前，在那裏主耶和華的靈（註：原文作"手"）降在我身上。²我觀看，見有像彷彿火的形狀，從他腰以下的形狀有火，從他腰以上有

¹⁴Though they blow the trumpet and get everything ready, no one will go into battle, for my wrath is upon the whole crowd.

¹⁵"Outside is the sword, inside are plague and famine; those in the country will die by the sword, and those in the city will be devoured by famine and plague. ¹⁶All who survive and escape will be in the mountains, moaning like doves of the valleys, each because of his sins. ¹⁷Every hand will go limp, and every knee will become as weak as water. ¹⁸They will put on sackcloth and be clothed with terror. Their faces will be covered with shame and their heads will be shaved. ¹⁹They will throw their silver into the streets, and their gold will be an unclean thing. Their silver and gold will not be able to save them in the day of the LORD's wrath. They will not satisfy their hunger or fill their stomachs with it, for it has made them stumble into sin. ²⁰They were proud of their beautiful jewelry and used it to make their detestable idols and vile images. Therefore I will turn these into an unclean thing for them. ²¹I will hand it all over as plunder to foreigners and as loot to the wicked of the earth, and they will defile it. ²²I will turn my face away from them, and they will desecrate my treasured place; robbers will enter it and desecrate it.

²³"Prepare chains, because the land is full of bloodshed and the city is full of violence. ²⁴I will bring the most wicked of the nations to take possession of their houses; I will put an end to the pride of the mighty, and their sanctuaries will be desecrated. ²⁵When terror comes, they will seek peace, but there will be none. ²⁶Calamity upon calamity will come, and rumor upon rumor. They will try to get a vision from the prophet; the teaching of the law by the priest will be lost, as will the counsel of the elders. ²⁷The king will mourn, the prince will be clothed with despair, and the hands of the people of the land will tremble. I will deal with them according to their conduct, and by their own standards I will judge them. Then they will know that I am the LORD."

Idolatry in the Temple

8 In the sixth year, in the sixth month on the fifth day, while I was sitting in my house and the elders of Judah were sitting before me, the hand of the Sovereign LORD came upon me there. ²I looked, and I saw a figure like that of a man.ᵃ From what appeared to be his waist down he was like fire, and from

a 2 Or saw a fiery figure

there up his appearance was as bright as glowing metal. [3]He stretched out what looked like a hand and took me by the hair of my head. The Spirit lifted me up between earth and heaven and in visions of God he took me to Jerusalem, to the entrance to the north gate of the inner court, where the idol that provokes to jealousy stood. [4]And there before me was the glory of the God of Israel, as in the vision I had seen in the plain.

[5]Then he said to me, "Son of man, look toward the north." So I looked, and in the entrance north of the gate of the altar I saw this idol of jealousy.

[6]And he said to me, "Son of man, do you see what they are doing—the utterly detestable things the house of Israel is doing here, things that will drive me far from my sanctuary? But you will see things that are even more detestable."

[7]Then he brought me to the entrance to the court. I looked, and I saw a hole in the wall. [8]He said to me, "Son of man, now dig into the wall." So I dug into the wall and saw a doorway there.

[9]And he said to me, "Go in and see the wicked and detestable things they are doing here." [10]So I went in and looked, and I saw portrayed all over the walls all kinds of crawling things and detestable animals and all the idols of the house of Israel. [11]In front of them stood seventy elders of the house of Israel, and Jaazaniah son of Shaphan was standing among them. Each had a censer in his hand, and a fragrant cloud of incense was rising.

[12]He said to me, "Son of man, have you seen what the elders of the house of Israel are doing in the darkness, each at the shrine of his own idol? They say, 'The LORD does not see us; the LORD has forsaken the land.' " [13]Again, he said, "You will see them doing things that are even more detestable."

[14]Then he brought me to the entrance to the north gate of the house of the LORD, and I saw women sitting there, mourning for Tammuz. [15]He said to me, "Do you see this, son of man? You will see things that are even more detestable than this."

[16]He then brought me into the inner court of the house of the LORD, and there at the entrance to the temple, between the portico and the altar, were about twenty-five men. With their backs toward the temple of the LORD and their faces toward the east, they were bowing down to the sun in the east.

[17]He said to me, "Have you seen this, son of man? Is it a trivial matter for the house of Judah

光輝的形狀，彷彿光耀的精金。[3]他伸出彷彿一隻手的樣式，抓住我的一綹頭髮，靈就將我舉到天地中間，在神的異象中，帶我到耶路撒冷朝北的內院門口，在那裏有觸動主怒偶像的坐位，就是惹動忌邪的。[4]誰知，在那裏有以色列神的榮耀，形狀與我在平原所見的一樣。

[5]神對我說：「人子啊，你舉目向北觀看。」我就舉目向北觀看，見祭壇門的北邊，在門口有這惹忌邪的偶像。

[6]又對我說：「人子啊，以色列家所行的，就是在此行這大可憎的事，使我遠離我的聖所，你看見了嗎？你還要看見另有大可憎的事。」

[7]他領我到院門口。我觀看，見牆上有個窟窿。[8]他對我說：「人子啊，你要挖牆。」我一挖牆，見有一門。

[9]他說：「你進去，看他們在這裏所行可憎的惡事。」[10]我進去一看，誰知，在四面牆上畫着各樣爬物和可憎的走獸，並以色列家一切的偶像。[11]在這些像前，有以色列家的七十個長老站立，沙番的兒子雅撒尼亞也站在其中。各人手拿香爐，煙雲的香氣上騰。

[12]他對我說：「人子啊，以色列家的長老暗中在各人畫像屋裏所行的，你看見了嗎？他們常說：『耶和華看不見我們，耶和華已經離棄這地。』」[13]他又說：「你還要看見他們另外行大可憎的事。」

[14]他領我到耶和華殿外院朝北的門口。誰知，在那裏有婦女坐着，為搭模斯哭泣。[15]他對我說：「人子啊，你看見了嗎？你還要看見比這更可憎的事。」

[16]他又領我到耶和華殿的內院。誰知，在耶和華的殿門口、廊子和祭壇中間，約有二十五個人，背向耶和華的殿，面向東方拜日頭。

[17]他對我說：「人子啊，你看見了嗎？猶大家在此行這可憎的事還算

為小嗎？他們在這地遍行強暴，再三惹我發怒，他們手拿枝條舉向鼻前。18因此，我也要以忿怒行事，我眼必不顧惜，也不可憐他們；他們雖向我耳中大聲呼求，我還是不聽。」

擊殺拜偶像者

9 他向我耳中大聲喊叫說：「要使那監管這城的人手中各拿滅命的兵器前來。」2忽然有六個人從朝北的上門而來，各人手拿殺人的兵器。內中有一人身穿細麻衣，腰間帶着墨盒子。他們進來，站在銅祭壇旁。

3以色列神的榮耀本在基路伯上，現今從那裏升到殿的門檻。神將那身穿細麻衣，腰間帶着墨盒子的人召來。4耶和華對他說：「你去走遍耶路撒冷全城，那些因城中所行可憎之事歎息哀哭的人，畫記號在額上。」

5我耳中聽見他對其餘的人說：「要跟隨他走遍全城，以行擊殺。你們的眼不要顧惜，也不要可憐他們。6要將年老的、年少的，並處女、嬰孩和婦女從聖所起全都殺盡，只是凡有記號的人不要挨近他。」於是他們從殿前的長老殺起。

7他對他們說：「要污穢這殿，使院中充滿被殺的人。你們出去吧！」他們就出去，在城中擊殺。8他們擊殺的時候，我被留下。我就俯伏在地，說：「哎！主耶和華啊，你將忿怒傾在耶路撒冷，豈要將以色列所剩下的人都滅絕嗎？」

9他對我說：「以色列家和猶大家的罪孽極其重大。遍地有流血的事，滿城有冤屈，因為他們說：『耶和華已經離棄這地，他看不見我們。』10故此，我眼必不顧惜，也不可憐他們，要照他們所行的報應在他們頭上。」

11那穿細麻衣，腰間帶着墨盒子的人將這事回覆說：「我已經照你所吩咐的行了。」

to do the detestable things they are doing here? Must they also fill the land with violence and continually provoke me to anger? Look at them putting the branch to their nose! 18Therefore I will deal with them in anger; I will not look on them with pity or spare them. Although they shout in my ears, I will not listen to them."

Idolaters Killed

9 Then I heard him call out in a loud voice, "Bring the guards of the city here, each with a weapon in his hand." 2And I saw six men coming from the direction of the upper gate, which faces north, each with a deadly weapon in his hand. With them was a man clothed in linen who had a writing kit at his side. They came in and stood beside the bronze altar.

3Now the glory of the God of Israel went up from above the cherubim, where it had been, and moved to the threshold of the temple. Then the LORD called to the man clothed in linen who had the writing kit at his side 4and said to him, "Go throughout the city of Jerusalem and put a mark on the foreheads of those who grieve and lament over all the detestable things that are done in it."

5As I listened, he said to the others, "Follow him through the city and kill, without showing pity or compassion. 6Slaughter old men, young men and maidens, women and children, but do not touch anyone who has the mark. Begin at my sanctuary." So they began with the elders who were in front of the temple.

7Then he said to them, "Defile the temple and fill the courts with the slain. Go!" So they went out and began killing throughout the city. 8While they were killing and I was left alone, I fell facedown, crying out, "Ah, Sovereign LORD! Are you going to destroy the entire remnant of Israel in this outpouring of your wrath on Jerusalem?"

9He answered me, "The sin of the house of Israel and Judah is exceedingly great; the land is full of bloodshed and the city is full of injustice. They say, 'The LORD has forsaken the land; the LORD does not see.' 10So I will not look on them with pity or spare them, but I will bring down on their own heads what they have done."

11Then the man in linen with the writing kit at his side brought back word, saying, "I have done as you commanded."

The Glory Departs From the Temple

10 I looked, and I saw the likeness of a throne of sapphire[a] above the expanse that was over the heads of the cherubim. [2]The LORD said to the man clothed in linen, "Go in among the wheels beneath the cherubim. Fill your hands with burning coals from among the cherubim and scatter them over the city." And as I watched, he went in.

[3]Now the cherubim were standing on the south side of the temple when the man went in, and a cloud filled the inner court. [4]Then the glory of the LORD rose from above the cherubim and moved to the threshold of the temple. The cloud filled the temple, and the court was full of the radiance of the glory of the LORD. [5]The sound of the wings of the cherubim could be heard as far away as the outer court, like the voice of God Almighty[b] when he speaks.

[6]When the LORD commanded the man in linen, "Take fire from among the wheels, from among the cherubim," the man went in and stood beside a wheel. [7]Then one of the cherubim reached out his hand to the fire that was among them. He took up some of it and put it into the hands of the man in linen, who took it and went out. [8](Under the wings of the cherubim could be seen what looked like the hands of a man.)

[9]I looked, and I saw beside the cherubim four wheels, one beside each of the cherubim; the wheels sparkled like chrysolite. [10]As for their appearance, the four of them looked alike; each was like a wheel intersecting a wheel. [11]As they moved, they would go in any one of the four directions the cherubim faced; the wheels did not turn about[c] as the cherubim went. The cherubim went in whatever direction the head faced, without turning as they went. [12]Their entire bodies, including their backs, their hands and their wings, were completely full of eyes, as were their four wheels. [13]I heard the wheels being called "the whirling wheels." [14]Each of the cherubim had four faces: One face was that of a cherub, the second face of a man, the third the face of a lion, and the fourth the face of an eagle.

[15]Then the cherubim rose upward. These were the living creatures I had seen by the Kebar River. [16]When the cherubim moved, the wheels beside them moved; and when the cherubim spread their wings to rise from the ground, the wheels did not leave their side. [17]When the cherubim stood still, they also stood still; and when the cherubim rose, they rose

榮耀離開聖殿

10 我觀看，見基路伯頭上的穹蒼之中顯出藍寶石的形狀，彷彿寶座的形像。[2]主對那穿細麻衣的人說：「你進去，在旋轉的輪內、基路伯以下，從基路伯中間將火炭取滿兩手，撒在城上。」我就見他進去。

[3]那人進去的時候，基路伯站在殿的右邊，雲彩充滿了內院。[4]耶和華的榮耀從基路伯那裏上升，停在門檻以上。殿內滿了雲彩，院宇也被耶和華榮耀的光輝充滿。[5]基路伯翅膀的響聲聽到外院，好像全能神說話的聲音。

[6]他吩咐那穿細麻衣的人說："要從旋轉的輪內、基路伯中間取火。"那人就進去站在一個輪子旁邊。[7]有一個基路伯從基路伯中伸手到基路伯中間的火那裏，取些放在那穿細麻衣的人兩手中，那人就拿出去了。[8]在基路伯翅膀之下顯出有人手的樣式。

[9]我又觀看，見基路伯旁邊有四個輪子，這基路伯旁有一個輪子，那基路伯旁有一個輪子，每基路伯都是如此；輪子的顏色（註：原文作"形狀"）彷彿水蒼玉。[10]至於四輪的形狀，都是一個樣式，彷彿輪中套輪。[11]輪行走的時候，向四方都能直行，並不掉轉。頭向何方，他們也隨向何方，行走的時候並不掉轉。[12]他們全身，連背帶手和翅膀，並輪周圍，都滿了眼睛。這四個基路伯的輪子都是如此。[13]至於這些輪子，我耳中聽見說是"旋轉的"。[14]基路伯各有四臉：第一是基路伯的臉，第二是人的臉，第三是獅子的臉，第四是鷹的臉。

[15]基路伯升上去了，這是我在迦巴魯河邊所見的活物。[16]基路伯行走，輪也在旁邊行走；基路伯展開翅膀，離地上升，輪也不轉離他們旁邊。[17]那些站住，這些也站住；那些

a 1 Or lapis lazuli   b 5 Hebrew El-Shaddai   c 11 Or aside

上升，這些也一同上升，因為活物的靈在輪中。¹⁸耶和華的榮耀從殿的門檻那裏出去，停在基路伯以上。¹⁹基路伯出去的時候，就展開翅膀，在我眼前離地上升。輪也在他們的旁邊，都停在耶和華殿的東門口。在他們以上有以色列神的榮耀。

²⁰這是我在迦巴魯河邊所見以色列神榮耀以下的活物，我就知道他們是基路伯。²¹他們各有四個臉面，四個翅膀，翅膀以下有人手的樣式。²²至於他們臉的模樣，並身體的形像，是我從前在迦巴魯河邊所看見的。他們俱各直往前行。

對以色列首領的審判

11 靈將我舉起，帶到耶和華殿向東的東門。誰知，在門口有二十五個人，我見其中有民間的首領押朔的兒子雅撒尼亞和比拿雅的兒子毘拉提。²耶和華對我說："人子啊，這就是圖謀罪孽的人，在這城中給人設惡謀。³他們說：'蓋房屋的時候尚未臨近，這城是鍋，我們是肉。'⁴人子啊，因此，你當說預言，說預言攻擊他們。"

⁵耶和華的靈降在我身上，對我說："你當說，耶和華如此說：以色列家啊，你們口中所說的，心裏所想的，我都知道。⁶你們在這城中殺人增多，使被殺的人充滿街道。

⁷ "所以主耶和華如此說：你們殺在城中的人就是肉，這城就是鍋，你們卻要從其中被帶出去。⁸你們怕刀劍，我必使刀劍臨到你們。這是主耶和華說的。⁹我必從這城中帶出你們去，交在外邦人的手中，且要在你們中間施行審判。¹⁰你們必倒在刀下，我必在以色列的境界審判你們，你們就知道我是耶和華。¹¹這城必不作你們的鍋，你們也不作其中的肉。我必在以色列的境界審判你們，¹²你們就知道我是耶和華。

with them, because the spirit of the living creatures was in them.

¹⁸Then the glory of the LORD departed from over the threshold of the temple and stopped above the cherubim. ¹⁹While I watched, the cherubim spread their wings and rose from the ground, and as they went, the wheels went with them. They stopped at the entrance to the east gate of the LORD's house, and the glory of the God of Israel was above them.

²⁰These were the living creatures I had seen beneath the God of Israel by the Kebar River, and I realized that they were cherubim. ²¹Each had four faces and four wings, and under their wings was what looked like the hands of a man. ²²Their faces had the same appearance as those I had seen by the Kebar River. Each one went straight ahead.

Judgment on Israel's Leaders

11 Then the Spirit lifted me up and brought me to the gate of the house of the LORD that faces east. There at the entrance to the gate were twenty-five men, and I saw among them Jaazaniah son of Azzur and Pelatiah son of Benaiah, leaders of the people. ²The LORD said to me, "Son of man, these are the men who are plotting evil and giving wicked advice in this city. ³They say, 'Will it not soon be time to build houses?ᵃ This city is a cooking pot, and we are the meat.' ⁴Therefore prophesy against them; prophesy, son of man."

⁵Then the Spirit of the LORD came upon me, and he told me to say: "This is what the LORD says: That is what you are saying, O house of Israel, but I know what is going through your mind. ⁶You have killed many people in this city and filled its streets with the dead.

⁷"Therefore this is what the Sovereign LORD says: The bodies you have thrown there are the meat and this city is the pot, but I will drive you out of it. ⁸You fear the sword, and the sword is what I will bring against you, declares the Sovereign LORD. ⁹I will drive you out of the city and hand you over to foreigners and inflict punishment on you. ¹⁰You will fall by the sword, and I will execute judgment on you at the borders of Israel. Then you will know that I am the LORD. ¹¹This city will not be a pot for you, nor will you be the meat in it; I will execute judgment on you at the borders of Israel. ¹²And you will know that I am the LORD, for you have not

---

a 3 Or This is not the time to build houses.

followed my decrees or kept my laws but have conformed to the standards of the nations around you."

¹³Now as I was prophesying, Pelatiah son of Benaiah died. Then I fell facedown and cried out in a loud voice, "Ah, Sovereign LORD! Will you completely destroy the remnant of Israel?"

¹⁴The word of the LORD came to me: ¹⁵"Son of man, your brothers—your brothers who are your blood relatives[a] and the whole house of Israel—are those of whom the people of Jerusalem have said, 'They are[b] far away from the LORD; this land was given to us as our possession.'

Promised Return of Israel

¹⁶"Therefore say: 'This is what the Sovereign LORD says: Although I sent them far away among the nations and scattered them among the countries, yet for a little while I have been a sanctuary for them in the countries where they have gone.'

¹⁷"Therefore say: 'This is what the Sovereign LORD says: I will gather you from the nations and bring you back from the countries where you have been scattered, and I will give you back the land of Israel again.'

¹⁸"They will return to it and remove all its vile images and detestable idols. ¹⁹I will give them an undivided heart and put a new spirit in them; I will remove from them their heart of stone and give them a heart of flesh. ²⁰Then they will follow my decrees and be careful to keep my laws. They will be my people, and I will be their God. ²¹But as for those whose hearts are devoted to their vile images and detestable idols, I will bring down on their own heads what they have done, declares the Sovereign LORD."

²²Then the cherubim, with the wheels beside them, spread their wings, and the glory of the God of Israel was above them. ²³The glory of the LORD went up from within the city and stopped above the mountain east of it. ²⁴The Spirit lifted me up and brought me to the exiles in Babylonia[c] in the vision given by the Spirit of God.

Then the vision I had seen went up from me, ²⁵and I told the exiles everything the LORD had shown me.

---

a 15 Or *are in exile with you* (see Septuagint and Syriac)
b 15 Or *those to whom the people of Jerusalem have said, 'Stay*
c 24 Or *Chaldea*

因為你們沒有遵行我的律例，也沒有順從我的典章，卻隨從你們四圍列國的惡俗。'"

¹³我正說預言的時候，比拿雅的兒子毘拉提死了。於是我俯伏在地，大聲呼叫說："哎！主耶和華啊，你要將以色列剩下的人滅絕淨盡嗎？"

¹⁴耶和華的話臨到我說：¹⁵"人子啊，耶路撒冷的居民對你的弟兄、你的本族、你的親屬、以色列全家，就是對大眾說：'你們遠離耶和華吧！這地是賜給我們為業的。'

應許以色列人得歸回

¹⁶"所以你當說：'耶和華如此說：我雖將以色列全家遠遠遷移到列國中，將他們分散在列邦內，我還要在他們所到的列邦，暫作他們的聖所。'

¹⁷"你當說：'主耶和華如此說：我必從萬民中招聚你們，從分散的列國內聚集你們，又要將以色列地賜給你們。'

¹⁸"他們必到那裏，也必從其中除掉一切可憎可厭的物。¹⁹我要使他們有合一的心，也要將新靈放在他們裏面，又從他們肉體中除掉石心，賜給他們肉心，²⁰使他們順從我的律例，謹守遵行我的典章。他們要作我的子民，我要作他們的神。²¹至於那些心中隨從可憎可厭之物的，我必照他們所行的報應在他們頭上。這是主耶和華說的。'"

²²於是基路伯展開翅膀，輪子都在他們旁邊；在他們以上，有以色列神的榮耀。²³耶和華的榮耀從城中上升，停在城東的那座山上。²⁴靈將我舉起，在異象中藉着神的靈，將我帶進迦勒底地，到被擄的人那裏。

我所見的異象就離我上升去了。²⁵我便將耶和華所指示我的一切事都說給被擄的人聽。

被擄的預兆

12 耶和華的話又臨到我說：²「人子啊，你住在悖逆的家中，他們有眼睛看不見、有耳朵聽不見，因為他們是悖逆之家。

³「所以，人子啊，你要預備擄去使用的物件，在白日，當他們眼前從你所住的地方移到別處去；他們雖是悖逆之家，或者可以揣摩思想。⁴你要在白日當他們眼前帶出你的物件去，好像預備擄去使用的物件。到了晚上，你要在他們眼前親自出去，像被擄的人出去一樣。⁵你要在他們眼前挖通了牆，從其中將物件帶出去。⁶到天黑時，你要當他們眼前搭在肩頭上帶出去，並要蒙住臉看不見地，因為我立你作以色列家的預兆。」

⁷我就照着所吩咐的去行，白日帶出我的物件，好像預備擄去使用的物件。到了晚上，我用手挖通了牆。天黑的時候，就當他們眼前搭在肩頭上帶出去。

⁸次日早晨，耶和華的話臨到我說：⁹「人子啊，以色列家，就是那悖逆之家，豈不是問你說：『你做甚麼呢？』

¹⁰「你要對他們說：『主耶和華如此說：這是關乎耶路撒冷的君王和他周圍以色列全家的預表（註：原文作「擔子」）。』¹¹你要說：『我作你們的預兆。我怎樣行，他們所遭遇的也必怎樣，他們必被擄去。』

¹²「他們中間的君王，也必在天黑的時候將物件搭在肩頭上帶出去。他們要挖通了牆，從其中帶出去。他必蒙住臉，眼看不見地。¹³我必將我的網撒在他身上，他必在我的網羅中纏住。我必帶他到迦勒底人之地的巴比倫；他雖死在那裏，卻看不見那地。¹⁴周圍一切幫助他的和他所有的軍隊，我必分散四方（註：「方」原文作「風」），也要拔刀追趕他們。

¹⁵「我將他們四散在列國，分散在列邦的時候，他們就知道我是耶和華。¹⁶我卻要留下他們幾個人得免刀劍、饑荒、瘟疫，使他們在所到的各國中，述說他們一切可憎的事。人就知道我是耶和華。」

¹⁷耶和華的話又臨到我說：¹⁸「人子啊，你吃飯必膽戰，喝水必惶惶憂慮。¹⁹你要對這地的百姓說：『主耶和華論耶路撒冷和以色列地

The Exile Symbolized

12 The word of the LORD came to me: ²"Son of man, you are living among a rebellious people. They have eyes to see but do not see and ears to hear but do not hear, for they are a rebellious people.

³"Therefore, son of man, pack your belongings for exile and in the daytime, as they watch, set out and go from where you are to another place. Perhaps they will understand, though they are a rebellious house. ⁴During the daytime, while they watch, bring out your belongings packed for exile. Then in the evening, while they are watching, go out like those who go into exile. ⁵While they watch, dig through the wall and take your belongings out through it. ⁶Put them on your shoulder as they are watching and carry them out at dusk. Cover your face so that you cannot see the land, for I have made you a sign to the house of Israel."

⁷So I did as I was commanded. During the day I brought out my things packed for exile. Then in the evening I dug through the wall with my hands. I took my belongings out at dusk, carrying them on my shoulders while they watched.

⁸In the morning the word of the LORD came to me: ⁹"Son of man, did not that rebellious house of Israel ask you, 'What are you doing?'

¹⁰"Say to them, 'This is what the Sovereign LORD says: This oracle concerns the prince in Jerusalem and the whole house of Israel who are there.' ¹¹Say to them, 'I am a sign to you.'

"As I have done, so it will be done to them. They will go into exile as captives.

¹²"The prince among them will put his things on his shoulder at dusk and leave, and a hole will be dug in the wall for him to go through. He will cover his face so that he cannot see the land. ¹³I will spread my net for him, and he will be caught in my snare; I will bring him to Babylonia, the land of the Chaldeans, but he will not see it, and there he will die. ¹⁴I will scatter to the winds all those around him—his staff and all his troops—and I will pursue them with drawn sword.

¹⁵"They will know that I am the LORD, when I disperse them among the nations and scatter them through the countries. ¹⁶But I will spare a few of them from the sword, famine and plague, so that in the nations where they go they may acknowledge all their detestable practices. Then they will know that I am the LORD."

¹⁷The word of the LORD came to me: ¹⁸"Son of man, tremble as you eat your food, and shudder in fear as you drink your water. ¹⁹Say to the people of the land: 'This is what the Sovereign

LORD says about those living in Jerusalem and in the land of Israel: They will eat their food in anxiety and drink their water in despair, for their land will be stripped of everything in it because of the violence of all who live there. ²⁰The inhabited towns will be laid waste and the land will be desolate. Then you will know that I am the LORD.' "

²¹The word of the LORD came to me: ²²"Son of man, what is this proverb you have in the land of Israel: 'The days go by and every vision comes to nothing'? ²³Say to them, 'This is what the Sovereign LORD says: I am going to put an end to this proverb, and they will no longer quote it in Israel.' Say to them, 'The days are near when every vision will be fulfilled. ²⁴For there will be no more false visions or flattering divinations among the people of Israel. ²⁵But I the LORD will speak what I will, and it shall be fulfilled without delay. For in your days, you rebellious house, I will fulfill whatever I say, declares the Sovereign LORD.' "

²⁶The word of the LORD came to me: ²⁷"Son of man, the house of Israel is saying, 'The vision he sees is for many years from now, and he prophesies about the distant future.'

²⁸"Therefore say to them, 'This is what the Sovereign LORD says: None of my words will be delayed any longer; whatever I say will be fulfilled, declares the Sovereign LORD.' "

False Prophets Condemned

13 The word of the LORD came to me: ²"Son of man, prophesy against the prophets of Israel who are now prophesying. Say to those who prophesy out of their own imagination: 'Hear the word of the LORD! ³This is what the Sovereign LORD says: Woe to the foolish^a prophets who follow their own spirit and have seen nothing! ⁴Your prophets, O Israel, are like jackals among ruins. ⁵You have not gone up to the breaks in the wall to repair it for the house of Israel so that it will stand firm in the battle on the day of the LORD. ⁶Their visions are false and their divinations a lie. They say, "The LORD declares," when the LORD has not sent them; yet they expect their words to be fulfilled. ⁷Have you not seen false visions and uttered lying divinations when you say, "The LORD declares," though I have not spoken?

⁸"Therefore this is what the Sovereign LORD says: Because of your false words and lying visions, I am against you, declares the Sovereign LORD. ⁹My hand will be against the prophets

a 3 Or *wicked*

的居民如此說：他們吃飯必憂慮，喝水必驚惶，因其中居住的眾人所行強暴的事，這地必荒廢，一無所存。²⁰有居民的城邑必變為荒場，地也必變為荒廢，你們就知道我是耶和華。' "

²¹耶和華的話臨到我說：²²"人子啊，在你們以色列地怎麼有這俗語說：'日子遲延，一切異象都落了空'呢？²³你要告訴他們說：'主耶和華如此說：我必使這俗語止息，以色列中不再用這俗語。'你卻要對他們說：'日子臨近，一切的異象必都應驗。²⁴從此，在以色列家中必不再有虛假的異象和奉承的占卜。²⁵我耶和華說話，所說的必定成就，不再躭延。你們這悖逆之家，我所說的話，必趁你們在世的日子成就。這是主耶和華說的。' "

²⁶耶和華的話又臨到我說：²⁷"人子啊，以色列家的人說：'他所見的異象是關乎後來許多的日子；所說的預言是指著極遠的時候。'

²⁸"所以你要對他們說：'主耶和華如此說：我的話沒有一句再躭延的，我所說的必定成就。這是主耶和華說的。' "

假先知受譴責

13 耶和華的話臨到我說：²"人子啊，你要說預言攻擊以色列中說預言的先知，對那些本己心發預言的說：'你們當聽耶和華的話！³主耶和華如此說：愚頑的先知有禍了！他們隨從自己的心意，卻一無所見。⁴以色列啊，你的先知好像荒場中的狐狸。⁵沒有上去堵擋破口，也沒有為以色列家重修牆垣，使他們當耶和華的日子在陣上站立得住。⁶這些人所見的是虛假，是謊詐的占卜。他們說：是耶和華說的。其實耶和華並沒有差遣他們，他們倒使人指望那話必然立定。⁷你們豈不是見了虛假的異象嗎？豈不是說了謊詐的占卜嗎？你們說：這是耶和華說的。其實我沒有說。

⁸"'所以主耶和華如此說：因你們說的是虛假，見的是謊詐，我就與你們反對。這是主耶和華說的。⁹我的手必攻擊那見虛假異象，用謊

詐占卜的先知，他們必不列在我百姓的會中，不錄在以色列家的冊上，也不進入以色列地。你們就知道我是主耶和華。

10 " '因為他們誘惑我的百姓，說：平安！其實沒有平安，就像有人立起牆壁，他們倒用未泡透的灰抹上。11所以你要對那些抹上未泡透灰的人說：牆要倒塌，必有暴雨漫過。大冰雹啊，你們要降下，狂風也要吹裂這牆。12這牆倒塌之後，人豈不問你們說：你們抹上未泡透的灰在哪裏呢？

13 " '所以主耶和華如此說：我要發怒，使狂風吹裂這牆，在怒中使暴雨漫過，又發怒降下大冰雹毀滅這牆。14我要這樣拆毀你們那未泡透灰所抹的牆，拆平到地，以致根基露出。牆必倒塌，你們也必在其中滅亡。你們就知道我是耶和華。15我要這樣向牆和用未泡透灰抹牆的人成就我怒中所定的，並要對你們說：牆和抹牆的人都沒有了。16這抹牆的就是以色列的先知，他們指著耶路撒冷說預言，為這城見了平安的異象，其實沒有平安。這是主耶和華說的。'

17 "人子啊，你要面向本民中，從己心發預言的女子說預言，攻擊她們。18說：'主耶和華如此說：這些婦女有禍了！她們為眾人的膀臂縫靠枕，給高矮之人做下垂的頭巾，為要獵取人的性命。難道你們要獵取我百姓的性命，為利己將人救活嗎？19你們為兩把大麥，為幾塊餅，在我民中褻瀆我，對肯聽謊言的民說謊，殺死不該死的人，救活不該活的人。

20 " '所以主耶和華如此說：看哪，我與你們的靠枕反對，就是你們用以獵取人，使人的性命如鳥飛的。我要將靠枕從你們的膀臂上扯去，釋放你們獵取如鳥飛的人。21我也必撕裂你們下垂的頭巾，救我百姓脫離你們的手，不再被獵取，落在你們手中。你們就知道我是耶和華。22我不使義人傷心，你們卻以謊

who see false visions and utter lying divinations. They will not belong to the council of my people or be listed in the records of the house of Israel, nor will they enter the land of Israel. Then you will know that I am the Sovereign LORD.

10 " 'Because they lead my people astray, saying, "Peace," when there is no peace, and because, when a flimsy wall is built, they cover it with whitewash, 11therefore tell those who cover it with whitewash that it is going to fall. Rain will come in torrents, and I will send hailstones hurtling down, and violent winds will burst forth. 12When the wall collapses, will people not ask you, "Where is the whitewash you covered it with?"

13 " 'Therefore this is what the Sovereign LORD says: In my wrath I will unleash a violent wind, and in my anger hailstones and torrents of rain will fall with destructive fury. 14I will tear down the wall you have covered with whitewash and will level it to the ground so that its foundation will be laid bare. When it*a* falls, you will be destroyed in it; and you will know that I am the LORD. 15So I will spend my wrath against the wall and against those who covered it with whitewash. I will say to you, "The wall is gone and so are those who whitewashed it, 16those prophets of Israel who prophesied to Jerusalem and saw visions of peace for her when there was no peace, declares the Sovereign LORD."

17"Now, son of man, set your face against the daughters of your people who prophesy out of their own imagination. Prophesy against them 18and say, 'This is what the Sovereign LORD says: Woe to the women who sew magic charms on all their wrists and make veils of various lengths for their heads in order to ensnare people. Will you ensnare the lives of my people but preserve your own? 19You have profaned me among my people for a few handfuls of barley and scraps of bread. By lying to my people, who listen to lies, you have killed those who should not have died and have spared those who should not live.

20" 'Therefore this is what the Sovereign LORD says: I am against your magic charms with which you ensnare people like birds and I will tear them from your arms; I will set free the people that you ensnare like birds. 21I will tear off your veils and save my people from your hands, and they will no longer fall prey to your power. Then you will know that I am the LORD. 22Because you disheartened the righteous with your lies, when I had brought them no grief,

a 14 Or the city

and because you encouraged the wicked not to turn from their evil ways and so save their lives, [23]therefore you will no longer see false visions or practice divination. I will save my people from your hands. And then you will know that I am the LORD.' "

Idolaters Condemned

14 Some of the elders of Israel came to me and sat down in front of me. [2]Then the word of the LORD came to me: [3]"Son of man, these men have set up idols in their hearts and put wicked stumbling blocks before their faces. Should I let them inquire of me at all? [4]Therefore speak to them and tell them, 'This is what the Sovereign LORD says: When any Israelite sets up idols in his heart and puts a wicked stumbling block before his face and then goes to a prophet, I the LORD will answer him myself in keeping with his great idolatry. [5]I will do this to recapture the hearts of the people of Israel, who have all deserted me for their idols.'

[6]"Therefore say to the house of Israel, 'This is what the Sovereign LORD says: Repent! Turn from your idols and renounce all your detestable practices!

[7]" 'When any Israelite or any alien living in Israel separates himself from me and sets up idols in his heart and puts a wicked stumbling block before his face and then goes to a prophet to inquire of me, I the LORD will answer him myself. [8]I will set my face against that man and make him an example and a byword. I will cut him off from my people. Then you will know that I am the LORD.

[9]" 'And if the prophet is enticed to utter a prophecy, I the LORD have enticed that prophet, and I will stretch out my hand against him and destroy him from among my people Israel. [10]They will bear their guilt—the prophet will be as guilty as the one who consults him. [11]Then the people of Israel will no longer stray from me, nor will they defile themselves anymore with all their sins. They will be my people, and I will be their God, declares the Sovereign LORD.' "

Judgment Inescapable

[12]The word of the LORD came to me: [13]"Son of man, if a country sins against me by being unfaithful and I stretch out my hand against it to cut off its food supply and send famine upon it and kill its men and their animals, [14]even if these three men—Noah, Daniel[a] and Job—were

a 14 Or Danel; the Hebrew spelling may suggest a person other than the prophet Daniel; also in verse 20.

話使他傷心，又堅固惡人的手，使他不回頭離開惡道得以救活。[23]你們就不再見虛假的異象，也不再行占卜的事；我必救我的百姓脫離你們的手。你們就知道我是耶和華。' "

拜偶像者受譴責

14 有幾個以色列長老到我這裏來，坐在我面前。[2]耶和華的話就臨到我說：[3]"人子啊，這些人已將他們的假神接到心裏，把陷於罪的絆腳石放在面前，我豈能絲毫被他們求問嗎？[4]所以你要告訴他們，主耶和華如此說：'以色列家的人中，凡將他的假神接到心裏，把陷於罪的絆腳石放在面前，又就了先知來的，我耶和華在他所求的事上，必按他眾多的假神回答他（註：或作"必按他拜許多假神的罪報應他"）'，[5]好在以色列家的心事上捉住他們，因為他們都藉着假神與我生疏。'

[6]"所以你要告訴以色列家說：'主耶和華如此說：回頭吧！離開你們的偶像，轉臉莫從你們一切可憎的事。

[7]" '因為以色列家的人，或在以色列中寄居的外人，凡與我隔絕，將他的假神接到心裏，把陷於罪的絆腳石放在面前，又就了先知來要為自己的事求問我的，我耶和華必親自回答他。[8]我必向那人變臉，使他作了警戒、笑談、令人驚駭，並且我要將他從我民中剪除。你們就知道我是耶和華！

[9]" '先知若被迷惑說一句預言，是我耶和華任那先知受迷惑，我也必向他伸手，將他從我民以色列中除滅。[10]他們必擔當自己的罪孽，先知的罪孽和求問之人的罪孽都是一樣，[11]好使以色列家不再走遠離開我，不再因各樣的罪過玷污自己，只要作我的子民，我作他們的神。這是主耶和華說的。' "

不可逃避的審判

[12]耶和華的話臨到我說：[13]"人子啊，若有一國犯罪干犯我，我也向他伸手折斷他們的杖，就是斷絕他們的糧，使饑荒臨到那地，將人民與牲畜從其中剪除。[14]其中雖有挪亞、但以理、約伯這三人，他們只能因他們的

義救自己的性命。這是主耶和華說的。

15 "我若使惡獸經過，糟踐那地，使地荒涼，以致因這些獸，人都不得經過，16雖有這三人在其中，主耶和華說：我指着我的永生起誓，他們連兒帶女都不能得救，只能自己得救，那地仍然荒涼。

17 "或者我使刀劍臨到那地，說：'刀劍哪，要經過那地'，以致我將人與牲畜從其中剪除。18雖有這三人在其中，主耶和華說：我指着我的永生起誓，他們連兒帶女都不能得救，只能自己得救。

19 "或者我叫瘟疫流行那地，使我滅命（註：原文作"帶血"）的忿怒傾在其上，好將人與牲畜從其中剪除；20雖有挪亞、但以理、約伯在其中，主耶和華說：我指着我的永生起誓，他們連兒帶女都不能救，只能因他們的義救自己的性命。

21 主耶和華如此說：我將這四樣大災，就是刀劍、饑荒、惡獸、瘟疫降在耶路撒冷，將人與牲畜從其中剪除，豈不更重嗎？22然而其中必有剩下的人，他們連兒帶女必帶到你們這裏來，你們看見他們所行所為的，要因我降給耶路撒冷的一切災禍，便得了安慰。23你們看見他們所行所為的，得了安慰，就知道我在耶路撒冷中所行的並非無故。這是主耶和華說的。"

耶路撒冷，無用的葡萄樹

15 耶和華的話臨到我說：2 "人子啊，葡萄樹比別樣樹有甚麼強處？葡萄枝比眾樹枝有甚麼好處？3其上可以取木料做甚麼工用？可以取來做釘子掛甚麼器皿嗎？4看哪，已經拋在火中當作柴燒，火既燒了兩頭，中間也被燒了，還有益於工用嗎？5完全的時候尚且不合乎甚麼工用，何況被火燒壞，還能合乎甚麼工用嗎？

6 "所以主耶和華如此說：眾樹以內的葡萄樹，我怎樣使它在火中當柴，也必照樣待耶路撒冷的居民。7我必向他們變臉，他們雖從火

in it, they could save only themselves by their righteousness, declares the Sovereign LORD.

15"Or if I send wild beasts through that country and they leave it childless and it becomes desolate so that no one can pass through it because of the beasts, 16as surely as I live, declares the Sovereign LORD, even if these three men were in it, they could not save their own sons or daughters. They alone would be saved, but the land would be desolate.

17"Or if I bring a sword against that country and say, 'Let the sword pass throughout the land,' and I kill its men and their animals, 18as surely as I live, declares the Sovereign LORD, even if these three men were in it, they could not save their own sons or daughters. They alone would be saved.

19"Or if I send a plague into that land and pour out my wrath upon it through bloodshed, killing its men and their animals, 20as surely as I live, declares the Sovereign LORD, even if Noah, Daniel and Job were in it, they could save neither son nor daughter. They would save only themselves by their righteousness.

21"For this is what the Sovereign LORD says: How much worse will it be when I send against Jerusalem my four dreadful judgments—sword and famine and wild beasts and plague—to kill its men and their animals! 22Yet there will be some survivors—sons and daughters who will be brought out of it. They will come to you, and when you see their conduct and their actions, you will be consoled regarding the disaster I have brought upon Jerusalem—every disaster I have brought upon it. 23You will be consoled when you see their conduct and their actions, for you will know that I have done nothing in it without cause, declares the Sovereign LORD."

Jerusalem, A Useless Vine

15 The word of the LORD came to me: 2"Son of man, how is the wood of a vine better than that of a branch on any of the trees in the forest? 3Is wood ever taken from it to make anything useful? Do they make pegs from it to hang things on? 4And after it is thrown on the fire as fuel and the fire burns both ends and chars the middle, is it then useful for anything? 5If it was not useful for anything when it was whole, how much less can it be made into something useful when the fire has burned it and it is charred?

6"Therefore this is what the Sovereign LORD says: As I have given the wood of the vine among the trees of the forest as fuel for the fire, so will I treat the people living in Jerusalem. 7I will set my face against them. Although they have come out of the fire, the fire will yet consume them. And when I set my face against them, you will know that I am the LORD. ⁸I will make the land desolate because they have been unfaithful, declares the Sovereign LORD."

An Allegory of Unfaithful Jerusalem

16 The word of the LORD came to me: ²"Son of man, confront Jerusalem with her detestable practices ³and say, 'This is what the Sovereign LORD says to Jerusalem: Your ancestry and birth were in the land of the Canaanites; your father was an Amorite and your mother a Hittite. ⁴On the day you were born your cord was not cut, nor were you washed with water to make you clean, nor were you rubbed with salt or wrapped in cloths. ⁵No one looked on you with pity or had compassion enough to do any of these things for you. Rather, you were thrown out into the open field, for on the day you were born you were despised.

⁶'Then I passed by and saw you kicking about in your blood, and as you lay there in your blood I said to you, "Live!"ᵃ ⁷I made you grow like a plant of the field. You grew up and developed and became the most beautiful of jewels.ᵇ Your breasts were formed and your hair grew, you who were naked and bare.

⁸'Later I passed by, and when I looked at you and saw that you were old enough for love, I spread the corner of my garment over you and covered your nakedness. I gave you my solemn oath and entered into a covenant with you, declares the Sovereign LORD, and you became mine.

⁹'I bathedᶜ you with water and washed the blood from you and put ointments on you. ¹⁰I clothed you with an embroidered dress and put leather sandals on you. I dressed you in fine linen and covered you with costly garments. ¹¹I adorned you with jewelry: I put bracelets on your arms and a necklace around your neck, ¹²and I put a ring on your nose, earrings on your ears and a beautiful crown on your head. ¹³So you were adorned with gold and silver; your clothes were of fine linen and costly fabric and embroidered cloth. Your food was fine flour, honey and olive oil. You became very beautiful and rose to be a queen. ¹⁴And your fame spread among the nations on account of

a 6 A few Hebrew manuscripts, Septuagint and Syriac; most Hebrew manuscripts "Live!" And as you lay there in your blood I said to you, "Live!"　b 7 Or became mature　c 9 Or I had bathed

中出來，火卻要燒滅他們。我向他們變臉的時候，你們就知道我是耶和華。⁸我必使地土荒涼，因為他們行事干犯我。這是主耶和華說的。"

不貞的耶路撒冷的寓意

16 耶和華的話又臨到我說：² "人子啊，你要使耶路撒冷知道她那些可憎的事，³說：'主耶和華對耶路撒冷如此說：你根本，你出世，是在迦南地；你父親是亞摩利人，你母親是赫人。⁴論到你出世的景況，在你初生的日子沒有為你斷臍帶，也沒有用水洗你，使你潔淨，絲毫沒有撒鹽在你身上，也沒有用布裹你。⁵誰的眼也不可憐你，為你做一件這樣的事憐卹你；但你初生的日子扔在田野，是因你被厭惡。

⁶ '我從你旁邊經過，見你滾在血中，就對你說：你雖在血中，仍可存活；你雖在血中，仍可存活。⁷我使你生長好像田間所長的，你就漸漸長大，以致極其俊美，兩乳成形，頭髮長成，你卻仍然赤身露體。

⁸ '我從你旁邊經過，看見你的時候正動愛情，便用衣襟搭在你身上，遮蓋你的赤體，又向你起誓，與你結盟，你就歸於我。這是主耶和華說的。

⁹ '那時我用水洗你，洗淨你身上的血，又用油抹你。¹⁰我也使你身穿繡花衣服，腳穿海狗皮鞋，並用細麻布給你束腰，用絲綢為衣披在你身上。¹¹又用妝飾打扮你，將鐲子戴在你手上，將金鏈戴在你項上。¹²我也將環子戴在你鼻子上，將耳環戴在你耳朵上，將華冠戴在你頭上。¹³這樣，你就有金銀的妝飾，你穿的是細麻衣和絲綢，並繡花衣；吃的是細麵、蜂蜜和油。你也極其美貌，發達到王后的尊榮。¹⁴你美貌的名聲傳在列邦

中，你十分美貌，是因我加在你身上的威榮。這是主耶和華說的。

15 「『只是你仗着自己的美貌，又因你的名聲就行邪淫。你縱情淫亂，使過路的任意而行。16你用衣服為自己在高處結彩，在其上行邪淫。這樣的事將來必沒有，也必不再行了。17你又將我所給你那華美的金銀、寶器為自己製造人像，與他行邪淫。18又用你的繡花衣服給他披上，並將我的膏油和香料擺在他跟前。19又將我賜給你的食物，就是我賜給你吃的細麵、油和蜂蜜都擺在他跟前為馨香的供物。這是主耶和華說的。

20 「『並且你將給我所生的兒女焚獻給他。21你行淫亂豈是小事，竟將我的兒女殺了，使他們經火歸與他嗎？22你行這一切可憎和淫亂的事，並未追念你幼年赤身露體滾在血中的日子。

23 「『你行這一切惡事之後，（主耶和華說：你有禍了！有禍了！）24又為自己建造圓頂花樓，在各街上做了高臺。25你在一切市口上建造高臺，使你的美貌變為可憎的，又與一切過路的多行淫亂。26你也和你鄰邦放縱情慾的埃及人行淫，加增你的淫亂，惹我發怒。27因此，我伸手攻擊你，減少你應用的糧食，又將你交給恨你的非利士眾女（註：“眾女”是“城邑”的意思。本章下同），使她們任意待你。她們見你的淫行，為你羞恥。28你因貪色無厭，又與亞述人行淫，與他們行淫之後，仍不滿意。29並且多行淫亂直到那貿易之地，就是迦勒底，你仍不滿意。

30 「『主耶和華說：你行這一切事，都是不知羞恥妓女所行的，可

your beauty, because the splendor I had given you made your beauty perfect, declares the Sovereign LORD.

15" 'But you trusted in your beauty and used your fame to become a prostitute. You lavished your favors on anyone who passed by and your beauty became his.[a] 16You took some of your garments to make gaudy high places, where you carried on your prostitution. Such things should not happen, nor should they ever occur. 17You also took the fine jewelry I gave you, the jewelry made of my gold and silver, and you made for yourself male idols and engaged in prostitution with them. 18And you took your embroidered clothes to put on them, and you offered my oil and incense before them. 19Also the food I provided for you—the fine flour, olive oil and honey I gave you to eat—you offered as fragrant incense before them. That is what happened, declares the Sovereign LORD.

20" 'And you took your sons and daughters whom you bore to me and sacrificed them as food to the idols. Was your prostitution not enough? 21You slaughtered my children and sacrificed them[b] to the idols. 22In all your detestable practices and your prostitution you did not remember the days of your youth, when you were naked and bare, kicking about in your blood.

23" 'Woe! Woe to you, declares the Sovereign LORD. In addition to all your other wickedness, 24you built a mound for yourself and made a lofty shrine in every public square. 25At the head of every street you built your lofty shrines and degraded your beauty, offering your body with increasing promiscuity to anyone who passed by. 26You engaged in prostitution with the Egyptians, your lustful neighbors, and provoked me to anger with your increasing promiscuity. 27So I stretched out my hand against you and reduced your territory; I gave you over to the greed of your enemies, the daughters of the Philistines, who were shocked by your lewd conduct. 28You engaged in prostitution with the Assyrians too, because you were insatiable; and even after that, you still were not satisfied. 29Then you increased your promiscuity to include Babylonia,[c] a land of merchants, but even with this you were not satisfied.

30" 'How weak-willed you are, declares the Sovereign LORD, when you do all these things,

a 15 Most Hebrew manuscripts; one Hebrew manuscript (see some Septuagint manuscripts) by. Such a thing should not happen   b 21 Or and made them pass through [the fire]   c 29 Or Chaldea

acting like a brazen prostitute! 31When you built your mounds at the head of every street and made your lofty shrines in every public square, you were unlike a prostitute, because you scorned payment.

32"'You adulterous wife! You prefer strangers to your own husband. 33Every prostitute receives a fee, but you give gifts to all your lovers, bribing them to come to you from everywhere for your illicit favors. 34So in your prostitution you are the opposite of others; no one runs after you for your favors. You are the very opposite, for you give payment and none is given to you.

35"'Therefore, you prostitute, hear the word of the LORD! 36This is what the Sovereign LORD says: Because you poured out your wealth*a* and exposed your nakedness in your promiscuity with your lovers, and because of all your detestable idols, and because you gave them your children's blood, 37therefore I am going to gather all your lovers, with whom you found pleasure, those you loved as well as those you hated. I will gather them against you from all around and will strip you in front of them, and they will see all your nakedness. 38I will sentence you to the punishment of women who commit adultery and who shed blood; I will bring upon you the blood vengeance of my wrath and jealous anger. 39Then I will hand you over to your lovers, and they will tear down your mounds and destroy your lofty shrines. They will strip you of your clothes and take your fine jewelry and leave you naked and bare. 40They will bring a mob against you, who will stone you and hack you to pieces with their swords. 41They will burn down your houses and inflict punishment on you in the sight of many women. I will put a stop to your prostitution, and you will no longer pay your lovers. 42Then my wrath against you will subside and my jealous anger will turn away from you; I will be calm and no longer angry.

43"'Because you did not remember the days of your youth but enraged me with all these things, I will surely bring down on your head what you have done, declares the Sovereign LORD. Did you not add lewdness to all your other detestable practices?

44"'Everyone who quotes proverbs will quote this proverb about you: "Like mother, like daughter." 45You are a true daughter of your mother, who despised her husband and her children; and you are a true sister of your sisters,

a 36 Or lust

見你的心是何等懦弱！31因你在一切市口上建造圓頂花樓，在各街上做了高臺，你卻藐視賞賜，不像妓女。

32"'哎！你這行淫的妻啊，寧肯接外人不接丈夫。33凡妓女是得人贈送，你反倒贈送你所愛的人，賄賂他們從四圍來與你行淫。34你行淫與別的婦女相反，因為不是人從你行淫；你既贈送人，人並不贈送你，所以你與別的婦女相反。

35"'你這妓女啊，要聽耶和華的話。36主耶和華如此說：因你的污穢傾洩了，你與你所愛的行淫露出下體。又因你拜一切可憎的偶像，流兒女的血獻給他，37我就要將你一切相歡相愛的和你一切所恨的都聚集來，從四圍攻擊你。又將你的下體露出，使他們看盡了。38我也要審判你，好像官長審判淫婦和流人血的婦女一樣。我因忿怒忌恨，使流血的罪歸到你身上。39我又要將你交在他們手中，他們必拆毀你的圓頂花樓，毀壞你的高臺，剝去你的衣服，奪取你的華美寶器，留下你赤身露體。40他們也必帶多人來攻擊你，用石頭打死你，用刀劍刺透你，41用火焚燒你的房屋，在許多婦人眼前向你施行審判。我必使你不再行淫，也不再贈送與人。42這樣，我就止息向你發的忿怒，我的忌恨也要離開你，我要安靜，不再惱怒。

43"'因你不追念你幼年的日子，在這一切的事上向我發烈怒，所以我必照你所行的報應在你頭上，你就不再貪淫，行那一切可憎的事。這是主耶和華說的。

44"'凡說俗語的必用俗語攻擊你，說：母親怎樣，女兒也怎樣。45你正是你母親的女兒，厭棄丈夫和兒女；你正是你姐妹的姐妹，厭棄丈夫和兒女。你母親是赫人，你父親是亞摩利人。46你的姐姐是撒馬利亞，她和她的眾女住在你左邊；你的妹妹是所多瑪，她和她的眾女住在你右邊。47你沒有效法她們的行為，也沒有照她們可憎的事去做，你以那為小事，你一切所行的倒比她們更壞。48主耶和華說：我指著我的永生起誓，你妹妹所多瑪與她的眾女，尚未行你和你眾女所行的事。

49“‘看哪，你妹妹所多瑪的罪孽是這樣：她和她的眾女都心驕氣傲，糧食飽足，大享安逸，並沒有扶助困苦和窮乏人的手。50她們狂傲，在我面前行可憎的事，我看見便將她們除掉。51撒馬利亞沒有犯你一半的罪，你行可憎的事比她更多，使你的姐妹因你所行一切可憎的事，倒顯為義。52你既斷定你姐妹為義（註：“為義”或作“當受羞辱”），就要擔當自己的羞辱，因你所犯的罪比她們更為可憎，她們就比你更顯為義；你既使你的姐妹顯為義，你就要抱愧擔當自己的羞辱。

53“‘我必叫她們被擄的歸回，就是叫所多瑪和她的眾女，撒馬利亞和她的眾女，並你們中間被擄的，都要歸回，54好使你擔當自己的羞辱，並因你一切所行的使她們得安慰，你就抱愧。55你的妹妹所多瑪和她的眾女必歸回原位；撒馬利亞和她的眾女，你和你的眾女也必歸回原位。56、57在你驕傲的日子，你的惡行沒有顯露以先，你的口就不提你的妹妹所多瑪。那受了凌辱的亞蘭眾女和亞蘭四圍非利士的眾女都恨惡你，藐視你。58耶和華說：你貪淫和可憎的事，你已經擔當了。

59“‘主耶和華如此說：你這輕看誓言，背棄盟約的，我必照你所行的待你。60然而我要追念在你幼年時與你所立的約，也要與你立定永約。61你接待你姐姐和你妹妹的時候，你要追念你所行的，自覺慚

who despised their husbands and their children. Your mother was a Hittite and your father an Amorite. 46Your older sister was Samaria, who lived to the north of you with her daughters; and your younger sister, who lived to the south of you with her daughters, was Sodom. 47You not only walked in their ways and copied their detestable practices, but in all your ways you soon became more depraved than they. 48As surely as I live, declares the Sovereign LORD, your sister Sodom and her daughters never did what you and your daughters have done.

49“‘Now this was the sin of your sister Sodom: She and her daughters were arrogant, overfed and unconcerned; they did not help the poor and needy. 50They were haughty and did detestable things before me. Therefore I did away with them as you have seen. 51Samaria did not commit half the sins you did. You have done more detestable things than they, and have made your sisters seem righteous by all these things you have done. 52Bear your disgrace, for you have furnished some justification for your sisters. Because your sins were more vile than theirs, they appear more righteous than you. So then, be ashamed and bear your disgrace, for you have made your sisters appear righteous.

53“‘However, I will restore the fortunes of Sodom and her daughters and of Samaria and her daughters, and your fortunes along with them, 54so that you may bear your disgrace and be ashamed of all you have done in giving them comfort. 55And your sisters, Sodom with her daughters and Samaria with her daughters, will return to what they were before; and you and your daughters will return to what you were before. 56You would not even mention your sister Sodom in the day of your pride, 57before your wickedness was uncovered. Even so, you are now scorned by the daughters of Edom[a] and all her neighbors and the daughters of the Philistines—all those around you who despise you. 58You will bear the consequences of your lewdness and your detestable practices, declares the LORD.

59“‘This is what the Sovereign LORD says: I will deal with you as you deserve, because you have despised my oath by breaking the covenant. 60Yet I will remember the covenant I made with you in the days of your youth, and I will establish an everlasting covenant with you. 61Then you will remember your ways and be ashamed when you receive your sisters, both

a 57 Many Hebrew manuscripts and Syriac; most Hebrew manuscripts, Septuagint and Vulgate *Aram*

those who are older than you and those who are younger. I will give them to you as daughters, but not on the basis of my covenant with you. ⁶²So I will establish my covenant with you, and you will know that I am the LORD. ⁶³Then, when I make atonement for you for all you have done, you will remember and be ashamed and never again open your mouth because of your humiliation, declares the Sovereign LORD.' "

Two Eagles and a Vine

17 The word of the LORD came to me: ²"Son of man, set forth an allegory and tell the house of Israel a parable. ³Say to them, 'This is what the Sovereign LORD says: A great eagle with powerful wings, long feathers and full plumage of varied colors came to Lebanon. Taking hold of the top of a cedar, ⁴he broke off its topmost shoot and carried it away to a land of merchants, where he planted it in a city of traders.

⁵" 'He took some of the seed of your land and put it in fertile soil. He planted it like a willow by abundant water, ⁶and it sprouted and became a low, spreading vine. Its branches turned toward him, but its roots remained under it. So it became a vine and produced branches and put out leafy boughs.

⁷" 'But there was another great eagle with powerful wings and full plumage. The vine now sent out its roots toward him from the plot where it was planted and stretched out its branches to him for water. ⁸It had been planted in good soil by abundant water so that it would produce branches, bear fruit and become a splendid vine.'

⁹"Say to them, 'This is what the Sovereign LORD says: Will it thrive? Will it not be uprooted and stripped of its fruit so that it withers? All its new growth will wither. It will not take a strong arm or many people to pull it up by the roots. ¹⁰Even if it is transplanted, will it thrive? Will it not wither completely when the east wind strikes it—wither away in the plot where it grew?' "

¹¹Then the word of the LORD came to me: ¹²"Say to this rebellious house, 'Do you not know what these things mean?' Say to them: 'The king of Babylon went to Jerusalem and carried off her king and her nobles, bringing them back with him to Babylon. ¹³Then he took a member of the royal family and made a treaty with him, putting him under oath. He also carried away the leading men of the land, ¹⁴so that the kingdom would be brought low, unable to rise again, surviving only by keeping his treaty.

愧。並且我要將她們賜你為女兒,卻不是按着前約。⁶²我要堅定與你所立的約(你就知道我是耶和華),⁶³好使你在我赦免你一切所行的時候,心裏追念,自覺抱愧,又因你的羞辱就不再開口。這是主耶和華說的。'"

兩鷹與一葡萄樹

17 耶和華的話臨到我說:²"人子啊,你要向以色列家出謎語,設比喻,³說:'主耶和華如此說:有一大鷹,翅膀大,翎毛長,羽毛豐滿,彩色俱備,來到黎巴嫩,將香柏樹梢擰去,⁴就是折去香柏樹儘尖的嫩枝,叼到貿易之地,放在買賣城中。

⁵"'又將以色列地的枝子栽於肥田裏,插在大水旁,如插柳樹。⁶就漸漸生長,成為蔓延矮小的葡萄樹。其枝轉向那鷹,其根在鷹以下,於是成了葡萄樹,生出枝子,發出小枝。

⁷"'又有一大鷹,翅膀大,羽毛多,這葡萄樹從栽種的畦中向這鷹彎過根來,發出枝子,好得他的澆灌。⁸這樹栽於肥田多水的旁邊,好生枝子,結果子,成為佳美的葡萄樹。'

⁹"你要說:'主耶和華如此說:這葡萄樹豈能發旺呢?鷹豈不拔出它的根來,芟除它的果子,使它枯乾,使它發的嫩葉都枯乾了嗎?也不用大力和多民,就拔出它的根來。¹⁰葡萄樹雖然栽種,豈能發旺呢?一經東風,豈不全然枯乾嗎?必在生長的畦中枯乾了。'"

¹¹耶和華的話臨到我說:¹²"你對那悖逆之家說:'你們不知道這些事是甚麼意思嗎?'你要告訴他們說:'巴比倫王曾到耶路撒冷,將其中的君王和首領帶到巴比倫自己那裏去。¹³從以色列的宗室中取一人與他立約,使他發誓,並將國中有勢力的人擄去,¹⁴使國低微不能自強,惟因

守盟約得以存立。15他卻背叛巴比倫王，打發使者往埃及去，要他們給他馬匹和多民。他豈能亨通呢？行這樣事的人豈能逃脫呢？他背約豈能逃脫呢？

16 "‘他輕看向王所起的誓，背棄王與他所立的約。主耶和華說：我指着我的永生起誓，他定要死在立他作王巴比倫王的京都。17敵人築壘造臺，與他打仗的時候，為要剪除多人，法老雖領大軍隊和大羣眾，還是不能幫助他。18他輕看誓言，背棄盟約，已經投降，卻又做這一切的事，他必不能逃脫。

19 "‘所以主耶和華如此說：我指着我的永生起誓，他既輕看指我所起的誓，背棄指我所立的約，我必使這罪歸在他頭上。20我必將我的網撒在他身上，他必在我的網羅中纏住。我必帶他到巴比倫，並要在那裏因他干犯我的罪刑罰他。21他的一切軍隊，凡逃跑的，都必倒在刀下；所剩下的，也必分散四方（註："方"原文作"風"）。你們就知道說這話的是我耶和華。

22 "‘主耶和華如此說：我要將香柏樹梢擰去栽上，就是從儘尖的嫩枝中折一嫩枝，栽於極高的山上；23在以色列高處的山栽上。它就生枝子，結果子，成為佳美的香柏樹，各類飛鳥都必宿在其下，就是宿在枝子的蔭下。24田野的樹木都必知道我耶和華使高樹矮小，矮樹高大；青樹枯乾，枯樹發旺。

"‘我耶和華如此說，也如此行了。’"

犯罪的必死亡

18 耶和華的話又臨到我說：2 "你們在以色列地怎麼用這俗語說：

"‘父親吃了酸葡萄，
　兒子的牙酸倒了’呢？

3 "主耶和華說：我指着我的永生起誓，你們在以色列中，必不再有用這俗語的因由。4看哪，世人都是屬我的：為父的怎樣屬我，為子的也照樣屬我。犯罪的他必死亡。

5 "人若是公義，
　且行正直與合理的事：

15But the king rebelled against him by sending his envoys to Egypt to get horses and a large army. Will he succeed? Will he who does such things escape? Will he break the treaty and yet escape?

16" ' As surely as I live, declares the Sovereign LORD, he shall die in Babylon, in the land of the king who put him on the throne, whose oath he despised and whose treaty he broke. 17Pharaoh with his mighty army and great horde will be of no help to him in war, when ramps are built and siege works erected to destroy many lives. 18He despised the oath by breaking the covenant. Because he had given his hand in pledge and yet did all these things, he shall not escape.

19" 'Therefore this is what the Sovereign LORD says: As surely as I live, I will bring down on his head my oath that he despised and my covenant that he broke. 20I will spread my net for him, and he will be caught in my snare. I will bring him to Babylon and execute judgment upon him there because he was unfaithful to me. 21All his fleeing troops will fall by the sword, and the survivors will be scattered to the winds. Then you will know that I the LORD have spoken.

22" 'This is what the Sovereign LORD says: I myself will take a shoot from the very top of a cedar and plant it; I will break off a tender sprig from its topmost shoots and plant it on a high and lofty mountain. 23On the mountain heights of Israel I will plant it; it will produce branches and bear fruit and become a splendid cedar. Birds of every kind will nest in it; they will find shelter in the shade of its branches. 24All the trees of the field will know that I the LORD bring down the tall tree and make the low tree grow tall. I dry up the green tree and make the dry tree flourish.

" 'I the LORD have spoken, and I will do it.' ' "

The Soul Who Sins Will Die

18 The word of the LORD came to me: 2"What do you people mean by quoting this proverb about the land of Israel:

" 'The fathers eat sour grapes,
　and the children's teeth are set on edge'?

3"As surely as I live, declares the Sovereign LORD, you will no longer quote this proverb in Israel. 4For every living soul belongs to me, the father as well as the son—both alike belong to me. The soul who sins is the one who will die.

5"Suppose there is a righteous man who does what is just and right.

⁶He does not eat at the mountain shrines
　　or look to the idols of the house of Israel.
He does not defile his neighbor's wife
　　or lie with a woman during her period.
⁷He does not oppress anyone,
　　but returns what he took in pledge for a loan.
He does not commit robbery
　　but gives his food to the hungry
　　and provides clothing for the naked.
⁸He does not lend at usury
　　or take excessive interest.^a
He withholds his hand from doing wrong
　　and judges fairly between man and man.
⁹He follows my decrees
　　and faithfully keeps my laws.
That man is righteous;
　　he will surely live,
　　　　　　declares the Sovereign LORD.

¹⁰"Suppose he has a violent son, who sheds blood or does any of these other things^b ¹¹(though the father has done none of them):

"He eats at the mountain shrines.
He defiles his neighbor's wife.
¹²He oppresses the poor and needy.
He commits robbery.
He does not return what he took in pledge.
He looks to the idols.
He does detestable things.
¹³He lends at usury and takes excessive interest.

Will such a man live? He will not! Because he has done all these detestable things, he will surely be put to death and his blood will be on his own head.

¹⁴"But suppose this son has a son who sees all the sins his father commits, and though he sees them, he does not do such things:

¹⁵"He does not eat at the mountain shrines
　　or look to the idols of the house of Israel.
He does not defile his neighbor's wife.
¹⁶He does not oppress anyone
　　or require a pledge for a loan.
He does not commit robbery
　　but gives his food to the hungry
　　and provides clothing for the naked.
¹⁷He withholds his hand from sin^c
　　and takes no usury or excessive interest.
He keeps my laws and follows my decrees.

---

⁶未曾在山上吃過祭偶像之物，
　　未曾仰望以色列家的偶像；
　未曾玷污鄰舍的妻，
　　未曾在婦人的經期內親近她；
⁷未曾虧負人，
　　乃將欠債之人的當頭還給他；
　未曾搶奪人的物件，
　　卻將食物給飢餓的人吃，
　　將衣服給赤身的人穿；
⁸未曾向借錢的弟兄取利，
　　也未曾向借糧的弟兄多要；
　縮手不作罪孽，
　　在兩人之間，按至理判斷；
⁹遵行我的律例，
　　謹守我的典章，按誠實行事，
　這人是公義的，
　　必定存活。
　　　　　　　這是主耶和華說的。

¹⁰、¹¹「他若生一個兒子作強盜，是流人血的，不行以上所說之善，反行其中之惡：

「乃在山上吃過祭偶像之物，
　　並玷污鄰舍的妻；
¹²虧負困苦和窮乏的人；
　搶奪人的物；
　未曾將當頭還給人；
　仰望偶像，
　　並行可憎的事；
¹³向借錢的弟兄取利，
　　向借糧的弟兄多要。
這人豈能存活呢？他必不能存活，他行這一切可憎的事，必要死亡，他的罪必歸到他身上（註：「罪」原文作「血」）。

¹⁴「他若生一個兒子，見父親所犯的一切罪，便懼怕（註：有古卷作「思量」），不照樣去做：

¹⁵「未曾在山上吃過祭偶像之物，
　　未曾仰望以色列家的偶像；
　未曾玷污鄰舍的妻；
¹⁶未曾虧負人，
　　未曾取人的當頭；
　未曾搶奪人的物件，
　　卻將食物給飢餓的人吃，
　　將衣服給赤身的人穿；
¹⁷縮手不害貧窮人，
　　未曾向借錢的弟兄取利，
　　也未曾向借糧的弟兄多要；
他順從我的典章，遵行我的律例。

---

^a 8 Or take interest; similarly in verses 13 and 17　　^b 10 Or things to a brother　　^c 17 Septuagint (see also verse 8); Hebrew from the poor

就不因父親的罪孽死亡，定要存活。18至於由父親，因為欺人太甚，搶奪弟兄，在本國的民中行不善，他必因自己的罪孽死亡。

19"你們還說：'兒子為何不擔當父親的罪孽呢？'兒子行正直與合理的事，謹守遵行我的一切律例，他必定存活。20惟有犯罪的，他必死亡。兒子不擔當父親的罪孽，父親也不擔當兒子的罪孽。義人的善果必歸自己，惡人的惡報也必歸自己。

21"惡人若回頭離開所作的一切罪惡，謹守我一切的律例，行正直與合理的事，他必定存活，不至死亡。22他所犯的一切罪過都不被記念，因所行的義，他必存活。23主耶和華說：惡人死亡，豈是我喜悅的嗎？不是喜悅他回頭離開所行的道存活嗎？

24"義人若轉離義行而作罪孽，照着惡人所行一切可憎的事而行，他豈能存活嗎？他所行的一切義都不被記念，他必因所犯的罪、所行的惡死亡。

25"你們還說：'主的道不公平！'以色列家啊，你們當聽，我的道豈不公平嗎？你們的道豈不是不公平嗎？26義人若轉離義行而作罪孽死亡，他是因所作的罪孽死亡。27再者，惡人若回頭離開所行的惡，行正直與合理的事，他必將性命救活了。28因為他思量，回頭離開所犯的一切罪過，必定存活不至死亡。29以色列家還說：'主的道不公平！'以色列家啊，我的道豈不公平嗎？你們的道豈不是不公平嗎？

30"所以主耶和華說：以色列家啊，我必按你們各人所行的審判你們。你們當回頭離開所犯的一切罪過。這樣，罪孽必不使你們敗亡。31你們要將所犯的一切罪過盡行拋棄，自做一個新心和新靈。以色列家啊，你們何必死亡呢？32主耶和華說：我不喜悅那死人之死，所以你們當回頭而存活！

He will not die for his father's sin; he will surely live. 18But his father will die for his own sin, because he practiced extortion, robbed his brother and did what was wrong among his people.

19"Yet you ask, 'Why does the son not share the guilt of his father?' Since the son has done what is just and right and has been careful to keep all my decrees, he will surely live. 20The soul who sins is the one who will die. The son will not share the guilt of the father, nor will the father share the guilt of the son. The righteousness of the righteous man will be credited to him, and the wickedness of the wicked will be charged against him.

21"But if a wicked man turns away from all the sins he has committed and keeps all my decrees and does what is just and right, he will surely live; he will not die. 22None of the offenses he has committed will be remembered against him. Because of the righteous things he has done, he will live. 23Do I take any pleasure in the death of the wicked? declares the Sovereign LORD. Rather, am I not pleased when they turn from their ways and live?

24"But if a righteous man turns from his righteousness and commits sin and does the same detestable things the wicked man does, will he live? None of the righteous things he has done will be remembered. Because of the unfaithfulness he is guilty of and because of the sins he has committed, he will die.

25"Yet you say, 'The way of the Lord is not just.' Hear, O house of Israel: Is my way unjust? Is it not your ways that are unjust? 26If a righteous man turns from his righteousness and commits sin, he will die for it; because of the sin he has committed he will die. 27But if a wicked man turns away from the wickedness he has committed and does what is just and right, he will save his life. 28Because he considers all the offenses he has committed and turns away from them, he will surely live; he will not die. 29Yet the house of Israel says, 'The way of the Lord is not just.' Are my ways unjust, O house of Israel? Is it not your ways that are unjust?

30"Therefore, O house of Israel, I will judge you, each one according to his ways, declares the Sovereign LORD. Repent! Turn away from all your offenses; then sin will not be your downfall. 31Rid yourselves of all the offenses you have committed, and get a new heart and a new spirit. Why will you die, O house of Israel? 32For I take no pleasure in the death of anyone, declares the Sovereign LORD. Repent and live!

A Lament for Israel's Princes

19 "Take up a lament concerning the princes of Israel ²and say:

" 'What a lioness was your mother
    among the lions!
She lay down among the young lions
    and reared her cubs.
³She brought up one of her cubs,
    and he became a strong lion.
He learned to tear the prey
    and he devoured men.
⁴The nations heard about him,
    and he was trapped in their pit.
They led him with hooks
    to the land of Egypt.

⁵" 'When she saw her hope unfulfilled,
    her expectation gone,
she took another of her cubs
    and made him a strong lion.
⁶He prowled among the lions,
    for he was now a strong lion.
He learned to tear the prey
    and he devoured men.
⁷He broke down[a] their strongholds
    and devastated their towns.
The land and all who were in it
    were terrified by his roaring.
⁸Then the nations came against him,
    those from regions round about.
They spread their net for him,
    and he was trapped in their pit.
⁹With hooks they pulled him into a cage
    and brought him to the king of Babylon.
They put him in prison,
    so his roar was heard no longer
    on the mountains of Israel.

¹⁰" 'Your mother was like a vine in your
    vineyard[b]
planted by the water;
it was fruitful and full of branches
    because of abundant water.
¹¹Its branches were strong,
    fit for a ruler's scepter.
It towered high
    above the thick foliage,
conspicuous for its height
    and for its many branches.
¹²But it was uprooted in fury
    and thrown to the ground.

a 7 Targum (see Septuagint); Hebrew *He knew*   *b 10* Two
Hebrew manuscripts; most Hebrew manuscripts *your blood*

為以色列王作哀歌

19 "你當為以色列的王作起哀歌。²說：

" '你的母親是甚麼呢？
  是個母獅子，
蹲伏在獅子中間，
  在少壯獅子中養育小獅子。
³在她小獅子中養大一個，
  成了少壯獅子，
學會抓食而吃人。
⁴列國聽見了，
  就把他捉在他們的坑中，
用鈎子
  拉到埃及地去。

⁵" '母獅見自己等候
  失了指望，
就從她小獅子中
  又將一個養為少壯獅子。
⁶他在眾獅子中走來走去，
  成了少壯獅子，
學會抓食而吃人。
⁷他知道列國的宮殿，
  又使他們的城邑變為荒場，
因他咆哮的聲音，
  遍地和其中所有的就都荒廢。
⁸於是四圍邦國各省的人
  來攻擊他，
將網撒在他身上，
  捉在他們的坑中。
⁹他們用鈎子鈎住他，
  將他放在籠中
  帶到巴比倫王那裏，
將他放入堅固之所，
  使他的聲音在以色列山上
  不再聽見。

¹⁰" '你的母親先前如葡萄樹，
  極其茂盛（註：原文作"在你血中"），
  栽於水旁。
因為水多，就多結果子，
  滿生枝子。
¹¹生出堅固的枝幹，
  可作掌權者的杖。
這枝幹高舉在茂密的枝中，
  而且它生長高大，
枝子繁多，
  遠遠可見。
¹²但這葡萄樹因忿怒被拔出
  摔在地上，

東風吹乾
　　其上的果子，
堅固的枝幹折斷枯乾，
　　被火燒燼了。
¹³如今栽於曠野
　　乾旱無水之地。
¹⁴火也從它枝幹中發出，
　　燒滅果子，
以致沒有堅固的枝幹
　　可作掌權者的杖。'

這是哀歌，也必用以作哀歌。"

The east wind made it shrivel,
　　it was stripped of its fruit;
its strong branches withered
　　and fire consumed them.
¹³Now it is planted in the desert,
　　in a dry and thirsty land.
¹⁴Fire spread from one of its main*a* branches
　　and consumed its fruit.
No strong branch is left on it
　　fit for a ruler's scepter.'

This is a lament and is to be used as a lament."

悖逆的以色列

20 第七年五月初十日，有以色列的幾個長老來求問耶和華，坐在我面前。

²耶和華的話臨到我說：³ "人子啊，你要告訴以色列的長老說：'主耶和華如此說：你們來是求問我嗎？主耶和華說：我指着我的永生起誓，我必不被你們求問。'

⁴ "人子啊，你要審問審問他們嗎？你當使他們知道他們列祖那些可憎的事！⁵對他們說，主耶和華如此說：'當日我揀選以色列，向雅各家的後裔起誓，在埃及地將自己向他們顯現，說：我是耶和華你們的神。⁶那日我向他們起誓，必領他們出埃及地，到我為他們察看的流奶與蜜之地。那地在萬國中是有榮耀的。⁷我對他們說：你們各人要拋棄眼所喜愛那可憎之物，不可因埃及的偶像玷污自己。我是耶和華你們的神。

⁸ "'他們卻悖逆我，不肯聽從我，不拋棄他們眼所喜愛那可憎之物，不離棄埃及的偶像。我就說：我要將我的忿怒傾在他們身上，在埃及地向他們成就我怒中所定的。⁹我卻為我名的緣故沒有這樣行，免得我名在他們所住的列國人眼前被褻瀆；我領他們出埃及地，在這列國人的眼前將自己向他們顯現。¹⁰這樣，我就使他們出埃及地，領他們到曠野。¹¹將我的律例賜給他們，將我的典章指示他們；人若遵行，就必因此活着。¹²又將我的安息日賜給他們，好在我

Rebellious Israel

20 In the seventh year, in the fifth month on the tenth day, some of the elders of Israel came to inquire of the LORD, and they sat down in front of me.

²Then the word of the LORD came to me: ³"Son of man, speak to the elders of Israel and say to them, 'This is what the Sovereign LORD says: Have you come to inquire of me? As surely as I live, I will not let you inquire of me, declares the Sovereign LORD.'

⁴"Will you judge them? Will you judge them, son of man? Then confront them with the detestable practices of their fathers ⁵and say to them: 'This is what the Sovereign LORD says: On the day I chose Israel, I swore with uplifted hand to the descendants of the house of Jacob and revealed myself to them in Egypt. With uplifted hand I said to them, "I am the LORD your God." ⁶On that day I swore to them that I would bring them out of Egypt into a land I had searched out for them, a land flowing with milk and honey, the most beautiful of all lands. ⁷And I said to them, "Each of you, get rid of the vile images you have set your eyes on, and do not defile yourselves with the idols of Egypt. I am the LORD your God."

⁸"'But they rebelled against me and would not listen to me; they did not get rid of the vile images they had set their eyes on, nor did they forsake the idols of Egypt. So I said I would pour out my wrath on them and spend my anger against them in Egypt. ⁹But for the sake of my name I did what would keep it from being profaned in the eyes of the nations they lived among and in whose sight I had revealed myself to the Israelites by bringing them out of Egypt. ¹⁰Therefore I led them out of Egypt and brought them into the desert. ¹¹I gave them my decrees and made known to them my laws, for the man who obeys them will live by them. ¹²Also I gave

a 14 Or from under its

them my Sabbaths as a sign between us, so they would know that I the LORD made them holy.

13" 'Yet the people of Israel rebelled against me in the desert. They did not follow my decrees but rejected my laws—although the man who obeys them will live by them—and they utterly desecrated my Sabbaths. So I said I would pour out my wrath on them and destroy them in the desert. 14But for the sake of my name I did what would keep it from being profaned in the eyes of the nations in whose sight I had brought them out. 15Also with uplifted hand I swore to them in the desert that I would not bring them into the land I had given them—a land flowing with milk and honey, most beautiful of all lands— 16because they rejected my laws and did not follow my decrees and desecrated my Sabbaths. For their hearts were devoted to their idols. 17Yet I looked on them with pity and did not destroy them or put an end to them in the desert. 18I said to their children in the desert, "Do not follow the statutes of your fathers or keep their laws or defile yourselves with their idols. 19I am the LORD your God; follow my decrees and be careful to keep my laws. 20Keep my Sabbaths holy, that they may be a sign between us. Then you will know that I am the LORD your God."

21" 'But the children rebelled against me: They did not follow my decrees, they were not careful to keep my laws—although the man who obeys them will live by them—and they desecrated my Sabbaths. So I said I would pour out my wrath on them and spend my anger against them in the desert. 22But I withheld my hand, and for the sake of my name I did what would keep it from being profaned in the eyes of the nations in whose sight I had brought them out. 23Also with uplifted hand I swore to them in the desert that I would disperse them among the nations and scatter them through the countries, 24because they had not obeyed my laws but had rejected my decrees and desecrated my Sabbaths, and their eyes ⌊lusted⌋ after their fathers' idols. 25I also gave them over to statutes that were not good and laws they could not live by; 26I let them become defiled through their gifts—the sacrifice of every firstborn[a] — that I might fill them with horror so they would know that I am the LORD.'

27"Therefore, son of man, speak to the people of Israel and say to them, 'This is what the Sovereign LORD says: In this also your fathers blasphemed me by forsaking me: 28When I

與他們中間為證據,使他們知道我耶和華是叫他們成為聖的。

13 " '以色列家卻在曠野悖逆我,不順從我的律例,厭棄我的典章(人若遵行,就必因此活著),大大干犯我的安息日。我就說:要在曠野將我的忿怒傾在他們身上,滅絕他們。14我卻為我名的緣故沒有這樣行,免得我的名在我領他們出埃及的列國人眼前被褻瀆。15並且我在曠野向他們起誓,必不領他們進入我所賜給他們流奶與蜜之地,那地在萬國中是有榮耀的;16因為他們厭棄我的典章,不順從我的律例,干犯我的安息日,他們的心隨從自己的偶像。17雖然如此,我眼仍顧惜他們,不毀滅他們,不在曠野將他們滅絕淨盡。18我在曠野對他們的兒女說:不要遵行你們父親的律例,不要謹守他們的惡規,也不要因他們的偶像玷污自己。19我是耶和華你們的神,你們要順從我的律例,謹守遵行我的典章,20且以我的安息日為聖。這日在我與你們中間為證據,使你們知道我是耶和華你們的神。

21 " '只是他們的兒女悖逆我,不順從我的律例,也不謹守遵行我的典章(人若遵行,就必因此活著),干犯我的安息日。我就說:要將我的忿怒傾在他們身上,在曠野向他們成就我怒中所定的。22雖然如此,我卻為我名的緣故縮手沒有這樣行,免得我的名在我領他們出埃及的列國人眼前被褻瀆。23並且我在曠野向他們起誓,必將他們分散在列國,四散在列邦!24因為他們不遵行我的典章,竟厭棄我的律例,干犯我的安息日,眼目仰望他們父親的偶像。25我也任他們遵行不美的律例,謹守不能使人活著的惡規。26因他們將一切頭生的經火,我就任憑他們在這供獻的事上玷污自己,好叫他們淒涼,使他們知道我是耶和華。'

27 "人子啊,你要告訴以色列家說:'主耶和華如此說:你們的列祖在得罪我的事上褻瀆我,28因為我領

---

a 26 Or —making every firstborn pass through ⌊the fire⌋

他們到了我起誓應許賜給他們的地，他們看見各高山、各茂密樹，就在那裏獻祭，奉上惹我發怒的供物，也在那裏焚燒馨香的祭牲，並澆上奠祭。²⁹我就對他們說：你們所上的那高處叫甚麼呢？』」那高處的名字叫巴麻，直到今日。

審判與復興

³⁰「所以你要對以色列家說：『主耶和華如此說：你們仍照你們列祖所行的玷污自己嗎？仍照他們可憎的事行邪淫嗎？³¹你們奉上供物使你們兒子經火的時候，仍將一切偶像玷污自己，直到今日嗎？以色列家啊，我豈被你們求問嗎？主耶和華說：我指著我的永生起誓，我必不被你們求問。

³²「你們說：我們要像外邦人和列國的宗族一樣，去侍奉木頭與石頭。你們所起的這心意萬不能成就。³³主耶和華說：我指著我的永生起誓：我總要作王，用大能的手和伸出來的膀臂，並傾出來的忿怒，治理你們。³⁴我必用大能的手和伸出來的膀臂，並傾出來的忿怒，將你們從萬民中領出來，從分散的列國內聚集你們。³⁵我必帶你們到外邦人的曠野，在那裏當面刑罰你們。³⁶我怎樣在埃及地的曠野刑罰你們的列祖，也必照樣刑罰你們。這是主耶和華說的。³⁷我必使你們從杖下經過，使你們被約拘束。³⁸我必從你們中間除淨叛逆和得罪我的人，將他們從所寄居的地方領出來，他們卻不得入以色列地，你們就知道我是耶和華。

³⁹「以色列家啊，至於你們，主耶和華如此說：從此以後若不聽從我，就任憑你們去侍奉偶像，只是不可再因你們的供物和偶像褻瀆我的聖名。⁴⁰主耶和華說：在我的聖山，就是以色列高處的山，所有以色列的全家都要侍奉我。我要在那裏悅納你們，向你們要供物和初熟的土產，並一切的聖物。⁴¹我從萬民中領你們出來，從分散的列國內聚

brought them into the land I had sworn to give them and they saw any high hill or any leafy tree, there they offered their sacrifices, made offerings that provoked me to anger, presented their fragrant incense and poured out their drink offerings. ²⁹Then I said to them: What is this high place you go to?' " (It is called Bamah[a] to this day.)

Judgment and Restoration

³⁰"Therefore say to the house of Israel: 'This is what the Sovereign LORD says: Will you defile yourselves the way your fathers did and lust after their vile images? ³¹When you offer your gifts—the sacrifice of your sons in[b] the fire—you continue to defile yourselves with all your idols to this day. Am I to let you inquire of me, O house of Israel? As surely as I live, declares the Sovereign LORD, I will not let you inquire of me.

³²" 'You say, "We want to be like the nations, like the peoples of the world, who serve wood and stone." But what you have in mind will never happen. ³³As surely as I live, declares the Sovereign LORD, I will rule over you with a mighty hand and an outstretched arm and with outpoured wrath. ³⁴I will bring you from the nations and gather you from the countries where you have been scattered—with a mighty hand and an outstretched arm and with outpoured wrath. ³⁵I will bring you into the desert of the nations and there, face to face, I will execute judgment upon you. ³⁶As I judged your fathers in the desert of the land of Egypt, so I will judge you, declares the Sovereign LORD. ³⁷I will take note of you as you pass under my rod, and I will bring you into the bond of the covenant. ³⁸I will purge you of those who revolt and rebel against me. Although I will bring them out of the land where they are living, yet they will not enter the land of Israel. Then you will know that I am the LORD.

³⁹" 'As for you, O house of Israel, this is what the Sovereign LORD says: Go and serve your idols, every one of you! But afterward you will surely listen to me and no longer profane my holy name with your gifts and idols. ⁴⁰For on my holy mountain, the high mountain of Israel, declares the Sovereign LORD, there in the land the entire house of Israel will serve me, and there I will accept them. There I will require your offerings and your choice gifts,[c] along with all your holy sacrifices. ⁴¹I will accept you as fragrant incense when I bring you out from the

a 29 Bamah means high place.　b 31 Or —making your sons pass through　c 40 Or and the gifts of your firstfruits

nations and gather you from the countries where you have been scattered, and I will show myself holy among you in the sight of the nations. ⁴²Then you will know that I am the LORD, when I bring you into the land of Israel, the land I had sworn with uplifted hand to give to your fathers. ⁴³There you will remember your conduct and all the actions by which you have defiled yourselves, and you will loathe yourselves for all the evil you have done. ⁴⁴You will know that I am the LORD, when I deal with you for my name's sake and not according to your evil ways and your corrupt practices, O house of Israel, declares the Sovereign LORD.' "

Prophecy Against the South

⁴⁵The word of the LORD came to me: ⁴⁶"Son of man, set your face toward the south; preach against the south and prophesy against the forest of the southland. ⁴⁷Say to the southern forest: 'Hear the word of the LORD. This is what the Sovereign LORD says: I am about to set fire to you, and it will consume all your trees, both green and dry. The blazing flame will not be quenched, and every face from south to north will be scorched by it. ⁴⁸Everyone will see that I the LORD have kindled it; it will not be quenched.' "

⁴⁹Then I said, "Ah, Sovereign LORD! They are saying of me, 'Isn't he just telling parables?' "

Babylon, God's Sword of Judgment

21 The word of the LORD came to me: ²"Son of man, set your face against Jerusalem and preach against the sanctuary. Prophesy against the land of Israel ³and say to her: 'This is what the LORD says: I am against you. I will draw my sword from its scabbard and cut off from you both the righteous and the wicked. ⁴Because I am going to cut off the righteous and the wicked, my sword will be unsheathed against everyone from south to north. ⁵Then all people will know that I the LORD have drawn my sword from its scabbard; it will not return again.'

⁶"Therefore groan, son of man! Groan before them with broken heart and bitter grief. ⁷And when they ask you, 'Why are you groaning?' you shall say, 'Because of the news that is coming. Every heart will melt and every hand go limp; every spirit will become faint and every knee become as weak as water.' It is coming! It will surely take place, declares the Sovereign LORD."

⁸The word of the LORD came to me: ⁹"Son of man, prophesy and say, 'This is what the Lord says:

集你們，那時我必悅納你們好像馨香之祭，要在外邦人眼前在你們身上顯為聖。⁴²我領你們進入以色列地，就是我起誓應許賜給你們列祖之地，那時你們就知道我是耶和華。⁴³你們在那裏要追念玷污自己的行動作為，又要因所做的一切惡事厭惡自己。⁴⁴主耶和華說：以色列家啊，我為我名的緣故，不照着你們的惡行和你們的壞事待你們，你們就知道我是耶和華。'"

論南方的預言

⁴⁵耶和華的話臨到我說：⁴⁶"人子啊，你要面向南方，向南滴下預言攻擊南方田野的樹林。⁴⁷對南方的樹林說：'要聽耶和華的話。主耶和華如此說：我必使火在你中間着起，燒滅你中間的一切青樹和枯樹，猛烈的火焰必不熄滅。從南到北，人的臉面都被燒焦。⁴⁸凡有血氣的，都必知道是我耶和華使火着起，這火必不熄滅。'"

⁴⁹於是我說："哎！主耶和華啊，人都指着我說：'他豈不是說比喻的嗎？'"

巴比倫，神的審判刀

21 耶和華的話臨到我說：²"人子啊，你要面向耶路撒冷和聖所滴下預言，攻擊以色列地。³對以色列地說：'耶和華如此說：我與你為敵，並要拔刀出鞘，從你中間將義人和惡人一併剪除。⁴我既要從你中間剪除義人和惡人，所以我的刀要出鞘，自南至北攻擊一切有血氣的。⁵一切有血氣的就知道我耶和華已經拔刀出鞘，必不再入鞘。'

⁶"人子啊，你要歎息，在他們眼前彎着腰，苦苦地歎息。⁷他們問你說：'為何歎息呢？'你就說：'因為有風聲，災禍要來。人心都必消化，手都發軟，精神衰敗，膝弱如水。'看哪！這災禍臨近，必然成就。這是主耶和華說的。"

⁸耶和華的話臨到我說：⁹"人子啊，你要預言。耶和華吩咐我如此說：

" '有刀、有刀，
　　是磨快擦亮的；
10磨快為要行殺戮，
　　擦亮為要像閃電。

　　" '我們豈可快樂嗎？罰我子
的杖藐視各樹。

11 " '這刀已經交給人擦亮，
　　為要應手使用；
這刀已經磨快擦亮，
　　好交在行殺戮的人手中。
12人子啊，你要呼喊哀號，
　　因為這刀臨到我的百姓
和以色列一切的首領，
他們和我的百姓
　　都交在刀下，
所以你要拍腿歎息。

13 " '有試驗的事，若那藐視的
杖歸於無有，怎麼樣呢？這是主耶
和華說的。'

14 "人子啊，
　　你要拍掌預言。
我耶和華要使這刀，
　　就是致死傷的刀，
　　一連三次加倍刺人，
進入他們的內屋，
　　使大人受死傷的就是這刀。
15我設立恐嚇人的刀，
　　攻擊他們的一切城門，
使他們的心消化，
　　加增他們跌倒的事。
哎！這刀造得像閃電，
　　磨得尖利要行殺戮。
16刀啊，你要歸在右邊，
　　擺在左邊，
　　你面向哪方，就向哪方殺戮。
17我也要拍掌，
　　並要使我的忿怒止息。
這是我耶和華說的。'"

18耶和華的話又臨到我說：
19 "人子啊，你要定出兩條路，好使
巴比倫王的刀來。這兩條路必從一
地分出來，又要在通城的路口上畫
出一隻手來。20你要定出一條路，使
刀來到亞捫人的拉巴；又要定出一
條路，使刀來到猶大的堅固城耶路
撒冷。21因為巴比倫王站在岔路那
裏，在兩條路口上要占卜。他搖籤

" 'A sword, a sword,
　　sharpened and polished—
10sharpened for the slaughter,
　　polished to flash like lightning!

" 'Shall we rejoice in the scepter of my son
Judah? The sword despises every such stick.

11" 'The sword is appointed to be polished,
　　to be grasped with the hand;
it is sharpened and polished,
　　made ready for the hand of the slayer.
12Cry out and wail, son of man,
　　for it is against my people;
it is against all the princes of Israel.
They are thrown to the sword
　　along with my people.
Therefore beat your breast.

13" 'Testing will surely come. And what if the
scepter of Judah, which the sword despises,
does not continue? declares the Sovereign LORD.'

14"So then, son of man, prophesy
　　and strike your hands together.
Let the sword strike twice,
　　even three times.
It is a sword for slaughter—
　　a sword for great slaughter,
　　closing in on them from every side.
15So that hearts may melt
　　and the fallen be many,
I have stationed the sword for slaughter^a
　　at all their gates.
Oh! It is made to flash like lightning,
　　it is grasped for slaughter.
16O sword, slash to the right,
　　then to the left,
　　wherever your blade is turned.
17I too will strike my hands together,
　　and my wrath will subside.
I the LORD have spoken."

18The word of the LORD came to me: 19"Son of
man, mark out two roads for the sword of the
king of Babylon to take, both starting from the
same country. Make a signpost where the road
branches off to the city. 20Mark out one road for
the sword to come against Rabbah of the
Ammonites and another against Judah and fortified Jerusalem. 21For the king of Babylon will
stop at the fork in the road, at the junction of the

---

a 15 Septuagint; the meaning of the Hebrew for this word is
uncertain.

two roads, to seek an omen: He will cast lots with arrows, he will consult his idols, he will examine the liver. ²²Into his right hand will come the lot for Jerusalem, where he is to set up battering rams, to give the command to slaughter, to sound the battle cry, to set battering rams against the gates, to build a ramp and to erect siege works. ²³It will seem like a false omen to those who have sworn allegiance to him, but he will remind them of their guilt and take them captive.

²⁴"Therefore this is what the Sovereign LORD says: 'Because you people have brought to mind your guilt by your open rebellion, revealing your sins in all that you do—because you have done this, you will be taken captive.

²⁵" 'O profane and wicked prince of Israel, whose day has come, whose time of punishment has reached its climax, ²⁶this is what the Sovereign LORD says: Take off the turban, remove the crown. It will not be as it was: The lowly will be exalted and the exalted will be brought low. ²⁷A ruin! A ruin! I will make it a ruin! It will not be restored until he comes to whom it rightfully belongs; to him I will give it.'

²⁸"And you, son of man, prophesy and say, 'This is what the Sovereign LORD says about the Ammonites and their insults:

" 'A sword, a sword,
    drawn for the slaughter,
    polished to consume
    and to flash like lightning!
²⁹Despite false visions concerning you
    and lying divinations about you,
    it will be laid on the necks
    of the wicked who are to be slain,
    whose day has come,
    whose time of punishment has reached its
        climax.
³⁰Return the sword to its scabbard.
    In the place where you were created,
    in the land of your ancestry,
    I will judge you.
³¹I will pour out my wrath upon you
    and breathe out my fiery anger against you;
    I will hand you over to brutal men,
    men skilled in destruction.
³²You will be fuel for the fire,
    your blood will be shed in your land,
    you will be remembered no more;
    for I the LORD have spoken.' "

（註：原文作"箭"）求問神像，察看犧牲的肝。²²在右手中拿着為耶路撒冷占卜的籤，使他安設撞城錘，張口叫殺，揚聲吶喊，築壘造臺，以撞城錘，攻打城門。²³據那些曾起誓的猶大人看來，這是虛假的占卜，但巴比倫王要使他們想起罪孽，以致將他們捉住。

²⁴"主耶和華如此說：'因你們的過犯顯露，使你們的罪孽被記念，以致你們的罪惡在行為上都彰顯出來。又因你們被記念，就被捉住。

²⁵" '你這受死傷行惡的以色列王啊，罪孽的盡頭到了，受報的日子已到。²⁶主耶和華如此說：當除掉冠，摘下冕，景況必不再像先前；要使卑者升為高，使高者降為卑。²⁷我要將這國傾覆，傾覆，而又傾覆，這國也必不再有，直等到那應得的人來到，我就賜給他。'

²⁸"人子啊，要發預言說：主耶和華論到亞捫人和他們的凌辱，吩咐我如此說：

"'有刀，有拔出來的刀，
    已經擦亮，
    為行殺戮，
    使它像閃電以行吞滅。
²⁹人為你見虛假的異象，
    行謊詐之惡人的頸項上。
    使你倒在
    受死傷之惡人的頸項上。
    他們罪孽到了盡頭，
    受報的日子已到。
³⁰你將刀收入鞘吧！
    在你受造之處、
    生長之地，
    我必刑罰你。
³¹我必將我的惱恨倒在你身上，
    將我烈怒的火噴在你身上；
    又將你交在善於殺滅的
    畜類人手中。
³²你必當柴被火焚燒，
    你的血必流在國中，
    你必不再被記念，
    因為這是我耶和華說的。' "

耶路撒冷的罪

22 耶和華的話又臨到我說：² "人子啊，你要審問審問這流人血的城嗎？當使她知道她一切可憎的事。³ 你要說：'主耶和華如此說：哎！這城有流人血的事在其中，叫她受報的日期來到，又做偶像玷污自己，陷害自己。⁴ 你因流了人的血，就為有罪；你做了偶像，就玷污自己，使你受報之日臨近，報應之年來到。所以我叫你受列國的凌辱和列邦的譏誚。⁵ 你這名臭、多亂的城啊，那些離你近、離你遠的都必譏誚你。

⁶ "'看哪，以色列的首領各逞其能，在你中間流人之血。⁷ 在你中間有輕慢父母的，有欺壓寄居的，有虧負孤兒寡婦的。⁸ 你藐視了我的聖物，干犯了我的安息日。⁹ 在你中間有讒謗人流人血的；有在山上吃過祭偶像之物的；有行淫亂的。¹⁰ 在你中間有露體母下體羞辱父親的；有玷辱月經不潔淨之婦人的。¹¹ 這人與鄰舍的妻行可憎的事；那人貪淫玷污兒婦；還有玷辱同父之姐妹的。¹² 在你中間有為流人血受賄賂的；有向借錢的弟兄取利、向借糧的弟兄多要的。且因貪得無厭，欺壓鄰舍奪取財物，竟忘了我。這是主耶和華說的。

¹³ "'看哪，我因你所得不義之財和你中間所流的血，就拍掌歎息。¹⁴ 到了我懲罰你的日子，你的心還能忍受嗎？你的手還能有力嗎？我耶和華說了這話，就必照着行。¹⁵ 我必將你分散在列國，四散在列邦。我也必從你中間除掉你的污穢。¹⁶ 你必在列國人的眼前因自己所行的被褻瀆，你就知道我是耶和華。'"

¹⁷ 耶和華的話臨到我說：¹⁸ "人子啊，以色列家在我看為渣滓，他們都是爐中的銅、錫、鐵、鉛，都是銀渣滓。¹⁹ 所以主耶和華如此說：

Jerusalem's Sins

22 The word of the LORD came to me: ²"Son of man, will you judge her? Will you judge this city of bloodshed? Then confront her with all her detestable practices ³and say: 'This is what the Sovereign LORD says: O city that brings on herself doom by shedding blood in her midst and defiles herself by making idols, ⁴you have become guilty because of the blood you have shed and have become defiled by the idols you have made. You have brought your days to a close, and the end of your years has come. Therefore I will make you an object of scorn to the nations and a laughingstock to all the countries. ⁵Those who are near and those who are far away will mock you, O infamous city, full of turmoil.

⁶ 'See how each of the princes of Israel who are in you uses his power to shed blood. ⁷In you they have treated father and mother with contempt; in you they have oppressed the alien and mistreated the fatherless and the widow. ⁸You have despised my holy things and desecrated my Sabbaths. ⁹In you are slanderous men bent on shedding blood; in you are those who eat at the mountain shrines and commit lewd acts. ¹⁰In you are those who dishonor their fathers' bed; in you are those who violate women during their period, when they are ceremonially unclean. ¹¹In you one man commits a detestable offense with his neighbor's wife, another shamefully defiles his daughter-in-law, and another violates his sister, his own father's daughter. ¹²In you men accept bribes to shed blood; you take usury and excessive interest* and make unjust gain from your neighbors by extortion. And you have forgotten me, declares the Sovereign LORD.

¹³" 'I will surely strike my hands together at the unjust gain you have made and at the blood you have shed in your midst. ¹⁴Will your courage endure or your hands be strong in the day I deal with you? I the LORD have spoken, and I will do it. ¹⁵I will disperse you among the nations and scatter you through the countries; and I will put an end to your uncleanness. ¹⁶When you have been defiled*b* in the eyes of the nations, you will know that I am the LORD.' "

¹⁷Then the word of the LORD came to me: ¹⁸"Son of man, the house of Israel has become dross to me; all of them are the copper, tin, iron and lead left inside a furnace. They are but the dross of silver. ¹⁹Therefore this is what the

---

a 12 Or usury and interest　　b 16 Or When I have allotted you your inheritance

Sovereign LORD says: 'Because you have all become dross, I will gather you into Jerusalem. [20]As men gather silver, copper, iron, lead and tin into a furnace to melt it with a fiery blast, so will I gather you in my anger and my wrath and put you inside the city and melt you. [21]I will gather you and I will blow on you with my fiery wrath, and you will be melted inside her. [22]As silver is melted in a furnace, so you will be melted inside her, and you will know that I the LORD have poured out my wrath upon you.' "

[23]Again the word of the LORD came to me: [24]"Son of man, say to the land, 'You are a land that has had no rain or showers[a] in the day of wrath.' [25]There is a conspiracy of her princes[b] within her like a roaring lion tearing its prey; they devour people, take treasures and precious things and make many widows within her. [26]Her priests do violence to my law and profane my holy things; they do not distinguish between the holy and the common; they teach that there is no difference between the unclean and the clean; and they shut their eyes to the keeping of my Sabbaths, so that I am profaned among them. [27]Her officials within her are like wolves tearing their prey; they shed blood and kill people to make unjust gain. [28]Her prophets whitewash these deeds for them by false visions and lying divinations. They say, 'This is what the Sovereign LORD says'—when the LORD has not spoken. [29]The people of the land practice extortion and commit robbery; they oppress the poor and needy and mistreat the alien, denying them justice.

[30]"I looked for a man among them who would build up the wall and stand before me in the gap on behalf of the land so I would not have to destroy it, but I found none. [31]So I will pour out my wrath on them and consume them with my fiery anger, bringing down on their own heads all they have done, declares the Sovereign LORD."

Two Adulterous Sisters

23 The word of the LORD came to me: [2]"Son of man, there were two women, daughters of the same mother. [3]They became prostitutes in Egypt, engaging in prostitution from their youth. In that land their breasts were fondled and their virgin bosoms caressed. [4]The older was named Oholah, and her sister was Oholibah. They were mine and gave birth to sons and daughters. Oholah is Samaria, and Oholibah is Jerusalem.

'因你們都成為渣滓，我必聚集你們在耶路撒冷中。[20]人怎樣將銀、銅、鐵、鉛、錫聚在爐中，吹火熔化，照樣，我也要發怒氣和忿怒，將你們聚集放在城中熔化你們。[21]我必聚集你們，把我烈怒的火吹在你們身上，你們就在其中熔化。[22]銀子怎樣熔化在爐中，你們也必照樣熔化在城中，你們就知道我耶和華是將忿怒倒在你們身上了。'"

[23]耶和華的話臨到我說：[24]"人子啊，你要對這地說：'你是未得潔淨之地，在惱恨的日子也沒有雨下在你以上。'[25]其中的先知同謀背叛，如咆哮的獅子抓撕掠物，他們吞滅人民，搶奪財寶，使這地多有寡婦。[26]其中的祭司強解我的律法，褻瀆我的聖物，不分別聖的和俗的，也不使人分辨潔淨的和不潔淨的，又遮眼不顧我的安息日，我也在他們中間被褻慢。[27]其中的首領彷彿豺狼抓撕掠物，殺人流血，傷害人命，要得不義之財。[28]其中的先知為百姓用未泡透的灰抹牆，就是為他們見虛假的異象，用謊詐的占卜，說：'主耶和華如此說'，其實耶和華沒有說。[29]國內眾民一味地欺壓，慣行搶奪，虧負困苦窮乏的，背理欺壓寄居的。

[30]"我在他們中間尋找一人重修牆垣，在我面前為這國站在破口防堵，使我不滅絕這國，卻找不著一個。[31]所以我將惱恨倒在他們身上，用烈怒的火滅了他們，照他們所行的報應在他們頭上。這是主耶和華說的。"

兩個行淫的姐妹

23 耶和華的話又臨到我說：[2]"人子啊，有兩個女子，是一母所生，[3]她們在埃及行邪淫，在幼年時行邪淫。她們在那裏作處女的時候，有人擁抱她們的懷，撫摸她們的乳。[4]她們的名字，姐姐名叫阿荷拉，妹妹名叫阿荷利巴。她們都歸於我，生了兒女。論到她們的名字，阿荷拉就是撒馬利亞，阿荷利巴就是耶路撒冷。

---

a 24 Septuagint; Hebrew *has not been cleansed or rained on*
b 25 Septuagint; Hebrew *prophets*

5 "阿荷拉歸我之後行邪淫，貪
戀所愛的人，就是她的鄰邦亞述
人。6這些人都穿藍衣，作省長、副
省長，都騎著馬，是可愛的少年
人。7阿荷拉就與亞述人中最美的男
子放縱淫行，她因所戀愛之人的一
切偶像玷污自己。8自從在埃及的時
候，她就沒有離開淫亂。因為她年
幼作處女的時候，埃及人與她行
淫，撫摸她的乳，縱慾與她行淫。

9 "因此，我將她交在她所愛的
人手中，就是她所戀愛的亞述人手
中。10他們就露了她的下體，擄掠她
的兒女，用刀殺了她，使她在婦女中
留下臭名，因他們向她施行審判。

11 "她妹妹阿荷利巴雖然看見
了，卻還貪戀，比她姐姐更醜，行
淫亂比她姐姐更多。12她貪戀鄰邦的
亞述人，就是穿極華美的衣服，騎
著馬的省長、副省長，都是可愛的
少年人。13我看見她被玷污了，她姐
妹二人同行一路。

14 "阿荷利巴又加增淫行，因她
看見人像畫在牆上，就是用丹色所
畫迦勒底人的像；15腰間繫著帶子，
頭上有下垂的裹頭巾，都是軍長的
形狀，仿照巴比倫人的形像；他們
的故土就是迦勒底。16阿荷利巴一看
見就貪戀他們，打發使者往迦勒底
去見他們。17巴比倫人就來登她愛情
的牀，與她行淫玷污她。她被玷
污，隨後心裏厭棄他們生疏。18這樣，
她顯露淫行，又顯露下體；我心就
與她生疏，像先前與她姐姐生疏一
樣。19她還加增她的淫行，追念她幼
年在埃及行邪淫的日子。20貪戀情
人身壯精足，如驢如馬。21這樣，你
就想起你幼年的淫行，那時，埃及
人擁抱你的懷，撫摸你的乳。

22 "阿荷利巴啊，主耶和華如此
說：我必激動你先愛而後生疏的人
來攻擊你。我必使他們來，在你四

5"Oholah engaged in prostitution while she
was still mine; and she lusted after her lovers,
the Assyrians—warriors 6clothed in blue, governors and commanders, all of them handsome
young men, and mounted horsemen. 7She gave
herself as a prostitute to all the elite of the
Assyrians and defiled herself with all the idols
of everyone she lusted after. 8She did not give
up the prostitution she began in Egypt, when
during her youth men slept with her, caressed
her virgin bosom and poured out their lust
upon her.

9"Therefore I handed her over to her lovers,
the Assyrians, for whom she lusted. 10They
stripped her naked, took away her sons and
daughters and killed her with the sword. She
became a byword among women, and punishment was inflicted on her.

11"Her sister Oholibah saw this, yet in her
lust and prostitution she was more depraved
than her sister. 12She too lusted after the Assyrians—governors and commanders, warriors in
full dress, mounted horsemen, all handsome
young men. 13I saw that she too defiled herself;
both of them went the same way.

14"But she carried her prostitution still further. She saw men portrayed on a wall, figures
of Chaldeans^a portrayed in red, 15with belts
around their waists and flowing turbans on
their heads; all of them looked like Babylonian
chariot officers, natives of Chaldea.^b 16As soon
as she saw them, she lusted after them and sent
messengers to them in Chaldea. 17Then the Babylonians came to her, to the bed of love, and in
their lust they defiled her. After she had been
defiled by them, she turned away from them in
disgust. 18When she carried on her prostitution
openly and exposed her nakedness, I turned
away from her in disgust, just as I had turned
away from her sister. 19Yet she became more
and more promiscuous as she recalled the days
of her youth, when she was a prostitute in Egypt.
20There she lusted after her lovers, whose geni-
tals were like those of donkeys and whose emission was like that of horses. 21So you longed for
the lewdness of your youth, when in Egypt your
bosom was caressed and your young breasts
fondled.^c

22"Therefore, Oholibah, this is what the
Sovereign LORD says: I will stir up your lovers
against you, those you turned away from in disgust, and I will bring them against you from

---

a 14 Or Babylonians　　*b 15 Or Babylonia; also in verse 16*
*c 21 Syriac (see also verse 3); Hebrew caressed because of your
young breasts*

every side— ²³the Babylonians and all the Chaldeans, the men of Pekod and Shoa and Koa, and all the Assyrians with them, handsome young men, all of them governors and commanders, chariot officers and men of high rank, all mounted on horses. ²⁴They will come against you with weapons,ᵃ chariots and wagons and with a throng of people; they will take up positions against you on every side with large and small shields and with helmets. I will turn you over to them for punishment, and they will punish you according to their standards. ²⁵I will direct my jealous anger against you, and they will deal with you in fury. They will cut off your noses and your ears, and those of you who are left will fall by the sword. They will take away your sons and daughters, and those of you who are left will be consumed by fire. ²⁶They will also strip you of your clothes and take your fine jewelry. ²⁷So I will put a stop to the lewdness and prostitution you began in Egypt. You will not look on these things with longing or remember Egypt anymore.

²⁸"For this is what the Sovereign LORD says: I am about to hand you over to those you hate, to those you turned away from in disgust. ²⁹They will deal with you in hatred and take away everything you have worked for. They will leave you naked and bare, and the shame of your prostitution will be exposed. Your lewdness and promiscuity ³⁰have brought this upon you, because you lusted after the nations and defiled yourself with their idols. ³¹You have gone the way of your sister; so I will put her cup into your hand.

³²"This is what the Sovereign LORD says:

"You will drink your sister's cup,
  a cup large and deep;
it will bring scorn and derision,
  for it holds so much.
³³You will be filled with drunkenness and
  sorrow,
the cup of ruin and desolation,
  the cup of your sister Samaria.
³⁴You will drink it and drain it dry;
  you will dash it to pieces
and tear your breasts.

I have spoken, declares the Sovereign LORD.

³⁵"Therefore this is what the Sovereign LORD says: Since you have forgotten me and thrust me

圍攻擊你。²³所來的就是巴比倫人、迦勒底的眾人、比割人、書亞人、哥亞人，同着他們的還有亞述眾人，乃是作省長、副省長、作軍長有名聲的，都騎着馬，是可愛的少年人。²⁴他們必帶兵器、戰車、輜重車，率領大眾來攻擊你。他們要拿大小盾牌，頂盔擺陣，在你四圍攻擊你。我要將審判的事交給他們，他們必按着自己的條例審判你。²⁵我必以忌恨攻擊你，他們必以忿怒辦你。他們必割去你的鼻子和耳朵，你遺留（註：或作"餘剩"。下同）的人必倒在刀下。他們必擄去你的兒女，你所遺留的必被火焚燒。²⁶他們必剝去你的衣服，奪取你華美的寶器。²⁷這樣，我必使你的淫行和你從埃及地染來的淫亂止息了，使你不再仰望亞述，也不再追念埃及。

²⁸"主耶和華如此說：我必將你交在你所恨惡的人手中，就是你心與他生疏的人手中。²⁹他們必以恨惡辦你，奪取你一切勞碌得來的，留下你赤身露體。你淫亂的下體，連你的淫行帶你的淫亂，都被顯露。³⁰人必向你行這些事，因為你隨從外邦人行邪淫，被他們的偶像玷污了。³¹你走了你姐姐所走的路，所以我必將她的杯交在你手中。

³²"主耶和華如此說：

"你必喝你姐姐所喝的杯；
  那杯又深又廣，
  盛得甚多，
  使你被人嗤笑譏刺。
³³你必酩酊大醉，
  滿有愁苦，
喝乾你姐姐撒馬利亞的杯，
  就是令人驚駭淒涼的杯。
³⁴你必喝這杯，以致喝盡。
  杯破又齦杯片，
  撕裂自己的乳，

因為這事我曾說過。這是主耶和華說的。

³⁵"主耶和華如此說：因你忘記

<hr>

ᵃ 24 The meaning of the Hebrew for this word is uncertain.

我，將我丟在背後，所以你要擔當你淫行和淫亂的報應。"

36耶和華又對我說："人子啊，你要審問阿荷拉與阿荷利巴嗎？當指出她們所行可憎的事。37她們行淫，手中有殺人的血，又與偶像行淫，並使她們為我所生的兒女經火燒給偶像。38此外，她們還有向我所行的，就是同日玷污我的聖所，干犯我的安息日。39她們殺了兒女獻與偶像，當天又入我的聖所，將聖所褻瀆了，她們在我殿中所行的乃是如此。

40"況且你們二婦打發使者去請遠方人，使者到他們那裏，他們就來了。你們為他們沐浴己身，粉飾眼目，佩戴妝飾，41坐在華美的牀上，前面擺設桌案，將我的香料、膏油擺在其上。

42"在那裏有羣眾安逸歡樂的聲音，並有粗俗的人和酒徒從曠野同來，把鐲子戴在二婦的手上，把華冠戴在她們的頭上。43我論這行淫衰老的婦人說：'現在人還要與她行淫，她也要與人行淫。'44人與阿荷拉，並阿荷利巴二淫婦苟合，好像與妓女苟合。45必有義人，照審判淫婦和流人血的婦人之例審判她們，因為她們是淫婦，手中有殺人的血。

46"主耶和華如此說：我必使多人來攻擊她們，使她們拋來拋去，被人搶奪。47這些人必用石頭打死她們，用刀劍殺害她們，又殺戮她們的兒女，用火焚燒她們的房屋。

48"這樣，我必使淫行從國內止息，好叫一切婦人都受警戒，不效法你們的淫行。49人必照着你們的淫行報應你們，你們要擔當拜偶像的罪，就知道我是主耶和華。"

behind your back, you must bear the consequences of your lewdness and prostitution."

36The LORD said to me: "Son of man, will you judge Oholah and Oholibah? Then confront them with their detestable practices, 37for they have committed adultery and blood is on their hands. They committed adultery with their idols; they even sacrificed their children, whom they bore to me,[a] as food for them. 38They have also done this to me: At that same time they defiled my sanctuary and desecrated my Sabbaths. 39On the very day they sacrificed their children to their idols, they entered my sanctuary and desecrated it. That is what they did in my house.

40"They even sent messengers for men who came from far away, and when they arrived you bathed yourself for them, painted your eyes and put on your jewelry. 41You sat on an elegant couch, with a table spread before it on which you had placed the incense and oil that belonged to me.

42"The noise of a carefree crowd was around her; Sabeans[b] were brought from the desert along with men from the rabble, and they put bracelets on the arms of the woman and her sister and beautiful crowns on their heads. 43Then I said about the one worn out by adultery, 'Now let them use her as a prostitute, for that is all she is.' 44And they slept with her. As men sleep with a prostitute, so they slept with those lewd women, Oholah and Oholibah. 45But righteous men will sentence them to the punishment of women who commit adultery and shed blood, because they are adulterous and blood is on their hands.

46"This is what the Sovereign LORD says: Bring a mob against them and give them over to terror and plunder. 47The mob will stone them and cut them down with their swords; they will kill their sons and daughters and burn down their houses.

48"So I will put an end to lewdness in the land, that all women may take warning and not imitate you. 49You will suffer the penalty for your lewdness and bear the consequences of your sins of idolatry. Then you will know that I am the Sovereign LORD."

---

a 37 Or *even made the children they bore to me pass through the fire*　b 42 Or *drunkards*

The Cooking Pot

24 In the ninth year, in the tenth month on the tenth day, the word of the LORD came to me: ²"Son of man, record this date, this very date, because the king of Babylon has laid siege to Jerusalem this very day. ³Tell this rebellious house a parable and say to them: This is what the Sovereign LORD says:

" 'Put on the cooking pot; put it on
　and pour water into it.
⁴Put into it the pieces of meat,
　all the choice pieces—the leg and the
　　shoulder.
　Fill it with the best of these bones;
⁵　take the pick of the flock.
　Pile wood beneath it for the bones;
　bring it to a boil
　and cook the bones in it.

⁶" 'For this is what the Sovereign LORD says:

" 'Woe to the city of bloodshed,
　to the pot now encrusted,
　whose deposit will not go away!
　Empty it piece by piece
　without casting lots for them.

⁷" 'For the blood she shed is in her midst:
　She poured it on the bare rock;
　she did not pour it on the ground,
　where the dust would cover it.
⁸To stir up wrath and take revenge
　I put her blood on the bare rock,
　so that it would not be covered.

⁹" 'Therefore this is what the Sovereign LORD says:

" 'Woe to the city of bloodshed!
　I, too, will pile the wood high.
¹⁰So heap on the wood
　and kindle the fire.
　Cook the meat well,
　mixing in the spices;
　and let the bones be charred.
¹¹Then set the empty pot on the coals
　till it becomes hot and its copper glows
　so its impurities may be melted
　and its deposit burned away.
¹²It has frustrated all efforts;
　its heavy deposit has not been removed,
　not even by fire.

煮食物的鍋

24 第九年十月初十日，耶和華的話又臨到我說：²"人子啊，今日正是巴比倫王就近耶路撒冷的日子，你要將這日記下。³要向這悖逆之家設比喻說：主耶和華如此說：

" '將鍋放在火上，放好了，
　就倒水在其中。
⁴將肉塊，
　就是一切肥美的肉塊，
　腿和肩都聚在其中，
　拿美好的骨頭把鍋裝滿；
⁵取羊羣中最好的，
　將柴堆在鍋下，
　使鍋開滾，
　好把骨頭煮在其中。

⁶" '主耶和華如此說：

" '禍哉！這流人血的城，
　就是長鏽的鍋。
　其中的鏽未曾除掉，
　須要將肉塊從其中一一取出來，
　不必為它拈鬮。

⁷" '城中所流的血
　倒在淨光的磐石上，
　不倒在地上，
　用土掩蓋。
⁸這城中所流的血倒在淨光的磐石上，
　不得掩蓋，乃是出於我，
　為要發忿施行報應。

⁹" '所以主耶和華如此說：

" '禍哉，這流人血的城！
　我也必大堆火柴。
¹⁰添上木柴，
　使火着旺，
　將肉煮爛，
　把湯熬濃，
　使骨頭烤焦。
¹¹把鍋倒空坐在炭火上，
　使鍋燒熱，使銅燒紅，
　熔化其中的污穢，
　除淨其上的鏽。
¹²這鍋勞碌疲乏，
　所長的大鏽仍未除掉，
　這鏽就是用火也不能除掉。

¹³ " '在你污穢中有淫行，我潔淨你，你卻不潔淨。你的污穢再不能潔淨，直等我向你發的忿怒止息。

¹⁴ " '我耶和華說過的必定成就，必照話而行，必不返回，必不顧惜，也不後悔。人必照你的舉動行為審判你。這是主耶和華說的。' "

以西結妻子死

¹⁵ 耶和華的話又臨到我說：¹⁶ "人子啊，我要將你眼目所喜愛的忽然取去，你卻不可悲哀哭泣，也不可流淚。¹⁷ 只可歎息，不可出聲，不可辦理喪事；頭上仍勒裹頭巾，腳上仍穿鞋，不可蒙着嘴唇，也不可吃弔喪的食物。"

¹⁸ 於是我將這事早晨告訴百姓，晚上我的妻就死了。次日早晨我便遵命而行。

¹⁹ 百姓問我說："你這樣行與我們有甚麼關係，你不告訴我們嗎？"

²⁰ 我回答他們："耶和華的話臨到我說：²¹ 你告訴以色列家：'主耶和華如此說：我必使我的聖所，就是你們勢力所誇耀，眼裏所喜愛，心中所愛惜的被褻瀆，並且你們所遺留的兒女，必倒在刀下。²² 那時，你們必行我僕人所行的；不蒙着嘴唇，也不吃弔喪的食物。²³ 你們仍要頭上勒裹頭巾，腳上穿鞋，不可悲哀哭泣。你們必因自己的罪孽相對歎息，漸漸消減。²⁴ 以西結必這樣為你們作預兆；凡他所行的，你們也必照樣行。那事來到，你們就知道我是主耶和華。'

²⁵ "人子啊，我除掉他們所倚靠、所歡喜的榮耀，並眼中所喜愛、心裏所看重的兒女。²⁶ 那日逃脫的人豈不來到你這裏，使你耳聞這事嗎？²⁷ 你必向逃脫的人開口說話，不再啞口。你必這樣為他們作預兆，他們就知道我是耶和華。"

¹³" 'Now your impurity is lewdness. Because I tried to cleanse you but you would not be cleansed from your impurity, you will not be clean again until my wrath against you has subsided.

¹⁴ 'I the LORD have spoken. The time has come for me to act. I will not hold back; I will not have pity, nor will I relent. You will be judged according to your conduct and your actions, declares the Sovereign LORD.' "

Ezekiel's Wife Dies

¹⁵ The word of the LORD came to me: ¹⁶"Son of man, with one blow I am about to take away from you the delight of your eyes. Yet do not lament or weep or shed any tears. ¹⁷Groan quietly; do not mourn for the dead. Keep your turban fastened and your sandals on your feet; do not cover the lower part of your face or eat the customary food ⌊of mourners⌋."

¹⁸So I spoke to the people in the morning, and in the evening my wife died. The next morning I did as I had been commanded.

¹⁹Then the people asked me, "Won't you tell us what these things have to do with us?"

²⁰So I said to them, "The word of the LORD came to me: ²¹Say to the house of Israel, 'This is what the Sovereign LORD says: I am about to desecrate my sanctuary—the stronghold in which you take pride, the delight of your eyes, the object of your affection. The sons and daughters you left behind will fall by the sword. ²²And you will do as I have done. You will not cover the lower part of your face or eat the customary food ⌊of mourners⌋. ²³You will keep your turbans on your heads and your sandals on your feet. You will not mourn or weep but will waste away because of*ᵃ* your sins and groan among yourselves. ²⁴Ezekiel will be a sign to you; you will do just as he has done. When this happens, you will know that I am the Sovereign LORD.'

²⁵"And you, son of man, on the day I take away their stronghold, their joy and glory, the delight of their eyes, their heart's desire, and their sons and daughters as well— ²⁶on that day a fugitive will come to tell you the news. ²⁷At that time your mouth will be opened; you will speak with him and will no longer be silent. So you will be a sign to them, and they will know that I am the LORD."

A Prophecy Against Ammon

25 The word of the LORD came to me: 2"Son of man, set your face against the Ammonites and prophesy against them. 3Say to them, 'Hear the word of the Sovereign LORD. This is what the Sovereign LORD says: Because you said "Aha!" over my sanctuary when it was desecrated and over the land of Israel when it was laid waste and over the people of Judah when they went into exile, 4therefore I am going to give you to the people of the East as a possession. They will set up their camps and pitch their tents among you; they will eat your fruit and drink your milk. 5I will turn Rabbah into a pasture for camels and Ammon into a resting place for sheep. Then you will know that I am the LORD. 6For this is what the Sovereign LORD says: Because you have clapped your hands and stamped your feet, rejoicing with all the malice of your heart against the land of Israel, 7therefore I will stretch out my hand against you and give you as plunder to the nations. I will cut you off from the nations and exterminate you from the countries. I will destroy you, and you will know that I am the LORD.' "

A Prophecy Against Moab

8"This is what the Sovereign LORD says: 'Because Moab and Seir said, "Look, the house of Judah has become like all the other nations," 9therefore I will expose the flank of Moab, beginning at its frontier towns—Beth Jeshimoth, Baal Meon and Kiriathaim—the glory of that land. 10I will give Moab along with the Ammonites to the people of the East as a possession, so that the Ammonites will not be remembered among the nations; 11and I will inflict punishment on Moab. Then they will know that I am the LORD.' "

A Prophecy Against Edom

12"This is what the Sovereign LORD says: 'Because Edom took revenge on the house of Judah and became very guilty by doing so, 13therefore this is what the Sovereign LORD says: I will stretch out my hand against Edom and kill its men and their animals. I will lay it waste, and from Teman to Dedan they will fall by the sword. 14I will take vengeance on Edom by the hand of my people Israel, and they will deal with Edom in accordance with my anger and my wrath; they will know my vengeance, declares the Sovereign LORD.' "

論亞捫的預言

25 耶和華的話臨到我說：2 "人子啊，你要面向亞捫人說預言攻擊他們，3說：'你們當聽主耶和華的話。主耶和華如此說：我的聖所被褻瀆，以色列地變荒涼，猶大家被擄掠，那時，你便因這些事說：啊哈！4所以我必將你的地交給東方人為業，他們必在你的地上安營居住，吃你的果子，喝你的奶。5我必使拉巴為駱駝場，使亞捫人的地為羊羣躺臥之處。你們就知道我是耶和華。6主耶和華如此說：因你拍手頓足，以滿心的恨惡，向以色列地歡喜，7所以我伸手攻擊你，將你交給列國作為擄物。我必從萬民中剪除你，使你從萬國中敗亡。我必除滅你，你就知道我是耶和華。'"

論摩押的預言

8 "主耶和華如此說：'因摩押和西珥人說：看哪，猶大家與列國無異。9所以我要破開摩押邊界上的城邑，就是摩押人看為本國之榮耀的伯耶西末、巴力免、基列亭，10好使東方人來攻擊亞捫人。我必將亞捫人之地交給他們為業，使亞捫人在列國中不再被記念。11我必向摩押施行審判，他們就知道我是耶和華。'"

論以東的預言

12 "主耶和華如此說：'因為以東報仇雪恨，攻擊猶大家，向他們報仇，大大有罪。13所以主耶和華如此說：我必伸手攻擊以東，剪除人與牲畜，使以東從提幔起，人必倒在刀下，地要變為荒涼，直到底但。14我必藉我民以色列的手報復以東；以色列民必照我的怒氣，按我的忿怒在以東施報，以東人就知道是我施報。這是主耶和華說的。'"

論非利士的預言

15 "主耶和華如此說：'因非利士人向猶大人報仇，就是以恨惡的心報仇雪恨，永懷仇恨，要毀滅他們。16所以主耶和華如此說：我必伸手攻擊非利士人，剪除基利提人，滅絕沿海剩下的居民。17我向他們大施報應，發怒斥責他們。我報復他們的時候，他們就知道我是耶和華。'"

論推羅的預言

26 第十一年十一月初一日，耶和華的話臨到我說：2 "人子啊，因推羅向耶路撒冷說：'阿哈！那作眾民之門的已經破壞，向我開放；她既變為荒場，我必豐盛。' 3所以主耶和華如此說：推羅啊，我必與你為敵，使許多國民上來攻擊你，如同海使波浪湧上來一樣。4他們必破壞推羅的牆垣，拆毀她的城樓。我也要刮淨塵土，使她成為淨光的磐石。5她必在海中作曬網的地方，也必成為列國的擄物。這是主耶和華說的。6屬推羅城邑的居民（註："城邑的居民"原文作"田間的眾女"。8節同）必被刀劍殺滅，他們就知道我是耶和華。

7 "主耶和華如此說：我必使諸王之王的巴比倫王尼布甲尼撒率領馬匹、車輛、馬兵、軍隊和許多人民，從北方來攻擊你推羅。8他必用刀劍殺滅屬你城邑的居民，也必造臺、築壘、舉盾牌攻擊你。9他必安設撞城錘攻破你的牆垣，用鐵器拆毀你的城樓。10因他的馬匹眾多，塵土揚起遮蔽你。他進入你的城門，好像人進入已有破口之城。那時，你的牆垣必因騎馬的和戰車、輜重車的響聲震動。11他的馬蹄必踐踏你一切的街道，他必用刀殺戮你的居民，你堅固的柱子（註：或作"柱像"）必倒在地上。12人必以你的財寶為擄物，以你的貨財為掠物，破壞你的牆垣，拆毀你華美的房屋，將你的

A Prophecy Against Philistia

15"This is what the Sovereign LORD says: 'Because the Philistines acted in vengeance and took revenge with malice in their hearts, and with ancient hostility sought to destroy Judah, 16therefore this is what the Sovereign LORD says: I am about to stretch out my hand against the Philistines, and I will cut off the Kerethites and destroy those remaining along the coast. 17I will carry out great vengeance on them and punish them in my wrath. Then they will know that I am the LORD, when I take vengeance on them.' "

A Prophecy Against Tyre

26 In the eleventh year, on the first day of the month, the word of the LORD came to me: 2"Son of man, because Tyre has said of Jerusalem, 'Aha! The gate to the nations is broken, and its doors have swung open to me; now that she lies in ruins I will prosper,' 3therefore this is what the Sovereign LORD says: I am against you, O Tyre, and I will bring many nations against you, like the sea casting up its waves. 4They will destroy the walls of Tyre and pull down her towers; I will scrape away her rubble and make her a bare rock. 5Out in the sea she will become a place to spread fishnets, for I have spoken, declares the Sovereign LORD. She will become plunder for the nations, 6and her settlements on the mainland will be ravaged by the sword. Then they will know that I am the LORD.

7"For this is what the Sovereign LORD says: From the north I am going to bring against Tyre Nebuchadnezzar[a] king of Babylon, king of kings, with horses and chariots, with horsemen and a great army. 8He will ravage your settlements on the mainland with the sword; he will set up siege works against you, build a ramp up to your walls and raise his shields against you. 9He will direct the blows of his battering rams against your walls and demolish your towers with his weapons. 10His horses will be so many that they will cover you with dust. Your walls will tremble at the noise of the war horses, wagons and chariots when he enters your gates as men enter a city whose walls have been broken through. 11The hoofs of his horses will trample all your streets; he will kill your people with the sword, and your strong pillars will fall to the ground. 12They will plunder your wealth and loot your merchandise; they will break down your walls and demolish your fine houses and throw your stones, timber and rubble into the

a 7 Hebrew Nebuchadrezzar, of which Nebuchadnezzar is a variant; here and often in Ezekiel and Jeremiah

sea. ¹³I will put an end to your noisy songs, and the music of your harps will be heard no more. ¹⁴I will make you a bare rock, and you will become a place to spread fishnets. You will never be rebuilt, for I the LORD have spoken, declares the Sovereign LORD.

¹⁵"This is what the Sovereign LORD says to Tyre: Will not the coastlands tremble at the sound of your fall, when the wounded groan and the slaughter takes place in you? ¹⁶Then all the princes of the coast will step down from their thrones and lay aside their robes and take off their embroidered garments. Clothed with terror, they will sit on the ground, trembling every moment, appalled at you. ¹⁷Then they will take up a lament concerning you and say to you:

" 'How you are destroyed, O city of renown,
    peopled by men of the sea!
You were a power on the seas,
    you and your citizens;
you put your terror
    on all who lived there.
¹⁸Now the coastlands tremble
    on the day of your fall;
the islands in the sea
    are terrified at your collapse.'

¹⁹"This is what the Sovereign LORD says: When I make you a desolate city, like cities no longer inhabited, and when I bring the ocean depths over you and its vast waters cover you, ²⁰then I will bring you down with those who go down to the pit, to the people of long ago. I will make you dwell in the earth below, as in ancient ruins, with those who go down to the pit, and you will not return or take your place*a* in the land of the living. ²¹I will bring you to a horrible end and you will be no more. You will be sought, but you will never again be found, declares the Sovereign LORD."

A Lament for Tyre

27 The word of the LORD came to me: ²"Son of man, take up a lament concerning Tyre. ³Say to Tyre, situated at the gateway to the sea, merchant of peoples on many coasts, 'This is what the Sovereign LORD says:

" 'You say, O Tyre,
    "I am perfect in beauty."
⁴Your domain was on the high seas;
    your builders brought your beauty to
        perfection.

a 20 Septuagint; Hebrew return, and I will give glory

石頭、木頭、塵土都拋在水中。¹³我必使你唱歌的聲音止息,人也不再聽見你彈琴的聲音。¹⁴我必使你成為淨光的磐石,作曬網的地方,你不得再被建造,因為這是主耶和華說的。

¹⁵ "主耶和華對推羅如此說:在你中間行殺戮,受傷之人唉哼的時候,因你傾倒的響聲,海島豈不都震動嗎?¹⁶那時靠海的君王必都下位,除去朝服,脫下花衣,披上戰兢,坐在地上,時刻發抖,為你驚駭。¹⁷他們必為你作起哀歌說:

" '你這有名之城,
    素為航海之人居住,
    在海上為最堅固的。
平日,你和居民使一切
      住在那裏的人無不驚恐,
    現在何竟毀滅了?
¹⁸如今在你這傾覆的日子,
    海島都必戰兢;
海中的羣島見你歸於無有,
    就都驚惶。'

¹⁹ "主耶和華如此說:推羅啊,我使你變為荒涼,如無人居住的城邑,又使深水漫過你,大水淹沒你。²⁰那時,我要叫你下入陰府,與古時的人一同在地的深處久已荒涼之地居住,使你不再有居民。我也要在活人之地顯榮耀(註:"我也云云"或作"在活人之地不再有榮耀")。²¹我必叫你令人驚恐,不再存留於世。人雖尋找你,卻永尋不見。這是主耶和華說的。"

為推羅作哀歌

27 耶和華的話又臨到我說:²"人子啊,要為推羅作起哀歌,³說:'你居住海口,是眾民的商埠,你的交易通到許多的海島。主耶和華如此說:

" '推羅啊,你曾說:
    我是全然美麗的。
⁴你的境界在海中,
    造你的
      使你全然美麗。

⁵他們用示尼珥的松樹
　　做你的一切板，
　用黎巴嫩的香柏樹
　　做桅杆，
⁶用巴珊的橡樹
　　做你的槳，
　用象牙鑲嵌基提海島的黃楊木
　　為坐板（註：“坐板”或作“艙板”）。
⁷你的篷帆
　　是用埃及繡花細麻布做的，
　　可以作你的大旗；
　你的涼棚是用以利沙島的藍色、
　　紫色布做的。
⁸西頓和亞發的居民作你盪槳的；
　推羅啊，
　　你中間的智慧人作掌舵的。
⁹迦巴勒的老者和聰明人，
　　都在你中間作補縫的；
　一切泛海的船隻和水手，
　　都在你中間經營交易的事。

¹⁰ “‘波斯人、路德人、弗人
　　在你軍營中作戰士。
　他們在你中間
　　懸掛盾牌和頭盔，
　　彰顯你的尊榮。
¹¹亞發人和你的軍隊
　　都在你四圍的牆上，
　你的望樓
　　也有勇士。
　他們懸掛盾牌，
　　成全你的美麗。

¹² “‘他施人因你多有各類的財
物，就作你的客商，拿銀、鐵、
錫、鉛兌換你的貨物。
¹³ “‘雅完人、土巴人、米設人
都與你交易；他們用人口和銅器兌
換你的貨物。
¹⁴ “‘陀迦瑪族用馬和戰馬並騾
子兌換你的貨物。

¹⁵ “‘底但人與你交易；許多海
島作你的碼頭，他們拿象牙、烏木
與你兌換（註：“兌換”或作“進貢”）。
¹⁶ “‘亞蘭人因你的工作很多，
就作你的客商；他們用綠寶石、紫
色布繡貨、細麻布、珊瑚、紅寶石
兌換你的貨物。

⁵They made all your timbers
　　of pine trees from Senir[a];
　they took a cedar from Lebanon
　　to make a mast for you.
⁶Of oaks from Bashan
　　they made your oars;
　of cypress wood[b] from the coasts of Cyprus[c]
　　they made your deck, inlaid with ivory.
⁷Fine embroidered linen from Egypt was your
　　sail
　　and served as your banner;
　your awnings were of blue and purple
　　from the coasts of Elishah.
⁸Men of Sidon and Arvad were your oarsmen;
　your skilled men, O Tyre, were aboard as
　　your seamen.
⁹Veteran craftsmen of Gebal[d] were on board
　　as shipwrights to caulk your seams.
　All the ships of the sea and their sailors
　　came alongside to trade for your wares.

¹⁰" 'Men of Persia, Lydia and Put
　　served as soldiers in your army.
　They hung their shields and helmets on your
　　walls,
　　bringing you splendor.
¹¹Men of Arvad and Helech
　　manned your walls on every side;
　men of Gammad
　　were in your towers.
　They hung their shields around your walls;
　　they brought your beauty to perfection.

¹²" 'Tarshish did business with you because
of your great wealth of goods; they exchanged
silver, iron, tin and lead for your merchandise.
¹³" 'Greece, Tubal and Meshech traded with
you; they exchanged slaves and articles of
bronze for your wares.
¹⁴" 'Men of Beth Togarmah exchanged work
horses, war horses and mules for your merchandise.
¹⁵" 'The men of Rhodes[e] traded with you, and
many coastlands were your customers; they
paid you with ivory tusks and ebony.
¹⁶" 'Aram[f] did business with you because of
your many products; they exchanged turquoise,
purple fabric, embroidered work, fine linen,
coral and rubies for your merchandise.

---

a 5 That is, Hermon   *b 6* Targum; the Masoretic Text has a
different division of the consonants.   *c 6* Hebrew *Kittim*
d 9 That is, Byblos   *e 15* Septuagint; Hebrew *Dedan*
f 16 Most Hebrew manuscripts; some Hebrew manuscripts
and Syriac *Edom*

17" 'Judah and Israel traded with you; they exchanged wheat from Minnith and confections,*ᵃ* honey, oil and balm for your wares.

18" 'Damascus, because of your many products and great wealth of goods, did business with you in wine from Helbon and wool from Zahar.

19" 'Danites and Greeks from Uzal bought your merchandise; they exchanged wrought iron, cassia and calamus for your wares.

20" 'Dedan traded in saddle blankets with you.

21" 'Arabia and all the princes of Kedar were your customers; they did business with you in lambs, rams and goats.

22" 'The merchants of Sheba and Raamah traded with you; for your merchandise they exchanged the finest of all kinds of spices and precious stones, and gold.

23" 'Haran, Canneh and Eden and merchants of Sheba, Asshur and Kilmad traded with you. 24In your marketplace they traded with you beautiful garments, blue fabric, embroidered work and multicolored rugs with cords twisted and tightly knotted.

25" 'The ships of Tarshish serve
as carriers for your wares.
You are filled with heavy cargo
in the heart of the sea.
26Your oarsmen take you
out to the high seas.
But the east wind will break you to pieces
in the heart of the sea.
27Your wealth, merchandise and wares,
your mariners, seamen and shipwrights,
your merchants and all your soldiers,
and everyone else on board
will sink into the heart of the sea
on the day of your shipwreck.
28The shorelands will quake
when your seamen cry out.
29All who handle the oars
will abandon their ships;
the mariners and all the seamen
will stand on the shore.
30They will raise their voice
and cry bitterly over you;
they will sprinkle dust on their heads
and roll in ashes.
31They will shave their heads because of you
and will put on sackcloth.
They will weep over you with anguish of soul
and with bitter mourning.

---

a 17 The meaning of the Hebrew for this word is uncertain.

17 "'猶大和以色列地的人都與你交易；他們用米匿的麥子、餅、蜜、油、乳香兌換你的貨物。

18 "'大馬士革人因你的工作很多，又因你多有各類的財物，就拿黑本酒和白羊毛與你交易。

19 "'威但人和雅完人拿紡成的線、亮鐵、桂皮、菖蒲兌換你的貨物。

20 "'底但人用高貴的毯子、鞍、韂與你交易。

21 "'阿拉伯人和基達的一切首領都作你的客商，用羊羔、公綿羊、公山羊與你交易。

22 "'示巴和拉瑪的商人與你交易，他們用各類上好的香料、各類的寶石和黃金兌換你的貨物。

23 "'哈蘭人、干尼人、伊甸人、示巴的商人和亞述人、基抹人與你交易。24這些商人以美好的貨物包在繡花藍色包袱內，又有華麗的衣服裝在香柏木的箱子裏，用繩捆着與你交易。

25 "'他施的船隻接連成幫
為你運貨，
你便在海中豐富，
極其榮華。
26盪槳的已經把你
盪到大水之處，
東風在海中
將你打破。
27你的資財、物件、貨物、
水手、掌舵的、補縫的、
經營交易的，
並你中間的戰士和人民，
在你破壞的日子
必都沉在海中。
28你掌舵的呼號之聲一發，
郊野都必震動。
29凡盪槳的
和水手，
並一切泛海掌舵的，
都必下船登岸。
30他們必為你
放聲痛哭，
把塵土撒在頭上，
在灰中打滾。
31又為你使頭上光禿，
用麻布束腰，
號咷痛哭，
苦苦悲哀。

32他們哀號的時候，
　　為你作起哀歌哀哭，說：
　　有何城如推羅？
　　有何城如她在海中成為寂寞的呢？
33你由海上運出貨物，
　　就使許多國民充足；
　　你以許多資財、貨物，
　　使地上的君王豐富。
34你在深水中
　　被海浪打破的時候，
　　你的貨物和你中間的一切人民，
　　就都沉下去了。
35海島的居民
　　為你驚奇，
　　他們的君王都甚恐慌，
　　面帶愁容。
36各國民中的客商都向你發嘶聲。
　　你令人驚恐，
　　不再存留於世，直到永遠。』"

論推羅王的預言

28 耶和華的話又臨到我說：
2"人子啊，你對推羅君王
說：'主耶和華如此說：

"'因你心裏高傲，說：
　　我是神，
　　我在海中坐神之位。

你雖然居心自比神，
　　也不過是人，並不是神！
（3看哪，你比但以理更有智慧，
　　甚麼秘事都不能向你隱藏。
4你靠自己的智慧聰明
　　得了金銀財寶，
　　收入庫中。

5你靠自己的大智慧和貿易
　　增添資財，
　　又因資財
　　心裏高傲。）

6"'所以主耶和華如此說：

"'因你居心
　　自比神，
7我必使外邦人，
　　就是列國中的強暴人臨到你這裏，
　　他們必拔刀
　　砍壞你用智慧得來的美物，
　　褻瀆你的榮光。

32As they wail and mourn over you,
　　they will take up a lament concerning you:
　　"Who was ever silenced like Tyre,
　　surrounded by the sea?"
33When your merchandise went out on the seas,
　　you satisfied many nations;
　　with your great wealth and your wares
　　you enriched the kings of the earth.
34Now you are shattered by the sea
　　in the depths of the waters;
　　your wares and all your company
　　have gone down with you.
35All who live in the coastlands
　　are appalled at you;
　　their kings shudder with horror
　　and their faces are distorted with fear.
36The merchants among the nations hiss at you;
　　you have come to a horrible end
　　and will be no more.' "

A Prophecy Against the King of Tyre

28 The word of the LORD came to me:
2"Son of man, say to the ruler of Tyre,
'This is what the Sovereign LORD says:

"'In the pride of your heart
　　you say, "I am a god;
　　I sit on the throne of a god
　　in the heart of the seas."
But you are a man and not a god,
　　though you think you are as wise as a god.
3Are you wiser than Daniel[a]?
　　Is no secret hidden from you?
4By your wisdom and understanding
　　you have gained wealth for yourself
　　and amassed gold and silver
　　in your treasuries.
5By your great skill in trading
　　you have increased your wealth,
　　and because of your wealth
　　your heart has grown proud.

6" 'Therefore this is what the Sovereign LORD
says:

" 'Because you think you are wise,
　　as wise as a god,
7I am going to bring foreigners against you,
　　the most ruthless of nations;
　　they will draw their swords against your
　　　　beauty and wisdom
　　and pierce your shining splendor.

*a 3 Or Danel; the Hebrew spelling may suggest a person other
than the prophet Daniel.*

⁸They will bring you down to the pit,
　　and you will die a violent death
　　　in the heart of the seas.
⁹Will you then say, "I am a god,"
　　in the presence of those who kill you?
　You will be but a man, not a god,
　　in the hands of those who slay you.
¹⁰You will die the death of the uncircumcised
　　at the hands of foreigners.

I have spoken, declares the Sovereign LORD.' "

¹¹The word of the LORD came to me: ¹²"Son of man, take up a lament concerning the king of Tyre and say to him: 'This is what the Sovereign LORD says:

" 'You were the model of perfection,
　　full of wisdom and perfect in beauty.
¹³You were in Eden,
　　the garden of God;
　every precious stone adorned you:
　　ruby, topaz and emerald,
　　chrysolite, onyx and jasper,
　　sapphire,^a turquoise and beryl.^b
　Your settings and mountings^c were made of gold;
　　on the day you were created they were prepared.
¹⁴You were anointed as a guardian cherub,
　　for so I ordained you.
　You were on the holy mount of God;
　　you walked among the fiery stones.
¹⁵You were blameless in your ways
　　from the day you were created
　　till wickedness was found in you.
¹⁶Through your widespread trade
　　you were filled with violence,
　　and you sinned.
　So I drove you in disgrace from the mount of God,
　　and I expelled you, O guardian cherub,
　　from among the fiery stones.
¹⁷Your heart became proud
　　on account of your beauty,
　and you corrupted your wisdom
　　because of your splendor.
　So I threw you to the earth;
　　I made a spectacle of you before kings.
¹⁸By your many sins and dishonest trade
　　you have desecrated your sanctuaries.

⁸他們必使你下坑，
　　你必死在海中，
　　　與被殺的人一樣。
⁹在殺你的人面前
　　你還能說「我是神」嗎？
　其實你在殺害你的人手中，
　　不過是人，並不是神。
¹⁰你必死在外邦人手中，
　　與未受割禮（註：或作"不潔"。下同）
　　　的人一樣，
因為這是主耶和華說的。'"

¹¹耶和華的話臨到我說：¹²"人子啊，你為推羅王作起哀歌說：'主耶和華如此說：

" '你無所不備，
　　智慧充足，全然美麗。
¹³你曾在伊甸
　　神的園中，
　佩戴各樣寶石，
　　就是紅寶石、紅璧璽、金鋼石、
　　水蒼玉、紅瑪瑙、碧玉、
　　藍寶石、綠寶石、紅玉和黃金，
　又有精美的鼓笛
　　在你那裏，
　都是在你受造之日
　　預備齊全的。
¹⁴你是那受膏
　　遮掩約櫃的基路伯，
　我將你安置在神的聖山上，
　　你在發光如火的寶石中間往來。
¹⁵你從受造之日所行的都完全，
　　後來在你中間又察出不義。
¹⁶因你貿易很多，
　　就被強暴的事充滿，
　　以致犯罪，
　所以我因你褻瀆聖地，
　　就從神的山驅逐你。
　遮掩約櫃的基路伯啊，
　　我已將你從發光如火的寶石中除滅。
¹⁷你因美麗心中高傲，
　　又因榮光敗壞智慧，
　我已將你摔倒在地，
　　使你倒在君王面前，
　　好叫他們目睹眼見。
¹⁸你因罪孽眾多，貿易不公，
　　就褻瀆你那裏的聖所。

a 13 Or *lapis lazuli*　　*b 13* The precise identification of some of these precious stones is uncertain.　　*c 13* The meaning of the Hebrew for this phrase is uncertain.

故此，我使火從你中間發出
　燒滅你，
使你在所有觀看的人眼前
　變為地上的爐灰。
¹⁹各國民中，
　凡認識你的都必為你驚奇。
你令人驚恐，
　不再存留於世，直到永遠。’”

So I made a fire come out from you,
　and it consumed you,
and I reduced you to ashes on the ground
　in the sight of all who were watching.
¹⁹All the nations who knew you
　are appalled at you;
you have come to a horrible end
　and will be no more.’ ”

論西頓的預言

²⁰耶和華的話臨到我說：²¹ “人子啊，你要向西頓預言攻擊她，²²說‘主耶和華如此說：

A Prophecy Against Sidon

²⁰The word of the LORD came to me: ²¹“Son of man, set your face against Sidon; prophesy against her ²²and say: ‘This is what the Sovereign LORD says:

“ ‘西頓哪，我與你為敵，
　我必在你中間得榮耀。
我在你中間施行審判、
　顯為聖的時候，
　人就知道我是耶和華。
²³我必使瘟疫進入西頓，
　使血流在她街上。
被殺的必在其中仆倒，
　四圍有刀劍臨到她，
　人就知道我是耶和華。

“ ‘I am against you, O Sidon,
　and I will gain glory within you.
They will know that I am the LORD,
　when I inflict punishment on her
　and show myself holy within her.
²³I will send a plague upon her
　and make blood flow in her streets.
The slain will fall within her,
　with the sword against her on every side.
Then they will know that I am the LORD.

²⁴ “ ‘四圍恨惡以色列家的人，必不再向他們作刺人的荊棘，傷人的蒺藜，人就知道我是主耶和華。

²⁴“ ‘No longer will the people of Israel have malicious neighbors who are painful briers and sharp thorns. Then they will know that I am the Sovereign LORD.

²⁵ “ ‘主耶和華如此說：我將分散在萬民中的以色列家招聚回來，向他們在列邦人眼前顯為聖的時候，他們就在我賜給我僕人雅各之地仍然居住。²⁶他們要在這地上安然居住。我向四圍恨惡他們的眾人施行審判以後，他們要蓋造房屋，栽種葡萄園，安然居住，就知道我是耶和華他們的神。’”

²⁵“ ‘This is what the Sovereign LORD says: When I gather the people of Israel from the nations where they have been scattered, I will show myself holy among them in the sight of the nations. Then they will live in their own land, which I gave to my servant Jacob. ²⁶They will live there in safety and will build houses and plant vineyards; they will live in safety when I inflict punishment on all their neighbors who maligned them. Then they will know that I am the LORD their God.’ ”

論埃及的預言

29 第十年十月十二日，耶和華的話臨到我說：² “人子啊，你要向埃及王法老預言攻擊他和埃及全地，³說：‘主耶和華如此說：

A Prophecy Against Egypt

29 In the tenth year, in the tenth month on the twelfth day, the word of the LORD came to me: ²“Son of man, set your face against Pharaoh king of Egypt and prophesy against him and against all Egypt. ³Speak to him and say: ‘This is what the Sovereign LORD says:

“ ‘埃及王法老啊，
　我與你這臥在自己河中的大魚
　　為敵。
你曾說：這河是我的，
　是我為自己造的。

“ ‘I am against you, Pharaoh king of Egypt,
　you great monster lying among your
　　streams.
You say, “The Nile is mine;
　I made it for myself.”

⁴But I will put hooks in your jaws
　　and make the fish of your streams stick to
　　　your scales.
　I will pull you out from among your streams,
　　with all the fish sticking to your scales.
⁵I will leave you in the desert,
　　you and all the fish of your streams.
　You will fall on the open field
　　and not be gathered or picked up.
　I will give you as food
　　to the beasts of the earth and the birds of the
　　　air.

⁶Then all who live in Egypt will know that I am
the LORD.

" 'You have been a staff of reed for the house
of Israel. ⁷When they grasped you with their
hands, you splintered and you tore open their
shoulders; when they leaned on you, you broke
and their backs were wrenched.ᵃ

⁸" 'Therefore this is what the Sovereign LORD
says: I will bring a sword against you and kill
your men and their animals. ⁹Egypt will become
a desolate wasteland. Then they will know that I
am the LORD.

" 'Because you said, "The Nile is mine; I made
it," ¹⁰therefore I am against you and against
your streams, and I will make the land of Egypt
a ruin and a desolate waste from Migdol to
Aswan, as far as the border of Cush.ᵇ ¹¹No foot
of man or animal will pass through it; no one
will live there for forty years. ¹²I will make the
land of Egypt desolate among devastated lands,
and her cities will lie desolate forty years among
ruined cities. And I will disperse the Egyptians
among the nations and scatter them through the
countries.

¹³" 'Yet this is what the Sovereign LORD says:
At the end of forty years I will gather the Egyptians from the nations where they were scattered. ¹⁴I will bring them back from captivity
and return them to Upper Egypt,ᶜ the land of
their ancestry. There they will be a lowly kingdom. ¹⁵It will be the lowliest of kingdoms and
will never again exalt itself above the other
nations. I will make it so weak that it will never
again rule over the nations. ¹⁶Egypt will no
longer be a source of confidence for the people
of Israel but will be a reminder of their sin in
turning to her for help. Then they will know
that I am the Sovereign LORD.' "

⁴我耶和華必用鈎子鈎住你的腮頰，
　　又使江河中的魚
　　　貼住你的鱗甲；
　我必將你和所有貼住你鱗甲的魚，
　　從江河中拉上來，
⁵把你並江河中的魚
　　都拋在曠野；
　你必倒在田間，
　　不被收殮，不被掩埋。
　我已將你給地上野獸、
　　空中飛鳥作食物。

⁶ " '埃及一切的居民，因向以
色列家成了蘆葦的杖，就知道我是耶
和華。

⁷ " '他們用手持住你，你就斷
折，傷了他們的肩；他們倚靠你，你
就斷折，閃了他們的腰。

⁸ " '所以主耶和華如此説：我
必使刀劍臨到你，從你中間將人與牲
畜剪除。⁹埃及地必荒廢淒涼，他們
就知道我是耶和華。

" '因為法老説：這河是我的，
是我所造的。¹⁰所以我必與你並你的
江河為敵，使埃及地從色弗尼塔直到
古實境界，全然荒廢淒涼。¹¹人的
腳，獸的蹄，都不經過，四十年之久
並無人居住。¹²我必使埃及地在荒涼
的國中成為荒涼，使埃及城在荒廢的
城中變成荒廢，共有四十年。我必將
埃及人分散在列國，四散在列邦。

¹³ " '主耶和華如此説：滿了四
十年，我必招聚分散在各國民中的埃
及人。¹⁴我必叫埃及被擄的人回來，
使他們歸回本地巴忒羅。在那裏也不成
為低微的國，¹⁵必為列國中最低微
的，也不再自高於列國之上。我必減
少他們，以致不再轄制列國。¹⁶埃及
必不再作以色列家所倚靠的；以色列
家仰望埃及人的時候，便思念罪孽，
他們就知道我是主耶和華。' "

a 7 Syriac (see also Septuagint and Vulgate); Hebrew and you
caused their backs to stand　　b 10 That is, the upper Nile region
c 14 Hebrew to Pathros

17二十七年正月初一日，耶和華的話臨到我說：18「人子啊，巴比倫王尼布甲尼撒使他的軍兵大大效勞，攻打推羅，以致頭都光禿，肩都磨破；然而他和他的軍兵攻打推羅，並沒有從那裏得甚麼酬勞。19所以主耶和華如此說：我必將埃及地賜給巴比倫王尼布甲尼撒。他必擄掠埃及羣眾，搶其中的財為擄物，奪其中的貨為掠物，這就可以作他軍兵的酬勞。20我將埃及地賜給他，酬他所效的勞，因王與軍兵是為我勤勞。這是主耶和華說的。

21「當那日，我必使以色列家的角發生，又必使你以西結在他們中間得以開口，他們就知道我是耶和華。」

為埃及作哀歌

30 耶和華的話又臨到我說：2「人子啊，你要發預言說：
『主耶和華如此說：

" 『哀哉這日！
　你們應當哭號。
3因為耶和華的日子臨近，
　就是密雲之日，
　列國受罰之期。

4必有刀劍臨到埃及，
　在埃及被殺之人仆倒的時候，
　古實人就有痛苦，
　人民必被擄掠，
　基址必被拆毀。

5古實人、弗人（註：又作「利比亞人」）、路德人、雜族的人民，並古巴人，以及同盟之地的人，都要與埃及人一同倒在刀下。
6 " 『耶和華如此說：

" 『扶助埃及的也必傾倒，
　埃及因勢力而有的驕傲必降低微，
　其中的人民從色弗尼塔起（註：見29章10節）必倒在刀下。
　　　　這是主耶和華說的。
7 " 『埃及地在荒涼的國中
　必成為荒涼；
　埃及城在荒廢的城中
　也變為荒廢。
8我在埃及中使火着起，
　幫助埃及的，都被滅絕，
　那時，他們就知道我是耶和華。

17In the twenty-seventh year, in the first month on the first day, the word of the LORD came to me: 18"Son of man, Nebuchadnezzar king of Babylon drove his army in a hard campaign against Tyre; every head was rubbed bare and every shoulder made raw. Yet he and his army got no reward from the campaign he led against Tyre. 19Therefore this is what the Sovereign LORD says: I am going to give Egypt to Nebuchadnezzar king of Babylon, and he will carry off its wealth. He will loot and plunder the land as pay for his army. 20I have given him Egypt as a reward for his efforts because he and his army did it for me, declares the Sovereign LORD. 21"On that day I will make a horn[a] grow for the house of Israel, and I will open your mouth among them. Then they will know that I am the LORD."

A Lament for Egypt

30 The word of the LORD came to me: 2"Son of man, prophesy and say: 'This is what the Sovereign LORD says:

" 'Wail and say,
　"Alas for that day!"
3For the day is near,
　the day of the LORD is near—
a day of clouds,
　a time of doom for the nations.
4A sword will come against Egypt,
　and anguish will come upon Cush.[b]
When the slain fall in Egypt,
　her wealth will be carried away
　and her foundations torn down.

5Cush and Put, Lydia and all Arabia, Libya[c] and the people of the covenant land will fall by the sword along with Egypt.

6" 'This is what the LORD says:

" 'The allies of Egypt will fall
　and her proud strength will fail.
From Migdol to Aswan
　they will fall by the sword within her,
　　　　declares the Sovereign LORD.
7" 'They will be desolate
　among desolate lands,
　and their cities will lie
　among ruined cities.
8Then they will know that I am the LORD,
　when I set fire to Egypt
　and all her helpers are crushed.

a 21 Horn here symbolizes strength.　　*b 4* That is, the upper Nile region; also in verses 5 and 9　　*c 5* Hebrew *Cub*

9" 'On that day messengers will go out from me in ships to frighten Cush out of her complacency. Anguish will take hold of them on the day of Egypt's doom, for it is sure to come.

10" 'This is what the Sovereign LORD says:

" 'I will put an end to the hordes of Egypt
　by the hand of Nebuchadnezzar king of
　　Babylon.
11He and his army—the most ruthless of
　　nations—
　will be brought in to destroy the land.
　They will draw their swords against Egypt
　and fill the land with the slain.
12I will dry up the streams of the Nile
　and sell the land to evil men;
　by the hand of foreigners
　I will lay waste the land and everything in it.

I the LORD have spoken.

13" 'This is what the Sovereign LORD says:

" 'I will destroy the idols
　and put an end to the images in Memphis.[a]
　No longer will there be a prince in Egypt,
　and I will spread fear throughout the land.
14I will lay waste Upper Egypt,[b]
　set fire to Zoan
　and inflict punishment on Thebes.[c]
15I will pour out my wrath on Pelusium,[d]
　the stronghold of Egypt,
　and cut off the hordes of Thebes.
16I will set fire to Egypt;
　Pelusium will writhe in agony.
　Thebes will be taken by storm;
　Memphis will be in constant distress.
17The young men of Heliopolis[e] and Bubastis[f]
　will fall by the sword,
　and the cities themselves will go into captivity.
18Dark will be the day at Tahpanhes
　when I break the yoke of Egypt;
　there her proud strength will come to an
　　end.
　She will be covered with clouds,
　and her villages will go into captivity.
19So I will inflict punishment on Egypt,
　and they will know that I am the LORD.' "

9 " '到那日，必有使者坐船從我面前出去，使安逸無慮的古實人驚懼；必有痛苦臨到他們，好像埃及遭災的日子一樣。看哪，這事臨近了。

10 " '主耶和華如此說：

" '我必藉巴比倫王
　尼布甲尼撒的手，
　除滅埃及眾人。
11他和隨從他的人，
　就是列國中強暴的，
　必進來毀滅這地。
　他們必拔刀攻擊埃及，
　使遍地有被殺的人。
12我必使江河乾涸，
　將地賣在惡人的手中，
　我必藉外邦人的手，
　使這地和其中所有的變為淒涼。

這是我耶和華說的。

13 " '主耶和華如此說：

" '我必毀滅偶像，
　從挪弗除滅神像，
　必不再有君王出自埃及地，
　我要使埃及地的人懼怕。
14我必使巴忒羅荒涼，
　在瑣安中使火著起，
　向挪施行審判。
15我必將我的忿怒
　倒在埃及的保障上，
　就是訓上，並要剪除挪的眾人。
16我必在埃及中使火著起，
　訓必大大痛苦，挪必被攻破，
　挪弗白日見仇敵（註："白日" 或作
　　"終日"）。
17亞文和比伯實的少年人
　必倒在刀下。
　這些城的人必被擄掠。
18我在答比匿折斷埃及的諸軛，
　使他因勢力而有的驕傲
　　在其中止息。
　那時，日光必退去。
　至於這城，必有密雲遮蔽，
　其中的女子必被擄掠。
19我必這樣向埃及施行審判，
　他們就知道我是耶和華。' "

---

a 13 Hebrew Noph; also in verse 16　　b 14 Hebrew waste
Pathros　　c 14 Hebrew No; also in verses 15 and 16
d 15 Hebrew Sin; also in verse 16　　e 17 Hebrew Awen (or On)
f 17 Hebrew Pi Beseth

²⁰十一年正月初七日，耶和華的話臨到我說：²¹「人子啊，我已打折<u>埃及</u>王法老的膀臂，沒有敷藥，也沒有用布纏好，使他有力持刀。²²所以主耶和華如此說：看哪，我與<u>埃及</u>王法老為敵，必將他有力的膀臂和已打折的膀臂全行打斷，使刀從他手中墜落。²³我必將<u>埃及</u>人分散在列國，四散在列邦。²⁴我必使<u>巴比倫</u>王的膀臂有力，將我的刀交在他手中；卻要打斷法老的膀臂，他就在<u>巴比倫</u>王面前唉哼，如同受死傷的人一樣。²⁵我必扶持<u>巴比倫</u>王的膀臂，法老的膀臂卻要下垂；我將我的刀交在<u>巴比倫</u>王手中，他必舉刀攻擊<u>埃及</u>地。他們就知道我是耶和華。²⁶我必將<u>埃及</u>人分散在列國，四散在列邦。他們就知道我是耶和華。」

黎巴嫩的香柏樹

31 十一年三月初一日，耶和華的話臨到我說：²「人子啊，你要向<u>埃及</u>王法老和他的眾人說：

「『在威勢上誰能與你相比呢？
³<u>亞述</u>王曾如<u>黎巴嫩</u>中的香柏樹，
　　枝條榮美，
　　影密如林，
　極其高大，
　　樹尖插入雲中。
⁴眾水使它生長，
　　深水使它長大。
　所栽之地
　　有江河圍流，
　汊出的水道
　　延到田野諸樹。
⁵所以它高大
　　超過田野諸樹；
　發旺的時候
　　枝子繁多，
　　因得大水之力枝條長長。
⁶空中的飛鳥
　　都在枝子上搭窩；
　田野的走獸
　　都在枝條下生子；
　所有大國的人民
　　都在它蔭下居住。
⁷樹大條長，
　　成為榮美，

²⁰In the eleventh year, in the first month on the seventh day, the word of the LORD came to me: ²¹"Son of man, I have broken the arm of Pharaoh king of Egypt. It has not been bound up for healing or put in a splint so as to become strong enough to hold a sword. ²²Therefore this is what the Sovereign LORD says: I am against Pharaoh king of Egypt. I will break both his arms, the good arm as well as the broken one, and make the sword fall from his hand. ²³I will disperse the Egyptians among the nations and scatter them through the countries. ²⁴I will strengthen the arms of the king of Babylon and put my sword in his hand, but I will break the arms of Pharaoh, and he will groan before him like a mortally wounded man. ²⁵I will strengthen the arms of the king of Babylon, but the arms of Pharaoh will fall limp. Then they will know that I am the LORD, when I put my sword into the hand of the king of Babylon and he brandishes it against Egypt. ²⁶I will disperse the Egyptians among the nations and scatter them through the countries. Then they will know that I am the LORD."

A Cedar in Lebanon

31 In the eleventh year, in the third month on the first day, the word of the LORD came to me: ²"Son of man, say to Pharaoh king of Egypt and to his hordes:

" 'Who can be compared with you in majesty?
³Consider Assyria, once a cedar in Lebanon,
　　with beautiful branches overshadowing the forest;
　it towered on high,
　　its top above the thick foliage.
⁴The waters nourished it,
　　deep springs made it grow tall;
　their streams flowed
　　all around its base
　and sent their channels
　　to all the trees of the field.
⁵So it towered higher
　　than all the trees of the field;
　its boughs increased
　　and its branches grew long,
　　spreading because of abundant waters.
⁶All the birds of the air
　　nested in its boughs,
　all the beasts of the field
　　gave birth under its branches;
　all the great nations
　　lived in its shade.
⁷It was majestic in beauty,
　　with its spreading boughs,

for its roots went down
  to abundant waters.
⁸The cedars in the garden of God
  could not rival it,
  nor could the pine trees
    equal its boughs,
  nor could the plane trees
    compare with its branches—
  no tree in the garden of God
    could match its beauty.
⁹I made it beautiful
  with abundant branches,
the envy of all the trees of Eden
  in the garden of God.

10" 'Therefore this is what the Sovereign LORD says: Because it towered on high, lifting its top above the thick foliage, and because it was proud of its height, ¹¹I handed it over to the ruler of the nations, for him to deal with according to its wickedness. I cast it aside, ¹²and the most ruthless of foreign nations cut it down and left it. Its boughs fell on the mountains and in all the valleys; its branches lay broken in all the ravines of the land. All the nations of the earth came out from under its shade and left it. ¹³All the birds of the air settled on the fallen tree, and all the beasts of the field were among its branches. ¹⁴Therefore no other trees by the waters are ever to tower proudly on high, lifting their tops above the thick foliage. No other trees so well-watered are ever to reach such a height; they are all destined for death, for the earth below, among mortal men, with those who go down to the pit.

15" 'This is what the Sovereign LORD says: On the day it was brought down to the grave*ᵃ* I covered the deep springs with mourning for it; I held back its streams, and its abundant waters were restrained. Because of it I clothed Lebanon with gloom, and all the trees of the field withered away. ¹⁶I made the nations tremble at the sound of its fall when I brought it down to the grave with those who go down to the pit. Then all the trees of Eden, the choicest and best of Lebanon, all the trees that were well-watered, were consoled in the earth below. ¹⁷Those who lived in its shade, its allies among the nations, had also gone down to the grave with it, joining those killed by the sword.

18" 'Which of the trees of Eden can be compared with you in splendor and majesty? Yet you, too, will be brought down with the trees of Eden to the earth below; you will lie among the uncircumcised, with those killed by the sword.

因為根在眾水之旁。

⁸神園中的香柏樹
  不能遮蔽它。
松樹
  不及它的枝子，
楓樹
  不及它的枝條，
神園中的樹
  都沒有它榮美。
⁹我使它的枝條蕃多，
  成為榮美，
以致神伊甸園中的樹
  都嫉妒它。

10 " '所以主耶和華如此說：因它高大，樹尖插入雲中，心驕氣傲，¹¹我就必將它交給列國中大有威勢的人。他必定辦它，我因它的罪惡，已經驅逐它。¹²外邦人，就是列邦中強暴的，將它砍斷棄掉。它的枝條落在山間和一切谷中；它的枝子折斷，落在地的一切河旁。地上的眾民已經走去，離開它的蔭下。¹³空中的飛鳥都要宿在這敗落的樹上；田野的走獸都要臥在它的枝條下。¹⁴好使水旁的諸樹不因高大而自尊，也不將樹尖插入雲中，並且那些得水滋潤有勢力的也不得高大自立。因為它們在世人中和下坑的人都被交與死亡，到陰府去了。

15 " '主耶和華如此說：它下陰間的那日，我便使人悲哀。我為它遮蓋深淵，使江河凝結，大水停流；我也使黎巴嫩為它悽慘，田野的諸樹都因它發昏。¹⁶我將它扔到陰間，與下坑的人一同下去。那時，列國聽見它墜落的響聲就都震動，並且伊甸的一切樹，就是黎巴嫩得水滋潤最佳最美的樹，都在陰府受了安慰。¹⁷它們也與它同下陰間，到被殺的人那裏。它們曾作它的膀臂，在列國中它的蔭下居住。

18 " '在這樣榮耀威勢上，在伊甸園諸樹中，誰能與你相比呢？然而你要與伊甸的諸樹一同下到陰府，在未受割禮的人中與被殺的人一同躺臥。

　　　"'法老和他的羣眾乃是如此。這是主耶和華說的。'"

為法老作哀歌

32 十二年十二月初一日，耶和華的話臨到我說：²"人子啊，你要為埃及王法老作哀歌，說：

"'從前你在列國中如同少壯獅子，
　現在你卻像海中的大魚。
你衝出江河，
　用爪攪動諸水，
　使江河渾濁。

³"'主耶和華如此說：

"'我必用多國的人民，
　將我的網撒在你身上，
　把你拉上來。
⁴我必將你丟在地上，
　拋在田野。
使空中的飛鳥都落在你身上，
　使遍地的野獸
　吃你得飽。
⁵我必將你的肉丟在山間，
　用你高大的屍首填滿山谷。
⁶我又必用你的血
　澆灌你所游泳之地，
　漫過山頂，河道都必充滿。
⁷我將你撲滅的時候，要把天遮蔽，
　使眾星昏暗，
以密雲遮掩太陽，
　月亮也不放光。
⁸我必使天上的亮光都在你以上
　變為昏暗，
　使你的地上黑暗。
　　　　　　　這是主耶和華說的。
⁹我使你敗亡的風聲
　傳到你所不認識的各國，
那時，
　我必使多民的心因你愁煩。
¹⁰我在許多國民和君王面前
　向你掄我的刀，
國民就必因你驚奇，
　君王也必因你
　極其恐慌。
在你仆倒的日子，
　他們各人為自己的性命
　時刻戰兢。

"'This is Pharaoh and all his hordes, declares the Sovereign LORD.'"

A Lament for Pharaoh

32 In the twelfth year, in the twelfth month on the first day, the word of the LORD came to me: ²"Son of man, take up a lament concerning Pharaoh king of Egypt and say to him:

"'You are like a lion among the nations;
　you are like a monster in the seas
thrashing about in your streams,
　churning the water with your feet
　and muddying the streams.

³"'This is what the Sovereign LORD says:

"'With a great throng of people
　I will cast my net over you,
　and they will haul you up in my net.
⁴I will throw you on the land
　and hurl you on the open field.
I will let all the birds of the air settle on you
　and all the beasts of the earth gorge
　　themselves on you.
⁵I will spread your flesh on the mountains
　and fill the valleys with your remains.
⁶I will drench the land with your flowing blood
　all the way to the mountains,
　and the ravines will be filled with your flesh.
⁷When I snuff you out, I will cover the heavens
　and darken their stars;
I will cover the sun with a cloud,
　and the moon will not give its light.
⁸All the shining lights in the heavens
　I will darken over you;
I will bring darkness over your land,
　　　　declares the Sovereign LORD.
⁹I will trouble the hearts of many peoples
　when I bring about your destruction among
　　the nations,
　among*a* lands you have not known.
¹⁰I will cause many peoples to be appalled at
　　you,
　and their kings will shudder with horror
　　because of you
when I brandish my sword before them.
On the day of your downfall
　each of them will tremble
　every moment for his life.

a 9 Hebrew; Septuagint bring you into captivity among the nations, / to

¹¹" 'For this is what the Sovereign LORD says:

" 'The sword of the king of Babylon
will come against you.
¹²I will cause your hordes to fall
by the swords of mighty men—
the most ruthless of all nations.
They will shatter the pride of Egypt,
and all her hordes will be overthrown.
¹³I will destroy all her cattle
from beside abundant waters
no longer to be stirred by the foot of man
or muddied by the hoofs of cattle.
¹⁴Then I will let her waters settle
and make her streams flow like oil,
                    declares the Sovereign LORD.
¹⁵When I make Egypt desolate
and strip the land of everything in it,
when I strike down all who live there,
then they will know that I am the LORD.'

¹⁶"This is the lament they will chant for her.
The daughters of the nations will chant it; for
Egypt and all her hordes they will chant it,
declares the Sovereign LORD."

¹⁷In the twelfth year, on the fifteenth day of
the month, the word of the LORD came to me:
¹⁸"Son of man, wail for the hordes of Egypt and
consign to the earth below both her and the
daughters of mighty nations, with those who go
down to the pit. ¹⁹Say to them, 'Are you more
favored than others? Go down and be laid
among the uncircumcised.' ²⁰They will fall
among those killed by the sword. The sword is
drawn; let her be dragged off with all her hordes.
²¹From within the grave^a the mighty leaders will
say of Egypt and her allies, 'They have come
down and they lie with the uncircumcised, with
those killed by the sword.'
²²"Assyria is there with her whole army; she
is surrounded by the graves of all her slain, all
who have fallen by the sword. ²³Their graves are
in the depths of the pit and her army lies around
her grave. All who had spread terror in the land
of the living are slain, fallen by the sword.
²⁴"Elam is there, with all her hordes around
her grave. All of them are slain, fallen by the
sword. All who had spread terror in the land of
the living went down uncircumcised to the
earth below. They bear their shame with those
who go down to the pit. ²⁵A bed is made for her
among the slain, with all her hordes around her
grave. All of them are uncircumcised, killed by

¹¹ " '主耶和華如此説：

" '巴比倫王的刀
必臨到你。
¹²我必藉勇士的刀
使你的眾民仆倒；
這勇士都是列國中強暴的。
他們必使埃及的驕傲歸於無有，
埃及的眾民必被滅絕。
¹³我必從埃及多水旁
除滅所有的走獸，
人腳獸蹄
必不再攪渾這水。
¹⁴那時，我必使埃及河澄清，
江河像油緩流。
              這是主耶和華説的。
¹⁵我使埃及地變為荒廢淒涼，
這地缺少從前所充滿的，
又擊殺其中一切的居民。
那時，他們就知道我是耶和華。'

¹⁶ "人必用這哀歌去哀哭，列國
的女子為埃及和她的羣眾，也必以此
悲哀。這是主耶和華説的。"

¹⁷十二年十二月十五日，耶和華
的話臨到我説：¹⁸ "人子啊，你要為
埃及羣眾哀號，又要將埃及和有名之
國的女子，並其坑的人一同扔到陰府
去。¹⁹你埃及的美麗勝過誰呢？你下
去與未受割禮的人一同躺臥吧！²⁰他
們必在被殺的人中仆倒。她被交給刀
劍，要把她和她的羣眾拉去。²¹強盛
的勇士，要在陰間對埃及王和幫助他
的説話：'他們是未受割禮被殺的
人，已經下去，躺臥不動。'

²² "亞述和她的眾民都在那裏，
她民的墳墓在她四圍，他們都是被殺
倒在刀下的。²³他們的墳墓在坑中極
深之處，她的眾民在她墳墓的四圍，
都是被殺倒在刀下的，他們曾在活人
之地使人驚恐。

²⁴ "以攔也在那裏。她的羣眾在
她墳墓的四圍，都是被殺倒在刀下，
未受割禮而下陰府的，他們曾在活人
之地使人驚恐，並且與下坑的人一同
擔當羞辱。²⁵人給她和她的羣眾在被
殺的人中設立牀榻。她民的墳墓在她

^a 21 Hebrew Sheol; also in verse 27

四圍，他們都是未受割禮被刀殺的，他們曾在活人之地使人驚恐，並且與下坑的人一同擔當羞辱。以攔已經放在被殺的人中。

26 "米設、土巴和他們的羣眾都在那裏。她民的墳墓在她四圍，他們都是未受割禮被刀殺的；他們曾在活人之地人人驚恐。27 他們不得與那未受割禮仆倒的勇士一同躺臥。這些勇士帶着兵器下陰間，頭枕刀劍，骨頭上有本身的罪孽；他們曾在活人之地使勇士驚恐。

28 "法老啊，你必在未受割禮的人中敗壞，與那些被殺的人一同躺臥。

29 "以東也在那裏。她君王和一切首領雖然仗着勢力，還是放在被殺的人中。他們必與未受割禮的和下坑的人一同躺臥。

30 "在那裏，有北方的眾王子和一切西頓人都與被殺的人下去。他們雖然仗着勢力使人驚恐，還是蒙羞。他們未受割禮和被刀殺的一同躺臥，與下坑的人一同擔當羞辱。

31 "法老看見他們，便為他被殺的軍隊受安慰。這是主耶和華說的。32 我任憑法老在活人之地使人驚恐，法老和他的羣眾必放在未受割禮和被殺的人中。這是主耶和華說的。"

以西結作守望者

33 耶和華的話臨到我說：2 "人子啊，你要告訴本國的子民說：'我使刀劍臨到哪一國，那一國的民從他們中間選立一人為守望的，3 他見刀劍臨到那地，若吹角警戒眾民，4 凡聽見角聲不受警戒的，刀劍若來除滅了他，他的罪就必歸到自己的頭上（註："罪"原文作"血"）。5 他聽見角聲，不受警戒，他的罪必歸到自己的身上；他若受警戒，便是救了自己的性命。6 倘若守望的人見刀劍臨到，不吹角，以致民不受警戒，刀劍來殺了他們中間的一個人；他雖然死在罪孽之中，我卻要

the sword. Because their terror had spread in the land of the living, they bear their shame with those who go down to the pit; they are laid among the slain.

26 "Meshech and Tubal are there, with all their hordes around their graves. All of them are uncircumcised, killed by the sword because they spread their terror in the land of the living. 27 Do they not lie with the other uncircumcised warriors who have fallen, who went down to the grave with their weapons of war, whose swords were placed under their heads? The punishment for their sins rested on their bones, though the terror of these warriors had stalked through the land of the living.

28 "You too, O Pharaoh, will be broken and will lie among the uncircumcised, with those killed by the sword.

29 "Edom is there, her kings and all her princes; despite their power, they are laid with those killed by the sword. They lie with the uncircumcised, with those who go down to the pit.

30 "All the princes of the north and all the Sidonians are there; they went down with the slain in disgrace despite the terror caused by their power. They lie uncircumcised with those killed by the sword and bear their shame with those who go down to the pit.

31 "Pharaoh—he and all his army—will see them and he will be consoled for all his hordes that were killed by the sword, declares the Sovereign LORD. 32 Although I had him spread terror in the land of the living, Pharaoh and all his hordes will be laid among the uncircumcised, with those killed by the sword, declares the Sovereign LORD."

Ezekiel a Watchman

33 The word of the LORD came to me: 2 "Son of man, speak to your countrymen and say to them: 'When I bring the sword against a land, and the people of the land choose one of their men and make him their watchman, 3 and he sees the sword coming against the land and blows the trumpet to warn the people, 4 then if anyone hears the trumpet but does not take warning and the sword comes and takes his life, his blood will be on his own head. 5 Since he heard the sound of the trumpet but did not take warning, his blood will be on his own head. If he had taken warning, he would have saved himself. 6 But if the watchman sees the sword coming and does not blow the trumpet to warn the people and the sword comes and takes the life of one of them, that man will be taken away because of his sin, but I will hold the watchman accountable for his blood.'

7"Son of man, I have made you a watchman for the house of Israel; so hear the word I speak and give them warning from me. 8When I say to the wicked, 'O wicked man, you will surely die,' and you do not speak out to dissuade him from his ways, that wicked man will die for*a* his sin, and I will hold you accountable for his blood. 9But if you do warn the wicked man to turn from his ways and he does not do so, he will die for his sin, but you will have saved yourself.

10"Son of man, say to the house of Israel, 'This is what you are saying: "Our offenses and sins weigh us down, and we are wasting away because of*b* them. How then can we live?" ' 11Say to them, 'As surely as I live, declares the Sovereign LORD, I take no pleasure in the death of the wicked, but rather that they turn from their ways and live. Turn! Turn from your evil ways! Why will you die, O house of Israel?'

12"Therefore, son of man, say to your countrymen, 'The righteousness of the righteous man will not save him when he disobeys, and the wickedness of the wicked man will not cause him to fall when he turns from it. The righteous man, if he sins, will not be allowed to live because of his former righteousness.' 13If I tell the righteous man that he will surely live, but then he trusts in his righteousness and does evil, none of the righteous things he has done will be remembered; he will die for the evil he has done. 14And if I say to the wicked man, 'You will surely die,' but he then turns away from his sin and does what is just and right— 15if he gives back what he took in pledge for a loan, returns what he has stolen, follows the decrees that give life, and does no evil, he will surely live; he will not die. 16None of the sins he has committed will be remembered against him. He has done what is just and right; he will surely live.

17"Yet your countrymen say, 'The way of the Lord is not just.' But it is their way that is not just. 18If a righteous man turns from his righteousness and does evil, he will die for it. 19And if a wicked man turns away from his wickedness and does what is just and right, he will live by doing so. 20Yet, O house of Israel, you say, 'The way of the Lord is not just.' But I will judge each of you according to his own ways."

Jerusalem's Fall Explained

21In the twelfth year of our exile, in the tenth month on the fifth day, a man who had escaped

向守望的人討他喪命的罪（註："罪"原文作"血"）。'

7"人子啊，我照樣立你作以色列家守望的人。所以你要聽我口中的話，替我警戒他們。 8我對惡人說：'惡人哪，你必要死！'你以西結若不開口警戒惡人，使他離開所行的道，這惡人必死在罪孽之中，我卻要向你討他喪命的罪（註："罪"原文作"血"）； 9倘若你警戒惡人轉離所行的道，他仍不轉離，他必死在罪孽之中，你卻救自己脫離了罪。

10"人子啊，你要對以色列家說：'你們常說：我們的過犯罪惡在我們身上，我們必因此消滅，怎能存活呢？' 11你對他們說：'主耶和華說：我指着我的永生起誓，我斷不喜悅惡人死亡，惟喜悅惡人轉離所行的道而活。以色列家啊，你們轉回，轉回吧！離開惡道，何必死亡呢？'

12"人子啊，你要對本國的子民說：'義人的義，在犯罪之日不能救他；至於惡人的惡，在他轉離惡行之日也不能使他傾倒；義人在犯罪之日也不能因他的義存活。' 13我對義人說：'你必定存活！'他若倚靠他的義而作罪孽，他所行的義都不被記念；他必因所作的罪孽死亡。 14再者，我對惡人說：'你必定死亡！'他若轉離他的罪，行正直與合理的事： 15還人的當頭和所搶奪的，遵行生命的律例，不作罪孽，他必定存活，不至死亡。 16他所犯的一切罪必不被記念；他行了正直與合理的事，必定存活。

17"你本國的子民還說：'主的道不公平。'其實他們的道不公平。 18義人轉離他的義而作罪孽，就必因此死亡。 19惡人轉離他的惡，行正直與合理的事，就必因此存活。 20你們還說：'主的道不公平。'以色列家啊，我必按你們各人所行的審判你們。"

解釋耶路撒冷的淪陷

21我們被擄之後十二年十月初五日，有人從耶路撒冷逃到我這裏，

---

a 8 Or in; also in verse 9   *b 10 Or away in*

説：“城已攻破。”²²逃來的人未到前一日的晚上，耶和華的靈（註：原文作“手”）降在我身上，開我的口。到第二日早晨，那人來到我這裏，我口就開了，不再緘默。

²³耶和華的話臨到我說：²⁴“人子啊，住在<u>以色列</u>荒廢之地的人說：‘<u>亞伯拉罕</u>獨自一人能得這地為業，我們人數眾多，這地更是給我們為業的。’²⁵所以你要對他們說：‘主耶和華如此說：你們吃帶血的物，仰望偶像，並且殺人流血，你們還能得這地為業嗎？²⁶你們倚仗自己的刀劍行可憎的事，人人玷污鄰舍的妻，你們還能得這地為業嗎？’

²⁷“你要對他們這樣說：‘主耶和華如此說：我指着我的永生起誓：在荒場中的必倒在刀下；在田野間的必交給野獸吞吃；在保障和洞裏的必遭瘟疫而死。²⁸我必使這地荒涼，令人驚駭；她因勢力而有的驕傲，也必止息。<u>以色列</u>的山都必荒涼，無人經過。²⁹我因他們所行一切可憎的事使地荒涼，令人驚駭。那時，他們就知道我是耶和華。’

³⁰“人子啊，你本國的子民在牆垣旁邊、在房屋門口談論你，弟兄對弟兄彼此說：‘來吧！聽聽有甚麼話從耶和華而出。’³¹他們來到你這裏如同民來聚會，坐在你面前彷彿是我的民；他們聽你的話卻不去行，因為他們的口多顯愛情，心卻追隨財利。³²他們看你如善於奏樂、聲音幽雅之人所唱的雅歌，他們聽你的話卻不去行。

³³“看哪，所說的快要應驗；應驗了，他們就知道在他們中間有了先知。”

牧人與羊

34 耶和華的話臨到我說：²“人子啊，你要向<u>以色列</u>的牧人發預言，攻擊他們說：‘主耶和華如此說：禍哉！<u>以色列</u>的牧人只知牧養自己。牧人豈不當牧養羣羊嗎？³你們吃脂油、穿羊毛，宰

from Jerusalem came to me and said, "The city has fallen!" ²²Now the evening before the man arrived, the hand of the LORD was upon me, and he opened my mouth before the man came to me in the morning. So my mouth was opened and I was no longer silent.

²³Then the word of the LORD came to me: ²⁴"Son of man, the people living in those ruins in the land of Israel are saying, 'Abraham was only one man, yet he possessed the land. But we are many; surely the land has been given to us as our possession.' ²⁵Therefore say to them, 'This is what the Sovereign LORD says: Since you eat meat with the blood still in it and look to your idols and shed blood, should you then possess the land? ²⁶You rely on your sword, you do detestable things, and each of you defiles his neighbor's wife. Should you then possess the land?'

²⁷"Say this to them: 'This is what the Sovereign LORD says: As surely as I live, those who are left in the ruins will fall by the sword, those out in the country I will give to the wild animals to be devoured, and those in strongholds and caves will die of a plague. ²⁸I will make the land a desolate waste, and her proud strength will come to an end, and the mountains of Israel will become desolate so that no one will cross them. ²⁹Then they will know that I am the LORD, when I have made the land a desolate waste because of all the detestable things they have done.'

³⁰"As for you, son of man, your countrymen are talking together about you by the walls and at the doors of the houses, saying to each other, 'Come and hear the message that has come from the LORD.' ³¹My people come to you, as they usually do, and sit before you to listen to your words, but they do not put them into practice. With their mouths they express devotion, but their hearts are greedy for unjust gain. ³²Indeed, to them you are nothing more than one who sings love songs with a beautiful voice and plays an instrument well, for they hear your words but do not put them into practice.

³³"When all this comes true—and it surely will—then they will know that a prophet has been among them."

Shepherds and Sheep

34 The word of the LORD came to me: ²"Son of man, prophesy against the shepherds of Israel; prophesy and say to them: 'This is what the Sovereign LORD says: Woe to the shepherds of Israel who only take care of themselves! Should not shepherds take care of the flock? ³You eat the curds, clothe yourselves with the wool and slaughter the choice animals, but you do not take care of the flock. ⁴You have not strengthened the weak or healed the sick or bound up the injured. You have not brought back the strays or searched for the lost. You have ruled them harshly and brutally. ⁵So they were scattered because there was no shepherd, and when they were scattered they became food for all the wild animals. ⁶My sheep wandered over all the mountains and on every high hill. They were scattered over the whole earth, and no one searched or looked for them.

⁷" 'Therefore, you shepherds, hear the word of the LORD: ⁸As surely as I live, declares the Sovereign LORD, because my flock lacks a shepherd and so has been plundered and has become food for all the wild animals, and because my shepherds did not search for my flock but cared for themselves rather than for my flock, ⁹therefore, O shepherds, hear the word of the LORD: ¹⁰This is what the Sovereign LORD says: I am against the shepherds and will hold them accountable for my flock. I will remove them from tending the flock so that the shepherds can no longer feed themselves. I will rescue my flock from their mouths, and it will no longer be food for them.

¹¹" 'For this is what the Sovereign LORD says: I myself will search for my sheep and look after them. ¹²As a shepherd looks after his scattered flock when he is with them, so will I look after my sheep. I will rescue them from all the places where they were scattered on a day of clouds and darkness. ¹³I will bring them out from the nations and gather them from the countries, and I will bring them into their own land. I will pasture them on the mountains of Israel, in the ravines and in all the settlements in the land. ¹⁴I will tend them in a good pasture, and the mountain heights of Israel will be their grazing land. There they will lie down in good grazing land, and there they will feed in a rich pasture on the mountains of Israel. ¹⁵I myself will tend my sheep and have them lie down, declares the Sovereign LORD. ¹⁶I will search for the lost and bring back the strays. I will bind up the injured and strengthen the weak, but the sleek and the strong I will destroy. I will shepherd the flock with justice.

¹⁷" 'As for you, my flock, this is what the Sovereign LORD says: I will judge between one sheep and another, and between rams and goats. ¹⁸Is it not enough for you to feed on the good pasture? Must you also trample the rest of your pasture with your feet? Is it not enough for you to drink clear water? Must you also muddy

肥壯的，卻不牧養羣羊。⁴瘦弱的，你們沒有養壯；有病的，你們沒有醫治；受傷的，你們沒有纏裹；被逐的，你們沒有領回；失喪的，你們沒有尋找；但用強暴嚴嚴地轄制。⁵因無牧人，羊就分散；既分散，便作了一切野獸的食物。⁶我的羊在諸山間，在各高岡上流離，在全地上分散，無人去尋，無人去找。

⁷" '所以，你們這些牧人要聽耶和華的話。⁸主耶和華說：我指着我的永生起誓，我的羊因無牧人就成為掠物，也作了一切野獸的食物。我的牧人不尋找我的羊，這些牧人只知牧養自己，並不牧養我的羊。⁹所以，你們這些牧人要聽耶和華的話。¹⁰主耶和華如此說：我必與牧人為敵，必向他們的手追討我的羊，使他們不再牧放羣羊，牧人也不再牧養自己。我必救我的羊脫離他們的口，不再作他們的食物。

¹¹" '主耶和華如此說：看哪，我必親自尋找我的羊，將他們尋見。¹²牧人在羊羣四散的日子，怎樣尋找他的羊，我必照樣尋找我的羊。這些羊在密雲黑暗的日子散到各處，我必從那裏救回他們來。¹³我必從萬民中領出他們，從各國內聚集他們，引導他們歸回故土，也必在以色列山上，一切溪水旁邊，境內一切可居之處牧養他們。¹⁴我必在美好的草場牧養他們；他們的圈必在以色列高處的山上。他們必在佳美之圈中躺臥，也在以色列山肥美的草場吃草。¹⁵主耶和華說：我必親自作牧養我羊的牧人，使他們得以躺臥。¹⁶失喪的，我必尋找；被逐的，我必領回；受傷的，我必纏裹；有病的，我必醫治；只是肥的壯的，我必除滅，也要秉公牧養他們。

¹⁷" '我的羊羣哪，論到你們，主耶和華如此說：我必在羊與羊中間、公綿羊與公山羊中間施行判斷。¹⁸你們這些肥壯的羊，在美好的草場吃草，還以為小事嗎？剩下的草，你們竟用蹄踐踏了；你們喝清水，剩下

的水，你們竟用蹄攪渾了。¹⁹至於我的羊，只得吃你們所踐踏的，喝你們所攪渾的。

²⁰ " '所以主耶和華如此說：我必在肥羊和瘦羊中間施行判斷。²¹因為你們用脅用肩擁擠一切瘦弱的，又用角牴觸，以致使他們四散。²²所以我必拯救我的羣羊不再作掠物，我也必在羊和羊中間施行判斷。²³我必立一牧人照管他們，牧養他們，就是我的僕人大衛。他必牧養他們，作他們的牧人。²⁴我耶和華必作他們的神，我的僕人大衛必在他們中間作王。這是耶和華說的。

²⁵ " '我必與他們立平安的約，使惡獸從境內斷絕，他們就必安居在曠野，躺臥在林中。²⁶我必使他們與我山的四圍成為福源，我也必叫時雨落下，必有福如甘霖而降。²⁷田野的樹必結果，地也必有出產。他們必在故土安然居住。我折斷他們所負的軛，救他們脫離那以他們為奴之人的手。那時，他們就知道我是耶和華。²⁸他們必不再作外邦人的掠物，地上的野獸也不再吞吃他們，卻要安然居住，無人驚嚇。²⁹我必給他們興起有名的植物，他們在境內不再為饑荒所滅，也不再受外邦人的羞辱。³⁰必知道我耶和華他們的神是與他們同在，並知道他們以色列家是我的民。這是主耶和華說的。³¹你們作我的羊，我草場上的羊，乃是以色列人，我也是你們的神。這是主耶和華說的。' "

論以東的預言

35 耶和華的話又臨到我說：² "人子啊，你要面向西珥山發預言攻擊他，³對他說：'主耶和華如此說：西珥山哪，我與你為敵，必向你伸手攻擊你，使你荒涼，令人驚駭。⁴我必使你的城邑變為荒場，成為淒涼，你就知道我是耶和華。

⁵ " '因為你永懷仇恨，在以色列人遭災，罪孽到了盡頭的時候，將他們交與刀劍。⁶所以主耶和華

the rest with your feet? ¹⁹Must my flock feed on what you have trampled and drink what you have muddied with your feet?

²⁰ " 'Therefore this is what the Sovereign LORD says to them: See, I myself will judge between the fat sheep and the lean sheep. ²¹Because you shove with flank and shoulder, butting all the weak sheep with your horns until you have driven them away, ²²I will save my flock, and they will no longer be plundered. I will judge between one sheep and another. ²³I will place over them one shepherd, my servant David, and he will tend them; he will tend them and be their shepherd. ²⁴I the LORD will be their God, and my servant David will be prince among them. I the LORD have spoken.

²⁵ " 'I will make a covenant of peace with them and rid the land of wild beasts so that they may live in the desert and sleep in the forests in safety. ²⁶I will bless them and the places surrounding my hill.ᵃ I will send down showers in season; there will be showers of blessing. ²⁷The trees of the field will yield their fruit and the ground will yield its crops; the people will be secure in their land. They will know that I am the LORD, when I break the bars of their yoke and rescue them from the hands of those who enslaved them. ²⁸They will no longer be plundered by the nations, nor will wild animals devour them. They will live in safety, and no one will make them afraid. ²⁹I will provide for them a land renowned for its crops, and they will no longer be victims of famine in the land or bear the scorn of the nations. ³⁰Then they will know that I, the LORD their God, am with them and that they, the house of Israel, are my people, declares the Sovereign LORD. ³¹You my sheep, the sheep of my pasture, are people, and I am your God, declares the Sovereign LORD.' "

A Prophecy Against Edom

35 The word of the LORD came to me: ²"Son of man, set your face against Mount Seir; prophesy against it ³and say: 'This is what the Sovereign LORD says: I am against you, Mount Seir, and I will stretch out my hand against you and make you a desolate waste. ⁴I will turn your towns into ruins and you will be desolate. Then you will know that I am the LORD.

⁵ " 'Because you harbored an ancient hostility and delivered the Israelites over to the sword at the time of their calamity, the time their punishment reached its climax, ⁶therefore as surely as I

---

a 26 Or I will make them and the places surrounding my hill a blessing

live, declares the Sovereign LORD, I will give you over to bloodshed and it will pursue you. Since you did not hate bloodshed, bloodshed will pursue you. ⁷I will make Mount Seir a desolate waste and cut off from it all who come and go. ⁸I will fill your mountains with the slain; those killed by the sword will fall on your hills and in your valleys and in all your ravines. ⁹I will make you desolate forever; your towns will not be inhabited. Then you will know that I am the LORD.

¹⁰"'Because you have said, "These two nations and countries will be ours and we will take possession of them," even though I the LORD was there, ¹¹therefore as surely as I live, declares the Sovereign LORD, I will treat you in accordance with the anger and jealousy you showed in your hatred of them and I will make myself known among them when I judge you. ¹²Then you will know that I the LORD have heard all the contemptible things you have said against the mountains of Israel. You said, "They have been laid waste and have been given over to us to devour." ¹³You boasted against me and spoke against me without restraint, and I heard it. ¹⁴This is what the Sovereign LORD says: While the whole earth rejoices, I will make you desolate. ¹⁵Because you rejoiced when the inheritance of the house of Israel became desolate, that is how I will treat you. You will be desolate, O Mount Seir, you and all of Edom. Then they will know that I am the LORD.'"

A Prophecy to the Mountains of Israel

36 "Son of man, prophesy to the mountains of Israel and say, 'O mountains of Israel, hear the word of the LORD. ²This is what the Sovereign LORD says: The enemy said of you, "Aha! The ancient heights have become our possession."' ³Therefore prophesy and say, 'This is what the Sovereign LORD says: Because they ravaged and hounded you from every side so that you became the possession of the rest of the nations and the object of people's malicious talk and slander, ⁴therefore, O mountains of Israel, hear the word of the Sovereign LORD: This is what the Sovereign LORD says to the mountains and hills, to the ravines and valleys, to the desolate ruins and the deserted towns that have been plundered and ridiculed by the rest of the nations around you— ⁵this is what the Sovereign LORD says: In my burning zeal I have spoken against the rest of the nations, and against all Edom, for with glee and with malice in their hearts they made my land their own possession so that they might plunder its pas-

說：我指着我的永生起誓，我必使你遭遇流血的報應，罪（註：原文作"血"。本節同）必追趕你；你既不恨惡殺人流血，所以這罪必追趕你。⁷我必使西珥山荒涼，令人驚駭，來往經過的人我必剪除。⁸我必使西珥山滿有被殺的人。被刀殺的，必倒在你小山和山谷，並一切的溪水中。⁹我必使你永遠荒涼，使你的城邑無人居住。你的民就知道我是耶和華。

¹⁰"'因為你曾說：這二國、這二邦必歸於我，我必得為業（其實耶和華仍在那裏）。¹¹所以主耶和華說：我指着我的永生起誓，我必照你的怒氣和你從仇恨中向他們所發的嫉妒待你。我審判你的時候，必將自己顯明在他們中間。¹²你也必知道我耶和華聽見了你的一切毀謗，就是你攻擊以色列山的話，說：這些山荒涼，是歸我們吞滅的。¹³你們也用口向我誇大，增添與我反對的話，我都聽見了。¹⁴主耶和華如此說：全地歡樂的時候，我必使你荒涼。¹⁵你怎樣因以色列家的地業荒涼而喜樂，我必照你所行的待你。西珥山哪，你和以東全地必都荒涼，你們就知道我是耶和華。'"

論以色列諸山的預言

36 "人子啊，你要對以色列山發預言說：'以色列山哪，要聽耶和華的話！²主耶和華如此說：因仇敵說：阿哈，這永久的山岡都歸我們為業了！'³所以要發預言說：'主耶和華如此說：因為敵人使你荒涼，四圍吞吃，好叫你歸與其餘的外邦人為業，並且多嘴多舌的人提起你來，百姓也說你有臭名。⁴故此，以色列山要聽主耶和華的話。大山小岡、水溝山谷、荒廢之地、被棄之城，為四圍其餘的外邦人所佔據、所譏刺的，⁵主耶和華對你們如此說：我真發憤恨如火，責備那其餘的外邦人和以東的眾人。他們快樂滿懷，心存恨惡，將我的地歸自己為業，又看為被棄的掠物。’ ⁶所以你要指着以色列地說預言，對大山小岡、水溝山谷說：主耶和華如此說：我發憤恨和忿怒說，因你們曾受外邦人的羞辱，⁷所以我起誓說：你們四圍的外邦人總要擔當自己的羞辱。這是主耶和華說的。

⁸ “ ‘以色列山哪，你必發枝條，為我的民以色列結果子，因為他們快要來到。⁹看哪，我是幫助你的，也必向你轉意，使你得以耕種。¹⁰我必使以色列全家的人數在你上面增多，城邑有人居住，荒場再被建造。¹¹我必使人和牲畜在你上面加增，他們必生養眾多。我要使你照舊有人居住，並要賜福與你比先前更多，你就知道我是耶和華。¹²我必使人，就是我的民以色列，行在你上面。他們必得你為業，你也不再使他們喪子。

¹³ “ ‘主耶和華如此說：因為人對你說：你是吞吃人的，又使國民喪子。¹⁴所以主耶和華說：你必不再吞吃人，也不再使國民喪子。¹⁵我使你不再聽見各國的羞辱，不再受萬民的辱罵，也不再使國民絆跌。這是主耶和華說的。’ ”

¹⁶耶和華的話又臨到我說：¹⁷“人子啊，以色列家住在本地的時候，在行動作為上玷污那地。他們的行為在我面前，好像正在經期的婦人那樣污穢。¹⁸所以我因他們在那地上流人的血，又因他們以偶像玷污那地，就把我的忿怒傾在他們身上。¹⁹我將他們分散在列國，四散在列邦，按他們的行動作為懲罰他們。²⁰他們到了所去的列國，就使我的聖名被褻瀆。因為人談論他們說：‘這是耶和華的民，是從耶和華的地出來的。’ ²¹我卻顧惜我的聖名，就是以色列家在所到的列國中所褻瀆的。

²²“所以你要對以色列家說：‘主耶和華如此說：以色列家啊，我行這事不是為你們，乃是為我的聖名，就是在你們到的列國中所褻

tureland.’ ⁶Therefore prophesy concerning the land of Israel and say to the mountains and hills, to the ravines and valleys: 'This is what the Sovereign LORD says: I speak in my jealous wrath because you have suffered the scorn of the nations. ⁷Therefore this is what the Sovereign LORD says: I swear with uplifted hand that the nations around you will also suffer scorn.

⁸ 'But you, O mountains of Israel, will produce branches and fruit for my people Israel, for they will soon come home. ⁹I am concerned for you and will look on you with favor; you will be plowed and sown, ¹⁰and I will multiply the number of people upon you, even the whole house of Israel. The towns will be inhabited and the ruins rebuilt. ¹¹I will increase the number of men and animals upon you, and they will be fruitful and become numerous. I will settle people on you as in the past and will make you prosper more than before. Then you will know that I am the LORD. ¹²I will cause people, my people Israel, to walk upon you. They will possess you, and you will be their inheritance; you will never again deprive them of their children.

¹³" 'This is what the Sovereign LORD says: Because people say to you, "You devour men and deprive your nation of its children," ¹⁴therefore you will no longer devour men or make your nation childless, declares the Sovereign LORD. ¹⁵No longer will I make you hear the taunts of the nations, and no longer will you suffer the scorn of the peoples or cause your nation to fall, declares the Sovereign LORD.' "

¹⁶Again the word of the LORD came to me: ¹⁷"Son of man, when the people of Israel were living in their own land, they defiled it by their conduct and their actions. Their conduct was like a woman's monthly uncleanness in my sight. ¹⁸So I poured out my wrath on them because they had shed blood in the land and because they had defiled it with their idols. ¹⁹I dispersed them among the nations, and they were scattered through the countries; I judged them according to their conduct and their actions. ²⁰And wherever they went among the nations they profaned my holy name, for it was said of them, 'These are the LORD's people, and yet they had to leave his land.' ²¹I had concern for my holy name, which the house of Israel profaned among the nations where they had gone.

²²"Therefore say to the house of Israel, 'This is what the Sovereign LORD says: It is not for your sake, O house of Israel, that I am going to do these things, but for the sake of my holy name, which you have profaned among the

nations where you have gone. 23I will show the holiness of my great name, which has been profaned among the nations, the name you have profaned among them. Then the nations will know that I am the LORD, declares the Sovereign LORD, when I show myself holy through you before their eyes.

24" 'For I will take you out of the nations; I will gather you from all the countries and bring you back into your own land. 25I will sprinkle clean water on you, and you will be clean; I will cleanse you from all your impurities and from all your idols. 26I will give you a new heart and put a new spirit in you; I will remove from you your heart of stone and give you a heart of flesh. 27And I will put my Spirit in you and move you to follow my decrees and be careful to keep my laws. 28You will live in the land I gave your forefathers; you will be my people, and I will be your God. 29I will save you from all your uncleanness. I will call for the grain and make it plentiful and will not bring famine upon you. 30I will increase the fruit of the trees and the crops of the field, so that you will no longer suffer disgrace among the nations because of famine. 31Then you will remember your evil ways and wicked deeds, and you will loathe yourselves for your sins and detestable practices. 32I want you to know that I am not doing this for your sake, declares the Sovereign LORD. Be ashamed and disgraced for your conduct, O house of Israel!

33" 'This is what the Sovereign LORD says: On the day I cleanse you from all your sins, I will resettle your towns, and the ruins will be rebuilt. 34The desolate land will be cultivated instead of lying desolate in the sight of all who pass through it. 35They will say, "This land that was laid waste has become like the garden of Eden; the cities that were lying in ruins, desolate and destroyed, are now fortified and inhabited." 36Then the nations around you that remain will know that I the LORD have rebuilt what was destroyed and have replanted what was desolate. I the LORD have spoken, and I will do it.'

37"This is what the Sovereign LORD says: Once again I will yield to the plea of the house of Israel and do this for them: I will make their people as numerous as sheep, 38as numerous as the flocks for offerings at Jerusalem during her appointed feasts. So will the ruined cities be filled with flocks of people. Then they will know that I am the LORD."

瀆的。23我要使我的大名顯為聖,這名在列國中已被褻瀆,就是你們在他們中間所褻瀆的。我在他們眼前、在你們身上顯為聖的時候,他們就知道我是耶和華。這是主耶和華說的。

24 " '我必從各國收取你們,從列邦聚集你們,引導你們歸回本地。25我必用清水灑在你們身上,你們就潔淨了。我要潔淨你們,使你們脫離一切的污穢,棄掉一切的偶像。26我也要賜給你們一個新心,將新靈放在你們裏面。又從你們的肉體中除掉石心,賜給你們肉心。27我必將我的靈放在你們裏面,使你們順從我的律例,謹守遵行我的典章。28你們必住在我所賜給你們列祖之地。你們要作我的子民,我要作你們的神。29我必救你們脫離一切的污穢,也必命五穀豐登,不使你們遭遇饑荒。30我必使樹木多結果子,田地多出土產,好叫你們不再因饑荒受外邦人的譏誚。31那時,你們必追想你們的惡行和你們不善的作為,就因你們的罪孽和可憎的事厭惡自己。32主耶和華說:你們要知道,我這樣行不是為你們。以色列家啊,當為自己的行為抱愧蒙羞!

33 " '主耶和華如此說:我潔淨你們,使你們脫離一切罪孽的日子,必使城邑有人居住,荒場再被建造。34過路的人雖看為荒廢之地,現今這荒廢之地仍得耕種。35他們必說:這先前為荒廢之地,現在成如伊甸園;這荒廢、淒涼、毀壞的城邑,現在堅固有人居住。36那時,在你們四圍其餘的外邦人,必知道我耶和華修造那毀壞之處,培植那荒廢之地。我耶和華說過,也必成就。'

37 "主耶和華如此說:我要加增以色列家的人數,多如羊羣。他們必為這事向我求問,我要給他們成就。38耶路撒冷在守節作祭物所獻的羊羣怎樣多,照樣,荒涼的城邑必被人羣充滿。他們就知道我是耶和華。"

遍滿枯骨的平原

37 耶和華的靈（註：原文作"手"）降在我身上，耶和華藉他的靈帶我出去，將我放在平原中，這平原遍滿骸骨。²他使我從骸骨的四圍經過，誰知在平原的骸骨甚多，而且極其枯乾。³他對我說："人子啊，這些骸骨能復活嗎？"

我說："主耶和華啊，你是知道的。"

⁴他又對我說："你向這些骸骨發預言說：'枯乾的骸骨啊，要聽耶和華的話！⁵主耶和華對這些骸骨如此說：我必使氣息進入你們裏面，你們就要活了。⁶我必給你們加上筋，使你們長肉，又將皮遮蔽你們，使氣息進入你們裏面，你們就要活了。你們便知道我是耶和華。'"

⁷於是我遵命說預言。正說預言的時候，不料，有響聲，有地震；骨與骨互相聯絡。⁸我觀看，見骸骨上有筋，也長了肉，又有皮遮蔽其上，只是還沒有氣息。

⁹主對我說："人子啊，你要發預言，向風發預言說：'主耶和華如此說：氣息啊，要從四方（註：原文作"風"）而來，吹在這些被殺的人身上，使他們活了。'"¹⁰於是我遵命說預言，氣息就進入骸骨，骸骨便活了，並且站起來，成為極大的軍隊。

¹¹主對我說："人子啊，這些骸骨就是以色列全家。他們說：'我們的骨頭枯乾了，我們的指望失去了，我們滅絕淨盡了。'¹²所以你要發預言對他們說：'主耶和華如此說：我的民哪，我必開你們的墳墓，使你們從墳墓中出來，領你們進入以色列地。¹³我的民哪，我開你們的墳墓，使你們從墳墓中出來，你們就知道我是耶和華。¹⁴我必將我的靈放在你們裏面，你們就要活了。我將你們安置在本地，你們就知道我耶和華如此說，也如此成就了。這是耶和華說的。'"

一國一王

¹⁵耶和華的話又臨到我說：¹⁶"人子啊，你要取一根木杖，在其上寫'為猶大和他的同伴以色列人'；又取一根木杖，在其上寫'為約瑟，就

The Valley of Dry Bones

37 The hand of the LORD was upon me, and he brought me out by the Spirit of the LORD and set me in the middle of a valley; it was full of bones. ²He led me back and forth among them, and I saw a great many bones on the floor of the valley, bones that were very dry. ³He asked me, "Son of man, can these bones live?"

I said, "O Sovereign LORD, you alone know."

⁴Then he said to me, "Prophesy to these bones and say to them, 'Dry bones, hear the word of the LORD! ⁵This is what the Sovereign LORD says to these bones: I will make breath[a] enter you, and you will come to life. ⁶I will attach tendons to you and make flesh come upon you and cover you with skin; I will put breath in you, and you will come to life. Then you will know that I am the LORD.'"

⁷So I prophesied as I was commanded. And as I was prophesying, there was a noise, a rattling sound, and the bones came together, bone to bone. ⁸I looked, and tendons and flesh appeared on them and skin covered them, but there was no breath in them.

⁹Then he said to me, "Prophesy to the breath; prophesy, son of man, and say to it, 'This is what the Sovereign LORD says: Come from the four winds, O breath, and breathe into these slain, that they may live.'" ¹⁰So I prophesied as he commanded me, and breath entered them; they came to life and stood up on their feet—a vast army.

¹¹Then he said to me: "Son of man, these bones are the whole house of Israel. They say, 'Our bones are dried up and our hope is gone; we are cut off.' ¹²Therefore prophesy and say to them: 'This is what the Sovereign LORD says: O my people, I am going to open your graves and bring you up from them; I will bring you back to the land of Israel. ¹³Then you, my people, will know that I am the LORD, when I open your graves and bring you up from them. ¹⁴I will put my Spirit in you and you will live, and I will settle you in your own land. Then you will know that I the LORD have spoken, and I have done it, declares the LORD.'"

One Nation Under One King

¹⁵The word of the LORD came to me: ¹⁶"Son of man, take a stick of wood and write on it, 'Belonging to Judah and the Israelites associated with him.' Then take another stick of wood, and

a 5 The Hebrew for this word can also mean wind or spirit (see verses 6-14).

write on it, 'Ephraim's stick, belonging to Joseph and all the house of Israel associated with him.' [17]Join them together into one stick so that they will become one in your hand.

[18]"When your countrymen ask you, 'Won't you tell us what you mean by this?' [19]say to them, 'This is what the Sovereign LORD says: I am going to take the stick of Joseph—which is in Ephraim's hand—and of the Israelite tribes associated with him, and join it to Judah's stick, making them a single stick of wood, and they will become one in my hand.' [20]Hold before their eyes the sticks you have written on [21]and say to them, 'This is what the Sovereign LORD says: I will take the Israelites out of the nations where they have gone. I will gather them from all around and bring them back into their own land. [22]I will make them one nation in the land, on the mountains of Israel. There will be one king over all of them and they will never again be two nations or be divided into two kingdoms. [23]They will no longer defile themselves with their idols and vile images or with any of their offenses, for I will save them from all their sinful backsliding,[a] and I will cleanse them. They will be my people, and I will be their God.

[24]" 'My servant David will be king over them, and they will all have one shepherd. They will follow my laws and be careful to keep my decrees. [25]They will live in the land I gave to my servant Jacob, the land where your fathers lived. They and their children and their children's children will live there forever, and David my servant will be their prince forever. [26]I will make a covenant of peace with them; it will be an everlasting covenant. I will establish them and increase their numbers, and I will put my sanctuary among them forever. [27]My dwelling place will be with them; I will be their God, and they will be my people. [28]Then the nations will know that I the LORD make Israel holy, when my sanctuary is among them forever.' "

A Prophecy Against Gog

38 The word of the LORD came to me: [2]"Son of man, set your face against Gog, of the land of Magog, the chief prince of[b] Meshech and Tubal; prophesy against him [3]and say: 'This is what the Sovereign LORD says: I am against you, O Gog, chief prince of[c] Meshech and Tubal. [4]I will turn you around, put hooks in your jaws and bring you out with your whole

a 23 Many Hebrew manuscripts (see also Septuagint); most Hebrew manuscripts *all their dwelling places where they sinned*
b 2 Or *the prince of Rosh,*   *c* 3 Or *Gog, prince of Rosh,*

是為以法蓮，又為他的同伴以色列全家」。[17]你要使這兩根木杖接連為一，在你手中成為一根。

[18]「你本國的子民問你說：『這是甚麼意思？你不指示我們嗎？』[19]你就對他們說：『主耶和華如此說：我要將約瑟和他同伴以色列支派的杖，就是那在以法蓮手中的，與猶大的杖一同接連為一，在我手中成為一根。』[20]你所寫的那兩根杖，要在他們眼前拿在手中，[21]要對他們說：『主耶和華如此說：我要將以色列人從他們所到的各國收取，又從四圍聚集他們，引導他們歸回本地。[22]我要使他們在那地，在以色列山上成為一國，有一王作他們眾民的王。他們不再為二國，決不再分為二國。[23]也不再因偶像和可憎的物，並一切的罪過玷污自己，我卻要救他們出離一切的住處，就是他們犯罪的地方，我要潔淨他們。如此，他們要作我的子民，我要作他們的神。

[24]「『我的僕人大衛必作他們的王，眾民必歸一個牧人。他們必順從我的典章，謹守遵行我的律例。[25]他們必住在我賜給我僕人雅各的地上，就是你們列祖所住之地。他們和他們的子孫，並子孫的子孫，都永遠住在那裏。我的僕人大衛必作他們的王，直到永遠。[26]並且我要與他們立平安的約，作為永約。我也要將他們安置在本地，使他們的人數增多，又在他們中間設立我的聖所，直到永遠。[27]我的居所必在他們中間。我要作他們的神，他們要作我的子民。[28]我的聖所在以色列人中間直到永遠，外邦人就必知道我是叫以色列成為聖的耶和華。』」

論歌革的預言

38 耶和華的話臨到我說：[2]「人子啊，你要面向瑪各地的歌革，就是羅施、米設、土巴的王發預言攻擊他，[3]說：『主耶和華如此說：羅施、米設、土巴的王歌革啊，我與你為敵。[4]我必用鈎子鈎住你的腮頰，調轉你，將你和你的軍兵、馬匹、馬兵帶出來，都披掛整齊，成了大隊，有大小盾牌，各拿刀劍。⁵波斯人、古實人和弗人（註：又作「利比亞人」），各拿盾牌，頭上戴盔，⁶歌篾人和他的軍隊，北方極處的陀迦瑪族和他的軍隊，這許多國的民都同着你。

⁷ "'那聚集到你這裏的各隊都當準備，你自己也要準備，作他們的大帥。⁸過了多日，你必被差派。到末後之年，你必來到脫離刀劍從列國收回之地，到以色列常久荒涼的山上，但那從列國中招聚出來的必在其上安然居住。⁹你和你的軍隊，並同着你許多國的民必如暴風上來，如密雲遮蓋地面。

10 "'主耶和華如此說：到那時，你心必起意念，圖謀惡計，¹¹說：我要上那無城牆的鄉村，我要到那安靜的民那裏，他們都沒有城牆，無門、無閂，安然居住。¹²我去要搶財為擄物，奪貨為掠物，反手攻擊那從前荒涼、現在有人居住之地，又攻擊那住世界中間、從列國招聚、得了牲畜財貨的民。¹³示巴人、底但人、他施的客商和其間的少壯獅子，都必問你說：你來要搶財為擄物嗎？你聚集軍隊要奪貨為掠物嗎？要奪取金銀，擄去牲畜財貨嗎？要搶奪許多財寶為擄物嗎？'

14 "人子啊，你要因此發預言，對歌革說：'主耶和華如此說：到我民以色列安然居住之日，你豈不知道嗎？¹⁵你必從本地、從北方的極處率領許多國的民來，都騎着馬，乃一大隊極多的軍兵。¹⁶歌革啊，你必上來攻擊我的民以色列，如密雲遮蓋地面。末後的日子，我必帶你來攻擊我的地，到我在外邦人眼前，在你身上顯為聖的時候，好叫他們認識我。

17 "'主耶和華如此說：我在古時藉我的僕人以色列的先知所說的，就是你嗎？當日他們多年預言我必帶你來攻擊以色列人。¹⁸主耶和華說：歌革上來攻擊以色列地的時

army—your horses, your horsemen fully armed, and a great horde with large and small shields, all of them brandishing their swords. ⁵Persia, Cush[d] and Put will be with them, all with shields and helmets, ⁶also Gomer with all its troops, and Beth Togarmah from the far north with all its troops—the many nations with you.

7 "'Get ready; be prepared, you and all the hordes gathered about you, and take command of them. ⁸After many days you will be called to arms. In future years you will invade a land that has recovered from war, whose people were gathered from many nations to the mountains of Israel, which had long been desolate. They had been brought out from the nations, and now all of them live in safety. ⁹You and all your troops and the many nations with you will go up, advancing like a storm; you will be like a cloud covering the land.

10" 'This is what the Sovereign LORD says: On that day thoughts will come into your mind and you will devise an evil scheme. ¹¹You will say, "I will invade a land of unwalled villages; I will attack a peaceful and unsuspecting people—all of them living without walls and without gates and bars. ¹²I will plunder and loot and turn my hand against the resettled ruins and the people gathered from the nations, rich in livestock and goods, living at the center of the land." ¹³Sheba and Dedan and the merchants of Tarshish and all her villages[b] will say to you, "Have you come to plunder? Have you gathered your hordes to loot, to carry off silver and gold, to take away livestock and goods and to seize much plunder?"'

14"Therefore, son of man, prophesy and say to Gog: 'This is what the Sovereign LORD says: In that day, when my people Israel are living in safety, will you not take notice of it? ¹⁵You will come from your place in the far north, you and many nations with you, all of them riding on horses, a great horde, a mighty army. ¹⁶You will advance against my people Israel like a cloud that covers the land. In days to come, O Gog, I will bring you against my land, so that the nations may know me when I show myself holy through you before their eyes.

17" 'This is what the Sovereign LORD says: Are you not the one I spoke of in former days by my servants the prophets of Israel? At that time they prophesied for years that I would bring you against them. ¹⁸This is what will happen in that day: When Gog attacks the land of Israel, my hot anger will be aroused, declares the Sovereign LORD. ¹⁹In my zeal and fiery wrath I declare that at that time there shall be a great earthquake in the land of Israel. ²⁰The fish of the sea, the birds of the air, the beasts of the field, every creature that moves along the ground, and all the people on the face of the earth will tremble at my presence. The mountains will be overturned, the cliffs will crumble and every wall will fall to the ground. ²¹I will summon a sword against Gog on all my mountains, declares the Sovereign LORD. Every man's sword will be against his brother. ²²I will execute judgment upon him with plague and bloodshed; I will pour down torrents of rain, hailstones and burning sulfur on him and on his troops and on the many nations with him. ²³And so I will show my greatness and my holiness, and I will make myself known in the sight of many nations. Then they will know that I am the LORD.'

39 "Son of man, prophesy against Gog and say: 'This is what the Sovereign LORD says: I am against you, O Gog, chief prince of[a] Meshech and Tubal. ²I will turn you around and drag you along. I will bring you from the far north and send you against the mountains of Israel. ³Then I will strike your bow from your left hand and make your arrows drop from your right hand. ⁴On the mountains of Israel you will fall, you and all your troops and the nations with you. I will give you as food to all kinds of carrion birds and to the wild animals. ⁵You will fall in the open field, for I have spoken, declares the Sovereign LORD. ⁶I will send fire on Magog and on those who live in safety in the coastlands, and they will know that I am the LORD.

⁷" 'I will make known my holy name among my people Israel. I will no longer let my holy name be profaned, and the nations will know that I the LORD am the Holy One in Israel. ⁸It is coming! It will surely take place, declares the Sovereign LORD. This is the day I have spoken of.

⁹" 'Then those who live in the towns of Israel will go out and use the weapons for fuel and burn them up—the small and large shields, the bows and arrows, the war clubs and spears. For seven years they will use them for fuel. ¹⁰They will not need to gather wood from the fields or cut it from the forests, because they will use the weapons for fuel. And they will plunder those who plundered them and loot those who looted them, declares the Sovereign LORD.

候，我的怒氣要從鼻孔裏發出。¹⁹我發憤恨和烈怒如火說：那日在以色列地必有大震動，²⁰甚至海中的魚、天空的鳥、田野的獸，並地上的一切昆蟲和其上的眾人，因見我的面，就都震動，山嶺必崩裂，陡巖必塌陷，牆垣都必坍倒。²¹主耶和華說：我必命我的諸山發刀劍來攻擊歌革，人都要用刀劍殺害弟兄。²²我必用瘟疫和流血的事刑罰他。我也必將暴雨、大雹與火，並硫磺降與他和他的軍隊，並他所率領的眾民。²³我必顯為大，顯為聖，在多國人的眼前顯現，他們就知道我是耶和華。'

39 "人子啊，你要向歌革發預言攻擊他說：'主耶和華如此說：羅施、米設、土巴的王歌革啊，我與你為敵。²我必調轉你，領你前往，使你從北方的極處上來，帶你到以色列的山上。³我必從你左手打落你的弓，從你右手打掉你的箭。⁴你和你的軍隊，並同着你的列國人，都必倒在以色列的山上。我必將你給各類的鷙鳥和田野的走獸作食物。⁵你必倒在田野，因為我曾說過，這是主耶和華說的。⁶我要降火在瑪各和海島安然居住的人身上，他們就知道我是耶和華。

⁷" '我要在我民以色列中顯出我的聖名，也不容我的聖名再被褻瀆，列國人就知道我是耶和華以色列中的聖者。⁸主耶和華說：這日事情臨近，也必成就，乃是我所說的日子。

⁹" '住以色列城邑的人必出去撿器械，就是大小盾牌、弓箭、梃杖、槍矛都當柴燒火，直燒七年。¹⁰甚至他們不必從田野撿柴，也不必從樹林伐木。因為他們要用器械燒火。並且搶奪那搶奪他們的人，擄掠那擄掠他們的人。這是主耶和華說的。

a 1 Or Gog, prince of Rosh,

11 "'當那日，我必將以色列地的谷，就是海東人所經過的谷，賜給歌革為墳地，使經過的人到此停步。在那裏，人必葬埋歌革和他的羣眾，就稱那地為哈們歌革谷。

12 "'以色列家的人必用七個月葬埋他們，為要潔淨全地。13全地的居民都必葬埋他們。當我得榮耀的日子，這事必叫他們得名聲，這是主耶和華說的。

14 "'他們必分派人時常巡查遍地，與過路的人一同葬埋那剩在地面上的屍首，好潔淨全地。過了七個月，他們還要巡查。15巡查遍地的人要經過全地，見有人的骸骨，就在旁邊立一標記，等葬埋的人來將骸骨葬在哈們歌革谷。16他們必這樣潔淨那地，並有一城名叫哈摩那。'

17 "人子啊，主耶和華如此說：你要對各類的飛鳥和田野的走獸說：'你們聚集來吧！要從四方聚到我為你們獻祭之地，就是在以色列山上獻大祭之地，好叫你們吃肉喝血。18你們必吃勇士的肉，喝地上首領的血，就如吃公綿羊、羊羔、公山羊、公牛，都是巴珊的肥畜。19你們吃我為你們所獻的祭，必吃飽了脂油，喝醉了血。20你們必在我席上飽吃馬匹和坐車的人，並勇士和一切的戰士。'這是主耶和華說的。

21 "我必顯我的榮耀在列國中，萬民就必看見我所行的審判與我在他們身上所加的手。22這樣，從那日以後，以色列家必知道我是耶和華他們的神。23列國人也必知道以色列家被擄掠，是因他們的罪孽。他們得罪我，我就掩面不顧，將他們交在敵人手中，他們便都倒在刀下。24並且我是照他們的污穢和罪過待他們，並且我掩面不顧他們。

25 "主耶和華如此說：我要使雅各被擄的人歸回，要憐憫以色列全

11" 'On that day I will give Gog a burial place in Israel, in the valley of those who travel east toward*a* the Sea.*b* It will block the way of travelers, because Gog and all his hordes will be buried there. So it will be called the Valley of Hamon Gog.*c*

12" 'For seven months the house of Israel will be burying them in order to cleanse the land. 13All the people of the land will bury them, and the day I am glorified will be a memorable day for them, declares the Sovereign LORD.

14" 'Men will be regularly employed to cleanse the land. Some will go throughout the land and, in addition to them, others will bury those that remain on the ground. At the end of the seven months they will begin their search. 15As they go through the land and one of them sees a human bone, he will set up a marker beside it until the gravediggers have buried it in the Valley of Hamon Gog. 16(Also a town called Hamonah*d* will be there.) And so they will cleanse the land.'

17"Son of man, this is what the Sovereign LORD says: Call out to every kind of bird and all the wild animals: 'Assemble and come together from all around to the sacrifice I am preparing for you, the great sacrifice on the mountains of Israel. There you will eat flesh and drink blood. 18You will eat the flesh of mighty men and drink the blood of the princes of the earth as if they were rams and lambs, goats and bulls—all of them fattened animals from Bashan. 19At the sacrifice I am preparing for you, you will eat fat till you are glutted and drink blood till you are drunk. 20At my table you will eat your fill of horses and riders, mighty men and soldiers of every kind,' declares the Sovereign LORD.

21"I will display my glory among the nations, and all the nations will see the punishment I inflict and the hand I lay upon them. 22From that day forward the house of Israel will know that I am the LORD their God. 23And the nations will know that the people of Israel went into exile for their sin, because they were unfaithful to me. So I hid my face from them and handed them over to their enemies, and they all fell by the sword. 24I dealt with them according to their uncleanness and their offenses, and I hid my face from them.

25"Therefore this is what the Sovereign LORD says: I will now bring Jacob back from captivity*e* and will have compassion on all the people of

---

a 11 Or of　　b 11 That is, the Dead Sea　　c 11 Hamon Gog
means hordes of Gog.　　d 16 Hamonah means horde.　　e 25 Or
now restore the fortunes of Jacob

Israel, and I will be zealous for my holy name. 26They will forget their shame and all the unfaithfulness they showed toward me when they lived in safety in their land with no one to make them afraid. 27When I have brought them back from the nations and have gathered them from the countries of their enemies, I will show myself holy through them in the sight of many nations. 28Then they will know that I am the LORD their God, for though I sent them into exile among the nations, I will gather them to their own land, not leaving any behind. 29I will no longer hide my face from them, for I will pour out my Spirit on the house of Israel, declares the Sovereign LORD."

The New Temple Area

40 In the twenty-fifth year of our exile, at the beginning of the year, on the tenth of the month, in the fourteenth year after the fall of the city—on that very day the hand of the LORD was upon me and he took me there. 2In visions of God he took me to the land of Israel and set me on a very high mountain, on whose south side were some buildings that looked like a city. 3He took me there, and I saw a man whose appearance was like bronze; he was standing in the gateway with a linen cord and a measuring rod in his hand. 4The man said to me, "Son of man, look with your eyes and hear with your ears and pay attention to everything I am going to show you, for that is why you have been brought here. Tell the house of Israel everything you see."

The East Gate to the Outer Court

5I saw a wall completely surrounding the temple area. The length of the measuring rod in the man's hand was six long cubits, each of which was a cubit[a] and a handbreadth.[b] He measured the wall; it was one measuring rod thick and one rod high.

6Then he went to the gate facing east. He climbed its steps and measured the threshold of the gate; it was one rod deep.[c] 7The alcoves for the guards were one rod long and one rod wide, and the projecting walls between the alcoves were five cubits thick. And the threshold of the gate next to the portico facing the temple was one rod deep.

---

a 5 The common cubit was about 1 1/2 feet (about 0.5 meter).

b 5 That is, about 3 inches (about 8 centimeters)

c 6 Septuagint; Hebrew deep, the first threshold, one rod deep

家，又為我的聖名發熱心。26、27他們在本地安然居住，無人驚嚇，是我將他們從萬民中領回，從仇敵之地召來。我在許多國的民眼前，在他們身上顯為聖的時候，他們要擔當自己的羞辱和干犯我的一切罪。28因我使他們被擄到外邦人中，後又聚集他們歸回本地，他們就知道我是耶和華他們的神，我必不再留他們一人在外邦。29我也不再掩面不顧他們，因我已將我的靈澆灌以色列家。這是主耶和華說的。"

新聖殿區域

40 我們被擄掠第二十五年，耶路撒冷城攻破後十四年，正在年初，月之初十日，耶和華的靈（註：原文作"手"）降在我身上，他把我帶到以色列地。2在神的異象中帶我到以色列地，安置在至高的山上；在山上的南邊有彷彿一座城建立。3他帶我到那裏，見有一人，顏色（註：原文作"形狀"）如銅，手拿麻繩和量度的竿站在門口。4那人對我說："人子啊，凡我所指示你的，你都要用眼看，用耳聽，並要放在心上。我帶你到這裏來，特為要指示你；凡你所見的，你都要告訴以色列家。"

東門至外院

5我見殿四圍有牆，那人手拿量度的竿，長六肘，每肘是一肘零一掌。他用竿量牆，厚一竿，高一竿。

6他到了朝東的門，就上門的臺階，量門的這檻，寬一竿；又量門的那檻，寬一竿。7又有衛房，每房長一竿，寬一竿，相隔五肘。門檻，就是挨着向殿的廊門檻，寬一竿。

⁸他又量向殿門的廊子，寬一竿。⁹又量門廊，寬八肘；牆柱厚二肘，那門的廊子向着殿。

¹⁰東門洞有衛房，這旁三間，那旁三間，都是一樣的尺寸；這邊的柱子和那邊的柱子，也是一樣的尺寸。¹¹他量門口，寬十肘，長十三肘。¹²衛房前展出的境界，這邊一肘，那邊一肘；衛房這邊六肘，那邊六肘。¹³又量門洞，從這衛房頂的後檐到那衛房頂的後檐，寬二十五肘，衛房門與門相對。¹⁴又量（註："量"原文作"造"）廊子六十肘（註：七十𧩙作二十肘）。牆柱外是院子，有廊為界，在門洞兩邊。¹⁵從大門口至內廊前，共五十肘。¹⁶衛房和門洞兩旁柱間並廊子，都有嚴緊的窗櫺，裏邊都有窗櫺，柱上有雕刻的棕樹。

外院

¹⁷他帶我到外院，見院的四圍有鋪石地，鋪石地上有屋子三十間。¹⁸鋪石地，就是矮鋪石地在各門洞兩旁，以門洞的長短為度。¹⁹他從下門量到內院外，共寬一百肘；東面、北面都是如此。

北門

²⁰他量外院朝北的門，長寬若干。²¹門洞的衛房，這旁三間，那旁三間。門洞的柱子和廊子與第一門的尺寸一樣。門洞長五十肘，寬二十五肘。²²其窗櫺和廊子，並雕刻的棕樹，與朝東的門尺寸一樣。登七

⁸Then he measured the portico of the gateway; ⁹it[a] was eight cubits deep and its jambs were two cubits thick. The portico of the gateway faced the temple.

¹⁰Inside the east gate were three alcoves on each side; the three had the same measurements, and the faces of the projecting walls on each side had the same measurements. ¹¹Then he measured the width of the entrance to the gateway; it was ten cubits and its length was thirteen cubits. ¹²In front of each alcove was a wall one cubit high, and the alcoves were six cubits square. ¹³Then he measured the gateway from the top of the rear wall of one alcove to the top of the opposite one; the distance was twenty-five cubits from one parapet opening to the opposite one. ¹⁴He measured along the faces of the projecting walls all around the inside of the gateway—sixty cubits. The measurement was up to the portico[b] facing the courtyard.[c] ¹⁵The distance from the entrance of the gateway to the far end of its portico was fifty cubits. ¹⁶The alcoves and the projecting walls inside the gateway were surmounted by narrow parapet openings all around, as was the portico; the openings all around faced inward. The faces of the projecting walls were decorated with palm trees.

The Outer Court

¹⁷Then he brought me into the outer court. There I saw some rooms and a pavement that had been constructed all around the court; there were thirty rooms along the pavement. ¹⁸It abutted the sides of the gateways and was as wide as they were long; this was the lower pavement. ¹⁹Then he measured the distance from the inside of the lower gateway to the outside of the inner court; it was a hundred cubits on the east side as well as on the north.

The North Gate

²⁰Then he measured the length and width of the gate facing north, leading into the outer court. ²¹Its alcoves—three on each side—its projecting walls and its portico had the same measurements as those of the first gateway. It was fifty cubits long and twenty-five cubits wide. ²²Its openings, its portico and its palm tree decorations had the same measurements as those of the gate facing east. Seven steps led up to it,

a 8,9 Many Hebrew manuscripts, Septuagint, Vulgate and Syriac; most Hebrew manuscripts *gateway facing the temple; it was one rod deep.* ⁹ *Then he measured the portico of the gateway; it* *b 14* Septuagint; Hebrew *projecting wall*   *c 14* The meaning of the Hebrew for this verse is uncertain.

with its portico opposite them. ²³There was a gate to the inner court facing the north gate, just as there was on the east. He measured from one gate to the opposite one; it was a hundred cubits.

The South Gate

²⁴Then he led me to the south side and I saw a gate facing south. He measured its jambs, its portico, and they had the same measurements as the others. ²⁵The gateway and its portico had narrow openings all around, like the openings of the others. It was fifty cubits long and twenty-five cubits wide. ²⁶Seven steps led up to it, with its portico opposite them; it had palm tree decorations on the faces of the projecting walls on each side. ²⁷The inner court also had a gate facing south, and he measured from this gate to the outer gate on the south side; it was a hundred cubits.

Gates to the Inner Court

²⁸Then he brought me into the inner court through the south gate, and he measured the south gate; it had the same measurements as the others. ²⁹Its alcoves, its projecting walls and its portico had the same measurements as the others. The gateway and its portico had openings all around. It was fifty cubits long and twenty-five cubits wide. ³⁰(The porticoes of the gateways around the inner court were twenty-five cubits wide and five cubits deep.) ³¹Its portico faced the outer court; palm trees decorated its jambs, and eight steps led up to it.

³²Then he brought me to the inner court on the east side, and he measured the gateway; it had the same measurements as the others. ³³Its alcoves, its projecting walls and its portico had the same measurements as the others. The gateway and its portico had openings all around. It was fifty cubits long and twenty-five cubits wide. ³⁴Its portico faced the outer court; palm trees decorated the jambs on either side, and eight steps led up to it.

³⁵Then he brought me to the north gate and measured it. It had the same measurements as the others, ³⁶as did its alcoves, its projecting walls and its portico, and it had openings all around. It was fifty cubits long and twenty-five cubits wide. ³⁷Its portico[a] faced the outer court; palm trees decorated the jambs on either side, and eight steps led up to it.

The Rooms for Preparing Sacrifices

³⁸A room with a doorway was by the portico

---

[a] 37 Septuagint (see also verses 31 and 34); Hebrew *jambs*

層臺階上到這門,前面有廊子。²³內院有門與這門相對,北面、東面都是如此。他從這門量到那門,共一百肘。

南門

²⁴他帶我往南去,見朝南有門。又照先前的尺寸量門洞的柱子和廊子。²⁵門洞兩旁與廊子的周圍都有窗櫺,和先量的窗櫺一樣。門洞長五十肘,寬二十五肘。²⁶登七層臺階上到這門,前面有廊子;柱上有雕刻的棕樹,這邊一棵,那邊一棵。²⁷內院朝南有門。從這門量到朝南的那門,共一百肘。

往內院的門

²⁸他帶我從南門到內院,就照先前的尺寸量南門。²⁹衛房和柱子,並廊子都照先前的尺寸。門洞兩旁與廊子的周圍都有窗櫺。門洞長五十肘,寬二十五肘。³⁰周圍有廊子,長二十五肘,寬五肘。³¹廊子朝着外院,柱上有雕刻的棕樹。登八層臺階上到這門。

³²他帶我到內院的東面,就照先前的尺寸量東門。³³衛房和柱子,並廊子都照先前的尺寸。門洞兩旁與廊子的周圍都有窗櫺。門洞長五十肘,寬二十五肘。³⁴廊子朝着外院。門洞兩旁的柱子,都有雕刻的棕樹。登八層臺階上到這門。

³⁵他帶我到北門,就照先前的尺寸量那門,³⁶就是量衛房和柱子,並廊子。門洞周圍都有窗櫺。門洞長五十肘,寬二十五肘。³⁷廊柱朝着外院。門洞兩旁的柱子都有雕刻的棕樹。登八層臺階上到這門。

預備祭牲的屋子

³⁸門洞的柱旁有屋子和門,祭司

（註：原文作"他們"）在那裏洗燔祭牲。³⁹在門廊內，這邊有兩張桌子，那邊有兩張桌子，在其上可以宰殺燔祭牲、贖罪祭牲和贖愆祭牲。⁴⁰上到朝北的門口，這邊有兩張桌子，門廊那邊也有兩張桌子。⁴¹門這邊有四張桌子，那邊有四張桌子，共八張。在其上祭司宰殺犧牲。⁴²為燔祭牲有四張桌子，是鑿過的石頭做成的：長一肘半，寬一肘半，高一肘。祭司將宰殺燔祭牲和平安祭牲所用的器皿放在其上。⁴³有鈎子，寬一掌，釘在廊內的四圍。桌子上有犧牲的肉。

祭司的屋子

⁴⁴在北門旁，內院裏有屋子，為歌唱的人而設。這屋子朝南，在南門旁，又有一間朝北（註："南"原文作"東"）。⁴⁵他對我說："這朝南的屋子是為看守殿宇的祭司；⁴⁶那朝北的屋子是為看守祭壇的祭司。這些祭司，是<u>利未人中撒督</u>的子孫，近前來侍奉耶和華的。"

⁴⁷他又量內院，長一百肘，寬一百肘，是見方的。祭壇在殿前。

聖殿

⁴⁸於是，他帶我到殿前的廊子，量廊子的牆柱。這面厚五肘，那面厚五肘。門兩旁，這邊三肘，那邊三肘。⁴⁹廊子長二十肘，寬十一肘。上廊子有臺階，靠近牆柱又有柱子，這邊一根，那邊一根。

41

他帶我到殿那裏量牆柱，這面厚六肘，那面厚六肘，寬

---

in each of the inner gateways, where the burnt offerings were washed. ³⁹In the portico of the gateway were two tables on each side, on which the burnt offerings, sin offerings and guilt offerings were slaughtered. ⁴⁰By the outside wall of the portico of the gateway, near the steps at the entrance to the north gateway were two tables, and on the other side of the steps were two tables. ⁴¹So there were four tables on one side of the gateway and four on the other—eight tables in all—on which the sacrifices were slaughtered. ⁴²There were also four tables of dressed stone for the burnt offerings, each a cubit and a half long, a cubit and a half wide and a cubit high. On them were placed the utensils for slaughtering the burnt offerings and the other sacrifices. ⁴³And double-pronged hooks, each a handbreadth long, were attached to the wall all around. The tables were for the flesh of the offerings.

Rooms for the Priests

⁴⁴Outside the inner gate, within the inner court, were two rooms, one[a] at the side of the north gate and facing south, and another at the side of the south[b] gate and facing north. ⁴⁵He said to me, "The room facing south is for the priests who have charge of the temple, ⁴⁶and the room facing north is for the priests who have charge of the altar. These are the sons of Zadok, who are the only Levites who may draw near to the LORD to minister before him."

⁴⁷Then he measured the court: It was square—a hundred cubits long and a hundred cubits wide. And the altar was in front of the temple.

The Temple

⁴⁸He brought me to the portico of the temple and measured the jambs of the portico; they were five cubits wide on either side. The width of the entrance was fourteen cubits and its projecting walls were[c] three cubits wide on either side. ⁴⁹The portico was twenty cubits wide, and twelve[d] cubits from front to back. It was reached by a flight of stairs,[e] and there were pillars on each side of the jambs.

41

Then the man brought me to the outer sanctuary and measured the jambs; the width of the jambs was six cubits[f] on

---

a 44 Septuagint; Hebrew were rooms for singers, which were
b 44 Septuagint; Hebrew east   c 48 Septuagint; Hebrew entrance was   d 49 Septuagint; Hebrew eleven   e 49 Hebrew; Septuagint Ten steps led up to it   f 1 The common cubit was about 1 1/2 feet (about 0.5 meter).

each side.*a* 2The entrance was ten cubits wide, and the projecting walls on each side of it were five cubits wide. He also measured the outer sanctuary; it was forty cubits long and twenty cubits wide.

3Then he went into the inner sanctuary and measured the jambs of the entrance; each was two cubits wide. The entrance was six cubits wide, and the projecting walls on each side of it were seven cubits wide. 4And he measured the length of the inner sanctuary; it was twenty cubits, and its width was twenty cubits across the end of the outer sanctuary. He said to me, "This is the Most Holy Place."

5Then he measured the wall of the temple; it was six cubits thick, and each side room around the temple was four cubits wide. 6The side rooms were on three levels, one above another, thirty on each level. There were ledges all around the wall of the temple to serve as supports for the side rooms, so that the supports were not inserted into the wall of the temple. 7The side rooms all around the temple were wider at each successive level. The structure surrounding the temple was built in ascending stages, so that the rooms widened as one went upward. A stairway went up from the lowest floor to the top floor through the middle floor.

8I saw that the temple had a raised base all around it, forming the foundation of the side rooms. It was the length of the rod, six long cubits. 9The outer wall of the side rooms was five cubits thick. The open area between the side rooms of the temple 10and the ⌊priests'⌋ rooms was twenty cubits wide all around the temple. 11There were entrances to the side rooms from the open area, one on the north and another on the south; and the base adjoining the open area was five cubits wide all around.

12The building facing the temple courtyard on the west side was seventy cubits wide. The wall of the building was five cubits thick all around, and its length was ninety cubits.

13Then he measured the temple; it was a hundred cubits long, and the temple courtyard and the building with its walls were also a hundred cubits long. 14The width of the temple courtyard on the east, including the front of the temple, was a hundred cubits.

15Then he measured the length of the building facing the courtyard at the rear of the temple, including its galleries on each side; it was a hundred cubits.

窄與會幕相同。2門口寬十肘。門兩旁，這邊五肘，那邊五肘。他量殿長四十肘，寬二十肘。

3他到內殿量牆柱，各厚二肘，門口寬六肘，門兩旁各寬七肘。4他量內殿，長二十肘，寬二十肘。他對我說："這是至聖所。"

5他又量殿牆，厚六肘；圍着殿有旁屋，各寬四肘。6旁屋有三層，層疊而上，每層排列三十間。旁屋的梁木擱在殿牆坎上，免得插入殿牆。7這圍殿的旁屋，越高越寬，因旁屋圍殿懸疊而上，所以越上越寬，從下一層，由中一層，到上一層。

8我又見圍着殿有高月臺。旁屋的根基，高足一竿，就是六大肘。9旁屋的外牆厚五肘。旁屋之外還有餘地。10在旁屋與對面的房屋中間有空地，寬二十肘。11旁屋的門都向餘地：一門向北，一門向南。周圍的餘地寬五肘。

12在西面空地之後有房子，寬七十肘，長九十肘，牆四圍厚五肘。

13這樣，他量殿，長一百肘；又量空地和那房子並牆，共長一百肘。14殿的前面和兩旁的空地，寬一百肘。

15他量空地後面的那房子，並兩旁的樓廊，共長一百肘。

<hr>

a 1 One Hebrew manuscript and Septuagint; most Hebrew manuscripts side, the width of the tent

16內殿、院廊、門檻，嚴緊的窗櫺，並對着門檻的三層樓廊，從地到窗櫺（窗櫺都有蔽子），17直到門以上，就是到內殿和外殿內外四圍牆壁，都按尺寸用木板遮蔽。18牆上雕刻基路伯和棕樹。每二基路伯中間有一棵棕樹，每基路伯有兩臉。19這邊有人臉向着棕樹，那邊有獅子臉向着棕樹，殿內周圍都是如此。20從地至門以上都有基路伯和棕樹。殿牆就是這樣。

21殿的門柱是方的。至聖所的前面，形狀和殿的形狀一樣。22壇是木頭做的，高三肘，長二肘。壇角和壇面並四旁，都是木頭做的。他對我說："這是耶和華面前的桌子。"23殿和至聖所的門各有兩扇。24每扇分兩扇，這兩扇是摺疊的。這邊門分兩扇，那邊門也分兩扇。25殿的門扇上雕刻基路伯和棕樹，與刻在牆上的一般。在外頭殿前有木檻。26廊這邊那邊都有嚴緊的窗櫺和棕樹，殿的旁屋和檻，就是這樣。

祭司用的聖屋

42 他帶我出來向北，到外院。又帶我進入聖屋，這聖屋一排順着空地，一排與北邊鋪石地之屋相對。2這聖屋長一百肘，寬五十肘，有向北的門。3對着內院那二十肘寬之空地，又對着外院的鋪石地，在第三層樓上有樓廊對着樓廊。4在聖屋前有一條夾道，寬十肘，長一百肘。房門都向北。5聖屋因為樓廊佔去些地方，所以上層比

The outer sanctuary, the inner sanctuary and the portico facing the court, 16as well as the thresholds and the narrow windows and galleries around the three of them—everything beyond and including the threshold was covered with wood. The floor, the wall up to the windows, and the windows were covered. 17In the space above the outside of the entrance to the inner sanctuary and on the walls at regular intervals all around the inner and outer sanctuary 18were carved cherubim and palm trees. Palm trees alternated with cherubim. Each cherub had two faces: 19the face of a man toward the palm tree on one side and the face of a lion toward the palm tree on the other. They were carved all around the whole temple. 20From the floor to the area above the entrance, cherubim and palm trees were carved on the wall of the outer sanctuary.

21The outer sanctuary had a rectangular doorframe, and the one at the front of the Most Holy Place was similar. 22There was a wooden altar three cubits high and two cubits square[a]; its corners, its base[b] and its sides were of wood. The man said to me, "This is the table that is before the LORD." 23Both the outer sanctuary and the Most Holy Place had double doors. 24Each door had two leaves—two hinged leaves for each door. 25And on the doors of the outer sanctuary were carved cherubim and palm trees like those carved on the walls, and there was a wooden overhang on the front of the portico. 26On the sidewalls of the portico were narrow windows with palm trees carved on each side. The side rooms of the temple also had overhangs.

Rooms for the Priests

42 Then the man led me northward into the outer court and brought me to the rooms opposite the temple courtyard and opposite the outer wall on the north side. 2The building whose door faced north was a hundred cubits[c] long and fifty cubits wide. 3Both in the section twenty cubits from the inner court and in the section opposite the pavement of the outer court, gallery faced gallery at the three levels. 4In front of the rooms was an inner passageway ten cubits wide and a hundred cubits[d] long. Their doors were on the north. 5Now the upper rooms were narrower, for the galleries took more space from them than from

a 22 Septuagint; Hebrew long   b 22 Septuagint; Hebrew length   c 2 The common cubit was about 1 1/2 feet (about 0.5 meter).   d 4 Septuagint and Syriac; Hebrew and one cubit

the rooms on the lower and middle floors of the building. ⁶The rooms on the third floor had no pillars, as the courts had; so they were smaller in floor space than those on the lower and middle floors. ⁷There was an outer wall parallel to the rooms and the outer court; it extended in front of the rooms for fifty cubits. ⁸While the row of rooms on the side next to the outer court was fifty cubits long, the row on the side nearest the sanctuary was a hundred cubits long. ⁹The lower rooms had an entrance on the east side as one enters them from the outer court.

¹⁰On the south side*a* along the length of the wall of the outer court, adjoining the temple courtyard and opposite the outer wall, were rooms ¹¹with a passageway in front of them. These were like the rooms on the north; they had the same length and width, with similar exits and dimensions. Similar to the doorways on the north ¹²were the doorways of the rooms on the south. There was a doorway at the beginning of the passageway that was parallel to the corresponding wall extending eastward, by which one enters the rooms.

¹³Then he said to me, "The north and south rooms facing the temple courtyard are the priests' rooms, where the priests who approach the LORD will eat the most holy offerings. There they will put the most holy offerings—the grain offerings, the sin offerings and the guilt offerings—for the place is holy. ¹⁴Once the priests enter the holy precincts, they are not to go into the outer court until they leave behind the garments in which they minister, for these are holy. They are to put on other clothes before they go near the places that are for the people."

¹⁵When he had finished measuring what was inside the temple area, he led me out by the east gate and measured the area all around: ¹⁶He measured the east side with the measuring rod; it was five hundred cubits.*b* ¹⁷He measured the north side; it was five hundred cubits*c* by the measuring rod. ¹⁸He measured the south side; it was five hundred cubits by the measuring rod. ¹⁹Then he turned to the west side and measured; it was five hundred cubits by the measuring rod. ²⁰So he measured the area on all four sides. It had a wall around it, five hundred cubits long and five hundred cubits wide, to separate the holy from the common.

中下兩層窄些。⁶聖屋有三層，卻無柱子，不像外院的屋子有柱子，所以上層比中下兩層更窄。⁷聖屋外，東邊有牆，靠着外院，長五十肘。⁸靠着外院的聖屋，長五十肘。殿北面的聖屋長一百肘。⁹在聖屋以下，東頭有進入之處，就是從外院進入之處。

¹⁰向南（註：原文作“東”）在內院牆裏有聖屋，一排與鋪石地之屋相對，一排順着空地。¹¹這聖屋前的夾道與北邊聖屋的夾道長寬一樣，出入之處與北屋門的樣式相同。¹²正在牆前、夾道的東頭，有門可以進入，與向南聖屋的門一樣。

¹³他對我說：“順着空地的南屋北屋都是聖屋。親近耶和華的祭司當在那裏吃至聖的物，也當在那裏放至聖的物，就是素祭、贖罪祭和贖愆祭，因此處為聖。¹⁴祭司進去出了聖所的時候，不可直到外院，但要在聖屋放下他們供職的衣服，因為是聖衣。要穿上別的衣服，才可以到屬民的外院。”

¹⁵他量完了內殿，就帶我出朝東的門，量院的四圍。¹⁶他用量度的竿量四圍，量東面五百肘（註：原文作“竿”。本章下同）。¹⁷用竿量北面五百肘，¹⁸用竿量南面五百肘。¹⁹又轉到西面，用竿量五百肘。²⁰他量四面，四圍有牆，長五百肘，寬五百肘，為要分別聖地與俗地。

---

a 10 Septuagint; Hebrew *Eastward*   *b 16* See Septuagint of verse *17;* Hebrew *rods;* also in verses 18 and 19.
c 17 Septuagint; Hebrew *rods*

榮光回到聖殿

43 以後，他帶我到一座門，就是朝東的門。²以色列神的榮光從東而來。他的聲音如同多水的聲音，地就因他的榮耀發光。³其狀如從前他來滅城的時候我所見的異象。那異象如我在迦巴魯河邊所見的異象，我就俯伏在地。⁴耶和華的榮光從朝東的門照入殿中。⁵靈將我舉起帶入內院，不料，耶和華的榮光充滿了殿。

⁶我聽見有一位從殿中對我說話。有一人站在我旁邊。⁷他對我說：「人子啊，這是我寶座之地，是我腳掌所踏之地。我要在這裏住，在以色列人中直到永遠。以色列家和他們的君王必不再玷污我的聖名，就是行邪淫，在錫安的高處葬埋他們君王的屍首。⁸使他們的門檻挨近我的門檻；他們的門框挨近我的門框。他們與我中間僅隔一牆，並且行可憎的事，玷污了我的聖名，所以我發怒滅絕他們。⁹現在他們當從我面前遠除邪淫和他們君王的屍首，我就住在他們中間直到永遠。

¹⁰「人子啊，你要將這殿指示以色列家，使他們因自己的罪孽慚愧，也要他們量殿的尺寸。¹¹他們若因自己所行的一切事慚愧，你就將殿的規模、樣式、出入之處和一切形狀、典章、禮儀、法則指示他們，在他們眼前寫上，使他們遵照殿的一切規模典章去做。

¹²「殿的法則乃是如此：殿在山頂上，四圍的全界要稱為至聖。這就是殿的法則。

祭壇

¹³「以下量祭壇，是以肘為度（這肘是一肘零一掌）。底座高一

The Glory Returns to the Temple

43 Then the man brought me to the gate facing east, ²and I saw the glory of the God of Israel coming from the east. His voice was like the roar of rushing waters, and the land was radiant with his glory. ³The vision I saw was like the vision I had seen when he*a* came to destroy the city and like the visions I had seen by the Kebar River, and I fell facedown. ⁴The glory of the LORD entered the temple through the gate facing east. ⁵Then the Spirit lifted me up and brought me into the inner court, and the glory of the LORD filled the temple.

⁶While the man was standing beside me, I heard someone speaking to me from inside the temple. ⁷He said: "Son of man, this is the place of my throne and the place for the soles of my feet. This is where I will live among the Israelites forever. The house of Israel will never again defile my holy name—neither they nor their kings—by their prostitution*b* and the lifeless idols*c* of their kings at their high places. ⁸When they placed their threshold next to my threshold and their doorposts beside my doorposts, with only a wall between me and them, they defiled my holy name by their detestable practices. So I destroyed them in my anger. ⁹Now let them put away from me their prostitution and the lifeless idols of their kings, and I will live among them forever.

¹⁰"Son of man, describe the temple to the people of Israel, that they may be ashamed of their sins. Let them consider the plan, ¹¹and if they are ashamed of all they have done, make known to them the design of the temple—its arrangement, its exits and entrances—its whole design and all its regulations*d* and laws. Write these down before them so that they may be faithful to its design and follow all its regulations.

¹²"This is the law of the temple: All the surrounding area on top of the mountain will be most holy. Such is the law of the temple.

The Altar

¹³"These are the measurements of the altar in long cubits, that cubit being a cubit*e* and a hand-

a 3 Some Hebrew manuscripts and Vulgate; most Hebrew manuscripts I　　b 7 Or their spiritual adultery; also in verse 9　　c 7 Or the corpses; also in verse 9　　d 11 Some Hebrew manuscripts and Septuagint; most Hebrew manuscripts regulations and its whole design　　e 13 The common cubit was about 1 1/2 feet (about 0.5 meter).

breadth[a]: Its gutter is a cubit deep and a cubit wide, with a rim of one span[b] around the edge. And this is the height of the altar: [14]From the gutter on the ground up to the lower ledge it is two cubits high and a cubit wide, and from the smaller ledge up to the larger ledge it is four cubits high and a cubit wide. [15]The altar hearth is four cubits high, and four horns project upward from the hearth. [16]The altar hearth is square, twelve cubits long and twelve cubits wide. [17]The upper ledge also is square, fourteen cubits long and fourteen cubits wide, with a rim of half a cubit and a gutter of a cubit all around. The steps of the altar face east."

[18]Then he said to me, "Son of man, this is what the Sovereign LORD says: These will be the regulations for sacrificing burnt offerings and sprinkling blood upon the altar when it is built: [19]You are to give a young bull as a sin offering to the priests, who are Levites, of the family of Zadok, who come near to minister before me, declares the Sovereign LORD. [20]You are to take some of its blood and put it on the four horns of the altar and on the four corners of the upper ledge and all around the rim, and so purify the altar and make atonement for it. [21]You are to take the bull for the sin offering and burn it in the designated part of the temple area outside the sanctuary.

[22]"On the second day you are to offer a male goat without defect for a sin offering, and the altar is to be purified as it was purified with the bull. [23]When you have finished purifying it, you are to offer a young bull and a ram from the flock, both without defect. [24]You are to offer them before the LORD, and the priests are to sprinkle salt on them and sacrifice them as a burnt offering to the LORD.

[25]"For seven days you are to provide a male goat daily for a sin offering; you are also to provide a young bull and a ram from the flock, both without defect. [26]For seven days they are to make atonement for the altar and cleanse it; thus they will dedicate it. [27]At the end of these days, from the eighth day on, the priests are to present your burnt offerings and fellowship offerings[c] on the altar. Then I will accept you, declares the Sovereign LORD."

肘，邊寬一肘，四圍起邊高一掌，這是壇的座。[14]從底座到下層磴臺，高二肘，邊寬一肘。從小磴臺到大磴臺，高四肘，邊寬一肘。[15]壇上的供臺，高四肘。供臺的四拐角上都有角。[16]供臺長十二肘，寬十二肘，四面見方；[17]磴臺長十四肘，寬十四肘，四面見方。四圍起邊高半肘，底座四圍的邊寬一肘。臺階朝東。"

[18]他對我說："人子啊，主耶和華如此說：建造祭壇，為要在其上獻燔祭灑血，造成的時候典章如下：[19]主耶和華說：你要將一隻公牛犢作為贖罪祭給祭司利未人撒督的後裔，就是那親近我、侍奉我的。[20]你要取些公牛的血，抹在壇的四角和磴臺的四拐角，並四圍所起的邊上。你這樣潔淨壇，壇就潔淨了。[21]你又要將那作贖罪祭的公牛犢燒在殿外——聖地之外預定之處。

[22]"次日，要將無殘疾的公山羊獻為贖罪祭，要潔淨壇，像用公牛犢潔淨的一樣。[23]潔淨了壇，就要將一隻無殘疾的公牛犢和羊羣中一隻無殘疾的公綿羊，[24]奉到耶和華前。祭司要撒鹽在其上，獻與耶和華為燔祭。

[25]"七日內，每日要預備一隻公山羊為贖罪祭，也要預備一隻公牛犢和羊羣中的一隻公綿羊，都要沒有殘疾的。[26]七日祭司潔淨壇，壇就潔淨了，要這樣把壇分別為聖。[27]滿了七日，自八日以後，祭司要在壇上獻你們的燔祭和平安祭，我必悅納你們。這是主耶和華說的。"

---

[a] 13 That is, about 3 inches (about 8 centimeters)　[b] 13 That is, about 9 inches (about 22 centimeters)　[c] 27 Traditionally peace offerings

君王，利未人，祭司

44 他又帶我回到聖地朝東的外門；那門關閉了。²耶和華對我說：「這門必須關閉，不可敞開，誰也不可由其中進入，因為耶和華以色列的神已經由其中進入，所以必須關閉。³至於王，他必按王的位分，坐在其內，在耶和華面前吃餅。他必由這門的廊而入，也必由此而出。」

⁴他又帶我由北門來到殿前。我觀看，見耶和華的榮光充滿耶和華的殿，我就俯伏在地。

⁵耶和華對我說：「人子啊，我對你所說耶和華殿中的一切典章法則，你要放在心上，用眼看，用耳聽，並要留心殿宇和聖地一切出入之處。⁶你要對那悖逆的以色列家說：『主耶和華如此說：以色列家啊，你們行一切可憎的事，當夠了吧！⁷你們把我的食物，就是脂油和血獻上的時候，將身心未受割禮的外邦人領進我的聖地，玷污了我的殿；又背了我的約，在你們一切可憎的事上，加上這一層。⁸你們也沒有看守我的聖物，卻派別人在聖地替你們看守我所吩咐你們的。⁹主耶和華如此說：以色列中的外邦人，就是身心未受割禮的，都不可入我的聖地。

¹⁰『當以色列人走迷的時候，有利未人遠離我，就是走迷離開我，隨從他們的偶像，他們必擔當自己的罪孽。¹¹然而他們必在我的聖地當僕役，照管殿門，在殿中供職；必為民宰殺燔祭牲和平安祭牲，必站在民前伺候他們。¹²因為這些利未人曾在偶像前伺候這民，成了以色列家罪孽的絆腳石。所以我向他們起誓：他們必擔當自己的罪孽。這是主耶和華說的。¹³他們不可親近我，給我供祭司的職分，也不可挨近我的一件聖物，就是至聖的物；他們卻要擔當自己的羞辱和所行可憎之事的報應。¹⁴然而我要使他們看守殿宇，辦理其中的一切事，並做其內一切當做之工。』

¹⁵「『以色列人走迷離開我的時候，祭司利未人撒督的子孫，仍看

The Prince, the Levites, the Priests

44 Then the man brought me back to the outer gate of the sanctuary, the one facing east, and it was shut. ²The LORD said to me, "This gate is to remain shut. It must not be opened; no one may enter through it. It is to remain shut because the LORD, the God of Israel, has entered through it. ³The prince himself is the only one who may sit inside the gateway to eat in the presence of the LORD. He is to enter by way of the portico of the gateway and go out the same way."

⁴Then the man brought me by way of the north gate to the front of the temple. I looked and saw the glory of the LORD filling the temple of the LORD, and I fell facedown.

⁵The LORD said to me, "Son of man, look carefully, listen closely and give attention to everything I tell you concerning all the regulations regarding the temple of the LORD. Give attention to the entrance of the temple and all the exits of the sanctuary. ⁶Say to the rebellious house of Israel, 'This is what the Sovereign LORD says: Enough of your detestable practices, O house of Israel! ⁷In addition to all your other detestable practices, you brought foreigners uncircumcised in heart and flesh into my sanctuary, desecrating my temple while you offered me food, fat and blood, and you broke my covenant. ⁸Instead of carrying out your duty in regard to my holy things, you put others in charge of my sanctuary. ⁹This is what the Sovereign LORD says: No foreigner uncircumcised in heart and flesh is to enter my sanctuary, not even the foreigners who live among the Israelites.

¹⁰" 'The Levites who went far from me when Israel went astray and who wandered from me after their idols must bear the consequences of their sin. ¹¹They may serve in my sanctuary, having charge of the gates of the temple and serving in it; they may slaughter the burnt offerings and sacrifices for the people and stand before the people and serve them. ¹²But because they served them in the presence of their idols and made the house of Israel fall into sin, therefore I have sworn with uplifted hand that they must bear the consequences of their sin, declares the Sovereign LORD. ¹³They are not to come near to serve me as priests or come near any of my holy things or my most holy offerings; they must bear the shame of their detestable practices. ¹⁴Yet I will put them in charge of the duties of the temple and all the work that is to be done in it.

¹⁵" 'But the priests, who are Levites and descendants of Zadok and who faithfully car-

12The shekel*a* is to consist of twenty gerahs. Twenty shekels plus twenty-five shekels plus fifteen shekels equal one mina.*b*

Offerings and Holy Days

13" 'This is the special gift you are to offer: a sixth of an ephah from each homer of wheat and a sixth of an ephah from each homer of barley. 14The prescribed portion of oil, measured by the bath, is a tenth of a bath from each cor (which consists of ten baths or one homer, for ten baths are equivalent to a homer). 15Also one sheep is to be taken from every flock of two hundred from the well-watered pastures of Israel. These will be used for the grain offerings, burnt offerings and fellowship offerings*c* to make atonement for the people, declares the Sovereign LORD. 16All the people of the land will participate in this special gift for the use of the prince in Israel. 17It will be the duty of the prince to provide the burnt offerings, grain offerings and drink offerings at the festivals, the New Moons and the Sabbaths—at all the appointed feasts of the house of Israel. He will provide the sin offerings, grain offerings, burnt offerings and fellowship offerings to make atonement for the house of Israel.

18" 'This is what the Sovereign LORD says: In the first month on the first day you are to take a young bull without defect and purify the sanctuary. 19The priest is to take some of the blood of the sin offering and put it on the doorposts of the temple, on the four corners of the upper ledge of the altar and on the gateposts of the inner court. 20You are to do the same on the seventh day of the month for anyone who sins unintentionally or through ignorance; so you are to make atonement for the temple.

21" 'In the first month on the fourteenth day you are to observe the Passover, a feast lasting seven days, during which you shall eat bread made without yeast. 22On that day the prince is to provide a bull as a sin offering for himself and for all the people of the land. 23Every day during the seven days of the Feast he is to provide seven bulls and seven rams without defect as a burnt offering to the LORD, and a male goat for a sin offering. 24He is to provide a grain offering an ephah for each bull and an ephah for each ram, along with a hin*d* of oil for each ephah.

---

a 12 A shekel weighed about 2/5 ounce (about 11.5 grams).
b 12 That is, 60 shekels; the common mina was 50 shekels.
c 15 Traditionally *peace offerings*; also in verse 17   *d 24* That is, probably about 4 quarts (about 4 liters)

賀梅珥的大小為準。12舍客勒是二十季拉。二十舍客勒，二十五舍客勒，十五舍客勒，為你們的彌那。

供物與聖日

13 ' '你們當獻的供物乃是這樣：一賀梅珥麥子要獻伊法六分之一；一賀梅珥大麥要獻伊法六分之一。14你們獻所分定的油，按油的罷特，一柯珥油要獻罷特十分之一（原來十罷特就是一賀梅珥）。15從以色列滋潤的草場上，每二百羊中要獻一隻羊羔。這都可作素祭、燔祭、平安祭，為民贖罪。這是主耶和華說的。16此地的民都要奉上這供物給以色列中的王。17王的本分，是在節期、月朔、安息日，就是以色列家一切的節期，奉上燔祭、素祭、奠祭。他要預備贖罪祭、素祭、燔祭和平安祭，為以色列家贖罪。

18 ' '主耶和華如此說：正月初一日，你要取無殘疾的公牛犢，潔淨聖所。19祭司要取些贖罪祭牲的血，抹在殿的門柱上和壇磴臺的四角上，並內院的門框上。20本月初七日（註：七十經作「七月初一日」）也要為誤犯罪的和愚蒙犯罪的如此行，為殿贖罪。

21 ' '正月十四日，你們要守逾越節，守節七日，要吃無酵餅。22當日，王要為自己和國內的眾民，預備一隻公牛作贖罪祭。23這節的七日，每日他要為耶和華預備無殘疾的公牛七隻、公綿羊七隻為燔祭。每日又要預備公山羊一隻為贖罪祭。24他也要預備素祭，就是為一隻公牛同獻一伊法細麵，為一隻公綿羊同獻一伊法細麵，每一伊法細麵加油一欣。

25 " '七月十五日守節的時候，七日他都要如此行，照逾越節的贖罪祭、燔祭、素祭和油的條例一樣。

46 " '主耶和華如此説：內院朝東的門，在辦理事務的六日內必須關閉，惟有安息日和月朔必須敞開。2王要從這門的廊進入，站在門框旁邊。祭司要為他預備燔祭和平安祭，他就要在門檻那裏敬拜，然後出去。這門直到晚上不可關閉。3在安息日和月朔，國內的居民要在這門口，耶和華面前敬拜。4安息日，王所獻與耶和華的燔祭，要用無殘疾的羊羔六隻，無殘疾的公綿羊一隻，5同獻的素祭要為公綿羊獻一伊法細麵，為羊羔照他的力量而獻，一伊法細麵加油一欣。6當月朔，要獻無殘疾的公牛犢一隻、羊羔六隻、公綿羊一隻，都要無殘疾的。7他也要預備素祭，為公牛獻一伊法細麵，為公綿羊獻一伊法細麵，為羊羔照他的力量而獻，一伊法細麵加油一欣。8王進入的時候必由這門的廊而入，也必由此而出。

9 " '在各節期，國內居民朝見耶和華的時候，從北門進入敬拜的，必由南門而出；從南門進入的，必由北門而出。不可從所入的門而出，必要直往前行，由對門而出。10民進入，王也要在民中進入；民出去，王也要一同出去。

11 " '在節期和聖會的日子同獻的素祭，要為一隻公牛獻一伊法細麵，為一隻公綿羊獻一伊法細麵，為羊羔照他的力量而獻，一伊法細麵加油一欣。12王預備甘心獻的燔祭或平安祭，就是向耶和華甘心獻的，當有人為他開朝東的門。他就預備燔祭和平安祭與安息日預備的一樣。獻畢就出去，他出去之後，當有人將門關閉。

25 " 'During the seven days of the Feast, which begins in the seventh month on the fifteenth day, he is to make the same provision for sin offerings, burnt offerings, grain offerings and oil.

46 " 'This is what the Sovereign LORD says: The gate of the inner court facing east is to be shut on the six working days, but on the Sabbath day and on the day of the New Moon it is to be opened. 2The prince is to enter from the outside through the portico of the gateway and stand by the gatepost. The priests are to sacrifice his burnt offering and his fellowship offerings.[a] He is to worship at the threshold of the gateway and then go out, but the gate will not be shut until evening. 3On the Sabbaths and New Moons the people of the land are to worship in the presence of the LORD at the entrance to that gateway. 4The burnt offering the prince brings to the LORD on the Sabbath day is to be six male lambs and a ram, all without defect. 5The grain offering given with the ram is to be an ephah,[b] and the grain offering with the lambs is to be as much as he pleases, along with a hin[c] of oil for each ephah. 6On the day of the New Moon he is to offer a young bull, six lambs and a ram, all without defect. 7He is to provide as a grain offering one ephah with the bull, one ephah with the ram, and with the lambs as much as he wants to give, along with a hin of oil with each ephah. 8When the prince enters, he is to go in through the portico of the gateway, and he is to come out the same way.

9 " 'When the people of the land come before the LORD at the appointed feasts, whoever enters by the north gate to worship is to go out the south gate; and whoever enters by the south gate is to go out the north gate. No one is to return through the gate by which he entered, but each is to go out the opposite gate. 10The prince is to be among them, going in when they go in and going out when they go out.

11 " 'At the festivals and the appointed feasts, the grain offering is to be an ephah with a bull, an ephah with a ram, and with the lambs as much as one pleases, along with a hin of oil for each ephah. 12When the prince provides a freewill offering to the LORD—whether a burnt offering or fellowship offerings—the gate facing east is to be opened for him. He shall offer his burnt offering or his fellowship offerings as he does on the Sabbath day. Then he shall go out, and after he has gone out, the gate will be shut.

---

a 2 Traditionally *peace offerings*; also in verse 12　　b 5 That is, probably about 3/5 bushel (about 22 liters)　　c 5 That is, probably about 4 quarts (about 4 liters)

13" 'Every day you are to provide a year-old lamb without defect for a burnt offering to the LORD; morning by morning you shall provide it. 14You are also to provide with it morning by morning a grain offering, consisting of a sixth of an ephah with a third of a hin of oil to moisten the flour. The presenting of this grain offering to the LORD is a lasting ordinance. 15So the lamb and the grain offering and the oil shall be provided morning by morning for a regular burnt offering.

16" 'This is what the Sovereign LORD says: If the prince makes a gift from his inheritance to one of his sons, it will also belong to his descendants; it is to be their property by inheritance. 17If, however, he makes a gift from his inheritance to one of his servants, the servant may keep it until the year of freedom; then it will revert to the prince. His inheritance belongs to his sons only; it is theirs. 18The prince must not take any of the inheritance of the people, driving them off their property. He is to give his sons their inheritance out of his own property, so that none of my people will be separated from his property.' "

19Then the man brought me through the entrance at the side of the gate to the sacred rooms facing north, which belonged to the priests, and showed me a place at the western end. 20He said to me, "This is the place where the priests will cook the guilt offering and the sin offering and bake the grain offering, to avoid bringing them into the outer court and consecrating the people."

21He then brought me to the outer court and led me around to its four corners, and I saw in each corner another court. 22In the four corners of the outer court were enclosed*a* courts, forty cubits long and thirty cubits wide; each of the courts in the four corners was the same size. 23Around the inside of each of the four courts was a ledge of stone, with places for fire built all around under the ledge. 24He said to me, "These are the kitchens where those who minister at the temple will cook the sacrifices of the people."

The River From the Temple

47 The man brought me back to the entrance of the temple, and I saw water coming out from under the threshold of the temple toward the east (for the temple faced east). The water was coming down from under the south side of the temple, south of the altar.

13 " '每日，你要預備無殘疾一歲的羊羔一隻，獻與耶和華為燔祭，要每早晨預備。14每早晨也要預備同獻的素祭，細麵一伊法六分之一，並油一欣三分之一，調和細麵。這素祭要常獻與耶和華為永遠的定例。15每早晨要這樣預備羊羔、素祭並油為常獻的燔祭。

16 " '主耶和華如此說：王若將產業賜給他的兒子，就成了他兒子的產業，那是他們承受為業的。17倘若王將一分產業賜給他的臣僕，就成了他臣僕的產業；到自由之年仍要歸與王。至於王的產業，必歸與他的兒子。18王不可奪取民的產業，以至驅逐他們離開所承受的；他要從自己的地業中，將產業賜給他兒子，免得我的民分散，各人離開所承受的。' "

19那帶我的，將我從門旁進入之處，領進為祭司預備的聖屋，是朝北的，見後頭西邊有一塊地。20他對我說："這是祭司煮贖愆祭、贖罪祭，烤素祭之地，免得帶到外院，使民成聖。"

21他又帶我到外院，使我經過院子的四拐角，見每拐角各有一個院子。22院子四拐角的院子，周圍有牆，每院長四十肘，寬三十肘。四拐角院子的尺寸都是一樣。23其中周圍有一排房子，房子內有煮肉的地方。24他對我說："這都是煮肉的房子，殿內的僕役要在這裏煮民的祭物。"

從聖殿流出的河

47 他帶我回到殿門，見殿的門檻下有水往東流出（原來殿面朝東）。這水從檻下，由殿的右邊，在祭壇的南邊往下流。

a 22 The meaning of the Hebrew for this word is uncertain.

2他帶我出北門，又領我從外邊轉到朝東的外門，見水從右邊流出。

3他手拿準繩往東出去的時候，量了一千肘，使我趟過水，水到踝子骨。4他又量了一千肘，使我趟過水，水就到膝。再量了一千肘，使我趟過水，水便到腰。5又量了一千肘，水便成了河，使我不能趟過；因為水勢漲起，成為可洑的水，不可趟的河。6他對我說："人子啊，你看見了甚麼？"

他就帶我回到河邊。7我回到河邊的時候，見在河這邊與那邊的岸上有極多的樹木。8他對我說："這水往東方流去，必下到亞拉巴，直到海。所發出來的水必流入鹽海，使水變甜（註：原文作"得醫治"。下同）。9這河水所到之處，凡滋生的動物都必生活，並且因這流來的水必有極多的魚，海水也變甜了。這河水所到之處，百物都必生活。10必有漁夫站在河邊，從隱基底直到隱以革蓮，都作曬（註：或作"張"）網之處。那魚各從其類，好像大海的魚甚多。11只是泥濘之地與窪濕之處不得治好，必為鹽地。12河這邊與那邊的岸上必生長各類的樹木。其果可作食物，葉子不枯乾，果子不斷絕。每月必結新果子，因為這水是從聖所流出來的。樹上的果子必作食物，葉子乃為治病。"

地界

13主耶和華如此說："你們要照地的境界，按以色列十二支派分地為業。約瑟必得兩分。14你們承受這地為業，要彼此均分，因為我曾起誓應許將這地賜與你們的列祖，這地必歸你們為業。

15 "地的四界乃是如此；

2He then brought me out through the north gate and led me around the outside to the outer gate facing east, and the water was flowing from the south side.

3As the man went eastward with a measuring line in his hand, he measured off a thousand cubits[a] and then led me through water that was ankle-deep. 4He measured off another thousand cubits and led me through water that was knee-deep. He measured off another thousand and led me through water that was up to the waist. 5He measured off another thousand, but now it was a river that I could not cross, because the water had risen and was deep enough to swim in—a river that no one could cross. 6He asked me, "Son of man, do you see this?"

Then he led me back to the bank of the river. 7When I arrived there, I saw a great number of trees on each side of the river. 8He said to me, "This water flows toward the eastern region and goes down into the Arabah,[b] where it enters the Sea.[c] When it empties into the Sea,[c] the water there becomes fresh. 9Swarms of living creatures will live wherever the river flows. There will be large numbers of fish, because this water flows there and makes the salt water fresh; so where the river flows everything will live. 10Fishermen will stand along the shore; from En Gedi to En Eglaim there will be places for spreading nets. The fish will be of many kinds—like the fish of the Great Sea.[d] 11But the swamps and marshes will not become fresh; they will be left for salt. 12Fruit trees of all kinds will grow on both banks of the river. Their leaves will not wither, nor will their fruit fail. Every month they will bear, because the water from the sanctuary flows to them. Their fruit will serve for food and their leaves for healing."

The Boundaries of the Land

13This is what the Sovereign LORD says: "These are the boundaries by which you are to divide the land for an inheritance among the twelve tribes of Israel, with two portions for Joseph. 14You are to divide it equally among them. Because I swore with uplifted hand to give it to your forefathers, this land will become your inheritance.

15"This is to be the boundary of the land:

---

a 3 That is, about 1,500 feet (about 450 meters)　b 8 Or the Jordan Valley　c 8 That is, the Dead Sea　d 10 That is, the Mediterranean; also in verses 15, 19 and 20

"On the north side it will run from the Great Sea by the Hethlon road past Lebo[a] Hamath to Zedad, [16]Berothah[b] and Sibraim (which lies on the border between Damascus and Hamath), as far as Hazer Hatticon, which is on the border of Hauran. [17]The boundary will extend from the sea to Hazar Enan,[c] along the northern border of Damascus, with the border of Hamath to the north. This will be the north boundary.

[18]"On the east side the boundary will run between Hauran and Damascus, along the Jordan between Gilead and the land of Israel, to the eastern sea and as far as Tamar.[d] This will be the east boundary.

[19]"On the south side it will run from Tamar as far as the waters of Meribah Kadesh, then along the Wadi [of Egypt] to the Great Sea. This will be the south boundary.

[20]"On the west side, the Great Sea will be the boundary to a point opposite Lebo[e] Hamath. This will be the west boundary.

[21]"You are to distribute this land among yourselves according to the tribes of Israel. [22]You are to allot it as an inheritance for yourselves and for the aliens who have settled among you and who have children. You are to consider them as native-born Israelites; along with you they are to be allotted an inheritance among the tribes of Israel. [23]In whatever tribe the alien settles, there you are to give him his inheritance," declares the Sovereign LORD.

The Division of the Land

48 "These are the tribes, listed by name: At the northern frontier, Dan will have one portion; it will follow the Hethlon road to Lebo[f] Hamath; Hazar Enan and the northern border of Damascus next to Hamath will be part of its border from the east side to the west side.

[2]"Asher will have one portion; it will border the territory of Dan from east to west.

[3]"Naphtali will have one portion; it will border the territory of Asher from east to west.

[4]"Manasseh will have one portion; it will border the territory of Naphtali from east to west.

[5]"Ephraim will have one portion; it will border the territory of Manasseh from east to west.

"北界從大海往希特倫直到西達達口。[16]又往哈馬、比羅他、西伯蓮（西伯蓮在大馬士革與哈馬兩界中間），到浩蘭邊界的哈撒哈提干。[17]這樣，境界從海邊往大馬士革地界上的哈薩以難，北邊以哈馬地為界。這是北界。

[18]"東界在浩蘭、大馬士革、基列和以色列地的中間，就是約旦河。你們要從北界量到東海。這是東界。

[19]"南界是從他瑪到米利巴加低斯的水，延到埃及小河，直到大海。這是南界。

[20]"西界就是大海，從南界直到哈馬口對面之地。這是西界。

[21]"你們要按着以色列的支派彼此分這地。[22]要拈鬮分這地為業，歸與自己和你們中間寄居的外人，就是在你們中間生養兒女的外人。你們要看他們如同以色列人中所生的一樣，他們在以色列支派中要與你們同得地業。[23]外人寄居在哪支派中，你們就在那裏分給他地業。"這是主耶和華說的。

分地

48 "眾支派按名所得之地記在下面：從北頭，由希特倫往哈馬口，到大馬士革地界上的哈薩以難。北邊靠着哈馬地（各支派的地都有東西的邊界），是但的一分。

[2]"挨着但的地界，從東到西，是亞設的一分。

[3]"挨着亞設的地界，從東到西，是拿弗他利的一分。

[4]"挨着拿弗他利的地界，從東到西，是瑪拿西的一分。

[5]"挨着瑪拿西的地界，從東到西，是以法蓮的一分。

---

a 15 Or *past the entrance to*   b 15,16 See Septuagint and Ezekiel 48:1; Hebrew *road to go into Zedad,* [16] *Hamath, Berothah*

c 17 Hebrew *Enon,* a variant of *Enan*   d 18 Septuagint and Syriac; Hebrew *Israel. You will measure to the eastern sea*

e 20 Or *opposite the entrance to*   f 1 Or *to the entrance to*

6 "挨着<u>以法蓮</u>的地界，從東到西，是<u>呂便</u>的一分。

7 "挨着<u>呂便</u>的地界，從東到西，是<u>猶大</u>的一分。"

8 "挨着<u>猶大</u>的地界，從東到西，必有你們所當獻的供地，寬二萬五千肘。從東界到西界，長短與各分之地相同，聖地當在其中。

9 "你們獻與耶和華的供地要長二萬五千肘，寬一萬肘。10這聖供地要歸與祭司，北長二萬五千肘，西寬一萬肘，東寬一萬肘，南長二萬五千肘。耶和華的聖地當在其中。11這地要歸與<u>撒督</u>的子孫中成為聖的祭司，就是那守我所吩咐的。當<u>以色列</u>人走迷的時候，他們不像那些<u>利未</u>人走迷了。12這要歸與供地，是全地中至聖的。供地挨着<u>利未</u>人的地界。

13 "<u>利未</u>人所得的地，要長二萬五千肘，寬一萬肘，與祭司的地界相等，都長二萬五千肘，寬一萬肘。14這地不可賣，不可換，初熟之物也不可歸與別人，因為是歸耶和華為聖的。

15 "這二萬五千肘前面所剩下五千肘寬之地要作俗用，作為造城蓋房郊野之地。城要在當中。16城的尺寸乃是如此：北面四千五百肘，南面四千五百肘，東面四千五百肘，西面四千五百肘。17城必有郊野，向北二百五十肘，向南二百五十肘，向東二百五十肘，向西二百五十肘。18靠着聖供地的餘地，東長一萬肘，西長一萬肘，要與聖供地相等；其中的土產要作城內工人的食物。19所有<u>以色列</u>支派中，在城內做工的，都要耕種這地。20你們所獻的聖供地連歸城之地，是四方的：長二萬五千肘，寬二萬五千肘。

21 "聖供地連歸城之地，兩邊的餘地要歸與王。供地東邊，南北二

6"Reuben will have one portion; it will border the territory of Ephraim from east to west.

7"Judah will have one portion; it will border the territory of Reuben from east to west.

8"Bordering the territory of Judah from east to west will be the portion you are to present as a special gift. It will be 25,000 cubits[a] wide, and its length from east to west will equal one of the tribal portions; the sanctuary will be in the center of it.

9"The special portion you are to offer to the LORD will be 25,000 cubits long and 10,000 cubits[b] wide. 10This will be the sacred portion for the priests. It will be 25,000 cubits long on the north side, 10,000 cubits wide on the west side, 10,000 cubits wide on the east side and 25,000 cubits long on the south side. In the center of it will be the sanctuary of the LORD. 11This will be for the consecrated priests, the Zadokites, who were faithful in serving me and did not go astray as the Levites did when the Israelites went astray. 12It will be a special gift to them from the sacred portion of the land, a most holy portion, bordering the territory of the Levites.

13"Alongside the territory of the priests, the Levites will have an allotment 25,000 cubits long and 10,000 cubits wide. Its total length will be 25,000 cubits and its width 10,000 cubits. 14They must not sell or exchange any of it. This is the best of the land and must not pass into other hands, because it is holy to the LORD.

15"The remaining area, 5,000 cubits wide and 25,000 cubits long, will be for the common use of the city, for houses and for pastureland. The city will be in the center of it 16and will have these measurements: the north side 4,500 cubits, the south side 4,500 cubits, the east side 4,500 cubits, and the west side 4,500 cubits. 17The pastureland for the city will be 250 cubits on the north, 250 cubits on the south, 250 cubits on the east, and 250 cubits on the west. 18What remains of the area, bordering on the sacred portion and running the length of it, will be 10,000 cubits on the east side and 10,000 cubits on the west side. Its produce will supply food for the workers of the city. 19The workers from the city who farm it will come from all the tribes of Israel. 20The entire portion will be a square, 25,000 cubits on each side. As a special gift you will set aside the sacred portion, along with the property of the city.

21"What remains on both sides of the area formed by the sacred portion and the city property will belong to the prince. It will extend east-

a 8 That is, about 7 miles (about 12 kilometers)　　*b 9* That is, about 3 miles (about 5 kilometers)

ward from the 25,000 cubits of the sacred portion to the eastern border, and westward from the 25,000 cubits to the western border. Both these areas running the length of the tribal portions will belong to the prince, and the sacred portion with the temple sanctuary will be in the center of them. ²²So the property of the Levites and the property of the city will lie in the center of the area that belongs to the prince. The area belonging to the prince will lie between the border of Judah and the border of Benjamin.

²³As for the rest of the tribes: Benjamin will have one portion; it will extend from the east side to the west side.

²⁴Simeon will have one portion; it will border the territory of Benjamin from east to west.

²⁵Issachar will have one portion; it will border the territory of Simeon from east to west.

²⁶Zebulun will have one portion; it will border the territory of Issachar from east to west.

²⁷Gad will have one portion; it will border the territory of Zebulun from east to west.

²⁸The southern boundary of Gad will run south from Tamar to the waters of Meribah Kadesh, then along the Wadi ⌊of Egypt⌋ to the Great Sea.*a*

²⁹This is the land you are to allot as an inheritance to the tribes of Israel, and these will be their portions," declares the Sovereign LORD.

The Gates of the City

³⁰"These will be the exits of the city: Beginning on the north side, which is 4,500 cubits long, ³¹the gates of the city will be named after the tribes of Israel. The three gates on the north side will be the gate of Reuben, the gate of Judah and the gate of Levi.

³²"On the east side, which is 4,500 cubits long, will be three gates: the gate of Joseph, the gate of Benjamin and the gate of Dan.

³³"On the south side, which measures 4,500 cubits, will be three gates: the gate of Simeon, the gate of Issachar and the gate of Zebulun.

³⁴"On the west side, which is 4,500 cubits long, will be three gates: the gate of Gad, the gate of Asher and the gate of Naphtali.

³⁵"The distance all around will be 18,000 cubits.

"And the name of the city from that time on will be:

THE LORD IS THERE."

萬五千肘，東至東界，西邊南北二萬五千肘，西至西界，與各分之地相同，都要歸王。聖供地和殿的聖地要在其中，²²並且利未人之地，與歸城之地的東西兩邊延長之地（這兩地在王地中間），就是在猶大和便雅憫兩界中間，要歸與王。

²³ "論到其餘的支派，從東到西，是便雅憫的一分。

²⁴ "挨着便雅憫的地界，從東到西，是西緬的一分。

²⁵ "挨着西緬的地界，從東到西，是以薩迦的一分。

²⁶ "挨着以薩迦的地界，從東到西，是西布倫的一分。

²⁷ "挨着西布倫的地界，從東到西，是迦得的一分。

²⁸ "迦得地的南界，是從他瑪到米利巴加低斯的水，延到埃及小河，直到大海。

²⁹ "這就是你們要拈鬮分給以色列支派為業之地，乃是他們各支派所得之分。" 這是主耶和華說的。

城門

³⁰ "城的北面四千五百肘，出城之處如下：³¹城的各門要按以色列支派的名字。北面有三門：一為呂便門，一為猶大門，一為利未門。

³² "東面四千五百肘，有三門：一為約瑟門，一為便雅憫門，一為但門。

³³ "南面四千五百肘，有三門：一為西緬門，一為以薩迦門，一為西布倫門。

³⁴ "西面四千五百肘，有三門：一為迦得門，一為亞設門，一為拿弗他利門。

³⁵ "城四圍共一萬八千肘。

"從此以後，這城的名字，必稱為：

耶和華的所在。"

---

a 28 That is, the Mediterranean

但以理書

Daniel

但以理在巴比倫受訓

1 猶大王約雅敬在位第三年，巴比倫王尼布甲尼撒來到耶路撒冷，將城圍困。² 主將猶大王約雅敬，並神殿中器皿的幾分交付他手，他就把這器皿帶到示拿地，收入他神的廟裏，放在他神的庫中。

³ 王吩咐太監長亞施毘拿從以色列人的宗室和貴冑中帶進幾個人來，⁴ 就是年少沒有殘疾、相貌俊美、通達各樣學問、知識聰明俱備、足能侍立在王宮裏的，要教他們迦勒底的文字言語。⁵ 王派定將自己所用的膳和所飲的酒，每日賜他們一分，養他們三年。滿了三年，好叫他們在王面前侍立。

⁶ 他們中間有猶大族的人：但以理、哈拿尼雅、米沙利、亞撒利雅。⁷ 太監長給他們起名，稱但以理為伯提沙撒，稱哈拿尼雅為沙得拉，稱米沙利為米煞，稱亞撒利雅為亞伯尼歌。

⁸ 但以理卻立志不以王的膳和王所飲的酒玷污自己，所以求太監長容他不玷污自己。⁹ 神使但以理在太監長眼前蒙恩惠，受憐憫。¹⁰ 太監長對但以理說：“我懼怕我主我王，他已經派定你們的飲食，倘若他見你們的面貌比你們同歲的少年人肌瘦，怎麼好呢？這樣，你們就使我的頭在王那裏難保。”

¹¹ 但以理對太監長所派管理但以理、哈拿尼雅、米沙利、亞撒利雅的委辦說：¹² “求你試試僕人們十天，給我們素菜吃，白水喝，¹³ 然後看看我們的面貌和用王膳那少年人的面貌，就照你所看的待僕人吧！”¹⁴ 委辦便允准他們這件事，試看他們十天。

Daniel's Training in Babylon

1 In the third year of the reign of Jehoiakim king of Judah, Nebuchadnezzar king of Babylon came to Jerusalem and besieged it. ²And the Lord delivered Jehoiakim king of Judah into his hand, along with some of the articles from the temple of God. These he carried off to the temple of his god in Babylonia^a and put in the treasure house of his god.

³Then the king ordered Ashpenaz, chief of his court officials, to bring in some of the Israelites from the royal family and the nobility— ⁴young men without any physical defect, handsome, showing aptitude for every kind of learning, well informed, quick to understand, and qualified to serve in the king's palace. He was to teach them the language and literature of the Babylonians.^b ⁵The king assigned them a daily amount of food and wine from the king's table. They were to be trained for three years, and after that they were to enter the king's service.

⁶Among these were some from Judah: Daniel, Hananiah, Mishael and Azariah. ⁷The chief official gave them new names: to Daniel, the name Belteshazzar; to Hananiah, Shadrach; to Mishael, Meshach; and to Azariah, Abednego.

⁸But Daniel resolved not to defile himself with the royal food and wine, and he asked the chief official for permission not to defile himself this way. ⁹Now God had caused the official to show favor and sympathy to Daniel, ¹⁰but the official told Daniel, "I am afraid of my lord the king, who has assigned your^c food and drink. Why should he see you looking worse than the other young men your age? The king would then have my head because of you."

¹¹Daniel then said to the guard whom the chief official had appointed over Daniel, Hananiah, Mishael and Azariah, ¹²"Please test your servants for ten days: Give us nothing but vegetables to eat and water to drink. ¹³Then compare our appearance with that of the young men who eat the royal food, and treat your servants in accordance with what you see." ¹⁴So he agreed to this and tested them for ten days.

---

^a 2 Hebrew *Shinar*　　^b 4 Or *Chaldeans*　　^c 10 The Hebrew for *your* and *you* in this verse is plural.

¹⁵At the end of the ten days they looked healthier and better nourished than any of the young men who ate the royal food. ¹⁶So the guard took away their choice food and the wine they were to drink and gave them vegetables instead.

¹⁷To these four young men God gave knowledge and understanding of all kinds of literature and learning. And Daniel could understand visions and dreams of all kinds.

¹⁸At the end of the time set by the king to bring them in, the chief official presented them to Nebuchadnezzar. ¹⁹The king talked with them, and he found none equal to Daniel, Hananiah, Mishael and Azariah; so they entered the king's service. ²⁰In every matter of wisdom and understanding about which the king questioned them, he found them ten times better than all the magicians and enchanters in his whole kingdom.

²¹And Daniel remained there until the first year of King Cyrus.

Nebuchadnezzar's Dream

2 In the second year of his reign, Nebuchadnezzar had dreams; his mind was troubled and he could not sleep. ²So the king summoned the magicians, enchanters, sorcerers and astrologers^a to tell him what he had dreamed. When they came in and stood before the king, ³he said to them, "I have had a dream that troubles me and I want to know what it means.^b"

⁴Then the astrologers answered the king in Aramaic,^c "O king, live forever! Tell your servants the dream, and we will interpret it."

⁵The king replied to the astrologers, "This is what I have firmly decided: If you do not tell me what my dream was and interpret it, I will have you cut into pieces and your houses turned into piles of rubble. ⁶But if you tell me the dream and explain it, you will receive from me gifts and rewards and great honor. So tell me the dream and interpret it for me."

⁷Once more they replied, "Let the king tell his servants the dream, and we will interpret it."

⁸Then the king answered, "I am certain that you are trying to gain time, because you realize that this is what I have firmly decided: ⁹If you do not tell me the dream, there is just one penalty for you. You have conspired to tell me misleading and wicked things, hoping the situation will change. So then, tell me the dream, and I will know that you can interpret it for me."

¹⁵過了十天，見他們的面貌比用王膳的一切少年人更加俊美肥胖。¹⁶於是委辦撒去派他們用的膳、飲的酒，給他們素菜吃。

¹⁷這四個少年人，神在各樣文字學問上（註：「學問」原文作「智慧」）賜給他們聰明知識，但以理又明白各樣的異象和夢兆。

¹⁸尼布甲尼撒王預定帶進少年人來的日期滿了，太監長就把他們帶到王面前。¹⁹王與他們談論，見少年人中無一人能比但以理、哈拿尼雅、米沙利、亞撒利雅，所以留他們在王面前侍立。²⁰王考問他們一切事，就見他們的智慧聰明比通國的術士和用法術的勝過十倍。

²¹到塞魯士王元年，但以理還在。

尼布甲尼撒的夢

2 尼布甲尼撒在位第二年，他做了夢，心裏煩亂，不能睡覺。²王吩咐人將術士、用法術的、行邪術的和迦勒底人召來，要他們將王的夢告訴王，他們就來站在王前。³王對他們說："我做了一夢，心裏煩亂，要知道這是甚麼夢。"

⁴迦勒底人用亞蘭的言語對王說："願王萬歲！請將那夢告訴僕人，僕人就可以講解。"

⁵王回答迦勒底人說："夢我已經忘了（註：或作"我已定命"。8節同），你們若不將夢和夢的講解告訴我，就必被凌遲，你們的房屋必成為糞堆；⁶你們若將夢和夢的講解告訴我，就必從我這裏得贈品和賞賜，並大尊榮。現在你們要將夢和夢的講解告訴我。"

⁷他們第二次對王說："請王將夢告訴僕人，僕人就可以講解。"

⁸王回答說："我準知道你們是故意遲延，因為你們知道那夢我已經忘了。⁹你們若不將夢告訴我，只有一法待你們，因為你們預備了謊言亂語向我說，要等候時勢改變。現在你們要將夢告訴我，因我知道你們能將夢的講解告訴我。"

---

^a 2 Or *Chaldeans;* also in verses 4, 5 and 10　　^b 3 Or *was*
^c 4 The text from here through chapter 7 is in Aramaic.

10迦勒底人在王面前回答説：
"世上沒有人能將王所問的事說出
來，因為沒有君王、大臣、掌權的
向術士，或用法術的，或迦勒底人
問過這樣的事。11王所問的事甚難，
除了不與世人同居的神明，沒有人
在王面前能説出來。"

12因此，王氣忿忿地大發烈怒，
吩咐滅絕巴比倫所有的哲士。13於是
命令發出，哲士將要見殺，人就尋
找但以理和他的同伴，要殺他們。

14王的護衛長亞略出來，要殺巴
比倫的哲士，但以理就用婉言回答
他，15向王的護衛長亞略説："王的
命令為何這樣緊急呢？"亞略就將
情節告訴但以理。16但以理遂進去求
王寬限，就可以將夢的講解告訴
王。

17但以理回到他的居所，將這事
告訴他的同伴哈拿尼雅、米沙利、
亞撒利雅，18要他們祈求天上的神施
憐憫，將這奧秘的事指明，免得但
以理和他的同伴與巴比倫其餘的哲
士一同滅亡。19這奧秘的事就在夜間
異象中給但以理顯明，但以理便稱
頌天上的神。20但以理説：

"神的名是應當稱頌的，
　　從亙古直到永遠！
　　因為智慧能力都屬乎他。
21他改變時候、日期、廢王、立王，
　　將智慧賜與智慧人，
　　將知識賜與聰明人。
22他顯明深奧隱秘的事，
　　知道暗中所有的，
　　光明也與他同居。
23我列祖的神啊，
　　我感謝你、讚美你，
　　因你將智慧才能賜給我，
　　允准我們所求的，
　　把王的事給我們指明。"

但以理解夢

24於是但以理進去見亞略，就是
王所派滅絕巴比倫哲士的，對他
説："不要滅絕巴比倫的哲士，求
你領我到王面前，我要將夢的講解
告訴王。"
25亞略就急忙將但以理領到王面
前，對王説："我在被擄的猶大人

10The astrologers answered the king, "There
is not a man on earth who can do what the king
asks! No king, however great and mighty, has
ever asked such a thing of any magician or
enchanter or astrologer. 11What the king asks is
too difficult. No one can reveal it to the king
except the gods, and they do not live among
men."

12This made the king so angry and furious
that he ordered the execution of all the wise men
of Babylon. 13So the decree was issued to put the
wise men to death, and men were sent to look
for Daniel and his friends to put them to death.

14When Arioch, the commander of the king's
guard, had gone out to put to death the wise men
of Babylon, Daniel spoke to him with wisdom
and tact. 15He asked the king's officer, "Why did
the king issue such a harsh decree?" Arioch then
explained the matter to Daniel. 16At this, Daniel
went in to the king and asked for time, so that he
might interpret the dream for him.

17Then Daniel returned to his house and
explained the matter to his friends Hananiah,
Mishael and Azariah. 18He urged them to plead
for mercy from the God of heaven concerning
this mystery, so that he and his friends might
not be executed with the rest of the wise men of
Babylon. 19During the night the mystery was
revealed to Daniel in a vision. Then Daniel
praised the God of heaven 20and said:

"Praise be to the name of God for ever and ever;
　　wisdom and power are his.
21He changes times and seasons;
　　he sets up kings and deposes them.
　　He gives wisdom to the wise
　　and knowledge to the discerning.
22He reveals deep and hidden things;
　　he knows what lies in darkness,
　　and light dwells with him.
23I thank and praise you, O God of my fathers:
　　You have given me wisdom and power,
　　you have made known to me what we asked
　　　of you,
　　you have made known to us the dream of
　　　the king."

Daniel Interprets the Dream

24Then Daniel went to Arioch, whom the king
had appointed to execute the wise men of Babylon, and said to him, "Do not execute the wise
men of Babylon. Take me to the king, and I will
interpret his dream for him."
25Arioch took Daniel to the king at once and
said, "I have found a man among the exiles from

Judah who can tell the king what his dream means."

²⁶The king asked Daniel (also called Belteshazzar), "Are you able to tell me what I saw in my dream and interpret it?"

²⁷Daniel replied, "No wise man, enchanter, magician or diviner can explain to the king the mystery he has asked about, ²⁸but there is a God in heaven who reveals mysteries. He has shown King Nebuchadnezzar what will happen in days to come. Your dream and the visions that passed through your mind as you lay on your bed are these:

²⁹"As you were lying there, O king, your mind turned to things to come, and the revealer of mysteries showed you what is going to happen. ³⁰As for me, this mystery has been revealed to me, not because I have greater wisdom than other living men, but so that you, O king, may know the interpretation and that you may understand what went through your mind.

³¹"You looked, O king, and there before you stood a large statue—an enormous, dazzling statue, awesome in appearance. ³²The head of the statue was made of pure gold, its chest and arms of silver, its belly and thighs of bronze, ³³its legs of iron, its feet partly of iron and partly of baked clay. ³⁴While you were watching, a rock was cut out, but not by human hands. It struck the statue on its feet of iron and clay and smashed them. ³⁵Then the iron, the clay, the bronze, the silver and the gold were broken to pieces at the same time and became like chaff on a threshing floor in the summer. The wind swept them away without leaving a trace. But the rock that struck the statue became a huge mountain and filled the whole earth.

³⁶"This was the dream, and now we will interpret it to the king. ³⁷You, O king, are the king of kings. The God of heaven has given you dominion and power and might and glory; ³⁸in your hands he has placed mankind and the beasts of the field and the birds of the air. Wherever they live, he has made you ruler over them all. You are that head of gold.

³⁹"After you, another kingdom will rise, inferior to yours. Next, a third kingdom, one of bronze, will rule over the whole earth. ⁴⁰Finally, there will be a fourth kingdom, strong as iron—for iron breaks and smashes everything—and as iron breaks things to pieces, so it will crush and break all the others. ⁴¹Just as you saw that the feet and toes were partly of baked clay and partly of iron, so this will be a divided kingdom; yet it will have some of the strength of iron in it,

中遇見一人，他能將夢的講解告訴王。"

²⁶王問稱為伯提沙撒的但以理說："你能將我所做的夢和夢的講解告訴我嗎？"

²⁷但以理在王面前回答說："王所問的那奧秘事，哲士、用法術的、術士、觀兆的都不能告訴王，²⁸只有一位在天上的神，能顯明奧秘的事，他已將日後必有的事指示尼布甲尼撒王。你的夢和你在牀上腦中的異象是這樣：

²⁹"王啊，你在牀上想到後來的事，那顯明奧秘事的主把將來必有的事指示你。³⁰至於那奧秘的事顯明給我，並非因我的智慧勝過一切活人，乃為使王知道夢的講解和心裏的思念。

³¹"王啊，你夢見一個大像，這像甚高，極其光耀，站在你面前，形狀甚是可怕。³²這像的頭是精金的，胸膛和膀臂是銀的，肚腹和腰是銅的，³³腿是鐵的，腳是半鐵半泥的。³⁴你觀看，見有一塊非人手鑿出來的石頭打在這像半鐵半泥的腳上，把腳砸碎，³⁵於是金、銀、銅、鐵、泥都一同砸得粉碎，成如夏天禾場上的糠粃，被風吹散，無處可尋。打碎這像的石頭變成一座大山，充滿天下。

³⁶"這就是那夢，我們在王面前要講解那夢。³⁷王啊，你是諸王之王，天上的神已將國度、權柄、能力、尊榮都賜給你。³⁸凡世人所住之地的走獸，並天空的飛鳥，他都交付你手，使你掌管這一切。你就是那金頭。

³⁹"在你以後必另興一國，不及於你。又有第三國，就是銅的，必掌管天下。⁴⁰第四國，必堅壯如鐵，鐵能打碎剋制百物，又能壓碎一切，那國也必打碎壓制列國。⁴¹你既見像的腳和腳指頭一半是窰匠的泥，一半是鐵，那國將來也必分開。你既見鐵與

泥攙雜，那國也必有鐵的力量。42那腳指頭既是半鐵半泥，那國也必半強半弱。43你既見鐵與泥攙雜，那國民也必與各種人攙雜，卻不能彼此相合，正如鐵與泥不能相合一樣。

44「當那列王在位的時候，天上的神必另立一國，永不敗壞，也不歸別國的人，卻要打碎滅絕那一切國，這國必存到永遠。45你既看見非人手鑿出來的一塊石頭從山而出，打碎金、銀、銅、鐵、泥。

「那就是至大的神把後來必有的事給王指明。這夢準是這樣，這講解也是確實的。」

46當時，尼布甲尼撒王俯伏在地，向但以理下拜，並且吩咐人給他奉上供物和香品。47王對但以理說：「你既能顯明這奧秘的事，你們的神誠然是萬神之神、萬王之主，又是顯明奧秘事的。」

48於是王高抬但以理，賞賜他許多上等禮物，派他管理巴比倫省，又立他為總理，掌管巴比倫的一切哲士。49但以理求王，王就派沙得拉、米煞、亞伯尼歌管理巴比倫省的事務，只是但以理常在朝中侍立。

金像與火窰

3 尼布甲尼撒王造了一個金像，高六十肘，寬六肘，立在巴比倫省杜拉平原。2尼布甲尼撒王差人將總督、欽差、巡撫、臬司、藩司、謀士、法官和各省的官員都召了來，為尼布甲尼撒王所立的像行開光之禮。3於是總督、欽差、巡撫、臬司、藩司、謀士、法官和各省的官員都聚集了來，要為尼布甲尼撒王所立的像行開光之禮，就站在尼布甲尼撒所立的像前。

4那時傳令的大聲呼叫說：「各方、各國、各族的人哪（註：「族」原文作「舌」。下同），有令傳與你們：5你們一聽見角、笛、琵琶、琴、

even as you saw iron mixed with clay. 42As the toes were partly iron and partly clay, so this kingdom will be partly strong and partly brittle. 43And just as you saw the iron mixed with baked clay, so the people will be a mixture and will not remain united, any more than iron mixes with clay.

44"In the time of those kings, the God of heaven will set up a kingdom that will never be destroyed, nor will it be left to another people. It will crush all those kingdoms and bring them to an end, but it will itself endure forever. 45This is the meaning of the vision of the rock cut out of a mountain, but not by human hands—a rock that broke the iron, the bronze, the clay, the silver and the gold to pieces.

"The great God has shown the king what will take place in the future. The dream is true and the interpretation is trustworthy."

46Then King Nebuchadnezzar fell prostrate before Daniel and paid him honor and ordered that an offering and incense be presented to him. 47The king said to Daniel, "Surely your God is the God of gods and the Lord of kings and a revealer of mysteries, for you were able to reveal this mystery."

48Then the king placed Daniel in a high position and lavished many gifts on him. He made him ruler over the entire province of Babylon and placed him in charge of all its wise men. 49Moreover, at Daniel's request the king appointed Shadrach, Meshach and Abednego administrators over the province of Babylon, while Daniel himself remained at the royal court.

The Image of Gold and the Fiery Furnace

3 King Nebuchadnezzar made an image of gold, ninety feet high and nine feet[a] wide, and set it up on the plain of Dura in the province of Babylon. 2He then summoned the satraps, prefects, governors, advisers, treasurers, judges, magistrates and all the other provincial officials to come to the dedication of the image he had set up. 3So the satraps, prefects, governors, advisers, treasurers, judges, magistrates and all the other provincial officials assembled for the dedication of the image that King Nebuchadnezzar had set up, and they stood before it.

4Then the herald loudly proclaimed, "This is what you are commanded to do, O peoples, nations and men of every language: 5As soon as you hear the sound of the horn, flute, zither,

a 1 Aramaic sixty cubits high and six cubits wide (about 27 meters high and 2.7 meters wide)

lyre, harp, pipes and all kinds of music, you must fall down and worship the image of gold that King Nebuchadnezzar has set up. 6Whoever does not fall down and worship will immediately be thrown into a blazing furnace."

7Therefore, as soon as they heard the sound of the horn, flute, zither, lyre, harp and all kinds of music, all the peoples, nations and men of every language fell down and worshiped the image of gold that King Nebuchadnezzar had set up.

8At this time some astrologers*a* came forward and denounced the Jews. 9They said to King Nebuchadnezzar, "O king, live forever! 10You have issued a decree, O king, that everyone who hears the sound of the horn, flute, zither, lyre, harp, pipes and all kinds of music must fall down and worship the image of gold, 11and that whoever does not fall down and worship will be thrown into a blazing furnace. 12But there are some Jews whom you have set over the affairs of the province of Babylon—Shadrach, Meshach and Abednego—who pay no attention to you, O king. They neither serve your gods nor worship the image of gold you have set up."

13Furious with rage, Nebuchadnezzar summoned Shadrach, Meshach and Abednego. So these men were brought before the king, 14and Nebuchadnezzar said to them, "Is it true, Shadrach, Meshach and Abednego, that you do not serve my gods or worship the image of gold I have set up? 15Now when you hear the sound of the horn, flute, zither, lyre, harp, pipes and all kinds of music, if you are ready to fall down and worship the image I made, very good. But if you do not worship it, you will be thrown immediately into a blazing furnace. Then what god will be able to rescue you from my hand?"

16Shadrach, Meshach and Abednego replied to the king, "O Nebuchadnezzar, we do not need to defend ourselves before you in this matter. 17If we are thrown into the blazing furnace, the God we serve is able to save us from it, and he will rescue us from your hand, O king. 18But even if he does not, we want you to know, O king, that we will not serve your gods or worship the image of gold you have set up."

19Then Nebuchadnezzar was furious with Shadrach, Meshach and Abednego, and his attitude toward them changed. He ordered the furnace heated seven times hotter than usual 20and commanded some of the strongest soldiers in his army to tie up Shadrach, Meshach and Abednego and throw them into the blazing furnace. 21So these men, wearing their robes, trousers,

a 8 Or Chaldeans

瑟、笙和各樣樂器的聲音，就當俯伏敬拜尼布甲尼撒王所立的金像。6凡不俯伏敬拜的，必立時扔在烈火的窰中。”

7因此各方、各國、各族的人民一聽見角、笛、琵琶、琴、瑟和各樣樂器的聲音，就都俯伏敬拜尼布甲尼撒王所立的金像。

8那時，有幾個迦勒底人進前來控告猶大人。9他們對尼布甲尼撒王說：“願王萬歲！10王啊，你曾降旨說，凡聽見角、笛、琵琶、琴、瑟、笙和各樣樂器聲音的都當俯伏敬拜金像；11凡不俯伏敬拜的，必立在烈火的窰中。12現在有幾個猶大人，就是王所派管理巴比倫省事務的沙得拉、米煞、亞伯尼歌，王啊，這些人不理你，不侍奉你的神，也不敬拜你所立的金像。”

13當時，尼布甲尼撒沖沖大怒，吩咐人把沙得拉、米煞、亞伯尼歌帶過來，他們就把那些人帶到王面前。14尼布甲尼撒問他們說：“沙得拉、米煞、亞伯尼歌，你們不侍奉我的神，也不敬拜我所立的金像，是故意的嗎？15你們再聽見角、笛、琵琶、琴、瑟、笙和各樣樂器的聲音，若俯伏敬拜我所造的像，卻還可以；若不敬拜，必立時扔在烈火的窰中！有何神能救你們脫離我手呢？”

16沙得拉、米煞、亞伯尼歌對王說：“尼布甲尼撒啊，這件事我們不必回答你。17即便如此，我們所侍奉的神，能將我們從烈火的窰中救出來。王啊，他也必救我們脫離你的手；18即或不然，王啊，你當知道我們決不侍奉你的神，也不敬拜你所立的金像！”

19當時尼布甲尼撒怒氣填胸，向沙得拉、米煞、亞伯尼歌變了臉色，吩咐人把窰燒熱，比尋常更加七倍。20又吩咐他軍中的幾個壯士，將沙得拉、米煞、亞伯尼歌捆起來，扔在烈火的窰中。21這三人穿着褲子、內袍、外衣和別的衣服，被捆起來扔在烈火的窰中。22因為王命緊急，窰又甚熱，那抬扔沙得拉、米煞、亞伯尼歌的人都被火焰燒死。23沙得拉、米煞、亞伯尼歌這三個人都被捆着落在烈火的窰中。

24那時，尼布甲尼撒王驚奇，急忙起來，對謀士說：「我們捆起來扔在火裏的不是三個人嗎？」

他們回答王說：「王啊，是。」

25王說：「看哪，我見有四個人，並沒有捆綁，在火中遊行，也沒有受傷，那第四個的相貌好像神子。」

26於是尼布甲尼撒就近烈火窰門，說：「至高神的僕人沙得拉、米煞、亞伯尼歌出來，上這裏來吧！」

沙得拉、米煞、亞伯尼歌就從火中出來了。27那些總督、欽差、巡撫和王的謀士，一同聚集看這三個人，見火無力傷他們的身體，頭髮也沒有燒焦，衣裳也沒有變色，並沒有火燎的氣味。

28尼布甲尼撒說：「沙得拉、米煞、亞伯尼歌的神是應當稱頌的！他差遣使者救護倚靠他的僕人，他們不遵王命，捨去己身，在他們神以外不肯事奉敬拜別神。29現在我降旨，無論何方、何國、何族的人，謗讟沙得拉、米煞、亞伯尼歌之神的，必被凌遲，他的房屋必成糞堆，因為沒有別神能這樣施行拯救。」

30那時王在巴比倫省，高升了沙得拉、米煞、亞伯尼歌。

尼布甲尼撒夢見大樹

4 尼布甲尼撒王，曉諭住在全地各方、各國、各族的人說：

願你們大享平安！

2我樂意將至高的神向我所行的神蹟奇事宣揚出來。

3他的神蹟何其大！
　他的奇事何其盛！

turbans and other clothes, were bound and thrown into the blazing furnace. 22The king's command was so urgent and the furnace so hot that the flames of the fire killed the soldiers who took up Shadrach, Meshach and Abednego, 23and these three men, firmly tied, fell into the blazing furnace.

24Then King Nebuchadnezzar leaped to his feet in amazement and asked his advisers, "Weren't there three men that we tied up and threw into the fire?"

They replied, "Certainly, O king."

25He said, "Look! I see four men walking around in the fire, unbound and unharmed, and the fourth looks like a son of the gods."

26Nebuchadnezzar then approached the opening of the blazing furnace and shouted, "Shadrach, Meshach and Abednego, servants of the Most High God, come out! Come here!"

So Shadrach, Meshach and Abednego came out of the fire, 27and the satraps, prefects, governors and royal advisers crowded around them. They saw that the fire had not harmed their bodies, nor was a hair of their heads singed; their robes were not scorched, and there was no smell of fire on them.

28Then Nebuchadnezzar said, "Praise be to the God of Shadrach, Meshach and Abednego, who has sent his angel and rescued his servants! They trusted in him and defied the king's command and were willing to give up their lives rather than serve or worship any god except their own God. 29Therefore I decree that the people of any nation or language who say anything against the God of Shadrach, Meshach and Abednego be cut into pieces and their houses be turned into piles of rubble, for no other god can save in this way."

30Then the king promoted Shadrach, Meshach and Abednego in the province of Babylon.

Nebuchadnezzar's Dream of a Tree

4 King Nebuchadnezzar,

To the peoples, nations and men of every language, who live in all the world:

May you prosper greatly!

2It is my pleasure to tell you about the miraculous signs and wonders that the Most High God has performed for me.

3How great are his signs,
　how mighty his wonders!

His kingdom is an eternal kingdom;
> his dominion endures from generation to
> generation.

[4]I, Nebuchadnezzar, was at home in my palace, contented and prosperous. [5]I had a dream that made me afraid. As I was lying in my bed, the images and visions that passed through my mind terrified me. [6]So I commanded that all the wise men of Babylon be brought before me to interpret the dream for me. [7]When the magicians, enchanters, astrologers[a] and diviners came, I told them the dream, but they could not interpret it for me. [8]Finally, Daniel came into my presence and I told him the dream. (He is called Belteshazzar, after the name of my god, and the spirit of the holy gods is in him.)

[9]I said, "Belteshazzar, chief of the magicians, I know that the spirit of the holy gods is in you, and no mystery is too difficult for you. Here is my dream; interpret it for me. [10]These are the visions I saw while lying in my bed: I looked, and there before me stood a tree in the middle of the land. Its height was enormous. [11]The tree grew large and strong and its top touched the sky; it was visible to the ends of the earth. [12]Its leaves were beautiful, its fruit abundant, and on it was food for all. Under it the beasts of the field found shelter, and the birds of the air lived in its branches; from it every creature was fed.

[13]"In the visions I saw while lying in my bed, I looked, and there before me was a messenger,[b] a holy one, coming down from heaven. [14]He called in a loud voice: 'Cut down the tree and trim off its branches; strip off its leaves and scatter its fruit. Let the animals flee from under it and the birds from its branches. [15]But let the stump and its roots, bound with iron and bronze, remain in the ground, in the grass of the field.

" 'Let him be drenched with the dew of heaven, and let him live with the animals among the plants of the earth. [16]Let his mind be changed from that of a man and let him be given the mind of an animal, till seven times[c] pass by for him.

[17]" 'The decision is announced by messengers, the holy ones declare the verdict, so that the living may know that the Most High is sovereign over the kingdoms of men and gives

他的國是永遠的！
他的權柄存到萬代！

[4]我尼布甲尼撒安居在宮中，平順在殿內。[5]我做了一夢，使我懼怕。我在牀上的思念，並腦中的異象，使我驚惶。[6]所以我降旨召巴比倫的一切哲士到我面前，叫他們把夢的講解告訴我。[7]於是那些術士、用法術的、迦勒底人、觀兆的都進來，我將那夢告訴了他們，他們卻不能把夢的講解告訴我。[8]末後，那照我神的名，稱為伯提沙撒的但以理來到我面前，他裏頭有聖神的靈，我將夢告訴他說：

[9]"術士的領袖伯提沙撒啊，因我知道你裏頭有聖神的靈，甚麼奧秘的事都不能使你為難，現在要把我夢中所見的異象和夢的講解告訴我。[10]我在牀上腦中的異象是這樣：我看見地當中有一棵樹，極其高大。[11]那樹漸長，而且堅固，高得頂天，從地極都能看見；[12]葉子華美，果子甚多，可作眾生的食物；田野的走獸臥在蔭下，天空的飛鳥宿在枝上；凡有血氣的都從這樹得食。

[13]"我在牀上腦中的異象，見有一位守望的聖者從天而降，[14]大聲呼叫說：'伐倒這樹！砍下枝子，搖掉葉子，拋散果子，使走獸離開樹下，飛鳥躲開樹枝。[15]樹不卻要留在地內，用鐵圈和銅圈箍住，在田野的青草中讓天露滴濕。

" '使他與地上的獸一同吃草，[16]使他的心改變，不如人心，給他一個獸心，使他經過七期
（註："期"或作"年"。本章同）。

[17]" '這是守望者所發的命，聖者所出的令，好叫世人知道至高者在人的國中掌權，要將國賜與

誰，就賜與誰，或立極卑微的人執掌國權。'

18 "這是我尼布甲尼撒王所做的夢。伯提沙撒啊，你要說明這夢的講解，因為我國中的一切哲士都不能將夢的講解告訴我，惟獨你能，因你裏頭有聖神的靈。"

但以理解夢

19 於是稱為伯提沙撒的但以理驚訝片時，心意驚惶。王說："伯提沙撒啊，不要因夢和夢的講解驚惶。"

伯提沙撒回答說："我主啊，願這夢歸與恨惡你的人，講解歸與你的敵人。20 你所見的樹漸長，而且堅固，高得頂天，從地極都能看見；21 葉子華美，果子甚多，可作眾生的食物；田野的走獸住在其下；天空的飛鳥宿在枝上。22 王啊，這漸長又堅固的樹就是你。你的威勢漸長及天，你的權柄管到地極。

23 "王既看見一位守望的聖者從天而降，說：'將這樹砍伐毀壞，樹不卻要留在地內，用鐵圈和銅圈箍住，在田野的青草中讓天露滴濕，使他與地上的獸一同吃草，直到經過七期。'

24 "王啊，講解就是這樣：臨到我主我王的事是出於至高者的命。25 你必被趕出離開世人，與野地的獸同居，吃草如牛，被天露滴濕，且要經過七期。等你知道至高者在人的國中掌權，要將國賜與誰就賜與誰。26 守望者既吩咐存留樹根，等你知道諸天掌權，以後你的國必定歸你。27 王啊，求你悅納我的諫言，以施行公義斷絕罪過，以憐憫窮人除掉罪孽，或者你的平安可以延長。"

夢兆應驗

28 這事都臨到尼布甲尼撒王。29 過了十二個月，他遊行在巴比倫

them to anyone he wishes and sets over them the lowliest of men.'

18"This is the dream that I, King Nebuchadnezzar, had. Now, Belteshazzar, tell me what it means, for none of the wise men in my kingdom can interpret it for me. But you can, because the spirit of the holy gods is in you."

Daniel Interprets the Dream

19Then Daniel (also called Belteshazzar) was greatly perplexed for a time, and his thoughts terrified him. So the king said, "Belteshazzar, do not let the dream or its meaning alarm you."

Belteshazzar answered, "My lord, if only the dream applied to your enemies and its meaning to your adversaries! 20The tree you saw, which grew large and strong, with its top touching the sky, visible to the whole earth, 21with beautiful leaves and abundant fruit, providing food for all, giving shelter to the beasts of the field, and having nesting places in its branches for the birds of the air— 22you, O king, are that tree! You have become great and strong; your greatness has grown until it reaches the sky, and your dominion extends to distant parts of the earth.

23"You, O king, saw a messenger, a holy one, coming down from heaven and saying, 'Cut down the tree and destroy it, but leave the stump, bound with iron and bronze, in the grass of the field, while its roots remain in the ground. Let him be drenched with the dew of heaven; let him live like the wild animals, until seven times pass by for him.'

24"This is the interpretation, O king, and this is the decree the Most High has issued against my lord the king: 25You will be driven away from people and will live with the wild animals; you will eat grass like cattle and be drenched with the dew of heaven. Seven times will pass by for you until you acknowledge that the Most High is sovereign over the kingdoms of men and gives them to anyone he wishes. 26The command to leave the stump of the tree with its roots means that your kingdom will be restored to you when you acknowledge that Heaven rules. 27Therefore, O king, be pleased to accept my advice: Renounce your sins by doing what is right, and your wickedness by being kind to the oppressed. It may be that then your prosperity will continue."

The Dream Is Fulfilled

28All this happened to King Nebuchadnezzar. 29Twelve months later, as the king was walking on the roof of the royal palace of Babylon, [30]he said, "Is not this the great Babylon I have built as the royal residence, by my mighty power and for the glory of my majesty?"

[31]The words were still on his lips when a voice came from heaven, "This is what is decreed for you, King Nebuchadnezzar: Your royal authority has been taken from you. [32]You will be driven away from people and will live with the wild animals; you will eat grass like cattle. Seven times will pass by for you until you acknowledge that the Most High is sovereign over the kingdoms of men and gives them to anyone he wishes."

[33]Immediately what had been said about Nebuchadnezzar was fulfilled. He was driven away from people and ate grass like cattle. His body was drenched with the dew of heaven until his hair grew like the feathers of an eagle and his nails like the claws of a bird.

[34]At the end of that time, I, Nebuchadnezzar, raised my eyes toward heaven, and my sanity was restored. Then I praised the Most High; I honored and glorified him who lives forever.

His dominion is an eternal dominion;
　his kingdom endures from generation to
　　generation.
[35]All the peoples of the earth
　are regarded as nothing.
He does as he pleases
　with the powers of heaven
　and the peoples of the earth.
No one can hold back his hand
　or say to him: "What have you done?"

[36]At the same time that my sanity was restored, my honor and splendor were returned to me for the glory of my kingdom. My advisers and nobles sought me out, and I was restored to my throne and became even greater than before. [37]Now I, Nebuchadnezzar, praise and exalt and glorify the King of heaven, because everything he does is right and all his ways are just. And those who walk in pride he is able to humble.

The Writing on the Wall

5 King Belshazzar gave a great banquet for a thousand of his nobles and drank wine with them. [2]While Belshazzar was drinking his wine, he gave orders to bring in the gold and silver goblets that Nebuchadnezzar his

---

王宮裏（註：原文作"上"）。[30]他說："這大巴比倫不是我用大能大力建為京都，要顯我威嚴的榮耀嗎？"

[31]這話在王口中尚未說完，有聲音從天降下，說："尼布甲尼撒王啊，有話對你說：你的國位離開你了。[32]你必被趕出離開世人，與野地的獸同居，吃草如牛，且要經過七期。等你知道至高者在人的國中掌權，要將國賜與誰，就賜與誰。"

[33]當時這話就應驗在尼布甲尼撒的身上，他被趕出離開世人，吃草如牛，身被天露滴濕，頭髮長長，好像鷹毛，指甲長長，如同鳥爪。

[34]日子滿足，我尼布甲尼撒舉目望天，我的聰明復歸於我，我便稱頌至高者，讚美尊敬活到永遠的神。

他的權柄是永有的，
　他的國存到萬代。
[35]世上所有的居民，
　都算為虛無。
在天上的萬軍
　和世上的居民中，
　他都憑自己的意旨行事。
無人能攔住他手，
　或問他說："你做甚麼呢？"

[36]那時，我的聰明復歸於我，為我國的榮耀威嚴和光耀也都復歸於我，並且我的謀士和大臣也來朝見我。我又得堅立在國位上，至大的權柄加增於我。[37]現在我尼布甲尼撒讚美、尊崇、恭敬天上的王，因為他所做的全都誠實，他所行的也都公平。那行動驕傲的，他能降為卑。

牆上見字

5 伯沙撒王為他的一千大臣設擺盛筵，與這一千人對面飲酒。[2]伯沙撒歡飲之間，吩咐人將他父（註："父"或作"祖"。下同）尼布甲尼撒從耶路撒冷殿中所掠的金銀器皿拿來，王與大臣、皇后、妃嬪好用這器皿飲酒。³於是他們把耶路撒冷神殿庫房中所掠的金器皿拿來，王和大臣、皇后、妃嬪就用這器皿飲酒。⁴他們飲酒，讚美金、銀、銅、鐵、木、石所造的神。

⁵當時，忽有人的指頭顯出，在王宮與燈臺相對的粉牆上寫字。王看見寫字的指頭，⁶就變了臉色，心意驚惶，腰骨好像脫節，雙膝彼此相碰。

⁷大聲吩咐將用法術的和迦勒底人，並觀兆的領進來，對巴比倫的哲士說：「誰能讀這文字，把講解告訴我，他必身穿紫袍，項帶金鏈，在我國中位列第三。」

⁸於是王的一切哲士都進來，卻不能讀那文字，也不能把講解告訴王。⁹伯沙撒王就甚驚惶。臉色改變，他的大臣也都驚奇。

¹⁰太后（註：或作「皇后」。下同）因王和他大臣所說的話，就進入宴宮，說：「願王萬歲！你心意不要驚惶，臉面不要變色。¹¹在你國中有一人，他裏頭有聖神的靈。你父在世的日子，這人心中光明，又有聰明智慧，好像神的智慧。你父尼布甲尼撒王，就是王的父，立他為術士、用法術的，和迦勒底人，並觀兆的領袖。¹²在他裏頭有美好的靈性，又有知識聰明，能圓夢、釋謎語，解疑惑。這人名叫但以理，尼布甲尼撒王又稱他為伯提沙撒；現在可以召他來，他必解明這意思。」

¹³但以理就被領到王前。王問但以理說：「你是被擄之猶大人中的但以理嗎？就是我父王從猶大擄來的嗎？¹⁴我聽說你裏頭有神的靈，心中光明，又有聰明和美好的智慧。¹⁵現在哲士和用法術的都領到我面前，為叫他們讀這文字，把講解告訴我，無奈他們都不能把講解說出來。¹⁶我聽說你善於講解，能解疑

father*ᵃ* had taken from the temple in Jerusalem, so that the king and his nobles, his wives and his concubines might drink from them. ³So they brought in the gold goblets that had been taken from the temple of God in Jerusalem, and the king and his nobles, his wives and his concubines drank from them. ⁴As they drank the wine, they praised the gods of gold and silver, of bronze, iron, wood and stone.

⁵Suddenly the fingers of a human hand appeared and wrote on the plaster of the wall, near the lampstand in the royal palace. The king watched the hand as it wrote. ⁶His face turned pale and he was so frightened that his knees knocked together and his legs gave way.

⁷The king called out for the enchanters, astrologers*ᵇ* and diviners to be brought and said to these wise men of Babylon, "Whoever reads this writing and tells me what it means will be clothed in purple and have a gold chain placed around his neck, and he will be made the third highest ruler in the kingdom."

⁸Then all the king's wise men came in, but they could not read the writing or tell the king what it meant. ⁹So King Belshazzar became even more terrified and his face grew more pale. His nobles were baffled.

¹⁰The queen,*ᶜ* hearing the voices of the king and his nobles, came into the banquet hall. "O king, live forever!" she said. "Don't be alarmed! Don't look so pale! ¹¹There is a man in your kingdom who has the spirit of the holy gods in him. In the time of your father he was found to have insight and intelligence and wisdom like that of the gods. King Nebuchadnezzar your father—your father the king, I say—appointed him chief of the magicians, enchanters, astrologers and diviners. ¹²This man Daniel, whom the king called Belteshazzar, was found to have a keen mind and knowledge and understanding, and also the ability to interpret dreams, explain riddles and solve difficult problems. Call for Daniel, and he will tell you what the writing means."

¹³So Daniel was brought before the king, and the king said to him, "Are you Daniel, one of the exiles my father the king brought from Judah? ¹⁴I have heard that the spirit of the gods is in you and that you have insight, intelligence and outstanding wisdom. ¹⁵The wise men and enchanters were brought before me to read this writing and tell me what it means, but they could not explain it. ¹⁶Now I have heard that you are able to give interpretations and to solve

a 2 Or ancestor; or predecessor; also in verses 11, 13 and 18
b 7 Or Chaldeans; also in verse 11　　*c 10 Or queen mother*

difficult problems. If you can read this writing and tell me what it means, you will be clothed in purple and have a gold chain placed around your neck, and you will be made the third highest ruler in the kingdom."

[17]Then Daniel answered the king, "You may keep your gifts for yourself and give your rewards to someone else. Nevertheless, I will read the writing for the king and tell him what it means.

[18]"O king, the Most High God gave your father Nebuchadnezzar sovereignty and greatness and glory and splendor. [19]Because of the high position he gave him, all the peoples and nations and men of every language dreaded and feared him. Those the king wanted to put to death, he put to death; those he wanted to spare, he spared; those he wanted to promote, he promoted; and those he wanted to humble, he humbled. [20]But when his heart became arrogant and hardened with pride, he was deposed from his royal throne and stripped of his glory. [21]He was driven away from people and given the mind of an animal; he lived with the wild donkeys and ate grass like cattle; and his body was drenched with the dew of heaven, until he acknowledged that the Most High God is sovereign over the kingdoms of men and sets over them anyone he wishes.

[22]"But you his son,[a] O Belshazzar, have not humbled yourself, though you knew all this. [23]Instead, you have set yourself up against the Lord of heaven. You had the goblets from his temple brought to you, and you and your nobles, your wives and your concubines drank wine from them. You praised the gods of silver and gold, of bronze, iron, wood and stone, which cannot see or hear or understand. But you did not honor the God who holds in his hand your life and all your ways. [24]Therefore he sent the hand that wrote the inscription.

[25]"This is the inscription that was written:

MENE, MENE, TEKEL, PARSIN[b]

[26]"This is what these words mean:

Mene[c]: God has numbered the days of your reign and brought it to an end.
[27]Tekel[d]: You have been weighed on the scales and found wanting.

惑；現在你若能讀這文字，把講解告訴我，就必身穿紫袍，項戴金鏈，在我國中位列第三。"

[17]但以理在王面前回答說："你的贈品可以歸你自己，你的賞賜可以歸給別人；我卻要為王讀這文字，把講解告訴王。

[18]"王啊，至高的神曾將國位、大權、榮耀、威嚴賜與你父尼布甲尼撒，[19]因神所賜他的大權，各方、各國、各族的人都在他面前戰兢恐懼。他可以隨意生殺，隨意升降。[20]但他心高氣傲，靈也剛愎，甚至行事狂傲，就被革去王位，奪去榮耀。[21]他被趕出離開世人，他的心變如獸心，與野驢同居，吃草如牛，身被天露滴濕，等他知道至高的神在人的國中掌權，憑自己的意旨立人治國。

[22]伯沙撒啊，你是他的兒子（註：或作"孫子"），你雖知道這一切，你心仍不自卑，[23]竟向天上的主自高，使人將他殿中的器皿拿到你面前，你和大臣、皇后、妃嬪用這器皿飲酒。你又讚美那不能看、不能聽、無知無識、金、銀、銅、鐵、木、石所造的神，卻沒有將榮耀歸與那手中有你氣息，管理你一切行動的神。[24]因此，從神那裏顯出指頭來寫這文字。

[25]"所寫的文字是：

彌尼，彌尼，提客勒，烏法珥新。

[26]"講解是這樣：
彌尼：就是神已經數算你國的年日到此完畢；

[27]提客勒：就是你被稱在天平裏，顯出你的虧欠；

a 22 Or descendant; or successor   b 25 Aramaic UPARSIN (that is, AND PARSIN)   c 26 Mene can mean numbered or mina (a unit of money).   d 27 Tekel can mean weighed or shekel.

28毘勒斯（註：與烏法珥新同義）：就是你的國分裂，歸與瑪代人和波斯人。”

29伯沙撒下令，人就把紫袍給但以理穿上，把金鏈給他戴在頸項上，又傳令使他在國中位列第三。

30當夜，迦勒底王伯沙撒被殺。31瑪代人大利烏年六十二歲，取了迦勒底國。

但以理在獅子坑中

6 大利烏隨心所願，立一百二十個總督治理通國。2又在他們以上立總長三人（但以理在其中），使總督在他們三人面前回覆事務，免得王受虧損。3因這但以理有美好的靈性，所以顯然超乎其餘的總長和總督，王又想立他治理通國。4那時總長和總督尋找但以理誤國的把柄，為要參他；只是找不着他的錯誤過失，因他忠心辦事，毫無錯誤過失。5那些人便説：“我們要找參這但以理的把柄，除非在他神的律法中就尋不着。”

6於是，總長和總督紛紛聚集來見王説：“願大利烏王萬歲！7國中的總長、欽差、總督、謀士和巡撫彼此商議，要立一條堅定的禁令（註：或作“求王下旨要立一條云云”），三十日內不拘何人，若在王以外或向神、或向人求甚麼，就必扔在獅子坑中。8王啊，現在求你立這禁令，加蓋玉璽，使禁令決不更改，照瑪代和波斯人的例，是不可更改的。”9於是大利烏王立這禁令，加蓋玉璽。

10但以理知道這禁令蓋了玉璽，就到自己家裏（他樓上的窗戶開向耶路撒冷），一日三次雙膝跪在他神面前，禱告感謝，與素常一樣。11那些人就紛紛聚集，見但以理在他神面前祈禱懇求，12他們便進到王前，提王的禁令説：“王啊，三十日內不拘何人，若在王以外或向

28*Peres*[a]: Your kingdom is divided and given to the Medes and Persians."

29Then at Belshazzar's command, Daniel was clothed in purple, a gold chain was placed around his neck, and he was proclaimed the third highest ruler in the kingdom.

30That very night Belshazzar, king of the Babylonians,[b] was slain, 31and Darius the Mede took over the kingdom, at the age of sixty-two.

Daniel in the Den of Lions

6 It pleased Darius to appoint 120 satraps to rule throughout the kingdom, 2with three administrators over them, one of whom was Daniel. The satraps were made accountable to them so that the king might not suffer loss. 3Now Daniel so distinguished himself among the administrators and the satraps by his exceptional qualities that the king planned to set him over the whole kingdom. 4At this, the administrators and the satraps tried to find grounds for charges against Daniel in his conduct of government affairs, but they were unable to do so. They could find no corruption in him, because he was trustworthy and neither corrupt nor negligent. 5Finally these men said, "We will never find any basis for charges against this man Daniel unless it has something to do with the law of his God."

6So the administrators and the satraps went as a group to the king and said: "O King Darius, live forever! 7The royal administrators, prefects, satraps, advisers and governors have all agreed that the king should issue an edict and enforce the decree that anyone who prays to any god or man during the next thirty days, except to you, O king, shall be thrown into the lions' den. 8Now, O king, issue the decree and put it in writing so that it cannot be altered—in accordance with the laws of the Medes and Persians, which cannot be repealed." 9So King Darius put the decree in writing.

10Now when Daniel learned that the decree had been published, he went home to his upstairs room where the windows opened toward Jerusalem. Three times a day he got down on his knees and prayed, giving thanks to his God, just as he had done before. 11Then these men went as a group and found Daniel praying and asking God for help. 12So they went to the king and spoke to him about his royal decree: "Did you not publish a decree that during the next thirty

a 28 Peres (the singular of *Parsin*) can mean *divided* or *Persia* or *a half mina* or *a half shekel*.　　*b 30* Or *Chaldeans*

days anyone who prays to any god or man except to you, O king, would be thrown into the lions' den?"

The king answered, "The decree stands—in accordance with the laws of the Medes and Persians, which cannot be repealed."

[13] Then they said to the king, "Daniel, who is one of the exiles from Judah, pays no attention to you, O king, or to the decree you put in writing. He still prays three times a day." [14] When the king heard this, he was greatly distressed; he was determined to rescue Daniel and made every effort until sundown to save him.

[15] Then the men went as a group to the king and said to him, "Remember, O king, that according to the law of the Medes and Persians no decree or edict that the king issues can be changed."

[16] So the king gave the order, and they brought Daniel and threw him into the lions' den. The king said to Daniel, "May your God, whom you serve continually, rescue you!"

[17] A stone was brought and placed over the mouth of the den, and the king sealed it with his own signet ring and with the rings of his nobles, so that Daniel's situation might not be changed. [18] Then the king returned to his palace and spent the night without eating and without any entertainment being brought to him. And he could not sleep.

[19] At the first light of dawn, the king got up and hurried to the lions' den. [20] When he came near the den, he called to Daniel in an anguished voice, "Daniel, servant of the living God, has your God, whom you serve continually, been able to rescue you from the lions?"

[21] Daniel answered, "O king, live forever! [22] My God sent his angel, and he shut the mouths of the lions. They have not hurt me, because I was found innocent in his sight. Nor have I ever done any wrong before you, O king."

[23] The king was overjoyed and gave orders to lift Daniel out of the den. And when Daniel was lifted from the den, no wound was found on him, because he had trusted in his God.

[24] At the king's command, the men who had falsely accused Daniel were brought in and thrown into the lions' den, along with their wives and children. And before they reached the floor of the den, the lions overpowered them and crushed all their bones.

[25] Then King Darius wrote to all the peoples, nations and men of every language throughout the land:

"May you prosper greatly!

神、或向人求甚麼,必被扔在獅子坑中,王不是在這禁令上蓋了玉璽嗎?"

王回答說:"實有這事,照瑪代和波斯人的例是不可更改的。"

[13] 他們對王說:"王啊,那被擄之猶大人中的但以理不理你,也不遵你蓋了玉璽的禁令,他竟一日三次祈禱。" [14] 王聽見這話,就甚愁煩,一心要救但以理,籌劃解救他,直到日落的時候。

[15] 那些人就紛紛聚集來見王說:"王啊,當知道瑪代人和波斯人有例,凡王所立的禁令和律例都不可更改。"

[16] 王下令,人就把但以理帶來,扔在獅子坑中。王對但以理說:"你所常侍奉的神,他必救你!"

[17] 有人搬石頭放在坑口,王用自己的璽和大臣的印封閉那坑,使懲辦但以理的事毫無更改。 [18] 王回宮,終夜禁食,無人拿樂器到他面前,並且睡不着覺。

[19] 次日黎明,王就起來,急忙往獅子坑那裏去。 [20] 臨近坑邊,哀聲呼叫但以理,對但以理說:"永生神的僕人但以理啊!你所常侍奉的神能救你脫離獅子嗎?"

[21] 但以理對王說:"願王萬歲! [22] 我的神差遣使者封住獅子的口,叫獅子不傷我;因我在神面前無辜,我在王面前也沒有行過虧損的事。"

[23] 王就甚喜樂,吩咐人將但以理從坑裏繫上來。於是但以理從坑裏被繫上來,身上毫無傷損,因為信靠他的神。

[24] 王下令,人就把那些控告但以理的人,連他們的妻子、兒女都帶來,扔在獅子坑中。他們還沒有到坑底,獅子就抓住(註:"抓住"原文作"勝了")他們,咬碎他們的骨頭。

[25] 那時,大利烏王傳旨,曉諭住在全地各方、各國、各族的人說:

"願你們大享平安!

²⁶ "現在我降旨曉諭我所統轄的全國人民,要在<u>但以理</u>的神面前戰兢恐懼。

"因為他是

永遠長存的活神,

他的國永不敗壞,

他的權柄永存無極!

²⁷他護庇人、搭救人,

在天上地下

施行神蹟奇事,

救了<u>但以理</u>

脫離獅子的口。"

²⁸如此,這<u>但以理</u>當<u>大利烏</u>王在位的時候和<u>波斯</u>王<u>塞魯士</u>在位的時候,大享亨通。

但以理夢見四獸

7 <u>巴比倫</u>王<u>伯沙撒</u>元年,<u>但以理</u>在牀上做夢,見了腦中的異象,就記錄這夢,述說其中的大意。

²<u>但以理</u>說:"我夜裏見異象,看見天的四風陡起,颳在大海之上。³有四個大獸從海中上來,形狀各有不同。

⁴ "頭一個像獅子,有鷹的翅膀。我正觀看的時候,獸的翅膀被拔去,獸從地上得立起來,用兩腳站立,像人一樣,又得了人心。

⁵ "又有一獸如熊,就是第二獸,旁跨而坐,口齒內啣着三根肋骨,有吩咐這獸的說:'起來吞吃多肉。'

⁶ "此後我觀看,又有一獸如豹,背上有鳥的四個翅膀;這獸有四個頭,又得了權柄。

⁷ "其後,我在夜間的異象中觀看,見第四獸甚是可怕,極其強壯,大有力量。有大鐵牙,吞吃嚼碎,所剩下的用腳踐踏。這獸與前三獸大不相同,頭有十角。

⁸ "我正觀看這些角,見其中又長起一個小角,先前的角中有三角

²⁶"I issue a decree that in every part of my kingdom people must fear and reverence the God of Daniel.

"For he is the living God
and he endures forever;
his kingdom will not be destroyed,
his dominion will never end.
²⁷He rescues and he saves;
he performs signs and wonders
in the heavens and on the earth.
He has rescued Daniel
from the power of the lions."

²⁸So Daniel prospered during the reign of Darius and the reign of Cyrus*ᵃ* the Persian.

Daniel's Dream of Four Beasts

7 In the first year of Belshazzar king of Babylon, Daniel had a dream, and visions passed through his mind as he was lying on his bed. He wrote down the substance of his dream.

²Daniel said: "In my vision at night I looked, and there before me were the four winds of heaven churning up the great sea. ³Four great beasts, each different from the others, came up out of the sea.

⁴"The first was like a lion, and it had the wings of an eagle. I watched until its wings were torn off and it was lifted from the ground so that it stood on two feet like a man, and the heart of a man was given to it.

⁵"And there before me was a second beast, which looked like a bear. It was raised up on one of its sides, and it had three ribs in its mouth between its teeth. It was told, 'Get up and eat your fill of flesh!'

⁶"After that, I looked, and there before me was another beast, one that looked like a leopard. And on its back it had four wings like those of a bird. This beast had four heads, and it was given authority to rule.

⁷"After that, in my vision at night I looked, and there before me was a fourth beast—terrifying and frightening and very powerful. It had large iron teeth; it crushed and devoured its victims and trampled underfoot whatever was left. It was different from all the former beasts, and it had ten horns.

⁸"While I was thinking about the horns, there before me was another horn, a little one, which came up among them; and three of the first

a 28 Or Darius, that is, the reign of Cyrus

horns were uprooted before it. This horn had eyes like the eyes of a man and a mouth that spoke boastfully.

⁹"As I looked,

"thrones were set in place,
    and the Ancient of Days took his seat.
His clothing was as white as snow;
    the hair of his head was white like wool.
His throne was flaming with fire,
    and its wheels were all ablaze.
¹⁰A river of fire was flowing,
    coming out from before him.
Thousands upon thousands attended him;
    ten thousand times ten thousand stood
        before him.
The court was seated,
    and the books were opened.

¹¹"Then I continued to watch because of the boastful words the horn was speaking. I kept looking until the beast was slain and its body destroyed and thrown into the blazing fire. ¹²(The other beasts had been stripped of their authority, but were allowed to live for a period of time.)

¹³"In my vision at night I looked, and there before me was one like a son of man, coming with the clouds of heaven. He approached the Ancient of Days and was led into his presence. ¹⁴He was given authority, glory and sovereign power; all peoples, nations and men of every language worshiped him. His dominion is an everlasting dominion that will not pass away, and his kingdom is one that will never be destroyed.

The Interpretation of the Dream

¹⁵"I, Daniel, was troubled in spirit, and the visions that passed through my mind disturbed me. ¹⁶I approached one of those standing there and asked him the true meaning of all this.

"So he told me and gave me the interpretation of these things: ¹⁷'The four great beasts are four kingdoms that will rise from the earth. ¹⁸But the saints of the Most High will receive the kingdom and will possess it forever—yes, for ever and ever.'

¹⁹"Then I wanted to know the true meaning of the fourth beast, which was different from all the others and most terrifying, with its iron teeth and bronze claws—the beast that crushed and devoured its victims and trampled underfoot whatever was left. ²⁰I also wanted to know about the ten horns on its head and about the other horn that came up, before which three of them fell—the horn that looked more imposing than the others and that had eyes and a mouth

在這角前，連根被它拔出來。這角有眼，像人的眼，有口說誇大的話。

⁹ 我觀看，

"見有寶座設立，
    上頭坐着亙古常在者，
他的衣服潔白如雪，
    頭髮如純淨的羊毛，
寶座乃火焰，
    其輪乃烈火。
¹⁰從他面前有火，
    像河發出，
侍奉他的有千千，
    在他面前侍立的有萬萬。

他坐着要行審判，
    案卷都展開了。

¹¹ 那時我觀看，見那獸因小角說誇大話的聲音被殺，身體損壞，扔在火中焚燒。¹²其餘的獸，權柄都被奪去，生命卻仍存留，直到所定的時候和日期。

¹³ "我在夜間的異象中觀看，見有一位像人子的，駕着天雲而來，被領到亙古常在者面前；¹⁴得了權柄、榮耀、國度，使各方、各國、各族的人都侍奉他。他的權柄是永遠的，不能廢去，他的國必不敗壞。

夢的講解

¹⁵ "至於我但以理，我的靈在我裏面愁煩，我腦中的異象使我驚惶。¹⁶我就近一位侍立者，問他這一切的真情。

"他就告訴我，將那事的講解給我說明：¹⁷'這四個大獸就是四王將要在世上興起，¹⁸然而，至高者的聖民，必要得國享受，直到永永遠遠。'

¹⁹ "那時我願知道第四獸的真情，牠為何與那三獸的真情大不相同，甚是可怕，有鐵牙銅爪，吞吃嚼碎，所剩下的用腳踐踏。²⁰頭有十角和那另長的一角，在這角前有三角被牠打落。這角有眼，有說誇大話的

口，形狀強橫，過於牠的同類。²¹我觀看，見這角與聖民爭戰，勝了他們，²²直到亙古常在者來給至高者的聖民伸冤，聖民得國的時候就到了。

²³「那侍立者這樣說：『第四獸就是世上必有的第四國，與一切國大不相同，必吞吃全地，並且踐踏嚼碎。²⁴至於那十角，就是從這國中必興起的十王，後來又興起一王，與先前的不同，他必制伏三王。²⁵他必向至高者說誇大的話，必折磨至高者的聖民，必想改變節期和律法。聖民必交付他手一載、二載、半載。

²⁶「『然而，審判者必坐着行審判，他的權柄必被奪去，毀壞，滅絕，一直到底。²⁷國度、權柄和天下諸國的大權，必賜給至高者的聖民。他的國是永遠的，一切掌權的都必侍奉他、順從他。』

²⁸「那事至此完畢。至於我但以理，心中甚是驚惶，臉色也改變了，卻將那事存記在心。」

但以理見綿羊公山羊的異象

8 伯沙撒王在位第三年，有異象現與我但以理，是在先前所見的異象之後。²我見了異象的時候，我以為在以攔省書珊城中（註：「城」或作「宮」），我見異象又如在烏萊河邊。³我舉目觀看，見有雙角的公綿羊站在河邊，兩角都高，這角高過那角，更高的是後長的。⁴我見那公綿羊往西、往北、往南牴觸，獸在牠面前都站立不住，也沒有能救護脫離牠手的，但牠任意而行，自高自大。

⁵我正思想的時候，見有一隻公山羊從西而來，遍行全地，腳不沾塵。這山羊兩眼當中有一非常的角。⁶牠往我所看見站在河邊有雙角的公綿羊那裏去，大發忿怒，向牠直闖。⁷我見公山羊就近公綿羊，向牠發烈怒，牴觸牠，折斷牠的兩角。綿羊在牠面前站立不住，牠將綿羊觸倒在地，用腳踐踏，沒有能

that spoke boastfully. ²¹As I watched, this horn was waging war against the saints and defeating them, ²²until the Ancient of Days came and pronounced judgment in favor of the saints of the Most High, and the time came when they possessed the kingdom.

²³"He gave me this explanation: 'The fourth beast is a fourth kingdom that will appear on earth. It will be different from all the other kingdoms and will devour the whole earth, trampling it down and crushing it. ²⁴The ten horns are ten kings who will come from this kingdom. After them another king will arise, different from the earlier ones; he will subdue three kings. ²⁵He will speak against the Most High and oppress his saints and try to change the set times and the laws. The saints will be handed over to him for a time, times and half a time.ᵃ

²⁶"'But the court will sit, and his power will be taken away and completely destroyed forever. ²⁷Then the sovereignty, power and greatness of the kingdoms under the whole heaven will be handed over to the saints, the people of the Most High. His kingdom will be an everlasting kingdom, and all rulers will worship and obey him.'

²⁸"This is the end of the matter. I, Daniel, was deeply troubled by my thoughts, and my face turned pale, but I kept the matter to myself."

Daniel's Vision of a Ram and a Goat

8 In the third year of King Belshazzar's reign, I, Daniel, had a vision, after the one that had already appeared to me. ²In my vision I saw myself in the citadel of Susa in the province of Elam; in the vision I was beside the Ulai Canal. ³I looked up, and there before me was a ram with two horns, standing beside the canal, and the horns were long. One of the horns was longer than the other but grew up later. ⁴I watched the ram as he charged toward the west and the north and the south. No animal could stand against him, and none could rescue from his power. He did as he pleased and became great.

⁵As I was thinking about this, suddenly a goat with a prominent horn between his eyes came from the west, crossing the whole earth without touching the ground. ⁶He came toward the two-horned ram I had seen standing beside the canal and charged at him in great rage. ⁷I saw him attack the ram furiously, striking the ram and shattering his two horns. The ram was powerless to stand against him; the goat knocked him to the ground and trampled on him, and none

a 25 Or for a year, two years and half a year

could rescue the ram from his power. [8]The goat became very great, but at the height of his power his large horn was broken off, and in its place four prominent horns grew up toward the four winds of heaven.

[9]Out of one of them came another horn, which started small but grew in power to the south and to the east and toward the Beautiful Land. [10]It grew until it reached the host of the heavens, and it threw some of the starry host down to the earth and trampled on them. [11]It set itself up to be as great as the Prince of the host; it took away the daily sacrifice from him, and the place of his sanctuary was brought low. [12]Because of rebellion, the host [a] of the saints[a] and the daily sacrifice were given over to it. It prospered in everything it did, and truth was thrown to the ground.

[13]Then I heard a holy one speaking, and another holy one said to him, "How long will it take for the vision to be fulfilled—the vision concerning the daily sacrifice, the rebellion that causes desolation, and the surrender of the sanctuary and of the host that will be trampled underfoot?"

[14]He said to me, "It will take 2,300 evenings and mornings; then the sanctuary will be reconsecrated."

The Interpretation of the Vision

[15]While I, Daniel, was watching the vision and trying to understand it, there before me stood one who looked like a man. [16]And I heard a man's voice from the Ulai calling, "Gabriel, tell this man the meaning of the vision."

[17]As he came near the place where I was standing, I was terrified and fell prostrate. "Son of man," he said to me, "understand that the vision concerns the time of the end."

[18]While he was speaking to me, I was in a deep sleep, with my face to the ground. Then he touched me and raised me to my feet.

[19]He said: "I am going to tell you what will happen later in the time of wrath, because the vision concerns the appointed time of the end.[b] [20]The two-horned ram that you saw represents the kings of Media and Persia. [21]The shaggy goat is the king of Greece, and the large horn between his eyes is the first king. [22]The four horns that replaced the one that was broken off represent four kingdoms that will emerge from his nation but will not have the same power.

[23]"In the latter part of their reign, when rebels have become completely wicked, a stern-faced

a 12 Or rebellion, the armies   b 19 Or because the end will be at the appointed time

救綿羊脱離牠手的。[8]這山羊極其自高自大,正強盛的時候,那大角折斷了,又在角根上向天的四方(註:"方"原文作"風")長出四個非常的角來。

[9]四角之中,有一角長出一個小角,向南、向東、向榮美之地,漸漸成為強大。[10]牠漸漸強大,高及天象,將些天象和星宿拋落在地,用腳踐踏。[11]並且牠自高自大,以為高及天象之君,除掉常獻給君的燔祭,毀壞君的聖所。[12]因罪過的緣故,有軍旅和常獻的燔祭交付牠。牠將真理拋在地上,任意而行,無不順利。

[13]我聽見有一位聖者說話,又有一位聖者問那說話的聖者說:"這除掉常獻的燔祭和施行毀壞的罪過,將聖所與軍旅踐踏的異象(註:"軍旅"或作"以色列的軍"),要到幾時才應驗呢?"

[14]他對我說:"到二千三百日,聖所就必潔淨。"

異象的解釋

[15]我但以理見了這異象,願意明白其中的意思,忽有一位形狀像人的站在我面前。[16]我又聽見烏萊河兩岸中有人聲呼叫說:"加百列啊,要使此人明白這異象。"

[17]他便來到我所站的地方。他一來,我就驚慌俯伏在地,他對我說:"人子啊,你要明白,因為這是關乎末後的異象。"

[18]他與我說話的時候,我面伏在地沉睡,他就摸我,扶我站起來。

[19]說:"我要指示你惱怒臨完必有的事,因為這是關乎末後的定期。[20]你所看見雙角的公綿羊,就是瑪代和波斯王。[21]那公山羊就是希臘王(註:"希臘"原文作"雅完"。下同),兩眼當中的大角,就是頭一王。[22]至於那折斷了的角,在其根上又長出四角,這四角就是四國,必從這國裏興起來,只是權勢都不及他。

[23]"這四國末時,犯法的人罪惡滿盈,必有一王興起,面貌兇惡,能

用雙關的詭語。24他的權柄必大，卻
不是因自己的能力，他必行非常的
毀滅。事情順利，任意而行，又必
毀滅有能力的和聖民。25他用權術成
就手中的詭計，心裏自高自大，在
人坦然無備的時候，毀滅多人。又
要站起來攻擊萬君之君，至終卻非
因人手而滅亡。"

26 "所說二千三百日的異象是真
的，但你要將這異象封住，因為關
乎後來許多的日子。"

27於是我但以理昏迷不醒，病了
數日，然後起來辦理王的事務。我
因這異象驚奇，卻無人能明白其中
的意思。

但以理的禱告

9 瑪代族亞哈隨魯的兒子大利
烏立為迦勒底國的王元年，
2就是他在位第一年，我但以
理從書上得知耶和華的話臨到先知
耶利米，論耶路撒冷荒涼的年數，
七十年為滿。3我便禁食，披麻蒙
灰，定意向主神祈禱懇求。

4我向耶和華我的神祈禱、認罪
說：

"主啊，大而可畏的神，向
愛主守主誡命的人，守約施慈
愛。5我們犯罪作孽，行惡叛逆，
偏離你的誡命典章。6沒有聽從你
僕人眾先知奉你名向我們君王、
首領、列祖和國中一切百姓所說
的話。

7 "主啊，你是公義的，我們
是臉上蒙羞的；因我們猶大人和
耶路撒冷的居民，並以色列眾
人，或在近處，或在遠處，被你
趕到各國的人，都得罪了你，正
如今日一樣。8主啊，我們和我們
的君王、首領、列祖因得罪了
你，就都臉上蒙羞。9主，我們的
神，是憐憫饒恕人的，我們卻違
背了他，10也沒有聽從耶和華我們
神的話，沒有遵行他藉僕人眾先
知向我們所陳明的律法。11以色列
眾人都犯了你的律法，偏行，不
聽從你的話。

king, a master of intrigue, will arise. 24He will become very strong, but not by his own power. He will cause astounding devastation and will succeed in whatever he does. He will destroy the mighty men and the holy people. 25He will cause deceit to prosper, and he will consider himself superior. When they feel secure, he will destroy many and take his stand against the Prince of princes. Yet he will be destroyed, but not by human power.

26"The vision of the evenings and mornings that has been given you is true, but seal up the vision, for it concerns the distant future."

27I, Daniel, was exhausted and lay ill for several days. Then I got up and went about the king's business. I was appalled by the vision; it was beyond understanding.

Daniel's Prayer

9 In the first year of Darius son of Xerxes[a] (a Mede by descent), who was made ruler over the Babylonian[b] kingdom— 2in the first year of his reign, I, Daniel, understood from the Scriptures, according to the word of the LORD given to Jeremiah the prophet, that the desolation of Jerusalem would last seventy years. 3So I turned to the Lord God and pleaded with him in prayer and petition, in fasting, and in sackcloth and ashes.

4I prayed to the LORD my God and confessed:

"O Lord, the great and awesome God, who keeps his covenant of love with all who love him and obey his commands, 5we have sinned and have done wrong. We have been wicked and have rebelled; we have turned away from your commands and laws. 6We have not listened to your servants the prophets, who spoke in your name to our kings, our princes and our fathers, and to all the people of the land.

7"Lord, you are righteous, but this day we are covered with shame—the men of Judah and people of Jerusalem and all Israel, both near and far, in all the countries where you have scattered us because of our unfaithfulness to you. 8O LORD, we and our kings, our princes and our fathers are covered with shame because we have sinned against you. 9The Lord our God is merciful and forgiving, even though we have rebelled against him; 10we have not obeyed the LORD our God or kept the laws he gave us through his servants the prophets. 11All Israel has transgressed your law and turned away, refusing to obey you.

a 1 Hebrew Ahasuerus　　b 1 Or Chaldean

"Therefore the curses and sworn judgments written in the Law of Moses, the servant of God, have been poured out on us, because we have sinned against you. [12]You have fulfilled the words spoken against us and against our rulers by bringing upon us great disaster. Under the whole heaven nothing has ever been done like what has been done to Jerusalem. [13]Just as it is written in the Law of Moses, all this disaster has come upon us, yet we have not sought the favor of the LORD our God by turning from our sins and giving attention to your truth. [14]The LORD did not hesitate to bring the disaster upon us, for the LORD our God is righteous in everything he does; yet we have not obeyed him.

[15]"Now, O Lord our God, who brought your people out of Egypt with a mighty hand and who made for yourself a name that endures to this day, we have sinned, we have done wrong. [16]O Lord, in keeping with all your righteous acts, turn away your anger and your wrath from Jerusalem, your city, your holy hill. Our sins and the iniquities of our fathers have made Jerusalem and your people an object of scorn to all those around us.

[17]"Now, our God, hear the prayers and petitions of your servant. For your sake, O Lord, look with favor on your desolate sanctuary. [18]Give ear, O God, and hear; open your eyes and see the desolation of the city that bears your Name. We do not make requests of you because we are righteous, but because of your great mercy. [19]O Lord, listen! O Lord, forgive! O Lord, hear and act! For your sake, O my God, do not delay, because your city and your people bear your Name."

The Seventy "Sevens"

[20]While I was speaking and praying, confessing my sin and the sin of my people Israel and making my request to the LORD my God for his holy hill— [21]while I was still in prayer, Gabriel, the man I had seen in the earlier vision, came to me in swift flight about the time of the evening sacrifice. [22]He instructed me and said to me, "Daniel, I have now come to give you insight and understanding. [23]As soon as you began to pray, an answer was given, which I have come to tell you, for you are highly esteemed. Therefore, consider the message and understand the vision:

[24]"Seventy 'sevens'[a] are decreed for your people and your holy city to finish[b] transgression, to

a 24 Or 'weeks'; also in verses 25 and 26   b 24 Or restrain

"因此，在你僕人摩西律法上所寫的咒詛和誓言，都傾在我們身上，因我們得罪了神。[12]他使大災禍臨到我們，成就了警戒我們和審判我們官長的話；原來在普天之下未曾行過像在耶路撒冷所行的。[13]這一切災禍臨到我們身上，是照摩西律法上所寫的，我們卻沒有求耶和華我們神的恩典，使我們回頭離開罪孽，明白你的真理。[14]所以耶和華留意使這災禍臨到我們身上，因為耶和華我們的神在他所行的事上都是公義，我們並沒有聽從他的話。

[15]"主，我們的神啊，你曾用大能的手領你的子民出埃及地，使自己得了名，正如今日一樣。我們犯了罪，作了惡。[16]主啊，求你按你的大仁大義，使你的怒氣和忿怒轉離你的城耶路撒冷，就是你的聖山。耶路撒冷和你的子民，因我們的罪惡和我們列祖的罪孽，被四圍的人羞辱。

[17]"我們的神啊，現在求你垂聽僕人的祈禱懇求，為自己使臉光照你荒涼的聖所。[18]我的神啊，求你側耳而聽，睜眼而看，眷顧我們荒涼之地和稱為你名下的城。我們在你面前懇求，原不是因自己的義，乃因你的大憐憫。[19]求主垂聽，求主赦免，求主應允而行，為你自己不要遲延。我的神啊，因這城和這民，都是稱為你名下的。"

七十個"七"

[20]我說話、禱告，承認我的罪和本國之民以色列的罪，為我神的聖山，在耶和華我神面前懇求。[21]我正禱告的時候，先前在異象中所見的那位加百列，奉命迅速飛來，約在獻晚祭的時候，按手在我身上。[22]他指教我說："但以理啊，現在我出來要使你有智慧、有聰明。[23]你初懇求的時候，就發出命令，我來告訴你，因你大蒙眷愛，所以你要思想明白這以下的事和異象：

[24]"為你本國之民和你聖城，已經定了七十個七，要止住罪過，除淨

罪惡，贖盡罪孽，引進 (註：或作 "彰顯") 永義，封住異象和預言，並膏至聖者 (註： "者" 或作 "所") 。

25 "你當知道、當明白，從出令重新建造耶路撒冷，直到有受膏君的時候，必有七個七和六十二個七。正在艱難的時候，耶路撒冷城連街帶濠都必重新建造。26 過了六十二個七，那受膏者 (註： "那" 或作 "有") 必被剪除，一無所有，必有一王的民來毀滅這城和聖所，至終必如洪水沖沒。必有爭戰，一直到底，荒涼的事已經定了。27 一七之內，他必與許多人堅定盟約；一七之半，他必使祭祀與供獻止息。那行毀壞可憎的 (註：或作 "使地荒涼的") 如飛而來，並且有忿怒傾在那行毀壞的身上 (註：或作 "傾在那荒涼之地") ，直到所定的結局。"

但以理見人子的異象

10 波斯王塞魯士第三年，有事顯給稱為伯提沙撒的但以理。這事是真的，是指着大爭戰。但以理通達這事，明白這異象。

2 當那時，我但以理悲傷了三個七日。3 美味我沒有吃，酒肉沒有入我的口，也沒有用油抹我的身，直到滿了三個七日。

4 正月二十四日，我在底格里斯大河邊。5 舉目觀看，見有一人身穿細麻衣，腰束烏法精金帶。6 他身體如水蒼玉，面貌如閃電，眼目如火把，手和腳如光明的銅，說話的聲音如大眾的聲音。

7 這異象惟有我但以理一人看見，同着我的人沒有看見，他們卻大大戰兢，逃跑隱藏，8 只剩下我一人。我見了這大異象便渾身無力，面貌失色，毫無氣力。9 我卻聽見他

put an end to sin, to atone for wickedness, to bring in everlasting righteousness, to seal up vision and prophecy and to anoint the most holy.[a]

25 "Know and understand this: From the issuing of the decree[b] to restore and rebuild Jerusalem until the Anointed One,[c] the ruler, comes, there will be seven 'sevens,' and sixty-two 'sevens.' It will be rebuilt with streets and a trench, but in times of trouble. 26 After the sixty-two 'sevens,' the Anointed One will be cut off and will have nothing.[d] The people of the ruler who will come will destroy the city and the sanctuary. The end will come like a flood: War will continue until the end, and desolations have been decreed. 27 He will confirm a covenant with many for one 'seven.'[e] In the middle of the 'seven'[e] he will put an end to sacrifice and offering. And on a wing [of the temple] he will set up an abomination that causes desolation, until the end that is decreed is poured out on him.[f]"[g]

Daniel's Vision of a Man

10 In the third year of Cyrus king of Persia, a revelation was given to Daniel (who was called Belteshazzar). Its message was true and it concerned a great war.[h] The understanding of the message came to him in a vision.

2 At that time I, Daniel, mourned for three weeks. 3 I ate no choice food; no meat or wine touched my lips; and I used no lotions at all until the three weeks were over.

4 On the twenty-fourth day of the first month, as I was standing on the bank of the great river, the Tigris, 5 I looked up and there before me was a man dressed in linen, with a belt of the finest gold around his waist. 6 His body was like chrysolite, his face like lightning, his eyes like flaming torches, his arms and legs like the gleam of burnished bronze, and his voice like the sound of a multitude.

7 I, Daniel, was the only one who saw the vision; the men with me did not see it, but such terror overwhelmed them that they fled and hid themselves. 8 So I was left alone, gazing at this great vision; I had no strength left, my face turned deathly pale and I was helpless. 9 Then I

a 24 Or Most Holy Place; or most holy One   b 25 Or word
c 25 Or an anointed one; also in verse 26   d 26 Or off and will
have no one; or off, but not for himself   e 27 Or 'week'   f 27 Or
it   g 27 Or And one who causes desolation will come upon the
pinnacle of the abominable [temple], until the end that is decreed is
poured out on the desolated [city]   h 1 Or true and burdensome

heard him speaking, and as I listened to him, I fell into a deep sleep, my face to the ground.

¹⁰A hand touched me and set me trembling on my hands and knees. ¹¹He said, "Daniel, you who are highly esteemed, consider carefully the words I am about to speak to you, and stand up, for I have now been sent to you." And when he said this to me, I stood up trembling.

¹²Then he continued, "Do not be afraid, Daniel. Since the first day that you set your mind to gain understanding and to humble yourself before your God, your words were heard, and I have come in response to them. ¹³But the prince of the Persian kingdom resisted me twenty-one days. Then Michael, one of the chief princes, came to help me, because I was detained there with the king of Persia. ¹⁴Now I have come to explain to you what will happen to your people in the future, for the vision concerns a time yet to come."

¹⁵While he was saying this to me, I bowed with my face toward the ground and was speechless. ¹⁶Then one who looked like a man*a* touched my lips, and I opened my mouth and began to speak. I said to the one standing before me, "I am overcome with anguish because of the vision, my lord, and I am helpless. ¹⁷How can I, your servant, talk with you, my lord? My strength is gone and I can hardly breathe."

¹⁸Again the one who looked like a man touched me and gave me strength. ¹⁹"Do not be afraid, O man highly esteemed," he said. "Peace! Be strong now; be strong."

When he spoke to me, I was strengthened and said, "Speak, my lord, since you have given me strength."

²⁰So he said, "Do you know why I have come to you? Soon I will return to fight against the prince of Persia, and when I go, the prince of Greece will come; ²¹but first I will tell you what is written in the Book of Truth. (No one supports me against them except Michael, your prince.

11 ¹And in the first year of Darius the Mede, I took my stand to support and protect him.)

The Kings of the South and the North

²"Now then, I tell you the truth: Three more kings will appear in Persia, and then a fourth, who will be far richer than all the others. When he has gained power by his wealth, he will stir

說話的聲音，一聽見就面伏在地沉睡了。

¹⁰忽然，有一手按在我身上，使我用膝和手掌支持微起。¹¹他對我說："大蒙眷愛的但以理啊，要明白我與你所說的話，只管站起來，因為我現在奉差遣來到你這裏。"他對我說這話，我便戰戰兢兢地立起來。

¹²他就說："但以理啊，不要懼怕！因為從你第一日專心求明白將來的事，又在你神面前刻苦己心，你的言語已蒙應允，我是因你的言語而來。¹³但波斯國的魔君攔阻我二十一日，忽然有大君（註：就是"天使長"。²¹節間）中的一位米迦勒來幫助我，我就停留在波斯諸王那裏。¹⁴現在我來要使你明白本國之民日後必遭遇的事，因為這異象關乎後來許多的日子。"

¹⁵他向我這樣說，我就臉面朝地，啞口無聲。¹⁶不料，有一位像人的摸我的嘴唇，我便開口向那站在我面前的說："我主啊，因見這異象我大大愁苦，毫無氣力。¹⁷我主的僕人怎能與我主說話呢？我一見異象就渾身無力，毫無氣息。"

¹⁸有一位形狀像人的又摸我，使我有力量。¹⁹他說："大蒙眷愛的人哪，不要懼怕，願你平安，你總要堅強！"

他一向我說話，我便覺得有力量，說："我主請說，因你使我有力量。"

²⁰他就說："你知道我為何來見你嗎？現在我要回去與波斯的魔君爭戰，我去後，希臘（註：原文作"雅完"）的魔君必來。²¹但我要將那錄在真確書上的事告訴你，除了你們的大君米迦勒之外，沒有幫助我抵擋這兩魔君的。"

11 ¹又說："當瑪代王大利烏元年，我曾起來扶助米迦勒，使他堅強。

南方王與北方王

²"現在我將真事指示你，波斯還有三王興起，第四王必富足遠勝諸王，他因富足成為強盛，就必激動大

---

a 16 Most manuscripts of the Masoretic Text; one manuscript of the Masoretic Text, Dead Sea Scrolls and Septuagint *Then something that looked like a man's hand*

眾攻擊希臘國。³必有一個勇敢的王興起，執掌大權，隨意而行。⁴他興起的時候，他的國必破裂，向天的四方（註：「方」原文作「風」）分開，卻不歸他的後裔，治國的權勢也都不及他，因為他的國必被拔出，歸與他後裔之外的人。

⁵「南方的王必強盛，他將帥中必有一個比他更強盛，執掌權柄，他的權柄甚大。⁶過些年後，他們必互相連合，南方王的女兒必就了北方王來立約，但這女子幫助之力存立不住，王和他所倚靠之力也不能存立，這女子和引導她來的，並生她的，以及當時扶助她的，都必交與死地。

⁷「但這女子的本家（註：「本家」原文作「根」）必另生一子（註：「子」原文作「枝」）繼續王位，他必率領軍隊進入北方王的保障，攻擊他們，而且得勝；⁸並將他們的神像和鑄成的偶像，與金銀的寶器掠到埃及去。數年之內，他不去攻擊北方的王。⁹北方的王（註：原文作「他」）必入南方王的國，卻要仍回本地。¹⁰北方王（註：原文作「他」）的二子必動干戈，招聚許多軍兵，這軍兵前去，如洪水氾濫，又必再去爭戰，直到南方王的保障。

¹¹「南方王必發烈怒，出來與北方王爭戰，擺列大軍，北方王的軍兵必交付他手。¹²他的眾軍高傲，他的心也必自高，他雖使數萬人仆倒，卻不得常勝。¹³北方王必回來擺列大軍，比先前的更多，滿了所定的年數，他必率領大軍，帶極多的軍裝來。

¹⁴「那時，必有許多人起來攻擊南方王，並且你本國的強暴人必興起，要應驗那異象，他們卻要敗亡。¹⁵北方王必來築壘，攻取堅固城，南方的軍兵必站立不住，就是選擇的精兵（註：「精兵」原文作「民」）也無力站住。¹⁶來攻擊他的必任意而行，無人在北方王（註：原文作「他」）面前站立得住。他必站在那榮美之地，用手施行毀滅。¹⁷他必定意用全

up everyone against the kingdom of Greece. ³Then a mighty king will appear, who will rule with great power and do as he pleases. ⁴After he has appeared, his empire will be broken up and parceled out toward the four winds of heaven. It will not go to his descendants, nor will it have the power he exercised, because his empire will be uprooted and given to others.

⁵"The king of the South will become strong, but one of his commanders will become even stronger than he and will rule his own kingdom with great power. ⁶After some years, they will become allies. The daughter of the king of the South will go to the king of the North to make an alliance, but she will not retain her power, and he and his power*ᵃ* will not last. In those days she will be handed over, together with her royal escort and her father*ᵇ* and the one who supported her.

⁷"One from her family line will arise to take her place. He will attack the forces of the king of the North and enter his fortress; he will fight against them and be victorious. ⁸He will also seize their gods, their metal images and their valuable articles of silver and gold and carry them off to Egypt. For some years he will leave the king of the North alone. ⁹Then the king of the North will invade the realm of the king of the South but will retreat to his own country. ¹⁰His sons will prepare for war and assemble a great army, which will sweep on like an irresistible flood and carry the battle as far as his fortress.

¹¹"Then the king of the South will march out in a rage and fight against the king of the North, who will raise a large army, but it will be defeated. ¹²When the army is carried off, the king of the South will be filled with pride and will slaughter many thousands, yet he will not remain triumphant. ¹³For the king of the North will muster another army, larger than the first; and after several years, he will advance with a huge army fully equipped.

¹⁴"In those times many will rise against the king of the South. The violent men among your own people will rebel in fulfillment of the vision, but without success. ¹⁵Then the king of the North will come and build up siege ramps and will capture a fortified city. The forces of the South will be powerless to resist; even their best troops will not have the strength to stand. ¹⁶The invader will do as he pleases; no one will be able to stand against him. He will establish himself in the Beautiful Land and will have the power to destroy it. ¹⁷He will determine to come with the

a 6 Or offspring   b 6 Or child (see Vulgate and Syriac)

might of his entire kingdom and will make an alliance with the king of the South. And he will give him a daughter in marriage in order to overthrow the kingdom, but his plans[a] will not succeed or help him. ¹⁸Then he will turn his attention to the coastlands and will take many of them, but a commander will put an end to his insolence and will turn his insolence back upon him. ¹⁹After this, he will turn back toward the fortresses of his own country but will stumble and fall, to be seen no more.

²⁰"His successor will send out a tax collector to maintain the royal splendor. In a few years, however, he will be destroyed, yet not in anger or in battle.

²¹"He will be succeeded by a contemptible person who has not been given the honor of royalty. He will invade the kingdom when its people feel secure, and he will seize it through intrigue. ²²Then an overwhelming army will be swept away before him; both it and a prince of the covenant will be destroyed. ²³After coming to an agreement with him, he will act deceitfully, and with only a few people he will rise to power. ²⁴When the richest provinces feel secure, he will invade them and will achieve what neither his fathers nor his forefathers did. He will distribute plunder, loot and wealth among his followers. He will plot the overthrow of fortresses—but only for a time.

²⁵"With a large army he will stir up his strength and courage against the king of the South. The king of the South will wage war with a large and very powerful army, but he will not be able to stand because of the plots devised against him. ²⁶Those who eat from the king's provisions will try to destroy him; his army will be swept away, and many will fall in battle. ²⁷The two kings, with their hearts bent on evil, will sit at the same table and lie to each other, but to no avail, because an end will still come at the appointed time. ²⁸The king of the North will return to his own country with great wealth, but his heart will be set against the holy covenant. He will take action against it and then return to his own country.

²⁹"At the appointed time he will invade the South again, but this time the outcome will be different from what it was before. ³⁰Ships of the western coastlands[b] will oppose him, and he will lose heart. Then he will turn back and vent his fury against the holy covenant. He will return and show favor to those who forsake the holy covenant.

國之力而來，立公正的約，照約而行，將自己的女兒給南方王為妻，想要敗壞他（註：或作“埃及”），這計卻不得成就，與自己毫無益處。¹⁸其後，他必轉回奪取了許多海島。但有一大帥，除掉他令人受的羞辱，並且使這羞辱歸他本身。¹⁹他就必轉向本地的保障，卻要絆跌仆倒，歸於無有。

²⁰“那時，必有一人興起接續他為王，使橫征暴斂的人通行國中的榮美地。這王不多日就必滅亡，卻不因忿怒，也不因爭戰。

²¹“必有一個卑鄙的人興起接續為王，人未曾將國的尊榮給他，他卻趁人坦然無備的時候，用諂媚的話得國。²²必有無數的軍兵勢如洪水，在他面前沖沒敗壞，同盟的君也必如此。²³與那君結盟之後，他必行詭詐，因為他必上來以微小的軍（註：原文作“民”）成為強盛。²⁴趁人坦然無備的時候，他必來到國中極肥美之地，行他列祖和他列祖之祖所未曾行的，將擄物、掠物和財寶散給眾人，又要設計攻打保障，然而這都是暫時的。

²⁵“他必奮勇向前，率領大軍攻擊南方王，南方王也必以極大極強的軍兵與他爭戰，卻站立不住，因為有人設計謀害南方王。²⁶吃王膳的，必敗壞他，他的軍隊必被沖沒，而且被殺的甚多。²⁷至於這二王，他們心懷惡計，同席說謊，計謀卻不成就，因為到了定期，事就了結。²⁸北方王（註：原文作“他”）必帶許多財寶回往本國，他的心反對聖約，任意而行，回到本地。

²⁹“到了定期，他必返回，來到南方，後一次卻不如前一次，³⁰因為基提戰船必來攻擊他，他就喪膽而回，又要惱恨聖約，任意而行。他必回來聯絡背棄聖約的人。

---

a 17 Or *but she*　　*b* 30 Hebrew of *Kittim*

31 "他必興兵，這兵必褻瀆聖地，就是保障。除掉常獻的燔祭，設立那行毀壞可憎的。32作惡違背聖約的人，他必用巧言勾引；惟獨認識神的子民必剛強行事。

33 "民間的智慧人必訓誨多人，然而他們多日必倒在刀下，或被火燒，或被擄掠搶奪。34他們仆倒的時候，稍得扶助，卻有許多人用諂媚的話親近他們。35智慧人中有些仆倒的，為要熬煉其餘的人，使他們清淨潔白，直到末了，因為到了定期，事就了結。

王自高自大

36 "王必任意而行，自高自大，超過所有的神，又用奇異的話攻擊萬神之神。他必行事亨通，直到主的忿怒完畢，因為所定的事必然成就。37他必不顧他列祖的神，也不顧婦女所羨慕的神，無論何神他都不顧，因為他必自大，高過一切。38他倒要敬拜保障的神，用金、銀、寶石和可愛之物敬奉他列祖所不認識的神。39他必靠外邦神的幫助，攻破最堅固的保障。凡承認他的，他必將榮耀加給他們，使他們管轄許多人，又為賄賂分地與他們。

40 "到末了，南方王要與他交戰，北方王必用戰車、馬兵和許多戰船，勢如暴風來攻擊他，也必進入列國如洪水氾濫。41又必進入那榮美之地，有許多國就被傾覆，但以東人、摩押人和一大半亞捫人必脫離他的手。42他必伸手攻擊列國，埃及地也不得脫離。43他必把持埃及的金銀財寶和各樣的寶物，利比亞人和古實人都必跟從他。44但從東方和北方必有消息擾亂他，他就大發烈怒出去，要將多人殺滅淨盡。45他必在海和榮美的聖山中間設立他如宮殿的帳幕；然而到了他的結局，必無人能幫助他。

31"His armed forces will rise up to desecrate the temple fortress and will abolish the daily sacrifice. Then they will set up the abomination that causes desolation. 32With flattery he will corrupt those who have violated the covenant, but the people who know their God will firmly resist him.

33"Those who are wise will instruct many, though for a time they will fall by the sword or be burned or captured or plundered. 34When they fall, they will receive a little help, and many who are not sincere will join them. 35Some of the wise will stumble, so that they may be refined, purified and made spotless until the time of the end, for it will still come at the appointed time.

The King Who Exalts Himself

36"The king will do as he pleases. He will exalt and magnify himself above every god and will say unheard-of things against the God of gods. He will be successful until the time of wrath is completed, for what has been determined must take place. 37He will show no regard for the gods of his fathers or for the one desired by women, nor will he regard any god, but will exalt himself above them all. 38Instead of them, he will honor a god of fortresses; a god unknown to his fathers he will honor with gold and silver, with precious stones and costly gifts. 39He will attack the mightiest fortresses with the help of a foreign god and will greatly honor those who acknowledge him. He will make them rulers over many people and will distribute the land at a price.[a]

40"At the time of the end the king of the South will engage him in battle, and the king of the North will storm out against him with chariots and cavalry and a great fleet of ships. He will invade many countries and sweep through them like a flood. 41He will also invade the Beautiful Land. Many countries will fall, but Edom, Moab and the leaders of Ammon will be delivered from his hand. 42He will extend his power over many countries; Egypt will not escape. 43He will gain control of the treasures of gold and silver and all the riches of Egypt, with the Libyans and Nubians in submission. 44But reports from the east and the north will alarm him, and he will set out in a great rage to destroy and annihilate many. 45He will pitch his royal tents between the seas at[b] the beautiful holy mountain. Yet he will come to his end, and no one will help him.

---

a 39 Or land for a reward   b 45 Or the sea and

The End Times

12 "At that time Michael, the great prince who protects your people, will arise. There will be a time of distress such as has not happened from the beginning of nations until then. But at that time your people—everyone whose name is found written in the book—will be delivered. ²Multitudes who sleep in the dust of the earth will awake: some to everlasting life, others to shame and everlasting contempt. ³Those who are wise*ᵃ* will shine like the brightness of the heavens, and those who lead many to righteousness, like the stars for ever and ever. ⁴But you, Daniel, close up and seal the words of the scroll until the time of the end. Many will go here and there to increase knowledge."

⁵Then I, Daniel, looked, and there before me stood two others, one on this bank of the river and one on the opposite bank. ⁶One of them said to the man clothed in linen, who was above the waters of the river, "How long will it be before these astonishing things are fulfilled?"

⁷The man clothed in linen, who was above the waters of the river, lifted his right hand and his left hand toward heaven, and I heard him swear by him who lives forever, saying, "It will be for a time, times and half a time.*ᵇ* When the power of the holy people has been finally broken, all these things will be completed."

⁸I heard, but I did not understand. So I asked, "My lord, what will the outcome of all this be?"

⁹He replied, "Go your way, Daniel, because the words are closed up and sealed until the time of the end. ¹⁰Many will be purified, made spotless and refined, but the wicked will continue to be wicked. None of the wicked will understand, but those who are wise will understand.

¹¹"From the time that the daily sacrifice is abolished and the abomination that causes desolation is set up, there will be 1,290 days. ¹²Blessed is the one who waits for and reaches the end of the 1,335 days.

¹³"As for you, go your way till the end. You will rest, and then at the end of the days you will rise to receive your allotted inheritance."

末時

12 "那時,保佑你本國之民的天使長(註:原文作"大君")米迦勒必站起來,並且有大艱難,從有國以來直到此時,沒有這樣的。你本國的民中,凡名錄在冊上的,必得拯救。²睡在塵埃中的,必有多人復醒,其中有得永生的,有受羞辱、永遠被憎惡的。³智慧人必發光,如同天上的光;那使多人歸義的,必發光如星,直到永永遠遠。⁴但以理啊,你要隱藏這話,封閉這書,直到末時。必有多人來往奔跑(註:或作"切心研究"),知識就必增長。"

⁵我但以理觀看,見另有兩個人站立,一個在河這邊,一個在河那邊。⁶有一個問那站在河水以上、穿細麻衣的說:"這奇異的事到幾時才應驗呢?"

⁷我聽見那站在河水以上、穿細麻衣的,向天舉起左右手,指着活到永遠的主起誓說:"要到一載、二載、半載,打破聖民權力的時候,這一切事就都應驗了。"

⁸我聽見這話,卻不明白,就說:"我主啊,這些事的結局是怎樣呢?"

⁹他說:"但以理啊,你只管去,因為這話已經隱藏封閉,直到末時。¹⁰必有許多人使自己清淨潔白,且被熬煉,但惡人仍必行惡,一切惡人都不明白,惟獨智慧人能明白。

¹¹"從除掉常獻的燔祭,並設立那行毀壞可憎之物的時候,必有一千二百九十日。¹²等到一千三百三十五日的,那人便為有福。

¹³"你且去等候結局,因為你必安歇。到了末期,你必起來,享受你的福分。"

---

a 3 Or who impart wisdom   b 7 Or a year, two years and half a year

何西阿書

1 當烏西雅、約坦、亞哈斯、希西家作猶大王，約阿施的兒子耶羅波安作以色列王的時候，耶和華的話臨到備利的兒子何西阿。

何西阿的妻子與兒女

2 耶和華初次與何西阿說話，對他說：“你去娶淫婦為妻，也收那從淫亂所生的兒女；因為這地大行淫亂，離棄耶和華。” 3 於是，何西阿去娶了滴拉音的女兒歌篾。這婦人懷孕，給他生了一個兒子。

4 耶和華對何西阿說：“給他起名叫耶斯列；因為再過片時，我必討耶戶家在耶斯列殺人流血的罪，也必使以色列家的國滅絕。5 到那日，我必在耶斯列平原折斷以色列的弓。”

6 歌篾又懷孕生了一個女兒，耶和華對何西阿說：“給她起名叫羅路哈瑪（註：就是“不蒙憐憫”的意思）；因為我必不再憐憫以色列家，決不赦免他們。7 我卻要憐憫猶大家，使他們靠耶和華他們的神得救，不使他們靠弓、刀、爭戰、馬匹與馬兵得救。”

8 歌篾給羅路哈瑪斷奶以後，又懷孕生了一個兒子。9 耶和華說：“給他起名叫羅阿米（註：就是“非我民”的意思）；因為你們不作我的子民，我也不作你們的神。

10 “然而，以色列的人數必如海沙，不可量、不可數。從前在甚麼地方對他們說：‘你們不是我的子民’，將來在那裏必對他們說：‘你們是永生神的兒子。’11 猶大人和以色列人必一同聚集，為自己立一個首領，從這地上去（註：或作“從被擄之地上來”），因為耶斯列的日子必為大日。

Hosea

1 The word of the LORD that came to Hosea son of Beeri during the reigns of Uzziah, Jotham, Ahaz and Hezekiah, kings of Judah, and during the reign of Jeroboam son of Jehoash[a] king of Israel:

Hosea's Wife and Children

2 When the LORD began to speak through Hosea, the LORD said to him, "Go, take to yourself an adulterous wife and children of unfaithfulness, because the land is guilty of the vilest adultery in departing from the LORD." 3 So he married Gomer daughter of Diblaim, and she conceived and bore him a son.

4 Then the LORD said to Hosea, "Call him Jezreel, because I will soon punish the house of Jehu for the massacre at Jezreel, and I will put an end to the kingdom of Israel. 5 In that day I will break Israel's bow in the Valley of Jezreel."

6 Gomer conceived again and gave birth to a daughter. Then the LORD said to Hosea, "Call her Lo-Ruhamah,[b] for I will no longer show love to the house of Israel, that I should at all forgive them. 7 Yet I will show love to the house of Judah; and I will save them—not by bow, sword or battle, or by horses and horsemen, but by the LORD their God."

8 After she had weaned Lo-Ruhamah, Gomer had another son. 9 Then the LORD said, "Call him Lo-Ammi,[c] for you are not my people, and I am not your God.

10 "Yet the Israelites will be like the sand on the seashore, which cannot be measured or counted. In the place where it was said to them, 'You are not my people,' they will be called 'sons of the living God.' 11 The people of Judah and the people of Israel will be reunited, and they will appoint one leader and will come up out of the land, for great will be the day of Jezreel.

---

a 1 Hebrew Joash, a variant of Jehoash   b 6 Lo-Ruhamah means not loved.   c 9 Lo-Ammi means not my people.

2

"Say of your brothers, 'My people,' and of your sisters, 'My loved one.'

Israel Punished and Restored

[2]"Rebuke your mother, rebuke her,
　for she is not my wife,
　and I am not her husband.
　Let her remove the adulterous look from her face
　and the unfaithfulness from between her breasts.

[3]Otherwise I will strip her naked
　and make her as bare as on the day she was born;
　I will make her like a desert,
　turn her into a parched land,
　and slay her with thirst.

[4]I will not show my love to her children,
　because they are the children of adultery.

[5]Their mother has been unfaithful
　and has conceived them in disgrace.
　She said, 'I will go after my lovers,
　who give me my food and my water,
　my wool and my linen, my oil and my drink.'

[6]Therefore I will block her path with thornbushes;
　I will wall her in so that she cannot find her way.

[7]She will chase after her lovers but not catch them;
　she will look for them but not find them.
　Then she will say,
　'I will go back to my husband as at first,
　for then I was better off than now.'

[8]She has not acknowledged that I was the one who gave her the grain, the new wine and oil,
　who lavished on her the silver and gold—
　which they used for Baal.

[9]"Therefore I will take away my grain when it ripens,
　and my new wine when it is ready.
　I will take back my wool and my linen,
　intended to cover her nakedness.

[10]So now I will expose her lewdness
　before the eyes of her lovers;
　no one will take her out of my hands.

[11]I will stop all her celebrations:
　her yearly festivals, her New Moons,
　her Sabbath days—all her appointed feasts.

[12]I will ruin her vines and her fig trees,
　which she said were her pay from her lovers;

2

"你們要稱你們的弟兄為阿米（註：就是"我民"的意思）；稱你們的姐妹為路哈瑪（註：就是"蒙憐憫"的意思）。

以色列受刑與復興

[2] "你們要與你們的母親大大爭辯，
　　因為她不是我的妻子，
　　我也不是她的丈夫。
　　叫她除掉臉上的淫像
　　和胸間的淫態。

[3]免得我剝去她的衣服，
　　使她赤體
　　與才生的時候一樣；
　　使她如曠野，
　　如乾旱之地，
　　因渴而死。

[4]我必不憐憫她的兒女，
　　因為他們是從淫亂而生的。

[5]他們的母親行了淫亂，
　　懷他們的母做了可羞恥的事，
　　因為她說：'我要隨從所愛的，
　　我的餅、水、羊毛、麻、油、酒
　　都是他們給的。'

[6]因此，我必用荊棘堵塞她的道，
　　築牆擋住她，
　　使她找不着路。

[7]她必追隨所愛的，
　　卻追不上；
　　她必尋找他們，卻尋不見。
　　便說：
　　'我要歸回前夫，
　　因我那時的光景比如今還好。'

[8]她不知道是我給她五穀、
　　新酒和油，
　　又加增她的金銀，
　　她卻以此供奉（註：或作"製造"）巴力。

[9] "因此，到了收割的日子，
　　出酒的時候，
　　我必將我的五穀、新酒收回，
　　也必將她應當遮體的羊毛和麻
　　奪回來。

[10]如今我必在她所愛的眼前
　　顯露她的醜態，
　　必無人能救她脫離我的手。

[11]我也必使她的宴樂、
　　節期、月朔、安息日，
　　並她的一切大會，都止息了。

[12]我也必毀壞她的葡萄樹
　　和無花果樹，
　　就是她說'這是我所愛的給我
　　為賞賜'的。

我必使這些樹變為荒林，
為田野的走獸所吃。
¹³我必追討
她素日給諸巴力燒香的罪，
那時她佩帶耳環和別樣妝飾，
隨從她所愛的，
卻忘記我。"

這是耶和華說的。

¹⁴ "後來我必勸導她，
領她到曠野，
對她說安慰的話。
¹⁵她從那裏出來，我必賜她葡萄園，
又賜她亞割谷作為指望的門。
她必在那裏應聲（註：或作 "歌唱"），
與幼年的日子一樣，
與從埃及地上來的時候相同。"

¹⁶耶和華說：
"那日你必稱呼我伊施（註：就是 "我
夫" 的意思），
不再稱呼我巴力（註：就是 "我主" 的
意思）。
¹⁷因為我必從我民的口中
除掉諸巴力的名號，
這名號不再提起。
¹⁸當那日，我必為我的民，
與田野的走獸和空中的飛鳥，
並地上的昆蟲立約。
又必在國中折斷弓刀，止息爭戰，
使他們安然躺臥。
¹⁹我必聘你永遠歸我為妻，
以仁義、公平、慈愛、憐憫
聘你歸我，
²⁰也以誠實聘你歸我，
你就必認識我耶和華。"

²¹耶和華說：
"那日我必應允，
我必應允天，
天必應允地。
²²地必應允五穀、新酒和油，
這些必應允耶斯列民（註："耶斯
列" 就是 "神栽種的" 意思）。
²³我必將她種在這地。
素不蒙憐憫的，我必憐憫；
本非我民的，我必對他說：
'你是我的民。'
他必說：
'你是我的神。'"

I will make them a thicket,
and wild animals will devour them.
¹³I will punish her for the days
she burned incense to the Baals;
she decked herself with rings and jewelry,
and went after her lovers,
but me she forgot,"
declares the LORD.

¹⁴"Therefore I am now going to allure her;
I will lead her into the desert
and speak tenderly to her.
¹⁵There I will give her back her vineyards,
and will make the Valley of Achor^a a door of
hope.
There she will sing^b as in the days of her youth,
as in the day she came up out of Egypt.

¹⁶"In that day," declares the LORD,
"you will call me 'my husband';
you will no longer call me 'my master.'^{c}
¹⁷I will remove the names of the Baals from her
lips;
no longer will their names be invoked.
¹⁸In that day I will make a covenant for them
with the beasts of the field and the birds of
the air
and the creatures that move along the ground.
Bow and sword and battle
I will abolish from the land,
so that all may lie down in safety.
¹⁹I will betroth you to me forever;
I will betroth you in^d righteousness and justice,
in^e love and compassion.
²⁰I will betroth you in faithfulness,
and you will acknowledge the LORD.

²¹"In that day I will respond,"
declares the LORD—
"I will respond to the skies,
and they will respond to the earth;
²²and the earth will respond to the grain,
the new wine and oil,
and they will respond to Jezreel.^{f}
²³I will plant her for myself in the land;
I will show my love to the one I called 'Not
my loved one.'^{g}
I will say to those called 'Not my people,'^{h}
'You are my people';
and they will say, 'You are my God.'"

---

a 15 *Achor* means *trouble*.　　b 15 Or *respond*　　c 16 Hebrew *baal*
d 19 Or *with*; also in verse 20　　e 19 Or *with*　　f 22 *Jezreel*
means *God plants*.　　g 23 Hebrew *Lo-Ruhamah*　　h 23 Hebrew
Lo-Ammi

Hosea's Reconciliation With His Wife

3 The Lord said to me, "Go, show your love to your wife again, though she is loved by another and is an adulteress. Love her as the Lord loves the Israelites, though they turn to other gods and love the sacred raisin cakes."

²So I bought her for fifteen shekels[a] of silver and about a homer and a lethek[b] of barley. ³Then I told her, "You are to live with[c] me many days; you must not be a prostitute or be intimate with any man, and I will live with[c] you."

⁴For the Israelites will live many days without king or prince, without sacrifice or sacred stones, without ephod or idol. ⁵Afterward the Israelites will return and seek the Lord their God and David their king. They will come trembling to the Lord and to his blessings in the last days.

The Charge Against Israel

4 Hear the word of the Lord, you Israelites, because the Lord has a charge to bring against you who live in the land:

"There is no faithfulness, no love,
 no acknowledgment of God in the land.
²There is only cursing,[d] lying and murder,
 stealing and adultery;
 they break all bounds,
 and bloodshed follows bloodshed.
³Because of this the land mourns,[e]
 and all who live in it waste away;
 the beasts of the field and the birds of the air
 and the fish of the sea are dying.

⁴"But let no man bring a charge,
 let no man accuse another,
 for your people are like those
 who bring charges against a priest.
⁵You stumble day and night,
 and the prophets stumble with you.
 So I will destroy your mother—
⁶ my people are destroyed from lack of knowledge.

"Because you have rejected knowledge,
 I also reject you as my priests;
because you have ignored the law of your God,
 I also will ignore your children.

何西阿與妻復合

3 耶和華對我說："你再去愛一個淫婦,就是她情人所愛的;好像以色列人,雖然偏向別神,喜愛葡萄餅,耶和華還是愛他們。"

²我便用銀子十五舍客勒,大麥一賀梅珥半,買她歸我。³我對她說:"你當多日為我獨居,不可行淫,不可歸別人為妻,我向你也必這樣。"

⁴以色列人也必多日獨居,無君王、無首領、無祭祀、無柱像、無以弗得、無家中的神像。⁵後來以色列人必歸回(註:或作"回心轉意"),尋求他們的神耶和華和他們的王大衛。在末後的日子,必以敬畏的心歸向耶和華,領受他的恩惠。

神對以色列的譴責

4 "以色列人哪,
 你們當聽耶和華的話。
 耶和華與這地的居民爭辯,
 因這地上無誠實,
 無良善,
 無人認識神。
²但起假誓、不踐前言、殺害、
 偷盜、姦淫、
 行強暴,
 殺人流血,接連不斷。
³因此,這地悲哀,
 其上的民、田野的獸、
 空中的鳥必都衰微,
 海中的魚也必消滅。

⁴ "然而,人都不必爭辯,
 也不必指責,
 因為這民
 與抗拒祭司的人一樣。
⁵你這祭司必日間跌倒;
 先知也必夜間與你一同跌倒。
 我必滅絕你的母親。
⁶我的民因無知識而滅亡。

"你棄掉知識,我也必棄掉你,
 使你不再給我作祭司;
 你既忘了你神的律法,
 我也必忘記你的兒女。

---

a 2 That is, about 6 ounces (about 170 grams)   b 2 That is, probably about 10 bushels (about 330 liters)   c 3 Or wait for   d 2 That is, to pronounce a curse upon   e 3 Or dries up

7祭司越發增多，
　　就越發得罪我；
　我必使他們的榮耀
　　變為羞辱。
8他們吃我民的贖罪祭，
　　滿心願意我民犯罪。
9將來民如何，祭司也必如何。
　　我必因他們所行的懲罰他們，
　　照他們所做的報應他們。

10 "他們吃，卻不得飽；
　　行淫，而不得立後；
　因為他們離棄耶和華，
　　不遵他的命。
11姦淫和酒，
　　並新酒，
　　奪去人的心。

12我的民求問木偶，
　　以為木杖能指示他們，
　因為他們的淫心使他們失迷，
　　他們就行淫離棄神，不守約束。
13在各山頂
　　各高岡的橡樹、楊樹、栗樹之下
　　獻祭燒香，
　　因為樹影美好。
　所以，你們的女兒淫亂，
　　你們的新婦 (註：或作 "兒婦"。下同)
　　行淫。

14 "你們的女兒淫亂，
　　你們的新婦行淫，
　我卻不懲罰她們，
　因為你們自己離羣
　　與娼妓同居，
　　與妓女一同獻祭。
　這無知的民
　　必致傾倒！

15 "以色列啊，你雖然行淫，
　　猶大卻不可犯罪。

　"不要往吉甲去，
　　不要上到伯亞文，
　　也不要指着永生的耶和華起誓。

16以色列倔強，
　　猶如倔強的母牛；
　現在耶和華要放他們，
　　如同放羊羔在寬闊之地。

7The more the priests increased,
　the more they sinned against me;
　they exchanged[a] their[b] Glory for something
　　disgraceful.
8They feed on the sins of my people
　and relish their wickedness.
9And it will be: Like people, like priests.
　I will punish both of them for their ways
　and repay them for their deeds.

10"They will eat but not have enough;
　they will engage in prostitution but not
　　increase,
because they have deserted the LORD
　to give themselves 11to prostitution,
　to old wine and new,
　which take away the understanding 12of my
　　people.
They consult a wooden idol
　and are answered by a stick of wood.
A spirit of prostitution leads them astray;
　they are unfaithful to their God.
13They sacrifice on the mountaintops
　and burn offerings on the hills,
under oak, poplar and terebinth,
　where the shade is pleasant.
Therefore your daughters turn to prostitution
　and your daughters-in-law to adultery.

14"I will not punish your daughters
　when they turn to prostitution,
nor your daughters-in-law
　when they commit adultery,
because the men themselves consort with
　　harlots
and sacrifice with shrine prostitutes—
　a people without understanding will come to
　　ruin!

15"Though you commit adultery, O Israel,
　let not Judah become guilty.

　"Do not go to Gilgal;
　do not go up to Beth Aven.[c]
　And do not swear, 'As surely as the Lord
　　lives!'
16The Israelites are stubborn,
　like a stubborn heifer.
　How then can the LORD pasture them
　like lambs in a meadow?

a 7 Syriac and an ancient Hebrew scribal tradition; Masoretic
Text I will exchange　　b 7 Masoretic Text; an ancient Hebrew
scribal tradition my　　c 15 Beth Aven means house of wickedness
(a name for Bethel, which means house of God).

¹⁷Ephraim is joined to idols;
　　leave him alone!
¹⁸Even when their drinks are gone,
　　they continue their prostitution;
　　their rulers dearly love shameful ways.
¹⁹A whirlwind will sweep them away,
　　and their sacrifices will bring them shame.

Judgment Against Israel

5 "Hear this, you priests!
　　Pay attention, you Israelites!
　　Listen, O royal house!
This judgment is against you:
　You have been a snare at Mizpah,
　　a net spread out on Tabor.
²The rebels are deep in slaughter.
　I will discipline all of them.
³I know all about Ephraim;
　Israel is not hidden from me.
Ephraim, you have now turned to prostitution;
　Israel is corrupt.

⁴"Their deeds do not permit them
　　to return to their God.
A spirit of prostitution is in their heart;
　they do not acknowledge the LORD.
⁵Israel's arrogance testifies against them;
　the Israelites, even Ephraim, stumble in their
　　sin;
Judah also stumbles with them.
⁶When they go with their flocks and herds
　to seek the LORD,
they will not find him;
　he has withdrawn himself from them.
⁷They are unfaithful to the LORD;
　they give birth to illegitimate children.
Now their New Moon festivals
　will devour them and their fields.

⁸"Sound the trumpet in Gibeah,
　　the horn in Ramah.
Raise the battle cry in Beth Aven^a;
　lead on, O Benjamin.
⁹Ephraim will be laid waste
　on the day of reckoning.
Among the tribes of Israel
　I proclaim what is certain.
¹⁰Judah's leaders are like those
　who move boundary stones.
I will pour out my wrath on them
　like a flood of water.

---

¹⁷以法蓮親近偶像，
　　任憑他吧！
¹⁸他們所喝的已經發酸，
　　他們時常行淫，
　　他們的官長最愛羞恥的事。
¹⁹風把他們裹在翅膀裏；
　　他們因所獻的祭必致蒙羞。

神對以色列的審判

5 "眾祭司啊，要聽我的話！
　　以色列家啊，要留心聽！
　　王家啊，要側耳而聽！
　　審判要臨到你們，
　　因你們在米斯巴如網羅，
　　在他泊山如鋪張的網。
²這些悖逆的人肆行殺戮，罪孽極深；
　　我卻斥責他們眾人。
³以法蓮為我所知，
　　以色列不能向我隱藏。
　　以法蓮哪，現在你行淫了，
　　以色列被玷污了。

⁴"他們所行的
　　使他們不能歸向神，
　　因有淫心在他們裏面，
　　他們也不認識耶和華。
⁵以色列的驕傲當面見證自己；
　　故此，以色列和以法蓮
　　必因自己的罪孽跌倒，
　　猶大也必與他們一同跌倒。
⁶他們必牽着羊羊
　　去尋求耶和華，
　　卻尋不見，
　　他已經轉去離開他們。
⁷他們向耶和華行事詭詐，
　　生了私子。
到了月朔，
　　他們與他們的地業必被吞滅。

⁸"你們當在基比亞吹角，
　　在拉瑪吹號，
在伯亞文吹出大聲說，
　　便雅憫哪，有仇敵在你後頭！
⁹在責罰的日子，
　　以法蓮必變為荒場。
我在以色列支派中，
　　指示將來必成的事。
¹⁰猶大的首領
　　如同挪移地界的人，
　　我必將忿怒倒在他們身上，
　　如水一般。

---

^a 8 Beth Aven means house of wickedness (a name for Bethel,
which means house of God).

11以法蓮因樂從人的命令，
　　就受欺壓，
　　被審判壓碎。
12我使以法蓮如蟲蛀之物，
　　使猶大家如朽爛之木。

13 "以法蓮見自己有病，
　　猶大見自己有瘡，
　　他們就打發人往亞述
　　去見耶雷布王，
　　他卻不能醫治你們，
　　不能治好你們的傷。
14我必向以法蓮如獅子，
　　向猶大家如少壯獅子。
　　我必撕裂而去，
　　我要奪去，無人搭救。
15我要回到原處，
　　等他們自覺有罪（註：或作 "承認己
　　罪"），尋求我面；
　　他們在急難的時候，
　　必切切尋求我。"

以色列人不肯悔改

6 "來吧，我們歸向耶和華！
　　他撕裂我們，
　　也必醫治；
　　他打傷我們，
　　也必纏裹。
2過兩天他必使我們甦醒，
　　第三天他必使我們興起，
　　我們就在他面前得以存活。
3我們務要認識耶和華，
　　竭力追求認識他。
　　他出現確如晨光；
　　他必臨到我們像甘雨，
　　像滋潤田地的春雨。"

4主說："以法蓮哪，
　　我可向你怎樣行呢？
　　猶大啊，我可向你怎樣做呢？
　　因為你們的良善如同早晨的雲霧，
　　又如速散的甘露。
5因此，我藉先知砍伐他們，
　　以我口中的話殺戮他們，
　　我施行的審判如光發出。
6我喜愛良善（註：或作 "憐恤"），
　　不喜愛祭祀；
　　喜愛認識神，勝於燔祭！
7他們卻如亞當背約，
　　在境內向我行事詭詐。
8基列是作孽之人的城，
　　被血沾染。

11Ephraim is oppressed,
　　trampled in judgment,
　　intent on pursuing idols.[a]
12I am like a moth to Ephraim,
　　like rot to the people of Judah.

13"When Ephraim saw his sickness,
　　and Judah his sores,
then Ephraim turned to Assyria,
　　and sent to the great king for help.
But he is not able to cure you,
　　not able to heal your sores.
14For I will be like a lion to Ephraim,
　　like a great lion to Judah.
I will tear them to pieces and go away;
　　I will carry them off, with no one to rescue
　　them.
15Then I will go back to my place
　　until they admit their guilt.
And they will seek my face;
　　in their misery they will earnestly seek me."

Israel Unrepentant

6 "Come, let us return to the LORD.
　　He has torn us to pieces
　　but he will heal us;
　he has injured us
　　but he will bind up our wounds.
2After two days he will revive us;
　　on the third day he will restore us,
　　that we may live in his presence.
3Let us acknowledge the LORD;
　　let us press on to acknowledge him.
　As surely as the sun rises,
　　he will appear;
　he will come to us like the winter rains,
　　like the spring rains that water the earth."

4"What can I do with you, Ephraim?
　　What can I do with you, Judah?
Your love is like the morning mist,
　　like the early dew that disappears.
5Therefore I cut you in pieces with my prophets,
　　I killed you with the words of my mouth;
　　my judgments flashed like lightning upon
　　you.
6For I desire mercy, not sacrifice,
　　and acknowledgment of God rather than
　　burnt offerings.
7Like Adam,[b] they have broken the covenant—
　　they were unfaithful to me there.
8Gilead is a city of wicked men,
　　stained with footprints of blood.

a 11 The meaning of the Hebrew for this word is uncertain.
b 7 Or As at Adam; or Like men

9As marauders lie in ambush for a man,
  so do bands of priests;
they murder on the road to Shechem,
  committing shameful crimes.
10I have seen a horrible thing
  in the house of Israel.
There Ephraim is given to prostitution
  and Israel is defiled.

11"Also for you, Judah,
  a harvest is appointed.

"Whenever I would restore the fortunes of my
  people,

7 1whenever I would heal Israel,
  the sins of Ephraim are exposed
  and the crimes of Samaria revealed.
They practice deceit,
  thieves break into houses,
  bandits rob in the streets;
2but they do not realize
  that I remember all their evil deeds.
Their sins engulf them;
  they are always before me.

3"They delight the king with their wickedness,
  the princes with their lies.
4They are all adulterers,
  burning like an oven
whose fire the baker need not stir
  from the kneading of the dough till it rises.
5On the day of the festival of our king
  the princes become inflamed with wine,
  and he joins hands with the mockers.
6Their hearts are like an oven;
  they approach him with intrigue.
Their passion smolders all night;
  in the morning it blazes like a flaming fire.
7All of them are hot as an oven;
  they devour their rulers.
All their kings fall,
  and none of them calls on me.

8"Ephraim mixes with the nations;
  Ephraim is a flat cake not turned over.
9Foreigners sap his strength,
  but he does not realize it.
His hair is sprinkled with gray,
  but he does not notice.
10Israel's arrogance testifies against him,
  but despite all this
he does not return to the LORD his God
  or search for him.

11"Ephraim is like a dove,
  easily deceived and senseless—

9強盜成羣，怎樣埋伏殺人；
  祭司結黨，
也照樣在示劍的路上殺戮，
  行了邪惡。
10在以色列家
  我見了可憎的事，
在以法蓮那裏有淫行，
  以色列被玷污。

11"猶大啊，
  我使被擄之民歸回的時候，

"必有為你所命定的收場。

7 1我想醫治以色列的時候，
  以法蓮的罪孽和撒馬利亞的
  罪惡就顯露出來。
他們行事虛謊，
  內有賊人入室偷竊；
  外有強盜成羣騷擾。
2他們心裏並不思想
  我記念他們的一切惡；
他們所行的現在纏繞他們，
  都在我面前。

3"他們行惡君王歡喜，
  說謊使首領喜樂。
4他們都是行淫的，
  像火爐被烤餅的燒熱，
從摶麵到發麵的時候，
  暫不使火着旺。
5在我們王宴樂的日子，
  首領因酒的烈性成病；
  王與褻慢人拉手。
6首領埋伏的時候，
  心中熱如火爐，
就如烤餅的整夜睡臥，
  到了早晨火氣炎炎。
7眾民也熱如火爐，
  燒滅他們的官長。
他們的君王都仆倒而死；
  他們中間無一人求告我。

8"以法蓮與列邦人攙雜，
  以法蓮是沒有翻過的餅。
9外邦人吞吃他勞力得來的，
  他卻不知道；
頭髮斑白，
  他也不覺得。
10以色列的驕傲當面見證自己，
  雖遭遇這一切，
他們仍不歸向耶和華他們的神，
  也不尋求他。

11"以法蓮好像鴿子
  愚蠢無知；

他們求告埃及，
　　投奔亞述。
12他們去的時候，
　　我必將我的網撒在他們身上，
　　我要打下他們如同空中的鳥。
　我必按他們會眾所聽見的
　　懲罰他們。
13他們因離棄我，必定有禍；
　　因違背我，必被毀滅。
　我雖要救贖他們，
　　他們卻向我說謊。

14他們並不誠心哀求我，
　　乃在牀上呼號。
　他們為求五穀新酒聚集，
　　仍然悖逆我。
15我雖教導他們，堅固他們的膀臂，
　　他們竟圖謀抗拒我。
16他們歸向，卻不歸向至上者；
　　他們如同翻背的弓。
　他們的首領
　　必因舌頭的狂傲倒在刀下，
　這在埃及地
　　必作人的譏笑。"

以色列所收的是暴風

8　"你用口吹角吧！
　　敵人如鷹
　　來攻打耶和華的家，
　因為這民違背我的約，
　　干犯我的律法。
2他們必呼叫我說："我的神啊！
　　我們以色列認識你了！"
3以色列丟棄良善（註：或作"福分"），
　　仇敵必追逼他。
4他們立君王，卻不由我；
　　他們立首領，我卻不認。
　他們用金銀為自己製造偶像，
　　以致被剪除。

5撒馬利亞啊！
　　耶和華已經丟棄你的牛犢；
　我的怒氣向拜牛犢的人發作，
　　他們到幾時方能無罪呢？
6這牛犢出於以色列，
　　是匠人所造的，
　　並不是神！
　撒馬利亞的牛犢必被打碎。

7　"他們所種的是風，
　　所收的是暴風；
　所種的不成禾稼，
　　就是發苗，也不結實；

now calling to Egypt,
　　now turning to Assyria.
12When they go, I will throw my net over them;
　　I will pull them down like birds of the air.
　When I hear them flocking together,
　　I will catch them.
13Woe to them,
　　because they have strayed from me!
　Destruction to them,
　　because they have rebelled against me!
　I long to redeem them
　　but they speak lies against me.
14They do not cry out to me from their hearts
　　but wail upon their beds.
　They gather together*a* for grain and new wine
　　but turn away from me.
15I trained them and strengthened them,
　　but they plot evil against me.
16They do not turn to the Most High;
　　they are like a faulty bow.
　Their leaders will fall by the sword
　　because of their insolent words.
　For this they will be ridiculed
　　in the land of Egypt.

Israel to Reap the Whirlwind

8　"Put the trumpet to your lips!
　　An eagle is over the house of the Lord
　　because the people have broken my
　　covenant
　and rebelled against my law.
2Israel cries out to me,
　　'O our God, we acknowledge you!'
3But Israel has rejected what is good;
　　an enemy will pursue him.
4They set up kings without my consent;
　　they choose princes without my approval.
　With their silver and gold
　　they make idols for themselves
　　to their own destruction.
5Throw out your calf-idol, O Samaria!
　　My anger burns against them.
　How long will they be incapable of purity?
6　They are from Israel!
　This calf—a craftsman has made it;
　　it is not God.
　It will be broken in pieces,
　　that calf of Samaria.

7"They sow the wind
　　and reap the whirlwind.
　The stalk has no head;
　　it will produce no flour.

*a 14 Most Hebrew manuscripts; some Hebrew manuscripts
and Septuagint They slash themselves*

Were it to yield grain,
　　foreigners would swallow it up.
[8]Israel is swallowed up;
　　now she is among the nations
　　like a worthless thing.
[9]For they have gone up to Assyria
　　like a wild donkey wandering alone.
　　Ephraim has sold herself to lovers.
[10]Although they have sold themselves among
　　　　the nations,
　　I will now gather them together.
　　They will begin to waste away
　　under the oppression of the mighty king.

[11]"Though Ephraim built many altars for sin
　　　offerings,
　　these have become altars for sinning.
[12]I wrote for them the many things of my law,
　　but they regarded them as something alien.
[13]They offer sacrifices given to me
　　and they eat the meat,
　　but the LORD is not pleased with them.
　　Now he will remember their wickedness
　　and punish their sins:
　　They will return to Egypt.
[14]Israel has forgotten his Maker
　　and built palaces;
　　Judah has fortified many towns.
　　But I will send fire upon their cities
　　that will consume their fortresses."

Punishment for Israel

9 Do not rejoice, O Israel;
　　do not be jubilant like the other nations.
　　For you have been unfaithful to your God;
　　you love the wages of a prostitute
　　at every threshing floor.
[2]Threshing floors and winepresses will not feed
　　　the people;
　　the new wine will fail them.
[3]They will not remain in the LORD's land;
　　Ephraim will return to Egypt
　　and eat unclean[a] food in Assyria.
[4]They will not pour out wine offerings to the
　　　LORD,
　　nor will their sacrifices please him.
　　Such sacrifices will be to them like the bread
　　　of mourners;
　　all who eat them will be unclean.
　　This food will be for themselves;
　　it will not come into the temple of the LORD.

即便結實，
　　外邦人必吞吃。
[8]以色列被吞吃，
　　現今在列國中，
　　好像人不喜悅的器皿。
[9]他們投奔亞述，
　　如同獨行的野驢。
　　以法蓮賄買朋黨。
[10]他們雖在列邦中賄買人，
　　現在我卻要聚集懲罰他們。
　　他們因君王和首領所加的重擔，
　　日漸衰微。

[11]"以法蓮增添祭壇取罪，
　　因此，祭壇使他犯罪。

[12]我為他寫了律法萬條，
　　他卻以為與他毫無關涉。
[13]至於獻給我的祭物，
　　他們自食其肉，
　　耶和華卻不悅納他們。
　　現在必記念他們的罪孽，
　　追討他們的罪惡；
　　他們必歸回埃及。
[14]以色列忘記造他的主，
　　建造宮殿；
　　猶大多造堅固城。
　　我卻要降火焚燒他的城邑，
　　燒滅其中的宮殿。"

對以色列的懲罰

9 以色列啊！
　　不要像外邦人歡喜快樂！
　　因為你行邪淫離棄你的神，
　　在各穀場上
　　如妓女喜愛賞賜。
[2]穀場和酒醡
　　都不夠以色列人使用，
　　新酒也必缺乏。
[3]他們必不得住耶和華的地；
　　以法蓮卻要歸回埃及，
　　必在亞述吃不潔淨的食物。
[4]他們必不得向耶和華奠酒，
　　即便奠酒，
　　也不蒙悅納。
　　他們的祭物，
　　必如居喪者的食物，
　　凡吃的必被玷污；
　　因他們的食物，只為自己的口腹，
　　必不奉入耶和華的殿。

---

a 3 That is, ceremonially unclean

⁵在大會的日子，
　　到耶和華的節期，
　　你們怎樣行呢？
⁶看哪！他們逃避災難，
　　埃及人必收殮他們的屍首；
　　摩弗人必葬埋他們的骸骨。
　他們用銀子做的美物上
　　必長蒺藜，
　他們的帳棚中必生荊棘。
⁷以色列人必知道降罰的日子臨近，
　　報應的時候來到。
　　（民說：
　　　作先知的是愚昧，
　　　受靈感的是狂妄。）
　皆因他們多多作孽，
　　大懷怨恨。
⁸以法蓮曾作我神守望的；
　　至於先知，在他一切的道上
　　　作為捕鳥人的網羅，
　　在他神的家中懷怨恨。
⁹以法蓮深深地敗壞，
　　如在基比亞的日子一樣。
　耶和華必記念他們的罪孽，
　　追討他們的罪惡。

¹⁰主說：
　　"我遇見以色列如葡萄在曠野；
　我看見你們的列祖如無花果樹上
　　春季初熟的果子。
　他們卻來到巴力毘珥
　　專拜那可羞恥的，
　　就成為可憎惡的，
　　與他們所愛的一樣。
¹¹至於以法蓮人，
　　他們的榮耀必如鳥飛去，
　　必不生產、不懷胎、不成孕。
¹²縱然養大兒女，
　　我卻必使他們喪子，
　　甚至不留一個。
　我離棄他們，他們就有禍了。
¹³我看以法蓮如推羅
　　栽於美地。
　以法蓮卻要將自己的兒女帶出來，
　　交與行殺戮的人。"

¹⁴耶和華啊，
　　求你加給他們，
　加甚麼呢？
　　要使他們胎墜乳乾。

¹⁵耶和華說：
　　"他們一切的惡事都在吉甲，
　　我在那裏憎惡他們，

⁵What will you do on the day of your appointed
　　feasts,
　　on the festival days of the LORD?
⁶Even if they escape from destruction,
　　Egypt will gather them,
　　and Memphis will bury them.
　Their treasures of silver will be taken over by
　　briers,
　　and thorns will overrun their tents.
⁷The days of punishment are coming,
　　the days of reckoning are at hand.
　　Let Israel know this.
　Because your sins are so many
　　and your hostility so great,
　the prophet is considered a fool,
　　the inspired man a maniac.
⁸The prophet, along with my God,
　　is the watchman over Ephraim,ᵃ
　yet snares await him on all his paths,
　　and hostility in the house of his God.
⁹They have sunk deep into corruption,
　　as in the days of Gibeah.
　God will remember their wickedness
　　and punish them for their sins.

¹⁰"When I found Israel,
　　it was like finding grapes in the desert;
　when I saw your fathers,
　　it was like seeing the early fruit on the fig
　　　tree.
　But when they came to Baal Peor,
　　they consecrated themselves to that
　　　shameful idol
　　and became as vile as the thing they loved.
¹¹Ephraim's glory will fly away like a bird—
　　no birth, no pregnancy, no conception.
¹²Even if they rear children,
　　I will bereave them of every one.
　Woe to them
　　when I turn away from them!
¹³I have seen Ephraim, like Tyre,
　　planted in a pleasant place.
　But Ephraim will bring out
　　their children to the slayer."

¹⁴Give them, O LORD—
　　what will you give them?
　Give them wombs that miscarry
　　and breasts that are dry.

¹⁵"Because of all their wickedness in Gilgal,
　　I hated them there.

ᵃ 8 Or *The prophet is the watchman over Ephraim, / the people of
my God*

Because of their sinful deeds,
  I will drive them out of my house.
I will no longer love them;
  all their leaders are rebellious.
¹⁶Ephraim is blighted,
  their root is withered,
  they yield no fruit.
Even if they bear children,
  I will slay their cherished offspring."

¹⁷My God will reject them
  because they have not obeyed him;
  they will be wanderers among the nations.

10 Israel was a spreading vine;
  he brought forth fruit for himself.
  As his fruit increased,
he built more altars;
as his land prospered,
  he adorned his sacred stones.
²Their heart is deceitful,
  and now they must bear their guilt.
The LORD will demolish their altars
  and destroy their sacred stones.

³Then they will say, "We have no king
  because we did not revere the LORD.
But even if we had a king,
  what could he do for us?"
⁴They make many promises,
  take false oaths
  and make agreements;
therefore lawsuits spring up
  like poisonous weeds in a plowed field.
⁵The people who live in Samaria fear
  for the calf-idol of Beth Aven.^a
Its people will mourn over it,
  and so will its idolatrous priests,
those who had rejoiced over its splendor,
  because it is taken from them into exile.
⁶It will be carried to Assyria
  as tribute for the great king.
Ephraim will be disgraced;
  Israel will be ashamed of its wooden idols.^b
⁷Samaria and its king will float away
  like a twig on the surface of the waters.
⁸The high places of wickedness^c will be
    destroyed—
  it is the sin of Israel.
Thorns and thistles will grow up
  and cover their altars.

因他們所行的惡，
  我必從我地上趕出他們去，
不再憐愛他們；
  他們的首領都是悖逆的。
¹⁶以法蓮受責罰，
  根本枯乾，
  必不能結果；
即或生產，
  我必殺他們所生的愛子。"

¹⁷我的神必棄絕他們，
  因為他們不聽從他；
  他們也必飄流在列國中。

10 以色列是茂盛的葡萄樹，
  結果繁多。
  果子越多，
  就越增添祭壇；
地土越肥美，
  就越造美麗的柱像。
²他們心懷二意，
  現今要定為有罪。
耶和華必拆毀他們的祭壇，
  毀壞他們的柱像。

³他們必說：
  "我們沒有王，
  因為我們不敬畏耶和華；
  王能為我們做甚麼呢？"
⁴他們為立約說謊言，
  起假誓；
因此，
  災罰如苦菜
  滋生在田間的犁溝中。
⁵撒馬利亞的居民，
  必因伯亞文的牛犢驚恐；
崇拜牛犢的民
  和喜愛牛犢的祭司，
都必因榮耀離開它，
  為它悲哀。
⁶人必將牛犢帶到亞述當作禮物，
  獻給耶雷布王。
以法蓮必蒙羞，
  以色列必因自己的計謀慚愧。
⁷至於撒馬利亞，他的王必滅沒，
  如水面的沫子一樣。
⁸伯亞文的邱壇——
  就是以色列取罪的地方，
  必被毀滅，
荊棘和蒺藜
  必長在他們的祭壇上。

---

a 5 Beth Aven means *house of wickedness* (a name for Bethel,
which means *house of God*).   *b 6* Or *its counsel*   *c 8* Hebrew
aven, a reference to Beth Aven (a derogatory name for Bethel)

他們必對大山說："遮蓋我們！"
　對小山說："倒在我們身上！"

9 "以色列啊，
　　你從基比亞的日子以來，時常犯罪。
　　你們的先人曾站在那裏，
　現今住基比亞的人，
　　以攻擊罪孽之輩的戰事
　　臨不到自己。
10我必隨意懲罰他們。
　　他們為兩樣的罪所纏，
　　列邦的民必聚集攻擊他們。
11以法蓮是馴良的母牛犢，
　　喜愛踹穀，
　我卻將軛加在牠肥美的頸項上，
　　我要使以法蓮拉套（註：或作"被
　　　騎"），
　猶大必耕田，
　　雅各必耙地。
12你們要為自己栽種公義，
　　就能收割慈愛。
　現今正是尋求耶和華的時候，
　　你們要開墾荒地，
　等他臨到，
　　使公義如雨降在你們身上。
13你們耕種的是奸惡，
　　收割的是罪孽，
　　吃的是謊話的果子。
　因你倚靠自己的行為，
　　仰賴勇士眾多。

14所以在這民中必有鬨嚷之聲，
　　你一切的保障必被拆毀，
　就如沙勒幔在爭戰的日子
　　拆毀伯亞比勒，
　將其中的母子
　　一同摔死。
15因他們的大惡，
　　伯特利必使你們遭遇如此。
　到了黎明，
　　以色列的王必全然滅絕。

神對以色列的愛

11 "以色列年幼的時候我愛他，
　　就從埃及召出我的兒子來。
　　2先知越發招呼他們，
　　他們越發走開，
　向諸巴力獻祭，
　　給雕刻的偶像燒香。
3我原教導以法蓮行走，
　　用膀臂抱着他們，
　他們卻不知道
　　是我醫治他們。

Then they will say to the mountains, "Cover us!"
　and to the hills, "Fall on us!"

9"Since the days of Gibeah, you have sinned, O
　　Israel,
　and there you have remained.[a]
Did not war overtake
　the evildoers in Gibeah?

10When I please, I will punish them;
　nations will be gathered against them
　to put them in bonds for their double sin.
11Ephraim is a trained heifer
　that loves to thresh;
　so I will put a yoke
　on her fair neck.
I will drive Ephraim,
　Judah must plow,
　and Jacob must break up the ground.
12Sow for yourselves righteousness,
　reap the fruit of unfailing love,
and break up your unplowed ground;
　for it is time to seek the LORD,
until he comes
　and showers righteousness on you.
13But you have planted wickedness,
　you have reaped evil,
　you have eaten the fruit of deception.
Because you have depended on your own
　　strength
　and on your many warriors,
14the roar of battle will rise against your people,
　so that all your fortresses will be devastated—
　as Shalman devastated Beth Arbel on the day
　　of battle,
　when mothers were dashed to the groun
　　with their children.
15Thus will it happen to you, O Bethel,
　because your wickedness is great.
When that day dawns,
　the king of Israel will be completely destroyed.

God's Love for Israel

11 "When Israel was a child, I loved him,
　　and out of Egypt I called my son.
　　2But the more I[b] called Israel,
　the further they went from me.[c]
They sacrificed to the Baals
　and they burned incense to images.
3It was I who taught Ephraim to walk,
　taking them by the arms;
but they did not realize
　it was I who healed them.

a 9 Or there a stand was taken　　*b 2 Some Septuagint*
manuscripts; Hebrew *they*　　*c 2 Septuagint; Hebrew them*

⁴I led them with cords of human kindness,
  with ties of love;
  I lifted the yoke from their neck
    and bent down to feed them.

⁵"Will they not return to Egypt
  and will not Assyria rule over them
  because they refuse to repent?
⁶Swords will flash in their cities,
  will destroy the bars of their gates
  and put an end to their plans.
⁷My people are determined to turn from me.
  Even if they call to the Most High,
  he will by no means exalt them.

⁸"How can I give you up, Ephraim?
  How can I hand you over, Israel?
  How can I treat you like Admah?
  How can I make you like Zeboiim?
  My heart is changed within me;
  all my compassion is aroused.
⁹I will not carry out my fierce anger,
  nor will I turn and devastate Ephraim.
  For I am God, and not man—
  the Holy One among you.
  I will not come in wrath.^a
¹⁰They will follow the LORD;
  he will roar like a lion.
  When he roars,
  his children will come trembling from the
     west.
¹¹They will come trembling
  like birds from Egypt,
  like doves from Assyria.
  I will settle them in their homes,"
  declares the LORD.

Israel's Sin

¹²Ephraim has surrounded me with lies,
  the house of Israel with deceit.
  And Judah is unruly against God,
  even against the faithful Holy One.

12 ¹Ephraim feeds on the wind;
  he pursues the east wind all day
  and multiplies lies and violence.
He makes a treaty with Assyria
  and sends olive oil to Egypt.
²The LORD has a charge to bring against Judah;
  he will punish Jacob^b according to his ways
  and repay him according to his deeds.
³In the womb he grasped his brother's heel;
  as a man he struggled with God.

⁴我用慈繩（註：「慈」原文作「人的」）
  愛索牽引他們，
  我待他們如人放鬆牛的兩腮夾板，
  把糧食放在他們面前。

⁵"他們必不歸回埃及地，
  亞述人卻要作他們的王，
  因他們不肯歸向我。
⁶刀劍必臨到他們的城邑，
  毀壞門閂，把人吞滅，
  都因他們隨從自己的計謀。
⁷我的民偏要背道離開我，
  眾先知雖然招呼他們
  歸向至上的主，卻無人尊崇主。

⁸"以法蓮哪，我怎能捨棄你？
  以色列啊，我怎能棄絕你？
  我怎能使你如押瑪？
  怎能使你如洗扁？
  我回心轉意，
  我的憐愛大大發動。
⁹我必不發猛烈的怒氣，
  也不再毀滅以法蓮；
  因我是神，並非世人；
  是你們中間的聖者，
  我必不在怒中臨到你們。
¹⁰耶和華必如獅子吼叫，
  子民必跟隨他。
  他一吼叫，
  他們就從西方
    急速而來。
¹¹他們必如雀鳥
  從埃及急速而來，
  又如鴿子從亞述地來到。
  我必使他們住自己的房屋。"
  這是耶和華說的。

以色列的罪

¹²以法蓮用謊話，
  以色列家用詭計圍繞我；
  猶大卻靠神掌權，向聖者有忠心。
（註：或作「猶大向神、向誠實的聖者猶疑不定」）

12 ¹以法蓮吃風，
  且追趕東風，
  時常增添虛謊和強暴，
與亞述立約，
  把油送到埃及。
²耶和華與猶大爭辯，
  必照雅各所行的懲罰他，
  按他所做的報應他。
³他在腹中抓住哥哥的腳跟，
  壯年的時候與神較力；

---

^a 9 Or *come against any city*   ^b 2 Jacob means *he grasps the heel*
(figuratively, *he deceives*).

4、5與天使較力並且得勝，
　　哭泣懇求，
　　在伯特利遇見耶和華。
　　　耶和華萬軍之神在那裏
　　　曉諭我們以色列人，
　　　耶和華是他可記念的名。
6所以你當歸向你的神，
　　謹守仁愛、公平，
　　常常等候你的神。

7以法蓮是商人，
　　手裏有詭詐的天平，愛行欺騙。
8以法蓮說：
　　"我果然成了富足，得了財寶，
　　我所勞碌得來的，
　　　人必不見有甚麼不義，
　　　可算為罪的。"

9 "自從你出埃及地以來，
　　我就是耶和華你的神，
　　我必使你再住帳棚，
　　　如在大會的日子一樣。
10我已曉諭眾先知，
　　並且加增默示，
　　　藉先知設立比喻。"

11基列人沒有罪孽嗎？
　　他們全然是虛假的。
　　人在吉甲獻牛犢為祭，
　　他們的祭壇
　　　好像田間犁溝中的亂堆。
12從前雅各逃到亞蘭地，
　　以色列為得妻服侍人，
　　為得妻與人放羊。
13耶和華藉先知
　　領以色列從埃及上來，
　　以色列也藉先知而得保存。
14以法蓮大大惹動主怒，
　　所以他流血的罪，
　　　必歸在他身上。
　　主必將那因以法蓮所受的羞辱
　　　歸還他。

主向以色列發的怒氣

13 從前以法蓮說話，人都戰兢，
　　他在以色列中居處高位；
　　但他在侍奉巴力的事上犯罪，
　　就死了。
2現今他們罪上加罪，
　　用銀子為自己鑄造偶像，
　　就是照自己的聰明製造，
　　都是匠人的工作。

4He struggled with the angel and overcame him;
　　he wept and begged for his favor.
　He found him at Bethel
　　and talked with him there—
5the LORD God Almighty,
　　the LORD is his name of renown!
6But you must return to your God;
　　maintain love and justice,
　　and wait for your God always.

7The merchant uses dishonest scales;
　　he loves to defraud.
8Ephraim boasts,
　　"I am very rich; I have become wealthy.
　With all my wealth they will not find in me
　　any iniquity or sin."

9"I am the LORD your God,
　　who brought you out of*a* Egypt;
　I will make you live in tents again,
　　as in the days of your appointed feasts.
10I spoke to the prophets,
　　gave them many visions
　　and told parables through them."

11Is Gilead wicked?
　　Its people are worthless!
　Do they sacrifice bulls in Gilgal?
　　Their altars will be like piles of stones
　　on a plowed field.
12Jacob fled to the country of Aram*b*;
　　Israel served to get a wife,
　　and to pay for her he tended sheep.
13The LORD used a prophet to bring Israel up
　　from Egypt,
　　by a prophet he cared for him.
14But Ephraim has bitterly provoked him to
　　anger;
　his Lord will leave upon him the guilt of his
　　bloodshed
　　and will repay him for his contempt.

The LORD's Anger Against Israel

13 When Ephraim spoke, men trembled;
　　he was exalted in Israel.
　　But he became guilty of Baal worship
　　and died.
2Now they sin more and more;
　　they make idols for themselves from their
　　　silver,
　cleverly fashioned images,
　　all of them the work of craftsmen.

---

a 9 Or God / ever since you were in　　*b 12 That is, Northwest
Mesopotamia*　　*c 2 Or "Men who sacrifice / kiss*

It is said of these people,
  "They offer human sacrifice
  and kiss[c] the calf-idols."
[3]Therefore they will be like the morning mist,
  like the early dew that disappears,
  like chaff swirling from a threshing floor,
  like smoke escaping through a window.

[4]"But I am the LORD your God,
  ⌊who brought you⌋ out of[a] Egypt.
  You shall acknowledge no God but me,
  no Savior except me.
[5]I cared for you in the desert,
  in the land of burning heat.
[6]When I fed them, they were satisfied;
  when they were satisfied, they became proud;
  then they forgot me.
[7]So I will come upon them like a lion,
  like a leopard I will lurk by the path.
[8]Like a bear robbed of her cubs,
  I will attack them and rip them open.
  Like a lion I will devour them;
  a wild animal will tear them apart.

[9]"You are destroyed, O Israel,
  because you are against me, against your
    helper.
[10]Where is your king, that he may save you?
  Where are your rulers in all your towns,
  of whom you said,
  'Give me a king and princes'?
[11]So in my anger I gave you a king,
  and in my wrath I took him away.
[12]The guilt of Ephraim is stored up,
  his sins are kept on record.
[13]Pains as of a woman in childbirth come to him,
  but he is a child without wisdom;
  when the time arrives,
  he does not come to the opening of the womb.

[14]"I will ransom them from the power of the
    grave[b];
  I will redeem them from death.
  Where, O death, are your plagues?
  Where, O grave,[b] is your destruction?

  "I will have no compassion,
[15] even though he thrives among his brothers.
  An east wind from the LORD will come,
  blowing in from the desert;
  his spring will fail
  and his well dry up.
  His storehouse will be plundered
  of all its treasures.

有人論説：
  "獻祭的人
    可以向牛犢親嘴。"
[3]因此，他們必如早晨的雲霧，
  又如速散的甘露，
  像場上的糠粃被狂風吹去，
  又像煙氣騰於窗外。

[4] "自從你出埃及地以來，
  我就是耶和華你的神。
  在我以外，你不可認識別神；
  除我以外並沒有救主。
[5]我曾在曠野
  乾旱之地認識你。
[6]這些民照我所賜的食物得了飽足；
  既得飽足，心就高傲，
  忘記了我。
[7]因此，我向他們如獅子，
  又如豹伏在道旁。
[8]我遇見他們必像丟崽子的母熊，
  撕裂他們的胸膛（註：或作"心膜"）。
  在那裏我必像母獅吞吃他們，
  野獸必撕裂他們。

[9] "以色列啊，你與我反對，
  就是反對幫助你的，
  自取敗壞。
[10]你曾求我說：'給我立王和首領。'
  現在你的王在哪裏呢？
  治理你的在哪裏呢？
  讓他在你所有的城中拯救你吧！
[11]我在怒氣中將王賜你，
  又在烈怒中將王廢去。
[12]以法蓮的罪孽包裹，
  他的罪惡收藏。
[13]產婦的疼痛必臨到他身上；
  他是無智慧之子，
  到了產期
  不當遲延。

[14] "我必救贖他們
  脫離陰間，
  救贖他們脫離死亡。
  死亡啊，你的災害在哪裏呢？
  陰間哪，你的毀滅在哪裏呢？

  "在我眼前決無後悔之事。
[15]他在弟兄中雖然茂盛，
  必有東風颳來，
  就是耶和華的風從曠野上來。
  他的泉源必乾，
  他的源頭必竭。
  仇敵必擄掠
  他所積蓄的一切寶器。

---

a 4 Or God / ever since you were in   *b 14 Hebrew Sheol*

16撒馬利亞必擔當自己的罪，
　　因為悖逆他的神。

他必倒在刀下，
　　嬰孩必被摔死，
　　孕婦必被剖開。"

悔改就可蒙福

14 以色列啊，
　　你要歸向耶和華你的神；
　　你是因自己的罪孽跌倒了。
2當歸向耶和華，
　　用言語禱告他說：
"求你除淨罪孽，悅納善行；
　　這樣，我們就把嘴唇的祭
　　代替牛犢獻上。
3我們不向亞述求救，不騎埃及的馬，
　　也不再對我們手所造的說：
'你是我們的神。'
　　因為孤兒在你耶和華那裏
　　得蒙憐憫。"

4"我必醫治他們背道的病，
　　甘心愛他們，
　　因為我的怒氣向他們轉消。
5我必向以色列如甘露，
　　他必如百合花開放，
　　如黎巴嫩的樹木扎根。
6他的枝條必延長，
　　他的榮華如橄欖樹，
　　他的香氣如黎巴嫩的香柏樹。
7曾住在他蔭下的必歸回，
　　發旺如五穀，
　　開花如葡萄樹。
　　他的香氣
　　如黎巴嫩的酒。
8以法蓮必說：
'我與偶像還有甚麼關涉呢？'
　　我耶和華回答他，也必顧念他。
　　我如青翠的松樹，
　　你的果子從我而得。"

9誰是智慧人，可以明白這些事；
　　誰是通達人，可以知道這一切。
因為耶和華的道是正直的，
　　義人必在其中行走；
　　罪人卻在其上跌倒。

16The people of Samaria must bear their guilt,
　　because they have rebelled against their
　　　God.
They will fall by the sword;
　　their little ones will be dashed to the ground,
　　their pregnant women ripped open."

Repentance to Bring Blessing

14 Return, O Israel, to the LORD your God.
　　Your sins have been your downfall!
　　2Take words with you
　　and return to the LORD.
Say to him:
"Forgive all our sins
and receive us graciously,
　　that we may offer the fruit of our lips.[a]
3Assyria cannot save us;
　　we will not mount war-horses.
We will never again say 'Our gods'
　　to what our own hands have made,
　　for in you the fatherless find compassion."

4"I will heal their waywardness
　　and love them freely,
　　for my anger has turned away from them.
5I will be like the dew to Israel;
　　he will blossom like a lily.
Like a cedar of Lebanon
　　he will send down his roots;
6　　his young shoots will grow.
His splendor will be like an olive tree,
　　his fragrance like a cedar of Lebanon.
7Men will dwell again in his shade.
　　He will flourish like the grain.
He will blossom like a vine,
　　and his fame will be like the wine from
　　　Lebanon.
8O Ephraim, what more have I[b] to do with
　　idols?
　　I will answer him and care for him.
I am like a green pine tree;
　　your fruitfulness comes from me."

9Who is wise? He will realize these things.
　　Who is discerning? He will understand them.
The ways of the LORD are right;
　　the righteous walk in them,
　　but the rebellious stumble in them.

a 2 Or offer our lips as sacrifices of bulls　　b 8 Or What more has Ephraim

Joel

約珥書

1 The word of the LORD that came to Joel son of Pethuel.

1 耶和華的話臨到<u>毘土珥</u>的兒子<u>約珥</u>。

An Invasion of Locusts

²Hear this, you elders;
  listen, all who live in the land.
 Has anything like this ever happened in your days
  or in the days of your forefathers?
³Tell it to your children,
  and let your children tell it to their children,
  and their children to the next generation.
⁴What the locust swarm has left
  the great locusts have eaten;
 what the great locusts have left
  the young locusts have eaten;
 what the young locusts have left
  other locusts*ᵃ* have eaten.

⁵Wake up, you drunkards, and weep!
  Wail, all you drinkers of wine;
 wail because of the new wine,
  for it has been snatched from your lips.
⁶A nation has invaded my land,
  powerful and without number;
 it has the teeth of a lion,
  the fangs of a lioness.
⁷It has laid waste my vines
  and ruined my fig trees.
 It has stripped off their bark
  and thrown it away,
  leaving their branches white.

⁸Mourn like a virgin*ᵇ* in sackcloth
  grieving for the husband*ᶜ* of her youth.
⁹Grain offerings and drink offerings
  are cut off from the house of the LORD.
 The priests are in mourning,
  those who minister before the LORD.
¹⁰The fields are ruined,
  the ground is dried up*ᵈ*;
 the grain is destroyed,
  the new wine is dried up,

蝗蟲侵犯

²老年人哪,當聽我的話;
  國中的居民哪,都要側耳而聽!
 在你們的日子,
  或你們列祖的日子,
  曾有這樣的事嗎?
³你們要將這事傳與子,
  子傳與孫,
  孫傳與後代。
⁴剪蟲剩下的,
  蝗蟲來吃;
 蝗蟲剩下的,
  蝻子來吃;
 蝻子剩下的,
  螞蚱來吃。

⁵酒醉的人哪,
  要清醒哭泣;
 好酒的人哪,都要為甜酒哀號;
  因為從你們的口中斷絕了。
⁶有一隊蝗蟲(註:原文作"民")
  又強盛,又無數,侵犯我的地。
 牠的牙齒如獅子的牙齒,
  大牙如母獅的大牙。
⁷牠毀壞我的葡萄樹,
  剝了我無花果樹的皮,
 剝盡而丟棄,
  使枝條露白。

⁸我的民哪,你當哀號!
  像處女腰束麻布,
  為幼年的丈夫哀號。
⁹素祭和奠祭
  從耶和華的殿中斷絕,
  侍奉耶和華的祭司都悲哀。
¹⁰田荒涼,
  地悲哀,
 因為五穀毀壞,
  新酒乾竭,

ᵃ 4 The precise meaning of the four Hebrew words used here for locusts is uncertain. *ᵇ 8 Or young woman* *ᶜ 8 Or betrothed* *ᵈ 10 Or ground mourns*

油也缺乏。
11 農夫啊，你們要慚愧；
　　修理葡萄園的啊，你們要哀號；
　　因為大麥小麥與田間的莊稼
　　都滅絕了。
12 葡萄樹枯乾，
　　無花果樹衰殘，
　　石榴樹、棕樹、蘋果樹，
　　連田野一切的樹木
　　也都枯乾；
　　眾人的喜樂
　　盡都消滅。

呼喚悔改

13 祭司啊，你們當腰束麻布痛哭；
　　伺候祭壇的啊，你們要哀號；
　　侍奉我神的啊，
　　　你們要來披上麻布過夜；
　　因為素祭和奠祭
　　　從你們神的殿中斷絕了。
14 你們要分定禁食的日子，
　　宣告嚴肅會，
　　招聚長老
　　　和國中的一切居民，
　　到耶和華你們神的殿，
　　　向耶和華哀求。

15 哀哉，
　　耶和華的日子臨近了！
　　這日來到，
　　好像毀滅從全能者來到。

16 糧食不是在我們眼前
　　斷絕了嗎？
　　歡喜快樂不是從我們神的殿中
　　止息了嗎？
17 穀種在土塊下朽爛，
　　倉也荒涼，
　　廩也破壞，
　　因為五穀枯乾了。
18 牲畜哀鳴；
　　牛羣混亂，
　　因為無草；
　　羊羣也受了困苦。

19 耶和華啊，我向你求告，
　　因為火燒滅曠野的草場；
　　火焰燒盡田野的樹木。

20 田野的走獸向你發喘，
　　因為溪水乾涸，
　　火也燒滅曠野的草場。

11 Despair, you farmers,
　　wail, you vine growers;
grieve for the wheat and the barley,
　　because the harvest of the field is destroyed.
12 The vine is dried up
　and the fig tree is withered;
the pomegranate, the palm and the apple
tree—
　all the trees of the field — are dried up.
Surely the joy of mankind
　is withered away.

A Call to Repentance

13 Put on sackcloth, O priests, and mourn;
　wail, you who minister before the altar.
Come, spend the night in sackcloth,
　you who minister before my God;
for the grain offerings and drink offerings
　are withheld from the house of your God.
14 Declare a holy fast;
　call a sacred assembly.
Summon the elders
　and all who live in the land
to the house of the LORD your God,
　and cry out to the LORD.

15 Alas for that day!
　For the day of the LORD is near;
　it will come like destruction from the
　　Almighty.[a]

16 Has not the food been cut off
　before our very eyes—
joy and gladness
　from the house of our God?
17 The seeds are shriveled
　beneath the clods.[b]
The storehouses are in ruins,
　the granaries have been broken down,
　for the grain has dried up.
18 How the cattle moan!
　The herds mill about
because they have no pasture;
　even the flocks of sheep are suffering.

19 To you, O LORD, I call,
　for fire has devoured the open pastures
　and flames have burned up all the trees of
　　the field.
20 Even the wild animals pant for you;
　the streams of water have dried up
　and fire has devoured the open pastures.

a 15 Hebrew *Shaddai*　　*b 17* The meaning of the Hebrew for
this word is uncertain.

An Army of Locusts

2 Blow the trumpet in Zion;
sound the alarm on my holy hill.
Let all who live in the land tremble,
for the day of the LORD is coming.
It is close at hand—
2 a day of darkness and gloom,
a day of clouds and blackness.
Like dawn spreading across the mountains
a large and mighty army comes,
such as never was of old
nor ever will be in ages to come.

3Before them fire devours,
behind them a flame blazes.
Before them the land is like the garden of Eden,
behind them, a desert waste—
nothing escapes them.
4They have the appearance of horses;
they gallop along like cavalry.
5With a noise like that of chariots
they leap over the mountaintops,
like a crackling fire consuming stubble,
like a mighty army drawn up for battle.

6At the sight of them, nations are in anguish;
every face turns pale.
7They charge like warriors;
they scale walls like soldiers.
They all march in line,
not swerving from their course.
8They do not jostle each other;
each marches straight ahead.
They plunge through defenses
without breaking ranks.
9They rush upon the city;
they run along the wall.
They climb into the houses;
like thieves they enter through the windows.

10Before them the earth shakes,
the sky trembles,
the sun and moon are darkened,
and the stars no longer shine.
11The LORD thunders
at the head of his army;
his forces are beyond number,
and mighty are those who obey his command.
The day of the LORD is great;
it is dreadful.
Who can endure it?

Rend Your Heart

12"Even now," declares the LORD,
"return to me with all your heart,
with fasting and weeping and mourning."

蝗蟲大軍

2 你們要在錫安吹角,
在我聖山吹出大聲;
國中的居民都要發顫;
因為耶和華的日子將到,
已經臨近。
2那日是黑暗、幽冥、
密雲、烏黑的日子,
好像晨光鋪滿山嶺。
有一隊蝗蟲(註:原文作"民")
又大又強,從來沒有這樣的,
以後直到萬代也必沒有。

3牠們前面如火燒滅,
後面如火焰燒盡;
未到以前,地如伊甸園;
過去以後,成了荒涼的曠野,
沒有一樣能躲避牠們的。
4牠們的形狀如馬,
奔跑如馬兵。
5在山頂蹦跳的響聲,
如車輛的響聲,
又如火焰燒碎稭的響聲,
好像強盛的民擺陣預備打仗。

6牠們一來,眾民傷慟,
臉都變色。
7牠們如勇士奔跑,
像戰士爬城。
各都步行,
不亂隊伍。
8彼此並不擁擠,
向前各行其路,
直闖兵器,
不偏左右。
9牠們蹦上城,
躍上牆,
爬上房屋,
進入窗戶如同盜賊。

10牠們一來,
地震天動,
日月昏暗,
星宿無光。
11耶和華在他軍旅前發聲,
他的隊伍甚大;
成就他命的,
是強盛者。
因為耶和華的日子
大而可畏,
誰能當得起呢?

要撕裂心腸

12耶和華說:"雖然如此,
你們應當禁食、哭泣、悲哀,
一心歸向我。"

13你們要撕裂心腸，
　　不撕裂衣服，
歸向耶和華你們的神；
　　因為他有恩典，有憐憫，
不輕易發怒，有豐盛的慈愛，
　　並且後悔不降所說的災。
14或者他轉意後悔，
　　留下餘福，
就是留下獻給耶和華你們神的
　　素祭和奠祭，也未可知。

15你們要在錫安吹角，
　　分定禁食的日子，
　　宣告嚴肅會。
16聚集眾民，
　　使會眾自潔；
招聚老者，
　　聚集孩童和吃奶的。
使新郎出離洞房，
　　新婦出離內室。

17侍奉耶和華的祭司，
　　要在廊子和祭壇中間
　　哭泣說：
“耶和華啊，
　　求你顧惜你的百姓，
不要使你的產業受羞辱，
　　列邦管轄他們。
為何容列國的人說：
　　‘他們的神在哪裏呢？’”

主的應允
18耶和華就為自己的地發熱心，
　　憐恤他的百姓。

19耶和華應允他的百姓說：

“我必賜給你們五穀、新酒和油，
　　使你們飽足；
我也不再使你們
　　受列國的羞辱，

20 “卻要使北方來的軍隊遠離你們，
　　將他們趕到乾旱荒廢之地：
前隊趕入東海，
　　後隊趕入西海；
因為他們所行的大惡（註：原文作“事”），
　　臭氣上升，
　　腥味騰空。”

21地土啊，不要懼怕！

13Rend your heart
　　and not your garments.
Return to the LORD your God,
　　for he is gracious and compassionate,
slow to anger and abounding in love,
　　and he relents from sending calamity.
14Who knows? He may turn and have pity
　　and leave behind a blessing—
grain offerings and drink offerings
　　for the LORD your God.

15Blow the trumpet in Zion,
　　declare a holy fast,
　　call a sacred assembly.
16Gather the people,
　　consecrate the assembly;
bring together the elders,
　　gather the children,
　　those nursing at the breast.
Let the bridegroom leave his room
　　and the bride her chamber.
17Let the priests, who minister before the LORD,
　　weep between the temple porch and the
　　altar.
Let them say, "Spare your people, O LORD.
　　Do not make your inheritance an object of
　　scorn,
　　a byword among the nations.
Why should they say among the peoples,
　　'Where is their God?' "

The LORD's Answer
18Then the LORD will be jealous for his land
　　and take pity on his people.

19The LORD will reply[a] to them:

"I am sending you grain, new wine and oil,
　　enough to satisfy you fully;
never again will I make you
　　an object of scorn to the nations.

20"I will drive the northern army far from you,
　　pushing it into a parched and barren land,
　　with its front columns going into the eastern
　　sea[b]
and those in the rear into the western sea.[c]
And its stench will go up;
　　its smell will rise."

Surely he has done great things.[d]
21　Be not afraid, O land;

---

a 18,19 Or LORD was jealous . . . | and took pity . . . | 19 The LORD
replied　　b 20 That is, the Dead Sea　　c 20 That is, the
Mediterranean　　d 20 Or rise. | Surely it has done great things."

be glad and rejoice.
Surely the LORD has done great things.
22 Be not afraid, O wild animals,
  for the open pastures are becoming green.
The trees are bearing their fruit;
  the fig tree and the vine yield their riches.
23Be glad, O people of Zion,
  rejoice in the LORD your God,
for he has given you
  the autumn rains in righteousness.[a]
He sends you abundant showers,
  both autumn and spring rains, as before.
24The threshing floors will be filled with grain;
  the vats will overflow with new wine and oil.

25"I will repay you for the years the locusts
    have eaten—
the great locust and the young locust,
  the other locusts and the locust swarm[b] —
my great army that I sent among you.
26You will have plenty to eat, until you are full,
  and you will praise the name of the LORD
    your God,
who has worked wonders for you;
  never again will my people be shamed.
27Then you will know that I am in Israel,
  that I am the LORD your God,
  and that there is no other;
never again will my people be shamed.

The Day of the LORD

28"And afterward,
  I will pour out my Spirit on all people.
Your sons and daughters will prophesy,
  your old men will dream dreams,
  your young men will see visions.
29Even on my servants, both men and women,
  I will pour out my Spirit in those days.
30I will show wonders in the heavens
  and on the earth,
  blood and fire and billows of smoke.
31The sun will be turned to darkness
  and the moon to blood
before the coming of the great and dreadful
  day of the LORD.
32And everyone who calls
  on the name of the LORD will be saved;
for on Mount Zion and in Jerusalem
  there will be deliverance,
  as the LORD has said,
among the survivors
  whom the LORD calls.

要歡喜快樂，
  因為耶和華行了大事。
22田野的走獸啊，不要懼怕！
  因為曠野的草發生，
樹木結果，
  無花果樹、葡萄樹也都効力。
23錫安的民哪，你們要快樂，
  為耶和華你們的神歡喜；
因他賜給你們合宜的秋雨，
  為你們降下甘霖，
就是秋雨、春雨，
  和先前一樣。
24禾場必滿了麥子，
  酒醡與油醡必有新酒和油盈溢。

25 "我打發到你們中間的
    大軍隊，
就是蝗蟲、蝻子、
  蟲蚱、剪蟲，
那些年所吃的我要補還你們。
26你們必多吃而得飽足，
  就讚美為你們行奇妙事之耶和華
    你們神的名。
我的百姓
  必永遠不至羞愧。
27你們必知道我是在以色列中間，
  又知道我是耶和華你們的神，
  在我以外並無別神。
我的百姓必永遠不至羞愧。

主的日子

28 "以後，
  我要將我的靈澆灌凡有血氣的。
你們的兒女要說預言，
  你們的老年人要做異夢，
  少年人要見異象。
29在那些日子，我要將我的靈
  澆灌我的僕人和使女。
30在天上地下，
  我要顯出奇事，
  有血、有火、有煙柱。
31日頭要變為黑暗，
  月亮要變為血，
這都在耶和華大而可畏的日子
  未到以前。
32到那時候，
  凡求告耶和華名的就必得救；
因為照耶和華所說的，
  在錫安山、耶路撒冷
  必有逃脫的人，
在剩下的人中
  必有耶和華所召的。

_a_ 23 Or / the teacher for righteousness: _b_ 25 The precise
meaning of the four Hebrew words used here for locusts is
uncertain.

列國受審

3

¹"到那日，
我使猶大和耶路撒冷被擄之
人歸回的時候，
²我要聚集萬民，
帶他們下到約沙法谷，
在那裏施行審判；
因為他們將我的百姓，
就是我的產業以色列，
分散在列國中，
又分取我的地土，

³且為我的百姓拈鬮，
將童子換妓女，
賣童女買酒喝。

⁴"推羅、西頓和非利士四境的
人哪，你們與我何干？你們要報復
我嗎？若報復我，我必使報應速速
歸到你們的頭上。⁵你們既然奪取我
的金銀，又將我可愛的寶物帶入你
們宮殿（註：或作「廟中」），⁶並將猶大
人和耶路撒冷人賣給希臘人（註：原文
作「雅完人」），使他們遠離自己的境
界。

⁷"我必激動他們離開你們所賣
到之地，又必使報應歸到你們的頭
上。⁸我必將你們的兒女賣在猶大人
的手中，他們必賣給遠方示巴國的
人。"這是耶和華說的。

⁹當在萬民中宣告說：
要預備打仗，
激動勇士，
使一切戰士上前來。

¹⁰要將犁頭打成刀劍，
將鐮刀打成戈矛。
軟弱的要說：
"我有勇力。"
¹¹四圍的列國啊，
你們要速速地來，
一同聚集。

耶和華啊，求你使你的大能者降臨！

¹²"萬民都當興起，
上到約沙法谷；
因為我必坐在那裏，
審判四圍的列國。

The Nations Judged

3

¹"In those days and at that time,
when I restore the fortunes of Judah and
Jerusalem,
²I will gather all nations
and bring them down to the Valley of
Jehoshaphat.^a
There I will enter into judgment against them
concerning my inheritance, my people Israel,
for they scattered my people among the
nations
and divided up my land.
³They cast lots for my people
and traded boys for prostitutes;
they sold girls for wine
that they might drink.

⁴"Now what have you against me, O Tyre
and Sidon and all you regions of Philistia? Are
you repaying me for something I have done? If
you are paying me back, I will swiftly and
speedily return on your own heads what you
have done. ⁵For you took my silver and my gold
and carried off my finest treasures to your
temples. ⁶You sold the people of Judah and Jerusalem to the Greeks, that you might send them
far from their homeland.

⁷"See, I am going to rouse them out of the
places to which you sold them, and I will return
on your own heads what you have done. ⁸I will
sell your sons and daughters to the people of
Judah, and they will sell them to the Sabeans, a
nation far away." The LORD has spoken.

⁹Proclaim this among the nations:
Prepare for war!
Rouse the warriors!
Let all the fighting men draw near and
attack.
¹⁰Beat your plowshares into swords
and your pruning hooks into spears.
Let the weakling say,
"I am strong!"
¹¹Come quickly, all you nations from every
side,
and assemble there.

Bring down your warriors, O LORD!

¹²"Let the nations be roused;
let them advance into the Valley of
Jehoshaphat,
for there I will sit
to judge all the nations on every side.

a 2 Jehoshaphat means the LORD judges; also in verse 12.

¹³Swing the sickle,
　　for the harvest is ripe.
Come, trample the grapes,
　　for the winepress is full
　　and the vats overflow—
so great is their wickedness!"

¹⁴Multitudes, multitudes
　　in the valley of decision!
For the day of the LORD is near
　　in the valley of decision.
¹⁵The sun and moon will be darkened,
　　and the stars no longer shine.
¹⁶The LORD will roar from Zion
　　and thunder from Jerusalem;
　　the earth and the sky will tremble.
But the LORD will be a refuge for his people,
　　a stronghold for the people of Israel.

Blessings for God's People

¹⁷"Then you will know that I, the LORD your God,
　　dwell in Zion, my holy hill.
Jerusalem will be holy;
　　never again will foreigners invade her.

¹⁸"In that day the mountains will drip new wine,
　　and the hills will flow with milk;
all the ravines of Judah will run with water.
A fountain will flow out of the LORD's house
　　and will water the valley of acacias.^a
¹⁹But Egypt will be desolate,
　　Edom a desert waste,
because of violence done to the people of Judah,
　　in whose land they shed innocent blood.
²⁰Judah will be inhabited forever
　　and Jerusalem through all generations.
²¹Their bloodguilt, which I have not pardoned,
　　I will pardon."

The LORD dwells in Zion!

¹³開鐮吧！
　　因為莊稼熟了；
踐踏吧！
　　因為酒醡滿了，
　　酒池盈溢，
他們的罪惡甚大。"

¹⁴許多許多的人
　　在斷定谷，
因為耶和華的日子
　　臨近斷定谷。
¹⁵日月昏暗，
　　星宿無光。
¹⁶耶和華必從錫安吼叫，
　　從耶路撒冷發聲，
　　天地就震動。
耶和華卻要作他百姓的避難所，
　　作以色列人的保障。

神子民的福氣

¹⁷"你們就知道
　　我是耶和華你們的神，
　　且又住在錫安我的聖山。
那時，耶路撒冷必成為聖，
　　外邦人不再從其中經過。

¹⁸"到那日，
　　大山要滴甜酒，
　　小山要流奶子，
　　猶大溪河都有水流。
必有泉源從耶和華的殿中流出來，
　　滋潤什亭谷。
¹⁹埃及必然荒涼，
　　以東變為悽涼的曠野，
都因向猶大人所行的強暴，
　　又因在本地流無辜人的血。

²⁰但猶大必存到永遠，
　　耶路撒冷必存到萬代。
²¹我未曾報復（註：或作"洗除"。下同）
　　流血的罪，現在我要報復。"

因為耶和華住在錫安。

---

^a 18 Or Valley of Shittim

阿摩司書

Amos

1 當猶大王烏西雅，以色列王約阿施的兒子耶羅波安在位的時候，大地震前二年，提哥亞牧人中的阿摩司得默示論以色列。

2 他說：

　　"耶和華必從錫安吼叫，
　　　　從耶路撒冷發聲；
　　牧人的草場要悲哀，
　　　　迦密的山頂要枯乾。"

以色列鄰國受的審判

3 耶和華如此說：

　　"大馬士革三番四次地犯罪，
　　　　我必不免去她的刑罰；
　　因為她以打糧食的鐵器
　　　　打過基列。
4 我卻要降火在哈薛的家中，
　　　　燒滅便哈達的宮殿。
5 我必折斷
　　　　大馬士革的門閂，
　　剪除亞文平原的居民
　　　　和伯伊甸掌權的。
　　亞蘭人必被擄到吉珥。"

　　　　　　　　　這是耶和華說的。

6 耶和華如此說：

　　"迦薩三番四次地犯罪，
　　　　我必不免去她的刑罰；
　　因為她擄掠眾民
　　　　交給以東。
7 我卻要降火在迦薩的城內，
　　　　燒滅其中的宮殿。
8 我必剪除亞實突的居民
　　　　和亞實基倫掌權的，

1 The words of Amos, one of the shepherds of Tekoa—what he saw concerning Israel two years before the earthquake, when Uzziah was king of Judah and Jeroboam son of Jehoash[a] was king of Israel.

2 He said:

"The LORD roars from Zion
　　and thunders from Jerusalem;
the pastures of the shepherds dry up,[b]
　　and the top of Carmel withers."

Judgment on Israel's Neighbors

3 This is what the LORD says:

"For three sins of Damascus,
　　even for four, I will not turn back ⌊my wrath⌋.
Because she threshed Gilead
　　with sledges having iron teeth,
4 I will send fire upon the house of Hazael
　　that will consume the fortresses of Ben-
　　　　Hadad.
5 I will break down the gate of Damascus;
　　I will destroy the king who is in[c] the Valley
　　　　of Aven[d]
and the one who holds the scepter in Beth
　　　　Eden.
The people of Aram will go into exile to Kir,"
　　　　　　　　　　　　says the LORD.

6 This is what the LORD says:

"For three sins of Gaza,
　　even for four, I will not turn back ⌊my wrath⌋.
Because she took captive whole communities
　　and sold them to Edom,
7 I will send fire upon the walls of Gaza
　　that will consume her fortresses.
8 I will destroy the king[e] of Ashdod
　　and the one who holds the scepter in
　　　　Ashkelon.

---

a 1 Hebrew Joash, a variant of Jehoash   *b 2 Or shepherds mourn*   *c 5 Or the inhabitants of*   *d 5 Aven means wickedness.*   *e 8 Or inhabitants*

I will turn my hand against Ekron,
till the last of the Philistines is dead,"
　　　　says the Sovereign LORD.

⁹This is what the LORD says:

"For three sins of Tyre,
even for four, I will not turn back ⌊my wrath⌋.
Because she sold whole communities of
captives to Edom,
disregarding a treaty of brotherhood,
¹⁰I will send fire upon the walls of Tyre
that will consume her fortresses."

¹¹This is what the LORD says:

"For three sins of Edom,
even for four, I will not turn back ⌊my wrath⌋.
Because he pursued his brother with a sword,
stifling all compassion,[a]
because his anger raged continually
and his fury flamed unchecked,
¹²I will send fire upon Teman
that will consume the fortresses of Bozrah."

¹³This is what the LORD says:

"For three sins of Ammon,
even for four, I will not turn back ⌊my wrath⌋.
Because he ripped open the pregnant women
of Gilead
in order to extend his borders,
¹⁴I will set fire to the walls of Rabbah
that will consume her fortresses
amid war cries on the day of battle,
amid violent winds on a stormy day.
¹⁵Her king[b] will go into exile,
he and his officials together,"
　　　　says the LORD.

2 This is what the LORD says:

"For three sins of Moab,
even for four, I will not turn back ⌊my wrath⌋.
Because he burned, as if to lime,
the bones of Edom's king,
²I will send fire upon Moab
that will consume the fortresses of Kerioth.[c]
Moab will go down in great tumult
amid war cries and the blast of the trumpet.
³I will destroy her ruler
and kill all her officials with him,"
　　　　says the LORD.

也必反手攻擊以革倫，
非利士人所餘剩的必都滅亡。"
　　　　這是主耶和華說的。

⁹耶和華如此說：

"推羅三番四次地犯罪，
我必不免去她的刑罰；
因為她將眾民交給以東，
並不記念弟兄的盟約。

¹⁰我卻要降火在推羅的城內，
燒滅其中的宮殿。"

¹¹耶和華如此說：

"以東三番四次地犯罪，
我必不免去她的刑罰；
因為她拿刀追趕兄弟，
毫無憐憫，
發怒撕裂，
永懷忿怒。

¹²我卻要降火在提幔，
燒滅波斯拉的宮殿。"

¹³耶和華如此說：

"亞捫人三番四次地犯罪，
我必不免去他們的刑罰；
因為他們剖開基列的孕婦，
擴張自己的境界。

¹⁴我卻要在爭戰吶喊的日子，
旋風狂暴的時候，
點火在拉巴的城內，
燒滅其中的宮殿。
¹⁵他們的王和首領
必一同被擄去。"
　　　　這是耶和華說的。

2 耶和華如此說：

"摩押三番四次地犯罪，
我必不免去她的刑罰；
因為她將以東王的骸骨
焚燒成灰。
²我卻要降火在摩押，
燒滅加略的宮殿。
摩押必在鬨嚷、
吶喊、吹角之中死亡。
³我必剪除摩押中的審判者，
將其中的一切首領和他一同殺戮。"
　　　　這是耶和華說的。

a 11 Or sword / and destroyed his allies　　b 15 Or / Molech;
Hebrew malcam　　c 2 Or of her cities

⁴耶和華如此説：

"猶大人三番四次地犯罪，
　　我必不免去他們的刑罰；
因為他們
　　厭棄耶和華的訓誨，
　　不遵守他的律例。
他們列祖
　　所隨從虛假的偶像，
　　使他們走迷了。
⁵我卻要降火在猶大，
　　燒滅耶路撒冷的宮殿。"

以色列受的審判

⁶耶和華如此説：

"以色列人三番四次地犯罪，
　　我必不免去他們的刑罰；
因他們為銀子賣了義人，
　　為一雙鞋賣了窮人。
⁷他們見窮人頭上所蒙的灰
　　也都垂涎；
　　阻礙謙卑人的道路；
父子同一個女子行淫，
　　褻瀆我的聖名。
⁸他們在各壇旁鋪人所當的衣服，
　　臥在其上，
又在他們神的廟中
　　喝受罰之人的酒。

⁹ "我從以色列人面前除滅亞摩利人。
他雖高大如香柏樹，
　　堅固如橡樹，
我卻上滅他的果子，
　　下絕他的根本。

¹⁰ "我也將你們從埃及地領上來，
在曠野引導你們四十年，
　　使你們得亞摩利人之地為業。
¹¹我從你們子弟中興起先知，
　　又從你們少年人中
　　興起拿細耳人。
以色列人哪，不是這樣嗎？"
　　　　　　　這是耶和華説的。
¹² "你們卻給拿細耳人酒喝，
　　囑咐先知説：'不要説預言。'

¹³ "看哪！在你們所住之地，
　　我必壓你們，
　　如同裝滿禾捆的車壓物一樣。
¹⁴快跑的不能逃脱，
　　有力的不能用力，
　　剛勇的也不能自救。

⁴This is what the LORD says:

"For three sins of Judah,
　　even for four, I will not turn back ⌊my wrath⌋.
Because they have rejected the law of the
　　　LORD
　　and have not kept his decrees,
because they have been led astray by false
　　　gods,ᵃ
　　the godsᵇ their ancestors followed,
⁵I will send fire upon Judah
　　that will consume the fortresses of
　　　Jerusalem."

Judgment on Israel

⁶This is what the LORD says:

"For three sins of Israel,
　　even for four, I will not turn back ⌊my wrath⌋.
They sell the righteous for silver,
　　and the needy for a pair of sandals.
⁷They trample on the heads of the poor
　　as upon the dust of the ground
　　and deny justice to the oppressed.
Father and son use the same girl
　　and so profane my holy name.
⁸They lie down beside every altar
　　on garments taken in pledge.
In the house of their god
　　they drink wine taken as fines.

⁹"I destroyed the Amorite before them,
　　though he was tall as the cedars
　　and strong as the oaks.
I destroyed his fruit above
　　and his roots below.

¹⁰"I brought you up out of Egypt,
　　and I led you forty years in the desert
　　to give you the land of the Amorites.
¹¹I also raised up prophets from among your
　　　sons
　　and Nazirites from among your young men.
Is this not true, people of Israel?"
　　　　　　declares the LORD.
¹²"But you made the Nazirites drink wine
　　and commanded the prophets not to prophesy.

¹³"Now then, I will crush you
　　as a cart crushes when loaded with grain.
¹⁴The swift will not escape,
　　the strong will not muster their strength,
　　and the warrior will not save his life.

a 4 Or *by lies*　　*b* 4 Or *lies*

¹⁵The archer will not stand his ground,
  the fleet-footed soldier will not get away,
  and the horseman will not save his life.
¹⁶Even the bravest warriors
  will flee naked on that day,"
                    declares the LORD.

Witnesses Summoned Against Israel

3 Hear this word the LORD has spoken
   against you, O people of Israel—against
   the whole family I brought up out of
Egypt:

²"You only have I chosen
  of all the families of the earth;
  therefore I will punish you
  for all your sins."

³Do two walk together
  unless they have agreed to do so?
⁴Does a lion roar in the thicket
  when he has no prey?
  Does he growl in his den
  when he has caught nothing?
⁵Does a bird fall into a trap on the ground
  where no snare has been set?
  Does a trap spring up from the earth
  when there is nothing to catch?
⁶When a trumpet sounds in a city,
  do not the people tremble?
  When disaster comes to a city,
  has not the LORD caused it?

⁷Surely the Sovereign LORD does nothing
  without revealing his plan
  to his servants the prophets.

⁸The lion has roared—
  who will not fear?
  The Sovereign LORD has spoken—
  who can but prophesy?

⁹Proclaim to the fortresses of Ashdod
  and to the fortresses of Egypt:
  "Assemble yourselves on the mountains of
    Samaria;
  see the great unrest within her
  and the oppression among her people."

¹⁰"They do not know how to do right," declares
    the LORD,
  "who hoard plunder and loot in their
    fortresses."

---

¹⁵拿弓的不能站立，
  腿快的不能逃脫，
  騎馬的也不能自救。
¹⁶到那日，勇士中最有膽量的
  必赤身逃跑。"
                    這是耶和華說的。

指證以色列的罪

3 以色列人哪，你們全家是我
   從埃及地領上來的，當聽耶
   和華攻擊你們的話：

² "在地上萬族中，
  我只認識你們；
  因此，我必追討你們的
    一切罪孽。"

³二人若不同心，
  豈能同行呢？
⁴獅子若非抓食，
  豈能在林中咆哮呢？
  少壯獅子若無所得，
  豈能從洞中發聲呢？
⁵若沒有機檻，
  雀鳥豈能陷在網羅裏呢？
  網羅若無所得，
  豈能從地上翻起呢？
⁶城中若吹角，
  百姓豈不驚恐呢？
  災禍若臨到一城，
  豈非耶和華所降的嗎？

⁷主耶和華若不將奧秘
  指示他的僕人眾先知，
  就一無所行。

⁸獅子吼叫，
  誰不懼怕呢？
  主耶和華發命，
  誰能不說預言呢？

⁹要在亞實突的宮殿中
  和埃及地的宮殿裏傳揚說：
  "你們要聚集在
  撒馬利亞的山上，
  就看見城中有何等大的擾亂
  與欺壓的事。"

¹⁰ "那些以強暴搶奪財物、
  積蓄在自己家中的人，
  不知道行正直的事。"
                    這是耶和華說的。

11所以主耶和華如此説：

"敵人必來圍攻這地，
　使你的勢力衰微，
　搶掠你的家宅。"

12耶和華如此説：

"牧人怎樣從獅子口中
　搶回兩條羊腿或半個耳朵，
　住撒馬利亞的以色列人
　躺臥在牀角上，
　或鋪繡花毯的榻上，
　他們得救也不過如此。"

13主耶和華萬軍之神説："當聽這話，警戒雅各家！"

14"我討以色列罪的日子，
　也要討伯特利祭壇的罪；
　壇角必被砍下，
　墜落於地。

15我要拆毀
　過冬和過夏的房屋，
　象牙的房屋也必毀滅，
　高大的房屋都歸無有。"

這是耶和華説的。

以色列還未歸向神

4 你們住撒馬利亞山如巴珊母牛的啊，當聽我的話！
你們欺負貧寒的，
壓碎窮乏的，
對家主説："拿酒來，
我們喝吧！"

2主耶和華指着自己的聖潔起誓説：
"日子快到，
人必用鈎子將你們鈎去，
用魚鈎將你們餘剩的鈎去。

3你們各人
必從破口直往前行，
投入哈門。"

這是耶和華説的。

4"以色列人哪，
任你們往伯特利去犯罪，
到吉甲加增罪過；
每日早晨獻上你們的祭物，
每三日奉上你們的十分之一。

11Therefore this is what the Sovereign LORD says:

"An enemy will overrun the land;
　he will pull down your strongholds
　and plunder your fortresses."

12This is what the LORD says:

"As a shepherd saves from the lion's mouth
　only two leg bones or a piece of an ear,
　so will the Israelites be saved,
those who sit in Samaria
　on the edge of their beds
　and in Damascus on their couches.a"

13"Hear this and testify against the house of Jacob," declares the Lord, the LORD God Almighty.

14"On the day I punish Israel for her sins,
　I will destroy the altars of Bethel;
　the horns of the altar will be cut off
　and fall to the ground.

15I will tear down the winter house
　along with the summer house;
　the houses adorned with ivory will be destroyed
　and the mansions will be demolished,"
　　　　　　　　　　declares the LORD.

Israel Has Not Returned to God

4 Hear this word, you cows of Bashan on Mount Samaria,
you women who oppress the poor and crush the needy
and say to your husbands, "Bring us some drinks!"

2The Sovereign LORD has sworn by his holiness:
"The time will surely come
when you will be taken away with hooks,
　the last of you with fishhooks.

3You will each go straight out
　through breaks in the wall,
　and you will be cast out toward Harmon,b"
　　　　　　　　　　declares the LORD.

4"Go to Bethel and sin;
　go to Gilgal and sin yet more.
　Bring your sacrifices every morning,
　your tithes every three years.c

a 12 The meaning of the Hebrew for this line is uncertain.
b 3 Masoretic Text; with a different word division of the Hebrew (see Septuagint) out, O mountain of oppression
c 4 Or tithes on the third day

⁵Burn leavened bread as a thank offering
    and brag about your freewill offerings—
  boast about them, you Israelites,
    for this is what you love to do,"
                declares the Sovereign LORD.

⁶"I gave you empty stomachs^a in every city
    and lack of bread in every town,
  yet you have not returned to me,"
                declares the LORD.

⁷"I also withheld rain from you
  when the harvest was still three months
    away.
I sent rain on one town,
  but withheld it from another.
One field had rain;
  another had none and dried up.
⁸People staggered from town to town for water
  but did not get enough to drink,
  yet you have not returned to me,"
                declares the LORD.

⁹"Many times I struck your gardens and
    vineyards,
  I struck them with blight and mildew.
Locusts devoured your fig and olive trees,
  yet you have not returned to me,"
                declares the LORD.

¹⁰"I sent plagues among you
  as I did to Egypt.
I killed your young men with the sword,
  along with your captured horses.
I filled your nostrils with the stench of your
    camps,
  yet you have not returned to me,"
                declares the LORD.

¹¹"I overthrew some of you
  as I^b overthrew Sodom and Gomorrah.
You were like a burning stick snatched from
    the fire,
  yet you have not returned to me,"
                declares the LORD.

¹²"Therefore this is what I will do to you, Israel,
  and because I will do this to you,
  prepare to meet your God, O Israel."

¹³He who forms the mountains,
  creates the wind,
  and reveals his thoughts to man,

---

⁵任你們獻有酵的感謝祭，
    把甘心祭宣傳報告給眾人，
    因為是你們所喜愛的。"
           這是主耶和華說的。

⁶"我使你們在一切城中牙齒乾淨，
    在你們各處糧食缺乏，
    你們仍不歸向我。"
           這是耶和華說的。

⁷"在收割的前三月，
    我使雨停止，
    不降在你們那裏；
  我降雨在這城，
    不降雨在那城；
  這塊地有雨，
    那塊地無雨，無雨的就枯乾了。
⁸這樣，兩三城的人湊到一城去找水，
    卻喝不足；
    你們仍不歸向我。"
           這是耶和華說的。

⁹"我以旱風、霉爛攻擊你們，
    你們園中許多菜蔬、
  葡萄樹、無花果樹、橄欖樹
    都被剪蟲所吃，
    你們仍不歸向我。"
           這是耶和華說的。

¹⁰"我降瘟疫在你們中間，
    像在埃及一樣。
  用刀殺戮你們的少年人，
    使你們的馬匹被擄掠，
  營中屍首的臭氣撲鼻，
    你們仍不歸向我。"

           這是耶和華說的。

¹¹"我傾覆你們中間的城邑，
    如同我從前傾覆所多瑪、
  蛾摩拉一樣，
  使你們好像從火中抽出來的一根柴，
    你們仍不歸向我。"
           這是耶和華說的。

¹²"以色列啊，我必向你如此行。
  以色列啊，我既這樣行，
    你當預備迎見你的神。"

¹³那創山、
  造風，
    將心意指示人，

---

^a 6 Hebrew *you cleanness of teeth*   ^b 11 Hebrew *God*

使晨光變為幽暗，
　腳踏在地之高處的——
　他的名是耶和華萬軍之神。

哀歌與悔改的呼喚

5 以色列家啊，要聽我為你們
　　所作的哀歌：

2 "以色列民（註："民"原文作"處女"）
　　跌倒，不得再起；
　躺在地上，
　　無人攙扶。"

3 主耶和華如此說：

"以色列家的城
　發出一千兵的，
　　只剩一百；
　發出一百的，
　　只剩十個。"

4 耶和華向以色列家如此說：

"你們要尋求我，就必存活。
5 不要往伯特利尋求，
　不要進入吉甲，
　不要過到別是巴；
因為吉甲必被擄掠，
　伯特利也必歸於無有。"
6 要尋求耶和華，就必存活，
　免得他在約瑟家
　　像火發出，
　在伯特利焚燒，
　　無人撲滅。

7 你們這使公平變為茵蔯，
　將公義丟棄於地的，
8 要尋求那造昴星和參星，
　使死蔭變為晨光，
　使白日變為黑夜，
　命海水來澆在地上的——
　耶和華是他的名——

9 他使力強的忽遭滅亡，
　以致保障遭遇毀壞。
10 你們怨恨那在城門口責備人的，
　憎惡那說正直話的。

11 你們踐踏貧民，
　向他們勒索麥子；

he who turns dawn to darkness,
　and treads the high places of the earth—
the LORD God Almighty is his name.

A Lament and Call to Repentance

5 Hear this word, O house of Israel, this
lament I take up concerning you:

2 "Fallen is Virgin Israel,
　never to rise again,
deserted in her own land,
　with no one to lift her up."

3 This is what the Sovereign LORD says:

"The city that marches out a thousand strong
　　for Israel
will have only a hundred left;
the town that marches out a hundred strong
　will have only ten left."

4 This is what the LORD says to the house of
Israel:

"Seek me and live;
5 　do not seek Bethel,
do not go to Gilgal,
　do not journey to Beersheba.
For Gilgal will surely go into exile,
　and Bethel will be reduced to nothing.*a*"
6 Seek the LORD and live,
　or he will sweep through the house of Joseph
　　like a fire;
it will devour,
　and Bethel will have no one to quench it.

7 You who turn justice into bitterness
　and cast righteousness to the ground
8 (he who made the Pleiades and Orion,
　who turns blackness into dawn
　and darkens day into night,
who calls for the waters of the sea
　and pours them out over the face of the
　　land—
　the LORD is his name—
9 he flashes destruction on the stronghold
　and brings the fortified city to ruin),
10 you hate the one who reproves in court
　and despise him who tells the truth.

11 You trample on the poor
　and force him to give you grain.

*a 5 Or grief; or wickedness; Hebrew aven, a reference to Beth
Aven (a derogatory name for Bethel)*

Therefore, though you have built stone
    mansions,
  you will not live in them;
though you have planted lush vineyards,
  you will not drink their wine.
¹²For I know how many are your offenses
    and how great your sins.

You oppress the righteous and take bribes
  and you deprive the poor of justice in the
    courts.
¹³Therefore the prudent man keeps quiet in
    such times,
  for the times are evil.

¹⁴Seek good, not evil,
  that you may live.
Then the LORD God Almighty will be with
    you,
  just as you say he is.
¹⁵Hate evil, love good;
  maintain justice in the courts.
Perhaps the LORD God Almighty will have
    mercy
  on the remnant of Joseph.

¹⁶Therefore this is what the Lord, the LORD
God Almighty, says:

"There will be wailing in all the streets
  and cries of anguish in every public square.
The farmers will be summoned to weep
  and the mourners to wail.
¹⁷There will be wailing in all the vineyards,
  for I will pass through your midst,"
                says the LORD.

The Day of the LORD
¹⁸Woe to you who long
  for the day of the LORD!
Why do you long for the day of the LORD?
  That day will be darkness, not light.
¹⁹It will be as though a man fled from a lion
  only to meet a bear,
as though he entered his house
  and rested his hand on the wall
  only to have a snake bite him.
²⁰Will not the day of the LORD be darkness, not
    light—
pitch-dark, without a ray of brightness?

²¹"I hate, I despise your religious feasts;
  I cannot stand your assemblies.
²²Even though you bring me burnt offerings
    and grain offerings,
  I will not accept them.

你們用鑿過的石頭
  建造房屋，
  卻不得住在其內；
栽種美好的葡萄園，
  卻不得喝所出的酒。
¹²我知道你們的罪愆何等多，
  你們的罪惡何等大。

你們苦待義人，收受賄賂，
  在城門口屈枉窮乏人。

¹³所以通達人見這樣的時勢，
  必靜默不言，
  因為時勢真惡。

¹⁴你們要求善，不要求惡，
  就必存活。
這樣，耶和華萬軍之神
  必照你們所說的，
  與你們同在。
¹⁵要惡惡好善，
  在城門口秉公行義，
  或者耶和華萬軍之神
  向約瑟的餘民施恩。

¹⁶主耶和華萬軍之神如此說：

"在一切寬闊處必有哀號的聲音，
  在各街市上必有人說：哀哉！哀哉！
又必叫農夫來哭號，
  叫善唱哀歌的來舉哀。
¹⁷在各葡萄園，必有哀號的聲音，
  因為我必從你們中間經過。"
            這是耶和華說的。

主的日子
¹⁸想望耶和華日子來到的，
  有禍了！
你們為何想望耶和華的日子呢？
  那日黑暗沒有光明，
¹⁹景況好像人躲避獅子
  又遇見熊，
或是進房屋
  以手靠牆，
  就被蛇咬。
²⁰耶和華的日子，
  不是黑暗沒有光明嗎？
  不是幽暗毫無光輝嗎？

²¹"我厭惡你們的節期，
  也不喜悅你們的嚴肅會。
²²你們雖然向我獻燔祭
  和素祭，
  我卻不悅納，

也不顧你們
　　用肥畜獻的平安祭。

23要使你們歌唱的聲音遠離我，
　　因為我不聽你們彈琴的響聲。
24惟願公平如大水滾滾，
　　使公義如江河滔滔！

25 "以色列家啊，你們在曠野四十年，
　　豈是將祭物和供物獻給我呢？
26你們抬着為自己所造之摩洛的帳幕
　　和偶像的龕，
　　並你們的神星。

27所以我要把你們
　　擄到大馬士革以外。"
　　這是耶和華名為萬軍之神說的。

安逸無慮的人有禍了

6 國為列國之首，
　　人最著名，
　　且為以色列家所歸向，
　在錫安和撒馬利亞山安逸無慮的，
　　有禍了！

2你們要過到甲尼察看，
　　從那裏往大城哈馬去，
　　又下到非利士人的迦特，
　看那些國比你們的國還強嗎？
　　境界比你們的境界還寬嗎？
3你們以為降禍的日子還遠，
　　坐在位上盡行強暴（註：或作"行強
　　暴使審判臨近"）。
4你們躺臥在象牙牀上，
　　舒身在榻上，
　　吃羣中的羊羔、棚裏的牛犢；
5彈琴鼓瑟唱消閑的歌曲，
　　為自己製造樂器，
　　如同大衛所造的；
6以大碗喝酒，
　　用上等的油抹身，
　　卻不為約瑟的苦難擔憂。
7所以這些人必在被擄的人中
　　首先被擄，
　　舒身的人荒宴之樂必消滅了。

主憎惡以色列的榮華

8主耶和華萬軍之神指着自己起
誓說：

Though you bring choice fellowship
　　offerings,[a]
　I will have no regard for them.
23Away with the noise of your songs!
　I will not listen to the music of your harps.
24But let justice roll on like a river,
　righteousness like a never-failing stream!

25"Did you bring me sacrifices and offerings
　forty years in the desert, O house of Israel?
26You have lifted up the shrine of your king,
　the pedestal of your idols,
　the star of your god[b] —
　which you made for yourselves.
27Therefore I will send you into exile beyond
　　Damascus,"
　says the Lord, whose name is God Almighty.

Woe to the Complacent

6 Woe to you who are complacent in
　　Zion,
　and to you who feel secure on Mount
　　Samaria,
you notable men of the foremost nation,
　to whom the people of Israel come!
2Go to Calneh and look at it;
　go from there to great Hamath,
　and then go down to Gath in Philistia.
　Are they better off than your two kingdoms?
　Is their land larger than yours?
3You put off the evil day
　and bring near a reign of terror.
4You lie on beds inlaid with ivory
　and lounge on your couches.
　You dine on choice lambs
　and fattened calves.
5You strum away on your harps like David
　and improvise on musical instruments.
6You drink wine by the bowlful
　and use the finest lotions,
　but you do not grieve over the ruin of
　　Joseph.
7Therefore you will be among the first to go
　　into exile;
　your feasting and lounging will end.

The Lord Abhors the Pride of Israel

8The Sovereign Lord has sworn by himself—
the Lord God Almighty declares:

---

a 22 Traditionally peace offerings　　b 26 Or lifted up Sakkuth
your king / and Kaiwan your idols, / your star-gods; Septuagint
lifted up the shrine of Molech / and the star of your god Rephan, /
their idols

"I abhor the pride of Jacob
　and detest his fortresses;
I will deliver up the city
　and everything in it."

⁹If ten men are left in one house, they too will die. ¹⁰And if a relative who is to burn the bodies comes to carry them out of the house and asks anyone still hiding there, "Is anyone with you?" and he says, "No," then he will say, "Hush! We must not mention the name of the LORD."

¹¹For the LORD has given the command,
　and he will smash the great house into pieces
　and the small house into bits.

¹²Do horses run on the rocky crags?
　Does one plow there with oxen?
But you have turned justice into poison
　and the fruit of righteousness into
　　bitterness—
¹³you who rejoice in the conquest of Lo Debar[a]
　and say, "Did we not take Karnaim[b] by our
　　own strength?"

¹⁴For the LORD God Almighty declares,
　"I will stir up a nation against you, O house
　　of Israel,
that will oppress you all the way
　from Lebo[c] Hamath to the valley of the
　　Arabah."

Locusts, Fire and a Plumb Line

7 This is what the Sovereign LORD showed me: He was preparing swarms of locusts after the king's share had been harvested and just as the second crop was coming up. ²When they had stripped the land clean, I cried out, "Sovereign LORD, forgive! How can Jacob survive? He is so small!"

³So the LORD relented.

"This will not happen," the LORD said.

⁴This is what the Sovereign LORD showed me: The Sovereign LORD was calling for judgment by fire; it dried up the great deep and devoured the land. ⁵Then I cried out, "Sovereign LORD, I beg you, stop! How can Jacob survive? He is so small!"

⁶So the LORD relented.

"This will not happen either," the Sovereign LORD said.

⁷This is what he showed me: The Lord was

"我憎惡雅各的榮華，
　厭棄他的宮殿；
因此，我必將城和其中所有的
　都交付敵人。"

⁹那時，若在一房之內剩下十個人，也都必死。¹⁰死人的伯叔，就是燒他屍首的，要將這屍首搬到房外，問房屋內間的人說："你那裏還有人沒有？"他必說："沒有。"又說："不要做聲，因為我們不可提耶和華的名。"

¹¹看哪，耶和華出令，
　大房就被攻破，
　小屋就被打裂。

¹²馬豈能在崖石上奔跑？
　人豈能在那裏用牛耕種呢？
你們卻使公平變為苦膽，
　使公義的果子變為茵蔯。

¹³你們喜愛虛浮的事，
　自誇說："我們不是憑自己的
　　力量取了角嗎？"

¹⁴耶和華萬軍之神說：
　"以色列家啊，
　我必興起一國攻擊你們；
他們必欺壓你們，
　從哈馬口直到亞拉巴的河。"

蝗蟲、火與準繩

7 主耶和華指示我一件事：為王割菜之後（註："菜"或作"草"），菜又發生，剛發生的時候，主造蝗蟲。²蝗蟲吃盡那地的青物，我就說："主耶和華啊，求你赦免！因為雅各微弱，他怎能站立得住呢？"

³耶和華就後悔說：
　"這災可以免了。"

⁴主耶和華又指示我一件事：他命火來懲罰以色列，火就吞滅深淵，險些將地燒滅。⁵我就說："主耶和華啊，求你止息！因為雅各微弱，他怎能站立得住呢？"

⁶耶和華就後悔說：
　"這災也可免了。"

⁷他又指示我一件事：有一道牆

是按準繩建築的，主手拿準繩站在
其上。⁸耶和華對我說：「阿摩司
啊，你看見甚麼？」

我說：「看見準繩。」

主說：「我要吊起準繩在我民
以色列中，我必不再寬恕他們。

⁹「以撒的邱壇必然淒涼，
　以色列的聖所必然荒廢。
我必興起，
　用刀攻擊耶羅波安的家。」

阿摩司與亞瑪謝

¹⁰伯特利的祭司亞瑪謝，打發人
到以色列王耶羅波安那裏，說：
「阿摩司在以色列家中圖謀背叛
你；他所說的一切話，這國擔當不
起。¹¹因為阿摩司如此說：

「『耶羅波安必被刀殺，
　以色列民定被擄去
　離開本地。』」

¹²亞瑪謝又對阿摩司說：「你這
先見哪，要逃往猶大地去，在那裏
餬口，在那裏說預言。¹³卻不要在伯
特利再說預言，因為這裏有王的聖
所，有王的宮殿。」

¹⁴阿摩司對亞瑪謝說：「我原不
是先知，也不是先知的門徒（註：原文
作「兒子」）；我是牧人，又是修理桑
樹的。¹⁵耶和華選召我，使我不跟從
羊羣，對我說：『你去向我民以色
列說預言。』¹⁶亞瑪謝啊，現在你要
聽耶和華的話。你說：

「『不要向以色列說預言，
　也不要向以撒家滴下預言。』

¹⁷「所以耶和華如此說：

「『你的妻子
　必在城中作妓女，
你的兒女
　必倒在刀下；
你的地必有人用繩子量了分取，
　你自己
　　必死在污穢之地。
以色列民定被擄去
　離開本地。』」

standing by a wall that had been built true to
plumb, with a plumb line in his hand. ⁸And the
LORD asked me, "What do you see, Amos?"

"A plumb line," I replied.

Then the Lord said, "Look, I am setting a
plumb line among my people Israel; I will spare
them no longer.

⁹"The high places of Isaac will be destroyed
　and the sanctuaries of Israel will be ruined;
　with my sword I will rise against the house
　　of Jeroboam."

Amos and Amaziah

¹⁰Then Amaziah the priest of Bethel sent a
message to Jeroboam king of Israel: "Amos is
raising a conspiracy against you in the very
heart of Israel. The land cannot bear all his
words. ¹¹For this is what Amos is saying:

"'Jeroboam will die by the sword,
　and Israel will surely go into exile,
　away from their native land.'"

¹²Then Amaziah said to Amos, "Get out, you
seer! Go back to the land of Judah. Earn your
bread there and do your prophesying there.
¹³Don't prophesy anymore at Bethel, because
this is the king's sanctuary and the temple of the
kingdom."

¹⁴Amos answered Amaziah, "I was neither a
prophet nor a prophet's son, but I was a shepherd, and I also took care of sycamore-fig trees.
¹⁵But the LORD took me from tending the flock
and said to me, 'Go, prophesy to my people
Israel.' ¹⁶Now then, hear the word of the LORD.
You say,

"'Do not prophesy against Israel,
　and stop preaching against the house of
　　Isaac.'

¹⁷"Therefore this is what the LORD says:

"'Your wife will become a prostitute in the
　city,
　and your sons and daughters will fall by the
　　sword.
Your land will be measured and divided up,
　and you yourself will die in a pagan^a
　　country.
And Israel will certainly go into exile,
　away from their native land.'"

a 17 Hebrew an unclean

A Basket of Ripe Fruit

8 This is what the Sovereign LORD showed me: a basket of ripe fruit. ²"What do you see, Amos?" he asked.

"A basket of ripe fruit," I answered.

Then the LORD said to me, "The time is ripe for my people Israel; I will spare them no longer.

³"In that day," declares the Sovereign LORD, "the songs in the temple will turn to wailing.ᵃ Many, many bodies—flung everywhere! Silence!"

⁴Hear this, you who trample the needy
    and do away with the poor of the land,

⁵saying,

"When will the New Moon be over
    that we may sell grain,
and the Sabbath be ended
    that we may market wheat?"—
skimping the measure,
    boosting the price
    and cheating with dishonest scales,
⁶buying the poor with silver
    and the needy for a pair of sandals,
    selling even the sweepings with the wheat.

⁷The LORD has sworn by the Pride of Jacob: "I will never forget anything they have done.

⁸"Will not the land tremble for this,
    and all who live in it mourn?
The whole land will rise like the Nile;
    it will be stirred up and then sink
    like the river of Egypt.

⁹"In that day," declares the Sovereign LORD,

"I will make the sun go down at noon
    and darken the earth in broad daylight.
¹⁰I will turn your religious feasts into mourning
    and all your singing into weeping.
I will make all of you wear sackcloth
    and shave your heads.
I will make that time like mourning for an
      only son
    and the end of it like a bitter day.

¹¹"The days are coming," declares the
    Sovereign LORD,
    "when I will send a famine through the
      land—

一筐夏天的果子

8 主耶和華又指示我一件事：我看見一筐夏天的果子。²他說："阿摩司啊，你看見甚麼？"

我說："看見一筐夏天的果子。"

耶和華說："我民以色列的結局到了，我必不再寬恕他們。"

³主耶和華說："那日，殿中的詩歌變為哀號，必有許多屍首在各處拋棄，無人做聲。"

⁴你們這些要吞吃窮乏人，
    使困苦人衰敗的，當聽我的話！

⁵你們說：

"月朔幾時過去？
    我們好賣糧；
安息日幾時過去？
    我們好擺開麥子。"
賣出用小升斗，
    收銀用大戥子，
    用詭詐的天平欺哄人，
⁶好用銀子買貧寒人，
    用一雙鞋換窮乏人，
    將壞了的麥子賣給人。

⁷耶和華指着雅各的榮耀起誓說："他們的一切行為，我必永遠不忘。

⁸"地豈不因這事震動？
    其上的居民不也悲哀嗎？
地必全然像尼羅河漲起，
    如同埃及河湧上落下。"

⁹主耶和華說："到那日，

"我必使日頭在午間落下，
    使地在白晝黑暗。
¹⁰我必使你們的節期變為悲哀，
    歌曲變為哀歌。
眾人腰束麻布，
    頭上光禿，
使這場悲哀
    如喪獨生子，
    至終如痛苦的日子一樣。"

¹¹主耶和華說：
    "日子將到，
    我必命飢荒降在地上。

---

a 3 Or "the temple singers will wail

人飢餓非因無餅，
　乾渴非因無水，
乃因不聽耶和華的話。
12他們必飄流，從這海到那海，
　從北邊到東邊，
往來奔跑尋求耶和華的話，
　卻尋不着。

13 "當那日，

"美貌的處女和少年的男子
　必因乾渴發昏。

14那指着撒馬利亞牛犢（註：原文作
　"罪"）起誓的說：
'但哪，我們指着
　　你那裏的活神起誓。'
又說：'我們指着別是巴的神道
　（註："神"原文作"活"）起誓。'
這些人都必仆倒，永不再起來。"

以色列必被毀滅

9 我看見主站在祭壇旁邊，他
　說：

"你要擊打柱頂，
　使門檻震動，
打碎柱頂落在眾人頭上；
　所剩下的人，
　我必用刀殺戮，
無一人能逃避，
　無一人能逃脫。
2他們雖然挖透陰間，
　我的手必取出他們來；
雖然爬上天去，
　我必拿下他們來。

3雖然藏在迦密山頂，
　我必搜尋，
　捉出他們來；
雖然從我眼前藏在海底，
　我必命蛇咬他們。

4雖被仇敵擄去，
　我必命刀劍殺戮他們；
我必向他們定住眼目，
　降禍不降福。"

5主萬軍之耶和華摸地，
　地就消化，
凡住在地上的都必悲哀。

not a famine of food or a thirst for water,
　but a famine of hearing the words of the
　　LORD.
12Men will stagger from sea to sea
　and wander from north to east,
searching for the word of the LORD,
　but they will not find it.

13"In that day

"the lovely young women and strong young
　men
　will faint because of thirst.
14They who swear by the shame[a] of Samaria,
　or say, 'As surely as your god lives, O Dan,'
　or, 'As surely as the god[b] of Beersheba
　　lives'—
they will fall,
　never to rise again."

Israel to Be Destroyed

9 I saw the Lord standing by the altar,
　and he said:

"Strike the tops of the pillars
　so that the thresholds shake.
Bring them down on the heads of all the
　people;
　those who are left I will kill with the sword.
Not one will get away,
　none will escape.
2Though they dig down to the depths of the
　grave,[c]
　from there my hand will take them.
Though they climb up to the heavens,
　from there I will bring them down.
3Though they hide themselves on the top of
　Carmel,
　there I will hunt them down and seize them.
Though they hide from me at the bottom of
　the sea,
　there I will command the serpent to bite
　　them.
4Though they are driven into exile by their
　enemies,
　there I will command the sword to slay
　　them.
I will fix my eyes upon them
　for evil and not for good."

5The Lord, the LORD Almighty,
　he who touches the earth and it melts,
　and all who live in it mourn—

<hr>

a 14 Or by Ashima; or by the idol　　b 14 Or power　　c 2 Hebrew
to Sheol

the whole land rises like the Nile,
  then sinks like the river of
    Egypt—
[6]he who builds his lofty palace[a] in the
    heavens
  and sets its foundation[b] on the earth,
who calls for the waters of the sea
  and pours them out over the face of the
    land—
    the LORD is his name.

[7]"Are not you Israelites
  the same to me as the Cushites[c]?"
                    declares the LORD.
"Did I not bring Israel up from Egypt,
  the Philistines from Caphtor[d]
  and the Arameans from Kir?

[8]"Surely the eyes of the Sovereign LORD
  are on the sinful kingdom.
I will destroy it
  from the face of the earth—
yet I will not totally destroy
  the house of Jacob,"
                    declares the LORD.
[9]"For I will give the command,
  and I will shake the house of Israel
    among all the nations
as grain is shaken in a sieve,
  and not a pebble will reach the ground.
[10]All the sinners among my people
  will die by the sword,
all those who say,
  'Disaster will not overtake or meet us.'

Israel's Restoration
[11]"In that day I will restore
  David's fallen tent.
I will repair its broken places,
  restore its ruins,
  and build it as it used to be,
[12]so that they may possess the remnant of
    Edom
  and all the nations that bear my name,[e]"
                    declares the LORD,
                    who will do these things.

[13]"The days are coming," declares the LORD,

"when the reaper will be overtaken by the
    plowman
  and the planter by the one treading grapes.

地必全然像尼羅河漲起，
  如同埃及河落下。
[6]那在天上建造樓閣，
  在地上安定穹蒼，
命海水澆在地上的，
  耶和華是他的名。

[7]耶和華說：
"以色列人哪，
  我豈不看你們如古實人嗎？"
"我豈不是領以色列人出埃及地，
  領非利士人出迦斐託，
  領亞蘭人出吉珥嗎？

[8]"主耶和華的眼目
  察看這有罪的國，
必將這國
  從地上滅絕；
卻不將雅各家
  滅絕淨盡。"
                    這是耶和華說的。
[9]"我必出令，
  將以色列家
    分散在列國中，
好像用篩子篩穀，
  連一粒也不落在地上。
[10]我民中的一切罪人說：
'災禍必追不上我們，
  也迎不著我們。'
  他們必死在刀下。

以色列的復興
[11]"到那日，
  我必建立大衛倒塌的帳幕，
  堵住其中的破口，
把那破壞的建立起來，
  重新修造，像古時一樣，
[12]使以色列人
  得以東所餘剩的
  和所有稱為我名下的國。"
                    此乃行這事的
                    耶和華說的。

[13]耶和華說："日子將到，

"耕種的必接續收割的，
  踹葡萄的必接續撒種的。

---

a 6 The meaning of the Hebrew for this phrase is uncertain.
b 6 The meaning of the Hebrew for this word is uncertain.
c 7 That is, people from the upper Nile region   *d* 7 That is,
Crete   *e* 12 Hebrew; Septuagint *so that the remnant of men /
and all the nations that bear my name may seek (the Lord)*

大山要滴下甜酒，
　　小山都必流奶（註：原文作"消化"。
　　見約珥書3章18節）。
¹⁴我必使我民以色列被擄的歸回，
　　他們必重修荒廢的城邑居住，
　　栽種葡萄園，喝其中所出的酒，
　　修造果木園，吃其中的果子。
¹⁵我要將他們栽於本地，
　　他們不再從我所賜給他們的地上
　　　拔出來。"

　　　　這是耶和華你的神說的。

New wine will drip from the mountains
and flow from all the hills.
¹⁴I will bring back my exiled[a] people Israel;
they will rebuild the ruined cities and live in
them.
They will plant vineyards and drink their
wine;
they will make gardens and eat their fruit.
¹⁵I will plant Israel in their own land,
never again to be uprooted
from the land I have given them,"

says the LORD your God.

表九：阿摩司所見的異象
TABLE 9 : AMOS'S VISIONS

異象 Vision	經文 Reference	重要性 Significance
蝗蟲 Swarm of locusts	7:1-3	神正要施行刑罰，因先知的代求而延遲臨到 God was preparing punishment, which he delayed only because of Amos's intervention.
火燒 Fire	7:4-6	神要命"火"燒滅全地，因先知為民續求而免 God was preparing devour the land, but Amos intervened on behalf of the people.
牆與準繩 Wall and plumb line	7:7-9	神要查看百姓是否彎曲，若然，必加判罰 God would see if the people were crooked, and, if they were, he would punish them.
一籃熟果 Basket of ripe fruit	8:1-14	雖然以民過去非常榮美，但今已變壞，無可救藥，他們實在需要受罰 The people were ripe for punishment; though once beautiful, they were now rotten.
主站壇旁 God standing by the altar	9:1-15	刑罰必然執行 Punishment was executed.

雖然先知一再代求而免刑，但以民的背道至終帶來審判。
Amos had a series of visions concerning God's judgement on Israel. God was planning to judge Israel by sending a swarm of locusts or by sending fire. In spite of Amos's intercession on Israel's behalf, God would still carry out his judgement because Israel persisted in her disobedience.

a 14 Or will restore the fortunes of my

Obadiah

¹The vision of Obadiah.

This is what the Sovereign LORD says about Edom—

> We have heard a message from the LORD:
> An envoy was sent to the nations to say,
> "Rise, and let us go against her for battle"—

²"See, I will make you small among the nations;
you will be utterly despised.
³The pride of your heart has deceived you,
you who live in the clefts of the rocks^a
and make your home on the heights,
you who say to yourself,
'Who can bring me down to the ground?'
⁴Though you soar like the eagle
and make your nest among the stars,
from there I will bring you down,"
declares the LORD.
⁵"If thieves came to you,
if robbers in the night—
Oh, what a disaster awaits you—
would they not steal only as much as they wanted?
If grape pickers came to you,
would they not leave a few grapes?
⁶But how Esau will be ransacked,
his hidden treasures pillaged!
⁷All your allies will force you to the border;
your friends will deceive and overpower you;
those who eat your bread will set a trap for you,^b
but you will not detect it.

⁸"In that day," declares the LORD,
"will I not destroy the wise men of Edom,
men of understanding in the mountains of Esau?
⁹Your warriors, O Teman, will be terrified,
and everyone in Esau's mountains
will be cut down in the slaughter.

俄巴底亞書

¹俄巴底亞得了耶和華的默示。

論以東說：

我從耶和華那裏聽見信息，
　並有使者被差往列國去，說：
　"起來吧，一同起來與以東爭戰。"

²"我使你以東在列國中為最小的，
　被人大大藐視。
³住在山穴中，
　居所在高處的啊，
　你因狂傲自欺，
　心裏說：
　'誰能將我拉下地去呢？'
⁴你雖如大鷹高飛，
　在星宿之間搭窩，
　我必從那裏拉下你來。"
　這是耶和華說的。
⁵"盜賊若來在你那裏，
　或強盜夜間而來
　(你何竟被剪除)，
　豈不偷竊，
　直到夠了呢？
　摘葡萄的若來到你那裏，
　豈不剩下些葡萄呢？
⁶以掃的隱密處何竟被搜尋？
　他隱藏的寶物何竟被查出？
⁷與你結盟的都送你上路，直到交界；
　與你和好的欺騙你，
　且勝過你；
　與你一同吃飯的，
　設下網羅陷害你；
　在你心裏毫無聰明。"

⁸耶和華說："到那日，
　我豈不從以東除滅智慧人、
　從以掃山除滅聰明人？
⁹提幔哪，
　你的勇士必驚惶，
　甚致以掃山的人都被殺戮剪除。

---

^a 3 Or of Sela   ^b 7 The meaning of the Hebrew for this clause is uncertain.

10因你向兄弟雅各行強暴，
　　羞愧必遮蓋你，
　　你也必永遠斷絕。

11當外人擄掠雅各的財物，
　　外邦人進入他的城門，
　　為耶路撒冷拈鬮的日子，
　　你竟站在一旁，
　　像與他們同夥。
12你兄弟遭難的日子，
　　你不當瞪眼看着；
　　猶大人被滅的日子，
　　你不當因此歡樂；
　　他們遭難的日子，
　　你不當說狂傲的話。
13我民遭災的日子，
　　你不當進他們的城門；
　　他們遭災的日子，
　　你不當瞪眼看着他們受苦；
　　他們遭災的日子，
　　你不當伸手搶他們的財物。

14你不當站在岔路口，
　　剪除他們中間逃脫的；
　　他們遭難的日子，
　　你不當將他們剩下的人交付仇敵。

15 "耶和華降罰的日子
　　臨近萬國。
　　你怎樣行，他也必照樣向你行，
　　你的報應必歸到你頭上。
16你們猶大人在我聖山
　　怎樣喝了苦杯，
　　萬國也必照樣常常地喝；
　　且喝且咽，他們就歸於無有。
17在錫安山必有逃脫的人，
　　那山也必成聖；
　　雅各家
　　必得原有的產業。
18雅各家必成為大火；
　　約瑟家必為火焰。
　　以掃家必如碎稭，
　　火必將他燒着吞滅；
　　以掃家必無餘剩的。"
　　　　　　　　這是耶和華說的。

19南地的人，
　　必得以掃山；
　　高原的人，
　　必得非利士地，
　　也得以法蓮地
　　和撒馬利亞地；
　　便雅憫人必得基列。
20在迦南人中被擄的以色列眾人，

10Because of the violence against your brother
　　Jacob,
　　you will be covered with shame;
　　you will be destroyed forever.
11On the day you stood aloof
　　while strangers carried off his wealth
　and foreigners entered his gates
　　and cast lots for Jerusalem,
　　you were like one of them.
12You should not look down on your brother
　　in the day of his misfortune,
　nor rejoice over the people of Judah
　　in the day of their destruction,
　nor boast so much
　　in the day of their trouble.
13You should not march through the gates of
　　my people
　　in the day of their disaster,
　nor look down on them in their calamity
　　in the day of their disaster,
　nor seize their wealth
　　in the day of their disaster.
14You should not wait at the crossroads
　　to cut down their fugitives,
　nor hand over their survivors
　　in the day of their trouble.

15"The day of the LORD is near
　　for all nations.
　　As you have done, it will be done to you;
　　your deeds will return upon your own head.
16Just as you drank on my holy hill,
　　so all the nations will drink continually;
　　they will drink and drink
　　and be as if they had never been.
17But on Mount Zion will be deliverance;
　　it will be holy,
　　and the house of Jacob
　　will possess its inheritance.
18The house of Jacob will be a fire
　　and the house of Joseph a flame;
　　the house of Esau will be stubble,
　　and they will set it on fire and consume it.
　There will be no survivors
　　from the house of Esau."
　　　　　　　　The LORD has spoken.

19People from the Negev will occupy
　　the mountains of Esau,
　　and people from the foothills will possess
　　the land of the Philistines.
　They will occupy the fields of Ephraim and
　　Samaria,
　　and Benjamin will possess Gilead.
20This company of Israelite exiles who are in
　　Canaan

will possess ⌊the land⌋ as far as Zarephath;
the exiles from Jerusalem who are in
Sepharad
will possess the towns of the Negev.
[21]Deliverers will go up on[a] Mount Zion
to govern the mountains of Esau.
And the kingdom will be the LORD's.

必得地直到撒勒法。
在西法拉中被擄的耶路撒冷人，
　必得南地的城邑。

[21]必有拯救者上到錫安山，
　審判以掃山；
　國度就歸耶和華了。

表十：以色列與以東相爭的歷史
TABLE 10 : HISTORY OF THE CONFLICT BETWEEN ISRAEL AND EDOM

以色列國由雅各而出，以東則由以掃而出 The nation of Israel descended from Jacob; the nation of Edom descended from Esau	創 Ge 25:23
雅各與以掃，在母腹中即已相爭 Jacob and Esau struggled in their mother's womb	創 Ge 25:21-26
以掃將長子名分賣給雅各 Esau sold his birthright and blessing to Jacob	創 Ge 25:29-34
以東拒絕以色列人經過其地 Edom refused to let the Israelites pass through its land	民 Nu 20:14-22
以色列諸王不斷與以東爭戰 Israel's kings had constant conflict with Edom	
· 掃羅 Saul	撒上 1Sa 14:47
· 大衛 David	撒下 2Sa 8:13, 14
· 所羅門 Solomon	王上 1Ki 11:14-22
· 約沙法 Jehoshaphat	代下 2Ch 20:2
· 約蘭 Jehoram	代下 2Ch 21:8-10
· 亞瑪謝 Amaziah	代下 2Ch 25:11-14
· 亞哈斯 Ahaz	代下 2Ch 28:16, 17
以東促使巴比倫人毀滅耶京 Edom urged Babylon to destroy Jerusalem	詩 Ps 137:7

約拿書

Jonah

約拿逃避主

1 耶和華的話臨到亞米太的兒子約拿，說：²"你起來往尼尼微大城去，向其中的居民呼喊，因為他們的惡達到我面前。"

³約拿卻起來逃往他施去躲避耶和華；下到約帕，遇見一隻船要往他施去，他就給了船價，上了船，要與船上的人同往他施去躲避耶和華。

⁴然而耶和華使海中起大風，海就狂風大作，甚至船幾乎破壞。⁵水手便懼怕，各人哀求自己的神。他們將船上的貨物拋在海中，為要使船輕些。

約拿已下到底艙躺臥沉睡。⁶船主到他那裏對他說："你這沉睡的人哪，為何這樣呢？起來，求告你的神，或者神顧念我們，使我們不至滅亡。"

⁷船上的人彼此說："來吧！我們掣籤，看看這災臨到我們是因誰的緣故。"於是他們掣籤，掣出約拿來。

⁸眾人對他說："請你告訴我們，這災臨到我們是因誰的緣故？你以何事為業？你從哪裏來？你是哪一國、屬哪一族的人？"

⁹他說："我是希伯來人。我敬畏耶和華那創造滄海旱地之天上的神。"

¹⁰他們就大大懼怕，對他說："你做的是甚麼事呢？"他們已經知道他躲避耶和華，因為他告訴了他們。

¹¹他們問他說："我們當向你怎樣行，使你浪平靜呢？"這話是因海浪越發翻騰。

¹²他對他們說："你們將我抬起來，拋在海中，海就平靜了。我知道你們遭這大風是因我的緣故。"

¹³然而那些人竭力盪槳，要把船攏岸，卻是不能，因為海浪越發向他們翻騰。¹⁴他們便求告耶和華說："耶和華啊，我們懇求你，不要因這人的性命使我們死亡，不要使流

Jonah Flees From the LORD

1 The word of the LORD came to Jonah son of Amittai: ²"Go to the great city of Nineveh and preach against it, because its wickedness has come up before me."

³But Jonah ran away from the LORD and headed for Tarshish. He went down to Joppa, where he found a ship bound for that port. After paying the fare, he went aboard and sailed for Tarshish to flee from the LORD.

⁴Then the LORD sent a great wind on the sea, and such a violent storm arose that the ship threatened to break up. ⁵All the sailors were afraid and each cried out to his own god. And they threw the cargo into the sea to lighten the ship.

But Jonah had gone below deck, where he lay down and fell into a deep sleep. ⁶The captain went to him and said, "How can you sleep? Get up and call on your god! Maybe he will take notice of us, and we will not perish."

⁷Then the sailors said to each other, "Come, let us cast lots to find out who is responsible for this calamity." They cast lots and the lot fell on Jonah.

⁸So they asked him, "Tell us, who is responsible for making all this trouble for us? What do you do? Where do you come from? What is your country? From what people are you?"

⁹He answered, "I am a Hebrew and I worship the LORD, the God of heaven, who made the sea and the land."

¹⁰This terrified them and they asked, "What have you done?" (They knew he was running away from the LORD, because he had already told them so.)

¹¹The sea was getting rougher and rougher. So they asked him, "What should we do to you to make the sea calm down for us?"

¹²"Pick me up and throw me into the sea," he replied, "and it will become calm. I know that it is my fault that this great storm has come upon you."

¹³Instead, the men did their best to row back to land. But they could not, for the sea grew even wilder than before. ¹⁴Then they cried to the LORD, "O LORD, please do not let us die for taking this man's life. Do not hold us accountable

for killing an innocent man, for you, O LORD, have done as you pleased." ¹⁵Then they took Jonah and threw him overboard, and the raging sea grew calm. ¹⁶At this the men greatly feared the LORD, and they offered a sacrifice to the LORD and made vows to him.

¹⁷But the LORD provided a great fish to swallow Jonah, and Jonah was inside the fish three days and three nights.

Jonah's Prayer

2 From inside the fish Jonah prayed to the LORD his God. ²He said:

"In my distress I called to the LORD,
    and he answered me.
From the depths of the grave^a I called for
        help,
    and you listened to my cry.
³You hurled me into the deep,
    into the very heart of the seas,
    and the currents swirled about me;
all your waves and breakers
    swept over me.
⁴I said, 'I have been banished
    from your sight;
yet I will look again
    toward your holy temple.'
⁵The engulfing waters threatened me,^{b}
    the deep surrounded me;
    seaweed was wrapped around my head.
⁶To the roots of the mountains I sank down;
    the earth beneath barred me in forever.
But you brought my life up from the pit,
    O LORD my God.

⁷"When my life was ebbing away,
    I remembered you, LORD,
and my prayer rose to you,
    to your holy temple.

⁸"Those who cling to worthless idols
    forfeit the grace that could be theirs.
⁹But I, with a song of thanksgiving,
    will sacrifice to you.
What I have vowed I will make good.
    Salvation comes from the LORD."

¹⁰And the LORD commanded the fish, and it vomited Jonah onto dry land.

無辜血的罪歸與我們,因為你耶和華是隨自己的意旨行事。"¹⁵他們遂將約拿抬起,拋在海中,海的狂浪就平息了。¹⁶那些人便大大敬畏耶和華,向耶和華獻祭,並且許願。

¹⁷耶和華安排一條大魚吞了約拿,他在魚腹中三日三夜。

約拿的禱告

2 約拿在魚腹中禱告耶和華他的神,²說:

"我遭遇患難求告耶和華,
    你就應允我;
從陰間的深處呼求,
    你就俯聽我的聲音。

³你將我投下深淵,
    就是海的深處;
大水環繞我,
    你的波浪洪濤
    都漫過我身。
⁴我說:
'我從你眼前雖被驅逐,
    我仍要仰望你的聖殿。'

⁵諸水環繞我,幾乎淹沒我;
    深淵圍住我,
    海草纏繞我的頭。
⁶我下到山根,
    地的門將我永遠關住。
耶和華我的神啊,
    你卻將我的性命從坑中救出來。

⁷"我心在我裏面發昏的時候,
    我就想念耶和華。
我的禱告進入你的聖殿,
    達到你的面前。

⁸"那信奉虛無之神的人,
    離棄憐愛他們的主;
⁹但我必用感謝的聲音
    獻祭與你。
我所許的願,我必償還。
    救恩出於耶和華。"

¹⁰耶和華吩咐魚,魚就把約拿吐在旱地上。

a 2 Hebrew Sheol   b 5 Or waters were at my throat

約拿往尼尼微去

3 耶和華的話二次臨到約拿說：² "你起來！往尼尼微大城去，向其中的居民宣告我所吩咐你的話。"

³約拿便照耶和華的話起來，往尼尼微去。這尼尼微是極大的城，有三日的路程。⁴約拿進城走了一日，宣告說："再等四十日，尼尼微必傾覆了！"⁵尼尼微人信服神，便宣告禁食，從最大的到至小的都穿麻衣（註：或作 "披上麻布"）。

⁶這信息傳到尼尼微王的耳中，他就下了寶座，脫下朝服，披上麻布，坐在灰中。⁷他又使人遍告尼尼微通城說：

"王和大臣有令：

人不可嘗甚麼，牲畜、牛羊不可吃草，也不可喝水。⁸人與牲畜都當披上麻布，人要切切求告神。各人回頭離開所行的惡道，丟棄手中的強暴。⁹或者神轉意後悔，不發烈怒，使我們不至滅亡，也未可知。"

¹⁰於是神察看他們的行為，見他們離開惡道，他就後悔，不把所說的災禍降與他們了。

約拿因主施憐憫而發怒

4 這事約拿大大不悅，且甚發怒，²就禱告耶和華說："耶和華啊，我在本國的時候豈不是這樣說嗎？我知道你是有恩典、有憐憫的神，不輕易發怒，有豐盛的慈愛，並且後悔不降所說的災，所以我急速逃往他施去。³耶和華啊，現在求你取我的命吧！因為我死了比活着還好。"

⁴耶和華說："你這樣發怒合乎理嗎？"

⁵於是約拿出城，坐在城的東邊，在那裏為自己搭了一座棚，坐在棚的蔭下，要看看那城究竟如何。⁶耶和華神安排一棵蓖麻，使其發生高過約拿，影兒遮蓋他的頭，救他脫離苦楚；約拿因這棵蓖麻大大喜樂。⁷次日黎明，神卻安排一條

Jonah Goes to Nineveh

3 Then the word of the LORD came to Jonah a second time: ²"Go to the great city of Nineveh and proclaim to it the message I give you."

³Jonah obeyed the word of the LORD and went to Nineveh. Now Nineveh was a very important city—a visit required three days. ⁴On the first day, Jonah started into the city. He proclaimed: "Forty more days and Nineveh will be overturned." ⁵The Ninevites believed God. They declared a fast, and all of them, from the greatest to the least, put on sackcloth.

⁶When the news reached the king of Nineveh, he rose from his throne, took off his royal robes, covered himself with sackcloth and sat down in the dust. ⁷Then he issued a proclamation in Nineveh:

"By the decree of the king and his nobles:

Do not let any man or beast, herd or flock, taste anything; do not let them eat or drink. ⁸But let man and beast be covered with sackcloth. Let everyone call urgently on God. Let them give up their evil ways and their violence. ⁹Who knows? God may yet relent and with compassion turn from his fierce anger so that we will not perish."

¹⁰When God saw what they did and how they turned from their evil ways, he had compassion and did not bring upon them the destruction he had threatened.

Jonah's Anger at the LORD's Compassion

4 But Jonah was greatly displeased and became angry. ²He prayed to the LORD, "O LORD, is this not what I said when I was still at home? That is why I was so quick to flee to Tarshish. I knew that you are a gracious and compassionate God, slow to anger and abounding in love, a God who relents from sending calamity. ³Now, O LORD, take away my life, for it is better for me to die than to live."

⁴But the LORD replied, "Have you any right to be angry?"

⁵Jonah went out and sat down at a place east of the city. There he made himself a shelter, sat in its shade and waited to see what would happen to the city. ⁶Then the LORD God provided a vine and made it grow up over Jonah to give shade for his head to ease his discomfort, and Jonah was very happy about the vine. ⁷But at dawn the next day God provided a worm, which chewed the vine so that it withered.

8When the sun rose, God provided a scorching east wind, and the sun blazed on Jonah's head so that he grew faint. He wanted to die, and said, "It would be better for me to die than to live."

9But God said to Jonah, "Do you have a right to be angry about the vine?"

"I do," he said. "I am angry enough to die."

10But the LORD said, "You have been concerned about this vine, though you did not tend it or make it grow. It sprang up overnight and died overnight. 11But Nineveh has more than a hundred and twenty thousand people who cannot tell their right hand from their left, and many cattle as well. Should I not be concerned about that great city?"

蟲子咬這蓖麻，以致枯槁。8日頭出來的時候，神安排炎熱的東風，日頭曝曬約拿的頭，使他發昏，他就為自己求死，說："我死了比活着還好！"

9神對約拿說："你因這棵蓖麻發怒合乎理嗎？"

他說："我發怒以至於死，都合乎理！"

10耶和華說："這蓖麻不是你栽種的，也不是你培養的，一夜發生，一夜乾死，你尚且愛惜；11何況這尼尼微大城，其中不能分辨左手右手的有十二萬多人，並有許多牲畜，我豈能不愛惜呢？"

圖七：約拿的旅程
MAP 7 : JONAH'S ROUNDABOUT JOURNEY

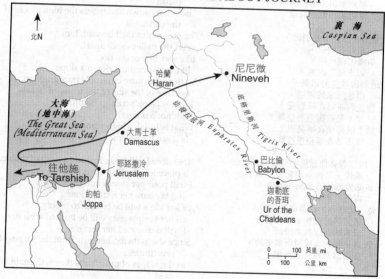

彌迦書

Micah

1 當猶大王約坦、亞哈斯、希西家在位的時候，摩利沙人彌迦得耶和華的默示，論撒馬利亞和耶路撒冷。

²萬民哪，你們都要聽！
　地和其上所有的，
　也都要側耳而聽！
　主耶和華從他的聖殿
　要見證你們的不是。

對撒馬利亞和耶路撒冷的審判
³看哪！
　耶和華出了他的居所，
　降臨步行地的高處。

⁴眾山在他以下必消化，
　諸谷必崩裂，
　如蠟化在火中，
　如水沖下山坡。
⁵這都因雅各的罪過，
　以色列家的罪惡。
　雅各的罪過在哪裏呢？
　豈不是在撒馬利亞嗎？
　猶大的邱壇在哪裏呢？
　豈不是在耶路撒冷嗎？

⁶ "所以我必使撒馬利亞變為田野的
　亂堆，又作為種葡萄之處；
　也必將她的石頭倒在谷中，
　露出根基來。
⁷她一切雕刻的偶像必被打碎，
　她所得的財物必被火燒，
　所有的偶像我必毀滅，
　因為是從妓女雇價所聚來的，
　後必歸為妓女的雇價。"

哭泣和哀號
⁸先知說：因此我必大聲哀號，
　赤腳露體而行；
　又要呼號如野狗，
　哀鳴如鴕鳥。
⁹因為撒馬利亞的傷痕無法醫治，
　延及猶大

1 The word of the LORD that came to Micah of Moresheth during the reigns of Jotham, Ahaz and Hezekiah, kings of Judah—the vision he saw concerning Samaria and Jerusalem.

²Hear, O peoples, all of you,
　listen, O earth and all who are in it,
that the Sovereign LORD may witness against you,
　the Lord from his holy temple.

Judgment Against Samaria and Jerusalem
³Look! The LORD is coming from his dwelling place;
　he comes down and treads the high places of the earth.
⁴The mountains melt beneath him
　and the valleys split apart,
like wax before the fire,
　like water rushing down a slope.
⁵All this is because of Jacob's transgression,
　because of the sins of the house of Israel.
What is Jacob's transgression?
　Is it not Samaria?
What is Judah's high place?
　Is it not Jerusalem?

⁶"Therefore I will make Samaria a heap of rubble,
　a place for planting vineyards.
I will pour her stones into the valley
　and lay bare her foundations.
⁷All her idols will be broken to pieces;
　all her temple gifts will be burned with fire;
　I will destroy all her images.
Since she gathered her gifts from the wages of prostitutes,
　as the wages of prostitutes they will again be used."

Weeping and Mourning
⁸Because of this I will weep and wail;
　I will go about barefoot and naked.
I will howl like a jackal
　and moan like an owl.
⁹For her wound is incurable;
　it has come to Judah.

It[a] has reached the very gate of my people,
   even to Jerusalem itself.
[10]Tell it not in Gath[b];
   weep not at all.[c]
In Beth Ophrah[d]
   roll in the dust.
[11]Pass on in nakedness and shame,
   you who live in Shaphir.[e]
Those who live in Zaanan[f]
   will not come out.
Beth Ezel is in mourning;
   its protection is taken from you.
[12]Those who live in Maroth[g] writhe in pain,
   waiting for relief,
because disaster has come from the LORD,
   even to the gate of Jerusalem.
[13]You who live in Lachish,[h]
   harness the team to the chariot.
You were the beginning of sin
   to the Daughter of Zion,
for the transgressions of Israel
   were found in you.
[14]Therefore you will give parting gifts
   to Moresheth Gath.
The town of Aczib[i] will prove deceptive
   to the kings of Israel.
[15]I will bring a conqueror against you
   who live in Mareshah.[j]
He who is the glory of Israel
   will come to Adullam.
[16]Shave your heads in mourning
   for the children in whom you delight;
make yourselves as bald as the vulture,
   for they will go from you into exile.

Man's Plans and God's

2 Woe to those who plan iniquity,
   to those who plot evil on their beds!
At morning's light they carry it out
   because it is in their power to do it.
[2]They covet fields and seize them,
   and houses, and take them.
They defraud a man of his home,
   a fellowman of his inheritance.

[3]Therefore, the LORD says:

和耶路撒冷我民的城門。

[10]不要在迦特報告這事，
   總不要哭泣。
我在伯亞弗拉
   滾於灰塵之中。
[11]沙斐的居民哪，
   你們要赤身蒙羞過去。
撒南的居民
   不敢出來。
伯以薛人的哀哭
   使你們無處可站。
[12]瑪律的居民心甚憂急，
   切望得好處，
因為災禍從耶和華那裏
   臨到耶路撒冷的城門。
[13]拉吉的居民哪，
   要用快馬套車；
錫安民（註："民"原文作"女子"）的罪
   由你而起；
以色列人的罪過
   在你那裏顯出。
[14]猶大啊，你要將禮物
   送給摩利設迦特。
亞革悉的眾族
   必用詭詐待以色列諸王。
[15]瑪利沙的居民哪，
   我必使那奪取你的來到你這裏；
以色列的尊貴人（註：原文作"榮耀"）
   必到亞杜蘭。
[16]猶大啊，要為你所喜愛的兒女
   剪除你的頭髮，使頭光禿；
要大大的光禿，如同禿鷹，
   因為他們都被擄去離開你。

人與神的計劃

2 禍哉！那些在牀上圖謀罪孽
   造作奸惡的，
天一發亮，
   因手有能力，就行出來了。
[2]他們貪圖田地就佔據，
   貪圖房屋便奪取。
他們欺壓人，
   霸佔房屋和產業。

[3]所以耶和華如此說：

---

a 9 Or *He*   *b 10 Gath* sounds like the Hebrew for *tell.*
c 10 Hebrew; Septuagint may suggest *not in Acco.* The Hebrew
for *in Acco* sounds like the Hebrew for *weep.*   *d 10 Beth
Ophrah* means *house of dust.*   *e 11 Shaphir* means *pleasant.*
f 11 Zaanan sounds like the Hebrew for *come out.*   *g 12 Maroth*
sounds like the Hebrew for *bitter.*   *h 13 Lachish* sounds like
the Hebrew for *team.*   *i 14 Aczib* means *deception.*
j 15 Mareshah sounds like the Hebrew for *conqueror.*

"我籌劃災禍降與這族，
　　這禍在你們的頸項上不能解脫；
你們也不能昂首而行，
　　因為這時勢是惡的。
4到那日，
　　必有人向你們提起悲慘的哀歌，
　　譏刺說：‘我們全然敗落了！
耶和華將我們的分轉歸別人，
　　何竟使這分離開我們？
他將我們的田地
　　分給悖逆的人。’”
5所以在耶和華的會中，
　　你必沒有人拈鬮、拉準繩。

假先知

6他們（註：或作“假先知”）說：
　　“你們不可說預言，
不可向這些人說預言，
　　不住地羞辱我們。”
7雅各家啊，
　　豈可說：“耶和華的心不忍耐嗎
　　（註：或作“心腸狹窄嗎”）？
　　這些事是他所行的嗎？”
　　“我耶和華的言語
豈不是與行動正直的人有益嗎？
8然而近來我的民
　　興起如仇敵，
從那些安然經過
　　不願打仗之人身上剝去外衣。
9你們將我民中的婦人
　　從安樂家中趕出，
又將我的榮耀從她們的小孩子
　　盡行奪去。
10你們起來去吧！
　　這不是你們安息之所，
因為污穢使人（註：或作“地”）毀滅，
　　而且大大毀滅。
11若有人心存虛假，用謊言說：
　　‘我要向你們預言得清酒和濃酒’，
那人就必作這民的先知！

應許拯救

12“雅各家啊，我必要聚集你們，
　　必要招聚以色列剩下的人，
安置在一處，如波斯拉的羊，
　　又如草場上的羊羣；
因為人數眾多，
　　就必大大喧嘩。
13開路的（註：或作“破城的”）
　　在他們前面上去，
他們直闖過城門，從城門出去。
　　他們的王在前面行，
耶和華引導他們。”

"I am planning disaster against this people,
from which you cannot save yourselves.
You will no longer walk proudly,
for it will be a time of calamity.
4In that day men will ridicule you;
they will taunt you with this mournful song:
'We are utterly ruined;
my people's possession is divided up.
He takes it from me!
He assigns our fields to traitors.' "

5Therefore you will have no one in the
assembly of the Lord
to divide the land by lot.

False Prophets

6"Do not prophesy," their prophets say.
"Do not prophesy about these things;
disgrace will not overtake us."
7Should it be said, O house of Jacob:
"Is the Spirit of the LORD angry?
Does he do such things?"

"Do not my words do good
to him whose ways are upright?
8Lately my people have risen up
like an enemy.
You strip off the rich robe
from those who pass by without a care,
like men returning from battle.
9You drive the women of my people
from their pleasant homes.
You take away my blessing
from their children forever.
10Get up, go away!
For this is not your resting place,
because it is defiled,
it is ruined, beyond all remedy.
11If a liar and deceiver comes and says,
'I will prophesy for you plenty of wine and
beer,'
he would be just the prophet for this people!

Deliverance Promised

12"I will surely gather all of you, O Jacob;
I will surely bring together the remnant of
Israel.
I will bring them together like sheep in a pen,
like a flock in its pasture;
the place will throng with people.
13One who breaks open the way will go up
before them;
they will break through the gate and go out.
Their king will pass through before them,
the LORD at their head."

Leaders and Prophets Rebuked

3 Then I said,

"Listen, you leaders of Jacob,
　you rulers of the house of Israel.
Should you not know justice,
[2] you who hate good and love evil;
who tear the skin from my people
　and the flesh from their bones;
[3]who eat my people's flesh,
　strip off their skin
　and break their bones in pieces;
who chop them up like meat for the pan,
　like flesh for the pot?"

[4]Then they will cry out to the LORD,
　but he will not answer them.
At that time he will hide his face from them
　because of the evil they have done.

[5]This is what the LORD says:

"As for the prophets
　who lead my people astray,
if one feeds them,
　they proclaim 'peace';
if he does not,
　they prepare to wage war against him.
[6]Therefore night will come over you, without
　visions,
and darkness, without divination.
The sun will set for the prophets,
　and the day will go dark for them.
[7]The seers will be ashamed
　and the diviners disgraced.
They will all cover their faces
　because there is no answer from God."

[8]But as for me, I am filled with power,
　with the Spirit of the LORD,
　and with justice and might,
to declare to Jacob his transgression,
　to Israel his sin.

[9]Hear this, you leaders of the house of Jacob,
　you rulers of the house of Israel,
who despise justice
　and distort all that is right;
[10]who build Zion with bloodshed,
　and Jerusalem with wickedness.
[11]Her leaders judge for a bribe,
　her priests teach for a price,
　and her prophets tell fortunes for money.
Yet they lean upon the LORD and say,
　"Is not the LORD among us?
　No disaster will come upon us."
[12]Therefore because of you,

斥責首領與先知

3 我說：

"雅各的首領、
　以色列家的官長啊，你們要聽！
你們不當知道公平嗎？
[2]你們惡善好惡，
　從人身上剝皮，
　從人骨頭上剔肉，
[3]吃我民的肉，
　剝他們的皮，
　打折他們的骨頭，
分成塊子像要下鍋，
　又像釜中的肉。"

[4]到了遭災的時候，這些人必哀求
　耶和華，他卻不應允他們；
那時他必照他們所行的惡事，
　向他們掩面。

[5]論到使我民走差路的先知：

"他們牙齒有所嚼的，
　他們就呼喊說：'平安了！'
凡不供給他們吃的，
　他們就預備攻擊他。（註："預備攻
　擊他"或作"說必遭遇刀兵"）"
耶和華如此說：
[6]"你們必遭遇黑夜，
　以致不見異象；
又必遭遇幽暗，以致不能占卜。
日頭必向你們沉落，
　白晝變為黑暗；
[7]先見必抱愧，
　占卜的必蒙羞，
都必搗著嘴唇，
　因為神不應允他們。"

[8]至於我，
　我藉耶和華的靈，
　滿有力量、公平、才能，
可以向雅各說明他的過犯，
　向以色列指出他的罪惡。
[9]雅各家的首領、
　以色列家的官長啊，當聽我的話！
你們厭惡公平，
　在一切事上屈枉正直；
[10]以人血建立錫安，
　以罪孽建造耶路撒冷。
[11]首領為賄賂行審判，
　祭司為雇價施訓誨，
　先知為銀錢行占卜。
他們卻倚賴耶和華，說：
　"耶和華不是在我們中間嗎？
　災禍必不臨到我們！"
[12]所以因你們的緣故，

錫安必被耕種像一塊田，
耶路撒冷必變為亂堆，
　　這殿的山必像叢林的高處。

主的山

4 末後的日子，

耶和華殿的山
必堅立，
超乎諸山，
高舉過於萬嶺；
萬民都要流歸這山。

2必有許多國的民前往，說：

"來吧！
我們登耶和華的山，
奔雅各神的殿。
主必將他的道教訓我們，
我們也要行他的路。"
因為訓誨必出於錫安，
耶和華的言語必出於耶路撒冷。
3他必在多國的民中施行審判，
為遠方強盛的國斷定是非。
他們要將刀打成犁頭，
把槍打成鐮刀。
這國不舉刀攻擊那國，
他們也不再學習戰事。

4人人都要坐在自己葡萄樹下
和無花果樹下，
無人驚嚇。
這是萬軍之耶和華親口說的。
5萬民各奉己神的名而行；
我們卻要永永遠遠奉耶和華
我們神的名而行。

主的計劃

6耶和華說："到那日，

我必聚集瘸腿的，
招聚被趕出的
和我所懲治的。
7我必使瘸腿的為餘剩之民，
使趕到遠方的為強盛之民。
耶和華要在錫安山作王治理他們，
從今直到永遠。
8你這羊群的高臺，錫安城（註："城"原
文作"女子"）的山哪，
從前的權柄，就是耶路撒冷民（註：
"民"原文作"女子"）的國權，
必歸與你。"

The Mountain of the LORD

4 In the last days

the mountain of the LORD's temple will
be established
as chief among the mountains;
it will be raised above the hills,
and peoples will stream to it.

2Many nations will come and say,

"Come, let us go up to the mountain of the
LORD,
to the house of the God of Jacob.
He will teach us his ways,
so that we may walk in his paths."
The law will go out from Zion,
the word of the LORD from Jerusalem.
3He will judge between many peoples
and will settle disputes for strong nations far
and wide.
They will beat their swords into plowshares
and their spears into pruning hooks.
Nation will not take up sword against nation,
nor will they train for war anymore.
4Every man will sit under his own vine
and under his own fig tree,
and no one will make them afraid,
for the LORD Almighty has spoken.
5All the nations may walk
in the name of their gods;
we will walk in the name of the LORD
our God for ever and ever.

The LORD's Plan

6"In that day," declares the LORD,

"I will gather the lame;
I will assemble the exiles
and those I have brought to grief.
7I will make the lame a remnant,
those driven away a strong nation.
The LORD will rule over them in Mount Zion
from that day and forever.
8As for you, O watchtower of the flock,
O stronghold[a] of the Daughter of Zion,
the former dominion will be restored to you;
kingship will come to the Daughter of
Jerusalem."

a 8 Or hill

[9]Why do you now cry aloud—
　　have you no king?
　Has your counselor perished,
　　that pain seizes you like that of a woman in
　　　labor?
[10]Writhe in agony, O Daughter of Zion,
　　like a woman in labor,
　for now you must leave the city
　　to camp in the open field.
　You will go to Babylon;
　　there you will be rescued.
　There the LORD will redeem you
　　out of the hand of your enemies.

[11]But now many nations
　　are gathered against you.
　They say, "Let her be defiled,
　　let our eyes gloat over Zion!"
[12]But they do not know
　　the thoughts of the LORD;
　they do not understand his plan,
　　he who gathers them like sheaves to the
　　　threshing floor.

[13]"Rise and thresh, O Daughter of Zion,
　　for I will give you horns of iron;
　I will give you hoofs of bronze
　　and you will break to pieces many nations."

You will devote their ill-gotten gains to the
　　LORD,
　their wealth to the Lord of all the earth.

A Promised Ruler From Bethlehem

5 Marshal your troops, O city of troops,[a]
　　for a siege is laid against us.
　　They will strike Israel's ruler
　on the cheek with a rod.

[2]"But you, Bethlehem Ephrathah,
　　though you are small among the clans[b] of
　　　Judah,
　out of you will come for me
　　one who will be ruler over Israel,
　whose origins[c] are from of old,
　　from ancient times.[d] "

[3]Therefore Israel will be abandoned
　　until the time when she who is in labor gives
　　　birth
　and the rest of his brothers return
　　to join the Israelites.

[9]現在你為何大聲哭號呢？
　疼痛抓住你彷彿產難的婦人，
　是因你中間沒有君王嗎？
　你的謀士滅亡了嗎？

[10]錫安的民（註：“民”原文作“女子”）哪，
　你要疼痛劬勞，
　彷彿產難的婦人；
　因為你必從城裏出來，住在田野，
　到巴比倫去。
　在那裏要蒙解救，
　在那裏耶和華必救贖你
　脫離仇敵的手。

[11]現在有許多國的民
　聚集攻擊你，
　說：“願錫安被玷污，
　願我們親眼見她遭報。”
[12]他們卻不知道
　耶和華的意念，
　也不明白他的籌劃。
　他聚集他們，
　好像把禾捆聚到禾場一樣。

[13]“錫安的民（註：“民”原文作“女子”）哪，
　起來踹穀吧！
　我必使你的角成為鐵，
　使你的蹄成為銅。
　你必打碎多國的民。”
　將他們的財獻與耶和華，
　將他們的貨獻與普天下的主。

應許掌權者由伯利恆而出

5 成羣的民（註：“民”原文作“女
　子”）哪，現在你要聚集成隊；
　因為仇敵圍攻我們，
　要用杖擊打以色列審判者的臉。

[2]“伯利恆、以法他啊，
　你在猶大諸城中為小，
　將來必有一位
　從你那裏出來，
　在以色列中為我作掌權的；
　他的根源從亙古、
　從太初就有。”

[3]耶和華必將以色列人交付敵人，
　直等那生產的婦人
　生下子來。
　那時，掌權者（註：原文作“他”）
　其餘的弟兄必歸到以色列人那裏。

---

a 1 Or Strengthen your walls, O walled city　b 2 Or rulers
c 2 Hebrew goings out　d 2 Or from days of eternity

4他必起來，
　　倚靠耶和華的大能，
　　並耶和華他神之名的威嚴，
　　牧養他的羊羣。
他們要安然居住；
　　因為他必日見尊大，
　　直到地極。
5這位必作我們的平安。

拯救與毀滅

當亞述人進入我們的地境，
　　踐踏宮殿的時候，
我們就立起七個牧者、
　　八個首領攻擊他。
6他們必用刀劍
　　毀壞亞述地
　　和寧錄地的關口。
亞述人進入我們的地境
　　踐踏的時候，
　　他必拯救我們。

7雅各餘剩的人
　　必在多國的民中，
如從耶和華那裏降下的露水，
　　又如甘霖降在草上；
不仗賴人力，
　　也不等候世人之功。
8雅各餘剩的人
　　必在多國多民中，
如林間百獸中的獅子，
　　又如少壯獅子在羊羣中。
他若經過，
　　就必踐踏撕裂，
　　無人搭救。
9願你的手舉起，
　　高過敵人！
　　願你的仇敵都被剪除！

10耶和華說："到那日，

我必從你中間剪除馬匹，
　　毀壞車輛。
11也必從你國中除滅城邑，
　　拆毀一切的保障，
12又必除掉你手中的邪術，
　　你那裏也不再有占卜的。
13我必從你中間
　　除滅雕刻的偶像和柱像，
你就不再跪拜
　　自己手所造的。
14我必從你中間拔出木偶，
　　又毀滅你的城邑。

4He will stand and shepherd his flock
　　in the strength of the LORD,
　　in the majesty of the name of the LORD his
　　　God.
And they will live securely, for then his
　　greatness
　　will reach to the ends of the earth.
5　And he will be their peace.

Deliverance and Destruction

When the Assyrian invades our land
　　and marches through our fortresses,
we will raise against him seven shepherds,
　　even eight leaders of men.
6They will rule[a] the land of Assyria with the
　　sword,
　　the land of Nimrod with drawn sword.[b]
He will deliver us from the Assyrian
　　when he invades our land
　　and marches into our borders.

7The remnant of Jacob will be
　　in the midst of many peoples
　　like dew from the LORD,
　　like showers on the grass,
which do not wait for man
　　or linger for mankind.
8The remnant of Jacob will be among the
　　nations,
　　in the midst of many peoples,
like a lion among the beasts of the forest,
　　like a young lion among flocks of sheep,
which mauls and mangles as it goes,
　　and no one can rescue.
9Your hand will be lifted up in triumph over
　　your enemies,
　　and all your foes will be destroyed.

10"In that day," declares the LORD,

"I will destroy your horses from among you
　　and demolish your chariots.
11I will destroy the cities of your land
　　and tear down all your strongholds.
12I will destroy your witchcraft
　　and you will no longer cast spells.
13I will destroy your carved images
　　and your sacred stones from among you;
you will no longer bow down
　　to the work of your hands.
14I will uproot from among you your Asherah
　　poles[c]
　　and demolish your cities.

*a 6 Or crush　b 6 Or Nimrod in its gates　c 14 That is, symbols
of the goddess Asherah*

¹⁵I will take vengeance in anger and wrath
　　upon the nations that have not obeyed me."

The LORD's Case Against Israel

6 Listen to what the LORD says:

"Stand up, plead your case before the
　　mountains;
let the hills hear what you have to say.
²Hear, O mountains, the LORD's accusation;
　　listen, you everlasting foundations of the
　　earth.
For the LORD has a case against his people;
　　he is lodging a charge against Israel.

³"My people, what have I done to you?
　　How have I burdened you? Answer me.
⁴I brought you up out of Egypt
　　and redeemed you from the land of slavery.
I sent Moses to lead you,
　　also Aaron and Miriam.
⁵My people, remember
　　what Balak king of Moab counseled
　　and what Balaam son of Beor answered.
Remember ⌊your journey⌋ from Shittim to
　　Gilgal,
that you may know the righteous acts of the
　　LORD."

⁶With what shall I come before the LORD
　　and bow down before the exalted God?
Shall I come before him with burnt offerings,
　　with calves a year old?
⁷Will the LORD be pleased with thousands of
　　rams,
　　with ten thousand rivers of oil?
Shall I offer my firstborn for my
　　transgression,
　　the fruit of my body for the sin of my soul?
⁸He has showed you, O man, what is good.
　　And what does the LORD require of you?
To act justly and to love mercy
　　and to walk humbly with your God.

Israel's Guilt and Punishment

⁹Listen! The LORD is calling to the city—
　　and to fear your name is wisdom—
"Heed the rod and the One who appointed
　　it.ᵃ
¹⁰Am I still to forget, O wicked house,
　　your ill-gotten treasures
and the short ephah,ᵇ which is accursed?
¹¹Shall I acquit a man with dishonest scales,

---

a 9 The meaning of the Hebrew for this line is uncertain.
b 10 An ephah was a dry measure.

---

¹⁵我也必在怒氣和忿怒中
　　向那不聽從的列國施報。"

主譴責以色列

6 以色列人哪，
　　當聽耶和華的話！
"要起來向山嶺爭辯，
　　使岡陵聽你的話。
²山嶺和地永久的根基啊，
　　要聽耶和華爭辯的話！
因為耶和華
　　要與他的百姓爭辯，
　　與以色列爭論。

³"我的百姓啊，我向你做了甚麼呢？
　　我在甚麼事上使你厭煩，
　　你可以對我證明。
⁴我曾將你從埃及地領出來，
　　從作奴僕之家救贖你，
我也差遣摩西、
　　亞倫和米利暗在你前面行。
⁵我的百姓啊，
　　你們當追念摩押王巴勒所設的謀
　　和比珥的兒子巴蘭回答他的話，
並你們從什亭到吉甲所遇見的事，
　　好使你們知道
　　耶和華公義的作為。"

⁶我朝見耶和華，
　　在至高神面前跪拜，
當獻上甚麼呢？
　　豈可獻一歲的牛犢為燔祭嗎？
⁷耶和華豈喜悅千千的公羊，
　　或是萬萬的油河嗎？
我豈可為自己的罪過
　　獻我的長子嗎？
為心中的罪惡
　　獻我身所生的嗎？
⁸世人哪，耶和華已指示你何為善，
　　他向你所要的是甚麼呢？
只要你行公義，好憐憫，
　　存謙卑的心，與你的神同行。

以色列的罪惡與懲罰

⁹耶和華向這城呼叫，
　　智慧人必敬畏他的名：
"你們當聽是誰派定刑杖的懲罰。

¹⁰惡人家中
　　不仍有非義之財
　　和可惡的小升斗嗎？
¹¹我若用不公道的天平
　　和囊中詭詐的法碼，

豈可算為清潔呢？
12城裏的富戶滿行強暴，
　　其中的居民也說謊言，
　　口中的舌頭是詭詐的。
13因此，我擊打你，使你的傷痕甚重，
　　使你因你的罪惡荒涼。
14你要吃，卻吃不飽；
　　你的虛弱必顯在你中間。
　你必挪去，卻不得救護；
　　所救護的，
　　我必交給刀劍。
15你必撒種，卻不得收割；
　　踹橄欖，卻不得油抹身；
　　踹葡萄，卻不得酒喝。

16因為你守暗利的惡規，
　　行亞哈家一切所行的，
　　順從他們的計謀；
　因此，我必使你荒涼，
　　使你的居民令人嗤笑，
　　你們也必擔當我民的羞辱。"

以色列的不幸

7 哀哉！我（註：或指"以色列"）
好像夏天的果子已被收盡，
又像摘了葡萄所剩下的，
沒有一掛可吃的。
我心羨慕初熟的無花果。
2地上虔誠人滅盡，
　　世間沒有正直人；
　各人埋伏要殺人流血，
　　都用網羅獵取弟兄。
3他們雙手作惡；
　　君王徇情面，
　審判官要賄賂，
　　位分大的吐出惡意，
　　都彼此結聯行惡。
4他們最好的，不過是蒺藜；
　　最正直的，不過是荊棘籬笆。
　你守望者說，
　　降罰的日子已經來到，
　　他們必擾亂不安。
5不要倚賴鄰舍，
　　不要信靠密友；
　要守住你的口，
　　不要向你懷中的妻提說。
6因為兒子藐視父親，
　　女兒抗拒母親，
　媳婦抗拒婆婆；
　人的仇敵
　　就是自己家裏的人。

with a bag of false weights?
12Her rich men are violent;
　her people are liars
　and their tongues speak deceitfully.
13Therefore, I have begun to destroy you,
　to ruin you because of your sins.
14You will eat but not be satisfied;
　your stomach will still be empty.[a]
You will store up but save nothing,
　because what you save I will give to the
　　sword.
15You will plant but not harvest;
　you will press olives but not use the oil on
　　yourselves,
　you will crush grapes but not drink the wine.
16You have observed the statutes of Omri
　and all the practices of Ahab's house,
　and you have followed their traditions.
Therefore I will give you over to ruin
　and your people to derision;
　you will bear the scorn of the nations.[b]"

Israel's Misery

7 What misery is mine!
I am like one who gathers summer fruit
　at the gleaning of the vineyard;
there is no cluster of grapes to eat,
　none of the early figs that I crave.
2The godly have been swept from the land;
　not one upright man remains.
All men lie in wait to shed blood;
　each hunts his brother with a net.
3Both hands are skilled in doing evil;
　the ruler demands gifts,
　the judge accepts bribes,
　the powerful dictate what they desire—
　they all conspire together.
4The best of them is like a brier,
　the most upright worse than a thorn hedge.
The day of your watchmen has come,
　the day God visits you.
Now is the time of their confusion.
5Do not trust a neighbor;
　put no confidence in a friend.
Even with her who lies in your embrace
　be careful of your words.
6For a son dishonors his father,
　a daughter rises up against her mother,
　a daughter-in-law against her
　　mother-in-law—
　a man's enemies are the members of his own
　　household.

<hr>

a 14 The meaning of the Hebrew for this word is uncertain.
b 16 Septuagint; Hebrew scorn due my people

⁷But as for me, I watch in hope for the LORD,
　I wait for God my Savior;
　my God will hear me.

Israel Will Rise

⁸Do not gloat over me, my enemy!
　Though I have fallen, I will rise.
　Though I sit in darkness,
　the LORD will be my light.
⁹Because I have sinned against him,
　I will bear the LORD's wrath,
until he pleads my case
　and establishes my right.
He will bring me out into the light;
　I will see his righteousness.
¹⁰Then my enemy will see it
　and will be covered with shame,
　she who said to me,
　"Where is the LORD your God?"
My eyes will see her downfall;
　even now she will be trampled underfoot
　like mire in the streets.

¹¹The day for building your walls will come,
　the day for extending your boundaries.
¹²In that day people will come to you
　from Assyria and the cities of Egypt,
　even from Egypt to the Euphrates
　and from sea to sea
　and from mountain to mountain.
¹³The earth will become desolate because of its
　inhabitants,
　as the result of their deeds.

Prayer and Praise

¹⁴Shepherd your people with your staff,
　the flock of your inheritance,
which lives by itself in a forest,
　in fertile pasturelands.ᵃ
Let them feed in Bashan and Gilead
　as in days long ago.

¹⁵"As in the days when you came out of Egypt,
　I will show them my wonders."

¹⁶Nations will see and be ashamed,
　deprived of all their power.
They will lay their hands on their mouths
　and their ears will become deaf.
¹⁷They will lick dust like a snake,
　like creatures that crawl on the ground.
They will come trembling out of their dens;
　they will turn in fear to the LORD our God
　and will be afraid of you.

ᵃ 14 Or in the middle of Carmel

⁷至於我，我要仰望耶和華，
　要等候那救我的神，
　我的神必應允我。

以色列必然興起

⁸我的仇敵啊，不要向我誇耀。
　我雖跌倒，卻要起來；
　我雖坐在黑暗裏，
　耶和華卻作我的光。
⁹我要忍受耶和華的惱怒，
　因我得罪了他，
　直等他為我辨屈，
　為我伸冤。
　他必領我到光明中，
　我必得見他的公義。
¹⁰那時我的仇敵，
　就是曾對我說：
　"耶和華你神在哪裏"的，
　她一看見這事，就被羞愧遮蓋。
　我必親眼見她遭報，
　她必被踐踏，
　如同街上的泥土。

¹¹以色列啊，日子必到，
　你的牆垣必重修；
　到那日，你的境界必開展
　　　（註：或作"命令必傳到遠方"）。
¹²當那日，
　人必從亞述，從埃及的城邑，
　從埃及到大河，從這海到那海，
　從這山到那山，都歸到你這裏來。
¹³然而這地因居民的緣故，
　又因他們行事的結果，必然荒涼。

禱告與讚美

¹⁴求耶和華在迦密山的樹林中，
　用你的杖
　牧放你獨居的民，
　就是你產業的羊羣。
求你容他們在巴珊和基列得食物，
　像古時一樣。

¹⁵耶和華說：
　"我要把奇事顯給他們看，
　好像出埃及地的時候一樣。"
¹⁶列國看見這事，
　就必為自己的勢力慚愧。
　他們必用手搗口，
　掩耳不聽。
¹⁷他們必舔土如蛇，
　又如土中腹行的物，
　戰戰兢兢地出他們的營寨。
　他們必戰懼投降耶和華，
　也必因我們的神而懼怕。

¹⁸神啊！
　　有何神像你，
　　赦免罪孽，
　　　饒恕你產業之餘民的罪過，
　　不永遠懷怒，
　　　喜愛施恩？
¹⁹必再憐憫我們，
　　　將我們的罪孽踏在腳下，
　　又將我們的一切罪
　　　投於深海。
²⁰你必按古時起誓
　　　應許我們列祖的話，
　　向雅各發誠實，
　　　向亞伯拉罕施慈愛。

¹⁸Who is a God like you,
　　who pardons sin and forgives the
　　　transgression
　of the remnant of his inheritance?
　You do not stay angry forever
　　but delight to show mercy.
¹⁹You will again have compassion on us;
　　you will tread our sins underfoot
　　and hurl all our iniquities into the depths of
　　　the sea.
²⁰You will be true to Jacob,
　　and show mercy to Abraham,
　as you pledged on oath to our fathers
　　in days long ago.

表十一：彌迦對不義之事的指證
TABLE 11 : MICAH'S CHARGES OF INJUSTICE

圖謀罪孽 Plotting evil	2:1
奪取，貪圖，霸佔 Fraud, coveting, violence	2:2
偷竊，不誠實 Stealing, dishonesty	2:8
侵吞寡婦家產 Driving widows from their homes	2:9
惡善好惡 Hating good, loving evil	3:1, 2
厭惡公平，屈枉正直 Despising justice, distorting what is right	3:9
流血謀殺 Murder	3:10
官長受賄 Taking bribes	3:11

Nahum

那鴻書

1 An oracle concerning Nineveh. The book of the vision of Nahum the Elkoshite.

1 論尼尼微的默示，就是伊勒歌斯人那鴻所得的默示。

The LORD's Anger Against Nineveh

²The LORD is a jealous and avenging God;
  the LORD takes vengeance and is filled with
    wrath.
The LORD takes vengeance on his foes
  and maintains his wrath against his enemies.
³The LORD is slow to anger and great in power;
  the LORD will not leave the guilty
    unpunished.
His way is in the whirlwind and the storm,
  and clouds are the dust of his feet.
⁴He rebukes the sea and dries it up;
  he makes all the rivers run dry.
Bashan and Carmel wither
  and the blossoms of Lebanon fade.
⁵The mountains quake before him
  and the hills melt away.
The earth trembles at his presence,
  the world and all who live in it.
⁶Who can withstand his indignation?
  Who can endure his fierce anger?
His wrath is poured out like fire;
  the rocks are shattered before him.

⁷The LORD is good,
  a refuge in times of trouble.
He cares for those who trust in him,
⁸ but with an overwhelming flood
  he will make an end of ⌊Nineveh⌋;
  he will pursue his foes into darkness.

⁹Whatever they plot against the LORD
  heᵃ will bring to an end;
  trouble will not come a second time.
¹⁰They will be entangled among thorns
  and drunk from their wine;
  they will be consumed like dry stubble.ᵇ
¹¹From you, ⌊O Nineveh,⌋has one come forth
  who plots evil against the LORD
  and counsels wickedness.

主向尼尼微發怒

²耶和華是忌邪施報的神；
  耶和華施報大有忿怒。
向他的敵人施報，
  向他的仇敵懷怒。
³耶和華不輕易發怒，
  大有能力，
  萬不以有罪的為無罪。
他乘旋風和暴風而來，
  雲彩為他腳下的塵土。
⁴他斥責海，使海乾了，
  使一切江河乾涸。
巴珊和迦密的樹林衰殘，
  黎巴嫩的花草也衰殘了。
⁵大山因他震動，
  小山也都消化；
大地在他面前突起，
  世界和住在其間的也都如此。
⁶他發忿恨，誰能立得住呢？
  他發烈怒，誰能當得起呢？
他的忿怒如火傾倒，
  磐石因他崩裂。

⁷耶和華本為善，
  在患難的日子為人的保障，
  並且認得那些投靠他的人。
⁸但他必以漲溢的洪水
  淹沒尼尼微，
  又驅逐仇敵進入黑暗。

⁹尼尼微人哪，設何謀攻擊耶和華呢？
  他必將你們滅絕淨盡，
  災難不再興起。
¹⁰你們像叢雜的荊棘，
  像喝醉了的人，
  又如枯乾的碎稭全然燒滅。
¹¹有一人從你那裏出來，
  圖謀邪惡，
  設惡計攻擊耶和華。

---

a 9 Or What do you foes plot against the LORD? / He   b 10 The meaning of the Hebrew for this verse is uncertain.

12耶和華如此說：

"尼尼微雖然勢力充足，
　　人數繁多，也被剪除，歸於無有。
<u>猶大</u>啊，我雖然使你受苦，
　　卻不再使你受苦。
13現在我必從你頸項上折斷他的軛，
　　扭開他的繩索。"

14耶和華已經出令，
　　指着<u>尼尼微</u>說：
　　　"你名下的人必不留後。
　我必從你神的廟中，
　　　除滅雕刻的偶像
　　　和鑄造的偶像，
　我必因你鄙陋，
　　　使你歸於墳墓。"

15看哪，
　　有報好信、
　　傳平安之人的腳登山，說：
　"<u>猶大</u>啊，可以守你的節期，
　　還你所許的願吧！
　因為那惡人不再從你中間經過，
　　他已滅絕淨盡了。"

尼尼微必要傾覆

2 　<u>尼尼微</u>啊，那打碎邦國的上
來攻擊你。
你要看守保障，
　謹防道路；
　使腰強壯，
　大大勉力。

2耶和華復興<u>雅各</u>的榮華，
　　好像<u>以色列</u>的榮華一樣，
　因為使地空虛的，
　　已經使<u>雅各</u>和<u>以色列</u>空虛，
　　將他們的葡萄枝毀壞了。
3他勇士的盾牌是紅的，
　　精兵都穿朱紅衣服。
　在他預備爭戰的日子，
　　戰車上的鋼鐵閃爍如火，
　　柏木把的槍也掄起來了。
4車輛在街上（註：或作"城外"）急行，
　　在寬闊處奔來奔去，
　形狀如火把，
　飛跑如閃電。

5<u>尼尼微</u>王招聚他的貴冑；
　　他們步行絆跌，
　速上城牆，
　預備擋牌。

12This is what the LORD says:

"Although they have allies and are numerous,
　they will be cut off and pass away.
Although I have afflicted you, ⌊O Judah,⌋
　I will afflict you no more.
13Now I will break their yoke from your neck
　and tear your shackles away."

14The LORD has given a command concerning
　　you, ⌊Nineveh⌋:
　"You will have no descendants to bear your
　　name.
I will destroy the carved images and cast idols
　that are in the temple of your gods.
I will prepare your grave,
　for you are vile."

15Look, there on the mountains,
　the feet of one who brings good news,
　who proclaims peace!
Celebrate your festivals, O Judah,
　and fulfill your vows.
No more will the wicked invade you;
　they will be completely destroyed.

Nineveh to Fall

2 　An attacker advances against you,
⌊Nineveh⌋.
Guard the fortress,
　watch the road,
　brace yourselves,
　marshal all your strength!

2The LORD will restore the splendor of Jacob
　like the splendor of Israel,
though destroyers have laid them waste
　and have ruined their vines.

3The shields of his soldiers are red;
　the warriors are clad in scarlet.
The metal on the chariots flashes
　on the day they are made ready;
　the spears of pine are brandished.a
4The chariots storm through the streets,
　rushing back and forth through the squares.
They look like flaming torches;
　they dart about like lightning.

5He summons his picked troops,
　yet they stumble on their way.
They dash to the city wall;
　the protective shield is put in place.

a 3 Hebrew; Septuagint and Syriac / the horsemen rush to and
fro

⁶The river gates are thrown open
　　and the palace collapses.
⁷It is decreed*a* that⌊the city⌋
　　be exiled and carried away.
　Its slave girls moan like doves
　　and beat upon their breasts.
⁸Nineveh is like a pool,
　　and its water is draining away.
　"Stop! Stop!" they cry,
　　but no one turns back.
⁹Plunder the silver!
　　Plunder the gold!
　The supply is endless,
　　the wealth from all its treasures!
¹⁰She is pillaged, plundered, stripped!
　　Hearts melt, knees give way,
　　bodies tremble, every face grows pale.

¹¹Where now is the lions' den,
　　the place where they fed their young,
　where the lion and lioness went,
　　and the cubs, with nothing to fear?
¹²The lion killed enough for his cubs
　　and strangled the prey for his mate,
　filling his lairs with the kill
　　and his dens with the prey.

¹³"I am against you,"
　　declares the LORD Almighty.
　"I will burn up your chariots in smoke,
　　and the sword will devour your young lions.
　I will leave you no prey on the earth.
　The voices of your messengers
　　will no longer be heard."

Woe to Nineveh

3 Woe to the city of blood,
　　full of lies,
　　full of plunder,
　never without victims!
²The crack of whips,
　　the clatter of wheels,
　galloping horses
　　and jolting chariots!
³Charging cavalry,
　　flashing swords
　　and glittering spears!
　Many casualties,
　　piles of dead,
　bodies without number,
　　people stumbling over the corpses—
⁴all because of the wanton lust of a harlot,
　　alluring, the mistress of sorceries,
　who enslaved nations by her prostitution

⁶河閘開放，
　　宮殿沖沒。
⁷王后蒙羞，
　　被人擄去；
　宮女搥胸，哀鳴如鴿。
　此乃命定之事。
⁸尼尼微自古以來充滿人民，
　　如同聚水的池子。
　現在居民都逃跑，
　　雖有人呼喊說："站住！站住！"
　卻無人回顧。
⁹你們搶掠金銀吧！
　　因為所積蓄的無窮，
　華美的寶器無數。
¹⁰尼尼微現在空虛荒涼，
　　人心消化，雙膝相碰，
　腰都疼痛，臉都變色。

¹¹獅子的洞和少壯獅子餵養之處
　　在哪裏呢？
　公獅、母獅、小獅遊行，
　　無人驚嚇之地在哪裏呢？
¹²公獅為小獅撕碎許多食物，
　　為母獅掐死活物，
　把撕碎的、掐死的
　　充滿牠的洞穴。

¹³萬軍之耶和華說：
　　"我與你為敵，
　必將你的車輛焚燒成煙，
　　刀劍也必吞滅你的少壯獅子。
　我必從地上除滅你所撕碎的，
　　你使者的聲音
　必不再聽見。"

尼尼微有禍了

3 禍哉！
　　這流人血的城，
　　充滿謊詐和強暴，
　搶奪的事總不止息。
²鞭聲響亮，
　　車輪轟轟，
　馬匹踢跳，
　　車輛奔騰，
³馬兵爭先，
　　刀劍發光，
　　槍矛閃爍，
　被殺的甚多，
　　屍首成了大堆，
　屍骸無數，
　　人碰著而跌倒；
⁴都因那美貌的妓女多有淫行，
　　慣行邪術，
　藉淫行誘惑列國，

---

a 7 The meaning of the Hebrew for this word is uncertain.

用邪術誘惑多族（註："誘惑"原文
作"賣"）。

5萬軍之耶和華說："我與你為敵。
　我必揭起你的衣襟，
　　蒙在你臉上，
　使列國看見你的赤體，
　　使列邦觀看你的醜陋。
6我必將可憎污穢之物拋在你身上，
　辱沒你，
　　為眾目所觀。
7凡看見你的，都必逃跑離開你，
　說：'尼尼微荒涼了！
　有誰為你悲傷呢？'
　我何處尋得安慰你的人呢？"

8你豈比挪亞們強呢？
　挪亞們坐落在眾河之間，
　　周圍有水，
　海（註："海"指"尼羅河"）作她的濠溝，
　　又作她的城牆。
9古實和埃及是她無窮的力量，
　弗人和路比族是她的幫手。
10但她被遷移，
　被擄去；
　她的嬰孩在各市口上
　　也被摔死。
　人為她的尊貴人拈鬮；
　她所有的大人都被鏈子鎖着。
11你也必喝醉，
　必被埋藏，
　並因仇敵的緣故尋求避難所。

12你一切保障，
　必像無花果樹上初熟的無花果，
　若一搖撼，
　　就落在想吃之人的口中。
13你地上的人民，
　如同婦女；
　你國中的關口
　　向仇敵敞開；
　你的門閂被火焚燒。

14你要打水預備受困，
　要堅固你的保障，
　踹土和泥，
　　修補磚窯。

15在那裏火必燒滅你，
　刀必殺戮你，
　吞滅你如同蝻子。
　任你加增人數多如蝻子、
　　多如蝗蟲吧！
16你增添商賈，

5"I am against you," declares the LORD
　　　Almighty.
　"I will lift your skirts over your face.
　I will show the nations your nakedness
　　and the kingdoms your shame.
6I will pelt you with filth,
　I will treat you with contempt
　　and make you a spectacle.
7All who see you will flee from you and say,
　　'Nineveh is in ruins—who will mourn for
　　　her?'
　Where can I find anyone to comfort you?"

8Are you better than Thebes,[a]
　situated on the Nile,
　　with water around her?
　The river was her defense,
　　the waters her wall.
9Cush[b] and Egypt were her boundless strength;
　Put and Libya were among her allies.
10Yet she was taken captive
　and went into exile.
　Her infants were dashed to pieces
　　at the head of every street.
　Lots were cast for her nobles,
　and all her great men were put in chains.
11You too will become drunk;
　you will go into hiding
　and seek refuge from the enemy.

12All your fortresses are like fig trees
　with their first ripe fruit;
　when they are shaken,
　the figs fall into the mouth of the eater.
13Look at your troops—
　they are all women!
　The gates of your land
　are wide open to your enemies;
　fire has consumed their bars.

14Draw water for the siege,
　strengthen your defenses!
　Work the clay,
　　tread the mortar,
　　repair the brickwork!
15There the fire will devour you;
　the sword will cut you down
　and, like grasshoppers, consume you.
　Multiply like grasshoppers,
　　multiply like locusts!
16You have increased the number of your
　　merchants

till they are more than the stars of the sky,
　　but like locusts they strip the land
　　　and then fly away.
¹⁷Your guards are like locusts,
　　your officials like swarms of locusts
　　that settle in the walls on a cold day—
　　but when the sun appears they fly away,
　　　and no one knows where.

¹⁸O king of Assyria, your shepherds^a slumber;
　　your nobles lie down to rest.
　　Your people are scattered on the mountains
　　with no one to gather them.
¹⁹Nothing can heal your wound;
　　your injury is fatal.
　　Everyone who hears the news about you
　　　claps his hands at your fall,
　　for who has not felt
　　　your endless cruelty?

多過天上的星；
　　蝻子吃盡而去。
¹⁷你的首領多如蝗蟲；
　　你的軍長彷彿成羣的螞蚱，
　　天涼的時候齊落在籬笆上，
　日頭一出便都飛去，
　　人不知道落在何處。

¹⁸亞述王啊，你的牧人睡覺，
　　你的貴冑安歇；
　你的人民散在山間，
　　無人招聚。
¹⁹你的損傷無法醫治，
　　你的傷痕極其重大；
　凡聽你信息的
　　必都因此向你拍掌。
　你所行的惡，
　　誰沒有時常遭遇呢？

哈巴谷書

Habakkuk

1
先知哈巴谷所得的默示。

1
The oracle that Habakkuk the prophet received.

哈巴谷的埋怨

2他說：耶和華啊，我呼求你，
　　你不應允，要到幾時呢？
我因強暴哀求你，
　　你還不拯救。
3你為何使我看見罪孽？
　　你為何看着奸惡而不理呢？
毀滅和強暴在我面前，
　　又起了爭端和相鬥的事。
4因此律法放鬆，
　　公理也不顯明；
惡人圍困義人，
　　所以公理顯然顛倒。

主的答覆

5耶和華說："你們要向列國中觀看，
　　大大驚奇；
因為在你們的時候，我行一件事，
　　雖有人告訴你們，
　　你們總是不信。
6我必興起迦勒底人，
　　就是那殘忍暴躁之民，
通行遍地，
　　佔據那不屬自己的住處。
7他威武可畏，
　　判斷和勢力
都任意發出。
8他的馬比豹更快，
　　比晚上的豺狼更猛。
馬兵踴躍爭先，
　　都從遠方而來；
他們飛跑如鷹抓食，
9都為行強暴而來，
　　定住臉面向前，
將擄掠的人聚集，多如塵沙。
10他們譏誚君王，
　　笑話首領，
嗤笑一切保障，
　　築壘攻取。
11他以自己的勢力為神，

Habakkuk's Complaint

2How long, O LORD, must I call for help,
　　but you do not listen?
Or cry out to you, "Violence!"
　　but you do not save?
3Why do you make me look at injustice?
　　Why do you tolerate wrong?
Destruction and violence are before me;
　　there is strife, and conflict abounds.
4Therefore the law is paralyzed,
　　and justice never prevails.
The wicked hem in the righteous,
　　so that justice is perverted.

The LORD's Answer

5"Look at the nations and watch—
　　and be utterly amazed.
For I am going to do something in your days
　　that you would not believe,
　　even if you were told.
6I am raising up the Babylonians,[a]
　　that ruthless and impetuous people,
who sweep across the whole earth
　　to seize dwelling places not their own.
7They are a feared and dreaded people;
　　they are a law to themselves
　　and promote their own honor.
8Their horses are swifter than leopards,
　　fiercer than wolves at dusk.
Their cavalry gallops headlong;
　　their horsemen come from afar.
They fly like a vulture swooping to devour;
9　they all come bent on violence.
Their hordes[b] advance like a desert wind
　　and gather prisoners like sand.
10They deride kings
　　and scoff at rulers.
They laugh at all fortified cities;
　　they build earthen ramps and capture them.
11Then they sweep past like the wind and go
　　on—

---

a 6 Or Chaldeans　　b 9 The meaning of the Hebrew for this
word is uncertain.

guilty men, whose own strength is their
    god."

Habakkuk's Second Complaint

¹²O LORD, are you not from everlasting?
    My God, my Holy One, we will not die.
  O LORD, you have appointed them to execute
    judgment;
  O Rock, you have ordained them to punish.
¹³Your eyes are too pure to look on evil;
    you cannot tolerate wrong.
  Why then do you tolerate the treacherous?
  Why are you silent while the wicked
  swallow up those more righteous than
    themselves?
¹⁴You have made men like fish in the sea,
    like sea creatures that have no ruler.
¹⁵The wicked foe pulls all of them up with hooks,
    he catches them in his net,
  he gathers them up in his dragnet;
    and so he rejoices and is glad.
¹⁶Therefore he sacrifices to his net
    and burns incense to his dragnet,
  for by his net he lives in luxury
    and enjoys the choicest food.
¹⁷Is he to keep on emptying his net,
    destroying nations without mercy?

2 I will stand at my watch
    and station myself on the ramparts;
  I will look to see what he will say to me,
  and what answer I am to give to this
    complaint.*a*

The LORD's Answer

²Then the LORD replied:

  "Write down the revelation
    and make it plain on tablets
  so that a herald*b* may run with it.
³For the revelation awaits an appointed time;
    it speaks of the end
    and will not prove false.
  Though it linger, wait for it;
    it*c* will certainly come and will not delay.

⁴"See, he is puffed up;
    his desires are not upright—
  but the righteous will live by his faith*d* —
⁵indeed, wine betrays him;
    he is arrogant and never at rest.
  Because he is as greedy as the grave*e*

---

*a 1 Or and what to answer when I am rebuked   b 2 Or so that
whoever reads it   c 3 Or Though he linger, wait for him; / he
d 4 Or faithfulness   e 5 Hebrew Sheol*

像風猛然掃過，
  顯為有罪。"

哈巴谷再次埋怨

¹²耶和華我的神、我的聖者啊！
  你不是從亙古而有嗎？
  我們必不致死。
  耶和華啊！你派定他為要刑罰人；
  磐石啊！你設立他為要懲治人。
¹³你眼目清潔不看邪僻，
  不看奸惡；
  行詭詐的，
  你為何看着不理呢？
  惡人吞滅比自己公義的，
  你為何靜默不語呢？
¹⁴你為何使人如海中的魚，
  又如沒有管轄的爬物呢？
¹⁵他用鈎鈎住，
  用網捕獲，
  用拉網聚集他們；
  因此，他歡喜快樂，
¹⁶就向網獻祭，
  向網燒香；
  因他由此得肥美的分
  和富裕的食物。
¹⁷他豈可屢次倒空網羅，
  將列國的人時常殺戮，
  毫不顧惜呢？

2 我要站在守望所，
    立在望樓上觀看，
  看耶和華對我說甚麼話，
  我可用甚麼話向他訴冤（註："向
    他訴冤"或作"回答所疑問的"）。

主的答覆

²他對我說：

  "將這默示明明地寫在版上，
    使讀的人容易讀（註：或作"隨跑隨
    讀"）。
³因為這默示有一定的日期，
    快要應驗，
    並不虛謊。
  雖然遲延，還要等候；
    因為必然臨到，不再遲延。

⁴"迦勒底人自高自大，
    心不正直；
  惟義人因信得生。
⁵迦勒底人因酒詭詐、
    狂傲，不住在家中，
    擴充心慾好像陰間。

他如死不能知足，
　聚集萬國，堆積萬民，
　都歸自己。

6 "這些國的民豈不都要題起詩
歌，並俗語譏刺他說：

　"'禍哉！迦勒底人，
　你增添不屬自己的財物，
　多多取人的當頭，
　要到幾時為止呢？'
7咬傷你的豈不忽然起來，
　擾害你的豈不興起，
　你就作他們的擄物嗎？
8因你搶奪許多的國，
　殺人流血，
　向國內的城並城中一切居民
　施行強暴，
　所以各國剩下的民都必搶奪你。

9 "為本家積蓄不義之財、
　在高處搭窩、
　指望免災的有禍了！
10你圖謀剪除多國的民，犯了罪，
　使你的家蒙羞，
　自害己命。
11牆裏的石頭必呼叫，
　房內的棟梁必應聲。

12 "以人血建城、
　以罪孽立邑的有禍了！
13眾民所勞碌得來的
　被火焚燒；
　列國由勞乏而得的
　歸於虛空，
　不都是出於萬軍之耶和華嗎？
14認識耶和華榮耀的知識，
　要充滿遍地，
　好像水充滿洋海一般。

15 "給人酒喝，
　又加上毒物，
　使他喝醉，
　好看見他下體的，
　有禍了！
16你滿受羞辱，不得榮耀，
　你也喝吧！顯出是未受割禮的。
　耶和華右手的杯
　必傳到你那裏，
　你的榮耀就變為大大的羞辱。
17你向黎巴嫩行強暴
　與殘害驚嚇野獸的事，

and like death is never satisfied,
　he gathers to himself all the nations
　and takes captive all the peoples.

6"Will not all of them taunt him with ridicule
and scorn, saying,

　" 'Woe to him who piles up stolen goods
　and makes himself wealthy by extortion!
　How long must this go on?'
7Will not your debtors[a] suddenly arise?
　Will they not wake up and make you
　　tremble?
　Then you will become their victim.
8Because you have plundered many nations,
　the peoples who are left will plunder you.
For you have shed man's blood;
　you have destroyed lands and cities and
　　everyone in them.

9"Woe to him who builds his realm by unjust
　　gain
　to set his nest on high,
　to escape the clutches of ruin!
10You have plotted the ruin of many peoples,
　shaming your own house and forfeiting your
　　life.
11The stones of the wall will cry out,
　and the beams of the woodwork will echo it.

12"Woe to him who builds a city with bloodshed
　and establishes a town by crime!
13Has not the LORD Almighty determined
　that the people's labor is only fuel for the
　　fire,
　that the nations exhaust themselves for
　　nothing?
14For the earth will be filled with the
　knowledge of the glory of the LORD,
　as the waters cover the sea.

15"Woe to him who gives drink to his
　　neighbors,
　pouring it from the wineskin till they are
　　drunk,
　so that he can gaze on their naked bodies.
16You will be filled with shame instead of glory.
　Now it is your turn! Drink and be exposed[b]!
　The cup from the LORD's right hand is coming
　　around to you,
　and disgrace will cover your glory.
17The violence you have done to Lebanon will
　　overwhelm you,

a 7 Or creditors   *b 16 Masoretic Text; Dead Sea Scrolls,
Aquila, Vulgate and Syriac (see also Septuagint) and stagger*

and your destruction of animals will terrify
　　you.
For you have shed man's blood;
　　you have destroyed lands and cities and
　　everyone in them.

18"Of what value is an idol, since a man has
　　carved it?
Or an image that teaches lies?
For he who makes it trusts in his own
　　creation;
he makes idols that cannot speak.
19Woe to him who says to wood, 'Come to life!'
Or to lifeless stone, 'Wake up!'
Can it give guidance?
It is covered with gold and silver;
　　there is no breath in it.
20But the LORD is in his holy temple;
　　let all the earth be silent before him."

Habakkuk's Prayer

3 A prayer of Habakkuk the prophet. On
　　shigionoth.[a]

2LORD, I have heard of your fame;
　　I stand in awe of your deeds, O LORD.
Renew them in our day,
　　in our time make them known;
　　in wrath remember mercy.

3God came from Teman,
　　the Holy One from Mount Paran.　　*Selah*[b]
His glory covered the heavens
　　and his praise filled the earth.
4His splendor was like the sunrise;
　　rays flashed from his hand,
　　where his power was hidden.
5Plague went before him;
　　pestilence followed his steps.
6He stood, and shook the earth;
　　he looked, and made the nations tremble.
The ancient mountains crumbled
　　and the age-old hills collapsed.
His ways are eternal.
7I saw the tents of Cushan in distress,
　　the dwellings of Midian in anguish.

8Were you angry with the rivers, O LORD?
　　Was your wrath against the streams?
Did you rage against the sea
　　when you rode with your horses
　　and your victorious chariots?

必遮蓋你；
因你殺人流血，
　　向國內的城並城中一切居民
　　施行強暴。

18　"雕刻的偶像，
　　人將它刻出來，
　　有甚麼益處呢？
　　鑄造的偶像，就是虛謊的師傅；
　　製造者倚靠這啞巴偶像
　　有甚麼益處呢？
19對木偶說：'醒起！'
　　對啞巴石像說：'起來！'
　　那人有禍了！
　　這個還能教訓人嗎？
　　看哪，是包裹金銀的，
　　其中毫無氣息。
20惟耶和華在他的聖殿中；
　　全地的人都當在他面前肅敬靜默。

哈巴谷的禱告

3 先知哈巴谷的禱告，
　　調用流離歌。

2耶和華啊，我聽見你的名聲（註："名
聲"或作"言語"）就懼怕。
耶和華啊，
　　求你在這些年間復興你的作為，
　　在這些年間顯明出來；
　　在發怒的時候以憐憫為念。
3神從提幔而來，
　　聖者從巴蘭山臨到。　　　　細拉
　　他的榮光遮蔽諸天，
　　頌讚充滿大地。
4他的輝煌如同日光；
　　從他手裏射出光線，
　　在其中藏着他的能力。
5在他前面有瘟疫流行，
　　在他腳下有熱症發出。
6他站立，
　　量了大地（註：或作"使地震動"）；
　　觀看，趕散萬民。
　　永久的山崩裂，長存的嶺塌陷，
　　他的作為與古時一樣。
7我見古珊的帳棚遭難，
　　米甸的幔子戰兢。

8耶和華啊，你乘在馬上，
　　坐在得勝的車上，
　　豈是不喜悅江河，
　　向江河發怒氣、
　　向洋海發憤恨嗎？

a 1 Probably a literary or musical term　　*b* 3 A word of
uncertain meaning; possibly a musical term; also in verses 9
and 13

9你的弓全然顯露，向眾支派
　　所起的誓都是可信的。　　　細拉
你以江河分開大地。
10山嶺見你，無不戰懼；
　　大水氾濫過去，
　　深淵發聲，洶湧翻騰（註：原文作
　　"向上舉手"）。

11因你的箭射出發光，
　　你的槍閃出光耀，
　　日月都在本宮停住。
12你發憤恨通行大地，
　　發怒氣責打列國，如同打糧。
13你出來要拯救你的百姓，
　　拯救你的受膏者，
　　打破惡人家長的頭，
　　露出他的腳（註："腳"原文作"根
　　基"），直到頸項。　　　細拉
14你用敵人的戈矛刺透他戰士的頭，
　　他們來如旋風，
　　要將我們分散，
　　他們所喜愛的是暗中吞吃貧民。
15你乘馬踐踏紅海，
　　就是踐踏洶湧的大水。

16我聽見耶和華的聲音，
　　身體戰兢，嘴唇發顫，
骨中朽爛；
　　我在所立之處戰兢。
　　我只可安靜等候災難之日臨到，
　　犯境之民上來。
17雖然無花果樹不發旺，
　　葡萄樹不結果，
橄欖樹也不效力，
　　田地不出糧食，
　　圈中絕了羊，
　　棚內也沒有牛；
18然而，我要因耶和華歡欣，
　　因救我的神喜樂。

19主耶和華是我的力量！
　　他使我的腳快如母鹿的蹄，
　　又使我穩行在高處。

這歌交與伶長，用絲弦的樂器。

9You uncovered your bow,
　　you called for many arrows.　　*Selah*
　　You split the earth with rivers;
10　the mountains saw you and writhed.
　　Torrents of water swept by;
　　the deep roared
　　and lifted its waves on high.

11Sun and moon stood still in the heavens
　　at the glint of your flying arrows,
　　at the lightning of your flashing spear.
12In wrath you strode through the earth
　　and in anger you threshed the nations.
13You came out to deliver your people,
　　to save your anointed one.
　　You crushed the leader of the land of
　　wickedness,
　　you stripped him from head to foot.　*Selah*
14With his own spear you pierced his head
　　when his warriors stormed out to scatter us,
　　gloating as though about to devour
　　the wretched who were in hiding.
15You trampled the sea with your horses,
　　churning the great waters.

16I heard and my heart pounded,
　　my lips quivered at the sound;
　　decay crept into my bones,
　　and my legs trembled.
　　Yet I will wait patiently for the day of calamity
　　to come on the nation invading us.
17Though the fig tree does not bud
　　and there are no grapes on the vines,
　　though the olive crop fails
　　and the fields produce no food,
　　though there are no sheep in the pen
　　and no cattle in the stalls,
18yet I will rejoice in the LORD,
　　I will be joyful in God my Savior.

19The Sovereign LORD is my strength;
　　he makes my feet like the feet of a deer,
　　he enables me to go on the heights.

For the director of music. On my stringed
instruments.

Zephaniah

西番雅書

1 The word of the LORD that came to Zephaniah son of Cushi, the son of Gedaliah, the son of Amariah, the son of Hezekiah, during the reign of Josiah son of Amon king of Judah:

Warning of Coming Destruction

2"I will sweep away everything
  from the face of the earth,"
                                    declares the LORD.
3"I will sweep away both men and animals;
  I will sweep away the birds of the air
  and the fish of the sea.
  The wicked will have only heaps of rubble[a]
  when I cut off man from the face of the
    earth,"
                                    declares the LORD.

Against Judah

4"I will stretch out my hand against Judah
  and against all who live in Jerusalem.
  I will cut off from this place every remnant of
    Baal,
  the names of the pagan and the idolatrous
    priests—
5those who bow down on the roofs
  to worship the starry host,
  those who bow down and swear by the LORD
  and who also swear by Molech,[b]
6those who turn back from following the LORD
  and neither seek the LORD nor inquire of
    him.
7Be silent before the Sovereign LORD,
  for the day of the LORD is near.
  The LORD has prepared a sacrifice;
  he has consecrated those he has invited.
8On the day of the LORD's sacrifice
  I will punish the princes
  and the king's sons
and all those clad
  in foreign clothes.
9On that day I will punish
  all who avoid stepping on the threshold,[c]
  who fill the temple of their gods

1 當猶大王亞們的兒子約西亞在位的時候，耶和華的話臨到希西家的玄孫、亞瑪利雅的曾孫、基大利的孫子、古示的兒子西番雅。

警告毀滅將臨

2耶和華說：
  "我必從地上除滅萬類。"

3 "我必除滅人和牲畜，
    與空中的鳥、
    海裏的魚，
  以及絆腳石和惡人；
  我必將人從地上剪除。"

                                    這是耶和華說的。

必攻擊猶大

4 "我必伸手攻擊猶大
    和耶路撒冷的一切居民，
  也必從這地方
    剪除所剩下的巴力，
  並基瑪林的名和祭司，

5與那些在房頂上
    敬拜天上萬象的，
  並那些敬拜耶和華指着他起誓，
    又指着瑪勒堪起誓的，
6與那些轉去不跟從耶和華的，
    和不尋求耶和華、
    也不訪問他的。
7你先要在主耶和華面前靜默無聲，
    因為耶和華的日子快到。
  耶和華已經預備祭物，
    將他的客分別為聖。
8到了我耶和華獻祭的日子，
    必懲罰首領和王子，
  並一切穿外邦衣服的。

9到那日，
  我必懲罰一切跳過門檻、
    將強暴和詭詐得來之物

a 3 The meaning of the Hebrew for this line is uncertain.
b 5 Hebrew Malcam, that is, Milcom   c 9 See 1 Samuel 5:5.

充滿主人房屋的。"

10耶和華說："當那日，
　　從魚門必發出悲哀的聲音，
　　從二城發出哀號的聲音，
　　從山間發出大破裂的響聲。
11瑪革提施的居民哪，你們要哀號！
　　因為迦南的商民都滅亡了；
　　凡搬運銀子的都被剪除。
12那時，
　　我必用燈巡查耶路撒冷，
　　我必懲罰那些如酒
　　在渣滓上澄清的。
　　他們心裏說：
　　'耶和華必不降福，也不降禍。'
13他們的財寶必成為掠物，
　　他們的房屋必變為荒場；
　　他們必建造房屋，
　　卻不得住在其內；
　　栽種葡萄園，
　　卻不得喝所出的酒。

主的大日子

14 "耶和華的大日臨近，
　　臨近而且甚快。
　　乃是耶和華日子的風聲，
　　勇士必痛痛地哭號。

15那日是忿怒的日子，
　　是急難困苦的日子，
　　是荒廢淒涼的日子，
　　是黑暗、幽冥、
　　密雲、烏黑的日子，
16是吹角吶喊的日子，
　　要攻擊堅固城
　　和高大的城樓。
17我必使災禍臨到人身上，
　　使他們行走如同瞎眼的，
　　因為得罪了我。
　　他們的血必倒出如灰塵；
　　他們的肉必拋棄如糞土。
18當耶和華發怒的日子，
　　他們的金銀
　　不能救他們。
　　他的忿怒如火，
　　必燒滅全地，
　　毀滅這地的一切居民，
　　而且大大毀滅。"

2 1、2不知羞恥的國民哪，
　　你們應當聚集！
　　趁命令沒有發出，
　　日子過去如風前的糠，
　　耶和華的烈怒未臨到你們，

with violence and deceit.

10"On that day," declares the LORD,
　　"a cry will go up from the Fish Gate,
　　wailing from the New Quarter,
　　and a loud crash from the hills.
11Wail, you who live in the market district[a];
　　all your merchants will be wiped out,
　　all who trade with[b] silver will be ruined.
12At that time I will search Jerusalem with
　　　lamps
　　and punish those who are complacent,
　　who are like wine left on its dregs,
　　who think, 'The LORD will do nothing,
　　either good or bad.'
13Their wealth will be plundered,
　　their houses demolished.
　　They will build houses
　　but not live in them;
　　they will plant vineyards
　　but not drink the wine.

The Great Day of the LORD

14"The great day of the LORD is near—
　　near and coming quickly.
　　Listen! The cry on the day of the LORD will be
　　　bitter,
　　the shouting of the warrior there.
15That day will be a day of wrath,
　　a day of distress and anguish,
　　a day of trouble and ruin,
　　a day of darkness and gloom,
　　a day of clouds and blackness,
16a day of trumpet and battle cry
　　against the fortified cities
　　and against the corner towers.
17I will bring distress on the people
　　and they will walk like blind men,
　　because they have sinned against the LORD.
　　Their blood will be poured out like dust
　　and their entrails like filth.
18Neither their silver nor their gold
　　will be able to save them
　　on the day of the LORD's wrath.
　　In the fire of his jealousy
　　the whole world will be consumed,
　　for he will make a sudden end
　　of all who live in the earth."

2 Gather together, gather together,
　　O shameful nation,
　　2before the appointed time arrives
　　and that day sweeps on like chaff,
　　before the fierce anger of the LORD comes

a 11 Or the Mortar　　b 11 Or in

upon you,
before the day of the LORD's wrath comes
upon you,

³Seek the LORD, all you humble of the land,
you who do what he commands.
Seek righteousness, seek humility;
perhaps you will be sheltered
on the day of the LORD's anger.

Against Philistia

⁴Gaza will be abandoned
and Ashkelon left in ruins.
At midday Ashdod will be emptied
and Ekron uprooted.
⁵Woe to you who live by the sea,
O Kerethite people;
the word of the LORD is against you,
O Canaan, land of the Philistines.

"I will destroy you,
and none will be left."

⁶The land by the sea, where the Kerethites^a
dwell,
will be a place for shepherds and sheep pens.
⁷It will belong to the remnant of the house of
Judah;
there they will find pasture.
In the evening they will lie down
in the houses of Ashkelon.
The LORD their God will care for them;
he will restore their fortunes.^b

Against Moab and Ammon

⁸"I have heard the insults of Moab
and the taunts of the Ammonites,
who insulted my people
and made threats against their land.
⁹Therefore, as surely as I live,"
declares the LORD Almighty, the God of
Israel,
"surely Moab will become like Sodom,
the Ammonites like Gomorrah—
a place of weeds and salt pits,
a wasteland forever.
The remnant of my people will plunder them;
the survivors of my nation will inherit their
land."

¹⁰This is what they will get in return for their
pride,
for insulting and mocking the people of the
LORD Almighty.

---

a 6 The meaning of the Hebrew for this word is uncertain.
b 7 Or *will bring back their captives*

他發怒的日子未到以先，
你們應當聚集前來。

³世上遵守耶和華典章的謙卑人哪，
你們都當尋求耶和華；
當尋求公義謙卑，
或者在耶和華發怒的日子
可以隱藏起來。

攻擊非利士

⁴迦薩必致見棄，
亞實基倫必然荒涼。
人在正午必趕出亞實突的民，
以革倫也被拔出根來。
⁵住沿海之地的基利提族有禍了！
迦南 非利士人之地啊，
耶和華的話與你反對，
說：

"我必毀滅你，
以致無人居住。"

⁶沿海之地要變為草場，
其上有牧人的住處
和羊羣的圈。
⁷這地必為猶大家剩下的人所得，
他們必在那裏牧放羣羊，
晚上必躺臥在
亞實基倫的房屋中；
因為耶和華他們的神
必眷顧他們，
使他們被擄的人歸回。

攻擊摩押與亞捫

⁸"我聽見摩押人的毀謗
和亞捫人的辱罵，
就是毀謗我的百姓，自誇自大，
侵犯他們的境界。"
⁹萬軍之耶和華以色列的神說：
我指着我的永生起誓：

"摩押必像所多瑪，
亞捫人必像蛾摩拉，
都變為刺草、鹽坑、
永遠荒廢之地。
我百姓所剩下的必擄掠他們；
我國中所餘剩的
必得着他們的地。"

¹⁰這事臨到他們是因他們驕傲，
自誇自大，
毀謗萬軍之耶和華的百姓。

11耶和華必向他們顯可畏之威；
　　因他必叫世上的諸神瘦弱，
　列國海島的居民
　　各在自己的地方敬拜他。

攻擊古實

12 "古實人哪，
　　你們必被我的刀所殺。"

攻擊亞述

13耶和華必伸手攻擊北方，
　　毀滅亞述，
　使尼尼微荒涼，
　　又乾旱如曠野。

14羣畜，
　　就是各國（註："國"或作"類"）的
　　　走獸必臥在其中，
　鵜鶘和箭豬要宿在柱頂上。
　在窗戶內有鳴叫的聲音；
　　門檻都已毀壞，
　香柏木已經露出。

15這是素來歡樂
　　安然居住的城，
　心裏說：
　　"惟有我，
　除我以外再沒有別的。"
　　現在何竟荒涼，
　成為野獸躺臥之處！
　凡經過的人都必搖手嗤笑他。

耶路撒冷的未來

3 這悖逆、污穢、
　　欺壓的城有禍了！
　2她不聽從命令，
　不領受訓誨，
　不倚靠耶和華，
　不親近她的神。

3她中間的首領是咆哮的獅子；
　　她的審判官是晚上的豺狼，
　一點食物也不留到早晨。

4她的先知是
　　虛浮詭詐的人；
　她的祭司褻瀆聖所，
　　強解律法。

5耶和華在她中間是公義的，
　　斷不做非義的事，
　每早晨顯明他的公義，
　　無日不然；
　只是不義的人不知羞恥。

6 "我耶和華已經除滅列國的民，
　　他們的城樓毀壞，
　我使他們的街道荒涼，
　　以致無人經過；

11The LORD will be awesome to them
　　when he destroys all the gods of the land.
　The nations on every shore will worship him,
　　every one in its own land.

Against Cush

12"You too, O Cushites,[a]
　　will be slain by my sword."

Against Assyria

13He will stretch out his hand against the north
　　and destroy Assyria,
　leaving Nineveh utterly desolate
　　and dry as the desert.
14Flocks and herds will lie down there,
　　creatures of every kind.
　The desert owl and the screech owl
　　will roost on her columns.
　Their calls will echo through the windows,
　　rubble will be in the doorways,
　　the beams of cedar will be exposed.
15This is the carefree city
　　that lived in safety.
　She said to herself,
　　"I am, and there is none besides me."
　What a ruin she has become,
　　a lair for wild beasts!
　All who pass by her scoff
　　and shake their fists.

The Future of Jerusalem

3 Woe to the city of oppressors,
　　rebellious and defiled!
　2She obeys no one,
　she accepts no correction.
　She does not trust in the LORD,
　　she does not draw near to her God.
3Her officials are roaring lions,
　　her rulers are evening wolves,
　who leave nothing for the morning.
4Her prophets are arrogant;
　　they are treacherous men.
　Her priests profane the sanctuary
　　and do violence to the law.
5The LORD within her is righteous;
　　he does no wrong.
　Morning by morning he dispenses his justice,
　　and every new day he does not fail,
　　yet the unrighteous know no shame.

6"I have cut off nations;
　　their strongholds are demolished.
　I have left their streets deserted,
　　with no one passing through.

a 12 That is, people from the upper Nile region

Their cities are destroyed;
  no one will be left—no one at all.
7I said to the city,
  'Surely you will fear me
  and accept correction!'
Then her dwelling would not be cut off,
  nor all my punishments come upon her.
But they were still eager
  to act corruptly in all they did.
8Therefore wait for me," declares the LORD,
  "for the day I will stand up to testify.[a]
I have decided to assemble the nations,
  to gather the kingdoms
and to pour out my wrath on them—
  all my fierce anger.
The whole world will be consumed
  by the fire of my jealous anger.

9"Then will I purify the lips of the peoples,
  that all of them may call on the name of the
    LORD
  and serve him shoulder to shoulder.
10From beyond the rivers of Cush[b]
  my worshipers, my scattered people,
  will bring me offerings.
11On that day you will not be put to shame
  for all the wrongs you have done to me,
because I will remove from this city
  those who rejoice in their pride.
Never again will you be haughty
  on my holy hill.
12But I will leave within you
  the meek and humble,
  who trust in the name of the LORD.
13The remnant of Israel will do no wrong;
  they will speak no lies,
  nor will deceit be found in their mouths.
They will eat and lie down
  and no one will make them afraid."

14Sing, O Daughter of Zion;
  shout aloud, O Israel!
Be glad and rejoice with all your heart,
  O Daughter of Jerusalem!
15The LORD has taken away your punishment,
  he has turned back your enemy.
The LORD, the King of Israel, is with you;
  never again will you fear any harm.
16On that day they will say to Jerusalem,
  "Do not fear, O Zion;
  do not let your hands hang limp.
17The LORD your God is with you,
  he is mighty to save.

a 8 Septuagint and Syriac; Hebrew will rise up to plunder
b 10 That is, the upper Nile region

他們的城邑毀滅，
  以致無人，也無居民。
7我說：
  你只要敬畏我，
  領受訓誨，
  如此，你的住處不致照我所擬定的
    除滅。
  只是你們從早起來，
  就在一切事上敗壞自己。"
8耶和華說："你們要等候我，
  直到我興起擄掠的日子。
因為我已定意招聚列國，
  聚集列邦，
將我的惱怒，就是我的烈怒，
  都傾在他們身上。
我的忿怒如火，
  必燒滅全地。

9"那時，
  我必使萬民用清潔的言語，
  好求告我耶和華的名，
  同心合意地侍奉我。
10祈禱我的，就是我所分散的民（註：
    原文作"女子"。下同），
  必從古實河外來，給我獻供物。
11當那日，
  你必不因你一切得罪我的事
  自覺羞愧；
  因為那時我必從你中間除掉
  矜誇高傲之輩，
  你也不再於我的聖山狂傲。
12我卻要在你中間
  留下困苦貧寒的民，
  他們必投靠我耶和華的名。
13以色列所剩下的人必不作罪孽，
  不說謊言，
  口中也沒有詭詐的舌頭；
  而且吃喝躺臥，
  無人驚嚇。"

14錫安的民哪，應當歌唱！
  以色列啊，應當歡呼！
耶路撒冷的民哪，
  應當滿心歡喜快樂！
15耶和華已經除去你的刑罰，
  趕出你的仇敵。
以色列的王耶和華在你中間，
  你必不再懼怕災禍。
16當那日，必有話向耶路撒冷說：
  "不要懼怕！
  錫安哪，不要手軟！
17耶和華你的神是施行拯救、
  大有能力的主！

他在你中間必因你歡欣喜樂，
　　默然愛你，
　　且因你喜樂而歡呼。"

18 "那些屬你、為無大會愁煩、
　　因你擔當羞辱的，
　　我必聚集他們。
19那時，
　　我必罰辦一切苦待你的人，
　　又拯救你瘸腿的，
　　聚集你被趕出的。
　　那些在全地受羞辱的，
　　我必使他們得稱讚，有名聲。
20那時，
　　我必領你們進來，聚集你們。
　　我使你們被擄之人歸回的時候，
　　就必使你們在地上的萬民中
　　有名聲，得稱讚。"

　　　　　　　　這是耶和華說的。

He will take great delight in you,
　　he will quiet you with his love,
　　he will rejoice over you with singing."
18"The sorrows for the appointed feasts
　　I will remove from you;
　　they are a burden and a reproach to you.*a*
19At that time I will deal
　　with all who oppressed you;
　I will rescue the lame
　　and gather those who have been scattered.
　I will give them praise and honor
　　in every land where they were put to shame.
20At that time I will gather you;
　　at that time I will bring you home.
　I will give you honor and praise
　　among all the peoples of the earth
　when I restore your fortunes*b*
　　before your very eyes,"
　　　　　　　　　　　　　says the LORD.

---

*a 18 Or "I will gather you who mourn for the appointed feasts;
/ your reproach is a burden to you　b 20 Or I bring back your
captives*

Haggai

哈該書

A Call to Build the House of the LORD

1 In the second year of King Darius, on the first day of the sixth month, the word of the LORD came through the prophet Haggai to Zerubbabel son of Shealtiel, governor of Judah, and to Joshua[a] son of Jehozadak, the high priest:

[2] This is what the LORD Almighty says: "These people say, 'The time has not yet come for the LORD's house to be built.' "

[3] Then the word of the LORD came through the prophet Haggai: [4]"Is it a time for you yourselves to be living in your paneled houses, while this house remains a ruin?"

[5] Now this is what the LORD Almighty says: "Give careful thought to your ways. [6]You have planted much, but have harvested little. You eat, but never have enough. You drink, but never have your fill. You put on clothes, but are not warm. You earn wages, only to put them in a purse with holes in it."

[7] This is what the LORD Almighty says: "Give careful thought to your ways. [8]Go up into the mountains and bring down timber and build the house, so that I may take pleasure in it and be honored," says the LORD. [9]"You expected much, but see, it turned out to be little. What you brought home, I blew away. Why?" declares the LORD Almighty. "Because of my house, which remains a ruin, while each of you is busy with his own house. [10]Therefore, because of you the heavens have withheld their dew and the earth its crops. [11]I called for a drought on the fields and the mountains, on the grain, the new wine, the oil and whatever the ground produces, on men and cattle, and on the labor of your hands."

[12] Then Zerubbabel son of Shealtiel, Joshua son of Jehozadak, the high priest, and the whole remnant of the people obeyed the voice of the LORD their God and the message of the prophet Haggai, because the LORD their God had sent him. And the people feared the LORD. [13]Then Haggai, the LORD's messenger, gave this message of the LORD to the people: "I am with you," declares the LORD. [14]So the LORD

建造主殿的呼召

1 大利烏王第二年六月初一日，耶和華的話藉先知哈該，向猶大省長撒拉鐵的兒子所羅巴伯，和約撒答的兒子大祭司約書亞說：

[2] 萬軍之耶和華如此說："這百姓說，'建造耶和華殿的時候尚未來到。' "

[3] 那時耶和華的話臨到先知哈該說：[4] "這殿仍然荒涼，你們自己還住天花板的房屋嗎？"

[5] 現在萬軍之耶和華如此說："你們要省察自己的行為。[6]你們撒的種多，收的卻少；你們吃，卻不得飽；喝，卻不得足；穿衣服，卻不得暖；得工錢的，將工錢裝在破漏的囊中。"

[7] 萬軍之耶和華如此說："你們要省察自己的行為。[8]你們要上山取木料建造這殿，我就因此喜樂，且得榮耀。"這是耶和華說的。[9] "你們盼望多得，所得的卻少；你們收到家中，我就吹去。這是為甚麼呢？因為我的殿荒涼，你們各人卻顧（註："顧"原文作"奔"）自己的房屋。"這是萬軍之耶和華說的。[10] "所以為你們的緣故，天就不降甘露，地也不出土產。[11]我命乾旱臨到地土、山岡、五穀、新酒和油，並地上的出產、人民、牲畜，以及人手一切勞碌得來的。"

[12] 那時，撒拉鐵的兒子所羅巴伯和約撒答的兒子大祭司約書亞，並剩下的百姓，都聽從耶和華他們神的話，和先知哈該奉耶和華他們神差來所說的話；百姓也在耶和華面前存敬畏的心。[13]耶和華的使者哈該奉耶和華差遣對百姓說："耶和華說：我與你們同在。"[14]耶和華激動猶大省長撒拉

---

a 1 A variant of *Jeshua*; here and elsewhere in Haggai

鐵的兒子<u>所羅巴伯</u>和<u>約撒答</u>的兒子大祭司<u>約書亞</u>，並剩下之百姓的心，他們就來為萬軍之耶和華他們神的殿做工。¹⁵這是在<u>大利烏</u>王第二年六月二十四日。

應許新殿的榮耀

2 七月二十一日，耶和華的話臨到先知哈該說：²"你要曉諭<u>猶大</u>省長撒拉鐵的兒子<u>所羅巴伯</u>和<u>約撒答</u>的兒子大祭司<u>約書亞</u>，並剩下的百姓，說：³'你們中間存留的，有誰見過這殿從前的榮耀呢？現在你們看着如何？豈不在眼中看如無有嗎？'⁴耶和華說：'<u>所羅巴伯</u>啊，雖然如此，你當剛強！你當剛強！這地的百姓，你們都當剛強做工，因為我與你們同在。'這是萬軍之耶和華說的。⁵'這是照着你們出<u>埃及</u>我與你們立約的話。那時，我的靈住在你們中間，你們不要懼怕。'

⁶"萬軍之耶和華如此說：'過不多時，我必再一次震動天地、滄海與旱地。⁷我必震動萬國，萬國的珍寶必都運來（註：或作"萬國所羨慕的必來到"），我就使這殿滿了榮耀。'這是萬軍之耶和華說的。⁸萬軍之耶和華說：'銀子是我的，金子也是我的。⁹這殿後來的榮耀必大過先前的榮耀。在這地方我必賜平安。'這是萬軍之耶和華說的。"

給污穢的子民祝福

¹⁰<u>大利烏</u>王第二年九月二十四日，耶和華的話臨到先知<u>哈該</u>說：¹¹"萬軍之耶和華如此說：'你要向祭司問律法說：¹²若有人用衣襟兜聖肉，這衣襟挨着餅，或湯，或酒，或油，或別的食物，便算為聖嗎？'"

祭司說："不算為聖。"
¹³<u>哈該</u>又說："若有人因摸死屍染了污穢，然後挨着這些物的哪一樣，這物算污穢嗎？"

祭司說："必算污穢。"

¹⁴於是<u>哈該</u>說："耶和華說：'這民這國，在我面前也是如此；他們手下的各樣工作都是如此；他

stirred up the spirit of Zerubbabel son of Shealtiel, governor of Judah, and the spirit of Joshua son of Jehozadak, the high priest, and the spirit of the whole remnant of the people. They came and began to work on the house of the LORD Almighty, their God, ¹⁵on the twenty-fourth day of the sixth month in the second year of King Darius.

The Promised Glory of the New House

2 On the twenty-first day of the seventh month, the word of the LORD came through the prophet Haggai: ²"Speak to Zerubbabel son of Shealtiel, governor of Judah, to Joshua son of Jehozadak, the high priest, and to the remnant of the people. Ask them, ³'Who of you is left who saw this house in its former glory? How does it look to you now? Does it not seem to you like nothing? ⁴But now be strong, O Zerubbabel,' declares the LORD. 'Be strong, O Joshua son of Jehozadak, the high priest. Be strong, all you people of the land,' declares the LORD, 'and work. For I am with you,' declares the LORD Almighty. ⁵'This is what I covenanted with you when you came out of Egypt. And my Spirit remains among you. Do not fear.'

⁶"This is what the LORD Almighty says: 'In a little while I will once more shake the heavens and the earth, the sea and the dry land. ⁷I will shake all nations, and the desired of all nations will come, and I will fill this house with glory,' says the LORD Almighty. ⁸'The silver is mine and the gold is mine,' declares the LORD Almighty. ⁹'The glory of this present house will be greater than the glory of the former house,' says the LORD Almighty. 'And in this place I will grant peace,' declares the LORD Almighty."

Blessings for a Defiled People

¹⁰On the twenty-fourth day of the ninth month, in the second year of Darius, the word of the LORD came to the prophet Haggai: ¹¹"This is what the LORD Almighty says: 'Ask the priests what the law says: ¹²If a person carries consecrated meat in the fold of his garment, and that fold touches some bread or stew, some wine, oil or other food, does it become consecrated?' "

The priests answered, "No."

¹³Then Haggai said, "If a person defiled by contact with a dead body touches one of these things, does it become defiled?"

"Yes," the priests replied, "it becomes defiled."

¹⁴Then Haggai said, " 'So it is with this people and this nation in my sight,' declares the LORD. 'Whatever they do and whatever they

offer there is defiled.

15" 'Now give careful thought to this from this day on[a]—consider how things were before one stone was laid on another in the LORD's temple. ¹⁶When anyone came to a heap of twenty measures, there were only ten. When anyone went to a wine vat to draw fifty measures, there were only twenty. ¹⁷I struck all the work of your hands with blight, mildew and hail, yet you did not turn to me,' declares the LORD. ¹⁸'From this day on, from this twenty-fourth day of the ninth month, give careful thought to the day when the foundation of the LORD's temple was laid. Give careful thought: ¹⁹Is there yet any seed left in the barn? Until now, the vine and the fig tree, the pomegranate and the olive tree have not borne fruit.

" 'From this day on I will bless you.' "

Zerubbabel the LORD's Signet Ring

²⁰The word of the LORD came to Haggai a second time on the twenty-fourth day of the month: ²¹"Tell Zerubbabel governor of Judah that I will shake the heavens and the earth. ²²I will overturn royal thrones and shatter the power of the foreign kingdoms. I will overthrow chariots and their drivers; horses and their riders will fall, each by the sword of his brother.

²³" 'On that day,' declares the LORD Almighty, 'I will take you, my servant Zerubbabel son of Shealtiel,' declares the LORD, 'and I will make you like my signet ring, for I have chosen you,' declares the LORD Almighty."

們在壇上所獻的也是如此。

¹⁵ " ' 現在你們要追想此日以前,耶和華的殿尚沒有一塊石頭疊在石頭上的光景。¹⁶在那一切日子,有人來到穀堆,想得二十斗,只得了十斗;有人來到酒池,想得五十桶,只得了二十桶。¹⁷在你們手下的各樣工作上,我以旱風、霉爛、冰雹攻擊你們,你們仍不歸向我。' 這是耶和華說的。¹⁸ '你們要追想此日以前,就是從這九月二十四日起,追想到立耶和華殿根基的日子。¹⁹倉裏有穀種嗎?葡萄樹、無花果樹、石榴樹、橄欖樹都沒有結果子。

" '從今日起,我必賜福與你們。' "

所羅巴伯為主的印

²⁰這月二十四日,耶和華的話二次臨到哈該說:²¹ "你要告訴猶大省長所羅巴伯說:我必震動天地;²²我必傾覆列國的寶座,除滅列邦的勢力,並傾覆戰車和坐在其上的。馬必跌倒,騎馬的敗落,各人被弟兄的刀所殺。

²³ " '萬軍之耶和華說:'我僕人撒拉鐵的兒子所羅巴伯啊,到那日,我必以你為印,因我揀選了你。' 這是萬軍之耶和華說的。' "

撒迦利亞書

呼籲百姓歸向主

1 大利烏王第二年八月，耶和華的話臨到易多的孫子、比利家的兒子先知撒迦利亞，說：

2 "耶和華曾向你們列祖大大發怒。3 所以你要對以色列人說：萬軍之耶和華如此說：'你們要轉向我，我就轉向你們。'這是萬軍之耶和華說的。4 不要效法你們列祖。從前的先知呼叫他們說：萬軍之耶和華如此說：'你們要回頭離開你們的惡道惡行！他們卻不聽，也不順從我。'這是耶和華說的。5 你們的列祖在哪裏呢？那些先知能永遠存活嗎？6 只是我的言語和律例，就是所吩咐我僕人眾先知的，豈不臨到你們列祖嗎？

"他們就回頭，說：'萬軍之耶和華定意按我們的行動作為向我們怎樣行，他已照樣行了。'"

站在番石榴樹中間的人

7 大利烏第二年十一月，就是細罷特月二十四日，耶和華的話臨到易多的孫子、比利家的兒子先知撒迦利亞，說：

8 "我夜間觀看，見一人騎着紅馬，站在窪地番石榴樹中間。在他身後，又有紅馬、黃馬和白馬。"

9 我對與我說話的天使說："主啊，這是甚麼意思？"

他說："我要指示你這是甚麼意思。"

10 那站在番石榴樹中間的人說："這是奉耶和華差遣，在遍地來來走去的。"

11 那些騎馬的對站在番石榴樹中間耶和華的使者說："我們已在遍地走來走去，見全地都安息平靜。"

12 於是，耶和華的使者說："萬軍之耶和華啊，你惱恨耶路撒冷和猶大的城邑已經七十年，你不施憐憫要到幾時呢？"13 耶和華就用美善

Zechariah

A Call to Return to the LORD

1 In the eighth month of the second year of Darius, the word of the LORD came to the prophet Zechariah son of Berekiah, the son of Iddo:

2 "The LORD was very angry with your forefathers. 3 Therefore tell the people: This is what the LORD Almighty says: 'Return to me,' declares the LORD Almighty, 'and I will return to you,' says the LORD Almighty. 4 Do not be like your forefathers, to whom the earlier prophets proclaimed: This is what the LORD Almighty says: 'Turn from your evil ways and your evil practices.' But they would not listen or pay attention to me, declares the LORD. 5 Where are your forefathers now? And the prophets, do they live forever? 6 But did not my words and my decrees, which I commanded my servants the prophets, overtake your forefathers?

"Then they repented and said, 'The LORD Almighty has done to us what our ways and practices deserve, just as he determined to do.'"

The Man Among the Myrtle Trees

7 On the twenty-fourth day of the eleventh month, the month of Shebat, in the second year of Darius, the word of the LORD came to the prophet Zechariah son of Berekiah, the son of Iddo.

8 During the night I had a vision—and there before me was a man riding a red horse! He was standing among the myrtle trees in a ravine. Behind him were red, brown and white horses.

9 I asked, "What are these, my lord?"

The angel who was talking with me answered, "I will show you what they are."

10 Then the man standing among the myrtle trees explained, "They are the ones the LORD has sent to go throughout the earth."

11 And they reported to the angel of the LORD, who was standing among the myrtle trees, "We have gone throughout the earth and found the whole world at rest and in peace."

12 Then the angel of the LORD said, "LORD Almighty, how long will you withhold mercy from Jerusalem and from the towns of Judah, which you have been angry with these seventy years?" 13 So the LORD spoke kind and comfort-

ing words to the angel who talked with me.

¹⁴Then the angel who was speaking to me said, "Proclaim this word: This is what the LORD Almighty says: 'I am very jealous for Jerusalem and Zion, ¹⁵but I am very angry with the nations that feel secure. I was only a little angry, but they added to the calamity.'

¹⁶"Therefore, this is what the LORD says: 'I will return to Jerusalem with mercy, and there my house will be rebuilt. And the measuring line will be stretched out over Jerusalem,' declares the LORD Almighty.

¹⁷"Proclaim further: This is what the LORD Almighty says: 'My towns will again overflow with prosperity, and the LORD will again comfort Zion and choose Jerusalem.' "

Four Horns and Four Craftsmen

¹⁸Then I looked up—and there before me were four horns! ¹⁹I asked the angel who was speaking to me, "What are these?"

He answered me, "These are the horns that scattered Judah, Israel and Jerusalem."

²⁰Then the LORD showed me four craftsmen. ²¹I asked, "What are these coming to do?"

He answered, "These are the horns that scattered Judah so that no one could raise his head, but the craftsmen have come to terrify them and throw down these horns of the nations who lifted up their horns against the land of Judah to scatter its people."

A Man With a Measuring Line

2 Then I looked up—and there before me was a man with a measuring line in his hand! ²I asked, "Where are you going?"

He answered me, "To measure Jerusalem, to find out how wide and how long it is."

³Then the angel who was speaking to me left, and another angel came to meet him ⁴and said to him: "Run, tell that young man, 'Jerusalem will be a city without walls because of the great number of men and livestock in it. ⁵And I myself will be a wall of fire around it,' declares the LORD, 'and I will be its glory within.'

⁶"Come! Come! Flee from the land of the north," declares the LORD, "for I have scattered you to the four winds of heaven," declares the LORD.

⁷"Come, O Zion! Escape, you who live in the Daughter of Babylon!" ⁸For this is what the LORD Almighty says: "After he has honored me and has sent me against the nations that have plundered you—for whoever touches you touches the apple of his eye— ⁹I will surely raise my hand against them so that their slaves will

的安慰話回答那與我說話的天使。

¹⁴與我說話的天使對我說："你要宣告說：萬軍之耶和華如此說：'我為耶路撒冷、為錫安，心裏極其火熱。¹⁵我甚惱怒那安逸的列國。因我從前稍微惱怒我民，他們就加害過分。'

¹⁶ "所以耶和華如此說：'現今我回到耶路撒冷，仍施憐憫。我的殿必重建在其中，準繩必拉在耶路撒冷之上。'這是萬軍之耶和華說的。

¹⁷ "你要再宣告說：萬軍之耶和華如此說：'我的城邑必再豐盛發達。耶和華必再安慰錫安，揀選耶路撒冷。'"

四角與四匠人

¹⁸我舉目觀看，見有四角。¹⁹我就問與我說話的天使說："這是甚麼意思？"

他回答說："這是打散猶大、以色列和耶路撒冷的角。"

²⁰耶和華又指四個匠人給我看。²¹我說："他們來做甚麼呢？"

他說："這是打散猶大的角，使人不敢抬頭；但這些匠人來威嚇列國，打掉他們的角，就是舉起打散猶大地的角。"

拿準繩的人

2 我又舉目觀看，見一人手拿準繩。²我說："你往哪裏去？"

他對我說："要去量耶路撒冷，看有多寬、多長。"

³與我說話的天使去的時候，又有一位天使迎着他來，⁴對他說："你跑去告訴那少年人，說：'耶路撒冷必有人居住，好像無城牆的鄉村，因為人民和牲畜甚多。⁵耶和華說：我要作耶路撒冷四圍的火城，並要作其中的榮耀。'"

⁶耶和華說："我從前分散你們在天的四方（註：原文作"猶如天的四風"），現在你們要從北方之地逃回。"這是耶和華說的。

⁷與巴比倫人同住的錫安民哪，應當逃脫。⁸萬軍之耶和華說："在顯出榮耀之後，差遣我去懲罰那擄掠你們的列國，摸你們的，就是摸他眼中的瞳人。⁹看哪，我（註：或作"他"）要向他們掄手，他們就必作服

侍他們之人的擄物，你們便知道萬軍之耶和華差遣我了。

10 "錫安城啊，應當歡樂歌唱，因為我來要住在你中間。這是耶和華說的。" 11 那時，必有許多國歸附耶和華，作他（註：原文作 "我"）的子民。他（註：原文作 "我"）要住在你中間，你就知道萬軍之耶和華差遣我到你那裏去了。12 耶和華必收回猶大作他聖地的分，也必再揀選耶路撒冷。13 凡有血氣的都當在耶和華面前靜默無聲。因為他興起，從聖所出來了。"

潔淨大祭司的衣服

3 天使（註：原文作 "他"）又指給我看，大祭司約書亞站在耶和華的使者面前，撒但也站在約書亞的右邊，與他作對。2 耶和華向撒但說："撒但哪，耶和華責備你，就是揀選耶路撒冷的耶和華責備你，這不是從火中抽出來的一根柴嗎？"

3 約書亞穿着污穢的衣服，站在使者面前。4 使者吩咐站在面前的說："你們要脫去他污穢的衣服。"又對約書亞說："我使你脫離罪孽，要給你穿上華美的衣服。"

5 我說："要將潔淨的冠冕戴在他頭上。"他們就把潔淨的冠冕戴在他頭上，給他穿上華美的衣服，耶和華的使者在旁邊站立。

6 耶和華的使者告誡約書亞說：7 "萬軍之耶和華如此說：'你若遵行我的道，謹守我的命令，你就可以管理我的家，看守我的院宇；我也要使你在這些站立的人中間來往。

8 " '大祭司約書亞啊，你和坐在你面前的同伴都當聽（他們是作預兆的）。我必使我僕人大衛的苗裔發出。9 看哪，我在約書亞面前所立的石頭，在一塊石頭上有七眼。'萬軍之耶和華說：'我要親自雕刻這石頭，並要在一日之間除掉這地的罪孽。

10 " '當那日，你們各人要請鄰舍坐在葡萄樹和無花果樹下。'這是萬軍之耶和華說的。"

---

plunder them.[a] Then you will know that the LORD Almighty has sent me.

10 "Shout and be glad, O Daughter of Zion. For I am coming, and I will live among you," declares the LORD. 11 "Many nations will be joined with the LORD in that day and will become my people. I will live among you and you will know that the LORD Almighty has sent me to you. 12 The LORD will inherit Judah as his portion in the holy land and will again choose Jerusalem. 13 Be still before the LORD, all mankind, because he has roused himself from his holy dwelling."

Clean Garments for the High Priest

3 Then he showed me Joshua[b] the high priest standing before the angel of the LORD, and Satan[c] standing at his right side to accuse him. 2 The LORD said to Satan, "The LORD rebuke you, Satan! The LORD, who has chosen Jerusalem, rebuke you! Is not this man a burning stick snatched from the fire?"

3 Now Joshua was dressed in filthy clothes as he stood before the angel. 4 The angel said to those who were standing before him, "Take off his filthy clothes."

Then he said to Joshua, "See, I have taken away your sin, and I will put rich garments on you."

5 Then I said, "Put a clean turban on his head." So they put a clean turban on his head and clothed him, while the angel of the LORD stood by.

6 The angel of the LORD gave this charge to Joshua: 7 "This is what the LORD Almighty says: 'If you will walk in my ways and keep my requirements, then you will govern my house and have charge of my courts, and I will give you a place among these standing here.

8 " 'Listen, O high priest Joshua and your associates seated before you, who are men symbolic of things to come: I am going to bring my servant, the Branch. 9 See, the stone I have set in front of Joshua! There are seven eyes[d] on that one stone, and I will engrave an inscription on it,' says the LORD Almighty, 'and I will remove the sin of this land in a single day.

10 " 'In that day each of you will invite his neighbor to sit under his vine and fig tree,' declares the LORD Almighty."

---

a 8,9 Or says after . . . eye: 9 "I . . . plunder them."　　b 1 A variant of Jeshua; here and elsewhere in Zechariah　　c 1 Satan means accuser.　　d 9 Or facets

The Gold Lampstand and the Two Olive Trees

4 Then the angel who talked with me returned and wakened me, as a man is wakened from his sleep. ²He asked me, "What do you see?"

I answered, "I see a solid gold lampstand with a bowl at the top and seven lights on it, with seven channels to the lights. ³Also there are two olive trees by it, one on the right of the bowl and the other on its left."

⁴I asked the angel who talked with me, "What are these, my lord?"

⁵He answered, "Do you not know what these are?"

"No, my lord," I replied.

⁶So he said to me, "This is the word of the LORD to Zerubbabel: 'Not by might nor by power, but by my Spirit,' says the LORD Almighty.

⁷"What*ᵃ* are you, O mighty mountain? Before Zerubbabel you will become level ground. Then he will bring out the capstone to shouts of 'God bless it! God bless it!'"

⁸Then the word of the LORD came to me: ⁹"The hands of Zerubbabel have laid the foundation of this temple; his hands will also complete it. Then you will know that the LORD Almighty has sent me to you.

¹⁰"Who despises the day of small things? Men will rejoice when they see the plumb line in the hand of Zerubbabel.

"(These seven are the eyes of the LORD, which range throughout the earth.)"

¹¹Then I asked the angel, "What are these two olive trees on the right and the left of the lampstand?"

¹²Again I asked him, "What are these two olive branches beside the two gold pipes that pour out golden oil?"

¹³He replied, "Do you not know what these are?"

"No, my lord," I said.

¹⁴So he said, "These are the two who are anointed to*ᵇ* serve the Lord of all the earth."

The Flying Scroll

5 I looked again—and there before me was a flying scroll!

²He asked me, "What do you see?"

I answered, "I see a flying scroll, thirty feet long and fifteen feet wide.*ᶜ*"

金燈臺與兩棵橄欖樹

4 那與我說話的天使又來叫醒我，好像人睡覺被喚醒一樣。²他問我說："你看見了甚麼？"

我說："我看見了一個純金的燈臺，頂上有燈盞，燈臺上有七盞燈，每盞有七個管子。³旁邊有兩棵橄欖樹，一棵在燈盞的右邊，一棵在燈盞的左邊。"

⁴我問與我說話的天使說："主啊，這是甚麼意思？"

⁵與我說話的天使回答我說："你不知道這是甚麼意思嗎？"

我說："主啊，我不知道。"

⁶他對我說："這是耶和華指示所羅巴伯的。萬軍之耶和華說：'不是倚靠勢力，不是倚靠才能，乃是倚靠我的靈方能成事。'

⁷"大山哪，你算甚麼呢？在所羅巴伯面前，你必成為平地。他必搬出一塊石頭，安在殿頂上。人且大聲歡呼說：'願恩惠恩惠歸與這殿（註："殿"或作"石"）！'"

⁸耶和華的話又臨到我說：⁹"所羅巴伯的手立了這殿的根基，他的手也必完成這工。你就知道萬軍之耶和華差遣我到你們這裏來了。

¹⁰"誰藐視這日的事為小呢？這七眼乃是耶和華的眼睛，遍察全地，見所羅巴伯手拿線鉈就歡喜。"

¹¹我又問天使說："這燈臺左右的兩棵橄欖樹是甚麼意思？"

¹²我二次問他說："這兩根橄欖枝在兩個流出金色油的金嘴旁邊是甚麼意思？"

¹³他對我說："你不知道這是甚麼意思嗎？"

我說："主啊，我不知道。"

¹⁴他說："這是兩個受膏者，站在普天下主的旁邊。"

飛行的書卷

5 我又舉目觀看，見有一飛行的書卷。

²他問我說："你看見甚麼？"

我回答說："我看見一飛行的書卷，長二十肘，寬十肘。"

---

a 7 Or *Who　b 14* Or *two who bring oil and　c 2* Hebrew *twenty cubits long and ten cubits wide* (about 9 meters long and 4.5 meters wide)

³他對我說：「這是發出行在遍地上的咒詛。凡偷竊的，必按卷上這面的話除滅；凡起假誓的，必按卷上那面的話除滅。⁴萬軍之耶和華說：『我必使這書卷出去，進入偷竊人的家和指我名起假誓人的家，必常在他家裏，連房屋帶木石都毀滅了。』」

量器中的婦人

⁵與我說話的天使出來，對我說：「你要舉目觀看，見所出來的是甚麼？」

⁶我說：「這是甚麼呢？」

他說：「這出來的是量器。」他又說：「這是惡人在遍地的形狀。」

⁷（我見有一片圓鉛被舉起來。）這坐在量器中的是個婦人。⁸天使說：「這是罪惡。」他就把婦人扔在量器中，將那片圓鉛扔在量器的口上。

⁹我又舉目觀看，見有兩個婦人出來，在她們翅膀中有風，飛得甚快，翅膀如同鸛鳥的翅膀。她們將量器抬起來，懸在天地中間。

¹⁰我問與我說話的天使說：「她們要將量器抬到哪裏去呢？」

¹¹他對我說：「要往示拿地去，為它蓋造房屋。等房屋齊備，就把它安置在自己的地方。」

四輛車

6

我又舉目觀看，見有四輛車從兩山中間出來，那山是銅山。²第一輛車套着紅馬，第二輛車套着黑馬，³第三輛車套着白馬，第四輛車套着有斑點的壯馬。⁴我就問與我說話的天使說：「主啊，這是甚麼意思？」

⁵天使回答我說：「這是天的四風，是從普天下的主面前出來的。⁶套着黑馬的車往北方去，白馬跟隨在後；有斑點的馬往南方去。」

⁷壯馬出來，要在遍地走來走去。天使說：「你們只管在遍地走來走去。」牠們就照樣行了。

³And he said to me, "This is the curse that is going out over the whole land; for according to what it says on one side, every thief will be banished, and according to what it says on the other, everyone who swears falsely will be banished. ⁴The Lord Almighty declares, 'I will send it out, and it will enter the house of the thief and the house of him who swears falsely by my name. It will remain in his house and destroy it, both its timbers and its stones.'"

The Woman in a Basket

⁵Then the angel who was speaking to me came forward and said to me, "Look up and see what this is that is appearing."

⁶I asked, "What is it?"

He replied, "It is a measuring basket.ᵃ" And he added, "This is the iniquityᵇ of the people throughout the land."

⁷Then the cover of lead was raised, and there in the basket sat a woman! ⁸He said, "This is wickedness," and he pushed her back into the basket and pushed the lead cover down over its mouth.

⁹Then I looked up—and there before me were two women, with the wind in their wings! They had wings like those of a stork, and they lifted up the basket between heaven and earth.

¹⁰"Where are they taking the basket?" I asked the angel who was speaking to me.

¹¹He replied, "To the country of Babyloniaᶜ to build a house for it. When it is ready, the basket will be set there in its place."

Four Chariots

6

I looked up again—and there before me were four chariots coming out from between two mountains—mountains of bronze! ²The first chariot had red horses, the second black, ³the third white, and the fourth dappled—all of them powerful. ⁴I asked the angel who was speaking to me, "What are these, my lord?"

⁵The angel answered me, "These are the four spiritsᵈ of heaven, going out from standing in the presence of the Lord of the whole world. ⁶The one with the black horses is going toward the north country, the one with the white horses toward the west,ᵉ and the one with the dappled horses toward the south."

⁷When the powerful horses went out, they were straining to go throughout the earth. And he said, "Go throughout the earth!" So they went throughout the earth.

---

a 6 Hebrew an ephah; also in verses 7-11　b 6 Or appearance
c 11 Hebrew Shinar　d 5 Or winds　e 6 Or horses after them

8Then he called to me, "Look, those going toward the north country have given my Spirit[a] rest in the land of the north."

A Crown for Joshua

9The word of the LORD came to me: 10"Take ⌊silver and gold⌋ from the exiles Heldai, Tobijah and Jedaiah, who have arrived from Babylon. Go the same day to the house of Josiah son of Zephaniah. 11Take the silver and gold and make a crown, and set it on the head of the high priest, Joshua son of Jehozadak. 12Tell him this is what the LORD Almighty says: 'Here is the man whose name is the Branch, and he will branch out from his place and build the temple of the LORD. 13It is he who will build the temple of the LORD, and he will be clothed with majesty and will sit and rule on his throne. And he will be a priest on his throne. And there will be harmony between the two.' 14The crown will be given to Heldai,[b] Tobijah, Jedaiah and Hen[c] son of Zephaniah as a memorial in the temple of the LORD. 15Those who are far away will come and help to build the temple of the LORD, and you will know that the LORD Almighty has sent me to you. This will happen if you diligently obey the LORD your God."

Justice and Mercy, Not Fasting

7 In the fourth year of King Darius, the word of the LORD came to Zechariah on the fourth day of the ninth month, the month of Kislev. 2The people of Bethel had sent Sharezer and Regem-Melech, together with their men, to entreat the LORD 3by asking the priests of the house of the LORD Almighty and the prophets, "Should I mourn and fast in the fifth month, as I have done for so many years?"

4Then the word of the LORD Almighty came to me: 5"Ask all the people of the land and the priests, 'When you fasted and mourned in the fifth and seventh months for the past seventy years, was it really for me that you fasted? 6And when you were eating and drinking, were you not just feasting for yourselves? 7Are these not the words the LORD proclaimed through the earlier prophets when Jerusalem and its surrounding towns were at rest and prosperous, and the Negev and the western foothills were settled?' "

8And the word of the LORD came again to Zechariah: 9"This is what the LORD Almighty says: 'Administer true justice; show mercy and

8他又呼叫我說："看哪，往北方去的，已在北方安慰我的心。"

為約書亞加冕

9耶和華的話臨到我說：10"你要從被擄之人中取黑玳、多比雅、耶大雅的金銀。這三人是從巴比倫來到西番雅的兒子約西亞的家裏。當日你要進他的家，11取這金銀作冠冕，戴在約撒答的兒子大祭司約書亞的頭上。12對他說，萬軍之耶和華如此說：'看哪，那名稱為大衛苗裔的，他要在本處長起來，並要建造耶和華的殿。13他要建造耶和華的殿，並擔負尊榮，坐在位上掌王權。又必在位上作祭司，使兩職之間籌定和平。'14這冠冕要歸希連(註：就是"黑玳")、多比雅、耶大雅和西番雅的兒子賢(註："賢"就是"約西亞")，放在耶和華的殿裏為紀念。15遠方的人也要來建造耶和華的殿，你們就知道萬軍之耶和華差遣我到你們這裏來。你們若留意聽從耶和華你們神的話，這事必然成就。"

公平憐憫，不在於禁食

7 大利烏王第四年九月，就是基斯流月初四日，耶和華的話臨到撒迦利亞。2那時伯特利人已經打發沙利色和利堅米勒，並跟從他們的人，去懇求耶和華的恩，3並問萬軍之耶和華殿中的祭司和先知說："我歷年以來，在五月間哭泣齋戒，現在還當這樣行嗎？"

4萬軍之耶和華的話就臨到我說：5"你要宣告國內的眾民和祭司，說：'你們這七十年，在五月、七月禁食悲哀，豈是絲毫向我禁食嗎？6你們吃喝，不是為自己吃、為自己喝嗎？7當耶路撒冷和四圍的城邑有居民，正興盛，南地高原有人居住的時候，耶和華藉從前的先知所宣告的話，你們不當聽嗎？'"

8耶和華的話又臨到撒迦利亞說：9"萬軍之耶和華曾對你們的列祖如此說：'要按至理判斷，各人以

a 8 Or spirit   b 14 Syriac; Hebrew Helem   c 14 Or and the gracious one, the

慈愛憐憫弟兄。10不可欺壓寡婦、孤兒、寄居的和貧窮人，誰都不可心裏謀害弟兄。’

11 “他們卻不肯聽從，扭轉肩頭，塞耳不聽，12使心硬如金鋼石，不聽律法和萬軍之耶和華用靈藉從前的先知所說的話。故此，萬軍之耶和華大發烈怒。

13 “萬軍之耶和華說：‘我曾呼喚他們，他們不聽；將來他們呼求我，我也不聽！14我必以旋風吹散他們到素不認識的萬國中。這樣，他們的地就荒涼，甚至無人來往經過，因為他們使美好之地荒涼了。’ ”

主應許賜福耶路撒冷

8 萬軍之耶和華的話臨到我說：2萬軍之耶和華如此說：“我為錫安心裏極其火熱。我為她火熱，向她的仇敵發烈怒。”

3耶和華如此說：“我現在回到錫安，要住在耶路撒冷中。耶路撒冷必稱為誠實的城，萬軍之耶和華的山必稱為聖山。”

4萬軍之耶和華如此說：“將來必有年老的男女坐在耶路撒冷街上，因為年紀老邁就手拿拐杖。5城中街上必滿有男孩女孩玩耍。”

6萬軍之耶和華如此說：“到那日，這事在餘剩的民眼中看為希奇，在我眼中也看為希奇嗎？”這是萬軍之耶和華說的。

7萬軍之耶和華如此說：“我要從東方、從西方救回我的民。8我要領他們來，使他們住在耶路撒冷中。他們要作我的子民，我要作他們的神，都憑誠實和公義。”

9萬軍之耶和華如此說：“當建造萬軍之耶和華的殿，立根基之日的先知所說的話，現在你們聽見，應當手裏強壯。10那日以先，人得不着雇價，牲畜也是如此；且因敵人的緣故，出入之人不得平安。乃因我使眾人互相攻擊。11但如今，我待這餘剩的民必不像從前。”這是萬軍之耶和華說的。

12 “因為他們必平安撒種，葡萄樹必結果子，地土必有出產，天也

compassion to one another. 10Do not oppress the widow or the fatherless, the alien or the poor. In your hearts do not think evil of each other.’

11“But they refused to pay attention; stubbornly they turned their backs and stopped up their ears. 12They made their hearts as hard as flint and would not listen to the law or to the words that the LORD Almighty had sent by his Spirit through the earlier prophets. So the LORD Almighty was very angry.

13“ ‘When I called, they did not listen; so when they called, I would not listen,’ says the LORD Almighty. 14‘I scattered them with a whirlwind among all the nations, where they were strangers. The land was left so desolate behind them that no one could come or go. This is how they made the pleasant land desolate.’ ”

The LORD Promises to Bless Jerusalem

8 Again the word of the LORD Almighty came to me. 2This is what the LORD Almighty says: “I am very jealous for Zion; I am burning with jealousy for her.”

3This is what the LORD says: “I will return to Zion and dwell in Jerusalem. Then Jerusalem will be called the City of Truth, and the mountain of the LORD Almighty will be called the Holy Mountain.”

4This is what the LORD Almighty says: “Once again men and women of ripe old age will sit in the streets of Jerusalem, each with cane in hand because of his age. 5The city streets will be filled with boys and girls playing there.”

6This is what the LORD Almighty says: “It may seem marvelous to the remnant of this people at that time, but will it seem marvelous to me?” declares the LORD Almighty.

7This is what the LORD Almighty says: “I will save my people from the countries of the east and the west. 8I will bring them back to live in Jerusalem; they will be my people, and I will be faithful and righteous to them as their God.”

9This is what the LORD Almighty says: “You who now hear these words spoken by the prophets who were there when the foundation was laid for the house of the LORD Almighty, let your hands be strong so that the temple may be built. 10Before that time there were no wages for man or beast. No one could go about his business safely because of his enemy, for I had turned every man against his neighbor. 11But now I will not deal with the remnant of this people as I did in the past,” declares the LORD Almighty.

12“The seed will grow well, the vine will yield its fruit, the ground will produce its crops, and the heavens will drop their dew. I will give all these things as an inheritance to the remnant of this people. [13]As you have been an object of cursing among the nations, O Judah and Israel, so will I save you, and you will be a blessing. Do not be afraid, but let your hands be strong."

[14]This is what the LORD Almighty says: "Just as I had determined to bring disaster upon you and showed no pity when your fathers angered me," says the LORD Almighty, [15]"so now I have determined to do good again to Jerusalem and Judah. Do not be afraid. [16]These are the things you are to do: Speak the truth to each other, and render true and sound judgment in your courts; [17]do not plot evil against your neighbor, and do not love to swear falsely. I hate all this," declares the LORD.

[18]Again the word of the LORD Almighty came to me. [19]This is what the LORD Almighty says: "The fasts of the fourth, fifth, seventh and tenth months will become joyful and glad occasions and happy festivals for Judah. Therefore love truth and peace.

[20]This is what the LORD Almighty says: "Many peoples and the inhabitants of many cities will yet come, [21]and the inhabitants of one city will go to another and say, 'Let us go at once to entreat the LORD and seek the LORD Almighty. I myself am going.' [22]And many peoples and powerful nations will come to Jerusalem to seek the LORD Almighty and to entreat him."

[23]This is what the LORD Almighty says: "In those days ten men from all languages and nations will take firm hold of one Jew by the hem of his robe and say, 'Let us go with you, because we have heard that God is with you.' "

Judgment on Israel's Enemies
An Oracle

9 The word of the LORD is against the land of Hadrach
and will rest upon Damascus —
for the eyes of men and all the tribes of Israel are on the LORD — [a]
[2]and upon Hamath too, which borders on it,
and upon Tyre and Sidon, though they are very skillful.
[3]Tyre has built herself a stronghold;
she has heaped up silver like dust,
and gold like the dirt of the streets.
[4]But the Lord will take away her possessions

---

a 1 Or Damascus. / For the eye of the LORD is on all mankind, / as well as on the tribes of Israel,

---

必降甘露。我要使這餘剩的民享受這一切的福。[13]猶大家和以色列家啊,你們從前在列國中怎樣成為可咒詛的;照樣,我要拯救你們,使人稱你們為有福的(註:或作「使你們叫人得福」)。你們不要懼怕,手要強壯!」

[14]萬軍之耶和華如此說:「你們列祖惹我發怒的時候,我怎樣定意降禍,並不後悔;[15]現在我照樣定意施恩與耶路撒冷和猶大家。你們不要懼怕。[16]你們所當行的是這樣:各人與鄰舍說話誠實,在城門口按至理判斷,使人和睦;[17]誰都不可心裏謀害鄰舍,也不可喜愛起假誓,因為這些事都為我所恨惡。」這是耶和華說的。

[18]萬軍之耶和華的話臨到我說:[19]萬軍之耶和華如此說:「四月、五月禁食的日子,七月、十月禁食的日子,必變為猶大家歡喜快樂的日子和歡樂的節期,所以你們要喜愛誠實與和平。」

[20]萬軍之耶和華如此說:「將來必有列國的人和多城的居民來到。[21]這城的居民必到那城,說:『我們要快去懇求耶和華的恩,尋求萬軍之耶和華,我也要去。』[22]必有列邦的人和強國的民,來到耶路撒冷尋求萬軍之耶和華,懇求耶和華的恩。」

[23]萬軍之耶和華如此說:「在那些日子,必有十個人從列國諸族(註:「族」原文作「方言」)中出來,拉住一個猶大人的衣襟,說:『我們要與你們同去,因為我們聽見神與你們同在了。』」

審判將臨以色列的仇敵

9 耶和華的默示應驗在哈得拉地大馬士革
(世人和以色列各支派的眼目都仰望耶和華),

[2]和靠近的哈馬,
並推羅、西頓,
因為這二城的人大有智慧。
[3]推羅為自己修築保障,
積蓄銀子如塵沙,
堆起精金如街上的泥土。
[4]主必趕出她,

打敗她海上的權力；
　她必被火燒滅。
5 亞實基倫看見必懼怕，
　迦薩看見甚痛苦；
　以革倫因失了盼望蒙羞。
　迦薩必不再有君王，
　亞實基倫也不再有居民。
6 私生子（註：或作「外族人」）必住在亞實
　突，我必除滅非利士人的驕傲。
7 我必除去他口中帶血之肉
　和牙齒內可憎之物。
　他必作為餘剩的人歸與我們的神；
　必在猶大像族長，
　以革倫人必如耶布斯人。
8 我必在我家的四圍安營，
　使敵軍不得任意往來，
　暴虐的人也不再經過，
　　因為我親眼看顧我的家。

要來的錫安君王

9 錫安的民哪，應當大大喜樂！
　耶路撒冷的民哪，應當歡呼！
　看哪，你的王來到你這裏！
　他是公義的，並且施行拯救，
　謙謙和和騎着驢，
　就是騎着驢的駒子。
10 我必除滅以法蓮的戰車
　和耶路撒冷的戰馬，
　爭戰的弓也必除滅。
　他必向列國講和平，
　他的權柄必從這海管到那海，
　從大河管到地極。
11 錫安哪，
　我因與你立約的血，
　將你中間被擄而囚的人，
　從無水的坑中釋放出來。
12 你們被囚而有指望的人，
　都要轉回保障。我今日說明，
　我必加倍賜福給你們。
13 我拿猶大作上弦的弓，
　我拿以法蓮為張弓的箭。
　錫安哪，我要激發你的眾子，
　攻擊希臘（註：原文作「雅完」）的
　眾子，使你如勇士的刀。

主必顯現

14 耶和華必顯現在他們以上，
　他的箭必射出像閃電。
　主耶和華必吹角，
　乘南方的旋風而行。
15 萬軍之耶和華必保護他們。
　他們必吞滅仇敵，

and destroy her power on the sea,
　and she will be consumed by fire.
5 Ashkelon will see it and fear;
　Gaza will writhe in agony,
　and Ekron too, for her hope will wither.
　Gaza will lose her king
　and Ashkelon will be deserted.
6 Foreigners will occupy Ashdod,
　and I will cut off the pride of the Philistines.
7 I will take the blood from their mouths,
　the forbidden food from between their teeth.
　Those who are left will belong to our God
　and become leaders in Judah,
　and Ekron will be like the Jebusites.
8 But I will defend my house
　against marauding forces.
　Never again will an oppressor overrun my people,
　for now I am keeping watch.

The Coming of Zion's King

9 Rejoice greatly, O Daughter of Zion!
　Shout, Daughter of Jerusalem!
　See, your king[a] comes to you,
　righteous and having salvation,
　gentle and riding on a donkey,
　on a colt, the foal of a donkey.
10 I will take away the chariots from Ephraim
　and the war-horses from Jerusalem,
　and the battle bow will be broken.
　He will proclaim peace to the nations.
　His rule will extend from sea to sea
　and from the River[b] to the ends of the earth.[c]
11 As for you, because of the blood of my
　covenant with you,
　I will free your prisoners from the waterless pit.
12 Return to your fortress, O prisoners of hope;
　even now I announce that I will restore twice
　as much to you.
13 I will bend Judah as I bend my bow
　and fill it with Ephraim.
　I will rouse your sons, O Zion,
　against your sons, O Greece,
　and make you like a warrior's sword.

The LORD Will Appear

14 Then the LORD will appear over them;
　his arrow will flash like lightning.
　The Sovereign LORD will sound the trumpet;
　he will march in the storms of the south,
15 and the LORD Almighty will shield them.
　They will destroy

a 9 Or King　　b 10 That is, the Euphrates　　c 10 Or the end of the land

and overcome with slingstones.
They will drink and roar as with wine;
   they will be full like a bowl
     used for sprinkling[a] the corners of the altar.
[16]The LORD their God will save them on that day
   as the flock of his people.
They will sparkle in his land
   like jewels in a crown.
[17]How attractive and beautiful they will be!
   Grain will make the young men thrive,
   and new wine the young women.

The LORD Will Care for Judah

10 Ask the LORD for rain in the springtime;
   it is the LORD who makes the storm clouds.
He gives showers of rain to men,
   and plants of the field to everyone.
[2]The idols speak deceit,
   diviners see visions that lie;
they tell dreams that are false,
   they give comfort in vain.
Therefore the people wander like sheep
   oppressed for lack of a shepherd.

[3]"My anger burns against the shepherds,
   and I will punish the leaders;
for the LORD Almighty will care
   for his flock, the house of Judah,
   and make them like a proud horse in battle.
[4]From Judah will come the cornerstone,
   from him the tent peg,
   from him the battle bow,
   from him every ruler.
[5]Together they[b] will be like mighty men
   trampling the muddy streets in battle.
Because the LORD is with them,
   they will fight and overthrow the horsemen.

[6]"I will strengthen the house of Judah
   and save the house of Joseph.
I will restore them
   because I have compassion on them.
They will be as though
   I had not rejected them,
for I am the LORD their God
   and I will answer them.
[7]The Ephraimites will become like mighty men,
   and their hearts will be glad as with wine.
Their children will see it and be joyful;
   their hearts will rejoice in the LORD.
[8]I will signal for them
   and gather them in.

a 15 Or bowl, / like   b 4,5 Or ruler, all of them together. / 5They

   踐踏彈石；
他們必喝血吶喊，猶如飲酒；
   他們必像盛滿血的碗，
   又像壇的四角滿了血。
[16]當那日，耶和華他們的神
   必看他的民，如羣羊拯救他們；
因為他們必像冠冕上的寶石，
   高舉在他的地以上。
（註："高舉云云"或作"在他的地上發光輝"）
[17]他的恩慈何等大！
   他的榮美何其盛！
   五穀健壯少男，新酒培養處女。

主必眷顧猶大

10 當春雨的時候，
   你們要向發閃電的耶和華求雨。
他必為眾人降下甘霖，
   使田園生長菜蔬。
[2]因為家神所言的是虛空，
   卜士所見的是虛假；
做夢者所說的是假夢，
   他們白白地安慰人。
所以眾人如羊流離，
   因無牧人就受苦。

[3] "我的怒氣向牧人發作，
   我必懲罰公山羊。
因我萬軍之耶和華
   眷顧自己的羊羣，就是猶大家，
   必使他們如駿馬在陣上。
[4]房角石、釘子、
   爭戰的弓，
   和一切掌權的
   都從他而出。
[5]他們必如勇士在陣上，
   將仇敵踐踏在街上的泥土中。
他們必爭戰，因為耶和華與他們
   同在，騎馬的也必羞愧。

[6] "我要堅固猶大家，
   拯救約瑟家，
   要領他們歸回。
我要憐恤他們，
   他們必像未曾棄絕的一樣。
都因我是耶和華他們的神，
   我必應允他們的禱告。
[7]以法蓮人必如勇士，
   他們心中暢快如同喝酒；
他們的兒女必看見而快活，
   他們的心必因耶和華喜樂。
[8]我要發嘶聲，
   聚集他們。

因我已經救贖他們。
他們的人數必加增，
　　如從前加增一樣。
9我雖然（註：或作"必"）播散他們
　　在列國中，他們必在遠方記念我。
他們與兒女都必存活，且得歸回。
10我必再領他們出埃及地，
　　招聚他們出亞述，
領他們到基列和黎巴嫩；
　　這地尚且不夠他們居住。
11耶和華必經過苦海，
　　擊打海浪，
使尼羅河的深處都枯乾。
　　亞述的驕傲必至卑微；
埃及的權柄必然滅沒。
12我必使他們倚靠我，得以堅固；
　　一舉一動必奉我的名。"
　　　　　　這是耶和華說的。

11 黎巴嫩哪，開開你的門，
　　　任火燒滅你的香柏樹。
　　2松樹啊，應當哀號，
因為香柏樹傾倒，
　　佳美的樹毀壞。
巴珊的橡樹啊，應當哀號，
　　因為茂盛的樹林已經倒了。
3聽啊，有牧人哀號的聲音，
　　因他們榮華的草場毀壞了；
有少壯獅子咆哮的聲音，
　　因約但河旁的叢林荒廢了。

兩個牧人

4耶和華我的神如此說："你撒
迦利亞要牧養這將宰的羣羊。5買他
們的宰了他們，以自己為無罪；賣
他們的說：'耶和華是應當稱頌
的，因我成為富足。'牧養他們的
並不憐恤他們。6耶和華說：我不再
憐恤這地的居民，必將這民交給各
人的鄰舍和他們王的手中。他們必
毀滅這地，我也不救這民脫離他們
的手。"
　　7於是，我牧養這將宰的羣羊，
就是羣中最困苦的羊。我拿著兩根
杖，一根我稱為榮美，一根我稱為
聯索。這樣，我牧養了羣羊。8一月
之內，我除滅三個牧人。
　　因為我的心厭煩他們；他們的心
也憎嫌我。9我就說："我不牧養你
們。要死的，由他死，要喪亡的，由他
喪亡；餘剩的，由他們彼此相食。"
　　10我折斷那稱為榮美的杖，表明
我廢棄與萬民所立的約。11當日就廢
棄了。這樣，那些仰望我的困苦
羊，就知道所說的是耶和華的話。

Surely I will redeem them;
　　they will be as numerous as before.
9Though I scatter them among the peoples,
　　yet in distant lands they will remember me.
They and their children will survive,
　　and they will return.
10I will bring them back from Egypt
　　and gather them from Assyria.
I will bring them to Gilead and Lebanon,
　　and there will not be room enough for them.
11They will pass through the sea of trouble;
　　the surging sea will be subdued
　　and all the depths of the Nile will dry up.
Assyria's pride will be brought down
　　and Egypt's scepter will pass away.
12I will strengthen them in the LORD
　　and in his name they will walk,"
　　　　　　　　declares the LORD.

11 Open your doors, O Lebanon,
　　　so that fire may devour your cedars!
　　2Wail, O pine tree, for the cedar has
fallen;
　　the stately trees are ruined!
Wail, oaks of Bashan,
　　the dense forest has been cut down!
3Listen to the wail of the shepherds;
　　their rich pastures are destroyed!
Listen to the roar of the lions;
　　the lush thicket of the Jordan is ruined!

Two Shepherds

4This is what the LORD my God says: "Pasture
the flock marked for slaughter. 5Their buyers
slaughter them and go unpunished. Those who
sell them say, 'Praise the LORD, I am rich!' Their
own shepherds do not spare them. 6For I will no
longer have pity on the people of the land,"
declares the LORD. "I will hand everyone over to
his neighbor and his king. They will oppress the
land, and I will not rescue them from their
hands."
　　7So I pastured the flock marked for slaughter,
particularly the oppressed of the flock. Then I
took two staffs and called one Favor and the
other Union, and I pastured the flock. 8In one
month I got rid of the three shepherds.
　　The flock detested me, and I grew weary of
them 9and said, "I will not be your shepherd.
Let the dying die, and the perishing perish. Let
those who are left eat one another's flesh."
　　10Then I took my staff called Favor and broke
it, revoking the covenant I had made with all the
nations. 11It was revoked on that day, and so the
afflicted of the flock who were watching me
knew it was the word of the LORD.

¹²I told them, "If you think it best, give me my pay; but if not, keep it." So they paid me thirty pieces of silver.

¹³And the LORD said to me, "Throw it to the potter"—the handsome price at which they priced me! So I took the thirty pieces of silver and threw them into the house of the LORD to the potter.

¹⁴Then I broke my second staff called Union, breaking the brotherhood between Judah and Israel.

¹⁵Then the LORD said to me, "Take again the equipment of a foolish shepherd. ¹⁶For I am going to raise up a shepherd over the land who will not care for the lost, or seek the young, or heal the injured, or feed the healthy, but will eat the meat of the choice sheep, tearing off their hoofs.

¹⁷"Woe to the worthless shepherd,
    who deserts the flock!
May the sword strike his arm and his right eye!
    May his arm be completely withered,
    his right eye totally blinded!"

Jerusalem's Enemies to Be Destroyed
An Oracle

12 This is the word of the LORD concerning Israel. The LORD, who stretches out the heavens, who lays the foundation of the earth, and who forms the spirit of man within him, declares: ²"I am going to make Jerusalem a cup that sends all the surrounding peoples reeling. Judah will be besieged as well as Jerusalem. ³On that day, when all the nations of the earth are gathered against her, I will make Jerusalem an immovable rock for all the nations. All who try to move it will injure themselves. ⁴On that day I will strike every horse with panic and its rider with madness," declares the LORD. "I will keep a watchful eye over the house of Judah, but I will blind all the horses of the nations. ⁵Then the leaders of Judah will say in their hearts, 'The people of Jerusalem are strong, because the LORD Almighty is their God.'

⁶"On that day I will make the leaders of Judah like a firepot in a woodpile, like a flaming torch among sheaves. They will consume right and left all the surrounding peoples, but Jerusalem will remain intact in her place.

⁷"The LORD will save the dwellings of Judah first, so that the honor of the house of David and of Jerusalem's inhabitants may not be greater than that of Judah. ⁸On that day the LORD will shield those who live in Jerusalem, so that the feeblest among them will be like David, and the

¹²我對他們說："你們若以為美，就給我工價。不然，就罷了！"於是他們給了三十塊錢，作為我的工價。

¹³耶和華吩咐我說："要把眾人所估定美好的價值丟給窰戶。"我便將這三十塊錢，在耶和華的殿中丟給窰戶了。

¹⁴我又折斷稱為聯索的那根杖，表明我廢棄猶大與以色列弟兄的情誼。

¹⁵耶和華又吩咐我說："你再取愚昧牧人所用的器具。¹⁶因我要在這地興起一個牧人，他不看顧喪亡的，不尋找分散的，不醫治受傷的，也不牧養強壯的；卻要吃肥羊的肉，撕裂牠的蹄子。

¹⁷"無用的牧人丟棄羊羣，
    有禍了！
刀必臨到他的膀臂和右眼上！
    他的膀臂必全然枯乾，
    他的右眼也必昏暗失明。"

耶路撒冷的仇敵要被毀滅

12 耶和華論以色列的默示。鋪張諸天，建立地基，造人裏面之靈的耶和華說：²"我必使耶路撒冷被圍困的時候，向四圍列國的民成為令人昏醉的杯；這默示也論到猶大（註：或作"猶大也是如此"）。³那日，我必使耶路撒冷向聚集攻擊她的萬民，當作一塊重石頭；凡舉起的必受重傷。"⁴耶和華說："到那日，我必使一切馬匹驚惶，使騎馬的顛狂。我必看顧猶大家，使列國的一切馬匹瞎眼。⁵猶大的族長必心裏說：'耶路撒冷的居民倚靠萬軍之耶和華他們的神，就作我們的能力。'

⁶"那日，我必使猶大的族長如火盆在木柴中，又如火把在禾捆裏。他們必左右燒滅四圍列國的民。耶路撒冷人必仍住本處，就是耶路撒冷。

⁷"耶和華必先拯救猶大的帳棚，免得大衛家的榮耀和耶路撒冷居民的榮耀勝過猶大。⁸那日，耶和華必保護耶路撒冷的居民。他們中間軟弱的必如大衛；大衛的家必如神，如

行在他們前面之耶和華的使者。⁹那日，我必定意滅絕來攻擊耶路撒冷各國的民。

他們要為所扎之人悲哀

¹⁰ "我必將那施恩叫人懇求的靈，澆灌大衛家和耶路撒冷的居民。他們必仰望我（註：或作「他」。本節同），就是他們所扎的；必為我悲哀，如喪獨生子，又為我愁苦，如喪長子。¹¹那日，耶路撒冷必有大大的悲哀，如米吉多平原之哈達臨門的悲哀。¹²境內一家一家的都必悲哀。大衛家，男的獨在一處，女的獨在一處；拿單家，男的獨在一處，女的獨在一處；¹³利未家，男的獨在一處，女的獨在一處；示每家，男的獨在一處，女的獨在一處。¹⁴其餘的各家，男的獨在一處，女的獨在一處。

洗除罪

13 "那日，必給大衛家和耶路撒冷的居民開一個泉源，洗除罪惡與污穢。"

²萬軍之耶和華說："那日，我必將地上除滅偶像的名，不再被人記念，也必使這地不再有假先知與污穢的靈。³若再有人說預言，生他的父母必對他說：'你不得存活，因為你託耶和華的名說假預言。'生他的父母在他說預言的時候，要將他刺透。

⁴ "那日，凡作先知說預言的，必因他所論的異象羞愧，不再穿毛衣哄騙人。⁵他必說：'我不是先知，我是耕地的，我從幼年作人的奴僕。'⁶必有人問他說：'你兩臂中間是甚麼傷呢？'他必回答說：'這是我在親友家中所受的傷。'"

擊打牧人，羊就分散

⁷萬軍之耶和華說：
　"刀劍哪，應當興起，
　　攻擊我的牧人和我的同伴，
　　擊打牧人，
　　羊就分散。

house of David will be like God, like the Angel of the LORD going before them. ⁹On that day I will set out to destroy all the nations that attack Jerusalem.

Mourning for the One They Pierced

¹⁰And I will pour out on the house of David and the inhabitants of Jerusalem a spirit*a* of grace and supplication. They will look on*b* me, the one they have pierced, and they will mourn for him as one mourns for an only child, and grieve bitterly for him as one grieves for a firstborn son. ¹¹On that day the weeping in Jerusalem will be great, like the weeping of Hadad Rimmon in the plain of Megiddo. ¹²The land will mourn, each clan by itself, with their wives by themselves: the clan of the house of David and their wives, the clan of the house of Nathan and their wives, ¹³the clan of the house of Levi and their wives, the clan of Shimei and their wives, ¹⁴and all the rest of the clans and their wives.

Cleansing From Sin

13 "On that day a fountain will be opened to the house of David and the inhabitants of Jerusalem, to cleanse them from sin and impurity.

²"On that day, I will banish the names of the idols from the land, and they will be remembered no more," declares the LORD Almighty. "I will remove both the prophets and the spirit of impurity from the land. ³And if anyone still prophesies, his father and mother, to whom he was born, will say to him, 'You must die, because you have told lies in the LORD's name.' When he prophesies, his own parents will stab him.

⁴"On that day every prophet will be ashamed of his prophetic vision. He will not put on a prophet's garment of hair in order to deceive. ⁵He will say, 'I am not a prophet. I am a farmer; the land has been my livelihood since my youth.*c*' ⁶If someone asks him, 'What are these wounds on your body*d*?' he will answer, 'The wounds I was given at the house of my friends.'

The Shepherd Struck, the Sheep Scattered

⁷"Awake, O sword, against my shepherd,
　against the man who is close to me!"
　　declares the LORD Almighty.
"Strike the shepherd,
　and the sheep will be scattered,

---

a 10 Or the Spirit   b 10 Or to   c 5 Or farmer; a man sold me in my youth   d 6 Or wounds between your hands

and I will turn my hand against the little
ones.

[8]In the whole land," declares the LORD,
"two-thirds will be struck down and perish;
yet one-third will be left in it.

[9]This third I will bring into the fire;
I will refine them like silver
and test them like gold.
They will call on my name
and I will answer them;
I will say, 'They are my people,'
and they will say, 'The LORD is our God.' "

The LORD Comes and Reigns

14 A day of the LORD is coming when your
plunder will be divided among you.
[2]I will gather all the nations to Jerusalem to fight against it; the city will be captured, the houses ransacked, and the women
raped. Half of the city will go into exile, but the
rest of the people will not be taken from the city.
[3]Then the LORD will go out and fight against
those nations, as he fights in the day of battle.
[4]On that day his feet will stand on the Mount of
Olives, east of Jerusalem, and the Mount of
Olives will be split in two from east to west,
forming a great valley, with half of the mountain moving north and half moving south. [5]You
will flee by my mountain valley, for it will
extend to Azel. You will flee as you fled from
the earthquake[a] in the days of Uzziah king of
Judah. Then the LORD my God will come, and all
the holy ones with him.

[6]On that day there will be no light, no cold or
frost. [7]It will be a unique day, without daytime
or nighttime—a day known to the LORD. When
evening comes, there will be light.

[8]On that day living water will flow out from
Jerusalem, half to the eastern sea[b] and half to the
western sea,[c] in summer and in winter.

[9]The LORD will be king over the whole earth.
On that day there will be one LORD, and his
name the only name.

[10]The whole land, from Geba to Rimmon,
south of Jerusalem, will become like the Arabah.
But Jerusalem will be raised up and remain in
its place, from the Benjamin Gate to the site of
the First Gate, to the Corner Gate, and from the
Tower of Hananel to the royal winepresses. [11]It
will be inhabited; never again will it be destroyed. Jerusalem will be secure.

[12]This is the plague with which the LORD will

我必反手
加在微小者的身上。"

[8]耶和華說："這全地的人,
三分之二必剪除而死;
三分之一仍必存留。
[9]我要使這三分之一經火,
熬煉他們,如熬煉銀子;
試煉他們,如試煉金子。
他們必求告我的名,
我必應允他們。
我要說:'這是我的子民。'
他們也要說:
'耶和華是我們的神。' "

主必降臨作全地之王

14 耶和華的日子臨近,你的財物
必被搶掠,在你中間分散。
[2]因為我必聚集萬國與<u>耶路撒
冷</u>爭戰,城必被攻取,房屋被搶奪,
婦女被玷污,城中的民一半被擄去;
剩下的民仍在城中,不致剪除。

[3]那時,耶和華必出去與那些國
爭戰,好像從前爭戰一樣。[4]那日,
他的腳必站在<u>耶路撒冷</u>前面朝東的<u>橄
欖山</u>上。這山必從中間分裂,自東至
西,成為極大的谷。山的一半向北挪
移,一半向南挪移。[5]你們要從我山
的谷中逃跑,因為山谷必延到<u>亞薩</u>。
你們逃跑,必如<u>猶大王烏西雅</u>年間的
人逃避大地震一樣。耶和華我的神必
降臨,有一切聖者同來。

[6]那日,必沒有光,三光必退
縮。[7]那日,必是耶和華所知道的。
不是白晝,也不是黑夜,到了晚上才
有光明。

[8]那日,必有活水從<u>耶路撒冷</u>出
來,一半往東海流,一半往西海流。
冬夏都是如此。

[9]耶和華必作全地的王,那日,
耶和華必為獨一無二的,他的名也是
獨一無二的。

[10]全地,從迦巴直到<u>耶路撒冷</u>南
方的<u>臨門</u>,要變為<u>亞拉巴</u>。<u>耶路撒冷</u>
必仍居高位,就是從<u>便雅憫</u>門到第一
門之處,又到<u>角門</u>,並從<u>哈楠業樓</u>,
直到王的酒醡。[11]人必住在其中,不
再有咒詛。<u>耶路撒冷</u>人必安然居住。

[12]耶和華用災殃攻擊那與<u>耶路撒

---

*a 5 Or [5]My mountain valley will be blocked and will extend to Azel.
It will be blocked as it was blocked because of the earthquake*
b 8 That is, the Dead Sea   c 8 That is, the Mediterranean

冷爭戰的列國人，必是這樣：他們兩腳站立的時候，肉必消沒，眼在眶中乾瘪，舌在口中潰爛。¹³那日，耶和華必使他們大大擾亂。他們各人彼此揪住，舉手攻擊。¹⁴猶大也必在耶路撒冷爭戰。那時四圍各國的財物，就是許多金銀衣服，必被收聚。¹⁵那臨到馬匹、騾子、駱駝、驢和營中一切牲畜的災殃，是與那災殃一般。

¹⁶所有來攻擊耶路撒冷列國中剩下的人，必年年上來敬拜大君王萬軍之耶和華，並守住棚節。¹⁷地上萬族中，凡不上耶路撒冷敬拜大君王萬軍之耶和華的，必無雨降在他們的地上。¹⁸埃及族若不上來，雨也不降在他們的地上；凡不上來守住棚節的列國人，耶和華也必用這災攻擊他們。¹⁹這就是埃及的刑罰，和那不上來守住棚節之列國的刑罰。

²⁰當那日，馬的鈴鐺上必有**歸耶和華為聖**的這句話。耶和華殿內的鍋必如祭壇前的碗一樣。²¹凡耶路撒冷和猶大的鍋，都必歸萬軍之耶和華為聖。凡獻祭的都必來取這鍋，煮肉在其中。當那日，在萬軍之耶和華的殿中，必不再有迦南人。

strike all the nations that fought against Jerusalem: Their flesh will rot while they are still standing on their feet, their eyes will rot in their sockets, and their tongues will rot in their mouths. ¹³On that day men will be stricken by the LORD with great panic. Each man will seize the hand of another, and they will attack each other. ¹⁴Judah too will fight at Jerusalem. The wealth of all the surrounding nations will be collected—great quantities of gold and silver and clothing. ¹⁵A similar plague will strike the horses and mules, the camels and donkeys, and all the animals in those camps.

¹⁶Then the survivors from all the nations that have attacked Jerusalem will go up year after year to worship the King, the LORD Almighty, and to celebrate the Feast of Tabernacles. ¹⁷If any of the peoples of the earth do not go up to Jerusalem to worship the King, the LORD Almighty, they will have no rain. ¹⁸If the Egyptian people do not go up and take part, they will have no rain. The LORDᵃ will bring on them the plague he inflicts on the nations that do not go up to celebrate the Feast of Tabernacles. ¹⁹This will be the punishment of Egypt and the punishment of all the nations that do not go up to celebrate the Feast of Tabernacles.

²⁰On that day HOLY TO THE LORD will be inscribed on the bells of the horses, and the cooking pots in the LORD's house will be like the sacred bowls in front of the altar. ²¹Every pot in Jerusalem and Judah will be holy to the LORD Almighty, and all who come to sacrifice will take some of the pots and cook in them. And on that day there will no longer be a Canaaniteᵇ in the house of the LORD Almighty.

a 18 Or part, then the LORD　　*b 21 Or merchant*

Malachi

1

An oracle: The word of the LORD to Israel through Malachi.[a]

Jacob Loved, Esau Hated

²"I have loved you," says the LORD.

"But you ask, 'How have you loved us?'

"Was not Esau Jacob's brother?" the LORD says. "Yet I have loved Jacob, ³but Esau I have hated, and I have turned his mountains into a wasteland and left his inheritance to the desert jackals."

⁴Edom may say, "Though we have been crushed, we will rebuild the ruins."

But this is what the LORD Almighty says: "They may build, but I will demolish. They will be called the Wicked Land, a people always under the wrath of the LORD. ⁵You will see it with your own eyes and say, 'Great is the LORD—even beyond the borders of Israel!'

Blemished Sacrifices

⁶"A son honors his father, and a servant his master. If I am a father, where is the honor due me? If I am a master, where is the respect due me?" says the LORD Almighty. "It is you, O priests, who show contempt for my name.

"But you ask, 'How have we shown contempt for your name?'

⁷"You place defiled food on my altar.

"But you ask, 'How have we defiled you?'

"By saying that the LORD's table is contemptible. ⁸When you bring blind animals for sacrifice, is that not wrong? When you sacrifice crippled or diseased animals, is that not wrong? Try offering them to your governor! Would he be pleased with you? Would he accept you?" says the LORD Almighty.

⁹"Now implore God to be gracious to us. With such offerings from your hands, will he accept you?"—says the LORD Almighty.

¹⁰"Oh, that one of you would shut the temple doors, so that you would not light useless fires on my altar! I am not pleased with you," says the LORD Almighty, "and I will accept no offering from your hands. ¹¹My name will be great among the nations, from the rising to the setting

a 1 Malachi means my messenger.

1

耶和華藉瑪拉基傳給以色列的默示。

愛雅各惡以掃

²耶和華說：「我曾愛你們。

「你們卻說：『你在何事上愛我們呢？』」

耶和華說：「以掃不是雅各的哥哥嗎？我卻愛雅各，³惡以掃，使他的山嶺荒涼，把他的地業交給曠野的野狗。」

⁴以東人說：「我們現在雖被毀壞，卻要重建荒廢之處。」

萬軍之耶和華如此說：「任他們建造，我必拆毀。人必稱他們的地為罪惡之境；稱他們的民為耶和華永遠惱怒之民。你們必親眼看見，也必說：『願耶和華在以色列境界之外被尊為大！』

殘疾的祭物

⁶「藐視我名的祭司啊，萬軍之耶和華對你們說：兒子尊敬父親，僕人敬畏主人；我既為父親，尊敬我的在哪裏呢？我既為主人，敬畏我的在哪裏呢？」

「你們卻說：『我們在何事上藐視你的名呢？』

⁷「你們將污穢的食物獻在我的壇上。

「且說：『我們在何事上污穢你呢？』

「因你們說，耶和華的桌子是可藐視的。⁸你們將瞎眼的獻為祭物，這不為惡嗎？將瘸腿的、有病的獻上，這不為惡嗎？你將給你的省長，他豈喜悅你，豈能看你的情面嗎？」這是萬軍之耶和華說的。

⁹「現在我勸你們懇求神，他好施恩與我們。這妄獻的事既由你們經手，他豈能看你們的情面嗎？」這是萬軍之耶和華說的。

¹⁰「甚願你們中間有一人關上殿門，免得你們徒然在我壇上燒火。」萬軍之耶和華說：「我不喜悅你們，也不從你們手中收納供物。」¹¹萬軍之耶和華說：「從日出之地到日落之

處，我的名在外邦中必尊為大。在各處，人必奉我的名燒香，獻潔淨的供物。因為我的名在外邦中必尊為大。」

12 「你們卻褻瀆我的名，說：『耶和華的桌子是污穢的，其上的食物是可藐視的。』13你們又說：『這些事何等煩瑣！』亞嗤之以鼻。」這是萬軍之耶和華說的。

「你們把搶奪的、瘸腿的、有病的拿來獻上為祭，我豈能從你們手中收納呢？」這是耶和華說的。14行詭詐的在羣中有公羊，他許願卻用有殘疾的獻給主，因為我是大君王，我的名在外邦中是可畏的。」這是萬軍之耶和華說的。

警告祭司

2 「眾祭司啊，這誡命是傳給你們的。」2萬軍之耶和華說：「你們若不聽從，也不放在心上，將榮耀歸與我的名，我就使咒詛臨到你們，使你們的福分變為咒詛；因為你們不把誡命放在心上，我已經咒詛你們了。

3 「我必斥責你們的種子，又把你們犧牲的糞抹在你們的臉上，你們要與糞一同除掉。4你們就知道我傳這誡命給你們，使我與利未（註：或作「利未人」）所立的約可以常存。」這是萬軍之耶和華說的。5「我曾與他立生命和平安的約，我將這兩樣賜給他，使他存敬畏的心；他就敬畏我，懼怕我的名。6真實的律法在他口中，他嘴裏沒有不義的話。他以平安和正直與我同行，使多人回頭離開罪孽。

7 「祭司的嘴裏當存知識，人也當由他口中尋求律法，因為他是萬軍之耶和華的使者。8你們卻偏離正道，使許多人在律法上跌倒；你們廢棄我與利未所立的約。」這是萬軍之耶和華說的。9「所以我使你們被眾人藐視，看為下賤，因為你們不守我的道，竟在律法上瞻徇情面。」

of the sun. In every place incense and pure offerings will be brought to my name, because my name will be great among the nations," says the LORD Almighty.

12"But you profane it by saying of the Lord's table, 'It is defiled,' and of its food, 'It is contemptible.' 13And you say, 'What a burden!' and you sniff at it contemptuously," says the LORD Almighty.

"When you bring injured, crippled or diseased animals and offer them as sacrifices, should I accept them from your hands?" says the LORD. 14"Cursed is the cheat who has an acceptable male in his flock and vows to give it, but then sacrifices a blemished animal to the Lord. For I am a great king," says the LORD Almighty, "and my name is to be feared among the nations.

Admonition for the Priests

2 "And now this admonition is for you, O priests. 2If you do not listen, and if you do not set your heart to honor my name," says the LORD Almighty, "I will send a curse upon you, and I will curse your blessings. Yes, I have already cursed them, because you have not set your heart to honor me.

3"Because of you I will rebuke[a] your descendants[b]; I will spread on your faces the offal from your festival sacrifices, and you will be carried off with it. 4And you will know that I have sent you this admonition so that my covenant with Levi may continue," says the LORD Almighty. 5"My covenant was with him, a covenant of life and peace, and I gave them to him; this called for reverence and he revered me and stood in awe of my name. 6True instruction was in his mouth and nothing false was found on his lips. He walked with me in peace and uprightness, and turned many from sin.

7"For the lips of a priest ought to preserve knowledge, and from his mouth men should seek instruction—because he is the messenger of the LORD Almighty. 8But you have turned from the way and by your teaching have caused many to stumble; you have violated the covenant with Levi," says the LORD Almighty. 9"So I have caused you to be despised and humiliated before all the people, because you have not followed my ways but have shown partiality in matters of the law."

---

a 3 Or cut off (see Septuagint)　　*b 3 Or will blight your grain*

Judah Unfaithful

[10]Have we not all one Father[a]? Did not one God create us? Why do we profane the covenant of our fathers by breaking faith with one another?

[11]Judah has broken faith. A detestable thing has been committed in Israel and in Jerusalem: Judah has desecrated the sanctuary the LORD loves, by marrying the daughter of a foreign god. [12]As for the man who does this, whoever he may be, may the LORD cut him off from the tents of Jacob[b]— even though he brings offerings to the LORD Almighty.

[13]Another thing you do: You flood the LORD's altar with tears. You weep and wail because he no longer pays attention to your offerings or accepts them with pleasure from your hands. [14]You ask, "Why?" It is because the LORD is acting as the witness between you and the wife of your youth, because you have broken faith with her, though she is your partner, the wife of your marriage covenant.

[15]Has not ⌊the LORD⌋ made them one? In flesh and spirit they are his. And why one? Because he was seeking godly offspring.[c] So guard yourself in your spirit, and do not break faith with the wife of your youth.

[16]"I hate divorce," says the LORD God of Israel, "and I hate a man's covering himself[d] with violence as well as with his garment," says the LORD Almighty.

So guard yourself in your spirit, and do not break faith.

The Day of Judgment

[17]You have wearied the LORD with your words.

"How have we wearied him?" you ask.

By saying, "All who do evil are good in the eyes of the LORD, and he is pleased with them" or "Where is the God of justice?"

3 "See, I will send my messenger, who will prepare the way before me. Then suddenly the Lord you are seeking will come to his temple; the messenger of the covenant, whom you desire, will come," says the LORD Almighty.

[2]But who can endure the day of his coming? Who can stand when he appears? For he will be like a refiner's fire or a launderer's soap. [3]He

猶大不忠

[10]我們豈不都是一位父嗎？豈不是一位神所造的嗎？我們各人怎麼以詭詐待弟兄，背棄了神與我們列祖所立的約呢？

[11]猶大人行事詭詐，並且在以色列和耶路撒冷中行一件可憎的事。因為猶大人褻瀆耶和華所喜愛的聖潔（註：或作「聖地」），娶侍奉外邦神的女子為妻。[12]凡行這事的，無論何人（註：「何人」原文作「叫醒的、答應的」），就是獻供物給萬軍之耶和華，耶和華也必從雅各的帳棚中剪除他。

[13]你們又行了一件這樣的事，使前妻歎息哭泣的眼淚遮蓋耶和華的壇，以致耶和華不再看顧那供物，也不樂意從你們手中收納。[14]你們還說：「這是為甚麼呢？」因耶和華在你和你幼年所娶的妻中間作見證。她雖是你的配偶，又是你盟約的妻，你卻以詭詐待她。

[15]雖然神有靈的餘力能造多人，他不是單造一人嗎？為何只造一人呢？乃是他願人得虔誠的後裔。所以當謹守你們的心，誰也不可以詭詐待幼年所娶的妻。

[16]耶和華以色列的神說：「休妻的事和以強暴待妻的人，都是我所恨惡的。」

所以當謹守你們的心，不可行詭詐。這是萬軍之耶和華說的。

審判之日

[17]你們用言語煩瑣耶和華。

你們還說：「我們在何事上煩瑣他呢？」

因為你們說：「凡行惡的，耶和華眼看為善，並且他喜悅他們。」或說：「公義的神在哪裏呢？」

3 萬軍之耶和華說：「我要差遣我的使者在我前面預備道路。你們所尋求的主，必忽然進入他的殿；立約的使者，就是你們所仰慕的，快要來到。」

[2]他來的日子，誰能當得起呢？他顯現的時候，誰能立得住呢？因為他如煉金之人的火，如漂布之人的鹼。[3]他必坐下如煉淨銀子的，必潔

---

[a] 10 Or *father*   [b] 12 Or [12]*May the LORD cut off from the tents of Jacob anyone who gives testimony in behalf of the man who does this*   [c] 15 Or [15]*But the one ⌊who is our father⌋ did not do this, not as long as life remained in him. And what was he seeking? An offspring from God*   [d] 16 Or *his wife*

淨利未人，熬煉他們像金銀一樣，他們就憑公義獻供物給耶和華。⁴那時，猶大和耶路撒冷所獻的供物，必蒙耶和華悅納，彷彿古時之日、上古之年。

⁵萬軍之耶和華說：「我必臨近你們，施行審判。我必速速作見證，警戒行邪術的、犯姦淫的、起假誓的、虧負人之工價的、欺壓寡婦孤兒的、屈枉寄居的，和不敬畏我的。

奪取神的供物

⁶因我耶和華是不改變的，所以你們雅各之子沒有滅亡。⁷萬軍之耶和華說：「從你們列祖的日子以來，你們常常偏離我的典章而不遵守。現在你們要轉向我，我就轉向你們。」

「你們卻問說：『我們如何才是轉向呢？』

⁸「人豈可奪取神之物呢？你們竟奪取我的供物。

「你們卻說：『我們在何事上奪取你的供物呢？』

「就是你們在當納的十分之一和當獻的供物上。⁹因你們通國的人都奪取我的供物，咒詛就臨到你們身上。⁰萬軍之耶和華說：「你們要將當納的十分之一全然送入倉庫，使我家有糧，以此試試我是否為你們敞開天上的窗戶，傾福與你們，甚至無處可容。」¹¹萬軍之耶和華說：「我必為你們斥責蝗蟲（註：「蝗蟲」原文作「吞噬者」），不容牠毀壞你們的土產。你們田間的葡萄樹在未熟之先，也不掉果子。」¹²萬軍之耶和華說：「萬國必稱你們為有福的，因為你們的地必成為喜樂之地！」

¹³耶和華說：「你們用話頂撞我。」

「你們還說：『我們用甚麼話頂撞了你呢？』

「你們說：『侍奉神是徒然的，遵守神所吩咐的，在萬軍之耶和華面前苦苦齋戒，有甚麼益處呢？¹⁵如今我們稱狂傲的人為有福，並且行惡的人得建立。他們雖然試探神，卻得脫離災難。』」

¹⁶那時，敬畏耶和華的彼此談論，耶和華側耳而聽，且有紀念冊在他面前，記錄那敬畏耶和華、思

will sit as a refiner and purifier of silver; he will purify the Levites and refine them like gold and silver. Then the LORD will have men who will bring offerings in righteousness, ⁴and the offerings of Judah and Jerusalem will be acceptable to the LORD, as in days gone by, as in former years.

⁵"So I will come near to you for judgment. I will be quick to testify against sorcerers, adulterers and perjurers, against those who defraud laborers of their wages, who oppress the widows and the fatherless, and deprive aliens of justice, but do not fear me," says the LORD Almighty.

Robbing God

⁶"I the LORD do not change. So you, O descendants of Jacob, are not destroyed. ⁷Ever since the time of your forefathers you have turned away from my decrees and have not kept them. Return to me, and I will return to you," says the LORD Almighty.

"But you ask, 'How are we to return?'

⁸"Will a man rob God? Yet you rob me.

"But you ask, 'How do we rob you?'

"In tithes and offerings. ⁹You are under a curse—the whole nation of you—because you are robbing me. ¹⁰Bring the whole tithe into the storehouse, that there may be food in my house. Test me in this," says the LORD Almighty, "and see if I will not throw open the floodgates of heaven and pour out so much blessing that you will not have room enough for it. ¹¹I will prevent pests from devouring your crops, and the vines in your fields will not cast their fruit," says the LORD Almighty. ¹²"Then all the nations will call you blessed, for yours will be a delightful land," says the LORD Almighty.

¹³"You have said harsh things against me," says the LORD.

"Yet you ask, 'What have we said against you?'

¹⁴"You have said, 'It is futile to serve God. What did we gain by carrying out his requirements and going about like mourners before the LORD Almighty? ¹⁵But now we call the arrogant blessed. Certainly the evildoers prosper, and even those who challenge God escape.' "

¹⁶Then those who feared the LORD talked with each other, and the LORD listened and heard. A scroll of remembrance was written in

his presence concerning those who feared the LORD and honored his name.

17"They will be mine," says the LORD Almighty, "in the day when I make up my treasured possession.*a* I will spare them, just as in compassion a man spares his son who serves him. 18And you will again see the distinction between the righteous and the wicked, between those who serve God and those who do not.

The Day of the LORD

4 "Surely the day is coming; it will burn like a furnace. All the arrogant and every evildoer will be stubble, and that day that is coming will set them on fire," says the LORD Almighty. "Not a root or a branch will be left to them. 2But for you who revere my name, the sun of righteousness will rise with healing in its wings. And you will go out and leap like calves released from the stall. 3Then you will trample down the wicked; they will be ashes under the soles of your feet on the day when I do these things," says the LORD Almighty.

4"Remember the law of my servant Moses, the decrees and laws I gave him at Horeb for all Israel.

5"See, I will send you the prophet Elijah before that great and dreadful day of the LORD comes. 6He will turn the hearts of the fathers to their children, and the hearts of the children to their fathers; or else I will come and strike the land with a curse."

念他名的人。

17萬軍之耶和華説："在我所定的日子，他們必屬我，特特歸我。我必憐恤他們，如同人憐恤、服侍自己的兒子。18那時，你們必歸回，將善人和惡人，侍奉神的和不侍奉神的分別出來。"

主的日子

4 萬軍之耶和華説："那日臨近，勢如燒着的火爐，凡狂傲的和行惡的必如碎稭，在那日必被燒盡，根本枝條一無存留。2但向你們敬畏我名的人，必有公義的日頭出現，其光線（註："光線"原文作"翅膀"）有醫治之能。你們必出來跳躍如圈裏的肥犢。3你們必踐踏惡人；在我所定的日子，他們必如灰塵在你們腳掌之下。"這是萬軍之耶和華説的。

4"你們當記念我僕人摩西的律法，就是我在何烈山為以色列眾人所吩咐他的律例典章。

5"看哪，耶和華大而可畏之日未到以前，我必差遣先知以利亞到你們那裏去！6他必使父親的心轉向兒女，兒女的心轉向父親，免得我來咒詛遍地。"

a 17 Or Almighty, "my treasured possession, in the day when I act

新約
NEW TESTAMENT

表一：舊約彌賽亞預言在新約中的應驗
TABLE 1 : MESSIANIC PROPHECIES AND FULFILMENTS

舊約預言 Prophecy in Old Testament	經文 Reference	新約的應驗 Fulfillment in New Testament
在伯利恆出生 Be born in Bethlehem	彌 Mic 5:2	太 Mt 2:1-6; 路 Lk 2:1-20
由童貞女所生 Be born of a virgin	賽 Isa 7:14	太 Mt 1:18-25; 路 Lk 1:26-38
像摩西一樣的先知 Be a prophet like Moses	申 Dt 18:15, 18, 19	約 Jn 7:40; 來 Heb 3:2
騎着驢駒進入耶路撒冷 Enter Jerusalem on donkey and colt	亞 Zec 9:9	太 Mt 21:1-9; 可 Mk 11:1-10; 路 Lk 19:28-39; 約 Jn 12:12-16
被自己的民所拒絕 Be rejected by his own people	賽 Isa 53:3; 詩 Ps 118:22	太 Mt 26:3,4; 路 Lk 4:28-30; 約 Jn 12:37-38; (徒 Ac 4:11)
潔淨聖殿 Clearing the temple	詩 Ps 69:9	太 Mt 21:12-13; 可 Mk 11:15-17; 路 Lk 19:45-46; 約 Jn 2:13-17
被自己的門徒出賣 Be betrayed by one of his followers	詩 Ps 41:9	太 Mt 26:14-16, 47-50; 可 Mk 14:10, 11, 45; 路 Lk 22:3-5, 47-48; 約 Jn 18:3-5
被審訊與判刑 Be tried and condemned	賽 Isa 53:8, 9	太 Mt 27:1-2,11-31可 Mk 15:1-15 路 Lk 23:1-25; 約 Jn 18:33-19:16
在控告者前沉默 Be silent before his accusers	賽 Isa 53:7	太 Mt 27:12-14; 可 Mk 15:3-5; 路 Lk 23:8-10
被敵人鞭打與吐涎 Be struck and spat at by his enemies	賽 Isa 50:6	太 Mt 26:67; 27:30; 可 Mk 14:65; 路 Lk 22:63; 約 Jn 18:22; 19:1
被人嗤笑譏誚 Be mocked and insulted	詩 Ps 22:7, 8	太 Mt 27:39-44; 可 Mk 15:29-32; 路 Lk 23:35; 約 Jn 19:2, 3
被殺 Be killed	詩 Ps 22:14, 16, 17	太 Mt 27:31; 可 Mk 15:20,25; 路 Lk 23:33; 約 Jn 19:17-19
與罪犯同列，為仇敵代禱 Suffer with criminals and pray for his enemies	賽 Isa 53:12	可 Mk 15:27; 路 Lk 23:32-34
給餵苦膽和醋 Be given vinegar and gall	詩 Ps 69:21	太 Mt 27:34, 48; 可 Mk 15:23,36; 路 Lk 23:36; 約 Jn 19:29-30
其衣服被拈鬮而分 His garments be divided up by casting lots	詩 Ps 22:18	太 Mt 27:35; 可 Mk 15:24; 路 Lk 23:34; 約 Jn 19:23-24
其骨頭一根也不折斷 His bones not be broken	出 Ex 12:46; 詩 Ps 34:20	約 Jn 19:31-32,36
肋旁被刺 His side be pierced	亞 Zec 12:10	約 Jn 19:34
為贖罪而代死 Die as a sacrifice for sin	賽 Isa 53:5-12	約 Jn 1:29; 11:49-53; 彼前 1Pe 1:18-19

表一：舊約彌賽亞預言在新約中的應驗（續）
TABLE 1 : MESSIANIC PROPHECIES AND FULFILMENTS (CONT.)

舊約預言 Prophecy in Old Testament	經文 Reference	新約的應驗 Fulfillment in New Testament
與財主同葬 Be buried with a rich man	賽 Isa 53:9	太 Mt 27:57-60
從死裏復活 Be raised from death	詩 Ps 16:10	太 Mt 28:1-10; 可 Mk 16:1-15; 路 Lk 24:1-49; 約 Jn 20:1-21:2; 徒 Ac 2:24,32
現今在神的右邊 Now at God's right hand	詩 Ps 110:1	可 Mk 16:19; 徒 Ac 7:55-56 來 Heb 1:3

表二：舊約中基督的預表
TABLE 2 : TYPOLOGY OF CHRIST IN OLD TESTAMENT

舊約中的預表　　Typology in O.T.	經文 O.T. Ref.	新約的引用 N.T. Ref.
挪亞的方舟 The ark of Noah	創 Ge 6:18-22	彼前 1Pe 3:20
撒冷王麥基洗德 Melchizedek, King of Salem	創 Ge 14:18-20	來 Heb7:1-4
代替以撒獻上的羔羊 The lamb substituting Isaac who being offered	創 Ge 22:13-14	約 Jn 1:29
約瑟被賣 Joseph being sold	創 Ge 37:28; 50:19-20	太 Mt 26:14-16
出埃及的事蹟 Exodus	出 Ex 12:41	
逾越節的羔羊 Passover lamb	出 Ex 12:1-14	約 Jn 1:29
嗎哪 Manna	出 Ex 16:14-15,31	約 Jn 6:31-35
磐石(供應食水) Rock (supplying water)	出 Ex 17:6	林前 1Co 10:3-4
銅蛇 Bronze snake	民 Nu 21:8-9	約 Jn 3:14-15
獻祭的禮儀 The sacrificial ritual	利 Lev Ch 1-5 章	
大祭司 High Priest	出 Ex. 29:1	來 Heb 9:11; 10:21
牛羊的血(立約的血) Blood of sheep/ox for covenant	出 Ex. 29:20; 利 Lev 8:23-24	來 Heb 9:12, 20, 25
以血潔淨 Purifying with blood	利 Lev 8:15, 19	來 Heb 9:21-22
進迦南 Entering Canaan ★約書亞 ★Joshua	申 Dt 31:23 書 Jos 1:6	來 Heb 2:10
大衛與所羅門受膏立為王 David's, Solomon's ordinations	撒上 1Sa 16:13; 王上 1Ki 1:39	路 Lk 1:32; 20:44

★ 希伯來文 "約書亞" 及希臘文 "耶穌" 同解作救主。
★ Both "Joshua" in Hebrew and "Jesus" in Greek mean savior.

表三：耶穌所行的神蹟
TABLE 3 : MIRACLES PERFORMED BY JESUS

神蹟 Miracle	地點 Place	太 Mt	可 Mk	路 Lk	約 Jn
1. 醫治病患 Healing the sick					
1. 大臣的兒子 Royal official's son	迦拿 Cana				4:46-54
2. 彼得的岳母 Peter's mother-in-law	迦百農 Capernaum	8:14-15	1:29-31	4:38-39	
3. 長大麻瘋的男人 A leper	加利利 Galilee	8:2-4	1:40-42	5:12-14	
4. 十個長大麻瘋的人 10 lepers				17:11-19	
5. 抬來的癱子 A paralytic	迦百農 Capernaum	9:2-7	2:1-12	5:18-25	
6. 畢士大池旁的病人 An invalid man	耶路撒冷 Jerusalem				5:1-9
7. 枯手的人 A shriveled-handed man	迦百農 Capernaum	12:9-13	3:1-5	6:6-10	
8. 血漏婦人 A bleeding woman	迦百農 Capernaum	9:20-22	5:25-34	8:43-48	
9. 兩個瞎子 2 blind men	迦百農 Capernaum	9:27-30			
10. 瞎子 A blind man	伯賽大 Bethsaida		8:22-26		
11. 生來瞎眼的人 A man born blind	耶路撒冷 Jerusalem				9:1-7
12. 耶利哥城郊的瞎子 Blind Bartimaeus	耶利哥 Jericho	20:29-34	10:46-52	18:35-43	
13. 百夫長的僕人 A centurion's servant	迦百農 Capernaum	8:5-13		7:1-10	
14. 駝背的婦人 A crippled woman				13:10-17	
15. 患水臌的人 A dropsy man				14:1-6	
16. 耳聾舌結的人 A deaf and mute man	迦百農 Capernaum		7:31-37		
17. 馬勒古的右耳朵 Malchus' right ear	耶路撒冷 Jerusalem			22:49-51	
2. 叫死人復活 Raising the dead					
1. 睚魯的女兒 Jairus' daughter	迦百農 Capernaum	9:18-19, 23-26	5:22-24, 35-43	8:41-42, 49-56	
2. 寡婦的兒子 A widow's son	拿因 Nain			7:11-16	
3. 拉撒路 Lazarus	伯大尼 Bethany				11:1-44

表三：耶穌所行的神蹟（續）

TABLE 3 : MIRACLES PERFORMED BY JESUS (CONTINUED)

神蹟 Miracles	地點 Place	太 Mt	可 Mk	路 Lk	約 Jn
3. 趕逐污鬼 Casting out demon					
1. 會堂裏的男人 A man in the synagogue	迦百農 Capernaum		1:21-28	4:31-35	
2. 被羣鬼附的人 Men with demons	加大拉 Gadara	8:28-34	5:1-20	8:26-39	
3. 啞巴 A mute man	迦百農 Capernaum	9:32-33		11:14	
4. 又瞎又啞的人 A blind and mute man	迦百農 Capernaum	12:22			
5. 迦南婦人之女 Canaanite woman's daughter	推羅 Tyre	15:21-28	7:24-30		
6. 變像山下的男孩 A boy	他泊山（或黑門山）下 Mt. Tabot/ Mt.Hermon	17:14-18	9:14-27	9:37-42	
4. 超自然能力的展示 Supernatural events					
1. 水變酒 Turning water into wine	迦拿 Cana				2:1-11
2. 平靜風浪 Calming storm	加利利湖 S. of Galilee	8:23-27	4:35-41	8:22-25	
3. 首次神奇魚穫 First catch of fish	加利利湖 S. of Galilee			5:4-11	
4. 給五千人吃飽 Five thousand being fed	近伯賽大 Bethsaida	14:15-21	6:35-44	9:12-17	6:5-14
5. 在水面上行走 Walking on water	加利利湖 S. of Galilee	14:22-23	6:45-52		6:17-21
6. 給四千人吃飽 Four thousand being fed	低加坡里 Decapolis	15:32-38	8:1-9		
7. 從魚口得稅銀 A coin in a fish's mouth	迦百農 Capernaum	17:24-27			
8. 咒詛不結果的無花果樹 Cursing the fig tree	耶路撒冷 Jerusalem	21:18-22	11:12-14, 20-24		
9. 第二次神奇魚穫 Second catch of fish	加利利湖 S. of Galilee				21:1-14
5. 無細節的記載 No detailed ones					
害各樣病及被鬼附的人 Many had various diseases, demon-processed people	各城鎮 Various places	4:23-24; 8:16-17	1:32-34; 3:10	4:40, 41; 6:19	21:25
6. 最大的神蹟 The greatest of all					
從死裏復活 Resurrect from death	墳墓 The tomb	28:6	16:6	24:6	20:18

表四：耶穌受難週大事記
TABLE 4 : MAJOR EVENTS IN PASSION WEEK

事蹟 Event	太 Mt	可 Mk	路 Lk	約 Jn
耶穌榮耀地進入耶路撒冷 Jesus entered Jerusalem in triumph	21:1-11	11:1-11	19:28-44	12:12-19
耶穌咒詛不結果的無花果樹 Jesus cursed the fruitless fig tree	21:18-19	11:12-14	(13:6-9)	
耶穌潔淨聖殿及在殿中治病 Jesus cleared the temple and healed the sick	21:12-17	11:15-19	19:45-48	(2:13-17)
無花果樹枯乾 The fig tree withered	21:20-22	11:20-26		
耶穌與宗教領袖的辯論 Jesus confronted with Jewish leaders	21:23-22:46	11:27-12:37	20:1-44	(2:18-22; 3:2)
耶穌責備法利賽人 Jesus rebuked the Pharisees	23:1-39	12:38-40	20:45-47	(13:4-5, 12-17)
耶穌稱讚窮寡婦的奉獻 Jesus praised the poor widow's offering		12:41-44	21:1-4	
希臘人求見耶穌，猶太人卻拒絕祂 Several Greeks visited Jesus, but the Jews rejected him				12:20-50
論末世預言及天國比喻 Revealed signs of the end of age	24:1-25:46	13:1-37	21:5-36	(16:2; 15:21; 14:26)
耶穌末次預言被釘十架 Jesus predicted crucifixion (last time)	26:1-2			
宗教領袖密謀殺耶穌，猶大賣主 Jewish leaders plotted, Judas bestrayed	26:3-5, 14-16	14:1-2, 10-11	22:1-6	13:2, 27 (6:70-71; 11:47-53)
耶穌在伯大尼受膏 Jesus was anointed in Bethany	26:6-13	14:3-9	(7:36-50)	12:1-8
最後晚餐（在耶路撒冷的馬可樓） Jesus had the last supper in Jerusalem	26:17-20	14:12-20	22:7-30	13:1-3
耶穌為門徒洗腳，勉勵彼此服侍相愛 Jesus washed disciples' feet as an example to serve and love one another				13:4-17, 31-35
耶穌預言被出賣 Jesus foretold his betrayal	26:21-25	14:18-21	22:21-23	13:18-30
耶穌預言彼得三次不認祂 Jesus predicted Peter's denial	26:34-35	14:29-31	22:31-34	13:36-38
耶穌臨別安慰、訓勉及代禱 Jesus gave farewell speech to disciples				14:1-17:26
耶穌在客西馬尼園禱告 Jesus prayed in Gethsemane	26:36-46	14:32-42	22:39-46	(18:1)
耶穌被賣與被捉拿 Jesus was betrayed and arrested	26:47-56	14:43-52	22:47-53	18:2-12

表四：耶穌受難週大事記（續）
TABLE 4 : MAJOR EVENTS IN PASSION WEEK (CONTINUED)

事蹟 Event	太 Mt	可 Mk	路 Lk	約 Jn
耶穌在公會前受審 Jesus stood the trial before Sanhedrin	26:57-68	14:53-65	22:54-71	18:13-24
彼得三次不認主 Peter disowned Jesus 3 times	26:69-75	14:66-72	22:54-62	18:15-18; 25-27
耶穌被解交彼拉多 Jesus was delivered to Pilate	27:1-2	15:1	23:1	18:28
猶大後悔自縊 Judas remorsed, returned the money and hanged himself	27:3-10			
耶穌在彼拉多前受審 Jesus stood the trial before Pilate	27:11-14	15:2-5	23:2-5	18:29-38
耶穌在希律前受審 Jesus stood the trial before Herod			23:6-12	
耶穌被解回彼拉多面前 Jesus stood the trial before Pilate again	27:15-26	15:6-15	23:13-25	18:39-40; 19:16
耶穌被羅馬兵丁戲虐 Jesus was flogged and mocked by Roman soldiers	27:27-31	15:16-20		19:1-15
古利奈人西門代背十字架往刑場 Simon from Cyrene carried the cross	27:32	15:21	23:26-32	
在各各他耶穌被釘在十字架上 Jesus was crucified at Calvary	27:33-44	15:22-32	23:33-44	19:17-29
耶穌在十字架上被嘲 Jesus was derided on the cross	27:38-43	15:27-32	23:35-38	(19:18-19, 29)
耶穌的十架七言 The Seven Saying of Jesus	(4)27:46	(4)15:34	(1)23:34 (2)23:43 (7)23:46	(3)19:26-27 (5)19:28 (6)19:30
耶穌死在十字架上 Jesus died on the cross	27:45-54	15:33-39	23:44-48	18:28-30
婦女見證耶穌被釘 Women witnessed the crucifixion	27:55-56	15:40-41	23:49	19:25-27
耶穌的肋旁被刺 Jesus was pierced at the side by a soldier's spear				19:31-37
屍身被亞利馬太人約瑟領去埋葬 Be buried by Joseph of Arimathea	27:57-61	15:42-47	23:50-55	19:38-42
眾人守安息日；兵丁把守墳墓 People observed sabbath, soldiers guarded the tomb	27:62-66		23:56	
耶穌在清早復活，向婦女、使徒顯現 Jesus resurrected at the dawn; appeared to the women, and the disciples	28:1-10 (28:16-20)	16:1-11 (16:12-18)	24:1-27 (24:36-49)	20:1-23 (19:24-21:23)

表五：四福音中所用的時間與現代時間對照表
TABLE 5 : COMPARISON OF TIME IN 4 GOSPELS AND MODERN TIME

四福音所 用的時間	Time in 4 Gospels	經文 References	現代時間 Modern Time	
巳初	3rd hour	太 Mt 20:3; 可 Mk 15:25	上午九時	9 am
午正	6th hour	太 Mt 20:5; 27:45; 可 Mk 15:33; 路 Lk 23:44; 約 Jn 4:6; 19:14	中午 十二時	noon
未時	7th hour	約 Jn 4:52	下午一時	1 pm
申初	9th hour	太 Mt 20:5, 6; 27:45, 46; 可 Mk 15:33, 34; 路 Lk 23:44; 10:3, 30	下午三時	3 pm
申正	10th hour	約 Jn 1:39	下午四時	4 pm
酉初	11th hour	太 Mt 20:6, 9	下午五時	5 pm

有些解經家認為馬太福音、馬可福音及路加福音，使用猶太人的計時方法：白天由日出（早上六時）起計至日落（下午六時），第一小時為早上六時至七時，由今天日落至明天日落為一天。 而約翰福音則使用羅馬人的計時方法（約11:9），一天由子夜起算，與現代的算法一樣。若是如此，則約翰福音的時間便會有不同的理解：安得烈跟隨主的時間應在上午十時（中譯"申正"即下午四時，參看1:39）；撒馬利亞婦人出來打水應在上午六時（中譯"午正"即中午十二時，參看4:6）；大臣兒子得醫治應在早上七時（中譯"未時"即下午一時，參看4:52）；彼拉多定耶穌死罪應約在早上六時（中譯"約有午正"即約中午十二時，參看19:14）。

至於猶太人的分夜法，則一夜分為四更， 每更三小時，以晚上（第一更，下午六時至九時）、半夜（第二更，下午九時至子夜十二時）、雞叫（第三更，子夜十二時至清晨三時）、早晨（第四更，清晨三時至早上六時）為名。

馬太福音、路加福音及約翰福音中耶穌預言彼得當夜嘜叫（名詞，指第三更）前，三次不認祂。而馬可福音則記載，雞叫（動詞，指雞啼）兩遍前，彼得三次不認耶穌。

Some expositors regard that the time in Matthew, Mark and Luke is used in Jewish way. "Daytime" is counted from sunrise (6 am) to sunset (6 pm). The first hour is 6 to 7 am. But in John, the Roman way, midnight as the beginning of a day, which is the same way as nowadays is adopted. If it is the case, John 1:39 would be at 10 am; 4:6, 6 am; 4:52, 7 am and 19:14, 6 am.

The Jews divide nighttime into 4 watches: the first watch, "evening", 6 to 9 pm; the second watch, "midnight", 9 pm to midnight; the third watch, "rooster crows", midnight to 3 am and the fourth watch, "dawn", 3 to 6 am.

In Matthew 26:34, Luke 22:34 and John 13:38 Jesus predicted Peter's denial before "rooster crows"(means the third watch), but in Mark 14:30, before "the rooster crows twice" (indicates the sequence).

圖一：耶穌時代的耶路撒冷
MAP 1 : JERUSALEM IN JESUS' TIMES

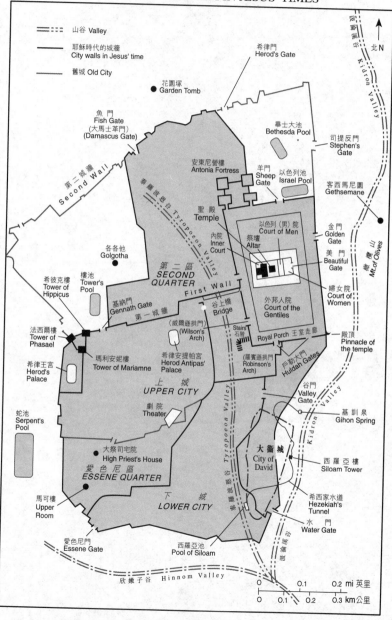

山谷 Valley

耶穌時代的城牆
City walls in Jesus' time

舊城 Old City

花園塚
Garden Tomb

魚 門
Fish Gate
(大馬士革門)
(Damascus Gate)

希律門
Herod's Gate

畢士大池
Bethesda Pool

司提反門
Stephen's Gate

第二城牆
Second Wall

安東尼營樓
Antonia Fortress

羊門
Sheep Gate

以色列池
Israel Pool

客西馬尼園
Gethsemane

泰羅波恩谷 Tyropoeon Valley

聖殿
Temple

各各他
Golgotha

樓池
Tower's
Pool

第二區
SECOND
QUARTER

First Wall 第一城牆

以色列（男）院
Court of Men

祭壇
Altar

內院
Inner
Court

金門
Golden Gate

美門
Beautiful
Gate

橄欖山
Mt. of Olives

希彼克樓
Tower of
Hippicus

基納門
Gennath Gate

谷上橋
Bridge

（威爾遜拱門）
(Wilson's
Arch)

外邦人院
Court of the
Gentiles

婦女院
Court of
Women

法西爾樓
Tower of
Phasael

瑪利安妮樓
Tower of Mariamne

希律安提帕宮
Herod Antipas'
Palace

石階
Stairs

王室走廊
Royal Porch

殿頂
Pinnacle
of the temple

希律王宮
Herod's
Palace

上 城
UPPER CITY

（羅賓遜拱門）
(Robinson's
Arch)

戶勒大門
Huldah Gates

谷門
Valley
Gate

蛇池
Serpent's
Pool

劇院
Theater

基訓泉
Gihon Spring

大祭司宅院
High Priest's House

大衛城
City of
David

西羅亞樓
Siloam Tower

馬可樓
Upper
Room

愛色尼區
ESSENE QUARTER

下 城
LOWER CITY

希西家水道
Hezekiah's
Tunnel

水 門
Water Gate

愛色尼門
Essene Gate

西羅亞池
Pool of Siloam

欣嫩子谷 Hinnom Valley

汲淪溪谷 Kidron Valley

泰羅波恩谷 Tyropoeon Valley

北 N

0   0.1   0.2 mi 英里

0   0.1   0.2   0.3 km 公里

xi

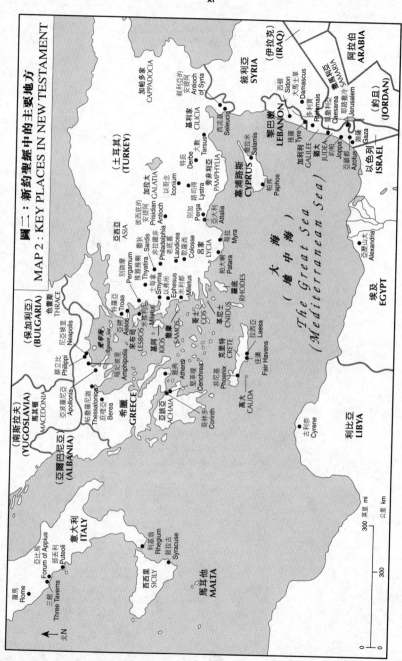

圖二：新約聖經中的主要地方
MAP 2 : KEY PLACES IN NEW TESTAMENT

Matthew

馬太福音

The Genealogy of Jesus

1 A record of the genealogy of Jesus Christ the son of David, the son of Abraham:

²Abraham was the father of Isaac,
  Isaac the father of Jacob,
  Jacob the father of Judah and his brothers,
³Judah the father of Perez and Zerah, whose mother was Tamar,
  Perez the father of Hezron,
  Hezron the father of Ram,
⁴Ram the father of Amminadab,
  Amminadab the father of Nahshon,
  Nahshon the father of Salmon,
⁵Salmon the father of Boaz, whose mother was Rahab,
  Boaz the father of Obed, whose mother was Ruth,
  Obed the father of Jesse,
⁶and Jesse the father of King David.

David was the father of Solomon, whose mother had been Uriah's wife,
⁷Solomon the father of Rehoboam,
  Rehoboam the father of Abijah,
  Abijah the father of Asa,
⁸Asa the father of Jehoshaphat,
  Jehoshaphat the father of Jehoram,
  Jehoram the father of Uzziah,
⁹Uzziah the father of Jotham,
  Jotham the father of Ahaz,
  Ahaz the father of Hezekiah,
¹⁰Hezekiah the father of Manasseh,
  Manasseh the father of Amon,
  Amon the father of Josiah,
¹¹and Josiah the father of Jeconiah*a* and his brothers at the time of the exile to Babylon.

¹²After the exile to Babylon:
  Jeconiah was the father of Shealtiel,
  Shealtiel the father of Zerubbabel,
¹³Zerubbabel the father of Abiud,
  Abiud the father of Eliakim,
  Eliakim the father of Azor,

a 11 That is, Jehoiachin; also in verse 12

耶穌的家譜

1 亞伯拉罕的後裔、大衛的子孫、耶穌基督的家譜（註："後裔"、"子孫"原文都作"兒子"。下同）：

²亞伯拉罕生以撒，
  以撒生雅各，
  雅各生猶大和他的弟兄，
³猶大從她瑪氏
  生法勒斯和謝拉，
  法勒斯生希斯崙，
  希斯崙生亞蘭，
⁴亞蘭生亞米拿達，
  亞米拿達生拿順，
  拿順生撒門，
⁵撒門從喇合氏
  生波阿斯，
  波阿斯從路得氏
  生俄備得，
  俄備得生耶西，
⁶耶西生大衛王。

大衛從烏利亞的妻子生所羅門，

⁷所羅門生羅波安，
  羅波安生亞比雅，
  亞比雅生亞撒，
⁸亞撒生約沙法，
  約沙法生約蘭，
  約蘭生烏西亞，
⁹烏西亞生約坦，
  約坦生亞哈斯，
  亞哈斯生希西家，
¹⁰希西家生瑪拿西，
  瑪拿西生亞們，
  亞們生約西亞。
¹¹百姓被遷到巴比倫的時候，
  約西亞生耶哥尼雅和他的弟兄。

¹²遷到巴比倫之後，
  耶哥尼雅生撒拉鐵，
  撒拉鐵生所羅巴伯，
¹³所羅巴伯生亞比玉，
  亞比玉生以利亞敬，
  以利亞敬生亞所，

14亞所生撒督，
撒督生亞金，
亞金生以律，
15以律生以利亞撒，
以利亞撒生馬但，
馬但生雅各，
16雅各生約瑟，就是馬利亞的丈
夫。那稱為基督的耶穌，是
從馬利亞生的。

17這樣，從亞伯拉罕到大衛，共
有十四代；從大衛到遷至巴比倫的
時候，也有十四代；從遷至巴比倫
的時候到基督，又有十四代。

耶穌基督的降生

18耶穌基督降生的事記在下面：
他母親馬利亞已經許配了約瑟，還
沒有迎娶，馬利亞就從聖靈懷了
孕。19她丈夫約瑟是個義人，不願意
明明地羞辱她，想要暗暗地把她休
了。

20正思念這事的時候，有主的使
者向他夢中顯現，說："大衛的子
孫約瑟，不要怕，只管娶過你的妻
子馬利亞來，因她所懷的孕是從聖
靈來的。21她將要生一個兒子，你要
給他起名叫耶穌，因他要將自己的
百姓從罪惡裏救出來。"

22這一切的事成就，是要應驗主
藉先知所說的話，23說："必有童女
懷孕生子，人要稱他的名為以馬內
利。"（"以馬內利"翻出來就是
"神與我們同在"。）

24約瑟醒了，起來，就遵着主使
者的吩咐，把妻子娶過來，25只是沒
有和她同房，等她生了兒子（註：有古
卷作"等她生了頭胎的兒子"），就給他起
名叫耶穌。

博士來朝拜聖嬰

2 當希律王的時候，耶穌生在
猶太的伯利恆。有幾個博士
從東方來到耶路撒冷，說：
2 "那生下來作猶太人之王的在哪
裏？我們在東方看見他的星，特來
拜他。"

14Azor the father of Zadok,
Zadok the father of Akim,
Akim the father of Eliud,
15Eliud the father of Eleazar,
Eleazar the father of Matthan,
Matthan the father of Jacob,
16and Jacob the father of Joseph, the husband of Mary, of whom was born Jesus,
who is called Christ.

17Thus there were fourteen generations in all
from Abraham to David, fourteen from David to
the exile to Babylon, and fourteen from the exile
to the Christ.*a*

The Birth of Jesus Christ

18This is how the birth of Jesus Christ came
about: His mother Mary was pledged to be married to Joseph, but before they came together,
she was found to be with child through the
Holy Spirit. 19Because Joseph her husband was a
righteous man and did not want to expose her
to public disgrace, he had in mind to divorce her
quietly.

20But after he had considered this, an angel of
the Lord appeared to him in a dream and said,
"Joseph son of David, do not be afraid to take
Mary home as your wife, because what is conceived in her is from the Holy Spirit. 21She will
give birth to a son, and you are to give him the
name Jesus,*b* because he will save his people
from their sins."

22All this took place to fulfill what the Lord
had said through the prophet: 23"The virgin will
be with child and will give birth to a son, and
they will call him Immanuel"*c* —which means,
"God with us."

24When Joseph woke up, he did what the
angel of the Lord had commanded him and took
Mary home as his wife. 25But he had no union
with her until she gave birth to a son. And he
gave him the name Jesus.

The Visit of the Magi

2 After Jesus was born in Bethlehem in
Judea, during the time of King Herod,
Magi*d* from the east came to Jerusalem
2and asked, "Where is the one who has been
born king of the Jews? We saw his star in the
east*e* and have come to worship him."

a 17 Or Messiah. "The Christ" (Greek) and "the Messiah"
(Hebrew) both mean "the Anointed One."　*b 21 Jesus is the*
Greek form of *Joshua, which means the LORD saves.*
c 23 Isaiah 7:14　d 1 Traditionally Wise Men　e 2 Or star
when it rose

3

³When King Herod heard this he was disturbed, and all Jerusalem with him. ⁴When he had called together all the people's chief priests and teachers of the law, he asked them where the Christ*a* was to be born. ⁵"In Bethlehem in Judea," they replied, "for this is what the prophet has written:

⁶" 'But you, Bethlehem, in the land of Judah,
 are by no means least among the rulers of
 Judah;
 for out of you will come a ruler
 who will be the shepherd of my people
 Israel.'*b* "

⁷Then Herod called the Magi secretly and found out from them the exact time the star had appeared. ⁸He sent them to Bethlehem and said, "Go and make a careful search for the child. As soon as you find him, report to me, so that I too may go and worship him."

⁹After they had heard the king, they went on their way, and the star they had seen in the east*c* went ahead of them until it stopped over the place where the child was. ¹⁰When they saw the star, they were overjoyed. ¹¹On coming to the house, they saw the child with his mother Mary, and they bowed down and worshiped him. Then they opened their treasures and presented him with gifts of gold and of incense and of myrrh. ¹²And having been warned in a dream not to go back to Herod, they returned to their country by another route.

The Escape to Egypt

¹³When they had gone, an angel of the Lord appeared to Joseph in a dream. "Get up," he said, "take the child and his mother and escape to Egypt. Stay there until I tell you, for Herod is going to search for the child to kill him."

¹⁴So he got up, took the child and his mother during the night and left for Egypt, ¹⁵where he stayed until the death of Herod. And so was fulfilled what the Lord had said through the prophet: "Out of Egypt I called my son."*d*

¹⁶When Herod realized that he had been outwitted by the Magi, he was furious, and he gave orders to kill all the boys in Bethlehem and its vicinity who were two years old and under, in accordance with the time he had learned from the Magi. ¹⁷Then what was said through the prophet Jeremiah was fulfilled:

³希律王聽見了，就心裏不安；耶路撒冷合城的人也都不安。⁴他就召齊了祭司長和民間的文士，問他們說："基督當生在何處？"⁵他們回答說："在猶太的伯利恆。因為有先知記着說：

⁶" '猶大地的伯利恆啊，
  你在猶大諸城中
  並不是最小的，
  因為將來有一位君王
  要從你那裏出來，
  牧養我以色列民。' "

⁷當下希律暗暗地召了博士來，細問那星是甚麼時候出現的，⁸就差他們往伯利恆去，說："你們去仔細尋訪那小孩子，尋到了，就來報信，我也好去拜他。"

⁹他們聽見王的話就去了。在東方所看見的那星，忽然在他們前頭行，直到小孩子的地方，就在上頭停住了。¹⁰他們看見那星，就大大地歡喜。¹¹進了房子，看見小孩子和他母親馬利亞，就俯伏拜那小孩子，揭開寶盒，拿黃金、乳香、沒藥為禮物獻給他。¹²博士因為在夢中被主指示，不要回去見希律，就從別的路回本地去了。

逃到埃及

¹³他們去後，有主的使者向約瑟夢中顯現，說："起來！帶着小孩子同他母親逃往埃及，住在那裏，等我吩咐你，因為希律必尋找小孩子，要除滅他。"

¹⁴約瑟就起來，夜間帶着小孩子和他母親往埃及去，¹⁵住在那裏，直到希律死了。這是要應驗主藉先知所說的話，說："我從埃及召出我的兒子來。"

¹⁶希律見自己被博士愚弄，就大大發怒，差人將伯利恆城裏並四境所有的男孩，照着他向博士仔細查問的時候，凡兩歲以裏的，都殺盡了。¹⁷這就應了先知耶利米的話，說：

---

a 4 Or *Messiah*   *b 6* Micah 5:2   *c 9* Or *seen when it rose*
d 15 Hosea 11:1

18 "在拉瑪聽見
　號咷大哭的聲音，
是拉結哭她兒女，
　不肯受安慰，
因為他們都不在了。"

回到拿撒勒

19 希律死了以後，有主的使者在埃及向約瑟夢中顯現，説：20 "起來！帶着小孩子和他母親往以色列地去，因為要害小孩子性命的人已經死了。"

21 約瑟就起來，把小孩子和他母親帶到以色列地去。22 只因聽見亞基老接着他父親希律作了猶太王，就怕往那裏去，又在夢中被主指示，便往加利利境內去了。23 到了一座城，名叫拿撒勒，就住在那裏。這是要應驗先知所説，他將稱為拿撒勒人的話了。

施洗約翰預備道路

3 那時，有施洗的約翰出來，在猶太的曠野傳道，説：2 "天國近了，你們應當悔改！" 3 這人就是先知以賽亞所説的，他説：

　"在曠野有人聲喊着説：
　'預備主的道，
　修直他的路！'"

4 這約翰身穿駱駝毛的衣服，腰束皮帶，吃的是蝗蟲、野蜜。5 那時，耶路撒冷和猶太全地，並約旦河一帶地方的人，都出去到約翰那裏，6 承認他們的罪，在約旦河裏受他的洗。

7 約翰看見許多法利賽人和撒都該人也來受洗，就對他們説："毒蛇的種類！誰指示你們逃避將來的忿怒呢？8 你們要結出果子來，與悔改的心相稱。9 不要自己心裏説："有亞伯拉罕為我們的祖宗。'我告訴你們：神能從這些石頭中給亞伯拉罕興起子孫來。10 現在斧子已經放在樹根上，凡不結好果子的樹，就砍下來，丟在火裏。

11 "我是用水給你們施洗，叫你們悔改；但那在我以後來的，能力比我更大，我就是給他提鞋也不

18 "A voice is heard in Ramah,
weeping and great mourning,
Rachel weeping for her children
and refusing to be comforted,
because they are no more."[a]

The Return to Nazareth

19 After Herod died, an angel of the Lord appeared in a dream to Joseph in Egypt 20 and said, "Get up, take the child and his mother and go to the land of Israel, for those who were trying to take the child's life are dead."

21 So he got up, took the child and his mother and went to the land of Israel. 22 But when he heard that Archelaus was reigning in Judea in place of his father Herod, he was afraid to go there. Having been warned in a dream, he withdrew to the district of Galilee, 23 and he went and lived in a town called Nazareth. So was fulfilled what was said through the prophets: "He will be called a Nazarene."

John the Baptist Prepares the Way

3 In those days John the Baptist came, preaching in the Desert of Judea 2 and saying, "Repent, for the kingdom of heaven is near." 3 This is he who was spoken of through the prophet Isaiah:

"A voice of one calling in the desert,
'Prepare the way for the Lord,
make straight paths for him.'"[b]

4 John's clothes were made of camel's hair, and he had a leather belt around his waist. His food was locusts and wild honey. 5 People went out to him from Jerusalem and all Judea and the whole region of the Jordan. 6 Confessing their sins, they were baptized by him in the Jordan River.

7 But when he saw many of the Pharisees and Sadducees coming to where he was baptizing, he said to them: "You brood of vipers! Who warned you to flee from the coming wrath? 8 Produce fruit in keeping with repentance. 9 And do not think you can say to yourselves, 'We have Abraham as our father.' I tell you that out of these stones God can raise up children for Abraham. 10 The ax is already at the root of the trees, and every tree that does not produce good fruit will be cut down and thrown into the fire.

11 "I baptize you with[c] water for repentance. But after me will come one who is more powerful than I, whose sandals I am not fit to carry.

a 18 Jer. 31:15　　b 3 Isaiah 40:3　　c 11 Or in

He will baptize you with the Holy Spirit and with fire. [12]His winnowing fork is in his hand, and he will clear his threshing floor, gathering his wheat into the barn and burning up the chaff with unquenchable fire."

The Baptism of Jesus

[13]Then Jesus came from Galilee to the Jordan to be baptized by John. [14]But John tried to deter him, saying, "I need to be baptized by you, and do you come to me?"

[15]Jesus replied, "Let it be so now; it is proper for us to do this to fulfill all righteousness." Then John consented.

[16]As soon as Jesus was baptized, he went up out of the water. At that moment heaven was opened, and he saw the Spirit of God descending like a dove and lighting on him. [17]And a voice from heaven said, "This is my Son, whom I love; with him I am well pleased."

The Temptation of Jesus

4 Then Jesus was led by the Spirit into the desert to be tempted by the devil. [2]After fasting forty days and forty nights, he was hungry. [3]The tempter came to him and said, "If you are the Son of God, tell these stones to become bread."

[4]Jesus answered, "It is written: 'Man does not live on bread alone, but on every word that comes from the mouth of God.'[a]"

[5]Then the devil took him to the holy city and had him stand on the highest point of the temple. [6]"If you are the Son of God," he said, "throw yourself down. For it is written:

" 'He will command his angels concerning you,

and they will lift you up in their hands,
so that you will not strike your foot against a stone.'[b]"

[7]Jesus answered him, "It is also written: 'Do not put the Lord your God to the test.'[c]"

[8]Again, the devil took him to a very high mountain and showed him all the kingdoms of the world and their splendor. [9]"All this I will give you," he said, "if you will bow down and worship me."

[10]Jesus said to him, "Away from me, Satan! For it is written: 'Worship the Lord your God, and serve him only.'[d]"

配。他要用聖靈與火給你們施洗。[12]他手裏拿着簸箕，要揚淨他的場，把麥子收在倉裏，把糠用不滅的火燒盡了。"

耶穌受洗

[13]當下，耶穌從加利利來到約旦河，見了約翰，要受他的洗。[14]約翰想要攔住他，說："我當受你的洗，你反倒上我這裏來嗎？"

[15]耶穌回答說："你暫且許我，因為我們理當這樣盡諸般的義（註：或作"禮"）。於是約翰許了他。

[16]耶穌受了洗，隨即從水裏上來。天忽然為他開了，他就看見神的靈彷彿鴿子降下，落在他身上。[17]從天上有聲音說："這是我的愛子，我所喜悅的。"

耶穌受試探

4 當時，耶穌被聖靈引到曠野，受魔鬼的試探。[2]他禁食四十晝夜，後來就餓了。[3]那試探人的進前來，對他說："你若是神的兒子，可以吩咐這些石頭變成食物。"

[4]耶穌卻回答說："經上記着說：'人活着，不是單靠食物，乃是靠神口裏所出的一切話。'"

[5]魔鬼就帶他進了聖城，叫他站在殿頂上（註："頂"原文作"翅"），[6]對他說："你若是神的兒子，可以跳下去，因為經上記着說：

" '主要為你
吩咐他的使者，
用手托着你，
免得你的腳碰在石頭上。'"

[7]耶穌對他說："經上又記着說：'不可試探主你的神。'"

[8]魔鬼又帶他上了一座最高的山，將世上的萬國與萬國的榮華，都指給他看，[9]對他說："你若俯伏拜我，我就把這一切都賜給你。"

[10]耶穌說："撒但（註："撒但"就是"抵擋"的意思，乃魔鬼的別名）退去吧！因為經上記着說：'當拜主你的神，單要侍奉他。'"

---

a 4 Deut. 8:3   b 6 Psalm 91:11,12   c 7 Deut. 6:16
d 10 Deut. 6:13

¹¹於是魔鬼離了耶穌，有天使來伺候他。

耶穌開始傳道

¹²耶穌聽見<u>約翰</u>下了監，就退到<u>加利利</u>去；¹³後又離開<u>拿撒勒</u>，往<u>迦百農</u>去，就住在那裏。那地方靠海，在<u>西布倫</u>和<u>拿弗他利</u>的邊界上。¹⁴這是要應驗先知<u>以賽亞</u>的話，

¹⁵說："<u>西布倫地</u>、<u>拿弗他利地</u>，
　　就是沿海的路，<u>約旦河外</u>，
　　外邦人的<u>加利利地</u>。
¹⁶那坐在黑暗裏的百姓，
　　看見了大光，
　　坐在死蔭之地的人，
　　有光發現照着他們。"

¹⁷從那時候，耶穌就傳起道來，說："天國近了，你們應當悔改！"

召第一批門徒

¹⁸耶穌在<u>加利利海</u>邊行走，看見弟兄二人，就是那稱呼<u>彼得</u>的<u>西門</u>和他兄弟<u>安得烈</u>，在海裏撒網；他們本是打魚的。¹⁹耶穌對他們說："來，跟從我！我要叫你們得人如得魚一樣。"²⁰他們就立刻捨了網，跟從了他。²¹從那裏往前走，又看見弟兄二人，就是<u>西庇太</u>的兒子<u>雅各</u>和他兄弟<u>約翰</u>，同他們的父親<u>西庇太</u>在船上補網，耶穌就招呼他們。²²他們立刻捨了船，別了父親，跟從了耶穌。

耶穌醫治病人

²³耶穌走遍<u>加利利</u>，在各會堂裏教訓人，傳天國的福音，醫治百姓各樣的病症。²⁴他的名聲就傳遍了<u>敍利亞</u>。那裏的人把一切害病的，就是害各樣疾病、各樣疼痛的和被鬼附的、癲癇的、癱瘓的，都帶了來，耶穌就治好了他們。²⁵當下，有許多人從<u>加利利</u>、<u>低加坡里</u>、<u>耶路撒冷</u>、<u>猶太</u>、<u>約旦河外</u>來跟着他。

¹¹Then the devil left him, and angels came and attended him.

Jesus Begins to Preach

¹²When Jesus heard that John had been put in prison, he returned to Galilee. ¹³Leaving Nazareth, he went and lived in Capernaum, which was by the lake in the area of Zebulun and Naphtali— ¹⁴to fulfill what was said through the prophet Isaiah:

¹⁵"Land of Zebulun and land of Naphtali,
　the way to the sea, along the Jordan,
　Galilee of the Gentiles—
¹⁶the people living in darkness
　have seen a great light;
　on those living in the land of the shadow of
　　death
　a light has dawned."^a

¹⁷From that time on Jesus began to preach, "Repent, for the kingdom of heaven is near."

The Calling of the First Disciples

¹⁸As Jesus was walking beside the Sea of Galilee, he saw two brothers, Simon called Peter and his brother Andrew. They were casting a net into the lake, for they were fishermen. ¹⁹"Come, follow me," Jesus said, "and I will make you fishers of men." ²⁰At once they left their nets and followed him.

²¹Going on from there, he saw two other brothers, James son of Zebedee and his brother John. They were in a boat with their father Zebedee, preparing their nets. Jesus called them, ²²and immediately they left the boat and their father and followed him.

Jesus Heals the Sick

²³Jesus went throughout Galilee, teaching in their synagogues, preaching the good news of the kingdom, and healing every disease and sickness among the people. ²⁴News about him spread all over Syria, and people brought to him all who were ill with various diseases, those suffering severe pain, the demon-possessed, those having seizures, and the paralyzed, and he healed them. ²⁵Large crowds from Galilee, the Decapolis,^b Jerusalem, Judea and the region across the Jordan followed him.

<hr/>

a 16 Isaiah 9:1,2　　*b 25* That is, the Ten Cities

The Beatitudes

5 Now when he saw the crowds, he went up on a mountainside and sat down. His disciples came to him, ²and he began to teach them, saying:

³"Blessed are the poor in spirit,
　for theirs is the kingdom of heaven.
⁴Blessed are those who mourn,
　for they will be comforted.
⁵Blessed are the meek,
　for they will inherit the earth.
⁶Blessed are those who hunger and thirst for righteousness,
　for they will be filled.
⁷Blessed are the merciful,
　for they will be shown mercy.
⁸Blessed are the pure in heart,
　for they will see God.
⁹Blessed are the peacemakers,
　for they will be called sons of God.
¹⁰Blessed are those who are persecuted because of righteousness,
　for theirs is the kingdom of heaven.

¹¹"Blessed are you when people insult you, persecute you and falsely say all kinds of evil against you because of me. ¹²Rejoice and be glad, because great is your reward in heaven, for in the same way they persecuted the prophets who were before you.

Salt and Light

¹³"You are the salt of the earth. But if the salt loses its saltiness, how can it be made salty again? It is no longer good for anything, except to be thrown out and trampled by men.

¹⁴"You are the light of the world. A city on a hill cannot be hidden. ¹⁵Neither do people light a lamp and put it under a bowl. Instead they put it on its stand, and it gives light to everyone in the house. ¹⁶In the same way, let your light shine before men, that they may see your good deeds and praise your Father in heaven.

The Fulfillment of the Law

¹⁷"Do not think that I have come to abolish the Law or the Prophets; I have not come to abolish them but to fulfill them. ¹⁸I tell you the truth, until heaven and earth disappear, not the smallest letter, not the least stroke of a pen, will by any means disappear from the Law until everything is accomplished. ¹⁹Anyone who breaks one of the least of these commandments and teaches others to do the same will be called least in the kingdom of heaven, but whoever

天國八福

5 耶穌看見這許多的人，就上了山，既已坐下，門徒到他跟前來。²他就開口教訓他們，說：

³「虛心的人有福了，
　因為天國是他們的。
⁴哀慟的人有福了，
　因為他們必得安慰。
⁵溫柔的人有福了，
　因為他們必承受地土。
⁶飢渴慕義的人有福了，
　因為他們必得飽足。

⁷憐恤人的人有福了，
　因為他們必蒙憐恤。
⁸清心的人有福了，
　因為他們必得見神。
⁹使人和睦的人有福了，
　因為他們必稱為神的兒子。
¹⁰為義受逼迫的人有福了，
　因為天國是他們的。

¹¹「人若因我辱罵你們，逼迫你們，捏造各樣壞話毀謗你們，你們就有福了。¹²應當歡喜快樂，因為你們在天上的賞賜是大的。在你們以前的先知，人也是這樣逼迫他們。

鹽和光

¹³「你們是世上的鹽。鹽若失了味，怎能叫它再鹹呢？以後無用，不過丟在外面，被人踐踏了。

¹⁴「你們是世上的光。城造在山上，是不能隱藏的。¹⁵人點燈，不放在斗底下，是放在燈臺上，就照亮一家的人。¹⁶你們的光也當這樣照在人前，叫他們看見你們的好行為，便將榮耀歸給你們在天上的父。

成全律法

¹⁷「莫想我來要廢掉律法和先知；我來不是要廢掉，乃是要成全。¹⁸我實在告訴你們：就是到天地都廢去了，律法的一點一畫也不能廢去，都要成全。¹⁹所以，無論何人廢掉這誡命中最小的一條，又教訓人這樣做，他在天國要稱為最小的；但無論

何人遵行這誡命，又教訓人遵行，他在天國要稱為大的。20我告訴你們：你們的義若不勝於文士和法利賽人的義，斷不能進天國。

論殺人

21 "你們聽見有吩咐古人的話，說：'不可殺人'，又說：'凡殺人的，難免受審判。' 22只是我告訴你們：凡向弟兄動怒的，難免受審判（註：有古卷在"凡"字下添"無緣無故地"五字）。凡罵弟兄是拉加的，難免公會的審斷；凡罵弟兄是魔利的，難免地獄的火。

23 "所以，你在祭壇上獻禮物的時候，若想起弟兄向你懷怨，24就把禮物留在壇前，先去同弟兄和好，然後來獻禮物。

25 "你同告你的對頭還在路上，就趕緊與他和息，恐怕他把你送給審判官，審判官交付衙役，你就下在監裏了。26我實在告訴你：若有一文錢沒有還清，你斷不能從那裏出來。

論姦淫

27 "你們聽見有話說：'不可姦淫。' 28只是我告訴你們：凡看見婦女就動淫念的，這人心裏已經與她犯姦淫了。29若是你的右眼叫你跌倒，就剜出來丟掉，寧可失去百體中的一體，不叫全身丟在地獄裏；30若是右手叫你跌倒，就砍下來丟掉，寧可失去百體中的一體，不叫全身下入地獄。

論休妻

31 "又有話說：'人若休妻，就當給她休書。' 32只是我告訴你們：凡休妻的，若不是為淫亂的緣故，就是叫她作淫婦了；人若娶這被休的婦人，也是犯姦淫了。

---

practices and teaches these commands will be called great in the kingdom of heaven. [20]For I tell you that unless your righteousness surpasses that of the Pharisees and the teachers of the law, you will certainly not enter the kingdom of heaven.

Murder

[21]"You have heard that it was said to the people long ago, 'Do not murder,[a] and anyone who murders will be subject to judgment.' [22]But I tell you that anyone who is angry with his brother[b] will be subject to judgment. Again, anyone who says to his brother, 'Raca,[c]' is answerable to the Sanhedrin. But anyone who says, 'You fool!' will be in danger of the fire of hell.

[23]"Therefore, if you are offering your gift at the altar and there remember that your brother has something against you, [24]leave your gift there in front of the altar. First go and be reconciled to your brother; then come and offer your gift.

[25]"Settle matters quickly with your adversary who is taking you to court. Do it while you are still with him on the way, or he may hand you over to the judge, and the judge may hand you over to the officer, and you may be thrown into prison. [26]I tell you the truth, you will not get out until you have paid the last penny.[d]

Adultery

[27]"You have heard that it was said, 'Do not commit adultery.'[e] [28]But I tell you that anyone who looks at a woman lustfully has already committed adultery with her in his heart. [29]If your right eye causes you to sin, gouge it out and throw it away. It is better for you to lose one part of your body than for your whole body to be thrown into hell. [30]And if your right hand causes you to sin, cut it off and throw it away. It is better for you to lose one part of your body than for your whole body to go into hell.

Divorce

[31]"It has been said, 'Anyone who divorces his wife must give her a certificate of divorce.'[f] [32]But I tell you that anyone who divorces his wife, except for marital unfaithfulness, causes her to become an adulteress, and anyone who marries the divorced woman commits adultery.

---

a 21 Exodus 20:13　*b 22* Some manuscripts *brother without cause*　*c 22* An Aramaic term of contempt　*d 26* Greek *kodrantes*　*e 27* Exodus 20:14　*f 31* Deut. 24:1

Oaths

33"Again, you have heard that it was said to the people long ago, 'Do not break your oath, but keep the oaths you have made to the Lord.' 34But I tell you, Do not swear at all: either by heaven, for it is God's throne; 35or by the earth, for it is his footstool; or by Jerusalem, for it is the city of the Great King. 36And do not swear by your head, for you cannot make even one hair white or black. 37Simply let your 'Yes' be 'Yes,' and your 'No,' 'No'; anything beyond this comes from the evil one.

An Eye for an Eye

38"You have heard that it was said, 'Eye for eye, and tooth for tooth.'*a* 39But I tell you, Do not resist an evil person. If someone strikes you on the right cheek, turn to him the other also. 40And if someone wants to sue you and take your tunic, let him have your cloak as well. 41If someone forces you to go one mile, go with him two miles. 42Give to the one who asks you, and do not turn away from the one who wants to borrow from you.

Love for Enemies

43"You have heard that it was said, 'Love your neighbor*b* and hate your enemy.' 44But I tell you: Love your enemies*c* and pray for those who persecute you, 45that you may be sons of your Father in heaven. He causes his sun to rise on the evil and the good, and sends rain on the righteous and the unrighteous. 46If you love those who love you, what reward will you get? Are not even the tax collectors doing that? 47And if you greet only your brothers, what are you doing more than others? Do not even pagans do that? 48Be perfect, therefore, as your heavenly Father is perfect.

Giving to the Needy

6 "Be careful not to do your 'acts of righteousness' before men, to be seen by them. If you do, you will have no reward from your Father in heaven.

2"So, when you give to the needy, do not announce it with trumpets, as the hypocrites do in the synagogues and on the streets, to be honored by men. I tell you the truth, they have received their reward in full. 3But when you give to the needy, do not let your left hand know what your right hand is doing, 4so that

---

論起誓

33 "你們又聽見有吩咐古人的話,說:'不可背誓,所起的誓,總要向主謹守。' 34只是我告訴你們:甚麼誓都不可起。不可指着天起誓,因為天是神的座位; 35不可指着地起誓,因為地是他的腳凳;也不可指着耶路撒冷起誓,因為耶路撒冷是大君的京城; 36又不可指着你的頭起誓,因為你不能使一根頭髮變黑變白了。 37你們的話,是,就說是;不是,就說不是;若再多說,就是出於那惡者

(註:或作"是從裏出來的")。

論以眼還眼

38 "你們聽見有話說:'以眼還眼,以牙還牙。' 39只是我告訴你們:不要與惡人作對。有人打你的右臉,連左臉也轉過來由他打; 40有人想要告你,要拿你的裏衣,連外衣也由他拿去; 41有人強逼你走一里路,你就同他走二里; 42有求你的,就給他;有向你借貸的,不可推辭。

論愛仇敵

43 "你們聽見有話說:'當愛你的鄰舍,恨你的仇敵。' 44只是我告訴你們:要愛你們的仇敵,為那逼迫你們的禱告。 45這樣,就可以作你們天父的兒子,因為他叫日頭照好人,也照歹人;降雨給義人,也給不義的人。 46你們若單愛那愛你們的人,有甚麼賞賜呢?就是稅吏不也是這樣行嗎? 47你們若單請你弟兄的安,比人有甚麼長處呢?就是外邦人不也是這樣行嗎? 48所以你們要完全,像你們的天父完全一樣。

論施捨

6 "你們要小心,不可將善事行在人的面前,故意叫他們看見;若是這樣,就不能得你們天父的賞賜了。

2 "所以,你施捨的時候,不可在你前面吹號,像那假冒為善的人在會堂裏和街道上所行的,故意要得人的榮耀。我實在告訴你們:他們已經得了他們的賞賜。 3你施捨的時候,不要叫左手知道右手所做的; 4要叫

---

a 38 Exodus 21:24; Lev. 24:20; Deut. 19:21   *b 43* Lev. 19:18
c 44 Some late manuscripts *enemies, bless those who curse you, do good to those who hate you*

你施捨的事行在暗中，你父在暗中察看，必然報答你（註：有古卷作 "必在明處報答你"）。

禱告

5 "你們禱告的時候，不可像那假冒為善的人，愛站在會堂裏和十字路口上禱告，故意叫人看見。我實在告訴你們：他們已經得了他們的賞賜。6你禱告的時候，要進你的內屋，關上門，禱告你在暗中的父，你父在暗中察看，必然報答你。7你們禱告，不可像外邦人，用許多重複話，他們以為話多了必蒙垂聽。8你們不可效法他們，因為你們沒有祈求以先，你們所需用的，你們的父早已知道了。

9 "所以，你們禱告要這樣說：

" '我們在天上的父，

願人都尊你的名為聖。

10願你的國降臨。

願你的旨意行在地上，

如同行在天上。

11我們日用的飲食，今日賜給我們。

12免我們的債，

如同我們免了人的債。

13不叫我們遇見試探，救我們

脫離兇惡（註：或作 "脫離惡者"）。

因為國度、權柄、榮耀，

全是你的，直到永遠。阿們！'

（註：有古卷無 "因為" 至 "阿們" 等字）

14你們饒恕人的過犯，你們的天父也必饒恕你們的過犯；15你們不饒恕人的過犯，你們的天父也必不饒恕你們的過犯。

禁食

16 "你們禁食的時候，不可像那假冒為善的人，臉上帶着愁容，因為他們把臉弄得難看，故意叫人看出他們是禁食。我實在告訴你們：他們已經得了他們的賞賜。17你禁食的時候，要梳頭洗臉，18不叫人看出你禁食來，只叫你暗中的父看見。你父在暗中察看，必然報答你。

積財寶在天

19 "不要為自己積攢財寶在地上，地上有蟲子咬，能銹壞，也有賊挖窟窿來偷；20只要積攢財寶在天上，天上沒有蟲子咬，不能銹壞，

your giving may be in secret. Then your Father, who sees what is done in secret, will reward you.

Prayer

5"And when you pray, do not be like the hypocrites, for they love to pray standing in the synagogues and on the street corners to be seen by men. I tell you the truth, they have received their reward in full. 6But when you pray, go into your room, close the door and pray to your Father, who is unseen. Then your Father, who sees what is done in secret, will reward you. 7And when you pray, do not keep on babbling like pagans, for they think they will be heard because of their many words. 8Do not be like them, for your Father knows what you need before you ask him.

9"This, then, is how you should pray:

" 'Our Father in heaven,

hallowed be your name,

10your kingdom come,

your will be done

on earth as it is in heaven.

11Give us today our daily bread.

12Forgive us our debts,

as we also have forgiven our debtors.

13And lead us not into temptation,

but deliver us from the evil one.*a*'

14For if you forgive men when they sin against you, your heavenly Father will also forgive you. 15But if you do not forgive men their sins, your Father will not forgive your sins.

Fasting

16"When you fast, do not look somber as the hypocrites do, for they disfigure their faces to show men they are fasting. I tell you the truth, they have received their reward in full. 17But when you fast, put oil on your head and wash your face, 18so that it will not be obvious to men that you are fasting, but only to your Father, who is unseen; and your Father, who sees what is done in secret, will reward you.

Treasures in Heaven

19"Do not store up for yourselves treasures on earth, where moth and rust destroy, and where thieves break in and steal. 20But store up for yourselves treasures in heaven, where moth and rust do not destroy, and where thieves do

a 13 Or from evil; some late manuscripts one, / for yours is the kingdom and the power and the glory forever. Amen.

not break in and steal. 21For where your treasure is, there your heart will be also.

22"The eye is the lamp of the body. If your eyes are good, your whole body will be full of light. 23But if your eyes are bad, your whole body will be full of darkness. If then the light within you is darkness, how great is that darkness!

24"No one can serve two masters. Either he will hate the one and love the other, or he will be devoted to the one and despise the other. You cannot serve both God and Money.

Do Not Worry

25"Therefore I tell you, do not worry about your life, what you will eat or drink; or about your body, what you will wear. Is not life more important than food, and the body more important than clothes? 26Look at the birds of the air; they do not sow or reap or store away in barns, and yet your heavenly Father feeds them. Are you not much more valuable than they? 27Who of you by worrying can add a single hour to his life*a*?

28"And why do you worry about clothes? See how the lilies of the field grow. They do not labor or spin. 29Yet I tell you that not even Solomon in all his splendor was dressed like one of these. 30If that is how God clothes the grass of the field, which is here today and tomorrow is thrown into the fire, will he not much more clothe you, O you of little faith? 31So do not worry, saying, 'What shall we eat?' or 'What shall we drink?' or 'What shall we wear?' 32For the pagans run after all these things, and your heavenly Father knows that you need them. 33But seek first his kingdom and his righteousness, and all these things will be given to you as well. 34Therefore do not worry about tomorrow, for tomorrow will worry about itself. Each day has enough trouble of its own.

Judging Others

7 "Do not judge, or you too will be judged. 2For in the same way you judge others, you will be judged, and with the measure you use, it will be measured to you.

3"Why do you look at the speck of sawdust in your brother's eye and pay no attention to the plank in your own eye? 4How can you say to your brother, 'Let me take the speck out of your eye,' when all the time there is a plank in your own eye? 5You hypocrite, first take the plank out of your own eye, and then you will see

a 27 Or single cubit to his height

也沒有賊挖窟窿來偷。21因為你的財寶在哪裏,你的心也在那裏。

22 "眼睛就是身上的燈。你的眼睛若瞭亮,全身就光明;23你的眼睛若昏花,全身就黑暗。你裏頭的光若黑暗了,那黑暗是何等大呢!

24 "一個人不能侍奉兩個主。不是惡這個愛那個,就是重這個輕那個。你們不能又侍奉神,又侍奉瑪門(註:"瑪門"是"財利"的意思)。

不要憂慮

25 "所以我告訴你們:不要為生命憂慮吃甚麼,喝甚麼;為身體憂慮穿甚麼。生命不勝於飲食嗎?身體不勝於衣裳嗎?26你們看那天上的飛鳥,也不種,也不收,也不積蓄在倉裏,你們的天父尚且養活牠。你們不比飛鳥貴重得多嗎?27你們哪一個能用思慮使壽數多加一刻呢(註:或作"使身量多加一肘呢")?

28 "何必為衣裳憂慮呢?你想,野地裏的百合花怎麼長起來?它也不勞苦,也不紡線。29然而我告訴你們:就是所羅門極榮華的時候,他所穿戴的還不如這花一朵呢!30你們這小信的人哪!野地裏的草今天還在,明天就丟在爐裏,神還給它這樣的妝飾,何況你們呢!31所以,不要憂慮說,'吃甚麼?喝甚麼?穿甚麼?'32這都是外邦人所求的。你們需用的這一切東西,你們的天父是知道的。33你們要先求他的國和他的義,這些東西都要加給你們了。34所以,不要為明天憂慮,因為明天自有明天的憂慮;一天的難處一天當就夠了。

不要論斷人

7 "你們不要論斷人,免得你們被論斷。2因為你們怎樣論斷人,也必怎樣被論斷;你們用甚麼量器量給人,也必用甚麼量器量給你們。

3 "為甚麼看見你弟兄眼中有刺,卻不想自己眼中有梁木呢?4你自己眼中有梁木,怎能對你弟兄說'容我去掉你眼中的刺'呢?5你這假冒為善的人!先去掉自己眼中的梁木，然後才能看得清楚，去掉你弟兄眼中的刺。

6 "不要把聖物給狗，也不要把你們的珍珠丟在豬前，恐怕牠踐踏了珍珠，轉過來咬你們。

祈求、尋找、叩門

7 "你們祈求，就給你們；尋找，就尋見；叩門，就給你們開門。8因為凡祈求的，就得着；尋找的，就尋見；叩門的，就給他開門。

9 "你們中間誰有兒子求餅，反給他石頭呢？10求魚，反給他蛇呢？11你們雖然不好，尚且知道拿好東西給兒女，何況你們在天上的父，豈不更把好東西給求他的人嗎？12所以，無論何事，你們願意人怎樣待你們，你們也要怎樣待人，因為這就是律法和先知的道理。

窄門與寬門

13 "你們要進窄門。因為引到滅亡，那門是寬的，路是大的，進去的人也多；14引到永生，那門是窄的，路是小的，找着的人也少。

樹和它的果子

15 "你們要防備假先知。他們到你們這裏來，外面披着羊皮，裏面卻是殘暴的狼。16憑着他們的果子，就可以認出他們來。荊棘上豈能摘葡萄呢？蒺藜裏豈能摘無花果呢？17這樣，凡好樹都結好果子，惟獨壞樹結壞果子。18好樹不能結壞果子，壞樹不能結好果子。19凡不結好果子的樹，就砍下來丟在火裏。20所以，憑着他們的果子，就可以認出他們來。

21 "凡稱呼我'主啊，主啊'的人，不能都進天國；惟獨遵行我天父旨意的人，才能進去。22當那日，必有許多人對我說：'主啊，主啊，我們不是奉你的名傳道，奉你的名趕鬼，奉你的名行許多異能嗎？'23我就明明地告訴他們說：'我從來不認識你們，你們這些作惡的人，離開我去吧！'

聰明和無知的蓋房者

24 "所以，凡聽見我這話就去行的，好比一個聰明人，把房子蓋在

clearly to remove the speck from your brother's eye.

6"Do not give dogs what is sacred; do not throw your pearls to pigs. If you do, they may trample them under their feet, and then turn and tear you to pieces.

Ask, Seek, Knock

7"Ask and it will be given to you; seek and you will find; knock and the door will be opened to you. 8For everyone who asks receives; he who seeks finds; and to him who knocks, the door will be opened.

9"Which of you, if his son asks for bread, will give him a stone? 10Or if he asks for a fish, will give him a snake? 11If you, then, though you are evil, know how to give good gifts to your children, how much more will your Father in heaven give good gifts to those who ask him! 12So in everything, do to others what you would have them do to you, for this sums up the Law and the Prophets.

The Narrow and Wide Gates

13"Enter through the narrow gate. For wide is the gate and broad is the road that leads to destruction, and many enter through it. 14But small is the gate and narrow the road that leads to life, and only a few find it.

A Tree and Its Fruit

15"Watch out for false prophets. They come to you in sheep's clothing, but inwardly they are ferocious wolves. 16By their fruit you will recognize them. Do people pick grapes from thornbushes, or figs from thistles? 17Likewise every good tree bears good fruit, but a bad tree bears bad fruit. 18A good tree cannot bear bad fruit, and a bad tree cannot bear good fruit. 19Every tree that does not bear good fruit is cut down and thrown into the fire. 20Thus, by their fruit you will recognize them.

21"Not everyone who says to me, 'Lord, Lord,' will enter the kingdom of heaven, but only he who does the will of my Father who is in heaven. 22Many will say to me on that day, 'Lord, Lord, did we not prophesy in your name, and in your name drive out demons and perform many miracles?' 23Then I will tell them plainly, 'I never knew you. Away from me, you evildoers!'

The Wise and Foolish Builders

24"Therefore everyone who hears these words of mine and puts them into practice is like a wise man who built his house on the rock.

²⁵The rain came down, the streams rose, and the winds blew and beat against that house; yet it did not fall, because it had its foundation on the rock. ²⁶But everyone who hears these words of mine and does not put them into practice is like a foolish man who built his house on sand. ²⁷The rain came down, the streams rose, and the winds blew and beat against that house, and it fell with a great crash."

²⁸When Jesus had finished saying these things, the crowds were amazed at his teaching, ²⁹because he taught as one who had authority, and not as their teachers of the law.

The Man With Leprosy

8 When he came down from the mountainside, large crowds followed him. ²A man with leprosy[a] came and knelt before him and said, "Lord, if you are willing, you can make me clean."

³Jesus reached out his hand and touched the man. "I am willing," he said. "Be clean!" Immediately he was cured[b] of his leprosy. ⁴Then Jesus said to him, "See that you don't tell anyone. But go, show yourself to the priest and offer the gift Moses commanded, as a testimony to them."

The Faith of the Centurion

⁵When Jesus had entered Capernaum, a centurion came to him, asking for help. ⁶"Lord," he said, "my servant lies at home paralyzed and in terrible suffering."

⁷Jesus said to him, "I will go and heal him."

⁸The centurion replied, "Lord, I do not deserve to have you come under my roof. But just say the word, and my servant will be healed. ⁹For I myself am a man under authority, with soldiers under me. I tell this one, 'Go,' and he goes; and that one, 'Come,' and he comes. I say to my servant, 'Do this,' and he does it."

¹⁰When Jesus heard this, he was astonished and said to those following him, "I tell you the truth, I have not found anyone in Israel with such great faith. ¹¹I say to you that many will come from the east and the west, and will take their places at the feast with Abraham, Isaac and Jacob in the kingdom of heaven. ¹²But the subjects of the kingdom will be thrown outside, into the darkness, where there will be weeping and gnashing of teeth."

¹³Then Jesus said to the centurion, "Go! It

²⁵雨淋，水沖，風吹，撞着那房子，房子總不倒塌，因為根基立在磐石上。²⁶凡聽見我這話不去行的，好比一個無知的人，把房子蓋在沙土上。²⁷雨淋，水沖，風吹，撞着那房子，房子就倒塌了，並且倒塌得很大。"

²⁸耶穌講完了這些話，眾人都希奇他的教訓。²⁹因為他教訓他們，正像有權柄的人，不像他們的文士。

長大痲瘋的人

8 耶穌下了山，有許多人跟着他。²有一個長大痲瘋的來拜他，說："主若肯，必能叫我潔淨了。"

³耶穌伸手摸他說："我肯，你潔淨了吧！"他的大痲瘋立刻就潔淨了。⁴耶穌對他說："你切不可告訴人，只要去把身體給祭司察看，獻上摩西所吩咐的禮物，對眾人作證據。"

百夫長的信心

⁵耶穌進了迦百農，有一個百夫長進前來，求他說：⁶"主啊，我的僕人害癱瘓病，躺在家裏，甚是疼苦。"

⁷耶穌說："我去醫治他。"

⁸百夫長回答說："主啊，你到我舍下，我不敢當；只要你說一句話，我的僕人就必好了。⁹因為我在人的權下，也有兵在我以下；對這個說，'去'，他就去；對那個說，'來'，他就來；對我的僕人說，'你做這事'，他就去做。"

¹⁰耶穌聽見就希奇，對跟從的人說："我實在告訴你們：這麼大的信心，就是在以色列中，我也沒有遇見過。¹¹我又告訴你們：從東從西，將有許多人來，在天國裏與亞伯拉罕、以撒、雅各一同坐席；¹²惟有本國的子民，竟被趕到外邊黑暗裏去，在那裏必要哀哭切齒了。"

¹³耶穌對百夫長說："你回去

---

a 2 The Greek word was used for various diseases affecting the skin—not necessarily leprosy.　b 3 Greek made clean

吧！照你的信心，給你成全了。"
那時，他的僕人就好了。

耶穌醫治許多病人

14耶穌到了彼得家裏，見彼得的
岳母害熱病躺着。15耶穌把她的手一
摸，熱就退了；她就起來服侍耶
穌。

16到了晚上，有人帶着許多被鬼
附的來到耶穌跟前，他只用一句
話，就把鬼都趕出去，並且治好了
一切有病的人。17這是要應驗先知以
賽亞的話，說：

　　"他代替我們的軟弱，
　　　擔當我們的疾病。"

跟從耶穌的代價

18耶穌見許多人圍着他，就吩咐
渡到那邊去。19有一個文士來，對他
說："夫子，你無論往哪裏去，我
要跟從你。"

20耶穌說："狐狸有洞，天空的
飛鳥有窩，人子卻沒有枕頭的地
方。"

21又有一個門徒對耶穌說："主
啊，容我先回去埋葬我的父親。"

22耶穌說："任憑死人埋葬他們
的死人，你跟從我吧！"

耶穌平靜風和海

23耶穌上了船，門徒跟着他。
24海裏忽然起了暴風，甚至船被波浪
掩蓋。耶穌卻睡着了。25門徒來叫醒
了他，說："主啊，救我們，我們
喪命啦！"

26耶穌說："你們這小信的人
哪！為甚麼膽怯呢？"於是起來，
斥責風和海，風和海就大大地平靜
了。

27眾人希奇說："這是怎樣的
人？連風和海也聽從他了！"

醫治兩個被鬼附着的人

28耶穌既渡到那邊去，來到加大
拉人的地方，就有兩個被鬼附的人
從墳塋裏出來迎着他，極其兇猛，
甚至沒有人能從那條路上經過。29他
們喊着說："神的兒子，我們與你
有甚麼相干？時候還沒有到，你就

will be done just as you believed it would." And
his servant was healed at that very hour.

Jesus Heals Many

14When Jesus came into Peter's house, he saw
Peter's mother-in-law lying in bed with a fever.
15He touched her hand and the fever left her,
and she got up and began to wait on him.

16When evening came, many who were
demon-possessed were brought to him, and he
drove out the spirits with a word and healed all
the sick. 17This was to fulfill what was spoken
through the prophet Isaiah:

　　"He took up our infirmities
　　　and carried our diseases."[a]

The Cost of Following Jesus

18When Jesus saw the crowd around him, he
gave orders to cross to the other side of the lake.
19Then a teacher of the law came to him and
said, "Teacher, I will follow you wherever you
go."

20Jesus replied, "Foxes have holes and birds
of the air have nests, but the Son of Man has no
place to lay his head."

21Another disciple said to him, "Lord, first let
me go and bury my father."

22But Jesus told him, "Follow me, and let the
dead bury their own dead."

Jesus Calms the Storm

23Then he got into the boat and his disciples
followed him. 24Without warning, a furious
storm came up on the lake, so that the waves
swept over the boat. But Jesus was sleeping.
25The disciples went and woke him, saying,
"Lord, save us! We're going to drown!"

26He replied, "You of little faith, why are you
so afraid?" Then he got up and rebuked the
winds and the waves, and it was completely
calm.

27The men were amazed and asked, "What
kind of man is this? Even the winds and the
waves obey him!"

The Healing of Two Demon-possessed Men

28When he arrived at the other side in the
region of the Gadarenes,[b] two demon-possessed
men coming from the tombs met him. They
were so violent that no one could pass that way.
29"What do you want with us, Son of God?"
they shouted. "Have you come here to torture

a 17 Isaiah 53:4　　*b 28* Some manuscripts *Gergesenes;* others
Gerasenes

us before the appointed time?"

³⁰Some distance from them a large herd of pigs was feeding. ³¹The demons begged Jesus, "If you drive us out, send us into the herd of pigs."

³²He said to them, "Go!" So they came out and went into the pigs, and the whole herd rushed down the steep bank into the lake and died in the water. ³³Those tending the pigs ran off, went into the town and reported all this, including what had happened to the demon-possessed men. ³⁴Then the whole town went out to meet Jesus. And when they saw him, they pleaded with him to leave their region.

Jesus Heals a Paralytic

9 Jesus stepped into a boat, crossed over and came to his own town. ²Some men brought to him a paralytic, lying on a mat. When Jesus saw their faith, he said to the paralytic, "Take heart, son; your sins are forgiven."

³At this, some of the teachers of the law said to themselves, "This fellow is blaspheming!"

⁴Knowing their thoughts, Jesus said, "Why do you entertain evil thoughts in your hearts? ⁵Which is easier: to say, 'Your sins are forgiven,' or to say, 'Get up and walk'? ⁶But so that you may know that the Son of Man has authority on earth to forgive sins. . . ." Then he said to the paralytic, "Get up, take your mat and go home." ⁷And the man got up and went home. ⁸When the crowd saw this, they were filled with awe; and they praised God, who had given such authority to men.

The Calling of Matthew

⁹As Jesus went on from there, he saw a man named Matthew sitting at the tax collector's booth. "Follow me," he told him, and Matthew got up and followed him.

¹⁰While Jesus was having dinner at Matthew's house, many tax collectors and "sinners" came and ate with him and his disciples. ¹¹When the Pharisees saw this, they asked his disciples, "Why does your teacher eat with tax collectors and 'sinners'?"

¹²On hearing this, Jesus said, "It is not the healthy who need a doctor, but the sick. ¹³But go and learn what this means: 'I desire mercy, not sacrifice.'ᵃ For I have not come to call the righteous, but sinners."

ᵃ 13 Hosea 6:6

上這裏來叫我們受苦嗎？"

　　³⁰離他們很遠，有一大羣豬吃食。³¹鬼就央求耶穌說："若把我們趕出去，就打發我們進入豬羣吧！"

　　³²耶穌說："去吧！"鬼就出來，進入豬羣。全羣忽然闖下山崖，投在海裏淹死了。³³放豬的就逃跑進城，將這一切事和被鬼附的人所遭遇的都告訴人。³⁴合城的人都出來迎見耶穌，既見了，就央求他離開他們的境界。

耶穌醫治癱子

9 耶穌上了船，渡過海，來到自己的城裏。²有人用褥子抬着一個癱子到耶穌跟前來。耶穌見他們的信心，就對癱子說："小子，放心吧！你的罪赦了。"

　　³有幾個文士心裏說："這個人說僭妄的話了。"

　　⁴耶穌知道他們的心意，就說："你們為甚麼心裏懷着惡念呢？⁵或說'你的罪赦了'，或說'你起來行走'，哪一樣容易呢？⁶但要叫你們知道，人子在地上有赦罪的權柄。"就對癱子說："起來，拿你的褥子回家去吧！"⁷那人就起來，回家去了。⁸眾人看見都驚奇，就歸榮耀與神，因為他將這樣的權柄賜給人。

召馬太

　　⁹耶穌從那裏往前走，看見一個人名叫馬太，坐在稅關上，就對他說："你跟從我來。"他就起來，跟從了耶穌。

　　¹⁰耶穌在屋裏坐席的時候，有好些稅吏和罪人來，與耶穌和他的門徒一同坐席。¹¹法利賽人看見，就對耶穌的門徒說："你們的先生為甚麼和稅吏並罪人一同吃飯呢？"

　　¹²耶穌聽見，就說："康健的人用不着醫生，有病的人才用得着。¹³經上說：'我喜愛憐恤，不喜愛祭祀。'這句話的意思，你們且去揣摩。我來，本不是召義人，乃是召罪人。"

耶穌被詢問禁食之事

14那時，約翰的門徒來見耶穌，說：「我們和法利賽人常常禁食，你的門徒倒不禁食，這是為甚麼呢？」

15耶穌對他們說：「新郎和陪伴之人同在的時候，陪伴之人豈能哀慟呢？但日子將到，新郎要離開他們，那時候他們就要禁食。

16「沒有人把新布補在舊衣服上，因為所補上的反帶壞了那衣服，破的就更大了。17也沒有人把新酒裝在舊皮袋裏，若是這樣，皮袋就裂開，酒漏出來，連皮袋也壞了。惟獨把新酒裝在新皮袋裏，兩樣就都保全了。」

死了的女孩和患血漏的女人

18耶穌說這話的時候，有一個管會堂的來拜他說：「我女兒剛才死了，求你去按手在她身上，她就必活了。」19耶穌便起來跟着他去，門徒也跟了去。

20有一個女人，患了十二年的血漏，來到耶穌背後，摸他的衣裳繸子，21因為她心裏說：「我只摸他的衣裳，就必痊愈。」

22耶穌轉過來看見她，就說：「女兒，放心！你的信救了你。」從那時候，女人就痊愈了。

23耶穌到了管會堂的家裏，看見有吹手，又有許多人亂嚷，24就說：「退去吧！這閨女不是死了，是睡着了。」他們就嗤笑他。25眾人既被攆出，耶穌就進去，拉着閨女的手，閨女便起來了。26於是這風聲傳遍了那地方。

耶穌醫治瞎子與啞巴

27耶穌從那裏往前走，有兩個瞎子跟着他，喊叫說：「大衛的子孫，可憐我們吧！」

28耶穌進了房子，瞎子就來到他跟前。耶穌說：「你們信我能做這事嗎？」

他們說：「主啊，我們信！」

29耶穌就摸他們的眼睛，說：「照着你們的信給你們成全了吧！」30他們的眼睛就開了。耶穌切切地囑咐他們說：「你們要小心，不可叫人知道。」31他們出去，竟把他的名聲傳遍了那地方。

32他們出去的時候，有人將鬼所附的一個啞巴帶到耶穌跟前來。33鬼

Jesus Questioned About Fasting

14Then John's disciples came and asked him, "How is it that we and the Pharisees fast, but your disciples do not fast?"

15Jesus answered, "How can the guests of the bridegroom mourn while he is with them? The time will come when the bridegroom will be taken from them; then they will fast.

16"No one sews a patch of unshrunk cloth on an old garment, for the patch will pull away from the garment, making the tear worse. 17Neither do men pour new wine into old wineskins. If they do, the skins will burst, the wine will run out and the wineskins will be ruined. No, they pour new wine into new wineskins, and both are preserved."

A Dead Girl and a Sick Woman

18While he was saying this, a ruler came and knelt before him and said, "My daughter has just died. But come and put your hand on her, and she will live." 19Jesus got up and went with him, and so did his disciples.

20Just then a woman who had been subject to bleeding for twelve years came up behind him and touched the edge of his cloak. 21She said to herself, "If I only touch his cloak, I will be healed."

22Jesus turned and saw her. "Take heart, daughter," he said, "your faith has healed you." And the woman was healed from that moment.

23When Jesus entered the ruler's house and saw the flute players and the noisy crowd, 24he said, "Go away. The girl is not dead but asleep." But they laughed at him. 25After the crowd had been put outside, he went in and took the girl by the hand, and she got up. 26News of this spread through all that region.

Jesus Heals the Blind and Mute

27As Jesus went on from there, two blind men followed him, calling out, "Have mercy on us, Son of David!"

28When he had gone indoors, the blind men came to him, and he asked them, "Do you believe that I am able to do this?"

"Yes, Lord," they replied.

29Then he touched their eyes and said, "According to your faith will it be done to you"; 30and their sight was restored. Jesus warned them sternly, "See that no one knows about this." 31But they went out and spread the news about him all over that region.

32While they were going out, a man who was demon-possessed and could not talk was brought to Jesus. 33And when the demon was driven out, the man who had been mute spoke. The crowd was amazed and said, "Nothing like this has ever been seen in Israel."

34But the Pharisees said, "It is by the prince of demons that he drives out demons."

The Workers Are Few

35Jesus went through all the towns and villages, teaching in their synagogues, preaching the good news of the kingdom and healing every disease and sickness. 36When he saw the crowds, he had compassion on them, because they were harassed and helpless, like sheep without a shepherd. 37Then he said to his disciples, "The harvest is plentiful but the workers are few. 38Ask the Lord of the harvest, therefore, to send out workers into his harvest field."

Jesus Sends Out the Twelve

10 He called his twelve disciples to him and gave them authority to drive out evil*a* spirits and to heal every disease and sickness.

2These are the names of the twelve apostles: first, Simon (who is called Peter) and his brother Andrew; James son of Zebedee, and his brother John; 3Philip and Bartholomew; Thomas and Matthew the tax collector; James son of Alphaeus, and Thaddaeus; 4Simon the Zealot and Judas Iscariot, who betrayed him.

5These twelve Jesus sent out with the following instructions: "Do not go among the Gentiles or enter any town of the Samaritans. 6Go rather to the lost sheep of Israel. 7As you go, preach this message: 'The kingdom of heaven is near.' 8Heal the sick, raise the dead, cleanse those who have leprosy,*b* drive out demons. Freely you have received, freely give. 9Do not take along any gold or silver or copper in your belts; 10take no bag for the journey, or extra tunic, or sandals or a staff; for the worker is worth his keep.

11"Whatever town or village you enter, search for some worthy person there and stay at his house until you leave. 12As you enter the home, give it your greeting. 13If the home is deserving, let your peace rest on it; if it is not, let your peace return to you. 14If anyone will not welcome you or listen to your words, shake the dust off your feet when you leave that home or town. 15I tell you the truth, it will be more bearable for Sodom and Gomorrah on the day of judgment than for that town. 16I am sending you out like sheep among wolves. Therefore be as

被趕出去,啞巴就說出話來。眾人都希奇說:"在<u>以色列</u>中,從來沒有見過這樣的事!"

34法利賽人卻說:"他是靠着鬼王趕鬼。"

做工的人少

35耶穌走遍各城各鄉,在會堂裏教訓人,宣講天國的福音,又醫治各樣的病症。36他看見許多的人,就憐憫他們,因為他們困苦流離,如同羊沒有牧人一般。37於是對門徒說:"要收的莊稼多,做工的人少。38所以,你們當求莊稼的主,打發工人出去收他的莊稼。"

耶穌差遣十二門徒

10 耶穌叫了十二個門徒來,給他們權柄,能趕逐污鬼,並醫治各樣的病症。

2這十二使徒的名:頭一個叫<u>西門</u>,又稱<u>彼得</u>,還有他兄弟<u>安得烈</u>,<u>西庇太</u>的兒子<u>雅各</u>和<u>雅各</u>的兄弟<u>約翰</u>,3<u>腓力</u>和<u>巴多羅買</u>,<u>多馬</u>和稅吏<u>馬太</u>,<u>亞勒腓</u>的兒子<u>雅各</u>,和<u>達太</u>,4<u>奮銳</u>黨的<u>西門</u>,還有賣耶穌的<u>加略人猶大</u>。

5耶穌差這十二個人去,吩咐他們說:"<u>外邦人</u>的路,你們不要走;<u>撒馬利亞</u>人的城,你們不要進;6寧可往<u>以色列</u>家迷失的羊那裏去。7隨走隨傳,說:'天國近了!'8醫治病人,叫死人復活,叫長大痲瘋的潔淨,把鬼趕出去。你們白白地得來,也要白白地捨去。9腰袋裏不要帶金銀銅錢。10行路不要帶口袋,不要帶兩件褂子,也不要帶鞋和枴杖,因為工人得飲食是應當的。

11"你們無論進哪一城,哪一村,要打聽那裏誰是好人,就住在他家,直住到走的時候。12進他家去,要請他的安。13那家若配得平安,你們所求的平安就必臨到那家;若不配得,你們所求的平安仍歸你們。14凡不接待你們、不聽你們話的人,你們離開那家或是那城的時候,就把腳上的塵土跺下去。15我實在告訴你們:當審判的日子,<u>所多瑪</u>和<u>蛾摩拉</u>所受的,比那城還容易受呢!16我差你們去,如同羊進入狼羣;所

a 1 Greek unclean   b 8 The Greek word was used for various diseases affecting the skin—not necessarily leprosy.

以你們要靈巧像蛇，馴良像鴿子。

17 "你們要防備人，因為他們要把你們交給公會，也要在會堂裏鞭打你們；18並且你們要為我的緣故，被送到諸侯君王面前，對他們和外邦人作見證。19你們被交的時候，不要思慮怎樣說話，或說甚麼話。到那時候，必賜給你們當說的話，20因為不是你們自己說的，乃是你們父的靈在你們裏頭說的。

21 "弟兄要把弟兄，父親要把兒子，送到死地；兒女要與父母為敵，害死他們。22並且你們要為我的名被眾人恨惡，惟有忍耐到底的必然得救。23有人在這城裏逼迫你們，就逃到那城裏去。我實在告訴你們：以色列的城邑，你們還沒有走遍，人子就到了。

24 "學生不能高過先生，僕人不能高過主人。25學生和先生一樣，僕人和主人一樣也就罷了。人既罵家主是別西卜（註："別西卜"是鬼王的名），何況他的家人呢！

26 "所以，不要怕他們。因為掩蓋的事，沒有不露出來的；隱藏的事，沒有不被人知道的。27我在暗中告訴你們的，你們要在明處說出來；你們耳中所聽的，要在房上宣揚出來。28那殺身體不能殺靈魂的，不要怕他們；惟有能把身體和靈魂都滅在地獄裏的，正要怕他。29兩個麻雀不是賣一分銀子嗎？若是你們的父不許，一個也不能掉在地上；30就是你們的頭髮也都被數過了。31所以，不要懼怕！你們比許多麻雀還貴重。

32 "凡在人面前認我的，我在我天上的父面前也必認他；33凡在人面前不認我的，我在我天上的父面前也必不認他。

34 "你們不要想，我來是叫地上太平；我來並不是叫地上太平，乃是叫地上動刀兵。35因為我來是叫

" '人與父親生疏，
　女兒與母親生疏，
　媳婦與婆婆生疏。

36人的仇敵就是自己家裏的人。'

shrewd as snakes and as innocent as doves.

17"Be on your guard against men; they will hand you over to the local councils and flog you in their synagogues. 18On my account you will be brought before governors and kings as witnesses to them and to the Gentiles. 19But when they arrest you, do not worry about what to say or how to say it. At that time you will be given what to say, 20for it will not be you speaking, but the Spirit of your Father speaking through you.

21"Brother will betray brother to death, and a father his child; children will rebel against their parents and have them put to death. 22All men will hate you because of me, but he who stands firm to the end will be saved. 23When you are persecuted in one place, flee to another. I tell you the truth, you will not finish going through the cities of Israel before the Son of Man comes.

24"A student is not above his teacher, nor a servant above his master. 25It is enough for the student to be like his teacher, and the servant like his master. If the head of the house has been called Beelzebub,*a* how much more the members of his household!

26"So do not be afraid of them. There is nothing concealed that will not be disclosed, or hidden that will not be made known. 27What I tell you in the dark, speak in the daylight; what is whispered in your ear, proclaim from the roofs. 28Do not be afraid of those who kill the body but cannot kill the soul. Rather, be afraid of the One who can destroy both soul and body in hell. 29Are not two sparrows sold for a penny*b*? Yet not one of them will fall to the ground apart from the will of your Father. 30And even the very hairs of your head are all numbered. 31So don't be afraid; you are worth more than many sparrows.

32"Whoever acknowledges me before men, I will also acknowledge him before my Father in heaven. 33But whoever disowns me before men, I will disown him before my Father in heaven.

34"Do not suppose that I have come to bring peace to the earth. I did not come to bring peace, but a sword. 35For I have come to turn

" 'a man against his father,
　a daughter against her mother,
　a daughter-in-law against her mother-in-law—
36 a man's enemies will be the members of his own household.'*c*

a 25 Greek Beezeboul or Beelzeboul　　*b 29 Greek an assarion*
c 36 Micah 7:6

37"Anyone who loves his father or mother more than me is not worthy of me; anyone who loves his son or daughter more than me is not worthy of me; 38and anyone who does not take his cross and follow me is not worthy of me. 39Whoever finds his life will lose it, and whoever loses his life for my sake will find it.

40"He who receives you receives me, and he who receives me receives the one who sent me. 41Anyone who receives a prophet because he is a prophet will receive a prophet's reward, and anyone who receives a righteous man because he is a righteous man will receive a righteous man's reward. 42And if anyone gives even a cup of cold water to one of these little ones because he is my disciple, I tell you the truth, he will certainly not lose his reward."

Jesus and John the Baptist

11 After Jesus had finished instructing his twelve disciples, he went on from there to teach and preach in the towns of Galilee.a

2When John heard in prison what Christ was doing, he sent his disciples 3to ask him, "Are you the one who was to come, or should we expect someone else?"

4Jesus replied, "Go back and report to John what you hear and see: 5The blind receive sight, the lame walk, those who have leprosyb are cured, the deaf hear, the dead are raised, and the good news is preached to the poor. 6Blessed is the man who does not fall away on account of me."

7As John's disciples were leaving, Jesus began to speak to the crowd about John: "What did you go out into the desert to see? A reed swayed by the wind? 8If not, what did you go out to see? A man dressed in fine clothes? No, those who wear fine clothes are in kings' palaces. 9Then what did you go out to see? A prophet? Yes, I tell you, and more than a prophet. 10This is the one about whom it is written:

" 'I will send my messenger ahead of you,
who will prepare your way before you.'c

11I tell you the truth: Among those born of women there has not risen anyone greater than John the Baptist; yet he who is least in the kingdom of heaven is greater than he. 12From the

---

37 "愛父母過於愛我的,不配作我的門徒;愛兒女過於愛我的,不配作我的門徒;38不背着他的十字架跟從我的,也不配作我的門徒。39得着生命的,將要失喪生命;為我失喪生命的,將要得着生命。

40 "人接待你們,就是接待我;接待我,就是接待那差我來的。41人因為先知的名接待先知,必得先知所得的賞賜;人因為義人的名接待義人,必得義人所得的賞賜。42無論何人,因為門徒的名,只把一杯涼水給這小子裏的一個喝,我實在告訴你們:這人不能不得賞賜。"

耶穌與施洗約翰

11 耶穌吩咐完了十二個門徒,就離開那裏,往各城去傳道教訓人。

2 約翰在監裏聽見基督所做的事,就打發兩個門徒去,3問他說:"那將要來的是你嗎?還是我們等候別人呢?"

4耶穌回答說:"你們去,把所聽見、所看見的事告訴約翰。5就是瞎子看見,瘸子行走,長大麻瘋的潔淨,聾子聽見,死人復活,窮人有福音傳給他們。6凡不因我跌倒的就有福了。"

7他們走的時候,耶穌就對眾人講論約翰說:"你們從前出到曠野是要看甚麼呢?要看風吹動的蘆葦嗎?8你們出去到底是要看甚麼?要看穿細軟衣服的人嗎?那穿細軟衣服的人是在王宮裏。9你們出去究竟是為甚麼?是要看先知嗎?我告訴你們:是的,他比先知大多了。10經上記着說:

" '我要差遣我的使者,
在你前面預備道路。'
所說的就是這個人。

11我實在告訴你們:凡婦人所生的,沒有一個興起來大過施洗約翰的;然而天國裏最小的比他還大。12從施洗

---

a 1 Greek *in their towns*   b 5 The Greek word was used for various diseases affecting the skin—not necessarily leprosy.
c 10 Mal. 3:1

約翰的時候到如今，天國是努力進入的，努力的人就得着了。13因為眾先知和律法說預言，到約翰為止。14你們若肯領受，這人就是那要當來的以利亞。15有耳可聽的，就應當聽！

16 "我可用甚麼比這世代呢？好像孩童坐在街市上招呼同伴，說：

17 " '我們向你們吹笛，
　　你們不跳舞；
　　我們向你們舉哀，
　　你們不捶胸。'

18約翰來了，也不吃，也不喝，人就說他是被鬼附着的。19人子來了，也吃也喝，人又說他是貪食好酒的人，是稅吏和罪人的朋友。但智慧之子，總以智慧為是 (註：有古卷作 "但智慧在行為上就顯為是") 。"

不悔改的城有禍了

20耶穌在諸城中行了許多異能，那些城的人終不悔改，就在那時候責備他們說：21 "哥拉汛哪，你有禍了！伯賽大啊，你有禍了！因為在你們中間所行的異能，若行在推羅、西頓，他們早已披麻蒙灰悔改了。22但我告訴你們：當審判的日子，推羅、西頓所受的比你們還容易受呢！23迦百農啊，你已經升到天上 (註：或作 "你將要升到天上嗎？") ，將來必墜落陰間，因為在你那裏所行的異能，若行在所多瑪，它還可以存到今日。24但我告訴你們：當審判的日子，所多瑪所受的，比你還容易受呢！"

勞苦者得安息

25那時，耶穌說："父啊，天地的主，我感謝你！因為你將這些事向聰明通達人就藏起來，向嬰孩就顯出來。26父啊，是的，因為你的美意本是如此。

27 "一切所有的，都是我父交付我的。除了父，沒有人知道子；除了子和子所願意指示的，沒有人知道父。

28 "凡勞苦擔重擔的人，可以到我這裏來，我就使你們得安息。29我心裏柔和謙卑，你們當負我的軛，

days of John the Baptist until now, the kingdom of heaven has been forcefully advancing, and forceful men lay hold of it. 13For all the Prophets and the Law prophesied until John. 14And if you are willing to accept it, he is the Elijah who was to come. 15He who has ears, let him hear.

16"To what can I compare this generation? They are like children sitting in the marketplaces and calling out to others:

17" 'We played the flute for you,
　　and you did not dance;
　we sang a dirge,
　　and you did not mourn.'

18For John came neither eating nor drinking, and they say, 'He has a demon.' 19The Son of Man came eating and drinking, and they say, 'Here is a glutton and a drunkard, a friend of tax collectors and "sinners." ' But wisdom is proved right by her actions."

Woe on Unrepentant Cities

20Then Jesus began to denounce the cities in which most of his miracles had been performed, because they did not repent. 21"Woe to you, Korazin! Woe to you, Bethsaida! If the miracles that were performed in you had been performed in Tyre and Sidon, they would have repented long ago in sackcloth and ashes. 22But I tell you, it will be more bearable for Tyre and Sidon on the day of judgment than for you. 23And you, Capernaum, will you be lifted up to the skies? No, you will go down to the depths.[a] If the miracles that were performed in you had been performed in Sodom, it would have remained to this day. 24But I tell you that it will be more bearable for Sodom on the day of judgment than for you."

Rest for the Weary

25At that time Jesus said, "I praise you, Father, Lord of heaven and earth, because you have hidden these things from the wise and learned, and revealed them to little children. 26Yes, Father, for this was your good pleasure.

27"All things have been committed to me by my Father. No one knows the Son except the Father, and no one knows the Father except the Son and those to whom the Son chooses to reveal him.

28"Come to me, all you who are weary and burdened, and I will give you rest. 29Take my yoke upon you and learn from me, for I am gentle and humble in heart, and you will find rest for your souls. [30]For my yoke is easy and my burden is light."

Lord of the Sabbath

12 At that time Jesus went through the grainfields on the Sabbath. His disciples were hungry and began to pick some heads of grain and eat them. [2]When the Pharisees saw this, they said to him, "Look! Your disciples are doing what is unlawful on the Sabbath."

[3]He answered, "Haven't you read what David did when he and his companions were hungry? [4]He entered the house of God, and he and his companions ate the consecrated bread— which was not lawful for them to do, but only for the priests. [5]Or haven't you read in the Law that on the Sabbath the priests in the temple desecrate the day and yet are innocent? [6]I tell you that one[a] greater than the temple is here. [7]If you had known what these words mean, 'I desire mercy, not sacrifice,'[b] you would not have condemned the innocent. [8]For the Son of Man is Lord of the Sabbath."

[9]Going on from that place, he went into their synagogue, [10]and a man with a shriveled hand was there. Looking for a reason to accuse Jesus, they asked him, "Is it lawful to heal on the Sabbath?"

[11]He said to them, "If any of you has a sheep and it falls into a pit on the Sabbath, will you not take hold of it and lift it out? [12]How much more valuable is a man than a sheep! Therefore it is lawful to do good on the Sabbath."

[13]Then he said to the man, "Stretch out your hand." So he stretched it out and it was completely restored, just as sound as the other. [14]But the Pharisees went out and plotted how they might kill Jesus.

God's Chosen Servant

[15]Aware of this, Jesus withdrew from that place. Many followed him, and he healed all their sick, [16]warning them not to tell who he was. [17]This was to fulfill what was spoken through the prophet Isaiah:

[18]"Here is my servant whom I have chosen,
the one I love, in whom I delight;
I will put my Spirit on him,
and he will proclaim justice to the nations.
[19]He will not quarrel or cry out;
no one will hear his voice in the streets.

學我的樣式,這樣,你們心裏就必得享安息。[30]因為我的軛是容易的,我的擔子是輕省的。"

安息日的主

12 那時,耶穌在安息日從麥地經過。他的門徒餓了,就掐起麥穗來吃。[2]法利賽人看見,就對耶穌說:"看哪,你的門徒做安息日不可做的事了!"

[3]耶穌對他們說:"經上記着大衞和跟從他的人飢餓之時所做的事,你們沒有念過嗎?[4]他怎麼進了神的殿,吃了陳設餅,這餅不是他和跟從他的人可以吃得,惟獨祭司才可以吃。[5]再者,律法上所記的,當安息日,祭司在殿裏犯了安息日,還是沒有罪,你們沒有念過嗎?[6]但我告訴你們:在這裏有一人比殿更大。[7]'我喜愛憐恤,不喜愛祭祀。'你們若明白這話的意思,就不將無罪的當作有罪的了。[8]因為人子是安息日的主。"

[9]耶穌離開那地方,進了一個會堂。[10]那裏有一個人枯乾了一隻手。有人問耶穌說:"安息日治病,可以不可以?"意思是要控告他。

[11]耶穌說:"你們中間誰有一隻羊,當安息日掉在坑裏,不把牠抓住拉上來呢?[12]人比羊何等貴重呢!所以,在安息日做善事是可以的。"

[13]於是對那人說:"伸出手來!"他把手一伸,手就復了原,和那隻手一樣。[14]法利賽人出去,商議怎樣可以除滅耶穌。

神所揀選的僕人

[15]耶穌知道了,就離開那裏。有許多人跟着他,他把其中有病的人都治好了,[16]又囑咐他們,不要給他傳名。[17]這是要應驗先知以賽亞的話,說:

[18]"看哪,我的僕人,我所揀選、所親愛、心裏所喜悅的;
我要將我的靈賜給他,
他必將公理傳給外邦。
[19]他不爭競,不喧嚷,
街上也沒有人聽見他的聲音。

---

a 6 Or *something;* also in verses 41 and 42　　*b* 7 Hosea 6:6

20壓傷的蘆葦，他不折斷；
　將殘的燈火，他不吹滅。
　等他施行公理，叫公理得勝；
21外邦人都要仰望他的名。”

耶穌與別西卜

22當下，有人將一個被鬼附着、又瞎又啞的人帶到耶穌那裏，耶穌就醫治他，甚至那啞巴又能說話，又能看見。23眾人都驚奇，說：“這不是大衛的子孫嗎？”

24但法利賽人聽見，就說：“這個人趕鬼，無非是靠着鬼王別西卜啊。”

25耶穌知道他們的意念，就對他們說：“凡一國自相紛爭，就成為荒場；一城一家自相紛爭，必站立不住。26若撒但趕逐撒但，就是自相紛爭，他的國怎能站得住呢？27我若靠着別西卜趕鬼，你們的子弟趕鬼又靠着誰呢？這樣，他們就要斷定你們的是非。28我若靠着神的靈趕鬼，這就是神的國臨到你們了。

29“人怎能進壯士家裏，搶奪他的家具呢？除非先捆住那壯士，才可以搶奪他的家財。

30“不與我相合的，就是敵我的；不同我收聚的，就是分散的。31所以我告訴你們：人一切的罪和褻瀆的話，都可得赦免；惟獨褻瀆聖靈，總不得赦免。32凡說話干犯人子的，還可得赦免；惟獨說話干犯聖靈的，今世、來世總不得赦免。

33“你們或以為樹好，果子也好；樹壞，果子也壞。因為看果子就可以知道樹。34毒蛇的種類！你們既是惡人，怎能說出好話來呢？因為心裏所充滿的，口裏就說出來。35善人從他心裏所存的善，就發出善來；惡人從他心裏所存的惡，就發出惡來。36我又告訴你們：凡人所說的閒話，當審判的日子，必要句句供出來。37因為要憑你的話定你為義，也要憑你的話定你有罪。”

20A bruised reed he will not break,
　and a smoldering wick he will not snuff out,
　till he leads justice to victory.
21 In his name the nations will put their hope."[a]

Jesus and Beelzebub

22Then they brought him a demon-possessed man who was blind and mute, and Jesus healed him, so that he could both talk and see. 23All the people were astonished and said, "Could this be the Son of David?"

24But when the Pharisees heard this, they said, "It is only by Beelzebub,[b] the prince of demons, that this fellow drives out demons."

25Jesus knew their thoughts and said to them, "Every kingdom divided against itself will be ruined, and every city or household divided against itself will not stand. 26If Satan drives out Satan, he is divided against himself. How then can his kingdom stand? 27And if I drive out demons by Beelzebub, by whom do your people drive them out? So then, they will be your judges. 28But if I drive out demons by the Spirit of God, then the kingdom of God has come upon you.

29"Or again, how can anyone enter a strong man's house and carry off his possessions unless he first ties up the strong man? Then he can rob his house.

30"He who is not with me is against me, and he who does not gather with me scatters. 31And so I tell you, every sin and blasphemy will be forgiven men, but the blasphemy against the Spirit will not be forgiven. 32Anyone who speaks a word against the Son of Man will be forgiven, but anyone who speaks against the Holy Spirit will not be forgiven, either in this age or in the age to come.

33"Make a tree good and its fruit will be good, or make a tree bad and its fruit will be bad, for a tree is recognized by its fruit. 34You brood of vipers, how can you who are evil say anything good? For out of the overflow of the heart the mouth speaks. 35The good man brings good things out of the good stored up in him, and the evil man brings evil things out of the evil stored up in him. 36But I tell you that men will have to give account on the day of judgment for every careless word they have spoken. 37For by your words you will be acquitted, and by your words you will be condemned."

a 21 Isaiah 42:1-4　　b 24 Greek Beezeboul or Beelzeboul; also in verse 27

The Sign of Jonah

³⁸Then some of the Pharisees and teachers of the law said to him, "Teacher, we want to see a miraculous sign from you."

³⁹He answered, "A wicked and adulterous generation asks for a miraculous sign! But none will be given it except the sign of the prophet Jonah. ⁴⁰For as Jonah was three days and three nights in the belly of a huge fish, so the Son of Man will be three days and three nights in the heart of the earth. ⁴¹The men of Nineveh will stand up at the judgment with this generation and condemn it; for they repented at the preaching of Jonah, and now one[a] greater than Jonah is here. ⁴²The Queen of the South will rise at the judgment with this generation and condemn it; for she came from the ends of the earth to listen to Solomon's wisdom, and now one greater than Solomon is here.

⁴³"When an evil[b] spirit comes out of a man, it goes through arid places seeking rest and does not find it. ⁴⁴Then it says, 'I will return to the house I left.' When it arrives, it finds the house unoccupied, swept clean and put in order. ⁴⁵Then it goes and takes with it seven other spirits more wicked than itself, and they go in and live there. And the final condition of that man is worse than the first. That is how it will be with this wicked generation."

Jesus' Mother and Brothers

⁴⁶While Jesus was still talking to the crowd, his mother and brothers stood outside, wanting to speak to him. ⁴⁷Someone told him, "Your mother and brothers are standing outside, wanting to speak to you."[c]

⁴⁸He replied to him, "Who is my mother, and who are my brothers?" ⁴⁹Pointing to his disciples, he said, "Here are my mother and my brothers. ⁵⁰For whoever does the will of my Father in heaven is my brother and sister and mother."

The Parable of the Sower

13 That same day Jesus went out of the house and sat by the lake. ²Such large crowds gathered around him that he got into a boat and sat in it, while all the people stood on the shore. ³Then he told them many things in parables, saying: "A farmer went out to sow his seed. ⁴As he was scattering the seed, some fell along the path, and the birds came and ate it up. ⁵Some fell on rocky places, where it

約拿的神蹟

³⁸當時,有幾個文士和法利賽人對耶穌說:"夫子,我們願意你顯個神蹟給我們看。"

³⁹耶穌回答說:"一個邪惡、淫亂的世代求看神蹟,除了先知約拿的神蹟以外,再沒有神蹟給他們看。⁴⁰約拿三日三夜在大魚肚腹中,人子也要這樣三日三夜在地裏頭。⁴¹當審判的時候,尼尼微人要起來定這世代的罪,因為尼尼微人聽了約拿所傳的,就悔改了;看哪,在這裏有一人比約拿更大。⁴²當審判的時候,南方的女王要起來定這世代的罪,因為她從地極而來,要聽所羅門的智慧話;看哪,在這裏有一人比所羅門更大。"

⁴³"污鬼離了人身,就在無水之地過來過去,尋求安歇之處,卻尋不着。⁴⁴於是說:'我要回到我所出來的屋裏去。'到了,就看見裏面空閒,打掃乾淨,修飾好了,⁴⁵便去另帶了七個比自己更惡的鬼來,都進去住在那裏。那人末後的景況比先前更不好了。這邪惡的世代也要如此。"

耶穌的母親和弟兄

⁴⁶耶穌還對眾人說話的時候,不料,他母親和他弟兄站在外邊,要與他說話。⁴⁷有人告訴他說:"看哪,你母親和你弟兄站在外邊,要與你說話。"

⁴⁸他卻回答那人說:"誰是我的母親?誰是我的弟兄?"⁴⁹就伸手指着門徒說:"看哪,我的母親,我的弟兄。⁵⁰凡遵行我天父旨意的人,就是我的弟兄、姐妹和母親了。"

撒種的比喻

13 當那一天,耶穌從房子裏出來,坐在海邊。²有許多人到他那裏聚集,他只得上船坐下,眾人都站在岸上。³他用比喻對他們講許多道理,說:"有一個撒種的出去撒種。⁴撒的時候,有落在路旁的,飛鳥來吃盡了。⁵有落在土淺

---

a 41 Or *something*; also in verse 42   b 43 Greek *unclean*

c 47 Some manuscripts do not have verse 47.

石頭地上的，土既不深，發苗最快，⁶日頭出來一曬，因為沒有根，就枯乾了。⁷有落在荊棘裏的，荊棘長起來，把它擠住了。⁸又有落在好土裏的，就結實，有一百倍的，有六十倍的，有三十倍的。⁹有耳可聽的，就應當聽！"

¹⁰門徒進前來，問耶穌說："對眾人講話為甚麼用比喻呢？"

¹¹耶穌回答說："因為天國的奧秘，只叫你們知道，不叫他們知道。¹²凡有的，還要加給他，叫他有餘；凡沒有的，連他所有的也要奪去。¹³所以我用比喻對他們講，是因：

"他們看也看不見，
　聽也聽不見，
　也不明白。

¹⁴在他們身上，正應了以賽亞的預言，說：
"'你們聽是要聽見，
　卻不明白；
　看是要看見，卻不曉得。
¹⁵因為這百姓油蒙了心，
　耳朵發沉，
　眼睛閉着；
　恐怕眼睛看見，
　耳朵聽見，
　心裏明白，
　回轉過來，我就醫治他們。'

¹⁶但你們的眼睛是有福的，因為看見了；你們的耳朵也是有福的，因為聽見了。¹⁷我實在告訴你們：從前有許多先知和義人要看你們所看的，卻沒有看見；要聽你們所聽的，卻沒有聽見。

¹⁸"所以，你們當聽這撒種的比喻：¹⁹凡聽見天國道理不明白的，那惡者就來，把所撒在他心裏的奪了去，這就是撒在路旁的了。²⁰撒在石頭地上的，就是人聽了道，當下歡喜領受，²¹只因心裏沒有根，不過是暫時的，及至為道遭了患難，或是受了逼迫，立刻就跌倒了。²²撒在荊棘裏的，就是人聽了道，後來有世

did not have much soil. It sprang up quickly, because the soil was shallow. ⁶But when the sun came up, the plants were scorched, and they withered because they had no root. ⁷Other seed fell among thorns, which grew up and choked the plants. ⁸Still other seed fell on good soil, where it produced a crop — a hundred, sixty or thirty times what was sown. ⁹He who has ears, let him hear."

¹⁰The disciples came to him and asked, "Why do you speak to the people in parables?"

¹¹He replied, "The knowledge of the secrets of the kingdom of heaven has been given to you, but not to them. ¹²Whoever has will be given more, and he will have an abundance. Whoever does not have, even what he has will be taken from him. ¹³This is why I speak to them in parables:

"Though seeing, they do not see;
　though hearing, they do not hear or
　　understand.

¹⁴In them is fulfilled the prophecy of Isaiah:

" 'You will be ever hearing but never
　　understanding;
　you will be ever seeing but never perceiving.
¹⁵For this people's heart has become calloused;
　they hardly hear with their ears,
　and they have closed their eyes.
Otherwise they might see with their eyes,
　hear with their ears,
　understand with their hearts
and turn, and I would heal them.'ᵃ

¹⁶But blessed are your eyes because they see, and your ears because they hear. ¹⁷For I tell you the truth, many prophets and righteous men longed to see what you see but did not see it, and to hear what you hear but did not hear it.

¹⁸"Listen then to what the parable of the sower means: ¹⁹When anyone hears the message about the kingdom and does not understand it, the evil one comes and snatches away what was sown in his heart. This is the seed sown along the path. ²⁰The one who received the seed that fell on rocky places is the man who hears the word and at once receives it with joy. ²¹But since he has no root, he lasts only a short time. When trouble or persecution comes because of the word, he quickly falls away. ²²The one who received the seed that fell among the thorns is the man who hears the word, but the worries of

_a 15_ Isaiah 6:9,10

this life and the deceitfulness of wealth choke it, making it unfruitful. 23But the one who received the seed that fell on good soil is the man who hears the word and understands it. He produces a crop, yielding a hundred, sixty or thirty times what was sown."

The Parable of the Weeds

24Jesus told them another parable: "The kingdom of heaven is like a man who sowed good seed in his field. 25But while everyone was sleeping, his enemy came and sowed weeds among the wheat, and went away. 26When the wheat sprouted and formed heads, then the weeds also appeared.

27"The owner's servants came to him and said, 'Sir, didn't you sow good seed in your field? Where then did the weeds come from?'

28" 'An enemy did this,' he replied.

"The servants asked him, 'Do you want us to go and pull them up?'

29" 'No,' he answered, 'because while you are pulling the weeds, you may root up the wheat with them. 30Let both grow together until the harvest. At that time I will tell the harvesters: First collect the weeds and tie them in bundles to be burned; then gather the wheat and bring it into my barn.' "

The Parables of the Mustard Seed and the Yeast

31He told them another parable: "The kingdom of heaven is like a mustard seed, which a man took and planted in his field. 32Though it is the smallest of all your seeds, yet when it grows, it is the largest of garden plants and becomes a tree, so that the birds of the air come and perch in its branches."

33He told them still another parable: "The kingdom of heaven is like yeast that a woman took and mixed into a large amount[a] of flour until it worked all through the dough."

34Jesus spoke all these things to the crowd in parables; he did not say anything to them without using a parable. 35So was fulfilled what was spoken through the prophet:

"I will open my mouth in parables,
I will utter things hidden since the creation of the world."[b]

The Parable of the Weeds Explained

36Then he left the crowd and went into the

a 33 Greek three satas (probably about 1/2 bushel or 22 liters)
b 35 Psalm 78:2

上的思慮，錢財的迷惑，把道擠住了，不能結實。23撒在好地上的，就是人聽道明白了，後來結實，有一百倍的，有六十倍的，有三十倍的。"

種子的比喻

24耶穌又設個比喻對他們說："天國好像人撒好種在田裏，25及至人睡覺的時候，有仇敵來，將稗子撒在麥子裏就走了。26到長苗吐穗的時候，稗子也顯出來。

27 "田主的僕人來告訴他說：'主啊，你不是撒好種在田裏嗎？從哪裏來的稗子呢？'

28 "主人說：'這是仇敵做的。'

僕人說：'你要我們去薅出來嗎？'

29 "主人說：'不必，恐怕薅稗子，連麥子也拔出來。30容這兩樣一齊長，等着收割。當收割的時候，我要對收割的人說：先將稗子薅出來，捆成捆，留着燒；惟有麥子要收在倉裏。' "

芥菜種與麵酵的比喻

31他又設個比喻對他們說："天國好像一粒芥菜種，有人拿去種在田裏。32這原是百種裏最小的，等到長起來，卻比各樣的菜都大，且成了樹，天上的飛鳥來宿在它的枝上。"

33他又對他們講個比喻說："天國好像麵酵，有婦人拿來，藏在三斗麵裏，直等全團都發起來。"

34這都是耶穌用比喻對眾人說的話；若不用比喻，就不對他們說甚麼。35這是要應驗先知的話，說：

"我要開口用比喻，
把創世以來所隱藏的事
發明出來。"

解釋稗子的比喻

36當下耶穌離開眾人，進了房

子。他的門徒進前來，說："請把田間稗子的比喻講給我們聽。"

37他回答說："那撒好種的就是人子，38田地就是世界，好種就是天國之子；稗子就是那惡者之子，39撒稗子的仇敵就是魔鬼；收割的時候就是世界的末了，收割的人就是天使。

40"將稗子薅出來用火焚燒，世界的末了也要如此。41人子要差遣使者，把一切叫人跌倒的和作惡的，從他國裏挑出來，42丟在火爐裏，在那裏必要哀哭切齒了。43那時，義人在他們父的國裏，要發出光來，像太陽一樣。有耳可聽的，就應當聽！

藏寶與尋珠的比喻

44"天國好像寶貝藏在地裏，人遇見了就把它藏起來，歡歡喜喜地去變賣一切所有的，買這塊地。

45"天國又好像買賣人尋找好珠子，46遇見一顆重價的珠子，就去變賣他一切所有的，買了這顆珠子。

撒網的比喻

47"天國又好像網撒在海裏，聚攏各樣水族。48網既滿了，人就拉上岸來；坐下，揀好的收在器具裏，將不好的丟棄了。49世界的末了也要這樣。天使要出來，從義人中把惡人分別出來，50丟在火爐裏，在那裏必要哀哭切齒了。"

51耶穌說："這一切的話你們都明白了嗎？"

他們說："我們明白了。"

52他說："凡文士受教作天國的門徒，就像一個家主，從他庫裏拿出新舊的東西來。"

不被尊敬的先知

53耶穌說完了這些比喻，就離開那裏，54來到自己的家鄉，在會堂裏

house. His disciples came to him and said, "Explain to us the parable of the weeds in the field."

37He answered, "The one who sowed the good seed is the Son of Man. 38The field is the world, and the good seed stands for the sons of the kingdom. The weeds are the sons of the evil one, 39and the enemy who sows them is the devil. The harvest is the end of the age, and the harvesters are angels.

40"As the weeds are pulled up and burned in the fire, so it will be at the end of the age. 41The Son of Man will send out his angels, and they will weed out of his kingdom everything that causes sin and all who do evil. 42They will throw them into the fiery furnace, where there will be weeping and gnashing of teeth. 43Then the righteous will shine like the sun in the kingdom of their Father. He who has ears, let him hear.

The Parables of the Hidden Treasure and the Pearl

44"The kingdom of heaven is like treasure hidden in a field. When a man found it, he hid it again, and then in his joy went and sold all he had and bought that field.

45"Again, the kingdom of heaven is like a merchant looking for fine pearls. 46When he found one of great value, he went away and sold everything he had and bought it.

The Parable of the Net

47"Once again, the kingdom of heaven is like a net that was let down into the lake and caught all kinds of fish. 48When it was full, the fishermen pulled it up on the shore. Then they sat down and collected the good fish in baskets, but threw the bad away. 49This is how it will be at the end of the age. The angels will come and separate the wicked from the righteous 50and throw them into the fiery furnace, where there will be weeping and gnashing of teeth.

51"Have you understood all these things?" Jesus asked.

"Yes," they replied.

52He said to them, "Therefore every teacher of the law who has been instructed about the kingdom of heaven is like the owner of a house who brings out of his storeroom new treasures as well as old."

A Prophet Without Honor

53When Jesus had finished these parables, he moved on from there. 54Coming to his hometown, he began teaching the people in their synagogue, and they were amazed. "Where did this man get this wisdom and these miraculous powers?" they asked. ⁵⁵"Isn't this the carpenter's son? Isn't his mother's name Mary, and aren't his brothers James, Joseph, Simon and Judas? ⁵⁶Aren't all his sisters with us? Where then did this man get all these things?" ⁵⁷And they took offense at him.

But Jesus said to them, "Only in his hometown and in his own house is a prophet without honor."

⁵⁸And he did not do many miracles there because of their lack of faith.

John the Baptist Beheaded

14 At that time Herod the tetrarch heard the reports about Jesus, ²and he said to his attendants, "This is John the Baptist; he has risen from the dead! That is why miraculous powers are at work in him."

³Now Herod had arrested John and bound him and put him in prison because of Herodias, his brother Philip's wife, ⁴for John had been saying to him: "It is not lawful for you to have her." ⁵Herod wanted to kill John, but he was afraid of the people, because they considered him a prophet.

⁶On Herod's birthday the daughter of Herodias danced for them and pleased Herod so much ⁷that he promised with an oath to give her whatever she asked. ⁸Prompted by her mother, she said, "Give me here on a platter the head of John the Baptist." ⁹The king was distressed, but because of his oaths and his dinner guests, he ordered that her request be granted ¹⁰and had John beheaded in the prison. ¹¹His head was brought in on a platter and given to the girl, who carried it to her mother. ¹²John's disciples came and took his body and buried it. Then they went and told Jesus.

Jesus Feeds the Five Thousand

¹³When Jesus heard what had happened, he withdrew by boat privately to a solitary place. Hearing of this, the crowds followed him on foot from the towns. ¹⁴When Jesus landed and saw a large crowd, he had compassion on them and healed their sick.

¹⁵As evening approached, the disciples came to him and said, "This is a remote place, and it's already getting late. Send the crowds away, so they can go to the villages and buy themselves some food."

¹⁶Jesus replied, "They do not need to go away. You give them something to eat."

教訓人,甚至他們都希奇,說:"這人從哪裏有這等智慧和異能呢?⁵⁵這不是木匠的兒子嗎?他母親不是叫馬利亞嗎?他弟兄們不是叫雅各、約西(註:有古卷作"約瑟")、西門、猶大嗎?⁵⁶他妹妹們不是都在我們這裏嗎?這人從哪裏有這一切的事呢?"⁵⁷他們就厭棄他(註:"厭棄他"原文作"因他跌倒")。

耶穌對他們說:"大凡先知,除了本地本家之外,沒有不被人尊敬的。"

⁵⁸耶穌因為他們不信,就在那裏不多行異能了。

施洗約翰被斬

14 那時,分封的王希律聽見耶穌的名聲,²就對臣僕說:"這是施洗的約翰從死裏復活,所以這些異能從他裏面發出來。"

³起先希律為他兄弟腓力的妻子希羅底的緣故,把約翰拿住鎖在監裏。⁴因為約翰曾對他說:"你娶這婦人是不合理的。"⁵希律就想要殺他,只是怕百姓,因為他們以約翰為先知。

⁶到了希律的生日,希羅底的女兒在眾人面前跳舞,使希律歡喜。⁷希律就起誓,應許隨她所求的給她。⁸女兒被母親所使,就說:"請把施洗約翰的頭放在盤子裏,拿來給我。"⁹王便憂愁,但因他所起的誓,又因同席的人,就吩咐給她。¹⁰於是打發人去,在監裏斬了約翰,¹¹把頭放在盤子裏,拿來給了女子,女子拿去給她母親。¹²約翰的門徒來,把屍首領去埋葬了,就去告訴耶穌。

耶穌給五千人吃飽

¹³耶穌聽見了,就上船從那裏獨自退到野地裏去。眾人聽見,就從各城裏步行跟隨他。¹⁴耶穌出來,見有許多的人,就憐憫他們,治好了他們的病人。

¹⁵天將晚的時候,門徒進前來說:"這是野地,時候已經過了,請叫眾人散開,他們好往村子裏去,自己買吃的。"

¹⁶耶穌說:"不用他們去,你們給他們吃吧!"

17門徒說："我們這裏只有五個餅、兩條魚。"

18耶穌說："拿過來給我。" 19於是吩咐眾人坐在草地上，就拿着這五個餅、兩條魚，望着天祝福，擘開餅，遞給門徒，門徒又遞給眾人。20他們都吃，並且吃飽了，把剩下的零碎收拾起來，裝滿了十二個籃子。21吃的人，除了婦女孩子，約有五千。

耶穌在水面上行走

22耶穌隨即催門徒上船，先渡到那邊去，等他叫眾人散開。23散了眾人以後，他就獨自上山去禱告。到了晚上，只有他一人在那裏。24那時，船在海中，因風不順，被浪搖撼。

25夜裏四更天，耶穌在海面上走，往門徒那裏去。26門徒看見他在海面上走，就驚慌了，說："是個鬼怪！"便害怕，喊叫起來。

27耶穌連忙對他們說："你們放心，是我，不要怕！"

28彼得說："主，如果是你，請叫我從水面上走到你那裏去。"

29耶穌說："你來吧！"

彼得就從船上下去，在水面上走，要到耶穌那裏去；30只因見風甚大，就害怕，將要沉下去，便喊着說："主啊，救我！"

31耶穌趕緊伸手拉住他，說："你這小信的人哪，為甚麼疑惑呢？"

32他們上了船，風就住了。33在船上的人都拜他，說："你真是神的兒子了。"

34他們過了海，來到革尼撒勒地方。35那裏的人一認出是耶穌，就打發人到周圍地方去，把所有的病人帶到他那裏，36只求耶穌准他們摸他的衣裳繸子，摸着的人就都好了。

17"We have here only five loaves of bread and two fish," they answered.

18"Bring them here to me," he said. 19And he directed the people to sit down on the grass. Taking the five loaves and the two fish and looking up to heaven, he gave thanks and broke the loaves. Then he gave them to the disciples, and the disciples gave them to the people. 20They all ate and were satisfied, and the disciples picked up twelve basketfuls of broken pieces that were left over. 21The number of those who ate was about five thousand men, besides women and children.

Jesus Walks on the Water

22Immediately Jesus made the disciples get into the boat and go on ahead of him to the other side, while he dismissed the crowd. 23After he had dismissed them, he went up on a mountainside by himself to pray. When evening came, he was there alone, 24but the boat was already a considerable distance*a* from land, buffeted by the waves because the wind was against it.

25During the fourth watch of the night Jesus went out to them, walking on the lake. 26When the disciples saw him walking on the lake, they were terrified. "It's a ghost," they said, and cried out in fear.

27But Jesus immediately said to them: "Take courage! It is I. Don't be afraid."

28"Lord, if it's you," Peter replied, "tell me to come to you on the water."

29"Come," he said.

Then Peter got down out of the boat, walked on the water and came toward Jesus. 30But when he saw the wind, he was afraid and, beginning to sink, cried out, "Lord, save me!"

31Immediately Jesus reached out his hand and caught him. "You of little faith," he said, "why did you doubt?"

32And when they climbed into the boat, the wind died down. 33Then those who were in the boat worshiped him, saying, "Truly you are the Son of God."

34When they had crossed over, they landed at Gennesaret. 35And when the men of that place recognized Jesus, they sent word to all the surrounding country. People brought all their sick to him 36and begged him to let the sick just touch the edge of his cloak, and all who touched him were healed.

a 24 Greek many stadia

Clean and Unclean

15 Then some Pharisees and teachers of the law came to Jesus from Jerusalem and asked, [2]"Why do your disciples break the tradition of the elders? They don't wash their hands before they eat!"

[3]Jesus replied, "And why do you break the command of God for the sake of your tradition? [4]For God said, 'Honor your father and mother'[a] and 'Anyone who curses his father or mother must be put to death.'[b] [5]But you say that if a man says to his father or mother, 'Whatever help you might otherwise have received from me is a gift devoted to God,' [6]he is not to 'honor his father'[c] with it. Thus you nullify the word of God for the sake of your tradition. [7]You hypocrites! Isaiah was right when he prophesied about you:

[8]" 'These people honor me with their lips,
　　but their hearts are far from me.
[9]They worship me in vain;
　　their teachings are but rules taught by men.'[d]"

[10]Jesus called the crowd to him and said, "Listen and understand. [11]What goes into a man's mouth does not make him 'unclean,' but what comes out of his mouth, that is what makes him 'unclean.' "

[12]Then the disciples came to him and asked, "Do you know that the Pharisees were offended when they heard this?"

[13]He replied, "Every plant that my heavenly Father has not planted will be pulled up by the roots. [14]Leave them; they are blind guides.[e] If a blind man leads a blind man, both will fall into a pit."

[15]Peter said, "Explain the parable to us."

[16]"Are you still so dull?" Jesus asked them. [17]"Don't you see that whatever enters the mouth goes into the stomach and then out of the body? [18]But the things that come out of the mouth come from the heart, and these make a man 'unclean.' [19]For out of the heart come evil thoughts, murder, adultery, sexual immorality, theft, false testimony, slander. [20]These are what make a man 'unclean'; but eating with unwashed hands does not make him 'unclean.' "

The Faith of the Canaanite Woman

[21]Leaving that place, Jesus withdrew to the region of Tyre and Sidon. [22]A Canaanite woman

---

a 4 Exodus 20:12; Deut. 5:16　　b 4 Exodus 21:17; Lev. 20:9
c 6 Some manuscripts *father or his mother*　　d 9 Isaiah 29:13
e 14 Some manuscripts *guides of the blind*

潔淨與污穢

15 那時，有法利賽人和文士從耶路撒冷來見耶穌，說：[2] "你的門徒為甚麼犯古人的遺傳呢？因為吃飯的時候，他們不洗手。"

[3]耶穌回答說："你們為甚麼因着你們的遺傳，犯神的誡命呢？[4]神說：'當孝敬父母'，又說：'咒罵父母的，必治死他。' [5]你們倒說：'無論何人對父母說，我所當奉給你的，已經作了供獻，[6]他就可以不孝敬父母。' 這就是你們藉着遺傳，廢了神的誡命。[7]假冒為善的人哪！以賽亞指着你們說的預言是不錯的。他說：

[8]" '這百姓用嘴唇尊敬我，
　　心卻遠離我；
[9]他們將人的吩咐當作道理教導人，
　　所以拜我也是枉然。' "

[10]耶穌就叫了眾人來，對他們說："你們要聽，也要明白。[11]入口的不能污穢人，出口的乃能污穢人。"

[12]當時，門徒進前來對他說："法利賽人聽見這話不服（註："不服"原文作"跌倒"），你知道嗎？"

[13]耶穌回答說："凡栽種的物，若不是我天父栽種的，必要拔出來。[14]任憑他們吧！他們是瞎眼領路的；若是瞎子領瞎子，兩個人都要掉在坑裏。"

[15]彼得對耶穌說："請將這比喻講給我們聽。"

[16]耶穌說："你們到如今還不明白嗎？[17]豈不知凡入口的，是運到肚子裏，又落在茅廁裏嗎？[18]惟獨出口的，是從心裏發出來的，這才污穢人。[19]因為從心裏發出來的，有惡念、兇殺、姦淫、苟合、偷盜、妄證、謗讟，[20]這都是污穢人的。至於不洗手吃飯，那卻不污穢人。"

迦南婦人的信心

[21]耶穌離開那裏，退到推羅、西頓的境內去。[22]有一個迦南婦人從那

地方出來，喊着説："主啊，<u>大衞</u>的子孫，可憐我！我女兒被鬼附得甚苦。"

23耶穌卻一言不答。門徒進前來，求他説："這婦人在我們後頭喊叫，請打發她走吧！"

24耶穌説："我奉差遣，不過是到以色列家迷失的羊那裏去。"

25那婦人來拜他，説："主啊，幫助我！"

26他回答説："不好拿兒女的餅丟給狗吃。"

27婦人説："主啊，不錯！但是狗也吃牠主人桌子上掉下來的碎渣兒。"

28耶穌説："婦人，你的信心是大的，照你所要的，給你成全了吧！"從那時候，她女兒就好了。

耶穌給四千人吃飽

29耶穌離開那地方，來到靠近<u>加利利</u>的海邊，就上山坐下。30有許多人到他那裏，帶着瘸子、瞎子、啞巴、有殘疾的和好些別的病人，都放在他腳前，他就治好了他們。31甚至眾人都希奇，因為看見啞巴説話，殘疾的痊愈，瘸子行走，瞎子看見，他們就歸榮耀給<u>以色列</u>的神。

32耶穌叫門徒來，説："我憐憫這眾人，因為他們同我在這裏已經三天，也沒有吃的了。我不願意叫他們餓着回去，恐怕在路上困乏。"

33門徒説："我們在這野地，哪裏有這麼多的餅叫這許多人吃飽呢？"

34耶穌説："你們有多少餅？"

他們説："有七個，還有幾條小魚。"

35他就吩咐眾人坐在地上，36拿着這七個餅和幾條魚，祝謝了，擘開，遞給門徒，門徒又遞給眾人。37眾人都吃，並且吃飽了，收拾剩下的零碎，裝滿了七個筐子。38吃的人，除了婦女孩子，共有四千。39耶穌叫眾人散去，就上船，來到<u>馬加丹</u>的境界。

求神蹟

16 <u>法利賽</u>人和<u>撒都該</u>人來試探耶穌，請他從天上顯個神蹟給他們看。

from that vicinity came to him, crying out, "Lord, Son of David, have mercy on me! My daughter is suffering terribly from demon-possession."

23Jesus did not answer a word. So his disciples came to him and urged him, "Send her away, for she keeps crying out after us."

24He answered, "I was sent only to the lost sheep of Israel."

25The woman came and knelt before him. "Lord, help me!" she said.

26He replied, "It is not right to take the children's bread and toss it to their dogs."

27"Yes, Lord," she said, "but even the dogs eat the crumbs that fall from their masters' table."

28Then Jesus answered, "Woman, you have great faith! Your request is granted." And her daughter was healed from that very hour.

Jesus Feeds the Four Thousand

29Jesus left there and went along the Sea of Galilee. Then he went up on a mountainside and sat down. 30Great crowds came to him, bringing the lame, the blind, the crippled, the mute and many others, and laid them at his feet; and he healed them. 31The people were amazed when they saw the mute speaking, the crippled made well, the lame walking and the blind seeing. And they praised the God of Israel.

32Jesus called his disciples to him and said, "I have compassion for these people; they have already been with me three days and have nothing to eat. I do not want to send them away hungry, or they may collapse on the way."

33His disciples answered, "Where could we get enough bread in this remote place to feed such a crowd?"

34"How many loaves do you have?" Jesus asked.

"Seven," they replied, "and a few small fish."

35He told the crowd to sit down on the ground. 36Then he took the seven loaves and the fish, and when he had given thanks, he broke them and gave them to the disciples, and they in turn to the people. 37They all ate and were satisfied. Afterward the disciples picked up seven basketfuls of broken pieces that were left over. 38The number of those who ate was four thousand, besides women and children. 39After Jesus had sent the crowd away, he got into the boat and went to the vicinity of Magadan.

The Demand for a Sign

16 The Pharisees and Sadducees came to Jesus and tested him by asking him to show them a sign from heaven.

[2]He replied,[a] "When evening comes, you say, 'It will be fair weather, for the sky is red,' [3]and in the morning, 'Today it will be stormy, for the sky is red and overcast.' You know how to interpret the appearance of the sky, but you cannot interpret the signs of the times. [4]A wicked and adulterous generation looks for a miraculous sign, but none will be given it except the sign of Jonah." Jesus then left them and went away.

The Yeast of the Pharisees and Sadducees

[5]When they went across the lake, the disciples forgot to take bread. [6]"Be careful," Jesus said to them. "Be on your guard against the yeast of the Pharisees and Sadducees."

[7]They discussed this among themselves and said, "It is because we didn't bring any bread."

[8]Aware of their discussion, Jesus asked, "You of little faith, why are you talking among yourselves about having no bread? [9]Do you still not understand? Don't you remember the five loaves for the five thousand, and how many basketfuls you gathered? [10]Or the seven loaves for the four thousand, and how many basketfuls you gathered? [11]How is it you don't understand that I was not talking to you about bread? But be on your guard against the yeast of the Pharisees and Sadducees." [12]Then they understood that he was not telling them to guard against the yeast used in bread, but against the teaching of the Pharisees and Sadducees.

Peter's Confession of Christ

[13]When Jesus came to the region of Caesarea Philippi, he asked his disciples, "Who do people say the Son of Man is?"

[14]They replied, "Some say John the Baptist; others say Elijah; and still others, Jeremiah or one of the prophets."

[15]"But what about you?" he asked. "Who do you say I am?"

[16]Simon Peter answered, "You are the Christ,[b] the Son of the living God."

[17]Jesus replied, "Blessed are you, Simon son of Jonah, for this was not revealed to you by man, but by my Father in heaven. [18]And I tell you that you are Peter,[c] and on this rock I will build my church, and the gates of Hades[d] will not overcome it.[e] [19]I will give you the keys of the kingdom of heaven; whatever you bind on earth will be[f] bound in heaven, and whatever

a 2 Some early manuscripts do not have the rest of verse 2 and all of verse 3.   b 16 Or Messiah; also in verse 20   c 18 Peter means rock.   d 18 Or hell   e 18 Or not prove stronger than it f 19 Or have been

[2]耶穌回答說："晚上天發紅，你們就說，'天必要晴'；[3]早晨天發紅，又發黑，你們就說，'今日必有風雨'。你們知道分辨天上的氣色，倒不能分辨這時候的神蹟。[4]一個邪惡淫亂的世代求神蹟，除了約拿的神蹟以外，再沒有神蹟給他看。"耶穌就離開他們去了。

法利賽人與撒都該人的酵

[5]門徒渡到那邊去，忘了帶餅。[6]耶穌對他們說："你們要謹慎，防備法利賽人和撒都該人的酵。"

[7]門徒彼此議論說："這是因為我們沒有帶餅吧！"

[8]耶穌看出來，就說："你們這小信的人，為甚麼因為沒有餅彼此議論呢？[9]你們還不明白嗎？不記得那五個餅分給五千人，又收拾了多少籃子的零碎嗎？[10]也不記得那七個餅分給四千人，又收拾了多少筐子的零碎嗎？[11]我對你們說：'要防備法利賽人和撒都該人的酵'，這話不是指着餅說的，你們怎麼不明白呢？"[12]門徒這才曉得他說的，不是叫他們防備餅的酵，乃是防備法利賽人和撒都該人的教訓。

彼得認基督

[13]耶穌到了凱撒利亞腓立比的境內，就問門徒說："人說我人子是誰（註：有古卷無"我"字）？"[14]他們說："有人說是施洗的約翰，有人說是以利亞，又有人說是耶利米或是先知裏的一位。"[15]耶穌說："你們說我是誰？"

[16]西門彼得回答說："你是基督，是永生神的兒子。"[17]耶穌對他說："西門巴約拿，你是有福的！因為這不是屬血肉的指示你的，乃是我在天上的父指示的。[18]我還告訴你：你是彼得，我要把我的教會建造在這磐石上，陰間的權柄不能勝過他（註："權柄"原文作"門"）。[19]我要把天國的鑰匙給你，凡你在地上所捆綁的，在天上也要捆

綁；凡你在地上所釋放的，在天上也要釋放。」20當下，耶穌囑咐門徒，不可對人說他是基督。

耶穌預言自己的死

21從此，耶穌才指示門徒，他必須上耶路撒冷去，受長老、祭司長、文士許多的苦，並且被殺，第三日復活。

22彼得就拉着他，勸他說：「主啊，萬不可如此！這事必不臨到你身上。」

23耶穌轉過來，對彼得說：「撒但，退我後邊去吧！你是絆我腳的，因為你不體貼神的意思，只體貼人的意思。」

24於是，耶穌對門徒說：「若有人要跟從我，就當捨己，背起他的十字架來跟從我。25因為凡要救自己生命的（註：「生命」或作「靈魂」。下同），必喪掉生命；凡為我喪掉生命的，必得着生命。26人若賺得全世界，賠上自己的生命，有甚麼益處呢？人還能拿甚麼換生命呢？27人子要在他父的榮耀裏，同着眾使者降臨；那時候，他要照各人的行為報應各人。28我實在告訴你們：站在這裏的，有人在沒嘗死味以前，必看見人子降臨在他的國裏。」

登山變像

17 過了六天，耶穌帶着彼得、雅各和雅各的兄弟約翰暗暗地上了高山，就在他們面前變了形像，臉面明亮如日頭，衣裳潔白如光。3忽然，有摩西、以利亞向他們顯現，同耶穌說話。

4彼得對耶穌說：「主啊，我們在這裏真好！你若願意，我就在這裏搭三座棚：一座為你，一座為摩西，一座為以利亞。」

5說話之間，忽然有一朵光明的雲彩遮蓋他們，且有聲音從雲彩裏出來說：「這是我的愛子，我所喜悅的，你們要聽他！」

6門徒聽見，就俯伏在地，極其害怕。7耶穌進前來，摸他們，說：

you loose on earth will be[a] loosed in heaven." 20Then he warned his disciples not to tell anyone that he was the Christ.

Jesus Predicts His Death

21From that time on Jesus began to explain to his disciples that he must go to Jerusalem and suffer many things at the hands of the elders, chief priests and teachers of the law, and that he must be killed and on the third day be raised to life.

22Peter took him aside and began to rebuke him. "Never, Lord!" he said. "This shall never happen to you!"

23Jesus turned and said to Peter, "Get behind me, Satan! You are a stumbling block to me; you do not have in mind the things of God, but the things of men."

24Then Jesus said to his disciples, "If anyone would come after me, he must deny himself and take up his cross and follow me. 25For whoever wants to save his life[b] will lose it, but whoever loses his life for me will find it. 26What good will it be for a man if he gains the whole world, yet forfeits his soul? Or what can a man give in exchange for his soul? 27For the Son of Man is going to come in his Father's glory with his angels, and then he will reward each person according to what he has done. 28I tell you the truth, some who are standing here will not taste death before they see the Son of Man coming in his kingdom."

The Transfiguration

17 After six days Jesus took with him Peter, James and John the brother of James, and led them up a high mountain by themselves. 2There he was transfigured before them. His face shone like the sun, and his clothes became as white as the light. 3Just then there appeared before them Moses and Elijah, talking with Jesus.

4Peter said to Jesus, "Lord, it is good for us to be here. If you wish, I will put up three shelters—one for you, one for Moses and one for Elijah."

5While he was still speaking, a bright cloud enveloped them, and a voice from the cloud said, "This is my Son, whom I love; with him I am well pleased. Listen to him!"

6When the disciples heard this, they fell facedown to the ground, terrified. 7But Jesus came and touched them. "Get up," he said. "Don't be

---

a 19 Or *have been*　*b 25* The Greek word means either *life* or *soul*; also in verse 26.

afraid." [8]When they looked up, they saw no one except Jesus.

[9]As they were coming down the mountain, Jesus instructed them, "Don't tell anyone what you have seen, until the Son of Man has been raised from the dead."

[10]The disciples asked him, "Why then do the teachers of the law say that Elijah must come first?"

[11]Jesus replied, "To be sure, Elijah comes and will restore all things. [12]But I tell you, Elijah has already come, and they did not recognize him, but have done to him everything they wished. In the same way the Son of Man is going to suffer at their hands." [13]Then the disciples understood that he was talking to them about John the Baptist.

The Healing of a Boy With a Demon

[14]When they came to the crowd, a man approached Jesus and knelt before him. [15]"Lord, have mercy on my son," he said. "He has seizures and is suffering greatly. He often falls into the fire or into the water. [16]I brought him to your disciples, but they could not heal him."

[17]"O unbelieving and perverse generation," Jesus replied, "how long shall I stay with you? How long shall I put up with you? Bring the boy here to me." [18]Jesus rebuked the demon, and it came out of the boy, and he was healed from that moment.

[19]Then the disciples came to Jesus in private and asked, "Why couldn't we drive it out?"

[20]He replied, "Because you have so little faith. I tell you the truth, if you have faith as small as a mustard seed, you can say to this mountain, 'Move from here to there' and it will move. Nothing will be impossible for you.[a]"

[22]When they came together in Galilee, he said to them, "The Son of Man is going to be betrayed into the hands of men. [23]They will kill him, and on the third day he will be raised to life." And the disciples were filled with grief.

The Temple Tax

[24]After Jesus and his disciples arrived in Capernaum, the collectors of the two-drachma tax came to Peter and asked, "Doesn't your teacher pay the temple tax[b]?"

[25]"Yes, he does," he replied.

When Peter came into the house, Jesus was the first to speak. "What do you think, Simon?" he asked. "From whom do the kings of the earth

"起來，不要害怕！"[8]他們舉目不見一人，只見耶穌在那裏。

[9]下山的時候，耶穌吩咐他們說："人子還沒有從死裏復活，你們不要將所看見的告訴人。"

[10]門徒問耶穌說："文士為甚麼說以利亞必須先來？"

[11]耶穌回答說："以利亞固然先來，並要復興萬事；[12]只是我告訴你們：以利亞已經來了，人卻不認識他，竟任意待他。人子也將要這樣受他們的害。"[13]門徒這才明白耶穌所說的，是指着施洗的約翰。

醫治被鬼附着的男孩

[14]耶穌和門徒到了眾人那裏，有一個人來見耶穌，跪下，[15]說："主啊，憐憫我的兒子！他害癲癇的病很苦，屢次跌在火裏，屢次跌在水裏。[16]我帶他到你門徒那裏，他們卻不能醫治他。"

[17]耶穌說："噯！這又不信、又悖謬的世代啊，我在你們這裏要到幾時呢？我忍耐你們要到幾時呢？把他帶到我這裏來吧！"[18]耶穌斥責那鬼，鬼就出來，從此孩子便痊愈了。

[19]門徒暗暗地到耶穌跟前說："我們為甚麼不能趕出那鬼呢？"

[20]耶穌說："是因你們的信心小。我實在告訴你們：你們若有信心像一粒芥菜種，就是對這座山說：'你從這邊挪到那邊'，它也必挪去，並且你們沒有一件不能做的事了。[21]至於這一類的鬼，若不禱告禁食，他就不出來（註：或作"不能趕他出來"）。"

[22]他們還住在加利利的時候，耶穌對門徒說："人子將要被交在人手裏。[23]他們要殺害他，第三日他要復活。"門徒就大大地憂愁。

聖殿稅

[24]到了迦百農，有收丁稅的人來見彼得說："你們的先生不納丁稅嗎（註：丁稅約有半塊錢）？"

[25]彼得說："納。"

他進了屋子，耶穌先向他說："西門，你的意思如何？世上的君王

---

a 20 Some manuscripts you. 21 But this kind does not go out except by prayer and fasting.   b 24 Greek the two drachmas

向誰徵收關稅、丁稅？是向自己的兒子呢，是向外人呢？"

26彼得說："是向外人。"

耶穌說："既然如此，兒子就可以免稅了。27但恐怕觸犯他們（註："觸犯"原文作"絆倒"），你且往海邊去釣魚，把先釣上來的魚拿起來，開了牠的口，必得一塊錢，可以拿去給他們，作你我的稅銀。"

天國裏最大的

18 當時，門徒進前來，問耶穌說："天國裏誰是最大的？"

2耶穌便叫一個小孩子來，使他站在他們當中，3說："我實在告訴你們：你們若不回轉，變成小孩子的樣式，斷不得進天國。4所以，凡自己謙卑像這小孩子的，他在天國裏就是最大的。

5"凡為我的名接待一個像這小孩子的，就是接待我。6凡使這信我的一個小子跌倒的，倒不如把大磨石拴在這人的頸項上，沉在深海裏。

7"這世界有禍了！因為將人絆倒；絆倒人的事是免不了的，但那絆倒人的有禍了！8倘若你一隻手或是一隻腳叫你跌倒，就砍下來丟掉；你缺一隻手或是一隻腳進入永生，強如有兩手兩腳被丟在永火裏。9倘若你一隻眼叫你跌倒，就把它剜出來丟掉；你只有一隻眼進入永生，強如有兩隻眼被丟在地獄的火裏。

失羊的比喻

10"你們要小心，不可輕看這小子裏的一個。我告訴你們：他們的使者在天上，常見我天父的面。（註：有古卷在此有11"人子來，為要拯救失喪的人。"）

12"一個人若有一百隻羊，一隻走迷了路，你們的意思如何？他豈不撇下這九十九隻，往山裏去找那隻迷路的羊嗎？13若是找着了，我實在告訴你們：他為這一隻羊歡喜，比為那沒有迷路的九十九隻歡喜還大呢！14你們在天上的父也是這樣，不願意這小子裏失喪一個。

collect duty and taxes—from their own sons or from others?"

26"From others," Peter answered.

"Then the sons are exempt," Jesus said to him. 27"But so that we may not offend them, go to the lake and throw out your line. Take the first fish you catch; open its mouth and you will find a four-drachma coin. Take it and give it to them for my tax and yours."

The Greatest in the Kingdom of Heaven

18 At that time the disciples came to Jesus and asked, "Who is the greatest in the kingdom of heaven?"

2He called a little child and had him stand among them. 3And he said: "I tell you the truth, unless you change and become like little children, you will never enter the kingdom of heaven. 4Therefore, whoever humbles himself like this child is the greatest in the kingdom of heaven.

5"And whoever welcomes a little child like this in my name welcomes me. 6But if anyone causes one of these little ones who believe in me to sin, it would be better for him to have a large millstone hung around his neck and to be drowned in the depths of the sea.

7"Woe to the world because of the things that cause people to sin! Such things must come, but woe to the man through whom they come! 8If your hand or your foot causes you to sin, cut it off and throw it away. It is better for you to enter life maimed or crippled than to have two hands or two feet and be thrown into eternal fire. 9And if your eye causes you to sin, gouge it out and throw it away. It is better for you to enter life with one eye than to have two eyes and be thrown into the fire of hell.

The Parable of the Lost Sheep

10"See that you do not look down on one of these little ones. For I tell you that their angels in heaven always see the face of my Father in heaven.[a]

12"What do you think? If a man owns a hundred sheep, and one of them wanders away, will he not leave the ninety-nine on the hills and go to look for the one that wandered off? 13And if he finds it, I tell you the truth, he is happier about that one sheep than about the ninety-nine that did not wander off. 14In the same way your Father in heaven is not willing that any of these little ones should be lost.

a 10 Some manuscripts heaven. 11 The Son of Man came to save what was lost.

A Brother Who Sins Against You

15"If your brother sins against you,[a] go and show him his fault, just between the two of you. If he listens to you, you have won your brother over. 16But if he will not listen, take one or two others along, so that 'every matter may be established by the testimony of two or three witnesses.'[b] 17If he refuses to listen to them, tell it to the church; and if he refuses to listen even to the church, treat him as you would a pagan or a tax collector.

18"I tell you the truth, whatever you bind on earth will be[c] bound in heaven, and whatever you loose on earth will be[c] loosed in heaven.

19"Again, I tell you that if two of you on earth agree about anything you ask for, it will be done for you by my Father in heaven. 20For where two or three come together in my name, there am I with them."

The Parable of the Unmerciful Servant

21Then Peter came to Jesus and asked, "Lord, how many times shall I forgive my brother when he sins against me? Up to seven times?"

22Jesus answered, "I tell you, not seven times, but seventy-seven times.[d]

23"Therefore, the kingdom of heaven is like a king who wanted to settle accounts with his servants. 24As he began the settlement, a man who owed him ten thousand talents[e] was brought to him. 25Since he was not able to pay, the master ordered that he and his wife and his children and all that he had be sold to repay the debt.

26"The servant fell on his knees before him. 'Be patient with me,' he begged, 'and I will pay back everything.' 27The servant's master took pity on him, canceled the debt and let him go.

28"But when that servant went out, he found one of his fellow servants who owed him a hundred denarii.[f] He grabbed him and began to choke him. 'Pay back what you owe me!' he demanded.

29"His fellow servant fell to his knees and begged him, 'Be patient with me, and I will pay you back.'

30"But he refused. Instead, he went off and had the man thrown into prison until he could pay the debt. 31When the other servants saw what had happened, they were greatly distressed and went and told their master everything that had happened.

得罪你的弟兄

15 倘若你的弟兄得罪你，你就去趁着只有他和你在一處的時候，指出他的錯來。他若聽你，你便得了你的弟兄。16他若不聽，你就另外帶一兩個人同去，要憑兩三個人的口作見證，句句都可定準。17若是不聽他們，就告訴教會；若是不聽教會，就看他像外邦人和稅吏一樣。

18 "我實在告訴你們：凡你們在地上所捆綁的，在天上也要捆綁；凡你們在地上所釋放的，在天上也要釋放。

19 "我又告訴你們：若是你們中間有兩個人在地上同心合意求甚麼事，我在天上的父必為他們成全。20因為無論在哪裏，有兩三個人奉我的名聚會，那裏就有我在他們中間。"

無憐憫心僕人的比喻

21那時，彼得進前來，對耶穌說："主啊，我弟兄得罪我，我當饒恕他幾次呢？到七次可以嗎？"

22耶穌說："我對你說：不是到七次，乃是到七十個七次。

23 "天國好像一個王要和他僕人算賬。24才算的時候，有人帶了一個欠一千萬銀子的來。25因為他沒有甚麼償還之物，主人吩咐把他和他妻子兒女，並一切所有的都賣了償還。

26 "那僕人就俯伏拜他，說：'主啊，寬容我！將來我都要還清。'27那僕人的主人就動了慈心，把他釋放了，並且免了他的債。

28 "那僕人出來，遇見他的一個同伴欠他十兩銀子，便揪着他，掐住他的喉嚨，說：'你把所欠的還我！'

29 "他的同伴就俯伏央求他說：'寬容我吧！將來我必還清。'

30 "他不肯，竟去把他下在監裏，等他還了所欠的債。31眾同伴看見他所做的事，就甚憂愁，去把這事都告訴了主人。

---

a 15 Some manuscripts do not have against you.   b 16 Deut. 19:15   c 18 Or have been   d 22 Or seventy times seven   e 24 That is, millions of dollars   f 28 That is, a few dollars

32 於是，主人叫了他來，對他說：『你這惡奴才！你央求我，我就把你所欠的都免了。33 你不應當憐恤你的同伴，像我憐恤你嗎？』34 主人就大怒，把他交給掌刑的，等他還清了所欠的債。

35 「你們各人若不從心裏饒恕你的弟兄，我天父也要這樣待你們了。」

論休妻

19 耶穌說完了這些話，就離開加利利，來到猶太的境界約旦河外。2 有許多人跟着他，他就在那裏把他們的病人治好了。

3 有法利賽人來試探耶穌說：「人無論甚麼緣故都可以休妻嗎？」4 耶穌回答說：「那起初造人的，是造男造女，5 並且說：『因此，人要離開父母，與妻子連合，二人成為一體。』這經你們沒有念過嗎？6 既然如此，夫妻不再是兩個人，乃是一體的了。所以，神配合的，人不可分開。」

7 法利賽人說：「這樣，摩西為甚麼吩咐給妻子休書，就可以休她呢？」

8 耶穌說：「摩西因為你們的心硬，所以許你們休妻，但起初並不是這樣。9 我告訴你們：凡休妻另娶的，若不是為淫亂的緣故，就是犯姦淫了；有人娶那被休的婦人，也是犯姦淫了。」

10 門徒對耶穌說：「人和妻子既是這樣，倒不如不娶。」

11 耶穌說：「這話不是人都能領受的，惟獨賜給誰，誰才能領受。12 因為有生來是閹人，也有被人閹的，並有為天國的緣故自閹的。這話誰能領受，就可以領受。」

小孩與耶穌

13 那時，有人帶着小孩子來見耶穌，要耶穌給他們按手禱告，門徒就責備那些人。

32 "Then the master called the servant in. 'You wicked servant,' he said, 'I canceled all that debt of yours because you begged me to. 33 Shouldn't you have had mercy on your fellow servant just as I had on you?' 34 In anger his master turned him over to the jailers to be tortured, until he should pay back all he owed.

35 "This is how my heavenly Father will treat each of you unless you forgive your brother from your heart."

Divorce

19 When Jesus had finished saying these things, he left Galilee and went into the region of Judea to the other side of the Jordan. 2 Large crowds followed him, and he healed them there.

3 Some Pharisees came to him to test him. They asked, "Is it lawful for a man to divorce his wife for any and every reason?"

4 "Haven't you read," he replied, "that at the beginning the Creator 'made them male and female,'[a] 5 and said, 'For this reason a man will leave his father and mother and be united to his wife, and the two will become one flesh'[b]? 6 So they are no longer two, but one. Therefore what God has joined together, let man not separate."

7 "Why then," they asked, "did Moses command that a man give his wife a certificate of divorce and send her away?"

8 Jesus replied, "Moses permitted you to divorce your wives because your hearts were hard. But it was not this way from the beginning. 9 I tell you that anyone who divorces his wife, except for marital unfaithfulness, and marries another woman commits adultery."

10 The disciples said to him, "If this is the situation between a husband and wife, it is better not to marry."

11 Jesus replied, "Not everyone can accept this word, but only those to whom it has been given. 12 For some are eunuchs because they were born that way; others were made that way by men; and others have renounced marriage[c] because of the kingdom of heaven. The one who can accept this should accept it."

The Little Children and Jesus

13 Then little children were brought to Jesus for him to place his hands on them and pray for them. But the disciples rebuked those who brought them.

---

a 4 Gen. 1:27　　*b* 5 Gen. 2:24　　*c* 12 Or *have made themselves eunuchs*

[14]Jesus said, "Let the little children come to me, and do not hinder them, for the kingdom of heaven belongs to such as these." [15]When he had placed his hands on them, he went on from there.

The Rich Young Man

[16]Now a man came up to Jesus and asked, "Teacher, what good thing must I do to get eternal life?"

[17]"Why do you ask me about what is good?" Jesus replied. "There is only One who is good. If you want to enter life, obey the commandments."

[18]"Which ones?" the man inquired.

Jesus replied, " 'Do not murder, do not commit adultery, do not steal, do not give false testimony, [19]honor your father and mother,'[a] and 'love your neighbor as yourself.'[b] "

[20]"All these I have kept," the young man said. "What do I still lack?"

[21]Jesus answered, "If you want to be perfect, go, sell your possessions and give to the poor, and you will have treasure in heaven. Then come, follow me."

[22]When the young man heard this, he went away sad, because he had great wealth.

[23]Then Jesus said to his disciples, "I tell you the truth, it is hard for a rich man to enter the kingdom of heaven. [24]Again I tell you, it is easier for a camel to go through the eye of a needle than for a rich man to enter the kingdom of God."

[25]When the disciples heard this, they were greatly astonished and asked, "Who then can be saved?"

[26]Jesus looked at them and said, "With man this is impossible, but with God all things are possible."

[27]Peter answered him, "We have left everything to follow you! What then will there be for us?"

[28]Jesus said to them, "I tell you the truth, at the renewal of all things, when the Son of Man sits on his glorious throne, you who have followed me will also sit on twelve thrones, judging the twelve tribes of Israel. [29]And everyone who has left houses or brothers or sisters or father or mother[c] or children or fields for my sake will receive a hundred times as much and will inherit eternal life. [30]But many who are first will be last, and many who are last will be first.

---

[14]耶穌說："讓小孩子到我這裏來，不要禁止他們，因為在天國的，正是這樣的人。"[15]耶穌給他們按手，就離開那地方去了。

富有的少年人

[16]有一個人來見耶穌說："夫子（註：有古卷作"良善的夫子"），我該做甚麼善事才能得永生？"

[17]耶穌對他說："你為甚麼以善事問我呢？只有一位是善的（註：有古卷作"你為甚麼稱我是良善的？除了神以外，沒有一個良善的"）。你若要進入永生，就當遵守誡命。"

[18]他說："甚麼誡命？"

耶穌說："就是'不可殺人，不可姦淫，不可偷盜，不可作假見證，[19]當孝敬父母，又當愛人如己。'"

[20]那少年人說："這一切我都遵守了，還缺少甚麼呢？"

[21]耶穌說："你若願意作完全人，可去變賣你所有的，分給窮人，就必有財寶在天上；你還要來跟從我。"

[22]那少年人聽見這話，就憂憂愁愁地走了，因為他的產業很多。

[23]耶穌對門徒說："我實在告訴你們：財主進天國是難的。[24]我又告訴你們：駱駝穿過針的眼，比財主進神的國還容易呢！"

[25]門徒聽見這話，就希奇得很，說："這樣誰能得救呢？"

[26]耶穌看着他們說："在人這是不能的，在神凡事都能！"

[27]彼得就對他說："看哪，我們已經撇下所有的跟從你，將來我們要得甚麼呢？"

[28]耶穌說："我實在告訴你們：你們這跟從我的人，到復興的時候，人子坐在他榮耀的寶座上，你們也要坐在十二個寶座上，審判以色列十二個支派。[29]凡為我的名撇下房屋或是弟兄、姐妹、父親、母親（註：有古卷添"妻子"）、兒女、田地的，必要得着百倍，並且承受永生。[30]然而，有許多在前的，將要在後；在後的，將要在前。

---

a 19 Exodus 20:12-16; Deut. 5:16-20   b 19 Lev. 19:18
c 29 Some manuscripts *mother or wife*

葡萄園工人的比喻

20 "因為天國好像家主清早去雇人，進他的葡萄園做工，²和工人講定一天一錢銀子，就打發他們進葡萄園去。

³約在巳初出去，看見市上還有閒站的人，⁴就對他們說：'你們也進葡萄園去，所當給的，我必給你們。'他們也進去了。

⁵約在午正和申初又出去，也是這樣行。⁶約在酉初出去，看見還有人站在那裏，就問他們說：'你們為甚麼整天在這裏閒站呢？'

⁷他們說：'因為沒有人雇我們。'

"他說：'你們也進葡萄園去。'

⁸到了晚上，園主對管事的說：'叫工人都來，給他們工錢，從後來的起，到先來的為止。'

⁹約在酉初雇的人來了，各人得了一錢銀子。¹⁰及至那先雇的來了，他們以為必要多得，誰知也是各得一錢。¹¹他們得了，就埋怨家主說：¹²'我們整天勞苦受熱，那後來的只做了一小時，你竟叫他們和我們一樣嗎？'

¹³家主回答其中的一人說：'朋友，我不虧負你，你與我講定的不是一錢銀子嗎？¹⁴拿你的走吧！我給那後來的和給你一樣，這是我願意的。¹⁵我的東西難道不可隨我的意思用嗎？因為我作好人，你就紅了眼嗎？'

¹⁶這樣，那在後的將要在前；在前的將要在後了（註：有古卷在此有"因為被召的人多，選上的人少"）。"

耶穌再預言自己的死

¹⁷耶穌上耶路撒冷去的時候，在路上把十二個門徒帶到一邊，對他們說：¹⁸"看哪，我們上耶路撒冷去，人子要被交給祭司長和文士。他們要定他死罪，¹⁹又交給外邦人，將他戲弄、鞭打、釘在十字架上，第三日他要復活。"

The Parable of the Workers in the Vineyard

20 "For the kingdom of heaven is like a landowner who went out early in the morning to hire men to work in his vineyard. ²He agreed to pay them a denarius for the day and sent them into his vineyard.

³"About the third hour he went out and saw others standing in the marketplace doing nothing. ⁴He told them, 'You also go and work in my vineyard, and I will pay you whatever is right.' ⁵So they went.

"He went out again about the sixth hour and the ninth hour and did the same thing. ⁶About the eleventh hour he went out and found still others standing around. He asked them, 'Why have you been standing here all day long doing nothing?'

⁷"'Because no one has hired us,' they answered.

"He said to them, 'You also go and work in my vineyard.'

⁸"When evening came, the owner of the vineyard said to his foreman, 'Call the workers and pay them their wages, beginning with the last ones hired and going on to the first.'

⁹"The workers who were hired about the eleventh hour came and each received a denarius. ¹⁰So when those came who were hired first, they expected to receive more. But each one of them also received a denarius. ¹¹When they received it, they began to grumble against the landowner. ¹²'These men who were hired last worked only one hour,' they said, 'and you have made them equal to us who have borne the burden of the work and the heat of the day.'

¹³"But he answered one of them, 'Friend, I am not being unfair to you. Didn't you agree to work for a denarius? ¹⁴Take your pay and go. I want to give the man who was hired last the same as I gave you. ¹⁵Don't I have the right to do what I want with my own money? Or are you envious because I am generous?'

¹⁶"So the last will be first, and the first will be last."

Jesus Again Predicts His Death

¹⁷Now as Jesus was going up to Jerusalem, he took the twelve disciples aside and said to them, ¹⁸"We are going up to Jerusalem, and the Son of Man will be betrayed to the chief priests and the teachers of the law. They will condemn him to death ¹⁹and will turn him over to the Gentiles to be mocked and flogged and crucified. On the third day he will be raised to life!"

A Mother's Request

²⁰Then the mother of Zebedee's sons came to Jesus with her sons and, kneeling down, asked a favor of him.

²¹"What is it you want?" he asked.

She said, "Grant that one of these two sons of mine may sit at your right and the other at your left in your kingdom."

²²"You don't know what you are asking," Jesus said to them. "Can you drink the cup I am going to drink?"

"We can," they answered.

²³Jesus said to them, "You will indeed drink from my cup, but to sit at my right or left is not for me to grant. These places belong to those for whom they have been prepared by my Father."

²⁴When the ten heard about this, they were indignant with the two brothers. ²⁵Jesus called them together and said, "You know that the rulers of the Gentiles lord it over them, and their high officials exercise authority over them. ²⁶Not so with you. Instead, whoever wants to become great among you must be your servant, ²⁷and whoever wants to be first must be your slave— ²⁸just as the Son of Man did not come to be served, but to serve, and to give his life as a ransom for many."

Two Blind Men Receive Sight

²⁹As Jesus and his disciples were leaving Jericho, a large crowd followed him. ³⁰Two blind men were sitting by the roadside, and when they heard that Jesus was going by, they shouted, "Lord, Son of David, have mercy on us!"

³¹The crowd rebuked them and told them to be quiet, but they shouted all the louder, "Lord, Son of David, have mercy on us!"

³²Jesus stopped and called them. "What do you want me to do for you?" he asked.

³³"Lord," they answered, "we want our sight."

³⁴Jesus had compassion on them and touched their eyes. Immediately they received their sight and followed him.

The Triumphal Entry

21 As they approached Jerusalem and came to Bethphage on the Mount of Olives, Jesus sent two disciples, ²saying to them, "Go to the village ahead of you, and at once you will find a donkey tied there, with her colt by her. Untie them and bring them to me. ³If anyone says anything to you, tell him that the Lord needs them, and he will send them right away."

⁴This took place to fulfill what was spoken through the prophet:

一個母親的請求

²⁰那時，西庇太兒子的母親同她兩個兒子上前來拜耶穌，求他一件事。

²¹耶穌說："你要甚麼呢？"

她說："願你叫我這兩個兒子在你國裏，一個坐在你右邊，一個坐在你左邊。"

²²耶穌回答說："你們不知道所求的是甚麼。我將要喝的杯，你們能喝嗎？"

他們說："我們能。"

²³耶穌說："我所喝的杯，你們必要喝；只是坐在我的左右，不是我可以賜的，乃是我父為誰預備的，就賜給誰。"

²⁴那十個門徒聽見，就惱怒他們弟兄二人。²⁵耶穌叫了他們來，說："你們知道外邦人有君王為主治理他們，有大臣操權管束他們。²⁶只是在你們中間不可這樣。你們中間誰願為大，就必作你們的用人；²⁷誰願為首，就必作你們的僕人。²⁸正如人子來，不是要受人的服侍，乃是要服侍人，並且要捨命，作多人的贖價。"

兩個瞎子得看見

²⁹他們出耶利哥的時候，有極多的人跟隨他。³⁰有兩個瞎子坐在路旁，聽說是耶穌經過，就喊着說："主啊，大衛的子孫，可憐我們吧！"

³¹眾人責備他們，不許他們做聲。他們卻越發喊着說："主啊，大衛的子孫，可憐我們吧！"

³²耶穌就站住，叫他們來，說："要我為你們做甚麼？"

³³他們說："主啊，要我們的眼睛能看見！"

³⁴耶穌就動了慈心，把他們的眼睛一摸，他們立刻看見，就跟從了耶穌。

光榮進聖城

21 耶穌和門徒將近耶路撒冷，到了伯法其，在橄欖山那裏。²耶穌就打發兩個門徒，對他們說："你們往對面村子裏去，必看見一匹驢拴在那裏，還有驢駒同在一處。你們解開，牽到我這裏來。³若有人對你們說甚麼，你們就說：'主要用牠。'那人必立時讓你們牽來。"

⁴這事成就，是要應驗先知的話，說：

5 "要對錫安的居民（註：原文作"女子"）說：

'看哪，你的王來到你這裏，
是溫柔的，又騎着驢，
就是騎着驢駒子。'"

6門徒就照耶穌所吩咐的去行，7牽了驢和驢駒來，把自己的衣服搭在上面，耶穌就騎上。8眾人多半把衣服鋪在路上，還有人砍下樹枝來鋪在路上。9前行後隨的眾人喊着說：

"和散那（註："和散那"原有"求救"的意思，在此乃稱頌的話）
歸於大衛的子孫！
奉主名來的，
是應當稱頌的！
高高在上和散那！"

10耶穌既進了耶路撒冷，合城都驚動了，說："這是誰？"
11眾人說："這是加利利 拿撒勒的先知耶穌。"

耶穌在聖殿中

12耶穌進了神的殿，趕出殿裏一切做買賣的人，推倒兌換銀錢之人的桌子和賣鴿子之人的凳子；13對他們說："經上記着說：'我的殿必稱為禱告的殿，你們倒使它成為賊窩了！'"

14在殿裏有瞎子、瘸子到耶穌跟前，他就治好了他們。15祭司長和文士看見耶穌所行的奇事，又見小孩子在殿裏喊着說："和散那歸於大衛的子孫！"就甚惱怒。

16對他說："這些人所說的，你聽見了嗎？"
耶穌說："是的。經上說：

"'你從嬰孩和吃奶的口中
完全了讚美的話。'
你們沒有念過嗎？"

17於是離開他們，出城到伯大尼去，在那裏住宿。

5"Say to the Daughter of Zion,
'See, your king comes to you,
gentle and riding on a donkey,
on a colt, the foal of a donkey.' "[a]

6The disciples went and did as Jesus had instructed them. 7They brought the donkey and the colt, placed their cloaks on them, and Jesus sat on them. 8A very large crowd spread their cloaks on the road, while others cut branches from the trees and spread them on the road. 9The crowds that went ahead of him and those that followed shouted,

"Hosanna[b] to the Son of David!"

"Blessed is he who comes in the name of the Lord!"[c]

"Hosanna[b] in the highest!"

10When Jesus entered Jerusalem, the whole city was stirred and asked, "Who is this?"
11The crowds answered, "This is Jesus, the prophet from Nazareth in Galilee."

Jesus at the Temple

12Jesus entered the temple area and drove out all who were buying and selling there. He overturned the tables of the money changers and the benches of those selling doves. 13"It is written," he said to them, " 'My house will be called a house of prayer,'[d] but you are making it a 'den of robbers.'[e]"

14The blind and the lame came to him at the temple, and he healed them. 15But when the chief priests and the teachers of the law saw the wonderful things he did and the children shouting in the temple area, "Hosanna to the Son of David," they were indignant.

16"Do you hear what these children are saying?" they asked him.
"Yes," replied Jesus, "have you never read,

" 'From the lips of children and infants
you have ordained praise'[f]?"

17And he left them and went out of the city to Bethany, where he spent the night.

---

a 5 Zech. 9:9　　b 9 A Hebrew expression meaning "Save!" which became an exclamation of praise; also in verse 15
c 9 Psalm 118:26　　d 13 Isaiah 56:7　　e 13 Jer. 7:11
f 16 Psalm 8:2

The Fig Tree Withers

18Early in the morning, as he was on his way back to the city, he was hungry. 19Seeing a fig tree by the road, he went up to it but found nothing on it except leaves. Then he said to it, "May you never bear fruit again!" Immediately the tree withered.

20When the disciples saw this, they were amazed. "How did the fig tree wither so quickly?" they asked.

21Jesus replied, "I tell you the truth, if you have faith and do not doubt, not only can you do what was done to the fig tree, but also you can say to this mountain, 'Go, throw yourself into the sea,' and it will be done. 22If you believe, you will receive whatever you ask for in prayer."

The Authority of Jesus Questioned

23Jesus entered the temple courts, and, while he was teaching, the chief priests and the elders of the people came to him. "By what authority are you doing these things?" they asked. "And who gave you this authority?"

24Jesus replied, "I will also ask you one question. If you answer me, I will tell you by what authority I am doing these things. 25John's baptism—where did it come from? Was it from heaven, or from men?"

They discussed it among themselves and said, "If we say, 'From heaven,' he will ask, 'Then why didn't you believe him?' 26But if we say, 'From men'—we are afraid of the people, for they all hold that John was a prophet."

27So they answered Jesus, "We don't know."

Then he said, "Neither will I tell you by what authority I am doing these things.

The Parable of the Two Sons

28"What do you think? There was a man who had two sons. He went to the first and said, 'Son, go and work today in the vineyard.'

29" 'I will not,' he answered, but later he changed his mind and went.

30"Then the father went to the other son and said the same thing. He answered, 'I will, sir,' but he did not go.

31"Which of the two did what his father wanted?"

"The first," they answered.

Jesus said to them, "I tell you the truth, the tax collectors and the prostitutes are entering the kingdom of God ahead of you. 32For John came to you to show you the way of righteousness, and you did not believe him, but the tax collectors and the prostitutes did. And even after you saw this, you did not repent and believe him.

無花果樹枯乾

18早晨回城的時候，他餓了，19看見路旁有一棵無花果樹，就走到跟前，在樹上找不着甚麼，不過有葉子，就對樹說：“從今以後，你永不結果子！”那無花果樹就立刻枯乾了。

20門徒看見了，便希奇說：“無花果樹怎麼立刻枯乾了呢？”

21耶穌回答說：“我實在告訴你們：你們若有信心，不疑惑，不但能行無花果樹上所行的事，就是對這座山說：‘你挪開此地，投在海裏！’也必成就。22你們禱告，無論求甚麼，只要信，就必得着。”

耶穌的權柄被質問

23耶穌進了殿，正教訓人的時候，祭司長和民間的長老來問他說：“你仗着甚麼權柄做這些事？給你這權柄的是誰呢？”

24耶穌回答說：“我也要問你們一句話，你們若告訴我，我就告訴你們我仗着甚麼權柄做這些事。25約翰的洗禮是從哪裏來的？是從天上來的？是從人間來的呢？”

他們彼此商議說：“我們若說‘從天上來’，他必對我們說，‘這樣，你們為甚麼不信他呢？’26若說‘從人間來’，我們又怕百姓，因為他們都以約翰為先知。”

27於是回答耶穌說：“我們不知道。”

耶穌說：“我也不告訴你們我仗着甚麼權柄做這些事。”

兩個兒子的比喻

28又說：“一個人有兩個兒子，他來對大兒子說：‘我兒，你今天到葡萄園裏去做工。’

29“他回答說：‘我不去’，以後自己懊悔，就去了。

30“又來對小兒子也是這樣說。他回答說：‘父啊，我去’，他卻不去。

31“你們想這兩個兒子，是哪一個遵行父命呢？”

他們說：“大兒子。”

耶穌說：“我實在告訴你們：稅吏和娼妓倒比你們先進神的國。32因為約翰遵着義路到你們這裏來，你們卻不信他；稅吏和娼妓倒信他。你們看見了，後來還是不懊悔去信他。

園戶的比喻

33 "你們再聽一個比喻:有個家主,栽了一個葡萄園,周圍圈上籬笆,裏面挖了一個壓酒池,蓋了一座樓,租給園戶,就往外國去了。34收果子的時候近了,就打發僕人到園戶那裏去收果子。

35 "園戶拿住僕人,打了一個,殺了一個,用石頭打死一個。36主人又打發別的僕人去,比先前更多,園戶還是照樣待他們。37後來打發他的兒子到他們那裏去,意思說:'他們必尊敬我的兒子。'

38 "不料,園戶看見他兒子,就彼此說:'這是承受產業的。來吧!我們殺他,佔他的產業!'39他們就拿住他,推出葡萄園外殺了。

40 "園主來的時候,要怎樣處治這些園戶呢?"

41他們說:"要下毒手除滅那些惡人,將葡萄園另租給那按着時候交果子的園戶。"

42耶穌說:"經上寫着:

" '匠人所棄的石頭,
　　已作了房角的頭塊石頭。
　　這是主所做的,
　　在我們眼中看為希奇。'
這經你們沒有念過嗎?

43 "所以我告訴你們:神的國必從你們奪去,賜給那能結果子的百姓。44誰掉在這石頭上,必要跌碎;這石頭掉在誰的身上,就要把誰砸得稀爛。"

45祭司長和法利賽人聽見他的比喻,就看出他是指着他們說的。46他們想要捉拿他,只是怕眾人,因為眾人以他為先知。

婚筵的比喻

22 耶穌又用比喻對他們說:2 "天國好比一個王為他兒子擺設娶親的筵席,3就打發僕人去,請那些被召的人來赴席;他們卻不肯來。

4 "王又打發別的僕人,說:'你們告訴那被召的人,我的筵席

The Parable of the Tenants

33"Listen to another parable: There was a landowner who planted a vineyard. He put a wall around it, dug a winepress in it and built a watchtower. Then he rented the vineyard to some farmers and went away on a journey. 34When the harvest time approached, he sent his servants to the tenants to collect his fruit.

35"The tenants seized his servants; they beat one, killed another, and stoned a third. 36Then he sent other servants to them, more than the first time, and the tenants treated them the same way. 37Last of all, he sent his son to them. 'They will respect my son,' he said.

38"But when the tenants saw the son, they said to each other, 'This is the heir. Come, let's kill him and take his inheritance.' 39So they took him and threw him out of the vineyard and killed him.

40"Therefore, when the owner of the vineyard comes, what will he do to those tenants?"

41"He will bring those wretches to a wretched end," they replied, "and he will rent the vineyard to other tenants, who will give him his share of the crop at harvest time."

42Jesus said to them, "Have you never read in the Scriptures:

" 'The stone the builders rejected
　has become the capstone[a];
　the Lord has done this,
　and it is marvelous in our eyes'[b]?

43"Therefore I tell you that the kingdom of God will be taken away from you and given to a people who will produce its fruit. 44He who falls on this stone will be broken to pieces, but he on whom it falls will be crushed."[c]

45When the chief priests and the Pharisees heard Jesus' parables, they knew he was talking about them. 46They looked for a way to arrest him, but they were afraid of the crowd because the people held that he was a prophet.

The Parable of the Wedding Banquet

22 Jesus spoke to them again in parables, saying: 2"The kingdom of heaven is like a king who prepared a wedding banquet for his son. 3He sent his servants to those who had been invited to the banquet to tell them to come, but they refused to come.

4"Then he sent some more servants and said, 'Tell those who have been invited that I have

a 42 Or *cornerstone*　　b 42 Psalm 118:22,23
c 44 Some manuscripts do not have verse 44.

prepared my dinner: My oxen and fattened cattle have been butchered, and everything is ready. Come to the wedding banquet.'

⁵"But they paid no attention and went off—one to his field, another to his business. ⁶The rest seized his servants, mistreated them and killed them. ⁷The king was enraged. He sent his army and destroyed those murderers and burned their city.

⁸"Then he said to his servants, 'The wedding banquet is ready, but those I invited did not deserve to come. ⁹Go to the street corners and invite to the banquet anyone you find.' ¹⁰So the servants went out into the streets and gathered all the people they could find, both good and bad, and the wedding hall was filled with guests.

¹¹"But when the king came in to see the guests, he noticed a man there who was not wearing wedding clothes. ¹²'Friend,' he asked, 'how did you get in here without wedding clothes?' The man was speechless.

¹³"Then the king told the attendants, 'Tie him hand and foot, and throw him outside, into the darkness, where there will be weeping and gnashing of teeth.'

¹⁴"For many are invited, but few are chosen."

Paying Taxes to Caesar

¹⁵Then the Pharisees went out and laid plans to trap him in his words. ¹⁶They sent their disciples to him along with the Herodians. "Teacher," they said, "we know you are a man of integrity and that you teach the way of God in accordance with the truth. You aren't swayed by men, because you pay no attention to who they are. ¹⁷Tell us then, what is your opinion? Is it right to pay taxes to Caesar or not?"

¹⁸But Jesus, knowing their evil intent, said, "You hypocrites, why are you trying to trap me? ¹⁹Show me the coin used for paying the tax." They brought him a denarius, ²⁰and he asked them, "Whose portrait is this? And whose inscription?"

²¹"Caesar's," they replied.

Then he said to them, "Give to Caesar what is Caesar's, and to God what is God's."

²²When they heard this, they were amazed. So they left him and went away.

Marriage at the Resurrection

²³That same day the Sadducees, who say there is no resurrection, came to him with a question. ²⁴"Teacher," they said, "Moses told us that if a man dies without having children, his brother must marry the widow and have chil-

已經預備好了，牛和肥畜已經宰了，各樣都齊備，請你們來赴席。'

⁵"那些人不理就走了：一個到自己田裏去，一個做買賣去，⁶其餘的拿住僕人，凌辱他們，把他們殺了。⁷王就大怒，發兵除滅那些兇手，燒燬他們的城。

⁸"於是對僕人說：'喜筵已經齊備，只是所召的人不配。⁹所以你們要往岔路口上去，凡遇見的，都召來赴席。'¹⁰那些僕人就出去到大路上，凡遇見的，不論善惡都召聚了來，筵席上就坐滿了客。

¹¹"王進來觀看賓客，見那裏有一個沒有穿禮服的，¹²就對他說：'朋友，你到這裏來，怎麼不穿禮服呢？'那人無言可答。

¹³"於是王對使喚的人說：'捆起他的手腳來，把他丟在外邊的黑暗裏，在那裏必要哀哭切齒了。'

¹⁴"因為被召的人多，選上的人少。"

納稅給凱撒

¹⁵當時，法利賽人出去，商議怎樣就着耶穌的話陷害他，¹⁶就打發他們的門徒同希律黨的人去見耶穌，說："夫子，我們知道你是誠實人，並且誠誠實實傳神的道，甚麼人你都不徇情面，因為你不看人的外貌。¹⁷請告訴我們，你的意見如何？納稅給凱撒可以不可以？"

¹⁸耶穌看出他們的惡意，就說："假冒為善的人哪，為甚麼試探我？¹⁹拿一個上稅的錢給我看。"他們就拿一個銀錢來給他。²⁰耶穌說："這像和這號是誰的？"

²¹他們說："是凱撒的。"耶穌說："這樣，凱撒的物當歸給凱撒；神的物當歸給神。"

²²他們聽見就希奇，離開他走了。

復活時的婚姻關係

²³撒都該人常說沒有復活的事。那天，他們來問耶穌說：²⁴"夫子，摩西說：'人若死了，沒有孩子，他兄弟當娶他的妻，為哥哥生子立

後。' 25從前，在我們這裏有弟兄七人。第一個娶了妻，死了，沒有孩子，撇下妻子給兄弟。26第二、第三，直到第七個，都是如此。27末後，婦人也死了。28這樣，當復活的時候，她是七個人中哪一個的妻子呢？因為他們都娶過她。"

29耶穌回答說："你們錯了，因為不明白聖經，也不曉得神的大能。30當復活的時候，人也不娶，也不嫁，乃像天上的使者一樣。31論到死人復活，神在經上向你們所說的，你們沒有念過嗎？32他說：'我是亞伯拉罕的神，以撒的神，雅各的神。' 神不是死人的神，乃是活人的神。"

33眾人聽見這話，就希奇他的教訓。

最大的誡命

34法利賽人聽見耶穌堵住了撒都該人的口，他們就聚集。35內中有一個人是律法師，要試探耶穌，就問他說：36"夫子，律法上的誡命，哪一條是最大的呢？"

37耶穌對他說："你要盡心、盡性、盡意，愛主你的神。38這是誡命中的第一，且是最大的。39其次也相倣，就是要愛人如己。40這兩條誡命是律法和先知一切道理的總綱。"

基督是誰的子孫？

41法利賽人聚集的時候，耶穌問他們說：42"論到基督，你們的意見如何？他是誰的子孫呢？"

他們回答說："是大衛的子孫。"

43耶穌說："這樣，大衛被聖靈感動，怎麼還稱他為主，說：

44"'主對我主說：
你坐在我的右邊，
等我把你仇敵
放在你的腳下。'

45大衛既稱他為主，他怎麼又是大衛的子孫呢？"46他們沒有一個人能回答一言。從那日以後也沒有人敢再問他甚麼。

dren for him. 25Now there were seven brothers among us. The first one married and died, and since he had no children, he left his wife to his brother. 26The same thing happened to the second and third brother, right on down to the seventh. 27Finally, the woman died. 28Now then, at the resurrection, whose wife will she be of the seven, since all of them were married to her?"

29Jesus replied, "You are in error because you do not know the Scriptures or the power of God. 30At the resurrection people will neither marry nor be given in marriage; they will be like the angels in heaven. 31But about the resurrection of the dead—have you not read what God said to you, 32'I am the God of Abraham, the God of Isaac, and the God of Jacob'[a]? He is not the God of the dead but of the living."

33When the crowds heard this, they were astonished at his teaching.

The Greatest Commandment

34Hearing that Jesus had silenced the Sadducees, the Pharisees got together. 35One of them, an expert in the law, tested him with this question: 36"Teacher, which is the greatest commandment in the Law?"

37Jesus replied: " 'Love the Lord your God with all your heart and with all your soul and with all your mind.'[b] 38This is the first and greatest commandment. 39And the second is like it: 'Love your neighbor as yourself.'[c] 40All the Law and the Prophets hang on these two commandments."

Whose Son Is the Christ?

41While the Pharisees were gathered together, Jesus asked them, 42"What do you think about the Christ[d]? Whose son is he?"

"The son of David," they replied.

43He said to them, "How is it then that David, speaking by the Spirit, calls him 'Lord'? For he says,

44" 'The Lord said to my Lord:
"Sit at my right hand
until I put your enemies
under your feet." '[e]

45If then David calls him 'Lord,' how can he be his son?" 46No one could say a word in reply, and from that day on no one dared to ask him any more questions.

---

a 32 Exodus 3:6   b 37 Deut. 6:5   c 39 Lev. 19:18
d 42 Or Messiah   e 44 Psalm 110:1

Seven Woes

23 Then Jesus said to the crowds and to his disciples: ²"The teachers of the law and the Pharisees sit in Moses' seat. ³So you must obey them and do everything they tell you. But do not do what they do, for they do not practice what they preach. ⁴They tie up heavy loads and put them on men's shoulders, but they themselves are not willing to lift a finger to move them.

⁵"Everything they do is done for men to see: They make their phylacteries*a* wide and the tassels on their garments long; ⁶they love the place of honor at banquets and the most important seats in the synagogues; ⁷they love to be greeted in the marketplaces and to have men call them 'Rabbi.'

⁸"But you are not to be called 'Rabbi,' for you have only one Master and you are all brothers. ⁹And do not call anyone on earth 'father,' for you have one Father, and he is in heaven. ¹⁰Nor are you to be called 'teacher,' for you have one Teacher, the Christ.*b* ¹¹The greatest among you will be your servant. ¹²For whoever exalts himself will be humbled, and whoever humbles himself will be exalted.

¹³"Woe to you, teachers of the law and Pharisees, you hypocrites! You shut the kingdom of heaven in men's faces. You yourselves do not enter, nor will you let those enter who are trying to.*c*

¹⁵"Woe to you, teachers of the law and Pharisees, you hypocrites! You travel over land and sea to win a single convert, and when he becomes one, you make him twice as much a son of hell as you are.

¹⁶"Woe to you, blind guides! You say, 'If anyone swears by the temple, it means nothing; but if anyone swears by the gold of the temple, he is bound by his oath.' ¹⁷You blind fools! Which is greater: the gold, or the temple that makes the gold sacred? ¹⁸You also say, 'If anyone swears by the altar, it means nothing; but if anyone swears by the gift on it, he is bound by his oath.' ¹⁹You blind men! Which is greater: the gift, or the altar that makes the gift sacred? ²⁰Therefore, he who swears by the altar swears by it and by everything on it. ²¹And he who swears by the temple swears by it and by the one who dwells in it. ²²And he who swears by heaven swears by

---

a 5 That is, boxes containing Scripture verses, worn on forehead and arm   b 10 Or Messiah   c 13 Some manuscripts to. 14 Woe to you, teachers of the law and Pharisees, you hypocrites! You devour widows' houses and for a show make lengthy prayers. Therefore you will be punished more severely.

七禍

23 那時，耶穌對眾人和門徒講論，²說："文士和法利賽人坐在摩西的位上，³凡他們所吩咐你們的，你們都要謹守遵行；但不要效法他們的行為，因為他們能說不能行。⁴他們把難擔的重擔捆起來，擱在人的肩上，但自己一個指頭也不肯動。

⁵"他們一切所做的事都是要叫人看見，所以將佩戴的經文做寬了，衣裳的繸子做長了；⁶喜愛筵席上的首座，會堂裏的高位；⁷又喜愛人在街市上問他安，稱呼他拉比（註："拉比"就是"夫子"）。

⁸"但你們不要受拉比的稱呼，因為只有一位是你們的夫子，你們都是弟兄。⁹也不要稱呼地上的人為父，因為只有一位是你們的父，就是在天上的父。¹⁰也不要受師尊的稱呼，因為只有一位是你們的師尊，就是基督。¹¹你們中間誰為大，誰就要作你們的用人。¹²凡自高的，必降為卑；自卑的，必升為高。

¹³"你們這假冒為善的文士和法利賽人有禍了！因為你們正當人前，把天國的門關了，自己不進去，正要進去的人，你們也不容他們進去。（註：有古卷在此有¹⁴"你們這假冒為善的文士和法利賽人有禍了！因為你們侵吞寡婦的家產，假意作很長的禱告，所以要受更重的刑罰。"）

¹⁵"你們這假冒為善的文士和法利賽人有禍了！因為你們走遍洋海陸地，勾引一個人入教，既入了教，卻使他作地獄之子，比你們還加倍。

¹⁶"你們這瞎眼領路的有禍了！你們說：'凡指着殿起誓的，這算不得甚麼；只是凡指着殿中金子起誓的，他就該謹守。'¹⁷你們這無知瞎眼的人哪！甚麼是大的？是金子呢，還是叫金子成聖的殿呢？¹⁸你們又說：'凡指着壇起誓的，這算不得甚麼；只是凡指着壇上禮物起誓的，他就該謹守。'¹⁹你們這瞎眼的人哪！甚麼是大的？是禮物呢，還是叫禮物成聖的壇呢？²⁰所以，人指着壇起誓，就是指着壇和壇上一切所有的起誓。²¹人指着殿起誓，就是指着殿和那住在殿裏的起誓。²²人指着天起誓，就是指着神的寶座和那坐在上面

的起誓。

23 "你們這假冒為善的文士和法利賽人有禍了！因為你們將薄荷、茴香、芹菜獻上十分之一，那律法上更重的事，就是公義、憐憫、信實，反倒不行了。這更重的是你們當行的，那也是不可不行的。24你們這瞎眼領路的，蠓蟲你們就濾出來，駱駝你們倒吞下去。

25 "你們這假冒為善的文士和法利賽人有禍了！因為你們洗淨杯盤的外面，裏面卻盛滿了勒索和放蕩。26你這瞎眼的法利賽人，先洗淨杯盤的裏面，好叫外面也乾淨了。

27 "你們這假冒為善的文士和法利賽人有禍了！因為你們好像粉飾的墳墓，外面好看，裏面卻裝滿了死人的骨頭和一切的污穢。28你們也是如此，在人前，外面顯出公義來，裏面卻裝滿了假善和不法的事。

29 "你們這假冒為善的文士和法利賽人有禍了！因為你們建造先知的墳，修飾義人的墓，說：30 '若是我們在我們祖宗的時候，必不和他們同流先知的血。'31這就是你們自己證明是殺害先知者的子孫了。你們去充滿你們祖宗的惡貫吧！

33 "你們這些蛇類、毒蛇之種啊！怎能逃脫地獄的刑罰呢？34所以我差遣先知和智慧人並文士到你們這裏來，有的你們要殺害，要釘十字架；有的你們要在會堂裏鞭打，從這城追逼到那城。35叫世上所流義人的血，都歸到你們身上，從義人亞伯的血起，直到你們在殿和壇中間所殺的巴拉加的兒子撒迦利亞的血為止。36我實在告訴你們：這一切的罪都要歸到這世代了。

37 "耶路撒冷啊，耶路撒冷啊！你常殺害先知，又用石頭打死那奉差遣到你這裏來的人。我多次願意聚集你的兒女，好像母雞把小雞聚集在翅膀底下，只是你們不願意。38看哪，你們的家成為荒場留給你們。39我告訴你們：從今以後，你們不得再見我，直等到你們說：'奉主名來的，是應當稱頌的！'"

23"Woe to you, teachers of the law and Pharisees, you hypocrites! You give a tenth of your spices—mint, dill and cummin. But you have neglected the more important matters of the law—justice, mercy and faithfulness. You should have practiced the latter, without neglecting the former. 24You blind guides! You strain out a gnat but swallow a camel.

25"Woe to you, teachers of the law and Pharisees, you hypocrites! You clean the outside of the cup and dish, but inside they are full of greed and self-indulgence. 26Blind Pharisee! First clean the inside of the cup and dish, and then the outside also will be clean.

27"Woe to you, teachers of the law and Pharisees, you hypocrites! You are like white-washed tombs, which look beautiful on the outside but on the inside are full of dead men's bones and everything unclean. 28In the same way, on the outside you appear to people as righteous but on the inside you are full of hypocrisy and wickedness.

29"Woe to you, teachers of the law and Pharisees, you hypocrites! You build tombs for the prophets and decorate the graves of the righteous. 30And you say, 'If we had lived in the days of our forefathers, we would not have taken part with them in shedding the blood of the prophets.' 31So you testify against yourselves that you are the descendants of those who murdered the prophets. 32Fill up, then, the measure of the sin of your forefathers!

33"You snakes! You brood of vipers! How will you escape being condemned to hell? 34Therefore I am sending you prophets and wise men and teachers. Some of them you will kill and crucify; others you will flog in your synagogues and pursue from town to town. 35And so upon you will come all the righteous blood that has been shed on earth, from the blood of righteous Abel to the blood of Zechariah son of Berekiah, whom you murdered between the temple and the altar. 36I tell you the truth, all this will come upon this generation.

37"O Jerusalem, Jerusalem, you who kill the prophets and stone those sent to you, how often I have longed to gather your children together, as a hen gathers her chicks under her wings, but you were not willing. 38Look, your house is left to you desolate. 39For I tell you, you will not see me again until you say, 'Blessed is he who comes in the name of the Lord.'*a* "

a 39 Psalm 118:26

Signs of the End of the Age

24 Jesus left the temple and was walking away when his disciples came up to him to call his attention to its buildings. ²"Do you see all these things?" he asked. "I tell you the truth, not one stone here will be left on another; every one will be thrown down."

³As Jesus was sitting on the Mount of Olives, the disciples came to him privately. "Tell us," they said, "when will this happen, and what will be the sign of your coming and of the end of the age?"

⁴Jesus answered: "Watch out that no one deceives you. ⁵For many will come in my name, claiming, 'I am the Christ,'ᵃ' and will deceive many. ⁶You will hear of wars and rumors of wars, but see to it that you are not alarmed. Such things must happen, but the end is still to come. ⁷Nation will rise against nation, and kingdom against kingdom. There will be famines and earthquakes in various places. ⁸All these are the beginning of birth pains.

⁹"Then you will be handed over to be persecuted and put to death, and you will be hated by all nations because of me. ¹⁰At that time many will turn away from the faith and will betray and hate each other, ¹¹and many false prophets will appear and deceive many people. ¹²Because of the increase of wickedness, the love of most will grow cold, ¹³but he who stands firm to the end will be saved. ¹⁴And this gospel of the kingdom will be preached in the whole world as a testimony to all nations, and then the end will come.

¹⁵"So when you see standing in the holy place 'the abomination that causes desolation,'ᵇ spoken of through the prophet Daniel—let the reader understand— ¹⁶then let those who are in Judea flee to the mountains. ¹⁷Let no one on the roof of his house go down to take anything out of the house. ¹⁸Let no one in the field go back to get his cloak. ¹⁹How dreadful it will be in those days for pregnant women and nursing mothers! ²⁰Pray that your flight will not take place in winter or on the Sabbath. ²¹For then there will be great distress, unequaled from the beginning of the world until now—and never to be equaled again. ²²If those days had not been cut short, no one would survive, but for the sake of the elect those days will be shortened. ²³At that time if anyone says to you, 'Look, here is the Christ!' or, 'There he is!' do not believe it. ²⁴For false Christs and false prophets will appear and perform great signs and miracles to deceive

---

末世的預兆

24 耶穌出了聖殿，正走的時候，門徒進前來，把殿宇指給他看。²耶穌對他們說："你們不是看見這殿宇嗎？我實在告訴你們：將來在這裏，沒有一塊石頭留在石頭上不被拆毀了。"

³耶穌在橄欖山上坐着，門徒暗暗地來說："請告訴我們，甚麼時候有這些事？你降臨和世界的末了，有甚麼預兆呢？"

⁴耶穌回答說："你們要謹慎，免得有人迷惑你們。⁵因為將來有好些人冒我的名來，說：'我是基督'，並且要迷惑許多人。⁶你們也要聽見打仗和打仗的風聲，總不要驚慌，因為這些事是必須有的，只是末期還沒有到。⁷民要攻打民，國要攻打國，多處必有饑荒、地震。⁸這都是災難的起頭（註："災難"原文作"生產之難"）。

⁹"那時，人要把你們陷在患難裏，也要殺害你們；你們又要為我的名被萬民恨惡。¹⁰那時，必有許多人跌倒，也要彼此陷害，彼此恨惡；¹¹且有好些假先知起來，迷惑多人。¹²只因不法的事增多，許多人的愛心才漸漸冷淡了。¹³惟有忍耐到底的必然得救。¹⁴這天國的福音要傳遍天下，對萬民作見證，然後末期才來到。

¹⁵"你們看見先知但以理所說的'那行毀壞可憎的'站在聖地（讀這經的人須要會意）。¹⁶那時，在猶太的，應當逃到山上；¹⁷在房上的，不要下來拿家裏的東西；¹⁸在田裏的，也不要回去取衣裳。¹⁹當那些日子，懷孕的和奶孩子的有禍了。²⁰你們應當祈求，叫你們逃走的時候，不遇見冬天或是安息日。²¹因為那時必有大災難，從世界的起頭直到如今，沒有這樣的災難，後來也必沒有。²²若不減少那日子，凡有血氣的，總沒有一個得救的；只是為選民，那日子必減少了。²³那時，若有人對你們說'基督在這裏'，或說'基督在那裏'，你們不要信。²⁴因為假基督、假先知將要起來，顯大神蹟、大奇事。倘若

---

a 5 Or Messiah; also in verse 23　　b 15 Daniel 9:27; 11:31; 12:11

能行，連選民也就迷惑了。25看哪，我預先告訴你們了。

26「若有人對你們說，『看哪，基督在曠野裏』，你們不要出去；或說，『看哪，基督在內屋中』，你們不要信。27閃電從東邊發出，直照到西邊；人子降臨，也要這樣。28屍首在哪裏，鷹也必聚在那裏。

29「那些日子的災難一過去，

> "『日頭就變黑了，
> 月亮也不放光，
> 眾星要從天上墜落，
> 天勢都要震動。』

30「那時，人子的兆頭要顯在天上，地上的萬族都要哀哭。他們要看見人子有能力，有大榮耀，駕着天上的雲降臨。31他要差遣使者，用號筒的大聲，將他的選民從四方（註：「方」原文作「風」），從天這邊到天那邊，都招聚了來。

32「你們可以從無花果樹學個比方：當樹枝發嫩長葉的時候，你們就知道夏天近了。33這樣，你們看見這一切的事，也該知道人子近了，正在門口了。34我實在告訴你們：這世代還沒有過去，這些事都要成就。35天地要廢去，我的話卻不能廢去。

那日子那時辰無人知道

36「但那日子、那時辰，沒有人知道，連天上的使者也不知道，子也不知道，惟獨父知道。37挪亞的日子怎樣，人子降臨也要怎樣。38當洪水以前的日子，人照常吃喝嫁娶，直到挪亞進方舟的那日，39不知不覺洪水來了，把他們全都沖去。人子降臨也要這樣。40那時，兩個人在田裏，取去一個，撇下一個；41兩個女人推磨，取去一個，撇下一個。

42「所以，你們要警醒，因為不知道你們的主是哪一天來到。43家主若知道幾更天有賊來，就必警醒，

even the elect—if that were possible. 25See, I have told you ahead of time.

26"So if anyone tells you, 'There he is, out in the desert,' do not go out; or, 'Here he is, in the inner rooms,' do not believe it. 27For as lightning that comes from the east is visible even in the west, so will be the coming of the Son of Man. 28Wherever there is a carcass, there the vultures will gather.

29"Immediately after the distress of those days

> " 'the sun will be darkened,
> and the moon will not give its light;
> the stars will fall from the sky,
> and the heavenly bodies will be shaken.'[a]

30"At that time the sign of the Son of Man will appear in the sky, and all the nations of the earth will mourn. They will see the Son of Man coming on the clouds of the sky, with power and great glory. 31And he will send his angels with a loud trumpet call, and they will gather his elect from the four winds, from one end of the heavens to the other.

32"Now learn this lesson from the fig tree: As soon as its twigs get tender and its leaves come out, you know that summer is near. 33Even so, when you see all these things, you know that it[b] is near, right at the door. 34I tell you the truth, this generation[c] will certainly not pass away until all these things have happened. 35Heaven and earth will pass away, but my words will never pass away.

The Day and Hour Unknown

36"No one knows about that day or hour, not even the angels in heaven, nor the Son,[d] but only the Father. 37As it was in the days of Noah, so it will be at the coming of the Son of Man. 38For in the days before the flood, people were eating and drinking, marrying and giving in marriage, up to the day Noah entered the ark; 39and they knew nothing about what would happen until the flood came and took them all away. That is how it will be at the coming of the Son of Man. 40Two men will be in the field; one will be taken and the other left. 41Two women will be grinding with a hand mill; one will be taken and the other left.

42"Therefore keep watch, because you do not know on what day your Lord will come. 43But understand this: If the owner of the house had

---

a 29 Isaiah 13:10; 34:4　　*b 33* Or *he*　　*c 34* Or *race*
d 36 Some manuscripts do not have *nor the Son.*

known at what time of night the thief was coming, he would have kept watch and would not have let his house be broken into. ⁴⁴So you also must be ready, because the Son of Man will come at an hour when you do not expect him.

⁴⁵"Who then is the faithful and wise servant, whom the master has put in charge of the servants in his household to give them their food at the proper time? ⁴⁶It will be good for that servant whose master finds him doing so when he returns. ⁴⁷I tell you the truth, he will put him in charge of all his possessions. ⁴⁸But suppose that servant is wicked and says to himself, 'My master is staying away a long time,' ⁴⁹and he then begins to beat his fellow servants and to eat and drink with drunkards. ⁵⁰The master of that servant will come on a day when he does not expect him and at an hour he is not aware of. ⁵¹He will cut him to pieces and assign him a place with the hypocrites, where there will be weeping and gnashing of teeth.

The Parable of the Ten Virgins

25 "At that time the kingdom of heaven will be like ten virgins who took their lamps and went out to meet the bridegroom. ²Five of them were foolish and five were wise. ³The foolish ones took their lamps but did not take any oil with them. ⁴The wise, however, took oil in jars along with their lamps. ⁵The bridegroom was a long time in coming, and they all became drowsy and fell asleep.

⁶"At midnight the cry rang out: 'Here's the bridegroom! Come out to meet him!'

⁷"Then all the virgins woke up and trimmed their lamps. ⁸The foolish ones said to the wise, 'Give us some of your oil; our lamps are going out.'

⁹" 'No,' they replied, 'there may not be enough for both us and you. Instead, go to those who sell oil and buy some for yourselves.'

¹⁰"But while they were on their way to buy the oil, the bridegroom arrived. The virgins who were ready went in with him to the wedding banquet. And the door was shut.

¹¹"Later the others also came. 'Sir! Sir!' they said. 'Open the door for us!'

¹²"But he replied, 'I tell you the truth, I don't know you.'

¹³"Therefore keep watch, because you do not know the day or the hour.

The Parable of the Talents

¹⁴"Again, it will be like a man going on a journey, who called his servants and entrusted his property to them. ¹⁵To one he gave five

不容人挖透房屋,這是你們所知道的。⁴⁴所以,你們也要預備,因為你們想不到的時候,人子就來了。

⁴⁵ "誰是忠心有見識的僕人,為主人所派,管理家裏的人,按時分糧給他們呢?⁴⁶主人來到,看見他這樣行,那僕人就有福了。⁴⁷我實在告訴你們:主人要派他管理一切所有的。⁴⁸倘若那惡僕心裏說:'我的主人必來得遲',⁴⁹就動手打他的同伴,又和酒醉的人一同吃喝。⁵⁰在想不到的日子,不知道的時候,那僕人的主人要來,⁵¹重重地處治他(註:或作"把他腰斬了"),定他和假冒為善的人同罪,在那裏必要哀哭切齒了。

十童女的比喻

25 "那時,天國好比十個童女拿着燈出去迎接新郎。²其中有五個是愚拙的,五個是聰明的。³愚拙的拿着燈,卻不預備油;⁴聰明的拿着燈,又預備油在器皿裏。⁵新郎遲延的時候,她們都打盹睡着了。

⁶ "半夜有人喊着說:'新郎來了,你們出來迎接他!'

⁷ "那些童女就都起來收拾燈。⁸愚拙的對聰明的說:'請分點油給我們,因為我們的燈要滅了。'

⁹ "聰明的回答說:'恐怕不夠你我用的,不如你們自己到賣油的那裏去買吧!'

¹⁰ "她們去買的時候,新郎到了,那預備好了的,同他進去坐席,門就關了。

¹¹ "其餘的童女隨後也來了,說:'主啊,主啊,給我們開門!'

¹² "他卻回答說:'我實在告訴你們:我不認識你們。'

¹³ "所以,你們要警醒,因為那日子、那時辰,你們不知道。

才幹的比喻

¹⁴ "天國又好比一個人要往外國去,就叫了僕人來,把他的家業交給他們,¹⁵按着各人的才幹,給他們銀

子，一個給了五千，一個給了二千，一個給了一千，就往外國去了。16那領五千的隨即拿去做買賣，另外賺了五千；17那領二千的也照樣另賺了二千；18但那一千的去掘開地，把主人的銀子埋藏了。

19"過了許久，那些僕人的主人來了，和他們算賬。20那領五千銀子的又帶着那另外的五千來，說：'主啊，你交給我五千銀子，請看，我又賺了五千。'

21"主人說：'好！你這又良善又忠心的僕人，你在不多的事上有忠心，我要把許多事派你管理；可以進來享受你主人的快樂。'

22"那領二千的也來，說：'主啊，你交給我二千銀子，請看，我又賺了二千。'

23"主人說：'好！你這又良善又忠心的僕人，你在不多的事上有忠心，我要把許多事派你管理；可以進來享受你主人的快樂。'

24"那領一千的也來，說：'主啊，我知道你是忍心的人，沒有種的地方要收割，沒有散的地方要聚斂，25我就害怕，去把你的一千銀子埋藏在地裏。請看，你的原銀子在這裏。'

26"主人回答說：'你這又惡又懶的僕人！你既知道我沒有種的地方要收割，沒有散的地方要聚斂，27就當把我的銀子放給兌換銀錢的人，到我來的時候，可以連本帶利收回。

28"奪過他這一千來，給那有一萬的！29因為凡有的，還要加給他，叫他有餘；沒有的，連他所有的也要奪過來。30把這無用的僕人丟在外面黑暗裏，在那裏必要哀哭切齒了。'"

綿羊與山羊

31"當人子在他榮耀裏，同着眾天使降臨的時候，要坐在他榮耀的

talents[a] of money, to another two talents, and to another one talent, each according to his ability. Then he went on his journey. 16The man who had received the five talents went at once and put his money to work and gained five more. 17So also, the one with the two talents gained two more. 18But the man who had received the one talent went off, dug a hole in the ground and hid his master's money.

19"After a long time the master of those servants returned and settled accounts with them. 20The man who had received the five talents brought the other five. 'Master,' he said, 'you entrusted me with five talents. See, I have gained five more.'

21"His master replied, 'Well done, good and faithful servant! You have been faithful with a few things; I will put you in charge of many things. Come and share your master's happiness!'

22"The man with the two talents also came. 'Master,' he said, 'you entrusted me with two talents; see, I have gained two more.'

23"His master replied, 'Well done, good and faithful servant! You have been faithful with a few things; I will put you in charge of many things. Come and share your master's happiness!'

24"Then the man who had received the one talent came. 'Master,' he said, 'I knew that you are a hard man, harvesting where you have not sown and gathering where you have not scattered seed. 25So I was afraid and went out and hid your talent in the ground. See, here is what belongs to you.'

26"His master replied, 'You wicked, lazy servant! So you knew that I harvest where I have not sown and gather where I have not scattered seed? 27Well then, you should have put my money on deposit with the bankers, so that when I returned I would have received it back with interest.

28"'Take the talent from him and give it to the one who has the ten talents. 29For everyone who has will be given more, and he will have an abundance. Whoever does not have, even what he has will be taken from him. 30And throw that worthless servant outside, into the darkness, where there will be weeping and gnashing of teeth.'

The Sheep and the Goats

31"When the Son of Man comes in his glory, and all the angels with him, he will sit on his

---

a 15 A talent was worth more than a thousand dollars.

throne in heavenly glory. 32All the nations will be gathered before him, and he will separate the people one from another as a shepherd separates the sheep from the goats. 33He will put the sheep on his right and the goats on his left.

34"Then the King will say to those on his right, 'Come, you who are blessed by my Father; take your inheritance, the kingdom prepared for you since the creation of the world. 35For I was hungry and you gave me something to eat, I was thirsty and you gave me something to drink, I was a stranger and you invited me in, 36I needed clothes and you clothed me, I was sick and you looked after me, I was in prison and you came to visit me.'

37"Then the righteous will answer him, 'Lord, when did we see you hungry and feed you, or thirsty and give you something to drink? 38When did we see you a stranger and invite you in, or needing clothes and clothe you? 39When did we see you sick or in prison and go to visit you?'

40"The King will reply, 'I tell you the truth, whatever you did for one of the least of these brothers of mine, you did for me.'

41"Then he will say to those on his left, 'Depart from me, you who are cursed, into the eternal fire prepared for the devil and his angels. 42For I was hungry and you gave me nothing to eat, I was thirsty and you gave me nothing to drink, 43I was a stranger and you did not invite me in, I needed clothes and you did not clothe me, I was sick and in prison and you did not look after me.'

44"They also will answer, 'Lord, when did we see you hungry or thirsty or a stranger or needing clothes or sick or in prison, and did not help you?'

45"He will reply, 'I tell you the truth, whatever you did not do for one of the least of these, you did not do for me.'

46"Then they will go away to eternal punishment, but the righteous to eternal life."

The Plot Against Jesus

26 When Jesus had finished saying all these things, he said to his disciples, 2"As you know, the Passover is two days away—and the Son of Man will be handed over to be crucified."

3Then the chief priests and the elders of the people assembled in the palace of the high priest, whose name was Caiaphas, 4and they plotted to arrest Jesus in some sly way and kill him. 5"But not during the Feast," they said, "or there may be a riot among the people."

寶座上。32萬民都要聚集在他面前。他要把他們分別出來，好像牧羊的分別綿羊山羊一般；33把綿羊安置在右邊，山羊在左邊。

34 "於是，王要向那右邊的說：'你們這蒙我父賜福的，可來承受那創世以來為你們所預備的國。35因為我餓了，你們給我吃；渴了，你們給我喝；我作客旅，你們留我住；36我赤身露體，你們給我穿；我病了，你們看顧我；我在監裏，你們來看我。'

37 "義人就回答說：'主啊，我們甚麼時候見你餓了，給你吃，渴了，給你喝？38甚麼時候見你作客旅，留你住，或是赤身露體，給你穿？39又甚麼時候見你病了，或是在監裏，來看你呢？'

40 "王要回答說：'我實在告訴你們：這些事你們既做在我這弟兄中一個最小的身上，就是做在我身上了。'

41 "王又要向那左邊的說：'你們這被咒詛的人，離開我，進入那為魔鬼和他的使者所預備的永火裏去！42因為我餓了，你們不給我吃；渴了，你們不給我喝；43我作客旅，你們不留我住；我赤身露體，你們不給我穿；我病了，我在監裏，你們不來看顧我。'

44 "他們也要回答說：'主啊，我們甚麼時候見你餓了，或渴了，或作客旅，或赤身露體，或病了，或在監裏，不伺候你呢？'

45 "王要回答說：'我實在告訴你們：這些事你們既不做在我這弟兄中一個最小的身上，就是不做在我身上了。'

46 "這些人，要往永刑裏去；那些義人，要往永生裏去。"

密謀害耶穌

26 耶穌說完了這一切的話，就對門徒說：

2 "你們知道，過兩天是逾越節，人子將要被交給人，釘在十字架上。"

3那時，祭司長和民間的長老，聚集在大祭司稱為該亞法的院裏。4大家商議要用詭計拿住耶穌殺他；5只是說："當節的日子不可，恐怕民間生亂。"

耶穌在伯大尼受膏

6耶穌在伯大尼長大痲瘋的西門家裏，7有一個女人拿着一玉瓶極貴的香膏來，趁耶穌坐席的時候，澆在他的頭上。

8門徒看見就很不喜悅，說：「何用這樣的枉費呢！9這香膏可以賣許多錢，賙濟窮人。」

10耶穌看出他們的意思，就說：「為甚麼難為這女人呢？她在我身上做的是一件美事。11因為常有窮人和你們同在，只是你們不常有我。12她將這香膏澆在我身上，是為我安葬做的。13我實在告訴你們：普天之下，無論在甚麼地方傳這福音，也要述說這女人所行的，作個記念。」

猶大約定出賣耶穌

14當下，十二門徒裏有一個稱為加略人猶大的，去見祭司長，說：15「我把他交給你們，你們願意給我多少錢？」他們就給了他三十塊錢。16從那時候，他就找機會要把耶穌交給他們。

主的晚餐

17除酵節的第一天，門徒來問耶穌說：「你吃逾越節的筵席，要我們在哪裏給你預備？」

18耶穌說：「你們進城去，到某人那裏，對他說：『夫子說：我的時候快到了，我與門徒要在你家裏守逾越節。』」19門徒遵着耶穌所吩咐的，就去預備了逾越節的筵席。

20到了晚上，耶穌和十二個門徒坐席。21正吃的時候，耶穌說：「我實在告訴你們：你們中間有一個人要賣我了。」

22他們就甚憂愁，一個一個地問他說：「主，是我嗎？」

23耶穌回答說：「同我蘸手在盤子裏的，就是他要賣我。24人子必要去世，正如經上指着他所寫的，但賣人子的人有禍了，那人不生在世上倒好！」

25賣耶穌的猶大問他說：「拉比，是我嗎？」

耶穌說：「你說的是。」

Jesus Anointed at Bethany

6While Jesus was in Bethany in the home of a man known as Simon the Leper, 7a woman came to him with an alabaster jar of very expensive perfume, which she poured on his head as he was reclining at the table.

8When the disciples saw this, they were indignant. "Why this waste?" they asked. 9"This perfume could have been sold at a high price and the money given to the poor."

10Aware of this, Jesus said to them, "Why are you bothering this woman? She has done a beautiful thing to me. 11The poor you will always have with you, but you will not always have me. 12When she poured this perfume on my body, she did it to prepare me for burial. 13I tell you the truth, wherever this gospel is preached throughout the world, what she has done will also be told, in memory of her."

Judas Agrees to Betray Jesus

14Then one of the Twelve—the one called Judas Iscariot—went to the chief priests 15and asked, "What are you willing to give me if I hand him over to you?" So they counted out for him thirty silver coins. 16From then on Judas watched for an opportunity to hand him over.

The Lord's Supper

17On the first day of the Feast of Unleavened Bread, the disciples came to Jesus and asked, "Where do you want us to make preparations for you to eat the Passover?"

18He replied, "Go into the city to a certain man and tell him, 'The Teacher says: My appointed time is near. I am going to celebrate the Passover with my disciples at your house.' " 19So the disciples did as Jesus had directed them and prepared the Passover.

20When evening came, Jesus was reclining at the table with the Twelve. 21And while they were eating, he said, "I tell you the truth, one of you will betray me."

22They were very sad and began to say to him one after the other, "Surely not I, Lord?"

23Jesus replied, "The one who has dipped his hand into the bowl with me will betray me. 24The Son of Man will go just as it is written about him. But woe to that man who betrays the Son of Man! It would be better for him if he had not been born."

25Then Judas, the one who would betray him, said, "Surely not I, Rabbi?"

Jesus answered, "Yes, it is you."[a]

a 25 Or "You yourself have said it"

26While they were eating, Jesus took bread, gave thanks and broke it, and gave it to his disciples, saying, "Take and eat; this is my body."

27Then he took the cup, gave thanks and offered it to them, saying, "Drink from it, all of you. 28This is my blood of the*a* covenant, which is poured out for many for the forgiveness of sins. 29I tell you, I will not drink of this fruit of the vine from now on until that day when I drink it anew with you in my Father's kingdom."

30When they had sung a hymn, they went out to the Mount of Olives.

Jesus Predicts Peter's Denial

31Then Jesus told them, "This very night you will all fall away on account of me, for it is written:

" 'I will strike the shepherd,
    and the sheep of the flock will be scattered.'*b*

32But after I have risen, I will go ahead of you into Galilee."

33Peter replied, "Even if all fall away on account of you, I never will."

34"I tell you the truth," Jesus answered, "this very night, before the rooster crows, you will disown me three times."

35But Peter declared, "Even if I have to die with you, I will never disown you." And all the other disciples said the same.

Gethsemane

36Then Jesus went with his disciples to a place called Gethsemane, and he said to them, "Sit here while I go over there and pray." 37He took Peter and the two sons of Zebedee along with him, and he began to be sorrowful and troubled. 38Then he said to them, "My soul is overwhelmed with sorrow to the point of death. Stay here and keep watch with me."

39Going a little farther, he fell with his face to the ground and prayed, "My Father, if it is possible, may this cup be taken from me. Yet not as I will, but as you will."

40Then he returned to his disciples and found them sleeping. "Could you men not keep watch with me for one hour?" he asked Peter. 41"Watch and pray so that you will not fall into temptation. The spirit is willing, but the body is weak."

42He went away a second time and prayed, "My Father, if it is not possible for this cup to be taken away unless I drink it, may your will be done."

26他們吃的時候，耶穌拿起餅來，祝福，就擘開遞給門徒，說："你們拿着吃，這是我的身體。"

27又拿起杯來，祝謝了，遞給他們，說："你們都喝這個，28因為這是我立約的血，為多人流出來，使罪得赦。29但我告訴你們：從今以後我不再喝這葡萄汁，直到我在我父的國裏同你們喝新的那日子。"

30他們唱了詩，就出來往橄欖山去。

耶穌預言彼得不認主

31那時，耶穌對他們說："今夜，你們為我的緣故都要跌倒。因為經上記着說：

" '我要擊打牧人，
    羊就分散了。'

32但我復活以後，要在你們以先往加利利去。"

33彼得說："眾人雖然為你的緣故跌倒，我卻永不跌倒。"

34耶穌說："我實在告訴你：今夜雞叫以先，你要三次不認我。"

35彼得說："我就是必須和你同死，也總不能不認你。"眾門徒都是這樣說。

客西馬尼

36耶穌同門徒來到一個地方，名叫客西馬尼，就對他們說："你們坐在這裏，等我到那邊去禱告。"37於是帶着彼得和西庇太的兩個兒子同去，就憂愁起來，極其難過，38便對他們說："我心裏甚是憂傷，幾乎要死；你們在這裏等候，和我一同警醒。"

39他就稍往前走，俯伏在地禱告說："我父啊，倘若可行，求你叫這杯離開我；然而，不要照我的意思，只要照你的意思。"

40來到門徒那裏，見他們睡着了，就對彼得說："怎麼樣，你們不能同我警醒片時嗎？41總要警醒禱告，免得入了迷惑。你們心靈固然願意，肉體卻軟弱了。"

42第二次又去禱告說："我父啊，這杯若不能離開我，必要我喝，就願你的意旨成全。"

a 28 Some manuscripts *the new*   *b 31* Zech. 13:7

43又來見他們睡着了，因為他們的眼睛困倦。44耶穌又離開他們去了。第三次禱告，說的話還是與先前一樣。

45於是來到門徒那裏，對他們說："現在你們仍然睡覺安歇吧（註："吧"或作"嗎"）？時候到了，人子被賣在罪人手裏了。46起來，我們走吧！看哪，賣我的人近了！"

耶穌被捕

47說話之間，那十二個門徒裏的猶大來了，並有許多人帶着刀棒，從祭司長和民間的長老那裏與他同來。48那賣耶穌的給了他們一個暗號，說："我與誰親嘴，誰就是他。你們可以拿住他。"49猶大隨即到耶穌跟前說："請拉比安。"就與他親嘴。

50耶穌對他說："朋友，你來要做的事，就做吧！"於是那些人上前，下手拿住耶穌。51有跟隨耶穌的一個人，伸手拔出刀來，將大祭司的僕人砍了一刀，削掉了他一個耳朵。

52耶穌對他說："收刀入鞘吧！凡動刀的，必死在刀下。53你想，我不能求我父現在為我差遣十二營多天使來嗎？54若是這樣，經上所說事情必須如此的話，怎麼應驗呢？"

55當時，耶穌對眾人說："你們帶着刀棒出來拿我，如同拿強盜嗎？我天天坐在殿裏教訓人，你們並沒有拿我。56但這一切的事成就了，為要應驗先知書上的話。"當下，門徒都離開他逃走了。

在公會前受審

57拿耶穌的人把他帶到大祭司該亞法那裏去，文士和長老已經在那裏聚會。58彼得遠遠地跟着耶穌，直到大祭司的院子，進到裏面，就和差役同坐，要看這事到底怎樣。

59祭司長和全公會尋找假見證控告耶穌，要治死他。60雖有好些人來作假見證，總得不着實據。

43When he came back, he again found them sleeping, because their eyes were heavy. 44So he left them and went away once more and prayed the third time, saying the same thing.

45Then he returned to the disciples and said to them, "Are you still sleeping and resting? Look, the hour is near, and the Son of Man is betrayed into the hands of sinners. 46Rise, let us go! Here comes my betrayer!"

Jesus Arrested

47While he was still speaking, Judas, one of the Twelve, arrived. With him was a large crowd armed with swords and clubs, sent from the chief priests and the elders of the people. 48Now the betrayer had arranged a signal with them: "The one I kiss is the man; arrest him." 49Going at once to Jesus, Judas said, "Greetings, Rabbi!" and kissed him.

50Jesus replied, "Friend, do what you came for."[a]

Then the men stepped forward, seized Jesus and arrested him. 51With that, one of Jesus' companions reached for his sword, drew it out and struck the servant of the high priest, cutting off his ear.

52"Put your sword back in its place," Jesus said to him, "for all who draw the sword will die by the sword. 53Do you think I cannot call on my Father, and he will at once put at my disposal more than twelve legions of angels? 54But how then would the Scriptures be fulfilled that say it must happen in this way?"

55At that time Jesus said to the crowd, "Am I leading a rebellion, that you have come out with swords and clubs to capture me? Every day I sat in the temple courts teaching, and you did not arrest me. 56But this has all taken place that the writings of the prophets might be fulfilled." Then all the disciples deserted him and fled.

Before the Sanhedrin

57Those who had arrested Jesus took him to Caiaphas, the high priest, where the teachers of the law and the elders had assembled. 58But Peter followed him at a distance, right up to the courtyard of the high priest. He entered and sat down with the guards to see the outcome.

59The chief priests and the whole Sanhedrin were looking for false evidence against Jesus so that they could put him to death. 60But they did not find any, though many false witnesses came forward.

a 50 Or "Friend, why have you come?"

Finally two came forward [61]and declared, "This fellow said, 'I am able to destroy the temple of God and rebuild it in three days.' "

[62]Then the high priest stood up and said to Jesus, "Are you not going to answer? What is this testimony that these men are bringing against you?" [63]But Jesus remained silent.

The high priest said to him, "I charge you under oath by the living God: Tell us if you are the Christ,[a] the Son of God."

[64]"Yes, it is as you say," Jesus replied. "But I say to all of you: In the future you will see the Son of Man sitting at the right hand of the Mighty One and coming on the clouds of heaven."

[65]Then the high priest tore his clothes and said, "He has spoken blasphemy! Why do we need any more witnesses? Look, now you have heard the blasphemy. [66]What do you think?"

"He is worthy of death," they answered.

[67]Then they spit in his face and struck him with their fists. Others slapped him [68]and said, "Prophesy to us, Christ. Who hit you?"

Peter Disowns Jesus

[69]Now Peter was sitting out in the courtyard, and a servant girl came to him. "You also were with Jesus of Galilee," she said.

[70]But he denied it before them all. "I don't know what you're talking about," he said.

[71]Then he went out to the gateway, where another girl saw him and said to the people there, "This fellow was with Jesus of Nazareth."

[72]He denied it again, with an oath: "I don't know the man!"

[73]After a little while, those standing there went up to Peter and said, "Surely you are one of them, for your accent gives you away."

[74]Then he began to call down curses on himself and he swore to them, "I don't know the man!"

Immediately a rooster crowed. [75]Then Peter remembered the word Jesus had spoken: "Before the rooster crows, you will disown me three times." And he went outside and wept bitterly.

Judas Hangs Himself

27 Early in the morning, all the chief priests and the elders of the people came to the decision to put Jesus to death. [2]They bound him, led him away and handed him over to Pilate, the governor.

末後，有兩個人前來，說：[61]"這個人曾說：'我能拆毀神的殿，三日內又建造起來。'"

[62]大祭司就站起來，對耶穌說："你甚麼都不回答嗎？這些人作見證告你的是甚麼呢？"[63]耶穌卻不言語。

大祭司對他說："我指着永生神叫你起誓告訴我們，你是神的兒子基督不是？"

[64]耶穌對他說："你說的是。然而，我告訴你們：後來你們要看見人子坐在那權能者的右邊，駕着天上的雲降臨。"

[65]大祭司就撕開衣服，說："他說了僭妄的話！我們何必再用見證人呢？這僭妄的話，現在你們都聽見了。[66]你們的意見如何？"

他們回答說："他是該死的。"

[67]他們就吐唾沫在他臉上，用拳頭打他；也有用手掌打他的，說：[68]"基督啊，你是先知，告訴我們打你的是誰？"

彼得不認耶穌

[69]彼得在外面院子裏坐着，有一個使女前來說："你素來也是同那加利利人耶穌一夥的。"

[70]彼得在眾人面前卻不承認，說："我不知道你說的是甚麼。"

[71]既出去，到了門口，又有一個使女看見他，就對那裏的人說："這個人也是同拿撒勒人耶穌一夥的。"

[72]彼得又不承認，並且起誓說："我不認得那個人！"

[73]過了不多的時候，旁邊站着的人前來對彼得說："你真是他們一黨的，你的口音把你露出來了。"

[74]彼得就發咒起誓地說："我不認得那個人！"

立時，雞就叫了。[75]彼得想起耶穌所說的話："雞叫以先，你要三次不認我。"他就出去痛哭。

猶大自縊

27 到了早晨，眾祭司長和民間的長老，大家商議要治死耶穌，[2]就把他捆綁，解去交給巡撫彼拉多。

---

a 63 Or Messiah; also in verse 68

³這時候，賣耶穌的<u>猶大</u>看見耶穌已經定了罪，就後悔，把那三十塊錢拿回來給祭司長和長老，說：⁴「我賣了無辜之人的血是有罪了。」

他們說：「那與我們有甚麼相干？你自己承當吧！」

⁵<u>猶大</u>就把那銀錢丟在殿裏，出去吊死了。

⁶祭司長拾起銀錢來說：「這是血價，不可放在庫裏。」⁷他們商議，就用那銀錢買了窰戶的一塊田，為要埋葬外鄉人。⁸所以那塊田直到今日還叫作「血田」。⁹這就應了先知<u>耶利米</u>的話，說：「他們用那三十塊錢，就是被估定之人的價錢，是<u>以色列</u>人中所估定的，¹⁰買了窰戶的一塊田；這是照着主所吩咐我的。」

耶穌在彼拉多面前

¹¹耶穌站在巡撫面前，巡撫問他說：「你是<u>猶太</u>人的王嗎？」

耶穌說：「你說的是。」

¹²他被祭司長和長老控告的時候，甚麼都不回答。¹³<u>彼拉多</u>就對他說：「他們作見證告你這麼多的事，你沒有聽見嗎？」¹⁴耶穌仍不回答，連一句話也不說，以致巡撫甚覺希奇。

¹⁵巡撫有一個常例，每逢這節期，隨眾人所要的，釋放一個囚犯給他們。¹⁶當時，有一個出名的囚犯叫<u>巴拉巴</u>。¹⁷眾人聚集的時候，<u>彼拉多</u>就對他們說：「你們要我釋放哪一個給你們？是<u>巴拉巴</u>呢？是稱為基督的耶穌呢？」¹⁸巡撫原知道，他們是因為嫉妒才把他解了來。

¹⁹正坐堂的時候，他的夫人打發人來說：「這義人的事你一點不可管，因為我今天在夢中為他受了許多的苦。」

²⁰祭司長和長老挑唆眾人，求釋放巴拉巴，除滅耶穌。

²¹巡撫對眾人說：「這兩個人，你們要我釋放哪一個給你們呢？」

他們說：「巴拉巴！」

²²<u>彼拉多</u>說：「這樣，那稱為基督的耶穌，我怎麼辦他呢？」

³When Judas, who had betrayed him, saw that Jesus was condemned, he was seized with remorse and returned the thirty silver coins to the chief priests and the elders. ⁴"I have sinned," he said, "for I have betrayed innocent blood."

"What is that to us?" they replied. "That's your responsibility."

⁵So Judas threw the money into the temple and left. Then he went away and hanged himself.

⁶The chief priests picked up the coins and said, "It is against the law to put this into the treasury, since it is blood money." ⁷So they decided to use the money to buy the potter's field as a burial place for foreigners. ⁸That is why it has been called the Field of Blood to this day. ⁹Then what was spoken by Jeremiah the prophet was fulfilled: "They took the thirty silver coins, the price set on him by the people of Israel, ¹⁰and they used them to buy the potter's field, as the Lord commanded me."*a*

Jesus Before Pilate

¹¹Meanwhile Jesus stood before the governor, and the governor asked him, "Are you the king of the Jews?"

"Yes, it is as you say," Jesus replied.

¹²When he was accused by the chief priests and the elders, he gave no answer. ¹³Then Pilate asked him, "Don't you hear the testimony they are bringing against you?" ¹⁴But Jesus made no reply, not even to a single charge—to the great amazement of the governor.

¹⁵Now it was the governor's custom at the Feast to release a prisoner chosen by the crowd. ¹⁶At that time they had a notorious prisoner, called Barabbas. ¹⁷So when the crowd had gathered, Pilate asked them, "Which one do you want me to release to you: Barabbas, or Jesus who is called Christ?" ¹⁸For he knew it was out of envy that they had handed Jesus over to him.

¹⁹While Pilate was sitting on the judge's seat, his wife sent him this message: "Don't have anything to do with that innocent man, for I have suffered a great deal today in a dream because of him."

²⁰But the chief priests and the elders persuaded the crowd to ask for Barabbas and to have Jesus executed.

²¹"Which of the two do you want me to release to you?" asked the governor.

"Barabbas," they answered.

²²"What shall I do, then, with Jesus who is called Christ?" Pilate asked.

a 10 See Zech. 11:12,13; Jer. 19:1-13; 32:6-9.

They all answered, "Crucify him!"

23"Why? What crime has he committed?" asked Pilate.

But they shouted all the louder, "Crucify him!"

24When Pilate saw that he was getting nowhere, but that instead an uproar was starting, he took water and washed his hands in front of the crowd. "I am innocent of this man's blood," he said. "It is your responsibility!"

25All the people answered, "Let his blood be on us and on our children!"

26Then he released Barabbas to them. But he had Jesus flogged, and handed him over to be crucified.

The Soldiers Mock Jesus

27Then the governor's soldiers took Jesus into the Praetorium and gathered the whole company of soldiers around him. 28They stripped him and put a scarlet robe on him, 29and then twisted together a crown of thorns and set it on his head. They put a staff in his right hand and knelt in front of him and mocked him. "Hail, king of the Jews!" they said. 30They spit on him, and took the staff and struck him on the head again and again. 31After they had mocked him, they took off the robe and put his own clothes on him. Then they led him away to crucify him.

The Crucifixion

32As they were going out, they met a man from Cyrene, named Simon, and they forced him to carry the cross. 33They came to a place called Golgotha (which means The Place of the Skull). 34There they offered Jesus wine to drink, mixed with gall; but after tasting it, he refused to drink it. 35When they had crucified him, they divided up his clothes by casting lots.a 36And sitting down, they kept watch over him there. 37Above his head they placed the written charge against him: THIS IS JESUS, THE KING OF THE JEWS.38Two robbers were crucified with him, one on his right and one on his left. 39Those who passed by hurled insults at him, shaking their heads 40and saying, "You who are going to destroy the temple and build it in three days, save yourself! Come down from the cross, if you are the Son of God!"

41In the same way the chief priests, the teachers of the law and the elders mocked him. 42"He saved others," they said, "but he can't save him-

a 35 A few late manuscripts lots that the word spoken by the prophet might be fulfilled: "They divided my garments among themselves and cast lots for my clothing" (Psalm 22:18)

他們都說:"把他釘十字架!"

23巡撫說:"為甚麼呢?他做了甚麼惡事呢?"

他們便極力地喊着說:"把他釘十字架!"

24彼拉多見說也無濟於事,反要生亂,就拿水在眾人面前洗手,說:"流這義人的血,罪不在我,你們承當吧!"

25眾人都回答說:"他的血歸到我們和我們的子孫身上。"

26於是彼拉多釋放巴拉巴給他們,把耶穌鞭打了,交給人釘十字架。

兵丁戲弄耶穌

27巡撫的兵就把耶穌帶進衙門,叫全營的兵都聚集在他那裏。28他們給他脫了衣服,穿上一件朱紅色袍子;29用荊棘編作冠冕,戴在他頭上;拿一根葦子放在他右手裏,跪在他面前,戲弄他說:"恭喜,猶太人的王啊!"30又吐唾沫在他臉上,拿葦子打他的頭。31戲弄完了,就給他脫了袍子,仍穿上他自己的衣服,帶他出去,要釘十字架。

釘十字架

32他們出來的時候,遇見一個古利奈人,名叫西門,就勉強他同去,好背着耶穌的十字架。33到了一個地方,名叫各各他,意思就是髑髏地。34兵丁拿苦膽調和的酒給耶穌喝。他嘗了,就不肯喝。35他們既將他釘在十字架上,就拈鬮分他的衣服,36又坐在那裏看守他。37在他頭以上安一個牌子,寫着他的罪狀說:"這是猶太人的王耶穌。"38當時,有兩個強盜和他同釘十字架,一個在右邊,一個在左邊。39從那裏經過的人譏誚他,搖着頭,說:40"你這拆毀聖殿,三日又建造起來的,可以救自己吧!你如果是神的兒子,就從十字架上下來吧!"

41祭司長和文士並長老也是這樣戲弄他,說:42"他救了別人,不能救自己。他是<u>以色列</u>的王，現在可以從十字架上下來，我們就信他。⁴³他倚靠神，神若喜悦他，現在可以救他，因為他曾説：'我是神的兒子。'" ⁴⁴那和他同釘的強盗也是這樣地譏誚他。

耶穌的死

⁴⁵從午正到申初，遍地都黑暗了。⁴⁶約在申初，耶穌大聲喊着説："以利！以利！拉馬撒巴各大尼？"就是説："我的神！我的神！為甚麼離棄我？"

⁴⁷站在那裏的人，有的聽見就説："這個人呼叫<u>以利亞</u>呢！"

⁴⁸内中有一個人趕緊跑去，拿海絨蘸滿了醋綁在葦子上，送給他喝。⁴⁹其餘的人説："且等着，看<u>以利亞</u>來救他不來。"

⁵⁰耶穌又大聲喊叫，氣就斷了。

⁵¹忽然，殿裏的幔子從上到下裂為兩半，地也震動，磐石也崩裂，⁵²墳墓也開了，已睡聖徒的身體，多有起來的。⁵³到耶穌復活以後，他們從墳墓裏出來，進了聖城，向許多人顯現。

⁵⁴百夫長和一同看守耶穌的人看見地震並所經歷的事，就極其害怕，説："這真是神的兒子了！"

⁵⁵有好些婦女在那裏，遠遠地觀看，她們是從<u>加利利</u>跟隨耶穌來服侍他的。⁵⁶内中有<u>抹大拉</u>的<u>馬利亞</u>，又有<u>雅各</u>和<u>約西</u>的母親<u>馬利亞</u>，並有<u>西庇太</u>兩個兒子的母親。

耶穌的安葬

⁵⁷到了晚上，有一個財主，名叫<u>約瑟</u>，是<u>亞利馬太</u>來的，他也是耶穌的門徒。⁵⁸這人去見<u>彼拉多</u>，求耶穌的身體，<u>彼拉多</u>就吩咐給他。⁵⁹<u>約瑟</u>取了身體，用乾淨細麻布裹好，⁶⁰安放在自己的新墳墓裏，就是他鑿在磐石裏的。他又把大石頭滾到墓門口，就去了。⁶¹有<u>抹大拉</u>的<u>馬利亞</u>和那個<u>馬利亞</u>在那裏，對着墳墓坐着。

self! He's the King of Israel! Let him come down now from the cross, and we will believe in him. ⁴³He trusts in God. Let God rescue him now if he wants him, for he said, 'I am the Son of God.'" ⁴⁴In the same way the robbers who were crucified with him also heaped insults on him.

The Death of Jesus

⁴⁵From the sixth hour until the ninth hour darkness came over all the land. ⁴⁶About the ninth hour Jesus cried out in a loud voice, *"Eloi, Eloi,[a] lama sabachthani?"*—which means, "My God, my God, why have you forsaken me?"[b]

⁴⁷When some of those standing there heard this, they said, "He's calling Elijah."

⁴⁸Immediately one of them ran and got a sponge. He filled it with wine vinegar, put it on a stick, and offered it to Jesus to drink. ⁴⁹The rest said, "Now leave him alone. Let's see if Elijah comes to save him."

⁵⁰And when Jesus had cried out again in a loud voice, he gave up his spirit.

⁵¹At that moment the curtain of the temple was torn in two from top to bottom. The earth shook and the rocks split. ⁵²The tombs broke open and the bodies of many holy people who had died were raised to life. ⁵³They came out of the tombs, and after Jesus' resurrection they went into the holy city and appeared to many people.

⁵⁴When the centurion and those with him who were guarding Jesus saw the earthquake and all that had happened, they were terrified, and exclaimed, "Surely he was the Son[c] of God!"

⁵⁵Many women were there, watching from a distance. They had followed Jesus from Galilee to care for his needs. ⁵⁶Among them were Mary Magdalene, Mary the mother of James and Joses, and the mother of Zebedee's sons.

The Burial of Jesus

⁵⁷As evening approached, there came a rich man from Arimathea, named Joseph, who had himself become a disciple of Jesus. ⁵⁸Going to Pilate, he asked for Jesus' body, and Pilate ordered that it be given to him. ⁵⁹Joseph took the body, wrapped it in a clean linen cloth, ⁶⁰and placed it in his own new tomb that he had cut out of the rock. He rolled a big stone in front of the entrance to the tomb and went away. ⁶¹Mary Magdalene and the other Mary were sitting there opposite the tomb.

a 46 Some manuscripts Eli, Eli   b 46 Psalm 22:1
c 54 Or a son

The Guard at the Tomb

62The next day, the one after Preparation Day, the chief priests and the Pharisees went to Pilate. 63"Sir," they said, "we remember that while he was still alive that deceiver said, 'After three days I will rise again.' 64So give the order for the tomb to be made secure until the third day. Otherwise, his disciples may come and steal the body and tell the people that he has been raised from the dead. This last deception will be worse than the first."

65"Take a guard," Pilate answered. "Go, make the tomb as secure as you know how." 66So they went and made the tomb secure by putting a seal on the stone and posting the guard.

The Resurrection

28 After the Sabbath, at dawn on the first day of the week, Mary Magdalene and the other Mary went to look at the tomb.

2There was a violent earthquake, for an angel of the Lord came down from heaven and, going to the tomb, rolled back the stone and sat on it. 3His appearance was like lightning, and his clothes were white as snow. 4The guards were so afraid of him that they shook and became like dead men.

5The angel said to the women, "Do not be afraid, for I know that you are looking for Jesus, who was crucified. 6He is not here; he has risen, just as he said. Come and see the place where he lay. 7Then go quickly and tell his disciples: 'He has risen from the dead and is going ahead of you into Galilee. There you will see him.' Now I have told you."

8So the women hurried away from the tomb, afraid yet filled with joy, and ran to tell his disciples. 9Suddenly Jesus met them. "Greetings," he said. They came to him, clasped his feet and worshiped him. 10Then Jesus said to them, "Do not be afraid. Go and tell my brothers to go to Galilee; there they will see me."

The Guards' Report

11While the women were on their way, some of the guards went into the city and reported to the chief priests everything that had happened. 12When the chief priests had met with the elders and devised a plan, they gave the soldiers a large sum of money, 13telling them, "You are to say, 'His disciples came during the night and stole him away while we were asleep.' 14If this report gets to the governor, we will satisfy him and keep you out of trouble." 15So the soldiers

兵丁守墳墓

62次日，就是預備日的第二天，祭司長和法利賽人聚集，來見彼拉多，說：63「大人，我們記得那誘惑人的還活着的時候，曾說：『三日後我要復活』。64因此，請吩咐人將墳墓把守妥當，直到第三日，恐怕他的門徒來把他偷了去，就告訴百姓說：『他從死裏復活了。』這樣，那後來的迷惑比先前的更利害了。」

65彼拉多說：「你們有看守的兵，去吧！盡你們所能的把守妥當。」66他們就帶着看守的兵同去，封了石頭，將墳墓把守妥當。

復活

28 安息日將盡，七日的頭一日，天快亮的時候，抹大拉的馬利亞和那個馬利亞來看墳墓。

2忽然，地大震動，因為有主的使者從天上下來，把石頭滾開，坐在上面。3他的像貌如同閃電，衣服潔白如雪。4看守的人就因他嚇得渾身亂戰，甚至和死人一樣。

5天使對婦女說：「不要害怕！我知道你們是尋找那釘十字架的耶穌。6他不在這裏，照他所說的，已經復活了。你們來看安放主的地方。7快去告訴他的門徒，說他從死裏復活了，並且在你們以先往加利利去，在那裏你們要見他。看哪，我已經告訴你們了。」

8婦女們就急忙離開墳墓，又害怕，又大大地歡喜，跑去要報給他的門徒。9忽然，耶穌遇見她們，說：「願你們平安！」她們就上前抱住他的腳拜他。10耶穌對她們說：「不要害怕！你們去告訴我的弟兄，叫他們往加利利去，在那裏必見我。」

兵丁的報告

11他們去的時候，看守的兵有幾個進城去，將所經歷的事都報給祭司長。12祭司長和長老聚集商議，就拿許多銀錢給兵丁，說：13「你們要這樣說：『夜間我們睡覺的時候，他的門徒來把他偷了去。』14倘若這話被巡撫聽見，有我們勸他，保你們無事。」15兵丁受了銀錢，就照所囑咐他們的去行。這話就傳說在<u>猶太</u>人中間，直到今日。

大使命

¹⁶十一個門徒往<u>加利利</u>去，到了耶穌約定的山上。¹⁷他們見了耶穌就拜他，然而還有人疑惑。¹⁸耶穌進前來，對他們說：「天上地下所有的權柄都賜給我了。¹⁹所以，你們要去，使萬民作我的門徒，奉父、子、聖靈的名給他們施洗（註：或作 "給他們施洗，歸於父、子、聖靈的名"）。²⁰凡我所吩咐你們的，都教訓他們遵守，我就常與你們同在，直到世界的末了。」

took the money and did as they were instructed. And this story has been widely circulated among the Jews to this very day.

The Great Commission

¹⁶Then the eleven disciples went to Galilee, to the mountain where Jesus had told them to go. ¹⁷When they saw him, they worshiped him; but some doubted. ¹⁸Then Jesus came to them and said, "All authority in heaven and on earth has been given to me. ¹⁹Therefore go and make disciples of all nations, baptizing them in^a the name of the Father and of the Son and of the Holy Spirit, ²⁰and teaching them to obey everything I have commanded you. And surely I am with you always, to the very end of the age."

圖三：馬太福音中的主要地方
MAP 3 : KEY PLACES IN MATTHEW

a 19 Or into; see Acts 8:16; 19:5; Romans 6:3; 1 Cor. 1:13; 10:2 and Gal. 3:27.

Mark

John the Baptist Prepares the Way

1 The beginning of the gospel about Jesus Christ, the Son of God.[a]

[2] It is written in Isaiah the prophet:

"I will send my messenger ahead of you,
   who will prepare your way"[b] —
[3] "a voice of one calling in the desert,
   'Prepare the way for the Lord,
   make straight paths for him.' "[c]

[4] And so John came, baptizing in the desert region and preaching a baptism of repentance for the forgiveness of sins. [5] The whole Judean countryside and all the people of Jerusalem went out to him. Confessing their sins, they were baptized by him in the Jordan River. [6] John wore clothing made of camel's hair, with a leather belt around his waist, and he ate locusts and wild honey. [7] And this was his message: "After me will come one more powerful than I, the thongs of whose sandals I am not worthy to stoop down and untie. [8] I baptize you with[d] water, but he will baptize you with the Holy Spirit."

The Baptism and Temptation of Jesus

[9] At that time Jesus came from Nazareth in Galilee and was baptized by John in the Jordan. [10] As Jesus was coming up out of the water, he saw heaven being torn open and the Spirit descending on him like a dove. [11] And a voice came from heaven: "You are my Son, whom I love; with you I am well pleased."

[12] At once the Spirit sent him out into the desert, [13] and he was in the desert forty days, being tempted by Satan. He was with the wild animals, and angels attended him.

The Calling of the First Disciples

[14] After John was put in prison, Jesus went into Galilee, proclaiming the good news of God. [15] "The time has come," he said. "The kingdom of God is near. Repent and believe the good news!"

---

a 1 Some manuscripts do not have *the Son of God*.
b 2 Mal. 3:1   c 3 Isaiah 40:3   d 8 Or *in*

施洗約翰預備道路

1 神的兒子，耶穌基督福音的起頭。

[2] 正如先知以賽亞（註：有古卷無"以賽亞"三字）書上記着說：

"看哪，我要差遣我的使者
   在你前面，預備道路。"
[3] "在曠野有人聲喊着說：
   '預備主的道，
   修直他的路。'"

[4] 照這話，約翰來了，在曠野施洗，傳悔改的洗禮，使罪得赦。[5] 猶太全地和耶路撒冷的人都出去到約翰那裏，承認他們的罪，在約旦河裏受他的洗。[6] 約翰穿駱駝毛的衣服，腰束皮帶，吃的是蝗蟲野蜜。[7] 他傳道說："有一位在我以後來的，能力比我更大，我就是彎腰給他解鞋帶也是不配的。[8] 我是用水給你們施洗，他卻要用聖靈給你們施洗。"

耶穌受洗並受試探

[9] 那時，耶穌從加利利的拿撒勒來，在約旦河裏受了約翰的洗。[10] 他從水裏一上來，就看見天裂開了，聖靈彷彿鴿子，降在他身上。[11] 又有聲音從天上來，說："你是我的愛子，我喜悅你。"

[12] 聖靈就把耶穌催到曠野裏去。[13] 他在曠野四十天，受撒但的試探，並與野獸同在一處，且有天使來伺候他。

召第一批門徒

[14] 約翰下監以後，耶穌來到加利利，宣傳神的福音，[15] 說："日期滿了，神的國近了！你們當悔改，信福音！"

¹⁶耶穌順着加利利的海邊走，看見西門和西門的兄弟安得烈在海裏撒網，他們本是打魚的。¹⁷耶穌對他們說：「來跟從我！我要叫你們得人如得魚一樣。」¹⁸他們就立刻捨了網，跟從了他。

¹⁹耶穌稍往前走，又見西庇太的兒子雅各和雅各的兄弟約翰在船上補網。²⁰耶穌隨即招呼他們，他們就把父親西庇太和雇工人留在船上，跟從耶穌去了。

耶穌趕出污鬼

²¹到了迦百農，耶穌就在安息日進了會堂教訓人。²²眾人很希奇他的教訓，因為他教訓他們，正像有權柄的人，不像文士。²³在會堂裏，有一個人被污鬼附着。他喊叫說：²⁴「拿撒勒人耶穌，我們與你有甚麼相干，你來滅我們嗎？我知道你是誰，乃是神的聖者！」

²⁵耶穌責備他說：「不要做聲，從這人身上出來吧！」²⁶污鬼叫那人抽了一陣風，大聲喊叫，就出來了。²⁷眾人都驚訝，以致彼此對問說：「這是甚麼事？是個新道理啊！他用權柄吩咐污鬼，連污鬼也聽從了他。」²⁸耶穌的名聲就傳遍了加利利的四方。

耶穌醫治許多病人

²⁹他們一出會堂，就同着雅各、約翰，進了西門和安得烈的家。³⁰西門的岳母正害熱病躺着，就有人告訴耶穌。³¹耶穌進前拉着她的手，扶她起來，熱就退了，她就服侍他們。

³²天晚日落的時候，有人帶着一切害病的和被鬼附的，來到耶穌跟前，³³合城的人都聚集在門前。³⁴耶穌治好了許多害各樣病的人，又趕出許多鬼，不許鬼說話，因為鬼認識他。

耶穌在曠野禱告

³⁵次日早晨，天未亮的時候，耶穌起來，到曠野地方去，在那裏禱告。³⁶西門和同伴追了他去，³⁷遇見

As Jesus walked beside the Sea of Galilee

¹⁶As Jesus walked beside the Sea of Galilee, he saw Simon and his brother Andrew casting a net into the lake, for they were fishermen. ¹⁷"Come, follow me," Jesus said, "and I will make you fishers of men." ¹⁸At once they left their nets and followed him.

¹⁹When he had gone a little farther, he saw James son of Zebedee and his brother John in a boat, preparing their nets. ²⁰Without delay he called them, and they left their father Zebedee in the boat with the hired men and followed him.

Jesus Drives Out an Evil Spirit

²¹They went to Capernaum, and when the Sabbath came, Jesus went into the synagogue and began to teach. ²²The people were amazed at his teaching, because he taught them as one who had authority, not as the teachers of the law. ²³Just then a man in their synagogue who was possessed by an evil^a spirit cried out, ²⁴"What do you want with us, Jesus of Nazareth? Have you come to destroy us? I know who you are—the Holy One of God!"

²⁵"Be quiet!" said Jesus sternly. "Come out of him!" ²⁶The evil spirit shook the man violently and came out of him with a shriek.

²⁷The people were all so amazed that they asked each other, "What is this? A new teaching—and with authority! He even gives orders to evil spirits and they obey him." ²⁸News about him spread quickly over the whole region of Galilee.

Jesus Heals Many

²⁹As soon as they left the synagogue, they went with James and John to the home of Simon and Andrew. ³⁰Simon's mother-in-law was in bed with a fever, and they told Jesus about her. ³¹So he went to her, took her hand and helped her up. The fever left her and she began to wait on them.

³²That evening after sunset the people brought to Jesus all the sick and demon-possessed. ³³The whole town gathered at the door, ³⁴and Jesus healed many who had various diseases. He also drove out many demons, but he would not let the demons speak because they knew who he was.

Jesus Prays in a Solitary Place

³⁵Very early in the morning, while it was still dark, Jesus got up, left the house and went off to a solitary place, where he prayed. ³⁶Simon and his companions went to look for him, ³⁷and

a 23 Greek unclean; also in verses 26 and 27

when they found him, they exclaimed: "Everyone is looking for you!"

[38]Jesus replied, "Let us go somewhere else—to the nearby villages—so I can preach there also. That is why I have come." [39]So he traveled throughout Galilee, preaching in their synagogues and driving out demons.

A Man With Leprosy

[40]A man with leprosy[a] came to him and begged him on his knees, "If you are willing, you can make me clean."

[41]Filled with compassion, Jesus reached out his hand and touched the man. "I am willing," he said. "Be clean!" [42]Immediately the leprosy left him and he was cured.

[43]Jesus sent him away at once with a strong warning: [44]"See that you don't tell this to anyone. But go, show yourself to the priest and offer the sacrifices that Moses commanded for your cleansing, as a testimony to them." [45]Instead he went out and began to talk freely, spreading the news. As a result, Jesus could no longer enter a town openly but stayed outside in lonely places. Yet the people still came to him from everywhere.

Jesus Heals a Paralytic

2 A few days later, when Jesus again entered Capernaum, the people heard that he had come home. [2]So many gathered that there was no room left, not even outside the door, and he preached the word to them. [3]Some men came, bringing to him a paralytic, carried by four of them. [4]Since they could not get him to Jesus because of the crowd, they made an opening in the roof above Jesus and, after digging through it, lowered the mat the paralyzed man was lying on. [5]When Jesus saw their faith, he said to the paralytic, "Son, your sins are forgiven."

[6]Now some teachers of the law were sitting there, thinking to themselves, [7]"Why does this fellow talk like that? He's blaspheming! Who can forgive sins but God alone?"

[8]Immediately Jesus knew in his spirit that this was what they were thinking in their hearts, and he said to them, "Why are you thinking these things? [9]Which is easier: to say to the paralytic, 'Your sins are forgiven,' or to say, 'Get up, take your mat and walk'? [10]But that you may know that the Son of Man has authority on earth

了就對他說:"眾人都找你。"

[38]耶穌對他們說:"我們可以往別處去,到鄰近的鄉村,我也好在那裏傳道,因為我是為這事出來的。" [39]於是在加利利全地,進了會堂,傳道,趕鬼。

長大痲瘋的人

[40]有一個長大痲瘋的來見耶穌,向他跪下,說:"你若肯,必能叫我潔淨了!"

[41]耶穌動了慈心,就伸手摸他,說:"我肯,你潔淨了吧!" [42]大痲瘋即時離開他,他就潔淨了。

[43]耶穌嚴嚴地囑咐他,就打發他走,[44]對他說:"你要謹慎,甚麼話都不可告訴人;只要去把身體給祭司察看,又因為你潔淨了,獻上摩西所吩咐的禮物,對眾人作證據。" [45]那人出去,倒說許多的話,把這件事傳揚開了,叫耶穌以後不得再明明的進城,只好在外邊曠野地方。人從各處都就了他來。

耶穌醫治癱子

2 過了些日子,耶穌又進了迦百農。人聽見他在房子裏,[2]就有許多人聚集,甚至連門前都沒有空地,耶穌就對他們講道。[3]有人帶着一個癱子來見耶穌,是用四個人抬來的。[4]因為人多,不得近前,就把耶穌所在的房子,拆了房頂,既拆通了,就把癱子連所躺臥的褥子都縋下來。[5]耶穌見他們的信心,就對癱子說:"小子,你的罪赦了。"

[6]有幾個文士坐在那裏,心裏議論,說:[7]"這個人為甚麼這樣說呢?他說僭妄的話了!除了神以外,誰能赦罪呢?"

[8]耶穌心中知道他們心裏這樣議論,就說:"你們心裏為甚麼這樣議論呢?[9]或對癱子說'你的罪赦了',或說'起來,拿你的褥子行走',哪一樣容易呢?[10]但要叫你們知道,人子在地上有赦罪的權柄。"就對癱子

---

a 40 The Greek word was used for various diseases affecting the skin—not necessarily leprosy.

說：¹¹「我吩咐你起來，拿你的褥子回家去吧！」¹²那人就起來，立刻拿着褥子，當眾人面前出去了。以致眾人都驚奇，歸榮耀與神，說：「我們從來沒有見過這樣的事。」

呼召利未

¹³耶穌又出到海邊去，眾人都就了他來，他便教訓他們。¹⁴耶穌經過的時候，看見亞勒腓的兒子利未坐在稅關上，就對他說：「你跟從我來！」他就起來，跟從了耶穌。

¹⁵耶穌在利未家裏坐席的時候，有好些稅吏和罪人與耶穌並門徒一同坐席，因為這樣的人多，他們也跟隨耶穌。¹⁶法利賽人中的文士（註：有古卷作「文士和法利賽人」）看見耶穌和罪人並稅吏一同吃飯，就對他門徒說：「他和稅吏並罪人一同吃喝嗎？」

¹⁷耶穌聽見，就對他們說：「康健的人用不着醫生，有病的人才用得着。我來本不是召義人，乃是召罪人。」

耶穌被詢問禁食的事

¹⁸當下，約翰的門徒和法利賽人禁食。他們來問耶穌說：「約翰的門徒和法利賽人的門徒禁食，你的門徒倒不禁食，這是為甚麼呢？」

¹⁹耶穌對他們說：「新郎和陪伴之人同在的時候，陪伴之人豈能禁食呢？新郎還同在，他們不能禁食。²⁰但日子將到，新郎要離開他們，那日他們就要禁食。」

²¹「沒有人把新布縫在舊衣服上，恐怕所補上的新布，帶壞了舊衣服，破的就更大了。²²也沒有人把新酒裝在舊皮袋裏，恐怕酒把皮袋裂開，酒和皮袋就都壞了；惟把新酒裝在新皮袋裏。」

安息日的主

²³耶穌當安息日從麥地經過。他門徒行路的時候，掐了麥穗。²⁴法利賽人對耶穌說：「看哪，他們在安息日為甚麼做不可做的事呢？」

to forgive sins . . . ." He said to the paralytic, ¹¹"I tell you, get up, take your mat and go home." ¹²He got up, took his mat and walked out in full view of them all. This amazed everyone and they praised God, saying, "We have never seen anything like this!"

The Calling of Levi

¹³Once again Jesus went out beside the lake. A large crowd came to him, and he began to teach them. ¹⁴As he walked along, he saw Levi son of Alphaeus sitting at the tax collector's booth. "Follow me," Jesus told him, and Levi got up and followed him.

¹⁵While Jesus was having dinner at Levi's house, many tax collectors and "sinners" were eating with him and his disciples, for there were many who followed him. ¹⁶When the teachers of the law who were Pharisees saw him eating with the "sinners" and tax collectors, they asked his disciples: "Why does he eat with tax collectors and 'sinners'?"

¹⁷On hearing this, Jesus said to them, "It is not the healthy who need a doctor, but the sick. I have not come to call the righteous, but sinners."

Jesus Questioned About Fasting

¹⁸Now John's disciples and the Pharisees were fasting. Some people came and asked Jesus, "How is it that John's disciples and the disciples of the Pharisees are fasting, but yours are not?"

¹⁹Jesus answered, "How can the guests of the bridegroom fast while he is with them? They cannot, so long as they have him with them. ²⁰But the time will come when the bridegroom will be taken from them, and on that day they will fast.

²¹"No one sews a patch of unshrunk cloth on an old garment. If he does, the new piece will pull away from the old, making the tear worse. ²²And no one pours new wine into old wineskins. If he does, the wine will burst the skins, and both the wine and the wineskins will be ruined. No, he pours new wine into new wineskins."

Lord of the Sabbath

²³One Sabbath Jesus was going through the grainfields, and as his disciples walked along, they began to pick some heads of grain. ²⁴The Pharisees said to him, "Look, why are they doing what is unlawful on the Sabbath?"

25He answered, "Have you never read what David did when he and his companions were hungry and in need? 26In the days of Abiathar the high priest, he entered the house of God and ate the consecrated bread, which is lawful only for priests to eat. And he also gave some to his companions."

27Then he said to them, "The Sabbath was made for man, not man for the Sabbath. 28So the Son of Man is Lord even of the Sabbath."

3 Another time he went into the synagogue, and a man with a shriveled hand was there. 2Some of them were looking for a reason to accuse Jesus, so they watched him closely to see if he would heal him on the Sabbath. 3Jesus said to the man with the shriveled hand, "Stand up in front of everyone."

4Then Jesus asked them, "Which is lawful on the Sabbath: to do good or to do evil, to save life or to kill?" But they remained silent.

5He looked around at them in anger and, deeply distressed at their stubborn hearts, said to the man, "Stretch out your hand." He stretched it out, and his hand was completely restored. 6Then the Pharisees went out and began to plot with the Herodians how they might kill Jesus.

Crowds Follow Jesus

7Jesus withdrew with his disciples to the lake, and a large crowd from Galilee followed. 8When they heard all he was doing, many people came to him from Judea, Jerusalem, Idumea, and the regions across the Jordan and around Tyre and Sidon. 9Because of the crowd he told his disciples to have a small boat ready for him, to keep the people from crowding him. 10For he had healed many, so that those with diseases were pushing forward to touch him. 11Whenever the evil[a] spirits saw him, they fell down before him and cried out, "You are the Son of God." 12But he gave them strict orders not to tell who he was.

The Appointing of the Twelve Apostles

13Jesus went up on a mountainside and called to him those he wanted, and they came to him. 14He appointed twelve—designating them apostles[b]—that they might be with him and that he might send them out to preach 15and to have authority to drive out demons. 16These are the twelve he appointed: Simon (to whom he gave the name Peter); 17James son of Zebedee and his

25耶穌對他們說："經上記着大衞和跟從他的人缺乏、飢餓之時所做的事，你們沒有念過嗎？26他當亞比亞他作大祭司的時候，怎麼進了神的殿，吃了陳設餅，又給跟從他的人吃。這餅除了祭司以外，人都不可吃。"

27又對他們說："安息日是為人設立的，人不是為安息日設立的。28所以，人子也是安息日的主。"

3 耶穌又進了會堂，在那裏有一個人枯乾了一隻手。2眾人窺探耶穌在安息日醫治不醫治，意思是要控告耶穌。3耶穌對那枯乾一隻手的人說："起來，站在當中。"

4又問眾人說："在安息日行善行惡，救命害命，哪樣是可以的呢？"他們都不做聲。

5耶穌怒目周圍看他們，憂愁他們的心剛硬，就對那人說："伸出手來！"他把手一伸，手就復了原。6法利賽人出去，同希律一黨的人商議怎樣可以除滅耶穌。

羣眾跟隨耶穌

7耶穌和門徒退到海邊去，有許多人從加利利跟隨他。8還有許多人聽見他所做的大事，就從猶太、耶路撒冷、以土買、約旦河外、並推羅、西頓的四方來到他那裏。9他因為人多，就吩咐門徒叫一隻小船伺候着，免得眾人擁擠他。10他治好了許多人，所以凡有災病的，都擠進來要摸他。11污鬼無論何時看見他，就俯伏在他面前，喊着說："你是神的兒子！"12耶穌再三地囑咐他們，不要把他顯露出來。

設立十二使徒

13耶穌上了山，隨自己的意思叫人來，他們便來到他那裏。14他就設立十二個人，要他們常和自己同在，也要差他們去傳道，15並給他們權柄趕鬼。16這十二個人有西門，耶穌又給他起名叫彼得；17還有西庇太的兒

---

a 11 Greek *unclean*; also in verse 30   b 14 Some manuscripts do not have *designating them apostles*.

子雅各和雅各的兄弟約翰，又給這兩個人起名叫半尼其，就是雷子的意思；¹⁸又有安得烈、腓力、巴多羅買、馬太、多馬、亞勒腓的兒子雅各，和達太，並奮銳黨的西門；¹⁹還有賣耶穌的加略人猶大。

耶穌與別西卜

²⁰耶穌進了一個屋子，眾人又聚集，甚至他連飯也顧不得吃。²¹耶穌的親屬聽見，就出來要拉住他，因為他們說他癲狂了。

²²從耶路撒冷下來的文士說：「他是被別西卜附着。」又說：「他是靠着鬼王趕鬼。」

²³耶穌叫他們來，用比喻對他們說：「撒但怎能趕出撒但呢？²⁴若一國自相紛爭，那國就站立不住；²⁵若一家自相紛爭，那家就站立不住。²⁶若撒但自相攻打紛爭，他就站立不住，必要滅亡。²⁷沒有人能進壯士家裏，搶奪他的家具；必先捆住那壯士，才可以搶奪他的家。²⁸我實在告訴你們：世人一切的罪和一切褻瀆的話都可得赦免；²⁹凡褻瀆聖靈的，卻永不得赦免，乃要擔當永遠的罪。」

³⁰這話是因為他們說：「他是被污鬼附着的。」

耶穌的母親和弟兄

³¹當下，耶穌的母親和弟兄來，站在外邊，打發人去叫他。³²有許多人在耶穌周圍坐着，他們就告訴他說：「看哪，你母親和你弟兄在外邊找你。」

³³耶穌回答說：「誰是我的母親？誰是我的弟兄？」

³⁴就四面觀看那周圍坐着的人，說：「看哪！我的母親，我的弟兄。³⁵凡遵行神旨意的人，就是我的弟兄姐妹和母親了。」

撒種的比喻

4 耶穌又在海邊教訓人。有許多人到他那裏聚集，他只得上船坐下。船在海裏，眾人都靠近海，站在岸上。²耶穌就用比喻教訓他們許多道理。在教訓之

brother John (to them he gave the name Boanerges, which means Sons of Thunder); ¹⁸Andrew, Philip, Bartholomew, Matthew, Thomas, James son of Alphaeus, Thaddaeus, Simon the Zealot ¹⁹and Judas Iscariot, who betrayed him.

Jesus and Beelzebub

²⁰Then Jesus entered a house, and again a crowd gathered, so that he and his disciples were not even able to eat. ²¹When his family heard about this, they went to take charge of him, for they said, "He is out of his mind."

²²And the teachers of the law who came down from Jerusalem said, "He is possessed by Beelzebub[a]! By the prince of demons he is driving out demons."

²³So Jesus called them and spoke to them in parables: "How can Satan drive out Satan? ²⁴If a kingdom is divided against itself, that kingdom cannot stand. ²⁵If a house is divided against itself, that house cannot stand. ²⁶And if Satan opposes himself and is divided, he cannot stand; his end has come. ²⁷In fact, no one can enter a strong man's house and carry off his possessions unless he first ties up the strong man. Then he can rob his house. ²⁸I tell you the truth, all the sins and blasphemies of men will be forgiven them. ²⁹But whoever blasphemes against the Holy Spirit will never be forgiven; he is guilty of an eternal sin."

³⁰He said this because they were saying, "He has an evil spirit."

Jesus' Mother and Brothers

³¹Then Jesus' mother and brothers arrived. Standing outside, they sent someone in to call him. ³²A crowd was sitting around him, and they told him, "Your mother and brothers are outside looking for you."

³³"Who are my mother and my brothers?" he asked.

³⁴Then he looked at those seated in a circle around him and said, "Here are my mother and my brothers! ³⁵Whoever does God's will is my brother and sister and mother."

The Parable of the Sower

4 Again Jesus began to teach by the lake. The crowd that gathered around him was so large that he got into a boat and sat in it out on the lake, while all the people were along the shore at the water's edge. ²He taught them many things by parables, and in his

a 22 Greek *Beezeboul* or *Beelzeboul*

teaching said: [3]"Listen! A farmer went out to sow his seed. [4]As he was scattering the seed, some fell along the path, and the birds came and ate it up. [5]Some fell on rocky places, where it did not have much soil. It sprang up quickly, because the soil was shallow. [6]But when the sun came up, the plants were scorched, and they withered because they had no root. [7]Other seed fell among thorns, which grew up and choked the plants, so that they did not bear grain. [8]Still other seed fell on good soil. It came up, grew and produced a crop, multiplying thirty, sixty, or even a hundred times."

[9]Then Jesus said, "He who has ears to hear, let him hear."

[10]When he was alone, the Twelve and the others around him asked him about the parables. [11]He told them, "The secret of the kingdom of God has been given to you. But to those on the outside everything is said in parables [12]so that,

" 'they may be ever seeing but never
    perceiving,
and ever hearing but never understanding;
otherwise they might turn and be forgiven!'[a] "

[13]Then Jesus said to them, "Don't you understand this parable? How then will you understand any parable? [14]The farmer sows the word. [15]Some people are like seed along the path, where the word is sown. As soon as they hear it, Satan comes and takes away the word that was sown in them. [16]Others, like seed sown on rocky places, hear the word and at once receive it with joy. [17]But since they have no root, they last only a short time. When trouble or persecution comes because of the word, they quickly fall away. [18]Still others, like seed sown among thorns, hear the word; [19]but the worries of this life, the deceitfulness of wealth and the desires for other things come in and choke the word, making it unfruitful. [20]Others, like seed sown on good soil, hear the word, accept it, and produce a crop—thirty, sixty or even a hundred times what was sown."

A Lamp on a Stand

[21]He said to them, "Do you bring in a lamp to put it under a bowl or a bed? Instead, don't you put it on its stand? [22]For whatever is hidden is meant to be disclosed, and whatever is concealed is meant to be brought out into the open. [23]If anyone has ears to hear, let him hear."

a 12 Isaiah 6:9,10

間，對他們說：[3]"你們聽啊！有一個撒種的出去撒種。[4]撒的時候，有落在路旁的，飛鳥來吃盡了。[5]有落在土淺石頭地上的，土既不深，發苗最快，[6]日頭出來一曬，因為沒有根，就枯乾了。[7]有落在荊棘裏的，荊棘長起來，把它擠住了，就不結實。[8]又有落在好土裏的，就發生長大，結實有三十倍的，有六十倍的，有一百倍的。"

[9]又說："有耳可聽的，就應當聽！"

[10]無人的時候，跟隨耶穌的人和十二個門徒，問他這比喻的意思。[11]耶穌對他們說："神國的奧秘，只叫你們知道，若是對外人講，凡事就用比喻，[12]叫

" '他們看是看見，卻不曉得；
  聽是聽見，卻不明白；
恐怕他們回轉過來，
    就得赦免。' "

[13]又對他們說："你們不明白這比喻嗎？這樣怎能明白一切的比喻呢？[14]撒種之人所撒的就是道。[15]那撒在路旁的，就是人聽了道，撒但立刻來，把撒在他心裏的道奪了去。[16]那撒在石頭地上的，就是人聽了道，立刻歡喜領受，[17]但他心裏沒有根，不過是暫時的，及至為道遭了患難，或是受了逼迫，立刻就跌倒了。[18]還有那撒在荊棘裏的，就是人聽了道，[19]後來有世上的思慮，錢財的迷惑，和別樣的私慾進來，把道擠住了，就不能結實。[20]那撒在好地上的，就是人聽道，又領受，並且結實，有三十倍的，有六十倍的，有一百倍的。"

燈放在燈臺上

[21]耶穌又對他們說："人拿燈來，豈是要放在斗底下，牀底下，不放在燈臺上嗎？[22]因為掩藏的事，沒有不顯出來的；隱瞞的事，沒有不露出來的。[23]有耳可聽的，就應當聽！"

24又說："你們所聽的要留心。你們用甚麼量器量給人，也必用甚麼量器量給你們，並且要多給你們。25因為有的，還要給他；沒有的，連他所有的也要奪去。"

種子生長的比喻

26又說："神的國，如同人把種撒在地上。27黑夜睡覺，白日起來，這種就發芽漸長，那人卻不曉得如何這樣。28地生五穀是出於自然的：先發苗，後長穗，再後穗上結成飽滿的子粒。29穀既熟了，就用鐮刀去割，因為收成的時候到了。"

芥菜種的比喻

30又說："神的國，我們可用甚麼比較呢？可用甚麼比喻表明呢？31好像一粒芥菜種，種在地裏的時候，雖比地上的百種都小，32但種上以後，就長起來，比各樣的菜都大，又長出大枝來，甚至天上的飛鳥可以宿在它的蔭下。"

33耶穌用許多這樣的比喻，照他們所能聽的，對他們講道。34若不用比喻，就不對他們講，沒有人的時候，就把一切的道講給門徒聽。

耶穌平靜風浪

35當那天晚上，耶穌對門徒說："我們渡到那邊去吧。"36門徒離開眾人，耶穌仍在船上，他們就把他一同帶去，也有別的船和他同行。37忽然起了暴風，波浪打入船內，甚至船要滿了水。38耶穌在船尾上，枕著枕頭睡覺。門徒叫醒了他，說："夫子！我們喪命，你不顧嗎？"

39耶穌醒了，斥責風，向海說："住了吧！靜了吧！"風就止住，大大地平靜了。

40耶穌對他們說："為甚麼膽怯，你們還沒有信心嗎？"

41他們就大大地懼怕，彼此說："這到底是誰，連風和海也聽從他了。"

24"Consider carefully what you hear," he continued. "With the measure you use, it will be measured to you—and even more. 25Whoever has will be given more; whoever does not have, even what he has will be taken from him."

The Parable of the Growing Seed

26He also said, "This is what the kingdom of God is like. A man scatters seed on the ground. 27Night and day, whether he sleeps or gets up, the seed sprouts and grows, though he does not know how. 28All by itself the soil produces grain—first the stalk, then the head, then the full kernel in the head. 29As soon as the grain is ripe, he puts the sickle to it, because the harvest has come."

The Parable of the Mustard Seed

30Again he said, "What shall we say the kingdom of God is like, or what parable shall we use to describe it? 31It is like a mustard seed, which is the smallest seed you plant in the ground. 32Yet when planted, it grows and becomes the largest of all garden plants, with such big branches that the birds of the air can perch in its shade."

33With many similar parables Jesus spoke the word to them, as much as they could understand. 34He did not say anything to them without using a parable. But when he was alone with his own disciples, he explained everything.

Jesus Calms the Storm

35That day when evening came, he said to his disciples, "Let us go over to the other side." 36Leaving the crowd behind, they took him along, just as he was, in the boat. There were also other boats with him. 37A furious squall came up, and the waves broke over the boat, so that it was nearly swamped. 38Jesus was in the stern, sleeping on a cushion. The disciples woke him and said to him, "Teacher, don't you care if we drown?"

39He got up, rebuked the wind and said to the waves, "Quiet! Be still!" Then the wind died down and it was completely calm.

40He said to his disciples, "Why are you so afraid? Do you still have no faith?"

41They were terrified and asked each other, "Who is this? Even the wind and the waves obey him!"

The Healing of a Demon-possessed Man

5 They went across the lake to the region of the Gerasenes.[a] 2When Jesus got out of the boat, a man with an evil[b] spirit came from the tombs to meet him. 3This man lived in the tombs, and no one could bind him any more, not even with a chain. 4For he had often been chained hand and foot, but he tore the chains apart and broke the irons on his feet. No one was strong enough to subdue him. 5Night and day among the tombs and in the hills he would cry out and cut himself with stones.

6When he saw Jesus from a distance, he ran and fell on his knees in front of him. 7He shouted at the top of his voice, "What do you want with me, Jesus, Son of the Most High God? Swear to God that you won't torture me!" 8For Jesus had said to him, "Come out of this man, you evil spirit!"

9Then Jesus asked him, "What is your name?"

"My name is Legion," he replied, "for we are many." 10And he begged Jesus again and again not to send them out of the area.

11A large herd of pigs was feeding on the nearby hillside. 12The demons begged Jesus, "Send us among the pigs; allow us to go into them." 13He gave them permission, and the evil spirits came out and went into the pigs. The herd, about two thousand in number, rushed down the steep bank into the lake and were drowned.

14Those tending the pigs ran off and reported this in the town and countryside, and the people went out to see what had happened. 15When they came to Jesus, they saw the man who had been possessed by the legion of demons, sitting there, dressed and in his right mind; and they were afraid. 16Those who had seen it told the people what had happened to the demon-possessed man—and told about the pigs as well. 17Then the people began to plead with Jesus to leave their region.

18As Jesus was getting into the boat, the man who had been demon-possessed begged to go with him. 19Jesus did not let him, but said, "Go home to your family and tell them how much the Lord has done for you, and how he has had mercy on you." 20So the man went away and began to tell in the Decapolis[c] how much Jesus

a 1 Some manuscripts Gadarenes; other manuscripts Gergesenes
b 2 Greek unclean; also in verses 8 and 13   c 20 That is, the Ten Cities

醫治被鬼附着的人

5 他們來到海那邊格拉森人的地方。2耶穌一下船，就有一個被污鬼附着的人從墳塋裏出來迎着他。3那人常住在墳塋裏，沒有人能捆住他，就是用鐵鏈也不能，4因為人屢次用腳鐐和鐵鏈捆鎖他，鐵鏈竟被他掙斷了，腳鐐也被他弄碎了。總沒有人能制伏他。5他晝夜常在墳塋裏和山中喊叫，又用石頭砍自己。

6他遠遠地看見耶穌，就跑過去拜他，7大聲呼叫說："至高神的兒子耶穌，我與你有甚麼相干？我指着神懇求你，不要叫我受苦！"8是因耶穌曾吩咐他說："污鬼啊，從這人身上出來吧！"

9耶穌問他說："你名叫甚麼？"

回答說："我名叫'羣'，因為我們多的緣故。"10就再三地求耶穌，不要叫他們離開那地方。

11在那裏山坡上，有一大羣豬吃食，12鬼就央求耶穌說："求你打發我們往豬羣裏，附着豬去。"13耶穌准了他們，污鬼就出來，進入豬裏去。於是那羣豬闖下山崖，投在海裏，淹死了。豬的數目約有二千。

14放豬的就逃跑了，去告訴城裏和鄉下的人。眾人就來，要看是甚麼事。15他們來到耶穌那裏，看見那被鬼附着的人，就是從前被羣鬼所附的，坐着，穿上衣服，心裏明白過來，他們就害怕。16看見這事的，便將鬼附之人所遇見的和那羣豬的事，都告訴了眾人，17眾人就央求耶穌離開他們的境界。

18耶穌上船的時候，那從前被鬼附着的人懇求和耶穌同在。19耶穌不許，卻對他說："你回家去，到你的親屬那裏，將主為你所做的是何等大的事，是怎樣憐憫你，都告訴他們。"20那人就走了，在低加坡里傳揚耶穌為他做了何等大的事，眾人就都希奇。

死了的女孩和患血漏的女人

21耶穌坐船又渡到那邊去，就有許多人到他那裏聚集。他正在海邊上。22有一個管會堂的人，名叫睚魯，來見耶穌，就俯伏在他腳前，23再三地求他，說：「我的小女兒快要死了，求你去按手在她身上，使她痊愈，得以活了。」24耶穌就和他同去。

有許多人跟隨擁擠他。25有一個女人，患了十二年的血漏，26在好些醫生手裏受了許多的苦，又花盡了她所有的，一點也不見好，病勢反倒更重了。27她聽見耶穌的事，就從後頭來，雜在眾人中間，摸耶穌的衣裳，28意思說：「我只摸他的衣裳，就必痊愈。」29於是她血漏的源頭立刻乾了，她便覺得身上的災病好了。

30耶穌頓時心裏覺得有能力從自己身上出去，就在眾人中間轉過來，說：「誰摸我的衣裳？」

31門徒對他說：「你看眾人擁擠你，還說『誰摸我』嗎？」

32耶穌周圍觀看，要見做這事的女人。33那女人知道在自己身上所成的事，就恐懼戰兢，來俯伏在耶穌跟前，將實情全告訴他。34耶穌對她說：「女兒，你的信救了你，平平安安地回去吧！你的災病痊愈了。」

35還說話的時候，有人從管會堂的家裏來，說：「你的女兒死了！何必還勞動先生呢？」

36耶穌聽見所說的話，就對管會堂的說：「不要怕，只要信！」

37於是帶着彼得，雅各，和雅各的兄弟約翰同去，不許別人跟隨他。38他們來到管會堂的家裏，耶穌看見那裏亂嚷，並有人大大地哭泣哀號，39進到裏面，就對他們說：「為甚麼亂嚷哭泣呢？孩子不是死了，是睡着了。」40他們就嗤笑耶穌。

耶穌把他們都攆出去，就帶着孩子的父母，和跟隨他人進了孩子所在的地方，41就拉着孩子的手，對

had done for him. And all the people were amazed.

A Dead Girl and a Sick Woman

21When Jesus had again crossed over by boat to the other side of the lake, a large crowd gathered around him while he was by the lake. 22Then one of the synagogue rulers, named Jairus, came there. Seeing Jesus, he fell at his feet 23and pleaded earnestly with him, "My little daughter is dying. Please come and put your hands on her so that she will be healed and live." 24So Jesus went with him.

A large crowd followed and pressed around him. 25And a woman was there who had been subject to bleeding for twelve years. 26She had suffered a great deal under the care of many doctors and had spent all she had, yet instead of getting better she grew worse. 27When she heard about Jesus, she came up behind him in the crowd and touched his cloak, 28because she thought, "If I just touch his clothes, I will be healed." 29Immediately her bleeding stopped and she felt in her body that she was freed from her suffering.

30At once Jesus realized that power had gone out from him. He turned around in the crowd and asked, "Who touched my clothes?"

31"You see the people crowding against you," his disciples answered, "and yet you can ask, 'Who touched me?'"

32But Jesus kept looking around to see who had done it. 33Then the woman, knowing what had happened to her, came and fell at his feet and, trembling with fear, told him the whole truth. 34He said to her, "Daughter, your faith has healed you. Go in peace and be freed from your suffering."

35While Jesus was still speaking, some men came from the house of Jairus, the synagogue ruler. "Your daughter is dead," they said. "Why bother the teacher any more?"

36Ignoring what they said, Jesus told the synagogue ruler, "Don't be afraid; just believe."

37He did not let anyone follow him except Peter, James and John the brother of James. 38When they came to the home of the synagogue ruler, Jesus saw a commotion, with people crying and wailing loudly. 39He went in and said to them, "Why all this commotion and wailing? The child is not dead but asleep." 40But they laughed at him.

After he put them all out, he took the child's father and mother and the disciples who were with him, and went in where the child was. 41He took her by the hand and said to her, "Talitha *koum!"* (which means, "Little girl, I say to you, get up!"). ⁴²Immediately the girl stood up and walked around (she was twelve years old). At this they were completely astonished. ⁴³He gave strict orders not to let anyone know about this, and told them to give her something to eat.

A Prophet Without Honor

6 Jesus left there and went to his home-town, accompanied by his disciples. ²When the Sabbath came, he began to teach in the synagogue, and many who heard him were amazed.

"Where did this man get these things?" they asked. "What's this wisdom that has been given him, that he even does miracles! ³Isn't this the carpenter? Isn't this Mary's son and the brother of James, Joseph,ᵃ Judas and Simon? Aren't his sisters here with us?" And they took offense at him.

⁴Jesus said to them, "Only in his hometown, among his relatives and in his own house is a prophet without honor." ⁵He could not do any miracles there, except lay his hands on a few sick people and heal them. ⁶And he was amazed at their lack of faith.

Jesus Sends Out the Twelve

Then Jesus went around teaching from village to village. ⁷Calling the Twelve to him, he sent them out two by two and gave them authority over evilᵇ spirits.

⁸These were his instructions: "Take nothing for the journey except a staff—no bread, no bag, no money in your belts. ⁹Wear sandals but not an extra tunic. ¹⁰Whenever you enter a house, stay there until you leave that town. ¹¹And if any place will not welcome you or listen to you, shake the dust off your feet when you leave, as a testimony against them."

¹²They went out and preached that people should repent. ¹³They drove out many demons and anointed many sick people with oil and healed them.

John the Baptist Beheaded

¹⁴King Herod heard about this, for Jesus' name had become well known. Some were say-ing,ᶜ "John the Baptist has been raised from the dead, and that is why miraculous powers are at work in him."

¹⁵Others said, "He is Elijah."

她説："大利大，古米！"翻出來就是説："閨女，我吩咐你起來！"⁴²那閨女立時起來走，他們就大大地驚奇；閨女已經十二歲了。⁴³耶穌切切地囑咐他們，不要叫人知道這事，又吩咐給她東西吃。

不被尊敬的先知

6 耶穌離開那裏，來到自己的家鄉，門徒也跟從他。²到了安息日，他在會堂裏教訓人。眾人聽見，就甚希奇，説：

"這人從哪裏有這些事呢？所賜給他的是甚麼智慧？他手所做的是何等的異能呢？³這不是那木匠嗎？不是<u>馬利亞</u>的兒子<u>雅各</u>、<u>約西</u>、<u>猶大</u>、<u>西門</u>的長兄嗎？他妹妹們不也是在我們這裏嗎？"他們就厭棄他（註："厭棄他"原文作"因他跌倒"）。

⁴耶穌對他們説："大凡先知，除了本地親屬、本家之外，沒有不被人尊敬的。"⁵耶穌就在那裏不得行甚麼異能，不過按手在幾個病人身上，治好他們。⁶他也詫異他們不信，就往周圍鄉村教訓人去了。

耶穌差遣十二門徒

⁷耶穌叫了十二個門徒來，差遣他們兩個兩個的出去，也賜給他們權柄，制伏污鬼。

⁸並且囑咐他們："行路的時候不要帶食物和口袋，腰袋裏也不要帶錢，除了拐杖以外，甚麼都不要帶；⁹只要穿鞋，也不要穿兩件褂子。"¹⁰又對他們説："你們無論到何處，進了人的家，就住在那裏，直到離開那地方。¹¹何處的人不接待你們，不聽你們，你們離開那裏的時候，就把腳上的塵土跺下去，對他們作見證。"

¹²門徒就出去傳道，叫人悔改；¹³又趕出許多的鬼，用油抹了許多病人，治好他們。

施洗約翰被斬

¹⁴耶穌的名聲傳揚出來。<u>希律</u>王聽見了，就説："施洗的<u>約翰</u>從死裏復活了，所以這些異能由他裏面發出來。"

¹⁵但別人説："是<u>以利亞</u>。"

ᵃ 3 Greek *Joses*, a variant of *Joseph*   ᵇ 7 Greek *unclean*

ᶜ 14 Some early manuscripts *He was saying*

又有人說：「是先知，正像先知中的一位。」

16希律聽見卻說：「是我所斬的約翰，他復活了。」

17先是希律為他兄弟腓力的妻子希羅底的緣故，差人去拿住約翰，鎖在監裏；因為希律已經娶了那婦人。18約翰曾對希律說：「你娶你兄弟的妻子是不合理的。」19於是希羅底懷恨他，想要殺他，只是不能。20因為希律知道約翰是義人，是聖人，所以敬畏他，保護他，聽他講論，就多照着行（註：「多照着行」有古卷作「游移不定」），並且樂意聽他。

21有一天，恰巧是希律的生日，希律擺設筵席，請了大臣和千夫長，並加利利作首領的。22希羅底的女兒進來跳舞，使希律和同席的人都歡喜。

王就對女子說：「你隨意向我求甚麼，我必給你。」23又對她起誓說：「隨你向我求甚麼，就是我國的一半，我也必給你！」

24她就出去對她母親說：「我可以求甚麼呢？」

她母親說：「施洗約翰的頭！」

25她就急忙進去見王，求他說：「我願王立時把施洗約翰的頭放在盤子裏給我。」

26王就甚憂愁，但因他所起的誓，又因同席的人，就不肯推辭，27隨即差一個護衛兵，吩咐拿約翰的頭來。護衛兵就去，在監裏斬了約翰，28把頭放在盤子裏，拿來給女子，女子就給她母親。29約翰的門徒聽見了，就來把他的屍首領去，葬在墳墓裏。

耶穌給五千人吃飽

30使徒聚集到耶穌那裏，將一切所做的事，所傳的道全告訴他。31他就說：「你們來，同我暗暗地到曠野地方去歇一歇。」這是因為來往的人多，他們連吃飯也沒有工夫。

32他們就坐船，暗暗地往曠野地方去。33眾人看見他們去，有許多認識他們的，就從各城步行，一同跑

And still others claimed, "He is a prophet, like one of the prophets of long ago."

16But when Herod heard this, he said, "John, the man I beheaded, has been raised from the dead!"

17For Herod himself had given orders to have John arrested, and he had him bound and put in prison. He did this because of Herodias, his brother Philip's wife, whom he had married. 18For John had been saying to Herod, "It is not lawful for you to have your brother's wife." 19So Herodias nursed a grudge against John and wanted to kill him. But she was not able to, 20because Herod feared John and protected him, knowing him to be a righteous and holy man. When Herod heard John, he was greatly puzzled[a]; yet he liked to listen to him.

21Finally the opportune time came. On his birthday Herod gave a banquet for his high officials and military commanders and the leading men of Galilee. 22When the daughter of Herodias came in and danced, she pleased Herod and his dinner guests.

The king said to the girl, "Ask me for anything you want, and I'll give it to you." 23And he promised her with an oath, "Whatever you ask I will give you, up to half my kingdom."

24She went out and said to her mother, "What shall I ask for?"

"The head of John the Baptist," she answered.

25At once the girl hurried in to the king with the request: "I want you to give me right now the head of John the Baptist on a platter."

26The king was greatly distressed, but because of his oaths and his dinner guests, he did not want to refuse her. 27So he immediately sent an executioner with orders to bring John's head. The man went, beheaded John in the prison, 28and brought back his head on a platter. He presented it to the girl, and she gave it to her mother. 29On hearing of this, John's disciples came and took his body and laid it in a tomb.

Jesus Feeds the Five Thousand

30The apostles gathered around Jesus and reported to him all they had done and taught. 31Then, because so many people were coming and going that they did not even have a chance to eat, he said to them, "Come with me by yourselves to a quiet place and get some rest."

32So they went away by themselves in a boat to a solitary place. 33But many who saw them leaving recognized them and ran on foot from all the towns and got there ahead of them.

a 20 Some early manuscripts he did many things

³⁴When Jesus landed and saw a large crowd, he had compassion on them, because they were like sheep without a shepherd. So he began teaching them many things.

³⁵By this time it was late in the day, so his disciples came to him. "This is a remote place," they said, "and it's already very late. ³⁶Send the people away so they can go to the surrounding countryside and villages and buy themselves something to eat."

³⁷But he answered, "You give them something to eat."

They said to him, "That would take eight months of a man's wages[a]! Are we to go and spend that much on bread and give it to them to eat?"

³⁸"How many loaves do you have?" he asked. "Go and see."

When they found out, they said, "Five—and two fish."

³⁹Then Jesus directed them to have all the people sit down in groups on the green grass. ⁴⁰So they sat down in groups of hundreds and fifties. ⁴¹Taking the five loaves and the two fish and looking up to heaven, he gave thanks and broke the loaves. Then he gave them to his disciples to set before the people. He also divided the two fish among them all. ⁴²They all ate and were satisfied, ⁴³and the disciples picked up twelve basketfuls of broken pieces of bread and fish. ⁴⁴The number of the men who had eaten was five thousand.

Jesus Walks on the Water

⁴⁵Immediately Jesus made his disciples get into the boat and go on ahead of him to Bethsaida, while he dismissed the crowd. ⁴⁶After leaving them, he went up on a mountainside to pray.

⁴⁷When evening came, the boat was in the middle of the lake, and he was alone on land. ⁴⁸He saw the disciples straining at the oars, because the wind was against them. About the fourth watch of the night he went out to them, walking on the lake. He was about to pass by them, ⁴⁹but when they saw him walking on the lake, they thought he was a ghost. They cried out, ⁵⁰because they all saw him and were terrified.

Immediately he spoke to them and said, "Take courage! It is I. Don't be afraid." ⁵¹Then he climbed into the boat with them, and the wind died down. They were completely amazed, ⁵²for they had not understood about the loaves; their hearts were hardened.

a 37 Greek take two hundred denarii

到那裏，比他們先趕到了。³⁴耶穌出來，見有許多的人，就憐憫他們，因為他們如同羊沒有牧人一般，於是開口教訓他們許多道理。

³⁵天已經晚了，門徒進前來，說："這是野地，天已經晚了，³⁶請叫眾人散開，他們好往四面鄉村裏去，自己買甚麼吃。"

³⁷耶穌回答說："你們給他們吃吧！"

門徒說："我們可以去買二十兩銀子的餅，給他們吃嗎？"

³⁸耶穌說："你們有多少餅，可以去看看。"

他們知道了，就說："五個餅，兩條魚。"

³⁹耶穌吩咐他們，叫眾人一幫一幫地坐在青草地上。⁴⁰眾人就一排一排地坐下，有一百一排的，有五十一排的。⁴¹耶穌拿着這五個餅，兩條魚，望着天祝福，擘開餅，遞給門徒，擺在眾人面前，也把那兩條魚分給眾人。⁴²他們都吃，並且吃飽了。⁴³門徒就把碎餅碎魚收拾起來，裝滿了十二個籃子。⁴⁴吃餅的男人共有五千。

耶穌在水面上行走

⁴⁵耶穌隨即催門徒上船，先渡到那邊伯賽大去，等他叫眾人散開。⁴⁶他既辭別了他們，就往山上去禱告。

⁴⁷到了晚上，船在海中，耶穌獨自在岸上，⁴⁸看見門徒因風不順，搖櫓甚苦。夜裏約有四更天，就在海面上走，往他們那裏去，意思要走過他們去。⁴⁹但門徒看見他在海面上走，以為是鬼怪，就喊叫起來。⁵⁰因為他們都看見了他，且甚驚慌。

耶穌連忙對他們說："你們放心，是我，不要怕！"⁵¹於是到他們那裏上了船，風就住了，他們心裏十分驚奇。⁵²這是因為他們不明白那分餅的事，心裏還是愚頑。

⁵³既渡過去,來到革尼撒勒地方,就靠了岸,⁵⁴一下船,眾人認得是耶穌,⁵⁵就跑遍那一帶地方,聽見他在何處,便將有病的人用褥子抬到那裏。⁵⁶凡耶穌所到的地方,或村中、或城裏、或鄉間,他們都將病人放在街市上,求耶穌只容他們摸他的衣裳繸子,凡摸着的人就都好了。

潔淨與污穢

7 有法利賽人和幾個文士從耶路撒冷來,到耶穌那裏聚集。²他們曾看見他的門徒中有人用俗手,就是沒有洗的手吃飯。(³原來法利賽人和猶太人都拘守古人的遺傳,若不仔細洗手就不吃飯;⁴從市上來,若不洗浴也不吃飯,還有好些別的規矩,他們歷代拘守,就是洗杯、罐、銅器等物。)

⁵法利賽人和文士問他說:「你的門徒為甚麼不照古人的遺傳,用俗手吃飯呢?」

⁶耶穌說:「以賽亞指着你們假冒為善之人所說的預言是不錯的。如經上說:

'這百姓用嘴唇尊敬我,
　心卻遠離我。
⁷他們將人的吩咐當做道理教導人,
　所以拜我也是枉然。'

⁸你們是離棄神的誡命,拘守人的遺傳。」

⁹又說:「你們誠然是廢棄神的誡命,要守自己的遺傳。¹⁰摩西說:'當孝敬父母',又說:'咒罵父母的,必治死他。'¹¹你們倒說:'人若對父母說:我所當奉給你的,已經做了各耳板'(各耳板就是供獻的意思),¹²以後你們就不容他再奉養父母。¹³這就是你們承接遺傳,廢了神的道。你們還做許多這樣的事。」

⁵³When they had crossed over, they landed at Gennesaret and anchored there. ⁵⁴As soon as they got out of the boat, people recognized Jesus. ⁵⁵They ran throughout that whole region and carried the sick on mats to wherever they heard he was. ⁵⁶And wherever he went—into villages, towns or countryside—they placed the sick in the marketplaces. They begged him to let them touch even the edge of his cloak, and all who touched him were healed.

Clean and Unclean

7 The Pharisees and some of the teachers of the law who had come from Jerusalem gathered around Jesus and ²saw some of his disciples eating food with hands that were "unclean," that is, unwashed. ³(The Pharisees and all the Jews do not eat unless they give their hands a ceremonial washing, holding to the tradition of the elders. ⁴When they come from the marketplace they do not eat unless they wash. And they observe many other traditions, such as the washing of cups, pitchers and kettles.^a)

⁵So the Pharisees and teachers of the law asked Jesus, "Why don't your disciples live according to the tradition of the elders instead of eating their food with 'unclean' hands?"

⁶He replied, "Isaiah was right when he prophesied about you hypocrites; as it is written:

" 'These people honor me with their lips,
　but their hearts are far from me.
⁷They worship me in vain;
　their teachings are but rules taught by
　men.'^b

⁸You have let go of the commands of God and are holding on to the traditions of men."

⁹And he said to them: "You have a fine way of setting aside the commands of God in order to observe^c your own traditions! ¹⁰For Moses said, 'Honor your father and your mother,'^d and, 'Anyone who curses his father or mother must be put to death.'^e ¹¹But you say that if a man says to his father or mother: 'Whatever help you might otherwise have received from me is Corban' (that is, a gift devoted to God), ¹²then you no longer let him do anything for his father or mother. ¹³Thus you nullify the word of God by your tradition that you have handed down. And you do many things like that."

a 4 Some early manuscripts pitchers, kettles and dining couches
b 6,7 Isaiah 29:13   c 9 Some manuscripts set up
d 10 Exodus 20:12; Deut. 5:16   e 10 Exodus 21:17; Lev. 20:9

¹⁴Again Jesus called the crowd to him and said, "Listen to me, everyone, and understand this. ¹⁵Nothing outside a man can make him 'unclean' by going into him. Rather, it is what comes out of a man that makes him 'unclean.'*a*"

¹⁷After he had left the crowd and entered the house, his disciples asked him about this parable. ¹⁸"Are you so dull?" he asked. "Don't you see that nothing that enters a man from the outside can make him 'unclean'? ¹⁹For it doesn't go into his heart but into his stomach, and then out of his body." (In saying this, Jesus declared all foods "clean.")

²⁰He went on: "What comes out of a man is what makes him 'unclean.' ²¹For from within, out of men's hearts, come evil thoughts, sexual immorality, theft, murder, adultery, ²²greed, malice, deceit, lewdness, envy, slander, arrogance and folly. ²³All these evils come from inside and make a man 'unclean.' "

The Faith of a Syrophoenician Woman

²⁴Jesus left that place and went to the vicinity of Tyre.*b* He entered a house and did not want anyone to know it; yet he could not keep his presence secret. ²⁵In fact, as soon as she heard about him, a woman whose little daughter was possessed by an evil*c* spirit came and fell at his feet. ²⁶The woman was a Greek, born in Syrian Phoenicia. She begged Jesus to drive the demon out of her daughter.

²⁷"First let the children eat all they want," he told her, "for it is not right to take the children's bread and toss it to their dogs."

²⁸"Yes, Lord," she replied, "but even the dogs under the table eat the children's crumbs."

²⁹Then he told her, "For such a reply, you may go; the demon has left your daughter."

³⁰She went home and found her child lying on the bed, and the demon gone.

The Healing of a Deaf and Mute Man

³¹Then Jesus left the vicinity of Tyre and went through Sidon, down to the Sea of Galilee and into the region of the Decapolis.*d* ³²There some people brought to him a man who was deaf and could hardly talk, and they begged him to place his hand on the man.

³³After he took him aside, away from the crowd, Jesus put his fingers into the man's ears. Then he spit and touched the man's tongue. ³⁴He looked up to heaven and with a deep sigh

---

a 15 Some early manuscripts 'unclean.' 16If anyone has ears to hear, let him hear.　b 24 Many early manuscripts Tyre and Sidon　c 25 Greek unclean　d 31 That is, the Ten Cities

---

¹⁴耶穌又叫眾人來，對他們說："你們都要聽我的話，也要明白：¹⁵從外面進去的，不能污穢人；惟有從裏面出來的，乃能污穢人。"（註：有古卷在此有¹⁶"有耳可聽的，就應當聽。"）

¹⁷耶穌離開眾人，進了屋子，門徒就問他這比喻的意思。¹⁸耶穌對他們說："你們也是這樣不明白嗎？豈不曉得凡從外面進入的，不能污穢人，¹⁹因為不是入他的心，乃是入他的肚腹，又落到茅廁裏。這是說，各樣的食物都是潔淨的。"

²⁰又說："從人裏面出來的，那才能污穢人，²¹因為從裏面，就是從人心裏發出惡念、苟合、²²偷盜、兇殺、姦淫、貪婪、邪惡、詭詐、淫蕩、嫉妒、謗讟、驕傲、狂妄。²³這一切的惡都是從裏面出來，且能污穢人。"

敘利腓尼基婦人的信心

²⁴耶穌從那裏起身，往推羅、西頓的境內去。進了一家，不願意人知道，卻隱藏不住。²⁵當下，有一個婦人，她的小女兒被污鬼附着，聽見耶穌的事，就來俯伏在他腳前。²⁶這婦人是希臘人，屬敘利腓尼基族。她求耶穌趕出那鬼離開她的女兒。

²⁷耶穌對她說："讓兒女們先吃飽，不好拿兒女的餅丟給狗吃。"

²⁸婦人回答說："主啊，不錯！但是狗在桌子底下也吃孩子們的碎渣兒。"

²⁹耶穌對她說："因這句話，你回去吧！鬼已經離開你的女兒了。"

³⁰她就回家去，見小孩子躺在牀上，鬼已經出去了。

醫治一個耳聾舌結的人

³¹耶穌又離了推羅的境界，經過西頓，就從低加坡里境內來到加利利海。³²有人帶着一個耳聾舌結的人來見耶穌，求他按手在他身上。

³³耶穌領他離開眾人，到一邊去，就用指頭探他的耳朵，吐唾沫抹他的舌頭，³⁴望天歎息，對他說：

"以法大！"就是説："開了吧！" 35他的耳朵就開了，舌結也解了，説話也清楚了。

36耶穌囑咐他們不要告訴人，但他越發囑咐，他們越發傳揚開了。37眾人分外希奇，説："他所做的事都好，他連聾子也叫他們聽見，啞巴也叫他們説話！"

耶穌給四千人吃飽

8 那時，又有許多人聚集，並沒有甚麼吃的。耶穌叫門徒來，説：2 "我憐憫這眾人，因為他們同我在這裏已經三天，也沒有吃的了。3我若打發他們餓着回家，就必在路上困乏，因為其中有從遠處來的。"

4門徒回答説："在這野地，從哪裏能得餅，叫這些人吃飽呢？"

5耶穌問他們説："你們有多少餅？"

他們説："七個。"

6他吩咐眾人坐在地上，就拿着這七個餅祝謝了，擘開，遞給門徒，叫他們擺開，門徒就擺在眾人面前。7又有幾條小魚，耶穌祝了福，就吩咐也擺在眾人面前。8眾人都吃，並且吃飽了，收拾剩下的零碎，有七筐子。9人數約有四千。耶穌打發他們走了，10隨即同門徒上船，來到大瑪努他境內。

11法利賽人出來盤問耶穌，求他從天上顯個神蹟給他們看，想要試探他。12耶穌心裏深深地歎息，説："這世代為甚麼求神蹟呢？我實在告訴你們：沒有神蹟給這世代看！"13他就離開他們，又上船往海那邊去了。

法利賽人與希律的酵

14門徒忘了帶餅，在船上除了一個餅，沒有別的食物。15耶穌囑咐他們説："你們要謹慎，防備法利賽人的酵和希律的酵。"

16他們彼此議論説："這是因為我們沒有餅吧？

said to him, *Ephphatha!*" (which means, "Be opened!"). 35At this, the man's ears were opened, his tongue was loosened and he began to speak plainly.

36Jesus commanded them not to tell anyone. But the more he did so, the more they kept talking about it. 37People were overwhelmed with amazement. "He has done everything well," they said. "He even makes the deaf hear and the mute speak."

Jesus Feeds the Four Thousand

8 During those days another large crowd gathered. Since they had nothing to eat, Jesus called his disciples to him and said, 2"I have compassion for these people; they have already been with me three days and have nothing to eat. 3If I send them home hungry, they will collapse on the way, because some of them have come a long distance."

4His disciples answered, "But where in this remote place can anyone get enough bread to feed them?"

5"How many loaves do you have?" Jesus asked.

"Seven," they replied.

6He told the crowd to sit down on the ground. When he had taken the seven loaves and given thanks, he broke them and gave them to his disciples to set before the people, and they did so. 7They had a few small fish as well; he gave thanks for them also and told the disciples to distribute them. 8The people ate and were satisfied. Afterward the disciples picked up seven basketfuls of broken pieces that were left over. 9About four thousand men were present. And having sent them away, 10he got into the boat with his disciples and went to the region of Dalmanutha.

11The Pharisees came and began to question Jesus. To test him, they asked him for a sign from heaven. 12He sighed deeply and said, "Why does this generation ask for a miraculous sign? I tell you the truth, no sign will be given to it." 13Then he left them, got back into the boat and crossed to the other side.

The Yeast of the Pharisees and Herod

14The disciples had forgotten to bring bread, except for one loaf they had with them in the boat. 15"Be careful," Jesus warned them. "Watch out for the yeast of the Pharisees and that of Herod."

16They discussed this with one another and said, "It is because we have no bread."

¹⁷Aware of their discussion, Jesus asked them: "Why are you talking about having no bread? Do you still not see or understand? Are your hearts hardened? ¹⁸Do you have eyes but fail to see, and ears but fail to hear? And don't you remember? ¹⁹When I broke the five loaves for the five thousand, how many basketfuls of pieces did you pick up?"

"Twelve," they replied.

²⁰"And when I broke the seven loaves for the four thousand, how many basketfuls of pieces did you pick up?"

They answered, "Seven."

²¹He said to them, "Do you still not understand?"

The Healing of a Blind Man at Bethsaida

²²They came to Bethsaida, and some people brought a blind man and begged Jesus to touch him. ²³He took the blind man by the hand and led him outside the village. When he had spit on the man's eyes and put his hands on him, Jesus asked, "Do you see anything?"

²⁴He looked up and said, "I see people; they look like trees walking around."

²⁵Once more Jesus put his hands on the man's eyes. Then his eyes were opened, his sight was restored, and he saw everything clearly. ²⁶Jesus sent him home, saying, "Don't go into the village.^a"

Peter's Confession of Christ

²⁷Jesus and his disciples went on to the villages around Caesarea Philippi. On the way he asked them, "Who do people say I am?"

²⁸They replied, "Some say John the Baptist; others say Elijah; and still others, one of the prophets."

²⁹"But what about you?" he asked. "Who do you say I am?"

Peter answered, "You are the Christ.^b"

³⁰Jesus warned them not to tell anyone about him.

Jesus Predicts His Death

³¹He then began to teach them that the Son of Man must suffer many things and be rejected by the elders, chief priests and teachers of the law, and that he must be killed and after three days rise again. ³²He spoke plainly about this, and Peter took him aside and began to rebuke him.

¹⁷耶穌看出來，就說："你們為甚麼因為沒有餅就議論呢？你們還不省悟，還不明白嗎？你們的心還是愚頑嗎？¹⁸你們有眼睛，看不見嗎？有耳朵，聽不見嗎？也不記得嗎？¹⁹我擘開那五個餅分給五千人，你們收拾的零碎裝滿了多少籃子呢？"

他們說："十二個。"

²⁰"又擘開那七個餅分給四千人，你們收拾的零碎裝滿了多少筐子呢？"

他們說："七個。"

²¹耶穌說："你們還是不明白嗎？"

在伯賽大治好瞎子

²²他們來到伯賽大，有人帶一個瞎子來，求耶穌摸他。²³耶穌拉着瞎子的手，領他到村外，就吐唾沫在他眼睛上，按手在他身上，問他說："你看見甚麼了？"

²⁴他就抬頭一看，說："我看見人了，他們好像樹木，並且行走。"

²⁵隨後又按手在他眼睛上，他定睛一看，就復了原，樣樣都看得清楚了。²⁶耶穌打發他回家，說："連這村子你也不要進去。"

彼得認基督

²⁷耶穌和門徒出去，往凱撒利亞腓立比的村莊去。在路上問門徒說："人說我是誰？"

²⁸他們說："有人說是施洗的約翰，有人說是以利亞，又有人說是先知裏的一位。"

²⁹又問他們說："你們說我是誰？"

彼得回答說："你是基督。"

³⁰耶穌就禁戒他們，不要告訴人。

耶穌預言自己的死

³¹從此，他教訓他們說："人子必須受許多的苦，被長老、祭司長和文士棄絕，並且被殺，過三天復活。"³²耶穌明明地說這話，彼得就拉着他勸他。

a 26 Some manuscripts Don't go and tell anyone in the village
b 29 Or Messiah. "The Christ" (Greek) and "the Messiah" (Hebrew) both mean "the Anointed One."

33耶穌轉過來，看着門徒，就責備彼得說：「撒但，退我後邊去吧！因為你不體貼神的意思，只體貼人的意思。」

34於是叫眾人和門徒來，對他們說：「若有人要跟從我，就當捨己，背起他的十字架來跟從我。35因為，凡要救自己生命（註：「生命」或作「靈魂」。下同）的，必喪掉生命；凡為我和福音喪掉生命的，必救了生命。36人就是賺得全世界，賠上自己的生命，有甚麼益處呢？37人還能拿甚麼換生命呢？38凡在這淫亂罪惡的世代，把我和我的道當作可恥的，人子在他父的榮耀裏，同聖天使降臨的時候，也要把那人當作可恥的。」

9 耶穌又對他們說：「我實在告訴你們：站在這裏的，有人在沒嘗死味以前，必要看見神的國大有能力臨到。」

登山變像

2過了六天，耶穌帶着彼得、雅各、約翰暗暗地上了高山，就在他們面前變了形像；3衣服放光，極其潔白，地上漂布的，沒有一個能漂得那樣白。4忽然，有以利亞同摩西向他們顯現，並且和耶穌說話。

5彼得對耶穌說：「拉比（註：「拉比」就是「夫子」），我們在這裏真好！可以搭三座棚，一座為你，一座為摩西，一座為以利亞。」6彼得不知道說甚麼才好，因為他們甚是懼怕。

7有一朵雲彩來遮蓋他們，也有聲音從雲彩裏出來，說：「這是我的愛子，你們要聽他！」

8門徒忽然周圍一看，不再見一人，只見耶穌同他們在那裏。

9下山的時候，耶穌囑咐他們說：「人子還沒有從死裏復活，你們不要將所看見的告訴人。」10門徒將這話存記在心，彼此議論從死裏復活是甚麼意思。

11他們就問耶穌說：「文士為甚麼說以利亞必須先來？」12耶穌說：「以利亞固然先來復興萬事，經上不是指着人子說，他要受許多的苦，被人輕慢呢？13我告訴你們：以利亞已經來了，他們也任意待他，正如經上所指着他的話。」

33But when Jesus turned and looked at his disciples, he rebuked Peter. "Get behind me, Satan!" he said. "You do not have in mind the things of God, but the things of men."

34Then he called the crowd to him along with his disciples and said: "If anyone would come after me, he must deny himself and take up his cross and follow me. 35For whoever wants to save his life*a* will lose it, but whoever loses his life for me and for the gospel will save it. 36What good is it for a man to gain the whole world, yet forfeit his soul? 37Or what can a man give in exchange for his soul? 38If anyone is ashamed of me and my words in this adulterous and sinful generation, the Son of Man will be ashamed of him when he comes in his Father's glory with the holy angels."

9 And he said to them, "I tell you the truth, some who are standing here will not taste death before they see the kingdom of God come with power."

The Transfiguration

2After six days Jesus took Peter, James and John with him and led them up a high mountain, where they were all alone. There he was transfigured before them. 3His clothes became dazzling white, whiter than anyone in the world could bleach them. 4And there appeared before them Elijah and Moses, who were talking with Jesus.

5Peter said to Jesus, "Rabbi, it is good for us to be here. Let us put up three shelters—one for you, one for Moses and one for Elijah." 6(He did not know what to say, they were so frightened.)

7Then a cloud appeared and enveloped them, and a voice came from the cloud: "This is my Son, whom I love. Listen to him!"

8Suddenly, when they looked around, they no longer saw anyone with them except Jesus.

9As they were coming down the mountain, Jesus gave them orders not to tell anyone what they had seen until the Son of Man had risen from the dead. 10They kept the matter to themselves, discussing what "rising from the dead" meant.

11And they asked him, "Why do the teachers of the law say that Elijah must come first?"

12Jesus replied, "To be sure, Elijah does come first, and restores all things. Why then is it written that the Son of Man must suffer much and be rejected? 13But I tell you, Elijah has come, and they have done to him everything they wished, just as it is written about him."

a 35 The Greek word means either life or soul; also in verse 36.

The Healing of a Boy With an Evil Spirit

[14]When they came to the other disciples, they saw a large crowd around them and the teachers of the law arguing with them. [15]As soon as all the people saw Jesus, they were overwhelmed with wonder and ran to greet him.

[16]"What are you arguing with them about?" he asked.

[17]A man in the crowd answered, "Teacher, I brought you my son, who is possessed by a spirit that has robbed him of speech. [18]Whenever it seizes him, it throws him to the ground. He foams at the mouth, gnashes his teeth and becomes rigid. I asked your disciples to drive out the spirit, but they could not."

[19]"O unbelieving generation," Jesus replied, "how long shall I stay with you? How long shall I put up with you? Bring the boy to me."

[20]So they brought him. When the spirit saw Jesus, it immediately threw the boy into a convulsion. He fell to the ground and rolled around, foaming at the mouth.

[21]Jesus asked the boy's father, "How long has he been like this?"

"From childhood," he answered. [22]"It has often thrown him into fire or water to kill him. But if you can do anything, take pity on us and help us."

[23]" 'If you can'?" said Jesus. "Everything is possible for him who believes."

[24]Immediately the boy's father exclaimed, "I do believe; help me overcome my unbelief!"

[25]When Jesus saw that a crowd was running to the scene, he rebuked the evil[a] spirit. "You deaf and mute spirit," he said, "I command you, come out of him and never enter him again."

[26]The spirit shrieked, convulsed him violently and came out. The boy looked so much like a corpse that many said, "He's dead." [27]But Jesus took him by the hand and lifted him to his feet, and he stood up.

[28]After Jesus had gone indoors, his disciples asked him privately, "Why couldn't we drive it out?"

[29]He replied, "This kind can come out only by prayer.[b]"

[30]They left that place and passed through Galilee. Jesus did not want anyone to know where they were, [31]because he was teaching his disciples. He said to them, "The Son of Man is going to be betrayed into the hands of men. They will kill him, and after three days he will rise." [32]But they did not understand what he meant and were afraid to ask him about it.

a 25 Greek unclean   b 29 Some manuscripts prayer and fasting

醫治被污鬼附着的男孩

[14]耶穌到了門徒那裏，看見有許多人圍着他們，又有文士和他們辯論。[15]眾人一見耶穌，都甚希奇，就跑上去問他的安。

[16]耶穌問他們說："你們和他們辯論的是甚麼？"

[17]眾人中間有一個人回答說："夫子，我帶了我的兒子到你這裏來，他被啞巴鬼附着。[18]無論在哪裏，鬼捉弄他，把他摔倒，他就口中流沫，咬牙切齒，身體枯乾。我請過你的門徒把鬼趕出去，他們卻是不能。"

[19]耶穌說："噯，不信的世代啊！我在你們這裏要到幾時呢？我忍耐你們要到幾時呢？把他帶到我這裏來吧。"

[20]他們就帶了他來。他一見耶穌，鬼便叫他重重地抽風，倒在地上，翻來覆去，口中流沫。

[21]耶穌問他父親說："他得這病有多少日子呢？"

回答說："從小的時候。[22]鬼屢次把他扔在火裏，水裏，要滅他。你若能做甚麼，求你憐憫我們，幫助我們！"

[23]耶穌對他說："你若能信，在信的人，凡事都能。"

[24]孩子的父親立時喊着說（註：有古卷作"立時流淚地喊着說"）："我信，但我信不足，求主幫助！"

[25]耶穌看見眾人都跑上來，就斥責那污鬼說："你這聾啞的鬼，我吩咐你從他裏頭出來，再不要進去！"

[26]那鬼喊叫，使孩子大大地抽了一陣風，就出來了。孩子好像死了一般。以致眾人多半說："他是死了。"[27]但耶穌拉着他的手，扶他起來，他就站起來了。

[28]耶穌進了屋子，門徒就暗暗地問他說："我們為甚麼不能趕出他去呢？"

[29]耶穌說："非用禱告（註：有古卷在此有"禁食"二字），這一類的鬼總不能出來（註：或作"不能趕他出來"）。"

[30]他們離開那地方，經過加利利，耶穌不願意人知道。[31]於是教訓門徒，說："人子將要被交在人手裏，他們要殺害他；被殺以後，過三天他要復活。"[32]門徒卻不明白這話，又不敢問他。

誰為大？

³³他們來到迦百農。耶穌在屋裏問門徒說：「你們在路上議論的是甚麼？」³⁴門徒不做聲，因為他們在路上彼此爭論誰為大。

³⁵耶穌坐下，叫十二個門徒來，說：「若有人願意作首先的，他必作眾人末後的，作眾人的用人。」

³⁶於是領過一個小孩子來，叫他站在門徒中間，又抱起他來，對他們說：³⁷「凡為我名接待一個像這小孩子的，就是接待我；凡接待我的，不是接待我，乃是接待那差我來的。」

不敵擋我們的就是幫助我們的

³⁸約翰對耶穌說：「夫子，我們看見一個人奉你的名趕鬼，我們就禁止他，因為他不跟從我們。」

³⁹耶穌說：「不要禁止他，因為沒有人奉我名行異能，反倒輕易毀謗我。⁴⁰不敵擋我們的，就是幫助我們的。⁴¹凡因你們是屬基督，給你們一杯水喝的，我實在告訴你們：他不能不得賞賜。

使人跌倒

⁴²「凡使這信我的一個小子跌倒的，倒不如把大磨石拴在這人的頸項上，扔在海裏。⁴³倘若你一隻手叫你跌倒，就把它砍下來；⁴⁴你缺了肢體進入永生，強如有兩隻手落到地獄，入那不滅的火裏去。⁴⁵倘若你一隻腳叫你跌倒，就把它砍下來；⁴⁶你瘸腿進入永生，強如有兩隻腳被丟在地獄裏。⁴⁷倘若你一隻眼叫你跌倒，就去掉它；你只有一隻眼進入神的國，強如有兩隻眼被丟在地獄裏。⁴⁸在那裏，

「『蟲是不死的，
　火是不滅的。』

⁴⁹因為必用火當鹽醃各人（註：有古卷在此有「凡祭物必用鹽醃」）。

⁵⁰「鹽本是好的，若失了味，可用甚麼叫它再鹹呢？你們裏頭應當有鹽，彼此和睦。」

Who Is the Greatest?

³³They came to Capernaum. When he was in the house, he asked them, "What were you arguing about on the road?" ³⁴But they kept quiet because on the way they had argued about who was the greatest.

³⁵Sitting down, Jesus called the Twelve and said, "If anyone wants to be first, he must be the very last, and the servant of all."

³⁶He took a little child and had him stand among them. Taking him in his arms, he said to them, ³⁷"Whoever welcomes one of these little children in my name welcomes me; and whoever welcomes me does not welcome me but the one who sent me."

Whoever Is Not Against Us Is for Us

³⁸"Teacher," said John, "we saw a man driving out demons in your name and we told him to stop, because he was not one of us."

³⁹"Do not stop him," Jesus said. "No one who does a miracle in my name can in the next moment say anything bad about me, ⁴⁰for whoever is not against us is for us. ⁴¹I tell you the truth, anyone who gives you a cup of water in my name because you belong to Christ will certainly not lose his reward.

Causing to Sin

⁴²"And if anyone causes one of these little ones who believe in me to sin, it would be better for him to be thrown into the sea with a large millstone tied around his neck. ⁴³If your hand causes you to sin, cut it off. It is better for you to enter life maimed than with two hands to go into hell, where the fire never goes out.^a ⁴⁵And if your foot causes you to sin, cut it off. It is better for you to enter life crippled than to have two feet and be thrown into hell.^b ⁴⁷And if your eye causes you to sin, pluck it out. It is better for you to enter the kingdom of God with one eye than to have two eyes and be thrown into hell, ⁴⁸where

"'their worm does not die,
　and the fire is not quenched.'^c

⁴⁹Everyone will be salted with fire.

⁵⁰"Salt is good, but if it loses its saltiness, how can you make it salty again? Have salt in yourselves, and be at peace with each other."

a 43 Some manuscripts out, ⁴⁴where | " 'their worm does not die, | and the fire is not quenched.' b 45 Some manuscripts hell, ⁴⁶where | " 'their worm does not die, | and the fire is not quenched.' c 48 Isaiah 66:24

Divorce

10 Jesus then left that place and went into the region of Judea and across the Jordan. Again crowds of people came to him, and as was his custom, he taught them.

[2] Some Pharisees came and tested him by asking, "Is it lawful for a man to divorce his wife?"

[3] "What did Moses command you?" he replied.

[4] They said, "Moses permitted a man to write a certificate of divorce and send her away."

[5] "It was because your hearts were hard that Moses wrote you this law," Jesus replied. [6] "But at the beginning of creation God 'made them male and female.'[a] [7] 'For this reason a man will leave his father and mother and be united to his wife,[b] [8] and the two will become one flesh.'[c] So they are no longer two, but one. [9] Therefore what God has joined together, let man not separate."

[10] When they were in the house again, the disciples asked Jesus about this. [11] He answered, "Anyone who divorces his wife and marries another woman commits adultery against her. [12] And if she divorces her husband and marries another man, she commits adultery."

The Little Children and Jesus

[13] People were bringing little children to Jesus to have him touch them, but the disciples rebuked them. [14] When Jesus saw this, he was indignant. He said to them, "Let the little children come to me, and do not hinder them, for the kingdom of God belongs to such as these. [15] I tell you the truth, anyone who will not receive the kingdom of God like a little child will never enter it." [16] And he took the children in his arms, put his hands on them and blessed them.

The Rich Young Man

[17] As Jesus started on his way, a man ran up to him and fell on his knees before him. "Good teacher," he asked, "what must I do to inherit eternal life?"

[18] "Why do you call me good?" Jesus answered. "No one is good—except God alone. [19] You know the commandments: 'Do not murder, do not commit adultery, do not steal, do not give false testimony, do not defraud, honor your father and mother.'[d]"

[20] "Teacher," he declared, "all these I have kept since I was a boy."

休妻

10 耶穌從那裏起身,來到猶太的境界<u>並約旦河外</u>。眾人又聚集到他那裏,他又照常教訓他們。

[2] 有法利賽人來問他說:"人休妻可以不可以?"意思要試探他。

[3] 耶穌回答說:"<u>摩西</u>吩咐你們的是甚麼?"

[4] 他們說:"<u>摩西</u>許人寫了休書便可以休妻。"

[5] 耶穌說:"<u>摩西</u>因為你們的心硬,所以寫這條例給你們。[6] 但從起初創造的時候,神造人是造男造女。[7] 因此,人要離開父母,與妻子連合,二人成為一體。[8] 既然如此,夫妻不再是兩個人,乃是一體的了。[9] 所以神配合的,人不可分開。"

[10] 到了屋裏,門徒就問他這事。[11] 耶穌對他們說:"凡休妻另娶的,就是犯姦淫,辜負他的妻子;[12] 妻子若離棄丈夫另嫁,也是犯姦淫了。"

小孩與耶穌

[13] 有人帶着小孩子來見耶穌,要耶穌摸他們,門徒便責備那些人。[14] 耶穌看見就惱怒,對門徒說:"讓小孩子到我這裏來,不要禁止他們,因為在神國的,正是這樣的人。[15] 我實在告訴你們:凡要承受神國的,若不像小孩子,斷不能進去。"[16] 於是抱着小孩子,給他們按手,為他們祝福。

富有的少年人

[17] 耶穌出來行路的時候,有一個人跑來,跪在他面前,問他說:"良善的夫子,我當做甚麼事才可以承受永生?"

[18] 耶穌對他說:"你為甚麼稱我是良善的?除了神一位之外,再沒有良善的。[19] 誡命你是曉得的:'不可殺人,不可姦淫,不可偷盜,不可作假見證,不可虧負人,當孝敬父母。'"

[20] 他對耶穌說:"夫子,這一切我從小都遵守了。"

---

a 6 Gen. 1:27   b 7 Some early manuscripts do not have *and be united to his wife.*   c 8 Gen. 2:24   d 19 Exodus 20:12-16; Deut. 5:16-20

²¹耶穌看着他，就愛他，對他說：「你還缺少一件，去變賣你所有的，分給窮人，就必有財寶在天上；你還要來跟從我。」

²²他聽見這話，臉上就變了色，憂憂愁愁地走了，因為他的產業很多。

²³耶穌周圍一看，對門徒說：「有錢財的人進神的國是何等地難哪！」

²⁴門徒希奇他的話。耶穌又對他們說：「小子，倚靠錢財的人進神的國是何等的難哪！²⁵駱駝穿過針的眼，比財主進神的國還容易呢。」

²⁶門徒就分外希奇，對他說：「這樣，誰能得救呢？」

²⁷耶穌看着他們，說：「在人是不能，在神卻不然，因為神凡事都能。」

²⁸彼得就對他說：「看哪，我們已經撇下所有的跟從你了。」

²⁹耶穌說：「我實在告訴你們：人為我和福音撇下房屋，或是弟兄、姐妹、父母、兒女、田地，³⁰沒有不在今世得百倍的，就是房屋、弟兄、姐妹、母親、兒女、田地，並且要受逼迫，在來世必得永生。³¹然而，有許多在前的，將要在後；在後的，將要在前。」

耶穌再預言自己的死

³²他們行路上耶路撒冷去。耶穌在前頭走，門徒就希奇，跟從的人也害怕。耶穌又叫過十二個門徒來，把自己將要遭遇的事告訴他們：³³「看哪，我們上耶路撒冷去，人子將要被交給祭司長和文士，他們要定他死罪，交給外邦人。³⁴他們要戲弄他，吐唾沫在他臉上，鞭打他，殺害他。過了三天，他要復活。」

雅各和約翰的請求

³⁵西庇太的兒子雅各、約翰進前來，對耶穌說：「夫子，我們無論求你甚麼，願你給我們做。」

³⁶耶穌說：「要我給你們做甚麼？」

²¹Jesus looked at him and loved him. "One thing you lack," he said. "Go, sell everything you have and give to the poor, and you will have treasure in heaven. Then come, follow me."

²²At this the man's face fell. He went away sad, because he had great wealth.

²³Jesus looked around and said to his disciples, "How hard it is for the rich to enter the kingdom of God!"

²⁴The disciples were amazed at his words. But Jesus said again, "Children, how hard it is*a* to enter the kingdom of God! ²⁵It is easier for a camel to go through the eye of a needle than for a rich man to enter the kingdom of God."

²⁶The disciples were even more amazed, and said to each other, "Who then can be saved?"

²⁷Jesus looked at them and said, "With man this is impossible, but not with God; all things are possible with God."

²⁸Peter said to him, "We have left everything to follow you!"

²⁹"I tell you the truth," Jesus replied, "no one who has left home or brothers or sisters or mother or father or children or fields for me and the gospel ³⁰will fail to receive a hundred times as much in this present age (homes, brothers, sisters, mothers, children and fields—and with them, persecutions) and in the age to come, eternal life. ³¹But many who are first will be last, and the last first."

Jesus Again Predicts His Death

³²They were on their way up to Jerusalem, with Jesus leading the way, and the disciples were astonished, while those who followed were afraid. Again he took the Twelve aside and told them what was going to happen to him. ³³"We are going up to Jerusalem," he said, "and the Son of Man will be betrayed to the chief priests and teachers of the law. They will condemn him to death and will hand him over to the Gentiles, ³⁴who will mock him and spit on him, flog him and kill him. Three days later he will rise."

The Request of James and John

³⁵Then James and John, the sons of Zebedee, came to him. "Teacher," they said, "we want you to do for us whatever we ask."

³⁶"What do you want me to do for you?" he asked.

---

a 24 Some manuscripts is for those who trust in riches

37They replied, "Let one of us sit at your right and the other at your left in your glory."

38"You don't know what you are asking," Jesus said. "Can you drink the cup I drink or be baptized with the baptism I am baptized with?"

39"We can," they answered.

Jesus said to them, "You will drink the cup I drink and be baptized with the baptism I am baptized with, 40but to sit at my right or left is not for me to grant. These places belong to those for whom they have been prepared."

41When the ten heard about this, they became indignant with James and John. 42Jesus called them together and said, "You know that those who are regarded as rulers of the Gentiles lord it over them, and their high officials exercise authority over them. 43Not so with you. Instead, whoever wants to become great among you must be your servant, 44and whoever wants to be first must be slave of all. 45For even the Son of Man did not come to be served, but to serve, and to give his life as a ransom for many."

Blind Bartimaeus Receives His Sight

46Then they came to Jericho. As Jesus and his disciples, together with a large crowd, were leaving the city, a blind man, Bartimaeus (that is, the Son of Timaeus), was sitting by the roadside begging. 47When he heard that it was Jesus of Nazareth, he began to shout, "Jesus, Son of David, have mercy on me!"

48Many rebuked him and told him to be quiet, but he shouted all the more, "Son of David, have mercy on me!"

49Jesus stopped and said, "Call him."

So they called to the blind man, "Cheer up! On your feet! He's calling you." 50Throwing his cloak aside, he jumped to his feet and came to Jesus.

51"What do you want me to do for you?" Jesus asked him.

The blind man said, "Rabbi, I want to see."

52"Go," said Jesus, "your faith has healed you." Immediately he received his sight and followed Jesus along the road.

The Triumphal Entry

11 As they approached Jerusalem and came to Bethphage and Bethany at the Mount of Olives, Jesus sent two of his disciples, 2saying to them, "Go to the village ahead of you, and just as you enter it, you will find a colt tied there, which no one has ever ridden. Untie it and bring it here. 3If anyone asks you, 'Why are you doing this?' tell him, 'The Lord needs it and will send it back here shortly.' "

37他們說："賜我們在你的榮耀裏，一個坐在你右邊，一個坐在你左邊。"

38耶穌說："你們不知道所求的是甚麼。我所喝的杯，你們能喝嗎？我所受的洗，你們能受嗎？"

39他們說："我們能。"

耶穌說："我所喝的杯，你們也要喝；我所受的洗，你們也要受。40只是坐在我的左右，不是我可以賜的，乃是為誰預備的，就賜給誰。"

41那十個門徒聽見，就惱怒雅各、約翰。42耶穌叫他們來，對他們說："你們知道，外邦人有尊為君王的，治理他們，有大臣操權管束他們。43只是在你們中間，不是這樣。你們中間，誰願為大，就必作你們的用人；44在你們中間，誰願為首，就必作眾人的僕人。45因為人子來，並不是要受人的服侍，乃是要服侍人，並且要捨命作多人的贖價。"

瞎子巴底買得看見

46到了耶利哥，耶穌同門徒並許多人出耶利哥的時候，有一個討飯的瞎子，是底買的兒子巴底買，坐在路旁。47他聽見是拿撒勒的耶穌，就喊着說："大衛的子孫耶穌啊，可憐我吧！"

48有許多人責備他，不許他做聲。他卻越發大聲喊着說："大衛的子孫哪，可憐我吧！"

49耶穌就站住，說："叫過他來。"

他們就叫那瞎子，對他說："放心！起來，他叫你啦。"50瞎子就丟下衣服，跳起來，走到耶穌那裏。

51耶穌說："要我為你做甚麼？"

瞎子說："拉波尼（註："拉波尼"就是"夫子"），我要能看見！"

52耶穌說："你去吧，你的信救了你了。"瞎子立刻看見了，就在路上跟隨耶穌。

光榮進聖城

11 耶穌和門徒將近耶路撒冷，到了伯法其和伯大尼，在橄欖山那裏。耶穌就打發兩個門徒，2對他們說："你們往對面村子裏去，一進去的時候，必看見一匹驢駒拴在那裏，是從來沒有人騎過的；可以解開，牽來。3若有人對你們說：'為甚麼做這事？'你們就說：'主要用牠。'那人必立時讓你們牽來。"

⁴他們去了，便看見一匹驢駒拴在門外街道上，就把牠解開。⁵在那裏站着的人，有幾個說：「你們解驢駒做甚麼？」⁶門徒照着耶穌所說的回答，那些人就任憑他們牽去了。⁷他們把驢駒牽到耶穌那裏，把自己的衣服搭在上面，耶穌就騎上。⁸有許多人把衣服鋪在路上，也有人把田間的樹枝砍下來，鋪在路上。⁹前行後隨的人都喊着說：

「和散那（註：「和散那」原在「求救」的意思，在此乃是稱頌的話）！」

「奉主名來的是應當稱頌的！」

10 「那將要來的我祖大衛之國是應當稱頌的！」

「高高在上和散那！」

11耶穌進了耶路撒冷，入了聖殿，周圍看了各樣物件。天色已晚，就和十二個門徒出城，往伯大尼去了。

耶穌潔淨聖殿

12第二天，他們從伯大尼出來，耶穌餓了。13遠遠地看見一棵無花果樹，樹上有葉子，就往那裏去，或者在樹上可以找着甚麼。到了樹下，竟找不着甚麼，不過有葉子，因為不是收無花果的時候。14耶穌就對樹說：「從今以後，永沒有人吃你的果子。」他的門徒也聽見了。

15他們來到耶路撒冷。耶穌進入聖殿，趕出殿裏做買賣的人，推倒兌換銀錢之人的桌子和賣鴿子之人的凳子，16也不許人拿着器具從殿裏經過。17便教訓他們說：「經上不是記着說：

「『我的殿必稱為萬國禱告的殿』嗎？

你們倒使它成為賊窩了。」

18祭司長和文士聽見這話，就想

⁴They went and found a colt outside in the street, tied at a doorway. As they untied it, ⁵some people standing there asked, "What are you doing, untying that colt?" ⁶They answered as Jesus had told them to, and the people let them go. ⁷When they brought the colt to Jesus and threw their cloaks over it, he sat on it. ⁸Many people spread their cloaks on the road, while others spread branches they had cut in the fields. ⁹Those who went ahead and those who followed shouted,

"Hosanna!ᵃ"

"Blessed is he who comes in the name of the Lord!"ᵇ

10"Blessed is the coming kingdom of our father David!"

"Hosanna in the highest!"

11Jesus entered Jerusalem and went to the temple. He looked around at everything, but since it was already late, he went out to Bethany with the Twelve.

Jesus Clears the Temple

12The next day as they were leaving Bethany, Jesus was hungry. 13Seeing in the distance a fig tree in leaf, he went to find out if it had any fruit. When he reached it, he found nothing but leaves, because it was not the season for figs. 14Then he said to the tree, "May no one ever eat fruit from you again." And his disciples heard him say it.

15On reaching Jerusalem, Jesus entered the temple area and began driving out those who were buying and selling there. He overturned the tables of the money changers and the benches of those selling doves, 16and would not allow anyone to carry merchandise through the temple courts. 17And as he taught them, he said, "Is it not written:

" 'My house will be called
a house of prayer for all nations'ᶜ?

But you have made it 'a den of robbers.'ᵈ "

18The chief priests and the teachers of the law heard this and began looking for a way to kill

---

a 9 A Hebrew expression meaning "Save!" which became an exclamation of praise; also in verse 10　　*b 9* Psalm 118:25,26　　*c 17* Isaiah 56:7　　*d 17* Jer. 7:11

him, for they feared him, because the whole crowd was amazed at his teaching.

[19]When evening came, they[a] went out of the city.

The Withered Fig Tree

[20]In the morning, as they went along, they saw the fig tree withered from the roots. [21]Peter remembered and said to Jesus, "Rabbi, look! The fig tree you cursed has withered!"

[22]"Have[b] faith in God," Jesus answered. [23]"I tell you the truth, if anyone says to this mountain, 'Go, throw yourself into the sea,' and does not doubt in his heart but believes that what he says will happen, it will be done for him. [24]Therefore I tell you, whatever you ask for in prayer, believe that you have received it, and it will be yours. [25]And when you stand praying, if you hold anything against anyone, forgive him, so that your Father in heaven may forgive you your sins.[c]"

The Authority of Jesus Questioned

[27]They arrived again in Jerusalem, and while Jesus was walking in the temple courts, the chief priests, the teachers of the law and the elders came to him. [28]"By what authority are you doing these things?" they asked. "And who gave you authority to do this?"

[29]Jesus replied, "I will ask you one question. Answer me, and I will tell you by what authority I am doing these things. [30]John's baptism— was it from heaven, or from men? Tell me!"

[31]They discussed it among themselves and said, "If we say, 'From heaven,' he will ask, 'Then why didn't you believe him?' [32]But if we say, 'From men' . . . ." (They feared the people, for everyone held that John really was a prophet.)

[33]So they answered Jesus, "We don't know."

Jesus said, "Neither will I tell you by what authority I am doing these things."

The Parable of the Tenants

12 He then began to speak to them in parables: "A man planted a vineyard. He put a wall around it, dug a pit for the winepress and built a watchtower. Then he rented the vineyard to some farmers and went away on a journey. [2]At harvest time he sent a servant to the tenants to collect from them some of the fruit of the vineyard. [3]But they seized him, beat

---

法子要除滅耶穌,卻又怕他,因為眾人都希奇他的教訓。

[19]每天晚上,耶穌出城去。

枯乾了的無花果樹

[20]早晨,他們從那裏經過,看見無花果樹連根都枯乾了。[21]彼得想起耶穌的話來,就對他說:"拉比,請看!你所咒詛的無花果樹,已經枯乾了。"[22]耶穌回答說:"你們當信服神。[23]我實在告訴你們:無論何人對這座山說:'你挪開此地,投在海裏!'他若心裏不疑惑,只信他所說的必成,就必給他成了。[24]所以我告訴你們:凡你們禱告祈求的,無論是甚麼,只要信是得着的,就必得着。[25]你們站着禱告的時候,若想起有人得罪你們,就當饒恕他,好叫你們在天上的父也饒恕你們的過犯。[26]你們若不饒恕人,你們在天上的父也不饒恕你們的過犯。(註:有古卷無此節)"

耶穌的權柄被質問

[27]他們又來到耶路撒冷。耶穌在殿裏行走的時候,祭司長和文士並長老進前來,[28]問他說:"你仗着甚麼權柄做這些事,給你這權柄的是誰呢?"

[29]耶穌對他們說:"我要問你們一句話,你們回答我,我就告訴你們我仗着甚麼權柄做這些事。[30]約翰的洗禮是從天上來的,是從人間來的呢?你們可以回答我。"

[31]他們彼此商議說:"我們若說'從天上來',他必說:'這樣,你們為甚麼不信他呢?'[32]若說'從人間來',卻又怕百姓,因為眾人真以約翰為先知。"

[33]於是回答耶穌說:"我們不知道。"耶穌說:"我也不告訴你們我仗着甚麼權柄做這些事。"

園戶的比喻

12 耶穌就用比喻對他們說:"有人栽了一個葡萄園,周圍圈上籬笆,挖了一個壓酒池,蓋了一座樓,租給園戶,就往外國去了。[2]到了時候,打發一個僕人到園戶那裏,要從園戶收葡萄園的果子。[3]園戶拿住他,打了他,叫他空

---

a 19 Some early manuscripts he   b 22 Some early manuscripts If you have   c 25 Some manuscripts sins. 26 But if you do not forgive, neither will your Father who is in heaven forgive your sins.

手回去。⁴再打發一個僕人到他們那裏，他們打傷他的頭，並且凌辱他。⁵又打發一個僕人去，他們就殺了他。後又打發好些僕人去，有被他們打的，有被他們殺的。

⁶「園主還有一位是他的愛子，末後又打發他去，意思說：『他們必尊敬我的兒子。』

⁷「不料，那些園戶彼此說：『這是承受產業的。來吧，我們殺他，產業就歸我們了！』⁸於是拿住他，殺了他，把他丟在園外。

⁹「這樣，葡萄園的主人要怎麼辦呢？他要來除滅那些園戶，將葡萄園轉給別人。¹⁰經上寫着說：

「「匠人所棄的石頭，
　　已作了房角的頭塊石頭。
¹¹這是主所做的，
　　在我們眼中看為希奇。』
這經你們沒有念過嗎？」

¹²他們看出這比喻是指着他們說的，就想要捉拿他，只是懼怕百姓，於是離開他走了。

納稅給凱撒

¹³後來，他們打發幾個法利賽人和幾個希律黨的人到耶穌那裏，要就着他的話陷害他。¹⁴他們來了，就對他說：「夫子，我們知道你是誠實的，甚麼人你都不徇情面，因為你不看人的外貌，乃是誠誠實實傳神的道。納稅給凱撒可以不可以？¹⁵我們該納不該納？」

耶穌知道他們的假意，就對他們說：「你們為甚麼試探我，拿一個銀錢來給我看。」¹⁶他們就拿了來。耶穌說：「這像和這號是誰的？」

他們說：「是凱撒的。」

¹⁷耶穌說：「凱撒的物當歸給凱撒，神的物當歸給神。」他們就很希奇他。

復活時的婚姻關係

¹⁸撒都該人常說沒有復活的事。他們來問耶穌說：¹⁹「夫子，摩西為我們寫着說：『人若死了，撇下妻子，沒有孩子，他兄弟當娶他的

---

him and sent him away empty-handed. ⁴Then he sent another servant to them; they struck this man on the head and treated him shamefully. ⁵He sent still another, and that one they killed. He sent many others; some of them they beat, others they killed.

⁶"He had one left to send, a son, whom he loved. He sent him last of all, saying, 'They will respect my son.'

⁷"But the tenants said to one another, 'This is the heir. Come, let's kill him, and the inheritance will be ours.' ⁸So they took him and killed him, and threw him out of the vineyard.

⁹"What then will the owner of the vineyard do? He will come and kill those tenants and give the vineyard to others. ¹⁰Haven't you read this scripture:

" 'The stone the builders rejected
　　has become the capstone*a*;
¹¹the Lord has done this,
　　and it is marvelous in our eyes'*b*?"

¹²Then they looked for a way to arrest him because they knew he had spoken the parable against them. But they were afraid of the crowd; so they left him and went away.

Paying Taxes to Caesar

¹³Later they sent some of the Pharisees and Herodians to Jesus to catch him in his words. ¹⁴They came to him and said, "Teacher, we know you are a man of integrity. You aren't swayed by men, because you pay no attention to who they are; but you teach the way of God in accordance with the truth. Is it right to pay taxes to Caesar or not? ¹⁵Should we pay or shouldn't we?"

But Jesus knew their hypocrisy. "Why are you trying to trap me?" he asked. "Bring me a denarius and let me look at it." ¹⁶They brought the coin, and he asked them, "Whose portrait is this? And whose inscription?"

"Caesar's," they replied.

¹⁷Then Jesus said to them, "Give to Caesar what is Caesar's and to God what is God's."

And they were amazed at him.

Marriage at the Resurrection

¹⁸Then the Sadducees, who say there is no resurrection, came to him with a question. ¹⁹"Teacher," they said, "Moses wrote for us that if a man's brother dies and leaves a wife but no children, the man must marry the widow and

---

a 10 Or *cornerstone*　　*b 11* Psalm 118:22,23

have children for his brother. 20Now there were seven brothers. The first one married and died without leaving any children. 21The second one married the widow, but he also died, leaving no child. It was the same with the third. 22In fact, none of the seven left any children. Last of all, the woman died too. 23At the resurrection[a] whose wife will she be, since the seven were married to her?"

24Jesus replied, "Are you not in error because you do not know the Scriptures or the power of God? 25When the dead rise, they will neither marry nor be given in marriage; they will be like the angels in heaven. 26Now about the dead rising—have you not read in the book of Moses, in the account of the bush, how God said to him, 'I am the God of Abraham, the God of Isaac, and the God of Jacob'[b]? 27He is not the God of the dead, but of the living. You are badly mistaken!"

The Greatest Commandment

28One of the teachers of the law came and heard them debating. Noticing that Jesus had given them a good answer, he asked him, "Of all the commandments, which is the most important?"

29"The most important one," answered Jesus, "is this: 'Hear, O Israel, the Lord our God, the Lord is one.[c] 30Love the Lord your God with all your heart and with all your soul and with all your mind and with all your strength.'[d] 31The second is this: 'Love your neighbor as yourself.'[e] There is no commandment greater than these."

32"Well said, teacher," the man replied. "You are right in saying that God is one and there is no other but him. 33To love him with all your heart, with all your understanding and with all your strength, and to love your neighbor as yourself is more important than all burnt offerings and sacrifices."

34When Jesus saw that he had answered wisely, he said to him, "You are not far from the kingdom of God." And from then on no one dared ask him any more questions.

Whose Son Is the Christ?

35While Jesus was teaching in the temple courts, he asked, "How is it that the teachers of the law say that the Christ[f] is the son of David? 36David himself, speaking by the Holy Spirit, declared:

妻，為哥哥生子立後。'20有弟兄七人，第一個娶了妻，死了，沒有留下孩子；21第二個娶了她，也死了，沒有留下孩子；第三個也是這樣。22那七個人都沒有留下孩子，末了，那婦人也死了。23當復活的時候，她是哪一個的妻子呢？因為他們七個人都娶過她。"

24耶穌說："你們所以錯了，豈不是因為不明白聖經，不曉得神的大能嗎？25人從死裏復活，也不娶也不嫁，乃像天上的使者一樣。26論到死人復活，你們沒有念過摩西的書荊棘篇上所載的嗎？神對摩西說：'我是亞伯拉罕的神，以撒的神，雅各的神。'27神不是死人的神，乃是活人的神。你們是大錯了。"

最大的誡命

28有一個文士來，聽見他們辯論，曉得耶穌回答得好，就問他說："誡命中哪是第一要緊的呢？"

29耶穌回答說："第一要緊的就是說：'以色列啊，你要聽！主我們神是獨一的主。30你要盡心、盡性、盡意、盡力愛主你的神。'31其次就是說：'要愛人如己。'再沒有比這兩條誡命更大的了。"

32那文士對耶穌說："夫子說，神是一位，實在不錯！除了他以外，再沒有別的神。33並且盡心、盡智、盡力愛他，又愛人如己，就比一切燔祭和各樣祭祀好得多。"

34耶穌見他回答得有智慧，就對他說："你離神的國不遠了。"從此以後，沒有人敢再問他甚麼。

基督是誰的子孫？

35耶穌在殿裏教訓人，就問他們說："文士怎麼說基督是大衛的子孫呢？36大衛被聖靈感動，說：

---

a 23 Some manuscripts resurrection, when men rise from the dead,
b 26 Exodus 3:6   c 29 Or the Lord our God is one Lord
d 30 Deut. 6:4,5   e 31 Lev. 19:18   f 35 Or Messiah

" '主對我主説:
　你坐在我的右邊,
等我使你仇敵
　作你的腳凳。'

³⁷大衛既自己稱他為主,他怎麼又是大衛的子孫呢?"

眾人都喜歡聽他。

³⁸耶穌在教訓之間,説:"你們要防備文士,他們好穿長衣遊行,喜愛人在街市上問他們的安,³⁹又喜愛會堂裏的高位,筵席上的首座;⁴⁰他們侵吞寡婦的家產,假意作很長的禱告。這些人要受更重的刑罰。"

寡婦的奉獻

⁴¹耶穌對着銀庫坐着,看眾人怎樣投錢入庫。有好些財主往裏投了若干的錢。⁴²有一個窮寡婦來,往裏投了兩個小錢,就是一個大錢。

⁴³耶穌叫門徒來,説:"我實在告訴你們:這窮寡婦投入庫裏的,比眾人所投的更多。⁴⁴因為,他們都是自己有餘,拿出來投在裏頭,但這寡婦是自己不足,把她一切養生的都投上了。"

末世的預兆

13 耶穌從殿裏出來的時候,有一個門徒對他説:"夫子,請看,這是何等的石頭,何等的殿宇!"

²耶穌對他説:"你看見這大殿宇嗎?將來在這裏沒有一塊石頭留在石頭上不被拆毀了。"

³耶穌在橄欖山上對聖殿而坐。彼得、雅各、約翰和安得烈暗暗地問他説:⁴"請告訴我們,甚麼時候有這些事呢?這一切事將成的時候有甚麼預兆呢?"

⁵耶穌説:"你們要謹慎,免得有人迷惑你們。⁶將來有好些人冒我的名來,説:'我是基督',並且要迷惑許多人。⁷你們聽見打仗和打仗的風聲,不要驚慌。這些事是必須有的,只是末期還沒有到。⁸民要攻打民,國要攻打國,多處必有地震、饑荒。這都是災難(註:"災難",原文作"生產之難")的起頭。

" 'The Lord said to my Lord:
　"Sit at my right hand
until I put your enemies
　under your feet." ' ᵃ

³⁷David himself calls him 'Lord.' How then can he be his son?"

The large crowd listened to him with delight.

³⁸As he taught, Jesus said, "Watch out for the teachers of the law. They like to walk around in flowing robes and be greeted in the market-places, ³⁹and have the most important seats in the synagogues and the places of honor at banquets. ⁴⁰They devour widows' houses and for a show make lengthy prayers. Such men will be punished most severely."

The Widow's Offering

⁴¹Jesus sat down opposite the place where the offerings were put and watched the crowd putting their money into the temple treasury. Many rich people threw in large amounts. ⁴²But a poor widow came and put in two very small copper coins,ᵇ worth only a fraction of a penny.ᶜ

⁴³Calling his disciples to him, Jesus said, "I tell you the truth, this poor widow has put more into the treasury than all the others. ⁴⁴They all gave out of their wealth; but she, out of her poverty, put in everything—all she had to live on."

Signs of the End of the Age

13 As he was leaving the temple, one of his disciples said to him, "Look, Teacher! What massive stones! What magnificent buildings!"

²"Do you see all these great buildings?" replied Jesus. "Not one stone here will be left on another; every one will be thrown down."

³As Jesus was sitting on the Mount of Olives opposite the temple, Peter, James, John and Andrew asked him privately, ⁴"Tell us, when will these things happen? And what will be the sign that they are all about to be fulfilled?"

⁵Jesus said to them: "Watch out that no one deceives you. ⁶Many will come in my name, claiming, 'I am he,' and will deceive many. ⁷When you hear of wars and rumors of wars, do not be alarmed. Such things must happen, but the end is still to come. ⁸Nation will rise against nation, and kingdom against kingdom. There will be earthquakes in various places, and famines. These are the beginning of birth pains.

a 36 Psalm 110:1　　b 42 Greek two lepta　　c 42 Greek kodrantes

9"You must be on your guard. You will be handed over to the local councils and flogged in the synagogues. On account of me you will stand before governors and kings as witnesses to them. 10And the gospel must first be preached to all nations. 11Whenever you are arrested and brought to trial, do not worry beforehand about what to say. Just say whatever is given you at the time, for it is not you speaking, but the Holy Spirit.

12"Brother will betray brother to death, and a father his child. Children will rebel against their parents and have them put to death. 13All men will hate you because of me, but he who stands firm to the end will be saved.

14"When you see 'the abomination that causes desolation'ᵃ standing where itᵇ does not belong—let the reader understand—then let those who are in Judea flee to the mountains. 15Let no one on the roof of his house go down or enter the house to take anything out. 16Let no one in the field go back to get his cloak. 17How dreadful it will be in those days for pregnant women and nursing mothers! 18Pray that this will not take place in winter, 19because those will be days of distress unequaled from the beginning, when God created the world, until now—and never to be equaled again. 20If the Lord had not cut short those days, no one would survive. But for the sake of the elect, whom he has chosen, he has shortened them. 21At that time if anyone says to you, 'Look, here is the Christᶜ!' or, 'Look, there he is!' do not believe it. 22For false Christs and false prophets will appear and perform signs and miracles to deceive the elect—if that were possible. 23So be on your guard; I have told you everything ahead of time.

24"But in those days, following that distress,

" 'the sun will be darkened,
    and the moon will not give its light;
25the stars will fall from the sky,
    and the heavenly bodies will be shaken.'ᵈ

26"At that time men will see the Son of Man coming in clouds with great power and glory. 27And he will send his angels and gather his elect from the four winds, from the ends of the earth to the ends of the heavens.

28"Now learn this lesson from the fig tree: As soon as its twigs get tender and its leaves come out, you know that summer is near. 29Even so,

9 "但你們要謹慎,因為人要把你們交給公會,並且你們在會堂裏要受鞭打;又為我的緣故站在諸侯與君王面前,對他們作見證。10然而,福音必須先傳給萬民。11人把你們拉去交官的時候,不要預先思慮說甚麼,到那時候,賜給你們甚麼話,你們就說甚麼,因為說話的不是你們,乃是聖靈。

12 "弟兄要把弟兄,父親要把兒子,送到死地;兒女要起來與父母為敵,害死他們。13並且你們要為我的名被眾人恨惡,惟有忍耐到底的,必然得救。

14 "你們看見那 '行毀壞可憎的',站在不當站的地方(讀這經的人須要會意)。那時,在猶太的,應當逃到山上;15在房上的,不要下來,也不要進去拿家裏的東西;16在田裏的,也不要回去取衣裳。17當那些日子,懷孕的和奶孩子的有禍了。18你們應當祈求,叫這些事不在冬天臨到。 19因為在那些日子必有災難,自從神創造萬物直到如今,並沒有這樣的災難,後來也必沒有。20若不是主減少那日子,凡有血氣的,總沒有一個得救的;只是為主的選民,他將那日子減少了。21那時若有人對你們說:'看哪,基督在這裏',或說:'基督在那裏',你們不要信。22因為假基督,假先知將要起來,顯神蹟奇事,倘若能行,就把選民迷惑了。 23你們要謹慎。看哪,凡事我都預先告訴你們了。

24 "在那些日子,那災難以後,

" '日頭要變黑了,
    月亮也不放光,
25眾星要從天上墜落,
    天勢都要震動。'

26 "那時,他們(註:馬太24章30節作"地上的萬族")要看見人子有大能力,大榮耀,駕雲降臨。27他要差遣天使,把他的選民,從四方(註:"方"原文作"風"),從地極直到天邊,都招聚了來。

28 "你們可以從無花果樹學個比方:當樹枝發嫩長葉的時候,你們就知道夏天近了。29這樣,你們幾時看

a 14 Daniel 9:27; 11:31; 12:11   b 14 Or he; also in verse 29
c 21 Or Messiah   d 25 Isaiah 13:10; 34:4

見這些事成就，也該知道人子（註：「人子」，或作「神的國」）近了，正在門口了。³⁰我實在告訴你們：這世代還沒有過去，這些事都要成就。³¹天地要廢去，我的話卻不能廢去！

那日子那時辰無人知道

³² "但那日子，那時辰，沒有人知道，連天上的使者也不知道，子也不知道，惟有父知道。³³你們要謹慎，警醒祈禱，因為你們不曉得那日期幾時來到。³⁴這事正如一個人離開本家，寄居外邦，把權柄交給僕人，分派各人當做的工，又吩咐看門的警醒。

³⁵ "所以，你們要警醒，因為你們不知道家主甚麼時候來，或晚上，或半夜，或雞叫，或早晨。³⁶恐怕他忽然來到，看見你們睡着了。³⁷我對你們所說的話，也是對眾人說：'要警醒！'"

耶穌在伯大尼受膏

14 過兩天是逾越節，又是除酵節，祭司長和文士想法子怎麼用詭計捉拿耶穌，殺他。²只是說："當節的日子不可，恐怕百姓生亂。"

³耶穌在伯大尼長大痲瘋的西門家裏坐席的時候，有一個女人拿着一玉瓶至貴的真哪噠香膏來，打破玉瓶，把膏澆在耶穌的頭上。

⁴有幾個人心中很不喜悅，說："何用這樣枉費香膏呢？⁵這香膏可以賣三十多兩銀子賙濟窮人。"他們就向那女人生氣。

⁶耶穌說："由她吧！為甚麼難為她呢？她在我身上做的是一件美事。⁷因為常有窮人和你們同在，要向他們行善隨時都可以；只是你們不常有我。⁸她所做的，是盡她所能的；她是為我安葬的事，把香膏預先澆在我身上。⁹我實在告訴你們：普天之下，無論在甚麼地方傳這福音，也要述說這女人所做的，以為記念。"

when you see these things happening, you know that it is near, right at the door. ³⁰I tell you the truth, this generation[a] will certainly not pass away until all these things have happened. ³¹Heaven and earth will pass away, but my words will never pass away.

The Day and Hour Unknown

³²"No one knows about that day or hour, not even the angels in heaven, nor the Son, but only the Father. ³³Be on guard! Be alert[b]! You do not know when that time will come. ³⁴It's like a man going away: He leaves his house and puts his servants in charge, each with his assigned task, and tells the one at the door to keep watch.

³⁵"Therefore keep watch because you do not know when the owner of the house will come back—whether in the evening, or at midnight, or when the rooster crows, or at dawn. ³⁶If he comes suddenly, do not let him find you sleeping. ³⁷What I say to you, I say to everyone: 'Watch!'"

Jesus Anointed at Bethany

14 Now the Passover and the Feast of Unleavened Bread were only two days away, and the chief priests and the teachers of the law were looking for some sly way to arrest Jesus and kill him. ²"But not during the Feast," they said, "or the people may riot."

³While he was in Bethany, reclining at the table in the home of a man known as Simon the Leper, a woman came with an alabaster jar of very expensive perfume, made of pure nard. She broke the jar and poured the perfume on his head.

⁴Some of those present were saying indignantly to one another, "Why this waste of perfume? ⁵It could have been sold for more than a year's wages[c] and the money given to the poor." And they rebuked her harshly.

⁶"Leave her alone," said Jesus. "Why are you bothering her? She has done a beautiful thing to me. ⁷The poor you will always have with you, and you can help them any time you want. But you will not always have me. ⁸She did what she could. She poured perfume on my body beforehand to prepare for my burial. ⁹I tell you the truth, wherever the gospel is preached throughout the world, what she has done will also be told, in memory of her."

a 30 Or race　　*b 33 Some manuscripts alert and pray*
c 5 Greek than three hundred denarii

¹⁰Then Judas Iscariot, one of the Twelve, went to the chief priests to betray Jesus to them. ¹¹They were delighted to hear this and promised to give him money. So he watched for an opportunity to hand him over.

The Lord's Supper

¹²On the first day of the Feast of Unleavened Bread, when it was customary to sacrifice the Passover lamb, Jesus' disciples asked him, "Where do you want us to go and make preparations for you to eat the Passover?"

¹³So he sent two of his disciples, telling them, "Go into the city, and a man carrying a jar of water will meet you. Follow him. ¹⁴Say to the owner of the house he enters, 'The Teacher asks: Where is my guest room, where I may eat the Passover with my disciples?' ¹⁵He will show you a large upper room, furnished and ready. Make preparations for us there."

¹⁶The disciples left, went into the city and found things just as Jesus had told them. So they prepared the Passover.

¹⁷When evening came, Jesus arrived with the Twelve. ¹⁸While they were reclining at the table eating, he said, "I tell you the truth, one of you will betray me—one who is eating with me."

¹⁹They were saddened, and one by one they said to him, "Surely not I?"

²⁰"It is one of the Twelve," he replied, "one who dips bread into the bowl with me. ²¹The Son of Man will go just as it is written about him. But woe to that man who betrays the Son of Man! It would be better for him if he had not been born."

²²While they were eating, Jesus took bread, gave thanks and broke it, and gave it to his disciples, saying, "Take it; this is my body."

²³Then he took the cup, gave thanks and offered it to them, and they all drank from it.

²⁴"This is my blood of the^a covenant, which is poured out for many," he said to them. ²⁵"I tell you the truth, I will not drink again of the fruit of the vine until that day when I drink it anew in the kingdom of God."

²⁶When they had sung a hymn, they went out to the Mount of Olives.

Jesus Predicts Peter's Denial

²⁷"You will all fall away," Jesus told them, "for it is written:

" 'I will strike the shepherd,
   and the sheep will be scattered.'^{b}

---

¹⁰十二門徒之中，有一個加略人猶大去見祭司長，要把耶穌交給他們。¹¹他們聽見就歡喜，又應許給他銀子。他就尋思如何得便，把耶穌交給他們。

主的晚餐

¹²除酵節的第一天，就是宰逾越羊羔的那一天，門徒對耶穌說："你吃逾越節的筵席要我們往哪裏去預備呢？"

¹³耶穌就打發兩個門徒，對他們說："你們進城去，必有人拿着一瓶水迎面而來，你們就跟着他。¹⁴他進哪家去，你們就對那家的主人說：'夫子說：客房在哪裏？我與門徒好在那裏吃逾越節的筵席。'¹⁵他必指給你們擺設整齊的一間大樓，你們就在那裏為我們預備。"

¹⁶門徒出去，進了城，所遇見的正如耶穌所說的。他們就預備了逾越節的筵席。

¹⁷到了晚上，耶穌和十二個門徒都來了。¹⁸他們坐席正吃的時候，耶穌說："我實在告訴你們：你們中間有一個與我同吃的人要賣我了。"

¹⁹他們就憂愁起來，一個一個地問他說："是我嗎？"

²⁰耶穌對他們說："是十二個門徒中同我蘸手在盤子裏的那個人。²¹人子必要去世，正如經上指着他所寫的；但賣人子的人有禍了！那人不生在世上倒好。"

²²他們吃的時候，耶穌拿起餅來，祝了福，就擘開遞給他們，說："你們拿着吃，這是我的身體。"

²³又拿起杯來，祝謝了，遞給他們，他們都喝了。

²⁴耶穌說："這是我立約的血，為多人流出來的。²⁵我實在告訴你們：我不再喝這葡萄汁，直到我在神的國裏喝新的那日子。"

²⁶他們唱了詩，就出來，往橄欖山去。

耶穌預言彼得不認主

²⁷耶穌對他們說："你們都要跌倒了，因為經上記着說：

" '我要擊打牧人，
   羊就分散了。'

---

a 24 Some manuscripts *the new*   *b* 27 Zech. 13:7

²⁸但我復活以後，要在你們以先往加利利去。」

²⁹彼得說：「眾人雖然跌倒，我總不能。」

³⁰耶穌對他說：「我實在告訴你：就在今天夜裏，雞叫兩遍以先，你要三次不認我。」

³¹彼得卻極力地說：「我就是必須和你同死，也總不能不認你！」眾門徒都是這樣說。

客西馬尼

³²他們來到一個地方，名叫客西馬尼。耶穌對門徒說：「你們坐在這裏，等我禱告。」³³於是帶着彼得、雅各、約翰同去，就驚恐起來，極其難過，³⁴對他們說：「我心裏甚是憂傷，幾乎要死，你們在這裏等候，警醒。」

³⁵他就稍往前走，俯伏在地，禱告說：「倘若可行，便叫那時候過去。」³⁶他說：「阿爸，父啊！在你凡事都能，求你將這杯撤去；然而，不要從我的意思，只要從你的意思。」

³⁷耶穌回來，見他們睡着了，就對彼得說：「西門，你睡覺嗎？不能警醒片時嗎？³⁸總要警醒禱告，免得入了迷惑。你們心靈固然願意，肉體卻軟弱了。」

³⁹耶穌又去禱告，說的話還是與先前一樣。⁴⁰又來見他們睡着了，因為他們的眼睛甚是困倦；他們也不知道怎麼回答。

⁴¹第三次來，對他們說：「現在你們仍然睡覺安歇吧（註：「吧」或作「嗎」）！夠了，時候到了。看哪，人子被賣在罪人手裏了。⁴²起來，我們走吧！看哪，那賣我的人近了！」

耶穌被捕

⁴³說話之間，忽然那十二個門徒裏的猶大來了，並有許多人帶着刀棒，從祭司長和文士並長老那裏與他同來。

⁴⁴賣耶穌的人曾給他們一個暗號，說：「我與誰親嘴，誰就是他！你們把他拿住，牢牢靠靠地帶去。」⁴⁵猶大來了，隨即到耶穌跟前，說：「拉比」，便與他親嘴。⁴⁶他們就下手拿住他。⁴⁷旁邊站着的人，有一個拔出刀來，將大祭司的僕人砍了一刀，削掉了他一個耳朵。

²⁸But after I have risen, I will go ahead of you into Galilee."

²⁹Peter declared, "Even if all fall away, I will not."

³⁰"I tell you the truth," Jesus answered, "today—yes, tonight—before the rooster crows twice[a] you yourself will disown me three times."

³¹But Peter insisted emphatically, "Even if I have to die with you, I will never disown you." And all the others said the same.

Gethsemane

³²They went to a place called Gethsemane, and Jesus said to his disciples, "Sit here while I pray." ³³He took Peter, James and John along with him, and he began to be deeply distressed and troubled. ³⁴"My soul is overwhelmed with sorrow to the point of death," he said to them. "Stay here and keep watch."

³⁵Going a little farther, he fell to the ground and prayed that if possible the hour might pass from him. ³⁶"Abba,[b] Father," he said, "everything is possible for you. Take this cup from me. Yet not what I will, but what you will."

³⁷Then he returned to his disciples and found them sleeping. "Simon," he said to Peter, "are you asleep? Could you not keep watch for one hour? ³⁸Watch and pray so that you will not fall into temptation. The spirit is willing, but the body is weak."

³⁹Once more he went away and prayed the same thing. ⁴⁰When he came back, he again found them sleeping, because their eyes were heavy. They did not know what to say to him.

⁴¹Returning the third time, he said to them, "Are you still sleeping and resting? Enough! The hour has come. Look, the Son of Man is betrayed into the hands of sinners. ⁴²Rise! Let us go! Here comes my betrayer!"

Jesus Arrested

⁴³Just as he was speaking, Judas, one of the Twelve, appeared. With him was a crowd armed with swords and clubs, sent from the chief priests, the teachers of the law, and the elders.

⁴⁴Now the betrayer had arranged a signal with them: "The one I kiss is the man; arrest him and lead him away under guard." ⁴⁵Going at once to Jesus, Judas said, "Rabbi!" and kissed him. ⁴⁶The men seized Jesus and arrested him. ⁴⁷Then one of those standing near drew his sword and struck the servant of the high priest, cutting off his ear.

---

a 30 Some early manuscripts do not have twice.
b 36 Aramaic for Father

⁴⁸"Am I leading a rebellion," said Jesus, "that you have come out with swords and clubs to capture me? ⁴⁹Every day I was with you, teaching in the temple courts, and you did not arrest me. But the Scriptures must be fulfilled." ⁵⁰Then everyone deserted him and fled.

⁵¹A young man, wearing nothing but a linen garment, was following Jesus. When they seized him, ⁵²he fled naked, leaving his garment behind.

Before the Sanhedrin

⁵³They took Jesus to the high priest, and all the chief priests, elders and teachers of the law came together. ⁵⁴Peter followed him at a distance, right into the courtyard of the high priest. There he sat with the guards and warmed himself at the fire.

⁵⁵The chief priests and the whole Sanhedrin were looking for evidence against Jesus so that they could put him to death, but they did not find any. ⁵⁶Many testified falsely against him, but their statements did not agree.

⁵⁷Then some stood up and gave this false testimony against him: ⁵⁸"We heard him say, 'I will destroy this man-made temple and in three days will build another, not made by man.' " ⁵⁹Yet even then their testimony did not agree.

⁶⁰Then the high priest stood up before them and asked Jesus, "Are you not going to answer? What is this testimony that these men are bringing against you?" ⁶¹But Jesus remained silent and gave no answer.

Again the high priest asked him, "Are you the Christ,ᵃ the Son of the Blessed One?"

⁶²"I am," said Jesus. "And you will see the Son of Man sitting at the right hand of the Mighty One and coming on the clouds of heaven."

⁶³The high priest tore his clothes. "Why do we need any more witnesses?" he asked. ⁶⁴"You have heard the blasphemy. What do you think?"

They all condemned him as worthy of death. ⁶⁵Then some began to spit at him; they blindfolded him, struck him with their fists, and said, "Prophesy!" And the guards took him and beat him.

Peter Disowns Jesus

⁶⁶While Peter was below in the courtyard, one of the servant girls of the high priest came by. ⁶⁷When she saw Peter warming himself, she looked closely at him.

⁴⁸耶穌對他們説："你們帶着刀棒出來拿我，如同拿強盜嗎？⁴⁹我天天教訓人，同你們在殿裏，你們並沒有拿我，但這事成就，為要應驗經上的話。"⁵⁰門徒都離開他，逃走了。

⁵¹有一個少年人，赤身披着一塊麻布，跟隨耶穌，眾人就捉拿他。⁵²他卻丟了麻布，赤身逃走了。

在公會前受審

⁵³他們把耶穌帶到大祭司那裏，又有眾祭司長和長老並文士都來和大祭司一同聚集。⁵⁴彼得遠遠地跟着耶穌，一直進入大祭司的院裏，和差役一同坐在火光裏烤火。

⁵⁵祭司長和全公會尋找見證控告耶穌，要治死他，卻尋不着。⁵⁶因為有好些人作假見證告他，只是他們的見證各不相合。

⁵⁷又有幾個人站起來作假見證告他，説：⁵⁸"我們聽見他説，'我要拆毀這人手所造的殿，三日內就另造一座不是人手所造的。' "⁵⁹他們就是這麼作見證，也是各不相合。

⁶⁰大祭司起來站在中間，問耶穌説："你甚麼都不回答嗎？這些人作見證告你的是甚麼呢？"⁶¹耶穌卻不言語，一句也不回答。

大祭司又問他説："你是那當稱頌者的兒子基督不是？"

⁶²耶穌説："我是。你們必看見人子坐在那權能者的右邊，駕着天上的雲降臨。"

⁶³大祭司就撕開衣服，説："我們何必再用見證人呢？⁶⁴你們已經聽見他這僭妄的話了。你們的意見如何？"

他們都定他該死的罪。⁶⁵就有人吐唾沫在他臉上，又蒙着他的臉，用拳頭打他，對他説："你説預言吧！"差役接過他來，用手掌打他。

彼得不認耶穌

⁶⁶彼得在下邊院子裏，來了大祭司的一個使女，⁶⁷見彼得烤火，就看着他，説：

a 61 Or *Messiah*

"你素來也是同拿撒勒人耶穌一夥的。"

68彼得卻不承認，說："我不知道，也不明白你說的是甚麼。"於是出來，到了前院，雞就叫了。

69那使女看見他，又對旁邊站着的人說："這也是他們一黨的。"70彼得又不承認。

過了不多的時候，旁邊站着的人又對彼得說："你真是他們一黨的，因為你是加利利人。"

71彼得就發咒起誓地說："我不認得你們說的這個人！"

72立時雞叫了第二遍。彼得想起耶穌對他所說的話："雞叫兩遍以先，你要三次不認我。"思想起來，就哭了。

耶穌在彼拉多面前

15 一到早晨，祭司長和長老、文士、全公會的人大家商議，就把耶穌捆綁，解去交給彼拉多。

2彼拉多問他說："你是猶太人的王嗎？"

耶穌回答說："你說的是。"

3祭司長告他許多的事。4彼拉多又問他說："你看，他們告你這麼多的事，你甚麼都不回答嗎？"

5耶穌仍不回答，以致彼拉多覺得希奇。

6每逢這節期，巡撫照眾人所求的，釋放一個囚犯給他們。7有一個人名叫巴拉巴，和作亂的人一同捆綁。他們作亂的時候，曾殺過人。8眾人上去求巡撫，照常例給他們辦。

9彼拉多說："你們要我釋放猶太人的王給你們嗎？"10他原曉得祭司長是因為嫉妒才把耶穌解了來。11只是祭司長挑唆眾人，寧可釋放巴拉巴給他們。

12彼拉多又說："那麼樣，你們所稱為猶太人的王，我怎麼辦他呢？"

13他們又喊着說："把他釘十字架！"

14彼拉多說："為甚麼呢？他做了甚麼惡事呢？"

"You also were with that Nazarene, Jesus," she said.

68But he denied it. "I don't know or understand what you're talking about," he said, and went out into the entryway.[a]

69When the servant girl saw him there, she said again to those standing around, "This fellow is one of them." 70Again he denied it.

After a little while, those standing near said to Peter, "Surely you are one of them, for you are a Galilean."

71He began to call down curses on himself, and he swore to them, "I don't know this man you're talking about."

72Immediately the rooster crowed the second time.[b] Then Peter remembered the word Jesus had spoken to him: "Before the rooster crows twice[c] you will disown me three times." And he broke down and wept.

Jesus Before Pilate

15 Very early in the morning, the chief priests, with the elders, the teachers of the law and the whole Sanhedrin, reached a decision. They bound Jesus, led him away and handed him over to Pilate.

2"Are you the king of the Jews?" asked Pilate.

"Yes, it is as you say," Jesus replied.

3The chief priests accused him of many things. 4So again Pilate asked him, "Aren't you going to answer? See how many things they are accusing you of."

5But Jesus still made no reply, and Pilate was amazed.

6Now it was the custom at the Feast to release a prisoner whom the people requested. 7A man called Barabbas was in prison with the insurrectionists who had committed murder in the uprising. 8The crowd came up and asked Pilate to do for them what he usually did.

9"Do you want me to release to you the king of the Jews?" asked Pilate, 10knowing it was out of envy that the chief priests had handed Jesus over to him. 11But the chief priests stirred up the crowd to have Pilate release Barabbas instead.

12"What shall I do, then, with the one you call the king of the Jews?" Pilate asked them.

13"Crucify him!" they shouted.

14"Why? What crime has he committed?" asked Pilate.

---

a 68 Some early manuscripts *entryway and the rooster crowed*

b 72 Some early manuscripts do not have *the second time.*

c 72 Some early manuscripts do not have *twice.*

But they shouted all the louder, "Crucify him!"

15Wanting to satisfy the crowd, Pilate released Barabbas to them. He had Jesus flogged, and handed him over to be crucified.

The Soldiers Mock Jesus

16The soldiers led Jesus away into the palace (that is, the Praetorium) and called together the whole company of soldiers. 17They put a purple robe on him, then twisted together a crown of thorns and set it on him. 18And they began to call out to him, "Hail, king of the Jews!" 19Again and again they struck him on the head with a staff and spit on him. Falling on their knees, they paid homage to him. 20And when they had mocked him, they took off the purple robe and put his own clothes on him. Then they led him out to crucify him.

The Crucifixion

21A certain man from Cyrene, Simon, the father of Alexander and Rufus, was passing by on his way in from the country, and they forced him to carry the cross. 22They brought Jesus to the place called Golgotha (which means The Place of the Skull). 23Then they offered him wine mixed with myrrh, but he did not take it. 24And they crucified him. Dividing up his clothes, they cast lots to see what each would get.

25It was the third hour when they crucified him. 26The written notice of the charge against him read: THE KING OF THE JEWS. 27They crucified two robbers with him, one on his right and one on his left.a 29Those who passed by hurled insults at him, shaking their heads and saying, "So! You who are going to destroy the temple and build it in three days, 30come down from the cross and save yourself!"

31In the same way the chief priests and the teachers of the law mocked him among themselves. "He saved others," they said, "but he can't save himself! 32Let this Christ,b this King of Israel, come down now from the cross, that we may see and believe." Those crucified with him also heaped insults on him.

The Death of Jesus

33At the sixth hour darkness came over the whole land until the ninth hour. 34And at the ninth hour Jesus cried out in a loud voice, "Eloi,

---

他們便極力地喊着說："把他釘十字架！"

15彼拉多要叫眾人喜悅，就釋放巴拉巴給他們，將耶穌鞭打了，交給人釘十字架。

兵丁戲弄耶穌

16兵丁把耶穌帶進衙門院裏，叫齊了全營的兵。17他們給他穿上紫袍，又用荊棘編做冠冕給他戴上，18就慶賀他說："恭喜，猶太人的王啊！"19又拿一根葦子打他的頭，吐唾沫在他臉上，屈膝拜他。20戲弄完了，就給他脫了紫袍，仍穿上他自己的衣服，帶他出去，要釘十字架。

釘十字架

21有一個古利奈人西門，就是亞歷山大和魯孚的父親，從鄉下來，經過那地方。他們就勉強他同去，好背着耶穌的十字架。22他們帶耶穌到了各各他地方（各各他翻出來就是髑髏地），23拿沒藥調和的酒給耶穌，他卻不受。24於是將他釘在十字架上，拈鬮分他的衣服，看是誰得甚麼。

25釘他在十字架上是巳初的時候。26在上面有他的罪狀，寫的是："猶太人的王"。27他們又把兩個強盜和他同釘十字架，一個在右邊，一個在左邊。（註：有古卷在此有28"這就應了經上的話說：'他被列在罪犯之中。'"）29從那裏經過的人辱罵他，搖着頭說："咳，你這拆毀聖殿，三日又建造起來的，30可以救自己，從十字架上下來吧！"

31祭司長和文士也是這樣戲弄他，彼此說："他救了別人，不能救自己。32以色列的王基督，現在可以從十字架上下來，叫我們看見，就信了！"那和他同釘的人也是譏誚他。

耶穌的死

33從午正到申初，遍地都黑暗了。34申初的時候，耶穌大聲喊着

---

a 27 Some manuscripts left, 28and the scripture was fulfilled which says, "He was counted with the lawless ones" (Isaiah 53:12)
b 32 Or Messiah

説："以羅伊！以羅伊！拉馬撒巴
各大尼？"翻出來就是："我的
神！我的神！為甚麼離棄我？"

³⁵旁邊站着的人，有的聽見就
説："看哪，他叫以利亞呢！"

³⁶有一個人跑去，把海絨蘸滿了
醋，綁在葦子上，送給他喝，説：
"且等着，看以利亞來不來把他取
下。"

³⁷耶穌大聲喊叫，氣就斷了。

³⁸殿裏的幔子從上到下裂為兩
半。³⁹對面站着的百夫長看見耶穌這
樣喊叫（註：有古卷無"喊叫"二字）斷
氣，就説："這人真是神的兒子！"

⁴⁰還有些婦女遠遠地觀看，內中
有抹大拉的馬利亞，又有小雅各和
約西的母親馬利亞，並有撒羅米，
⁴¹就是耶穌在加利利的時候，跟隨
他、服侍他的那些人，還有同耶穌
上耶路撒冷的好些婦女在那裏觀
看。

耶穌的安葬

⁴²到了晚上，因為這是預備日，
就是安息日的前一日，⁴³有亞利馬太
的約瑟前來，他是尊貴的議士，也
是等候神國的。他放膽進去見彼拉
多，求耶穌的身體。⁴⁴彼拉多詫異耶
穌已經死了，便叫百夫長來，問他
耶穌死了久不久。⁴⁵既從百夫長得知
實情，就把耶穌的屍首賜給約瑟。
⁴⁶約瑟買了細麻布，把耶穌取下來，
用細麻布裹好，安放在磐石中鑿出
來的墳墓裏，又滾過一塊石頭來擋
住墓門。⁴⁷抹大拉的馬利亞和約西的
母親馬利亞都看見安放他的地方。

復活

16 過了安息日，抹大拉的馬利
亞和雅各的母親馬利亞並撒
羅米，買了香膏要去膏耶穌
的身體。²七日的第一日清早，出太
陽的時候，她們來到墳墓那裏，³彼
此説："誰給我們把石頭從墓門滾
開呢？"

⁴那石頭原來很大，她們抬頭一
看，卻見石頭已經滾開了。⁵她們進

Eloi, lama sabachthani?"—which means, "My
God, my God, why have you forsaken me?"^a

³⁵When some of those standing near heard
this, they said, "Listen, he's calling Elijah."

³⁶One man ran, filled a sponge with wine
vinegar, put it on a stick, and offered it to Jesus
to drink. "Now leave him alone. Let's see if
Elijah comes to take him down," he said.

³⁷With a loud cry, Jesus breathed his last.

³⁸The curtain of the temple was torn in two
from top to bottom. ³⁹And when the centurion,
who stood there in front of Jesus, heard his cry
and^b saw how he died, he said, "Surely this man
was the Son^c of God!"

⁴⁰Some women were watching from a dis-
tance. Among them were Mary Magdalene,
Mary the mother of James the younger and of
Joses, and Salome. ⁴¹In Galilee these women had
followed him and cared for his needs. Many
other women who had come up with him to
Jerusalem were also there.

The Burial of Jesus

⁴²It was Preparation Day (that is, the day
before the Sabbath). So as evening approached,
⁴³Joseph of Arimathea, a prominent member of
the Council, who was himself waiting for the
kingdom of God, went boldly to Pilate and
asked for Jesus' body. ⁴⁴Pilate was surprised to
hear that he was already dead. Summoning the
centurion, he asked him if Jesus had already
died. ⁴⁵When he learned from the centurion that
it was so, he gave the body to Joseph. ⁴⁶So
Joseph bought some linen cloth, took down the
body, wrapped it in the linen, and placed it in a
tomb cut out of rock. Then he rolled a stone
against the entrance of the tomb. ⁴⁷Mary
Magdalene and Mary the mother of Joses saw
where he was laid.

The Resurrection

16 When the Sabbath was over, Mary
Magdalene, Mary the mother of James,
and Salome bought spices so that they
might go to anoint Jesus' body. ²Very early on
the first day of the week, just after sunrise, they
were on their way to the tomb ³and they asked
each other, "Who will roll the stone away from
the entrance of the tomb?"

⁴But when they looked up, they saw that the
stone, which was very large, had been rolled
away. ⁵As they entered the tomb, they saw a

*a 34 Psalm 22:1　　b 39 Some manuscripts do not have heard his
cry and　　c 39 Or a son*

young man dressed in a white robe sitting on the right side, and they were alarmed.

6"Don't be alarmed," he said. "You are looking for Jesus the Nazarene, who was crucified. He has risen! He is not here. See the place where they laid him. 7But go, tell his disciples and Peter, 'He is going ahead of you into Galilee. There you will see him, just as he told you.' "

8Trembling and bewildered, the women went out and fled from the tomb. They said nothing to anyone, because they were afraid.

[The most reliable early manuscripts and other ancient witnesses do not have Mark 16:9-20.]

9When Jesus rose early on the first day of the week, he appeared first to Mary Magdalene, out of whom he had driven seven demons. 10She went and told those who had been with him and who were mourning and weeping. 11When they heard that Jesus was alive and that she had seen him, they did not believe it.

12Afterward Jesus appeared in a different form to two of them while they were walking in the country. 13These returned and reported it to the rest; but they did not believe them either.

14Later Jesus appeared to the Eleven as they were eating; he rebuked them for their lack of faith and their stubborn refusal to believe those who had seen him after he had risen.

15He said to them, "Go into all the world and preach the good news to all creation. 16Whoever believes and is baptized will be saved, but whoever does not believe will be condemned. 17And these signs will accompany those who believe: In my name they will drive out demons; they will speak in new tongues; 18they will pick up snakes with their hands; and when they drink deadly poison, it will not hurt them at all; they will place their hands on sick people, and they will get well."

19After the Lord Jesus had spoken to them, he was taken up into heaven and he sat at the right hand of God. 20Then the disciples went out and preached everywhere, and the Lord worked with them and confirmed his word by the signs that accompanied it.

了墳墓，看見一個少年人坐在右邊，穿着白袍，就甚驚恐。

6那少年人對她們說："不要驚恐，你們尋找那釘十字架的拿撒勒人耶穌，他已經復活了，不在這裏。請看安放他的地方。7你們可以去告訴他的門徒和彼得，說：'他在你們以先往加利利去。在那裏你們要見他，正如他從前所告訴你們的。'"

8她們就出來，從墳墓那裏逃跑，又發抖又驚奇，甚麼也不告訴人，因為她們害怕。

9在七日的第一日清早，耶穌復活了，就先向抹大拉的馬利亞顯現，耶穌從她身上曾趕出七個鬼。10她去告訴那向來跟隨耶穌的人，那時他們正哀慟哭泣。11他們聽見耶穌活了，被馬利亞看見，卻是不信。

12這事以後，門徒中間有兩個人往鄉下去。走路的時候，耶穌變了形像，向他們顯現。13他們就去告訴其餘的門徒，其餘的門徒也是不信。

14後來，十一個門徒坐席的時候，耶穌向他們顯現，責備他們不信，心裏剛硬，因為他們不信那些在他復活以後看見他的人。

15他又對他們說："你們往普天下去，傳福音給萬民（註："萬民"原文作"凡受造的"）聽。16信而受洗的，必然得救，不信的，必被定罪。17信的人必有神蹟隨着他們：就是奉我的名趕鬼，說新方言；18手能拿蛇；若喝了甚麼毒物，也必不受害；手按病人，病人就必好了。"

19主耶穌和他們說完了話，後來被接到天上，坐在神的右邊。20門徒出去，到處宣傳福音。主和他們同工，用神蹟隨着，證實所傳的道。阿們！

路加福音

Luke

引言

1 ^{1、2}提阿非羅大人哪，有好些人提筆作書，述說在我們中間所成就的事，是照傳道的人從起初親眼看見又傳給我們的。³這些事我既從起頭都詳細考察了，就定意要按着次序寫給你，⁴使你知道所學之道都是確實的。

預告施洗約翰出生

⁵當猶太王希律的時候，亞比雅班裏有一個祭司，名叫撒迦利亞。他妻子是亞倫的後人，名叫伊利沙伯。⁶他們二人在神面前都是義人，遵行主的一切誡命禮儀，沒有可指摘的；⁷只是沒有孩子，因為伊利沙伯不生育，兩個人又年紀老邁了。

⁸撒迦利亞按班次在神面前供祭司的職分，⁹照祭司的規矩掣籤，得進主殿燒香。¹⁰燒香的時候，眾百姓在外面禱告。

¹¹有主的使者站在香壇的右邊向他顯現。¹²撒迦利亞看見，就驚慌害怕。¹³天使對他說：「撒迦利亞，不要害怕，因為你的祈禱已經被聽見了。你的妻子伊利沙伯要給你生一個兒子，你要給他起名叫約翰。¹⁴你必歡喜快樂；有許多人因他出世，也必喜樂。¹⁵他在主面前將要為大，淡酒濃酒都不喝，從母腹裏就被聖靈充滿了。¹⁶他要使許多以色列人回轉，歸於主他們的神。¹⁷他必有以利亞的心志能力，行在主的前面，叫為父的心

Introduction

1 Many have undertaken to draw up an account of the things that have been fulfilled^a among us, ²just as they were handed down to us by those who from the first were eyewitnesses and servants of the word. ³Therefore, since I myself have carefully investigated everything from the beginning, it seemed good also to me to write an orderly account for you, most excellent Theophilus, ⁴so that you may know the certainty of the things you have been taught.

The Birth of John the Baptist Foretold

⁵In the time of Herod king of Judea there was a priest named Zechariah, who belonged to the priestly division of Abijah; his wife Elizabeth was also a descendant of Aaron. ⁶Both of them were upright in the sight of God, observing all the Lord's commandments and regulations blamelessly. ⁷But they had no children, because Elizabeth was barren; and they were both well along in years.

⁸Once when Zechariah's division was on duty and he was serving as priest before God, ⁹he was chosen by lot, according to the custom of the priesthood, to go into the temple of the Lord and burn incense. ¹⁰And when the time for the burning of incense came, all the assembled worshipers were praying outside.

¹¹Then an angel of the Lord appeared to him, standing at the right side of the altar of incense. ¹²When Zechariah saw him, he was startled and was gripped with fear. ¹³But the angel said to him: "Do not be afraid, Zechariah; your prayer has been heard. Your wife Elizabeth will bear you a son, and you are to give him the name John. ¹⁴He will be a joy and delight to you, and many will rejoice because of his birth, ¹⁵for he will be great in the sight of the Lord. He is never to take wine or other fermented drink, and he will be filled with the Holy Spirit even from birth.^b ¹⁶Many of the people of Israel will he bring back to the Lord their God. ¹⁷And he will go on before the Lord, in the spirit and power of Elijah, to turn the hearts of the fathers to their

a 1 Or been surely believed　　b 15 Or from his mother's womb

children and the disobedient to the wisdom of the righteous—to make ready a people prepared for the Lord."

¹⁸Zechariah asked the angel, "How can I be sure of this? I am an old man and my wife is well along in years."

¹⁹The angel answered, "I am Gabriel. I stand in the presence of God, and I have been sent to speak to you and to tell you this good news. ²⁰And now you will be silent and not able to speak until the day this happens, because you did not believe my words, which will come true at their proper time."

²¹Meanwhile, the people were waiting for Zechariah and wondering why he stayed so long in the temple. ²²When he came out, he could not speak to them. They realized he had seen a vision in the temple, for he kept making signs to them but remained unable to speak.

²³When his time of service was completed, he returned home. ²⁴After this his wife Elizabeth became pregnant and for five months remained in seclusion. ²⁵"The Lord has done this for me," she said. "In these days he has shown his favor and taken away my disgrace among the people."

The Birth of Jesus Foretold

²⁶In the sixth month, God sent the angel Gabriel to Nazareth, a town in Galilee, ²⁷to a virgin pledge to be married to a man named Joseph, a descendant of David. The virgin's name was Mary. ²⁸The angel went to her and said, "Greetings, you who are highly favored! The Lord is with you."

²⁹Mary was greatly troubled at his words and wondered what kind of greeting this might be. ³⁰But the angel said to her, "Do not be afraid, Mary, you have found favor with God. ³¹You will be with child and give birth to a son, and you are to give him the name Jesus. ³²He will be great and will be called the Son of the Most High. The Lord God will give him the throne of his father David, ³³and he will reign over the house of Jacob forever; his kingdom will never end."

³⁴"How will this be," Mary asked the angel, "since I am a virgin?"

³⁵The angel answered, "The Holy Spirit will come upon you, and the power of the Most High will overshadow you. So the holy one to be born will be called^a the Son of God. ³⁶Even Elizabeth your relative is going to have a child in her old age, and she who was said to be bar-

a 35 Or So the child to be born will be called holy,

轉向兒女，叫悖逆的人轉從義人的智慧，又為主預備合用的百姓。"

¹⁸撒迦利亞對天使說："我憑着甚麼可知道這事呢？我已經老了，我的妻子也年紀老邁了。"

¹⁹天使回答說："我是站在神面前的加百列，奉差而來對你說話，將這好信息報給你。²⁰到了時候，這話必然應驗。只因你不信，你必啞巴，不能說話，直到這事成就的日子。"

²¹百姓等候撒迦利亞，詫異他許久在殿裏。²²及至他出來，不能和他們說話，他們就知道他在殿裏見了異象。因為他直向他們打手式，竟成了啞巴。

²³他供職的日子已滿，就回家去了。²⁴這些日子以後，他的妻子伊利沙伯懷了孕，就隱藏了五個月，²⁵說："主在眷顧我的日子，這樣看待我，要把我在人間的羞恥除掉。"

預告耶穌降生

²⁶到了第六個月，天使加百列奉神的差遣往加利利的一座城去，這城名叫拿撒勒，²⁷到一個童女那裏，是已經許配大衛家的一個人，名叫約瑟，童女的名字叫馬利亞。²⁸天使進去，對她說："蒙大恩的女子，我問你安，主和你同在了！"

²⁹馬利亞因這話就很驚慌，又反復思想這樣問安是甚麼意思。³⁰天使對她說："馬利亞，不要怕！你在神面前已經蒙恩了。³¹你要懷孕生子，可以給他起名叫耶穌。³²他要為大，稱為至高者的兒子，主神要把他祖大衛的位給他。³³他要作雅各家的王，直到永遠；他的國也沒有窮盡。"

³⁴馬利亞對天使說："我沒有出嫁，怎麼有這事呢？"

³⁵天使回答說："聖靈要臨到你身上，至高者的能力要蔭庇你，因此所要生的聖者必稱為神的兒子（註：或作："所要生的，必稱為聖，稱為神的兒子"）。³⁶況且你的親戚伊利沙伯，在年老的時候також懷了男胎，就是那素來稱為不

生育的，現在有孕六個月了。³⁷因為出於神的話，沒有一句不帶能力的。"

³⁸馬利亞說："我是主的使女，情願照你的話成就在我身上。"天使就離開她去了。

馬利亞探望伊利沙伯

³⁹那時候馬利亞起身，急忙往山地裏去，來到猶大的一座城。⁴⁰進了撒迦利亞的家，問伊利沙伯安。⁴¹伊利沙伯一聽馬利亞問安，所懷的胎就在腹裏跳動。伊利沙伯且被聖靈充滿，⁴²高聲喊着說："你在婦女中是有福的！你所懷的胎也是有福的！⁴³我主的母到我這裏來，這是從哪裏得的呢？⁴⁴因為你問安的聲音一入我耳，我腹裏的胎就歡喜跳動。⁴⁵這相信的女子是有福的！因為主對她所說的話都要應驗。"

馬利亞的頌歌

⁴⁶馬利亞說：
"我心尊主為大；
⁴⁷我靈以神我的救主為樂。
⁴⁸因為他顧念他使女的卑微，
　　從今以後，
　　萬代要稱我有福。

⁴⁹那有權能的，
　　為我成就了大事，
　　他的名為聖。
⁵⁰他憐憫敬畏他的人，
　　直到世世代代。
⁵¹他用膀臂施展大能；
　　那狂傲的人正心裏妄想
　　就被他趕散了。
⁵²他叫有權柄的失位，
　　叫卑賤的升高；
⁵³叫飢餓的得飽美食，
　　叫富足的空手回去。
⁵⁴他扶助了他的僕人以色列，

⁵⁵為要記念亞伯拉罕和他的後裔，
　　施憐憫直到永遠，
　　正如從前對我們列祖所說的話。"
⁵⁶馬利亞和伊利沙伯同住，約有三個月，就回家去了。

施洗約翰誕生

⁵⁷伊利沙伯的產期到了，就生了一個兒子。⁵⁸鄰里親族聽見主向她大施憐憫，就和她一同歡樂。

ren is in her sixth month. ³⁷For nothing is impossible with God."

³⁸"I am the Lord's servant," Mary answered. "May it be to me as you have said." Then the angel left her.

Mary Visits Elizabeth

³⁹At that time Mary got ready and hurried to a town in the hill country of Judea, ⁴⁰where she entered Zechariah's home and greeted Elizabeth. ⁴¹When Elizabeth heard Mary's greeting, the baby leaped in her womb, and Elizabeth was filled with the Holy Spirit. ⁴²In a loud voice she exclaimed: "Blessed are you among women, and blessed is the child you will bear! ⁴³But why am I so favored, that the mother of my Lord should come to me? ⁴⁴As soon as the sound of your greeting reached my ears, the baby in my womb leaped for joy. ⁴⁵Blessed is she who has believed that what the Lord has said to her will be accomplished!"

Mary's Song

⁴⁶And Mary said:
"My soul glorifies the Lord
⁴⁷　and my spirit rejoices in God my Savior,
⁴⁸for he has been mindful
　　of the humble state of his servant.
From now on all generations will call me
　　blessed,
⁴⁹　for the Mighty One has done great things
　　for me—
　　holy is his name.
⁵⁰His mercy extends to those who fear him,
　　from generation to generation.
⁵¹He has performed mighty deeds with his arm;
　　he has scattered those who are proud in
　　their inmost thoughts.
⁵²He has brought down rulers from their
　　thrones
　　but has lifted up the humble.
⁵³He has filled the hungry with good things
　　but has sent the rich away empty.
⁵⁴He has helped his servant Israel,
　　remembering to be merciful
⁵⁵to Abraham and his descendants forever,
　　even as he said to our fathers."

⁵⁶Mary stayed with Elizabeth for about three months and then returned home.

The Birth of John the Baptist

⁵⁷When it was time for Elizabeth to have her baby, she gave birth to a son. ⁵⁸Her neighbors and relatives heard that the Lord had shown her great mercy, and they shared her joy.

⁵⁹On the eighth day they came to circumcise the child, and they were going to name him after his father Zechariah, ⁶⁰but his mother spoke up and said, "No! He is to be called John."

⁶¹They said to her, "There is no one among your relatives who has that name."

⁶²Then they made signs to his father, to find out what he would like to name the child. ⁶³He asked for a writing tablet, and to everyone's astonishment he wrote, "His name is John." ⁶⁴Immediately his mouth was opened and his tongue was loosed, and he began to speak, praising God. ⁶⁵The neighbors were all filled with awe, and throughout the hill country of Judea people were talking about all these things. ⁶⁶Everyone who heard this wondered about it, asking, "What then is this child going to be?" For the Lord's hand was with him.

Zechariah's Song

⁶⁷His father Zechariah was filled with the Holy Spirit and prophesied:

⁶⁸"Praise be to the Lord, the God of Israel,
  because he has come and has redeemed his people.
⁶⁹He has raised up a hornᵃ of salvation for us
  in the house of his servant David
⁷⁰(as he said through his holy prophets of long ago),
⁷¹salvation from our enemies
  and from the hand of all who hate us—
⁷²to show mercy to our fathers
  and to remember his holy covenant,
⁷³ the oath he swore to our father Abraham:
⁷⁴to rescue us from the hand of our enemies,
  and to enable us to serve him without fear
⁷⁵ in holiness and righteousness before him all our days.

⁷⁶And you, my child, will be called a prophet of the Most High;
  for you will go on before the Lord to prepare the way for him,
⁷⁷to give his people the knowledge of salvation
  through the forgiveness of their sins,
⁷⁸because of the tender mercy of our God,
  by which the rising sun will come to us from heaven
⁷⁹to shine on those living in darkness
  and in the shadow of death,
  to guide our feet into the path of peace."

⁵⁹到了第八日,他們來要給孩子行割禮,並要照他父親的名字叫他撒迦利亞。⁶⁰他母親說:"不可!要叫他約翰。"

⁶¹他們說:"你親族中沒有叫這名字的。"

⁶²他們就向他父親打手式,問他要叫這孩子甚麼名字。⁶³他要了一塊寫字的板,就寫上說:"他的名字是約翰。"他們便都希奇。⁶⁴撒迦利亞的口立時開了,舌頭也舒展了,就說出話來,稱頌神。⁶⁵周圍居住的人都懼怕;這一切的事就傳遍了猶太的山地。⁶⁶凡聽見的人都將這事放在心裏,說:"這個孩子將來怎麼樣呢?"因為有主與他同在。

撒迦利亞的頌歌

⁶⁷他父親撒迦利亞被聖靈充滿了,就預言說:

⁶⁸"主以色列的神是應當稱頌的。
  因他眷顧他的百姓,
  為他們施行救贖,
⁶⁹在他僕人大衛家中,
  為我們興起了拯救的角,
⁷⁰(正如主藉着從創世以來聖先知的口所說的話。)
⁷¹拯救我們脫離仇敵
  和一切恨我們之人的手,
⁷²向我們列祖施憐憫,
  記念他的聖約,
⁷³就是他對我們祖宗亞伯拉罕所起的誓,
⁷⁴叫我們既從仇敵手中
  被救出來,
⁷⁵就可以終身在他面前,
  坦然無懼地用聖潔、公義侍奉他。

⁷⁶孩子啊!
  你要稱為至高者的先知;
  因為你要行在主的前面,
  預備他的道路,
⁷⁷叫他的百姓因罪得赦,
  就知道救恩;
⁷⁸因我們神憐憫的心腸,
  叫清晨的日光從高天臨到我們,
⁷⁹要照亮坐在黑暗中死蔭裏的人,
  把我們的腳引到平安的路上。"

---

a 69 Horn here symbolizes strength.

⁸⁰那孩子漸漸長大，心靈強健，住在曠野，直到他顯明在以色列人面前的日子。

耶穌降生

2 當那些日子，凱撒亞古士督有旨意下來，叫天下人民都報名上冊。²這是居里扭作敍利亞巡撫的時候，頭一次行報名上冊的事。³眾人各歸各城，報名上冊。

⁴約瑟也從加利利的拿撒勒城上猶太去，到了大衛的城，名叫伯利恆。因他本是大衛一族一家的人，⁵要和他所聘之妻馬利亞一同報名上冊。那時馬利亞的身孕已經重了。⁶他們在那裏的時候，馬利亞的產期到了，⁷就生了頭胎的兒子，用布包起來，放在馬槽裏，因為客店裏沒有地方。

牧羊人與天使

⁸在伯利恆之野地裏有牧羊的人，夜間按着更次看守羊羣。⁹有主的使者站在他們旁邊，主的榮光四面照着他們，牧羊的人就甚懼怕。¹⁰那天使對他們說：“不要懼怕！我報給你們大喜的信息，是關乎萬民的。¹¹因今天在大衛的城裏，為你們生了救主，就是主基督。¹²你們要看見一個嬰孩，包着布，臥在馬槽裏，那就是記號了。”

¹³忽然，有一大隊天兵同那天使讚美神說：

¹⁴ “在至高之處榮耀歸與神！
　　在地上平安歸與他所喜悅的人
　　（註：有古卷作“喜悅歸與人”）！”

¹⁵眾天使離開他們，升天去了。牧羊的人彼此說：“我們往伯利恆去，看看所成的事，就是主所指示我們的。”

¹⁶他們急忙去了，就尋見馬利亞和約瑟，又有那嬰孩臥在馬槽裏；¹⁷既然看見，就把天使論這孩子的話傳開了。¹⁸凡聽見的，就詫異牧羊之

⁸⁰And the child grew and became strong in spirit; and he lived in the desert until he appeared publicly to Israel.

The Birth of Jesus

2 In those days Caesar Augustus issued a decree that a census should be taken of the entire Roman world. ²(This was the first census that took place while Quirinius was governor of Syria.) ³And everyone went to his own town to register.

⁴So Joseph also went up from the town of Nazareth in Galilee to Judea, to Bethlehem the town of David, because he belonged to the house and line of David. ⁵He went there to register with Mary, who was pledged to be married to him and was expecting a child. ⁶While they were there, the time came for the baby to be born, ⁷and she gave birth to her firstborn, a son. She wrapped him in cloths and placed him in a manger, because there was no room for them in the inn.

The Shepherds and the Angels

⁸And there were shepherds living out in the fields nearby, keeping watch over their flocks at night. ⁹An angel of the Lord appeared to them, and the glory of the Lord shone around them, and they were terrified. ¹⁰But the angel said to them, “Do not be afraid. I bring you good news of great joy that will be for all the people. ¹¹Today in the town of David a Savior has been born to you; he is Christᵃ the Lord. ¹²This will be a sign to you: You will find a baby wrapped in cloths and lying in a manger.”

¹³Suddenly a great company of the heavenly host appeared with the angel, praising God and saying,

¹⁴“Glory to God in the highest,
　　and on earth peace to men on whom his
　　favor rests.”

¹⁵When the angels had left them and gone into heaven, the shepherds said to one another, “Let's go to Bethlehem and see this thing that has happened, which the Lord has told us about.”

¹⁶So they hurried off and found Mary and Joseph, and the baby, who was lying in the manger. ¹⁷When they had seen him, they spread the word concerning what had been told them about this child, ¹⁸and all who heard it were amazed at what the shepherds said to them.

ᵃ 11 Or Messiah. “The Christ” (Greek) and “the Messiah” (Hebrew) both mean “the Anointed One”; also in verse 26.

19But Mary treasured up all these things and pondered them in her heart. 20The shepherds returned, glorifying and praising God for all the things they had heard and seen, which were just as they had been told.

Jesus Presented in the Temple

21On the eighth day, when it was time to circumcise him, he was named Jesus, the name the angel had given him before he had been conceived.

22When the time of their purification according to the Law of Moses had been completed, Joseph and Mary took him to Jerusalem to present him to the Lord 23(as it is written in the Law of the Lord, "Every firstborn male is to be consecrated to the Lord"[a]), 24and to offer a sacrifice in keeping with what is said in the Law of the Lord: "a pair of doves or two young pigeons."[b]

25Now there was a man in Jerusalem called Simeon, who was righteous and devout. He was waiting for the consolation of Israel, and the Holy Spirit was upon him. 26It had been revealed to him by the Holy Spirit that he would not die before he had seen the Lord's Christ. 27Moved by the Spirit, he went into the temple courts. When the parents brought in the child Jesus to do for him what the custom of the Law required, 28Simeon took him in his arms and praised God, saying:

29"Sovereign Lord, as you have promised,
　　you now dismiss[c] your servant in peace.
30For my eyes have seen your salvation,
31　which you have prepared in the sight of all people,
32a light for revelation to the Gentiles
　　and for glory to your people Israel."

33The child's father and mother marveled at what was said about him. 34Then Simeon blessed them and said to Mary, his mother: "This child is destined to cause the falling and rising of many in Israel, and to be a sign that will be spoken against, 35so that the thoughts of many hearts will be revealed. And a sword will pierce your own soul too."

36There was also a prophetess, Anna, the daughter of Phanuel, of the tribe of Asher. She was very old; she had lived with her husband seven years after her marriage, 37and then was a widow until she was eighty-four.[d] She never left the temple but worshiped night and day, fasting

a 23 Exodus 13:2,12　　b 24 Lev. 12:8　　c 29 Or promised, / now dismiss　　d 37 Or widow for eighty-four years

人對他們所説的話。19馬利亞卻把這一切的事存在心裏，反復思想。20牧羊的人回去了，因所聽見所看見的一切事，正如天使向他們所説的，就歸榮耀與神，讚美他。

在聖殿中獻上小耶穌

21滿了八天，就給孩子行割禮，與他起名叫耶穌；這就是沒有成胎以前，天使所起的名。

22按摩西律法滿了潔淨的日子，他們帶着孩子上耶路撒冷去，要把他獻與主。23（正如主的律法上所記："凡頭生的男子必稱聖歸主。"）24又要照着主的律法上所説，或用一對斑鳩，或用兩隻雛鴿獻祭。

25在耶路撒冷有一個人，名叫西面。這人又公義又虔誠，素常盼望以色列的安慰者來到，又有聖靈在他身上。26他得了聖靈的啟示，知道自己未死以前，必看見主所立的基督。27他受了聖靈的感動，進入聖殿，正遇見耶穌的父母抱着孩子進來，要照律法的規矩辦理。28西面就用手接過他來，稱頌神説：

29"主啊！如今可以照你的話，
　　釋放僕人安然去世。
30因為我的眼睛已經看見你的救恩，
31就是你在萬民面前所預備的，

32是照亮外邦人的光，
　　又是你民以色列的榮耀。"

33孩子的父母因這論耶穌的話就希奇。34、35西面給他們祝福，又對孩子的母親馬利亞説："這孩子被立，是要叫以色列中許多人跌倒，許多人興起；又要作毀謗的話柄，叫許多人心裏的意念顯露出來；你自己的心也要被刀刺透。"

36又有女先知，名叫亞拿，是亞設支派法內力的女兒，年紀已經老邁，從作童女出嫁的時候，同丈夫住了七年就寡居了，37現在已經八十四歲（註：或作"就寡居了八十四年"），並不離開聖殿，禁食祈求，晝夜侍奉神。³⁸正當那時,她進前來稱謝神,將孩子的事對一切盼望耶路撒冷得救贖的人講說。

³⁹約瑟和馬利亞照主的律法辦完了一切的事,就回加利利,到自己的城拿撒勒去了。⁴⁰孩子漸漸長大,強健起來,充滿智慧,又有神的恩在他身上。

孩童耶穌在聖殿中

⁴¹每年到逾越節,他父母就上耶路撒冷去。⁴²當他十二歲的時候,他們按著節期的規矩上去。⁴³守滿了節期,他們回去,孩童耶穌仍舊在耶路撒冷。他的父母並不知道,⁴⁴以為他在同行的人中間,走了一天的路程,就在親族和熟識的人中找他,⁴⁵既找不著,就回耶路撒冷去找他。⁴⁶過了三天,就遇見他在殿裏,坐在教師中間,一面聽,一面問。⁴⁷凡聽見他的,都希奇他的聰明和他的應對。⁴⁸他父母看見就很希奇。他母親對他說:「我兒,為甚麼向我們這樣行呢?看哪,你父親和我傷心來找你!」

⁴⁹耶穌說:「為甚麼找我呢?豈不知我應當以我父的事為念嗎?(註:或作「豈不知我應當在我父的家裏嗎?」)」⁵⁰他所說的這話,他們不明白。

⁵¹他就同他們下去,回到拿撒勒,並且順從他們。他母親把這一切的事都存在心裏。⁵²耶穌的智慧和身量(註:「身量」或作:「年紀」),並神和人喜愛他的心,都一齊增長。

施洗約翰預備道路

3 凱撒提庇留在位第十五年,本丟彼拉多作猶太巡撫,希律作加利利分封的王,他兄弟腓力作以土利亞和特拉可尼地方分封的王,²呂撒聶作亞比利尼分封的王,²亞那和該亞法作大祭司。那時,撒迦利亞的兒子約翰在曠野裏,神的話臨到他。³他就來到約旦河一帶地方,宣講悔改的洗禮,使罪得赦。⁴正如先知以賽亞書上所記的話,說:

and praying. ³⁸Coming up to them at that very moment, she gave thanks to God and spoke about the child to all who were looking forward to the redemption of Jerusalem.

³⁹When Joseph and Mary had done everything required by the Law of the Lord, they returned to Galilee to their own town of Nazareth. ⁴⁰And the child grew and became strong; he was filled with wisdom, and the grace of God was upon him.

The Boy Jesus at the Temple

⁴¹Every year his parents went to Jerusalem for the Feast of the Passover. ⁴²When he was twelve years old, they went up to the Feast, according to the custom. ⁴³After the Feast was over, while his parents were returning home, the boy Jesus stayed behind in Jerusalem, but they were unaware of it. ⁴⁴Thinking he was in their company, they traveled on for a day. Then they began looking for him among their relatives and friends. ⁴⁵When they did not find him, they went back to Jerusalem to look for him. ⁴⁶After three days they found him in the temple courts, sitting among the teachers, listening to them and asking them questions. ⁴⁷Everyone who heard him was amazed at his understanding and his answers. ⁴⁸When his parents saw him, they were astonished. His mother said to him, "Son, why have you treated us like this? Your father and I have been anxiously searching for you."

⁴⁹"Why were you searching for me?" he asked. "Didn't you know I had to be in my Father's house?" ⁵⁰But they did not understand what he was saying to them.

⁵¹Then he went down to Nazareth with them and was obedient to them. But his mother treasured all these things in her heart. ⁵²And Jesus grew in wisdom and stature, and in favor with God and men.

John the Baptist Prepares the Way

3 In the fifteenth year of the reign of Tiberius Caesar—when Pontius Pilate was governor of Judea, Herod tetrarch of Galilee, his brother Philip tetrarch of Iturea and Traconitis, and Lysanias tetrarch of Abilene— ²during the high priesthood of Annas and Caiaphas, the word of God came to John son of Zechariah in the desert. ³He went into all the country around the Jordan, preaching a baptism of repentance for the forgiveness of sins. ⁴As is written in the book of the words of Isaiah the prophet:

"A voice of one calling in the desert,
　'Prepare the way for the Lord,
　　make straight paths for him.
[5]Every valley shall be filled in,
　every mountain and hill made low.
The crooked roads shall become straight,
　the rough ways smooth.
[6]And all mankind will see God's salvation.' "[a]

[7]John said to the crowds coming out to be baptized by him, "You brood of vipers! Who warned you to flee from the coming wrath? [8]Produce fruit in keeping with repentance. And do not begin to say to yourselves, 'We have Abraham as our father.' For I tell you that out of these stones God can raise up children for Abraham. [9]The ax is already at the root of the trees, and every tree that does not produce good fruit will be cut down and thrown into the fire."

[10]"What should we do then?" the crowd asked.

[11]John answered, "The man with two tunics should share with him who has none, and the one who has food should do the same."

[12]Tax collectors also came to be baptized. "Teacher," they asked, "what should we do?"

[13]"Don't collect any more than you are required to," he told them.

[14]Then some soldiers asked him, "And what should we do?"

He replied, "Don't extort money and don't accuse people falsely—be content with your pay."

[15]The people were waiting expectantly and were all wondering in their hearts if John might possibly be the Christ.[b] [16]John answered them all, "I baptize you with[c] water. But one more powerful than I will come, the thongs of whose sandals I am not worthy to untie. He will baptize you with the Holy Spirit and with fire. [17]His winnowing fork is in his hand to clear his threshing floor and to gather the wheat into his barn, but he will burn up the chaff with unquenchable fire." [18]And with many other words John exhorted the people and preached the good news to them.

[19]But when John rebuked Herod the tetrarch because of Herodias, his brother's wife, and all the other evil things he had done, [20]Herod added this to them all: He locked John up in prison.

The Baptism and Genealogy of Jesus

[21]When all the people were being baptized, Jesus was baptized too. And as he was praying, heaven was opened [22]and the Holy Spirit de-

"在曠野有人聲喊着說：
　'預備主的道，
　修直他的路！
[5]一切山窪都要填滿，
　大小山岡都要削平！
彎彎曲曲的地方要改為正直，
　高高低低的道路要改為平坦！
[6]凡有血氣的，都要見神的救恩！' "

[7]約翰對那出來要受他洗的眾人說："毒蛇的種類！誰指示你們逃避將來的忿怒呢？[8]你們要結出果子來，與悔改的心相稱。不要自己心裏說：'有亞伯拉罕為我們的祖宗。'我告訴你們：神能從這些石頭中，給亞伯拉罕興起子孫來。[9]現在斧子已經放在樹根上，凡不結好果子的樹就砍下來，丟在火裏。"

[10]眾人問他說："這樣，我們當做甚麼呢？"

[11]約翰回答說："有兩件衣裳的，就分給那沒有的；有食物的，也當這樣行。"

[12]又有稅吏來要受洗，問他說："夫子，我們當做甚麼呢？"

[13]約翰說："除了例定的數目，不要多取。"

[14]又有兵丁問他說："我們當做甚麼呢？"

約翰說："不要以強暴待人，也不要訛詐人，自己有錢糧就當知足。"

[15]百姓指望基督來的時候，人都心裏猜疑，或者約翰是基督。[16]約翰說："我是用水給你們施洗，但有一位能力比我更大的要來，我就是給他解鞋帶也不配。他要用聖靈與火給你們施洗。[17]他手裏拿着簸箕，要揚淨他的場，把麥子收在倉裏，把糠用不滅的火燒盡了。"[18]約翰又用許多別的話勸百姓，向他們傳福音。

[19]只是分封的王希律，因他兄弟之妻希羅底的緣故，並因他所行的一切惡事，受了約翰的責備；[20]又另外添了一件，就是把約翰收在監裏。

耶穌的洗禮和家譜

[21]眾百姓都受了洗，耶穌也受了洗。正禱告的時候，天就開了，[22]聖

靈降臨在他身上，形狀彷彿鴿子；又
有聲音從天上來，說：「你是我的愛
子，我喜悅你。」

²³耶穌開頭傳道，年紀約有三十
歲。依人看來，他是約瑟的兒子，

約瑟是希里的兒子，²⁴希里是瑪塔
的兒子，瑪塔是利未的兒子，利未
是麥基的兒子，麥基是雅拿的兒
子，雅拿是約瑟的兒子，

²⁵約瑟是瑪他提亞的兒子，瑪他提亞
是亞摩斯的兒子，亞摩斯是拿鴻的
兒子，拿鴻是以斯利的兒子，以斯
利是拿該的兒子，²⁶拿該是瑪押的
兒子，瑪押是瑪他提亞的兒子，瑪
他提亞是西美的兒子，西美是約瑟
的兒子，約瑟是猶大的兒子，猶大
是約但拿的兒子，

²⁷約亞拿是利撒的兒子，利撒是所羅
巴伯的兒子，所羅巴伯是撒拉鐵的
兒子，撒拉鐵是尼利的兒子，尼利
是麥基的兒子，²⁸麥基是亞底的兒
子，亞底是哥桑的兒子，哥桑是以
摩當的兒子，以摩當是瑪的兒子，
瑪是約細的兒子，

²⁹約細是以利以謝的兒子，以利以謝
是約令的兒子，約令是瑪塔的兒
子，瑪塔是利未的兒子，³⁰利未是
西緬的兒子，西緬是猶大的兒子，
猶大是約瑟的兒子，約瑟是約南的
兒子，約南是以利亞敬的兒子，

³¹以利亞敬是米利亞的兒子，米利亞
是買南的兒子，買南是瑪達他的兒
子，瑪達他是拿單的兒子，拿單是
大衛的兒子，³²大衛是耶西的兒
子，耶西是俄備得的兒子，俄備得
是波阿斯的兒子，波阿斯是撒門的
兒子，撒門是拿順的兒子，

³³拿順是亞米拿達的兒子，亞米拿達
是亞蘭的兒子，亞蘭是希斯崙的兒
子，希斯崙是法勒斯的兒子，法勒
斯是猶大的兒子，³⁴猶大是雅各的
兒子，雅各是以撒的兒子，以撒是
亞伯拉罕的兒子，亞伯拉罕是他拉
的兒子，他拉是拿鶴的兒子，

³⁵拿鶴是西鹿的兒子，西鹿是拉吳的
兒子，拉吳是法勒的兒子，法勒是
希伯的兒子，希伯是沙拉的兒子，
³⁶沙拉是該南的兒子，該南是亞法
撒的兒子，亞法撒是閃的兒子，閃
是挪亞的兒子，挪亞是拉麥的兒
子，

scended on him in bodily form like a dove. And
a voice came from heaven: "You are my Son,
whom I love; with you I am well pleased."

²³Now Jesus himself was about thirty years
old when he began his ministry. He was the son,
so it was thought, of Joseph,

the son of Heli, ²⁴the son of Matthat,
the son of Levi, the son of Melki,
the son of Jannai, the son of Joseph,

²⁵the son of Mattathias, the son of Amos,
the son of Nahum, the son of Esli,
the son of Naggai, ²⁶the son of Maath,
the son of Mattathias, the son of Semein,
the son of Josech, the son of Joda,

²⁷the son of Joanan, the son of Rhesa,
the son of Zerubbabel, the son of Shealtiel,
the son of Neri, ²⁸the son of Melki,
the son of Addi, the son of Cosam,
the son of Elmadam, the son of Er,

²⁹the son of Joshua, the son of Eliezer,
the son of Jorim, the son of Matthat,
the son of Levi, ³⁰the son of Simeon,
the son of Judah, the son of Joseph,
the son of Jonam, the son of Eliakim,

³¹the son of Melea, the son of Menna,
the son of Mattatha, the son of Nathan,
the son of David, ³²the son of Jesse,
the son of Obed, the son of Boaz,
the son of Salmon,ᵃ the son of Nahshon,

³³the son of Amminadab, the son of Ram,ᵇ
the son of Hezron, the son of Perez,
the son of Judah, ³⁴the son of Jacob,
the son of Isaac, the son of Abraham,
the son of Terah, the son of Nahor,

³⁵the son of Serug, the son of Reu,
the son of Peleg, the son of Eber,
the son of Shelah, ³⁶the son of Cainan,
the son of Arphaxad, the son of Shem,
the son of Noah, the son of Lamech,

ᵃ 32 Some early manuscripts Sala　　ᵇ 33 Some manuscripts
Amminadab, the son of Admin, the son of Arni; other manuscripts
vary widely.

37the son of Methuselah, the son of Enoch, the son of Jared, the son of Mahalalel, the son of Kenan, 38the son of Enosh, the son of Seth, the son of Adam, the son of God.

The Temptation of Jesus

4 Jesus, full of the Holy Spirit, returned from the Jordan and was led by the Spirit in the desert, 2where for forty days he was tempted by the devil. He ate nothing during those days, and at the end of them he was hungry.

3The devil said to him, "If you are the Son of God, tell this stone to become bread."

4Jesus answered, "It is written: 'Man does not live on bread alone.'*a*"

5The devil led him up to a high place and showed him in an instant all the kingdoms of the world. 6And he said to him, "I will give you all their authority and splendor, for it has been given to me, and I can give it to anyone I want to. 7So if you worship me, it will all be yours."

8Jesus answered, "It is written: 'Worship the Lord your God and serve him only.'*b*"

9The devil led him to Jerusalem and had him stand on the highest point of the temple. "If you are the Son of God," he said, "throw yourself down from here. 10For it is written:

" 'He will command his angels concerning
　　you
　to guard you carefully;
11they will lift you up in their hands,
　so that you will not strike your foot against
　　a stone.'*c*"

12Jesus answered, "It says: 'Do not put the Lord your God to the test.'*d*"

13When the devil had finished all this tempting, he left him until an opportune time.

Jesus Rejected at Nazareth

14Jesus returned to Galilee in the power of the Spirit, and news about him spread through the whole countryside. 15He taught in their synagogues, and everyone praised him.

16He went to Nazareth, where he had been brought up, and on the Sabbath day he went into the synagogue, as was his custom. And he stood up to read. 17The scroll of the prophet

a 4 Deut. 8:3　　*b 8* Deut. 6:13　　*c 11* Psalm 91:11,12
d 12 Deut. 6:16

37拉麥是瑪土撒拉的兒子，瑪土撒拉是以諾的兒子，以諾是雅列的兒子，雅列是瑪勒列的兒子，瑪勒列是該南的兒子，該南是以挪士的兒子，38以挪士是塞特的兒子，塞特是亞當的兒子，亞當是神的兒子。

耶穌受試探

4 耶穌被聖靈充滿，從約旦河回來，聖靈將他引到曠野，四十天受魔鬼的試探。2那些日子沒有吃甚麼，日子滿了，他就餓了。

3魔鬼對他說："你若是神的兒子，可以吩咐這塊石頭變成食物。"

4耶穌回答說："經上記着說：'人活着不是單靠食物，乃是靠神口裏所出的一切話。'"

5魔鬼又領他上了高山，霎時間把天下的萬國都指給他看，6對他說："這一切權柄、榮華，我都要給你，因為這原是交付我的，我願意給誰就給誰。7你若在我面前下拜，這都要歸你。"

8耶穌說："經上記着說：'當拜主你的神，單要侍奉他。'"

9魔鬼又領他到耶路撒冷去，叫他站在殿頂（註："頂"原文作"翅"）上，對他說："你若是神的兒子，可以從這裏跳下去；10因為經上記着說：

" '主要為你
　吩咐他的使者
　　保護你。
11他們要用手托着你，
　免得你的腳
　　碰在石頭上。' "

12耶穌對他說："經上說：'不可試探主你的神。'"

13魔鬼用完了各樣的試探，就暫時離開耶穌。

耶穌在拿撒勒被拒

14耶穌滿有聖靈的能力，回到加利利，他的名聲就傳遍了四方。15他在各會堂裏教訓人，眾人都稱讚他。

16耶穌來到拿撒勒，就是他長大的地方。在安息日，照他平常的規矩進了會堂，站起來要念聖經。17有人把先知以賽亞的書交給他，他就打開，找到一處寫着說：

18 "主的靈在我身上，
　　因為他用膏膏我，
　　叫我傳福音給貧窮的人；
　差遣我報告
　　被擄的得釋放，
　　瞎眼的得看見，
　　叫那受壓制的得自由，
19 報告神悅納人的禧年。"

20 於是把書捲起來，交還執事，就坐下。會堂裏的人都定睛看他。21 耶穌對他們說："今天這經應驗在你們耳中了。"

22 眾人都稱讚他，並希奇他口中所出的恩言。又說："這不是約瑟的兒子嗎？"

23 耶穌對他們說："你們必引這俗語向我說：'醫生，你醫治自己吧！我們聽見你在迦百農所行的事，也當行在你自己家鄉裏。'"

24 又說："我實在告訴你們：沒有先知在自己家鄉被人悅納的。25 我對你們說實話，當以利亞的時候，天閉塞了三年零六個月，遍地有大饑荒，那時，以色列中有許多寡婦，26 以利亞並沒有奉差往她們一個人那裏去，只奉差往西頓的撒勒法一個寡婦那裏去。27 先知以利沙的時候，以色列中有許多長大痲瘋的，但內中除了敘利亞國的乃縵，沒有一個得潔淨的。"

28 會堂裏的人聽見這話，都怒氣滿胸，29 就起來攆他出城。他們的城造在山上，他們帶他到山崖，要把他推下去。30 他卻從他們中間直行，過去了。

耶穌趕出污鬼

31 耶穌下到迦百農，就是加利利的一座城，在安息日教訓眾人。32 他們很希奇他的教訓，因為他的話裏有權柄。

33 在會堂裏有一個人，被污鬼的精氣附着，大聲喊叫說：34 "唉！拿撒勒的耶穌，我們與你有甚麼相干？

Isaiah was handed to him. Unrolling it, he found the place where it is written:

18 "The Spirit of the Lord is on me,
　　because he has anointed me
　　　to preach good news to the poor.
　He has sent me to proclaim freedom for the
　　prisoners
　　and recovery of sight for the blind,
　to release the oppressed,
19 　to proclaim the year of the Lord's favor."[a]

20 Then he rolled up the scroll, gave it back to the attendant and sat down. The eyes of everyone in the synagogue were fastened on him, 21 and he began by saying to them, "Today this scripture is fulfilled in your hearing."

22 All spoke well of him and were amazed at the gracious words that came from his lips. "Isn't this Joseph's son?" they asked.

23 Jesus said to them, "Surely you will quote this proverb to me: 'Physician, heal yourself! Do here in your hometown what we have heard that you did in Capernaum.'"

24 "I tell you the truth," he continued, "no prophet is accepted in his hometown. 25 I assure you that there were many widows in Israel in Elijah's time, when the sky was shut for three and a half years and there was a severe famine throughout the land. 26 Yet Elijah was not sent to any of them, but to a widow in Zarephath in the region of Sidon. 27 And there were many in Israel with leprosy[b] in the time of Elisha the prophet, yet not one of them was cleansed—only Naaman the Syrian."

28 All the people in the synagogue were furious when they heard this. 29 They got up, drove him out of the town, and took him to the brow of the hill on which the town was built, in order to throw him down the cliff. 30 But he walked right through the crowd and went on his way.

Jesus Drives Out an Evil Spirit

31 Then he went down to Capernaum, a town in Galilee, and on the Sabbath began to teach the people. 32 They were amazed at his teaching, because his message had authority.

33 In the synagogue there was a man possessed by a demon, an evil[c] spirit. He cried out at the top of his voice, 34 "Ha! What do you want with us, Jesus of Nazareth? Have you come to

---

a 19 Isaiah 61:1,2　　b 27 The Greek word was used for various diseases affecting the skin—not necessarily leprosy.
c 33 Greek unclean; also in verse 36

destroy us? I know who you are—the Holy One of God!"

35"Be quiet!" Jesus said sternly. "Come out of him!" Then the demon threw the man down before them all and came out without injuring him.

36All the people were amazed and said to each other, "What is this teaching? With authority and power he gives orders to evil spirits and they come out!" 37And the news about him spread throughout the surrounding area.

Jesus Heals Many

38Jesus left the synagogue and went to the home of Simon. Now Simon's mother-in-law was suffering from a high fever, and they asked Jesus to help her. 39So he bent over her and rebuked the fever, and it left her. She got up at once and began to wait on them.

40When the sun was setting, the people brought to Jesus all who had various kinds of sickness, and laying his hands on each one, he healed them. 41Moreover, demons came out of many people, shouting, "You are the Son of God!" But he rebuked them and would not allow them to speak, because they knew he was the Christ.*a*

42At daybreak Jesus went out to a solitary place. The people were looking for him and when they came to where he was, they tried to keep him from leaving them. 43But he said, "I must preach the good news of the kingdom of God to the other towns also, because that is why I was sent." 44And he kept on preaching in the synagogues of Judea.*b*

The Calling of the First Disciples

5 One day as Jesus was standing by the Lake of Gennesaret,*c* with the people crowding around him and listening to the word of God, 2he saw at the water's edge two boats, left there by the fishermen, who were washing their nets. 3He got into one of the boats, the one belonging to Simon, and asked him to put out a little from shore. Then he sat down and taught the people from the boat.

4When he had finished speaking, he said to Simon, "Put out into deep water, and let down*d* the nets for a catch."

5Simon answered, "Master, we've worked hard all night and haven't caught anything. But because you say so, I will let down the nets."

a 41 Or Messiah   b 44 Or the land of the Jews; some manuscripts Galilee   c 1 That is, Sea of Galilee   d 4 The Greek verb is plural.

你來滅我們嗎？我知道你是誰，乃是神的聖者！"

35耶穌責備他說："不要做聲，從這人身上出來吧！"鬼把那人摔倒在眾人中間，就出來了，卻也沒有害他。

36眾人都驚訝，彼此對問說："這是甚麼道理呢？因為他用權柄能力吩咐污鬼，污鬼就出來。"37於是耶穌的名聲傳遍了周圍地方。

耶穌醫治許多病人

38耶穌出了會堂，進了西門的家。西門的岳母害熱病甚重，有人為她求耶穌。39耶穌站在她旁邊，斥責那熱病，熱就退了。她立刻起來服侍他們。

40日落的時候，凡有病人的，不論害甚麼病，都帶到耶穌那裏。耶穌按手在他們各人身上，醫好他們。41又有鬼從好些人身上出來，喊着說："你是神的兒子！"耶穌斥責他們，不許他們說話，因為他們知道他是基督。

42天亮的時候，耶穌出來，走到曠野地方。眾人去找他，到了他那裏，要留住他，不要他離開他們。43但耶穌對他們說："我也必須在別城傳神國的福音，因我奉差原是為此。"44於是耶穌在加利利的各會堂傳道。

召第一批門徒

5 耶穌站在革尼撒勒湖邊，眾人擁擠他，要聽神的道。2他見有兩隻船灣在湖邊，打魚的人卻離開船洗網去了。3有一隻船是西門的，耶穌就上去，請他把船撐開，稍微離岸，就坐下，從船上教訓眾人。

4講完了，對西門說："把船開到水深之處，下網打魚。"

5西門說："夫子，我們整夜勞力，並沒有打着甚麼。但依從你的話，我就下網。"

⁶他們下了網，就圈住許多魚，網險些裂開，⁷便招呼那隻船的同伴來幫助。他們就來把魚裝滿了兩隻船，甚至船要沉下去。

⁸西門彼得看見，就俯伏在耶穌膝前，說："主啊，離開我，我是個罪人！"⁹他和一切同在的人都驚訝這一網所打的魚。¹⁰他的夥伴西庇太的兒子雅各、約翰，也是這樣。

耶穌對西門說："不要怕！從今以後，你要得人了。"¹¹他們把兩隻船攏了岸，就撇下所有的，跟從了耶穌。

長大痲瘋的人

¹²有一回，耶穌在一個城裏，有人滿身長了大痲瘋，看見他，就俯伏在地，求他說："主若肯，必能叫我潔淨了。"

¹³耶穌伸手摸他，說："我肯，你潔淨了吧！"大痲瘋立刻就離了他的身。

¹⁴耶穌囑咐他："你切不可告訴人，只要去把身體給祭司察看，又要為你得了潔淨，照摩西所吩咐的獻上禮物，對眾人作證據。"

¹⁵但耶穌的名聲越發傳揚出去。有極多的人聚集來聽道，也指望醫治他們的病。¹⁶耶穌卻退到曠野去禱告。

耶穌醫治癱子

¹⁷有一天，耶穌教訓人，有法利賽人和教法師在旁邊坐着，他們是從加利利各鄉村和猶太並耶路撒冷來的。主的能力與耶穌同在，使他能醫治病人。¹⁸有人用褥子抬着一個癱子，要抬進去放在耶穌面前，¹⁹卻因人多，尋不出法子抬進去，就上了房頂，從瓦間把他連褥子縋到當中，正在耶穌面前。

²⁰耶穌見他們的信心，就對癱子說："你的罪赦了。"

²¹文士和法利賽人就議論說："這說僭妄話的是誰？除了神以外，誰能赦罪呢？"

⁶When they had done so, they caught such a large number of fish that their nets began to break. ⁷So they signaled their partners in the other boat to come and help them, and they came and filled both boats so full that they began to sink.

⁸When Simon Peter saw this, he fell at Jesus' knees and said, "Go away from me, Lord; I am a sinful man!" ⁹For he and all his companions were astonished at the catch of fish they had taken, ¹⁰and so were James and John, the sons of Zebedee, Simon's partners.

Then Jesus said to Simon, "Don't be afraid; from now on you will catch men." ¹¹So they pulled their boats up on shore, left everything and followed him.

The Man With Leprosy

¹²While Jesus was in one of the towns, a man came along who was covered with leprosy.^a When he saw Jesus, he fell with his face to the ground and begged him, "Lord, if you are willing, you can make me clean."

¹³Jesus reached out his hand and touched the man. "I am willing," he said. "Be clean!" And immediately the leprosy left him.

¹⁴Then Jesus ordered him, "Don't tell anyone, but go, show yourself to the priest and offer the sacrifices that Moses commanded for your cleansing, as a testimony to them."

¹⁵Yet the news about him spread all the more, so that crowds of people came to hear him and to be healed of their sicknesses. ¹⁶But Jesus often withdrew to lonely places and prayed.

Jesus Heals a Paralytic

¹⁷One day as he was teaching, Pharisees and teachers of the law, who had come from every village of Galilee and from Judea and Jerusalem, were sitting there. And the power of the Lord was present for him to heal the sick. ¹⁸Some men came carrying a paralytic on a mat and tried to take him into the house to lay him before Jesus. ¹⁹When they could not find a way to do this because of the crowd, they went up on the roof and lowered him on his mat through the tiles into the middle of the crowd, right in front of Jesus.

²⁰When Jesus saw their faith, he said, "Friend, your sins are forgiven."

²¹The Pharisees and the teachers of the law began thinking to themselves, "Who is this fellow who speaks blasphemy? Who can forgive sins but God alone?"

---

a 12 The Greek word was used for various diseases affecting the skin—not necessarily leprosy.

22Jesus knew what they were thinking and asked, "Why are you thinking these things in your hearts? 23Which is easier: to say, 'Your sins are forgiven,' or to say, 'Get up and walk'? 24But that you may know that the Son of Man has authority on earth to forgive sins. . . ." He said to the paralyzed man, "I tell you, get up, take your mat and go home." 25Immediately he stood up in front of them, took what he had been lying on and went home praising God. 26Everyone was amazed and gave praise to God. They were filled with awe and said, "We have seen remarkable things today."

The Calling of Levi

27After this, Jesus went out and saw a tax collector by the name of Levi sitting at his tax booth. "Follow me," Jesus said to him, 28and Levi got up, left everything and followed him.

29Then Levi held a great banquet for Jesus at his house, and a large crowd of tax collectors and others were eating with them. 30But the Pharisees and the teachers of the law who belonged to their sect complained to his disciples, "Why do you eat and drink with tax collectors and 'sinners'?"

31Jesus answered them, "It is not the healthy who need a doctor, but the sick. 32I have not come to call the righteous, but sinners to repentance."

Jesus Questioned About Fasting

33They said to him, "John's disciples often fast and pray, and so do the disciples of the Pharisees, but yours go on eating and drinking."

34Jesus answered, "Can you make the guests of the bridegroom fast while he is with them? 35But the time will come when the bridegroom will be taken from them; in those days they will fast."

36He told them this parable: "No one tears a patch from a new garment and sews it on an old one. If he does, he will have torn the new garment, and the patch from the new will not match the old. 37And no one pours new wine into old wineskins. If he does, the new wine will burst the skins, the wine will run out and the wineskins will be ruined. 38No, new wine must be poured into new wineskins. 39And no one after drinking old wine wants the new, for he says, 'The old is better.' "

22耶穌知道他們所議論的，就說："你們心裏議論的是甚麼呢？23或說'你的罪赦了'，或說'你起來行走'，哪一樣容易呢？24但要叫你們知道，人子在地上有赦罪的權柄。"就對癱子說："我吩咐你起來，拿你的褥子回家去吧！"25那人當眾人面前立刻起來，拿着他所躺臥的褥子回家去，歸榮耀與神。26眾人都驚奇，也歸榮耀與神，並且滿心懼怕，說："我們今日看見非常的事了。"

召利未

27這事以後，耶穌出去，看見一個稅吏，名叫利未，坐在稅關上，就對他說："你跟從我來！"28他就撇下所有的，起來，跟從了耶穌。

29利未在自己家裏為耶穌大擺筵席，有許多稅吏和別人與他們一同坐席。30法利賽人和文士就向耶穌的門徒發怨言說："你們為甚麼和稅吏並罪人一同吃喝呢？"

31耶穌對他們說："無病的人用不着醫生，有病的人才用得着；32我來本不是召義人悔改，乃是召罪人悔改。"

向耶穌詢問禁食之事

33他們說："約翰的門徒屢次禁食祈禱，法利賽人的門徒也是這樣；惟獨你的門徒又吃又喝。"

34耶穌對他們說："新郎和陪伴之人同在的時候，豈能叫陪伴之人禁食呢？35但日子將到，新郎要離開他們，那日他們就要禁食了。"

36耶穌又設一個比喻，對他們說："沒有人把新衣服撕下一塊來補在舊衣服上；若是這樣，就把新的撕破了，並且所撕下來的那塊新的和舊的也不相稱。37也沒有人把新酒裝在舊皮袋裏；若是這樣，新酒必將皮袋裂開，酒便漏出來，皮袋也就壞了。38但新酒必須裝在新皮袋裏。39沒有人喝了陳酒又想喝新的，他總說陳的好。"

安息日的主

6 有一個安息日，耶穌從麥地經過。他的門徒掐了麥穗，用手搓着吃。²有幾個法利賽人說：「你們為甚麼做安息日不可做的事呢？」

³耶穌對他們說：「經上記着<u>大衛</u>和跟從他的人飢餓之時所做的事，連這個你們也沒有念過嗎？⁴他怎麼進了神的殿，拿陳設餅吃，又給跟從的人吃？這餅除了祭司以外，別人都不可吃。」⁵又對他們說：「人子是安息日的主。」

⁶又有一個安息日，耶穌進了會堂教訓人，在那裏有一個人右手枯乾了。⁷文士和法利賽人窺探耶穌，在安息日治病不治病，要得把柄去告他。⁸耶穌卻知道他們的意念，就對那枯乾一隻手的人說：「起來！站在當中。」那人就起來，站着。

⁹耶穌對他們說：「我問你們，在安息日行善行惡，救命害命，哪樣是可以的呢？」

¹⁰他就周圍看着他們眾人，對那人說：「伸出手來！」他把手一伸，手就復了原。¹¹他們就滿心大怒，彼此商議怎樣處治耶穌。

十二使徒

¹²那時，耶穌出去，上山禱告，整夜禱告神。¹³到了天亮，叫他的門徒來，就從他們中間挑選十二個人，稱他們為使徒。¹⁴這十二個人有<u>西門</u>，耶穌又給他起名叫<u>彼得</u>，還有他兄弟<u>安得烈</u>，又有<u>雅各</u>和<u>約翰</u>，<u>腓力</u>和<u>巴多羅買</u>，¹⁵<u>馬太</u>和<u>多馬</u>，<u>亞勒腓</u>的兒子<u>雅各</u>和奮銳黨的<u>西門</u>，¹⁶<u>雅各</u>的兒子（註：「兒子」或作「兄弟」）<u>猶大</u>和賣主的<u>加略人猶大</u>。

福與禍

¹⁷耶穌和他們下了山，站在一塊平地上；同站的有許多門徒，又有許多百姓，從<u>猶太</u>全地和<u>耶路撒冷</u>，並<u>推羅</u>、<u>西頓</u>的海邊來，都要聽他講道，又指望醫治他們的病；¹⁸還有被污鬼纏磨的，也得了醫治。¹⁹眾人都

Lord of the Sabbath

6 One Sabbath Jesus was going through the grainfields, and his disciples began to pick some heads of grain, rub them in their hands and eat the kernels. ²Some of the Pharisees asked, "Why are you doing what is unlawful on the Sabbath?"

³Jesus answered them, "Have you never read what David did when he and his companions were hungry? ⁴He entered the house of God, and taking the consecrated bread, he ate what is lawful only for priests to eat. And he also gave some to his companions." ⁵Then Jesus said to them, "The Son of Man is Lord of the Sabbath."

⁶On another Sabbath he went into the synagogue and was teaching, and a man was there whose right hand was shriveled. ⁷The Pharisees and the teachers of the law were looking for a reason to accuse Jesus, so they watched him closely to see if he would heal on the Sabbath. ⁸But Jesus knew what they were thinking and said to the man with the shriveled hand, "Get up and stand in front of everyone." So he got up and stood there.

⁹Then Jesus said to them, "I ask you, which is lawful on the Sabbath: to do good or to do evil, to save life or to destroy it?"

¹⁰He looked around at them all, and then said to the man, "Stretch out your hand." He did so, and his hand was completely restored. ¹¹But they were furious and began to discuss with one another what they might do to Jesus.

The Twelve Apostles

¹²One of those days Jesus went out to a mountainside to pray, and spent the night praying to God. ¹³When morning came, he called his disciples to him and chose twelve of them, whom he also designated apostles: ¹⁴Simon (whom he named Peter), his brother Andrew, James, John, Philip, Bartholomew, ¹⁵Matthew, Thomas, James son of Alphaeus, Simon who was called the Zealot, ¹⁶Judas son of James, and Judas Iscariot, who became a traitor.

Blessings and Woes

¹⁷He went down with them and stood on a level place. A large crowd of his disciples was there and a great number of people from all over Judea, from Jerusalem, and from the coast of Tyre and Sidon, ¹⁸who had come to hear him and to be healed of their diseases. Those troubled by evil^a spirits were cured, ¹⁹and the people

a 18 Greek *unclean*

all tried to touch him, because power was coming from him and healing them all.

²⁰Looking at his disciples, he said:

"Blessed are you who are poor,
    for yours is the kingdom of God.
²¹Blessed are you who hunger now,
    for you will be satisfied.
Blessed are you who weep now,
    for you will laugh.
²²Blessed are you when men hate you,
    when they exclude you and insult you
    and reject your name as evil,
       because of the Son of Man.

²³"Rejoice in that day and leap for joy, because great is your reward in heaven. For that is how their fathers treated the prophets.

²⁴"But woe to you who are rich,
    for you have already received your comfort.
²⁵Woe to you who are well fed now,
    for you will go hungry.
Woe to you who laugh now,
    for you will mourn and weep.
²⁶Woe to you when all men speak well of you,
    for that is how their fathers treated the false
      prophets.

Love for Enemies

²⁷"But I tell you who hear me: Love your enemies, do good to those who hate you, ²⁸bless those who curse you, pray for those who mistreat you. ²⁹If someone strikes you on one cheek, turn to him the other also. If someone takes your cloak, do not stop him from taking your tunic. ³⁰Give to everyone who asks you, and if anyone takes what belongs to you, do not demand it back. ³¹Do to others as you would have them do to you.

³²"If you love those who love you, what credit is that to you? Even 'sinners' love those who love them. ³³And if you do good to those who are good to you, what credit is that to you? Even 'sinners' do that. ³⁴And if you lend to those from whom you expect repayment, what credit is that to you? Even 'sinners' lend to 'sinners,' expecting to be repaid in full. ³⁵But love your enemies, do good to them, and lend to them without expecting to get anything back. Then your reward will be great, and you will be sons of the Most High, because he is kind to the ungrateful and wicked. ³⁶Be merciful, just as your Father is merciful.

想要摸他，因為有能力從他身上發出來，醫好了他們。

²⁰耶穌舉目看着門徒，說：

"你們貧窮的人有福了，
    因為神的國是你們的！
²¹你們飢餓的人有福了，
    因為你們將要飽足！
你們哀哭的人有福了，
    因為你們將要喜笑！
²²人為人子恨惡你們，
    拒絕你們，辱罵你們，
    棄掉你們的名，以為是惡，
      你們就有福了。

²³"當那日，你們要歡喜跳躍，因為你們在天上的賞賜是大的！他們的祖宗待先知也是這樣。

²⁴"但你們富足的人有禍了，
    因為你們受過你們的安慰！
²⁵你們飽足的人有禍了，
    因為你們將要飢餓！
你們喜笑的人有禍了，
    因為你們將要哀慟哭泣！
²⁶人都說你們好的時候，
    你們就有禍了，
    因為他們的祖宗待假先知
      也是這樣！

愛仇敵

²⁷"只是我告訴你們這聽道的人，你們的仇敵，要愛他！恨你們的，要待他好！²⁸咒詛你們的，要為他祝福！凌辱你們的，要為他禱告！²⁹有人打你這邊的臉，連那邊的臉也由他打。有人奪你的外衣，連裏衣也由他拿去。³⁰凡求你的，就給他。有人奪你的東西去，不用再要回來。³¹你們願意人怎樣待你們，你們也要怎樣待人。

³²"你們若單愛那愛你們的人，有甚麼可酬謝的呢？就是罪人也愛那愛他們的人。³³你們若善待那善待你們的人，有甚麼可酬謝的呢？就是罪人也是這樣行。³⁴你們若借給人，指望從他收回，有甚麼可酬謝的呢？就是罪人也借給罪人，要如數收回。³⁵你們倒要愛仇敵，也要善待他們，並要借給人不指望償還，你們的賞賜就必大了，你們也必作至高者的兒子，因為他恩待那忘恩的和作惡的。³⁶你們要慈悲，像你們的父慈悲一樣。

論斷別人

³⁷「你們不要論斷人，就不被論斷；你們不要定人的罪，就不被定罪；你們要饒恕人，就必蒙饒恕（註：「饒恕」原文作「釋放」）；³⁸你們要給人，就必有給你們的，並且用十足的升斗，連搖帶按，上尖下流地倒在你們懷裏；因為你們用甚麼量器量給人，也必用甚麼量器量給你們。」

³⁹耶穌又用比喻對他們說：「瞎子豈能領瞎子，兩個人不是都要掉在坑裏嗎？⁴⁰學生不能高過先生；凡學成了的不過和先生一樣。

⁴¹「為甚麼看見你弟兄眼中有刺，卻不想自己眼中有梁木呢？⁴²你不見自己眼中有梁木，怎能對你弟兄說：『容我去掉你眼中的刺』呢？你這假冒為善的人！先去掉自己眼中的梁木，然後才能看得清楚，去掉你弟兄眼中的刺。

樹和它的果子

⁴³「因為，沒有好樹結壞果子，也沒有壞樹結好果子。⁴⁴凡樹木看果子，就可以認出它來。人不是從荊棘上摘無花果，也不是從蒺藜裏摘葡萄。⁴⁵善人從他心裏所存的善就發出善來；惡人從他心裏所存的惡就發出惡來；因為心裏所充滿的，口裏就說出來。

聰明和無知的蓋房者

⁴⁶「你們為甚麼稱呼我『主啊，主啊』卻不遵我的話行呢？⁴⁷凡到我這裏來，聽見我的話就去行的，我要告訴你們他像甚麼人：⁴⁸他像一個人蓋房子，深深地挖地，把根基安在磐石上。到發大水的時候，水沖那房子，房子總不能搖動，因為根基立在磐石上（註：有古卷作「因為蓋造得好」）。⁴⁹惟有聽見不去行的，就像一個人在土地上蓋房子，沒有根基，水一沖，隨即倒塌了，並且那房子壞得很大。」

百夫長的信心

7 耶穌對百姓講完了這一切的話，就進了迦百農。²有一個百夫長所寶貴的僕人，害病快要死了。³百夫長風聞耶穌的事，就託猶太人的幾個長老去求耶穌來救

Judging Others

³⁷"Do not judge, and you will not be judged. Do not condemn, and you will not be condemned. Forgive, and you will be forgiven. ³⁸Give, and it will be given to you. A good measure, pressed down, shaken together and running over, will be poured into your lap. For with the measure you use, it will be measured to you."

³⁹He also told them this parable: "Can a blind man lead a blind man? Will they not both fall into a pit? ⁴⁰A student is not above his teacher, but everyone who is fully trained will be like his teacher.

⁴¹"Why do you look at the speck of sawdust in your brother's eye and pay no attention to the plank in your own eye? ⁴²How can you say to your brother, 'Brother, let me take the speck out of your eye,' when you yourself fail to see the plank in your own eye? You hypocrite, first take the plank out of your eye, and then you will see clearly to remove the speck from your brother's eye.

A Tree and Its Fruit

⁴³"No good tree bears bad fruit, nor does a bad tree bear good fruit. ⁴⁴Each tree is recognized by its own fruit. People do not pick figs from thornbushes, or grapes from briers. ⁴⁵The good man brings good things out of the good stored up in his heart, and the evil man brings evil things out of the evil stored up in his heart. For out of the overflow of his heart his mouth speaks.

The Wise and Foolish Builders

⁴⁶"Why do you call me, 'Lord, Lord,' and do not do what I say? ⁴⁷I will show you what he is like who comes to me and hears my words and puts them into practice. ⁴⁸He is like a man building a house, who dug down deep and laid the foundation on rock. When a flood came, the torrent struck that house but could not shake it, because it was well built. ⁴⁹But the one who hears my words and does not put them into practice is like a man who built a house on the ground without a foundation. The moment the torrent struck that house, it collapsed and its destruction was complete."

The Faith of the Centurion

7 When Jesus had finished saying all this in the hearing of the people, he entered Capernaum. ²There a centurion's servant, whom his master valued highly, was sick and about to die. ³The centurion heard of Jesus and sent some elders of the Jews to him, asking him to come and heal his servant. 4When they came to Jesus, they pleaded earnestly with him, "This man deserves to have you do this, 5because he loves our nation and has built our synagogue." 6So Jesus went with them.

He was not far from the house when the centurion sent friends to say to him: "Lord, don't trouble yourself, for I do not deserve to have you come under my roof. 7That is why I did not even consider myself worthy to come to you. But say the word, and my servant will be healed. 8For I myself am a man under authority, with soldiers under me. I tell this one, 'Go,' and he goes; and that one, 'Come,' and he comes. I say to my servant, 'Do this,' and he does it."

9When Jesus heard this, he was amazed at him, and turning to the crowd following him, he said, "I tell you, I have not found such great faith even in Israel." 10Then the men who had been sent returned to the house and found the servant well.

Jesus Raises a Widow's Son

11Soon afterward, Jesus went to a town called Nain, and his disciples and a large crowd went along with him. 12As he approached the town gate, a dead person was being carried out—the only son of his mother, and she was a widow. And a large crowd from the town was with her. 13When the Lord saw her, his heart went out to her and he said, "Don't cry."

14Then he went up and touched the coffin, and those carrying it stood still. He said, "Young man, I say to you, get up!" 15The dead man sat up and began to talk, and Jesus gave him back to his mother.

16They were all filled with awe and praised God. "A great prophet has appeared among us," they said. "God has come to help his people." 17This news about Jesus spread throughout Judea*a* and the surrounding country.

Jesus and John the Baptist

18John's disciples told him about all these things. Calling two of them, 19he sent them to the Lord to ask, "Are you the one who was to come, or should we expect someone else?"

20When the men came to Jesus, they said, "John the Baptist sent us to you to ask, 'Are you the one who was to come, or should we expect someone else?'"

21At that very time Jesus cured many who had diseases, sicknesses and evil spirits, and gave sight to many who were blind. 22So he

a 17 Or *the land of the Jews*

他的僕人。4他們到了耶穌那裏，就切切地求他說：「你給他行這事是他所配得的，5因為他愛我們的百姓，給我們建造會堂。」6耶穌就和他們同去。

離那家不遠，百夫長託幾個朋友去見耶穌，對他說：「主啊，不要勞動，因你到我舍下，我不敢當！7我也自以為不配去見你，只要你說一句話，我的僕人就必好了。8因為我在人的權下，也有兵在我以下，對這個說：『去！』他就去；對那個說：『來！』他就來；對我的僕人說：『你做這事！』他就去做。」

9耶穌聽見這話，就希奇他，轉身對跟隨的眾人說：「我告訴你們，這麼大的信心，就是在以色列中，我也沒有遇見過。」10那託來的人回到百夫長家裏，看見僕人已經好了。

耶穌使寡婦之子復活

11過了不多時（註：有古卷作「次日」），耶穌往一座城去，這城名叫拿因。他的門徒和極多的人與他同行。12將近城門，有一個死人被抬出來。這人是他母親獨生的兒子，他母親又是寡婦，有城裏的許多人同着寡婦送殯。13主看見那寡婦，就憐憫她，對她說：「不要哭。」

14於是進前按着杠，抬的人就站住了。耶穌說：「少年人，我吩咐你起來！」15那死人就坐起，並且說話。耶穌便把他交給他母親。

16眾人都驚奇，歸榮耀與神，說：「有大先知在我們中間興起來了！」又說：「神眷顧了他的百姓！」17他這事的風聲就傳遍了猶太和周圍地方。

耶穌與施洗約翰

18約翰的門徒把這些事都告訴約翰。19他便叫了兩個門徒來，打發他們到主那裏去，說：「那將要來的是你嗎？還是我們等候別人呢？」

20那兩個人來到耶穌那裏，說：「施洗的約翰打發我們來問你：『那將要來的是你嗎？還是我們等候別人呢？』」

21正當那時候，耶穌治好了許多有疾病的，受災患的，被惡鬼附着的，又開恩叫好些瞎子能看見。22耶穌回答說：“你們去，把所看見所聽見的事告訴約翰，就是瞎子看見，瘸子行走，長大痲瘋的潔淨，聾子聽見，死人復活，窮人有福音傳給他們。 ²³凡不因我跌倒的，就有福了！”

²⁴約翰所差來的人既走了，耶穌就對眾人講論約翰說：“你們從前出去到曠野，是要看甚麼呢？要看風吹動的蘆葦嗎？ ²⁵你們出去，到底是要看甚麼？要看穿細軟衣服的人嗎？那穿華麗衣服、宴樂度日的人是在王宮裏。 ²⁶你們出去，究竟是要看甚麼？要看先知嗎？我告訴你們，是的，他比先知大多了。 ²⁷經上記着說：

“‘我要差遣我的使者
　　在你前面預備道路。’
　所說的就是這個人。
²⁸我告訴你們，凡婦人所生的，沒有一個大過約翰的；然而神國裏最小的比他還大。”

²⁹眾百姓和稅吏既受過約翰的洗，聽見這話，就以神為義； ³⁰但法利賽人和律法師沒有受過約翰的洗，竟為自己廢棄了神的旨意。（註：29、30兩節或作“眾百姓和稅吏聽見了約翰的話，就受了他的洗，便以神為義；但法利賽人和律法師不受約翰的洗，竟為自己廢棄了神的旨意”）。

³¹主又說：“這樣，我可用甚麼比這世代的人呢？他們好像甚麼呢？ ³²好像孩童坐在街市上，彼此呼叫說：

“‘我們向你們吹笛，
　你們不跳舞；
　我們向你們舉哀，
　你們不啼哭。’

³³施洗的約翰來，不吃餅，不喝酒，你們說他是被鬼附着的。 ³⁴人子來，也吃也喝，你們說他是貪食好酒的人，是稅吏和罪人的朋友。 ³⁵但智慧之子都以智慧為是。”

有罪的女人膏抹耶穌

³⁶有一個法利賽人請耶穌和他吃飯，耶穌就到法利賽人家裏去坐席。 ³⁷那城裏有一個女人，是個罪人，知

replied to the messengers, "Go back and report to John what you have seen and heard: The blind receive sight, the lame walk, those who have leprosy[a] are cured, the deaf hear, the dead are raised, and the good news is preached to the poor. ²³Blessed is the man who does not fall away on account of me."

²⁴After John's messengers left, Jesus began to speak to the crowd about John: "What did you go out into the desert to see? A reed swayed by the wind? ²⁵If not, what did you go out to see? A man dressed in fine clothes? No, those who wear expensive clothes and indulge in luxury are in palaces. ²⁶But what did you go out to see? A prophet? Yes, I tell you, and more than a prophet. ²⁷This is the one about whom it is written:

" 'I will send my messenger ahead of you,
　who will prepare your way before you.'[b]

²⁸I tell you, among those born of women there is no one greater than John; yet the one who is least in the kingdom of God is greater than he."

²⁹(All the people, even the tax collectors, when they heard Jesus' words, acknowledged that God's way was right, because they had been baptized by John. ³⁰But the Pharisees and experts in the law rejected God's purpose for themselves, because they had not been baptized by John.)

³¹"To what, then, can I compare the people of this generation? What are they like? ³²They are like children sitting in the marketplace and calling out to each other:

" 'We played the flute for you,
　and you did not dance;
　we sang a dirge,
　and you did not cry.'

³³For John the Baptist came neither eating bread nor drinking wine, and you say, 'He has a demon.' ³⁴The Son of Man came eating and drinking, and you say, 'Here is a glutton and a drunkard, a friend of tax collectors and "sinners." ' ³⁵But wisdom is proved right by all her children."

Jesus Anointed by a Sinful Woman

³⁶Now one of the Pharisees invited Jesus to have dinner with him, so he went to the Pharisee's house and reclined at the table. ³⁷When a woman who had lived a sinful life in that town learned

a 22 The Greek word was used for various diseases affecting the skin—not necessarily leprosy.　*b 27* Mal. 3:1

that Jesus was eating at the Pharisee's house, she brought an alabaster jar of perfume, 38and as she stood behind him at his feet weeping, she began to wet his feet with her tears. Then she wiped them with her hair, kissed them and poured perfume on them.

39When the Pharisee who had invited him saw this, he said to himself, "If this man were a prophet, he would know who is touching him and what kind of woman she is—that she is a sinner."

40Jesus answered him, "Simon, I have something to tell you."

"Tell me, teacher," he said.

41"Two men owed money to a certain moneylender. One owed him five hundred denarii,*a* and the other fifty. 42Neither of them had the money to pay him back, so he canceled the debts of both. Now which of them will love him more?"

43Simon replied, "I suppose the one who had the bigger debt canceled."

"You have judged correctly," Jesus said.

44Then he turned toward the woman and said to Simon, "Do you see this woman? I came into your house. You did not give me any water for my feet, but she wet my feet with her tears and wiped them with her hair. 45You did not give me a kiss, but this woman, from the time I entered, has not stopped kissing my feet. 46You did not put oil on my head, but she has poured perfume on my feet. 47Therefore, I tell you, her many sins have been forgiven—for she loved much. But he who has been forgiven little loves little."

48Then Jesus said to her, "Your sins are forgiven."

49The other guests began to say among themselves, "Who is this who even forgives sins?"

50Jesus said to the woman, "Your faith has saved you; go in peace."

The Parable of the Sower

8 After this, Jesus traveled about from one town and village to another, proclaiming the good news of the kingdom of God. The Twelve were with him, 2and also some women who had been cured of evil spirits and diseases: Mary (called Magdalene) from whom seven demons had come out; 3Joanna the wife of Cuza, the manager of Herod's household; Susanna; and many others. These women were helping to support them out of their own means.

道耶穌在法利賽人家裏坐席，就拿着盛香膏的玉瓶，38站在耶穌背後，挨着他的腳哭，眼淚濕了耶穌的腳，就用自己的頭髮擦乾，又用嘴連連親他的腳，把香膏抹上。

39請耶穌的法利賽人看見這事，心裏說："這人若是先知，必知道摸他的是誰，是個怎樣的女人，乃是個罪人。"

40耶穌對他說："<u>西門</u>，我有句話要對你說。"

西門說："夫子，請說。"

41耶穌說："一個債主有兩個人欠他的債：一個欠五十兩銀子，一個欠五兩銀子，42因為他們無力償還，債主就開恩免了他們兩個人的債。這兩個人哪一個更愛他呢？"

43<u>西門</u>回答說："我想是那多得恩免的人。"

耶穌說："你斷的不錯。"

44於是轉過來向着那女人，便對<u>西門</u>說："你看見這女人嗎？我進了你的家，你沒有給我水洗腳，但這女人用眼淚濕了我的腳，用頭髮擦乾。45你沒有與我親嘴，但這女人從我進來的時候就不住地用嘴親我的腳。46你沒有用油抹我的頭，但這女人用香膏抹我的腳。47所以我告訴你，她許多的罪都赦免了，因為她的愛多；但那赦免少的，他的愛就少。"

48於是對那女人說："你的罪赦免了！"

49同席的人心裏說："這是甚麼人，竟赦免人的罪呢？"

50耶穌對那女人說："你的信救了你，平平安安地回去吧！"

撒種的比喻

8 過了不多日，耶穌周遊各城各鄉傳道，宣講神國的福音。和他同去的有十二個門徒，2還有被惡鬼所附、被疾病所累、已經治好的幾個婦女，內中有稱為<u>抹大拉</u>的<u>馬利亞</u>，曾有七個鬼從她身上趕出來；3又有<u>希律</u>的家宰<u>苦撒</u>的妻子<u>約亞拿，並蘇撒拿</u>，和好些別的婦女，都是用自己的財物供給耶穌和門徒。

---

a 41 A denarius was a coin worth about a day's wages.

4當許多人聚集、又有人從各城裏出來見耶穌的時候，耶穌就用比喻說：5"有一個撒種的出去撒種。撒的時候，有落在路旁的，被人踐踏，天上的飛鳥又來吃盡了。6有落在磐石上的，一出來就枯乾了，因為得不著滋潤。7有落在荊棘裏的，荊棘一同生長，把它擠住了。8又有落在好土裏的，生長起來，結實百倍。"

耶穌說了這些話，就大聲說："有耳可聽的，就應當聽！"

9門徒問耶穌說："這比喻是甚麼意思呢？"10他說："神國的奧秘只叫你們知道；至於別人，就用比喻，

" '叫他們看也看不見，
　聽也聽不明。'

11 "這比喻乃是這樣：種子就是神的道。12那些在路旁的，就是人聽了道，隨後魔鬼來，從他們心裏把道奪去，恐怕他們信了得救。13那些在磐石上的，就是人聽道，歡喜領受，但心中沒有根，不過暫時相信，及至遇見試煉就退後了。14那落在荊棘裏的，就是人聽了道，走開以後，被今生的思慮、錢財、宴樂擠住了，便結不出成熟的子粒來。15那落在好土裏的，就是人聽了道，持守在誠實善良的心裏，並且忍耐著結實。

燈放在燈臺上

16 "沒有人點燈用器皿蓋上，或放在牀底下，乃是放在燈臺上，叫進來的人看見亮光。17因為掩藏的事沒有不顯出來的；隱瞞的事沒有不露出來被人知道的。18所以，你們應當小心怎樣聽。因為凡有的，還要加給他；凡沒有的，連他自以為有的，也要奪去。"

耶穌的母親和弟兄

19耶穌的母親和他弟兄來了，因為人多，不得到他跟前。20有人告訴

4While a large crowd was gathering and people were coming to Jesus from town after town, he told this parable: 5"A farmer went out to sow his seed. As he was scattering the seed, some fell along the path; it was trampled on, and the birds of the air ate it up. 6Some fell on rock, and when it came up, the plants withered because they had no moisture. 7Other seed fell among thorns, which grew up with it and choked the plants. 8Still other seed fell on good soil. It came up and yielded a crop, a hundred times more than was sown."

When he said this, he called out, "He who has ears to hear, let him hear."

9His disciples asked him what this parable meant. 10He said, "The knowledge of the secrets of the kingdom of God has been given to you, but to others I speak in parables, so that,

" 'though seeing, they may not see;
　though hearing, they may not understand.'[a]

11"This is the meaning of the parable: The seed is the word of God. 12Those along the path are the ones who hear, and then the devil comes and takes away the word from their hearts, so that they may not believe and be saved. 13Those on the rock are the ones who receive the word with joy when they hear it, but they have no root. They believe for a while, but in the time of testing they fall away. 14The seed that fell among thorns stands for those who hear, but as they go on their way they are choked by life's worries, riches and pleasures, and they do not mature. 15But the seed on good soil stands for those with a noble and good heart, who hear the word, retain it, and by persevering produce a crop.

A Lamp on a Stand

16"No one lights a lamp and hides it in a jar or puts it under a bed. Instead, he puts it on a stand, so that those who come in can see the light. 17For there is nothing hidden that will not be disclosed, and nothing concealed that will not be known or brought out into the open. 18Therefore consider carefully how you listen. Whoever has will be given more; whoever does not have, even what he thinks he has will be taken from him."

Jesus' Mother and Brothers

19Now Jesus' mother and brothers came to see him, but they were not able to get near him because of the crowd. 20Someone told him,

a 10 Isaiah 6:9

"Your mother and brothers are standing outside, wanting to see you."

[21]He replied, "My mother and brothers are those who hear God's word and put it into practice."

Jesus Calms the Storm

[22]One day Jesus said to his disciples, "Let's go over to the other side of the lake." So they got into a boat and set out. [23]As they sailed, he fell asleep. A squall came down on the lake, so that the boat was being swamped, and they were in great danger.

[24]The disciples went and woke him, saying, "Master, Master, we're going to drown!"

He got up and rebuked the wind and the raging waters; the storm subsided, and all was calm. [25]"Where is your faith?" he asked his disciples.

In fear and amazement they asked one another, "Who is this? He commands even the winds and the water, and they obey him."

The Healing of a Demon-possessed Man

[26]They sailed to the region of the Gerasenes,[a] which is across the lake from Galilee. [27]When Jesus stepped ashore, he was met by a demon-possessed man from the town. For a long time this man had not worn clothes or lived in a house, but had lived in the tombs. [28]When he saw Jesus, he cried out and fell at his feet, shouting at the top of his voice, "What do you want with me, Jesus, Son of the Most High God? I beg you, don't torture me!" [29]For Jesus had commanded the evil[b] spirit to come out of the man. Many times it had seized him, and though he was chained hand and foot and kept under guard, he had broken his chains and had been driven by the demon into solitary places.

[30]Jesus asked him, "What is your name?"

"Legion," he replied, because many demons had gone into him. [31]And they begged him repeatedly not to order them to go into the Abyss.

[32]A large herd of pigs was feeding there on the hillside. The demons begged Jesus to let them go into them, and he gave them permission. [33]When the demons came out of the man, they went into the pigs, and the herd rushed down the steep bank into the lake and was drowned.

[34]When those tending the pigs saw what had happened, they ran off and reported this in the town and countryside, [35]and the people went out to see what had happened. When they came

a 26 Some manuscripts Gadarenes; other manuscripts Gergesenes; also in verse 37   b 29 Greek unclean

---

他說:"你母親和你弟兄站在外邊,要見你。"

[21]耶穌回答說:"聽了神之道而遵行的人就是我的母親,我的弟兄了。"

耶穌平靜風浪

[22]有一天,耶穌和門徒上了船,對門徒說:"我們可以渡到湖那邊去。"他們就開了船。[23]正行的時候,耶穌睡着了。湖上忽然起了暴風,船將滿了水,甚是危險。

[24]門徒來叫醒了他,說:"夫子!夫子!我們喪命啦!"

耶穌醒了,斥責那狂風大浪,風浪就止住,平靜了。[25]耶穌對他們說:"你們的信心在哪裏呢?"

他們又懼怕又希奇,彼此說:"這到底是誰?他吩咐風和水,連風和水也聽從他了。"

醫治被鬼附着的人

[26]他們到了格拉森(註:有古卷作"加大拉")人的地方,就是加利利的對面。[27]耶穌上了岸,就有城裏一個被鬼附着的人迎面而來。這個人許久不穿衣服,不住房子,只住在墳塋裏。[28]他見了耶穌,就俯伏在他面前,大聲喊叫,說:"至高神的兒子耶穌,我與你有甚麼相干?求你不要叫我受苦!"[29]是因耶穌曾吩咐污鬼從那人身上出來。原來這鬼屢次抓住他;他常被人看守,又被鐵鍊和腳鐐捆鎖,他竟把鎖鏈掙斷,被鬼趕到曠野去。

[30]耶穌問他說:"你名叫甚麼?"他說:"我名叫'羣'。"這是因為附着他的鬼多。[31]鬼就央求耶穌,不要吩咐他們到無底坑裏去。

[32]那裏有一大羣豬在山上吃食。鬼央求耶穌,准他們進入豬裏去。耶穌准了他們,[33]鬼就從那人出來,進入豬裏去。於是那羣豬闖下山崖,投在湖裏淹死了。

[34]放豬的看見這事就逃跑了,去告訴城裏和鄉下的人。[35]眾人出來要看是甚麼事。到了耶穌那裏,看見鬼

所離開的那人，坐在耶穌腳前，穿着衣服，心裏明白過來，他們就害怕。36看見這事的便將被鬼附着的人怎麼得救告訴他們。37格拉森四圍的人，因為害怕得很，都求耶穌離開他們；耶穌就上船回去了。

38鬼所離開的那人懇求和耶穌同在，耶穌卻打發他回去，說：39"你回家去，傳說神為你做了何等大的事。"他就去，滿城裏傳揚耶穌為他做了何等大的事。

死了的女孩和患血漏的女人

40耶穌回來的時候，眾人迎接他，因為他們都等候他。41有一個管會堂的，名叫睚魯，來俯伏在耶穌腳前，求耶穌到他家裏去。42因他有一個獨生女兒，約有十二歲，快要死了。

耶穌去的時候，眾人擁擠他。43有一個女人，患了十二年的血漏，在醫生手裏花盡了她一切養生的，並沒有一人能醫好她。44她來到耶穌背後，摸他的衣裳繸子，血漏立刻就止住了。

45耶穌說："摸我的是誰？"眾人都不承認。彼得和同行的人都說："夫子，眾人擁擠擠緊靠着你。（註：有古卷在此有"你還問摸我的是誰嗎？"）"

46耶穌說："總有人摸我，因我覺得有能力從我身上出去。"

47那女人知道不能隱藏，就戰戰兢兢地來俯伏在耶穌腳前，把摸他的緣故和怎樣立刻得好了，當着眾人都說出來。48耶穌對她說："女兒，你的信救了你，平平安安地去吧！"

49還說話的時候，有人從管會堂的家裏來，說："你的女兒死了，不要勞動夫子。"

50耶穌聽見就對他說："不要怕，只要信！你的女兒就必得救。"

51耶穌到了他的家，除了彼得、約翰、雅各和女兒的父母，不許別人同他進去。52眾人都為這女兒哀哭捶胸。耶穌說："不要哭！她不是死了，是睡着了。"

to Jesus, they found the man from whom the demons had gone out, sitting at Jesus' feet, dressed and in his right mind; and they were afraid. 36Those who had seen it told the people how the demon-possessed man had been cured. 37Then all the people of the region of the Gerasenes asked Jesus to leave them, because they were overcome with fear. So he got into the boat and left.

38The man from whom the demons had gone out begged to go with him, but Jesus sent him away, saying, 39"Return home and tell how much God has done for you." So the man went away and told all over town how much Jesus had done for him.

A Dead Girl and a Sick Woman

40Now when Jesus returned, a crowd welcomed him, for they were all expecting him. 41Then a man named Jairus, a ruler of the synagogue, came and fell at Jesus' feet, pleading with him to come to his house 42because his only daughter, a girl of about twelve, was dying.

As Jesus was on his way, the crowds almost crushed him. 43And a woman who had been subject to bleeding for twelve years,*a* but no one could heal her. 44She came up behind him and touched the edge of his cloak, and immediately her bleeding stopped.

45"Who touched me?" Jesus asked.

When they all denied it, Peter said, "Master, the people are crowding and pressing against you."

46But Jesus said, "Someone touched me; I know that power has gone out from me."

47Then the woman, seeing that she could not go unnoticed, came trembling and fell at his feet. In the presence of all the people, she told why she had touched him and how she had been instantly healed. 48Then he said to her, "Daughter, your faith has healed you. Go in peace."

49While Jesus was still speaking, someone came from the house of Jairus, the synagogue ruler. "Your daughter is dead," he said. "Don't bother the teacher any more."

50Hearing this, Jesus said to Jairus, "Don't be afraid; just believe, and she will be healed."

51When he arrived at the house of Jairus, he did not let anyone go in with him except Peter, John and James, and the child's father and mother. 52Meanwhile, all the people were wailing and mourning for her. "Stop wailing," Jesus said. "She is not dead but asleep."

a 43 Many manuscripts years, and she had spent all she had on doctors

53They laughed at him, knowing that she was dead. 54But he took her by the hand and said, "My child, get up!" 55Her spirit returned, and at once she stood up. Then Jesus told them to give her something to eat. 56Her parents were astonished, but he ordered them not to tell anyone what had happened.

Jesus Sends Out the Twelve

9 When Jesus had called the Twelve together, he gave them power and authority to drive out all demons and to cure diseases, 2and he sent them out to preach the kingdom of God and to heal the sick. 3He told them: "Take nothing for the journey—no staff, no bag, no bread, no money, no extra tunic. 4Whatever house you enter, stay there until you leave that town. 5If people do not welcome you, shake the dust off your feet when you leave their town, as a testimony against them." 6So they set out and went from village to village, preaching the gospel and healing people everywhere.

7Now Herod the tetrarch heard about all that was going on. And he was perplexed, because some were saying that John had been raised from the dead, 8others that Elijah had appeared, and still others that one of the prophets of long ago had come back to life. 9But Herod said, "I beheaded John. Who, then, is this I hear such things about?" And he tried to see him.

Jesus Feeds the Five Thousand

10When the apostles returned, they reported to Jesus what they had done. Then he took them with him and they withdrew by themselves to a town called Bethsaida, 11but the crowds learned about it and followed him. He welcomed him and spoke to them about the kingdom of God, and healed those who needed healing.

12Late in the afternoon the Twelve came to him and said, "Send the crowd away so they can go to the surrounding villages and countryside and find food and lodging, because we are in a remote place here."

13He replied, "You give them something to eat."

They answered, "We have only five loaves of bread and two fish—unless we go and buy food for all this crowd." 14(About five thousand men were there.)

But he said to his disciples, "Have them sit down in groups of about fifty each." 15The disciples did so, and everybody sat down. 16Taking the five loaves and the two fish and looking up to heaven, he gave thanks and broke them. Then

53他們曉得女兒已經死了，就嗤笑耶穌。54耶穌拉着她的手，呼叫說："女兒，起來吧！"55她的靈魂便回來，她就立刻起來了。耶穌吩咐給她東西吃。56她的父母驚奇得很。耶穌囑咐他們，不要把所做的事告訴人。

耶穌差遣十二門徒

9 耶穌叫齊了十二個門徒，給他們能力、權柄，制伏一切的鬼，醫治各樣的病，2又差遣他們去宣傳神國的道，醫治病人。3對他們說："行路的時候，不要帶枴杖和口袋，不要帶食物和銀子，也不要帶兩件褂子。4無論進哪一家，就住在那裏，也從那裏起行。5凡不接待你們的，你們離開那城的時候，要把腳上的塵土跺下去，見證他們的不是。"6門徒就出去，走遍各鄉宣傳福音，到處治病。

7分封的王希律聽見耶穌所做的一切事，就游移不定，因為有人說是約翰從死裏復活；8又有人說是以利亞顯現；還有人說是古時的一個先知又活了。9希律說："約翰我已經斬了，這卻是甚麼人？我竟聽見他這樣的事呢？"就想要見他。

耶穌給五千人吃飽

10使徒回來，將所做的事告訴耶穌，耶穌就帶他們暗暗地離開那裏，往一座城去，那城名叫伯賽大。11但眾人知道了，就跟着他去。耶穌便接待他們，對他們講論神國的道，醫治那些需醫的人。

12日頭快要平西，十二個門徒來對他說："請叫眾人散開，他們好往四面鄉村裏去借宿找吃的，因為我們這裏是野地。"

13耶穌說："你們給他們吃吧！"

門徒說："我們不過有五個餅，兩條魚，若不去為這許多人買食物就不夠。"14那時，人數約有五千。

耶穌對門徒說："叫他們一排一排地坐下，每排大約五十個人。"15門徒就如此行，叫眾人都坐下。16耶穌拿着這五個餅，兩條魚，望着天祝福，擘開，遞給門徒，擺在眾人面前。¹⁷他們就吃，並且都吃飽了；把剩下的零碎收拾起來，裝滿了十二籃子。

彼得認基督

¹⁸耶穌自己禱告的時候，門徒也同他在那裏。耶穌問他們說：「眾人說我是誰？」¹⁹他們說：「有人說是施洗的約翰，有人說是以利亞，還有人說是古時的一個先知又活了。」²⁰耶穌說：「你們說我是誰？」彼得回答說：「是神所立的基督。」

²¹耶穌切切地囑咐他們，不可將這事告訴人，²²又說：「人子必須受許多的苦，被長老、祭司長和文士棄絕，並且被殺，第三日復活。」

²³耶穌又對眾人說：「若有人要跟從我，就當捨己，天天背起他的十字架來跟從我。²⁴因為，凡要救自己生命（註：「生命」或作「靈魂」。下同）的，必喪掉生命；凡為我喪掉生命的，必救了生命。²⁵人若賺得全世界，卻喪了自己，賠上自己，有甚麼益處呢？²⁶凡把我和我的道當作可恥的，人子在自己的榮耀裏，並天父與聖天使的榮耀降臨的時候，也要把那人當作可恥的。²⁷我實在告訴你們：站在這裏的，有人在沒嘗死味以前，必看見神的國。」

登山變像

²⁸說了這話以後約有八天，耶穌帶着彼得、約翰、雅各上山去禱告。²⁹正禱告的時候，他的面貌就改變了，衣服潔白放光。³⁰忽然有摩西、以利亞兩個人同耶穌說話；³¹他們在榮光裏顯現，談論耶穌去世的事，就是他在耶路撒冷將要成的事。³²彼得和他的同伴都打盹，既清醒了，就看見耶穌的榮光，並同他站着的那兩個人。³³二人正要和耶穌分離的時候，彼得對耶穌說：「夫子，我們在這裏真好！可以搭三座棚，一座為你，一座為摩西，一座為以利亞。」他卻不知道所說的是甚麼。

³⁴說這話的時候，有一朵雲彩來遮蓋他們；他們進入雲彩裏就懼怕。

he gave them to the disciples to set before the people. ¹⁷They all ate and were satisfied, and the disciples picked up twelve basketfuls of broken pieces that were left over.

Peter's Confession of Christ

¹⁸Once when Jesus was praying in private and his disciples were with him, he asked them, "Who do the crowds say I am?"

¹⁹They replied, "Some say John the Baptist; others say Elijah; and still others, that one of the prophets of long ago has come back to life."

²⁰"But what about you?" he asked. "Who do you say I am?"

Peter answered, "The Christ[a] of God."

²¹Jesus strictly warned them not to tell this to anyone. ²²And he said, "The Son of Man must suffer many things and be rejected by the elders, chief priests and teachers of the law, and he must be killed and on the third day be raised to life."

²³Then he said to them all: "If anyone would come after me, he must deny himself and take up his cross daily and follow me. ²⁴For whoever wants to save his life will lose it, but whoever loses his life for me will save it. ²⁵What good is it for a man to gain the whole world, and yet lose or forfeit his very self? ²⁶If anyone is ashamed of me and my words, the Son of Man will be ashamed of him when he comes in his glory and in the glory of the Father and of the holy angels. ²⁷I tell you the truth, some who are standing here will not taste death before they see the kingdom of God."

The Transfiguration

²⁸About eight days after Jesus said this, he took Peter, John and James with him and went up onto a mountain to pray. ²⁹As he was praying, the appearance of his face changed, and his clothes became as bright as a flash of lightning. ³⁰Two men, Moses and Elijah, ³¹appeared in glorious splendor, talking with Jesus. They spoke about his departure, which he was about to bring to fulfillment at Jerusalem. ³²Peter and his companions were very sleepy, but when they became fully awake, they saw his glory and the two men standing with him. ³³As the men were leaving Jesus, Peter said to him, "Master, it is good for us to be here. Let us put up three shelters—one for you, one for Moses and one for Elijah." (He did not know what he was saying.)

³⁴While he was speaking, a cloud appeared and enveloped them, and they were afraid as

a 20 Or Messiah

they entered the cloud. 35A voice came from the cloud, saying, "This is my Son, whom I have chosen; listen to him." 36When the voice had spoken, they found that Jesus was alone. The disciples kept this to themselves, and told no one at that time what they had seen.

The Healing of a Boy With an Evil Spirit

37The next day, when they came down from the mountain, a large crowd met him. 38A man in the crowd called out, "Teacher, I beg you to look at my son, for he is my only child. 39A spirit seizes him and he suddenly screams; it throws him into convulsions so that he foams at the mouth. It scarcely ever leaves him and is destroying him. 40I begged your disciples to drive it out, but they could not."

41"O unbelieving and perverse generation," Jesus replied, "how long shall I stay with you and put up with you? Bring your son here."

42Even while the boy was coming, the demon threw him to the ground in a convulsion. But Jesus rebuked the evil*a* spirit, healed the boy and gave him back to his father. 43And they were all amazed at the greatness of God.

While everyone was marveling at all that Jesus did, he said to his disciples, 44"Listen carefully to what I am about to tell you: The Son of Man is going to be betrayed into the hands of men." 45But they did not understand what this meant. It was hidden from them, so that they did not grasp it, and they were afraid to ask him about it.

Who Will Be the Greatest?

46An argument started among the disciples as to which of them would be the greatest. 47Jesus, knowing their thoughts, took a little child and had him stand beside him. 48Then he said to them, "Whoever welcomes this little child in my name welcomes me; and whoever welcomes me welcomes the one who sent me. For he who is least among you all—he is the greatest."

49"Master," said John, "we saw a man driving out demons in your name and we tried to stop him, because he is not one of us."

50"Do not stop him," Jesus said, "for whoever is not against you is for you."

Samaritan Opposition

51As the time approached for him to be taken up to heaven, Jesus resolutely set out for Jerusalem. 52And he sent messengers on ahead, who went into a Samaritan village to get things ready for him; 53but the people there did not welcome

a 42 Greek unclean

35有聲音從雲彩裏出來，說：「這是我的兒子，我所揀選的（註：有古卷作「這是我的愛子」），你們要聽他。」36聲音住了，只見耶穌一人在那裏。當那些日子，門徒不提所看見的事，一樣也不告訴人。

醫治被污鬼附着的男孩

37第二天，他們下了山，就有許多人迎見耶穌。38其中有一人喊叫說：「夫子！求你看顧我的兒子，因為他是我的獨生子。39他被鬼抓住就忽然喊叫；鬼又叫他抽風，口中流沫，並且重重地傷害他，難以離開他。40我求過你的門徒把鬼趕出去，他們卻是不能。」

41耶穌說：「噯！這又不信又悖謬的世代啊，我在你們這裏，忍耐你們要到幾時呢？將你的兒子帶到這裏來吧！」

42正來的時候，鬼把他摔倒，叫他重重地抽風。耶穌就斥責那污鬼，把孩子治好了，交給他父親。43眾人都詫異神的大能（註：「大能」或作「威榮」）。

耶穌所做的一切事，眾人正希奇的時候，耶穌對門徒說：44「你們要把這些話存在耳中，因為人子將要被交在人手裏。」45他們不明白這話，意思乃是隱藏的，叫他們不能明白，他們也不敢問這話的意思。

誰為大？

46門徒中間起了議論，誰將為大。47耶穌看出他們心中的議論，就領一個小孩子來，叫他站在自己旁邊，48對他們說：「凡為我名接待這小孩子的，就是接待我；凡接待我的，就是接待那差我來的。你們中間最小的，他便為大。」

49約翰說：「夫子，我們看見一個人奉你的名趕鬼，我們就禁止他，因為他不與我們一同跟從你。」

50耶穌說：「不要禁止他，因為不敵擋你們的，就是幫助你們的。」

撒馬利亞人不接待主

51耶穌被接上升的日子將到，他就定意向耶路撒冷去，52便打發使者在他前頭走。他們到了撒馬利亞的一個村莊，要為他預備。53那裏的人不接待他，因他面向耶路撒冷去。54他的門徒雅各、約翰看見了，就說："主啊，你要我們吩咐火從天上降下來燒滅他們，像以利亞所做的（註：有古卷無"像以利亞所做的"數字）嗎？" 55耶穌轉身責備兩個門徒，說："你們的心如何，你們並不知道。56人子來不是要滅人的性命（註："性命"或作"靈魂"，下同），是要救人的性命。" 說着就往別的村莊去了（註：有古卷只有55節首句，56節末句）。

跟從耶穌的代價

57他們走路的時候，有一人對耶穌說："你無論往哪裏去，我要跟從你。"

58耶穌說："狐狸有洞，天空的飛鳥有窩，只是人子沒有枕頭的地方。"

59又對一個人說："跟從我來！"

那人說："主，容我先回去埋葬我的父親。"

60耶穌說："任憑死人埋葬他們的死人，你只管去傳揚神國的道。"

61又有一人說："主，我要跟從你，但容我先去辭別我家裏的人。"

62耶穌說："手扶着犁向後看的，不配進神的國。"

耶穌差遣七十人

10 這事以後，主又設立七十個人，差遣他們兩個兩個的在他前面，往自己所要到的各城、各地方去，2就對他們說："要收的莊稼多，做工的人少。所以，你們當求莊稼的主打發工人出去收他的莊稼。3你們去吧！我差你們出去，如同羊羔進入狼羣。4不要帶錢囊，不要帶口袋，不要帶鞋，在路上也不要問人的安。

5 "無論進哪一家，先要說：'願這一家平安！' 6那裏若有當得平安的人（註："當得平安的人"原文作"平安之子"），你們所求的平安就必臨到那家；不然，就歸與你們了。7你們要住在那家，吃喝他們所供給的，因為工人得工價是應當的。不要從這家搬到那家。

him, because he was heading for Jerusalem. 54When the disciples James and John saw this, they asked, "Lord, do you want us to call fire down from heaven to destroy them[a]?" 55But Jesus turned and rebuked them, 56and[b] they went to another village.

The Cost of Following Jesus

57As they were walking along the road, a man said to him, "I will follow you wherever you go."

58Jesus replied, "Foxes have holes and birds of the air have nests, but the Son of Man has no place to lay his head."

59He said to another man, "Follow me."

But the man replied, "Lord, first let me go and bury my father."

60Jesus said to him, "Let the dead bury their own dead, but you go and proclaim the kingdom of God."

61Still another said, "I will follow you, Lord; but first let me go back and say good-by to my family."

62Jesus replied, "No one who puts his hand to the plow and looks back is fit for service in the kingdom of God."

Jesus Sends Out the Seventy-two

10 After this the Lord appointed seventy-two[c] others and sent them two by two ahead of him to every town and place where he was about to go. 2He told them, "The harvest is plentiful, but the workers are few. Ask the Lord of the harvest, therefore, to send out workers into his harvest field. 3Go! I am sending you out like lambs among wolves. 4Do not take a purse or bag or sandals; and do not greet anyone on the road.

5"When you enter a house, first say, 'Peace to this house.' 6If a man of peace is there, your peace will rest on him; if not, it will return to you. 7Stay in that house, eating and drinking whatever they give you, for the worker deserves his wages. Do not move around from house to house.

---

a 54 Some manuscripts them, even as Elijah did　b 55,56 Some manuscripts them. And he said, "You do not know what kind of spirit you are of, for the Son of Man did not come to destroy men's lives, but to save them." 56 And　c 1 Some manuscripts seventy; also in verse 17

8"When you enter a town and are welcomed, eat what is set before you. 9Heal the sick who are there and tell them, 'The kingdom of God is near you.' 10But when you enter a town and are not welcomed, go into its streets and say, 11'Even the dust of your town that sticks to our feet we wipe off against you. Yet be sure of this: The kingdom of God is near.' 12I tell you, it will be more bearable on that day for Sodom than for that town.

13"Woe to you, Korazin! Woe to you, Bethsaida! For if the miracles that were performed in you had been performed in Tyre and Sidon, they would have repented long ago, sitting in sackcloth and ashes. 14But it will be more bearable for Tyre and Sidon at the judgment than for you. 15And you, Capernaum, will you be lifted up to the skies? No, you will go down to the depths.*a*

16"He who listens to you listens to me; he who rejects you rejects me; but he who rejects me rejects him who sent me."

17The seventy-two returned with joy and said, "Lord, even the demons submit to us in your name."

18He replied, "I saw Satan fall like lightning from heaven. 19I have given you authority to trample on snakes and scorpions and to overcome all the power of the enemy; nothing will harm you. 20However, do not rejoice that the spirits submit to you, but rejoice that your names are written in heaven."

21At that time Jesus, full of joy through the Holy Spirit, said, "I praise you, Father, Lord of heaven and earth, because you have hidden these things from the wise and learned, and revealed them to little children. Yes, Father, for this was your good pleasure.

22"All things have been committed to me by my Father. No one knows who the Son is except the Father, and no one knows who the Father is except the Son and those to whom the Son chooses to reveal him."

23Then he turned to his disciples and said privately, "Blessed are the eyes that see what you see. 24For I tell you that many prophets and kings wanted to see what you see but did not see it, and to hear what you hear but did not hear it."

The Parable of the Good Samaritan

25On one occasion an expert in the law stood up to test Jesus. "Teacher," he asked, "what must I do to inherit eternal life?"

8 "無論進哪一城,人若接待你們,給你們擺上甚麼,你們就吃甚麼。9要醫治那城裏的病人,對他們說:'神的國臨近你們了。'10無論進哪一城,人若不接待你們,你們就到街上去,11說:'就是你們城裏的塵土粘在我們的腳上,我們也當着你們擦去。雖然如此,你們該知道神的國臨近了。12我告訴你們:當審判的日子,所多瑪所受的,比那城還容易受呢!

13 "哥拉汛哪,你有禍了!伯賽大啊,你有禍了!因為在你們中間所行的異能若行在推羅、西頓,他們早已披麻蒙灰,坐在地上悔改了。14當審判的日子,推羅、西頓所受的,比你們還容易受呢!15迦百農啊!你已經升到天上(註:或作"你將要升到天上嗎?"),將來必推下陰間。"

16 又對門徒說:"聽從你們的就是聽從我;棄絕你們的就是棄絕我;棄絕我的就是棄絕那差我來的。"

17 那七十個人歡歡喜喜地回來,說:"主啊!因你的名,就是鬼也服了我們。"

18耶穌對他們說:"我曾看見撒但從天上墜落,像閃電一樣。19我已經給你們權柄可以踐踏蛇和蠍子,又勝過仇敵一切的能力,斷沒有甚麼能害你們。20然而,不要因鬼服了你們就歡喜,要因你們的名記錄在天上歡喜。"

21正當那時,耶穌被聖靈感動就歡樂,說:"父啊,天地的主,我感謝你!因為你將這些事向聰明通達人就藏起來,向嬰孩就顯出來。父啊,是的,因為你的美意本是如此。

22 "一切所有的都是我父交付我的。除了父,沒有人知道子是誰;除了子和子所願意指示的,沒有人知道父是誰。"

23耶穌轉身暗暗地對門徒說:"看見你們所看見的,那眼睛就有福了。24我告訴你們:從前有許多先知和君王要看你們所看的,卻沒有看見;要聽你們所聽的,卻沒有聽見。"

好撒馬利亞人的比喻

25有一個律法師起來試探耶穌,說:"夫子,我該做甚麼才可以承受永生?"

²⁶耶穌對他說：「律法上寫的是甚麼？你念的是怎樣呢？」

²⁷他回答說：「你要盡心、盡性、盡力、盡意愛主你的神；又要愛鄰舍如同自己。」

²⁸耶穌說：「你回答的是。你這樣行，就必得永生。」

²⁹那人要顯明自己有理，就對耶穌說：「誰是我的鄰舍呢？」

³⁰耶穌回答說：「有一個人從耶路撒冷下耶利哥去，落在強盜手中。他們剝去他的衣裳，把他打個半死，就丟下他走了。³¹偶然有一個祭司從這條路下來，看見他就從那邊過去了。³²又有一個利未人來到這地方，看見他，也照樣從那邊過去了。³³惟有一個撒瑪利亞人行路來到那裏，看見他就動了慈心，³⁴上前用油和酒倒在他的傷處，包裹好了，扶他騎上自己的牲口，帶到店裏去照應他。³⁵第二天拿出二錢銀子來，交給店主，說：『你且照應他，此外所費用的，我回來必還你。』

³⁶「你想，這三個人哪一個是落在強盜手中的鄰舍呢？」

³⁷他說：「是憐憫他的。」

耶穌說：「你去照樣行吧。」

在馬大、馬利亞家裏

³⁸他們走路的時候，耶穌進了一個村莊。有一個女人，名叫馬大，接他到自己家裏。³⁹她有一個妹子，名叫馬利亞，在耶穌腳前坐着聽他的道。⁴⁰馬大伺候的事多，心裏忙亂，就進前來說：「主啊，我的妹子留下我一個人伺候，你不在意嗎？請吩咐她來幫助我。」

⁴¹耶穌回答說：「馬大！馬大！你為許多的事思慮煩擾，⁴²但是不可少的只有一件，馬利亞已經選擇那上好的福分，是不能奪去的。」

²⁶"What is written in the Law?" he replied. "How do you read it?"

²⁷He answered: " 'Love the Lord your God with all your heart and with all your soul and with all your strength and with all your mind'*a*; and, 'Love your neighbor as yourself.'*b*"

²⁸"You have answered correctly," Jesus replied. "Do this and you will live."

²⁹But he wanted to justify himself, so he asked Jesus, "And who is my neighbor?"

³⁰In reply Jesus said: "A man was going down from Jerusalem to Jericho, when he fell into the hands of robbers. They stripped him of his clothes, beat him and went away, leaving him half dead. ³¹A priest happened to be going down the same road, and when he saw the man, he passed by on the other side. ³²So too, a Levite, when he came to the place and saw him, passed by on the other side. ³³But a Samaritan, as he traveled, came where the man was; and when he saw him, he took pity on him. ³⁴He went to him and bandaged his wounds, pouring on oil and wine. Then he put the man on his own donkey, took him to an inn and took care of him. ³⁵The next day he took out two silver coins*c* and gave them to the innkeeper. 'Look after him,' he said, 'and when I return, I will reimburse you for any extra expense you may have.'

³⁶"Which of these three do you think was a neighbor to the man who fell into the hands of robbers?"

³⁷The expert in the law replied, "The one who had mercy on him."

Jesus told him, "Go and do likewise."

At the Home of Martha and Mary

³⁸As Jesus and his disciples were on their way, he came to a village where a woman named Martha opened her home to him. ³⁹She had a sister called Mary, who sat at the Lord's feet listening to what he said. ⁴⁰But Martha was distracted by all the preparations that had to be made. She came to him and asked, "Lord, don't you care that my sister has left me to do the work by myself? Tell her to help me!"

⁴¹"Martha, Martha," the Lord answered, "you are worried and upset about many things, ⁴²but only one thing is needed.*d* Mary has chosen what is better, and it will not be taken away from her."

---

a 27 Deut. 6:5　　*b* 27 Lev. 19:18　　*c* 35 Greek *two denarii*
d 42 Some manuscripts *but few things are needed—or only one*

Jesus' Teaching on Prayer

11 One day Jesus was praying in a certain place. When he finished, one of his disciples said to him, "Lord, teach us to pray, just as John taught his disciples."

²He said to them, "When you pray, say:

" 'Father,*a*
hallowed be your name,
  your kingdom come.*b*
³Give us each day our daily bread.
⁴Forgive us our sins,
  for we also forgive everyone who sins
    against us.*c*
And lead us not into temptation.*d* ' "

⁵Then he said to them, "Suppose one of you has a friend, and he goes to him at midnight and says, 'Friend, lend me three loaves of bread, ⁶because a friend of mine on a journey has come to me, and I have nothing to set before him.'

⁷"Then the one inside answers, 'Don't bother me. The door is already locked, and my children are with me in bed. I can't get up and give you anything.' ⁸I tell you, though he will not get up and give him the bread because he is his friend, yet because of the man's boldness*e* he will get up and give him as much as he needs.

⁹"So I say to you: Ask and it will be given to you; seek and you will find; knock and the door will be opened to you. ¹⁰For everyone who asks receives; he who seeks finds; and to him who knocks, the door will be opened.

¹¹"Which of you fathers, if your son asks for*f* a fish, will give him a snake instead? ¹²Or if he asks for an egg, will give him a scorpion? ¹³If you then, though you are evil, know how to give good gifts to your children, how much more will your Father in heaven give the Holy Spirit to those who ask him!"

Jesus and Beelzebub

¹⁴Jesus was driving out a demon that was mute. When the demon left, the man who had been mute spoke, and the crowd was amazed.

a 2 Some manuscripts Our Father in heaven　　b 2 Some manuscripts come. May your will be done on earth as it is in heaven.　　c 4 Greek everyone who is indebted to us　　d 4 Some manuscripts temptation but deliver us from the evil one　　e 8 Or persistence　　f 11 Some manuscripts for bread, will give him a stone; or if he asks for

耶穌教導禱告

11 耶穌在一個地方禱告。禱告完了，有個門徒對他説："求主教導我們禱告，像約翰教導他的門徒。"

²耶穌説："你們禱告的時候，要説：

" '我們在天上的父 (註：有古卷只作 "父啊")：
願人都尊你的名為聖。
願你的國降臨；
願你的旨意行在地上，如同行在天上
(註：有古卷無 "願你的旨意云云") 。
³我們日用的飲食，天天賜給我們。
⁴赦免我們的罪，
  因為我們也赦免凡虧欠我們的人。
不叫我們遇見試探；
救我們脫離兇惡 (註：有古卷無末句) 。' "

⁵耶穌又説："你們中間誰有一個朋友半夜到他那裏去，説：'朋友，請借給我三個餅，⁶因為我有一個朋友行路，來到我這裏，我沒有甚麼給他擺上。'

⁷ '那人在裏面回答説：'不要攪擾我，門已經關閉，孩子們也同我在牀上了，我不能起來給你。' ⁸我告訴你們：雖不因他是朋友起來給他，但因他情詞迫切地直求，就必起來照他所需用的給他。

⁹ "我又告訴你們：你們祈求，就給你們；尋找，就尋見；叩門，就給你們開門。¹⁰因為，凡祈求的，就得着；尋找的，就尋見；叩門的，就給他開門。

¹¹ "你們中間作父親的，誰有兒子求餅，反給他石頭呢？求魚，反拿蛇當魚給他呢？¹²求雞蛋，反給他蠍子呢？¹³你們雖然不好，尚且知道拿好東西給兒女，何況天父，豈不更將聖靈給求他的人嗎？"

耶穌與別西卜

¹⁴耶穌趕出一個叫人啞巴的鬼。鬼出去了，啞巴就説出話來，眾都

希奇。¹⁵內中卻有人說："他是靠着鬼王別西卜趕鬼。"¹⁶又有人試探耶穌，向他求從天上來的神蹟。

¹⁷他曉得他們的意念，便對他們說："凡一國自相紛爭，就成為荒場；凡一家自相紛爭，就必敗落。¹⁸若撒但自相紛爭，他的國怎能站得住呢？因為你們說我是靠着別西卜趕鬼。¹⁹我若靠着別西卜趕鬼，你們的子弟趕鬼又靠着誰呢？這樣，他們就要斷定你們的是非。²⁰我若靠着神的能力趕鬼，這就是神的國臨到你們了。

²¹"壯士披掛整齊，看守自己的住宅，他所有的都平安無事；²²但有一個比他更壯的來，勝過他，就奪去他所倚靠的盔甲兵器，又分了他的贓。

²³"不與我相合的，就是敵我的；不同我收聚的，就是分散的。

²⁴"污鬼離了人身，就在無水之地過來過去，尋求安歇之處；既尋不着，便說：'我要回到我所出來的屋裏去。'²⁵到了，就看見裏面打掃乾淨，修飾好了，²⁶便去另帶了七個比自己更惡的鬼來，都進去住在那裏。那人末後的景況比先前更不好了。"

²⁷耶穌正說這話的時候，眾人中間有一個女人大聲說："懷你胎的和乳養你的有福了！"

²⁸耶穌說："是，卻還不如聽神之道而遵守的人有福。"

約拿的神蹟

²⁹當眾人聚集的時候，耶穌開講說："這世代是一個邪惡的世代。他們求看神蹟，除了約拿的神蹟以外，再沒有神蹟給他們看。³⁰約拿怎樣為尼尼微人成了神蹟，人子也要照樣為這世代的人成了神蹟。³¹當審判的時候，南方的女王要起來定這世代的罪，因為她從地極而來，要聽所羅門的智慧話。看哪！在這裏有一人比所羅門更大。³²當審判的時候，尼尼微人要起來定這世代的罪，因為尼尼微人聽了約拿所傳的就悔改了。看哪！在這裏有一人比約拿更大。

¹⁵But some of them said, "By Beelzebub,ᵃ the prince of demons, he is driving out demons." ¹⁶Others tested him by asking for a sign from heaven.

¹⁷Jesus knew their thoughts and said to them: "Any kingdom divided against itself will be ruined, and a house divided against itself will fall. ¹⁸If Satan is divided against himself, how can his kingdom stand? I say this because you claim that I drive out demons by Beelzebub. ¹⁹Now if I drive out demons by Beelzebub, by whom do your followers drive them out? So then, they will be your judges. ²⁰But if I drive out demons by the finger of God, then the kingdom of God has come to you.

²¹"When a strong man, fully armed, guards his own house his possessions are safe. ²²But when someone stronger attacks and overpowers him, he takes away the armor in which the man trusted and divides up the spoils.

²³"He who is not with me is against me, and he who does not gather with me, scatters.

²⁴"When an evilᵇ spirit comes out of a man, it goes through arid places seeking rest and does not find it. Then it says, 'I will return to the house I left.' ²⁵When it arrives, it finds the house swept clean and put in order. ²⁶Then it goes and takes seven other spirits more wicked than itself, and they go in and live there. And the final condition of that man is worse than the first."

²⁷As Jesus was saying these things, a woman in the crowd called out, "Blessed is the mother who gave you birth and nursed you."

²⁸He replied, "Blessed rather are those who hear the word of God and obey it."

The Sign of Jonah

²⁹As the crowds increased, Jesus said, "This is a wicked generation. It asks for a miraculous sign, but none will be given it except the sign of Jonah. ³⁰For as Jonah was a sign to the Ninevites, so also will the Son of Man be to this generation. ³¹The Queen of the South will rise at the judgment with the men of this generation and condemn them; for she came from the ends of the earth to listen to Solomon's wisdom, and now oneᶜ greater than Solomon is here. ³²The men of Nineveh will stand up at the judgment with this generation and condemn it; for they repented at the preaching of Jonah, and now one greater than Jonah is here.

a 15 Greek Beezeboul or Beelzeboul; also in verses 18 and 19
b 24 Greek unclean　　c 31 Or something; also in verse 32

The Lamp of the Body

33"No one lights a lamp and puts it in a place where it will be hidden, or under a bowl. Instead he puts it on its stand, so that those who come in may see the light. 34Your eye is the lamp of your body. When your eyes are good, your whole body also is full of light. But when they are bad, your body also is full of darkness. 35See to it, then, that the light within you is not darkness. 36Therefore, if your whole body is full of light, and no part of it dark, it will be completely lighted, as when the light of a lamp shines on you."

Six Woes

37When Jesus had finished speaking, a Pharisee invited him to eat with him; so he went in and reclined at the table. 38But the Pharisee, noticing that Jesus did not first wash before the meal, was surprised.

39Then the Lord said to him, "Now then, you Pharisees clean the outside of the cup and dish, but inside you are full of greed and wickedness. 40You foolish people! Did not the one who made the outside make the inside also? 41But give what is inside the dish*a* to the poor, and everything will be clean for you.

42"Woe to you Pharisees, because you give God a tenth of your mint, rue and all other kinds of garden herbs, but you neglect justice and the love of God. You should have practiced the latter without leaving the former undone.

43"Woe to you Pharisees, because you love the most important seats in the synagogues and greetings in the marketplaces.

44"Woe to you, because you are like unmarked graves, which men walk over without knowing it."

45One of the experts in the law answered him, "Teacher, when you say these things, you insult us also."

46Jesus replied, "And you experts in the law, woe to you, because you load people down with burdens they can hardly carry, and you yourselves will not lift one finger to help them.

47"Woe to you, because you build tombs for the prophets, and it was your forefathers who killed them. 48So you testify that you approve of what your forefathers did; they killed the prophets, and you build their tombs. 49Because of this, God in his wisdom said, 'I will send them prophets and apostles, some of whom they will kill and others they will persecute.' 50Therefore this generation will be held responsible for the blood of all the prophets that has been shed since

身上的燈

33"沒有人點燈放在地窨子裏或是斗底下,總是放在燈臺上,使進來的人得見亮光。34你眼睛就是身上的燈。你的眼睛若瞭亮,全身就光明;眼睛若昏花,全身就黑暗。35所以,你要省察,恐怕你裏頭的光或者黑暗了。36若是你全身光明,毫無黑暗,就必全然光明,如同燈的明光照亮你。"

六禍

37說話的時候,有一個法利賽人請耶穌同他吃飯,耶穌就進去坐席。38這法利賽人看見耶穌飯前不洗手便詫異。

39主對他說:"如今你們法利賽人洗淨杯盤的外面,你們裏面卻滿了勒索和邪惡。40無知的人哪,造外面的,不也造裏面嗎?41只要把裏面的施捨給人,凡物於你們就都潔淨了。

42"你們法利賽人有禍了!因為你們將薄荷、芸香並各樣菜蔬獻上十分之一,那公義和愛神的事反倒不行了。這原是你們當行的,那也是不可不行的。

43"你們法利賽人有禍了!因為你們喜愛會堂裏的首位,又喜愛人在街市上問你們的安。

44"你們有禍了!因為你們如同不顯露的墳墓,走在上面的人並不知道。"

45律法師中有一個回答耶穌說:"夫子,你這樣說也把我們糟蹋了!"

46耶穌說:"你們律法師也有禍了!因為你們把難擔的擔子放在人身上,自己一個指頭卻不肯動。

47"你們有禍了!因為你們修造先知的墳墓,那先知正是你們的祖宗所殺的。48可見你們祖宗所做的事,你們又證明又喜歡,因為他們殺了先知,你們修造先知的墳墓。49所以神用智慧(註:"用智慧"或作"的智者")曾說:'我要差遣先知和使徒到他們那裏去,有的他們要殺害,有的他們要逼迫。'50使創世以來所流眾先知血的罪,都要問在這世代的人身上,

a 41 Or what you have

⁵¹就是從亞伯的血起，直到被殺在壇和殿中間撒迦利亞的血為止。我實在告訴你們：這都要問在這世代的人身上。

⁵²"你們律法師有禍了！因為你們把知識的鑰匙奪了去，自己不進去，正要進去的人你們也阻擋他們。"

⁵³耶穌從那裏出來，文士和法利賽人就極力地催逼他，引動他多說話，⁵⁴私下窺聽，要拿他的話柄。

警戒與勉勵

12 這時，有幾萬人聚集，甚至彼此踐踏。耶穌開講，先對門徒說："你們要防備法利賽人的酵，就是假冒為善。²掩蓋的事，沒有不露出來的；隱藏的事，沒有不被人知道的。³因此，你們在暗中所說的，將要在明處被人聽見；在內室附耳所說的，將要在房上被人宣揚。

⁴"我的朋友，我對你們說：那殺身體以後不能再做甚麼的，不要怕他們。⁵我要指示你們當怕的是誰，當怕那殺了以後又有權柄丟在地獄裏的。我實在告訴你們：正要怕他。⁶五個麻雀不是賣二分銀子嗎？但在神面前，一個也不忘記；⁷就是你們的頭髮，也都被數過了。不要懼怕，你們比許多麻雀還貴重！

⁸"我又告訴你們：凡在人面前認我的，人子在神的使者面前也必認他；⁹在人面前不認我的，人子在神的使者面前也必不認他。¹⁰凡說話干犯人子的，還可得赦免；惟獨褻瀆聖靈的，總不得赦免。

¹¹"人帶你們到會堂，並官府和有權柄的人面前，不要思慮怎麼分訴，說甚麼話，¹²因為正在那時候，聖靈要指教你們當說的話。"

無知財主的比喻

¹³眾人中有一個人對耶穌說："夫子，請你吩咐我的兄長和我分開家業。"

the beginning of the world, ⁵¹from the blood of Abel to the blood of Zechariah, who was killed between the altar and the sanctuary. Yes, I tell you, this generation will be held responsible for it all.

⁵²"Woe to you experts in the law, because you have taken away the key to knowledge. You yourselves have not entered, and you have hindered those who were entering."

⁵³When Jesus left there, the Pharisees and the teachers of the law began to oppose him fiercely and to besiege him with questions, ⁵⁴waiting to catch him in something he might say.

Warnings and Encouragements

12 Meanwhile, when a crowd of many thousands had gathered, so that they were trampling on one another, Jesus began to speak first to his disciples, saying: "Be on your guard against the yeast of the Pharisees, which is hypocrisy. ²There is nothing concealed that will not be disclosed, or hidden that will not be made known. ³What you have said in the dark will be heard in the daylight, and what you have whispered in the ear in the inner rooms will be proclaimed from the roofs.

⁴"I tell you, my friends, do not be afraid of those who kill the body and after that can do no more. ⁵But I will show you whom you should fear: Fear him who, after the killing of the body, has power to throw you into hell. Yes, I tell you, fear him. ⁶Are not five sparrows sold for two pennies^a? Yet not one of them is forgotten by God. ⁷Indeed, the very hairs of your head are all numbered. Don't be afraid; you are worth more than many sparrows.

⁸"I tell you, whoever acknowledges me before men, the Son of Man will also acknowledge him before the angels of God. ⁹But he who disowns me before men will be disowned before the angels of God. ¹⁰And everyone who speaks a word against the Son of Man will be forgiven, but anyone who blasphemes against the Holy Spirit will not be forgiven.

¹¹"When you are brought before synagogues, rulers and authorities, do not worry about how you will defend yourselves or what you will say, ¹²for the Holy Spirit will teach you at that time what you should say."

The Parable of the Rich Fool

¹³Someone in the crowd said to him, "Teacher, tell my brother to divide the inheritance with me."

---

a 6 Greek two assaria

14Jesus replied, "Man, who appointed me a judge or an arbiter between you?" 15Then he said to them, "Watch out! Be on your guard against all kinds of greed; a man's life does not consist in the abundance of his possessions."

16And he told them this parable: "The ground of a certain rich man produced a good crop. 17He thought to himself, 'What shall I do? I have no place to store my crops.'

18"Then he said, 'This is what I'll do. I will tear down my barns and build bigger ones, and there I will store all my grain and my goods. 19And I'll say to myself, "You have plenty of good things laid up for many years. Take life easy; eat, drink and be merry." '

20"But God said to him, 'You fool! This very night your life will be demanded from you. Then who will get what you have prepared for yourself?'

21"This is how it will be with anyone who stores up things for himself but is not rich toward God."

Do Not Worry

22Then Jesus said to his disciples: "Therefore I tell you, do not worry about your life, what you will eat; or about your body, what you will wear. 23Life is more than food, and the body more than clothes. 24Consider the ravens: They do not sow or reap, they have no storeroom or barn; yet God feeds them. And how much more valuable you are than birds! 25Who of you by worrying can add a single hour to his life*a*? 26Since you cannot do this very little thing, why do you worry about the rest?

27"Consider how the lilies grow. They do not labor or spin. Yet I tell you, not even Solomon in all his splendor was dressed like one of these. 28If that is how God clothes the grass of the field, which is here today, and tomorrow is thrown into the fire, how much more will he clothe you, O you of little faith! 29And do not set your heart on what you will eat or drink; do not worry about it. 30For the pagan world runs after all such things, and your Father knows that you need them. 31But seek his kingdom, and these things will be given to you as well.

32"Do not be afraid, little flock, for your Father has been pleased to give you the kingdom. 33Sell your possessions and give to the poor. Provide purses for yourselves that will not wear out, a treasure in heaven that will not be exhausted, where no thief comes near and no moth destroys. 34For where your treasure is, there your heart will be also.

14耶穌說："你這個人！誰立我作你們斷事的官，給你們分家業呢？" 15於是對眾人說："你們要謹慎自守，免去一切的貪心，因為人的生命不在乎家道豐富。"

16就用比喻對他們說："有一個財主田產豐盛，17自己心裏思想說：'我的出產沒有地方收藏，怎麼辦呢？'

18"又說：'我要這麼辦：要把我的倉房拆了，另蓋更大的，在那裏好收藏我一切的糧食和財物，19然後要對我的靈魂說：靈魂哪，你有許多財物積存，可作多年的費用，只管安安逸逸地吃喝快樂吧！'

20"神卻對他說：'無知的人哪，今夜必要你的靈魂，你所預備的要歸誰呢？'

21"凡為自己積財，在神面前卻不富足的，也是這樣。"

勿憂慮

22耶穌又對門徒說："所以我告訴你們：不要為生命憂慮吃甚麼，為身體憂慮穿甚麼；23因為生命勝於飲食，身體勝於衣裳。24你想，烏鴉也不種，也不收，又沒有倉又沒有庫，神尚且養活牠。你們比飛鳥是何等的貴重呢！25你們哪一個能用思慮使壽數多加一刻呢（註：或作"使身量多加一肘呢"）？26這最小的事，你們尚且不能做，為甚麼還憂慮其餘的事呢？

27"你想，百合花怎麼長起來？它也不勞苦，也不紡線。然而我告訴你們：就是所羅門極榮華的時候，他所穿戴的，還不如這花一朵呢！28你們這小信的人哪，野地裏的草今天還在，明天就丟在爐裏，神還給它這樣的妝飾，何況你們呢！29你們不要求吃甚麼，喝甚麼，也不要掛心，30這都是外邦人所求的。你們必須用這些東西，你們的父是知道的。31你們只要求他的國，這些東西就必加給你們了。

32"你們這小羣，不要懼怕，因為你們的父樂意把國賜給你們。33你們要變賣所有的賙濟人，為自己預備永不壞的錢囊，用不盡的財寶在天上，就是賊不能近、蟲不能蛀的地方。34因為，你們的財寶在哪裏，你們的心也在那裏。

a 25 Or single cubit to his height

警醒

35 "你們腰裏要束上帶，燈也要點着，36 自己好像僕人等候主人從婚姻的筵席上回來。他來到叩門，就立刻給他開門。37 主人來了，看見僕人警醒，那僕人就有福了。我實在告訴你們：主人必叫他們坐席，自己束上帶，進前伺候他們。38 或是二更天來，或是三更天來，看見僕人這樣，那僕人就有福了。39 家主若知道賊甚麼時候來，就必警醒，不容賊挖透房屋，這是你們所知道的。40 你們也要預備，因為你們想不到的時候，人子就來了。"

41 彼得說："主啊，這比喻是為我們說的呢，還是為眾人呢？"

42 主說："誰是那忠心有見識的管家，主人派他管理家裏的人，按時分糧給他們呢？43 主人來到，看見僕人這樣行，那僕人就有福了。44 我實在告訴你們：主人要派他管理一切所有的。45 那僕人若心裏說：'我的主人必來得遲'，就動手打僕人和使女，並且吃喝醉酒。46 在他想不到的日子，不知道的時辰，那僕人的主人要來，重重地處治他（註：或作"把他腰斬了"），定他和不忠心的人同罪。

47 "僕人知道主人的意思，卻不預備，又不順他的意思行，那僕人必多受責打；48 惟有那不知道的，做了當受責打的事，必少受責打。因為多給誰，就向誰多取；多託誰，就向誰多要。

不是太平乃是紛爭

49 "我來要把火丟在地上，倘若已經着起來，不也是我所願意的嗎？50 我有當受的洗還沒有成就，我是何等的迫切呢！51 你們以為我來，是叫地上太平嗎？我告訴你們：不是，乃是叫人紛爭。52 從今以後，一家五個人將要紛爭：三個人和兩個人相爭，兩個人和三個人相爭；53 父親和兒子相爭，兒子和父親相爭；母親和女兒

Watchfulness

35"Be dressed ready for service and keep your lamps burning, 36like men waiting for their master to return from a wedding banquet, so that when he comes and knocks they can immediately open the door for him. 37It will be good for those servants whose master finds them watching when he comes. I tell you the truth, he will dress himself to serve, will have them recline at the table and will come and wait on them. 38It will be good for those servants whose master finds them ready, even if he comes in the second or third watch of the night. 39But understand this: If the owner of the house had known at what hour the thief was coming, he would not have let his house be broken into. 40You also must be ready, because the Son of Man will come at an hour when you do not expect him."

41Peter asked, "Lord, are you telling this parable to us, or to everyone?"

42The Lord answered, "Who then is the faithful and wise manager, whom the master puts in charge of his servants to give them their food allowance at the proper time? 43It will be good for that servant whom the master finds doing so when he returns. 44I tell you the truth, he will put him in charge of all his possessions. 45But suppose the servant says to himself, 'My master is taking a long time in coming,' and he then begins to beat the menservants and maidservants and to eat and drink and get drunk. 46The master of that servant will come on a day when he does not expect him and at an hour he is not aware of. He will cut him to pieces and assign him a place with the unbelievers.

47"That servant who knows his master's will and does not get ready or does not do what his master wants will be beaten with many blows. 48But the one who does not know and does things deserving punishment will be beaten with few blows. From everyone who has been given much, much will be demanded; and from the one who has been entrusted with much, much more will be asked.

Not Peace but Division

49"I have come to bring fire on the earth, and how I wish it were already kindled! 50But I have a baptism to undergo, and how distressed I am until it is completed! 51Do you think I came to bring peace on earth? No, I tell you, but division. 52From now on there will be five in one family divided against each other, three against two and two against three. 53They will be divided, father against son and son against father, mother against daughter and daughter against mother, mother-in-law against daughter-in-law and daughter-in-law against mother-in-law."

Interpreting the Times

54He said to the crowd: "When you see a cloud rising in the west, immediately you say, 'It's going to rain,' and it does. 55And when the south wind blows, you say, 'It's going to be hot,' and it is. 56Hypocrites! You know how to interpret the appearance of the earth and the sky. How is it that you don't know how to interpret this present time?

57"Why don't you judge for yourselves what is right? 58As you are going with your adversary to the magistrate, try hard to be reconciled to him on the way, or he may drag you off to the judge, and the judge turn you over to the officer, and the officer throw you into prison. 59I tell you, you will not get out until you have paid the last penny.*a*"

Repent or Perish

13 Now there were some present at that time who told Jesus about the Galileans whose blood Pilate had mixed with their sacrifices. 2Jesus answered, "Do you think that these Galileans were worse sinners than all the other Galileans because they suffered this way? 3I tell you, no! But unless you repent, you too will all perish. 4Or those eighteen who died when the tower in Siloam fell on them—do you think they were more guilty than all the others living in Jerusalem? 5I tell you, no! But unless you repent, you too will all perish."

6Then he told this parable: "A man had a fig tree, planted in his vineyard, and he went to look for fruit on it, but did not find any. 7So he said to the man who took care of the vineyard, 'For three years now I've been coming to look for fruit on this fig tree and haven't found any. Cut it down! Why should it use up the soil?'

8"'Sir,' the man replied, 'leave it alone for one more year, and I'll dig around it and fertilize it. 9If it bears fruit next year, fine! If not, then cut it down.'"

A Crippled Woman Healed on the Sabbath

10On a Sabbath Jesus was teaching in one of the synagogues, 11and a woman was there who had been crippled by a spirit for eighteen years. She was bent over and could not straighten up at all. 12When Jesus saw her, he called her forward and said to her, "Woman, you are set free

a 59 Greek lepton

相爭，女兒和母親相爭；婆婆和媳婦相爭，媳婦和婆婆相爭。"

分辨時候

54耶穌又對眾人說："你們看見西邊起了雲彩，就說：'要下一陣雨'，果然就有。55起了南風，就說：'將要燥熱'，也就有了。56假冒為善的人哪，你們知道分辨天地的氣色，怎麼不知道分辨這時候呢？

57"你們又為何不自己審量甚麼是合理的呢？58你同告你的對頭去見官，還在路上，務要盡力地和他了結；恐怕他拉你到官面前，官交付差役，差役把你下在監裏。59我告訴你：若有半文錢沒有還清，你斷不能從那裏出來。"

悔改或滅亡

13 正當那時，有人將彼拉多使加利利人的血攙雜在他們祭物中的事告訴耶穌。2耶穌說："你們以為這些加利利人比眾加利利人更有罪，所以受這害嗎？3我告訴你們：不是的！你們若不悔改，都要如此滅亡！4從前西羅亞樓倒塌了，壓死十八個人，你們以為那些人比一切住在耶路撒冷的人更有罪嗎？5我告訴你們：不是的！你們若不悔改，都要如此滅亡！"

6於是用比喻說："一個人有一棵無花果樹栽在葡萄園裏。他來到樹前找果子，卻找不着。7就對管園的說：'看哪，我這三年來到這無花果樹前找果子，竟找不着。把它砍了吧，何必白佔地土呢？'

8"管園的說：'主啊，今年且留着，等我周圍掘開土，加上糞，9以後若結果子便罷，不然再把它砍了。'"

安息日醫治駝背的女人

10安息日，耶穌在會堂裏教訓人。11有一個女人被鬼附着，病了十八年，腰彎得一點直不起來。12耶穌看見，便叫過她來，對她說："女人，你脫離這病了！」 13 於是用兩隻手按着她，她立刻直起腰來，就歸榮耀與神。

14 管會堂的因為耶穌在安息日治病，就氣忿忿地對眾人說：「有六日應當做工，那六日之內可以來求醫，在安息日卻不可！」

15 主說：「假冒為善的人哪，難道你們各人在安息日不解開槽上的牛、驢，牽去飲嗎？ 16 況且這女人本是亞伯拉罕的後裔，被撒但捆綁了這十八年，不當在安息日解開她的綁嗎？」

17 耶穌說這話，他的敵人都慚愧了；眾人因他所行一切榮耀的事，就都歡喜了。

芥菜種和麵酵的比喻

18 耶穌說：「神的國好像甚麼？我拿甚麼來比較呢？ 19 好像一粒芥菜種，有人拿去種在園子裏，長大成樹，天上的飛鳥宿在它的枝上。」

20 又說：「我拿甚麼來比神的國呢？ 21 好比麵酵，有婦人拿來藏在三斗麵裏，直等全團都發起來。」

窄門

22 耶穌往耶路撒冷去，在所經過的各城各鄉教訓人。 23 有一個人問他說：「主啊，得救的人少嗎？」

24 耶穌對眾人說：「你們要努力進窄門。我告訴你們：將來有許多人想要進去，卻是不能。 25 及至家主起來關了門，你們站在外面叩門，說：『主啊，給我們開門！』

「他就回答說：『我不認識你們，不曉得你們是哪裏來的！』

26 「那時，你們要說：『我們在你面前吃過、喝過，你也在我們的街上教訓過人。』

27 「他要說：『我告訴你們：我不曉得你們是哪裏來的。你們這一切作惡的人，離開我去吧！』

28 「你們要看見亞伯拉罕、以撒、雅各，和眾先知都在神的國裏，你們卻被趕到外面，在那裏必要哀哭切齒了。 29 從東、從西、從南、從

---

from your infirmity." [13]Then he put his hands on her, and immediately she straightened up and praised God.

[14]Indignant because Jesus had healed on the Sabbath, the synagogue ruler said to the people, "There are six days for work. So come and be healed on those days, not on the Sabbath."

[15]The Lord answered him, "You hypocrites! Doesn't each of you on the Sabbath untie his ox or donkey from the stall and lead it out to give it water? [16]Then should not this woman, a daughter of Abraham, whom Satan has kept bound for eighteen long years, be set free on the Sabbath day from what bound her?"

[17]When he said this, all his opponents were humiliated, but the people were delighted with all the wonderful things he was doing.

The Parables of the Mustard Seed and the Yeast

[18]Then Jesus asked, "What is the kingdom of God like? What shall I compare it to? [19]It is like a mustard seed, which a man took and planted in his garden. It grew and became a tree, and the birds of the air perched in its branches."

[20]Again he asked, "What shall I compare the kingdom of God to? [21]It is like yeast that a woman took and mixed into a large amount[a] of flour until it worked all through the dough."

The Narrow Door

[22]Then Jesus went through the towns and villages, teaching as he made his way to Jerusalem. [23]Someone asked him, "Lord, are only a few people going to be saved?"

He said to them, [24]"Make every effort to enter through the narrow door, because many, I tell you, will try to enter and will not be able to. [25]Once the owner of the house gets up and closes the door, you will stand outside knocking and pleading, 'Sir, open the door for us.'

"But he will answer, 'I don't know you or where you come from.'

[26]"Then you will say, 'We ate and drank with you, and you taught in our streets.'

[27]"But he will reply, 'I don't know you or where you come from. Away from me, all you evildoers!'

[28]"There will be weeping there, and gnashing of teeth, when you see Abraham, Isaac and Jacob and all the prophets in the kingdom of God, but you yourselves thrown out. [29]People will come from east and west and north and south, and will take their places at the feast in the kingdom

---

a 21 Greek three satas (probably about 1/2 bushel or 22 liters)

sand men to oppose the one coming against him with twenty thousand? ³²If he is not able, he will send a delegation while the other is still a long way off and will ask for terms of peace. ³³In the same way, any of you who does not give up everything he has cannot be my disciple.

³⁴"Salt is good, but if it loses its saltiness, how can it be made salty again? ³⁵It is fit neither for the soil nor for the manure pile; it is thrown out.

"He who has ears to hear, let him hear."

The Parable of the Lost Sheep

15 Now the tax collectors and "sinners" were all gathering around to hear him. ²But the Pharisees and the teachers of the law muttered, "This man welcomes sinners and eats with them."

³Then Jesus told them this parable: ⁴"Suppose one of you has a hundred sheep and loses one of them. Does he not leave the ninety-nine in the open country and go after the lost sheep until he finds it? ⁵And when he finds it, he joyfully puts it on his shoulders ⁶and goes home. Then he calls his friends and neighbors together and says, 'Rejoice with me; I have found my lost sheep.' ⁷I tell you that in the same way there will be more rejoicing in heaven over one sinner who repents than over ninety-nine righteous persons who do not need to repent.

The Parable of the Lost Coin

⁸"Or suppose a woman has ten silver coins^a and loses one. Does she not light a lamp, sweep the house and search carefully until she finds it? ⁹And when she finds it, she calls her friends and neighbors together and says, 'Rejoice with me; I have found my lost coin.' ¹⁰In the same way, I tell you, there is rejoicing in the presence of the angels of God over one sinner who repents."

The Parable of the Lost Son

¹¹Jesus continued: "There was a man who had two sons. ¹²The younger one said to his father, 'Father, give me my share of the estate.' So he divided his property between them.

¹³"Not long after that, the younger son got together all he had, set off for a distant country and there squandered his wealth in wild living. ¹⁴After he had spent everything, there was a severe famine in that whole country, and he began to be in need. ¹⁵So he went and hired himself out to a citizen of that country, who sent him to his fields to feed pigs. ¹⁶He longed to fill his

---

敵那領二萬兵來攻打他的嗎？³²若是不能，就趁敵人還遠的時候，派使者去求和息的條款。³³這樣，你們無論甚麼人，若不撇下一切所有的，就不能作我的門徒。

³⁴"鹽本是好的，鹽若失了味，可用甚麼叫它再鹹呢？³⁵或用在田裏，或堆在糞裏，都不合式，只好丟在外面。

"有耳可聽的，就應當聽！"

失羊的比喻

15 眾稅吏和罪人都挨近耶穌，要聽他講道。²法利賽人和文士私下議論說："這個人接待罪人，又同他們吃飯。"

³耶穌就用比喻說：⁴"你們中間誰有一百隻羊失去一隻，不把這九十九隻撇在曠野，去找那失去的羊，直到找着呢？⁵找着了，就歡歡喜喜地扛在肩上，⁶回到家裏，就請朋友鄰舍來，對他們說：'我失去的羊已經找着了，你們和我一同歡喜吧！'⁷我告訴你們：一個罪人悔改，在天上也要這樣為他歡喜，較比為九十九個不用悔改的義人歡喜更大。

失錢的比喻

⁸"或是一個婦人有十塊錢，若失落一塊，豈不點上燈，打掃屋子，細細地找，直到找着嗎？⁹找着了，就請朋友鄰舍來，對他們說：'我失落的那塊錢已經找着了，你們和我一同歡喜吧！'¹⁰我告訴你們：一個罪人悔改，在神的使者面前也是這樣為他歡喜。"

浪子的比喻

¹¹耶穌又說："一個人有兩個兒子。¹²小兒子對父親說：'父親，請你把我應得的家業分給我。'他父親就把產業分給他們。

¹³"過了不多幾日，小兒子就把他一切所有的都收拾起來，往遠方去了。在那裏任意放蕩，浪費資財。¹⁴既耗盡了一切所有的，又遇着那地方大遭饑荒，就窮苦起來。¹⁵於是去投靠那地方的一個人，那人打發他到田裏去放豬。¹⁶他恨不得拿豬所吃的

---

a 8 Greek ten drachmas, *each worth about a day's wages*

豆莢充飢，也沒有人給他。

17 "他醒悟過來，就說：'我父親有多少的雇工，口糧有餘，我倒在這裏餓死嗎？18我要起來，到我父親那裏去，向他說：父親！我得罪了天，又得罪了你。19從今以後，我不配稱為你的兒子，把我當作一個雇工吧！' 20於是起來，往他父親那裏去。

"相離還遠，他父親看見，就動了慈心，跑去抱着他的頸項，連連與他親嘴。

21 "兒子說：'父親！我得罪了天，又得罪了你。從今以後，我不配稱為你的兒子。'

22 "父親卻吩咐僕人說：'把那上好的袍子快拿出來給他穿，把戒指戴在他指頭上，把鞋穿在他腳上，23把那肥牛犢牽來宰了，我們可以吃喝快樂。24因為我這個兒子是死而復活，失而又得的。'他們就快樂起來。

25 "那時，大兒子正在田裏。他回來，離家不遠，聽見作樂跳舞的聲音，26便叫過一個僕人來，問是甚麼事。27僕人說：'你兄弟來了。你父親因為得他無災無病地回來，把肥牛犢宰了。'

28 "大兒子卻生氣，不肯進去。他父親就出來勸他。29他對父親說：'我服侍你這多年，從來沒有違背過你的命，你並沒有給我一隻山羊羔，叫我和朋友一同快樂。30但你這個兒子和娼妓吞盡了你的產業，他一來了，你倒為他宰了肥牛犢！'

31 "父親對他說：'兒啊！你常和我同在，我一切所有的都是你的；32只是你這個兄弟是死而復活、失而又得的，所以我們理當歡喜快樂。'"

精明管家的比喻

16 耶穌又對門徒說："有一個財主的管家，別人向他主人告他浪費主人的財物。2主人叫他來，對他說：'我聽見你這事怎麼樣呢？把你所經管的交代明白，因你不能再作我的管家。'

stomach with the pods that the pigs were eating, but no one gave him anything.

17"When he came to his senses, he said, 'How many of my father's hired men have food to spare, and here I am starving to death! 18I will set out and go back to my father and say to him: Father, I have sinned against heaven and against you. 19I am no longer worthy to be called your son; make me like one of your hired men.' 20So he got up and went to his father.

"But while he was still a long way off, his father saw him and was filled with compassion for him; he ran to his son, threw his arms around him and kissed him.

21"The son said to him, 'Father, I have sinned against heaven and against you. I am no longer worthy to be called your son.a'

22"But the father said to his servants, 'Quick! Bring the best robe and put it on him. Put a ring on his finger and sandals on his feet. 23Bring the fattened calf and kill it. Let's have a feast and celebrate. 24For this son of mine was dead and is alive again; he was lost and is found.' So they began to celebrate.

25"Meanwhile, the older son was in the field. When he came near the house, he heard music and dancing. 26So he called one of the servants and asked him what was going on. 27'Your brother has come,' he replied, 'and your father has killed the fattened calf because he has him back safe and sound.'

28"The older brother became angry and refused to go in. So his father went out and pleaded with him. 29But he answered his father, 'Look! All these years I've been slaving for you and never disobeyed your orders. Yet you never gave me even a young goat so I could celebrate with my friends. 30But when this son of yours who has squandered your property with prostitutes comes home, you kill the fattened calf for him!'

31" 'My son,' the father said, 'you are always with me, and everything I have is yours. 32But we had to celebrate and be glad, because this brother of yours was dead and is alive again; he was lost and is found.' "

The Parable of the Shrewd Manager

16 Jesus told his disciples: "There was a rich man whose manager was accused of wasting his possessions. 2So he called him in and asked him, 'What is this I hear about you? Give an account of your management, because you cannot be manager any longer.'

---

a 21 Some early manuscripts son. Make me like one of your hired men.

3"The manager said to himself, 'What shall I do now? My master is taking away my job. I'm not strong enough to dig, and I'm ashamed to beg— 4I know what I'll do so that, when I lose my job here, people will welcome me into their houses.'

5"So he called in each one of his master's debtors. He asked the first, 'How much do you owe my master?'

6" 'Eight hundred gallons*a* of olive oil,' he replied.

"The manager told him, 'Take your bill, sit down quickly, and make it four hundred.'

7"Then he asked the second, 'And how much do you owe?'

" 'A thousand bushels*b* of wheat,' he replied.

"He told him, 'Take your bill and make it eight hundred.'

8"The master commended the dishonest manager because he had acted shrewdly. For the people of this world are more shrewd in dealing with their own kind than are the people of the light. 9I tell you, use worldly wealth to gain friends for yourselves, so that when it is gone, you will be welcomed into eternal dwellings.

10"Whoever can be trusted with very little can also be trusted with much, and whoever is dishonest with very little will also be dishonest with much. 11So if you have not been trustworthy in handling worldly wealth, who will trust you with true riches? 12And if you have not been trustworthy with someone else's property, who will give you property of your own?

13"No servant can serve two masters. Either he will hate the one and love the other, or he will be devoted to the one and despise the other. You cannot serve both God and Money."

14The Pharisees, who loved money, heard all this and were sneering at Jesus. 15He said to them, "You are the ones who justify yourselves in the eyes of men, but God knows your hearts. What is highly valued among men is detestable in God's sight.

Additional Teachings

16"The Law and the Prophets were proclaimed until John. Since that time, the good news of the kingdom of God is being preached, and everyone is forcing his way into it. 17It is easier for heaven and earth to disappear than for the least stroke of a pen to drop out of the Law.

3 "那管家心裏說:'主人辭我,不用我再作管家,我將來做甚麼?鋤地呢?無力;討飯呢?怕羞。4我知道怎麼行,好叫人在我不作管家之後,接我到他們家裏去。'

5 "於是把欠他主人債的,一個一個地叫了來,問頭一個說:'你欠我主人多少?'

6 "他說:'一百簍(註:每簍約五十斤)油。'

"管家說:'拿你的賬,快坐下,寫五十。'

7 "又問一個說:'你欠多少?'

"他說:'一百石麥子。'

"管家說:'拿你的賬,寫八十。'

8 "主人就誇獎這不義的管家做事聰明,因為今世之子,在世事之上,較比光明之子更加聰明。9我又告訴你們:要藉着那不義的錢財結交朋友,到了錢財無用的時候,他們可以接你們到永存的帳幕裏去。

10 "人在最小的事上忠心,在大事上也忠心;在最小的事上不義,在大事上也不義。11倘若你們在不義的錢財上不忠心,誰還把那真實的錢財託付你們呢?12倘若你們在別人的東西上不忠心,誰還把你們自己的東西給你們呢?

13 "一個僕人不能侍奉兩個主,不是惡這個愛那個,就是重這個輕那個。你們不能又侍奉神,又侍奉瑪門。"

14法利賽人是貪愛錢財的,他們聽見這一切話,就嗤笑耶穌。15耶穌對他們說:"你們是在人面前自稱為義的,你們的心,神卻知道;因為人所尊貴的,是神看為可憎惡的。

其他的教訓

16 "律法和先知到約翰為止,從此神國的福音傳開了,人人努力要進去。17天地廢去較比律法的一點一畫落空還容易。

---

a 6 Greek *one hundred batous* (probably about 3 kiloliters)

b 7 Greek *one hundred korous* (probably about 35 kiloliters)

18 "凡休妻另娶的就是犯姦淫；娶被休之妻的也是犯姦淫。

財主和拉撒路

19 "有一個財主，穿着紫色袍和細麻布衣服，天天奢華宴樂。20 又有一個討飯的，名叫拉撒路，渾身生瘡，被人放在財主門口，21 要得財主桌子上掉下來的零碎充飢，並且狗來舐他的瘡。

22 "後來那討飯的死了，被天使帶去放在亞伯拉罕的懷裏。財主也死了，並且埋葬了。23 他在陰間受痛苦，舉目遠遠地望見亞伯拉罕，又望見拉撒路在他懷裏，24 就喊着說：'我祖亞伯拉罕哪，可憐我吧！打發拉撒路來，用指頭尖蘸點水，涼涼我的舌頭，因為我在這火焰裏，極其痛苦。'

25 "亞伯拉罕說：'兒啊，你該回想你生前享過福，拉撒路也受過苦；如今他在這裏得安慰，你倒受痛苦。26 不但這樣，並且在你我之間，有深淵限定，以致人要從這邊過到你們那邊是不能的；要從那邊過到我們這邊也是不能的。'

27 "財主說：'我祖啊！既是這樣，求你打發拉撒路到我父家去，28 因為我還有五個弟兄，他可以對他們作見證，免得他們也來到這痛苦的地方。'

29 "亞伯拉罕說：'他們有摩西和先知的話可以聽從。'

30 "他說：'我祖亞伯拉罕哪，不是的，若有一個從死裏復活的，到他們那裏去的，他們必要悔改。'

31 "亞伯拉罕說：'若不聽從摩西和先知的話，就是有一個從死裏復活的，他們也是不聽勸。'"

罪，信心，本分

17 耶穌又對門徒說："絆倒人的事是免不了的，但那絆倒人的有禍了。2 就是把磨石拴在這人的頸項上，丟在海裏，還強如他把這小子裏的一個絆倒了。3 你們要謹慎！

"若是你的弟兄得罪你，就勸戒他；他若懊悔，就饒恕他。4 倘若他一天七次得罪你，又七次回轉，說：'我懊悔了'，你總要饒恕他。"

18 "Anyone who divorces his wife and marries another woman commits adultery, and the man who marries a divorced woman commits adultery.

The Rich Man and Lazarus

19 "There was a rich man who was dressed in purple and fine linen and lived in luxury every day. 20 At his gate was laid a beggar named Lazarus, covered with sores 21 and longing to eat what fell from the rich man's table. Even the dogs came and licked his sores.

22 "The time came when the beggar died and the angels carried him to Abraham's side. The rich man also died and was buried. 23 In hell,ᵃ where he was in torment, he looked up and saw Abraham far away, with Lazarus by his side. 24 So he called to him, 'Father Abraham, have pity on me and send Lazarus to dip the tip of his finger in water and cool my tongue, because I am in agony in this fire.'

25 "But Abraham replied, 'Son, remember that in your lifetime you received your good things, while Lazarus received bad things, but now he is comforted here and you are in agony. 26 And besides all this, between us and you a great chasm has been fixed, so that those who want to go from here to you cannot, nor can anyone cross over from there to us.'

27 "He answered, 'Then I beg you, father, send Lazarus to my father's house, 28 for I have five brothers. Let him warn them, so that they will not also come to this place of torment.'

29 "Abraham replied, 'They have Moses and the Prophets; let them listen to them.'

30 " 'No, father Abraham,' he said, 'but if someone from the dead goes to them, they will repent.'

31 "He said to him, 'If they do not listen to Moses and the Prophets, they will not be convinced even if someone rises from the dead.' "

Sin, Faith, Duty

17 Jesus said to his disciples: "Things that cause people to sin are bound to come, but woe to that person through whom they come. 2 It would be better for him to be thrown into the sea with a millstone tied around his neck than for him to cause one of these little ones to sin. 3 So watch yourselves.

"If your brother sins, rebuke him, and if he repents, forgive him. 4 If he sins against you seven times in a day, and seven times comes back to you and says, 'I repent,' forgive him."

a 23 Greek Hades

⁵The apostles said to the Lord, "Increase our faith!"

⁶He replied, "If you have faith as small as a mustard seed, you can say to this mulberry tree, 'Be uprooted and planted in the sea,' and it will obey you.

⁷"Suppose one of you had a servant plowing or looking after the sheep. Would he say to the servant when he comes in from the field, 'Come along now and sit down to eat'? ⁸Would he not rather say, 'Prepare my supper, get yourself ready and wait on me while I eat and drink; after that you may eat and drink'? ⁹Would he thank the servant because he did what he was told to do? ¹⁰So you also, when you have done everything you were told to do, should say, 'We are unworthy servants; we have only done our duty.' "

Ten Healed of Leprosy

¹¹Now on his way to Jerusalem, Jesus traveled along the border between Samaria and Galilee. ¹²As he was going into a village, ten men who had leprosy*a* met him. They stood at a distance ¹³and called out in a loud voice, "Jesus, Master, have pity on us!"

¹⁴When he saw them, he said, "Go, show yourselves to the priests." And as they went, they were cleansed.

¹⁵One of them, when he saw he was healed, came back, praising God in a loud voice. ¹⁶He threw himself at Jesus' feet and thanked him—and he was a Samaritan.

¹⁷Jesus asked, "Were not all ten cleansed? Where are the other nine? ¹⁸Was no one found to return and give praise to God except this foreigner?" ¹⁹Then he said to him, "Rise and go; your faith has made you well."

The Coming of the Kingdom of God

²⁰Once, having been asked by the Pharisees when the kingdom of God would come, Jesus replied, "The kingdom of God does not come with your careful observation, ²¹nor will people say, 'Here it is,' or 'There it is,' because the kingdom of God is within*b* you."

²²Then he said to his disciples, "The time is coming when you will long to see one of the days of the Son of Man, but you will not see it. ²³Men will tell you, 'There he is!' or 'Here he is!' Do not go running off after them. ²⁴For the Son of Man in his day*c* will be like the lightning, which flashes and lights up the sky from one

---

a 12 The Greek word was used for various diseases affecting the skin—not necessarily leprosy.　　*b 21* Or *among*
c 24 Some manuscripts do not have *in his day*.

⁵使徒對主說："求主加增我們的信心。"

⁶主說："你們若有信心像一粒芥菜種，就是對這棵桑樹說：'你要拔起根來，栽在海裏'，它也必聽從你們。

⁷"你們誰有僕人耕地或是放羊，從田裏回來，就對他說，'你快來坐下吃飯'呢？⁸豈不對他說，'你給我預備晚飯，束上帶子伺候我，等我吃喝完了，你才可以吃喝'嗎？⁹僕人照所吩咐的去做，主人還謝謝他嗎？¹⁰這樣，你們做完了一切所吩咐的，只當說：'我們是無用的僕人，所做的本是我們應分做的。'"

十個被治好的痲瘋病人

¹¹耶穌往耶路撒冷去，經過撒馬利亞和加利利。¹²進入一個村子，有十個長大痲瘋的，迎面而來，遠遠地站着，¹³高聲說："耶穌，夫子，可憐我們吧！"

¹⁴耶穌看見，就對他們說："你們去，把身體給祭司察看！"他們去的時候就潔淨了。

¹⁵內中有一個見自己已經好了，就回來大聲歸榮耀與神，¹⁶又俯伏在耶穌腳前感謝他；這人是撒馬利亞人。

¹⁷耶穌說："潔淨了的不是十個人嗎？那九個在哪裏呢？¹⁸除了這外族人，再沒有別人回來歸榮耀與神嗎？"¹⁹就對那人說："起來，走吧！你的信救了你了。"

神國的來臨

²⁰法利賽人問神的國幾時來到，耶穌回答說："神的國來到不是眼所能見的。²¹人也不得說：'看哪，在這裏！看哪，在那裏！'因為神的國就在你們心裏（註："心裏"或作"中間"）。"

²²他又對門徒說："日子將到，你們巴不得看見人子的一個日子，卻不得看見。²³人將要對你們說：'看哪，在那裏！看哪，在這裏！'你們不要出去，也不要跟隨他們。²⁴因為人子在他降臨的日子，好像閃電從天

這邊一閃直照到天那邊。25只是他必須先受許多苦，又被這世代棄絕。

26 "挪亞的日子怎樣，人子的日子也要怎樣。27那時候的人又吃又喝，又娶又嫁，到挪亞進方舟的那日，洪水就來，把他們全都滅了。

28 "又好像羅得的日子，人又吃又喝，又買又賣，又耕種又蓋造。29到羅得出所多瑪的那日，就有火與硫磺從天上降下來，把他們全都滅了。

30 "人子顯現的日子也要這樣。31當那日，人在房上，器具在屋裏，不要下來拿；人在田裏，也不要回家。32你們要回想羅得的妻子。33凡想要保全生命的，必喪掉生命；凡喪掉生命的，必救活生命。34我對你們說，當那一夜，兩個人在一個牀上，要取去一個，撇下一個。35兩個女人一同推磨，要取去一個，撇下一個。

(註：有古卷在此有36 "兩個人在田裏，要取去一個，撇下一個。")"

37門徒說："主啊，在哪裏有這事呢？"耶穌說："屍首在哪裏，鷹也必聚在那裏。"

切求的寡婦的比喻

18 耶穌設一個比喻，是要人常常禱告，不可灰心。2說："某城裏有一個官，不懼怕神，也不尊重世人。3那城裏有個寡婦，常到他那裏，說：'我有一個對頭，求你給我伸冤。'

4 "他多日不准。後來心裏說：'我雖不懼怕神，也不尊重世人，5只因這寡婦煩擾我，我就給她伸冤吧，免得她常來纏磨我！'"

6主說："你們聽這不義之官所說的話。7神的選民晝夜呼籲他，他縱然為他們忍了多時，豈不終久給他們伸冤嗎？8我告訴你們：要快快地給他們伸冤了。然而，人子來的時候，遇得見世上有信德嗎？"

法利賽人和稅吏的比喻

9耶穌向那些仗著自己是義人，藐視別人的，設一個比喻，10說："有兩個人上殿裏去禱告：一個是法

end to the other. 25But first he must suffer many things and be rejected by this generation.

26"Just as it was in the days of Noah, so also will it be in the days of the Son of Man. 27People were eating, drinking, marrying and being given in marriage up to the day Noah entered the ark. Then the flood came and destroyed them all.

28"It was the same in the days of Lot. People were eating and drinking, buying and selling, planting and building. 29But the day Lot left Sodom, fire and sulfur rained down from heaven and destroyed them all.

30"It will be just like this on the day the Son of Man is revealed. 31On that day no one who is on the roof of his house, with his goods inside, should go down to get them. Likewise, no one in the field should go back for anything. 32Remember Lot's wife! 33Whoever tries to keep his life will lose it, and whoever loses his life will preserve it. 34I tell you, on that night two people will be in one bed; one will be taken and the other left. 35Two women will be grinding grain together; one will be taken and the other left.*a*"

37"Where, Lord?" they asked.

He replied, "Where there is a dead body, there the vultures will gather."

The Parable of the Persistent Widow

18 Then Jesus told his disciples a parable to show them that they should always pray and not give up. 2He said: "In a certain town there was a judge who neither feared God nor cared about men. 3And there was a widow in that town who kept coming to him with the plea, 'Grant me justice against my adversary.'

4"For some time he refused. But finally he said to himself, 'Even though I don't fear God or care about men, 5yet because this widow keeps bothering me, I will see that she gets justice, so that she won't eventually wear me out with her coming!' "

6And the Lord said, "Listen to what the unjust judge says. 7And will not God bring about justice for his chosen ones, who cry out to him day and night? Will he keep putting them off? 8I tell you, he will see that they get justice, and quickly. However, when the Son of Man comes, will he find faith on the earth?"

The Parable of the Pharisee and the Tax Collector

9To some who were confident of their own righteousness and looked down on everybody else, Jesus told this parable: 10"Two men went

a 35 Some manuscripts left. 36Two men will be in the field; one will be taken and the other left.

up to the temple to pray, one a Pharisee and the other a tax collector. [11]The Pharisee stood up and prayed about[a] himself: 'God, I thank you that I am not like other men—robbers, evildoers, adulterers—or even like this tax collector. [12]I fast twice a week and give a tenth of all I get.'

[13]"But the tax collector stood at a distance. He would not even look up to heaven, but beat his breast and said, 'God, have mercy on me, a sinner.'

[14]"I tell you that this man, rather than the other, went home justified before God. For everyone who exalts himself will be humbled, and he who humbles himself will be exalted."

The Little Children and Jesus

[15]People were also bringing babies to Jesus to have him touch them. When the disciples saw this, they rebuked them. [16]But Jesus called the children to him and said, "Let the little children come to me, and do not hinder them, for the kingdom of God belongs to such as these. [17]I tell you the truth, anyone who will not receive the kingdom of God like a little child will never enter it."

The Rich Ruler

[18]A certain ruler asked him, "Good teacher, what must I do to inherit eternal life?"

[19]"Why do you call me good?" Jesus answered. "No one is good—except God alone. [20]You know the commandments: 'Do not commit adultery, do not murder, do not steal, do not give false testimony, honor your father and mother.'[b]"

[21]"All these I have kept since I was a boy," he said.

[22]When Jesus heard this, he said to him, "You still lack one thing. Sell everything you have and give to the poor, and you will have treasure in heaven. Then come, follow me."

[23]When he heard this, he became very sad, because he was a man of great wealth. [24]Jesus looked at him and said, "How hard it is for the rich to enter the kingdom of God! [25]Indeed, it is easier for a camel to go through the eye of a needle than for a rich man to enter the kingdom of God."

[26]Those who heard this asked, "Who then can be saved?"

[27]Jesus replied, "What is impossible with men is possible with God."

[28]Peter said to him, "We have left all we had to follow you!"

利賽人，一個是稅吏。[11]法利賽人站着，自言自語地禱告說：'神啊，我感謝你，我不像別人勒索、不義、姦淫，也不像這個稅吏。[12]我一個禮拜禁食兩次，凡我所得的都捐上十分之一。'

[13]"那稅吏遠遠地站着，連舉目望天也不敢，只捶着胸說：'神啊，開恩可憐我這個罪人！'

[14]"我告訴你們：這人回家去比那人倒算為義了。因為凡自高的，必降為卑；自卑的，必升為高。"

小孩和耶穌

[15]有人抱着自己的嬰孩來見耶穌，要他摸他們；門徒看見就責備那些人。[16]耶穌卻叫他們來，說："讓小孩子到我這裏來，不要禁止他們，因為在神國的正是這樣的人。[17]我實在告訴你們：凡要承受神國的，若不像小孩子，斷不能進去。"

富有的官

[18]有一個官問耶穌說："良善的夫子，我該做甚麼事才可以承受永生？"

[19]耶穌對他說："你為甚麼稱我是良善的？除了神一位之外，再沒有良善的。[20]誡命你是曉得的：'不可姦淫，不可殺人，不可偷盜，不可作假見證，當孝敬父母。'"

[21]那人說："這一切我從小都遵守了。"

[22]耶穌聽見了，就說："你還缺少一件：要變賣你一切所有的，分給窮人，就必有財寶在天上；你還要來跟從我。"

[23]他聽見這話，就甚憂愁，因為他很富足。[24]耶穌看見他，就說："有錢財的人進神的國是何等的難哪！[25]駱駝穿過針的眼比財主進神的國還容易呢！"

[26]聽見的人說："這樣，誰能得救呢？"

[27]耶穌說："在人所不能的事，在神卻能。"

[28]彼得說："看哪！我們已經撇下自己所有的跟從你了。"

---

a 11 Or *to*　　*b 20* Exodus 20:12-16; Deut. 5:16-20

29耶穌説：「我實在告訴你們：人為神的國撇下房屋，或是妻子、弟兄、父母、兒女，30沒有在今世不得百倍，在來世不得永生的。」

耶穌再預言自己的死

31耶穌帶着十二個門徒，對他們說：「看哪，我們上耶路撒冷去，先知所寫的一切事都要成就在人子身上。32他將要被交給外邦人。他們要戲弄他，凌辱他，吐唾沫在他臉上，33並要鞭打他，殺害他。第三日他要復活。」

34這些事門徒一樣也不懂得，意思乃是隱藏的，他們不曉得所説的是甚麼。

盲丐得看見

35耶穌將近耶利哥的時候，有一個瞎子坐在路旁討飯。36聽見許多人經過，就問是甚麼事。37他們告訴他，是拿撒勒人耶穌經過。

38他就呼叫説：「大衞的子孫耶穌啊，可憐我吧！」

39在前頭走的人就責備他，不許他做聲；他卻越發喊叫説：「大衞的子孫，可憐我吧！」

40耶穌站住，吩咐把他領過來，到了跟前，就問他説：41「你要我為你做甚麼？」

他説：「主啊，我要能看見！」

42耶穌説：「你可以看見！你的信救了你了。」43瞎子立刻看見了，就跟隨耶穌，一路歸榮耀與神。眾人看見這事，也讚美神。

税吏撒該

19 耶穌進了耶利哥，正經過的時候，2有一個人名叫撒該，作税吏長，是個財主。3他要看看耶穌是怎樣的人，只因人多，他的身量又矮，所以不得看見。4就跑到前頭，爬上桑樹，要看耶穌，因為耶穌必從那裏經過。

5耶穌到了那裏，抬頭一看，對他説：「撒該，快下來！今天我必住在你家裏。」6他就急忙下來，歡歡喜喜地接待耶穌。

7眾人看見，都私下議論説：「他竟到罪人家裏去住宿。」

29"I tell you the truth," Jesus said to them, "no one who has left home or wife or brothers or parents or children for the sake of the kingdom of God 30will fail to receive many times as much in this age and, in the age to come, eternal life."

Jesus Again Predicts His Death

31Jesus took the Twelve aside and told them, "We are going up to Jerusalem, and everything that is written by the prophets about the Son of Man will be fulfilled. 32He will be handed over to the Gentiles. They will mock him, insult him, spit on him, flog him and kill him. 33On the third day he will rise again."

34The disciples did not understand any of this. Its meaning was hidden from them, and they did not know what he was talking about.

A Blind Beggar Receives His Sight

35As Jesus approached Jericho, a blind man was sitting by the roadside begging. 36When he heard the crowd going by, he asked what was happening. 37They told him, "Jesus of Nazareth is passing by."

38He called out, "Jesus, Son of David, have mercy on me!"

39Those who led the way rebuked him and told him to be quiet, but he shouted all the more, "Son of David, have mercy on me!"

40Jesus stopped and ordered the man to be brought to him. When he came near, Jesus asked him, 41"What do you want me to do for you?"

"Lord, I want to see," he replied.

42Jesus said to him, "Receive your sight; your faith has healed you." 43Immediately he received his sight and followed Jesus, praising God. When all the people saw it, they also praised God.

Zacchaeus the Tax Collector

19 Jesus entered Jericho and was passing through. 2A man was there by the name of Zacchaeus; he was a chief tax collector and was wealthy. 3He wanted to see who Jesus was, but being a short man he could not, because of the crowd. 4So he ran ahead and climbed a sycamore-fig tree to see him, since Jesus was coming that way.

5When Jesus reached the spot, he looked up and said to him, "Zacchaeus, come down immediately. I must stay at your house today." 6So he came down at once and welcomed him gladly.

7All the people saw this and began to mutter, "He has gone to be the guest of a 'sinner.' "

⁸But Zacchaeus stood up and said to the Lord, "Look, Lord! Here and now I give half of my possessions to the poor, and if I have cheated anybody out of anything, I will pay back four times the amount."

⁹Jesus said to him, "Today salvation has come to this house, because this man, too, is a son of Abraham. ¹⁰For the Son of Man came to seek and to save what was lost."

The Parable of the Ten Minas

¹¹While they were listening to this, he went on to tell them a parable, because he was near Jerusalem and the people thought that the kingdom of God was going to appear at once. ¹²He said: "A man of noble birth went to a distant country to have himself appointed king and then to return. ¹³So he called ten of his servants and gave them ten minas.ᵃ 'Put this money to work,' he said, 'until I come back.'

¹⁴"But his subjects hated him and sent a delegation after him to say, 'We don't want this man to be our king.'

¹⁵"He was made king, however, and returned home. Then he sent for the servants to whom he had given the money, in order to find out what they had gained with it.

¹⁶"The first one came and said, 'Sir, your mina has earned ten more.'

¹⁷" 'Well done, my good servant!' his master replied. 'Because you have been trustworthy in a very small matter, take charge of ten cities.'

¹⁸"The second came and said, 'Sir, your mina has earned five more.'

¹⁹"His master answered, 'You take charge of five cities.'

²⁰"Then another servant came and said, 'Sir, here is your mina; I have kept it laid away in a piece of cloth. ²¹I was afraid of you, because you are a hard man. You take out what you did not put in and reap what you did not sow.'

²²"His master replied, 'I will judge you by your own words, you wicked servant! You knew, did you, that I am a hard man, taking out what I did not put in, and reaping what I did not sow? ²³Why then didn't you put my money on deposit, so that when I came back, I could have collected it with interest?'

²⁴"Then he said to those standing by, 'Take his mina away from him and give it to the one who has ten minas.'

²⁵" 'Sir,' they said, 'he already has ten!'

ᵃ 13 A mina was about three months' wages.

⁸撒該站着對主說："主啊,我把所有的一半給窮人;我若訛詐了誰,就還他四倍。"

⁹耶穌說:"今天救恩到了這家,因為他也是亞伯拉罕的子孫。¹⁰人子來,為要尋找、拯救失喪的人。"

十錠銀子的比喻

¹¹眾人正在聽見這些話的時候,耶穌因為將近耶路撒冷,又因他們以為神的國快要顯出來,就另設一個比喻,說:¹²"有一個貴胄往遠方去,要得國回來,¹³便叫了他的十個僕人來,交給他們十錠(註:"錠"原文作"彌拿",一彌拿約銀十兩)銀子,說:'你們去做生意,直等我回來。'

¹⁴"他本國的人卻恨他,打發使者隨後去,說:'我們不願意這個人作我們的王。'

¹⁵"他既得國回來,就吩咐叫那領銀子的僕人來,要知道他們做生意賺了多少。

¹⁶"頭一個上來,說:'主啊,你的一錠銀子已經賺了十錠。'

¹⁷"主人說:'好!良善的僕人,你既在最小的事上有忠心,可以有權柄管十座城。'

¹⁸"第二個來,說:'主啊,你的一錠銀子已經賺了五錠。'

¹⁹"主人說:'你也可以管五座城。'

²⁰"又有一個來說:'主啊,看哪,你的一錠銀子在這裏,我把它包在手巾裏存着。²¹我原是怕你,因為你是嚴厲的人;沒有放下的,還要去拿;沒有種下的,還要去收。'

²²"主人對他說:'你這惡僕,我要憑你的口定你的罪!你既知道我是嚴厲的人,沒有放下的,還要去拿,沒有種下的,還要去收,²³為甚麼不把我的銀子交給銀行,等我來的時候,連本帶利都可以要回來呢?'

²⁴"就對旁邊站着的人說:'奪過他這一錠來,給那有十錠的。'

²⁵"他們說:'主啊,他已經有十錠了!'

26 "主人説：'我告訴你們：凡有的，還要加給他；沒有的，連他所有的也要奪過來。27 至於我那些仇敵，不要我作他們王的，把他們拉來，在我面前殺了吧！'"

光榮進聖城

28 耶穌説完了這話，就在前面走，上耶路撒冷去。29 將近伯法其和伯大尼，在一座山名叫橄欖山那裏，就打發兩個門徒，説：30 "你們往對面村子裏去，進去的時候，必看見一匹驢駒拴在那裏，是從來沒有人騎過的，可以解開牽來。31 若有人問為甚麼解牠，你們就説：'主要用牠。'"

32 打發的人去了，所遇見的正如耶穌所説的。33 他們解驢駒的時候，主人問他們説："解驢駒做甚麼？"

34 他們説："主要用牠。"

35 他們牽到耶穌那裏，把自己的衣服搭在上面，扶着耶穌騎上。36 走的時候，眾人把衣服鋪在路上。

37 將近耶路撒冷，正下橄欖山的時候，眾門徒因所見過的一切異能，都歡樂起來，大聲讚美神，

38 説："奉主名來的王
　　　是應當稱頌的！"
　　 "在天上有和平；
　　　在至高之處有榮光！"

39 眾人中有幾個法利賽人對耶穌説："夫子，責備你的門徒吧！"40 耶穌説："我告訴你們：若是他們閉口不説，這些石頭必要呼叫起來。"

41 耶穌快到耶路撒冷，看見城，就為它哀哭，42 説："巴不得你在這日子知道關係你平安的事；無奈這事現在是隱藏的，叫你的眼看不出來。43 因為日子將到，你的仇敵必築起土壘，周圍環繞你，四面困住你，44 並要掃滅你和你裏頭的兒女，連一塊石頭也不留在石頭上，因你不知道眷顧你的時候。"

耶穌在聖殿中

45 耶穌進了殿，趕出裏頭做買賣的人，46 對他們説："經上説：'我

26 "He replied, 'I tell you that to everyone who has, more will be given, but as for the one who has nothing, even what he has will be taken away. 27 But those enemies of mine who did not want me to be king over them—bring them here and kill them in front of me.' "

The Triumphal Entry

28 After Jesus had said this, he went on ahead, going up to Jerusalem. 29 As he approached Bethphage and Bethany at the hill called the Mount of Olives, he sent two of his disciples, saying to them, 30 "Go to the village ahead of you, and as you enter it, you will find a colt tied there, which no one has ever ridden. Untie it and bring it here. 31 If anyone asks you, 'Why are you untying it?' tell him, 'The Lord needs it.' "

32 Those who were sent ahead went and found it just as he had told them. 33 As they were untying the colt, its owners asked them, "Why are you untying the colt?"

34 They replied, "The Lord needs it."

35 They brought it to Jesus, threw their cloaks on the colt and put Jesus on it. 36 As he went along, people spread their cloaks on the road.

37 When he came near the place where the road goes down the Mount of Olives, the whole crowd of disciples began joyfully to praise God in loud voices for all the miracles they had seen:

38 "Blessed is the king who comes in the name of the Lord!" [a]

"Peace in heaven and glory in the highest!"

39 Some of the Pharisees in the crowd said to Jesus, "Teacher, rebuke your disciples!"

40 "I tell you," he replied, "if they keep quiet, the stones will cry out."

41 As he approached Jerusalem and saw the city, he wept over it 42 and said, "If you, even you, had only known on this day what would bring you peace—but now it is hidden from your eyes. 43 The days will come upon you when your enemies will build an embankment against you and encircle you and hem you in on every side. 44 They will dash you to the ground, you and the children within your walls. They will not leave one stone on another, because you did not recognize the time of God's coming to you."

Jesus at the Temple

45 Then he entered the temple area and began driving out those who were selling. 46 "It is writ-

a 38 Psalm 118:26

ten," he said to them, " 'My house will be a house of prayer'[a]; but you have made it 'a den of robbers.'[b]"

47Every day he was teaching at the temple. But the chief priests, the teachers of the law and the leaders among the people were trying to kill him. 48Yet they could not find any way to do it, because all the people hung on his words.

The Authority of Jesus Questioned

20 One day as he was teaching the people in the temple courts and preaching the gospel, the chief priests and the teachers of the law, together with the elders, came up to him. 2"Tell us by what authority you are doing these things," they said. "Who gave you this authority?"

3He replied, "I will also ask you a question. Tell me, 4John's baptism—was it from heaven, or from men?"

5They discussed it among themselves and said, "If we say, 'From heaven,' he will ask, 'Why didn't you believe him?' 6But if we say, 'From men,' all the people will stone us, because they are persuaded that John was a prophet."

7So they answered, "We don't know where it was from."

8Jesus said, "Neither will I tell you by what authority I am doing these things."

The Parable of the Tenants

9He went on to tell the people this parable: "A man planted a vineyard, rented it to some farmers and went away for a long time. 10At harvest time he sent a servant to the tenants so they would give him some of the fruit of the vineyard. But the tenants beat him and sent him away empty-handed. 11He sent another servant, but that one also they beat and treated shamefully and sent away empty-handed. 12He sent still a third, and they wounded him and threw him out.

13"Then the owner of the vineyard said, 'What shall I do? I will send my son, whom I love; perhaps they will respect him.'

14"But when the tenants saw him, they talked the matter over. 'This is the heir,' they said. 'Let's kill him, and the inheritance will be ours.' 15So they threw him out of the vineyard and killed him.

"What then will the owner of the vineyard do to them? 16He will come and kill those tenants and give the vineyard to others."

When the people heard this, they said, "May this never be!"

的殿必作禱告的殿' ，你們倒使它成為賊窩了。"

47耶穌天天在殿裏教訓人。祭司長和文士與百姓的尊長都想要殺他，48但尋不出法子來，因為百姓都側耳聽他。

耶穌的權柄被質問

20 有一天，耶穌在殿裏教訓百姓，講福音的時候，祭司長和文士並長老上前來，2問他說："你告訴我們，你仗着甚麼權柄做這些事？給你這權柄的是誰呢？"

3耶穌回答說："我也要問你們一句話，你們且告訴我，4約翰的洗禮是從天上來的，是從人間來的呢？"

5他們彼此商議說："我們若說'從天上來'，他必說：'你們為甚麼不信他呢？' 6若說'從人間來'，百姓都要用石頭打死我們，因為他們信約翰是先知。"

7於是回答說："不知道是從哪裏來的。"

8耶穌說："我也不告訴你們，我仗着甚麼權柄做這些事。"

兇惡園戶的比喻

9耶穌就設比喻對百姓說："有人栽了一個葡萄園，租給園戶，就往外國去住了許久。10到了時候，打發一個僕人到園戶那裏去，叫他們把園中當納的果子交給他。園戶竟打了他，叫他空手回去。11又打發一個僕人去，他們也打了他，並且凌辱他，叫他空手回去。12又打發第三個僕人去，他們也打傷了他，把他推出去了。

13 "園主說：'我怎麼辦呢？我要打發我的愛子去，或者他們尊敬他。'

14 "不料，園戶看見他，就彼此商量說：'這是承受產業的，我們殺他吧，使產業歸於我們！' 15於是把他推出葡萄園外殺了。

"這樣，葡萄園的主人要怎樣處治他們呢？16他要來除滅這些園戶，將葡萄園轉給別人。"

聽見的人說："這是萬不可的！"

---

a 46 Isaiah 56:7   b 46 Jer. 7:11

17耶穌看着他們說："經上記着：

" '匠人所棄的石頭
已作了房角的頭塊石頭。'
這是甚麼意思呢？
18凡掉在那石頭上的，必要跌碎；那石頭掉在誰的身上，就要把誰砸得稀爛。"

19文士和祭司長看出這比喻是指着他們說的，當時就想要下手拿他，只是懼怕百姓。

納稅給凱撒

20於是窺探耶穌，打發奸細裝作好人，要在他的話上得把柄，好將他交在巡撫的政權之下。21奸細就問耶穌說："夫子，我們曉得你所講所傳都是正道，也不取人的外貌，乃是誠誠實實傳神的道。22我們納稅給凱撒，可以不可以？"

23耶穌看出他們的詭詐，就對他們說：24"拿一個銀錢來給我看。這像和這號是誰的？"

他們說："是凱撒的。"

25耶穌說："這樣，凱撒的物當歸給凱撒，神的物當歸給神。"

26他們當着百姓，在這話上得不着把柄，又希奇他的應對，就閉口無言了。

復活與婚姻

27撒都該人常說沒有復活的事。有幾個來問耶穌說：28"夫子！摩西為我們寫着說："人若有妻無子就死了，他兄弟當娶他的妻，為哥哥生子立後。'29有弟兄七人，第一個娶了妻，沒有孩子死了；30第二個、第三個也娶過她；31那七個人都娶過她，沒有留下孩子就死了。32後來婦人也死了。33這樣，當復活的時候，她是哪一個的妻子呢？因為他們七個人都娶過她。"

34耶穌說："這世界的人有娶有嫁。35惟有算為配得那世界，與從死

17Jesus looked directly at them and asked, "Then what is the meaning of that which is written:

" 'The stone the builders rejected
has become the capstone[a][b]?

18Everyone who falls on that stone will be broken to pieces, but he on whom it falls will be crushed."

19The teachers of the law and the chief priests looked for a way to arrest him immediately, because they knew he had spoken this parable against them. But they were afraid of the people.

Paying Taxes to Caesar

20Keeping a close watch on him, they sent spies, who pretended to be honest. They hoped to catch Jesus in something he said so that they might hand him over to the power and authority of the governor. 21So the spies questioned him: "Teacher, we know that you speak and teach what is right, and that you do not show partiality but teach the way of God in accordance with the truth. 22Is it right for us to pay taxes to Caesar or not?"

23He saw through their duplicity and said to them, 24"Show me a denarius. Whose portrait and inscription are on it?"

25"Caesar's," they replied.

He said to them, "Then give to Caesar what is Caesar's, and to God what is God's."

26They were unable to trap him in what he had said there in public. And astonished by his answer, they became silent.

The Resurrection and Marriage

27Some of the Sadducees, who say there is no resurrection, came to Jesus with a question. 28"Teacher," they said, "Moses wrote for us that if a man's brother dies and leaves a wife but no children, the man must marry the widow and have children for his brother. 29Now there were seven brothers. The first one married a woman and died childless. 30The second 31and then the third married her, and in the same way the seven died, leaving no children. 32Finally, the woman died too. 33Now then, at the resurrection whose wife will she be, since the seven were married to her?"

34Jesus replied, "The people of this age marry and are given in marriage. 35But those who are considered worthy of taking part in that age and in the resurrection from the dead will neither

a 17 Or cornerstone   b 17 Psalm 118:22

marry nor be given in marriage, ³⁶and they can no longer die; for they are like the angels. They are God's children, since they are children of the resurrection. ³⁷But in the account of the bush, even Moses showed that the dead rise, for he calls the Lord 'the God of Abraham, and the God of Isaac, and the God of Jacob.'^a ³⁸He is not the God of the dead, but of the living, for to him all are alive."

³⁹Some of the teachers of the law responded, "Well said, teacher!" ⁴⁰And no one dared to ask him any more questions.

Whose Son Is the Christ?

⁴¹Then Jesus said to them, "How is it that they say the Christ^b is the Son of David? ⁴²David himself declares in the Book of Psalms:

" 'The Lord said to my Lord:
    "Sit at my right hand
⁴³until I make your enemies
    a footstool for your feet." '^c

⁴⁴David calls him 'Lord.' How then can he be his son?"

⁴⁵While all the people were listening, Jesus said to his disciples, ⁴⁶"Beware of the teachers of the law. They like to walk around in flowing robes and love to be greeted in the marketplaces and have the most important seats in the synagogues and the places of honor at banquets. ⁴⁷They devour widows' houses and for a show make lengthy prayers. Such men will be punished most severely."

The Widow's Offering

21 As he looked up, Jesus saw the rich putting their gifts into the temple treasury. ²He also saw a poor widow put in two very small copper coins.^d ³"I tell you the truth," he said, "this poor widow has put in more than all the others. ⁴All these people gave their gifts out of their wealth; but she out of her poverty put in all she had to live on."

Signs of the End of the Age

⁵Some of his disciples were remarking about how the temple was adorned with beautiful stones and with gifts dedicated to God. But Jesus said, ⁶"As for what you see here, the time will come when not one stone will be left on another; every one of them will be thrown down."

裏復活的人，也不娶也不嫁，³⁶因為他們不能再死，和天使一樣；既是復活的人，就為神的兒子。³⁷至於死人復活，<u>摩西</u>在荊棘篇上，稱主是<u>亞伯拉罕</u>的神，<u>以撒</u>的神，<u>雅各</u>的神，就指示明白了。³⁸神原不是死人的神，乃是活人的神，因為在他那裏（註："那裏"或作"看來"），人都是活的。"

³⁹有幾個文士說："夫子，你說得好！" ⁴⁰以後他們不敢再問他甚麼。

基督是誰的子孫？

⁴¹耶穌對他們說："人怎麼說基督是<u>大衛</u>的子孫呢？⁴²詩篇上<u>大衛</u>自己說：

" '主對我主說：
    你坐在我的右邊，
⁴³等我使你仇敵
    作你的腳凳。'

⁴⁴<u>大衛</u>既稱他為主，他怎麼又是<u>大衛</u>的子孫呢？"

⁴⁵眾百姓聽的時候，耶穌對門徒說：⁴⁶"你們要防備文士。他們好穿長衣遊行，喜愛人在街市上問他們安，又喜愛會堂裏的高位，筵席上的首座；⁴⁷他們侵吞寡婦的家產，假意作很長的禱告。這些人要受更重的刑罰！"

寡婦的奉獻

21 耶穌抬頭觀看，見財主把捐項投在庫裏，²又見一個窮寡婦投了兩個小錢，³就說："我實在告訴你們：這窮寡婦所投的比眾人還多。⁴因為眾人都是自己有餘，拿出來投在捐項裏；但這寡婦是自己不足，把她一切養生的都投上了。"

末世的預兆

⁵有人談論聖殿是用美石和供物妝飾的，⁶耶穌就說："論到你們所看見的這一切，將來日子到了，在這裏沒有一塊石頭留在石頭上不被拆毀了。"

---

^a 37 Exodus 3:6   ^b 41 Or Messiah   ^c 43 Psalm 110:1
^d 2 Greek two lepta

7他們問他説：“夫子，甚麼時候有這事呢？這事將到的時候有甚麼預兆呢？”

8耶穌説：“你們要謹慎，不要受迷惑，因為將來有好些人冒我的名來，説：‘我是基督’，又説：‘時候近了’，你們不要跟從他們！9你們聽見打仗和擾亂的事，不要驚惶，因為這些事必須先有，只是末期不能立時就到。”

10當時，耶穌對他們説：“民要攻打民，國要攻打國，11地要大大震動，多處必有饑荒、瘟疫，又有可怕的異象和大神蹟從天上顯現。

12“但這一切的事以先，人要下手拿住你們，逼迫你們，把你們交給會堂，並且收在監裏，又為我的名拉你們到君王諸侯面前。13但這些事終必為你們的見證。14所以，你們當立定心意，不要預先思想怎樣分訴，15因為我必賜你們口才、智慧，是你們一切敵人所敵不住、駁不倒的。16連你們的父母、弟兄、親族、朋友也要把你們交official；你們也有被他們害死的。17你們要為我的名被眾人恨惡，18然而，你們連一根頭髮也必不損壞。19你們常存忍耐，就必保全靈魂（註：或作“必得生命”）。

20“你們看見耶路撒冷被兵圍困，就可知道它成荒場的日子近了。21那時，在猶太的應當逃到山上，在城裏的應當出來，在鄉下的不要進城，22因為這是報應的日子，使經上所寫的都得應驗。23當那些日子，懷孕的和奶孩子的有禍了！因為將有大災難降在這地方，也有震怒臨到這百姓。24他們要倒在刀下，又被擄到各國去。耶路撒冷要被外邦人踐踏，直到外邦人的日期滿了。

25“日、月、星辰要顯出異兆，地上的邦國也有困苦，因海中波浪的響聲，就慌慌不定。26天勢都要震動，人想起那將要臨到世界的事，就都嚇得魂不附體。27那時，他們要看見人子有能力，有大榮耀駕雲降臨。28一有這些事，你們就當挺身昂首，因為你們得贖的日子近了。”

29、30耶穌又設比喻對他們説：“你們看無花果樹和各樣的樹：它發

7"Teacher," they asked, "when will these things happen? And what will be the sign that they are about to take place?"

8He replied: "Watch out that you are not deceived. For many will come in my name, claiming, 'I am he,' and, 'The time is near.' Do not follow them. 9When you hear of wars and revolutions, do not be frightened. These things must happen first, but the end will not come right away."

10Then he said to them: "Nation will rise against nation, and kingdom against kingdom. 11There will be great earthquakes, famines and pestilences in various places, and fearful events and great signs from heaven.

12"But before all this, they will lay hands on you and persecute you. They will deliver you to synagogues and prisons, and you will be brought before kings and governors, and all on account of my name. 13This will result in your being witnesses to them. 14But make up your mind not to worry beforehand how you will defend yourselves. 15For I will give you words and wisdom that none of your adversaries will be able to resist or contradict. 16You will be betrayed even by parents, brothers, relatives and friends, and they will put some of you to death. 17All men will hate you because of me. 18But not a hair of your head will perish. 19By standing firm you will gain life.

20"When you see Jerusalem being surrounded by armies, you will know that its desolation is near. 21Then let those who are in Judea flee to the mountains, let those in the city get out, and let those in the country not enter the city. 22For this is the time of punishment in fulfillment of all that has been written. 23How dreadful it will be in those days for pregnant women and nursing mothers! There will be great distress in the land and wrath against this people. 24They will fall by the sword and will be taken as prisoners to all the nations. Jerusalem will be trampled on by the Gentiles until the times of the Gentiles are fulfilled.

25"There will be signs in the sun, moon and stars. On the earth, nations will be in anguish and perplexity at the roaring and tossing of the sea. 26Men will faint from terror, apprehensive of what is coming on the world, for the heavenly bodies will be shaken. 27At that time they will see the Son of Man coming in a cloud with power and great glory. 28When these things begin to take place, stand up and lift up your heads, because your redemption is drawing near."

29He told them this parable: "Look at the fig tree and all the trees. 30When they sprout leaves, you can see for yourselves and know that summer is near. [31]Even so, when you see these things happening, you know that the kingdom of God is near.

[32]"I tell you the truth, this generation[a] will certainly not pass away until all these things have happened. [33]Heaven and earth will pass away, but my words will never pass away.

[34]"Be careful, or your hearts will be weighed down with dissipation, drunkenness and the anxieties of life, and that day will close on you unexpectedly like a trap. [35]For it will come upon all those who live on the face of the whole earth. [36]Be always on the watch, and pray that you may be able to escape all that is about to happen, and that you may be able to stand before the Son of Man."

[37]Each day Jesus was teaching at the temple, and each evening he went out to spend the night on the hill called the Mount of Olives, [38]and all the people came early in the morning to hear him at the temple.

Judas Agrees to Betray Jesus

22 Now the Feast of Unleavened Bread, called the Passover, was approaching, [2]and the chief priests and the teachers of the law were looking for some way to get rid of Jesus, for they were afraid of the people. [3]Then Satan entered Judas, called Iscariot, one of the Twelve. [4]And Judas went to the chief priests and the officers of the temple guard and discussed with them how he might betray Jesus. [5]They were delighted and agreed to give him money. [6]He consented, and watched for an opportunity to hand Jesus over to them when no crowd was present.

The Last Supper

[7]Then came the day of Unleavened Bread on which the Passover lamb had to be sacrificed. [8]Jesus sent Peter and John, saying, "Go and make preparations for us to eat the Passover."

[9]"Where do you want us to prepare for it?" they asked.

[10]He replied, "As you enter the city, a man carrying a jar of water will meet you. Follow him to the house that he enters, [11]and say to the owner of the house, 'The Teacher asks: Where is the guest room, where I may eat the Passover with my disciples?' [12]He will show you a large upper room, all furnished. Make preparations there."

芽的時候，你們一看見，自然曉得夏天近了。[31]這樣，你們看見這些事漸漸地成就，也該曉得神的國近了。

[32]「我實在告訴你們：這世代還沒有過去，這些事都要成就。[33]天地要廢去，我的話卻不能廢去。

[34]「你們要謹慎，恐怕因貪食、醉酒，並今生的思慮累住你們的心，那日子就如同網羅忽然臨到你們，[35]因為那日子要這樣臨到全地上一切居住的人。[36]你們要時時警醒，常常祈求，使你們能逃避這一切要來的事，得以站立在人子面前。」

[37]耶穌每日在殿裏教訓人，每夜出城在一座山，名叫橄欖山住宿。[38]眾百姓清早上聖殿，到耶穌那裏，要聽他講道。

猶大約定出賣耶穌

22 除酵節又名逾越節近了。[2]祭司長和文士想法子怎麼才能殺害耶穌，是因他們懼怕百姓。[3]這時，撒但入了那稱為加略人猶大的心，他本是十二門徒裏的一個。[4]他去和祭司長並守殿官商量，怎麼可以把耶穌交給他們。[5]他們歡喜，就約定給他銀子。[6]他應允了，就找機會，要趁眾人不在跟前的時候把耶穌交給他們。

最後的晚餐

[7]除酵節，須宰逾越羊羔的那一天到了。[8]耶穌打發彼得、約翰，說：「你們去為我們預備逾越節的筵席，好叫我們吃。」

[9]他們問他說：「要我們在哪裏預備？」

[10]耶穌說：「你們進了城，必有人拿着一瓶水迎面而來，你們就跟着他，到他所進的房子裏去，[11]對那家的主人說：『夫子說：客房在哪裏？我與門徒好在那裏吃逾越節的筵席。』[12]他必指給你們擺設整齊的一間大樓，你們就在那裏預備。」

¹³他們去了，所遇見的正如耶穌所說的。他們就預備了逾越節的筵席。

¹⁴時候到了，耶穌坐席，使徒也和他同坐。¹⁵耶穌對他們說："我很願意在受害以先和你們吃這逾越節的筵席。¹⁶我告訴你們：我不再吃這筵席，直到成就在神的國裏。"

¹⁷耶穌接過杯來，祝謝了，說："你們拿這個，大家分着喝。¹⁸我告訴你們：從今以後，我不再喝這葡萄汁，直等神的國來到。"

¹⁹又拿起餅來，祝謝了，就擘開，遞給他們，說："這是我的身體，為你們捨的，你們也應當如此行，為的是記念我。"

²⁰飯後也照樣拿起杯來，說："這杯是用我血所立的新約，是為你們流出來的。²¹看哪，那賣我之人的手與我一同在桌子上。²²人子固然要照所預定的去世，但賣人子的人有禍了！"²³他們就彼此對問，是哪一個要做這事。

²⁴門徒起了爭論，他們中間哪一個可算為大。²⁵耶穌說："外邦人有君王為主治理他們，那掌權管他們的稱為恩主。²⁶但你們不可這樣。你們裏頭為大的，倒要像年幼的；為首領的，倒要像服侍人的。²⁷是誰為大？是坐席的呢？是服侍人的呢？不是坐席的大嗎？然而，我在你們中間如同服侍人的。²⁸我在磨煉之中，常和我同在的就是你們。²⁹我將國賜給你們，正如我父賜給我一樣，³⁰叫你們在我國裏，坐在我的席上吃喝，並且坐在寶座上，審判以色列十二個支派。"

³¹主又說："西門！西門！撒但想要得着你們，好篩你們像篩麥子一樣；³²但我已經為你祈求，叫你不至於失了信心。你回頭以後，要堅固你的弟兄。"

³³彼得說："主啊，我就是同你下監，同你受死，也是甘心！"

³⁴耶穌說："彼得，我告訴你，今日雞還沒有叫，你要三次說不認得我。"

³⁵耶穌又對他們說："我差你們出去的時候，沒有錢囊，沒有口袋，沒有鞋，你們缺少甚麼沒有？"

他們說："沒有。"

¹³They left and found things just as Jesus had told them. So they prepared the Passover.

¹⁴When the hour came, Jesus and his apostles reclined at the table. ¹⁵And he said to them, "I have eagerly desired to eat this Passover with you before I suffer. ¹⁶For I tell you, I will not eat it again until it finds fulfillment in the kingdom of God."

¹⁷After taking the cup, he gave thanks and said, "Take this and divide it among you. ¹⁸For I tell you I will not drink again of the fruit of the vine until the kingdom of God comes."

¹⁹And he took bread, gave thanks and broke it, and gave it to them, saying, "This is my body given for you; do this in remembrance of me."

²⁰In the same way, after the supper he took the cup, saying, "This cup is the new covenant in my blood, which is poured out for you. ²¹But the hand of him who is going to betray me is with mine on the table. ²²The Son of Man will go as it has been decreed, but woe to that man who betrays him." ²³They began to question among themselves which of them it might be who would do this.

²⁴Also a dispute arose among them as to which of them was considered to be greatest. ²⁵Jesus said to them, "The kings of the Gentiles lord it over them; and those who exercise authority over them call themselves Benefactors. ²⁶But you are not to be like that. Instead, the greatest among you should be like the youngest, and the one who rules like the one who serves. ²⁷For who is greater, the one who is at the table or the one who serves? Is it not the one who is at the table? But I am among you as one who serves. ²⁸You are those who have stood by me in my trials. ²⁹And I confer on you a kingdom, just as my Father conferred one on me, ³⁰so that you may eat and drink at my table in my kingdom and sit on thrones, judging the twelve tribes of Israel.

³¹"Simon, Simon, Satan has asked to sift you*a* as wheat. ³²But I have prayed for you, Simon, that your faith may not fail. And when you have turned back, strengthen your brothers."

³³But he replied, "Lord, I am ready to go with you to prison and to death."

³⁴Jesus answered, "I tell you, Peter, before the rooster crows today, you will deny three times that you know me."

³⁵Then Jesus asked them, "When I sent you without purse, bag or sandals, did you lack anything?"

"Nothing," they answered.

a31 The Greek is plural.

36He said to them, "But now if you have a purse, take it, and also a bag; and if you don't have a sword, sell your cloak and buy one. 37It is written: 'And he was numbered with the transgressors'*a*; and I tell you that this must be fulfilled in me. Yes, what is written about me is reaching its fulfillment."

38The disciples said, "See, Lord, here are two swords."

"That is enough," he replied.

Jesus Prays on the Mount of Olives

39Jesus went out as usual to the Mount of Olives, and his disciples followed him. 40On reaching the place, he said to them, "Pray that you will not fall into temptation." 41He withdrew about a stone's throw beyond them, knelt down and prayed, 42"Father, if you are willing, take this cup from me; yet not my will, but yours be done." 43An angel from heaven appeared to him and strengthened him. 44And being in anguish, he prayed more earnestly, and his sweat was like drops of blood falling to the ground.*b*

45When he rose from prayer and went back to the disciples, he found them asleep, exhausted from sorrow. 46"Why are you sleeping?" he asked them. "Get up and pray so that you will not fall into temptation."

Jesus Arrested

47While he was still speaking a crowd came up, and the man who was called Judas, one of the Twelve, was leading them. He approached Jesus to kiss him, 48but Jesus asked him, "Judas, are you betraying the Son of Man with a kiss?"

49When Jesus' followers saw what was going to happen, they said, "Lord, should we strike with our swords?" 50And one of them struck the servant of the high priest, cutting off his right ear.

51But Jesus answered, "No more of this!" And he touched the man's ear and healed him.

52Then Jesus said to the chief priests, the officers of the temple guard, and the elders, who had come for him, "Am I leading a rebellion, that you have come with swords and clubs? 53Every day I was with you in the temple courts, and you did not lay a hand on me. But this is your hour—when darkness reigns."

Peter Disowns Jesus

54Then seizing him, they led him away and took him into the house of the high priest. Peter followed at a distance. 55But when they had kin-

36耶穌說：「但如今有錢囊的可以帶着，有口袋的也可以帶着，沒有刀的要賣衣服買刀。37我告訴你們，經上寫着說：'他被列在罪犯之中。'這話必應驗在我身上，因為那關係我的事必然成就。」

38他們說：「主啊，請看！這裏有兩把刀。」

耶穌說：「夠了。」

耶穌在橄欖山上禱告

39耶穌出來，照常往橄欖山去，門徒也跟隨他。40到了那地方，就對他們說：「你們要禱告，免得入了迷惑。」41於是離開他們約有扔一塊石頭那麼遠，跪下禱告，42說：「父啊！你若願意，就把這杯撤去；然而，不要成就我的意思，只要成就你的意思。」43有一位天使從天上顯現，加添他的力量。44耶穌極其傷痛，禱告更加懇切，汗珠如大血點滴在地上。

45禱告完了，就起來，到門徒那裏，見他們因為憂愁都睡着了，46就對他們說：「你們為甚麼睡覺呢？起來禱告，免得入了迷惑！」

耶穌被捕

47說話之間，來了許多人。那十二個門徒裏名叫猶大的，走在前頭，就近耶穌，要與他親嘴。48耶穌對他說：「猶大！你用親嘴的暗號賣人子嗎？」

49左右的人見光景不好，就說：「主啊！我們拿刀砍可以不可以？」50內中有一個人把大祭司的僕人砍了一刀，削掉了他的右耳。

51耶穌說：「到了這個地步，由他們吧！」就摸那人的耳朵，把他治好了。

52耶穌對那些來拿他的祭司長和守殿官並長老說：「你們帶着刀棒出來拿我，如同拿強盜嗎？53我天天同你們在殿裏，你們不下手拿我。現在卻是你們的時候，黑暗掌權了。」

彼得不認耶穌

54他們拿住耶穌，把他帶到大祭司的宅裏。彼得遠遠地跟着。55他們

a 37 Isaiah 53:12   b 44 Some early manuscripts do not have verses 43 and 44.

在院子裏生了火，一同坐着；<u>彼得也坐在他們中間</u>。56有一個使女看見<u>彼得坐在火光裏</u>，就定睛看他，說："這個人素來也是同那人一夥的。"

57<u>彼得卻不承認</u>，說："女子，我不認得他。"

58過了不多的時候，又有一個人看見他，說："你也是他們一黨的。"

<u>彼得說</u>："你這個人！我不是。"

59約過了一小時，又有一個人極力地說："他實在是同那人一夥的，因為他也是<u>加利利人</u>。"

60<u>彼得說</u>："你這個人！我不曉得你說的是甚麼！"正說話之間，雞就叫了。61<u>主轉過身來看彼得，彼得</u>便想起主對他所說的話："今日雞叫以先，你要三次不認我。"62他就出去痛哭。

兵丁戲弄耶穌

63看守耶穌的人戲弄他，打他，64又蒙着他的眼，問他說："你是先知，告訴我們打你的是誰？"65他們還用許多別的話辱罵他。

耶穌在彼拉多與希律面前

66天一亮，民間的眾長老連祭司長帶文士都聚會，把耶穌帶到他們的公會裏，67說："你若是基督，就告訴我們。"

耶穌說："我若告訴你們，你們也不信；68我若問你們，你們也不回答。69從今以後，人子要坐在神權能的右邊。"

70他們都說："這樣，你是神的兒子嗎？"

耶穌說："你們所說的是。"

71他們說："何必再用見證呢？他親口所說的，我們都親自聽見了。"

23 眾人都起來，把耶穌解到<u>彼拉多面前</u>，2就告他說："我們見這人誘惑國民，禁止納稅給凱撒，並說自己是基督，是王。"

3<u>彼拉多問耶穌說</u>："你是<u>猶太人的王嗎</u>？"

耶穌回答說："你說的是。"

dled a fire in the middle of the courtyard and had sat down together, Peter sat down with them. 56A servant girl saw him seated there in the firelight. She looked closely at him and said, "This man was with him."

57But he denied it. "Woman, I don't know him," he said.

58A little later someone else saw him and said, "You also are one of them."

"Man, I am not!" Peter replied.

59About an hour later another asserted, "Certainly this fellow was with him, for he is a Galilean."

60Peter replied, "Man, I don't know what you're talking about!" Just as he was speaking, the rooster crowed. 61The Lord turned and looked straight at Peter. Then Peter remembered the word the Lord had spoken to him: "Before the rooster crows today, you will disown me three times." 62And he went outside and wept bitterly.

The Guards Mock Jesus

63The men who were guarding Jesus began mocking and beating him. 64They blindfolded him and demanded, "Prophesy! Who hit you?" 65And they said many other insulting things to him.

Jesus Before Pilate and Herod

66At daybreak the council of the elders of the people, both the chief priests and teachers of the law, met together, and Jesus was led before them. 67"If you are the Christ,a" they said, "tell us."

Jesus answered, "If I tell you, you will not believe me, 68and if I asked you, you would not answer. 69But from now on, the Son of Man will be seated at the right hand of the mighty God."

70They all asked, "Are you then the Son of God?"

He replied, "You are right in saying I am."

71Then they said, "Why do we need any more testimony? We have heard it from his own lips."

23 Then the whole assembly rose and led him off to Pilate. 2And they began to accuse him, saying, "We have found this man subverting our nation. He opposes payment of taxes to Caesar and claims to be Christ,b a king."

3So Pilate asked Jesus, "Are you the king of the Jews?"

"Yes, it is as you say," Jesus replied.

---

a 67 Or Messiah   b 2 Or Messiah; also in verses 35 and 39

⁴Then Pilate announced to the chief priests and the crowd, "I find no basis for a charge against this man."

⁵But they insisted, "He stirs up the people all over Judea*a* by his teaching. He started in Galilee and has come all the way here."

⁶On hearing this, Pilate asked if the man was a Galilean. ⁷When he learned that Jesus was under Herod's jurisdiction, he sent him to Herod, who was also in Jerusalem at that time.

⁸When Herod saw Jesus, he was greatly pleased, because for a long time he had been wanting to see him. From what he had heard about him, he hoped to see him perform some miracle. ⁹He plied him with many questions, but Jesus gave him no answer. ¹⁰The chief priests and the teachers of the law were standing there, vehemently accusing him. ¹¹Then Herod and his soldiers ridiculed and mocked him. Dressing him in an elegant robe, they sent him back to Pilate. ¹²That day Herod and Pilate became friends—before this they had been enemies.

¹³Pilate called together the chief priests, the rulers and the people, ¹⁴and said to them, "You brought me this man as one who was inciting the people to rebellion. I have examined him in your presence and have found no basis for your charges against him. ¹⁵Neither has Herod, for he sent him back to us; as you can see, he has done nothing to deserve death. ¹⁶Therefore, I will punish him and then release him.*b*"

¹⁸With one voice they cried out, "Away with this man! Release Barabbas to us!" ¹⁹(Barabbas had been thrown into prison for an insurrection in the city, and for murder.)

²⁰Wanting to release Jesus, Pilate appealed to them again. ²¹But they kept shouting, "Crucify him! Crucify him!"

²²For the third time he spoke to them: "Why? What crime has this man committed? I have found in him no grounds for the death penalty. Therefore I will have him punished and then release him."

²³But with loud shouts they insistently demanded that he be crucified, and their shouts prevailed. ²⁴So Pilate decided to grant their demand. ²⁵He released the man who had been thrown into prison for insurrection and murder, the one they asked for, and surrendered Jesus to their will.

---

⁴彼拉多對祭司長和眾人說："我查不出這人有甚麼罪來。"

⁵但他們越發極力地說:"他煽惑百姓,在猶太遍地傳道,從加利利起,直到這裏了。"

⁶彼拉多一聽見,就問:"這人是加利利人嗎?"⁷既曉得耶穌屬希律所管,就把他送到希律那裏去。那時希律正在耶路撒冷。

⁸希律看見耶穌,就很歡喜,因為聽見過他的事,久已想要見他,並且指望看他行一件神蹟,⁹於是問他許多的話,耶穌卻一言不答。¹⁰祭司長和文士都站着,極力地告他。¹¹希律和他的兵丁就藐視耶穌,戲弄他,給他穿上華麗衣服,把他送回彼拉多那裏去。¹²從前希律和彼拉多彼此有仇,在那一天就成了朋友。

¹³彼拉多傳齊了祭司長和官府並百姓,¹⁴就對他們說:"你們解這人到我這裏,說他是誘惑百姓的。看哪,我也曾將你們告他的事,在你們面前審問他,並沒有查出他甚麼罪來;¹⁵就是希律也是如此,所以把他送回來。可見他沒有做甚麼該死的事。¹⁶故此,我要責打他,把他釋放了。"(註:有古卷在此有¹⁷"每逢這節期,巡撫必須釋放一個囚犯給他們"。)

¹⁸眾人卻一齊喊着說:"除掉這個人!釋放巴拉巴給我們!"¹⁹這巴拉巴是因在城裏作亂殺人,下在監裏的。

²⁰彼拉多願意釋放耶穌,就又勸解他們。²¹無奈他們喊着說:"釘他十字架!釘他十字架!"

²²彼拉多第三次對他們說:"為甚麼呢?這人做了甚麼惡事呢?我並沒有查出他甚麼該死的罪來。所以,我要責打他,把他釋放了。"

²³他們大聲催逼彼拉多,求他把耶穌釘在十字架上。他們的聲音就得了勝。²⁴彼拉多這才照他們所求的定案,²⁵把他們所求的那個亂殺人、下在監裏的釋放了,把耶穌交給他們,任憑他們的意思行。

---

a 5 Or over the land of the Jews   *b 16 Some manuscripts him." 17Now he was obliged to release one man to them at the Feast.*

釘十字架

²⁶帶耶穌去的時候，有一個古利奈人西門，從鄉下來，他們就抓住他，把十字架擱在他身上，叫他背着跟隨耶穌。²⁷有許多百姓跟隨耶穌，內中有好些婦女，婦女們為他號咷痛哭。²⁸耶穌轉身對她們說：「耶路撒冷的女子，不要為我哭，當為自己和自己的兒女哭。²⁹因為日子要到，人必說：『不生育的和未曾懷胎的，未曾乳養嬰孩的，有福了！』³⁰那時，

"　'人要向大山說：倒在我們身上！
　　向小山說：遮蓋我們！'

³¹這些事既行在有汁水的樹上，那枯乾的樹將來怎麼樣呢？」

³²又有兩個犯人，和耶穌一同帶來處死。³³到了一個地方，名叫髑髏地，就在那裏把耶穌釘在十字架上，又釘了兩個犯人：一個在左邊，一個在右邊。³⁴當下耶穌說：「父啊，赦免他們！因為他們所做的，他們不曉得。」兵丁就拈鬮分他的衣服。

³⁵百姓站在那裏觀看。官府也嗤笑他，說：「他救了別人，他若是基督，神所揀選的，可以救自己吧！」

³⁶兵丁也戲弄他，上前拿醋送給他喝，³⁷說：「你若是猶太人的王，可以救自己吧！」

³⁸在耶穌以上有一個牌子（註：有古卷在此有「用希臘、羅馬、希伯來的文字」）寫着：「這是猶太人的王。」

³⁹那同釘的兩個犯人，有一個譏誚他，說：「你不是基督嗎？可以救自己和我們吧！」

⁴⁰那一個就應聲責備他，說：「你既是一樣受刑的，還不怕神嗎？⁴¹我們是應該的，因為我們所受的與我們所做的相稱，但這個人沒有做過一件不好的事。」

⁴²就說：「耶穌啊，你得國降臨的時候，求你記念我！」

⁴³耶穌對他說：「我實在告訴你：今日你要同我在樂園裏了。」

耶穌的死

⁴⁴那時約有午正，遍地都黑暗

The Crucifixion

²⁶As they led him away, they seized Simon from Cyrene, who was on his way in from the country, and put the cross on him and made him carry it behind Jesus. ²⁷A large number of people followed him, including women who mourned and wailed for him. ²⁸Jesus turned and said to them, "Daughters of Jerusalem, do not weep for me; weep for yourselves and for your children. ²⁹For the time will come when you will say, 'Blessed are the barren women, the wombs that never bore and the breasts that never nursed!' ³⁰Then

"　'they will say to the mountains, "Fall on us!"
　　and to the hills, "Cover us!" '^a

³¹For if men do these things when the tree is green, what will happen when it is dry?"

³²Two other men, both criminals, were also led out with him to be executed. ³³When they came to the place called the Skull, there they crucified him, along with the criminals—one on his right, the other on his left. ³⁴Jesus said, "Father, forgive them, for they do not know what they are doing."^b And they divided up his clothes by casting lots.

³⁵The people stood watching, and the rulers even sneered at him. They said, "He saved others; let him save himself if he is the Christ of God, the Chosen One."

³⁶The soldiers also came up and mocked him. They offered him wine vinegar ³⁷and said, "If you are the king of the Jews, save yourself."

³⁸There was a written notice above him, which read: THIS IS THE KING OF THE JEWS.

³⁹One of the criminals who hung there hurled insults at him: "Aren't you the Christ? Save yourself and us!"

⁴⁰But the other criminal rebuked him. "Don't you fear God," he said, "since you are under the same sentence? ⁴¹We are punished justly, for we are getting what our deeds deserve. But this man has done nothing wrong."

⁴²Then he said, "Jesus, remember me when you come into your kingdom.^c"

⁴³Jesus answered him, "I tell you the truth, today you will be with me in paradise."

Jesus' Death

⁴⁴It was now about the sixth hour, and darkness came over the whole land until the ninth

a 30 Hosea 10:8   *b 34* Some early manuscripts do not have this sentence.   *c 42* Some manuscripts *come with your kingly power*

hour, [45]for the sun stopped shining. And the curtain of the temple was torn in two. [46]Jesus called out with a loud voice, "Father, into your hands I commit my spirit." When he had said this, he breathed his last.

[47]The centurion, seeing what had happened, praised God and said, "Surely this was a righteous man." [48]When all the people who had gathered to witness this sight saw what took place, they beat their breasts and went away. [49]But all those who knew him, including the women who had followed him from Galilee, stood at a distance, watching these things.

Jesus' Burial

[50]Now there was a man named Joseph, a member of the Council, a good and upright man, [51]who had not consented to their decision and action. He came from the Judean town of Arimathea and he was waiting for the kingdom of God. [52]Going to Pilate, he asked for Jesus' body. [53]Then he took it down, wrapped it in linen cloth and placed it in a tomb cut in the rock, one in which no one had yet been laid. [54]It was Preparation Day, and the Sabbath was about to begin.

[55]The women who had come with Jesus from Galilee followed Joseph and saw the tomb and how his body was laid in it. [56]Then they went home and prepared spices and perfumes. But they rested on the Sabbath in obedience to the commandment.

The Resurrection

24 On the first day of the week, very early in the morning, the women took the spices they had prepared and went to the tomb. [2]They found the stone rolled away from the tomb, [3]but when they entered, they did not find the body of the Lord Jesus. [4]While they were wondering about this, suddenly two men in clothes that gleamed like lightning stood beside them. [5]In their fright the women bowed down with their faces to the ground, but the men said to them, "Why do you look for the living among the dead? [6]He is not here; he has risen! Remember how he told you, while he was still with you in Galilee: [7]'The Son of Man must be delivered into the hands of sinful men, be crucified and on the third day be raised again.' " [8]Then they remembered his words.

[9]When they came back from the tomb, they told all these things to the Eleven and to all the others. [10]It was Mary Magdalene, Joanna, Mary the mother of James, and the others with them who told this to the apostles. [11]But they did not believe the women, because their words seemed

了，直到申初，[45]日頭變黑了。殿裏的幔子從當中裂為兩半。[46]耶穌大聲喊着說："父啊！我將我的靈魂交在你手裏。"說了這話，氣就斷了。

[47]百夫長看見所成的事，就歸榮耀與神，說："這真是個義人！"[48]聚集觀看的眾人見了這所成的事，都捶着胸回去了。[49]還有一切與耶穌熟識的人和加利利跟着他來的婦女們，都遠遠地站着看這些事。

耶穌的安葬

[50]有一個人名叫約瑟，是個議士，為人善良公義。[51]眾人所謀所為，他並沒有附從。他本是猶太亞利馬太城裏素常盼望神國的人。[52]這人去見彼拉多，求耶穌的身體，[53]就取下來，用細麻布裹好，安放在石頭鑿成的墳墓裏；那裏頭從來沒有葬過人。[54]那日是預備日，安息日也快到了。

[55]那些從加利利和耶穌同來的婦女跟在後面，看見了墳墓和他的身體怎樣安放。[56]她們就回去，預備了香料香膏。她們在安息日，便遵着誡命安息了。

復活

24 七日的頭一日，黎明的時候，那些婦女帶着所預備的香料來到墳墓前，[2]看見石頭已經從墳墓滾開了，[3]她們就進去，只是不見主耶穌的身體。[4]正在猜疑之間，忽然有兩個人站在旁邊，衣服放光。[5]婦女們驚怕，將臉伏地。那兩個人就對她們說："為甚麼在死人中找活人呢？[6]他不在這裏，已經復活了。當記念他還在加利利的時候怎樣告訴你們，[7]說：'人子必須被交在罪人手裏，釘在十字架上，第三日復活。'"[8]她們就想起耶穌的話來。

[9]便從墳墓那裏回去，把這一切事告訴十一個使徒和其餘的人。[10]那告訴使徒的就是抹大拉的馬利亞和約亞拿，並雅各的母親馬利亞，還有與她們在一處的婦女。[11]她們這些話，

使徒以為是胡言，就不相信。¹²彼得起來，跑到墳墓前，低頭往裏看，見細麻布獨在一處，就回去了，心裏希奇所成的事。

在以馬忤斯路上

¹³正當那日，門徒中有兩個人往一個村子去；這村子名叫以馬忤斯，離耶路撒冷約有二十五里。¹⁴他們彼此談論所遇見的這一切事。¹⁵正談論相問的時候，耶穌親自就近他們，和他們同行；¹⁶只是他們的眼睛迷糊了，不認識他。

¹⁷耶穌對他們說："你們走路彼此談論的是甚麼事呢？"

他們就站住，臉上帶著愁容。¹⁸二人中有一個名叫革流巴的回答說："你在耶路撒冷作客，還不知道這幾天在那裏所出的事嗎？"

¹⁹耶穌說："甚麼事呢？"

他們說："就是拿撒勒人耶穌的事。他是個先知，在神和眾百姓面前說話行事都有大能。²⁰祭司長和我們的官府竟把他解去，定了死罪，釘在十字架上。²¹但我們素來所盼望、要贖以色列民的就是他！不但如此，而且這事成就，現在已經三天了。²²再者，我們中間有幾個婦女使我們驚奇，她們清早到了墳墓那裏，²³不見他的身體，就回來告訴我們說，看見天使顯現，說他活了。²⁴又有我們的幾個人往墳墓那裏去，所遇見的正如婦女們所說的，只是沒有看見他。"

²⁵耶穌對他們說："無知的人哪，先知所說的一切話，你們的心信得太遲鈍了。²⁶基督這樣受害，又進入他的榮耀，豈不是應當的嗎？"²⁷於是從摩西和眾先知起，凡經上所指著自己的話都給他們講解明白了。

²⁸將近他們所去的村子，耶穌好像還要往前行。²⁹他們卻強留他，說："時候晚了，日頭已經平西了，請你同我們住下吧！"耶穌就進去，要同他們住下。

³⁰到了坐席的時候，耶穌拿起餅來，祝謝了，擘開，遞給他們。³¹他們的眼睛明亮了，這才認出他來。忽然耶

On the Road to Emmaus

¹³Now that same day two of them were going to a village called Emmaus, about seven miles[a] from Jerusalem. ¹⁴They were talking with each other about everything that had happened. ¹⁵As they talked and discussed these things with each other, Jesus himself came up and walked along with them; ¹⁶but they were kept from recognizing him.

¹⁷He asked them, "What are you discussing together as you walk along?"

They stood still, their faces downcast. ¹⁸One of them, named Cleopas, asked him, "Are you only a visitor to Jerusalem and do not know the things that have happened there in these days?"

¹⁹"What things?" he asked.

"About Jesus of Nazareth," they replied. "He was a prophet, powerful in word and deed before God and all the people. ²⁰The chief priests and our rulers handed him over to be sentenced to death, and they crucified him; ²¹but we had hoped that he was the one who was going to redeem Israel. And what is more, it is the third day since all this took place. ²²In addition, some of our women amazed us. They went to the tomb early this morning ²³but didn't find his body. They came and told us that they had seen a vision of angels, who said he was alive. ²⁴Then some of our companions went to the tomb and found it just as the women had said, but him they did not see."

²⁵He said to them, "How foolish you are, and how slow of heart to believe all that the prophets have spoken! ²⁶Did not the Christ[b] have to suffer these things and then enter his glory?" ²⁷And beginning with Moses and all the Prophets, he explained to them what was said in all the Scriptures concerning himself.

²⁸As they approached the village to which they were going, Jesus acted as if he were going farther. ²⁹But they urged him strongly, "Stay with us, for it is nearly evening; the day is almost over." So he went in to stay with them.

³⁰When he was at the table with them, he took bread, gave thanks, broke it and began to give it to them. ³¹Then their eyes were opened and they recognized him, and he disappeared from their

a 13 Greek sixty stadia (about 11 kilometers)　　b 26 Or Messiah; also in verse 46 sight. 32They asked each other, "Were not our hearts burning within us while he talked with us on the road and opened the Scriptures to us?"

33They got up and returned at once to Jerusalem. There they found the Eleven and those with them, assembled together 34and saying, "It is true! The Lord has risen and has appeared to Simon." 35Then the two told what had happened on the way, and how Jesus was recognized by them when he broke the bread.

Jesus Appears to the Disciples

36While they were still talking about this, Jesus himself stood among them and said to them, "Peace be with you."

37They were startled and frightened, thinking they saw a ghost. 38He said to them, "Why are you troubled, and why do doubts rise in your minds? 39Look at my hands and my feet. It is I myself! Touch me and see; a ghost does not have flesh and bones, as you see I have."

40When he had said this, he showed them his hands and feet. 41And while they still did not believe it because of joy and amazement, he asked them, "Do you have anything here to eat?" 42They gave him a piece of broiled fish, 43and he took it and ate it in their presence.

44He said to them, "This is what I told you while I was still with you: Everything must be fulfilled that is written about me in the Law of Moses, the Prophets and the Psalms."

45Then he opened their minds so they could understand the Scriptures. 46He told them, "This is what is written: The Christ will suffer and rise from the dead on the third day, 47and repentance and forgiveness of sins will be preached in his name to all nations, beginning at Jerusalem. 48You are witnesses of these things. 49I am going to send you what my Father has promised; but stay in the city until you have been clothed with power from on high."

The Ascension

50When he had led them out to the vicinity of Bethany, he lifted up his hands and blessed them. 51While he was blessing them, he left them and was taken up into heaven. 52Then they worshiped him and returned to Jerusalem with great joy. 53And they stayed continually at the temple, praising God.

穌不見了。32他們彼此說:"在路上,他和我們說話,給我們講解聖經的時候,我們的心豈不是火熱的嗎?"

33他們就立時起身,回耶路撒冷去,正遇見十一個使徒和他們的同人聚集在一處,34說:"主果然復活,已經現給西門看了。"35兩個人就把路上所遇見,和擘餅的時候怎麼被他們認出來的事,都述說了一遍。

耶穌向門徒顯現

36正說這話的時候,耶穌親自站在他們當中,說;"願你們平安!"

37他們卻驚慌害怕,以為所看見的是魂。38耶穌說:"你們為甚麼愁煩?為甚麼心裏起疑念呢?39你們看我的手,我的腳,就知道實在是我了。摸我看看!魂無骨無肉,你們看,我是有的。"

40說了這話,就把手和腳給他們看。41他們正喜得不敢信,並且希奇,耶穌就說:"你們這裏有甚麼吃的沒有?"42他們便給他一片燒魚。(註:有古卷在此有"和一塊蜜房")43他接過來,在他們面前吃了。

44耶穌對他們說:"這就是我從前與你們同在之時所告訴你們的話說:摩西的律法、先知的書和詩篇上所記的,凡指着我的話都必須應驗。"

45於是耶穌開他們的心竅,使他們能明白聖經,46又對他們說:"照經上所寫的,基督必受害,第三日從死裏復活,47並且人要奉他的名傳悔改、赦罪的道,從耶路撒冷起直傳到萬邦。48你們就是這些事的見證。49我要將我父所應許的降在你們身上,你們要在城裏等候,直到你們領受從上頭來的能力。"

升天

50耶穌領他們到伯大尼的對面,就舉手給他們祝福。51正祝福的時候,他就離開他們,被帶到天上去了。52他們就拜他,大大地歡喜,回耶路撒冷去,53常在殿裏稱頌神。

約翰福音

道成肉身

1 太初有道，道與神同在，道就是神。²這道太初與神同在。

³萬物是藉着他造的；凡被造的，沒有一樣不是藉着他造的。⁴生命在他裏頭，這生命就是人的光。⁵光照在黑暗裏，黑暗卻不接受光。

⁶有一個人，是從神那裏差來的，名叫<u>約翰</u>。⁷這人來，為要作見證，就是為光作見證，叫眾人因他可以信。⁸他不是那光，乃是要為光作見證。⁹那光是真光，照亮一切生在世上的人。

¹⁰他在世界，世界也是藉着他造的，世界卻不認識他。¹¹他到自己的地方來，自己的人倒不接待他。¹²凡接待他的，就是信他名的人，他就賜他們權柄，作神的兒女。¹³這等人不是從血氣生的，不是從情慾生的，也不是從人意生的，乃是從神生的。

¹⁴道成了肉身，住在我們中間，充充滿滿地有恩典有真理。我們也見過他的榮光，正是父獨生子的榮光。

¹⁵<u>約翰</u>為他作見證，喊着說："這就是我曾說：'那在我以後來的，反成了在我以前的，因他本來在我以前。'"¹⁶從他豐滿的恩典裏，我們都領受了，而且恩上加恩。¹⁷律法本是藉着<u>摩西</u>傳的，恩典和真理都是由<u>耶穌基督</u>來的。¹⁸從來沒有人看見神，只有在父懷裏的獨生子將他表明出來。

施洗約翰否認自己是基督

¹⁹<u>約翰</u>所作的見證記在下面：<u>猶太</u>人從<u>耶路撒冷</u>差祭司和<u>利未</u>人到<u>約翰</u>那

John

The Word Became Flesh

1 In the beginning was the Word, and the Word was with God, and the Word was God. ²He was with God in the beginning.

³Through him all things were made; without him nothing was made that has been made. ⁴In him was life, and that life was the light of men. ⁵The light shines in the darkness, but the darkness has not understood[a] it.

⁶There came a man who was sent from God; his name was John. ⁷He came as a witness to testify concerning that light, so that through him all men might believe. ⁸He himself was not the light; he came only as a witness to the light. ⁹The true light that gives light to every man was coming into the world.[b]

¹⁰He was in the world, and though the world was made through him, the world did not recognize him. ¹¹He came to that which was his own, but his own did not receive him. ¹²Yet to all who received him, to those who believed in his name, he gave the right to become children of God— ¹³children born not of natural descent,[c] nor of human decision or a husband's will, but born of God.

¹⁴The Word became flesh and made his dwelling among us. We have seen his glory, the glory of the One and Only,[d] who came from the Father, full of grace and truth.

¹⁵John testifies concerning him. He cries out, saying, "This was he of whom I said, 'He who comes after me has surpassed me because he was before me.' " ¹⁶From the fullness of his grace we have all received one blessing after another. ¹⁷For the law was given through Moses; grace and truth came through Jesus Christ. ¹⁸No one has ever seen God, but God the One and Only,[d] [e] who is at the Father's side, has made him known.

John the Baptist Denies Being the Christ

¹⁹Now this was John's testimony when the Jews of Jerusalem sent priests and Levites to ask

a 5 Or *darkness, and the darkness has not overcome*　*b 9* Or *This was the true light that gives light to every man who comes into the world*　*c 13* Greek *of bloods*　*d 14 ,18* Or *the Only Begotten*　*e 18* Some manuscripts *but the only* (or *only begotten*) *Son*

him who he was. [20]He did not fail to confess, but confessed freely, "I am not the Christ.[a]"

[21]They asked him, "Then who are you? Are you Elijah?"

He said, "I am not."

"Are you the Prophet?"

He answered, "No."

[22]Finally they said, "Who are you? Give us an answer to take back to those who sent us. What do you say about yourself?"

[23]John replied in the words of Isaiah the prophet, "I am the voice of one calling in the desert, 'Make straight the way for the Lord.' "[b]

[24]Now some Pharisees who had been sent [25]questioned him, "Why then do you baptize if you are not the Christ, nor Elijah, nor the Prophet?"

[26]"I baptize with[c] water," John replied, "but among you stands one you do not know. [27]He is the one who comes after me, the thongs of whose sandals I am not worthy to untie."

[28]This all happened at Bethany on the other side of the Jordan, where John was baptizing.

Jesus the Lamb of God

[29]The next day John saw Jesus coming toward him and said, "Look, the Lamb of God, who takes away the sin of the world! [30]This is the one I meant when I said, 'A man who comes after me has surpassed me because he was before me.' [31]I myself did not know him, but the reason I came baptizing with water was that he might be revealed to Israel."

[32]Then John gave this testimony: "I saw the Spirit come down from heaven as a dove and remain on him. [33]I would not have known him, except that the one who sent me to baptize with water told me, 'The man on whom you see the Spirit come down and remain is he who will baptize with the Holy Spirit.' [34]I have seen and I testify that this is the Son of God."

Jesus' First Disciples

[35]The next day John was there again with two of his disciples. [36]When he saw Jesus passing by, he said, "Look, the Lamb of God!"

[37]When the two disciples heard him say this, they followed Jesus. [38]Turning around, Jesus saw them following and asked, "What do you want?"

裏，問他說："你是誰？"[20]他就明說，並不隱瞞；明說："我不是基督。"

[21]他們又問他說："這樣，你是誰呢？是<u>以利亞</u>嗎？"

他說："我不是。"

"是那先知嗎？"

他回答說："不是。"

[22]於是他們說："你到底是誰？叫我們好回覆差我們來的人。你自己說，你是誰？"

[23]他說："我就是那在曠野有人聲喊着說：'修直主的道路'，正如先知<u>以賽亞</u>所說的。"

[24]那些人是法利賽人差的（註：或作"那差來的是法利賽人"）。[25]他們就問他說："你既不是基督，不是<u>以利亞</u>，也不是那先知，為甚麼施洗呢？"

[26]<u>約翰</u>回答說："我是用水施洗，但有一位站在你們中間，是你們不認識的，[27]就是那在我以後來的，我給他解鞋帶也不配。"

[28]這些是在<u>約旦河</u>外<u>伯大尼</u>（註：有古卷作"伯大巴喇"），<u>約翰</u>施洗的地方作的見證。

耶穌是神的羔羊

[29]次日，<u>約翰</u>看見耶穌來到他那裏，就說："看哪，神的羔羊，除去（註：或作"背負"）世人罪孽的。[30]這就是我曾說'有一位在我以後來，反成了在我以前的，因為他本來在我以前。'[31]我先前不認識他，如今我來用水施洗，為要叫他顯明給<u>以色列</u>人。"

[32]<u>約翰</u>又作見證說："我曾看見聖靈彷彿鴿子從天降下，住在他的身上。[33]我先前不認識他，只是那差我來用水施洗的，對我說：'你看見聖靈降下來，住在誰的身上，誰就是用聖靈施洗的。'[34]我看見了，就證明這是神的兒子。"

耶穌的第一批門徒

[35]再次日，<u>約翰</u>同兩個門徒站在那裏。[36]他見耶穌行走，就說："看哪，這是神的羔羊！"

[37]兩個門徒聽見他的話，就跟從了耶穌。[38]耶穌轉過身來，看見他們跟着，就問他們說："你們要甚麼？"

---

a 20 Or *Messiah.* "The Christ" (Greek) and "the Messiah" (Hebrew) both mean "the Anointed One"; also in verse 25.
b 23 Isaiah 40:3   *c* 26 Or *in*; also in verses 31 and 33

他們說：「拉比（「拉比」翻出來就是「夫子」），在哪裏住？」

39耶穌說：「你們來看。」

他們就去看他在哪裏住，這一天便與他同住。那時約有申正了。

40聽見約翰的話，跟從耶穌的那兩個人，一個是西門彼得的兄弟安得烈。41他先找着自己的哥哥西門，對他說：「我們遇見彌賽亞了（「彌賽亞」翻出來就是「基督」）！」42於是領他去見耶穌。

耶穌看着他說：「你是約翰的兒子西門（註：「約翰」在馬太16章17節稱「約拿」），你要稱為磯法（「磯法」翻出來就是「彼得」）。」

耶穌呼召腓力與拿但業

43又次日，耶穌想要往加利利去，遇見腓力，就對他說：「來，跟從我吧！」

44這腓力是伯賽大人，和安得烈、彼得同城。45腓力找着拿但業，對他說：「摩西在律法上所寫的和眾先知所記的那一位，我們遇見了，就是約瑟的兒子拿撒勒人耶穌。」

46拿但業對他說：「拿撒勒還能出甚麼好的嗎？」

腓力說：「你來看！」

47耶穌看見拿但業來，就指着他說：「看哪，這是個真以色列人，他心裏是沒有詭詐的。」

48拿但業對耶穌說：「你從哪裏知道我呢？」耶穌回答說：「腓力還沒有招呼你，你在無花果樹底下，我就看見你了。」

49拿但業說：「拉比，你是神的兒子，你是以色列的王！」

50耶穌對他說：「因為我說在無花果樹底下看見你，你就信嗎？你將要看見比這更大的事。」51又說：「我實實在在地告訴你們：你們將要看見天開了，神的使者上去下來在人子身上。」

耶穌變水為酒

2 第三日，在加利利的迦拿有娶親的筵席，耶穌的母親在那裏。2耶穌和他的門徒也被請去赴席。3酒用盡了，耶穌的母親對他說：「他們沒有酒了。」

They said, "Rabbi" (which means Teacher), "where are you staying?"

39"Come," he replied, "and you will see."

So they went and saw where he was staying, and spent that day with him. It was about the tenth hour.

40Andrew, Simon Peter's brother, was one of the two who heard what John had said and who had followed Jesus. 41The first thing Andrew did was to find his brother Simon and tell him, "We have found the Messiah" (that is, the Christ). 42And he brought him to Jesus.

Jesus looked at him and said, "You are Simon son of John. You will be called Cephas" (which, when translated, is Peter*a*).

Jesus Calls Philip and Nathanael

43The next day Jesus decided to leave for Galilee. Finding Philip, he said to him, "Follow me."

44Philip, like Andrew and Peter, was from the town of Bethsaida. 45Philip found Nathanael and told him, "We have found the one Moses wrote about in the Law, and about whom the prophets also wrote—Jesus of Nazareth, the son of Joseph."

46"Nazareth! Can anything good come from there?" Nathanael asked.

"Come and see," said Philip.

47When Jesus saw Nathanael approaching, he said of him, "Here is a true Israelite, in whom there is nothing false."

48"How do you know me?" Nathanael asked.

Jesus answered, "I saw you while you were still under the fig tree before Philip called you."

49Then Nathanael declared, "Rabbi, you are the Son of God; you are the King of Israel."

50Jesus said, "You believe*b* because I told you I saw you under the fig tree. You shall see greater things than that." 51He then added, "I tell you*c* the truth, you*c* shall see heaven open, and the angels of God ascending and descending on the Son of Man."

Jesus Changes Water to Wine

2 On the third day a wedding took place at Cana in Galilee. Jesus' mother was there, 2and Jesus and his disciples had also been invited to the wedding. 3When the wine was gone, Jesus' mother said to him, "They have no more wine."

---

a 42 Both *Cephas* (Aramaic) and *Peter* (Greek) mean *rock.*
b 50 Or *Do you believe . . . ?*　　*c 51* The Greek is plural.

4"Dear woman, why do you involve me?" Jesus replied. "My time has not yet come."

5His mother said to the servants, "Do whatever he tells you."

6Nearby stood six stone water jars, the kind used by the Jews for ceremonial washing, each holding from twenty to thirty gallons.*a*

7Jesus said to the servants, "Fill the jars with water"; so they filled them to the brim.

8Then he told them, "Now draw some out and take it to the master of the banquet."

They did so, 9and the master of the banquet tasted the water that had been turned into wine. He did not realize where it had come from, though the servants who had drawn the water knew. Then he called the bridegroom aside 10and said, "Everyone brings out the choice wine first and then the cheaper wine after the guests have had too much to drink; but you have saved the best till now."

11This, the first of his miraculous signs, Jesus performed at Cana in Galilee. He thus revealed his glory, and his disciples put their faith in him.

Jesus Clears the Temple

12After this he went down to Capernaum with his mother and brothers and his disciples. There they stayed for a few days.

13When it was almost time for the Jewish Passover, Jesus went up to Jerusalem. 14In the temple courts he found men selling cattle, sheep and doves, and others sitting at tables exchanging money. 15So he made a whip out of cords, and drove all from the temple area, both sheep and cattle; he scattered the coins of the money changers and overturned their tables. 16To those who sold doves he said, "Get these out of here! How dare you turn my Father's house into a market!"

17His disciples remembered that it is written: "Zeal for your house will consume me."*b*

18Then the Jews demanded of him, "What miraculous sign can you show us to prove your authority to do all this?"

19Jesus answered them, "Destroy this temple, and I will raise it again in three days."

20The Jews replied, "It has taken forty-six years to build this temple, and you are going to raise it in three days?" 21But the temple he had spoken of was his body. 22After he was raised from the dead, his disciples recalled what he had said. Then they believed the Scripture and the words that Jesus had spoken.

4耶穌說：「母親（註：原文作「婦人」），我與你有甚麼相干？我的時候還沒有到。」

5他母親對用人說：「他告訴你們甚麼，你們就做甚麼。」

6照猶太人潔淨的規矩，有六口石缸擺在那裏，每口可以盛兩三桶水。

7耶穌對用人說：「把缸倒滿了水。」他們就倒滿了，直到缸口。

8耶穌又說：「現在可以舀出來，送給管筵席的。」

他們就送了去。9管筵席的嘗了那水變的酒，並不知道是哪裏來的，只有舀水的用人知道。管筵席的便叫新郎來，10對他說：「人都是先擺上好酒，等客喝足了，才擺上次的；你倒把好酒留到如今！」

11這是耶穌所行的頭一件神蹟，是在加利利的迦拿行的，顯出他的榮耀來，他的門徒就信他了。

耶穌潔淨聖殿

12這事以後，耶穌與他的母親、弟兄和門徒都下迦百農去，在那裏住了不多幾日。

13猶太人的逾越節近了，耶穌就上耶路撒冷去。14看見殿裏有賣牛、羊、鴿子的，並有兌換銀錢的人坐在那裏。15耶穌就拿繩子做成鞭子，把牛羊都趕出殿去，倒出兌換銀錢之人的銀錢，推翻他們的桌子。16又對賣鴿子的說：「把這些東西拿去！不要將我父的殿當作買賣的地方。」

17他的門徒就想起經上記着說：「我為你的殿，心裏焦急，如同火燒。」

18因此猶太人問他說：「你既做這些事，還顯甚麼神蹟給我們看呢？」

19耶穌回答說：「你們拆毀這殿，我三日內要再建立起來。」

20猶太人便說：「這殿是四十六年才造成的，你三日內就再建立起來嗎？」21但耶穌這話，是以他的身體為殿。22所以到他從死裏復活以後，門徒就想起他說過這話，便信了聖經和耶穌所說的。

---

a 6 Greek *two to three metretes* (probably about 75 to 115 liters)
b 17 Psalm 69:9

²³當耶穌在耶路撒冷過逾越節的時候，有許多人看見他所行的神蹟，就信了他的名。²⁴耶穌卻不將自己交託他們，因為他知道萬人；²⁵也用不著誰見證人怎樣，因他知道人心裏所存的。

耶穌教導尼哥德慕

3 有一個法利賽人，名叫尼哥德慕，是猶太人的官。²這人夜裏來見耶穌，說：「拉比，我們知道你是由神那裏來作師傅的，因為你所行的神蹟，若沒有神同在，無人能行。」

³耶穌回答說：「我實實在在地告訴你：人若不重生，就不能見神的國。」

⁴尼哥德慕說：「人已經老了，如何能重生呢？豈能再進母腹生出來嗎？」

⁵耶穌說：「我實實在在地告訴你：人若不是從水和聖靈生的，就不能進神的國。⁶從肉身生的，就是肉身；從靈生的，就是靈。⁷我說『你們必須重生』，你不要以為希奇。⁸風隨著意思吹，你聽見風的響聲，卻不曉得從哪裏來，往哪裏去；凡從聖靈生的，也是如此。」

⁹尼哥德慕問他說：「怎能有這事呢？」

¹⁰耶穌回答說：「你是以色列人的先生，還不明白這事嗎？¹¹我實實在在地告訴你：我們所說的，是我們知道的；我們所證的，是我們見過的；你們卻不領受我們的見證。¹²我對你們說地上的事，你們尚且不信；若說天上的事，如何能信呢？¹³除了從天降下仍舊在天的人子，沒有人升過天。¹⁴摩西在曠野怎樣舉蛇，人子也必照樣被舉起來，¹⁵叫一切信他的都得永生（註：或作「叫一切信的人在他裏面得永生」）。

¹⁶「神愛世人，甚至將他的獨生子賜給他們，叫一切信他的，不至滅亡，反得永生。¹⁷因為神差他的兒子降世，不是要定世人的罪（註：或作「審判世人」。下同），乃是要叫世人因他得救。¹⁸信他的人，不被定罪；不

²³Now while he was in Jerusalem at the Passover Feast, many people saw the miraculous signs he was doing and believed in his name.[a] ²⁴But Jesus would not entrust himself to them, for he knew all men. ²⁵He did not need man's testimony about man, for he knew what was in a man.

Jesus Teaches Nicodemus

3 Now there was a man of the Pharisees named Nicodemus, a member of the Jewish ruling council. ²He came to Jesus at night and said, "Rabbi, we know you are a teacher who has come from God. For no one could perform the miraculous signs you are doing if God were not with him."

³In reply Jesus declared, "I tell you the truth, no one can see the kingdom of God unless he is born again.[b]"

⁴"How can a man be born when he is old?" Nicodemus asked. "Surely he cannot enter a second time into his mother's womb to be born!"

⁵Jesus answered, "I tell you the truth, no one can enter the kingdom of God unless he is born of water and the Spirit. ⁶Flesh gives birth to flesh, but the Spirit[c] gives birth to spirit. ⁷You should not be surprised at my saying, 'You[d] must be born again.' ⁸The wind blows wherever it pleases. You hear its sound, but you cannot tell where it comes from or where it is going. So it is with everyone born of the Spirit."

⁹"How can this be?" Nicodemus asked.

¹⁰"You are Israel's teacher," said Jesus, "and do you not understand these things? ¹¹I tell you the truth, we speak of what we know, and we testify to what we have seen, but still you people do not accept our testimony. ¹²I have spoken to you of earthly things and you do not believe; how then will you believe if I speak of heavenly things? ¹³No one has ever gone into heaven except the one who came from heaven—the Son of Man.[e] ¹⁴Just as Moses lifted up the snake in the desert, so the Son of Man must be lifted up, ¹⁵that everyone who believes in him may have eternal life.[f]

¹⁶"For God so loved the world that he gave his one and only Son,[g] that whoever believes in him shall not perish but have eternal life. ¹⁷For God did not send his Son into the world to condemn the world, but to save the world through him. ¹⁸Whoever believes in him is not condemned, but whoever does not believe stands

---

a 23 Or and believed in him　*b 3 Or born from above; also in verse 7*　*c 6 Or but spirit*　*d 7 The Greek is plural.*
e 13 Some manuscripts Man, who is in heaven　*f 15 Or believes may have eternal life in him*　*g 16 Or his only begotten Son*

condemned already because he has not believed in the name of God's one and only Son.[a] [19]This is the verdict: Light has come into the world, but men loved darkness instead of light because their deeds were evil. [20]Everyone who does evil hates the light, and will not come into the light for fear that his deeds will be exposed. [21]But whoever lives by the truth comes into the light, so that it may be seen plainly that what he has done has been done through God."[b]

John the Baptist's Testimony About Jesus

[22]After this, Jesus and his disciples went out into the Judean countryside, where he spent some time with them, and baptized. [23]Now John also was baptizing at Aenon near Salim, because there was plenty of water, and people were constantly coming to be baptized. [24](This was before John was put in prison.) [25]An argument developed between some of John's disciples and a certain Jew[c] over the matter of ceremonial washing. [26]They came to John and said to him, "Rabbi, that man who was with you on the other side of the Jordan—the one you testified about—well, he is baptizing, and everyone is going to him."

[27]To this John replied, "A man can receive only what is given him from heaven. [28]You yourselves can testify that I said, 'I am not the Christ[d] but am sent ahead of him.' [29]The bride belongs to the bridegroom. The friend who attends the bridegroom waits and listens for him, and is full of joy when he hears the bridegroom's voice. That joy is mine, and it is now complete. [30]He must become greater; I must become less.

[31]"The one who comes from above is above all; the one who is from the earth belongs to the earth, and speaks as one from the earth. The one who comes from heaven is above all. [32]He testifies to what he has seen and heard, but no one accepts his testimony. [33]The man who has accepted it has certified that God is truthful. [34]For the one whom God has sent speaks the words of God, for God[e] gives the Spirit without limit. [35]The Father loves the Son and has placed everything in his hands. [36]Whoever believes in the Son has eternal life, but whoever rejects the Son will not see life, for God's wrath remains on him."[f]

信的人，罪已經定了，因為他不信神獨生子的名。[19]光來到世間，世人因自己的行為是惡的，不愛光倒愛黑暗，定他們的罪就是在此。[20]凡作惡的便恨光，並不來就光，恐怕他的行為受責備；[21]但行真理的必來就光，要顯明他所行的是靠神而行。"

施洗約翰為耶穌作見證

[22]這事以後，耶穌和門徒到了猶太地，在那裏居住施洗。[23]約翰在靠近撒冷的哀嫩也施洗，因為那裏水多，眾人都去受洗。[24]那時約翰還沒有下在監裏。[25]約翰的門徒和一個猶太人辯論潔淨的禮，[26]就來見約翰說："拉比，從前同你在約旦河外、你所見證的那位，現在施洗，眾人都往他那裏去了。"

[27]約翰說："若不是從天上賜的，人就不能得甚麼。[28]我曾說'我不是基督，是奉差遣在他前面的'，你們自己可以給我作見證。[29]娶新婦的就是新郎，新郎的朋友站著聽見新郎的聲音就甚喜樂，故此我這喜樂滿足了。[30]他必興旺，我必衰微。

[31]"從天上來的，是在萬有之上；從地上來的，是屬乎地，他所說的也是屬乎地。從天上來的是在萬有之上。[32]他將所見所聞的見證出來，只是沒有人領受他的見證。[33]那領受他見證的，就印上印，證明神是真的。[34]神所差來的，就說神的話，因為神賜聖靈給他，是沒有限量的。[35]父愛子，已將萬有交在他手裏。[36]信子的人有永生；不信子的人得不著永生（註：原文作"不得見永生"），神的震怒常在他身上。"

---

a 18 Or God's only begotten Son   b 21 Some interpreters end the quotation after verse 15.   c 25 Some manuscripts and certain Jews   d 28 Or Messiah   e 34 Greek he   f 36 Some interpreters end the quotation after verse 30.

耶穌與撒馬利亞婦人談道

4 主知道法利賽人聽見他收門徒施洗比約翰還多，²（其實不是耶穌親自施洗，乃是他的門徒施洗。）³他就離了猶太，又往加利利去。

⁴必須經過撒馬利亞，⁵於是到了撒馬利亞的一座城，名叫敘加，靠近雅各給他兒子約瑟的那塊地。⁶在那裏有雅各井。耶穌因走路困乏，就坐在井旁。那時約有午正。

⁷有一個撒馬利亞的婦人來打水，耶穌對她說：「請你給我水喝。」⁸那時門徒進城買食物去了。

⁹撒馬利亞的婦人對他說：「你既是猶太人，怎麼向我一個撒馬利亞婦人要水喝呢？」原來猶太人和撒馬利亞人沒有來往。

¹⁰耶穌回答說：「你若知道神的恩賜和對你說『給我水喝』的是誰，你必早求他，他也必早給了你活水。」

¹¹婦人說：「先生，沒有打水的器具，井又深，你從哪裏得活水呢？¹²我們的祖宗雅各將這井留給我們，他自己和兒子並牲畜也都喝這井裏的水，難道你比他還大嗎？」

¹³耶穌回答說：「凡喝這水的，還要再渴；¹⁴人若喝我所賜的水，就永遠不渴。我所賜的水要在他裏頭成為泉源，直湧到永生。」

¹⁵婦人說：「先生，請把這水賜給我，叫我不渴，也不用來這麼遠打水。」

¹⁶耶穌說：「你去叫你丈夫也到這裏來。」

¹⁷婦人說：「我沒有丈夫。」

耶穌說：「你說沒有丈夫，是不錯的。¹⁸你已經有五個丈夫，你現在有的，並不是你的丈夫，你這話是真的。」

¹⁹婦人說：「先生，我看出你是先知。²⁰我們的祖宗在這山上禮拜，你們倒說，應當禮拜的地方是在耶路撒冷。」

²¹耶穌說：「婦人，你當信我。時候將到，你們拜父也不在這山上，也不在耶路撒冷。²²你們所拜

Jesus Talks With a Samaritan Woman

4 The Pharisees heard that Jesus was gaining and baptizing more disciples than John, ²although in fact it was not Jesus who baptized, but his disciples. ³When the Lord learned of this, he left Judea and went back once more to Galilee.

⁴Now he had to go through Samaria. ⁵So he came to a town in Samaria called Sychar, near the plot of ground Jacob had given to his son Joseph. ⁶Jacob's well was there, and Jesus, tired as he was from the journey, sat down by the well. It was about the sixth hour.

⁷When a Samaritan woman came to draw water, Jesus said to her, "Will you give me a drink?" ⁸(His disciples had gone into the town to buy food.)

⁹The Samaritan woman said to him, "You are a Jew and I am a Samaritan woman. How can you ask me for a drink?" (For Jews do not associate with Samaritans.[a])

¹⁰Jesus answered her, "If you knew the gift of God and who it is that asks you for a drink, you would have asked him and he would have given you living water."

¹¹"Sir," the woman said, "you have nothing to draw with and the well is deep. Where can you get this living water? ¹²Are you greater than our father Jacob, who gave us the well and drank from it himself, as did also his sons and his flocks and herds?"

¹³Jesus answered, "Everyone who drinks this water will be thirsty again, ¹⁴but whoever drinks the water I give him will never thirst. Indeed, the water I give him will become in him a spring of water welling up to eternal life."

¹⁵The woman said to him, "Sir, give me this water so that I won't get thirsty and have to keep coming here to draw water."

¹⁶He told her, "Go, call your husband and come back."

¹⁷"I have no husband," she replied.

Jesus said to her, "You are right when you say you have no husband. ¹⁸The fact is, you have had five husbands, and the man you now have is not your husband. What you have just said is quite true."

¹⁹"Sir," the woman said, "I can see that you are a prophet. ²⁰Our fathers worshiped on this mountain, but you Jews claim that the place where we must worship is in Jerusalem."

²¹Jesus declared, "Believe me, woman, a time is coming when you will worship the Father neither on this mountain nor in Jerusalem. ²²You

a 9 Or do not use dishes Samaritans have used

Samaritans worship what you do not know; we worship what we do know, for salvation is from the Jews. 23Yet a time is coming and has now come when the true worshipers will worship the Father in spirit and truth, for they are the kind of worshipers the Father seeks. 24God is spirit, and his worshipers must worship in spirit and in truth."

25The woman said, "I know that Messiah" (called Christ) "is coming. When he comes, he will explain everything to us."

26Then Jesus declared, "I who speak to you am he."

The Disciples Rejoin Jesus

27Just then his disciples returned and were surprised to find him talking with a woman. But no one asked, "What do you want?" or "Why are you talking with her?"

28Then, leaving her water jar, the woman went back to the town and said to the people, 29"Come, see a man who told me everything I ever did. Could this be the Christ^a?" 30They came out of the town and made their way toward him.

31Meanwhile his disciples urged him, "Rabbi, eat something."

32But he said to them, "I have food to eat that you know nothing about."

33Then his disciples said to each other, "Could someone have brought him food?"

34"My food," said Jesus, "is to do the will of him who sent me and to finish his work. 35Do you not say, 'Four months more and then the harvest'? I tell you, open your eyes and look at the fields! They are ripe for harvest. 36Even now the reaper draws his wages, even now he harvests the crop for eternal life, so that the sower and the reaper may be glad together. 37Thus the saying 'One sows and another reaps' is true. 38I sent you to reap what you have not worked for. Others have done the hard work, and you have reaped the benefits of their labor."

Many Samaritans Believe

39Many of the Samaritans from that town believed in him because of the woman's testimony, "He told me everything I ever did." 40So when the Samaritans came to him, they urged him to stay with them, and he stayed two days. 41And because of his words many more became believers.

42They said to the woman, "We no longer believe just because of what you said; now we

的,你們不知道;我們所拜的,我們知道,因為救恩是從猶太人出來的。23時候將到,如今就是了。那真正拜父的,要用心靈和誠實拜他,因為父要這樣的人拜他。24神是個靈(註:或無"個"字),所以拜他的,必須用心靈和誠實拜他。"

25婦人說:"我知道彌賽亞(就是那稱為基督的)要來,他來了,必將一切的事都告訴我們。"

26耶穌說:"這和你說話的就是他。"

門徒與耶穌會合

27當下門徒回來,就希奇耶穌和一個婦人說話。只是沒有人說:"你是要甚麼?"或說:"你為甚麼和她說話?"

28那婦人就留下水罐子,往城裏去,對眾人說:29"你們來看!有一個人將我素來所行的一切事都給我說出來了,莫非這就是基督嗎?"30眾人就出城往耶穌那裏去。

31這其間,門徒對耶穌說:"拉比,請吃。"

32耶穌說:"我有食物吃,是你們不知道的。"

33門徒就彼此對問說:"莫非有人拿甚麼給他吃嗎?"

34耶穌說:"我的食物就是遵行差我來者的旨意,做成他的工。35你們豈不說'到收割的時候還有四個月'嗎?我告訴你們:舉目向田觀看,莊稼已經熟了(註:原文作"發白"),可以收割了。36收割的人得工價,積蓄五穀到永生,叫撒種的和收割的一同快樂。37俗語說'那人撒種,這人收割',這話可見是真的。38我差你們去收你們所沒有勞苦的,別人勞苦,你們享受他們所勞苦的。"

許多撒馬利亞人信主

39那城裏有好些撒馬利亞人信了耶穌,因為那婦人作見證說:"他將我素來所行的一切事都給我說出來了。"40於是撒馬利亞人來見耶穌,求他在他們那裏住下,他便在那裏住了兩天。41因耶穌的話,信的人就更多了。

42便對婦人說:"現在我們信,不是因為你的話,是我們親自聽見

a 29 Or Messiah

了，知道這真是救世主。"

耶穌治好大臣的兒子

43過了那兩天，耶穌離了那地方，往加利利去。44因為耶穌自己作過見證說："先知在本地是沒有人尊敬的。"45到了加利利，加利利人既然看見他在耶路撒冷過節所行的一切事，就接待他，因為他們也是上去過節。

46耶穌又到了加利利的迦拿，就是他從前變水為酒的地方。有一個大臣，他的兒子在迦百農患病。47他聽見耶穌從猶太到了加利利，就來見他，求他下去醫治他的兒子，因為他兒子快要死了。

48耶穌就對他說："若不看見神蹟奇事，你們總是不信。"

49那大臣說："先生，求你趁着我的孩子還沒有死就下去。"

50耶穌對他說："回去吧！你的兒子活了。"

那人信耶穌所說的話，就回去了。51正下去的時候，他的僕人迎見他，說他的兒子活了。52他就問甚麼時候見好的。他們說："昨日未時熱就退了。"

53他便知道這正是耶穌對他說"你兒子活了"的時候，他自己和全家就都信了。

54這是耶穌在加利利行的第二件神蹟，是他從猶太回去以後行的。

在池邊治病

5 這事以後，到了猶太人的一個節期，耶穌就上耶路撒冷去。2在耶路撒冷，靠近羊門有一個池子，希伯來話叫作畢士大，旁邊有五個廊子。3裏面躺着瞎眼的、瘸腿的、血氣枯乾的許多病人。(註：有古卷在此有"等候水動，4因為有天使按時下池子攪動那水，水動之後，誰先下去，無論害甚麼病就痊愈了。")5在那裏有一個人，病了三十八年。6耶穌看

have heard for ourselves, and we know that this man really is the Savior of the world."

Jesus Heals the Official's Son

43After the two days he left for Galilee. 44(Now Jesus himself had pointed out that a prophet has no honor in his own country.) 45When he arrived in Galilee, the Galileans welcomed him. They had seen all that he had done in Jerusalem at the Passover Feast, for they also had been there.

46Once more he visited Cana in Galilee, where he had turned the water into wine. And there was a certain royal official whose son lay sick at Capernaum. 47When this man heard that Jesus had arrived in Galilee from Judea, he went to him and begged him to come and heal his son, who was close to death.

48"Unless you people see miraculous signs and wonders," Jesus told him, "you will never believe."

49The royal official said, "Sir, come down before my child dies."

50Jesus replied, "You may go. Your son will live."

The man took Jesus at his word and departed. 51While he was still on the way, his servants met him with the news that his boy was living. 52When he inquired as to the time when his son got better, they said to him, "The fever left him yesterday at the seventh hour."

53Then the father realized that this was the exact time at which Jesus had said to him, "Your son will live." So he and all his household believed.

54This was the second miraculous sign that Jesus performed, having come from Judea to Galilee.

The Healing at the Pool

5 Some time later, Jesus went up to Jerusalem for a feast of the Jews. 2Now there is in Jerusalem near the Sheep Gate a pool, which in Aramaic is called Bethesda[a] and which is surrounded by five covered colonnades. 3Here a great number of disabled people used to lie—the blind, the lame, the paralyzed.[b] 5One who was there had been an invalid for thirty-eight years. 6When Jesus saw him lying there

---

a 2 Some manuscripts Bethzatha; other manuscripts Bethsaida
b 3 Some less important manuscripts paralyzed—and they waited for the moving of the waters. 4 From time to time an angel of the Lord would come down and stir up the waters. The first one into the pool after each such disturbance would be cured of whatever disease he had.

and learned that he had been in this condition for a long time, he asked him, "Do you want to get well?"

7"Sir," the invalid replied, "I have no one to help me into the pool when the water is stirred. While I am trying to get in, someone else goes down ahead of me."

8Then Jesus said to him, "Get up! Pick up your mat and walk." 9At once the man was cured; he picked up his mat and walked.

The day on which this took place was a Sabbath, 10and so the Jews said to the man who had been healed, "It is the Sabbath; the law forbids you to carry your mat."

11But he replied, "The man who made me well said to me, 'Pick up your mat and walk.' "

12So they asked him, "Who is this fellow who told you to pick it up and walk?"

13The man who was healed had no idea who it was, for Jesus had slipped away into the crowd that was there.

14Later Jesus found him at the temple and said to him, "See, you are well again. Stop sinning or something worse may happen to you." 15The man went away and told the Jews that it was Jesus who had made him well.

Life Through the Son

16So, because Jesus was doing these things on the Sabbath, the Jews persecuted him. 17Jesus said to them, "My Father is always at his work to this very day, and I, too, am working." 18For this reason the Jews tried all the harder to kill him; not only was he breaking the Sabbath, but he was even calling God his own Father, making himself equal with God.

19Jesus gave them this answer: "I tell you the truth, the Son can do nothing by himself; he can do only what he sees his Father doing, because whatever the Father does the Son also does. 20For the Father loves the Son and shows him all he does. Yes, to your amazement he will show him even greater things than these. 21For just as the Father raises the dead and gives them life, even so the Son gives life to whom he is pleased to give it. 22Moreover, the Father judges no one, but has entrusted all judgment to the Son, 23that all may honor the Son just as they honor the Father. He who does not honor the Son does not honor the Father, who sent him.

24"I tell you the truth, whoever hears my word and believes him who sent me has eternal life and will not be condemned; he has crossed over from death to life. 25I tell you the truth, a time is coming and has now come when the dead will hear the voice of the Son of God and

見他躺着，知道他病了許久，就問他說：「你要痊愈嗎？」

7病人回答說：「先生，水動的時候，沒有人把我放在池子裏；我正去的時候，就有別人比我先下去。」

8耶穌對他說：「起來，拿你的褥子走吧！」9那人立刻痊愈，就拿起褥子來走了。

10那天是安息日，所以猶太人對那醫好的人說：「今天是安息日，你拿褥子是不可的！」

11他卻回答說：「那使我痊愈的對我說：『拿你的褥子走吧！』」

12他們問他說：「對你說『拿褥子走』的是甚麼人？」

13那醫好的人不知道是誰，因為那裏的人多，耶穌已經躲開了。

14後來耶穌在殿裏遇見他，對他說：「你已經痊愈了，不要再犯罪，恐怕你遭遇的更加利害。」15那人就去告訴猶太人，使他痊愈的是耶穌。

從子得生命

16所以猶太人逼迫耶穌，因為他在安息日做了這事。17耶穌就對他們說：「我父做事直到如今，我也做事。」18所以猶太人越發想要殺他，因他不但犯了安息日，並且稱神為他的父，將自己和神當作平等。

19耶穌對他們說：「我實實在在地告訴你們：子憑着自己不能做甚麼，惟有看見父所做的，子才能做；父所做的事，子也照樣做。20父愛子，將自己所做的一切事指給他看，還要將比這更大的事指給他看，叫你們希奇。21父怎樣叫死人起來，使他們活着，子也照樣隨自己的意思使人活着。22父不審判甚麼人，乃將審判的事全交與子，23叫人都尊敬子如同尊敬父一樣。不尊敬的，就是不尊敬差子來的父。

24「我實實在在地告訴你們：那聽我話、又信差我來者的，就有永生，不至於定罪，是已經出死入生了。25我實實在在地告訴你們：時候將到，現在就是了，死人要聽見神兒子

的聲音，聽見的人就要活了。26因為
父怎樣在自己有生命，就賜給他兒子
也照樣在自己有生命，27並且因為他
是人子，就賜給他行審判的權柄。

28 "你們不要把這事看作希奇。
時候要到，凡在墳墓裏的，都要聽
見他的聲音，就出來。29行善的，復
活得生；作惡的，復活定罪。30我憑
着自己不能做甚麼，我怎麼聽見，
就怎麼審判。我的審判也是公平
的，因為我不求自己的意思，只求
那差我來者的意思。

為耶穌作的見證

31 "我若為自己作見證，我的見
證就不真；32另有一位給我作見證，
我也知道他給我作的見證是真的。

33 "你們曾差人到約翰那裏，他
為真理作過見證。34其實我所受的見
證不是從人來的；然而我說這些話，
為要叫你們得救。35約翰是點着的明
燈，你們情願暫時喜歡他的光。

36 "但我有比約翰更大的見證，
因為父交給我要我成就的事，就是
我所做的事，這便見證我是父所差
來的。37差我來的父也為我作過見
證。你們從來沒有聽見他的聲音，
也沒有看見他的形像，38你們並沒有
他的道存在心裏，因為他所差來
的，你們不信。39你們查考聖經（註：
或作「應當查考聖經」），因你們以為內
中有永生；給我作見證的就是這
經。40然而你們不肯到我這裏來得生
命。

41 "我不受從人來的榮耀，42但
我知道，你們心裏沒有神的愛。43我
奉我父的名來，你們並不接待我；
若有別人奉自己的名來，你們倒要
接待他。44你們互相受榮耀，卻不求
從獨一之神來的榮耀，怎能信我
呢？

45 "不要想我在父面前要告你
們，有一位告你們的，就是你們所
仰賴的摩西。46你們如果信摩西，也
必信我，因為他書上有指着我寫的
話。47你們若不信他的書，怎能信我
的話呢？"

those who hear will live. 26For as the Father has life in himself, so he has granted the Son to have life in himself. 27And he has given him authority to judge because he is the Son of Man.

28"Do not be amazed at this, for a time is coming when all who are in their graves will hear his voice 29and come out—those who have done good will rise to live, and those who have done evil will rise to be condemned. 30By myself I can do nothing; I judge only as I hear, and my judgment is just, for I seek not to please myself but him who sent me.

Testimonies About Jesus

31"If I testify about myself, my testimony is not valid. 32There is another who testifies in my favor, and I know that his testimony about me is valid.

33"You have sent to John and he has testified to the truth. 34Not that I accept human testimony; but I mention it that you may be saved. 35John was a lamp that burned and gave light, and you chose for a time to enjoy his light.

36"I have testimony weightier than that of John. For the very work that the Father has given me to finish, and which I am doing, testifies that the Father has sent me. 37And the Father who sent me has himself testified concerning me. You have never heard his voice nor seen his form, 38nor does his word dwell in you, for you do not believe the one he sent. 39You diligently study*a* the Scriptures because you think that by them you possess eternal life. These are the Scriptures that testify about me, 40yet you refuse to come to me to have life.

41"I do not accept praise from men, 42but I know you. I know that you do not have the love of God in your hearts. 43I have come in my Father's name, and you do not accept me; but if someone else comes in his own name, you will accept him. 44How can you believe if you accept praise from one another, yet make no effort to obtain the praise that comes from the only God*b*?

45"But do not think I will accuse you before the Father. Your accuser is Moses, on whom your hopes are set. 46If you believed Moses, you would believe me, for he wrote about me. 47But since you do not believe what he wrote, how are you going to believe what I say?"

a 39 Or Study diligently (the imperative)   b 44 Some early manuscripts the Only One

Jesus Feeds the Five Thousand

6 Some time after this, Jesus crossed to the far shore of the Sea of Galilee (that is, the Sea of Tiberias), ²and a great crowd of people followed him because they saw the miraculous signs he had performed on the sick. ³Then Jesus went up on a mountainside and sat down with his disciples. ⁴The Jewish Passover Feast was near.

⁵When Jesus looked up and saw a great crowd coming toward him, he said to Philip, "Where shall we buy bread for these people to eat?" ⁶He asked this only to test him, for he already had in mind what he was going to do.

⁷Philip answered him, "Eight months' wages*a* would not buy enough bread for each one to have a bite!"

⁸Another of his disciples, Andrew, Simon Peter's brother, spoke up, ⁹"Here is a boy with five small barley loaves and two small fish, but how far will they go among so many?"

¹⁰Jesus said, "Have the people sit down." There was plenty of grass in that place, and the men sat down, about five thousand of them. ¹¹Jesus then took the loaves, gave thanks, and distributed to those who were seated as much as they wanted. He did the same with the fish.

¹²When they had all had enough to eat, he said to his disciples, "Gather the pieces that are left over. Let nothing be wasted." ¹³So they gathered them and filled twelve baskets with the pieces of the five barley loaves left over by those who had eaten.

¹⁴After the people saw the miraculous sign that Jesus did, they began to say, "Surely this is the Prophet who is to come into the world." ¹⁵Jesus, knowing that they intended to come and make him king by force, withdrew again to a mountain by himself.

Jesus Walks on the Water

¹⁶When evening came, his disciples went down to the lake, ¹⁷where they got into a boat and set off across the lake for Capernaum. By now it was dark, and Jesus had not yet joined them. ¹⁸A strong wind was blowing and the waters grew rough. ¹⁹When they had rowed three or three and a half miles,*b* they saw Jesus approaching the boat, walking on the water; and they were terrified. ²⁰But he said to them, "It is I; don't be afraid." ²¹Then they were willing to take him into the boat, and immediately the boat reached the shore where they were heading.

a 7 Greek two hundred denarii   b 19 Greek rowed twenty-five or thirty stadia (about 5 or 6 kilometers)

耶穌給五千人吃飽

6 這事以後，耶穌渡過加利利海，就是提比哩亞海。²有許多人因為看見他在病人身上所行的神蹟，就跟隨他。³耶穌上了山，和門徒一同坐在那裏。⁴那時猶太人的逾越節近了。

⁵耶穌舉目看見許多人來，就對腓力說："我們從哪裏買餅叫這些人吃呢？"⁶他說這話是要試驗腓力，他自己原知道要怎樣行。

⁷腓力回答說："就是二十兩銀子的餅，叫他們各人吃一點，也是不夠的。"

⁸有一個門徒，就是西門彼得的兄弟安得烈，對耶穌說：⁹"在這裏有一個孩童，帶着五個大麥餅、兩條魚，只是分給這許多人，還算甚麼呢？"

¹⁰耶穌說："你們叫眾人坐下。"原來那地方的草多，眾人就坐下，數目約有五千。¹¹耶穌拿起餅來，祝謝了，就分給那坐着的人，分魚也是這樣，都隨着他們所要的。

¹²他們吃飽了，耶穌對門徒說："把剩下的零碎收拾起來，免得有糟蹋的。"¹³他們便將那五個大麥餅的零碎，就是眾人吃了剩下來，裝滿了十二個籃子。

¹⁴眾人看見耶穌所行的神蹟，就說："這真是那要到世間來的先知。"¹⁵耶穌既知道眾人要來強逼他作王，就獨自又退到山上去了。

耶穌在水面上行走

¹⁶到了晚上，他的門徒下海邊去，¹⁷上了船，要過海往迦百農去。天已經黑了，耶穌還沒有來到他們那裏。¹⁸忽然狂風大作，海就翻騰起來。¹⁹門徒搖櫓約行了十里多路，看見耶穌在海面上走，漸漸近了船，他們就害怕。²⁰耶穌對他們說："是我，不要怕！"²¹門徒就喜歡接他上船，船立時到了他們所要去的地方。

22第二日，站在海那邊的眾人，知道那裏沒有別的船，只有一隻小船；又知道耶穌沒有同他的門徒上船，乃是門徒自己去的。23然而，有幾隻小船從提比哩亞來，靠近主祝謝後分餅給人吃的地方。24眾人見耶穌和門徒都不在那裏，就上了船，往迦百農去找耶穌。

耶穌是生命的糧

25既在海那邊找着了，就對他說："拉比，是幾時到這裏來的？"

26耶穌回答說："我實實在在地告訴你們：你們找我，並不是因見了神蹟，乃是因吃餅得飽。27不要為那必壞的食物勞力，要為那存到永生的食物勞力，就是人子要賜給你們的，因為人子是父神所印證的。"

28眾人問他說："我們當行甚麼，才算做神的工呢？"

29耶穌回答說："信神所差來的，這就是做神的工。"

30他們又說："你行甚麼神蹟，叫我們看見就信你？你到底做甚麼事呢？31我們的祖宗在曠野吃過嗎哪，如經上寫着說：'他從天上賜下糧來給他們吃。'"

32耶穌說："我實實在在地告訴你們：那從天上來的糧，不是摩西賜給你們的，乃是我父將天上來的真糧賜給你們。33因為神的糧，就是那從天上降下來賜生命給世界的。"

34他們說："主啊，常將這糧賜給我們。"

35耶穌說："我就是生命的糧，到我這裏來的，必定不餓；信我的，永遠不渴。36只是我對你們說過，你們已經看見我，還是不信。37凡父所賜給我的人，必到我這裏來；到我這裏來的，我總不丟棄他。38因為我從天上降下來，不是要按自己的意思行，乃是要按那差我來者的意思行。39差我來者的意思就是：他所賜給我的，叫我一個也不失落，在末日卻叫他復活。40因為我父的意思是叫一切見子而信的人得永生，並且在末日我要叫他復活。"

22The next day the crowd that had stayed on the opposite shore of the lake realized that only one boat had been there, and that Jesus had not entered it with his disciples, but that they had gone away alone. 23Then some boats from Tiberias landed near the place where the people had eaten the bread after the Lord had given thanks. 24Once the crowd realized that neither Jesus nor his disciples were there, they got into the boats and went to Capernaum in search of Jesus.

Jesus the Bread of Life

25When they found him on the other side of the lake, they asked him, "Rabbi, when did you get here?"

26Jesus answered, "I tell you the truth, you are looking for me, not because you saw miraculous signs but because you ate the loaves and had your fill. 27Do not work for food that spoils, but for food that endures to eternal life, which the Son of Man will give you. On him God the Father has placed his seal of approval."

28Then they asked him, "What must we do to do the works God requires?"

29Jesus answered, "The work of God is this: to believe in the one he has sent."

30So they asked him, "What miraculous sign then will you give that we may see it and believe you? What will you do? 31Our forefathers ate the manna in the desert; as it is written: 'He gave them bread from heaven to eat.'a"

32Jesus said to them, "I tell you the truth, it is not Moses who has given you the bread from heaven, but it is my Father who gives you the true bread from heaven. 33For the bread of God is he who comes down from heaven and gives life to the world."

34"Sir," they said, "from now on give us this bread."

35Then Jesus declared, "I am the bread of life. He who comes to me will never go hungry, and he who believes in me will never be thirsty. 36But as I told you, you have seen me and still you do not believe. 37All that the Father gives me will come to me, and whoever comes to me I will never drive away. 38For I have come down from heaven not to do my will but to do the will of him who sent me. 39And this is the will of him who sent me, that I shall lose none of all that he has given me, but raise them up at the last day. 40For my Father's will is that everyone who looks to the Son and believes in him shall have eternal life, and I will raise him up at the last day."

a 31 Exodus 16:4; Neh. 9:15; Psalm 78:24,25

41At this the Jews began to grumble about him because he said, "I am the bread that came down from heaven." 42They said, "Is this not Jesus, the son of Joseph, whose father and mother we know? How can he now say, 'I came down from heaven'?"

43"Stop grumbling among yourselves," Jesus answered. 44"No one can come to me unless the Father who sent me draws him, and I will raise him up at the last day. 45It is written in the Prophets: 'They will all be taught by God.'a Everyone who listens to the Father and learns from him comes to me. 46No one has seen the Father except the one who is from God; only he has seen the Father. 47I tell you the truth, he who believes has everlasting life. 48I am the bread of life. 49Your forefathers ate the manna in the desert, yet they died. 50But here is the bread that comes down from heaven, which a man may eat and not die. 51I am the living bread that came down from heaven. If anyone eats of this bread, he will live forever. This bread is my flesh, which I will give for the life of the world."

52Then the Jews began to argue sharply among themselves, "How can this man give us his flesh to eat?"

53Jesus said to them, "I tell you the truth, unless you eat the flesh of the Son of Man and drink his blood, you have no life in you. 54Whoever eats my flesh and drinks my blood has eternal life, and I will raise him up at the last day. 55For my flesh is real food and my blood is real drink. 56Whoever eats my flesh and drinks my blood remains in me, and I in him. 57Just as the living Father sent me and I live because of the Father, so the one who feeds on me will live because of me. 58This is the bread that came down from heaven. Your forefathers ate manna and died, but he who feeds on this bread will live forever." 59He said this while teaching in the synagogue in Capernaum.

Many Disciples Desert Jesus

60On hearing it, many of his disciples said, "This is a hard teaching. Who can accept it?"

61Aware that his disciples were grumbling about this, Jesus said to them, "Does this offend you? 62What if you see the Son of Man ascend to where he was before! 63The Spirit gives life; the flesh counts for nothing. The words I have spoken to you are spiritb and they are life. 64Yet there are some of you who do not believe." For Jesus had known from the beginning which of

41猶太人因為耶穌說 "我是從天上降下來的糧", 就私下議論他, 42說: "這不是約瑟的兒子耶穌嗎? 他的父母我們豈不認得嗎? 他如今怎麼說 '我是從天上降下來的' 呢?"

43耶穌回答說: "你們不要大家議論。44若不是差我來的父吸引人, 就沒有能到我這裏來的; 到我這裏來的, 在末日我要叫他復活。45在先知書上寫着說: '他們都要蒙神的教訓。' 凡聽見父之教訓又學習的, 就到我這裏來。46這不是說有人看見過父, 惟獨從神來的, 他看見過父。47我實實在在告訴你們: 信的人有永生。48我就是生命的糧。49你們的祖宗在曠野吃過嗎哪, 還是死了。50這是從天上降下來的糧, 叫人吃了就不死。51我是從天上降下來生命的糧; 人若吃這糧, 就必永遠活着。我所要賜的糧, 就是我的肉, 為世人之生命所賜的。"

52因此, 猶太人彼此爭論說: "這個人怎能把他的肉給我們吃呢?"

53耶穌說: "我實實在在告訴你們: 你們若不吃人子的肉, 不喝人子的血, 就沒有生命在你們裏面。54吃我肉喝我血的人就有永生, 在末日我要叫他復活。55我的肉真是可吃的, 我的血真是可喝的。56吃我肉喝我血的人常在我裏面, 我也常在他裏面。57永活的父怎樣差我來, 我又因父活着; 照樣, 吃我肉的人也要因我活着。58這就是從天上降下來的糧。吃這糧的人, 就永遠活着, 不像你們的祖宗吃過嗎哪還是死了。"59這些話是耶穌在迦百農會堂裏教訓人說的。

許多門徒離開耶穌

60他的門徒中有好些人聽見了, 就說: "這話甚難, 誰能聽呢?"

61耶穌心裏知道門徒為這話議論, 就對他們說: "這話是叫你們厭棄嗎(註: "厭棄" 原文作 "跌倒") ? 62倘或你們看見人子升到他原來所在之處, 怎麼樣呢? 63叫人活着的乃是靈, 肉體是無益的。我對你們所說的話就是靈, 就是生命。64只是你們中間有不信的人。"耶穌從起頭就知道

a 45 Isaiah 54:13   b 63 Or Spirit

誰不信他，誰要賣他。⁶⁵耶穌又説：
"所以我對你們説過，若不是蒙我父
的恩賜，沒有人能到我這裏來。"

⁶⁶從此，他門徒中多有退去的，
不再和他同行。

⁶⁷耶穌就對那十二個門徒説：
"你們也要去嗎？"

⁶⁸西門彼得回答説："主啊，你
有永生之道，我們還歸從誰呢？⁶⁹我
們已經信了，又知道你是神的聖
者。"

⁷⁰耶穌説："我不是揀選了你們
十二個門徒嗎？但你們中間有一個是
魔鬼。"⁷¹耶穌這話是指着加略人西
門的兒子猶大説的，他本是十二個門
徒裏的一個，後來要賣耶穌的。

耶穌去守住棚節

7 這事以後，耶穌在加利利遊
行，不願在猶太遊行，因為
猶太人想要殺他。²當時，猶
太人的住棚節近了，³耶穌的弟兄就
對他説："你離開這裏上猶太去
吧！叫你的門徒也看見你所行的
事。⁴人要顯揚名聲，沒有在暗處行
事的，你如果行這些事，就當將自
己顯明給世人看。"⁵因為連他的弟
兄説這話，是因為不信他。

⁶耶穌就對他們説："我的時候還
沒有到，你們的時候常是方便的。
⁷世人不能恨你們，卻是恨我，因為
我指證他們所做的事是惡的。⁸你們
上去過節罷！我現在不上去過這
節，因為我的時候還沒有滿。"⁹耶
穌説了這話，仍舊住在加利利。

¹⁰但他弟兄上去以後，他也上去
過節，不是明去，似乎是暗去的。
¹¹正在節期，猶太人尋找耶穌説：
"他在哪裏？"

¹²眾人為他紛紛議論，有的説：
"他是好人。"

有的説："不然，他是迷惑眾
人的。"¹³只是沒有人明明地講論
他，因為怕猶太人。

耶穌在節期教訓人

¹⁴到了節期，耶穌上殿裏去教訓
人。¹⁵猶太人就希奇説："這個人沒
有學過，怎麼明白書呢？"

them did not believe and who would betray him.
⁶⁵He went on to say, "This is why I told you that
no one can come to me unless the Father has
enabled him."

⁶⁶From this time many of his disciples turned
back and no longer followed him.

⁶⁷"You do not want to leave too, do you?"
Jesus asked the Twelve.

⁶⁸Simon Peter answered him, "Lord, to whom
shall we go? You have the words of eternal life.
⁶⁹We believe and know that you are the Holy
One of God."

⁷⁰Then Jesus replied, "Have I not chosen you,
the Twelve? Yet one of you is a devil!" ⁷¹(He
meant Judas, the son of Simon Iscariot, who,
though one of the Twelve, was later to betray
him.)

Jesus Goes to the Feast of Tabernacles

7 After this, Jesus went around in Galilee,
purposely staying away from Judea
because the Jews there were waiting to
take his life. ²But when the Jewish Feast of Tabernacles was near, ³Jesus' brothers said to him,
"You ought to leave here and go to Judea, so that
your disciples may see the miracles you do. ⁴No
one who wants to become a public figure acts in
secret. Since you are doing these things, show
yourself to the world." ⁵For even his own brothers did not believe in him.

⁶Therefore Jesus told them, "The right time
for me has not yet come; for you any time is
right. ⁷The world cannot hate you, but it hates
me because I testify that what it does is evil.
⁸You go to the Feast. I am not yet[a] going up to
this Feast, because for me the right time has not
yet come." ⁹Having said this, he stayed in Galilee.

¹⁰However, after his brothers had left for the
Feast, he went also, not publicly, but in secret.
¹¹Now at the Feast the Jews were watching for
him and asking, "Where is that man?"

¹²Among the crowds there was widespread
whispering about him. Some said, "He is a good
man."

Others replied, "No, he deceives the people."
¹³But no one would say anything publicly about
him for fear of the Jews.

Jesus Teaches at the Feast

¹⁴Not until halfway through the Feast did
Jesus go up to the temple courts and begin to
teach. ¹⁵The Jews were amazed and asked,
"How did this man get such learning without
having studied?"

---

a 8 Some early manuscripts do not have *yet*.

¹⁶Jesus answered, "My teaching is not my own. It comes from him who sent me. ¹⁷If anyone chooses to do God's will, he will find out whether my teaching comes from God or whether I speak on my own. ¹⁸He who speaks on his own does so to gain honor for himself, but he who works for the honor of the one who sent him is a man of truth; there is nothing false about him. ¹⁹Has not Moses given you the law? Yet not one of you keeps the law. Why are you trying to kill me?"

²⁰"You are demon-possessed," the crowd answered. "Who is trying to kill you?"

²¹Jesus said to them, "I did one miracle, and you are all astonished. ²²Yet, because Moses gave you circumcision (though actually it did not come from Moses, but from the patriarchs), you circumcise a child on the Sabbath. ²³Now if a child can be circumcised on the Sabbath so that the law of Moses may not be broken, why are you angry with me for healing the whole man on the Sabbath? ²⁴Stop judging by mere appearances, and make a right judgment."

Is Jesus the Christ?

²⁵At that point some of the people of Jerusalem began to ask, "Isn't this the man they are trying to kill? ²⁶Here he is, speaking publicly, and they are not saying a word to him. Have the authorities really concluded that he is the Christ^a? ²⁷But we know where this man is from; when the Christ comes, no one will know where he is from."

²⁸Then Jesus, still teaching in the temple courts, cried out, "Yes, you know me, and you know where I am from. I am not here on my own, but he who sent me is true. You do not know him, ²⁹but I know him because I am from him and he sent me."

³⁰At this they tried to seize him, but no one laid a hand on him, because his time had not yet come. ³¹Still, many in the crowd put their faith in him. They said, "When the Christ comes, will he do more miraculous signs than this man?"

³²The Pharisees heard the crowd whispering such things about him. Then the chief priests and the Pharisees sent temple guards to arrest him.

³³Jesus said, "I am with you for only a short time, and then I go to the one who sent me. ³⁴You will look for me, but you will not find me; and where I am, you cannot come."

³⁵The Jews said to one another, "Where does this man intend to go that we cannot find him?

a 26 Or Messiah; also in verses 27, 31, 41 and 42

¹⁶耶穌說："我的教訓不是我自己的，乃是那差我來者的。¹⁷人若立志遵着他的旨意行，就必曉得這教訓或是出於神，或是我憑着自己說的。¹⁸人憑着自己說，是求自己的榮耀；惟有求那差他來者的榮耀，這人是真的，在他心裏沒有不義。¹⁹摩西豈不是傳律法給你們嗎？你們卻沒有一個人守律法。為甚麼想要殺我呢？"

²⁰眾人回答說："你是被鬼附着了！誰想要殺你？"

²¹耶穌說："我做了一件事，你們都以為希奇。²²摩西傳割禮給你們（其實不是從摩西起的，乃是從祖先起的），因此你們也在安息日給人行割禮。²³人若在安息日受割禮，免得違背摩西的律法，我在安息日叫一個人全然好了，你們就向我生氣嗎？²⁴不可按外貌斷定是非，總要按公平斷定是非。"

耶穌是基督？

²⁵耶路撒冷人中有的說："這不是他們想要殺的人嗎？²⁶你看他還明明地講道，他們也不向他說甚麼，難道官長真知道這是基督嗎？²⁷然而我們知道這個人從哪裏來；只是基督來的時候，沒有人知道他從哪裏來。"

²⁸那時，耶穌在殿裏教訓人，大聲說："你們也知道我，也知道我從哪裏來；我來並不是由於自己，但那差我來的是真的。你們不認識他，²⁹我卻認識他，因為我是從他來的，他也是差了我來。"

³⁰他們就想要捉拿耶穌，只是沒有人下手，因為他的時候還沒有到。³¹但眾人中間有好些信他的，說："基督來的時候，他所行的神蹟豈能比這人所行的更多嗎？"

³²法利賽人聽見眾人為耶穌這樣紛紛議論，祭司長和法利賽人就打發差役去捉拿他。

³³於是耶穌說："我還有不多的時候和你們同在，以後就回到差我來的那裏去。³⁴你們要找我，卻找不着；我所在的地方，你們不能到。"

³⁵猶太人就彼此對問說："這人要往哪裏去，叫我們找不着呢？難道

他要往散住希臘中的猶太人那裏去教訓希臘人嗎？³⁶他說‘你們要找我，卻找不着；我所在的地方，你們不能到。’這話是甚麼意思呢？"

³⁷節期的末日，就是最大之日，耶穌站着高聲說："人若渴了，可以到我這裏來喝！³⁸信我的人，就如經上所說：‘從他腹中要流出活水的江河來。’"³⁹耶穌這話是指着信他之人要受聖靈說的。那時還沒有賜下聖靈來，因為耶穌尚未得着榮耀。

⁴⁰眾人聽見這話，有的說："這真是那先知。"

⁴¹有的說："這是基督。"

但也有的說："基督豈是從加利利出來的嗎？⁴²經上豈不是說‘基督是大衞的後裔，從大衞本鄉伯利恆出來的’嗎？"⁴³於是眾人因着耶穌起了紛爭。⁴⁴其中有人要捉拿他，只是無人下手。

猶太領袖們不信

⁴⁵差役回到祭司長和法利賽人那裏，他們對差役說："你們為甚麼沒有帶他來呢？"

⁴⁶差役回答說："從來沒有像他這樣說話的。"

⁴⁷法利賽人說："你們也受了迷惑嗎？⁴⁸官長或是法利賽人豈有信他的呢？⁴⁹但這些不明白律法的百姓是被咒詛的。"

⁵⁰內中有尼哥德慕，就是從前去見耶穌的，對他們說：⁵¹"不先聽本人的口供，不知道他所做的事，難道我們的律法還定他的罪嗎？"

⁵²他們回答說："你也是出於加利利嗎？你且去查考，就可知道加利利沒有出過先知。"

---

8 於是各人都回家去了，耶穌卻往橄欖山去。²清早又回到殿裏，眾百姓都到他那裏

Will he go where our people live scattered among the Greeks, and teach the Greeks? ³⁶What did he mean when he said, 'You will look for me, but you will not find me,' and 'Where I am, you cannot come'?"

³⁷On the last and greatest day of the Feast, Jesus stood and said in a loud voice, "If anyone is thirsty, let him come to me and drink. ³⁸Whoever believes in me, as^a the Scripture has said, streams of living water will flow from within him." ³⁹By this he meant the Spirit, whom those who believed in him were later to receive. Up to that time the Spirit had not been given, since Jesus had not yet been glorified.

⁴⁰On hearing his words, some of the people said, "Surely this man is the Prophet."

⁴¹Others said, "He is the Christ."

Still others asked, "How can the Christ come from Galilee? ⁴²Does not the Scripture say that the Christ will come from David's family^b and from Bethlehem, the town where David lived?" ⁴³Thus the people were divided because of Jesus. ⁴⁴Some wanted to seize him, but no one laid a hand on him.

Unbelief of the Jewish Leaders

⁴⁵Finally the temple guards went back to the chief priests and Pharisees, who asked them, "Why didn't you bring him in?"

⁴⁶"No one ever spoke the way this man does," the guards declared.

⁴⁷"You mean he has deceived you also?" the Pharisees retorted. ⁴⁸"Has any of the rulers or of the Pharisees believed in him? ⁴⁹No! But this mob that knows nothing of the law—there is a curse on them."

⁵⁰Nicodemus, who had gone to Jesus earlier and who was one of their own number, asked, ⁵¹"Does our law condemn anyone without first hearing him to find out what he is doing?"

⁵²They replied, "Are you from Galilee, too? Look into it, and you will find that a prophet^c does not come out of Galilee."

[The earliest and most reliable manuscripts and other ancient witnesses do not have John 7:53-8:11.]

⁵³Then each went to his own home.

8 But Jesus went to the Mount of Olives. ²At dawn he appeared again in the temple courts, where all the people gath-

---

a 37,38 Or / If anyone is thirsty, let him come to me. / And let him drink, ³⁸ who believes in me. / As　　b 42 Greek seed
c 52 Two early manuscripts the Prophet

ered around him, and he sat down to teach them. [3]The teachers of the law and the Pharisees brought in a woman caught in adultery. They made her stand before the group [4]and said to Jesus, "Teacher, this woman was caught in the act of adultery. [5]In the Law Moses commanded us to stone such women. Now what do you say?" [6]They were using this question as a trap, in order to have a basis for accusing him.

But Jesus bent down and started to write on the ground with his finger. [7]When they kept on questioning him, he straightened up and said to them, "If any one of you is without sin, let him be the first to throw a stone at her." [8]Again he stooped down and wrote on the ground.

[9]At this, those who heard began to go away one at a time, the older ones first, until only Jesus was left, with the woman still standing there. [10]Jesus straightened up and asked her, "Woman, where are they? Has no one condemned you?"

[11]"No one, sir," she said.

"Then neither do I condemn you," Jesus declared. "Go now and leave your life of sin."

The Validity of Jesus' Testimony

[12]When Jesus spoke again to the people, he said, "I am the light of the world. Whoever follows me will never walk in darkness, but will have the light of life."

[13]The Pharisees challenged him, "Here you are, appearing as your own witness; your testimony is not valid."

[14]Jesus answered, "Even if I testify on my own behalf, my testimony is valid, for I know where I came from and where I am going. But you have no idea where I come from or where I am going. [15]You judge by human standards; I pass judgment on no one. [16]But if I do judge, my decisions are right, because I am not alone. I stand with the Father, who sent me. [17]In your own Law it is written that the testimony of two men is valid. [18]I am one who testifies for myself; my other witness is the Father, who sent me."

[19]Then they asked him, "Where is your father?"

"You do not know me or my Father," Jesus replied. "If you knew me, you would know my Father also." [20]He spoke these words while teaching in the temple area near the place where the offerings were put. Yet no one seized him, because his time had not yet come.

去，他就坐下教訓他們。[3]文士和法利賽人帶着一個行淫時被拿的婦人來，叫她站在當中。[4]就對耶穌說："夫子，這婦人是正行淫之時被拿的。[5]摩西在律法上吩咐我們，把這樣的婦人用石頭打死。你說該把她怎麼樣呢？"[6]他們說這話，乃試探耶穌，要得着告他的把柄。

耶穌卻彎着腰用指頭在地上畫字。[7]他們還是不住地問他，耶穌就直起腰來，對他們說："你們中間誰是沒有罪的，誰就可以先拿石頭打她。"[8]於是又彎着腰用指頭在地上畫字。

[9]他們聽見這話，就從老到少一個一個地都出去了，只剩下耶穌一人，還有那婦人仍然站在當中。[10]耶穌就直起腰來，對她說："婦人，那些人在哪裏呢？沒有人定你的罪嗎？"

[11]她說："主啊，沒有。"

耶穌說："我也不定你的罪，去吧！從此不要再犯罪了。"

耶穌見證的真確性

[12]耶穌又對眾人說："我是世界的光。跟從我的，就不在黑暗裏走，必要得着生命的光。"

[13]法利賽人對他說："你是為自己作見證，你的見證不真。"

[14]耶穌說："我雖然為自己作見證，我的見證還是真的。因我知道我從哪裏來，往哪裏去；你們卻不知道我從哪裏來，往哪裏去。[15]你們是以外貌（註：原文作"憑肉身"）判斷人，我卻不判斷人。[16]就是判斷人，我的判斷也是真的，因為不是我獨自在這裏，還有差我來的父與我同在。[17]你們的律法上也記着說：'兩個人的見證是真的。'[18]我是為自己作見證，還有差我來的父也是為我作見證。"

[19]他們就問他說："你的父在哪裏？"

耶穌回答說："你們不認識我，也不認識我的父；若是認識我，也就認識我的父。[20]這些話是耶穌在殿裏的庫房教訓人時所說的，也沒有人拿他，因為他的時候還沒有到。

21耶穌又對他們說："我要去了，你們要找我，並且你們要死在罪中；我所去的地方，你們不能到。"

22猶太人說："他說'我所去的地方，你們不能到'，難道他要自盡嗎？"

23耶穌對他們說："你們是從下頭來的，我是從上頭來的；你們是屬這世界的，我不是屬這世界的。24所以我對你們說，你們要死在罪中；你們若不信我是基督，必要死在罪中。"

25他們就問他說："你是誰？"

耶穌對他們說："就是我從起初所告訴你們的。26我有許多事講論你們，判斷你們；但那差我來的是真的，我在他那裏所聽見的，我就傳給世人。"

27他們不明白耶穌是指着父說的。28所以耶穌說："你們舉起人子以後，必知道我是基督，並且知道我沒有一件事是憑着自己做的。我說這些話，乃是照着父所教訓我的。29那差我來的，是與我同在；他沒有撇下我獨自在這裏，因為我常做他所喜悅的事。"30耶穌說這話的時候，就有許多人信他。

亞伯拉罕的子孫

31耶穌對信他的猶太人說："你們若常常遵守我的道，就真是我的門徒。32你們必曉得真理，真理必叫你們得以自由。"

33他們回答說："我們是亞伯拉罕的後裔，從來沒有作過誰的奴僕，你怎麼說'你們必得以自由'呢？"

34耶穌回答說："我實實在在地告訴你們：所有犯罪的，就是罪的奴僕。35奴僕不能永遠住在家裏，兒子是永遠住在家裏。36所以天父的兒子若叫你們自由，你們就真自由了。37我知道你們是亞伯拉罕的子孫，你們卻想要殺我，因為你們心裏容不下我的道。38我所說的，是在我父那裏看見的；你們所行的，是在你們的父那裏聽見的。"

39他們說："我們的父就是亞伯拉罕。"

耶穌說："你們若是亞伯拉罕的兒子，就必行亞伯拉罕所行的事。40我將在神那裏所聽見的真理告

21Once more Jesus said to them, "I am going away, and you will look for me, and you will die in your sin. Where I go, you cannot come."

22This made the Jews ask, "Will he kill himself? Is that why he says, 'Where I go, you cannot come'?"

23But he continued, "You are from below; I am from above. You are of this world; I am not of this world. 24I told you that you would die in your sins; if you do not believe that I am ⌊the one I claim to be⌋,[a] you will indeed die in your sins."

25"Who are you?" they asked.

"Just what I have been claiming all along," Jesus replied. 26"I have much to say in judgment of you. But he who sent me is reliable, and what I have heard from him I tell the world."

27They did not understand that he was telling them about his Father. 28So Jesus said, "When you have lifted up the Son of Man, then you will know that I am ⌊the one I claim to be⌋ and that I do nothing on my own but speak just what the Father has taught me. 29The one who sent me is with me; he has not left me alone, for I always do what pleases him." 30Even as he spoke, many put their faith in him.

The Children of Abraham

31To the Jews who had believed him, Jesus said, "If you hold to my teaching, you are really my disciples. 32Then you will know the truth, and the truth will set you free."

33They answered him, "We are Abraham's descendants[b] and have never been slaves of anyone. How can you say that we shall be set free?"

34Jesus replied, "I tell you the truth, everyone who sins is a slave to sin. 35Now a slave has no permanent place in the family, but a son belongs to it forever. 36So if the Son sets you free, you will be free indeed. 37I know you are Abraham's descendants. Yet you are ready to kill me, because you have no room for my word. 38I am telling you what I have seen in the Father's presence, and you do what you have heard from your father.[c]"

39"Abraham is our father," they answered.

"If you were Abraham's children," said Jesus, "then you would[d] do the things Abraham did. 40As it is, you are determined to kill me, a man

a 24 Or I am he; also in verse 28　　b 33 Greek seed; also in verse 37　　c 38 Or presence. Therefore do what you have heard from the Father.　　d 39 Some early manuscripts "If you are Abraham's children," said Jesus, "then

who has told you the truth that I heard from God. Abraham did not do such things. [41]You are doing the things your own father does."

"We are not illegitimate children," they protested. "The only Father we have is God himself."

The Children of the Devil

[42]Jesus said to them, "If God were your Father, you would love me, for I came from God and now am here. I have not come on my own; but he sent me. [43]Why is my language not clear to you? Because you are unable to hear what I say. [44]You belong to your father, the devil, and you want to carry out your father's desire. He was a murderer from the beginning, not holding to the truth, for there is no truth in him. When he lies, he speaks his native language, for he is a liar and the father of lies. [45]Yet because I tell the truth, you do not believe me! [46]Can any of you prove me guilty of sin? If I am telling the truth, why don't you believe me? [47]He who belongs to God hears what God says. The reason you do not hear is that you do not belong to God."

The Claims of Jesus About Himself

[48]The Jews answered him, "Aren't we right in saying that you are a Samaritan and demon-possessed?"

[49]"I am not possessed by a demon," said Jesus, "but I honor my Father and you dishonor me. [50]I am not seeking glory for myself; but there is one who seeks it, and he is the judge. [51]I tell you the truth, if anyone keeps my word, he will never see death."

[52]At this the Jews exclaimed, "Now we know that you are demon-possessed! Abraham died and so did the prophets, yet you say that if anyone keeps your word, he will never taste death. [53]Are you greater than our father Abraham? He died, and so did the prophets. Who do you think you are?"

[54]Jesus replied, "If I glorify myself, my glory means nothing. My Father, whom you claim as your God, is the one who glorifies me. [55]Though you do not know him, I know him. If I said I did not, I would be a liar like you, but I do know him and keep his word. [56]Your father Abraham rejoiced at the thought of seeing my day; he saw it and was glad."

[57]"You are not yet fifty years old," the Jews said to him, "and you have seen Abraham!"

[58]"I tell you the truth," Jesus answered, "before Abraham was born, I am!" [59]At this, they picked up stones to stone him, but Jesus hid himself, slipping away from the temple grounds.

訴了你們，現在你們卻想要殺我！這不是亞伯拉罕所行的事，[41]你們是行你們父所行的事。"

他們說："我們不是從淫亂生的，我們只有一位父，就是神。"

魔鬼的子孫

[42]耶穌說："倘若神是你們的父，你們就必愛我，因為我本是出於神，也是從神而來，並不是由着自己來，乃是他差我來。[43]你們為甚麼不明白我的話呢？無非是因你們不能聽我的道。[44]你們是出於你們的父魔鬼，你們父的私慾，你們偏要行。他從起初是殺人的，不守真理，因他心裏沒有真理；他說謊是出於自己，因他本來是說謊的，也是說謊之人的父。[45]我將真理告訴你們，你們就因此不信我。[46]你們中間誰能指證我有罪呢？我既然將真理告訴你們，為甚麼不信我呢？[47]出於神的，必聽神的話；你們不聽，因為你們不是出於神。"

耶穌對自己的宣稱

[48]猶太人回答說："我們說你是撒馬利亞人，並且是鬼附着的，這話豈不正對嗎？"

[49]耶穌說："我不是鬼附着的，我尊敬我的父，你們倒輕慢我。[50]我不求自己的榮耀，有一位為我求榮耀、定是非的。[51]我實實在在地告訴你們：人若遵守我的道，就永遠不見死。"

[52]猶太人對他說："現在我們知道你是鬼附着的。亞伯拉罕死了，眾先知也死了，你還說'人若遵守我的道，就永遠不嘗死味'。[53]難道你比我們的祖宗亞伯拉罕還大嗎？他死了，眾先知也死了！你將自己當作甚麼人呢？"

[54]耶穌回答說："我若榮耀自己，我的榮耀就算不得甚麼；榮耀我的乃是我的父，就是你們所說是你們的神。[55]你們未曾認識他，我卻認識他。我若說不認識他，我就是說謊的，像你們一樣；但我認識他，也遵守他的道。[56]你們的祖宗亞伯拉罕歡歡喜喜地仰望我的日子，既看見了，就快樂。"

[57]猶太人說："你還沒有五十歲，豈見過亞伯拉罕呢？"

[58]耶穌說："我實實在在地告訴你們：還沒有亞伯拉罕就有了我。"[59]於是他們拿石頭要打他，耶穌卻躲藏，從殿裏出去了。

耶穌醫治來瞎眼的人

9 耶穌過去的時候，看見一個人生來是瞎眼的。²門徒問耶穌說：「拉比，這人生來是瞎眼的，是誰犯了罪？是這人呢？是他父母呢？」

³耶穌回答說：「也不是這人犯了罪，也不是他父母犯了罪，是要在他身上顯出神的作為來。⁴趁著白日，我們必須做那差我來者的工；黑夜將到，就沒有人能做工了。⁵我在世上的時候，是世上的光。」

⁶耶穌說了這話，就吐唾沫在地上，用唾沫和泥抹在瞎子的眼睛上，⁷對他說：「你往西羅亞池子裏去洗。」（「西羅亞」翻出來，就是「奉差遣」）他去一洗，回頭就看見了。

⁸他的鄰舍和那素常見他是討飯的，就說：「這不是那從前坐著討飯的人嗎？」⁹有人說：「是他。」

又有人說：「不是，卻是像他。」

他自己說：「是我。」

¹⁰他們對他說：「你的眼睛是怎麼開的呢？」

¹¹他回答說：「有一個人名叫耶穌，他和泥抹我的眼睛，對我說『你往西羅亞池子去洗』；我去一洗，就看見了。」

¹²他們說：「那個人在哪裏？」

他說：「我不知道。」

法利賽人調查醫治的事

¹³他們把從前瞎眼的人帶到法利賽人那裏。¹⁴耶穌和泥開他眼睛的日子是安息日。¹⁵法利賽人也問他是怎麼得看見的。瞎子對他們說：「他把泥抹在我的眼睛上，我去一洗，就看見了。」

¹⁶法利賽人中有的說：「這個人不是從神來的，因為他不守安息日。」

又有人說：「一個罪人怎能行這樣的神蹟呢？」他們就起了紛爭。

¹⁷他們又對瞎子說：「他既然開了你的眼睛，你說他是怎樣的人呢？」

他說：「是個先知。」

¹⁸猶太人不信他從前是瞎眼，後來能看見，等到叫了他的父母來，¹⁹問他們說：「這是你們的兒子嗎？你們說他生來是瞎眼的，如今怎麼能看見了呢？」

Jesus Heals a Man Born Blind

9 As he went along, he saw a man blind from birth. ²His disciples asked him, "Rabbi, who sinned, this man or his parents, that he was born blind?"

³"Neither this man nor his parents sinned," said Jesus, "but this happened so that the work of God might be displayed in his life. ⁴As long as it is day, we must do the work of him who sent me. Night is coming, when no one can work. ⁵While I am in the world, I am the light of the world."

⁶Having said this, he spit on the ground, made some mud with the saliva, and put it on the man's eyes. ⁷"Go," he told him, "wash in the Pool of Siloam" (this word means Sent). So the man went and washed, and came home seeing.

⁸His neighbors and those who had formerly seen him begging asked, "Isn't this the same man who used to sit and beg?" ⁹Some claimed that he was.

Others said, "No, he only looks like him."

But he himself insisted, "I am the man."

¹⁰"How then were your eyes opened?" they demanded.

¹¹He replied, "The man they call Jesus made some mud and put it on my eyes. He told me to go to Siloam and wash. So I went and washed, and then I could see."

¹²"Where is this man?" they asked him.

"I don't know," he said.

The Pharisees Investigate the Healing

¹³They brought to the Pharisees the man who had been blind. ¹⁴Now the day on which Jesus had made the mud and opened the man's eyes was a Sabbath. ¹⁵Therefore the Pharisees also asked him how he had received his sight. "He put mud on my eyes," the man replied, "and I washed, and now I see."

¹⁶Some of the Pharisees said, "This man is not from God, for he does not keep the Sabbath."

But others asked, "How can a sinner do such miraculous signs?" So they were divided.

¹⁷Finally they turned again to the blind man, "What have you to say about him? It was your eyes he opened."

The man replied, "He is a prophet."

¹⁸The Jews still did not believe that he had been blind and had received his sight until they sent for the man's parents. ¹⁹"Is this your son?" they asked. "Is this the one you say was born blind? How is it that now he can see?"

20"We know he is our son," the parents answered, "and we know he was born blind. 21But how he can see now, or who opened his eyes, we don't know. Ask him. He is of age; he will speak for himself." 22His parents said this because they were afraid of the Jews, for already the Jews had decided that anyone who acknowledged that Jesus was the Christ*a* would be put out of the synagogue. 23That was why his parents said, "He is of age; ask him."

24A second time they summoned the man who had been blind. "Give glory to God,*b*" they said. "We know this man is a sinner."

25He replied, "Whether he is a sinner or not, I don't know. One thing I do know. I was blind but now I see!"

26Then they asked him, "What did he do to you? How did he open your eyes?"

27He answered, "I have told you already and you did not listen. Why do you want to hear it again? Do you want to become his disciples, too?"

28Then they hurled insults at him and said, "You are this fellow's disciple! We are disciples of Moses! 29We know that God spoke to Moses, but as for this fellow, we don't even know where he comes from."

30The man answered, "Now that is remarkable! You don't know where he comes from, yet he opened my eyes. 31We know that God does not listen to sinners. He listens to the godly man who does his will. 32Nobody has ever heard of opening the eyes of a man born blind. 33If this man were not from God, he could do nothing."

34To this they replied, "You were steeped in sin at birth; how dare you lecture us!" And they threw him out.

Spiritual Blindness

35Jesus heard that they had thrown him out, and when he found him, he said, "Do you believe in the Son of Man?"

36"Who is he, sir?" the man asked. "Tell me so that I may believe in him."

37Jesus said, "You have now seen him; in fact, he is the one speaking with you."

38Then the man said, "Lord, I believe," and he worshiped him.

39Jesus said, "For judgment I have come into this world, so that the blind will see and those who see will become blind."

40Some Pharisees who were with him heard him say this and asked, "What? Are we blind too?"

20他父母回答說：“他是我們的兒子，生來就瞎眼，這是我們知道的。21至於他如今怎麼能看見，我們卻不知道；是誰開了他的眼睛，我們也不知道。他已經成了人，你們問他吧！他自己必能說。”22他父母說這話，是怕猶太人，因為猶太人已經商議定了，若有認耶穌是基督的，要把他趕出會堂。23因此他父母說：“他已經成了人，你們問他吧！”

24所以法利賽人第二次叫那從前瞎眼的人來，對他說：“你該將榮耀歸給神，我們知道這人是個罪人。”

25他說：“他是個罪人不是，我不知道；有一件事我知道：從前我是眼瞎的，如今能看見了！”

26他們就問他說：“他向你做甚麼？是怎麼開了你的眼睛呢？”

27他回答說：“我方才告訴你們，你們不聽，為甚麼又要聽呢？莫非你們也要作他的門徒嗎？”

28他們就罵他說：“你是他的門徒，我們是摩西的門徒！29神對摩西說話，是我們知道的；只是這個人，我們不知道他從哪裏來。”

30那人回答說：“他開了我的眼睛，你們竟不知道他從哪裏來，這真是奇怪！31我們知道神不聽罪人，惟有敬奉神、遵行他旨意的，神才聽他。32從創世以來，未曾聽見有人把生來是瞎子的眼睛開了。33這人若不是從神來的，甚麼也不能做。”

34他們回答說：“你全然生在罪孽中，還要教訓我們嗎？”於是把他趕出去了。

靈性的瞎眼

35耶穌聽說他們把他趕出去，後來遇見他，就說：“你信神的兒子嗎？”

36他回答說：“主啊，誰是神的兒子，叫我信他呢？”

37耶穌說：“你已經看見他，現在和你說話的就是他。”

38他說：“主啊，我信！”就拜耶穌。

39耶穌說：“我為審判到這世上來，叫不能看見的，可以看見；能看見的，反瞎了眼。”

40同他在那裏的法利賽人聽見這話，就說：“難道我們也瞎了眼嗎？”

---

a 22 Or *Messiah*　　*b* 24 A solemn charge to tell the truth (see Joshua 7:19)

41耶穌對他們說：「你們若瞎了眼，就沒有罪了；但如今你們說『我們能看見』，所以你們的罪還在。

牧人與羊羣

10 「我實實在在地告訴你們：人進羊圈，不從門進去，倒從別處爬進去，那人就是賊，就是強盜。2從門進去的，才是羊的牧人。3看門的就給他開門，羊也聽他的聲音。他按着名叫自己的羊，把羊領出來。4既放出自己的羊來，就在前頭走，羊也跟着他，因為認得他的聲音。5羊不跟着生人，因為不認得他的聲音，必要逃跑。」6耶穌將這比喻告訴他們，但他們不明白所說的是甚麼意思。

7所以耶穌又對他們說：「我實實在在地告訴你們：我就是羊的門。8凡在我以先來的，都是賊，是強盜，羊都不聽他們。9我就是門，凡從我進來的，必然得救，並且出入得草吃。10盜賊來，無非要偷竊、殺害、毀壞；我來了，是要叫羊（註：或作「人」）得生命，並且得的更豐盛。

11「我是好牧人，好牧人為羊捨命。12若是雇工，不是牧人，羊也不是他自己的，他看見狼來，就撇下羊逃走；狼抓住羊，趕散了羊羣。13雇工逃走，因他是雇工，並不顧念羊。

14「我是好牧人，我認識我的羊，我的羊也認識我。15正如父認識我，我也認識父一樣，並且我為羊捨命。16我另外有羊，不是這圈裏的；我必須領他們來，他們也要聽我的聲音，並且要合成一羣，歸一個牧人了。17我父愛我，因我將命捨去，好再取回來。18沒有人奪我的命去，是我自己捨的。我有權柄捨了，也有權柄取回來，這是我從我父所受的命令。」

19猶太人為這些話又起了紛爭。20內中有好些人說：「他是被鬼附着，而且瘋了，為甚麼聽他呢？」

41Jesus said, "If you were blind, you would not be guilty of sin; but now that you claim you can see, your guilt remains.

The Shepherd and His Flock

10 "I tell you the truth, the man who does not enter the sheep pen by the gate, but climbs in by some other way, is a thief and a robber. 2The man who enters by the gate is the shepherd of his sheep. 3The watchman opens the gate for him, and the sheep listen to his voice. He calls his own sheep by name and leads them out. 4When he has brought out all his own, he goes on ahead of them, and his sheep follow him because they know his voice. 5But they will never follow a stranger; in fact, they will run away from him because they do not recognize a stranger's voice." 6Jesus used this figure of speech, but they did not understand what he was telling them.

7Therefore Jesus said again, "I tell you the truth, I am the gate for the sheep. 8All who ever came before me were thieves and robbers, but the sheep did not listen to them. 9I am the gate; whoever enters through me will be saved.*a* He will come in and go out, and find pasture. 10The thief comes only to steal and kill and destroy; I have come that they may have life, and have it to the full.

11"I am the good shepherd. The good shepherd lays down his life for the sheep. 12The hired hand is not the shepherd who owns the sheep. So when he sees the wolf coming, he abandons the sheep and runs away. Then the wolf attacks the flock and scatters it. 13The man runs away because he is a hired hand and cares nothing for the sheep.

14"I am the good shepherd; I know my sheep and my sheep know me— 15just as the Father knows me and I know the Father—and I lay down my life for the sheep. 16I have other sheep that are not of this sheep pen. I must bring them also. They too will listen to my voice, and there shall be one flock and one shepherd. 17The reason my Father loves me is that I lay down my life—only to take it up again. 18No one takes it from me, but I lay it down of my own accord. I have authority to lay it down and authority to take it up again. This command I received from my Father."

19At these words the Jews were again divided. 20Many of them said, "He is demon-possessed and raving mad. Why listen to him?"

a 9 Or kept safe

21But others said, "These are not the sayings of a man possessed by a demon. Can a demon open the eyes of the blind?"

The Unbelief of the Jews

22Then came the Feast of Dedication*a* at Jerusalem. It was winter, 23and Jesus was in the temple area walking in Solomon's Colonnade. 24The Jews gathered around him, saying, "How long will you keep us in suspense? If you are the Christ,*b* tell us plainly."

25Jesus answered, "I did tell you, but you do not believe. The miracles I do in my Father's name speak for me, 26but you do not believe because you are not my sheep. 27My sheep listen to my voice; I know them, and they follow me. 28I give them eternal life, and they shall never perish; no one can snatch them out of my hand. 29My Father, who has given them to me, is greater than all*c*; no one can snatch them out of my Father's hand. 30I and the Father are one."

31Again the Jews picked up stones to stone him, 32but Jesus said to them, "I have shown you many great miracles from the Father. For which of these do you stone me?"

33"We are not stoning you for any of these," replied the Jews, "but for blasphemy, because you, a mere man, claim to be God."

34Jesus answered them, "Is it not written in your Law, 'I have said you are gods'*d*? 35If he called them 'gods,' to whom the word of God came—and the Scripture cannot be broken—36what about the one whom the Father set apart as his very own and sent into the world? Why then do you accuse me of blasphemy because I said, 'I am God's Son'? 37Do not believe me unless I do what my Father does. 38But if I do it, even though you do not believe me, believe the miracles, that you may know and understand that the Father is in me, and I in the Father." 39Again they tried to seize him, but he escaped their grasp.

40Then Jesus went back across the Jordan to the place where John had been baptizing in the early days. Here he stayed 41and many people came to him. They said, "Though John never performed a miraculous sign, all that John said about this man was true." 42And in that place many believed in Jesus.

21又有人説："這不是鬼附之人所説的話，鬼豈能叫瞎子的眼睛開了呢？"

猶太人的不信

22在耶路撒冷有修殿節，是冬天的時候。23耶穌在殿裏所羅門的廊下行走。24猶太人圍着他説："你叫我們猶疑不定到幾時呢？你若是基督，就明明地告訴我們。"

25耶穌回答説："我已經告訴你們，你們不信。我奉我父之名所行的事可以為我作見證；26只是你們不信，因為你們不是我的羊。27我的羊聽我的聲音，我也認識他們，他們也跟着我；28我又賜給他們永生，他們永不滅亡，誰也不能從我手裏把他們奪去。29我父把羊賜給我，他比萬有都大，誰也不能從我父手裏把他們奪去。30我與父原為一。"

31猶太人又拿起石頭來要打他。32耶穌對他們説："我從父顯出許多善事給你們看，你們是為哪一件拿石頭打我呢？"

33猶太人回答説："我們不是為善事拿石頭打你，是為你説僭妄的話；又為你是個人，反將自己當作神。"

34耶穌説："你們的律法上豈不是寫着'我曾説你們是神'嗎？35經上的話是不能廢的。若那些承受神道的人，尚且稱為神；36父所分別為聖，又差到世間來的，他自稱是神的兒子，你們還向他説'你説僭妄的話'嗎？37我若不行我父的事，你們就不必信我；38我若行了，你們縱然不信我，也當信這些事，叫你們又知道又明白：父在我裏面，我也在父裏面。"39他們又要拿他，他卻逃出他們的手走了。

40耶穌又往約旦河外去，到了約翰起初施洗的地方，就住在那裏。41有許多人來到他那裏，他們説："約翰一件神蹟沒有行過，但約翰指着這人所説的一切話都是真的。"42在那裏信耶穌的人就多了。

---

a 22 That is, Hanukkah   *b* 24 Or *Messiah*   *c* 29 Many early manuscripts *What my Father has given me is greater than all*   *d* 34 Psalm 82:6

拉撒路的死

11 有一個患病的人，名叫拉撒路，住在伯大尼，就是馬利亞和她姐姐馬大的村莊。²這馬利亞就是那用香膏抹主，又用頭髮擦他腳的，患病的拉撒路是她的兄弟。³他姊妹兩個就打發人去見耶穌說：「主啊，你所愛的人病了。」

⁴耶穌聽見就說：「這病不至於死，乃是為神的榮耀，叫神的兒子因此得榮耀。」⁵耶穌素來愛馬大和她妹子並拉撒路，⁶聽見拉撒路病了，就在所居之地仍住了兩天。

⁷然後對門徒說：「我們再往猶太去吧！」

⁸門徒說：「拉比，猶太人近來要拿石頭打你，你還往那裏去嗎？」

⁹耶穌回答說：「白日不是有十二小時嗎？人在白日走路，就不至跌倒，因為看見這世上的光；¹⁰若在黑夜走路，就必跌倒，因為他沒有光。」

¹¹耶穌說了這話，隨後對他們說：「我們的朋友拉撒路睡了，我去叫醒他。」

¹²門徒說：「主啊，他若睡了，就必好了。」¹³耶穌這話是指著他死說的，他們卻以為是說照常睡了。

¹⁴耶穌就明明地告訴他們說：「拉撒路死了。¹⁵我沒有在那裏就歡喜，這是為你們的緣故，好叫你們相信。如今我們可以往他那裏去吧！」

¹⁶多馬，又稱為低土馬，就對那同作門徒的說：「我們也去和他同死吧。」

耶穌安慰姐妹二人

¹⁷耶穌到了，就知道拉撒路在墳墓裏已經四天了。¹⁸伯大尼離耶路撒冷不遠，約有六里路。¹⁹有好些猶太人來看馬大和馬利亞，要為她們的兄弟安慰她們。²⁰馬大聽見耶穌來了，就出去迎接他；馬利亞卻仍然坐在家裏。

²¹馬大對耶穌說：「主啊，你若早在這裏，我兄弟必不死！²²就是現在，我也知道，你無論向神求甚麼，神也必賜給你。」

²³耶穌說：「你兄弟必然復活。」

The Death of Lazarus

11 Now a man named Lazarus was sick. He was from Bethany, the village of Mary and her sister Martha. ²This Mary, whose brother Lazarus now lay sick, was the same one who poured perfume on the Lord and wiped his feet with her hair. ³So the sisters sent word to Jesus, "Lord, the one you love is sick."

⁴When he heard this, Jesus said, "This sickness will not end in death. No, it is for God's glory so that God's Son may be glorified through it." ⁵Jesus loved Martha and her sister and Lazarus. ⁶Yet when he heard that Lazarus was sick, he stayed where he was two more days.

⁷Then he said to his disciples, "Let us go back to Judea."

⁸"But Rabbi," they said, "a short while ago the Jews tried to stone you, and yet you are going back there?"

⁹Jesus answered, "Are there not twelve hours of daylight? A man who walks by day will not stumble, for he sees by this world's light. ¹⁰It is when he walks by night that he stumbles, for he has no light."

¹¹After he had said this, he went on to tell them, "Our friend Lazarus has fallen asleep; but I am going there to wake him up."

¹²His disciples replied, "Lord, if he sleeps, he will get better." ¹³Jesus had been speaking of his death, but his disciples thought he meant natural sleep.

¹⁴So then he told them plainly, "Lazarus is dead, ¹⁵and for your sake I am glad I was not there, so that you may believe. But let us go to him."

¹⁶Then Thomas (called Didymus) said to the rest of the disciples, "Let us also go, that we may die with him."

Jesus Comforts the Sisters

¹⁷On his arrival, Jesus found that Lazarus had already been in the tomb for four days. ¹⁸Bethany was less than two miles*a* from Jerusalem, ¹⁹and many Jews had come to Martha and Mary to comfort them in the loss of their brother. ²⁰When Martha heard that Jesus was coming, she went out to meet him, but Mary stayed at home.

²¹"Lord," Martha said to Jesus, "if you had been here, my brother would not have died. ²²But I know that even now God will give you whatever you ask."

²³Jesus said to her, "Your brother will rise again."

a 18 Greek *fifteen stadia* (about 3 kilometers)

[24]Martha answered, "I know he will rise again in the resurrection at the last day."

[25]Jesus said to her, "I am the resurrection and the life. He who believes in me will live, even though he dies; [26]and whoever lives and believes in me will never die. Do you believe this?"

[27]"Yes, Lord," she told him, "I believe that you are the Christ,[a] the Son of God, who was to come into the world."

[28]And after she had said this, she went back and called her sister Mary aside. "The Teacher is here," she said, "and is asking for you." [29]When Mary heard this, she got up quickly and went to him. [30]Now Jesus had not yet entered the village, but was still at the place where Martha had met him. [31]When the Jews who had been with Mary in the house, comforting her, noticed how quickly she got up and went out, they followed her, supposing she was going to the tomb to mourn there.

[32]When Mary reached the place where Jesus was and saw him, she fell at his feet and said, "Lord, if you had been here, my brother would not have died."

[33]When Jesus saw her weeping, and the Jews who had come along with her also weeping, he was deeply moved in spirit and troubled. [34]"Where have you laid him?" he asked.

"Come and see, Lord," they replied.

[35]Jesus wept.

[36]Then the Jews said, "See how he loved him!"

[37]But some of them said, "Could not he who opened the eyes of the blind man have kept this man from dying?"

Jesus Raises Lazarus From the Dead

[38]Jesus, once more deeply moved, came to the tomb. It was a cave with a stone laid across the entrance. [39]"Take away the stone," he said.

"But, Lord," said Martha, the sister of the dead man, "by this time there is a bad odor, for he has been there four days."

[40]Then Jesus said, "Did I not tell you that if you believed, you would see the glory of God?"

[41]So they took away the stone. Then Jesus looked up and said, "Father, I thank you that you have heard me. [42]I knew that you always hear me, but I said this for the benefit of the people standing here, that they may believe that you sent me."

[24]馬大說："我知道在末日復活的時候，他必復活。"

[25]耶穌對她說："復活在我，生命也在我！信我的人，雖然死了，也必復活。[26]凡活着信我的人必永遠不死。你信這話嗎？"

[27]馬大說："主啊，是的，我信你是基督，是神的兒子，就是那要臨到世界的。"

[28]馬大說了這話，就回去暗暗地叫她妹子馬利亞來："夫子來了，叫你。"[29]馬利亞聽見了，就急忙起來，到耶穌那裏去。[30]那時，耶穌還沒有進村子，仍在馬大迎接他的地方。[31]那些同馬利亞在家裏安慰她的猶太人，見她急忙起來出去，就跟着她，以為她要往墳墓那裏去哭。

[32]馬利亞到了耶穌那裏，看見他，就俯伏在他腳前，說："主啊，你若早在這裏，我兄弟必不死。"

[33]耶穌看見她哭，並看見與她同來的猶太人也哭，就心裏悲歎，又甚憂愁，[34]便說："你們把他安放在哪裏？"

他們回答說："請主來看。"

[35]耶穌哭了。

[36]猶太人就說："你看他愛這人是何等懇切。"

[37]其中有人說："他既然開了瞎子的眼睛，豈不能叫這人不死嗎？"

耶穌使拉撒路復活

[38]耶穌又心裏悲歎，來到墳墓前；那墳墓是個洞，有一塊石頭擋着。[39]耶穌說："你們把石頭挪開！"

那死人的姐姐馬大對他說："主啊，他現在必是臭了，因為他死了已經四天了。"

[40]耶穌說："我不是對你說過，你若信，就必看見神的榮耀嗎？"

[41]他們就把石頭挪開。耶穌舉目望天說："父啊，我感謝你，因為你已經聽我；[42]我也知道你常聽我。但我說這話，是為周圍站着的眾人，叫他們信是你差了我來。"

43說了這話，就大聲呼叫說："拉撒路出來！"44那死人就出來了，手腳裹着布，臉上包着手巾。

耶穌對他們說："解開，叫他走！"

密謀殺害耶穌

45那些來看馬利亞的猶太人，見了耶穌所做的事，就多有信他的。46但其中也有去見法利賽人的，將耶穌所做的事告訴他們。47祭司長和法利賽人聚集公會，說：

"這人行好些神蹟，我們怎麼辦呢？48若這樣由着他，人人都要信他，羅馬人也要來奪我們的地土和我們的百姓。"

49內中有一個人，名叫該亞法，本年作大祭司，對他們說："你們不知道甚麼。50獨不想一個人替百姓死，免得通國滅亡，就是你們的益處。"

51他這話不是出於自己，是因他本年作大祭司，所以預言耶穌將要替這一國死。52也不但替這一國死，並要將神四散的子民都聚集歸一。53從那日起他們就商議要殺耶穌。

54所以耶穌不再顯然行在猶太人中間，就離開那裏往靠近曠野的地方去。到了一座城，名叫以法蓮，就在那裏和門徒同住。

55猶太人的逾越節近了，有許多人從鄉下上耶路撒冷去，要在節前潔淨自己。56他們就尋找耶穌，站在殿裏彼此說："你們的意思如何？他不來過節嗎？"57那時，祭司長和法利賽人早已吩咐說："若有人知道耶穌在哪裏，就要報明，好去拿他。"

耶穌在伯大尼受膏

12 逾越節前六日，耶穌來到伯大尼，就是他叫拉撒路從死裏復活之處。2有人在那裏給耶穌預備筵席，馬大伺候，拉撒路也在那同耶穌坐席的人中。3馬利亞就拿着一斤極貴的真哪噠香膏抹耶穌

43When he had said this, Jesus called in a loud voice, "Lazarus, come out!" 44The dead man came out, his hands and feet wrapped with strips of linen, and a cloth around his face.

Jesus said to them, "Take off the grave clothes and let him go."

The Plot to Kill Jesus

45Therefore many of the Jews who had come to visit Mary, and had seen what Jesus did, put their faith in him. 46But some of them went to the Pharisees and told them what Jesus had done. 47Then the chief priests and the Pharisees called a meeting of the Sanhedrin.

"What are we accomplishing?" they asked. "Here is this man performing many miraculous signs. 48If we let him go on like this, everyone will believe in him, and then the Romans will come and take away both our place*a* and our nation."

49Then one of them, named Caiaphas, who was high priest that year, spoke up, "You know nothing at all! 50You do not realize that it is better for you that one man die for the people than that the whole nation perish."

51He did not say this on his own, but as high priest that year he prophesied that Jesus would die for the Jewish nation, 52and not only for that nation but also for the scattered children of God, to bring them together and make them one. 53So from that day on they plotted to take his life.

54Therefore Jesus no longer moved about publicly among the Jews. Instead he withdrew to a region near the desert, to a village called Ephraim, where he stayed with his disciples.

55When it was almost time for the Jewish Passover, many went up from the country to Jerusalem for their ceremonial cleansing before the Passover. 56They kept looking for Jesus, and as they stood in the temple area they asked one another, "What do you think? Isn't he coming to the Feast at all?" 57But the chief priests and Pharisees had given orders that if anyone found out where Jesus was, he should report it so that they might arrest him.

Jesus Anointed at Bethany

12 Six days before the Passover, Jesus arrived at Bethany, where Lazarus lived, whom Jesus had raised from the dead. 2Here a dinner was given in Jesus' honor. Martha served, while Lazarus was among those reclining at the table with him. 3Then Mary took about a pint*b* of pure nard, an expensive perfume; she poured it on Jesus' feet and wiped his

---

a 48 Or temple　b 3 Greek a litra (probably about 0.5 liter)

feet with her hair. And the house was filled with the fragrance of the perfume.

⁴But one of his disciples, Judas Iscariot, who was later to betray him, objected, ⁵"Why wasn't this perfume sold and the money given to the poor? It was worth a year's wages.ᵃ" ⁶He did not say this because he cared about the poor but because he was a thief; as keeper of the money bag, he used to help himself to what was put into it.

⁷"Leave her alone," Jesus replied. "⌞It was intended⌟ that she should save this perfume for the day of my burial. ⁸You will always have the poor among you, but you will not always have me."

⁹Meanwhile a large crowd of Jews found out that Jesus was there and came, not only because of him but also to see Lazarus, whom he had raised from the dead. ¹⁰So the chief priests made plans to kill Lazarus as well, ¹¹for on account of him many of the Jews were going over to Jesus and putting their faith in him.

The Triumphal Entry

¹²The next day the great crowd that had come for the Feast heard that Jesus was on his way to Jerusalem. ¹³They took palm branches and went out to meet him, shouting,

"Hosanna!ᵇ"

"Blessed is he who comes in the name of the Lord!"ᶜ

"Blessed is the King of Israel!"

¹⁴Jesus found a young donkey and sat upon it, as it is written,

¹⁵"Do not be afraid, O Daughter of Zion;
see, your king is coming,
seated on a donkey's colt."ᵈ

¹⁶At first his disciples did not understand all this. Only after Jesus was glorified did they realize that these things had been written about him and that they had done these things to him.

¹⁷Now the crowd that was with him when he called Lazarus from the tomb and raised him from the dead continued to spread the word. ¹⁸Many people, because they had heard that he had done this miraculous sign, went out to meet

---

的腳，又用自己頭髮去擦，屋裏就滿了膏的香氣。

⁴有一個門徒，就是那將要賣耶穌的<u>加略人猶大</u>，⁵說：「這香膏為甚麼不賣三十兩銀子賙濟窮人呢？」⁶他說這話，並不是掛念窮人，乃因他是個賊，又帶着錢囊，常取其中所存的。

⁷耶穌說：「由她吧！她是為我安葬之日存留的。⁸因為常有窮人和你們同在，只是你們不常有我。」

⁹有許多<u>猶太</u>人知道耶穌在那裏，就來了，不但是為耶穌的緣故，也是要看他從死裏所復活的<u>拉撒路</u>。¹⁰但祭司長商議連<u>拉撒路</u>也要殺了，¹¹因有好些<u>猶太</u>人為<u>拉撒路</u>的緣故，回去信了耶穌。

光榮進聖城

¹²第二天，有許多上來過節的人，聽見耶穌將到<u>耶路撒冷</u>，¹³就拿着棕樹枝，出去迎接他，喊着說：

「和散那！」

「奉主名來的<u>以色列</u>王是應當稱頌的！」

¹⁴耶穌得了一個驢駒，就騎上，如經上所記的說：

¹⁵「<u>錫安</u>的民哪（註：「民」原文作「女子」），不要懼怕！你的王騎着驢駒來了。」

¹⁶這些事門徒起先不明白，等到耶穌得了榮耀以後，才想起這話是指着他寫的，並且眾人果然向他這樣行了。

¹⁷當耶穌呼喚<u>拉撒路</u>，叫他從死復活出墳墓的時候，同耶穌在那裏的眾人就作見證。¹⁸眾人因聽見耶穌行

---

a 5 Greek three hundred denarii   b 13 A Hebrew expression meaning "Save!" which became an exclamation of praise   c 13 Psalm 118:25, 26   d 15 Zech. 9:9

了這神蹟，就去迎接他。¹⁹法利賽人彼此説：「看哪，你們是徒勞無益，世人都隨從他去了。」

耶穌預言自己的死

²⁰那時，上來過節禮拜的人中，有幾個希臘人。²¹他們來見加利利 伯賽大的腓力，求他説：「先生，我們願意見耶穌。」²²腓力去告訴安得烈，安得烈同腓力去告訴耶穌。

²³耶穌説：「人子得榮耀的時候到了。²⁴我實實在在地告訴你們：一粒麥子不落在地裏死了，仍舊是一粒；若是死了，就結出許多子粒來。²⁵愛惜自己生命的，就失喪生命；在這世上恨惡自己生命的，就要保守生命到永生。²⁶若有人服侍我，就當跟從我；我在哪裏，服侍我的人也要在那裏；若有人服侍我，我父必尊重他。

²⁷「我現在心裏憂愁，我説甚麼才好呢？父啊，救我脱離這時候，但我原是為這時候來的。²⁸父啊，願你榮耀你的名。」

當時就有聲音從天上來説：「我已經榮耀了我的名，還要再榮耀。」²⁹站在旁邊的眾人聽見，就説：「打雷了。」還有人説：「有天使對他説話。」

³⁰耶穌説：「這聲音不是為我，是為你們來的。³¹現在這世界受審判，這世界的王要被趕出去。³²我若從地上被舉起來，就要吸引萬人來歸我。」³³耶穌這話原是指着自己將要怎樣死説的。

³⁴眾人回答説：「我們聽見律法上有話説『基督是永存的』，你怎麼説『人子必須被舉起來』呢？這人子是誰呢？」

³⁵耶穌對他們説：「光在你們中間還有不多的時候，應當趁着有光行走，免得黑暗臨到你們；那在黑暗裏行走的，不知道往何處去。³⁶你們應當趁着有光，信從這光，使你們成為光明之子。」耶穌説了這話，就離開他們，隱藏了。

猶太人仍舊不信

³⁷他雖然在他們面前行了許多神蹟，他們還是不信他。³⁸這是要應驗先知以賽亞的話，説：

him. ¹⁹So the Pharisees said to one another, "See, this is getting us nowhere. Look how the whole world has gone after him!"

Jesus Predicts His Death

²⁰Now there were some Greeks among those who went up to worship at the Feast. ²¹They came to Philip, who was from Bethsaida in Galilee, with a request. "Sir," they said, "we would like to see Jesus." ²²Philip went to tell Andrew; Andrew and Philip in turn told Jesus.

²³Jesus replied, "The hour has come for the Son of Man to be glorified. ²⁴I tell you the truth, unless a kernel of wheat falls to the ground and dies, it remains only a single seed. But if it dies, it produces many seeds. ²⁵The man who loves his life will lose it, while the man who hates his life in this world will keep it for eternal life. ²⁶Whoever serves me must follow me; and where I am, my servant also will be. My Father will honor the one who serves me.

²⁷"Now my heart is troubled, and what shall I say? 'Father, save me from this hour'? No, it was for this very reason I came to this hour. ²⁸Father, glorify your name!"

Then a voice came from heaven, "I have glorified it, and will glorify it again." ²⁹The crowd that was there and heard it said it had thundered; others said an angel had spoken to him.

³⁰Jesus said, "This voice was for your benefit, not mine. ³¹Now is the time for judgment on this world; now the prince of this world will be driven out. ³²But I, when I am lifted up from the earth, will draw all men to myself." ³³He said this to show the kind of death he was going to die.

³⁴The crowd spoke up, "We have heard from the Law that the Christ*ᵃ* will remain forever, so how can you say, 'The Son of Man must be lifted up'? Who is this 'Son of Man'?"

³⁵Then Jesus told them, "You are going to have the light just a little while longer. Walk while you have the light, before darkness overtakes you. The man who walks in the dark does not know where he is going. ³⁶Put your trust in the light while you have it, so that you may become sons of light." When he had finished speaking, Jesus left and hid himself from them.

The Jews Continue in Their Unbelief

³⁷Even after Jesus had done all these miraculous signs in their presence, they still would not believe in him. ³⁸This was to fulfill the word of Isaiah the prophet:

a 34 Or Messiah

"Lord, who has believed our message
and to whom has the arm of the Lord been
revealed?"[a]

[39] For this reason they could not believe,
because, as Isaiah says elsewhere:

[40] "He has blinded their eyes
and deadened their hearts,
so they can neither see with their eyes,
nor understand with their hearts,
nor turn—and I would heal them."[b]

[41] Isaiah said this because he saw Jesus' glory and
spoke about him.

[42] Yet at the same time many even among the
leaders believed in him. But because of the Pharisees they would not confess their faith for fear
they would be put out of the synagogue; [43] for
they loved praise from men more than praise
from God.

[44] Then Jesus cried out, "When a man believes
in me, he does not believe in me only, but in the
one who sent me. [45] When he looks at me, he
sees the one who sent me. [46] I have come into the
world as a light, so that no one who believes in
me should stay in darkness.

[47] "As for the person who hears my words but
does not keep them, I do not judge him. For I
did not come to judge the world, but to save it.
[48] There is a judge for the one who rejects me
and does not accept my words; that very word
which I spoke will condemn him at the last day.
[49] For I did not speak of my own accord, but the
Father who sent me commanded me what to say
and how to say it. [50] I know that his command
leads to eternal life. So whatever I say is just
what the Father has told me to say."

Jesus Washes His Disciples' Feet

13 It was just before the Passover Feast.
Jesus knew that the time had come for
him to leave this world and go to the
Father. Having loved his own who were in the
world, he now showed them the full extent of
his love.[c]

[2] The evening meal was being served, and the
devil had already prompted Judas Iscariot, son
of Simon, to betray Jesus. [3] Jesus knew that the
Father had put all things under his power, and
that he had come from God and was returning
to God; [4] so he got up from the meal, took off his

"主啊，
我們所傳的有誰信呢？
主的膀臂向誰顯露呢？"

[39] 他們所以不能信，因為以賽亞
又說：

[40] "主叫他們瞎了眼、
硬了心，
免得他們眼睛看見，
心裏明白，回轉過來，
我就醫治他們。"

[41] 以賽亞因為看見他的榮耀，就指着
他說這話。

[42] 雖然如此，官長中卻有好些信
他的，只因法利賽人的緣故，就不承
認，恐怕被趕出會堂。[43] 這是因他們
愛人的榮耀過於愛神的榮耀。

[44] 耶穌大聲說："信我的，不是
信我，乃是信那差我來的。[45] 人看見
我，就是看見那差我來的。[46] 我到世
上來，乃是光，叫凡信我的，不住在
黑暗裏。

[47] "若有人聽見我的話不遵守，
我不審判他。我來本不是要審判世
界，乃是要拯救世界。[48] 棄絕我、不
領受我話的人，有審判他的，就是我
所講的道，在末日要審判他。[49] 因為
我沒有憑着自己講，惟有差我來的
父，已經給我命令，叫我說甚麼、講
甚麼。[50] 我也知道他的命令就是永
生。故此，我所講的話正是照着父對
我所說的。"

耶穌洗門徒的腳

13 逾越節以前，耶穌知道自己
離世歸父的時候到了，他既
然愛世間屬自己的人，就愛
他們到底。

[2] 吃晚飯的時候（魔鬼已將賣耶
穌的意思放在西門的兒子加略人猶大
心裏），[3] 耶穌知道父已將萬有交在
他手裏，且知道自己是從神出來的，
又要歸到神那裏去，[4] 就離席站起來

---

a 38 Isaiah 53:1   *b 40* Isaiah 6:10   *c 1* Or *he loved them to the
last*

脫了衣服，拿一條手巾束腰，5隨後把水倒在盆裏，就洗門徒的腳，並用自己所束的手巾擦乾。

6挨到西門彼得，彼得對他說："主啊，你洗我的腳嗎？"

7耶穌回答說："我所做的，你如今不知道，後來必明白。"

8彼得說："你永不可洗我的腳！"

耶穌說："我若不洗你，你就與我無分了。"

9西門彼得說："主啊，不但我的腳，連手和頭也要洗！。"

10耶穌說："凡洗過澡的人，只要把腳一洗，全身就乾淨了；你們是乾淨的，然而不都是乾淨的。"11耶穌原知道要賣他的是誰，所以說："你們不都是乾淨的。"

12耶穌洗完了他們的腳，就穿上衣服，又坐下，對他們說："我向你們所做的，你們明白嗎？13你們稱呼我夫子，稱呼我主，你們說的不錯，我本來是。14我是你們的主，你們的夫子，尚且洗你們的腳，你們也當彼此洗腳。15我給你們作了榜樣，叫你們照着我向你們所做的去做。16我實實在在地告訴你們：僕人不能大於主人，差人也不能大於差他的人。17你們既知道這事，若是去行就有福了。

耶穌預言自己被出賣

18"我這話不是指着你們眾人說的，我知道我所揀選的是誰。現在要應驗經上的話，說：'同我吃飯的人，用腳踢我。'

19"如今事情還沒有成就，我要先告訴你們，叫你們到事情成就的時候，可以信我是基督。20我實實在在地告訴你們：有人接待我所差遣的，就是接待我；接待我，就是接待那差遣我的。"

21耶穌說了這話，心裏憂愁，就明說："我實實在在地告訴你們：你們中間有一個人要賣我了。"

22門徒彼此對看，猜不透所說的是誰。23有一個門徒，是耶穌所愛的，側身挨近耶穌的懷裏。24西門彼得點頭對他說："你告訴我們，主是指着誰說的。"

outer clothing, and wrapped a towel around his waist. 5After that, he poured water into a basin and began to wash his disciples' feet, drying them with the towel that was wrapped around him.

6He came to Simon Peter, who said to him, "Lord, are you going to wash my feet?"

7Jesus replied, "You do not realize now what I am doing, but later you will understand."

8"No," said Peter, "you shall never wash my feet."

Jesus answered, "Unless I wash you, you have no part with me."

9"Then, Lord," Simon Peter replied, "not just my feet but my hands and my head as well!"

10Jesus answered, "A person who has had a bath needs only to wash his feet; his whole body is clean. And you are clean, though not every one of you." 11For he knew who was going to betray him, and that was why he said not every one was clean.

12When he had finished washing their feet, he put on his clothes and returned to his place. "Do you understand what I have done for you?" he asked them. 13"You call me 'Teacher' and 'Lord,' and rightly so, for that is what I am. 14Now that I, your Lord and Teacher, have washed your feet, you also should wash one another's feet. 15I have set you an example that you should do as I have done for you. 16I tell you the truth, no servant is greater than his master, nor is a messenger greater than the one who sent him. 17Now that you know these things, you will be blessed if you do them.

Jesus Predicts His Betrayal

18"I am not referring to all of you; I know those I have chosen. But this is to fulfill the scripture: 'He who shares my bread has lifted up his heel against me.'[a]

19"I am telling you now before it happens, so that when it does happen you will believe that I am He. 20I tell you the truth, whoever accepts anyone I send accepts me; and whoever accepts me accepts the one who sent me."

21After he had said this, Jesus was troubled in spirit and testified, "I tell you the truth, one of you is going to betray me."

22His disciples stared at one another, at a loss to know which of them he meant. 23One of them, the disciple whom Jesus loved, was reclining next to him. 24Simon Peter motioned to this disciple and said, "Ask him which one he means."

a 18 Psalm 41:9

25Leaning back against Jesus, he asked him, "Lord, who is it?"

26Jesus answered, "It is the one to whom I will give this piece of bread when I have dipped it in the dish." Then, dipping the piece of bread, he gave it to Judas Iscariot, son of Simon. 27As soon as Judas took the bread, Satan entered into him.

"What you are about to do, do quickly," Jesus told him, 28but no one at the meal understood why Jesus said this to him. 29Since Judas had charge of the money, some thought Jesus was telling him to buy what was needed for the Feast, or to give something to the poor. 30As soon as Judas had taken the bread, he went out. And it was night.

Jesus Predicts Peter's Denial

31When he was gone, Jesus said, "Now is the Son of Man glorified and God is glorified in him. 32If God is glorified in him,a God will glorify the Son in himself, and will glorify him at once.

33"My children, I will be with you only a little longer. You will look for me, and just as I told the Jews, so I tell you now: Where I am going, you cannot come.

34"A new command I give you: Love one another. As I have loved you, so you must love one another. 35By this all men will know that you are my disciples, if you love one another."

36Simon Peter asked him, "Lord, where are you going?"

Jesus replied, "Where I am going, you cannot follow now, but you will follow later."

37Peter asked, "Lord, why can't I follow you now? I will lay down my life for you."

38Then Jesus answered, "Will you really lay down your life for me? I tell you the truth, before the rooster crows, you will disown me three times!

Jesus Comforts His Disciples

14 "Do not let your hearts be troubled. Trust in Godb; trust also in me. 2In my Father's house are many rooms; if it were not so, I would have told you. I am going there to prepare a place for you. 3And if I go and prepare a place for you, I will come back and take you to be with me that you also may be where I am. 4You know the way to the place where I am going."

25那門徒便就勢靠着耶穌的胸膛，問他說："主啊，是誰呢？"

26耶穌回答說："我蘸一點餅給誰，就是誰。"耶穌就蘸了一點餅，遞給加略人西門的兒子猶大。27他吃了以後，撒但就入了他的心。

耶穌便對他說："你所做的，快做吧！"28同席的人，沒有一個知道是為甚麼對他說這話。29有人因猶大帶着錢囊，以為耶穌是對他說"你去買我們過節所應用的東西"，或是叫他拿甚麼賙濟窮人。30猶大受了那點餅，立刻就出去。那時候是夜間了。

耶穌預言彼得不認主

31他既出去，耶穌就說："如今人子得了榮耀，神在人子身上也得了榮耀。32神要因自己榮耀人子，並且要快快地榮耀他。

33"小子們，我還有不多的時候與你們同在，後來你們要找我，但我所去的地方你們不能到。這話我曾對猶太人說過，如今也照樣對你們說。

34"我賜給你們一條新命令，乃是叫你們彼此相愛；我怎樣愛你們，你們也要怎樣相愛。35你們若有彼此相愛的心，眾人因此就認出你們是我的門徒了。"

36西門彼得問耶穌說："主往哪裏去？"耶穌回答說："我所去的地方，你現在不能跟我去，後來卻要跟我去。"

37彼得說："主啊，我為甚麼現在不能跟你去？我願意為你捨命。"

38耶穌說："你願意為我捨命嗎？我實實在在地告訴你：雞叫以先，你要三次不認我。

耶穌安慰門徒

14 "你們心裏不要憂愁，你們信神，也當信我。2在我父的家裏有許多住處；若是沒有，我就早已告訴你們了；我去原是為你們預備地方去。3我若去為你們預備了地方，就必再來接你們到我那裏去；我在哪裏，叫你們也在那裏。4我往哪裏去，你們知道；那條路，你們也知道（註：有古卷作"我往哪裏去，你們知道那條路"）。"

---

a 32 Many early manuscripts do not have If God is glorified in him.   b 1 Or You trust in God

耶穌是到父那裏去的路

5多馬對他說："主啊，我們不知道你往哪裏去，怎麼知道那條路呢？"

6耶穌說："我就是道路、真理、生命；若不藉着我，沒有人能到父那裏去。7你們若認識我，也就認識我的父。從今以後，你們認識他，並且已經看見他。"

8腓力對他說："求主將父顯給我們看，我們就知足了。"

9耶穌對他說："腓力，我與你們同在這樣長久，你還不認識我嗎？人看見了我，就是看見了父，你怎麼說'將父顯給我們看'呢？10我在父裏面，父在我裏面，你不信嗎？我對你們所說的話，不是憑着自己說的，乃是住在我裏面的父做他自己的事。11你們當信我，我在父裏面，父在我裏面；即或不信，也當因我所做的事信我。12我實實在在地告訴你們：我所做的事，信我的人也要做；並且要做比這更大的事，因為我往父那裏去。13你們奉我的名無論求甚麼，我必成就，叫父因兒子得榮耀。14你們若奉我的名求甚麼，我必成就。

耶穌應許賜聖靈

15"你們若愛我，就必遵守我的命令。16我要求父，父就另外賜給你們一位保惠師（註：或作"訓慰師"。下同），叫他永遠與你們同在，17就是真理的聖靈，乃世人不能接受的，因為不見他，也不認識他；你們卻認識他，因他常與你們同在，也要在你們裏面。18我不撇下你們為孤兒，我必到你們這裏來。19還有不多的時候，世人不再看見我；你們卻看見我，因為我活着，你們也要活着。20到那日你們就知道我在父裏面，你們在我裏面，我也在你們裏面。21有了我的命令又遵守的，這人就是愛我的；愛我的必蒙我父愛他，我也要愛他，並且要向他顯現。"

22猶大（不是加略人猶大）問耶穌說："主啊，為甚麼要向我們顯現，不向世人顯現呢？"

23耶穌回答說："人若愛我，就必遵守我的道，我父也必愛他，並且我們要到他那裏去，與他同住。

Jesus the Way to the Father

5Thomas said to him, "Lord, we don't know where you are going, so how can we know the way?"

6Jesus answered, "I am the way and the truth and the life. No one comes to the Father except through me. 7If you really knew me, you would know[a] my Father as well. From now on, you do know him and have seen him."

8Philip said, "Lord, show us the Father and that will be enough for us."

9Jesus answered: "Don't you know me, Philip, even after I have been among you such a long time? Anyone who has seen me has seen the Father. How can you say, 'Show us the Father'? 10Don't you believe that I am in the Father, and that the Father is in me? The words I say to you are not just my own. Rather, it is the Father, living in me, who is doing his work. 11Believe me when I say that I am in the Father and the Father is in me; or at least believe on the evidence of the miracles themselves. 12I tell you the truth, anyone who has faith in me will do what I have been doing. He will do even greater things than these, because I am going to the Father. 13And I will do whatever you ask in my name, so that the Son may bring glory to the Father. 14You may ask me for anything in my name, and I will do it.

Jesus Promises the Holy Spirit

15"If you love me, you will obey what I command. 16And I will ask the Father, and he will give you another Counselor to be with you forever— 17the Spirit of truth. The world cannot accept him, because it neither sees him nor knows him. But you know him, for he lives with you and will be[b] in you. 18I will not leave you as orphans; I will come to you. 19Before long, the world will not see me anymore, but you will see me. Because I live, you also will live. 20On that day you will realize that I am in my Father, and you are in me, and I am in you. 21Whoever has my commands and obeys them, he is the one who loves me. He who loves me will be loved by my Father, and I too will love him and show myself to him."

22Then Judas (not Judas Iscariot) said, "But, Lord, why do you intend to show yourself to us and not to the world?"

23Jesus replied, "If anyone loves me, he will obey my teaching. My Father will love him, and we will come to him and make our home with

---

a 7 Some early manuscripts *If you really have known me, you will know*　b 17 Some early manuscripts *and is* him. 24He who does not love me will not obey my teaching. These words you hear are not my own; they belong to the Father who sent me.

25"All this I have spoken while still with you. 26But the Counselor, the Holy Spirit, whom the Father will send in my name, will teach you all things and will remind you of everything I have said to you. 27Peace I leave with you; my peace I give you. I do not give to you as the world gives. Do not let your hearts be troubled and do not be afraid.

28"You heard me say, 'I am going away and I am coming back to you.' If you loved me, you would be glad that I am going to the Father, for the Father is greater than I. 29I have told you now before it happens, so that when it does happen you will believe. 30I will not speak with you much longer, for the prince of this world is coming. He has no hold on me, 31but the world must learn that I love the Father and that I do exactly what my Father has commanded me.

"Come now; let us leave.

The Vine and the Branches

15 "I am the true vine, and my Father is the gardener. 2He cuts off every branch in me that bears no fruit, while every branch that does bear fruit he prunes[a] so that it will be even more fruitful. 3You are already clean because of the word I have spoken to you. 4Remain in me, and I will remain in you. No branch can bear fruit by itself; it must remain in the vine. Neither can you bear fruit unless you remain in me.

5"I am the vine; you are the branches. If a man remains in me and I in him, he will bear much fruit; apart from me you can do nothing. 6If anyone does not remain in me, he is like a branch that is thrown away and withers; such branches are picked up, thrown into the fire and burned. 7If you remain in me and my words remain in you, ask whatever you wish, and it will be given you. 8This is to my Father's glory, that you bear much fruit, showing yourselves to be my disciples.

9"As the Father has loved me, so have I loved you. Now remain in my love. 10If you obey my commands, you will remain in my love, just as I have obeyed my Father's commands and remain in his love. 11I have told you this so that my joy may be in you and that your joy may be complete. 12My command is this: Love each other as I have loved you. 13Greater love has no one than this, that he lay down his life for his friends.

a 2 The Greek for prunes also means cleans.

24不愛我的人就不遵守我的道，你們所聽見的道不是我的，乃是差我來之父的道。

25 "我還與你們同住的時候，已將這些話對你們說了。26但保惠師，就是父因我的名所要差來的聖靈，他要將一切的事指教你們，並且要叫你們想起我對你們所說的一切話。27我留下平安給你們，我將我的平安賜給你們。我所賜的，不像世人所賜的；你們心裏不要憂愁，也不要膽怯。

28 "你們聽見我對你們說了，我去還要到你們這裏來。你們若愛我，因我到父那裏去，就必喜樂，因為父是比我大的。29現在事情還沒有成就，我預先告訴你們，叫你們到事情成就的時候，就可以信。30以後我不再和你們多說話，因為這世界的王將到，他在我裏面是毫無所有；31但要叫世人知道我愛父，並且父怎樣吩咐我，我就怎樣行。

"起來，我們走吧！

葡萄樹與枝子

15 "我是真葡萄樹，我父是栽培的人。2凡屬我不結果子的枝子，他就剪去；凡結果子的，他就修理乾淨，使枝子結果子更多。3現在你們因我講給你們的道，已經乾淨了。4你們要常在我裏面，我也常在你們裏面。枝子若不常在葡萄樹上，自己就不能結果子；你們若不常在我裏面，也是這樣。

5 "我是葡萄樹，你們是枝子；常在我裏面的，我也常在他裏面，這人就多結果子。因為離了我，你們就不能做甚麼。6人若不常在我裏面，就像枝子丟在外面枯乾，人拾起來扔在火裏燒了。7你們若常在我裏面，我的話也常在你們裏面；凡你們所願意的，祈求就給你們成就。8你們多結果子，我父就因此得榮耀，你們也就是我的門徒了。

9 "我愛你們，正如父愛我一樣，你們要常在我的愛裏。10你們若遵守我的命令，就常在我的愛裏；正如我遵守了我父的命令，常在他的愛裏。11這些事我已經對你們說了，是要叫我的喜樂存在你們心裏，並叫你們的喜樂可以滿足。12你們要彼此相愛，像我愛你們一樣，這就是我的命令。13人為朋友捨命，人的愛心沒有比這個大的。¹⁴你們若遵行我所吩咐的，就是我的朋友了。¹⁵以後我不再稱你們為僕人，因僕人不知道主人所做的事；我乃稱你們為朋友，因我從我父所聽見的，已經都告訴你們了。¹⁶不是你們揀選了我，是我揀選了你們；並且分派你們去結果子，叫你們的果子常存，使你們奉我的名，無論向父求甚麼，他就賜給你們。¹⁷我這樣吩咐你們，是要叫你們彼此相愛。

世人恨門徒

¹⁸ "世人若恨你們，你們須知道（註：或作"該知道"）恨你們以先，已經恨我了。¹⁹你們若屬世界，世界必愛屬自己的；只因你們不屬世界，乃是我從世界中揀選了你們，所以世界就恨你們。²⁰你們要記念我從前對你們所說的話：'僕人不能大於主人。' 他們若逼迫了我，也要逼迫你們；若遵守了我的話，也要遵守你們的話。²¹但他們因我的名要向你們行這一切的事，因為他們不認識那差我來的。²²我若沒有來教訓他們，他們就沒有罪；但如今他們的罪無可推諉了。²³恨我的，也恨我的父。²⁴我若沒有在他們中間行過別人未曾行的事，他們就沒有罪；但如今連我與我的父，他們也看見也恨惡了。²⁵這要應驗他們律法上所寫的話，說：'他們無故地恨我。'

²⁶ "但我要從父那裏差保惠師來，就是從父出來真理的聖靈，他來了，就要為我作見證。²⁷你們也要作見證，因為你們從起頭就與我同在。

16 "我已將這些事告訴你們，使你們不至於跌倒。²人要把你們趕出會堂，並且時候將到，凡殺你們的，就以為是侍奉神。³他們這樣行，是因未曾認識父，也未曾認識我。⁴我將這事告訴你們，是叫你們到了時候，可以想起我對你們說過了。我起先沒有將這事告訴你們，因為我與你們同在。

聖靈的工作

⁵ "現今我往差我來的父那裏去，你們中間並沒有人問我：'你往哪裏去？' ⁶只因我將這事告訴你們，你們就滿心憂愁。⁷然而我將真

¹⁴You are my friends if you do what I command. ¹⁵I no longer call you servants, because a servant does not know his master's business. Instead, I have called you friends, for everything that I learned from my Father I have made known to you. ¹⁶You did not choose me, but I chose you and appointed you to go and bear fruit—fruit that will last. Then the Father will give you whatever you ask in my name. ¹⁷This is my command: Love each other.

The World Hates the Disciples

¹⁸"If the world hates you, keep in mind that it hated me first. ¹⁹If you belonged to the world, it would love you as its own. As it is, you do not belong to the world, but I have chosen you out of the world. That is why the world hates you. ²⁰Remember the words I spoke to you: 'No servant is greater than his master.'ᵃ If they persecuted me, they will persecute you also. If they obeyed my teaching, they will obey yours also. ²¹They will treat you this way because of my name, for they do not know the One who sent me. ²²If I had not come and spoken to them, they would not be guilty of sin. Now, however, they have no excuse for their sin. ²³He who hates me hates my Father as well. ²⁴If I had not done among them what no one else did, they would not be guilty of sin. But now they have seen these miracles, and yet they have hated both me and my Father. ²⁵But this is to fulfill what is written in their Law: 'They hated me without reason.'ᵇ

²⁶"When the Counselor comes, whom I will send to you from the Father, the Spirit of truth who goes out from the Father, he will testify about me. ²⁷And you also must testify, for you have been with me from the beginning.

16 "All this I have told you so that you will not go astray. ²They will put you out of the synagogue; in fact, a time is coming when anyone who kills you will think he is offering a service to God. ³They will do such things because they have not known the Father or me. ⁴I have told you this, so that when the time comes you will remember that I warned you. I did not tell you this at first because I was with you.

The Work of the Holy Spirit

⁵"Now I am going to him who sent me, yet none of you asks me, 'Where are you going?' ⁶Because I have said these things, you are filled with grief. ⁷But I tell you the truth: It is for your

a 20 John 13:16   b 25 Psalms 35:19; 69:4

good that I am going away. Unless I go away, the Counselor will not come to you; but if I go, I will send him to you. [8]When he comes, he will convict the world of guilt[a] in regard to sin and righteousness and judgment: [9]in regard to sin, because men do not believe in me; [10]in regard to righteousness, because I am going to the Father, where you can see me no longer; [11]and in regard to judgment, because the prince of this world now stands condemned.

[12]"I have much more to say to you, more than you can now bear. [13]But when he, the Spirit of truth, comes, he will guide you into all truth. He will not speak on his own; he will speak only what he hears, and he will tell you what is yet to come. [14]He will bring glory to me by taking from what is mine and making it known to you. [15]All that belongs to the Father is mine. That is why I said the Spirit will take from what is mine and make it known to you.

[16]"In a little while you will see me no more, and then after a little while you will see me."

The Disciples' Grief Will Turn to Joy

[17]Some of his disciples said to one another, "What does he mean by saying, 'In a little while you will see me no more, and then after a little while you will see me,' and 'Because I am going to the Father'?" [18]They kept asking, "What does he mean by 'a little while'? We don't understand what he is saying."

[19]Jesus saw that they wanted to ask him about this, so he said to them, "Are you asking one another what I meant when I said, 'In a little while you will see me no more, and then after a little while you will see me'? [20]I tell you the truth, you will weep and mourn while the world rejoices. You will grieve, but your grief will turn to joy. [21]A woman giving birth to a child has pain because her time has come; but when her baby is born she forgets the anguish because of her joy that a child is born into the world. [22]So with you: Now is your time of grief, but I will see you again and you will rejoice, and no one will take away your joy. [23]In that day you will no longer ask me anything. I tell you the truth, my Father will give you whatever you ask in my name. [24]Until now you have not asked for anything in my name. Ask and you will receive, and your joy will be complete.

[25]"Though I have been speaking figuratively, a time is coming when I will no longer use this kind of language but will tell you plainly about my Father. [26]In that day you will ask in my name.

情告訴你們,我去是與你們有益的。我若不去,保惠師就不到你們這裏來;我若去,就差他來。[8]他既來了,就要叫世人為罪、為義、為審判,自己責備自己。[9]為罪,是因他們不信我;[10]為義,是因我往父那裏去,你們就不再見我;[11]為審判,是因這世界的王受了審判。

[12]"我還有好些事要告訴你們,但你們現在擔當不了(註:或作"不能領會")。[13]只等真理的聖靈來了,他要引導你們明白(註:原文作"進入")一切的真理,因為他不是憑自己說的,乃是把他所聽見的都說出來,並要把將來的事告訴你們。[14]他要榮耀我,因為他要將受於我的告訴你們。[15]凡父所有的,都是我的,所以我說,他要將受於我的告訴你們。

[16]"等不多時,你們就不得見我;再等不多時,你們還要見我。"

門徒的憂愁要變為喜樂

[17]有幾個門徒就彼此說:"他對我們說'等不多時,你們就不得見我;再等不多時,你們還要見我';又說'因我往父那裏去',這是甚麼意思呢?"[18]門徒彼此說:"他說'等不多時'到底是甚麼意思呢?我們不明白他所說的話。"

[19]耶穌看出他們要問他,就說:"我說'等不多時,你們就不得見我;再等不多時,你們還要見我',你們為這話彼此相問嗎?[20]我實實在在地告訴你們:你們將要痛哭、哀號,世人倒要喜樂;你們將要憂愁,然而你們的憂愁要變為喜樂。[21]婦人生產的時候就憂愁,因為她的時候到了;既生了孩子,就不再記念那苦楚,因為歡喜世上生了一個人。[22]你們現在也是憂愁,但我要再見你們,你們的心就喜樂了;這喜樂也沒有人能奪去。[23]到那日,你們甚麼也就不問我了。我實實在在地告訴你們:你們若向父求甚麼,他必因我的名賜給你們。[24]向來你們沒有奉我的名求甚麼,如今你們求就必得着,叫你們的喜樂可以滿足。

[25]"這些事,我是用比喻對你們說的;時候將到,我不再用比喻對你們說,乃要將父明明地告訴你們。[26]到那日,你們要奉我的名求;我

a 8 Or will expose the guilt of the world

並不對你們說，我要為你們求父。²⁷父自己愛你們，因為你們已經愛我，又信我是從父出來的。²⁸我從父出來，到了世界；我又離開世界，往父那裏去。"

²⁹門徒說："如今你是明說，並不用比喻了。³⁰現在我們曉得你凡事都知道，也不用人問你，因此我們信你是從神出來的。"

³¹耶穌說："現在你們信嗎？³²看哪，時候將到，且是已經到了，你們要分散，各歸自己的地方去，留下我獨自一人；其實我不是獨自一人，因為有父與我同在。

³³"我將這些事告訴你們，是要叫你們在我裏面有平安。在世上你們有苦難，但你們可以放心，我已經勝了世界。"

耶穌為自己禱告

17 耶穌說了這話，就舉目望天說：

"父啊，時候到了，願你榮耀你的兒子，使兒子也榮耀你；²正如你曾賜給他權柄，管理凡有血氣的，叫他將永生賜給你所賜給他的人。³認識你獨一的真神，並且認識你所差來的耶穌基督，這就是永生。⁴我在地上已經榮耀你，你所託付我的事，我已成全了。⁵父啊，現在求你使我同你享榮耀，就是未有世界以先，我同你所有的榮耀。

耶穌為門徒禱告

⁶"你從世上賜給我的人，我已將你的名顯明與他們。他們本是你的，你將他們賜給我，他們也遵守了你的道。⁷如今他們知道，凡你所賜給我的，都是從你那裏來的；⁸因為你所賜給我的道，我已經賜給他們。他們也領受了，又確實知道，我是從你出來的，並且信你差了我來。⁹我為他們祈求，不為世人祈求，卻為你所賜給我的人祈求，因他們本是你的。¹⁰凡是我的都是你的，你的也是我的，並且我因他們得了榮耀。¹¹從今以後，我不在世上，他

I am not saying that I will ask the Father on your behalf. ²⁷No, the Father himself loves you because you have loved me and have believed that I came from God. ²⁸I came from the Father and entered the world; now I am leaving the world and going back to the Father."

²⁹Then Jesus' disciples said, "Now you are speaking clearly and without figures of speech. ³⁰Now we can see that you know all things and that you do not even need to have anyone ask you questions. This makes us believe that you came from God."

³¹"You believe at last!"[a] Jesus answered. ³²"But a time is coming, and has come, when you will be scattered, each to his own home. You will leave me all alone. Yet I am not alone, for my Father is with me.

³³"I have told you these things, so that in me you may have peace. In this world you will have trouble. But take heart! I have overcome the world."

Jesus Prays for Himself

17 After Jesus said this, he looked toward heaven and prayed:

"Father, the time has come. Glorify your Son, that your Son may glorify you. ²For you granted him authority over all people that he might give eternal life to all those you have given him. ³Now this is eternal life: that they may know you, the only true God, and Jesus Christ, whom you have sent. ⁴I have brought you glory on earth by completing the work you gave me to do. ⁵And now, Father, glorify me in your presence with the glory I had with you before the world began.

Jesus Prays for His Disciples

⁶"I have revealed you[b] to those whom you gave me out of the world. They were yours; you gave them to me and they have obeyed your word. ⁷Now they know that everything you have given me comes from you. ⁸For I gave them the words you gave me and they accepted them. They knew with certainty that I came from you, and they believed that you sent me. ⁹I pray for them. I am not praying for the world, but for those you have given me, for they are yours. ¹⁰All I have is yours, and all you have is mine. And glory has come to me through them. ¹¹I will remain in the world no longer, but they are still in the world, and I

---

a 31 Or *"Do you now believe?"*　　*b* 6 Greek *your name;* also in verse 26 am coming to you. Holy Father, protect them by the power of your name—the name you gave me—so that they may be one as we are one. ¹²While I was with them, I protected them and kept them safe by that name you gave me. None has been lost except the one doomed to destruction so that Scripture would be fulfilled.

¹³"I am coming to you now, but I say these things while I am still in the world, so that they may have the full measure of my joy within them. ¹⁴I have given them your word and the world has hated them, for they are not of the world any more than I am of the world. ¹⁵My prayer is not that you take them out of the world but that you protect them from the evil one. ¹⁶They are not of the world, even as I am not of it. ¹⁷Sanctify*a* them by the truth; your word is truth. ¹⁸As you sent me into the world, I have sent them into the world. ¹⁹For them I sanctify myself, that they too may be truly sanctified.

Jesus Prays for All Believers

²⁰"My prayer is not for them alone. I pray also for those who will believe in me through their message, ²¹that all of them may be one, Father, just as you are in me and I am in you. May they also be in us so that the world may believe that you have sent me. ²²I have given them the glory that you gave me, that they may be one as we are one: ²³I in them and you in me. May they be brought to complete unity to let the world know that you sent me and have loved them even as you have loved me.

²⁴"Father, I want those you have given me to be with me where I am, and to see my glory, the glory you have given me because you loved me before the creation of the world.

²⁵"Righteous Father, though the world does not know you, I know you, and they know that you have sent me. ²⁶I have made you known to them, and will continue to make you known in order that the love you have for me may be in them and that I myself may be in them."

Jesus Arrested

18 When he had finished praying, Jesus left with his disciples and crossed the Kidron Valley. On the other side there was an olive grove, and he and his disciples went into it.

們卻在世上；我往你那裏去。聖父啊，求你因你所賜給我的名保守他們，叫他們合而為一，像我們一樣。¹²我與他們同在的時候，因你所賜給我的名保守了他們，我也護衞了他們；其中除了那滅亡之子，沒有一個滅亡的，好叫經上的話得應驗。

¹³"現在我往你那裏去，我還在世上說這話，是叫他們心裏充滿我的喜樂。¹⁴我已將你的道賜給他們。世界又恨他們，因為他們不屬世界，正如我不屬世界一樣。¹⁵我不求你叫他們離開世界，只求你保守他們脫離那惡者（註：或作"脫離罪惡"）。¹⁶他們不屬世界，正如我不屬世界一樣。¹⁷求你用真理使他們成聖，你的道就是真理。¹⁸你怎樣差我到世上，我也照樣差他們到世上。¹⁹我為他們的緣故，自己分別為聖，叫他們也因真理成聖。

耶穌為所有信徒禱告

²⁰ "我不但為這些人祈求，也為那些因他們的話信我的人祈求，²¹使他們都合而為一。正如你父在我裏面，我在你裏面，使他們也在我們裏面，叫世人可以信你差了我來。²²你所賜給我的榮耀，我已賜給他們，使他們合而為一，像我們合而為一。²³我在他們裏面，你在我裏面，使他們完完全全地合而為一，叫世人知道你差了我來，也知道你愛他們如同愛我一樣。

²⁴ "父啊，我在哪裏，願你所賜給我的人也同我在那裏，叫他們看見你所賜給我的榮耀。因為創立世界以前，你已經愛我了。

²⁵ "公義的父啊，世人未曾認識你，我卻認識你，這些人也知道你差了我來。²⁶我已將你的名指示他們，還要指示他們，使你所愛我的愛在他們裏面，我也在他們裏面。"

耶穌被捕

18 耶穌說了這話，就同門徒出去，過了汲淪溪，在那裏有一個園子，他和門徒進去了。

---

a 17 Greek *hagiazo* (*set apart for sacred use* or *make holy*); also in verse 19

²賣耶穌的<u>猶大</u>也知道那地方，因為耶穌和門徒屢次上那裏去聚集。³<u>猶大</u>領了一隊兵和祭司長並法利賽人的差役，拿着燈籠、火把、兵器，就來到園裏。

⁴耶穌知道將要臨到自己的一切事，就出來對他們說：「你們找誰？」

⁵他們回答說：「找<u>拿撒勒</u>人耶穌。」

耶穌說：「我就是！」賣他的<u>猶大</u>也同他們站在那裏。⁶耶穌一說「我就是」，他們就退後倒在地上。

⁷他又問他們說：「你們找誰？」他們說：「找<u>拿撒勒</u>人耶穌。」

⁸耶穌說：「我已經告訴你們，我就是。你們若找我，就讓這些人去吧！」⁹這要應驗耶穌從前的話，說：「你所賜給我的人，我沒有失落一個。」

¹⁰<u>西門彼得</u>帶着一把刀，就拔出來，將大祭司的僕人砍了一刀，削掉他的右耳，那僕人名叫<u>馬勒古</u>。

¹¹耶穌就對<u>彼得</u>說：「收刀入鞘吧！我父所給我的那杯，我豈不可不喝呢？」

耶穌被帶到亞那面前

¹²那隊兵和千夫長並<u>猶太</u>人的差役就拿住耶穌，把他捆綁了，¹³先帶到<u>亞那</u>面前，因為<u>亞那</u>是本年作大祭司<u>該亞法</u>的岳父。¹⁴這<u>該亞法</u>就是從前向<u>猶太</u>人發議論說「一個人替百姓死是有益的」那位。

彼得第一次不認主

¹⁵<u>西門彼得</u>跟着耶穌，還有一個門徒跟着。那門徒是大祭司所認識的，他就同耶穌進了大祭司的院子，¹⁶<u>彼得</u>卻站在門外。大祭司所認識的那個門徒出來，和看門的使女說了一聲，就領<u>彼得</u>進去。

¹⁷那看門的使女對<u>彼得</u>說：「你不也是這人的門徒嗎？」

他說：「我不是。」

¹⁸僕人和差役因為天冷，就生了炭火，站在那裏烤火，<u>彼得</u>也同他們站着烤火。

²Now Judas, who betrayed him, knew the place, because Jesus had often met there with his disciples. ³So Judas came to the grove, guiding a detachment of soldiers and some officials from the chief priests and Pharisees. They were carrying torches, lanterns and weapons.

⁴Jesus, knowing all that was going to happen to him, went out and asked them, "Who is it you want?"

⁵"Jesus of Nazareth," they replied.

"I am he," Jesus said. (And Judas the traitor was standing there with them.) ⁶When Jesus said, "I am he," they drew back and fell to the ground.

⁷Again he asked them, "Who is it you want?"

And they said, "Jesus of Nazareth."

⁸"I told you that I am he," Jesus answered. "If you are looking for me, then let these men go." ⁹This happened so that the words he had spoken would be fulfilled: "I have not lost one of those you gave me."[a]

¹⁰Then Simon Peter, who had a sword, drew it and struck the high priest's servant, cutting off his right ear. (The servant's name was Malchus.)

¹¹Jesus commanded Peter, "Put your sword away! Shall I not drink the cup the Father has given me?"

Jesus Taken to Annas

¹²Then the detachment of soldiers with its commander and the Jewish officials arrested Jesus. They bound him ¹³and brought him first to Annas, who was the father-in-law of Caiaphas, the high priest that year. ¹⁴Caiaphas was the one who had advised the Jews that it would be good if one man died for the people.

Peter's First Denial

¹⁵Simon Peter and another disciple were following Jesus. Because this disciple was known to the high priest, he went with Jesus into the high priest's courtyard, ¹⁶but Peter had to wait outside at the door. The other disciple, who was known to the high priest, came back, spoke to the girl on duty there and brought Peter in.

¹⁷"You are not one of his disciples, are you?" the girl at the door asked Peter.

He replied, "I am not."

¹⁸It was cold, and the servants and officials stood around a fire they had made to keep warm. Peter also was standing with them, warming himself.

a 9 John 6:39

The High Priest Questions Jesus

[19]Meanwhile, the high priest questioned Jesus about his disciples and his teaching.

[20]"I have spoken openly to the world," Jesus replied. "I always taught in synagogues or at the temple, where all the Jews come together. I said nothing in secret. [21]Why question me? Ask those who heard me. Surely they know what I said."

[22]When Jesus said this, one of the officials nearby struck him in the face. "Is this the way you answer the high priest?" he demanded.

[23]"If I said something wrong," Jesus replied, "testify as to what is wrong. But if I spoke the truth, why did you strike me?" [24]Then Annas sent him, still bound, to Caiaphas the high priest.[a]

Peter's Second and Third Denials

[25]As Simon Peter stood warming himself, he was asked, "You are not one of his disciples, are you?"

He denied it, saying, "I am not."

[26]One of the high priest's servants, a relative of the man whose ear Peter had cut off, challenged him, "Didn't I see you with him in the olive grove?" [27]Again Peter denied it, and at that moment a rooster began to crow.

Jesus Before Pilate

[28]Then the Jews led Jesus from Caiaphas to the palace of the Roman governor. By now it was early morning, and to avoid ceremonial uncleanness the Jews did not enter the palace; they wanted to be able to eat the Passover. [29]So Pilate came out to them and asked, "What charges are you bringing against this man?"

[30]"If he were not a criminal," they replied, "we would not have handed him over to you."

[31]Pilate said, "Take him yourselves and judge him by your own law."

"But we have no right to execute anyone," the Jews objected. [32]This happened so that the words Jesus had spoken indicating the kind of death he was going to die would be fulfilled.

[33]Pilate then went back inside the palace, summoned Jesus and asked him, "Are you the king of the Jews?"

[34]"Is that your own idea," Jesus asked, "or did others talk to you about me?"

[35]"Am I a Jew?" Pilate replied. "It was your people and your chief priests who handed you over to me. What is it you have done?"

a 24 Or (*Now Annas had sent him, still bound, to Caiaphas the high priest.*)

大祭司盤問耶穌

[19]大祭司就以耶穌的門徒和他的教訓盤問他。

[20]耶穌回答說："我從來是明明地對世人說話。我常在會堂和殿裏，就是猶太人聚集的地方教訓人，我在暗地裏並沒有說甚麼。[21]你為甚麼問我呢？可以問那聽見的人，我對他們說的是甚麼；我所說的，他們都知道。"

[22]耶穌說了這話，旁邊站着的一個差役用手掌打他，說："你這樣回答大祭司嗎？"

[23]耶穌說："我若說得不是，你可以指證那不是；我若說得是，你為甚麼打我呢？"[24]亞那就把耶穌解到大祭司該亞法那裏，仍是捆着解去的。

彼得二次三次不認主

[25]西門彼得正站着烤火，有人對他說："你不也是他的門徒嗎？"

彼得不承認，說："我不是！"

[26]有大祭司的一個僕人，是彼得削掉耳朵那人的親屬，說："我不是看見你同他在園子裏嗎？"[27]彼得又不承認。立時雞就叫了。

耶穌在彼拉多面前

[28]眾人將耶穌從該亞法那裏往衙門內解去，那時天還早，他們自己卻不進衙門，恐怕染了污穢，不能吃逾越節的筵席。[29]彼拉多就出來，到他們那裏，說："你們告這人是為甚麼事呢？"

[30]他們回答說："這人若不是作惡的，我們就不把他交給你。"

[31]彼拉多說："你們自己帶他去，按着你們的律法審問他吧！"

猶太人說："我們沒有殺人的權柄。"[32]這要應驗耶穌所說自己將要怎樣死的話了。

[33]彼拉多又進了衙門，叫耶穌來，對他說："你是猶太人的王嗎？"

[34]耶穌回答說："這話是你自己說的，還是別人論我對你說的呢？"

[35]彼拉多說："我豈是猶太人呢？你本國的人和祭司長把你交給我，你做了甚麼事呢？"

³⁶耶穌回答說：「我的國不屬這世界。我的國若屬這世界，我的臣僕必要爭戰，使我不至於被交給猶太人；只是我的國不屬這世界。」

³⁷彼拉多就對他說：「這樣，你是王嗎？」

耶穌回答說：「你說我是王，我為此而生，也為此來到世間，特為給真理作見證。凡屬真理的人就聽我的話。」

³⁸彼拉多說：「真理是甚麼呢？」說了這話，又出來到猶太人那裏，對他們說：「我查不出他有甚麼罪來，³⁹但你們有個規矩，在逾越節要我給你們釋放一個人，你們要我給你們釋放猶太人的王嗎？」

⁴⁰他們又喊着說：「不要這人，要巴拉巴！」這巴拉巴是個強盜。

耶穌被判釘十字架

19 當下彼拉多將耶穌鞭打了。²兵丁用荊棘編作冠冕戴在他頭上，給他穿上紫袍，³又挨近他說：「恭喜猶太人的王啊！」他們就用手掌打他。

⁴彼拉多又出來對眾人說：「我帶他出來見你們，叫你們知道我查不出他有甚麼罪來。」⁵耶穌出來，戴着荊棘冠冕，穿着紫袍。彼拉多對他們說：「你們看這個人！」

⁶祭司長和差役看見他，就喊着說：「釘他十字架！釘他十字架！」

彼拉多說：「你們自己把他釘十字架吧！我查不出他有甚麼罪來。」

⁷猶太人回答說：「我們有律法，按那律法，他是該死的！因他以自己為神的兒子。」

⁸彼拉多聽見這話，越發害怕，⁹又進衙門，對耶穌說：「你是哪裏來的？」耶穌卻不回答。¹⁰彼拉多說：「你不對我說話嗎？你豈不知我有權柄釋放你，也有權柄把你釘十字架嗎？」

¹¹耶穌回答說：「若不是從上頭賜給你的，你就毫無權柄辦我，所以把我交給你的那人，罪更重了。」

¹²從此彼拉多想要釋放耶穌，無奈猶太人喊着說：「你若釋放這個人，就不是凱撒的忠臣（註：原文作「朋友」）。凡以自己為王的，就是背叛凱撒了。」

³⁶Jesus said, "My kingdom is not of this world. If it were, my servants would fight to prevent my arrest by the Jews. But now my kingdom is from another place."

³⁷"You are a king, then!" said Pilate.

Jesus answered, "You are right in saying I am a king. In fact, for this reason I was born, and for this I came into the world, to testify to the truth. Everyone on the side of truth listens to me."

³⁸"What is truth?" Pilate asked. With this he went out again to the Jews and said, "I find no basis for a charge against him. ³⁹But it is your custom for me to release to you one prisoner at the time of the Passover. Do you want me to release 'the king of the Jews'?"

⁴⁰They shouted back, "No, not him! Give us Barabbas!" Now Barabbas had taken part in a rebellion.

Jesus Sentenced to be Crucified

19 Then Pilate took Jesus and had him flogged. ²The soldiers twisted together a crown of thorns and put it on his head. They clothed him in a purple robe ³and went up to him again and again, saying, "Hail, king of the Jews!" And they struck him in the face.

⁴Once more Pilate came out and said to the Jews, "Look, I am bringing him out to you to let you know that I find no basis for a charge against him." ⁵When Jesus came out wearing the crown of thorns and the purple robe, Pilate said to them, "Here is the man!"

⁶As soon as the chief priests and their officials saw him, they shouted, "Crucify! Crucify!"

But Pilate answered, "You take him and crucify him. As for me, I find no basis for a charge against him."

⁷The Jews insisted, "We have a law, and according to that law he must die, because he claimed to be the Son of God."

⁸When Pilate heard this, he was even more afraid, ⁹and he went back inside the palace. "Where do you come from?" he asked Jesus, but Jesus gave him no answer. ¹⁰"Do you refuse to speak to me?" Pilate said. "Don't you realize I have power either to free you or to crucify you?"

¹¹Jesus answered, "You would have no power over me if it were not given to you from above. Therefore the one who handed me over to you is guilty of a greater sin."

¹²From then on, Pilate tried to set Jesus free, but the Jews kept shouting, "If you let this man go, you are no friend of Caesar. Anyone who claims to be a king opposes Caesar."

¹³When Pilate heard this, he brought Jesus out and sat down on the judge's seat at a place known as the Stone Pavement (which in Aramaic is Gabbatha). ¹⁴It was the day of Preparation of Passover Week, about the sixth hour.

"Here is your king," Pilate said to the Jews.

¹⁵But they shouted, "Take him away! Take him away! Crucify him!"

"Shall I crucify your king?" Pilate asked.

"We have no king but Caesar," the chief priests answered.

¹⁶Finally Pilate handed him over to them to be crucified.

The Crucifixion

So the soldiers took charge of Jesus. ¹⁷Carrying his own cross, he went out to the place of the Skull (which in Aramaic is called Golgotha). ¹⁸Here they crucified him, and with him two others—one on each side and Jesus in the middle.

¹⁹Pilate had a notice prepared and fastened to the cross. It read: JESUS OF NAZARETH, THE KING OF THE JEWS. ²⁰Many of the Jews read this sign, for the place where Jesus was crucified was near the city, and the sign was written in Aramaic, Latin and Greek. ²¹The chief priests of the Jews protested to Pilate, "Do not write 'The King of the Jews,' but that this man claimed to be king of the Jews."

²²Pilate answered, "What I have written, I have written."

²³When the soldiers crucified Jesus, they took his clothes, dividing them into four shares, one for each of them, with the undergarment remaining. This garment was seamless, woven in one piece from top to bottom.

²⁴"Let's not tear it," they said to one another. "Let's decide by lot who will get it."

This happened that the scripture might be fulfilled which said,

"They divided my garments among them
    and cast lots for my clothing."ᵃ

So this is what the soldiers did.

²⁵Near the cross of Jesus stood his mother, his mother's sister, Mary the wife of Clopas, and Mary Magdalene. ²⁶When Jesus saw his mother there, and the disciple whom he loved standing nearby, he said to his mother, "Dear woman, here is your son," ²⁷and to the disciple, "Here is your mother." From that time on, this disciple took her into his home.

a 24 Psalm 22:18

¹³彼拉多聽見這話，就帶耶穌出來，到了一個地方，名叫鋪華石處，希伯來話叫厄巴大，就在那裏坐堂。¹⁴那日是預備逾越節的日子。約有午正，彼拉多對猶太人說：

"看哪，這是你們的王！"

¹⁵他們喊着說："除掉他！除掉他！釘他在十字架上！"彼拉多說："我可以把你們的王釘十字架嗎？"祭司長回答說："除了凱撒，我們沒有王！"

¹⁶於是，彼拉多將耶穌交給他們去釘十字架。

釘十字架

¹⁷他們就把耶穌帶了去。耶穌背着自己的十字架出來，到了一個地方，名叫髑髏地，希伯來話叫各各他。¹⁸他們就在那裏釘他在十字架上，還有兩個人和他一同釘着，一邊一個，耶穌在中間。

¹⁹彼拉多又用牌子寫了一個名號，安在十字架上，寫的是："猶太人的王，拿撒勒人耶穌。"²⁰有許多猶太人念這名號，因為耶穌被釘十字架的地方，與城相近，並且是用希伯來、羅馬、希臘三樣文字寫的。²¹猶太人的祭司長就對彼拉多說："不要寫'猶太人的王'，要寫'他自己說我是猶太人的王'。"

²²彼拉多說："我所寫的，我已經寫上了。"

²³兵丁既然將耶穌釘在十字架上，就拿他的衣服分為四分，每兵一分；又拿他的裏衣，這件裏衣原來沒有縫兒，是上下一片織成的。

²⁴他們就彼此說："我們不要撕開，只要拈鬮，看誰得着。"

這要應驗經上的話說：

"他們分了我的外衣，
    為我的裏衣拈鬮。"

兵丁果然做了這事。

²⁵站在耶穌十字架旁邊的，有他母親與他母親的姊妹，並革羅罷的妻子馬利亞和抹大拉的馬利亞。²⁶耶穌見母親和他所愛的那門徒站在旁邊，就對他母親說："母親（註：原文作"婦人"），看，你的兒子！"²⁷又對那門徒說："看，你的母親！"從此那門徒就接她到自己家裏去了。

耶穌的死

28這事以後，耶穌知道各樣的事已經成了，為要使經上的話應驗，就說：「我渴了。」 29有一個器皿盛滿了醋，放在那裏，他們就拿海絨蘸滿了醋，綁在牛膝草上，送到他口。 30耶穌嘗（註：原文作「受」）了那醋，就說：「成了！」，便低下頭，將靈魂交付神了。

31猶太人因這日是預備日，又因那安息日是個大日，就求彼拉多叫人打斷他們的腿，把他們拿去，免得屍首當安息日留在十字架上。 32於是兵丁來，把頭一個人的腿，並與耶穌同釘第二個人的腿都打斷了。 33只是來到耶穌那裏，見他已經死了，就不打斷他的腿。 34惟有一個兵拿槍扎他的肋旁，隨即有血和水流出來。 35看見這事的那人就作見證，他的見證也是真的，並且他知道自己所說的是真的，叫你們也可以信。 36這些事成了，為要應驗經上的話說：「他的骨頭一根也不可折斷。」 37經上又有一句說：「他們要仰望自己所扎的人。」

耶穌的安葬

38這些事以後，有亞利馬太人約瑟，是耶穌的門徒，只因怕猶太人，就暗暗地作門徒。他來求彼拉多，要把耶穌的身體領去。彼拉多允准，他就把耶穌的身體領去了。 39又有尼哥德慕，就是先前夜裏去見耶穌的，帶着沒藥和沉香約有一百斤前來。 40他們就照猶太人殯葬的規矩，把耶穌的身體用細麻布加上香料裹好了。 41在耶穌釘十字架的地方有一個園子，園子裏有一座新墳墓，是從來沒有葬過人的。 42只因為猶太人的預備日，又因那墳墓近，他們就把耶穌安放在那裏。

空墳墓

20 七日的第一日清早，天還黑的時候，抹大拉的馬利亞來到墳墓那裏，看見石頭從墳墓挪開了， 2就跑來見西門彼得和耶

The Death of Jesus

28Later, knowing that all was now completed, and so that the Scripture would be fulfilled, Jesus said, "I am thirsty." 29A jar of wine vinegar was there, so they soaked a sponge in it, put the sponge on a stalk of the hyssop plant, and lifted it to Jesus' lips. 30When he had received the drink, Jesus said, "It is finished." With that, he bowed his head and gave up his spirit.

31Now it was the day of Preparation, and the next day was to be a special Sabbath. Because the Jews did not want the bodies left on the crosses during the Sabbath, they asked Pilate to have the legs broken and the bodies taken down. 32The soldiers therefore came and broke the legs of the first man who had been crucified with Jesus, and then those of the other. 33But when they came to Jesus and found that he was already dead, they did not break his legs. 34Instead, one of the soldiers pierced Jesus' side with a spear, bringing a sudden flow of blood and water. 35The man who saw it has given testimony, and his testimony is true. He knows that he tells the truth, and he testifies so that you also may believe. 36These things happened so that the scripture would be fulfilled: "Not one of his bones will be broken,"[a] 37and, as another scripture says, "They will look on the one they have pierced."[b]

The Burial of Jesus

38Later, Joseph of Arimathea asked Pilate for the body of Jesus. Now Joseph was a disciple of Jesus, but secretly because he feared the Jews. With Pilate's permission, he came and took the body away. 39He was accompanied by Nicodemus, the man who earlier had visited Jesus at night. Nicodemus brought a mixture of myrrh and aloes, about seventy-five pounds.[c] 40Taking Jesus' body, the two of them wrapped it, with the spices, in strips of linen. This was in accordance with Jewish burial customs. 41At the place where Jesus was crucified, there was a garden, and in the garden a new tomb, in which no one had ever been laid. 42Because it was the Jewish day of Preparation and since the tomb was nearby, they laid Jesus there.

The Empty Tomb

20 Early on the first day of the week, while it was still dark, Mary Magdalene went to the tomb and saw that the stone had been removed from the entrance. 2So she came

---

a 36 Exodus 12:46; Num. 9:12; Psalm 34:20　　b 37 Zech. 12:10
c 39 Greek *a hundred litrai* (about 34 kilograms)

running to Simon Peter and the other disciple, the one Jesus loved, and said, "They have taken the Lord out of the tomb, and we don't know where they have put him!"

3So Peter and the other disciple started for the tomb. 4Both were running, but the other disciple outran Peter and reached the tomb first. 5He bent over and looked in at the strips of linen lying there but did not go in. 6Then Simon Peter, who was behind him, arrived and went into the tomb. He saw the strips of linen lying there, 7as well as the burial cloth that had been around Jesus' head. The cloth was folded up by itself, separate from the linen. 8Finally the other disciple, who had reached the tomb first, also went inside. He saw and believed. 9(They still did not understand from Scripture that Jesus had to rise from the dead.)

Jesus Appears to Mary Magdalene

10Then the disciples went back to their homes, 11but Mary stood outside the tomb crying. As she wept, she bent over to look into the tomb 12and saw two angels in white, seated where Jesus' body had been, one at the head and the other at the foot.

13They asked her, "Woman, why are you crying?"

"They have taken my Lord away," she said, "and I don't know where they have put him." 14At this, she turned around and saw Jesus standing there, but she did not realize that it was Jesus.

15"Woman," he said, "why are you crying? Who is it you are looking for?"

Thinking he was the gardener, she said, "Sir, if you have carried him away, tell me where you have put him, and I will get him."

16Jesus said to her, "Mary."

She turned toward him and cried out in Aramaic, "Rabboni!" (which means Teacher).

17Jesus said, "Do not hold on to me, for I have not yet returned to the Father. Go instead to my brothers and tell them, 'I am returning to my Father and your Father, to my God and your God.'"

18Mary Magdalene went to the disciples with the news: "I have seen the Lord!" And she told them that he had said these things to her.

Jesus Appears to His Disciples

19On the evening of that first day of the week, when the disciples were together, with the doors locked for fear of the Jews, Jesus came and stood among them and said, "Peace be with you!" 20After he said this, he showed them his hands

穌所愛的那個門徒，對他們說："有人把主從墳墓裏挪了去，我們不知道放在哪裏！"

3彼得和那門徒就出來，往墳墓那裏去。4兩個人同跑，那門徒比彼得跑的更快，先到了墳墓，5低頭往裏看，就見細麻布還放在那裏，只是沒有進去。6西門彼得隨後也到了，進墳墓裏去，就看見細麻布還放在那裏，7又看見耶穌的裹頭巾沒有和細麻布放在一處，是另在一處捲着。8先到墳墓的那門徒也進去，看見就信了。9因為他們還不明白聖經的意思，就是耶穌必要從死裏復活。

耶穌向抹大拉的馬利亞顯現

10於是兩個門徒回自己的住處去了。11馬利亞卻站在墳墓外面哭，哭的時候，低頭往墳墓裏看，12就見兩個天使，穿着白衣，在安放耶穌身體的地方坐着，一個在頭，一個在腳。

13天使對她說："婦人，你為甚麼哭？"

她說："因為有人把我主挪了去，我不知道放在哪裏。"14說了這話，就轉過身來，看見耶穌站在那裏，卻不知道是耶穌。

15耶穌問她說："婦人，為甚麼哭？你找誰呢？"

馬利亞以為是看園的，就對他說："先生，若是你把他移了去，請告訴我你把他放在哪裏，我便去取他。"

16耶穌說："馬利亞！"

馬利亞就轉過來，用希伯來話對他說："拉波尼（拉波尼就是夫子的意思）！"

17耶穌說："不要摸我，因我還沒有升上去見我的父。你往我弟兄那裏去，告訴他們說：我要升上去見我的父，也是你們的父；見我的神，也是你們的神。"

18抹大拉的馬利亞就去告訴門徒說："我已經看見了主！"她又將主對她說的這話告訴他們。

耶穌向門徒顯現

19那日（就是七日的第一日）晚上，門徒所在的地方，因怕猶太人，門都關了。耶穌來站在當中，對他們說："願你們平安！"20說了這話，就把手和肋旁指給他們看。門徒看見主，就喜樂了。

21耶穌又對他們說：「願你們平安！父怎樣差遣了我，我也照樣差遣你們。」22說了這話，就向他們吹一口氣，說：「你們受聖靈。23你們赦免誰的罪，誰的罪就赦免了；你們留下誰的罪，誰的罪就留下了。」

耶穌向多馬顯現

24那十二個門徒中，有稱為低土馬的多馬，耶穌來的時候，他沒有和他們同在。25那些門徒就對他說：「我們已經看見主了！」

多馬卻說：「我非看見他手上的釘痕，用指頭探入那釘痕，又用手探入他的肋旁，我總不信。」

26過了八日，門徒又在屋裏，多馬也和他們同在。門都關了。耶穌來站在當中說：「願你們平安！」27就對多馬說：「伸過你的指頭來，摸（註：「摸」原文作「看」）我的手；伸出你的手來，探入我的肋旁。不要疑惑，總要信！」

28多馬說：「我的主，我的神！」

29耶穌對他說：「你因看見了我才信，那沒有看見就信的有福了！」

30耶穌在門徒面前另外行了許多神蹟，沒有記在這書上。31但記這些事，要叫你們信耶穌是基督，是神的兒子，並且叫你們信了他，就可以因他的名得生命。

耶穌與網魚的神蹟

21 這些事以後，耶穌在提比哩亞海邊又向門徒顯現。他怎樣顯現記在下面：2有西門彼得和稱為低土馬的多馬，並加利利的迦拿人拿但業，還有西庇太的兩個兒子，又有兩個門徒，都在一處。3西門彼得對他們說：「我打魚去。」他們說：「我們也和你同去。」他們就出去，上了船，那一夜並沒有打着甚麼。

4天將亮的時候，耶穌站在岸上，門徒卻不知道是耶穌。

5耶穌就對他們說：「小子！你們有吃的沒有？」

他們回答說：「沒有！」

and side. The disciples were overjoyed when they saw the Lord.

21Again Jesus said, "Peace be with you! As the Father has sent me, I am sending you." 22And with that he breathed on them and said, "Receive the Holy Spirit. 23If you forgive anyone his sins, they are forgiven; if you do not forgive them, they are not forgiven."

Jesus Appears to Thomas

24Now Thomas (called Didymus), one of the Twelve, was not with the disciples when Jesus came. 25So the other disciples told him, "We have seen the Lord!"

But he said to them, "Unless I see the nail marks in his hands and put my finger where the nails were, and put my hand into his side, I will not believe it."

26A week later his disciples were in the house again, and Thomas was with them. Though the doors were locked, Jesus came and stood among them and said, "Peace be with you!" 27Then he said to Thomas, "Put your finger here; see my hands. Reach out your hand and put it into my side. Stop doubting and believe."

28Thomas said to him, "My Lord and my God!"

29Then Jesus told him, "Because you have seen me, you have believed; blessed are those who have not seen and yet have believed."

30Jesus did many other miraculous signs in the presence of his disciples, which are not recorded in this book. 31But these are written that you may*a* believe that Jesus is the Christ, the Son of God, and that by believing you may have life in his name.

Jesus and the Miraculous Catch of Fish

21 Afterward Jesus appeared again to his disciples, by the Sea of Tiberias.*b* It happened this way: 2Simon Peter, Thomas (called Didymus), Nathanael from Cana in Galilee, the sons of Zebedee, and two other disciples were together. 3"I'm going out to fish," Simon Peter told them, and they said, "We'll go with you." So they went out and got into the boat, but that night they caught nothing.

4Early in the morning, Jesus stood on the shore, but the disciples did not realize that it was Jesus.

5He called out to them, "Friends, haven't you any fish?"

"No," they answered.

a 31 Some manuscripts may continue to　*b 1 That is, Sea of Galilee*

6He said, "Throw your net on the right side of the boat and you will find some." When they did, they were unable to haul the net in because of the large number of fish.

7Then the disciple whom Jesus loved said to Peter, "It is the Lord!" As soon as Simon Peter heard him say, "It is the Lord," he wrapped his outer garment around him (for he had taken it off) and jumped into the water. 8The other disciples followed in the boat, towing the net full of fish, for they were not far from shore, about a hundred yards.ᵃ 9When they landed, they saw a fire of burning coals there with fish on it, and some bread.

10Jesus said to them, "Bring some of the fish you have just caught."

11Simon Peter climbed aboard and dragged the net ashore. It was full of large fish, 153, but even with so many the net was not torn. 12Jesus said to them, "Come and have breakfast." None of the disciples dared ask him, "Who are you?" They knew it was the Lord. 13Jesus came, took the bread and gave it to them, and did the same with the fish. 14This was now the third time Jesus appeared to his disciples after he was raised from the dead.

Jesus Reinstates Peter

15When they had finished eating, Jesus said to Simon Peter, "Simon son of John, do you truly love me more than these?"

"Yes, Lord," he said, "you know that I love you."

Jesus said, "Feed my lambs."

16Again Jesus said, "Simon son of John, do you truly love me?"

He answered, "Yes, Lord, you know that I love you."

Jesus said, "Take care of my sheep."

17The third time he said to him, "Simon son of John, do you love me?"

Peter was hurt because Jesus asked him the third time, "Do you love me?" He said, "Lord, you know all things; you know that I love you."

Jesus said, "Feed my sheep. 18I tell you the truth, when you were younger you dressed yourself and went where you wanted; but when you are old you will stretch out your hands, and someone else will dress you and lead you where you do not want to go." 19Jesus said this to indicate the kind of death by which Peter would glorify God. Then he said to him, "Follow me!"

6耶穌説："你們把網撒在船的右邊，就必得着。"他們便撒下網去，竟拉不上來了，因為魚甚多。

7耶穌所愛的那門徒對彼得説："是主！"那時西門彼得赤着身子，一聽見是主，就束上一件外衣，跳在海裏。8其餘的門徒（離岸不遠，約有二百肘（註：古代以肘為尺，一肘約有今時尺半。））就在小船上把那網魚拉過來。9他們上了岸，就看見那裏有炭火，上面有魚，又有餅。

10耶穌對他們説："把剛才打的魚拿幾條來。"

11西門彼得就去（註：或作"上船"），把網拉到岸上，那網滿了大魚，共一百五十三條。魚雖這樣多，網卻沒有破。12耶穌説："你們來吃早飯。"門徒中沒有一個敢問他"你是誰"，因為知道是主。13耶穌就來拿餅和魚給他們。14耶穌從死裏復活以後向門徒顯現，這是第三次。

耶穌使彼得復興

15他們吃完了早飯，耶穌對西門彼得説："約翰的兒子西門（註："約翰"在馬太16章17節稱"約拿"），你愛我比這些更深嗎？"

彼得説："主啊，是的，你知道我愛你。"

耶穌對他説："你餵養我的小羊。"

16耶穌第二次又對他説："約翰的兒子西門，你愛我嗎？"彼得説："主啊，是的，你知道我愛你。"

耶穌説："你牧養我的羊。"

17第三次對他説："約翰的兒子西門，你愛我嗎？"

彼得因為耶穌第三次對他説："你愛我嗎"，就憂愁，對耶穌説："主啊，你是無所不知的，你知道我愛你。"

耶穌説："你餵養我的羊。18我實實在在地告訴你：你年少的時候，自己束上帶子，隨意往來；但年老的時候，你要伸出手來，別人要把你束上，帶你到不願意去的地方。"19耶穌説這話，是指着彼得要怎樣死，榮耀神。説了這話，就對他説："你跟從我吧！"

---

a 8 Greek about two hundred cubits (about 90 meters)

20彼得轉過來，看見耶穌所愛的那門徒跟着，就是在晚飯的時候，靠着耶穌胸膛說"主啊，賣你的是誰"的那門徒。21彼得看見他，就問耶穌說："主啊，這人將來如何？"

22耶穌對他說："我若要他等到我來的時候，與你何干？你跟從我吧！"23於是這話傳在弟兄中間，說那門徒不死；其實耶穌不是說他不死，乃是說："我若要他等到我來的時候，與你何干？"

24為這些事作見證，並且記載這些事的，就是這門徒。我們也知道他的見證是真的。

25耶穌所行的事還有許多，若是一一地都寫出來，我想，所寫的書就是世界也容不下了。

20Peter turned and saw that the disciple whom Jesus loved was following them. (This was the one who had leaned back against Jesus at the supper and had said, "Lord, who is going to betray you?") 21When Peter saw him, he asked, "Lord, what about him?"

22Jesus answered, "If I want him to remain alive until I return, what is that to you? You must follow me." 23Because of this, the rumor spread among the brothers that this disciple would not die. But Jesus did not say that he would not die; he only said, "If I want him to remain alive until I return, what is that to you?"

24This is the disciple who testifies to these things and who wrote them down. We know that his testimony is true.

25Jesus did many other things as well. If every one of them were written down, I suppose that even the whole world would not have room for the books that would be written.

圖四：約翰福音中的主要地方
MAP 4 : KEY PLACES IN JOHN

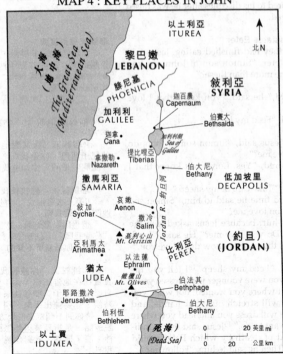

Acts

Jesus Taken Up Into Heaven

1 In my former book, Theophilus, I wrote about all that Jesus began to do and to teach ²until the day he was taken up to heaven, after giving instructions through the Holy Spirit to the apostles he had chosen. ³After his suffering, he showed himself to these men and gave many convincing proofs that he was alive. He appeared to them over a period of forty days and spoke about the kingdom of God. ⁴On one occasion, while he was eating with them, he gave them this command: "Do not leave Jerusalem, but wait for the gift my Father promised, which you have heard me speak about. ⁵For John baptized with*ᵃ* water, but in a few days you will be baptized with the Holy Spirit."

⁶So when they met together, they asked him, "Lord, are you at this time going to restore the kingdom to Israel?"

⁷He said to them: "It is not for you to know the times or dates the Father has set by his own authority. ⁸But you will receive power when the Holy Spirit comes on you; and you will be my witnesses in Jerusalem, and in all Judea and Samaria, and to the ends of the earth."

⁹After he said this, he was taken up before their very eyes, and a cloud hid him from their sight.

¹⁰They were looking intently up into the sky as he was going, when suddenly two men dressed in white stood beside them. ¹¹"Men of Galilee," they said, "why do you stand here looking into the sky? This same Jesus, who has been taken from you into heaven, will come back in the same way you have seen him go into heaven."

Matthias Chosen to Replace Judas

¹²Then they returned to Jerusalem from the hill called the Mount of Olives, a Sabbath day's walk*ᵇ* from the city. ¹³When they arrived, they went upstairs to the room where they were staying. Those present were Peter, John, James and Andrew; Philip and Thomas, Bartholomew and Matthew; James son of Alphaeus and Simon the

使徒行傳

耶穌被接升天

1 提阿非羅啊，我已經作了前書，論到耶穌開頭一切所行所教訓的，²直到他藉着聖靈吩咐所揀選的使徒，以後被接上升的日子為止。³他受害之後，用許多的憑據將自己活活地顯給使徒看，四十天之久向他們顯現，講說神國的事。⁴耶穌和他們聚集的時候，囑咐他們說："不要離開耶路撒冷，要等候父所應許的，就是你們聽見我說過的。⁵約翰是用水施洗，但不多幾日，你們要受聖靈的洗。"

⁶他們聚集的時候，問耶穌說："主啊，你復興以色列國就在這時候嗎？"

⁷耶穌對他們說："父憑着自己的權柄所定的時候、日期，不是你們可以知道的。⁸但聖靈降臨在你們身上，你們就必得着能力；並要在耶路撒冷、猶太全地和撒馬利亞，直到地極，作我的見證。"

⁹說了這話，他們正看的時候，他就被取上升，有一朵雲彩把他接去，便看不見他了。

¹⁰當他往上去，他們定睛望天的時候，忽然有兩個人身穿白衣，站在旁邊，說：¹¹ "加利利人哪，你們為甚麼站着望天呢？這離開你們被接升天的耶穌，你們見他怎樣往天上去，他還要怎樣來。"

揀選馬提亞代替猶大

¹²有一座山，名叫橄欖山，離耶路撒冷不遠，約有安息日可走的路程。當下，門徒從那裏回耶路撒冷去，¹³進了城，就上了所住的一間樓房。在那裏有彼得、約翰、雅各、安得烈、腓力、多馬、巴多羅買、馬太、亞勒腓的兒子雅各、奮銳黨的西

---

a 5 Or in   b 12 That is, about 3/4 mile (about 1,100 meters)

門和雅各的兒子 (註：或作 "兄弟") 猶大。14這些人同着幾個婦人和耶穌的母親馬利亞，並耶穌的弟兄，都同心合意地恆切禱告。

15那時，有許多人聚會，約有一百二十名，彼得就在弟兄中間站起來，16說：「弟兄們，聖靈藉大衛的口，在聖經上預言領人捉拿耶穌的猶大，這話是必須應驗的。17他本來列在我們數中，並且在使徒的職任上得了一分。

18這人用他作惡的工價買了一塊田，以後身子仆倒，肚腹崩裂，腸子都流出來。19住在耶路撒冷的眾人都知道這事，所以按着他們那裏的話給那塊田起名叫亞革大馬，就是血田的意思。

20因為詩篇上寫着說：

"　'願他的住處變為荒場，
　　無人在內居住，'

又說：

"　'願別人得他的職分。'

21所以主耶穌在我們中間始終出入的時候，22就是從約翰施洗起，直到主離開我們被接上升的日子為止，必須從那常與我們作伴的人中，立一位與我們同作耶穌復活的見證。」

23於是選舉兩個人，就是那叫做巴撒巴，又稱呼猶士都的約瑟和馬提亞。24、25眾人就禱告說：「主啊，你知道萬人的心。求你從這兩個人中，指明你所揀選的是誰，叫他得這使徒的位分。這位分猶大已經丟棄，往自己的地方去了。」26於是眾人為他們搖籤，搖出馬提亞來；他就和十一個使徒同列。

五旬節聖靈降臨

2 五旬節到了，門徒都聚集在一處。2忽然，從天上有響聲下來，好像一陣大風吹過，充滿了他們所坐的屋子；3又有舌頭如火焰顯現出來，分開落在他們各人頭上。4他們就都被聖靈充滿，按着聖靈所賜的口才說起別國的話來。

Zealot, and Judas son of James. 14They all joined together constantly in prayer, along with the women and Mary the mother of Jesus, and with his brothers.

15In those days Peter stood up among the believers[a] (a group numbering about a hundred and twenty) 16and said, "Brothers, the Scripture had to be fulfilled which the Holy Spirit spoke long ago through the mouth of David concerning Judas, who served as guide for those who arrested Jesus— 17he was one of our number and shared in this ministry."

18(With the reward he got for his wickedness, Judas bought a field; there he fell headlong, his body burst open and all his intestines spilled out. 19Everyone in Jerusalem heard about this, so they called that field in their language Akeldama, that is, Field of Blood.)

20"For," said Peter, "it is written in the book of Psalms,

"　'May his place be deserted;
　　let there be no one to dwell in it,'[b]

and,

"　'May another take his place of leadership.'[c]

21Therefore it is necessary to choose one of the men who have been with us the whole time the Lord Jesus went in and out among us, 22beginning from John's baptism to the time when Jesus was taken up from us. For one of these must become a witness with us of his resurrection."

23So they proposed two men: Joseph called Barsabbas (also known as Justus) and Matthias. 24Then they prayed, "Lord, you know everyone's heart. Show us which of these two you have chosen 25to take over this apostolic ministry, which Judas left to go where he belongs." 26Then they cast lots, and the lot fell to Matthias; so he was added to the eleven apostles.

The Holy Spirit Comes at Pentecost

2 When the day of Pentecost came, they were all together in one place. 2Suddenly a sound like the blowing of a violent wind came from heaven and filled the whole house where they were sitting. 3They saw what seemed to be tongues of fire that separated and came to rest on each of them. 4All of them were filled with the Holy Spirit and began to speak in other tongues[d] as the Spirit enabled them.

a 15 Greek brothers　　b 20 Psalm 69:25　　c 20 Psalm 109:8
d 4 Or languages; also in verse 11

⁵Now there were staying in Jerusalem God-fearing Jews from every nation under heaven. ⁶When they heard this sound, a crowd came together in bewilderment, because each one heard them speaking in his own language. ⁷Utterly amazed, they asked: "Are not all these men who are speaking Galileans? ⁸Then how is it that each of us hears them in his own native language? ⁹Parthians, Medes and Elamites; residents of Mesopotamia, Judea and Cappadocia, Pontus and Asia, ¹⁰Phrygia and Pamphylia, Egypt and the parts of Libya near Cyrene; visitors from Rome ¹¹(both Jews and converts to Judaism); Cretans and Arabs—we hear them declaring the wonders of God in our own tongues!" ¹²Amazed and perplexed, they asked one another, "What does this mean?"

¹³Some, however, made fun of them and said, "They have had too much wine.^a"

Peter Addresses the Crowd

¹⁴Then Peter stood up with the Eleven, raised his voice and addressed the crowd: "Fellow Jews and all of you who live in Jerusalem, let me explain this to you; listen carefully to what I say. ¹⁵These men are not drunk, as you suppose. It's only nine in the morning! ¹⁶No, this is what was spoken by the prophet Joel:

¹⁷" 'In the last days, God says,
　　I will pour out my Spirit on all people.
　Your sons and daughters will prophesy,
　　your young men will see visions,
　　your old men will dream dreams.
¹⁸Even on my servants, both men and women,
　　I will pour out my Spirit in those days,
　　and they will prophesy.
¹⁹I will show wonders in the heaven above
　　and signs on the earth below,
　　blood and fire and billows of smoke.
²⁰The sun will be turned to darkness
　　and the moon to blood
　　before the coming of the great and glorious
　　　　day of the Lord.
²¹And everyone who calls
　　on the name of the Lord will be saved.'^b

²²"Men of Israel, listen to this: Jesus of Nazareth was a man accredited by God to you by miracles, wonders and signs, which God did among you through him, as you yourselves know. ²³This man was handed over to you by God's set purpose and foreknowledge; and you,

⁵那時，有虔誠的<u>猶太</u>人從天下各國來，住在<u>耶路撒冷</u>。⁶這聲音一響，眾人都來聚集。各人聽見門徒用眾人的鄉談說話，就甚納悶，⁷都驚訝希奇說：「看哪，這說話的不都是<u>加利利</u>人嗎？⁸我們各人怎麼聽見他們說我們生來所用的鄉談呢？⁹我們<u>帕提亞</u>人、<u>瑪代</u>人、<u>以攔</u>人，和住在<u>美索不達米亞</u>、<u>猶太</u>、<u>加帕多家</u>、<u>本都</u>、<u>亞西亞</u>、¹⁰<u>弗呂家</u>、<u>旁非利亞</u>、<u>埃及</u>的人，並靠近<u>古利奈</u>的<u>利比亞</u>一帶地方的人，從<u>羅馬</u>來的客旅中，或是<u>猶太</u>人，或是進<u>猶太</u>教的人，¹¹<u>克里特</u>和<u>阿拉伯</u>人，都聽見他們用我們的鄉談，講說神的大作為。」¹²眾人就都驚訝猜疑，彼此說：「這是甚麼意思呢？」

¹³還有人譏誚說：「他們無非是新酒灌滿了。」

彼得向羣眾講道

¹⁴<u>彼得</u>和十一個使徒站起，高聲說：「<u>猶太</u>人和一切住在<u>耶路撒冷</u>的人哪，這件事你們當知道，也當側耳聽我的話。¹⁵你們想這些人是醉了？其實不是醉了，因為時候剛到巳初。¹⁶這正是先知<u>約珥</u>所說的：

¹⁷" 『神說：在末後的日子，
　　我要將我的靈澆灌凡有血氣的。
　你們的兒女要說預言；
　　你們的少年人要見異象；
　　老年人要做異夢。
¹⁸在那些日子，
　　我要將我的靈澆灌我的僕人和使女，
　　他們就要說預言。
¹⁹在天上我要顯出奇事；
　　在地下我要顯出神蹟，
　　有血、有火、有煙霧。
²⁰日頭要變為黑暗，
　　月亮要變為血；
　　這都在主大而明顯的日子
　　　　未到以前。
²¹到那時候，
　　凡求告主名的，就必得救。』

²²「<u>以色列</u>人哪，請聽我的話：神藉着<u>拿撒勒</u>人耶穌在你們中間施行異能、奇事、神蹟，將他證明出來，這是你們自己知道的。²³他既按着神的定旨、先見被交與人，你們就藉着

_{a 13 Or sweet wine　b 21 Joel 2:28-32}

無法之人的手，把他釘在十字架上殺了。24神卻將死的痛苦解釋了，叫他復活，因為他原不能被死拘禁。25大衛指着他說：

" '我看見主常在我眼前，
　　他在我右邊，
　　叫我不至於搖動。
26所以我心裏歡喜，
　　我的靈（註：原文作"舌"）快樂；
　　並且我的肉身要安居在指望中。
27因你必不將我的靈魂撇在陰間，
　　也不叫你的聖者見朽壞。

28你已將生命的道路指示我，
　　必叫我因見你的面（註：或作"叫我在你面前"），得着滿足的快樂。'

29"弟兄們，先祖大衛的事，我可以明明地對你們說，他死了，也葬埋了，並且他的墳墓直到今日還在我們這裏。30大衛既是先知，又曉得神曾向他起誓，要從他的後裔中立一位坐在他的寶座上，31就預先看明這事，講論基督復活說：'他的靈魂不撇在陰間；他的肉身也不見朽壞。'32這耶穌，神已經叫他復活了，我們都為這事作見證。33他既被神的右手高舉（註：或作"他既高舉在神的右邊"），又從父受了所應許的聖靈，就把你們所看見、所聽見的澆灌下來。34大衛並沒有升到天上，但自己說：

" '主對我主說：
　　你坐在我的右邊，
35等我使你仇敵
　　作你的腳凳。'

36"故此，以色列全家當確實地知道，你們釘在十字架上的這位耶穌，神已經立他為主，為基督了。"

37眾人聽見這話，覺得扎心，就對彼得和其餘的使徒說："弟兄們，我們當怎樣行？"

38彼得說："你們各人要悔改，奉耶穌基督的名受洗，叫你們的罪得赦，就必領受所賜的聖靈；39因為這應許是給你們和你們的兒女，並一切在遠方的人，就是主我們神所召來的。"

with the help of wicked men,[a] put him to death by nailing him to the cross. 24But God raised him from the dead, freeing him from the agony of death, because it was impossible for death to keep its hold on him. 25David said about him:

" 'I saw the Lord always before me.
　Because he is at my right hand,
　　I will not be shaken.
26Therefore my heart is glad and my tongue rejoices;
　　my body also will live in hope,
27because you will not abandon me to the grave,
　　nor will you let your Holy One see decay.
28You have made known to me the paths of life;
　　you will fill me with joy in your presence.'[b]

29"Brothers, I can tell you confidently that the patriarch David died and was buried, and his tomb is here to this day. 30But he was a prophet and knew that God had promised him on oath that he would place one of his descendants on his throne. 31Seeing what was ahead, he spoke of the resurrection of the Christ,[c] that he was not abandoned to the grave, nor did his body see decay. 32God has raised this Jesus to life, and we are all witnesses of the fact. 33Exalted to the right hand of God, he has received from the Father the promised Holy Spirit and has poured out what you now see and hear. 34For David did not ascend to heaven, and yet he said,

" 'The Lord said to my Lord:
　"Sit at my right hand
35until I make your enemies
　　a footstool for your feet." '[d]

36"Therefore let all Israel be assured of this: God has made this Jesus, whom you crucified, both Lord and Christ."

37When the people heard this, they were cut to the heart and said to Peter and the other apostles, "Brothers, what shall we do?"

38Peter replied, "Repent and be baptized, every one of you, in the name of Jesus Christ for the forgiveness of your sins. And you will receive the gift of the Holy Spirit. 39The promise is for you and your children and for all who are far off—for all whom the Lord our God will call."

---

a 23 Or of those not having the law (that is, Gentiles)
b 28 Psalm 16:8-11   c 31 Or Messiah. "The Christ" (Greek) and "the Messiah" (Hebrew) both mean "the Anointed One"; also in verse 36.   d 35 Psalm 110:1

[40]With many other words he warned them; and he pleaded with them, "Save yourselves from this corrupt generation." [41]Those who accepted his message were baptized, and about three thousand were added to their number that day.

The Fellowship of the Believers

[42]They devoted themselves to the apostles' teaching and to the fellowship, to the breaking of bread and to prayer. [43]Everyone was filled with awe, and many wonders and miraculous signs were done by the apostles. [44]All the believers were together and had everything in common. [45]Selling their possessions and goods, they gave to anyone as he had need. [46]Every day they continued to meet together in the temple courts. They broke bread in their homes and ate together with glad and sincere hearts, [47]praising God and enjoying the favor of all the people. And the Lord added to their number daily those who were being saved.

Peter Heals the Crippled Beggar

3 One day Peter and John were going up to the temple at the time of prayer—at three in the afternoon. [2]Now a man crippled from birth was being carried to the temple gate called Beautiful, where he was put every day to beg from those going into the temple courts. [3]When he saw Peter and John about to enter, he asked them for money. [4]Peter looked straight at him, as did John. Then Peter said, "Look at us!" [5]So the man gave them his attention, expecting to get something from them.

[6]Then Peter said, "Silver or gold I do not have, but what I have I give you. In the name of Jesus Christ of Nazareth, walk." [7]Taking him by the right hand, he helped him up, and instantly the man's feet and ankles became strong. [8]He jumped to his feet and began to walk. Then he went with them into the temple courts, walking and jumping, and praising God. [9]When all the people saw him walking and praising God, [10]they recognized him as the same man who used to sit begging at the temple gate called Beautiful, and they were filled with wonder and amazement at what had happened to him.

Peter Speaks to the Onlookers

[11]While the beggar held on to Peter and John, all the people were astonished and came running to them in the place called Solomon's Colonnade. [12]When Peter saw this, he said to them: "Men of Israel, why does this surprise you? Why do you stare at us as if by our own

[40]彼得還用許多話作見證，勸勉他們說：「你們當救自己脫離這彎曲的世代。」[41]於是，領受他話的人就受了洗。那一天，門徒約添了三千人。

信徒彼此相交

[42]都恆心遵守使徒的教訓，彼此交接、擘餅、祈禱。[43]眾人都懼怕。使徒又行了許多奇事、神蹟。[44]信的人都在一處，凡物公用，[45]並且賣了田產、家業，照各人所需用的分給各人。[46]他們天天同心合意恆切地在殿裏，且在家中擘餅，存着歡喜、誠實的心用飯，[47]讚美神，得眾民的喜愛。主將得救的人天天加給他們。

彼得醫治瘸腿的乞丐

3 申初禱告的時候，彼得、約翰上聖殿去。[2]有一個人，生來是瘸腿的，天天被人抬來，放在殿的一個門口（那門名叫美門），要求進殿的人賙濟。[3]他看見彼得、約翰將要進殿，就求他們賙濟。[4]彼得、約翰定睛看他。彼得說：「你看我們！」[5]那人就留意看他們，指望得着甚麼。

[6]彼得說：「金銀我都沒有，只把我所有的給你。我奉拿撒勒人耶穌基督的名，叫你起來行走！」[7]於是拉着他的右手，扶他起來。他的腳和踝子骨立刻健壯了，[8]就跳起來，站着，又行走，同他們進了殿，走着，跳着，讚美神。[9]百姓都看見他行走，讚美神，[10]認得他是那素常坐在殿的美門口求賙濟的，就因他所遇着的事，滿心希奇驚訝。

彼得向圍觀的人講道

[11]那人正在稱為所羅門的廊下，拉着彼得、約翰，眾百姓一齊跑到他們那裏，很覺希奇。[12]彼得看見，就對百姓說：「以色列人哪，為甚麼把這事當作奇奇呢？為甚麼定睛看我

們，以為我們憑自己的能力和虔誠使這人行走呢？¹³亞伯拉罕、以撒、雅各的神，就是我們列祖的神，已經榮耀了他的僕人耶穌（註："僕人"或作"兒子"）；你們卻把他交付彼拉多。彼拉多定意要釋放他，你們竟在彼拉多面前棄絕了他。¹⁴你們棄絕了那聖潔公義者，反求着釋放一個兇手給你們。¹⁵你們殺了那生命的主，神卻叫他從死裏復活了。我們都是為這事作見證。¹⁶我們因信他的名，他的名便叫你們所看見、所認識的這人健壯了。正是他所賜的信心，叫這人在你們眾人面前全然好了。

¹⁷"弟兄們，我曉得你們做這事是出於不知，你們的官長也是如此。¹⁸但神曾藉眾先知的口，預言基督將要受害，就這樣應驗了。¹⁹所以你們當悔改歸正，使你們的罪得以塗抹。這樣，那安舒的日子就必從主面前來到，²⁰主也必差遣所預定給你們的基督耶穌降臨。²¹天必留他，等到萬物復興的時候，就是神從創世以來，藉着聖先知的口所說的。²²摩西曾說：'主神要從你們弟兄中間給你們興起一位先知像我，凡他向你們所說的，你們都要聽從。²³凡不聽從那先知的，必要從民中全然滅絕。'

²⁴"從撒母耳以來的眾先知，凡說預言的，也都說到這些日子。²⁵你們是先知的子孫，也承受神與你們祖宗所立的約，就是對亞伯拉罕說：'地上萬族都要因你的後裔得福。'²⁶神既興起他的僕人（註：或作"兒子"），就先差他到你們這裏來，賜福給你們，叫你們各人回轉，離開罪惡。"

彼得約翰在公會前

4 使徒對百姓說話的時候，祭司們和守殿官，並撒都該人忽然來了。²因他們教訓百姓，本着耶穌，傳說死人復活，就很煩惱，³於是下手拿住他們。因為天已經晚了，就把他們押到第二天。⁴但聽道之人有許多信的，男丁數目約到五千。

power or godliness we had made this man walk? ¹³The God of Abraham, Isaac and Jacob, the God of our fathers, has glorified his servant Jesus. You handed him over to be killed, and you disowned him before Pilate, though he had decided to let him go. ¹⁴You disowned the Holy and Righteous One and asked that a murderer be released to you. ¹⁵You killed the author of life, but God raised him from the dead. We are witnesses of this. ¹⁶By faith in the name of Jesus, this man whom you see and know was made strong. It is Jesus' name and the faith that comes through him that has given this complete healing to him, as you can all see.

¹⁷"Now, brothers, I know that you acted in ignorance, as did your leaders. ¹⁸But this is how God fulfilled what he had foretold through all the prophets, saying that his Christ[a] would suffer. ¹⁹Repent, then, and turn to God, so that your sins may be wiped out, that times of refreshing may come from the Lord, ²⁰and that he may send the Christ, who has been appointed for you—even Jesus. ²¹He must remain in heaven until the time comes for God to restore everything, as he promised long ago through his holy prophets. ²²For Moses said, 'The Lord your God will raise up for you a prophet like me from among your own people; you must listen to everything he tells you. ²³Anyone who does not listen to him will be completely cut off from among his people.'[b]

²⁴"Indeed, all the prophets from Samuel on, as many as have spoken, have foretold these days. ²⁵And you are heirs of the prophets and of the covenant God made with your fathers. He said to Abraham, 'Through your offspring all peoples on earth will be blessed.'[c] ²⁶When God raised up his servant, he sent him first to you to bless you by turning each of you from your wicked ways."

Peter and John Before the Sanhedrin

4 The priests and the captain of the temple guard and the Sadducees came up to Peter and John while they were speaking to the people. ²They were greatly disturbed because the apostles were teaching the people and proclaiming in Jesus the resurrection of the dead. ³They seized Peter and John, and because it was evening, they put them in jail until the next day. ⁴But many who heard the message believed, and the number of men grew to about five thousand.

a 18 Or *Messiah; also in verse 20　　b 23* Deut. 18:15,18,19
c 25 Gen. 22:18; 26:4

5The next day the rulers, elders and teachers of the law met in Jerusalem. 6Annas the high priest was there, and so were Caiaphas, John, Alexander and the other men of the high priest's family. 7They had Peter and John brought before them and began to question them: "By what power or what name did you do this?"

8Then Peter, filled with the Holy Spirit, said to them: "Rulers and elders of the people! 9If we are being called to account today for an act of kindness shown to a cripple and are asked how he was healed, 10then know this, you and all the people of Israel: It is by the name of Jesus Christ of Nazareth, whom you crucified but whom God raised from the dead, that this man stands before you healed. 11He is

" 'the stone you builders rejected,
     which has become the capstone.a'b

12Salvation is found in no one else, for there is no other name under heaven given to men by which we must be saved."

13When they saw the courage of Peter and John and realized that they were unschooled, ordinary men, they were astonished and they took note that these men had been with Jesus. 14But since they could see the man who had been healed standing there with them, there was nothing they could say. 15So they ordered them to withdraw from the Sanhedrin and then conferred together. 16"What are we going to do with these men?" they asked. "Everybody living in Jerusalem knows they have done an outstanding miracle, and we cannot deny it. 17But to stop this thing from spreading any further among the people, we must warn these men to speak no longer to anyone in this name."

18Then they called them in again and commanded them not to speak or teach at all in the name of Jesus. 19But Peter and John replied, "Judge for yourselves whether it is right in God's sight to obey you rather than God. 20For we cannot help speaking about what we have seen and heard."

21After further threats they let them go. They could not decide how to punish them, because all the people were praising God for what had happened. 22For the man who was miraculously healed was over forty years old.

The Believers' Prayer

23On their release, Peter and John went back to their own people and reported all that the

5第二天，官府、長老和文士在耶路撒冷聚會，6又有大祭司亞那和該亞法、約翰、亞歷山大，並大祭司的親族都在那裏；7叫使徒站在當中，就問他們說：「你們用甚麼能力，奉誰的名做這事呢？」

8那時，彼得被聖靈充滿，對他們說：9「治民的官府和長老啊，倘若今日因為在殘疾人身上所行的善事，查問我們他是怎麼得了痊愈，10你們眾人和以色列百姓都當知道，站在你們面前的這人得痊愈，是因你們所釘十字架，神叫他從死裏復活的拿撒勒人耶穌基督的名。11他是

" '你們匠人所棄的石頭，
     已成了房角的頭塊石頭。'

12除他以外，別無拯救，因為在天下人間，沒有賜下別的名，我們可以靠着得救。」

13他們見彼得、約翰的膽量，又看出他們原是沒有學問的小民，就希奇，認明他們是跟過耶穌的。14又看見那治好了的人和他們一同站着，就無話可駁。15於是吩咐他們從公會出去，就彼此商議說：16「我們當怎樣辦這兩個人呢？因為他們誠然行了一件明顯的神蹟，凡住耶路撒冷的人都知道，我們也不能說沒有。17惟恐這事越發傳揚在民間，我們必須恐嚇他們，叫他們不再奉這名對人講論。」

18於是叫了他們來，禁止他們，總不可奉耶穌的名講論、教訓人。19彼得、約翰說：「聽從你們，不聽從神，這在神面前合理不合理，你們自己酌量吧！20我們所看見、所聽見的，不能不說。」

21官長為百姓的緣故，想不出法子刑罰他們，又恐嚇一番，把他們釋放了。這是因眾人為所行的奇事，都歸榮耀與神。22原來藉着神蹟醫好的那人有四十多歲了。

信徒的禱告

23二人既被釋放，就到會友那裏去，把祭司長和長老所說的話都告訴

a 11 Or cornerstone   b 11 Psalm 118:22

他們。²⁴他們聽見了，就同心合意地高聲向神說：「主啊，你是造天、地、海和其中萬物的，²⁵你曾藉着聖靈託你僕人——我們祖宗大衛的口說：

「『外邦為甚麼爭鬧？
　萬民為甚麼謀算虛妄的事？
²⁶世上的君王一齊起來，
　臣宰也聚集，
　要敵擋主，
　並主的受膏者（註：或作「基督」）。』

²⁷希律和本丟彼拉多、外邦人和以色列民果然在這城裏聚集，要攻打你所膏的聖僕耶穌（註：「僕」或作「子」），²⁸成就你手和你意旨所預定必有的事。²⁹他們恐嚇我們，現在求主鑒察。一面叫你僕人大放膽量，講你的道；一面伸出你的手來醫治疾病，並且使神蹟奇事因着你聖僕耶穌的名行出來（註：「僕」或作「子」）。³¹禱告完了，聚會的地方震動，他們就都被聖靈充滿，放膽講論神的道。

信徒凡物公用

³²那許多信的人都是一心一意的，沒有一人說他的東西有一樣是自己的，都是大家公用。³³使徒大有能力，見證主耶穌復活，眾人也都蒙大恩。³⁴內中也沒有一個缺乏的，因為人人將田產房屋都賣了，把所賣的價銀拿來，³⁵放在使徒腳前，照各人所需用的，分給各人。

³⁶有一個利未人，生在塞浦路斯，名叫約瑟，使徒稱他為巴拿巴（巴拿巴翻出來就是勸慰子）。³⁷他有田地也賣了，把價銀拿來，放在使徒腳前。

亞拿尼亞和撒非喇

5 有一個人，名叫亞拿尼亞，同他的妻子撒非喇賣了田產，²把價銀私自留下幾分，他的妻子也知道，其餘的幾分拿來放在使徒腳前。

---

chief priests and elders had said to them. ²⁴When they heard this, they raised their voices together in prayer to God. "Sovereign Lord," they said, "you made the heaven and the earth and the sea, and everything in them. ²⁵You spoke by the Holy Spirit through the mouth of your servant, our father David:

"'Why do the nations rage
　and the peoples plot in vain?
²⁶The kings of the earth take their stand
　and the rulers gather together
　against the Lord
　and against his Anointed One.[a,b]

²⁷Indeed Herod and Pontius Pilate met together with the Gentiles and the people[c] of Israel in this city to conspire against your holy servant Jesus, whom you anointed. ²⁸They did what your power and will had decided beforehand should happen. ²⁹Now, Lord, consider their threats and enable your servants to speak your word with great boldness. ³⁰Stretch out your hand to heal and perform miraculous signs and wonders through the name of your holy servant Jesus."

³¹After they prayed, the place where they were meeting was shaken. And they were all filled with the Holy Spirit and spoke the word of God boldly.

The Believers Share Their Possessions

³²All the believers were one in heart and mind. No one claimed that any of his possessions was his own, but they shared everything they had. ³³With great power the apostles continued to testify to the resurrection of the Lord Jesus, and much grace was upon them all. ³⁴There were no needy persons among them. For from time to time those who owned lands or houses sold them, brought the money from the sales ³⁵and put it at the apostles' feet, and it was distributed to anyone as he had need.

³⁶Joseph, a Levite from Cyprus, whom the apostles called Barnabas (which means Son of Encouragement), ³⁷sold a field he owned and brought the money and put it at the apostles' feet.

Ananias and Sapphira

5 Now a man named Ananias, together with his wife Sapphira, also sold a piece of property. ²With his wife's full knowledge he kept back part of the money for himself, but brought the rest and put it at the apostles' feet.

a 26 That is, Christ or Messiah　　*b 26* Psalm 2:1,2　　*c 27* The Greek is plural.

³Then Peter said, "Ananias, how is it that Satan has so filled your heart that you have lied to the Holy Spirit and have kept for yourself some of the money you received for the land? ⁴Didn't it belong to you before it was sold? And after it was sold, wasn't the money at your disposal? What made you think of doing such a thing? You have not lied to men but to God."

⁵When Ananias heard this, he fell down and died. And great fear seized all who heard what had happened. ⁶Then the young men came forward, wrapped up his body, and carried him out and buried him.

⁷About three hours later his wife came in, not knowing what had happened. ⁸Peter asked her, "Tell me, is this the price you and Ananias got for the land?"

"Yes," she said, "that is the price."

⁹Peter said to her, "How could you agree to test the Spirit of the Lord? Look! The feet of the men who buried your husband are at the door, and they will carry you out also."

¹⁰At that moment she fell down at his feet and died. Then the young men came in and, finding her dead, carried her out and buried her beside her husband. ¹¹Great fear seized the whole church and all who heard about these events.

The Apostles Heal Many

¹²The apostles performed many miraculous signs and wonders among the people. And all the believers used to meet together in Solomon's Colonnade. ¹³No one else dared join them, even though they were highly regarded by the people. ¹⁴Nevertheless, more and more men and women believed in the Lord and were added to their number. ¹⁵As a result, people brought the sick into the streets and laid them on beds and mats so that at least Peter's shadow might fall on some of them as he passed by. ¹⁶Crowds gathered also from the towns around Jerusalem, bringing their sick and those tormented by evil*ᵃ* spirits, and all of them were healed.

The Apostles Persecuted

¹⁷Then the high priest and all his associates, who were members of the party of the Sadducees, were filled with jealousy. ¹⁸They arrested the apostles and put them in the public jail. ¹⁹But during the night an angel of the Lord opened the doors of the jail and brought them out. ²⁰"Go, stand in the temple courts," he said, "and tell the people the full message of this new life."

a16 Greek unclean

³彼得說："亞拿尼亞,為甚麼撒但充滿了你的心,叫你欺哄聖靈,把田地的價銀私自留下幾分呢?⁴田地還沒有賣,不是你自己的嗎?既賣了,價銀不是你做主嗎?你怎麼心裏起這意念呢?你不是欺哄人,是欺哄神了!"

⁵亞拿尼亞聽見這話,就仆倒,斷了氣。聽見的人都甚懼怕。⁶有些少年人起來,把他包裹,抬出去埋葬了。

⁷約過了三小時,他的妻子進來,還不知道這事。⁸彼得對她說:"你告訴我,你們賣田地的價銀就是這些嗎?"

她說:"就是這些。"

⁹彼得說:"你們為甚麼同心試探主的靈呢?埋葬你丈夫之人的腳已到門口,他們也要把你抬出去。"

¹⁰婦人立刻仆倒在彼得腳前,斷了氣。那些少年人進來,見她已經死了,就抬出去,埋在她丈夫旁邊。¹¹全教會和聽見這事的人都甚懼怕。

使徒醫好許多病人

¹²主藉使徒的手在民間行了許多神蹟奇事。(他們(註:或作"信的人")都同心合意地在所羅門的廊下;¹³其餘的人沒有一個敢貼近他們,百姓卻尊重他們。¹⁴信而歸主的人越發增添,連男帶女很多。)¹⁵甚至有人將病人抬到街上,放在牀上或褥子上,指望彼得過來的時候,或者得他的影兒照在甚麼人身上。¹⁶還有許多人帶着病人和被污鬼纏磨的,從耶路撒冷四圍的城邑來,全都得了醫治。

使徒受逼迫

¹⁷大祭司和他的一切同人,就是撒都該教門的人,都起來,滿心忌恨,¹⁸就下手拿住使徒,收在外監。¹⁹但主的使者夜間開了監門,領他們出來,²⁰說:"你們去站在殿裏,把這生命的道都講給百姓聽。"

²¹使徒聽了這話，天將亮的時候就進殿裏去教訓人。

大祭司和他的同人來了，叫齊公會的人和以色列族的眾長老，就差人到監裏去，要把使徒提出來。²²但差役到了，不見他們在監裏，就回來稟報說：²³ "我們看見監牢關得極妥當，看守的人也站在門外，及至開了門，裏面一個人都不見！" ²⁴守殿官和祭司長聽見這話，心裏犯難，不知這事將來如何。

²⁵有一個人來稟報說："你們收在監裏的人，現在站在殿裏教訓百姓。" ²⁶於是守殿官和差役去帶使徒來，並沒有用強暴，因為怕百姓用石頭打他們。

²⁷帶到了，便叫使徒站在公會前。大祭司問他們說：²⁸ "我們不是嚴嚴地禁止你們，不可奉這名教訓人嗎？你們倒把你們的道理充滿了耶路撒冷，想要叫這人的血歸到我們身上。"

²⁹彼得和眾使徒回答說："順從神，不順從人，是應當的！³⁰你們掛在木頭上殺害的耶穌，我們祖宗的神已經叫他復活。³¹神且用右手將他高舉（註：或作 "他就是神高舉在自己的右邊"），叫他作君王、作救主，將悔改的心和赦罪的恩賜給以色列人。³²我們為這事作見證，神賜給順從之人的聖靈也為這事作見證。"

³³公會的人聽見就極其惱怒，想要殺他們。³⁴但有一個法利賽人，名叫迦瑪列，是眾百姓所敬重的教法師，在公會中站起來，吩咐人把使徒暫且帶到外面去，³⁵就對眾人說："以色列人哪，論到這些人，你們應當小心怎樣辦理。³⁶從前丟大起來，自誇為大，附從他的人約有四百。他被殺後，附從他的全都散了，歸於無有。³⁷此後，報名上冊的時候，又有加利利的猶大起來，引誘些百姓跟從他。他也滅亡，附從他的人也都四散了。³⁸現在，我勸你們不要管這些人，任憑他們吧！他們所謀的、所行的，若是出於人，必要敗壞；³⁹若是出於神，你們就不能敗壞他們，恐怕你們倒是攻擊神了。"

²¹At daybreak they entered the temple courts, as they had been told, and began to teach the people.

When the high priest and his associates arrived, they called together the Sanhedrin—the full assembly of the elders of Israel—and sent to the jail for the apostles. ²²But on arriving at the jail, the officers did not find them there. So they went back and reported, ²³"We found the jail securely locked, with the guards standing at the doors; but when we opened them, we found no one inside." ²⁴On hearing this report, the captain of the temple guard and the chief priests were puzzled, wondering what would come of this.

²⁵Then someone came and said, "Look! The men you put in jail are standing in the temple courts teaching the people." ²⁶At that, the captain went with his officers and brought the apostles. They did not use force, because they feared that the people would stone them.

²⁷Having brought the apostles, they made them appear before the Sanhedrin to be questioned by the high priest. ²⁸"We gave you strict orders not to teach in this name," he said. "Yet you have filled Jerusalem with your teaching and are determined to make us guilty of this man's blood."

²⁹Peter and the other apostles replied: "We must obey God rather than men! ³⁰The God of our fathers raised Jesus from the dead—whom you had killed by hanging him on a tree. ³¹God exalted him to his own right hand as Prince and Savior that he might give repentance and forgiveness of sins to Israel. ³²We are witnesses of these things, and so is the Holy Spirit, whom God has given to those who obey him."

³³When they heard this, they were furious and wanted to put them to death. ³⁴But a Pharisee named Gamaliel, a teacher of the law, who was honored by all the people, stood up in the Sanhedrin and ordered that the men be put outside for a little while. ³⁵Then he addressed them: "Men of Israel, consider carefully what you intend to do to these men. ³⁶Some time ago Theudas appeared, claiming to be somebody, and about four hundred men rallied to him. He was killed, all his followers were dispersed, and it all came to nothing. ³⁷After him, Judas the Galilean appeared in the days of the census and led a band of people in revolt. He too was killed, and all his followers were scattered. ³⁸Therefore, in the present case I advise you: Leave these men alone! Let them go! For if their purpose or activity is of human origin, it will fail. ³⁹But if it is from God, you will not be able to stop these men; you will only find yourselves fighting against God."

[40]His speech persuaded them. They called the apostles in and had them flogged. Then they ordered them not to speak in the name of Jesus, and let them go.

[41]The apostles left the Sanhedrin, rejoicing because they had been counted worthy of suffering disgrace for the Name. [42]Day after day, in the temple courts and from house to house, they never stopped teaching and proclaiming the good news that Jesus is the Christ.[a]

The Choosing of the Seven

6 In those days when the number of disciples was increasing, the Grecian Jews among them complained against the Hebraic Jews because their widows were being overlooked in the daily distribution of food. [2]So the Twelve gathered all the disciples together and said, "It would not be right for us to neglect the ministry of the word of God in order to wait on tables. [3]Brothers, choose seven men from among you who are known to be full of the Spirit and wisdom. We will turn this responsibility over to them [4]and will give our attention to prayer and the ministry of the word."

[5]This proposal pleased the whole group. They chose Stephen, a man full of faith and of the Holy Spirit; also Philip, Procorus, Nicanor, Timon, Parmenas, and Nicolas from Antioch, a convert to Judaism. [6]They presented these men to the apostles, who prayed and laid their hands on them.

[7]So the word of God spread. The number of disciples in Jerusalem increased rapidly, and a large number of priests became obedient to the faith.

Stephen Seized

[8]Now Stephen, a man full of God's grace and power, did great wonders and miraculous signs among the people. [9]Opposition arose, however, from members of the Synagogue of the Freedmen (as it was called)—Jews of Cyrene and Alexandria as well as the provinces of Cilicia and Asia. These men began to argue with Stephen, [10]but they could not stand up against his wisdom or the Spirit by whom he spoke.

[11]Then they secretly persuaded some men to say, "We have heard Stephen speak words of blasphemy against Moses and against God."

[12]So they stirred up the people and the elders and the teachers of the law. They seized Stephen and brought him before the Sanhedrin. [13]They produced false witnesses, who testified, "This

a 42 Or Messiah

---

[40]公會的人聽從了他，便叫使徒來，把他們打了，又吩咐他們不可奉耶穌的名講道，就把他們釋放了。

[41]他們離開公會，心裏歡喜，因被算是配為這名受辱。[42]他們就每日在殿裏、在家裏不住地教訓人，傳耶穌是基督。

揀選七人

6 那時，門徒增多，有說希臘話的猶太人向希伯來人發怨言，因為在天天的供給上忽略了他們的寡婦。[2]十二使徒叫眾門徒來，對他們說："我們撇下神的道去管理飯食，原是不合宜的。[3]所以，弟兄們，當從你們中間選出七個有好名聲、被聖靈充滿、智慧充足的人，我們就派他們管理這事。[4]但我們要專心以祈禱傳道為事。"

[5]大眾都喜悅這話，就揀選了司提反，乃是大有信心、聖靈充滿的人；又揀選腓利、伯羅哥羅、尼迦挪、提門、巴米拿，並進猶太教的安提阿人尼哥拉，[6]叫他們站在使徒面前。使徒禱告了，就按手在他們頭上。

[7]神的道興旺起來。在耶路撒冷門徒數目加增的甚多，也有許多祭司信從了這道。

司提反被捉拿

[8]司提反滿得恩惠能力，在民間行了大奇事和神蹟。[9]當時有稱利百地拿會堂的幾個人，並有古利奈、亞歷山太、基利家、亞西亞各處會堂的幾個人，都起來和司提反辯論。[10]司提反是以智慧和聖靈說話，眾人敵擋不住。

[11]就買出人來說："我們聽見他說謗讟摩西和神的話。"

[12]他們又聳動了百姓、長老並文士，就忽然來捉拿他，把他帶到公會去，[13]設下假見證說："這個人說話

不住地糟踐聖所和律法，14我們曾聽見他說：這拿撒勒人耶穌要毀壞此地，也要改變摩西所交給我們的規條。"

15在公會裏坐着的人都定睛看他，見他的面貌好像天使的面貌。

司提反向公會的陳述

7 大祭司就說："這些事果然有嗎？"

2司提反說："諸位父兄請聽！當日我們的祖宗亞伯拉罕在美索不達米亞還未住哈蘭的時候，榮耀的神向他顯現，3對他說：'你要離開本地和親族，往我所要指示你的地方去。'

4"他就離開迦勒底人之地，住在哈蘭。他父親死了以後，神使他從那裏搬到你們現在所住之地。5在這地方神並沒有給他產業，連立足之地也沒有給他；但應許要將這地賜給他和他的後裔為業。那時他還沒有兒子。6神說：'他的後裔必寄居外邦，那裏的人要叫他們作奴僕，苦待他們四百年。'7神又說：'使他們作奴僕的那國，我要懲罰。以後他們要出來，在這地方侍奉我。'8神又賜他割禮的約。於是亞伯拉罕生了以撒，第八日給他行了割禮。以撒生雅各，雅各生十二位先祖。

9"先祖嫉妒約瑟，把他賣到埃及去。神卻與他同在，10救他脫離一切苦難，又使他在埃及王法老面前得恩典，有智慧。法老就派他作埃及國的宰相兼管全家。

11"後來埃及和迦南全地遭遇饑荒，大受艱難，我們的祖宗就絕了糧。12雅各聽見在埃及有糧，就打發我們的祖宗初次往那裏去。13第二次約瑟與弟兄們相認，他的親族也被法老知道了。14約瑟就打發弟兄請父親雅各和全家七十五個人都來。15於是雅各下了埃及，後來他和我們的

fellow never stops speaking against this holy place and against the law. 14For we have heard him say that this Jesus of Nazareth will destroy this place and change the customs Moses handed down to us."

15All who were sitting in the Sanhedrin looked intently at Stephen, and they saw that his face was like the face of an angel.

Stephen's Speech to the Sanhedrin

7 Then the high priest asked him, "Are these charges true?"

2To this he replied: "Brothers and fathers, listen to me! The God of glory appeared to our father Abraham while he was still in Mesopotamia, before he lived in Haran. 3'Leave your country and your people,' God said, 'and go to the land I will show you.'a

4"So he left the land of the Chaldeans and settled in Haran. After the death of his father, God sent him to this land where you are now living. 5He gave him no inheritance here, not even a foot of ground. But God promised him that he and his descendants after him would possess the land, even though at that time Abraham had no child. 6God spoke to him in this way: 'Your descendants will be strangers in a country not their own, and they will be enslaved and mistreated four hundred years. 7But I will punish the nation they serve as slaves,' God said, 'and afterward they will come out of that country and worship me in this place.'b 8Then he gave Abraham the covenant of circumcision. And Abraham became the father of Isaac and circumcised him eight days after his birth. Later Isaac became the father of Jacob, and Jacob became the father of the twelve patriarchs.

9"Because the patriarchs were jealous of Joseph, they sold him as a slave into Egypt. But God was with him 10and rescued him from all his troubles. He gave Joseph wisdom and enabled him to gain the goodwill of Pharaoh king of Egypt; so he made him ruler over Egypt and all his palace.

11"Then a famine struck all Egypt and Canaan, bringing great suffering, and our fathers could not find food. 12When Jacob heard that there was grain in Egypt, he sent our fathers on their first visit. 13On their second visit, Joseph told his brothers who he was, and Pharaoh learned about Joseph's family. 14After this, Joseph sent for his father Jacob and his whole family, seventy-five in all. 15Then Jacob went down to Egypt, where he and our fathers died.

a 3 Gen. 12:1　b 7 Gen. 15:13,14

¹⁶Their bodies were brought back to Shechem and placed in the tomb that Abraham had bought from the sons of Hamor at Shechem for a certain sum of money.

¹⁷"As the time drew near for God to fulfill his promise to Abraham, the number of our people in Egypt greatly increased. ¹⁸Then another king, who knew nothing about Joseph, became ruler of Egypt. ¹⁹He dealt treacherously with our people and oppressed our forefathers by forcing them to throw out their newborn babies so that they would die.

²⁰"At that time Moses was born, and he was no ordinary child.*^a* For three months he was cared for in his father's house. ²¹When he was placed outside, Pharaoh's daughter took him and brought him up as her own son. ²²Moses was educated in all the wisdom of the Egyptians and was powerful in speech and action.

²³"When Moses was forty years old, he decided to visit his fellow Israelites. ²⁴He saw one of them being mistreated by an Egyptian, so he went to his defense and avenged him by killing the Egyptian. ²⁵Moses thought that his own people would realize that God was using him to rescue them, but they did not. ²⁶The next day Moses came upon two Israelites who were fighting. He tried to reconcile them by saying, 'Men, you are brothers; why do you want to hurt each other?'

²⁷"But the man who was mistreating the other pushed Moses aside and said, 'Who made you ruler and judge over us? ²⁸Do you want to kill me as you killed the Egyptian yesterday?'*^b* ²⁹When Moses heard this, he fled to Midian, where he settled as a foreigner and had two sons.

³⁰"After forty years had passed, an angel appeared to Moses in the flames of a burning bush in the desert near Mount Sinai. ³¹When he saw this, he was amazed at the sight. As he went over to look more closely, he heard the Lord's voice: ³²'I am the God of your fathers, the God of Abraham, Isaac and Jacob.'*^c* Moses trembled with fear and did not dare to look.

³³"Then the Lord said to him, 'Take off your sandals; the place where you are standing is holy ground. ³⁴I have indeed seen the oppression of my people in Egypt. I have heard their groaning and have come down to set them free. Now come, I will send you back to Egypt.'*^d*

³⁵"This is the same Moses whom they had rejected with the words, 'Who made you ruler and judge?' He was sent to be their ruler and

---

¹⁶祖宗都死在那裏；¹⁶又被帶到示劍，葬於亞伯拉罕在示劍用銀子從哈抹子孫買來的墳墓裏。

¹⁷ "及至神應許亞伯拉罕的日期將到，以色列民在埃及興盛眾多，¹⁸直到有不曉得約瑟的新王興起。¹⁹他用詭計待我們的宗族，苦害我們的祖宗，叫他們丟棄嬰孩，使嬰孩不能存活。

²⁰ "那時，摩西生下來，俊美非凡，在他父親家裏撫養了三個月。²¹他被丟棄的時候，法老的女兒拾了去，養為自己的兒子。²²摩西學了埃及人一切的學問，說話行事都有才能。

²³ "他將到四十歲，心中起意，去看望他的弟兄以色列人。²⁴到了那裏，見他們一個人受冤屈，就護庇他，為那受欺壓的人報仇，打死了那埃及人。²⁵他以為弟兄必明白神是藉他的手搭救他們，他們卻不明白。²⁶第二天，遇見兩個以色列人爭鬥，就勸他們和睦，說：'你們二位是弟兄，為甚麼彼此欺負呢？'

²⁷ "那欺負鄰舍的把他推開說：'誰立你作我們的首領和審判官呢？²⁸難道你要殺我，像昨天殺那埃及人嗎？' ²⁹摩西聽見這話就逃走了，寄居於米甸，在那裏生了兩個兒子。

³⁰ "過了四十年，在西奈山的曠野，有一位天使從荊棘火焰中向摩西顯現。³¹摩西見了那異象，便覺希奇，正進前觀看的時候，有主的聲音說：³² '我是你列祖的神，就是亞伯拉罕的神、以撒的神、雅各的神。' 摩西戰戰兢兢，不敢觀看。

³³ "主對他說：'把你腳上的鞋脫下來，因為你所站之地是聖地。³⁴我的百姓在埃及所受的困苦，我實在看見了；他們悲歎的聲音，我也聽見了。我下來要救他們。你來！我要差你往埃及去。'

³⁵ "這摩西，就是百姓棄絕說'誰立你作我們的首領和審判官'的，神卻藉那在荊棘中顯現之使者的

---

a 20 Or was fair in the sight of God   b 28 Exodus 2:14
c 32 Exodus 3:6   d 34 Exodus 3:5,7,8,10

手，差派他作首領、作救贖的。36這人領百姓出來，在埃及、在紅海、在曠野，四十年間行了奇事神蹟。

37"那曾對以色列人說：'神要從你們弟兄中間給你們興起一位先知像我的'，就是這位摩西。38這人曾在曠野會中西奈山上與那對他說話的天使同在，又與我們的祖宗同在，並且領受活潑的聖言傳給我們。

39"我們的祖宗不肯聽從，反棄絕他，心裏歸向埃及，40對亞倫說：'你且為我們造些神像，在我們前面引路；因為領我們出埃及地的那個摩西，我們不知道他遭了甚麼事。'41那時，他們造了一個牛犢，又拿祭物獻給那像，歡喜自己手中的工作。42神就轉臉不顧，任憑他們侍奉天上的日月星辰，正如先知書上所寫的說：

" '以色列家啊，
　你們四十年間在曠野，
　豈是將犧牲和祭物獻給我嗎？
43你們抬着摩洛的帳幕和理番神的星，
　就是你們所造，為要敬拜的像。
因此，我要把你們
　遷到巴比倫外去。'

44"我們的祖宗在曠野有法櫃的帳幕，是神吩咐摩西叫他照所看見的樣式做的。45這帳幕，我們的祖宗相繼承受。當神在他們面前趕出外邦人去的時候，他們同約書亞把帳幕搬進承受為業之地，直存到大衛的日子。46大衛在神面前蒙恩，祈求為雅各的神預備居所，47卻是所羅門為神造成殿宇。

48"其實，至高者並不住人手所造的，就如先知所言：

49" '主說，
　天是我的座位，
　　地是我的腳凳，
　你們要為我造何等的殿宇？
　　哪裏是我安息的地方呢？
50這一切不都是我手所造的嗎？'

deliverer by God himself, through the angel who appeared to him in the bush. 36He led them out of Egypt and did wonders and miraculous signs in Egypt, at the Red Sea[a] and for forty years in the desert.

37"This is that Moses who told the Israelites, 'God will send you a prophet like me from your own people.'[b] 38He was in the assembly in the desert, with the angel who spoke to him on Mount Sinai, and with our fathers; and he received living words to pass on to us.

39"But our fathers refused to obey him. Instead, they rejected him and in their hearts turned back to Egypt. 40They told Aaron, 'Make us gods who will go before us. As for this fellow Moses who led us out of Egypt—we don't know what has happened to him!'[c] 41That was the time they made an idol in the form of a calf. They brought sacrifices to it and held a celebration in honor of what their hands had made. 42But God turned away and gave them over to the worship of the heavenly bodies. This agrees with what is written in the book of the prophets:

" 'Did you bring me sacrifices and offerings
　　forty years in the desert, O house of Israel?
43You have lifted up the shrine of Molech
　　and the star of your god Rephan,
　　the idols you made to worship.
Therefore I will send you into exile[d] beyond
　　Babylon.

44"Our forefathers had the tabernacle of the Testimony with them in the desert. It had been made as God directed Moses, according to the pattern he had seen. 45Having received the tabernacle, our fathers under Joshua brought it with them when they took the land from the nations God drove out before them. It remained in the land until the time of David, 46who enjoyed God's favor and asked that he might provide a dwelling place for the God of Jacob.[e] 47But it was Solomon who built the house for him.

48"However, the Most High does not live in houses made by men. As the prophet says:

49" 'Heaven is my throne,
　　and the earth is my footstool.
　What kind of house will you build for me?
　　　　　　　　　　　　　　says the Lord.
　Or where will my resting place be?
50Has not my hand made all these things?'[f]

51"You stiff-necked people, with uncircumcised hearts and ears! You are just like your fathers: You always resist the Holy Spirit! 52Was there ever a prophet your fathers did not persecute? They even killed those who predicted the coming of the Righteous One. And now you have betrayed and murdered him— 53you who have received the law that was put into effect through angels but have not obeyed it."

The Stoning of Stephen

54When they heard this, they were furious and gnashed their teeth at him. 55But Stephen, full of the Holy Spirit, looked up to heaven and saw the glory of God, and Jesus standing at the right hand of God. 56"Look," he said, "I see heaven open and the Son of Man standing at the right hand of God."

57At this they covered their ears and, yelling at the top of their voices, they all rushed at him, 58dragged him out of the city and began to stone him. Meanwhile, the witnesses laid their clothes at the feet of a young man named Saul.

59While they were stoning him, Stephen prayed, "Lord Jesus, receive my spirit." 60Then he fell on his knees and cried out, "Lord, do not hold this sin against them." When he had said this, he fell asleep.

8 And Saul was there, giving approval to his death.

The Church Persecuted and Scattered

On that day a great persecution broke out against the church at Jerusalem, and all except the apostles were scattered throughout Judea and Samaria. 2Godly men buried Stephen and mourned deeply for him. 3But Saul began to destroy the church. Going from house to house, he dragged off men and women and put them in prison.

Philip in Samaria

4Those who had been scattered preached the word wherever they went. 5Philip went down to a city in Samaria and proclaimed the Christ[b] there. 6When the crowds heard Philip and saw the miraculous signs he did, they all paid close attention to what he said. 7With shrieks, evil[c] spirits came out of many, and many paralytics and cripples were healed. 8So there was great joy in that city.

---

51 "你們這硬着頸項，心與耳未受割禮的人，常時抗拒聖靈；你們的祖宗怎樣，你們也怎樣！52哪一個先知不是你們祖宗逼迫呢？他們也把那預先傳說那義者要來的人殺了；如今你們又把那義者賣了、殺了。53你們受了天使所傳的律法，竟不遵守。"

司提反被石頭打死

54眾人聽見這話，就極其惱怒，向司提反咬牙切齒。55但司提反被聖靈充滿，定睛望天，看見神的榮耀，又看見耶穌站在神的右邊，56就說："我看見天開了，人子站在神的右邊！"

57眾人大聲喊叫，摀着耳朵，齊心擁上前去，58把他推到城外，用石頭打他。作見證的人把衣裳放在一個少年人名叫掃羅的腳前。

59他們正用石頭打的時候，司提反呼籲主說："求主耶穌接收我的靈魂！"60又跪下大聲喊着說："主啊，不要將這罪歸於他們！"說了這話，就睡了。

8 掃羅也喜悅他被害。

教會受逼迫分散

從這日起，耶路撒冷的教會大遭逼迫。除了使徒以外，門徒都分散在猶太和撒馬利亞各處。2有虔誠的人把司提反埋葬了，為他捶胸大哭。3掃羅卻殘害教會，進各人的家，拉着男女下在監裏。

腓利在撒馬利亞

4那些分散的人往各處去傳道。5腓利下撒馬利亞城去宣講基督。6眾人聽見了，又看見腓利所行的神蹟，就同心合意地聽從他的話。7因為有許多人被污鬼附着，那些鬼大聲呼叫，從他們身上出來；還有許多癱瘓的、瘸腿的，都得了醫治。8在那城裏就大有歡喜。

---

a 5 Or Messiah　　b 7 Greek unclean

行邪術的西門

9有一個人，名叫西門，向來在那城裏行邪術，妄自尊大，使撒馬利亞的百姓驚奇；10無論大小都聽從他，說：「這人就是那稱為神的大能者。」11他們聽從他，因他久用邪術，使他們驚奇。12及至他們信了腓利所傳神國的福音和耶穌基督的名，連男帶女就受了洗。13西門自己也信了，既受了洗，就常與腓利在一處，看見他所行的神蹟和大異能，就甚驚奇。

14使徒在耶路撒冷聽見撒馬利亞人領受了神的道，就打發彼得、約翰往他們那裏去。15兩個人到了，就為他們禱告，要叫他們受聖靈。16因為聖靈還沒有降在他們一個人身上，他們只奉主耶穌的名受了洗。17於是使徒按手在他們頭上，他們就受了聖靈。

18西門看見使徒按手，便有聖靈賜下，就拿錢給使徒，19說：「把這權柄也給我，叫我手按着誰，誰就可以受聖靈。」

20彼得說：「你的銀子和你一同滅亡吧！因你想神的恩賜是可以用錢買的。21你在這道上無分無關，因為在神面前，你的心不正。22你當懊悔你這罪惡，祈求主，或者你心裏的意念可得赦免。23我看出你正在苦膽之中，被罪惡捆綁。」

24西門說：「願你們為我求主，叫你們所說的，沒有一樣臨到我身上。」

25使徒既證明主道，而且傳講，就回耶路撒冷去，一路在撒馬利亞好些村莊傳揚福音。

腓利與埃提阿伯太監

26有主的一個使者對腓利說：「起來！向南走，往那從耶路撒冷下迦薩的路上去。那路是曠野。」27腓利就起身去了。不料，有一個埃提阿伯（註：即古實，見以賽亞書18章1節）人，是個有大權的太監，在埃提阿

Simon the Sorcerer

9Now for some time a man named Simon had practiced sorcery in the city and amazed all the people of Samaria. He boasted that he was someone great, 10and all the people, both high and low, gave him their attention and exclaimed, "This man is the divine power known as the Great Power." 11They followed him because he had amazed them for a long time with his magic. 12But when they believed Philip as he preached the good news of the kingdom of God and the name of Jesus Christ, they were baptized, both men and women. 13Simon himself believed and was baptized. And he followed Philip everywhere, astonished by the great signs and miracles he saw.

14When the apostles in Jerusalem heard that Samaria had accepted the word of God, they sent Peter and John to them. 15When they arrived, they prayed for them that they might receive the Holy Spirit, 16because the Holy Spirit had not yet come upon any of them; they had simply been baptized into[a] the name of the Lord Jesus. 17Then Peter and John placed their hands on them, and they received the Holy Spirit.

18When Simon saw that the Spirit was given at the laying on of the apostles' hands, he offered them money 19and said, "Give me also this ability so that everyone on whom I lay my hands may receive the Holy Spirit."

20Peter answered: "May your money perish with you, because you thought you could buy the gift of God with money! 21You have no part or share in this ministry, because your heart is not right before God. 22Repent of this wickedness and pray to the Lord. Perhaps he will forgive you for having such a thought in your heart. 23For I see that you are full of bitterness and captive to sin."

24Then Simon answered, "Pray to the Lord for me so that nothing you have said may happen to me."

25When they had testified and proclaimed the word of the Lord, Peter and John returned to Jerusalem, preaching the gospel in many Samaritan villages.

Philip and the Ethiopian

26Now an angel of the Lord said to Philip, "Go south to the road—the desert road—that goes down from Jerusalem to Gaza." 27So he started out, and on his way he met an Ethiopian[b] eunuch, an important official in charge of all the treasury of Candace, queen of the Ethiopians.

a 16 Or in　b 27 That is, from the upper Nile region

This man had gone to Jerusalem to worship, [28]and on his way home was sitting in his chariot reading the book of Isaiah the prophet. [29]The Spirit told Philip, "Go to that chariot and stay near it."

[30]Then Philip ran up to the chariot and heard the man reading Isaiah the prophet. "Do you understand what you are reading?" Philip asked.

[31]"How can I," he said, "unless someone explains it to me?" So he invited Philip to come up and sit with him.

[32]The eunuch was reading this passage of Scripture:

"He was led like a sheep to the slaughter,
    and as a lamb before the shearer is silent,
    so he did not open his mouth.
[33]In his humiliation he was deprived of justice.
    Who can speak of his descendants?
    For his life was taken from the earth."[a]

[34]The eunuch asked Philip, "Tell me, please, who is the prophet talking about, himself or someone else?" [35]Then Philip began with that very passage of Scripture and told him the good news about Jesus.

[36]As they traveled along the road, they came to some water and the eunuch said, "Look, here is water. Why shouldn't I be baptized?"[b] [38]And he gave orders to stop the chariot. Then both Philip and the eunuch went down into the water and Philip baptized him. [39]When they came up out of the water, the Spirit of the Lord suddenly took Philip away, and the eunuch did not see him again, but went on his way rejoicing. [40]Philip, however, appeared at Azotus and traveled about, preaching the gospel in all the towns until he reached Caesarea.

Saul's Conversion

9 Meanwhile, Saul was still breathing out murderous threats against the Lord's disciples. He went to the high priest [2]and asked him for letters to the synagogues in Damascus, so that if he found any there who belonged to the Way, whether men or women, he might take them as prisoners to Jerusalem. [3]As he neared Damascus on his journey, suddenly a light from heaven flashed around him. [4]He fell to the ground and heard a voice say to him, "Saul, Saul, why do you persecute me?"

a 33 Isaiah 53:7,8   b 36 Some late manuscripts baptized?" [37] Philip said, "If you believe with all your heart, you may." The eunuch answered, "I believe that Jesus Christ is the Son of God."

伯女王干大基的手下總管銀庫,他上耶路撒冷禮拜去了。[28]現在回來,在車上坐着,念先知以賽亞的書。[29]聖靈對腓利說:"你去貼近那車走。"

[30]腓利就跑到太監那裏,聽見他念先知以賽亞的書,便問他說:"你所念的,你明白嗎?"

[31]他說:"沒有人指教我,怎能明白呢?"於是請腓利上車,與他同坐。

[32]他所念的那段經,說:

"他像羊被牽到宰殺之地,
    又像羊羔在剪毛的人手下無聲,
    他也是這樣不開口。
[33]他卑微的時候,人不按公義審判他
    (註:原文作"他的審判被奪去");
    誰能述說他的世代?
    因為他的生命從地上奪去。"

[34]太監對腓利說:"請問先知說這話,是指着誰?是指着自己呢?是指着別人呢?"[35]腓利就開口從這經上起,對他傳講耶穌。

[36]二人正往前走,到了有水的地方,太監說:"看哪,這裏有水,我受洗有甚麼妨礙呢?"(註:有古卷在此有[37]腓利說:"你若是一心相信,就可以。"他回答說:"我信耶穌基督是神的兒子。")[38]於是吩咐車站住,腓利和太監二人同下水裏去,腓利就給他施洗。[39]從水裏上來,主的靈把腓利提了去。太監也不再見他了,就歡歡喜喜地走路。[40]後來有人在亞鎖都遇見腓利。他走遍那地方,在各城宣傳福音,直到凱撒利亞。

掃羅的悔改

9 掃羅仍然向主的門徒口吐威嚇兇殺的話,去見大祭司,[2]求文書給大馬士革的各會堂,若是找着信奉這道的人,無論男女,都准他捆綁帶到耶路撒冷。[3]掃羅行路,將到大馬士革,忽然從天上發光,四面照着他。[4]他就仆倒在地,聽見有聲音對他說:"掃羅,掃羅!你為甚麼逼迫我?"

5他說："主啊，你是誰？"

主說："我就是你所逼迫的耶穌。6起來！進城去，你所當做的事，必有人告訴你。"

7同行的人站在那裏，說不出話來，聽見聲音，卻看不見人。8掃羅從地上起來，睜開眼睛，竟不能看見甚麼。有人拉他的手，領他進了大馬士革。9三日不能看見，也不吃，也不喝。

10當下，在大馬士革有一個門徒，名叫亞拿尼亞。主在異象中對他說："亞拿尼亞。"

他說："主，我在這裏。"

11主對他說："起來！往直街去，在猶大的家裏，訪問一個大數人，名叫掃羅，他正禱告。12又看見了一個人，名叫亞拿尼亞，進來按手在他身上，叫他能看見。"

13亞拿尼亞回答說："主啊，我聽見許多人說，這人怎樣在耶路撒冷多多苦害你的聖徒，14並且他在這裏有從祭司長得來的權柄，捆綁一切求告你名的人。"

15主對亞拿尼亞說："你只管去。他是我所揀選的器皿，要在外邦人和君王並以色列人面前宣揚我的名。16我也要指示他，為我的名必須受許多的苦難。"

17亞拿尼亞就去了，進入那家，把手按在掃羅身上說："兄弟掃羅，在你來的路上向你顯現的主，就是耶穌，打發我來，叫你能看見，又被聖靈充滿。"18掃羅的眼睛上好像有鱗立刻掉下來，他就能看見，於是起來受了洗，19吃過飯就健壯了。

掃羅在大馬士革和耶路撒冷

掃羅和大馬士革的門徒同住了些日子，20就在各會堂裏宣傳耶穌，說他是神的兒子。21凡聽見的人都驚奇，說："在耶路撒冷殘害求告這名的，不是這人嗎？並且他到這裏來，特要捆綁他們，帶到祭司長那裏。"22但掃羅越發有能力，駁倒住大馬士革的猶太人，證明耶穌是基督。

23過了好些日子，猶太人商議要殺掃羅，24但他們的計謀被掃羅知道

5"Who are you, Lord?" Saul asked.

"I am Jesus, whom you are persecuting," he replied. 6"Now get up and go into the city, and you will be told what you must do."

7The men traveling with Saul stood there speechless; they heard the sound but did not see anyone. 8Saul got up from the ground, but when he opened his eyes he could see nothing. So they led him by the hand into Damascus. 9For three days he was blind, and did not eat or drink anything.

10In Damascus there was a disciple named Ananias. The Lord called to him in a vision, "Ananias!"

"Yes, Lord," he answered.

11The Lord told him, "Go to the house of Judas on Straight Street and ask for a man from Tarsus named Saul, for he is praying. 12In a vision he has seen a man named Ananias come and place his hands on him to restore his sight."

13"Lord," Ananias answered, "I have heard many reports about this man and all the harm he has done to your saints in Jerusalem. 14And he has come here with authority from the chief priests to arrest all who call on your name."

15But the Lord said to Ananias, "Go! This man is my chosen instrument to carry my name before the Gentiles and their kings and before the people of Israel. 16I will show him how much he must suffer for my name."

17Then Ananias went to the house and entered it. Placing his hands on Saul, he said, "Brother Saul, the Lord—Jesus, who appeared to you on the road as you were coming here—has sent me so that you may see again and be filled with the Holy Spirit." 18Immediately, something like scales fell from Saul's eyes, and he could see again. He got up and was baptized, 19and after taking some food, he regained his strength.

Saul in Damascus and Jerusalem

Saul spent several days with the disciples in Damascus. 20At once he began to preach in the synagogues that Jesus is the Son of God. 21All those who heard him were astonished and asked, "Isn't he the man who raised havoc in Jerusalem among those who call on this name? And hasn't he come here to take them as prisoners to the chief priests?" 22Yet Saul grew more and more powerful and baffled the Jews living in Damascus by proving that Jesus is the Christ.ª

23After many days had gone by, the Jews conspired to kill him, 24but Saul learned of their

a 22 Or Messiah

plan. Day and night they kept close watch on the city gates in order to kill him. 25But his followers took him by night and lowered him in a basket through an opening in the wall.

26When he came to Jerusalem, he tried to join the disciples, but they were all afraid of him, not believing that he really was a disciple. 27But Barnabas took him and brought him to the apostles. He told them how Saul on his journey had seen the Lord and that the Lord had spoken to him, and how in Damascus he had preached fearlessly in the name of Jesus. 28So Saul stayed with them and moved about freely in Jerusalem, speaking boldly in the name of the Lord. 29He talked and debated with the Grecian Jews, but they tried to kill him. 30When the brothers learned of this, they took him down to Caesarea and sent him off to Tarsus.

31Then the church throughout Judea, Galilee and Samaria enjoyed a time of peace. It was strengthened; and encouraged by the Holy Spirit, it grew in numbers, living in the fear of the Lord.

Aeneas and Dorcas

32As Peter traveled about the country, he went to visit the saints in Lydda. 33There he found a man named Aeneas, a paralytic who had been bedridden for eight years. 34"Aeneas," Peter said to him, "Jesus Christ heals you. Get up and take care of your mat." Immediately Aeneas got up. 35All those who lived in Lydda and Sharon saw him and turned to the Lord.

36In Joppa there was a disciple named Tabitha (which, when translated, is Dorcas*a*), who was always doing good and helping the poor. 37About that time she became sick and died, and her body was washed and placed in an upstairs room. 38Lydda was near Joppa; so when the disciples heard that Peter was in Lydda, they sent two men to him and urged him, "Please come at once!"

39Peter went with them, and when he arrived he was taken upstairs to the room. All the widows stood around him, crying and showing him the robes and other clothing that Dorcas had made while she was still with them.

40Peter sent them all out of the room; then he got down on his knees and prayed. Turning toward the dead woman, he said, "Tabitha, get up." She opened her eyes, and seeing Peter she sat up. 41He took her by the hand and helped her to her feet. Then he called the believers and the widows and presented her to them alive.

了。他們又晝夜在城門守候，要殺他。25他的門徒就在夜間用筐子把他從城牆上縋下去。

26掃羅到了耶路撒冷，想與門徒結交。他們卻都怕他，不信他是門徒。27惟有巴拿巴接待他，領去見使徒，把他在路上怎麼看見主，主怎麼向他說話，他在大馬士革怎麼奉耶穌的名放膽傳道，都述說出來。28於是掃羅在耶路撒冷和門徒出入來往，29奉主的名放膽傳道，並與說希臘話的猶太人講論辯駁。他們卻想法子要殺他。30弟兄們知道了，就送他下凱撒利亞，打發他往大數去。

31那時，猶太、加利利、撒馬利亞各處的教會都得平安，被建立；凡事敬畏主，蒙聖靈的安慰，人數就增多了。

以尼雅和多加

32彼得周流四方的時候，也到了居住呂大的聖徒那裏，33遇見一個人，名叫以尼雅，得了癱瘓，在褥子上躺臥八年。34彼得對他說："以尼雅，耶穌基督醫好你了！起來，收拾你的褥子！"他就立刻起來了。35凡住呂大和沙崙的人都看見了他，就歸服主。

36在約帕有一個女徒，名叫大比大，翻希臘話就是多加（註："多加"就是"羚羊"的意思）。她廣行善事，多施賙濟。37當時，她患病而死，有人把她洗了，停在樓上。38呂大原與約帕相近；門徒聽見彼得在那裏，就打發兩個人去見他，央求他說："快到我們那裏去，不要躭延！"

39彼得就起身和他們同去。到了，便有人領他上樓。眾寡婦都站在彼得旁邊哭，拿多加與她們同在時所做的裏衣外衣給他看。

40彼得叫她們都出去，就跪下禱告，轉身對着死人說："大比大，起來！"她就睜開眼睛，見了彼得，便坐起來。41彼得伸手扶她起來，叫眾聖徒和寡婦進去，把多加活活地交給他們。

a 36 Both *Tabitha* (Aramaic) and *Dorcas* (Greek) mean *gazelle.*

42這事傳遍了<u>約帕</u>，就有許多人信了主。43此後，<u>彼得</u>在<u>約帕</u>一個硝皮匠<u>西門</u>的家裏住了多日。

哥尼流邀請彼得

10 在<u>凱撒利亞</u>有一個人，名叫<u>哥尼流</u>，是<u>意大利</u>營的百夫長。2他是個虔誠人，他和全家都敬畏神，多多賙濟百姓，常常禱告神。3有一天，約在申初，他在異象中明明看見神的一個使者進去，到他那裏，說：「<u>哥尼流</u>。」

4<u>哥尼流</u>定睛看他，驚怕說：「主啊，甚麼事呢？」

天使說：「你的禱告和你的賙濟達到神面前，已蒙記念了。5現在你當打發人往<u>約帕</u>去，請那稱呼<u>彼得</u>的<u>西門</u>來。6他住在海邊一個硝皮匠<u>西門</u>的家裏，房子在海邊上。」

7向他說話的天使去後，<u>哥尼流</u>叫了兩個家人和常伺候他的一個虔誠兵來，8把這事都述說給他們聽，就打發他們往<u>約帕</u>去。

彼得見異象

9第二天，他們行路將近那城，<u>彼得</u>約在午正上房頂去禱告。10覺得餓了，想要吃。那家的人正預備飯的時候，<u>彼得</u>魂遊象外，11看見天開了，有一物降下，好像一塊大布，繫着四角，縋在地上。12裏面有地上各樣四足的走獸和昆蟲，並天上的飛鳥。13又有聲音向他說：「<u>彼得</u>，起來，宰了吃！」

14<u>彼得</u>卻說：「主啊，這是不可的！凡俗物和不潔淨的物，我從來沒有吃過。」

15第二次有聲音向他說：「神所潔淨的，你不可當作俗物。」

16這樣一連三次，那物隨即收回天上去了。

17<u>彼得</u>心裏正在猜疑之間，不知所看見的異象是甚麼意思。<u>哥尼流</u>所差來的人已經訪問到<u>西門</u>的家，站在門外，18喊着問：「有稱呼<u>彼得</u>的<u>西門</u>住在這裏沒有？」

42This became known all over Joppa, and many people believed in the Lord. 43Peter stayed in Joppa for some time with a tanner named Simon.

Cornelius Calls for Peter

10 At Caesarea there was a man named Cornelius, a centurion in what was known as the Italian Regiment. 2He and all his family were devout and God-fearing; he gave generously to those in need and prayed to God regularly. 3One day at about three in the afternoon he had a vision. He distinctly saw an angel of God, who came to him and said, "Cornelius!"

4Cornelius stared at him in fear. "What is it, Lord?" he asked.

The angel answered, "Your prayers and gifts to the poor have come up as a memorial offering before God. 5Now send men to Joppa to bring back a man named Simon who is called Peter. 6He is staying with Simon the tanner, whose house is by the sea."

7When the angel who spoke to him had gone, Cornelius called two of his servants and a devout soldier who was one of his attendants. 8He told them everything that had happened and sent them to Joppa.

Peter's Vision

9About noon the following day as they were on their journey and approaching the city, Peter went up on the roof to pray. 10He became hungry and wanted something to eat, and while the meal was being prepared, he fell into a trance. 11He saw heaven opened and something like a large sheet being let down to earth by its four corners. 12It contained all kinds of four-footed animals, as well as reptiles of the earth and birds of the air. 13Then a voice told him, "Get up, Peter. Kill and eat."

14"Surely not, Lord!" Peter replied. "I have never eaten anything impure or unclean."

15The voice spoke to him a second time, "Do not call anything impure that God has made clean."

16This happened three times, and immediately the sheet was taken back to heaven.

17While Peter was wondering about the meaning of the vision, the men sent by Cornelius found out where Simon's house was and stopped at the gate. 18They called out, asking if Simon who was known as Peter was staying there.

¹⁹While Peter was still thinking about the vision, the Spirit said to him, "Simon, three^a men are looking for you. ²⁰So get up and go downstairs. Do not hesitate to go with them, for I have sent them."

²¹Peter went down and said to the men, "I'm the one you're looking for. Why have you come?"

²²The men replied, "We have come from Cornelius the centurion. He is a righteous and God-fearing man, who is respected by all the Jewish people. A holy angel told him to have you come to his house so that he could hear what you have to say." ²³Then Peter invited the men into the house to be his guests.

Peter at Cornelius' House

The next day Peter started out with them, and some of the brothers from Joppa went along. ²⁴The following day he arrived in Caesarea. Cornelius was expecting them and had called together his relatives and close friends. ²⁵As Peter entered the house, Cornelius met him and fell at his feet in reverence. ²⁶But Peter made him get up. "Stand up," he said, "I am only a man myself."

²⁷Talking with him, Peter went inside and found a large gathering of people. ²⁸He said to them: "You are well aware that it is against our law for a Jew to associate with a Gentile or visit him. But God has shown me that I should not call any man impure or unclean. ²⁹So when I was sent for, I came without raising any objection. May I ask why you sent for me?"

³⁰Cornelius answered: "Four days ago I was in my house praying at this hour, at three in the afternoon. Suddenly a man in shining clothes stood before me ³¹and said, 'Cornelius, God has heard your prayer and remembered your gifts to the poor. ³²Send to Joppa for Simon who is called Peter. He is a guest in the home of Simon the tanner, who lives by the sea.' ³³So I sent for you immediately, and it was good of you to come. Now we are all here in the presence of God to listen to everything the Lord has commanded you to tell us."

³⁴Then Peter began to speak: "I now realize how true it is that God does not show favoritism ³⁵but accepts men from every nation who fear him and do what is right. ³⁶You know the message God sent to the people of Israel, telling the good news of peace through Jesus Christ, who is Lord of all. ³⁷You know what has happened

a 19 One early manuscript *two*; other manuscripts do not have the number.

¹⁹彼得還思想那異象的時候，聖靈向他說：「有三個人來找你。²⁰起來，下去，和他們同往，不要疑惑！因為是我差他們來的。」

²¹於是彼得下去見那些人，說：「我就是你們所找的人。你們來是為甚麼緣故？」²²他們說：「百夫長哥尼流是個義人，敬畏神，為猶太通國所稱讚。他蒙一位聖天使指示，叫他請你到他家裏去，聽你的話。」²³彼得就請他們進去，住了一宿。

彼得在哥尼流家

次日起身和他們同去，還有約帕的幾個弟兄同着他去。²⁴又次日，他們進入凱撒利亞。哥尼流已經請了他的親屬、密友等候他們。²⁵彼得一進去，哥尼流就迎接他。俯伏在他腳前拜他。²⁶彼得卻拉他，說：「你起來，我也是人。」

²⁷彼得和他說着話進去，見有好些人在那裏聚集，²⁸就對他們說：「你們知道，猶太人和別國的人親近來往，本是不合例的，但神已經指示我，無論甚麼人都不可看作俗而不潔淨的。²⁹所以我被請的時候，就不推辭而來。現在請問：你們叫我來有甚麼意思呢？」

³⁰哥尼流說：「前四天這個時候，我在家中守着申初的禱告，忽然有一個人穿着光明的衣裳，站在我面前，³¹說：『哥尼流，你的禱告已蒙垂聽，你的賙濟達到神面前，已蒙記念了。³²你當打發人往約帕去，請那稱呼彼得的西門來，他住在海邊一個硝皮匠西門的家裏。』³³所以我立時打發人去請你。你來了很好，現今我們都在神面前，要聽主所吩咐你的一切話。」

³⁴彼得就開口說：「我真看出神是不偏待人。³⁵原來各國中，那敬畏主、行義的人都為主所悅納。³⁶神藉着耶穌基督（他是萬有的主）傳和平的福音，將這道賜給以色列人。³⁷這話在約翰宣傳洗禮以後，從加利利

起，傳遍了猶太。38神怎樣以聖靈和能力膏拿撒勒人耶穌，這都是你們知道的。他周流四方，行善事，醫好凡被魔鬼壓制的人，因為神與他同在。

39 "他在猶太人之地並耶路撒冷所行的一切事，有我們作見證。他們竟把他掛在木頭上殺了。40第三日，神叫他復活，顯現出來；41不是顯現給眾人看，乃是顯現給神預先所揀選為他作見證的人看，就是我們這些在他從死裏復活以後，和他同吃同喝的人。42他吩咐我們傳道給眾人，證明他是神所立定的，要作審判活人死人的主。43眾先知也為他作見證，說：'凡信他的人，必因他的名得蒙赦罪。'"

44彼得還說這話的時候，聖靈降在一切聽道的人身上。45那些奉割禮和彼得同來的信徒，見聖靈的恩賜也澆在外邦人身上，就都希奇，46因聽見他們說方言，稱讚神為大。

47於是彼得說："這些人既受了聖靈，與我們一樣，誰能禁止用水給他們施洗呢？"48就吩咐奉耶穌基督的名給他們施洗。他們又請彼得住了幾天。

彼得解釋他的行動

11 使徒和在猶太的眾弟兄聽說外邦人也領受了神的道。2及至彼得上了耶路撒冷，那些奉割禮的門徒和他爭辯說：3 "你進入未受割禮之人的家和他們一同吃飯了。"

4彼得就開口把這事挨次給他們講解，說：5 "我在約帕城裏禱告的時候，魂遊象外，看見異象，有一物降下，好像一塊大布，繫着四角，從天縋下，直來到我跟前。6我定睛觀看，見內中有地上四足的牲畜和野獸、昆蟲並天上的飛鳥。7我且聽見有聲音向我說：'彼得，起來，宰了吃！'

8 "我說：'主啊，這是不可的！凡俗而不潔淨的物從來沒有入過我的口。'

9 "第二次，有聲音從天上說：'神所潔淨的，你不可當作俗物。'

---

throughout Judea, beginning in Galilee after the baptism that John preached— 38how God anointed Jesus of Nazareth with the Holy Spirit and power, and how he went around doing good and healing all who were under the power of the devil, because God was with him.

39"We are witnesses of everything he did in the country of the Jews and in Jerusalem. They killed him by hanging him on a tree, 40but God raised him from the dead on the third day and caused him to be seen. 41He was not seen by all the people, but by witnesses whom God had already chosen—by us who ate and drank with him after he rose from the dead. 42He commanded us to preach to the people and to testify that he is the one whom God appointed as judge of the living and the dead. 43All the prophets testify about him that everyone who believes in him receives forgiveness of sins through his name."

44While Peter was still speaking these words, the Holy Spirit came on all who heard the message. 45The circumcised believers who had come with Peter were astonished that the gift of the Holy Spirit had been poured out even on the Gentiles. 46For they heard them speaking in tongues[a] and praising God.

Then Peter said, 47"Can anyone keep these people from being baptized with water? They have received the Holy Spirit just as we have." 48So he ordered that they be baptized in the name of Jesus Christ. Then they asked Peter to stay with them for a few days.

Peter Explains His Actions

11 The apostles and the brothers throughout Judea heard that the Gentiles also had received the word of God. 2So when Peter went up to Jerusalem, the circumcised believers criticized him 3and said, "You went into the house of uncircumcised men and ate with them."

4Peter began and explained everything to them precisely as it had happened: 5"I was in the city of Joppa praying, and in a trance I saw a vision. I saw something like a large sheet being let down from heaven by its four corners, and it came down to where I was. 6I looked into it and saw four-footed animals of the earth, wild beasts, reptiles, and birds of the air. 7Then I heard a voice telling me, 'Get up, Peter. Kill and eat.'

8"I replied, 'Surely not, Lord! Nothing impure or unclean has ever entered my mouth.'

9"The voice spoke from heaven a second time, 'Do not call anything impure that God has

a 46 Or other languages

made clean.' ¹⁰This happened three times, and then it was all pulled up to heaven again.

¹¹"Right then three men who had been sent to me from Caesarea stopped at the house where I was staying. ¹²The Spirit told me to have no hesitation about going with them. These six brothers also went with me, and we entered the man's house. ¹³He told us how he had seen an angel appear in his house and say, 'Send to Joppa for Simon who is called Peter. ¹⁴He will bring you a message through which you and all your household will be saved.'

¹⁵"As I began to speak, the Holy Spirit came on them as he had come on us at the beginning. ¹⁶Then I remembered what the Lord had said: 'John baptized with*ᵃ* water, but you will be baptized with the Holy Spirit.' ¹⁷So if God gave them the same gift as he gave us, who believed in the Lord Jesus Christ, who was I to think that I could oppose God?"

¹⁸When they heard this, they had no further objections and praised God, saying, "So then, God has granted even the Gentiles repentance unto life."

The Church in Antioch

¹⁹Now those who had been scattered by the persecution in connection with Stephen traveled as far as Phoenicia, Cyprus and Antioch, telling the message only to Jews. ²⁰Some of them, however, men from Cyprus and Cyrene, went to Antioch and began to speak to Greeks also, telling them the good news about the Lord Jesus. ²¹The Lord's hand was with them, and a great number of people believed and turned to the Lord.

²²News of this reached the ears of the church at Jerusalem, and they sent Barnabas to Antioch. ²³When he arrived and saw the evidence of the grace of God, he was glad and encouraged them all to remain true to the Lord with all their hearts. ²⁴He was a good man, full of the Holy Spirit and faith, and a great number of people were brought to the Lord.

²⁵Then Barnabas went to Tarsus to look for Saul, ²⁶and when he found him, he brought him to Antioch. So for a whole year Barnabas and Saul met with the church and taught great numbers of people. The disciples were called Christians first at Antioch.

²⁷During this time some prophets came down from Jerusalem to Antioch. ²⁸One of them, named Agabus, stood up and through the Spirit predicted that a severe famine would spread

a 16 Or in

---

¹⁰這樣一連三次，就都收回天上去了。

¹¹"正當那時，有三個人站在我們所住的房門前，是從凱撒利亞差來見我的。¹²聖靈吩咐我和他們同去，不要疑惑（註：或作"不要分別等類"）。同着我去的，還有這六位弟兄，我們都進了那人的家。¹³那人就告訴我們，他如何看見一位天使站在他屋裏，說：'你打發人往約帕去，請那稱呼彼得的西門來，¹⁴他有話告訴你，可以叫你和你的全家得救。'

¹⁵"我一開講，聖靈便降在他們身上，正像當初降在我們身上一樣。¹⁶我就想起主的話說：'約翰是用水施洗，但你們要受聖靈的洗。'¹⁷神既然給他們恩賜，像在我們信主耶穌基督的時候給了我們一樣，我是誰，能攔阻神呢？"

¹⁸眾人聽見這話，就不言語了，只歸榮耀與神，說："這樣看來，神也賜恩給外邦人，叫他們悔改得生命了。"

在安提阿的教會

¹⁹那些因司提反的事遭患難四散的門徒，直走到腓尼基和塞浦路斯並安提阿。他們不向別人講道，只向猶太人講。²⁰但內中有塞浦路斯和古利奈人，他們到了安提阿，也向希臘人傳講主耶穌（註：有古卷作"也向說希臘話的猶太人傳講主耶穌"）。²¹主與他們同在，信而歸主的人就很多了。

²²這風聲傳到耶路撒冷教會人的耳中，他們就打發巴拿巴出去，走到安提阿為止。²³他到了那裏，看見神所賜的恩就歡喜，勸勉眾人，立定心志，恆久靠主。²⁴這巴拿巴原是個好人，被聖靈充滿，大有信心。於是，有許多人歸服了主。

²⁵他又往大數去找掃羅，²⁶找着了，就帶他到安提阿去。他們足有一年的工夫和教會一同聚集，教訓了許多人。門徒稱為基督徒是從安提阿起首。

²⁷當那些日子，有幾位先知從耶路撒冷下到安提阿。²⁸內中有一位名叫亞迦布，站起來，藉着聖靈指明天下將有大饑荒。這事到革老丟年間果

然有了。²⁹於是門徒定意照各人的力量捐錢，送去供給住在<u>猶太</u>的弟兄。³⁰他們就這樣行，把捐項託<u>巴拿巴</u>和<u>掃羅</u>送到眾長老那裏。

彼得神奇地出監

12 那時，<u>希律</u>王下手苦害教會中幾個人，²用刀殺了<u>約翰</u>的哥哥<u>雅各</u>。³他見<u>猶太</u>人喜歡這事，又去捉拿<u>彼得</u>。那時正是除酵的日子。⁴<u>希律</u>拿了<u>彼得</u>，收在監裏，交付四班兵丁看守，每班四個人，意思要在逾越節後，把他提出來，當着百姓辦他。

⁵於是<u>彼得</u>被囚在監裏；教會卻為他切切地禱告神。

⁶<u>希律</u>將要提他出來的前一夜，<u>彼得</u>被兩條鐵鍊鎖着，睡在兩個兵丁當中。看守的人也在門外看守。⁷忽然有主的一個使者站在旁邊，屋裏有光照耀。天使拍<u>彼得</u>的肋旁，拍醒了他，說："快快起來！"那鐵鍊就從他手上脫落下來。

⁸天使對他說："束上帶子，穿上鞋！"他就那樣做。天使又說："披上外衣，跟着我來。"⁹<u>彼得</u>就出來跟着他，不知道天使所做是真的，只當見了異象。¹⁰過了第一層、第二層監牢，就來到臨街的鐵門，那門自己開了。他們出來，走過一條街，天使便離開他去了。

¹¹<u>彼得</u>醒悟過來，說："我現在真知道主差遣他的使者，救我脫離<u>希律</u>的手和<u>猶太</u>百姓一切所盼望的。"

¹²想了一想，就往那稱呼<u>馬可</u>的<u>約翰</u>他母親<u>馬利亞</u>家去，在那裏有好些人聚集禱告。¹³<u>彼得</u>敲外門，有一個使女名叫<u>羅大</u>，出來探聽，¹⁴聽得是<u>彼得</u>的聲音，就歡喜的顧不得開門，跑進去告訴眾人說："<u>彼得</u>站在門外！"

¹⁵他們說："你是瘋了！"使女極力地說："真是他！"他們說："必是他的天使。"

Peter's Miraculous Escape From Prison

over the entire Roman world. (This happened during the reign of Claudius.) ²⁹The disciples, each according to his ability, decided to provide help for the brothers living in Judea. ³⁰This they did, sending their gift to the elders by Barnabas and Saul.

12 It was about this time that King Herod arrested some who belonged to the church, intending to persecute them. ²He had James, the brother of John, put to death with the sword. ³When he saw that this pleased the Jews, he proceeded to seize Peter also. This happened during the Feast of Unleavened Bread. ⁴After arresting him, he put him in prison, handing him over to be guarded by four squads of four soldiers each. Herod intended to bring him out for public trial after the Passover.

⁵So Peter was kept in prison, but the church was earnestly praying to God for him.

⁶The night before Herod was to bring him to trial, Peter was sleeping between two soldiers, bound with two chains, and sentries stood guard at the entrance. ⁷Suddenly an angel of the Lord appeared and a light shone in the cell. He struck Peter on the side and woke him up. "Quick, get up!" he said, and the chains fell off Peter's wrists.

⁸Then the angel said to him, "Put on your clothes and sandals." And Peter did so. "Wrap your cloak around you and follow me," the angel told him. ⁹Peter followed him out of the prison, but he had no idea that what the angel was doing was really happening; he thought he was seeing a vision. ¹⁰They passed the first and second guards and came to the iron gate leading to the city. It opened for them by itself, and they went through it. When they had walked the length of one street, suddenly the angel left him.

¹¹Then Peter came to himself and said, "Now I know without a doubt that the Lord sent his angel and rescued me from Herod's clutches and from everything the Jewish people were anticipating."

¹²When this had dawned on him, he went to the house of Mary the mother of John, also called Mark, where many people had gathered and were praying. ¹³Peter knocked at the outer entrance, and a servant girl named Rhoda came to answer the door. ¹⁴When she recognized Peter's voice, she was so overjoyed she ran back without opening it and exclaimed, "Peter is at the door!"

¹⁵"You're out of your mind," they told her. When she kept insisting that it was so, they said, "It must be his angel."

¹⁶But Peter kept on knocking, and when they opened the door and saw him, they were astonished. ¹⁷Peter motioned with his hand for them to be quiet and described how the Lord had brought him out of prison. "Tell James and the brothers about this," he said, and then he left for another place.

¹⁸In the morning, there was no small commotion among the soldiers as to what had become of Peter. ¹⁹After Herod had a thorough search made for him and did not find him, he cross-examined the guards and ordered that they be executed.

Herod's Death

Then Herod went from Judea to Caesarea and stayed there a while. ²⁰He had been quarreling with the people of Tyre and Sidon; they now joined together and sought an audience with him. Having secured the support of Blastus, a trusted personal servant of the king, they asked for peace, because they depended on the king's country for their food supply.

²¹On the appointed day Herod, wearing his royal robes, sat on his throne and delivered a public address to the people. ²²They shouted, "This is the voice of a god, not of a man." ²³Immediately, because Herod did not give praise to God, an angel of the Lord struck him down, and he was eaten by worms and died.

²⁴But the word of God continued to increase and spread.

²⁵When Barnabas and Saul had finished their mission, they returned from^a Jerusalem, taking with them John, also called Mark.

Barnabas and Saul Sent Off

13 In the church at Antioch there were prophets and teachers: Barnabas, Simeon called Niger, Lucius of Cyrene, Manaen (who had been brought up with Herod the tetrarch) and Saul. ²While they were worshiping the Lord and fasting, the Holy Spirit said, "Set apart for me Barnabas and Saul for the work to which I have called them." ³So after they had fasted and prayed, they placed their hands on them and sent them off.

On Cyprus

⁴The two of them, sent on their way by the Holy Spirit, went down to Seleucia and sailed from there to Cyprus. ⁵When they arrived at Salamis, they proclaimed the word of God in the Jewish synagogues. John was with them as their helper.

a 25 Some manuscripts to

¹⁶彼得不住地敲門。他們開了門，看見他，就甚驚奇。¹⁷彼得擺手，不要他們做聲，就告訴他們主怎樣領他出監。又說："你們把這事告訴雅各和眾弟兄。"於是出去往別處去了。

¹⁸到了天亮，兵丁擾亂得很，不知道彼得往哪裏去了。¹⁹希律找他，找不着，就審問看守的人，吩咐把他們拉去殺了。

希律的死

後來希律離開猶太，下凱撒利亞去，住在那裏。²⁰希律惱怒推羅、西頓的人。他們那一帶地方是從王的地土得糧，因此就託了王的內侍臣伯拉斯都的情，一心來求和。

²¹希律在所定的日子，穿上朝服，坐在位上，對他們講論一番。²²百姓喊着說："這是神的聲音，不是人的聲音。"²³希律不歸榮耀給神，所以主的使者立刻罰他，他被蟲所咬，氣就絕了。

²⁴神的道日見興旺，越發廣傳。

²⁵巴拿巴和掃羅辦完了他們供給的事，就從耶路撒冷回來，帶着稱呼馬可的約翰同去。

巴拿巴和掃羅被差派

13 在安提阿的教會中有幾位先知和教師，就是巴拿巴和稱呼尼結的西面、古利奈人路求，與分封之王希律同養的馬念，並掃羅。²他們侍奉主，禁食的時候，聖靈說："要為我分派巴拿巴和掃羅，去做我召他們所做的工。"³於是禁食禱告，按手在他們頭上，就打發他們去了。

在塞浦路斯

⁴他們既被聖靈差遣，就下到西流基，從那裏坐船往塞浦路斯去。⁵到了撒拉米，就在猶太人各會堂裏傳講神的道，也有約翰作他們的幫手。

⁶經過全島，直到帕弗，在那裏遇見一個有法術、假充先知的猶太人，名叫巴耶穌。⁷這人常和方伯士求保羅同在。士求保羅是個通達人，他請了巴拿巴和掃羅來，要聽神的道。⁸只是那行法術的以呂馬（這名翻出來就是"行法術"的意思）敵擋使徒，要叫方伯不信真道。⁹掃羅又名保羅，被聖靈充滿，定睛看他，¹⁰說："你這充滿各樣詭詐奸惡，魔鬼的兒子，眾善的仇敵，你混亂主的正道還不止住嗎？¹¹現在主的手加在你身上，你要瞎眼，暫且不見日光。"

他的眼睛立刻昏蒙黑暗，四下裏求人拉着手領他。¹²方伯看見所做的事，很希奇主的道，就信了。

在彼西底的安提阿

¹³保羅和他的同人從帕弗開船，來到旁非利亞的別加，約翰就離開他們，回耶路撒冷去。¹⁴他們離了別加往前行，來到彼西底的安提阿，在安息日進會堂坐下。¹⁵讀完了律法和先知的書，管會堂的叫人過去，對他們說："二位兄台，若有甚麼勸勉眾人的話，請說。"

¹⁶保羅就站起來，舉手說："以色列人和一切敬畏神的人，請聽。¹⁷這以色列民的神揀選了我們的祖宗，當民寄居埃及的時候，抬舉他們，用大能的手領他們出來；¹⁸又在曠野容忍他們約有四十年（註："容忍"或作"撫養"）。¹⁹既滅了迦南地七族的人，就把那地分給他們為業。²⁰此後給他們設立士師，約有四百五十年，直到先知撒母耳的時候。

²¹後來他們求一個王，神就將便雅憫支派中基士的兒子掃羅給他們作王四十年。²²既廢了掃羅，就選立大衛作他們的王，又為他作見證說：'我尋得耶西的兒子大衛，他是合我心意的人，凡事要遵行我的旨意。'

⁶They traveled through the whole island until they came to Paphos. There they met a Jewish sorcerer and false prophet named Bar-Jesus, ⁷who was an attendant of the proconsul, Sergius Paulus. The proconsul, an intelligent man, sent for Barnabas and Saul because he wanted to hear the word of God. ⁸But Elymas the sorcerer (for that is what his name means) opposed them and tried to turn the proconsul from the faith. ⁹Then Saul, who was also called Paul, filled with the Holy Spirit, looked straight at Elymas and said, ¹⁰"You are a child of the devil and an enemy of everything that is right! You are full of all kinds of deceit and trickery. Will you never stop perverting the right ways of the Lord? ¹¹Now the hand of the Lord is against you. You are going to be blind, and for a time you will be unable to see the light of the sun."

Immediately mist and darkness came over him, and he groped about, seeking someone to lead him by the hand. ¹²When the proconsul saw what had happened, he believed, for he was amazed at the teaching about the Lord.

In Pisidian Antioch

¹³From Paphos, Paul and his companions sailed to Perga in Pamphylia, where John left them to return to Jerusalem. ¹⁴From Perga they went on to Pisidian Antioch. On the Sabbath they entered the synagogue and sat down. ¹⁵After the reading from the Law and the Prophets, the synagogue rulers sent word to them, saying, "Brothers, if you have a message of encouragement for the people, please speak."

¹⁶Standing up, Paul motioned with his hand and said: "Men of Israel and you Gentiles who worship God, listen to me! ¹⁷The God of the people of Israel chose our fathers; he made the people prosper during their stay in Egypt, with mighty power he led them out of that country, ¹⁸he endured their conduct*a* for about forty years in the desert, ¹⁹he overthrew seven nations in Canaan and gave their land to his people as their inheritance. ²⁰All this took about 450 years.

"After this, God gave them judges until the time of Samuel the prophet. ²¹Then the people asked for a king, and he gave them Saul son of Kish, of the tribe of Benjamin, who ruled forty years. ²²After removing Saul, he made David their king. He testified concerning him: 'I have found David son of Jesse a man after my own heart; he will do everything I want him to do.'

a 18 Some manuscripts and cared for them

23"From this man's descendants God has brought to Israel the Savior Jesus, as he promised. 24Before the coming of Jesus, John preached repentance and baptism to all the people of Israel. 25As John was completing his work, he said: 'Who do you think I am? I am not that one. No, but he is coming after me, whose sandals I am not worthy to untie.'

26"Brothers, children of Abraham, and you God-fearing Gentiles, it is to us that this message of salvation has been sent. 27The people of Jerusalem and their rulers did not recognize Jesus, yet in condemning him they fulfilled the words of the prophets that are read every Sabbath. 28Though they found no proper ground for a death sentence, they asked Pilate to have him executed. 29When they had carried out all that was written about him, they took him down from the tree and laid him in a tomb. 30But God raised him from the dead, 31and for many days he was seen by those who had traveled with him from Galilee to Jerusalem. They are now his witnesses to our people.

32"We tell you the good news: What God promised our fathers 33he has fulfilled for us, their children, by raising up Jesus. As it is written in the second Psalm:

" 'You are my Son;
    today I have become your Father.'*a'b*

34The fact that God raised him from the dead, never to decay, is stated in these words:

" 'I will give you the holy and sure blessings promised to David.'*c*

35So it is stated elsewhere:

" 'You will not let your Holy One see decay.'*d*

36"For when David had served God's purpose in his own generation, he fell asleep; he was buried with his fathers and his body decayed. 37But the one whom God raised from the dead did not see decay.

38"Therefore, my brothers, I want you to know that through Jesus the forgiveness of sins is proclaimed to you. 39Through him everyone who believes is justified from everything you could not be justified from by the law of Moses. 40Take care that what the prophets have said does not happen to you:

a 33 Or have begotten you   b 33 Psalm 2:7   c 34 Isaiah 55:3
d 35 Psalm 16:10

---

23 "從這人的後裔中,神已經照着所應許的,為以色列人立了一位救主,就是耶穌。24在他沒有出來以先,約翰向以色列眾民宣講悔改的洗禮。25約翰將行盡他的程途說:'你們以為我是誰?我不是基督;只是有一位在我以後來的,我解他腳上的鞋帶也是不配的。'

26 "弟兄們,亞伯拉罕的子孫和你們中間敬畏神的人哪,這救世的道是傳給我們的。27耶路撒冷居住的人和他們的官長,因為不認識基督,也不明白每安息日所讀眾先知的書,就把基督定了死罪,正應了先知的預言。28雖然查不出他有當死的罪來,還是求彼拉多殺他。29既成就了經上指着他所記的一切話,就把他從木頭上取下來,放在墳墓裏。30神卻叫他從死裏復活。31那從加利利同他上耶路撒冷的人多日看見他,這些人如今在民間是他的見證。

32 "我們也報好信息給你們,就是那應許祖宗的話,33神已經向我們這些兒女的應驗,叫耶穌復活了。正如詩篇第二篇上記着說:

" '你是我的兒子,
     我今日生你。'

34論到神叫他從死裏復活,不再歸於朽壞,就這樣說:

" '我必將所應許大衛
     那聖潔可靠的恩典,
     賜給你們。'

35又有一篇上說:

" '你必不叫你的聖者見朽壞。'

36 "大衛在世的時候遵行了神的旨意,就睡了(註:或作"大衛按神的旨意服侍了他那一世的人,就睡了。"),歸到他祖宗那裏,已見朽壞;37惟獨神所復活的,他並未見朽壞。

38 "所以弟兄們,你們當曉得:赦罪的道是由這人傳給你們的。39你們靠摩西的律法,在一切不得稱義的事上信靠這人,就都得稱義了。40所以,你們務要小心,免得先知書上所說的臨到你們。

41 "主說：'你們這輕慢的人
　　要觀看、要驚奇、要滅亡，
　因為在你們的時候，
　　我行一件事，雖有人告訴你們，
　　你們總是不信。'"

42他們出會堂的時候，眾人請他們到下安息日再講這話給他們聽。43散會以後，猶太人和敬虔進猶太教的人多有跟從保羅、巴拿巴的。二人對他們講道，勸他們務要恆久在神的恩中。

44到下安息日，合城的人幾乎都來聚集，要聽神的道。45但猶太人看見人這樣多，就滿心嫉妒，硬駁保羅所說的話，並且毀謗。

46保羅和巴拿巴放膽說："神的道先講給你們，原是應當的，只因你們棄絕這道，斷定自己不配得永生，我們就轉向外邦人去。47因為主曾這樣吩咐我們說：

" '我已經立你作外邦人的光，
　叫你施行救恩，
　直到地極。' "

48外邦人聽見這話，就歡喜了，讚美神的道；凡預定得永生的人都信了。
49於是主的道傳遍了那一帶地方。50但猶太人挑唆虔敬尊貴的婦女和城內有名望的人，逼迫保羅、巴拿巴，將他們趕出境外。51二人對着眾人跺下腳上的塵土，就往以哥念去了。52門徒滿心喜樂，又被聖靈充滿。

在以哥念

14 二人在以哥念同進猶太人的會堂，在那裏講的，叫猶太人和希臘人信的很多。2但那不順從的猶太人聳動外邦人，叫他們心裏惱恨弟兄。3二人在那裏住了多日，倚靠主放膽講道，主藉他們的手施行神蹟奇事，證明他的恩道。4城裏的眾人就分了黨：有附從

41 " 'Look, you scoffers,
　　wonder and perish,
　for I am going to do something in your days
　　that you would never believe,
　　even if someone told you.'[a]"

42As Paul and Barnabas were leaving the synagogue, the people invited them to speak further about these things on the next Sabbath. 43When the congregation was dismissed, many of the Jews and devout converts to Judaism followed Paul and Barnabas, who talked with them and urged them to continue in the grace of God.

44On the next Sabbath almost the whole city gathered to hear the word of the Lord. 45When the Jews saw the crowds, they were filled with jealousy and talked abusively against what Paul was saying.

46Then Paul and Barnabas answered them boldly: "We had to speak the word of God to you first. Since you reject it and do not consider yourselves worthy of eternal life, we now turn to the Gentiles. 47For this is what the Lord has commanded us:

" 'I have made you[b] a light for the Gentiles,
　that you[b] may bring salvation to the ends of
　　the earth.'[c]"

48When the Gentiles heard this, they were glad and honored the word of the Lord; and all who were appointed for eternal life believed.

49The word of the Lord spread through the whole region. 50But the Jews incited the God-fearing women of high standing and the leading men of the city. They stirred up persecution against Paul and Barnabas, and expelled them from their region. 51So they shook the dust from their feet in protest against them and went to Iconium. 52And the disciples were filled with joy and with the Holy Spirit.

In Iconium

14 At Iconium Paul and Barnabas went as usual into the Jewish synagogue. There they spoke so effectively that a great number of Jews and Gentiles believed. 2But the Jews who refused to believe stirred up the Gentiles and poisoned their minds against the brothers. 3So Paul and Barnabas spent considerable time there, speaking boldly for the Lord, who confirmed the message of his grace by enabling them to do miraculous signs and wonders. 4The people of the city were divided; some

a 41 Hab. 1:5　　*b 47* The Greek is singular.　　*c 47* Isaiah 49:6

sided with the Jews, others with the apostles. [5]There was a plot afoot among the Gentiles and Jews, together with their leaders, to mistreat them and stone them. [6]But they found out about it and fled to the Lycaonian cities of Lystra and Derbe and to the surrounding country, [7]where they continued to preach the good news.

In Lystra and Derbe

[8]In Lystra there sat a man crippled in his feet, who was lame from birth and had never walked. [9]He listened to Paul as he was speaking. Paul looked directly at him, saw that he had faith to be healed [10]and called out, "Stand up on your feet!" At that, the man jumped up and began to walk.

[11]When the crowd saw what Paul had done, they shouted in the Lycaonian language, "The gods have come down to us in human form!" [12]Barnabas they called Zeus, and Paul they called Hermes because he was the chief speaker. [13]The priest of Zeus, whose temple was just outside the city, brought bulls and wreaths to the city gates because he and the crowd wanted to offer sacrifices to them.

[14]But when the apostles Barnabas and Paul heard of this, they tore their clothes and rushed out into the crowd, shouting: [15]"Men, why are you doing this? We too are only men, human like you. We are bringing you good news, telling you to turn from these worthless things to the living God, who made heaven and earth and sea and everything in them. [16]In the past, he let all nations go their own way. [17]Yet he has not left himself without testimony: He has shown kindness by giving you rain from heaven and crops in their seasons; he provides you with plenty of food and fills your hearts with joy." [18]Even with these words, they had difficulty keeping the crowd from sacrificing to them.

[19]Then some Jews came from Antioch and Iconium and won the crowd over. They stoned Paul and dragged him outside the city, thinking he was dead. [20]But after the disciples had gathered around him, he got up and went back into the city. The next day he and Barnabas left for Derbe.

The Return to Antioch in Syria

[21]They preached the good news in that city and won a large number of disciples. Then they returned to Lystra, Iconium and Antioch, [22]strengthening the disciples and encouraging them to remain true to the faith. "We must go through many hardships to enter the kingdom

猶太人的，有附從使徒的。[5]那時，外邦人和猶太人並他們的官長一齊擁上來，要凌辱使徒，用石頭打他們。[6]使徒知道了，就逃往呂高尼的路司得、特庇兩個城和周圍地方去，[7]在那裏傳福音。

在路司得與特庇

[8]路司得城裏坐着一個兩腳無力的人，生來是瘸腿的，從來沒有走過。[9]他聽保羅講道，保羅定睛看他，見他有信心，可得痊愈，[10]就大聲說："你起來，兩腳站直！"那人就跳起來，而且行走。

[11]眾人看見保羅所做的事，就用呂高尼的話大聲說："有神藉着人形降臨在我們中間了！"[12]於是稱巴拿巴為宙斯，稱保羅為希耳米，因為他說話領首。[13]有城外宙斯廟的祭司，牽着牛，拿着花圈來到門前，要同眾人向使徒獻祭。

[14]巴拿巴、保羅二使徒聽見，就撕開衣裳，跳進眾人中間，喊着說：[15]"諸君，為甚麼做這事呢？我們也是人，性情和你們一樣！我們傳福音給你們，是叫你們離棄這些虛妄，歸向那創造天、地、海和其中萬物的永生神。[16]他在從前的世代，任憑萬國各行其道；[17]然而為自己未嘗不顯出證據來，就如常施恩惠，從天降雨，賞賜豐年，叫你們飲食飽足，滿心喜樂。"[18]二人說了這些話，僅僅地攔住眾人不獻祭與他們。

[19]但有些猶太人從安提阿和以哥念來，挑唆眾人，用石頭打保羅，以為他是死了，便拖到城外。[20]門徒正圍着他，他就起來，走進城去。第二天，同巴拿巴往特庇去。

回敍利亞的安提阿

[21]對那城裏的人傳了福音，使好些人作門徒，就回路司得、以哥念、安提阿去，[22]堅固門徒的心，勸他們恆守所信的道，又說："我們進入神

的國，必須經歷許多艱難。」²³二人在各教會中選立了長老，又禁食禱告，就把他們交託所信的主。²⁴二人經過彼西底，來到旁非利亞。²⁵在別加講了道，就下亞大利去。

²⁶從那裏坐船，往安提阿去。當初他們被眾人所託，蒙神之恩，要辦現在所做之工，就是在這地方。²⁷到了那裏，聚集了會眾，就述說神藉他們所行的一切事，並神怎樣為外邦人開了信道的門。²⁸二人就在那裏同門徒住了多日。

耶路撒冷的會議

15 有幾個人從猶太下來，教訓弟兄們說：「你們若不按摩西的規條受割禮，不能得救。」²保羅、巴拿巴與他們大大地紛爭辯論；眾門徒就定規，叫保羅、巴拿巴和本會中幾個人，為所辯論的上耶路撒冷去見使徒和長老。³於是教會送他們起行。他們經過腓尼基、撒馬利亞，隨處傳說外邦人歸主的事，叫眾弟兄都甚歡喜。⁴到了耶路撒冷，教會和使徒並長老都接待他們，他們就述說神同他們所行的一切事。

⁵惟有幾個信徒是法利賽教門的人，起來說：「必須給外邦人行割禮，吩咐他們遵守摩西的律法。」

⁶使徒和長老聚會商議這事。⁷辯論已經多了，彼得就起來，說：「諸位弟兄，你們知道神早已在你們中間揀選了我，叫外邦人從我口中得聽福音之道，而且相信。⁸知道人心的神也為他們作了見證，賜聖靈給他們，正如給我們一樣；⁹又藉着信潔淨了他們的心，並不分他們、我們。¹⁰現在為甚麼試探神，要把我們祖宗和我們所不能負的軛放在門徒的頸項上呢？¹¹我們得救乃是因主耶穌的恩，和他們一樣，這是我們所信的。」

of God," they said. ²³Paul and Barnabas appointed elders*ᵃ* for them in each church and, with prayer and fasting, committed them to the Lord, in whom they had put their trust. ²⁴After going through Pisidia, they came into Pamphylia, ²⁵and when they had preached the word in Perga, they went down to Attalia.

²⁶From Attalia they sailed back to Antioch, where they had been committed to the grace of God for the work they had now completed. ²⁷On arriving there, they gathered the church together and reported all that God had done through them and how he had opened the door of faith to the Gentiles. ²⁸And they stayed there a long time with the disciples.

The Council at Jerusalem

15 Some men came down from Judea to Antioch and were teaching the brothers: "Unless you are circumcised, according to the custom taught by Moses, you cannot be saved." ²This brought Paul and Barnabas into sharp dispute and debate with them. So Paul and Barnabas were appointed, along with some other believers, to go up to Jerusalem to see the apostles and elders about this question. ³The church sent them on their way, and as they traveled through Phoenicia and Samaria, they told how the Gentiles had been converted. This news made all the brothers very glad. ⁴When they came to Jerusalem, they were welcomed by the church and the apostles and elders, to whom they reported everything God had done through them.

⁵Then some of the believers who belonged to the party of the Pharisees stood up and said, "The Gentiles must be circumcised and required to obey the law of Moses."

⁶The apostles and elders met to consider this question. ⁷After much discussion, Peter got up and addressed them: "Brothers, you know that some time ago God made a choice among you that the Gentiles might hear from my lips the message of the gospel and believe. ⁸God, who knows the heart, showed that he accepted them by giving the Holy Spirit to them, just as he did to us. ⁹He made no distinction between us and them, for he purified their hearts by faith. ¹⁰Now then, why do you try to test God by putting on the necks of the disciples a yoke that neither we nor our fathers have been able to bear? ¹¹No! We believe it is through the grace of our Lord Jesus that we are saved, just as they are."

a 23 Or Barnabas ordained elders; or Barnabas had elders elected

12The whole assembly became silent as they listened to Barnabas and Paul telling about the miraculous signs and wonders God had done among the Gentiles through them. 13When they finished, James spoke up: "Brothers, listen to me. 14Simon[a] has described to us how God at first showed his concern by taking from the Gentiles a people for himself. 15The words of the prophets are in agreement with this, as it is written:

16" 'After this I will return
    and rebuild David's fallen tent.
  Its ruins I will rebuild,
    and I will restore it,
17that the remnant of men may seek the Lord,
    and all the Gentiles who bear my name,
  says the Lord, who does these things'[b]
18 that have been known for ages.[c]

19"It is my judgment, therefore, that we should not make it difficult for the Gentiles who are turning to God. 20Instead we should write to them, telling them to abstain from food polluted by idols, from sexual immorality, from the meat of strangled animals and from blood. 21For Moses has been preached in every city from the earliest times and is read in the synagogues on every Sabbath."

The Council's Letter to Gentile Believers

22Then the apostles and elders, with the whole church, decided to choose some of their own men and send them to Antioch with Paul and Barnabas. They chose Judas (called Barsabbas) and Silas, two men who were leaders among the brothers. 23With them they sent the following letter:

The apostles and elders, your brothers,

To the Gentile believers in Antioch, Syria and Cilicia:

Greetings.

24We have heard that some went out from us without our authorization and disturbed you, troubling your minds by what they said. 25So we all agreed to choose some men and send them to you with our dear friends Barnabas and Paul— 26men who have risked

a 14 Greek Simeon, a variant of Simon; that is, Peter
b 17 Amos 9:11,12   c 17,18 Some manuscripts things'—
/ 18 known to the Lord for ages is his work

12眾人都默默無聲，聽巴拿巴和保羅述說神藉他們在外邦人中所行的神蹟奇事。13他們住了聲，雅各就說：「諸位弟兄，請聽我的話。14方才西門述說神當初怎樣眷顧外邦人，從他們中間選取百姓歸於自己的名下；15眾先知的話也與這意思相合。

16正如經上所寫的：
「『此後，我要回來，
    重新修造大衛倒塌的帳幕，
  把那破壞的，
    重新修造建立起來。
17叫餘剩的人，
    就是凡稱為我名下的外邦人，
    都尋求主。』
18這話是從創世以來
    顯明這事的主說的。

19「所以據我的意見，不可難為那歸服神的外邦人，20只要寫信吩咐他們禁戒偶像的污穢和姦淫，並勒死的牲畜和血。21因為從古以來，摩西的書在各城有人傳講，每逢安息日在會堂裏誦讀。」

會議給外邦信徒的信

22那時，使徒和長老並全教會定意從他們中間揀選人，差他們和保羅、巴拿巴同往安提阿去。所揀選的就是稱呼巴撒巴的猶大和西拉，這兩個人在弟兄中是作首領的。23於是寫信交付他們，內中說：

使徒和作長老的弟兄們

問安提阿、敍利亞、基利家外邦眾弟兄的安！

24我們聽說有幾個人從我們這裏出去，用言語擾擾你們，惑亂你們的心。（註：有古卷在此有「你們必須受割禮，守摩西的律法。」）其實我們並沒有吩咐他們。25所以我們同心定意揀選幾個人，差他們同我們所親愛的巴拿巴和保羅往你們那裏去。26這二人是為我主耶穌基督的名不顧性命的。27我們就差了猶大和西拉，他們也要親口訴說這些事。28因為聖靈和我們定意不將別的重擔放在你們身上，惟有幾件事是不可少的，29就是禁戒祭偶像的物和血，並勒死的牲畜和姦淫。這幾件你們若能自己禁戒不犯就好了。

願你們平安！

30他們既奉了差遣，就下安提阿去，聚集眾人，交付書信。31眾人念了，因為信上安慰的話就歡喜了。32猶大和西拉也是先知，就用許多話勸勉弟兄，堅固他們。33住了些日子，弟兄們打發他們平平安安地回到差遣他們的人那裏去。（註：有古卷在此有34"惟有西拉定意仍住在那裏。"）35但保羅和巴拿巴仍住在安提阿，和許多別人一同教訓人，傳主的道。

保羅與巴拿巴之間的爭論

36過了些日子，保羅對巴拿巴說："我們可以回到從前宣傳主道的各城，看望弟兄們景況如何。"37巴拿巴有意要帶稱呼馬可的約翰同去，38但保羅因為馬可從前在旁非利亞離開他們，不和他們同去做工，就以為不可帶他去。39於是二人起了爭論，甚至彼此分開。巴拿巴帶着馬可坐船往塞浦路斯去；40保羅揀選了西拉也出去，蒙弟兄們把他交於主的恩中。41他就走遍敘利亞、基利家，堅固眾教會。

提摩太加入保羅與西拉的工作

16 保羅來到特庇，又到路司得。在那裏有一個門徒，名叫提摩太，是信主之猶太婦人的兒子，他父親卻是希臘人。2路司得和以哥念的弟兄都稱讚他。3保羅要帶他同去，只因那些地方的猶太人都知道他父親是希臘人，就給他行了割禮。4他們經過各城，把耶路撒冷使徒和長老所定的條規交給

their lives for the name of our Lord Jesus Christ. 27Therefore we are sending Judas and Silas to confirm by word of mouth what we are writing. 28It seemed good to the Holy Spirit and to us not to burden you with anything beyond the following requirements: 29You are to abstain from food sacrificed to idols, from blood, from the meat of strangled animals and from sexual immorality. You will do well to avoid these things.

Farewell.

30The men were sent off and went down to Antioch, where they gathered the church together and delivered the letter. 31The people read it and were glad for its encouraging message. 32Judas and Silas, who themselves were prophets, said much to encourage and strengthen the brothers. 33After spending some time there, they were sent off by the brothers with the blessing of peace to return to those who had sent them.*a* 35But Paul and Barnabas remained in Antioch, where they and many others taught and preached the word of the Lord.

Disagreement Between Paul and Barnabas

36Some time later Paul said to Barnabas, "Let us go back and visit the brothers in all the towns where we preached the word of the Lord and see how they are doing." 37Barnabas wanted to take John, also called Mark, with them, 38but Paul did not think it wise to take him, because he had deserted them in Pamphylia and had not continued with them in the work. 39They had such a sharp disagreement that they parted company. Barnabas took Mark and sailed for Cyprus, 40but Paul chose Silas and left, commended by the brothers to the grace of the Lord. 41He went through Syria and Cilicia, strengthening the churches.

Timothy Joins Paul and Silas

16 He came to Derbe and then to Lystra, where a disciple named Timothy lived, whose mother was a Jewess and a believer, but whose father was a Greek. 2The brothers at Lystra and Iconium spoke well of him. 3Paul wanted to take him along on the journey, so he circumcised him because of the Jews who lived in that area, for they all knew that his father was a Greek. 4As they traveled from town to town, they delivered the decisions reached by the apostles and elders in Jerusalem for the peo-

a 33 Some manuscripts them, 34 but Silas decided to remain there ple to obey. [5]So the churches were strengthened in the faith and grew daily in numbers.

Paul's Vision of the Man of Macedonia

[6]Paul and his companions traveled throughout the region of Phrygia and Galatia, having been kept by the Holy Spirit from preaching the word in the province of Asia. [7]When they came to the border of Mysia, they tried to enter Bithynia, but the Spirit of Jesus would not allow them to. [8]So they passed by Mysia and went down to Troas. [9]During the night Paul had a vision of a man of Macedonia standing and begging him, "Come over to Macedonia and help us." [10]After Paul had seen the vision, we got ready at once to leave for Macedonia, concluding that God had called us to preach the gospel to them.

Lydia's Conversion in Philippi

[11]From Troas we put out to sea and sailed straight for Samothrace, and the next day on to Neapolis. [12]From there we traveled to Philippi, a Roman colony and the leading city of that district of Macedonia. And we stayed there several days.

[13]On the Sabbath we went outside the city gate to the river, where we expected to find a place of prayer. We sat down and began to speak to the women who had gathered there. [14]One of those listening was a woman named Lydia, a dealer in purple cloth from the city of Thyatira, who was a worshiper of God. The Lord opened her heart to respond to Paul's message. [15]When she and the members of her household were baptized, she invited us to her home. "If you consider me a believer in the Lord," she said, "come and stay at my house." And she persuaded us.

Paul and Silas in Prison

[16]Once when we were going to the place of prayer, we were met by a slave girl who had a spirit by which she predicted the future. She earned a great deal of money for her owners by fortune-telling. [17]This girl followed Paul and the rest of us, shouting, "These men are servants of the Most High God, who are telling you the way to be saved." [18]She kept this up for many days. Finally Paul became so troubled that he turned around and said to the spirit, "In the name of Jesus Christ I command you to come out of her!" At that moment the spirit left her.

[19]When the owners of the slave girl realized that their hope of making money was gone, they seized Paul and Silas and dragged them into the marketplace to face the authorities. [20]They

門徒遵守。[5]於是眾教會信心越發堅固，人數天天加增。

保羅見馬其頓人的異象

[6]聖靈既然禁止他們在亞西亞講道，他們就經過弗呂家、加拉太一帶地方，[7]到了每西亞的邊界，他們想要往庇推尼去，耶穌的靈卻不許。[8]他們就越過每西亞下到特羅亞去。[9]在夜間有異象現與保羅：有一個馬其頓人站着求他說："請你過到馬其頓來幫助我們！"[10]保羅既看見這異象，我們隨即想要往馬其頓去，以為神召我們傳福音給那裏的人聽。

呂底亞在腓立比信主

[11]於是從特羅亞開船，一直行到撒摩特喇，第二天到了尼亞坡里。[12]從那裏來到腓立比，就是馬其頓這一方的頭一個城，也是羅馬的駐防城。我們在這城裏住了幾天。

[13]當安息日，我們出城門，到了河邊，知道那裏有一個禱告的地方，我們就坐下對那聚會的婦女講道。[14]有一個賣紫色布疋的婦人，名叫呂底亞，是推雅推喇城的人，素來敬拜神。她聽見了，主就開導她的心，叫她留心聽保羅所講的話。[15]她和她一家既領了洗，便求我們說："你們若以為我是真信主的（註：或作"你們若以為我是忠心侍主的"），請到我家裏來住。"於是強留我們。

保羅與西拉在監獄中

[16]後來，我們往那禱告的地方去。有一個使女迎着面來，她被巫鬼所附，用法術叫她主人們大得財利。[17]她跟隨保羅和我們，喊着說："這些人是至高神的僕人，對你們傳說救人的道！"[18]她一連多日這樣喊叫，保羅就心中厭煩，轉身對那鬼說："我奉耶穌基督的名，吩咐你從她身上出來！"那鬼當時就出來了。

[19]使女的主人們見得利的指望沒有了，便揪住保羅和西拉，拉他們到市上去見首領，[20]又帶到官長面前

說：“這些人原是猶太人，竟騷擾我們的城，21傳我們羅馬人所不可受、不可行的規矩。”

22眾人就一同起來攻擊他們。官長吩咐剝了他們的衣裳，用棍打。23打了許多棍，便將他們下在監裏，囑咐禁卒嚴緊看守。24禁卒領了這樣的命，就把他們下在內監裏，兩腳上了木狗。

25約在半夜，保羅和西拉禱告唱詩讚美神，眾囚犯也側耳而聽。26忽然地大震動，甚至監牢的地基都搖動了，監門立刻全開，眾囚犯的鎖鏈也都鬆開了。27禁卒一醒，看見監門全開，以為囚犯已經逃走，就拔刀要自殺。28保羅大聲呼叫說：“不要傷害自己！我們都在這裏。”

29禁卒叫人拿燈來，就跳進去，戰戰兢兢地俯伏在保羅、西拉面前，30又領他們出來，說：“二位先生，我當怎樣行才可以得救？”
31他們說：“當信主耶穌，你和你一家都必得救。”32他們就把主的道講給他和他全家的人聽。33當夜，就在那時候，禁卒把他們帶去，洗他們的傷；他和屬乎他的人立時都受了洗。34於是禁卒領他們上自己家裏去，給他們擺上飯。他和全家，因為信了神，都很喜樂。

35到了天亮，官長打發差役來，說：“釋放那兩個人吧！”36禁卒就把這話告訴保羅，說：“官長打發人來叫釋放你們。如今可以出監，平平安安地去吧！”
37保羅卻說：“我們是羅馬人，並沒有定罪，他們就在眾人面前打了我們，又把我們下在監裏，現在要私下攆我們出去嗎？這是不行的。叫他們自己來領我們出去吧！”
38差役把這話回稟官長。官長聽見他們是羅馬人，就害怕了，39於是來勸他們，領他們出來，請他們離開那城。40二人出了監，往呂底亞家裏去，見了弟兄們，勸慰他們一番，就走了。

brought them before the magistrates and said, "These men are Jews, and are throwing our city into an uproar 21by advocating customs unlawful for us Romans to accept or practice."

22The crowd joined in the attack against Paul and Silas, and the magistrates ordered them to be stripped and beaten. 23After they had been severely flogged, they were thrown into prison, and the jailer was commanded to guard them carefully. 24Upon receiving such orders, he put them in the inner cell and fastened their feet in the stocks.

25About midnight Paul and Silas were praying and singing hymns to God, and the other prisoners were listening to them. 26Suddenly there was such a violent earthquake that the foundations of the prison were shaken. At once all the prison doors flew open, and everybody's chains came loose. 27The jailer woke up, and when he saw the prison doors open, he drew his sword and was about to kill himself because he thought the prisoners had escaped. 28But Paul shouted, "Don't harm yourself! We are all here!"

29The jailer called for lights, rushed in and fell trembling before Paul and Silas. 30He then brought them out and asked, "Sirs, what must I do to be saved?"

31They replied, "Believe in the Lord Jesus, and you will be saved—you and your household." 32Then they spoke the word of the Lord to him and to all the others in his house. 33At that hour of the night the jailer took them and washed their wounds; then immediately he and all his family were baptized. 34The jailer brought them into his house and set a meal before them; he was filled with joy because he had come to believe in God—he and his whole family.

35When it was daylight, the magistrates sent their officers to the jailer with the order: "Release those men." 36The jailer told Paul, "The magistrates have ordered that you and Silas be released. Now you can leave. Go in peace."

37But Paul said to the officers: "They beat us publicly without a trial, even though we are Roman citizens, and threw us into prison. And now do they want to get rid of us quietly? No! Let them come themselves and escort us out."

38The officers reported this to the magistrates, and when they heard that Paul and Silas were Roman citizens, they were alarmed. 39They came to appease them and escorted them from the prison, requesting them to leave the city. 40After Paul and Silas came out of the prison, they went to Lydia's house, where they met with the brothers and encouraged them. Then they left.

In Thessalonica

17 When they had passed through Amphipolis and Apollonia, they came to Thessalonica, where there was a Jewish synagogue. ²As his custom was, Paul went into the synagogue, and on three Sabbath days he reasoned with them from the Scriptures, ³explaining and proving that the Christ*ᵃ* had to suffer and rise from the dead. "This Jesus I am proclaiming to you is the Christ,*ᵃ*" he said. ⁴Some of the Jews were persuaded and joined Paul and Silas, as did a large number of God-fearing Greeks and not a few prominent women.

⁵But the Jews were jealous; so they rounded up some bad characters from the marketplace, formed a mob and started a riot in the city. They rushed to Jason's house in search of Paul and Silas in order to bring them out to the crowd.*ᵇ* ⁶But when they did not find them, they dragged Jason and some other brothers before the city officials, shouting: "These men who have caused trouble all over the world have now come here, ⁷and Jason has welcomed them into his house. They are all defying Caesar's decrees, saying that there is another king, one called Jesus." ⁸When they heard this, the crowd and the city officials were thrown into turmoil. ⁹Then they made Jason and the others post bond and let them go.

In Berea

¹⁰As soon as it was night, the brothers sent Paul and Silas away to Berea. On arriving there, they went to the Jewish synagogue. ¹¹Now the Bereans were of more noble character than the Thessalonians, for they received the message with great eagerness and examined the Scriptures every day to see if what Paul said was true. ¹²Many of the Jews believed, as did also a number of prominent Greek women and many Greek men.

¹³When the Jews in Thessalonica learned that Paul was preaching the word of God at Berea, they went there too, agitating the crowds and stirring them up. ¹⁴The brothers immediately sent Paul to the coast, but Silas and Timothy stayed at Berea. ¹⁵The men who escorted Paul brought him to Athens and then left with instructions for Silas and Timothy to join him as soon as possible.

In Athens

¹⁶While Paul was waiting for them in Athens, he was greatly distressed to see that the city was

在帖撒羅尼迦

17 保羅和西拉經過暗妃坡里、亞波羅尼亞，來到帖撒羅尼迦，在那裏有猶太人的會堂。²保羅照他素常的規矩進去，一連三個安息日，本着聖經與他們辯論，³講解陳明基督必須受害，從死裏復活；又說："我所傳與你們的這位耶穌，就是基督。"他說。⁴他們中間有些人聽了勸，就附從保羅和西拉，並有許多虔敬的希臘人，尊貴的婦女也不少。

⁵但那不信的猶太人心裏嫉妒，招聚了些市井匪類，搭夥成羣，聳動合城的人闖進耶孫的家，要將保羅、西拉帶到百姓那裏。⁶找不着他們，就把耶孫和幾個弟兄拉到地方官那裏，喊叫說："那攪亂天下的也到這裏來了！⁷耶孫收留他們。這些人都違背凱撒的命令，說另有一個王耶穌。"⁸眾人和地方官聽見這話，就驚慌了，⁹於是取了耶孫和其餘之人的保狀，就釋放了他們。

在庇哩亞

¹⁰弟兄們隨即在夜間打發保羅和西拉往庇哩亞去。二人到了，就進入猶太人的會堂。¹¹這地方的人賢於帖撒羅尼迦的人，甘心領受這道，天天考查聖經，要曉得這道是與不是。¹²所以他們中間多有相信的，又有希臘尊貴的婦女，男子也不少。

¹³但帖撒羅尼迦的猶太人知道保羅又在庇哩亞傳神的道，也就往那裏去，聳動攪擾眾人。¹⁴當時弟兄們便打發保羅往海邊去；西拉和提摩太仍住在庇哩亞。¹⁵送保羅的人帶他到了雅典，既領了保羅的命，叫西拉和提摩太速速到他這裏來，就回去了。

在雅典

¹⁶保羅在雅典等候他們的時候，看見滿城都是偶像，就心裏着急，

---

a 3 Or Messiah　　b 5 Or the assembly of the people

17於是在會堂裏與猶太人和虔敬的人，並每日在市上所遇見的人辯論。18還有伊壁鳩魯和斯多亞兩門的學士與他爭論。有的說：「這胡言亂語的要說甚麼？」有的說：「他似乎是傳說外邦鬼神的。」這話是因保羅傳耶穌與復活的道。19他們就把他帶到亞略巴古，說：「你所講的這新道，我們也可以知道嗎？20因為你有些奇怪的事，傳到我們耳中，我們願意知道這些事是甚麼意思。」21（雅典人和住在那裏的客人都不顧別的事，只將新聞說說聽聽。）

22保羅站在亞略巴古當中，說：「眾位雅典人哪，我看你們凡事很敬畏鬼神。23我遊行的時候，觀看你們所敬拜的，遇見一座壇，上面寫着『未識之神』；你們所不認識而敬拜的，我現在告訴你們：

24「創造宇宙和其中萬物的神，既是天地的主，就不住人手所造的殿，25也不用人手服侍，好像缺少甚麼；自己倒將生命、氣息、萬物，賜給萬人。26他從一本造出萬族的人（註：「本」有古卷作「血脈」），住在全地上，並且預先定準他們的年限和所住的疆界；27要叫他們尋求神，或者可以揣摩而得。其實他離我們各人不遠，28我們生活、動作、存留，都在乎他。就如你們作詩的，有人說：『我們也是他所生的。』

29「我們既是神所生的，就不當以為神的神性像人用手藝、心思所雕刻的金、銀、石。30世人蒙昧無知的時候，神並不監察，如今卻吩咐各處的人都要悔改。31因為他已經定了日子，要藉着他所設立的人按公義審判天下，並且叫他從死裏復活，給萬人作可信的憑據。」

32眾人聽見從死裏復活的話，就有譏誚他的；又有人說：「我們再

full of idols. 17So he reasoned in the synagogue with the Jews and the God-fearing Greeks, as well as in the marketplace day by day with those who happened to be there. 18A group of Epicurean and Stoic philosophers began to dispute with him. Some of them asked, "What is this babbler trying to say?" Others remarked, "He seems to be advocating foreign gods." They said this because Paul was preaching the good news about Jesus and the resurrection. 19Then they took him and brought him to a meeting of the Areopagus, where they said to him, "May we know what this new teaching is that you are presenting? 20You are bringing some strange ideas to our ears, and we want to know what they mean." 21(All the Athenians and the foreigners who lived there spent their time doing nothing but talking about and listening to the latest ideas.)

22Paul then stood up in the meeting of the Areopagus and said: "Men of Athens! I see that in every way you are very religious. 23For as I walked around and looked carefully at your objects of worship, I even found an altar with this inscription: TO AN UNKNOWN GOD. Now what you worship as something unknown I am going to proclaim to you.

24"The God who made the world and everything in it is the Lord of heaven and earth and does not live in temples built by hands. 25And he is not served by human hands, as if he needed anything, because he himself gives all men life and breath and everything else. 26From one man he made every nation of men, that they should inhabit the whole earth; and he determined the times set for them and the exact places where they should live. 27God did this so that men would seek him and perhaps reach out for him and find him, though he is not far from each one of us. 28For in him we live and move and have our being.' As some of your own poets have said, 'We are his offspring.'

29"Therefore since we are God's offspring, we should not think that the divine being is like gold or silver or stone—an image made by man's design and skill. 30In the past God overlooked such ignorance, but now he commands all people everywhere to repent. 31For he has set a day when he will judge the world with justice by the man he has appointed. He has given proof of this to all men by raising him from the dead."

32When they heard about the resurrection of the dead, some of them sneered, but others said, "We want to hear you again on this subject."

³³At that, Paul left the Council. ³⁴A few men became followers of Paul and believed. Among them was Dionysius, a member of the Areopagus, also a woman named Damaris, and a number of others.

In Corinth

18 After this, Paul left Athens and went to Corinth. ²There he met a Jew named Aquila, a native of Pontus, who had recently come from Italy with his wife Priscilla, because Claudius had ordered all the Jews to leave Rome. Paul went to see them, ³and because he was a tentmaker as they were, he stayed and worked with them. ⁴Every Sabbath he reasoned in the synagogue, trying to persuade Jews and Greeks.

⁵When Silas and Timothy came from Macedonia, Paul devoted himself exclusively to preaching, testifying to the Jews that Jesus was the Christ.ᵃ ⁶But when the Jews opposed Paul and became abusive, he shook out his clothes in protest and said to them, "Your blood be on your own heads! I am clear of my responsibility. From now on I will go to the Gentiles."

⁷Then Paul left the synagogue and went next door to the house of Titius Justus, a worshiper of God. ⁸Crispus, the synagogue ruler, and his entire household believed in the Lord; and many of the Corinthians who heard him believed and were baptized.

⁹One night the Lord spoke to Paul in a vision: "Do not be afraid; keep on speaking, do not be silent. ¹⁰For I am with you, and no one is going to attack and harm you, because I have many people in this city." ¹¹So Paul stayed for a year and a half, teaching them the word of God.

¹²While Gallio was proconsul of Achaia, the Jews made a united attack on Paul and brought him into court. ¹³"This man," they charged, "is persuading the people to worship God in ways contrary to the law."

¹⁴Just as Paul was about to speak, Gallio said to the Jews, "If you Jews were making a complaint about some misdemeanor or serious crime, it would be reasonable for me to listen to you. ¹⁵But since it involves questions about words and names and your own law—settle the matter yourselves. I will not be a judge of such things." ¹⁶So he had them ejected from the court. ¹⁷Then they all turned on Sosthenes the synagogue ruler and beat him in front of the court. But Gallio showed no concern whatever.

聽你講這個吧！" ³³於是保羅從他們當中出去了。³⁴但有幾個人貼近他，信了主，其中有亞略巴古的官丟尼修，並一個婦人，名叫大馬哩，還有別人一同信從。

在哥林多

18 這事以後，保羅離了雅典，來到哥林多。²遇見一個猶太人，名叫亞居拉，他生在本都；因為革老丟命猶太人都離開羅馬，新近帶着妻百基拉從意大利來。保羅就投奔了他們。³他們本是製造帳棚為業。保羅因與他們同業，就和他們同住做工。⁴每逢安息日，保羅在會堂裏辯論，勸化猶太人和希臘人。

⁵西拉和提摩太從馬其頓來的時候，保羅為道迫切，向猶太人證明耶穌是基督。⁶他們既抗拒、毀謗，保羅就抖着衣裳，說："你們的罪歸到你們自己頭上（註："罪"原文作"血"），與我無干（註：原文作"我卻乾淨"）！從今以後，我要往外邦人那裏去。"

⁷於是離開那裏，到了一個人的家中，這人名叫提多猶士都，是敬拜神的，他的家靠近會堂。⁸管會堂的基利司布和全家都信了主，還有許多哥林多人聽了，就相信受洗。

⁹夜間，主在異象中對保羅說："不要怕，只管講，不要閉口。¹⁰有我與你同在，必沒有人下手害你，因為在這城裏，我有許多的百姓。"¹¹保羅在那裏住了一年零六個月，將神的道教訓他們。

¹²到迦流作亞該亞方伯的時候，猶太人同心起來攻擊保羅，拉他到公堂，¹³說："這個人，勸人不按着律法敬拜神。"

¹⁴保羅剛要開口，迦流就對猶太人說："你們這些猶太人！如果是為冤枉或奸惡的事，我理當耐性聽你們。¹⁵但所爭論的，若是關乎言語、名目，和你們的律法，你們自己去辦吧！這樣的事我不願意審判。"¹⁶就把他們攆出公堂。¹⁷眾人便揪住管會堂的所提尼，在堂前打他。這些事迦流都不管。

ᵃ 5 Or *Messiah*; also in verse 28

百基拉、亞居拉與亞波羅

18保羅又住了多日，就辭別了弟兄，坐船往敘利亞去，百基拉、亞居拉和他同去。他因為許過願，就在堅革哩剪了頭髮。19到了以弗所，保羅就把他們留在那裏，自己進了會堂，和猶太人辯論。20眾人請他多住些日子，他卻不允，21就辭別他們，說："神若許我，我還要回到你們這裏。"於是開船離了以弗所。22在凱撒利亞下了船，就上耶路撒冷去問教會安，隨後下安提阿去。

23住了些日子，又離開那裏，挨次經過加拉太和弗呂家地方，堅固眾門徒。

24有一個猶太人，名叫亞波羅，來到以弗所。他生在亞歷山太，是有學問的，最能講解聖經（註："學問"或作"口才"）。25這人已經在主的道上受了教訓，心裏火熱，將耶穌的事詳細講論教訓人；只是他單曉得約翰的洗禮。26他在會堂裏放膽講道，百基拉、亞居拉聽見，就接他來，將神的道給他講解更加詳細。

27他想要往亞該亞去，弟兄們就勉勵他，並寫信請門徒接待他（註：或作"弟兄們就寫信勸門徒接待他"）。他到了那裏，多幫助那蒙恩信主的人，28在眾人面前極有能力駁倒猶太人，引聖經證明耶穌是基督。

保羅在以弗所

19 亞波羅在哥林多的時候，保羅經過了上邊一帶地方，就來到以弗所；在那裏遇見幾個門徒，2問他們說："你們信的時候，受了聖靈沒有？"

他們回答說："沒有，也未曾聽見有聖靈賜下來。"

3保羅說："這樣，你們受的是甚麼洗呢？"

他們說："是約翰的洗。"

4保羅說："約翰所行的是悔改的洗，告訴百姓當信那在他以後要來的，就是耶穌。"5他們聽見這話，就奉主耶穌的名受洗。6保羅按

Priscilla, Aquila and Apollos

18Paul stayed on in Corinth for some time. Then he left the brothers and sailed for Syria, accompanied by Priscilla and Aquila. Before he sailed, he had his hair cut off at Cenchrea because of a vow he had taken. 19They arrived at Ephesus, where Paul left Priscilla and Aquila. He himself went into the synagogue and reasoned with the Jews. 20When they asked him to spend more time with them, he declined. 21But as he left, he promised, "I will come back if it is God's will." Then he set sail from Ephesus. 22When he landed at Caesarea, he went up and greeted the church and then went down to Antioch.

23After spending some time in Antioch, Paul set out from there and traveled from place to place throughout the region of Galatia and Phrygia, strengthening all the disciples.

24Meanwhile a Jew named Apollos, a native of Alexandria, came to Ephesus. He was a learned man, with a thorough knowledge of the Scriptures. 25He had been instructed in the way of the Lord, and he spoke with great fervor[a] and taught about Jesus accurately, though he knew only the baptism of John. 26He began to speak boldly in the synagogue. When Priscilla and Aquila heard him, they invited him to their home and explained to him the way of God more adequately.

27When Apollos wanted to go to Achaia, the brothers encouraged him and wrote to the disciples there to welcome him. On arriving, he was a great help to those who by grace had believed. 28For he vigorously refuted the Jews in public debate, proving from the Scriptures that Jesus was the Christ.

Paul in Ephesus

19 While Apollos was at Corinth, Paul took the road through the interior and arrived at Ephesus. There he found some disciples 2and asked them, "Did you receive the Holy Spirit when[b] you believed?"

They answered, "No, we have not even heard that there is a Holy Spirit."

3So Paul asked, "Then what baptism did you receive?"

"John's baptism," they replied.

4Paul said, "John's baptism was a baptism of repentance. He told the people to believe in the one coming after him, that is, in Jesus." 5On hearing this, they were baptized into[c] the name of the Lord Jesus. 6When Paul placed his hands

a 25 Or with fervor in the Spirit   b 2 Or after   c 5 Or in

on them, the Holy Spirit came on them, and they spoke in tongues*a* and prophesied. ⁷There were about twelve men in all.

⁸Paul entered the synagogue and spoke boldly there for three months, arguing persuasively about the kingdom of God. ⁹But some of them became obstinate; they refused to believe and publicly maligned the Way. So Paul left them. He took the disciples with him and had discussions daily in the lecture hall of Tyrannus. ¹⁰This went on for two years, so that all the Jews and Greeks who lived in the province of Asia heard the word of the Lord.

¹¹God did extraordinary miracles through Paul, ¹²so that even handkerchiefs and aprons that had touched him were taken to the sick, and their illnesses were cured and the evil spirits left them.

¹³Some Jews who went around driving out evil spirits tried to invoke the name of the Lord Jesus over those who were demon-possessed. They would say, "In the name of Jesus, whom Paul preaches, I command you to come out." ¹⁴Seven sons of Sceva, a Jewish chief priest, were doing this. ¹⁵⌈One day⌉ the evil spirit answered them, "Jesus I know, and I know about Paul, but who are you?" ¹⁶Then the man who had the evil spirit jumped on them and overpowered them all. He gave them such a beating that they ran out of the house naked and bleeding.

¹⁷When this became known to the Jews and Greeks living in Ephesus, they were all seized with fear, and the name of the Lord Jesus was held in high honor. ¹⁸Many of those who believed now came and openly confessed their evil deeds. ¹⁹A number who had practiced sorcery brought their scrolls together and burned them publicly. When they calculated the value of the scrolls, the total came to fifty thousand drachmas.*b* ²⁰In this way the word of the Lord spread widely and grew in power.

²¹After all this had happened, Paul decided to go to Jerusalem, passing through Macedonia and Achaia. "After I have been there," he said, "I must visit Rome also." ²²He sent two of his helpers, Timothy and Erastus, to Macedonia, while he stayed in the province of Asia a little longer.

The Riot in Ephesus

²³About that time there arose a great disturbance about the Way. ²⁴A silversmith named Demetrius, who made silver shrines of Artemis,

手在他們頭上，聖靈便降在他們身上，他們就說方言，又說預言（註：或作"又講道"）。⁷一共約有十二個人。

⁸保羅進會堂放膽講道，一連三個月，辯論神國的事，勸化眾人。⁹後來，有些人心裏剛硬不信，在眾人面前毀謗這道。保羅就離開他們，也叫門徒與他們分離，便在推喇奴的學房天天辯論。¹⁰這樣有兩年之久，叫一切住在亞西亞的，無論是猶太人，是希臘人，都聽見主的道。

¹¹神藉保羅的手行了些非常的奇事，¹²甚至有人從保羅身上拿手巾或圍裙放在病人身上，病就退了，惡鬼也出去了。

¹³那時，有幾個遊行各處，念咒趕鬼的猶太人，向那被惡鬼附的人擅自稱主耶穌的名，說："我奉保羅所傳的耶穌，勅令你們出來！"¹⁴做這事的，有猶太祭司長士基瓦的七個兒子。¹⁵惡鬼回答他們說："耶穌我認識，保羅我也知道。你們卻是誰呢？"¹⁶惡鬼所附的人就跳在他們身上，勝了其中二人，制伏他們，叫他們赤着身子受了傷，從那房子裏逃出去了。

¹⁷凡住在以弗所的，無論是猶太人，是希臘人，都知道這事，也都懼怕，主耶穌的名從此就尊大了。¹⁸那已經信的，多有人來承認訴說自己所行的事。¹⁹平素行邪術的，也有許多人把書拿來，堆積在眾人面前焚燒。他們算計書價，便知道共合五萬塊錢。²⁰主的道大大興旺，而且得勝，就是這樣。

²¹這些事完了，保羅心裏定意，經過了馬其頓、亞該亞，就往耶路撒冷去；又說："我到了那裏以後，也必須往羅馬去看看。"²²於是從幫助他的人中，打發提摩太、以拉都二人往馬其頓去，自己暫時等在亞西亞。

以弗所的騷亂

²³那時，因為這道起的擾亂不小。²⁴有一個銀匠，名叫底米丟，是製造亞底米神銀龕的，他使這樣手藝

---

a 6 Or *other languages*　　*b* 19 A drachma was a silver coin worth about a day's wages.

人生意發達。25他聚集他們和同行的工人，說："眾位，你們知道我們是倚靠這生意發財。26這保羅不但在<u>以弗所</u>，也幾乎在<u>亞西亞</u>全地，引誘迷惑許多人，說：'人手所做的，不是神。'這是你們所看見、所聽見的。27這樣，不獨我們這事業被人藐視，就是大女神<u>亞底米</u>的廟也要被人輕忽，連<u>亞西亞</u>全地和普天下所敬拜的大女神之威榮也要消滅了。"

28眾人聽見，就怒氣填胸，喊着說："大哉，<u>以弗所</u>人的<u>亞底米</u>啊！"29滿城都轟動起來。眾人拿住與保羅同行的<u>馬其頓</u>人<u>該猶</u>和<u>亞里達古</u>，齊心擁進戲園裏去。30保羅想要進去，到百姓那裏，門徒卻不許他去。31還有<u>亞西亞</u>幾位首領，是<u>保羅</u>的朋友，打發人來勸他，不要冒險到戲園裏去。

32聚集的人紛紛亂亂，有喊叫這個的，有喊叫那個的，大半不知道是為甚麼聚集。33有人把<u>亞歷山大</u>從眾人中帶出來，<u>猶太</u>人推他往前。<u>亞歷山大</u>就擺手，要向百姓分訴，34只因他們認出他是<u>猶太</u>人，就大家同聲喊着說："大哉，<u>以弗所</u>人的<u>亞底米</u>啊！"如此約有兩小時。

35那城裏的書記安撫了眾人，就說："<u>以弗所</u>人哪，誰不知道<u>以弗所</u>人的城是看守大<u>亞底米</u>的廟，和從<u>宙斯</u>那裏落下來的像呢？36這事既是駁不倒的，你們就當安靜，不可造次。37你們把這些人帶來，他們並沒有偷竊廟中之物，也沒有謗讟我們的女神。38若是<u>底米丟</u>和他同行的人有控告人的事，自有放告的日子（註：或作"自有公堂"），也有方伯可以彼此對告。39你們若問別的事，就可以照常例聚集斷定。40今日的擾亂本是無緣無故，我們難免被查問。論到這樣聚眾，我們也說不出所以然來。"41說了這話，便叫眾人散去。

brought in no little business for the craftsmen. 25He called them together, along with the workmen in related trades, and said: "Men, you know we receive a good income from this business. 26And you see and hear how this fellow Paul has convinced and led astray large numbers of people here in Ephesus and in practically the whole province of Asia. He says that man-made gods are no gods at all. 27There is danger not only that our trade will lose its good name, but also that the temple of the great goddess Artemis will be discredited, and the goddess herself, who is worshiped throughout the province of Asia and the world, will be robbed of her divine majesty."

28When they heard this, they were furious and began shouting: "Great is Artemis of the Ephesians!" 29Soon the whole city was in an uproar. The people seized Gaius and Aristarchus, Paul's traveling companions from Macedonia, and rushed as one man into the theater. 30Paul wanted to appear before the crowd, but the disciples would not let him. 31Even some of the officials of the province, friends of Paul, sent him a message begging him not to venture into the theater.

32The assembly was in confusion: Some were shouting one thing, some another. Most of the people did not even know why they were there. 33The Jews pushed Alexander to the front, and some of the crowd shouted instructions to him. He motioned for silence in order to make a defense before the people. 34But when they realized he was a Jew, they all shouted in unison for about two hours: "Great is Artemis of the Ephesians!"

35The city clerk quieted the crowd and said: "Men of Ephesus, doesn't all the world know that the city of Ephesus is the guardian of the temple of the great Artemis and of her image, which fell from heaven? 36Therefore, since these facts are undeniable, you ought to be quiet and not do anything rash. 37You have brought these men here, though they have neither robbed temples nor blasphemed our goddess. 38If, then, Demetrius and his fellow craftsmen have a grievance against anybody, the courts are open and there are proconsuls. They can press charges. 39If there is anything further you want to bring up, it must be settled in a legal assembly. 40As it is, we are in danger of being charged with rioting because of today's events. In that case we would not be able to account for this commotion, since there is no reason for it." 41After he had said this, he dismissed the assembly.

Through Macedonia and Greece

20 When the uproar had ended, Paul sent for the disciples and, after encouraging them, said good-by and set out for Macedonia. ²He traveled through that area, speaking many words of encouragement to the people, and finally arrived in Greece, ³where he stayed three months. Because the Jews made a plot against him just as he was about to sail for Syria, he decided to go back through Macedonia. ⁴He was accompanied by Sopater son of Pyrrhus from Berea, Aristarchus and Secundus from Thessalonica, Gaius from Derbe, Timothy also, and Tychicus and Trophimus from the province of Asia. ⁵These men went on ahead and waited for us at Troas. ⁶But we sailed from Philippi after the Feast of Unleavened Bread, and five days later joined the others at Troas, where we stayed seven days.

Eutychus Raised From the Dead at Troas

⁷On the first day of the week we came together to break bread. Paul spoke to the people and, because he intended to leave the next day, kept on talking until midnight. ⁸There were many lamps in the upstairs room where we were meeting. ⁹Seated in a window was a young man named Eutychus, who was sinking into a deep sleep as Paul talked on and on. When he was sound asleep, he fell to the ground from the third story and was picked up dead. ¹⁰Paul went down, threw himself on the young man and put his arms around him. "Don't be alarmed," he said. "He's alive!" ¹¹Then he went upstairs again and broke bread and ate. After talking until daylight, he left. ¹²The people took the young man home alive and were greatly comforted.

Paul's Farewell to the Ephesian Elders

¹³We went on ahead to the ship and sailed for Assos, where we were going to take Paul aboard. He had made this arrangement because he was going there on foot. ¹⁴When he met us at Assos, we took him aboard and went on to Mitylene. ¹⁵The next day we set sail from there and arrived off Kios. The day after that we crossed over to Samos, and on the following day arrived at Miletus. ¹⁶Paul had decided to sail past Ephesus to avoid spending time in the province of Asia, for he was in a hurry to reach Jerusalem, if possible, by the day of Pentecost.

¹⁷From Miletus, Paul sent to Ephesus for the elders of the church. ¹⁸When they arrived, he said to them: "You know how I lived the whole time I was with you, from the first day I came into the province of Asia. ¹⁹I served the Lord

經過馬其頓和希臘

20 亂定之後，保羅請門徒來，勸勉他們，就辭別起行，往馬其頓去。²走遍了那一帶地方，用許多話勸勉門徒（註：或作“眾人”），然後來到希臘。³在那裏住了三個月，將要坐船往敘利亞去，猶太人設計要害他，他就定意從馬其頓回去。⁴同他到亞西亞去的，有庇哩亞人畢羅斯的兒子所巴特，帖撒羅尼迦人亞里達古和西公都，還有特庇人該猶，並提摩太，又有亞西亞人推基古和特羅非摩。⁵這些人先走，在特羅亞等候我們。⁶過了除酵的日子，我們從腓立比開船，五天到了特羅亞，和他們相會，在那裏住了七天。

在特羅亞使猶古復活

⁷七日的第一日，我們聚會擘餅的時候，保羅因為要次日起行，就與他們講論，直講到半夜。⁸我們聚會的那座樓上，有好些燈燭。⁹有一個少年人，名叫猶推古，坐在窗臺上困倦沉睡。保羅講了多時，少年人睡熟了，就從三層樓上掉下去；扶起他來，已經死了。¹⁰保羅下去，伏在他身上，抱着他，說：“你們不要發慌，他的靈魂還在身上。”¹¹保羅又上去，擘餅，吃了，談論許久，直到天亮，這才走了。¹²有人把那童子活活地領來，得的安慰不小。

保羅向以弗所長老告別

¹³我們先上船開往亞朔去，意思要在那裏接保羅，因為他是這樣安排的，他自己打算要步行。¹⁴他既在亞朔與我們相會，我們就接他上船，來到米推利尼。¹⁵從那裏開船，次日到了基阿的對面；又次日，在撒摩靠岸；又次日，來到米利都。¹⁶乃因保羅早已定意越過以弗所，免得在亞西亞躭延。他急忙前走，巴不得趕五旬節能到耶路撒冷。

¹⁷保羅從米利都打發人往以弗所去，請教會的長老來。¹⁸他們來了，保羅就說：“你們知道，自從我到亞西亞的日子以來，在你們中間始終為人如何，¹⁹服侍主凡事謙卑，眼中流

淚，又因<u>猶太</u>人的謀害，經歷試煉。²⁰你們也知道，凡與你們有益的，我沒有一樣避諱不說的。或在眾人面前，或在各人家裏，我都教導你們。²¹又對<u>猶太</u>人和<u>希臘</u>人證明當向神悔改，信靠我主耶穌基督。

²²"現在我往<u>耶路撒冷</u>去，心甚迫切（註：原文作"心被捆綁"），不知道在那裏要遇見甚麼事。²³但知道聖靈在各城裏向我指證，說有捆鎖與患難等待我。²⁴我卻不以性命為念，也不看為寶貴，只要行完我的路程，成就我從主耶穌所領受的職事，證明神恩惠的福音。

²⁵"我素常在你們中間來往，傳講神國的道。如今我曉得，你們以後都不得再見我的面了。²⁶所以我今日向你們證明，你們中間無論何人死亡，罪不在我身上（註：原文作"我於眾人的血是潔淨的"）。²⁷因為神的旨意，我並沒有一樣避諱不傳給你們的。²⁸聖靈立你們作全羣的監督，你們就當為自己謹慎，也為全羣謹慎，牧養神的教會，就是他用自己血所買來的（註：或作"救贖的"）。²⁹我知道我去之後，必有兇暴的豺狼進入你們中間，不愛惜羊羣。³⁰就是你們中間，也必有人起來，說悖謬的話，要引誘門徒跟從他們。³¹所以你們應當警醒，記念我三年之久晝夜不住地流淚，勸戒你們各人。

³²"如今我把你們交託神和他恩惠的道；這道能建立你們，叫你們和一切成聖的人同得基業。³³我未曾貪圖一個人的金、銀、衣服。³⁴我這兩隻手常供給我和同人的需用，這是你們自己知道的。³⁵我凡事給你們作榜樣，叫你們知道應當這樣勞苦，扶助軟弱的人，又當記念主耶穌的話，說：'施比受更為有福。'"

³⁶<u>保羅</u>說完了這話，就跪下同眾人禱告。³⁷眾人痛哭，抱着<u>保羅</u>的頸項，和他親嘴。³⁸叫他們最傷心的，就是他說"以後不能再見我的面"那句話，於是送他上船去了。

with great humility and with tears, although I was severely tested by the plots of the Jews. ²⁰You know that I have not hesitated to preach anything that would be helpful to you but have taught you publicly and from house to house. ²¹I have declared to both Jews and Greeks that they must turn to God in repentance and have faith in our Lord Jesus.

²²"And now, compelled by the Spirit, I am going to Jerusalem, not knowing what will happen to me there. ²³I only know that in every city the Holy Spirit warns me that prison and hardships are facing me. ²⁴However, I consider my life worth nothing to me, if only I may finish the race and complete the task the Lord Jesus has given me—the task of testifying to the gospel of God's grace.

²⁵"Now I know that none of you among whom I have gone about preaching the kingdom will ever see me again. ²⁶Therefore, I declare to you today that I am innocent of the blood of all men. ²⁷For I have not hesitated to proclaim to you the whole will of God. ²⁸Keep watch over yourselves and all the flock of which the Holy Spirit has made you overseers.[a] Be shepherds of the church of God,[b] which he bought with his own blood. ²⁹I know that after I leave, savage wolves will come in among you and will not spare the flock. ³⁰Even from your own number men will arise and distort the truth in order to draw away disciples after them. ³¹So be on your guard! Remember that for three years I never stopped warning each of you night and day with tears.

³²"Now I commit you to God and to the word of his grace, which can build you up and give you an inheritance among all those who are sanctified. ³³I have not coveted anyone's silver or gold or clothing. ³⁴You yourselves know that these hands of mine have supplied my own needs and the needs of my companions. ³⁵In everything I did, I showed you that by this kind of hard work we must help the weak, remembering the words the Lord Jesus himself said: 'It is more blessed to give than to receive.'"

³⁶When he had said this, he knelt down with all of them and prayed. ³⁷They all wept as they embraced him and kissed him. ³⁸What grieved them most was his statement that they would never see his face again. Then they accompanied him to the ship.

a 28 Traditionally *bishops*　　*b 28* Many manuscripts *of the Lord*

On to Jerusalem

21 After we had torn ourselves away from them, we put out to sea and sailed straight to Cos. The next day we went to Rhodes and from there to Patara. ²We found a ship crossing over to Phoenicia, went on board and set sail. ³After sighting Cyprus and passing to the south of it, we sailed on to Syria. We landed at Tyre, where our ship was to unload its cargo. ⁴Finding the disciples there, we stayed with them seven days. Through the Spirit they urged Paul not to go on to Jerusalem. ⁵But when our time was up, we left and continued on our way. All the disciples and their wives and children accompanied us out of the city, and there on the beach we knelt to pray. ⁶After saying good-by to each other, we went aboard the ship, and they returned home.

⁷We continued our voyage from Tyre and landed at Ptolemais, where we greeted the brothers and stayed with them for a day. ⁸Leaving the next day, we reached Caesarea and stayed at the house of Philip the evangelist, one of the Seven. ⁹He had four unmarried daughters who prophesied.

¹⁰After we had been there a number of days, a prophet named Agabus came down from Judea. ¹¹Coming over to us, he took Paul's belt, tied his own hands and feet with it and said, "The Holy Spirit says, 'In this way the Jews of Jerusalem will bind the owner of this belt and will hand him over to the Gentiles.' "

¹²When we heard this, we and the people there pleaded with Paul not to go up to Jerusalem. ¹³Then Paul answered, "Why are you weeping and breaking my heart? I am ready not only to be bound, but also to die in Jerusalem for the name of the Lord Jesus." ¹⁴When he would not be dissuaded, we gave up and said, "The Lord's will be done."

¹⁵After this, we got ready and went up to Jerusalem. ¹⁶Some of the disciples from Caesarea accompanied us and brought us to the home of Mnason, where we were to stay. He was a man from Cyprus and one of the early disciples.

Paul's Arrival at Jerusalem

¹⁷When we arrived at Jerusalem, the brothers received us warmly. ¹⁸The next day Paul and the rest of us went to see James, and all the elders were present. ¹⁹Paul greeted them and reported in detail what God had done among the Gentiles through his ministry.

²⁰When they heard this, they praised God. Then they said to Paul: "You see, brother, how

上耶路撒冷

21 我們離別了眾人，就開船一直行到哥士。第二天到了羅底，從那裏到帕大喇，²遇見一隻船要往腓尼基去，就上船起行。³望見塞浦路斯，就從南邊行過，往敍利亞去。我們就在推羅上岸，因為船要在那裏卸貨。⁴找著了門徒，就在那裏住了七天。他們被聖靈感動，對保羅說：“不要上耶路撒冷去。”⁵過了這幾天，我們就起身前行，他們眾人同妻子兒女送我們到城外。我們都跪在岸上禱告，彼此辭別。⁶我們上了船，他們就回家去了。

⁷我們從推羅行盡了水路，來到多利買，就問那裏的弟兄安，和他們同住了一天。⁸第二天，我們離開那裏，來到凱撒利亞，就進了傳福音的腓利家裏，和他同住。他是那七個執事裏的一個。⁹他有四個女兒，都是處女，是說預言的。

¹⁰我們在那裏多住了幾天。有一個先知，名叫亞迦布，從猶太下來，¹¹到了我們這裏，就拿保羅的腰帶捆上自己的手腳，說：“聖靈說，猶太人在耶路撒冷要如此捆綁這腰帶的主人，把他交在外邦人手裏。”

¹²我們和那本地的人聽見這話，都苦勸保羅不要上耶路撒冷去。¹³保羅說：“你們為甚麼這樣痛哭，使我心碎呢？我為主耶穌的名，不但被人捆綁，就是死在耶路撒冷也是願意的。”¹⁴保羅既不聽勸，我們便住了口，只說：“願主的旨意成就”便了。

¹⁵過了幾日，我們收拾行李上耶路撒冷去。¹⁶有凱撒利亞的幾個門徒和我們同去，帶我們到一個久為（註：“久為”或作“老”）門徒的家裏，叫我們與他同住。他名叫拿孫，是塞浦路斯人。

保羅抵達耶路撒冷

¹⁷到了耶路撒冷，弟兄們歡歡喜喜地接待我們。¹⁸第二天，保羅同我們去見雅各，長老們也都在那裏。¹⁹保羅問了他們安，便將神用他傳教，在外邦人中間所行之事一一地述說了。

²⁰他們聽見，就歸榮耀與神，對保羅說：“兄台，你看猶太人中信主

的有多少萬，並且都為律法熱心。 21他們聽見人說，你教訓一切在外邦的猶太人離棄摩西，對他們說，不要給孩子行割禮，也不要遵行條規。 22眾人必聽見你來了，這可怎麼辦呢？ 23你就照着我們的話行吧！我們這裏有四個人，都有願在身。 24你帶他們去，與他們一同行潔淨的禮，替他們拿出規費，叫他們得以剃頭。這樣，眾人就可知道，先前所聽見你的事都是虛的；並可知道，你自己為人循規蹈矩，遵行律法。 25至於信主的外邦人，我們已經寫信擬定，叫他們謹忌那祭偶像之物和血，並勒死的牲畜，與姦淫。”

26於是，保羅帶着那四個人，第二天與他們一同行了潔淨的禮，進了殿，報明潔淨的日期滿足，只等祭司為他們各人獻祭。

保羅被捕

27那七日將完，從亞西亞來的猶太人，看見保羅在殿裏，就聳動了眾人下手拿他， 28喊叫說：“以色列人來幫助！這就是在各處教訓眾人，糟踐我們百姓和律法並這地方的。他又帶着希臘人進殿，污穢了這聖地。” 29因他們曾看見以弗所人特羅非摩同保羅在城裏，以為保羅帶他進了殿。

30合城都震動，百姓一齊跑來，拿住保羅，拉他出殿，殿門立刻都關了。 31他們正想要殺他，有人報信給營裏的千夫長說：“耶路撒冷合城都亂了！” 32千夫長立時帶着兵丁和幾個百夫長跑下去，到了他們那裏。他們見了千夫長和兵丁，就止住不打保羅。

33於是千夫長上前拿住他，吩咐用兩條鐵鏈捆鎖；又問他是甚麼人，做的是甚麼事。 34眾人有喊叫這個的，有喊叫那個的。千夫長因為這樣亂嚷，得不着實情，就吩咐人將保羅帶進營樓去。 35到了臺階上，眾人擠得兇猛，兵丁只得將保羅抬

many thousands of Jews have believed, and all of them are zealous for the law. 21They have been informed that you teach all the Jews who live among the Gentiles to turn away from Moses, telling them not to circumcise their children or live according to our customs. 22What shall we do? They will certainly hear that you have come, 23so do what we tell you. There are four men with us who have made a vow. 24Take these men, join in their purification rites and pay their expenses, so that they can have their heads shaved. Then everybody will know there is no truth in these reports about you, but that you yourself are living in obedience to the law. 25As for the Gentile believers, we have written to them our decision that they should abstain from food sacrificed to idols, from blood, from the meat of strangled animals and from sexual immorality."

26The next day Paul took the men and purified himself along with them. Then he went to the temple to give notice of the date when the days of purification would end and the offering would be made for each of them.

Paul Arrested

27When the seven days were nearly over, some Jews from the province of Asia saw Paul at the temple. They stirred up the whole crowd and seized him, 28shouting, "Men of Israel, help us! This is the man who teaches all men everywhere against our people and our law and this place. And besides, he has brought Greeks into the temple area and defiled this holy place." 29(They had previously seen Trophimus the Ephesian in the city with Paul and assumed that Paul had brought him into the temple area.)

30The whole city was aroused, and the people came running from all directions. Seizing Paul, they dragged him from the temple, and immediately the gates were shut. 31While they were trying to kill him, news reached the commander of the Roman troops that the whole city of Jerusalem was in an uproar. 32He at once took some officers and soldiers and ran down to the crowd. When the rioters saw the commander and his soldiers, they stopped beating Paul.

33The commander came up and arrested him and ordered him to be bound with two chains. Then he asked who he was and what he had done. 34Some in the crowd shouted one thing and some another, and since the commander could not get at the truth because of the uproar, he ordered that Paul be taken into the barracks. 35When Paul reached the steps, the violence of the mob was so great he had to be carried by the soldiers. ³⁶The crowd that followed kept shouting, "Away with him!"

Paul Speaks to the Crowd

³⁷As the soldiers were about to take Paul into the barracks, he asked the commander, "May I say something to you?"

"Do you speak Greek?" he replied. ³⁸"Aren't you the Egyptian who started a revolt and led four thousand terrorists out into the desert some time ago?"

³⁹Paul answered, "I am a Jew, from Tarsus in Cilicia, a citizen of no ordinary city. Please let me speak to the people."

⁴⁰Having received the commander's permission, Paul stood on the steps and motioned to the crowd. When they were all silent, he said to

22 them in Aramaic*ᵃ*:¹"Brothers and fathers, listen now to my defense."

²When they heard him speak to them in Aramaic, they became very quiet.

Then Paul said: ³"I am a Jew, born in Tarsus of Cilicia, but brought up in this city. Under Gamaliel I was thoroughly trained in the law of our fathers and was just as zealous for God as any of you are today. ⁴I persecuted the followers of this Way to their death, arresting both men and women and throwing them into prison, ⁵as also the high priest and all the Council can testify. I even obtained letters from them to their brothers in Damascus, and went there to bring these people as prisoners to Jerusalem to be punished.

⁶"About noon as I came near Damascus, suddenly a bright light from heaven flashed around me. ⁷I fell to the ground and heard a voice say to me, 'Saul! Saul! Why do you persecute me?'

⁸" 'Who are you, Lord?' I asked.

" 'I am Jesus of Nazareth, whom you are persecuting,' he replied. ⁹My companions saw the light, but they did not understand the voice of him who was speaking to me.

¹⁰" 'What shall I do, Lord?' I asked.

" 'Get up,' the Lord said, 'and go into Damascus. There you will be told all that you have been assigned to do.' ¹¹My companions led me by the hand into Damascus, because the brilliance of the light had blinded me.

¹²"A man named Ananias came to see me. He was a devout observer of the law and highly respected by all the Jews living there. ¹³He stood beside me and said, 'Brother Saul, receive your sight!' And at that very moment I was able to see him.

a 40 Or possibly Hebrew; also in 22:2

起來。³⁶眾人跟在後面，喊着說：
"除掉他！"

保羅向羣眾解釋

³⁷將要帶他進營樓，<u>保羅</u>對千夫長說："我對你說句話，可以不可以？"

他說："你懂得<u>希臘</u>話嗎？³⁸你莫非是從前作亂、帶領四千兇徒往曠野去的那<u>埃及</u>人嗎？"

³⁹<u>保羅</u>說："我本是<u>猶太</u>人，生在<u>基利家</u>的<u>大數</u>，並不是無名小城的人。求你准我對百姓說話。"

⁴⁰千夫長准了。<u>保羅</u>就站在臺階上，向百姓擺手，他們都靜默無聲。<u>保羅</u>便用<u>希伯來</u>話對他們說：

22｜¹"諸位父兄請聽，我現在對你們分訴。"²眾人聽他說的是<u>希伯來</u>話，就更加安靜了。

³<u>保羅</u>說："我原是<u>猶太</u>人，生在<u>基利家</u>的<u>大數</u>，長在這城裏，在<u>迦瑪列</u>門下，按着我們祖宗嚴緊的律法受教，熱心侍奉神，像你們眾人今日一樣。⁴我也曾逼迫奉這道的人直到死地，無論男女都鎖拿下監。⁵這是大祭司和眾長老都可以給我作見證的。我又領了他們達與弟兄的書信，往<u>大馬士革</u>去，要把在那裏奉這道的人鎖拿，帶到<u>耶路撒冷</u>受刑。

⁶"我將到<u>大馬士革</u>，正走的時候，約在晌午，忽然從天上發大光，四面照着我。⁷我就仆倒在地，聽見有聲音對我說：'<u>掃羅</u>，<u>掃羅</u>！你為甚麼逼迫我？'

⁸我回答說：'主啊，你是誰？'

"他說：'我就是你所逼迫的<u>拿撒勒</u>人耶穌。'⁹與我同行的人看見了那光，卻沒有聽明那位對我說話的聲音。

¹⁰"我說：'主啊，我當做甚麼？'主說：'起來！進<u>大馬士革</u>去，在那裏，要將所派你做的一切事告訴你。'¹¹我因那光的榮耀不能看見，同行的人就拉着我手進了<u>大馬士革</u>。

¹²"那裏有一個人，名叫<u>亞拿尼亞</u>，按着律法是虔誠人，為一切住在那裏的<u>猶太</u>人所稱讚。¹³他來見我，站在旁邊對我說：'兄弟<u>掃羅</u>，你可以看見。'我當時往上一看，就看見了他。

14 "他又説：'我們祖宗的神揀選了你，叫你明白他的旨意，又得見那義者，聽他口中所出的聲音。15因為你要將所看見的、所聽見的對着萬人為他作見證。16現在你為甚麼耽延呢？起來！求告他的名受洗，洗去你的罪。'

17 "後來，我回到耶路撒冷，在殿裏禱告的時候，魂游象外，18看見主向我説：'你趕緊地離開耶路撒冷，不可遲延，因你為我作的見證，這裏的人必不領受。'

19 "我就説：'主啊，他們知道我從前把信你的人收在監裏，又在各會堂裏鞭打他們。20並且你的見證人司提反被害流血的時候，我也站在旁邊歡喜，又看守害死他之人的衣裳。'

21 "主向我説：'你去吧！我要差你遠遠地往外邦人那裏去。'"

羅馬公民保羅

22眾人聽他説到這句話，就高聲説："這樣的人，從世上除掉他吧！他是不當活着的！"

23眾人喧嚷，摔掉衣裳，把塵土向空中揚起來。24千夫長就吩咐將保羅帶進營樓去，叫人用鞭子拷問他，要知道他們向他這樣喧嚷是為甚麼緣故。25剛用皮條捆上，保羅對旁邊站着的百夫長説："人是羅馬人，又沒有定罪，你們就鞭打他，有這個例嗎？"

26百夫長聽見這話，就去見千夫長，告訴他説："你要做甚麼？這人是羅馬人！"

27千夫長就來問保羅説："你告訴我，你是羅馬人嗎？"

保羅説："是。"

28千夫長説："我用許多銀子，才入了羅馬的民籍。"

保羅説："我生來就是。"

29於是那些要拷問保羅的人，就離開他去了。千夫長既知道他是羅馬人，又因為捆綁了他，也害怕了。

在公會前答辯

30第二天，千夫長為要知道猶太人控告保羅的實情，便解開他，吩

14"Then he said: 'The God of our fathers has chosen you to know his will and to see the Righteous One and to hear words from his mouth. 15You will be his witness to all men of what you have seen and heard. 16And now what are you waiting for? Get up, be baptized and wash your sins away, calling on his name.'

17"When I returned to Jerusalem and was praying at the temple, I fell into a trance 18and saw the Lord speaking. 'Quick!' he said to me. 'Leave Jerusalem immediately, because they will not accept your testimony about me.'

19" 'Lord,' I replied, 'these men know that I went from one synagogue to another to imprison and beat those who believe in you. 20And when the blood of your martyr*a* Stephen was shed, I stood there giving my approval and guarding the clothes of those who were killing him.'

21"Then the Lord said to me, 'Go; I will send you far away to the Gentiles.' "

Paul the Roman Citizen

22The crowd listened to Paul until he said this. Then they raised their voices and shouted, "Rid the earth of him! He's not fit to live!"

23As they were shouting and throwing off their cloaks and flinging dust into the air, 24the commander ordered Paul to be taken into the barracks. He directed that he be flogged and questioned in order to find out why the people were shouting at him like this. 25As they stretched him out to flog him, Paul said to the centurion standing there, "Is it legal for you to flog a Roman citizen who hasn't even been found guilty?"

26When the centurion heard this, he went to the commander and reported it. "What are you going to do?" he asked. "This man is a Roman citizen."

27The commander went to Paul and asked, "Tell me, are you a Roman citizen?"

"Yes, I am," he answered.

28Then the commander said, "I had to pay a big price for my citizenship."

"But I was born a citizen," Paul replied.

29Those who were about to question him withdrew immediately. The commander himself was alarmed when he realized that he had put Paul, a Roman citizen, in chains.

Before the Sanhedrin

30The next day, since the commander wanted to find out exactly why Paul was being accused by the Jews, he released him and ordered the

a 20 Or witness

chief priests and all the Sanhedrin to assemble. Then he brought Paul and had him stand before them.

23 Paul looked straight at the Sanhedrin and said, "My brothers, I have fulfilled my duty to God in all good conscience to this day." ²At this the high priest Ananias ordered those standing near Paul to strike him on the mouth. ³Then Paul said to him, "God will strike you, you whitewashed wall! You sit there to judge me according to the law, yet you yourself violate the law by commanding that I be struck!"

⁴Those who were standing near Paul said, "You dare to insult God's high priest?"

⁵Paul replied, "Brothers, I did not realize that he was the high priest; for it is written: 'Do not speak evil about the ruler of your people.'ᵃ"

⁶Then Paul, knowing that some of them were Sadducees and the others Pharisees, called out in the Sanhedrin, "My brothers, I am a Pharisee, the son of a Pharisee. I stand on trial because of my hope in the resurrection of the dead." ⁷When he said this, a dispute broke out between the Pharisees and the Sadducees, and the assembly was divided. ⁸(The Sadducees say that there is no resurrection, and that there are neither angels nor spirits, but the Pharisees acknowledge them all.)

⁹There was a great uproar, and some of the teachers of the law who were Pharisees stood up and argued vigorously. "We find nothing wrong with this man," they said. "What if a spirit or an angel has spoken to him?" ¹⁰The dispute became so violent that the commander was afraid Paul would be torn to pieces by them. He ordered the troops to go down and take him away from them by force and bring him into the barracks.

¹¹The following night the Lord stood near Paul and said, "Take courage! As you have testified about me in Jerusalem, so you must also testify in Rome."

The Plot to Kill Paul

¹²The next morning the Jews formed a conspiracy and bound themselves with an oath not to eat or drink until they had killed Paul. ¹³More than forty men were involved in this plot. ¹⁴They went to the chief priests and elders and said, "We have taken a solemn oath not to eat anything until we have killed Paul. ¹⁵Now then, you and the Sanhedrin petition the commander to bring him before you on the pretext of wanting more accurate information about his case. We are ready to kill him before he gets here."

a 5 Exodus 22:28

咐祭司長和全公會的人都聚集,將保羅帶下來,叫他站在他們面前。

23 保羅定睛看着公會的人,說:"弟兄們,我在神面前行事為人都是憑着良心,直到今日。" ²大祭司亞拿尼亞就吩咐旁邊站着的人打他的嘴。³保羅對他說:"你這粉飾的牆,神要打你!你坐堂為的是按律法審問我,你竟違背律法,吩咐人打我嗎?"

⁴站在旁邊的人說:"你辱罵神的大祭司嗎?"

⁵保羅說:"弟兄們,我不曉得他是大祭司。經上記着說:'不可毀謗你百姓的官長。'"

⁶保羅看出大眾一半是撒都該人,一半是法利賽人,就在公會中大聲說:"弟兄們,我是法利賽人,也是法利賽人的子孫。我現在受審問,是為盼望死人復活。" ⁷說了這話,法利賽人和撒都該人就爭論起來,會眾分為兩黨。⁸因為撒都該人說沒有復活,也沒有天使和鬼魂;法利賽人卻說兩樣都有。

⁹於是大大地喧嚷起來。有幾個法利賽黨的文士站起來爭辯說:"我們看不出這人有甚麼惡處,倘若有鬼魂或是天使對他說過話,怎麼樣呢?" ¹⁰那時大起爭吵,千夫長恐怕保羅被他們扯碎了,就吩咐兵丁下去,把他從眾人當中搶出來,帶進營樓去。

¹¹當夜,主站在保羅旁邊,說:"放心吧!你怎樣在耶路撒冷為我作見證,也必怎樣在羅馬為我作見證。"

殺害保羅的計謀

¹²到了天亮,猶太人同謀起誓說:"若不先殺保羅,就不吃不喝!" ¹³這樣同心起誓的有四十多人。¹⁴他們來見祭司長和長老,說:"我們已經起了一個大誓,若不先殺保羅,就不吃甚麼。¹⁵現在你們和公會要知會千夫長,叫他帶下保羅到你們這裏來,假作要詳細察考他的事。我們已經預備好了,不等他來到跟前就殺他。"

16保羅的外甥聽見他們設下埋伏，就來到營樓裏告訴保羅。

17保羅請一個百夫長來，說："你這少年人去見千夫長，他有事告訴他。"18於是把他領去見千夫長，說：

"被囚的保羅請我到他那裏，求我領這少年人來見你，他有事告訴你。"

19千夫長就拉着他的手，走到一旁，私下問他說："你有甚麼事告訴我呢？"

20他說："猶太人已經約定，要求你明天帶下保羅到公會裏去，假作要詳細查問他的事。21你切不要隨從他們，因為他們有四十多人埋伏，已經起誓說，若不先殺保羅，就不吃不喝。現在預備好了，只等你應允。"

22於是千夫長打發少年人走，囑咐他說："不要告訴人你將這事報給我了。"

保羅被解往凱撒利亞

23千夫長便叫了兩個百夫長來，說："預備步兵二百，馬兵七十，長槍手二百，今夜亥初往凱撒利亞去；24也要預備牲口叫保羅騎上，護送到巡撫腓力斯那裏去。"

25千夫長又寫了文書，

26大略說：革老丟呂西亞

請巡撫腓力斯大人安。

27這人被猶太人拿住，將要殺害，我得知他是羅馬人，就帶兵丁下去救他出來。28因為要知道他們告他的緣故，我就帶他下到他們的公會去，29便查知他被告是因他們律法的辯論，並沒有甚麼該死、該綁的罪名。30後來有人把要害他的計謀告訴我，我就立時解他到你那裏去，又吩咐告他的人在你面前告他（註：有古卷在此有"願你平安！"）。

16But when the son of Paul's sister heard of this plot, he went into the barracks and told Paul.

17Then Paul called one of the centurions and said, "Take this young man to the commander; he has something to tell him." 18So he took him to the commander.

The centurion said, "Paul, the prisoner, sent for me and asked me to bring this young man to you because he has something to tell you."

19The commander took the young man by the hand, drew him aside and asked, "What is it you want to tell me?"

20He said: "The Jews have agreed to ask you to bring Paul before the Sanhedrin tomorrow on the pretext of wanting more accurate information about him. 21Don't give in to them, because more than forty of them are waiting in ambush for him. They have taken an oath not to eat or drink until they have killed him. They are ready now, waiting for your consent to their request."

22The commander dismissed the young man and cautioned him, "Don't tell anyone that you have reported this to me."

Paul Transferred to Caesarea

23Then he called two of his centurions and ordered them, "Get ready a detachment of two hundred soldiers, seventy horsemen and two hundred spearmen*a* to go to Caesarea at nine tonight. 24Provide mounts for Paul so that he may be taken safely to Governor Felix.

25He wrote a letter as follows:

26Claudius Lysias,

To His Excellency, Governor Felix:

Greetings.

27This man was seized by the Jews and they were about to kill him, but I came with my troops and rescued him, for I had learned that he is a Roman citizen. 28I wanted to know why they were accusing him, so I brought him to their Sanhedrin. 29I found that the accusation had to do with questions about their law, but there was no charge against him that deserved death or imprisonment. 30When I was informed of a plot to be carried out against the man, I sent him to you at once. I also ordered his accusers to present to you their case against him.

---

a 23 The meaning of the Greek for this word is uncertain.

³¹So the soldiers, carrying out their orders, took Paul with them during the night and brought him as far as Antipatris. ³²The next day they let the cavalry go on with him, while they returned to the barracks. ³³When the cavalry arrived in Caesarea, they delivered the letter to the governor and handed Paul over to him. ³⁴The governor read the letter and asked what province he was from. Learning that he was from Cilicia, ³⁵he said, "I will hear your case when your accusers get here." Then he ordered that Paul be kept under guard in Herod's palace.

The Trial Before Felix

24 Five days later the high priest Ananias went down to Caesarea with some of the elders and a lawyer named Tertullus, and they brought their charges against Paul before the governor. ²When Paul was called in, Tertullus presented his case before Felix: "We have enjoyed a long period of peace under you, and your foresight has brought about reforms in this nation. ³Everywhere and in every way, most excellent Felix, we acknowledge this with profound gratitude. ⁴But in order not to weary you further, I would request that you be kind enough to hear us briefly.

⁵"We have found this man to be a troublemaker, stirring up riots among the Jews all over the world. He is a ringleader of the Nazarene sect ⁶and even tried to desecrate the temple; so we seized him. ⁸By*ᵃ* examining him yourself you will be able to learn the truth about all these charges we are bringing against him."

⁹The Jews joined in the accusation, asserting that these things were true.

¹⁰When the governor motioned for him to speak, Paul replied: "I know that for a number of years you have been a judge over this nation; so I gladly make my defense. ¹¹You can easily verify that no more than twelve days ago I went up to Jerusalem to worship. ¹²My accusers did not find me arguing with anyone at the temple, or stirring up a crowd in the synagogues or anywhere else in the city. ¹³And they cannot prove to you the charges they are now making against me. ¹⁴However, I admit that I worship the God of our fathers as a follower of the Way, which they call a sect. I believe everything that agrees

a 6-8 Some manuscripts him and wanted to judge him according to our law. 7 But the commander, Lysias, came and with the use of much force snatched him from our hands 8 and ordered his accusers to come before you. By

³¹於是兵丁照所吩咐他們的，將保羅夜裏帶到安提帕底。³²第二天讓馬兵護送，他們就回營樓去。³³馬兵來到凱撒利亞，把文書呈給巡撫，便叫保羅站在他面前。³⁴巡撫看了文書，問保羅是哪省的人。既曉得他是基利家人，³⁵就說："等告你的人來到，我要細聽你的事。"便吩咐人把他看守在希律的衙門裏。

在腓力斯面前受審

24 過了五天，大祭司亞拿尼亞同幾個長老和一個辯士帖土羅下來，向巡撫控告保羅。²保羅被提了來，帖土羅就告他說：³"腓力斯大人，我們因你得以大享太平，並且這一國的弊病，因着你的先見得以更正了，我們隨時隨地滿心感謝不盡。⁴惟恐多說，你嫌煩絮，只求你寬容聽我們說幾句話。

⁵"我們看這個人，如同瘟疫一般，是鼓動普天下眾猶太人生亂的，又是拿撒勒教黨裏的一個頭目，⁶連聖殿他也想要污穢。我們把他捉住了（註：有古卷在此有"要按我們的律法審問，⁷不料，千夫長呂西亞前來，甚是強橫，從我們手中把他奪去，吩咐告他的人到你這裏來。"）。⁸你自己究問他，就可以知道我們告他的一切事了。"

⁹眾猶太人也隨着告他說："事情誠然是這樣。"

¹⁰巡撫點頭叫保羅說話。他就說："我知道你在這國裏斷事多年，所以我樂意為自己分訴。¹¹你查問就可以知道，從我上耶路撒冷禮拜到今日，不過有十二天。¹²他們並沒有看見我在殿裏，或是在會堂裏，或是在城裏，和人辯論，聳動眾人。¹³他們現在所告我的事並不能對你證實了。¹⁴但有一件事，我向你承認，就是他們所稱為異端的道，我正按着那道侍奉我祖宗的神，又信合乎律法的和先

知書上一切所記載的，¹⁵並且靠着神，盼望死人，無論善惡，都要復活，就是他們自己也有這個盼望。¹⁶我因此自己勉勵，對神、對人，常存無虧的良心。

¹⁷ "過了幾年，我帶着賙濟本國的捐項和供獻的物上去。¹⁸正獻的時候，他們看見我在殿裏已經潔淨了，並沒有聚眾，也沒有吵嚷，惟有幾個從亞西亞來的猶太人。¹⁹他們若有告我的事，應當到你面前來告我。²⁰即或不然，這些人若看出我站在公會前有妄為的地方，他們自己也可以說明。²¹縱然有，也不過一句話，就是我站在他們中間大聲說：'我今日在你們面前受審，是為死人復活的道理。'"

²²腓力斯本是詳細曉得這道，就支吾他們說："且等千夫長呂西亞下來，我要審斷你們的事。"²³於是吩咐百夫長看守保羅，並且寬待他，也不攔阻他的親友來供給他。

²⁴過了幾天，腓力斯和他夫人——猶太的女子土西拉一同來到，就叫了保羅來，聽他講論信基督耶穌的道。²⁵保羅講論公義、節制和將來的審判。腓力斯甚覺恐懼，說："你暫且去吧！等我得便再叫你來。"²⁶腓力斯又指望保羅送他銀錢，所以屢次叫他來，和他談論。

²⁷過了兩年，波求非斯都接了腓力斯的任。腓力斯要討猶太人的喜歡，就留保羅在監裏。

在非斯都面前受審

25 非斯都到了任，過了三天，就從凱撒利亞上耶路撒冷去。²祭司長和猶太人的首領向他控告保羅，³又央告他，求他的情，將保羅提到耶路撒冷來，他們要在路上埋伏殺害他。⁴非斯都卻回答說："保羅押在凱撒利亞，我自己快要往那裏去。"⁵又說："你們中間有權勢的人與我一同下去，那人若有甚麼不是，就可以告他。"

with the Law and that is written in the Prophets, ¹⁵and I have the same hope in God as these men, that there will be a resurrection of both the righteous and the wicked. ¹⁶So I strive always to keep my conscience clear before God and man.

¹⁷"After an absence of several years, I came to Jerusalem to bring my people gifts for the poor and to present offerings. ¹⁸I was ceremonially clean when they found me in the temple courts doing this. There was no crowd with me, nor was I involved in any disturbance. ¹⁹But there are some Jews from the province of Asia, who ought to be here before you and bring charges if they have anything against me. ²⁰Or these who are here should state what crime they found in me when I stood before the Sanhedrin— ²¹unless it was this one thing I shouted as I stood in their presence: 'It is concerning the resurrection of the dead that I am on trial before you today.'"

²²Then Felix, who was well acquainted with the Way, adjourned the proceedings. "When Lysias the commander comes," he said, "I will decide your case." ²³He ordered the centurion to keep Paul under guard but to give him some freedom and permit his friends to take care of his needs.

²⁴Several days later Felix came with his wife Drusilla, who was a Jewess. He sent for Paul and listened to him as he spoke about faith in Christ Jesus. ²⁵As Paul discoursed on righteousness, self-control and the judgment to come, Felix was afraid and said, "That's enough for now! You may leave. When I find it convenient, I will send for you." ²⁶At the same time he was hoping that Paul would offer him a bribe, so he sent for him frequently and talked with him.

²⁷When two years had passed, Felix was succeeded by Porcius Festus, but because Felix wanted to grant a favor to the Jews, he left Paul in prison.

The Trial Before Festus

25 Three days after arriving in the province, Festus went up from Caesarea to Jerusalem, ²where the chief priests and Jewish leaders appeared before him and presented the charges against Paul. ³They urgently requested Festus, as a favor to them, to have Paul transferred to Jerusalem, for they were preparing an ambush to kill him along the way. ⁴Festus answered, "Paul is being held at Caesarea, and I myself am going there soon. ⁵Let some of your leaders come with me and press charges against the man there, if he has done anything wrong."

6After spending eight or ten days with them, he went down to Caesarea, and the next day he convened the court and ordered that Paul be brought before him. 7When Paul appeared, the Jews who had come down from Jerusalem stood around him, bringing many serious charges against him, which they could not prove.

8Then Paul made his defense: "I have done nothing wrong against the law of the Jews or against the temple or against Caesar."

9Festus, wishing to do the Jews a favor, said to Paul, "Are you willing to go up to Jerusalem and stand trial before me there on these charges?"

10Paul answered: "I am now standing before Caesar's court, where I ought to be tried. I have not done any wrong to the Jews, as you yourself know very well. 11If, however, I am guilty of doing anything deserving death, I do not refuse to die. But if the charges brought against me by these Jews are not true, no one has the right to hand me over to them. I appeal to Caesar!"

12After Festus had conferred with his council, he declared: "You have appealed to Caesar. To Caesar you will go!"

Festus Consults King Agrippa

13A few days later King Agrippa and Bernice arrived at Caesarea to pay their respects to Festus. 14Since they were spending many days there, Festus discussed Paul's case with the king. He said: "There is a man here whom Felix left as a prisoner. 15When I went to Jerusalem, the chief priests and elders of the Jews brought charges against him and asked that he be condemned.

16"I told them that it is not the Roman custom to hand over any man before he has faced his accusers and has had an opportunity to defend himself against their charges. 17When they came here with me, I did not delay the case, but convened the court the next day and ordered the man to be brought in. 18When his accusers got up to speak, they did not charge him with any of the crimes I had expected. 19Instead, they had some points of dispute with him about their own religion and about a dead man named Jesus who Paul claimed was alive. 20I was at a loss how to investigate such matters; so I asked if he would be willing to go to Jerusalem and stand trial there on these charges. 21When Paul made his appeal to be held over for the Emperor's decision, I ordered him held until I could send him to Caesar."

22Then Agrippa said to Festus, "I would like to hear this man myself."

He replied, "Tomorrow you will hear him."

6非斯都在他們那裏住了不過十天八天，就下凱撒利亞去。第二天坐堂，吩咐將保羅提上來。7保羅來了，那些從耶路撒冷下來的猶太人周圍站着，將許多重大的事控告他，都是不能證實的。

8保羅分訴說：“無論猶太人的律法、或是聖殿、或是凱撒，我都沒有干犯。”

9但非斯都要討猶太人的喜歡，就問保羅說：“你願意上耶路撒冷去，在那裏聽我審斷這事嗎？”

10保羅說：“我站在凱撒的堂前，這就是我應當受審的地方。我向猶太人並沒有行過甚麼不義的事，這也是你明明知道的。11我若行了不義的事，犯了甚麼該死的罪，就是死，我也不辭！他們所告我的事若都不實，就沒有人可以把我交給他們。我要上告於凱撒。”

12非斯都和議會商量了，就說：“你既上告於凱撒，可以往凱撒那裏去。”

非斯都諮詢亞基帕王

13過了些日子，亞基帕王和百妮基氏來到凱撒利亞，問非斯都安。14在那裏住了多日，非斯都將保羅的事告訴王，說：“這裏有一個人，是腓力斯留在監裏的。15我在耶路撒冷的時候，祭司長和猶太的長老將他的事稟報了我，求我定他的罪。

16“我對他們說：無論甚麼人，被告還沒有和原告對質，未得機會分訴所告他的事，就先定他的罪，這不是羅馬人的條例。17及至他們都來到這裏，我就不就延，第二天便坐堂，吩咐把那人提上來。18告他的人站着告他，所告的，並沒有我所逆料的那等惡事，19不過是有幾樣辯論，為他們自己敬鬼神的事，又為一個人名叫耶穌，是已經死了，保羅卻說他是活着的。20這些事當怎樣究問，我心裏作難，所以問他說：‘你願意上耶路撒冷去，在那裏為這些事聽審嗎？’21但保羅求我留下他，要聽皇上審斷，我就吩咐把他留下，等我解他到凱撒那裏去。”

22亞基帕對非斯都說：“我自己也願聽這人辯論。”

非斯都說：“明天你可以聽。”

保羅在亞基帕面前

²³第二天，<u>亞基帕</u>和<u>百妮基</u>大張威勢而來，同着眾千夫長和城裏的尊貴人進了公廳。<u>非斯都</u>吩咐一聲，就有人將<u>保羅</u>帶進來。²⁴<u>非斯都</u>說：「<u>亞基帕</u>王和在這裏的諸位啊，你們看這人，就是一切<u>猶太人</u>在<u>耶路撒冷</u>和這裏，曾向我懇求呼叫說：『不可容他再活着！』²⁵但我查明他沒有犯甚麼該死的罪，並且他自己上告於皇帝，所以我定意把他解去。²⁶論到這人，我沒有確實的事可以奏明主上。因此，我帶他到你們面前，也特意帶他到你<u>亞基帕</u>王面前，為要在查問之後有所陳奏。²⁷據我看來，解送囚犯，不指明他的罪案是不合理的。」

26 <u>亞基帕</u>對<u>保羅</u>說：「准你為自己辯明。」

於是<u>保羅</u>伸手分訴說：²「<u>亞基帕</u>王啊，<u>猶太人</u>所告我的一切事，今日得在你面前分訴，實為萬幸！³更可幸的，是你熟悉<u>猶太人</u>的規矩和他們的辯論，所以求你耐心聽我。

⁴「我從起初在本國的民中，並在<u>耶路撒冷</u>，自幼為人如何，<u>猶太人</u>都知道。⁵他們若肯作見證，就曉得我從起初是按着我們教中最嚴緊的教門作了法利賽人。⁶現在我站在這裏受審，是因為指望神向我們祖宗所應許的。⁷這應許，我們十二個支派，晝夜切切地侍奉神，都指望得着。王啊，我被<u>猶太人</u>控告，就是因這指望。⁸神叫死人復活，你們為甚麼看作不可信的呢？

⁹「從前我自己以為應當多方攻擊<u>拿撒勒人耶穌</u>的名，¹⁰我在<u>耶路撒冷</u>也曾這樣行了。既從祭司長得了權柄，我就把許多聖徒囚在監裏；他們被殺，我也出名定案。¹¹在各會堂，我屢次用刑強逼他們說褻瀆的話，又分外惱恨他們，甚至追逼他們直到外邦的城邑。

Paul Before Agrippa

²³The next day Agrippa and Bernice came with great pomp and entered the audience room with the high ranking officers and the leading men of the city. At the command of Festus, Paul was brought in. ²⁴Festus said: "King Agrippa, and all who are present with us, you see this man! The whole Jewish community has petitioned me about him in Jerusalem and here in Caesarea, shouting that he ought not to live any longer. ²⁵I found he had done nothing deserving of death, but because he made his appeal to the Emperor I decided to send him to Rome. ²⁶But I have nothing definite to write to His Majesty about him. Therefore I have brought him before all of you, and especially before you, King Agrippa, so that as a result of this investigation I may have something to write. ²⁷For I think it is unreasonable to send on a prisoner without specifying the charges against him."

26 Then Agrippa said to Paul, "You have permission to speak for yourself."

So Paul motioned with his hand and began his defense: ²"King Agrippa, I consider myself fortunate to stand before you today as I make my defense against all the accusations of the Jews, ³and especially so because you are well acquainted with all the Jewish customs and controversies. Therefore, I beg you to listen to me patiently.

⁴"The Jews all know the way I have lived ever since I was a child, from the beginning of my life in my own country, and also in Jerusalem. ⁵They have known me for a long time and can testify, if they are willing, that according to the strictest sect of our religion, I lived as a Pharisee. ⁶And now it is because of my hope in what God has promised our fathers that I am on trial today. ⁷This is the promise our twelve tribes are hoping to see fulfilled as they earnestly serve God day and night. O king, it is because of this hope that the Jews are accusing me. ⁸Why should any of you consider it incredible that God raises the dead?

⁹"I too was convinced that I ought to do all that was possible to oppose the name of Jesus of Nazareth. ¹⁰And that is just what I did in Jerusalem. On the authority of the chief priests I put many of the saints in prison, and when they were put to death, I cast my vote against them. ¹¹Many a time I went from one synagogue to another to have them punished, and I tried to force them to blaspheme. In my obsession against them, I even went to foreign cities to persecute them.

12"On one of these journeys I was going to Damascus with the authority and commission of the chief priests. 13About noon, O king, as I was on the road, I saw a light from heaven, brighter than the sun, blazing around me and my companions. 14We all fell to the ground, and I heard a voice saying to me in Aramaic,ᵃ 'Saul, Saul, why do you persecute me? It is hard for you to kick against the goads.'

15"Then I asked, 'Who are you, Lord?'

" 'I am Jesus, whom you are persecuting,' the Lord replied. 16'Now get up and stand on your feet. I have appeared to you to appoint you as a servant and as a witness of what you have seen of me and what I will show you. 17I will rescue you from your own people and from the Gentiles. I am sending you to them 18to open their eyes and turn them from darkness to light, and from the power of Satan to God, so that they may receive forgiveness of sins and a place among those who are sanctified by faith in me.'

19"So then, King Agrippa, I was not disobedient to the vision from heaven. 20First to those in Damascus, then to those in Jerusalem and in all Judea, and to the Gentiles also, I preached that they should repent and turn to God and prove their repentance by their deeds. 21That is why the Jews seized me in the temple courts and tried to kill me. 22But I have had God's help to this very day, and so I stand here and testify to small and great alike. I am saying nothing beyond what the prophets and Moses said would happen— 23that the Christᵇ would suffer and, as the first to rise from the dead, would proclaim light to his own people and to the Gentiles."

24At this point Festus interrupted Paul's defense. "You are out of your mind, Paul!" he shouted. "Your great learning is driving you insane."

25"I am not insane, most excellent Festus," Paul replied. "What I am saying is true and reasonable. 26The king is familiar with these things, and I can speak freely to him. I am convinced that none of this has escaped his notice, because it was not done in a corner. 27King Agrippa, do you believe the prophets? I know you do."

28Then Agrippa said to Paul, "Do you think that in such a short time you can persuade me to be a Christian?"

29Paul replied, "Short time or long—I pray God that not only you but all who are listening to me today may become what I am, except for these chains."

¹²“那時，我領了祭司長的權柄和命令，往大馬士革去。”¹³王啊，我在路上，晌午的時候，看見從天發光，比日頭還亮，四面照着我並與我同行的人。¹⁴我們都仆倒在地，我就聽見有聲音用希伯來話向我說：‘掃羅，掃羅！為甚麼逼迫我？你用腳踢刺是難的！’

¹⁵“我說：‘主啊，你是誰？’

“主說：‘我就是你所逼迫的耶穌。¹⁶你起來站着！我特意向你顯現，要派你作執事，作見證，將你所看見的事和我將要指示你的事證明出來。¹⁷我也要救你脫離百姓和外邦人的手。¹⁸我差你到他們那裏去，要叫他們的眼睛得開，從黑暗中歸向光明，從撒但權下歸向神；又因信我，得蒙赦罪，和一切成聖的人同得基業。’

¹⁹“亞基帕王啊，我故此沒有違背那從天上來的異象，²⁰先在大馬士革，後在耶路撒冷和猶太全地，以及外邦，勸勉他們應當悔改歸向神，行事與悔改的心相稱。²¹因此，猶太人在殿裏拿住我，想要殺我。²²然而我蒙神的幫助，直到今日還站得住，對着尊貴、卑賤、老幼作見證。所講的並不外乎眾先知和摩西所說將來必成的事，²³就是基督必須受害，並且因從死裏復活，要首先把光明的道傳給百姓和外邦人。”

²⁴保羅這樣分訴，非斯都大聲說：“保羅，你癲狂了吧！你的學問太大，反叫你癲狂了。”

²⁵保羅說：“非斯都大人，我不是癲狂，我說的乃是真實明白話。²⁶王也曉得這些事，所以我向王放膽直言。我深信這些事沒有一件向王隱藏的，因都不是在背地裏做的。²⁷亞基帕王啊，你信先知嗎？我知道你是信的。”

²⁸亞基帕對保羅說：“你想少微一勸，便叫我作基督徒嗎？”（註：或作：“你這樣勸我，幾乎叫我作基督徒了。”）

²⁹保羅說：“無論是少勸，是多勸，我向神所求的，不但你一個人，就是今天一切聽我的，都要像我一樣，只是不要像我有這些鎖鏈。”

a 14 Or Hebrew   b 23 Or Messiah

30於是，王和巡撫並百妮基與同坐的人都起來，31退到裏面，彼此談論說：「這人並沒有犯甚麼該死、該綁的罪。」

32亞基帕又對非斯都說：「這人若沒有上告於凱撒，就可以釋放了。」

保羅坐船往羅馬

27 非斯都既然定規了，叫我們坐船往意大利去，便將保羅和別的囚犯交給御營裏的一個百夫長，名叫猶流。2有一隻亞大米田的船要沿着亞西亞一帶地方的海邊走，我們就上了那船開行，有馬其頓的帖撒羅尼迦人亞里達古和我們同去。

3第二天，到了西頓，猶流寬待保羅，准他往朋友那裏去，受他們的照應。4從那裏又開船，因為風不順，就貼着塞浦路斯背風岸行去。5過了基利家、旁非利亞前面的海，就到了呂家的每拉。6在那裏，百夫長遇見一隻亞歷山太的船要往意大利去，便叫我們上了那船。7一連多日，船行得慢，僅僅來到革尼土的對面。因為被風攔阻，就貼着克里特背風岸，從撒摩尼對面行過。8我們沿岸行走，僅僅來到一個地方，名叫佳澳。離那裏不遠，有拉西亞城。

9走的日子多了，已經過了禁食的節期，行船又危險，保羅就勸眾人說：10「眾位，我看這次行船，不但貨物和船要受傷損，大遭破壞，連我們的性命也難保。」11但百夫長信從掌船的和船主，不信從保羅所說的；12且因在這海口過冬不便，船上的人就多半說，不如開船離開這地方，或者能到非尼基過冬。非尼基是克里特的一個海口，一面朝東北，一面朝東南。

風暴

13這時微微起了南風，他們以為得意，就起了錨，貼近克里特行去。14不多幾時，狂風從島上撲下

30The king rose, and with him the governor and Bernice and those sitting with them. 31They left the room, and while talking with one another, they said, "This man is not doing anything that deserves death or imprisonment."

32Agrippa said to Festus, "This man could have been set free if he had not appealed to Caesar."

Paul Sails for Rome

27 When it was decided that we would sail for Italy, Paul and some other prisoners were handed over to a centurion named Julius, who belonged to the Imperial Regiment. 2We boarded a ship from Adramyttium about to sail for ports along the coast of the province of Asia, and we put out to sea. Aristarchus, a Macedonian from Thessalonica, was with us.

3The next day we landed at Sidon; and Julius, in kindness to Paul, allowed him to go to his friends so they might provide for his needs. 4From there we put out to sea again and passed to the lee of Cyprus because the winds were against us. 5When we had sailed across the open sea off the coast of Cilicia and Pamphylia, we landed at Myra in Lycia. 6There the centurion found an Alexandrian ship sailing for Italy and put us on board. 7We made slow headway for many days and had difficulty arriving off Cnidus. When the wind did not allow us to hold our course, we sailed to the lee of Crete, opposite Salmone. 8We moved along the coast with difficulty and came to a place called Fair Havens, near the town of Lasea.

9Much time had been lost, and sailing had already become dangerous because by now it was after the Fast.[a] So Paul warned them, 10"Men, I can see that our voyage is going to be disastrous and bring great loss to ship and cargo, and to our own lives also." 11But the centurion, instead of listening to what Paul said, followed the advice of the pilot and of the owner of the ship. 12Since the harbor was unsuitable to winter in, the majority decided that we should sail on, hoping to reach Phoenix and winter there. This was a harbor in Crete, facing both southwest and northwest.

The Storm

13When a gentle south wind began to blow, they thought they had obtained what they wanted; so they weighed anchor and sailed along the shore of Crete. 14Before very long, a wind of hurricane force, called the "northeaster," swept

a 9 That is, the Day of Atonement (Yom Kippur)

down from the island. ¹⁵The ship was caught by the storm and could not head into the wind; so we gave way to it and were driven along. ¹⁶As we passed to the lee of a small island called Cauda, we were hardly able to make the lifeboat secure. ¹⁷When the men had hoisted it aboard, they passed ropes under the ship itself to hold it together. Fearing that they would run aground on the sandbars of Syrtis, they lowered the sea anchor and let the ship be driven along. ¹⁸We took such a violent battering from the storm that the next day they began to throw the cargo overboard. ¹⁹On the third day, they threw the ship's tackle overboard with their own hands. ²⁰When neither sun nor stars appeared for many days and the storm continued raging, we finally gave up all hope of being saved.

²¹After the men had gone a long time without food, Paul stood up before them and said: "Men, you should have taken my advice not to sail from Crete; then you would have spared yourselves this damage and loss. ²²But now I urge you to keep up your courage, because not one of you will be lost; only the ship will be destroyed. ²³Last night an angel of the God whose I am and whom I serve stood beside me ²⁴and said, 'Do not be afraid, Paul. You must stand trial before Caesar; and God has graciously given you the lives of all who sail with you.' ²⁵So keep up your courage, men, for I have faith in God that it will happen just as he told me. ²⁶Nevertheless, we must run aground on some island."

The Shipwreck

²⁷On the fourteenth night we were still being driven across the Adriatic[a] Sea, when about midnight the sailors sensed they were approaching land. ²⁸They took soundings and found that the water was a hundred and twenty feet[b] deep. A short time later they took soundings again and found it was ninety feet[c] deep. ²⁹Fearing that we would be dashed against the rocks, they dropped four anchors from the stern and prayed for daylight. ³⁰In an attempt to escape from the ship, the sailors let the lifeboat down into the sea, pretending they were going to lower some anchors from the bow. ³¹Then Paul said to the centurion and the soldiers, "Unless these men stay with the ship, you cannot be saved." ³²So the soldiers cut the ropes that held the lifeboat and let it fall away.

---

a 27 In ancient times the name referred to an area extending well south of Italy.   b 28 Greek twenty orguias (about 37 meters)   c 28 Greek fifteen orguias (about 27 meters)

來。那風名叫"友拉革羅"。¹⁵船被風抓住，敵不住風，我們就任風颳去。¹⁶貼着一個小島的背風岸奔行。那島名叫高大，在那裏僅僅收住了小船。¹⁷既然把小船拉上來，就用纜索捆綁船底，又恐怕在賽耳底沙灘上擱了淺，就落下篷來，任船飄去。¹⁸我們被風浪逼得甚急，第二天，眾人就把貨物拋在海裏。¹⁹到第三天，他們又親手把船上的器具拋棄了。²⁰太陽和星辰多日不顯露，又有狂風大浪催逼，我們得救的指望就都絕了。

²¹眾人多日沒有吃甚麼，保羅就出來站在他們中間，說："眾位，你們本該聽我的話，不離開克里特，免得遭這樣的傷損破壞。²²現在我還勸你們放心，你們的性命一個也不失喪，惟獨失喪這船。²³因我所屬、所侍奉的神，他的使者昨夜站在我旁邊，說：²⁴'保羅，不要害怕！你必定站在凱撒面前；並且與你同船的人，神都賜給你了。'²⁵所以眾位可以放心，我信神他怎樣對我說，事情也要怎樣成就。²⁶只是我們必要撞在一個島上。"

海難

²⁷到了第十四天夜間，船在亞得里亞海飄來飄去。約到半夜，水手以為漸近旱地，²⁸就探深淺，探得有十二丈；稍往前行，又探深淺，探得有九丈。²⁹恐怕撞在石頭上，就從船尾拋下四個錨，盼望天亮。³⁰水手想要逃出船去，把小船放在海裏，假作要從船頭拋錨的樣子。³¹保羅對百夫長和兵丁說："這些人若不等在船上，你們必不能得救。"³²於是兵丁砍斷小船的繩子，由它飄去。

33天漸亮的時候，保羅勸眾人都吃飯，說："你們懸望忍餓不吃甚麼已經十四天了。34所以我勸你們吃飯，這是關乎你們救命的事；因為你們各人一根頭髮也不至於損壞。"35保羅說了這話，就拿着餅，在眾人面前祝謝了神，擘開吃。36於是他們都放下心，也就吃了。37我們在船上的共有二百七十六個人。38他們吃飽了，就把船上的麥子拋在海裏，為要叫船輕一點。

39到了天亮，他們不認識那地方，但見一個海灣，有岸可登，就商議能把船攏進去不能。40於是砍斷纜索，棄錨在海裏，同時也鬆開舵繩，拉起頭篷，順着風向岸行去。41但遇着兩水夾流的地方，就把船擱了淺。船頭膠住不動，船尾被浪的猛力衝壞。

42兵丁的意思要把囚犯殺了，恐怕有洑水脫逃的。43但百夫長要救保羅，不准他們任意而行，就吩咐會洑水的，跳下水去先上岸，44其餘的人可以用板子或船上的零碎東西上岸。這樣，眾人都得了救，上了岸。

在馬耳他島登陸

28 我們既已得救，才知道那島名叫馬耳他。2土人看待我們，有非常的情分；因為當時下雨，天氣又冷，就生火接待我們眾人。3那時，保羅拾起一捆柴，放在火上，有一條毒蛇，因為熱了出來，咬住他的手。4土人看見那毒蛇懸在他手上，就彼此說："這人必是個兇手，雖然從海裏救上來，天理還不容他活着。"5保羅竟把那毒蛇甩在火裏，並沒有受傷。6土人想他必要腫起來，或是忽然仆倒死了；看了多時，見他無害，就轉念說："他是個神！"

7離那地方不遠，有田產是島長部百流的。他接納我們，盡情款待三日。8當時，部百流的父親患熱病

33Just before dawn Paul urged them all to eat. "For the last fourteen days," he said, "you have been in constant suspense and have gone without food—you haven't eaten anything. 34Now I urge you to take some food. You need it to survive. Not one of you will lose a single hair from his head." 35After he said this, he took some bread and gave thanks to God in front of them all. Then he broke it and began to eat. 36They were all encouraged and ate some food themselves. 37Altogether there were 276 of us on board. 38When they had eaten as much as they wanted, they lightened the ship by throwing the grain into the sea.

39When daylight came, they did not recognize the land, but they saw a bay with a sandy beach, where they decided to run the ship aground if they could. 40Cutting loose the anchors, they left them in the sea and at the same time untied the ropes that held the rudders. Then they hoisted the foresail to the wind and made for the beach. 41But the ship struck a sandbar and ran aground. The bow stuck fast and would not move, and the stern was broken to pieces by the pounding of the surf.

42The soldiers planned to kill the prisoners to prevent any of them from swimming away and escaping. 43But the centurion wanted to spare Paul's life and kept them from carrying out their plan. He ordered those who could swim to jump overboard first and get to land. 44The rest were to get there on planks or on pieces of the ship. In this way everyone reached land in safety.

Ashore on Malta

28 Once safely on shore, we found out that the island was called Malta. 2The islanders showed us unusual kindness. They built a fire and welcomed us all because it was raining and cold. 3Paul gathered a pile of brushwood and, as he put it on the fire, a viper, driven out by the heat, fastened itself on his hand. 4When the islanders saw the snake hanging from his hand, they said to each other, "This man must be a murderer; for though he escaped from the sea, Justice has not allowed him to live." 5But Paul shook the snake off into the fire and suffered no ill effects. 6The people expected him to swell up or suddenly fall dead, but after waiting a long time and seeing nothing unusual happen to him, they changed their minds and said he was a god.

7There was an estate nearby that belonged to Publius, the chief official of the island. He welcomed us to his home and for three days entertained us hospitably. 8His father was sick in bed, suffering from fever and dysentery. Paul went in to see him and, after prayer, placed his hands on him and healed him. [9]When this had happened, the rest of the sick on the island came and were cured. [10]They honored us in many ways and when we were ready to sail, they furnished us with the supplies we needed.

Arrival at Rome

[11]After three months we put out to sea in a ship that had wintered in the island. It was an Alexandrian ship with the figurehead of the twin gods Castor and Pollux. [12]We put in at Syracuse and stayed there three days. [13]From there we set sail and arrived at Rhegium. The next day the south wind came up, and on the following day we reached Puteoli. [14]There we found some brothers who invited us to spend a week with them. And so we came to Rome. [15]The brothers there had heard that we were coming, and they traveled as far as the Forum of Appius and the Three Taverns to meet us. At the sight of these men Paul thanked God and was encouraged. [16]When we got to Rome, Paul was allowed to live by himself, with a soldier to guard him.

Paul Preaches at Rome Under Guard

[17]Three days later he called together the leaders of the Jews. When they had assembled, Paul said to them: "My brothers, although I have done nothing against our people or against the customs of our ancestors, I was arrested in Jerusalem and handed over to the Romans. [18]They examined me and wanted to release me, because I was not guilty of any crime deserving death. [19]But when the Jews objected, I was compelled to appeal to Caesar—not that I had any charge to bring against my own people. [20]For this reason I have asked to see you and talk with you. It is because of the hope of Israel that I am bound with this chain."

[21]They replied, "We have not received any letters from Judea concerning you, and none of the brothers who have come from there has reported or said anything bad about you. [22]But we want to hear what your views are, for we know that people everywhere are talking against this sect."

[23]They arranged to meet Paul on a certain day, and came in even larger numbers to the place where he was staying. From morning till evening he explained and declared to them the kingdom of God and tried to convince them about Jesus from the Law of Moses and from the Prophets. [24]Some were convinced by what he

和痢疾躺着。保羅進去為他禱告，按手在他身上，治好了他。[9]從此，島上其餘的病人也來得了醫治。[10]他們又多方地尊敬我們，到了開船的時候，也把我們所需用的送到船上。

抵達羅馬

[11]過了三個月，我們上了亞歷山太的船往前行。這船以"宙斯雙子"為記，是在那海島過了冬的。[12]到了敘拉古，我們停泊三日，[13]又從那裏繞行，來到利基翁。過了一天，起了南風，第二天就來到部丟利。[14]在那裏遇見弟兄們，請我們與他們同住了七天。這樣，我們來到羅馬。[15]那裏的弟兄們一聽見我們的信息，就出來到亞比烏市和三館地方迎接我們。保羅見了他們，就感謝神，放心壯膽。[16]進了羅馬城，（註：有古卷在此有"百夫長把眾囚犯交給御營的統領，惟有"）保羅蒙准，和一個看守他的兵另住在一處。

保羅在羅馬受監管下傳道

[17]過了三天，保羅請猶太人的首領來。他們來了，就對他們說："弟兄們，我雖沒有做甚麼事干犯本國的百姓和我們祖宗的規條，卻被鎖綁，從耶路撒冷解在羅馬人的手裏。[18]他們審問了我，就願意釋放我，因為在我身上並沒有該死的罪。[19]無奈猶太人不服，我不得已，只好上告於凱撒，並非有甚麼要控告我本國的百姓。[20]因此，我請你們來見面說話。我原為以色列人所指望的，被這鏈子捆鎖。"

[21]他們說："我們並沒有接着從猶太來論你的信，也沒有弟兄到這裏來，報給我們說你有甚麼不好處。[22]但我們願意聽你的意見如何，因為這教門，我們曉得是到處被毀謗的。"

[23]他們和保羅約定了日子，就有許多人到他的寓處來。保羅從早到晚對他們講論這事，證明神國的道，引摩西的律法和先知的書，以耶穌的事勸勉他們。[24]他所說的話，有信的，

有不信的。²⁵他們彼此不合，就散了。未散以先，保羅說了一句話，說：「聖靈藉先知以賽亞向你們祖宗所說的話是不錯的。

²⁶「他說：『你去告訴這百姓說：
你們聽是要聽見，
　卻不明白；
看是要看見，
　卻不曉得。
²⁷因為這百姓油蒙了心，
　耳朵發沉，
　眼睛閉着；
恐怕眼睛看見，
　耳朵聽見，
　心裏明白，
回轉過來，我就醫治他們。』

²⁸「所以你們當知道，神這救恩如今傳給外邦人，他們也必聽受。」

（註：有古卷在此有²⁹「保羅說了這話，猶太人議論紛紛地就走了。」）

³⁰保羅在自己所租的房子裏住了足足兩年。凡來見他的人，他全都接待，³¹放膽傳講神國的道，將主耶穌基督的事教導人，並沒有人禁止。

said, but others would not believe. ²⁵They disagreed among themselves and began to leave after Paul had made this final statement: "The Holy Spirit spoke the truth to your forefathers when he said through Isaiah the prophet:

²⁶" 'Go to this people and say,
　"You will be ever hearing but never
　　understanding;
　you will be ever seeing but never
　　perceiving."
²⁷For this people's heart has become calloused;
　they hardly hear with their ears,
　and they have closed their eyes.
Otherwise they might see with their eyes,
　hear with their ears,
　understand with their hearts
and turn, and I would heal them.'ᵃ

²⁸"Therefore I want you to know that God's salvation has been sent to the Gentiles, and they will listen!"ᵇ

³⁰For two whole years Paul stayed there in his own rented house and welcomed all who came to see him. ³¹Boldly and without hindrance he preached the kingdom of God and taught about the Lord Jesus Christ.

---

a 27 Isaiah 6:9,10　　b 28 Some manuscripts listen!" ²⁹ After he said this, the Jews left, arguing vigorously among themselves.

Romans

羅馬書

1 Paul, a servant of Christ Jesus, called to be an apostle and set apart for the gospel of God—²the gospel he promised beforehand through his prophets in the Holy Scriptures ³regarding his Son, who as to his human nature was a descendant of David, ⁴and who through the Spirit*a* of holiness was declared with power to be the Son of God*b* by his resurrection from the dead: Jesus Christ our Lord. ⁵Through him and for his name's sake, we received grace and apostleship to call people from among all the Gentiles to the obedience that comes from faith. ⁶And you also are among those who are called to belong to Jesus Christ.

⁷To all in Rome who are loved by God and called to be saints:

Grace and peace to you from God our Father and from the Lord Jesus Christ.

Paul's Longing to Visit Rome

⁸First, I thank my God through Jesus Christ for all of you, because your faith is being reported all over the world. ⁹God, whom I serve with my whole heart in preaching the gospel of his Son, is my witness how constantly I remember you ¹⁰in my prayers at all times; and I pray that now at last by God's will the way may be opened for me to come to you.

¹¹I long to see you so that I may impart to you some spiritual gift to make you strong— ¹²that is, that you and I may be mutually encouraged by each other's faith. ¹³I do not want you to be unaware, brothers, that I planned many times to come to you (but have been prevented from doing so until now) in order that I might have a harvest among you, just as I have had among the other Gentiles.

¹⁴I am obligated both to Greeks and non-Greeks, both to the wise and the foolish. ¹⁵That is why I am so eager to preach the gospel also to you who are at Rome.

1 耶穌基督的僕人保羅，奉召為使徒，特派傳神的福音。²這福音是神從前藉眾先知在聖經上所應許的。³論到他兒子我主耶穌基督，按肉體說，是從大衛後裔生的；⁴按聖善的靈說，因從死裏復活，以大能顯明是神的兒子。⁵我們從他受了恩惠並使徒的職分，在萬國之中叫人為他的名信服真道；⁶其中也有你們這蒙召屬耶穌基督的人。

⁷我寫信給你們在羅馬為神所愛、奉召作聖徒的眾人：

願恩惠、平安從我們的父神並主耶穌基督歸與你們！

保羅切望去羅馬探訪

⁸第一，我靠着耶穌基督，為你們眾人感謝我的神，因你們的信德傳遍了天下。⁹我在他兒子福音上，用心靈所侍奉的神，可以見證我怎樣不住地提到你們。¹⁰在禱告之間常常懇求，或者照神的旨意，終能得平坦的道路往你們那裏去。

¹¹因為我切切地想見你們，要把些屬靈的恩賜分給你們，使你們可以堅固。¹²這樣，我在你們中間，因你與我彼此的信心，就可以同得安慰。¹³弟兄們，我不願意你們不知道，我屢次定意往你們那裏去，要在你們中間得些果子，如同在其餘的外邦人中一樣，只是到如今仍有阻隔。

¹⁴無論是希臘人、化外人、聰明人、愚拙人，我都欠他們的債。¹⁵所以情願盡我的力量，將福音也傳給你們在羅馬的人。

---

a 4 Or who as to his spirit　　*b 4 Or was appointed to be the Son of God with power*

16我不以福音為恥；這福音本是神的大能，要救一切相信的，先是猶太人，後是希臘人。17因為神的義，正在這福音上顯明出來；這義是本於信，以至於信。如經上所記："義人必因信得生。"

神對人類的忿怒

18原來，神的忿怒，從天上顯明在一切虔不義的人身上，就是那些行不義阻擋真理的人。19神的事情，人所能知道的，原顯明在人心裏，因為神已經給他們顯明。20自從造天地以來，神的永能和神性是明明可知的，雖是眼不能見，但藉着所造之物就可以曉得，叫人無可推諉。

21因為，他們雖然知道神，卻不當作神榮耀他，也不感謝他。他們的思念變為虛妄，無知的心就昏暗了。22自稱為聰明，反成了愚拙；23將不能朽壞之神的榮耀變為偶像，彷彿必朽壞的人和飛禽、走獸、昆蟲的樣式。

24所以，神任憑他們逞着心裏的情慾行污穢的事，以致彼此玷辱自己的身體。25他們將神的真實變為虛謊，去敬拜侍奉受造之物，不敬奉那造物的主。主乃是可稱頌的，直到永遠。阿們！

26因此，神任憑他們放縱可羞恥的情慾。他們的女人把順性的用處變為逆性的用處；27男人也是如此，棄了女人順性的用處，慾火攻心，彼此貪戀，男和男行可羞恥的事，就在自己身上受這妄為當得的報應。

28他們既然故意不認識神，神就任憑他們存邪僻的心，行那些不合理的事；29裝滿了各樣不義、邪惡、貪婪、惡毒（註：或作"陰毒"），滿心是嫉妒、兇殺、爭競、詭詐、毒恨；30又是讒毀的、背後說人的、怨恨神的（註：或作"被神所憎惡的"）、侮慢人的、狂傲的、自誇的、捏造惡事的、違背父母的、31無知的、背約的、無親情的、不憐憫人的。32他們雖知道神判定行這樣事的人是當死

16I am not ashamed of the gospel, because it is the power of God for the salvation of everyone who believes: first for the Jew, then for the Gentile. 17For in the gospel a righteousness from God is revealed, a righteousness that is by faith from first to last,[a] just as it is written: "The righteous will live by faith."[b]

God's Wrath Against Mankind

18The wrath of God is being revealed from heaven against all the godlessness and wickedness of men who suppress the truth by their wickedness, 19since what may be known about God is plain to them, because God has made it plain to them. 20For since the creation of the world God's invisible qualities—his eternal power and divine nature—have been clearly seen, being understood from what has been made, so that men are without excuse.

21For although they knew God, they neither glorified him as God nor gave thanks to him, but their thinking became futile and their foolish hearts were darkened. 22Although they claimed to be wise, they became fools 23and exchanged the glory of the immortal God for images made to look like mortal man and birds and animals and reptiles.

24Therefore God gave them over in the sinful desires of their hearts to sexual impurity for the degrading of their bodies with one another. 25They exchanged the truth of God for a lie, and worshiped and served created things rather than the Creator—who is forever praised. Amen.

26Because of this, God gave them over to shameful lusts. Even their women exchanged natural relations for unnatural ones. 27In the same way the men also abandoned natural relations with women and were inflamed with lust for one another. Men committed indecent acts with other men, and received in themselves the due penalty for their perversion.

28Furthermore, since they did not think it worthwhile to retain the knowledge of God, he gave them over to a depraved mind, to do what ought not to be done. 29They have become filled with every kind of wickedness, evil, greed and depravity. They are full of envy, murder, strife, deceit and malice. They are gossips, 30slanderers, God-haters, insolent, arrogant and boastful; they invent ways of doing evil; they disobey their parents; 31they are senseless, faithless, heartless, ruthless. 32Although they know God's righteous decree that those who do such things deserve

a 17 Or is from faith to faith　　b 17 Hab. 2:4

death, they not only continue to do these very things but also approve of those who practice them.

God's Righteous Judgment

2 You, therefore, have no excuse, you who pass judgment on someone else, for at whatever point you judge the other, you are condemning yourself, because you who pass judgment do the same things. ²Now we know that God's judgment against those who do such things is based on truth. ³So when you, a mere man, pass judgment on them and yet do the same things, do you think you will escape God's judgment? ⁴Or do you show contempt for the riches of his kindness, tolerance and patience, not realizing that God's kindness leads you toward repentance?

⁵But because of your stubbornness and your unrepentant heart, you are storing up wrath against yourself for the day of God's wrath, when his righteous judgment will be revealed. ⁶God "will give to each person according to what he has done."*a* ⁷To those who by persistence in doing good seek glory, honor and immortality, he will give eternal life. ⁸But for those who are self-seeking and who reject the truth and follow evil, there will be wrath and anger. ⁹There will be trouble and distress for every human being who does evil: first for the Jew, then for the Gentile; ¹⁰but glory, honor and peace for everyone who does good: first for the Jew, then for the Gentile. ¹¹For God does not show favoritism.

¹²All who sin apart from the law will also perish apart from the law, and all who sin under the law will be judged by the law. ¹³For it is not those who hear the law who are righteous in God's sight, but it is those who obey the law who will be declared righteous. ¹⁴(Indeed, when Gentiles, who do not have the law, do by nature things required by the law, they are a law for themselves, even though they do not have the law, ¹⁵since they show that the requirements of the law are written on their hearts, their consciences also bearing witness, and their thoughts now accusing, now even defending them.) ¹⁶This will take place on the day when God will judge men's secrets through Jesus Christ, as my gospel declares.

The Jews and the Law

¹⁷Now you, if you call yourself a Jew; if you rely on the law and brag about your relationship to God; ¹⁸if you know his will and approve of

a 6 Psalm 62:12; Prov. 24:12

的，然而他們不但自己去行，還喜歡別人去行。

神的公義審判

2 你這論斷人的，無論你是誰，也無可推諉。你在甚麼事上論斷人，就在甚麼事上定自己的罪，因你這論斷人的，自己所行卻和別人一樣。²我們知道這樣行的人，神必照真理審判他。³你這人哪，你論斷行這樣事的人，自己所行的卻和別人一樣！你以為能逃脫神的審判嗎？⁴還是你藐視他豐富的恩慈、寬容、忍耐，不曉得他的恩慈是領你悔改呢？

⁵你竟任着你剛硬不悔改的心，為自己積蓄忿怒，以致神震怒，顯他公義審判的日子來到。⁶他 "必照各人的行為報應各人。" ⁷凡恆心行善，尋求榮耀、尊貴和不能朽壞之福的，就以永生報應他們；⁸惟有結黨不順從真理，反順從不義的，就以忿怒、惱恨報應他們。⁹將患難、困苦加給一切作惡的人，先是猶太人，後是希臘人；¹⁰卻將榮耀、尊貴、平安加給一切行善的人，先是猶太人，後是希臘人。¹¹因為神不偏待人。

¹²凡沒有律法犯了罪的，也必不按律法滅亡；凡在律法以下犯了罪的，也必按律法受審判。（¹³原來，在神面前不是聽律法的為義，乃是行律法的稱義。¹⁴沒有律法的外邦人，若順着本性行律法上的事，他們雖然沒有律法，自己就是自己的律法。¹⁵這是顯出律法的功用刻在他們心裏，他們是非之心同作見證，並且他們的思念互相較量，或以為是，或以為非。）¹⁶就在神藉耶穌基督審判人隱秘事的日子，照着我的福音所言。

猶太人與律法

¹⁷你稱為猶太人，又倚靠律法，且指着神誇口；¹⁸既從律法中受了教

訓，就曉得神的旨意，也能分別是非（註：或作"也喜愛那美好的事"）；19又深信自己是給瞎子領路的，是黑暗中人的光，20是蠢笨人的師傅，是小孩子的先生，在律法上有知識和真理的模範。21你既是教導別人，還不教導自己嗎？你講說人不可偷竊，自己還偷竊嗎？22你說人不可姦淫，自己還姦淫嗎？你厭惡偶像，自己還偷竊廟中之物嗎？23你指著律法誇口，自己倒犯律法玷辱神嗎？24"神的名在外邦人中，因你們受了褻瀆"，正如經上所記的。

25你若是行律法的，割禮固然於你有益；若是犯律法的，你的割禮就算不得割禮。26所以那未受割禮的，若遵守律法的條例，他雖然未受割禮，豈不算是有割禮嗎？27而且那本來未受割禮的，若能全守律法，豈不是要審判你這有儀文和割禮竟犯律法的人嗎？

28因為外面作猶太人的，不是真猶太人；外面肉身的割禮，也不是真割禮。29惟有裏面作的，才是真猶太人；真割禮也是心裏的，在乎靈，不在乎儀文。這人的稱讚不是從人來的，乃是從神來的。

神的信實

3 這樣說來，猶太人有甚麼長處，割禮有甚麼益處呢？2凡事大有好處，第一是神的聖言交託他們。

3即便有不信的，這有何妨呢？難道他們的不信，就廢掉神的信嗎？4斷乎不能！不如說，神是真實的，人都是虛謊的。如經上所記：

"你責備人的時候，顯為公義；
　被人議論的時候，可以得勝。"

5我且照著人的常話說，我們的不義若顯出神的義來，我們可以怎麼說呢？神降怒，是他不義嗎？6斷乎不是！若是這樣，神怎能審判世

what is superior because you are instructed by the law; 19if you are convinced that you are a guide for the blind, a light for those who are in the dark, 20an instructor of the foolish, a teacher of infants, because you have in the law the embodiment of knowledge and truth— 21you, then, who teach others, do you not teach yourself? You who preach against stealing, do you steal? 22You who say that people should not commit adultery, do you commit adultery? You who abhor idols, do you rob temples? 23You who brag about the law, do you dishonor God by breaking the law? 24As it is written: "God's name is blasphemed among the Gentiles because of you."[a]

25Circumcision has value if you observe the law, but if you break the law, you have become as though you had not been circumcised. 26If those who are not circumcised keep the law's requirements, will they not be regarded as though they were circumcised? 27The one who is not circumcised physically and yet obeys the law will condemn you who, even though you have the[b] written code and circumcision, are a lawbreaker.

28A man is not a Jew if he is only one outwardly, nor is circumcision merely outward and physical. 29No, a man is a Jew if he is one inwardly; and circumcision is circumcision of the heart, by the Spirit, not by the written code. Such a man's praise is not from men, but from God.

God's Faithfulness

3 What advantage, then, is there in being a Jew, or what value is there in circumcision? 2Much in every way! First of all, they have been entrusted with the very words of God.

3What if some did not have faith? Will their lack of faith nullify God's faithfulness? 4Not at all! Let God be true, and every man a liar. As it is written:

" So that you may be proved right when you speak
　and prevail when you judge."[c]

5But if our unrighteousness brings out God's righteousness more clearly, what shall we say? That God is unjust in bringing his wrath on us? (I am using a human argument.) 6Certainly not! If that were so, how could God judge the world?

a 24 Isaiah 52:5; Ezek. 36:22　　b 27 Or who, by means of a
c 4 Psalm 51:4

[7]Someone might argue, "If my falsehood enhances God's truthfulness and so increases his glory, why am I still condemned as a sinner?" [8]Why not say—as we are being slanderously reported as saying and as some claim that we say—"Let us do evil that good may result"? Their condemnation is deserved.

No One Is Righteous

[9]What shall we conclude then? Are we any better[a]? Not at all! We have already made the charge that Jews and Gentiles alike are all under sin. [10]As it is written:

"There is no one righteous, not even one;
[11] there is no one who understands,
    no one who seeks God.
[12]All have turned away,
    they have together become worthless;
there is no one who does good,
    not even one."[b]
[13]"Their throats are open graves;
    their tongues practice deceit."[c]
"The poison of vipers is on their lips."[d]
[14] "Their mouths are full of cursing and
    bitterness."[e]
[15]"Their feet are swift to shed blood;
[16] ruin and misery mark their ways,
[17]and the way of peace they do not know."[f]
[18] "There is no fear of God before their eyes."[g]

[19]Now we know that whatever the law says, it says to those who are under the law, so that every mouth may be silenced and the whole world held accountable to God. [20]Therefore no one will be declared righteous in his sight by observing the law; rather, through the law we become conscious of sin.

Righteousness Through Faith

[21]But now a righteousness from God, apart from law, has been made known, to which the Law and the Prophets testify. [22]This righteousness from God comes through faith in Jesus Christ to all who believe. There is no difference, [23]for all have sinned and fall short of the glory of God, [24]and are justified freely by his grace through the redemption that came by Christ Jesus. [25]God presented him as a sacrifice of atonement,[h] through faith in his blood. He did this to demonstrate his justice, because in his

---

界呢？[7]"若神的真實，因我的虛謊越發顯出他的榮耀，為甚麼我還受審判，好像罪人呢？"[8]為甚麼不說："我們可以作惡以成善呢"？這是毀謗我們的人說我們有這話。這等人定罪是該當的。

沒有義人

[9]這卻怎麼樣呢？我們比他們強嗎？決不是的！因我們已經證明：<u>猶太人</u>和<u>希臘人</u>都在罪惡之下。[10]就如經上所記：

"沒有義人，連一個也沒有！
[11]沒有明白的，
    沒有尋求神的；
[12]都是偏離正路，
    一同變為無用。
沒有行善的，
    連一個也沒有！"
[13] "他們的喉嚨是敞開的墳墓；
    他們用舌頭弄詭詐。"
"嘴唇裏有虺蛇的毒氣。"
[14] "滿口是咒罵苦毒。"

[15] "殺人流血，他們的腳飛跑，
[16]所經過的路，便行殘害暴虐的事；
[17]平安的路，他們未曾知道。"
[18] "他們眼中不怕神。"

[19]我們曉得律法上的話，都是對律法以下之人說的，好塞住各人的口，叫普世的人都伏在神審判之下。[20]所以凡有血氣的，沒有一個因行律法能在神面前稱義，因為律法本是叫人知罪。

因信稱義

[21]但如今，神的義在律法以外已經顯明出來，有律法和先知為證。[22]就是神的義，因信耶穌基督加給一切相信的人，並沒有分別。[23]因為世人都犯了罪，虧缺了神的榮耀，[24]如今卻蒙神的恩典，因基督耶穌的救贖，就白白地稱義。[25]神設立耶穌作挽回祭，是憑着耶穌的血，藉着人的信，要顯明神的義。因為他用忍耐的

---

a 9 Or *worse*   *b* 12 Psalms 14:1-3; 53:1-3; Eccles. 7:20
c 13 Psalm 5:9   *d* 13 Psalm 140:3   *e* 14 Psalm 10:7
f 17 Isaiah 59:7,8   *g* 18 Psalm 36:1
h 25 Or *as the one who would turn aside his wrath, taking away sin*

心，寬容人先時所犯的罪，²⁶好在今時顯出他的義，使人知道他自己為義，也稱信耶穌的人為義。

²⁷既是這樣，哪裏能誇口呢？沒有可誇的了！用何法沒有的呢？是用立功之法嗎？不是，乃用信主之法。²⁸所以（註：有古卷作「因為」）我們看定了：人稱義是因着信，不在乎遵行律法。²⁹難道神只作猶太人的神嗎？不也是作外邦人的神嗎？是的，也作外邦人的神。³⁰神既是一位，他就要因信稱那受割禮的為義，也要因信稱那未受割禮的為義。³¹這樣，我們因信廢了律法嗎？斷乎不是！更是堅固律法。

亞伯拉罕因信稱義

4 如此說來，我們的祖宗亞伯拉罕憑着肉體得了甚麼呢？²倘若亞伯拉罕是因行為稱義，就有可誇的，只是在神面前並無可誇。³經上說甚麼呢？說："亞伯拉罕信神，這就算為他的義。"

⁴做工的得工價，不算恩典，乃是該得的；⁵惟有不做工的，只信稱罪人為義的神，他的信就算為義。⁶正如大衛稱那在行為以外蒙神算為義的人是有福的。

⁷他說：
"得赦免其過、遮蓋其罪的，
    這人是有福的！
⁸主不算為有罪的，
    這人是有福的！"

⁹如此看來，這福是單加給那受割禮的人嗎？不也是加給那未受割禮的人嗎？因我們所說，亞伯拉罕的信，就算為他的義。¹⁰是怎麼算的呢？是在他受割禮的時候呢？是在他未受割禮的時候呢？不是在受割禮的時候，乃是在未受割禮的時候。¹¹並且他受了割禮的記號，作他未受割禮的時候因信稱義的印證，叫他作一切未受割禮而信之人的父，使他們也算為義；¹²又作受割禮之人的父，就是那些不但受割禮，

forbearance he had left the sins committed beforehand unpunished— ²⁶he did it to demonstrate his justice at the present time, so as to be just and the one who justifies those who have faith in Jesus.

²⁷Where, then, is boasting? It is excluded. On what principle? On that of observing the law? No, but on that of faith. ²⁸For we maintain that a man is justified by faith apart from observing the law. ²⁹Is God the God of Jews only? Is he not the God of Gentiles too? Yes, of Gentiles too, ³⁰since there is only one God, who will justify the circumcised by faith and the uncircumcised through that same faith. ³¹Do we, then, nullify the law by this faith? Not at all! Rather, we uphold the law.

Abraham Justified by Faith

4 What then shall we say that Abraham, our forefather, discovered in this matter? ²If, in fact, Abraham was justified by works, he had something to boast about—but not before God. ³What does the Scripture say? "Abraham believed God, and it was credited to him as righteousness."[a]

⁴Now when a man works, his wages are not credited to him as a gift, but as an obligation. ⁵However, to the man who does not work but trusts God who justifies the wicked, his faith is credited as righteousness. ⁶David says the same thing when he speaks of the blessedness of the man to whom God credits righteousness apart from works:

⁷"Blessed are they
    whose transgressions are forgiven,
    whose sins are covered.
⁸Blessed is the man
    whose sin the Lord will never count against
      him."[b]

⁹Is this blessedness only for the circumcised, or also for the uncircumcised? We have been saying that Abraham's faith was credited to him as righteousness. ¹⁰Under what circumstances was it credited? Was it after he was circumcised, or before? It was not after, but before! ¹¹And he received the sign of circumcision, a seal of the righteousness that he had by faith while he was still uncircumcised. So then, he is the father of all who believe but have not been circumcised, in order that righteousness might be credited to them. ¹²And he is also the father of the circumcised who not only are circumcised but who also

a 3 Gen. 15:6; also in verse 22   b 8 Psalm 32:1,2

walk in the footsteps of the faith that our father Abraham had before he was circumcised.

[13]It was not through law that Abraham and his offspring received the promise that he would be heir of the world, but through the righteousness that comes by faith. [14]For if those who live by law are heirs, faith has no value and the promise is worthless, [15]because law brings wrath. And where there is no law there is no transgression.

[16]Therefore, the promise comes by faith, so that it may be by grace and may be guaranteed to all Abraham's offspring—not only to those who are of the law but also to those who are of the faith of Abraham. He is the father of us all. [17]As it is written: "I have made you a father of many nations."[a] He is our father in the sight of God, in whom he believed—the God who gives life to the dead and calls things that are not as though they were.

[18]Against all hope, Abraham in hope believed and so became the father of many nations, just as it had been said to him, "So shall your offspring be."[b] [19]Without weakening in his faith, he faced the fact that his body was as good as dead—since he was about a hundred years old—and that Sarah's womb was also dead. [20]Yet he did not waver through unbelief regarding the promise of God, but was strengthened in his faith and gave glory to God, [21]being fully persuaded that God had power to do what he had promised. [22]This is why "it was credited to him as righteousness." [23]The words "it was credited to him" were written not for him alone, [24]but also for us, to whom God will credit righteousness—for us who believe in him who raised Jesus our Lord from the dead. [25]He was delivered over to death for our sins and was raised to life for our justification.

Peace and Joy

5 Therefore, since we have been justified through faith, we[c] have peace with God through our Lord Jesus Christ, [2]through whom we have gained access by faith into this grace in which we now stand. And we[c] rejoice in the hope of the glory of God. [3]Not only so, but we[c] also rejoice in our sufferings, because we know that suffering produces perseverance; [4]perseverance, character; and character, hope. [5]And hope does not disappoint us, because God has poured out his love into our hearts by the Holy Spirit, whom he has given us.

並且按我們的祖宗<u>亞伯拉罕</u>，未受割禮而信之蹤跡去行的人。

[13]因為神應許<u>亞伯拉罕</u>和他後裔必得承受世界，不是因律法，乃是因信而得的義。[14]若是屬乎律法的人才得為後嗣，信就歸於虛空，應許也就廢棄了。[15]因為律法是惹動忿怒的（註：或作「叫人受刑的」），哪裏沒有律法，那裏就沒有過犯。

[16]所以人得為後嗣是本乎信，因此就屬乎恩，叫應許定然歸給一切後裔，不但歸給那屬乎律法的，也歸給那效法<u>亞伯拉罕</u>之信的。[17]<u>亞伯拉罕</u>所信的，是那叫死人復活、使無變為有的神，他在主面前作我們世人的父。如經上所記：「我已經立你作多國的父。」

[18]他在無可指望的時候，因信仍有指望，就得以作多國的父，正如先前所說：「你的後裔將要如此。」[19]他將近百歲的時候，雖然想到自己的身體如同已死，<u>撒拉</u>的生育已經斷絕，他的信心還是不軟弱。[20]並且仰望神的應許，總沒有因不信，心裏起疑惑，反倒因信，心裏得堅固，將榮耀歸給神。[21]且滿心相信神所應許的必能作成。[22]所以這就「算為他的義」。[23]「算為他義」的這句話，不是單為他寫的，[24]也是為我們將來得算為義之人寫的，就是我們這信神使我們的主耶穌從死裏復活的人。[25]耶穌被交給人，是為我們的過犯；復活，是為叫我們稱義（註：或作「耶穌是為我們的過犯交付了；是為我們稱義復活了」）。

平安與喜樂

5 我們既因信稱義，就藉着我們的主耶穌基督得與神相和。[2]我們又藉着他，因信得進入現在所站的這恩典中，並且歡歡喜喜盼望神的榮耀。[3]不但如此，就是在患難中也是歡歡喜喜的。因為知道患難生忍耐，[4]忍耐生老練，老練生盼望，[5]盼望不至於羞恥；因為所賜給我們的聖靈將神的愛澆灌在我們心裏。

a 17 Gen. 17:5   *b* 18 Gen. 15:5   *c* 1 ,2,3 Or let us

6因我們還軟弱的時候，基督就按所定的日期為罪人死。7為義人死，是少有的；為仁人死，或者有敢係的；8惟有基督在我們還作罪人的時候為我們死，神的愛就在此向我們顯明了。

9現在我們既靠着他的血稱義，就更要藉着他免去神的忿怒。10因為我們作仇敵的時候，且藉着神兒子的死，得與神和好；既已和好，就更要因他的生得救了。11不但如此，我們既藉着我主耶穌基督得與神和好，也就藉着他以神為樂。

死由亞當來，生命由基督來

12這就如罪是從一人入了世界，死又是從罪來的，於是死就臨到眾人，因為眾人都犯了罪。13沒有律法之先，罪已經在世上，但沒有律法，罪也不算罪。14然而從亞當到摩西，死就作了王，連那些不與亞當一樣罪過的，也在他的權下。亞當乃是那以後要來之人的預像。

15只是過犯不如恩賜。若因一人的過犯，眾人都死了，何況神的恩典，與那因耶穌基督一人恩典中的賞賜，豈不更加倍地臨到眾人嗎？16因一人犯罪就定罪，也不如恩賜；原來審判是由一人而定罪，恩賜乃是由許多過犯而稱義。17若因一人的過犯，死就因這一人作了王，何況那些受洪恩又蒙所賜之義的，豈不更要因耶穌基督一人在生命中作王嗎？

18如此說來，因一次的過犯，眾人都被定罪；照樣，因一次的義行，眾人也就被稱義得生命了。19因一人的悖逆，眾人成為罪人；照樣，因一人的順從，眾人也成為義了。

20律法本是外添的，叫過犯顯多；只是罪在哪裏顯多，恩典就更顯多了。21就如罪作王叫人死；照

6You see, at just the right time, when we were still powerless, Christ died for the ungodly. 7Very rarely will anyone die for a righteous man, though for a good man someone might possibly dare to die. 8But God demonstrates his own love for us in this: While we were still sinners, Christ died for us.

9Since we have now been justified by his blood, how much more shall we be saved from God's wrath through him! 10For if, when we were God's enemies, we were reconciled to him through the death of his Son, how much more, having been reconciled, shall we be saved through his life! 11Not only is this so, but we also rejoice in God through our Lord Jesus Christ, through whom we have now received reconciliation.

Death Through Adam, Life Through Christ

12Therefore, just as sin entered the world through one man, and death through sin, and in this way death came to all men, because all sinned— 13for before the law was given, sin was in the world. But sin is not taken into account when there is no law. 14Nevertheless, death reigned from the time of Adam to the time of Moses, even over those who did not sin by breaking a command, as did Adam, who was a pattern of the one to come.

15But the gift is not like the trespass. For if the many died by the trespass of the one man, how much more did God's grace and the gift that came by the grace of the one man, Jesus Christ, overflow to the many! 16Again, the gift of God is not like the result of the one man's sin: The judgment followed one sin and brought condemnation, but the gift followed many trespasses and brought justification. 17For if, by the trespass of the one man, death reigned through that one man, how much more will those who receive God's abundant provision of grace and of the gift of righteousness reign in life through the one man, Jesus Christ.

18Consequently, just as the result of one trespass was condemnation for all men, so also the result of one act of righteousness was justification that brings life for all men. 19For just as through the disobedience of the one man the many were made sinners, so also through the obedience of the one man the many will be made righteous.

20The law was added so that the trespass might increase. But where sin increased, grace increased all the more, 21so that, just as sin reigned in death, so also grace might reign through righteousness to bring eternal life through Jesus Christ our Lord.

Dead to Sin, Alive in Christ

6 What shall we say, then? Shall we go on sinning so that grace may increase? [2]By no means! We died to sin; how can we live in it any longer? [3]Or don't you know that all of us who were baptized into Christ Jesus were baptized into his death? [4]We were therefore buried with him through baptism into death in order that, just as Christ was raised from the dead through the glory of the Father, we too may live a new life.

[5]If we have been united with him like this in his death, we will certainly also be united with him in his resurrection. [6]For we know that our old self was crucified with him so that the body of sin might be done away with,[a] that we should no longer be slaves to sin— [7]because anyone who has died has been freed from sin.

[8]Now if we died with Christ, we believe that we will also live with him. [9]For we know that since Christ was raised from the dead, he cannot die again; death no longer has mastery over him. [10]The death he died, he died to sin once for all; but the life he lives, he lives to God.

[11]In the same way, count yourselves dead to sin but alive to God in Christ Jesus. [12]Therefore do not let sin reign in your mortal body so that you obey its evil desires. [13]Do not offer the parts of your body to sin, as instruments of wickedness, but rather offer yourselves to God, as those who have been brought from death to life; and offer the parts of your body to him as instruments of righteousness. [14]For sin shall not be your master, because you are not under law, but under grace.

Slaves to Righteousness

[15]What then? Shall we sin because we are not under law but under grace? By no means! [16]Don't you know that when you offer yourselves to someone to obey him as slaves, you are slaves to the one whom you obey—whether you are slaves to sin, which leads to death, or to obedience, which leads to righteousness? [17]But thanks be to God that, though you used to be slaves to sin, you wholeheartedly obeyed the form of teaching to which you were entrusted. [18]You have been set free from sin and have become slaves to righteousness.

[19]I put this in human terms because you are weak in your natural selves. Just as you used to

a 6 Or be rendered powerless

樣，恩典也藉着義作王，叫人因我們的主耶穌基督得永生。

向罪死，在基督裏活

6 這樣，怎麼說呢？我們可以仍在罪中，叫恩典顯多嗎？ [2]斷乎不可！我們在罪上死了的人豈可仍在罪中活着呢？ [3]豈不知我們這受洗歸入基督耶穌的人，是受洗歸入他的死嗎？ [4]所以我們藉着洗禮歸入死，和他一同埋葬，原是叫我們一舉一動有新生的樣式，像基督藉着父的榮耀從死裏復活一樣。

[5]我們若在他死的形狀上與他聯合，也要在他復活的形狀上與他聯合。 [6]因為知道我們的舊人和他同釘十字架，使罪身滅絕，叫我們不再作罪的奴僕， [7]因為已死的人是脫離了罪。

[8]我們若是與基督同死，就信必與他同活， [9]因為知道基督既從死裏復活，就不再死，死也不再作他的主了。 [10]他死是向罪死了，只有一次；他活是向神活着。

[11]這樣，你們向罪也當看自己是死的；向神在基督耶穌裏，卻當看自己是活的。 [12]所以，不要容罪在你們必死的身上作王，使你們順從身子的私慾。 [13]也不要將你們的肢體獻給罪作不義的器具；倒要像從死裏復活的人，將自己獻給神，並將肢體作義的器具獻給神。 [14]罪必不能作你們的主，因你們不在律法之下，乃在恩典之下。

作義的奴僕

[15]這卻怎麼樣呢？我們在恩典之下，不在律法之下，就可以犯罪嗎？斷乎不可！ [16]豈不曉得你們獻上自己作奴僕，順從誰，就作誰的奴僕嗎？或作罪的奴僕，以至於死；或作順命的奴僕，以至成義。 [17]感謝神！因為你們從前雖然作罪的奴僕，現今卻從心裏順服了所傳給你們道理的模範。 [18]你們既從罪裏得了釋放，就作了義的奴僕。

[19]我因你們肉體的軟弱，就照人的常話對你們說：你們從前怎樣將肢

體獻給不潔、不法作奴僕，以至於不法；現今也要照樣將肢體獻給義作奴僕，以至於成聖。20因為你們作罪之奴僕的時候，就不被義約束了。21你們現今所看為羞恥的事，當日有甚麼果子呢？那些事的結局就是死！22但現今你們既從罪裏得了釋放，作了神的奴僕，就有成聖的果子，那結局就是永生！23因為罪的工價乃是死；惟有神的恩賜，在我們的主基督耶穌裏，乃是永生。

以婚姻作比方

7 弟兄們，我現在對明白律法的人說：你們豈不曉得律法管人是在活着的時候嗎？2就如女人有了丈夫，丈夫還活着，就被律法約束；丈夫若死了，就脫離了丈夫的律法。3所以丈夫活着，她若歸於別人，便叫淫婦；丈夫若死了，她就脫離了丈夫的律法，雖然歸於別人，也不是淫婦。

4我的弟兄們，這樣說來，你們藉着基督的身體，在律法上也是死了，叫你們歸於別人，就是歸於那從死裏復活的，叫我們結果子給神。5因為我們屬肉體的時候，那因律法而生的惡慾就在我們肢體中發動，以致結成死亡的果子。6但我們既然在捆我們的律法上死了，現今就脫離了律法，叫我們服侍主，要按着心靈的新樣（註：“心靈”或作“聖靈”），不按着儀文的舊樣。

與罪爭戰

7這樣，我們可說甚麼呢？律法是罪嗎？斷乎不是！只是非因律法，我就不知何為罪。非律法說：“不可起貪心”，我就不知何為貪心。8然而罪趁着機會，就藉着誡命叫諸般的貪心在我裏頭發動，因為沒有律法，罪是死的。9我以前沒有律法，是活着的；但是誡命來到，罪又活了，我就死了。10那本來叫人活的誡命，反倒叫我死，11因為罪趁

offer the parts of your body in slavery to impurity and to ever-increasing wickedness, so now offer them in slavery to righteousness leading to holiness. 20When you were slaves to sin, you were free from the control of righteousness. 21What benefit did you reap at that time from the things you are now ashamed of? Those things result in death! 22But now that you have been set free from sin and have become slaves to God, the benefit you reap leads to holiness, and the result is eternal life. 23For the wages of sin is death, but the gift of God is eternal life in[a] Christ Jesus our Lord.

An Illustration From Marriage

7 Do you not know, brothers—for I am speaking to men who know the law—that the law has authority over a man only as long as he lives? 2For example, by law a married woman is bound to her husband as long as he is alive, but if her husband dies, she is released from the law of marriage. 3So then, if she marries another man while her husband is still alive, she is called an adulteress. But if her husband dies, she is released from that law and is not an adulteress, even though she marries another man.

4So, my brothers, you also died to the law through the body of Christ, that you might belong to another, to him who was raised from the dead, in order that we might bear fruit to God. 5For when we were controlled by the sinful nature,[b] the sinful passions aroused by the law were at work in our bodies, so that we bore fruit for death. 6But now, by dying to what once bound us, we have been released from the law so that we serve in the new way of the Spirit, and not in the old way of the written code.

Struggling With Sin

7What shall we say, then? Is the law sin? Certainly not! Indeed I would not have known what sin was except through the law. For I would not have known what coveting really was if the law had not said, "Do not covet."[c] 8But sin, seizing the opportunity afforded by the commandment, produced in me every kind of covetous desire. For apart from law, sin is dead. 9Once I was alive apart from law; but when the commandment came, sin sprang to life and I died. 10I found that the very commandment that was intended to bring life actually brought death. 11For sin, seizing the opportunity afforded

a 23 Or through   b 5 Or the flesh; also in verse 25
c 7 Exodus 20:17; Deut. 5:21

by the commandment, deceived me, and through the commandment put me to death. [12]So then, the law is holy, and the commandment is holy, righteous and good.

[13]Did that which is good, then, become death to me? By no means! But in order that sin might be recognized as sin, it produced death in me through what was good, so that through the commandment sin might become utterly sinful.

[14]We know that the law is spiritual; but I am unspiritual, sold as a slave to sin. [15]I do not understand what I do. For what I want to do I do not do, but what I hate I do. [16]And if I do what I do not want to do, I agree that the law is good. [17]As it is, it is no longer I myself who do it, but it is sin living in me. [18]I know that nothing good lives in me, that is, in my sinful nature.[a] For I have the desire to do what is good, but I cannot carry it out. [19]For what I do is not the good I want to do; no, the evil I do not want to do—this I keep on doing. [20]Now if I do what I do not want to do, it is no longer I who do it, but it is sin living in me that does it.

[21]So I find this law at work: When I want to do good, evil is right there with me. [22]For in my inner being I delight in God's law; [23]but I see another law at work in the members of my body, waging war against the law of my mind and making me a prisoner of the law of sin at work within my members. [24]What a wretched man I am! Who will rescue me from this body of death? [25]Thanks be to God — through Jesus Christ our Lord!

So then, I myself in my mind am a slave to God's law, but in the sinful nature a slave to the law of sin.

Life Through the Spirit

8 Therefore, there is now no condemnation for those who are in Christ Jesus,[b] [2]because through Christ Jesus the law of the Spirit of life set me free from the law of sin and death. [3]For what the law was powerless to do in that it was weakened by the sinful nature,[c] God did by sending his own Son in the likeness of sinful man to be a sin offering.[d] And so he condemned sin in sinful man,[e] [4]in order that the righteous requirements of the law might be fully met in us, who do not live according to the sinful nature but according to the Spirit.

a 18 Or my flesh b 1 Some later manuscripts Jesus, who do not live according to the sinful nature but according to the Spirit, c 3 Or the flesh; also in verses 4, 5, 8, 9, 12 and 13 d 3 Or man, for sin e 3 Or in the flesh

着機會，就藉着誡命引誘我，並且殺了我。[12]這樣看來，律法是聖潔的，誡命也是聖潔、公義、良善的。

[13]既然如此，那良善的是叫我死嗎？斷乎不是！叫我死的乃是罪。但罪藉着那良善的叫我死，就顯出真是罪，叫罪因着誡命更顯出是惡極了。

[14]我們原曉得律法是屬乎靈的，但我是屬乎肉體的，是已經賣給罪了。[15]因為我所做的，我自己不明白；我所願意的，我並不做；我所恨惡的，我倒去做。[16]若我所做的，是我所不願意的，我就應承律法是善的。[17]既是這樣，就不是我做的，乃是住在我裏頭的罪做的。[18]我也知道在我裏頭，就是我肉體之中，沒有良善。因為立志為善由得我，只是行出來由不得我。[19]故此，我所願意的善，我反不不做；我所不願意的惡，我倒去做。[20]若我去做所不願意做的，就不是我做的，乃是住在我裏頭的罪做的。

[21]我覺得有個律，就是我願意為善的時候，便有惡ryong我同在。[22]因為按着我裏面的意思（註：原文作"人"），我是喜歡神的律，[23]但我覺得肢體中另有個律和我心裏的律交戰，把我擄去，叫我附從那肢體中犯罪的律。[24]我真是苦啊！誰能救我脫離這取死的身體呢？[25]感謝神！靠着我們的主耶穌基督就能脫離了。

這樣看來，我以內心順服神的律，我肉體卻順服罪的律了。

從聖靈得生命

8 如今，那些在基督耶穌裏的就不定罪了。[2]因為賜生命聖靈的律在基督耶穌裏釋放了我，使我脫離罪和死的律了。[3]律法既因肉體軟弱，有所不能行的，神就差遣自己的兒子成為罪身的形狀，作了贖罪祭，在肉體中定了罪案，[4]使律法的義成就在我們這不隨從肉體，只隨從聖靈的人身上。

5因為隨從肉體的人，體貼肉體的事；隨從聖靈的人，體貼聖靈的事。6體貼肉體的就是死；體貼聖靈的乃是生命平安。7原來體貼肉體的，是與神為仇，因為不服神的律法，也是不能服。8而且屬肉體的人不能得神的喜歡。

9如果神的靈住在你們心裏，你們就不屬肉體，乃屬聖靈了。人若沒有基督的靈，就不是屬基督的。10基督若在你們心裏，身體就因罪而死，心靈卻因義而活。11然而叫耶穌從死裏復活者的靈，若住在你們心裏，那叫基督耶穌從死裏復活的，也必藉着住在你們心裏的聖靈，使你們必死的身體又活過來。

12弟兄們，這樣看來，我們並不是欠肉體的債，去順從肉體活着。13你們若順從肉體活着，必要死；若靠着聖靈治死身體的惡行，必要活着。14因為凡被神的靈引導的，都是神的兒子。15你們所受的不是奴僕的心，仍舊害怕；所受的乃是兒子的心，因此我們呼叫：「阿爸，父！」16聖靈與我們的心同證我們是神的兒女；17既是兒女，便是後嗣，就是神的後嗣，和基督同作後嗣。如果我們和他一同受苦，也必和他一同得榮耀。

將來的榮耀

18我想，現在的苦楚若比起將來要顯於我們的榮耀，就不足介意了。19受造之物切望等候神的眾子顯出來。20因為受造之物服在虛空之下，不是自己願意，乃是因那叫他如此的。21但受造之物仍然指望脫離敗壞的轄制，得享神兒女自由的榮耀（註：「享」原文作「入」）。

22我們知道一切受造之物一同歎息、勞苦，直到如今。23不但如此，就是我們這有聖靈初結果子的，也是自己心裏歎息，等候得着兒子的

5Those who live according to the sinful nature have their minds set on what that nature desires; but those who live in accordance with the Spirit have their minds set on what the Spirit desires. 6The mind of sinful man[a] is death, but the mind controlled by the Spirit is life and peace; 7the sinful mind[b] is hostile to God. It does not submit to God's law, nor can it do so. 8Those controlled by the sinful nature cannot please God.

9You, however, are controlled not by the sinful nature but by the Spirit, if the Spirit of God lives in you. And if anyone does not have the Spirit of Christ, he does not belong to Christ. 10But if Christ is in you, your body is dead because of sin, yet your spirit is alive because of righteousness. 11And if the Spirit of him who raised Jesus from the dead is living in you, he who raised Christ from the dead will also give life to your mortal bodies through his Spirit, who lives in you.

12Therefore, brothers, we have an obligation—but it is not to the sinful nature, to live according to it. 13For if you live according to the sinful nature, you will die; but if by the Spirit you put to death the misdeeds of the body, you will live, 14because those who are led by the Spirit of God are sons of God. 15For you did not receive a spirit that makes you a slave again to fear, but you received the Spirit of sonship.[c] And by him we cry, "Abba,[d] Father." 16The Spirit himself testifies with our spirit that we are God's children. 17Now if we are children, then we are heirs—heirs of God and co-heirs with Christ, if indeed we share in his sufferings in order that we may also share in his glory.

Future Glory

18I consider that our present sufferings are not worth comparing with the glory that will be revealed in us. 19The creation waits in eager expectation for the sons of God to be revealed. 20For the creation was subjected to frustration, not by its own choice, but by the will of the one who subjected it, in hope 21that[e] the creation itself will be liberated from its bondage to decay and brought into the glorious freedom of the children of God.

22We know that the whole creation has been groaning as in the pains of childbirth right up to the present time. 23Not only so, but we ourselves, who have the firstfruits of the Spirit, groan

---

a 6 Or mind set on the flesh　b 7 Or the mind set on the flesh
c 15 Or adoption　d 15 Aramaic for Father
e 20,21 Or subjected it in hope. 21For

inwardly as we wait eagerly for our adoption as sons, the redemption of our bodies. 24For in this hope we were saved. But hope that is seen is no hope at all. Who hopes for what he already has? 25But if we hope for what we do not yet have, we wait for it patiently.

26In the same way, the Spirit helps us in our weakness. We do not know what we ought to pray for, but the Spirit himself intercedes for us with groans that words cannot express. 27And he who searches our hearts knows the mind of the Spirit, because the Spirit intercedes for the saints in accordance with God's will.

More Than Conquerors

28And we know that in all things God works for the good of those who love him,[a] who[b] have been called according to his purpose. 29For those God foreknew he also predestined to be conformed to the likeness of his Son, that he might be the firstborn among many brothers. 30And those he predestined, he also called; those he called, he also justified; those he justified, he also glorified.

31What, then, shall we say in response to this? If God is for us, who can be against us? 32He who did not spare his own Son, but gave him up for us all—how will he not also, along with him, graciously give us all things? 33Who will bring any charge against those whom God has chosen? It is God who justifies. 34Who is he that condemns? Christ Jesus, who died—more than that, who was raised to life—is at the right hand of God and is also interceding for us. 35Who shall separate us from the love of Christ? Shall trouble or hardship or persecution or famine or nakedness or danger or sword? 36As it is written:

"For your sake we face death all day long;
　we are considered as sheep to be
　　slaughtered."[c]

37No, in all these things we are more than conquerors through him who loved us. 38For I am convinced that neither death nor life, neither angels nor demons,[d] neither the present nor the future, nor any powers, 39neither height nor depth, nor anything else in all creation, will be able to separate us from the love of God that is in Christ Jesus our Lord.

名分，乃是我們的身體得贖。24我們得救是在乎盼望；只是所見的盼望不是盼望，誰還盼望他所見的呢？（註：有古卷作「人所看見的何必再盼望呢？」）25但我們若盼望那所不見的，就必忍耐等候。

26況且，我們的軟弱有聖靈幫助，我們本不曉得當怎樣禱告，只是聖靈親自用說不出來的歎息替我們禱告。27鑒察人心的，曉得聖靈的意思，因為聖靈照着神的旨意替聖徒祈求。

得勝有餘

28我們曉得萬事都互相效力，叫愛神的人得益處，就是按他旨意被召的人。29因為他預先所知道的人，就預先定下效法他兒子的模樣，使他兒子在許多弟兄中作長子。30預先所定下的人又召他們來；所召來的人又稱他們為義；所稱為義的人又叫他們得榮耀。

31既是這樣，還有甚麼說的呢？神若幫助我們，誰能敵擋我們呢？32神既不愛惜自己的兒子為我們眾人捨了，豈不也把萬物和他一同白白地賜給我們嗎？33誰能控告神所揀選的人呢？有神稱他們為義了。（註：或作「是稱他們為義的神嗎？」）34誰能定他們的罪呢？有基督耶穌已經死了，而且從死裏復活，現今在神的右邊，也替我們祈求。（註：「有基督云云」，或作「是已經死了，而且從死裏復活，現今在神的右邊，也替我們祈求的基督耶穌嗎？」）35誰能使我們與基督的愛隔絕呢？難道是患難嗎？是困苦嗎？是逼迫嗎？是飢餓嗎？是赤身露體嗎？是危險嗎？是刀劍嗎？36如經上所記：
「我們為你的緣故終日被殺，
　人看我們如將宰的羊。」

37然而，靠着愛我們的主，在這一切的事上已經得勝有餘了。38因為我深信無論是死、是生，是天使、是掌權的，是有能的，是現在的事，是將來的事，39是高處的、是低處的，是別的受造之物，都不能叫我們與神的愛隔絕；這愛是在我們的主基督耶穌裏的。

---

a 28 Some manuscripts And we know that all things work together for good to those who love God   b 28 Or works together with those who love him to bring about what is good—with those who   c 36 Psalm 44:22   d 38 Or nor heavenly rulers

神全權的揀選

9 我在基督裏說真話，並不謊言，有我良心被聖靈感動，給我作見證。²我是大有憂愁，心裏時常傷痛。³為我弟兄、我骨肉之親，就是自己被咒詛，與基督分離，我也願意。⁴他們是以色列人，那兒子的名分、榮耀、諸約、律法、禮儀、應許，都是他們的。⁵列祖就是他們的祖宗，按肉體說，基督也是從他們出來的，他是在萬有之上，永遠可稱頌的神。阿們！

⁶這不是說神的話落了空，因為從以色列生的，不都是以色列人；⁷也不因為是亞伯拉罕的後裔，就都作他的兒女；惟獨「從以撒生的，才要稱為你的後裔。」⁸這就是說，肉身所生的兒女不是神的兒女，惟獨那應許的兒女才算是後裔。⁹因為所應許的話是這樣說：「到明年這時候我要來，撒拉必生一個兒子。」

¹⁰不但如此，還有利百加，既從一個人，就是從我們的祖宗以撒懷了孕，（¹¹雙子還沒有生下來，善惡還沒有作出來，只因要顯明神揀選人的旨意，不在乎人的行為，乃在乎召人的主。）¹²神就對利百加說：「將來大的要服侍小的。」¹³正如經上所記：「雅各是我所愛的，以掃是我所惡的。」

¹⁴這樣，我們可說甚麼呢？難道神有甚麼不公平嗎？斷乎沒有！¹⁵因他對摩西說：

「我要憐憫誰，就憐憫誰；
　要恩待誰，就恩待誰。」

¹⁶據此看來，這不在乎那定意的，也不在乎那奔跑的，只在乎發憐憫的神。¹⁷因為經上有話向法老說：「我將你興起來，特要在你身上彰顯我的權能，並要使我的名傳遍天下。」¹⁸如此看來，神要憐憫誰，就憐憫誰；要叫誰剛硬，就叫誰剛硬。

¹⁹這樣，你必對我說：「他為甚麼還指責人呢？有誰抗拒他的旨意呢？」²⁰你這個人哪，你是誰，竟敢

God's Sovereign Choice

9 I speak the truth in Christ—I am not lying, my conscience confirms it in the Holy Spirit— ²I have great sorrow and unceasing anguish in my heart. ³For I could wish that I myself were cursed and cut off from Christ for the sake of my brothers, those of my own race, ⁴the people of Israel. Theirs is the adoption as sons; theirs the divine glory, the covenants, the receiving of the law, the temple worship and the promises. ⁵Theirs are the patriarchs, and from them is traced the human ancestry of Christ, who is God over all, forever praised![a] Amen.

⁶It is not as though God's word had failed. For not all who are descended from Israel are Israel. ⁷Nor because they are his descendants are they all Abraham's children. On the contrary, "It is through Isaac that your offspring will be reckoned."[b] ⁸In other words, it is not the natural children who are God's children, but it is the children of the promise who are regarded as Abraham's offspring. ⁹For this was how the promise was stated: "At the appointed time I will return, and Sarah will have a son."[c]

¹⁰Not only that, but Rebekah's children had one and the same father, our father Isaac. ¹¹Yet, before the twins were born or had done anything good or bad—in order that God's purpose in election might stand: ¹²not by works but by him who calls—she was told, "The older will serve the younger."[d] ¹³Just as it is written: "Jacob I loved, but Esau I hated."[e]

¹⁴What then shall we say? Is God unjust? Not at all! ¹⁵For he says to Moses,

"I will have mercy on whom I have mercy,
　and I will have compassion on whom I have
　　compassion."[f]

¹⁶It does not, therefore, depend on man's desire or effort, but on God's mercy. ¹⁷For the Scripture says to Pharaoh: "I raised you up for this very purpose, that I might display my power in you and that my name might be proclaimed in all the earth."[g] ¹⁸Therefore God has mercy on whom he wants to have mercy, and he hardens whom he wants to harden.

¹⁹One of you will say to me: "Then why does God still blame us? For who resists his will?" ²⁰But who are you, O man, to talk back to God?

---

a 5 Or Christ, who is over all. God be forever praised! Or Christ.
God who is over all be forever praised!　b 7 Gen. 21:12
c 9 Gen. 18:10,14　d 12 Gen. 25:23　e 13 Mal. 1:2,3
f 15 Exodus 33:19　g 17 Exodus 9:16

"Shall what is formed say to him who formed it, 'Why did you make me like this?' *a* 21Does not the potter have the right to make out of the same lump of clay some pottery for noble purposes and some for common use?

22What if God, choosing to show his wrath and make his power known, bore with great patience the objects of his wrath—prepared for destruction? 23What if he did this to make the riches of his glory known to the objects of his mercy, whom he prepared in advance for glory— 24even us, whom he also called, not only from the Jews but also from the Gentiles? 25As he says in Hosea:

"I will call them 'my people' who are not my people;
    and I will call her 'my loved one' who is not my loved one,"*b*

26and,

"It will happen that in the very place where it was said to them,
    'You are not my people,'
they will be called 'sons of the living God.' "*c*

27Isaiah cries out concerning Israel:

"Though the number of the Israelites be like the sand by the sea,
    only the remnant will be saved.
28For the Lord will carry out
    his sentence on earth with speed and finality."*d*

29It is just as Isaiah said previously:

"Unless the Lord Almighty
    had left us descendants,
we would have become like Sodom,
    we would have been like Gomorrah."*e*

Israel's Unbelief

30What then shall we say? That the Gentiles, who did not pursue righteousness, have obtained it, a righteousness that is by faith; 31but Israel, who pursued a law of righteousness, has not attained it. 32Why not? Because they pursued it not by faith but as if it were by works. They stumbled over the "stumbling stone." 33As it is written:

向神強嘴呢？受造之物豈能對造他的說："你為甚麼這樣造我呢？" 21窰匠難道沒有權柄從一團泥裏拿一塊做成貴重的器皿，又拿一塊做成卑賤的器皿嗎？

22倘若神要顯明他的忿怒，彰顯他的權能，就多多忍耐寬容那可怒、預備遭毀滅的器皿，23又要將他豐盛的榮耀彰顯在那蒙憐憫、早預備得榮耀的器皿上。24這器皿就是我們被神所召的，不但是從猶太人中，也是從外邦人中。這有甚麼不可呢？25就像神在何西阿書上說：

"那本來不是'我子民的'，
    我要稱為我的子民；
本來不是'蒙愛的'，
    我要稱為蒙愛的。

26 "從前在甚麼地方對他們說：
    '你們不是我的子民'，
將來就在那裏
    稱他們為'永生神的兒子'。"

27以賽亞指着以色列人喊着說：

"以色列人
    雖多如海沙，
    得救的不過是剩下的餘數。
28因為主要在世上施行他的話，
    叫他的話都成全，
    速速地完結。"

29又如以賽亞先前說過：

"若不是萬軍之主
    給我們存留餘種，
我們早已像所多瑪、
    蛾摩拉的樣子了。"

以色列人的不信

30這樣，我們可說甚麼呢？那本來不追求義的外邦人反得了義，就是因信而得的義；31但以色列人追求律法的義，反得不着律法的義。32這是甚麼緣故呢？是因為他們不憑着信心求，只憑着行為求，他們正跌在那絆腳石上。33就如經上所記：

a 20 Isaiah 29:16; 45:9   *b* 25 Hosea 2:23   *c* 26 Hosea 1:10
d 28 Isaiah 10:22,23   *e* 29 Isaiah 1:9

"我在錫安放一塊
　絆腳的石頭，
　跌人的磐石，
信靠他的人
　必不至於羞愧。"

10 弟兄們，我心裏所願的，向神所求的，是要以色列人得救。²我可以證明他們向神有熱心，但不是按着真知識。³因為不知道神的義，想要立自己的義，就不服神的義了。⁴律法的總結就是基督，使凡信他的都得義。

⁵摩西寫着說："人若行那出於律法的義，就必因此活着。"⁶惟有出於信心的義如此說："你不要心裏說，'誰要升到天上去呢？'（就是要領下基督來。）⁷'誰要下到陰間去呢？'（就是要領基督從死裏上來。）⁸他到底怎麼說呢？他說："這道離你不遠，正在你口裏，在你心裏。"就是我們所傳信主的道。⁹你若口裏認耶穌為主，心裏信神叫他從死裏復活，就必得救。¹⁰因為人心裏相信，就可以稱義；口裏承認，就可以得救。¹¹經上說："凡信他的人，必不至於羞愧。"¹²猶太人和希臘人並沒有分別；因為眾人同有一位主，他也厚待一切求告他的人。¹³因為"凡求告主名的，就必得救。"

¹⁴然而人未曾信他，怎能求他呢？未曾聽見他，怎能信他呢？沒有傳道的，怎能聽見呢？¹⁵若沒有奉差遣，怎能傳道呢？如經上所記："報福音傳喜信的人，他們的腳蹤何等佳美！"

¹⁶只是人沒有都聽從福音。因為以賽亞說："主啊，我們所傳的有誰信呢？"¹⁷可見信道是從聽道來的，聽道是從基督的話來的。¹⁸但我說，人沒有聽見嗎？誠然聽見了。

"See, I lay in Zion a stone that causes men to
　stumble
and a rock that makes them fall,
and the one who trusts in him will never be
　put to shame."[a]

10 Brothers, my heart's desire and prayer to God for the Israelites is that they may be saved. ²For I can testify about them that they are zealous for God, but their zeal is not based on knowledge. ³Since they did not know the righteousness that comes from God and sought to establish their own, they did not submit to God's righteousness. ⁴Christ is the end of the law so that there may be righteousness for everyone who believes.

⁵Moses describes in this way the righteousness that is by the law: "The man who does these things will live by them."[b] ⁶But the righteousness that is by faith says: "Do not say in your heart, 'Who will ascend into heaven?'[c] (that is, to bring Christ down) ⁷"or 'Who will descend into the deep?'[d] (that is, to bring Christ up from the dead). ⁸But what does it say? "The word is near you; it is in your mouth and in your heart,"[e] that is, the word of faith we are proclaiming: ⁹That if you confess with your mouth, "Jesus is Lord," and believe in your heart that God raised him from the dead, you will be saved. ¹⁰For it is with your heart that you believe and are justified, and it is with your mouth that you confess and are saved. ¹¹As the Scripture says, "Anyone who trusts in him will never be put to shame."[f] ¹²For there is no difference between Jew and Gentile—the same Lord is Lord of all and richly blesses all who call on him, ¹³for, "Everyone who calls on the name of the Lord will be saved."[g]

¹⁴How, then, can they call on the one they have not believed in? And how can they believe in the one of whom they have not heard? And how can they hear without someone preaching to them? ¹⁵And how can they preach unless they are sent? As it is written, "How beautiful are the feet of those who bring good news!"[h]

¹⁶But not all the Israelites accepted the good news. For Isaiah says, "Lord, who has believed our message?"[i] ¹⁷Consequently, faith comes from hearing the message, and the message is heard through the word of Christ. ¹⁸But I ask: Did they not hear? Of course they did:

---

a 33 Isaiah 8:14; 28:16　　*b 5* Lev. 18:5　　*c 6* Deut. 30:12
d 7 Deut. 30:13　　*e 8* Deut. 30:14　　*f 11* Isaiah 28:16
g 13 Joel 2:32　　*h 15* Isaiah 52:7　　*i 16* Isaiah 53:1

"Their voice has gone out into all the earth,
　their words to the ends of the world."[a]

[19]Again I ask: Did Israel not understand? First,
Moses says,

"I will make you envious by those who are
　not a nation;
I will make you angry by a nation that has
　no understanding."[b]

[20]And Isaiah boldly says,

"I was found by those who did not seek me;
I revealed myself to those who did not ask
　for me."[c]

[21]But concerning Israel he says,

"All day long I have held out my hands
　to a disobedient and obstinate people."[d]

The Remnant of Israel

11 I ask then: Did God reject his people?
By no means! I am an Israelite myself, a
descendant of Abraham, from the tribe
of Benjamin. [2]God did not reject his people,
whom he foreknew. Don't you know what the
Scripture says in the passage about Elijah—how
he appealed to God against Israel: [3]"Lord, they
have killed your prophets and torn down your
altars; I am the only one left, and they are trying
to kill me"[e]? [4]And what was God's answer to
him? "I have reserved for myself seven thousand who have not bowed the knee to Baal."[f]
[5]So too, at the present time there is a remnant
chosen by grace. [6]And if by grace, then it is no
longer by works; if it were, grace would no longer
be grace.[g]

[7]What then? What Israel sought so earnestly
it did not obtain, but the elect did. The others
were hardened, [8]as it is written:

"God gave them a spirit of stupor,
　eyes so that they could not see
　and ears so that they could not hear,
to this very day."[h]

[9]And David says:

"他們的聲音傳遍天下，
　他們的言語傳到地極。"

[19]我再說，以色列人不知道嗎？先有
摩西說：

"我要用那不成子民的，
　惹動你們的憤恨；
我要用那無知的民，
　觸動你們的怒氣。"

[20]又有以賽亞放膽說：

"沒有尋找我的，我叫他們遇見；
沒有訪問我的，我向他們顯現。"

[21]至於以色列人，他說：

"我整天伸手
　招呼那悖逆、頂嘴的百姓。"

以色列的餘民

11 我且說，神棄絕了他的百姓
嗎？斷乎沒有！因為我也是
以色列人，亞伯拉罕的後
裔，屬便雅憫支派的。[2]神並沒有棄
絕他預先所知道的百姓。你們豈不曉
得經上論到以利亞是怎麼說的呢？他
在神面前怎樣控告以色列人說：
[3]"主啊，他們殺了你的先知，拆了
你的祭壇，只剩下我一個人，他們還
要尋索我的命。"[4]神的回話是怎麼
說的呢？他說："我為自己留下七千
人，是未曾向巴力屈膝的。"[5]如今
也是這樣，照着揀選的恩典，還有所
留的餘數。[6]既是出於恩典，就不在
乎行為，不然，恩典就不是恩典了。

[7]這是怎麼樣呢？以色列人所求
的，他們沒有得着，惟有蒙揀選的人
得着了，其餘的就成了頑梗不化的。
[8]如經上所記：
"神給他們昏迷的心，
　眼睛不能看見，
耳朵不能聽見，
　直到今日。"

[9]大衛也說：

a 18 Psalm 19:4　　b 19 Deut. 32:21　　c 20 Isaiah 65:1
d 21 Isaiah 65:2　　e 3 1 Kings 19:10,14　　f 4 1 Kings 19:18
g 6 Some manuscripts by grace. But if by works, then it is no
longer grace; if it were, work would no longer be work.
h 8 Deut. 29:4; Isaiah 29:10

"願他們的筵席變為網羅，變為機檻，
　　變為絆腳石，作他們的報應；
10願他們的眼睛昏矇，
　　　不得看見；
　　願你時常彎下他們的腰。"

被接上的枝子

11我且說，他們失腳是要他們跌倒嗎？斷乎不是！反倒因他們的過失，救恩便臨到外邦人，要激動他們發憤。12若他們的過失，為天下的富足，他們的缺乏，為外邦人的富足，何況他們的豐滿呢？

13我對你們外邦人說這話，因我是外邦人的使徒，所以敬重我的職分（註："敬重"原文作"榮耀"）。14或者可以激動我骨肉之親發憤，好救他們一些人。15若他們被丟棄，天下就得與神和好，他們被收納，豈不是死而復生嗎？16所獻的新麵若是聖潔，全團也就聖潔了；樹根若是聖潔，樹枝也就聖潔了。

17若有幾根枝子被折下來，你這野橄欖得接在其中，一同得着橄欖根的肥汁；18你就不可向舊枝子誇口；若是誇口，當知道不是你托着根，乃是根托着你。19你若說："那枝子被折下來是特為叫我接上。"20不錯！他們因為不信，所以被折下來；你因為信，所以立得住。你不可自高，反要懼怕。21神既不愛惜原來的枝子，也必不愛惜你。

22可見神的恩慈和嚴厲，向那跌倒的人是嚴厲的，向你是有恩慈的。只要你長久在他的恩慈裏，不然，你也要被砍下來。23而且他們若不是長久不信，仍要被接上，因為神能夠把他們從新接上。24你是從那天生的野橄欖上砍下來的，尚且逆着性得接在好橄欖上，何況這本樹的枝子要接在本樹上呢！

以色列全家都要得救

25弟兄們，我不願意你們不知道這奧秘（恐怕你們自以為聰明）：就是以色列人有幾分是硬心的，等到外邦人的數目添滿了，26於是以色列全家都要得救。如經上所記：

"May their table become a snare and a trap,
　a stumbling block and a retribution for them.
10May their eyes be darkened so they cannot
　see,
　and their backs be bent forever."[a]

Ingrafted Branches

11Again I ask: Did they stumble so as to fall beyond recovery? Not at all! Rather, because of their transgression, salvation has come to the Gentiles to make Israel envious. 12But if their transgression means riches for the world, and their loss means riches for the Gentiles, how much greater riches will their fullness bring!

13I am talking to you Gentiles. Inasmuch as I am the apostle to the Gentiles, I make much of my ministry 14in the hope that I may somehow arouse my own people to envy and save some of them. 15For if their rejection is the reconciliation of the world, what will their acceptance be but life from the dead? 16If the part of the dough offered as firstfruits is holy, then the whole batch is holy; if the root is holy, so are the branches.

17If some of the branches have been broken off, and you, though a wild olive shoot, have been grafted in among the others and now share in the nourishing sap from the olive root, 18do not boast over those branches. If you do, consider this: You do not support the root, but the root supports you. 19You will say then, "Branches were broken off so that I could be grafted in." 20Granted. But they were broken off because of unbelief, and you stand by faith. Do not be arrogant, but be afraid. 21For if God did not spare the natural branches, he will not spare you either.

22Consider therefore the kindness and sternness of God: sternness to those who fell, but kindness to you, provided that you continue in his kindness. Otherwise, you also will be cut off. 23And if they do not persist in unbelief, they will be grafted in, for God is able to graft them in again. 24After all, if you were cut out of an olive tree that is wild by nature, and contrary to nature were grafted into a cultivated olive tree, how much more readily will these, the natural branches, be grafted into their own olive tree!

All Israel Will Be Saved

25I do not want you to be ignorant of this mystery, brothers, so that you may not be conceited: Israel has experienced a hardening in part until the full number of the Gentiles has come in. 26And so all Israel will be saved, as it is written:

a 10 Psalm 69:22,23

"The deliverer will come from Zion;
he will turn godlessness away from Jacob.
[27] And this is[a] my covenant with them
when I take away their sins."[b]

[28] As far as the gospel is concerned, they are enemies on your account; but as far as election is concerned, they are loved on account of the patriarchs, [29] for God's gifts and his call are irrevocable. [30] Just as you who were at one time disobedient to God have now received mercy as a result of their disobedience, [31] so they too have now become disobedient in order that they too may now[c] receive mercy as a result of God's mercy to you. [32] For God has bound all men over to disobedience so that he may have mercy on them all.

Doxology

[33] Oh, the depth of the riches of the wisdom and[d] knowledge of God!
How unsearchable his judgments,
and his paths beyond tracing out!
[34] "Who has known the mind of the Lord?
Or who has been his counselor?"[e]
[35] "Who has ever given to God,
that God should repay him?"[f]
[36] For from him and through him and to him are all things.
To him be the glory forever! Amen.

Living Sacrifices

12 Therefore, I urge you, brothers, in view of God's mercy, to offer your bodies as living sacrifices, holy and pleasing to God—this is your spiritual[g] act of worship. [2] Do not conform any longer to the pattern of this world, but be transformed by the renewing of your mind. Then you will be able to test and approve what God's will is—his good, pleasing and perfect will.

[3] For by the grace given me I say to every one of you: Do not think of yourself more highly than you ought, but rather think of yourself with sober judgment, in accordance with the measure of faith God has given you. [4] Just as each of us has one body with many members, and these members do not all have the same function, [5] so in Christ we who are many form one body, and each member belongs to all the others. [6] We have different gifts, according to the grace given us. If

"必有一位救主從錫安出來，
要消除雅各家的一切罪惡。"
[27] 又說："我除去他們罪的時候，
這就是我與他們所立的約。"

[28] 就着福音說，他們為你們的緣故是仇敵；就着揀選說，他們為列祖的緣故是蒙愛的。[29] 因為神的恩賜和選召是沒有後悔的。[30] 你們從前不順服神，如今因他們的不順服，你們倒蒙了憐恤。[31] 這樣，他們也是不順服，叫他們因着施給你們的憐恤，現在也就蒙憐恤。[32] 因為神將眾人都圈在不順服之中，特意要憐恤眾人。

頌讚

[33] 深哉，神豐富的智慧和知識！
他的判斷何其難測！
他的蹤跡何其難尋！

[34] "誰知道主的心？
誰作過他的謀士呢？"
[35] "誰是先給了他，
使他後來償還呢？"
[36] 因為萬有都是本於他，
倚靠他，歸於他。
願榮耀歸給他，直到永遠。阿們！

活祭

12 所以弟兄們，我以神的慈悲勸你們，將身體獻上，當作活祭，是聖潔的，是神所喜悅的，你們如此侍奉，乃是理所當然的。[2] 不要效法這個世界，只要心意更新而變化，叫你們察驗何為神的善良、純全、可喜悅的旨意。

[3] 我憑着所賜我的恩，對你們各人說：不要看自己過於所當看的，要照着神所分給各人信心的大小，看得合乎中道。[4] 正如我們一個身子上有好些肢體，肢體也不都是一樣的用處。[5] 我們這許多人，在基督裏成為一身，互相聯絡作肢體，也是如此。[6] 按我們所得的恩賜，各有不同：或

a 27 Or will be   b 27 Isaiah 59:20,21; 27:9; Jer. 31:33,34
c 31 Some manuscripts do not have now.   d 33 Or riches and
the wisdom and the   e 34 Isaiah 40:13   f 35 Job 41:11
g 1 Or reasonable

說預言，就當照着信心的程度說預言；⁷或作執事，就當專一執事；或作教導的，就當專一教導；⁸或作勸化的，就當專一勸化；施捨的，就當誠實；治理的，就當殷勤；憐憫人的，就當甘心。

愛

⁹愛人不可虛假，惡要厭惡，善要親近。¹⁰愛弟兄，要彼此親熱；恭敬人，要彼此推讓。¹¹殷勤不可懶惰。要心裏火熱，常常服侍主。¹²在指望中要喜樂，在患難中要忍耐，禱告要恆切。¹³聖徒缺乏要幫補，客要一味地款待。

¹⁴逼迫你們的，要給他們祝福；只要祝福，不可咒詛。¹⁵與喜樂的人要同樂；與哀哭的人要同哭。¹⁶要彼此同心，不要志氣高大，倒要俯就卑微的人（註："人"或作"事"）。不要自以為聰明。

¹⁷不要以惡報惡。眾人以為美的事，要留心去做。¹⁸若是能行，總要盡力與眾人和睦。¹⁹親愛的弟兄，不要自己伸冤，寧可讓步，聽憑主怒（註：或作"讓人發怒"）。因為經上記着："主說：伸冤在我，我必報應。"²⁰所以，

"你的仇敵若餓了，就給他吃；
　　若渴了，就給他喝。
　因為你這樣行，
　　就是把炭火堆在他的頭上。"

²¹你不可為惡所勝，反要以善勝惡。

順服掌權者

13 在上有權柄的，人人當順服他，因為沒有權柄不是出於神的，凡掌權的都是神所命的。²所以抗拒掌權的，就是抗拒神的命；抗拒的必自取刑罰。³作官的原不是叫行善的懼怕，乃是叫作惡的懼怕。你願意不懼怕掌權的嗎？你只要行善，就可得他的稱讚，⁴因為他是神的用人，是與你有益的。

a man's gift is prophesying, let him use it in proportion to his[a] faith. ⁷If it is serving, let him serve; if it is teaching, let him teach; ⁸if it is encouraging, let him encourage; if it is contributing to the needs of others, let him give generously; if it is leadership, let him govern diligently; if it is showing mercy, let him do it cheerfully.

Love

⁹Love must be sincere. Hate what is evil; cling to what is good. ¹⁰Be devoted to one another in brotherly love. Honor one another above yourselves. ¹¹Never be lacking in zeal, but keep your spiritual fervor, serving the Lord. ¹²Be joyful in hope, patient in affliction, faithful in prayer. ¹³Share with God's people who are in need. Practice hospitality.

¹⁴Bless those who persecute you; bless and do not curse. ¹⁵Rejoice with those who rejoice; mourn with those who mourn. ¹⁶Live in harmony with one another. Do not be proud, but be willing to associate with people of low position.[b] Do not be conceited.

¹⁷Do not repay anyone evil for evil. Be careful to do what is right in the eyes of everybody. ¹⁸If it is possible, as far as it depends on you, live at peace with everyone. ¹⁹Do not take revenge, my friends, but leave room for God's wrath, for it is written: "It is mine to avenge; I will repay,"[c] says the Lord. ²⁰On the contrary:

"If your enemy is hungry, feed him;
　if he is thirsty, give him something to drink.
In doing this, you will heap burning coals on
　his head."[d]

²¹Do not be overcome by evil, but overcome evil with good.

Submission to the Authorities

13 Everyone must submit himself to the governing authorities, for there is no authority except that which God has established. The authorities that exist have been established by God. ²Consequently, he who rebels against the authority is rebelling against what God has instituted, and those who do so will bring judgment on themselves. ³For rulers hold no terror for those who do right, but for those who do wrong. Do you want to be free from fear of the one in authority? Then do what is right and he will commend you. ⁴For he is God's servant to do you good. But if you do

---

a 6 Or in agreement with the   b 16 Or willing to do menial work
c 19 Deut. 32:35   d 20 Prov. 25:21,22

wrong, be afraid, for he does not bear the sword for nothing. He is God's servant, an agent of wrath to bring punishment on the wrongdoer. [5]Therefore, it is necessary to submit to the authorities, not only because of possible punishment but also because of conscience.

[6]This is also why you pay taxes, for the authorities are God's servants, who give their full time to governing. [7]Give everyone what you owe him: If you owe taxes, pay taxes; if revenue, then revenue; if respect, then respect; if honor, then honor.

Love, for the Day Is Near

[8]Let no debt remain outstanding, except the continuing debt to love one another, for he who loves his fellowman has fulfilled the law. [9]The commandments, "Do not commit adultery," "Do not murder," "Do not steal," "Do not covet,"[a] and whatever other commandment there may be, are summed up in this one rule: "Love your neighbor as yourself."[b] [10]Love does no harm to its neighbor. Therefore love is the fulfillment of the law.

[11]And do this, understanding the present time. The hour has come for you to wake up from your slumber, because our salvation is nearer now than when we first believed. [12]The night is nearly over; the day is almost here. So let us put aside the deeds of darkness and put on the armor of light. [13]Let us behave decently, as in the daytime, not in orgies and drunkenness, not in sexual immorality and debauchery, not in dissension and jealousy. [14]Rather, clothe yourselves with the Lord Jesus Christ, and do not think about how to gratify the desires of the sinful nature.[c]

The Weak and the Strong

14 Accept him whose faith is weak, without passing judgment on disputable matters. [2]One man's faith allows him to eat everything, but another man, whose faith is weak, eats only vegetables. [3]The man who eats everything must not look down on him who does not, and the man who does not eat everything must not condemn the man who does, for God has accepted him. [4]Who are you to judge someone else's servant? To his own master he stands or falls. And he will stand, for the Lord is able to make him stand.

[5]One man considers one day more sacred than another; another man considers every day alike. Each one should be fully convinced in his

你若作惡，卻當懼怕，因為他不是空空地佩劍。他是神的用人，是伸冤的，刑罰那作惡的。[5]所以你們必須順服，不但是因為刑罰，也是因為良心。

[6]你們納糧也為這個緣故，因他們是神的差役，常常特管這事。[7]凡人所當得的，就給他；當得糧的，給他納糧；當得稅的，給他上稅；當懼怕的，懼怕他；當恭敬的，恭敬他。

當彼此相愛，因白晝將近

[8]凡事都不可虧欠人，惟有彼此相愛，要常以為虧欠，因為愛人的就完全了律法。[9]像那「不可姦淫」，「不可殺人」，「不可偷盜」，「不可貪婪」，或有別的誡命，都包在「愛人如己」這一句話之內了。[10]愛是不加害與人的，所以愛就完全了律法。

[11]再者，你們曉得現今就是該趁早睡醒的時候，因為我們得救，現今比初信的時候更近了。[12]黑夜已深，白晝將近，我們就當脫去暗昧的行為，帶上光明的兵器。[13]行事為人要端正，好像行在白晝。不可荒宴醉酒，不可好色邪蕩，不可爭競嫉妒。[14]總要披戴主耶穌基督，不要為肉體安排，去放縱私慾。

軟弱的與剛強的

14 信心軟弱的，你們要接納，但不要辯論所疑惑的事。[2]有人信百物都可吃，但那軟弱的，只吃蔬菜。[3]吃的人不可輕看不吃的人，不吃的人不可論斷吃的人，因為神已經收納他了。[4]你是誰，竟論斷別人的僕人呢？他或站住，或跌倒，自有他的主人在，而且他也必要站住，因為主能使他站住。

[5]有人看這日比那日強，有人看日日都是一樣，只是各人心裏要意見

---

a 9 Exodus 20:13-15,17; Deut. 5:17-19,21   *b 9* Lev. 19:18
c 14 Or *the flesh*

堅定。6守日的人，是為主守的。吃的人，是為主吃的，因他感謝神；不吃的人，是為主不吃的，也感謝神。7我們沒有一個人為自己活，也沒有一個人為自己死。8我們若活着，是為主而活；若死了，是為主而死。所以我們或活或死，總是主的人。

9因此基督死了，又活了，為要作死人並活人的主。10你這個人，為甚麼論斷弟兄呢？又為甚麼輕看弟兄呢？因我們都要站在神的臺前。11經上寫着：

“主說：‘我憑着我的永生起誓，
萬膝必向我跪拜，
萬口必向我承認。’”

12這樣看來，我們各人必要將自己的事在神面前說明。

13所以我們不可再彼此論斷，寧可定意，誰也不給弟兄放下絆腳跌人之物。14我憑着主耶穌確知深信，凡物本來沒有不潔淨的，惟獨人以為不潔淨的，在他就不潔淨了。15你若因食物叫弟兄憂愁，就不是按着愛人的道理行。基督已經替他死，你不可因你的食物叫他敗壞。16不可叫你的善被人毀謗，17因為神的國不在乎吃喝，只在乎公義、和平並聖靈中的喜樂。18在這幾樣上服侍基督的，就為神所喜悅，又為人所稱許。

19所以，我們務要追求和睦的事與彼此建立德行的事。20不可因食物毀壞神的工程。凡物固然潔淨，但有人因食物叫人跌倒，就是他的罪了。21無論是吃肉，是喝酒，是甚麼別的事，叫弟兄跌倒，一概不做才好。

22你有信心，就當在神面前守着。人在自己以為可行的事上能不自責，就有福了。23若有疑心而吃的，就必有罪。因為他吃，不是出於信心；凡不出於信心的都是罪。

own mind. 6He who regards one day as special, does so to the Lord. He who eats meat, eats to the Lord, for he gives thanks to God; and he who abstains, does so to the Lord and gives thanks to God. 7For none of us lives to himself alone and none of us dies to himself alone. 8If we live, we live to the Lord; and if we die, we die to the Lord. So, whether we live or die, we belong to the Lord.

9For this very reason, Christ died and returned to life so that he might be the Lord of both the dead and the living. 10You, then, why do you judge your brother? Or why do you look down on your brother? For we will all stand before God's judgment seat. 11It is written:

" 'As surely as I live,' says the Lord,
'every knee will bow before me;
every tongue will confess to God.' "*a*

12So then, each of us will give an account of himself to God.

13Therefore let us stop passing judgment on one another. Instead, make up your mind not to put any stumbling block or obstacle in your brother's way. 14As one who is in the Lord Jesus, I am fully convinced that no food*b* is unclean in itself. But if anyone regards something as unclean, then for him it is unclean. 15If your brother is distressed because of what you eat, you are no longer acting in love. Do not by your eating destroy your brother for whom Christ died. 16Do not allow what you consider good to be spoken of as evil. 17For the kingdom of God is not a matter of eating and drinking, but of righteousness, peace and joy in the Holy Spirit, 18because anyone who serves Christ in this way is pleasing to God and approved by men.

19Let us therefore make every effort to do what leads to peace and to mutual edification. 20Do not destroy the work of God for the sake of food. All food is clean, but it is wrong for a man to eat anything that causes someone else to stumble. 21It is better not to eat meat or drink wine or to do anything else that will cause your brother to fall.

22So whatever you believe about these things keep between yourself and God. Blessed is the man who does not condemn himself by what he approves. 23But the man who has doubts is condemned if he eats, because his eating is not from faith; and everything that does not come from faith is sin.

a 11 Isaiah 45:23　　*b 14* Or *that nothing*

15

We who are strong ought to bear with the failings of the weak and not to please ourselves. [2]Each of us should please his neighbor for his good, to build him up. [3]For even Christ did not please himself but, as it is written: "The insults of those who insult you have fallen on me."[a] [4]For everything that was written in the past was written to teach us, so that through endurance and the encouragement of the Scriptures we might have hope.

[5]May the God who gives endurance and encouragement give you a spirit of unity among yourselves as you follow Christ Jesus, [6]so that with one heart and mouth you may glorify the God and Father of our Lord Jesus Christ.

[7]Accept one another, then, just as Christ accepted you, in order to bring praise to God. [8]For I tell you that Christ has become a servant of the Jews[b] on behalf of God's truth, to confirm the promises made to the patriarchs [9]so that the Gentiles may glorify God for his mercy, as it is written:

"Therefore I will praise you among the
    Gentiles;
I will sing hymns to your name."[c]

[10]Again, it says,

"Rejoice, O Gentiles, with his people."[d]

[11]And again,

"Praise the Lord, all you Gentiles,
    and sing praises to him, all you peoples."[e]

[12]And again, Isaiah says,

"The Root of Jesse will spring up,
    one who will arise to rule over the nations;
    the Gentiles will hope in him."[f]

[13]May the God of hope fill you with all joy and peace as you trust in him, so that you may overflow with hope by the power of the Holy Spirit.

Paul the Minister to the Gentiles

[14]I myself am convinced, my brothers, that you yourselves are full of goodness, complete in knowledge and competent to instruct one anoth-

15

我們堅固的人應該擔代不堅固人的軟弱，不求自己的喜悅。[2]我們各人務要叫鄰舍喜悅，使他得益處，建立德行。[3]因為基督也不求自己的喜悅，如經上所記：「辱罵你人的辱罵都落在我身上。」[4]從前所寫的聖經都是為教訓我們寫的，叫我們因聖經所生的忍耐和安慰，可以得着盼望。

[5]但願賜忍耐、安慰的神，叫你們彼此同心，效法基督耶穌，[6]一心一口榮耀神、我們主耶穌基督的父。

[7]所以你們要彼此接納，如同基督接納你們一樣，使榮耀歸與神。[8]我說，基督是為神真理作了受割禮人的執事，要證實所應許列祖的話，[9]並叫外邦人因他的憐憫榮耀神。如經上所記：

「因此我要在外邦中稱讚你，
    歌頌你的名。」

[10]又說：

「你們外邦人當與主的百姓一同歡樂。」

[11]又說：

「外邦啊，你們當讚美主！
    萬民哪，你們都當頌讚他！」

[12]又有以賽亞說：

「將來有耶西的根，
    就是那興起來要治理外邦的，
    外邦人要仰望他。」

[13]但願使人有盼望的神，因信將諸般的喜樂平安充滿你們的心，使你們藉着聖靈的能力大有盼望。

保羅為外邦人作僕役

[14]弟兄們，我自己也深信你們是滿有良善，充足了諸般的知識，也能

---

a 3 Psalm 69:9   b 8 Greek circumcision   c 9 2 Samuel 22:50; Psalm 18:49   d 10 Deut. 32:43   e 11 Psalm 117:1
f 12 Isaiah 11:10

彼此勸戒。¹⁵但我稍微放膽寫信給你們，是要提醒你們的記性，特因神所給我的恩典，¹⁶使我為外邦人作基督耶穌的僕役，作神福音的祭司，叫所獻上的外邦人，因着聖靈成為聖潔，可蒙悅納。

¹⁷所以論到神的事，我在基督耶穌裏有可誇的。¹⁸除了基督藉我做的那些事，我甚麼都不敢提，只提他藉我言語作為，用神蹟奇事的能力，並聖靈的能力，使外邦人順服。¹⁹甚至我從耶路撒冷，直轉到以利哩古，到處傳了基督的福音。²⁰我立了志向，不在基督的名被稱過的地方傳福音，免得建造在別人的根基上。²¹就如經上所記：

"未曾聞知他信息的，將要看見；
　　未曾聽過的，將要明白。"

²²我因多次被攔阻，總不得到你們那裏去。

保羅計劃去羅馬探訪

²³但如今在這裏再沒有可傳的地方，而且這好幾年，我切心想望到西班牙去的時候，可以到你們那裏，²⁴盼望從你們那裏經過，得見你們，先與你們彼此交往，心裏稍微滿足，然後蒙你們送行。²⁵但現在，我往耶路撒冷去供給聖徒。²⁶因為馬其頓和亞該亞人樂意湊出捐項給耶路撒冷聖徒中的窮人。²⁷這固然是他們樂意的，其實也算是所欠的債。因外邦人既然在他們屬靈的好處上有分，就當把養身之物供給他們。²⁸等我辦完了這事，把這善果向他們交付明白，我就要路過你們那裏，往西班牙去。²⁹我也曉得去的時候，必帶着基督豐盛的恩典而去。

³⁰弟兄們，我藉着我們主耶穌基督，又藉着聖靈的愛，勸你們與我一同竭力，為我祈求神，³¹叫我脫離在猶太不順從的人，也叫我為耶路撒冷所辦的捐項可蒙聖徒悅納，³²並

er. ¹⁵I have written you quite boldly on some points, as if to remind you of them again, because of the grace God gave me ¹⁶to be a minister of Christ Jesus to the Gentiles with the priestly duty of proclaiming the gospel of God, so that the Gentiles might become an offering acceptable to God, sanctified by the Holy Spirit.

¹⁷Therefore I glory in Christ Jesus in my service to God. ¹⁸I will not venture to speak of anything except what Christ has accomplished through me in leading the Gentiles to obey God by what I have said and done— ¹⁹by the power of signs and miracles, through the power of the Spirit. So from Jerusalem all the way around to Illyricum, I have fully proclaimed the gospel of Christ. ²⁰It has always been my ambition to preach the gospel where Christ was not known, so that I would not be building on someone else's foundation. ²¹Rather, as it is written:

"Those who were not told about him will see,
　　and those who have not heard will
　　understand."[a]

²²This is why I have often been hindered from coming to you.

Paul's Plan to Visit Rome

²³But now that there is no more place for me to work in these regions, and since I have been longing for many years to see you, ²⁴I plan to do so when I go to Spain. I hope to visit you while passing through and to have you assist me on my journey there, after I have enjoyed your company for a while. ²⁵Now, however, I am on my way to Jerusalem in the service of the saints there. ²⁶For Macedonia and Achaia were pleased to make a contribution for the poor among the saints in Jerusalem. ²⁷They were pleased to do it, and indeed they owe it to them. For if the Gentiles have shared in the Jews' spiritual blessings, they owe it to the Jews to share with them their material blessings. ²⁸So after I have completed this task and have made sure that they have received this fruit, I will go to Spain and visit you on the way. ²⁹I know that when I come to you, I will come in the full measure of the blessing of Christ.

³⁰I urge you, brothers, by our Lord Jesus Christ and by the love of the Spirit, to join me in my struggle by praying to God for me. ³¹Pray that I may be rescued from the unbelievers in Judea and that my service in Jerusalem may be acceptable to the saints there, ³²so that by God's

a 21 Isaiah 52:15

will I may come to you with joy and together with you be refreshed. ³³The God of peace be with you all. Amen.

Personal Greetings

16 I commend to you our sister Phoebe, a servant^a of the church in Cenchrea. ²I ask you to receive her in the Lord in a way worthy of the saints and to give her any help she may need from you, for she has been a great help to many people, including me.

³Greet Priscilla^b and Aquila, my fellow workers in Christ Jesus. ⁴They risked their lives for me. Not only I but all the churches of the Gentiles are grateful to them.

⁵Greet also the church that meets at their house.

Greet my dear friend Epenetus, who was the first convert to Christ in the province of Asia.

⁶Greet Mary, who worked very hard for you.

⁷Greet Andronicus and Junias, my relatives who have been in prison with me. They are outstanding among the apostles, and they were in Christ before I was.

⁸Greet Ampliatus, whom I love in the Lord.

⁹Greet Urbanus, our fellow worker in Christ, and my dear friend Stachys.

¹⁰Greet Apelles, tested and approved in Christ.

Greet those who belong to the household of Aristobulus.

¹¹Greet Herodion, my relative.

Greet those in the household of Narcissus who are in the Lord.

¹²Greet Tryphena and Tryphosa, those women who work hard in the Lord.

Greet my dear friend Persis, another woman who has worked very hard in the Lord.

¹³Greet Rufus, chosen in the Lord, and his mother, who has been a mother to me, too.

¹⁴Greet Asyncritus, Phlegon, Hermes, Patrobas, Hermas and the brothers with them.

¹⁵Greet Philologus, Julia, Nereus and his sister, and Olympas and all the saints with them.

¹⁶Greet one another with a holy kiss.

All the churches of Christ send greetings.

¹⁷I urge you, brothers, to watch out for those who cause divisions and put obstacles in your way that are contrary to the teaching you have learned. Keep away from them. ¹⁸For such people are not serving our Lord Christ, but their

---

叫我順着神的旨意，歡歡喜喜地到你們那裏，與你們同得安息。³³願賜平安的神常和你們眾人同在。阿們！

個人間安

16 我對你們舉薦我們的姊妹非比，她是堅革哩教會中的女執事。²請你們為主接待她，合乎聖徒的體統。她在何事上要你們幫助，你們就幫助她，因她素來幫助許多人，也幫助了我。

³問百基拉和亞居拉安。他們在基督耶穌裏與我同工，⁴也為我的命將自己的頸項置之度外。不但我感謝他們，就是外邦的眾教會也感謝他們。

⁵又問在他們家中的教會安。

問我所親愛的以弗尼土安，他在亞西亞是歸基督初結的果子。

⁶又問馬利亞安，她為你們多受勞苦。

⁷又問我親屬與我一同坐監的安多尼古和猶尼亞安，他們在使徒中是有名望的，也是比我先在基督裏。

⁸又問我在主裏面所親愛的暗伯利安。

⁹又問在基督裏與我們同工的耳巴奴並我所親愛的士大古安。

¹⁰又問在基督裏經過試驗的亞比利安。

問亞利多布家裏的人安。

¹¹又問我親屬希羅天安。

問拿其數家在主裏的人安。

¹²又問為主勞苦的土非拿氏和土富撒氏安。

問可親愛為主多受勞苦的彼息氏安。

¹³又問在主蒙揀選的魯孚和他母親安；他的母親就是我的母親。

¹⁴又問亞遜其土、弗勒干、黑米、八羅巴、黑馬，並與他們在一處的弟兄們安。

¹⁵又問非羅羅古和猶利亞、尼利亞和他姊妹，同阿林巴，並與他們在一處的眾聖徒安。

¹⁶你們親嘴問安，彼此務要聖潔。

基督的眾教會都問你們安。

¹⁷弟兄們，那些離間你們，叫你們跌倒，背乎所學之道的人，我勸你們要留意躲避他們。¹⁸因為這樣的人不服侍我們的主基督，只服侍自己的

---

a 1 Or deaconess   b 3 Greek Prisca, a variant of Priscilla

肚腹，用花言巧語誘惑那些老實人的心。19你們的順服已經傳於眾人，所以我為你們歡喜，但我願意你們在善上聰明，在惡上愚拙。

20賜平安的神，快要將撒但踐踏在你們腳下。願我主耶穌基督的恩常和你們同在！

21與我同工的提摩太和我的親屬路求、耶孫、所西巴德問你們安。

22我這代筆寫信的德丟，在主裏面問你們安。

23那接待我，也接待全教會的該猶問你們安。

24城內管銀庫的以拉都和兄弟括土問你們安。

25惟有神能照我所傳的福音和所講的耶穌基督，並照永古隱藏不言的奧秘，堅固你們的心。26這奧秘如今顯明出來，而且按着永生神的命，藉眾先知的書指示萬國的民，使他們信服真道。27願榮耀因耶穌基督歸與獨一全智的神，直到永遠。阿們！

own appetites. By smooth talk and flattery they deceive the minds of naive people. [19]Everyone has heard about your obedience, so I am full of joy over you; but I want you to be wise about what is good, and innocent about what is evil.

[20]The God of peace will soon crush Satan under your feet.

The grace of our Lord Jesus be with you.

[21]Timothy, my fellow worker, sends his greetings to you, as do Lucius, Jason and Sosipater, my relatives.

[22]I, Tertius, who wrote down this letter, greet you in the Lord.

[23]Gaius, whose hospitality I and the whole church here enjoy, sends you his greetings.

Erastus, who is the city's director of public works, and our brother Quartus send you their greetings.[a]

[25]Now to him who is able to establish you by my gospel and the proclamation of Jesus Christ, according to the revelation of the mystery hidden for long ages past, [26]but now revealed and made known through the prophetic writings by the command of the eternal God, so that all nations might believe and obey him— [27]to the only wise God be glory forever through Jesus Christ! Amen.

---

a 23 Some manuscripts their greetings. [24]May the grace of our Lord Jesus Christ be with all of you. Amen.

1 Corinthians

哥林多前書

1 Paul, called to be an apostle of Christ Jesus by the will of God, and our brother Sosthenes,

2 To the church of God in Corinth, to those sanctified in Christ Jesus and called to be holy, together with all those everywhere who call on the name of our Lord Jesus Christ—their Lord and ours:

3 Grace and peace to you from God our Father and the Lord Jesus Christ.

Thanksgiving

4 I always thank God for you because of his grace given you in Christ Jesus. **5** For in him you have been enriched in every way—in all your speaking and in all your knowledge— **6** because our testimony about Christ was confirmed in you. **7** Therefore you do not lack any spiritual gift as you eagerly wait for our Lord Jesus Christ to be revealed. **8** He will keep you strong to the end, so that you will be blameless on the day of our Lord Jesus Christ. **9** God, who has called you into fellowship with his Son Jesus Christ our Lord, is faithful.

Divisions in the Church

10 I appeal to you, brothers, in the name of our Lord Jesus Christ, that all of you agree with one another so that there may be no divisions among you and that you may be perfectly united in mind and thought. **11** My brothers, some from Chloe's household have informed me that there are quarrels among you. **12** What I mean is this: One of you says, "I follow Paul"; another, "I follow Apollos"; another, "I follow Cephas*a*"; still another, "I follow Christ."

13 Is Christ divided? Was Paul crucified for you? Were you baptized into*b* the name of Paul? **14** I am thankful that I did not baptize any of you except Crispus and Gaius, **15** so no one can say that you were baptized into my name. **16** (Yes, I also baptized the household of Stephanas; beyond that, I don't remember if I baptized any-

1 奉神旨意，蒙召作耶穌基督使徒的保羅同兄弟所提尼，

2 寫信給在哥林多神的教會，就是在基督耶穌裏成聖，蒙召作聖徒的，以及所有在各處求告我主耶穌基督之名的人。基督是他們的主，也是我們的主。

3 願恩惠、平安從神我們的父並主耶穌基督歸與你們！

感恩

4 我常為你們感謝我的神，因神在基督耶穌裏所賜給你們的恩惠，**5** 又因你們在他裏面凡事富足，口才、知識都全備。**6** 正如我為基督作的見證在你們心裏得以堅固，**7** 以至你們在恩賜上沒有一樣不及人的，等候我們的主耶穌基督顯現。**8** 他也必堅固你們到底，叫你們在我們主耶穌基督的日子無可責備。**9** 神是信實的，你們原是被他所召，好與他兒子——我們的主耶穌基督一同得分。

教會分黨紛爭

10 弟兄們，我藉我們主耶穌基督的名，勸你們都說一樣的話。你們中間也不可分黨，只要一心一意，彼此相合。**11** 因為革來氏家裏的人曾對我提起弟兄們來，說你們中間有爭分。**12** 我的意思就是你們各人說："我是屬保羅的"，"我是屬亞波羅的"，"我是屬磯法的"，"我是屬基督的"。

13 基督是分開的嗎？保羅為你們釘了十字架嗎？你們是奉保羅的名受了洗嗎？**14** 我感謝神，除了基利司布並該猶以外，我沒有給你們一個人施洗，**15** 免得有人說，你們是奉我的名受洗。**16** 我也給司提反家施過洗，此外給別人施洗沒有，我卻記不清。

---

a 12 That is, Peter   *b* 13 Or *in*; also in verse 15

17基督差遣我，原不是為施洗，乃是為傳福音，並不用智慧的言語，免得基督的十字架落了空。

基督是神的智慧和大能

18因為十字架的道理，在那滅亡的人為愚拙；在我們得救的人卻為神的大能。19就如經上所記：

"我要滅絕智慧人的智慧，
　廢棄聰明人的聰明。"

20智慧人在哪裏？文士在哪裏？這世上的辯士在哪裏？神豈不是叫這世上的智慧變成愚拙嗎？21世人憑自己的智慧，既不認識神，神就樂意用人所當作愚拙的道理拯救那些信的人，這就是神的智慧了。22猶太人是要神蹟，希臘人是求智慧；23我們卻是傳釘十字架的基督。在猶太人為絆腳石，在外邦人為愚拙；24但在那蒙召的，無論是猶太人、希臘人，基督總為神的能力，神的智慧。25因神的愚拙總比人智慧，神的軟弱總比人強壯。

26弟兄們哪，可見你們蒙召的，按着肉體有智慧的不多，有能力的不多，有尊貴的也不多。27神卻揀選了世上愚拙的，叫有智慧的羞愧；又揀選了世上軟弱的，叫那強壯的羞愧。28神也揀選了世上卑賤的，以及那無有的，為要廢掉那有的，29使一切有血氣的，在神面前一個也不能自誇。30但你們得在基督耶穌裏是本乎神，神又使他成為我們的智慧、公義、聖潔、救贖。31如經上所記："誇口的，當指着主誇口。"

2 弟兄們，從前我到你們那裏去，並沒有用高言大智對你們宣傳神的奧秘。2因為我曾定了主意，在你們中間不知道別的，只知道耶穌基督並他釘十字架。3我在你們那裏，又軟弱，又懼怕，又甚戰兢。4我說的話、講的道，不是用智慧委婉的言語，乃是

one else.) 17For Christ did not send me to baptize, but to preach the gospel—not with words of human wisdom, lest the cross of Christ be emptied of its power.

Christ the Wisdom and Power of God

18For the message of the cross is foolishness to those who are perishing, but to us who are being saved it is the power of God. 19For it is written:

"I will destroy the wisdom of the wise;
　the intelligence of the intelligent I will
　frustrate."[a]

20Where is the wise man? Where is the scholar? Where is the philosopher of this age? Has not God made foolish the wisdom of the world? 21For since in the wisdom of God the world through its wisdom did not know him, God was pleased through the foolishness of what was preached to save those who believe. 22Jews demand miraculous signs and Greeks look for wisdom, 23but we preach Christ crucified: a stumbling block to Jews and foolishness to Gentiles, 24but to those whom God has called, both Jews and Greeks, Christ the power of God and the wisdom of God. 25For the foolishness of God is wiser than man's wisdom, and the weakness of God is stronger than man's strength.

26Brothers, think of what you were when you were called. Not many of you were wise by human standards; not many were influential; not many were of noble birth. 27But God chose the foolish things of the world to shame the wise; God chose the weak things of the world to shame the strong. 28He chose the lowly things of this world and the despised things—and the things that are not—to nullify the things that are, 29so that no one may boast before him. 30It is because of him that you are in Christ Jesus, who has become for us wisdom from God—that is, our righteousness, holiness and redemption. 31Therefore, as it is written: "Let him who boasts boast in the Lord."[b]

2 When I came to you, brothers, I did not come with eloquence or superior wisdom as I proclaimed to you the testimony about God.[c] 2For I resolved to know nothing while I was with you except Jesus Christ and him crucified. 3I came to you in weakness and fear, and with much trembling. 4My message and my preaching were not with wise and per-

a 19 Isaiah 29:14　b 31 Jer. 9:24　c 1 Some manuscripts as I proclaimed to you God's mystery

suasive words, but with a demonstration of the Spirit's power, [5]so that your faith might not rest on men's wisdom, but on God's power.

Wisdom From the Spirit

[6]We do, however, speak a message of wisdom among the mature, but not the wisdom of this age or of the rulers of this age, who are coming to nothing. [7]No, we speak of God's secret wisdom, a wisdom that has been hidden and that God destined for our glory before time began. [8]None of the rulers of this age understood it, for if they had, they would not have crucified the Lord of glory. [9]However, as it is written:

"No eye has seen,
  no ear has heard,
  no mind has conceived
  what God has prepared for those who love
    him"[a] —

[10]but God has revealed it to us by his Spirit.

The Spirit searches all things, even the deep things of God. [11]For who among men knows the thoughts of a man except the man's spirit within him? In the same way no one knows the thoughts of God except the Spirit of God. [12]We have not received the spirit of the world but the Spirit who is from God, that we may understand what God has freely given us. [13]This is what we speak, not in words taught us by human wisdom but in words taught by the Spirit, expressing spiritual truths in spiritual words.[b] [14]The man without the Spirit does not accept the things that come from the Spirit of God, for they are foolishness to him, and he cannot understand them, because they are spiritually discerned. [15]The spiritual man makes judgments about all things, but he himself is not subject to any man's judgment:

[16]"For who has known the mind of the Lord
  that he may instruct him?"[c]

But we have the mind of Christ.

On Divisions in the Church

3 Brothers, I could not address you as spiritual but as worldly—mere infants in Christ. [2]I gave you milk, not solid food, for you were not yet ready for it. Indeed, you are still not ready. [3]You are still worldly. For since there is jealousy and quarreling among you,

---

a 9 Isaiah 64:4   b 13 Or Spirit, interpreting spiritual truths to spiritual men   c 16 Isaiah 40:13

用聖靈和大能的明證，[5]叫你們的信不在乎人的智慧，只在乎神的大能。

從聖靈來的智慧

[6]然而，在完全的人中，我們也講智慧。但不是這世上的智慧，也不是這世上有權有位將要敗亡之人的智慧。[7]我們講的，乃是從前所隱藏、神奧秘的智慧，就是神在萬世以前預定使我們得榮耀的。[8]這智慧，世上有權有位的人沒有一個知道的；他們若知道，就不把榮耀的主釘在十字架上了。[9]如經上所記：

"神為愛他的人所預備的，
  是眼睛未曾看見，
  耳朵未曾聽見，
  人心也未曾想到的。"

[10]只有神藉着聖靈向我們顯明了。
  因為聖靈參透萬事，就是神深奧的事也參透了。[11]除了在人裏頭的靈，誰知道人的事？像這樣，除了神的靈，也沒有人知道神的事。[12]我們所領受的，並不是世上的靈，乃是從神來的靈，叫我們能知道神開恩賜給我們的事。[13]並且我們講說這些事，不是用人智慧所指教的言語，乃是用聖靈所指教的言語，將屬靈的話解釋屬靈的事（註：或作"將屬靈的事講與屬靈的人"）。[14]然而，屬血氣的人不領會神聖靈的事，反倒以為愚拙，並且不能知道，因為這些事惟有屬靈的人才能看透。[15]屬靈的人能看透萬事，卻沒有一人能看透了他。

[16]"誰曾知道主的心
  去教導他呢？"

但我們是有基督的心了。

論教會中的紛爭

3 弟兄們，我從前對你們說話，不能把你們當作屬靈的，只得把你們當作屬肉體，在基督裏為嬰孩的。[2]我是用奶餵你們，沒有用飯餵你們。那時你們不能吃，就是如今還是不能。[3]你們仍是屬肉體的，因為在你們中間有嫉妒、紛爭，這豈不是屬乎肉體、照着世人的樣子行嗎？⁴有說：「我是屬保羅的。」有說：「我是屬亞波羅的。」這豈不是你們和世人一樣嗎？

⁵亞波羅算甚麼？保羅算甚麼？無非是執事，照主所賜給他們各人的，引導你們相信。⁶我栽種了，亞波羅澆灌了；惟有神叫他生長。⁷可見栽種的算不得甚麼，澆灌的也算不得甚麼；只在那叫他生長的神。⁸栽種的和澆灌的，都是一樣。但將來各人要照自己的工夫得自己的賞賜。⁹因為我們是與神同工的；你們是神所耕種的田地，所建造的房屋。

¹⁰我照神所給我的恩，好像一個聰明的工頭，立好了根基，有別人在上面建造，只是各人要謹慎怎樣在上面建造。¹¹因為那已經立好的根基就是耶穌基督，此外沒有人能立別的根基。¹²若有人用金、銀、寶石、草木、禾稭在這根基上建造，¹³各人的工程必然顯露，因為那日子要將它表明出來，有火發現，這火要試驗各人的工程怎樣。¹⁴人在那根基上所建造的工程若存得住，他就要得賞賜；¹⁵人的工程若被燒了，他就要受虧損，自己卻要得救；雖然得救，乃像從火裏經過的一樣。

¹⁶豈不知你們是神的殿，神的靈住在你們裏頭嗎？¹⁷若有人毀壞神的殿，神必要毀壞那人，因為神的殿是聖的，這殿就是你們。

¹⁸人不可自欺。你們中間若有人在這世界自以為有智慧，倒不如變作愚拙，好成為有智慧的。¹⁹因這世界的智慧，在神看是愚拙。如經上記着說：「主叫有智慧的，中了自己的詭計。」²⁰又說：「主知道智慧人的意念是虛妄的。」²¹所以無論誰，都不可拿人誇口，因為萬有全是你們的。²²或保羅，或亞波羅，或磯法，或世界，或生，或死，或現今的事，或將來的事，全是你們的。²³並且你們是屬基督的，基督又是屬神的。

基督的使徒

4 人應當以我們為基督的執事，為神奧秘事的管家。²所求於管家的，是要他有忠心。³我被你們論斷，或被別人論

are you not worldly? Are you not acting like mere men? ⁴For when one says, "I follow Paul," and another, "I follow Apollos," are you not mere men?

⁵What, after all, is Apollos? And what is Paul? Only servants, through whom you came to believe—as the Lord has assigned to each his task. ⁶I planted the seed, Apollos watered it, but God made it grow. ⁷So neither he who plants nor he who waters is anything, but only God, who makes things grow. ⁸The man who plants and the man who waters have one purpose, and each will be rewarded according to his own labor. ⁹For we are God's fellow workers; you are God's field, God's building.

¹⁰By the grace God has given me, I laid a foundation as an expert builder, and someone else is building on it. But each one should be careful how he builds. ¹¹For no one can lay any foundation other than the one already laid, which is Jesus Christ. ¹²If any man builds on this foundation using gold, silver, costly stones, wood, hay or straw, ¹³his work will be shown for what it is, because the Day will bring it to light. It will be revealed with fire, and the fire will test the quality of each man's work. ¹⁴If what he has built survives, he will receive his reward. ¹⁵If it is burned up, he will suffer loss; he himself will be saved, but only as one escaping through the flames.

¹⁶Don't you know that you yourselves are God's temple and that God's Spirit lives in you? ¹⁷If anyone destroys God's temple, God will destroy him; for God's temple is sacred, and you are that temple.

¹⁸Do not deceive yourselves. If any one of you thinks he is wise by the standards of this age, he should become a "fool" so that he may become wise. ¹⁹For the wisdom of this world is foolishness in God's sight. As it is written: "He catches the wise in their craftiness"[a]; ²⁰and again, "The Lord knows that the thoughts of the wise are futile."[b] ²¹So then, no more boasting about men! All things are yours, ²²whether Paul or Apollos or Cephas[c] or the world or life or death or the present or the future—all are yours, ²³and you are of Christ, and Christ is of God.

Apostles of Christ

4 So then, men ought to regard us as servants of Christ and as those entrusted with the secret things of God. ²Now it is required that those who have been given a trust must prove faithful. ³I care very little if I am

---

a 19 Job 5:13　　*b 20* Psalm 94:11　　*c 22* That is, Peter

judged by you or by any human court; indeed, I do not even judge myself. [4]My conscience is clear, but that does not make me innocent. It is the Lord who judges me. [5]Therefore judge nothing before the appointed time; wait till the Lord comes. He will bring to light what is hidden in darkness and will expose the motives of men's hearts. At that time each will receive his praise from God.

[6]Now, brothers, I have applied these things to myself and Apollos for your benefit, so that you may learn from us the meaning of the saying, "Do not go beyond what is written." Then you will not take pride in one man over against another. [7]For who makes you different from anyone else? What do you have that you did not receive? And if you did receive it, why do you boast as though you did not?

[8]Already you have all you want! Already you have become rich! You have become kings—and that without us! How I wish that you really had become kings so that we might be kings with you! [9]For it seems to me that God has put us apostles on display at the end of the procession, like men condemned to die in the arena. We have been made a spectacle to the whole universe, to angels as well as to men. [10]We are fools for Christ, but you are so wise in Christ! We are weak, but you are strong! You are honored, we are dishonored! [11]To this very hour we go hungry and thirsty, we are in rags, we are brutally treated, we are homeless. [12]We work hard with our own hands. When we are cursed, we bless; when we are persecuted, we endure it; [13]when we are slandered, we answer kindly. Up to this moment we have become the scum of the earth, the refuse of the world.

[14]I am not writing this to shame you, but to warn you, as my dear children. [15]Even though you have ten thousand guardians in Christ, you do not have many fathers, for in Christ Jesus I became your father through the gospel. [16]Therefore I urge you to imitate me. [17]For this reason I am sending to you Timothy, my son whom I love, who is faithful in the Lord. He will remind you of my way of life in Christ Jesus, which agrees with what I teach everywhere in every church.

[18]Some of you have become arrogant, as if I were not coming to you. [19]But I will come to you very soon, if the Lord is willing, and then I will find out not only how these arrogant people are talking, but what power they have. [20]For the kingdom of God is not a matter of talk but of power. [21]What do you prefer? Shall I come to you with a whip, or in love and with a gentle spirit?

斷，我都以為極小的事，連我自己也不論斷自己。[4]我雖不覺得自己有錯，卻也不能因此得以稱義；但判斷我的乃是主。[5]所以，時候未到，甚麼都不要論斷，只等主來，他要照出暗中的隱情，顯明人心的意念。那時，各人要從神那裏得着稱讚。

[6]弟兄們，我為你們的緣故，拿這些事轉比自己和亞波羅，叫你們效法我們不可過於聖經所記，免得你們自高自大，貴重這個，輕看那個。[7]使你與人不同的是誰呢？你有甚麼不是領受的呢？若是領受的，為何自誇，彷彿不是領受的呢？

[8]你們已經飽足了，已經豐富了，不用我們，自己就作王了。我願意你們果真作王，叫我們也得與你們一同作王。[9]我想神把我們使徒明明列在末後，好像定死罪的囚犯；因為我們成了一臺戲，給世人和天使觀看。[10]我們為基督的緣故算是愚拙的，你們在基督裏倒是聰明的；我們軟弱，你們倒強壯；你們有榮耀，我們倒被藐視。[11]直到如今，我們還是又飢、又渴、又赤身露體、又挨打、又沒有一定的住處，[12]並且勞苦，親手做工。被人咒罵，我們就祝福；被人逼迫，我們就忍受；[13]被人毀謗，我們就善勸。直到如今，人還把我們看作世界上的污穢，萬物中的渣滓。

[14]我寫這話，不是叫你們羞愧，乃是警戒你們，好像我所親愛的兒女一樣。[15]你們學基督的，師傅雖有一萬，為父的卻是不多，因我在基督耶穌裏用福音生了你們。[16]所以，我求你們效法我。[17]因此我已打發提摩太到你們那裏去；他在主裏面，是我所親愛、有忠心的兒子。他必提醒你們，記念我在基督裏怎樣行事，在各處各教會中怎樣教導人。

[18]有些人自高自大，以為我不到你們那裏去；[19]然而主若許我，我必快到你們那裏去；並且我所要知道的，不是那些自高自大之人的言語，乃是他們的權能。[20]因為神的國不在乎言語，乃在乎權能。[21]你們願意怎麼樣呢？是願意我帶着刑杖到你們那裏去呢？還是要我存慈愛溫柔的心呢？

逐出淫亂的弟兄！

5 風聞在你們中間有淫亂的事。這樣的淫亂連外邦人中也沒有，就是有人收了他的繼母。²你們還是自高自大，並不哀痛，把行這事的人從你們中間趕出去。³我身子雖不在你們那裏，心卻在你們那裏，好像我親自與你們同在，已經判斷了行這事的人。⁴就是你們聚會的時候，我的心也同在。奉我們主耶穌的名，並用我們主耶穌的權能，⁵要把這樣的人交給撒但，敗壞他的肉體，使他的靈魂在主耶穌的日子可以得救。

⁶你們這自誇是不好的，豈不知一點麵酵能使全團發起來嗎？⁷你們既是無酵的麵，應當把舊酵除淨，好使你們成為新團；因為我們逾越節的羔羊基督，已經被殺獻祭了。⁸所以我們守這節不可用舊酵，也不可用惡毒（註：或作「陰毒」）、邪惡的酵，只用誠實真正的無酵餅。

⁹我先前寫信給你們說：不可與淫亂的人相交。¹⁰此話不是指這世上一概行淫亂的，或貪婪的、勒索的，或拜偶像的；若是這樣，你們除非離開世界方可。¹¹但如今我寫信給你們說：若有稱為弟兄是行淫亂的，或貪婪的，或拜偶像的，或辱罵的，或醉酒的，或勒索的，這樣的人不可與他相交，就是與他吃飯都不可。

¹²因為審判教外的人與我何干？教內的人豈不是你們審判的嗎？¹³至於外人，有神審判他們。你們應當把那惡人從你們中間趕出去。

信徒彼此告狀

6 你們中間有彼此相爭的事，怎敢在不義的人面前求審，不在聖徒面前求審呢？²豈不知聖徒要審判世界嗎？若世界為你們所審，難道你們不配審判這最小的事嗎？³豈不知我們要審判天使嗎？何況今生的事呢！⁴既是這樣，你們若有今生的事當審判，是派教

Expel the Immoral Brother!

5 It is actually reported that there is sexual immorality among you, and of a kind that does not occur even among pagans: A man has his father's wife. ²And you are proud! Shouldn't you rather have been filled with grief and have put out of your fellowship the man who did this? ³Even though I am not physically present, I am with you in spirit. And I have already passed judgment on the one who did this, just as if I were present. ⁴When you are assembled in the name of our Lord Jesus and I am with you in spirit, and the power of our Lord Jesus is present, ⁵hand this man over to Satan, so that the sinful nature[a] may be destroyed and his spirit saved on the day of the Lord.

⁶Your boasting is not good. Don't you know that a little yeast works through the whole batch of dough? ⁷Get rid of the old yeast that you may be a new batch without yeast—as you really are. For Christ, our Passover lamb, has been sacrificed. ⁸Therefore let us keep the Festival, not with the old yeast, the yeast of malice and wickedness, but with bread without yeast, the bread of sincerity and truth.

⁹I have written you in my letter not to associate with sexually immoral people— ¹⁰not at all meaning the people of this world who are immoral, or the greedy and swindlers, or idolaters. In that case you would have to leave this world. ¹¹But now I am writing you that you must not associate with anyone who calls himself a brother but is sexually immoral or greedy, an idolater or a slanderer, a drunkard or a swindler. With such a man do not even eat.

¹²What business is it of mine to judge those outside the church? Are you not to judge those inside? ¹³God will judge those outside. "Expel the wicked man from among you."[b]

Lawsuits Among Believers

6 If any of you has a dispute with another, dare he take it before the ungodly for judgment instead of before the saints? ²Do you not know that the saints will judge the world? And if you are to judge the world, are you not competent to judge trivial cases? ³Do you not know that we will judge angels? How much more the things of this life! ⁴Therefore, if you have disputes about such matters, appoint as judges even men of little account in the church!*a* 5I say this to shame you. Is it possible that there is nobody among you wise enough to judge a dispute between believers? 6But instead, one brother goes to law against another—and this in front of unbelievers!

7The very fact that you have lawsuits among you means you have been completely defeated already. Why not rather be wronged? Why not rather be cheated? 8Instead, you yourselves cheat and do wrong, and you do this to your brothers.

9Do you not know that the wicked will not inherit the kingdom of God? Do not be deceived: Neither the sexually immoral nor idolaters nor adulterers nor male prostitutes nor homosexual offenders 10nor thieves nor the greedy nor drunkards nor slanderers nor swindlers will inherit the kingdom of God. 11And that is what some of you were. But you were washed, you were sanctified, you were justified in the name of the Lord Jesus Christ and by the Spirit of our God.

Sexual Immorality

12"Everything is permissible for me"—but not everything is beneficial. "Everything is permissible for me"—but I will not be mastered by anything. 13"Food for the stomach and the stomach for food"—but God will destroy them both. The body is not meant for sexual immorality, but for the Lord, and the Lord for the body. 14By his power God raised the Lord from the dead, and he will raise us also. 15Do you not know that your bodies are members of Christ himself? Shall I then take the members of Christ and unite them with a prostitute? Never! 16Do you not know that he who unites himself with a prostitute is one with her in body? For it is said, "The two will become one flesh."*b* 17But he who unites himself with the Lord is one with him in spirit.

18Flee from sexual immorality. All other sins a man commits are outside his body, but he who sins sexually sins against his own body. 19Do you not know that your body is a temple of the Holy Spirit, who is in you, whom you have received from God? You are not your own; 20you were bought at a price. Therefore honor God with your body.

會所輕看的人審判嗎？5我說這話是要叫你們羞恥。難道你們中間沒有一個智慧人能審斷弟兄們的事嗎？6你們竟是弟兄與弟兄告狀，而且告在不信主的人面前。

7你們彼此告狀，這已經是你們的大錯了。為甚麼不情願受欺呢？為甚麼不情願吃虧呢？8你們倒是欺壓人、虧負人，況且所欺壓、所虧負的就是弟兄！

9你們豈不知不義的人不能承受神的國嗎？不要自欺！無論是淫亂的、拜偶像的、姦淫的、作變童的、親男色的、10偷竊的、貪婪的、醉酒的、辱罵的、勒索的，都不能承受神的國。11你們中間也有人從前是這樣；但如今你們奉主耶穌基督的名，並藉着我們神的靈，已經洗淨、成聖、稱義了。

淫行

12凡事我都可行，但不都有益處；凡事我都可行，但無論哪一件，我總不受它的轄制。13食物是為肚腹，肚腹是為食物；但神要叫這兩樣都廢壞。身子不是為淫亂，乃是為主；主也是為身子。14並且神已經叫主復活，也要用自己的能力叫我們復活。15豈不知你們的身子是基督的肢體嗎？我可以將基督的肢體作為娼妓的肢體嗎？斷乎不可！16豈不知與娼妓聯合的，便是與她成為一體嗎？因為主說："二人要成為一體。"17但與主聯合的，便是與主成為一靈。

18你們要逃避淫行。人所犯的，無論甚麼罪，都在身子以外；惟有行淫的，是得罪自己的身子。19豈不知你們的身子就是聖靈的殿嗎？這聖靈是從神而來，住在你們裏頭的；並且你們不是自己的人，20因為你們是重價買來的，所以要在你們的身子上榮耀神。

a 4 Or *matters, do you appoint as judges men of little account in the church?* *b* 16 Gen. 2:24

婚姻

7 論到你們信上所提的事，我說男不近女倒好。²但要免淫亂的事，男子當各有自己的妻子，女子也當各有自己的丈夫。³丈夫當用合宜之分待妻子，妻子待丈夫也要如此。⁴妻子沒有權柄主張自己的身子，乃在丈夫；丈夫也沒有權柄主張自己的身子，乃在妻子。⁵夫妻不可彼此虧負，除非兩相情願，暫時分房，為要專心禱告方可；以後仍要同房，免得撒但趁着你們情不自禁引誘你們。⁶我說這話，原是准你們的，不是命你們的。⁷我願意眾人像我一樣，只是各人領受神的恩賜，一個是這樣，一個是那樣。

⁸我對着沒有嫁娶的和寡婦說，若他們常像我就好。⁹倘若自己禁止不住，就可以嫁娶。與其慾火攻心，倒不如嫁娶為妙。

¹⁰至於那已經嫁娶的，我吩咐他們，其實不是我吩咐，乃是主吩咐說："妻子不可離開丈夫。¹¹若是離開了，不可再嫁，或是仍同丈夫和好。丈夫也不可離棄妻子。"

¹²我對其餘的人說，不是主說，倘若某弟兄有不信的妻子，妻子也情願和他同住，他就不要離棄妻子。¹³妻子有不信的丈夫，丈夫也情願和她同住，她就不要離棄丈夫。¹⁴因為不信的丈夫就因着妻子成了聖潔，並且不信的妻子就因着丈夫成了聖潔（註："丈夫"原文作"弟兄"）。不然，你們的兒女就不潔淨，但如今他們是聖潔的了。

¹⁵倘若那不信的人要離去，就由他離去吧！無論是弟兄、是姐妹，遇着這樣的事都不必拘束。神召我們原是要我們和睦。¹⁶你這作妻子的，怎麼知道不能救你的丈夫呢？你這作丈夫的，怎麼知道不能救你的妻子呢？

¹⁷只要照主所分給各人的，和神所召各人的而行。我吩咐各教會都是這樣。¹⁸有人已受割禮蒙召呢，就不要廢割禮；有人未受割禮蒙召

Marriage

7 Now for the matters you wrote about: It is good for a man not to marry.ᵃ ²But since there is so much immorality, each man should have his own wife, and each woman her own husband. ³The husband should fulfill his marital duty to his wife, and likewise the wife to her husband. ⁴The wife's body does not belong to her alone but also to her husband. In the same way, the husband's body does not belong to him alone but also to his wife. ⁵Do not deprive each other except by mutual consent and for a time, so that you may devote yourselves to prayer. Then come together again so that Satan will not tempt you because of your lack of self-control. ⁶I say this as a concession, not as a command. ⁷I wish that all men were as I am. But each man has his own gift from God; one has this gift, another has that.

⁸Now to the unmarried and the widows I say: It is good for them to stay unmarried, as I am. ⁹But if they cannot control themselves, they should marry, for it is better to marry than to burn with passion.

¹⁰To the married I give this command (not I, but the Lord): A wife must not separate from her husband. ¹¹But if she does, she must remain unmarried or else be reconciled to her husband. And a husband must not divorce his wife.

¹²To the rest I say this (I, not the Lord): If any brother has a wife who is not a believer and she is willing to live with him, he must not divorce her. ¹³And if a woman has a husband who is not a believer and he is willing to live with her, she must not divorce him. ¹⁴For the unbelieving husband has been sanctified through his wife, and the unbelieving wife has been sanctified through her believing husband. Otherwise your children would be unclean, but as it is, they are holy.

¹⁵But if the unbeliever leaves, let him do so. A believing man or woman is not bound in such circumstances; God has called us to live in peace. ¹⁶How do you know, wife, whether you will save your husband? Or, how do you know, husband, whether you will save your wife?

¹⁷Nevertheless, each one should retain the place in life that the Lord assigned to him and to which God has called him. This is the rule I lay down in all the churches. ¹⁸Was a man already circumcised when he was called? He should not become uncircumcised. Was a man uncircum-

---

a 1 Or "It is good for a man not to have sexual relations with a woman."

cised when he was called? He should not be circumcised. [19]Circumcision is nothing and uncircumcision is nothing. Keeping God's commands is what counts. [20]Each one should remain in the situation which he was in when God called him. [21]Were you a slave when you were called? Don't let it trouble you—although if you can gain your freedom, do so. [22]For he who was a slave when he was called by the Lord is the Lord's freedman; similarly, he who was a free man when he was called is Christ's slave. [23]You were bought at a price; do not become slaves of men. [24]Brothers, each man, as responsible to God, should remain in the situation God called him to.

[25]Now about virgins: I have no command from the Lord, but I give a judgment as one who by the Lord's mercy is trustworthy. [26]Because of the present crisis, I think that it is good for you to remain as you are. [27]Are you married? Do not seek a divorce. Are you unmarried? Do not look for a wife. [28]But if you do marry, you have not sinned; and if a virgin marries, she has not sinned. But those who marry will face many troubles in this life, and I want to spare you this.

[29]What I mean, brothers, is that the time is short. From now on those who have wives should live as if they had none; [30]those who mourn, as if they did not; those who are happy, as if they were not; those who buy something, as if it were not theirs to keep; [31]those who use the things of the world, as if not engrossed in them. For this world in its present form is passing away.

[32]I would like you to be free from concern. An unmarried man is concerned about the Lord's affairs—how he can please the Lord. [33]But a married man is concerned about the affairs of this world—how he can please his wife— [34]and his interests are divided. An unmarried woman or virgin is concerned about the Lord's affairs: Her aim is to be devoted to the Lord in both body and spirit. But a married woman is concerned about the affairs of this world—how she can please her husband. [35]I am saying this for your own good, not to restrict you, but that you may live in a right way in undivided devotion to the Lord.

[36]If anyone thinks he is acting improperly toward the virgin he is engaged to, and if she is getting along in years and he feels he ought to marry, he should do as he wants. He is not sinning. They should get married. [37]But the man who has settled the matter in his own mind, who is under no compulsion but has control over his own will, and who has made up his mind not to marry the virgin—this man also does the right

呢，就不要受割禮。[19]受割禮算不得甚麼，不受割禮也算不得甚麼，只要守神的誡命就是了。[20]各人蒙召的時候是甚麼身分，仍要守住這身分。[21]你是作奴隸蒙召的嗎？不要因此憂慮。若能以自由，就求自由更好。[22]因為作奴僕蒙召於主的，就是主所釋放的人；作自由之人蒙召的，就是基督的奴僕。[23]你們是重價買來的，不要作人的奴僕。[24]弟兄們，你們各人蒙召的時候是甚麼身分，仍要在神面前守住這身分。

[25]論到童身的人，我沒有主的命令，但我既蒙主憐恤能作忠心的人，就把自己的意見告訴你們。[26]因現今的艱難，據我看來，人不如守素安常才好。[27]你有妻子纏着呢，就不要求脫離；你沒有妻子纏着呢，就不要求妻子。[28]你若娶妻，並不是犯罪；處女若出嫁，也不是犯罪。然而這等人肉身必受苦難，我卻願意你們免這苦難。

[29]弟兄們，我對你們說，時候減少了。從此以後，那有妻子的，要像沒有妻子；[30]哀哭的，要像不哀哭；快樂的，要像不快樂；置買的，要像無有所得；[31]用世物的，要像不用世物；因為這世界的樣子將要過去了。

[32]我願你們無所掛慮。沒有娶妻的，是為主的事掛慮，想怎樣叫主喜悅；[33]娶了妻的，是為世上的事掛慮，想怎樣叫妻子喜悅。[34]婦人和處女也有分別。沒有出嫁的，是為主的事掛慮，要身體、靈魂都聖潔；已經出嫁的，是為世上的事掛慮，想怎樣叫丈夫喜悅。[35]我說這話是為你們的益處，不是要牢籠你們，乃是要叫你們行合宜的事，得以殷勤服侍主，沒有分心的事。

[36]若有人以為自己待他的女兒不合宜，女兒也過了年歲，事又當行，他就可隨意辦理，不算有罪，叫二人成親就是了。[37]倘若人心裏堅定，沒有不得已的事，並且由得自己作主，心裏又決定了留下女兒不出嫁，如此

行也好。³⁸這樣看來，叫自己的女兒出嫁是好，不叫她出嫁更是好。

³⁹丈夫活着的時候，妻子是被約束的；丈夫若死了，妻子就可以自由，隨意再嫁，只是要嫁這在主裏面的人。⁴⁰然而按我的意見，若常守節更有福氣。我也想自己是被神的靈感動了。

祭偶像的食物

8 論到祭偶像之物，我們曉得我們都有知識。但知識是叫人自高自大，惟有愛心能造就人。²若有人以為自己知道甚麼，按他所當知道的，他仍是不知道。³若有人愛神，這人乃是神所知道的。

⁴論到吃祭偶像之物，我們知道偶像在世上算不得甚麼，也知道神只有一位，再沒有別的神。⁵雖有稱為神的，或在天、或在地，就如那許多的神，許多的主；⁶然而我們只有一位神，就是父，萬物都本於他，我們也歸於他；並有一位主，就是耶穌基督，萬物都是藉着他有的，我們也是藉着他有的。

⁷但人不都有這等知識。有人到如今因拜慣了偶像，就以為所吃的是祭偶像之物，他們的良心既然軟弱，也就污穢了。⁸其實食物不能叫神看中我們，因為我們不吃也無損，吃也無益。

⁹只是你們要謹慎，恐怕你們這自由竟成了那軟弱人的絆腳石。¹⁰若有人見你這有知識的在偶像的廟裏坐席，這人的良心若是軟弱，豈不放膽去吃那祭偶像之物嗎？¹¹因此，基督為他死的那軟弱弟兄，也就因你的知識沉淪了。¹²你們這樣得罪弟兄們，傷了他們軟弱的良心，就是得罪基督。¹³所以，食物若叫我弟兄

thing. ³⁸So then, he who marries the virgin does right, but he who does not marry her does even better.[a]

³⁹A woman is bound to her husband as long as he lives. But if her husband dies, she is free to marry anyone she wishes, but he must belong to the Lord. ⁴⁰In my judgment, she is happier if she stays as she is—and I think that I too have the Spirit of God.

Food Sacrificed to Idols

8 Now about food sacrificed to idols: We know that we all possess knowledge.[b] Knowledge puffs up, but love builds up. ²The man who thinks he knows something does not yet know as he ought to know. ³But the man who loves God is known by God.

⁴So then, about eating food sacrificed to idols: We know that an idol is nothing at all in the world and that there is no God but one. ⁵For even if there are so-called gods, whether in heaven or on earth (as indeed there are many "gods" and many "lords"), ⁶yet for us there is but one God, the Father, from whom all things came and for whom we live; and there is but one Lord, Jesus Christ, through whom all things came and through whom we live.

⁷But not everyone knows this. Some people are still so accustomed to idols that when they eat such food they think of it as having been sacrificed to an idol, and since their conscience is weak, it is defiled. ⁸But food does not bring us near to God; we are no worse if we do not eat, and no better if we do.

⁹Be careful, however, that the exercise of your freedom does not become a stumbling block to the weak. ¹⁰For if anyone with a weak conscience sees you who have this knowledge eating in an idol's temple, won't he be emboldened to eat what has been sacrificed to idols? ¹¹So this weak brother, for whom Christ died, is destroyed by your knowledge. ¹²When you sin against your brothers in this way and wound their weak conscience, you sin against Christ. ¹³Therefore, if what I eat causes my brother to fall into sin, I

---

a 36-38 Or ³⁶ If anyone thinks he is not treating his daughter properly, and if she is getting along in years, and he feels she ought to marry, he should do as he wants. He is not sinning. He should let her get married. ³⁷ But the man who has settled the matter in his own mind, who is under no compulsion but has control over his own will, and who has made up his mind to keep the virgin unmarried— this man also does the right thing. ³⁸ So then, he who gives his virgin in marriage does right, but he who does not give her in marriage does even better.   b 1 Or "We all possess knowledge," as you say

will never eat meat again, so that I will not cause him to fall.

The Rights of an Apostle

9 Am I not free? Am I not an apostle? Have I not seen Jesus our Lord? Are you not the result of my work in the Lord? ²Even though I may not be an apostle to others, surely I am to you! For you are the seal of my apostleship in the Lord.

³This is my defense to those who sit in judgment on me. ⁴Don't we have the right to food and drink? ⁵Don't we have the right to take a believing wife along with us, as do the other apostles and the Lord's brothers and Cephas[a]? ⁶Or is it only I and Barnabas who must work for a living?

⁷Who serves as a soldier at his own expense? Who plants a vineyard and does not eat of its grapes? Who tends a flock and does not drink of the milk? ⁸Do I say this merely from a human point of view? Doesn't the Law say the same thing? ⁹For it is written in the Law of Moses: "Do not muzzle an ox while it is treading out the grain."[b] Is it about oxen that God is concerned? ¹⁰Surely he says this for us, doesn't he? Yes, this was written for us, because when the plowman plows and the thresher threshes, they ought to do so in the hope of sharing in the harvest. ¹¹If we have sown spiritual seed among you, is it too much if we reap a material harvest from you? ¹²If others have this right of support from you, shouldn't we have it all the more?

But we did not use this right. On the contrary, we put up with anything rather than hinder the gospel of Christ. ¹³Don't you know that those who work in the temple get their food from the temple, and those who serve at the altar share in what is offered on the altar? ¹⁴In the same way, the Lord has commanded that those who preach the gospel should receive their living from the gospel.

¹⁵But I have not used any of these rights. And I am not writing this in the hope that you will do such things for me. I would rather die than have anyone deprive me of this boast. ¹⁶Yet when I preach the gospel, I cannot boast, for I am compelled to preach. Woe to me if I do not preach the gospel! ¹⁷If I preach voluntarily, I have a reward; if not voluntarily, I am simply discharging the trust committed to me. ¹⁸What then is my reward? Just this: that in preaching the gospel I may offer it free of charge, and so not make use of my rights in preaching it.

跌倒，我就永遠不吃肉，免得叫我弟兄跌倒了。

使徒的權柄

9 我不是自由的嗎？我不是使徒嗎？我不是見過我們的主耶穌嗎？你們不是我在主裏面所做之工嗎？²假若在別人我不是使徒，在你們我總是使徒。因為你們在主裏正是我作使徒的印證。

³我對那盤問我的人就是這樣分訴。⁴難道我們沒有權柄靠福音吃喝嗎？⁵難道我們沒有權柄娶信主的姊妹為妻，帶着一同往來，彷彿其餘的使徒和主的弟兄，並<u>磯法</u>一樣嗎？⁶獨有我與<u>巴拿巴</u>沒有權柄不做工嗎？

⁷有誰當兵自備糧餉呢？有誰栽葡萄園不吃園裏的果子呢？有誰牧養牛羊不吃牛羊的奶呢？⁸我說這話，豈是照人的意見？律法不也是這樣說嗎？⁹就如<u>摩西</u>的律法記着說："牛在場上踹穀的時候，不可籠住牠的嘴。"難道神所掛念的是牛嗎？¹⁰不全是為我們說的嗎？分明是為我們說的。因為耕種的當存着指望去耕種；打場的也當存得糧的指望去打場。¹¹我們若把屬靈的種子撒在你們中間，就是從你們收割奉養肉身之物，這還算大事嗎？¹²若別人在你們身上有這權柄，何況我們呢？

然而，我們沒有用過這權柄，倒凡事忍受，免得基督的福音被阻隔。¹³你們豈不知為聖事勞碌的，就吃殿中的物嗎？伺候祭壇的，就分領壇上的物嗎？¹⁴主也是這樣命定，叫傳福音的靠着福音養生。

¹⁵但這權柄我全沒有用過。我寫這話，並非要你們這樣待我，因為我寧可死，也不叫人使我所誇的落了空！¹⁶我傳福音原沒有可誇的，因為我是不得已的；若不傳福音，我便有禍了。¹⁷我若甘心做這事，就有賞賜；若不甘心，責任卻已經託付我了。¹⁸既是這樣，我的賞賜是甚麼呢？就是我傳福音的時候，叫人不花錢得福音，免得用盡我傳福音的權柄。

---

a 5 That is, Peter   *b* 9 Deut. 25:4

19我雖是自由的，無人轄管，然而我甘心作了眾人的僕人，為要多得人。20向猶太人，我就作猶太人，為要得猶太人；向律法以下的人，我雖不在律法以下，還是作律法以下的人，為要得律法以下的人；21向沒有律法的人，我就作沒有律法的人，為要得沒有律法的人。其實我在神面前，不是沒有律法；在基督面前，正在律法之下。22向軟弱的人，我就作軟弱的人，為要得軟弱的人；向甚麼樣的人，我就作甚麼樣的人。無論如何總要救些人。23凡我所行的，都是為福音的緣故，為要與人同得這福音的好處。

24豈不知在場上賽跑的都跑，但得獎賞的只有一人？你們也當這樣跑，好叫你們得着獎賞。25凡較力爭勝的，諸事都有節制，他們不過是要得能壞的冠冕；我們卻是要得不能壞的冠冕。26所以，我奔跑，不像無定向的；我鬥拳，不像打空氣的。27我是攻克己身，叫身服我，恐怕我傳福音給別人，自己反被棄絕了。

以色列歷史的鑑戒

10 弟兄們，我不願意你們不曉得，我們的祖宗從前都在雲下，都經海而過，2都在雲裏、海裏受洗歸了摩西，3並且都吃了一樣的靈食，4也都喝了一樣的靈水；所喝的是出於隨着他們的靈磐石，那磐石就是基督。5但他們中間多半是神不喜歡的人，所以在曠野倒斃。

6這些事都是我們的鑑戒，叫我們不要貪戀惡事，像他們那樣貪戀的；7也不要拜偶像，像他們有人拜的。如經上所記："百姓坐下吃喝，起來玩耍。"8我們也不要行姦淫，像他們有人行的，一天就倒斃了二萬三千人；9也不要試探主（註："主"有古卷作"基督"），像他們有人試探的，就被蛇所滅；10你們也不要發怨言，像他們有發怨言的，就被滅命的所滅。

11他們遭遇這些事都要作為鑑戒，並且寫在經上，正是警戒我們這末世的人。12所以，自己以為站得

19Though I am free and belong to no man, I make myself a slave to everyone, to win as many as possible. 20To the Jews I became like a Jew, to win the Jews. To those under the law I became like one under the law (though I myself am not under the law), so as to win those under the law. 21To those not having the law I became like one not having the law (though I am not free from God's law but am under Christ's law), so as to win those not having the law. 22To the weak I became weak, to win the weak. I have become all things to all men so that by all possible means I might save some. 23I do all this for the sake of the gospel, that I may share in its blessings.

24Do you not know that in a race all the runners run, but only one gets the prize? Run in such a way as to get the prize. 25Everyone who competes in the games goes into strict training. They do it to get a crown that will not last; but we do it to get a crown that will last forever. 26Therefore I do not run like a man running aimlessly; I do not fight like a man beating the air. 27No, I beat my body and make it my slave so that after I have preached to others, I myself will not be disqualified for the prize.

Warnings From Israel's History

10 For I do not want you to be ignorant of the fact, brothers, that our forefathers were all under the cloud and that they all passed through the sea. 2They were all baptized into Moses in the cloud and in the sea. 3They all ate the same spiritual food 4and drank the same spiritual drink; for they drank from the spiritual rock that accompanied them, and that rock was Christ. 5Nevertheless, God was not pleased with most of them; their bodies were scattered over the desert.

6Now these things occurred as examples[a] to keep us from setting our hearts on evil things as they did. 7Do not be idolaters, as some of them were; as it is written: "The people sat down to eat and drink and got up to indulge in pagan revelry."[b] 8We should not commit sexual immorality, as some of them did—and in one day twenty-three thousand of them died. 9We should not test the Lord, as some of them did—and were killed by snakes. 10And do not grumble, as some of them did—and were killed by the destroying angel.

11These things happened to them as examples and were written down as warnings for us, on whom the fulfillment of the ages has come. 12So,

a 6 Or types; also in verse 11　*b 7 Exodus 32:6*

if you think you are standing firm, be careful that you don't fall! [13]No temptation has seized you except what is common to man. And God is faithful; he will not let you be tempted beyond what you can bear. But when you are tempted, he will also provide a way out so that you can stand up under it.

Idol Feasts and the Lord's Supper

[14]Therefore, my dear friends, flee from idolatry. [15]I speak to sensible people; judge for yourselves what I say. [16]Is not the cup of thanksgiving for which we give thanks a participation in the blood of Christ? And is not the bread that we break a participation in the body of Christ? [17]Because there is one loaf, we, who are many, are one body, for we all partake of the one loaf.

[18]Consider the people of Israel: Do not those who eat the sacrifices participate in the altar? [19]Do I mean then that a sacrifice offered to an idol is anything, or that an idol is anything? [20]No, but the sacrifices of pagans are offered to demons, not to God, and I do not want you to be participants with demons. [21]You cannot drink the cup of the Lord and the cup of demons too; you cannot have a part in both the Lord's table and the table of demons. [22]Are we trying to arouse the Lord's jealousy? Are we stronger than he?

The Believer's Freedom

[23]"Everything is permissible"—but not everything is beneficial. "Everything is permissible"—but not everything is constructive. [24]Nobody should seek his own good, but the good of others.

[25]Eat anything sold in the meat market without raising questions of conscience, [26]for, "The earth is the Lord's, and everything in it."[a]

[27]If some unbeliever invites you to a meal and you want to go, eat whatever is put before you without raising questions of conscience. [28]But if anyone says to you, "This has been offered in sacrifice," then do not eat it, both for the sake of the man who told you and for conscience' sake[b] — [29]the other man's conscience, I mean, not yours. For why should my freedom be judged by another's conscience? [30]If I take part in the meal with thankfulness, why am I denounced because of something I thank God for?

[31]So whether you eat or drink or whatever you do, do it all for the glory of God. [32]Do not

穩的，須要謹慎，免得跌倒。[13]你們所遇見的試探，無非是人所能受的。神是信實的，必不叫你們受試探過於所能受的。在受試探的時候，總要給你們開一條出路，叫你們能忍受得住。

偶像的筵席與主的晚餐

[14]我所親愛的弟兄啊，你們要逃避拜偶像的事。[15]我好像對明白人說的，你們要審察我的話。[16]我們所祝福的杯，豈不是同領基督的血嗎？我們所擘開的餅，豈不是同領基督的身體嗎？[17]我們雖多，仍是一個餅、一個身體，因為我們都是分受這一個餅。

[18]你們看屬肉體的<u>以色列</u>人，那吃祭物的豈不是在祭壇上有分嗎？[19]我是怎麼說呢？豈是說祭偶像之物算得甚麼呢？或說偶像算得甚麼呢？[20]我乃是說：外邦人所獻的祭是祭鬼，不是祭神，我不願意你們與鬼相交。[21]你們不能喝主的杯，又喝鬼的杯；不能吃主的筵席又吃鬼的筵席。[22]我們可惹主的憤恨嗎？我們比他還有能力嗎？

信徒的自由

[23]凡事都可行，但不都有益處。凡事都可行，但不都造就人。[24]無論何人，不要求自己的益處，乃要求別人的益處。

[25]凡市上所賣的，你們只管吃，不要為良心的緣故問甚麼話，[26]因為地和其中所充滿的都屬乎主。

[27]倘有一個不信的人請你們赴席，你們若願意去，凡擺在你們面前的，只管吃，不要為良心的緣故問甚麼話。[28]若有人對你們說："這是獻過祭的物"，就要為那告訴你們的人，並為良心的緣故不吃。[29]我說的良心不是你的，乃是他的。我這自由為甚麼被別人的良心論斷呢？[30]我若謝恩而吃，為甚麼因我謝恩的物被人毀謗呢？

[31]所以，你們或吃或喝，無論做甚麼，都要為榮耀神而行。[32]不拘是

---

a 26 Psalm 24:1   *b* 28 Some manuscripts *conscience' sake, for* "*the earth is the Lord's and everything in it*"

猶太人，是希臘人，是神的教會，你們都不要使他跌倒，³³就好像我凡事都叫眾人喜歡，不求自己的益處，只求眾人的益處，叫他們得救。

11 ¹你們該效法我，像我效法基督一樣。

敬拜的規矩

²我稱讚你們，因為你們凡事記念我，又堅守我所傳給你們的。

³我願意你們知道，基督是各人的頭，男人是女人的頭，神是基督的頭。⁴凡男人禱告或是講道（註："講道"或作"說預言"。下同），若蒙着頭，就羞辱自己的頭。⁵凡女人禱告或是講道，若不蒙着頭，就羞辱自己的頭，因為這就如同剃了頭髮一樣。⁶女人若不蒙着頭，就該剪了頭髮；女人若以剪髮剃髮為羞愧，就該蒙着頭。⁷男人本不該蒙着頭，因為他是神的形像和榮耀，但女人是男人的榮耀。⁸起初，男人不是由女人而出，女人乃是由男人而出。⁹並且男人不是為女人造的，女人乃是為男人造的。¹⁰因此，女人為天使的緣故，應當在頭上有服權柄的記號。

¹¹然而照主的安排，女也不是無男，男也不是無女。¹²因為女人原是由男人而出，男人也是由女人而出；但萬有都是出乎神。¹³你們自己審察，女人禱告神，不蒙着頭是合宜的嗎？¹⁴你們的本性不也指示你們，男人若有長頭髮，便是他的羞辱嗎？¹⁵但女人有長頭髮，乃是她的榮耀，因為這頭髮是給她作蓋頭的。¹⁶若有人想要辯駁，我們卻沒有這樣的規矩，神的眾教會也是沒有的。

主的晚餐

¹⁷我現今吩咐你們的話，不是稱讚你們，因為你們聚會不是受益，

11 ¹Follow my example, as I follow the example of Christ.

Propriety in Worship

²I praise you for remembering me in everything and for holding to the teachings,[a] just as I passed them on to you.

³Now I want you to realize that the head of every man is Christ, and the head of the woman is man, and the head of Christ is God. ⁴Every man who prays or prophesies with his head covered dishonors his head. ⁵And every woman who prays or prophesies with her head uncovered dishonors her head—it is just as though her head were shaved. ⁶If a woman does not cover her head, she should have her hair cut off; and if it is a disgrace for a woman to have her hair cut or shaved off, she should cover her head. ⁷A man ought not to cover his head,[b] since he is the image and glory of God; but the woman is the glory of man. ⁸For man did not come from woman, but woman from man; ⁹neither was man created for woman, but woman for man. ¹⁰For this reason, and because of the angels, the woman ought to have a sign of authority on her head.

¹¹In the Lord, however, woman is not independent of man, nor is man independent of woman. ¹²For as woman came from man, so also man is born of woman. But everything comes from God. ¹³Judge for yourselves: Is it proper for a woman to pray to God with her head uncovered? ¹⁴Does not the very nature of things teach you that if a man has long hair, it is a disgrace to him, ¹⁵but that if a woman has long hair, it is her glory? For long hair is given to her as a covering. ¹⁶If anyone wants to be contentious about this, we have no other practice—nor do the churches of God.

The Lord's Supper

¹⁷In the following directives I have no praise for you, for your meetings do more harm than

a 2 Or traditions　b 4-7 Or ⁴ Every man who prays or prophesies with long hair dishonors his head. ⁵ And every woman who prays or prophesies with no covering [of hair] on her head dishonors her head—she is just like one of the "shorn women." ⁶ If a woman has no covering, let her be for now with short hair, but since it is a disgrace for a woman to have her hair shorn or shaved, she should grow it again. ⁷ A man ought not to have long hair

good. 18In the first place, I hear that when you come together as a church, there are divisions among you, and to some extent I believe it. 19No doubt there have to be differences among you to show which of you have God's approval. 20When you come together, it is not the Lord's Supper you eat, 21for as you eat, each of you goes ahead without waiting for anybody else. One remains hungry, another gets drunk. 22Don't you have homes to eat and drink in? Or do you despise the church of God and humiliate those who have nothing? What shall I say to you? Shall I praise you for this? Certainly not!

23For I received from the Lord what I also passed on to you: The Lord Jesus, on the night he was betrayed, took bread, 24and when he had given thanks, he broke it and said, "This is my body, which is for you; do this in remembrance of me." 25In the same way, after supper he took the cup, saying, "This cup is the new covenant in my blood; do this, whenever you drink it, in remembrance of me." 26For whenever you eat this bread and drink this cup, you proclaim the Lord's death until he comes.

27Therefore, whoever eats the bread or drinks the cup of the Lord in an unworthy manner will be guilty of sinning against the body and blood of the Lord. 28A man ought to examine himself before he eats of the bread and drinks of the cup. 29For anyone who eats and drinks without recognizing the body of the Lord eats and drinks judgment on himself. 30That is why many among you are weak and sick, and a number of you have fallen asleep. 31But if we judged ourselves, we would not come under judgment. 32When we are judged by the Lord, we are being disciplined so that we will not be condemned with the world.

33So then, my brothers, when you come together to eat, wait for each other. 34If anyone is hungry, he should eat at home, so that when you meet together it may not result in judgment.

And when I come I will give further directions.

Spiritual Gifts

12 Now about spiritual gifts, brothers, I do not want you to be ignorant. 2You know that when you were pagans, somehow or other you were influenced and led astray to mute idols. 3Therefore I tell you that no one who is speaking by the Spirit of God says, "Jesus be cursed," and no one can say, "Jesus is Lord," except by the Holy Spirit.

4There are different kinds of gifts, but the same Spirit. 5There are different kinds of service,

乃是招損。18第一，我聽說你們聚會的時候，彼此分門別類，我也稍微地信這話。19在你們中間不免有分門結黨的事，好叫那些有經驗的人顯明出來。20你們聚會的時候，算不得吃主的晚餐；21因為吃的時候，各人先吃自己的飯，甚至這個飢餓，那個酒醉。22你們要吃喝，難道沒有家嗎？還是藐視神的教會，叫那沒有的羞愧呢？我向你們可怎麼說呢？可因此稱讚你們嗎？我不稱讚！

23我當日傳給你們的，原是從主領受的，就是主耶穌被賣的那一夜，拿起餅來，24祝謝了，就擘開，說："這是我的身體，為你們捨的（註："捨"有古卷作"擘開"）。你們應當如此行，為的是記念我。"25飯後，也照樣拿起杯來，說："這杯是用我的血所立的新約。你們每逢喝的時候，要如此行，為的是記念我。"26你們每逢吃這餅，喝這杯，是表明主的死，直等到他來。

27所以，無論何人不按理吃主的餅、喝主的杯，就是干犯主的身、主的血了。28人應當自己省察，然後吃這餅、喝這杯。29因為人吃喝，若不分辨是主的身體，就是吃喝自己的罪了。30因此，在你們中間有好些軟弱的與患病的，死的也不少（註："死"原文作"睡"）。31我們若是先分辨自己，就不至於受審。32我們受審的時候，乃是被主懲治，免得我們和世人一同定罪。

33所以我弟兄們，你們聚會吃的時候，要彼此等待。34若有人飢餓，可以在家裏先吃，免得你們聚會，自己取罪。

其餘的事，我來的時候再安排。

屬靈的恩賜

12 弟兄們，論到屬靈的恩賜，我不願意你們不明白。2你們作外邦人的時候，隨事被牽引、受迷惑，去服侍那啞巴偶像，這是你們知道的。3所以我告訴你們：被神的靈感動的，沒有說耶穌是可咒詛的；若不是被聖靈感動的，也沒有能說耶穌是主的。

4恩賜原有分別，聖靈卻是一位；5職事也有分別，主卻是一位；

⁶功用也有分別，神卻是一位，在眾人裏面運行一切的事。

⁷聖靈顯在各人身上，是叫人得益處。⁸這人蒙聖靈賜他智慧的言語，那人也蒙這位聖靈賜他知識的言語，⁹又有一人蒙這位聖靈賜他信心，還有一人蒙這位聖靈賜他醫病的恩賜，¹⁰又叫一人能行異能，又叫一人能作先知，又叫一人能辨別諸靈，又叫一人能說方言，又叫一人能翻方言。¹¹這一切都是這位聖靈所運行、隨己意分給各人的。

一個身子，許多肢體

¹²就如身子是一個，卻有許多肢體；而且肢體雖多，仍是一個身子。基督也是這樣。¹³我們不拘是猶太人，是希臘人，是為奴的，是自主的，都從一位聖靈受洗，成了一個身體，飲於一位聖靈。

¹⁴身子原不是一個肢體，乃是許多肢體。¹⁵設若腳說：「我不是手，所以不屬乎身子。」它不能因此就不屬乎身子。¹⁶設若耳說：「我不是眼，所以不屬乎身子。」它也不能因此就不屬乎身子。¹⁷若全身是眼，從哪裏聽聲呢？若全身是耳，從哪裏聞味呢？¹⁸但如今神隨自己的意思把肢體俱各安排在身上了。¹⁹若都是一個肢體，身子在哪裏呢？²⁰但如今肢體是多的，身子卻是一個。

²¹眼不能對手說：「我用不着你。」頭也不能對腳說：「我用不着你。」²²不但如此，身上肢體，人以為軟弱的，更是不可少的。²³身上肢體，我們看為不體面的，越發給它加上體面；不俊美的，越發得着俊美。²⁴我們俊美的肢體，自然用不着裝飾；但神配搭這身子，把加倍的體面給那有缺欠的肢體，²⁵免得身上分門別類，總要肢體彼此相顧。²⁶若一個肢體受苦，所有的肢體就一同受苦；若一個肢體得榮耀，所有的肢體就一同快樂。

but the same Lord. ⁶There are different kinds of working, but the same God works all of them in all men.

⁷Now to each one the manifestation of the Spirit is given for the common good. ⁸To one there is given through the Spirit the message of wisdom, to another the message of knowledge by means of the same Spirit, ⁹to another faith by the same Spirit, to another gifts of healing by that one Spirit, ¹⁰to another miraculous powers, to another prophecy, to another distinguishing between spirits, to another speaking in different kinds of tongues,*ᵃ* and to still another the interpretation of tongues.*ᵃ* ¹¹All these are the work of one and the same Spirit, and he gives them to each one, just as he determines.

One Body, Many Parts

¹²The body is a unit, though it is made up of many parts; and though all its parts are many, they form one body. So it is with Christ. ¹³For we were all baptized by*ᵇ* one Spirit into one body—whether Jews or Greeks, slave or free—and we were all given the one Spirit to drink.

¹⁴Now the body is not made up of one part but of many. ¹⁵If the foot should say, "Because I am not a hand, I do not belong to the body," it would not for that reason cease to be part of the body. ¹⁶And if the ear should say, "Because I am not an eye, I do not belong to the body," it would not for that reason cease to be part of the body. ¹⁷If the whole body were an eye, where would the sense of hearing be? If the whole body were an ear, where would the sense of smell be? ¹⁸But in fact God has arranged the parts in the body, every one of them, just as he wanted them to be. ¹⁹If they were all one part, where would the body be? ²⁰As it is, there are many parts, but one body.

²¹The eye cannot say to the hand, "I don't need you!" And the head cannot say to the feet, "I don't need you!" ²²On the contrary, those parts of the body that seem to be weaker are indispensable, ²³and the parts that we think are less honorable we treat with special honor. And the parts that are unpresentable are treated with special modesty, ²⁴while our presentable parts need no special treatment. But God has combined the members of the body and has given greater honor to the parts that lacked it, ²⁵so that there should be no division in the body, but that its parts should have equal concern for each other. ²⁶If one part suffers, every part suffers with it; if one part is honored, every part rejoices with it.

a 10 Or languages; also in verse 28   b 13 Or with; or in

27Now you are the body of Christ, and each one of you is a part of it. 28And in the church God has appointed first of all apostles, second prophets, third teachers, then workers of miracles, also those having gifts of healing, those able to help others, those with gifts of administration, and those speaking in different kinds of tongues. 29Are all apostles? Are all prophets? Are all teachers? Do all work miracles? 30Do all have gifts of healing? Do all speak in tongues*a*? Do all interpret? 31But eagerly desire*b* the greater gifts.

Love

And now I will show you the most excellent way.

13 If I speak in the tongues*c* of men and of angels, but have not love, I am only a resounding gong or a clanging cymbal. 2If I have the gift of prophecy and can fathom all mysteries and all knowledge, and if I have a faith that can move mountains, but have not love, I am nothing. 3If I give all I possess to the poor and surrender my body to the flames,*d* but have not love, I gain nothing.

4Love is patient, love is kind. It does not envy, it does not boast, it is not proud. 5It is not rude, it is not self-seeking, it is not easily angered, it keeps no record of wrongs. 6Love does not delight in evil but rejoices with the truth. 7It always protects, always trusts, always hopes, always perseveres.

8Love never fails. But where there are prophecies, they will cease; where there are tongues, they will be stilled; where there is knowledge, it will pass away. 9For we know in part and we prophesy in part, 10but when perfection comes, the imperfect disappears. 11When I was a child, I talked like a child, I thought like a child, I reasoned like a child. When I became a man, I put childish ways behind me. 12Now we see but a poor reflection as in a mirror; then we shall see face to face. Now I know in part; then I shall know fully, even as I am fully known.

13And now these three remain: faith, hope and love. But the greatest of these is love.

Gifts of Prophecy and Tongues

14 Follow the way of love and eagerly desire spiritual gifts, especially the gift of prophecy. 2For anyone who speaks in a tongue*e* does not speak to men but to God.

*a 30 Or other languages　b 31 Or But you are eagerly desiring
c 1 Or languages　d 3 Some early manuscripts body that I may boast　e 2 Or another language; also in verses 4, 13, 14, 19, 26 and 27*

27你們就是基督的身子，並且各自作肢體。28神在教會所設立的：第一是使徒，第二是先知，第三是教師，其次是行異能的，再次是得恩賜醫病的，幫助人的，治理事的，說方言的。29豈都是使徒嗎？豈都是先知嗎？豈都是教師嗎？豈都是行異能的嗎？30豈都是得恩賜醫病的嗎？豈都是說方言的嗎？豈都是翻方言的嗎？31你們要切切地求那更大的恩賜。

愛

我現今把最妙的道指示你們。

13 我若能說萬人的方言，並天使的話語，卻沒有愛，我就成了鳴的鑼、響的鈸一般。2我若有先知講道之能，也明白各樣的奧秘、各樣的知識，而且有全備的信，叫我能夠移山，卻沒有愛，我就算不得甚麼。3我若將所有的賙濟窮人，又捨己身叫人焚燒，卻沒有愛，仍然與我無益。

4愛是恆久忍耐，又有恩慈；愛是不嫉妒；愛是不自誇，不張狂，5不做害羞的事，不求自己的益處，不輕易發怒，不計算人的惡，6不喜歡不義，只喜歡真理；7凡事包容，凡事相信，凡事盼望，凡事忍耐。

8愛是永不止息。先知講道之能，終必歸於無有；說方言之能，終必停止；知識也終必歸於無有。9我們現在所知道的有限，先知所講的也有限，10等那完全的來到，這有限的必歸於無有了。11我做孩子的時候，話語像孩子，心思像孩子，意念像孩子；既成了人，就把孩子的事丟棄了。12我們如今彷彿對著鏡子觀看，模糊不清（註："模糊不清"原文作"如同猜謎"），到那時，就要面對面了。我如今所知道的有限，到那時就全知道，如同主知道我一樣。

13如今常存的有信，有望，有愛；這三樣，其中最大的是愛。

先知講道與說方言的恩賜

14 你們要追求愛，也要切慕屬靈的恩賜，其中更要羨慕的，是作先知講道（註：原文作"是說預言"。下同）。2那說方言的，原不是對人說，乃是對神說，因為沒有人聽出來。然而他在心靈裏，卻是講說各樣的奧秘。3但作先知講道的，是對人說，要造就、安慰、勸勉人。4說方言的，是造就自己；作先知講道的，乃是造就教會。5我願意你們都說方言，更願意你們作先知講道，因為說方言的，若不翻出來，使教會被造就，那作先知講道的，就比他強了。

6弟兄們，我到你們那裏去，若只說方言，不用啟示、或知識、或預言、或教訓，給你們講解，我與你們有甚麼益處呢？7就是那有聲無氣的物，或簫、或琴，若發出來的聲音沒有分別，怎能知道所吹、所彈的是甚麼呢？8若吹無定的號聲，誰能預備打仗呢？9你們也是如此，舌頭若不說容易明白的話，怎能知道所說的是甚麼呢？這就是向空說話了。10世上的聲音或者甚多，卻沒有一樣是無意思的。11我若不明白那聲音的意思，這說話的人必以我為化外之人，我也以他為化外之人。12你們也是如此，既是切慕屬靈的恩賜，就當求多得造就教會的恩賜。

13所以那說方言的，就當求着能翻出來。14我若用方言禱告，是我的靈禱告，但我的悟性沒有果效。15這卻怎麼樣呢？我要用靈禱告，也要用悟性禱告；我要用靈歌唱，也要用悟性歌唱。16不然，你用靈祝謝，那在座不通方言的人，既然不明白你的話，怎能在你感謝的時候說"阿們"呢？17你感謝的固然是好，無奈不能造就別人。

18我感謝神，我說方言比你們眾人還多。19但在教會中，寧可用悟性說五句教導人的話，強如說萬句方言。

20弟兄們，在心志上不要作小孩子；然而，在惡事上要作嬰孩，在心志上總要作大人。21律法上記着：

Indeed, no one understands him; he utters mysteries with his spirit.*a* 3But everyone who prophesies speaks to men for their strengthening, encouragement and comfort. 4He who speaks in a tongue edifies himself, but he who prophesies edifies the church. 5I would like every one of you to speak in tongues,*b* but I would rather have you prophesy. He who prophesies is greater than one who speaks in tongues,*b* unless he interprets, so that the church may be edified.

6Now, brothers, if I come to you and speak in tongues, what good will I be to you, unless I bring you some revelation or knowledge or prophecy or word of instruction? 7Even in the case of lifeless things that make sounds, such as the flute or harp, how will anyone know what tune is being played unless there is a distinction in the notes? 8Again, if the trumpet does not sound a clear call, who will get ready for battle? 9So it is with you. Unless you speak intelligible words with your tongue, how will anyone know what you are saying? You will just be speaking into the air. 10Undoubtedly there are all sorts of languages in the world, yet none of them is without meaning. 11If then I do not grasp the meaning of what someone is saying, I am a foreigner to the speaker, and he is a foreigner to me. 12So it is with you. Since you are eager to have spiritual gifts, try to excel in gifts that build up the church.

13For this reason anyone who speaks in a tongue should pray that he may interpret what he says. 14For if I pray in a tongue, my spirit prays, but my mind is unfruitful. 15So what shall I do? I will pray with my spirit, but I will also pray with my mind; I will sing with my spirit, but I will also sing with my mind. 16If you are praising God with your spirit, how can one who finds himself among those who do not understand*c* say "Amen" to your thanksgiving, since he does not know what you are saying? 17You may be giving thanks well enough, but the other man is not edified.

18I thank God that I speak in tongues more than all of you. 19But in the church I would rather speak five intelligible words to instruct others than ten thousand words in a tongue.

20Brothers, stop thinking like children. In regard to evil be infants, but in your thinking be adults. 21In the Law it is written:

---

a 2 Or by the Spirit　　b 5 Or other languages; also in verses 6, 18, 22, 23 and 39　　c 16 Or among the inquirers

"Through men of strange tongues
and through the lips of foreigners
I will speak to this people,
but even then they will not listen to me,"[a]
says the Lord.

22Tongues, then, are a sign, not for believers
but for unbelievers; prophecy, however, is for
believers, not for unbelievers. 23So if the whole
church comes together and everyone speaks in
tongues, and some who do not understand[b] or
some unbelievers come in, will they not say that
you are out of your mind? 24But if an unbeliever
or someone who does not understand[c] comes in
while everybody is prophesying, he will be convinced by all that he is a sinner and will be
judged by all, 25and the secrets of his heart will
be laid bare. So he will fall down and worship
God, exclaiming, "God is really among you!"

Orderly Worship

26What then shall we say, brothers? When you
come together, everyone has a hymn, or a word
of instruction, a revelation, a tongue or an interpretation. All of these must be done for the
strengthening of the church. 27If anyone speaks
in a tongue, two—or at the most three—should
speak, one at a time, and someone must interpret. 28If there is no interpreter, the speaker
should keep quiet in the church and speak to
himself and God.

29Two or three prophets should speak, and
the others should weigh carefully what is said.
30And if a revelation comes to someone who is
sitting down, the first speaker should stop. 31For
you can all prophesy in turn so that everyone
may be instructed and encouraged. 32The spirits
of prophets are subject to the control of prophets.
33For God is not a God of disorder but of peace.

As in all the congregations of the saints,
34women should remain silent in the churches.
They are not allowed to speak, but must be in
submission, as the Law says. 35If they want to
inquire about something, they should ask their
own husbands at home; for it is disgraceful for a
woman to speak in the church.

36Did the word of God originate with you?
Or are you the only people it has reached? 37If
anybody thinks he is a prophet or spiritually
gifted, let him acknowledge that what I am writing to you is the Lord's command. 38If he ignores
this, he himself will be ignored.[d]

主說："我要用外邦人的舌頭
和外邦人的嘴唇，
向這百姓說話，
雖然如此，
他們還是不聽從我。"

22這樣看來，說方言不是為信的
人作證據，乃是為不信的人；作先知
講道不是為不信的人作證據，乃是為
信的人。23所以全教會聚在一處的時
候，若都說方言，偶然有不通方言
的，或是不信的人進來，豈不說你們
癲狂了嗎？24若都作先知講道，偶然
有不信的，或是不通方言的人進來，
就被眾人勸醒，被眾人審明，25他心
裏的隱情顯露出來，就必將臉伏地，
敬拜神，說："神真是在你們中間
了。"

有秩序地敬拜

26弟兄們，這卻怎麼樣呢？你們
聚會的時候，各人或有詩歌，或有教
訓，或有啟示，或有方言，或有翻出
來的話，凡事都當造就人。27若有說
方言的，只好兩個人，至多三個人，
且要輪流着說，也要一個人翻出來。
28若沒有人翻，就當在會中閉口，只
對自己和神說就是了。

29至於作先知講道的，只好兩個
人，或是三個人，其餘的就當慎思明
辨。30若旁邊坐着的得了啟示，那先
說話的就當閉口不言。31因為你們都
可以一個一個地作先知講道，叫眾人
學道理，叫眾人得勸勉。32先知的靈
原是順服先知的，33因為神不是叫人
混亂，乃是叫人安靜。

34婦女在會中要閉口不言，像在
聖徒的眾教會一樣，因為不准他們說
話。他們總要順服，正如律法所說
的。35他們若要學甚麼，可以在家裏
問自己的丈夫，因為婦女在會中說話
原是可恥的。

36神的道理豈是從你們出來嗎？
豈是單臨到你們嗎？37若有人以為自
己是先知，或是屬靈的，就該知道我
所寫給你們的是主的命令。38若有不
知道的，就由他不知道吧！

<hr>

a 21 Isaiah 28:11,12   b 23 Or some inquirers   c 24 Or or some
inquirer   d 38 Some manuscripts If he is ignorant of this, let him
be ignorant

³⁹所以我弟兄們，你們要切慕作先知講道，也不要禁止說方言。⁴⁰凡事都要規規矩矩地按着次序行。

基督的復活

15 弟兄們，我如今把先前所傳給你們的福音，告訴你們知道。這福音你們也領受了，又靠着站立得住；²並且你們若不是徒然相信，能以持守我所傳給你們的，就必因這福音得救。

³我當日所領受又傳給你們的，第一，就是基督照聖經所說，為我們的罪死了，⁴而且埋葬了，又照聖經所說，第三天復活了，⁵並且顯給磯法看，然後顯給十二使徒看，⁶後來一時顯給五百多弟兄看，其中一大半到如今還在，卻也有已經睡了的。⁷以後顯給雅各看，再顯給眾使徒看，⁸末了，也顯給我看；我如同未到產期而生的人一般。

⁹我原是使徒中最小的，不配稱為使徒，因為我從前逼迫神的教會。¹⁰然而我今日成了何等人，是蒙神的恩才成的；並且他所賜我的恩不是徒然的。我比眾使徒格外勞苦，這原不是我，乃是神的恩與我同在。¹¹不拘是我，是眾使徒，我們如此傳，你們也如此信了。

死人的復活

¹²既傳基督是從死裏復活了，怎麼在你們中間有人說沒有死人復活的事呢？¹³若沒有死人復活的事，基督也就沒有復活了。¹⁴若基督沒有復活，我們所傳的便是枉然，你們所信的也是枉然！¹⁵並且明顯我們是為神妄作見證的，因我們見證神是叫基督復活了。若死人真不復活，神也就沒有叫基督復活了。¹⁶因為死人若不復活，基督也就沒有復活了。¹⁷基督若沒有復活，你們的信便是徒然，你們仍在罪裏；¹⁸就是在基督裏睡了的人也滅亡了。¹⁹我們若靠基督只在今生有指望，就算比眾人更可憐。

²⁰但基督已經從死裏復活，成為睡了之人初熟的果子。²¹死既是因一

The Resurrection of Christ

15 Now, brothers, I want to remind you of the gospel I preached to you, which you received and on which you have taken your stand. ²By this gospel you are saved, if you hold firmly to the word I preached to you. Otherwise, you have believed in vain.

³For what I received I passed on to you as of first importance*a*: that Christ died for our sins according to the Scriptures, ⁴that he was buried, that he was raised on the third day according to the Scriptures, ⁵and that he appeared to Peter,*b* and then to the Twelve. ⁶After that, he appeared to more than five hundred of the brothers at the same time, most of whom are still living, though some have fallen asleep. ⁷Then he appeared to James, then to all the apostles, ⁸and last of all he appeared to me also, as to one abnormally born.

⁹For I am the least of the apostles and do not even deserve to be called an apostle, because I persecuted the church of God. ¹⁰But by the grace of God I am what I am, and his grace to me was not without effect. No, I worked harder than all of them—yet not I, but the grace of God that was with me. ¹¹Whether, then, it was I or they, this is what we preach, and this is what you believed.

The Resurrection of the Dead

¹²But if it is preached that Christ has been raised from the dead, how can some of you say that there is no resurrection of the dead? ¹³If there is no resurrection of the dead, then not even Christ has been raised. ¹⁴And if Christ has not been raised, our preaching is useless and so is your faith. ¹⁵More than that, we are then found to be false witnesses about God, for we have testified about God that he raised Christ from the dead. But he did not raise him if in fact the dead are not raised. ¹⁶For if the dead are not raised, then Christ has not been raised either. ¹⁷And if Christ has not been raised, your faith is futile; you are still in your sins. ¹⁸Then those also who have fallen asleep in Christ are lost. ¹⁹If only for this life we have hope in Christ, we are to be pitied more than all men.

²⁰But Christ has indeed been raised from the dead, the firstfruits of those who have fallen asleep. ²¹For since death came through a man,

a 3 Or you at the first   b 5 Greek Cephas

the resurrection of the dead comes also through a man. [22]For as in Adam all die, so in Christ all will be made alive. [23]But each in his own turn: Christ, the firstfruits; then, when he comes, those who belong to him. [24]Then the end will come, when he hands over the kingdom to God the Father after he has destroyed all dominion, authority and power. [25]For he must reign until he has put all his enemies under his feet. [26]The last enemy to be destroyed is death. [27]For he "has put everything under his feet."[a] Now when it says that "everything" has been put under him, it is clear that this does not include God himself, who put everything under Christ. [28]When he has done this, then the Son himself will be made subject to him who put everything under him, so that God may be all in all.

[29]Now if there is no resurrection, what will those do who are baptized for the dead? If the dead are not raised at all, why are people baptized for them? [30]And as for us, why do we endanger ourselves every hour? [31]I die every day—I mean that, brothers—just as surely as I glory over you in Christ Jesus our Lord. [32]If I fought wild beasts in Ephesus for merely human reasons, what have I gained? If the dead are not raised,

"Let us eat and drink,
　for tomorrow we die."[b]

[33]Do not be misled: "Bad company corrupts good character." [34]Come back to your senses as you ought, and stop sinning; for there are some who are ignorant of God—I say this to your shame.

The Resurrection Body

[35]But someone may ask, "How are the dead raised? With what kind of body will they come?" [36]How foolish! What you sow does not come to life unless it dies. [37]When you sow, you do not plant the body that will be, but just a seed, perhaps of wheat or of something else. [38]But God gives it a body as he has determined, and to each kind of seed he gives its own body. [39]All flesh is not the same: Men have one kind of flesh, animals have another, birds another and fish another. [40]There are also heavenly bodies and there are earthly bodies; but the splendor of the heavenly bodies is one kind, and the splendor of the earthly bodies is another. [41]The sun has one kind of splendor, the moon another and the stars another; and star differs from star in splendor.

人而來，死人復活也是因一人而來。 [22]在亞當裏眾人都死了；照樣，在基督裏眾人也都要復活。 [23]但各人是按着自己的次序復活，初熟的果子是基督，以後在他來的時候，是那些屬基督的。 [24]再後，末期到了，那時，基督既將一切執政的、掌權的、有能的都毀滅了，就把國交與父神。 [25]因為基督必要作王，等神把一切仇敵都放在他的腳下。 [26]儘末了所毀滅的仇敵就是死。 [27]因為經上說：「神叫萬物都服在他的腳下。」既說萬物都服了他，明顯那叫萬物服他的，不在其內了。 [28]萬物既服了他，那時，子也要自己服那叫萬物服他的，叫神在萬物之上，為萬物之主。

[29]不然，那些為死人受洗的，將來怎樣呢？若死人總不復活，因何為他們受洗呢？ [31]弟兄們，我在我主基督耶穌裏指着你們所誇的口極力地說，我是天天冒死。 [32]我若當日像尋常人在以弗所同野獸戰鬥，那於我有甚益處呢？若死人不復活，

「我們就吃吃喝喝吧！
　因為明天要死了。」

[33]你們不要自欺，濫交是敗壞善行。 [34]你們要醒悟為善，不要犯罪，因為有人不認識神。我說這話是要叫你們羞愧。

復活的身體

[35]或有人問：「死人怎樣復活，帶着甚麼身體來呢？」 [36]無知的人哪，你所種的，若不死，就不能生！ [37]並且你所種的，不是那將來的形體，不過是子粒，即如麥子，或是別樣的穀。 [38]但神隨自己的意思給它一個形體，並叫各等子粒各有自己的形體。 [39]凡肉體各有不同：人是一樣，獸又是一樣，鳥又是一樣，魚又是一樣。 [40]有天上的形體，也有地上的形體。但天上形體的榮光是一樣，地上形體的榮光又是一樣。 [41]日有日的榮光，月有月的榮光，星有星的榮光；這星和那星的榮光也有分別。

a 27 Psalm 8:6　　*b* 32 Isaiah 22:13

⁴²死人復活也是這樣：所種的是必朽壞的，復活的是不朽壞的；⁴³所種的是羞辱的，復活的是榮耀的；所種的是軟弱的，復活的是強壯的；⁴⁴所種的是血氣的身體，復活的是靈性的身體。

若有血氣的身體，也必有靈性的身體。⁴⁵經上也是這樣記着說："首先的人亞當成了有靈的活人（註："靈"或作"血氣"）"；末後的亞當成了叫人活的靈。⁴⁶但屬靈的不在先，屬血氣的在先，以後才有屬靈的。⁴⁷頭一個人是出於地，乃屬土；第二個人是出於天。⁴⁸那屬土的怎樣，凡屬土的也就怎樣；屬天的怎樣，凡屬天的也就怎樣。⁴⁹我們既有屬土的形狀，將來也必有屬天的形狀。

⁵⁰弟兄們，我告訴你們說，血肉之體不能承受神的國，必朽壞的不能承受不朽壞的。⁵¹我如今把一件奧秘的事告訴你們：我們不是都要睡覺，乃是都要改變，⁵²就在一霎時，眨眼之間，號筒末次吹響的時候。因號筒要響，死人要復活，成為不朽壞的，我們也要改變。⁵³這必朽壞的總要變成（註："變成"原文作"穿"。下同）不朽壞的，這必死的總要變成不死的。⁵⁴這必朽壞的既變成不朽壞的，這必死的既變成不死的，那時經上所記"死被得勝吞滅"的話就應驗了。

⁵⁵"死啊，你得勝的權勢在哪裏？　死啊，你的毒鈎在哪裏？"

⁵⁶死的毒鈎就是罪，罪的權勢就是律法。⁵⁷感謝神，使我們藉着我們的主耶穌基督得勝。

⁵⁸所以，我親愛的弟兄們，你們務要堅固，不可搖動，常常竭力多做主工，因為知道你們的勞苦，在主裏面不是徒然的。

為聖徒捐錢

16 論到為聖徒捐錢，我從前怎樣吩咐加拉太的眾教會，你們也當怎樣行。²每逢七日的第一日，各人要照自己的進項抽出來留着，免得我來的時候現湊。³及至我來到了，你們寫信舉薦誰，我就打發他們，把你們的捐資送到耶

⁴²So will it be with the resurrection of the dead. The body that is sown is perishable, it is raised imperishable; ⁴³it is sown in dishonor, it is raised in glory; it is sown in weakness, it is raised in power; ⁴⁴it is sown a natural body, it is raised a spiritual body.

If there is a natural body, there is also a spiritual body. ⁴⁵So it is written: "The first man Adam became a living being"^a; the last Adam, a life-giving spirit. ⁴⁶The spiritual did not come first, but the natural, and after that the spiritual. ⁴⁷The first man was of the dust of the earth, the second man from heaven. ⁴⁸As was the earthly man, so are those who are of the earth; and as is the man from heaven, so also are those who are of heaven. ⁴⁹And just as we have borne the likeness of the earthly man, so shall we^b bear the likeness of the man from heaven.

⁵⁰I declare to you, brothers, that flesh and blood cannot inherit the kingdom of God, nor does the perishable inherit the imperishable. ⁵¹Listen, I tell you a mystery: We will not all sleep, but we will all be changed— ⁵²in a flash, in the twinkling of an eye, at the last trumpet. For the trumpet will sound, the dead will be raised imperishable, and we will be changed. ⁵³For the perishable must clothe itself with the imperishable, and the mortal with immortality. ⁵⁴When the perishable has been clothed with the imperishable, and the mortal with immortality, then the saying that is written will come true: "Death has been swallowed up in victory."^c

⁵⁵"Where, O death, is your victory?　Where, O death, is your sting?"^d

⁵⁶The sting of death is sin, and the power of sin is the law. ⁵⁷But thanks be to God! He gives us the victory through our Lord Jesus Christ.

⁵⁸Therefore, my dear brothers, stand firm. Let nothing move you. Always give yourselves fully to the work of the Lord, because you know that your labor in the Lord is not in vain.

The Collection for God's People

16 Now about the collection for God's people: Do what I told the Galatian churches to do. ²On the first day of every week, each one of you should set aside a sum of money in keeping with his income, saving it up, so that when I come no collections will have to be made. ³Then, when I arrive, I will give letters of introduction to the men you approve and send

<hr>

a 45 Gen. 2:7　　*b 49* Some early manuscripts *so let us*
c 54 Isaiah 25:8　　*d 55* Hosea 13:14

them with your gift to Jerusalem. [4]If it seems advisable for me to go also, they will accompany me.

Personal Requests

[5]After I go through Macedonia, I will come to you—for I will be going through Macedonia. [6]Perhaps I will stay with you awhile, or even spend the winter, so that you can help me on my journey, wherever I go. [7]I do not want to see you now and make only a passing visit; I hope to spend some time with you, if the Lord permits. [8]But I will stay on at Ephesus until Pentecost, [9]because a great door for effective work has opened to me, and there are many who oppose me.

[10]If Timothy comes, see to it that he has nothing to fear while he is with you, for he is carrying on the work of the Lord, just as I am. [11]No one, then, should refuse to accept him. Send him on his way in peace so that he may return to me. I am expecting him along with the brothers.

[12]Now about our brother Apollos: I strongly urged him to go to you with the brothers. He was quite unwilling to go now, but he will go when he has the opportunity.

[13]Be on your guard; stand firm in the faith; be men of courage; be strong. [14]Do everything in love.

[15]You know that the household of Stephanas were the first converts in Achaia, and they have devoted themselves to the service of the saints. I urge you, brothers, [16]to submit to such as these and to everyone who joins in the work, and labors at it. [17]I was glad when Stephanas, Fortunatus and Achaicus arrived, because they have supplied what was lacking from you. [18]For they refreshed my spirit and yours also. Such men deserve recognition.

Final Greetings

[19]The churches in the province of Asia send you greetings. Aquila and Priscilla[a] greet you warmly in the Lord, and so does the church that meets at their house. [20]All the brothers here send you greetings. Greet one another with a holy kiss.

[21]I, Paul, write this greeting in my own hand.

[22]If anyone does not love the Lord—a curse be on him. Come, O Lord[b]!

[23]The grace of the Lord Jesus be with you.

[24]My love to all of you in Christ Jesus. Amen.[c]

a 19 Greek *Prisca,* a variant of *Priscilla*   *b 22* In Aramaic the expression *Come, O Lord* is *Marana tha.*   *c 24* Some manuscripts do not have *Amen.*

路撒冷去。[4]若我也該去,他們可以和我同去。

個人的請求

[5]我要從馬其頓經過,既經過了,就要到你們那裏去,[6]或者和你們同住幾時,或者也過冬。無論我往哪裏去,你們就可以給我送行。[7]我如今不願意路過見你們,主若許我,我就指望和你們同住幾時。[8]但我要仍舊住在以弗所,直等到五旬節,[9]因為有寬大又有功效的門為我開了,並且反對的人也多。

[10]若是提摩太來到,你們要留心,叫他在你們那裏無所懼怕,因為他勞力做主的工,像我一樣。[11]所以無論誰,都不可藐視他,只要送他平安前行,叫他到我這裏來,因為我指望他和弟兄們同來。

[12]至於兄弟亞波羅,我再三地勸他同弟兄們到你們那裏去;但這時他決不願意去,幾時有了機會他必去。

[13]你們務要警醒,在真道上站立得穩,要作大丈夫,要剛強。[14]凡你們所做的,都要憑愛心而做。

[15]弟兄們,你們曉得司提反一家是亞該亞初結的果子,並且他們專以服侍聖徒為念。[16]我勸你們順服這樣的人,並一切同工同勞的人。[17]司提反和福徒拿都並亞該古到這裏來,我很喜歡,因為你們待我有不及之處,他們補上了。[18]他們叫我和你們心裏都快活。這樣的人,你們務要敬重。

最後的問安

[19]亞西亞的眾教會問你們安。亞居拉和百基拉並在他們家裏的教會,因主多多地問你們安。[20]眾弟兄都問你們安。你們要親嘴問安,彼此務要聖潔。

[21]我保羅親筆問安。

[22]若有人不愛主,這人可詛可咒。主必要來!

[23]願主耶穌基督的恩常與你們眾人同在!

[24]我在基督耶穌裏的愛與你們眾人同在。阿們!

哥林多後書

1 奉神旨意，作基督耶穌使徒的<u>保羅</u>和兄弟<u>提摩太</u>，

寫信給在<u>哥林多</u>神的教會，並<u>亞該亞</u>遍處的眾聖徒：

² 願恩惠、平安從神我們的父和主耶穌基督歸與你們！

賜各樣安慰的神

³ 願頌讚歸與我們的主耶穌基督的父神，就是發慈悲的父，賜各樣安慰的神。⁴ 我們在一切患難中，他就安慰我們，叫我們能用神所賜的安慰去安慰那遭各樣患難的人。⁵ 我們既多受基督的苦楚，就靠基督多得安慰。⁶ 我們受患難呢，是為叫你們得安慰、得拯救；我們得安慰呢，也是為叫你們得安慰；這安慰能叫你們忍受我們所受的那樣苦楚。⁷ 我們為你們所存的盼望是確定的，因為知道你們既是同受苦楚，也必同得安慰。

⁸ 弟兄們，我們不要你們不曉得，我們從前在<u>亞西亞</u>遭遇苦難，被壓太重，力不能勝，甚至連活命的指望都絕了。⁹ 自己心裏也斷定是必死的，叫我們不靠自己，只靠叫死人復活的神。¹⁰ 他曾救我們脫離那極大的死亡，現在仍要救我們，並且我們指望他將來還要救我們。¹¹ 你們以祈禱幫助我們，好叫許多人為我們謝恩，就是為我們因許多人所得的恩。

保羅改變計劃

¹² 我們所誇的是自己的良心，見證我們憑着神的聖潔和誠實；在世為人，不靠人的聰明，乃靠神的恩

2 Corinthians

1 Paul, an apostle of Christ Jesus by the will of God, and Timothy our brother,

To the church of God in Corinth, together with all the saints throughout Achaia:

²Grace and peace to you from God our Father and the Lord Jesus Christ.

The God of All Comfort

³Praise be to the God and Father of our Lord Jesus Christ, the Father of compassion and the God of all comfort, ⁴who comforts us in all our troubles, so that we can comfort those in any trouble with the comfort we ourselves have received from God. ⁵For just as the sufferings of Christ flow over into our lives, so also through Christ our comfort overflows. ⁶If we are distressed, it is for your comfort and salvation; if we are comforted, it is for your comfort, which produces in you patient endurance of the same sufferings we suffer. ⁷And our hope for you is firm, because we know that just as you share in our sufferings, so also you share in our comfort.

⁸We do not want you to be uninformed, brothers, about the hardships we suffered in the province of Asia. We were under great pressure, far beyond our ability to endure, so that we despaired even of life. ⁹Indeed, in our hearts we felt the sentence of death. But this happened that we might not rely on ourselves but on God, who raises the dead. ¹⁰He has delivered us from such a deadly peril, and he will deliver us. On him we have set our hope that he will continue to deliver us, ¹¹as you help us by your prayers. Then many will give thanks on our*a* behalf for the gracious favor granted us in answer to the prayers of many.

Paul's Change of Plans

¹²Now this is our boast: Our conscience testifies that we have conducted ourselves in the world, and especially in our relations with you, in the holiness and sincerity that are from God. We have done so not according to worldly wis-

a 11 Many manuscripts your

dom but according to God's grace. ¹³For we do not write you anything you cannot read or understand. And I hope that, ¹⁴as you have understood us in part, you will come to understand fully that you can boast of us just as we will boast of you in the day of the Lord Jesus.

¹⁵Because I was confident of this, I planned to visit you first so that you might benefit twice. ¹⁶I planned to visit you on my way to Macedonia and to come back to you from Macedonia, and then to have you send me on my way to Judea. ¹⁷When I planned this, did I do it lightly? Or do I make my plans in a worldly manner so that in the same breath I say, "Yes, yes" and "No, no"?

¹⁸But as surely as God is faithful, our message to you is not "Yes" and "No." ¹⁹For the Son of God, Jesus Christ, who was preached among you by me and Silas*a* and Timothy, was not "Yes" and "No," but in him it has always been "Yes." ²⁰For no matter how many promises God has made, they are "Yes" in Christ. And so through him the "Amen" is spoken by us to the glory of God. ²¹Now it is God who makes both us and you stand firm in Christ. He anointed us, ²²set his seal of ownership on us, and put his Spirit in our hearts as a deposit, guaranteeing what is to come.

²³I call God as my witness that it was in order to spare you that I did not return to Corinth. ²⁴Not that we lord it over your faith, but we work with you for your joy, because it is by faith

2 you stand firm. ¹So I made up my mind that I would not make another painful visit to you. ²For if I grieve you, who is left to make me glad but you whom I have grieved? ³I wrote as I did so that when I came I should not be distressed by those who ought to make me rejoice. I had confidence in all of you, that you would all share my joy. ⁴For I wrote you out of great distress and anguish of heart and with many tears, not to grieve you but to let you know the depth of my love for you.

Forgiveness for the Sinner

⁵If anyone has caused grief, he has not so much grieved me as he has grieved all of you, to some extent—not to put it too severely. ⁶The punishment inflicted on him by the majority is sufficient for him. ⁷Now instead, you ought to forgive and comfort him, so that he will not be overwhelmed by excessive sorrow. ⁸I urge you, therefore, to reaffirm your love for him. ⁹The reason I wrote you was to see if you would stand the test and be obedient in everything. ¹⁰If

惠，向你們更是這樣。¹³我們現在寫給你們的話，並不外乎你們所念的、所認識的，我也盼望你們到底還是要認識，¹⁴正如你們已經有幾分認識我們，以我們誇口，好像我們在我們主耶穌的日子以你們誇口一樣。

¹⁵我既然這樣深信，就早有意到你們那裏去，叫你們再得益處。¹⁶也要從你們那裏經過，往<u>馬其頓</u>去，再從<u>馬其頓</u>回到你們那裏，叫你們給我送行往<u>猶太</u>去。¹⁷我有此意，豈是反覆不定嗎？我所起的意，豈是從情慾起的，叫我忽是忽非嗎？

¹⁸我指着信實的神說，我們向你們所傳的道，並沒有是而又非的。¹⁹因為我和<u>西拉</u>並<u>提摩太</u>，在你們中間所傳神的兒子耶穌基督，總沒有是而又非的，在他只有一是。²⁰神的應許不論有多少，在基督都是是的，所以藉着他也都是實在的（註：「實在」原文作「阿們」），叫神因我們得榮耀。²¹那在基督裏堅固我們和你們，並且膏我們的就是神。²²他又用印印了我們，並賜聖靈在我們心裏作憑據（註：原文作「質」）。

²³我呼籲神給我的心作見證，我沒有往<u>哥林多</u>去是為要寬容你們。²⁴我們並不是轄管你們的信心，乃是幫助你們的快樂，因為你們憑信才站

2 立得住。¹我自己定了主意，再到你們那裏去，必須大家沒有憂愁。²倘若我叫你們憂愁，除了我叫那憂愁的人以外，誰能叫我快樂呢？³我曾把這事寫給你們，恐怕我到的時候，應該叫我快樂的那些人，反倒叫我憂愁。我也深信，你們眾人都以我的快樂為自己的快樂。⁴我先前心裏難過痛苦，多多地流淚，寫信給你們，不是叫你們憂愁，乃是叫你們知道我格外也疼愛你們。

赦免犯過錯的人

⁵若有叫人憂愁的，他不但叫我憂愁，也是叫你們眾人有幾分憂愁。我說幾分，恐怕說得太重。⁶這樣的人，受了眾人的責罰也就夠了；⁷倒不如赦免他，安慰他，免得他憂愁太過，甚至沉淪了。⁸所以我勸你們，要向他顯出堅定不移的愛心來。⁹為此我先前也寫信給你們，要試驗你們，看你們凡事順從不順從。¹⁰你們

a 19 Greek *Silvanus*, a variant of *Silas*

赦免誰，我也赦免誰。我若有所赦免的，是在基督面前為你們赦免的，¹¹免得撒但趁着機會勝過我們，因我們並非不曉得他的詭計。

新約的執事

¹²我從前為基督的福音到了<u>特羅亞</u>，主也給我開了門。¹³那時因為沒有遇見兄弟<u>提多</u>，我心裏不安，便辭別那裏的人往<u>馬其頓</u>去了。

¹⁴感謝神！常帥領我們在基督裏誇勝，並藉着我們在各處顯揚那因認識基督而有的香氣。¹⁵因為我們在神面前，無論在得救的人身上，或滅亡的人身上，都有基督馨香之氣。¹⁶在這等人，就作了死的香氣叫他死；在那等人，就作了活的香氣叫他活。這事誰能當得起呢？¹⁷我們不像那許多人，為利混亂神的道，乃是由於誠實、由於神，在神面前憑着基督講道。

3 我們豈是又舉薦自己嗎？豈像別人，用人的薦信給你們或用你們的薦信給人嗎？²你們就是我們的薦信，寫在我們的心裏，被眾人所知道、所念誦的。³你們明顯是基督的信，藉着我們修成的。不是用墨寫的，乃是用永生神的靈寫的；不是寫在石版上，乃是寫在心版上。

⁴我們因基督，所以在神面前才有這樣的信心。⁵並不是我們憑自己能承擔甚麼事，我們所能承擔的，乃是出於神。⁶他叫我們能承當這新約的執事，不是憑着字句，乃是憑着精意。因為那字句是叫人死，精意是叫人活（註："精意"或作"聖靈"）。

新約的榮光

⁷那用字刻在石頭上屬死的職事，尚且有榮光，甚至<u>以色列</u>人因<u>摩西</u>面上的榮光，不能定睛看他的臉；這榮光原是漸漸退去的，⁸何況那屬靈的職事，豈不更有榮光嗎？⁹若是定罪的職事有榮光，那稱義的職事，榮光就越發大了。¹⁰那從前有榮光的，因這極大的榮光就算不得有榮光了。¹¹若那廢掉的有榮光，這長存的就更有榮光了。

you forgive anyone, I also forgive him. And what I have forgiven—if there was anything to forgive—I have forgiven in the sight of Christ for your sake, ¹¹in order that Satan might not outwit us. For we are not unaware of his schemes.

Ministers of the New Covenant

¹²Now when I went to Troas to preach the gospel of Christ and found that the Lord had opened a door for me, ¹³I still had no peace of mind, because I did not find my brother Titus there. So I said good-by to them and went on to Macedonia.

¹⁴But thanks be to God, who always leads us in triumphal procession in Christ and through us spreads everywhere the fragrance of the knowledge of him. ¹⁵For we are to God the aroma of Christ among those who are being saved and those who are perishing. ¹⁶To the one we are the smell of death; to the other, the fragrance of life. And who is equal to such a task? ¹⁷Unlike so many, we do not peddle the word of God for profit. On the contrary, in Christ we speak before God with sincerity, like men sent from God.

3 Are we beginning to commend ourselves again? Or do we need, like some people, letters of recommendation to you or from you? ²You yourselves are our letter, written on our hearts, known and read by everybody. ³You show that you are a letter from Christ, the result of our ministry, written not with ink but with the Spirit of the living God, not on tablets of stone but on tablets of human hearts.

⁴Such confidence as this is ours through Christ before God. ⁵Not that we are competent in ourselves to claim anything for ourselves, but our competence comes from God. ⁶He has made us competent as ministers of a new covenant—not of the letter but of the Spirit; for the letter kills, but the Spirit gives life.

The Glory of the New Covenant

⁷Now if the ministry that brought death, which was engraved in letters on stone, came with glory, so that the Israelites could not look steadily at the face of Moses because of its glory, fading though it was, ⁸will not the ministry of the Spirit be even more glorious? ⁹If the ministry that condemns men is glorious, how much more glorious is the ministry that brings righteousness! ¹⁰For what was glorious has no glory now in comparison with the surpassing glory. ¹¹And if what was fading away came with glory, how much greater is the glory of that which lasts!

12Therefore, since we have such a hope, we are very bold. 13We are not like Moses, who would put a veil over his face to keep the Israelites from gazing at it while the radiance was fading away. 14But their minds were made dull, for to this day the same veil remains when the old covenant is read. It has not been removed, because only in Christ is it taken away. 15Even to this day when Moses is read, a veil covers their hearts. 16But whenever anyone turns to the Lord, the veil is taken away. 17Now the Lord is the Spirit, and where the Spirit of the Lord is, there is freedom. 18And we, who with unveiled faces all reflect[a] the Lord's glory, are being transformed into his likeness with ever-increasing glory, which comes from the Lord, who is the Spirit.

Treasures in Jars of Clay

4 Therefore, since through God's mercy we have this ministry, we do not lose heart. 2Rather, we have renounced secret and shameful ways; we do not use deception, nor do we distort the word of God. On the contrary, by setting forth the truth plainly we commend ourselves to every man's conscience in the sight of God. 3And even if our gospel is veiled, it is veiled to those who are perishing. 4The god of this age has blinded the minds of unbelievers, so that they cannot see the light of the gospel of the glory of Christ, who is the image of God. 5For we do not preach ourselves, but Jesus Christ as Lord, and ourselves as your servants for Jesus' sake. 6For God, who said, "Let light shine out of darkness,"[b] made his light shine in our hearts to give us the light of the knowledge of the glory of God in the face of Christ.

7But we have this treasure in jars of clay to show that this all-surpassing power is from God and not from us. 8We are hard pressed on every side, but not crushed; perplexed, but not in despair; 9persecuted, but not abandoned; struck down, but not destroyed. 10We always carry around in our body the death of Jesus, so that the life of Jesus may also be revealed in our body. 11For we who are alive are always being given over to death for Jesus' sake, so that his life may be revealed in our mortal body. 12So then, death is at work in us, but life is at work in you.

13It is written: "I believed; therefore I have spoken."[c] With that same spirit of faith we also believe and therefore speak, 14because we know

12我們既有這樣的盼望，就大膽講說，13不像摩西將帕子蒙在臉上，叫以色列人不能定睛看到那將廢者的結局。14但他們的心地剛硬，直到今日誦讀舊約的時候，這帕子還沒有揭去；這帕子在基督裏已經廢去了。15然而直到今日，每逢誦讀摩西書的時候，帕子還在他們心上。16但他們的心幾時歸向主，帕子就幾時除去了。17主就是那靈，主的靈在哪裏，那裏就得以自由。18我們眾人既然敞着臉得以看見主的榮光，好像從鏡子裏返照，就變成主的形狀，榮上加榮，如同從主的靈變成的。

寶貝放在瓦器裏

4 我們既然蒙憐憫，受了這職分，就不喪膽，2乃將那些暗昧可恥的事棄絕了，不行詭詐，不謬講神的道理，只將真理表明出來，好在神面前把自己薦與各人的良心。3如果我們的福音蒙蔽，就是蒙蔽在滅亡的人身上。4此等不信之人，被這世界的神弄瞎了心眼，不叫基督榮耀福音的光照着他們。基督本是神的像。5我們原不是傳自己，乃是傳基督耶穌為主，並且自己因耶穌作你們的僕人。6那吩咐光從黑暗裏照出來的神，已經照在我們心裏，叫我們得知神榮耀的光，顯在耶穌基督的面上。

7我們有這寶貝放在瓦器裏，要顯明這莫大的能力，是出於神，不是出於我們。8我們四面受敵，卻不被困住；心裏作難，卻不至失望；9遭逼迫，卻不被丟棄；打倒了，卻不至死亡。10身上常帶着耶穌的死，使耶穌的生也顯明在我們身上。11因為我們這活着的人，是常為耶穌被交於死地，使耶穌的生，在我們這必死的身上顯明出來。12這樣看來，死是在我們身上發動，生卻在你們身上發動。

13但我們既有信心，正如經上記着說："我因信，所以如此說話。"我們也信，所以也說話。14自己知道

a 18 Or contemplate　　b 6 Gen. 1:3　　c 13 Psalm 116:10

那叫主耶穌復活的，也必叫我們與耶穌一同復活，並且叫我們與你們一同站在他面前。¹⁵凡事都是為你們，好叫恩惠因人多越發加增，感謝格外顯多，以致榮耀歸與神。

¹⁶所以，我們不喪膽。外體雖然毀壞，內心卻一天新似一天。¹⁷我們這至暫至輕的苦楚，要為我們成就極重無比永遠的榮耀。¹⁸原來我們不是顧念所見的，乃是顧念所不見的；因為所見的是暫時的，所不見的是永遠的。

天上的房屋

5 我們原知道，我們這地上的帳棚若拆毀了，必得神所造，不是人手所造，在天上永存的房屋。²我們在這帳棚裏歎息，深想得那從天上來的房屋，好像穿上衣服。³倘若穿上，被遇見的時候就不至於赤身了。⁴我們在這帳棚裏歎息勞苦，並非願意脫下這個，乃是願意穿上那個，好叫這必死的被生命吞滅了。⁵為此培植我們的就是神，他又賜給我們聖靈作憑據（註：原文作“質”）。

⁶所以，我們時常坦然無懼，並且曉得我們住在身內，便與主相離。⁷因我們行事為人是憑着信心，不是憑着眼見。⁸我們坦然無懼，是更願意離開身體與主同住。⁹所以，無論是住在身內，離開身外，我們立了志向，要得主的喜悅。¹⁰因為我們眾人必要在基督臺前顯露出來，叫各人按着本身所行的，或善或惡受報。

和好的職分

¹¹我們既知道主是可畏的，所以勸人。但我們在神面前是顯明的，盼望在你們的良心裏也是顯明的。¹²我們不是向你們再舉薦自己，乃是叫你們因我們有可誇之處，好對那憑外貌不憑內心誇口的人，有言可答。¹³我們若果顛狂，是為神；若果謹守，是為你們。¹⁴原來基督的愛激勵我們。因我們想，一人既替眾人死，眾人就都死了；¹⁵並且他替眾人

that the one who raised the Lord Jesus from the dead will also raise us with Jesus and present us with you in his presence. ¹⁵All this is for your benefit, so that the grace that is reaching more and more people may cause thanksgiving to overflow to the glory of God.

¹⁶Therefore we do not lose heart. Though outwardly we are wasting away, yet inwardly we are being renewed day by day. ¹⁷For our light and momentary troubles are achieving for us an eternal glory that far outweighs them all. ¹⁸So we fix our eyes not on what is seen, but on what is unseen. For what is seen is temporary, but what is unseen is eternal.

Our Heavenly Dwelling

5 Now we know that if the earthly tent we live in is destroyed, we have a building from God, an eternal house in heaven, not built by human hands. ²Meanwhile we groan, longing to be clothed with our heavenly dwelling, ³because when we are clothed, we will not be found naked. ⁴For while we are in this tent, we groan and are burdened, because we do not wish to be unclothed but to be clothed with our heavenly dwelling, so that what is mortal may be swallowed up by life. ⁵Now it is God who has made us for this very purpose and has given us the Spirit as a deposit, guaranteeing what is to come.

⁶Therefore we are always confident and know that as long as we are at home in the body we are away from the Lord. ⁷We live by faith, not by sight. ⁸We are confident, I say, and would prefer to be away from the body and at home with the Lord. ⁹So we make it our goal to please him, whether we are at home in the body or away from it. ¹⁰For we must all appear before the judgment seat of Christ, that each one may receive what is due him for the things done while in the body, whether good or bad.

The Ministry of Reconciliation

¹¹Since, then, we know what it is to fear the Lord, we try to persuade men. What we are is plain to God, and I hope it is also plain to your conscience. ¹²We are not trying to commend ourselves to you again, but are giving you an opportunity to take pride in us, so that you can answer those who take pride in what is seen rather than in what is in the heart. ¹³If we are out of our mind, it is for the sake of God; if we are in our right mind, it is for you. ¹⁴For Christ's love compels us, because we are convinced that one died for all, and therefore all died. ¹⁵And he

died for all, that those who live should no longer live for themselves but for him who died for them and was raised again.

[16]So from now on we regard no one from a worldly point of view. Though we once regarded Christ in this way, we do so no longer. [17]Therefore, if anyone is in Christ, he is a new creation; the old has gone, the new has come! [18]All this is from God, who reconciled us to himself through Christ and gave us the ministry of reconciliation: [19]that God was reconciling the world to himself in Christ, not counting men's sins against them. And he has committed to us the message of reconciliation. [20]We are therefore Christ's ambassadors, as though God were making his appeal through us. We implore you on Christ's behalf: Be reconciled to God. [21]God made him who had no sin to be sin[a] for us, so that in him we might become the righteousness of God.

6 As God's fellow workers we urge you not to receive God's grace in vain. [2]For he says,

"In the time of my favor I heard you,
and in the day of salvation I helped you."[b]

I tell you, now is the time of God's favor, now is the day of salvation.

Paul's Hardships

[3]We put no stumbling block in anyone's path, so that our ministry will not be discredited. [4]Rather, as servants of God we commend ourselves in every way: in great endurance; in troubles, hardships and distresses; [5]in beatings, imprisonments and riots; in hard work, sleepless nights and hunger; [6]in purity, understanding, patience and kindness; in the Holy Spirit and in sincere love; [7]in truthful speech and in the power of God; with weapons of righteousness in the right hand and in the left; [8]through glory and dishonor, bad report and good report; genuine, yet regarded as impostors; [9]known, yet regarded as unknown; dying, and yet we live on; beaten, and yet not killed; [10]sorrowful, yet always rejoicing; poor, yet making many rich; having nothing, and yet possessing everything.

[11]We have spoken freely to you, Corinthians, and opened wide our hearts to you. [12]We are not withholding our affection from you, but you are withholding yours from us. [13]As a fair exchange—I speak as to my children—open wide your hearts also.

死，是叫那些活着的人不再為自己活，乃為替他們死而復活的主活。

[16]所以，我們從今以後，不憑着外貌（註：原文作「肉體」。本節同）認人了。雖然憑着外貌認過基督，如今卻不再這樣認他了。[17]若有人在基督裏，他就是新造的人，舊事已過，都變成新的了。[18]一切都是出於神，他藉着基督使我們與他和好，又將勸人與他和好的職分賜給我們。[19]這就是神在基督裏叫世人與自己和好，不將他們的過犯歸到他們身上，並且將這和好的道理託付了我們。[20]所以，我們作基督的使者，就好像神藉我們勸你們一般。我們替基督求你們與神和好。[21]神使那無罪的（註：「無罪」原文作「不知罪」），替我們成為罪，好叫我們在他裏面成為神的義。

6 我們與神同工的也勸你們，不可徒受他的恩典。[2]因為他說：

"在悅納的時候，我應允了你；
　在拯救的日子，我搭救了你。"

看哪，現在正是悅納的時候，現在正是拯救的日子。

保羅的艱苦

[3]我們凡事都不叫人有妨礙，免得這職分被人毀謗；[4]反倒在各樣的事上表明自己是神的用人，就如在許多的忍耐、患難、窮乏、困苦、[5]鞭打、監禁、擾亂、勤勞、警醒、不食、[6]廉潔、知識、恒忍、慈慈、聖靈的感化、無偽的愛心、[7]真實的道理、神的大能；仁義的兵器在左在右。[8]榮耀、羞辱、惡名、美名；似乎是誘惑人的，卻是誠實的；[9]似乎不為人所知，卻是人所共知的；似乎要死，卻是活着的；似乎受責罰，卻是不至喪命的；[10]似乎憂愁，卻是常常快樂的；似乎貧窮，卻是叫許多人富足的；似乎一無所有，卻是樣樣都有的。

[11]哥林多人哪，我們向你們，口是張開的，心是寬宏的。[12]你們狹窄，原不在乎我們，是在乎自己的心腸狹窄。[13]你們也要照樣用寬宏的心報答我。我這話正像對自己的孩子說的。

a 21 Or be a sin offering   b 2 Isaiah 49:8

不要與不信者同負一軛

14你們和不信的原不相配，不要同負一軛。義和不義有甚麼相交呢？光明和黑暗有甚麼相通呢？15基督和彼列（註："彼列" 就是撒但的別名）有甚麼相和呢？信主的和不信主的有甚麼相干呢？16神的殿和偶像有甚麼相同呢？因為我們是永生神的殿，就如神曾說："我要在他們中間居住，在他們中間來往；我要作他們的神，他們要作我的子民。"

17又說：
"你們務要從他們中間出來，
　與他們分別，
不要沾不潔淨的物，
　我就收納你們。"
18 "我要作你們的父，
　你們要作我的兒女。"
　　　這是全能的主說的。

7 親愛的弟兄啊，我們既有這等應許，就當潔淨自己，除去身體、靈魂一切的污穢，敬畏神，得以成聖。

保羅的喜樂

2你們要心地寬大收納我們。我們未曾虧負誰，未曾敗壞誰，未曾佔誰的便宜。3我說這話，不是要定你們的罪。我已經說過，你們常在我們心裏，情願與你們同生同死。4我大大地放膽，向你們說話；我因你們多多誇口，滿得安慰；我們在一切患難中分外的快樂。

5我們從前就是到了馬其頓的時候，身體也不得安寧，周圍遭患難，外有爭戰、內有懼怕。6但那安慰喪氣之人的神，藉着提多來安慰了我們。7不但藉着他來，也藉着他從你們所得的安慰，安慰了我們。因他把你們的想念、哀慟和向我的熱心，都告訴了我，叫我更加歡喜。

8我先前寫信叫你們憂愁，我後來雖然懊悔，如今卻不懊悔，因我知道那信叫你們憂愁，不過是暫時的。9如今我歡喜，不是因你們憂愁，是因你們從憂愁中生出懊悔來。你們依着神的意思憂愁，凡事

Do Not Be Yoked With Unbelievers

14Do not be yoked together with unbelievers. For what do righteousness and wickedness have in common? Or what fellowship can light have with darkness? 15What harmony is there between Christ and Belial[a]? What does a believer have in common with an unbeliever? 16What agreement is there between the temple of God and idols? For we are the temple of the living God. As God has said: "I will live with them and walk among them, and I will be their God, and they will be my people."[b]

17"Therefore come out from them
　and be separate,
　　　　　　　　　　　　says the Lord.
Touch no unclean thing,
　and I will receive you."[c]
18"I will be a Father to you,
　and you will be my sons and daughters,
　　　　　　　　says the Lord Almighty."[d]

7 Since we have these promises, dear friends, let us purify ourselves from everything that contaminates body and spirit, perfecting holiness out of reverence for God.

Paul's Joy

2Make room for us in your hearts. We have wronged no one, we have corrupted no one, we have exploited no one. 3I do not say this to condemn you; I have said before that you have such a place in our hearts that we would live or die with you. 4I have great confidence in you; I take great pride in you. I am greatly encouraged; in all our troubles my joy knows no bounds.

5For when we came into Macedonia, this body of ours had no rest, but we were harassed at every turn—conflicts on the outside, fears within. 6But God, who comforts the downcast, comforted us by the coming of Titus, 7and not only by his coming but also by the comfort you had given him. He told us about your longing for me, your deep sorrow, your ardent concern for me, so that my joy was greater than ever.

8Even if I caused you sorrow by my letter, I do not regret it. Though I did regret it—I see that my letter hurt you, but only for a little while— 9yet now I am happy, not because you were made sorry, but because your sorrow led you to repentance. For you became sorrowful as

God intended and so were not harmed in any way by us. [10]Godly sorrow brings repentance that leads to salvation and leaves no regret, but worldly sorrow brings death. [11]See what this godly sorrow has produced in you: what earnestness, what eagerness to clear yourselves, what indignation, what alarm, what longing, what concern, what readiness to see justice done. At every point you have proved yourselves to be innocent in this matter. [12]So even though I wrote to you, it was not on account of the one who did the wrong or of the injured party, but rather that before God you could see for yourselves how devoted to us you are. [13]By all this we are encouraged.

In addition to our own encouragement, we were especially delighted to see how happy Titus was, because his spirit has been refreshed by all of you. [14]I had boasted to him about you, and you have not embarrassed me. But just as everything we said to you was true, so our boasting about you to Titus has proved to be true as well. [15]And his affection for you is all the greater when he remembers that you were all obedient, receiving him with fear and trembling. [16]I am glad I can have complete confidence in you.

Generosity Encouraged

8 And now, brothers, we want you to know about the grace that God has given the Macedonian churches. [2]Out of the most severe trial, their overflowing joy and their extreme poverty welled up in rich generosity. [3]For I testify that they gave as much as they were able, and even beyond their ability. Entirely on their own, [4]they urgently pleaded with us for the privilege of sharing in this service to the saints. [5]And they did not do as we expected, but they gave themselves first to the Lord and then to us in keeping with God's will. [6]So we urged Titus, since he had earlier made a beginning, to bring also to completion this act of grace on your part. [7]But just as you excel in everything—in faith, in speech, in knowledge, in complete earnestness and in your love for us[a] —see that you also excel in this grace of giving.

[8]I am not commanding you, but I want to test the sincerity of your love by comparing it with the earnestness of others. [9]For you know the grace of our Lord Jesus Christ, that though he was rich, yet for your sakes he became poor, so that you through his poverty might become rich.

a 7 Some manuscripts in our love for you

就不至於因我們受虧損了。[10]因為依着神的意思憂愁，就生出沒有後悔的懊悔來，以至得救；但世俗的憂愁是叫人死。[11]你看，你們依着神的意思憂愁，從此就生出何等的殷勤、自訴、自恨、恐懼、想念、熱心、責罰（註：或作"自責"）。在這一切事上，你們都表明自己是潔淨的。[12]我雖然從前寫信給你們，卻不是為那虧我負人的，也不是為那受人虧負的，乃要在神面前把你們顧念我們的熱心表明出來。[13]故此我們得了安慰。

並且在安慰之中，因你們眾人使提多心裏暢快歡喜，我們就更加歡喜了。[14]我若對提多誇獎了你們甚麼，也覺得沒有慚愧，但我對提多誇獎你們的話成了真的，正如我對你們所說的話也都是真的。[15]並且提多想起你們眾人的順服，是怎樣恐懼戰兢地接待他，他愛你們的心腸就越發熱了。[16]我如今歡喜，能在凡事上為你們放心。

鼓勵慷慨捐助

8 弟兄們，我把神賜給馬其頓眾教會的恩告訴你們，[2]就是他們在患難中受大試煉的時候，仍有滿足的快樂；在極窮之間，還格外顯出他們樂捐的厚恩。[3]我可以證明他們是按着力量，而且也過了力量，自己甘心樂意地捐助，[4]再三地求我們，准他們在這供給聖徒的恩情上有分。[5]並且他們所做的，不但照我們所想望的，更照神的旨意，先把自己獻給主，又歸附了我們。[6]因此我就勸提多，既然在你們中間開辦這慈惠的事，就當辦成了。[7]你們既然在信心、口才、知識、熱心和待我們的愛心上，都格外顯出滿足來，就當在這慈惠的事上也格外顯出滿足來。

[8]我說這話，不是吩咐你們，乃是藉着別人的熱心試驗你們愛心的實在。[9]你們知道我們主耶穌基督的恩典：他本來富足，卻為你們成了貧窮，叫你們因他的貧窮，可以成為富足。

¹⁰我在這事上把我的意見告訴你們，是與你們有益。因為你們下手辦這事，而且起此心意已經有一年了，¹¹如今就當辦成這事。既有願做的心，也當照你們所有的去辦成，¹²因為人若有願做的心，必蒙悅納，乃是照他所有的，並不是照他所無的。

¹³我原不是要別人輕省，你們受累，¹⁴乃要均平，就是要你們的富餘，現在可以補他們的不足，使他們的富餘，將來也可以補你們的不足，這就均平了。¹⁵如經上所記：「多收的也沒有餘，少收的也沒有缺。」

差提多去哥林多

¹⁶多謝神，感動提多的心，叫他待你們殷勤，像我一樣。¹⁷他固然是聽了我的勸，但自己更是熱心，情願往你們那裏去。¹⁸我們還打發一位兄弟和他同去，這人在福音上得了眾教會的稱讚。¹⁹不但這樣，他也被眾教會挑選，和我們同行，把所託與我們的這捐資送到了，可以榮耀主，又表明我們樂意的心。²⁰這就免得有人因我們收的捐銀很多，就挑我們的不是。²¹我們留心行光明的事，不但在主面前，就在人面前，也是這樣。

²²我們又打發一位兄弟同去，這人的熱心，我們在許多事上屢次試驗過。現在他因為深信你們，就更加熱心了。²³論到提多，他是我的同伴，一同為你們勞碌的。論到那兩位兄弟，他們是眾教會的使者，是基督的榮耀。²⁴所以，你們務要在眾教會面前顯明你們愛心的憑據，並我所誇獎你們的憑據。

9 論到供給聖徒的事，我不必寫信給你們，²因為我知道你們樂意的心，常對馬其頓人誇獎你們，說亞該亞人預備好了，已經有一年了，並且你們的熱心激動了許多人。³但我打發那幾位弟兄去，要叫你們照我的話預備妥當，免得我們在這事上誇獎你們的話落

¹⁰And here is my advice about what is best for you in this matter: Last year you were the first not only to give but also to have the desire to do so. ¹¹Now finish the work, so that your eager willingness to do it may be matched by your completion of it, according to your means. ¹²For if the willingness is there, the gift is acceptable according to what one has, not according to what he does not have.

¹³Our desire is not that others might be relieved while you are hard pressed, but that there might be equality. ¹⁴At the present time your plenty will supply what they need, so that in turn their plenty will supply what you need. Then there will be equality, ¹⁵as it is written: "He who gathered much did not have too much, and he who gathered little did not have too little."[a]

Titus Sent to Corinth

¹⁶I thank God, who put into the heart of Titus the same concern I have for you. ¹⁷For Titus not only welcomed our appeal, but he is coming to you with much enthusiasm and on his own initiative. ¹⁸And we are sending along with him the brother who is praised by all the churches for his service to the gospel. ¹⁹What is more, he was chosen by the churches to accompany us as we carry the offering, which we administer in order to honor the Lord himself and to show our eagerness to help. ²⁰We want to avoid any criticism of the way we administer this liberal gift. ²¹For we are taking pains to do what is right, not only in the eyes of the Lord but also in the eyes of men.

²²In addition, we are sending with them our brother who has often proved to us in many ways that he is zealous, and now even more so because of his great confidence in you. ²³As for Titus, he is my partner and fellow worker among you; as for our brothers, they are representatives of the churches and an honor to Christ. ²⁴Therefore show these men the proof of your love and the reason for our pride in you, so that the churches can see it.

9 There is no need for me to write to you about this service to the saints. ²For I know your eagerness to help, and I have been boasting about it to the Macedonians, telling them that since last year you in Achaia were ready to give; and your enthusiasm has stirred most of them to action. ³But I am sending the brothers in order that our boasting about you in this matter should not prove hollow, but that you may be ready, as I said you would be.

a 15 Exodus 16:18

⁴For if any Macedonians come with me and find you unprepared, we—not to say anything about you—would be ashamed of having been so confident. ⁵So I thought it necessary to urge the brothers to visit you in advance and finish the arrangements for the generous gift you had promised. Then it will be ready as a generous gift, not as one grudgingly given.

Sowing Generously

⁶Remember this: Whoever sows sparingly will also reap sparingly, and whoever sows generously will also reap generously. ⁷Each man should give what he has decided in his heart to give, not reluctantly or under compulsion, for God loves a cheerful giver. ⁸And God is able to make all grace abound to you, so that in all things at all times, having all that you need, you will abound in every good work. ⁹As it is written:

"He has scattered abroad his gifts to the poor;
　his righteousness endures forever."ᵃ

¹⁰Now he who supplies seed to the sower and bread for food will also supply and increase your store of seed and will enlarge the harvest of your righteousness. ¹¹You will be made rich in every way so that you can be generous on every occasion, and through us your generosity will result in thanksgiving to God.

¹²This service that you perform is not only supplying the needs of God's people but is also overflowing in many expressions of thanks to God. ¹³Because of the service by which you have proved yourselves, men will praise God for the obedience that accompanies your confession of the gospel of Christ, and for your generosity in sharing with them and with everyone else. ¹⁴And in their prayers for you their hearts will go out to you, because of the surpassing grace God has given you. ¹⁵Thanks be to God for his indescribable gift!

Paul's Defense of His Ministry

10 By the meekness and gentleness of Christ, I appeal to you—I, Paul, who am "timid" when face to face with you, but "bold" when away! ²I beg you that when I come I may not have to be as bold as I expect to be toward some people who think that we live by the standards of this world. ³For though we live in the world, we do not wage war as the world does. ⁴The weapons we fight with are not the weapons of the world. On the contrary, they have

ᵃ 9 Psalm 112:9

了空。⁴萬一有馬其頓人與我同去，見你們沒有預備，就叫我們所確信的，反成了羞愧；你們羞愧，更不用說了。⁵因此，我想不得不求那幾位弟兄先到你們那裏去，把從前所應許的捐資預備妥當，就顯出你們所捐的，是出於樂意，不是出於勉強。

慷慨撒種

⁶ "少種的少收，多種的多收"，這話是真的。⁷各人要隨本心所酌定的，不要作難、不要勉強，因為捐得樂意的人是神所喜愛的。⁸神能將各樣的恩惠多多地加給你們，使你們凡事常常充足，能多行各樣善事。⁹如經上所記：

"他施捨錢財，賙濟貧窮；
　他的仁義存到永遠。"

¹⁰那賜種給撒種的，賜糧給人吃的，必多多加給你們種地的種子，又增添你們仁義的果子；¹¹叫你們凡事富足，可以多多施捨，就藉着我們使感謝歸於神。

¹²因為辦這供給的事，不但補聖徒的缺乏，而且叫許多人越發感謝神。¹³他們從這供給的事上得了憑據，知道你們承認基督，順服他的福音，多多地捐錢給他們和眾人，便將榮耀歸與神。¹⁴他們也因神極大的恩賜顯在你們心裏，就切切地想念你們，為你們祈禱。¹⁵感謝神，因他有說不盡的恩賜！

保羅為自己的職分辯護

10 我保羅，就是與你們見面的時候是謙卑的，不在你們那裏的時候向你們們是勇敢的，如今親自藉着基督的溫柔、和平勸你們。²有人以為我是憑着血氣行事，我也以為必須用勇敢待這等人；求你們不要叫我在你們那裏的時候，有這樣的勇敢。³因為我們雖然在血氣中行事，卻不憑着血氣爭戰。⁴我們爭戰的兵器，本不是屬血氣的，乃是在神面前有能力，可以攻破堅固的營壘，5將各樣的計謀，各樣攔阻人認識神的那些自高之事一概攻破了，又將人所有的心意奪回，使他都順服基督。6並且我已經預備好了，等你們十分順服的時候，要責罰那一切不順服的人。

7你們是看眼前的嗎？倘若有人自信是屬基督的，他要再想想，他如何屬基督，我們也是如何屬基督的。8主賜給我們權柄，是要造就你們，並不是要敗壞你們。我就是為這權柄稍微誇口，也不至於慚愧。9我說這話，免得你們以為我寫信是要威嚇你們。10因為有人說：「他的信又沉重、又利害，及至見面，卻是氣貌不揚、言語粗俗的。」11這等人當想，我們不在那裏的時候，信上的言語如何，見面的時候，行事也必如何。

12因為我們不敢將自己和那自薦的人同列相比。他們用自己度量自己，用自己比較自己，乃是不通達的。13我們不願意分外誇口，只要照神所量給我們的界限撐到你們那裏。14我們並非過了自己的界限，好像撐不到你們那裏，因為我們早到你們那裏，傳了基督的福音。15我們不仗着別人所勞碌的分外誇口；但指望你們信心增長的時候，所量給我們的界限，就可以因着你們更加開展，16得以將福音傳到你們以外的地方，並不是在別人界限之內，藉着他現成的事誇口。17但誇口的，當指着主誇口。18因為蒙悅納的，不是自己稱許的，乃是主所稱許的。

保羅與假使徒

11 但願你們寬容我這一點愚妄；其實，你們原是寬容我的。2我為你們起的憤恨，原是神那樣的憤恨。因為我曾把你們許配一個丈夫，要把你們如同貞潔

divine power to demolish strongholds. ⁵We demolish arguments and every pretension that sets itself up against the knowledge of God, and we take captive every thought to make it obedient to Christ. ⁶And we will be ready to punish every act of disobedience, once your obedience is complete.

⁷You are looking only on the surface of things.ᵃ If anyone is confident that he belongs to Christ, he should consider again that we belong to Christ just as much as he. ⁸For even if I boast somewhat freely about the authority the Lord gave us for building you up rather than pulling you down, I will not be ashamed of it. ⁹I do not want to seem to be trying to frighten you with my letters. ¹⁰For some say, "His letters are weighty and forceful, but in person he is unimpressive and his speaking amounts to nothing." ¹¹Such people should realize that what we are in our letters when we are absent, we will be in our actions when we are present.

¹²We do not dare to classify or compare ourselves with some who commend themselves. When they measure themselves by themselves and compare themselves with themselves, they are not wise. ¹³We, however, will not boast beyond proper limits, but will confine our boasting to the field God has assigned to us, a field that reaches even to you. ¹⁴We are not going too far in our boasting, as would be the case if we had not come to you, for we did get as far as you with the gospel of Christ. ¹⁵Neither do we go beyond our limits by boasting of work done by others.ᵇ Our hope is that, as your faith continues to grow, our area of activity among you will greatly expand, ¹⁶so that we can preach the gospel in the regions beyond you. For we do not want to boast about work already done in another man's territory. ¹⁷But, "Let him who boasts boast in the Lord."ᶜ ¹⁸For it is not the one who commends himself who is approved, but the one whom the Lord commends.

Paul and the False Apostles

11 I hope you will put up with a little of my foolishness; but you are already doing that. ²I am jealous for you with a godly jealousy. I promised you to one husband, to Christ, so that I might present you as a pure vir-

---

a 7 Or Look at the obvious facts   b 13-15 Or ¹³ We, however, will not boast about things that cannot be measured, but we will boast according to the standard of measurement that the God of measure has assigned us—a measurement that relates even to you. ¹⁴ . . . . ¹⁵ Neither do we boast about things that cannot be measured in regard to the work done by others.   c 17 Jer. 9:24

gin to him. ³But I am afraid that just as Eve was deceived by the serpent's cunning, your minds may somehow be led astray from your sincere and pure devotion to Christ. ⁴For if someone comes to you and preaches a Jesus other than the Jesus we preached, or if you receive a different spirit from the one you received, or a different gospel from the one you accepted, you put up with it easily enough. ⁵But I do not think I am in the least inferior to those "super-apostles." ⁶I may not be a trained speaker, but I do have knowledge. We have made this perfectly clear to you in every way.

⁷Was it a sin for me to lower myself in order to elevate you by preaching the gospel of God to you free of charge? ⁸I robbed other churches by receiving support from them so as to serve you. ⁹And when I was with you and needed something, I was not a burden to anyone, for the brothers who came from Macedonia supplied what I needed. I have kept myself from being a burden to you in any way, and will continue to do so. ¹⁰As surely as the truth of Christ is in me, nobody in the regions of Achaia will stop this boasting of mine. ¹¹Why? Because I do not love you? God knows I do! ¹²And I will keep on doing what I am doing in order to cut the ground from under those who want an opportunity to be considered equal with us in the things they boast about.

¹³For such men are false apostles, deceitful workmen, masquerading as apostles of Christ. ¹⁴And no wonder, for Satan himself masquerades as an angel of light. ¹⁵It is not surprising, then, if his servants masquerade as servants of righteousness. Their end will be what their actions deserve.

Paul Boasts About His Sufferings

¹⁶I repeat: Let no one take me for a fool. But if you do, then receive me just as you would a fool, so that I may do a little boasting. ¹⁷In this self-confident boasting I am not talking as the Lord would, but as a fool. ¹⁸Since many are boasting in the way the world does, I too will boast. ¹⁹You gladly put up with fools since you are so wise! ²⁰In fact, you even put up with anyone who enslaves you or exploits you or takes advantage of you or pushes himself forward or slaps you in the face. ²¹To my shame I admit that we were too weak for that!

What anyone else dares to boast about—I am speaking as a fool—I also dare to boast about. ²²Are they Hebrews? So am I. Are they Israelites? So am I. Are they Abraham's descendants? So am I. ²³Are they servants of Christ? (I am out

的童女獻給基督；³我只怕你們的心或偏於邪，失去那向基督所存純一清潔的心，就像蛇用詭詐誘惑了夏娃一樣。⁴假如有人來另傳一個耶穌，不是我們所傳過的，或者你們另受一個靈，不是你們所受過的；或者另得一個福音，不是你們所得過的，你們容讓他也就罷了。⁵但我想，我一點不在那些最大的使徒以下。⁶我的言語雖然粗俗，我的知識卻不粗俗。這是我們在凡事上向你們眾人顯明出來的。

⁷我因為白白傳神的福音給你們，就自居卑微，叫你們高升，這算是我犯罪嗎？⁸我虧負了別的教會，向他們取了工價來給你們効力。⁹我在你們那裏缺乏的時候，並沒有累着你們一個人，因我所缺乏的，那從馬其頓來的弟兄們都補足了。我向來凡事謹守，後來也必謹守，總不至於累着你們。¹⁰既有基督的誠實在我裏面，就無人能在亞該亞一帶地方阻擋我這自誇。¹¹為甚麼呢？是因我不愛你們嗎？有神知道。¹²我現在所做的，後來還要做，為要斷絕那些尋機會人的機會，使他們在所誇的事上也不過與我們一樣。

¹³那等人是假使徒，行事詭詐，裝作基督使徒的模樣。¹⁴這也不足為怪，因為連撒但也裝作光明的天使。¹⁵所以，他的差役若裝作仁義的差役，也不算希奇。他們的結局必然照着他們的行為。

保羅以所受的苦誇口

¹⁶我再說，人不可把我看作愚妄的；縱然如此，也要把我當作愚妄人接納，叫我可以略略自誇。¹⁷我說的話不是奉主命說的，乃是像愚妄人放膽自誇；¹⁸既有好些人憑着血氣自誇，我也要自誇了。¹⁹你們既是精明人，就能甘心忍耐愚妄人。²⁰假若有人強你們作奴僕，或侵吞你們，或擄掠你們，或侮慢你們，或打你們的臉，你們都能忍耐他。²¹我說這話是羞辱自己，好像我們從前是軟弱的！

然而人在何事上勇敢，（我說句愚妄話）我也勇敢。²²他們是希伯來人嗎？我也是。他們是以色列人嗎？我也是。他們是亞伯拉罕的後裔嗎？我也是。²³他們是基督的僕人嗎？

（我説句狂話）我更是！我比他們多受勞苦，多下監牢；受鞭打是過重的，冒死是屢次有的。²⁴被猶太人鞭打五次，每次四十，減去一下；²⁵被棍打了三次，被石頭打了一次；遇着船壞三次，一晝一夜在深海裏。²⁶又屢次行遠路，遭江河的危險、盜賊的危險、同族的危險、外邦人的危險、城裏的危險、曠野的危險、海中的危險、假弟兄的危險。²⁷受勞碌、受困苦、多次不得睡；又飢又渴，多次不得食；受寒冷，赤身露體。²⁸除了這外面的事，還有為眾教會掛心的事，天天壓在我身上。²⁹有誰軟弱我不軟弱呢？有誰跌倒我不焦急呢？

³⁰我若必須自誇，就誇那關乎我軟弱的事便了。³¹那永遠可稱頌之主耶穌的父神知道我不説謊。³²在大馬士革亞哩達王手下的提督，把守大馬士革城要捉拿我，³³我就從窗戶中，在筐子裏，從城牆上被人縋下去，脱離了他的手。

保羅的異象與他的刺

12 我自誇固然無益，但我是不得已的。如今我要説到主的顯現和啓示。²我認得一個在基督裏的人，他前十四年被提到第三層天上去。或在身內，我不知道；或在身外，我也不知道，只有神知道。³我認得這人，或在身內、或在身外，我都不知道，只有神知道。⁴他被提到樂園裏，聽見隱秘的言語，是人不可説的。⁵為這人，我要誇口；但是為我自己，除了我的軟弱以外，我並不誇口！⁶我就是願意誇口，也不算狂，因為我必説實話；只是我禁止不説，恐怕有人把我看高了，過於他在我身上所看見、所聽見的。

⁷又恐怕我因所得的啓示甚大，就過於自高，所以有一根刺加在我肉體上，就是撒但的差役要攻擊我，免得我過於自高。⁸為這事，我三次求過主，叫這刺離開我。⁹他對我説："我的恩典夠你用的，因為我的能力是在人的軟弱上顯得完全。"所以，我更喜歡誇自己的軟

of my mind to talk like this.) I am more. I have worked much harder, been in prison more frequently, been flogged more severely, and been exposed to death again and again. ²⁴Five times I received from the Jews the forty lashes minus one. ²⁵Three times I was beaten with rods, once I was stoned, three times I was shipwrecked, I spent a night and a day in the open sea, ²⁶I have been constantly on the move. I have been in danger from rivers, in danger from bandits, in danger from my own countrymen, in danger from Gentiles; in danger in the city, in danger in the country, in danger at sea; and in danger from false brothers. ²⁷I have labored and toiled and have often gone without sleep; I have known hunger and thirst and have often gone without food; I have been cold and naked. ²⁸Besides everything else, I face daily the pressure of my concern for all the churches. ²⁹Who is weak, and I do not feel weak? Who is led into sin, and I do not inwardly burn?

³⁰If I must boast, I will boast of the things that show my weakness. ³¹The God and Father of the Lord Jesus, who is to be praised forever, knows that I am not lying. ³²In Damascus the governor under King Aretas had the city of the Damascenes guarded in order to arrest me. ³³But I was lowered in a basket from a window in the wall and slipped through his hands.

Paul's Vision and His Thorn

12 I must go on boasting. Although there is nothing to be gained, I will go on to visions and revelations from the Lord. ²I know a man in Christ who fourteen years ago was caught up to the third heaven. Whether it was in the body or out of the body I do not know—God knows. ³And I know that this man—whether in the body or apart from the body I do not know, but God knows— ⁴was caught up to paradise. He heard inexpressible things, things that man is not permitted to tell. ⁵I will boast about a man like that, but I will not boast about myself, except about my weaknesses. ⁶Even if I should choose to boast, I would not be a fool, because I would be speaking the truth. But I refrain, so no one will think more of me than is warranted by what I do or say.

⁷To keep me from becoming conceited because of these surpassingly great revelations, there was given me a thorn in my flesh, a messenger of Satan, to torment me. ⁸Three times I pleaded with the Lord to take it away from me. ⁹But he said to me, "My grace is sufficient for you, for my power is made perfect in weakness." Therefore I will boast all the more gladly

about my weaknesses, so that Christ's power may rest on me. [10]That is why, for Christ's sake, I delight in weaknesses, in insults, in hardships, in persecutions, in difficulties. For when I am weak, then I am strong.

Paul's Concern for the Corinthians

[11]I have made a fool of myself, but you drove me to it. I ought to have been commended by you, for I am not in the least inferior to the "super-apostles," even though I am nothing. [12]The things that mark an apostle—signs, wonders and miracles—were done among you with great perseverance. [13]How were you inferior to the other churches, except that I was never a burden to you? Forgive me this wrong!

[14]Now I am ready to visit you for the third time, and I will not be a burden to you, because what I want is not your possessions but you. After all, children should not have to save up for their parents, but parents for their children. [15]So I will very gladly spend for you everything I have and expend myself as well. If I love you more, will you love me less? [16]Be that as it may, I have not been a burden to you. Yet, crafty fellow that I am, I caught you by trickery! [17]Did I exploit you through any of the men I sent you? [18]I urged Titus to go to you and I sent our brother with him. Titus did not exploit you, did he? Did we not act in the same spirit and follow the same course?

[19]Have you been thinking all along that we have been defending ourselves to you? We have been speaking in the sight of God as those in Christ; and everything we do, dear friends, is for your strengthening. [20]For I am afraid that when I come I may not find you as I want you to be, and you may not find me as you want me to be. I fear that there may be quarreling, jealousy, outbursts of anger, factions, slander, gossip, arrogance and disorder. [21]I am afraid that when I come again my God will humble me before you, and I will be grieved over many who have sinned earlier and have not repented of the impurity, sexual sin and debauchery in which they have indulged.

Final Warnings

13 | This will be my third visit to you. "Every matter must be established by the testimony of two or three witnesses."[a] [2]I already gave you a warning when I was with you the second time. I now repeat it while

弱，好叫基督的能力覆庇我。[10]我為基督的緣故，就以軟弱、凌辱、急難、逼迫、困苦為可喜樂的，因我甚麼時候軟弱，甚麼時候就剛強了！

保羅關心哥林多

[11]我成了愚妄人，是被你們強逼的，我本該被你們稱許才是。我雖算不了甚麼，卻沒有一件事在那些最大的使徒以下。[12]我在你們中間，用百般的忍耐，藉着神蹟、奇事、異能，顯出使徒的憑據來。[13]除了我不累着你們這一件事，你們還有甚麼事不及別的教會呢？這不公之處，求你們饒恕我吧！

[14]如今，我打算第三次到你們那裏去，也必不累着你們，因我所求的是你們，不是你們的財物。兒女不該為父母積財，父母該為兒女積財。[15]我也甘心樂意為你們的靈魂費財費力。難道我越發愛你們，就越發少得你們的愛嗎？[16]罷了！我自己並沒有累着你們，你們卻有人說我是詭詐，用心計牢籠你們。[17]我所差到你們那裏去的人，我藉着他們一個人佔過你們的便宜嗎？[18]我勸了提多到你們那裏去，又差那位兄弟與他同去，提多佔過你們的便宜嗎？我們行事不同是一個心靈（註："心靈"或作"聖靈"）嗎？不同是一個腳蹤嗎？

[19]你們到如今，還想我們是向你們分訴；我們本是在基督裏當神面前說話。親愛的弟兄啊，一切的事都是為造就你們。[20]我怕我再來的時候，見你們不合我所望的，你們見我也不合你們所想望的；又怕有紛爭、嫉妒、惱怒、結黨、毀謗、讒言、狂傲、混亂的事；[21]且怕我來的時候，我的神叫我在你們面前慚愧；又因許多人從前犯罪，行污穢、姦淫、邪蕩的事，不肯悔改，我就憂愁。

最後的警告

13 | 這是我第三次要到你們那裏去。憑兩三個人的口作見證，句句都要定準。[2]我從前說過，如今不在你們那裏又說，正如我第二次見你們的時候所說的一樣，就是對那犯了罪的和其餘的人說：

a 1 Deut. 19:15

"我若再來，必不寬容！" ³你們既然尋求基督在我裏面說話的憑據，我必不寬容。因為基督在你們身上不是軟弱的，在你們裏面是有大能的。⁴他因軟弱被釘在十字架上，卻因神的大能仍然活着。我們也是這樣同他軟弱，但因神向你們所顯的大能，也必與他同活。

⁵你們總要自己省察有信心沒有，也要自己試驗。豈不知，你們若不是可棄絕的，就有耶穌基督在你們心裏嗎？⁶我卻盼望你們曉得，我們不是可棄絕的人。⁷我們求神叫你們一件惡事都不做。這不是要顯明我們是蒙悅納的，是要你們行事端正，任憑人看我們是被棄絕的吧！⁸我們凡事不能敵擋真理，只能扶助真理。⁹即使我們軟弱，你們剛強，我們也歡喜；並且我們所求的，就是你們作完全人。¹⁰所以，我不在你們那裏的時候，把這話寫給你們，好叫我見你們的時候，不用照主所給我的權柄嚴厲地待你們。這權柄原是為造就人，並不是為敗壞人。

最後的問安

¹¹還有末了的話：願弟兄們都喜樂！要作完全人，要受安慰，要同心合意，要彼此和睦。如此，仁愛和平的神必常與你們同在。

¹²你們親嘴問安，彼此務要聖潔。¹³眾聖徒都問你們安。

¹⁴願主耶穌基督的恩惠、神的慈愛、聖靈的感動，常與你們眾人同在！

---

absent: On my return I will not spare those who sinned earlier or any of the others, ³since you are demanding proof that Christ is speaking through me. He is not weak in dealing with you, but is powerful among you. ⁴For to be sure, he was crucified in weakness, yet he lives by God's power. Likewise, we are weak in him, yet by God's power we will live with him to serve you.

⁵Examine yourselves to see whether you are in the faith; test yourselves. Do you not realize that Christ Jesus is in you—unless, of course, you fail the test? ⁶And I trust that you will discover that we have not failed the test. ⁷Now we pray to God that you will not do anything wrong. Not that people will see that we have stood the test but that you will do what is right even though we may seem to have failed. ⁸For we cannot do anything against the truth, but only for the truth. ⁹We are glad whenever we are weak but you are strong; and our prayer is for your perfection. ¹⁰This is why I write these things when I am absent, that when I come I may not have to be harsh in my use of authority—the authority the Lord gave me for building you up, not for tearing you down.

Final Greetings

¹¹Finally, brothers, good-by. Aim for perfection, listen to my appeal, be of one mind, live in peace. And the God of love and peace will be with you.

¹²Greet one another with a holy kiss. ¹³All the saints send their greetings.

¹⁴May the grace of the Lord Jesus Christ, and the love of God, and the fellowship of the Holy Spirit be with you all.

Galatians

加拉太書

1 Paul, an apostle—sent not from men nor by man, but by Jesus Christ and God the Father, who raised him from the dead— ²and all the brothers with me,

To the churches in Galatia:

³Grace and peace to you from God our Father and the Lord Jesus Christ, ⁴who gave himself for our sins to rescue us from the present evil age, according to the will of our God and Father, ⁵to whom be glory for ever and ever. Amen.

No Other Gospel

⁶I am astonished that you are so quickly deserting the one who called you by the grace of Christ and are turning to a different gospel— ⁷which is really no gospel at all. Evidently some people are throwing you into confusion and are trying to pervert the gospel of Christ. ⁸But even if we or an angel from heaven should preach a gospel other than the one we preached to you, let him be eternally condemned! ⁹As we have already said, so now I say again: If anybody is preaching to you a gospel other than what you accepted, let him be eternally condemned!

¹⁰Am I now trying to win the approval of men, or of God? Or am I trying to please men? If I were still trying to please men, I would not be a servant of Christ.

Paul Called by God

¹¹I want you to know, brothers, that the gospel I preached is not something that man made up. ¹²I did not receive it from any man, nor was I taught it; rather, I received it by revelation from Jesus Christ.

¹³For you have heard of my previous way of life in Judaism, how intensely I persecuted the church of God and tried to destroy it. ¹⁴I was advancing in Judaism beyond many Jews of my own age and was extremely zealous for the traditions of my fathers. ¹⁵But when God, who set me apart from birth[a] and called me by his grace, was pleased ¹⁶to reveal his Son in me so that I

a 15 Or from my mother's womb

1 作使徒的保羅（不是由於人，也不是藉着人，乃是藉着耶穌基督，與叫他從死裏復活的父神），²和一切與我同在的眾弟兄，

寫信給加拉太的各教會：

³願恩惠、平安從父神與我們的主耶穌基督歸與你們。⁴基督照我們父神的旨意為我們的罪捨己，要救我們脫離這罪惡的世代。⁵但願榮耀歸於神，直到永永遠遠。阿們！

沒有別的福音

⁶我希奇你們這麼快離開那藉着基督之恩召你們的，去從別的福音。⁷那並不是福音，不過有些人攪擾你們，要把基督的福音更改了。⁸但無論是我們，是天上來的使者，若傳福音給你們，與我們所傳給你們的不同，他就應當被咒詛。⁹我們已經說了，現在又說：若有人傳福音給你們，與你們所領受的不同，他就應當被咒詛！

¹⁰我現在是要得人的心呢？還是要得神的心呢？我豈是討人的喜歡嗎？若仍舊討人的喜歡，我就不是基督的僕人了。

保羅蒙神所召

¹¹弟兄們，我告訴你們，我素來所傳的福音，不是出於人的意思，¹²因為我不是從人領受的，也不是人教導我的，乃是從耶穌基督啓示來的。

¹³你們聽見我從前在猶太教中所行的事，怎樣極力逼迫、殘害神的教會；¹⁴我又在猶太教中，比我本國許多同歲的人更有長進，為我祖宗的遺傳更加熱心。¹⁵然而那把我從母腹裏分別出來、又施恩召我的神，¹⁶既然樂意將他兒子啓示在我心裏，叫我把

他傳在外邦人中，我就沒有與屬血氣的人商量，17也沒有上耶路撒冷去見那些比我先作使徒的，惟獨往阿拉伯去，後又回到大馬士革。

18過了三年，才上耶路撒冷去見磯法，和他同住了十五天。19至於別的使徒，除了主的兄弟雅各，我都沒有看見。20我寫給你們的不是謊話，這是在神面前說的。21以後我到了敘利亞和基利家境內。22那時，猶太信基督的各教會都沒有見過我的面，23不過聽說那從前逼迫我們的，現在傳揚他原先所殘害的真道。24他們就為我的緣故，歸榮耀給神。

眾使徒接納保羅

2 過了十四年，我同巴拿巴又上耶路撒冷去，並帶着提多同去。2我是奉啟示上去的，把我在外邦人中所傳的福音對弟兄們陳說，卻是背地裏對那有名望之人說的，惟恐我現在或是從前徒然奔跑。3但與我同去的提多雖是希臘人，也沒有勉強他受割禮。4因為有偷着引進來的假弟兄，私下窺探我們在基督耶穌裏的自由，要叫我們作奴僕。5我們就是一刻的工夫也沒有容讓順服他們，為要叫福音的真理仍存在你們中間。

6至於那些有名望的，不論他是何等人，都與我無干。神不以外貌取人。那些有名望的，並沒有加增我甚麼，7反倒看見了主託我傳福音給那未受割禮的人，正如託彼得傳福音給那受割禮的人。（那感動彼得叫他為受割禮之人作使徒的，也感動我，叫我為外邦人作使徒。）9又知道所賜給我的恩典，那稱為教會柱石的雅各、磯法、約翰，就向我和巴拿巴用右手行相交之禮，叫我們往外邦人那裏去，他們往受割禮的人那裏去。10只是願意我們記念窮人，這也是我本來熱心去行的。

might preach him among the Gentiles, I did not consult any man, 17nor did I go up to Jerusalem to see those who were apostles before I was, but I went immediately into Arabia and later returned to Damascus.

18Then after three years, I went up to Jerusalem to get acquainted with Peter[a] and stayed with him fifteen days. 19I saw none of the other apostles—only James, the Lord's brother. 20I assure you before God that what I am writing you is no lie. 21Later I went to Syria and Cilicia. 22I was personally unknown to the churches of Judea that are in Christ. 23They only heard the report: "The man who formerly persecuted us is now preaching the faith he once tried to destroy." 24And they praised God because of me.

Paul Accepted by the Apostles

2 Fourteen years later I went up again to Jerusalem, this time with Barnabas. I took Titus along also. 2I went in response to a revelation and set before them the gospel that I preach among the Gentiles. But I did this privately to those who seemed to be leaders, for fear that I was running or had run my race in vain. 3Yet not even Titus, who was with me, was compelled to be circumcised, even though he was a Greek. 4This matter arose because some false brothers had infiltrated our ranks to spy on the freedom we have in Christ Jesus and to make us slaves. 5We did not give in to them for a moment, so that the truth of the gospel might remain with you.

6As for those who seemed to be important— whatever they were makes no difference to me; God does not judge by external appearance— those men added nothing to my message. 7On the contrary, they saw that I had been entrusted with the task of preaching the gospel to the Gentiles,[b] just as Peter had been to the Jews.[c] 8For God, who was at work in the ministry of Peter as an apostle to the Jews, was also at work in my ministry as an apostle to the Gentiles. 9James, Peter[d] and John, those reputed to be pillars, gave me and Barnabas the right hand of fellowship when they recognized the grace given to me. They agreed that we should go to the Gentiles, and they to the Jews. 10All they asked was that we should continue to remember the poor, the very thing I was eager to do.

a 18 Greek Cephas　b 7 Greek uncircumcised　c 7 Greek circumcised; also in verses 8 and 9　d 9 Greek Cephas; also in verses 11 and 14

Paul Opposes Peter

[11]When Peter came to Antioch, I opposed him to his face, because he was clearly in the wrong. [12]Before certain men came from James, he used to eat with the Gentiles. But when they arrived, he began to draw back and separate himself from the Gentiles because he was afraid of those who belonged to the circumcision group. [13]The other Jews joined him in his hypocrisy, so that by their hypocrisy even Barnabas was led astray.

[14]When I saw that they were not acting in line with the truth of the gospel, I said to Peter in front of them all, "You are a Jew, yet you live like a Gentile and not like a Jew. How is it, then, that you force Gentiles to follow Jewish customs?

[15]"We who are Jews by birth and not 'Gentile sinners' [16]know that a man is not justified by observing the law, but by faith in Jesus Christ. So we, too, have put our faith in Christ Jesus that we may be justified by faith in Christ and not by observing the law, because by observing the law no one will be justified.

[17]"If, while we seek to be justified in Christ, it becomes evident that we ourselves are sinners, does that mean that Christ promotes sin? Absolutely not! [18]If I rebuild what I destroyed, I prove that I am a lawbreaker. [19]For through the law I died to the law so that I might live for God. [20]I have been crucified with Christ and I no longer live, but Christ lives in me. The life I live in the body, I live by faith in the Son of God, who loved me and gave himself for me. [21]I do not set aside the grace of God, for if righteousness could be gained through the law, Christ died for nothing!"[a]

Faith or Observance of the Law

3 You foolish Galatians! Who has bewitched you? Before your very eyes Jesus Christ was clearly portrayed as crucified. [2]I would like to learn just one thing from you: Did you receive the Spirit by observing the law, or by believing what you heard? [3]Are you so foolish? After beginning with the Spirit, are you now trying to attain your goal by human effort? [4]Have you suffered so much for nothing—if it really was for nothing? [5]Does God give you his Spirit and work miracles among you because you observe the law, or because you believe what you heard?

保羅抵擋磯法

[11]後來磯法到了安提阿，因他有可責之處，我就當面抵擋他。[12]從雅各那裏來的人未到以先，他和外邦人一同吃飯；及至他們來到，他因怕奉割禮的人，就退去與外邦人隔開了。[13]其餘的猶太人也都隨着他裝假，甚至連巴拿巴也隨夥裝假。

[14]但我一看見他們行得不正，與福音的真理不合，就在眾人面前對磯法說："你既是猶太人，若隨外邦人行事，不隨猶太人行事，怎麼還勉強外邦人隨猶太人呢？

[15]"我們這生來的猶太人，不是外邦的罪人，[16]既知道人稱義不是因行律法，乃是因信耶穌基督，連我們也信了基督耶穌，使我們因信基督稱義，不因行律法稱義，因為凡有血氣的，沒有一人因行律法稱義。

[17]"我們若求在基督裏稱義，卻仍舊是罪人，難道基督是叫人犯罪的嗎？斷乎不是！[18]我素來所拆毀的，若重新建造，這就證明自己是犯罪的人。[19]我因律法，就向律法死了，叫我可以向神活着。[20]我已經與基督同釘十字架，現在活着的不再是我，乃是基督在我裏面活着；並且我如今在肉身活着，是因信神的兒子而活，他是愛我，為我捨己。[21]我不廢掉神的恩；義若是藉着律法得的，基督就是徒然死了。"

信心或行律法

3 無知的加拉太人哪，耶穌基督釘十字架，已經活畫在你們眼前，誰又迷惑了你們呢？[2]我只要問你們這一件：你們受了聖靈，是因行律法呢？是因聽信福音呢？[3]你們既靠聖靈入門，如今還靠肉身成全嗎？你們是這樣的無知嗎？[4]你們受苦如此之多，都是徒然的嗎？難道果真是徒然的嗎？[5]那賜給你們聖靈，又在你們中間行異能的，是因你們行律法呢？是因你們聽信福音呢？

---

[a] 21 Some interpreters end the quotation after verse 14.

6正如“亞伯拉罕信神，這就算為他的義。”7所以你們要知道，那以信為本的人，就是亞伯拉罕的子孫。8並且聖經既然預先看明，神要叫外邦人因信稱義，就早已傳福音給亞伯拉罕，說：“萬國都必因你得福。”9可見那以信為本的人和有信心的亞伯拉罕一同得福。

10凡以行律法為本的，都是被咒詛的，因為經上記着：“凡不常照律法書上所記一切之事去行的，就被咒詛。”11沒有一個人靠着律法在神面前稱義，這是明顯的，因為經上說：“義人必因信得生。”12律法原不本乎信，只說：“行這些事的，就必因此活着。”13基督既為我們受了咒詛（註：“受”原文作“成”），就贖出我們脫離律法的咒詛，因為經上記着：“凡掛在木頭上都是被咒詛的。”14這便叫亞伯拉罕的福，因基督耶穌可以臨到外邦人，使我們因信得着所應許的聖靈。

律法和應許

15弟兄們，我且照着人的常話說：雖然是人的文約，若已經立定了，就沒有能廢棄或加增的。16所應許的原是向亞伯拉罕和他子孫說的；神並不是說“眾子孫”，指着許多人，乃是說“你那一個子孫”，指着一個人，就是基督。17我是這麼說：神預先所立的約，不能被那四百三十年以後的律法廢掉，叫應許歸於虛空。18因為承受產業，若本乎律法，就不本乎應許；但神是憑着應許，把產業賜給亞伯拉罕。

19這樣說來，律法是為甚麼有的呢？原是為過犯添上的，等候那蒙應許的子孫來到，並且是藉天使經中保之手設立的。20但中保不是為一面作的，神卻是一位。

21這樣，律法是與神的應許反對嗎？斷乎不是！若曾傳一個能叫人得生的律法，義就誠然本乎律法了。22但聖經把眾人都圈在罪裏，使

6Consider Abraham: "He believed God, and it was credited to him as righteousness."[a] 7Understand, then, that those who believe are children of Abraham. 8The Scripture foresaw that God would justify the Gentiles by faith, and announced the gospel in advance to Abraham: "All nations will be blessed through you."[b] 9So those who have faith are blessed along with Abraham, the man of faith.

10All who rely on observing the law are under a curse, for it is written: "Cursed is everyone who does not continue to do everything written in the Book of the Law."[c] 11Clearly no one is justified before God by the law, because, "The righteous will live by faith."[d] 12The law is not based on faith; on the contrary, "The man who does these things will live by them."[e] 13Christ redeemed us from the curse of the law by becoming a curse for us, for it is written: "Cursed is everyone who is hung on a tree."[f] 14He redeemed us in order that the blessing given to Abraham might come to the Gentiles through Christ Jesus, so that by faith we might receive the promise of the Spirit.

The Law and the Promise

15Brothers, let me take an example from everyday life. Just as no one can set aside or add to a human covenant that has been duly established, so it is in this case. 16The promises were spoken to Abraham and to his seed. The Scripture does not say "and to seeds," meaning many people, but "and to your seed,"[g] meaning one person, who is Christ. 17What I mean is this: The law, introduced 430 years later, does not set aside the covenant previously established by God and thus do away with the promise. 18For if the inheritance depends on the law, then it no longer depends on a promise; but God in his grace gave it to Abraham through a promise.

19What, then, was the purpose of the law? It was added because of transgressions until the Seed to whom the promise referred had come. The law was put into effect through angels by a mediator. 20A mediator, however, does not represent just one party; but God is one.

21Is the law, therefore, opposed to the promises of God? Absolutely not! For if a law had been given that could impart life, then righteousness would certainly have come by the law. 22But the Scripture declares that the whole world is a prisoner of sin, so that what was

a 6 Gen. 15:6　　*b 8* Gen. 12:3; 18:18; 22:18　　*c 10* Deut. 27:26
d 11 Hab. 2:4　　*e 12* Lev. 18:5　　*f 13* Deut. 21:23
g 16 Gen. 12:7; 13:15; 24:7

promised, being given through faith in Jesus Christ, might be given to those who believe.

²³Before this faith came, we were held prisoners by the law, locked up until faith should be revealed. ²⁴So the law was put in charge to lead us to Christ*ᵃ* that we might be justified by faith. ²⁵Now that faith has come, we are no longer under the supervision of the law.

Sons of God

²⁶You are all sons of God through faith in Christ Jesus, ²⁷for all of you who were baptized into Christ have clothed yourselves with Christ. ²⁸There is neither Jew nor Greek, slave nor free, male nor female, for you are all one in Christ Jesus. ²⁹If you belong to Christ, then you are Abraham's seed, and heirs according to the promise.

4 What I am saying is that as long as the heir is a child, he is no different from a slave, although he owns the whole estate. ²He is subject to guardians and trustees until the time set by his father. ³So also, when we were children, we were in slavery under the basic principles of the world. ⁴But when the time had fully come, God sent his Son, born of a woman, born under law, ⁵to redeem those under law, that we might receive the full rights of sons. ⁶Because you are sons, God sent the Spirit of his Son into our hearts, the Spirit who calls out, "Abba,*ᵇ* Father." ⁷So you are no longer a slave, but a son; and since you are a son, God has made you also an heir.

Paul's Concern for the Galatians

⁸Formerly, when you did not know God, you were slaves to those who by nature are not gods. ⁹But now that you know God—or rather are known by God—how is it that you are turning back to those weak and miserable principles all over again? Do you wish to be enslaved by them all over again? ¹⁰You are observing special days and months and seasons and years! ¹¹I fear for you, that somehow I have wasted my efforts on you.

¹²I plead with you, brothers, become like me, for I became like you. You have done me no wrong. ¹³As you know, it was because of an illness that I first preached the gospel to you. ¹⁴Even though my illness was a trial to you, you did not treat me with contempt or scorn. Instead, you welcomed me as if I were an angel of God, as if I were Christ Jesus himself. ¹⁵What has happened to all your joy? I can testify that, if

a 24 Or charge until Christ came   b 6 Aramaic for Father

所應許的福因信耶穌基督歸給那信的人。

²³但這因信得救的理還未來以先，我們被看守在律法之下，直圈到那將來的真道顯明出來。²⁴這樣，律法是我們訓蒙的師傅，引我們到基督那裏，使我們因信稱義。²⁵但這因信得救的理既然來到，我們從此就不在師傅的手下了。

神的兒子

²⁶所以，你們因信基督耶穌，都是神的兒子。²⁷你們受洗歸入基督的，都是披戴基督了。²⁸並不分猶太人、希臘人、自主的、為奴的，或男或女，因為你們在基督耶穌裏，都成為一了。²⁹你們既屬乎基督，就是亞伯拉罕的後裔，是照着應許承受產業的了。

4 我說那承受產業的，雖然是全業的主人，但為孩童的時候，卻與奴僕毫無分別，²乃在師傅和管家的手下，直等他父親預定的時候來到。³我們為孩童的時候，受管於世俗小學之下，也是如此。⁴及至時候滿足，神就差遣他的兒子，為女子所生，且生在律法以下，⁵要把律法以下的人贖出來，叫我們得着兒子的名分。⁶你們既為兒子，神就差他兒子的靈進入你們（註：原文作「我們」）的心，呼叫："阿爸，父！"⁷可見，從此以後，你不是奴僕，乃是兒子了。既是兒子，就靠着神為後嗣。

保羅關心加拉太人

⁸但從前你們不認識神的時候，是給那些本來不是神的作奴僕。⁹現在你們既然認識神，更可說是被神所認識的，怎麼還要歸回那懦弱無用的小學，情願再給他作奴僕呢？¹⁰你們謹守日子、月份、節期、年份，¹¹我為你們害怕，惟恐我在你們身上是枉費了工夫。

¹²弟兄們，我勸你們要像我一樣，因為我也像你們一樣，你們一點沒有虧負我。¹³你們知道，我頭一次傳福音給你們，是因為身體有疾病。¹⁴你們為我身體的緣故受試煉，沒有輕看我，也沒有厭棄我，反倒接待我，如同神的使者，如同基督耶穌。¹⁵你們當日所誇的福氣在哪裏呢？那

時，你們若能行，就是把自己的眼睛剜出來給我，也都情願。這是我可以給你們作見證的！ 16如今，我將真理告訴你們，就成了你們的仇敵嗎？

17那些人熱心待你們，卻不是好意，是要離間你們（註：原文作「把你們關在外面」），叫你們熱心待他們。 18在善事上常用熱心待人，原是好的，卻不單我與你們同在的時候才這樣。 19我小子啊，我為你們再受生產之苦，直等到基督成形在你們心裏。 20我巴不得現今在你們那裏，改換口氣，因我為你們心裏作難。

夏甲與撒拉

21你們這願意在律法以下的人，請告訴我，你們豈沒有聽見律法嗎？ 22因為律法上記着，<u>亞伯拉罕</u>有兩個兒子，一個是使女生的，一個是自主之婦人生的。 23然而那使女所生的，是按着血氣生的；那自主之婦人所生的，是憑着應許生的。 24這都是比方，那兩個婦人就是兩約。一約是出於<u>西奈山</u>，生子為奴，乃是<u>夏甲</u>。 25這<u>夏甲</u>二字是指着<u>阿拉伯</u>的<u>西奈山</u>，與現在的<u>耶路撒冷</u>同類，因<u>耶路撒冷</u>和她的兒女都是為奴的。 26但那在上的<u>耶路撒冷</u>是自主的，她是我們的母。 27因為經上記着：

"不懷孕、不生養的，
　你要歡樂；
未曾經過產難的，
　你要高聲歡呼，
因為沒有丈夫的，
　比有丈夫的兒女更多。"

28弟兄們，我們是憑着應許作兒女，如同<u>以撒</u>一樣。 29當時，那按着血氣生的，逼迫了那按着聖靈生的，現在也是這樣。 30然而經上是怎麼說的呢？是說："把使女和她兒子趕出去，因為使女的兒子不可與自主婦人的兒子一同承受產業。" 31弟兄們，這樣看來，我們不是使女的兒女，乃是自主婦人的兒女了。

you could have done so, you would have torn out your eyes and given them to me. [16]Have I now become your enemy by telling you the truth?

[17]Those people are zealous to win you over, but for no good. What they want is to alienate you ⌊from us⌋, so that you may be zealous for them. [18]It is fine to be zealous, provided the purpose is good, and to be so always and not just when I am with you. [19]My dear children, for whom I am again in the pains of childbirth until Christ is formed in you, [20]how I wish I could be with you now and change my tone, because I am perplexed about you!

Hagar and Sarah

[21]Tell me, you who want to be under the law, are you not aware of what the law says? [22]For it is written that Abraham had two sons, one by the slave woman and the other by the free woman. [23]His son by the slave woman was born in the ordinary way; but his son by the free woman was born as the result of a promise. [24]These things may be taken figuratively, for the women represent two covenants. One covenant is from Mount Sinai and bears children who are to be slaves: This is Hagar. [25]Now Hagar stands for Mount Sinai in Arabia and corresponds to the present city of Jerusalem, because she is in slavery with her children. [26]But the Jerusalem that is above is free, and she is our mother. [27]For it is written:

"Be glad, O barren woman,
　who bears no children;
break forth and cry aloud,
　you who have no labor pains;
because more are the children of the desolate
　woman
　than of her who has a husband."[a]

[28]Now you, brothers, like Isaac, are children of promise. [29]At that time the son born in the ordinary way persecuted the son born by the power of the Spirit. It is the same now. [30]But what does the Scripture say? "Get rid of the slave woman and her son, for the slave woman's son will never share in the inheritance with the free woman's son."[b] [31]Therefore, brothers, we are not children of the slave woman, but of the free woman.

a 27 Isaiah 54:1　b 30 Gen. 21:10

Freedom in Christ

5 It is for freedom that Christ has set us free. Stand firm, then, and do not let yourselves be burdened again by a yoke of slavery.

²Mark my words! I, Paul, tell you that if you let yourselves be circumcised, Christ will be of no value to you at all. ³Again I declare to every man who lets himself be circumcised that he is obligated to obey the whole law. ⁴You who are trying to be justified by law have been alienated from Christ; you have fallen away from grace. ⁵But by faith we eagerly await through the Spirit the righteousness for which we hope. ⁶For in Christ Jesus neither circumcision nor uncircumcision has any value. The only thing that counts is faith expressing itself through love.

⁷You were running a good race. Who cut in on you and kept you from obeying the truth? ⁸That kind of persuasion does not come from the one who calls you. ⁹"A little yeast works through the whole batch of dough." ¹⁰I am confident in the Lord that you will take no other view. The one who is throwing you into confusion will pay the penalty, whoever he may be. ¹¹Brothers, if I am still preaching circumcision, why am I still being persecuted? In that case the offense of the cross has been abolished. ¹²As for those agitators, I wish they would go the whole way and emasculate themselves!

¹³You, my brothers, were called to be free. But do not use your freedom to indulge the sinful nature*ᵃ*; rather, serve one another in love. ¹⁴The entire law is summed up in a single command: "Love your neighbor as yourself."*ᵇ* ¹⁵If you keep on biting and devouring each other, watch out or you will be destroyed by each other.

Life by the Spirit

¹⁶So I say, live by the Spirit, and you will not gratify the desires of the sinful nature. ¹⁷For the sinful nature desires what is contrary to the Spirit, and the Spirit what is contrary to the sinful nature. They are in conflict with each other, so that you do not do what you want. ¹⁸But if you are led by the Spirit, you are not under law.

¹⁹The acts of the sinful nature are obvious: sexual immorality, impurity and debauchery; ²⁰idolatry and witchcraft; hatred, discord, jealousy, fits of rage, selfish ambition, dissensions, factions ²¹and envy; drunkenness, orgies, and the like. I warn you, as I did before, that those

a 13 Or the flesh; also in verses 16, 17, 19 and 24
b 14 Lev. 19:18

在基督裏的自由

5 基督釋放了我們，叫我們得以自由，所以要站立得穩，不要再被奴僕的軛挾制。

²我保羅告訴你們：若受割禮，基督就與你們無益了。³我再指着凡受割禮的人確實地說，他是欠着行全律法的債。⁴你們這要靠律法稱義的，是與基督隔絕，從恩典中墜落了。⁵我們靠着聖靈，憑着信心，等候所盼望的義。⁶原來在基督耶穌裏，受割禮不受割禮全無功效；惟獨使人生發仁愛的信心才有功效。

⁷你們向來跑得好，有誰攔阻你們，叫你們不順從真理呢？⁸這樣的勸導不是出於那召你們的。⁹"一點麵酵能使全團都發起來。"¹⁰我在主裏很信你們必不懷別樣的心，但攪擾你們的，無論是誰，必擔當他的罪名！¹¹弟兄們，我若仍舊傳割禮，為甚麼還受逼迫呢？若是這樣，那十字架討厭的地方就沒有了。¹²恨不得那攪亂你們的人，把自己割絕了。

¹³弟兄們，你們蒙召是要得自由，只是不可將你們的自由當作放縱情慾的機會，總要用愛心互相服侍。¹⁴因為全律法都包在"愛人如己"這一句話之內了。¹⁵你們要謹慎，若相咬相吞，只怕要彼此消滅了。

順着聖靈而行

¹⁶我說：你們當順着聖靈而行，就不放縱肉體的情慾了。¹⁷因為情慾和聖靈相爭，聖靈和情慾相爭，這兩個是彼此相敵，使你們不能做所願意做的。¹⁸但你們若被聖靈引導，就不在律法以下。

¹⁹情慾的事都是顯而易見的，就如姦淫、污穢、邪蕩、²⁰拜偶像、邪術、仇恨、爭競、忌恨、惱怒、結黨、紛爭、異端、²¹嫉妒（註：有古卷在此有"兇殺"二字）、醉酒、荒宴等類。我從前告訴你們，現在又告訴你們，

行這樣事的人必不能承受神的國。

22聖靈所結的果子，就是仁愛、喜樂、和平、忍耐、恩慈、良善、信實、23溫柔、節制。這樣的事，沒有律法禁止。24凡屬基督耶穌的人，是已經把肉體連肉體的邪情私慾同釘在十字架上了。25我們若是靠聖靈得生，就當靠聖靈行事。26不要貪圖虛名，彼此惹氣，互相嫉妒。

向眾人行善

6 弟兄們，若有人偶然被過犯所勝，你們屬靈的人，就當用溫柔的心把他挽回過來；又當自己小心，恐怕也被引誘。2你們各人的重擔要互相擔當，如此，就完全了基督的律法。3人若無有，自己還以為有，就是自欺了。4各人應當察驗自己的行為。這樣，他所誇的就專在自己，不在別人了，5因為各人必擔當自己的擔子。

6在道理上受教的，當把一切需用的供給施教的人。

7不要自欺，神是輕慢不得的。人種的是甚麼，收的也是甚麼。8順着情慾撒種的，必從情慾收敗壞；順着聖靈撒種的，必從聖靈收永生。9我們行善，不可喪志；若不灰心，到了時候就要收成。10所以，有了機會，就當向眾人行善，向信徒一家的人更當這樣。

不在於割禮而在於作新造的人

11請看我親手寫給你們的字是何等的大呢！

12凡希圖外貌體面的人，都勉強你們受割禮，無非是怕自己為基督的十字架受逼迫。13他們那些受割禮的，連自己也不守律法。他們願意你們受割禮，不過要藉着你們的肉體誇口。14但我斷不以別的誇口，只誇我們主耶穌基督的十字架。因這十字架，就我而論，世界已經釘在十字架上；就世界而論，我已經釘在十字架上。15受割禮不受割禮都無關緊要，要緊的就是作新造的人。16凡照此理而行的，願平安、憐憫加

who live like this will not inherit the kingdom of God.

22But the fruit of the Spirit is love, joy, peace, patience, kindness, goodness, faithfulness, 23gentleness and self-control. Against such things there is no law. 24Those who belong to Christ Jesus have crucified the sinful nature with its passions and desires. 25Since we live by the Spirit, let us keep in step with the Spirit. 26Let us not become conceited, provoking and envying each other.

Doing Good to All

6 Brothers, if someone is caught in a sin, you who are spiritual should restore him gently. But watch yourself, or you also may be tempted. 2Carry each other's burdens, and in this way you will fulfill the law of Christ. 3If anyone thinks he is something when he is nothing, he deceives himself. 4Each one should test his own actions. Then he can take pride in himself, without comparing himself to somebody else, 5for each one should carry his own load.

6Anyone who receives instruction in the word must share all good things with his instructor.

7Do not be deceived: God cannot be mocked. A man reaps what he sows. 8The one who sows to please his sinful nature, from that nature*a* will reap destruction; the one who sows to please the Spirit, from the Spirit will reap eternal life. 9Let us not become weary in doing good, for at the proper time we will reap a harvest if we do not give up. 10Therefore, as we have opportunity, let us do good to all people, especially to those who belong to the family of believers.

Not Circumcision but a New Creation

11See what large letters I use as I write to you with my own hand!

12Those who want to make a good impression outwardly are trying to compel you to be circumcised. The only reason they do this is to avoid being persecuted for the cross of Christ. 13Not even those who are circumcised obey the law, yet they want you to be circumcised that they may boast about your flesh. 14May I never boast except in the cross of our Lord Jesus Christ, through which*b* the world has been crucified to me, and I to the world. 15Neither circumcision nor uncircumcision means anything; what counts is a new creation. 16Peace and mercy

---

a 8 Or his flesh, from the flesh　　b 14 Or whom

to all who follow this rule, even to the Israel of God.

¹⁷Finally, let no one cause me trouble, for I bear on my body the marks of Jesus.

¹⁸The grace of our Lord Jesus Christ be with your spirit, brothers. Amen.

給他們和神的<u>以色列</u>民。

¹⁷從今以後，人都不要攪擾我，因為我身上帶着耶穌的印記。

¹⁸弟兄們，願我主耶穌基督的恩常在你們心裏。阿們！

圖五：加拉太書中的主要地方
MAP 5 : KEY PLACES IN GALATIANS

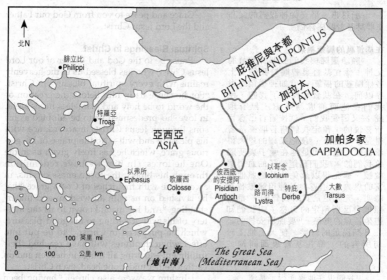

以弗所書

Ephesians

1 奉神旨意，作基督耶穌使徒的<u>保羅</u>，

1 Paul, an apostle of Christ Jesus by the will of God,

寫信給在<u>以弗所</u>的聖徒，就是在基督耶穌裏有忠心的人：

To the saints in Ephesus,*a* the faithful*b* in Christ Jesus:

² 願恩惠、平安從神我們的父和主耶穌基督歸與你們！

²Grace and peace to you from God our Father and the Lord Jesus Christ.

在基督裏的屬靈福氣

Spiritual Blessings in Christ

³ 願頌讚歸與我們主耶穌基督的父神！他在基督裏曾賜給我們天上各樣屬靈的福氣。⁴就如神從創立世界以前，在基督裏揀選了我們，使我們在他面前成為聖潔，無有瑕疵；⁵又因愛我們，就按着自己意旨所喜悅的，預定我們藉着耶穌基督得兒子的名分，⁶使他榮耀的恩典得着稱讚。這恩典是他在愛子裏所賜給我們的。⁷我們藉這愛子的血得蒙救贖，過犯得以赦免，乃是照他豐富的恩典。⁸這恩典是神用諸般智慧聰明，充充足足賞給我們的，⁹都是照他自己所預定的美意，叫我們知道他旨意的奧秘，¹⁰要照所安排的，在日期滿足的時候，使天上地上一切所有的，都在基督裏面同歸於一。

³Praise be to the God and Father of our Lord Jesus Christ, who has blessed us in the heavenly realms with every spiritual blessing in Christ. ⁴For he chose us in him before the creation of the world to be holy and blameless in his sight. In love ⁵he*c* predestined us to be adopted as his sons through Jesus Christ, in accordance with his pleasure and will— ⁶to the praise of his glorious grace, which he has freely given us in the One he loves. ⁷In him we have redemption through his blood, the forgiveness of sins, in accordance with the riches of God's grace ⁸that he lavished on us with all wisdom and understanding. ⁹And he*d* made known to us the mystery of his will according to his good pleasure, which he purposed in Christ, ¹⁰to be put into effect when the times will have reached their fulfillment—to bring all things in heaven and on earth together under one head, even Christ.

¹¹我們也在他裏面得了基業（註："得"或作"成"），這原是那位隨己意行做萬事的，照着他旨意所預定的，¹²叫他的榮耀，從我們這首先在基督裏有盼望的人，可以得着稱讚。¹³你們既聽見真理的道，就是那叫你們得救的福音，也信了基督，既然信他，就受了所應許的聖靈為印記。（註：原文作"質"），直等到神之民（註："民"原文作"產業"）被贖，使他的榮耀得着稱讚。

¹¹In him we were also chosen,*e* having been predestined according to the plan of him who works out everything in conformity with the purpose of his will, ¹²in order that we, who were the first to hope in Christ, might be for the praise of his glory. ¹³And you also were included in Christ when you heard the word of truth, the gospel of your salvation. Having believed, you were marked in him with a seal, the promised Holy Spirit, ¹⁴who is a deposit guaranteeing our inheritance until the redemption of those who are God's possession—to the praise of his glory.

---

a 1 Some early manuscripts do not have in Ephesus.   b 1 Or believers who are   c 4,5 Or sight in love. ⁵ He   d 8,9 Or us. With all wisdom and understanding, ⁹ he   e 11 Or were made heirs

Thanksgiving and Prayer

¹⁵For this reason, ever since I heard about your faith in the Lord Jesus and your love for all the saints, ¹⁶I have not stopped giving thanks for you, remembering you in my prayers. ¹⁷I keep asking that the God of our Lord Jesus Christ, the glorious Father, may give you the Spirit*a* of wisdom and revelation, so that you may know him better. ¹⁸I pray also that the eyes of your heart may be enlightened in order that you may know the hope to which he has called you, the riches of his glorious inheritance in the saints, ¹⁹and his incomparably great power for us who believe. That power is like the working of his mighty strength, ²⁰which he exerted in Christ when he raised him from the dead and seated him at his right hand in the heavenly realms, ²¹far above all rule and authority, power and dominion, and every title that can be given, not only in the present age but also in the one to come. ²²And God placed all things under his feet and appointed him to be head over everything for the church, ²³which is his body, the fullness of him who fills everything in every way.

Made Alive in Christ

2 As for you, you were dead in your transgressions and sins, ²in which you used to live when you followed the ways of this world and of the ruler of the kingdom of the air, the spirit who is now at work in those who are disobedient. ³All of us also lived among them at one time, gratifying the cravings of our sinful nature*b* and following its desires and thoughts. Like the rest, we were by nature objects of wrath. ⁴But because of his great love for us, God, who is rich in mercy, ⁵made us alive with Christ even when we were dead in transgressions—it is by grace you have been saved. ⁶And God raised us up with Christ and seated us with him in the heavenly realms in Christ Jesus, ⁷in order that in the coming ages he might show the incomparable riches of his grace, expressed in his kindness to us in Christ Jesus. ⁸For it is by grace you have been saved, through faith—and this not from yourselves, it is the gift of God— ⁹not by works, so that no one can boast. ¹⁰For we are God's workmanship, created in Christ Jesus to do good works, which God prepared in advance for us to do.

感恩與禱告

¹⁵因此，我既聽見你們信從主耶穌，親愛眾聖徒，¹⁶就為你們不住地感謝神，禱告的時候，常提到你們，¹⁷求我們主耶穌基督的神，榮耀的父，將那賜人智慧和啓示的靈賞給你們，使你們真知道他。¹⁸並且照明你們心中的眼睛，使你們知道他的恩召有何等指望；他在聖徒中得的基業有何等豐盛的榮耀，¹⁹並知道他向我們這信的人所顯的能力是何等浩大，²⁰就是照他在基督身上所運行的大能大力，使他從死裏復活，叫他在天上坐在自己的右邊，²¹遠超過一切執政的、掌權的、有能的、主治的和一切有名的，不但是今世的，連來世的也都超過了。²²又將萬有服在他的腳下，使他為教會作萬有之首。²³教會是他的身體，是那充滿萬有者所充滿的。

在基督裏活過來

2 你們死在過犯罪惡之中，他叫你們活過來。²那時，你們在其中行事為人，隨從今世的風俗，順服空中掌權者的首領，就是現今在悖逆之子心中運行的邪靈。³我們從前也都在他們中間，放縱肉體的私慾，隨着肉體和心中所喜好的去行，本為可怒之子，和別人一樣。⁴然而神既有豐富的憐憫，因他愛我們的大愛，⁵當我們死在過犯中的時候，便叫我們與基督一同活過來（你們得救是本乎恩）。⁶他又叫我們與基督耶穌一同復活，一同坐在天上，⁷要將他極豐富的恩典，就是他在基督耶穌裏向我們所施的恩慈，顯明給後來的世代看。⁸你們得救是本乎恩，也因着信。這並不是出於自己，乃是神所賜的；⁹也不是出於行為，免得有人自誇。¹⁰我們原是他的工作，在基督耶穌裏造成的，為要叫我們行善，就是神所預備叫我們行的。

---

a 17 Or a spirit   *b 3 Or our flesh*

在基督裏合而為一

11 所以你們應當記念，你們從前按肉體是外邦人，是稱為沒受割禮的，這名原是那些憑人手在肉身上稱為受割禮之人所起的。12 那時，你們與基督無關，在以色列國民以外，在所應許的諸約上是局外人，並且活在世上沒有指望，沒有神。13 你們從前遠離神的人，如今卻在基督耶穌裏，靠着他的血，已經得親近了。

14 因他使我們和睦（註：原文作"因他是我們的和睦"），將兩下合而為一，拆毀了中間隔斷的牆，15 而且以自己的身體廢掉冤仇，就是那記在律法上的規條，為要將兩下藉着自己造成一個新人，如此便成就了和睦。16 既在十字架上滅了冤仇，便藉這十字架使兩下歸為一體，與神和好了，17 並且來傳和平的福音給你們遠處的人，也給那近處的人。18 因為我們兩下藉着他被一個聖靈所感，得以進到父面前。

19 這樣，你們不再作外人和客旅，是與聖徒同國，是神家裏的人了。20 並且被建造在使徒和先知的根基上，有基督耶穌自己為房角石，21 各（註：或作"全"）房靠他聯絡得合式，漸漸成為主的聖殿。22 你們也靠他同被建造，成為神藉着聖靈居住的所在。

保羅為外邦人的傳道人

3 因此，我保羅為你們外邦人作了基督耶穌被囚的，替你們祈禱（註：此句乃照對14節所加）。2 諒必你們曾聽見神賜恩給我，將關切你們的職分託付我，3 用啟示使我知道福音的奧秘，正如我以前略略寫過的。4 你們念了，就能曉得我深知基督的奧秘，5 這奧秘在以前的世代沒有叫人知道，像如今藉着聖靈啟示他的聖使徒和先知一樣。6 這奧秘就是外邦人在基督耶穌裏，藉着福音，得以同為後嗣，同為一體，同蒙應許。

7 我作了這福音的執事，是照神的恩賜，這恩賜是照他運行的大能賜給我的。8 我本來比眾聖徒中最小的還小，然而他還賜我這恩典，叫

One in Christ

11 Therefore, remember that formerly you who are Gentiles by birth and called "uncircumcised" by those who call themselves "the circumcision" (that done in the body by the hands of men)— 12 remember that at that time you were separate from Christ, excluded from citizenship in Israel and foreigners to the covenants of the promise, without hope and without God in the world. 13 But now in Christ Jesus you who once were far away have been brought near through the blood of Christ.

14 For he himself is our peace, who has made the two one and has destroyed the barrier, the dividing wall of hostility, 15 by abolishing in his flesh the law with its commandments and regulations. His purpose was to create in himself one new man out of the two, thus making peace, 16 and in this one body to reconcile both of them to God through the cross, by which he put to death their hostility. 17 He came and preached peace to you who were far away and peace to those who were near. 18 For through him we both have access to the Father by one Spirit.

19 Consequently, you are no longer foreigners and aliens, but fellow citizens with God's people and members of God's household, 20 built on the foundation of the apostles and prophets, with Christ Jesus himself as the chief cornerstone. 21 In him the whole building is joined together and rises to become a holy temple in the Lord. 22 And in him you too are being built together to become a dwelling in which God lives by his Spirit.

Paul the Preacher to the Gentiles

3 For this reason I, Paul, the prisoner of Christ Jesus for the sake of you Gentiles— 2 Surely you have heard about the administration of God's grace that was given to me for you, 3 that is, the mystery made known to me by revelation, as I have already written briefly. 4 In reading this, then, you will be able to understand my insight into the mystery of Christ, 5 which was not made known to men in other generations as it has now been revealed by the Spirit to God's holy apostles and prophets. 6 This mystery is that through the gospel the Gentiles are heirs together with Israel, members together of one body, and sharers together in the promise in Christ Jesus.

7 I became a servant of this gospel by the gift of God's grace given me through the working of his power. 8 Although I am less than the least of all God's people, this grace was given me: to

preach to the Gentiles the unsearchable riches of Christ, ⁹and to make plain to everyone the administration of this mystery, which for ages past was kept hidden in God, who created all things. ¹⁰His intent was that now, through the church, the manifold wisdom of God should be made known to the rulers and authorities in the heavenly realms, ¹¹according to his eternal purpose which he accomplished in Christ Jesus our Lord. ¹²In him and through faith in him we may approach God with freedom and confidence. ¹³I ask you, therefore, not to be discouraged because of my sufferings for you, which are your glory.

A Prayer for the Ephesians

¹⁴For this reason I kneel before the Father, ¹⁵from whom his whole family*a* in heaven and on earth derives its name. ¹⁶I pray that out of his glorious riches he may strengthen you with power through his Spirit in your inner being, ¹⁷so that Christ may dwell in your hearts through faith. And I pray that you, being rooted and established in love, ¹⁸may have power, together with all the saints, to grasp how wide and long and high and deep is the love of Christ, ¹⁹and to know this love that surpasses knowledge—that you may be filled to the measure of all the fullness of God.

²⁰Now to him who is able to do immeasurably more than all we ask or imagine, according to his power that is at work within us, ²¹to him be glory in the church and in Christ Jesus throughout all generations, for ever and ever! Amen.

Unity in the Body of Christ

4 As a prisoner for the Lord, then, I urge you to live a life worthy of the calling you have received. ²Be completely humble and gentle; be patient, bearing with one another in love. ³Make every effort to keep the unity of the Spirit through the bond of peace. ⁴There is one body and one Spirit— just as you were called to one hope when you were called— ⁵one Lord, one faith, one baptism; ⁶one God and Father of all, who is over all and through all and in all.

⁷But to each one of us grace has been given as Christ apportioned it. ⁸This is why it*b* says:

"When he ascended on high,
    he led captives in his train
    and gave gifts to men."*c*

我把基督那測不透的豐富傳給外邦人。⁹又使眾人都明白，這歷代以來隱藏在創造萬物之神裏的奧秘，是如何安排的，¹⁰為要藉着教會使天上執政的、掌權的，現在得知神百般的智慧。¹¹這是照神從萬世以前，在我們主基督耶穌裏所定的旨意。¹²我們因信耶穌，就在他裏面放膽無懼，篤信不疑地來到神面前。¹³所以，我求你們不要因我為你們所受的患難喪膽，這原是你們的榮耀。

為以弗所人禱告

¹⁴因此，我在父面前屈膝，（¹⁵天上地上的各（註：或作"全"）家，都是從他得名。）¹⁶求他按着他豐盛的榮耀，藉着他的靈，叫你們心裏的力量剛強起來。¹⁷使基督因你們的信，住在你們心裏，叫你們的愛心有根有基，¹⁸能以和眾聖徒一同明白基督的愛是何等長闊高深！¹⁹並知道這愛是過於人所能測度的，便叫神一切所充滿的，充滿了你們。

²⁰神能照着運行在我們心裏的大力，充充足足地成就一切，超過我們所求所想的。²¹但願他在教會中，並在基督耶穌裏，得着榮耀，直到世世代代，永永遠遠。阿們！

在基督身體裏的合一

4 我為主被囚的勸你們：既然蒙召，行事為人就當與蒙召的恩相稱。²凡事謙虛、溫柔、忍耐，用愛心互相寬容，³用和平彼此聯絡，竭力保守聖靈所賜合而為一的心。⁴身體只有一個，聖靈只有一個，正如你們蒙召，同有一個指望。⁵一主，一信，一洗，⁶一神，就是眾人的父，超乎眾人之上，貫乎眾人之中，也住在眾人之內。

⁷我們各人蒙恩，都是照基督所量給各人的恩賜。⁸所以經上說：

"他升上高天的時候，
擄掠了仇敵，
將各樣的恩賜賞給人。"

---

a 15 Or whom all fatherhood   *b 8 Or God*   *c 8 Psalm 68:18*

（⁹既說升上，豈不是先降在地下嗎？¹⁰那降下的，就是遠升諸天之上要充滿萬有的。）¹¹他所賜的有使徒，有先知，有傳福音的，有牧師和教師。¹²為要成全聖徒，各盡其職，建立基督的身體，¹³直等到我們眾人在真道上同歸於一，認識神的兒子，得以長大成人，滿有基督長成的身量。

¹⁴使我們不再作小孩子，中了人的詭計和欺騙的法術，被一切異教之風搖動，飄來飄去，就隨從各樣的異端。¹⁵惟用愛心說誠實話，凡事長進，連於元首基督。¹⁶全身都靠他聯絡得合式，百節各按各職，照着各體的功用彼此相助，便叫身體漸漸增長，在愛中建立自己。

行事為人當像光明之子

¹⁷所以我說，且在主裏確實地說，你們行事，不要再像外邦人存虛妄的心行事。¹⁸他們心地昏昧，與神所賜的生命隔絕了，都因自己無知，心裏剛硬；¹⁹良心既然喪盡，就放縱私慾，貪行種種的污穢。

²⁰你們學了基督，卻不是這樣。²¹如果你們聽過他的道，領了他的教，學了他的真理，²²就要脫去你們從前行為上的舊人，這舊人是因私慾的迷惑漸漸變壞的。²³又要將你們的心志改換一新，²⁴並且穿上新人，這新人是照着神的形像造的，有真理的仁義和聖潔。

²⁵所以你們要棄絕謊言，各人與鄰舍說實話，因為我們是互相為肢體。²⁶生氣卻不要犯罪，不可含怒到日落；²⁷也不可給魔鬼留地步。²⁸從前偷竊的，不要再偷；總要勞力，親手做正經事，就可有餘，分給那缺少的人。

⁹(What does "he ascended" mean except that he also descended to the lower, earthly regions*a*? ¹⁰He who descended is the very one who ascended higher than all the heavens, in order to fill the whole universe.) ¹¹It was he who gave some to be apostles, some to be prophets, some to be evangelists, and some to be pastors and teachers, ¹²to prepare God's people for works of service, so that the body of Christ may be built up ¹³until we all reach unity in the faith and in the knowledge of the Son of God and become mature, attaining to the whole measure of the fullness of Christ.

¹⁴Then we will no longer be infants, tossed back and forth by the waves, and blown here and there by every wind of teaching and by the cunning and craftiness of men in their deceitful scheming. ¹⁵Instead, speaking the truth in love, we will in all things grow up into him who is the Head, that is, Christ. ¹⁶From him the whole body, joined and held together by every supporting ligament, grows and builds itself up in love, as each part does its work.

Living as Children of Light

¹⁷So I tell you this, and insist on it in the Lord, that you must no longer live as the Gentiles do, in the futility of their thinking. ¹⁸They are darkened in their understanding and separated from the life of God because of the ignorance that is in them due to the hardening of their hearts. ¹⁹Having lost all sensitivity, they have given themselves over to sensuality so as to indulge in every kind of impurity, with a continual lust for more.

²⁰You, however, did not come to know Christ that way. ²¹Surely you heard of him and were taught in him in accordance with the truth that is in Jesus. ²²You were taught, with regard to your former way of life, to put off your old self, which is being corrupted by its deceitful desires; ²³to be made new in the attitude of your minds; ²⁴and to put on the new self, created to be like God in true righteousness and holiness.

²⁵Therefore each of you must put off falsehood and speak truthfully to his neighbor, for we are all members of one body. ²⁶"In your anger do not sin"*b*: Do not let the sun go down while you are still angry, ²⁷and do not give the devil a foothold. ²⁸He who has been stealing must steal no longer, but must work, doing something useful with his own hands, that he may have something to share with those in need.

a 9 Or the depths of the earth   b 26 Psalm 4:4

²⁹Do not let any unwholesome talk come out of your mouths, but only what is helpful for building others up according to their needs, that it may benefit those who listen. ³⁰And do not grieve the Holy Spirit of God, with whom you were sealed for the day of redemption. ³¹Get rid of all bitterness, rage and anger, brawling and slander, along with every form of malice. ³²Be kind and compassionate to one another, forgiving each other, just as in Christ God forgave you.

5 Be imitators of God, therefore, as dearly loved children ²and live a life of love, just as Christ loved us and gave himself up for us as a fragrant offering and sacrifice to God.

³But among you there must not be even a hint of sexual immorality, or of any kind of impurity, or of greed, because these are improper for God's holy people. ⁴Nor should there be obscenity, foolish talk or coarse joking, which are out of place, but rather thanksgiving. ⁵For of this you can be sure: No immoral, impure or greedy person—such a man is an idolater—has any inheritance in the kingdom of Christ and of God.ª ⁶Let no one deceive you with empty words, for because of such things God's wrath comes on those who are disobedient. ⁷Therefore do not be partners with them.

⁸For you were once darkness, but now you are light in the Lord. Live as children of light ⁹(for the fruit of the light consists in all goodness, righteousness and truth) ¹⁰and find out what pleases the Lord. ¹¹Have nothing to do with the fruitless deeds of darkness, but rather expose them. ¹²For it is shameful even to mention what the disobedient do in secret. ¹³But everything exposed by the light becomes visible, ¹⁴for it is light that makes everything visible. This is why it is said:

"Wake up, O sleeper,
　rise from the dead,
and Christ will shine on you."

¹⁵Be very careful, then, how you live—not as unwise but as wise, ¹⁶making the most of every opportunity, because the days are evil. ¹⁷Therefore do not be foolish, but understand what the Lord's will is. ¹⁸Do not get drunk on wine, which leads to debauchery. Instead, be filled with the Spirit. ¹⁹Speak to one another with psalms, hymns and spiritual songs. Sing and make music

²⁹污穢的言語，一句不可出口，只要隨事說造就人的好話，叫聽見的人得益處。³⁰不要叫神的聖靈擔憂；你們原是受了他的印記，等候得贖的日子來到。³¹一切苦毒、惱恨、忿怒、嚷鬧、毀謗，並一切的惡毒（註：或作"陰毒"），都當從你們中間除掉。³²並要以恩慈相待，存憐憫的心，彼此饒恕，正如神在基督裏饒恕了你們一樣。

5 所以你們該效法神，好像蒙慈愛的兒女一樣。²也要憑愛心行事，正如基督愛我們，為我們捨了自己，當作馨香的供物和祭物獻與神。

³至於淫亂並一切污穢，或是貪婪，在你們中間連提都不可，方合聖徒的體統。⁴淫詞、妄語和戲笑的話都不相宜，總要說感謝的話。⁵因為你們確實地知道，無論是淫亂的，是污穢的，是有貪心的，在基督和神的國裏都是無分的。有貪心的，就與拜偶像的一樣。⁶不要被人虛浮的話欺哄，因這些事，神的忿怒必臨到那悖逆之子。⁷所以你們不要與他們同夥。

⁸從前你們是暗昧的，但如今在主裏面是光明的，行事為人就當像光明的子女。⁹光明所結的果子就是一切良善、公義、誠實。¹⁰總要察驗何為主所喜悅的事。¹¹那暗昧無益的事，不要與人同行，倒要責備行這事的人。¹²因為他們暗中所行的，就是提起來也是可恥的。¹³凡事受了責備，就被光顯明出來，因為一切能顯明的就是光。¹⁴所以主說：

"你這睡着的人，當醒過來，
　從死裏復活，
基督就要光照你了。"

¹⁵你們要謹慎行事，不要像愚昧人，當像智慧人。¹⁶要愛惜光陰，因為現今的世代邪惡。¹⁷不要作糊塗人，要明白主的旨意如何。¹⁸不要醉酒，酒能使人放蕩，乃要被聖靈充滿。¹⁹當用詩章、頌詞、靈歌彼此對

ª 5 Or kingdom of the Christ and God

說，口唱心和地讚美主。²⁰凡事要奉我們主耶穌基督的名，常常感謝父神。

²¹又當存敬畏基督的心，彼此順服。

妻子與丈夫

²²你們作妻子的，當順服自己的丈夫，如同順服主。²³因為丈夫是妻子的頭，如同基督是教會的頭，他又是教會全體的救主。²⁴教會怎樣順服基督，妻子也要怎樣凡事順服丈夫。

²⁵你們作丈夫的，要愛你們的妻子，正如基督愛教會，為教會捨己。²⁶要用水藉着道把教會洗淨，成為聖潔，²⁷可以獻給自己，作個榮耀的教會，毫無玷污、皺紋等類的病，乃是聖潔沒有瑕疵的。²⁸丈夫也當照樣愛妻子，如同愛自己的身子，愛妻子便是愛自己了。²⁹從來沒有人恨惡自己的身子，總是保養顧惜，正像基督待教會一樣，³⁰因我們是他身上的肢體（註：有古卷在此有"就是他的骨、他的肉"）。³¹為這個緣故，人要離開父母，與妻子連合，二人成為一體。³²這是極大的奧秘，但我是指着基督和教會說的。³³然而你們各人都當愛妻子，如同愛自己一樣；妻子也當敬重她的丈夫。

兒女與父母

6 你們作兒女的，要在主裏聽從父母，這是理所當然的。²、³要孝敬父母，使你得福，在世長壽。這是第一條帶應許的誡命。

⁴你們作父親的，不要惹兒女的氣，只要照着主的教訓和警戒養育他們。

奴僕與主人

⁵你們作僕人的，要懼怕戰兢，用誠實的心聽從你們肉身的主人，好像聽從基督一般。⁶不要只在眼前侍奉，像是討人喜歡的，要像基督的僕人，從心裏遵行神的旨意，⁷甘心侍奉，好像服侍主，不像服侍人。⁸因為曉得各人所行的善事，不論是為奴的、是自主的，都必按所行的，得主的賞賜。

in your heart to the Lord, ²⁰always giving thanks to God the Father for everything, in the name of our Lord Jesus Christ.

²¹Submit to one another out of reverence for Christ.

Wives and Husbands

²²Wives, submit to your husbands as to the Lord. ²³For the husband is the head of the wife as Christ is the head of the church, his body, of which he is the Savior. ²⁴Now as the church submits to Christ, so also wives should submit to their husbands in everything.

²⁵Husbands, love your wives, just as Christ loved the church and gave himself up for her ²⁶to make her holy, cleansing*ᵃ* her by the washing with water through the word, ²⁷and to present her to himself as a radiant church, without stain or wrinkle or any other blemish, but holy and blameless. ²⁸In this same way, husbands ought to love their wives as their own bodies. He who loves his wife loves himself. ²⁹After all, no one ever hated his own body, but he feeds and cares for it, just as Christ does the church— ³⁰for we are members of his body. ³¹"For this reason a man will leave his father and mother and be united to his wife, and the two will become one flesh."*ᵇ* ³²This is a profound mystery—but I am talking about Christ and the church. ³³However, each one of you also must love his wife as he loves himself, and the wife must respect her husband.

Children and Parents

6 Children, obey your parents in the Lord, for this is right. ²"Honor your father and mother"—which is the first commandment with a promise— ³"that it may go well with you and that you may enjoy long life on the earth."*ᶜ*

⁴Fathers, do not exasperate your children; instead, bring them up in the training and instruction of the Lord.

Slaves and Masters

⁵Slaves, obey your earthly masters with respect and fear, and with sincerity of heart, just as you would obey Christ. ⁶Obey them not only to win their favor when their eye is on you, but like slaves of Christ, doing the will of God from your heart. ⁷Serve wholeheartedly, as if you were serving the Lord, not men, ⁸because you know that the Lord will reward everyone for whatever good he does, whether he is slave or free.

a 26 Or having cleansed　b 31 Gen. 2:24　c 3 Deut. 5:16

9And masters, treat your slaves in the same way. Do not threaten them, since you know that he who is both their Master and yours is in heaven, and there is no favoritism with him.

The Armor of God

10Finally, be strong in the Lord and in his mighty power. 11Put on the full armor of God so that you can take your stand against the devil's schemes. 12For our struggle is not against flesh and blood, but against the rulers, against the authorities, against the powers of this dark world and against the spiritual forces of evil in the heavenly realms. 13Therefore put on the full armor of God, so that when the day of evil comes, you may be able to stand your ground, and after you have done everything, to stand. 14Stand firm then, with the belt of truth buckled around your waist, with the breastplate of righteousness in place, 15and with your feet fitted with the readiness that comes from the gospel of peace. 16In addition to all this, take up the shield of faith, with which you can extinguish all the flaming arrows of the evil one. 17Take the helmet of salvation and the sword of the Spirit, which is the word of God. 18And pray in the Spirit on all occasions with all kinds of prayers and requests. With this in mind, be alert and always keep on praying for all the saints.

19Pray also for me, that whenever I open my mouth, words may be given me so that I will fearlessly make known the mystery of the gospel, 20for which I am an ambassador in chains. Pray that I may declare it fearlessly, as I should.

Final Greetings

21Tychicus, the dear brother and faithful servant in the Lord, will tell you everything, so that you also may know how I am and what I am doing. 22I am sending him to you for this very purpose, that you may know how we are, and that he may encourage you.

23Peace to the brothers, and love with faith from God the Father and the Lord Jesus Christ. 24Grace to all who love our Lord Jesus Christ with an undying love.

9你們作主人的待僕人也是一理，不要威嚇他們，因為知道他們和你們同有一位主在天上，他並不偏待人。

神的軍裝

10我還有末了的話：你們要靠着主，倚賴他的大能大力，作剛強的人。11要穿戴神所賜的全副軍裝，就能抵擋魔鬼的詭計。12因我們並不是與屬血氣的爭戰，乃是與那些執政的、掌權的、管轄這幽暗世界的，以及天空屬靈氣的惡魔爭戰（註：兩“爭戰”原文都作“摔跤”）。13所以，要拿起神所賜的全副軍裝，好在磨難的日子抵擋仇敵，並且成就了一切，還能站立得住。14所以要站穩了，用真理當作帶子束腰，用公義當作護心鏡遮胸，15又用平安的福音當作預備走路的鞋穿在腳上。16此外，又拿着信德當作籐牌，可以滅盡那惡者一切的火箭。17並戴上救恩的頭盔，拿着聖靈的寶劍，就是神的道。18靠着聖靈，隨時多方禱告祈求，並要在此警醒不倦，為眾聖徒祈求。

19也為我祈求，使我得着口才，能以放膽開口講明福音的奧秘，20（我為這福音的奧秘作了帶鎖鏈的使者）並使我照着當盡的本分放膽講論。

最後的問安

21今有所親愛、忠心侍奉主的兄弟推基古，他要把我的事情並我的景況如何全告訴你們，叫你們知道。22我特意打發他到你們那裏去，好叫你們知道我們的光景，又叫他安慰你們的心。

23願平安、仁愛、信心從父神和主耶穌基督歸與弟兄們！24並願所有誠心愛我們主耶穌基督的人都蒙恩惠！

腓立比書

1

基督耶穌的僕人保羅和提摩太，

寫信給凡住腓立比、在基督耶穌裏的眾聖徒和諸位監督、諸位執事：

2願恩惠、平安從神我們的父並主耶穌基督歸與你們！

感恩與禱告

3我每逢想念你們，就感謝我的神；（4每逢為你們眾人祈求的時候，常是歡歡喜喜地祈求。）5因為從頭一天直到如今，你們是同心合意地興旺福音。6我深信那在你們心裏動了善工的，必成全這工，直到耶穌基督的日子。

7我為你們眾人有這樣的意念，原是應當的，因你們常在我心裏，無論我是在捆鎖之中，是辯明證實福音的時候，你們都與我一同得恩。8我體會基督耶穌的心腸，切切地想念你們眾人，這是神可以給我作見證的。

9我所禱告的，就是要你們的愛心，在知識和各樣見識上多而又多，10使你們能分別是非（註：或作"喜愛那美好的事"），作誠實無過的人，直到基督的日子；11並靠著耶穌基督結滿了仁義的果子，叫榮耀稱讚歸與神。

保羅的捆鎖叫福音興旺

12弟兄們，我願意你們知道，我所遭遇的事更是叫福音興旺，13以致我受的捆鎖，在御營全軍和其餘的人中，已經顯明是為基督的緣故。14並且那在主裏的弟兄，多半因我受的捆鎖，就篤信不疑，越發放膽傳神的道，無所懼怕。

15有的傳基督是出於嫉妒紛爭，也有的是出於好意。16這一等是出於愛心，知道我是為辯明福音設立的；17那一等傳基督是出於結黨，並

Philippians

1

Paul and Timothy, servants of Christ Jesus,

To all the saints in Christ Jesus at Philippi, together with the overseers[a] and deacons:

2Grace and peace to you from God our Father and the Lord Jesus Christ.

Thanksgiving and Prayer

3I thank my God every time I remember you. 4In all my prayers for all of you, I always pray with joy 5because of your partnership in the gospel from the first day until now, 6being confident of this, that he who began a good work in you will carry it on to completion until the day of Christ Jesus.

7It is right for me to feel this way about all of you, since I have you in my heart; for whether I am in chains or defending and confirming the gospel, all of you share in God's grace with me. 8God can testify how I long for all of you with the affection of Christ Jesus.

9And this is my prayer: that your love may abound more and more in knowledge and depth of insight, 10so that you may be able to discern what is best and may be pure and blameless until the day of Christ, 11filled with the fruit of righteousness that comes through Jesus Christ—to the glory and praise of God.

Paul's Chains Advance the Gospel

12Now I want you to know, brothers, that what has happened to me has really served to advance the gospel. 13As a result, it has become clear throughout the whole palace guard[b] and to everyone else that I am in chains for Christ. 14Because of my chains, most of the brothers in the Lord have been encouraged to speak the word of God more courageously and fearlessly.

15It is true that some preach Christ out of envy and rivalry, but others out of goodwill. 16The latter do so in love, knowing that I am put here for the defense of the gospel. 17The former preach Christ out of selfish ambition, not sin-

a 1 Traditionally bishops   b 13 Or whole palace

cerely, supposing that they can stir up trouble for me while I am in chains.[a] [18]But what does it matter? The important thing is that in every way, whether from false motives or true, Christ is preached. And because of this I rejoice.

Yes, and I will continue to rejoice, [19]for I know that through your prayers and the help given by the Spirit of Jesus Christ, what has happened to me will turn out for my deliverance.[b] [20]I eagerly expect and hope that I will in no way be ashamed, but will have sufficient courage so that now as always Christ will be exalted in my body, whether by life or by death. [21]For to me, to live is Christ and to die is gain. [22]If I am to go on living in the body, this will mean fruitful labor for me. Yet what shall I choose? I do not know! [23]I am torn between the two: I desire to depart and be with Christ, which is better by far; [24]but it is more necessary for you that I remain in the body. [25]Convinced of this, I know that I will remain, and I will continue with all of you for your progress and joy in the faith, [26]so that through my being with you again your joy in Christ Jesus will overflow on account of me.

[27]Whatever happens, conduct yourselves in a manner worthy of the gospel of Christ. Then, whether I come and see you or only hear about you in my absence, I will know that you stand firm in one spirit, contending as one man for the faith of the gospel [28]without being frightened in any way by those who oppose you. This is a sign to them that they will be destroyed, but that you will be saved—and that by God. [29]For it has been granted to you on behalf of Christ not only to believe on him, but also to suffer for him, [30]since you are going through the same struggle you saw I had, and now hear that I still have.

Imitating Christ's Humility

2 If you have any encouragement from being united with Christ, if any comfort from his love, if any fellowship with the Spirit, if any tenderness and compassion, [2]then make my joy complete by being like-minded, having the same love, being one in spirit and purpose. [3]Do nothing out of selfish ambition or vain conceit, but in humility consider others better than yourselves. [4]Each of you should look not only to your own interests, but also to the interests of others.

[5]Your attitude should be the same as that of Christ Jesus:

a 16,17 Some late manuscripts have verses 16 and 17 in reverse order.   b 19 Or salvation

---

不誠實,意思要加增我捆鎖的苦楚。[18]這有何妨呢?或是假意,或是真心,無論怎樣,基督究竟被傳開了。

為此,我就歡喜,並且還要歡喜。[19]因為我知道,這事藉着你們的祈禱和耶穌基督之靈的幫助,終必叫我得救。[20]照着我所切慕、所盼望的,沒有一事叫我羞愧。只要凡事放膽,無論是生是死,總叫基督在我身上照常顯大。[21]因我活着就是基督,我死了就有益處。[22]但我在肉身活着,若成就我工夫的果子,我就不知道該挑選甚麼。[23]我正在兩難之間,情願離世與基督同在,因為這是好得無比的。[24]然而,我在肉身活着,為你們更是要緊的。[25]我既然這樣深信,就知道仍要住在世間,且與你們眾人同住,使你們在所信的道上又長進、又喜樂。[26]叫你們在基督耶穌裏的歡樂,因我再到你們那裏去,就越發加增。

[27]只要你們行事為人與基督的福音相稱,叫我或來見你們,或不在你們那裏,可以聽見你們的景況,知道你們同有一個心志,站立得穩,為所信的福音齊心努力。[28]凡事不怕敵人的驚嚇,這是證明他們沉淪,你們得救,都是出於神。[29]因為你們蒙恩,不但得以信服基督,並要為他受苦。[30]你們的爭戰,就與你們在我身上從前所看見、現在所聽見的一樣。

效法基督的謙卑

2 所以,你們在基督裏若有甚麼勸勉,愛心有甚麼安慰,聖靈有甚麼交通,心中有甚麼慈悲憐憫,[2]你們就要意念相同,愛心相同,有一樣的心思,有一樣的意念,使我的喜樂可以滿足。[3]凡事不可結黨,不可貪圖虛浮的榮耀;只要存心謙卑,各人看別人比自己強。[4]各人不要單顧自己的事,也要顧別人的事。

[5]你們當以基督耶穌的心為心。

⁶他本有神的形像，
　　不以自己與神同等為強奪的，

⁷反倒虛己，
　　取了奴僕的形像，
　　成為人的樣式。
⁸既有人的樣子，
　　就自己卑微，
　　存心順服，以至於死，
　　且死在十字架上。
⁹所以神將他升為至高，
　　又賜給他那超乎萬名之上的名，

¹⁰叫一切在天上的、
　　地上的和地底下的，
　　因耶穌的名無不屈膝，
¹¹無不口稱耶穌基督為主，
　　使榮耀歸與父神。

像明光照耀

¹²這樣看來，我親愛的弟兄，你們既是常順服的，不但我在你們那裏，就是我如今不在你們那裏，更是順服的，就當恐懼戰兢，做成你們得救的工夫。¹³因為你們立志行事，都是神在你們心裏運行，為要成就他的美意。

¹⁴凡所行的，都不要發怨言、起爭論，¹⁵使你們無可指摘，誠實無偽，在這彎曲悖謬的世代，作神無瑕疵的兒女。你們顯在這世代中，好像明光照耀，¹⁶將生命的道表明出來，叫我在基督的日子好誇我沒有空跑，也沒有徒勞。¹⁷我以你們的信心為供獻的祭物，我若被澆奠在其上，也是喜樂，並且與你們眾人一同喜樂；¹⁸你們也要照樣喜樂，並且與我一同喜樂。

提摩太與以巴弗提

¹⁹我靠主耶穌指望快打發提摩太去見你們，叫我知道你們的事，心裏就得着安慰。²⁰因為我沒有別人與我同心，實在掛念你們的事。²¹別人都求自己的事，並不求耶穌基督的事。²²但你們知道提摩太的明證，他興旺福音，與我同勞，待我像兒子待父親一樣。²³所以我一看出我的事要怎樣了結，就盼望立刻打發他去；²⁴但我靠着主，自信我也必快去。

⁶Who, being in very nature*ᵃ* God,
　　did not consider equality with God
　　something to be grasped,
⁷but made himself nothing,
　　taking the very nature*ᵇ* of a servant,
　　being made in human likeness.
⁸And being found in appearance as a man,
　　he humbled himself
　　and became obedient to death—
　　even death on a cross!
⁹Therefore God exalted him to the highest place
　　and gave him the name that is above every
　　name,
¹⁰that at the name of Jesus every knee should
　　bow,
　　in heaven and on earth and under the earth,
¹¹and every tongue confess that Jesus Christ is
　　Lord,
　　to the glory of God the Father.

Shining as Stars

¹²Therefore, my dear friends, as you have always obeyed—not only in my presence, but now much more in my absence—continue to work out your salvation with fear and trembling, ¹³for it is God who works in you to will and to act according to his good purpose.

¹⁴Do everything without complaining or arguing, ¹⁵so that you may become blameless and pure, children of God without fault in a crooked and depraved generation, in which you shine like stars in the universe ¹⁶as you hold out*ᶜ* the word of life—in order that I may boast on the day of Christ that I did not run or labor for nothing. ¹⁷But even if I am being poured out like a drink offering on the sacrifice and service coming from your faith, I am glad and rejoice with all of you. ¹⁸So you too should be glad and rejoice with me.

Timothy and Epaphroditus

¹⁹I hope in the Lord Jesus to send Timothy to you soon, that I also may be cheered when I receive news about you. ²⁰I have no one else like him, who takes a genuine interest in your welfare. ²¹For everyone looks out for his own interests, not those of Jesus Christ. ²²But you know that Timothy has proved himself, because as a son with his father he has served with me in the work of the gospel. ²³I hope, therefore, to send him as soon as I see how things go with me. ²⁴And I am confident in the Lord that I myself will come soon.

---

a 6 Or in the form of　　b 7 Or the form　　c 16 Or hold on to

²⁵But I think it is necessary to send back to you Epaphroditus, my brother, fellow worker and fellow soldier, who is also your messenger, whom you sent to take care of my needs. ²⁶For he longs for all of you and is distressed because you heard he was ill. ²⁷Indeed he was ill, and almost died. But God had mercy on him, and not on him only but also on me, to spare me sorrow upon sorrow. ²⁸Therefore I am all the more eager to send him, so that when you see him again you may be glad and I may have less anxiety. ²⁹Welcome him in the Lord with great joy, and honor men like him, ³⁰because he almost died for the work of Christ, risking his life to make up for the help you could not give me.

No Confidence in the Flesh

3 Finally, my brothers, rejoice in the Lord! It is no trouble for me to write the same things to you again, and it is a safeguard for you.

²Watch out for those dogs, those men who do evil, those mutilators of the flesh. ³For it is we who are the circumcision, we who worship by the Spirit of God, who glory in Christ Jesus, and who put no confidence in the flesh— ⁴though I myself have reasons for such confidence.

If anyone else thinks he has reasons to put confidence in the flesh, I have more: ⁵circumcised on the eighth day, of the people of Israel, of the tribe of Benjamin, a Hebrew of Hebrews; in regard to the law, a Pharisee; ⁶as for zeal, persecuting the church; as for legalistic righteousness, faultless.

⁷But whatever was to my profit I now consider loss for the sake of Christ. ⁸What is more, I consider everything a loss compared to the surpassing greatness of knowing Christ Jesus my Lord, for whose sake I have lost all things. I consider them rubbish, that I may gain Christ ⁹and be found in him, not having a righteousness of my own that comes from the law, but that which is through faith in Christ—the righteousness that comes from God and is by faith. ¹⁰I want to know Christ and the power of his resurrection and the fellowship of sharing in his sufferings, becoming like him in his death, ¹¹and so, somehow, to attain to the resurrection from the dead.

Pressing on Toward the Goal

¹²Not that I have already obtained all this, or have already been made perfect, but I press on to take hold of that for which Christ Jesus took hold of me. ¹³Brothers, I do not consider myself yet to have taken hold of it. But one thing I do: Forgetting what is behind and straining toward

²⁵然而，我想必須打發以巴弗提到你們那裏去。他是我的兄弟，與我一同做工、一同當兵，是你們所差遣的，也是供給我需用的。²⁶他很想念你們眾人，並且極其難過，因為你們聽見他病了。²⁷他實在是病了，幾乎要死，然而，神憐恤他，不但憐恤他，也憐恤我，免得我憂上加憂。²⁸所以我越發急速打發他去，叫你們再見他，就可以喜樂，我也可以少些憂愁。²⁹故此，你們要在主裏歡歡樂樂地接待他，而且要尊重這樣的人，³⁰因他為做基督的工夫，幾乎至死，不顧性命，要補足你們供給我的不及之處。

不靠肉體

3 弟兄們，我還有話說：你們要靠主喜樂。我把這話再寫給你們，於我並不為難，於你們卻是妥當。

²應當防備犬類，防備作惡的，防備妄自行割的。³因為真受割禮的，乃是我們這以神的靈敬拜、在基督耶穌裏誇口、不靠着肉體的。⁴其實我也可以靠肉體。

若是別人想他可以靠肉體，我更可以靠着了；⁵我第八天受割禮，我是以色列族、便雅憫支派的人，是希伯來人所生的希伯來人；就律法說，我是法利賽人；⁶就熱心說，我是逼迫教會的；就律法上的義說，我是無可指摘的。

⁷只是我先前以為與我有益的，我現在因基督都當作有損的。⁸不但如此，我也將萬事當作有損的，因我以認識我主基督耶穌為至寶。我為他已經丟棄萬事，看作糞土，為要得着基督，⁹並且得以在他裏面，不是有自己因律法而得的義，乃是有信基督的義，就是因信神而來的義，¹⁰使我認識基督，曉得他復活的大能，並且曉得和他一同受苦，效法他的死，¹¹或者我也得以從死裏復活。

向標竿直跑

¹²這不是說我已經得着了，已經完全了，我乃是竭力追求，或者可以得着基督耶穌所以得着我的（註："所以得着我的"或作 "所要我得的"）。¹³弟兄們，我不是以為自己已經得着了，我只有一件事，就是忘記背後，努力面

前的，¹⁴向着標竿直跑，要得神在基督耶穌裏從上面召我來得的獎賞。

¹⁵所以我們中間凡是完全人，總要存這樣的心；若在甚麼事上存別樣的心，神也必以此指示你們。¹⁶然而我們到了甚麼地步，就當照着甚麼地步行。

¹⁷弟兄們，你們要一同效法我，也當留意看那些照我們榜樣行的人。¹⁸因為有許多人行事是基督十字架的仇敵。我屢次告訴你們，現在又流淚地告訴你們：¹⁹他們的結局就是沉淪，他們的神就是自己的肚腹，他們以自己的羞辱為榮耀，專以地上的事為念。²⁰我們卻是天上的國民，並且等候救主，就是主耶穌基督從天上降臨。²¹他要按着那能叫萬有歸服自己的大能，將我們這卑賤的身體改變形狀，和他自己榮耀的身體相似。

4 我所親愛、所想念的弟兄們，你們就是我的喜樂，我的冠冕！我親愛的弟兄，你們應當靠主站立得穩。

勸勉

²我勸友阿蝶和循都基要在主裏同心。³我也求你這真實同負一軛的，幫助這兩個女人，因為她們在福音上曾與我一同勞苦；還有革利免，並其餘和我一同做工的，他們的名字都在生命冊上。

⁴你們要靠主常常喜樂！我再說，你們要喜樂！⁵當叫眾人知道你們謙讓的心。主已經近了。⁶應當一無掛慮，只要凡事藉着禱告、祈求和感謝，將你們所要的告訴神。⁷神所賜出人意外的平安，必在基督耶穌裏，保守你們的心懷意念。

⁸弟兄們，我還有未盡的話：凡是真實的、可敬的、公義的、清潔的、可愛的、有美名的，若有甚麼德行，若有甚麼稱讚，這些事你們都要思念。⁹你們在我身上所學習的、所領受的、所聽見的、所看見的，這些事你們都要去行，賜平安的神就必與你們同在。

what is ahead, ¹⁴I press on toward the goal to win the prize for which God has called me heavenward in Christ Jesus.

¹⁵All of us who are mature should take such a view of things. And if on some point you think differently, that too God will make clear to you. ¹⁶Only let us live up to what we have already attained.

¹⁷Join with others in following my example, brothers, and take note of those who live according to the pattern we gave you. ¹⁸For, as I have often told you before and now say again even with tears, many live as enemies of the cross of Christ. ¹⁹Their destiny is destruction, their god is their stomach, and their glory is in their shame. Their mind is on earthly things. ²⁰But our citizenship is in heaven. And we eagerly await a Savior from there, the Lord Jesus Christ, ²¹who, by the power that enables him to bring everything under his control, will transform our lowly bodies so that they will be like his glorious body.

4 Therefore, my brothers, you whom I love and long for, my joy and crown, that is how you should stand firm in the Lord, dear friends!

Exhortations

²I plead with Euodia and I plead with Syntyche to agree with each other in the Lord. ³Yes, and I ask you, loyal yokefellow,*^a* help these women who have contended at my side in the cause of the gospel, along with Clement and the rest of my fellow workers, whose names are in the book of life.

⁴Rejoice in the Lord always. I will say it again: Rejoice! ⁵Let your gentleness be evident to all. The Lord is near. ⁶Do not be anxious about anything, but in everything, by prayer and petition, with thanksgiving, present your requests to God. ⁷And the peace of God, which transcends all understanding, will guard your hearts and your minds in Christ Jesus.

⁸Finally, brothers, whatever is true, whatever is noble, whatever is right, whatever is pure, whatever is lovely, whatever is admirable—if anything is excellent or praiseworthy—think about such things. ⁹Whatever you have learned or received or heard from me, or seen in me—put it into practice. And the God of peace will be with you.

---

a 3 Or loyal *Syzygus*

Thanks for Their Gifts

[10]I rejoice greatly in the Lord that at last you have renewed your concern for me. Indeed, you have been concerned, but you had no opportunity to show it. [11]I am not saying this because I am in need, for I have learned to be content whatever the circumstances. [12]I know what it is to be in need, and I know what it is to have plenty. I have learned the secret of being content in any and every situation, whether well fed or hungry, whether living in plenty or in want. [13]I can do everything through him who gives me strength.

[14]Yet it was good of you to share in my troubles. [15]Moreover, as you Philippians know, in the early days of your acquaintance with the gospel, when I set out from Macedonia, not one church shared with me in the matter of giving and receiving, except you only; [16]for even when I was in Thessalonica, you sent me aid again and again when I was in need. [17]Not that I am looking for a gift, but I am looking for what may be credited to your account. [18]I have received full payment and even more; I am amply supplied, now that I have received from Epaphroditus the gifts you sent. They are a fragrant offering, an acceptable sacrifice, pleasing to God. [19]And my God will meet all your needs according to his glorious riches in Christ Jesus.

[20]To our God and Father be glory for ever and ever. Amen.

Final Greetings

[21]Greet all the saints in Christ Jesus. The brothers who are with me send greetings. [22]All the saints send you greetings, especially those who belong to Caesar's household.

[23]The grace of the Lord Jesus Christ be with your spirit. Amen.[a]

感謝餽贈

[10]我靠主大大地喜樂，因為你們思念我的心如今又發生；你們向來就思念我，只是沒得機會。[11]我並不是因缺乏說這話，我無論在甚麼景況都可以知足，這是我已經學會了。[12]我知道怎樣處卑賤，也知道怎樣處豐富，或飽足、或飢餓、或有餘、或缺乏，隨事隨在，我都得了秘訣。[13]我靠着那加給我力量的，凡事都能做。

[14]然而你們和我同受患難，原是美事。[15]腓立比人哪，你們也知道我初傳福音，離了馬其頓的時候，論到授受的事，除了你們以外，並沒有別的教會供給我。[16]就是我在帖撒羅尼迦，你們也一次兩次地打發人供給我的需用。[17]我並不求甚麼餽送，所求的就是你們的果子漸漸增多，歸在你們的賬上。[18]但我樣樣都有，並且有餘；我已經充足，因我從以巴弗提受了你們的餽送，當作極美的香氣，為神所收納、所喜悅的祭物。[19]我的神必照他榮耀的豐富，在基督耶穌裏使你們一切所需用的都充足。

[20]願榮耀歸給我們的父神，直到永永遠遠。阿們！

最後的問安

[21]請問在基督耶穌裏的各位聖徒安。在我這裏的眾弟兄都問你們安。[22]眾聖徒都問你們安。在凱撒家裏的人特特地問你們安。

[23]願主耶穌基督的恩常在你們心裏！

---

a 23 Some manuscripts do not have Amen.

歌羅西書

Colossians

1 奉神旨意，作基督耶穌使徒的<u>保羅</u>和兄弟<u>提摩太</u>，

2寫信給<u>歌羅西</u>的聖徒，在基督裏有忠心的弟兄：

願恩惠、平安從神我們的父歸與你們！

感恩與禱告

3我們感謝神、我們主耶穌基督的父，常常為你們禱告，4因聽見你們在基督耶穌裏的信心，並向眾聖徒的愛心，5是為那給你們存在天上的盼望；這盼望就是你們從前在福音真理的道上所聽見的。6這福音傳到你們那裏，也傳到普天之下，並且結果、增長，如同在你們中間，自從你們聽見福音，真知道神恩惠的日子一樣。7正如你們從我們所親愛、一同作僕人的<u>以巴弗</u>所學的。他為我們（註：有古卷作"你們"）作了基督忠心的執事，8也把你們因星靈所存的愛心告訴了我們。

9因此，我們自從聽見的日子，也就為你們不住地禱告祈求，願你們在一切屬靈的智慧悟性上，滿心知道神的旨意，10好叫你們行事為人對得起主，凡事蒙他喜悅，在一切善事上結果子，漸漸地多知道神；11照他榮耀的權能，得以在各樣的力上加力，好叫你們凡事歡歡喜喜地忍耐寬容；12又感謝父，叫我們能與眾聖徒在光明中同得基業。13他救了我們脫離黑暗的權勢，把我們遷到他愛子的國裏；14我們在愛子裏得蒙救贖，罪過得以赦免。

1 Paul, an apostle of Christ Jesus by the will of God, and Timothy our brother,

2To the holy and faithful[a] brothers in Christ at Colosse:

Grace and peace to you from God our Father.[b]

Thanksgiving and Prayer

3We always thank God, the Father of our Lord Jesus Christ, when we pray for you, 4because we have heard of your faith in Christ Jesus and of the love you have for all the saints— 5the faith and love that spring from the hope that is stored up for you in heaven and that you have already heard about in the word of truth, the gospel 6that has come to you. All over the world this gospel is bearing fruit and growing, just as it has been doing among you since the day you heard it and understood God's grace in all its truth. 7You learned it from Epaphras, our dear fellow servant, who is a faithful minister of Christ on our[c] behalf, 8and who also told us of your love in the Spirit.

9For this reason, since the day we heard about you, we have not stopped praying for you and asking God to fill you with the knowledge of his will through all spiritual wisdom and understanding. 10And we pray this in order that you may live a life worthy of the Lord and may please him in every way: bearing fruit in every good work, growing in the knowledge of God, 11being strengthened with all power according to his glorious might so that you may have great endurance and patience, and joyfully 12giving thanks to the Father, who has qualified you[d] to share in the inheritance of the saints in the kingdom of light. 13For he has rescued us from the dominion of darkness and brought us into the kingdom of the Son he loves, 14in whom we have redemption,[e] the forgiveness of sins.

---

a 2 Or believing　b 2 Some manuscripts Father and the Lord Jesus Christ　c 7 Some manuscripts your　d 12 Some manuscripts us　e 14 A few late manuscripts redemption through his blood

The Supremacy of Christ

[15]He is the image of the invisible God, the firstborn over all creation. [16]For by him all things were created: things in heaven and on earth, visible and invisible, whether thrones or powers or rulers or authorities; all things were created by him and for him. [17]He is before all things, and in him all things hold together. [18]And he is the head of the body, the church; he is the beginning and the firstborn from among the dead, so that in everything he might have the supremacy. [19]For God was pleased to have all his fullness dwell in him, [20]and through him to reconcile to himself all things, whether things on earth or things in heaven, by making peace through his blood, shed on the cross.

[21]Once you were alienated from God and were enemies in your minds because of[a] your evil behavior. [22]But now he has reconciled you by Christ's physical body through death to present you holy in his sight, without blemish and free from accusation— [23]if you continue in your faith, established and firm, not moved from the hope held out in the gospel. This is the gospel that you heard and that has been proclaimed to every creature under heaven, and of which I, Paul, have become a servant.

Paul's Labor for the Church

[24]Now I rejoice in what was suffered for you, and I fill up in my flesh what is still lacking in regard to Christ's afflictions, for the sake of his body, which is the church. [25]I have become its servant by the commission God gave me to present to you the word of God in its fullness— [26]the mystery that has been kept hidden for ages and generations, but is now disclosed to the saints. [27]To them God has chosen to make known among the Gentiles the glorious riches of this mystery, which is Christ in you, the hope of glory.

[28]We proclaim him, admonishing and teaching everyone with all wisdom, so that we may present everyone perfect in Christ. [29]To this end I labor, struggling with all his energy, which so powerfully works in me.

2 I want you to know how much I am struggling for you and for those at Laodicea, and for all who have not met me personally. [2]My purpose is that they may be encouraged in heart and united in love, so that they may have the full riches of complete understanding, in order that they may know the mystery of God, namely, Christ, [3]in whom are hid-

a 21 Or minds, as shown by

基督的超越

[15]愛子是那不能看見之神的像，是首生的，在一切被造的以先。[16]因為萬有都是靠他造的，無論是天上的、地上的、能看見的、不能看見的，或是有位的、主治的、執政的、掌權的，一概都是藉着他造的，又是為他造的。[17]他在萬有之先，萬有也靠他而立。[18]他也是教會全體之首，他是元始，是從死裏首先復生的，使他可以在凡事上居首位。[19]因為父喜歡叫一切的豐盛在他裏面居住。[20]既然藉着他在十字架上所流的血成就了和平，便藉着他叫萬有，無論是地上的、天上的，都與自己和好了。

[21]你們從前與神隔絕，因着惡行，心裏與他為敵；[22]但如今他藉着基督的肉身受死，叫你們與自己和好，都成了聖潔，沒有瑕疵，無可責備，把你們引到自己面前。[23]只要你們在所信的道上恆心，根基穩固，堅定不移，不至被引動失去（註：原文作"離開"）福音的盼望，這福音就是你們所聽過的，已經傳與普天下萬人聽的（註："萬人"原文作"凡受造的"）。我保羅也作了這福音的執事。

保羅為教會勞苦

[24]現在我為你們受苦，倒覺歡樂，並且為基督的身體，就是為教會，要在我肉身上補滿基督患難的缺欠。[25]我照神為你們所賜我的職分作了教會的執事，要把神的道理傳得全備。[26]這道理就是歷世歷代所隱藏的奧秘，但如今向他的聖徒顯明了。[27]神願意叫他們知道，這奧秘在外邦人中有何等豐盛的榮耀，就是基督在你們心裏成了有榮耀的盼望。

[28]我們傳揚他，是用諸般的智慧勸戒各人、教導各人，要把各人在基督裏完完全全地引到神面前。[29]我也為此勞苦，照着他在我裏面運用的大能，盡心竭力。

2 我願意你們曉得我為你們和老底嘉人，並一切沒有與我親自見面的人，是何等地盡心竭力，[2]要叫他們的心得安慰，因愛心互相聯絡，以致豐豐足足在悟性中有充足的信心，使他們真知神的奧秘就是基督；[3]所積蓄的一切智慧知識，都在他裏面藏着。⁴我說這話，免得有人用花言巧語迷惑你們。⁵我身子雖與你們相離，心卻與你們同在，見你們循規蹈矩，信基督的心也堅固，我就歡喜了。

藉與基督同活在人類規條上得自由

⁶你們既然接受了主基督耶穌，就當遵他而行；⁷在他裏面生根建造，信心堅固，正如你們所領的教訓，感謝的心也更增長了。

⁸你們要謹慎，恐怕有人用他的理學和虛空的妄言，不照着基督，乃照人間的遺傳和世上的小學，就把你們擄去。

⁹因為神本性一切的豐盛，都有形有體地居住在基督裏面，¹⁰你們在他裏面也得了豐盛。他是各樣執政掌權者的元首。¹¹你們在他裏面，也受了不是人手所行的割禮，乃是基督使你們脫去肉體情慾的割禮。¹²你們既受洗與他一同埋葬，也就在此與他一同復活，都因信那叫他從死裏復活神的功用。

¹³你們從前在過犯和未受割禮的肉體中死了，神赦免了你們（註：或作"我們"）一切過犯，便叫你們與基督一同活過來；¹⁴又塗抹了在律例上所寫攻擊我們、有礙於我們的字據，把它撤去，釘在十字架上。¹⁵既將一切執政的、掌權的擄來，明顯給眾人看，就仗着十字架誇勝。

¹⁶所以不拘在飲食上，或節期、月朔、安息日，都不可讓人論斷你們。¹⁷這些原是後事的影兒，那形體卻是基督。¹⁸不可讓人因着故意謙虛和敬拜天使，就奪去你們的獎賞。這等人拘泥在所見過的（註：有古卷作"這等人窺察所沒有見過的"），隨着自己的慾心，無故地自高自大，¹⁹不持定元首。全身既然靠着他，筋節得以相助聯絡，就因神大得長進。

²⁰-²¹你們若是與基督同死，脫離了世上的小學，為甚麼仍像在世俗中活着，服從那"不可拿、不可

den all the treasures of wisdom and knowledge. ⁴I tell you this so that no one may deceive you by fine-sounding arguments. ⁵For though I am absent from you in body, I am present with you in spirit and delight to see how orderly you are and how firm your faith in Christ is.

Freedom From Human Regulations Through Life With Christ

⁶So then, just as you received Christ Jesus as Lord, continue to live in him, ⁷rooted and built up in him, strengthened in the faith as you were taught, and overflowing with thankfulness.

⁸See to it that no one takes you captive through hollow and deceptive philosophy, which depends on human tradition and the basic principles of this world rather than on Christ.

⁹For in Christ all the fullness of the Deity lives in bodily form, ¹⁰and you have been given fullness in Christ, who is the head over every power and authority. ¹¹In him you were also circumcised, in the putting off of the sinful nature,ᵃ not with a circumcision done by the hands of men but with the circumcision done by Christ, ¹²having been buried with him in baptism and raised with him through your faith in the power of God, who raised him from the dead.

¹³When you were dead in your sins and in the uncircumcision of your sinful nature,ᵇ God made youᶜ alive with Christ. He forgave us all our sins, ¹⁴having canceled the written code, with its regulations, that was against us and that stood opposed to us; he took it away, nailing it to the cross. ¹⁵And having disarmed the powers and authorities, he made a public spectacle of them, triumphing over them by the cross.ᵈ

¹⁶Therefore do not let anyone judge you by what you eat or drink, or with regard to a religious festival, a New Moon celebration or a Sabbath day. ¹⁷These are a shadow of the things that were to come; the reality, however, is found in Christ. ¹⁸Do not let anyone who delights in false humility and the worship of angels disqualify you for the prize. Such a person goes into great detail about what he has seen, and his unspiritual mind puffs him up with idle notions. ¹⁹He has lost connection with the Head, from whom the whole body, supported and held together by its ligaments and sinews, grows as God causes it to grow.

²⁰Since you died with Christ to the basic principles of this world, why, as though you still belonged to it, do you submit to its rules: ²¹"Do

a 11 Or *the flesh*   *b 13* Or *your flesh*   *c 13* Some manuscripts *us*   *d 15* Or *them in him*

not handle! Do not taste! Do not touch!"? [22]These are all destined to perish with use, because they are based on human commands and teachings. [23]Such regulations indeed have an appearance of wisdom, with their self-imposed worship, their false humility and their harsh treatment of the body, but they lack any value in restraining sensual indulgence.

Rules for Holy Living

3 Since, then, you have been raised with Christ, set your hearts on things above, where Christ is seated at the right hand of God. [2]Set your minds on things above, not on earthly things. [3]For you died, and your life is now hidden with Christ in God. [4]When Christ, who is your[a] life, appears, then you also will appear with him in glory.

[5]Put to death, therefore, whatever belongs to your earthly nature: sexual immorality, impurity, lust, evil desires and greed, which is idolatry. [6]Because of these, the wrath of God is coming.[b] [7]You used to walk in these ways, in the life you once lived. [8]But now you must rid yourselves of all such things as these: anger, rage, malice, slander, and filthy language from your lips. [9]Do not lie to each other, since you have taken off your old self with its practices [10]and have put on the new self, which is being renewed in knowledge in the image of its Creator. [11]Here there is no Greek or Jew, circumcised or uncircumcised, barbarian, Scythian, slave or free, but Christ is all, and is in all.

[12]Therefore, as God's chosen people, holy and dearly loved, clothe yourselves with compassion, kindness, humility, gentleness and patience. [13]Bear with each other and forgive whatever grievances you may have against one another. Forgive as the Lord forgave you. [14]And over all these virtues put on love, which binds them all together in perfect unity.

[15]Let the peace of Christ rule in your hearts, since as members of one body you were called to peace. And be thankful. [16]Let the word of Christ dwell in you richly as you teach and admonish one another with all wisdom, and as you sing psalms, hymns and spiritual songs with gratitude in your hearts to God. [17]And whatever you do, whether in word or deed, do it all in the name of the Lord Jesus, giving thanks to God the Father through him.

嘗、不可摸"等類的規條呢？[22]這都是照人所吩咐、所教導的。說到這一切，正用的時候就都敗壞了。[23]這些規條使人徒有智慧之名，用私意崇拜，自表謙卑，苦待己身，其實在克制肉體的情慾上是毫無功效。

聖潔生活準則

3 所以你們若真與基督一同復活，就當求在上面的事；那裏有基督坐在神的右邊。[2]你們要思念上面的事，不要思念地上的事。[3]因為你們已經死了，你們的生命與基督一同藏在神裏面。[4]基督是我們的生命，他顯現的時候，你們也要與他一同顯現在榮耀裏。

[5]所以要治死你們在地上的肢體，就如淫亂、污穢、邪情、惡慾和貪婪，貪婪就與拜偶像一樣。[6]因這些事，神的忿怒必臨到那悖逆之子。[7]當你們在這些事中活着的時候，也曾這樣行過。[8]但現在你們要棄絕這一切的事，以及惱恨、忿怒、惡毒（註：或作"陰毒"）、毀謗，並口中污穢的言語。[9]不要彼此說謊，因你們已經脫去舊人和舊人的行為，[10]穿上了新人。這新人在知識上漸漸更新，正如造他主的形像。[11]在此並不分希臘人、猶太人、受割禮的、未受割禮的、化外人、西古提人、為奴的、自主的，惟有基督是包括一切，又住在各人之內。

[12]所以，你們既是神的選民、聖潔蒙愛的人，就要存（註：原文作"穿"。下同）憐憫、恩慈、謙虛、溫柔、忍耐的心。[13]倘若這人與那人有嫌隙，總要彼此包容，彼此饒恕；主怎樣饒恕了你們，你們也要怎樣饒恕人。[14]在這一切之外，要存着愛心，愛心就是聯絡全德的。

[15]又要叫基督的平安在你們心裏做主，你們也為此蒙召，歸為一體；且要存感謝的心。[16]當用各樣的智慧，把基督的道理豐豐富富地存在心裏（註：或作"當把基督的道理豐豐富富地存在心裏，以各樣的智慧"），用詩章、頌詞、靈歌，彼此教導，互相勸戒，心被恩感，歌頌神。[17]無論做甚麼，或說話、或行事，都要奉主耶穌的名，藉着他感謝神。

---

a 4 Some manuscripts *our*   *b* 6 Some early manuscripts *coming on those who are disobedient*

基督徒家庭的準則

¹⁸你們作妻子的，當順服自己的丈夫，這在主裏面是相宜的。¹⁹你們作丈夫的，要愛你們的妻子，不可苦待她們。²⁰你們作兒女的，要凡事聽從父母，因為這是主所喜悅的。²¹你們作父親的，不要惹兒女的氣，恐怕他們失了志氣。²²你們作僕人的，要凡事聽從你們肉身的主人，不要只在眼前侍奉，像是討人喜歡的，總要存心誠實敬畏主。²³無論做甚麼，都要從心裏做，像是給主做的，不是給人做的，²⁴因為你們知道從主那裏必得着基業為賞賜。你們所侍奉的乃是主基督。²⁵那行不義的，必受不義的報應；主並不偏待人。

4 你們作主人的，要公平平地待僕人，因為知道你們也有一位主在天上。

進一步的教導

²你們要恆切禱告，在此警醒感恩；³也要為我們禱告，求神給我們開傳道的門，能以講基督的奧秘（我為此被捆鎖），⁴叫我按着所該說的話將這奧秘發明出來。⁵你們要愛惜光陰，用智慧與外人交往。⁶你們的言語要常常帶着和氣，好像用鹽調和，就可知道該怎樣回答各人。

最後的問安

⁷有我親愛的兄弟<u>推基古</u>要將我一切的事告訴你們。他是忠心的執事，和我一同作主的僕人。⁸我特意打發他到你們那裏去，好叫你們知道我們的光景，又叫他安慰你們的心。⁹我又打發一位親愛忠心的兄弟<u>阿尼西謀</u>同去，他也是你們那裏的人。他們要把這裏一切的事都告訴你們。

¹⁰與我一同坐監的<u>亞里達古</u>問你們安。<u>巴拿巴</u>的表弟<u>馬可</u>也問你們安。（說到這<u>馬可</u>，你們已經受了吩咐，他若到了你們那裏，你們就接待他。）¹¹<u>耶數</u>又稱為<u>猶士都</u>，也問你們安。奉割禮的人中，只有這三個人是為神的國與我一同做工的，也是叫我心裏得安慰的。¹²有你們那裏的人，作基督耶穌僕人的<u>以</u>

Rules for Christian Households

¹⁸Wives, submit to your husbands, as is fitting in the Lord.

¹⁹Husbands, love your wives and do not be harsh with them.

²⁰Children, obey your parents in everything, for this pleases the Lord.

²¹Fathers, do not embitter your children, or they will become discouraged.

²²Slaves, obey your earthly masters in everything; and do it, not only when their eye is on you and to win their favor, but with sincerity of heart and reverence for the Lord. ²³Whatever you do, work at it with all your heart, as working for the Lord, not for men, ²⁴since you know that you will receive an inheritance from the Lord as a reward. It is the Lord Christ you are serving. ²⁵Anyone who does wrong will be repaid for his wrong, and there is no favoritism.

4 Masters, provide your slaves with what is right and fair, because you know that you also have a Master in heaven.

Further Instructions

²Devote yourselves to prayer, being watchful and thankful. ³And pray for us, too, that God may open a door for our message, so that we may proclaim the mystery of Christ, for which I am in chains. ⁴Pray that I may proclaim it clearly, as I should. ⁵Be wise in the way you act toward outsiders; make the most of every opportunity. ⁶Let your conversation be always full of grace, seasoned with salt, so that you may know how to answer everyone.

Final Greetings

⁷Tychicus will tell you all the news about me. He is a dear brother, a faithful minister and fellow servant in the Lord. ⁸I am sending him to you for the express purpose that you may know about our^a circumstances and that he may encourage your hearts. ⁹He is coming with Onesimus, our faithful and dear brother, who is one of you. They will tell you everything that is happening here.

¹⁰My fellow prisoner Aristarchus sends you his greetings, as does Mark, the cousin of Barnabas. (You have received instructions about him; if he comes to you, welcome him.) ¹¹Jesus, who is called Justus, also sends greetings. These are the only Jews among my fellow workers for the kingdom of God, and they have proved a comfort to me. ¹²Epaphras, who is one of you and a servant of Christ Jesus, sends greetings.

a 8 Some manuscripts that he may know about your

He is always wrestling in prayer for you, that you may stand firm in all the will of God, mature and fully assured. ¹³I vouch for him that he is working hard for you and for those at Laodicea and Hierapolis. ¹⁴Our dear friend Luke, the doctor, and Demas send greetings. ¹⁵Give my greetings to the brothers at Laodicea, and to Nympha and the church in her house.

¹⁶After this letter has been read to you, see that it is also read in the church of the Laodiceans and that you in turn read the letter from Laodicea.

¹⁷Tell Archippus: "See to it that you complete the work you have received in the Lord."

¹⁸I, Paul, write this greeting in my own hand. Remember my chains. Grace be with you.

巴弗問你們安。他在禱告之間，常為你們竭力地祈求，願你們在神一切的旨意上得以完全，信心充足，能站立得穩。¹³他為你們和老底嘉並希拉波立的弟兄多多地勞苦，這是我可以給他作見證的。¹⁴所親愛的醫生路加和底馬問你們安。¹⁵請問老底嘉的弟兄和寧法，並她家裏的教會安。

¹⁶你們念了這書信，便交給老底嘉的教會，叫他們也念；你們也要念從老底嘉來的書信。

¹⁷要對亞基布說："務要謹慎，盡你從主所受的職分。"

¹⁸我保羅親筆問你們安。你們要記念我的捆鎖。願恩惠常與你們同在！

圖六：歌羅西書中的主要地方
MAP 6 : KEY PLACES IN COLOSSIANS

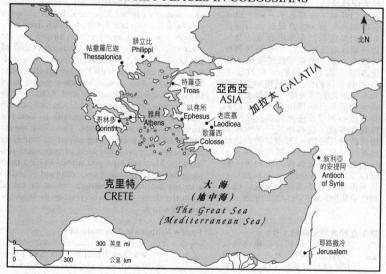

帖撒羅尼迦前書

1 保羅、西拉、提摩太，

寫信給帖撒羅尼迦在父神和主耶穌基督裏的教會：

願恩惠、平安歸與你們！

為帖撒羅尼迦人的信心感恩

2 我們為你們眾人常常感謝神，禱告的時候提到你們。3 在神我們的父面前，不住地記念你們因信心所做的工夫，因愛心所受的勞苦，因盼望我們主耶穌基督所存的忍耐。

4 被神所愛的弟兄啊，我知道你們是蒙揀選的，5 因為我們的福音傳到你們那裏，不獨在乎言語，也在乎權能和聖靈，並充足的信心。正如你們知道我們在你們那裏，為你們的緣故是怎樣為人；6 並且你們在大遭大難中蒙了聖靈所賜的喜樂，領受真道，就效法我們，也效法了主，7 甚至你們作了馬其頓和亞該亞所有信主之人的榜樣。8 因為主的道從你們那裏已經傳揚出來，你們向神的信心不但在馬其頓和亞該亞，就是在各處，也都傳開了，所以不用我們說甚麼話。9 因為他們自己已經報明我們是怎樣進到你們那裏，你們是怎樣離棄偶像，歸向神，要服侍那又真又活的神，10 等候他兒子從天降臨，就是他從死裏復活的，那位救我們脫離將來忿怒的耶穌。

保羅在帖撒羅尼迦的工作

2 弟兄們，你們自己原曉得我們進到你們那裏並不是徒然的。2 我們從前在腓立比被害受辱，這是你們知道的；然而還是靠我們的神放開膽量，在大爭戰中把神的福音傳給你們。3 我們的勸勉，不是出於錯誤，不是出於污穢，也不是用詭詐。4 但神既然驗中了我們，把福音託付我們，我們就

1 Thessalonians

1 Paul, Silas[a] and Timothy,

To the church of the Thessalonians in God the Father and the Lord Jesus Christ:

Grace and peace to you.[b]

Thanksgiving for the Thessalonians' Faith

2 We always thank God for all of you, mentioning you in our prayers. 3 We continually remember before our God and Father your work produced by faith, your labor prompted by love, and your endurance inspired by hope in our Lord Jesus Christ.

4 For we know, brothers loved by God, that he has chosen you, 5 because our gospel came to you not simply with words, but also with power, with the Holy Spirit and with deep conviction. You know how we lived among you for your sake. 6 You became imitators of us and of the Lord; in spite of severe suffering, you welcomed the message with the joy given by the Holy Spirit. 7 And so you became a model to all the believers in Macedonia and Achaia. 8 The Lord's message rang out from you not only in Macedonia and Achaia—your faith in God has become known everywhere. Therefore we do not need to say anything about it, 9 for they themselves report what kind of reception you gave us. They tell how you turned to God from idols to serve the living and true God, 10 and to wait for his Son from heaven, whom he raised from the dead—Jesus, who rescues us from the coming wrath.

Paul's Ministry in Thessalonica

2 You know, brothers, that our visit to you was not a failure. 2 We had previously suffered and been insulted in Philippi, as you know, but with the help of our God we dared to tell you his gospel in spite of strong opposition. 3 For the appeal we make does not spring from error or impure motives, nor are we trying to trick you. 4 On the contrary, we speak as men approved by God to be

---

a 1 Greek *Silvanus*, a variant of *Silas*　*b 1* Some early manuscripts *you from God our Father and the Lord Jesus Christ*

entrusted with the gospel. We are not trying to please men but God, who tests our hearts. ⁵You know we never used flattery, nor did we put on a mask to cover up greed—God is our witness. ⁶We were not looking for praise from men, not from you or anyone else.

As apostles of Christ we could have been a burden to you, ⁷but we were gentle among you, like a mother caring for her little children. ⁸We loved you so much that we were delighted to share with you not only the gospel of God but our lives as well, because you had become so dear to us. ⁹Surely you remember, brothers, our toil and hardship; we worked night and day in order not to be a burden to anyone while we preached the gospel of God to you.

¹⁰You are witnesses, and so is God, of how holy, righteous and blameless we were among you who believed. ¹¹For you know that we dealt with each of you as a father deals with his own children, ¹²encouraging, comforting and urging you to live lives worthy of God, who calls you into his kingdom and glory.

¹³And we also thank God continually because, when you received the word of God, which you heard from us, you accepted it not as the word of men, but as it actually is, the word of God, which is at work in you who believe. ¹⁴For you, brothers, became imitators of God's churches in Judea, which are in Christ Jesus: You suffered from your own countrymen the same things those churches suffered from the Jews, ¹⁵who killed the Lord Jesus and the prophets and also drove us out. They displease God and are hostile to all men ¹⁶in their effort to keep us from speaking to the Gentiles so that they may be saved. In this way they always heap up their sins to the limit. The wrath of God has come upon them at last.ᵃ

Paul's Longing to See the Thessalonians

¹⁷But, brothers, when we were torn away from you for a short time (in person, not in thought), out of our intense longing we made every effort to see you. ¹⁸For we wanted to come to you—certainly I, Paul, did, again and again—but Satan stopped us. ¹⁹For what is our hope, our joy, or the crown in which we will glory in the presence of our Lord Jesus when he comes? Is it not you? ²⁰Indeed, you are our glory and joy.

照樣講，不是要討人喜歡，乃是要討那察驗我們心的神喜歡。⁵因為我們從來沒有用過諂媚的話，這是你們知道的；也沒有藏着貪心，這是神可以作見證的。

⁶我們作基督的使徒，雖然可以叫人尊重，卻沒有向你們或向別人求榮耀，⁷只在你們中間存心溫柔，如同母親乳養自己的孩子。⁸我們既是這樣愛你們，不但願意將神的福音給你們，連自己的性命也願意給你們，因你們是我們所疼愛的。⁹弟兄們，你們記念我們的辛苦勞碌，晝夜做工，傳神的福音給你們，免得叫你們一人受累。

¹⁰我們向你們信主的人，是何等聖潔、公義，無可指摘，有你們作見證，也有神作見證。¹¹你們也曉得我們怎樣勸勉你們，安慰你們，囑咐你們各人，好像父親待自己的兒女一樣。¹²要叫你們行事對得起那召你們進他國、得他榮耀的神。

¹³為此，我們也不住地感謝神，因你們聽見我們所傳神的道，就領受了；不以為是人的道，乃以為是神的道。這道實在是神的，並且運行在你們信主的人心中。¹⁴弟兄們，你們曾效法猶太中，在基督耶穌裏神的各教會，因為你們也受了本地人的苦害，像他們受了猶太人的苦害一樣。¹⁵這猶太人殺了主耶穌和先知，又把我們趕出去；他們不得神的喜悅，且與眾人為敵；¹⁶不許我們傳道給外邦人，使外邦人得救，常常充滿自己的罪惡。神的忿怒臨在他們身上已經到了極處。

保羅渴望見帖撒羅尼迦人

¹⁷弟兄們，我們暫時與你們離別，是面目離別，心裏卻不離別；我們極力地想法子，很願意見你們的面，¹⁸所以我們有意到你們那裏。我保羅有一兩次要去，只是撒但阻擋了我們。¹⁹我們的盼望和喜樂並所誇的冠冕是甚麼呢？豈不是我們主耶穌來的時候，你們在他面前站立得住嗎？²⁰因為你們就是我們的榮耀，我們的喜樂。

---

a 16 Or them fully

3 我們既不能再忍，就願意獨自等在雅典，²打發我們的兄弟在基督福音上作神執事的提摩太前去（註："作神執事的"有古卷作"與神同工的"）堅固你們，並在你們所信的道上勸慰你們，³免得有人被諸般患難搖動，因為你們自己知道，我們受患難原是命定的。⁴我們在你們那裏的時候預先告訴你們，我們必受患難，以後果然應驗了，你們也知道。⁵為此，我既不能再忍，就打發人去，要曉得你們的信心如何，恐怕那誘惑人的到底誘惑了你們，叫我們的勞苦歸於徒然。

令人鼓舞的好消息

⁶但提摩太剛才從你們那裏回來，將你們信心和愛心的好消息報給我們，又說你們常常記念我們，切切地想見我們，如同我們想見你們一樣。⁷所以弟兄們，我們在一切困苦患難之中，因着你們的信心就得了安慰。⁸你們若靠主站立得穩，我們就活了。⁹我們在神面前，因着你們甚是喜樂，為這一切喜樂，可用何等的感謝為你們報答神呢？¹⁰我們晝夜切切地祈求，要見你們的面，補滿你們信心的不足。

¹¹願神我們的父和我們的主耶穌，一直引領我們到你們那裏去；¹²又願主叫你們彼此相愛的心，並愛眾人的心，都能增長、充足，如同我們愛你們一樣；¹³好使你們當我們主耶穌同他眾聖徒來的時候，在我們父神面前心裏堅固，成為聖潔，無可責備。

為討神喜悅而活

4 弟兄們，我還有話說：我們靠着主耶穌求你們、勸你們，你們既然受了我們的教訓，知道該怎樣行，可以討神的喜悅，就要照你們現在所行的，更加勉勵。²你們原曉得我們憑主耶穌傳給你們甚麼命令。

³神的旨意就是要你們成為聖潔，遠避淫行；⁴要你們各人曉得怎樣用聖潔、尊貴守着自己的身體，⁵不

---

3 So when we could stand it no longer, we thought it best to be left by ourselves in Athens. ²We sent Timothy, who is our brother and God's fellow worker*a* in spreading the gospel of Christ, to strengthen and encourage you in your faith, ³so that no one would be unsettled by these trials. You know quite well that we were destined for them. ⁴In fact, when we were with you, we kept telling you that we would be persecuted. And it turned out that way, as you well know. ⁵For this reason, when I could stand it no longer, I sent to find out about your faith. I was afraid that in some way the tempter might have tempted you and our efforts might have been useless.

Timothy's Encouraging Report

⁶But Timothy has just now come to us from you and has brought good news about your faith and love. He has told us that you always have pleasant memories of us and that you long to see us, just as we also long to see you. ⁷Therefore, brothers, in all our distress and persecution we were encouraged about you because of your faith. ⁸For now we really live, since you are standing firm in the Lord. ⁹How can we thank God enough for you in return for all the joy we have in the presence of our God because of you? ¹⁰Night and day we pray most earnestly that we may see you again and supply what is lacking in your faith.

¹¹Now may our God and Father himself and our Lord Jesus clear the way for us to come to you. ¹²May the Lord make your love increase and overflow for each other and for everyone else, just as ours does for you. ¹³May he strengthen your hearts so that you will be blameless and holy in the presence of our God and Father when our Lord Jesus comes with all his holy ones.

Living to Please God

4 Finally, brothers, we instructed you how to live in order to please God, as in fact you are living. Now we ask you and urge you in the Lord Jesus to do this more and more. ²For you know what instructions we gave you by the authority of the Lord Jesus.

³It is God's will that you should be sanctified: that you should avoid sexual immorality; ⁴that each of you should learn to control his own body*b* in a way that is holy and honorable, ⁵not

a 2 Some manuscripts brother and fellow worker; other manuscripts brother and God's servant b 4 Or learn to live with his own wife; or learn to acquire a wife in passionate lust like the heathen, who do not know God; 6and that in this matter no one should wrong his brother or take advantage of him. The Lord will punish men for all such sins, as we have already told you and warned you. 7For God did not call us to be impure, but to live a holy life. 8Therefore, he who rejects this instruction does not reject man but God, who gives you his Holy Spirit.

9Now about brotherly love we do not need to write to you, for you yourselves have been taught by God to love each other. 10And in fact, you do love all the brothers throughout Macedonia. Yet we urge you, brothers, to do so more and more.

11Make it your ambition to lead a quiet life, to mind your own business and to work with your hands, just as we told you, 12so that your daily life may win the respect of outsiders and so that you will not be dependent on anybody.

The Coming of the Lord

13Brothers, we do not want you to be ignorant about those who fall asleep, or to grieve like the rest of men, who have no hope. 14We believe that Jesus died and rose again and so we believe that God will bring with Jesus those who have fallen asleep in him. 15According to the Lord's own word, we tell you that we who are still alive, who are left till the coming of the Lord, will certainly not precede those who have fallen asleep. 16For the Lord himself will come down from heaven, with a loud command, with the voice of the archangel and with the trumpet call of God, and the dead in Christ will rise first. 17After that, we who are still alive and are left will be caught up together with them in the clouds to meet the Lord in the air. And so we will be with the Lord forever. 18Therefore encourage each other with these words.

5 Now, brothers, about times and dates we do not need to write to you, 2for you know very well that the day of the Lord will come like a thief in the night. 3While people are saying, "Peace and safety," destruction will come on them suddenly, as labor pains on a pregnant woman, and they will not escape.

4But you, brothers, are not in darkness so that this day should surprise you like a thief. 5You are all sons of the light and sons of the day. We do not belong to the night or to the darkness. 6So then, let us not be like others, who are asleep, but let us be alert and self-controlled. 7For those who sleep, sleep at night, and those who get drunk, get drunk at night. 8But since we belong to the day, let us be self-controlled,

放縱私慾的邪情，像那不認識神的外邦人。6不要一個人在這事上越分，欺負他的弟兄，因為這一類的事，主必報應，正如我預先對你們說過，又切切囑咐你們的。7神召我們，本不是要我們沾染污穢，乃是要我們成為聖潔。8所以，那棄絕的，不是棄絕人，乃是棄絕那賜聖靈給我們的神。

9論到弟兄們相愛，不用人寫信給你們，因為你們自己蒙了神的教訓，叫你們彼此相愛。10你們向馬其頓全地的眾弟兄固然是這樣行，但我勸弟兄們要更加勉勵。

11又要立志作安靜人，辦自己的事，親手做工，正如我們從前所吩咐你們的，12叫你們可以向外人行事端正，自己也就沒有甚麼缺乏了。

主的降臨

13論到睡了的人，我們不願意弟兄們不知道，恐怕你們憂傷，像那些沒有指望的人一樣。14我們若信耶穌死而復活了，那已經在耶穌裏睡了的人，神也必將他與耶穌一同帶來。15我們現在照主的話告訴你們一件事：我們這活着還存留到主降臨的人，斷不能在那已經睡了的人之先，16因為主必親自從天降臨，有呼叫的聲音和天使長的聲音，又有神的號吹響；那在基督裏死了的人必先復活。17以後我們這活着還存留的人必和他們一同被提到雲裏，在空中與主相遇。這樣，我們就要和主永遠同在。18所以，你們當用這些話彼此勸慰。

5 弟兄們，論到時候、日期，不用寫信給你們，2因為你們自己明明曉得，主的日子來到，好像夜間的賊一樣。3人正說平安穩妥的時候，災禍忽然臨到他們，如同產難臨到懷胎的婦人一樣；他們絕不能逃脫。

4弟兄們，你們卻不在黑暗裏，叫那日子臨到你們像賊一樣。5你們都是光明之子，都是白晝之子；我們不是屬黑夜的，也不是屬幽暗的。6所以，我們不要睡覺，像別人一樣，總要警醒謹守。7因為睡了的人是在夜間睡，醉了的人是在夜間醉。8但我們既然屬乎白晝，就應當謹守，把信和愛當作護心鏡遮胸，把得救的盼望當作頭盔戴上。⁹因為神不是預定我們受刑，乃是預定我們藉着我們主耶穌基督得救。¹⁰他替我們死，叫我們無論醒着、睡着，都與他同活。¹¹所以，你們該彼此勸慰，互相建立，正如你們素常所行的。

最後的勸戒

¹²弟兄們，我們勸你們敬重那在你們中間勞苦的人，就是在主裏面治理你們們、勸戒你們的。¹³又因他們所做的工，用愛心格外尊重他們。你們也要彼此和睦。¹⁴我們又勸弟兄們，要警戒不守規矩的人，勉勵灰心的人，扶助軟弱的人，也要向眾人忍耐。¹⁵你們要謹慎，無論是誰都不可以惡報惡；或是彼此相待，或是待眾人，常要追求良善。

¹⁶要常常喜樂，¹⁷不住地禱告，¹⁸凡事謝恩，因為這是神在基督耶穌裏向你們所定的旨意。

¹⁹不要消滅聖靈的感動，²⁰不要藐視先知的講論；²¹但要凡事察驗，善美的要持守，²²各樣的惡事要禁戒不做。

²³願賜平安的神親自使你們全然成聖。又願你們的靈與魂與身子得蒙保守，在我主耶穌基督降臨的時候，完全無可指摘。²⁴那召你們的本是信實的，他必成就這事。

²⁵請弟兄們為我們禱告。²⁶與眾弟兄親嘴問安，務要聖潔。²⁷我指着主囑咐你們，要把這信念給眾弟兄聽。

²⁸願我主耶穌基督的恩常與你們同在！

putting on faith and love as a breastplate, and the hope of salvation as a helmet. ⁹For God did not appoint us to suffer wrath but to receive salvation through our Lord Jesus Christ. ¹⁰He died for us so that, whether we are awake or asleep, we may live together with him. ¹¹Therefore encourage one another and build each other up, just as in fact you are doing.

Final Instructions

¹²Now we ask you, brothers, to respect those who work hard among you, who are over you in the Lord and who admonish you. ¹³Hold them in the highest regard in love because of their work. Live in peace with each other. ¹⁴And we urge you, brothers, warn those who are idle, encourage the timid, help the weak, be patient with everyone. ¹⁵Make sure that nobody pays back wrong for wrong, but always try to be kind to each other and to everyone else.

¹⁶Be joyful always; ¹⁷pray continually; ¹⁸give thanks in all circumstances, for this is God's will for you in Christ Jesus.

¹⁹Do not put out the Spirit's fire; ²⁰do not treat prophecies with contempt. ²¹Test everything. Hold on to the good. ²²Avoid every kind of evil.

²³May God himself, the God of peace, sanctify you through and through. May your whole spirit, soul and body be kept blameless at the coming of our Lord Jesus Christ. ²⁴The one who calls you is faithful and he will do it.

²⁵Brothers, pray for us. ²⁶Greet all the brothers with a holy kiss. ²⁷I charge you before the Lord to have this letter read to all the brothers.

²⁸The grace of our Lord Jesus Christ be with you.

2 Thessalonians

帖撒羅尼迦後書

1 Paul, Silas*ᵃ* and Timothy,

To the church of the Thessalonians in God our Father and the Lord Jesus Christ:

1 保羅、西拉、提摩太，

寫信給帖撒羅尼迦在神我們的父與主耶穌基督裏的教會：

²Grace and peace to you from God the Father and the Lord Jesus Christ.

² 願恩惠、平安從父神和主耶穌基督歸與你們！

Thanksgiving and Prayer

³We ought always to thank God for you, brothers, and rightly so, because your faith is growing more and more, and the love every one of you has for each other is increasing. ⁴Therefore, among God's churches we boast about your perseverance and faith in all the persecutions and trials you are enduring.

⁵All this is evidence that God's judgment is right, and as a result you will be counted worthy of the kingdom of God, for which you are suffering. ⁶God is just: He will pay back trouble to those who trouble you ⁷and give relief to you who are troubled, and to us as well. This will happen when the Lord Jesus is revealed from heaven in blazing fire with his powerful angels. ⁸He will punish those who do not know God and do not obey the gospel of our Lord Jesus. ⁹They will be punished with everlasting destruction and shut out from the presence of the Lord and from the majesty of his power ¹⁰on the day he comes to be glorified in his holy people and to be marveled at among all those who have believed. This includes you, because you believed our testimony to you.

¹¹With this in mind, we constantly pray for you, that our God may count you worthy of his calling, and that by his power he may fulfill every good purpose of yours and every act prompted by your faith. ¹²We pray this so that the name of our Lord Jesus may be glorified in you, and you in him, according to the grace of our God and the Lord Jesus Christ.*ᵇ*

感恩與禱告

³ 弟兄們，我們該為你們常常感謝神，這本是合宜的，因你們的信心格外增長，並且你們眾人彼此相愛的心也都充足。⁴ 甚至我們在神的各教會裏為你們誇口，都因你們在所受的一切逼迫患難中，仍舊存忍耐和信心。

⁵ 這正是神公義判斷的明證，叫你們可算配得神的國，你們就是為這國受苦。⁶ 神既是公義的，就必將患難報應那加患難給你們的人；⁷ 也必使你們這受患難的人與我們同得平安。那時，主耶穌同他有能力的天使從天上在火焰中顯現，⁸ 要報應那不認識神和那不聽從我主耶穌福音的人。⁹ 他們要受刑罰，就是永遠沉淪，離開主的面和他權能的榮光。¹⁰ 這正是主降臨，要在他聖徒的身上得榮耀，又在一切信的人身上顯為希奇的那日子。（我們對你們作的見證，你們也信了。）

¹¹ 因此，我們常為你們禱告，願我們的神看你們配得過所蒙的召，又用大能成就你們一切所羨慕的良善和一切因信心所做的工夫；¹² 叫我們主耶穌的名在你們身上得榮耀，你們也在他身上得榮耀，都照着我們的神並主耶穌基督的恩。

---

a 1 Greek *Silvanus*, a variant of *Silas*   *b* 12 Or *God and Lord, Jesus Christ*

不法的人

2 弟兄們，論到我們主耶穌基督降臨和我們到他那裏聚集，2我勸你們：無論有靈、有言語、有冒我名的書信，說主的日子現在到了（註："現在"或作"就"），不要輕易動心，也不要驚慌。3人不拘用甚麼法子，你們總不要被他誘惑！因為那日子以前，必有離道反教的事，並有那大罪人，就是沉淪之子，顯露出來。4他是抵擋主，高抬自己，超過一切稱為神的和一切受人敬拜的，甚至坐在神的殿裏自稱是神。

5我還在你們那裏的時候，曾把這些事告訴你們，你們不記得嗎？6現在你們也知道那攔阻他的是甚麼，是叫他到了的時候，才可以顯露。7因為那不法的隱意已經發動，只是現在有一個攔阻的，等到那攔阻的被除去，8那時這不法的人必顯露出來，主耶穌要用口中的氣滅絕他，用降臨的榮光廢掉他。9這不法的人來，是照撒但的運動，行各樣的異能、神蹟和一切虛假的奇事，10並且在那沉淪的人身上，行各樣出於不義的詭詐，因他們不領受愛真理的心，使他們得救。11故此，神就給他們一個生發錯謬的心，叫他們信從虛謊，12使一切不信真理、倒喜愛不義的人都被定罪。

要站立得穩

13主所愛的弟兄們哪，我們本該常為你們感謝神，因為他從起初揀選了你們，叫你們因信真道，又被聖靈感動，成為聖潔，能以得救。14神藉我們所傳的福音召你們到這地步，好得着我們主耶穌基督的榮光。15所以弟兄們，你們要站立得穩，凡所領受的教訓，不拘是我們口傳的，是信上寫的，都要堅守。

16但願我們主耶穌基督和那愛我們、開恩將永遠的安慰並美好的盼望賜給我們的父神，17安慰你們的心，並且在一切善行善言上堅固你們。

The Man of Lawlessness

2 Concerning the coming of our Lord Jesus Christ and our being gathered to him, we ask you, brothers, 2not to become easily unsettled or alarmed by some prophecy, report or letter supposed to have come from us, saying that the day of the Lord has already come. 3Don't let anyone deceive you in any way, for ⌊that day will not come⌋ until the rebellion occurs and the man of lawlessness[a] is revealed, the man doomed to destruction. 4He will oppose and will exalt himself over everything that is called God or is worshiped, so that he sets himself up in God's temple, proclaiming himself to be God.

5Don't you remember that when I was with you I used to tell you these things? 6And now you know what is holding him back, so that he may be revealed at the proper time. 7For the secret power of lawlessness is already at work; but the one who now holds it back will continue to do so till he is taken out of the way. 8And then the lawless one will be revealed, whom the Lord Jesus will overthrow with the breath of his mouth and destroy by the splendor of his coming. 9The coming of the lawless one will be in accordance with the work of Satan displayed in all kinds of counterfeit miracles, signs and wonders, 10and in every sort of evil that deceives those who are perishing. They perish because they refused to love the truth and so be saved. 11For this reason God sends them a powerful delusion so that they will believe the lie 12and so that all will be condemned who have not believed the truth but have delighted in wickedness.

Stand Firm

13But we ought always to thank God for you, brothers loved by the Lord, because from the beginning God chose you[b] to be saved through the sanctifying work of the Spirit and through belief in the truth. 14He called you to this through our gospel, that you might share in the glory of our Lord Jesus Christ. 15So then, brothers, stand firm and hold to the teachings[c] we passed on to you, whether by word of mouth or by letter.

16May our Lord Jesus Christ himself and God our Father, who loved us and by his grace gave us eternal encouragement and good hope, 17encourage your hearts and strengthen you in every good deed and word.

a 3 Some manuscripts *sin*　　b 13 Some manuscripts *because God chose you as his firstfruits*　　c 15 Or *traditions*

Request for Prayer

3 Finally, brothers, pray for us that the message of the Lord may spread rapidly and be honored, just as it was with you. ²And pray that we may be delivered from wicked and evil men, for not everyone has faith. ³But the Lord is faithful, and he will strengthen and protect you from the evil one. ⁴We have confidence in the Lord that you are doing and will continue to do the things we command. ⁵May the Lord direct your hearts into God's love and Christ's perseverance.

Warning Against Idleness

⁶In the name of the Lord Jesus Christ, we command you, brothers, to keep away from every brother who is idle and does not live according to the teaching*a* you received from us. ⁷For you yourselves know how you ought to follow our example. We were not idle when we were with you, ⁸nor did we eat anyone's food without paying for it. On the contrary, we worked night and day, laboring and toiling so that we would not be a burden to any of you. ⁹We did this, not because we do not have the right to such help, but in order to make ourselves a model for you to follow. ¹⁰For even when we were with you, we gave you this rule: "If a man will not work, he shall not eat."

¹¹We hear that some among you are idle. They are not busy; they are busybodies. ¹²Such people we command and urge in the Lord Jesus Christ to settle down and earn the bread they eat. ¹³And as for you, brothers, never tire of doing what is right.

¹⁴If anyone does not obey our instruction in this letter, take special note of him. Do not associate with him, in order that he may feel ashamed. ¹⁵Yet do not regard him as an enemy, but warn him as a brother.

Final Greetings

¹⁶Now may the Lord of peace himself give you peace at all times and in every way. The Lord be with all of you.

¹⁷I, Paul, write this greeting in my own hand, which is the distinguishing mark in all my letters. This is how I write.

¹⁸The grace of our Lord Jesus Christ be with you all.

a 6 Or tradition

請求代禱

3 弟兄們，我還有話說：請你們為我們禱告，好叫主的道理快快行開，得着榮耀，正如在你們中間一樣；²也叫我們脫離無理之惡人的手，因為人不都是有信心。³但主是信實的，要堅固你們，保護你們脫離那惡者（註：或作"脫離兇惡"）。⁴我們靠主深信，你們現在是遵行我們所吩咐的，後來也必要遵行。⁵願主引導你們的心，叫你們愛神，並學基督的忍耐。

警告閒懶的人

⁶弟兄們，我們奉主耶穌基督的名吩咐你們：凡有弟兄不按規矩而行，不遵守從我們所受的教訓，就當遠離他。⁷你們自己原知道應當怎樣效法我們。因為我們在你們中間，未嘗不按規矩而行，⁸也未嘗白吃人的飯，倒是辛苦勞碌，晝夜做工，免得叫你們一人受累。⁹這並不是因我們沒有權柄，乃是要給你們作榜樣，叫你們效法我們。¹⁰我們在你們那裏的時候，曾吩咐你們說："若有人不肯做工，就不可吃飯。"

¹¹因我們聽說，在你們中間有人不按規矩而行，甚麼工都不做，反倒專管閒事。¹²我們靠主耶穌基督，吩咐、勸戒這樣的人，要安靜做工，吃自己的飯。¹³弟兄們，你們行善不可喪志。

¹⁴若有人不聽從我們這信上的話，要記下他，不和他交往，叫他自覺羞愧；¹⁵但不要以他為仇人，要勸他如弟兄。

最後的問安

¹⁶願賜平安的主隨時隨事親自給你們平安。願主常與你們眾人同在！

¹⁷我保羅親筆問你們安。凡我的信都以此為記，我的筆跡就是這樣。

¹⁸願我們主耶穌基督的恩常與你們眾人同在！

提摩太前書

1 Timothy

1 奉我們救主神和我們的盼望基督耶穌之命，作基督耶穌使徒的保羅，

² 寫信給那因信主作我真兒子的提摩太：

願恩惠、憐憫、平安從父神和我們主基督耶穌歸與你！

提醒防備假教法師

³ 我往馬其頓去的時候，曾勸你仍住在以弗所，好囑咐那幾個人不可傳異教，⁴ 也不可聽從荒渺無憑的話語和無窮的家譜。這等事只生辯論，並不發明神在信上所立的章程。⁵ 但命令的總歸就是愛，這愛是從清潔的心和無虧的良心、無偽的信心生出來的。⁶ 有人偏離這些，反去講虛浮的話，⁷ 想要作教法師，卻不明白自己所講說的、所論定的。

⁸ 我們知道律法原是好的，只要人用得合宜。⁹ 因為律法不是為義人設立的，乃是為不法和不服的、不虔誠和犯罪的，不聖潔和戀世俗的，弒父母和殺人的，¹⁰ 行淫和親男色的，搶人口和說謊話的，並起假誓的，或是為別樣敵正道的事設立的。¹¹ 這是照著可稱頌之神交託我榮耀福音說的。

主對保羅的恩典

¹² 我感謝那給我力量的我們主基督耶穌，因他以我有忠心，派我服侍他。¹³ 我從前是褻瀆神的，逼迫人的，侮慢人的，然而我還蒙了憐憫，因我是不信、不明白的時候而做的。¹⁴ 並且我主的恩是格外豐盛，使我在基督耶穌裏有信心和愛心。

¹⁵ "基督耶穌降世，為要拯救罪人。" 這話是可信的，是十分可佩服的。在罪人中我是個罪魁。¹⁶ 然而

1 Paul, an apostle of Christ Jesus by the command of God our Savior and of Christ Jesus our hope,

²To Timothy my true son in the faith:

Grace, mercy and peace from God the Father and Christ Jesus our Lord.

Warning Against False Teachers of the Law

³As I urged you when I went into Macedonia, stay there in Ephesus so that you may command certain men not to teach false doctrines any longer ⁴nor to devote themselves to myths and endless genealogies. These promote controversies rather than God's work—which is by faith. ⁵The goal of this command is love, which comes from a pure heart and a good conscience and a sincere faith. ⁶Some have wandered away from these and turned to meaningless talk. ⁷They want to be teachers of the law, but they do not know what they are talking about or what they so confidently affirm.

⁸We know that the law is good if one uses it properly. ⁹We also know that law*ª* is made not for the righteous but for lawbreakers and rebels, the ungodly and sinful, the unholy and irreligious; for those who kill their fathers or mothers, for murderers, ¹⁰for adulterers and perverts, for slave traders and liars and perjurers—and for whatever else is contrary to the sound doctrine ¹¹that conforms to the glorious gospel of the blessed God, which he entrusted to me.

The Lord's Grace to Paul

¹²I thank Christ Jesus our Lord, who has given me strength, that he considered me faithful, appointing me to his service. ¹³Even though I was once a blasphemer and a persecutor and a violent man, I was shown mercy because I acted in ignorance and unbelief. ¹⁴The grace of our Lord was poured out on me abundantly, along with the faith and love that are in Christ Jesus.

¹⁵Here is a trustworthy saying that deserves full acceptance: Christ Jesus came into the world to save sinners—of whom I am the worst. ¹⁶But

a 9 Or that the law

for that very reason I was shown mercy so that in me, the worst of sinners, Christ Jesus might display his unlimited patience as an example for those who would believe on him and receive eternal life. [17]Now to the King eternal, immortal, invisible, the only God, be honor and glory for ever and ever. Amen.

[18]Timothy, my son, I give you this instruction in keeping with the prophecies once made about you, so that by following them you may fight the good fight, [19]holding on to faith and a good conscience. Some have rejected these and so have shipwrecked their faith. [20]Among them are Hymenaeus and Alexander, whom I have handed over to Satan to be taught not to blaspheme.

Instructions on Worship

2 I urge, then, first of all, that requests, prayers, intercession and thanksgiving be made for everyone— [2]for kings and all those in authority, that we may live peaceful and quiet lives in all godliness and holiness. [3]This is good, and pleases God our Savior, [4]who wants all men to be saved and to come to a knowledge of the truth. [5]For there is one God and one mediator between God and men, the man Christ Jesus, [6]who gave himself as a ransom for all men—the testimony given in its proper time. [7]And for this purpose I was appointed a herald and an apostle—I am telling the truth, I am not lying—and a teacher of the true faith to the Gentiles.

[8]I want men everywhere to lift up holy hands in prayer, without anger or disputing.

[9]I also want women to dress modestly, with decency and propriety, not with braided hair or gold or pearls or expensive clothes, [10]but with good deeds, appropriate for women who profess to worship God.

[11]A woman should learn in quietness and full submission. [12]I do not permit a woman to teach or to have authority over a man; she must be silent. [13]For Adam was formed first, then Eve. [14]And Adam was not the one deceived; it was the woman who was deceived and became a sinner. [15]But women[a] will be saved[b] through childbearing—if they continue in faith, love and holiness with propriety.

我蒙了憐憫，是因耶穌基督要在我這罪魁身上顯明他一切的忍耐，給後來信他得永生的人作榜樣。[17]但願尊貴、榮耀歸與那不能朽壞、不能看見、永世的君王、獨一的神，直到永永遠遠。阿們！

[18]我兒提摩太啊，我照從前指着你的預言，將這命令交託你，叫你因此可以打那美好的仗，[19]常存信心和無虧的良心；有人丟棄良心，就在真道上如同船破壞了一般。[20]其中有許米乃和亞歷山大，我已經把他們交給撒但，使他們受責罰，就不再謗瀆了。

對敬拜的指示

2 我勸你第一要為萬人懇求、禱告、代求、祝謝；[2]為君王和一切在位的，也該如此，使我們可以敬虔、端正，平安無事地度日。[3]這是好的，在神我們救主面前可蒙悅納。[4]他願意萬人得救，明白真道。[5]因為只有一位神，在神和人中間，只有一位中保，乃是降世為人的基督耶穌。[6]他捨自己作萬人的贖價，到了時候，這事必證明出來。[7]我為此奉派作傳道的，作使徒，作外邦人的師傅，教導他們相信，學習真道。我說的是真話，並不是謊言。

[8]我願男人無忿怒，無爭論（註："爭論"或作"疑惑"），舉起聖潔的手，隨處禱告。

[9]又願女人廉恥、自守，以正派衣裳為妝飾，不以編髮、黃金、珍珠和貴價的衣裳為妝飾；[10]只要有善行，這才與自稱是敬神的女人相宜。

[11]女人要沉靜學道，一味地順服。[12]我不許女人講道，也不許她轄管男人，只要沉靜。[13]因為先造的是亞當，後造的是夏娃；[14]且不是亞當被引誘，乃是女人被引誘，陷在罪裏。[15]然而，女人若常存信心、愛心，又聖潔自守，就必在生產上得救。

a 15 Greek she　　b 15 Or restored

監督與執事

3 "人若想要得監督的職分，就是羨慕善工。" 這話是可信的。²作監督的，必須無可指責，只作一個婦人的丈夫，有節制，自守、端正，樂意接待遠人，善於教導；³不因酒滋事、不打人，只要溫和，不爭競、不貪財；⁴好好管理自己的家，使兒女凡事端莊、順服（註：或作"端端莊莊地使兒女順服"）。⁵人若不知道管理自己的家，焉能照管神的教會呢？⁶初入教的不可作監督，恐怕他自高自大，就落在魔鬼所受的刑罰裏。⁷監督也必須在教外有好名聲，恐怕被人毀謗，落在魔鬼的網羅裏。

⁸作執事的也是如此：必須端莊，不一口兩舌，不好喝酒，不貪不義之財；⁹要存清潔的良心，固守真道的奧秘。¹⁰這等人也要先受試驗，若沒有可責之處，然後叫他們作執事。

¹¹女執事（註：原文作"女人"）也是如此：必須端莊，不說讒言，有節制，凡事忠心。

¹²執事只要作一個婦人的丈夫，好好管理兒女和自己的家。¹³因為善作執事的，自己就得到美好的地步，並且在基督耶穌裏的真道上大有膽量。

¹⁴我指望快到你那裏去，所以先將這些事寫給你。¹⁵倘若我躭延日久，你也可以知道在神的家中當怎樣行；這家就是永生神的教會，真理的柱石和根基。¹⁶大哉，敬虔的奧秘！無人不以為然，就是：

神在肉身顯現，
　　被聖靈稱義
　　（註：或作"在靈性稱義"），
被天使看見，
　　被傳於外邦，
被世人信服，
　　被接在榮耀裏。

對提摩太的教導

4 聖靈明說：在後來的時候，必有人離棄真道，聽從那引誘人的邪靈和鬼魔的道理。²這是因為說謊之人的假冒，這等人

Overseers and Deacons

3 Here is a trustworthy saying: If anyone sets his heart on being an overseer,[a] he desires a noble task. ²Now the overseer must be above reproach, the husband of but one wife, temperate, self-controlled, respectable, hospitable, able to teach, ³not given to drunkenness, not violent but gentle, not quarrelsome, not a lover of money. ⁴He must manage his own family well and see that his children obey him with proper respect. ⁵(If anyone does not know how to manage his own family, how can he take care of God's church?) ⁶He must not be a recent convert, or he may become conceited and fall under the same judgment as the devil. ⁷He must also have a good reputation with outsiders, so that he will not fall into disgrace and into the devil's trap.

⁸Deacons, likewise, are to be men worthy of respect, sincere, not indulging in much wine, and not pursuing dishonest gain. ⁹They must keep hold of the deep truths of the faith with a clear conscience. ¹⁰They must first be tested; and then if there is nothing against them, let them serve as deacons.

¹¹In the same way, their wives[b] are to be women worthy of respect, not malicious talkers but temperate and trustworthy in everything.

¹²A deacon must be the husband of but one wife and must manage his children and his household well. ¹³Those who have served well gain an excellent standing and great assurance in their faith in Christ Jesus.

¹⁴Although I hope to come to you soon, I am writing you these instructions so that, ¹⁵if I am delayed, you will know how people ought to conduct themselves in God's household, which is the church of the living God, the pillar and foundation of the truth. ¹⁶Beyond all question, the mystery of godliness is great:

He[c] appeared in a body,[d]
　　was vindicated by the Spirit,
was seen by angels,
　　was preached among the nations,
was believed on in the world,
　　was taken up in glory.

Instructions to Timothy

4 The Spirit clearly says that in later times some will abandon the faith and follow deceiving spirits and things taught by demons. ²Such teachings come through hypo-

---

a 1 Traditionally *bishop*; also in verse 2　　*b 11* Or *way, deaconesses*　　*c 16* Some manuscripts *God*　　*d 16* Or *in the flesh* critical liars, whose consciences have been seared as with a hot iron. [3]They forbid people to marry and order them to abstain from certain foods, which God created to be received with thanksgiving by those who believe and who know the truth. [4]For everything God created is good, and nothing is to be rejected if it is received with thanksgiving, [5]because it is consecrated by the word of God and prayer.

[6]If you point these things out to the brothers, you will be a good minister of Christ Jesus, brought up in the truths of the faith and of the good teaching that you have followed. [7]Have nothing to do with godless myths and old wives' tales; rather, train yourself to be godly. [8]For physical training is of some value, but godliness has value for all things, holding promise for both the present life and the life to come.

[9]This is a trustworthy saying that deserves full acceptance [10](and for this we labor and strive), that we have put our hope in the living God, who is the Savior of all men, and especially of those who believe.

[11]Command and teach these things. [12]Don't let anyone look down on you because you are young, but set an example for the believers in speech, in life, in love, in faith and in purity. [13]Until I come, devote yourself to the public reading of Scripture, to preaching and to teaching. [14]Do not neglect your gift, which was given you through a prophetic message when the body of elders laid their hands on you.

[15]Be diligent in these matters; give yourself wholly to them, so that everyone may see your progress. [16]Watch your life and doctrine closely. Persevere in them, because if you do, you will save both yourself and your hearers.

Advice About Widows, Elders and Slaves

5 Do not rebuke an older man harshly, but exhort him as if he were your father. Treat younger men as brothers, [2]older women as mothers, and younger women as sisters, with absolute purity.

[3]Give proper recognition to those widows who are really in need. [4]But if a widow has children or grandchildren, these should learn first of all to put their religion into practice by caring for their own family and so repaying their parents and grandparents, for this is pleasing to God. [5]The widow who is really in need and left all alone puts her hope in God and continues night and day to pray and to ask God for help. [6]But the widow who lives for pleasure is dead even while she lives. [7]Give the people these instructions, too, so that no one may be open to

的良心如同被熱鐵烙慣了一般。[3]他們禁止嫁娶，又禁戒食物（註：或作"又叫人戒葷"），就是神所造，叫那信而明白真道的人感謝着領受的。[4]凡神所造的物都是好的，若感謝着領受，就沒有一樣可棄的，[5]都因神的道和人的祈求成為聖潔了。

[6]你若將這些事提醒弟兄們，便是基督耶穌的好執事，在真道的話語和你向來所服從的善道上得了教育。[7]只是要棄絕那世俗的言語和老婦荒渺的話，在敬虔上操練自己。[8]操練身體，益處還少；惟獨敬虔，凡事都有益處，因有今生和來生的應許。

[9]這話是可信的，是十分可佩服的，[10]我們勞苦努力，正是為此，因我們的指望在乎永生的神；他是萬人的救主，更是信徒的救主。

[11]這些事，你要吩咐人，也要教導人。[12]不可叫人小看你年輕，總要在言語、行為、愛心、信心、清潔上，都作信徒的榜樣。[13]你要以宣讀、勸勉、教導為念，直等到我來。[14]你不要輕忽所得的恩賜，就是從前藉着預言，在眾長老按手的時候賜給你的。

[15]這些事你要殷勤去做，並要在此專心，使眾人看出你的長進來。[16]你要謹慎自己和自己的教訓，要在這些事上恆心；因為這樣行，又能救自己，又能救聽你的人。

有關對寡婦、長老和奴僕的勸告

5 不可嚴責老年人，只要勸他如同父親；勸少年人如同弟兄；[2]勸老年婦女如同母親；勸少年婦女如同姐妹；總要清清潔潔的。

[3]要尊敬那真為寡婦的。[4]若寡婦有兒女，或有孫子、孫女，便叫他們先在自己家中學着行孝，報答親恩，因為這在神面前是可悅納的。[5]那獨居無靠真為寡婦的，是仰賴神，晝夜不住地祈求禱告。[6]但那好宴樂的寡婦，正活着的時候也是死的。[7]這些事你要囑咐她們，叫她們無可指責。

8人若不看顧親屬，就是背了真道，比不信的人還不好。不看顧自己家裏的人更是如此。

9寡婦記在冊子上，必須年紀到六十歲，從來只作一個丈夫的妻子，10又有行善的名聲，就如養育兒女，接待遠人，洗聖徒的腳，救濟遭難的人，竭力行各樣善事。

11至於年輕的寡婦，就可以辭她，因為她們的情慾發動，違背基督的時候，就想要嫁人。12她們被定罪，是因廢棄了當初所許的願；13並且她們又習慣懶惰，挨家閒遊；不但是懶惰，又說長道短，好管閒事，說些不當說的話。14所以我願意年輕的寡婦嫁人，生養兒女，治理家務，不給敵人辱罵的把柄，15因為已經有轉去隨從撒但的。

16信主的婦女，若家中有寡婦，自己就當救濟她們，不可累着教會，好使教會能救濟那真無倚靠的寡婦。

17那善於管理教會的長老，當以為配受加倍的敬奉；那勞苦傳道教導人的，更當如此。18因為經上說："牛在場上踹穀的時候，不可籠住牠的嘴。"又說："工人得工價是應當的。"19控告長老的呈子，非有兩三個見證就不要收。20犯罪的人，當在眾人面前責備他，叫其餘的人也可以懼怕。

21我在神和基督耶穌並蒙揀選的天使面前囑咐你：要遵守這些話，不可存成見，行事也不可有偏心。

22給人行按手的禮，不可急促；不要在別人的罪上有分，要保守自己清潔。

23因你胃口不清，屢次患病，再不要照常喝水，可以稍微用點酒。

24有些人的罪是明顯的，如同先到審判案前；有些人的罪是隨後跟了去的。25這樣，善行也有明顯的；

blame. 8If anyone does not provide for his relatives, and especially for his immediate family, he has denied the faith and is worse than an unbeliever.

9No widow may be put on the list of widows unless she is over sixty, has been faithful to her husband,[a] 10and is well known for her good deeds, such as bringing up children, showing hospitality, washing the feet of the saints, helping those in trouble and devoting herself to all kinds of good deeds.

11As for younger widows, do not put them on such a list. For when their sensual desires overcome their dedication to Christ, they want to marry. 12Thus they bring judgment on themselves, because they have broken their first pledge. 13Besides, they get into the habit of being idle and going about from house to house. And not only do they become idlers, but also gossips and busybodies, saying things they ought not to. 14So I counsel younger widows to marry, to have children, to manage their homes and to give the enemy no opportunity for slander. 15Some have in fact already turned away to follow Satan.

16If any woman who is a believer has widows in her family, she should help them and not let the church be burdened with them, so that the church can help those widows who are really in need.

17The elders who direct the affairs of the church well are worthy of double honor, especially those whose work is preaching and teaching. 18For the Scripture says, "Do not muzzle the ox while it is treading out the grain,"[b] and "The worker deserves his wages."[c] 19Do not entertain an accusation against an elder unless it is brought by two or three witnesses. 20Those who sin are to be rebuked publicly, so that the others may take warning.

21I charge you, in the sight of God and Christ Jesus and the elect angels, to keep these instructions without partiality, and to do nothing out of favoritism.

22Do not be hasty in the laying on of hands, and do not share in the sins of others. Keep yourself pure.

23Stop drinking only water, and use a little wine because of your stomach and your frequent illnesses.

24The sins of some men are obvious, reaching the place of judgment ahead of them; the sins of others trail behind them. 25In the same way, good deeds are obvious, and even those that are not cannot be hidden.

6 All who are under the yoke of slavery should consider their masters worthy of full respect, so that God's name and our teaching may not be slandered. ²Those who have believing masters are not to show less respect for them because they are brothers. Instead, they are to serve them even better, because those who benefit from their service are believers, and dear to them. These are the things you are to teach and urge on them.

Love of Money

³If anyone teaches false doctrines and does not agree to the sound instruction of our Lord Jesus Christ and to godly teaching, ⁴he is conceited and understands nothing. He has an unhealthy interest in controversies and quarrels about words that result in envy, strife, malicious talk, evil suspicions ⁵and constant friction between men of corrupt mind, who have been robbed of the truth and who think that godliness is a means to financial gain.

⁶But godliness with contentment is great gain. ⁷For we brought nothing into the world, and we can take nothing out of it. ⁸But if we have food and clothing, we will be content with that. ⁹People who want to get rich fall into temptation and a trap and into many foolish and harmful desires that plunge men into ruin and destruction. ¹⁰For the love of money is a root of all kinds of evil. Some people, eager for money, have wandered from the faith and pierced themselves with many griefs.

Paul's Charge to Timothy

¹¹But you, man of God, flee from all this, and pursue righteousness, godliness, faith, love, endurance and gentleness. ¹²Fight the good fight of the faith. Take hold of the eternal life to which you were called when you made your good confession in the presence of many witnesses. ¹³In the sight of God, who gives life to everything, and of Christ Jesus, who while testifying before Pontius Pilate made the good confession, I charge you ¹⁴to keep this command without spot or blame until the appearing of our Lord Jesus Christ, ¹⁵which God will bring about in his own time—God, the blessed and only Ruler, the King of kings and Lord of lords, ¹⁶who alone is immortal and who lives in unapproachable light, whom no one has seen or can see. To him be honor and might forever. Amen.

那不明顯的也不能隱藏。

6 凡在軛下作僕人的，當以自己主人配受十分的恭敬，免得神的名和道理被人褻瀆。²僕人有信道的主人，不可因為與他是弟兄就輕看他；更要加意服侍他，因為得服侍之益處的，是信道蒙愛的。你要以此教訓人、勸勉人。

貪愛錢財

³若有人傳異教，不服從我們主耶穌基督純正的話與那合乎敬虔的道理，⁴他是自高自大，一無所知，專好問難，爭辯言詞，從此就生出嫉妒、紛爭、毀謗、妄疑，⁵並那壞了心術、失喪真理之人的爭競。他們以敬虔為得利的門路。

⁶然而，敬虔加上知足的心便是大利了。⁷因為我們沒有帶甚麼到世上來，也不能帶甚麼去，⁸只要有衣有食，就當知足。⁹但那些想要發財的人，就陷在迷惑、落在網羅和許多無知有害的私慾裏，叫人沉在敗壞和滅亡中。¹⁰貪財是萬惡之根！有人貪戀錢財，就被引誘離了真道，用許多愁苦把自己刺透了。

保羅對提摩太的囑咐

¹¹但你這屬神的人要逃避這些事，追求公義、敬虔、信心、愛心、忍耐、溫柔。¹²你要為真道打那美好的仗，持定永生。你為此被召，也在許多見證人面前已經作了那美好的見證。¹³我在叫萬物生活的神面前，並在向本丟彼拉多作過那美好見證的基督耶穌面前囑咐你：¹⁴要守這命令，毫不玷污，無可指責，直到我們的主耶穌基督顯現。¹⁵到了日期，那可稱頌、獨有權能的萬王之王、萬主之主，¹⁶就是那獨一不死，住在人不能靠近的光裏，是人未曾看見，也是不能看見的，要將他顯明出來。但願尊貴和永遠的權能都歸給他。阿們！

¹⁷你要囑咐那些今世富足的人，不要自高，也不要倚靠無定的錢財；只要倚靠那厚賜百物給我們享受的神。¹⁸又要囑咐他們行善，在好事上富足，甘心施捨，樂意供給人（註："供給"或作"體貼"），¹⁹為自己積成美好的根基，預備將來，叫他們持定那真正的生命。

²⁰提摩太啊，你要保守所託付你的，躲避世俗的虛談和那敵真道、似是而非的學問。²¹已經有人自稱有這學問，就偏離了真道。

願恩惠常與你們同在！

¹⁷Command those who are rich in this present world not to be arrogant nor to put their hope in wealth, which is so uncertain, but to put their hope in God, who richly provides us with everything for our enjoyment. ¹⁸Command them to do good, to be rich in good deeds, and to be generous and willing to share. ¹⁹In this way they will lay up treasure for themselves as a firm foundation for the coming age, so that they may take hold of the life that is truly life.

²⁰Timothy, guard what has been entrusted to your care. Turn away from godless chatter and the opposing ideas of what is falsely called knowledge, ²¹which some have professed and in so doing have wandered from the faith.

Grace be with you.

圖七：提摩太書中的主要地方
MAP 7 : KEY PLACES IN 1 & 2 TIMOTHY

2 Timothy

1 Paul, an apostle of Christ Jesus by the will of God, according to the promise of life that is in Christ Jesus,

²To Timothy, my dear son:

Grace, mercy and peace from God the Father and Christ Jesus our Lord.

Encouragement to Be Faithful

³I thank God, whom I serve, as my forefathers did, with a clear conscience, as night and day I constantly remember you in my prayers. ⁴Recalling your tears, I long to see you, so that I may be filled with joy. ⁵I have been reminded of your sincere faith, which first lived in your grandmother Lois and in your mother Eunice and, I am persuaded, now lives in you also. ⁶For this reason I remind you to fan into flame the gift of God, which is in you through the laying on of my hands. ⁷For God did not give us a spirit of timidity, but a spirit of power, of love and of self-discipline.

⁸So do not be ashamed to testify about our Lord, or ashamed of me his prisoner. But join with me in suffering for the gospel, by the power of God, ⁹who has saved us and called us to a holy life—not because of anything we have done but because of his own purpose and grace. This grace was given us in Christ Jesus before the beginning of time, ¹⁰but it has now been revealed through the appearing of our Savior, Christ Jesus, who has destroyed death and has brought life and immortality to light through the gospel. ¹¹And of this gospel I was appointed a herald and an apostle and a teacher. ¹²That is why I am suffering as I am. Yet I am not ashamed, because I know whom I have believed, and am convinced that he is able to guard what I have entrusted to him for that day.

¹³What you heard from me, keep as the pattern of sound teaching, with faith and love in Christ Jesus. ¹⁴Guard the good deposit that was entrusted to you—guard it with the help of the Holy Spirit who lives in us.

¹⁵You know that everyone in the province of Asia has deserted me, including Phygelus and Hermogenes.

提摩太後書

1 奉神旨意，照着在基督耶穌裏生命的應許，作基督耶穌使徒的<u>保羅</u>，

²寫信給我親愛的兒子<u>提摩太</u>：

願恩惠、憐憫、平安從父神和我們主基督耶穌歸與你！

激勵要忠心

³我感謝神，就是我接續祖先，用清潔的良心所侍奉的神。祈禱的時候，不住地想念你，⁴記念你的眼淚，晝夜切切地想要見你，好叫我滿心快樂。⁵想到你心裏無偽之信，這信是先在你外祖母<u>羅以</u>和你母親<u>友妮基</u>心裏的，我深信也在你的心裏。⁶為此我提醒你，使你將神藉我按手所給你的恩賜，再如火挑旺起來。⁷因為神賜給我們不是膽怯的心，乃是剛強、仁愛、謹守的心。

⁸你不要以給我們的主作見證為恥，也不要以我這為主被囚的為恥。總要按神的能力，與我為福音同受苦難。⁹神救了我們，以聖召召我們，不是按我們的行為，乃是按他的旨意和恩典；這恩典是萬古之先在基督耶穌裏賜給我們的。¹⁰但如今藉着我們救主基督耶穌的顯現，才表明出來了。他已經把死廢去，藉着福音，將不能壞的生命彰顯出來。¹¹我為這福音奉派作傳道的，作使徒，作師傅。¹²為這緣故，我也受這些苦難，然而我不以為恥。因為知道我所信的是誰，也深信他能保全我所交付他的（註：或作"他所交託我的"），直到那日。

¹³你從我聽的那純正話語的規模，要用在基督耶穌裏的信心和愛心，常常守着。¹⁴從前所交託你的善道，你要靠着那住在我們裏面的聖靈牢牢地守着。

¹⁵凡在<u>亞西亞</u>的人都離棄我，這是你知道的，其中有<u>腓吉路</u>和<u>黑摩其尼</u>。

16願主憐憫阿尼色弗一家的人，因他屢次使我暢快，不以我的鎖鏈為恥，17反倒在羅馬的時候殷勤地找我，並且找着了。18願主使他在那日得主的憐憫。他在以弗所怎樣多多地服侍我，是你明明知道的。

2 我兒啊，你要在基督耶穌的恩典上剛強起來。2你在許多見證人面前聽見我所教訓的，也要交託那忠心能教導別人的人。3你要和我同受苦難，好像基督耶穌的精兵。4凡在軍中當兵的，不將世務纏身，好叫那招他當兵的人喜悅。5人若在場上比武，非按規矩，就不能得冠冕。6勞力的農夫理當先得糧食。7我所說的話你要思想，因為凡事主必給你聰明。

8你要記念耶穌基督乃是大衛的後裔，他從死裏復活，正合乎我所傳的福音。9我為這福音受苦難，甚至被捆綁，像犯人一樣；然而，神的道卻不被捆綁。10所以我為選民凡事忍耐，叫他們也可以得着那在基督耶穌裏的救恩和永遠的榮耀。

11有可信的話說：

我們若與基督同死，
　也必與他同活；
12我們若能忍耐，
　也必和他一同作王；
我們若不認他，
　他也必不認我們；
13我們縱然失信，
　他仍是可信的，
　因為他不能背乎自己。

蒙神喜悅的工人

14你要使眾人回想這些事，在主面前囑咐他們：不可為言語爭辯，這是沒有益處的，只能敗壞聽見的人。15你當竭力在神面前得蒙喜悅，作無愧的工人，按着正意分解真理的道。16但要遠避世俗的虛談，因為這等人必進到不更虔的地步。17他們的話如同毒瘡，越爛越大；其中有許米乃和腓理徒，18他們偏離了真道，說復活的事已過，就敗壞好些

16May the Lord show mercy to the household of Onesiphorus, because he often refreshed me and was not ashamed of my chains. 17On the contrary, when he was in Rome, he searched hard for me until he found me. 18May the Lord grant that he will find mercy from the Lord on that day! You know very well in how many ways he helped me in Ephesus.

2 You then, my son, be strong in the grace that is in Christ Jesus. 2And the things you have heard me say in the presence of many witnesses entrust to reliable men who will also be qualified to teach others. 3Endure hardship with us like a good soldier of Christ Jesus. 4No one serving as a soldier gets involved in civilian affairs—he wants to please his commanding officer. 5Similarly, if anyone competes as an athlete, he does not receive the victor's crown unless he competes according to the rules. 6The hardworking farmer should be the first to receive a share of the crops. 7Reflect on what I am saying, for the Lord will give you insight into all this.

8Remember Jesus Christ, raised from the dead, descended from David. This is my gospel, 9for which I am suffering even to the point of being chained like a criminal. But God's word is not chained. 10Therefore I endure everything for the sake of the elect, that they too may obtain the salvation that is in Christ Jesus, with eternal glory.

11Here is a trustworthy saying:

If we died with him,
　we will also live with him;
12if we endure,
　we will also reign with him.
If we disown him,
　he will also disown us;
13if we are faithless,
　he will remain faithful,
　for he cannot disown himself.

A Workman Approved by God

14Keep reminding them of these things. Warn them before God against quarreling about words; it is of no value, and only ruins those who listen. 15Do your best to present yourself to God as one approved, a workman who does not need to be ashamed and who correctly handles the word of truth. 16Avoid godless chatter, because those who indulge in it will become more and more ungodly. 17Their teaching will spread like gangrene. Among them are Hymenaeus and Philetus, 18who have wandered away from the truth. They say that the resurrection has already taken place, and they destroy the faith of some. [19]Nevertheless, God's solid foundation stands firm, sealed with this inscription: "The Lord knows those who are his,"[a] and, "Everyone who confesses the name of the Lord must turn away from wickedness."

[20]In a large house there are articles not only of gold and silver, but also of wood and clay; some are for noble purposes and some for ignoble. [21]If a man cleanses himself from the latter, he will be an instrument for noble purposes, made holy, useful to the Master and prepared to do any good work.

[22]Flee the evil desires of youth, and pursue righteousness, faith, love and peace, along with those who call on the Lord out of a pure heart. [23]Don't have anything to do with foolish and stupid arguments, because you know they produce quarrels. [24]And the Lord's servant must not quarrel; instead, he must be kind to everyone, able to teach, not resentful. [25]Those who oppose him he must gently instruct, in the hope that God will grant them repentance leading them to a knowledge of the truth, [26]and that they will come to their senses and escape from the trap of the devil, who has taken them captive to do his will.

Godlessness in the Last Days

3 But mark this: There will be terrible times in the last days. [2]People are lovers of themselves, lovers of money, boastful, proud, abusive, disobedient to their parents, ungrateful, unholy, [3]without love, unforgiving, slanderous, without self-control, brutal, not lovers of the good, [4]treacherous, rash, conceited, lovers of pleasure rather than lovers of God— [5]having a form of godliness but denying its power. Have nothing to do with them.

[6]They are the kind who worm their way into homes and gain control over weak-willed women, who are loaded down with sins and are swayed by all kinds of evil desires, [7]always learning but never able to acknowledge the truth. [8]Just as Jannes and Jambres opposed Moses, so also these men oppose the truth—men of depraved minds, who, as far as the faith is concerned, are rejected. [9]But they will not get very far because, as in the case of those men, their folly will be clear to everyone.

Paul's Charge to Timothy

[10]You, however, know all about my teaching, my way of life, my purpose, faith, patience, love,

人的信心。[19]然而，神堅固的根基立住了。上面有這印記說："主認識誰是他的人。"又說："凡稱呼主名的人總要離開不義。"

[20]在大戶人家，不但有金器銀器，也有木器瓦器；有作為貴重的，有作為卑賤的。[21]人若自潔，脫離卑賤的事，就必作貴重的器皿，成為聖潔，合乎主用，預備行各樣的善事。

[22]你要逃避少年的私慾，同那清心禱告主的人追求公義、信德、仁愛、和平。[23]惟有那愚拙無學問的辯論，總要棄絕，因為知道這等事是起爭競的。[24]然而主的僕人不可爭競；只要溫溫和和待眾人，善於教導，存心忍耐，[25]用溫柔勸戒那抵擋的人，或者神給他們悔改的心，可以明白真道，[26]叫他們這已經被魔鬼任意擄去的，可以醒悟，脫離他的網羅。

末世不敬虔的情形

3 你該知道，末世必有危險的日子來到。[2]因為那時人要專顧自己、貪愛錢財、自誇、狂傲、謗讟、違背父母、忘恩負義、心不聖潔、[3]無親情、不解怨、好說讒言、不能自約、性情兇暴、不愛良善、[4]賣主賣友、任意妄為、自高自大、愛宴樂、不愛神，[5]有敬虔的外貌，卻背了敬虔的實意，這等人你要躲開。

[6]那偷進人家，牢籠無知婦女的，正是這等人。這些婦女擔負罪惡，被各樣的私慾引誘，[7]常常學習，終久不能明白真道。[8]從前雅尼和佯庇怎樣敵擋摩西，這等人也怎樣敵擋真道。他們的心地壞了，在真道上是可廢棄的。[9]然而他們不能再這樣敵擋，因為他們的愚昧必在眾人面前顯露出來，像那二人一樣。

保羅對提摩太的囑咐

[10]但你已經服從了我的教訓、品行、志向、信心、寬容、愛心、忍

a 19 Num. 16:5 (see Septuagint)

耐，¹¹以及我在安提阿、以哥念、路司得所遭遇的逼迫、苦難。我所忍受是何等的逼迫！但從這一切苦難中，主都把我救出來了。¹²不但如此，凡立志在基督耶穌裏敬虔度日的，也都要受逼迫。¹³只是作惡的和迷惑人的，必越久越惡，他欺哄人，也被人欺哄。¹⁴但你所學習的、所確信的，要存在心裏，因為你知道是跟誰學的。¹⁵並且知道你是從小明白聖經；這聖經能使你因信基督耶穌有得救的智慧。¹⁶聖經都是神所默示的（註：或作「凡神所默示的聖經」），於教訓、督責、使人歸正、教導人學義都是有益的，¹⁷叫屬神的人得以完全，預備行各樣的善事。

4 我在神面前，並在將來審判活人死人的基督耶穌面前，憑着他的顯現和他的國度囑咐你：²務要傳道！無論得時不得時，總要專心，並用百般的忍耐，各樣的教訓，責備人，警戒人，勸勉人。³因為時候要到，人必厭煩純正的道理，耳朵發癢，就隨從自己的情慾，增添好些師傅，⁴並且掩耳不聽真道，偏向荒渺的言語。⁵你卻要凡事謹慎，忍受苦難，做傳道的工夫，盡你的職分。

⁶我現在被澆奠，我離世的時候到了。⁷那美好的仗我已經打過了，當跑的路我已經跑盡了，所信的道我已經守住了。⁸從此以後，有公義的冠冕為我存留，就是按着公義審判的主到了那日要賜給我的；不但賜給我，也賜給凡愛慕他顯現的人。

個人的吩咐

⁹你要趕緊到我這裏來。¹⁰因為底馬貪愛現今的世界，就離棄我往帖撒羅尼迦去了，革勒士往加拉太去，提多往撻馬太去，¹¹獨有路加在我這裏。你來的時候，要把馬可帶來，因為他在傳道的事上於我有益處（註：「傳道」或作「服侍我」）。¹²我已經打發推基古往以弗所去。¹³我在特羅亞留於加布的那件外衣，你來的時候可以帶來，那些書也要帶來，更要緊的是那些皮卷。

endurance, ¹¹persecutions, sufferings—what kinds of things happened to me in Antioch, Iconium and Lystra, the persecutions I endured. Yet the Lord rescued me from all of them. ¹²In fact, everyone who wants to live a godly life in Christ Jesus will be persecuted, ¹³while evil men and impostors will go from bad to worse, deceiving and being deceived. ¹⁴But as for you, continue in what you have learned and have become convinced of, because you know those from whom you learned it, ¹⁵and how from infancy you have known the holy Scriptures, which are able to make you wise for salvation through faith in Christ Jesus. ¹⁶All Scripture is God-breathed and is useful for teaching, rebuking, correcting and training in righteousness, ¹⁷so that the man of God may be thoroughly equipped for every good work.

4 In the presence of God and of Christ Jesus, who will judge the living and the dead, and in view of his appearing and his kingdom, I give you this charge: ²Preach the Word; be prepared in season and out of season; correct, rebuke and encourage—with great patience and careful instruction. ³For the time will come when men will not put up with sound doctrine. Instead, to suit their own desires, they will gather around them a great number of teachers to say what their itching ears want to hear. ⁴They will turn their ears away from the truth and turn aside to myths. ⁵But you, keep your head in all situations, endure hardship, do the work of an evangelist, discharge all the duties of your ministry.

⁶For I am already being poured out like a drink offering, and the time has come for my departure. ⁷I have fought the good fight, I have finished the race, I have kept the faith. ⁸Now there is in store for me the crown of righteousness, which the Lord, the righteous Judge, will award to me on that day—and not only to me, but also to all who have longed for his appearing.

Personal Remarks

⁹Do your best to come to me quickly, ¹⁰for Demas, because he loved this world, has deserted me and has gone to Thessalonica. Crescens has gone to Galatia, and Titus to Dalmatia. ¹¹Only Luke is with me. Get Mark and bring him with you, because he is helpful to me in my ministry. ¹²I sent Tychicus to Ephesus. ¹³When you come, bring the cloak that I left with Carpus at Troas, and my scrolls, especially the parchments.

14Alexander the metalworker did me a great deal of harm. The Lord will repay him for what he has done. 15You too should be on your guard against him, because he strongly opposed our message.

16At my first defense, no one came to my support, but everyone deserted me. May it not be held against them. 17But the Lord stood at my side and gave me strength, so that through me the message might be fully proclaimed and all the Gentiles might hear it. And I was delivered from the lion's mouth. 18The Lord will rescue me from every evil attack and will bring me safely to his heavenly kingdom. To him be glory for ever and ever. Amen.

Final Greetings

19Greet Priscilla*a* and Aquila and the household of Onesiphorus. 20Erastus stayed in Corinth, and I left Trophimus sick in Miletus. 21Do your best to get here before winter. Eubulus greets you, and so do Pudens, Linus, Claudia and all the brothers.

22The Lord be with your spirit. Grace be with you.

14銅匠亞歷山大多多地害我，主必照他所行的報應他。15你也要防備他，因為他極力敵擋了我們的話。

16我初次申訴，沒有人前來幫助，竟都離棄我；但願這罪不歸與他們。17惟有主站在我旁邊，加給我力量，使福音被我盡都傳明，叫外邦人都聽見。我也從獅子口裏被救出來。18主必救我脫離諸般的兇惡，也必救我進他的天國。願榮耀歸給他，直到永永遠遠。阿們！

最後的問安

19問百基拉、亞居拉和阿尼色弗一家的人安。20以拉都在哥林多住下了。特羅非摩病了，我就留他在米利都。21你要趕緊在冬天以前到我這裏來。有友布羅、布田、利奴、革老底亞和眾弟兄都問你安。

22願主與你的靈同在！願恩惠常與你們同在！

---

a 19 Greek *Prisca*, a variant of *Priscilla*

提多書

1 神的僕人、耶穌基督的使徒保羅，憑着神選民的信心與敬虔真理的知識，²盼望那無謊言的神在萬古之先所應許的永生，³到了日期，藉着傳揚的工夫，把他的道顯明了；這傳揚的責任是按着神我們救主的命令交託了我。

⁴現在寫信給提多，就是照着我們共信之道作我真兒子的：

願恩惠、平安從父神和我們的救主基督耶穌歸與你！

提多在克里特的任務

⁵我從前留你在克里特，是要你將那沒有辦完的事都辦整齊了，又照我所吩咐你的，在各城設立長老。⁶若有無可指責的人，只作一個婦人的丈夫，兒女也是信主的，沒有人告他們是放蕩不服約束的，就可以設立。⁷監督既是神的管家，必須無可指責，不任性、不暴躁、不因酒滋事、不打人、不貪無義之財；⁸樂意接待遠人，好善、莊重、公平、聖潔、自持；⁹堅守所教真實的道理，就能將純正的教訓勸化人，又能把爭辯的人駁倒了。

¹⁰因為有許多人不服約束，說虛空話欺哄人，那奉割禮的更是這樣。¹¹這些人的口總要堵住。他們因貪不義之財，將不該教導的教導人，敗壞人的全家。¹²有克里特人中的一個本地先知說：「克里特人常說謊話，乃是惡獸，又饞又懶！」¹³這個見證是真的。所以，你要嚴嚴地責備他們，使他們在真道上純全無疵，¹⁴不聽猶太人荒渺的言語和離棄真道之人的誡命。¹⁵在潔淨的人，凡物都潔淨；在污穢不信的人，甚麼都不潔淨，連心地和天良也都污

Titus

1 Paul, a servant of God and an apostle of Jesus Christ for the faith of God's elect and the knowledge of the truth that leads to godliness— ²a faith and knowledge resting on the hope of eternal life, which God, who does not lie, promised before the beginning of time, ³and at his appointed season he brought his word to light through the preaching entrusted to me by the command of God our Savior,

⁴To Titus, my true son in our common faith:

Grace and peace from God the Father and Christ Jesus our Savior.

Titus' Task on Crete

⁵The reason I left you in Crete was that you might straighten out what was left unfinished and appoint[a] elders in every town, as I directed you. ⁶An elder must be blameless, the husband of but one wife, a man whose children believe and are not open to the charge of being wild and disobedient. ⁷Since an overseer[b] is entrusted with God's work, he must be blameless—not overbearing, not quick-tempered, not given to drunkenness, not violent, not pursuing dishonest gain. ⁸Rather he must be hospitable, one who loves what is good, who is self-controlled, upright, holy and disciplined. ⁹He must hold firmly to the trustworthy message as it has been taught, so that he can encourage others by sound doctrine and refute those who oppose it.

¹⁰For there are many rebellious people, mere talkers and deceivers, especially those of the circumcision group. ¹¹They must be silenced, because they are ruining whole households by teaching things they ought not to teach—and that for the sake of dishonest gain. ¹²Even one of their own prophets has said, "Cretans are always liars, evil brutes, lazy gluttons." ¹³This testimony is true. Therefore, rebuke them sharply, so that they will be sound in the faith ¹⁴and will pay no attention to Jewish myths or to the commands of those who reject the truth. ¹⁵To the pure, all things are pure, but to those who are corrupted and do not believe, nothing is pure.

a 5 Or ordain　　*b 7* Traditionally *bishop*

In fact, both their minds and consciences are corrupted. [16]They claim to know God, but by their actions they deny him. They are detestable, disobedient and unfit for doing anything good.

What Must Be Taught to Various Groups

2 You must teach what is in accord with sound doctrine. [2]Teach the older men to be temperate, worthy of respect, self-controlled, and sound in faith, in love and in endurance.

[3]Likewise, teach the older women to be reverent in the way they live, not to be slanderers or addicted to much wine, but to teach what is good. [4]Then they can train the younger women to love their husbands and children, [5]to be self-controlled and pure, to be busy at home, to be kind, and to be subject to their husbands, so that no one will malign the word of God.

[6]Similarly, encourage the young men to be self-controlled. [7]In everything set them an example by doing what is good. In your teaching show integrity, seriousness [8]and soundness of speech that cannot be condemned, so that those who oppose you may be ashamed because they have nothing bad to say about us.

[9]Teach slaves to be subject to their masters in everything, to try to please them, not to talk back to them, [10]and not to steal from them, but to show that they can be fully trusted, so that in every way they will make the teaching about God our Savior attractive.

[11]For the grace of God that brings salvation has appeared to all men. [12]It teaches us to say "No" to ungodliness and worldly passions, and to live self-controlled, upright and godly lives in this present age, [13]while we wait for the blessed hope—the glorious appearing of our great God and Savior, Jesus Christ, [14]who gave himself for us to redeem us from all wickedness and to purify for himself a people that are his very own, eager to do what is good.

[15]These, then, are the things you should teach. Encourage and rebuke with all authority. Do not let anyone despise you.

Doing What Is Good

3 Remind the people to be subject to rulers and authorities, to be obedient, to be ready to do whatever is good, [2]to slander no one, to be peaceable and considerate, and to show true humility toward all men.

[3]At one time we too were foolish, disobedient, deceived and enslaved by all kinds of passions and pleasures. We lived in malice and envy, being hated and hating one another. [4]But

穢了。[16]他們説是認識神，行事卻和他相背；本是可憎惡的，是悖逆的，在各樣善事上是可廢棄的。

對各種人應有的教導

2 但你所講的，總要合乎那純正的道理。[2]勸老年人要有節制、端莊、自守，在信心、愛心、忍耐上都要純全無疵。

[3]又勸老年婦人，舉止行動要恭敬，不說讒言，不給酒作奴僕，用善道教訓人，[4]好指教少年婦人愛丈夫，愛兒女，[5]謹守、貞潔，料理家務，待人有恩，順服自己的丈夫，免得神的道理被毀謗。

[6]又勸少年人要謹守。[7]你自己凡事要顯出善行的榜樣，在教訓上要正直端莊，[8]言語純全，無可指責，叫那反對的人，既無處可説我們的不是，便自覺羞愧。

[9]勸僕人要順服自己的主人，凡事討他的喜歡，不可頂撞他，[10]不可私拿東西，要顯為忠誠，以至凡事尊榮我們救主神的道。

[11]因為神救眾人的恩典已經顯明出來，[12]教訓我們除去不敬虔的心和世俗的情慾，在今世自守、公義、敬虔度日，[13]等候所盼望的福，並等候至大的神和（註：或作「和」字）我們救主耶穌基督的榮耀顯現。[14]他為我們捨了自己，要贖我們脫離一切罪惡，又潔淨我們，特作自己的子民，熱心為善。

[15]這些事你要講明，勸戒人，用各等權柄責備人，不可叫人輕看你。

行各樣的善事

3 你要提醒眾人，叫他們順服作官的、掌權的，遵他的命，預備行各樣的善事。[2]不要毀謗，不要爭競，總要和平，向眾人大顯溫柔。

[3]我們從前也是無知、悖逆、受迷惑，服侍各樣私慾和宴樂，常存惡毒（註：或作「陰毒」）、嫉妒的心，是可恨的，又是彼此相恨。[4]但到了

神我們救主的恩慈和他向人所施的慈愛顯明的時候，⁵他便救了我們，並不是因我們自己所行的義，乃是照他的憐憫，藉着重生的洗和聖靈的更新。⁶聖靈就是神藉着耶穌基督，我們救主厚厚澆灌在我們身上的，⁷好叫我們因他的恩得稱為義，可以憑着永生的盼望成為後嗣（註：或作「可以憑着盼望承受永生」）。⁸這話是可信的。我也願你把這些事切切實實地講明，使那些已信神的人留心做正經事業（註：或作「留心行善」）。這都是美事，並且與人有益。

⁹要遠避無知的辯論和家譜的空談以及紛爭，並因律法而起的爭競，因為這都是虛妄無益的。¹⁰分門結黨的人，警戒過一兩次，就要棄絕他。¹¹因為知道這等人已經背道，犯了罪，自己明知不是，還是去做。

最後的囑咐

¹²我打發亞提馬或是推基古到你那裏去的時候，你要趕緊往尼哥波立去見我，因為我已經定意在那裏過冬。¹³你要趕緊給律師西納和亞波羅送行，叫他們沒有缺乏。¹⁴並且我們的人要學習正經事業（註：或作「要學習行善」），預備所需用的，免得不結果子。

¹⁵同我在一處的人都問你安。請代問那些因有信心愛我們的人安。願恩惠常與你們眾人同在！

when the kindness and love of God our Savior appeared, ⁵he saved us, not because of righteous things we had done, but because of his mercy. He saved us through the washing of rebirth and renewal by the Holy Spirit, ⁶whom he poured out on us generously through Jesus Christ our Savior, ⁷so that, having been justified by his grace, we might become heirs having the hope of eternal life. ⁸This is a trustworthy saying. And I want you to stress these things, so that those who have trusted in God may be careful to devote themselves to doing what is good. These things are excellent and profitable for everyone.

⁹But avoid foolish controversies and genealogies and arguments and quarrels about the law, because these are unprofitable and useless. ¹⁰Warn a divisive person once, and then warn him a second time. After that, have nothing to do with him. ¹¹You may be sure that such a man is warped and sinful; he is self-condemned.

Final Remarks

¹²As soon as I send Artemas or Tychicus to you, do your best to come to me at Nicopolis, because I have decided to winter there. ¹³Do everything you can to help Zenas the lawyer and Apollos on their way and see that they have everything they need. ¹⁴Our people must learn to devote themselves to doing what is good, in order that they may provide for daily necessities and not live unproductive lives.

¹⁵Everyone with me sends you greetings. Greet those who love us in the faith.

Grace be with you all.

Philemon

腓利門書

¹Paul, a prisoner of Christ Jesus, and Timothy our brother,

To Philemon our dear friend and fellow worker, ²to Apphia our sister, to Archippus our fellow soldier and to the church that meets in your home:

³Grace to you and peace from God our Father and the Lord Jesus Christ.

Thanksgiving and Prayer

⁴I always thank my God as I remember you in my prayers, ⁵because I hear about your faith in the Lord Jesus and your love for all the saints. ⁶I pray that you may be active in sharing your faith, so that you will have a full understanding of every good thing we have in Christ. ⁷Your love has given me great joy and encouragement, because you, brother, have refreshed the hearts of the saints.

Paul's Plea for Onesimus

⁸Therefore, although in Christ I could be bold and order you to do what you ought to do, ⁹yet I appeal to you on the basis of love. I then, as Paul—an old man and now also a prisoner of Christ Jesus— ¹⁰I appeal to you for my son Onesimus,ᵃ who became my son while I was in chains. ¹¹Formerly he was useless to you, but now he has become useful both to you and to me.

¹²I am sending him—who is my very heart—back to you. ¹³I would have liked to keep him with me so that he could take your place in helping me while I am in chains for the gospel. ¹⁴But I did not want to do anything without your consent, so that any favor you do will be spontaneous and not forced. ¹⁵Perhaps the reason he was separated from you for a little while was that you might have him back for good— ¹⁶no longer as a slave, but better than a slave, as a dear brother. He is very dear to me but even dearer to you, both as a man and as a brother in the Lord.

¹為基督耶穌被囚的保羅同兄弟提摩太，

寫信給我們所親愛的同工腓利門，²和妹子亞腓亞，並與我們同當兵的亞基布，以及在你家的教會：

³願恩惠、平安從神我們的父和主耶穌基督歸與你們！

感恩與禱告

⁴我禱告的時候提到你，常為你感謝我的神，⁵因聽說你的愛心並你向主耶穌和眾聖徒的信心（註：或作"因聽說你向主耶穌和眾聖徒有愛心、有信心"）。⁶願你與人所同有的信心顯出功效，使人知道你們各樣善事都是為基督做的。⁷兄弟啊，我為你的愛心大有快樂，大得安慰，因眾聖徒的心從你得了暢快。

保羅為阿尼西謀求情

⁸我雖然靠着基督能放膽吩咐你合宜的事，⁹然而像我這有年紀的保羅，現在又是為基督耶穌被囚的，寧可憑着愛心求你，¹⁰就是為我在捆鎖中所生的兒子阿尼西謀（註：此名就是"有益處"的意思）求你。¹¹他從前與你沒有益處，但如今與你我都有益處。

¹²我現在打發他親自回你那裏去，他是我心上的人。¹³我本來有意將他留下，在我為福音所受的捆鎖中替你伺候我。¹⁴但不知道你的意思，我就不願意這樣行，叫你的善行不是出於勉強，乃是出於甘心。¹⁵他暫時離開你，或者是叫你永遠得着他；¹⁶不再是奴僕，乃是高過奴僕，是親愛的兄弟。在我實在是如此，何況在你呢！這也不拘是按肉體說，是按主說。

ᵃ 10 Onesimus means useful.

¹⁷你若以我為同伴,就收納他,如同收納我一樣。¹⁸他若虧負你,或欠你甚麼,都歸在我的賬上,¹⁹我必償還。這是我保羅親筆寫的。我並不用對你説,連你自己也是虧欠於我。²⁰兄弟啊,望你使我在主裏因你得快樂(註:或作「益處」),並望你使我的心在基督裏得暢快。²¹我寫信給你,深信你必順服,知道你所要行的,必過於我所説的。

²²此外,你還要給我預備住處,因為我盼望藉着你們的禱告,必蒙恩到你們那裏去。

²³為基督耶穌與我同坐監的以巴弗問你安。²⁴與我同工的馬可、亞里達古、底馬、路加也都問你安。

²⁵願我們主耶穌基督的恩常在你的心裏。阿們!

¹⁷So if you consider me a partner, welcome him as you would welcome me. ¹⁸If he has done you any wrong or owes you anything, charge it to me. ¹⁹I, Paul, am writing this with my own hand. I will pay it back—not to mention that you owe me your very self. ²⁰I do wish, brother, that I may have some benefit from you in the Lord; refresh my heart in Christ. ²¹Confident of your obedience, I write to you, knowing that you will do even more than I ask.

²²And one thing more: Prepare a guest room for me, because I hope to be restored to you in answer to your prayers.

²³Epaphras, my fellow prisoner in Christ Jesus, sends you greetings. ²⁴And so do Mark, Aristarchus, Demas and Luke, my fellow workers.

²⁵The grace of the Lord Jesus Christ be with your spirit.

Hebrews

The Son Superior to Angels

1 In the past God spoke to our forefathers through the prophets at many times and in various ways, ²but in these last days he has spoken to us by his Son, whom he appointed heir of all things, and through whom he made the universe. ³The Son is the radiance of God's glory and the exact representation of his being, sustaining all things by his powerful word. After he had provided purification for sins, he sat down at the right hand of the Majesty in heaven. ⁴So he became as much superior to the angels as the name he has inherited is superior to theirs.

⁵For to which of the angels did God ever say,

"You are my Son;
today I have become your Father ᵃ"ᵇ?

Or again,

"I will be his Father,
and he will be my Son"ᶜ?

⁶And again, when God brings his firstborn into the world, he says,

"Let all God's angels worship him."ᵈ

⁷In speaking of the angels he says,

"He makes his angels winds,
his servants flames of fire."ᵉ

⁸But about the Son he says,

"Your throne, O God, will last for ever and
ever,
and righteousness will be the scepter of
your kingdom.
⁹You have loved righteousness and hated
wickedness;

---

a 5 Or have begotten you   b 5 Psalm 2:7   c 5 2 Samuel 7:14;
1 Chron. 17:13   d 6 Deut. 32:43 (see Dead Sea Scrolls and
Septuagint)   e 7 Psalm 104:4

希伯來書

聖子超過天使

1 神既在古時藉着眾先知多次多方地曉諭列祖，²就在這末世，藉着他兒子曉諭我們，又早已立他為承受萬有的，也曾藉着他創造諸世界。³他是神榮耀所發的光輝，是神本體的真像，常用他權能的命令托住萬有。他洗淨了人的罪，就坐在高天至大者的右邊。⁴他所承受的名，既比天使的名更尊貴，就遠超過天使。

⁵所有的天使，神從來對哪一個說：
"你是我的兒子，
我今日生你"？

又指着哪一個說：

"我要作他的父，
他要作我的子"？

⁶再者，神使長子到世上來的時候（註：或作"神再使長子到世上來的時候"），就說：
"神的使者都要拜他。"

⁷論到使者，又說：

"神以風為使者，
以火焰為僕役。"

⁸論到子卻說：

"神啊，你的寶座
是永永遠遠的，
你的國權
是正直的。
⁹你喜愛公義，
恨惡罪惡，

所以神，就是你的神，
　　用喜樂油膏你，
　　勝過膏你的同伴。"

¹⁰又説：

"主啊，
　　你起初立了地的根基，
　　天也是你手所造的。
¹¹天地都要滅沒，你卻要長存；
　　天地都要像衣服漸漸舊了。
¹²你要將天地捲起來，像一件外衣，
　　天地就都改變了。
惟有你永不改變，
　　你的年數沒有窮盡。"

¹³所有的天使，神從來對哪一個説：

"你坐在我的右邊，
等我使你仇敵
　　作你的腳凳"？

¹⁴天使豈不都是服役的靈、奉差遣為
那將要承受救恩的人効力嗎？

警告要鄭重留心

2 所以，我們當越發鄭重所聽
見的道理，恐怕我們隨流失
去。²那藉着天使所傳的話，
既是確定的，凡干犯悖逆的，都受
了該受的報應。³我們若忽略這麼大
的救恩，怎能逃罪呢？這救恩起先
是主親自講的，後來是聽見的人給
我們證實了。⁴神又按自己的旨意，
用神蹟奇事和百般的異能，並聖靈
的恩賜，同他們作見證。

耶穌與他的弟兄相同

⁵我們所説將來的世界，神原沒
有交給天使管轄。⁶但有人在經上某
處證明説：

"人算甚麼，你竟顧念他？
　　世人算甚麼，你竟眷顧他？
⁷你叫他比天使微小一點（註：或作"你叫
　　他暫時比天使小"），
　　賜他榮耀、尊貴為冠冕，
　　並將你手所造的都派他管理，
⁸　　叫萬物都服在他的腳下。"

therefore God, your God, has set you above
　　your companions
by anointing you with the oil of joy."ᵃ

¹⁰He also says,

"In the beginning, O Lord, you laid the
　　foundations of the earth,
and the heavens are the work of your hands.
¹¹They will perish, but you remain;
　　they will all wear out like a garment.
¹²You will roll them up like a robe;
　　like a garment they will be changed.
But you remain the same,
　　and your years will never end."ᵇ

¹³To which of the angels did God ever say,

"Sit at my right hand
until I make your enemies
　　a footstool for your feet"ᶜ?

¹⁴Are not all angels ministering spirits sent to
serve those who will inherit salvation?

Warning to Pay Attention

2 We must pay more careful attention,
therefore, to what we have heard, so that
we do not drift away. ²For if the message spoken by angels was binding, and every
violation and disobedience received its just punishment, ³how shall we escape if we ignore such
a great salvation? This salvation, which was first
announced by the Lord, was confirmed to us by
those who heard him. ⁴God also testified to it by
signs, wonders and various miracles, and gifts
of the Holy Spirit distributed according to his
will.

Jesus Made Like His Brothers

⁵It is not to angels that he has subjected the
world to come, about which we are speaking.
⁶But there is a place where someone has testified:

"What is man that you are mindful of him,
　　the son of man that you care for him?
⁷You made him a littleᵈ lower than the angels;
　　you crowned him with glory and honor
⁸　　and put everything under his feet."ᵉ

---

a 9 Psalm 45:6,7　　*b 12* Psalm 102:25-27　　*c 13* Psalm 110:1
d 7 Or *him for a little while*; also in verse 9　　*e 8* Psalm 8:4-6

In putting everything under him, God left nothing that is not subject to him. Yet at present we do not see everything subject to him. [9]But we see Jesus, who was made a little lower than the angels, now crowned with glory and honor because he suffered death, so that by the grace of God he might taste death for everyone.

[10]In bringing many sons to glory, it was fitting that God, for whom and through whom everything exists, should make the author of their salvation perfect through suffering. [11]Both the one who makes men holy and those who are made holy are of the same family. So Jesus is not ashamed to call them brothers. [12]He says,

"I will declare your name to my brothers;
　in the presence of the congregation I will
　　sing your praises."[a]

[13]And again,

"I will put my trust in him."[b]

And again he says,

"Here am I, and the children God has given
　me."[c]

[14]Since the children have flesh and blood, he too shared in their humanity so that by his death he might destroy him who holds the power of death—that is, the devil— [15]and free those who all their lives were held in slavery by their fear of death. [16]For surely it is not angels he helps, but Abraham's descendants. [17]For this reason he had to be made like his brothers in every way, in order that he might become a merciful and faithful high priest in service to God, and that he might make atonement for[d] the sins of the people. [18]Because he himself suffered when he was tempted, he is able to help those who are being tempted.

Jesus Greater Than Moses

3 Therefore, holy brothers, who share in the heavenly calling, fix your thoughts on Jesus, the apostle and high priest whom we confess. [2]He was faithful to the one who appointed him, just as Moses was faithful in all God's house. [3]Jesus has been found worthy of greater honor than Moses, just as the builder of a house has greater honor than the house itself. [4]For every house is built by some-

既叫萬物都服他，就沒有剩下一樣不服他的。只是如今我們還不見萬物都服他，[9]惟獨見那成為比天使小一點的耶穌（註：或作"惟獨見耶穌暫時比天使小"），因為受死的苦，就得了尊貴、榮耀為冠冕，叫他因着神的恩，為人人嘗了死味。

[10]原來那為萬物所屬、為萬物所本的，要領許多的兒子進榮耀裏去，使救他們的元帥因受苦難得以完全，本是合宜的。[11]因那使人成聖的和那些得以成聖的，都是出於一。所以他稱他們為弟兄，也不以為恥，[12]說：

"我要將你的名傳與我的弟兄，
　在會中我要頌揚你。"

[13]又說：

"我要倚賴他。"

又說：

"看哪，我與神所給我的兒女。"

[14]兒女既同有血肉之體，他也照樣親自成了血肉之體，特要藉着死，敗壞那掌死權的，就是魔鬼，[15]並要釋放那些一生因怕死而為奴僕的人。[16]他並不救拔天使，乃是救拔亞伯拉罕的後裔。[17]所以，他凡事該與他的弟兄相同，為要在神的事上成為慈悲忠信的大祭司，為百姓的罪獻上挽回祭。[18]他自己既然被試探而受苦，就能搭救被試探的人。

耶穌大過摩西

3 同蒙天召的聖潔弟兄啊，你們應當思想我們所認為使者、為大祭司的耶穌。[2]他為那設立他的盡忠，如同摩西在神的全家盡忠一樣。[3]他比摩西算是更配多得榮耀，好像建造房屋的比房屋更尊榮。[4]因為房屋都必有人建造，但建

---

a 12 Psalm 22:22　　*b 13* Isaiah 8:17　　*c 13* Isaiah 8:18
d 17 Or *and that he might turn aside God's wrath, taking away*

造萬物的就是神。5摩西為僕人，在神的全家誠然盡忠，為要證明將來必傳說的事。6但基督為兒子，治理神的家；我們若將可誇的盼望和膽量堅持到底，便是他的家了。

警戒硬心不信

7聖靈有話說：

"你們今日若聽他的話，
8就不可硬着心，
　　像在曠野惹他發怒、
　　試探他的時候一樣。
9在那裏，你們的祖宗試我探我，
　　並且觀看我的作為有四十年之久。
10所以我厭煩那世代的人，說：
　　'他們心裏常常迷糊，
　　竟不曉得我的作為！'

11我就在怒中起誓說：
　　'他們斷不可進入我的安息。'"

12弟兄們，你們要謹慎，免得你們中間或有人存着不信的惡心，把永生神離棄了。13總要趁着還有今日，天天彼此相勸，免得你們中間有人被罪迷惑，心裏就剛硬了。14我們若將起初確實的信心堅持到底，就在基督裏有分了。15經上說：

"你們今日若聽他的話，
　　就不可硬着心，
　　像惹他發怒的日子一樣。"

16那時聽見他話、惹他發怒的是誰呢？豈不是跟着摩西從埃及出來的眾人嗎？17神四十年之久又厭煩誰呢？豈不是那些犯罪、屍首倒在曠野的人嗎？18又向誰起誓，不容他們進入他的安息呢？豈不是向那些不信從的人嗎？19這樣看來，他們不能進入安息是因為不信的緣故了。

為神子民存留一安息日的安息

4 我們既蒙留下有進入他安息的應許，就當畏懼，免得我們中間（註："我們"原文作"你們"）或有人似乎是趕不上了。2因為有福音傳給我們，像傳給他們一樣；只是所聽見的道與他們無益，

one, but God is the builder of everything. 5Moses was faithful as a servant in all God's house, testifying to what would be said in the future. 6But Christ is faithful as a son over God's house. And we are his house, if we hold on to our courage and the hope of which we boast.

Warning Against Unbelief

7So, as the Holy Spirit says:

"Today, if you hear his voice,
8　do not harden your hearts
　as you did in the rebellion,
　during the time of testing in the desert,
9where your fathers tested and tried me
　and for forty years saw what I did.
10That is why I was angry with that generation,
　and I said, 'Their hearts are always going astray,
　and they have not known my ways.'
11So I declared on oath in my anger,
　'They shall never enter my rest.'"[a]

12See to it, brothers, that none of you has a sinful, unbelieving heart that turns away from the living God. 13But encourage one another daily, as long as it is called Today, so that none of you may be hardened by sin's deceitfulness. 14We have come to share in Christ if we hold firmly till the end the confidence we had at first. 15As has just been said:

"Today, if you hear his voice,
　do not harden your hearts
　as you did in the rebellion."[b]

16Who were they who heard and rebelled? Were they not all those Moses led out of Egypt? 17And with whom was he angry for forty years? Was it not with those who sinned, whose bodies fell in the desert? 18And to whom did God swear that they would never enter his rest if not to those who disobeyed[c]? 19So we see that they were not able to enter, because of their unbelief.

A Sabbath-Rest for the People of God

4 Therefore, since the promise of entering his rest still stands, let us be careful that none of you be found to have fallen short of it. 2For we also have had the gospel preached to us, just as they did; but the message they heard was of no value to them, because

a 11 Psalm 95:7-11　　b 15 Psalm 95:7,8　　c 18 Or disbelieved

387

those who heard did not combine it with faith.[a] [3]Now we who have believed enter that rest, just as God has said,

"So I declared on oath in my anger,
'They shall never enter my rest.' "[b]

And yet his work has been finished since the creation of the world. [4]For somewhere he has spoken about the seventh day in these words: "And on the seventh day God rested from all his work."[c] [5]And again in the passage above he says, "They shall never enter my rest."

[6]It still remains that some will enter that rest, and those who formerly had the gospel preached to them did not go in, because of their disobedience. [7]Therefore God again set a certain day, calling it Today, when a long time later he spoke through David, as was said before:

"Today, if you hear his voice,
do not harden your hearts."[d]

[8]For if Joshua had given them rest, God would not have spoken later about another day. [9]There remains, then, a Sabbath-rest for the people of God; [10]for anyone who enters God's rest also rests from his own work, just as God did from his. [11]Let us, therefore, make every effort to enter that rest, so that no one will fall by following their example of disobedience.

[12]For the word of God is living and active. Sharper than any double-edged sword, it penetrates even to dividing soul and spirit, joints and marrow; it judges the thoughts and attitudes of the heart. [13]Nothing in all creation is hidden from God's sight. Everything is uncovered and laid bare before the eyes of him to whom we must give account.

Jesus the Great High Priest

[14]Therefore, since we have a great high priest who has gone through the heavens,[e] Jesus the Son of God, let us hold firmly to the faith we profess. [15]For we do not have a high priest who is unable to sympathize with our weaknesses, but we have one who has been tempted in every way, just as we are—yet was without sin. [16]Let us then approach the throne of grace with confidence, so that we may receive mercy and find grace to help us in our time of need.

因為他們沒有信心與所聽見的道調和。[3]但我們已經相信的人得以進入那安息，正如神所說：

"我在怒中起誓說：
　'他們斷不可進入我的安息！'"

其實造物之工，從創世以來已經成全了。[4]論到第七日，有一處說："到第七日，神就歇了他一切的工。"[5]又有一處說："他們斷不可進入我的安息！"

[6]既有必進安息的人，那先前聽見福音的，因為不信從，不得進去。[7]所以過了多年，就在大衛的書上，又限定一日，如以上所引的說：

"你們今日若聽他的話，
　就不可硬著心。"

[8]若是約書亞已叫他們享了安息，後來神就不再提別的日子了。[9]這樣看來，必另有一安息日的安息，為神的子民存留。[10]因為那進入安息的，乃是歇了自己的工，正如神歇了他的工一樣。[11]所以，我們務必竭力進入那安息，免得有人學那不信從的樣子跌倒了。

[12]神的道是活潑的，是有功效的，比一切兩刃的劍更快，甚至魂與靈、骨節與骨髓，都能刺入、剖開，連心中的思念和主意都能辨明。[13]並且被造的沒有一樣在他面前不顯然的；原來萬物在那與我們有關係的主眼前，都是赤露敞開的。

尊榮的大祭司耶穌

[14]我們既然有一位已經升入高天尊榮的大祭司，就是神的兒子耶穌，便當持定所承認的道。[15]因我們的大祭司並非不能體恤我們的軟弱，他也曾凡事受過試探，與我們一樣；只是他沒有犯罪。[16]所以我們只管坦然無懼地來到施恩的寶座前，為要得憐恤，蒙恩惠，作隨時的幫助。

---

a 2 Many manuscripts *because they did not share in the faith of those who obeyed*　b 3 Psalm 95:11; also in verse 5
c 4 Gen. 2:2　d 7 Psalm 95:7,8　e 14 Or *gone into heaven*

5 凡從人間挑選的大祭司，是奉派替人辦理屬神的事，為要獻上禮物和贖罪祭（註：或作「要為罪獻上禮物和祭物」）。²他能體諒那愚蒙的和失迷的人，因為他自己也是被軟弱所困。³故此，他理當為百姓和自己獻祭贖罪。

⁴這大祭司的尊榮，沒有人自取，惟要蒙神所召，像亞倫一樣。⁵如此，基督也不是自取榮耀作大祭司，乃是在乎向他說：

"你是我的兒子，
　我今日生你" 的那一位。

⁶就如經上又有一處說：

"你是照着麥基洗德的等次
　永遠為祭司。"

⁷基督在肉體的時候既大聲哀哭，流淚禱告，懇求那能救他免死的主，就因他的虔誠蒙了應允。⁸他雖然為兒子，還是因所受的苦難學了順從。⁹他既得以完全，就為凡順從他的人成了永遠得救的根源，¹⁰並蒙神照着麥基洗德的等次稱他為大祭司。

警告不可離棄真道

¹¹論到麥基洗德，我們有好些話，並且難以解明，因為你們聽不進去。¹²看你們學習的工夫，本該作師傅，誰知還得有人將神聖言小學的開端另教導你們，並且成了那必須吃奶、不能吃乾糧的人！¹³凡只能吃奶的，都不熟練仁義的道理，因為他是嬰孩；¹⁴惟獨長大成人的，才能吃乾糧，他們的心竅習練得通達，就能分辨好歹了。

6 所以，我們應當離開基督道理的開端，竭力進到完全的地步，不必再立根基，就如那懊悔死行、信靠神，²各樣洗禮、按手之禮、死人復活，以及永遠審判各等教訓。³神若許我們，我們必如此行。

5 Every high priest is selected from among men and is appointed to represent them in matters related to God, to offer gifts and sacrifices for sins. ²He is able to deal gently with those who are ignorant and are going astray, since he himself is subject to weakness. ³This is why he has to offer sacrifices for his own sins, as well as for the sins of the people.

⁴No one takes this honor upon himself; he must be called by God, just as Aaron was. ⁵So Christ also did not take upon himself the glory of becoming a high priest. But God said to him,

"You are my Son;
　today I have become your Father."ᵃᵇ

⁶And he says in another place,

"You are a priest forever,
　in the order of Melchizedek."ᶜ

⁷During the days of Jesus' life on earth, he offered up prayers and petitions with loud cries and tears to the one who could save him from death, and he was heard because of his reverent submission. ⁸Although he was a son, he learned obedience from what he suffered ⁹and, once made perfect, he became the source of eternal salvation for all who obey him ¹⁰and was designated by God to be high priest in the order of Melchizedek.

Warning Against Falling Away

¹¹We have much to say about this, but it is hard to explain because you are slow to learn. ¹²In fact, though by this time you ought to be teachers, you need someone to teach you the elementary truths of God's word all over again. You need milk, not solid food! ¹³Anyone who lives on milk, being still an infant, is not acquainted with the teaching about righteousness. ¹⁴But solid food is for the mature, who by constant use have trained themselves to distinguish good from evil.

6 Therefore let us leave the elementary teachings about Christ and go on to maturity, not laying again the foundation of repentance from acts that lead to death,ᵈ and of faith in God, ²instruction about baptisms, the laying on of hands, the resurrection of the dead, and eternal judgment. ³And God permitting, we will do so.

---

a 5 Or have begotten you　　b 5 Psalm 2:7　　c 6 Psalm 110:4
d 1 Or from useless rituals

[4]It is impossible for those who have once been enlightened, who have tasted the heavenly gift, who have shared in the Holy Spirit, [5]who have tasted the goodness of the word of God and the powers of the coming age, [6]if they fall away, to be brought back to repentance, because[a] to their loss they are crucifying the Son of God all over again and subjecting him to public disgrace.

[7]Land that drinks in the rain often falling on it and that produces a crop useful to those for whom it is farmed receives the blessing of God. [8]But land that produces thorns and thistles is worthless and is in danger of being cursed. In the end it will be burned.

[9]Even though we speak like this, dear friends, we are confident of better things in your case— things that accompany salvation. [10]God is not unjust; he will not forget your work and the love you have shown him as you have helped his people and continue to help them. [11]We want each of you to show this same diligence to the very end, in order to make your hope sure. [12]We do not want you to become lazy, but to imitate those who through faith and patience inherit what has been promised.

The Certainty of God's Promise

[13]When God made his promise to Abraham, since there was no one greater for him to swear by, he swore by himself, [14]saying, "I will surely bless you and give you many descendants."[b] [15]And so after waiting patiently, Abraham received what was promised.

[16]Men swear by someone greater than themselves, and the oath confirms what is said and puts an end to all argument. [17]Because God wanted to make the unchanging nature of his purpose very clear to the heirs of what was promised, he confirmed it with an oath. [18]God did this so that, by two unchangeable things in which it is impossible for God to lie, we who have fled to take hold of the hope offered to us may be greatly encouraged. [19]We have this hope as an anchor for the soul, firm and secure. It enters the inner sanctuary behind the curtain, [20]where Jesus, who went before us, has entered on our behalf. He has become a high priest forever, in the order of Melchizedek.

Melchizedek the Priest

7 This Melchizedek was king of Salem and priest of God Most High. He met Abraham returning from the defeat of the kings and blessed him, [2]and Abraham gave

[4]論到那些已經蒙了光照，嘗過天恩的滋味，又於聖靈有分，[5]並嘗過神善道的滋味，覺悟來世權能的人，[6]若是離棄道理，就不能叫他們從新懊悔了。因為他們把神的兒子重釘十字架，明明地羞辱他。

[7]就如一塊田地，吃過屢次下的雨水，生長菜蔬，合乎耕種的人用，就從神得福；[8]若長荊棘和蒺藜，必被廢棄，近於咒詛，結局就是焚燒。

[9]親愛的弟兄們，我們雖是這樣說，卻深信你們的行為強過這些，而且近乎得救。[10]因為神並非不公義，竟忘記你們所做的工和你們為他名所顯的愛心，就是先前伺候聖徒，如今還是伺候。[11]我們願你們各人都顯出這樣的殷勤，使你們有滿足的指望，一直到底。[12]並且不懈怠，總要效法那些憑信心和忍耐承受應許的人。

神應許的確實

[13]當初神應許亞伯拉罕的時候，因為沒有比自己更大可以指着起誓的，就指着自己起誓，說：[14]"論福，我必賜大福給你；論子孫，我必叫你的子孫多起來。" [15]這樣，亞伯拉罕既恆久忍耐，就得了所應許的。

[16]人都是指着比自己大的起誓，並且以起誓為實據，了結各樣的爭論。[17]照樣，神願意為那承受應許的人，格外顯明他的旨意是不更改的，就起誓為證。[18]藉這兩件不更改的事，神決不能說謊，好叫我們這逃往避難所、持定擺在我們前頭指望的人可以大得勉勵。[19]我們有這指望，如同靈魂的錨，又堅固、又牢靠，且通入幔內。[20]作先鋒的耶穌，既照着麥基洗德的等次成了永遠的大祭司，就為我們進入幔內。

大祭司麥基洗德

7 這麥基洗德就是撒冷王，又是至高神的祭司，本是長遠為祭司的。他當亞伯拉罕殺敗諸王回來的時候，就迎接他，給他祝福。[2]亞伯拉罕也將自己所得來的，取十分之一給他。他頭一個名翻出來就是仁義王，他又名撒冷王，就是平安王的意思。³他無父、無母、無族譜、無生之始、無命之終，乃是與神的兒子相似。

⁴你們想一想，先祖亞伯拉罕將自己所擄來上等之物取十分之一給他，這人是何等尊貴呢！⁵那得祭司職任的利未子孫，領命照例向百姓取十分之一，這百姓是自己的弟兄，雖是從亞伯拉罕身中生的（註：「身」原文作「腰」），還是照例取十分之一。⁶獨有麥基洗德，不與他們同譜，倒收納亞伯拉罕的十分之一，為那蒙應許的亞伯拉罕祝福。⁷從來位分大的給位分小的祝福，這是駁不倒的理。⁸在這裏收十分之一的都是必死的人；但在那裏收十分之一的，有為他作見證的說，他是活的。⁹並且可說那受十分之一的利未，也是藉著亞伯拉罕納了十分之一。¹⁰因為麥基洗德迎接亞伯拉罕的時候，利未已經在他先祖的身中（註：「身」原文作「腰」）。

耶穌像麥基洗德

¹¹從前百姓在利未人祭司職任以下受律法，倘若藉這職任能得完全，又何用另外興起一位祭司，照麥基洗德的等次，不照亞倫的等次呢？¹²祭司的職任既已更改，律法也必須更改。¹³因為這話所指的人本屬別的支派，那支派裏從來沒有一人伺候祭壇。¹⁴我們的主分明是從猶大出來的，但這支派，摩西並沒有提到祭司。¹⁵倘若照麥基洗德的樣式，另外興起一位祭司來，我的話更是顯而易見的了。¹⁶他成為祭司，並不是照屬肉體的條例，乃是照無窮之生命的大能（註：「無窮」原文作「不能毀壞」）。¹⁷因為有給他作見證的說：

「你是照著麥基洗德的等次永遠為祭司。」

¹⁸先前的條例因軟弱無益，所以廢掉了，¹⁹（律法原來一無所成）就引進了更美的指望，靠這指望，我們便可以進到神面前。

²⁰再者，耶穌為祭司，並不是不起誓立的。²¹至於那些祭司，原不是起誓立的，只有耶穌是起誓立的。因為那立他的對他說：

him a tenth of everything. First, his name means "king of righteousness"; then also, "king of Salem" means "king of peace." ³Without father or mother, without genealogy, without beginning of days or end of life, like the Son of God he remains a priest forever.

⁴Just think how great he was: Even the patriarch Abraham gave him a tenth of the plunder! ⁵Now the law requires the descendants of Levi who become priests to collect a tenth from the people—that is, their brothers—even though their brothers are descended from Abraham. ⁶This man, however, did not trace his descent from Levi, yet he collected a tenth from Abraham and blessed him who had the promises. ⁷And without doubt the lesser person is blessed by the greater. ⁸In the one case, the tenth is collected by men who die; but in the other case, by him who is declared to be living. ⁹One might even say that Levi, who collects the tenth, paid the tenth through Abraham, ¹⁰because when Melchizedek met Abraham, Levi was still in the body of his ancestor.

Jesus Like Melchizedek

¹¹If perfection could have been attained through the Levitical priesthood (for on the basis of it the law was given to the people), why was there still need for another priest to come—one in the order of Melchizedek, not in the order of Aaron? ¹²For when there is a change of the priesthood, there must also be a change of the law. ¹³He of whom these things are said belonged to a different tribe, and no one from that tribe has ever served at the altar. ¹⁴For it is clear that our Lord descended from Judah, and in regard to that tribe Moses said nothing about priests. ¹⁵And what we have said is even more clear if another priest like Melchizedek appears, ¹⁶one who has become a priest not on the basis of a regulation as to his ancestry but on the basis of the power of an indestructible life. ¹⁷For it is declared:

"You are a priest forever,
 in the order of Melchizedek."*a*

¹⁸The former regulation is set aside because it was weak and useless ¹⁹(for the law made nothing perfect), and a better hope is introduced, by which we draw near to God.

²⁰And it was not without an oath! Others became priests without any oath, ²¹but he became a priest with an oath when God said to him:

a 17 Psalm 110:4

"The Lord has sworn
and will not change his mind:
'You are a priest forever.' "[a]

[22]Because of this oath, Jesus has become the guarantee of a better covenant.

[23]Now there have been many of those priests, since death prevented them from continuing in office; [24]but because Jesus lives forever, he has a permanent priesthood. [25]Therefore he is able to save completely[b] those who come to God through him, because he always lives to intercede for them.

[26]Such a high priest meets our need—one who is holy, blameless, pure, set apart from sinners, exalted above the heavens. [27]Unlike the other high priests, he does not need to offer sacrifices day after day, first for his own sins, and then for the sins of the people. He sacrificed for their sins once for all when he offered himself. [28]For the law appoints as high priests men who are weak; but the oath, which came after the law, appointed the Son, who has been made perfect forever.

The High Priest of a New Covenant

8 The point of what we are saying is this: We do have such a high priest, who sat down at the right hand of the throne of the Majesty in heaven, [2]and who serves in the sanctuary, the true tabernacle set up by the Lord, not by man.

[3]Every high priest is appointed to offer both gifts and sacrifices, and so it was necessary for this one also to have something to offer. [4]If he were on earth, he would not be a priest, for there are already men who offer the gifts prescribed by the law. [5]They serve at a sanctuary that is a copy and shadow of what is in heaven. This is why Moses was warned when he was about to build the tabernacle: "See to it that you make everything according to the pattern shown you on the mountain."[c] [6]But the ministry Jesus has received is as superior to theirs as the covenant of which he is mediator is superior to the old one, and it is founded on better promises.

[7]For if there had been nothing wrong with that first covenant, no place would have been sought for another. [8]But God found fault with the people and said[d]:

"主起了誓，
決不後悔，
你是永遠為祭司。"

[22]既是起誓立的，耶穌就作了更美之約的中保。

[23]那些成為祭司的，數目本來多，是因為有死阻隔，不能長久。[24]這位既是永遠常存的，他祭司的職任就長久不更換。[25]凡靠着他進到神面前的人，他都能拯救到底，因為他是長遠活着，替他們祈求。

[26]像這樣聖潔、無邪惡、無玷污、遠離罪人、高過諸天的大祭司，原是與我們合宜的。[27]他不像那些大祭司，每日必須先為自己的罪，後為百姓的罪獻祭，因為他只一次將自己獻上，就把這事成全了。[28]律法本是立軟弱的人為大祭司；但在律法以後起誓的話，是立兒子為大祭司，乃是成全到永遠的。

新約的大祭司

8 我們所講的事，其中第一要緊的，就是我們有這樣的大祭司，已經坐在天上至大者寶座的右邊，[2]在聖所，就是真帳幕裏作執事；這帳幕是主所支的，不是人所支的。

[3]凡大祭司都是為獻禮物和祭物設立的，所以這位大祭司也必須有所獻的。[4]他若在地上，必不得為祭司，因為已經有照律法獻禮物的祭司。[5]他們供奉的事，本是天上事的形狀和影像，正如摩西將要造帳幕的時候，蒙神警戒他，說："你要謹慎，做各樣的物件都要照着在山上指示你的樣式。"[6]如今耶穌所得的職任是更美的，正如他作更美之約的中保；這約原是憑更美之應許立的。

[7]那前約若沒有瑕疵，就無處尋求後約了。[8]所以主指責他的百姓說
(註：或作"所以主指前約的缺欠說")：

---

a 21 Psalm 110:4   *b* 25 Or *forever*   *c* 5 Exodus 25:40
d 8 Some manuscripts may be translated *fault and said to the people.*

"日子將到,
　我要與以色列家
和猶大家
　另立新約。
9不像我拉着他們祖宗的手,
　領他們出埃及的時候,
　與他們所立的約。
因為他們不恆心守我的約,
　我也不理他們。"
　　　　　　　　這是主說的。

10主又說:
"那些日子以後,
　我與以色列家所立的約乃是這樣:
我要將我的律法放在他們裏面,
　寫在他們心上;
我要作他們的神,
　他們要作我的子民。
11他們不用各人教導自己的鄉鄰
　和自己的弟兄說:
　'你該認識主,'
因為他們從最小的到至大的,
　都必認識我。
12我要寬恕他們的不義,
　不再記念他們的罪愆。"

13既說新約,就以前約為舊了;
但那漸舊漸衰的,就必快歸無有
了。

屬世界帳幕中的敬拜

9 原來前約有禮拜的條例和屬
世界的聖幕。2因為有預備的
帳幕,頭一層叫作聖所,裏
面有燈臺、桌子和陳設餅。3第二幔
子後又有一層帳幕,叫作至聖所,
4有金香爐(註:"爐"或作"壇"),有
包金的約櫃,櫃裏有盛嗎哪的金罐
和亞倫發過芽的杖並兩塊約版。5櫃
上面有榮耀基路伯的影罩着施恩座
(註:"施恩"原文作"蔽罪")。這幾件
我現在不能一一細說。

6這些物件既如此預備齊了,眾
祭司就常進頭一層帳幕,行拜神的
禮。7至於第二層帳幕,惟有大祭司
一年一次獨自進去,沒有不帶着血
為自己和百姓的過錯獻上。8聖靈用
此指明,頭一層帳幕仍存的時候,

"The time is coming, declares the Lord,
　when I will make a new covenant
with the house of Israel
　and with the house of Judah.
9It will not be like the covenant
　I made with their forefathers
when I took them by the hand
　to lead them out of Egypt,
because they did not remain faithful to my
　covenant,
　and I turned away from them,
　　　　　　　　　　declares the Lord.
10This is the covenant I will make with the
　house of Israel
　after that time, declares the Lord.
I will put my laws in their minds
　and write them on their hearts.
I will be their God,
　and they will be my people.
11No longer will a man teach his neighbor,
　or a man his brother, saying, 'Know the
　Lord,'
because they will all know me,
　from the least of them to the greatest.
12For I will forgive their wickedness
　and will remember their sins no more."[a]

13By calling this covenant "new," he has
made the first one obsolete; and what is obsolete
and aging will soon disappear.

Worship in the Earthly Tabernacle

9 Now the first covenant had regulations
for worship and also an earthly sanctuary. 2A tabernacle was set up. In its first
room were the lampstand, the table and the consecrated bread; this was called the Holy Place.
3Behind the second curtain was a room called
the Most Holy Place, 4which had the golden altar
of incense and the gold-covered ark of the
covenant. This ark contained the gold jar of
manna, Aaron's staff that had budded, and the
stone tablets of the covenant. 5Above the ark
were the cherubim of the Glory, overshadowing
the atonement cover.[b] But we cannot discuss
these things in detail now.

6When everything had been arranged like
this, the priests entered regularly into the outer
room to carry on their ministry. 7But only the
high priest entered the inner room, and that
only once a year, and never without blood,
which he offered for himself and for the sins the
people had committed in ignorance. 8The Holy
Spirit was showing by this that the way into the

a 12 Jer. 31:31-34　　b 5 Traditionally the mercy seat

Most Holy Place had not yet been disclosed as long as the first tabernacle was still standing. 9This is an illustration for the present time, indicating that the gifts and sacrifices being offered were not able to clear the conscience of the worshiper. 10They are only a matter of food and drink and various ceremonial washings—external regulations applying until the time of the new order.

The Blood of Christ

11When Christ came as high priest of the good things that are already here,*a* he went through the greater and more perfect tabernacle that is not man-made, that is to say, not a part of this creation. 12He did not enter by means of the blood of goats and calves; but he entered the Most Holy Place once for all by his own blood, having obtained eternal redemption. 13The blood of goats and bulls and the ashes of a heifer sprinkled on those who are ceremonially unclean sanctify them so that they are outwardly clean. 14How much more, then, will the blood of Christ, who through the eternal Spirit offered himself unblemished to God, cleanse our consciences from acts that lead to death,*b* so that we may serve the living God!

15For this reason Christ is the mediator of a new covenant, that those who are called may receive the promised eternal inheritance—now that he has died as a ransom to set them free from the sins committed under the first covenant.

16In the case of a will,*c* it is necessary to prove the death of the one who made it, 17because a will is in force only when somebody has died; it never takes effect while the one who made it is living. 18This is why even the first covenant was not put into effect without blood. 19When Moses had proclaimed every commandment of the law to all the people, he took the blood of calves, together with water, scarlet wool and branches of hyssop, and sprinkled the scroll and all the people. 20He said, "This is the blood of the covenant, which God has commanded you to keep."*d* 21In the same way, he sprinkled with the blood both the tabernacle and everything used in its ceremonies. 22In fact, the law requires that nearly everything be cleansed with blood, and without the shedding of blood there is no forgiveness.

23It was necessary, then, for the copies of the heavenly things to be purified with these sacrifices, but the heavenly things themselves with

進入至聖所的路還未顯明。那頭一層帳幕作現今的一個表樣，所獻的禮物和祭物，就着良心說，都不能叫禮拜的人得以完全。10這些事，連那飲食和諸般洗濯的規矩，都不過是屬肉體的條例，命定到振興的時候為止。

基督的血

11但現在基督已經來到，作了將來美事的大祭司，經過那更大、更全備的帳幕，不是人手所造，也不是屬乎這世界的。12並且不用山羊和牛犢的血，乃用自己的血，只一次進入聖所，成了永遠贖罪的事。13若山羊和公牛的血，並母牛犢的灰，灑在不潔的人身上，尚且叫人成聖，身體潔淨，14何況基督藉着永遠的靈，將自己無瑕無疵獻給神，他的血豈不更能洗淨你們的心（註：原文作「良心」），除去你們的死行，使你們侍奉那永生神嗎？

15為此，他作了新約的中保，既然受死贖了人在前約之時所犯的罪過，便叫蒙召之人得着所應許永遠的產業。

16凡有遺命，必須等到留遺命的人死了（註：「遺命」原文與「約」字同）。17因為人死了，遺命才有效力；若留遺命的尚在，那遺命還有用處嗎？18所以，前約也不是不用血立的。19因為摩西當日照着律法將各樣誡命傳給眾百姓，就拿朱紅色絨和牛膝草，把牛犢、山羊的血和水灑在書上，又灑在眾百姓身上，說：20「這血就是神與你們立約的憑據。」21他又照樣把血灑在帳幕和各樣器皿上。22按着律法，凡物差不多都是用血潔淨的，若不流血，罪就不得赦免了。

23照着天上樣式做的物件，必須用這些祭物去潔淨；但那天上的本物

---

a 11 Some early manuscripts *are to come   b 14* Or *from useless rituals   c 16* Same Greek word as *covenant*; also in verse 17
d 20 Exodus 24:8

自然當用更美的祭物去潔淨。²⁴因為基督並不是進了人手所造的聖所（這不過是真聖所的影像），乃是進了天堂，如今為我們顯在神面前；²⁵也不是多次將自己獻上，像那大祭司每年帶着牛羊的血進入聖所（註：“牛羊的血”原文作“不是自己的血”）。²⁶如果這樣，他從創世以來，就必多次受苦了。但如今在這末世顯現一次，把自己獻為祭，好除掉罪。²⁷按着定命，人人都有一死，死後且有審判。²⁸像這樣，基督既然一次被獻，擔當了多人的罪，將來要向那等候他的人第二次顯現，並與罪無關，乃是為拯救他們。

基督一次永遠的贖罪祭

10 律法既是將來美事的影兒，不是本物的真像，總不能藉着每年常獻一樣的祭物，叫那近前來的人得以完全。²若不然，獻祭的事豈不早已止住了嗎？因為禮拜的人，良心既被潔淨，就不再覺得有罪了。³但這些祭物是叫人每年想起罪來，⁴因為公牛和山羊的血斷不能除罪。

⁵所以，基督到世上來的時候，就說：

“神啊，祭物和禮物是你不願意的；
　你曾給我預備了身體。
⁶燔祭和贖罪祭
　是你不喜歡的。
⁷那時我說：‘神啊！我來了，
　為要照你的旨意行；
　我的事在經卷上已經記載了。’”

⁸以上說：“祭物和禮物，燔祭和贖罪祭，是你不願意的，也是你不喜歡的”（這都是按着律法獻的）。⁹後又說：“我來了為要照你的旨意行。”可見他是除去在先的，為要立定在後的。¹⁰我們憑這旨意，靠耶穌基督只一次獻上他的身體，就得以成聖。

¹¹凡祭司天天站着侍奉神，屢次獻上一樣的祭物，這祭物永不能除

better sacrifices than these. ²⁴For Christ did not enter a man-made sanctuary that was only a copy of the true one; he entered heaven itself, now to appear for us in God's presence. ²⁵Nor did he enter heaven to offer himself again and again, the way the high priest enters the Most Holy Place every year with blood that is not his own. ²⁶Then Christ would have had to suffer many times since the creation of the world. But now he has appeared once for all at the end of the ages to do away with sin by the sacrifice of himself. ²⁷Just as man is destined to die once, and after that to face judgment, ²⁸so Christ was sacrificed once to take away the sins of many people; and he will appear a second time, not to bear sin, but to bring salvation to those who are waiting for him.

Christ's Sacrifice Once for All

10 The law is only a shadow of the good things that are coming—not the realities themselves. For this reason it can never, by the same sacrifices repeated endlessly year after year, make perfect those who draw near to worship. ²If it could, would they not have stopped being offered? For the worshipers would have been cleansed once for all, and would no longer have felt guilty for their sins. ³But those sacrifices are an annual reminder of sins, ⁴because it is impossible for the blood of bulls and goats to take away sins.

⁵Therefore, when Christ came into the world, he said:

"Sacrifice and offering you did not desire,
　but a body you prepared for me;
⁶with burnt offerings and sin offerings
　you were not pleased.
⁷Then I said, 'Here I am—it is written about me in the scroll—
　I have come to do your will, O God.' "[a]

⁸First he said, "Sacrifices and offerings, burnt offerings and sin offerings you did not desire, nor were you pleased with them" (although the law required them to be made). ⁹Then he said, "Here I am, I have come to do your will." He sets aside the first to establish the second. ¹⁰And by that will, we have been made holy through the sacrifice of the body of Jesus Christ once for all.

¹¹Day after day every priest stands and performs his religious duties; again and again he offers the same sacrifices, which can never take

a 7 Psalm 40:6-8 (see Septuagint)

away sins. [12]But when this priest had offered for all time one sacrifice for sins, he sat down at the right hand of God. [13]Since that time he waits for his enemies to be made his footstool, [14]because by one sacrifice he has made perfect forever those who are being made holy.

[15]The Holy Spirit also testifies to us about this. First he says:

[16]"This is the covenant I will make with them after that time, says the Lord.
I will put my laws in their hearts,
and I will write them on their minds."[a]

[17]Then he adds:

"Their sins and lawless acts
I will remember no more."[b]

[18]And where these have been forgiven, there is no longer any sacrifice for sin.

A Call to Persevere

[19]Therefore, brothers, since we have confidence to enter the Most Holy Place by the blood of Jesus, [20]by a new and living way opened for us through the curtain, that is, his body, [21]and since we have a great priest over the house of God, [22]let us draw near to God with a sincere heart in full assurance of faith, having our hearts sprinkled to cleanse us from a guilty conscience and having our bodies washed with pure water. [23]Let us hold unswervingly to the hope we profess, for he who promised is faithful. [24]And let us consider how we may spur one another on toward love and good deeds. [25]Let us not give up meeting together, as some are in the habit of doing, but let us encourage one another—and all the more as you see the Day approaching.

[26]If we deliberately keep on sinning after we have received the knowledge of the truth, no sacrifice for sins is left, [27]but only a fearful expectation of judgment and of raging fire that will consume the enemies of God. [28]Anyone who rejected the law of Moses died without mercy on the testimony of two or three witnesses. [29]How much more severely do you think a man deserves to be punished who has trampled the Son of God under foot, who has treated as an unholy thing the blood of the covenant that sanctified him, and who has insulted the Spirit of grace? [30]For we know him who said, "It is mine to avenge; I will repay,"[c] and again, "The

罪。[12]但基督獻了一次永遠的贖罪祭，就在神的右邊坐下了。[13]從此等候他仇敵成了他的腳凳。[14]因為他一次獻祭，便叫那得以成聖的人永遠完全。

[15]聖靈也對我們作見證，因為他既已說過：

[16]"主說，那些日子以後，
我與他們所立的約乃是這樣：
我要將我的律法寫在他們心上，
又要放在他們的裏面。"

[17]以後就說：

"我不再記念他們的罪愆
和他們的過犯。"

[18]這些罪過既已赦免，就不用再為罪獻祭了。

勸勉要堅忍

[19]弟兄們，我們既因耶穌的血，得以坦然進入至聖所，[20]是藉着他給我們開了一條又新又活的路，從幔子經過，這幔子就是他的身體。[21]又有一位大祭司治理神的家。[22]並我們心中天良的虧欠已經灑去，身體用清水洗淨了，就當存着誠心和充足的信心來到神面前；[23]也要堅守我們所承認的指望，不至搖動，因為那應許我們的是信實的。[24]又要彼此相顧，激發愛心，勉勵行善。[25]你們不可停止聚會，好像那些停止慣了的人，倒要彼此勸勉。既知道（註：原文作"看見"）那日子臨近，就更當如此。

[26]因為我們得知真道以後，若故意犯罪，贖罪的祭就再沒有了，[27]惟有戰懼等候審判和那燒滅眾敵人的烈火。[28]人干犯摩西的律法，憑兩三個見證人尚且不得憐恤而死；[29]何況人踐踏神的兒子，將那使他成聖之約的血當作平常，又褻慢施恩的聖靈，你們想，他要受的刑罰該怎樣加重呢？[30]因為我們知道誰說："伸冤在我，我必報應。"又說："主要審判他的

a 16 Jer. 31:33   b 17 Jer. 31:34   c 30 Deut. 32:35

百姓。" 31落在永生神的手裏，真是可怕的！

32你們要追念往日，蒙了光照以後，所忍受大爭戰的各樣苦難。33一面被毀謗，遭患難，成了戲景，叫眾人觀看；一面陪伴那些受這樣苦難的人。34因為你們體恤了那些被捆鎖的人，並且你們的家業被人搶去，也甘心忍受，知道自己有更美長存的家業。

35所以，你們不可丟棄勇敢的心，存這樣的心必得大賞賜。36你們必須忍耐，使你們行完了神的旨意，就可以得着所應許的。37因為還有一點點時候，

"那要來的就來，
　並不遲延。
38只是義人必因信得生（註："義人"有古卷作"我的義人"）；
　他若退後，我心裏就不喜歡他。"

39我們卻不是退後入沉淪的那等人，乃是有信心以至靈魂得救的人。

因着信

11 信就是所望之事的實底，是未見之事的確據。2古人在這信上得了美好的證據。

3我們因着信，就知道諸世界是藉神話造成的，這樣，所看見的，並不是從顯然之物造出來的。

4亞伯因着信，獻祭與神，比該隱所獻的更美，因此便得了稱義的見證，就是神指他禮物作的見證。他雖然死了，卻因這信，仍舊說話。

5以諾因着信，被接去，不至於見死，人也找不着他，因為神已經把他接了去。只是他被接去以先，已經得了神喜悅他的明證。6人非有信，就不能得神的喜悅；因為到神面前來的人，必須信有神，且信他賞賜那尋求他的人。

7挪亞因着信，既蒙神指示他未見的事，動了敬畏的心，預備了一隻方舟，使他全家得救。因此就定

Lord will judge his people."[a] 31It is a dreadful thing to fall into the hands of the living God.

32Remember those earlier days after you had received the light, when you stood your ground in a great contest in the face of suffering. 33Sometimes you were publicly exposed to insult and persecution; at other times you stood side by side with those who were so treated. 34You sympathized with those in prison and joyfully accepted the confiscation of your property, because you knew that you yourselves had better and lasting possessions.

35So do not throw away your confidence; it will be richly rewarded. 36You need to persevere so that when you have done the will of God, you will receive what he has promised. 37For in just a very little while,

"He who is coming will come and will not
　delay.
38　But my righteous one[b] will live by faith.
　And if he shrinks back,
　　I will not be pleased with him."[c]

39But we are not of those who shrink back and are destroyed, but of those who believe and are saved.

By Faith

11 Now faith is being sure of what we hope for and certain of what we do not see. 2This is what the ancients were commended for.

3By faith we understand that the universe was formed at God's command, so that what is seen was not made out of what was visible.

4By faith Abel offered God a better sacrifice than Cain did. By faith he was commended as a righteous man, when God spoke well of his offerings. And by faith he still speaks, even though he is dead.

5By faith Enoch was taken from this life, so that he did not experience death; he could not be found, because God had taken him away. For before he was taken, he was commended as one who pleased God. 6And without faith it is impossible to please God, because anyone who comes to him must believe that he exists and that he rewards those who earnestly seek him.

7By faith Noah, when warned about things not yet seen, in holy fear built an ark to save his family. By his faith he condemned the world

---

a 30 Deut. 32:36; Psalm 135:14　　b 38 One early manuscript
But the righteous　　c 38 Hab. 2:3,4

and became heir of the righteousness that comes by faith.

⁸By faith Abraham, when called to go to a place he would later receive as his inheritance, obeyed and went, even though he did not know where he was going. ⁹By faith he made his home in the promised land like a stranger in a foreign country; he lived in tents, as did Isaac and Jacob, who were heirs with him of the same promise. ¹⁰For he was looking forward to the city with foundations, whose architect and builder is God.

¹¹By faith Abraham, even though he was past age—and Sarah herself was barren—was enabled to become a father because he*a* considered him faithful who had made the promise. ¹²And so from this one man, and he as good as dead, came descendants as numerous as the stars in the sky and as countless as the sand on the seashore.

¹³All these people were still living by faith when they died. They did not receive the things promised; they only saw them and welcomed them from a distance. And they admitted that they were aliens and strangers on earth. ¹⁴People who say such things show that they are looking for a country of their own. ¹⁵If they had been thinking of the country they had left, they would have had opportunity to return. ¹⁶Instead, they were longing for a better country—a heavenly one. Therefore God is not ashamed to be called their God, for he has prepared a city for them.

¹⁷By faith Abraham, when God tested him, offered Isaac as a sacrifice. He who had received the promises was about to sacrifice his one and only son, ¹⁸even though God had said to him, "It is through Isaac that your offspring*b* will be reckoned."*c* ¹⁹Abraham reasoned that God could raise the dead, and figuratively speaking, he did receive Isaac back from death.

²⁰By faith Isaac blessed Jacob and Esau in regard to their future.

²¹By faith Jacob, when he was dying, blessed each of Joseph's sons, and worshiped as he leaned on the top of his staff.

²²By faith Joseph, when his end was near, spoke about the exodus of the Israelites from Egypt and gave instructions about his bones.

²³By faith Moses' parents hid him for three months after he was born, because they saw he was no ordinary child, and they were not afraid of the king's edict.

了那世代的罪，自己也承受了那從信而來的義。

⁸亞伯拉罕因着信，蒙召的時候，就遵命出去，往將來要得為業的地方去；出去的時候，還不知往哪裏去。⁹他因着信，就在所應許之地作客，好像在異地居住帳棚，與那同蒙一個應許的以撒、雅各一樣。¹⁰因為他等候那座有根基的城，就是神所經營、所建造的。

¹¹因着信，連撒拉自己，雖然過了生育的歲數，還能懷孕，因她以為那應許她的是可信的。¹²所以從一個彷彿已死的人就生出子孫，如同天上的星那樣眾多，海邊的沙那樣無數。

¹³這些人都是存着信心死的，並沒有得着所應許的，卻從遠處望見，且歡喜迎接，又承認自己在世上是客旅，是寄居的。¹⁴說這樣話的人，是表明自己要找一個家鄉。¹⁵他們若想念所離開的家鄉，還有可以回去的機會。¹⁶他們卻羨慕一個更美的家鄉，就是在天上的。所以神被稱為他們的神，並不以為恥，因為他已經給他們預備了一座城。

¹⁷亞伯拉罕因着信，被試驗的時候，就把以撒獻上；這便是那歡喜領受應許的，將自己獨生的兒子獻上。¹⁸論到這兒子，曾有話說："從以撒生的才要稱為你的後裔。"¹⁹他以為神還能叫人從死裏復活，他也彷彿從死中得回他的兒子來。

²⁰以撒因着信，就指着將來的事給雅各、以掃祝福。

²¹雅各因着信，臨死的時候，給約瑟的兩個兒子各自祝福，扶着杖頭敬拜神。

²²約瑟因着信，臨終的時候，提到以色列族將來要出埃及，並為自己的骸骨留下遺命。

²³摩西生下來，他的父母見他是個俊美的孩子，就因着信，把他藏了三個月，並不怕王命。

---

a 11 Or *By faith even Sarah, who was past age, was enabled to bear children because she*   *b* 18 Greek *seed*   *c* 18 Gen. 21:12

24摩西因着信，長大了就不肯稱為法老女兒之子。25他寧可和神的百姓同受苦害，也不願暫時享受罪中之樂。26他看為基督受的凌辱比埃及的財物更寶貴，因他想望所要得的賞賜。27他因着信，就離開埃及，不怕王怒；因為他恆心忍耐，如同看見那不能看見的主。28他因着信，就守逾越節（註："守"或作"立"），行灑血的禮，免得那滅長子的臨近以色列人。

29他們因着信，過紅海如行乾地；埃及人試着要過去，就被吞滅了。

30以色列人因着信，圍繞耶利哥城七日，城牆就倒塌了。

31妓女喇合因着信，曾和平平地接待探子，就不與那些不順從的人一同滅亡。

32我又何必再說呢？若要一一細說，基甸、巴拉、參孫、耶弗他、大衛、撒母耳和眾先知的事，時候就不夠了。33他們因着信，制伏了敵國，行了公義，得了應許；堵了獅子的口，34滅了烈火的猛勢，脫了刀劍的鋒刃；軟弱變為剛強，爭戰顯出勇敢，打退外邦的全軍。35有婦人得自己的死人復活，又有人忍受嚴刑，不肯苟且得釋放（註："釋放"原文作"贖"），為要得着更美的復活。36又有人忍受戲弄、鞭打、捆鎖、監禁各等的磨煉，37被石頭打死，被鋸鋸死，受試探，被刀殺，被着綿羊、山羊的皮各處奔跑，受窮乏、患難、苦害，38在曠野、山嶺、山洞、地穴飄流無定，本是世界不配有的人。

39這些人都是因信得了美好的證據，卻仍未得着所應許的。40因為神給我們預備了更美的事，叫他們若不與我們同得，就不能完全。

神管教其兒女

12 我們既有這許多的見證人，如同雲彩圍着我們，就當放下各樣的重擔，脫去容易纏

24By faith Moses, when he had grown up, refused to be known as the son of Pharaoh's daughter. 25He chose to be mistreated along with the people of God rather than to enjoy the pleasures of sin for a short time. 26He regarded disgrace for the sake of Christ as of greater value than the treasures of Egypt, because he was looking ahead to his reward. 27By faith he left Egypt, not fearing the king's anger; he persevered because he saw him who is invisible. 28By faith he kept the Passover and the sprinkling of blood, so that the destroyer of the firstborn would not touch the firstborn of Israel.

29By faith the people passed through the Red Sea[a] as on dry land; but when the Egyptians tried to do so, they were drowned.

30By faith the walls of Jericho fell, after the people had marched around them for seven days.

31By faith the prostitute Rahab, because she welcomed the spies, was not killed with those who were disobedient.[b]

32And what more shall I say? I do not have time to tell about Gideon, Barak, Samson, Jephthah, David, Samuel and the prophets, 33who through faith conquered kingdoms, administered justice, and gained what was promised; who shut the mouths of lions, 34quenched the fury of the flames, and escaped the edge of the sword; whose weakness was turned to strength; and who became powerful in battle and routed foreign armies. 35Women received back their dead, raised to life again. Others were tortured and refused to be released, so that they might gain a better resurrection. 36Some faced jeers and flogging, while still others were chained and put in prison. 37They were stoned[c]; they were sawed in two; they were put to death by the sword. They went about in sheepskins and goatskins, destitute, persecuted and mistreated— 38the world was not worthy of them. They wandered in deserts and mountains, and in caves and holes in the ground.

39These were all commended for their faith, yet none of them received what had been promised. 40God had planned something better for us so that only together with us would they be made perfect.

God Disciplines His Sons

12 Therefore, since we are surrounded by such a great cloud of witnesses, let us throw off everything that hinders and

a 29 That is, Sea of Reeds   b 31 Or unbelieving
c 37 Some early manuscripts stoned; they were put to the test;

the sin that so easily entangles, and let us run with perseverance the race marked out for us. [2]Let us fix our eyes on Jesus, the author and perfecter of our faith, who for the joy set before him endured the cross, scorning its shame, and sat down at the right hand of the throne of God. [3]Consider him who endured such opposition from sinful men, so that you will not grow weary and lose heart.

[4]In your struggle against sin, you have not yet resisted to the point of shedding your blood. [5]And you have forgotten that word of encouragement that addresses you as sons:

"My son, do not make light of the Lord's
　　discipline,
　　and do not lose heart when he rebukes you,
[6]because the Lord disciplines those he loves,
　　and he punishes everyone he accepts as a
　　son."[a]

[7]Endure hardship as discipline; God is treating you as sons. For what son is not disciplined by his father? [8]If you are not disciplined (and everyone undergoes discipline), then you are illegitimate children and not true sons. [9]Moreover, we have all had human fathers who disciplined us and we respected them for it. How much more should we submit to the Father of our spirits and live! [10]Our fathers disciplined us for a little while as they thought best; but God disciplines us for our good, that we may share in his holiness. [11]No discipline seems pleasant at the time, but painful. Later on, however, it produces a harvest of righteousness and peace for those who have been trained by it.

[12]Therefore, strengthen your feeble arms and weak knees. [13]"Make level paths for your feet,"[b] so that the lame may not be disabled, but rather healed.

Warning Against Refusing God

[14]Make every effort to live in peace with all men and to be holy; without holiness no one will see the Lord. [15]See to it that no one misses the grace of God and that no bitter root grows up to cause trouble and defile many. [16]See that no one is sexually immoral, or is godless like Esau, who for a single meal sold his inheritance rights as the oldest son. [17]Afterward, as you know, when he wanted to inherit this blessing, he was rejected. He could bring about no change of mind, though he sought the blessing with tears.

累我們的罪，存心忍耐，奔那擺在我們前頭的路程，[2]仰望為我們信心創始成終的耶穌（註：或作"仰望那將真道創始成終的耶穌"）。他因那擺在前面的喜樂，就輕看羞辱，忍受了十字架的苦難，便坐在神寶座的右邊。[3]那忍受罪人這樣頂撞的，你們要思想，免得疲倦灰心。

[4]你們與罪惡相爭，還沒有抵擋到流血的地步。[5]你們又忘了那勸你們如同勸兒子的話，說：

"我兒，你不可輕看主的管教，
　被他責備的時候，
　也不可灰心。
[6]因為主所愛的，他必管教，
　又鞭打凡所收納的兒子。"

[7]你們所忍受的，是神管教你們，待你們如同待兒子。焉有兒子不被父親管教的呢？[8]管教原是眾子所共受的，你們若不受管教，就是私子，不是兒子了。[9]再者，我們曾有生身的父管教我們，我們尚且敬重他；何況萬靈的父，我們豈不更當順服他得生嗎？[10]生身的父都是暫隨己意管教我們；惟有萬靈的父管教我們，是要我們得益處，使我們在他的聖潔上有分。[11]凡管教的事，當時不覺得快樂，反覺得愁苦，後來卻為那經練過的人結出平安的果子，就是義。

[12]所以，你們要把下垂的手、發酸的腿挺起來，[13]也要為自己的腳，把道路修直了，使瘸子不至歪腳，反得痊愈（註："歪腳"或作"差路"）。

警告不可棄絕神

[14]你們要追求與眾人和睦，並要追求聖潔；非聖潔沒有人能見主。[15]又要謹慎，恐怕有人失了神的恩；恐怕有毒根生出來擾亂你們，因此叫眾人沾染污穢。[16]恐怕有淫亂的，有貪戀世俗如以掃的；他因一點食物把自己長子的名分賣了。[17]後來想要承受父所祝的福，竟被棄絕，雖然號哭切求，卻得不着門路使他父親的心意回轉。這是你們知道的。

a 6 Prov. 3:11,12   b 13 Prov. 4:26

¹⁸你們原不是來到那能摸的山；此山有火焰、密雲、黑暗、暴風、¹⁹角聲與說話的聲音。那些聽見這聲音的，都求不要再向他們說話。²⁰因為他們當不起所命他們的話，說："靠近這山的，即便是走獸，也要用石頭打死。"²¹所見的極其可怕，甚至摩西說："我甚是恐懼戰兢。"

²²你們乃是來到錫安山、永生神的城邑，就是天上的耶路撒冷。那裏有千萬的天使，²³有名錄在天上諸長子之會所共聚的總會，有審判眾人的神和被成全之義人的靈魂，²⁴並新約的中保耶穌，以及所灑的血。這血所說的比亞伯的血所說的更美。

²⁵你們總要謹慎，不可棄絕那向你們說話的。因為那些棄絕在地上警戒他們的，尚且不能逃罪，何況我們違背那從天上警戒我們的呢？²⁶當時他的聲音震動了地，但如今他應許說："再一次我不單要震動地，還要震動天。"²⁷這再一次的話，是指明被震動的，就是受造之物都要挪去，使那不被震動的常存。

²⁸所以，我們既得了不能震動的國，就當感恩，照神所喜悅的，用虔誠、敬畏的心侍奉神。²⁹因為我們的神乃是烈火。

結束的勸勉

13 你們務要常存弟兄相愛的心。²不可忘記用愛心接待客旅，因為曾有接待客旅的，不知不覺就接待了天使。³你們要記念被捆綁的人，好像與他們同受捆綁；也要記念遭苦害的人，想到自己也在肉身之內。

⁴婚姻，人人都當尊重，牀也不可污穢，因為苟合行淫的人，神必要審判。⁵你們存心不可貪愛錢財，要以自己所有的為足。因為主曾說：

"我總不撇下你，
也不丟棄你。"

¹⁸You have not come to a mountain that can be touched and that is burning with fire; to darkness, gloom and storm; ¹⁹to a trumpet blast or to such a voice speaking words that those who heard it begged that no further word be spoken to them, ²⁰because they could not bear what was commanded: "If even an animal touches the mountain, it must be stoned."^a ²¹The sight was so terrifying that Moses said, "I am trembling with fear."^b

²²But you have come to Mount Zion, to the heavenly Jerusalem, the city of the living God. You have come to thousands upon thousands of angels in joyful assembly, ²³to the church of the firstborn, whose names are written in heaven. You have come to God, the judge of all men, to the spirits of righteous men made perfect, ²⁴to Jesus the mediator of a new covenant, and to the sprinkled blood that speaks a better word than the blood of Abel.

²⁵See to it that you do not refuse him who speaks. If they did not escape when they refused him who warned them on earth, how much less will we, if we turn away from him who warns us from heaven? ²⁶At that time his voice shook the earth, but now he has promised, "Once more I will shake not only the earth but also the heavens."^c ²⁷The words "once more" indicate the removing of what can be shaken—that is, created things—so that what cannot be shaken may remain.

²⁸Therefore, since we are receiving a kingdom that cannot be shaken, let us be thankful, and so worship God acceptably with reverence and awe, ²⁹for our "God is a consuming fire."^d

Concluding Exhortations

13 Keep on loving each other as brothers. ²Do not forget to entertain strangers, for by so doing some people have entertained angels without knowing it. ³Remember those in prison as if you were their fellow prisoners, and those who are mistreated as if you yourselves were suffering.

⁴Marriage should be honored by all, and the marriage bed kept pure, for God will judge the adulterer and all the sexually immoral. ⁵Keep your lives free from the love of money and be content with what you have, because God has said,

"Never will I leave you;
never will I forsake you."^e

a 20 Exodus 19:12,13　　*b 21* Deut. 9:19　　*c 26* Haggai 2:6
d 29 Deut. 4:24　　*e 5* Deut. 31:6

[6]So we say with confidence,

> "The Lord is my helper; I will not be afraid.
> What can man do to me?"[a]

[7]Remember your leaders, who spoke the word of God to you. Consider the outcome of their way of life and imitate their faith. [8]Jesus Christ is the same yesterday and today and forever.

[9]Do not be carried away by all kinds of strange teachings. It is good for our hearts to be strengthened by grace, not by ceremonial foods, which are of no value to those who eat them. [10]We have an altar from which those who minister at the tabernacle have no right to eat.

[11]The high priest carries the blood of animals into the Most Holy Place as a sin offering, but the bodies are burned outside the camp. [12]And so Jesus also suffered outside the city gate to make the people holy through his own blood. [13]Let us, then, go to him outside the camp, bearing the disgrace he bore. [14]For here we do not have an enduring city, but we are looking for the city that is to come.

[15]Through Jesus, therefore, let us continually offer to God a sacrifice of praise—the fruit of lips that confess his name. [16]And do not forget to do good and to share with others, for with such sacrifices God is pleased.

[17]Obey your leaders and submit to their authority. They keep watch over you as men who must give an account. Obey them so that their work will be a joy, not a burden, for that would be of no advantage to you.

[18]Pray for us. We are sure that we have a clear conscience and desire to live honorably in every way. [19]I particularly urge you to pray so that I may be restored to you soon.

[20]May the God of peace, who through the blood of the eternal covenant brought back from the dead our Lord Jesus, that great Shepherd of the sheep, [21]equip you with everything good for doing his will, and may he work in us what is pleasing to him, through Jesus Christ, to whom be glory for ever and ever. Amen.

[22]Brothers, I urge you to bear with my word of exhortation, for I have written you only a short letter.

[23]I want you to know that our brother Timothy has been released. If he arrives soon, I will come with him to see you.

[6]所以我們可以放膽説：

> "主是幫助我的，我必不懼怕；
> 人能把我怎麼樣呢？"

[7]從前引導你們、傳神之道給你們的人，你們要想念他們，效法他們的信心，留心看他們為人的結局。[8]耶穌基督，昨日、今日、一直到永遠是一樣的。

[9]你們不要被那諸般怪異的教訓勾引了去。因為人心靠恩得堅固才是好的，並不是靠飲食；那在飲食上專心的，從來沒有得着益處。[10]我們有一祭壇，上面的祭物是那些在帳幕中供職的人不可吃的。

[11]原來牲畜的血被大祭司帶入聖所作贖罪祭，牲畜的身子被燒在營外。[12]所以耶穌要用自己的血叫百姓成聖，也就在城門外受苦。[13]這樣，我們也當出到營外，就了他去，忍受他所受的凌辱。[14]我們在這裏本沒有常存的城，乃是尋求那將來的城。

[15]我們應當靠着耶穌，常常以頌讚為祭獻給神，這就是那承認主名之人嘴唇的果子。[16]只是不可忘記行善和捐輸的事，因為這樣的祭是神所喜悦的。

[17]你們要依從那些引導你們的，且要順服，因他們為你們的靈魂時刻警醒，好像那將來交賬的人。你們要使他們交的時候有快樂，不至憂愁；若憂愁就與你們無益了。

[18]請你們為我們禱告，因我們自覺良心無虧，願意凡事按正道而行。[19]我更求你們為我禱告，使我快些回到你們那裏去。

[20]但願賜平安的神，就是那憑永約之血使羣羊的大牧人——我主耶穌從死裏復活的神，[21]在各樣善事上成全你們，叫你們遵行他的旨意；又藉着耶穌基督在你們心裏行他所喜悦的事。願榮耀歸給他，直到永永遠遠。阿們！

[22]弟兄們，我略略寫信給你們，望你們聽我勸勉的話。

[23]你們該知道，我們的兄弟提摩太已經釋放了。他若快來，我必同他去見你們。

---

a 6 Psalm 118:6,7

²⁴請你們問引導你們的諸位和眾聖徒安。從義大利來的人也問你們安。

²⁵願恩惠常與你們眾人同在。阿們！

²⁴Greet all your leaders and all God's people. Those from Italy send you their greetings.

²⁵Grace be with you all.

表六：舊約與新約的對比

TABLE 6 : COMPARISON OF THE OLD AND NEW CONVENANTS

舊約 O.C. under Moses	新約 N.C. in Christ	應用 Application
有罪的人須獻上祭與禮 Gifts and sacrifices by those guilty of sin	無罪的基督自我犧牲 Self-sacrifice by the guiltless Christ	基督為你而死 Christ died for you
敬拜時專注於物質的殿 Focused on a physical building where one goes to worship	注重基督在信徒心中的統領 Focuses on reign of Christ in the hearts of believers	神直接介入你的生命中 God directly involved in your life
影兒 A shadow	實體、真像 A reality	不是短暫的，乃是永恆的 Not temporal, but eternal
有限的應許 Limited promises	無盡的應許 Limitless promises	我們可以信靠神的諸應許 We can trust God's promises to us
人守不了諾言或約章 Failed agreement by people	基督信實地守住其諾言 Faithful agreement by Christ	人不能守約，基督卻能 Christ can kept the agreement where people couldn't
外表的標準與規條 External standards and rules	內裏的標準 — 新心 Internal standards — a new heart	神看行為與動機 — 我們是向神不是向規條交賬 God sees both actions and motives — we are accountable to God, not rules
有限制地親近神 Limited access to God	無限制地親近神 Unlimited access to God	神是可親近、隨時都在的 God is personally avaiable
出於懼怕 Based on fear	出於愛與寬恕 Based on love and forgiveness	神的赦免，使我們的失敗不至將約廢去 Forgiveness keeps our failures from destroying the agreement
法制上潔淨 Legal cleansing	個人得以潔淨 Personal cleansing	神的潔淨，最為完全 God's cleansing is complete
不斷的獻祭 Continual sacrifice	決定性的獻祭 Conclusive sacrifice	基督的犧牲是完美且是最後的 Christ's sacrifice is perfect and final
服從規條 Obey the rules	服侍永活神 Serve the living God	我們有的是與神的關係而不是教條 We have a relationship, not regulations
赦免是賺取回來的 Forgiveness earned	赦免是白白賞賜給人的 Forgiveness freely given	我們有真正且完全的赦免 We have true and complete forgiveness
要每年重申 Repeated yearly	由基督的死成全 Completed by Christ's death	基督的死可適用於你的罪上 Christ's death can be applied to your sin
人為的努力 Human effort	神的恩惠 God's grace	由神的愛為你而發動 Initiated by God's love for you
只適用於某些人 Available to some	凡人均可得 Available to all	你也可以得到 Available to you

James

雅各書

1 James, a servant of God and of the Lord Jesus Christ,

To the twelve tribes scattered among the nations:

Greetings.

Trials and Temptations

²Consider it pure joy, my brothers, whenever you face trials of many kinds, ³because you know that the testing of your faith develops perseverance. ⁴Perseverance must finish its work so that you may be mature and complete, not lacking anything. ⁵If any of you lacks wisdom, he should ask God, who gives generously to all without finding fault, and it will be given to him. ⁶But when he asks, he must believe and not doubt, because he who doubts is like a wave of the sea, blown and tossed by the wind. ⁷That man should not think he will receive anything from the Lord; ⁸he is a double-minded man, unstable in all he does.

⁹The brother in humble circumstances ought to take pride in his high position. ¹⁰But the one who is rich should take pride in his low position, because he will pass away like a wild flower. ¹¹For the sun rises with scorching heat and withers the plant; its blossom falls and its beauty is destroyed. In the same way, the rich man will fade away even while he goes about his business.

¹²Blessed is the man who perseveres under trial, because when he has stood the test, he will receive the crown of life that God has promised to those who love him.

¹³When tempted, no one should say, "God is tempting me." For God cannot be tempted by evil, nor does he tempt anyone; ¹⁴but each one is tempted when, by his own evil desire, he is dragged away and enticed. ¹⁵Then, after desire has conceived, it gives birth to sin; and sin, when it is full-grown, gives birth to death.

¹⁶Don't be deceived, my dear brothers. ¹⁷Every good and perfect gift is from above, coming down from the Father of the heavenly lights, who does not change like shifting shadows. ¹⁸He chose to give us birth through the

1 作神和主耶穌基督僕人的雅各,

請散住十二個支派之人的安。

試煉與試探

²我的弟兄們,你們落在百般試煉中,都要以為大喜樂;³因為知道你們的信心經過試驗,就生忍耐。⁴但忍耐也當成功,使你們成全完備,毫無缺欠。⁵你們中間若有缺少智慧的,應當求那厚賜與眾人、也不斥責人的神,主就必賜給他。⁶只要憑着信心求,一點不疑惑;因為那疑惑的人,就像海中的波浪,被風吹動翻騰。⁷這樣的人不要想從主那裏得甚麼。⁸心懷二意的人,在他一切所行的路上都沒有定見。

⁹卑微的弟兄升高,就該喜樂;¹⁰富足的降卑,也該如此。因為他必要過去,如同草上的花一樣,¹¹太陽出來,熱風颳起,草就枯乾,花也凋謝,美容就消沒了;那富足的人在他所行的事上,也要這樣衰殘。

¹²忍受試探的人是有福的,因為他經過試驗以後,必得生命的冠冕,這是主應許給那些愛他之人的。

¹³人被試探,不可說:"我是被神試探",因為神不能被惡試探,他也不試探人。¹⁴但各人被試探,乃是被自己的私慾牽引、誘惑的。¹⁵私慾既懷了胎,就生出罪來;罪既長成,就生出死來。

¹⁶我親愛的弟兄們,不要看錯了。¹⁷各樣美善的恩賜和各樣全備的賞賜都是從上頭來的,從眾光之父那裏降下來的;在他並沒有改變,也沒有轉動的影兒。¹⁸他按自己的旨意,

用真道生了我們，叫我們在他所造的萬物中，好像初熟的果子。

聽道與行道

19我親愛的弟兄們，這是你們所知道的。但你們各人要快快地聽，慢慢地說，慢慢地動怒，20因為人的怒氣並不成就神的義。21所以，你們要脫去一切的污穢和盈餘的邪惡，存溫柔的心領受那所栽種的道，就是能救你們靈魂的道。

22只是你們要行道，不要單單聽道，自己欺哄自己。23因為聽道而不行道的，就像人對着鏡子看自己本來的面目，24看見，走後，隨即忘了他的相貌如何。25惟有詳細察看那全備、使人自由之律法的，並且時常如此，這人既不是聽了就忘，乃是實在行出來，就在他所行的事上必然得福。

26若有人自以為虔誠，卻不勒住他的舌頭，反欺哄自己的心，這人的虔誠是虛的。27在神我們的父面前，那清潔沒有玷污的虔誠，就是看顧在患難中的孤兒寡婦，並且保守自己不沾染世俗。

不可偏心待人

2 我的弟兄們，你們信奉我們榮耀的主耶穌基督，便不可按着外貌待人。2若有一個人戴着金戒指，穿着華美衣服，進你們的會堂去，又有一個窮人，穿着骯髒衣服也進去；3你們就重看那穿華美衣服的人，說："請坐在這好位上"，又對那窮人說："你站在那裏"，或"坐在我腳凳下邊"，4這豈不是你們偏心待人，用惡意斷定人嗎？

5我親愛的弟兄們，請聽！神豈不是揀選了世上的貧窮人，叫他們在信上富足，並承受他所應許給那些愛他之人的國嗎？6你們反倒羞辱貧窮人！那富足人豈不是欺壓你們，拉你們到公堂去嗎？7他們不是褻瀆你們所敬奉（註："所敬奉"或作"被稱"）的尊名嗎？

8經上記着說："要愛人如己。"你們若全守這至尊的律法，才是好的；9但你們若按外貌待人，便是犯

word of truth, that we might be a kind of first-fruits of all he created.

Listening and Doing

19My dear brothers, take note of this: Everyone should be quick to listen, slow to speak and slow to become angry, 20for man's anger does not bring about the righteous life that God desires. 21Therefore, get rid of all moral filth and the evil that is so prevalent and humbly accept the word planted in you, which can save you.

22Do not merely listen to the word, and so deceive yourselves. Do what it says. 23Anyone who listens to the word but does not do what it says is like a man who looks at his face in a mirror 24and, after looking at himself, goes away and immediately forgets what he looks like. 25But the man who looks intently into the perfect law that gives freedom, and continues to do this, not forgetting what he has heard, but doing it—he will be blessed in what he does.

26If anyone considers himself religious and yet does not keep a tight rein on his tongue, he deceives himself and his religion is worthless. 27Religion that God our Father accepts as pure and faultless is this: to look after orphans and widows in their distress and to keep oneself from being polluted by the world.

Favoritism Forbidden

2 My brothers, as believers in our glorious Lord Jesus Christ, don't show favoritism. 2Suppose a man comes into your meeting wearing a gold ring and fine clothes, and a poor man in shabby clothes also comes in. 3If you show special attention to the man wearing fine clothes and say, "Here's a good seat for you," but say to the poor man, "You stand there" or "Sit on the floor by my feet," 4have you not discriminated among yourselves and become judges with evil thoughts?

5Listen, my dear brothers: Has not God chosen those who are poor in the eyes of the world to be rich in faith and to inherit the kingdom he promised those who love him? 6But you have insulted the poor. Is it not the rich who are exploiting you? Are they not the ones who are dragging you into court? 7Are they not the ones who are slandering the noble name of him to whom you belong?

8If you really keep the royal law found in Scripture, "Love your neighbor as yourself,"*a* you are doing right. 9But if you show favoritism,

a 8 Lev. 19:18

you sin and are convicted by the law as law-breakers. [10]For whoever keeps the whole law and yet stumbles at just one point is guilty of breaking all of it. [11]For he who said, "Do not commit adultery,"[a] also said, "Do not murder."[b] If you do not commit adultery but do commit murder, you have become a lawbreaker.

[12]Speak and act as those who are going to be judged by the law that gives freedom, [13]because judgment without mercy will be shown to anyone who has not been merciful. Mercy triumphs over judgment!

Faith and Deeds

[14]What good is it, my brothers, if a man claims to have faith but has no deeds? Can such faith save him? [15]Suppose a brother or sister is without clothes and daily food. [16]If one of you says to him, "Go, I wish you well; keep warm and well fed," but does nothing about his physical needs, what good is it? [17]In the same way, faith by itself, if it is not accompanied by action, is dead.

[18]But someone will say, "You have faith; I have deeds."

Show me your faith without deeds, and I will show you my faith by what I do. [19]You believe that there is one God. Good! Even the demons believe that—and shudder.

[20]You foolish man, do you want evidence that faith without deeds is useless[c]? [21]Was not our ancestor Abraham considered righteous for what he did when he offered his son Isaac on the altar? [22]You see that his faith and his actions were working together, and his faith was made complete by what he did. [23]And the scripture was fulfilled that says, "Abraham believed God, and it was credited to him as righteousness,"[d] and he was called God's friend. [24]You see that a person is justified by what he does and not by faith alone.

[25]In the same way, was not even Rahab the prostitute considered righteous for what she did when she gave lodging to the spies and sent them off in a different direction? [26]As the body without the spirit is dead, so faith without deeds is dead.

Taming the Tongue

3 Not many of you should presume to be teachers, my brothers, because you know that we who teach will be judged more strictly. [2]We all stumble in many ways. If

罪，被律法定為犯法的。[10]因為凡遵守全律法的，只在一條上跌倒，他就是犯了眾條。[11]原來那說"不可姦淫"的，也說"不可殺人"。你就是不姦淫，卻殺人，仍是成了犯律法的。

[12]你們既然要按使人自由的律法受審判，就該照這律法說話行事。[13]因為那不憐憫人的，也要受無憐憫的審判，憐憫原是向審判誇勝。

信心與行為

[14]我的弟兄們，若有人說自己有信心，卻沒有行為，有甚麼益處呢？這信心能救他嗎？[15]若是弟兄或是姐妹，赤身露體，又缺了日用的飲食，[16]你們中間有人對他們說："平平安安地去吧！願你們穿得暖吃得飽"，卻不給他們身體所需用的，這有甚麼益處呢？[17]這樣，信心若沒有行為就是死的。

[18]必有人說："你有信心，我有行為。"

你將你沒有行為的信心指給我看，我便藉着我的行為，將我的信心指給你看。[19]你信神只有一位，你信的不錯！鬼魔也信，卻是戰驚。

[20]虛浮的人哪，你願意知道沒有行為的信心是死的嗎？[21]我們的祖宗亞伯拉罕把他兒子以撒獻在壇上，豈不是因行為稱義嗎？[22]可見信心是與他的行為並行，而且信心因着行為才得成全。[23]這就應驗經上所說："亞伯拉罕信神，這就算為他的義。"他又得稱為神的朋友。[24]這樣看來，人稱義是因着行為，不是單因着信。

[25]妓女喇合接待使者，又放他們從別的路上出去，不也是一樣因行為稱義嗎？[26]身體沒有靈魂是死的，信心沒有行為也是死的。

制伏舌頭

3 我的弟兄們，不要多人作師傅，因為曉得我們要受更重的判斷。[2]原來我們在許多事上都有過失；若有人在話語上沒有過

失，他就是完全人，也能勒住自己的全身。

3我們若把嚼環放在馬嘴裏，叫牠順服，就能調動牠的全身。4看哪，船隻雖然甚大，又被大風催逼，只用小小的舵，就隨着掌舵的意思轉動。5這樣，舌頭在百體裏也是最小的，卻能說大話。看哪，最小的火能點着最大的樹林；6舌頭就是火，在我們百體中，舌頭是個罪惡的世界，能污穢全身，也能把生命的輪子點起來，並且是從地獄裏點着的。

7各類的走獸、飛禽、昆蟲、水族，本來都可以制伏，也已經被人制伏了；8惟獨舌頭沒有人能制伏，是不止息的惡物，滿了害死人的毒氣。9我們用舌頭頌讚那為主、為父的，又用舌頭咒詛那照着神形像被造的人。10頌讚和咒詛從一個口裏出來，我的弟兄們，這是不應當的。11泉源從一個眼裏能發出甜苦兩樣的水嗎？12我的弟兄們，無花果樹能生橄欖嗎？葡萄樹能結無花果嗎？鹹水裏也不能發出甜水來。

兩種智慧

13你們中間誰是有智慧、有見識的呢？他就當在智慧的溫柔上顯出他的善行來。14你們心裏若懷着苦毒的嫉妒和紛爭，就不可自誇，也不可說謊話抵擋真道。15這樣的智慧不是從上頭來的，乃是屬地的、屬情慾的、屬鬼魔的。16在何處有嫉妒紛爭，就在何處有擾亂和各樣的壞事。

17惟獨從上頭來的智慧，先是清潔，後是和平，溫良柔順，滿有憐憫，多結善果，沒有偏見，沒有假冒。18並且使人和平的，是用和平所栽種的義果。

你們要順服神

4 你們中間的爭戰、鬥毆，是從哪裏來的呢？不是從你們百體中戰鬥之私慾來的嗎？2你們貪戀，還是得不着；你們殺害嫉妒，又鬥毆爭戰，也不能得。你

anyone is never at fault in what he says, he is a perfect man, able to keep his whole body in check.

3When we put bits into the mouths of horses to make them obey us, we can turn the whole animal. 4Or take ships as an example. Although they are so large and are driven by strong winds, they are steered by a very small rudder wherever the pilot wants to go. 5Likewise the tongue is a small part of the body, but it makes great boasts. Consider what a great forest is set on fire by a small spark. 6The tongue also is a fire, a world of evil among the parts of the body. It corrupts the whole person, sets the whole course of his life on fire, and is itself set on fire by hell.

7All kinds of animals, birds, reptiles and creatures of the sea are being tamed and have been tamed by man, 8but no man can tame the tongue. It is a restless evil, full of deadly poison.

9With the tongue we praise our Lord and Father, and with it we curse men, who have been made in God's likeness. 10Out of the same mouth come praise and cursing. My brothers, this should not be. 11Can both fresh water and salt*a* water flow from the same spring? 12My brothers, can a fig tree bear olives, or a grapevine bear figs? Neither can a salt spring produce fresh water.

Two Kinds of Wisdom

13Who is wise and understanding among you? Let him show it by his good life, by deeds done in the humility that comes from wisdom. 14But if you harbor bitter envy and selfish ambition in your hearts, do not boast about it or deny the truth. 15Such "wisdom" does not come down from heaven but is earthly, unspiritual, of the devil. 16For where you have envy and selfish ambition, there you find disorder and every evil practice.

17But the wisdom that comes from heaven is first of all pure; then peace-loving, considerate, submissive, full of mercy and good fruit, impartial and sincere. 18Peacemakers who sow in peace raise a harvest of righteousness.

Submit Yourselves to God

4 What causes fights and quarrels among you? Don't they come from your desires that battle within you? 2You want something but don't get it. You kill and covet, but you cannot have what you want. You quarrel and fight. You do not have, because you do not

a 11 Greek *bitter* (see also verse 14)

ask God. ³When you ask, you do not receive, because you ask with wrong motives, that you may spend what you get on your pleasures.

⁴You adulterous people, don't you know that friendship with the world is hatred toward God? Anyone who chooses to be a friend of the world becomes an enemy of God. ⁵Or do you think Scripture says without reason that the spirit he caused to live in us envies intensely?ᵃ ⁶But he gives us more grace. That is why Scripture says:

> "God opposes the proud
> but gives grace to the humble."ᵇ

⁷Submit yourselves, then, to God. Resist the devil, and he will flee from you. ⁸Come near to God and he will come near to you. Wash your hands, you sinners, and purify your hearts, you double-minded. ⁹Grieve, mourn and wail. Change your laughter to mourning and your joy to gloom. ¹⁰Humble yourselves before the Lord, and he will lift you up.

¹¹Brothers, do not slander one another. Anyone who speaks against his brother or judges him speaks against the law and judges it. When you judge the law, you are not keeping it, but sitting in judgment on it. ¹²There is only one Lawgiver and Judge, the one who is able to save and destroy. But you—who are you to judge your neighbor?

Boasting About Tomorrow

¹³Now listen, you who say, "Today or tomorrow we will go to this or that city, spend a year there, carry on business and make money." ¹⁴Why, you do not even know what will happen tomorrow. What is your life? You are a mist that appears for a little while and then vanishes. ¹⁵Instead, you ought to say, "If it is the Lord's will, we will live and do this or that." ¹⁶As it is, you boast and brag. All such boasting is evil. ¹⁷Anyone, then, who knows the good he ought to do and doesn't do it, sins.

Warning to Rich Oppressors

5 Now listen, you rich people, weep and wail because of the misery that is coming upon you. ²Your wealth has rotted, and moths have eaten your clothes. ³Your gold and silver are corroded. Their corrosion will testify against you and eat your flesh like fire. You

---

a 5 Or that God jealously longs for the spirit that he made to live in us; or that the Spirit he caused to live in us longs jealously
b 6 Prov. 3:34

們得不着，是因為你們不求；³你們求也得不着，是因為你們妄求，要浪費在你們的宴樂中。

⁴你們這些淫亂的人哪（註："淫亂的人"原文作"淫婦"），豈不知與世俗為友就是與神為敵嗎？所以凡想要與世俗為友的，就是與神為敵了。⁵你們想經上所說是徒然的嗎？神所賜住在我們裏面的靈，是戀愛至於嫉妒嗎？⁶但他賜更多的恩典，所以經上說：

> "神阻擋驕傲的人，
> 賜恩給謙卑的人。"

⁷故此，你們要順服神。務要抵擋魔鬼，魔鬼就必離開你們逃跑了。⁸你們親近神，神就必親近你們。有罪的人哪，要潔淨你們的手；心懷二意的人哪，要清潔你們的心。⁹你們要愁苦、悲哀、哭泣，將喜笑變作悲哀，歡樂變作愁悶。¹⁰務要在主面前自卑，主就必叫你們升高。

¹¹弟兄們，你們不可彼此批評。人若批評弟兄，論斷弟兄，就是批評律法，論斷律法。你若論斷律法，就不是遵行律法，乃是判斷人的。¹²設立律法和判斷人的，只有一位，就是那能救人也能滅人的。你是誰，竟敢論斷別人呢？

勿為明天誇口

¹³嗐！你們有話說："今天、明天我們要往某城裏去，在那裏住一年，做買賣得利。"¹⁴其實明天如何，你們還不知道。你們的生命是甚麼呢？你們原來是一片雲霧，出現少時就不見了。¹⁵你們只當說："主若願意，我們就可以活着，也可以做這事，或做那事。"¹⁶現今你們竟以張狂誇口；凡這樣誇口都是惡的。¹⁷人若知道行善，卻不去行，這就是他的罪了。

警告富足的壓迫者

5 嗐！你們這些富足人哪，應當哭泣、號咷，因為將有苦難臨到你們身上。²你們的財物壞了，衣服也被蟲子咬了。³你們的金銀都長了銹；那銹要證明你們的不是，又要吃你們的肉，如同火燒。

你們在這末世只知積攢錢財。⁴工人給你們收割莊稼，你們虧欠他們的工錢；這工錢有聲音呼叫，並且那收割之人的冤聲已經入了萬軍之主的耳了。⁵你們在世上享美福，好宴樂，當宰殺的日子竟嬌養你們的心。⁶你們定了義人的罪，把他殺害，他也不抵擋你們。

在苦難中忍耐

⁷弟兄們哪，你們要忍耐，直到主來。看哪，農夫忍耐等候地裏寶貴的出產，直到得了秋雨春雨。⁸你們也當忍耐，堅固你們的心，因為主來的日子近了。⁹弟兄們，你們不要彼此埋怨，免得受審判。看哪，審判的主站在門前了！

¹⁰弟兄們，你們要把那先前奉主名說話的眾先知，當作能受苦能忍耐的榜樣。¹¹那先前忍耐的人，我們稱他們是有福的。你們聽見過約伯的忍耐，也知道主給他的結局，明顯主是滿心憐憫，大有慈悲。

¹²我的弟兄們，最要緊的是不可起誓。不可指着天起誓，也不可指着地起誓，無論何誓都不可起。你們說話，是就說是，不是就說不是，免得你們落在審判之下。

信心的禱告

¹³你們中間有受苦的呢，他就該禱告；有喜樂的呢，他就該歌頌。¹⁴你們中間有病了的呢，他就請教會的長老來，他們可以奉主的名用油抹他，為他禱告。¹⁵出於信心的祈禱要救那病人，主必叫他起來；他若犯了罪，也必蒙赦免。¹⁶所以你們要彼此認罪，互相代求，使你們可以得醫治。義人祈禱所發的力量是大有功效的。

¹⁷以利亞與我們是一樣性情的人，他懇切禱告，求不要下雨，雨就三年零六個月不下在地上。¹⁸他又禱告，天就降下雨來，地也生出土產。

¹⁹我的弟兄們，你們中間若有失迷真道的，有人使他回轉，²⁰這人該知道，叫一個罪人從迷路上轉回，便是救一個靈魂不死，並且遮蓋許多的罪。

have hoarded wealth in the last days. ⁴Look! The wages you failed to pay the workmen who mowed your fields are crying out against you. The cries of the harvesters have reached the ears of the Lord Almighty. ⁵You have lived on earth in luxury and self-indulgence. You have fattened yourselves in the day of slaughter.ª ⁶You have condemned and murdered innocent men, who were not opposing you.

Patience in Suffering

⁷Be patient, then, brothers, until the Lord's coming. See how the farmer waits for the land to yield its valuable crop and how patient he is for the autumn and spring rains. ⁸You too, be patient and stand firm, because the Lord's coming is near. ⁹Don't grumble against each other, brothers, or you will be judged. The Judge is standing at the door!

¹⁰Brothers, as an example of patience in the face of suffering, take the prophets who spoke in the name of the Lord. ¹¹As you know, we consider blessed those who have persevered. You have heard of Job's perseverance and have seen what the Lord finally brought about. The Lord is full of compassion and mercy.

¹²Above all, my brothers, do not swear—not by heaven or by earth or by anything else. Let your "Yes" be yes, and your "No," no, or you will be condemned.

The Prayer of Faith

¹³Is any one of you in trouble? He should pray. Is anyone happy? Let him sing songs of praise. ¹⁴Is any one of you sick? He should call the elders of the church to pray over him and anoint him with oil in the name of the Lord. ¹⁵And the prayer offered in faith will make the sick person well; the Lord will raise him up. If he has sinned, he will be forgiven. ¹⁶Therefore confess your sins to each other and pray for each other so that you may be healed. The prayer of a righteous man is powerful and effective.

¹⁷Elijah was a man just like us. He prayed earnestly that it would not rain, and it did not rain on the land for three and a half years. ¹⁸Again he prayed, and the heavens gave rain, and the earth produced its crops.

¹⁹My brothers, if one of you should wander from the truth and someone should bring him back, ²⁰remember this: Whoever turns a sinner from the error of his way will save him from death and cover over a multitude of sins.

a 5 Or yourselves as in a day of feasting

1 Peter

1 Peter, an apostle of Jesus Christ,

To God's elect, strangers in the world, scattered throughout Pontus, Galatia, Cappadocia, Asia and Bithynia, ²who have been chosen according to the foreknowledge of God the Father, through the sanctifying work of the Spirit, for obedience to Jesus Christ and sprinkling by his blood:

Grace and peace be yours in abundance.

Praise to God for a Living Hope

³Praise be to the God and Father of our Lord Jesus Christ! In his great mercy he has given us new birth into a living hope through the resurrection of Jesus Christ from the dead, ⁴and into an inheritance that can never perish, spoil or fade—kept in heaven for you, ⁵who through faith are shielded by God's power until the coming of the salvation that is ready to be revealed in the last time. ⁶In this you greatly rejoice, though now for a little while you may have had to suffer grief in all kinds of trials. ⁷These have come so that your faith—of greater worth than gold, which perishes even though refined by fire—may be proved genuine and may result in praise, glory and honor when Jesus Christ is revealed. ⁸Though you have not seen him, you love him; and even though you do not see him now, you believe in him and are filled with an inexpressible and glorious joy, ⁹for you are receiving the goal of your faith, the salvation of your souls.

¹⁰Concerning this salvation, the prophets, who spoke of the grace that was to come to you, searched intently and with the greatest care, ¹¹trying to find out the time and circumstances to which the Spirit of Christ in them was pointing when he predicted the sufferings of Christ and the glories that would follow. ¹²It was revealed to them that they were not serving themselves but you, when they spoke of the things that have now been told you by those who have preached the gospel to you by the Holy Spirit sent from heaven. Even angels long to look into these things.

彼得前書

1 耶穌基督的使徒彼得，

寫信給那分散在本都、加拉太、加帕多家、亞西亞、庇推尼寄居的，²就是照父神的先見被揀選，藉着聖靈得成聖潔，以至順服耶穌基督，又蒙他血所灑的人：

願恩惠、平安多多地加給你們！

因活潑的盼望頌讚神

³願頌讚歸與我們主耶穌基督的父神。他曾照自己的大憐憫，藉耶穌基督從死裏復活，重生了我們，叫我們有活潑的盼望，⁴可以得着不能朽壞、不能玷污、不能衰殘、為你們存留在天上的基業。⁵你們這因信蒙神能力保守的人，必能得着所預備、到末世要顯現的救恩。⁶因此，你們是大有喜樂。但如今在百般的試煉中暫時憂愁，⁷叫你們的信心既被試驗，就比那被火試驗仍然能壞的金子更顯寶貴，可以在耶穌基督顯現的時候，得着稱讚、榮耀、尊貴。⁸你們雖然沒有見過他，卻是愛他；如今雖不得看見，卻因信他就有說不出來、滿有榮光的大喜樂，⁹並且得着你們信心的果效，就是靈魂的救恩。

¹⁰論到這救恩，那預先說你們要得恩典的眾先知早已詳細地尋求考察，¹¹就是考察在他們心裏基督的靈，預先證明基督受苦難，後來得榮耀，是指着甚麼時候，並怎樣的時候。¹²他們得了啟示，知道他們所傳講的一切事（註："傳講"原文作"服侍"），不是為自己，乃是為你們。那靠着從天上差來的聖靈傳福音給你們的人，現在將這些事報給你們，天使也願意詳細察看這些事。

務要聖潔

13所以要約束你們的心（註：原文作"束上你們心中的腰"），謹慎自守，專心盼望耶穌基督顯現的時候所帶來給你們的恩。14你們既作順命的兒女，就不要效法從前蒙昧無知的時候那放縱私慾的樣子。15那召你們的既是聖潔，你們在一切所行的事上也要聖潔。16因為經上記着說："你們要聖潔，因為我是聖潔的。"

17你們既稱那不偏待人、按各人行為審判人的主為父，就當存敬畏的心，度你們在世寄居的日子，18知道你們得贖、脫去你們祖宗所傳流虛妄的行為，不是憑着能壞的金銀等物，19乃是憑着基督的寶血，如同無瑕疵、無玷污的羔羊之血。20基督在創世以前是預先被神知道的，卻在這末世才為你們顯現。21你們也因着他，信那叫他從死裏復活，又給他榮耀的神，叫你們的信心和盼望都在於神。

22你們既因順從真理，潔淨了自己的心，以致愛弟兄沒有虛假，就當從心裏彼此切實相愛（註："從心裏"有古卷作"從清潔的心"）。23你們蒙了重生，不是由於能壞的種子，乃是由於不能壞的種子，是藉着神活潑常存的道。24因為：

"凡有血氣的，盡都如草，
　他的美榮都像草上的花。
草必枯乾，
　花必凋謝；
25惟有主的道是永存的。"

所傳給你們的福音就是這道。

2 所以，你們既除去一切的惡毒（註：或作"陰毒"）、詭詐並假善、嫉妒和一切毀謗的話，2就要愛慕那純淨的靈奶，像才生的嬰孩愛慕奶一樣，叫你們因此漸長，以至得救。3你們若嘗過主恩的滋味，就必如此。

活石與被揀選的族類

4主乃活石，固然是被人所棄的，卻是被神所揀選、所寶貴的。5你們來到主面前，也就像活石，被建造成為靈宮，作聖潔的祭司，藉着耶穌基督奉獻神所悅納的靈祭。6因為經上說：

Be Holy

13Therefore, prepare your minds for action; be self-controlled; set your hope fully on the grace to be given you when Jesus Christ is revealed. 14As obedient children, do not conform to the evil desires you had when you lived in ignorance. 15But just as he who called you is holy, so be holy in all you do; 16for it is written: "Be holy, because I am holy."[a]

17Since you call on a Father who judges each man's work impartially, live your lives as strangers here in reverent fear. 18For you know that it was not with perishable things such as silver or gold that you were redeemed from the empty way of life handed down to you from your forefathers, 19but with the precious blood of Christ, a lamb without blemish or defect. 20He was chosen before the creation of the world, but was revealed in these last times for your sake. 21Through him you believe in God, who raised him from the dead and glorified him, and so your faith and hope are in God.

22Now that you have purified yourselves by obeying the truth so that you have sincere love for your brothers, love one another deeply, from the heart.[b] 23For you have been born again, not of perishable seed, but of imperishable, through the living and enduring word of God. 24For,

"All men are like grass,
　and all their glory is like the flowers of the field;
the grass withers and the flowers fall,
25　but the word of the Lord stands forever."[c]

And this is the word that was preached to you.

2 Therefore, rid yourselves of all malice and all deceit, hypocrisy, envy, and slander of every kind. 2Like newborn babies, crave pure spiritual milk, so that by it you may grow up in your salvation, 3now that you have tasted that the Lord is good.

The Living Stone and a Chosen People

4As you come to him, the living Stone—rejected by men but chosen by God and precious to him— 5you also, like living stones, are being built into a spiritual house to be a holy priesthood, offering spiritual sacrifices acceptable to God through Jesus Christ. 6For in Scripture it says:

a 16 Lev. 11:44,45; 19:2; 20:7　　b 22 Some early manuscripts from a pure heart　　c 25 Isaiah 40:6-8

"See, I lay a stone in Zion,
   a chosen and precious cornerstone,
and the one who trusts in him
   will never be put to shame."[a]

[7]Now to you who believe, this stone is precious. But to those who do not believe,

"The stone the builders rejected
   has become the capstone,"[b][c]

[8]and,

"A stone that causes men to stumble
   and a rock that makes them fall."[d]

They stumble because they disobey the message—which is also what they were destined for. [9]But you are a chosen people, a royal priesthood, a holy nation, a people belonging to God, that you may declare the praises of him who called you out of darkness into his wonderful light. [10]Once you were not a people, but now you are the people of God; once you had not received mercy, but now you have received mercy.

[11]Dear friends, I urge you, as aliens and strangers in the world, to abstain from sinful desires, which war against your soul. [12]Live such good lives among the pagans that, though they accuse you of doing wrong, they may see your good deeds and glorify God on the day he visits us.

Submission to Rulers and Masters

[13]Submit yourselves for the Lord's sake to every authority instituted among men: whether to the king, as the supreme authority, [14]or to governors, who are sent by him to punish those who do wrong and to commend those who do right. [15]For it is God's will that by doing good you should silence the ignorant talk of foolish men. [16]Live as free men, but do not use your freedom as a cover-up for evil; live as servants of God. [17]Show proper respect to everyone: Love the brotherhood of believers, fear God, honor the king.

[18]Slaves, submit yourselves to your masters with all respect, not only to those who are good and considerate, but also to those who are harsh. [19]For it is commendable if a man bears up under the pain of unjust suffering because he is

"看哪,我把所揀選、所寶貴的
   房角石安放在錫安,
信靠他的人
   必不至於羞愧。"

[7]所以,他在你們信的人就為寶貴,在那不信的人有話說:

"匠人所棄的石頭,
   已作了房角的頭塊石頭。"

[8]又說:

"作了絆腳的石頭,
   跌人的磐石。"

他們既不順從,就在道理上絆跌(註:或作"他們絆跌都因不順從道理")。他們這樣絆跌,也是豫定的。[9]惟有你們是被揀選的族類,是有君尊的祭司,是聖潔的國度,是屬神的子民,要叫你們宣揚那召你們出黑暗、入奇妙光明者的美德。[10]你們從前算不得子民,現在卻作了神的子民;從前未曾蒙憐恤,現在卻蒙了憐恤。

[11]親愛的弟兄啊,你們是客旅,是寄居的。我勸你們要禁戒肉體的私慾;這私慾是與靈魂爭戰的。[12]你們在外邦人中,應當品行端正,叫那些毀謗你們是作惡的,因看見你們的好行為,便在鑒察的日子(註:"鑒察"或作"眷顧")歸榮耀給神。

順服掌權者及主人

[13]你們為主的緣故,要順服人的一切制度,或是在上的君王,[14]或是君王所派罰惡賞善的臣宰。[15]因為神的旨意原是要你們行善,可以堵住那糊塗無知人的口。[16]你們雖是自由的,卻不可藉著自由遮蓋惡毒(註:或作"陰毒"),總要作神的僕人。[17]務要尊敬眾人,親愛教中的弟兄,敬畏神,尊敬君王。

[18]你們作僕人的,凡事要存敬畏的心順服主人;不但順服那善良溫和的,就是那乖僻的也要順服。[19]倘若人為叫良心對得住神,就忍受冤屈的

---

a 6 Isaiah 28:16   *b 7* Or *cornerstone*   *c 7* Psalm 118:22
d 8 Isaiah 8:14

苦楚，這是可喜愛的。²⁰你們若因犯罪受責打，能忍耐，有甚麼可誇的呢？但你們若因行善受苦，能忍耐，這在神看是可喜愛的。²¹你們蒙召原是為此，因基督也為你們受過苦，給你們留下榜樣，叫你們跟隨他的腳蹤行。

²² "他並沒有犯罪，
　　口裏也沒有詭詐。"

²³他被罵不還口，受害不說威嚇的話，只將自己交託那按公義審判人的主。²⁴他被掛在木頭上，親身擔當了我們的罪，使我們既然在罪上死，就得以在義上活。因他受的鞭傷，你們便得了醫治。²⁵你們從前好像迷路的羊，如今卻歸到你們靈魂的牧人監督了。

妻子與丈夫

3 你們作妻子的，要順服自己的丈夫。這樣，若有不信從道理的丈夫，他們雖然不聽道，也可以因妻子的品行被感化過來。²這正是因看見你們有貞潔的品行和敬畏的心。³你們不要以外面的辮頭髮、戴金飾、穿美衣為妝飾，⁴只要以裏面存着長久溫柔、安靜的心為妝飾，這在神面前是極寶貴的。⁵因為古時仰賴神的聖潔婦人，正是以此為妝飾，順服自己的丈夫，⁶就如撒拉聽從亞伯拉罕，稱他為主。你們若行善，不因恐嚇而害怕，便是撒拉的女兒了。

⁷你們作丈夫的，也要按情理和妻子同住（註："情理" 原文作 "知識"），因她比你軟弱（註："比你軟弱" 原文作 "是軟弱的器皿"），與你一同承受生命之恩的，所以要敬重她。這樣，便叫你們的禱告沒有阻礙。

因行善受苦

⁸總而言之，你們都要同心，彼此體恤，相愛如弟兄，存慈憐謙卑的心；⁹不以惡報惡、以辱罵還辱罵，倒要祝福；因你們是為此蒙召，好叫你們承受福氣。¹⁰因為經上說：

conscious of God. ²⁰But how is it to your credit if you receive a beating for doing wrong and endure it? But if you suffer for doing good and you endure it, this is commendable before God. ²¹To this you were called, because Christ suffered for you, leaving you an example, that you should follow in his steps.

²²"He committed no sin,
　　and no deceit was found in his mouth."[a]

²³When they hurled their insults at him, he did not retaliate; when he suffered, he made no threats. Instead, he entrusted himself to him who judges justly. ²⁴He himself bore our sins in his body on the tree, so that we might die to sins and live for righteousness; by his wounds you have been healed. ²⁵For you were like sheep going astray, but now you have returned to the Shepherd and Overseer of your souls.

Wives and Husbands

3 Wives, in the same way be submissive to your husbands so that, if any of them do not believe the word, they may be won over without words by the behavior of their wives, ²when they see the purity and reverence of your lives. ³Your beauty should not come from outward adornment, such as braided hair and the wearing of gold jewelry and fine clothes. ⁴Instead, it should be that of your inner self, the unfading beauty of a gentle and quiet spirit, which is of great worth in God's sight. ⁵For this is the way the holy women of the past who put their hope in God used to make themselves beautiful. They were submissive to their own husbands, ⁶like Sarah, who obeyed Abraham and called him her master. You are her daughters if you do what is right and do not give way to fear.

⁷Husbands, in the same way be considerate as you live with your wives, and treat them with respect as the weaker partner and as heirs with you of the gracious gift of life, so that nothing will hinder your prayers.

Suffering for Doing Good

⁸Finally, all of you, live in harmony with one another; be sympathetic, love as brothers, be compassionate and humble. ⁹Do not repay evil with evil or insult with insult, but with blessing, because to this you were called so that you may inherit a blessing. ¹⁰For,

a 22 Isaiah 53:9

"Whoever would love life
　　and see good days
must keep his tongue from evil
　　and his lips from deceitful speech.
[11]He must turn from evil and do good;
　　he must seek peace and pursue it.
[12]For the eyes of the Lord are on the righteous
　　and his ears are attentive to their prayer,
but the face of the Lord is against those who
　　do evil."[a]

[13]Who is going to harm you if you are eager to do good? [14]But even if you should suffer for what is right, you are blessed. "Do not fear what they fear[b]; do not be frightened."[c] [15]But in your hearts set apart Christ as Lord. Always be prepared to give an answer to everyone who asks you to give the reason for the hope that you have. But do this with gentleness and respect, [16]keeping a clear conscience, so that those who speak maliciously against your good behavior in Christ may be ashamed of their slander. [17]It is better, if it is God's will, to suffer for doing good than for doing evil. [18]For Christ died for sins once for all, the righteous for the unrighteous, to bring you to God. He was put to death in the body but made alive by the Spirit, [19]through whom[d] also he went and preached to the spirits in prison [20]who disobeyed long ago when God waited patiently in the days of Noah while the ark was being built. In it only a few people, eight in all, were saved through water, [21]and this water symbolizes baptism that now saves you also—not the removal of dirt from the body but the pledge[e] of a good conscience toward God. It saves you by the resurrection of Jesus Christ, [22]who has gone into heaven and is at God's right hand—with angels, authorities and powers in submission to him.

Living for God

4 Therefore, since Christ suffered in his body, arm yourselves also with the same attitude, because he who has suffered in his body is done with sin. [2]As a result, he does not live the rest of his earthly life for evil human desires, but rather for the will of God. [3]For you have spent enough time in the past doing what pagans choose to do—living in debauchery, lust, drunkenness, orgies, carousing and detestable idolatry. [4]They think it strange that you do not plunge with them into

"人若愛生命，
　　願享美福，
須要禁止舌頭不出惡言，
　　嘴唇不説詭詐的話；
[11]也要離惡行善，
　　尋求和睦，一心追趕。
[12]因為主的眼看顧義人，
　　主的耳聽他們的祈禱；
惟有行惡的人，
　　主向他們變臉。"

[13]你們若是熱心行善，有誰害你們呢？[14]你們就是為義受苦，也是有福的。不要怕人的威嚇，也不要驚慌（註："的威嚇"或作"所怕的"），[15]只要心裏尊主基督為聖。有人問你們心中盼望的緣由，就要常作準備，以溫柔、敬畏的心回答各人。[16]存着無虧的良心，叫你們在何事上被毀謗，就在何事上可以叫那誣賴你們在基督裏有好品行的人自覺羞愧。[17]神的旨意若是叫你們因行善受苦，總強如因行惡受苦。[18]因基督也曾一次為罪受苦（註："受苦"有古卷作"受死"），就是義的代替不義的，為要引我們到神面前。按着肉體説，他被治死；按着靈性説，他復活了。[19]他藉這靈曾去傳道給那些在監獄裏的靈聽，[20]就是那從前在挪亞預備方舟、神容忍等待的時候，不信從的人。當時進入方舟，藉着水得救的不多，只有八個人。[21]這水所表明的洗禮，現在藉着耶穌基督復活，也拯救你們；這洗禮本不在乎除掉肉體的污穢，只求在神面前有無虧的良心。[22]耶穌已經進入天堂，在神的右邊，眾天使和有權柄的，並有能力的，都服從了他。

為神而活

4 基督既在肉身受苦，你們也當將這樣的心志作為兵器，因為在肉身受過苦的，就已經與罪斷絕了。[2]你們存這樣的心，從今以後，就可以不從人的情慾，只從神的旨意在世度餘下的光陰。[3]因為往日隨從外邦人的心意行邪淫、惡慾、醉酒、荒宴、羣飲，並可惡拜偶像的事，時候已經夠了。[4]他們在這些事上，見你們不與他們同奔那放蕩

a 12 Psalm 34:12-16　　b 14 Or not fear their threats　　c 14 Isaiah 8:12　　d 18,19 Or alive in the spirit, 19 through which　　e 21 Or response

無度的路，就以為怪，毀謗你們。5他們必在那將要審判活人死人的主面前交賬。6為此，就是死人也曾有福音傳給他們，要叫他們的肉體按着人受審判，他們的靈性卻靠神活着。

7萬物的結局近了，所以你們要謹慎自守，警醒禱告。8最要緊的是彼此切實相愛，因為愛能遮掩許多的罪。9你們要互相款待，不發怨言。10各人要照所得的恩賜彼此服侍，作神百般恩賜的好管家。11若有講道的，要按着神的聖言講；若有服侍人的，要按着神所賜的力量服侍，叫神在凡事上因耶穌基督得榮耀。原來榮耀、權能都是他的，直到永永遠遠。阿們！

因作基督徒受苦

12親愛的弟兄啊，有火煉的試驗臨到你們，不要以為奇怪（似乎是遭遇非常的事），13倒要歡喜。因為你們是與基督一同受苦，使你們在他榮耀顯現的時候，也可以歡喜快樂。14你們若為基督的名受辱罵，便是有福的，因為神榮耀的靈常住在你們身上。15你們中間卻不可有人因為殺人、偷竊、作惡、好管閒事而受苦；16若為作基督徒受苦，卻不要羞恥，倒要因這名歸榮耀給神。17因為時候到了，審判要從神的家起首。若是先從我們起首，那不信從神福音的人將有何等的結局呢？

18 "若是義人僅僅得救，
　　那不虔敬和犯罪的人
　　將有何地可站呢？"

19所以，那照神旨意受苦的人要一心為善，將自己靈魂交與那信實的造化之主。

致長老和年幼的

5 我這作長老、作基督受苦的見證、同享後來所要顯現之榮耀的，勸你們中間與我同作長老的人：2務要牧養你們中間

the same flood of dissipation, and they heap abuse on you. 5But they will have to give account to him who is ready to judge the living and the dead. 6For this is the reason the gospel was preached even to those who are now dead, so that they might be judged according to men in regard to the body, but live according to God in regard to the spirit.

7The end of all things is near. Therefore be clear minded and self-controlled so that you can pray. 8Above all, love each other deeply, because love covers over a multitude of sins. 9Offer hospitality to one another without grumbling. 10Each one should use whatever gift he has received to serve others, faithfully administering God's grace in its various forms. 11If anyone speaks, he should do it as one speaking the very words of God. If anyone serves, he should do it with the strength God provides, so that in all things God may be praised through Jesus Christ. To him be the glory and the power for ever and ever. Amen.

Suffering for Being a Christian

12Dear friends, do not be surprised at the painful trial you are suffering, as though something strange were happening to you. 13But rejoice that you participate in the sufferings of Christ, so that you may be overjoyed when his glory is revealed. 14If you are insulted because of the name of Christ, you are blessed, for the Spirit of glory and of God rests on you. 15If you suffer, it should not be as a murderer or thief or any other kind of criminal, or even as a meddler. 16However, if you suffer as a Christian, do not be ashamed, but praise God that you bear that name. 17For it is time for judgment to begin with the family of God; and if it begins with us, what will the outcome be for those who do not obey the gospel of God? 18And,

"If it is hard for the righteous to be saved,
　　what will become of the ungodly and the
　　sinner?"[a]

19So then, those who suffer according to God's will should commit themselves to their faithful Creator and continue to do good.

To Elders and Young Men

5 To the elders among you, I appeal as a fellow elder, a witness of Christ's sufferings and one who also will share in the glory to be revealed: 2Be shepherds of God's

a 18 Prov. 11:31

flock that is under your care, serving as over-seers—not because you must, but because you are willing, as God wants you to be; not greedy for money, but eager to serve; ³not lording it over those entrusted to you, but being examples to the flock. ⁴And when the Chief Shepherd appears, you will receive the crown of glory that will never fade away.

⁵Young men, in the same way be submissive to those who are older. All of you, clothe yourselves with humility toward one another, because,

"God opposes the proud
  but gives grace to the humble."ᵃ

⁶Humble yourselves, therefore, under God's mighty hand, that he may lift you up in due time. ⁷Cast all your anxiety on him because he cares for you.

⁸Be self-controlled and alert. Your enemy the devil prowls around like a roaring lion looking for someone to devour. ⁹Resist him, standing firm in the faith, because you know that your brothers throughout the world are undergoing the same kind of sufferings.

¹⁰And the God of all grace, who called you to his eternal glory in Christ, after you have suffered a little while, will himself restore you and make you strong, firm and steadfast. ¹¹To him be the power for ever and ever. Amen.

Final Greetings

¹²With the help of Silas,ᵇ whom I regard as a faithful brother, I have written to you briefly, encouraging you and testifying that this is the true grace of God. Stand fast in it.

¹³She who is in Babylon, chosen together with you, sends you her greetings, and so does my son Mark. ¹⁴Greet one another with a kiss of love.

Peace to all of you who are in Christ.

神的羣羊，按着神旨意照管他們；不是出於勉強，乃是出於甘心；也不是因為貪財，乃是出於樂意；³也不是轄制所託付你們的，乃是作羣羊的榜樣。⁴到了牧長顯現的時候，你們必得那永不衰殘的榮耀冠冕。

⁵你們年幼的也要順服年長的。就是你們眾人也都要以謙卑束腰，彼此順服，

"因為神阻擋驕傲的人，
  賜恩給謙卑的人。"

⁶所以你們要自卑，服在神大能的手下，到了時候，他必叫你們升高。⁷你們要將一切的憂慮卸給神，因為他顧念你們。

⁸務要謹守、警醒，因為你們的仇敵魔鬼，如同吼叫的獅子，遍地游行，尋找可吞吃的人。⁹你們要用堅固的信心抵擋他，因為知道你們在世上的眾弟兄也是經歷這樣的苦難。

¹⁰那賜諸般恩典的神曾在基督裏召你們，得享他永遠的榮耀，等你們暫受苦難之後，必要親自成全你們，堅固你們，賜力量給你們。¹¹願權能歸給他，直到永永遠遠。阿們！

最後的問安

¹²我略略地寫了這信，託我所看為忠心的兄弟西拉轉交你們，勸勉你們，又證明這恩是神的真恩。你們務要在這恩上站立得住。

¹³在巴比倫與你們同蒙揀選的教會問你們安。我兒子馬可也問你們安。¹⁴你們要用愛心彼此親嘴問安。

願平安歸與你們凡在基督裏的人！

ᵃ 5 Prov. 3:34   ᵇ 12 Greek *Silvanus,* a variant of *Silas*

彼得後書

1

作耶穌基督僕人和使徒的西門彼得，

寫信給那因我們的神和（註：有古卷無"和"字）救主耶穌基督之義，與我們同得一樣寶貴信心的人：

2 願恩惠、平安因你們認識神和我們主耶穌，多多地加給你們！

使蒙召與揀選堅定不移

3 神的神能已將一切關乎生命和虔敬的事賜給我們，皆因我們認識那用自己榮耀和美德召我們的主。4 因此，他已將又寶貴、又極大的應許賜給我們，叫我們既脫離世上從情慾來的敗壞，就得與神的性情有分。

5 正因這緣故，你們要分外地殷勤。有了信心，又要加上德行；有了德行，又要加上知識；6 有了知識，又要加上節制；有了節制，又要加上忍耐；有了忍耐，又要加上虔敬；7 有了虔敬，又要加上愛弟兄的心；有了愛弟兄的心，又要加上愛眾人的心。8 你們若充充足足地有這幾樣，就必使你們在認識我們的主耶穌基督上，不至於閒懶不結果子了。9 人若沒有這幾樣，就是眼瞎，只看見近處的，忘了他舊日的罪已經得了潔淨。

10 所以弟兄們，應當更加殷勤，使你們所蒙的恩召和揀選堅定不移。你們若行這幾樣，就永不失腳。11 這樣，必叫你們豐豐富富地得以進入我們主救主耶穌基督永遠的國。

經上的預言

12 你們雖然曉得這些事，並且在你們已有的真道上堅固，我卻要將這些事常常提醒你們。13 我以為應當趁我還在這帳棚的時候提醒你們，激發你們。14 因為知道我脫離這帳棚的時候快到了，正如我們主耶穌基督所指示我的。15 並且我要盡心竭

2 Peter

1

Simon Peter, a servant and apostle of Jesus Christ,

To those who through the righteousness of our God and Savior Jesus Christ have received a faith as precious as ours:

2 Grace and peace be yours in abundance through the knowledge of God and of Jesus our Lord.

Making One's Calling and Election Sure

3 His divine power has given us everything we need for life and godliness through our knowledge of him who called us by his own glory and goodness. 4 Through these he has given us his very great and precious promises, so that through them you may participate in the divine nature and escape the corruption in the world caused by evil desires.

5 For this very reason, make every effort to add to your faith goodness; and to goodness, knowledge; 6 and to knowledge, self-control; and to self-control, perseverance; and to perseverance, godliness; 7 and to godliness, brotherly kindness; and to brotherly kindness, love. 8 For if you possess these qualities in increasing measure, they will keep you from being ineffective and unproductive in your knowledge of our Lord Jesus Christ. 9 But if anyone does not have them, he is nearsighted and blind, and has forgotten that he has been cleansed from his past sins.

10 Therefore, my brothers, be all the more eager to make your calling and election sure. For if you do these things, you will never fall, 11 and you will receive a rich welcome into the eternal kingdom of our Lord and Savior Jesus Christ.

Prophecy of Scripture

12 So I will always remind you of these things, even though you know them and are firmly established in the truth you now have. 13 I think it is right to refresh your memory as long as I live in the tent of this body, 14 because I know that I will soon put it aside, as our Lord Jesus Christ has made clear to me. 15 And I will make

every effort to see that after my departure you will always be able to remember these things.

16We did not follow cleverly invented stories when we told you about the power and coming of our Lord Jesus Christ, but we were eyewitnesses of his majesty. 17For he received honor and glory from God the Father when the voice came to him from the Majestic Glory, saying, "This is my Son, whom I love; with him I am well pleased."*a* 18We ourselves heard this voice that came from heaven when we were with him on the sacred mountain.

19And we have the word of the prophets made more certain, and you will do well to pay attention to it, as to a light shining in a dark place, until the day dawns and the morning star rises in your hearts. 20Above all, you must understand that no prophecy of Scripture came about by the prophet's own interpretation. 21For prophecy never had its origin in the will of man, but men spoke from God as they were carried along by the Holy Spirit.

False Teachers and Their Destruction

2 But there were also false prophets among the people, just as there will be false teachers among you. They will secretly introduce destructive heresies, even denying the sovereign Lord who bought them—bringing swift destruction on themselves. 2Many will follow their shameful ways and will bring the way of truth into disrepute. 3In their greed these teachers will exploit you with stories they have made up. Their condemnation has long been hanging over them, and their destruction has not been sleeping.

4For if God did not spare angels when they sinned, but sent them to hell,*b* putting them into gloomy dungeons*c* to be held for judgment; 5if he did not spare the ancient world when he brought the flood on its ungodly people, but protected Noah, a preacher of righteousness, and seven others; 6if he condemned the cities of Sodom and Gomorrah by burning them to ashes, and made them an example of what is going to happen to the ungodly; 7and if he rescued Lot, a righteous man, who was distressed by the filthy lives of lawless men 8(for that righteous man, living among them day after day, was tormented in his righteous soul by the lawless deeds he saw and heard)— 9if this is so, then the Lord knows how to rescue godly men from trials and

力，使你們在我去世以後時常記念這些事。

16我們從前將我們主耶穌基督的大能，和他降臨的事告訴你們，並不是隨從乖巧捏造的虛言，乃是親眼見過他的威榮。17我們從父神得尊貴榮耀的時候，從極大榮光之中有聲音出來向他說：“這是我的愛子，我所喜悅的。”18我們同他在聖山的時候，親自聽見這聲音從天上出來。

19我們並有先知更確的預言，如同燈照在暗處。你們在這預言上留意，直等到天發亮，晨星在你們心裏出現的時候，才是好的。20第一要緊的，該知道經上所有的預言沒有可隨私意解說的；21因為預言從來沒有出於人意的，乃是人被聖靈感動，說出神的話來。

假師傅與他們的滅亡

2 從前在百姓中有假先知起來，將來在你們中間也必有假師傅，私自引進陷害人的異端，連買他們的主他們也不承認，自取速速的滅亡。2將有許多人隨從他們邪淫的行為，便叫真道因他們的緣故被毀謗。3他們因有貪心，要用捏造的言語在你們身上取利。他們的刑罰，自古以來並不遲延；他們的滅亡，也必速速來到（註：原文作“也不打盹”）。

4就是天使犯了罪，神也沒有寬容，曾把他們丟在地獄，交在黑暗坑中，等候審判；5神也沒有寬容上古的世代，曾叫洪水臨到那不敬虔的世代，卻保護了傳義道的挪亞一家八口；6又判定所多瑪、蛾摩拉，將二城傾覆，焚燒成灰，作為後世不敬虔人的鑑戒；7只搭救了那常為惡人淫行憂傷的義人羅得。8因為那義人住在他們中間，看見聽見他們不法的事，他的義心就天天傷痛。9主知道搭救敬虔的人脫離試探，把不義的人

---

a 17 Matt. 17:5; Mark 9:7; Luke 9:35　　*b 4* Greek *Tartarus*

c 4 Some manuscripts *into chains of darkness*

留在刑罰之下，等候審判的日子。10那些隨肉身縱污穢的情慾、輕慢主治之人的，更是如此。

他們膽大任性，毀謗在尊位的也不知懼怕。11就是天使，雖然力量權能更大，還不用毀謗的話在主面前告他們。12但這些人好像沒有靈性，生來就是畜類，以備捉拿宰殺的。他們毀謗所不曉得的事，正在敗壞人的時候，自己必遭遇敗壞。

13行的不義，就得了不義的工價。這些人喜愛白晝宴樂，他們已被玷污，又有瑕疵，正與你們一同坐席，就以自己的詭詐為快樂。14他們滿眼是淫色（註：“淫色”原文作“淫婦”），止不住犯罪，引誘那心不堅固的人，心中習慣了貪婪，正是被咒詛的種類。15他們離棄正路，就走差了，隨從比珥之子巴蘭的路。巴蘭就是那貪愛不義之工價的先知，16他卻為自己的過犯受了責備；那不能說話的驢，以人言攔阻先知的狂妄。

17這些人是無水的井，是狂風催逼的霧氣，有墨黑的幽暗為他們存留。18他們說虛妄矜誇的大話，用肉身的情慾和邪淫的事引誘那些剛才脫離妄行的人。19他們應許人得以自由，自己卻作敗壞的奴僕，因為人被誰制伏，就是誰的奴僕。20倘若他們因認識主救主耶穌基督，得以脫離世上的污穢，後來又在其中被纏住制伏，他們末後的景況就比先前更不好了。21他們曉得義路，竟背棄了傳給他們的聖命，倒不如不曉得為妙。22俗語說得真不錯：“狗所吐的，牠轉過來又吃；豬洗淨了，又回到泥裏去滾。”這話在他們身上正合式。

to hold the unrighteous for the day of judgment, while continuing their punishment.[a] 10This is especially true of those who follow the corrupt desire of the sinful nature[b] and despise authority.

Bold and arrogant, these men are not afraid to slander celestial beings; 11yet even angels, although they are stronger and more powerful, do not bring slanderous accusations against such beings in the presence of the Lord. 12But these men blaspheme in matters they do not understand. They are like brute beasts, creatures of instinct, born only to be caught and destroyed, and like beasts they too will perish.

13They will be paid back with harm for the harm they have done. Their idea of pleasure is to carouse in broad daylight. They are blots and blemishes, reveling in their pleasures while they feast with you.[c] 14With eyes full of adultery, they never stop sinning; they seduce the unstable; they are experts in greed—an accursed brood! 15They have left the straight way and wandered off to follow the way of Balaam son of Beor, who loved the wages of wickedness. 16But he was rebuked for his wrongdoing by a donkey—a beast without speech—who spoke with a man's voice and restrained the prophet's madness.

17These men are springs without water and mists driven by a storm. Blackest darkness is reserved for them. 18For they mouth empty, boastful words and, by appealing to the lustful desires of sinful human nature, they entice people who are just escaping from those who live in error. 19They promise them freedom, while they themselves are slaves of depravity—for a man is a slave to whatever has mastered him. 20If they have escaped the corruption of the world by knowing our Lord and Savior Jesus Christ and are again entangled in it and overcome, they are worse off at the end than they were at the beginning. 21It would have been better for them not to have known the way of righteousness, than to have known it and then to turn their backs on the sacred command that was passed on to them. 22Of them the proverbs are true: "A dog returns to its vomit,"[d] and, "A sow that is washed goes back to her wallowing in the mud."

a 9 Or unrighteous for punishment until the day of judgment
b 10 Or the flesh　　c 13 Some manuscripts in their love feasts
d 22 Prov. 26:11

The Day of the Lord

3 Dear friends, this is now my second letter to you. I have written both of them as reminders to stimulate you to wholesome thinking. [2]I want you to recall the words spoken in the past by the holy prophets and the command given by our Lord and Savior through your apostles.

[3]First of all, you must understand that in the last days scoffers will come, scoffing and following their own evil desires. [4]They will say, "Where is this 'coming' he promised? Ever since our fathers died, everything goes on as it has since the beginning of creation." [5]But they deliberately forget that long ago by God's word the heavens existed and the earth was formed out of water and by water. [6]By these waters also the world of that time was deluged and destroyed. [7]By the same word the present heavens and earth are reserved for fire, being kept for the day of judgment and destruction of ungodly men.

[8]But do not forget this one thing, dear friends: With the Lord a day is like a thousand years, and a thousand years are like a day. [9]The Lord is not slow in keeping his promise, as some understand slowness. He is patient with you, not wanting anyone to perish, but everyone to come to repentance.

[10]But the day of the Lord will come like a thief. The heavens will disappear with a roar; the elements will be destroyed by fire, and the earth and everything in it will be laid bare.[a]

[11]Since everything will be destroyed in this way, what kind of people ought you to be? You ought to live holy and godly lives [12]as you look forward to the day of God and speed its coming.[b] That day will bring about the destruction of the heavens by fire, and the elements will melt in the heat. [13]But in keeping with his promise we are looking forward to a new heaven and a new earth, the home of righteousness.

[14]So then, dear friends, since you are looking forward to this, make every effort to be found spotless, blameless and at peace with him. [15]Bear in mind that our Lord's patience means salvation, just as our dear brother Paul also wrote you with the wisdom that God gave him. [16]He writes the same way in all his letters, speaking in them of these matters. His letters contain some things that are hard to understand, which ignorant and unstable people distort, as they do the other Scriptures, to their own destruction.

主的日子

3 親愛的弟兄啊，我現在寫給你們的是第二封信。這兩封都是提醒你們，激發你們誠實的心，[2]叫你們記念聖先知預先所說的話和主救主的命令，就是使徒所傳給你們的。

[3]第一要緊的，該知道在末世必有好譏誚的人，隨從自己的私慾出來譏誚說：[4]"主要降臨的應許在哪裏呢？因為從列祖睡了以來，萬物與起初創造的時候仍是一樣。"[5]他們故意忘記，從太古憑神的命有了天，並從水而出藉水而成的地。[6]故此，當時的世界被水淹沒就消滅了。[7]但現在的天地還是憑着那命存留，直留到不敬虔之人受審判遭沉淪的日子，用火焚燒。

[8]親愛的弟兄啊，有一件事你們不可忘記，就是主看一日如千年，千年如一日。[9]主所應許的尚未成就，有人以為他是躭延，其實不是躭延，乃是寬容你們，不願有一人沉淪，乃願人人都悔改。

[10]但主的日子要像賊來到一樣。那日，天必大有響聲廢去，有形質的都要被烈火銷化，地和其上的物都要燒盡了。

[11]這一切既然都要如此銷化，你們為人該當怎樣聖潔、怎樣敬虔，[12]切切仰望神的日子來到。在那日，天被火燒就銷化了，有形質的都要被烈火熔化。[13]但我們照他的應許，盼望新天新地，有義居在其中。

[14]親愛的弟兄啊，你們既盼望這些事，就當殷勤，使自己沒有玷污，無可指摘，安然見主。[15]並且要以我主長久忍耐為得救的因由，就如我們所親愛的兄弟保羅，照着所賜給他的智慧寫了信給你們。[16]他一切的信上也都是講論這事。信中有些難明白的，那無學問、不堅固的人強解，如強解別的經書一樣，就自取沉淪。

---

a 10 Some manuscripts *be burned up*　　*b 12* Or *as you wait eagerly for the day of God to come*

17親愛的弟兄啊，你們既然預先知道這事，就當防備，恐怕被惡人的錯謬誘惑，就從自己堅固的地步上墜落。18你們卻要在我們主救主耶穌基督的恩典和知識上有長進。願榮耀歸給他，從今直到永遠。阿們！

17Therefore, dear friends, since you already know this, be on your guard so that you may not be carried away by the error of lawless men and fall from your secure position. 18But grow in the grace and knowledge of our Lord and Savior Jesus Christ. To him be glory both now and forever! Amen.

圖八：彼得書信中的主要地方
MAP 8 : KEY PLACES IN 1 & 2 PETER

1 John

The Word of Life

1 That which was from the beginning, which we have heard, which we have seen with our eyes, which we have looked at and our hands have touched—this we proclaim concerning the Word of life. ²The life appeared; we have seen it and testify to it, and we proclaim to you the eternal life, which was with the Father and has appeared to us. ³We proclaim to you what we have seen and heard, so that you also may have fellowship with us. And our fellowship is with the Father and with his Son, Jesus Christ. ⁴We write this to make our[a] joy complete.

Walking in the Light

⁵This is the message we have heard from him and declare to you: God is light; in him there is no darkness at all. ⁶If we claim to have fellowship with him yet walk in the darkness, we lie and do not live by the truth. ⁷But if we walk in the light, as he is in the light, we have fellowship with one another, and the blood of Jesus, his Son, purifies us from all[b] sin.

⁸If we claim to be without sin, we deceive ourselves and the truth is not in us. ⁹If we confess our sins, he is faithful and just and will forgive us our sins and purify us from all unrighteousness. ¹⁰If we claim we have not sinned, we make him out to be a liar and his word has no place in our lives.

2 My dear children, I write this to you so that you will not sin. But if anybody does sin, we have one who speaks to the Father in our defense—Jesus Christ, the Righteous One. ²He is the atoning sacrifice for our sins, and not only for ours but also for[c] the sins of the whole world.

³We know that we have come to know him if we obey his commands. ⁴The man who says, "I know him," but does not do what he commands is a liar, and the truth is not in him. ⁵But if anyone obeys his word, God's love[d] is truly made complete in him. This is how we know we are in

約翰一書

生命之道

1 論到從起初原有的生命之道，就是我們所聽見，所看見，親眼看過，親手摸過的。²（這生命已經顯現出來，我們也看見過，現在又作見證，將原與父同在，且顯現與我們那永遠的生命傳給你們。）³我們將所看見、所聽見的傳給你們，使你們與我們相交。我們乃是與父並他兒子耶穌基督相交的。⁴我們將這些話寫給你們，使你們（註：有古卷作"我們"）的喜樂充足。

在光明中行

⁵神就是光，在他毫無黑暗！這是我們從主所聽見，又報給你們的信息。⁶我們若說是與神相交，卻仍在黑暗裏行，就是說謊話，不行真理了。⁷我們若在光明中行，如同神在光明中，就彼此相交，他兒子耶穌的血也洗淨我們一切的罪。

⁸我們若說自己無罪，便是自欺，真理不在我們心裏了；⁹我們若認自己的罪，神是信實的，是公義的，必要赦免我們的罪，洗淨我們一切的不義；¹⁰我們若說自己沒有犯過罪，便是以神為說謊的，他的道也不在我們心裏了。

2 我小子們哪，我將這些話寫給你們，是要叫你們不犯罪。若有人犯罪，在父那裏我們有一位中保，就是那義者耶穌基督。²他為我們的罪作了挽回祭，不是單為我們的罪，也是為普天下人的罪。

³我們若遵守他的誡命，就曉得是認識他。⁴人若說"我認識他"，卻不遵守他的誡命，便是說謊話的，真理也不在他心裏了。⁵凡遵守主道的，愛神的心在他裏面實在是完全的，從此我們知道我們是在主裏面。

---

a 4 Some manuscripts *your*　　b 7 Or *every*　　c 2 Or *He is the one who turns aside God's wrath, taking away our sins, and not only ours but also*　　d 5 Or *word, love for God*

⁶人若說他住在主裏面，就該自己照主所行的去行。

⁷親愛的弟兄啊，我寫給你們的，不是一條新命令，乃是你們從起初所受的舊命令；這舊命令就是你們所聽見的道。⁸再者，我寫給你們的是一條新命令，在主是真的，在你們也是真的；因為黑暗漸漸過去，真光已經照耀。

⁹人若說自己在光明中，卻恨他的弟兄，他到如今還是在黑暗裏。¹⁰愛弟兄的，就是住在光明中，在他並沒有絆跌的緣由。¹¹惟獨恨弟兄的是在黑暗裏，且在黑暗裏行，也不知道往哪裏去，因為黑暗叫他眼睛瞎了。

¹²小子們哪，我寫信給你們，
　　因為你們的罪藉着主名
　　得了赦免。
¹³父老啊，我寫信給你們，
　　因為你們認識那從起初原有的。
　少年人哪，我寫信給你們，
　　因為你們勝了那惡者。
　小子們哪，我曾寫信給你們，
　　因為你們認識父。

¹⁴父老啊，我曾寫信給你們，
　　因為你們認識那從起初原有的。
　少年人哪，我曾寫信給你們，
　　因為你們剛強，
　　神的道常存在你們心裏，
　　你們也勝了那惡者。

不要愛世界

¹⁵不要愛世界和世界上的事；人若愛世界，愛父的心就不在他裏面了。¹⁶因為凡世界上的事，就像肉體的情慾，眼目的情慾，並今生的驕傲，都不是從父來的，乃是從世界來的。¹⁷這世界和其上的情慾都要過去，惟獨遵行神旨意的，是永遠常存。

警告提防敵基督

¹⁸小子們哪，如今是末時了。你們曾聽見說，那敵基督的要來。現在已經有好些敵基督的出來了，從此我們就知道如今是末時了。¹⁹他們從我們中間出去，卻不是屬我們的；若是屬我們的，就必仍舊與我

---

him: ⁶Whoever claims to live in him must walk as Jesus did.

⁷Dear friends, I am not writing you a new command but an old one, which you have had since the beginning. This old command is the message you have heard. ⁸Yet I am writing you a new command; its truth is seen in him and you, because the darkness is passing and the true light is already shining.

⁹Anyone who claims to be in the light but hates his brother is still in the darkness. ¹⁰Whoever loves his brother lives in the light, and there is nothing in him^a to make him stumble. ¹¹But whoever hates his brother is in the darkness and walks around in the darkness; he does not know where he is going, because the darkness has blinded him.

¹²I write to you, dear children,
　　because your sins have been forgiven on
　　account of his name.
¹³I write to you, fathers,
　　because you have known him who is from
　　the beginning.
　I write to you, young men,
　　because you have overcome the evil one.
　I write to you, dear children,
　　because you have known the Father.
¹⁴I write to you, fathers,
　　because you have known him who is from
　　the beginning.
　I write to you, young men,
　　because you are strong,
　　and the word of God lives in you,
　　and you have overcome the evil one.

Do Not Love the World

¹⁵Do not love the world or anything in the world. If anyone loves the world, the love of the Father is not in him. ¹⁶For everything in the world—the cravings of sinful man, the lust of his eyes and the boasting of what he has and does—comes not from the Father but from the world. ¹⁷The world and its desires pass away, but the man who does the will of God lives forever.

Warning Against Antichrists

¹⁸Dear children, this is the last hour; and as you have heard that the antichrist is coming, even now many antichrists have come. This is how we know it is the last hour. ¹⁹They went out from us, but they did not really belong to us. For if they had belonged to us, they would have

a 10 Or it

remained with us; but their going showed that none of them belonged to us.

²⁰But you have an anointing from the Holy One, and all of you know the truth.*ᵃ* ²¹I do not write to you because you do not know the truth, but because you do know it and because no lie comes from the truth. ²²Who is the liar? It is the man who denies that Jesus is the Christ. Such a man is the antichrist—he denies the Father and the Son. ²³No one who denies the Son has the Father; whoever acknowledges the Son has the Father also.

²⁴See that what you have heard from the beginning remains in you. If it does, you also will remain in the Son and in the Father. ²⁵And this is what he promised us—even eternal life.

²⁶I am writing these things to you about those who are trying to lead you astray. ²⁷As for you, the anointing you received from him remains in you, and you do not need anyone to teach you. But as his anointing teaches you about all things and as that anointing is real, not counterfeit—just as it has taught you, remain in him.

Children of God

²⁸And now, dear children, continue in him, so that when he appears we may be confident and unashamed before him at his coming.

²⁹If you know that he is righteous, you know that everyone who does what is right has been born of him.

3 How great is the love the Father has lavished on us, that we should be called children of God! And that is what we are! The reason the world does not know us is that it did not know him. ²Dear friends, now we are children of God, and what we will be has not yet been made known. But we know that when he appears,*ᵇ* we shall be like him, for we shall see him as he is. ³Everyone who has this hope in him purifies himself, just as he is pure.

⁴Everyone who sins breaks the law; in fact, sin is lawlessness. ⁵But you know that he appeared so that he might take away our sins. And in him is no sin. ⁶No one who lives in him keeps on sinning. No one who continues to sin has either seen him or known him.

⁷Dear children, do not let anyone lead you astray. He who does what is right is righteous, just as he is righteous. ⁸He who does what is sinful is of the devil, because the devil has been sinning from the beginning. The reason the Son of God appeared was to destroy the devil's work.

們同在;他們出去顯明都不是屬我們的。

²⁰你們從那聖者受了恩膏,並且知道這一切的事(註:或作"都有知識")。²¹我寫信給你們,不是因你們不知道真理,正是因你們知道,並且知道沒有虛謊是從真理出來的。²²誰是說謊話的呢?不是那不認耶穌為基督的嗎?不認父與子的,這就是敵基督的。²³凡不認子的,就沒有父;認子的,連父也有了。

²⁴論到你們,務要將那從起初所聽見的常存在心裏。若將從起初所聽見的存在心裏,你們就必住在子裏面,也必住在父裏面。²⁵主所應許我們的就是永生。

²⁶我將這些話寫給你們,是指着那引誘你們的人說的。²⁷你們從主所受的恩膏常存在你們心裏,並不用人教訓你們,自有主的恩膏在凡事上教訓你們。這恩膏是真的,不是假的,你們要按這恩膏的教訓住在主裏面。

神的兒女

²⁸小子們哪,你們要住在主裏面。這樣,他若顯現,我們就可以坦然無懼;當他來的時候,在他面前也不至於慚愧。

²⁹你們若知道他是公義的,就知道凡行公義之人都是他所生的。

3 你看父賜給我們是何等的慈愛,使我們得稱為神的兒女!我們也真是他的兒女。世人所以不認識我們,是因未曾認識他。²親愛的弟兄啊,我們現在是神的兒女,將來如何,還未顯明;但我們知道,主若顯現,我們必要像他,因為必得見他的真體。³凡向他有這指望的,就潔淨自己,像他潔淨一樣。

⁴凡犯罪的,就是違背律法;違背律法,就是罪。⁵你們知道主曾顯現,是要除掉人的罪,在他並沒有罪。⁶凡住在他裏面的,就不犯罪;凡犯罪的,是未曾看見他,也未曾認識他。

⁷小子們哪,不要被人誘惑。行義的才是義人,正如主是義的一樣。⁸犯罪的是屬魔鬼,因為魔鬼從起初就犯罪。神的兒子顯現出來,為要除

---

a 20 Some manuscripts and you know all things   b 2 Or when it is made known

滅魔鬼的作為。9凡從神生的，就不犯罪，因神的道（註：原文作“種”）存在他心裏；他也不能犯罪，因為他是由神生的。10從此就顯出誰是神的兒女，誰是魔鬼的兒女。凡不行義的就不屬神，不愛弟兄的也是如此。

彼此相愛

11我們應當彼此相愛，這就是你們從起初所聽見的命令。12不可像該隱，他是屬那惡者，殺了他的兄弟。為甚麼殺了他呢？因自己的行為是惡的，兄弟的行為是善的。13弟兄們哪，世人若恨你們，不要以為希奇。14我們因為愛弟兄，就曉得是已經出死入生了。沒有愛心的，仍住在死中。15凡恨他弟兄的，就是殺人的；你們曉得凡殺人的，沒有永生存在他裏面。

16主為我們捨命，我們從此就知道何為愛，我們也當為弟兄捨命。17凡有世上財物的，看見弟兄窮乏，卻塞住憐恤的心，愛神的心怎能存在他裏面呢？18小子們哪，我們相愛，不要只在言語和舌頭上，總要在行為和誠實上。19從此，就知道我們是屬真理的，並且我們的心在神面前可以安穩。20我們的心若責備我們，神比我們的心大，一切事沒有不知道的。

21親愛的弟兄啊，我們的心若不責備我們，就可以向神坦然無懼了。22並且我們一切所求的，就從他得着，因為我們遵守他的命令，行他所喜悅的事。23神的命令就是叫我們信他兒子耶穌基督的名，且照他所賜給我們的命令彼此相愛。24遵守神命令的，就住在神裏面，神也住在他裏面。我們所以知道神住在我們裏面，是因他所賜給我們的聖靈。

試驗諸靈

4 親愛的弟兄啊，一切的靈，你們不可都信，總要試驗那些靈是出於神的不是，因為世上有許多假先知已經出來了。2凡靈認耶穌基督是成了肉身來的，就是出於神的，從此你們可以認出神的靈來。3凡靈不認耶穌，就不是出於神，這是那敵基督者的靈。你們

Love One Another

9No one who is born of God will continue to sin, because God's seed remains in him; he cannot go on sinning, because he has been born of God. 10This is how we know who the children of God are and who the children of the devil are: Anyone who does not do what is right is not a child of God; nor is anyone who does not love his brother.

Love One Another

11This is the message you heard from the beginning: We should love one another. 12Do not be like Cain, who belonged to the evil one and murdered his brother. And why did he murder him? Because his own actions were evil and his brother's were righteous. 13Do not be surprised, my brothers, if the world hates you. 14We know that we have passed from death to life, because we love our brothers. Anyone who does not love remains in death. 15Anyone who hates his brother is a murderer, and you know that no murderer has eternal life in him.

16This is how we know what love is: Jesus Christ laid down his life for us. And we ought to lay down our lives for our brothers. 17If anyone has material possessions and sees his brother in need but has no pity on him, how can the love of God be in him? 18Dear children, let us not love with words or tongue but with actions and in truth. 19This then is how we know that we belong to the truth, and how we set our hearts at rest in his presence 20whenever our hearts condemn us. For God is greater than our hearts, and he knows everything.

21Dear friends, if our hearts do not condemn us, we have confidence before God 22and receive from him anything we ask, because we obey his commands and do what pleases him. 23And this is his command: to believe in the name of his Son, Jesus Christ, and to love one another as he commanded us. 24Those who obey his commands live in him, and he in them. And this is how we know that he lives in us: We know it by the Spirit he gave us.

Test the Spirits

4 Dear friends, do not believe every spirit, but test the spirits to see whether they are from God, because many false prophets have gone out into the world. 2This is how you can recognize the Spirit of God: Every spirit that acknowledges that Jesus Christ has come in the flesh is from God, 3but every spirit that does not acknowledge Jesus is not from God. This is the spirit of the antichrist, which

you have heard is coming and even now is already in the world.

⁴You, dear children, are from God and have overcome them, because the one who is in you is greater than the one who is in the world. ⁵They are from the world and therefore speak from the viewpoint of the world, and the world listens to them. ⁶We are from God, and whoever knows God listens to us; but whoever is not from God does not listen to us. This is how we recognize the Spirit*a* of truth and the spirit of falsehood.

God's Love and Ours

⁷Dear friends, let us love one another, for love comes from God. Everyone who loves has been born of God and knows God. ⁸Whoever does not love does not know God, because God is love. ⁹This is how God showed his love among us: He sent his one and only Son*b* into the world that we might live through him. ¹⁰This is love: not that we loved God, but that he loved us and sent his Son as an atoning sacrifice for*c* our sins. ¹¹Dear friends, since God so loved us, we also ought to love one another. ¹²No one has ever seen God; but if we love one another, God lives in us and his love is made complete in us.

¹³We know that we live in him and he in us, because he has given us of his Spirit. ¹⁴And we have seen and testify that the Father has sent his Son to be the Savior of the world. ¹⁵If anyone acknowledges that Jesus is the Son of God, God lives in him and he in God. ¹⁶And so we know and rely on the love God has for us.

God is love. Whoever lives in love lives in God, and God in him. ¹⁷In this way, love is made complete among us so that we will have confidence on the day of judgment, because in this world we are like him. ¹⁸There is no fear in love. But perfect love drives out fear, because fear has to do with punishment. The one who fears is not made perfect in love.

¹⁹We love because he first loved us. ²⁰If anyone says, "I love God," yet hates his brother, he is a liar. For anyone who does not love his brother, whom he has seen, cannot love God, whom he has not seen. ²¹And he has given us this command: Whoever loves God must also love his brother.

從前聽見他要來，現在已經在世上了。

⁴小子們哪，你們是屬神的，並且勝了他們，因為那在你們裏面的，比那在世界上的更大。⁵他們是屬世界的，所以論世界的事，世人也聽從他們。⁶我們是屬神的，認識神的就聽從我們；不屬神的，就不聽從我們。從此我們可以認出真理的靈和謬妄的靈來。

神的愛和我們的愛

⁷親愛的弟兄啊，我們應當彼此相愛，因為愛是從神來的。凡有愛心的，都是由神而生，並且認識神。⁸沒有愛心的，就不認識神，因為神就是愛。⁹神差他獨生子到世間來，使我們藉着他得生，神愛我們的心在此就顯明了。¹⁰不是我們愛神，乃是神愛我們，差他的兒子，為我們的罪作了挽回祭，這就是愛了。¹¹親愛的弟兄啊，神既是這樣愛我們，我們也當彼此相愛。¹²從來沒有人見過神，我們若彼此相愛，神就住在我們裏面，愛他的心在我們裏面得以完全了。

¹³神將他的靈賜給我們，從此就知道我們是住在他裏面，他也住在我們裏面。¹⁴父差子作世人的救主，這是我們所看見且作見證的。¹⁵凡認耶穌為神兒子的，神就住在他裏面，他也住在神裏面。¹⁶神愛我們的心，我們也知道、也信。

神就是愛！住在愛裏面的，就是住在神裏面，神也住在他裏面。¹⁷這樣，愛在我們裏面得以完全，我們就可以在審判的日子坦然無懼。因為他如何，我們在這世上也如何。¹⁸愛裏沒有懼怕；愛既完全，就把懼怕除去，因為懼怕裏含着刑罰，懼怕的人在愛裏未得完全。

¹⁹我們愛，因為神先愛我們。²⁰人若説"我愛神"，卻恨他的弟兄，就是説謊話的；不愛他所看見的弟兄，就不能愛沒有看見的神 (註：有古卷作"怎能愛沒有看見的神呢？")。²¹愛神的，也當愛弟兄，這是我們從神所受的命令。

---

a 6 Or spirit   *b* 9 Or his only begotten Son   *c* 10 Or as the one who would turn aside his wrath, taking away

在神兒子裏的信心

5 凡信耶穌是基督的，都是從神而生，凡愛生他之神的，也必愛從神生的。²我們若愛神，又遵守他的誡命，從此就知道我們愛神的兒女。³我們遵守神的誡命，這就是愛他了，並且他的誡命不是難守的。⁴因為凡從神生的，就勝過世界；使我們勝了世界的，就是我們的信心。⁵勝過世界的是誰呢？不是那信耶穌是神兒子的嗎？

⁶這藉着水和血而來的，就是耶穌基督；不是單用水，乃是用水又用血，並且有聖靈作見證，因為聖靈就是真理。⁸作見證的原來有三：就是聖靈、水與血，這三樣也都歸於一。⁹我們既領受人的見證，神的見證就該領受了（註："該領受"原文作"大"）。因神的見證是為他兒子作的。¹⁰信神兒子的，就有這見證在他心裏；不信神的，就是將神當作說謊的，因不信神為他兒子作的見證。¹¹這見證就是神賜給我們永生，這永生也是在他兒子裏面。¹²人有了神的兒子就有生命；沒有神的兒子就沒有生命。

結束的囑咐

¹³我將這些話寫給你們信奉神兒子之名的人，要叫你們知道自己有永生。¹⁴我們若照他的旨意求甚麼，他就聽我們，這是我們向他所存坦然無懼的心。¹⁵既然知道他聽我們一切所求的，就知道我們所求於他的，無不得着。

¹⁶人若看見弟兄犯了不至於死的罪，就當為他祈求，神必將生命賜給他；有至於死的罪，我不說當為這罪祈求。¹⁷凡不義的事都是罪，也有不至於死的罪。

¹⁸我們知道凡從神生的，必不犯罪，從神生的，必保守自己（註：有古卷作"那從神生的必保護他"），那惡者也就無法害他。¹⁹我們知道我們是屬神

Faith in the Son of God

5 Everyone who believes that Jesus is the Christ is born of God, and everyone who loves the father loves his child as well. ²This is how we know that we love the children of God: by loving God and carrying out his commands. ³This is love for God: to obey his commands. And his commands are not burdensome, ⁴for everyone born of God overcomes the world. This is the victory that has overcome the world, even our faith. ⁵Who is it that overcomes the world? Only he who believes that Jesus is the Son of God.

⁶This is the one who came by water and blood — Jesus Christ. He did not come by water only, but by water and blood. And it is the Spirit who testifies, because the Spirit is the truth. ⁷For there are three that testify: ⁸the[a] Spirit, the water and the blood; and the three are in agreement. ⁹We accept man's testimony, but God's testimony is greater because it is the testimony of God, which he has given about his Son. ¹⁰Anyone who believes in the Son of God has this testimony in his heart. Anyone who does not believe God has made him out to be a liar, because he has not believed the testimony God has given about his Son. ¹¹And this is the testimony: God has given us eternal life, and this life is in his Son. ¹²He who has the Son has life; he who does not have the Son of God does not have life.

Concluding Remarks

¹³I write these things to you who believe in the name of the Son of God so that you may know that you have eternal life. ¹⁴This is the confidence we have in approaching God: that if we ask anything according to his will, he hears us. ¹⁵And if we know that he hears us — whatever we ask—we know that we have what we asked of him.

¹⁶If anyone sees his brother commit a sin that does not lead to death, he should pray and God will give him life. I refer to those whose sin does not lead to death. There is a sin that leads to death. I am not saying that he should pray about that. ¹⁷All wrongdoing is sin, and there is sin that does not lead to death.

¹⁸We know that anyone born of God does not continue to sin; the one who was born of God keeps him safe, and the evil one cannot harm him. ¹⁹We know that we are children of God,

a 7,8 Late manuscripts of the Vulgate testify in heaven: the Father, the Word and the Holy Spirit, and these three are one. 8 And there are three that testify on earth: the (not found in any Greek manuscript before the sixteenth century)

and that the whole world is under the control of the evil one. 20We know also that the Son of God has come and has given us understanding, so that we may know him who is true. And we are in him who is true—even in his Son Jesus Christ. He is the true God and eternal life.

21Dear children, keep yourselves from idols.

的，全世界都臥在那惡者手下。20我們也知道神的兒子已經來到，且將智慧賜給我們，使我們認識那位真實的，我們也在那位真實的裏面，就是在他兒子耶穌基督裏面。這是真神，也是永生。

21小子們哪，你們要自守，遠避偶像。

表七：約翰一書中的對比
TABLE 7 : CONTRASTS IN 1 JOHN

對比 Contrast between	經文 Reference
光明與黑暗 Light and darkness	1:5
新命令與舊命令 The new command and the old command	2:7, 8
愛天父與愛世界 Loving the Father and loving the world	2:15, 16
基督與敵基督 Christ and antichrist	2:18
真理與虛謊 Truth and lies	2:20, 21
神的兒女與魔鬼的兒女 Children of God and children of devil	3:1-10
永生與永死 Eternal life and eternal death	3:14
愛與恨 Love and hatred	3:15, 16
真教訓與假教訓 (真先知與假先知) True teaching and false teaching	4:1-3
愛與懼怕 Love and fear	4:18, 19
有生命與沒生命 Having life and not having life	5:11, 12

約翰二書

¹作長老的，

寫信給蒙揀選的太太（註："太太"或作"教會"。下同）和她的兒女，就是我誠心所愛的，也是一切知道真理之人所愛的。²愛你們是為真理的緣故，這真理存在我們裏面，也必永遠與我們同在。

³恩惠、憐憫、平安從父神和他兒子耶穌基督，在真理和愛心上必常與我們同在！

⁴我見你的兒女，有照我們從父所受之命令遵行真理的，就甚歡喜。⁵太太啊，我現在勸你，我們大家要彼此相愛。這並不是我寫一條新命令給你，乃是我們從起初所受的命令。⁶我們若照他的命令行，這就是愛。你們從起初所聽見當行的，就是這命令。

⁷因為世上有許多迷惑人的出來，他們不認耶穌基督是成了肉身來的，這就是那迷惑人、敵基督的。⁸你們要小心，不要失去你們（註：有古卷作"我們"）所做的工，乃要得着滿足的賞賜。⁹凡越過基督的教訓不常守着的，就沒有神；常守這教訓的，就有父又有子。¹⁰若有人到你們那裏，不是傳這教訓，不要接他到家裏，也不要問他的安。¹¹因為問他安的，就在他的惡行上有分。

¹²我還有許多事要寫給你們，卻不願意用紙墨寫出來，但盼望到你們那裏，與你們當面談論，使你們的喜樂滿足。

¹³你那蒙揀選之姊妹的兒女都問你安。

2 John

¹The elder,

To the chosen lady and her children, whom I love in the truth—and not I only, but also all who know the truth— ²because of the truth, which lives in us and will be with us forever:

³Grace, mercy and peace from God the Father and from Jesus Christ, the Father's Son, will be with us in truth and love.

⁴It has given me great joy to find some of your children walking in the truth, just as the Father commanded us. ⁵And now, dear lady, I am not writing you a new command but one we have had from the beginning. I ask that we love one another. ⁶And this is love: that we walk in obedience to his commands. As you have heard from the beginning, his command is that you walk in love.

⁷Many deceivers, who do not acknowledge Jesus Christ as coming in the flesh, have gone out into the world. Any such person is the deceiver and the antichrist. ⁸Watch out that you do not lose what you have worked for, but that you may be rewarded fully. ⁹Anyone who runs ahead and does not continue in the teaching of Christ does not have God; whoever continues in the teaching has both the Father and the Son. ¹⁰If anyone comes to you and does not bring this teaching, do not take him into your house or welcome him. ¹¹Anyone who welcomes him shares in his wicked work.

¹²I have much to write to you, but I do not want to use paper and ink. Instead, I hope to visit you and talk with you face to face, so that our joy may be complete.

¹³The children of your chosen sister send their greetings.

3 John

約翰三書

[1]The elder,

To my dear friend Gaius, whom I love in the truth.

[2]Dear friend, I pray that you may enjoy good health and that all may go well with you, even as your soul is getting along well. [3]It gave me great joy to have some brothers come and tell about your faithfulness to the truth and how you continue to walk in the truth. [4]I have no greater joy than to hear that my children are walking in the truth.

[5]Dear friend, you are faithful in what you are doing for the brothers, even though they are strangers to you. [6]They have told the church about your love. You will do well to send them on their way in a manner worthy of God. [7]It was for the sake of the Name that they went out, receiving no help from the pagans. [8]We ought therefore to show hospitality to such men so that we may work together for the truth.

[9]I wrote to the church, but Diotrephes, who loves to be first, will have nothing to do with us. [10]So if I come, I will call attention to what he is doing, gossiping maliciously about us. Not satisfied with that, he refuses to welcome the brothers. He also stops those who want to do so and puts them out of the church.

[11]Dear friend, do not imitate what is evil but what is good. Anyone who does what is good is from God. Anyone who does what is evil has not seen God. [12]Demetrius is well spoken of by everyone—and even by the truth itself. We also speak well of him, and you know that our testimony is true.

[13]I have much to write you, but I do not want to do so with pen and ink. [14]I hope to see you soon, and we will talk face to face.

Peace to you. The friends here send their greetings. Greet the friends there by name.

[1]作長老的，

寫信給親愛的該猶，就是我誠心所愛的。

[2]親愛的兄弟啊，我願你凡事興盛，身體健壯，正如你的靈魂興盛一樣。[3]有弟兄來證明你心裏存的真理，正如你按真理而行，我就甚喜樂。[4]我聽見我的兒女們按真理而行，我的喜樂就沒有比這個大的。

[5]親愛的兄弟啊，凡你向作客旅之弟兄所行的，都是忠心的。[6]他們在教會面前證明了你的愛。你若配得過神，幫助他們往前行，這就好了；[7]因他們是為主的名（註：原文作“那名”）出外，對於外邦人一無所取。[8]所以我們應該接待這樣的人，叫我們與他們一同為真理做工。

[9]我曾略略地寫信給教會，但那在教會中好為首的丟特腓不接待我們。[10]所以我若去，必要提說他所行的事，就是他用惡言妄論我們。還不以此為足，他自己不接待弟兄，有人願意接待，他也禁止，並且將接待弟兄的人趕出教會。

[11]親愛的兄弟啊，不要效法惡，只要效法善。行善的屬乎神，行惡的未曾見過神。[12]低米丟行善，有眾人給他作見證，又有真理給他作見證，就是我們也給他作見證。你也知道我們的見證是真的。

[13]我原有許多事要寫給你，卻不願意用筆墨寫給你，[14]但盼望快快的見你，我們就當面談論。

[15]願你平安！眾位朋友都問你安。請你替我按着姓名問眾位朋友安。

猶大書

¹耶穌基督的僕人、<u>雅各</u>的弟兄<u>猶大</u>，

寫信給那被召、在父神裏蒙愛、為耶穌基督保守的人：

²願憐恤、平安、慈愛多多地加給你們！

不虔誠人的罪惡與滅亡

³親愛的弟兄啊，我想盡心寫信給你們，論我們同得救恩的時候，就不得不寫信勸你們，要為從前一次交付聖徒的真道竭力地爭辯。⁴因為有些人偷着進來，就是自古被定受刑罰的，是不虔誠的，將我們神的恩變作放縱情慾的機會，並且不認獨一的主宰、我們（註："我們"或作"和我們"）主耶穌基督。

⁵從前主救了他的百姓出<u>埃及</u>地，後來就把那些不信的滅絕了。這一切的事你們雖然都知道，我卻仍要提醒你們。⁶又有不守本位、離開自己住處的天使，主用鎖鏈把他們永遠拘留在黑暗裏，等候大日的審判。⁷又如<u>所多瑪</u>、<u>蛾摩拉</u>和周圍城邑的人，也照他們一味的行淫，隨從逆性的情慾，就受永火的刑罰，作為鑑戒。

⁸這些做夢的人也像他們污穢身體，輕慢主治的，毀謗在尊位的。⁹天使長米迦勒為<u>摩西</u>的屍首與魔鬼爭辯的時候，尚且不敢用毀謗的話罪責他，只說："主責備你吧！"¹⁰但這些人毀謗他們所不知道的。他們本性所知道的事與那沒有靈性的畜類一樣，在這事上竟敗壞了自己。

¹¹他們有禍了！因為走了<u>該隱</u>的道路，又為利往<u>巴蘭</u>的錯謬裏直

Jude

¹Jude, a servant of Jesus Christ and a brother of James,

To those who have been called, who are loved by God the Father and kept by^a Jesus Christ:

²Mercy, peace and love be yours in abundance.

The Sin and Doom of Godless Men

³Dear friends, although I was very eager to write to you about the salvation we share, I felt I had to write and urge you to contend for the faith that was once for all entrusted to the saints. ⁴For certain men whose condemnation was written about^b long ago have secretly slipped in among you. They are godless men, who change the grace of our God into a license for immorality and deny Jesus Christ our only Sovereign and Lord.

⁵Though you already know all this, I want to remind you that the Lord^c delivered his people out of Egypt, but later destroyed those who did not believe. ⁶And the angels who did not keep their positions of authority but abandoned their own home—these he has kept in darkness, bound with everlasting chains for judgment on the great Day. ⁷In a similar way, Sodom and Gomorrah and the surrounding towns gave themselves up to sexual immorality and perversion. They serve as an example of those who suffer the punishment of eternal fire.

⁸In the very same way, these dreamers pollute their own bodies, reject authority and slander celestial beings. ⁹But even the archangel Michael, when he was disputing with the devil about the body of Moses, did not dare to bring a slanderous accusation against him, but said, "The Lord rebuke you!" ¹⁰Yet these men speak abusively against whatever they do not understand; and what things they do understand by instinct, like unreasoning animals—these are the very things that destroy them.

¹¹Woe to them! They have taken the way of Cain; they have rushed for profit into Balaam's

---

a 1 Or *for; or in*   *b* 4 Or *men who were marked out for condemnation*   *c* 5 Some early manuscripts *Jesus*

error; they have been destroyed in Korah's rebellion.

[12]These men are blemishes at your love feasts, eating with you without the slightest qualm—shepherds who feed only themselves. They are clouds without rain, blown along by the wind; autumn trees, without fruit and uprooted—twice dead. [13]They are wild waves of the sea, foaming up their shame; wandering stars, for whom blackest darkness has been reserved forever.

[14]Enoch, the seventh from Adam, prophesied about these men: "See, the Lord is coming with thousands upon thousands of his holy ones [15]to judge everyone, and to convict all the ungodly of all the ungodly acts they have done in the ungodly way, and of all the harsh words ungodly sinners have spoken against him." [16]These men are grumblers and faultfinders; they follow their own evil desires; they boast about themselves and flatter others for their own advantage.

A Call to Persevere

[17]But, dear friends, remember what the apostles of our Lord Jesus Christ foretold. [18]They said to you, "In the last times there will be scoffers who will follow their own ungodly desires." [19]These are the men who divide you, who follow mere natural instincts and do not have the Spirit.

[20]But you, dear friends, build yourselves up in your most holy faith and pray in the Holy Spirit. [21]Keep yourselves in God's love as you wait for the mercy of our Lord Jesus Christ to bring you to eternal life.

[22]Be merciful to those who doubt; [23]snatch others from the fire and save them; to others show mercy, mixed with fear—hating even the clothing stained by corrupted flesh.

Doxology

[24]To him who is able to keep you from falling and to present you before his glorious presence without fault and with great joy— [25]to the only God our Savior be glory, majesty, power and authority, through Jesus Christ our Lord, before all ages, now and forevermore! Amen.

奔，並在可拉的背叛中滅亡了。

[12]這樣的人在你們的愛席上與你們同吃的時候，正是礁石（註：或作"玷污"）。他們作牧人，只知餵養自己，無所懼怕；是沒有雨的雲彩，被風飄蕩；是秋天沒有果子的樹，死而又死，連根被拔出來；[13]是海裏的狂浪，湧出自己可恥的沫子來；是流蕩的星，有墨黑的幽暗為他們永遠存留。

[14]亞當的七世孫以諾曾預言這些人說：「看哪，主帶着他的千萬聖者降臨，[15]要在眾人身上行審判，證實那一切不敬虔的人所妄行一切不敬虔的事，又證實不敬虔之罪人所說頂撞他的剛愎話。」[16]這些人是私下議論，常發怨言的，隨從自己的情慾而行，口中說誇大的話，為得便宜諂媚人。

要堅持忍耐

[17]親愛的弟兄啊，你們要記念我們主耶穌基督之使徒從前所說的話。[18]他們曾對你們說過，末世必有好譏誚的人隨從自己不敬虔的私慾而行。[19]這就是那些引人結黨、屬乎血氣、沒有聖靈的人。

[20]親愛的弟兄啊，你們卻要在至聖的真道上造就自己，在聖靈裏禱告，[21]保守自己常在神的愛中，仰望我們主耶穌基督的憐憫，直到永生。

[22]有些人存疑心，你們要憐憫他們；[23]有些人你們要從火中搶出來，搭救他們；有些人你們要存懼怕的心憐憫他們，連那被情慾沾染的衣服也當厭惡。

頌讚

[24]那能保守你們不失腳，叫你們無瑕無疵、歡歡喜喜站在他榮耀之前的我們的救主、獨一的神，[25]願榮耀、威嚴、能力、權柄，因我們的主耶穌基督歸與他，從萬古以前並現今，直到永永遠遠。阿們！

啓示錄

前言

1 耶穌基督的啓示，就是神賜給他，叫他將必要快成的事指示他的眾僕人。他就差遣使者曉諭他的僕人約翰。²約翰便將神的道和耶穌基督的見證，凡自己所看見的都證明出來。³念這書上預言的和那些聽見又遵守其中所記載的，都是有福的，因為日期近了。

問安與頌讚

⁴約翰，

寫信給亞西亞的七個教會：

但願從那昔在、今在、以後永在的神和他寶座前的七靈，⁵並那誠實作見證的，從死裏首先復活，為世上君王元首的耶穌基督，有恩惠、平安歸與你們！

他愛我們，用自己的血使我們脫離罪惡（註：“脫離”有古卷作“洗去”），⁶又使我們成為國民，作他父神的祭司。但願榮耀、權能歸給他，直到永永遠遠。阿們！

⁷看哪！他駕雲降臨，
  眾目要看見他，
連刺他的人也要看見他，
  地上的萬族都要因他哀哭。

              這話是真實的。阿們！

⁸主神說：“我是阿拉法，我是俄梅戛（註：“阿拉法”、“俄梅戛”乃希臘字母首末二字），是昔在、今在、以後永在的全能者。”

像人子的一位

⁹我約翰就是你們的弟兄，和你們在耶穌的患難、國度、忍耐裏一同有分，為神的道，並為給耶穌作的見證，曾在那名叫拔摩的海島

Revelation

Prologue

1 The revelation of Jesus Christ, which God gave him to show his servants what must soon take place. He made it known by sending his angel to his servant John, ²who testifies to everything he saw—that is, the word of God and the testimony of Jesus Christ. ³Blessed is the one who reads the words of this prophecy, and blessed are those who hear it and take to heart what is written in it, because the time is near.

Greetings and Doxology

⁴John,

To the seven churches in the province of Asia:

Grace and peace to you from him who is, and who was, and who is to come, and from the seven spirits*a* before his throne, ⁵and from Jesus Christ, who is the faithful witness, the firstborn from the dead, and the ruler of the kings of the earth.

To him who loves us and has freed us from our sins by his blood, ⁶and has made us to be a kingdom and priests to serve his God and Father—to him be glory and power for ever and ever! Amen.

⁷Look, he is coming with the clouds,
  and every eye will see him,
even those who pierced him;
  and all the peoples of the earth will mourn
  because of him.
           So shall it be! Amen.

⁸"I am the Alpha and the Omega," says the Lord God, "who is, and who was, and who is to come, the Almighty."

One Like a Son of Man

⁹I, John, your brother and companion in the suffering and kingdom and patient endurance that are ours in Jesus, was on the island of Patmos because of the word of God and the tes-

a 4 Or the sevenfold Spirit

timony of Jesus. [10]On the Lord's Day I was in the Spirit, and I heard behind me a loud voice like a trumpet, [11]which said: "Write on a scroll what you see and send it to the seven churches: to Ephesus, Smyrna, Pergamum, Thyatira, Sardis, Philadelphia and Laodicea."

[12]I turned around to see the voice that was speaking to me. And when I turned I saw seven golden lampstands, [13]and among the lampstands was someone "like a son of man,"[a] dressed in a robe reaching down to his feet and with a golden sash around his chest. [14]His head and hair were white like wool, as white as snow, and his eyes were like blazing fire. [15]His feet were like bronze glowing in a furnace, and his voice was like the sound of rushing waters. [16]In his right hand he held seven stars, and out of his mouth came a sharp double-edged sword. His face was like the sun shining in all its brilliance.

[17]When I saw him, I fell at his feet as though dead. Then he placed his right hand on me and said: "Do not be afraid. I am the First and the Last. [18]I am the Living One; I was dead, and behold I am alive for ever and ever! And I hold the keys of death and Hades.

[19]"Write, therefore, what you have seen, what is now and what will take place later. [20]The mystery of the seven stars that you saw in my right hand and of the seven golden lampstands is this: The seven stars are the angels[b] of the seven churches, and the seven lampstands are the seven churches.

To the Church in Ephesus

2 "To the angel[c] of the church in Ephesus write:

These are the words of him who holds the seven stars in his right hand and walks among the seven golden lampstands: [2]I know your deeds, your hard work and your perseverance. I know that you cannot tolerate wicked men, that you have tested those who claim to be apostles but are not, and have found them false. [3]You have persevered and have endured hardships for my name, and have not grown weary.

[4]Yet I hold this against you: You have forsaken your first love. [5]Remember the height from which you have fallen! Repent and do the things you did at first. If you do not repent, I will come to you and remove your lampstand from its place. [6]But you

上。[10]當主日，我被聖靈感動，聽見在我後面有大聲音如吹號，說：[11]"你所看見的，當寫在書上，達與<u>以弗所</u>、<u>士每拿</u>、<u>別迦摩</u>、<u>推雅推喇</u>、<u>撒狄</u>、<u>非拉鐵非</u>、<u>老底嘉</u>那七個教會。"

[12]我轉過身來，要看是誰發聲與我說話。既轉過來，就看見七個金燈臺。[13]燈臺中間有一位好像人子，身穿長衣，直垂到腳，胸間束着金帶。[14]他的頭與髮皆白，如白羊毛，如雪，眼目如同火焰，[15]腳好像在爐中煅煉光明的銅，聲音如同眾水的聲音。[16]他右手拿着七星，從他口中出來一把兩刃的利劍，面貌如同烈日放光。

[17]我一看見，就仆倒在他腳前，像死了一樣。他用右手按着我說："不要懼怕！我是首先的，我是末後的，[18]又是那存活的；我曾死過，現在又活了，直活到永永遠遠，並且拿着死亡和陰間的鑰匙。

[19]"所以你要把所看見的和現在的事，並將來必成的事都寫出來。[20]論到你所看見、在我右手中的七星和七個金燈臺的奧秘，那七星就是七個教會的使者，七燈臺就是七個教會。

寫信給以弗所教會

2 "你要寫信給<u>以弗所</u>教會的使者說：

那右手拿着七星，在七個金燈臺中間行走的說：[2]我知道你的行為、勞碌、忍耐，也知道你不能容忍惡人。你也曾試驗那自稱為使徒卻不是使徒的，看出他們是假的來。[3]你也能忍耐，曾為我的名勞苦，並不乏倦。

[4]然而，有一件事我要責備你，就是你把起初的愛心離棄了。[5]所以應當回想你是從哪裏墜落的，並要悔改，行起初所行的事。你若不悔改，我就臨到你那裏，把你的燈臺從原處挪去。[6]然而，你還有一件可取的事，就

---

a 13 Daniel 7:13   *b 20* Or *messengers*   *c 1* Or *messenger*; also in verses 8, 12 and 18

是你恨惡尼哥拉一黨人的行為，
這也是我所恨惡的。

7聖靈向眾教會所說的話，
凡有耳的，就應當聽！得勝的，
我必將神樂園中生命樹的果子賜
給他吃。

寫信給士每拿教會

8 "你要寫信給士每拿教會的使者說：

那首先的、末後的、死過
又活的說：9我知道你的患難，也
你的貧窮（你卻是富足的），也
知道那自稱是猶太人所說的毀謗
話，其實他們不是猶太人，乃是
撒但一會的人。10你將要受的苦
你不用怕。魔鬼要把你們中間幾
個人下在監裏，叫你們被試煉，
你們必受患難十日。你務要至死
忠心，我就賜給你那生命的冠
冕。

11聖靈向眾教會所說的話，
凡有耳的，就應當聽！得勝的，
必不受第二次死的害。

寫信給別迦摩教會

12 "你要寫信給別迦摩教會的使者
說：

那有兩刃利劍的說：13我知
道你的居所，就是有撒但座位之
處。當我忠心的見證人安提帕在
你們中間、撒但所住的地方被殺
之時，你還堅守我的名，沒有棄
絕我的道。

14然而，有幾件事我要責備
你，因為在你那裏，有人服從了
巴蘭的教訓；這巴蘭曾教導巴勒
將絆腳石放在以色列人面前，叫
他們吃祭偶像之物，行姦淫的
事。15你那裏也有人照樣服從了
尼哥拉一黨人的教訓。16所以你
當悔改！若不悔改，我就快臨到
你那裏，用我口中的劍攻擊他
們。

17聖靈向眾教會所說的話，
凡有耳的，就應當聽！得勝的，
我必將那隱藏的嗎哪賜給他，並
賜他一塊白石，石上寫着新名，
除了那領受的以外，沒有人能認
識。

have this in your favor: You hate the practices of the Nicolaitans, which I also hate.
7He who has an ear, let him hear what the Spirit says to the churches. To him who overcomes, I will give the right to eat from the tree of life, which is in the paradise of God.

To the Church in Smyrna

8"To the angel of the church in Smyrna write:

These are the words of him who is the First and the Last, who died and came to life again. 9I know your afflictions and your poverty—yet you are rich! I know the slander of those who say they are Jews and are not, but are a synagogue of Satan. 10Do not be afraid of what you are about to suffer. I tell you, the devil will put some of you in prison to test you, and you will suffer persecution for ten days. Be faithful, even to the point of death, and I will give you the crown of life.

11He who has an ear, let him hear what the Spirit says to the churches. He who overcomes will not be hurt at all by the second death.

To the Church in Pergamum

12"To the angel of the church in Pergamum write:

These are the words of him who has the sharp, double-edged sword. 13I know where you live—where Satan has his throne. Yet you remain true to my name. You did not renounce your faith in me, even in the days of Antipas, my faithful witness, who was put to death in your city—where Satan lives.

14Nevertheless, I have a few things against you: You have people there who hold to the teaching of Balaam, who taught Balak to entice the Israelites to sin by eating food sacrificed to idols and by committing sexual immorality. 15Likewise you also have those who hold to the teaching of the Nicolaitans. 16Repent therefore! Otherwise, I will soon come to you and will fight against them with the sword of my mouth.

17He who has an ear, let him hear what the Spirit says to the churches. To him who overcomes, I will give some of the hidden manna. I will also give him a white stone with a new name written on it, known only to him who receives it.

在我神面前，沒有一樣是完□的。³所以要回想你是怎樣領□，怎樣聽見的，又要遵守，並□悔改。若不警醒，我必臨到你□裏，如同賊一樣。我幾時臨□，你也決不能知道。

⁴然而在撒狄，你還有幾名是未曾污穢自己衣服的；他們要穿白衣與我同行，因為他們是配得過的。⁵凡得勝的，必這樣穿白衣，我也必不從生命冊上塗抹他的名，且要在我父面前和我父眾使者面前認他的名。⁶聖靈向眾教會所說的話，凡有耳的，就應當聽！

寫信給非拉鐵非教會

⁷ "你要寫信給非拉鐵非教會的使者說：

那聖潔、真實，拿着大衛的鑰匙，開了就沒有人能關，關了就沒有人能開的，說：⁸我知道你的行為，你略有一點力量，也曾遵守我的道，沒有棄絕我的名。看哪，我在你面前給你一個敞開的門，是無人能關的。⁹那撒但一會的，自稱是猶太人，其實不是猶太人，乃是說謊話的，我要使他們來在你腳前下拜，也使他們知道我是已經愛你了。¹⁰你既遵守我忍耐的道，我必在普天下人受試煉的時候，保守你免去你的試煉。

¹¹我必快來，你要持守你所有的，免得人奪去你的冠冕。¹²得勝的，我要叫他在我神殿中作柱子，他也必不再從那裏出去。我又要將我神的名和我神城的名（這城就是從天上、從我神那裏降下來的新耶路撒冷），並我的新名，都寫在他上面。¹³聖靈向眾教會所說的話，凡有耳的，就應當聽！

寫信給老底嘉教會

¹⁴ "你要寫信給老底嘉教會的使者說：

那為阿們的，為誠信真實見證的，在神創造萬物之上為元首的，說：¹⁵我知道你的行為，你也不冷也不熱；我巴不得你或

deeds complete in the sight of my God. ³Remember, therefore, what you have received and heard; obey it, and repent. But if you do not wake up, I will come like a thief, and you will not know at what time I will come to you.

⁴Yet you have a few people in Sardis who have not soiled their clothes. They will walk with me, dressed in white, for they are worthy. ⁵He who overcomes will, like them, be dressed in white. I will never blot out his name from the book of life, but will acknowledge his name before my Father and his angels. ⁶He who has an ear, let him hear what the Spirit says to the churches.

To the Church in Philadelphia

⁷"To the angel of the church in Philadelphia write:

These are the words of him who is holy and true, who holds the key of David. What he opens no one can shut, and what he shuts no one can open. ⁸I know your deeds. See, I have placed before you an open door that no one can shut. I know that you have little strength, yet you have kept my word and have not denied my name. ⁹I will make those who are of the synagogue of Satan, who claim to be Jews though they are not, but are liars—I will make them come and fall down at your feet and acknowledge that I have loved you. ¹⁰Since you have kept my command to endure patiently, I will also keep you from the hour of trial that is going to come upon the whole world to test those who live on the earth.

¹¹I am coming soon. Hold on to what you have, so that no one will take your crown. ¹²Him who overcomes I will make a pillar in the temple of my God. Never again will he leave it. I will write on him the name of my God and the name of the city of my God, the new Jerusalem, which is coming down out of heaven from my God; and I will also write on him my new name. ¹³He who has an ear, let him hear what the Spirit says to the churches.

To the Church in Laodicea

¹⁴"To the angel of the church in Laodicea write:

These are the words of the Amen, the faithful and true witness, the ruler of God's creation. ¹⁵I know your deeds, that you are neither cold nor hot. I wish you were either

To the Church in Thyatira

¹⁸"To the angel of the church in Thyatira write:

These are the words of the Son of God, whose eyes are like blazing fire and whose feet are like burnished bronze. ¹⁹I know your deeds, your love and faith, your service and perseverance, and that you are now doing more than you did at first.

²⁰Nevertheless, I have this against you: You tolerate that woman Jezebel, who calls herself a prophetess. By her teaching she misleads my servants into sexual immorality and the eating of food sacrificed to idols. ²¹I have given her time to repent of her immorality, but she is unwilling. ²²So I will cast her on a bed of suffering, and I will make those who commit adultery with her suffer intensely, unless they repent of her ways. ²³I will strike her children dead. Then all the churches will know that I am he who searches hearts and minds, and I will repay each of you according to your deeds. ²⁴Now I say to the rest of you in Thyatira, to you who do not hold to her teaching and have not learned Satan's so-called deep secrets (I will not impose any other burden on you): ²⁵Only hold on to what you have until I come.

²⁶To him who overcomes and does my will to the end, I will give authority over the nations—

²⁷'He will rule them with an iron scepter;
    he will dash them to pieces like pottery'^a—

just as I have received authority from my Father. ²⁸I will also give him the morning star. ²⁹He who has an ear, let him hear what the Spirit says to the churches.

To the Church in Sardis

3 "To the angel^b of the church in Sardis write:

These are the words of him who holds the seven spirits^c of God and the seven stars. I know your deeds; you have a reputation of being alive, but you are dead. ²Wake up! Strengthen what remains and is about to die, for I have not found your

a 27 Psalm 2:9   b 1 Or *messenger;* also in verses 7 and 14
c 1 Or *the sevenfold Spirit*

寫信給推雅推啊

¹⁸「你要寫信給□□□ 說：

那眼目如火□□□ 的 神之子說：¹⁹□□□ 為、愛心、信心、□□□ 又知道你末後所行的□□□ 初所行的更多。

²⁰然而，有一件事□□□ 你，就是你容讓那自稱□□□ 婦人耶洗別教導我的僕人□□□ 他們行姦淫，吃祭偶像□□□ ²¹我曾給她悔改的機會，如□□□ 肯悔改她的淫行。²²看哪，□□□ 叫她病臥在牀；那些與她行□□□ 人，若不悔改所行的，我也要□□□ 他們同受大患難。²³我又要殺□□□ 她的黨類（註：「黨類」原文作□□□ 女」），叫眾教會知道，我是那□□□ 察看人肺腑心腸的，並要照你們□□□ 的行為報應你們各人。²⁴至於你□□□ 們推雅推喇其餘的人，就是一切□□□ 不從那教訓，不曉得他們素常所□□□ 說撒但深奧之理的人，我告訴你□□□ 們：我不將別的擔子放在你們身□□□ 上，²⁵但你們已經有的，總要持□□□ 守，直等到我來。

²⁶那得勝又遵守我命令到底□□□ 的，我要賜給他權柄制伏列國。□□□

²⁷「他必用鐵杖轄管他們（註：「轄□□□ 管」原文作「牧」），將他們□□□ 如同窯戶的瓦器打得粉碎。」

像我從我父領受的權柄一樣。□□□ ²⁸我又要把晨星賜給他。²⁹聖靈向□□□ 眾教會所說的話，凡有耳的，就□□□ 應當聽！

寫信給撒狄教會

3 「你要寫信給撒狄教會的使□□□ 者說：

那有神的七靈和七星的說：□□□ 我知道你的行為，按名你是活□□□ 的，其實是死的。²你要警醒！□□□ 堅固那剩下將要衰微的（註：「衰□□□ 微」原文作「死」），因我見你的行

one or the other! ¹⁶So, because you are luke-warm—neither hot nor cold—I am about to spit you out of my mouth. ¹⁷You say, 'I am rich; I have acquired wealth and do not need a thing.' But you do not realize that you are wretched, pitiful, poor, blind and naked. ¹⁸I counsel you to buy from me gold refined in the fire, so you can become rich; and white clothes to wear, so you can cover your shameful nakedness; and salve to put on your eyes, so you can see.

¹⁹Those whom I love I rebuke and discipline. So be earnest, and repent. ²⁰Here I am! I stand at the door and knock. If anyone hears my voice and opens the door, I will come in and eat with him, and he with me.

²¹To him who overcomes, I will give the right to sit with me on my throne, just as I overcame and sat down with my Father on his throne. ²²He who has an ear, let him hear what the Spirit says to the churches."

The Throne in Heaven

4 After this I looked, and there before me was a door standing open in heaven. And the voice I had first heard speaking to me like a trumpet said, "Come up here, and I will show you what must take place after this." ²At once I was in the Spirit, and there before me was a throne in heaven with someone sitting on it. ³And the one who sat there had the appearance of jasper and carnelian. A rainbow, resembling an emerald, encircled the throne. ⁴Surrounding the throne were twenty-four other thrones, and seated on them were twenty-four elders. They were dressed in white and had crowns of gold on their heads. ⁵From the throne came flashes of lightning, rumblings and peals of thunder. Before the throne, seven lamps were blazing. These are the seven spirits^a of God. ⁶Also before the throne there was what looked like a sea of glass, clear as crystal.

In the center, around the throne, were four living creatures, and they were covered with eyes, in front and in back. ⁷The first living creature was like a lion, the second was like an ox, the third had a face like a man, the fourth was like a flying eagle. ⁸Each of the four living creatures had six wings and was covered with eyes all around, even under his wings. Day and night they never stop saying:

冷或熱。¹⁶你既如溫水，也不冷也不熱，所以我必從我口中把你吐出去。¹⁷你說：'我是富足，已經發了財，一樣都不缺。'卻不知道你是那困苦、可憐、貧窮、瞎眼、赤身的。¹⁸我勸你向我買火煉的金子，叫你富足；又買白衣穿上，叫你赤身的羞恥不露出來；又買眼藥擦你的眼睛，使你能看見。

¹⁹凡我所疼愛的，我就責備管教他，所以你要發熱心，也要悔改。²⁰看哪，我站在門外叩門，若有聽見我聲音就開門的，我要進到他那裏去，我與他，他與我一同坐席。

²¹得勝的，我要賜他在我寶座上與我同坐，就如我得了勝，在我父的寶座上與他同坐一般。²²聖靈向眾教會所說的話，凡有耳的，就應當聽！"

天上的寶座

4 此後，我觀看，見天上有門開了。我初次聽見好像吹號的聲音，對我說："你上到這裏來！我要將以後必成的事指示你。"²我立刻被聖靈感動，見有一個寶座安置在天上，又有一位坐在寶座上。³看那坐者的，好像碧玉和紅寶石，又有虹圍着寶座，好像綠寶石。⁴寶座的周圍又有二十四個座位，其上坐着二十四位長老，身穿白衣，頭上戴着金冠冕。⁵有閃電、聲音、雷轟從寶座中發出。又有七盞火燈在寶座前點着，這七燈就是神的七靈。⁶寶座前好像一個玻璃海，如同水晶。

寶座中和寶座周圍有四個活物，前後遍體都滿了眼睛。⁷第一個活物像獅子，第二個像牛犢，第三個臉面像人，第四個像飛鷹。⁸四活物各有六個翅膀，遍體內外都滿了眼睛。它們晝夜不住地說：

---

^a 5 Or the sevenfold Spirit

"聖哉！聖哉！聖哉！
　　主神是昔在、今在、
　　以後永在的全能者！"

9每逢四活物將榮耀、尊貴、感謝歸給那坐在寶座上、活到永永遠遠者的時候，10那二十四位長老就俯伏在坐寶座的面前，敬拜那活到永永遠遠的，又把他們的冠冕放在寶座前，說：

11 "我們的主，我們的神，
　　你是配得榮耀、尊貴、權柄的！
　　因為你創造了萬物，
　　並且萬物是因你的旨意
　　　被創造而有的。"

書卷和羔羊

5 我看見坐寶座的右手中有書卷，裏外都寫着字，用七印封嚴了。2我又看見一位大力的天使大聲宣傳說："有誰配展開那書卷，揭開那七印呢？"3在天上、地上、地底下，沒有能展開、能觀看那書卷的。4因為沒有配展開、配觀看那書卷的，我就大哭。5長老中有一位對我說："不要哭！看哪，猶大支派中的獅子、大衛的根，他已得勝，能以展開那書卷，揭開那七印。"

6我又看見寶座與四活物並長老之中，有羔羊站立，像是被殺過的，有七角七眼，就是神的七靈，奉差遣往普天下去的。7這羔羊前來，從坐寶座的右手裏拿了書卷。8他既拿了書卷，四活物和二十四位長老就俯伏在羔羊面前，各拿着琴和盛滿了香的金爐；這香就是眾聖徒的祈禱。9他們唱新歌，說：

"你配拿書卷，
　　配揭開七印。
　因為你曾被殺，
　　用自己的血
　從各族、各方、各民、各國中
　　買了人來，
　叫他們歸於神，

"Holy, holy, holy
　is the Lord God Almighty,
　who was, and is, and is to come."

9Whenever the living creatures give glory, honor and thanks to him who sits on the throne and who lives for ever and ever, 10the twenty-four elders fall down before him who sits on the throne, and worship him who lives for ever and ever. They lay their crowns before the throne and say:

11"You are worthy, our Lord and God,
　to receive glory and honor and power,
　for you created all things,
　and by your will they were created
　and have their being."

The Scroll and the Lamb

5 Then I saw in the right hand of him who sat on the throne a scroll with writing on both sides and sealed with seven seals. 2And I saw a mighty angel proclaiming in a loud voice, "Who is worthy to break the seals and open the scroll?" 3But no one in heaven or on earth or under the earth could open the scroll or even look inside it. 4I wept and wept because no one was found who was worthy to open the scroll or look inside. 5Then one of the elders said to me, "Do not weep! See, the Lion of the tribe of Judah, the Root of David, has triumphed. He is able to open the scroll and its seven seals."

6Then I saw a Lamb, looking as if it had been slain, standing in the center of the throne, encircled by the four living creatures and the elders. He had seven horns and seven eyes, which are the seven spirits[a] of God sent out into all the earth. 7He came and took the scroll from the right hand of him who sat on the throne. 8And when he had taken it, the four living creatures and the twenty-four elders fell down before the Lamb. Each one had a harp and they were holding golden bowls full of incense, which are the prayers of the saints. 9And they sang a new song:

"You are worthy to take the scroll
　and to open its seals,
　because you were slain,
　and with your blood you purchased men for God
　　from every tribe and language and people and nation.

a 6 Or the sevenfold Spirit

¹⁰You have made them to be a kingdom and
   priests to serve our God,
   and they will reign on the earth."

¹¹Then I looked and heard the voice of many
angels, numbering thousands upon thousands,
and ten thousand times ten thousand. They
encircled the throne and the living creatures and
the elders. ¹²In a loud voice they sang:

"Worthy is the Lamb, who was slain,
   to receive power and wealth and wisdom
      and strength
   and honor and glory and praise!"

¹³Then I heard every creature in heaven and
on earth and under the earth and on the sea, and
all that is in them, singing:

"To him who sits on the throne and to the
      Lamb
   be praise and honor and glory and power,
      for ever and ever!"

¹⁴The four living creatures said, "Amen," and
the elders fell down and worshiped.

The Seals

6 I watched as the Lamb opened the first
   of the seven seals. Then I heard one of
   the four living creatures say in a voice
like thunder, "Come!" ²I looked, and there
before me was a white horse! Its rider held a
bow, and he was given a crown, and he rode out
as a conqueror bent on conquest.

³When the Lamb opened the second seal, I
heard the second living creature say, "Come!"
⁴Then another horse came out, a fiery red one.
Its rider was given power to take peace from the
earth and to make men slay each other. To him
was given a large sword.

⁵When the Lamb opened the third seal, I
heard the third living creature say, "Come!" I
looked, and there before me was a black horse!
Its rider was holding a pair of scales in his hand.
⁶Then I heard what sounded like a voice among
the four living creatures, saying, "A quart[a] of
wheat for a day's wages,[b] and three quarts of
barley for a day's wages,[b] and do not damage
the oil and the wine!"

⁷When the Lamb opened the fourth seal, I
heard the voice of the fourth living creature say,
"Come!" ⁸I looked, and there before me was a

¹⁰又叫他們成為國民，
    作祭司，歸於神，
    在地上執掌王權。"

¹¹我又看見且聽見寶座與活物並
長老的周圍，有許多天使的聲音；他
們的數目有千千萬萬，¹²大聲說：

"曾被殺的羔羊
    是配得權柄、豐富、
    智慧、能力、
    尊貴、榮耀、頌讚的！"

¹³我又聽見在天上、地上、地底
下、滄海裏和天地間一切所有被造之
物都說：

"但願頌讚、尊貴、
    榮耀、權勢
    都歸給坐寶座的和羔羊，
    直到永永遠遠！"

¹⁴四活物就說："阿們！"眾長老也
俯伏敬拜。

七印

6 我看見羔羊揭開七印中第一
   印的時候，就聽見四活物中
   的一個活物，聲音如雷，
說："你來！"²我就觀看，見有一
匹白馬！騎在馬上的拿着弓，並有冠
冕賜給他。他便出來，勝了又要勝。

³揭開第二印的時候，我聽見第
二個活物說："你來！"⁴就另有一
匹馬出來，是紅的，有權柄給了那騎
馬的，可以從地上奪去太平，使人彼
此相殺，又有一把大刀賜給他。

⁵揭開第三印的時候，我聽見第
三個活物說："你來！"我就觀看，
見有一匹黑馬；騎在馬上的，手裏拿
着天平。⁶我聽見在四活物中似乎有
聲音說："一錢銀子買一升麥子，一
錢銀子買三升大麥，油和酒不可糟
蹋。"

⁷揭開第四印的時候，我聽見第
四個活物說："你來！"⁸我就觀

a 6 Greek a choinix (probably about a liter)   b 6 Greek a
denarius

看，見有一匹灰色馬！騎在馬上的，名字叫作死，陰府也隨着他。有權柄賜給他們，可以用刀劍、饑荒、瘟疫（註：“瘟疫”或作“死亡”）、野獸，殺害地上四分之一的人。

9揭開第五印的時候，我看見在祭壇底下，有為神的道並為作見證被殺之人的靈魂，10大聲喊着說：“聖潔真實的主啊！你不審判住在地上的人給我們伸流血的冤，要等到幾時呢？”11於是有白衣賜給他們各人，又有話對他們說：“還要安息片時，等着一同作僕人的和他們的弟兄，也像他們被殺，滿了數目。”

12揭開第六印的時候，我又看見地大震動，日頭變黑像毛布，滿月變紅像血；13天上的星辰墜落於地，如同無花果樹被大風搖動，落下末熟的果子一樣。14天就挪移，好像書卷被捲起來；山嶺海島都被挪移，離開本位。

15地上的君王、臣宰、將軍、富戶、壯士和一切為奴的、自主的，都藏在山洞和巖石穴裏，16向山和巖石說：“倒在我們身上吧！把我們藏起來，躲避坐寶座者的面目和羔羊的忿怒，17因為他們忿怒的大日到了，誰能站得住呢？”

十四萬四千人受印

7 此後，我看見四位天使站在地的四角，執掌地上四方的風，叫風不吹在地上、海上和樹上。2我又看見另有一位天使，從日出之地上來，拿着永生神的印。他就向那держ着權柄能傷害地和海的四位天使大聲喊着說：3“地與海並樹木，你們不可傷害，等我們印了我們神眾僕人的額。”4我聽見以色列人各支派中受印的數目有十四萬四千：

5猶大支派中受印的有一萬二千；
　呂便支派中有一萬二千；
　迦得支派中有一萬二千；
6亞設支派中有一萬二千；
　拿弗他利支派中有一萬二千；
　瑪拿西支派中有一萬二千；

pale horse! Its rider was named Death, and Hades was following close behind him. They were given power over a fourth of the earth to kill by sword, famine and plague, and by the wild beasts of the earth.

9When he opened the fifth seal, I saw under the altar the souls of those who had been slain because of the word of God and the testimony they had maintained. 10They called out in a loud voice, "How long, Sovereign Lord, holy and true, until you judge the inhabitants of the earth and avenge our blood?" 11Then each of them was given a white robe, and they were told to wait a little longer, until the number of their fellow servants and brothers who were to be killed as they had been was completed.

12I watched as he opened the sixth seal. There was a great earthquake. The sun turned black like sackcloth made of goat hair, the whole moon turned blood red, 13and the stars in the sky fell to earth, as late figs drop from a fig tree when shaken by a strong wind. 14The sky receded like a scroll, rolling up, and every mountain and island was removed from its place.

15Then the kings of the earth, the princes, the generals, the rich, the mighty, and every slave and every free man hid in caves and among the rocks of the mountains. 16They called to the mountains and the rocks, "Fall on us and hide us from the face of him who sits on the throne and from the wrath of the Lamb! 17For the great day of their wrath has come, and who can stand?"

144,000 Sealed

7 After this I saw four angels standing at the four corners of the earth, holding back the four winds of the earth to prevent any wind from blowing on the land or on the sea or on any tree. 2Then I saw another angel coming up from the east, having the seal of the living God. He called out in a loud voice to the four angels who had been given power to harm the land and the sea: 3"Do not harm the land or the sea or the trees until we put a seal on the foreheads of the servants of our God." 4Then I heard the number of those who were sealed: 144,000 from all the tribes of Israel.

5From the tribe of Judah 12,000 were sealed,
　from the tribe of Reuben 12,000,
　from the tribe of Gad 12,000,
6from the tribe of Asher 12,000,
　from the tribe of Naphtali 12,000,
　from the tribe of Manasseh 12,000,

7from the tribe of Simeon 12,000,
  from the tribe of Levi 12,000,
  from the tribe of Issachar 12,000,
8from the tribe of Zebulun 12,000,
  from the tribe of Joseph 12,000,
  from the tribe of Benjamin 12,000.

The Great Multitude in White Robes

9After this I looked and there before me was a great multitude that no one could count, from every nation, tribe, people and language, standing before the throne and in front of the Lamb. They were wearing white robes and were holding palm branches in their hands. 10And they cried out in a loud voice:

> "Salvation belongs to our God,
> who sits on the throne,
> and to the Lamb."

11All the angels were standing around the throne and around the elders and the four living creatures. They fell down on their faces before the throne and worshiped God, 12saying:

> "Amen!
> Praise and glory
> and wisdom and thanks and honor
> and power and strength
> be to our God for ever and ever.
> Amen!"

13Then one of the elders asked me, "These in white robes—who are they, and where did they come from?"

14I answered, "Sir, you know."

And he said, "These are they who have come out of the great tribulation; they have washed their robes and made them white in the blood of the Lamb. 15Therefore,

> "they are before the throne of God
> and serve him day and night in his temple;
> and he who sits on the throne will spread his
> tent over them.
16Never again will they hunger;
> never again will they thirst.
> The sun will not beat upon them,
> nor any scorching heat.
17For the Lamb at the center of the throne will
> be their shepherd;
> he will lead them to springs of living water.
> And God will wipe away every tear from
> their eyes."

7西緬支派中有一萬二千;
  利未支派中有一萬二千;
  以薩迦支派中有一萬二千;
8西布倫支派中有一萬二千;
  約瑟支派中有一萬二千;
  便雅憫支派中受印的有一萬二千。

無數身穿白衣的羣眾

9此後,我觀看,見有許多的人,沒有人能數過來,是從各國、各族、各民、各方來的,站在寶座和羔羊面前,身穿白衣,手拿棕樹枝,10大聲喊着說:

> "願救恩歸與坐在
> 寶座上我們的神,
> 也歸與羔羊。"

11眾天使都站在寶座和眾長老並四活物的周圍,在寶座前,面伏於地敬拜神,12說:

> "阿們!
> 頌讚、榮耀、
> 智慧、感謝、尊貴、
> 權柄、大力
> 都歸與我們的神,直到永永遠遠。
> 阿們!"

13長老中有一位問我說:"這些穿白衣的是誰?是從哪裏來的?"

14我對他說:"我主,你知道。"
他向我說:"這些人是從大患難中出來的,曾用羔羊的血把衣裳洗白淨了。15所以,

> "他們在神寶座前,
> 晝夜在他殿中侍奉他。
> 坐寶座的要
> 用帳幕覆庇他們。
16他們不再飢、
> 不再渴,
> 日頭和炎熱
> 也必不傷害他們。
17因為寶座中的羔羊
> 必牧養他們,
> 領他們到生命水的泉源;
神也必擦去
> 他們一切的眼淚。"

第七印和金香爐

8 羔羊揭開第七印的時候，天上寂靜約有二刻。

²我看見那站在神面前的七位天使，有七枝號賜給他們。

³另有一位天使拿着金香爐，來站在祭壇旁邊。有許多香賜給他，要和眾聖徒的祈禱一同獻在寶座前的金壇上。⁴那香的煙和眾聖徒的祈禱，從天使的手中一同升到神面前。⁵天使拿着香爐，盛滿了壇上的火，倒在地上，隨有雷轟、大聲、閃電、地震。

七號

⁶拿着七枝號的七位天使就預備要吹。

⁷第一位天使吹號，就有雹子與火攙着血丟在地上。地的三分之一和樹的三分之一被燒了，一切的青草也被燒了。

⁸第二位天使吹號，就有彷彿火燒着的大山扔在海中。海的三分之一變成血，⁹海中的活物死了三分之一，船隻也壞了三分之一。

¹⁰第三位天使吹號，就有燒着的大星好像火把從天上落下來，落在江河的三分之一和眾水的泉源上。¹¹這星名叫"茵蔯"。眾水的三分之一變為茵蔯，因水變苦，就死了許多人。

¹²第四位天使吹號，日頭的三分之一，月亮的三分之一，星辰的三分之一都被擊打，以致日月星的三分之一黑暗了，白晝的三分之一沒有光，黑夜也是這樣。

¹³我又看見一個鷹飛在空中，並聽見牠大聲說："三位天使要吹那其餘的號，你們住在地上的民，禍哉！禍哉！禍哉！"

9 第五位天使吹號，我就看見一個星從天落到地上，有無底坑的鑰匙賜給它。²它開了無底坑，便有煙從坑裏往上冒，好像大火爐的煙，日頭和天空都因這

The Seventh Seal and the Golden Censer

8 When he opened the seventh seal, there was silence in heaven for about half an hour.

²And I saw the seven angels who stand before God, and to them were given seven trumpets.

³Another angel, who had a golden censer, came and stood at the altar. He was given much incense to offer, with the prayers of all the saints, on the golden altar before the throne. ⁴The smoke of the incense, together with the prayers of the saints, went up before God from the angel's hand. ⁵Then the angel took the censer, filled it with fire from the altar, and hurled it on the earth; and there came peals of thunder, rumblings, flashes of lightning and an earthquake.

The Trumpets

⁶Then the seven angels who had the seven trumpets prepared to sound them.

⁷The first angel sounded his trumpet, and there came hail and fire mixed with blood, and it was hurled down upon the earth. A third of the earth was burned up, a third of the trees were burned up, and all the green grass was burned up.

⁸The second angel sounded his trumpet, and something like a huge mountain, all ablaze, was thrown into the sea. A third of the sea turned into blood, ⁹a third of the living creatures in the sea died, and a third of the ships were destroyed.

¹⁰The third angel sounded his trumpet, and a great star, blazing like a torch, fell from the sky on a third of the rivers and on the springs of water— ¹¹the name of the star is Wormwood.ᵃ A third of the waters turned bitter, and many people died from the waters that had become bitter.

¹²The fourth angel sounded his trumpet, and a third of the sun was struck, a third of the moon, and a third of the stars, so that a third of them turned dark. A third of the day was without light, and also a third of the night.

¹³As I watched, I heard an eagle that was flying in midair call out in a loud voice: "Woe! Woe! Woe to the inhabitants of the earth, because of the trumpet blasts about to be sounded by the other three angels!"

9 The fifth angel sounded his trumpet, and I saw a star that had fallen from the sky to the earth. The star was given the key to the shaft of the Abyss. ²When he opened the Abyss, smoke rose from it like the smoke from a gigantic furnace. The sun and sky were darkened by the smoke from the Abyss.

a 11 That is, Bitterness

³And out of the smoke locusts came down upon the earth and were given power like that of scorpions of the earth. ⁴They were told not to harm the grass of the earth or any plant or tree, but only those people who did not have the seal of God on their foreheads. ⁵They were not given power to kill them, but only to torture them for five months. And the agony they suffered was like that of the sting of a scorpion when it strikes a man. ⁶During those days men will seek death, but will not find it; they will long to die, but death will elude them.

⁷The locusts looked like horses prepared for battle. On their heads they wore something like crowns of gold, and their faces resembled human faces. ⁸Their hair was like women's hair, and their teeth were like lions' teeth. ⁹They had breastplates like breastplates of iron, and the sound of their wings was like the thundering of many horses and chariots rushing into battle. ¹⁰They had tails and stings like scorpions, and in their tails they had power to torment people for five months. ¹¹They had as king over them the angel of the Abyss, whose name in Hebrew is Abaddon, and in Greek, Apollyon.ᵃ

¹²The first woe is past; two other woes are yet to come.

¹³The sixth angel sounded his trumpet, and I heard a voice coming from the hornsᵇ of the golden altar that is before God. ¹⁴It said to the sixth angel who had the trumpet, "Release the four angels who are bound at the great river Euphrates." ¹⁵And the four angels who had been kept ready for this very hour and day and month and year were released to kill a third of mankind. ¹⁶The number of the mounted troops was two hundred million. I heard their number.

¹⁷The horses and riders I saw in my vision looked like this: Their breastplates were fiery red, dark blue, and yellow as sulfur. The heads of the horses resembled the heads of lions, and out of their mouths came fire, smoke and sulfur. ¹⁸A third of mankind was killed by the three plagues of fire, smoke and sulfur that came out of their mouths. ¹⁹The power of the horses was in their mouths and in their tails; for their tails were like snakes, having heads with which they inflict injury.

²⁰The rest of mankind that were not killed by these plagues still did not repent of the work of their hands; they did not stop worshiping demons, and idols of gold, silver, bronze, stone and wood—idols that cannot see or hear or

---

煙昏暗了。³有蝗蟲從煙中出來，飛到地上，有能力賜給牠們，好像地上蠍子的能力一樣。⁴並且吩咐牠們說，不可傷害地上的草和各樣青物，並一切樹木，惟獨要傷害額上沒有神印記的人。⁵但不許蝗蟲害死他們，只叫他們受痛苦五個月，這痛苦就像蠍子螫人的痛苦一樣。⁶在那些日子，人要求死，決不得死；願意死，死卻遠避他們。

⁷蝗蟲的形狀好像預備出戰的馬一樣，頭上戴的好像金冠冕，臉面好像男人的臉面，⁸頭髮像女人的頭髮，牙齒像獅子的牙齒。⁹胸前有甲，好像鐵甲。牠們翅膀的聲音，好像許多車馬奔跑上陣的聲音。¹⁰有尾巴像蠍子，尾巴上的毒鉤能傷人五個月。¹¹有無底坑的使者作牠們的王，按著<u>希伯來</u>話，名叫<u>亞巴頓</u>；<u>希臘</u>話，名叫<u>亞玻倫</u>。

¹²第一樣災禍過去了，還有兩樣災禍要來。

¹³第六位天使吹號，我就聽見有聲音從神面前金壇的四角出來，¹⁴吩咐那吹號的第六位天使，說：「把那捆綁在<u>幼發拉底</u>大河的四個使者釋放了。」¹⁵那四個使者就被釋放。他們原是預備好了，到某年某月某日某時，要殺人的三分之一。¹⁶馬軍有二萬萬，他們的數目我聽見了。

¹⁷我在異象中看見那些馬和騎馬的，騎馬的胸前有甲如火，與紫瑪瑙並硫磺。馬的頭好像獅子頭，有火、有煙、有硫磺，從馬的口中出來。¹⁸口中所出來的火與煙，並硫磺，這三樣災殺了人的三分之一。¹⁹這馬的能力是在口裏和尾巴上，因這尾巴像蛇，並且有頭用以害人。

²⁰其餘未曾被這些災所殺的人，仍舊不悔改自己手所做的，還是去拜鬼魔和那些不能看、不能聽、不能走，金、銀、銅、木、石的偶像；

ᵃ 11 *Abaddon* and *Apollyon* mean *Destroyer.*   ᵇ 13 That is, projections

21又不悔改他們那些凶殺、邪術、姦淫、偷竊的事。

天使與小書卷

10 我又看見另有一位大力的天使從天降下，披着雲彩，頭上有虹，臉面像日頭，兩腳像火柱。²他手裏拿着小書卷，是展開的。他右腳踏海，左腳踏地，³大聲呼喊，好像獅子吼叫。呼喊完了，就有七雷發聲。⁴七雷發聲之後，我正要寫出來，就聽見從天上有聲音說：「七雷所說的你要封上，不可寫出來。」

⁵我所看見的那踏海踏地的天使向天舉起右手來，⁶指着那創造天和天上之物、地和地上之物、海和海中之物，直活到永永遠遠的，起誓說：「不再有時日了（註：或作「不再躭延了」）！⁷但在第七位天使吹號發聲的時候，神的奧秘就成全了，正如神所傳給他僕人眾先知的佳音。」

⁸我先前從天上所聽見的那聲音又吩咐我說：「你去，把那踏海踏地之天使手中展開的小書卷取過來。」⁹我就走到天使那裏，對他說：「請你把小書卷給我。」他對我說：「你拿着吃盡了，便叫你肚子發苦，然而在你口中要甜如蜜。」¹⁰我從天使手中把小書卷接過來，吃盡了，在我口中果然甜如蜜，吃了以後，肚子覺得發苦了。¹¹天使（註：原文作「他們」）對我說：「你必指着多民、多國、多方、多王再說預言。」

兩位見證人

11 有一根葦子賜給我，當作量度的杖，且有話說：「起來，將神的殿和祭壇，並在殿中禮拜的人都量一量。²只是殿外的院子要留下不用量，因為這是給了外邦人的，他們要踐踏聖城四十二個月。³我要使我那兩個見證人，穿着毛衣，傳道一千二百六十天。」⁴他們就是那兩棵橄欖樹，兩個燈臺，立在世界之主面前的。⁵若有人想要害他們，就有火從他們口中出來，燒滅仇敵。凡想要害他們

The Angel and the Little Scroll

10 Then I saw another mighty angel coming down from heaven. He was robed in a cloud, with a rainbow above his head; his face was like the sun, and his legs were like fiery pillars. ²He was holding a little scroll, which lay open in his hand. He planted his right foot on the sea and his left foot on the land, ³and he gave a loud shout like the roar of a lion. When he shouted, the voices of the seven thunders spoke. ⁴And when the seven thunders spoke, I was about to write; but I heard a voice from heaven say, "Seal up what the seven thunders have said and do not write it down."

⁵Then the angel I had seen standing on the sea and on the land raised his right hand to heaven. ⁶And he swore by him who lives for ever and ever, who created the heavens and all that is in them, the earth and all that is in it, and the sea and all that is in it, and said, "There will be no more delay! ⁷But in the days when the seventh angel is about to sound his trumpet, the mystery of God will be accomplished, just as he announced to his servants the prophets."

⁸Then the voice that I had heard from heaven spoke to me once more: "Go, take the scroll that lies open in the hand of the angel who is standing on the sea and on the land."

⁹So I went to the angel and asked him to give me the little scroll. He said to me, "Take it and eat it. It will turn your stomach sour, but in your mouth it will be as sweet as honey." ¹⁰I took the little scroll from the angel's hand and ate it. It tasted as sweet as honey in my mouth, but when I had eaten it, my stomach turned sour. ¹¹Then I was told, "You must prophesy again about many peoples, nations, languages and kings."

The Two Witnesses

11 I was given a reed like a measuring rod and was told, "Go and measure the temple of God and the altar, and count the worshipers there. ²But exclude the outer court; do not measure it, because it has been given to the Gentiles. They will trample on the holy city for 42 months. ³And I will give power to my two witnesses, and they will prophesy for 1,260 days, clothed in sackcloth." ⁴These are the two olive trees and the two lampstands that stand before the Lord of the earth. ⁵If anyone tries to harm them, fire comes from their mouths and devours their enemies. This is how anyone who wants to harm them must die. [6]These men have power to shut up the sky so that it will not rain during the time they are prophesying; and they have power to turn the waters into blood and to strike the earth with every kind of plague as often as they want.

[7]Now when they have finished their testimony, the beast that comes up from the Abyss will attack them, and overpower and kill them. [8]Their bodies will lie in the street of the great city, which is figuratively called Sodom and Egypt, where also their Lord was crucified. [9]For three and a half days men from every people, tribe, language and nation will gaze on their bodies and refuse them burial. [10]The inhabitants of the earth will gloat over them and will celebrate by sending each other gifts, because these two prophets had tormented those who live on the earth.

[11]But after the three and a half days a breath of life from God entered them, and they stood on their feet, and terror struck those who saw them. [12]Then they heard a loud voice from heaven saying to them, "Come up here." And they went up to heaven in a cloud, while their enemies looked on.

[13]At that very hour there was a severe earthquake and a tenth of the city collapsed. Seven thousand people were killed in the earthquake, and the survivors were terrified and gave glory to the God of heaven.

[14]The second woe has passed; the third woe is coming soon.

The Seventh Trumpet

[15]The seventh angel sounded his trumpet, and there were loud voices in heaven, which said:

"The kingdom of the world has become the
    kingdom of our Lord and of his Christ,
and he will reign for ever and ever."

[16]And the twenty-four elders, who were seated on their thrones before God, fell on their faces and worshiped God, [17]saying:

"We give thanks to you, Lord God Almighty,
    the One who is and who was,
because you have taken your great power
    and have begun to reign.
[18]The nations were angry;
    and your wrath has come.

的，都必這樣被殺。[6]這二人有權柄，在他們傳道的日子叫天閉塞不下雨；又有權柄叫水變為血，並且能隨時隨意用各樣的災殃攻擊世界。

[7]他們作完見證的時候，那從無底坑裏上來的獸必與他們交戰，並且得勝，把他們殺了。[8]他們的屍首就倒在大城裏的街上，這城按着靈意叫所多瑪，又叫埃及，就是他們的主釘十字架之處。[9]從各民、各族、各方、各國中，有人觀看他們的屍首三天半，又不許把屍首放在墳墓裏。[10]住在地上的人就為他們歡喜快樂，互相餽送禮物，因這兩位先知曾叫住在地上的人受痛苦。

[11]過了這三天半，有生氣從神那裏進入他們裏面，他們就站起來，看見他們的人甚是害怕。[12]兩位先知聽見有大聲音從天上來，對他們說："上到這裏來！"他們就駕着雲上了天，他們的仇敵也看見了。

[13]正在那時候，地大震動，城就倒塌了十分之一，因地震而死的有七千人，其餘的都恐懼，歸榮耀給天上的神。

[14]第二樣災禍過去，第三樣災禍快到了。

第七號

[15]第七位天使吹號，天上就有大聲音說：

"世上的國，
    成了我主和主基督的國，
他要作王，直到永永遠遠。"

[16]在神面前，坐在自己位上的二十四位長老，就面伏於地敬拜神，[17]說：

"昔在、今在的主神，
    全能者啊，我們感謝你！
因你執掌大權
    作王了。
[18]外邦發怒，
    你的忿怒也臨到了，

審判死人的時候也到了；
你的僕人眾先知和眾聖徒，
凡敬畏你名的人，
連大帶小得賞賜的時候也到了；
你敗壞那些敗壞世界之人的時候
也就到了。」

19當時，神天上的殿開了，在他殿中現出他的約櫃，隨後有閃電、聲音、雷轟、地震、大雹。

婦人和龍

12 天上現出大異象來：有一個婦人，身披日頭，腳踏月亮，頭戴十二星的冠冕。2她懷了孕，在生產的艱難中疼痛呼叫。3天上又現出異象來：有一條大紅龍，七頭十角，七頭上戴著七個冠冕。4牠的尾巴拖拉著天上星辰的三分之一，摔在地上。龍就站在那將要生產的婦人面前，等她生產之後，要吞吃她的孩子。5婦人生了一個男孩子，是將來要用鐵杖轄管萬國的（註：「轄管」原文作「牧」）。她的孩子被提到神寶座那裏去了。6婦人就逃到曠野，在那裏有神給她預備的地方，使她被養活一千二百六十天。

7在天上就有了爭戰。米迦勒同他的使者與龍爭戰，龍也同牠的使者去爭戰，8並沒有得勝，天上再沒有牠們的地方。9大龍就是那古蛇，名叫魔鬼，又叫撒但，是迷惑普天下的。牠被摔在地上，牠的使者也一同被摔下去。

10我聽見在天上有大聲音說：

「我神的救恩、能力、國度，
並他基督的權柄，
現在都來到了，
因為那在我們神面前
晝夜控告
我們弟兄的，
已經被摔下去了。
11弟兄勝過牠，
是因羔羊的血
和自己所見證的道。
他們雖至於死，
也不愛惜性命。
12所以諸天和住在其中的，
你們都快樂吧！

The time has come for judging the dead,
and for rewarding your servants the prophets
and your saints and those who reverence your
name,
both small and great—
and for destroying those who destroy the earth."

19Then God's temple in heaven was opened,
and within his temple was seen the ark of his
covenant. And there came flashes of lightning,
rumblings, peals of thunder, an earthquake and
a great hailstorm.

The Woman and the Dragon

12 A great and wondrous sign appeared in
heaven: a woman clothed with the sun,
with the moon under her feet and a
crown of twelve stars on her head. 2She was
pregnant and cried out in pain as she was about
to give birth. 3Then another sign appeared in
heaven: an enormous red dragon with seven
heads and ten horns and seven crowns on his
heads. 4His tail swept a third of the stars out of
the sky and flung them to the earth. The dragon
stood in front of the woman who was about to
give birth, so that he might devour her child the
moment it was born. 5She gave birth to a son, a
male child, who will rule all the nations with an
iron scepter. And her child was snatched up to
God and to his throne. 6The woman fled into the
desert to a place prepared for her by God, where
she might be taken care of for 1,260 days.

7And there was war in heaven. Michael and
his angels fought against the dragon, and the
dragon and his angels fought back. 8But he was
not strong enough, and they lost their place in
heaven. 9The great dragon was hurled down—
that ancient serpent called the devil, or Satan,
who leads the whole world astray. He was hurled
to the earth, and his angels with him.

10Then I heard a loud voice in heaven say:

"Now have come the salvation and the power
and the kingdom of our God,
and the authority of his Christ.
For the accuser of our brothers,
who accuses them before our God day and
night,
has been hurled down.
11They overcame him
by the blood of the Lamb
and by the word of their testimony;
they did not love their lives so much
as to shrink from death.
12Therefore rejoice, you heavens
and you who dwell in them!

But woe to the earth and the sea,
  because the devil has gone down to you!
He is filled with fury,
  because he knows that his time is short."

¹³When the dragon saw that he had been hurled to the earth, he pursued the woman who had given birth to the male child. ¹⁴The woman was given the two wings of a great eagle, so that she might fly to the place prepared for her in the desert, where she would be taken care of for a time, times and half a time, out of the serpent's reach. ¹⁵Then from his mouth the serpent spewed water like a river, to overtake the woman and sweep her away with the torrent. ¹⁶But the earth helped the woman by opening its mouth and swallowing the river that the dragon had spewed out of his mouth. ¹⁷Then the dragon was enraged at the woman and went off to make war against the rest of her offspring—those who obey God's commandments and hold to the testimony of Jesus. ¹And the dragon[a] stood on the shore of the sea.

The Beast out of the Sea

And I saw a beast coming out of the sea. He had ten horns and seven heads, with ten crowns on his horns, and on each head a blasphemous name. ²The beast I saw resembled a leopard, but had feet like those of a bear and a mouth like that of a lion. The dragon gave the beast his power and his throne and great authority. ³One of the heads of the beast seemed to have had a fatal wound, but the fatal wound had been healed. The whole world was astonished and followed the beast. ⁴Men worshiped the dragon because he had given authority to the beast, and they also worshiped the beast and asked, "Who is like the beast? Who can make war against him?"

⁵The beast was given a mouth to utter proud words and blasphemies and to exercise his authority for forty-two months. ⁶He opened his mouth to blaspheme God, and to slander his name and his dwelling place and those who live in heaven. ⁷He was given power to make war against the saints and to conquer them. And he was given authority over every tribe, people, language and nation. ⁸All inhabitants of the earth will worship the beast—all whose names have not been written in the book of life belonging to the Lamb that was slain from the creation of the world.[a]

a 1 Some late manuscripts And I   b 8 Or written from the creation of the world in the book of life belonging to the Lamb that was slain

只是地與海有禍了，
  因為魔鬼知道自己的時候不多，
就氣忿忿地
  下到你們那裏去了。"

¹³龍見自己被摔在地上，就逼迫那生男孩子的婦人。¹⁴於是有大鷹的兩個翅膀賜給婦人，叫她能飛到曠野，到自己的地方躲避那蛇；她在那裏被養活一載二載半載。¹⁵蛇就在婦人身後，從口中吐出水來，像河一樣，要將婦人沖去。¹⁶地卻幫助婦人，開口吞了從龍口吐出來的水（註：原文作"河"）。¹⁷龍向婦人發怒，去與她其餘的兒女爭戰，這兒女就是那守神誡命，為耶穌作見證的。那時龍就站在海邊的沙上。

¹我又看見一個獸從海中上來，

從海中上來的獸

有十角七頭，在十角上戴着十個冠冕，七頭上有褻瀆的名號。²我所看見的獸，形狀像豹，腳像熊的腳，口像獅子的口。那龍將自己的能力、座位和大權柄都給了牠。³我看見獸的七頭中，有一個似乎受了死傷，那死傷卻醫好了。全地的人都希奇跟從那獸，⁴又拜那龍，因為牠將自己的權柄給了獸，也拜獸說："誰能比這獸，誰能與牠交戰呢？"

⁵又賜給牠說誇大褻瀆話的口，又有權柄賜給牠，可以任意而行四十二個月。⁶獸就開口向神說褻瀆的話，褻瀆神的名並他的帳幕，以及那些住在天上的。⁷又任憑牠與聖徒爭戰，並且得勝。也把權柄賜給牠，制伏各族、各民、各方、各國。⁸凡住在地上，名字從創世以來沒有記在被殺之羔羊生命冊上的人，都要拜牠。

⁹凡有耳的，就應當聽！

¹⁰擄掠人的，
　　必被擄掠；
　用刀殺人的，
　　必被刀殺。

聖徒的忍耐和信心就是在此。

從地中上來的獸

¹¹我又看見另有一個獸從地中上來，有兩角如同羊羔，說話好像龍。¹²牠在頭一個獸面前，施行頭一個獸所有的權柄，並且叫地和住在地上的人，拜那死傷醫好的頭一個獸。¹³又行大奇事，甚至在人面前，叫火從天降在地上。¹⁴牠因賜給牠權柄在獸面前能行奇事，就迷惑住在地上的人，說：「要給那受刀傷還活着的獸做個像。」¹⁵又有權柄賜給牠，叫獸像有生氣，並且能說話，又叫所有不拜獸像的人都被殺害。¹⁶牠又叫眾人，無論大小、貧富、自主的、為奴的，都在右手上或是在額上受一個印記。¹⁷除了那受印記、有了獸名或有獸名數目的，都不得作買賣。

¹⁸在這裏有智慧。凡有聰明的，可以算計獸的數目，因為這是人的數目，他的數目是六百六十六。

羔羊與十四萬四千人

14 我又觀看，見羔羊站在錫安山，同他又有十四萬四千人，都有他的名和他父的名寫在額上。²我聽見從天上有聲音，像眾水的聲音和大雷的聲音，並且我所聽見的好像彈琴的所彈的琴聲。³他們在寶座前，並在四活物和眾長老前唱歌，彷彿是新歌，除了從地上買來的那十四萬四千人以外，沒有人能學這歌。⁴這些人未曾沾染婦女，他們原是童身。羔羊無論往哪裏去，他們都跟隨他。他們是從人間買來的，作初熟的果子歸

⁹He who has an ear, let him hear.

¹⁰If anyone is to go into captivity,
　　into captivity he will go.
If anyone is to be killed^a with the sword,
　　with the sword he will be killed.

This calls for patient endurance and faithfulness on the part of the saints.

The Beast out of the Earth

¹¹Then I saw another beast, coming out of the earth. He had two horns like a lamb, but he spoke like a dragon. ¹²He exercised all the authority of the first beast on his behalf, and made the earth and its inhabitants worship the first beast, whose fatal wound had been healed. ¹³And he performed great and miraculous signs, even causing fire to come down from heaven to earth in full view of men. ¹⁴Because of the signs he was given power to do on behalf of the first beast, he deceived the inhabitants of the earth. He ordered them to set up an image in honor of the beast who was wounded by the sword and yet lived. ¹⁵He was given power to give breath to the image of the first beast, so that it could speak and cause all who refused to worship the image to be killed. ¹⁶He also forced everyone, small and great, rich and poor, free and slave, to receive a mark on his right hand or on his forehead, ¹⁷so that no one could buy or sell unless he had the mark, which is the name of the beast or the number of his name.

¹⁸This calls for wisdom. If anyone has insight, let him calculate the number of the beast, for it is man's number. His number is 666.

The Lamb and the 144,000

14 Then I looked, and there before me was the Lamb, standing on Mount Zion, and with him 144,000 who had his name and his Father's name written on their foreheads. ²And I heard a sound from heaven like the roar of rushing waters and like a loud peal of thunder. The sound I heard was like that of harpists playing their harps. ³And they sang a new song before the throne and before the four living creatures and the elders. No one could learn the song except the 144,000 who had been redeemed from the earth. ⁴These are those who did not defile themselves with women, for they kept themselves pure. They follow the Lamb wherever he goes. They were purchased from among men and offered as firstfruits to God and the

a 10 Some manuscripts anyone kills

Lamb. [5]No lie was found in their mouths; they are blameless.

The Three Angels

[6]Then I saw another angel flying in midair, and he had the eternal gospel to proclaim to those who live on the earth—to every nation, tribe, language and people. [7]He said in a loud voice, "Fear God and give him glory, because the hour of his judgment has come. Worship him who made the heavens, the earth, the sea and the springs of water."

[8]A second angel followed and said, "Fallen! Fallen is Babylon the Great, which made all the nations drink the maddening wine of her adulteries."

[9]A third angel followed them and said in a loud voice: "If anyone worships the beast and his image and receives his mark on the forehead or on the hand, [10]he, too, will drink of the wine of God's fury, which has been poured full strength into the cup of his wrath. He will be tormented with burning sulfur in the presence of the holy angels and of the Lamb. [11]And the smoke of their torment rises for ever and ever. There is no rest day or night for those who worship the beast and his image, or for anyone who receives the mark of his name." [12]This calls for patient endurance on the part of the saints who obey God's commandments and remain faithful to Jesus.

[13]Then I heard a voice from heaven say, "Write: Blessed are the dead who die in the Lord from now on."

"Yes," says the Spirit, "they will rest from their labor, for their deeds will follow them."

The Harvest of the Earth

[14]I looked, and there before me was a white cloud, and seated on the cloud was one "like a son of man"[a] with a crown of gold on his head and a sharp sickle in his hand. [15]Then another angel came out of the temple and called in a loud voice to him who was sitting on the cloud, "Take your sickle and reap, because the time to reap has come, for the harvest of the earth is ripe." [16]So he who was seated on the cloud swung his sickle over the earth, and the earth was harvested.

[17]Another angel came out of the temple in heaven, and he too had a sharp sickle. [18]Still another angel, who had charge of the fire, came from the altar and called in a loud voice to him who had the sharp sickle, "Take your sharp

a 14 Daniel 7:13

與神和羔羊。[5]在他們口中察不出謊言來,他們是沒有瑕疵的。

三位天使

[6]我又看見另有一位天使飛在空中,有永遠的福音要傳給住在地上的人,就是各國、各族、各方、各民。[7]他大聲說:"應當敬畏神,將榮耀歸給他,因他施行審判的時候已經到了!應當敬拜那創造天、地、海和眾水泉源的。"

[8]又有第二位天使接着說:"叫萬民喝邪淫、大怒之酒的巴比倫大城傾倒了,傾倒了!"

[9]又有第三位天使接着他們,大聲說:"若有人拜獸和獸像,在額上或在手上受了印記,[10]這人也必喝神大怒的酒,此酒斟在神忿怒的杯中純一不雜。他要在聖天使和羔羊面前,在火與硫磺之中受痛苦。[11]他受痛苦的煙往上冒,直到永永遠遠。那些拜獸和獸像,受牠名之印記的,晝夜不得安寧。"[12]聖徒的忍耐就在此,他們是守神誡命和耶穌真道的。

[13]我聽見從天上有聲音說:"你要寫下:從今以後,在主裏面而死的人有福了!"

聖靈說:"是的,他們息了自己的勞苦,做工的果效也隨着他們。"

地上的莊稼

[14]我又觀看,見一片白雲,雲上坐着一位好像人子,頭上戴着金冠冕,手裏拿着快鐮刀。[15]又有一位天使從殿中出來,向那坐在雲上的大聲喊着說:"伸出你的鐮刀來收割!因為收割的時候已經到了,地上的莊稼已經熟透了。"[16]那坐在雲上的,就把鐮刀扔在地上,地上的莊稼就被收割了。

[17]又有一位天使從天上的殿中出來,他也拿着快鐮刀。[18]又有一位天使從祭壇中出來,是有權柄管火的,向拿着快鐮刀的大聲喊着說:"伸出快鐮刀來!收取地上葡萄樹的果子,

因為葡萄熟透了。" 19那天使就把鐮刀扔在地上，收取了地上的葡萄，丟在神忿怒的大酒醡中。 20那酒醡踹在城外，就有血從酒醡裏流出來，高到馬的嚼環，遠有六百里。

掌管七災的七位天使

15 我又看見在天上有異象，大而且奇，就是七位天使掌管末了的七災，因為神的大怒在這七災中發盡了。 2我看見彷彿有玻璃海，其中有火攙雜。又看見那些勝了獸和獸的像，並牠名字數目的人，都站在玻璃海上，拿着神的琴， 3唱神僕人摩西的歌和羔羊的歌，說：

"主神，全能者啊，
　　你的作為大哉，奇哉！
萬世之王啊（註："世"或作"國"），
　　你的道途義哉，誠哉！
4主啊，誰敢不敬畏你，
　　不將榮耀歸與你的名呢？
因為獨有你是聖的，
　　萬民都要來
　　在你面前敬拜，
　　因你公義的作為已經顯出來了。"

5此後，我看見在天上那存法櫃的殿開了。 6那掌管七災的七位天使從殿中出來，穿着潔白光明的細麻衣（註："細麻衣"有古卷作"寶石"），胸間束着金帶。 7四活物中有一個把盛滿了活到永永遠遠之神大怒的七個金碗給了那七位天使。 8因神的榮耀和能力，殿中充滿了煙。於是沒有人能以進殿，直等到那七位天使所降的七災完畢了。

盛神大怒的七碗

16 我聽見有大聲音從殿中出來，向那七位天使說："你們去，把盛神大怒的七碗倒在地上！"

2第一位天使便去，把碗倒在地上，就有惡而且毒的瘡生在那些有獸印記、拜獸像的人身上。

sickle and gather the clusters of grapes from the earth's vine, because its grapes are ripe." [19]The angel swung his sickle on the earth, gathered its grapes and threw them into the great winepress of God's wrath. [20]They were trampled in the winepress outside the city, and blood flowed out of the press, rising as high as the horses' bridles for a distance of 1,600 stadia.[a]

Seven Angels With Seven Plagues

15 I saw in heaven another great and marvelous sign: seven angels with the seven last plagues—last, because with them God's wrath is completed. [2]And I saw what looked like a sea of glass mixed with fire and, standing beside the sea, those who had been victorious over the beast and his image and over the number of his name. They held harps given them by God [3]and sang the song of Moses the servant of God and the song of the Lamb:

"Great and marvelous are your deeds,
　　Lord God Almighty.
Just and true are your ways,
　　King of the ages.
[4]Who will not fear you, O Lord,
　　and bring glory to your name?
For you alone are holy.
All nations will come
　　and worship before you,
for your righteous acts have been revealed."

[5]After this I looked and in heaven the temple, that is, the tabernacle of the Testimony, was opened. [6]Out of the temple came the seven angels with the seven plagues. They were dressed in clean, shining linen and wore golden sashes around their chests. [7]Then one of the four living creatures gave to the seven angels seven golden bowls filled with the wrath of God, who lives for ever and ever. [8]And the temple was filled with smoke from the glory of God and from his power, and no one could enter the temple until the seven plagues of the seven angels were completed.

The Seven Bowls of God's Wrath

16 Then I heard a loud voice from the temple saying to the seven angels, "Go, pour out the seven bowls of God's wrath on the earth."

[2]The first angel went and poured out his bowl on the land, and ugly and painful sores broke out on the people who had the mark of the beast and worshiped his image.

a 20 That is, about 180 miles (about 300 kilometers)

³The second angel poured out his bowl on the sea, and it turned into blood like that of a dead man, and every living thing in the sea died.

⁴The third angel poured out his bowl on the rivers and springs of water, and they became blood. ⁵Then I heard the angel in charge of the waters say:

"You are just in these judgments,
  you who are and who were, the Holy One,
  because you have so judged;
⁶for they have shed the blood of your saints and prophets,
  and you have given them blood to drink as they deserve."

⁷And I heard the altar respond:

"Yes, Lord God Almighty,
  true and just are your judgments."

⁸The fourth angel poured out his bowl on the sun, and the sun was given power to scorch people with fire. ⁹They were seared by the intense heat and they cursed the name of God, who had control over these plagues, but they refused to repent and glorify him.

¹⁰The fifth angel poured out his bowl on the throne of the beast, and his kingdom was plunged into darkness. Men gnawed their tongues in agony ¹¹and cursed the God of heaven because of their pains and their sores, but they refused to repent of what they had done.

¹²The sixth angel poured out his bowl on the great river Euphrates, and its water was dried up to prepare the way for the kings from the East. ¹³Then I saw three evil*ᵃ* spirits that looked like frogs; they came out of the mouth of the dragon, out of the mouth of the beast and out of the mouth of the false prophet. ¹⁴They are spirits of demons performing miraculous signs, and they go out to the kings of the whole world, to gather them for the battle on the great day of God Almighty.

¹⁵"Behold, I come like a thief! Blessed is he who stays awake and keeps his clothes with him, so that he may not go naked and be shamefully exposed."

¹⁶Then they gathered the kings together to the place that in Hebrew is called Armageddon.

¹⁷The seventh angel poured out his bowl into the air, and out of the temple came a loud voice from the throne, saying, "It is done!" ¹⁸Then there came flashes of lightning, rumblings, peals

³第二位天使把碗倒在海裏，海就變成血，好像死人的血，海中的活物都死了。

⁴第三位天使把碗倒在江河與眾水的泉源裏，水就變成血了。⁵我聽見掌管眾水的天使說：

"昔在、今在的聖者啊，
  你這樣判斷是公義的！

⁶他們曾流聖徒
  與先知的血，
現在你給他們血喝，
  這是他們所該受的。"

⁷我又聽見祭壇中有聲音說：

"是的，主神，全能者啊！
  你的判斷義哉！誠哉！"

⁸第四位天使把碗倒在日頭上，叫日頭能用火烤人。⁹人被大熱所烤，就褻瀆那有權掌管這些災的神之名，並不悔改將榮耀歸給神。

¹⁰第五位天使把碗倒在獸的座位上，獸的國就黑暗了。人因疼痛就咬自己的舌頭；¹¹又因所受的疼痛和生的瘡，就褻瀆天上的神，並不悔改所行的。

¹²第六位天使把碗倒在<u>幼發拉底</u>大河上，河水就乾了，要給那從日出之地所來的眾王預備道路。¹³我又看見三個污穢的靈，好像青蛙，從龍口、獸口並假先知的口中出來。¹⁴他們本是鬼魔的靈，施行奇事，出去到普天下眾王那裏，叫他們在神全能者的大日聚集爭戰。

¹⁵（"看哪！我來像賊一樣。那警醒、看守衣服、免得赤身而行、叫人見他羞恥的有福了！"）

¹⁶那三個鬼魔便叫眾王聚集在一處，<u>希伯來</u>話叫作<u>哈米吉多頓</u>。

¹⁷第七位天使把碗倒在空中，就有大聲音從殿中的寶座上出來，說："成了！"¹⁸又有閃電、聲音、雷轟、大地震，自從地上有人以來，沒

---

a 13 Greek *unclean*

有這樣大、這樣厲害的地震。¹⁹那大城裂為三段，列國的城也都倒塌了。神也想起巴比倫大城來，要把那盛自己烈怒的酒杯遞給他。²⁰各海島都逃避了，眾山也不見了。²¹又有大雹子從天落在人身上，每一個約重一他連得（註：一他連得約有九十斤）。為這雹子的災極大，人就褻瀆神。

騎在獸上的女人

17 拿着七碗的七位天使中，有一位前來對我說：「你到這裏來，我將將坐在眾水上的大淫婦所要受的刑罰指給你看。²地上的君王與她行淫，住在地上的人喝醉了她淫亂的酒。」

³我被聖靈感動，天使帶我到曠野去，我就看見一個女人騎在朱紅色的獸上；那獸有七頭十角，遍體有褻瀆的名號。⁴那女人穿着紫色和朱紅色的衣服，用金子、寶石、珍珠為妝飾；手拿金杯，杯中盛滿了可憎之物，就是她淫亂的污穢。⁵在她額上有名寫着說：

奧秘哉！
大巴比倫，
作世上的淫婦
和一切可憎之物的母。

⁶我又看見那女人喝醉了聖徒的血和為耶穌作見證之人的血。

我看見她，就大大地希奇。⁷天使對我說：「你為甚麼希奇呢？我要將這女人和馱着她的那七頭十角獸的奧秘告訴你。⁸你所看見的獸，先前有、如今沒有，將要從無底坑裏上來，又要歸於沉淪。凡住在地上，名字從創世以來沒有記在生命冊上的，見先前有、如今沒有、以後再有的獸，就必希奇。

⁹「智慧的心在此可以思想。那七頭就是女人所坐的七座山，¹⁰又是七位王：五位已經傾倒了，一位還

of thunder and a severe earthquake. No earthquake like it has ever occurred since man has been on earth, so tremendous was the quake. ¹⁹The great city split into three parts, and the cities of the nations collapsed. God remembered Babylon the Great and gave her the cup filled with the wine of the fury of his wrath. ²⁰Every island fled away and the mountains could not be found. ²¹From the sky huge hailstones of about a hundred pounds each fell upon men. And they cursed God on account of the plague of hail, because the plague was so terrible.

The Woman on the Beast

17 One of the seven angels who had the seven bowls came and said to me, "Come, I will show you the punishment of the great prostitute, who sits on many waters. ²With her the kings of the earth committed adultery and the inhabitants of the earth were intoxicated with the wine of her adulteries."

³Then the angel carried me away in the Spirit into a desert. There I saw a woman sitting on a scarlet beast that was covered with blasphemous names and had seven heads and ten horns. ⁴The woman was dressed in purple and scarlet, and was glittering with gold, precious stones and pearls. She held a golden cup in her hand, filled with abominable things and the filth of her adulteries. ⁵This title was written on her forehead:

MYSTERY
BABYLON THE GREAT
THE MOTHER OF PROSTITUTES
AND OF THE ABOMINATIONS OF THE EARTH.

⁶I saw that the woman was drunk with the blood of the saints, the blood of those who bore testimony to Jesus.

When I saw her, I was greatly astonished. ⁷Then the angel said to me: "Why are you astonished? I will explain to you the mystery of the woman and of the beast she rides, which has the seven heads and ten horns. ⁸The beast, which you saw, once was, now is not, and will come up out of the Abyss and go to his destruction. The inhabitants of the earth whose names have not been written in the book of life from the creation of the world will be astonished when they see the beast, because he once was, now is not, and yet will come.

⁹"This calls for a mind with wisdom. The seven heads are seven hills on which the woman sits. ¹⁰They are also seven kings. Five have fallen,

one is, the other has not yet come; but when he does come, he must remain for a little while. [11]The beast who once was, and now is not, is an eighth king. He belongs to the seven and is going to his destruction.

[12]"The ten horns you saw are ten kings who have not yet received a kingdom, but who for one hour will receive authority as kings along with the beast. [13]They have one purpose and will give their power and authority to the beast. [14]They will make war against the Lamb, but the Lamb will overcome them because he is Lord of lords and King of kings—and with him will be his called, chosen and faithful followers."

[15]Then the angel said to me, "The waters you saw, where the prostitute sits, are peoples, multitudes, nations and languages. [16]The beast and the ten horns you saw will hate the prostitute. They will bring her to ruin and leave her naked; they will eat her flesh and burn her with fire. [17]For God has put it into their hearts to accomplish his purpose by agreeing to give the beast their power to rule, until God's words are fulfilled. [18]The woman you saw is the great city that rules over the kings of the earth."

The Fall of Babylon

18 After this I saw another angel coming down from heaven. He had great authority, and the earth was illuminated by his splendor. [2]With a mighty voice he shouted:

"Fallen! Fallen is Babylon the Great!
 She has become a home for demons
and a haunt for every evil[a] spirit,
 a haunt for every unclean and detestable bird.
[3]For all the nations have drunk
 the maddening wine of her adulteries.
The kings of the earth committed adultery
 with her,
and the merchants of the earth grew rich
 from her excessive luxuries."

[4]Then I heard another voice from heaven say:

"Come out of her, my people,
 so that you will not share in her sins,
 so that you will not receive any of her
 plagues;
[5]for her sins are piled up to heaven,
 and God has remembered her crimes.
[6]Give back to her as she has given;
 pay her back double for what she has done.
 Mix her a double portion from her own cup.

a 2 Greek unclean

在，一位還沒有來到；他來的時候，必須暫時存留。[11]那先前有、如今沒有的獸，就是第八位，他也和那七位同列，並且歸於沉淪。

[12] "你所看見的那十角就是十王，他們還沒有得國，但他們一時之間要和獸同得權柄，與王一樣。[13]他們同心合意將自己的能力權柄給那獸。[14]他們與羔羊爭戰，羔羊必勝過他們，因為羔羊是萬主之主，萬王之王。同着羔羊的，就是蒙召、被選、有忠心的，也必得勝。"

[15]天使又對我說："你所看見那淫婦坐的眾水，就是多民、多人、多國、多方。[16]你所看見的那十角與獸必恨這淫婦，使她冷落赤身，又要吃她的肉，用火將她燒盡。[17]因為神使諸王同心合意，遵行他的旨意，把自己的國給那獸，直等到神的話都應驗了。[18]你所看見的那女人就是管轄地上眾王的大城。"

巴比倫傾倒

18 此後，我看見另有一位有大權柄的天使從天降下，地就因他的榮耀發光。[2]他大聲喊着說：

"巴比倫大城傾倒了！傾倒了！
 成了鬼魔的住處和各樣污穢
 之靈的巢穴（註：或作"牢獄"。下同），
 並各樣污穢可憎之雀鳥的巢穴。
[3]因為列國
 都被她邪淫大怒的酒傾倒了。
地上的君王
 與她行淫，
地上的客商
 因她奢華太過就發了財。"

[4]我又聽見從天上有聲音說：

"我的民哪，你們要從那城出來，
 免得與她一同有罪，
 受她所受的災殃；
[5]因她的罪惡滔天，
 她的不義，神已經想起來了。
[6]她怎樣待人，也要怎樣待她，
 按她所行的加倍地報應她，
 用她調酒的杯加倍地調給她喝。

7她怎樣榮耀自己，怎樣奢華，
　　也當叫她照樣痛苦悲哀，
　因她心裏說：
　　『我坐了皇后的位，
　　並不是寡婦，決不至於悲哀。』
8所以在一天之內，
　　她的災殃要一齊來到，
　　就是死亡、悲哀、饑荒。
　她又要被火燒盡了，
　　因為審判她的主神大有能力。

　　9 "地上的君王，素來與她行淫，一同奢華的，看見燒她的煙，就必為她哭泣哀號。10因怕她的痛苦，就遠遠地站着說：

　"　'哀哉！哀哉！
　　巴比倫大城，堅固的城啊！
　　一時之間你的刑罰就來到了！'

　　11 "地上的客商也都為她哭泣悲哀，因為沒有人再買他們的貨物了。12這貨物就是金、銀、寶石、珍珠、細麻布、紫色料、綢子、朱紅色料、各樣香木，各樣象牙的器皿，各樣極寶貴的木頭和銅、鐵、漢白玉的器皿，13並肉桂、荳蔻、香料、香膏、乳香、酒、油、細麵、麥子、牛、羊、車、馬和奴僕、人口。

　　14 "巴比倫哪，你所貪愛的果子離開了你！你一切的珍饈美味和華美的物件也從你中間毀滅，決不能再見了！15販賣這些貨物、藉着她發了財的客商，因怕她的痛苦，就遠遠地站着哭泣悲哀，16說：

　"　'哀哉！哀哉！這大城啊！
　　素常穿着細麻、紫色、
　　　朱紅色的衣服，
　　又用金子、寶石和珍珠為妝飾！
17一時之間，
　　這麼大的富厚就歸於無有了！'

　　"凡船主和坐船往各處去的並眾水手，連所有靠海為業的，都遠遠地站着，18看見燒她的煙，就喊着說：'有何城能比這大城呢？'19他們又把塵土撒在頭上，哭泣悲哀，喊着說：

7Give her as much torture and grief
　as the glory and luxury she gave herself.
In her heart she boasts,
　'I sit as queen; I am not a widow,
　and I will never mourn.'
8Therefore in one day her plagues will overtake her:
　death, mourning and famine.
She will be consumed by fire,
　for mighty is the Lord God who judges her.

　9"When the kings of the earth who committed adultery with her and shared her luxury see the smoke of her burning, they will weep and mourn over her. 10Terrified at her torment, they will stand far off and cry:

　"'Woe! Woe, O great city,
　O Babylon, city of power!
　In one hour your doom has come!'

　11"The merchants of the earth will weep and mourn over her because no one buys their cargoes any more— 12cargoes of gold, silver, precious stones and pearls; fine linen, purple, silk and scarlet cloth; every sort of citron wood, and articles of every kind made of ivory, costly wood, bronze, iron and marble; 13cargoes of cinnamon and spice, of incense, myrrh and frankincense, of wine and olive oil, of fine flour and wheat; cattle and sheep; horses and carriages; and bodies and souls of men.

　14"They will say, 'The fruit you longed for is gone from you. All your riches and splendor have vanished, never to be recovered.' 15The merchants who sold these things and gained their wealth from her will stand far off, terrified at her torment. They will weep and mourn 16and cry out:

　"'Woe! Woe, O great city,
　dressed in fine linen, purple and scarlet,
　and glittering with gold, precious stones and pearls!
17In one hour such great wealth has been brought to ruin!'

　"Every sea captain, and all who travel by ship, the sailors, and all who earn their living from the sea, will stand far off. 18When they see the smoke of her burning, they will exclaim, 'Was there ever a city like this great city?' 19They will throw dust on their heads, and with weeping and mourning cry out:

" 'Woe! Woe, O great city,
   where all who had ships on the sea
     became rich through her wealth!
   In one hour she has been brought to ruin!
20Rejoice over her, O heaven!
   Rejoice, saints and apostles and prophets!
   God has judged her for the way she treated
     you.' "

   21Then a mighty angel picked up a boulder
the size of a large millstone and threw it into the
sea, and said:

"With such violence
   the great city of Babylon will be thrown down,
   never to be found again.
22The music of harpists and musicians, flute
     players and trumpeters,
   will never be heard in you again.
No workman of any trade
   will ever be found in you again.
The sound of a millstone
   will never be heard in you again.
23The light of a lamp
   will never shine in you again.
The voice of bridegroom and bride
   will never be heard in you again.
Your merchants were the world's great men.
By your magic spell all the nations were led
   astray.
24In her was found the blood of prophets and of
     the saints,
   and of all who have been killed on the
     earth."

Hallelujah!

19

After this I heard what sounded like the
roar of a great multitude in heaven
shouting:

"Hallelujah!
   Salvation and glory and power belong to our
     God,
2 for true and just are his judgments.
He has condemned the great prostitute
   who corrupted the earth by her adulteries.
He has avenged on her the blood of his
     servants."

   3And again they shouted:

"Hallelujah!
The smoke from her goes up for ever and
   ever."

" '哀哉！哀哉！這大城啊！
   凡有船在海中的，
   都因她的珍寶成了富足，
   她在一時之間就成了荒場！
20天哪！眾聖徒、眾使徒、眾先知啊！
   你們都要因她歡喜，
   因為神已經在她身上
   伸了你們的冤！' "

   21有一位大力的天使舉起一塊石
頭，好像大磨石，扔在海裏，說：

"巴比倫大城
   也必這樣猛力地被扔下去，
   決不能再見了！
22彈琴、作樂、
     吹笛、吹號的聲音，
   在你中間決不能再聽見。
各行手藝人，
   在你中間決不能再遇見。
推磨的聲音，
   在你中間決不能再聽見。
23燈光在你中間
   決不能再照耀。
新郎和新婦的聲音，
   在你中間決不能再聽見。
你的客商原來是地上的尊貴人，
萬國也被你的邪術迷惑了。

24先知和聖徒
   並地上一切被殺之人的血，
   都在這城裏看見了。"

哈利路亞！

19

此後，我聽見好像羣眾在天
上大聲說：

"哈利路亞（註：就是"要讚美耶和華"的
     意思）！
   救恩、榮耀、權能都屬乎我們的神！
2他的判斷是真實、公義的，
   因他判斷了
   那用淫行敗壞世界的大淫婦，
   並且向淫婦討流僕人血的罪，
   給他們伸冤。"

   3又說：

"哈利路亞！
   燒淫婦的煙往上冒，
   直到永永遠遠。"

4那二十四位長老與四活物就俯
伏敬拜坐寶座的神，說：

"阿們，哈利路亞！"

5有聲音從寶座出來說：

"神的眾僕人哪，
　凡敬畏他的，
無論大小，
　都要讚美我們的神！"

6我聽見好像羣眾的聲音，眾水
的聲音，大雷的聲音，說：

"哈利路亞！
　因為主我們的神，全能者作王了。
7我們要歡喜快樂，
　將榮耀歸給他！
因為羔羊婚娶的時候到了，
　新婦也自己備好了，
8就蒙恩
　得穿光明潔白的細麻衣。"

這細麻衣就是聖徒所行的義。

9天使吩咐我說："你要寫上：
'凡被請赴羔羊之婚筵的有福
了！'"又對我說："這是神真實
的話。"

10我就俯伏在他腳前要拜他。他
說："千萬不可！我和你，並你那
些為耶穌作見證的弟兄同是作僕人
的。你要敬拜神。因為預言中的靈
意乃是為耶穌作見證。"

騎白馬的

11我觀看，見天開了。有一匹白
馬，騎在馬上的稱為誠信真實，他
審判、爭戰都按着公義。12他的眼睛
如火焰，他頭上戴着許多冠冕，又
有寫着的名字，除了他自己沒有人
知道。13他穿着濺了血的衣服，他的
名稱為神之道。14在天上的眾軍騎着
白馬，穿着細麻衣，又白又潔，跟
隨他。15有利劍從他口中出來，可以
擊殺列國。他必用鐵杖轄管他們
（註："轄管"原文作"牧"），並要踹全

4The twenty-four elders and the four living
creatures fell down and worshiped God, who
was seated on the throne. And they cried:

"Amen, Hallelujah!"

5Then a voice came from the throne, saying:

"Praise our God,
all you his servants,
you who fear him,
both small and great!"

6Then I heard what sounded like a great multitude, like the roar of rushing waters and like
loud peals of thunder, shouting:

"Hallelujah!
For our Lord God Almighty reigns.
7Let us rejoice and be glad
and give him glory!
For the wedding of the Lamb has come,
and his bride has made herself ready.
8Fine linen, bright and clean,
was given her to wear."

(Fine linen stands for the righteous acts of the
saints.)

9Then the angel said to me, "Write: 'Blessed
are those who are invited to the wedding supper of the Lamb!' " And he added, "These are
the true words of God."

10At this I fell at his feet to worship him. But
he said to me, "Do not do it! I am a fellow servant with you and with your brothers who hold
to the testimony of Jesus. Worship God! For the
testimony of Jesus is the spirit of prophecy."

The Rider on the White Horse

11I saw heaven standing open and there
before me was a white horse, whose rider is
called Faithful and True. With justice he judges
and makes war. 12His eyes are like blazing fire,
and on his head are many crowns. He has a
name written on him that no one knows but he
himself. 13He is dressed in a robe dipped in
blood, and his name is the Word of God. 14The
armies of heaven were following him, riding on
white horses and dressed in fine linen, white
and clean. 15Out of his mouth comes a sharp
sword with which to strike down the nations.
"He will rule them with an iron scepter."[a] He
treads the winepress of the fury of the wrath of

a 15 Psalm 2:9

God Almighty. [16]On his robe and on his thigh he has this name written:

KING OF KINGS AND LORD OF LORDS.

[17]And I saw an angel standing in the sun, who cried in a loud voice to all the birds flying in midair, "Come, gather together for the great supper of God, [18]so that you may eat the flesh of kings, generals, and mighty men, of horses and their riders, and the flesh of all people, free and slave, small and great."

[19]Then I saw the beast and the kings of the earth and their armies gathered together to make war against the rider on the horse and his army. [20]But the beast was captured, and with him the false prophet who had performed the miraculous signs on his behalf. With these signs he had deluded those who had received the mark of the beast and worshiped his image. The two of them were thrown alive into the fiery lake of burning sulfur. [21]The rest of them were killed with the sword that came out of the mouth of the rider on the horse, and all the birds gorged themselves on their flesh.

The Thousand Years

20 And I saw an angel coming down out of heaven, having the key to the Abyss and holding in his hand a great chain. [2]He seized the dragon, that ancient serpent, who is the devil, or Satan, and bound him for a thousand years. [3]He threw him into the Abyss, and locked and sealed it over him, to keep him from deceiving the nations anymore until the thousand years were ended. After that, he must be set free for a short time.

[4]I saw thrones on which were seated those who had been given authority to judge. And I saw the souls of those who had been beheaded because of their testimony for Jesus and because of the word of God. They had not worshiped the beast or his image and had not received his mark on their foreheads or their hands. They came to life and reigned with Christ a thousand years. [5](The rest of the dead did not come to life until the thousand years were ended.) This is the first resurrection. [6]Blessed and holy are those who have part in the first resurrection. The second death has no power over them, but they will be priests of God and of Christ and will reign with him for a thousand years.

Satan's Doom

[7]When the thousand years are over, Satan will be released from his prison [8]and will go out

能神烈怒的酒醡。[16]在他衣服和大腿上有名寫着說：

萬王之王，萬主之主。

[17]我又看見一位天使站在日頭中，向天空所飛的鳥大聲喊着說："你們聚集來赴神的大筵席！[18]可以吃君王與將軍的肉，壯士與馬和騎馬者的肉，並一切自主的、為奴的，以及大小人民的肉。"

[19]我看見那獸和地上的君王，並他們的眾軍都聚集，要與騎白馬的並他的軍兵爭戰。[20]那獸被擒拿，那在獸面前曾行奇事、迷惑受獸印記和拜獸像之人的假先知，也與獸同被擒拿。他們兩個就活活地被扔在燒着硫磺的火湖裏。[21]其餘的被騎白馬者口中出來的劍殺了。飛鳥都吃飽了他們的肉。

一千年

20 我又看見一位天使從天降下，手裏拿着無底坑的鑰匙和一條大鏈子。[2]他捉住那龍，就是古蛇，又叫魔鬼，也叫撒但，把牠捆綁一千年，[3]扔在無底坑裏，將無底坑關閉，用印封上，使牠不得再迷惑列國。等到那一千年完了，以後必須暫時釋放牠。

[4]我又看見幾個寶座，也有坐在上面的，並有審判的權柄賜給他們。我又看見那些因為給耶穌作見證，並為神之道被斬者的靈魂，和那沒有拜過獸與獸像，也沒有在額上和手上受過牠印記之人的靈魂，他們都復活了，與基督一同作王一千年。[5]這是頭一次的復活。其餘的死人還沒有復活，直等那一千年完了。[6]在頭一次復活有分的有福了、聖潔了。第二次的死在他們身上沒有權柄。他們必作神和基督的祭司，並要與基督一同作王一千年。

撒但的下場

[7]那一千年完了，撒但必從監牢裏被釋放，[8]出來要迷惑地上四方的

列國（註："方"原文作"角"），就是歌革和瑪各，叫他們聚集爭戰。他們的人數多如海沙。⁹他們上來遍滿了全地，圍住聖徒的營與蒙愛的城，就有火從天降下，燒滅了他們。¹⁰那迷惑他們的魔鬼被扔在硫磺的火湖裏，就是獸和假先知所在的地方。他們必晝夜受痛苦，直到永永遠遠。

死人受審判

¹¹我又看見一個白色的大寶座與坐在上面的，從他面前天地都逃避，再無可見之處了。¹²我又看見死了的人，無論大小，都站在寶座前。案卷展開了，並且另有一卷展開，就是生命冊。死了的人都憑着這些案卷所記載的，照他們所行的受審判。¹³於是海交出其中的死人，死亡和陰間也交出其中的死人。他們都照各人所行的受審判。¹⁴死亡和陰間也被扔在火湖裏，這火湖就是第二次的死。¹⁵若有人名字沒記在生命冊上，他就被扔在火湖裏。

新耶路撒冷

21 我又看見一個新天新地。因為先前的天地已經過去了，海也不再有了。²我又看見聖城新耶路撒冷由神那裏出天而降，預備好了，就如新婦妝飾整齊，等候丈夫。³我聽見有大聲音從寶座出來說："看哪！神的帳幕在人間。他要與人同住，他們要作他的子民；神要親自與他們同在，作他們的神。⁴神要擦去他們一切的眼淚。不再有死亡，也不再有悲哀、哭號、疼痛，因為以前的事都過去了。"

⁵坐寶座的說："看哪！我將一切都更新了。"又說："你要寫上，因這些話是可信的，是真實的。"

⁶他又對我說："都成了。我是阿拉法，我是俄梅戛；我是初，我是終。我要將生命泉的水白白賜給那口渴的人喝。⁷得勝的，必承受這些為業。我要作他的神，他要作我的兒子。⁸惟有膽怯的、不信的、可憎的、殺人的、淫亂的、行邪術

to deceive the nations in the four corners of the earth—Gog and Magog—to gather them for battle. In number they are like the sand on the seashore. ⁹They marched across the breadth of the earth and surrounded the camp of God's people, the city he loves. But fire came down from heaven and devoured them. ¹⁰And the devil, who deceived them, was thrown into the lake of burning sulfur, where the beast and the false prophet had been thrown. They will be tormented day and night for ever and ever.

The Dead Are Judged

¹¹Then I saw a great white throne and him who was seated on it. Earth and sky fled from his presence, and there was no place for them. ¹²And I saw the dead, great and small, standing before the throne, and books were opened. Another book was opened, which is the book of life. The dead were judged according to what they had done as recorded in the books. ¹³The sea gave up the dead that were in it, and death and Hades gave up the dead that were in them, and each person was judged according to what he had done. ¹⁴Then death and Hades were thrown into the lake of fire. The lake of fire is the second death. ¹⁵If anyone's name was not found written in the book of life, he was thrown into the lake of fire.

The New Jerusalem

21 Then I saw a new heaven and a new earth, for the first heaven and the first earth had passed away, and there was no longer any sea. ²I saw the Holy City, the new Jerusalem, coming down out of heaven from God, prepared as a bride beautifully dressed for her husband. ³And I heard a loud voice from the throne saying, "Now the dwelling of God is with men, and he will live with them. They will be his people, and God himself will be with them and be their God. ⁴He will wipe every tear from their eyes. There will be no more death or mourning or crying or pain, for the old order of things has passed away."

⁵He who was seated on the throne said, "I am making everything new!" Then he said, "Write this down, for these words are trustworthy and true."

⁶He said to me: "It is done. I am the Alpha and the Omega, the Beginning and the End. To him who is thirsty I will give to drink without cost from the spring of the water of life. ⁷He who overcomes will inherit all this, and I will be his God and he will be my son. ⁸But the cowardly, the unbelieving, the vile, the murderers, the

sexually immoral, those who practice magic arts, the idolaters and all liars—their place will be in the fiery lake of burning sulfur. This is the second death."

⁹One of the seven angels who had the seven bowls full of the seven last plagues came and said to me, "Come, I will show you the bride, the wife of the Lamb." ¹⁰And he carried me away in the Spirit to a mountain great and high, and showed me the Holy City, Jerusalem, coming down out of heaven from God. ¹¹It shone with the glory of God, and its brilliance was like that of a very precious jewel, like a jasper, clear as crystal. ¹²It had a great, high wall with twelve gates, and with twelve angels at the gates. On the gates were written the names of the twelve tribes of Israel. ¹³There were three gates on the east, three on the north, three on the south and three on the west. ¹⁴The wall of the city had twelve foundations, and on them were the names of the twelve apostles of the Lamb.

¹⁵The angel who talked with me had a measuring rod of gold to measure the city, its gates and its walls. ¹⁶The city was laid out like a square, as long as it was wide. He measured the city with the rod and found it to be 12,000 stadia*ᵃ* in length, and as wide and high as it is long. ¹⁷He measured its wall and it was 144 cubits*ᵇ* thick,*ᶜ* by man's measurement, which the angel was using. ¹⁸The wall was made of jasper, and the city of pure gold, as pure as glass. ¹⁹The foundations of the city walls were decorated with every kind of precious stone. The first foundation was jasper, the second sapphire, the third chalcedony, the fourth emerald, ²⁰the fifth sardonyx, the sixth carnelian, the seventh chrysolite, the eighth beryl, the ninth topaz, the tenth chrysoprase, the eleventh jacinth, and the twelfth amethyst.*ᵈ* ²¹The twelve gates were twelve pearls, each gate made of a single pearl. The great street of the city was of pure gold, like transparent glass.

²²I did not see a temple in the city, because the Lord God Almighty and the Lamb are its temple. ²³The city does not need the sun or the moon to shine on it, for the glory of God gives it light, and the Lamb is its lamp. ²⁴The nations will walk by its light, and the kings of the earth will bring their splendor into it. ²⁵On no day will its gates ever be shut, for there will be no night there. ²⁶The glory and honor of the nations

---

的、拜偶像的和一切說謊話的，他們的分就在燒着硫磺的火湖裏，這是第二次的死。"

⁹拿着七個金碗、盛滿末後七災的七位天使中，有一位來對我說："你到這裏來，我要將新婦，就是羔羊的妻，指給你看。" ¹⁰我被聖靈感動，天使就帶我到一座高大的山，將那由神那裏從天而降的聖城耶路撒冷指示我。¹¹城中有神的榮耀，城的光輝如同極貴的寶石，好像碧玉，明如水晶。¹²有高大的牆，有十二個門，門上有十二位天使，門上又寫着以色列十二個支派的名字。¹³東邊有三門，北邊有三門，南邊有三門，西邊有三門。¹⁴城牆有十二根基，根基上有羔羊十二使徒的名字。

¹⁵對我說話的，拿着金葦子當尺，要量那城和城門、城牆。¹⁶城是四方的，長寬一樣。天使用葦子量那城，共有四千里，長、寬、高都是一樣；¹⁷又量了城牆，按着人的尺寸，就是天使的尺寸，共有一百四十四肘。¹⁸牆是碧玉造的，城是精金的，如同明淨的玻璃。¹⁹城牆的根基是用各樣寶石修飾的：第一根基是碧玉，第二是藍寶石，第三是綠瑪瑙，第四是綠寶石，²⁰第五是紅瑪瑙，第六是紅寶石，第七是黃璧璽，第八是水蒼玉，第九是紅璧璽，第十是翡翠，第十一是紫瑪瑙，第十二是紫晶。²¹十二個門是十二顆珍珠，每門是一顆珍珠。城內的街道是精金，好像明透的玻璃。

²²我未見城內有殿，因主神全能者和羔羊為城的殿。²³那城內又不用日月光照，因有神的榮耀光照，又有羔羊為城的燈。²⁴列國要在城的光裏行走，地上的君王必將自己的榮耀歸與那城。²⁵城門白晝總不關閉，在那裏原沒有黑夜。²⁶人必將列國的榮

---

a 16 That is, about 1,400 miles (about 2,200 kilometers)
b 17 That is, about 200 feet (about 65 meters)　　*c 17* Or *high*
d 20 The precise identification of some of these precious stones is uncertain.

耀、尊貴歸與那城。²⁷凡不潔淨的，並那行可憎與虛謊之事的，總不得進那城，只有名字寫在羔羊生命冊上的才得進去。

生命河

22 天使又指示我在城內街道當中一道生命水的河，明亮如水晶，從神和羔羊的寶座流出來。²在河這邊與那邊有生命樹，結十二樣果子（註："樣"或作"回"），每月都結果子，樹上的葉子乃為醫治萬民。³以後再沒有咒詛。在城裏有神和羔羊的寶座，他的僕人都要侍奉他，⁴也要見他的面。他的名字必寫在他們的額上。⁵不再有黑夜，他們也不用燈光、日光，因為主神要光照他們。他們要作王，直到永永遠遠。

⁶天使又對我說："這些話是真實可信的。主就是眾先知被靈之靈的神，差遣他的使者，將那必要快成的事指示他僕人。"

耶穌必快來

⁷"看哪，我必快來！凡遵守這書上預言的有福了。"

⁸這些事是我約翰所聽見、所看見的，我既聽見、看見了，就在指示我的天使腳前俯伏要拜他。⁹他對我說："千萬不可！我與你和你的弟兄眾先知，並那些守這書上言語的人，同是作僕人的。你要敬拜神。"

¹⁰他又對我說："不可封了這書上的預言，因為日期近了。¹¹不義的，叫他仍舊不義；污穢的，叫他仍舊污穢；為義的，叫他仍舊為義；聖潔的，叫他仍舊聖潔。"

¹²"看哪，我必快來！賞罰在我，要照各人所行的報應他。¹³我是阿拉法，我是俄梅戛；我是首先的，我是末後的；我是初，我是終。

¹⁴"那些洗淨自己衣服的有福了。可得權柄能到生命樹那裏，也

will be brought into it. ²⁷Nothing impure will ever enter it, nor will anyone who does what is shameful or deceitful, but only those whose names are written in the Lamb's book of life.

The River of Life

22 Then the angel showed me the river of the water of life, as clear as crystal, flowing from the throne of God and of the Lamb ²down the middle of the great street of the city. On each side of the river stood the tree of life, bearing twelve crops of fruit, yielding its fruit every month. And the leaves of the tree are for the healing of the nations. ³No longer will there be any curse. The throne of God and of the Lamb will be in the city, and his servants will serve him. ⁴They will see his face, and his name will be on their foreheads. ⁵There will be no more night. They will not need the light of a lamp or the light of the sun, for the Lord God will give them light. And they will reign for ever and ever.

⁶The angel said to me, "These words are trustworthy and true. The Lord, the God of the spirits of the prophets, sent his angel to show his servants the things that must soon take place."

Jesus Is Coming

⁷"Behold, I am coming soon! Blessed is he who keeps the words of the prophecy in this book."

⁸I, John, am the one who heard and saw these things. And when I had heard and seen them, I fell down to worship at the feet of the angel who had been showing them to me. ⁹But he said to me, "Do not do it! I am a fellow servant with you and with your brothers the prophets and of all who keep the words of this book. Worship God!"

¹⁰Then he told me, "Do not seal up the words of the prophecy of this book, because the time is near. ¹¹Let him who does wrong continue to do wrong; let him who is vile continue to be vile; let him who does right continue to do right; and let him who is holy continue to be holy."

¹²"Behold, I am coming soon! My reward is with me, and I will give to everyone according to what he has done. ¹³I am the Alpha and the Omega, the First and the Last, the Beginning and the End.

¹⁴"Blessed are those who wash their robes, that they may have the right to the tree of life and may go through the gates into the city.

15Outside are the dogs, those who practice magic arts, the sexually immoral, the murderers, the idolaters and everyone who loves and practices falsehood.

16"I, Jesus, have sent my angel to give you*a* this testimony for the churches. I am the Root and the Offspring of David, and the bright Morning Star."

17The Spirit and the bride say, "Come!" And let him who hears say, "Come!" Whoever is thirsty, let him come; and whoever wishes, let him take the free gift of the water of life.

18I warn everyone who hears the words of the prophecy of this book: If anyone adds anything to them, God will add to him the plagues described in this book. 19And if anyone takes words away from this book of prophecy, God will take away from him his share in the tree of life and in the holy city, which are described in this book.

20He who testifies to these things says, "Yes, I am coming soon."

Amen. Come, Lord Jesus.

21The grace of the Lord Jesus be with God's people. Amen.

能從門進城。15城外有那些犬類、行邪術的、淫亂的、殺人的、拜偶像的,並一切喜好說謊言編造虛謊的。

16 "我耶穌差遣我的使者為眾教會將這些事向你們證明。我是大衛的根,又是他的後裔。我是明亮的晨星。"

17聖靈和新婦都說:"來!"聽見的人也該說:"來!"口渴的人也當來;願意的,都可以白白取生命的水喝。

18我向一切聽見這書上預言的作見證,若有人在這預言上加添甚麼,神必將寫在這書上的災禍加在他身上;19這書上的預言,若有人刪去甚麼,神必從這書上所寫的生命樹和聖城,刪去他的分。

20證明這事的說:"是了,我必快來。"

阿們!主耶穌啊,我願你來!

21願主耶穌的恩惠常與眾聖徒同在。阿們!

圖九:啟示錄中的主要地方
MAP 9 : KEY PLACES IN REVELATION

表八：啟示錄中耶穌的名
TABLE 8 : NAMES OF JESUS IN REVELATION

名稱	Name	經文 Reference
阿拉法，首先的，初	Alpha, First, Beginning	1:8, 17; 2:8; 21:6
俄梅戛，末後的，終	Omega, Last, End	1:8, 17; 2:8; 21:6
全能者	Almighty	1:8; 19:6; 11:17; 15:3
主神	Lord God	1:8; 19:6; 11:17; 15:3
存活的	Living One	1:18
神之子	Son of God	2:18
阿們的	Amen	3:14
猶大支派中的獅子	Lion of the tribe of Judah	5:5
大衛的根，大衛的後裔	Root of David, Offspring of David	5:5; 22:16
羔羊	Lamb	5:6, 8, 12, 13; 6:1, 3, 5, 7, 16; 7:9, 10, 14, 17; 13:8; 14:1, 4, 10; 15:3; 17:14; 19:7, 9; 21:9, 14, 22, 23, 27; 22:1
聖潔真實的主	Sovereign Lord, holy and true	6:10
牧人	Shepherd	7:17
基督	Christ	12:10; 20:4, 6
聖者	Holy One	16:5
誠信真實	Faithful and True	19:11
神之道	Word of God	19:13
萬王之王	King of Kings	17:14; 19:16
萬主之主	Lord of Lord	17:14; 19:16
晨星	Morning Star	22:16

工作人員名單

統籌＼謝陸麗儀

編輯＼白耀華　謝陸麗儀　周約彼　麥偉儀

校對＼謝陸麗儀　白耀華　麥偉儀
黃盧容弟　李玉燕　曾堅貞
李美玲　張敏敏　柯子明
袁熙羣　范約翰　沈珪

設計＼張潤明

製作＼張添英　唐建華　張潤明
丁堅德　陳俊成　翁鳳玲

技術顧問＼Creation Technology

我們的事工

"**聖經傳萬家，救恩臨天下**"是國際聖經協會的使命。當然，這使命是源自耶穌基督升天前所頒佈的大使命。實現這個理想，方法林林總總，用聖經作為福音工具，卻是最具策略性的一種。我們從五個方面進發，組織了五個部門：譯經部、贈經部、事工部、出版部和行政部。這五個部門雖然是獨立工作，但也是相輔相成的。通過彼此緊密合作，履行大使命，使人能從聖經中得着永恆的益處。

聖經翻譯

聖經原來是用希伯來文、亞蘭文和希臘文寫成的，因此，翻譯聖經是福音進入一個新的語言羣體時，宣教士或當地的教會必須進行的工作。隨着語言的轉變，聖經考古學的新發現和聖經研究的新方向帶來經文意義更高的清晰度，都促使翻譯聖經或修訂舊版本聖經成為一項生生不息的工作，與教會的延續和成長並駕齊驅。因此我們邀約了一批華人聖經學者，組織成一獨立的譯經委員會，參考英文新國際版聖經（NIV）的翻譯原則，根據原文聖經，在下一世紀來臨之前，重新翻譯一本既準確，可讀性又高的現代化中文聖經譯本——新漢語譯本。

聖經贈送

聖經記載了傳福音的命令，也記載了福音的內容：讓聖經存留在萬千的家庭中，救恩也就有機會遍臨天下。這是贈經部配合教會福音工作的一個重要信念。

我們的目標是要聯絡各教會、機構和個人，透過他們把聖經送到香港、中國和海外地區華人福音對象和初信者手上。贈經部長遠的目標是將聖經中的事蹟和教訓普及化，達到人盡皆知，為香港福音化、中國福音化、海外華人福音化鋪路。

贈經計劃包括：大陸贈經計劃、金蘋果贈經計劃、醫院贈經計劃、邊緣羣體贈經計劃、老人羣體贈經計劃、新葡贈經計劃……

活動事工

透過活動，把聖經信息深印在人心中。

活動事工包括：聖經朗誦節、聖經佈道隊、學校聖經科獎學金、聖誕贈經大使、聖經圖畫填色比賽、聖經專題講座……

聖經出版

配合譯經和贈經工作，出版部肩負了最重要的"生產"過程，為着不同背景、年齡、知識水平羣體的需要，編寫多項適合他們的聖經讀本、聖經教材、電子聖經和錄音帶，讓他們直接從聖經中認識真理。

行政拓展

在譯經部、贈經部、事工部和出版部的背後，是默默耕耘、扮演支援角色的行政拓展部，工作包括辦公室管理、人事及會計工作、對外聯絡、籌募經費、聖經銷售、運輸和電腦操作等。

IBS'S MINISTRY

"TO EVANGELISE THE CHINESE WORLD WITH THE CHINESE WORD" is our mission statement in responding to the Great Commission. Five departments representing five approaches are constructed, namely Bible Translation Department, Free Bible Distribution Department, Out-reach Department, Bible Publicating Department and Administration Department. These five departments work closely with one another in order to maximise both the effectiveness and efficiency of using the Bible in evangelism and discipleship.

BIBLE TRANSLATION

Bible means so much to believers and non-believers. To make the Bible be available and understandable to people is the key of all. Since the Bible is written in Hebrew, Aramaic and Greek, Bible translating is an all time job. That is, to preach the gospel to Chinese, Chinese Bible is needed.

Drawing on the experience of NIV, dozens of Chinese Bible scholars and stylists are gathered to form a Bible translating committee for the translation of CNIV to provide an accurate and reliable Chinese version of the Bible.

FREE BIBLE DISTRIBUTION

Bible is one of the most powerful evangelistic tool. It is strongly believed that salvation would be in places wherever Bible is available. The mission of Free Bible Distribution Department is, then, to enhance the availibility of the Bible to every Chinese. Christians in Mainland China, patients in hospital, youth, elderly, new believers, etc. are our specific target groups of receiving the gift of the Bible.

OUT-REACH

The Bible messages are provided to the public or special target groups, such as students, children, elderly, etc. through activities or mass programmes including Bible Recitation Festival, Evangelistic Team, Bible class, scholarship, colouring competition...

BIBLE PUBLICATION

Bible Publication Department is essential in making the Bible translation available in all media. All possible forms of medium such as printed matter, cassette and compact disc are used in order to maximize the effectiveness. Our publications are not only useful within the church but also helpful in evangelism. Besides publicating for people in general, evangelical Bible and materials are even produced with special target groups. Students, children, working adults, elderly etc, for instance.

ADMINISTRATION

As a backup of Bible Translation, Bible Free Distribution, Bible Out-reach and Bible Publication, Adminstration Department works hard for office management, personel and accounting, liaison, fund raising, book distribution, etc.